T3-BNQ-065

Who's Who in America®

Who'sWho in America®

2008

62nd Edition
Volume 1 ✦ A-L

890 Mountain Avenue, Suite 300
New Providence, NJ 07974 U.S.A.
www.marquiswhoswho.com

Who'sWho in America®

Marquis Who's Who®

For information, contact: Marquis Who's Who, 890 Mountain Avenue, Suite 300
New Providence, New Jersey 07974
1-908-673-1001; www.marquiswhoswho.com

International Standard Book Number	978-0-0-8379-7011-0	(Classic Edition, Set)
	978-0-0-8379-7007-3	(Classic Edition, Volume 1)
	978-0-0-8379-7012-7	(Deluxe Edition, Set)
	978-0-8379-7009-7	(Deluxe Edition, Volume 1)
International Standard Serial Number	0083-9396	

Manufactured in the United States of America.

Table of Contents

Preface

"WHO'S WHO IN AMERICA *shall endeavor to list those individuals who are of current national reference interest and inquiry either because of meritorious achievement or because of the position they hold."*

Albert Nelson Marquis
Founder, 1899

Marquis Who's Who is proud to present the 62nd Edition of *Who's Who in America.* This edition features over 100,000 profiles of prominent individuals representing virtually every major field of endeavor. This edition also honors a group of "difference makers", men and women who have made profound contributions to America and the world.

In 1899, our first year of publication, Marquis biographees numbered 8,602. While the number of individuals profiled in *Who's Who in America* has grown substantially, our selection standards remain stringent. Fewer than one in 2,900 Americans are included in the 2008 edition of *Who's Who in America.*

While the vast majority of the individuals profiled on the following pages are American, *Who's Who in America* also includes the biographies of select individuals from around the world whose lives have had considerable impact and influence in America.

On the pages that follow, you will find Olympic champions, Nobel and Pulitzer Prize winners, university presidents, accomplished artists, renowned entertainers, entrepreneurs, and leaders representing hundreds of industries. Our 2008 Edition includes some long-established biographees like Bill Gates, Walter Cronkite and Meryl Streep, as well as many intriguing first-time listees. *Who's Who in America* also includes the profiles of thousands of remarkable achievers who, despite extraordinary accomplishments in everything from breakthrough medical research to cutting-edge technological innovations, have not as yet become household names.

Our profiles provide you with critical biographical information, including educational background, family history, work history, civic activity, memberships, honors, and awards. In many cases, hobbies and special interests are also listed.

One Principle Governs Selection

As in all Marquis Who's Who biographical volumes, the individuals profiled in *Who's Who in America* are selected on the basis of current reference value. Factors such as position, noteworthy accomplishments, visibility, and prominence in a field are all taken into account. An individual's desire to be listed is not sufficient reason for inclusion. Similarly, wealth and social position are not relevant criteria. Of course, Marquis Who's Who has never charged a fee for publishing a biography, nor is purchase of the book ever a factor in the selection of biographees. Final decisions concerning inclusion or exclusion are made following extensive discussion, evaluation, and deliberation.

Biographical information is gathered in a variety of manners. In most cases, we invite our biographees to submit their biographical details. In many cases, though, the information is collected independently by our research and editorial staffs, which use a wide assortment of tools to gather the most complete, accurate, and up-to-date information available. Sketches researched by Marquis Who's Who are followed by an asterisk (*).

Responding to Your Reference Needs

As a complement to the biographical profiles, the Geographic and Professional Indexes featured in Volume 2 make *Who's Who in America* an even more productive research tool. Through these indexes, users can identify and locate individuals in any of thirty-eight professional categories, as well as by country, state, or city. Each entry contains name and occupation description.

The Geographic Index lists names in the United States under state and city designations, as well as biographees in American territories. Canadian listings include provinces and cities. Names in Mexico and other countries appear by city. Biographees whose addresses are not published in their sketches are found under Address Unpublished.

The Professional Index includes categories ranging alphabetically from Agriculture to Social Science. Within each area, the names appear under geographic subheadings. Names without published addresses appear at the end of each professional area listing under Address Unpublished. If the occupation does not fall within one of the specified areas, the name is listed under Unclassified.

Some biographees have professions encompassing more than one area; each of these appears under the field best suited to the biographee's occupation. Thus, while most bankers are listed under Finance: Banking Services, investment bankers are found in Finance: Investment Services. A biographee with two or more diverse occupations is found under the area that best fits his or her professional profile.

Our Challenge

While the Marquis Who's Who editors exercise the utmost care in preparing each biographical sketch for publication, it is inevitable in a publication involving so many profiles that occasional errors will appear. Users of this publication are urged to notify the publisher of any issues so that adjustments can be made, which will not only be reflected in all subsequent editions of the book but which can now be immediately displayed via Marquis Who's Who on the Web.

We sincerely hope that this volume will be an indispensable reference tool for you. We are always looking for ways to better serve you and welcome your ideas for improvements. In addition, we continue to welcome your Marquis Who's Who nominations. Feel free to submit these via our Web site (www.marquiswhoswho.com) or by e-mail and postal mail.

Our Utmost Thanks

Without the cooperation and assistance of those profiled on the pages that follow, *Who's Who in America* would not be possible. We would like to specifically thank our biographees for reviewing and editing their profiles. As a consequence, *Who's Who in America* remains the unchallenged leader in the field of biographical reference works. For this we are truly grateful.

Key to Information

[1] GIBSON, OSCAR JULIUS, [2] physician, educator; **[3]** b. Syracuse, NY, Aug. 31, 1937; **[4]** s. Paul Oliver and Elizabeth H. (Thrun) G.; **[5]** m. Judith S. Gonzalez, Apr. 28, 1968; **[6]** children: Richard Gary, Matthew Lucas, Samuel Perry. **[7]** BA magna cum laude, U. Pa., 1960; MD, Harvard U., 1964. **[8]** Diplomate Am. Bd. Internal Medicine, Am. Bd. Preventive Medicine. **[9]** Intern Barnes Hosp., St. Louis, 1964-65, resident, 1965-66; clin. assoc. Nat. Heart Inst., NIH, Bethesda, Md., 1966-68; chief resident medicine U. Okla. Hosps., 1968-69; asst. prof. cmty. health Okla. Med. Ctr., 1969-70, assoc. prof., 1970-74, prof., chmn. dept., 1974-80; dean Coll. Medicine U. Okla., 1978-82; v.p. med. staff affairs Bapt. Med. Ctr., Oklahoma City, 1982-86, exec. v.p., 1986-88, chmn., 1988-95, chmn., CEO, 1995—; **[10]** mem. governing bd. Ambulatory Health Care Consortium, Inc., 1979-80; mem. Okla. Bd. Medicolegal Examiners, 1985—, Okla. Bd. Med. Ethics, 1994—. **[11]** Contbr. articles to profl. jours. **[12]** Bd. dirs., v.p. Okla. Arthritis Found., 1982—; trustee N. Ctrl. Mental Health Ctr., 1985—. **[13]** Served to lt. US Army, 1954-56. **[14]** Recipient R.T. Chadwick award Overlook Hosp., 1968; grantee Am. Heart Assn., 1985-86, 88, 1995-96. **[15]** Fellow Assn. Tchrs. Preventive Medicine; mem. AAAS, AMA, Am. Fedn. Clin. Rsch., Assn. Med. Colls., Masons, Shriners, Sigma Xi. **[16]** Republican. **[17]** Roman Catholic. **[18]** Achievements include research in the role of MMP inhibitors in the prevention of skin aging. **[19]** Avocations: swimming, weight lifting, traveling. **[20]** Home: 6060 N Ridge Ave Oklahoma City OK 73126 **[21]** Office: Bapt Med Ctr 1986 Cuba Hwy Oklahoma City OK 73120*

KEY

[1]	Name
[2]	Occupation
[3]	Vital statistics
[4]	Parents
[5]	Marriage
[6]	Children
[7]	Education
[8]	Professional certifications
[9]	Career
[10]	Career-related
[11]	Writings and creative works
[12]	Civic and political activities
[13]	Military
[14]	Awards and fellowships
[15]	Professional and association memberships, clubs and lodges
[16]	Political affiliation
[17]	Religion
[18]	Achievements
[19]	Avocations
[20]	Home address
[21]	Office address
[*]	Researched by Marquis Who's Who

Table of Abbreviations

The following is a list of some of the most frequently used Marquis abbreviations:

A

A Associate (used with academic degrees)
AA Associate in Arts
AAAL American Academy of Arts and Letters
AAAS American Association for the Advancement of Science
AACD American Association for Counseling and Development
AACN American Association of Critical Care Nurses
AAHA American Academy of Health Administrators
AAHP American Association of Hospital Planners
AAHPERD American Alliance for Health, Physical Education, Recreation, and Dance
AAS Associate of Applied Science
AASL American Association of School Librarians
AASPA American Association of School Personnel Administrators
AAU Amateur Athletic Union
AAUP American Association of University Professors
AAUW American Association of University Women
AB Arts, Bachelor of
AB Alberta
ABA American Bar Association
AC Air Corps
acad. academy
acct. accountant
acctg. accounting
ACDA Arms Control and Disarmament Agency
ACHA American College of Hospital Administrators
ACLS Advanced Cardiac Life Support
ACLU American Civil Liberties Union
ACOG American College of Ob-Gyn
ACP American College of Physicians
ACS American College of Surgeons
ADA American Dental Association
adj. adjunct, adjutant
adm. admiral
adminstr. administrator
adminstrn. administration
adminstrv. administrative
ADN Associate's Degree in Nursing
ADP Automatic Data Processing
adv. advocate, advisory
advt. advertising
AE Agricultural Engineer
AEC Atomic Energy Commission
aero. aeronautical, aeronautic
aerodyn. aerodynamic
AFB Air Force Base
AFTRA American Federation of Television and Radio Artists
agr. agriculture
agrl. agricultural
agt. agent
AGVA American Guild of Variety Artists
agy. agency
A&I Agricultural and Industrial
AIA American Institute of Architects
AIAA American Institute of Aeronautics and Astronautics
AIChE American Institute of Chemical Engineers
AICPA American Institute of Certified Public Accountants
AID Agency for International Development
AIDS Acquired Immune Deficiency Syndrome
AIEE American Institute of Electrical Engineers
AIME American Institute of Mining, Metallurgy, and Petroleum Engineers
AK Alaska
AL Alabama
ALA American Library Association
Ala. Alabama
alt. alternate
Alta. Alberta
A&M Agricultural and Mechanical
AM Arts, Master of
Am. American, America
AMA American Medical Association
amb. ambassador
AME African Methodist Episcopal
Amtrak National Railroad Passenger Corporation
AMVETS American Veterans
ANA American Nurses Association
anat. anatomical
ANCC American Nurses Credentialing Center
ann. annual
anthrop. anthropological
AP Associated Press
APA American Psychological Association
APHA American Public Health Association
APO Army Post Office
apptd. appointed
Apr. April
apt. apartment
AR Arkansas
ARC American Red Cross
arch. architect
archeol. archeological
archtl. architectural
Ariz. Arizona
Ark. Arkansas
ArtsD Arts, Doctor of
arty. artillery
AS Associate in Science, American Samoa
ASCAP American Society of Composers, Authors and Publishers
ASCD Association for Supervision and Curriculum Development
ASCE American Society of Civil Engineers
ASME American Society of Mechanical Engineers
ASPA American Society for Public Administration
ASPCA American Society for the Prevention of Cruelty to Animals
assn. association
assoc. associate
asst. assistant
ASTD American Society for Training and Development
ASTM American Society for Testing and Materials
astron. astronomical
astrophys. astrophysical
ATLA Association of Trial Lawyers of America
ATSC Air Technical Service Command
atty. attorney
Aug. August
aux. auxiliary
Ave. Avenue
AVMA American Veterinary Medical Association
AZ Arizona

B

B Bachelor
b. born
BA Bachelor of Arts
BAgr Bachelor of Agriculture
Balt. Baltimore
Bapt. Baptist
BArch Bachelor of Architecture
BAS Bachelor of Agricultural Science
BBA Bachelor of Business Administration
BBB Better Business Bureau
BC British Columbia
BCE Bachelor of Civil Engineering
BChir Bachelor of Surgery
BCL Bachelor of Civil Law
BCS Bachelor of Commercial Science
BD Bachelor of Divinity
bd. board
BE Bachelor of Education
BEE Bachelor of Electrical Engineering
BFA Bachelor of Fine Arts
bibl. biblical
bibliog. bibliographical
biog. biographical
biol. biological
BJ Bachelor of Journalism
Bklyn. Brooklyn
BL Bachelor of Letters
bldg. building
BLS Bachelor of Library Science
Blvd. Boulevard

BMI Broadcast Music, Inc.
bn. battalion
bot. botanical
BPE Bachelor of Physical Education
BPhil Bachelor of Philosophy
br. branch
BRE Bachelor of Religious Education
brig. gen. brigadier general
Brit. British
Bros. Brothers
BS Bachelor of Science
BSA Bachelor of Agricultural Science
BSBA Bachelor of Science in Business Administration
BSChemE Bachelor of Science in Chemical Engineering
BSD Bachelor of Didactic Science
BSEE Bachelor of Science in Electrical Engineering
BSN Bachelor of Science in Nursing
BST Bachelor of Sacred Theology
BTh Bachelor of Theology
bull. bulletin
bur. bureau
bus. business
BWI British West Indies

C

CA California
CAD-CAM Computer Aided Design–Computer Aided Model
Calif. California
Can. Canada, Canadian
CAP Civil Air Patrol
capt. captain
cardiol. cardiological
cardiovasc. cardiovascular
Cath. Catholic
cav. cavalry
CBI China, Burma, India Theatre of Operations
CC Community College
CCC Commodity Credit Corporation
CCNY City College of New York
CCRN Critical Care Registered Nurse
CCU Cardiac Care Unit
CD Civil Defense
CE Corps of Engineers, Civil Engineer
CEN Certified Emergency Nurse
CENTO Central Treaty Organization
CEO chief executive officer
CERN European Organization of Nuclear Research
cert. certificate, certification, certified
CETA Comprehensive Employment Training Act
CFA Chartered Financial Analyst
CFL Canadian Football League
CFO chief financial officer
CFP Certified Financial Planner
ch. church
ChD Doctor of Chemistry
chem. chemical
ChemE Chemical Engineer
ChFC Chartered Financial Consultant
Chgo. Chicago
chirurg., der surgeon
chmn. chairman
chpt. chapter
CIA Central Intelligence Agency
Cin. Cincinnati
cir. circle, circuit
CLE Continuing Legal Education
Cleve. Cleveland
climatol. climatological
clin. clinical
clk. clerk
CLU Chartered Life Underwriter
CM Master in Surgery
CM Northern Mariana Islands
cmty. community
CO Colorado
Co. Company
COF Catholic Order of Foresters
C. of C. Chamber of Commerce
col. colonel
coll. college
Colo. Colorado
com. committee
comd. commanded
comdg. commanding
comdr. commander
comdt. commandant
comm. communications
commd. commissioned
comml. commercial
commn. commission
commr. commissioner
compt. comptroller
condr. conductor
conf. Conference
Congl. Congregational, Congressional
Conglist. Congregationalist
Conn. Connecticut
cons. consultant, consulting
consol. consolidated
constl. constitutional
constn. constitution
constrn. construction
contbd. contributed
contbg. contributing
contbn. contribution
contbr. contributor
contr. controller
Conv. Convention
COO chief operating officer
coop. cooperative
coord. coordinator
corp. corporation, corporate
corr. correspondent, corresponding, correspondence
coun. council
CPA Certified Public Accountant
CPCU Chartered Property and Casualty Underwriter
CPH Certificate of Public Health
cpl. corporal
CPR Cardio-Pulmonary Resuscitation
CS Christian Science
CSB Bachelor of Christian Science
CT Connecticut
ct. court
ctr. center
ctrl. central

D

D Doctor
d. daughter of
DAgr Doctor of Agriculture
DAR Daughters of the American Revolution
dau. daughter
DAV Disabled American Veterans
DC District of Columbia
DCL Doctor of Civil Law
DCS Doctor of Commercial Science
DD Doctor of Divinity
DDS Doctor of Dental Surgery
DE Delaware
Dec. December
dec. deceased
def. defense
Del. Delaware
del. delegate, delegation
Dem. Democrat, Democratic
DEng Doctor of Engineering
denom. denomination, denominational
dep. deputy
dept. department
dermatol. dermatological
desc. descendant
devel. development, developmental
DFA Doctor of Fine Arts
DHL Doctor of Hebrew Literature
dir. director
dist. district
distbg. distributing
distbn. distribution
distbr. distributor
disting. distinguished
div. division, divinity, divorce
divsn. division
DLitt Doctor of Literature
DMD Doctor of Dental Medicine
DMS Doctor of Medical Science
DO Doctor of Osteopathy
docs. documents
DON Director of Nursing
DPH Diploma in Public Health
DPhil, Doctor of Philosophy
DR Daughters of the Revolution
Dr. Drive, Doctor
DRE Doctor of Religious Education
DrPH Doctor of Public Health
DSc Doctor of Science
DSChemE Doctor of Science in Chemical Engineering
DSM Distinguished Service Medal
DST Doctor of Sacred Theology
DTM Doctor of Tropical Medicine
DVM Doctor of Veterinary Medicine
DVS Doctor of Veterinary Surgery

E

E East
ea. eastern
Eccles. Ecclesiastical
ecol. ecological

econ. economic
ECOSOC UN Economic and Social Council
ED Doctor of Engineering
ed. educated
EdB Bachelor of Education
EdD Doctor of Education
edit. edition
editl. editorial
EdM Master of Education
edn. education
ednl. educational
EDP Electronic Data Processing
EdS Specialist in Education
EE Electrical Engineer
EEC European Economic Community
EEG Electroencephalogram
EEO Equal Employment Opportunity
EEOC Equal Employment Opportunity Commission
EKG electrocardiogram
elec. electrical
electrochem. electrochemical
electrophys. electrophysical
elem. elementary
EM Engineer of Mines
EMT Emergency Medical Technician
ency. encyclopedia
Eng. England
engr. engineer
engring. engineering
entomol. entomological
environ. environmental
EPA Environmental Protection Agency
epidemiol. epidemiological
Episc. Episcopalian
ERA Equal Rights Amendment
ERDA Energy Research and Development Administration
ESEA Elementary and Secondary Education Act
ESL English as Second Language
ESSA Environmental Science Services Administration
ethnol. ethnological
ETO European Theatre of Operations
EU European Union
Evang. Evangelical
exam. examination, examining
Exch. Exchange
exec. executive
exhbn. exhibition
expdn. expedition
expn. exposition
expt. experiment
exptl. experimental
Expy. Expressway
Ext. Extension

F

FAA Federal Aviation Administration
FAO UN Food and Agriculture Organization
FBA Federal Bar Association
FBI Federal Bureau of Investigation
FCA Farm Credit Administration
FCC Federal Communications Commission
FCDA Federal Civil Defense Administration
FDA Food and Drug Administration
FDIA Federal Deposit Insurance Administration
FDIC Federal Deposit Insurance Corporation
FEA Federal Energy Administration
Feb. February
fed. federal
fedn. federation
FERC Federal Energy Regulatory Commission
fgn. foreign
FHA Federal Housing Administration
fin. financial, finance
FL Florida
Fl. Floor
Fla. Florida
FMC Federal Maritime Commission
FNP Family Nurse Practitioner
FOA Foreign Operations Administration
found. foundation
FPC Federal Power Commission
FPO Fleet Post Office
frat. fraternity
FRS Federal Reserve System
FSA Federal Security Agency
Ft. Fort
FTC Federal Trade Commission
Fwy. Freeway

G

GA, Ga. Georgia
GAO General Accounting Office
gastroent. gastroenterological
GATT General Agreement on Tariffs and Trade
GE General Electric Company
gen. general
geneal. genealogical
geog. geographic, geographical
geol. geological
geophys. geophysical
geriat. geriatrics
gerontol. gerontological
GHQ General Headquarters
gov. governor
govt. government
govtl. governmental
GPO Government Printing Office
grad. graduate, graduated
GSA General Services Administration
Gt. Great
GU Guam
gynecol. gynecological

H

hdqs. headquarters
HEW Department of Health, Education and Welfare
HHD Doctor of Humanities
HHFA Housing and Home Finance Agency
HHS Department of Health and Human Services
HI Hawaii
hist. historical, historic
HM Master of Humanities
homeo. homeopathic
hon. honorary, honorable
House of Dels. House of Delegates
House of Reps. House of Representatives
hort. horticultural
hosp. hospital
HS High School
HUD Department of Housing and Urban Development
Hwy. Highway
hydrog. hydrographic

I

IA Iowa
IAEA International Atomic Energy Agency
IBRD International Bank for Reconstruction and Development
ICA International Cooperation Administration
ICC Interstate Commerce Commission
ICCE International Council for Computers in Education
ICU Intensive Care Unit
ID Idaho
IEEE Institute of Electrical and Electronics Engineers
IFC International Finance Corporation
IL, Ill. Illinois
illus. illustrated
ILO International Labor Organization
IMF International Monetary Fund
IN Indiana
Inc. Incorporated
Ind. Indiana
ind. independent
Indpls. Indianapolis
indsl. industrial
inf. infantry
info. information
ins. insurance
insp. inspector
inst. institute
instl. institutional
instn. institution
instr. instructor
instrn. instruction
instrnl. instructional
internat. international
intro. introduction
IRE Institute of Radio Engineers
IRS Internal Revenue Service

J

JAG Judge Advocate General
JAGC Judge Advocate General Corps
Jan. January
Jaycees Junior Chamber of Commerce
JB Jurum Baccalaureus
JCB Juris Canonici Baccalaureus
JCD Juris Canonici Doctor, Juris Civilis Doctor
JCL Juris Canonici Licentiatus
JD Juris Doctor

jg. junior grade
jour. journal
jr. junior
JSD Juris Scientiae Doctor
JUD Juris Utriusque Doctor
jud. judicial

K

Kans. Kansas
KC Knights of Columbus
KS Kansas
KY, Ky. Kentucky

L

LA, La. Louisiana
LA Los Angeles
lab. laboratory
L.Am. Latin America
lang. language
laryngol. laryngological
LB Labrador
LDS Latter Day Saints
lectr. lecturer
legis. legislation, legislative
LHD Doctor of Humane Letters
LI Long Island
libr. librarian, library
lic. licensed, license
lit. literature
litig. litigation
LittB Bachelor of Letters
LittD Doctor of Letters
LLB Bachelor of Laws
LLD Doctor of Laws
LLM Master of Laws
Ln. Lane
LPGA Ladies Professional Golf Association
LPN Licensed Practical Nurse
lt. lieutenant
Ltd. Limited
Luth. Lutheran
LWV League of Women Voters

M

M Master
m. married
MA Master of Arts
MA Massachusetts
MADD Mothers Against Drunk Driving
mag. magazine
MAgr Master of Agriculture
maj. major
Man. Manitoba
Mar. March
MArch Master in Architecture
Mass. Massachusetts
math. mathematics, mathematical
MB Bachelor of Medicine, Manitoba
MBA Master of Business Administration
MC Medical Corps
MCE Master of Civil Engineering
mcht. merchant
mcpl. municipal
MCS Master of Commercial Science
MD Doctor of Medicine
MD, Md. Maryland
MDiv Master of Divinity
MDip Master in Diplomacy
mdse. merchandise
MDV Doctor of Veterinary Medicine
ME Mechanical Engineer
ME Maine
M.E.Ch. Methodist Episcopal Church
mech. mechanical
MEd. Master of Education
med. medical
MEE Master of Electrical Engineering
mem. member
meml. memorial
merc. mercantile
met. metropolitan
metall. metallurgical
MetE Metallurgical Engineer
meteorol. meteorological
Meth. Methodist
Mex. Mexico
MF Master of Forestry
MFA Master of Fine Arts
mfg. manufacturing
mfr. manufacturer
mgmt. management
mgr. manager
MHA Master of Hospital Administration
MI Military Intelligence, Michigan
Mich. Michigan
micros. microscopic
mid. middle
mil. military
Milw. Milwaukee
Min. Minister
mineral. mineralogical
Minn. Minnesota
MIS Management Information Systems
Miss. Mississippi
MIT Massachusetts Institute of Technology
mktg. marketing
ML Master of Laws
MLA Modern Language Association
MLitt Master of Literature, Master of Letters
MLS Master of Library Science
MME Master of Mechanical Engineering
MN Minnesota
mng. managing
MO, Mo. Missouri
moblzn. mobilization
Mont. Montana
MP Member of Parliament
MPA Master of Public Administration
MPE Master of Physical Education
MPH Master of Public Health
MPhil Master of Philosophy
MPL Master of Patent Law
Mpls. Minneapolis
MRE Master of Religious Education
MRI Magnetic Resonance Imaging
MS Master of Science
MS, Ms. Mississippi
MSc Master of Science
MSChemE Master of Science in Chemical Engineering
MSEE Master of Science in Electrical Engineering
MSF Master of Science of Forestry
MSN Master of Science in Nursing
MST Master of Sacred Theology
MSW Master of Social Work
MT Montana
Mt. Mount
mus. museum, musical
MusB Bachelor of Music
MusD Doctor of Music
MusM Master of Music
mut. mutual
MVP Most Valuable Player
mycol. mycological

N

N North
NAACOG Nurses Association of the American College of Obstetricians and Gynecologists
NAACP National Association for the Advancement of Colored People
NACA National Advisory Committee for Aeronautics
NACDL National Association of Criminal Defense Lawyers
NACU National Association of Colleges and Universities
NAD National Academy of Design
NAE National Academy of Engineering, National Association of Educators
NAESP National Association of Elementary School Principals
NAFE National Association of Female Executives
N.Am. North America
NAM National Association of Manufacturers
NAMH National Association for Mental Health
NAPA National Association of Performing Artists
NARAS National Academy of Recording Arts and Sciences
NAREB National Association of Real Estate Boards
NARS National Archives and Record Service
NAS National Academy of Sciences
NASA National Aeronautics and Space Administration
NASP National Association of School Psychologists
NASW National Association of Social Workers
nat. national
NATAS National Academy of Television Arts and Sciences
NATO North Atlantic Treaty Organization

nav. navigation
NB, N.B. New Brunswick
NBA National Basketball Association
NC North Carolina
NCAA National College Athletic Association
NCCJ National Conference of Christians and Jews
ND North Dakota
NDEA National Defense Education Act
NE Nebraska
NE Northeast
NEA National Education Association
Nebr. Nebraska
NEH National Endowment for Humanities
neurol. neurological
Nev. Nevada
NF Newfoundland
NFL National Football League
Nfld. Newfoundland
NG National Guard
NH New Hampshire
NHL National Hockey League
NIH National Institutes of Health
NIMH National Institute of Mental Health
NJ New Jersey
NLRB National Labor Relations Board
NM, N.Mex. New Mexico
No. Northern
NOAA National Oceanographic and Atmospheric Administration
NORAD North America Air Defense
Nov. November
NOW National Organization for Women
nr. near
NRA National Rifle Association
NRC National Research Council
NS Nova Scotia
NSC National Security Council
NSF National Science Foundation
NSTA National Science Teachers Association
NSW New South Wales
nuc. nuclear
numis. numismatic
NV Nevada
NW Northwest
NWT Northwest Territories
NY New York
NYC New York City
NYU New York University
NZ New Zealand

O

ob-gyn obstetrics-gynecology
obs. observatory
obstet. obstetrical
occupl. occupational
oceanog. oceanographic
Oct. October
OD Doctor of Optometry
OECD Organization for Economic Cooperation and Development
OEEC Organization of European Economic Cooperation
OEO Office of Economic Opportunity
ofcl. official
OH Ohio
OK, Okla. Oklahoma
ON, Ont. Ontario
oper. operating
ophthal. ophthalmological
ops. operations
OR Oregon
orch. orchestra
Oreg. Oregon
orgn. organization
orgnl. organizational
ornithol. ornithological
orthop. orthopedic
OSHA Occupational Safety and Health Administration
OSRD Office of Scientific Research and Development
OSS Office of Strategic Services
osteo. osteopathic
otol. otological
otolaryn. otolaryngological

P

PA, Pa. Pennsylvania
paleontol. paleontological
path. pathological
pediat. pediatrics
PEI Prince Edward Island
PEN Poets, Playwrights, Editors, Essayists and Novelists
penol. penological
pers. personnel
PGA Professional Golfers' Association of America
PHA Public Housing Administration
pharm. pharmaceutical
PharmD Doctor of Pharmacy
PharmM Master of Pharmacy
PhB Bachelor of Philosophy
PhD Doctor of Philosophy
PhDChemE Doctor of Science in Chemical Engineering
PhM Master of Philosophy
Phila. Philadelphia
philharm. philharmonic
philol. philological
philos. philosophical
photog. photographic
phys. physical
physiol. physiological
Pitts. Pittsburgh
Pk. Park
Pky. Parkway
Pl. Place
Plz. Plaza
PO Post Office
polit. political
poly. polytechnic, polytechnical
PQ Province of Quebec
PR Puerto Rico
prep. preparatory
pres. president
Presbyn. Presbyterian
presdl. presidential
prin. principal
procs. proceedings
prod. produced
prodn. production
prodr. producer
prof. professor
profl. professional
prog. progressive
propr. proprietor
pros. prosecuting
pro tem. pro tempore
psychiat. psychiatric
psychol. psychological
PTA Parent-Teachers Association
ptnr. partner
PTO Pacific Theatre of Operations, Parent Teacher Organization
pub. publisher, publishing, published, public
publ. publication
pvt. private

Q

quar. quarterly
qm. quartermaster
Que. Quebec

R

radiol. radiological
RAF Royal Air Force
RCA Radio Corporation of America
RCAF Royal Canadian Air Force
Rd. Road
R&D Research & Development
REA Rural Electrification Administration
rec. recording
ref. reformed
regt. regiment
regtl. regimental
rehab. rehabilitation
rels. relations
Rep. Republican
rep. representative
Res. Reserve
ret. retired
Rev. Reverend
rev. review, revised
RFC Reconstruction Finance Corporation
RI Rhode Island
Rlwy. Railway
Rm. Room
RN Registered Nurse
roentgenol. roentgenological
ROTC Reserve Officers Training Corps
RR rural route, railroad
rsch. research
rschr. researcher
Rt. Route

S

S South
s. son
SAC Strategic Air Command
SAG Screen Actors Guild
S.Am. South America
san. sanitary

SAR Sons of the American Revolution
Sask. Saskatchewan
savs. savings
SB Bachelor of Science
SBA Small Business Administration
SC South Carolina
ScB Bachelor of Science
SCD Doctor of Commercial Science
ScD Doctor of Science
sch. school
sci. science, scientific
SCV Sons of Confederate Veterans
SD South Dakota
SE Southeast
SEC Securities and Exchange Commission
sec. secretary
sect. section
seismol. seismological
sem. seminary
Sept. September
s.g. senior grade
sgt. sergeant
SI Staten Island
SJ Society of Jesus
SJD Scientiae Juridicae Doctor
SK Saskatchewan
SM Master of Science
SNP Society of Nursing Professionals
So. Southern
soc. society
sociol. sociological
spkr. speaker
spl. special
splty. specialty
Sq. Square
SR Sons of the Revolution
sr. senior
SS Steamship
St. Saint, Street
sta. station
stats. statistics
statis. statistical
STB Bachelor of Sacred Theology
stblzn. stabilization
STD Doctor of Sacred Theology
std. standard
Ste. Suite
subs. subsidiary
SUNY State University of New York
supr. supervisor
supt. superintendent
surg. surgical
svc. service
SW Southwest
sys. system

T

Tb. tuberculosis
tchg. teaching
tchr. teacher
tech. technical, technology
technol. technological
tel. telephone
telecom. telecommunications
temp. temporary
Tenn. Tennessee
TESOL Teachers of English to Speakers of Other Languages
Tex. Texas
ThD Doctor of Theology
theol. theological
ThM Master of Theology
TN Tennessee
tng. training
topog. topographical
trans. transaction, transferred
transl. translation, translated
transp. transportation
treas. treasurer
TV television
twp. township
TX Texas
typog. typographical

U

U. University
UAW United Auto Workers
UCLA University of California at Los Angeles
UK United Kingdom
UN United Nations
UNESCO United Nations Educational, Scientific and Cultural Organization
UNICEF United Nations International Children's Emergency Fund
univ. university
UNRRA United Nations Relief and Rehabilitation Administration
UPI United Press International
urol. urological
US, USA United States of America
USAAF United States Army Air Force
USAF United States Air Force
USAFR United States Air Force Reserve
USAR United States Army Reserve
USCG United States Coast Guard
USCGR United States Coast Guard Reserve
USES United States Employment Service
USIA United States Information Agency
USMC United States Marine Corps
USMCR United States Marine Corps Reserve
USN United States Navy
USNG United States National Guard
USNR United States Naval Reserve
USO United Service Organizations
USPHS United States Public Health Service
USS United States Ship
USSR Union of the Soviet Socialist Republics
USTA United States Tennis Association
UT Utah

V

VA Veterans Administration
VA, Va. Virginia
vet. veteran, veterinary
VFW Veterans of Foreign Wars
VI Virgin Islands
vis. visiting
VISTA Volunteers in Service to America
vocat. vocational
vol. volunteer, volume
v.p. vice president
vs. versus
VT, Vt. Vermont

W

W West
WA, Wash. Washington (state)
WAC Women's Army Corps
WAVES Women's Reserve, US Naval Reserve
WCTU Women's Christian Temperance Union
we. western
WHO World Health Organization
WI Wisconsin, West Indies
Wis. Wisconsin
WV, W.Va. West Virginia
WY, Wyo. Wyoming

X, Y, Z

YK Yukon Territory
YMCA Young Men's Christian Association
YMHA Young Men's Hebrew Association
YM & YWHA Young Men's and Young Women's Hebrew Association
yr. year
YT Yukon Territory
YWCA Young Women's Christian Association

Alphabetical Practices

Names are arranged alphabetically according to the surnames, and under identical surnames according to the first given name. If both surname and first given name are identical, names are arranged alphabetically according to the second given name.

Surnames beginning with De, Des, Du, however capitalized or spaced, are recorded with the prefix preceding the surname and arranged alphabetically under the letter D.

Surnames beginning with Mac and Mc are arranged alphabetically under M.

Surnames beginning with Saint or St. appear after names that begin Sains, and are arranged according to the second part of the name, e.g., St. Clair before Saint Dennis.

Surnames beginning with Van, Von, or von are arranged alphabetically under the letter V.

Compound surnames are arranged according to the first member of the compound.

Many hyphenated Arabic names begin Al-, El-, or al-. These names are alphabetized according to each biographee's designation of last name. Thus Al-Bahar, Neta may be listed either under Al- or under Bahar, depending on the preference of the listee.

Also, Arabic names have a variety of possible spellings when transposed to English. Spelling of these names is always based on the practice of the biographee. Some biographees use a Western form of word order, while others prefer the Arabic word sequence.

Similarly, Asian names may have no comma between family and given names, but some biographees have chosen to add the comma. In each case, punctuation follows the preference of the biographee.

Parentheses used in connection with a name indicate which part of the full name is usually omitted in common usage. Hence, Chambers, E(lizabeth) Anne indicates that the first name, Elizabeth, is generally recorded as an initial. In such a case, the parentheses are ignored in alphabetizing and the name would be arranged as Chambers, Elizabeth Anne.

However, if the entire first name appears in parentheses, for example, Chambers, (Elizabeth) Anne, the first name is not commonly used, and the alphabetizing is therefore arranged as though the name were Chambers, Anne.

If the entire middle name is in parentheses, it is still used in alphabetical sorting. Hence, Belamy, Katherine (Lucille) would sort as Belamy, Katherine Lucille. The same occurs if the entire last name is in parentheses, e.g., (Brandenberg), Howard Keith would sort as Brandenberg, Howard Keith.

For visual clarification:

Smith, H(enry) George: Sorts as Smith, Henry George
Smith, (Henry) George: Sorts as Smith, George
Smith, Henry (George): Sorts as Smith, Henry George
(Smith), Henry George: Sorts as Smith, Henry George

Who'sWho in America®

Biographees A - L

AABERG, THOMAS MARSHALL, SR., academic administrator; b. St. Paul, Sept. 5, 1936; m. Judith S. Young, June 17, 1961; children: Thomas M. Jr., Leigh, Sarah. BA, Dartmouth Coll., 1958, MS, 1959; MD, Harvard U., 1961; MSPH in Preventive Medicine, U. Okla., 1967. Diplomate Am. Bd. Ophthalmology. Asst. prof. ophthalmology Med. Coll. Wis., Milw., 1969-71, assoc. prof. ophthalmology, 1971-76, prof. ophthalmology, 1976-88; chmn. dept. ophthalmology Sch. Medicine Emory U., Atlanta, 1988—. Surgeon USPHS, 1966-68. Office: Emory Eye Ctr Ste B 4405 1365-B Clifton Rd NE Atlanta GA 30322-1013 Office Phone: 404-778-4456. Business E-Mail: ophttma@emory.edu.

AADLAND, THOMAS VERNON, minister; b. Mpls., Dec. 24, 1950; s. Otto Sidney and Dorothy Jean (Holmquist) A.; m. Mary Joanne Pratt, June 27, 1981; children: Evangeline Faith, Brigitta Hope, Andrew Paul, Marian Joy. AB in Philosophy, Wheaton Coll., 1973; MDiv, Luther Theol. Sem., 1980. Ordained to ministry Am. Luth. Ch., 1980. Assoc. pastor Christ Luth. Ch., Duluth, Minn., 1980-91, sr. pastor, 1991—99; sec. Am. Assn. Luth. Chs., Mpls., 1987-93; min. Christ. Luth. Ch., 1980—99. Presiding pastor, Amer. Assn. of Lutheran Chs., 1999—, bd. dirs. Lake Superior Life Care Ctr., Duluth, Minn., 1987-90, pres. Lake Superior chpt. Luths. for Life, 1996—99, nat. bd. dirs., 2003—, sec., 2004—. Lutheran. Home: 13986 Dallas Ave Rosemount MN 55068-7108 Office Phone: 952-884-7784. E-mail: aadland@aol.com. *I believe Americans cannot escape the religous question. The enjoyment of our freedoms—in some vitally important sense—depends upon a humble and grateful recognition that the source of our fundamental rights to life, liberty and property is transcendent: they derive not from the generosity of the State but from the magnanimity of God, in Whose image we are created.*

AADNESEN, CHRISTOPHER, rail transportation executive, consultant; b. Salt Lake City, Nov. 2, 1948; s. Grant C. and Helen Jane (Ray) Aadnesen; m. Helen Elizabeth Twelves, Aug. 14, 1973 (div. 1988); children: Aric Paul, Brian James, Nicholas Twelves; m. Betty Jean DeLeon, Aug. 19, 1988; stepchildren: Brooke Bingham, Brad Bingham. BA in English, U. Utah, 1971, MBA, 1973; PMD, Harvard U., 1990. Gen. mgr., founder Thaddeus Duncan Co., Salt Lake City, 1968-72; divsn. supt. Western Pacific RR, Sacramento, 1978-82; gen. supt. of transp. Mo. Pacific RR, Spring, Tex., 1983-84; asst. gen. mgr. So. Region Union Pacific RR, Spring, Tex., 1984-88, gen. dir. pers. svcs. Omaha, 1988-89, asst. v.p. ops. adminstrn., 1989-90, asst. v.p. employee devel. and involvement, 1990-91, sr. asst. v.p. field ops., 1992-93, sr. asst. v.p. transp., 1993-95, pres. capitol city group, pres. capitol city mgmt. assocs., 1996—; COO Transp. Ferroviara Mexicana, S.A. de C.V., 1996-99, exec. v.p., 1999-2000; exec. v.p., COO Tex. Mexican Rlwy. Co., 1999-2000; chmn. Port Terminal RR Assn., 2000-01; dir. freight rail ctrl. divsn. HNTB, Austin, Tex., 2007—. Chmn. of bd. dirs. Georgetown Rail Equipment Co., 2002—; bd. dirs. Cmty. European Railways, 2005—07; CEO Estonian Railways Ltd., Tallinn, 2004—07; v.p. Am. C. of C. of Estonia, 2004—07. Campaign mgr. County Commr., Quincy, Calif., 1978; commr. planning and zoning Georgetown, 2001—04; bd. dirs. Palace Theatre, Georgetown, Tex., 2001—04. With USN, 1967—69. Mem.: Am. Assn. RR Supts., Georgetown C. of C., Cimarron Hills Country Club, Berry Creek Country Club, Field Club Omaha, Happy Hollow Country Club, Rotary, Beta Theta Pi. Republican. Episcopalian. Avocations: guitar, golf, fishing, music. Home: 30102 Briarcrest Ct Georgetown TX 78628-1154 Office: 361 Congress Ave Ste 600 Austin TX 78701 Home Phone: 512-868-0033; Office Phone: 512-691-2251. Personal E-mail: caadnesen@hotmail.com.

AALL, CHRISTIAN BERGENGREN, entrepreneur; b. St. Louis, Dec. 7, 1955; s. Christian Hiorth Aall and Ruth (Bergengren) Perkins; m. Esther Drugowitsch, Aug. 5, 1983; children: Christian Daniel, Nathalie Caroline. MME, Swiss Fed. Inst. Tech., Zürich, 1980; MBA, Internat. Mgmt. Devel. Inst., Lausanne, Switzerland, 1987. Project mgr. Cementos Apasco S.A., Apasco, Mexico, 1981-82; cons. Holderbank (Switzerland) Mgmt. & Cons. Ltd., 1982-86; mgr. systems and strategic planning GM Europe Parts and Accessories, Zürich, 1988-91; comptr. GM Europe Parts & Accessories, Ruesselsheim, Germany, 1991-92; comptr. sales Adam Opel AG, Ruesselsheim, 1992-95; mng. dir. Opel Master Lease GmbH, Ruesselsheim, 1996-98; pres. Daidalos Cons., Wellesley, Mass., 1998-2001; dir. internat. ops. Daidalos Unternehmensberatung GmbH, Wolfratshausen, Germany, 1998—2001; CEO C2 Remktg., Inc., Los Altos, Calif., 2001—02; pres. Aall Devel., Inc., Wellesley, 2003—. Bd. trustees Frankfurt Internat. Sch., 1995-97, chmn. bldgs. and grounds com., treas., chmn. fin. com. 1997-98; treas. IMD Alumni Deutschland e.V., 1995-99. E-mail: caall@comcast.net.

AAMODT, ROGER LOUIS, retired federal agency administrator; b. San Francisco, Dec. 9, 1941; s. Rodney Lee and Barbara Helen (Quinn) A.; m. Janet Roberta Hall, Sept. 15, 1962 (div. 1995); children: Sandra Marie, Aaron Lee; m. Diane Sue Dwyer, Apr. 27, 1997. Student, Antioch Coll., 1959-60; BS cum laude, U. Utah, 1966; PhD, U. Rochester, 1972. Rsch. asst. dept. radiol. health U. Utah, Salt Lake City, 1965-66; sect. chief dept. nuclear medicine Clin. Ctr., NIH, Bethesda, Md., 1971-83; grants assoc. NIH, Bethesda, 1983-84; program dir. cancer diagnosis br. Nat. Cancer Inst., NIH, Rockville, Md., 1984-96, chief resources devel. br. cancer diagnosis program, 1997—2005; ret., 2005. Pres. Internat. Soc. for Biol. and Environ. Repositories, 2002—03; cons. Aamodt Enterprises, 2005—. Author (with others): Textbook of Nuclear Medicine, 1978; contbr. refence tables to Human Health and Disease, 1977, more than 50 articles to profl. jours. Pres. Calvin Park Civic Assn., Rockville, 1974-94.—. Spl. Health Physics fellow U.S. Atomic Energy Commn., 1966-69, NDEA fellow, 1969-71. Mem. AAAS, Am. Soc. Investigative Pathology, Internat. Soc. Analytical Cytology, NIH Microcomputer Club (sec.-treas. 1983-84). Democrat. Methodist. Achievements include research on zinc absorption and metabolism in humans; organization of the NCI Cooperative Human Tissue Network, Cooperative Breast Cancer Tissue Resource, and Cooperative Prostate Cancer Tissue Network. Personal E-mail: aamodtr@starpower.net.

AAMOTH, GORDON M., medical association administrator; b. Apr. 12, 1940; MD, Northwestern U., 1966. Intern U. Calif., San Francisco, 1966—67, fellow, 1968—69, residency, 1969—73; clinical prof. of orthopaedic surgery U. Minn.; dir. private rotation in dept. orthopaedic surgery Abbott Northwestern Hosp., pres., med. staf; faculty mem. Hennepin County Gen. Hosp., Mpls.; private practice Mpls. Orthopaedics. Spkr. in field; vis. prof. for several universities. Assoc. editor Clinical Orthopaedics and Related Research, consulting reviewer Journal of Bone and Joint Surgery. Recipient Charles Bowles-Bowles Rogers award, Hennepin County Med. Soc., 2004. Mem.: Am. Bd. Med. Specialties, Am. Orthopaedic Assn., Assn. Bone and Joint Surgeons, Am. Acad. Orthopaedic Surgeons (mem-at-large bd. dirs. 2005—), Am. Bd. of Orthopaedic Surgery (past pres., bd. dir.). Office: U Minn Depart of Orthopaedic Surgery 2512 S 7th St R200 Minneapolis MN 55454 also: 825 S 8th St Ste 550 Minneapolis MN 55404-1293 Office Phone: 612-333-5000.

AARDSMA, DAVID A., waste management executive; With Waste Mgmt., Inc., 1977—, v.p. sales Western Group, v.p. sales, 2000—05, sr. v.p. sales and mktg., 2005—. Office: Waste Mgmt Inc 1001 Fannin Ste 4000 Houston TX 77002 Office Phone: 713-512-6200.*

AARON, BERTRAM DONALD, engineering executive, management consultant; b. Newport News, Va., Jan. 10, 1922; s. Harry and Lillian (Blackman) A.; children: Harry, Cynthia, Jill; m. Marcia Kurke, 1952 (dec. Nov. 1974); m. Judith Goldstein, Dec. 28, 1985 (dec. May 1993); m. Gladys Cohen, June, 1998. BSEE, Va. Poly. Inst., 1943. Registered profl. engr., NY, Pa., Va. Aero. rsch. scientist Nat. Adv. Com. for Aeros., Langley AFB, Va., 1946-50; pres. Aaron Investors, Inc., 1948-98, Pres., 2000—; elec. engr. Signal Corps Supply Agy., Phila., 1950-53; propr. Bertram D. Aaron and Co., LA, 1953-58, pres. Plainview, N.Y., 1958-91, Aaron Tech. Cons., Williamsburg, Va., 1990—. Pres. Microwave Instrumentation Labs., 1959-80, AWS Visucal Aids Inc., 1960-64, HAL Antenna Products, Inc., Aaron Tech. Market, Inc., 1991-2004 Author: Hydrogen Thyratron Circuitry Considerations, 1953, Surveillance Under Low Light Level Conditions, 1971; editor Procs. Integration Com. on Hydrogen Thyratrons, 1951-53; patentee antenna. Dir. devel. Va. Breast Cancer Found., 1993, organizer, chmn. symposium Primary Care Perspectives, 1995; founder, chmn. Williamsburg Va. Symphony Soc., 1998-2003; bd. dirs. Va. Symphony, 1998—; mem. Williamsburg Area Arts Commn., 2002; chmn. Williamsburg Area Arts Com., 2001-05; bd. dirs. Williamsburg Area Performing Arts Ctr., 2002—05. Capt. Signal Corps, U.S. Army, 1943-46. Mem. IEEE (sr.), Electronic Reps. Assn. (past pres. NY chpt., chmn. bd., nat. del. N.Y. chpt.), Assn. Old Crows (pres. Tidewater Va. chpt. 1993-95), Kiwanis (bd. dirs. 1998-2000, organizer Williamsburg Colonial Polo Cup). Jewish. Home and Office: Aaron Tech Cons Inc 212 Burtcher Ct Williamsburg VA 23185-8905

AARON, DAVID L., diplomat, author; b. Chgo., Aug. 21, 1938; m. Chloe W. Aaron; 1 child. BA, Occidental Coll., PhD (hon.); MA, Princeton U. With Fgn. Svc., 1962—, polit. and econ. officer Guayaquil, Ecuador; internat. rels. officer Dept. of State, 1964-66; polit. officer NATO, Paris, 1966; with Arms Control and Disarmament Agy.; sr. staff mem. Nat. Security Coun., 1972-74; legis. asst. Senator Walter F. Mondale, Minn., 1974-75; task force leader select com. intelligence U.S. Senate, 1975-76; dep. asst. to pres. for nat. security, 1977-81; v.p. Oppenheimer and Co., Inc., 1981-85; writer, lectr. Lantz-Harris Agy., 1985-93. Sr. advisor Mondale Presdl. Campaign, 1984; cons. 20th Century Fund, 1990-92, sr. fellow, 1992-93; bd. dirs. quest value dual purpose fund Oppenheimer Capital Corp.; amb., U.S. rep. Orgn. Econ. Cooperation and Devel., Paris, 1996.; presdl. spl. envoy for cryptography, 1996; undersec. internat. trade dept. Commerce, 1997-00; sr. internat. adv. Dorsey & Whitney, 2000-2003; sr. fellow, dir. Ctr. for Middle East Pub. Policy, RAND, 2003—. Author: State Scarlet, Agent of Influence, Crossing By Night; contbr. articles to profl. jours. Staff mem. Carter-Mondale Presdl. Campaign; bd. dirs. Atlantic Coun. Decorated Nat. Def. medal. Mem. Nat. Dem. Inst. Internat. Affairs (bd. dirs.), Coun. Fgn. Rels., Internat. League Human Rights (bd. dirs.), Authors Guild, Pacific Coun. on Internat. Policy. Office: RAND Corp 1776 Main St Santa Monica CA 90407-2138 Office Phone: 310-393-0411. E-mail: daaron@rand.org.

AARON, HANK (HENRY L. AARON), professional baseball team executive; b. Mobile, Ala., Feb. 5, 1934; s. Herbert and Estella A. Aaron; m. Billye Suber Aaron, Nov. 1973; 1 child, Ceci; children: Gail, Hank, Lary, Gary(dec.). Student pub. schs. Former semi-pro baseball player; baseball player Milw. Braves (became Atlanta Braves 1966), 1954—76; v.p. player devel. Atlanta Braves, 1976—89, sr. v.p., asst. to pres., 1989—, also bd. dirs.; owner Hank Aaron Automotive Group, 1999—. Mem. Nat. League All-Star Team, 1955—74, Am. League All-Star Team, 1975, World Series Championship Team, 1957; broke Babe Ruth's career home run record with 715th home run, April 8, 1974; holder major league record for most home runs (755), most runs batted in (2297). Author: (autobiography) I Had A Hammer: The Hank Aaron Story, 1991. Pres. No Greater Love, 1974; nat. chmn. Friends of Fisk for Athletics; organizer Hank Aaron Scholarship Fund; sponsor Hank Aaron Celebrity Bowling Tournament for Sickle Cell Anemia, 1972; mem. exec. bd. PUSH; mem. nat. bd. Big Bros./Big Sisters Am., NAACP; state chmn. Wis. Easter Seal Soc., 1975; nat. sports chmn. Nat. Easter Seal Soc., 1974; mem. Atlanta bd. Am. Cancer Soc. Named Most Valuable Player, Nat. League, 1957, Player of Yr., Sporting News, 1956, 1963, MLB All-Century Team, 1999; named to Baseball Hall of Fame, 1982; recipient Nat. League Gold Glove Award, 1958—60. Office: Atlanta Braves PO Box 4064 Atlanta GA 30302-4064

AARON, HENRY JACOB J., economics professor; b. Chgo., June 16, 1936; s. David and Betty (Cooper) A.; m. Ruth Kotell, May 5, 1963; children: Jeffrey, Melissa. AB, UCLA, 1958; MA, Harvard U., 1960, PhD, 1963. Assoc. prof. econs. U. Md., 1967-75, prof., 1975-77, 79-89; sr. fellow Brookings Instn., 1968-78, 96—, 1996—, dir. econ. studies, 1990-96; asst. sec. planning and evaluation HEW, Washington, 1977-78. Sr. staff economist Pres.'s Coun. Econ. Advisers, 1966-67; mem. Gov. Md. Coun. Econ. Advisers, 1968-75; vis. prof. econs. Harvard U., 1974; mem. bd. dirs. Abt Assocs., 1979—, Ctr. on Budget and Policy Priorities, 1994—; chmn. Adv. Coun. on Social Security, 1978-79; trustee Tchrs. Ins. and Annuity Assn., 1984-87; trustee Georgetown U., 1995-97, bd. dirs.; mem. vis. com. dept. econs. Harvard U., 1985-89; mem. Inst. Medicine, 1986—, mem. com. on econ. future of baseball, 1990-92; rsch. adv. coun. Joint Ctr. Polit. Studies, 1984-89; v.p. Nat. Acad. Social Ins., 1986-96, chmn. bd. dirs., 1998—; rsch. adv. bd. Com. Econ. Devel., 1988-92; mem. adv. com. Stanford Inst. Econ. Policy Rsch. Stanford U., 1991—; mem. vis. com. Harvard Med. and Dental Schs., 2006-. Author: Who Pays the Property Tax?, 1974, Politics and the Professors, 1978, Serious and Unstable Condition: Financing America's Health Care; co-author: The Peculiar Problem of Taxing Life Insurance Companies, 1983, The Economic Effects of Social Security, 1984, The Painful Prescription: Rationing Hospital Care, 1984, Assessing Tax Reform, 1985, Can America Afford To Grow Old?, 1988, (with Robert Reischauer) Countdown to Reform: The Great Social Security Debate; editor: Setting National Priorities: Policies for the Nineties, 1990, Serious and Unstable Condition: Financing America's Health Care, 1991; co-editor: Setting Domestic Priorities: What Can Government Do?, 1992, Values and Public Policy, 1994. Economic Effects of Fundamental Tax Reform (edited with William Gale), 1996, (with Robert D. Reischaver) Countdown to Reform: The Great Social Security Debate, 1998, Jour. Econ. Perspectives, Jour. Pub. Econs., Jour. Health Econs.; contbr. articles to profl. jours. Mem. adv. com. Ctr. Econ. Policy Rsch., Stanford U. Ctr. for Advanced Study in the Behavioral Scis. fellow, 1996-97, Guggenheim fellow, 1996-97. Mem. Am. Econ. Assn. (exec. com. 1978-81, v.p. 1991), Am. Acad. Arts and Scis., Assn. Pub. Policy and Mgmt. (pres. 1998-99). Home: Apt #41 2101 Connecticut Ave NW Washington DC 20008 Office: 1775 Massachusetts Ave NW Washington DC 20036-2103 Office Phone: 202-797-6128. Business E-Mail: haaron@brookings.edu.

AARON, KENNETH ELLYOT, lawyer; b. Phila., Nov. 3, 1948; s. Neal L. and Dorothea G. Aaron; m. Phyllis A. Carroll, May 29, 1969; children: Seth Joel, Joshua Scott. BS in Econs., U. Pa., 1970, JD, 1973. Bar: Pa. 1973, Del. 2001, Fla. 2001, US Dist. Ct. (ea. dist.) Pa. 1973, US Dist. Ct. (we. dist.) Md. 1993, US Dist. Ct. (ea. dist.) Pa. 1993, US Dist. Ct. Del. 2001, US Dist. Ct. (so., mid. and no. dists.) Fla. 2001, US Ct. Appeals (3d cir.) 1974, US Ct. Appeals (7th cir.) 1995, US Ct. Appeals (6th cir.) 2000, US Supreme Ct. 1977; cert. bus. bankruptcy law specialist Am. Bankruptcy Bd. Cert. Assoc. Astor & Weiss, Phila., 1973-76; ptnr. Casper & Davidson, P.C., Phila., 1976-80; pvt. practice Phila., 1980-83; ptnr. Garfinkel & Volpicelli, Phila., 1983-86, Mesirov, Gelman, Jaffe, Cramer & Jamieson, Phila., 1986-91, Buchanan Ingersoll P.C., Phila., 1991-2001, Weir & Ptnrs., Phila., 2001—. Mem. Ea. Dist. Pa. Bankruptcy Conf., vice chmn. edn. com. 1991, co-chmn. 1992, co-chmn. legis com., 1993; trustee Phila. Bar Found., 1997-2000. Author: Foreclosure and Repossession, 1989; contbr. chpts. to books Commr. Haverford (Pa.) Twp. Planning Bd., 1978—80; chmn. Lower Merion Zoning Bd., 1993—; planning commr. Lower Merion Twp. Planning Bd., Ardmore, Pa., 1992. Recipient Tax Writing award Nat. Assn. Accts., 1970, Am. Jr. award in Creditors' Rights, 1973. Mem.: Phila. Bar Found. (trustee 1997—2000), Phila. Bar Assn. (chmn. commn. on insolvency issues in real estate 1989—), Hias & Coun. (v.p. 1999—2002), Rotary (pres. Haverford Twp. 1982—83). Avocations: sports, camping, golf. Office: Weir & Ptnrs 1339 Chestnut St Ste 500 Philadelphia PA 19107 Office Phone: 215-665-8181. Business E-Mail: kaaron@weirpartners.com.

AARON, LARRY GENE, secondary school educator, writer, minister; b. Danville, Va., Oct. 10, 1945; s. Conley Lee and Virginia Evelyn Aaron; m. Bonita Louise Becker (div.); m. Nancy Cody Ikenberry, June 3, 1989; children: Lori Cramton, Christie Wright, John. B in Biology, Va. Tech., 1968; B in Religious Edn., Midwestern Bapt. Coll., 1974; MDiv, Liberty Bapt. Theol. Sem., 1986; D in Ministry, Luther Rice Sem., 1999. Assoc. pastor, interim Christian Heritage Ch., Danville, 1993—94; tchr., chair dept. sci. Chatham HS, Va., 1997—. Adj. faculty Nat. Coll. Bus. Tech., Danville, Va., 1996—2004; instr. Piedmont Regional Govs. Sch., 2003—. Author: Barefoot Boy: An Anthology of Blue Ridge Poems 2d edit., 2006, The Race to the Dan, 2007; co-author (with Capt. John Kepchar): Keppy's War, 2005. Named State Tchr. of Yr., Aerospace Edn. Found. Va., 2004, Chatham H.S., 2004—05, H.S. Educator of Yr., Pittsylvania County Schs., 2004—05; recipient First pl. Feature Writing Series award, Va. Press Assn., 2000, 2002. Mem.: Va. Soc. SAR (founder, past pres. Dan River chpt., Liberty medal, Virginia medal, Meritorious Svc. medal, Bronze Citizenship medal), Va. Assn. Sci. Tchrs., Halifax County Hist. Soc., Danville Mus. Fine Arts and History, Pittsylvania County Hist. Soc. Avocations: backpacking, biking. Home: 185 Martindale Dr Danville VA 24541 Office Phone: 434-432-8305. Personal E-mail: larry.aaron@gmail.com.

AARON, M. ROBERT, electrical engineer; b. Phila., Aug. 21, 1922; s. Edward A. and Beatrice A.; m. Wilma Spiegelman, Nov. 18, 1944; children: Richard (dec.), James. BSEE, U. Pa., 1949, MSEE, 1951. Research engr. Franklin Inst. Research Labs., Phila., 1949-51; with Bell Telephone Labs. Inc., Murray Hill, NJ, 1951-89, supr., 1954-68, dept. head, 1968-89; ret., 1989; cons., 1989—. Lectr., tchr. in field. Mem. adv. com. Whippany (N.J.) Sch. Bd., 1950's. Guest editor for tech. jours., 1971-99; contbr. articles to profl. jours., poems to various jours.; patentee in field. Tutor NAACP Program, Red Bank, N.J., 1966-68. Served to lt. (j.g.) USCG, 1942-45. Co-recipient computers and communications prize Found. for Computers and Communications Promotion, 1988. Fellow IEEE (mem. fin. bd. 1976-77, awards bd. 1987-89, 93, co-recipient Alexander Graham Bell medal 1978, Centennial medal 1984, Millenium medal 2000), Internat. Engrng. Consortium; mem. Nat. Acad. Engrng., IEEE Circuits and Systems Soc. (assoc. editor 1969-71, pres. 1973), IEEE Comm. Soc. (chmn. awards bd. 1975-79, 80-84, bd. govs. 1986-89, Meritorious Svc. award 1985, fellow evaluation 1992-96, disting. lectr. 1995, lifetime svc. award 1997, Christopher Columbus internat. telecomms. award 1999), Student Soc. for Stem Cell Rsch. (mem. adv. bd. 2004—, internet libr. named Robert Aaron Libr.), Internat. Myeloma Found. Home and Office: 2427 Presidential Way Apt 901 West Palm Beach FL 33401-1359 E-mail: b.aaron@ieee.org.

AARON, MERIK ROY, financial executive, lawyer, judge, educator; b. NYC, May 22, 1947; s. Harry and Gertrude S. (Scherl) A.; m. Karen M. Snyder, 1984; children: Stacey Lynn, Lauren Jill. BA, L.I. U., 1969, MA, 1971; profl. diploma, Hofstra U., 1975; EdD, Nova Southeastern U., 1982; JD, Touro Coll., 1991. Bar: N.J. 1992, U.S. Dist. Ct. N.J. 1992, Conn. 1992, U.S. Dist. Ct. (so. and ea. dists.) N.Y. 1992, D.C. 1993, Minn. 1993, N.Y. 1994, U.S. Ct. Appeals (fed. cir.) 1995, U.S. Ct. Appeals Armed Forces 1995, U.S. Ct. Fed. Claims 1995, U.S. Supreme Ct. 1995. Dist. sci. supr. Carle Place Pub. Schs., NY, 1969-80; dist. dir. sci. Lawrence Pub. Schs., NY, 1980-84; dir. curriculum, asst. prin. Bellmore-Merrick Ctrl. HS dist., NY, 1984—91; law clk. Liotti & Skelos, Garden City, NY, 1991—92; gen. counsel Cliff Data Sys., Lyndhurst, NJ, 1992-94; prin. dep. town atty. Town of Hempstead, NY, 1994—2006, 2007—; judge family ct. County Nassau, Westbury, NY, 2006—07. Pres. Mervic Enterprises, Smithtown, N.Y., 1980—; adj. prof. Nassau C.C., 1975—, Syracuse U., 1974-80; bd. dirs. Joseph C. Zoller meml. scholarship fund Fordham U., 2007—. Trustee Carle Place Bd. Edn., 1981—86; exec. bd. Five Towns Cmty. Coun., Woodmere, NY, 1998—99; commr. Storm Water Drainage Com., Inc., Village of Hewlett Harbor, NY, 2003—04; village atty. Village of Hewlett Harbor, 2004—06, 2007—; Rep. candidate NY State Assembly, 20th Assembly Dist., 1996, Nassau County Legislature, 7th Legis. Dist., 2001; exec. leader North Woodmere Rep. Com., 1999—2006; bd. dirs. Joseph C. Zollor Meml. Scholarship Fund, Fordham U., 2007—. Recipient Outstanding Contbrns. to Edn. award, Nassau County, 1981, Outstanding Sci. Supr. award, State of N.Y., 1986, Nation's Outstanding Sci. Supr. award, 1991, Profl. Excellence award Nassau C.C., 2000. Mem.: ABA, Woodmere Mchts. Assn. (v.p. 2000—), Nassau Lawyers Assn. LI (pres. 2004—05, chmn. bd. 2007—), NY State Bar Assn., Bar Assn. Nassau County (chmn. fee conciliation com. 2000—02, grievance com. 2002—06, 2007—), Am. Assn. Sex Educators, Counselors and Therapists (cert.), Nassau County Sci. Suprs. Assn. (pres. 1979), NY State Sci. Suprs. Assn. (pres. 1982—83), Nat. Sci. Suprs. Assn. (exec. bd. 1983—88, pres. 1986—87), Nat. Sci. Tchrs. Assn. (exec. bd. 1986), NY Acad. Scis. (life), LI U./C.W. Post Campus Alumni Assn. (bd. dirs. 1997—99), North Woodmere Rep. Club (pres. 1992—99), Civic Club, Shriners, Masons, Kiwanis (life; pres. Westbury, NY club 1982—83, pres. Five Towns NY Club 1998—99), Phi Delta Kappa (exec. bd. 1988). Office: Town of Hempstead 1 Washington St Hempstead NY 11550 Office Phone: 516-489-5000 3176. Personal E-mail: eddjd@aol.com.

AARON, ROGER S., lawyer; b. Cleve., 1942; AB magna cum laude, Dartmouth Coll., 1964; MBA with high distinction, Dartmouth Coll., Amos Tuck School of Business Adminstrn., 1965; LLB, JD, Yale U., 1968. Bar: NY 1969. Sr. ptnr. for corporate Skadden, Arps, Slate, Meagher & Flom,

NYC, serves on Policy Com. Lectr. in field. Mem.: ABA. Office: Skadden Arps Slate Meagher Flom 4 Times Sq New York NY 10036-6522 Office Phone: 212-735-3300. Office Fax: 917-777-3300. Business E-Mail: raaron@skadden.com.

AARON, STEWART D., lawyer; b. 1958; m. Christine Aaron; children: Harrison, Caroline, Elizabeth. BS, Cornell Univ., 1980; JD summa cum laude, Syracuse Univ., 1983. Bar: NY 1984, US Supreme Ct. 1988. Ptnr., securities enforcement, litig. Arnold & Porter LLP, NYC, 2005—. Notes and comments editor Syracuse Law Rev., 1982—83. Named one of NY Super Lawyers Bus. Litigation, 2006. Fellow: NY Bar Found.; mem.: Assn. of Bar of City of NY, NY County Lawyers Assn., NY State Bar Assn., Order of Coif. Office: Arnold & Porter LLP 399 Park Ave New York NY 10022-4690 Office Phone: 212-715-1114. Office Fax: 212-715-1399. Business E-Mail: Stewart.Aaron@aporter.com.

AARONS, STEPHEN D., lawyer; b. St. Louis, Nov. 23, 1954; s. Donald E. and Teddye W. Costello; m. Doris A. Valdez, Apr. 12, 1993; 1 child, Ian. BA, George Washington U., 1976; JD, St. Louis U., 1979; student, Oxford U., Eng., 1984. Bar: Mo. 1980, N.Mex. 1985, US Dist. Ct. (we. dist.) Mo. 1980, US Dist. Ct. N.Mex. 1985, US Dist. Ct. Mont. 1996, US Dist. Ct. (ea. dist.) Mich. 1997, US Ct. Appeals (10th cir.) 1985, US Ct. Appeals (5th cir.) 1992, US Mil. Ct. 1981, US Supreme Ct. 1983. VISTA lawyer Mont. Legal Svcs., Gt. Falls, 1979-80; judge advocate U.S. Army Intelligence Command, Augsburg, Germany, 1980-83; chief capital trial def. counsel N.Mex. Pub. Defender Dept., Santa Fe, 1984-89; assoc. Jones, Snead, Wertheim, Santa Fe, 1989-92; mng. atty. Aarons Law Firm, PC, Santa Fe, 1992—. Mem. faculty Nat. Inst. Trial Advocacy. Nat. pres. Coll. Dems. of Am., Washington, 1975-77. Lt. col. USAR, 1980—. Office: Aarons Law Firm PC 300 Catron St Santa Fe NM 87501-1807 Office Phone: 505-984-1100. E-mail: aar095@yahoo.com.

AARONSON, DAVID ERNEST, lawyer, educator; b. Washington, Sept. 19, 1940; s. Edward Allan and May (Rosett) A.; m. Laura Dine, 1991; stepchildren: Dara Prushansky, Jared Prushansky. BA in Econs, George Washington U., 1961, MA, 1964, PhD, 1970; LL.B., Harvard U., 1964; LL.M. (E. Barrett Prettyman fellow), Georgetown U., 1965. Bar: D.C. bar 1965, Md. bar 1975, U.S. Supreme Ct. bar 1969. Research asst. Office of Commr., Bur. Labor Stats., U.S. Dept. Labor, Washington, 1961; staff atty. legal intern program Georgetown Grad. Law Ctr., Washington, 1964-65; rsch. assoc. patent rsch. project dept. econ. George Washington U., Washington, 1966; assoc. firm Aaronson and Aaronson, Washington, 1965-67, ptnr., 1967-70; prof., B.J. Tennery Scholar Am. U. Law Sch., Washington, 1970—; prof. Sch. Justice, Coll. Pub. and Internat. Affairs, 1981-92; dep. dir. Law and Policy Inst., Jerusalem, summer, 1978. Interim dir. clin. programs Md. Criminal Justice Clinic, 1971-73, founder prosecutor criminal litigation clinic, 1972, co-dir. trial advocacy program, 1982-2004, dir. trial advocacy program, 2004—; vis. prof. Law Sch. of Hebrew U., Jerusalem, 1978; trustee Montgomery-Prince George's Continuing Legal Edn. Inst., 1983-1997. Author: Maryland Criminal Jury Instructions and Commentary, 1975, (with N.N. Kittrie and D. Saari) Alternatives to Conventional Criminal Adjudication: Guidebook for Planners and Practitioners, 1977, (with B. Hoff, P. Jaszi, N.N. Kittrie and D. Saari) The New Justice: Alternatives to Conventional Criminal Adjudication, 1977, (with C.T. Dienes and M.C. Musheno) Decriminalization of Public Drunkenness: Tracing the Implementation of a Public Policy, 1981, Public Policy and Police Discretion: Processes of Decriminalization, 1984, (with R. Simon) The Insanity Defense: A Critical Assessment of Law and Policy in the Post-Hinckley Era, 1988, Maryland Criminal Jury Instructions and Commentary, 2d rev. edit., 1988; contbr. articles to profl. jours. Mem. Friendship Heights Village Coun., 1979. Recipient Outstanding Cmty. Svc. award, 1980; Outstanding Tchr. award Am. U. Law Sch., 1978, 81, Scholar/Tchr. of Yr. award Am. U., 1989; Pauline Ruyle Moore scholar in Pub. Law, 1983; B.J. Tennery scholar, 1990—. Mem. ABA (criminal justice sect. rules of ct. prof. and evid. com. 1991—), D.C. Bar Assn. (chmn. criminal code rev. com. 1971-73), Md. State Bar Assn. (criminal law sect. coun. 1984—, chmn. 1989-90, Robert C. Heeney award 1999), Assn. Am. Law Schs. (elected to sect. coun., criminal justice sect. 1999—), Montgomery County (Md.) Bar Assn., Am. Law Inst., Phi Beta Kappa. Office: Am U Law Sch 4801 Massachusetts Ave NW Washington DC 20016-8196 Office Phone: 202-274-4201. E-mail: daarons@wcl.american.edu.

AARONSON, ROBERT JAY, air transportation executive; b. Temple, Tex., June 8, 1942; s. Leonard and Ruth (Lader) A.; m. Louise Elaine Loia, June 6, 1967; children: Steven Bradford, Suzanne Denise. AB, Brown U., 1964; M in Govtl. Adminstrn., Wharton Sch., U. Pa., 1965. Spl. asst. Southeastern Pa. Transp. Authority, Phila., 1965-67; transp. rep. Urban Mass Transp. Adminstrn., Washington, 1967-69; transp. adviser HUD, 1969-71; aviation adminstr. Md. Dept. Transp., Balt., 1972-78; asso. adminstr. for airports FAA, Washington, 1978-81; dir. aviation Port Authority of N.Y. and N.J., NYC, 1981-89; pres. Air Transport Assn. Am., Washington, 1989-92; exec. v.p. Lockheed Air Terminal, Inc., Burbank, Calif., 1993-94, Airport Group Internat., Inc., Glendale, Calif., 1995-97; pres. Strategies For Airports, Inc., Encino, Calif., 1997-98; exec. v.p. Lufthansa Cons. GmbH, Encino, Calif., 1999—2002; dir. gen. Airports Coun. Internat., Geneva, 2002—. Lectr. Royal Aero. Transport Course, Oxford U. Samuel S. Fels fellow, 1964-65 Mem. Nat. Assn. State Aviation Ofcls. (pres. 1978), Airport Operators Coun. Internat. (chmn. 1987-88), Am. Assn. Airport Execs., Wings Club (pres. 1992). Office: Geneva Airport PO Box 4 1215 Geneva 15 Switzerland Office Phone: 41 22 717 8585. Business E-Mail: raaronson@aci.aero.

AARSLEFF, HANS, linguistics educator; b. Rungsted Kyst, Denmark, July 19, 1925; came to U.S., 1948, naturalized, 1964; s. Einar Faber and Inger (Lotz) A. BA, U. Copenhagen, 1945; PhD, U. Minn., 1960. Instr. English U. Minn., 1952-56; instr. Princeton U., 1956-60, asst. prof., 1960-65, assoc. prof., 1965-72, prof., 1972-97. Author: The Study of Language in England 1780-1860, 1967, From Locke to Saussure: Essays on the Study of Language and Intellectual History, 1982, Introduction to Wilhelm von Humboldt, On Language, 1988, Philosophy of Language, in Cambridge History of Eighteenth-Century Philosophy, 2006; editor, translator: Condillac, Essay on the Origin of Human Knowledge, 2001;; assoc. editor: The Historiography of Linguistics, bd. editors: Jour. History Ideas, 1979—; contbr. articles to jours. and books. Jr. fellow Council of Humanities Princeton U., fall 1962; fellow Am. Council Learned Socs., 1964-65, 72-73, NEH, 1975-76 Fellow Am. Acad. Arts and Scis.; mem. Am. Philos. Soc., Royal Danish Acad. Scis. and Letters (fgn.). Office: Princeton U Dept English Princeton NJ 08544-0001

ABAKANOWICZ, MAGDALENA, artist, sculptor; b. Falenty, Poland, June 20, 1930; d. Konstanty and Helena (Domaszowska) A.; m. Jan Kosmowski, Sept. 22, 1956 Grad., Warsaw Acad. Fine Arts, 1954; D (hon.), Royal Coll. Art, London, 1974, RI Sch. Design, 1992, Acad. Fine Arts, Lódz, Poland, 1998, Pratt Inst., 2000, Mass. Coll. Art, 2001; DHC (hon.), Sch. of the Art Inst. Chgo., 2002; Dr. (hon.), Acad. Fine Arts, Poznan, Poland, 2002. Prof. Acad. Fine Art, Poznan, Poland, 1965, 1979. Prin. works include monumental space forms of woven fibres , circles of figurative sculptures of burlap, wood, metals, stone and clay drawings, paintings , exhibited in group shows at Internat. Biennale de Tapisserie, Lausanne, 1962—79 , Biennale of Art, São Paulo, 1965 , Venice Biennale, 1968 , Biennale of Art, São Paulo, 1979 , Venice Biennale, 1980 , ROSC, Dublin, 1980 , Nat. Gallery, Berlin, 1983 , ARS '83, Helsinki, 1983 , Mus. Moderner Kunst Vienne, 1984 , Nürnberg Triennale of Drawing, 1985 , Sydney Biennale of Art, 1986 , Mus. Modern Art, NYC, 1987 , County Mus., 1987 , Hirshorn Mus., Washington, 1988 , Olympic Pk., Seoul, 1988 , Mus. Nacional Belas Artes, Rio de Janeiro, 1992 , Fuji San Kei Biennial, Japan, 1993 , Europa-Europa, Bonn, Germany, 1994 , Muzeum Narodove, Warsaw, 1994 , Centro Galego de Arte Conteporanea Santiago de Compostela, 1994 , Royal Festival Hall, London, 1995 , Mus. Ludwig, Cologne, Germany, 1995 , Les Champs Elysees, Paris, 1996 , The Nasher Collection, Guggenheim Mus., NYC, 1997 , Guggenheim Mus., Bilbao, Spain, 1997—98 , Mus. D'Art Moderne Ville de Paris, 1997 , Arco, Madrid, 1998 , Mus. Würth Künzelsau, Germany, 2000 , Nat. Gallery Jeu de Paume, Paris, 2000 , Mus. Würth, Germany, 2000 , Open 2002, Venice, 2002 , one-woman shows include Museo Reina Sofia, Madrid, 2004 , Three Rivers Art Festival, 2001 , exhibited in group shows at Les Jardins Du Palais Royal, Paris, 2000 , Europalia, 201, Musee D'Art Moderne, France, 2001 , Den Haag Sculpture, Haque, Holland, 2001 , Maque, Holland, 2001 , La Parade des Animaux, Monte Carlo, Monaco, 2002 , Open 2002, Lido, Italy , Museo Nacional Centro de Arte Reina Sofia, Madrid, 2004 , one-woman shows include Kunsthaus Zurich, 1968 , Nationalmuseum Stockholm, 1970 , Pasadena Art Mus., Calif., 1971 , Art Mus., 1971 , Dusseldorf Kunsthalle, 1972 , Whitechapel Art Gallery, London, 1975 , Nat. Gallery of Victoria, Melbourne, 1976 , Muzeum Sztuki, Lodz, Poland, 1978 , Mus. d'Art Moderne de la Ville de Paris, 1982 , Mus. Contemporary Art, Chgo., 1982 , Mus. d'Art Contemporain, Montreal, 1983 , Portland Art Mus., Oreg., 1984 , Dallas Mus. Fine Arts, 1984 , Xavier Fourcade Gallery, NYC, 1985 , Turske & Turske Gallery, Zürich , Mücsarnok Palace, Budapest, Hungary, 1988 , Städel Kunstinstitut, Frankfurt, 1989 , Marlborough Gallery, NYC, 1989 , Sezon Mus., Tokyo, 1991 , Mus.Modern Art, Shiga, 1991 , Art Tower, Mito, 1991 , Hiroshima Art Mus., 1991 , Walker Art Ctr., Mpls., 1992 , Inst. Contemporary Art P.S. 1 Mus., NY, 1993 , BWH Kraków, 1993 , Hiroshima City Mus. Contemporary Art, 1993 , Kordegarda, Warsaw, 1994 , Marlborough Gallery, Madrid, 1994 , Fundacio Miro a Mallorca, 1994 , Ctr. Polish Sculpture, Oronsko, 1995 , Yorkshire Sculpture Park, 1995 , Manchester City Art Galleries, 1995 , Ujazdowski Castle, Warsaw, 1995 , Galerie Marwan Hoss, Paris, 1996 , Charlottenborg Exhbn. Hall, Copenhagen, 1996 , Oriel Mostyn, Wales, 1996 , Marlborough Gallery, NYC, 1997 , Doris Freedman Plz., NY , Galerie Marvan Moss, Paris, 1997 , Gallery Starmach, Krakow, 1998 , Muzeum Sztuki, Lodz, Poland, 1994 , Met. Mus. Art, NYC, 1999 , Jardins du Palais Royal, Paris, 1999 , Marlborough Gallery, NY, 2000 , NYC, 2000 , Pillsbury and Peters Fine Art, Dallas, 2001 , Grant Selwyn Fine Arts, LA, 2001 , Gerald Peters Gallery, Santa Fe, N.Mex., 2001 , Muzeum Narodowe (Nat. Mus.), Poznan, Poland, 2002 , Mart, Museo di Arte Moderna e Contemporaranem, Trento, Rovereto, Italy, 2003 , Beck & Eggeling, Inst. Fine Art, Dusseldorf, Germany, 2003 , Mus. Beelden Aan Zee, Germany, Holland, 2003 , Marlborough Fine Art, London, Eng., 2003 , Marlborough Gallery, NY, 2003 , Mus. of Art, Lucerne, Switzerland, 2003 , Savannah Mus. of Art and Designe, Georgia, 2004 , Schleswig Holstein Mus., Schloss-Gottorf, Germany, 2004 , Represented in permanent collections Galerie Saint Severin, Paris , Muzeum Sztuki, Lodz , Mus. Modern Art, N.Y.C. , Kyoto, Japan , Stedelijk Mus., Amsterdam , Australian Nat. Collection, Canberra , Ctr. Georges Pompidou, Paris , Mus. Contemprary Art, Chgo. , Nat. Mus., Stockholm , Met. Mus., NYC , LA County Mus. , Israel Mus., Jerusalem , Mus. Moderner Kunst, Vienna , Spazzi d'Arte, Italy , Va. Mus. Fine Art, Richmond , W. Lehmbruck Mus., Duisburg , Storm King Art Ctr., N.Y. , Mus. Ludwig, Cologne , Hess Collection, Napa, Calif. , Nasher Collection, Tex. , Mus. Nacional Centro Arte Reina Sofia, Madrid , Mus. D'Art Moderne Ville Paris, Paris , Nelson-Atkins Mus. Art, Mo. , Nat. Gallery Art, Washington , exhibitions include Open, exhi. of Sculptures and Installation, Venice and Lido, Italy, 2002. Mem. Presdl. Coun. for Culture, 1992—. Decorated officier, comdr. Order Arts and Letters (France), comdr. cross with star Order Polonia Restituta, cavaliere Order of Merit of Republic of Italy; recipient prize 1st class Min. of Culture, Poland, 1965, Gold medal VIII Biennale of Art, Sao Paulo, 1965, Polish State prize Stiftung F.V.S. Hamburg, Vienna, 1979, Alfred Jurzykowski prize, 1982, award for distinction in sculpture, NY, 1993, Leonardo da Vinci World award of Arts, 1997, award for the entire Creative Culture, 2005. Mem. Am. Acad. Arts and Letters (hon.), Polish Assn. Authors., Akademie der Kunste (hon.), Sachsische Akademie der Kunste, Dresden, Germany (hon.), Orden Pour le merite fur Wissenschaften und Kunste, Berlin. Address: Bzowa 1 02-708 Warsaw Poland E-mail: magdalena@abakanowicz.art.pl.

ABATE, ANNE KATHERINE, librarian, consultant, educator; b. Cleve., Mar. 10, 1958; d. Frank M. and Cecelia (Homic) Abate; m. George S. Maley, May 17, 1980. HAB with honors, Xavier U., Cin., 1980; MSLS, U. Ky., 1986; PhD, Nova Southeastern U., Ft. Lauderdale, Fla., 1998. Asst. dept. head Kenton County Pub. Libr., Covington, Ky., 1985-87; asst. dir. Lloyd Libr. and Mus., Cin., 1987-88; libr. Dinsmore & Shohl, 1988-99; asst. prof. Xavier U., 1999—2000; mktg. dir. GovConnect, 2000—04; exec. dir. Greater Cin. Libr. Consortium, SWON Libraries, 2004—. Part time faculty Xavier U., Cin., 1997—, U. Ky., 1998—; mem. adj. faculty Nova Southeastern U., Ft. Lauderdale, Fla., 1999—; mem. adv. bd. West Pub. Corp., Eagan, Minn., 1992-95. Contbr. articles to profl. jours.; cons./author video package: Managing Emerging Technologies, 1994. Mem. Spl. Librs. Assn. (bd. dirs. 1997-99, chpt. pres. 1992-93, chair pub. rels. com. 1993-95), Am. Libr. Assn., Beta Phi Mu. Roman Catholic. Avocations: reading, cooking, world travel. Office: SWON Libraries 10815 Indeco Dr Ste 200 Cincinnati OH 45241 Office Phone: 513-751-4422. Business E-Mail: anne@swonlibraries.org.

ABATE, CATHERINE M., retired state legislator; b. Margate, NJ, Dec. 8, 1947; d. Joseph and Carolyn (Fiore) A.; m. Ronald E. Kliegerman, Oct. 28, 1978; 1 child, Kyle. BA, Vassar Coll., 1969; JD, Boston U., 1972. Bar: N.Y. 1973, U.S. Dist. Ct. (so. dist.) N.Y. 1976. Staff atty. Legal Aid Soc., NYC, 1972-74, 75-78, supervising atty., 1979-81, dir. tng., 1981-85, acting chairperson Gov.'s Taskforce Criminal Justice, 1983; chairperson NY State Platform Criminal Justice, 1984, NY Crime Victims Bd., 1988-90; exec. dep. commr. NY State Div. Human Rights, 1986-88; commr. NYC Dept. Probation, 1990-92, NYC Dept. Correction, 1992-94; mem. NY State Senate, Albany, 1995-98; pres., CEO Cmty. Healthcare Network, 1999—. Dist. leader Dem. Party, 1981-86; 1st vice chmn. county com. Dem. Party, N.Y. County; bd. dirs. Village Nursing Home, 1987-99; bd. mem. Naral, 1999—, Correctional Assn., 1999—, Eleanor Roosevelt Legacy Com., 2003, Citizen Action, 2001—; chair 2001—; pres. bd. Family Planning Advs., 2004—. Mem. Bar Assn. City N.Y. (criminal cts. com. 1982-86), Nat. Assn. Crime Victims Compensation Bd. (bd. dirs. 1989-90), Nat. Orgn. Italian-Am. Women (bd. dirs. 1986-2003, chief judge's CPL com., 1999—, prisoner legal svcs. com., 1999—). Roman Catholic. Avocation: tennis. Home: 303 Mercer St New York NY 10003-6706 Office Phone: 212-366-4500 ext. 262. Business E-Mail: cabate@chnnyc.org.

ABATE, JOHN E., electrical engineer, consultant; b. Paterson, NJ, July 25, 1931; s. Joseph and Lucy Abate; m. Mary Ann Parrillo, July 9, 1955; children: John F., Robert J., Mark J., Holly A. BSEE, NCE, 1954; MSEE, Stevens Inst. Tech., 1960; ScD in Elec. Engring., N.J. Inst. Tech., 1967. Registered profl. engr., N.J. Astronautic engr. Kearfott Inc., Little Falls, NJ, 1956—63; tech. mgr., mem. tech. staff Bell Labs., Holmdel, NJ, 1963—98; comm. cons. AT&T Labs., Holmdel, 1998—2001. Chmn. synchronization stds. group Am. Nat. Stds. Inst. T1X1.3, 1983-86; mem. U.S. Nat. Bur. Stds. Panel for Basic Stds., 1986-89; expert in field of comm. network synchronization. Contbr. over 20 articles to profl. jours., conf. procs. and mags. Cubmaster Cub Scouts, Holmdel, 1968-70; chmn. ch. coms., Holmdel, 1968-70. 1st lt. USAF, 1954-56. Bell Labs. fellow, 1991, AT&T fellow, 1996; named to Alumni Honor Roll, N.J. Inst. Tech. Alumni Assn., Newark, 1992, Disting. Alumni, NCE, Newark, 1964; recipient commendation Nat. Security Agy., Washington, 1956. Mem. IEEE (sr., life). Roman Catholic. Achievements include invention of adaptive delta modulator used in NASA space shuttle communications system, Bell Labs fellow in 1991 for fundamental contributions national and international in area digital synchonization planning for public and private communication networks and AT&T fellow in 1996. Office: PO Box 664 Manasquan NJ 08736 Home: 2421 Riverside Terr Manasquan NJ 08736

ABATEMARCO, TRACY J., lawyer; BA summa cum laude, SUNY, Albany, 1988; JD, Georgetown U., 1991. Bar: NY 1991, Conn. 1992, US Dist. Ct. So. Dist. NY, US Dist. Ct. Ea. Dist. NY. Ptnr. Wilson, Elser, Moskowitz, Edelman & Dicker LLP, NYC. Mem.: NY State Bar Assn., Phi Beta Kappa. Office: Wilson Elser Moskowitz Edelman & Dicker LLP 23rd Fl 150 E 42nd St New York NY 10017-5639 Office Phone: 212-490-3000 ext. 2613. Office Fax: 212-490-3038. Business E-Mail: abatemarcot@wemed.com.

ABAUNZA, DONALD RICHARD, lawyer; b. New Orleans, Oct. 25, 1945; s. Alfred E. and Virginia (White) A.; m. Carolyn Thompson; 1 child, Richard. BA, Vanderbilt U., 1966; JD, Tulane U., 1969. Bar: La. 1969, U.S. Dist. Ct. (ea. dist.) La. 1969, U.S. Dist. Ct. (we. dist.) La. 1980, U.S. Supreme Ct. 1986. Ptnr. Liskow & Lewis, New Orleans, 1977—, mng. ptnr., 1996—2003. Adj. faculty Tulane Sch. Law, 1981-89. Named one of Best Lawyers in Am., 2007. Fellow Am. Coll. Trial Lawyers; mem. La. Bar Assn. (Pres.'s award 1988). Office: Liskow & Lewis 1 Shell Sq 50th Fl 701 Poydras St New Orleans LA 70139-5099 Office Phone: 504-556-4110. Business E-Mail: drabaunza@liskow.com.

ABBAS BORHAN, RICHAT, research and development company executive; arrived in US, 1989, naturalized, 1999; s. Abbas Borhan and Maria Abliz; m. Hamra Borhan Turahmat; children: Zerina Richat Borhan, Tilman Jon Borhan, Davron Richat Borhan. PhD in Pharmaceutical Sci., Ohio State U., Columbus, 1994. Rsch. asst. Coll. Pharmacy, Ohio State U., Columbus, 1990—94; pharmacokineticist Toxicology Divsn., Armstrong Lab., Wright-Patterson AFB, Dayton, Ohio, 1994—96; mgr., sr. pharmacokineticist Otsuka Am. Pharm., Inc., Rockville, Md., 1996—2000; dir., staff scientist Emisphere Techs., Inc., Tarrytown, NY, 2000—02; assoc. clin. dir., clin. pharmacologist Hoffmann-La Roche, Inc., Nutley, 2002—04; dir., lead investigator clin. pharmacology R&D Wyeth Rsch., Collegeville, 2004—. Contbr. over 90 articles to profl. jours. Recipient Sci. and Tech. Achievement award, US Dept. Defense, 1996, Sci. Achievement award, Dept. Air Force, 1996; Rsch. Assistantship scholar, Ohio State U., 1990 - 1994. Mem.: Am. Soc. Clin. Pharmacology and Therapeutics, Am. Assn. Pharm. Scientists (assoc.). Achievements include development of new drug; patents for oral insulin and oral cromolyn; research in pharmacokinetics; design clinical trials for new drug development. Home Phone: 610-631-2090; Office Phone: 484-865-8577.

ABBASSIAN, ASSAD, urologist; b. Tehran, Iran, Mar. 4, 1933; s. Ali Akbar Abbassian and Fatemeh Khanbabaee; MD, Tehran Med. Sch., Iran, 1958; MD (hon.), Minn. Sch. Medicine, Mayo Clinic, 1965. Diplomate Am. Coll. Surgeons, 1971. Surgeon urologist Harper Hosp., Detroit, 1962; cancer, pediat. urologist London Ins. Urology, London, 1964—65; surgeon gen. Oakwood Hosp., Dearborn, Mich., 1965—66; intern, resident Deaconess Hosp., Cleve., 1958—60; chief surgery Annapolis Hosp., Wayne, Mich., 1978—80, chief staff, 1981—82; staff mem. Oakwood Hosp., 1966—71; ret., 1971. Urologist Urology Ctr., Garden City, Mich., 1965—86. Contbr. articles various profl. jours.; author: The Story of New Years, 2002, The Set Up, 2007. Docent Tucson Botanical Garden, Tucson Botanical Garden Libr. Mem.: Am. Urol. Assn. (diplomate). Avocations: gardening, painting, sculpting. Home: 1920 E Pole Star Pl Oro Valley AZ 85737 Personal E-mail: abbassian20@wmconnect.com.

ABBE, ALEXANDER, lawyer; b. Bethesda, Md., Mar. 16, 1972; BA with distinction, Swarthmore Coll., 1994; JD cum laude, Univ. Pa., 1994. Bar: Calif. 1999. Assoc. Richards, Watson & Gershon, LA. Editor (exec.): Univ. Pa. Law Rev.; contbr. articles to profl. jours. Named a Rising Star, So. Calif. Super Lawyers, 2006. Mem.: LA County Bar Assn., Phi Beta Kappa. Office: Richards Watson & Gershon 40th Fl 355 S Grand Ave Los Angeles CA 90071-3101 Office Phone: 213-626-8484. Office Fax: 213-626-0078. Business E-Mail: aabbe@rwglaw.com.

ABBE, COLMAN, investment banker; b. NYC, Sept. 24, 1932; s. Leo Theodore and Beatrice (Shiff) A.; m. Nancy Adele Hyams, June 23, 1963; children: Elizabeth, Leo, Richard. BS in Acctg., Bucknell U., 1953; MBA, NYU, 1962. CPA NY. Ptnr. Belsky & Abbe CPA, NYC, 1960—70; stockbroker Loeb Rhoades, NYC, 1971—72; pres. Sagittarius Fund, NYC, 1973, OCG Tech. Inc., NYC, 1973, Profl. Mediquip Inc., Scarsdale, NY, 1974—80, Abbe & Co., Inc., 1984—; mng. dir. corp. fin. Evans & Co. Inc., NYC, 1985—87, Reich & Co., Inc., NYC, 1988—90; vice chmn., sr. mgr., dir. investment banking Laidlaw Internat. Inc., NYC, 1991—93; chmn. AB Capital Markets, NYC, 1993—94. Trustee Heart Rsch. Found., N.Y.C., 1982-92, pres., 1986; pres. Am. Friends of HAIFA Med. Ctr., 1989-93. Mem. AICPA, N.Y. State Soc. CPA Democrat. Jewish. Office: Abbe & Co Inc 26 Lawrence Rd Scarsdale NY 10583-7209 Home Phone: 914-723-3736. Personal E-mail: colman26@verizon.net.

ABBE, ELFRIEDE MARTHA, sculptor, graphics designer; b. Washington; d. Cleveland Jr. and Frieda (Dauer) A. Student, Art Inst. Chgo., 1937; B.F.A., Cornell U., 1940; postgrad., Syracuse U., 1947. Author and illustrator: books including The Plants of Virgil's Georgics, 1965; One-woman exhbns. include Carnegie-Mellon U., 1962, 69, Cornell U., 1963, Trinity Coll., Hartford, 1964, Arts Club of Washington, 1972, Cornell Club of N.Y., 1977, Copley Soc. Boston, 1978, Woods-Gerry Gallery, R.I. Sch. Design, 1983; represented in permanent collections Met. Mus. Art., Watson Library, Boston Mus. Fine Arts, Cin. Art Mus., Dumbarton Oaks, Washington, Houghton Library, Harvard U., Hunt Library, Carnegie-Mellon U., N.Y. Pub. Library, Rosenwald Collection Nat. Gallery, Kew Gardens Library, Royal Bot. Garden, Edinburgh, Nat. Library, Canberra, Australia; sculpture placed in Mann Library, Kroch Library and Morrison Hall, Cornell U., McGill U., N.Y. Bot. Gardens, Hunt Library, Pitts., Pres.'s Office, Keene (N.H.) State Coll., Herzog August Bibliothek, Wolfenbüttel, Fed. Republic Germany (bronze bust of founder), Abbe Mus., Bar Harbor, Maine (bronze bust of founder Dr. Robert Abbe). Recipient Gold medals Pen and Brush, N.Y.C., 1964, Margaret Sussman Meml. award 1987, Gold medals Nat. Arts Club, 1970, Gold medals Acad. Artists Assn., Springfield, Mass., 1976, Founders' Prize Pen and Brush, 1977; Bd. Dirs. award Salmagundi Club N.Y., 1978; Elliot Liskin award, 1979, Catherine Lorillard Wolfe Club award, 1993. Fellow Nat. Sculpture Soc. (Barrett-Colea prize 1984); mem. Nat. Soc. Mural Painters, Phi Kappa Phi.

ABBETT, ROBERT KENNEDY, artist, writer; b. Hammond, Ind., Jan. 5, 1926; s. Clarence Corodon and Vere Kennedy Abbett; m. Marilyn Kay Smith; children: Robert Smith, Linda J. BS, Prudue Univ., W. Lafayette, Ind., 1946; BA, Univ. Mo., Cloumbia, Mo., 1947. Illustrator Stevens-Gross Studio, Chgo., 1947—49, Bielefeld Studios, Chgo., 1952—53, Chaite Studios, NYC, 1953—54; freelance illustrator Darien, Conn., 1954—70; gallery painting, 1970—. Career cons., country wide, 1998—; writing freelance, 1983—; tchg. Scotdale Artists Sch., 1986—96. Represented in permanent collections Mus. of Nat History, Norman, Okla., Nat. Cowboy and Western Heritage Mus., Okla. City, Genesco County Mus. of Wildlife Art, Mumford, N.Y., Dog Mus. of Am., St. Louis, Mo., Soc. of Illustrators, N.Y.C., Nat. Bird Dog Mus., Grand Junction, Tenn., over 120 ltd. edit. prints, exhibitions include Nat. Cowboy and Western Heritage Mus., Oklahoma City, 1974—2004, Artists of Am., Denever Rotary, 1982—85, 1990—93, Soc. of Am. Impressionists, 1984, Nat. Western & Wildlife Art Collectors Annual, 1984 (Wildlife Artist of the Yr., 1984), Birds in Art, Leigh Yawkey Woodson Mus., 1984—87, The Era of the Pet, Univ. Pa.,

1984, Thomas Gilcrease Mus., Tulsa, 1984—88, 1995—96, Cheyenne Frontier Days, Old West Mus., 1985, 1990, The Dog in Art, Acad. of the Arts, Md., 1999, exhibitions include 20th annv. Sports Edge King Gallery, N.Y., 1992, sculputer bronze edit., Grey Water, sculputer brone edit., Whoa!, Dare, T.V. special, Robert K. Abbett, Conn. Profile, WVIT TV Hartford, 1987, The Fall Colors of Robert Abbett, Pub. TV, Okla. City; author: The Outdoor Paintings of Robert K. Abbett, 1976, ABBETT, Masters of the Wild Series, by Michael McIntosh, 1989, Wings from Cover, The Upland Images of Robert K. Abbett and Ed Gray, 1996, A Season for Painting, 2001; contbr. articles numerous pub. to profl. jour. Air cadet USN, 1943—45. Recipient First prize, Salmagundi Summer Exhibit, NYC, 1972, Top Ten Wildlife Artists, 100th Anniversary issue of Sport's Afield Mag., 2004, Wildlife Artists Award of Excellence, Sporting Classics Mag., 2004. Mem.: Soc. Animal Artist. Republican. Achievements include protraitures of Jimmy Stewart, Sam Walton, Margaret Meade. Avocations: photography, maintaining 56 rural acres.

ABBEY, G(EORGE) MARSHALL, lawyer, retired health facility administrator; b. Dunkirk, NY, July 24, 1933; s. Ralph Ambrose and Grace A. (Fisher) A.; m. Sue Carroll, July 13, 1974; children: Mark, Steven, Michael, Lincoln. BA with high distinction, U. Rochester, 1954; JD with distinction, Cornell U., 1957. Bar: N.H. 1957, Ill. 1965. Atty. McLane, Carleton, Graf, Greene & Brown, Manchester, N.H., 1957-65, Baxter Internat. Inc., Deerfield, Ill., 1965-69, gen. counsel, 1969-72, sec., gen. counsel, 1972-75, v.p., sec., gen. counsel, 1975-82, sr. v.p., gen. counsel, 1985-90, sr. v.p., sec., gen. counsel, 1990-93; of counsel Bell Boyd & Lloyd, Chgo., 1997—2000; pvt. practice, 1993-97, 2000—. Editor Cornell Law Rev., 1956-57. Mem. vis. com. Law Sch., U. Chgo., 1978-81; dir. Coun. Puerto Rico-U.S. Affairs, 1988-92; mem. indsl. adv. coun. U. P.R.; dir. P.R.-USA Found., 1975-93, B.U.I.L.D., Chgo., 1980-84, bus. adv. com. B.U.I.L.D. Inc.; bd. dirs. Hundred Club of Lake County, Ill., 1976-86; dir. Food and Drug Law Inst., 1975-93; bd. dirs. Evanston Inventure, 1986-88; former trustee Winnetka Congl. Ch.; dir. Nat. Com. for Quality Health Care, 1988-93; mem. Northwestern U. Corp. Coun. adv. bd., 1976-93; dir. P.R. Cmty. Found., 1986-94; bd. dirs. Better Bus. Bur. Chgo. and No. Ill., 1991-93; mem. Conf. Bd's. Coun. Chief Legal Officers and Legal Quality Coun., 1991-93. Mem. ABA, Ill. Bar Assn., Lake County Bar Assn., Chgo. Bar Assn., Health Industry Mfrs. Assn. (chmn. legal/regulatory affairs 1976-78, bd. dirs. 1978-80, chmn. govt. affairs com. 1980-81), Univ. Club, Exmoor Country Club, Bankers Club (P.R.), Order of the Coif, Phi Beta Kappa. Office: 836 Skokie Blvd Northbrook IL 60062-4001

ABBEY, GEORGE W. S., space center executive; b. Seattle, Aug. 21, 1932; children: George, Joyce, Suzanne, James, Andrew. BS in Gen. Sci., U.S. Naval Acad., 1954; MSEE, Air Force Inst. Tech., 1959. Commd. 2d lt. USAF, 1954, advanced through grades to maj., 1965; detailed to Johnson Space Ctr. (formerly Manned Spacecraft Ctr.), Houston, 1964-67, tech. asst. to mgr. Apollo Spacecraft program, 1967-69, tech. asst. to dir., 1969-76, dir. flight ops., 1976-85, dir. flight crew ops., 1985-88; dep. assoc. adminstr. for space flight NASA Hdqs., Washington, 1988-90, dep. for ops. for synthesis group, 1990-91; sr. dir. for civil space policy Nat. Space Coun., Exec. Office Pres., Washington, 1991-92; spl. asst. to adminstr. NASA, Washington, 1992-94; dep. dir. Johnson Space Ctr., 1994-95, acting dir., 1995, dir., 1996—2001. Sr. fellow James A. Baker III Inst. for Pub. Policy, Rice U., 2001—. Recipient Medal of Freedom, Pres. of U.S., 1970, Exceptional Performance award Fed. Women Program, 1973, Civil Servant of Yr. award managerial and exec. category Fed. Bus. Assn., 1974, Space Flight award Am. Astron. Soc., 1983, Al Merito Della Repulica Italiana award, 1996, Quasar award, 1997, Clear Lake Econ. Devel. Found. award for excellence, 1997, Rotary Nat. award for Space Achievement Found., 1997, NASA Disting. Svc. medal, 1973, 81, 2000; named Sr. Exec. Svc. Presdl. rank, meritorious, 1989, disting., 1994, Nassau Bay Citizen of Yr., 1999. Fellow Am. Astronautical Soc.; mem. U.S. Naval Inst. Office: Baker Inst Rice U MS 40 6100 Main St Houston TX 77005

ABBOT, WILLIAM WRIGHT, history professor; b. Louisville, Ga., May 20, 1922; s. William Wright and Lillian (Carswell) A.; m. Eleanor Pearre, Mar. 31, 1958; children— William Wright, John Pearre. Student, Davidson Coll., NC, 1939-41; AB, U. Ga., 1943; MA, Duke U., 1949, PhD, 1953; LHD, Coll. William and Mary, 1998. Tchr. Louisville Acad., 1946-47, McCallie Sch., 1951-52; from asst. prof. to prof. history Coll. William and Mary, 1953—61, 1963—66; assoc. prof. Northwestern U., 1958-59, Rice U., 1961-63; James Madison prof. history U. Va., 1966-92, emeritus, 1992—, chmn. history dept., 1972—74. Author: The Royal Governors of Georgia, 1754-1775, 1957, The Colonial Origins of the United States, 1607-1763, 1975, In Search of George Washington, 2006; editor in chief: The Papers of George Washington, 1977-92 , Colonial Series, Vols. I-X, Revolutionary War Series, Vols. I-VI, Confederation, Vols. I-VI, 1992-97, Presidential, Vols. I-V, Retirement Series, Vols. I-IV, 1998; editor Jour. So. History, 1961-63; book rev. editor William and Mary Quar., 1955-61, editor, 1963-66; bd. editors Va. Quarterly Rev., 1971-90. Served to lt. USNR, 1943-46. Mem. Inst. Early Am. History and Culture (coun. 1976-79), So. Hist. Assn. (exec. coun. 1978-81), Mass. Hist. Soc., Am. Antiquarian Soc., Va. Hist. Soc. (hon.), Gridiron Club (U. Ga.), Raven Soc. (U. Va.), Phi Beta Kappa (pres. Alpha chpt. 1984-87). Home: 804 Rugby Rd Charlottesville VA 22903-1629

ABBOTT, A. DWIGHT, retired astronautical engineer; BS in Aero. Engring., Purdue U., 1958, MS in Indsl. Mgmt., 1964. Gen. mgr. sys. engring., gen. mgr. bus. mgmt. space tech. applications, prin. dir. design engring., prin. dir. space transp. devel. space launch ops. Aerospace Corp., LA, 1960—2000; with Aeronautics and Space Engring. Bd. Nat. Academies, Washington, 1997—2003. Mem. dean's vis. com. sch. engring. Purdue U., West Lafayette, Ind. Mayor Palos Verdes Estates (Calif.) City Coun., 2003—07; bd. dirs. So. Calif. Coun. Govts. Fellow: AIAA (assoc.; mem. pub. policy com.); mem.: AAAS (assoc.), Planetary Soc. Avocation: flying. Home: 1825 Via Estudillo Palos Verdes Estates CA 90274

ABBOTT, ALDEN FRANCIS, lawyer, federal official; b. Bethesda, Md., Nov. 10, 1951; s. Roger Sloane and Suzanne Jeanne (Dupuy) Abbott; m. Ljubica Visich, May 3, 1980; 1 child, Roger Visich. Cert., U. Madrid, 1972; BA, U. Va., 1974; JD, Harvard U., 1977; MA in Econs., Georgetown U., 1984. Bar: DC 1977, US Supreme Ct. 1992. Atty. Office of Legal Policy FTC, Washington, 1977-80; atty. Fried, Frank, Harris, Shriver & Kampelman, Washington, 1980-82; spl. counsel Office of Legal Policy U.S. Dept. Justice, Washington, 1982-84, spl. asst. to asst. atty. gen. antitrust divsn., 1984-86, sr. counsel Office of Legal Counsel, 1987-89; counselor to gen. counsel U.S. Dept. Commerce, Washington, 1989-92, chief counsel Nat. Telecom. and Info. Adminstrn., 1992-94, asst. gen. counsel fin. and litig., 1994-2001, acting gen. counsel, 2001; asst. dir. for policy evaluation, Bur. of Competition FTC, Washington, 2001—, assoc. dir. for policy and coordination, 2004—05; assoc. dir. Bureau Competition, 2006—. Adj. prof. Sch. Law George Mason U., Arlington, Va., 1991—; vis. fellow All Souls Coll., Oxford, England, 2005. Comment and note editor: Harvard Internat. Law Jour.; contbr. articles to profl. jours. Mem.: Henry Simons Soc., US Supreme Ct. Bar, Fed. Comm. Bar Assn. (internat. sect.), Phi Beta Kappa, Phi Eta Sigma. Avocations: languages, swimming, reading, skiing, travel. Home: 1611 Westmoreland St Mc Lean VA 22101-5166 Office: US Fed Trade Commn 6th & Penn Ave NW Washington DC 20580 Office Phone: 202-326-2881. Business E-Mail: aabbott@ftc.gov.

ABBOTT, BARRY ALEXANDER, lawyer; b. New Haven, Aug. 20, 1950; s. Harold and Norma (Kaufman) A.; 1 child, Anne Stewart. AB, Dartmouth Coll., 1972; JD, U. Fla., 1975; MBA, Stanford U., 1977. Bar: Fla. 1975, Calif. 1976, US Dist. Ct. (so. dist.) Fla. 1976, US Dist. Ct. (no. dist.) Calif. 1976, US Ct. Appeals (9th cir.) 1976, US Supreme Ct. 1979, DC 1985, NY 1986. Assoc. Morrison & Foerster, San Francisco, 1977-83, ptnr., 1983-94; dir. Howard Rice Nemerovski Canady Falk & Rabkin, San Francisco, 1994—2006, of counsel, 2006—; chief legal officer, dir. govt. rels. Rex Group, San Francisco, 2006—. Adj. faculty mem. Boalt Hall Sch. Law, U. Calif., Berkeley, 1998; lectr. corp., comml. and fin. inst. law various orgns.; mem. Fed. Res. Bd. Consumer Adv. Coun., 1992-94, chmn. consumer credit com., 1993-94, mem. governing com. Conf. on Consumer Fin. Law; mem. Am. Coll. Consumer Fin. Svcs. Attys., 1995—, bd. regents, 1995-98, sec., 2002-05, treas., 2005-07. Co-author: Truth in Lending: A Comprehensive Guide; contbr. articles to profl. jours. Named one of Outstanding Young Men of Am., U.S. Jaycees, 1980. Fellow Royal Soc. Arts (Silver medal 1972); mem. ABA (chmn. young lawyers divsn. bus. law com. 1987-88, chmn. ins. products subcom. 1987-92, vice chmn. consumer fin. svcs. commn. 1995-96, active various coms.), Calif. Bar Assn. (vice chair fin. instns. com. 1991-92, chair 1992-93, mem. ins. law com. 1994-96, mem. bus. law sect. exec. com. 1996-99, treas. 1997-98, vice chair 1998-99), Fla. Bar Assn., D.C. Bar Assn., N.Y. State Bar Assn., San Francisco Bar Assn. (chmn. membership com. 1984-86, bd. dirs. 1982, 87-88, Merit award 1985, 2004), Commonwealth Club (Calif.), Barristers Club (bd. dirs. 1981-83, treas., pres. 1982), Order of Coif, Phi Beta Kappa, Phi Kappa Phi. Republican. Office: The Rex Group 101 California St Ste 1950 San Francisco CA 94111 Office Phone: 415-992-4200.

ABBOTT, BEVERLY STUBBLEFIELD, artist; b. Greensboro, NC, Dec. 12, 1940; d. Robert L. and Helen W. Stubblefield; m. Ira H. A. Abbott, May 7, 1960; children: Ira Robert, Leslie Ann. Represented by Seaside Art Gallery, Nags Head, NC. Exhibitions include Leigh Yawkey Woodson Art Mus., 1996—97, Seaside Art Gallery, 1996—2007, Village Gallery, 1997—99, Germantown Gallery, 1999—2004, Fla. Wildlife Art Expo, 1999—2005, Southeastern Wildlife Expo, 2002, Miniature Art Soc. Fla., 2003—07, Miniature Art Soc. NJ, 2005, Pawprints on My Heart, 2000, Paw Prints through the Years, 2004, prin. works include Va. Living Mus. Wildlife Arts Festival, 2003, World Federation of Miniaturists, Smithsonian Inst., 2004, Paper Mill Internat. Miniature art exhbn., 2004—05, Miniature Painters, Sculptors and Gravers Soc. Washington, 2004—06. Grantee, Susan K. Black Found., 2002. Mem.: Hampton Arts League (Merit award 1997), Miniature Painters, Sculptors, and Gravers Soc. (assoc.), Atlantic Wildfowl Heritage Mus., James River Camera Club (pres. 1994), Langley Kennel Club (life; show chmn. 1977, 1984). Avocations: travel, photography. Home: 13 Delta Cir Newport News VA 23601-3117

ABBOTT, CHARLES FAVOUR, lawyer; b. Sedro-Wolley, Wash., Oct. 12, 1937; s. Charles Favour and Violette Doris Abbott; m. Oranee Harward, Sept. 19, 1958; children: Patricia, Stephen, Nelson, Cynthia, Lisa, Alyson. BA in Econs., U. Wash., Seattle, 1959, JD, 1962. Bar: Calif. 1962, Utah 1981, Wash. 2005. Law clk. Judge M. Oliver Koelsch, US Ct. Appeals (9th cir.), San Francisco, 1963; assoc. Jones, Hatfield & Abbott, Escondido, 1964; pvt. practice Escondido, 1964-77, Provo, Utah, 1983-93; of counsel Mueller & Abbott, Escondido, 1997—; ptnr. Abbott, Thorn & Hill, Provo, 1981-83, Abbott & Abbott, 1993—98; pres. Charles F. Abbott PC, 1998—; of counsel Abbott & Walker, PC, 1998—. Presenter in field. Author: How to Do Your Own Legal Work, 1976, 2d edit., 1981, How to Win in Small Claims Court, 1981, How to Be Free of Debt in 24 Hours, 1981, How to Hire the Best Lawyer at the Lowest Fee, 1981, The Lawyers's Inside Method of Making Money, 1979, The Millionaire Mindset, 1987, How to Make Big Money in the Next 30 Days, 1989, Business Legal Manual and Forms, 1990, How to Make Millions in Marketing, 1990, Telemarketing Training Course, 1990, How to Form A Corporation in Any State, 1990, The Complete Asset Protection Plan, 1990, Personal Injury and the Law, 1997, Fen-Phen Fallout--The Medical and Legal Crisis, 1998; mem. editl. bd. Wash. Law Rev. and State Bar Assn. Jour., 1961-62; bd. editors Phen-fen Litigation Strategist, 1998-2000; contbr. articles to profl. jours. Pres. HHT Found. Internat., 2006—. Mem. ATLA, Utah Bar Assn., Calif. Bar Assn., US Supreme Ct. Bar Assn., Wash. State Bar Assn. Office Phone: 801-426-6902. Business E-Mail: charles@abbott-abbott.com.

ABBOTT, CHARLES WARREN, retired lawyer; b. Miami, Jan. 16, 1930; s. Voyle E. and Katherine (Paschall) A.; m. Betty Jo Eckholdt, Jan. 9, 1959; children: Brenda Jean, Katherine Louise, Abigail Jill. BS in Bus. Adminstrn., U. Fla., 1951, JD, 1953. Bar: Fla. 1955, U.S. Dist. Ct. (so. dist.) Fla. 1955, U.S. Dist. Ct. (ctrl. dist.) Fla., U.S. Supreme Ct. 1960, U.S. Ct. Appeals (11th cir.) 1981, U.S. Dist. Ct. (no. dist.) Fla. 1981; cert. mediator Supreme Ct. Fla. Assoc. Maguire, Voorhis & Wells, P.A., Orlando, Fla., 1955-59, ptnr., 1959-68, dir., 1968—95, of counsel, 1995—98; ptnr. Holland & Knight LLP, Orlando, Fla., 1998—2006; ret., 2006. Mem. judicial nominating commn. Fifth Appellate Dist., 1984-88, chmn. 1987-88. Chmn. Goldenrod Fire Control Dist., 1966-79; mem. Orange County Emergency Med. Svcs. Coun., 1984, 91-94; dir. Fla. Found. for Spl. Children; trustee U. Fla. Law Ctr. Assn, 2002—. Served with JAGC, USAF, 1953-55; served to capt. USAFR, 1951-62. Fellow Am. Coll. Trial Lawyers; mem. ABA, Fla. Bar Assn., Orange County Bar Assns., Fla. Def. Lawyers Assn. (sec.-treas. 1983, v.p. 1984, pres. 1985), Def. Rsch. Inst. (state chmn. 1981-85, so. regional v.p. 1986-88, nat. dir. 1988-91), Fedn. Ins. Corp. Counsel, Am. Bd. Trial Advs. (charter, treas. 1991-92, sec. 1992-93), First Ctrl. Fla. Am. Inns of Ct. (charter mem., treas., pres. 1992-93), Phi Delta Phi. Democrat. Methodist. Home: 2035 Summerland Ave Winter Park FL 32789-1453 Office: Holland & Knight LLP PO Box 1526 200 S Orange Ave Ste 2600 Orlando FL 32801 Office Phone: 407-244-1124. Business E-Mail: charles.abbott@hklaw.com.

ABBOTT, DAVID HENRY, manufacturing executive; b. Milton, Ky., July 6, 1936; s. Carl and Rachael (Miles) A.; m. Joan Shefchik, Aug. 14, 1976; children— Kristine, Gina, Beth, Linsey BS, U. Ky., 1960, MBA, 1961. With Ford Motor Co., Louisville, Mpls. and Dearborn, Mich., 1961-69; div. controller J I Case Co., Racine, Wis., 1970-73, gen. mgr. service parts supply div., 1973-75, v.p., 1975, v.p. and gen. mgr. constrn. equipment div., 1975-77, v.p., gen. mgr. Drott div. Wausau, Wis., 1977-79, exec. v.p. worldwide constrn. equipment, 1979-81; pres., chief operating officer Portec, Inc., Oak Brook, Ill., 1981-87, also dir.; pres., chief exec. officer, dir. E.D. Etnyre & Co., Oregon, Ill., 1988—2002, ret., 2002. Dir. Oak Brook Bank, 1982-88. Served with U.S. Army, 1958 Mem. Constrn. Industry Mfrs. Assn. (bd. dirs. 1979-81, 82-2002, chmn. 1992), Am. Rd. and Transpn. Builders Assn. (dir. 1988—2002). Republican. Home: 2461 Saddlewood Ct Lanark IL 61046

ABBOTT, DAVID L., agricultural products executive; BS, Univ. Vt. CEO Purina Mills, St. Louis; pres., CEO E-markets Inc., Ames, Iowa. Mem.: Nat. FFA Found. (bd. mem.), Am. Feed Ind. Assn. (past pres.). Office: E-markets Inc Ste 108 1606 Golden Aspen Dr Ames IA 50010-8011

ABBOTT, DOUGLAS EUGENE, engineering educator; b. Glendale, Calif., Apr. 20, 1934; s. Richard Edward and Eva (Pogue) A.; m. Doris Bernice Newmark, Dec. 16, 1956; children: Sandra Lee, Jodi Frances, Shari Evalinis, Traci Bernice. B.M.E., Stanford U., 1956, M.M.E., 1957, PhD, 1961. Asst. head fluid mechanics sect. Vidya div. Itek Corp., Palo Alto, Calif., 1960-64; lectr. Stanford U., 1963-64; asso. prof. Purdue U., 1964-69, prof., 1969-77, dir. thermal scis. and propulsion center, 1972-77; prof., chmn. dept. mech. engring. and mechanics, dir. computer-aided design/computer-aided mfg. ednl. program Lehigh U., Bethlehem, Pa., 1977-83, vice provost for computing and info. services, 1983-85; assoc. vice chancellor for info. technologies U. Mass.-Amherst, 1985-96; cons. in comms. technologies Amherst, 1996—. Staff cons. Midwest Applied Sci. Corp., Lafayette, Ind., 1964-72; energy controls div. Bendix Corp., South Bend, Ind., 1967-75, Westinghouse Research and Devel. Center, Pitts., 1970-75, ERDA, 1975-77; chmn. air breathing propulsion adv. com. Air Force Office of Sci. Research, 1973-83, Tech. Concepts, Inc., Sudbury, Mass., 1985-88; bd. dirs. Univ. Programs in Computer Aided Engring., Design and Mfg., 1984-91. Mem. governing bd. Five Coll. Libr., 1991-96. Hon. research fellow Sci. Research Council, U.K., 1971-72 Fellow AAAS, Am. Phys. Soc.; mem. ASME, AIAA, N.Y. Acad. Scis., Nat. Computer Graphics Assn. (bd. dirs. 1985-87, treas. 1987-89), Nat. Computer Graphics Assn. Ednl. Found. (bd. dirs. 1989-92, stewardship coun. 2004—), Trout Unltd. (bd. dirs. Pioneer Valley chpt. 1995—2004), Pi Tau Sigma. Home: 150 Wendell Rd Shutesbury MA 01072-9754 Office Phone: 413-253-9422. Business E-Mail: abbott@oit.umass.edu.

ABBOTT, EDWARD LEROY, finance executive; b. Dayton, Ohio, Dec. 18, 1930; s. Roy Edward and Mildred Eileen (Filler) A.; m. Elizabeth Joan Grahame, June 8, 1957; children: Jay Edward, Julie Beth Abbott Holland. AB, Wittenberg U., 1952; postgrad., Ohio State U., 1952-53. With Northwestern Mut. Life Ins. Co., 1956-73, regional mgr. Washington, 1970-73; with Acacia Mut. Life Ins. Co., Washington, 1973-83, exec. v.p., treas., 1978-83; vice chmn., exec. v.p. CenTrust Savs. Bank, Miami, Fla., 1983-87; chmn., pres., CEO Capital-Union Savs., Baton Rouge, 1987-90; pres. CEO, dir. Firstate Fin., Orlando, Fla., 1992-97, Heritage Hill Farm, 1998—. Served with U.S. Army, 1954-55. Mem. Alpha Tau Omega. Republican.

ABBOTT, GAY O., bank executive; BBA, Emory U., Atlanta, 1983. Comml. banking tng. assoc. SunTrust Banks, Inc., Atlanta, 1983, exec. v.p., retail banking line of bus. mgr. Ctrl. Group, corp. exec. v.p. comml. line of bus. Bd. trustees Agnes Scott Coll., 2006—. Office: SunTrust Banks Inc PO Box 4418 Atlanta GA 30302-4418 Office Phone: 404-588-7711. Office Fax: 404-827-6173.*

ABBOTT, GEOFFREY WINSTON, physiologist, researcher; b. Bradford-On-Avon, Wiltshire, Eng., June 14, 1970; arrived in U.S., 1997; s. Ronald and Helen Mary (Black) Abbott. BSc in Zoology (hon.), Durham U., Eng., 1991; MSc in Molecular Pathology, Toxicology, U. Leicester, Eng., 1993; PhD in Biochemistry, U. London, 1997. Wellcome trust prize travelling postdoctoral rsch. fellow Yale U. Sch. Medicine, New Haven, 1997—99, assoc., 1999—2001; asst. prof. dept. medicine Cornell U. Weill Med. Coll., NYC, 2001—, asst. prof. dept. pharmacology, 2001—. Mem. editl. bd. Jour. Pharmacology and Exptl. Therapeutics, 2004—, Jour. Cardiovascular Pharmacology and Therapeutics, 2006—; dir. grad. program pharmacology Weill Cornell Med. Coll., 2007. Contbr. chapters to books, articles to profl. jours. Recipient Cornell U. Weill Med. Coll. Investigator award, Michael Wolk Found., 2002; grantee, Am. Heart Assn., 2002—, NIH, 2004—. Mem.: Am. Heart Assn., Biophysical Soc., Soc. for Neuroscience. Achievements include patents for MinK-related genes, formation of potassium channels and association with cardiac arrhythmia; novel small molecule modulators of ion channels; first to use RNA interference technique in Xenopus oocytes; co-discoverer of the KCNE gene family of potassium channel beta subunits; co-discoverer of the first example of a molecular genetic basis for acquired cardiac arrhythmia; co-discoverer of novel roles for potassium channel ancillary subunits in mammalian brain; co-discoverer of the molecular basis for bradycardia in patients under propofol general anesthesia; co-discoverer of genetic evidence of requirement for KCNE2 in gastric acid secretion. Home: 1161 York Avenue Apt 8K New York NY 10021 Office: Cornell University Weill Med College Starr 463 520 East 70th Street New York NY 10021 Home Phone: 212-842-8714; Office Phone: 212-746-6275. Office Fax: 212-746-7984. Personal E-mail: gwa2001@med.cornell.edu.

ABBOTT, GEORGE LINDELL, retired librarian; b. Rutland, Vt., July 11, 1941; s. F. George and Eva Marie (Fields) A.; m. Sandra Jean Baker, Aug. 6, 1966; 1 child, Brian George. BA in Math., St. Michael's Coll., 1963; MLS, Syracuse U., 1966. Cataloguer St. Michael's Coll., Winooski, Vt., 1963-64; cataloguer libr. Syracuse U., NY, 1966-70, media librarian, 1970-80, head dept. media svcs., 1980—2005; ret., 2005. Cons. in field. Contbr. articles to various publs.; editor Videodisc/VideoTex jour., 1980-82. Recipient Watson Davis award, Am. Soc. for Info. Sci. and Tech., 1987. Mem. ALA, Am. Soc. Info. Sci. (bd. dirs. 1981-85), Internat. Fedn. of Libr. Assns. and Instns. (standing com. audiovisual and multimedia sect., 2003—), Libr. and Info. Tech. Assn. (bd. dirs. 1985-88), Soc. Motion Picture and TV Engrs., Beta Phi Mu. Avocations: microcomputing, cinema.

ABBOTT, GINA, municipal government executive; b. Patuxent River, Md., Oct. 12, 1954; d. Ralph Orlando Pivero and Nancy Dinicola; m. Winthrop S. Abbott, Jr., Nov. 13, 1977 (dec. Aug. 1996). BSBA, U. Phoenix, 1989. Cert. profl. pub. buyer. From purchasing asst. to small order buyer Tex. Instruments, Colorado Springs, 1984-89; from buyer to procurement & contracts dir. El Paso County Govt., Colorado Springs, 1990—. Recipient cert. of achievement Fed. Emergency Mgmt. Assn. Mem. Nat. Inst. Govtl. Purchasing, Rocky Mtn. Govtl. Purchasing Assn. (v.p. 2001). Avocations: cooking, baking, travel, watching sports. Office: El Paso County Govt 27 E Vermijo Ave Colorado Springs CO 80903-2208 Home: 14 Anita Rd Colorado Springs CO 80906-3110

ABBOTT, GREG, state attorney general, former state supreme court justice; b. Wichita Falls, Tex., Nov. 13, 1957; s. Calvin Roger and Doris Lacristia (Jacks) Rowley A.; m. Cecilia Therese Phalen, Aug. 15, 1981; 1 child, Audrey. BBA, U. Tex., 1981; JD, Vanderbilt U., 1984. Bar: Tex. 1985, US Dist. Ct. (so. dist.) Tex. 1985. Atty. Butler & Binion, Houston, 1984-92; judge 12th State Dist. Ct., Houston, 1992-96; justice Texas Supreme Ct., 1996—2000; ptnr. Bracewell & Patterson, LLP; atty. gen. State of Tex., 2003—. Prof. U. Tex. Law Sch.; mem. com. on Pub. Trust and Confidence in Tex. Cts., Jury Task Force Implementation Project; mem. cert. bd. Tex. Ct. Reporters; exec. com. Family Law 2000 Task Force. Dir. Houston Ctr. for Barrier Free Living, 1986-87; capt. March of Dimes Team Walk, Houston, 1986-87; mem. Gov.'s Com. to Promote Adoption; bd. dirs. Tex. Inst. Rehab. and Rsch., Maywood Children and Family Svcs.; bd. trustees Ctrl. Tex. Goodwill Industries; adv. bd. Career and Recovery Resources Inc. Named Disabled Person of Yr. Harris County Com. on Employment of Disabled Persons, 1985, Outstanding Young Texan Tex. Jaycees, 1995; recipient Am. Jurisprudence award Am. Jur, 1983, Named Outstanding Trial Judge, Texas Assn. of Civil Trial and Appellate Specialists, 1995. Mem. State Bar Tex. (com. on legal advt. 1988, Supreme Ct. liason for com. on jud. ethics, jud. conduct commn., code of jud. conduct), Houston Bar Assn. (Houston's Outstanding Young Lawyer 1994), Houston Young Lawyers Assn., Tex. Assn. State Judges (exec. com.). Republican. Roman Catholic. Avocations: snow-skiing, travel, swimming. Office: Office of Atty Gen Capitol Sta PO Box 12548 Austin TX 78711-2548 Office Phone: 512-463-2100.*

ABBOTT, HIRSCHEL THERON, JR., lawyer; b. Clarksdale, Miss., Jan. 11, 1942; s. Hirschel Theron Sr. and Ona Belle (Williamson) A.; m. Mimi Eugenia DuPre, June 14, 1969; children: Barkley, Chip. BBA in Acct., U. Miss., Oxford, 1964; JD, U. Va., Charlottesville, 1971. Bar: La. 1971, Miss. 1971, U.S. Dist. Ct. (ea. dist.) La. 1971, U.S. Ct. Appeals (5th cir.) 1981, U.S. Tax Ct. 1988; bd. cert. tax law specialist. Lawyer Stone Pigman Walther Wittmann LLP, New Orleans, 1971—75, ptnr., 1975—. Former bd. dirs. Episcopal Housing for Srs., Inc., Lambeth House, Inc.; past trustee, sec. Preservation Resource Ctr., New Orleans; past bd. mem., chmn. Trinity Episcopal Sch. Bd. Trustees; past trustee, treas. La. Civil Svc. League; past bd. mem. Uptown Neighborhood Improvement Assn.; past mem., chmn. La. Jefferson Scholarship Selection Com. U. Va.; past regional chmn. La. U. Va. Law Sch. Annual Giving Fund; chancellor, past mem. vestry Trinity Episcopal Ch.; past mem. Adv. Bd. Jr. League New Orleans. Recipient Monte M. Lemann award, La. Civil Svc. League, 1989. Fellow Am. Coll. Trust and Estate Counsel (past mem. charitable planning and exempt orgns. com.), La. Bar Found.; mem. ABA (tax sect., bus. law sect., real property trusts probate sect.), La. Bar Assn. (past chmn. tax law specialization commn., tax sect., corp. sect., successions, donations and trusts sect.), Miss. State Bar Assn., New Orleans Estate Planning Coun., Assn. Employee Benefit Planners. Epicopalian. Office: Stone Pigman Walther et al 546 Carondelet St New Orleans LA 70130-3588 Office Phone: 504-593-0809. Business E-Mail: habbott@stonepigman.com.

ABBOTT, HORACE PORTER, English literature educator; b. Balt., Nov. 21, 1940; s. Horace P. and Barbara Ann (Trueblood) A.; m. Anita Vaivods, June 25, 1966; children: Jason, Byram. BA, Reed Coll., Portland, Oreg., 1962; MA, U. Toronto, Ont., Can., 1964, PhD, 1968. From asst. prof. to assoc. prof. U. Calif., Santa Barbara, 1966-82, prof., 1982—2005, prof. emeritus, 2005—, chair English, 1983-87, 90, acting dean humanities and fine arts, 1992-94, acting dir. Interdisciplinary Humanities Ctr., 1999—2001. Lectr., instr. Yeats Summer Sch., Sligo, Ireland, 1989. Author: The Fiction of Samuel Beckett, 1973, Diary Fiction, 1984, Beckett Writing Beckett, 1996, The Cambridge Introduction to Narrative, 2002; (poetry) Cold Certainties and Changes Beyond Measure, 1988; editor On the Origin of Fictions, 2001. Pres. Foothill Preservation League, Santa Barbara, 1996-2004. Recipient William Stafford award Poetry Assn. Wash., 1977. Mem. MLA, Samuel Beckett Soc. (pres. 1962-64), Soc. for the Study of Narrative Lit., Soc. for Lit. Sci. and the Arts, Modernist Studies Assn. Office: U of Calif Dept English Santa Barbara CA 93106 Office Phone: 805-893-3791. Business E-Mail: pabbott@english.ucsb.edu.

ABBOTT, ISABELLA AIONA, retired biology educator; b. Hana, Maui, Hawaii, June 20, 1919; d. Loo Yuen and Annie Patseu (Chung) Aiona; m. Donald P. Abbott, Mar. 3, 1943 (dec.); 1 dau., Ann Kaiue Abbott. AB, U. Hawaii, 1941; MS, U. Mich., 1942; PhD, U. Calif., Berkeley, 1950. Prof. biology Stanford U., 1972-82; G.P. Wilder prof. botany U. Hawaii, 1978-98, G.P. Wilder emerita prof. botany, 1998—. Vis. rsch. biologist and tchr., Japan and Chile. Co-author: (with G.J. Hollenberg) Marine Algae of Calif., 1976, La'au Hawaii, traditional Hawaiian uses of plants, 1992; contbr. articles to profl. jours. Co-recipient NY Bot. Garden award for best book in botany, 1978; recipient Merit award Bot. Soc. Am., 1995, G.M. Smith medal NAS, 1997, Spl. Award for Ethnobotany Wings WorldQuest Women of Discovery Awards, 2006. Fellow AAAS; mem. Internat. Phycological Soc. (treas. 1964-68), Western Soc. Naturalists (sec. 1962-64, pres. 1977), Phycological Soc. Am., Bishop Mus. (bd. trustees), Hawaiian Bot. Soc. Office: U Hawaii Manoa Botany Dept 3190 Maile Way Honolulu HI 96822-2232

ABBOTT, JAMES EDWARD, lawyer; b. Bklyn., June 26, 1959; s. Ralph Rawley and Ethel Mildred (Maguire) A.; m. Jennifer Ann Hocking, Dec. 29, 1984. BA, Colgate U., 1981; JD, NYU, 1984. Bar: NY 1985, US Dist. Ct. (so. dist.) NY 1985. Ptnr. Carter, Ledyard & Milburn, NYC, 1984—86, 1987—2007; assoc. Withers, London, 1986-87, Ashurst, Morris, Crisp, London, 1987; ptnr. Seward & Kissel LLP, NYC, 2007—, chief, bus. transaction grp., 2007—. Mem. NY State Bar Assn. (internat. law and practice sect., com. fgn. investment in US bus.), Phi Beta Kappa. Avocations: golf, softball. Office: Seward & Kissel LLP One Battery Park Plz New York NY 10004 Office Phone: 212-574-1226. Office Fax: 212-480-8421.*

ABBOTT, JAMES SAMUEL, III, marketing executive; b. Cleve., Nov. 19, 1918; s. James Samuel and Dorothy (Wilbor) A.; m. Mary Margaret Torrance, Oct. 13, 1957; 1 child, James Samuel. Student, Cornell U., 1941. Sales engr. Nat. Acme Co., Cleve., Chgo., 1945-63, chief sales engr. Cleve., 1963-67, sales mgr., 1967-69; mktg. mgr. Cleveland Twist Drill Co., Cleve., 1969-83; pres. James S. Abbott Consulting, Inc., Gates Mills, Ohio, 1983—. Contbr. articles to profl. jours. Mem. pk. bd. Village of Gates Mills, Ohio, 1979-86. Capt. USAF, 1941-45. Mem. Soc. Founders-Patriots (gov. 1968-69), Soc. Colonial Wars, Western Res. Hist. Soc., Clev. Mus. Natural History, U.S. Horse Cavalry Assn., Mayfield Country Club. Avocations: history, antiques, fly fishing, golf, tennis. Home: 7059 Hillcreek Ln Gates Mills OH 44040-9629 Personal E-mail: jsageninde@aol.com.

ABBOTT, KEVIN CHARLES, lawyer; b. Pitts., May 7, 1956; BA in Polit. Sci. magna cum laude, Ind. U. of Pa., 1978; JD magna cum laude, U. Pitts., 1981. Bar: Pa. 1981, W.Va. 1997, Commonwealth Ct. Pa. 1981, US Ct. Appeals 3rd Cir. 1982, US Ct. Appeals 6th Cir. 1982, US Dist. Ct. No. Dist. Ohio 1982, US Dist. Ct. We. Dist. Pa. 1983, US Dist. Ct. Mid. Dist. Pa. 1991, US Dist. Ct. No. Dist. W.Va. 1997, US Dist. Ct. So. Dist. W.Va. 1999, US Dist. Ct. Ea. Dist. Pa. 1999. Law clk. to Honorable Leroy Contie, Jr US Dist. Ct. No. Dist. Ohio, 1981-82, US Ct. Appeals 6th Cir., 1982-83; assoc. Thorp, Reed & Armstrong, Pitts., 1983-90, ptnr., 1990—2000, Reed Smith LLP, Pitts., 2000—, Pitts. practice group leader litig. group, head energy & natural resources group. Case note editor U. Pitts. Law Rev., 1981. Bd. trustees Energy and Mineral Law Found. Recipient Fed. Bar Assn. prize, 1981; Provost's scholar U. Pitts., 1981; Owens fellow U. Pitts., 1978. Mem. ABA, Pa. Bar Assn., Allegheny County Bar Assn., Am. Arbitration Assn., Order of Coif. Office: Reed Smith LLP 435 Sixth Ave Pittsburgh PA 15219 Office Phone: 412-288-3804. Office Fax: 412-288-3063. Business E-Mail: kabbott@reedsmith.com.

ABBOTT, LAURENCE FREDERICK, physics educator; b. Toronto, Ont., Can., May 15, 1950; came to U.S., 1957; s. Norman John and Ursula (Herbst) A.; m. Catherine Mitchell Davis, Apr. 6, 1974; children: Paul Davis, Karen Chapin. Student, Oberlin Coll., 1968-71; PhD in Physics, Brandeis U., 1977. Rsch. assoc. Stanford (Calif.) Linear Accelerator, 1977-79; asst. prof. Brandeis U., Waltham, Mass., 1979-80, assoc. prof., 1982-88, prof., 1988—, sabbatical leave, 2005—06; prof., dept. physiology and cellular biophysics Columbia U. Coll. Physicians and Surgeons, NY. Sci. assoc. European Orgn. for Nuclear Rsch. (CERN), Geneva, 1980-81; mem. adv. bd. Theoretical Advanced Summer Inst., Dept. Energy, Washington, 1988—. Editor: Inflationary Cosmology, 1986, (with Terrence J. Sejnowski) Neural Codes and Distributed Representations: Foundations of Neural Computation (Computational Neuroscience), 1999; mem. editl. bd. Phys. Rev., 1987—; editorial adv. bd. Network, England, 1989—; contbr. numerous articles to profl. jours.; patentee in field. Sloan Found. fellow, 1983-85; rsch. grantee Dept. Energy, 1979—; recipient Pioneer award, NIH, 2004. Fellow: Am. Acad. Arts and Sciences. Achievements include research in analytic techniques and computer simulation to study the electrical characteristics of single neurons. Office: Brandeis U 415 South St Waltham MA 02454 also: Columbia U Dept Physiology and Biophysics Kolb Research Annex Rm 759 630 W 168th St New York NY 10032 Office Phone: 212-543-5070. Office Fax: 212-543-5010. Business E-Mail: abbott@brandeis.edu, lfa2103@columbia.edu.

ABBOTT, LAWRENCE E., lawyer; b. Miami, Fla., May 18, 1944; BA, St. Edward's U., 1967; JD, Tulane U. La., 1972. Bar: La. 1972, U.S. Dist. Ct. (ea. dist.) La. 1972, U.S. Dist. Ct. (we. dist.) La. 1974, U.S. Dist. Ct. (mid. dist.) La. 1975, U.S. Supreme Ct. 1979, U.S. Ct. Appeals (5th cir.) 1981, U.S. Ct. Appeals (11th cir.) 1984, Tex. 1996. D.C. 1996. Mem. Abbott, Simses & Kuchler, Houston, New Orleans and Covington, La. Mem. ABA (products, gen. liability and consumer law com., rail and motor carrier law com., toxic and hazardous substances and environ. law com. 1995—), Maritime Law Assn. U.S. (mem. internat. law sea com. 1984—, mem. subcom. offshore exploration and devel. 1984—, mem. com. river and ocean towing 1985—), Average Adjusters Assn. U.S. (assoc.), La. State Bar Assn. (asst. examiner com. on bar admissions 1994—), La. Assn. Def. Counsel, New Orleans Bar Assn., New Orleans Def. Counsel Assn., Southeastern Admiralty Law Inst., Def. Rsch. Inst., Inc., La. Bar Found., La. Assn. R.R. Trial Counsel, Am. Arbitration Assn., La. Assn. Bus. and Industry, Phi Delta Phi. Office Phone: 985-893-2991. Business E-Mail: larry-abbott@abbott-simses.com.

ABBOTT, MICHAEL LEHMAN, environmental scientist; b. Valdosta, Ga., Apr. 23, 1953; s. Clark Johnson and Gloria Mae Abbott; m. Julia Mary Falkenstern, Oct. 10, 1960; children: Sarah Mary, Hannah Mae. BS, USAF Acad., Colorado, 1975; MS, Colo. State U., 1989. Sr. engr. Naval Reactors Facility, Idaho Falls, Idaho, 1980—86; adv. scientist Idaho Nat. Lab., 1989—. Contbr. articles to profl. jours. Capt. USAF, 1978—80. Decorated Air Force Commendation medal USAF. Achievements include patents for submersible purification system for radioactive water. Avocations: mountain climbing, skiing. Office: Idaho Nat Lab PO Box 1625 Idaho Falls ID 83415 Home Phone: 208-524-0514; Office Phone: 208-526-8596.

ABBOTT, PAUL SCOTT, writer, public relations executive, consultant; b. Chgo., Nov. 15, 1956; s. Thomas Charles and Shirley May (Schuette) A.; 1 child: Ashleigh Danielle. BS in Journalism, Northwestern U., Evanston, Ill., 1978. Bus. reporter The Cin. Enquirer, 1978; staff writer The Richmond (Va.) News Leader, 1978-84; editor, pub. The County Line, Richmond, 1984-86; bus. writer Albuquerque Jour., 1986-87; mng. editor Carlsbad (N.Mex.) Current Argus, 1987; bur. mgr. PR Newswire, Miami, Fla., 1987-89; exec. v.p. Stuart Newman Assocs., Miami, 1989-93; independent writer, cons. Paul Scott Abbott Pub. Rels./Comm., Miramar, Fla., 1993—. Cons. Nat. Assn. Chiefs of Police, Miami, 1989—, Port of Miami, 1993—. Author: Hot Pursuit, 1996; contbr. numerous articles to Ft. Lauderdale Sun-Sentinel, 1996; contbr. numerous articles, contbg. editor World Wide Shipping, 1993—; contbr. articles, weekly columnist Fla. Shipper Mag., 1993—. Founder Miramar Tower Power Com., 1994—; wildlife rescuer Duck Haven, Margate, Fla., 1994—. Recipient Cert. of Merit Va. Press Assn., Richmond, 1983, Red Ribbon award Informed Families of Dade County, Miami, 1990. Mem. Propeller Club of U.S. (pres. Port of Miami chpt. 1996-97), Soc. Prof. Journalists (pres. South Fla. chpt. 1994-95), Fla. Pub. Rels. Assn. (accredited pub. rels. profl., pres. Greater Miami chpt. 1993-95). Republican. Lutheran. Avocations: cats, baseball, cooking, crosswords. Home: 7130 Granada Blvd Miramar FL 33023-5922

ABBOTT, REBECCA PHILLIPS, art historian, consultant, photographer, director; b. Giessen, Germany, Jan. 10, 1950; d. Charles Leonard and Janet Alice (Praeger) Phillips. BA, Emory and Henry Coll., 1973; postgrad., Georgetown U., 1975, Am. U., 1982-88. Assoc. univ. registrar Am. U., Washington, 1977-81, assoc. dir. adminstrv. computing, 1981-84, dir. adminstrv. computing, 1984-88; dir. membership Nat. Mus. of Women in the Arts, Washington, 1988-89, dir., 1989-98; cons. in fine arts, 1998—. Fine arts photographer. Selected solo exhbns., Includes Anton Gallery, Public Places Private Views, 1992, The Wind, 1994, Canal Views, 1996, Burton Marinkovich Fine Art, Shadows at 18th and K, 1998; Selected group exhbns. includes The Annex Gallery, Metaphysical Landscapes,1989, Embassy of Japan: East Meets West, 1995, Nippon Gallery, Assimilations, 1997. Mem.: Coll. Art Assn., Mus. Art Table, Am. Assn. Mus. Personal E-mail: rphillipsabbott@netscape.net, rphillipsabbott@yahoo.com.

ABBOTT, REGINA A., neurodiagnostic technologist, consultant, business owner; b. Haverhill, Mass., Mar. 5, 1950; d. Frank A. and Ann (Drelick) A. Student, Pierce Bus. Sch., Boston, 1967-70, Seizure Unit Children's Hosp. Med. Ctr. Sch. EEG Tech., 1970-71. Registered electroneurodiagnostic technologist Advanced Fuller Sch. Massage Therapy, 2001, nat. cert. massage therapist Nat. Cert. Bd. Therapeutic Massage and Bodywork. Tech. dir. electrodiagnostic labs. Salem Hosp., 1972-76; lab. dir. clin. neurophysiology Tufts U. New Eng. Med. Ctr., Boston, 1976-78; clin. instr. EEG program Laboure Coll., Boston, 1977-81; adminstrv. dir. dept. Neurology Mt. Auburn Hosp., Cambridge, Mass., 1978-81; tech. dir. clin. neurophysiology Drs. Diagnostic Service, Virginia Beach, Va.; tech. dir. neurodiagnostic ctr. Portsmouth Psychiatric Ctr., 1981-87; founder, pres., owner Commonwealth Neurodiagnostic Services, Inc., 1986—, Hands on HealthCare, 2001—, Hands On-Site, LLC, 2004—. Co-dir. continuing edn. program EEG Tech., Boston, 1977-78; mem. adv. com. sch. neurodiagnostic tech. Laboure Coll., 1977-81, Sch. EEG Tech. Children's Hosp. Med. Ctr., Boston, 1980-81; assoc. examiner Am. Bd. Registration of Electroencephalographic Technologists, 1977-83; mem. guest faculty Oxford Medilog Co.; cons. Nihon Kohden Am., 1981-83, Teca Corp., Pleasantville, N.Y., 1981-87, educator; clin. evaluator Calif. Coll. for Health Scis., 1995—; mem. adv. bd. Tidewater Tech. Massage Therapy Program, Chesapeake, Virginia Beach, 2006. Contbr. articles to profl. jours. EIL scholar, Poland/USSR, 1970; recipient Internat. Woman of Yr. award in bus. and sci. Internat. Biographical Ctr., London, 1993-94. Mem.: NAFE, Am. Soc. Electroneurodiagnostic Technologists, Am. Massage Therapy Assn. Avocations: running, art collecting, photography, reading, investing.

ABBOTT, RICHARD LEE, academic administrator; s. Joseph C. and Anne Abbott; m. Cecilia V. BrundelRe, June 19, 1971; children: Galen Alexander, Alison Abbott Chassin, Lauren Abbott Maucere. BS, Tufts U., Medford, Mass., 1967; MD, George Washington U., Washington, 1971. Diplomate Am. Bd. of Ophthalmology, 1978. Dir. corneal diseases Calif. Pacific Med. Ctr., San Francisco, 1985—95; prof., dir. cornea svc. U. Calif. San Francisco, 1995—2003, Thomas W. Boyden endowed chair, 2003—. Bd. dirs. Internat. Coun. Ophthalmology, San Francisco; bd. dirs., chair of underwriting Ophthalmic Mut. Ins. Co., San Francisco. Author: (medical text book) Surgical Intervention in Corneal and External Diseases. Rsch. assoc. Francis I. Proctor Found.; pres. Pan Am. Assn. Ophthalmology Found., 2003—06; adv. capacity for ednl. activities Project ORBIS, NYC, 2003—. Capt. US Indian Pub. Health Svc., 1972—74, Gallup, N.Mex. Fellow Heed Ophthalmic fellow, Heed Found., 1977—78; grantee Rsch. grantee, Fight for Sight, Inc, 1977—78. Fellow: Am. Acad. Ophthalmology (licentiate; sec. 1995—, bd. trustees 1996—2001, sec. quality of care 2002—, sec. for knowledge base devel. 2002—); mem.: Pan Am. Assn. Ophthalmology (pres. 2007—), Am. Ophthal. Soc. (life). Independent. Avocations: travel, photography, tennis, hiking. Office: University of California San Francisco 10 Koret Way K301 San Francisco CA 94143 Office Fax: 415-502-7418. Business E-Mail: richard.abbott@ucsf.edu.

ABBOTT, RICK, pediatric neurosurgeon, educator; b. Schnectady, NY, Aug. 31, 1950; s. Ira Richmond and Anne Elizabeth Abbott; m. Elaine L. Luckadoo, June 5, 1975; children: Richmond, John. BA, Colo. Coll., Colorado Springs, 1972; MD, Baylor U., Houston, 1980. Diplomate Am. Bd. Neurol. Surgery, 1991, Am. Bd. Pediatric Neurol. Surgery, 1996. Intern Baylor Affiliated Hosps., 1980—81; resident neurosurgery Baylor Hosps., 1981—86; fellow pediat. neurosurgery NYU Med. Ctr., 1986—87; asst. prof. dept. neurosurgery NYU, NYC, 1989—94, assoc. prof., 1994—96, Albert Einstein Coll. Medicine, Bronx, NY, 1996—2006, prof. clin. neurosurgery, 2006—; physician Montefiore Med. Ctr., NY, 2007—. Chmn. credential com. Am. Bd. Pediat. Neurol. Surgery, 2004—. Contbr. more than 50 articles to profl. jours., 15 chpts. to books. Sgt. USAF, 1973—76. Fellow: Am. Acad. Pediats.; mem.: Congress of Neurol. Surgeons, Am. Assn. Neurol. Surgeons (chmn. joint sect. pediat. neurosurgery congress neurol. surgeons 2005—), Am. Soc. Pediat. Neurosurgery (treas. 2005), Internation Soc. Pediat. Neurosurgery (chmn.-elect 2006). Home: 30 Standish Dr Scarsdale NY 10583 Office: Montefiore Med Cnt Dept Neurosurgery 111 E 210th St Bronx NY 10467 Home Phone: 914-725-2858; Office Phone: 718-920-8512. Business E-Mail: rabbott@montefiore.org.

ABBOTT, WILLIAM SAUNDERS, lawyer; b. Medford, Mass., June 2, 1938; s. Charles Theodoric and Evelyn (Saunders) A.; m. Susan Shaw, June 24, 1961; children: Cathryn, Stephen, David. AB, Harvard U., 1960, LLB, 1966. Bar: Mass. 1967, U.S. Dist. Ct. Mass., U.S. Ct. Appeals (D.C. cir.). White House fellow, 1966-67; regional coord. U.S. Agrl. Programs Asia USDA, 1967-68; gen. counsel Cabot, Cabot & Forbes Co., Boston, 1968-77; prin. Simonds, Winslow, Willis & Abbott, Boston, 1977—. Mem. Harvard Law Review. Pres. The Wildlands Trust Southeastern Mass., 1984—90, 1996—97, Nat. Found. to Improve TV, 1970—2003; mem., chmn. Arlington Bd. Selectmen, 1970—73. Lt. USN, 1960—63. Mem.: Boston Bar Assn., Mass. Bar Assn., Phi Beta Kappa. Home: 33 Herring Way Plymouth MA 02360-3225 Office: Simonds Winslow Willis & Abbott 50 Congress St Ste 925 Boston MA 02109-4075 Office Phone: 617-523-5520. E-mail: wabbott1@aol.com.

ABBOTT, WILLIAM THOMAS, private investigator; b. Guthrie, Okla., Jan. 6, 1938; s. Benjamin Franklin and Eva Mae (Lattin) Abbott; m. Jerri Evelyn Stacy, Apr. 20, 1974. BS, Ctrl. State U., Okla., 1960; casualty claim law assoc., Am. Ednl. Inst., 1975. Cert. fraud examiner. Claim adjuster Crawford and Co., Lubbock, Tex., 1964-67, Tulsa, 1967-70; sr. claim specialist State Farm Ins. Co., Tulsa, 1970-2000; pvt. investigator Abbott Investigations, Inc., Tulsa, 2000—. Bd. dirs. Okla. Arson Adv. Coun., chmn., 1996—; mem. Tulsa Mental Health Hotline, 1971—73, Okla. Hist. Soc.; pres., bd. dirs. Vis. Nurse Assn., Tulsa, 2003—05; mem. Young Reps., 1967, Tulsa Met. Ministries, 1971—75. With USMC, 1960—64. Mem.: Santa Fe Trail Assn., Internat. Assn. Spl. Investigation Units, Mt. Carmel Cemetery Assn., Tulsa Claims Assn., Assn. Cert. Fraud Examiners, Internat. Assn. Arson Investigators, Noble Co., Nat. Off-Rd. Bicycle Assn., Adventure Cyclists, League Am. Bicyclists (life), Tulsa Bicycle Club, Am. Legion. Republican. Methodist. Avocations: bicycling, history, writing. Office: Abbott Investigations Inc PMB 631 4306 S Peoria Ave Tulsa OK 74105-3922 Personal E-mail: tulsatracker@aol.com.

ABBOTT-RYAN, PAT, painter, writer; b. Bloomington, Ind., Aug. 2, 1932; d. John Carl Abbott and Martha Louise Stone; m. James Herbert Ryan, June 7, 1955; 1 child, Pamela Louise. BA cum laude, U. Md., 1981. Coll. bd. mem. Mademoiselle Mag., NYC, 1952. Exhibits chmn. Petersburg (Va.) Area Art League, 2000—04. Editor: Silver-Burdett Time/Life, 1967; assoc. editor: Detective Mag., 1960—62; contbr. columns in newspapers, chapters to books, articles to popular mags.; one-woman shows include Touchstone Gallery, Washington, 1985, Foundry Gallery, 1985, PAAL Gallery, Petersburg, Va., 1999, others, exhibited in group shows at Rawls Mus. Arts, Courtland, Va., 2000, 1708 Gallery, Richmond, Va., 2000, St. Paul's Ch. and St. Stephen's Ch., 2001, Zenith Gallery, Washington, 2002—03, Olde Towne Pet Resort, Springfield, Va., 2002—03, others. Scholar, Skowhegan (Maine) Sch. Painting & Sculpture, 1981. Mem.: Petersburg (Va.) Area Art League (bd. dirs. 2000—04). Home: 1221 Woodland Road Petersburg VA 23805 Personal E-mail: ryancqrt@msn.com.

ABBOUD, ALFRED ROBERT, banker, investor, consultant, director; b. Boston, May 29, 1929; s. Alfred and Victoria (Karam) A.; m. Joan Grover, June 11, 1955; children: Robert G., Jeanne Frances, Katherine Jane. BS cum laude, Harvard U., 1951, LL.B., 1956, MBA, 1958. Bar: Mass. 1957, Ill. 1959. Asst. cashier First Nat. Bank of Chgo., 1960-62, asst. v.p., 1962-64, v.p., 1964-69, sr. v.p., 1969-72, exec. v.p., 1972-73, vice chmn. bd., 1973-74, dep. chmn. bd., 1974-75, chmn. bd., CEO, 1975-80; pres., COO Occidental Petroleum Corp., LA, 1980-84; pres. A. Robert Abboud & Co., Fox River Grove, Ill., 1984—; chmn., CEO First City Bancorp. of Tex. Inc., Houston, 1988-91. Co-chmn., lead dir. Ivanhoe Energy, Inc., 2006—. Author: Money in the Bank: How Safe Is It?, 1988. Capt. USMC, 1951-53. Decorated Purple Heart, Bronze Star; Baker scholar, 1958. Mem. Econ. Comml. Club, The Chgo. Club, Harvard Club Chgo., Harvard Club N.Y.C., Barrington Hills Country Club. Home: 209 Braeburn Rd Barrington IL 60010-9637 Office: PO Box 33 212 Stone Hill Ctr Fox River Grove IL 60021-0033 Home Phone: 847-658-4808; Office Phone: 847-639-0101.

ABBOUD, FRANCOIS MITRY, physician, educator; b. Cairo, Jan. 5, 1931; arrived in U.S., 1955, naturalized, 1963; s. Mitry Y. and Asma (Habac) Abboud; m. Doris Evelyn Khal, June 5, 1955; children: Mary Agnese, Susan Marie, Nancy Louise, Anthony Lawrence. Student, U. Cairo, 1948—52; MBBCh, Ains Chams U., 1955; D (hon.), U. Lyon, France, 1991; DSc (hon.), Med. Coll. Wis., 1994. Diplomate Am. Bd. Internal Medicine, Am. Bd. Cardiovasc. Disease (bd. govs. 1987-93). Intern Demerdash Govt. Hosp., Cairo, 1955; resident Milw. County Hosp., 1955—58; Am. Heart Assn. rsch. fellow cardiovasc. labs. Marquette U., 1958—60; Am. Heart Assn. advanced rsch. fellow U. Iowa, 1960—62, asst. prof., 1961—65, assoc. prof. medicine, 1965—68, prof. medicine, 1968—, prof. physiology and biophysics, 1975—, Edith King Pearson chair of cardiovascular rsch., 1988—, dir. cardiovasc. divsn., 1970—76, chmn. dept. internal medicine, 1976—2002, dir. cardiovasc. rsch. ctr., 1974—, assoc. v.p. for rsch., 2003—. Attending physician U. Iowa Hosps., 1961—; VA Hosp., Iowa City, 1963—; chmn. rsch. rev. com. Nat. Heart, Lung and Blood Inst., 1978—80, adv. coun., 1995—99. Editor Circulation Rsch., 1981—86, Procs. Assn. Am. Physicians, 1995—2000, assoc. editor Advances in Internal Medicine, 1991—95, Physiology in Medicine, 2002—, editl. bd. Medicine, 1992—. Recipient European Traveling fellowship, French govt., 1948, NIH Career Devel. award, 1962—71, Disting. Rsch. award, Assn. Am. Med. Colls., 2006. Master: ACP (award for outstanding work in sci. related to medicine 2000); mem.: AMA, Am. Coll. Cardiology (Disting. Scientist award 2004), Assn. Patient Oriented Rsch. (founding mem.), Am. Acad. Arts and Scis., Internat. Soc. Hypertension (Merck Sharp & Dohme Internat. award for rsch. in hypertension 1994), Am. Soc. Pharmacology and Exptl. Therapeutics (award exptl. therapeutics 1972), Am. Clin. and Climatol. Assn. (councillor 1993—96), Am. Physiol. Soc. (chmn. clin. physiology sect. 1979—83, chmn. circulation group 1980, publ. com. 1987—90, Wiggers award 1988, Carl Ludwig lecture award 2000), Assn. Am. Physicians (treas. 1979—84, councillor 1984—89, pres.-elect 1989—90, pres. 1990—91), Assn. Profs. Medicine (bd. dirs. 1993—97, Robert H. Williams Disting. Chmn. of Medicine award 1993), Assn. Univ. Cardiologists, Am. Fedn. Clin. Rsch. (pres. 1971—72), Am. Heart Assn. (bd. dirs. 1977—80, pres.-elect 1989—90, pres. 1990—91, past chmn. rsch. coms., bd. dirs. 1988—91, award of merit 1982, Disting. Achievement award 1987, CIBA award for hypertension rsch. 1990, Gold Heart award 1995, Rsch. Achievement award 1999), Soc. Exptl. Biology and Medicine, Ctrl. Soc. for Clin. Rsch. (pres. elect 1984—85, pres. 1985—86), Am. Soc. Clin. Investigation, Inst. Medicine NAS, Alpha Omega Alpha (bd. dirs. 1989—92), Sigma Xi. Achievements include research and publications in cardiovascular physiology on neurohumoral control of circulation and molecular mechanisms and gene regulation of baroreceptor activation. Home: 24 Kennedy Pky Iowa City IA 52246-2780 Office: Carver Coll Medicine U Iowa Assoc Vice pres Rsch 318 CMAB Iowa City IA 52242-1101

ABBOUD, JOSEPH M., fashion designer; b. Boston, May 5, 1950; s. Joseph and Lila (Sallah) A.; m. Lynn Weinstein, June 6, 1976. BA cum laude, U. Mass. 1972. Buyer, merchandiser Louis of Boston, 1972-80; salesman, designer Polo-Ralph Lauren, NYC, 1980-84; designer, cons. Chanel, Paris, 1984-86; designer, prin. Joseph Abboud Co., NYC, 1986—. Recipient men's knitwear design award Woolknit Assocs., 1986, Cutty Sark award as most promising menswear designer, 1987, Woolmark award as best designer of menswear, 1988, Spl. Achievement award Neckwear Assn. Am., Inc., 1994; named Menswear Designer of Yr., Coun. Fashion Designers Am., 1989, 90. Avocations: tennis, squash, running, fiction. Office: 650 5th Ave Fl 27 New York NY 10019-6108

ABCARIAN, HERAND, surgeon, educator; b. Ahvaz, Iran, Jan. 23, 1941; arrived in U.S., 1966; s. Joseph and Stella (Banki) A.; m. Karen Jane Berger, May 10, 1969; children: Gregory, Ariane, Margot. MD, Teheran U., 1965. Intern Cook County Hosp., Chgo., 1966—67, resident in gen. surgery, 1967—71, resident in colon and rectal surgery, 1971—72, chmn. colon and rectal surgery, 1972—93; head dept. surgery, Turi Josefson prof. U. Ill. Coll. Med., Chgo., 1989—; exec. dir./sec. treas. Am. Bd. Colon & Rectal Surgery, Taylor, Mich. Assoc. editor: Diseases of Colon and Rectum, 1981—95. Fellow ACS (various coms. and offices), Am. Soc. Colon and Rectal Surgeons (sec. 1985-87, pres. 1988-89), Can. Soc. Colon and Rectal Surgeons (hon.); mem. Am. Surg. Assn., Soc. Am. Gastroendoscopic Surgeons (founder), Sydney Soc. Colon and Rectal Surgeons (hon.), Assn. Coloprotology of Gt. Britain (hon. fellow). Republican. Roman Catholic. Avocations: visual arts, music, philately. Office: U Ill 840 S Wood St 518 Chicago IL 60612-7317 Address: Am Bd Colon & Rectal Surgery 20600 Eureka Rd Ste 713 Taylor MI 48180-5376 Home Phone: 708-366-5065; Office Phone: 312-996-2061. Business E-Mail: abcarian@uic.edu.

ABDEL DAYEM, HUSSEIN MAHMOUD, nuclear medicine physician, radiology educator; b. Cairo, Apr. 5, 1934; s. Mahamaud and Shafika (El Sayed) A.D.; m. Ayda M. El-Shirbiny, Sept. 19, 1968; children: Amani, Essmaeel. MB, BChir, Cairo U., 1959, MD in Radiology, 1967. Diplomate Am. Bd. Nuclear Medicine, Am. Bd. Radio Therapy. Instr. radiology Faculty of Medicine Cairo U., Egypt, 1967-70; resident, fellow Roswell Park Cancer Inst., Buffalo, 1970-72; dir. nuc. medicine Erie County Med. Ctr., Buffalo, 1972-81; assoc. prof. radiology SUNY, Buffalo, 1972-81; prof., chmn. dept. nuc. medicine Kuwait U., 1981-90; adj. mem. Meml. Sloan Kettering Cancer Ctr., NYC, 1990-92; dir. nuc. medicine St. Vincent's Hosp., NYC, 1992—; prof. radiology N.Y. Med. Coll., NYC, 1992—. Sr. registrar Cancer Ctr. Kuwait, 1969-70; vis. prof. Med. Coll. Wis., 1990. Contbr. articles to profl. jours. and chpts. to books; mem. editl. bd. European Jour. Nuc. Medicine. Fellow: N.Y. Acad. Medicine (pres. nuc. medicine sect. 2001—03), Am. Coll. Nuc. Medicine (v.p. 2006), Am. Coll. Nuc. Physicians; mem.: Radiol. Soc. N.Am. (bd. trustees), Soc. Nuc. Medicine (pres. Asia and Oceana fedn. 1988—92, vice chmn. sci. program 1994, pres. N.E. chpt. 2001—03, 1st prize nuc. medicine rsch. 1984, 3rd prize 1986). Muslim. Achievements include research in nuc. medicine. Home: 71 Hoover Dr Cresskill NJ 07626-1705 Office: St Vincent's Hosp 153 W 11th St New York NY 10011-8305 Business E-Mail: dayem@njir.us.

ABDEL-HAKIM M. ALY, ALAA EL-DIN, engineer, researcher; s. Abdel-Hakim Mohamed Aly; children: Ahd Alaa El-Din Abdel-Hakim, Karim Alaa El-Din Abdel-Hakim, Hamzah Alaa El-Din Abdel-Hakim. BSc, Assiut U., 1996, MSc, 2000; PhD, U. Louisville, 2007. Rsch. & tchg. asst. Assiut U., 1996—2002; rsch. asst. U. Louisville, 2002—. Mem.: IEEE, Egyptian Syndicate Engrs., Tau Beta Pi. Office: Elec Enging Dept Assiut Univ Assiut 74111 Egypt Business E-Mail: alaa.hakim@ieee.org.

ABDELKHALIK, OSSAMA, computer science educator, researcher; s. Mohamed Omar and Hanem Elwasifi; m. Doaa Abdelrasoul, Aug. 5, 2000; children: Ganna Omar, Noureddean Omar. BS, Cairo U., 1996, MSc, 2000; PhD, Tex. A&M U., College Station, 2005. Instr. High Inst. Computers and Mgmt. Tech., Cairo, 1996—98; design engr. ORASCOM Engring., Giza, Egypt, 1998—99; vis. rschr. Carlo Gavvazi Space Co., Milan, 1998—99; rsch. engr. Nat. Auth. Remote Sensing and Space Scis., Cairo, 1999—2001; rsch. assoc. Tex. A&M U., College Station, 2005—06; asst. prof. Embry-Riddle Aero. U., Daytona Beach, Fla., 2006—. Contbr. articles to profl. jours. Pres. Egyptian Student Assn., College Station, 2004—05; judge Tex. A&M U. Undergrad. Summer Rsch. Grant Poster Presentation, College Station, 2006. Mem.: Am. Astronautical Soc., Sigma Xi. Achievements include research in two-way orbits: developed an analytical method to find orbits in which two satellites intesect at a nadir point at the same time parallel to each other; optimal orbit design for ground surveillance missions. This research aims at developing a method to find to the optimal orbit in space in which a spacecraft is able to achieve given requirements; space surveillance using star trackers: estimating the trajectory of an object in space using a camera onboard another satellite; engineering feasibility and trade studies for the NASA/VSGC micromaps space mission; orbit control of MITA-class satellites with FEEP electric propulsion system. Avocations: soccer, chess. Office: Mich Tech Univ Mech Engring and Enging Mechanics Dept 1400 Townsend Dr Houghton MI 49931 Home Phone: 386-671-9485; Office Phone: 906-487-2911.

ABDEL-KHALIK, SAID IBRAHIM, nuclear and mechanical engineering educator; b. Alexandria, Egypt, Aug. 9, 1948; came to U.S., 1969; s. Ibrahim Saad and Esha Farag (Ahmad) A.-K.; m. Sharon Lora Duncan; 1 child, Faith Austen Khalik. BS summa cum laude, Alexandria U., 1967; MS in Mech. Engring., U. Wis.-Madison, 1971, PhD in Mech. Engring., 1973. Postdoctoral fellow in chem. engring. U. Wis., Madison, 1973-74, asst. prof. nuclear engring., 1976-78, assoc. prof., 1978-82, prof., 1982-87; Ga. Power disting. prof. nuclear engring. Ga. Inst. Tech., Atlanta, 1987-89, assoc. dir. sch. mech. engring., 1990-92, so. nuclear disting. prof., 1993—; instr. Alexandria U., 1967-69; sr. engr. Babcock & Wilcox, Lynchburg, Va., 1975. Guest rsch. scientist Nuclear Rsch. Ctr., Karlsruhe, Fed. Republic Germany, 1979; vis. prof. EPFL, Inst. de Genie Atomique, Lausanne, Switzerland, 1982; cons. Kewaunee Nuclear Plant, Green Bay, Wis., 1983—93, So. Nuclear Vogtle, Hatch, and Farley Nuclear Plants, 1999-, numerous rsch. orgns. and govtl. agys.; adv. com. reactor safeguards U.S. Nuc. Regulatory Commn., 2006—. Contbr. articles to profl. jours. Fellow Am. Nuclear Soc., ASME; chair Fusion Energy Divsn. Am. Nuclear Soc. 2005; mem. Am. Soc. Engring. Edn. (Glenn Murphy award 1999), Profl. Reactor Operators Soc., Am. Inst. Physics, Assn. Egyptian-Am. Scholars, Sigma Xi, Phi Kappa Phi. Achievements include patents in field. Avocations: sailing, chess. Home: 3579 Midvale Cove Tucker GA 30084-3210 Office: Sch Mech Engring Ga Inst Tech Atlanta GA 30332-0405 Home Phone: 770-493-4027; Office Phone: 404-894-3719. Business E-Mail: said.abdelkhalik@me.gatech.edu.

ABDELLAH, FAYE GLENN, retired public health service officer; d. H. B. and Margaret (Glenn) Abdellah. BS in Tchg., Columbia U., 1945; MA in Tchg., Rutgers U., NJ, 1947, EdD, 1955; LLD (hon.), Case Western Res. U., 1967, Rutgers U., 1973; DSc in Nursing (hon.), U. Akron, 1978; DSc (hon.), Cath. U. Am., 1981; DSc in Public Svc. (hon.), Monmouth Coll., 1982; DSc (hon.), Ea. Mich U., 1987, U. Bridgeport, 1987, Georgetown U., 1989; D in Pub. Svc. (hon.), Am. U., 1987; LHD (hon.), Georgetown U., 1989, U. SC, 1991, D in Pub. Svc., 1991; D, Norwich U., Vt., 1996; D in Mil. Nursing (hon.), USUHS, 2002. RN NY, DC. Commd. officer USPHS, Rockville, Md., 1949, advanced through grades to rear adm., 1970, dep. Surgeon Gen., chief nurse officer, 1970—87, dep. Surgeon Gen., 1981—89, chief nursing edn. br., divsn. nursing, 1949—59, Surgeon Gen., 1989; chief rsch. grants br. Bur. Health Manpower Edn., NIH, HEW, Rockville, 1959—69; dir. Office Rsch. Tng. Nat. Ctr. for Health Svcs. R & D, Health Svcs. Mental Health Adminstrn., Rockville, 1969; acting dep. dir. Nat. Ctr. Health Svcs. R & D, Rockville, 1971, Bur. Health Svcs. Rsch. and Evaluation, Health Resources Adminstrn., Rockville, 1973; dir. Office Long-Term Care, Office Asst. Sec. for Health, HEW, Rockville, 1973—80; exec. dir. Grad. Sch. Nursing Uniformed Svcs. U. Health Scis., Bethesda, Md., 1993—, founding dean, prof. emeritus, 2001—. Prof. nursing, Emily Myrtle Smith chair U. SC, Columbia, 1990—91; dean, prof. Grad. Sch. Nursing, Uniformed Svcs. U. Health Scis., 1993—2002, founding dean, prof. emerita, 1993—2002; mem. US Dels. Exchange Missions to USSA, Yugoslavia and France; coord. nursing US-Argentia Cooperation Health and Med. Rsch. Project. Author: Effect of Nurse Staffing on Satisfactions with Nursing Care, 1959, Patient Centered Approaches to Nursing, 1960, Better Patient Care Through Nursing Research, 1965, 2d edit., 1979, 3d edit., 1986, Intensive Care, Concepts and Practices for Clinical Nurse Specialists, 1969, New Directions in Patient Centered Nursing, 1972, Preparing Nursing Research for the 21st Century, 1994; contbr. over 152 articles to profl. pubs.:. Named to TC Nursing Hall of Fame, Columbia U., 1999, Nat. Women's Hall of Fame, 2000; recipient Mary Adelaide Nutting award, 1983, Oustanding Leadership award, U. Pa., 1987, 1999, Disting. Svc. award, 1973—89, Surgeon Gen.'s medal and medallion, 1989, Achievement award in aging, Allied-Signal, 1989, Gustav O. Lienhard award, Inst. Medicine NAS, 1992, Breaking Ground in Women's Health award, 2001, G.W. "Sonny" Montgomery award, Dept. Vets. Affairs, 2002, Centennial award for Achievements in Nursing, Ohio State U., 1970. Fellow: Am. Acad. Nursing (charter, past v.p., pres., Living Legend award); mem.: AAAS, ANA (hon.), APA, Assn. Mil. Surgeons US, Douglas Soc., Phi Lambda Theta, Sigma Theta Tau (Disting. Rsch. Fellow award 1989, Nells Watt Lifetime Achievement Nursing award 2005, Life Time award 2006). Achievements include established first military school of nursing at Uniformed Services University of Health Sciences 1993; received congressional tributes for United States Senator Daniel K. Inouye in 2000 and 2002. Home: 3713 Chanel Rd Annandale VA 22003-2024

ABDEL-MALEK, KARIM A., biomedical engineer, educator; b. Cairo, Apr. 25, 1965; s. Antoun Abel-Malek and Josette Abdel-Malek; m. Mary Abdel-Malek; children: Tony, Ella. BS, U. Jordan, Amman, 1988; MS, U. Pa., 1990, PhD, 1993. Asst. prof. U. Iowa, Iowa City, 1994—2001, assoc. prof., 2001—05, prof. biomed. engring., 2005—, dir. Ctr. Computer-Aided Design, 2005—; pres. Viztek, Inc., Iowa City, 2001—05. Author: Human Modeling and Simulation, 2006. Named Outstanding Young Mfg. Engr.; Fulbright scholar, 1988—90. Mem.: ASME (chmn. med. symposium, Best Paper award), SAM, SAE (chmn. conf. 2005). Office: U Iowa 330 S Madison Iowa City IA 52242

ABDEL-MISIH, RAAFAT Z., surgeon, educator; b. Egypt; m. Mona Abdel-Misih; children: Sherif, Rami. MD, Assuit U., Egypt, 1971, MBBCh (hon.), 1972. Diplomate Am. Bd. Surgery. Pvt. practice R.Z. Abdel-Misih, MD, PA, Wilmington, Del., 1981—. Sr. attending Christiana Care Health Sys., Newark, 1992—, vice chmn. dept. surgery, 1993—; clin. asst. prof. Jefferson Med. Coll., Phila., 1992—. Named Outstanding Tchr. of Yr., Christiana Care Health Sys., 1990, 2000, 2003, 2006. Fellow: ACS (pres. elect Del. chpt.); mem.: Am. Soc. Gen. Surgeons, Am. Soc. Laparascopic Surgeons, Am. Hepato-Biliary Pancreatic Assn., Soc. Surg. Oncology, Del. Soc. Oncology, Del. Med. Soc. Avocations: tennis, swimming, golf, skiing. Office: RZ Abdel-Misih MD PA 1021 Gilpin Ave Ste 203 Wilmington DE 19806 Office Phone: 302-658-7533. Office Fax: 302-658-7205.

ABDELRAHMAN, TALAAT AHMAD MOHAMMAD, financial executive; b. Kafr Saqr, Sharkia, Egypt, Sept. 13, 1940; came to US, 1970; s. Ahmad Mohammad and Zeen Elmahdi (Hassan) A.; m. Soher T. Ali (Dec. Feb. 1979); children: Manar, Neven, Nancy, Amon; m. Ekram T. Kandil (div. May 1994); m. Moushira El Shafei, Jan. 1996 (div. Jan. 2005). BS in Mgmt., Cairo U., 1965, BA in Law, 1969, PhD in Fin., 1987; MBA in Acctg., NYU, 1974. Fin. analyst Nat. Bank Egypt, Cairo, 1965—70; Euro-dollar specialist Bankers Trust Co., NYC, 1970—74; sr. cost acct. Phelps Dodge Cable & Wire, Yonkers, NY, 1974—75; fin. cons. East Orange, NJ, 1975—76; asst. treas. ITT Fed. Electric, Paramus, NJ, 1976—82, mgr. fin. Jed, Saudi Arabia, 1982—86, mgr. corp. fin. Paramus, 1987—91; gen. dir., chmn., pres., co-owner Franconia Pediat. & Family Med. Ctrs., Alexandria, Va., 1997—2003; real estate investor, 2003—. Bd. dirs. ITT Howard/Egypt, Cairo, Talkan USA, Inc., Morganville, NJ; owner 7-Eleven Franchise, Wood Ridge, NJ, 1991-96, Hackensack, NJ, 1992-96, Family Food Store Inc., T/A Broadway Stop & Shop, Fair Lawn, NJ, 1993-95. Contbr. articles to profl. jours. Pres. Bergen County Islamic Ctr., 1995-96. Avocations: windsurfing, swimming. Office Phone: 813-961-0846. Fax: 813-964-9757. E-mail: talaatgroup@gmail.com.

ABDELSAMAD, MOUSTAFA HASSAN, dean; b. Mar. 12, 1941; B in Commerce with honors, Cairo U., 1961; MBA, George Washington U., 1965, DBA, 1970. Assoc. dean Va. Commonwealth U., Richmond, Va., 1977-88; dean, finance prof. U. Mass., N. Dartmouth, Mass., 1988-91; prof. fin. Tex. A&M U., Corpus Christi, Tex., 1991—, dean Coll. Bus., 1991—. Cons. in field Editor-in-chief SAM Advanced Mgmt. jour., 1985—. Mem. Fin. Mgmt. Assoc., Soc. Advancement Mgmt. (mgmt. excellence award, 1991, 1998, pres. excellence award, 1996, Phil Carroll Advancement Mgmt. finance award, 1989, internat. pres. 1983-86, 96—), Tex. Coun. Coll. Bus. Edn., So. Bus. Adminstrn. Assoc. Office: Dean Coll Business Tex A&M U Corpus Christi Corpus Christi TX 78412 E-mail: moustafa@cob.tamucc.edu.

ABDELSAYED, WAFEEK HAKIM, accounting educator; b. Fayoum, Egypt, Aug. 16, 1958; came to U.S., 1970; s. Fr. Gabriel H. and Tahani (Mikhael) A. BBA, Hofstra U., 1979; MBA, Adelphi U., 1983, MS, 1984; PhD, U. Conn., 1996. CPA Fla., N.Y.; cert. fraud examiner Assn. of Cert Fraud Examiners; cert. fin. mgr; cert. control assesment, Inst. Internal Auditors, 2002, cert. gov. auditing profl., 2003. Staff acct. KPMG Peat Marwick, LI, N.Y., 1981-82, Deloitte & Touche, LI, 1983-84; prof. acctg. dept. So. Conn. State U., New Haven, 1984—. Contbr. rsch. papers to profl. publs. (Competitive Paper award 1991, Becker's Outstanding Rsch. award 1991). Mem. bd. deacons Virgin Mary Coptic Orthodox Ch., treas. Scholar N.Y. State Soc. CPA's, 1983. Mem. AICPA, N.E. Bus. and Econs. Assn. (bd. dir.), Am. Acctg. Assn., Inst. Mgmt. Accts. (cert. mgmt. acct., cert. fin. mgmt.), Inst. Internal Auditors (cert. internal auditor), Cert. Govt. Financial Mgr., Assn. Govt. Accts, Conn. Soc. CPAs, Beta Gamma Sigma, Beta Alpha Psi. Egyptian/Christian Orthodox. Avocations: coin and stamp collecting, photography. Home: PO Box 170 North Haven CT 06473-0170 Office: So Conn State U Sch Bus 501 Crescent St New Haven CT 06515-1330 Office Phone: 203-392-5690. E-mail: abdelsayedw1@southernct.edu.

ABDENUR, ROBERTO MAMERI PINTO, ambassador; b. Rio de Janeiro, May 5, 1942; married; 3 children. B in Econs., London Sch. of Econs.; law student, Pontifical Cath. U. of Rio de Janeiro. Div. of comm. and archives Brazilian Min. of External Rels., 1964—65, trade policy divsn., 1966—67, acting head Tech. Sect. of Analysis and Planning to under sec. for Policy Planning, 1968, cabinet staff mem., 1969, asst. to sec.-gen, 1975—78; econ. trade chief Brazilian Min. of External Relations, 1979—84; dep. min. Brazilian Min. of External Rels., 1993—95; Brazilian dep. consulate gen. to consulate gen. London, 1969—73; first sec. Washington, 1973—75; amb. to Equador Quito, 1985—88; amb. to China Beijing, 1989—93; amb. to Germany Berlin, 1995—2002; amb. to Austria Vienna, 2002—04; amb. to US Washington, 2004—. Fluent in Portuguese, Spanish, English, French, German. Office: Embassy of Brazil 3006 Mass Ave NW Washington DC 20008

ABDO, VIRGINIA RICHIE, retired secondary school educator; b. Dallas, Mar. 11, 1929; d. James Logan and Sara Virginia (Ogletree) Richie; m. Milton Kalil Abdo, June 2, 1956; children: Anthony Logan, David Kalil, Ernest Alan. BA cum laude, So. Meth. U., Dallas, 1954, MA, 1979. Cert. tchr. Tchr. El Centro Jr. Coll., Dallas, 1968-70, Berkner H.S., Richardson, Tex., 1970—98; ret., 1998. Musician Mesquite Symphony Orch., New Philharm. Symphony, Irving. Contbr. reviews to music mags. Bd. dirs. Dallas Opera, Dallas Chamber Music Soc., Greater Dallas Youth Orchestras; active Dallas Symphony, So. Meth. U. Conservatory, Met. Opera, Santa Fe Opera, Seattle Opera, Lyric Opera of Chgo., San Francisco Opera, Gesellschaft Der Freunde von Bayreuth, Germany, Houston Grand Opera, Wagner Soc. NY, Wagner Soc. Am., Dallas Mus. of Art, Kimbell Art Mus., Art Inst. Chgo., Met. Mus. Art., MEadows Mus. Art, Women's Mus. Art, Washington, Friends of So. Meth. U. Librs., Friends of Sta. WRR. Mem. Am. Assn. Tchrs. of German, Tex. Fgn. Lang. Assn., Dallas Goethe Ctr., Alliance Francaise, So. Meth. U. Alumni Assn., Highland Park High Sch. Alumni Assn., Wagner Soc. of Dallas (founder, pres. 1990, bd. dirs.), Phi Beta Kappa (sec., treas. North Tex. chpt. 1988-90), Mu Phi Epsilon, Alpha Lambda Delta, Delta Phi Alpha, Phi Beta Kappa. Avocations: music, playing viola and violin in amateur groups and chamber music groups. Home: 3234 Amherst Ave Dallas TX 75225-7620

ABDOO, ELIZABETH A., lawyer; b. Apr. 1958; BA, JD, Georgetown U. Bar: 1987. Sr. v.p., asst. gen. counsel Orbital Sciences Corp., 1996—2001; sr. v.p., gen. counsel Host Hotels & Resorts, Inc. (formerly Host Marriott Corp.), Bethesda, Md., 2001—03, corp. sec., 2001—, exec. v.p., gen. counsel, 2003—. Office: Host Hotels & Resorts, Inc 6903 Rockledge Dr Ste 1500 Bethesda MD 20817*

ABDUL, PAULA (PAULA JULIE ABDUL), singer, dancer, choreographer; b. San Fernando, Calif., June 19, 1963; d. Harry and Lorraine A.; m. Emilio Estevez, Apr. 29, 1992 (div. 1994); m. Brad Beckerman, Oct. 14, 1996 (div. 1998). Student, Calif. State Univ., Northridge; studied tap, jazz with Joe Tramine, the Bella Lewitzky Co. Laker Girls head cheerleader, head choreographer L.A. Lakers basketball team; choreography for Jacksons singing group, Janet Jackson, ZZ Top, Arnold Schwarzenegger, Tom Hanks, The Tracey Ullman Show, others; judge American Idol, 2002—. Albums: Forever Your Girl, 1988, Shut Up and Dance, 1990, Spellbound, 1991, Head Over Heels, 1995, Greatest Hits: Straight Up!, 2007; Actress (TV films) Junior High School, 1978, Touched By Evil, 1997, Amy Fuentes, The Waiting Game, 1998, Denise Walton, Mr. Rock 'n' Roll: The Alan Freed Story, 1999; (voice) Robots, 2005; choreographer (films) Private School, 1983, A Smoky Mountain Christmas, 1986, Dragnet, 1987, Can't Buy Me Love, 1987, The Running Man, 1987, Coming to America, 1988, Bull Durham, 1988, Action Jackson, 1988, Dance to Win, 1989, The Karate Kid Part III, 1989, She's Out of Control, 1989, The Doors, 1991, Jerry Maguire, 1996, American Beauty, 1999, Black Knight, 2001, The Master of Disguise, 2002, (TV series) The Tracy Ullman Show, 1987, (TV) The 17th Annual Am. Music Awards, 1990, 62nd Annual Academy Awards, 1990, (video) ZZ Top: Greatest Hits (Velcro Fly), 1992; singer, Side Out, 1990; exec. prodr. (video) Straight Up, 1989, Under My Spell Live, 1993, Cardio Dance, 1998, Cardio Cheer, 2005; TV guest appearances include: Top of the Pops, 1989, 1990, 1995, Spin City, 1998, The Wayans Bros., 1999, Sabrina, the Teenage Witch, 1999, Mad TV, 2002, The Bernie Mac Show, 2004, Fashion In Focus, 2005, Less Than Perfect, 2005, The Contender, 2005, So You Think You Can Dance, 2005 and several others. Recipient Soul Train award for best video, 1989, best choreography, 1989, Am. Video Arts award choreographer of yr. 1990, Nat. Acad. Video Arts and Scis., 1987, Emmy awards: best choreography for the Tracy Ullman Show, 1988-89, Outstanding Achievement in Choreography for Am. Music Awards, 1990; MTV awards: best choreography, Janet Jackson's Nasty video, 1986, best female video, best dance video, best choreography in a video, best editing in a video for hit Straight Up, 1989, Am. Music awards: for choreography on ZZ Top's Velcro Fly video, 1987, Favorite Pop-Rock Female, 1990, 1992, Favorite Dance artist, 1990; People's Choice awards: Favorite Female Musical Performer, 1990, 1991; named to Nickelodeon's Kids Choice Hall of Fame; represented by star on Hollywood Blvd. Mailing: American Idol Fox Broadcasting PO Box 900 Beverly Hills CA 90213-0900

ABDUL-JABBAR, KAREEM (LEW ALCINDOR, LEWIS FERDINAND ALCINDOR), professional basketball coach, retired professional basketball player; b. NYC, Apr. 16, 1947; s. Ferdinand Lewis and Cora Alcindor; m. Habiba (Janice Brown), 1971 (div. 1973); children: Habiba, Kareem, Sutana, Amir. BA, UCLA, 1969. Basketball player with Milw. Bucks, 1969—75, L.A. Lakers, 1975—89; owner Kareem Productions; asst. coach L.A. Clippers, 2000—01; cons. Ind. Pacers, 2001—02; head coach, Okla. Storm U.S. Basketball League, 2002; cons., scout NY Knicks, 2004—05; spl. asst. to coach Phil Jackson L.A. Lakers, 2005—. Commentator ESPN, Bristol, Conn. Actor: (films) Game of Death, 1978, The Fish that Saved Pittsburgh, 1979, Airplane, 1980, Fletch, 1985; (TV miniseries) The Stand, 1994, (TV appearances) Mannix, 1971, Emergency!, 1974, The Man from Atlantis, 1977, Dinah!, 1977, The Way It Was, 1977, Diff'rent Strokes, 1982, Pryor's Place, 1984, Tales from the Darkside, 1985, Stingray, 1987, 21 Jump Street, 1990, Good Sports, 1991, Uncle Buck, 1991, Amen, 1991, Matrix, 1993, The Critic, 1994, The Fresh Prince of Bel-Air, 1994, Full House, 1995, Martin, 1996, Everybody Loves Raymond, 1996, Living Single, 1997, Boston Common, 1997; author (with Peter Knobler): Giant Steps: An Autobiography of Kareem Abdul-Jabbar, 1983; author: (with Mignon McCarthy) Kareem, 1990; author: (with Stephen Singular) A Season on the Reservation: My Soujourn with the White Mountain Apaches, 2000; author: (with Alan Steinburg) Black Profiles in Courage: A Legacy of African-American Achievement, 2000; author: (with Anthony Walton) Brothers in Arms: The Epic Story of the 761st Tank Battalion, WWII's Forgotten Heroes, 2004; author: (with Raymond Obstfeld) On the Shoulders of Giants: My Personal Journey Through the Harlem Renaissance, 2007. Named NBA Rookie of the Yr., 1970, NBA Most Valuable Player, 1971, 1972, 1974, 1976, 1977, 1980, NBA Playoff Most Valuable Player, 1971, 1985, NCAA Tournament Most Outstanding Player, 1967, 1968, 1969; named to NBA All-Star Game, 1970—87, 35th Anniversary All-Time Team, NBA, 1980, NBA Hall of Fame, 1995; recipient Maurice Podoloff Cup. Muslim. Achievements include being the NBA career leader in points scored (38,387), field goals attempted (28,307), field goals made (15,837), minutes played (57,446) and personal fouls (4,657); being a mem. of 6 NBA Championship Teams, 1971, 80, 82, 85, 87, 88; being a mem. 3 NCAA Championship Teams, 1967, 68, 69. Avocation: jazz. Office: LA Lakers 555 N Nash St El Segundo CA 90245*

ABDULLAEV, YALCHIN, neuroscientist, educator; b. Baku, Azerbaijan, Aug. 19, 1960; s. Gulhuseyn and Almas Abdullaev; m. Naida Velieva, Nov. 24, 1987 (div. June 20, 2003); 1 child, Mikail. MS, Azerbaijan State U., Baku, 1982; PhD, Inst. Exptl. Medicine, St. Petersburg, Russia, 1987; MD, St. Petersburg Med. Acad., 1994. Rsch. asst. Inst. Physiology, Azerbaijan Acad. Scis., Baku, 1982-84; grad. stud. Inst. Exptl. Medicine, St. Petersburg, 1984-87, jr. rsch. scientist, 1987-89, sr. rsch. scientist, 1989-90, Brain Ctr., St. Petersburg, 1990-94; asst. prof. U. Oreg., Eugene, 1994-96, U. Louisville, 1996—2005; rsch. scientist U. Oreg., 2005—. Mem. grad. faculty U. Louisville, 1996—2005; rsch. dir. Cognitive Neurosci. Lab., 1996—2005. Mem. editl. bd.: Internat. Jour. Psychophysiology, 1992—96; mem. editl. bd. The Sci. World, 2002—, Med. Sci. Monitor, 2003—; contbr. more than 60 rsch. articles to profl. jours. Mem.: Internat. Orgn. Psychophysiology, Internat. Orgn. Human Brain Mapping, Soc. Neurosci., Am. Psychol. Soc. Avocations: swimming, running, Judo, reading. Personal E-mail: yabdullaev@yahoo.com.

ABDUR-RAHIM, SHAREEF (JULIUS SHAREEF ABDUL-RAHIM), professional basketball player; b. Marietta, Ga., Dec. 11, 1976; s. William and Aminah Abdur-Rahim; m. Delicia (DeeDee) Abdur-Rahim; 1 child, Jabri. Forward, guard Vancouver Grizzlies NBA, 1996—2001, Altanta Hawks NBA, 2001—03, Portland Trail Blazers, 2003—05; forward Sacramento Kings NBA, 2005—. Guest Jamie Foxx Show. Founder The Future Found., Rebound America (to raise funds for 9/11 victims), 2001. Named one of Good Guys in Sports, The Sporting News; named to NBA All-Rookie First Team, 1996—97, Third Team All-Am., AP. Achievements include third overall draft pick, NBA Draft, 1996. Avocations: pool, collecting basketball jerseys, movies. Mailing: c/o Sacramento Kings Arco Arena One Sports Plz Sacramento CA 95834

ABDY, PAMELA, film producer; b. Nov. 23, 1973; Grad., Emerson Coll., Boston, 1995. Receptionist Jersey Films, LA, asst. to Danny DeVito, 1996—99, pres. prodn.; v.p. prodn. Paramount Pictures, 2003—04, sr. v.p. prodn., 2004—06, exec. v.p. prodn., 2006—. Assoc. prodr.: (films) Man on the Moon, 1999; co-prodr.: The Caveman's Valentine, 2001; exec. prodr.: How High, 2001; prodr.: Garden State, 2004, Babel, 2006. Office: Paramount Pictures 5555 Melrose Ave Los Angeles CA 90038*

ABE, NOBUYASU, ambassador; b. Akita, Japan, Sept. 9, 1945; m. Akiko Sugawara; 2 children. Studied, U. Tokyo, Japan, 1964—67; BA, Amherst Coll., 1969. Joined Japanese Fgn. Svc., 1967; served in embassy Washington, 1969—71, Tel Aviv, 1979—81, Manila, Philippines, 1990—92; served in UN missions and other internat. orgns. Geneva, 1977—79; served in mission NYC, 1987—90, 1996—97; dep. dir.-gen. econ. affairs, 1992—94; consul-gen. Boston, 1994—96; dir.-gen. Arms Control and Sci. Affairs, Tokyo, 1997—99; amb. Internat. Orgn. Vienna, 1999—2001, Kingdom Saudi Arabia, 2001—03; under-sec.-gen. UN Disarmament Affairs, 2003—06; amb. of Japan to Switzerland, 2006—. Internat. fellow, Weatherhead Ctr. for Internat. Affairs Harvard U., 1986—87. Internat. fellow, Weatherhead Ctr. Internat. Affairs, Harvard U., 1986—87. Mem.: Internat. Inst. Strategic Studies. Achievements include helping organize the Tokyo Forum for Nuclear Nonproliferation and Disarmament and particpated in mnay internat. activities for disarmament and nonproliferation; instrumental in bringing about the Japanese ratification of the Ottawa Conv. to Ban Anti-personnel Landmines; in Vienna, leading the efforts to promote the entry into force of the Comprehensive Test Ban Treaty and to conclude the negotiation on the FIrearms Protocol of the Anti-Organized Crime Conv. Office: Embassy of Japan Engestrasse 53 3012 Bern Switzerland Home Phone: 41-31-309-7111. Personal E-mail: nobieabee@aol.com.

ABEGG, MARTIN GERALD, retired academic administrator; b. Alliance, Nebr., Oct. 3, 1925; s. Frank and Mary Anna (Newberry) A.; m. Barbara Louise Chamberlain, June 29, 1946; children: Martin Gerald, Robert Miles. BS in Gen. Engring, Bradley U., 1947; MS in Civil Engring, U. Colo., 1951; PhD in Civil Engring, Rensselaer Poly. Inst., 1960; LL.D. (hon.), Ill. Coll., 1982; L.H.D. (hon.), Bradley U., 1993. Registered profl. engr., Ill. registered land surveyor, Ill. Instr. engring. Bradley U., 1947-50, asst. prof., 1950-55, asso. prof., 1955-60, prof., 1960—, head dept. civil engring., 1960-63, dean Coll. Engring. and Tech., 1963-70, pres., 1971-92, pres. emeritus, 1992—. Engring. aide Ill. Div. Hwys., Dixon, 1946, civil engr., Peoria, Ill., 1948; park dist. engr., Peoria, 1953-55; cons. engr. Norman Porter & Assos., N.Y.C., 1956-57, 59. Served to lt. (j.g.) USNR, 1943-46. Recipient Putnam award Bradley U., 1961, Disting. Engring Alumnus award U. Colo., 1986, Disting. Alumnus award Bradley U., 1992. Mem. Am. Soc. C.E., Sigma Xi, Sigma Tau, Phi Kappa Phi, Omicron Delta Kappa, Tau Beta Pi, Chi Epsilon. Home: PO Box 429 Fish Creek WI 54212 Home Phone: 920-868-2983.

ABEL, BARBARA ELLEN, photographer; d. Robert and Virginia Buckley; m. Ernest Abel, Sept. 20; children: Jason Robert, Rebecca Abel Salama. BS in Edn., Salem State U., Winston-Salem, NC, 1966; MA, SUNY, Amherst, 1980; student, Oakland C.C., 1994—2005. Tchr. Gloucester Pub. Sch., Mass., 1966—68, Oakland Pub. Sch., Calif., 1968—70, Toronto Pvt. Sch., 1970—71, Durham County Pub. Sch., NC, 1971—73; substitute tchr. Amherst Pub. Sch., NY, 1973—75; pvt. reading specialist Amherst, 1980—83; rsch. asst. Rsch. Inst. Alcohol, Buffalo, 1983—85, Wayne State U., Detroit, 1985—95; pres. Babel's Dreamcatcher Photography, Inc., West Bloomfield, Mich., 1996—. Exhibitions include Bloomfield Art Assn., 1997 (1st pl. award), City Hall Gallery, Dearborn, Mich., 1997 (Best of Show award), 1998, Erector Sq. Gallery, New Haven, Conn., 1998 (Curator's Choice award), Stamford Art Assn., Conn., 1998, Masuer Mus. Art, Monroe, La., 0199 (Juror's award), Albercrombie Gallery, La., 1999 (Purchase award), Chautauqua Nat. Exhbn. Am. Art., 1999 (William S. Holmes award), Arts Coun. SE, Mo., 1999 (Juror's award), Loudon House Gallery, Lexington, Ky., 1999, Paint Creek Ctr. Arts, Rochester, Mich., 1999, Janice Charach Epstein Gallery, West Bloomfield, 2000, Mem. Gallery, Soc. Contemporary Photography, Kansas City, 2000, Dennos Mus., Traverse City, Mich., 2000, Veridian Gallery, NYC, 2000 (Show Competition All Media award), Rice/Polak Gallery, Provincetown, Mass., 2002, 2004—06, Air Gallery, NYC, 2005, Brighton Mus., England, 2005, photography, published in Sleek Mag., Berlin, 2006. Pres. Maple West Sch. PTA, Williamsville, NY, 1984—85; vol. Bloomfield Hills Sch., Mich., 1986—94; vol. photographer calendar Mich. Humane Soc., Mich., 1995. Mem.: Women of Bloomfield (bd. mem. 2005—). Office Phone: 248-872-8513. Personal E-mail: abel55@comcast.net, abel55@comast.net.

ABEL, CARLOS ALBERTO, immunologist; b. Buenos Aires, May 7, 1930; came to U.S., 1959, naturalized, 1969; s. Carlos Alberto and Rosa Blanca (Molinero) A.; m. Amalia Carmen Minieri, June 15, 1959. BS, M. Belgrano Coll., 1948; MD, U. Buenos Aires, 1957. Intern St. Joseph's Hosp., Providence, 1959-60; fellow in pediatrics U. Md., Balt., 1960-64, resident in pediatrics, 1964-66; advanced rsch. fellow Scripps Clinic, La Jolla, Calif., 1966-69; vis. scientist U. Oxford, England, 1969-70; mem. div. basic immunology Nat. Jewish Hosp., Denver, 1970-84; sr. scientist Med. Rsch. Inst., San Francisco, 1984-92; dir. immunochemistry ICR/Med. Rsch. Inst., 1986-89; chmn. sci. coun. Med. Rsch. Inst., 1993—. Biotech. cons.; vis. scholar U. Calif.-Berkeley, 1982. Contbr. articles to profl. jours. Mem. Am. Assn. Immunologists, Am. Assn. Pathologists, Biochem. Soc. (Eng.), British Soc. for Immunology, Sociedad Argentina de Immunologia, Assn. Latino Americana Immunologia, Soc. Clin. Immunology. Democrat. Roman Catholic. Achievements include research in structure and function of glycoproteins from the surfaces of lymphocytes; study of their role in cell-cell interactions, structure of antibodies, glycobiology. Home: 523 Cragmont Ave Berkeley CA 94708-1205 E-mail: carlosabel@comcast.net.

ABEL, ELIZABETH ANN, dermatologist; b. Hartford, Conn., Mar. 16, 1940; d. Frederick A. and Rose (Borovicka) Abel; m. Barton Lane; children: Barton F. Lane, Geoffrey Lane, Suzanne Lane Franklin. Student, Colby-Sawyer Coll., 1957-60; BS, Wash. Hosp. Ctr. Sch. Med. Tech., 1961, U. Md., 1965, MD cum laude, 1967. Diplomate Am. Bd. Dermatology. Intern San Francisco Gen. Hosp., 1967-68; resident in medicine, fellow in oncology U. Calif. Med. Ctr., San Francisco, 1968-69; resident in dermatology NYU Med. Ctr., 1969-72, chief resident, 1971-72, USPHS research trainee in immunology, 1972-73; dep. chief dept. dermatology USPHS Hosp., SI, NY, 1973-74; instr. clin. dermatology Columbia U. Coll. Physicians and Surgeons, NYC, 1974-75, Stanford (Calif.) U. Sch. Medicine, 1975-77, clin. asst. prof. dermatology, 1977-82, asst. prof. dermatology, 1982-90, clin. assoc. prof., 1990-96, clin. prof., 1996—. Asst. editor Jour. Am. Acad. Dermatology, 1993-98; mem. med. adv. bd. The Nat. Psoriasis Found., 1993-95. Contbr. articles to profl. sci. jours. Mellon Found. fellow, 1983, 87. Fellow Am. Acad. Dermatology; mem. N.Am. Clin. Dermatologic Soc., San Francisco Dermatologic Soc., Internat. Soc. Dermatology, Pacific Dermatologic Assn., Women's Dermatologic Soc., Noah Worcester Dermatologic Soc., Alpha Omega Alpha. Avocations: piano, golf, travel, reading. Office: 2660 Grant Rd Ste D Mountain View CA 94040-4315 Office Phone: 650-938-6244. Personal E-mail: eaabelmd@aol.com.

ABEL, GREGORY E., utility company executive; B in Commerce with honors, U. Alberta, Can. Chartered acct., Can. With Price Waterhouse, San Francisco, Calif. Energy Co., Inc., 1992, sr. v.p.; pres., COO MidAm. Energy Holdings Co., Des Moines, 1997—. CEO CE Electric UK, England, MidAmerican Funding, LLC., Kern River Gas Transmission Co., Northern Natural Gas Co.; dir. MidAmerican Energy Holdings Co., HomeServices Am., Inc., Mpls.; bd. dir. Edison Electric Inst. Bd., exec. com. Greater Des Moines Partnership; Iowa Bus. Coun.; bd. dir. Wells Fargo, Iowa; exec. bd. Mid-Iowa Coun. Boy Scouts Am. Mem.: Alberta Inst. Chartered Accts., Canadian Inst. Chartered Accts. Office: Mid Am Energy Holdings Co 666 Grand Ave Des Moines IA 50309

ABEL, JAMES E., treasurer; b. Phila. BA with honors, Lehigh U., MA in Fin. Joined PPL Corp., Allentown, Pa., 1972, treasury mgr., 1984—95, mgr. corp. audit svcs., 1995—96, treas., 1996—99, v.p. fin., treas., 1999—. Mem.: Assn. of Fin. Profls. Office: PPL Corp Two N Ninth St Allentown PA 18101*

ABEL, MICHAEL L., marketing executive; b. New London, Wis., Jan. 15, 1952; s. William A. and Delores R. (Shuey) A.; m. Monica L. Miller, Dec. 18, 1971; children: Richard M., David M. AAS, Joliet Jr. Coll., Ill., 1975; BA in Bus. Adminstrn., Lewis U., 1977, MBA, 1979. Lab. technician No. Petrochem. Co., Morris, Ill., 1975-76, tech. specialist, 1976-80, nat. account rep. Des Plaines, Ill., 1980-82; product mgr. Enron Chem. Co., Omaha, 1982-85, mktg. mgr., 1985-87; sr. account exec. Quantum Chem. Co., Rancho Mirage, Calif., 1987-89; sr. v.p. N.Am. ops. Intac Automotive Products, Inc., Lemont, Ill., 1989—; pres., chief exec. officer Desert Leisure Devel. Corp., Palm Springs, 1991—, bd. dirs. Bd. dirs. Palm Cts. Assn., Rancho Mirage, 1988-97, The Kids Business, Inc., Rancho Mirage, 1996—. Patentee in chem. engring. field. Pres. Palm Ct. Owners Assn., Rancho Mirage, 1988-97; mem. Rep. Presdl. Task Force, 1990—. Mem. ASTM, Soc. Automotive Engrs., Nat. Assn. Corrosion Engrs. (sec. 1981-82), Internat. Platform Assn. Republican. Lutheran. Home: 36845 Palm Ct Rancho Mirage CA 92270-2206

ABEL, ROBERT BERGER, science administrator; b. Providence, July 21, 1926; s. Abraham Lincoln and Betty Ruth (Berger) A.; m. Nancy Marilyn Klein, Oct. 4, 1953; children: Alan Stewart, Deborah Jane. BS in Chemistry, Brown U., 1947; MEA, George Washington U., 1961; PhD, Am. U., 1972. Chemist Woods Hole (Mass.) Oceanographic Inst., 1947-50; oceanographer U.S. Navy Hydrographic Office, Suitland, Md., 1950-55; asst. to dir. U.S. Navy Hydrog. Office, 1955-60; asst. research coordinator Office Naval Research, Washington, 1961-64; exec. sec. Interagy. Com. Oceanography, 1960-67; asst. exec. sec. Nat. Council Marine Resources and Engring. Devel., 1967-68; dir. Nat. Sea Grant Program, Dept. Commerce, 1966-77; asst. v.p. Tex. A&M U., 1977—80; v.p. N.J. Marine Scis. Consortium, Fort. Hancock, 1979-81, pres., 1981-93; sr. sci. Stevens Inst. Tech., Hoboken, N.J., 1993—. Instr. oceanography USNR Officers Sch., 1960-65, Fairleigh Dickinson U., 1966-83, U. Va., 1976-77; instr. ocean mgmt. Rutgers U., 1980-84; dir. Israel Oceanographic and Limnol. Rsch. Ltd., Inc.; mem. panel Nat. Acad. Scis.; mgr. Cooperative Marine Tech. Program for Middle East, 1980—; mem. N.J. Marine Fisheries Coun., 1993—; mem. N.J. Aquaculture Adv. Coun.; chmn. adv. com. Jersey Shore Partnership; cruise lectr. Cunard, Crystal, Holland Am., Celebrity, Lindblad and Seabourne Lines. Pres. Cris-Mar Manor Civic Assn., 1957-61; bd. dirs. Tantallon Civic Assn., 1973-74, Ctr. Ocean Law and Policy; v.p. Jewish Congregation; chmn. Zoning Bd., Shrewsbury, N.J., 1990-2001. Active duty USN, 1945—46, recruiting officer USN, 1946—47, RI, instr. Naval Reserve Officers Sch. USN, 1960—66, active USNR, 1945—65. Recipient Spl. award Prince of Monaco, 1952, Superior Civilian Svc. award Navy Dept., 1963, Disting. Svc. award, 1967, Disting. Alumnus award George Washington U., 1983, Compass Disting. Svc. award, 1987, Disting. Svc. award Egyptian Nat. Inst. Oceanography and Fisheries; Gold medal Dept. Commerce, 1973; named Man of Yr. Nat. Sea Grant Program, 1977; decorated Order Jules Richard, Monaco, 1951. Mem. Am. Chem. Soc., Rsch. Soc. Am. (past pres. chpt.), Marine Tech. Soc. (pres. 1974-75), Am. Geophys. Union, Am. Soc. Oceanography (pres. 1971-72), Cosmos Club (Washington), Brown Club NJ, B'Nai Israel Congregation (bd. trustees). Jewish. Home: 55 Queen Ann Dr Shrewsbury NJ 07702-4127 Office: Stevens Inst Tech Davidson Labs 711 Hudson St Hoboken NJ 07030 Office Phone: 201-216-5314. Personal E-mail: rbanka@aol.com.

ABEL, WILLIAM EDWARD, applied physicist, consultant; b. Great Falls, Mont., May 23, 1928; s. Ernest Edward and Anna Lucille (Rempel) A.; m. Theodora Louise Hartho, Mar. 24, 1964; children: Stephen Edward, Jeffrey William. BA, Whitman Coll., Walla Walla, Wash., 1952; MFA, Cranbrook Acad. Art, Bloomfield Hills, Mich., 1954. Owner William Abel Design, Portland, Oreg., 1955-76, Lake Oswego, Oreg., 1976—. Co-founder Audiotrainer, Inc., Mountain View, Calif., 1967, dir., 1967-85; cons. in field, 1965—. Dir. Riverdale RFPD, Portland, 1983—, chmn., 1999-2001; chmn. bldg. and bonding com. Riverdale Sch. Dist., 1988. Served to sgt. USAF, 1946-48. Achievements include 16 patents in field. Home and Office: 12203 SW Tryon Hill Rd Portland OR 97219-8314 Office Phone: 503-636-0759.

ABELE, JOHN E., medical products executive; m. Mary Abele; 3 children. BS in Physics and Philosophy, Amherst Coll., 1959. With Advanced Instruments, Inc.; co-founder, chmn., dir. Boston Sci., Natick, Mass., 1979—. Founder Kingbridge Centre, Canada. Trustee Mus. of Sci., Boston; chmn. First Orgn.; founder Argosy Found. (formerly known as Abele Family Charitable Trust), 1995, trustee. Named one of Forbes' Richest Americans, 2006. Achievements include first to develop medical technology and products that reduce risk, trauma, cost and recovery time; invention of steerable catheter in 1969; patents in field. Office: Boston Sci One Boston Scientific Pl Natick MA 01760-1537

ABELES, KIM VICTORIA, artist; b. Richmond Heights, Mo., Aug. 28, 1952; d. Burton Noel Wright and Frances Elizabeth (Sander) Hoffman. BFA in Painting, Ohio U., 1974; MFA in Studio Art, U. Calif., Irvine, 1980. Free-lance artist, LA, 1975—. Lectr. varius schs. and art ctrs., 1980—; vis. disting. artist Calif. State U., Fullerton, 1985-87; assoc. prof. Calif. State U., Northridge, 1998—; artist-in-residence Art Mill, Czech Republic, 2005; commissions Cmty. Magnet Sch., Bel Air, Calif., 2006, LA Unified Sch. Dist., 2007. Author, illustrator Crafts, Cookery and 'Country Living, 1976, Kim Abeles, 1988, Kim Abeles: Encyclopedia Persona, 1993, author, photographer: Impressions, 1979; co-author: Surface tension Problematics of Site, 2003; work featured in Artery, 1979, Pacific Poetry and Fiction Review, 1980, Fiction Internat., 1985; one-woman shows include U. Calif., Irvine, 1979—80, Mcpl. Art Gallery, LA, 1981, LA City Hall, 1982, Phyllis Kind Gallery, Chgo., 1983, Karl Bornstein Gallery, Santa Monica, Calif., 1983, 1985, 1987, Pepperdine U., Malibu, Calif., 1985, A.I.R. Gallery, NYC, 1986, Chapman Coll., Orange, Calif., 1986, Mount St. Mary's Coll., LA, 1987, Atlanta Pavilion, 1990, Calif. Mus. of Sci. and Industry, LA, 1991, Laguna Art Mus. Satellite Gallery, Costa Mesa, Calif., 1991, Turner-Krull Gallery, LA, 1992, Lawrence Miller Gallery, NYC, 1992, Santa Monica Mus. Art, LA, 1993, Nat. Mus. Fine Arts, Santiago, Chile, 1996, Mus. Modern Art, Rio de Janeiro, 1996, Cmplejo Cultural Recoleta, Buenos Aires, 1986, Centro Cutural Consolidado, Caracas, 1997, Cepa Gallery, Buffalo, 1998, A.R.T., Inc., NYC, 1989, Contemporary Arts Ctr., Cin., 2000, Art Resources Transfer, NYC, 2001, Intersection, San Francisco, 2001, Calif. Sci. Ctr., LA, 2000—01, Coll. Environ. Design, Calif. Poly. U., Pomona, 2002, El Camino Coll., LA, 2003, SCAPE, Carona del Mar, Calif., 2007, The Shed, Newport Beach, Calif., 2007, exhibitions include Mus. of Contemporary Art, LA, LA County Mus. Art, Calif. African-Am. Mus., Allen Meml. Art Mus., Ohio, Songzhuang Festival, Beijing, Represented in permanent collections Marriott Hotels, City of Pasadena, San Fernando Valley Constituent Svc. Ctr., Marvin Braude San Fernando Valley Constituent Svc. Ctr., Dept. Transp., LA, Cmty. Magnet Sch., exhibited in group shows at Mus. Kampa, Czech Republic, Silpakorn U., Bangkok, 2002, Nat. History Mus., LA, 2005, Hanoi U. Fine Arts, Vietnam, 2005, Sun Valley Ctr. Arts, Idaho, 2006, Boulder Mus. Contemporary Art, Colo., 2007, U. Berkeley Art Mus., Calif., 2007. Honored for Outstanding Student Rsch. & Creative Achievement U. Calif., 1979; recipient U.S. Steel award Exhbn. of the Associated Artists of pitts., 1977, Clean Air award Air Quality Mgmt. Dist., Calif., 1992; Hand Hollow Found. fellow, 1984, Design Team fellow Panorama City Libr., Calif., 1992-93, J. Paul Getty Trust Fund for the Visual Arts fellow, 1994; Pollock-Krasner Found. grantee, 1990, Calif. Arts Coun. grantee, 1990, L.A. Cultural Affairs grantee, 1991, 95, 96, U.S. Info. Agy. grantee, 1995-97, Art Mill residency, Czech Republic, 2005; commissioned by Panorama City Pub. Libr., L.A., 1993, Met. Transp. Authority, L.A., 1995, Dept. Transp., L.A., 2000, Cmty. Magnet Sch., Bel Air, Calif., 2007, LA Unified Sch. Dist., 2007; recipient Richard Neutra award for Profl. Excellence, 2001. Office Phone: 213-626-4623. Personal E-mail: kimabeles@earthlink.net.

ABELES, NORMAN, psychologist, educator; came to U.S., 1939, naturalized, 1944; s. Felix and Bertha (Gronich) A.; m. Jeanette Bueller, Apr. 14, 1957; children: Linda, Mark. BA, NYU, 1949; MA, U. Tex., 1952, PhD, 1958. Diplomate: Am. Bd. Profl. Psychology (Midwest regional bd. 1972-78, chmn. regional bd. 1975-77; nat. trustee 1975-77). Fellow in counseling U. Tex., Austin, 1956-57; instr. Mich. State U., East Lansing, 1957-59, asst. prof., 1959-64, asso. prof., 1964-67, prof. psychology, 1968—, dir. psychol. clinic, 1978—2004, co-dir. clin. tng., 1981-96, asst. dir. counseling center, 1965-71. U.S. State Dept. ednl. exch. prof. U. Utrecht, Netherlands, 1969, vis. prof., 1975; cons. Peace Corps, 1965-69; vocat. cons. Social Security Office of Hearings and Appeals, 1962—; med. advisor Social Security Office of Hearings and Appeals, 1986—; mem. Mich. Commn. Cert. of Psychologists, 1962-77, chmn., 1966-68; mem. coun. Nat. Register Health Svc. Providers in Psychology, 1974—, vice chmn., 1975-80; del. White House Conf. on Aging, 1995, 2005; mem. geriatric and gerontology adv. com. to Sec. of VA, 2002—. Editor: Acad. Psychology bull., 1978-82; cons. editor Am. Jour. Alzheimers Disease and other Dementias, Jour. Personality Assessment, 1988—, Clin. Psychology: Sci. and Practice, 1994-2004, Clin. Psychology Rev., 1995-98, Profl. Psychology: Rsch. and Practice, 1979-81, 89—, editor, 1983-88; contbr. articles to profl. jours. Served with U.S. Army, 1954-56. Fulbright-Hays grantee, 1969; recipient Disting. Psychologist award Mich. Soc. Clin. Psychologists, 1984; Disting. Practitioner, Nat. Acad. Practice, 1982; Arthur Furst Ethics Lectureship medal Pacific Grad. Sch. Psychology, 1996; Dept. Vets. Affairs Spl. Contbns. award, Battle Creek Mich., 1997. Fellow APA (coun. reps. 1972-75, 77-79, 89-91, 93-95, 99—, policy and planning bd. 1975-79, chmn. 1976, rec. sec. 1980-86, chmn. edn. and tng. bd. 1988, bd. ednl. affairs 1999-2001, com. on internat. rels. in psychology 2002-04, pres. divsn. psychotherapy and divsn. clin. psychology 1990, publs. and comm. bd. 1990-96, chmn. 1995, pres.-elect 1996, pres. 1997, bd. dirs. divsn. psychotherapy 2000—2005, pres. divsn. 7 geropsychology/internat. psychology 2005, pres. sect. IX assessment divsn. clin. psychology 2004, ethics com. 2005—), Am. Psychol. Found. (sec. 2002—), Coun. Sci. Socs. Pres.; mem. Midwestern Psychol. Assn., Mich. Psychol. Assn. (legis. chmn. 1964-72, pres. 1971-72, Disting. Psychologist 1974), Internat. Union Psychol. Scis. (U.S. com. 1999-2005), Sigma Xi. Home: 953 Rosewood Ave East Lansing MI 48823-3126 Office: Mich State U Dept Psychology 110C Psychology Bldg East Lansing MI 48824-1117 Home Phone: 517-337-0853; Office Phone: 517-353-7274. Business E-Mail: abeles@msu.edu.

ABELES, SIGMUND M., painter, sculptor, printmaker; b. Bklyn., Nov. 6, 1934; s. Samuel and Henrietta (Banner) A.; m. Anne Merck (div. 1998); children: David Paul, Shoshanna Lynn, Maxwell Merck Abeles. Student, Pratt Inst., 1952-53, Art Students' League, 1954, Skowhegan Sch., 1955-56, Bklyn. Mus. Sch. (Graphics scholar), 1956-57; AB in Art, U. SC, 1955; MFA, Columbia U., 1957; DA (hon.), Coastal Carolina U., 2000. Faculty Swain Sch. Design, New Bedford, Mass., 1961-64; resident artist Wellesley (Mass.) Coll., 1964-69; asst. prof. art Boston U., 1969-70; prof. U. N.H., 1970-87, prof. emeritus, 1987—; artist-in-residence U. So. Maine, Gorham, 1990. Instr. workshop Acad. Realist Art, Seattle, 1995, Art Students League, N.Y.C., 1997-2000; instr. advanced drawing workshop Nat. Acad. Sch. Fine Arts, N.Y.C., 1997-98; bd. dirs. Artist Fellowship, N.Y.C.; represented by Spaneirman Modern, NYC. One man shows include Bates Coll. Mus., Lewiston, Maine, 1999, Thomas Williams Fine Arts, London, 2000, Art 2003, London, Thomas Williams Fine Arts and Drawing Studio, Tucson, Burroughs/Chapin Art Mus., Portland Mus. Art, others; group shows include Pinkard Gallery, Bunting Ctr., Md., Coll. Art, Balt., 2001, Randall Bryan Art Gallery, 2001, S.C. State Mus., Columbia, 1999, Denise Bibro Gallery, N.Y.C., 1999, Atrium Gallery U. Conn., 1992, John Szoke Gallery, N.Y.C., 1989, Am. Artists Galleries, 1986, others; represented in permanent collections including Albert & Victoria Mus., London, The Brit. Mus., London, Libr. Congress, Washington, Mus. Modern Art, N.Y.C., Met. Mus. Art, N.Y.C., Museo de Arte, Ponce, P.R., Phila. Mus. Art, Mus. Find Art, Boston, Fitz William Mus., Cambridge, England, Munson-Proctor-Williams Inst., Ithaca, N.Y., Whitney Mus. Am. Art, N.Y.C., The Old Print Shop, Whilliam P. Carl Fine Prints, Northampton, Mass., Portfolio Art Gallery, Columbia, SC, Yale U. Art Gallery, New Haven, Conn., Brookgreen Gardens, Munells Inlet, SC, others; vis. sculptor Johnson Atelier, Tech. Inst. for Sculpture, 1977; traveling retrospective exhbn. New Eng. Coll., Henniker, N.H., McKissick Mus., U. S.C., Columbia, Checkwood Mus. Art, Nashville, Fitchburg (Mass.) Mus. Art, 1992-93; (subject of) The Observant Hand, Forty Years of the Drawing of Sigmund Abeles, So. Meth. U. Gallery, Dallas, 1998; archive for his papers set up at South Carolinian Libr., U. S.C., 1998—, study archive for prints at Bates Coll. Mus. Art, 1998—, grant to paint Chateau Rochefort-en-tene-France, 2000. Nat. Inst. Arts and Letters grantee, 1965, Nat. Coun. Arts and Humanities sabbatical grantee, 1966, Louis Comfort Tiffany Found. grantee, 1967, U. N.H. Grad. Sch. Sculpture grantee, 1973, Am. Jewish Com. grantee for acad. seminar in Israel, 1981, Florsheim Found. grantee, 1992, residency grantee Chateau Rochefort en Terre, Brittany, France, 2000; recipient Am. Master/Printmaking award Am. Artist mag., 1996; subject of "Sigmund Abeles, A Monograph" essays by Charles Simic and Robert Doty, 1992. Mem. NAD (Leo Meisner prize 1983, academician 1990, mem. coun., corr. sec. 1991—), Soc. Am. Graphic Artists, Pastel Soc. Am. (Hall of Fame honoree 2004). E-mail: sabelesart@aol.com. *I strive to observe life with a penetrating eye that I hope can go beyond surface reality to reveal psychological and visual truth, even some magic.*

ABELL, CHARLES S., federal official; b. Sayre, PA, Dec. 20, 1946; m. Cathy McCaffrey, July 24, 1982; 1 child. BS in Polit. Sci. & Social Sci., U. Tampa, 1976; MS in Human Resource Mgmt., Columbus U. Enlisted US Army, 1966, advanced through ranks to lt. col., dep. chief of staff for personnel, 1989—91, ret., 1993; profl. staff mem. Senate Armed Svcs. Com., 1993—2001, staff dir., 2005—; asst. sec. for force mgmt. policy US Dept. Def., Washington, 2001—02, prin. dep. under sec. for personnel & readiness, 2002—05. Decorated Bronze Star with "V" device (2), Purple Heart, Combat Infantryman's Badge, Legion of Merit, Meritorious Svc. medal with 4 oak leaf cluster, Air medals (14), Amy Commendation medal. Roman Catholic. Office: US Armed Services Com Senate Russell Office Bldg Washington DC 20510

ABELL, NANCY L., lawyer; b. LA, July 19, 1950; BA with honors, Pitzer Coll., 1972; JD, UCLA, 1979. Bar: Calif. 1979. Extern clk. to Hon. Shirley Hufstedler U.S. Ct. Appeals (9th cir.), 1978; ptnr. Paul, Hastings, Janofsky & Walker LLP, LA, 1986—, chairperson employment law dept. Bd. govs. Inst. Corp. Counsel, 1989—, chairperson, 1994-95; bd. advisors UCLA Sch. Law. Author: (with P.W. Cane) An Employer's Guide to the Americans with Disabilities Act, 1991, An Employer's Guide for Preparing Affirmative Action Programs. Bd. advisors UCLA Sch. Law. Fellow Coll. Labor and Employment Lawyers, Inc.; mem. ABA (mgmt. co-chair trial advocacy subcom., employee rights and responsibilities com., labor and employment law sect. 1991-94); Order of Barristers, Order of Coif. Office:

Paul Hastings Janofsky & Walker LLP 515 S Flower St Fl 23 Los Angeles CA 90071-2300 Office Phone: 213-683-6162. Office Fax: 213-996-3162. Business E-Mail: nancyabell@paulhastings.com.

ABELL, RICHARD BENDER, federal judicial officer, lawyer; b. Phila., Dec. 2, 1943; s. Lon Edward Welch, Jr. and Charlotte Amelia (Bender) A., stepfather Ernest George Abell; m. Lucia del Carmen Lombana-Cadavid, Dec. 2, 1968; children: David, Christian, Rachel. BA in Internat. Affairs, George Washington U., 1966, JD, 1974. Bar: Pa. 1974. Vol. Peace Corps, Colombia, 1967-69; assoc. Reilly & Fogwell, West Chester, Pa., 1974-80; asst. dist. atty. Chester County, Pa., 1974-79; staff mem. to US Senator Richard Schweiker US Senate, Washington, 1979-80; dir. Office of Prog. Devel. Peace Corp., Washington, 1981-83; dep. asst. atty. gen. US Dept. Justice, Washington, 1983-86, asst. atty. gen., 1986-90; spl. master, spl. trial judge US Ct. Fed. Claims, Washington, 1991—. Mem. adj. faculty Del. Law Sch., Wilmington, 1975-77, West Chester State U., 1976; bd. dirs. Fed. Prison Industries, Inc., 1985-91; chmn. Nat. Crime Prevention Coalition, 1986-90; mem. adv. bd. Nat. Inst. Corrections, 1986-90; co-chmn. adv. com. Nat. Ctr. for State and Local Law Enforcement Tng., 1987-90; vice chmn. rsch. and devel. rev. bd. Dept. Justice, 1987-89; mem. nat. drug policy bd. Enforcement Coordinating Group and Coordinating Group for Drug Abuse Prevention and Health, The White House, Washington, 1988-89. Author: Peter Smith of Westmoreland County, Va. (Died 1741) and Some Descendents, 1996, Sojourns of a Patriot: Field and Prison Papers of An Unreconstructed Confederate, 1998. Chmn. Young Rep. Nat. Fedn., Washington, 1979-81; mem. exec. com. Rep. Nat. Com., 1979-81; mem. fed. coordinating coun. on Juvenile Justice and Delinquency Prevention, 1986-90; mem. Pres.'s Task Force on Adoption, 1987-88; mem. Pres.'s Commn. on Agrl. Workers, 1988-93. Served in US Army, 1969—71. Decorated Purple Heart, Army Commendation medal for heroism, Air medal; recipient Jefferson Davis Hist. gold medal, 2000. Mem.: Order Indian Wars US, Sons of Revolution, Soc. Colonial Wars, Soc. Cin., Aztec Club of 1847. Anglican Catholic. Office: US Ct Fed Claims Office of Spl Masters Ste 200 1440 New York Ave NW Washington DC 20005 Office Phone: 202-357-6349. Personal E-mail: richard_bender_abell@yahoo.com.

ABELLAN, JOSÉ LUIS, humanities educator; b. Madrid, May 19, 1933; s. José M. Abellan and Angela M. Gonzalez. M. U. Complutense, Madrid, 1960; PhD, U. Complutense, 1961. Prof. U. PR, 1961—63, U. Belfast, Ireland, 1963-65, U. Madrid, 1966—. Corr. N. Am. Acad. Spanish Lang., 1993—; rep. of Spain to exec. bd. UNESCO, 1983—85; pres. Atheneum of Madrid, 2001. Author: (7 vols.) History of Spanish Thought, 1979-82, Nat. Essay prize, 1981, Erasmism in Spain, 1976, Theldea of America, 1972; editor: (5 vols.) Spanish Exile of 1939, 1976-78. Grantee Juan March Found., 1976. Fellow Soc. Spanish and Spanish-Am. Studies Nebr. U., pres., Athenenum of Madrid, 2001. Avocations: walking, photography. Home: Gravina 7 28004 Madrid Spain Office: Facultad de Filosofia Univ Complutense 28040 Madrid Spain Office Phone: 34-91-429-1750. Business E-Mail: presidenciaateneo@telefonica.net.

ABELMAN, ARTHUR F., lawyer; b. NYC, June 12, 1933; s. Bert and Myra (Dickoff) A. AB, Harvard U., 1954, JD, 1957. Bar: N.Y. 1958, U.S. Dist. Ct. (so. and ea. dist.) N.Y. 1958, U.S. Ct. Appeals (2d cir.) 1958. Assoc. Casey Lane & Mittendorf, NYC, 1957-59; counsel Am. Petroleum Inst., NYC, 1959-61; corp. sec. Pocket Books, Inc., NYC, 1961-65; assoc. Weil Gotshal Manges, NYC, 1965-79; counsel Moses & Singer, NYC, 1979—; pres. Millan House, Inc., NYC, 1982—. Pres. Sculpture Ctr., Inc., N.Y.C., 1979-85, trustee, 1971-2000, exec. com., 1988-2000, treas., 1991-2000; trustee Norman Rockwell Art Collection Trust, E.E. Cummings Trust. Mem. ABA, N.Y. Bar Assn., Assn. of Bar of City of N.Y. Clubs: Harvard. Republican. Jewish. Home: 116 E 68th St New York NY 10021-5955 Business E-Mail: aabelman@mosessinger.com.

ABELOFF, MARTIN DAVID, medical administrator, educator, researcher; b. Shenandoah, Pa., Apr. 4, 1942; s. Aaron Harry and Cele (Freid) A.; m. Diane Kaufman, Jan. 7, 1967; children: Elisa, Jennifer. Student, Franklin and Marshall Coll., 1959-61; AB, Johns Hopkins U., 1963, MD, 1966. Diplomate Am. Bd. Internal Medicine, subspecialty in med. oncology. Intern U. Chgo. Hosps. and Clinics, 1966-67; clin. assoc. Balt. Cancer Rsch. Ctr., 1967-69; sr. asst. resident in medicine Beth Israel Hosp., Boston, 1969-70; fellow in clin. hematology New Eng. Med. Ctr., Boston, 1970-71; fellow in clin. oncology Sch. Medicine Johns Hopkins U., Balt., 1971-72, instr. in medicine, 1972-75, asst. prof. oncology, 1974-79, asst. prof. medicine, 1975-80, prof. medicine, 1990—, Eli Kennerly Mashall Jr. prof. oncology, dir.; Sidney Kimmel Comprehensive Cancer Ctr., 2000—; prof. & dir. Johns Hopkins Oncology Ctr., Balt., 1992—. Numerous vis. professorships and lectrs. including INstitut Jules Bordet, Brussels, Milton S. Hershey Med. Ctr., Nat. Cancer Inst., U. Ariz., SUNY, Stony Brook, U. So. Calif., U. Chgo., U. Md., Boston U., Mayo Clinic, others; advisor St. George's Soc., Am. Cancer Soc., 1974-84; chmn. psychosocial com. Ea. Coop. Oncology Group, 1979-83; cons. reviewer for clin. oncology rev. com. divsn. cancer treatment Nat. Cancer Inst., Bethesda, Md., 1980—. Editorial bd. Lung Cancer, 1985—, PDQ, NCI, 1986-88, Cancer Rsch., 1993; assoc. editor Jour. Clin. Oncology, 1987-96, Oncology, 1987—; assoc. editor, editorial bd. Cancer Treatment Reports, 1980-83; editor Clin. Oncology, 1992—, Oncology News Internat.; sect. editor Annals of Surg. Oncology, 1993—; adv. bd. The Med. Letter, 1991—; mem. editorial adv. bd. Health After 50, 1989—; contbr. numerous articles to profl. jours., chpts. to books. Bd. dirs. Md. divsn. Am. Cancer Soc., 1985-86. Mem. Am. Soc. Clin. Oncology (mem. ednl. com. 1978-80, mem. program com. 1981-83; chmn. program 1983-84, bd. dirs. 1984-87, chmn. com. on patterns of care 1986-87, chmn. ad-hoc com. for FDA liaison 1988-89, pres. 1991-92), Am. Assn. Cancer Rsch., Internat. Assn. for Study of Lung Cancer, Am. Assn. Cancer Edn., Phi Beta Kappa. Office: Johns Hopkins Oncology Ctr 600 N Wolfe St Rm 157 Baltimore MD 21287-0005*

ABELOW, BRADLEY, state official; b. June 9, 1958; m. Carolyn Abelow; children: Sarah, Hannah, Daniel. BA, Northwestern U., 1983; M in Pub. and Pvt. Mgmt., Yale U., 1989. Program officer Urban Coalition, Mpls.; mng. dir. Goldman Sachs & Co., 1997, ptnr., 1998, head ops., tech. and fin. in Asia Hong Kong; head global ops. The Goldman Sachs Group, Inc., NYC, 2000—04; treas. State of NJ, Trenton, 2006—. Bd. dirs. Depository Trust & Clearing Corp (DTCC) Thomson Fin. Office: Office of Gov PO Box 001 Trenton NJ 08625 Office Phone: 609-292-6000.*

ABELSON, ALAN, columnist; b. NYC, Oct. 12, 1925; s. Harry Carl and Vivian (Finkelstein) A.; m. Virginia Eloise Peterson, Sept. 1, 1951; children— Justin Adams, Reed Vivian. BS in Chemistry and English, CCNY, 1946; MA in Creative Writing, U. Iowa, 1947. Reporter N.Y. Jour. Am., NYC, 1949-56, stock market columnist, 1952-56; with Barron's, The Dow Jones Bus. and Fin. Weekly, NYC, 1956—, mng. editor, 1965-81, editor, 1981-93; columnist Up & Down Wall St., 1966—. Bus. corres. NBC-TV News at Sunrise, 1982-90. Office: Barron's 200 Liberty St New York NY 10281-1003

ABELSON, HERBERT TRAUB, pediatrician, educator; b. St. Louis, Feb. 19, 1941; s. Benjamin J. and Ann (Traub) Abelson; m. Constance Faye Caldwell, May 17, 1968; children: Matthew, Rebecca, Jonathan, Daniel. AB with high honors, U. Ill., 1962; MD, Washington U., St. Louis, 1966. Diplomate Am. Bd. Pediat., Am. Bd. Pediatric Hematology-Oncology. Intern pediat. U Colo. Med. Ctr., Denver, 1966—67; resident Boston Children's Hosp., 1969—71; staff assoc. Nat. Cancer Inst. NIH, Bethesda, Md., 1967—69; Jane Childs Meml. Fund for Med. Rsch. fellow NIH, 1971, spl. postdoctoral fellow, 1972; teaching fellow Med. Sch. Harvard Coll., Boston, 1970—71, instr. pediat., 1973—74, asst. prof., 1974—79; tutor in med. scis., 1977—79; assoc. prof. Harvard Coll., Boston, 1979—83; vis. prof., Ctr. for Cancer Rsch. MIT, Cambridge, 1982—83; prof., chmn. dept. pediat. Med. Sch. U. Wash., Seattle, 1983—95; prof., chmn., physician-in-chief dept. pediat. U. Chgo., 1995—2004, assoc. dean. admissions Pritzker Sch. Medicine, 2005—. Rsch. fellow in hematology Children's Hosp. Med. Ctr., Boston, 1971—73; rsch. assoc. in biology MIT, 1971—73; mem. exec. com. Am. Med. Sch. Pediatric Dept. Chairmen, 1989—91; lectr. U. Wash., 1990; mem. pediatric residency rev. com. Accreditation Coun. for Grad. Med. Edn., 1992—97; examiner Am. Bd. Pediatrics, 1988—, bd. dirs., 1992—97, sec.-treas., 1995, chmn. elect., 1995—96, chmn., 1996—97; endowed chair U. Chgo., 2004. Contbr. articles to profl. jours. Lt. comdr. USPHS, 1967—69. Recipient Rsch. Career Devel. award, NIH, 1975—80, Alumni achievement award, Washington U., 2001. Fellow: Am. Acad. Pediat.; mem.: Am. Soc. Pediat. Hematology (fin. com.), Am. Bd. Med. Spltys. (fin. com.), Am. Pediatric Soc., Soc. Pediatric Rsch., Am. Soc. Clin. Oncology, Am. Assn. Cancer Rsch., Am. Soc. Hematology (mem. sci. subcom. on pediatric hematology 1987—91). Avocations: aviation, squash, cooking. Office: Univ Chgo Office Medical Edn 924 E 57th St BSLC104 MC1000 Chicago IL 60637-1455 Office Phone: 773-702-3650. Business E-Mail: habelson@bsd.uchicago.edu.

ABELSON, REED, reporter; Healthcare bus. reporter NY Times. Office: NY Times 229 W 43rd St New York NY 10036 Office Phone: 212-556-1477. Office Fax: 212-556-1448. E-mail: abelson@nytimes.com.

ABELSON, ROBERT PAUL, cantor, singer; b. Nov. 16, 1929; BBA, CCNY, NYC, 1950; B Sacred Music, Hebrew Union Coll., NYC, 1957, D (hon.). Cantor Temple Beth Sholom, Flushing, NY, 1957—70, Temple of Covenant, 1970—80, Temple Israel, NYC, 1980—; solo baritone NYC Opera, 1978, various orchs. and opera cos. Mem.: Am. Guild Mus. Artists, Actors Equity, Am. Soc. Jewish Music. Office: 112 E 75th St New York NY 10021

ABELT, RALPH WILLIAM, bank executive; b. Elmhurst, Ill., Feb. 16, 1929; s. P. Alfred and Clara S. (Springhorn) A.; m. Patricia Mitchell, Feb. 2, 1952; children: Susan E., Christopher M., Leslie A. BS, U. Colo., 1952; MBA, Ind. U., 1953. Acct. Marion Hutchinson, C.P.A., Denver, 1952; v.p. comml. banking Continental Ill., Chgo., 1953-77; pres., chief exec. officer, dir. Bank One of Northeastern Ohio, NA, Painesville, 1977-83; chmn., chief exec. officer Bank One Cleve., NA, 1983-86; pres., chief exec. officer Work in N.E. Ohio Council, 1988-91. Past pres., mem. exec. bd., area v.p. N.E. Ohio coun. Boy Scouts Am., Painesville, 1981; dir. Holden Arboretum, Kirtland, Ohio, 1986-2005; dir. Knowledgeworks Found., Cin., 1987-2007. With USMC, 1946-48. Home: 13500 N Rancho Vistoso #511 Tucson AZ 85721 Personal E-mail: custcraft@aol.com.

ABER, JOHN WILLIAM (JACK), finance educator, consultant; b. Canonsburg, Pa., Sept. 9, 1937; s. John William and Rose (Lauda) A.; m. Cynthia Louise Sousa, Nov. 24, 1962; children: John, Valerie, Alexander. BS, Pa. State U., 1959; MBA, Columbia U., 1965; DBA, Harvard U., 1972. Cons. Univ. Affiliates, Inc., Boston, 1969-71; asst. prof. fin. Ga. State U., Atlanta, 1971-72, Boston U., 1972-78, assoc. prof., 1978-97, prof., 1997—, chmn. dept. fin. and econs., 2004—. Bd. dirs. Managers Funds, Appleton Growth Fund, Third Ave. Funds. McKinsey scholar Columbia U.; fellow Harvard U. Home: 51 Columbia St Brookline MA 02446-2407 Office: Boston U 595 Commonwealth Ave Boston MA 02215-1704 Business E-Mail: jackaber@bu.edu.

ABERBACH, JOEL DAVID, political science professor, writer; b. NYC, June 19, 1940; s. Isidore and Miriam (Meltzer) A.; m. Joan F. Gross, June 17, 1962; Children: Ian Mark, Amy Aberbach Arbreton, Matthew Daniel, Rachel Aberbach Metz. AB, Cornell U., 1961; MA, Ohio State U., 1963, Yale U., 1965, PhD, 1967. Asst. prof. U. Mich., Ann Arbor, 1967-72, research scientist, 1967-88, assoc. prof., 1972-78, prof., 1978-88; sr. fellow Brookings Inst., Washington, 1977-80; dir. Ctr. for Am. Politics and Pub. Policy, UCLA, 1986—; disting. prof. UCLA, 2004—; Winant prof. U. Oxford, 2006—07. Cons. Commn. on the Op. of the Senate, Washington, 1976, U.S. Office of Pers. Mgmt., Washington, 1983, Nat. Pub. Radio, Washington, 1983-84, U.S. Govt. Accountability Office, 2004—; vis. fellow U. Bologna, Inst. Advanced Study. Author: Keeping a Watchful Eye, 1990; co-author: Race in the City, 1973, Bureaucrats and Politicians in Western Democracies, 1981, In the Web of Politics, 2000; co-editor: The Role of the State in Taiwan's Development, 1994, Institutions of American Democracy: The Executive Branch, 2005. Del. Mich. Dem. Conv., Detroit, 1972; editorial bd. Congress and the Presidency, Washington, 1981—, Governance, Oxford, Eng., 1987-98, 2006-, Italian Rev. of Pub. Policy, 2001-, Pub. Orgn. Rev., 2000-; mem. internat. adv. bd. Pub. Policy and Adminstrn., 2007-; external adv. bd. Sociology, Politics, Internat. Relations, and Econs., U. Oxford, 2007-. Recipient Richard E. Neustadt award Best Reference Book on Presidency, Presidency Resch. Sect. Am. Polit. Sci. Assn., 2006; grantee, NSF, 1969—73, 1978—81, 1986—89, 1993—98. Fellow Brookings Inst., Ctr. Advanced Study in Behavioral Scis., Swedish Collegium Advanced Study in the Social Scis., Nat. Acad. Pub. Adminstrn.; mem. Am. Polit. Sci. Assn., Rsch. Com. on Structure and Orgn. Govt. of Internat. Polit. Sci. Assn. (exec. bd. 1985-89, co-chmn. 1989—), Annenberg Found. Insts. of Democracy Project (co-chair exec. br. commn. 2003—), Phi Beta Kappa. Jewish. Home: 10453 Colina Way Los Angeles CA 90077-2041 Office: UCLA 4250 Public Affairs Bldg Los Angeles CA 90095-1484 Home Phone: 310-474-7675; Office Phone: 310-206-5720. Business E-Mail: aberbach@polisci.ucla.edu.

ABERCROMBIE, NEIL, congressman; b. Buffalo, June 26, 1938; s. G. Don and Vera June (Giersdorf) Abercrombie; m. Nancie Ellen Caraway, July 18, 1981. BA, Union Coll., 1959; MA, U. Hawaii, 1964, PhD in Am. studies, 1974. Mem. Hawaii Ho. Reps., 1974—86, Hawaii Senate, 1978—86, US Congress from 1st Hawaiian dist., 1986—87, 1991—, mem. resources com., armed svcs. com., nat. security com. Mem. Honolulu City Coun., 1988—90. Co-author: Blood of Patriots. Democrat. Office: US Ho Reps 1502 Longworth Ho Office Bldg Washington DC 20515-1101 also: Prince Kuhio Fed Bldg Rm 4104 300 Ala Moana Blvd Honolulu HI 96850 Office Phone: 202-225-2726. Office Fax: 202-225-4580. E-mail: neil.abercrombie@mail.house.gov.*

ABERG, GILBERT S., retired writer; b. Chgo., May 28, 1922; s. Samuel and Rose Aberg; m. Blossom Zelda Fisher, July 17, 1943; children: Miriam, Jerrold, Steven, Ethan, Rachel. BA, U. Wis., Madison, 1947. Writer Ency. Britannica, Wilmette, Ill., 1949—52; writer, prodr. Pa. State U., State College, 1955—76, sci. info. officer, 1970—76. Author: (play) Esther, 1969, Encyclopedia Britannica Films, numerous ednl. films, comml. and documentary films, 1976—2000. Mil. intelligence specialist US Army, 1943—46. Recipient award, Cleve. Film Festival, Forestry Film Festival, Coun. Advancement Secondary Edn. Mem.: Nat. Assn. Sci. Writers, Congregation Brit Shalom. Avocations: tennis, racquetball, ping pong/table tennis, acting. Home: 704 McKee St State College PA 16803 Personal E-mail: gilabrg@aol.com.

ABERLIN, BETTY KAY, actor, poet; b. NYC, Dec. 30, 1942; d. Harry Ageloff and Daisy Kinstein. BA in Creative Writing, Bennington Coll. Actor: (musical theater) Sandhog, I'm Getting My Act Together; (TV series) Mr. Rogers' Neighborhood, 1969—2001, The Smothers Brothers; (films) Dogma, Jersey Girl; co-founder, on-air talent Sta. WYEP-FM, Pitts.; author: Stop Me Before I Love Again, Girl Steps Out of Car - Gets Blown Up, The Blonding of America, Nightclub, Potter's Field, The White Pages, Zossima Press; contr. to websites including: PoetsAgainstTheWar-.com, FreshYarn.com. Vol. chaplain's office Rikers Island, NYC; vol. Children's Hosp., LA; organizer Save the Theaters. Jewish Christian. Avocations: writing, art. Personal E-mail: bettykayday@earthlink.net.

ABERMAN, HAROLD MARK, veterinarian; b. Chgo., Aug. 5, 1956; s. Howard Oscar and Goldie Esther Aberman. BS, Purdue U., 1979, MSE, 1987, BSE, 1986, DVM, 1983. NIH postdoctoral fellow Purdue U., West Lafayette, 1983-87; dir. sci. and biol. affairs Howmedica div. Pfizer, Rutherford, 1987-99; pres. Applied Biol. Concepts, Los Alamitos, Calif., 1996—; dir. devel. Orthop. Rsch. Inst., Long Beach, Calif., 1999-2001, med. device cons., 2001—; dir. sci. affairs, chief sci. officer Synthes Spine, West Chester, Pa., 2003—. Adj. prof. N.C. State U., Raleigh, 1988—, Miss. State U., Starkville, Miss., 1990—, Purdue U., 1991—. Contbr. articles to profl. jours. Mem. ASME, AVMA, Am. Animal Hosp. Assn., Ortho. Rsch. Soc., Soc. Biomechanics, Acad. Surg. Rsch. Jewish. Office: Applied Biol Concepts 12581 Silver Fox Rd Los Alamitos CA 90720-5234 also: Synthes Spine 1302 Wrights Ln E West Chester PA 19380 Office Phone: 610-719-5682. Personal E-mail: haroldabc@aol.com.

ABERNATHY, FREDERICK HENRY, mechanical engineering educator; b. Denver, June 19, 1930; s. Henry James and Irene Sarah (Lehman) A.; m. AnnaMaria Herbert, June 18, 1961; children: Sarah, Marian, Pauline. BSME, Newark Coll. Engring., 1951; postgrad., Oak Ridge Sch. Reactor Tech., 1952; SM, Harvard U., 1954, PhD, 1959. Gordon McKay prof. engring. Harvard U., Cambridge, Mass., 1963—, Abbott and James Lawrence prof. mech. engring., 1995—; dir. engring. divsn. NSF, Washington, 1972-73, dir. energy-realted rsch., 1973-74; prof. engring. Harvard U. Dir. Textile/Clothing Tech. Corp., Cambridge, 1985-87, Harvard Ctr. for Textile and Apparel Rsch., 1991—. Fellow Am. Phys. Soc., Am. Acad. Arts and Scis.; mem. ASME, Am. Soc. Engring. Edn., Sigma Xi. Office: Harvard Univ Divsn Engring/Applied Scis Pierce Hall Cambridge MA 02138 E-mail: fha@deas.harvard.edu.

ABERNATHY, GEORGE THOMAS, cardiologist, consultant; b. Atlanta, Oct. 31, 1943; s. Ira Raulston and Stella Eulalia Abernathy. BA, Emory Coll. Arts and Scis., Atlanta, 1964; MD, Emory U. Sch. Medicine, Atlanta, 1968. Diplomate internal medicine and cardiovasc. diseases Am. Bd. Internal Medicine. Intern Emory U. Sch. Medicine, Atlanta, 1968—69; resident U. Minn., Mpls., 1971—73; cardiology fellow Emory U. Sch. Medicine, Atlanta, 1973—75; pvt. practice cardiologist Ft. Lauderdale, Fla., 1975—78, Tampa, Fla., 1986—91, Ruskin, Fla., 1991—96, Venice, Fla., 1996—. Col. USAF, 1978—86, US, Germany. Fellow: Am. Heart Assn., Am. Coll. Cardiology; mem.: ASNC, ASE. Avocations: boating, fishing, scuba diving, horse breeding. Office: Heart Inst Venice 1370 E Venice Ave Ste102 Venice FL 34285

ABERNATHY, JAMES LOGAN, public relations executive; b. Kansas City, Mo., Jan. 23, 1941; s. James Logan and Caryl (Nicolson) A.; m. Kevin Kearns, Sept. 12, 1981; 1 child, Nell Logan. Student, Brown U., 1959-64. Assoc. dir. investor relations CBS Inc., NYC, 1967-72; v.p. investor relations Warner Communications Inc., NYC, 1972-74, ABC Inc., NYC, 1974-79, v.p. corp. affairs, 1979-84; chmn. Abernathy/MacGregor Group Inc., NYC, 1984—. Trustee, chmn., dir. Caron Found., Wernersville, Pa., 19836; trustee Hackley Sch., Tarrytown, N.Y., 1982-89; overseer Brown U. Sch. Medicine, 1996—; dir. Nat. Coun. on Alcoholism and Drug Addiction, 2000. Mem. Investor Relations Assn. (pres. 1979-80), Nat. Investor Relations Inst., Knickerbocker Club (N.Y.C.), Doubles Club (N.Y.C.), Devon Yacht Club (L.I.). Home: 130 E End Ave New York NY 10028-7553 Office: Abernathy MacGregor Group Inc 501 Madison Ave New York NY 10022-5602

ABERNATHY, JENNIFER P., music educator; b. Naperville, Ill., Nov. 12, 1980; d. Beatrice J. and Robert P. Abernathy. AA, Lincoln Trail Coll., Robinson, Ill., 2000; MusB, Ea. Ill. U., Charleston, 2003. Dir. bands, choral dir. Hutsonville CUSD No. 1, Ill., 2003—05; dir. bands, kindergarten music tchr. Oblong CUSD No. 4, Ill., 2005—06; dir. bands Princeton H.S., Ill., 2006—. Named Outstanding Young Career Woman of the Yr., Crawford County Bus. and Profl. Women's Orgn., 2004. Mem.: NEA, Nat. Band Assn., Music Educator's Nat. Conf. Home Phone: 618-553-5362; Office Phone: 815-875-3308 ext. 250. Personal E-mail: jennabernathy@gmail.com.

ABERNATHY, ROBERT E., health products executive; b. San Marcos, Tex., 1954; m. Laura Abernathy; 2 children. BS in Chemistry, U. Ala., 1976; MS, Inst. Paper Chemistry, 1978. Rsch. scientist Kimberly-Clark Corp., 1982, v.p. North Am. Diaper ops., 1992—94, mng. dir. Kimberly-Clark Australia Pty. Ltd., 1994—96, group pres., 1996—98, group pres. bus.-to-bus. segment, 1998—2004, group pres. developing and emerging markets, 2004—. Bd. dirs. Lubrizol Corp., 2006—. Office: Kimberly Clark Corp 1400 Holcomb Bridge Rd Roswell GA 30076*

ABERNATHY, SHIELDS B., allergist, immunologist, internist; b. Bronxville, NY, Mar. 14, 1951; m. Leslie Abernathy; children: Amelia, Camille, Lant. BA, Ohio Wesleyan U., 1973; MS, Harvard U., 1975; MD, Med. Coll. Pa., 1979. Diplomate Am. Bd. Internal Medicine, Am. Bd. Allergy and Immunology, eligible Am. Preventive Medicine, Nat. Bd. Med. Examiners; Qualified Med. Examiner Calif.; Fed. Aviation Med. Examiner; ACLS Am. Heart Assn. Intern in internal medicine L.A. County/U. So. Calif. Med. Ctr., LA, 1979-80; resident in internal medicine Hosp. of Good Samaritan, LA, 1980-81; resident UCLA Wadsworth VA Med. Ctr., 1981-82, fellow allergy and immunology, 1982-84. Med. philanthropic facilitator, Philippines, 2000, India, 2001, Indochina, 2001, Amazon, 2002, Africa, 2004; vis. lectr. in allergy/immunology U. Mongolia, 2007; lectr., rschr. in field. Fellow Am. Coll. Allergy and Immunology, Am. Acad. Allergy and Immunology; mem. Am. Med. Health Assn., Am. Pub. Health Assn. (internat. health sect.). Office: 1050 Las Tablas Rd Ste 3 Templeton CA 93465-9792 Office Phone: 805-434-1000. E-mail: sabernats@sbcglobal.net.

ABERNETHY, ROBERT JOHN, real estate developer; b. Indpls., Feb. 28, 1940; s. George Lawrence and Helen Sarah (McLandress) A. BA, Johns Hopkins U., 1962; MBA, Harvard U., 1968; cert. in real estate fin. and constrn., UCLA, 1974. Asst. to chief scientist Phoenix missile program Hughes Aircraft Co., LA, 1968-69, asst. program mgr. Iroquois night fighter and night tracker program, 1969-71, asst. to contr. space and comm. group, 1971-72, contr. tech. divsn., 1972-74; pres. Am. Std. Devel. Co., LA, 1074—, Transit Cmty. Devel. Corp., 1997-2001. Bd. dirs., chmn. audit com. Pub. Storage, Inc., Glendale, Calif., Marathon Nat. Bank, LA, 1984-2003, Tech Net, LA Bancorp, Met. Water Dist., So. Calif., Met. Transp. Authority, LA County; pres. Self Svc. Storage Assn., San Francisco, 1978-83. Active Albert Schweitzer Found.; asst. to dep. campaign mgr. Humphrey for Pres., Washington, 1968; commr. LA Planning Commn., 1984—88, LA Telecom. Commn., 1992—93, Calif. Transp. Commn., 1998—2001, Calif. State Bd. Edn., 2000—04; vice chmn. LA Econ. Devel. Coun., 1988—93; chmn. Calif. Tech. Adv. Com. on Aeronautics, Ctr. for Study Dem. Inst., Santa Barbara, Calif., 1986—; bd. dirs. Met. Transp. Authority LA County, South Bay Civic Light Opera, LA Children's Mus., World Children's Transplant Fund, French Found. for Alzheimers Rsch., Pacific Coun. on Internat. Policy; adv. bd. mem. Peabody Conservatory, 1992—, Ctr. Talented Youth, 1992—, Nitze Sch. Advanced Internat. Studies, 1993—, Harvard Ptnrs., 1996—, Inst. Acad. Achievement of Youth, 1999—; bd. vis. Davidson Coll.; bd. dirs. LA Theatre Ctr., 1986—92, YMCA; mem. Coun. on Fgn. Rels., LA Com. on Fgn. Rels., Calif Arts Coun., 2001—; trustee Johns Hopkins U., 1991—. Lt. USNR, 1962—66. Mem. So. Calif. Planning Congress (bd. dirs.),

Parker Found. (bd. dirs.), California Club, St. Francis Yacht Club, Jonathan Club, Calif. Yacht Club, Alpha Lambda. Address: PO Box 834 Redondo Beach CA 90277 E-mail: rabernethy@techcenter.net.

ABERSON, LESLIE DONALD, lawyer; b. St. Louis, May 30, 1936; s. Hillard and Adele (Wenneker) A.; m. Regene Jo Lowenstein, Oct. 16, 1960; children: Karen, Angie, Leslie. BS, U. Ky., 1957, JD, 1960. Bar: Ky. 1960, U.S. Dist. Ct. (we. dist.) Ky. 1964, U.S. Tax Ct. 1968, U.S. Supreme Ct. 1975. Dir. Bank of Louisville. Bd. dirs. Ky. Athletic Hall of Fame, 1965—2003, NCCJ; past bd. dirs. Jewish Hosp. Louisville, Louisville Med. Rsch. Found.; past pres. B'rith Sholom Temple; bd. dirs., past v.p. Jewish Cmty. Fedn. Louisville; bd. dirs. Louisville Free Pub. Libr. Found. Recipient Louis Cole Young Leadership award. Mem.: Louisville Bar Assn., Ky. Bar Assn., U. Ky. Law Sch. Alumni Assn. (bd. dirs.). Home: 5431 Harbortown Cir Prospect KY 40059-9257 Office: Ste 102 5940 Timber Ridge Dr Prospect KY 40059

ABETTI, PIER ANTONIO, electrical engineer, management consultant, educator; b. Florence, Italy, Feb. 7, 1921; came to U.S., 1946; s. Giorgio and Anna (Garino) A.; m. Elizabeth Burr Nelson, June 11, 1948; children: George E., Frank A. Student, Poly. Inst., Turin, Italy, 1940—44; D of Indsl. Engring., U. Pisa, 1945; MSEE, Ill. Inst. Tech., 1948, PhD in Elec. Engring., 1953. Registered profl. engr., Mass. Engr. advanced devel. GE, Pittsfield, Mass., 1948—56, mgr. project EHV, 1957—62, mgr. pvt. telephone sys. Lynchburg, Va., 1971—73, mgr. Europe strategic planning Brussels, 1974—79, cons. R & D Schenectady, NY, 1980—81; dep. gen. mgr. UNIVAC-Europe, Lausanne, Switzerland, 1963—64; prof. mgmt. of tech. and entrepreneurship Rensselaer Poly. Inst., Troy, NY, 1982—, dir. Ctr. for Entrepreneurship New Tech. Ventures, 1988—92. Adj. prof. MIT, Troy, NY, 1951—52, Berkshire CC, Pittsfield, 1958—60; vis. prof. U. Calgary, Canada, 1986—87, U. Tech., Compiègne, France, 1988—92, Internat. U., Japan, 1991, 93, Elec. Rsch. Inst., Cuernavaca, Mexico, 1992, Helsinki Sch. Econs. and Bus. Adminstrn., Finland, 1994—2007, U. Oulu, Finland, 1997, Korean Advanced Inst. Sci. and Tech., 1995—97, U. Stellenbosch, South Africa, 1994, Gordon Inst. Tufts U., 1987—2007, Duxx Sch. Bus. Leadership, Monterrey, Mexico, 1997—2000, Queensland U. Tech., Brisbane, Australia, 1998, 2000—03, Nat. Coll. Ireland, Dublin, 1998—2004, Danish U. Tech., 1999—2001, Technol. Inst. Costa Rica, 1999—2000, U. Udine, Italy, 2001, Help Inst., Malaysia, 2002—03, Nat. U. Singapore, 2003, Inst. Hautes Etudes Commls. Bus. Sch. 10 Nov. U., Tunisia, 2004—05, Mediterranean Sch. Bus., Tunisia, 2006, IPADE, Pan Am. U., Mexico, 2006, Turku Sch. Econs., Finland, 2005—06, Swedish Sch. Econs., Hanken, 2007; cons. in field. Author: Linking Technology and Business Strategy, 1990, (with J. Maldifassi) The Defense Industries of Argentina, Brazil, Chile, 1994; assoc. editor Internat. Jour. Entrepreneurship and Innovation Mgmt., 2001—; contbr. articles to profl. jours Pres. Berkshire Mycol. Soc., Pittsfield, 1954-59; pres. Berkshire Film Soc., 1955-58. Recipient Coffin award GE, 1952, Internat. prize Montefiore Inst., 1953, Recognition award Italian Hist. Soc. Am., 1953, Kaufmann Found. award Entrepreurship Educator of Yr. Finalist, 1993. Fellow IEEE (chmn. Volta scholarship 1961-66, awards bd. 1984-86, chmn. scholarship awards 1984-86); mem. Am. Mgmt. Assn. (R&D coun. 1985-92), Italian Soc. for Sci. Progress (hon.), Eta Kappa Nu (Recognition award 1953), Tau Beta Pi. Office Phone: 518-276-6834. Business E-Mail: abettp@rpi.edu. *In my life I have always tried to learn from my predecessors in science and technology and innovate based on their teaching and my original thinking.*

ABHYANKAR, SHREERAM SHANKAR, mathematics professor; b. Ujjain, India, July 22, 1930; came to U.S., 1951, naturalized, 1989; s. Shankar Keshav and Uma (Tamhankar) A.; m. Yvonne Margit Kraft, June 5, 1958; children: Hari Shreeram, Kashi Shreeram. BSc, Bombay U., 1951; AM, Harvard U., 1952, PhD, 1955; DHD (hon.), U. Angers, 1998. Rsch. instr. Columbia U., NYC, 1955-56, vis. asst. prof., 1956-57; asst. prof. Cornell U., Ithaca, NY, 1957-58; vis. asst. prof. Princeton (N.J.) U., 1958-59; assoc. prof. Johns Hopkins U., Balt., 1959-63; pres. math. Purdue U., West Lafayette, Ind., 1963-67, Marshall disting. prof. math., 1967—, prof. indsl. engring., 1987—, prof. computer scis., 1988—. Vis. lectr. Harvard U., 1960-61; vis. prof. Munster U., Erlangen U., summer 1963, Matsci., Madras, India, fall 1963, Tata Inst., Bombay, 1969-70, 75-76, spring 1974, Kyoto U., fall 1976, U. Ky., fall 1978, U. Paris, spring 1980, ENS St. Cloud, France, spring 1982, U. Nice, spring 1983, U. Sydney, spring 1986, U. Strasbourg, spring 1991, Ohio State U., spring 1995; vis. assoc. prof. Yale U., spring 1963; spkr. numerous profl. meetings, univ., insts., symposia, confs., and congresses, 1960—. Author: Ramification Theoretic Methods in Algebraic Geometry, 1959, Local Analytic Geometry, 1964, Resolution of Singularities of Embedded Algebraic Surfaces, 1966, 2d enlarged edit. 1998, A Glimpse of Algebraic Geometry, 1971, Algebraic Space Curves, 1971, Lectures on Expansion Techniques in Algebraic Geometry, 1977, Weighted Expansions for Canonical Desingularization, 1982, Enumerative Combinatorics of Young Tableaux, 1988, Algebraic Geometry for Scientists and Engineers, 1990; also over 150 articles. Recipient Herbert Newby McCoy award Purdue U., 1973, Medal of Honor, U. Valliadolid, Spain, 1990; grantee NSF, 1960-87, 89-91, 89-2002, Office Naval Rsch., 1986-90, Army Rsch. Office, 1988-90, Nat. Security Agy., 1992-99; rsch. fellow Alfred P. Sloan Found., 1958-60. Fellow Indian Nat. Sci. Acad., Indian Acad. Scis.; mem. Am. Math. Soc., Math. Assn. Am. (Lester R. Ford prize 1977, Chauvenet award 1978), Phi Beta Kappa. Achievements include research in algebraic geometry, commutative and local algebra, theory of functions of several complex variables, quantum electrodynamics, circuit and invariant theory, combinatorics, computer aided design, and robotics. Home: 111 Waldron St West Lafayette IN 47906-2836 Office: Purdue U Div Math Sci West Lafayette IN 47907 Business E-Mail: ram@cs.purdue.edu.

ABICH, YVETTE M., lawyer; BA, Loyola Marymount U., 1990; JD, Loyola Law Sch., 1994. Bar: Calif., US Dist. Ct. Ctrl. Calif., US Ct. Appeals Ninth Cir. Sr. counsel Colantuono & Levin, LA; city atty., Redevelopment Agy. counsel City of Barstow, Calif.; asst. city atty. Sierra Madre & Calabasas, Calif. Named a Rising Star, So. Calif. Super Lawyers, 2004—06; named an Amazing Woman, Mexican-Am. Bar Assn., 2003. Office: Colantuono & Levin 31st Fl 555 W 5th St Los Angeles CA 90013-1018 Office Phone: 213-533-4201. Office Fax: 213-533-4191. Business E-Mail: yabich@cllaw.us.

ABID, ANN B., art librarian; b. St. Louis, Mar. 17, 1942; d. Clarence Frederick and Luella (Niehaus) Bartelsmeyer; m. Amor Abid (div. 1969); children: Rod, Kady; m. Cleon R. Yohe, Aug. 10, 1974 (div.); m. Roldo S. Bartimole, Feb. 1, 1991. Cert. in Librarianship, Washington U., St. Louis, 1976. Asst. to libr. St. Louis Art Mus., 1963-68, libr., 1968-85; head libr. Cleve. Mus. Art, 1985—2004; ret., 2004. Vis. com. univ. librs. Case We. Res.U., 1987-90, co-chairperson, 1990. Author: Introduction, Art Museum Libraries and Librarianship, 2007; co-author: Documents of Surrealism, 1918-1942, 1981, Planning for Automation of the Slide and Photograph Collections at the Cleveland Museum of Art: A Draft Marc Visual Materials Record, 1998; contbr. articles to profl. jours. Grantee Mo. Coun. Arts, 1978, Mo. Com. Humanities, 1980, Nat. Hist. Pubs. and Records Commn., 1981, Reinberger Found., 1987, Japan Found., 1996. Mem. ALA, Art Librs. Soc. N.Am. (chmn. mus.-type-of-libr. group nat. chpt. 1979-81, chmn. New Orleans 1980, nominating com. 1980, 84, Wittenborn awards com. 1981, 90, v.p., pres.-elect 1987-88, pres. 1988-89, past pres. 1989-90, chmn. N.Am. art libr. resources com. 1991-93, search com. new exec. dir. 1993-94. chmn. fin. com. 1996-98, presenter numerous papers, chmn. nominating com. 1999-2000, co-chair conf. program com. 1999-2000), Soc. Am. Archivists, Midwest Mus. Conf. (co-chmn. program com. ann. meeting 1982), Spl. Librs. Assn., Rsch. Librs. Group (shares exec. group 1996-98, shares participation com. 1997-99). Personal E-mail: annaoh@adelphia.net.

ABIDI, ASAD ALI, electrical engineer, educator; BSEE with honors, Imperial Coll. Sci. and Tech., London, 1976; MSEE, U. Calif., Berkeley, 1978, PhD in Elec. Engring., 1981. Mem. tech. staff Advanced LSI Devel. Lab. Bell Labs., Murray Hill, NJ, 1981—84; asst. prof. elec. engring. dept. UCLA, 1985—88, assoc. prof., 1988—93, prof., 1993—. Vis. faculty rschr. high-speed electronics dept. Hewlett Packard Labs., Palo Alto, Calif., 1989; adv. Teranetics, Santa Clara, Calif. Contbr. articles to sci. jours.; editor: IEEE Jour. Solid-State Cir., 1992—95; co-editor: Integrated Circuits for Wireless Communications, 1998. Recipient TRW award for Innovative Tchg., 1988, Design Contest award, Design Automation Conf., 1998. Fellow: IEEE (Donald G. Fink award 1997, Millennium medal 2000); mem.: NAE. Office: UCLA Dept Elec Engring Box 951594 53-141 Engr IV Los Angeles CA 90095-1594 Office Phone: 310-825-9490. Office Fax: 310-206-8495. E-mail: abidi@icsl.ucla.edu.*

ABIDI, BESMA ROUI, information scientist, educator; arrived in US, 1988; d. Abdallah Roui and Chedlia Chemingui; m. Mongi A Abidi, Jan. 29, 1988; children: Samy A, Ramzy. BS in Elec. Engring., Nat. Engring. Sch. Tunis, 1983, MS in Remote Sensing, 1986; PhD, U. Tenn., Knoxville, 1995. Adj. asst. prof. Mil. Acad. of Tunisia, Fondouk Djedid, Tunisia, 1985—87; asst. prof. Nat. Engring. Sch. of Tunis, Tunis, Tunisia, 1985—88; rsch. scientist Oak Ridge Nat. Lab., Oak Ridge, Tenn., 1998—2001; rsch. asst. prof. Univ. Tenn., Knoxville, Tenn., 1998—. Cons. Informatics and Telecom. Rsch. Inst., Tunis, Tunisia, 1985—88. Co-editor: Face Biometrics for Personal Identification, 2007; contbr. scientific papers pub. to profl. jour. (Best Paper Award, 2004). Treas. Internat. Assn. for the Exchange of Students for Tech. Experience, Tunis, Tunisia, 1983—85; organizer Robotics competition, Knoxville, Tenn., 2004—06; active homeowners assn., Knoxville, Tenn., 1995—98; mgr. soccer team Falcons Soccer Club, Knoxville, Tenn., 1999—2000; com. mem. Regional Sci. Fair, Knoxville, Tenn., 2000—05. Recipient Most Cited Paper award, Computer Vision and Image Understanding. Mem.: SPIE, IEEE (sr.), Order of the Engr. (life), Phi Kappa Phi. Achievements include patents pending for New method for fully automatic image contrast enhancement; development of Sys. for automatic intrusion detection; research in Fusion of thermal and visible data for face recognition improvement. Office: Univ Tenn 317 Ferris Hall Knoxville TN 37996-2100 Home Phone: 865-690-6399; Office Phone: 865-974-9918. Office Fax: 865-974-5459. Business E-Mail: besma@utk.edu.

ABIERA, ROBERTO, mechanical engineer; b. Manila, Philippines, Oct. 18, 1932; s. Pedro Sr. and Francisca (Gonzales) A.; m. Leticia Ferraren, Oct. 26, 1958; children: Arturo, Luis, Miguel, Joselito, Francisco, Mary Angeline. BS in Mech. Engring., U. So. Philippines, 1960; BS in Indsl. Engring., Colegio de San Jose, 1962, postgrad., 1964. Founder, chmn. Ralf Mgmt. Corp.; founder, chmn., pres. Roblett Internat. Constrn. Corp.; founder, chmn. OMS Philippines Corp. Cons. and speaker in field. Named Most Outstanding Mech. Engr. Philippines Profl. Regulation Commn., 1984, Outstanding Achievement Internat. Contracting Cebu Contractors Assn., 1983, Ten Exemplary Young Citizens Cebu, 1971, Ten Outstanding Young Men, 1970, Engr. of Yr., Rotary Club, 1968; recipient Most Outstanding Buisnessman award Jaycees, 1974, Outstanding award Exemplary Performance in Field of Industry, Cebu C. of C., 1974, Excellence award Philippine Fedn. Profl. Assn., 2005. Mem. Philipoine Constructors Assn. (dir. 1983), Registered Overseas Constructors Assn. Philippines (dir. 1983), Philippine Soc. Mech. Engrs. (pres. 1977, 78), Most Outstanding Mech. Engr. Overseas Contracting 1984, Mgmt. Assn. Philippines, Am. Inst. Constructors, ASME, Am. Assn. Cost Engrs., Am. Mgmt. Assn., Philippine Inventors Commn. (bd. judges). Office: Roblett Internat Constrn OMS Bldg 837 Maria Clara St Mondaluyong City Philippines Home Phone: 63-2-8247791; Office Phone: 63-2-5339624. Business E-Mail: roberto.abiera@roblett.ph.

ABI-GHANEM, GEORGES VICTOR, civil engineer, environmental engineer; b. Dakar, Senegal, Feb. 16, 1954; Came to U.S. 1976. s. Victor and Souad (Syriani) Abi-G. Maitrise Es-Science with honors, Universite Claude-Bernard, Academie de Lyon, France, 1975; Diplome d'Ingénieur Civil, ESIB, Lebanon, 1976; MS in Water Resources Engring., Stanford U., 1977; MS in Structures and Mechanics, Princeton U., 1980, PhD in Continuum Physics, 1982. Rsch. engr. U. Delft, The Netherlands, 1975; rsch. assoc. U. Ariz., 1977-78; rsch. and teaching asst. Sch. of Engring. and Applied Sci. Princeton U., 1978-82; chief engr., gen. mgr. EWA, Inc., Mpls., 1983-87, prin. scientist, 1987-90, ARDI Corp., Mpls., 1983—. Cons. to fed. and state agys. and various corps. in U.S. and abroad, 1977—; tech. reviewer Water Resources Rsch., Soc. Petroleum Engrs. Jour. and SIAM, 1982-92; observer Audits of U.S. DOE Contracts on High-Level Nuclear Waste Disposal Projects, 1987; tech. reviewer R&D grant applications Nat. Scis. and Engring. Rsch. Coun. of Canada, 1987—, Oversight of US DOE Environ. Restoration and Waste Mgmt. Activites, 1988-90; peer reviewer Hanford Environ. Dose Reconstruction Project, Hanford, Wash., 1990-94. Co-author: (with V. V. Nguyen and H. O. Pfannkuch) Practical Solutions to Chemical Spillages and Groundwater Contamination; contbr. articles to Water Resources Research, Physical Review, Jour. of Physics, Jour. of Mathematical Physics, others; author numerous publs. in conf. proceedings and tech. reports. Recipient grad. studies scholarship, 1976-77. Mem. Am. Math. Soc., Am. Phys. Soc., Am. Geophys. Union. Achievements include development of models for simulation of flow and transport of chemicals and radionuclides in air, water and geological media, of stochastic based criteria for the evaluation of environmental/health monitoring network designs, of remedial action strategies for hazardous/nuclear wastes site clean-up; characterization of scale dependent rock properties for analysis and survivability of deep underground structures subject to shock wave impulses; structural stability criteria for the construction and performance of new and improved materials; modelling of surface physics processes and thin film growth; Neuromorphic Systems design & stability criteria; research in hazardous/nuclear waste technology and monitoring design for environmental systems, in atmospheric chemistry and physics of air pollution, in physics of state transition in solids, and in image formation, compression of complex information, and associative memory in neural webworks. Address: PO Box 50058 Minneapolis MN 55405-0058

ABISH, CECILE, artist; b. NYC; m. Walter Abish. BFA, Bklyn. Coll., 1953. Instr. art Queens Coll. Vis. artist U. Mass, Amherst, Cooper Union, Harvard U. Solo exhbns. include Newark Coll. Engring., 1968, Inst. Contemporary Art, Boston, 1974, U. Md., 1975, Alessandra Gallery, N.Y.C., 1977, Wright State U., Dayton, Ohio, 1978, Carpenter Ctr., Cambridge, Mass., 1979, Anderson Gallery, Va. Commonwealth U., Richmond, 1981, SUNY-Stony Brook, 1982, Ctr. for Creative Photography, Tucson, 1984, Books & Co., N.Y.C., 1996; group exhbns.: Detroit Inst. Art, 1969, Aldrich Mus. Art, 1971, 10 Bleecker St., N.Y.C., 1972, Lakeview Ctr. Arts, Peoria, Ill., 1972, Bykert Gallery, N.Y.C., 1971-74, Michael Walls Gallery, N.Y.C., 1975, Fine Arts Bldg. Gallery, N.Y.C., 1976, Mus. Modern Art, N.Y.C., 1976, Hudson River Mus., 1979, Atlanta Arts Festival, 1980, New Mus., N.Y.C., 1980, 81, Kuntsgebaude, Stuttgart, Fed. Republic Germany, 1981, Long Beach (Calif.) Mus., 1983, Edith C. Blum Art Inst., Bard Coll., Annandale-on-Hudson, N.Y., 1984, Mus. Modern Kunst, Vienna, Austria, 1985, U. R.I., Kingston, 1985, Art Defense Galleries, Paris, 1993, Architektur Zentrum, Vienna, 1993, Artists Space, N.Y.C., 1994, Islip Art Mus., N.Y., 1995, P.S. 1 Contemporary Art Ctr., N.Y., 1999; numerous commns.; represented in permanent collections; published photo works: Firsthand, 1978, Chinese Crossing, 1986, 99: The New Meaning, 1990. Nat. Endowment Arts fellow, 1975, 77, 80; CAPS fellow, 1975. Mem. Coll. Art Assn. Office: Cooper Station PO Box 485 New York NY 10276-0485

ABIZAID, JOHN PHILIP, retired military officer; b. Redwood City, Calif., Apr. 1, 1951; m. Kathleen Denton; children: Sharon, Christine, David. Grad., US Mil. Acad., 1973; Infantry Officer Basic & Advanced Training, Armed Forces Staff Coll.; MA in Area Studies, Harvard U.; Olmsted scholar, U. Jordan, Amman. Commd. 2nd lt. US Army, 1973, advanced through grades to gen., 2003; comdt. cadets US Mil. Acad., West Point, NY, 1997-99; comdr. First Infantry Divsn., Wurzburg, Germany, 1999—2000; dir. strategic plans and policy Joint Staff, The Pentagon, Washington, 2000—01, dir., 2001—03; dep. comdr. Combined Forces Command, MacDill AFB, Fla., 2003; comdr. US Ctrl. Command, 2003—07. Decorated Def. Disting Svc. medal with Oak Leaf Cluster, Disting. Svc. medal with Oak Leaf Cluster, Def. Superior Svc. medal, Legion of Merit with 5 Oak Leaf Clusters, Def. Meritorious Svc. medal, Meritorious Svc. medal with 2 Oak Leaf Clusters, Army Commendation medal with 2 Oak Leaf Clusters, Army Achievement medal, Bronze Star, Combat Infantryman's Badge, Master Parachutist Badge with Gold Star, Expert Infantryman's Badge, Ranger Tab, Joint Chiefs of Staff Identification Badge, Army Staff Identification Badge.*

ABLARD, CHARLES DAVID, administrative judge; b. Enid, Okla., Oct. 25, 1930; s. Charles Ross and Mary M. (Pattie) Ablard; m. Doris Maria Perl, Nov. 14, 1959; children— Jennifer, Jonathan, Catherine BA, U. Okla., 1952, JD, 1954; LLM, George Washington U., 1959. Bar: DC. Jud. officer US Post Office Dept., Washington, 1958-60; ptnr. Ablard and Harrison, Washington, 1960-63; v.p., counsel Mag. Pubs. Assn., Washington, 1963-69; gen. counsel USIA, Washington, 1969-72; assoc. dep. atty. gen. Dept. Justice, Washington, 1972-74; assoc. dean Vt. Law Sch., South Royalton, 1974; gen. counsel Dept. Army, Washington, 1975-77; ptnr. Gage and Tucker, Washington, 1979-92, Faegre and Benson, Washington and Mpls., 1992-97, Perkins, Smith, Cohen & Crowe, Washington and Boston, 1997—2003; administrv. judge Office Hearings and Appeals US Dept. Def., Arlington, Va., 2003—. Adj. prof. Cath. U., Washington, 1984; mem. Fgn. Svc. Grievance Bd., 1998—. Contbr. articles to profl. jours. Bd. dirs. Hist. Alexandria Found., Pub. Diplomacy Coun.; commr. Alexandria Hist. Restoration and Preservation Commn.; mem. coun. Adminstrv. Conf. US, Washington, 1970-73; mem. Bd. Internat. Broadcasting, Washington, 1980-84; bd. dirs. Radio Free Europe/Radio Liberty, Washington, 1983-84. Col. USAF, 1954-56, ret. Fellow Ctr. Internat. Studies, Downing Coll., Cambridge U., Eng., 1974; recipient Profl. Achievement award George Washington U., 1976, Disting. Civilian Svc. award Dept. Army, 1975, 76 Fellow Am. Bar Found. (life); mem. ABA (chmn. adminstrv. law sect. 1984-85), English Speaking Union US (bd. dirs.). Clubs: Cosmos (Washington); Army-Navy Country (Arlington, Va.); Small Point (Maine). Republican. Episcopalian. Office: Dept Def Office of Hearings & Appeals Liberty Ctr 875 N Randolph Arlington VA 22203 Home Phone: 703-751-8590; Office Phone: 703-696-1838.

ABLE, EDWARD H., association executive; BA in Chemistry, Emory U., 1967; MBA, George Washington U., 1973. Cert. assn. exec. Staff aide to U.S. Senator Richard B. Russell, 1967-68; staff aide to U.S. Senator Mike Mansfield, 1968; acct. exec. Exec. Cons., Inc., Washington, 1971-73; asst. dir. resident assoc. program Smithsonian Instn., Washington, 1973-77; exec. v.p. Am. Soc. Landscape Architects, Washington, 1977-86; pres., CEO Am. Assn. Mus., Washington, 1986—2006. Lectr. in field. Author: (with others) Principles of Association Management, 1988. Bd. dirs. Nat. Humanities Alliance, 1986—, officer, 1990—, Nat. Cultural Alliance, 1991—; mem. founding bd. dirs. Nat. Ctr. Non-profit Bds., 1987—, vice chair, 1993-99; coun. mem. U.S. Com. World Heritage, 1988—; bd. mem. Nat. Ctr. for Non-Profit Enterprise. Capt. U.S. Army, 1968-71. Decorated Bronze Star. Fellow Am. Soc. Assn. Execs. (bd. dirs. 1987-90, chmn. mgmt. conf. 1988, instr. 1985—, frequent speaker meetings and convs. 1981—, chmn. grad. studies commn. 1986-87, mem. nat. edn. com. 1984-86, vice-chmn. 1985, chmn. 1986, bd. dirs. membership dirs. sect. 1982-83, Key award 1990, vice-chmn. fellows 1987-88, chmn. 1988-89), bd. dirs., 1994—; Greater Washington Soc. Assn. Execs. (chief exec. officer conf. com. 1982-83), Univ. Club (Washington). Office: Am Assn Museums 1575 I St NW Ste 400 Washington DC 20005-1113*

ABLE, KENNETH PAUL, biology professor; b. Louisville, Feb. 5, 1944; s. William Morris and Viola (Bridwell) A.; m. Mary Allen, Jan. 28, 1967; 1 child, Joshua. BS, U. Louisville, 1966, MS, 1968; PhD, U. Ga., 1971. Asst. prof. SUNY, Albany, 1971-77, assoc. prof., 1977-84, prof., 1984—2003, prof. emeritus, 2003—. NSF grantee, 1974-2000. Fellow Animal Behavior Soc., Am. Ornithologists' Union (treas. 1981-85, elective councilor 1999-2002, William Brewster medal 1996); mem. Internat. Soc. Behavioral Ecology, Am. Soc. Naturalists, Am. Birding Assn. (dir. 1986-95, 99—2003). Business E-Mail: KenAble@hughes.net.

ABLE, WARREN WALTER, natural resource company executive, physician; b. Seymour, Ind., Mar. 3, 1932; s. Walter Cudwith and Edith (Harmon) A.; m. Joan Graham, May 6, 1956; children: Susan, Nancy, Cynthia, Wally. AB, Ind. U., 1953, MD, 1956, JD, 1968. Bar: Ind. 1968. Intern Indpls. Gen. Hosp., 1956-57; surgeon USPHS, 1957-59; pres. Able Ventures, Inc., Columbus, Ind., 1968—. Bd. dirs. Salin Bank & Trust. Editor: Lawyer's Medical Cyclopedia, 1967-68. Bd. dirs. Bartholomew Consol. Sch. Corp., Columbus, 1970-74; trustee Christian Theol. Sem., 1991—2003. Mem. AMA, Ind. Med. Soc., ABA, Ind. Bar Soc., Nat. Benevolent Assn. (bd. dirs. 1983-90). Democrat. Mem. Christian Ch. (Disciples Of Christ). Avocations: aviation, farming. Home and Office: 4253 E Windsor Ln Columbus IN 47201-9681

ABLER, RONALD FRANCIS, geography educator; b. Milw., May 30, 1939; s. Ambrose Francis and Lucille Bernice A.; m. Barbara Ruth Bailey, Apr. 23, 1983; children: Frederick F., Kenneth J. BA, U. Minn., Mpls., 1963, MA, 1966, PhD, 1968. Prof. Pa. State U., University Park, 1967-95; exec. dir. Assn. Am. Geographers, Washington, 1990—2002; sr. scientist Nat. Acad. Sci., Nat. Rsch. Coun., 2003—. Dir. geography program NSF, Washington, 1984-88; vis. prof. Stockholm Sch. Econs., 1982-83, U. Minn., Mpls., 1972-74, U. B.C., Vancouver, 1971; sec. gen., treas. Internat. Geographical Union, 2000-06, v.p. 2007-. Editor: A Comparative Atlas of America's Great Cities, 1976; co-editor: Atlas of Pennsylvania, 1989, Geography's Inner Worlds, 1992, Global Change and Local Places: Estimating, Understanding, and Reducing Greenhouse Gases, 2003. Councilman State College (Pa.) Borough, 1978-82. Recipient Publ. award Geog. Soc. Chgo., 1976, Centenary medal Royal Scottish Geog. Soc., 1990, Spl. Recognition award NSF, Washington, 1988, Victoria medal Royal Geog. Soc./Inst. Brit. Geographers, 1996, Samuel Finley Breese Morse medal Am. Geog. Soc., 2004. Fellow AAAS, Assn. Am. Geographers (pres. 1985-86, exec. dir. 1990—2002, Honors 1995), Cosmos Club. Avocation: beekeeping. Home: 2246 N Pollard St Arlington VA 22207-3805 Office: Internat Geog Union 525 Pennsylvania Ave Unit 301 Sheboygan WI 53081-4666 Home Phone: 920-208-3452.

ABLIN, RICHARD JOEL, immunologist, educator; b. Chgo., May 15, 1940; s. Robert Benjamin and Minnie Edith (Gordon) A.; m. Linda Lee Lutwack; 1 son, Michael David. AB, Lake Forest Coll., 1962; PhD in Microbiology, SUNY, Buffalo, 1967; DSc (hon.), Lake Forest Coll., 2005. Diplomate Am. Bd. Clin. Immunology and Allergy; cert. specialist in pub. health and med. lab. microbiology Nat. Registry Microbiologists of Am. Acad. Microbiology, Am. Soc. Clin. Pathology Bd. Registry. Grad. asst. dept. biology SUNY-Buffalo, 1963-65, rsch. asst., summer 1963, rsch.

fellow, 1965-66; USPHS postdoctoral fellow dept. microbiology Sch. Medicine, lectr., lab instr., 1966-68; instr., rsch. asst. Rosary Hill Coll., 1965-66; rsch. cons. program med. edn. AID, Paraguay, 1968; dir. divsn. immunology Millard Fillmore Hosp. Rsch. Inst., Buffalo, 1968-70; head sect. immunology, renal unit Meml. Hosp. Springfield, 1970-73; dir. sect. immunobiology div. urology dept. surgery Cook County Hosp. and Hektoen Inst. Med. Rsch., Chgo., 1973-75, sr. sci. officer divsn. immunology, 1976-83; sr. mem. sci. staff, clin. immunologist Cook County Hosp., 1973-75; asst. prof. medicine So. Ill. U., 1971-73; assoc. prof. microbiology Univ. Health Sci. (Chgo. Med. Sch.), 1973-74; pres., dir. Robert Benjamin Ablin Found. for Cancer Rsch., Evergreen Park, Ill., 1979—; rsch. assoc. prof. urology, dir. immunology unit dept. urology SUNY, Stony Brook, 1983—89, mem. U. Senate, 1986—89, 1989—92, mem. U. Gov. Coms., 1984—92; acad. del. United U. Professions, 1986—88, 1988—90; dir. sci. investigation Tetragenex Pharms., Inc., Park Ridge, NJ, 1991—2003, consulting scientist, 2003—. Vis. rsch. prof. Coll. Medicine U. Ariz., Tucson, 2001-04; rsch. prof. dept. immunobiology Ariz. Coll. Medicine, Ariz. Cancer Ctr. and B105 Inst., Tucson, 2005—; organizer, presenter, instr., participant numerous nat. and internat. profl. meetings, symposia, seminars. Editor: Allergologia et Immunopathologia, 1980—84; co-editor: Cancer Metastasis-Biology and Treatment, 2000—; contbg. editor: Allergologia et Immunopathologia, 1974—84, Seminars in Immunopathology and Oncology, Ill. Med. Jour., 1975—88, Cancer Watch, 2001—; adv. editor: Jour. Cancer, 1976—89; adv. editor Jour. Translational Medicine, 2006—; assoc. editor: Low Temperature Medicine, 1975—, Jour. Investigational Allergology and Clin. Immunology (formerly Allergologia et Immunopathologia), 1985—95, Jour. Exptl. Therapeutics and Oncology, 2003—, Cancer Science, 2007—, mem. editl. adv. bd.: Med. Sci. Rsch., 1984—2000, Cancer Detection and Prevention, 2006—; mem. editl. bd. Medikon, 1974—80, Immunology and Allergy Practice, 1979—95, Tumor Diagnostik and Therapie, 1980—98, Am. Jour. Reproductive Immunology and Microbiology, 1980—91, Cellular and Molecular Biology, 1985—87, Chemistry Today, 1991—97, Early Pregnancy: Biology and Medicine, 1995—, Internat. Jour. Oncology, 1996—, Current Oncology, 1998—, Advances in Therapy, 1999—, Prostate Jour., 1999—2001, Bratislava Med. Jour., 1999—, Exptl. Biology and Medicine, 2000—06, UroOncology, 2000—, Annals Clin. and Lab.Sci., 2000—, Clin. and Applied Immunology Revs., 2001—, Clin. and Vaccine Immunology (formerly Clin. and Diagnostic Lab. Immunology), 2002—, Expert Rev. Anticancer Therapy, 2002—, Cancer Therapy, 2003—, Internat. Jour. Cancer Prevention, 2003—, Current Opinion in Oncology, 2005—; contbr. chapters to books, articles to profl. jours. Chief Sangamo Nation Y-Indian Guides, Springfield, 1972-73; mgr. Skokie Indians' Boys' Baseball, Ill., 1973-74, 77, 80, 81, bd. dirs., 1979-83, exec. v.p., 1981-82; mgr. Little League Three Villages, Setauket, N.Y., 1986; cubmaster N.W. Suburban coun. Boy Scouts Am., 1974-78, asst. scoutmaster, 1975-77; mem. exploring divsn. Suffolk County coun. Boy Scouts Am., 1985-88; pres., dir. Spirit of Chgo. Hockey Club Found., Evergreen Park, Ill., 1982—. Recipient Nat. Pres. Leader's Dist. Boy Scouts Am., 1975; named Cubmaster of Yr. Boy Scouts Am., 1977 Fellow: Assn. Clin. Scientists, Am. Coll. Cryosurgery (adv. bd. 1977—78, v.p. 1977—79, parliamentarian 1977—79, adv. bd. 1980—81, 1984—99), Am. Coll. Allergy and Immunology (bd. registry), Indian Cryogenics Coun. (hon.); mem.: AAAS, Anticancer Therapeutics and Oncology Soc., Am. Soc. Clin. Pathology, Metastasis Rsch. Soc., Am. Assn. Cancer Rsch., Am. Assn. Immunologists, Am. Soc. Microbiology, Assn. Med. Lab Immunologists, Brit. Assn. Surg. Oncology, Buffalo Collegium Immunology, Internat. Soc. Andrology, Internat. Soc. Chronobiology, Internat. Soc. Immunology Reprodn., N.Y. Acad. Scis., Soc. Cryobiology, Soc. Exptl. Biology and Medicine, Soc. Leukocyte Biology, Soc. Protozoologists, Japan Soc. Low Temperature Medicine (hon.), Internat. Soc. Cryosurgery (hon.; pres. 1977—80, bd. dirs. 1980—, hon. life pres.), Soc. Study Reprodn., Transplantation Soc., Cryoimmunotherapeutic Study Group (chmn.), Witebsky Ctr. Microbial Pathogenesis and Immunology, Sigma Xi, Phi Beta Kappa. Achievements include identification of prostate specific antigen (PSA), used as tumor marker in prostate cancer, and of human thymic specific antigen providing means for differentiation of thymic lymphocytes from other lymphoid cells and the development of antithymocyte globulin (selectively immunosuppressive for thymocytes) used in renal allograft (transplant) recipients; development of concept of cryoimmunotherapy for treatment of cancer. Office: Univ Ariz Coll Medicine Health Scis Ctr Dept Immunobiology 1501 N Campbell Ave PO Box 245049 Tucson AZ 85724-5049 Office Phone: 520-622-8319. Business E-Mail: ablinrj@email.arizona.edu. *One of the saddest things in life is to have the opportunity to do something and not to take advantage of it.*

ABLOW, KEITH RUSSELL, writer; b. Boston, Nov. 23, 1961; s. Allan Murray and Jeanette Norma (Mezansky) A. ScB, Brown U., 1983; MD, Johns Hopkins U., 1987. Reporter Newsweek, NYC, 1984; columnist Balt. Evening Sun, Boston Herald, 1985-89, Washington Post, 1990—; intern in psychiatry Tufts U.-New Eng. Med. Ctr. Hosps., Boston, 1987-88, resident, 1988-91; chief resident 1991—, 1991-92; columnist Washington Post, 1990—; cons. psychiatrist WCVB TV, Boston, 1992—; med. dir. Tri-City Mental Health Ctr., 1992-94; assoc. med. dir. Heritage Health Systems, 1993-94; corr. Med. News Network, 1993—; med. dir. FHC New Eng., 1994-96; outpatient psychiatrist Boston Regional Med. Ctr., 1996—. Med. editor Lifetime Med. TV, L.A. and Astoria, N.Y., 1986-89; founder, CEO, memorymountain.com. Author: (novels) Denial, 1997, Projection, 1999, Compulsion, 2002, Psychopath, 2003, Murder Suicide, 2004, The Architect, 2005, (non-fiction) Medical School: Getting In, Staying In, Staying Human, 1987, How to Cope With Depression, 1989, To Wrestle With Demons, 1992, Anatomy of a Psychiatric Illness, 1993, The Strange Case of Dr. Kappler, 1994, Without Mercy: The Shocking True Story of a Doctor Who Murdered, 1996, Inside the Mind of Scott Peterson, 2005; columnist Mental Health Infosource Website, 1996—. Trustee White Pines Coll., Chester, N.H., 1989-91. Recipient Optimate award Am. Soc. Profl. Italians, 1990. Mem. AAAS, AMA (sr. editor, creative cons. Pulse 1986-87, Jerry L. Pettis award 1987), Am. Psychiat. Assn., Am. Med. Writers Assn. (Will Solimene award 1991, 92, Best Trade Book, 1993). Democrat. Avocation: writing fiction.

ABLOW, ROZ KAROL (ROSELYN KAROL ABLOW), painter, curator; b. Allentown, Pa. BA, Bennington Coll., 1954; student, Boston U. Fellow Bunting Inst., 1988; instr. Newton Arts Ctr., Mass., 1989-92, New Arts Ctr., Newton, Mass., 1993-95. Curator New Arts Ctr., Newton, Mass., 1994. One-person shows at Amherst (Mass.) Coll., 1976, Impressions Gallery, Mass., 1979, Clark Gallery, Lincoln, Mass., 1984, Pine Manor Coll., Brookline, Mass., 1991, Miami U., Oxford, Ohio, 1995, Art Guild of Old Forge, NY, 2002; group shows include Smithsonian Traveling Exhbn., 1978-80, Fitchburg Art Mus., 1988, Bunting Inst., Radcliffe Coll., 1988, David Brown Gallery, Provincetown, Mass., 1988, Pratt Graphic Ctr. Internat. Monotype Show, 1989, Gallery 30, Burlingame, Calif., 1993, New Art Ctr., Newton, Mass., 1994, Pucker Gallery, 2004, 05, 06, others; represented in permanent collections Mobil Corp., Chemical Bank, NY, New Eng. Mutual Life Ins. Co., Boston, Conn. Gen. Life, Hartford, Sears, Roebuck & Co., Chgo., Philip Morris, NYC, Odell Assocs., Charlotte, NC, Conn. Gen. Life, Hartford, Broadway Crown Plaza Hotel, NY, Pucker Gallery, Boston, Boston Pub. Libr. Bunting Inst. fellow Radcliffe Coll., 1988; grantee Mass. Arts Lottery Coun., 1990-91. Address: Pucker Gallery Boston MA 02116 Office Phone: 617-734-3652.

ABNER, HAROLD LOYD, military officer, consultant; b. Fort Walton Beach, Fla., Mar. 23, 1962; s. Harold L. and Linda L. Abner; m. Denise L. Hughes, Mar. 28, 1987; children: Natasha L., Nicole L. BA, William Jennings Bryan Coll., 1984; MA, Webster U., 1996; PhD, Capella U., 2005. Army officer US Army Spl. Ops. Cmd., Fayetteville, NC, 1997—2004; chief, leadership and staff devel. br. Dept. of Healthcare Ops., San Antonio, 1994—97. Martial arts instr. (instruction, tournaments, exhbns.). Min., evangelist Covenant Love Family Ch., Fayetteville, NC, 2001—03. Maj. Med. Svc. Corps, 1984—2004. Mem.: DAV (life), Internat. Good Will Tang Soo Do (life), Agapy Christian Martial Arts (life), San Kil Tang Soo Do (life), Mil. Officers Assn. of Am. (life). Pentecostal. Achievements include design of Soldier's Coin. Avocations: aviation, martial arts. Home: 106 Farmington Blvd Hampton VA 23666-1812 Home Phone: 757-224-8613; Office Phone: 757-660-1397. Personal E-mail: haroldabner@cox.net.

ABNEY, DAVID P., delivery service executive; m. Sherry Abney; children: Valerie, Matt. BBA in Mktg., Delta State U. Various positions UPS, Inc., Atlanta, 1974—95, mgr. SonicAir, 1995—2000, Fritz cos. integration mgr., 2001—02, sr. v.p., pres. Internat., 2003—07, COO, 2007—, pres. UPS Airlines, 2007—. Bd. mem. Air Courier Conf. Am. Trustee UPS Found.; bd. mem. U.S. Japan Bus. Council, Southern Ctr. for Internat. Studies, Coalition Svc. Industries, Delta State Univ. Alumni Found. Office: UPS 55 Glenlake Pky NE Atlanta GA 30328*

ABNEY, MARTHA MCEACHERN, music educator; b. Bremen, Ga., Dec. 6, 1957; d. James Sterling and Nancy Hughes McEachern; m. Jeffrey Robert Abney, June 8, 2002; children: Laura, Steve, Ginger, Sam, Ellen, Peter. B of Music Edn., West Ga. Coll., 1987, M of Music Edn., 1992. Tchr. music Bremen City Schs., Ga., 1987—98, Carroll County Schs., Villa Rica, 1998—, State U. West Ga., Carrollton, 1999—. Music dir. Bremen 1st United Meth. Ch., 1992—95, Tallapoosa 1st United Meth. Ch., 2005—. Mem.: Ga. Music Educators Assn., Am. Choral Dirs. Assn., Spirit Atlanta Alumni Assn. (assoc.). Republican. Methodist. Home: 34 Woodstream Ln Tallapoosa GA 30176 Office: Villa Rica High Sch 600 Rocky Branch Rd Villa Rica GA 30180 Office Phone: 770-459-5185. Business E-Mail: martie.abney@carrollcountyschools.com.

ABNEY, WILLIAM K., lawyer; b. Marshall, Tex., Apr. 26, 1975; BBA cum laude in Fin., So. Meth. U., 1997; JD, U. Tex., Austin, 2000. Bar: Tex. 2000, N.Mex. 2002. Atty. Lynch, Chappell & Alsup, P.C., Midland, Tex., 2002—, shareholder, 2005—. Vice chmn. bd. dirs. High Sky Children's Ranch; bd. dirs. High Sky Children's Ranch Endowment; trustee Mus. of S.W. Named a Rising Star, Tex. Super Lawyers mag., 2006. Mem.: ABA, Midland County Bar Assn., Travis County Bar Assn. Office: Lynch Chappell & Alsup PC 300 N Marienfeld Ste 700 Midland TX 79701 Office Phone: 432-683-3351. E-mail: wabney@lcalawfirm.com.*

ABO, RONALD KENT, freelance/self-employed architect; b. Rupert, Idaho, July 10, 1946; s. Isamu and Ameria (Hachiya) A.; m. Lisa A. Wiesley; children: Tamiko N., Reiko D., Ryan A., Emily A., Ian Y. BArch, U. Colo., 1969. Lic. architect, Colo. Designer SLP & Ptnrs., Denver, 1968-71; dir. Community Design Ctr., Denver, 1971-72; assoc. Barker, Rinker, Seacat, Denver, 1972-76; pvt. practice Denver, 1976-80; pres. Abo Gude Architects, Denver, 1980-84, Ron Abo Architects, Denver, 1984-91, Abo Architects PC, Denver, 1991-94, Abo Copeland Architecture, 1995—2002, ACLP Architecture, Inc., 2002—04, The ABO Group, Inc., 2005—. Design instr., thesis advisor U. Colo., Denver. Prin. works include Morrison Horticultre Ctr., 1983 (W.O.O.D. Inc. citation 1983), Highland Square, 1982 (AIA citation 1983), Roxborough Elem. Sch., 1990, Tropical Discovery Ctr. Denver Zoo, 1992, New Denver Internat. Airport Concourse Bldgs., 1993, Nederland Middle/H.S., 1996, Julesburg Welcome Ctr., 1997, Rocky Mountain Mfg. Acad., 1998. Active Denver Comty. Leadership Forum, 1986, Colfax-on-the-Hill, 1988—, U. Colo. Alumni Bd., Workforce Devel. Bd., 1990—, Savid House. Recipient Design Excellence award W.O.O.D. Inc., Denver, 1982, Martin Luther King Bus. Social Responsibility award, 1998. Mem. AIA (bd. dirs., pres.-elect Denver chpt. 1990, pres. 1991, pres.-elect Colo. chpt. 1997, pres. 1998), Asian C. of C. (pres. 1998), Colo. Aikido Assn. (head instr. Denver Buddhist Temple Aikido), Lions Club (bd. dirs.). Democrat. Avocation: 5th degree black belt. Office: The ABO Group Inc 1660 Wynkoop St Ste 900 Denver CO 80202 Business E-Mail: ron@theabogroup.com.

ABOLHODA, AMIR, surgeon; b. Langroud, Iran, Aug. 18, 1962; arrived in US, 1980; s. Shamsedine Abolhuda and Khadijeh Habibi. BS summa cum laude, U. Calif., Irvine, 1984, MD, 1988. Diplomate Am. Bd. Surgery, Am. Bd. Thoracic Surgery. Cardiothoracic surgeon Pat D. Daily, Inc., San Diego, 2000—03; cardiothoracic surgeon, asst. clin. prof. U. Calif. Irvine Med. Ctr., Orange, 2003—. Fellow: ACS; mem.: Soc. Thoracic Surgeons, Phi Beta Kappa. Office: U Calif Irvine 100 City Dr Orange CA 92868

ABOLINS, MARIS ARVIDS, physicist, educator; b. Liepaja, Latvia, Feb. 5, 1938; came to U.S., 1949, naturalized, 1956; s. Arvids Gustavs and Olga Elizabete (Grintals) A.; m. Frances Delano, Dec. 19, 1959 BS magna cum laude, U. Wash., 1960; MS, U. Calif.-San Diego, 1962, PhD, 1965. Research asst. U. Calif.-San Diego, 1960-65; physicist Lawrence Berkeley Lab., 1965-68; assoc. prof. physics Mich. State U., East Lansing, 1968-73, prof. physics, 1973—. Cons. U.S. Dept. Energy; sci. assoc. CERN, Geneva, 1976-77; vis. research scientist, Saclay, France, 1977, Fermi Nat. Accelerator Lab., 1990-92, Saclay, France, 1997; mem. tech. adv. com. Argonne Nat. Lab., 1971-72; mem. prep. com. Fermilab, 1978-79; chmn. Fermilab Users' Exec. Com., 1982-83; mem. SSC Users Exec. Com., 1988-91; chmn. bd. dirs. ATLAS Trigger/DAQ Instnl., 1997-99. NSF research grantee, 1971—; Disting. Faculty award 1998. Fellow Am. Phys. Soc. (exec. com. div. particles and fields 1984-86); mem. AAAS, Patria, Phi Beta Kappa, Sigma Xi. Home: 1430 Fairoaks Ct East Lansing MI 48823-1812 Office: Mich State U Dept Physics And Astro East Lansing MI 48824 Home Phone: 517-351-7376; Office Phone: 517-355-9200 x2121. Business E-Mail: abolins@pa.msu.edu.

ABOOLIAN, ANDRE, plastic surgeon; BS, UCLA; MD, Mt. Sinai Sch. Medicine. Intern, then resident, in gen. surgery Mt. Sinai Sch. Medicine, NYC; resident in plastic & reconstructive surgery U. Tex., M.D. Anderson Cancer Ctr., Houston; fellow in aesthetic/cosmetic surgery Garth D. Fisher, MD, Beverly Hills, Calif., assoc. Appears on (TV series) Extreme Makeover, ABC. Recipient Rsch. award, Am. Heart Assn. of Southern Calif., 1988, Aux. award, UCLA Med. Ctr., 1989. Fellow: Am. Coll. Surgeons (assoc.); mem.: Calif. Med. Assn., Calif. Med. Assn., LA Soc. Plastic Surgeons. Office: 120 S Spalding Dr Ste 222 Beverly Hills CA 90212 Office Phone: 310-888-8862. Office Fax: 310-273-9079.*

ABORN, FOSTER LITCHFIELD, insurance company executive; b. Providence, July 8, 1934; s. John Russell and Helene Cecile (Hesse) A.; m. Sara Holbrook; children: Justin, Hilary. BA, Dartmouth Coll., 1956, MBA, 1957; exec. prog., 1978. Asst. v.p. Mellon Bank N.A., Pitts., 1957-68; asst. investment officer John Hancock Ins. Co., 1968—72, second v.p., 1972—78, v.p., 1978—84, sr. v.p., Treas. & Fin. Services, 1984—87, sr. v.p., Corp. Mktg. Rsch., 1984, sector head, Investment & Pension Group, 1987—92; vice chmn. & chief investment officer John Hancock Fin. Svcs., Inc., 1992—2000; bd. dir. John Hancock Life Ins., 2000—. Dir.,mem. of com. of fin., John Hancock Life Insurance Co.; mem. adv. com. One Liberty Ventures; mem. investment com., Kairos Fund, L.P.; adv. dir., Debt Exchange, LLC; dir., Seniorlink Incorp., cMarket, Inc. Trustee, dir., & chmn. fin. com. Beth Israel Deaconess Med. Ctr.; chmn. investment com. Controlled Risk Ins. Co.; chmn. exec. adv. bd. & capital campaign steering com. Bay Cove Human Services; dir. SquashBusters; overseer Huntington Theatre Co. Mem. Univ. Club Boston. Office: John Hancock Finl Svcs PO Box 111 C-02-01 Boston MA 02117-0111

ABOTT, MICHAEL LARRY, physician; b. Bklyn., Mar. 22, 1952; s. Jerome and Lynn A.; m. Beth Ellen Friedberg, Aug. 10, 1975; children: Stephen, Richard. BS, Bklyn. Coll., 1974; MD, Autonomous U. de Guadalajara, Mex., 1978. Diplomate Am. Bd. Internal Medicine, Am. Bd. Pulmonary Diseases, Am. Bd. Critical Care, Am. Bd. Geriatrics. Pvt. practice, Bklyn., 1984—; assoc. attending physician N.Y. Meth. Hosp., Bklyn., 1984—, Victory Meml. Hosp., Bklyn., 1984—, Maimonides Med. Ctr., Bklyn., 1995—; CEO, United Med. Assocs., 1998—. Med. dir. Lily Pond Nursing Home, S.I., 1984—, Garden of Eden Home, Bklyn., 1984-2001; dir. pulmonary Medspect Imaging, Bklyn., 1990—; mem. steering utility com. Bklyn. Physicians, Ind. Physicians Assn., 1995, mem. exec. com. Meth. Hosp., 1995; chmn. quality assurance N.Y. Meth. Hosp., 2001—. Fellow ACP, Am. Coll. Chest Physicians; mem. AMA, Am. Acad. Geriatrics, Soc. Critical Care Medicine, N.Y. State Soc. Internal Medicine, Thoracic Soc., Kings County Med. Soc. Office: 7124 18th Ave Brooklyn NY 11204 also: 263 7th Ave Brooklyn NY 11215 Office Phone: 718-234-3333. Personal E-mail: abottuma@aol.com.

ABOUD, JOHN ANTHONY, music educator; b. Cedar Rapids, Iowa, Apr. 10, 1955; s. George Zach and Mary LaVonne Aboud; m. Dianne Kay Johnson; children: Leslie, Johnny. B Music Edn., U. No. Iowa, 1977, M Music Edn., 1989. Cert. tchr. Nat. Bd. Cert. Tchr., 2006. Instrumental music tchr. grades 5-12 Bennett (Iowa) Cmty. Schs., 1977—78; HS band dir. Belmond (Iowa) Cmty. Schs., 1978—79, Algona (Iowa) Cmty. Schs., 1980—. Mem. Iowa State Bd. Ednl. Examiners, 2002—. Mem.: Iowa Bandmasters Assn. (mem. found. bd. 2004—, Karl King svc. award 2004), Iowa Music Educators Assn. (chmn. All State Band 1999—2004, pres.-elect 2005—06, pres. 2006—, svc. award 2004). Home: 825 S Minnesota St Algona IA 50511 Office: Algona HS 600 S Hale St Algona IA 50511 Office Phone: 515-295-7207.

ABOUFAKHER, RABEEA, cardiologist; b. Swaida, Syria, Apr. 14, 1975; s. Naif and Hayat Aboufakher; m. Rasha Hatem, Sept. 24, 1999; children: Sarah, Hala. MD, Damascus U., Syria, 1998. Resident Oakwood Hosp. and Med. Ctr., Dearborn, Mich., 2000—03, med. chief resident, 2003—04; geriatric fellow Beaumont Hosp., Royal Oak, 2004—05; cardiology fellow St. John Hosp. and Med. Ctr., Detroit, 2005—. CEO resident-run clinic Oakwood Hosp. and Med. Ctr., 2003—04. Lectr. Am. Druze Soc., Detroit, 2002—07. Mem.: ACP (assoc.), Am. Coll. Cardiology (assoc.), Am. Geriatric Assn. (assoc.). Druze. Achievements include research in incidence, risk factors, and prognosis of inhospital heart failure after percutaneous coronary intervention; recurrent syncope in a patient with an implantable loop recorder. Avocations: philosophy, soccer. Home Phone: 313-565-4386.

ABOULAFIA, ELIE DAVID, vascular surgeon; b. Jerusalem, June 16, 1928; arrived in US, 1953, naturalized, 1958; s. David and Mathilda (Yeshaya) Aboulafia. BSc in Medicine, U. Geneva, 1949, MD, 1953; MSc in Surgery, Tufts U., 1960. Diplomate Am. Bd. Surgery, Am. Bd. Gen. Vascular Surgery. Intern Michael Reese Hosp., Chgo., 1953-54; resident in surgery NYU-Bellevue Med. Ctr., NYC, 1954-56; surg. rsch. fellow Tufts-New Eng. Med. Ctr., Boston, 1958-59, chief surg. resident, 1959-61; dir. surg. rsch. Sinai Hosp., Detroit, 1961-63; head sect. vascular surgery Botsford Gen. Hosp., Farmington Hills, Mich., 1963-95; dir. surg. edn. Highland Park (Mich.) Gen. Hosp., Detroit, 1969-73; dir. vascular med. svcs. DMC/Sinai-Grace Hosp., Detroit, 1995—2006. Clin. prof. surgery Mich. State U., East Lansing, 1977—; clin. prof. medicine Wayne State U., Detroit, 1998—. Mem. editl. bd. Internat. Jour. Surgery, 1972—95, Itnernat. Jour. Angiology, 1992—; contbr. articles to profl. jours. Trustee Jewish Mus. Greece, Athens, 1991—, Friends of Israel Def. Forces, NYC, 1997—. Lt. comdr. USNR, 1956—58. Fellow: Mich. Vascular Surg. Soc., Midwest Vasular Surg. Soc., Soc. Vascular Surgery, Internat. Coll. Surgeons (pres. 1991, Disting. Svc. award 1992, emeritus fellow 1995), Internat. Soc. Vascular Surgery, Soc. Clin. Vascular Surgery; mem.: Maimonides Med. Soc. (pres. 1966—68), Southeastern Mich. Surg. Soc. (pres. 1984—85), Mich. State Med. Soc. (Spl. Recognition Leadership award 1991, 2005), Internat. Coll. Angiology (vice chair sci. coun. 1994—, sec. 2002, pres. 2003), US/Internat. Coll. Surgeons (pres. 1991), Sigma Xi. Home: 27501 W 14 Mile Rd Farmington Hills MI 48334 Personal E-mail: vascelie@sbcglobal.net.

ABOU-SAYED, HATEM, plastic surgeon; s. Ahmed S. and Kadreya E. Abou-Sayed. BS, U. Calif., Berkeley, 1992; MD, U. Calif. San Francisco, 1996. Diplomate Am. Bd. of Surgery, 2002, Am. Bd. of Plastic Surgery, 2004. Intern dept. surgery Mass. Gen. Hosp., Boston, 1996—97, resident dept. surgery, 1997—2001; resident divsn. plastic surgery U. Calif., 2001—03; plastic surgeon Plastic Surgery of Palm Beach, Palm Springs, Fla., 2003—. Musician: (popular music) Hookah Smoke. Recipient Academic Excellence award, UCSF Alumni Faculty Assn., 1996; scholar Regents scholar, U. Calif.-Berkeley, 1988—92; Nat. Merit Scholar Edward Frank Kraft, 1988. Mem.: Am. Soc. Plastic Surgeons, Palm Beach County Med. Soc., AMA, ACS (assoc.), Alpha Omega Alpha, Phi Beta Kappa, Eta Kappa Nu, Tau Beta Pi. Office: Plastic Surgery of Palm Beach PA 1620 South Congress Ave Ste 100 Palm Springs FL 33461 Office Phone: 561-968-7111. Office Fax: 561-968-1800.

ABOUSSIE, MARILYN, retired judge; b. Wichita Falls, Tex., June 9, 1948; m. John A. Hay, Jr., Dec. 9, 1973; 1 child, John A. III. BA, Midwestern U., 1969; JD, U. Tex., 1974. Bar: Tex. 1974. Assoc. Foreman, Dyess, Prewett, Rosenberg & Henderson, Houston, 1974-76; pvt. practice San Angelo, Tex., 1976-78; ptnr. Smith, Davis, Rose, Finley & Hofmann, San Angelo, Tex., 1978-83; judge 340th Dist. Ct., San Angelo, 1983-86; justice Tex. Ct. Appeals, Austin, 1986-98, chief justice, 1998—2003; ret., 2003; sr. judge Tex., 2003—. Mem.: ABA, State Bar Assn. of Tex. Episcopalian. Office Phone: 325-658-9758.

ABRAHAM, ALFRED JUDE, lawyer; b. Warren, Ohio, Oct. 12, 1978; s. Francis Vincent and Mary Jo Anne Abraham. BA magna cum laude, John Carroll U., University Hts., Ohio, 1996—99; JD cum laude, U. Notre Dame, S.Bend, Ind., 2000—03. Bar: Ohio 2003. Atty. Alfred J. Abraham, Atty. at Law, Warren, Ohio, 2004—. Mem.: Trumbull County Bar Assn., John Carroll U. Alumni-in-Admission Program, Mensa. Roman Cath. Avocation: history. Home Phone: 330-372-7061.

ABRAHAM, F. MURRAY (FAHRID MURRAY ABRAHAM), actor, educator; b. Pitts., Oct. 24, 1939; s. Fahrid and Josephine Abraham; m. Kate Hannan, 1962; two children. Student, U. Tex., El Paso, 1959-61. Actor Broadway, Off-Broadway, children's theater, musicals, film, TV; prof. Bklyn. Coll., 1985—. Dir. No Smoking Please, N.Y.C., Time & Space Ltd. Theatre, N.Y.C. Profl. stage debut in The Wonderful Ice Cream Suit, Coronet Theatre, L.A., 1965; Broadway debut in The Man in the Glass Booth, Royale Theatre, 1968; appeared in numerous Broadway plays including 6 Rms RivVu, 1972-73, Bad Habits, 1974, The Ritz, 1976, Teibele and Her Demon, 1979; other stage appearances include Landscape of the Body, 1977, The Master and Margarita, 1978, The Golem, 1984, King Lear, 1981, Frankie and Johnny in the Claire de Lune, 1987, A Month in the Country, 1995, Merchant of Venice, 2007; films include: They Might Be Giants, 1971, Serpico, 1974, The Sunshine Boys, 1975, All the President's Men, 1976, The Ritz, 1976, The Big Fix, 1979, Scarface, 1983, Amadeus, 1984 (Academy award best actor 1984, Golden Globe award best actor 1984), The Name of the Rose, 1986, Russicum, 1989, An Innocent Man, 1989, Bonfire of the Vanities, 1990, Cadence, 1991, Mobsters, 1991, National Lampoon's Loaded Weapon I, 1993, By the Sword, 1993, Last Action Hero, 1993, Surviving The Game, 1994, The Case, 1994, Nostradamus, 1994, Jamila, 1994, Fresh, 1994, Mighty Aphrodite, 1995, Dillinger and Capone, 1995, Baby Face Nelson, 1995,

Looking for Richard, 1996, Children of the Revolution, 1996, Mimic, 1997, Eruption, 1997, Laurel and Hardy: For Love or Mummy, 1998, Star Trex IX, 1998, Falcone, 1999, Esther, 1999, Muppets From Space, 1999, Finding Forrester, 2000; narrator Herman Melville, Damned in Paradise, PBS, 1985; appeared in PBS Masterpiece Theatre prodn.: Silas Marner, 1987, Noah's Ark, 1999, Star Trek: Insurrection, 1998; TV mini-series Larry McMurtry's Dead Man's Walk, 1996; TV spl. Einstein Revealed (voice), 1996, TV movie Sex and the Married Woman, 1978, Color of Justice, 1997, Noah's Ark, 1999, Esther, 1999; TV series Love of Life. Recipient Obie award for Uncle Vanya 1984; Los Angeles Film Critics award, 1985. Mem. Actors Equity, AFTRA, Screen Actors Guild*

ABRAHAM, HENRY JULIAN, retired political science professor; b. Offenbach am Main, Germany, Aug. 25, 1921; s. Frederick and Louise Kullmann Abraham; m. Mildred Kosches; children: Philip F., Peter D. AB summa cum laude, Kenyon Coll., 1948, LHD (hon.), 1972; MA, Columbia U., 1949; PhD, U. Pa., 1952; LLD (hon.), U. Hartford, 1982, Knox Coll., 1982; LittD (hon.), St. Joseph's U., 1987; LLD (hon.), Old Dominion U., 1996. Faculty U. Pa., 1949-72, prof. polit. sci., 1962-72; Doherty prof. govt. and fgn. affairs U. Va., 1972—78, James Hart prof., 1978-97, James Hart prof. emeritus, 1997—. Vis. prof. Swarthmore Coll., CCNY, Colo. U., Columbia U., Richmond Law Sch., Copenhagen U., U. Stockhholm, Aarhus U., Lund U., Goteborg U., U. Oslo, U. Helsinki, U. Uppsala, U. Amsterdam, U. London, univs. in India and Iran, 1978, univs. in Peru, Bolivia, Brazil, Paraguay, Argentina, 1979, univs. in Japan, China, Taiwan, The Philippines, New Zealand, and Australia, 1982, univs. in Republic of Korea, 1982, 84. Author: Compulsory Voting, 1955, Government as Entrepreneur, 1956, Courts and Judges, 1959, Elements of Democratic Government, 1964, Essentials of National Government, 1971, Justices & Presidents, 1992, American Democracy, 1990, The Judiciary, 1997, The Judicial Process, 1997, Freedom and the Court, 2003. Mem. com. on non-discriminition Phila. Bd. Edn., 1962; mem. vis. com. on govt. Lehigh U., 1967-71; trustee fedn. Jewish Agys. Greater Phila., 1970-72, Kenyon Coll., 1987-93; mem. Va. Commn. on Bicentennial of Constn. of US, 1985-92, Va. Coun. on Human Rights, 1999-2002. Recipient award excellence undergrad. teaching U. Pa., 1959, 67, Kite and Key Tchg. award, 1967, award excellence undergrad. teaching U. Va., 1978, Thomas Jefferson award U. Va., 1983, Alumni Tchg. award, 1986, Disting. Svc. award Va. Social Sci. Assn., 1982, Disting. Prof. award U. Va. Alumni Assn., 1986, First Lifetime Achievement award, org. sec. on law & courts, Am. polit., sci. Assn., 1993, others; NEH, 1975-76, 78, 80-81, NSF fellow, 1965, fellow Am. Philos. Soc., 1961-67, 79, Rockefeller Found. fellow, 1978, Earhart fellow, 1984, Bradley Found., 1989-97. Mem. Fellows in Am. Studies (pres. 1966), Am. Polit. Sci. Assn. (v.p. 1980-82), Raven Soc., Am. Soc. for Legal History, So. Polit. Sci. Ass. (rec. sec. 1980-81), Soc. of Fellows, English-Speaking Union, Met. Opera Guild, Nat. Trust, Golden Key, Greencroft Club (v.p. 1985-87, Charlottesville, Va.), Z Club, Imp Club, Yale Club (NYC), Capitol Hill Club (Washington), Oliver Turner Soc., Phi Beta Kappa (vis. scholar 1970-71), Pi Sigma Alpha, Pi Gamma Mu, Omicron Delta Kappa. Home: 250 Pantops Mountain Rd Apt 5311 Charlottesville VA 22911 Office Phone: 434-924-3192. *Basically—a commitment to hard work; to discipline; to a maintenance of a sense of humour; to a rejection of pompousness and egomania; to a resolute embrace of merit. Above all, an abiding faith in drawing a viable line between the rights and obligations of individuals and those of society without which the democratic process can neither work nor survive.*

ABRAHAM, JACOB A., computer engineering educator, consultant; b. Kerala, India, Dec. 8, 1948; came to U.S., 1970; s. Jacob and Annamma (Chacko) A.; m. Ruth Anne Dick, July 19, 1975; children— Nathan Thomas, Sarah Anne BS, U. Kerala, 1970; MS, Stanford U., 1971, PhD, 1974. Acting asst. prof. Stanford U., Calif., 1974-75; asst. prof. computer engrng. U. Ill., Urbana, 1975-80, assoc. prof., 1980-83, prof., 1983-88; prof. and Cockrell Family Regents Chair in Engrng. #8 U. Tex., Austin, 1988—, dir. Computer Engrng. Rsch. Ctr., 1989—. Cons. Aerospace Corp., Digital Equipment Corp., GE, GTE, Hewlett-Packard Co., IBM Corp., Intel, Sperry, 1979—; dir. rsch. program in reliable very large scale integration architectures U. Ill., 1984-88. Assoc. editor JETTA, 1992—; adv. editor Asken Assocs. Pub., 1987-89; contbr. over 200 articles to profl. confs., jours. and books. Recipient Best Paper award IEEE-Assn., IEEE Emanuel R. Piore award, 2005, Computing Machinery Design Automation Conf., 1993. Fellow IEEE (assoc. editor transactions on computer-aided design of integrated circuits and systems 1984-86, assoc. editor transactions on very large scale integration systems 1992-93, chair Computer Sci. Tech. Com. on Fault-Tolerant Computing, 1991-92); fellow Assn. Computing Machinery, Sigma Xi. Mem. Ch. of S. India Achievements include 1 patent. Office: U Tex Computer Engrng Rsch Ctr 1 University Sta C8800 Austin TX 78712-0323

ABRAHAM, JOHN, professional football player; b. Timmonsville, SC, May 6, 1978; m. Tunisia Abraham; 3 children. Grad., U. of SC. Linebacker New York Jets, 2000—06, Atlanta Falcons, 2006—. Named to NFL Pro Bowl team, 2001, 2003. Office: Atlanta Falcons 4400 Falcons Pkwy Flowery Branch GA 30542

ABRAHAM, JOHN PATRICK, mechanical engineer, educator; b. Bklyn. Ctr., Minn., Oct. 27, 1973; s. Jerry Joseph and Lois Louis Abraham; m. Molly Katherine Rolfsmeier, Aug. 12, 2001; children: Lilith Ann children: Olivia Milawnn. BS in Mech. Engring., U. Minn., Mpls., 1997, MS in Mech. Engring., 1999, PhD in Mech. Engring., 2001. Prof. engring. U. St. Thomas, St. Paul, 2001—. Achievements include patents pending for related to novel ways of cooling high-power electronics; research in modeling of heat transfer within living tissue; numerical simulation of fluid flow and heat transfer within electronic devices; new methods of performing numerical simulations. Office: Univ St Thomas 2115 Summit Ave Saint Paul MN 55105-1079 Home Phone: 612-722-6717; Office Phone: 651-962-5766. Business E-Mail: jpabraham@stthomas.edu.

ABRAHAM, KENNETH SAMUEL, law educator; b. Kearny, NJ, June 19, 1946; s. Saul Jerome and Helen Beverly (Godin) A.; m. Susan R. Stein, Apr. 5, 1981. AB, Ind. U., 1967; JD, Yale U., 1971. Bar: Md. 1977, Va. 1988. Assoc. Mazer & Lesemann, Hackensack, NJ, 1971-73; asst. prof. law U. Md., Balt., 1974-77, assoc. prof., 1977-80, prof., 1980-84; prof. law U. Va., Charlottesville, 1984—, Class 1962 prof., 1988—2002, Robert E. Scott Disting. prof & Class 1966 Rsch. prof., 2002—. Assoc. reporter ALI, Phila., 1986—91; vis. asst. prof. Case Western Res. U., Cleve., 1974, Johns Hopkins U., 1976; vis. prof. U. Va., 1983—84, Harvard U., 2003. Author: Distributing Risk: Insurance, Legal Theory, and Pub. Policy, 1986, Insurance Law and Regulation, 4th edit., 2005, Environmental Liability Insurance Law, 1991, The Forms and Functions of Tort Law, 2d edit., 2002; also articles. Mem. Am. Law Inst. (coun.), Phi Beta Kappa. Home: 770 Covey Hill Rd Charlottesville VA 22901-3268 Office: U Va Sch Law 580 Massie Rd Charlottesville VA 22903-1738

ABRAHAM, MAGID M., Internet company executive; PhD in Ops. Rsch., MIT, MBA; holds an engrng. degree, Ecole Polytechnique. Pres., COO Information Resources, Inc.; founder, CEO Paragren Technologies, Inc. (now part of Siebel Systems); pres., CEO, co-founder comScore Networks, Inc., Reston, Va., 1999—. Spkr. in field. Author: (several articles) Harvard Business Review and Marketing Science. Co-recipient Paul Green award, Am. Mktg. Assn., 1996, William F. O'Dell award, 2000. Office: comScore Networks Inc 11465 Sunset Hills Rd Ste 200 Reston VA 20190 Office Phone: 203-438-2000. Office Fax: 203-438-2051.*

ABRAHAM, MANOJ TIMOTHY, plastic surgeon, educator; m. Kavita Aggarwal; children: Kiran Abraham-Aggarwal, Minali Abraham-Aggarwal. BS, Brown U., Providence; MD, Cornell U., NYC. Diplomate Am. Bd. Facial Plastic Surgery, Am. Bd. Otolaryngology - Head & Neck Surgery, Nat. Bd. Med. Examiners, NY State Medicine & Surgery, Calif. State Physician & Surgeon, Drug Enforcement Agy. Gen. surgery internship Lenox Hill Hosp., NYC; resident otolaryngology Manhattan Eye, Ear & Throat Hosp., NYC; chief resident otolaryngology NYU Medical Ctr., NYC; fellow facial plastic & reconstructive surgery UCLA Med. Ctr.; tchg. asst. dept. physiology Brown U., Providence, 1992—93; papanicolaou fellow dept. cell biology & anatomy Cornell U., NYC, clin. assoc. dept. otorhinolaryngology Weill Med. Coll.; tchg. asst. dept. otolaryngology NYU Sch. Medicine; clin. instr. divsn. head & neck surgery U. Calif., LA Sch. Medicine; clin. asst. prof. dept. otolaryngology NY Med. Coll., Valhalla; active med. staff dept. otolaryngology Vassar Bros. Med. Ctr., Poughkeepsie, NY; clin. instr. facial plastic & reconstructive surgery NY Eye & Ear Infirmary, NYC. Com. mem. Vassar Bros. Med. Ctr., Continuing Med. Edn. Com., Poughkeepsie. Contbr. articles to profl. jours. Surgeon on humanitarian mission CRISP, Mazatenango, Guatemala, 2003—06; com. mem. Brendon Montessori, Poughkeepsie. Nominee Facutly Scholar award, Brown U., 1992; recipient Albert Arnold Bennett award, 1993, James A. Moore scholarship for excellence in otorhinoloaryngology, Cornell U. Med. Coll., 1997, 1st prize, NY Acad. Medicine, 2001, Ea. Sect. prize, Triological Soc., 2001; grantee Rsch. fellowship, NIH, 1995, Solon Summerfield Found., 1996, Scudder Meml. scholarship, Cornell U. Med. Coll., 1997; scholar George E. Hall Funding for rsch. in head & neck oncology, NYU Med. Ctr., Dept. Otolaryngology, 2000; Immunology Rsch. grant, Max and Leila Stern Fund, 1993. Fellow: ACS; mem.: AMA, Am. Rhinologic Soc., Med. Soc. State NY, Dutchess County Med. Soc. (com. mem., conf. chmn. 2003—06), Am. Acad. Otolaryngology (com. mem., conf. chmn. 2004—06), NY Facial Plastic Surgery Soc. (sec. 2006), Am. Acad. Facial Plastics & Reconstructive Surgery (com. mem. 2001—06), Sigma Xi. Avocation: photography. Office: Facial Plastic Reconstructive & Laser Surgery PO Box 2179 Poughkeepsie NY 12601 Office Fax: 845-454-8026. Business E-Mail: info@nyfacemd.com.

ABRAHAM, NATHAN SAMUEL, advertising agency and public relations executive, marketing and management consultant; b. Worcester, Mass., Mar. 8, 1946; s. Israel and Ethel (Zellon) Tighe; 1 child, Joshua D. BA, U. Mass., 1968. Sales rep. IBM Corp., Springfield, Mass., 1968—69; sales rep., trainer Mut. Benefit Life, Springfield, 1969—71, NCOA, Portsmouth, NH, 1974—75; owner, prin. Nathan Abraham & Assocs., Worcester and Springfield, 1971—74, Brookline, Mass., 1975—77; ptnr. Abraham & Abraham Inc., Brookline, 1977—89; pres. Nathan Abraham & Assocs., 1989—. Trustee Temple Ohabei Shalom, Brookline, 1987-88; bd. dirs., mem. publicity com. Early Childhood Ctr., Brookline, 1987-88; founder Footprints for Peace TM Internat., 1984. Recipient Leadership tng. award, Bus. People, Ctrl. Mass., 1971, Jaycees for Course award, 1971. Jewish. Avocations: fishing, camping. Office Phone: 413-552-3530. E-mail: nathan@nathanabraham.com.

ABRAHAM, (EDWARD) SPENCER, former Secretary of Energy; b. East Lansing, Mich., June 12, 1952; s. Eddie and Julie Abraham; m. Jane Hershey, 1990; children: Julie, Betsy, Spencer. BA in Social Sci.and Polit. Sci., Mich. State U., 1974; JD, Harvard U., 1979. Asst. prof. law Thomas M. Cooley Law Sch., 1981-83; chmn. Mich. Republican Party, 1983-90; dep. chief of staff to Vice President Dan Quayle The White House, Washington, 1990-91; co-chmn. Nat. Republican Congressional Com., 1991-93; of counsel Miller, Canfield, Paddock & Stone, 1993-94; U.S. senator from Mich., 1995-2001; mem. budget, commerce, sci., transp., judiciary, and small bus. committees; sec. U.S. Dept. Energy, Washington, 2001—05. Disting. vis. fellow Hoover Inst., 2005—; bd. dirs. Occidental Petroleum Corp., LA, 2005—. Mem.: Electricity Advisory Bd. (also secretary), 2001. Republican. Office: Hoover Inst Stanford U Stanford CA 94305

ABRAHAM, TERRY, school librarian; b. Portland, Oreg., Oct. 6, 1944; BA, U. Wash., 1965; MFA, Wash. State U., 1968; MLS, U. Oreg., 1970. Cert. archivist, 1989. Libr. Wash. State U., Pullman, 1967-68, manuscript-archives libr., 1970-84; head, spl. collections and archives U. Idaho, Moscow, 1984—2005. Projects editor Soc. Am. Archivists, Chgo., 1981-85; program officer Nat. Endowment for Humanities, Washington, 1987-88. Author: Austin Mires, 1968, Selected Manuscript Resources in the Washington State University Library, 1974, A Union List of the Papers of Members of Congress from the Pacific Northwest, 1976, Mountains So Sublime: Nineteenth-Century British Travellers and the Lure of the Rocky Mountain West, 2006; compiler (with R. Davis) Day to Day: A Guide to the Records of the Historic Day Minervs Group in the University of Idaho Library, 1992; editor: Chinese Servants in the West, 2007. Mem. adv. bd. Wash. State Hist. Records, Olympia, 1981-84, Idaho Hist. Records, Boise, 1984-92, 97-2003, Idaho Ctr. for The Book, Boise, 1993—2005. Recipient Hard-Rock Mining in the Coeur d'Alenes Nat. Hist. Publs. and Records Commn., 1986-88, Idaho Archives and Manuscripts Database, 1989-91, Nat. Hist. Publs. and Records Commn., Mining Records Appraisal and Description U.S. Dept. Edn., 1991-92. Address: 735 E 6th St Moscow ID 83843-3562 Business E-Mail: tabraham@uidaho.edu.

ABRAHAM, WILLIAM JOHN, JR., lawyer; b. Jan. 17, 1948; s. William John and Constance (Dudley) A.; m. Linda Omeis, Aug. 31, 1968; children: Richard W., Heidi K. BA with honors, U. Ill., 1969; JD magna cum laude, U. Mich., Ann Arbor, 1972. Bar: Wis. 1973, U.S. Supreme Ct. 1975. Jud. clk. U.S. Ct. Appeals (D.C. cir.), Washington, 1972-73; ptnr. Foley & Lardner, Milw., 1973—. Former mem. mgmt. com., former chmn. bus. law dept; bd. dirs. The Vollrath Co., Windway Capital Corp., Phillips Plastics Corp., Quad/Graphics, Inc., Park Bank, L'eft Bank Wine Co., Ltd., Proliance, Inc.; Hi-Liter, LLC lectr. MBA program U. Wis.; prin. Lakeview Equity Ptnrs. LLC; prin. Lakeview Eqity Ptrs. Mem. adv. bd. Wis. Policy Rsch. Inst.; mem. Greater Milw. Com.; chmn. Children's Rsch. Inst.; bd. dirs. Children's Health Sys. of Milw.; past bd. dirs. United Way of Greater Milw., Family Svc. of Milw., Milw. Zool. Soc.; bd. dirs., former chmn. Children's Hosp. Found. Named All-Am. Big 10 Fencing Champion, 1968—69. Mem. ABA, State Bar of Wis. (former chmn. legis. com.), Milw. Bar Assn., Barristers, Tripoli Country Club (bd. dirs., pres.), Milw. Athletic Club, Milw. Club, Desert Mountain Country Club. Office: Foley & Lardner 777 E Wisconsin Ave Ste 3800 Milwaukee WI 53202-5367 Office Phone: 414-297-5667. Business E-Mail: wabraham@foley.com.

ABRAHAMS, ROBERT M., lawyer; b. NYC, Nov. 21, 1948; s. Ralph M. and Mathilda (Moses) Abrahams; m. Carol J. Popkin, Aug. 8, 1970; children: Kathryn, Emily, Daniel. BA, Hobart Coll., 1969; JD, Hofstra U., 1976. Bar: NY 1977, registered: US Dist. Ct. (So. Dist.) NY 1977, US Dist. Ct. (Ea. Dist.) NY 1977, US Ct. Appeals (2nd Cir.) 1980, US Supreme Ct. 1980, US Ct. Appeals (3rd Cir.) 1984, US Tax Ct. Assoc. Paul, Weiss, Rifkind, Wharton & Garrison, NYC, 1976—80, Schulte Roth & Zabel LLP, NYC, 1980—83, ptnr., 1984—, co-chair, litigation dept., 2002—. Instr. trial advocacy program Hofstra U., 1984—88. Editor-in-chief Hofstra U. Law Rev., 1975. Bd zoning appeals Village of Thomaston, NY, 1982—97; mem. Mediation Panel US Dist. Ct. (So. Dist.) NY, 1998—. Fellow: NY Bar Found.; mem.: NY Bar Assn. (Task Force on Foreclosure Reform, Real Property Sect., Litig. Sect.), ABA (Litig. Sect., trial practice com., RICO subcom 1984—). Office: Schulte Roth & Zabel 919 Third Ave New York NY 10022-4774 Office Phone: 212-756-2355. Office Fax: 212-593-5955. Business E-Mail: robert.abrahams@srz.com.

ABRAHAMS, SIDNEY CYRIL, physicist, crystallographer; b. London, May 28, 1924; arrived in U.S., 1948; s. Aaron Harry and Freda (Cohen) A.; m. Rhoda Banks, May 1, 1950; children: David Mark, Peter Brian, Jennifer Anne. BSc, U. Glasgow, Scotland, 1946, PhD, 1949, DSc, 1957; Doctor honoris causa, U. Uppsala, Sweden, 1981, U. Bordeaux, 1997. Rsch. fellow U. Minn., Mpls., 1949-50; mem. staff MIT, Cambridge, 1950-54; rsch. fellow U. Glasgow, 1954-57; mem. tech. staff Bell Labs., Murray Hill, NJ, 1957-82; disting. mem. tech. staff AT&T Bell Labs., Murray Hill, 1982-88; Humboldt sr. scientist Inst. Crystallography, U. Tübingen, Germany, 1989-90. Guest scientist Brookhaven Nat. Lab., Upton, N.Y., 1957-90; vis. prof. U. Bordeaux, France, 1979, 90; Humboldt sr. scientist U. Tübingen, 1995; adj. prof. physics So. Oreg. U., 1990—. Mem. editl. bd. Rev. Sci. Instruments, 1963-65; co-editor Anomalous Scattering, 1975; editor World Directory of Crystallographers, 1977; editor-in-chief Acta Crystallographica, 1978-87; book rev. editor Ferroelectrics, 1975—. Recipient Sr. U.S. Scientist award, Alexander von Humboldt Found., 1989-90. Fellow AAAS, Am. Phys. Soc., Internat. Union Pure and Applied Chemistry (rep. interdivsnl. com. on nomenclature and symbols 1978-2004); mem. Am. Crystallographic Assn. (pres. 1968, mng. editor 1965-90), Royal Soc. Chemistry, Am. Inst. Physics (chmn. pub. policy com. 1981-91), Internat. Union Crystallography (chmn. commn. on crystallographic apparatus 1972-75, commn. on jours. 1978-87, commn. on crystallographic nomenclature 1978-2004), Sigma Xi (founding pres. S. Oreg. U. chpt. 1993-95). Avocations: photography, hiking. Home: 89 Mallard St Ashland OR 97520-7316 Office: So Oreg U Physics Dept Ashland OR 97520 Business E-Mail: sca@sou.edu.

ABRAHAMSON, A. CRAIG, lawyer; b. Washington, May 24, 1954; s. Joseph Labe and Helen Dorothy (Selis) A.; m. Mary Ellen Bernard, Dec. 29, 1979; children: Nicholas Eric, Amy Nicole. BA, U. Minn., 1976; JD, U. Tulsa, 1979. Bar: Minn. 1979, US Dist. Ct. Minn. 1979, Okla. 1982, US Dist. Ct. (no. and ea. dists.) Okla. 1983, US Ct. Appeals (10th cir.) 1990, Mo. 1991. Assoc. Law Office of Joseph L. Abrahamson, Mpls., 1979-82, Freese & March, Tulsa, 1982-83, Barlow & Cox, Tulsa, 1983-86; pvt. practice Tulsa, 1986-95, 2000—; ptnr. Levinson, Smith & Abrahamson, Tulsa, 1995-2000; gen. counsel, v.p. Sandman Property Svcs., Inc. & The Sanditen Cos., 2001—04. V.p. program com. Youth Svcs., Tulsa, Inc., Leadership Tulsa Class XVII, 1989-92; sec. Great Expectations Educators, Inc., 1995-99; mem. bd. trustees Am. Theatre Co., 1999—. Recipient Am. Jurisprudence Evidence award Lawyers Co-operative Pub. Co. Bancroft-Whitney Co., 1978. Mem. Okla. Bar Assn. (family law sect., bankruptcy sect.), Tulsa County Bar Assn. (family law sect., bankruptcy sect.), Rotary Internat. Democrat. Jewish. Avocations: fishing, camping, travel, tennis. Home: 7518 S 107th East Ave Tulsa OK 74133-2530 Office: A Craig Abrahamson 406 S Boulder Ave Ste 706 Tulsa OK 74103 Office Phone: 918-584-0318. Business E-Mail: craiga@abrahamsonlaw.com.

ABRAHAMSON, SHIRLEY SCHLANGER, state supreme court chief justice; b. NYC, Dec. 17, 1933; d. Leo and Ceil (Sauerteig) Schlanger; m. Seymour Abrahamson, Aug. 26, 1953; 1 son, Daniel Nathan. AB, NYU, 1953; JD, Ind. U., 1956; SJD, U. Wis., 1962. Bar: Ind. 1956, N.Y. 1961, Wis. 1962. Asst. dir. Legis. Drafting Research Fund, Columbia U. Law Sch., 1957-60; since practiced in Madison, Wis., 1962-76; mem. firm LaFollette, Sinykin, Anderson & Abrahamson, 1962-76; justice Wis. Supreme Ct., Madison, 1976-96, chief justice, 1996—. Bd. visitors Ind. U. Sch. Law, 1972-02, U. Miami Sch. Law, 1982-97, U. Chgo. Law Sch., 1988-92, Brigham Young U., Sch. Law, 1986-88, Northwestern U. Law Sch., 1989-94; chmn. Wis. Rhodes Scholarship Com., 1992-95; chmn. nat. adv. com. on ct.-adjudicated and ct.-ordered health care George Washington U. Ctr. Health Policy, Washington, 1993-95; mem. DNA adv. bd. FBI, U.S. Dept. Justice, 1995-2001; bd. dirs. Inst. Jud. Adminstrn., Inc., NYU Sch. Law; chair Nat. Inst. Justice's Commn. Future DNA Evidence, 1997-2001; prof. U. Wis. Sch. Law, 1966-92; v.p. Conference of Chief Justices, 2002-. Editor: Constitutions of the United States (National and State) 2 vols, 1962. Mem. study group program of rsch., mental health and the law John D. and Catherine T. MacArthur Found., 1988-96; mem. coun. fund for rsch. on dispute resolution Ford Found., 1987-91; bd. dirs. Wis. Civil Liberties Union, 1968-72; mem. ct. reform adv. panel Internat. Human Rights Law Group Cambodia Project, 1995-97. Recipient Dwight D. Opperman award, Am. Judicature Soc., 2004. Mem. ABA (coun., sect. legal edn. and admissions to bar 1976-86, mem. commn. on undergrad. edn. in law and the humanities 1978-79, standing com. on pub. edn. 1991-95, mem. commn. on access to justice/2000 1993-02, mem. adv. bd. Ctrl. and East European law initiative 1994-99, mem. consortium on legal svcs. and the public 1995-2001, vice-chair ABA Coalition for Justice 1997-2000), Wis. Bar Assn., Dane County Bar Assn., 7th Cir. Bar Assn., Nat. Assn. Women Judges, Am. Law Inst. (mem. coun. 1985-), Am. Philos. Soc., Am. Acad. Arts and Scis. Office: Wis Supreme Ct PO Box 1688 Madison WI 53702-1688*

ABRAHM, JANET LEE, hematologist, oncologist, educator, palliative care specialist; b. San Francisco, Mar. 14, 1949; d. Paul Milton and Helen Lesser Abrahm; m. David Rytman Slavitt, Apr. 16, 1978. Student, U. Calif., Berkeley, 1969; BA, U. Calif., San Francisco, 1970, MD, 1973. Diplomate in internal medicine, hematology and oncology Am. Bd. Internal Medicine; diplomate Am. Bd. Hospice and Palliative Medicine. Intern and resident medicine Mass. Gen. Hosp., Boston, 1973-75, hematology fellow, 1975-76; chief resident medicine Moffitt Hosp. U. Calif., San Francisco, 1976-77; hematology/oncology fellow Hosp. U. Pa., Phila., 1977-80; postdoctoral fellow medicine U. Pa., Phila., 1977-78, postdoctoral trainee medicine, 1977-80, asst. prof. medicine, 1980-86, Hosp. U. Pa. and VA Med. Ctr., Phila., 1986-89, assoc. prof. medicine, 1989-2000; attending physician Hosp. U. Pa., Phila., 1980-93; from staff physician to assoc. chief of staff, primary care and consultation medicine Phila. VA Med. Ctr., 1982—97, faculty scholar Project Death in Am., 1997—2000; med. dir. Wissahickon Hospice UPHS, 1998-2000; assoc. prof. medicine and anesthesia Harvard Med. Sch., 2001—; attending physician Dana-Farber Cancer Inst., Brigham and Women's Hosp., Boston, 2001—. Prin. investigator Palliative Care Fellowship Grant, 1996-2001, 03-; mem. concensus panel on End-of-Life Care, ACP, 1997—; chmn. adv. com. Cancer Care VA Dist. 4, 1987-90; sec. subsplty. bd. hematology Am. Bd. Internal Medicine, 1987-92, sec. SEP subcom. hematology, 1993-95; 01—; mem. test writing com. hospice and palliative medicine exam. Am. Bd. Internal Medicine, 2007—; dir. palliative fellowship Dana-Farber Cancer Inst., Boston, 2001-07. Author: Pain Management and Antiemetic Therapy in Hematologic Disorders in Hematology: Basic Principles and Practice, 1994, 2005, Anemia, Pain Management in Geriatric Secrets, 1996, 2000, 2004, A Physician's Guide to Pain and Symptom Management in Cancer Patients, 2000, 2d edit., 2005, Caring For Patients at the End of Life Clinical Oncology, 2004, Specialized Care of the Terminally Ill, In Cancer, Principles & Practices of Oncology, 2005; reviewer New Eng. Jour. Medicine, JAMA, Cancer, Archives Internal Medicine, Annals Internal Medicine; mem. editl. bd.: Jour. Palliative Medicine, 2004—, Jour. Clin. Oncology, 2005—, Cancer, 2007—; contbr. numerous articles to profl. jours. Fellow: ACP, Am. Acad. Hospice and Palliative Medicine (bd. dirs. 2002—07, sec. 2007—); mem.: Am. Pain Soc., Am. Assn. Cancer Edn. (program com. 1993), Am. Soc. Clin. Oncology, Am. Soc. Clin. Hypnosis, Am. Soc. Hematology, Alpha Omega Alpha, Phi Beta Kappa. Home: 35 West St #5 Cambridge MA 02139 Office: Dana Farber Cancer Inst 44 Binney St Boston MA 02115 Office Phone: 617-632-6464. Business E-Mail: jabrahm@partners.org.

ABRAM, MONROE J., athletic trainer, educator; b. Macon, Ga., May 4, 1964; s. Monroe E. and Avis P. Abram; m. Kimberly R. Woods; children: Maye, Arianna, Jamison, Ella. BE, U. Ga., Athnes, 1986; MEd, Springfield Coll., Mass., 1988. Cert. athletic trainer. Staff athletic trainer Piedmont Sports Med. Clinic, Macon, 1988—92, Grecter Atlanta Sports Medicine, Atlanta, 1992—95; head atlantic trainer Savanah State U., Ga., 1995—98; head athletic trainer Morohowe Coll., Atlanta, 1998—99; head atlantic trainer Tenn. State U., Nashville, 1999—. Bd. mem. Ethic Diveristy Com.,

Dallas, 2004—, Tenn. Bd. Athletic Trainers, Nashville, 2007—; instr. phys. edn. dept. Tenn. State U. Sponsor US Olympic Tng. Ctr., 1997; athletic trainer Olympic Games, Atlanta, 1996. Recipient Coll. Athletic Trainer Yr., Tenn. Atlanta Trainers Soc., 2004, Above Call award, Tng. and Consulting Mag., 2005. Office: Tenn State Univ 3500 John Merritt Blvd Nashville TN 37209

ABRAM, RUTH JACOBETH, museum administrator and founder; b. Orange County, Calif., Sept. 19, 1945; d. Morris B. and Jane (Maguire) A.; m. Herbert Teitelbaum, June 4, 1967; children: Anna Kaye, Noah Abram Teitelbaum. BA, Sarah Lawrence Coll., 1967; MSW, Brandeis U., 1970; MA in Am. History, NYU, 1983; D Pub. Svc. (hon.), Russell Sage Coll.; D (hon.), Muhlenberg Coll., 2007. Title VII coord. NAACP Legal Def. and Edn. Fund; exec. dir. Norman Found., NYC, 1971-72; program dir. ACLU Found., NYC, 1972-74; exec. dir. Women's Action Alliance, NYC, 1974-79; pres., founder Paraphrase, Inc., NYC, 1983—, Lower East Side Hist. Conservancy, NYC, 1984-88, Lower East Side Tenement Mus., NYC, 1988—. Commr. Internat. Women's Yr., 1975; mem. bd. trustees Lower East Side Tenement Mus., NYC. Author: Send Us a Lady Physician. Recipient Encore award, Arts & Bus. Coun. of NY, 1999, Camille Mermod award, Am. Med. Women's Assn., Disting. Alumni award, NYU, Alumnae of Yr. award, Sarah Lawrence Coll., Women in Preservation award, Briscoe award, Emerald Isle Immigration Ctr. Mem. Am. Assn. State and Local History, Am. Assn. Museums (named to Centennial Honor Roll, 2006)

ABRAM, STEPHEN, librarian, writer; m. Stephanie Smith Abram; children: Zachary, Sydney. BA in Anthropology (hon.), U. Toronto, 1978, MLS Faculty Libr. & Info. Sci., 1980. Head libr. Nat. Info. Ctr. Coopers & Lybrand/Currie Coopers & Lybrand (auditing, taxation, consulting), 1980—85; dir. info. resources Hay Mgmt. Cons./Hay Group, 1985—89, dir. info. & mktg. resources, dir. adminstrn., 1989—91; sr. product mgr., electronic info. Thomson Electronic Publishing, 1991; pub. electronic info. Carswell, Thomson Profl. Pub., 1992—94; v.p., corp. develop. Micromedia ProQuest/IHS Can., 1999—2004; v.p. innovation SirsiDyniz Corp., Huntsville, Ala., 2004—. Frequent keynote spkr. at librs. and info. industry confs.; co-chair Toronto Libr. Continuing Edn. Group, 1984—99; founding chair Toronto Inmagic User's Group, 1985—88; founding ptnr. Can. Online/Can. Info. Congress, 1985—86; lectr. Ryerson Polytechnic U., 1989—95; faculty info. studies, student coun. dir. U. Toronto, 1979—80, adj. prof. faculty info. studies, 1989—98, mem. FLIS Grad. Sch. coun., 1991—92; mem. conf. adv. bds. Internat. World Can., Online, & Computers in Librs. Confs., Internet Libr., ASIS, Internet Libr. Internat., 1990—2000. Writer (columns and articles) Information Outlook, Feliciter, Access, Multimedia & Internet@ Schools and Library Journal; contbr. SirsiDynix Corp OneSource e-letter. Named Canadian Spl. Librarian of Yr., 1998; named one of the first Movers and Shakers, Libr. Jour., the Key People Who Are Influencing The Future of Libraries and Librarianship, 2002; recipient U. Toronto Libr. Sci. Kathleen Reeves award, 1980, Mecklermedia.Internet World Can. Best Bus. Website Info. Industry Assn. (US) New Product Achievement, 1992, Canadian Online Product award, 1997, U. Toronto Faculty of Info. Studies Jubilee award, 2001. Fellow: Spl. Librs. Assn. (bus. & fin. divsn. directory com. 1985, President's internat. inter-assn. task force enhance image info. profl 1988—90, mem. pub. relations, nominations, continuing edn. Toronto chpt. 1988—95, pres.-elect Toronto chpt. 1989—90, mem. bus. & fin. divsn. roundtable 1990, pres. Toronto chpt. 1990—91, past pres. Toronto chpt. 1991—92, chair-elect, chair, past-chair libr. mgmt. divsn. 1991—93, President's visioning com. mem. 1992—94, nominations com. chair libr. mgmt. divsn. 1993—94, pub. relations com. chair 1995—96, bd. dir. 1996—99, strategic planning com. chair 1997—98, pub. relations com. chair Toronto chpt. 1999—2000, libr. mgmt. divsn. bylaws chair 1999—2000, com. on com. mems. 1999—2000, pres.-elect candidate 2006, pres-elect 2007—, John Cotton Dana award 2003, Libr. Mgmt. Divsn. Leadership award 1999, (Toronto Chpt.) Mem. of Yr. 1992); mem.: Can. Assn. Spl. Librs. and Info. Svcs. (program coord. Toronto chpt. 1983—84, pres. Toronto chpt. 1984—86, nat. treas. 1985—88), Info. Tech. Assn. Can., Ont. Libr. Assn. (pres. 2002, mem. internat. bd. dir.), Can. Libr. Assn. (pres., immediate past pres.), Beta Phi Mu (info. industries com. chair 1994—96). Achievements include being the leading international librarian and lighthouse thinker in the North American library community. Office: SirsiDynix Corp 101 Washington St SE Huntsville AL 35801-4827*

ABRAMOWITZ, ELKAN, lawyer; b. NYC, Mar. 10, 1940; S. Harry and Claire L. (Liebreich) A.; m. Susan Isaacs, Dec. 7, 1943; children: Andrew, Elizabeth. AB, Brown U., 1961; LLB, N.Y. U., 1964. Bar: N.Y. 1964. Law clk. U.S. Dist. Ct. (so. dist.) N.Y., 1964-66; asst. U.S. atty. So. Dist. N.Y., 1966-70, chief criminal divsn., 1976-77; pvt. practice NYC, 1970-76, 77-79; with Morvillo Abramowitz Grand Iason, Anello & Bohrer, NYC, 1979—. Mem. ABA, N.Y. State Bar Assn., Assn. Bar City of N.Y., Fed. Bar Coun. Office: 565 5th Ave New York NY 10017 Office Phone: 212-880-9500. Business E-Mail: eabramowitz@magislaw.com.*

ABRAMOWITZ, MORTON I., former ambassador; b. Lakewood, NJ, Jan. 20, 1933; s. Mendel and Dora (Smith) Abramowitz; m. Sheppie Glass, Sept. 13, 1959; children: Michael, Rachel. BA, Stanford U.; MA, Harvard U., 1955; DD (hon.), U. Edinburg, 2004. Joined U.S. Fgn. Service, 1960; 3d sec., vice consul Taipei, Formosa, 1960-62; with Fgn. Area and Lang. Tng. Ctr., Taichung, Taiwan, 1962-63; consul, polit. officer Hong Kong, 1963-66; assigned Bur. Econ. Affairs, 1966-68; Sr. Inter dept. Group, 1968-69; spl. asst. under-sec. state, 1969-71; research assoc. Inst. for Strategic Studies, 1971; asst. to sec. of def., 1972-73; polit. adviser to Comdr.-in-Chief Pacific, 1973-78; also dep. asst. sec. def. for Inter-Am., E. Asia and Pacific, 1974-78; amb. to Thailand, Bangkok, 1978-83; U.S. rep. to Mutual and Balanced Force Reduction Negotiations Vienna, 1983-85; dir., asst. sec. Bur. of Intelligence and Rsch., 1985-89; amb. to Turkey, 1989-91. Author (with Richard Moorsteen): Remaking China Policy, 1972; author: Moving the Glacier, the Two Koreas and the Powers, 1972, East Asian Actors and Issues, China, Can We Have a Policy, 1997, Turkey's Transformation and American Policy, 2000, Turkey and the United States - Allies in Need, 2003; contbr. articles to jours. and newspapers; author (with Stephen Bosworth): Chasing the Sun--Rethinking East Asian Policy. Pres. Carnegie Endowment for Internat. Peace, Washington, 1991—97; bd. dirs. Internat. Crisis Group, 1995—, Internat. Rescue Com., Nat. Endowment for Democracy. With AUS, 1957. Recipient Disting. Pub. Svc. award, Dept. Def., 1976, Sec. Def. Disting. Svc. award, 1978, Joseph C. Wilson award, 1980, Pres.'s award for Disting. Fed. Svc., 1981, 1985, 1988, Nat. Intelligence Disting. medal, 1989, Lifetime Contbn. award Am. Diplomacy, Am. Fgn. Svc. Assn., 2006. Mem.: Am. Acad. Arts and Scis., Phi Beta Kappa. Home Phone: 202-338-9167; Office Phone: 202-745-5468.

ABRAMOWITZ, ROBERT LESLIE, lawyer; b. Phila., May 1, 1950; s. Nathan P. and Lucille H. (Rader) A.; m. Susan Margaret Stewart, Dec. 1, 1974; children: David, Catherine. BA, Yale U., 1971; JD, Harvard U., 1974. Bar: Pa. 1974, N.J. 1975. Assoc. Ballard, Spahr, Andrews & Ingersoll, Phila., 1974-81, ptnr., 1981-90; ptnr. Morgan Lewis & Bockius, LLP, Phila., 1990—. Adj. prof. law Villanova U., 1986—2001. Trustee Moorestown (N.J.) Friends Sch., 1981-90, Rock Sch. of Pa. Ballet, 1990—; pres. Harvard Law Sch. Assn. Greater Phila., 1999-2001. Mem. ABA, Am. Coll. Employee Benefits Counsel, Phila. Bar Assn. (exec. com. probate sect. 1982-85, pension com. 1985-94, chair 1987-89), Am. Coll. Tax Counsel, Athenaeum Phila., Yale Club, Merion Cricket Club. Home: 623 Pembroke Rd Bryn Mawr PA 19010-3613 Office: Morgan Lewis & Bockius LLP 1701 Market St Philadelphia PA 19103-2903

ABRAMS, ARTHUR JAY, retired physician; b. Camden, NJ, Apr. 9, 1938; s. Morris and Sophia Sarah (Kates) A.; m. Marianne Ritto Abrams, June 8, 1963; children: Suzanne Beth, Cheryl Lyn, Robert Dwight. BA, Rutgers U., Camden, NJ, 1959; MD, Hahnemann U., 1963. Diplomate Am. Bd. Dermatology. Intern Madigan Army Med. Ctr., Tacoma, 1963-64; resident, chief resident Letterman Army Med. Ctr., San Francisco, 1964-67; dermatologist, Far East cons. 249th Gen. Hosp. U.S. Army, Tokyo, 1967-69; asst. chief dermatologist Tripler Army Med. Ctr., Honolulu, 1969-70; staff dermatologist El Camino Hosp., Mountain View, Calif., 1970—2005; clin. assoc. prof. dermatology emeritus Stanford U. Med. Ctr., 1979—; dermatology cons. San Jose State U., Calif., 1994—; maj. U.S. Army, 1963-70. Mem. AMA, Calif. Med. Assn., Pacific Dermatol. Assn., San Francisco Dermatol. Soc. Avocations: volleyball, walking.

ABRAMS, DAN, broadcast executive, news correspondent; b. NYC, May 20, 1966; s. Floyd and Efrat Abrams. BA in Polit. Sci., Duke U., 1988; JD, Columbia U., 1992; LLM (hon.), Stetson U. Anchor, reporter Court TV, New York, NY, 1992—97, Teen Court TV; news cons. NBC News, 1995—97, gen. assignment corr., 1997—2006, chief legal corr.; host, The Abrams Report MSNBC, 2002—07, gen. mgr., 2006—. Contbr. Jewish World Review, host The Abrams Report, MSNBC, 2001—06. Jewish. Office: MSNBC 1 MSNBC Plz Secaucus NJ 07094 E-mail: abramsreport@msnbc.com.*

ABRAMS, DAVID B., federal agency administrator; BSc in computer sci. and psychology, U. Witwatersrand, Johannesburg, South Africa; MS in clin. psychology, Rutgers U., PhD. Prof. psychiatry and human behavior Brown U. Med. Sch., Providence, prof. cmty. health, founding dir. Centers for Behavioral and Preventive Medicine; co-dir. Transdisciplinary Rsch. Butler Hosp., Providence; dir. Office of Behavioral and Social Sciences Rsch., NIH, Bethesda, Md., 2005—. Fellow: Am. Psychol. Assn., Soc. Behavioral Medicine (Disting. Scientist Award). Office: OBSSR 31 Cente Dr Rm B2B37 Bldg 31 Bethesda MD 20892-2027 Office Phone: 301-402-1146. Office Fax: 301-402-1150. E-mail: AbramsD@od.nih.gov.

ABRAMS, ELLIOTT, federal official; b. NYC, Jan. 24, 1948; s. Joseph and Mildred (Kauder) Abrams; m. Rachel Decter, Mar. 9, 1980; children: Jacob, Sarah, Joseph BA, Harvard U., 1969, JD, 1973; MS in Internat. Rels., London Sch. Economics, 1970. Atty. Breed, Abbott & Morgan, Boston, 1973—75; asst. counsel US Senate Permanent Subcom. on Investigations, Washington, 1975; spl. counsel Sen. Henry M. Jackson, 1975-76, Sen. Daniel P. Moynihan, 1977-78, chief of staff, 1978-79; atty. Verner, Liipfert, Bernhard & McPherson, Washington, 1979—81; asst. sec. for internat. orgn. affairs US Dept. State, Washington, 1981, asst. sec. for human rights and humanitarian affairs, 1981-85, asst. sec. for Inter-Am. affairs, 1985-89; sr. fellow Hudson Inst., Washington, 1990-96; pres. Ethics and Pub. Policy Ctr., Washington, 1996-2001; spl. asst. to Pres., sr. dir. for democracy, human rights, and internat ops. NSC, Washington, 2001—02, spl. asst. to Pres., sr. dir. for Near East and North African Affairs, 2002—05; dep. asst. to pres. The White House, Washington, 2005—; dep. nat. security advisor for global democracy strategy NSC, Washington, 2005—. Bd. dirs. Inter-Am. Found., 1985—90; commr. US Commn. on Internat. Religious Freedom, 1999—2001, chmn., 2000—01; columnist Beliefnet. Author: Undue Process, 1992, Security and Sacrifice, 1995, Faith or Fear: How Jews Can Survive in a Christian America, 1997. Mem.: Coun. Fgn. Rels. Republican. Office: Nat Security Coun 347 Old Exec Office Bldg Washington DC 20504

ABRAMS, FLOYD, lawyer, educator; b. NYC, July 9, 1936; s. Isidore and Rae (Eberlin) A.; m. Efrat Surasky, Dec. 25, 1963; children: Daniel, Ronnie. BA, Cornell U., 1956; LL.B., Yale U., 1960. Bar: NY 1961. Research asst. dept. politics Princeton U., 1960-61; law clk. to Paul Leahy US Dist. Ct., Wilmington, Del., 1961-63; assoc. firm Cahill Gordon & Reindel, NYC, 1963-70, ptnr., 1970—. Mem. first amendment adv. coun. The Media Inst., 2004-; vis. lectr. Yale U., 1974-80, 86-89, Columbia U., 1981-85; assoc. in journalism Grad. Sch. Journalism, Columbia U., 1980, William J. Brennan Jr. vis. prof., 1993—. Author: Speaking Freely: Trials of the First Amendment, 2005; Mem. bd editors: N.Y. Law Jour., 1983—, Legal Times, 1989—. Bd. dirs. Mexican Am. Legal Def. and Edn. Fund, Dalton Sch., 1978-81; bd. dirs. Dalton Sch., 1978-84, v.p., 1982-83; bd. dirs. media and soc. seminars, 1980-90, vice chmn., 1983-90. Named one of 100 Most Influential Lawyers, Nat. Law Jour., 2006; recipient Anvil of Freedom award, Estlow Internat. Ctr. Journalism and New Media, 2003—04, Hubert H. Humphrey First Amendment Freedoms Prize, Anti-Defamation League, 2003. Mem. ABA (chmn. rights of expression com. individual rights sect. 1976-79, Ross essay prize, chmn. freedom of speech and press com. litigation sect. 1977-79, mem. forum com. 1979-80, amicus curiae com. 1980-82), Assn. Bar City NY (state legis. com. 1965-67, chmn. comm. com. 1992-94), US Dept Defense Tech. & Privacy Adv. Com., 2002-03, NY State Commn. on Pub. Access to Ct. Records (chmn. 2002-04); Fellow, Am. Coll. Trial Lawyers.; fellow Am. Acad. Arts and Sciences Office: Cahill Gordon & Reindel LLP 80 Pine St Fl 17 New York NY 10005-1790 Office Phone: 212-701-3621. Office Fax: 212-269-5420.

ABRAMS, FREDRICK RALPH, physician, clinical ethicist; b. NYC, June 18, 1928; s. David and Jane R. (Rein) A.; m. Alice Marilyn Engelhard, Nov. 25, 1949; children: Reid, Glenn, Hal. BA, Cornell U., 1950, MD, 1954. Diplomate Am. Bd. Ob-Gyn. Intern Letterman Army Hosp., San Francisco, 1954-55; pvt. practice gynecology Denver, 1962-96; ret.; resident Fitzsimons Army Hosp., Denver, 1956-59; prof. U. Colo. Grad. Sch. Pub. Affairs, Denver, 1987—; dir. biomed. ethics Ctr. for Health Ethics and Policy, U. Colo., 1987-92; commr. Govs. Commn. on Life and the Law, State of Colo., 1991—. Vis. prof. Iliff Sch. Theology; founder Ctr. for Applied Biomed. Ethics Rose Med. Ctr., Denver, 1982-87; assoc. med. dir. Colo. Found. for Med. Care, 1992—; Lectr. for pub. edn. in med. ethics; mem. Nat. Adv. Bd. on Ethics in Reproduction, 1995—; sr. rsch. assoc. Denver U. Ctr. Health Policy and Contemporary Affairs. Contbr. chpts. to book and articles to profl. jours. Maj. U.S. Army, 1955-62. Grantee Robert Wood Johnson, 1988-89, Colo. Trust, 1987-90, Rose Found., 1982-87, Issac Hays, MD and John Bell, MD award for Leadership in Med. Ethics and Professionalism, AMA, 2006. Mem. Internat. Soc. for Advancement of Humanistic Studies in Gynecology (past pres.), Denver Med. Soc. (past v.p.), Colo. Med. Soc., Am. Coll. Ob-Gyn. (past chmn. ethics com.). Avocations: sculpture, jewelry, fly fishing, poetry, gardening.*

ABRAMS, GERALD DAVID, pathologist, educator; b. Detroit, Apr. 27, 1932; s. Arthur and Esther (Kushner) A.; m. Gloria Sandra Turner, June 6, 1954; children— Kathryn, Nancy AB, Wayne U., 1951; MD, U. Mich., 1955. Diplomate Am. Bd. Pathology. House officer pathology U. Mich., Ann Arbor, 1955-59, instr. pathology, 1959-60, asst. prof. pathology, 1963-66, assoc. prof. Ann Arbor, Mich., 1966-69, prof., 1969—2002, prof. emeritus, 2002—, dir. anatomic pathology, 1985-89; asst. chief dept. exptl. pathology Walter Reed Army Inst. Rsch., 1961-62. Dep. med. examiner Washtenaw County, Mich., 1963—; cons. physician Ann Arbor VA Hosp., 1970—2002. Served to capt. M.C., US Army, 1961-62 Markle scholar John and Mary Markle Found., 1963-68; recipient Elizabeth Crosby Teaching award U. Mich., 1969, 87, 96, Kaiser-Permanente Teaching award U. Mich., 1978, Lifetime Achievement award in Med. Edn., 2002, Disting. Svc. award U. Mich. Med. Ctr. Alumni Soc., 2005. Mem. AAAS, US-Can. Acad. Pathology, Mich. Soc. Pathologists Office: U Mich Dept Pathology Ann Arbor MI 48109 Home Phone: 734-663-5433; Office Phone: 734-936-6770. Business E-Mail: gabrams@umich.edu.

ABRAMS, HAROLD EUGENE, lawyer; b. Pensacola, Fla., Jan. 18, 1933; s. Samuel Ralph and Sadie (Gerhardt) A.; m. Nancy Gray, June 22, 1958; children: Shari Abrams Marx, Eric Gray. BA, U. Mich., 1954; JD, Harvard U., 1957. Bar: Ga. 1958, D.C. 1976, U.S. Supreme Ct. 1970. Law clk. to presiding judge U.S. Ct. Appeals (5th cir.), Atlanta, 1957-58; assoc. Kilpatrick & Cody, Atlanta, 1958-63; ptnr. Kilpatrick Stockton, Atlanta, 1963—. Pres. Atlanta Tax Forum, 1990-91, Atlanta Estate Planning Coun., 1991-92; bd. dirs. Randall Bros., Inc., Atlanta, Selig Enterprises, Inc., Atlanta. Contbr. articles on tax and estate planning to profl. publs. Pres. Buckhead Little League, Atlanta, 1972-73; bd. dir. Atlanta chpt. Am. Jewish Com., 1987-2001, Atlanta Jewish Fedn., 1996-2006; sec. Ronald McDonald's Children's Charities, Atlanta, 1988. With U.S. Army, 1957-58. Fellow Am. Coll. Tax Counsel; mem. State Bar of Ga. (chmn. tax sect. 1964-65), So. Fed. Tax Inst. (trustee 1964-2001, pres. 1970-71, treas. 1986-95), Atlanta Lawyers Club. Avocations: tennis, travel. Office: Kilpatrick Stockton LLP 1100 Peachtree St NE Ste 2800 Atlanta GA 30309-4530 Home Phone: 404-760-0727; Office Phone: 404-815-6600. Business E-Mail: habrams@kilpatrickstockton.com.

ABRAMS, HERBERT LEROY, radiologist, educator; b. NYC, Aug. 16, 1920; s. Morris and Freda (Sugarman) Abrams; m. Marilyn Spitz, Mar. 23, 1943; children: Nancy, John. BA, Cornell U., 1941; MD, Downstate Med. Ctr., NYC, 1946. Diplomate Am. Bd. Radiology. Intern L.I. Coll. Hosp., 1946—47; resident in internal medicine Montefiore Hosp., Bronx, NY, 1947—48; resident in radiology Stanford (Calif.) U. Hosp., 1948—51; practice medicine specializing in radiology Stanford U., Calif., 1951—67, mem. faculty Sch. Medicine, 1951—67, dir. divsn. diagnostic roentgenology Sch. Medicine, 1961—67, prof. radiology Sch. Medicine, 1962—67; Philip H. Cook prof. radiology Harvard U., 1967—85, now prof. emeritus, chmn. dept. radiology, 1967—80; prof. radiology Stanford U. Sch. Medicine, 1985—90, prof. emeritus, 1990—; clin. prof. U. Calif. Sch. Medicine, San Francisco, 1986—. Radiologist-in-chief Peter Bent Brigham Hosp., Boston, 1967—80; chmn. dept. radiology Brigham and Women's Hosp., Boston, 1981—85; radiologist-in-chief Sidney Farber Cancer Inst., Boston, 1974—85; R.H. Nimmo vis. prof. U. Adelaide, Australia; mem.-in-residence Ctr. for Internat. Security and Cooperation, Stanford U., 1985—; mem. radiation study sect. NIH, 1962—66; cons. to hosps., profl. socs. Author (with others): Angiocardiography in Congenital Heart Disease, 1956, Congenital Heart Disease, 1965, Coronary Arteriography: A Practical Approach, 1983, Brigham Guide to Diagnostic Imaging, 1986, Assessment of Diagnostic Technology in Health Care; editor: Abrams' Angiography, 3d edit., 1983; author: The President Has Been Shot: Confusion, Disability and the 25th Amendment, 1992, 1994, The History of Cardiac Radiology, 1996; mem. editl. bd.: Investigative Radiology, editor-in-chief, founder: Cardiovasc. and Interventional Radiology, 1978—88, Postgrad. Radiology, 1983—99. Named David M. Gould Meml. lectr., Johns Hopkins, 1964, William R. Whitman Meml. lectr., 1968, Leo G. Rigler lectr., Tel Aviv U., 1969, Holmes lectr., New Eng. Roentgen Ray Soc., Boston, 1970, Ross Golden lectr., N.Y. Roentgen Ray Soc., N.Y.C., 1971, Stauffer Meml. lectr., Phila. Roentgen Ray Soc., 1971, J.M.T. Finney Fund lectr., Md. Radiol. Soc., Ocean City, 1972, Aubrey Hampton lectr., Mass. Gen. Hosp., Boston, 1974, Kirklin-Weber lectr., Mayo Clinic, 1974, Crookshank lectr., Royal Coll. Radiology, 1980, Alpha Omega Alpha lectr., vis. prof., U. Calif. Med. Sch., San Francisco, 1961—65, W.H. Herbert lectr., U. Calif., Caldwell lectr., Am. Roentgen Ray Soc., 1982, Percy lectr., McMaster Med. Sch., 1983, Charles Dotter lectr., Soc. Cardiovasc. and Interventional Radiology, 1988, Philip Hodes lectr., Jefferson Med. Coll., 1988, David Gould Meml. lectr., Johns Hopkins U., 1991, Hymer Friedell lectr., Western Res. Sch. Medicine, 1993, Felix Fheischner Meml. lectr., Harvard Med. Sch., 1997, Charles Dotter Meml. lectr., Am. Heart Assn., 1998; fellow, Nat. Cancer Inst., 1950, Spl. Rsch. fellow, Nat. Heart Inst., 1960, 1973—74, Henry J. Kaiser sr. fellow, Ctr. for Advanced Study in Behavioral Sci., 1980—81. Fellow: Am. Coll. Cardiology, Am. Coll. Radiology, Royal Coll. Radiology (Gt. Britain) (hon.), Royal Coll. Surgery (Ireland) (hon.); mem.: NIH (working group on disability of U.S. pres. 1995—98, internat. blue ribbon panel radiation effects rsch. found. Hiroshima 1996, chmn. consensus panel on MRI), NAS (com. biol. effects of low-level ionizing radiation BEIR VII 1999—2005), Nat. Coun. Health Tech. Assessment, Soc. Chmn. Acad. Radiology Depts. (pres. 1970—71), Soc. Cardiovasc. Radiology (Gold medal 2000), Internat. Physicians for Prevention of Nuc. War (founding v.p., participant Nobel Peace prize 1985), N.Am. Soc. Cardiac Radiology (pres. 1979—80), Radiol. Soc. N.Am. (Gold medal 1995), Am. Soc. Nephrology, Am. Heart Assn., Inst. Medicine, Assn. Univ. Radiologists (Gold medal 1984), Alpha Omega Alpha, Phi Beta Kappa. Achievements include Naming of Abrams Conf. Rm. in radiology and Women's Hosp., 1984; establishment of Herbert L. Abrams ann. lectures of Harvard Med. Sch., 1985; dedication of endowed Herbert L. Abrams Directorship of Vascular and Interventional Radiology at Brigham and Women's, 2002. Office: Stanford U Sch Medicine 300 Pasteur Dr Stanford CA 94305-5105 Home: 620 Sand Hill Rd Apt 109G Palo Alto CA 94304 Business E-Mail: hlabrams@stanford.edu.

ABRAMS, JACKIE, artist, educator; b. NYC, Jan. 19, 1949; d. Moe Werner and Eleanor Borhak; children: Dani Mariasha, Rina Rose Tobias. BS in Child Devel., U. Mass., Amherst, 1970, MEd in Humanistic Edn., 1973; studied ash basketry with Ben Higgins, Chesterfield, Mass., 1975. Staff Internat. Fiber Forum, Geelong, Australia, 2004. Chairperson North Country Basketmakers Guild, 1985—86, newsletter editor, 1986—88; founder, planning com. North Country Studio Workshops, Hanover, NH, 1990—2003, pres., 2001—03; juror Am. Craft Coun., 2001; curator Brookfield Craft Ctr., Conn., 2002; bd. trustees Am. Craft Coun., 2002—05; scribe Handweavers Guild Am., 2002; co-curator hanging com. Windham Art Gallery, Brattleboro, 2003—05; adv. coun. mem. Arrowmont Sch. Arts and Crafts, Gatlinburg, Tenn., 2004—; assoc. dir. Cross Cultural Collaborative, Ghana, 2006—. Represented in permanent collections League NH Craftsmen, Concord, Mich. State U. Mus., Lansing, Wustum Mus. Fine Arts, Racine, Wis., selected exhbn., The Works Gallery, Phila., 1998, 2001, Brookfield Craft Ctr., Conn., 1998, 2002, 2004, Gallery at Phil. Mus. Art, 1998, Am. Craft Enterprises, Balt., 1998, 1999, 2001, Am. Craft Expn., Evanston, Ill., 1998, 2000, 2001, Northeast Basketmakers Guild, Lexington, Mass., 1998, Creative Arts Workshop, New Haven, Conn., 1998, Washington Craft Show, DC, 1998, 1999, 2004, Arrowmont Sch. Arts and Crafts, 1999, 2001, 2003, 2005, Westchester Craft Show, NY, 1999, SOFA, Mobilia Gallery, Chgo., 1999, 2000, Crafts at the Castle, Boston, 1999, 2003, John Michael Kohler Arts Ctr., Treasures, Wis., 1999, 2000, 2001, New Eng. Artists' Trust Congress Juried Show, New Haven, Conn., 1999, Guild.com, 1999—, Fountainhead Gallery, Seattle, 2000, Rutledge Gallery, Dayton, Ohio, 2000, Wustum Mus. Fine Arts, Racine, Wis., 2000, 2003, 2005, Am. Craft Coun., Balt., 2000, 2001, 2002, 2004, 2005, Phila. Mus. Art Craft Show, 2000, 2002, 2003, 2006, Smithsonian Craft Show, Washington, DC, 1997, 2000, 2002, delMano Gallery, LA, 2001, SOFA, Katie Gingrass Gallery, Chgo., 2001, 2002, 2003, 2004, NYC, 2005, 2006, Dane Gallery, Nantucket, Mass., 2001, Nat. Basketry Orgn., Abiquiu, N.Mex, 2002, 2005, Fiber Art Ctr., Amherst, 2002, NH Inst. Art, 2002, 2004, Handweavers Guild Am., Vancouver, Can., 2002, Boulder, Colo., 2004, Am. Art Co., Tacoma, Wash., 2002, 2003, 2005, Soc. Arts and Crafts, Boston, 2002, Ark. Art Ctr., 2002, U. Conn., Storrs, 2003, Windham Art Gallery, Brattleboro, 2003, 2005, 2004, The Carnegie, Cin., 2003, Craft Alliance, St. Louis, 2003, Yeiser Art Ctr., Paducah, Ky., 2003, Penland Gallery, NC, 2003, Allied Arts Assn. Gallery, Richland, Wash., 2004, Dairy Ctr. Arts, Boulder, 2004, Brookfield Craft Ctr., Conn., 2004, Gallery 205, Concord, 2004, Convergence, HGA, Boulder, 2004, Dairy Barn Arts Ctr., Athens, Ohio, 2004, Goldstein Mus. Design, Mpls., 2004, Grubbs Gallery, Easthampton, Mass., 2004, U. So. Maine, Gorham, 2005. Sunapee Fair com. League NH Craftsmen, Concord, 1983—85, trustee, 1987—90; charter bd. mem. Vt. Crafts Coun., Montpelier, 1990—93; edn. com. Brattleboro Mus. Art, Vt., 2001—; assoc. dir. Cross Cultural Collaborative, Ghana, 2006—; bd. dirs. Women's Crisis Ctr., Brattlebror, Vt., 2006—. Finalist Niche award, 2001; recipient Edith Grodin award,

Annual Juried Exhibit, League NH Craftsmen, 1988, Janeway Fellowship award, Stratton Arts Festival, Vt., 1990, Juror's award of Distinction, 1995, Merit award for Outstanding Work of Art, Paper/Fiber XVII, Iowa City, 1994, Honorable Mention award, Am. Craft Enterprises, Balt., 2000, Craft Emergency Relief Fund Artist, CERF Life Boats, 2002, Third Place award, Small Expressions, Handweavers Guild Am., 2004; grantee, League NH Craftsmen, 1984, 1987; scholar, 1992, 1997; Study Grant, Vermont Arts Coun., 1995, Artist Devel. Grant, 1996, Opportunity Grant, 1999, 2003, 2005, Creation Grant, Vt. Arts Coun., 2001, Vt. Cmty. Found., 2002, Residency Grant, Cross Cultural Collaboratives, Ghana, West Africa, 2005. Avocations: gardening, walking, yoga, knitting, travel. Home: 21 Howard St Brattleboro VT 05301 Office Phone: 802-257-2688. Personal E-mail: jackiabrams@verizon.net. E-mail: jackie@jackieabrams.com.

ABRAMS, J.J. (JEFFREY JACOB ABRAMS), television producer, scriptwriter; b. NYC, June 27, 1966; s. Gerald W. Abrams; m. Katie McGrath; children: Henry, Gracie, August. Attended, Sarah Lawrence Coll. Actor: (films) Six Degrees of Separation, 1993, Diabolique, 1996; prodr., writer, actor: Regarding Henry, 1991; exec. prodr., dir., writer: (TV series) Felicity, 1998—2002; Alias, 2001—06; Lost, 2004— (Emmy award for outstanding directing for a drama series, 2005, best TV series, drama, Producers Guild Am., 2006); exec. prodr.: What About Brian, 2006, Six Degrees, 2006; exec. prodr., writer: (films) Forever Young, 1992; prodr.: The Pallbearer, 1996; actor, prodr.: (films) The Suburbans, 1999; writer, prodr.: Joy Ride, 2001; writer, dir. Mission: Impossible III, 2006; writer Gone Fishin', 1997; (screenplay) Armageddon, 1998. Named one of 100 People in Hollywood You Need to Know, Fade In mag., 2005, 100 Most Influential People, Time Mag., 2006, 100 Most Powerful Celebrities, Forbes.com, 2007. Office: William Morris Agency 1 William Morris Place Beverly Hills CA 90212*

ABRAMS, LEE NORMAN, lawyer; b. Chgo., Feb. 28, 1935; s. Saul E. and Evelyn (Cohen) A.; m. Myrna Parker, Dec. 26, 1965; 1 dau., Elana Shira. AB, U. Mich., 1955, JD, 1957. Bar: Ill. 1957, U.S. Supreme Ct. 1961, U.S. Tax Ct. 1972. Assoc. firm Mayer, Brown, Rowe & Maw and predecessors, Chgo., 1957-66, ptnr., 1966—. Mem. visitors com. U. Mich. Law Sch., 1970—; bd. assocs. Nat. Coll. Edn., Chgo., 1973-80. Recipient Gold medal AICPA, 1958. Mem. ABA (coun. antitrust sect. 1975-77, fin. officer 1977-81, program chair antitrust sect. 1988-91, vice chair antitrust sect. 1991-92, chmn. forum on franchising 1982-85, chmn. antitrust com. sect. bus. law 1995-99), Chgo. Bar Assn. (antitrust law com. 1970-85), Ill. State Bar Assn. (antitrust section coun. 1994-2001), U.S. C. of C. (antitrust and trade regulation com. 1974-80), Briarwood Country Club, Royal and Ancient Golf Club of St. Andrews (Scotland). Office: Mayer Brown Rowe & Maw & predecessors 71 S Wacker Dr Chicago IL 60606 Home Phone: 847-256-6262; Office Phone: 312-701-7083. Business E-Mail: labrams@mayerbrownrowe.com.

ABRAMS, LEIGH JEFFREY, manufacturing executive; b. NYC, July 28, 1942; BBA, Baruch Coll., 1964. CPA, N.Y. Sr. auditor Ernest & Whinney, NYC, 1964—68; exec. v.p. Drew Industries Inc., White Plains, NY, 1969—78, pres., CEO, dir., 1989—, LBP, Inc., 1994—2002. Bd. dirs. Impac Mortgage Holdings, Inc. Past chmn. bd. dirs. YMCA; past chmn. Jr. Achievement of the Hudson Valley, Inc., bd. dirs. Mem. AICPA, NY Soc. CPAs. Office: Drew Industries Inc 200 Mamaroneck Ave White Plains NY 10601 Home: 631 Long Ridge Rd Unit 47 Stamford CT 69021-1263 Office Phone: 914-428-9098. Business E-Mail: leigh@drewindustries.com.

ABRAMS, MARC, lawyer, political organization worker; b. NYC, Mar. 23, 1957; s. Stephen Robert and Virginia Ornstein Abrams; 1 child, Lawrence Christopher. BA magna cum laude, Wesleyan U., Middletown, Conn., 1978; MA, JD, U. Mich., 1981. Bar: Conn. 1982, N.Y. 1986, D.C. 1987, Pa. 1987, Oreg. 1989, U.S. Dist Ct. (so. dist.) N.Y. 1986, U.S. Dist. Co. (ea. dist.) Pa. 1988, U.S. Dist. Ct. Mont. 1989, U.S. Cir. Ct. (3d, 4th and 9th cirs.), U.S. Dist. Ct. Oreg. 1989, U.S. Supreme Ct. Asst. prof. U. Oreg., 1981-83; exec. dir. Student Press Law Ctr., 1983-85; pvt. practice, 1985—2002; sr. asst. atty. gen. State of Oreg., 2002—. Talk show host KXL-AM, 2002—; commentator KATU-TV, 2005—. Co-author: Law of the Student Press, 1983, Confronting Wrongful Discharge Under Oregon and Washington Law, 1989. Vice chair Lane County (Oreg.) Dem. Ctrl. Com., 1981-82, Multnomah County (Oreg.) Dem. Ctrl. Com., 1991-92; mem. Oreg. Dem. State Ctrl. Com., 1981-82, 91—, Multnomah Edn. Svc. Dist. Bd., 1993-97, chmn., 1996-97; fin. chair Oreg. State Dem. Party, 1993-95, vice chair, 1994-97, chmn., 1997-99; mem. Portland Sch. Bd., 1995-2003, vice chair, 1998-2002; treas. Assn. State Dem. Chairs, 1998-99. Recipient Johnnie Phelps medal Vets. for Human Rights, 1995. Jewish. Office: 1162 Court St NE Salem OR 97301 Business E-Mail: marc.abrams@state.or.us.

ABRAMS, MEYER HOWARD, language educator; b. Long Branch, NJ, July 23, 1912; s. Joseph and Sarah (Shanes) A.; m. Ruth Gaynes, Sept. 1, 1937; children: Jane, Judith. AB, Harvard U., 1934, MA, 1937, PhD, 1940; postgrad. (Henry fellow), Cambridge U., Eng., 1934-35; DHL (hon.), U. Rochester, 1978, Northwestern U., 1981, U. Chgo., 1982, Western Md. Coll., 1985, Le Moyne Coll., 1993, Carleton Coll., 2003, Yale U., 2007. Instr. Harvard, 1938-42; research asso. psycho-acoustic lab. Harvard U., 1942-45; asst. prof. English, Cornell U., Ithaca, NY, 1945-47, asso. prof., 1947-53, prof., 1953-60, Frederic J. Whiton prof. English, 1960-73, Class of 1916 prof. English, 1973-83, prof. emeritus, 1983—. Adv. editor W.W. Norton & Co., Inc., 1961—; bd. editors various Cornell publs. Hon. sr. fellow Sch. Criticism and Theory, Cornell U., Fulbright lectr. Royal U. Malta, Cambridge U., 1953; Roache lectr. U. Ind., 1963; Alexander lectr. U. Toronto, 1964; Ewing lectures UCLA, 1975; Cecil Green lectr. U B.C., 1980; Lamont lectures Union Coll., 1995; Mem. founders group Nat. Humanities Ctr.; mem. coun. of scholars Libr. of Congress, 1980-94, chmn. coun. of scholars, 1984-94. Author: The Milk of Paradise, 1934, 2d edit., 1970, The Mirror and the Lamp: Romantic Theory and the Critical Tradition, 1953, A Glossary of Literary Terms, 1957, 8th edit., 2005, Natural Supernaturalism: Tradition and Revolution in Romantic Literature, 1971, The Correspondent Breeze: Essays on English Romanticism, 1984, Doing Things with Texts: Essays in Criticism and Critical Theory, 1989, also publs. on mil. communications; editor: The Poetry of Pope, 1954; Editor: Literature and Belief, 1958, The Romantic Poets: Modern Essays in Criticism, 1960, rev. edit., 1975, The Norton Anthology of English Literature, 1962, 7th edit., 1999, Wordsworth: A Collection of Critical Essays, 1972, (with others) Wordsworth's Prelude: Norton Critical Edition, 1979. Recipient Christian Gauss prize Phi Beta Kappa, 1954, James Russell Lowell prize, 1971, Am. Acad. award humanistic studies, 1984, Disting. Scholar award Keats-Shelley Assn., 1987, Am. Acad. and Inst. Arts and Letters award for lit., 1990; Rockefeller fellow, 1946; Ford fellow, 1952; Guggenheim fellow, 1958, 60-61; fellow Center for Advanced Study in the Behavioral Scis., Palo Alto, Calif., 1967-68; vis. fellow All Soul's Coll., Oxford, 1977. Mem. AAUP, MLA (exec. council 1961-64), Am. Acad. Arts and Scis., Am. Acad. Arts and Letters, Am. Philos. Soc., Brit. Acad. (corr. fellow), Phi Beta Kappa, Sigma Xi. Home: 378 Savage Farm Dr Ithaca NY 14850-6505 Office Phone: 607-255-3428. Business E-Mail: mha5@cornell.edu.

ABRAMS, NORMAN, retired law educator, former academic administrator; b. Chgo., July 7, 1933; s. Harry A. and Gertrude (Dick) A.; m. Toshka Alster, 1977; children: Marshall David, Julie, Hanna, Naomi. AB, U. Chgo., 1952, JD, 1955. Bar: Ill. 1956, US Supreme Ct. 1967. Assoc. in law Columbia U., 1955-57; rsch. assoc. Harvard U., 1957-59; sec. Harvard-Brandeis Coop. Rsch. for Israel's Legal Devel., 1957-58, dir., 1959; mem. faculty law sch. UCLA, 1959—, prof. law, 1964—2005, prof. law emeritus, 2005—06, 2007—, co-dir. Ctr. for internat. and strategic studies, 1982-83, chmn. steering com., 1985-87, 88-89, assoc. dean law, 1989-91, vice chancellor acad. pers., 1991-2001, interim exec. vice chancellor, 1998, interim dean law, 2003—04, acting chancellor, 2006—07, prof. law emeritus, 2007—. Reporter for So. Calif. indigent accused persons study Am. Bar Found., 1963; cons. Gov. Calif. Commn. LA Riots, 1965, Pres.'s Commn. Law Enforcement and Adminstrn. Justice, 1966-67, Nat. Commn. on Reform of Fed. Criminal Laws, 1967-69, Rand Corp., 1968-74, Ctr. for Adminstrv. Justice, ABA, 1973-77, Nat. Adv. Commn. on Criminal Justice Stds., Organized Crime Task Force, 1976; spl. hearing officer conscientious objector cases Dept. Justice, 1967-68; vis. scholar Inst. for Advanced Studies, Hebrew U., summer, 1994; vis. prof. Hebrew U., 1969-70, 86, Bar Ilan U., 1970-71, 78, U. So. Calif., 1972, Stanford U., 1977, U. Calif., Berkeley, Calif., 1977; spl. asst. to U.S. atty. gen. Dept. Justice, 1966-67, prof.-in-residence Criminal Divsn., 1966-67. Author: (with others) Evidence, Cases and Materials, 7th edit., 1983, 8th edit., 1988, 9th edit., 1997, Federal Criminal Law and Its Enforcement, 1986, (with S. Beale), 2d edit., 1993, 3d edit, 2000, 4th edit., 2006, Anti-terrorism and Criminal Enforcement, 2003, 2d edit., 2005; mem. editl. bd. Criminal Law Forum, 1990—, Jour. Nat. Security Law and Policy, 2004—. Chmn. Jewish Conciliation Bd., LA, 1975-81; bd. dir. Bet Tzedek, 1975-85, LA Hillel Coun., 1979-82, Shalhevet HS, 1998—; chmn. So. Calif. region Am. Prof. for Peace in Middle East, 1981-83; bd. dir. met. region Jewish Fedn., 1982-88, v.p. 1982-83; pres. Westwood Kehillah Congregation, 1985. Mem. Internat. Soc. for Reform of Criminal Law (mem. exec. com. 1994—), Phi Beta Kappa. Office: UCLA Law School 405 Hilgard Ave Los Angeles CA 90095-9000 Office Phone: 310-794-4056. Business E-Mail: abrams@law.ucla.edu.

ABRAMS, ROBERT, lawyer, state attorney general; b. Bronx, NY, July 4, 1938; BA, Columbia U., 1960; JD, NYU, 1963; LLD (hon.), Hofstra U., 1979, Yeshiva U., 1984, L.I. U., 1989, Pace U., 1991. Mem. N.Y. State Assembly, 1965-69; pres. Borough of Bronx, 1970-78; atty. gen. State of N.Y., 1979-93; ptnr. Stroock & Stroock & Lavan, NYC, 1994—. Panel mem. of disting. neutrals CPR Inst.; dir. Sterling Nat. Bank, Sterling Bancorp.; commr. NYC Charter Revision Commn.; chmn. Atty. Gen. Cuomo's transition com.; co-chair Gov. Spitzer's policy adv. com. on govtl. reform; lectr. NYU Sch. Law. Contbr. articles to profl. publs.; writer column Nat. Law Jour., NY Law Jour., NY Times, NY Newsday, NY Post, NY Daily News, Buffalo News, Albany Times Union, Ganette Suburban Newspapers, The Harvard Environ. Law Rev., NYU Law Rev., Columbia Jour. Environ. Law, Pace Environ. Law Rev., Washburn Law Rev., Albany Law Rev., Pace Law Rev., The Jour. of State Gov. Pres. Citizens Union Found., Help Am. Vote Act - Impact and Potential for NY, Century Found.; del. Dem. Nat. Conv., 1972, 76, 80, 84, mem. platform com., 1988; elector Electoral Coll., 1988; co-chair Nat. Jewish Dem. Coun., N.Y. State; apptd. mem. Charter Revision Commn., 2004. Recipient Adam Clayton Powell Pub. Svc. award, Interfaith award Coun. Chs., NYC, Bronx CC Svc. medallion, Scroll of Honor plaque United Jewish Appeal, Benjamin Cardozo award for legal excellence Jewish Lawyers Guild, Brotherhood award B'nai B'rith, Man of Yr. award NAACP, Alumni Achievement award NYU Sch. Law, Environmentalist of Yr. award Environ. Planning Lobby NY, Disting. Pub. Svc. Citation Bus. Coun. NY State, NY State Sheriff's Assn. award, Nat. Crime Victims award, Torch of Liberty award Anti-Defamation League, Anatoly Scharansky Freedom award NY Conf. Soviet Jewry, Environmentalist of Yr. award LI Pine Barrens Soc., Il Leone de San Marco Hon. Italian Am. award, Cavaliere medal Pres. Italy, Pres. award Marist Coll., Hubert Humphrey Humanitarian award United Fedn. Tchrs., Law Day award NY State Trial Lawyers Assn., Contbns. to Urban Law award Fordham Law Jour., Deans medal Law Sch. NYU, Margaret Sanger award NY State Family Planning Advocates, Lehman/LaGuardia Civic Achievement award Anti-Defamation League B'nai B'rith and Commn. on Social Justice of Order of Sons of Italy, Father of Yr. award Nat. Father's Day Com., B'nai Zion Bill of Rights award, Avodah award Jewish Tchr's. Assn., Man of Yr. award NY State Consumer Assembly, Rodef Tzedek Pursuer of Justice award Restructionist Rabbinical Coll., Humanitarian award Rochester Labor and Religious Coalition, Special Recognition award Profl. Women in Construction and Allied Industries, Humanitarian award LI Assn. Children with Learning Disabilities, Man of Yr. award Mental Illness Found., NY State Ct's. Man of Yr. award Shamrai Tzedek Soc., Grand Marshall award Schenectady Labor Coun. Labor Day Parade, Louis Brandeis award Zionist Orgn. Am., Lubavich Tzivos Hashem award, Chassidius in Am. Exemplary Leadership award Bostoner Chassidum, Recognition for Pub. Svc. award Greater Buffalo AFL-CIO Coun., Effort on Behalf of Elderly award Workmen's Circle Home & Infirmary For the Aged, Dedication Concerning Reproductive Rights award NY Coun. Jewish Women, Citation of Appreciation NY State Assn. of Architects, Pesach-Tikvah Hope Developer award, Pub. Svc. award NY Soc. Clin. Psychologists, Cmty. Achievement award Am. Orthodox Fedn., State Svc. award Nat. Columbus Day Com., Environmentalist of Yr. award Sierra Club, Svc. award NY State Jewish War Veterans, Cadet award NYC Mission Soc., Disting. Achievement award AMIT Women, Man of Yr. award Nassau County Police Res. Assn., Ann. award Lubavitch Youth Orgn., Appreciation award Japanese C. of C. NY, Friend of Cmty. award Empire State Pride Agenda, Roland Smith award Capital Region chpt. NY Civil Liberties Union, Scharansky Freedom award LI Com. on Soviet Jewry, Cert. of Honor award NY League of Histadrut, Scouting For Handicapped Outstanding Svc. award Greater NY Coun. of Boy Scouts Am., Citizen of Yr. award Western NY Labor Coalition, Svc. award Citizen's Coun. for Cmty. of Mentally Retarded, Rockland Hosp. Guild, Man of Yr. award Shield Inst. for Retarded Children, Maccabean Svc. award NY Bd. Rabbis, Thurgood Marshall award Bridge Builders Albany, Pro Choice award Naral NY, Dist. Humanitarian award Insts. Applied Human Dynamics, Life-Long Dedication award Holocaust Meml. Com., Disting. Cmty. Svc. award Am. Friends of Bnei Akiva; named Man of Yr. St. Patrick's Home Aged and Infirm, Man of Yr. State Israel Bonds; named an Outstanding New Yorker NYC Coun. Mem. NY State Bar Assn. (Environ. Acheivement award), Nat. Assn. of Attys. Gen. (pres. 1988-89, chmn. environ. protection com. 1982-85, chmn. antitrust com. 1985-88, chmn. civil rights com. 1990-92, chmn. ea. regional conf. of attys. gen. 1983-84, Wyman award for Outstanding Atty. Gen. in the Nation 1991, Bellotti award, 2005), Assn. Bar City of NY (spl. commn. campaign fin. reform). Democrat. Office: Stroock & Stroock & Lavan 180 Maiden Ln Ste 3989 New York NY 10038-4937 Office Phone: 212-806-5546. Office Fax: 212-806-6006. Business E-Mail: rabrams@stroock.com.

ABRAMS, ROGER IAN, lawyer, educator; b. Newark, July 30, 1945; s. Avel S. and Myrna (Posner) A.; m. Frances Elise Kovitz, June 1, 1969; children: Jason, Seth. BA, Cornell U., 1967; JD, Harvard U., 1970. Bar: Mass. 1970, U.S. Dist. Ct. Mass. 1971, U.S. Ct. Appeals (1st cir.) 1971. Law clk. to Judge Frank M. Coffin U.S. Ct. Appeals (1st cir.), Boston, 1970—71; assoc. Foley, Hoag & Eliot, Boston, 1971—74; prof. law Law. Sch. Case We. Res. U., Cleve., 1974—86; dean Law Ctr. Nova U., Ft. Lauderdale, Fla., 1986—93; dean Law Sch. Rutgers U., Newark, 1993—98; prof. law sch. Rutger U., Newark, 1993—99; Herbert J. Hannuch scholar Rutgers U., Newark, 1998—99; dean Northeastern U., Boston, 1999—2002, Richardson prof. law, 1999—. Labor arbitrator Fed. Mediation Svc., 1975—; vis. prof. law sch. Harvard U., 2006; scholar-in-residence Nat. Baseball Hall of Fame, 2006. Author: Legal Bases: Baseball and the Law, 1998, The Money Pitch: Baseball Free Agency and Salary Arbitration, 2000, The First World Scenes and the Baseball Fanatics of 1903, 2003; contbr. articles to law jours. Recipient Gen. Counsel's Advocacy award NAACP, Boston, 1974; inductee Union N.J. Hall of Fame, 1995. Fellow Mass. Hist. Soc.; mem. Am. Law Inst., Am. Bar Found., Am. Arbitration Assn. (labor arbitrator). Democrat. Jewish. Avocations: swimming, distance walking, reading. Office: Northeastern Univ Sch Law 400 Huntington Ave Boston MA 02115-5005 Office Phone: 617-373-2068. Business E-Mail: r.abrams@neu.edu.

ABRAMS, RONALD LAWRENCE, state legislator; b. Apr. 1952; m. Joanne Abrams; two children. BA summa cum laude, U. Minn., 1974; JD, Harvard U., 1977. Atty. Briggs and Morgan, St. Paul, 1977—80; atty. and area mgr. Grp. W. Cable TV, Mpls., 1980—84; asst. minority leader Minn. Ho. of Reps., 1992-99, state rep. Dist. 45A, 1989—2006; judge Minn. Jud. Ctr., St. Paul, 2006—. Mem. Fin. Instn. & Ins. Com., Gen. Legislation Com., Vet. Affairs & Elections Com., Rules & Legis. Adminstrn. Com., Ways & Means & Taxes Coms.; chair tax com. 1999—; spkr. pro tem Minn. Ho. of Reps., 1999—. Office: Minn Jud Ctr 25 Rev Dr Martin Luther King Jr Blvd Saint Paul MN 55155 Office Phone: 651-297-7650.

ABRAMS, ROSALIE SILBER, retired state agency official; b. Balt., June 2, 1916; d. Isaac and Dora (Rodbell) Silber; 1 child, Elizabeth Joan. RN, Sinai Hosp.; postgrad., Columbia U.; BS, Johns Hopkins U., 1963, MA in Polit. Sci. Pub. health nurse USNR, 1945-46; bus. mgr. Sequoia Med. Group, Calif., 1946-47; asst. bus. mgr. Silber's Bakery, Balt., 1947-53; mem. Md. Ho. of Dels., 1967-70, Md. Senate, 1970-83, majority leader, 1978-82; chmn. Dem. Party of Md., 1978-83, chmn. fin. com., 1982-83; dir. Office on Aging, State of Md., 1983-95, ret., 1995. Chair World War II Meml. Commn., 1996-2000; mem. Balt. City Commn. on Aging, 1997—2000; host Outlook TV show, 1983-90; guest lectr., witness before congl. coms. Platform com. on nat. healthcare Dem. Nat., Com., 1979—; chmn. Md. Humane Practices Commn., 1978-83, mem., 1971-74; mem. New Coalition, 1979-83, State-Fed. Assembly Com. on Human Resources, 1977-83, Md. Comprehensive Health Planning Agy., 1972-75, Md. Commn. on Status of Women, 1968—, Am. Jewish Com. Chair Med. Supplies Com. for Needy and Elderly in Odessa, Ukraine; chair dept. human resources, dept. health and mental hygiene, transp., housing and cmty. devel., econ. and employment devel., Interagy. Com., 1984-95; bd. dirs. Sinai Hosp., Balt., 1973-2000, Balt. Jewish Coun., Cross Country Improvement Assn., 1969—2000, Fifth Dist. Reform Dems., 1967—2000; chmn. legis. com. Balt. Area Coun. on Alcoholism, 1973-75; mem. adv. bd. long term care project U. Md., Balt., 1986; mem. Md. Adv. Com. for Adult and Cmty. Svcs., 1984; mem. nat. adv. bd. Pre-Retirement Edn. Planning, 1986—93; mem. State Adv. Coun. on Nutrition, 1988—; spl. trustee Sheppard-Pratt Hosp., 1992-2000. With Nurse Corps USN, 1944-46. Recipient Louise Waterman Wise Cmty. Svc. award, 1969, award Am. Acad. Comprehensive Health Planning, 1971, Balt. News Am. award, Women of Distinction in Medicine, 1971, traffic safety award, Safety First Club of Md., 1971, an London Scott Meml. award for legis. excellence, Md. chpt. NOW, 1975, Md. Nurses Assn., 1975, svc. award Balt. Area Coun. on Alcoholism, 1975, First Citizens award Md. Senate Pres., 1999, named to Md. Women's Hall of Fame, Md. Commn. for Women and Women Legislators of Md. Gen. Assembly, 1994, numerous others; 1st ann. Rosalie S. Abrams Firsts award awarded by Women Legislators of Md., 2004, Nursing Spectrum award, 2005. Mem. AAUW, AARP, Md. Order Women Legislators (pres. 1973-75), Nat. Conf. State Legislatures (human resources and urban affairs steering com. 1977-83), Nat. Legis. Conf. (human resources task force, intergovtl. rels. com. 1975-83), Md. Gerontol. Assn. (bd. dirs. 1984—), Nat. Fedn. Dem. Women, Am. Jewish Congress, Am. Soc. on Aging, Md. Gerontol. Assn., Sigma Theta Tau Nursing Soc., Balta City Hist. Soc. (trustee 2000—). Home: North Oaks 725 Mt Wilson Ln Apt 729 Baltimore MD 21208

ABRAMS, WILLIAM F., lawyer; b. Indpls., Sept. 21, 1954; AB with honors, Stanford U., 1976; JD, U. Santa Clara, 1979. Bar: Calif. 1979, U.S. Dist. Ct. (all Calif. dist., Md., Del.), U.S. Tax Ct., U.S. Ct. Appeals (8th, 9th cir.), U.S. Supreme Ct. 1983. Past mem. Orrick, Herrington & Sutcliffe, San Francisco; ptnr. Intellectual Property practice, head IP Litigation team Pillsbury Winthrop Shaw Pittman, Palo Alto, Calif.; ptrnr. Bingham McCutcheon LLP, Palo Alto, Calif., 2006—. Instr. Stanford Univ. Mng. editor Santa Clara Law Rev., 1978; contbr. articles to profl. jours.; frequent legal commentator in print & broadcast media. Bd. dir. Youth Law Ctr., San Francisco, Silicon Valley Campaign for Legal Svcs., Hear My Voice, Ann Arbor, Palo Alto Babe Ruth League. Named a No. Calif. Super lawyer, San Francisco Mag., 2004; named one of Silicon Valley's Top 300 Lawyers, San Jose Mag., 2001—04; recipient Human Biology Excellence in Advising award, 2004. Mem. ABA, Am. Intellectual Property Law Assn., State Bar Calif., Santa Clara County Bar Assn. (trustee), Fed. Cir. Bar Assn., Intellectual Property Owners Assn., INTA, Bar Assn. San Francisco, Assn. Bus. Trial Lawyers, William A. Ingram Inn of Ct. Office: Bingham McCutcheon LLP 1900 University Ave Palo Alto CA 94303 E-mail: bill.abrams@bingham.com.

ABRAMSKY, ODED, neurologist; b. Jerusalem, Nov. 2, 1940; s. Shmuel and Mina (Brodowsky) A.; m. Henia Kligman, Nov. 1, 1960; children: Yael, Assa, Dan, Haim. MD, Hebrew U., Jerusalem, 1969, PhD, 1978. Bd. cert. in neurology. Acad. physician Hadassah U. Hosp., Jerusalem, 1974—, head neuroimmunology unit, 1982-88, chmn. dept. neurology, 1988—; prof. neurology Hebrew U., Jerusalem, 1982—, dean faculty of medicine, 1992—96, Israel S. Wechsler chair neurology; chief scientist Israel Ministry of Health, Jerusalem, 1988-92; dir. Agnes Ginges Ctr. Human Neurogenetics Hadassah Med. Org., Jerusalem. Chmn. com. for basic medicine Israel Acad. Scis. and Humanities, Jerusalem, 1980-81; chmn. com. for neuroscis. Israel Nat. Coun. for R & D, 1985-90; chmn. bd. govs. U.S.-Israel Binat. Sci. Found., 1990-91. Co-author: Neurosciences in Israel, 1989, Medical Research in Israel, 1996; editl. bd. Jour. Neuroimmunology, 1988-92, Jour. Neurol. Sci., 1990—. Col. Israel Def. Forces, 1978-88. Recipient Lions Israel award Distinction in Medicine, 2000. Mem. Israel Soc. Neuroimmunology (hon. pres.), European Neurol. Soc. (exec. com. 1986-95), Internat. Soc. Neuroimmunology (internat. adv. bd. 1986—), European Coun. for Treatment and Rsch. in Multiple Sclerosis (pres. 1994-95), Assoc. Med. Schs. in Europe (exec. com. 1995—), Inst. Medicine (fgn. assoc.), Am. Assn. Neurology (hon.). Home: Ramat Moza 11 Hamitnahlim-Bahar St Jerusalem Israel Office: Hadassah Med Org Kiryat Hadassah pob 12000 91120 Jerusalem Israel Office Phone: 02 6777111. Office Fax: 02 6434434. E-mail: pr1@hadassah.org.il.

ABRAMSON, ALEXIS R., mechanical engineering educator; BS, Tufts U., 1995, MS, 1998; PhD, U. Calif., Berkeley, 2002. Asst. prof. mech. engrng. Case Western Res. U., Cleve., 2003—. Office: Case Western Res U 10900 Euclid Ave Cleveland OH 44106-7222 Office Fax: 216-368-3007. Business E-Mail: alexis.abramson@case.edu.

ABRAMSON, ARTHUR SEYMOUR, linguistics educator, researcher; b. Jersey City, Jan. 26, 1925; s. Seymour Vallie (Olshan) A.; m. Ruby Melamed, June 27, 1952 (div. May 1985); children: Joseph B., David N. Student, Rutgers U., 1942-43; BA, Yeshiva U., NYC, 1949; MA, Columbia U., NYC, 1950, PhD, 1960. Tchr. English and French Pub. High Schs., Jersey City, 1950-53; research staff Haskins Labs., NYC and New Haven, 1959-63, 64-65, research assoc., 1963-64, 65—, also bd. dirs., corp. sec., 2005—; assoc. prof. speech CUNY, 1963-64, prof. communication arts and scis., 1965-67; prof. linguistics U. Conn., Storrs, 1967-92, prof. emeritus, 1992—, head dept. linguistics, 1967-74. Fulbright tchr. Bangkok and Songkhla, Thailand, 1953-55; vis. prof. Lady Davis Fellowship Trust, Jerusalem, 1981. Author: The Vowels and Tones of Standard Thai: Acoustical Measurements and Experiments; editor Language and Speech, 1975-87; contbr. numerous articles to profl. jours. With US Army, 1943-46, ETO. Am. Coun. Learned Socs. fellow, 1973-74, Ford Found. fellow, Thailand, 1973-74. Fellow Acoustical Soc. Am., Internat. Soc. Phonetic Scis. (v.p. 1985-91), Linguistic Soc. Am. (sec.-treas. 1974-78, v.p. 1982, pres. 1983); mem. MLA, Internat. Phonetic Assn. (coun. 1986-90), Am.

Soc. Phonetic Scis., S.E. Asian Linguistics Soc., Siam Soc., Conn. Acad. Arts. and Scis., Phi Kappa Phi. Democrat. Jewish. Office: Haskins Labs 300 George St New Haven CT 06511-6624 also: U Conn Dept Linguistics 337 Mansfield Rd Unit 1145 Storrs Mansfield CT 06269-1145 Home: 49A Middle Tpke Mansfield Depot CT 06251-5109 Office Phone: 203-865-6163, 860-450-6341. Business E-Mail: arthur.abramson@uconn.edu.

ABRAMSON, DAVID LAWRENCE, plastic surgeon, educator; b. NYC, Sept. 1, 1962; s. Paul Richard and Adele Francis Abramson; m. Karen Waite, May 27, 1995. BA in Natural Scis., Johns Hopkins U., 1984; MD, NYU, 1988. Diplomate Am. Bd. Plastic Surgery, Am. Bd. Surgery, Nat. Bd. Med. Examiners. Resident dept. surgery SUNY Health Sci. Ctr., Bklyn., 1988-92, chief resident dept. surgery, 1992-93, clin. asst. prof. surgery/plastic surgery, 1996-98, assoc. prof. surgery/plastic surgery, 2000—06, chief divsn. plastic and reconstructive surgery, 1997—2000, program dir. plastic surgery residency, 1998—; resident plastic surgery dept. surgery Harvard/Brigham/Children's Divsn. Plastic Surgery, 1993-94, chief resident plastic surgery dept. surgery, 1994-95, craniofacial fellow dept. surgery, 1995-96. Clin. asst. instr. SUNY Health Sci. Ctr., Bklyn., 1988-93; clin. fellow surgery Harvard U., 1993-96; cons. physician Mariner Health Care, 1995-96; cons. Marinen Health Care, Boston, 1994-96; attending surgeon Englewood Hosp. and Med. Ctr., 1996—, U. Hosp. Bklyn., 1996—, Kings County Hosp. Ctr., 1997—; assoc. attending physician L.I. Coll. Hosp., 1996—, Manhattan Eye, Ear and Throat Hosp., 1996—; attending physician Lenox Hill Hosp., 1998—; presenter and lectr. in field. Contbr. chpts. to books and articles to profl. jours. Recipient 1st prize Soc. for Gastrointestinal Endoscopic Surgeons, 1991. Fellow ACS (assoc.); mem. AMA, Am. Soc. Plastic and Reconstructive Surgeons (govt. rels. com. 1998—), Am. Soc. Plastic Surgery, Assn. Acad. Chmn. in Plastic Surgery, Am. Soc. for Laser Medicine and Surgery, N.Y. Regional Soc. Plastic and Reconstructive Surgery, Phi Beta Kappa. Avocations: tennis, golf, theater. Office: 363 Grand Ave Englewood NJ 07631-4104 also: 42A E 74th St New York NY 10021 Office Phone: 212-426-7200. E-mail: plasticsurgerydoc@yahoo.com.*

ABRAMSON, HANLEY NORMAN, pharmacy educator; b. Detroit, June 10, 1940; s. Frederick Jacob and Lillian (Kampner) A.; m. Young Hee Kim, Aug. 4, 1967; children: Nathaniel, Deborah, Stephen. BS in Pharmacy, Wayne State U., 1962; MS in Pharm. Chemistry, U. Mich., 1963, PhD in Pharm. Chemistry, 1966. Registered pharmacist. Rsch. assoc. The Hebrew U., Jerusalem, 1966-67; asst. prof. Wayne State U., Detroit, 1967-73, assoc. prof., 1973-78, prof., 1978—, chmn. dept. pharm. sci., 1986-95, interim dean Eugene Applebaum Coll. of Pharmacy and Health Scis., 1987—88, assoc. provost, 1991-95, assoc. dean, 1996-99, dep. dean pharmacy, 2000—02. Author numerous published articles in field of medicinal chemistry. Bd. trustees 1st Bapt. Ch. of Oak Park, Mich., 1974-78; deacon Bloomfield Hills (Mich.) Bapt. Ch., 1986-89; dir. Met. Detroit Alliance for Minority Participation, 1994-2000. Recipient rsch. grants Mich. Heart Assn., Detroit, 1967-76, Nat. Cancer Inst., Bethesda, Md., 1982-91. Mem. AAAS, Am. Chem. Soc., Am. Pharm. Assn., Am. Assn. Colls. Pharmacy. Baptist. Avocations: astronomy, coin collecting/numismatics, baseball history, classical music. Home: 5530 Hammersmith Dr West Bloomfield MI 48322-1452 Office: Wayne State U 3607 Applebaum Bldg Detroit MI 48201 Home Phone: 248-661-0419; Office Phone: 313-577-1711. Business E-Mail: ac2531@wayne.edu.

ABRAMSON, HYMAN NORMAN, engineering and science research executive; b. San Antonio, Mar. 4, 1926; s. Nathan and Pearl (Westerman) A.; m. Idelle Rebecca Ringel, Apr. 20, 1947; children: Phillip David, Mark Donald. BSME, Stanford U., 1950, MS in Engring. Mechanics, 1951; PhD in Engring. Mechanics (So. Fellowship Fund fellow), U. Tex., Austin, 1956. Engr. U.S. Naval Air Missile Test Center, Point Mugu, Calif., 1947—48; project engr. Chance Vought Aircraft Co., Dallas, 1951-52; assoc. prof. aero. engring. Tex. A&M U., 1952-55; sect. mgr., dept. dir. S.W. Research Inst., San Antonio, 1956-72, v.p. div. engring. scis., 1972-85, exec. v.p., 1985-91, also bd. dirs. Mem. many research adv. coms. U.S. Govt.; bd. dirs. Broadway Nat. Bank. Author: An Intro to the Dynamics of Airplanes, 1958, reprinted, 1971; contbr. numerous articles to profl. publs.; editor: (with others) Applied Mechanics Surveys, 1966, The Dynamic Behavior of Liquids in Moving Containers, 1966; assoc. editor: (with others) Applied Mechanics Revs, 1954-85; editorial adv. bd.: (with others) Jour. Computers and Structures, 1970—, Aeros. and Astronautics, 1975-80. Mem. Greater San Antonio C. of C., and City of San Antonio Market Sq. Adv. Com., 1973-77; mem. U.S. Bicentennial Com. of San Antonio, 1975-76; mem. adv. bd. dirs. U.S. Alamo, Inc., 1985-90; mem. adv. bd. Karta Techs., 1991—. Served with USN, 1943-45. Fellow AIAA (Disting. Service award 1973, dir., Structures, Structural Dynamics and Materials medal 1991), ASME (v.p., gov., hon. mem. 1979, Gold medal 1999); mem. Nat. Acad. Engring., Soc. Naval Architects and Marine Engrs., Nat. Acad. Engring. Mexico, AAAS, Sigma Xi. Republican. Jewish. Home: 1511 Spanish Oaks San Antonio TX 78213-1635 Office: SW Research Inst PO Box 28510 San Antonio TX 78228-0510 Home Phone: 210-342-5764; Office Phone: 210-522-2207.

ABRAMSON, JILL, newspaper publishing executive; AB in History and Lit., Harvard U., 1976. Stringer Time mag., 1974-76, Boston bur. mgr., reporter, 1976-77; with NBC News Election Unit, 1979-81; sr. writer Am. Lawyer, 1981-88; editor Legal Times, 1986-88; with New York Times, Washington, 1988—, Chernoff Silver, 1988-97; dep. bur. chief The Wall Street Jour., 1993-97; enterprise editor Washington bur. New York Times, 1997—2003, mng. editor, 2003—. Co-author: Where They Are Now: The Story of Women of Harvard Law 1974, 1976, Strange Justice, 1994. Recipient Matrix award for newspaper work, NY Women in Comm. Inc., 2006. Office: NY Times 229 W 43rd St New York NY 10036

ABRAMSON, LESLIE HOPE, lawyer; b. Queens, NY, 1943; 1 child, Laine. Grad., Queens Coll.; JD, UCLA. Bar: Calif. 1970. Lawyer L.A. County Pub. Defender's Office, 1970—77; pvt. practice, 1977—. Co-author: (with Richard Flaste) The Defense is Ready: My Life in Crime, 1997. Recipient award for outstanding trial atty., Criminal Cts. Bar Assn., 1985. Mem.: Calif. Attys. for Criminal Justice (pres.). Office: 4929 Wilshire Blvd Los Angeles CA 90010*

ABRAMSON, NORMAN, retired engineering educator, electronics executive; b. Boston, Apr. 1, 1932; s. Edward and Esther (Vaslavsky) Abramson; m. Joan Freulich, July 4, 1954; children: Mark David, Carin Lynn. AB, Harvard U., 1953; MA, UCLA, 1955; PhD, Stanford U., 1958. Asst. prof. to assoc. prof. Stanford U., Calif., 1958—65; vis. prof. U. Calif., Berkeley, 1965, Harvard U., Cambridge, Mass., 1965-66; prof. U. Hawaii, Honolulu, 1966-94, emeritus prof., 2005—; v.p. Aloha Networks, Inc., San Francisco, 1994-2001, SkyWare, Inc., San Francisco, 2002—06, bd. dirs. Vis. prof. MIT, 1981—82; cons. Internat. Telecom. Union, Geneva, UNESCO, Paris, UN Devel. Prog., NYC. Author: Information Theory and Coding, 1963; co-editor: Computer Communication Networks, 1973; editor: Multiple Access Communications, Foundations for Emerging Technologies, 1993. Recipient Tech. award, Rhein Found., 2000. Fellow: IEEE (Koji Kobayshi Computers and Comm. award 1995, Alexander Graham Bell medal 2007), Internat. Engring. Consortium, IEEE Info. Theory Soc. (Golden Jubilee award for Tech. Innovation 1998). Achievements include patents in field. Home: 521 Lake St San Francisco CA 94118-1216 Personal E-mail: norm@hawaii.edu.

ABRAMSON, NORMAN M., lawyer; b. Mpls. BA cum laude, Boston U., 1990; JD cum laude, U. Minn. Sch. Law, 1993. Bar: Minn. 1993, US Dist. Ct. (dist. Minn.) 1993. Law clk. to Hon. Margaret M. Marrinan Ramsey County Dist. Ct.; assoc. Doherty, Rumble & Butler; ptnr. Patterson, Thuente, Skaar & Christensen, P.A., Mpls.; atty. Gray, Plant & Mooty, Mpls. Named a Rising Star, Minn. Super Lawyers mag., 2006. Mem.: Minn. State Bar Assn., Ramsey County Bar Assn. Office: Gray Plant Mooty 500 IDS Ctr 80 S 8th St Minneapolis MN 55402 Office Phone: 612-632-3342. Office Fax: 612-632-4342. E-mail: norman.abramson@gpmlaw.com.*

ABRAMSON, PAUL ROBERT, political scientist, educator; b. St. Louis, Nov. 28, 1937; s. Harry Benjamin and Hattie Abramson; m. Janet Carolyn Schwartz, Sept. 11, 1966; children: Lee Jacob, Heather Lyn. BA, Washington U., St. Louis, 1959; MA, U. Calif.-Berkeley, 1961, PhD, 1967. Asst. prof. polit. sci. Mich. State U., East Lansing, 1967-71, assoc. prof. polit. sci., 1971-77, prof. polit. sci., 1977—. Lady Davis vis. prof. Hebrew U. Jerusalem, 1994. Author: Generational Change in American Politics, 1975, The Political Socialization of Black Americans, 1977, Political Attitudes in America, 1983; co-author: Change and Continuity in the 1980 Elections, 1982, rev. edit., 1983, Change and Continuity in the 1984 Elections, 1986, rev. edit., 1987, Change and Continuity in the 1988 Elections, 1990, rev. edit., 1991, Change and Continuity in the 1992 Elections, 1994, rev. edit., 1995, Value Change in Global Perspective, 1995, Change and Continuity in the 1996 Elections, 1998, Change and Continuity in the 1996 and 1998 Elections, 1999, Change and Continuity in the 2000 Elections, 2002, Change and Continuity in the 2000 and 2002 Elections, 2003, Change and Continuity in the 2004 Elections, 2006, Change and Continuity in the 2004 and 2006 Elections, 2007; contbr. articles to profl. jours. Served to lt. US Army, 1960—62. Woodrow Wilson fellow, 1959-60; Ford Found. faculty research fellow, 1972-73; Fulbright grantee sr. lectr. Hebrew U. of Jerusalem, 1987-88. Mem. Am. Polit. Sci. Assn., Midwest Polit. Sci. Assn., So. Polit. Sci. Assn., Am. Sociol. Assn., Internat. Polit. Sci. Assn., Phi Beta Kappa Home: 2830 Turtlecreek Dr East Lansing MI 48823-6333 Office: Mich State U Dept Polit Sci East Lansing MI 48824-1032 Office Phone: 517-353-3285. E-mail: abramson@msu.edu.

ABRAVANEL, ALLAN RAY, lawyer; b. NYC, Mar. 11, 1947; s. Leon and Sydelle (Berenson) A.; m. Susan Ava Paikin, Dec. 28, 1971; children: Karen, David. BA magna cum laude, Yale U., 1968; JD cum laude, Harvard U., 1971. Bar: N.Y. 1972, Oreg. 1976. Assoc. Paul, Weiss, Rifkind, Wharton & Garrison, NYC, 1971-72, 74-76; fellow Internat. Legal Ctr., Lima, Peru, 1972-74; from assoc. to ptnr. Stoel, Rives, Boley, Fraser & Wyse, Portland, Oreg., 1976-83; ptnr. Perkins Coie, Portland, 1983—. Editor, pub. Abravanel Family Newsletter. Chair Oreg. Internat. Trade Com., Oreg. Dist. Export Coun. Mem.: ABA. Office: Perkins Coie LLP 1120 NW Couch St Portland OR 97209-4125 Office Phone: 503-727-2000. E-mail: aabravanel@perkinscoie.com.

ABREU, BOBBY, professional baseball player; b. Aragua, Venezuela, Mar. 11, 1974; 1 child, Emily Paola. With Astros, 1990-97, right fielder, 1997-98; outfielder Phila. Phillies, 1998—2006, New York Yankees, 2006—. Named Home Run Derby Champion, MLB All-Star Game, 2005; named to Nat. League All-Star Team, 2004—05. Office: New York Yankees Yankee Stadium E 161st St and River Ave Bronx NY 10452

ABREU, LUIS ALBERTO, lawyer; b. Pinar Del Rio, Cuba, Apr. 20, 1956; came to U.S., 1961; s. Arnaldo Jesus and Justa (Villar) A.; m. Sallie Brown Shadrick, Aug. 23, 1980; children: Sarah, Maria. BA, Davidson Coll., 1978; JD, U. Fla., 1981. Bar: Va. 1981, U.S. Bankruptcy Ct. 1981, U.S. Ct. Appeals (4th cir.) 1981. From assoc. to ptnr. Clement & Wheatley, Danville, Va., 1981—2003; prin. Carter Craig, Attys. at Law, Danville, Va., 2003—. Mng. mem. Sunset Ridge, LLC, 2005—. Chmn. Local Human Rights Com., Danville, Va., 1986—89; commr. Commn. Archtl. Rev.; bd. dirs., pres. YMCA, 1992; mem. planning and budget com. United Way; bd. dirs. Danville Sci. Ctr. Recipient Bob Greine award Miami Touchdown Club, 1976; named one of Va.'s Legal Elite bus. mag., 2002-06; Alex Hemby scholar Davidson Coll., 1974-78. Mem.: ABA, Mental Health Assn. (bd. dirs.), Va. Bar Assn., Danville Mus. Fine Arts, Hist. Soc., Lions (pres. 1984—85). Republican. Roman Catholic. Home: 250 Shoreham Dr Danville VA 24541-5149 Office: Carter Craig 126 S Union St Danville VA 24541 Office Phone: 434-792-9311. Business E-Mail: labreu@ccbbk.com.

ABRIKOSOV, ALEXEI ALEXEYEVICH, physicist; b. Moscow, June 25, 1928; s. Aleksey Ivanovich and Fanny Davidovna (Vulf) Abrikosov; m. Svetlana Yuriyevna Bun-kova, 1977; 3 children. Degree, Moscow U., 1948; DS in Physics and Math., Inst. Phys. Problems, Moscow, 1955; DS, DS, Slovak Acad. Scis., 2007. Rsch. assoc., sr. scientist Inst. Phys. Problems USSR Acad. Scis., Moscow, 1948-65, head dept. L.D. Landau Inst. Theoretical Physics, 1965-88; dir. Inst. High Pressure Physics, Moscow, 1988-91; disting. sci. Argonne Nat. Lab., Ill., 1991—. Prof. Moscow Univ, 1951—68, Gorky Univ, 1971—72, Moscow Physical Eng Inst, 1974—75; head chair theoretical physics Moscow Inst Steel and Alloys, 1976—92. Author: Quantum Field Theory Methods in Statistical Physics, 1962, Introduction to the Theory of Normal Metals, 1972, Fundamentals of the Theory of Metals, 1987; contbr. articles to profl jours. Recipient Lenin Prize, 1966, Fritz London Award, 1972, State Prize, 1982, Landau Prize, Acad Sci USSR, 1989, Int John Bardeen Award, 1991, Nobel prize in physics, 2003, Golden Plate award, Acad. Achievement, 2004. Fellow: Am. Acad. Arts and Scis., Am. Physics Soc.; mem.: NAS, Royal Soc. London (fgn.), Hungarian Acad. Scis. (hon.), Russian Acad. Scis. Office: Argonne Nat Lab 9700 Cass Ave Argonne IL 60439-4803 Home Phone: 630-257-0742; Office Phone: 630-252-5482. E-mail: abrikosov@anl.gov.

ABRIOLA, LINDA MARIE, civil and environmental engineer; BS in Civil Engring., Drexel U., 1976; MS in Civil Engring., Princeton U., 1979, MA in Civil Engring., 1980, PhD in Civil Engring., 1983. Project engr. Procter and Gamble Mfg. Co., SI, NY, 1976—78; rsch. asst. dept. civil engring. Princeton U., NJ, 1979—83, postdoctoral rschr. dept. civil engring., 1983—84; vis. assoc. prof. dept. petroleum engring. U. Tex., Austin, 1991; vis. scientist dept. geotech. engring. Universitat Politecnica de Cataluna, Barcelona, 1992; asst. prof. dept. civil and environ. engring. U. Mich., Ann Arbor, 1984—90, assoc. prof. dept. civil and environ. engring., 1990—96, prof., dir. Environ. and Water Resources Engring. Program, 1996—2003; dean engring., prof. civil and environ. engring. Tufts U., 2003—. Mem. environ. engring. com. USEPA Sci. Adv. Bd., 1990—96; mem. com. on groundwater clean-up alternatives NRC, 1991—94, mem. water sci and tech. bd., 1994—97; mem. sci. adv. com. Western Region Hazardous Substance Rsch. Ctr., 1995—. Contbr. articles to profl. jours. Recipient Presdl. Young Investigator award, NSF, 1985, Faculty award for Women Scientists and Engrs., 1991, Outstanding Educator award, Assn. for Women Geoscientists, 1996; Vis. Scientist's grant, Spanish Ministry of Edn. and Sci., 1992, Disting. Darcy lectr., Nat. Groundwater Assn., 1996. Fellow: Am. Acad. Arts and Sciences; mem.: NAE (councillor 2007—), Am. Geophys. Union (hydrology divsn. 1992—94), Assn. Environ. Engring. Profs. (bd. dirs. 1990—92). Office: Dean Engring Tufts U Medford MA 02155*

ABRON, LILIA A., chemical engineer; b. Memphis, Mar. 8, 1945; d. Ernest and Bernice (Wise) A.; children: Fredeick, Ernest, David. BS in Chemistry, Lemoyne Coll., 1966; MS in Sanitary Engring., Washington U., 1968; PhD in Chem. Engring., U. Iowa, 1971. Profl. engr. Free lance cons., Washington, 1971-74; asst. prof. Howard U., Washington, 1974-81; chief environ. div. Delon Hampton & Assocs., Washington, 1975-78; pres., CEO Peer Cons., Rockville, Md., 1978—. Com. mem. Nat. Coun. Examiners, Clemson, S.C. Pres. Jack & Jill Am., Inc., D.C. Chpt., 1990-92; bd. dirs. Bapt. Home for Children, Washington. Recipient Women Owned Bus. Enterprise award DOT, 1988, Balti. Outstanding Minority Bus. award Fed. Exec. Bd., 1987; named Alumnus of Yr. Lemoyne Owen Coll., 1988. Fellow Am. Acad. Arts & Scis.; mem. AAAS, Water Environ. Fedn., Am. Soc. Civil Engrs., Am. Water Works Assn., Sigma Xi Office: PEER Cons 12300 Twinbrook Pkwy Ste 410 Rockville MD 20852-1650

ABSHIRE, DAVID MANKER, former ambassador, research executive; b. Chattanooga, Apr. 11, 1926; s. James Ernest and Phyllis (Patten) A.; m. Carolyn Lamar Sample, Sept. 7, 1957; children: Lupton Patten, Anna Lamra Abshire Bowman, Mary Lee Sample Abshire Jensvold, Phyllis Anderson Abshire d'Hoop, Carolyn Abshire Hall. Student, U. Chattanooga, 1945; BS, U.S. Mil. Acad., 1951; PhD, Georgetown U., 1959; DHL, Va. Theol. Sem., 1992; DCL (hon.), U. of the South, 1994; DHL, Georgetown U., Washington. Mem. minority staff U.S. Ho. Reps., 1958-60; dir. spl. projects Am. Enterprise Inst., Washington, 1961-62; from exec. dir. to pres. and co-founder Center Strategic and Internat. Studies Georgetown U., 1962-99; vice chmn. Center Strategic and Internat. Studies, 1999—; ambassador, U.S. permanent rep. North Atlantic Council, 1983-87; spl. counsellor to pres. The White House, 1987, vice chmn., bd. trustees; pres. Ctr. for the Study of the Presidency, 1999—, Richard Lounsbery Found., 2002—. Asst. sec. state for congl. rels., 1970-73; presdl. appointee Congl. Commn. on Orgn. of Govt. for Conduct of Fgn. Policy, 1973-75; chmn. U.S. Bd. for Internat. Broadcasting, 1974-77; dir. nat. security group Transition Office of Pres.-Elect Reagan, 1980-81; dir. Ogden Corp., 1987-96; mem. adv. bd. BP Am., President's Task Force on U.S. Government Internat. Broadcasting, 1991, bd. Procter and Gamble; adj. prof. Georgetown U., 1973-83. Author: The South Rejects a Prophet: The Life of Senator D.M. Key, 1967, International Broadcasting: A New Dimension of Western Diplomacy, 1976, Foreign Policy Makers: President vs. Congress, 1979, The Growing Power of Congress, 1981, Preventing World War III: A Realistic Grand Strategy, 1988, Saving The Reagan Presidency: Trust Is The Coin Of The Realm, 2005 (with others), Detente, 1965, Vietnam Legacy, 1976, The Global Economy, 1990; editor: National Security, 1963, Portuguese Africa, 1969, Research Resources for the Seventies, 1971, Triumphs and Tragedies of the Modern Presidency: Seventy-Six Case Studies in Presidential Leadership, 2001; co-editor Washington Quar., 1977-83; co-author: Putting America's House in Order, 1996; editor-in-chief: Report to the President-elect 2000: Triumphs and Tragedies of the Modern Presidency, 2000, Saving the Reagan Presidency, 2005. Mem. adv. bd. Naval War Coll., 1975-79; vice-chmn. bd. Youth for Understanding, 1979-80; trustee Baylor Sch., 1980—; mem. Pres.'s Fgn. Intelligence Adv. Bd., 1981-83; bd. dirs. Spaak Found., Brussels; trustee George W. Marshall Found. With AUS, 1945-46; 1st lt. 1951-56; capt. Res. ret. Decorated Bronze Star with oak leaf cluster, with V for Valor, V commendation ribbon with metal pendant; Order of Crown, comdr. Order of Leopold (Belgium); grand ofcl. Order of Republic of Italy; recipient medal of Pres. of Italian Republic, Senate, Parliament and Govt. and of Pio Manzu Ctr.; recipient John Carroll award, Dept. Def. disting. pub. svc. medal, 1988, Presdl. Citizens medal, 1989, medal of diplomatic merit Republic of Korea, 1993; First Class Order of The Lion of Finland insignia of the Comdr., 1994, U.S. Military Acad. Castle award, 1994, Order of the Liberator, Argentina, 1999, Order of Sacred Treasure Gold and Silver Star, Japan, 2001. Mem. Coun. Am. Ambs., Coun. on Competitiveness, Coun. Fgn. Rels., Inst. Strategic Studies, Trinity Nat. Leadership Roundtable (co-founder), Gold Key Soc., Alfalfa Club, Met. Club, Cosmos Club, Alibi Club, Phi Alpha Theta. Republican. Episcopalian. Home: 311 S St Asaph St Alexandria VA 22314-3745 Office: Ctr for Study of the Presidency 1020 19th St NW Ste 250 Washington DC 20036

ABSTON, DUNBAR, JR., management consultant; b. Memphis, Jan. 26, 1931; s. Dunbar and Esther (Cook) A.; m. Constance Condon, Apr. 29, 1978; children— Lauri Abston Arnold, Dunbar III, Linda Abston Larsen, Frank Norfleet; stepchildren— Selden Early Popwell, Martha McKellar Early, William Cole Early III, Elizabeth Early Gore. AB, Princeton U., 1953; MBA, Harvard U., 1955; M.Phil., Oxford U., 1989. Joined Parts Inc., Memphis, 1959, chmn., 1979; pres. parent co. Parts Industries Corp., Memphis, 1981-83, pres., chief exec. officer, 1983-87; pres., proprieter Abston Mgmt. Co., Memphis, 1987—. Pres. Tract-O-Land Plantation; ptnr. Abston Farms, Lake Comorant, Miss., Abston-Norfleet Realty Co., Memphis, Abston Sod Farm LLC, Lake Comorant, Miss., 2000—. Past chmn. Memphis Symphony Orch., Memphis Plough Community Found.; trustee Rhodes Coll., Lawrenceville Sch. Baker scholar Harvard U., 1954. Mem. Automotive Warehouse Distbrs. Assn. (past chmn.), Memphis Econ. Club (past chmn.), Phi Beta Kappa. Republican. Presbyterian. Home: 4010 Dumaine Way Memphis TN 38117 Office: Abston Mgmt Co 4727 Spottswood Ave Memphis TN 38117-4818

ABT, JEFFREY, art educator, art historian, artist, writer; b. Kansas City, Mo., Feb. 27, 1949; s. Arthur and Lottie (Weinman) A.; m. Mary Kathleen Paquette, July 16, 1972; children: Uriel, Danya. BFA, Drake U., 1971, MFA, 1977. Curator collections Wichita (Kans.) Art Mus., 1977-78; gen. mgr. Billy Hork Galleries, Ltd., Chgo., 1978-80; exhbns. coordinator U. Chgo. Libr., 1980-86; asst. dir. Smart Mus. of Art, U. Chgo., 1986—87, acting dir., 1987—89; assoc. prof. dept. art and art history Wayne State U., Detroit, 1989—, dept. chair, 1989-94, mem. adv. bd. Humanities Ctr., 1993-95. Author: A Museum on the Verge: A Socioeconomic History of the Detroit Institute of Arts, 1882-2000, 001; exhbn. catalogues The Printer's Craft, 1982, The Book Made Art, 1986; one-man shows include Cliff Dwellers, 1997, Cary Gallery, 1998, Wayne State U., 1999, 2003, Worthington Arts Coun. Gallery, 2000; editor ann. Book and Paper Group Am. Inst. for Conservation, 1985-86; editor exhbn. catalogue Up From the Streets: Detroit Art from the Duffy Warehouse Collection, 2001; mem. editl. bd. Wayne State U. Press, 1990-96, 2002—, chmn. editl. bd., 1996—2001; mem. editl. bd. Museum History Jour., 2006-; illustrator: Water: Sheba's Story, 1997; contbr. articles and book revs. to profl. jours., chpts. to books and encys. Bd. dir. Hyde Pk. Jewish Cmty. Ctr., Chgo., 1988-89, Detroit Artists Market, 1994—, sec., 1996-99, pres., chmn. bd. dir., 1999-2001, hon. dir., 2004—; trustee Ragdale Found., Lake Forest, Ill., 1985-96, nat. adv. coun., 1996—; intercultural programs com., 1990-92, libr. adv. com., 1990-96, edn. adv. com., 1992-95, Detroit Inst. Arts; visual arts com. Detroit Festival of the Arts, 1989-92; juror art exhbns., 1986—; dir. Reva and David Logan Found., Chgo., 2003—. Recipient numerous purchase prizes, awards and commns. for artistic work, 1974—, award of merit Mich. Hist. Soc., 2002, Bd. Govs. award Wayne State U., 2003; Hebrew Union Coll.-Jewish Inst. Religion fellow, Jerusalem, 1971-72; grantee IMS, NEA, NEH, Rockefeller Archive Ctr., Rockefeller U., Logan Found., Wayne State U. Humanities Ctr., Kaufman Meml. Trust, Woodrow Wilson Nat. Fellowship Found. Mem. Am. Assn. Mus., Coll. Art Assn., Assn. Mus. History (co-founder), Mus. and Galleries History Group. Office: Wayne State U Dept Art and Art History 150 Art Bldg Detroit MI 48202 Office Phone: 313-993-6785. Business E-Mail: j_abt@wayne.edu.

ABT, RALPH EDWIN, lawyer; b. Chgo., Apr. 9, 1960; s. Wendel Peter and Hedi Lucie (Wieder) A. BA, Loyola U., Chgo., 1982; JD, John Marshall Law Sch., Chgo., 1987. Bar: Ill. 1987, US Dist. Ct. (no. dist.) Ill. 1987, US Ct. Appeals (7th cir.) Ill. 1988. Pvt. practice, Chgo., 1987—88; staff atty. Sec. of State's Office, Chgo., 1988—95, Ill. Dept. Healthcare and Family Svcs. (formerly Ill. Dept. Pub. Aid), Chgo., 1995—. Poll watcher, Chgo., 1981, 83, precinct capt., 1983, 93-2000. Mem.: ABA, Ill. Bar Assn., Chgo. Bar Assn., Trade Law Assn. (charter mem., chmn. charter membership drive 1986), Phi Alpha Delta. Lutheran. Avocations: reading, tennis, bicycling, weightlifting. Home: 5067 W Balmoral Ave Chicago IL 60630-1547 Office: Ill Dept Healthcare and Family Svcs Ste 1200 32 W Randolph St Chicago IL 60601-3470

ABT, STEVEN R., civil engineer, educator; b. Cheyenne Wells, Colo. BCE, Colo. State U., 1973, MSCE, 1976, PhDCE, 1980. Hydraulics staff engr. Leonard Rice Engring., Denver, 1974-76; instr. Colo. State U., Ft. Collins, 1976-80, from asst. prof. to assoc. prof., 1980-88, prof., 1988—, exec. asst. dean, 1997—2004, interim dean, 2004—05. Cons., Ft. Collins, 1976—. Editor, co-editor Proceedings; contbr. more than 78 articles to profl. jour. 2d lt. C.E., US Army, 1973, major gen. USAR, 1973—. Fellow ASCE; mem. Transp. Rsch. Bd., Internat. Erosion Control Assn. Office: Colo State U Engring and Rsch Ctr Fort Collins CO 80523-1372 Office Phone: 970-491-8203. E-mail: sabt@engr.colostate.edu.

ABTS, HENRY WILLIAM, retired banker; b. Columbus, Nebr., July 3, 1918; s. Matthew C. and Irene (Xanders) A.; m. Virginia Lung, Nov. 7, 1942; children: Bruce M., Susan A. (Mrs. J. Farnham). BS, Butler U., 1941. Asst. mgr. indsl. relations Union Carbide Co., Kokomo, Ind., 1945-54, personnel mgr. NYC, 1954-56, dir. indsl. relations South Charleston, W.Va., 1956-60; v.p. personnel Cummins Engine Co., Inc., Columbus, Ind., 1960-68, v.p. adminstrn., sec., 1968-82, ret., 1982; v.p. Columbus Bank and Trust, 1982-87, pres., chief exec. officer, 1987-88; ret., 1988. Mem. regional adv. bd. Liberty Mut. Ins. Co. Served to capt. USAAF, 1941-45. Recipient Disting. Alumnus award Butler U., 1981, Cmty. Svc. award Columbus C. of C., 1985; named Outstanding Young Man Kokomo Jr. C. of C., 1951, Boss of Year Columbus Jr. C. of C., 1963, Athletic Hall of Fame, Butler U., 1996. Mem. Ind. C. of C., Ind. Golf Assn. (past pres., dir.), Phi Delta Theta. Mem. Christian Ch. Clubs: Otter Creek Golf (past pres.), Harrison Lakes Country (past pres.); Columbus Rotary (past pres.). Home: 9544 Raintree Dr S Columbus IN 47201-4817

ABU-DEEB, KAMAL MIKHA'IL, humanities educator; b. Safita, Syria, May 23, 1942; m. Ruth Ena Marjorie; children: Umayya, Riham. Grad., Damascus U.; postgrad., Trinity Coll., Oxford, St. John's Coll.; PhD, Oxford U. Prof. Arabic Lit. Columbia U., NYC, 1990—92; prof. Arabic U. London, 1992—. Instr. Oxford U.; prof. Berkeley U., Pa. U., Yarmouk U., Jordan, San'a U., Yemen; vis. prof. Princeton U., Princeton, NJ, U. Bahrain; lectr. in field. Contbr. articles to profl. jours.; author: Poetry: Elegies of Jeremaya; Beirut, 1972, On the Rhythmic Structure of Arabic Poetry: Towards a Radical Alternative to al-Khalil's Prosody and an Introduction to Comparative Rhythmics, 1974 (Soc. of Friends of the Book -Beirut prize, 1975), Al-Jurjani's Theory of Poetic Imagery, 1979, The Dialectics of the Hidden and the Manifest, 1979, Masquerading Visions, 1986 (Baghdad Internat. Book Fair prize, 1987), On Poeticality, 1987, The Perplexity of the All Knowing, 1987, Generative Structures in Pre-Islamic Poetry, 1989, In Celebration of Difference, 1995, The Aesthetics of Contiguity or The Interlacing of Creative Spaces, 1997, In Search of the Orphan Pearl, 2000. Home: 45 Saint John St Oxford 0X1 2LH England Office: Sch Oriental and African Studies Lang-Cultures of Near Mid East Thornhaugh St Russell Sq London WC1H 0XG England

ABUDULMAJID, IMAN See IMAN

ABUEIDA, ATIF, mathematics professor; PhD, Auburn U., Ala., 2000. Assoc. prof. math. U. Dayton, 2000—. Office: Univ Dayton 300 College Park Dayton OH 45469-2316 Office Phone: 937-229-2687.

ABU-ELENIN, SHERIF MOHAMED, electrical engineer, educator; arrived in US, 2000; s. Mohamed Aly Abu-Elenin and Tahany Badr Abdel-Rahman; m. Rabab Farouk Abdel-Kader, July 20, 2000; children: Nour, Malak. BS, Suez Canal U., Port-Said, Egypt, 1999; MS, Tuskegee U., Ala., 2002; PhD, Auburn U., Ala., 2005. Rsch. asst. Auburn U., 2002—05; asst. prof. Tuskegee U., 2005—. Session chmn. NSF Elec. and Communication Sys. Divsn. Grantees Workshop, Tuskegee, 2006; presenter in field. Translator poetry. Presdl. Grad. fellow, Auburn U. Coll. Engring., 2002—05. Mem.: IEEE, IEEE Comm. Soc. Islam. Achievements include development of model and a prototype for the new concept of magnetic ring spinning; assess control strategies for magnetic levitation systems; new method for noise reduction in digital images, by combining spatial filtering methods and matrix rank-reducing singular value decomposition analysis; research in magnetic suspention systems that incorporates permanent magnets. Office: Tuskegee U 303 Luther Foster Hall CEAPS Tuskegee AL 36088 Home Phone: 334-502-6508; Office Phone: 334-727-8989. Business E-Mail: sabu-elenin@tuskegee.edu.

ABUHOFF, DANIEL MARK, lawyer; b. Westbury, NY, Jan. 7, 1954; s. Ralph Leo and Fleur (Karastoff) A.; m. Tamsen Carol Granger, Oct. 16, 1982; children: Granger, Sadie, Ezekiel. AB, Princeton U., 1975; JD, Columbia U., 1978. Bar: NY 1979. Assoc. Debevoise & Plimpton LLP, NYC, 1978-88, ptnr., mem. litig. dept., 1988—. Mem. non-profit coord. com. NY Real Property Task Force. Mem. ABA (litigation sect., antitrust sect.), Assn. Bar City NY Office: Debevoise & Plimpton LLP 919 Third Ave New York NY 10022 Office Phone: 212-909-6381. Office Fax: 212-909-6836. E-mail: dmabuhoff@debevoise.com.

ABU-KHADER, NABIL, electrical engineer, educator; s. Adnan Abu-Khader. PhD in Elec. Engring., Wayne State U., Detroit, 2005. Registered profl. engr., Mich., 2005. Tchg. asst. Wayne State U., 2000—05; asst. prof. The Hashemite U., Zarka, Jordan, 2006—. Contbr. articles to profl. jours. Office: The Hashemite Univ PO Box 150459 The Hashemite Univ Zarka 13115 Jordan Home Phone: +96265237670; Office Phone: +96253903333. Personal E-mail: nabil_abukhader@hotmail.com. Business E-Mail: nkhader@hu.edu.jo.

ABU-KHALAF, MURAD, researcher; b. Jerusalem, Palestine, July 29, 1977; s. Muhammad Samir and Suzan Abu-Khalaf. BS in Electronics and Elec. Engring., Bogazici U., Istanbul, Turkey, 1998; MSEE, U. Tex., Arlington, 2000, PhD, 2005. Rsch. asst. Automation & Robotics Rsch. Inst., Ft. Worth, 2000—05, postdoctoral fellow, 2005—06; with devel. controls and estimation group Math Works Inc., Natick, Mass., 2006—. Adj. asst. prof. U. Tex., Arlington, 2005—; panelist, grant reviewer NSF, 2006. Author: Nonlinear H2/H-Infinity Constrained Feedback Control: A Practical Design Approach Using Neural Networks, 2006. Recipient Inst. Outstanding PhD Dissertation award, Automation & Robotics Rsch. Inst., 2005. Mem.: Internat. Neural Network Soc., IEEE Robotics and Automation Soc., IEEE Control Systems Soc., Eta Kappa Nu. Muslim. Achievements include research in advanced designs of control systems for complex mechanical and aerospace systems.

ABUL-HAJ, SULEIMAN KAHIL, pathologist; b. Palestine, Apr. 20, 1925; came to U.S., 1946, naturalized, 1955; s. Sheik Khalil and S. Buteina (Oda) Abul-H.; m. Elizabeth Abood, Feb. 11, 1948; children: Charles, Alan, Cary. *The roots of the Abul-Haj family date back to the 7th century, A.D. Arab armies invaded North Africa and intermarried with local inhabitants, the Berbers. The Berbers were Barbarian Germanic hordes who invaded Rome and then moved into and settled in North Africa. Tarique Bin Ziyad, born to a Berber mother and an Arab father, was the founding ancestor. Tarique commanded the Arab armies that conquered Spain in 711 A.D. Jabal Tarique, anglicized to Gibralter, was named after him, which means the Mount of Tarique. The name Abul-Haj, father of the pilgrims, was dubbed in the 12th century following the treaty between Saladdin and the Crusaders.* BS, U. Calif., Berkeley, 1949; MS, U. Calif., San Francisco, 1951, MD, 1955. Intern Cook County Hosp., Chgo., 1955-56; resident U. Calif. Hosp., San Francisco, 1949, Brooke Gen Hosp., 1957-59; chief clin. and anatomic pathology Walter Reed Army Hosp., Washington, 1959-62; assoc. prof. U. So. Calif. Sch. Medicine, LA, 1963-96; sr. surg. pathologist Los Angeles County Gen. Hosp., 1963; dir. dept. pathology Cmty. Meml. Hosp., Ventura, Calif., 1964-80, Gen. Hosp. Ventura County, 1966-74; dir. Pathology Svc. Med. Group, 1970—. Cons. Calif. Tumor Tissue Registry, 1962-96, Camarillo State Hosp., 1964-70, Tripler Gen. Hosp., Hawaii, 1963-67, Armed Forces Inst. Pathology, 1960-69. Contbr. articles to profl. jours. Bd. dirs. Tri-Counties Blood Bank, Am. Cancer Soc. Maj., M.C., US Army, 1956-65. Recipient Calif. Honor Soc. award, 1949, Borden award, 1955, Achievement cert. Surgeon Gen. Army, 1962, Internat. medal of Honor, Am. medal of Honor, Internat. Living Legends Leading Scientists of the World. Fellow Coll. Am. Pathologists; mem. AAAS, AMA, Inte rnat. Coll. Surgeons, World Affairs Coun., World Peace and Diplomacy Forum. Achievements include research in cancer, cardiovascular disease, endocrine, renal, and skin diseases. Home and Office: 105 Encinal Way Ventura CA 93001-3317 Office Phone: 805-648-1232. Personal E-mail: eabulhaj@earthlink.net.

ABU-MOSTAFA, AYMAN SAID, application developer, consultant; b. Giza, Egypt, June 1, 1953; came to U.S., 1978; s. Said S. Abu-Mostafa and Faiza A. Ibrahim. BME, Cairo U., 1976; MS in Mech. and Aerospace Engring., Okla. State U., 1980, PhD, 1984. Tchg. asst. Cairo U., Giza, Egypt, 1978, Okla. State U., Stillwater, 1978-79, rsch. assoc., 1979-81; software engr. SEAM Internat. Corp., Palos Verdes, Calif., 1984-87; computing and networking cons. Calif. State U., Los Alamitos, 1987-92; sr. sys. analyst Allied Signal Aerospace, Torrance, Calif., 1992-93; pres., CEO NeuroDollars, Inc., Huntington Beach, Calif., 1993-97; sr. programmer analyst Softnet Systems, Irvine, Calif., 1997-99; software solutions cons. Borland Software Corp. (formerly known as StarBase Corp.), Santa Ana, Calif., 1999—2003; freelance software solutions cons., 2003—. Author papers, articles in field. Undergrad. fellow Ministry of Higher Edn., Cairo, 1971, 72, 76; NASA/Ames grantee, 1979-81. Mem. AIAA, IEEE, Assn. for Computing Machinery. Avocations: reading, computers, languages, music. Personal E-mail: ayman1@aol.com.

ABU-MOUSTAFA, ADEL H., medical educator, dean; b. Cairo, Nov. 18, 1939; came to U.S., 1962; s. Abdulhamid and Zanab (Ayad) Abu-moustafa; m. Magda Ismail Kabbany, Oct. 10, 1962; children: Heidi, Sally, Sherief. BSc, Cairo U., 1960; MA, Harvard U., 1964; PhD, Boston U., 1969. Instr. Boston Coll., Chestnut Hill, Mass., 1964-67; from asst. prof. to assoc. prof. Salem (Mass.) State Coll., 1967-70, prof., 19770-72, dean undergrad studies, 1972-74, acting acad. dean, 1974-76, dean acad. svcs., 1976-79, exec. v.p., 1979-83; adminstrv. counselor King Faisal U., Saudi Arabia, 1983-86; dir. svcs. to higher edn. Acad. for Ednl. Devel., Washington, 1983-87; dir. assoc. dean internat. health affairs Tufts U. Sch. Medicine, Boston, 1987—, dean internat. health affairs, 1997—. Team leader consortium of U.S. Univs. and U.S. Dept. Treasury, U.S. Saudi Commn. on Econ. Cooperation to assist King Faisal U., Saudi Arabia, 1983-87. Contbr. articles to profl. jours. Mem. exec. com. Fletcher Sch. Law and Diplomacy, 1987—. Mem. Arab Am. Physicians. Muslim. Avocation: politics. Office: Tufts U Sch Medicine 136 Harrison Ave Boston MA 02111-1817 Office Phone: 617-636-0355. Business E-Mail: adel.abu-moustafa@tufts.edu.

ABU-OMAR, MAHDI M., chemistry professor; b. Jerusalem, Oct. 18, 1970; s. Muhammad and Naema Abu-Omar; m. Kristen Loraine Fritz, May 23, 1992; children: Jasmine Shareen, Moeen Michael, Jamila Eman. BS summa cum laude in Chemistry, Hampden-Sydney Coll., Va., 1992; PhD in Inorganic Chemistry, Iowa State U. Sci. & Tech., Ames, 1996. NIH postdoctoral scholar Calif. Inst. Tech., Pasadena, 1996—97; asst. prof. U. Calif., LA, 1997—2003; assoc. prof. Purdue U., West Lafayette, Ind., 2003—. Contbr. articles to profl. jours. Recipient Faculty Early Career Devel. award, NSF, 1999—2003, Beckman Young Investigator award, Beckman Found., 1999—2001, Basil O'Connor Starter Scholar Rsch. award, March Dimes, 1999—2001, Faculty Career Devel. award, UCLA, 1999, 2001, Coll. Engring. Team Excellence award, Purdue U., 2007. Mem.: AAAS, Am. Chemcial Soc. Islam. Achievements include patents pending for chemical storage of hydrogen. Avocations: soccer, travel, hiking. Office: Purdue Univ 560 Oval Dr West Lafayette IN 47907

ABU-RADDAD, LAITH JAMAL, mathematical epidemiologist, educator; b. Amman, Jordan, 1970; m. Mercedes Elvira Rivera, 1996; children: Ommar Laith Aburaddad, Alnaser Laith Aburaddad. BSc, U. Jordan, Amman, 1992; MSc, Miami U., Oxford, Ohio, 1994; PhD, Fla. State U., Tallahassee, 2000. Rsch. assoc. Osaka U., Japan, 2000—02, Imperial Coll. London, London, 2002—04; rsch. scientist U. Wash., 2004—. Recipient Dirac-Hellmann Theoret. Physics award, Fla. State U., 2000; fellow, Thomas Jefferson Nat. Accelerator Facility, 1996, NSF, Japan Soc. Promotion Sci., 2000. Independent. Muslim. Achievements include research in HIV epidemiology. Home: 9502 179th PL NE Unit 3 Redmond WA 98052 Office: Fred Hutchinson Cancer Rsch Ctr 1100 Fairview Ave N LE-400 Seattle WA 98109 Office Phone: 206-667-5076. Personal E-mail: laithbus@hotmail.com. Business E-Mail: laith@scharp.org.

ABUT, CHARLES C., lawyer; BA, Columbia U., 1969; JD, Cornell U., 1972. Bar: NJ 1972, DC 1979, NY 1980, U.S. Supreme Ct. 1976, cert.: (matrimonial atty.), accredited family law mediator:. Arbitrator Am. Arbitration Assn., 1978—. Lectr. CLE, 1989-2006. Author: Celebrity Goodwill, 1989. With Mil. Police, U.S. Army, 1964-67. Fellow Am. Acad. Matrimonial Attys.; mem. ABA, ATLA, N.J. Trial Lawyers Assn., Masons, Psi Upsilon. Office: 21 Main St Ste 155 Hackensack NJ 07601 Office Phone: 201-342-0404. Personal E-mail: ccaesq@att.net.

ACAIN, MICHAEL P., lawyer; b. Harbor City, Calif., June 16, 1974; BA cum laude, Loyola Marymount Univ., 1996, JD, 1999. Bar: Calif. 1999, US Dist. Ct. So. Calif. Assoc., civil litigation practice McKay, Byrne & Graham, LA. Editor (exec.): Loyola of LA Entertainment Law Jour.; contbr. articles to profl. jours. Named a Rising Star, So. Calif. Super Lawyers, 2006; recipient Am. Jurisprudence award in criminal procedure. Mem.: ABA, State Bar Calif., LA County Bar Assn. Office: McKay Byrne & Graham Ste 603 3250 Wilshire Blvd Los Angeles CA 90010 Office Phone: 213-386-6900. Office Fax: 213-381-1762.

ACAMPORA, RALPH JOSEPH, brokerage firm executive; b. NYC, Oct. 2, 1941; s. Ralph J. and Teresa (Fusco) Acampora; m. Rosemary Sherlock; stepchildren: Ross J., Matthew. BA, St. Joseph's Sem., Yonkers, NY, Iona Coll. With Harris, Upham & Co. (merged with Smith Barney), NYC, 1969-80; sr. v.p., tech. analyst Kidder Peabody & Co., NYC, 1980-90, Prudential Equity Group, NYC, 1990—, mng. dir. tech. rsch. Tchr. N.Y. Inst. Fin., 1970—. Author: The Fourth Mega Market, 2000. Bd. dirs. Hudson River Performing Arts Ctr. Mem.: Security Industry Assn. (bd. dirs.), Security Traders Assn. (bd. dirs.), NY Soc. Security Analysts (bd. dirs.), Internat. Fedn. Technician Analysts (founder, 1st chmn. 1986—92), Market Technicians Assn. (founder assn. libr. 1975, pres. 1979—80, 2001—03, chartered, founder 1970s, Hon. award 1987). Republican. Roman Catholic. Avocation: study of World War II. Home: 350 Albany St Ph 1 New York NY 10280-1415 Office: Prudential Equity Group 1 New York Plz New York NY 10004-1901

ACAR, EVRIM, computer scientist; b. Erzurum, Turkey, Dec. 16, 1980; BS with honors, Bogazici U., Istanbul, Turkey, 1999—2003; MS in Computer Sci., Rensselaer Poly. Inst., Troy, NY, 2006. Lic. computer engr., Bogazici U., 2003. Rsch. asst. Rensselaer Poly. Inst., 2003—; vis. rschr. Faculty Life Scis., Copenhagen U. Vis. rschr. Chemometrics Group, U. Copenhagen. Contbr. scientific papers. Office: Rensselaer Poly Inst Computer Sci 110 8th St Troy NY 12180 Office Phone: 518-276-8489. Office Fax: 518-276-4033. Business E-Mail: acare@cs.rpi.edu.

ACCARDI, JOSEPH RONALD, accountant; b. Bklyn., July 29, 1960; s. Joseph Anthony and Mary Catherine (Masotti) A.; m. Colette Possert, Oct. 9, 1988; children: Joseph Theodore, Nicolette Barbara. BS, St. John's U., 1982. CPA N.Y., N.J. Staff acct. Pannell Kerr Forster, NYC, 1982-84; sr. acct. KPMG, NYC, 1984-87, Siemens Corp., NYC, 1987-90, mgr. fin. acctg., 1990-92, mgr. bus. adminstrn. Iselin, N.J., 1992-97; mgr. bus. planning & fin. analysis Siemens Transp. Systems, Inc., Iselin, N.J., 1998-99; vp., asst. contr., asst. sec. Siemens Capital Co. LLC, Iselin, NJ, 1999—. Mem. AICPA, N.J. State Soc. CPAs, St. John's Alumni Assn., Inst. Mgmt. Accts., Fin. Execs. Networking Group. Roman Catholic. Avocations: football, baseball, music. Office: 170 Wood Ave S Iselin NJ 08830 Home: 28 Burnet Walk Robbinsville NJ 08691 Office Phone: 732-590-2552. Business E-Mail: joseph.accardi@siemens.com.

ACCATINO, STEVEN C., instrumental music educator, orchestra conductor; s. Charles B and Ruth E Accatino; m. Carolyn S Vanderbilt, Sept. 1, 2002; children: Megan E, Adrienne A, Kimberly E Vanderbilt, Peter C, Emily N. AA, Diablo Valley Coll., 1968—70; BA, Calif. State U., 1970—72; MS, So. Oreg. U., 1993—95. California State Teaching Credential Calif. Dept. of Edn., 1973. Dir., instrumental music Ygnacio Valley H.S., Concord, Calif., 1980—; music dir., condr. Young Artists Symphony Orch., Walnut Creek, Calif., 1997—. Treas. Contra Costa County Band Directors Assn., Concord, Calif., 2003—. Musician: Western Internat. Band Clinic (Order of the Phoenix, 1995). Scout leader Boy Scouts of Am., Concord, Calif., 1996—99. Recipient Eagle Scout award, Boy Scouts of Am., 1967. Mem.: Music Educators Nat. Conf. (assoc. Nationally Registered Music Educator 1997), Assn. of Calif. Symphony Orch. (assoc.), Calif. Band Directors Assn. (assoc.). Avocations: travel, music, model railroading. Office: Ygnacio Valley HS 755 Oak Grove Rd Concord CA 94518 Home Phone: 925-825-6231; Office Phone: 925-685-8414. Office Fax: 925-685-1435. Personal E-mail: saccatino@earthlink.net.

ACCORDINO, FRANK JOSEPH, architect; b. Bklyn., July 14, 1946; s. Carmine Anthony and Elvira Saccone) A.; m. Sheila May Lloyd, Sept. 6, 1969. BS, SUNY, N.Y. Inst. Tech., 1969; MArch, U. N.Mex., 1971. Registered architect, N.Y., Ill., Fla.; cert. Nat. Coun. Archtl. Registration Bds. Project architect Gencorelli & Salo Architects, Mineola, N.Y., 1971-74, Grove Haack & Assocs., P.C., Architects, Engrs., Planners, Ft. Lauderdale, Fla., 1974-76; v.p., dir. Cashin Assocs., P.C., Architects, Engrs., Planners, Mineola, N.Y., 1976-79; prin. architect Frank Accordino, AIA, Merrick, NY, 1979-80; sr. architect, facilities devel. Eastern Airlines, Inc., Miami, Fla., 1980-83; sr. architect Dean Witter Reynolds, Inc., NYC, 1983-84; regional dir. constrn. and engring. Avis Rent A Car System, Inc., Garden City, NY, 1984-87, v.p. corp. facilities, 1987—2002; prin. architect Frank Accordino, AIA, Palm City, Fla., 2004—. Mem.: AIA. Republican. Roman Catholic. Personal E-mail: frankala@comcast.net.

ACCORSI, ERNIE (ERNEST WILLIAM ACCORSI JR.), retired professional sports team executive; b. Hershey, Pa., Oct. 29, 1941; s. Ernest William Sr. and Mary Doris (Nardi) A.; m. Judy Ann Nangle, Sept. 9, 1967 (div. Aug. 1985); children: Michael Ryan, Sherlyn Paige, Patrick Vincent. BA, Wake Forest U., 1963; postgrad., Temple U., 1967. News dir. St. Joseph's U., Phila.; sportswriter Phila. Inquirer, 1966-69; with sports info. dept. Pa. State U., University Park, 1969-70; pub. relations dir. Balt. Colts, Owings Mill, Md., 1970-75, asst. gen. mgr., 1977-82, gen. mgr., 1982-84; asst. to pres. NFL, NYC, 1975-77, Cleve. Browns, 1984-85, exec. v.p. football ops., 1985—92; exec. mgr. bus. affairs Balt. Orioles, 1992—94; asst. gen. mgr. NY Giants, 1994—98, gen. mgr., 1998—2007. Bd. dirs. Nat. Football Found., N.Y.C., 1983. Served with U.S. Army N.G., 1964. Recipient Columbia award Italian-Am. Orgns. Md., Balt., 1982; named Grand Marshall Conv. Council Colts' Corrals, 1983. Mem. Advt. Club Balt. (bd. dirs.) Democrat. Roman Catholic.*

ACEMOGLU, DARON (K. DARON ACEMOGLU), economics professor; b. Istanbul, Turkey, Sept. 3, 1967; s. Kevork and Irma Acemoglu; m. Asuman Ozdaglar, May 29, 2004. BA in Econs., U. York, 1989; MSc in Econometrics and Math. Econs., London Sch. Econs., 1990, PhD in Econs., 1992. Lectr. econs. London Sch. Econs., London, 1992—93; asst. prof. econs. MIT, Cambridge, Mass., 1993—97, Penti Kouri assoc. prof. econs., 1997—2000, prof. econs., 2000—04, Charles P. Kindleberger prof. applied econs., 2004—. Lectr. in field. Co-author (with James Robinson): (book) Economic Origins of Dictatorship and Democracy, 2006; editor: Nat. Bur. of Econs. Rsch., Macroeconomic Ann., Review of Econs. and Stats., 2003—; mem. editl. bd. Journal of Econ. Growth; contbr. articles to profl. jours., chapters to books. Recipient John Bates Clark medal, Am. Econ. Assn., 2005, Sherwin Rosen award for outstanding contbns. to labor econs., Soc. of Labor Economists, 2004, T.W. Shultz prize, U. Chgo., 2004, John Bates Clark medal, Am. Econ. Assn., 2005, Disting. Sci. award, Turkish Sciences Assn., 2006; Rsch. Assoc., Canadian Inst. Advanced Rsch., Toulouse Info. Tech. Network, Nat. Bur. Econ. Rsch., Centre for Econ. Policy Rsch., Fellow, Bur. Rsch. and Econ. Analysis in Develop. Fellow: European Econ. Assn., Am. Acad. Arts & Sciences, Econometric Soc. (life). Mailing: MIT E52-380b 50 Memorial Dr Cambridge MA 02142-1347 Office Phone: 617-253-1330. Business E-Mail: daron@mit.edu.

ACERRA, MICHELE (MIKE ACERRA), engineering and construction company executive; b. Messina, Italy, Apr. 15, 1937; came to U.S., 1978; s. Luigi and Matilde Mazzullo A.; m. Elena Fino, May 31, 1975; children—Marco Eugenio, Matilde Enrica Jennifer. Dr. Chem. Engring., Politecnico, Milan, Italy, 1962. Vessels designer Foster Wheeler Italiana, Milan, 1962, asst. mgr. drawing office, 1963, project engr., 1963-70, project mgr., 1970-74; pres. Glitsch Italiana, Rome, 1974-78; pres., chief oper. officer, dir. 8 subs. cos. Glitsch, Inc., Dallas, 1978-86; pres., chief exec. officer Foster Wheeler USA Corp., Perryville, NJ, 1986-89; corp. v.p. indsl. and environ. group Foster Wheeler Corp., Perryville, NJ, 1989-94; v.p. Foster Wheeler Energy Internat. Inc., 1994-97; dir. 4 subs.; v.p., mgr. BOC JV Foster Wheeler Power Sys., 1997-99; pres. Tray, Inc., Clinton, NJ, 2000—04; cons. in worldwide engring. and constrn., mfg., internat. arbitrator, 2004—. Roman Catholic. Avocations: reading, gardening, travel. Office Phone: 908-832-9290. E-mail: meacerra@embarq.net.

ACETO, VINCENT JOHN, librarian, educator; b. Schenectady, NY, Feb. 5, 1932; s. Henry and Gilda (Maietta) Aceto; m. Jean Louise Rasey, Aug. 27, 1955 (div. 1974); children: David, Paul Andrew; m. Kveta Urbanova, June 16, 1993. AB, MA, SUNY, 1953, MLS, 1959; postgrad., Case Western Res. U., 1959, 62, 65-66. Tchr. Scotia (N.Y.)-Glenville Ctrl. Schs., 1956-57; high sch. libr. Burnt Hills (N.Y.)-Ballston Lake Ctrl. Schs., 1957-59; libr. dir. Town of Ballston Pub. Libr., Burnt Hills, 1958-60; Fulbright lectr. U. Dacca, East Pakistan, 1964-65; asst. prof. Sch. Libr. Sci., SUNY, Albany, 1959-62, assoc. prof. libr. sci., 1963-69, prof., 1969—, assoc. dean, 1987-93, interim dean, 1993-95, co-dir. film and TV documentation ctr., 1983—, Disting. Svc. prof., 2000—. Libr. cons. various pub. schs., N.Y. State Edn. Dept., U.S. Dept. Edn., USA Govt. of Bangladesh, 1965, Govt. of Cyprus, 1992, 94; dir. U.S. Office Edn. insts. and traineeships. Joint Editor: Film Lit. Index; contbr. articles to profl. jours. Pres., Filmdex Par II, Inc., 1973-90; bd. dirs. Freedom Forum, Schenectady, 1970-78, chmn., 1976-78; trustee Clifton Park Halfmoon Pub. Libr., 1995—, v.p., 1996-97, 2000, pres., 1997-99, pres., 2002-; mem. Shenendehowa Ctrl. Pub. Schs. Bd. of Edn., 2002—05, v.p., 2004—05. Served with AUS, 1954-56. Collins fellow U. Albany, 1997. Mem.: NEA, ALA, Soc. Cinema Studies, Am. Soc. Info. Scis., Am. Soc. Indexers, Hudson-Mohawk Libr. Assn. (v.p. 1964—66), N.Y. Libr. Assn., East Pakistan Libr. Assn., Pakistan Libr. Assn., Idaka Forum, Shenendehowa Rotary Club, Rotary, Phi Delta Kappa, Kappa Phi Kappa. Democrat.

Unitarian Universalist. Office: SUNY Albany Sch Info Sci and Policy 1400 Washington Ave Albany NY 12222-0100 Home: 27 Wheeler Dr Clifton Park NY 12065 Personal E-mail: vacetol@nycap.rr.com. Business E-Mail: aceto@albany.edu.

ACEVEDO-VILÁ, ANÍBAL, governor, former congressional representative; b. Hato Rey, PR, Feb. 13, 1962; s. Salvador Acevedo-Colón and Elba Vilá; m. Luisa Gándara, June 29, 1987; children: Gabriela, Juan-Carlos. BA, U. P.R., 1982, JD, 1985; LLM, Harvard U., 1987. Law clk. to Hon. Federico Hernández-Denton Supreme Ct. of P.R., San Juan, 1985-86; law clk. to Hon. Levin H. Campbell U.S. Ct. Appeals (1st cir.), Boston, 1987-88; legis. affairs aide to Gov. Rafael Hernandez Colon San Juan, 1989-92; mem. at-large P.R. Ho. of Reps., San Juan, 1991—2001, ho. minority leader, 1997-2001; pres. Popular Dem. Party, 1997-99, v.p., 1999—; resident commr. U.S. Ho. Reps from P. R., 2001—05; gov. Commonwealth of PR, San Juan, 2005—. Editor-in chief U. P.R. Law Jour., 1984—85, columnist El Nuevo Dia, 1993—96; author: En Honor a la Verdad. Mem. governing bd. Popular Dem. Party, San Juan, 1995-. Mem.: P.R. Bar Assn. Democrat. Avocation: reading. Office: La Fortaleza PO Box 9020082 San Juan PR 00902-0082*

ACHAMPONG, FRANCIS KOFI, academic administrator; b. Kumasi, Ghana, Feb. 18, 1955; came to U.S., 1981; s. John Wilberforce and Salome (Mensa) A.; m. Nicole Victoria Blache. LLB, U. Ghana, 1976; LLM, U. London, 1977, PhD, 1981; LLM, Georgetown U., 1985. Bar: N.Y. 1986, Va. 1988, U.S. Dist. Ct. (ea. dist.) Va. 1988, U.S. Ct. Appeals (4th cir.) 1988, U.S. Supreme Ct. 1990. Adj. lectr. George Washington U., Washington, 1981-82; asst. prof. Howard U., Washington, 1981-85; assoc. prof. Norfolk State U., Va., 1985—92, prof., 1992—2002, chair dept. entrepreneurial studies, 1998—2001, interim dean Sch. Bus., 2001—02; of counsel Jones, Shelton, Kmetz & Malone, P.C, Norfolk, 1998—; dir. acad. affairs Pa. State U. at Mont Alto, 2002—. Cons. Aetna Life & Casualty, Hartford, Conn., 1981-82, Profl. Ins. Assn. of Md., Pa., 1986, Shapiro, Meiselman & Greene, P.C., Rockville, Md., 1987, Crowell & Moring, Washington, 1988, Clark & Stant, Virginia Beach, Va., 1988. Author: Workplace Sexual Harassment, 1999; contbr. articles to profl. jours. Mem. Am. Risk and Ins. Assn., Acad. Legal Studies in Bus. Avocations: gospel music, exercise, reading, movies. Office: Pa State U at Mont Alto One Campus Dr Mont Alto PA 17237 Home: 6132 Winged Foot Ct Fayetteville PA 17222-9650 Office Phone: 717-749-6050. E-mail: fka3@psu.edu.

ACHATZ, GRANT, chef; b. Mich., 1974; m. Angela Snell; 1 child, Kaden. Grad., Culinary Inst. Am., Hyde Park, NY, 1996. Chef French Laundry, Napa Valley, 1996—98, sous chef, 1998—2000; asst. winemaker La Jota Vineyards; exec. chef Trio, Evanston, Ill., 2001—05; exec. chef., mng. ptnr. Alinea, Chgo., 2005—. Guest appearances on Today Show, CBS Sunday Morning, The Food Network, The Discovery Channel, PBS. Named Rising Star Chef in Am., James Beard Found., 2003, Best Chef: Great Lakes, 2007, Next Great Am. Chef, NY Times, 2005; named one of Best New Chefs in Am., Food & Wine mag., 2002. Office: Alinea 1723 N Halsted Chicago IL 60614 Office Phone: 312-867-0110.*

ACHAUER, BRUCE MICHAEL, plastic surgeon; MD, Baylor U., 1967. Intern San Francisco Gen. Hosp., 1967-68; resident in gen. surgery U. Calif., Irvine, 1970-74, rsch. in plastic surgery, 1974-76, adj. prof. surgery, 1994—; fellow in plastic surgery Queen Victoria Hosp., East Grinstead, U.K., 1976; pvt. practice U. Calif. Irvine Med. Ctr., Orange, 1977—; mem. staff St. Joseph Hosp., 1977—; mem. active staff Children's Hosp. of Orange County, 1977—; pvt. practice plastic surgery Orange. Mem. courtesy staff Med. Ctr. of GGG, 1985—; dir. Am. Bd. Plastic Surgery, 1995—. Fellow Am. Acad. Pediatrics; mem. AMA, Am. Assn. Plastic Surgeons, Am. Cleft Palate Assn., Am. Soc. for Surgery of Hand, Am. Soc. Plastic and Reconstructive Surgeons (sec. edtl. found.).

ACHEBE, CHINUA, writer, humanities educator; b. Ogidi, Nigeria, Nov. 16, 1930; s. Isaiah Okafo and Janet N. (Iloegbunam) A.; m. Christie Chinwe Okoli, Sept. 10, 1961; children: Chinelo, Ikechukwu, Chidi, Nwando. Student, Univ. Coll., Ibadan, Nigeria, 1948—52; BA, U. London, 1953; DLitt (hon.), Dartmouth Coll., 1972; DUniv, Stirling U., Scotland, 1975; DLitt (hon.), U. Southampton, Eng., 1975; LLD (hon.), U. Prince Edward Isl., Can., 1976; LHD (hon.), U. Mass., 1977; DLitt (hon.), U. Ife, Nigeria, 1978, U. Nigeria, Nsukka, 1981, U. Kent, Canterbury, Eng., 1982, Mt. Allison U., Sackville, Can., 1984, U. Guelph, Can., 1984, Franklin Pierce Coll., 1985, Ibadan U., 1989; DUniv, Open U., Eng., 1989; LLD (hon.), Georgetown U., 1990, Port Harcourt U., Nigeria, 1991; DLitt (hon.), Skidmore Coll., 1991, CCNY, 1992, Fitchburg State Coll., 1994; DLitt, Harvard U., 1996, Binghamton U., 1996, Bates Coll., 1996, Fairleigh Dickinson U., 2002; LHD (hon.), Westfield Coll., 1989, New Sch. for Social Rsch., 1991, Hobart and William Smith Coll., 1991; LHD, Marymount Manhattan Coll., 1991; LHD (hon.), Colgate U., 1993; DLitt, Syracuse U., 1997, Trinity Coll., 1999, Ohio Wesleyan U., 1999, U. Witwatersrand, South Africa, 2000; LHD, Cape Town U., South Africa, 2002; DLitt, Haverford Coll., 2001; DLitt (hon.), Toronto U., 2006, Sokoto U., Nigeria, 2006. Prodr., contr., dir. Nigerian Broadcasting Co., Lagos, 1954-66; sr. rsch. fellow in African studies U. Nigeria, 1967-72, prof. dept. English, 1976-81, emeritus prof., 1985—. Vis. prof. English U. Mass., Amherst, 1972-75, U. Conn, Storrs, 1975-76, Afro-Am. studies U. Mass., Amherst, 1987-88; pro-chancellor Anambra State U. Tech., Enugu, Nigeria, 1986-88; Regent's lectr. UCLA, 1984; dir. Heinemann Ednl. Books (Nigeria) Ltd.; vis. fellow and Ashby lectr. Clare Hall, Cambridge (Eng.) U., 1993. Author: (novels) Things Fall Apart, 1958, No Longer at Ease, 1960, Arrow of God, 1964, A Man of the People, 1966, Anthills of the Savannah, 1988; (poetry) Christmas in Biafra, 1975, Collected Poems, 2004; (short stories) Girls at War, 1972; (essays) Morning Yet on Creation Day, 1975; The Trouble with Nigeria, 1983, Hopes and Impediments-Selected Essays, 1965-87, 1988; (essay and poems) Another Africa, 1998; (non-fiction) Home and Exile, 2000, (children's stories) The Flute, 1978, The Drum 1978. Mem. com. Lagos (Nigeria) U., 1966; mem. East Ctrl. State Libr. Bd., 1971-72, Anambra State Arts Coun., 1977-79; Goodwill amb. UN Population Fund, 1998-06. Recipient Lit. award New Statesman, 1965, Commonwealth Poetry prize, 1973, Nat. Creativity award Nigeria, 1999, St. Louis Lit. award 1999, Man Booker Internat. prize, 2007; Rockefeller fellow, 1960-61; UNESCO fellow, 1963. Friedenspreis (Peace Prize) Germany, 2002, Man Booker Internat. prize, 2007. Fellow: MLA (hon.), Nigerian Acad. Letters, Royal Soc. Lit. (hon.); mem.: Royal African Soc. (v.p. London 1998), Nonino Risit D'Aur, Am. Acad. Arts and Scis. Office: Bard Coll Dept Lang and Lit Annandale On Hudson NY 12504

ACHELPOHL, STEVEN EDWARD, lawyer; b. Wichita, Kans., July 15, 1950; s. Ray Edward and Juanita J. (Barnes) A.; m. Shelley R. Kiel (div. Sept. 1987); m. Sara K. Nabity, Nov. 24, 1989; children: Joseph E., Samuel B., Raechel A., Ryan Sullivan, Peter Sullivan. BA, U. Nebr., 1972, JD with distinction, 1975. Bar: Nebr. 1975, US Dist. Ct. Nebr. 1975, US Ct. Appeals (8th cir.) 1981. Law clk. hon. Donald R. Ross US Ct. Appeals (8th cir.), 1975-77; atty. McGrath, North, O'Mally, Kratz, Omaha, 1977-80, Dwyer, O'Leary & Martin, Omaha, 1980-83; ptnr. Schumacher & Achelpohl, Omaha, 1983-92, Smith Peterson, Omaha, 1992-93; pvt. practice Omaha, 1994—. Mem. Dem. Nat. Com., 2001—; chair Neb. Dem. Party, 2001—. Recipient Robert M. Spire Pub. Svc. award, Omaha Bar Assn., 2006. Fellow: Neb. State Bar Found., Am. Coll. Trial Lawyers. Avocations: golf, baseball, politics. Home: 6420 Underwood Ave Omaha NE 68132-1812 Office: 1823 Harney St Ste 1010 Omaha NE 68102-1900 Office Phone: 402-346-1900. Personal E-mail: achelpohl@usa.net.

ACHENBACH, JAN DREWES, engineering scientist; b. Leeuwarden, Netherlands, Aug. 20, 1935; arrived in U.S., 1959, naturalized, 1978; s. Johannes and Elizabeth (Schipper) Achenbach; m. Marcia Graham Fee, July 15, 1961. Candidate engr., Tech. U. Delft, 1959; PhD, Stanford U., Calif., 1962. Preceptor Columbia U., 1962-63; asst. prof. Northwestern U., Evanston, Ill., 1963, assoc. prof., 1966-69, prof. dept. civil engring., 1969—, Walter P. Murphy prof. civil engring., mech. engring. and applied math., 1981—, dir. Ctr. for Quality Engring. and Failure Prevention, 1986—2006; vis. assoc. prof. U. Calif., San Diego, 1969; vis. prof. Tech. U. Delft, 1970-71; prof. Huazhong Inst. Sci. and Tech., 1981. Mem. at large US Nat. Com. Theoretical and Applied Mechanics, 1972—78, 1986—. Author: Wave Propagation in Elastic Solids, 1973, A Theory of Elasticity with Microstructure for Directionally Reinforced Composites, 1975; author: (with A. K. Gautesen and H. McMaken) Ray Methods for Waves in Elastic Solids, 1982; author: (with Y. Rajapakse) Solid Mechanics Research for Quantitative Non-Destructive Evaluation, 1987, Reciprocity in Elastodynamics, 2004; editor (with J. Miklowitz): Modern Problems in Elastic Wave Propagation, 1978; editor: (with S. K. Datta and Y. S. Rajapakse) Elastic Waves and Ultrasonic Nondestructive Testing, 1990; editor-in-chief: Wave Motion, 1979—. Named to Tempo All-Prof. Team Scis., Chgo. Tribune, 1993; recipient award, C. Gelderman Found., 1970, C. W. McGraw Rsch. award, Am. Soc. Engring. Edn., 1975, Model of Excellence award, McDonnell-Douglas, 1996, DSM, Am. Acad. Mechanics, 1997, Nat. medal Tech., 2003, Ultrasonics Lifetime Achievement award, SPIE, 2005, 2005 Nat. Medal Sci., NSF, 2007. Fellow: AAAS, ASME (hon. Timoshenko medal 1992), Soc. Engring. Sci., Acoustical Soc. Am., Soc. Engring. Sci. (Prager medal 2001), Am. Acad. Arts Scis.; mem.: Am. Soc. Nondestructive Testing (Tutorial citation 2004), US Nat. Acad. Engring., Royal Dutch Acad. Scis. (corr.), US Nat. Acad. Scis. Home: 711 Roslyn Ter Evanston IL 60201-1721 Office: Northwestern U Room 324 2137 N Sheridan Catalysis Bldg Evanston IL 60208 Office Phone: 847-491-5527. Business E-Mail: achenbach@northwestern.edu.

ACHENBAUM, ALVIN ALLEN, marketing and management consultant; b. NYC, Dec. 11, 1925; s. Benjamin and Dora (Dworin) A.; m. Barbara Ann Greenwald, June 24, 1951 (dec. Apr. 1992); children: Jonathan Peter, Lisa Jane, Martha Beth; m. Leila Lebendig, June 6, 1993. BS, UCLA, 1950; MS, Columbia U., 1951. Mgr. market rsch. McCann-Erickson, NYC, 1951-57; exec. v.p., sec., dir. Grey Advt., Inc., NYC, 1957-71; exec. v.p. J. Walter Thompson Co., 1971-74; chmn. bd. dirs. Canter, Achenbaum, Assocs., Inc., NYC, 1974-89; vice chmn. bd. dirs. Backer, Spielvogel, Bates Worldwide, NYC, 1989-93; pres. Achenbaum Assocs. Inc., NYC, 1992-95; chmn. Achenbaum Bogda Assocs. Inc., NYC, 1996—. Bd. dirs. MARC, Inc. Mem. edit. bd. Jour. Advt. Rsch. Mem. Citizens Adv. Com. of Irvington, 1970—; mem. Middle Eastern affairs com. Anti-Defamation League; adv. com. Assn. Consumer Research.; Trustee Mktg. Sci. Inst.; Am. Mktg. Assn. Found.; editl. bd. Mktg. Mgmt. Mag. Named to Market Research Hall of Fame. Mem. Market Rsch. Coun. N.Y., Copy Rsch. Coun. N.Y., Am. Mktg. Assn. (v.p. global mktg. div., bd. dirs., found. trustee), Am. Econ. Assn., Assn. Pub. Opinion Rsch., Beta Gamma Sigma. Home: 225 Central Park W New York NY 10024-6026 Office: Achenbaum Bogda Assocs Inc 225 Central Park W Apt 723 New York NY 10024-6033 Home Phone: 212-787-9444; Office Phone: 212-579-3333. Business E-Mail: al@abaconsulting.com. E-mail: alvinache@aol.com.

ACHENBAUM, W(ILBERT) ANDREW, historian, gerontologist; b. Phila., Mar. 2, 1947; s. Wilbert Andrew and Muriel Maine Achenbaum; children: Emily Schieve, Laura Schieve. BA, Amherst Coll., Mass., 1968; MA, U. Pa., Phila., 1970; PhD, U. Mich., Ann Arbor, 1976. Asst. prof. history Canisius Coll., Buffalo, 1976—80; asst. to prof. of history Carnegie Mellon U., Pitts., 1980—87; prof. history U. Mich., Ann Arbor, 1987—99; prof. history and social work U. Houston, 2002—. Assoc. v.p. for academic affairs Carnegie Mellon U., Pitts., 1984—87; dep. dir., inst. of gerontology U. Mich., Ann Arbor, 1989—99; dean, coll. of liberal arts and social sciences U. Houston, 1999—2002; adj. prof. U. Tex. Health Sci. Ctr., Houston, 2005—. Author: (books on hist. gerontology) Old Age in the New Land, 1978, Shades of Gray, 1983, Social Security, 1986, Crossing Frontiers: Gerontology Becomes a Science, 1995, Older Americans, Vital Communities, 2005; editor: Pub. Policy and Aging e-Newsletter, 2007. Mem. Interfaith Ministries, Houston, 2005—07; mem. planning com. Alzheimer's Assn., Houston, 2004—07; chair Ctr., Christ Ch. Cathedral; chair and leadership coun. Nat. Coun. on the Aging, Washington, 1993—2007; sec., policy chair Gerontol. Soc. of Am., Washington, 2001—07; academic Holocaust Mus., Houston, 2001—07. Sgt. US Army, 1970—72. Named Outstanding Educator of Yr., Mich., 1992, Gerontological Profl. Yr., Houston, 2006. Fellow: Assn. Gerontology in Higher Edn.; mem.: Nat. Coun. Aging, Am. Soc. Aging, Houston Philosophical Soc. Democrat. Episcopalian. Home: 425 Westmoreland St Houston TX 77006 Office: Grad Coll Social Work Univ of Houston Houston TX 77204 Business E-Mail: achenbaum@uh.edu.

ACHESON, ALLEN MORROW, retired engineering executive; b. Tanta, Egypt, June 12, 1926; s. Samuel Irvine and Hazel Lenore (Welker) A.; m. Mary Jean Baird, Aug. 5, 1950 (div. May 1978); children: Rebecca R., Jennifer E., Scott A., Jon M. BS in Mech. Engring., Iowa State U., Ames, 1950; LLD, Tarkio Coll., 1985. Registered profl. engr., Mo. Sta. supt. Iowa Pub. Svc. Co., Carroll, 1950—54; engr. Proctor & Gamble Co., 1954—55, Iowa-Ill. Gas & Electric Co., 1955—56; mgr. City Power & Light Co., Independence, Mo., 1956—60; mgmt. adviser Yanhee Electricity Authority, Bangkok, 1960—63; exec. v.p. Black & Veatch Internat., Kansas City, Mo., 1964—73, pres., 1973—88, chmn., 1989—91; gen. ptnr. Black & Veatch, Kansas City, 1974—75, exec. ptnr., 1975—91; ret., 1991. Trustee Tarkio (Mo.) Coll., 1964-77, chmn., 1975-77; elder Trinity and Rolling Hills Presbyn. Ch. With USNR, 1944-46. Recipient Profl. Achievement citation Coll. Engring., Iowa State U., 1976, Marston Gold medal, 1992. Mem. Am. Cons. Engrs. Coun. (chmn. internat. engring. divsn., past pres. award 1992); mem. ASME (life). Home: 224 W 124th St Kansas City MO 64145-1704 Personal E-mail: aacheson@hotmail.com.

ACHESON, AMY J., lawyer; b. Pitts., July 16, 1963; d. Willard Phillips and Patricia Louise (Marshall) A. BA, Haverford Coll., 1984; JD cum laude, U. S.C., 1987. Bar: Pa. 1987, U.S. Dist. Ct. (we. dist.) Pa. 1987, U.S. Ct. Appeals (10th cir.) 1989, U.S. Ct. Appeals (3d cir.) 1988, U.S. Ct. Appeals (4th cir.) 1993. Atty. Reed, Smith, Shaw & McClay, Pitts., 1987—95; shareholder Berger Law Firm, Pitts., 1995—99; of counsel Ogg, Jones, Cordes & Ignelzi, Pitts., 1999—2005; pvt. practice, 2006—. Mem. S.C. Law Rev., 1985-87. Fin. officer Ret. Sr. Vol. Program Allegheny County, Pitts., 1990-91; treas. Parents League for Emotional Adjustments, Pitts., 1990-91; mem. adv. bd. Pa. Dept. Correction, Community Svc. Ctr. No. 1, Pitts., 1990-97; bd. mgrs. The Woodwell, Pitts., 1992-97, v.p., 1998-2000; bd. dirs. Presbyn. Seniorcare Network, Inc., 2000—; bd. trustees Shadyside Presbyn. Ch. Nursery Sch., 2001-03. Mem. ABA (jud. adminstrn. div. com., chmn. subcom. on discipline of fed. judges, 1990-91), ATLA (life mem.), Allegheny County Bar Assn. (young lawyers sect. coun. 1990-91), Order of the Coif, Order of the Wig and Robe. Office: One Oxford Centre Ste 4300 Pittsburgh PA 15219 Office Phone: 412-255-3739. Personal E-mail: amyacheson@aol.com.

ACHESON, DAVID CAMPION, retired lawyer, policy analyst, writer; b. Washington, Nov. 4, 1921; s. Dean G. and Alice (Stanley) Acheson; m. Patricia Castles, May 1, 1943 (dec. 2000); children: Eleanor Dean, David Campion, Peter Wesley. BA, Yale U., 1942; LLB, Harvard U., 1948. Bar: DC, Pa., U.S. Supreme Ct. With Office Gen. Counsel AEC, 1948—49; with firm Covington & Burling, Washington, 1950—61, mem. firm, 1958—61; US atty. Washington, 1961—65; spl. asst. to sec. treasury, 1965—67; v.p., sr. v.p., gen. counsel Comm. Satellite Corp., 1967—74; ptnr. Jones, Day, Reavis & Pogue, Washington, 1974—78, Drinker Biddle & Reath, Phila., Washington, 1978—87. Author (with others): Effective Washington Representation, 1983, Acheson Country: A Memoir, 1993; co-author (CSIS report): A More Effective Civil Space Program, 1988; editor: This Vast External Realm, 1973; editor: (with David McLellan) Among Friends, 1980. Mem. presdl. commn. on Challenger accident, 1986; pres. Atlantic Coun. U.S., 1993—99. Mem.: Met. Club. Episcopalian. Home: 2700 Calvert St NW Washington DC 20008-2621 Personal E-mail: dcampach@aol.com.

ACHI, MAY IFEOMA, pharmacist, consultant; d. Peter Uche and Chinyere Pricilla Achi. PharmD, U. Scis., Phila., 1997—2003. Cert. advance cardiac life support Am. Heart Assn., 2005, pharmacotheray specialist Bd. Pharm. Specialties, 2006. Pharmacy practice resident Christiana Care Hosp., Newark, Del., 2003—04; cardiovasc. pharmacotherapy resident U. Scis., 2004—05; clin. pharmacy cardiology specialist Meth. Hosp., Houston, 2005—. Clin. pharmacy cons. Machie, Inc., Houston, 2006—. Partnership patron Christian Children's Fund, 2002. Recipient Florence Fisherman award, CC Phila., 1998, All Am. Basketball award, 1999. Mem.: Am. Coll. Clin. Pharmacy, Am. Soc. Health-Sys. Pharmacy. Avocations: dance, sports, travel, fashion design, movies. Home Phone: 215-760-4418.

ACHINSTEIN, PETER JACOB, philosopher, educator; b. NYC, June 30, 1935; s. Asher and Betty (Comras) A.; children: Jonathan, Sharon, Betty, married L. Suzanne Brown, June 16, 2005. AB, Harvard, 1956, AM, 1958, PhD, 1961; postgrad. (Knox Traveling fellow), Oxford U., Eng., 1959-60. Asst. prof. U. Iowa, Iowa City, 1961-62; asst. prof. philosophy Johns Hopkins Balt., 1962-64; asso. prof., 1964-68; prof., 1968—; chmn. dept. philosophy, 1968-77; vis. prof. M.I.T., Cambridge, 1965-66, Stanford (Calif.) U., 1967, City U. N.Y., 1973; mem. adv. panel NSF, 1968-70, 79-81; Lady Davis vis. prof. Hebrew U., Jerusalem, spring 1976. Author: Concepts of Science, 1968, Law and Explanation, 1971, The Nature of Explanation, 1983, Particles and Waves: Historical Essays in the Philosophy of Science, 1991 (Lakatos award 1993); The Book of Evidence, 2001; editor: (with Stephen Barker) The Legacy of Logical Positivism, 1969, The Concept of Evidence, 1983, (with Laura J. Snyder) Scientific Methods, 1994; Science Rules, 2004, Scientific Evidence, 2005; mem. editl. bd. Philosophy of Sci., 1973-2000. Guggenheim fellow, 1966-67 Fellow AAAS (chair history and philosophy of sci. sect. L 1995); mem. Philosophy of Sci. Assn. (bd. govs.), Internat. Union History and Philosophy (del. U.S. 1967-73, 79-86), Phi Beta Kappa. Office: Johns Hopkins U Dept Philosophy Baltimore MD 21218 E-mail: peter.achinstein@jhu.edu.

ACHOLONU, WILFRED W., JR., clinical pharmacy specialist, educator; b. Owerri, Imo, Nigeria, July 18, 1953; arrived in U.S., 1974; s. Wilfred W. and Esther Rose Acholonu; m. Ezioma G. Onwuchekwa, May 25, 1991; children: Ikenna Colin, Ezioge Celest. BS in Pharmacy, Oreg. State U., 1980, MS in Pharmacology and Toxicology, 1984; PharmD, U. Fla., 1994. Cert. Bd. Pharm. Spltys. Resident hosp. pharm. VA Med. Ctr., Portland, Oreg., 1983—84; staff pharmacist Olin E. Teague VA Med. Ctr., Temple, Tex., 1984—89, VA Med. Ctr., Gainesville, Fla., 1989—94; assoc. clin. prof. pharmacy practice U. Fla., Gainesville, 1996—; clin. pharmacy specialist VA Med. Ctr., Gainesville, 1994—. Mem. PET com. VA Med. Ctr., Gainesville. Contbr. articles to profl. jours. Mem.: Am. Soc. Health Sys. Pharmacists, Am. Coll. Clin. Pharmacy, Coll. Psychiatric and Neurologic Pharmacists. Avocations: tennis, racquetball, basketball. Office: North Fla/South Ga VHS 1601 SW Archer Rd Gainesville FL 32608 Office Phone: 352-376-1611 ext. 6459. E-mail: wilfred.acholonu@med.va.gov.

ACHON, RAQUEL ANDREA, music educator, consultant; b. Ctrl. Preston, Cuba, May 5, 1927; arrived in U.S., 1947; d. Crescencio Gutierrez and Basilisa Semorile; m. David Achon, Dec. 25, 1957; 1 child, David. BA, Instituto Santiago, 1947; diploma, Martin Coll., 1949; BS in Arts, Peabody Coll., 1951. Pvt. music tchr., Downey, Calif., 1968—. Cons. in field. Editor: Celebrenos II, 1983, El Himnario, 1998, 1999. Pianist Crusader's Class, 2004; vice-chair, editor United Meth. Hymnal, 1989; pianist Downey (Calif.) United Meth. Ch., 1995. Named to Hall of Fame, Am. Coll. Musicians, 1990. Mem.: Am. Coll. Musicians. Republican. Methodist. Avocations: collecting angels, collecting boxes. Home: 12029 Gurley Ave Downey CA 90242

ACHORD, JAMES LEE, retired gastroenterologist; b. Dayton, Ohio, Sept. 24, 1931; s. Lonnie M. and Ethel E. (Collins) A.; m. Patsy Jane Moore, Dec. 18, 1954; children: J. Michael, Ann Elizabeth, Andrew P. DMD, Emory U., 1952, MD, 1956. Intern Emory Hosp., 1956-57; resident Emory U., Atlanta, 1959-62, instr., assoc. prof., 1962-71; med. dir. Med. Ctr. Cen. Ga., Macon, 1971-75; assoc. dean, prof. East Tenn. State Sch. Medicine, Johnson City, 1975-76; prof., dir. div. digestive diseases U. Miss. Med. Ctr., Jackson, 1976-98, prof. emeritus, 1998. Editor book revs. Am. Jour. Gastroenterology, 1985-91, Dig. Dis. Sci., 1994-96; mem. editl. bd. Am. Jour. Clin. Gastroenterology, 1999—; contbr. numerous articles and edits. to profl. jours. and chpts. to books. Capt. U.S. Army, 1957-59. Master ACP (gov. Miss. chpt. 1993-97), Am. Coll. Gastroenterology (pres. 1983-84), Am. Soc. Gastroenterologic Endoscopy; mem. Am. Assn. Study Liver Disease, Am. Gastroent. Assn.

ACHORN, ROBERT COMEY, retired newspaper publisher; b. Westboro, Mass., Mar. 31, 1922; s. Edward Welt and Mabel (Comey) A.; m. Jean Mary Berlo, Sept. 23, 1950 (dec. 1980); children: Nancy Louise (Mrs. Eric Engberg), Susan Jean, Edward Christopher, Judith Joyce (Mrs. Albert Berry), Carole Lee (Mrs. Ralph Abislaiman); m. Ann Bouvier, Aug. 20, 1982. AB, Brown U., 1943. Reporter Worcester (Mass.) Telegram, 1946-53; editorial writer Evening Gazette, Worcester, 1953-60, mng. editor, 1964-67; editor editorial pages Worcester Telegram & Gazette, 1964-67, assoc. editor, 1967-70, editor, 1970-73, v.p., editor, 1973-81, assoc. pub., exec. v.p., 1981-82, pub., 1982-87, dir., 1982-88, pres., 1986-87, Beacon Communications Corp., 1984-85, vice chmn., 1985-87; pres. Worcester Telegram & Gazette, Inc., 1985-87. Bd. dirs. Blackstone Valley Regional Devel. Corp., 1991-95; mem. newspaper adv. bd. UPI, 1974-78. Pres. United Way of Ctrl. Mass., Worcester, 1973—75; v.p. The Meml. Hosp., 1976; vice chmn. Ctrl. Mass. chpt. ARC, 1976—84, chmn., 1984—86; media chmn. Mass. Bar-Press Com., 1976—77; chmn. trustees Worcester Found. Exptl. Biology, 1984—87; trustee Old Sturbridge Village, 1986—2001, hon. trustee, 2001—; trustee U. Mass. Med. Ctr. Found., 1991—2002, Sutton Coun. on Aging, 1993—99, U. Mass. Meml. Found., 1998—2002. Fellow Acad. New Eng. Journalists; mem. UPI New Eng. Newspaper Editors (pres. 1969), Am. Soc. Newspaper Editors, New Eng. Newspaper Assn. (pres. 1986-87), New Eng. Soc. Newspaper Editors (pres. 1968), New Eng. AP News Execs. Assn. (pres. 1971), Am. Antiquarian Soc., Soc. Profl. Journalists, Worcester Club, Worcester Econ. Club (pres. 1975), Bohemian Club, Nat. Press Club, St. Wulstan Soc., Worcester Torch Club, Phi Beta Kappa.

ACHUFF, STEPHEN CHARLES, cardiologist; b. St. Louis, Mar. 12, 1943; m. Cary Williams Lipscomb, Dec. 27, 1970; children: Catherine Elise, Jeanne Ann, Charles Walter. BA in Religion, Philosophy, Wesleyan U., 1964; MD, U. Mo., 1969. Diplomate Am. Bd. Internal Medicine, Am. Bd. Cardiovasc., Am. Bd. Med. Examiners. Intern, jr. asst. resident John Hopkins Hosp., 1969-71, fellow medicine, 1971-73, chief resident medicine, 1973-74, asst. dir. Adult Cardia Catheterization Lab., 1975-77, cardiologist Lipid Rsch. Clinic, 1975-84, dir. Adult Cardiology Clin. Program, 1980—2000; instr. medicine John Hopkins U., 1973-74, from asst. prof. to assoc. prof., 1975-90, prof. medicine, 1990—. Rsch. fellow Am. Heart Assn., 1971-73; rsch. fellow, hon. sr. registrar dept. cardiology Royal Infirmary Edinburgh, Scotland, 1974-75; mem. adv. bd. John Hopkins U., 1979-80, Pinnaclecare; vis. prof. Guy's Hosp., London, 1990. Mem. editl. bd. Audiovisual Programs Continuing Edn., John Hopkins U.,

1976-92; contbr. articles to profl. jours. Recipient Oustanding Grad. award Mo. State Med. Assn., 1969, Pfizer award U. Mo., 1968; USPHS fellow U. Mo., 1966-67. Fellow Am. Coll. Cardiology, Am. Heart Assn. (mem. coun. clin. cardiology 1979, v.p., bd. dirs. 1979-80); mem. Internat. Soc. Heart Tranplantation, Alpha Omega Alpha. Office: Cardiology Johns Hopkins Hosp 600 N Wolfe St Baltimore MD 21287 Office Phone: 410-955-7670. Business E-Mail: sachuff@jhmi.edu.*

ACKER, ALAN SCOTT, lawyer; b. Chgo., Mar. 14, 1953; s. Isreal and Loretta (Alter) A.; m. Lillian Grace Kacyn, Aug. 12, 1973; children: Steven, Kenneth, Jennifer, Daniel. BS, U. Ill., 1974; JD, Chgo.-Kent Coll. Law, 1977. Bar: Ill. 1977, Va. 1986, Ohio 1990. 2nd v.p. AM. Nat. and Trust Co., Chgo., 1978-81; assoc. Reuben & Procter, Chgo., 1981-86, Hofheimer, Nusbaum, McPhaul & Samuels, Norfolk, Va.; ptnr. Schottenstein, Zox & Dunn, Columbus, Ohio; sole practice atty. Columbus. Adj. prof. law DePaul U., Chgo., 1984-85; adj. prof. income taxation of trusts and estates, Capital Law Sch., Columbus, Ohio, 1992-2003. Contbr. articles to profl. jours. Named one of Top 100 Attys., Worth mag., 2005. Fellow Am. Coll. Trusts and Estates Counsel; mem. ABA, Ill. State Bar Assn., Chgo. Bar Assn. (David C. Hilliard award 1985), Va. Bar Assn., Norfolk-Portsmouth Bar Assn., Tidewater Estate Planning Coun., Va. CPA Soc., AICPA, Ill. CPA Soc., Columbus Bar Assn., Ohio State Bar Assn., Ohio Soc. CPA. Jewish. Office: 145 E Rich St 4th Fl Columbus OH 43215 Office Phone: 614-220-8877. Office Fax: 614-220-8876. E-mail: alansacker@aol.com.*

ACKER, ANN E., lawyer; b. Chgo., July 21, 1948; BA magna cum laude, St. Mary's Coll., 1970; JD cum laude, Loyola U., 1973. Bar: Ill. 1973. Asst. corp. counsel City of Chgo.; partner Chapman and Cutler, Chgo. Fellow: Am. Bar Found.; mem.: Nat. Assoc. of Bond Lawyers, Chicago Bar Assoc., Amer. Bar Assoc. Office: Chapman and Cutler 111 W Monroe St Ste 1700 Chicago IL 60603-4006 Office Phone: 312-845-3710. Office Fax: 312-701-2361. Business E-Mail: acker@chapman.com.

ACKER, FREDERICK GEORGE, lawyer; b. Defiance, Ohio, May 7, 1934; s. Julius William and Orah Louise (Dowler) A.; m. Cynthia Ann Wayne, Dec. 1, 1962; children: Frederick Wayne, Mary Katherine, Richard Hoghton, Jennifer Ruth. Student, Ind. U., 1952-54; BA, Valparaiso U., 1956; MA, Harvard U., 1957, JD, 1961; postgrad., U. Manchester, Eng., 1957-58. Bar: Ill. 1961, Ind. 1961. Ptnr. Winston & Strawn, Chgo., 1961-88, McDermott, Will & Emery, Chgo., 1988—2003, counsel, 2003—. Co-chmn. Joint Prin. and Income Act. com., Chgo., 1976-81. Co-author: (portfolio) Generation-Skipping Tax, 1991; contbr. articles to profl. jours. Bd. dirs. Max McGraw Wildlife Found., Dundee, Ill., 1984-03, chmn., pres. 1997-01; trustee L.S. Wood Ednl. Trust, Chgo., 1975—, Ill. chpt. The Nature Conservancy, Chgo., 1981-90, chmn., 1986-90. Danforth Found. fellow, 1956; Fulbright scholar, 1957. Mem. Trout Unlimited, Fulbright Assn. (bd. dirs. 1994-2000, pres. 2000), Met. Chgo. Club, Anglers Club, Coleman Lake Club. Lutheran. Avocations: hunting, fishing. Home: 543 N Madison St Hinsdale IL 60521-3213 Office: McDermott Will & Emery 227 W Monroe St Ste 3100 Chicago IL 60606-5096

ACKER, LOREN CALVIN, medical products executive; b. Lamar, Colo., Mar. 3, 1934; s. John C. and Ada M. (Ecton) Acker; m. Judy N. Willms, Sept. 17, 1955 (dec. Oct. 1968); children: Cheryl Acker Hoge, Keith B., Karen Acker Kime; m. Darla S. Copeland, July 24, 1976. BSME, Fresno State Coll., 1956; cert. in bus. and mgmt., U. Calif., Berkeley, 1961; MBA, U. Santa Clara, 1966. Flight test NASA, Edwards, Calif., 1954-56; engring. mgr. Westinghouse, Sunnyvale, Calif., 1956—68; engring. mgr., assoc. dir. Kitt Peak Nat. Obs., Assn. U. Rsch. in Astronomy, Ariz., 1968—73; founder, bd. dirs. Engr. & Rsch. Assocs., Inc. (Sebra), Tucson, 1973—. Founder Winged Foot Assocs., Tucson, 1974—, ERA LLC, Tucson, 1999, WoofSpa and Resort, NYC, 2003, Electrophysiology LLC, Tucson, 2000; co-founder NYPA Inc., Tucson, 1986, Acker Mgmt. Group LLC, Tucson, 2006. Chmn. pk. and recreation City of Cupertino, Calif., 1968; founder, mem. So. Ariz. Leadership Coun., 1997—; bd. dirs. Sonoran Sea Aquarium, 1999—; chmn. bioindustry Greater Tucson Econ. Coun., 1994—99; mem. master engring. Ariz. U./Indsl. Partnership, 2000—06; mem. agrl. and biosystem coun. U. Ariz., 1999—. Entrepreneurial fellow, U. Ariz., 1999. Mem.: Internat. Soc. Cellular Therapy, Am. Soc. Apherises, Am. Assn. Blood Banks, Audubon Soc., Nature Conservancy, Sierra Club. Republican. Achievements include patents in field. Avocations: skiing, tennis. Home: 4831 E Winged Foot Pl Tucson AZ 85718-1727 Office: 100 N Tucson Blvd Tucson AZ 85716-4740

ACKER, MARTIN HERBERT, psychotherapist, educator; b. NYC, Dec. 15, 1921; s. Irving and Rose Martha (Katz) A.; m. Joan Elise Robinson, Apr. 29, 1948; children— Michael Christopher, David, Jonathon, Steven Anthony; m. Julia Ann Payne, Feb. 14, 1976 PhD, NYU, 1963. Lic. psychologist, Oreg. Prof. counseling and psychology U. Oreg., Eugene, 1961-86, prof. emeritus, 1986—, chmn. counseling, 1963-68. Vis. prof. Fed. City Coll., Washington, 1968-69, U. Victoria, B.C., Can., 1974, Fredrich Karls U., Tübingen, Germany, 1987; psychotherapist, Eugene, 1974—; dir. BeBusk Meml. Clinic, 1983-85. Mem. adv. com. Lane County Adult Corrections; bd. dirs. Lane Mental Health Assn., Pearl Buck Ctr.; mem. budget com. Sch. Dist. 4J, Eugene, 1994—. Mem. Am. Pers. and Guidance Assn. (bd. dirs. 1967-68), Soc. Sci. Study Sex, Oreg. Psychol. Assn. (chair 1995, dir. northwest men's symposium 1990-93), Am. Rehab. Counselors Assn. (pres. 1968-69), Men's Studies Assn. (co-chair 1986-90), Lane County Psychologists Assn. (pres. 1985-86), Friars Club. Home: 2733 Kismet Way Eugene OR 97405-1284 E-mail: macker@comcast.net.

ACKER, MICHAEL A., thoracic surgeon, educator; b. Phila., May 15, 1956; MD, Brown U., 1981. Cert. Thoracic Surgery. Intern, surgery U. Pa. Hosp., 1981—82, resident, cardiothoracic surgery, 1982—88, attending, thoracic cardiological surgery, 1993, surgical dir. cardio transplant prog., 1994, asst. prof., surgery, 1993, asst. prof., 1997; resident, cardiac surgery John Hopkins Hosp., Balt., 1988—91; attending, cardiac surgery John Hopkins U. Med. Sch., Balt., 1991, asst. prof., surgery, 1991; attending, thoracic cardiological surgery Sinai Hosp., Balt., 1991—93; attending Vet. Affairs, Phila., 1994; chief, cardiac surgery divsn. U. Pa. Med. Ctr.; asst. instr. surgery U. Pa. Sch. Medicine, 1982—87, prof. surgery; lab. dir. U. Pa; dir. Heart Transplatation and Ventricular Assist Prog. Office: Hosp Univ Pa 3400 Spruce St 6 Silverstein Pavilion Philadelphia PA 19104 Address: Penn Presbyn Med Ctr Dept Surgery 39th & Market St 101 Medical Arts Building Philadelphia PA 19104 Office Phone: 215-349-8305, 215-662-9595. Office Fax: 215-349-5798, 215-243-3243. Business E-Mail: michael.acker@uphs.upenn.edu.

ACKER, ROBERT FLINT, retired microbiologist; b. Chgo., Aug. 24, 1920; s. Robert Booth and Mary (Flint) A.; m. Phyllis Catharine Fry, Jan. 2, 1948 (dec. Apr. 2005); children: Catharine Elizabeth, Barbara Fenner, Robert Macdonald, James Christopher; m. Helen Crawford Stephens, Apr. 8, 2006. BA, Ind. U., 1942, MA, 1947; PhD, Rutgers U., 1953. Asst. prof. Iowa State U., Ames, 1954-59; asst. chief cancer chemotherapy dept., chief quality control dept. Microbiol. Assocs., Inc., Bethesda, Md., 1959-61, chief dept. cell and media prodn., 1961-62; dir. microbiology program Office of Naval Research, Dept. Navy, Washington, 1962-69; dir. office of rsch. coord., asst. dean faculties for research, prof. biol. scis. Northwestern U., Evanston, Ill., 1969-74; exec. dir. Am. Soc. Microbiology, Washington, 1974-81, Nat. Found. Infectious Diseases, Bethesda, Md., 1981-86; pres. Bionox Corp., Tucson, 1985-92. Mem. bacteriology and mycology study sect. NIH, 1964. Author: (with R.R. Jennings) The Protistan Kingdom, 1970; editor: Proc. 24th Internat. Congress on Marine Corrosion and Fouling, 1972; editorial bd.: Applied Microbiology, 1962-73. V.p., bd. dirs. Iona House Sr. Svc. Ctr., Washington, 1978-79, pres., 1979-81; trustee Massanetta Conf. Ctr., 1983-86; bd. dirs. Am. Type Culture Collection, 1983-89; pres. Sunrise Mountain Ridge Homeowners Assn., 1994-95; bd. elders Potomac United Presbyn. Ch., Md., 1967-69, Winnetka (Ill.) Presbyn. Ch., 1972-74, Nat. Presbyn. Ch., Washington, 1983-86, St. Andrew's Presbyn. Ch., Tucson, 1989-91, 1998-2000. Eli Lilly & Co. postdoctoral fellow, 1953—54. Fellow Am. Acad. Microbiology, Soc. for Indsl. Microbiology (pres. 1986-87, Charles Porter award 2001); mem. Am. Soc. for Microbiology, Am. Inst. Biol. Sci. (coun. 1983-91), Cosmos Club. Personal E-mail: rfacker@msn.com.

ACKER, RODNEY, lawyer; b. Jacksonville, Tex., Sept. 29, 1949; s. Mike and Dorothy (Kennedy) Acker; m. Judy Bruyere, Sept. 2, 1972; children: Amy, Shelley, Rachel, Sam. BBA, U. Tex., Arlington, 1971; JD with honors, Tex. Tech, 1974. Bar: Tex. 1974, US Dist. Ct. No., So., Ea., We. Districts Tex., US Ct. Appeals 5th & 11th Circuits, US Supreme Ct.; cert. in civil trial law. Law clk. to Hon. Eldon Mahon, US Dist. Ct., Ft. Worth, 1974-76; assoc. Kendrick, Kendrick & Bradley, Dallas, 1976, Jenkens & Gilchrist, P.C., Dallas, 1976-79, ptnr., then shareholder, 1979—, mng. shareholder Dallas office; with Fulbright & Jaworski L.L.P., Dallas, 2007—. Fellow Am. Bar Found., Tex. Bar Found., Dallas Bar Found., Am. Coll. Trial Lawyers; mem. ABA, State Bar Tex., Dallas Bar Assn., Am. Bd. Trial Advocates, State Bar Coll., Patrick E. Higginbotham Am. Inns of Ct., Securities Industry Assn., Tex. Assn. Bank Counsel, Tex. Assn. Defense Counsel, Tex. Judicature Soc., Phi Delta Phi. Baptist. Office: Fulbright & Jaworski LLP 2200 Ross Ave Ste 2800 Dallas TX 75201 Office Phone: 214-855-7466. Office Fax: 214-855-8200. Business E-Mail: racker@fulbright.com.

ACKERLY, WENDY SAUNDERS, construction company executive; b. Chgo., July 23, 1960; d. Robert S. Jr. and Linda Ackerly. BS in Atmospheric Sci., U. Calif., Davis, 1982; postgrad., U. Nev., Reno, 1985. Programmer U. Calif, Davis, 1982-83; cons. software Tesco, Sacramento, 1983; software engr. Bently Nev. Corp., Minden, Nev., 1984-85; mgr. computer scis. Jensen Electric Co., Reno, 1985-86, software engr. Cameron Park, Calif., 1986-89; sr. engr. Aerojet, Sacramento, 1989-96, test ops. specialist, 1996-98; dir. design and devel. Kerry King Constrn., Inc., 1998—, sec.-treas., 1991—. Mem. Nat. Space Soc., Planetary Soc., U.S. Tennis Assn., Calif. Aggie Alumni Assn. Republican. Avocations: tennis, hiking, travel, piano. Office: PO Box 269 Rescue CA 95672-0269

ACKERMAN, ARLENE, education professor, former school system administrator; BA in Elem. Edn., Harris Stowe Tchrs. Coll.; MA in Ednl. Adminstrn. an dpolicy, Washington U.; MA in Edn., Harvard U., EdD in Adminstrn., Planning and Social Policy. Supt. Washington (D.C.) Pub. Schs., 1997—99, San Francisco United Sch. Dist., 1999—2005; Christian A. Johnson prof. Teachers Coll., Columbia Univ., NYC, 2006—. Bd. mem. WestEd Regional Edn. Lab., 2003—; mem. Bay Area Sch. Reform Collaboration; program advisor BROAD-Urban Supts. Acad. Trustee San Francisco Fine Arts; bd. govs. San Francisco Symphony; active San Francisco Workforce Investment Bd. Recipient Apple for the Tchr. award, Iota Lambda Sorority, Disting. Alumni award, Harris Stowe Tchrs. Coll.; McDonnell Douglas fellow. Mem.: ASCD, Presdl. Commn. on Hist. Black Colls. and Univs., Nat. Assn. Black Sch. Educators, Coun. of the Great City Schs. (chair), Am. Assn. Sch. Adminstrs., Phi Delta Kappa. Office: Teachers College 525 W 120th St New York NY 10027 Office Phone: 212-678-3715. Business E-Mail: ackerman@exchange.tc.columbia.edu.*

ACKERMAN, BRUCE ARNOLD, law educator; b. NYC, Aug. 19, 1943; s. Nathan and Jean (Rosenberg) A.; m. Susan Gould Rose, May 29, 1967; children: Sybil Rose, John Mill. BA summa cum laude, Harvard U., 1964; LLB with honors, Yale U., 1967. Bar: Pa. 1970. Law clk. US Ct. Appeals (2d cir.), New York, 1967-68; law clk. to assoc. justice John M. Harlan US Supreme Ct., Washington, 1968-69; prof. law and public policy analysis U. Pa., Phila., 1969-74; prof. law Yale U., New Haven, 1974-82, Sterling prof. law and polit. sci., 1987—; Beekman prof. law and philosophy Columbia U., NYC, 1982-87. Holmes lectr. Law Sch. Harvard U. Author: Private Property and the Constitution, 1977, Social Justice in the Liberal State, 1980 (Gavel award ABA), (with Hassler) Clean Coal/Dirty Air, 1981, Reconstructing American Law, 1984, We the People: Foundations, 1991, The Future of Liberal Revolution, 1992, (with Golove) Is NAFTA Constitutional?, 1995, We the People: Transformations, 1998, The Failure of the Founding Fathers: Jefferson, Marshall, and the Rise of Presidential Democracy, 2005, (with others) The Uncertain Search for Environmental Quality, 1974 (Henderson prize Harvard Law Sch.). Named Cmdr. French Order Merit Henry Phillips prize in Jurisprudence, Am. Philol. Soc.; Guggenheim fellow, 1985. Fellow Am. Acad. Arts and Scis.; mem. Am. Law Inst. Office: Yale U Law Sch PO Box 208215 New Haven CT 06520-8215

ACKERMAN, DAVID P., lawyer; b. Wilmington, Del., Feb. 22, 1957; BA with honors, Bucknell Univ., 1979; JD, George Washington Univ., 1982. Bar: Fla. 1983, US Dist. Ct. (so., no., middle dist. Fla.), US Ct. Appeals (11th cir.). Law clk. Judge James C. Paine, US Dist. Ct.; ptnr. Gunster Yoakley & Stewart, 1983—96; founding ptnr., bus. litigation Ackerman Link & Sartory, West Palm Beach, Fla., 1996—. Past chmn. Judicial Nominating Commn. for 15th Judicial Cir., Palm Beach County, Fla.; trustee, past pres. Legal Aid Soc., Palm Beach County, Fla. Contbr. articles to CLE publ. Named one of Fla. Legal Elite, Fla. Trend mag., 2004; recipient Pro Bono Svc award, Legal Aid Soc. Palm Beach County. Fellow: Am. Coll. Trial Lawyers; mem.: ABA, Fla. Bar (mem. exec. council Bus. Law sect.), Palm Beach County Bar Assn. Office: Ackerman Link & Sartory LLP Suite 1250 Esperante 220 Lakeview Ave West Palm Beach FL 33401 Office Phone: 561-838-4100. Office Fax: 561-838-5305. Business E-Mail: dackerman@alslaw.com.

ACKERMAN, DEBORAH, lawyer; b. Santa Monica, CA, 1950; children: Laura, Melissa. BA, So. Meth. U., 1972; JD, St. Mary's U., 1979. Ptnr. Oppenheimer, Rosenberg, Kelleher & Wheatley, 1979—87, Cauthorn & Tobin, 1987—88; asst. gen. counsel Southwest Airlines Co., Dallas, 1988—2001, v.p., gen. counsel, asst. sec., 2001—. Mem.: ABA. Office: Southwest Airlines Customer Rels PO Box 36647 1CR Dallas TX 75235-1647 also: Southwest Airlines 2702 Love Field Dr Dallas TX 75346 Office Phone: 214-792-4000. Office Fax: 214-792-5015.*

ACKERMAN, EUGENE, biophysics professor; b. Bklyn., July 8, 1920; s. Saul Benton and Dorothy (Salwen) A.; m. Dorothy Hopkirk, June 5, 1943; children— Francis H., Emmanuel T., Amy R. Ackerman de Canésie. BA, Swarthmore Coll., 1941; Sc.M., Brown U., 1943; PhD, U. Wis., 1949; postgrad., U. Pa., 1949-51, fellow, 1957-58. Instr. Brown U., 1943; from asst. prof. to prof. biophysics Pa. State U., 1951-60; mem. faculty U. Minn. Mayo Grad. Sch. Medicine, 1960-67, prof. biophysics, 1965-91, Hill Family Found. prof. biomed. computing, prof. biometry also computer scis. Mpls., 1967-79, prof. dept. lab. medicine and pathology, 1969-91, prof. emeritus, 1991—, dir. div. health computer sci., 1969-79; staff cons. biophysics Mayo Found. and Mayo Clinic, 1960-67; dir. computer facility Mayo Found., 1964-65. Cons. bioacoustics USAF, 1957-62; mem. epidemiology and biometry tng. com. NIH, 1963-67, spl. study sect. ultrasonic applications, 1965-67, spl. study sect. lab. med. scis., 1967-69, computer and biomath. sci. study sect., 1969-73; dir. nat. resource for simulation of stochastic micropopulation models, 1983-90 Author: Biophysical Science, 1962, (with L. Ellis and L. Williams), 2d edit., 1979; (with L. Gatewood) Math Models in the Health Sciences, 1979, (with L. Elveback and J. Fox) Infectious Disease: Simulation of Epidemics and Vaccination Strategies, 1984; editor Biophys. Jour., 1983-87; also articles, tech. reports, chpts. in books. Rsch. grantee Am. Cancer Soc., 1953-56, NSF, 1958-64, NIH, 1954-90 Mem. Biophys. Soc., Am. Physiol. Soc., Assn. Computing Machinery, IEEE, Phi Beta Kappa, Sigma Xi, Gamma Alpha. Mem. Soc. Of Friends. Home: 11301 Park Ridge Dr W Minnetonka MN 55305-2551 Office: U Minn Health Ctr Box 511 MMC 420 Delaware St SE Minneapolis MN 55455-0374 Business E-Mail: acker004@umn.edu.

ACKERMAN, FELICIA NIMUE, philosophy educator, writer; b. Bklyn., June 23, 1947; d. Arthur and Zelda (Sondack) A. AB summa cum laude, Cornell U., 1968; PhD, U. Mich., 1976. Asst. prof. philosophy Brown U., Providence, 1974-79, assoc. prof., 1979-91, prof., 1991—. Vis. asst. prof. philosophy UCLA, 1976; vis. hon. lectr. logic and metaphysics U. St. Andrews, Scotland, 1983; sr. Fulbright lectr. Hebrew U., 1985. Contbr. articles and short stories to various mags. Recipient O. Henry award for short story pub. in Prize Stories, 1990; fellow Ctr. for Advanced Study in Behavioral Scis., NEH, 1988-89. Mem. ACLU, NAACP (asst. sec. Providence br.), Am. Philos. Assn., Amnesty Internat. Office: Brown U Dept Philosophy PO Box 1918 Providence RI 02912-1918 Office Phone: 401-863-3240. Business E-Mail: felicia_ackerman@brown.edu.

ACKERMAN, GARY LEONARD, congressman; b. Bklyn., Nov. 19, 1942; s. Max and Eva (Barnett) Ackerman; m. Rita Tewel, May 27, 1967; children: Lauren Meredith, Corey Brian, Ari David. BA, CUNY Queens Coll., 1965; student, St. John's U., NY, 1966. Tchr. NYC Pub. Schs., 1965—70; founder, editor, pub. Queens Tribune, NY, 1970—89; owner Multi-Media Advt., Queens, 1972—78; mem. NY State Senate, 1979-83, US Congress from 5th NY dist., 1983—, mem. fin. svcs. com., mem. fgn. affairs com., chmn. subcommittee on the Mid. East and South Asia, chmn. Congl. caucus on India and Indian Ams. Recipient Loyalty award, Ministerial Coun. Race Rels., 1977, Edn. award, Nat. Conf. Christians and Jews, 1977, Friend of Farm Animals award, Farm Sanctuary, 2001. Mem. Queens Coll. Alumni Assn. Democrat. Jewish. Office: US House Reps 2243 Rayburn House Office Bldg Washington DC 20515-3205 Office Phone: 202-225-2601.*

ACKERMAN, GERALD MARTIN, art historian, consultant; b. Alameda, Calif., Aug. 21, 1928; s. Alois M. and Eva L. Ackerman. BA, U. Calif.-Berkeley, 1952; postgrad., U. Munich, Germany, 1955-58; PhD, Princeton U., 1964. Instr. Bryn Mawr Coll., Pa., 1960-64; asst. prof. Stanford U., Calif., 1964-70; assoc. prof. dept. art Pomona Coll., Claremont, Calif., 1970-75, prof., 1975-89, chmn. dept. art, 1972-82; prof. emeritus, 1989—. Fulbright prof. U. Leningrad, 1980; prof. Florence (Italy) Acad. Art, 1996—. Author: The Life and Work of J.L. Gerome, 1986, American Orientalists, 1994, Gerome, 2000, Les Orientalistes de l'Ecole britannique, 1991, The Barque-Gerome Drawing Course, 2003. Named Appleton eminent scholar, Fla. State U., 1994. Democrat. Home: 360 S Mills Ave Claremont CA 91711-5331 Office Phone: 909-626-6594. Personal E-mail: gackerman@pomona.edu.

ACKERMAN, JACK ROSSIN, investment banker; b. NYC, Feb. 8, 1931; s. Robert M. and Florence (Rossin) Ackerman; m. Dana Lowenthal, Nov. 29, 1974; children: Ellen, Jay, Robin, Bradley. BA, Harvard U., 1953, MBA, 1955. With Bache Halsey Stuart Shields, Inc., NYC, 1955-80; mng. dir. Drexel Burnham Lambert, Inc., NYC, 1980-88; pres. Bond Review Inc., NYC, 1988-91; mng. dir. Ladenburg Thalmann & Co. Inc., NYC, 1991-93, Brill Securities, 1993-94, Burnham Securities, Inc., 1994-96. Bd. dirs. Jewish Found. Edn. Women, 1980; trustee, v.p. Jewish Bd. Family and Children's Svcs. Mem.: Harvard Club N.Y.C., Century Country Club (Purchase, N.Y.). E-mail: jack_ackerman2@verizon.net.

ACKERMAN, JACOB LEWIS, ophthalmologist; b. Berlin, July 22, 1947; s. Joseph and Pearl (Ziment) A.; m. Elaine Marsha Horowitz, Aug. 10, 1969 (dec. Mar. 2002); children: Rita, Karen, Steven, Julie; m. Judith Fay Rosenfeld, Oct. 6, 2002. MD, Albert Einstein Coll. Medicine, 1971. Assoc. dir. Brook Plaza Ophthalmology, Bklyn., 1975—, Brook Plaza Ambulatory Surgery Ctr., Bklyn., 1989—; asst. prof. of ophthalmology SUNY Health Sci. Ctr., Down State Med. Ctr., 1981—. Exec. bd. dirs. Met. Ophthalmic Ambulatory Surg. Ctr. Assn., Bronx. Contbr. articles to profl. jours. Sec. Young Israel of Lawrence-Cedarhurst, 1993. Avocations: tennis, writing, talmud, art, torah. Office: Brook Plaza Ophthalmology Assocs 1901 Utica Ave Brooklyn NY 11234-3213 Home: 138-15 Union Turnpike Flushing NY 11367-3250 Home Phone: 718-969-1589; Office Phone: 718-968-8700. Personal E-mail: jfjamd2000@yahoo.com.

ACKERMAN, JAMES, fine arts educator; b. San Francisco, Nov. 8, 1919; s. Lloyd S. and Louise (Sloss) A.; m. Mildred Rosenbaum, Apr. 11, 1947 (dec. Jan. 10, 1986); children: Anne, Anthony, Sarah; m. Jill Slosburg, Aug. 1987; 1 child, Jesse August. AB, Yale U., 1941; MA, NYU, 1947, PhD, 1952; LHD, Kenyon Coll., 1961; DFA, Md. Inst., 1972, Mass. Coll. Art, 1984; LHD, U. Md., 1976; DArch, U. Venice, 1985. Part-time instr. Yale U., 1946-48; rsch. fellow Am. Acad. in Rome, 1949-52; from asst. prof. to prof. U. Calif., 1952-60; editor in chief Art Bull., 1956-60; prof. fine arts Harvard U., 1960—, chmn. dept. fine arts, 1963-68, 82-84, Arthur Kingsley Porter prof. fine arts, 1984-90, prof. emeritus, 1990. Slade prof. fine art, fellow King's Coll., Cambridge U., 1969-70; vis. fellow Coun. Humanities, Princeton, 1960-61; fellow Am. Coun. Learned Socs., 1964-65, N.Y. Humanities Inst., spring 1992; Mellon sr. scholar Can. Ctr. for Architecture, 2001; vis. prof. fine arts NYU, 1992; sr. fellow NEH, 1974-75; Mellon lectr. Nat. Gallery Art, 1985; Schapiro prof. art history Columbia U., 1989-90, 91; vis. prof. architecture MIT, 1996, Harvard, 1996-97. Author: The Cortile del Belvedere, 1954, The Architecture of Michelangelo, 1961 (winner Alice D. Hitchcock award Soc. Archtl. Historians 1961, Charles R. Morey award 1963), (with Rhys Carpenter) Art and Archaeology, 1963, Palladio, 1967, Palladio's Villas, 1967, The Villa: Form and Ideology of Country Houses, 1990, Distance Points, 1991, Origins, Imitation, Conventions, 2002; co-editor: Annali d'Architettura, 1992-95, Conventions of Architectural Drawing, 2000; films Looking for Renaissance Rome (with Kathleen Weil-Garris), 1975, Palladio the Architect and His Influence in America. Trustee The Artists Found., pres., 1977-79; mem. council of scholars Library of Congress, 1980-82. Recipient medal for svc. in art edn. Nat. Gallery Art, 1966, Centennial citation U. Calif., 1968, Honors AIA 1987, Gold medal Inst. per la Storia dell'Arte Lombarda, 1987, Archtl. History award AIA, 1991, Paul Oskar Kristeller Lifetime Achievement award Renaissance Soc. Am., 1998, Internat. Balzan prize, 2001; decorated grand officer Order of Merit, Republic of Italy, 1985, Premio Daria Borghese, 1995; Guggenheim fellow, 1992-93. Fellow Am. Acad. Arts and Scis., Am. Philos. Soc., Brit. Acad., Accademia Olimpica (corr.), Royal Acad. Arts and Scis., Academia of St. Luca (Rome, hon.), Ateneo Veneto, Royal Acad. Uppsala (corr.), Bavarian Acad. Scis. (corr.). Home: 12 Coolidge Hill Rd Cambridge MA 02138-5510 Office: Harvard U Sackler Mus Cambridge MA 02138 E-mail: jsackerm@fas.harvard.edu.

ACKERMAN, JASON, food products executive; Former fin. investor Food Prods. Industry; co-founder, CFO FreshDirect Grocery, 2001—. Office: FreshDirect 20-30 Borden Ave Long Island City NY 11101*

ACKERMAN, JEROME LEONARD, biomedical researcher; BS in Chemistry cum laude, SUNY, Stony Brook, 1971; PhD in Physical Chemistry, MIT, Cambridge, 1976. Postdoctoral fellow U. Calif., Berkeley, 1976-77; asst. prof. chemistry U. Cin., 1977-82, assoc. prof. chemistry, 1982-85; asst. prof. radiology Harvard Med. Sch., Boston, 1985-95, assoc. prof. radiology, 1995—; dir. NMR spectroscopy Mass. Gen. Hosp., Charlestown, 1985—. Co-founder SkelScan, Inc.; cons. in field. Editor: (book) Advanced Tomographic Imaging Methods for the Analysis of Materials, 1991; contbr. numerous articles to profl. jours. Mem. Internat. Soc. for Magnetic Resonance in Medicine, Exptl. Nuclear Magnetic Resonance Conf. (mem. exec. com. 1991—, conf. chair 1999). Achievements include research in magnetic resonance studies of bone and synthetic biomaterials. Office: Biomaterials Lab Matinos Ctr Mass Gen Hosp Rm 2320 149 13th St Charlestown MA 02129-2000 E-mail: jerry@nmr.mgh.harvard.edu.

ACKERMAN, KENNETH EDWARD, retired lawyer, educator; b. Bronx, NY, May 25, 1946; s. Kenneth L. and Anna (McCarthy) A.; m. Kathryn H. Hartnett, July 8, 1972; children: Andrew, Carl, Sheila, Edward, Daniel, Kenneth. Student, Talladega Coll., 1966; BA, Fordham Coll., 1968; JD, Cornell U., 1971. Bar: N.Y. 1972, Pa. 1994, U.S. Ct. Appeals (2d cir.) 1975, U.S. Supreme Ct. 1976; cert tchr., N.Y. State, 2002. Clk. legal dept. Port Authority N.Y. and N.J., 1969, IBM, 1970; ptnr. Mackenzie Hughes LLP, Syracuse, NY, 1971—2006; ret., 2006. Adj. prof. banking law and negotiable instruments Am. Inst. Banking program Onondaga Community Coll., 1984—, Syracuse U. Coll., lectr.; adj. prof. white collar crime Ithaca Coll., 2002-03. Author: Alcoholism-Prognosis for Recovery in the Reconstituted Soviet Republics, 1991; contbr. articles to profl. jours. Chmn. Ctrl. N.Y. chpt. March of Dimes, 1972-82; mem. A.A.-USSR Travel Group, 1987; bd. dirs. Ctrl. N.Y. Health Systems Agy., Inc., 1982-83, Syracuse Sr. Citizens Housing Project Corp., 1992—; trustee N.Y. State Lawyers Assistance Trust, 2003—; mem. Bellacosa Commn. Alcohol and Drug Abuse in the Profession, 1999-2001. Mem.: ABA, Onondaga County Bar Assn. (bd. dirs. 1990—93), N.Y. State Bar Assn. (chmn. com. lawyer alcoholism and drug abuse 1993—95). Office: 600 M & T Bldg PO Box 4967 Syracuse NY 13221-4967

ACKERMAN, LENNIS CAMPBELL, retired management consultant; b. LA, July 28, 1917; s. Lennis Howard and Ethel (Campbell) A.; m. Barbara Bohlken, July 27, 1941; children: Nancy (Mrs. Michael H. Burnaugh), Janet (Mrs. Robert W. Lesser), John, Barbara (Mrs. H.D. Arnold), George. AB, UCLA, 1940. With Texaco Co., LA, 1940-43, Schenley Distillers, San Francisco, 1945-48; merchandiser Richfield Oil Corp., San Francisco, 1949-52; sales rep. Walker Mfg. Co., 1952-56, mktg. adminstr., 1956-58; v.p., gen. mgr. Can. subs. Galt Metal Industries, 1958-63, v.p. internat. ops. parent co., 1963-65, v.p. mktg., 1965, pres., 1966-68; pres., chief exec. officer Newport News Shipbldg. and Dry Dock Co., 1969-73; exec. v.p. Tenneco, Inc., 1972-73; group v.p. Questor Corp., 1973-78; assoc. dean Sch. Bus. Adminstrn. Coll. William and Mary, Williamsburg, Va., 1978-83. Sec. Va. Port Authority, 1971-73; mem. Sch. Bus. Adminstrn. Sponsors, Inc., Coll. William and Mary, 1970-79, chmn., 1970-72. Served with USAAF, 1943-45. Mem. Soc. Automotive Engrs., Pine Valley Golf Club, Beta Gamma Sigma (hon.), Alpha Sigma Phi. Episcopalian. Home and Office: Apt 129 5700 Williamsburg Landing Dr Williamsburg VA 23185-8077 Personal E-mail: budackman1@cox.net.

ACKERMAN, LISA MARILYN, foundation administrator, consultant; b. Danville, Pa., May 19, 1960; d. Bruce David and Jean Mamie (Pedevill) A. BA, Middlebury Coll., Vt., 1982; MBA, NYU, 1986. Intern Internat. Found. for Art Rsch., NYC, 1982; adminstrv. asst. Samuel H. Kress Found., NYC, 1982-84, program adminstr., 1984-87, chief adminstrv. officer, 1987-93, v.p., 1993—2003, exec. v.p., 2003—; bd. mem. Hist. House Trust, NYC, 2003—. Cons. Internat. Found. for Art Rsch., 1985-86; rsch. cons. survey on art-deco comm. architecture, 1987-93; bd. dirs. U.S. chpt. Internat. Coun. of Monuments and Sites, 1998-2005; mem. adv. coun. The Gallery of the Am. Bible Soc., 2003-05. Contbr. articles to profl. jours. Vol. Planned Parenthood, NYC, 1982-83, Middlebury Coll. Alumni Assn., 1982-86, edn. dept. Mus. Modern Art, NYC, 1989-94; bd. dirs. St. Ann Ctr. for Restoration and the Arts, 1992-97, Jewish Heritage Coun., 1993-95; active Middlebury Coll. Arts Coun., 1998—; bd. advisors Neighborhood Preservation Ctr., 1999—07; pres. Friends of Roberto Longhi Found., 2000-06, NY Preservation Archive Project, 2000—, Ptnrs. for Sacred Places, 1997-2003. Avocation: dance. Office: Samuel H Kress Found 174 E 80th St New York NY 10021-0439 Office Phone: 212-861-4993. Business E-Mail: lisa@shkf.org.

ACKERMAN, MARSHALL, publishing executive; b. NYC, Jan. 22, 1925; s. Albert and Beatrice (Munstuk) A.; m. Carol Lipman, June 8, 1948; children: Stark, Scott, A. Marc. AB, Harvard U., 1949; MS in Journalism, Northwestern U., 1950. Dir. employee relations Gimbel Bros., NYC, 1950-51; account exec. Leonard Wolf & Assoc. (advt. agy.), NYC, 1951-54; with Rodale Press, Inc., 1954-91, exec. v.p., 1967-91, vice chmn. bd., 1978-91; pub. Prevention mag., 1977-86, Theatre Crafts mag., 1967-78, vice chmn., Western divsn., 1986-91; ind. cons. health food industry, health media, 1992—2002. Pres. bd. assocs. Cedar Crest Coll., Allentown, Pa., 1976—78, trustee, 1983—87; pres. Pa. Stage Co., Allentown, 1978—80; chmn. Santa Barbara chpt. Am. Inst. Wine and Food, 1998—2003. Charge de Presse, Confrerie de la Chaine des Rotisseurs, Bailliage de Santa Barbara, 1998-2003; Decorated Bronze Star, Purple Heart. Home and Office: 894 Toro Canyon Rd Santa Barbara CA 93108-1642 E-mail: mackermanm@aol.com.

ACKERMAN, MELVIN, investment company executive; b. Bronx, NY, Feb. 6, 1937; s. Norman Ackerman and Lilly (Ostreicher) Warshaw; m. Jennie Wang, Sept. 19, 1964; children: Lori, Julie, Melissa. Student, Bklyn. Coll., 1956-59. Trader Myron A. Lomasney & Co., NYC, 1960-62; sr. v.p. E.F. Hutton & Co., NYC, 1963-88. Exch. arbitrator Am. Stock Exch., N.Y.C., 1984-88; mem. options adv. com. Phila. Stock Exch., 1980-88, Am. Stock Exch., 1975-88; ind. cons., 1988—; dir. BBFD Investment Co.; ptnr. Breckenridge Holding Co. With USMC, 1956-58. Mem. Securities Traders Assn. N.Y., Securities Industry Assn. (credit div., options and derivative products com., 1983-88). Jewish.

ACKERMAN, PHILIP CHARLES, utilities executive, lawyer; b. Kenmore, NY, Feb. 14, 1944; s. Harold Lewis and Marion (Ehrhardt) Ackerman; m. Nancy Margaret Weig, Sept. 11, 1967; children: David Philip, Kathryn Elizabeth. BS in Acctg., SUNY, Buffalo, 1965; LLB, Harvard U., 1968. Bar: N.Y. 1968. Atty. Iroquois Gas Corp., Buffalo, 1968-72, asst. sec., 1972-74; sec. Nat. Fuel Gas Distbn. Corp., Buffalo, 1975—84, gen. counsel, 1978—84, sr. v.p., 1983—84, exec. v.p., 1989—95, pres., 1995—99, bd. dirs.; sr. v.p. Nat. Fuel Gas Supply Corp., 1984—88, exec. v.p., 1988—90, 1994—2002; v.p. Nat. Fuel Gas. Co., Buffalo, 1980—89, sr. v.p., 1989—99, dir., 1994—, pres., 1999—2006, CEO, 2001—, chmn. bd., 2002—. V.p. Seneca Resource Corp., 1978—89, pres., 1989—96, also bd. dirs.; mem. regional adv. bd. J. P. Morgan Chase. Mem.: Gas Tech. Inst. (bd. dirs. 2002—), Bus. Coun. N.Y. State (bd. dirs. 2002—), Buffalo Soc. Natural Sci. (bd. mgrs. 1982—, vice chmn. 1990—99, chmn. 1999—), Am. Gas Assn. (bd. dirs. 1999—, chmn. security, integrity and reliability com. 2001—04). Office: Nat Fuel Gas Co 6363 Main St Williamsville NY 14221*

ACKERMAN, RAYMOND BASIL, advertising executive; b. Pitts., Aug. 7, 1922; s. Charles Raymond and Teresa Jane (Grasinger) A.; m. Lucille Frances Flanagan, June 14, 1948; children: Patricia Ann Mehring, Ann Carol Adams, Ray K., Susan Marie Fuller, Mark, Amy Lou Shaver. BS, Oklahoma City U., 1951, PhD (hon.) in Comml. Sci., 1996. Mem. display advt. staff Okla. Pub. Co., Oklahoma City, 1947-52; account exec. Knox-Ackerman Advt., Oklahoma City, 1952-53; pres. Ackerman Assos., Oklahoma City, 1954-74; chmn. bd. Ackerman McQueen, Inc., advt. agy., Oklahoma City, Tulsa, Dallas, Washington, 1975-92; chmn. emeritus Ackerman McQueen, Inc., 1992—. Bd. dirs. LSB Industries; past internat. pres. Worldwide Ptnrs. affil. Author: Tomorrow Belongs to Oklahoma, 1964; subject of biography Old Man River by Bob Burke with Joan Gilmore, 2002. Pres., campaign chmn. Oklahoma City United Appeal, 1964-66, trustee, 1967—; chmn. Oklahoma City Salvation Army, 1968; pres. Oklahoma City Better Bus. Bur., 1966; gen. chmn. Nat. Finals Rodeo Oklahoma City, 1965-84; past bd. dirs. Jr. Achievement, Oklahoma City, Okla. Water Devel. Found., Redlands Coun. of Girl Scouts, Urban League, Mercy Hosp.; past pres., bd. dirs. St. Anthony Hosp. Found.; past pres. Omniplex Sci. Mus., Oklahoma City; past trustee Oklahoma City Youth Park; campaign chmn., pres. Allied Arts Found., Oklahoma City, 1986-88, mem. exec. com., 1989—, Oklahoma City Cmty. Coun., 1989-2003; bd. dirs. Kirkpatrick Ctr. Mus. Complex, Oklahoma City, 1973-2004, pres. 1990-92; trustee, mem. exec. com., Oklahoma City U., 1988—; bd. dirs. Red Earth Indian Ctr., 1987-2004, Oklahoma City Pub. Sch. Found., 1990—; adv. bd. Enterprise Sq., 1994—; mem. last frontier coun. Boy Scouts Am. Rear Adm. USNR, ret. Recipient Silver medal Am. Adv. Fedn., 1982, Lifetime Svc. award Oklahoma City United Appeal, 1992, Pathfinder award Oklahoma County Hist. Soc., 1992, Outstanding Grad. award, Oklahoma City U., 1964, Disting. Alumnus award, 1991, Leadership Okla. award, 2001, Dean A. McGee award Downtown Now, Oklahoma City, 2000, Archbishop Beltran Cmty. Svc. award, 2000, Gov. Okla.'s Arts award, 2000, Lifetime Achievement award Nat. Assn. Fund Raising Execs., 2000, Sales and Mktg. Execs. Internat. Acad. Achievement award, 2000, Leadership Okla., 2001, Father of Yr. award Am. Diabetes Assn., 2003; named Humanitarian of Yr. Oklahoma County Arthritis Found., 1992, Okla. Living Treasures for Tomorrow Okla. Health Ctr. Found., 2004; named to Okla. Hall of Fame, 1993, Okla. Commerce and Industry Hall of Honor, 1998; named Ray Ackerman Leadership award in his honor United Way of Ctr. Okla., 2004. Mem. Naval Res. Assn. (nat. pres. 1969-71), Navy League (nat. bd. dirs. 1972-76, pres. Okla. chpt. 1974-76), Okla. Heritage Assn. (bd. dirs.), Oklahoma City C. of C. (bd. dirs., chmn. 1991, creation of Ray Ackerman award 1993), Oklahoma City Advt. Club (pres. 1954, Disting. Svc. award 1964), Am. Assn. of Advt. Agys. (past chmn. southwest coun.), Quail Creek Golf and Country Club, Rotary, Fortune Club, others. Office Phone: 405-843-7777.

ACKERMAN, RICHARD CHARLES, lawyer, state legislator; b. Long Beach, Calif., Dec. 5, 1942; s. Jay Fuller and Marge Mae (Lyon) A.; m. Linda Irene Vranesic, May 4, 1968; children: Lauren, Marc, Brett. AB in Math., U. Calif., Berkeley, 1964; JD, Hastings Sch. Law, 1967. Ptnr. Ackerman, Mordock & Bowen, Fullerton, Calif., 1982—. Mem. city coun. City of Fullerton, 1980-92; pres. Orange County Waste Mgmt., Santa Ana, Calif., 1982-95; v.p. So. Calif. Hazardous Waste Mgmt., L.A., 1982-95; mem. Calif. State Assembly, 1994-2000, mem. Calif. State Sen., 2000-. Named Ofcl. of Yr., O.C. Com. Persons with Disabilities, 1996. Mem. Orange County Bar Assn., Fullerton C. of C. (pres., Man of Yr. 1983, Educator of Yr. 1996), Fullerton Rotary Club (pres.), Elks, Fullerton Yacht Club (commodore 1976—). Republican. Presbyterian. Avocations: sailing, racquetball, reading. Office: Ackerman Mordock & Bowen 305 N Harbor Blvd Ste 303 Fullerton CA 92832-1901

ACKERMAN, ROBERT WALLACE, private equity manager; b. NYC, Sept. 14, 1938; s. Emory Graham and Margaret Wallace A.; m. Margaret Tracy Dealy, Dec. 30, 1964; children: Ashley, Graham, Todd. BS, Yale U., 1960; MBA, Harvard U., 1962, DBA, 1968. CPA, N.Y. Cons. Arthur Young & Co., NYC, 1962-66; asst. prof. Harvard Bus. Sch., Boston, 1968-72, lectr., 1972-74; v.p. fin. and adminstrn. Preco, Inc., West Springfield, Mass., 1974-78; pres. and bd. dir. Premoid Corp., West Springfield, 1979—86, Whitman Products Ltd., West Warwick, RI, 1977—86; sr. research fellow Harvard Bus. Sch., 1986-88; pres. and CEO Lincoln Pulp & Paper, Inc., 1988—92, Sheffield Steel Corp., 1992—99, chmn. and CEO Sand Springs, Okla., 1999—2000; ptnr. Watermill Group, Waltham, Mass., 2000—. Bd. dir. WGI Heavy Minerals, Inc., Litecontrol, Inc.; pres, CEO Multulayer Coating Techs., LLC, 2006—. Author: The Social Challenge to Business, 1975, (with Hugo Uyterhoeven and John Rosenblum) Strategy and Organization, Text and Cases, General Management, 1973, 2d. edit., 1977, (with Raymond Bauer) Corporate Social Responsiveness, 1976. Deacon 1st Ch. in Cambridge Congl., 1970—; bd. dir. Wildlife Conservation Trust, 1977—; chair adv. bd. Nature Conservancy, Mass., 1994—. Served with AUS, 1963 Mem.: AICPA, Steel Mfrs. Assn. (chmn. 1998—2000), N.Y. State Soc. CPA's, Am. Acad. Mgmt. (gov. 1972—73), Timber Owners of New Eng. (pres. 1977—, bd. dirs.), Harvard Club (Boston), The Kittansett Club (Maron, Mass.), Yale Club (N.Y.C.). Home: 274 Beacon St Boston MA 02116- Office: Watermill Ctr 800 South St Waltham MA 02453-1435

ACKERMAN, ROGER G., ceramics engineer; m. Maureen Ackerman; 4 children. Grad., D, Rutgers U.; PMD program, Harvard U. Engr., sales, mgmt. positions Corning (N.Y.) Inc., 1962—72, pres. Corhart Refractories Co., 1972—75, gen. mgr., v.p. Ceramic Products Divsn., 1975—80, sr. v.p., 1980—81, dir. Mfg. and Engring. Divsn., 1981—83, pres. MetPath Inc., 1983—85, pres. Specialty Materials, 1985—90, pres., COO, 1990—96, chmn., CEO, 1996—2001; ret., 2001. Bd. dirs. The Brinks Co., Mass. Mut. Life Ins. Co. Trustee Corning Inc. Found., Corning Mus. Glass; mem. bd. overseers Rutgers U. Found. Office: Corning Inc PO Box 45 Phoenix NY 13135 Office Phone: 877-867-7970. E-mail: ackermanrg@corning.com.

ACKERMAN, SIGURD HOWARD, psychiatrist; b. Millville, NJ, Feb. 25, 1940; s. William H. and Ethel (Kessler) A.; m. Cecelia M. McCarton, Apr. 25, 1983; children: Elizabeth, Rebecca, McCarton. BA, Harvard U., 1962; MD, Tufts U., 1966. Intern Kings County Hosp., Bklyn., 1966-67, resident in medicine, 1967-68; resident in psychiatry Montefiore Med. Ctr., Bronx, NY, 1970-73; dir. psychiatry St. Luke's Roosevelt Hosp. Ctr., NYC, 1989—98, med. dir., exec. v.p., 1991-93; prof. clin. psychiatry Columbia U. Coll. Physicians and Surgeons, NYC, 1989—, assoc. dean, 1991-93; pres., CEO St. Luke's-Roosevelt Med. Ctr., NYC, 1998—2001; pres., med. dir. Silver Hill Hosp., Inc., New Canaan, Conn., 2003—. Rsch. Scientist Devel. award level I and II, NIMH, 1976-84. Home: 97 Sagamore Rd Stamford CT 06902-8007 Office: Silver Hill Hosp 208 Valley Rd New Canaan CT 06840 Office Phone: 203-801-2215. Business E-Mail: sackerman@silverhillhospital.org.

ACKERMAN, VALERIE B., former sports association executive; b. Nov. 7, 1959; m. Charlie Rappaport; children: Emily, Sally. Grad., U. Va., 1981, UCLA Sch. Law, 1985. Assoc. Simpson, Thacher & Bartlett, NYC; staff atty. NBA, 1988, spl. asst. to commr., 1990-92, dir. bus. affairs, 1992—94, v.p. bus. affairs, 1994—96; pres. WNBA, 1996—2005. Bd. dirs. USA Basketball; exec. com. Naismith Meml. Basketball Hall of Fame. Trustee March of Dimes. Named to, GTE Acad. All-Am. Hall of Fame, 1999, Scholar Athlete Hall Fame, Inst. for Internat. Sport, 2003; recipient Disting. Alumna award, U. Va. Women's Ctr., 1997.

ACKERMANN, BARBARA BOGEL, counselor; b. Bay Shore, NY, Nov. 16, 1940; d. Charles Henry Jurgens and Marjorie (Stevens) Bogel; children: Erika, Stefan. BS in Polit. Sci., Ursinus Coll., 1962; MS in Counseling Edn., L.I. U., 1978, profl. diploma in counseling, 1982, postgrad., 1991. Lic. sch. adminstr., NY. Child protective worker Suffolk County Social Svc., NY, 1962-65; med. social worker St. Joseph's Hosp., Syracuse, NY, 1965-69; child protective worker Tallahassee Social Svc., Fla., 1967-68; RSVP coord. Suffolk County Ret. Sr. Vol. Program, 1975; sch. counselor Hampton Bays HS, NY, 1978-86; guidance dir., counselor Southold HS, NY, 1986—2002; ret. Treas. Human Understanding and Growth Seminars, Laurel, NY, 1987-89, bd. dirs., 1984-90. Alt. committeewoman Southold Town Rep. Com., 1976-83; deacon Presbyn. Ch., Mattituck, NY, 1977—. Named NY State HS Counselor of Yr., 1995, Educator of Yr. Suffolk Times, 2002-. Mem. East End Counselors Assn. (pres. 1982, bd. dirs. 1979—), LI Counselors Ann. Conf. (co-chairperson 1985, 94, 98), NY State Assn. for Counseling and Devel. (v.p. 1983-85, North Atlantic region rep. 1985-87), NY Counseling Assn., Am. Counseling Assn., Nat. Assn. Coll. Admission Counselors, Am. Sch. Counselor Assn., NY State Sch. Counselors Assn. (dist. gov. 1989-92), Southold Rotary (bd. dirs., pres. 2003-, asst. gov. Dist. 7260, 2005-, scholarship chmn., 2005-, Paul Harris fellow), Delta Kappa Gamma. Personal E-mail: back56@aol.com.

ACKERS, GARY KEITH, biophysical chemistry educator, researcher; b. Dodge City, Kans., Oct. 25, 1939; s. Leo Finley and Mabel Ida (Hostetler) A.; children: Lisa, Sandra, Keith. BS in Chemistry and Math., Harding Coll., Searcy, Ark., 1961; PhD in Physiol. Chemistry, Johns Hopkins U., 1964. Instr. physiol. chemistry Johns Hopkins U. Sch. Medicine, Balt., 1965-66, prof. biology and biophysics, 1977-89, dir. Inst. Biophys. Rsch., 1987-89; asst. prof. biochemistry U. Va. Sch. Medicine, Charlottesville, 1966-67, assoc. prof., 1967-72, prof. biochemistry and biophysics, 1972-77; prof. biochemistry and molecular biophysics Washington U., St. Louis, 1989—, head dept. biochemistry and molecular biophysics, 1989-96. Instr. physiology Marine Biol. Labs., Woods Hole, Mass., 1974-76; chmn. Gordon Conf. on Proteins, 1985; disting. lectr. Red Cell Club, 1997—. Mem. editorial bd. Analytical Biochemistry, 1970-79, Biophys. Chemistry, 1973-78, Proteins, Structures, Functional Genetics, 1991—; contbr. over 150 articles to sci. jours. Guggenheim fellow, 1972-73; recipient NIH Merit award, 1987. Fellow Biophys. Soc. (coun. 1972-74, 80-83, pres. 1984-85, Cole rsch. award 1994); mem. Am. Chem. Soc. (program chair biol. chem. divsn. 1994), Am. Soc. Biochem. Molecular Biology. Office: Washington U Med Sch Dept Biochem and Molecular Biophysics 660 S Euclid Ave Saint Louis MO 63110-1010

ACKERSON, CHARLES STANLEY, minister, educator, social worker; b. St. Louis, June 19, 1935; s. Charles Albert and Glenda Mae (Brown) A.; m. Carol Jean Stehlick, Aug. 18, 1957; children: Debra Lynn, Charles Mark, Heather Sue. AB, William Jewell Coll., Liberty, Mo., 1957; MDiv, Colgate Rochester Crozier Div. Sch., 1961. Ordained to ministry Am. Bapt. Ch., 1961; LCSW. Pastor Glens Falls (NY) Friends Meeting, 1961-65; assoc. pastor Delmar Bapt. Ch., St. Louis, 1965-68; resource dir. Block Partnership, 1968-71; group home dir. Northside YMCA, 1971—72; group home supr. St. Louis Juvenile Ct., 1973-74; program dir. Youth Opportunities Unltd., casework supr. St. Louis County Juvenile Ct., 1974-83; pastor St. Jordan's and St. John's United Chs. of Christ, 1976—; youth svcs. specialist St. Louis County Dept. Human Svcs., 1985-94; assoc. dir. Gen. Protestant Children's Home, 1994-99; residential dir. Mo. Bapt. Children's Home, 1999-2000; instr. sociology, adminstrn. of justice and human svcs. Mo. Bapt. U., 1980—. Exhibit coord. Dog Mus., 1989—91; cons. Am. Youth Found., 1990—2001; mem. ordination coun. area V Great Rivers region Am. Bapt. Chs. U.S.A., 1982—84; chmn. youth focus group Interfaith Partnership Met. St. Louis, 1985—88; chmn. St. Louis Area Youth Svcs. Network, 1987—89. Chmn. group home com. Mo. Coun. on Criminal Justice, 1973-75; chmn. cts. and instns. subcom. Juvenile Delinquency Task Force for Gov. Mo. Action Plan for Pub. Safety, 1976. Mem.: Nat. Juvenile Ct. Svcs. Assn., Soc. for the Sci. Study Religion, Am. Correctional Assn., Mo. Juvenile Justice Assn., Nat. Coun. Juvenile and Family Ct. Judges (mem. faith law and morality com.), Mo. Conservation Fedn., Nat. Audubon Soc., Smithsonian Instn. Assn., Three Rivers Kennel Club of Mo. (past pres.), Cairn Terrier Club Am., Lambda Chi Alpha. Democrat. Baptist. Home: 1221 Havenhurst Rd Ballwin MO 63011-4402 Personal E-mail: cackersn@swbell.net.

ACKERSON, REX DAVID, science educator, museum director; b. Blackwell, Okla., Nov. 24, 1943; s. Marion Ethmur Ackerson and Leona Olive Frazier-Ackerson; m. Roberta Irene Woodson, July 28, 1980; children: Richard Jeffrey Jones, Philip Russell Jones. AS, No. Okla. Coll., Tonkawa, 1963; BS, Okla. State U., Stillwater, 1971, MS, 1973. Tchr. US Peace Corps, Monduli, Tanzania, 1966—68; asst. agr. officer Shimba Ashs, Kenya, 1968—69; tchr. McAlester H.S., Okla., 1973—75; chemistry tchr. Altus H.S., Okla., 1975—80; chemistry prof. No. Okla. Coll., Tonkawa, 1980—, mus. dir., 1986—, chair divsn. sci., math. and engring., 2004—. Bd. dirs. Pioneer Woman Mus., Ponca City, Okla., 2001—06, pres., 2001—06, chair, 2004—06. Contbr. articles to profl. jours. including Jour. Chem. Edn. Pres., bd. dirs. Tonkawa United Way, 1981—92; pub. libr. bd. dirs. Tonkawa, Okla., 2000—02; chair Wesley Ho. Student Union, Tonkawa, 1980—96; bd. dirs., chair Tonkawa Hist. Soc., 1986—92; bd. dirs. Okla. Mus. Assn., Oklahoma City, 1990—96. Named Band Parent of Yr., Tonkawa Pub. Schs., 1988; recipient Commendation award, Internat. Sci. and Engring. Fair, 1980, Legislative Citation, Okla. State Legislature, 1984, Outstanding Svc. award, Kiwanis, 1984, 1986, Excellence award, Nat. Inst. for Staff and Orgnl. Devel., 1999, Edn. Leadership award, NOC, 2006, 2007. Mem.: Phi Theta Kappa (adv. 1996—2002). Democrat. Methodist. Avocations: reading, gardening. Home: 103 N Cherry Tonkawa OK 74653 Office Phone: 580-628-6477. Personal E-mail: chemagic@yahoo.com.

ACKERT, T(ERRENCE) W(ILLIAM), lawyer; b. NYC, June 8, 1946; s. T.W. and M. Ackert; m. MP. Ackert, July 4, 1970. BA in History, U. West Fla., 1969; JD, U. Fla., 1972. Bar: Fla. 1972, U.S. Dist. Ct. (mid. dist.) Fla. 1972, U.S. Supreme Ct. 1977, U.S. Ct. Appeals (fed. cir.) 1981. Pvt. practice, Orlando, Fla., 1972—; counsel Sharks Success, Inc., 1988-93, U.S. Ct. Internat. Trade, 2001—. Adj. prof. U. Cen. Fla., Orlando, 1988-93; gen. counsel (Fla.) Morgran Stiftung, Liechtenstein, 1991-95; law lectr. Profl. Skills Inst., Fla., 1981-85. Co-author: Florida Dissolution Manual, 1991; contbr. articles to profl. jours. Chmn. 9th Cir. Grievance Com., Orlando, 1989; mem. Human Svc. Planning Com., Orange County, Fla., 1984. Mem. Seminole County Bar (LAS pres. 1979, Pres. award 1980-83), Orange County Bar (LAS dir. 1980), Fla. Bar (trial lawyers sect., chmn. bar delivery of legal svc. com. 1986-88, chmn. mid-yr. conv. family law 1981, Pres.'s Svc. award 1985, 87). Avocation: travel. Office: PO Box 2548 Winter Park FL 32790-2548

ACKLEY, DANIEL, music educator, conductor, composer; s. Dennis Ackley and Barbara Landis; m. Elizabeth Hartleb, June 28, 1980; children: Alaina, Tristan. BFA, U. Wis., Milw., 1991, MusM, 1993; D Mus. Arts, U. Wis., Madison, 2002. Assoc. lectr. U. Wis. Washington County, West Bend, 1993—2002, sr. lectr., 2002—. Dir. River City Irregulars Cmty. Band, West Bend, 2005—; condr. Wash. County Youth Orch., West Bend, 2006—. Composer: (symphony) The Seven Seals; arranger: band Mussorgsky-Pictures At An Exhibition, Dies Irae from Verdi's Requiem, Mozart's Requiem, Mussorgsky-Prologue from Boris Godunov, composer various songs, worksfor percussion and quintets. Recipient Highly Meritorious Tchg. award, U. Wis.-Washington County; Advanced Opportunity fellow, U. Wis.-Madison. Mem.: Coll. Band Dirs. Nat. Assn., Nat. Band Assn., Phi Kappa Phi (life). Home: 4150 Hidden Creek Ct Jackson WI 53037 Office: U Wis Washington County 400 University Dr West Bend WI 53095 Home Phone: 262-677-0234; Office Phone: 262-335-5200. Business E-Mail: daniel.ackley@uwc.edu.

ACKLEY, ROBERT ARTHUR, mathematics educator, retired military officer; b. Bremerton, Wash., Dec. 2, 1946; s. Joe and Helen Betty Ackley; children: Rodney Shawn, John Thomas, Cheryl Rebecca Miles, Victoria Elizabeth Hicks. BAE in Math., Ariz. State U., Tempe, 1974, BS in Sociology, 1974; MPA, Golden Gate U., San Francisco, 1988. Cert. tchr. Ariz., Mo. Math tchr. Sunnyside Unified Sch. Dist., Tucson, 1995—2006, McCluer N. HS, Ferguson Florissant Sch. Dist., Mo., 2006—. With USAF, 1967—71, re-enlisted and advanced through ranks to capt. USAF, 1979—95. Decorated DSM USAF, Viet Nam Svc. medal, Viet Nam Campaign medal, Humanitarian Svc. medal; named Dist. Tchr. of Yr., Sunnyside Unified Sch., Tucson, 2004, 2005. Mem.: VFW, SAR (chpt. pres. 1999, Best Chpt. award 1999), Math. Assn. Am., Nat. Coun. Tchrs. of Math. Office: Ferguson-Florissant Sch Dist Adminstrn Ctr 1005 Waterford Dr Florissant MO 63033

ACKLEY, ROBERT O., lawyer; b. Chgo., July 24, 1952; s. William O. and Jeannette E. (Mitchell) A.; m. Patricia Ann Cerney, May 24, 1980; children: Matthew, Allison, Elizabeth, Anne, Kathryn, Kimberly. BA, No. Ill. U., 1974; MA., No. Mich. U., 1977; JD, John Marshall Law Sch., Chgo., 1988. Bar: Ill. 1988, U.S. Dist. Ct. (no. dist.) Ill. 1988, U.S. Ct. Appeals (7th cir.), 2003. Adminstrv. intern, asst. to city mgr. City of Marquette, Mich., 1976—77; adminstrv. asst. to town mgr. Town of Glastonbury, Conn., 1978; supr. Continental Bank, Chgo., 1979; chief methods analyst dept. fin. City of Chgo., 1980—81, chief supr. ops. dept. revenue, 1981—84; pres. Ackley & Assocs., Chgo., 1984—88; law clk., adminstrv. asst. to chief justice Thomas J. Moran Supreme Ct. of Ill., Lake Forest, 1988—90; atty. Cassiday, Schade & Gloor, Chgo., 1990—91; pvt. practice Chgo., 1991—2002; ptnr. Sarles & Ouimet, Chgo., 2003—, Woodstock & Dallas. Bd. dirs. Ill. Pro Bono Ctr., 1997-2002; adj. prof. Roosevelt U., Chgo., 1989-90; mem. panel arbitrators Cir. Ctr. of 19th Jud. Cir., 1991-97, Cir. Ct. Cook County, 1993-97; detention screening atty. pretrial svcs. Cir. Ct. of Cook County, 1991—; drugs panel atty. Office of State Appellate Defender, 1992—. Bd. dirs. Bryn Mawr-Broadway Ridge Mchts. Assn., Chgo., 1984-87; panel mem. Capital Resource Ctr., 1991, Community Econ. Devel. Law Project. Fellow Ill. Bar Found.; mem. Nat. Assn. Counsel Children, Ill. Bar Assn., Chgo. Bar Assn., Lake County Bar Assn. (pro bono svc. award 2000), Ill. Appellate Lawyers Assn., Acad. Polit. Sci. (life), Nat. Coun. Juvenile and Family Ct. Judges, McHenry County Bar Assn. (Pro Bono Svc. award, 2004), Assn. Family & Conciliation Courts. Home: 606 Buckingham Pl Libertyville IL 60048-3326 Office: 500 N Lake St Mundelein IL 60060 Home Phone: 847-816-0108; Office Phone: 847-566-7101. Personal E-mail: ackley.robert@gmail.com. Business E-Mail: ackley@mundeleinlaw.com.

ACKMAN, WILLIAM ALBERT, investment company executive; b. May 11, 1966; s. Lawrence D. Ackman; m. Karen Ann Herskovitz, July 10, 1994. BA magna cum laude, Harvard Coll.; MBA, Harvard U. Co-founder Gotham Ptnrs. Mgmt. Co., LLC, NYC, 1992—2003; mng. ptnr., founder & pres. Pershing Sq. Capital Mgmt., L.P., NYC, 2003—. Named one of 40 Under 40 Rising Stars, Crain's NY Bus., 1998. Office: Pershing Sq Capital Mgmt 29th Fl 888 7th Ave New York NY 10019 Office Phone: 212-813-3700.*

ACKOFF, RUSSELL LINCOLN, social systems designer, educator; b. Phila., Feb. 12, 1919; s. Jack and Fannie (Weitz) A.; m. Alexandra Makar, July 17, 1949 (dec. Feb. 1987); children: Alan W., Karen B., Karla S.; m. Helen Wald, Dec. 20, 1987. BArch, U. Pa., 1941, PhD in Philosophy, 1947; DSc, U. Lancaster, 1967; DSc (hon.), Washington U., St. Louis, 1993, U. Lincolnshire and Humberside, UK, 1999, Fla. Internat. U., 2001, U. Hull, Eng., 2007; DL (hon.), U. New Haven, 1997; Dr. (hon.), Pontificia U. Cath. del Peru, Lima, 1999. Asst. instr. philosophy U. Pa., Phila., 1941-42, 46-47; asst. prof. philosophy and math. Wayne U., Detroit, 1947-51; assoc. prof., prof. ops. rsch. Case Inst. Tech., Cleve., 1951-64; Silberberg prof. systems scis. U. Pa., 1964-86, chmn. dept. stats. and ops. rsch., 1964-66, chmn. grad. faculty ops. rsch., 1964-69, dir. Mgmt. Sci. Ctr., 1964-67, 69-70, chmn. Busch Ctr., 1970-74, 76-79, chmn. social systems sci. unit, 1974-78, 86—, Anheuser-Busch prof. emeritus of mgmt. scis., 1986—. Chmn. INTERACT: The Inst. Interactive Mgmt., 1986—; methodological cons. U.S. Bur. Census, 1950-51; cons. Eastern Airlines, Emerson Electric Co., Gen. Foods Co., Mobil Oil Co., Nat. Acad. Scis., Nat. U. Mex., Sci. and Tech. Rsch. Coun., Turkey, Western Electric Co.; bd. dirs. Mantua Indsl. Devel. Corp.; August A. Busch Jr. vis. prof. mktg. Washington U., St. Louis, 1989-95; mem. core faculty Union Inst., Cin., 1989-91, Ackoff Ctr. Advanced Sys. Approaches Univ. Penn., 2000—; vis. prof. U. Hull, U.K., 2005—. Author: (with C.W. Churchman) Psychologistics, 1946, Methods of Inquiry, 1950, (with C.W. Churchman and M. Wax) Measurement of Consumer Interest, 1947, The Design of Social Research, 1953, (with C.W. Churchman and E.L. Arnoff) Introduction to Operations Research, 1957, Progress in Operations Research, I, 1961, Scientific Method, 1962, (with P. Rivett) A Manager's Guide to Operations Research, 1963, (with M. Sasieni) Fundamentals of Operations Research, 1968, A Concept of Corporate Planning, 1970, (with F.E. Emery) On Purposeful Systems, 1972, Redesigning The Future, 1974, (with T.A. Cowan et al) Designing a National Scientific and Technological Communication System, 1976, The Art of Problem Solving, 1978, Creating the Corporate Future, 1981, (with E. V. Finnel, J. Gharajedaghi) A Guide to Controlling Your Corporation's Future, 1984, (with P. Broholm and R. Snow) Revitalizing Western Economics, 1984, Management in Small Doses, 1986, Ackoff's Fables, 1991, The Democratic Corporation, 1994, Exploring Personality: An Intellectual Odyssey, 1998, Ackoff's Best, 1999, Re-Creating the Corporation, 1999, (with Sheldon Rovin) Redesigning Society, 2003, Beating the System, 2004; (with Jason Magidson and Herbert Addison) Idealized Design, 2006, (with Herbert J. Addison and Sally Bibb) Management f-laws, 2007; (with Herbert J. addison and Sally Bibb) Management f-Laws, 2007; editor: Management Science, 1965-70, Systems and Mgmt. Ann, 1974; assoc. editor Ops. Rsch., 1953-65, Conflict Resolution, 1964-70; book rev. editor Philosophy of Science, 1947-53; mem. abstracting staff: Biological Abstracts, 1950-51; adv. editor mgmt. sci. John Wiley & Sons, 1964-86; adv. bd. Math. Spectrum, 1968-86; mem. editl. bd. Management Decision, 1968-86, Reflections, 2001-03, European Jour. Operational Rsch.; contbr. articles to profl. jours. Bd. dirs. Tallberg Found., Sweden, 1997—2000, Ctr. for Quality Mgmt., Cambridge, Mass., 1996—2004; mem. UN Devel. Adv. Coun., 1996—. Recipient award ASTD, 1993, award for outstanding achievement in sys. thinking and practice U.K. Sys. Soc., 1999, The Tallberg Found. and SupdBank Leadership award, 2005. Fellow Am. Statis. Assn., Ops. Rsch. Soc. Am. (v.p., pres. 1956-57), Internat. Acad. Mgmt., Inst. Mgmt. Cons.; mem. Internat. Acad. Mgmt., Russian Acad. Natural Scis. (fgn. mem.), Inst. Mgmt. Scis. (v.p. 1965), Operational Rsch. Soc. (U.K.) (Silver medal 1971), Soc. Gen. Systems Rsch. (pres. 1987-88), Oprational Rsch. Soc. India, Peace Rsch. Soc., Sigma Xi, Tau Sigma Delta. Achievements include Ackoff Ctr. for Advancement of Sys. Approaches (2000) the Russell L. Ackoff Endowment (2001) established at U. Pa. Home: Benson House 101 930 Montgomery Ave Bryn Mawr PA 19010-3044 Office: # 201 1021 W Lancaster Ave Ste 201 Bryn Mawr PA 19010-2635 Home Phone: 610-525-8019; Office Phone: 610-526-9374. Personal E-mail: rlackoff@aol.com.

ACKOUREY, PETER PAUL, lawyer; b. Scranton, Pa., Dec. 18, 1954; s. Paul Peter and Regina Helene (Dorris) A.; m. Christine Marie Van Wert, Aug. 6, 1977; children: Abigail Regina, Kenneth Jamal, Jemeille Irene, Mary Rose. BA in History, U. Scranton, 1974; JD, Harvard U., 1977. Bar: Pa. 1977, N.J. 1989. Assoc. Drinker Biddle & Reath, Phila., 1977-83; assoc. counsel Mellon Bank Corp., Phila., 1983-88; ptnr. Drinker Biddle & Reath LLP, Princeton, NJ, Florham Park, NJ, 1988—2005; shareholder Buchanan Ingersoll Rooney P.C., Princeton, 2005—, Phila., 2005—. Co-ptnr. in charge of Princeton office Drinker Biddle & Reath LLP, 1995—2000, bd. mem. mng. ptnrs., 1996—2000. Mem. ABA, Pa. Bar Assn., N.J. Bar Assn., Phila. Bar Assn. Avocations: U.S. history, baseball. Office: Buchanan Ingersoll Rooney PC 700 Alexander Pk Princeton NJ 08540-6347 Home Phone: 215-322-7295; Office Phone: 609-987-6807. Business E-Mail: peter.ackourey@bipc.com.

ACOBA, SIMEON RIVERA, JR., state supreme court justice, educator; b. Honolulu, Mar. 11, 1944; s. Simeon R. and Martina (Domingo) A. BA, U. Hawaii, 1966; JD, Northwestern U., Chgo., 1969. Bar: Hawaii 1969, U.S. Dist. Ct. Hawaii, U.S. Ct. Appeals (9th cir.). Law clk. Hawaii Supreme Ct., Honolulu, 1969-70; housing officer U. Hawaii, Honolulu, 1970-71; dep. atty. gen. State of Hawaii, Honolulu, 1971-73; pvt. practice, Honolulu, 1973-80; judge 1st Circuit Ct. Hawaii, Honolulu, 1980-94, Intermediate Ct. Appeals Hawaii, Honolulu, 1994-2000; assoc. justice Hawaii Supreme Ct., 2000—. Atty. on spl. contract divsn. OSHA, Dept. Labor, Honolulu, 1975—77, Pub. Utilities divsn., State of Hawaii, 1976—77; campaign spending com. State of Hawaii, 1976; staff atty. Hawaii State Legislature, 1975; instr. criminal law Hawaii Pacific U., 1992—. Bd. dirs. Hawaii Mental Health Assn., 1975—77, Nuuanu YMCA, 1975—78, Hawaii Youth at Risk, 1990—91; mem. Gov.'s Conf. on Yr. 2000, Honolulu, 1970, Citizens Com. on Adminstrn. of Justice, 1972, State Drug Abuse Commn., 1975—76, Com. to Consider the Adoption of ABA Model Rules of Profl. Conduct, 1989—91; mem. Judicial Edn. Com., 1992—93, Hawaii State Bar Assn. Jud. Adminstrn. Com., 1992—94, Permanent Com. Rules Penal Procedure and Cir. Ct. Rules, 1992—96; subcom. chmn. Supreme Ct. Com. Pattern Jury Instrns., 1990—91; mem. Hawaii Supreme Ct. Ad Hoc Com. Jury Master List, 1991—92. Recipient Liberty Bell award, 1964. Mem.: Am. Judicature Soc. (mem. ct. security com. Hawaii chpt. 2006—), Hawaii State Bar Assn., Hawaii Bar Assn. (dir. young lawyers sect. 1973, ethics award com. 2005—). Office: Hawaii Supreme Ct 417 S King St Honolulu HI 96813-2912

ACOMB, ROBERT BAILEY, JR., lawyer, educator; b. New Orleans, July 28, 1930; s. Robert Bailey and Catherine (Ryan) Acomb; m. Greta LeBlanc, Apr. 25, 1953; children: Robert III, Dwight J., Greta, William Ryan, John. BBA, Tulane U., New Orleans, 1951, JD, 1953. Bar: La. 1953, US Dist. Ct. (ea. and mid. dist.) La. 1953, US Ct. Appeals (5th cir.) 1955, US Supreme Ct. 1967, US Ct. Appeals (7th cir.) 1976, US Ct. Appeals (11th cir.) 1981, US Dist. Ct. (we. dist.) La. 1989. Assoc. Jones, Walker, Waechter, Poitevent, Carrere & Denegre, New Orleans, 1953-56, ptnr., 1956, sr. ptnr., 1968—. Adj. prof. law Tulane U., New Orleans, 1969—; pres. bd. dirs. Christian Bros. Found., Inc., New Orleans, 1989—. Author: Collision and Limitation of Liability, 1997, Transportation Contracts, Charter Parties, Towing Contracts and Affreightment Contracts, 2002, Maritime Personal Injury & Death, 4th edit., 2005; editor: Damages Recoverable in Maritime Matters, 1984; contbr. articles to profl. jours., chapters to books; chmn. adv. editors Tulane Maritime Law Jour., 1976—, mem. editl. bd. Benedicts Maritime Bull., 2003—. Chmn. Archbishop's Cmty. Appeal, New Orleans, 1993; pres. Tulane U. Assocs., New Orleans, 1990—92; mem. bd. adminstrs. Tulane Edn. Fund, 1996—2000. Decorated knight grand cross Equestrian Order of Holy Sepulchre of Jerusalem, knight of St. Gregory Pope Johna Paul II; named Outstanding Alumnus, Emeritus Club U. Tulane, 2003; named one of 50 Top Lawyers, New Orleans City Bus., 2005; named to Best Lawyers in Am., 1983—85; recipient Boisfontaine Trial Advocacy award, La. Bar Assn., 2002. Fellow: Am. Bar Found., Am. Coll. Trial Lawyers (state chair 1978—81); mem.: ABA (mem. standing com. admiralty, chmn. 1979—83), Assn. Average Adjusters US (chmn. 1992—93), Tulane Maritime Law Inst., Maritime Law Assn. US (proctor, meme. exec. com. 1981—84), Tulane Maritime Law Ctr. (chmn. 1982—), New Orleans Bar Assn. (Disting. Maritime Lawyer 1996, Pres. award 2002), Navy League US (pres. New Orleans chpt. 1987—88, state pres. 1990—94), Tulane U. Alumni Assn. (pres. 1989—90, Vol. or the Yr. 1992), Stratford Club, Pickwick Club, Cornell Club, Boston Club, New Orleans Country Club, Order of St. Louis, Mil. Order Fgn. Wars (comdr. La Commandery). Roman Catholic. Avocations: photography, travel, sports. Office: Jones Walker Waechter Poitevent Carrere & Denegre 201 Saint Charles Ave Fl 48 New Orleans LA 70170-1000 Office Phone: 504-582-8112. Office Fax: 504-582-8010. Business E-Mail: bacomb@joneswalker.com.

ACOSTA, ALEX (RENE ALEXANDER ACOSTA), prosecutor, former federal agency administrator; b. Miami; BA, JD, Harvard U. Law clk. US Ct. Appeals (3rd cir.); assoc. Kirkland & Ellis, 1995—97; sr. fellow Ethics & Pub. Policy Ctr., 1997—2000; prin. dep. asst. atty. gen. civil rights divsn. US Dept. Justice, Washington, 2001—02, asst. atty. gen. civil rights divsn., 2003—05, interim US atty. (so. dist.) Fla. Miami, 2005—06, US atty. (so. dist.) Fla., 2006—. Mem. NLRB, 2002—03. Recipient Disting. Leadership award, Arab Am. Anti-Discrimination Com. Mich., 2004, Excellence in Govt. Svc. award, Mex.-Am. Legal Def. and Edn. Fund, 2003, Hugh A. Johnson, Jr. Meml. award, DC Hispanic Bar Assn., 2003, Friend in Govt. award, Am.-Arab Anti-Discrimination Com., 2005. Office: US Attys Office 99 N E 4th St Miami FL 33132*

ACOSTA, EDUARDO G., physiatrist, director; BS, U. of the East, 1965, MD, 1970. Diplomate Am. Bd. Phys. Medicine and Rehab. Intern Booth Meml. Hosp., 1971—72; resident NYU, 1972—75, fellow, 1975—76; med. dir. rehab. unit Med. Ctr., McKinney, Tex., 1991—. Mem.: Tex. Med. Assn. Mailing: Ste 134 375 Mcpl Dr Richardson TX 75080-3543

ACOSTA, LYDIA M., library director; AA, Brevard CC, 1968; BA, U. South Fla., Tampa, 1970, MA in Libr. Sci., 1973. Dir., sec. libr. bd. control East Baton Rouge Parish Libr., 2003—. Mem. Children's Coalition, Vols. in Pub. Schs. Mem.: La. Libr. Assn., Baton Rouge Area Libr. Club (former pres.). Office: East Baton Rouge Parish Libr 7711 Goodwood Blvd Baton Rouge LA 70806 Office Phone: 225-231-3700. E-mail: lacosta@ebr.lib.la.us.

ACOSTA, MARITONI A., lawyer; BA, UCLA, 1991; JD, Loyola Law Sch., 1994. Bar: Calif., cert.: (Family Law Specialist). Ptnr., head family law mediation dept. Feinberg, Mindel, Brandt, Klein & Kline, LA, 2000—. Named a Rising Star, So. Calif. Super Lawyers, 2004—06. Mem.: Santa Monica Bar Assn. (chmn. family law sect.), Philippine Am. Bar Assn. (bd. dir.). Office: Feinberg Mindel Brandt Klein & Kline Ste 900 12400 Wilshire Bldv Los Angeles CA 90025 Office Phone: 310-447-8675 ext 115. Office Fax: 310-447-8678. Business E-Mail: macosta@fmbklaw.com.

ACOSTA, RAYMOND LUIS, federal judge; b. NYC, May 31, 1925; s. Ramon J. and Carmen J. (Acha-Jimenez) Acosta-Colon; m. Marie Hatcher, Nov. 2, 1957; children: Regina, Gregory, Ann Marie. Student, Princeton U., 1948; JD, Rutgers U., 1951. Bar: N.J. 1953, U.S. Supreme Ct. 1956, P.R. 1959. Sole practice, Hackensack, NJ, 1953-54; spl. agt. FBI, San Diego, Washington, Miami, Fla., 1954-58; asst. U.S. atty. San Juan, 1958-61; sole practice, 1961-67; trust officer Banco Credito y Ahorro Ponceno, San Juan, 1967-80; U.S. atty. Dist. P.R., Hato Rey, 1980-82; judge U.S. Dist. Ct. P.R., San Juan, 1982—. Alt. del. U.S.-P.R. Commn. on Status, 1962-63; mem. Gov.'s Spl. Com. to Study Structure and Orgn. Police Dept., P.R., 1969 Contbr. articles to profl. jours. Pres. United Fund, P.R., 1979. Served with USN, 1943-46, Normandy. Recipient Merit cert. Mayor of San Juan, 1973. Mem. Fed. Bar Assn. (pres., P.R. 1967), P.R. Bankers Assn. (chmn. trust div. 1971, 75, 77), P.R. Bar Assn., Soc. Former Spl. Agts. FBI. Office: US Courthouse & PO Bldg Ste 348 300 Recinto Sur St San Juan PR 00901

ACREE, G. HARDY, airport executive; Previous positions with Anchorage Internat. Airport, Alaska, Phila., Indpls. , and Riverside/San Bernardino area airports; mgr., dep. dir. aviation Bush Intercontinental Airport, Houston, 1995—99; dir. Sacramento County Airport Sys., Sacramento Internat. Airport, Calif., 1999—. Office: Sacramento County Airport Sys Sacramento Internat Airport 6900 Airport Blvd Sacramento CA 95837 Office Phone: 916-874-0719. E-mail: Acreeh@saccounty.net.

ACRIVOS, ANDREAS, chemical engineering professor; b. Athens, Greece, June 13, 1928; m. Juana Vivo, Sept. 1, 1956. BSChemE, Syracuse U., 1950; MS, U. Minn., 1951, PhD, 1954. Instr. U. Calif., Berkeley, 1954-55, asst. prof., 1955-59, assoc. prof., 1959-62; prof. Stanford (Calif.) U., 1962-88; Einstein prof. CCNY, 1988-2001. Prof. emeritus, CCNY, 2001—. Contbr. articles to profl. jours. Guggenheim Found. fellow, 1959, 76; recipient Bingham Medal, 1994, Soc. Rheology, Nat. medal of Science, 2001. Fellow AIChE (awards 1963, 68, 84), Am. Phys. Soc. (Fluid Dynamics prize 1991); mem. NAS, NAE, Am. Acad. Arts and Scis., Am. Chem. Soc., Soc. Rheology. Office: CCNY Levich Inst 138th St at Convent Ave New York NY 10031 Business E-Mail: acrivos@sci.ccny.cuny.edu.

ACTA, MANNY (MANUEL ELIAS ACTA), professional baseball manager; b. San Pedro de Macoris, Dominican Republic, Jan. 11, 1969; Profl. baseball player minor league sys. Houston Astros, 1986—91, player-coach A-level team, 1991; coach Asheville (South Atlantic League), NC, 1992, Houston Astros New Orleans AAA Team (Pacific Coast League), 2001; mgr. Auburn (NY-Pa. League), 1993—96, Quad City River Bandits (Houston Astros Midwest League affiliate), 1997, Kissimmee (Fla. State League), 1998—2000, Caracas (Venezuelan Winter League), 1999—2001, Estrellas Orientales (Dominican Winter League), Dominican Republic, 2002—03, Licey Tigers (Dominican Winter League), Dominican Republic, 2003—04; third base & infield coach Montreal Expos, 2002—04, NY Mets, 2005—06; mgr. Washington Nationals, 2006—. Mgr. Dominican Republic Team (World Baseball Classic), 2006. Named Mgr. of Yr., Fla. State League, 1999, Dominican Winter League, 2004. Achievements include winning the Dominican Winter League's Championship and Caribbean World Series as manager of the Licey Tigers. Office: Washington Nats Baseball Club RFK Stadium 2400 E Capitol St SE Washington DC 20003*

ACTON, DAVID, lawyer; b. Phila., Feb. 13, 1933; s. Kenneth Davis and Mary (Musselman) A.; m. Barbara Ann Sullivan, June 18, 1955; children: Lauren Doane, Paul Bodine; m. Jane Thomas Young, June 24, 1978. AB, Yale, 1955; JD, U. Pa., 1960. Assoc. Krusen, Evans & Byrne, Phila., 1960-63; asst. sec., asst. gen. counsel Leeds & Northrup Co., Phila., 1963-65, sec., gen. counsel North Wales, Pa., 1965-71; v.p., gen. counsel K.S. Sweet Assos., King of Prussia, Pa., 1971-75; practice in Bryn Mawr, Pa., 1975-77; v.p. Crockett Mortgage Co., Valley Forge, Pa.; gen. mgr. Hershey's Mill, 1977-82; exec. v.p. Ultec, Inc., Exton, Pa., 1982-85; arbitrator and mediator, 1986—. Mem. Phila. panel Internat. Inst. for Conflict Prevention and Resolution; mem. comml. and constrn. panels Am. Arbitration Assn. Bd. dirs. Nat. Ctr. for the Am. Revolution. Mem. Phila. Bar Assn., Colonial Soc. Pa., Assn. for Conflict Resolution, Mensa, Union League Club, Merion Cricket Club, Yale Club (Phila.), Chevaliers du Tastevin. Home and Office: 233 Righters Mill Rd Gladwyne PA 19035-1532 Home Phone: 610-649-5254; Office Phone: 610-649-4972. Personal E-mail: d.acton1326@comcast.net.

ACTON, DAVID L(AWRENCE), automobile company executive; b. Detroit, Apr. 12, 1949; s. Lawrence E. and Johannah (Cassimatis) A.; m. Dianne Patience McNeill, Sept. 5, 1981; children: Andrew, Stephen, Amy. BME, Gen. Motors Inst., Flint, Mich., 1973; MBA, U. Mich., 1978. Assoc. engr. Hydra-matic div. GM, Ypsilanti, Mich., 1973-74, project engr., 1974-77, supr. indsl. engring., 1977-78, asst. supt. indsl. engring., 1978-81, asst. supt. progress tracking, quality and reliability Detroit, 1981-83, sr. adminstr., 1983-85, mgr. program planning B-O-C- car group, 1985, program mgr. Allanté elec. test system, 1985-87; mgr. elec. design and processing Cadillac Motor Car Co., Detroit, 1987-91, mgr. electrical product systems, 1991-93; chief engr. elec./electronics Cadillac luxury car divsn. GM, Flint, Mich., 1993-96, dir. elec. engring. mid-luxury car group, 1996-97, dir. elec. engring. N.Am. ops. Warren, Mich., 1997-98, chief vehicle engr. OnStar divsn. Troy, Mich., 1998-2000, exec. dir. global telematics, 2000—02, dir. global telematics portfolio planning, 2002—04; pres., CEO Charter Mobile Info. Inc., Owosso, 2004—05; v.p. Connexis LLC, Owosso, 2005—. Bd. dirs. Its Am. Mem.: SAE, Convergence Transp. Electronics Assn. (bd. dirs.). Office: 120 Exchange St Ste 200C Owosso MI 48867

ACUFF, A. MARSHALL, JR., retired investment company executive; Grad., Coll. William & Mary, 1962, U. Mich. Grad. Sch. of Bus. Admin., 1966. Various positions including sr. v.p., mng. dir. & mem. investment policy com. Salomon Smith Barney Inc., 1966—2001; pres. AMA Investment Counsel, LLC. Mem. Inst. of Chartered Financial Analysts; columnist Japan Economic Jour., Handelsblatt; bd. dirs. Owens and Minor Corp. Trustee Charles Stewart Mott Found., 2002—, mem. investment com.; bd. dirs. Jamestown-Yorktown Found., Inc., Episcopal Church Found., William & Mary Endowment Assn., Va. Inst. of Marine Sci. Found., Va. Found. for Independent Coll. Fellow: Assn. for Investment Mgmt. and Rsch.; mem.: Assn. of Governing Bds. of Coll. and U. (chair), NY Soc. of Security Analysts. Office: Charles Stewart Mott Found 503 S Saginaw Str Ste 1200 Flint MI 48502 also: AMA Investment Counsel 50 Bellona Arsenal Midlothian VA 23113

ACUÑA, MARIO H., astrophysicist; b. Córdoba, Argentina, 1940; Grad., U. Córdoba; MSEE, U. Tucumán, Argentina, 1967; PhD in Space Sci., Cath. U., Washington, 1974. Tchg. and rsch. assoc. U. Tucuman Elec. Engring. Dept. and Ionospheric Rsch. Lab. and Argentine Nat. Space Rsch. Commn., 1963—67; with Fairchild-Hiller Corp., Germantown, Md., 1967, head electronic systems divsn., 1968; with NASA Goddard Space Flight Ctr., Greenbelt, Md., 1969—, sr. astrophysicist Planetary Magnetospheres Lab. US project scientist Internat. Solar Terrestrial Physics prog.; instrument scientist, co-investigator or prin.investigator multiple NASA and European Space Agy. missions such as Pioneer, Voyager, Mariner, Giotto, Tether and others; prin. investigator or lead scientist magnetometer investigations Near Earth Asteroid Rendezvous Mission, Mars Global Surveyor, Lunar Prospector, Messenger and STEREO. Contbr. articles to sci. jours. Recipient Exceptional Svc. medal, NASA, 1986, Disting. Svc. medal, 1996, Medal for Exceptional Sci. Achievement, John C. Lindsay award for Space Sci., Moe I. Schneebaum Meml. award, Presdl. Rank Meritorious award, 2003, Outstanding Engring. Achievement award, Cath. U. Alumni Assn., 1991, Outstanding Tech. Contbn. award, Soc. Hispanic Profl. Engrs. Fellow: Am. Geophys. Union; mem.: IEEE, NAS, Internat. Assn. Geomagnetism and Aeronomy, Latin Am. Assn. Space Geophysics (ALAGE) (founding mem.), Sigma Xi. Office: Planetary Magnetospheres Lab NASA Goddard Space Flight Ctr Code 695 Greenbelt MD 20771 Office Phone: 301-286-7258. Office Fax: 301-286-1433. E-mail: mario.acuna@nasa.gov.

ACZÉL, JÁNOS DEZSŐ, mathematician; b. Budapest, Hungary, Dec. 26, 1924; s. Dezső and Irén (Adler) A.; m. Susan Kende, Dec. 14, 1946; children: Catherine, Julie. MA, PhD, U. Budapest, 1947; DSc, Hungarian Acad. Sci., 1957; Dr. honoris causa, U. Karlsruhe, 1990, U. Graz, 1995, Silesian U. Katowice, 1996, U. Miskolc, 1999, U. Debrecen, 2003. Faculty U. Szeged, Hungary, 1948-50; prof. math. Tech. U., Miskolc, 1950-52, Kossuth U., Debrecen, Hungary, 1952-65, U. Waterloo, Ont., Canada, 1965-93, disting. prof., 1969-93, disting. prof. emeritus, 1993—; vis. prof. U. Fla., Gainesville, 1963-64, 81, Stanford U., 1964, U. Köln, Germany, 1965, U. Giessen, 1966, 70, Ruhr U., Bochum, 1968, Fla. Atlantic U., 1968, U. Pavia, 1968, 69, Ist. Naz. Alta Matematica, Rome, 1971, Monash U., Clayton, Victoria, Australia, 1972, Ahmadu Bello U., Zaria, Nigeria, 1975-76, U. Lecce, Italy, 1976, Calif. Inst. Tech., 1978, Karl-Franzens U., Graz, Austria, 1979, 1986, 1991, 1993, 1999, 2003, Okayama U., Japan, 1984, U. Milan, 1985, 91, U. Hamburg, 1985, U. Politécnica Catalunya, Barcelona, 1986, 92, U. Bern, Switzerland, 1986, U. Karlsruhe, Germany, 1992, 98, U. Calif., Irvine, 1994, 1996—2002, 2004—. Cons. Naval Ocean Systems Ctr., San Diego, 1979-81; chmn. Internat. Symposium on Functional Equations, 1962-96, hon. chmn., 1997—; Jeffrey lectr. Acadia U., 1984, Marshak lectr. UCLA, 1998. Author (with S. Gołąb): Funktionalgleichungen der Theorie der geometrischen Objekte, 1960; author: Vorlesungen über Funktionalgleichungen und ihre Anwendungen, 1961, Ein Blick auf Funktionalgleichungen und ihre Anwendungen, 1962, Lectures on Functional Equations and Their Applications, 1966, Dover re-edition, 2006, On Applications and Theory of Functional Equations, 1969; author:

(with Z. Daróczy) On Measures of Information and Their Characterizations, 1975; author: A Short Course on Functional Equations Based Upon Recent Applications to Social and Behavioral Sciences, 1987; author: (with J. Dhombres) Functional Equations in Several Variables with Applications to Mathematics, Information Theory and to the Natural and Social Sciences, 1989, Russian trans., 2003; editor: Functional Equations: History, Applications and Theory, 1984, Aggregating Clones, Colors, Equations, Iterates, Numbers and Tiles, 1995, Rendiconti di Matematica e delle sue Applicazioni, Inequalities and their Applications, Scientiae Mathematicae Japonicae, Results of Mathematics, Mathware and Soft Computing, Publications Mathematicae Debrecen, Comptes Rendus Mathématiques de l'Académie des Sciences Can.; editor-in-chief Theory and Decision Libr.-Math. and Methods Series, hon. editor-in-chief Aequationes Mathematicae. Recipient M. Beke award J. Bolyai Math. Soc., 1961, Hungarian Acad. Scis. award, 1958, 62, Cajal medal Spanish Nat. Coun. Sci. Rsch., 1988, J. Kampé de Feriet award Internat. Conf. on Info. Processing and Mgmt. of Uncertainty in Knowledge-based Sys., 2004. Fellow Royal Soc. Can., Hungarian Acad. Scis. (fgn.); mem. Can. Math. Soc., Am. Math. Soc., N.Y. Acad. Scis. Achievements include rsch. in modern theory of functional equations; gen. theorems and applications to geometry, algebra, analysis, econs., mathematical psychology, utility, decision, probability and info. theory; theories of mean values, measurement, and webs. Office: Univ Waterloo Pure Math Dept Waterloo ON Canada N2L 3G1 E-mail: jdaczel@math.uwaterloo.ca.

ADAIKKALAVAN, RAMAN, computer scientist, educator; b. Pudukkottai, Tamil Nadu, India, 1978; s. Adaikkalavan Meyyappan and Soundaram Adaikkalavan. B of Engring. in Computer Sci. and Engring., Bharathidasan U., Tiruchirapalli, Tamilnadu, India, 1999; MS in Computer Sci. and Engring., U. Tex., Arlington, 2002, PhD in Computer Sci. and Engring., 2006. Rsch. assoc. info. tech. lab., CSE Dept, U. Tex., Arlington, 2000—06, grad. tchg./rsch. asst., faculty assoc. computer sci. and engring. dept., 2001—06, instr. computer sci. and engring. dept., 2006; asst. prof. computer sci. dept. Ind. U., South Bend, 2006—. Contbr. articles to profl. jours. Active mem., fund raiser and vol. Fine Arts Soc. India, U. Tex., Arlington, 2001; vol. Vibha.org (For Underprivileged Children), Dallas, 2004, DFW Hindu Temple, Irving, 2003. Scholar, U. Tex., 2004—05, 2005—06; Rudolf Hermanns Grad. fellow, 2002—06. Mem.: IEEE, ACM, Upsilon Pi Epsilon, Tau Beta Pi. Home Phone: 214-293-8468; Office Phone: 574-520-4295.

ADAIR, DONALD ROBERT, lawyer; b. Rochester, NY, July 24, 1943; s. Robert Voigt and Esca Lois (Naas) A.; m. Susanne Jonsson, Nov. 1969 (div. 1974); 1 child, Emily Elsebeth; m. Judith Ann Jameson, Nov. 29, 1975 (div. Nov. 1995); children: Thomas, Abigail, Kathryn Carrie. BA, Harvard U., 1965; JD, Cornell U., 1968. Bar: N.Y. 1968, U.S. Dist. Ct. (we. dist.) N.Y. 1968. Assoc. Nixon, Hargrave, Devans & Doyle, Rochester, 1968-76, ptnr., 1977-87; prin. Adair Law Firm LLP and predecessor firms, Rochester, 1988—. Bd. dirs. Stone Constrn. Equip., Inc., Honeoye, N.Y., Victor Insulators, Inc., Victor, N.Y. Contbr. chpt. to book New York Limited Liability Companies and Partnerships, 1995. Active Greater Rochester chpt. ARC, 1973—, chair, 1991-93; mem. Consumer Credit Counseling Svc. of Rochester, Inc., 1972—, chair, 1994-96. Recipient Spl. Citation for Exceptional Vol. Svc., Greater Rochester chpt. ARC, 1991. Fellow Am. Bar Found. (life); mem. ABA, N.Y. State Bar Assn., Monroe County Bar Assn. Office: Adair Law Firm LLP 300 Linden Oaks 220 Rochester NY 14625-2805

ADAIR, ELEANOR REED, environmental biologist; b. Arlington, Mass., Nov. 28, 1926; d. Kenneth Clarke and Margaret Reed; m. Robert Kemp Adair, June 21, 1952; children: Douglas, Margaret, James(dec.). BA, Mt. Holyoke Coll., 1948; MA, U. Wis., 1951, PhD, 1955. From rsch. asst. to lectr., sr. scientist Yale U., New Haven, 1960—. From asst. fellow to fellow John B. Pierce Lab., New Haven, 1966—96; cons. sci. adv. bd. EPA, 1983—89; sr. scientist Electromagnetic Radiation Effects, Air Force Rsch. Lab., Brooks AFB, Tex., 1996—2001, sr. scientist emeritus, 2001—. Editor: Microwaves & Thermoregulation, 1983; contbr. articles to profl. jours. Bd. dirs. Am. Himalayan Found., 1990—. Fellow: IEEE, APA, AAAS, N.Y. Acad. Scis., Am. Inst. Med. and Biol. Engring.; mem.: Bioelectromagnetics Soc. Avocations: birdwatching, gardening, Buddhism. Home: 50 Deepwood Dr Hamden CT 06517

ADAIR, IRMALEE TRAYLOR, social worker; b. Portsmouth, Ohio, Jan. 5, 1920; d. Finley Arving and Lora Alice (Nickell) Traylor; m. James Russell Adair; children: Jacqueline, Robert, Celeste, Marquita. AA in Social Work, Chipola Jr. Coll., 1980; BA in Social Work, U. West Fla., 1983; MSW, Fla. State U., 1985. Cert. gerontologist, community info. counselor. Sr. aide Guardian Office ESSH, Trevose, Pa.; interviewer, subcontractor Nat. Analysts, Phila.; social worker Hill House Manor, Bensalem, Pa.; ret. Mem. NASW, Fla. State U. Alumni Assn., U. West. Fla. Alumni Assn., Am. Assn. Retired Persons.

ADAIR, ROBERT KEMP, physicist, educator; b. Ft. Wayne, Ind., Aug. 14, 1924; s. Robert Cleland and Margaret (Wiegman) Adair; m. Eleanor Reed, June 21, 1952; children: Douglas McVeigh, Margaret Guthrie, James Cleland. Ph.B., U. Wis., 1947, PhD, 1951, DSc (hon.), 1994. Instr. physics U. Wis., Madison, 1950-53; physicist Brookhaven Nat. Lab., Upton, NY, 1953-58, assoc. dir. high energy and nuc. physics, 1987-88; mem. faculty Yale U., New Haven, 1958—, prof. physics, 1961-72, Eugene Higgins prof. physics, 1972-88, Sterling prof. physics, 1988—94, Sterling prof. emeritus, 1994—, chmn. dept. physics, 1967-70, dir. divsn. phys. scis., 1977-80, sr. rsch. scientist, 1994—. Physicist Nat. Baseball League, 1987—89. Author (with Earle C. Fowler): (book) Strange Particles, 1963; author: Concepts in Physics, 1969, The Great Design, 1987, The Physics of Baseball, 1990; assoc. editor: Phys. Rev., 1963—66, Phys. Rev. Letters, 1974—76; editor, 1978—84. With inf. US Army, 1943—46. Guggenheim fellow, 1954, Ford Found. fellow, 1962—63, Sloan Found. fellow, 1962—63. Fellow: Am. Acad. Arts and Scis., Am. Phys. Soc. (chmn. divsn. particles and fields 1972—73); mem.: NAS (chmn. physics sect. 1986—89, sec. class phys. scis. 1989—92, chmn. class phys. scis. 1992—94). Home: 50 Deepwood Dr Hamden CT 06517-3415 Office: Yale U Dept Physics Sloane Physics Lab PO Box 208121 New Haven CT 06520-8121 Business E-Mail: adair@hepmail.physics.yale.edu.

ADAIR, STEFAN RENE, plastic surgeon; BA cum laude, Johns Hopkins U., 1988; MD, Tulane U., 1993. Diplomate Am. Bd. Plastic Surgery. Residency Santa Barbara Cottage Hosp., Calif., 1998; rotation Sherman Oaks Burn Ctr., Calif., 1994, Cedars-Sinai Hosp., LA, 1995, LA Children's Hosp., 1996, LA County Hosp., 1996; fellowship in plastic surgery U. Calif. Irvine, 1998—2000; pvt. practice Beverly Hills, 2000—, Atlanta, 2005—, Macon, Ga., 2005—. Externship in reconstructive surgery Oxford Med. Sch., England, 1993; staff privileges Cedars Sinai Hosp., Century City Hosp. Contbr. articles to profl. jours. Lt. comdr. USNR. Fellow: ACS.

ADAM, JOHN, JR., insurance company executive emeritus; b. Braintree, Mass., Dec. 14, 1914; s. John and Harriet E. (Hubley) A.; m. Ruth E. Maddock, Dec. 27, 1945. AB, Oberlin Coll., 1937; LL.D. (hon.), Clark U., 1974. Underwriter Glens Falls Ins. Co., 1938-39, mgr. inland marine dept., 1939-40; with Central Mut. Ins. Co., 1940-60, v.p., 1957-60, Worcester Mut. Ins. Co., 1960, pres., 1960-79; also dir. pres., dir. Hanover Ins. Cos., 1969-79, dir., 1979, pres. emeritus, 1979—; pres. Heald, Inc., 1979-87. Chmn. adv. com. Mich. Investment Fund, M.B.W. Venture Ptnrs. Author: More Sales for You, 1949, also articles. Chmn. Mass. Bd. Higher Edn., 1972-77; past pres. Greater Worcester Community Found. Mem. Worcester C. of C. (past pres., dir.), Worcester County Music Assn. (past pres.), C.P.C.U. Soc. (nat. pres. 1967, dir.), Worcester Econ. Club (past pres.), Boston Sales Execs. Club (past pres.)

ADAM, THOMAS, humanities educator; b. Hennigsdorf, Brandenburg, Germany, Feb. 3, 1968; s. Peter G. Adam; Degree, U. Leipzig, Germany, 1994, PhD, 1998. Vis. scholar U. Toronto, 1999—2001; assoc. prof. U. Tex., Arlington, 2001—. Editor: (edited volume) Philanthropy, Patronage, and Civil Society: Experiences from Germany, Great Britain, and North America, 2004, (three-volume encyclopedia) Germany and the Americas: Culture, Politics, and History, 2005; co-editor (edited volume) Traveling between Worlds: German-American Encounters, 2006. Fellow, Alexander von Humboldt Found., 1999—2001. Mem.: Am. Hist. Assn. Office: Box 19529 University Hall Rm 320 Arlington TX 76019-0529 Home Phone: 817-860-0945. Office Fax: 817-272-2852. Business E-Mail: adam@uta.edu.

ADAMANY, DAVID WALTER, law and political science educator, former academic administrator; b. Janesville, Wis., Sept. 23, 1936; s. Walter Joseph and Dora Marie (Mutter) Adamany. AB, Harvard U., 1958, JD, 1961; MS, U. Wis., 1963, PhD in Polit. Sci., 1967; LLD (hon.), Adrian Coll., 1984; AAS (hon.), Schoolcraft Coll., 1986; D. Engring. (hon.), Mich. Tech. U., 1987; D in Pub. Svc. (hon.), Eastern Mich. U., 1997. Bar: Wis. 1961. Spl. asst. to atty. gen. State of Wis., Madison, 1961—63, exec. pardon counsel, 1963; commr. Wis. Pub. Svc. Commn., 1963—65; instr. polit. sci. Wis. State U., Whitewater, 1965—67; asst. prof., then assoc. prof. Wesleyan U., Middletown, Conn., 1967—72, dean coll., 1969—71; assoc. prof., then prof. polit. sci. U. Wis., Madison, 1972—77; v.p. acad. affairs, prof. Calif. State U., Long Beach, 1977—80, U. Md., College Park, 1980—82; disting. prof. law and polit. sci. Wayne State U., Detroit, 1982—2000, pres., 1982—97, pres. emeritus, 1997—; CEO Detroit Pub. Schs., 1999—2000; pres. Temple U., Phila., 2000—06, Laura Carnell prof. law and polit. sci., 2006—, chancellor, 2006—. Chmn. Wis. Coun. Criminal Justice, 1973—75, Wis. Elections Bd., 1976—77; sec. Wis. Dept. Revenue, 1973—75. Author: Financing Politics, 1969, Campaign Finance in America, 1972; co-author: Borzoi Reader in American Politics, 1972, American Government: Democracy and Liberty in Balance, 1975, Political Money, 1975; editl. bd.: Social Sci. Quarterly, 1973—, State and Local Govt. Rev., 1974—80; contbr. articles to profl. jours. Mem. exec. com. Detroit Med. Ctr., 1982—97; chmn. Mich. Bicentennial of U.S. Constrn. Commn., 1986—88; mem. Mich. Civil Svc. Commn., 1996—99; bd. dirs. Greater Phila. First, 2001—, African Am. Mus. Phila., 2001—; mem. Wis. Gov.'s Commn. on Campaign Fin. Reform, 1996—97; bd. dirs. Detroit Inst. Arts Founders Soc., 1983—92, Detroit Symphony Orch., 1983—89, Detroit Econ. Growth Corp., 1984—92, Karmanos Cancer Inst., 1982—97, New Detroit, 1982—95, Blue Cross Blue Shield Found. Mich., 1995—2000, Gilmour Fund, 1996—, HOPE Fund of Cmty. Found. of S.E. Mich., 1995—2000, Temple U. Health Sys., 2000—. Mem.: ABA (commn. on coll. and univ. legal studies 1992—95), ACLU, Pres.'s Coun. State Univs. (chmn. 1982—97), Am. Polit. Sci. Assn., Wis. Bar Assn., Greater Phila. C of C (exec. com. 2000—), Nat. Adv. Com. on Instl. Quality and Integrity (U.S. dept. edn. 1994—2000), Can.-U.S. Fulbright Commn. (bd. dirs. 1993—97). Democrat. Office: Temple U 1801 N Broad St Philadelphia PA 19122 Office Phone: 215-204-3737. E-mail: David.Adamany@temple.edu.*

ADAMCIK, JOE ALFRED, retired chemistry professor, lawyer; b. Taylor, Tex., June 28, 1930; s. Joseph John Adamcik and Pearle Mae Offield. BS, U. Tex., Austin, 1951, MA, 1954; PhD, U. Ill., 1958; JD, Tex. Tech. U., 1991. Bar: Tex. 1991. Asst. prof. chemistry Tex. Tech. U., Lubbock, 1957-61, assoc. prof. chemistry, 1961-88; ret., 1988; practiced in Lubbock, 1991-95; ret., 1995. Mediator Dispute Resolution Ctr., Lubbock, 1991—2004. Contbr. articles to profl. chemistry jours. Fellow AAAS, Tex. Acad. Sci. (v.p.); mem. Am. Chem. Soc. (dir. 1981-88), Am. Geophys. Union, Royal Soc. Chemistry. Avocation: computers. Home: 5223 42d St Lubbock TX 79414 E-mail: jadamcik@aol.com.

ADAMEK, CHARLES ANDREW, lawyer; b. Chgo., Dec. 24, 1944; s. Stanley Charles and Virginia Marie (Budzban) A.; m. Lori Merriel Klein; children: Donald Steven, Elizabeth Jean. BA with honors, U. Mich., 1966, JD, 1969. Bar: Ill. 1969, Calif. 1978. Clk. U.S. Dist. Judge U.S. Fed. Cts., Chgo., 1969-71; assoc. atty. Lord Bissell & Brook, Chgo., 1971-77, ptnr., 1977-78, LA, 1978—2006, of counsel, 2007—. Mem. ABA, Ill. State Bar Assn., State Bar Calif., Nat. Assn. Railroad Trial Counsel(emeritus mem.). Roman Catholic. Avocations: banjo, hockey. Office: Lord Bissell & Brook 300 S Grand Ave Ste 800 Los Angeles CA 90071-3119 Home Phone: 818-790-3941; Office Phone: 213-687-6721. Business E-Mail: cadamek@lordbissell.com.

ADAMI, NORMAN J., brewery executive; b. Kroonstad, S. Africa, Aug. 12, 1954; children: Kelly, Simon. Honors degree in Bus. Sci., U. Cape Town, 1977; MBA, U. Witwatersrand, 1979. Projects officer, various sr. level positions SABMiller plc The South African Breweries Ltd., 1979—94, mng. dir., 1994—95, chmn., mem. exec. com., 1995—; pres., CEO Miller Brewing Co., 2003—06, SABMiller Americas, 2006—. Office: Miller Brewing Co 3939 W Highland Blvd Milwaukee WI 53208

ADAMIAN, GREGORY HARRY, academic administrator; b. Somerville, Mass., Sept. 17, 1926; s. Adam K. and Sandy (Martin) Adamian; m. June Mouradian, July 6, 1958 (dec. Jan. 1967); children: Douglas, Daniel; m. Deborah Murdza, Jan. 1, 1978. AB, Harvard, 1947; MPA, JD, Boston U., 1951, LLD (hon.), 1991; DCS (hon.), Bentley Coll., 1991. Bar: Mass. 1951. Since practiced in, Cambridge; lectr. law and econs. Suffolk U., 1953-54; prof. law Bentley Coll., Waltham, Mass., 1955-67, chmn. dept. law, 1968-70, pres. coll., 1970-91, chancellor, 1991—. Lectr. real estate law Am. Savs. and Loan Inst. Pres. and trustee emeritus Bentley Coll. Lt. USN, 1944—47. Recipient Boyan Humanity award, Armenian Students Assn., 1973, Silver Shingle Disting. Svc. award, Boston U. Law Sch., 1986, Humanities award, 1990, Significant SIG medal, 1997, St. Sahag & St. Mesrob medal, Armenian Ch., 1998. Mem.: ABA, Am. Bus. Law Assn., Boston Bar Assn., Mass. Bar Assn., Nat. Assn. Armenian Studies and Rsch., Oakley Country Club, Shriners, Masons. Mem. Armenian Apostolic Ch. Office: Bentley Coll Office of Chancellor Waltham MA 02452

ADAMIEC, JEAN KRAUS, retired advertising executive; b. NYC; d. Henry Fred and Florence (Dulfer) Kraus; m. Robert John Adamiec, July 23, 1966 (dec. 2001); 1 child, Tracy Christine. BA, Syracuse U., NY; AS, Del. Co. CC, Media, Pa., 1987. Shopping editor, "What's New" editor Outdoor Life Mag., NYC, 1955—58; merchandising mgr. Field & Stream Mag., NYC, 1958—61; advt. promotions mgr. Internat. Sci. and Tech. Mag., NYC, 1961—63; merchandising mgr. True Mag., NYC, 1963—66; tchr. Taipei Am. Sch., Taiwan, 1966—68; tax preparer, cons. Paperworkers Union, Phila., 1995—97; estates executrix, fin. adminstr. Wallingford, Pa., 2001—. Mem.: Syracuse U. Alumni Assn., Newcomers & Neighbors, Phi Mu Alumnae Assn. Presbyterian. Avocations: travel, theater, investing, animal welfare. Home and Office: 106 Brent Dr Wallingford PA 19086 Office Phone: 610-876-2962.

ADAMO, KENNETH ROBERT, lawyer; b. SI, NY, Sept. 27, 1950; BS, ChE, Rensselaer Polytech. Inst., 1972; JD, Union U., Albany, 1975; LLM, John Marshall Law Sch., 1989. Bar: Ill. 1975, N.Y. 1976, Ohio 1984, Tex. 1988, U.S. Patent and Trademark Office. Ptnr. Jones, Day, Reavis & Pogue, Cleve. Mem.: Internat. Bar Assn. Office: Jones Day Reavis & Pogue N Point 901 Lakeside Ave Cleveland OH 44114 Address: 2727 N Harwood Dallas TX 75201 Office Phone: 216-586-7120, 214-969-4856. Business E-Mail: kradamo@jonesday.com.

ADAMS, A. JOHN BERTRAND, public affairs consultant, director; b. Liverpool, Eng., Nov. 22, 1931; came to U.S., 1962, naturalized, 1971; s. Wilfrid and Francine Sophia (Bertrand) A.; m. Vibeke Dinsen, June 3, 1963 (div. 1975); m. Judith Ann Duff, Oct. 15, 1978; 1 dau., Caroline Louise. Corr. London Daily Telegraph, 1952-56; editor, bur. chief, asst. dir. news Radio Free Europe, Bonn and Munich, W.Ger., 1956-62; Africa corr. ABC News, 1963; writer, exec. CBS News, NYC, 1964-70; assoc. dir. advt. and pub. rels. Investment Co. Inst., 1971-72; dir. pub. affairs U.S. Price Commn., Washington, 1972-73; pres. John Adams Assocs., Inc., Washington, 1973—; founding chmn. The WORLDCOM Group, NYC, London, Tokyo, 1987. Bd. dirs. King Comm. Group, Washington. Author: (with J.M. Burke) Civil Rights: A Current Guide to the People, Organizations and Events, 1970; editor: Energy Policy: Industry Perspectives, 1975. Bd. dirs. Psychiat. Inst. Found., Washington, 1974-79, Nat. Coun. Fireworks Safety, 1986-96, Radio Free Europe Radio Liberty Fund, 1987—, Am. Com. for Aid to Poland, 1989-97, Am. Friends of Queen Mary Coll., U. London, 1990—, Friends of Benjamin Franklin House, London, 1990—; exec. dir. Eviron. Industry Coun., 1975-80; mem adv. bd. Gallaudet Coll. for Deaf, Washington, 1977-79. Lt. King's Shropshire Light Inf., Brit. Army, 1951-52, Korea. Recipient Knight's Cross, Order of Merit, Govt. of Poland, 1998, Disting. Svc. award U.S. Price Commn., 1973. Mem. Pub. Rels. Soc. Am. (Silver Anvil award 1978, 84, Hall of Fame, 1999), Nat. Press Club, Fed. City Club, Univ. Club (Washington), Severn River Yacht Club (Annapolis, Md.). Office: John Adams Assocs 807 National Press Building Washington DC 20045 Home: Oakleigh Farm 38065 Kite Ln Lovettsville VA 20180 Office Phone: 202-737-8400. Business E-Mail: jadams@johnadams.com.

ADAMS, ALBERT T., lawyer; b. Cleve., Dec. 20, 1950; BA, Harvard Coll., 1973; MBA, Harvard Bus. Sch., 1977; JD, Harvard Law Sch., 1977. Bar: Ohio 1977, US Tax Ct., 1977. Ptnr. Baker & Hostetler, Cleve., chmn. Cleve. office, 1996—, mem. policy com. Mem.: ABA (mem. bus. law section, mem. com. on developments in bus. financing), Cleve. Bar Assn., Ohio Bar Assn. Office: Baker & Hostetler 3200 Nat City Ctr 1900 E 9th St Ste 3200 Cleveland OH 44114-3475 Office Phone: 261-861-7499. Office Fax: 216-696-0740. Business E-Mail: aadams@bakerlaw.com.

ADAMS, ALFRED GRAY, lawyer; b. Winston-Salem, NC, Feb. 28, 1946; s. Carlton Noble and Elizabeth (Walker) A.; m. Elizabeth Lark; children: Alfred Gray Jr., Amanda Laing. BA, Wake Forest U., 1968, JD, 1973. Bar: NC 1973; cert. specialist bus., comml., indsl. real estate property transactions. Ptnr. Van Winkle, Buck, Wall, Starnes & Davis, P.A., Asheville, NC, 1973-94, Kilpatrick Stockton L.L.P., Winston-Salem, 1994—2001, Womble, Carlyle, Sandridge & Rice, PLLC, Winston-Salem, 2001—. Adj. prof. law Wake Forest U., 1996-2005. Assoc. editor: Wake Forest Law Rev., 1972. Chmn. Buncombe County Tax. Adv. Com., Asheville, 1983; Leadership Cir. chair United Way, 2000; pres. Wake Forest U. Alumni Coun., 2003—04; mem. Centenary United Meth. Ch., bd. trustees, 2004—, chmn. bd. trustees, 2007; bd. dir. Downtown Winston-Salem Partnership, Winston-Salem, 2002—, Downtown Winston-Salem Found., 2003—, chair, 2006—; bd. dirs. Piedmont Triad Rsch. Park, 2005—. Named Top Real Estate Atty. NC Legal Elite NC Bus. Mag., 2004; James Mason scholar Wake Forest U., 1972. Mem. NC Bar Assn. (bd. govs. 1987-90, real property sect. vice chmn. 1982-83, chmn. 1983-84, writer, lectr. real property and future interests bar rev. course 1981-83, real property curriculum adv. com. 1984-91, chmn. 1988-91, seminar planner and lectr. real property 1987-03, chmn. cont. legal edn. com. 1991-93), Am. Coll. Real Estate Lawyers, Am. Coll. Mortgage Attys. (state chair 1995-02, bd. regents 1996-98, sec. 1998, pres. 2000-01), Biltmore Forest Country Club (bd. govs. 1993-94), Forsyth Country Club (bd. dirs. 2003-05, pres. 2005), Old North State Club. Republican. Methodist. Home: 115 Sullivan Way Winston Salem NC 27104-4911 Office: One W Fourth St Winston Salem NC 27101 Home Phone: 336-760-2674; Office Phone: 336-721-3642. Business E-Mail: aadams@wcsr.com.

ADAMS, ALICE, sculptor; b. NYC, Nov. 16, 1930; d. Charles P. and Loretto G. (Tobin) Adams; m. William D. Gordy, Feb. 7, 1969; 1 child, Katherine Adams Gordy. Student, Adelphi Coll., 1948—50; BFA, Columbia U., 1953; postgrad. (French Govt. fellow), 1953—54; postgrad. Fulbright Travel grantee, L'Ecole Nat d'Art Decoratif, Aubusson, France, 1953—54. Lectr. Manhattanville Coll., Purchase, NY, 1960—79; instr. sculpture Sch. Visual Arts, 1980—87. One-woman shows include Hall Bromm Gallery, NYC, 1979, 1980, Lehman Coll. Gallery, 2000—01, exhibited in group shows at Whitney Mus. Am. Art, 1971, 1973, Indpls. Mus. Art, 1974, Nassau County Mus. Fine Arts, Roslyn, NY, 1977, Wave Hill, Riverdale, NY, 1979, Mus. Modern Art, NYC, 1984, Represented in permanent collections Weatherspoon Gallery U. NC, Greensboro, U. Nebr., Everson Mus., Syracuse, NY, Haags Gemetemuseum, The Hague, Netherlands, Am. Crafts Mus., NYC, Edwin I. Ulrich Mus., Wichita, prin. works include Bot. Garden, Toledo, Port Authority NY and NJ, Thomas Jefferson U., Phila., NYC Bd. Edn., State of Conn., Denver Internat. Airport, NYC Met. Transp. Authority, U. Tex., San Antonio, Broward County, Fla., U. Del., Newark, Montclair State U., Station NJ Transit, Vets. Meml. Home, Vineland, NJ; mem. design team Seattle Transit Project, St. Louis Metro-Link Project, Midland Metro, Brimingham, Eng., Charlotte Area Transit Sys., NC, 2003—05. Creative Artists Pub. Svc. grantee, 1973—74, 1976—77, Nat. Endowment Arts Artists grantee, 1978—79, AM. Acad. Arts and Letters grantee, 1984, Richard Florsheim grantee, 1999, Guggenheim fellow, 1981—82, Rockefeller Found. resident, Bellagio, Italy, 2002. Home: 3370 Fort Independence St Bronx NY 10463-4502 Office Phone: 718-543-4658.

ADAMS, ARLIN MARVIN, lawyer, retired judge, arbitrator, mediator; b. Phila., Apr. 16, 1921; s. Aaron M. and Mathilda (Landau) A.; m. Neysa Cristol, Nov. 10, 1942; children: Carol (Mrs. Howard Kirshner), Judith A., Jane C. BS in Econs. with highest honors, Temple U., 1941; LLB with honors, U. Pa., 1947, MA in Econs., 1950; DHL (hon.), Temple U., 1964; DSc (hon.), Phila. Coll. Optometry, 1965; LLD (hon.), Phila. Coll., 1966, Susquehanna U., 1985, Muhlenberg Coll., 1986, Villanova U., 1987, U. Pa., 1998. Bar: Pa. 1947; U.S. Ct. Appeals (3rd cir.), 1947. Law clk., Chief Justice Horace Stern Pa. Supreme Ct., 1947; assoc. firm Schnader, Harrison, Segal & Lewis, Phila., 1947-50, sr. ptnr., 1950-63, 66-69; sec. pub. welfare Commonwealth of Pa., Phila., 1963-66; judge U.S. Ct. Appeals (3d cir.), Phila., 1969-87; counsel Schnader, Harrison, Segal & Lewis, Phila., 1987—. Apptd. ind. counsel to investigate Dept. HUD, 1990-95; apptd. spl. counsel Pa. Commn. of Police, 1994-95; instr. Am. Inst. Banking, Phila., 1949-52; lectr. fed. practice Law Sch., U. Pa., Phila., 1952-56, lectr. constl. law, 1972-97; endowed chair Arlin M. Adams Professorship Constl. Law, U. Pa. Law Sch., 2004. Author: Law and Religion, 2 vols., 1991, A Nation Dedicated to Religious Liberty, 1990; Editor-in-chief Law Review U. Penn., 1947; contbr. articles to profl. jours. Pres. Annenberg Inst., 1988—91; chmn. bd. dirs. Moss Rehab. Hosp., Phila., 1962—63; trustee U. Pa., 1985—; chmn. U.S. Supreme Ct. Jud. Fellows Commn., 1987—93, Fels Inst. Govt., Phila., 1967—77, Sch. of Social Work, Bryn Mawr (Pa.) Coll., 1967—78, Diagnostic and Rehab. Ctr., Phila., 1971—72; chmn. overseers U. Pa. Law Sch., 1985—92; trustee Med. Coll. of Pa., 1974—80, hon. trustee, 1981—98; trustee German Marshall Meml. Fund, 1972—84, Lewis H. Stevens Trust, Bryn Mawr Coll., 1972—78, Columbia U. Ctr. for Law and Econ. Studies, U. Pa. Inst. for Law and Econs., William Penn Found.; hon. trustee Phila. Mus. Art, 1998—; mem. Cardinal's Commn. re Abuse of Children, 2002. With

USNR, 1942—45, North Pacific. Recipient Disting. Service award U. Pa. Law Sch., 1981, Justice award Am. Jud. Soc., 1982, John Courtney Murray award DePaul U., 1987, Cresset award Rosemont Coll., 1988, Gold Medallion award Chapel of Four Chaplains, Founders award Temple U., 1997, Phila. award, 1997. Mem. ABA (del. ho. of dels. 1966-67, 75-77, chmn. trade assn. com.), Am. Law Inst., Am. Bar Found., Pa. Bar Assn. (pres. jr. bar 1950, ho. of dels. 1967-71, pres.'s award 2005), Phila. Bar Assn. (chancellor 1967, Gold Medal award 1999), Am. Judicature Soc. (pres. 1975-77, Justice award), Am. Philos. Soc. (sec. 1980-83, v.p. 1987-92, pres. 1993-99), Am. Acad. Arts and Scis., Arlin Adams Law and Soc. Inst., Phila. Club, Union League, Sun. Breakfast Club, Legal Club (pres. 1986-91), Jr. Legal Club, Order of Coif, Beta Gamma Sigma. Office Phone: 215-751-2072. E-mail: aadams@schnader.com.

ADAMS, AUSTIN A., bank executive; b. NC, 1943; Grad., Appalachian State Univ., 1965. Head of operations and automation First Union Corp., 1985—2001; exec. v.p., head of technology and operation Bank One Corp., 2001, exec. v.p., chief info. officer, 2001—04, JPMorgan Chase (acquired Bank One), 2004—. Named a Premier 100 IT Leader, Computerworld mag., 2004; recipient Disting. Alumni award, Appalachian State Univ., 1996. Office: JPMorgan Chase 1 Bank One Plz Chicago IL 60670

ADAMS, BARBARA, language educator, poet, writer; b. NYC, Mar. 23, 1932; d. David S. Block and Helen (Taxter) Block Tyler; m. Elwood Adams, June 6, 1952; (dec. 1993); children: Steven, Amy, Anne, Samuel. BS, SUNY, New Paltz, 1962, MA, 1970; PhD, NYU, 1981. Prof. English Pace U., NYC, 1984—2000, dir. bus. comm., 1984—2001. Poet in residence Cape Cod Writers' Conf., 1988. Author: Double Solitaire, 1982, The Enemy Self: The Poetry & Criticism of Laura Riding, 1990, Hapax Legomena, 1990, Negative Capability, 1999 (1st Prize for Fiction); (poetry) The Ordinary Living, 2004; (play) God's Lioness and the Crow: Sylvia Plath and Ted Hughes, 2000; author numerous poems; contbr. articles to profl. jours. Recipient 1st prize for poetry NYU and Acad. Am. Poets, 1975, 1st prize for fiction Negative Capability contest, 1999; Penfield fellow NYU, 1977. Mem. PEN, Poetry Soc. Am., Poets and Writers. Home: 59 Coach Ln Newburgh NY 12550-3818 Personal E-mail: bbadams323@verizon.net.

ADAMS, BARBARA, lawyer; b. Hutchinson, Kans., Nov. 17, 1951; d. Robert Thomas and MaryJane (Lewis) Adams; m. John B. Rosenthal, Apr. 22, 1983 (div. 1986); children: Anna Adams-Sarthou, Kari Torp, Sian Torp. BA, Smith Coll., 1973; JD, Temple U., 1978. Bar: Pa. 1978, US Dist. Ct. Ea. Dist. Pa. 1978, US Ct. Appeals 3rd Cir. 1978. Rsch. ofcl. Schuylkill County Office Tech. Assistance, Pottsville, Pa., 1974-75; mgr. First Valley Bank, Bethlehem, Pa., 1975-77; clk. Duane Morris LLP, Phila., 1977—78, assoc., 1978—85, ptnr., 1986—2005, chair firm fin. practice group; gen. counsel for Commonwealth of Pa., 2005—. Co-author booklet: Business Political Action in Pennsylvania, 1977; editor PABL Update newsletter, 1991-92. Coord. housing task force Rendell Transition Team, Phila., 1991-92; policy com. co-chair of housing Gov.-elect Rendell Transition Team, 2002; commr. Ind. Charter Commn. of City of Phila., 1992—94, Phila. Gas Commn., 1995-98; bd. mem. & sec. Phila. Neighborhood Enterprise, 1989-93; treas. Reading Terminal Market Corp., 1994-2001, bd. mem., 1997-2001; co-founder Pa. Energy Buyers Forum, 1997-, mem. mgmt. com., sec./treas.; bd. mem. Phila. Assn. Cmty. Devel. Corporations, 1998-2005, People's Emergency Ctr., 2003-05. Mem. ABA (sect. pub. utility; charter mem. forum on affordable housing and cmty. devel. law), Pa. Bar Assn., Phila. Bar Assn. (bus. law sect.), Nat. Assn. Bond Lawyers, Pa. Assn. Bond Lawyers (bd. dirs. 1991-97). Avocations: interior decorating, travel, violin, yoga. Office: Office Gen Counsel 225 Main Capitol Harrisburg PA 17120

ADAMS, BERNARD SCHRODER, retired college president; b. Lancaster, Pa., July 20, 1928; s. Martin Ray and Charlotte (Schroder) A.; m. Natalie Virginia Stout, June 2, 1951; children: Deborah Rowland, David Schroder. BA, Princeton, 1950; MA, Yale, 1951; PhD, U. Pitts., 1964; LL.D. (hon.), Lawrence U., 1967; cert., Inst. for Ednl. Mgmt., Harvard U., 1975. Asst. dir. admissions, instr. English Princeton, 1953-57; dir. admissions and student aid U. Pitts., 1957-60, spl. asst. to chancellor, 1960-64; dean students, lectr. English Oberlin (Ohio) Coll., 1964-66; pres. Ripon (Wis.) Coll., 1966-85, Ft. Lewis Coll., Colo., 1985-87; ednl. cons. pvt. practice, Colo. Springs, 1987-88; v.p. resources Goodwill Industries, Colorado Springs, Colo., 1988-96; ret. Dir. Wis. Power & Light Co., Newton Funds, 1970-85; cons., examiner Commn. on Instns. Higher Edn., North Cen. Assn. Colls. and Secondary Schs., 1972-87, exec. commr., 1981-86; bd. dirs. Four Corners Opera Assn., 1985-87, pres., 1986-87. Contbr. articles to profl. jours. Bd. dirs. Keep Colorado Springs Beautiful, 1990—99; bd. dirs. Colo. chpt. Nat. Assn. Fundraising Execs., 1990—94; bd. dirs. Colorado Springs Music Vols., 1992—98, 2000—, Ctr. Prevention Domestic Violence, 1995—2001. 1st lt. USAF, 1951—53. Woodrow Wilson fellow, 1951 Mem. Assoc. Colls. Midwest (bd. dirs. 1966-85, pres. 1973-75), Wis. Assn. Ind. Colls. and Univs. (bd. dirs. 1966-85, pres. 1969-71, 83-85). Home: 90 Ellsworth St Colorado Springs CO 80906-7954

ADAMS, BRYAN, vocalist, composer, photographer; b. Kingston, Ont., Can., Nov. 5, 1959; Vocalist, 1976—; composer various bands including Prism, Bachman-Turner Overdrive, Bob Welch, Kiss, 1977—. Albums include Bryan Adams, 1980, You Want It, You Got It, 1981, Cuts Like a Knife, 1983, Reckless, 1984, Into the Fire, 1987, Live! Live! Live!, 1988, Waking Up the Neighbors, 1991, So Far, So Good, 1993, 18 Til I Die, 1996, Bryan Adams MTV Unplugged, 1997, On A Day Like Today, 1998, The Best of Me, 1999, (soundtrack) Spirit: Stallion of the Cimarron, 2002, Spirit: l'etalon des plaines, 2002, Room Service, 2004, Byran Adams: The Anthology 1980-2005, 2005; singles include Straight from the Heart, Cuts Like a Knife, 1983, Heaven, One Night Love Affair, It's Only Love, 1985, Heat of the Night, Victim of Love, Only the Strong Survive, Hearts On Fire, 1987, Thought I Died and Gone to Heaven, 1991, (Everything I Do) I Do It for You (Acad. award nominee for best original song 1992), Can't Stop This Thing We Started, There Will Never Be Another Tonight, (with Michael Kamen and Robert John Lange, from Don Juan DeMarco) Have You Ever Loved a Woman, 1995 (Acad. award nominee for best original song 1996); contbr. to soundtracks: Robin Hood: Prince of Thieves, The Three Musketeers (with Rod Stewart & Sting), Don Juan DeMarco; photographer (books) Made in Canada, 1999, Haven, 1999, American Women, 2005. Decorated with Order of B.C., Order of Canada; recipient multi-platinum record, #1 single in Am., Can., U.K., Sweden, Finland, Denmark, Norway; named Artist of Decade, Canadian Recording Industry; nominated for 6 Grammys and 7 Juno awards, 1992, many other awards in music. Office: ICM 40 W 57th St New York NY 10019

ADAMS, C. LEE, marketing executive; b. Houston, Dec. 5, 1940; s. Carl Adams and Ruth (Carroll) Adams McGraw; m. Betty Leatherwood, June 1, 1963; children: Diana, Carroll Ann. BBA, Tex. A&M U., 1963. Export sales svc. asst. Comet Rice Mills, Inc., Houston, 1963-64, asst. export sales mgr., 1964-67, export sales mgr., 1967-68, gen. mgr. Country Cupboard Foods Divsn., 1968-71; sales mgr. Childers Mfg. Co., Houston, 1971-75; export sales mgr. Am. Rice, Inc., Houston, 1975-76, v.p. internat. mktg., 1976-80, group v.p. mktg., 1980-85, group v.p. internat. mktg., 1986-93, sr. v.p., 1993-99, sr. v.p., COO, 1999—2003, pres., 2004—. Bd. dirs. USA Rice Fedn., chmn., 2004-2006; mem. rice com. New Orleans Commodity Exchange, 1981-84. Bd. dirs. Harris County Water Control and Improvement Dist. 93, 1974-76; mem. Chelford One Mcpl. Utility Dist. Appraisal Rev. Bd., 1982-85. Served with USMCR, 1960-66. Mem. Am. Arab C. of C. (bd. dirs. 1978-81), TAMU 12th Man Found. (bd. dirs. 1987—), USA Rice Coun. (bd. dirs. 1995—), Rice Millers Assn. (bd. dirs. 1983—, pres. 1986-87), Assn. Former Students Tex. A&M U., Elsik H.S. Ram Rods Club (pres. 1984-85), Sweetwater Country Club, KC, Am. Legion. Roman Catholic. Office: Am Rice Inc PO Box 2587 Houston TX 77252-2587 E-mail: ladams@amrice.com.

ADAMS, CAROL H., dean; d. Wilfred L. and Sadie Dean Hoskins; m. John W. Adams, Apr. 10, 1966; children: Craig J., Dina R. BA in Edn., Mich. State U., 1965; MS in Edn., CUNY, Queens, 1975. Tchr. K-6 N.Y.C. Bd. Edn., 1965—72; tech. cons. Green Leigh Assocs., NYC, 1972—74; instr. tchr. edn. York Coll. CUNY, Jamaica, 1974—75; instr. SUNY Brockport, Rochester, 1975—77; prof. devel. edn. Monroe C.C., Rochester, 1977—91, acad. dean, 1991—. Cons. Greenleigh Assn., NYC, 1972—74; cons. tchr. edn. Corning C.C., NY, 2003. Bd. dirs. YWCA, Rochester, 1989—; mem. steering com. AALDP United Way, Rochester, 1992—93; mem. adv. bd. youth/family project U. Rochester, 2000. Recipient Women's History award, Rochester City Sch. Dist., 1997, Chancellor's award for excellence, SUNY, 2000. Mem.: AAUW, Nat. Inst. Leadership Devel., Am. Assn. Women in Cmty. and Jr. Colls., Nat. Assn. Devel. Edn., The Links (v.p. 2002), Leaders League for Innovation, Phi Delta Kappa. Office: Monroe Community Coll 1000 E Henrietta Rd Rochester NY 14623

ADAMS, CHARLES FRANCIS, advertising and real estate company executive; b. Detroit, Sept. 26, 1927; s. James R. and Bertha C. (DeChant) A.; m. Helen R. Harrell, Nov. 12, 1949; children: Charles Francis, Amy Ann, James Randolph, Patricia Duncan. BA, U. Mich., 1948; postgrad., U. Calif., Berkeley, 1949; student additional study, Oxford U., 1996. With D'Arcy-MacManus & Masius, Inc., 1947-80, exec. v.p., dir., 1970-76, pres., chief operating officer, 1976-80; pres. Adams Enterprises, 1971—; exec. v.p., dir. Washington Office, Am. Assn. Advt. Agys., 1980-84. Chmn., chief exec. officer Wajim Corp., Detroit; past mem. steering com. Nat. Advt. Rev. Bd.; mem. mktg. com. U.S. Info. Agy.; pres. Internat. Visitors Ctr. of the Bay Area, 1988-89. Author: Common Sense in Advertising, 1965, Heroes of the Golden Gate, 1987, California of the Year 2000, 1992, The Magnificent Rogues, 1999, Murder By The Bay, 2005 Past chmn. exec. com. Oakland U. Mem. Am. Assn. Advt. Agys. (dir., mem. govt. rels. com.), Advt. Fedn. Am. (past dir.), Nat. Outdoor Advt. Bur. (past chmn.), Nat. Golf Links Am. Club (Southampton, LI), Olympic Club, The Family Club, Theta Chi, hon. mem. Alpha Delta Sigma, (hon.). Republican. Roman Catholic. Home: 2240 Hyde St # 5 San Francisco CA 94109-1509 Office: 10 W Long Lake Rd Bloomfield Hills MI 48304-2707

ADAMS, CHARLES GILCHRIST, theology studies educator, pastor; b. Detroit, Dec. 13, 1936; Student, Fisk U., 1954-56; BA with honors, U. Mich., 1958; MDiv. with honors, Harvard U., 1964; DD (hon.), Birmingham Bapt. Coll., 1976, Shaw Coll., Detroit, 1980, Morris Coll., 1980, Morehouse Coll., 1984; LHD (hon.), Marygrove Coll., 1985; LLD (hon.), Dillard U., 1985; D Hum (hon.), U. Mich., 1986; DD (hon.), Edward Waters Coll., 1987; LHD (hon.), Kalamazoo Coll., 1994. Pastor Concord Bapt. Ch., Boston, 1962-69, Hartford Meml. Bapt. Ch., Detroit, 1970—; Williams and Lucille Nickerson prof. of practice of ethics and ministry Harvard Div. Sch., 2007—. Instr. theology Boston U., Andover Newton Sch. Theology, Ctrl. Bapt. Sem., Kansas City, Iliff Sch. Theology, Denver; invited speaker UN, 1989, World Congress of Bapt. World Alliance, Seoul, Korea, 1990, 7th Gen. assembly of World Coun. Chs., Canberra, Australia, 1991, Evian, France, 1992; conf. preacher Hampton (Va.) U. Ministers Conf., 1993-94. Doctoral fellow Union Theol. Sem., N.Y.C.; named One of Ebony's Top 100 Influential Black Ams., 1990-94, One of 15 Greatest Black Preachers, 1993-94. Office: Harvard Div Sch Andover Hall 45 Francis Ave Cambridge MA 02138*

ADAMS, CHARLES P., JR., lawyer; b. Jackson, Miss., Feb. 28, 1949; BSBA cum laude, Georgetown U., 1971; JD, Georgetown U. Law Ctr., 1974. Bar: Miss. 1975. Mng. ptnr. Adams and Reese, LLP, Jackson, Miss. Mem.: Miss. Bar, Hinds County Bar Assn. Office: Adams and Reese LLP 111 Capitol Bldg 111 E Capitol St Ste 350 Jackson MS 39201 Office Phone: 601-292-0720. Office Fax: 601-355-9708. Business E-Mail: charles.adams@arlaw.com.

ADAMS, CHRISTOPHER STEVE, JR., retired electronics executive, military officer; b. Shreveport, La., July 8, 1930; s. Christopher Steve and Armenda Lee (Tanner) A.; m. Mary Alene Mitchell, Aug. 22, 1953; children: Cynthia, Charlotte, Cheri, Christopher III. AS, Tarleton State U., 1950; BS, Tex. A&M U., 1952. Commd. U.S. Air Force, 1952, advanced through grades to maj. gen., 1979, B-36, B-52 pilot Ramey AFB, P.R.; dir. plans and policy J-5, Def. Nuclear Agy., Washington, 1970-73; comdr. 90th Strategic Missile Wing, 1973-75; comdr. 12th Air Div., 1975-78; chief of staff SAC, 1982-83; ret., 1983; assoc. dir. Los Alamos Nat. Lab., 1983—86; v.p. bus. devel. Andrew Corp., Dallas, 1987-94, ret., 1994. Author: The Cold War Series, 6 books, 1999—2004. Decorated D.S.M., Def. Superior Service medal, Legion of Merit (2), Air Force Commendation medal, Air medal (2); recipient Disting. Alumnus award Tarleton State U., 1990, Disting. Alumnus award Tex. A&M U., 1991. Presbyterian. Home: 9408 Gimmee Ct Granbury TX 76049 Personal E-mail: cadams@itexas.net. *America the beautiful. I have dedicated my life through service to preserve our freedom. There is no better place on earth— I know, I've been there.*

ADAMS, CINDY, journalist; b. NYC, Apr. 24; d. Harry and Jessica (Sugar); m. Joey Adams, Feb. 14 (dec. Dec. 2, 1999). News commentator Sta. WABC-TV, NYC, 1967-70; interviewer NBC-TV, 1970-73, 2007—; dir., asst. to pres. Miss Universe, Inc., NYC, 1970-77, Good Morning Am., 1996—98; columnist N.Y. Post, NYC, 1981—. Interviewer of celebrities for Fox-TV's "A Current Affair", 1986-91, Lifetime Cable, 1991—; commentator fashion show Bonds for Israel, N.Y., 1970-85; lectr. Keedick Lectr. Service, N.Y., 1970-80. Author: Sukarno of Indonesia, 1965, Lee Strasberg: The Imperfect Genius of the Actor's Studio, 1980, Jolie Gabor, 1978, The Gift of Jazzy, 2003, Living a Dog's Life: Jazzy, Juicy and Me, 2005; co-author (with Susan Crimp): Iron Rose: The Story of Rose Fitzgerald Kennedy and Her Dynasty, 1995; contbr. articles to mags.; designer jewelry Cartier, N.Y. 1971. Recipient Matrix award, 2007. Avocation: travel. Office: NY Post 1211 Avenue Of The Americas New York NY 10036-8790

ADAMS, CYNTHIA ANN, librarian, media specialist, language educator; b. Thomaston, Ga., Nov. 27, 1942; d. Emory Ellis and Marian (Moseley) A. AB, Mercer U., 1964; MEd, U. Ga., 1972; EdS, Ga. State U., 1994. Cert. English tchr., career libr. media specialist, Ga. Libr. media specialist Upson County Bd. Edn., Thomaston, Ga., 1971—72, Walton County Bd. Edn., Monroe, Ga., 1972-74, Madison County Bd. Edn., Danielsville, Ga., 1974-80; tchr. English, libr. media specialist Westwood Bd. Trustees, Thomaston, 1981-82; libr. media specialist Harris County Bd. Edn., Hamilton, Ga., 1983—97; instr. writing, coord. computer lab. Gordon Coll., Barnesville, Ga., 1997—. Book reviewer Sch. Libr. Jour., 1973-74; crafts exhibited at Nat. Mus. Women in the Arts, Washington, TUAC Gallery, Thomaston; poet. Mem. visual arts com. Thomaston Upson Arts Coun.; vol. Am. Heart Assn., St. John Lutheran Ch. Food Program, Griffin, Ga. Grad. study scholar. Mem. Kappa Delta Pi. Achievements include research in preservation of paper collections in archives. Home: 630 S Center St Thomaston GA 30286-4133 Office: Gordon Coll 419 Coll Dr Barnesville GA 30204 Business E-Mail: c_adams@gdn.edu.

ADAMS, DANIEL FENTON, law educator; b. Reading, Pa., July 29, 1922; s. Daniel Snyder and Carrie Betsy (Vought) A.; m. Eloise Williams, Sept. 6, 1968. AB, Dickinson Coll., 1947; LL.B., Dickinson Sch. Law, 1949. Bar: Pa. 1951, Ark. 1984. Prof. law Dickinson Sch. Law, Carlisle, Pa., 1949-65, asst. to dean, 1952-54, 56-60, acting dean, 1954-56, asst. dean, 1960-65; prof. Sch. Law U. Ark., Little Rock, 1965-70, 77-93, prof. emeritus, 1993—; asst. dean U. Ark. Sch. Law, Little Rock, 1966-70, acting dean, 1981-82, interim dean, 1989-91; prof. U. Miss. Sch. Law, Oxford, 1970-77. Vis. prof. Stetson U. Sch. Law, St. Petersburg, Fla., 1976-77, 99-00, U. Tenn. Coll. Law, 1993. Contbr. articles to profl. jours. Served with U.S. Army, 1943-44 Mem. ABA, Pa. Bar Assn., Ark. Bar Assn. Personal E-mail: condodfa@aol.com.

ADAMS, DAVID FRANKLYN, music educator; b. Albuquerque, May 17, 1939; adopted s. John Marian and s. Mary Louise Adams, s. Kenneth Jewell and Peggy Crowther (Stepmother); m. Vickie Sharon Mobley, June 8, 1998; m. Gail Lenore Ingraham, June 10, 1966 (div. Oct. 28, 1983); children: Christina Ann Cox, Tamara Gail Olarte, Wendy Michelle Swoope. Diploma, Mesa Coll., 1974. Musician Denver Affair, Las Vegas, 1969—73; band dir. Burlington H.S., Colo., 1967—68; pianist USAF Bicentennial Band, Fort Meade, Md., 1974—76, US Army Field Band, 1977—79; stage band dir. 1st Army Band, Fort Carson, Colo., 1979—80; rhythm vocal br. head Armed Forces Sch. of Music, Norfolk, Va., 1980—86; acting band comdr. US Army Band, Fort Hamilton, NY, 1986—87; counselor Army Cmty. Services, 1988—90; pvt. tchr., musician Albuquerque, 1990—95; band dir., tchr. Bosque Prep. Sch., 1996—98; dir. jazz studies Acad. Music, Norfolk, Va., 1999—2000; band dir. An Achievable Dream Acad., Newport News, 2001—. Resident jazz musician Va. Beach Pub. Schs., Virginia Beach, 2001—01, all-city jazz band dir., 2002—02; founder, dir., prodr. Young Razzcals Jazz Project, 1992—. Composer: (music) The Magic of Christmas; author: (poetry book) The Reason for the Rhyme. Squadron comdr. CAP, Fort Meade, 1977—79, mission pilot Norfolk, Va., 1980—90, dir. aerospace edn. Albuquerque, 1990—95. With US Army, 1974—90. Recipient Grover Loening Aerospace award, CAP, 1991, Frank G. Brewer Aerospace award, Regional CAP, 1995, Nat. CAP, 1995, Cmty. Svc. award, Arts Coun. Coop., 1997, Outstanding Leadership and Performance, Young Razzcals Jazz Project, 2001, 2002. Mem.: Internat. Assn. Jazz Educators, Nat. Assn. Music Edn. Achievements include development of Jazz for the very young, see website www.youngrazzcalsjazzproject.com. Avocations: flying, running, writing, scuba diving, hang-gliding. Home: 5228 Dundee Ln Virginia Beach VA 23464 Home Phone: 757-479-9316; Office Phone: 757-373-6622. Office Fax: 757-247-1720; Home Fax: 757-479-1454. Personal E-mail: darazzcaljazz@cs.com.

ADAMS, DAVID G., lawyer; b. Monroe, La., Jan. 30, 1952; BA, U. Southwestern La., 1973; JD, NYU, 1977. Bar: Ga. 1977, US Dist. Ct. (no. dist.) Ga. 1977, US Dist. Ct., DC 1995, US Ct. Appeals (4th and 10th cirs.) 1999, US Dist. Ct., Dist. Md. 1999. Dir. Policy Develop. and Coordination Staff, assoc. chief counsel for drugs/litig. atty. FDA, 1978—94; ptnr., chmn. Food & Drug Group Venable LLP, Washington, DC. Tchr. food & drug law George Washington U. Law Sch. Contbr. articles to profl. jours. Root-Tilden Scholar. Mem.: ABA (chmn Food & Drug Law Comt., Bus. Law Sect.), DC Bar. Office: Venable LLP 575 7th St NW Washington DC 20004 Office Phone: 202-344-8014. Office Fax: 202-344-8300. E-mail: dgadams@venable.com.

ADAMS, DAVID HUNTINGTON, judge; b. Cleve., May 30, 1942; s. Donald Croxton and Nancy Adams; m. Mary Watson, Dec. 4, 1982; children from previous marriage: Ann Arendell, David Huntington, Susanna Camp. AB, Washington and Lee U., 1965, JD, 1968. Bar: Va. 1968, U.S. Dist. Ct. (ea. dist.) Va. 1968, U.S. Ct. Appeals (4th cir.) 1968, U.S. Supreme Ct. 1973. Law clk. U.S. Dist. Ct., Norfolk, Va., 1968-69; assoc. law firm Willcox, Savage, Norfolk, 1969-72; ptnr. law firm Agelasto, Bernard & Adams, Norfolk, 1972-74, Taylor, Walker, Bernard & Adams, Norfolk, 1974-78, Taylor, Walker & Adams, Norfolk, 1974-87, Clark & Stant, P.C., 1987-93; judge U.S. Bankruptcy Ct. (ea. dist. Va.), 1993—. Master of the bench James Kent Am. Inn of Ct., 1994-99, pres., 1995; lectr. bankruptcy practice joint com. on cont. legal edn. Va. Bar Found., 1981, 89, 93—; adminstrv. hearing officer Commonwealth of Va., 1974-89; mem. 4th Cir. Jud. Coun., 2003-2005, Adminstrv. Office Bankruptcy Judges Adv. Coun., 2001—04, Bankruptcy Judges Adv. Group, 2001—04, Adminstrv. Office Joint Adv. Com., 2003-2005 Author: Virginia Landlord/Tenant Law, 1980. Bd. dir. Heritage Mus., Norfolk, 1991-94, Virginia Beach Neptune Fest., 1997—, King Neptune XXVI; chmn. Neptune Found., 2002; pres. Bay Colony Civic League, Virginia Beach, 1978, Princess Anne Hills Civic League, Virginia Beach, 1988; mem. 4th Cir. Jud. Conf., 1974—;, 4th Cir. Jud. Coun., 2002—; mem. 2d dist. ethics com. Va. State Bar, 1983-84. Recipient Superior Pub. Svc. award, Sec. of Navy, 2004. Mem.: ABA, Va. Bar Assn. (bd. dir. bankruptcy sect. 1990—93, mem. coun. jud. sect. 1995—, chmn. 1997), Virginia Beach Bar Assn., Norfolk-Portsmouth Bar Assn., Nat. Conf. Bankruptcy Judges (bd. govs. 1996—2000, sec. 2000, pres. 2004—05), Am. Bankruptcy Inst., Hampton Roads Naval Historical Found. (bd. dir. 2005—), Hampton Roads Coun. Navy League U.S. (life; pres. 2000—04, nat. dir. 2002—04), N.Y. Yacht Club, Cavalier Golf and Yacht Club (bd. dir. 1993—98, commodore 1994). Episcopalian. Avocations: yachting, swimming, bicycling. Office: United States Bankruptcy Ct Walter E Hoffman US Courthouse 600 Granby St Norfolk VA 23510-1915 Business E-Mail: david_adams@vaeb.uscourts.gov.

ADAMS, DAVID PARRISH, historian, epidemiologist, educator; b. Jacksonville, Fla., Aug. 2, 1958; s. David Parrish and Gloria Ann (Nesmith) A.; m. Teri Ann Becker, Aug. 31, 1985; 1 child, Morgan Becker. BA, Emory U., 1980; AM, Washington U., St. Louis, 1982; PhD, U. Fla., 1987; MPH, Ohio State U., 1994. Resource faculty dept. family medicine U. Fla., Gainesville, 1983-87; assoc. prof. dept. humanities Columbus (Ohio) State C.C., 1987-95; rsch. dir. Cabarrus Family Medicine Residence Program, Concord, N.C., 1995—; cons. assoc. dept. cmty. and family medicine Duke Med. Ctr., Durham, N.C., 1996—; assoc. prof. dept. health sci. Armstrong Atlantic State U., 2001—. Adj. faculty dept. history Ohio Dominican Coll., Columbus, 1987-95; adj. asst. prof. dept. family medicine Ohio State U., Columbus, 1990-95, post-doctoral rschr. AHEC program, 1995, lectr. dept. history, 1995; adj. asst. prof. dept. family medicine Ponce (P.R.) Sch. Medicine, 1993; rsch. dir. Cabarrus Family Practice Residence program Cabarrus Meml. Hosp., Concord, N.C.; cons. assoc. dept. cmty. and family medicine Duke U., 1995—; vis. asst. prof. med. humanities program Davidson Coll., 1996—; adj. asst. prof. Coll. Nursing, U. Tenn.-Knoxville; adj. asst. prof. dept. family medicine Quillen Coll. Medicine, Ea. Tenn. State U., 1998—; cons. in field; assoc. prof. Atlantic State U; clin. asst. prof. Med. Coll. Ga Dept. Family Medicine. Author: The Greatest Good to the Greatest Number: Penicillin Rationing on the American Home Front, 1940-45, 1991, American Board of Family Practice: A History, 1999; contbr. articles to profl. jours. Med. Humanities fellow U. Ill., Chgo., 1992; grant-in-aid U. Wis., 1985; grantee NIH, 1989, Ohio Acad. Family Physicians, 1991. Mem. APHA, Am. Assn. History of Medicine, Am. Hist. Assn., Orgn. Am. Historians, Soc. Tchrs. Family Medicine, Am. Soc. Tropical Medicine and Hygiene. Democrat. Mem. United Ch. of Christ. Achievements include research in general and family practice; evolution of family practice; penicillin, dentistry and SBE; wartime penicillin policy; community oriented primary care.

ADAMS, DEAN (LEWIS ADAMS), theater director; b. Seattle, July 22, 1957; s. Brockman and Mary Elizabeth (Scott) A.; m. Kristin Cook Gilbert, June 20, 1981. BA in Drama and English, Tufts U., 1980; MA in TV-Film, U. Md., 1986; MFA in Directing, Fla. State U., 2002. Mgr. stage prodn. Shakespeare and Co., Washington, 1975—79; asst. stage mgr. Arena Stage, Washington, 1976; tech. dir. St. Albans Sch., Washington, 1980—82; dir. theater Loomis Chaffee Sch., Windsor, Conn., 1982—88, Westminster Sch., Simsbury, Conn., 1989—99; freelance theater dir. Artistic dir. Conn.

Theater Festival, Simsbury, 1989—; assoc. prof. theater, artistic dir., Kennesaw State U., Ga., 2002—. Dir. (U.K. tour) Dining Room, 1985; dir., producer (1st Chinese tour of Am. mus.) Once Upon a Mattress, 1987. Grantee Ford Found., 1984; scholar Tufts U., 1978-80. Mem. Internat. Brotherhood Magicians, Soc. Am. Magicians, Soc. of Stage Dirs. and Choreographers, Actors Equity Assn., Assn. of Performing Arts Presenters. Democrat. Episcopalian. Home and Office: 1512 Tennessee Walker Dr Roswell GA 30075 Office: Kennesaw State Univ 1000 Chastain Rd Kennesaw GA 30144 Office Phone: 770-420-4408. Personal E-mail: deanadams@msn.com. Business E-Mail: dadams@kennesaw.edu.

ADAMS, DEBORAH ROWLAND, lawyer; b. Princeton, NJ, July 28, 1952; d. Bernard S. and Natalie S. Adams; m. Charles L. Campbell, June 16, 1990. BA, Colo. Coll., Colorado Springs, 1974; JD, U. Colo., 1978. Bar: Ind. 1978, Colo. 1978, U.S. Dist. Ct. Colo. 1978. Atty. Legal Svcs. Orgn. Ind., Indpls., 1978-79, Pikes Peak Legal Svcs., Colorado Springs, 1979-80, Pub. Defender's Office, Colorado Springs, 1980-81; assoc. Ranson, Thomas, Cook and Livingston, Colorado Springs, 1982-84; pvt. practice Colorado Springs, 1985—. Mem. state Jud. Nominating Commn. for 4th Jud. Dist., 1994-99; Colo. State Grievance Com., 1997-98, Atty. Regulation Com., 1999. Bd. dirs. Domestic Violence Prevention Ctr., 1980-86, pres., 1982-84; bd. dirs. Pikes Peak Legal Svcs., 1983-88, pres., 1986-87, Colo. Coll. Bus. and Cmty. Alliance Bd., 1998-2002, Citizens Project Bd., 1999-2002, CASA, 1999-2004, Emily Griffith Ctr., 2002—, v.p., 2003-06, Colo. Bar Found., 1993-2006, pres 2003-04; bd. dirs. Chins Up, 1991-97, state bd. dirs. Legal Aid Found., 1994-2000, v.p., 1997-99; mem. Colorado Springs Leadership Inst., 1997, mem. adv. bd., 1998-2003. Recipient Pro Bono award Pikes Peak Legal Svcs., 1988, Portia award Women's Lawyers of the Fourth Judicial Dist., 1992, Outstanding Affiliate Mem. of Colo. Women Lawyers Assn., 1996; named Atty of Yr. El Paso County Legal Secs. Assn., 1990, Wagon Wheel Girl Scouts Cmty. Svc. award, 2004. Mem. Colo. Bar Assn. (family law sect. 1991-2005, bd. govs. 1994-97, exec. counsel 1995-97, nominating com. 1996), El Paso County Bar Assn. (pres. 1995-96), El Paso County Bar Found. (founding mem.), Colo. Bar Assn., Colo. Women's Bar Assn., Women Lawyers Assn. of the 4th Jud. Dist., Zonta Club Colorado Springs (pres. 1989-90, co-chair dist. 12 regional conf. 1991-92, Zontian of Yr. 1990-91). Democrat. Avocations: tennis, mountain biking, travel, snowboarding. Office: 2 N Cascade Ave Ste 1010 Colorado Springs CO 80903-1629 Home Phone: 719-471-9346; Office Phone: 719-471-7727. Personal E-mail: dradams@pcisys.net.

ADAMS, DIRK STANDLEY, lawyer; b. Lynch, Nebr., May 19, 1951; s. Howard W. and Marilyn (Standley) A.; m. Anita Low, Feb. 14, 1984. BS, U. Tex., 1972; JD, Harvard U., 1976. Bar: N.Y. 1977, Calif. 1985. Ptnr. Sullivan, Johnson, Peters, Burns, Adams & Mullin, P.C., Rochester, N.Y., 1981-82; exec. v.p., treas., gen. counsel Suffolk County Fed. Savs & Loan Assn., Centereach, N.Y., 1982; ptnr. Phillips, Lytle, Hitchcock, Blaine & Huber, Rochester, 1982-83; sr. v.p., gen. counsel, corp. sec. Fed. Home Loan Bank of San Francisco, 1983—; pvt. practice Wilsall, Mont. Acting counsel Fed. Asset Disposition Assn., San Francisco, 1985-86. Bd. dirs. Vol. Legal Services Project, Inc., Rochester, 1983. Mem. ABA (com. savs. and loan assns. sect. corp., banking and bus. 1983—), Calif. Bar Assn. (fin. instns. com. 1985). Office: 729 Shields River Rd Wilsall MT 59086-9431 Office Phone: 406-578-2330. Business E-Mail: dirksadams@mcn.net.

ADAMS, DONALD E., physiatrist; s. Robert Reith and Marlene Beth Adams; m. Theresa Ann Orturo, June 14, 1998; children: Jacob, Elizabeth, Jackson. BS in Biochemistry, Pacific Union Coll., Angwin, Calif., 1993; MD, Loma Linda U., Calif., 1997. Diplomate Am. Bd. Phys. Medicine and Rehab. Internship San Bernardino County Med. Ctr., 1997—98; residency divsn. phys. medicine & rehab. U. Utah, 1998—2001, chief resident Slat Lake City, 2001—02; ptnr., attending Okla. Sports Sci. & Orhtop., Oklahoma City, 2003—. Asst. physician N. Pacific Union Conf., Mindinao, Philippines, 1997, med. dir., Zambia, 99; mem. exec. com. N.W. Surg. Hosp., Oklahoma City, 2005—. Mem.: Internat. Spine Intervention Soc., Am. Soc. Intervention Pain Physicians, Am. Acad. Phys. Medicine and Rehab. Seventh-Day Adventist. Office: Physicians Group 1616 S Kelly Edmond OK 73013

ADAMS, EARL WILLIAM, JR., retired economics professor; b. Lansing, Mich., Nov. 13, 1937; s. Earl William and V. Crystal (Woodruff) A.; m. Barbara Joan Charlton, Aug. 4, 1964; children: Earl William, III, Nicholas Charlton. BA, U. Mich., 1959; PhD, MIT, 1971. Asst. prof. econs. Amherst Coll., 1963-66, U. Pitts., 1966-72; Andrew Wells Robertson prof. econs. Allegheny Coll., Meadville, Pa., 1972—2005. Vis. asst. prof. U. Mass., 1966; rsch. dir. bus. taxation Pa. Tax Commn., 1979-81; mem. adv. coun. Pa. Blue Shield, 1980-82, mem. corp., 1982; mem. bd. trustees Allegheny Coll., 2007—. Contbr. to profl. publs. Woodrow Wilson fellow, 1959 Mem. Am. Econs. Assn., Pa. Econs. Assn., Phi Beta Kappa, Phi Kappa Phi. Home: 187 Grandview Ave Meadville PA 16335-1415

ADAMS, EDMUND JOHN, lawyer; b. Lansing, Mich., June 6, 1938; s. John Edmund and Helen Kathryn (Pavlick) A.; m. Mary Louise Riegler, Aug. 11, 1962 (dec. May 2004); m. Cynthia A.Howell, May 20, 2006. BA, Xavier U., 1960; LLB, U. Notre Dame, 1963. Bar: Ohio 1963. Assoc. Paxton & Seasongood, Cin., 1965-70, Frost & Jacobs (now Frost Brown Todd), 1970-71, ptnr., 1971-2000, mem. exec. com., 1985-88, 90-96, mng. ptnr., 1994-96, chmn., 1996-2000, of counsel, 2000—; tournament counsel Western & Southern Fin. Group Tennis Masters Tournament, 2003—05. Author: Catholic Trails West, The Founding Catholic Families of Pennsylvania, Vol. 1, 1988, Vol. 2, 1989. Mem. Ohio Bd. Regents, 1999—, sec., 2002-03, vice-chmn., 2003-04, chmn, 2005-06; mem., com. co-chair Ohio Gov.'s Commn. on Higher Edn. and the Economy, 2003-04; mem. Gov.'s Partnership for Continued Learning, 2005—; trustee Jewish Hosp., 1995-2001, Cin. Internat. Visitors Ctr., 1989-91, Japan Am. Soc. Greater Cin., 1988-96, Ursuline Acad., 1992-94; trustee S.W. Ohio Regional Transit Authority, 1980-91, pres., 1983, 88; trustee Sister Cities Assn. Greater Cin., 1984-91, chmn., 1984-90; trustee Econ. Ctr. for Edn. and Rsch., 1996—, exec. com., 1999-, vice-chmn., 2002-04, chmn., 2005-06; chmn. USTA Nat. Father and Son Clay Ct. Tennis Championships, 1990-92; exec. com. Hamilton County Rep., 1982—, fin. com., 1990-04, chmn., 1992-94, ctrl. com., 2000—, adv. bd. Elder HS, 2002—, Ohio Coll. Access Network, 2005-07; mem. adv. bd. Global Ctr., 2007—.; bd. dirs. Elder HS Altiora Found., 2007—. 1st lt. U.S. Army, 1963-65. Fellow Am. Coll. Bankruptcy; mem. ABA, Ohio Bar Assn., Cin. Bar Assn., Cin. Tennis Club (trustee 1990-98, treas. 1992-93, sec. 1994-95, pres. 1996-98, historian 2001—), Met. Club, (bd. dirs. 1996-2001), Friendly Sons St. Patrick of Cin. (historian 2006—). Roman Catholic. Home: 3210 Columbia Pky Cincinnati OH 45226-1042 Office: Frost Brown Todd 2500 PNC Ctr 201 E 5th St Cincinnati OH 45202-4182 E-mail: eadams@fbtlaw.com.

ADAMS, EDWARD A., legal journalist; b. South Bend, Ind., Sept. 28, 1963; s. Richard E. and Louise M. (Augustine) A.; m. Eliza A. Dolin, Dec. 31, 1988. PhB, Miami U., Oxford, Ohio, 1985; JD, Columbia U., 1988. Metro intern Cin. Enquirer, summer 1983; reporter intern Am. Lawyer, NYC, winter 1984; rschr. intern Cable News Network, Washington, summer 1984; features intern Cleve. Plain Dealer, summer 1985; reporter intern Nat. Law Jour., NYC, summers 1986-87; bus. intern U.S. News & World Report, Washington, summer 1988; TV reporter N.Y. Post, NYC, 1988; law firm reporter N.Y. Law Jour., NYC, 1989-97, on line editor, 1997; publisher and editor ABA Jour., 2006—. Co-editor book: Inside the Law Schools, 1991. Mem. Investigative Reporters and Editors. Office: ABA Jour 15th Fl 321 N Clark St Chicago IL 60610

ADAMS, EDWIN MELVILLE, retired diplomat, actor, writer; b. Gridley, Ill., Sept. 28, 1914; s. Edwin Melville and Crystal (Montgomery) A. AB, U. Ill., Champaign-Urbana, 1936, LL.B., 1939; postgrad., The Hague Acad. Internat. Law, summer 1951. Bar: Ill. 1939. Atty. State Farm Ins. Cos., Bloomington, Ill., 1939-42; officer charge Brazil area World Trade intelligence div., State Dept., Washington, 1942-43, negotiator German external assets agreements with neutral countries, 1946-48; successively assigned by State Dept. to, London, Paris, Bern and Frankfort; as U.S. negotiator at internat. econ. confs., 1948-50; econ. attache Am. embassy, The Hague, 1950-52; charge Italian econ. affairs State Dept., 1952-55; dep. chief mut. def. affairs, 2d sec. Am. embassy, Rome, Italy, 1955-58, chief mut. def. affairs, 1st sec., 1958-61; officer in charge econ. affairs for N. Africa Dept. State, 1961-64, career mgmt. officer, 1964-65; spl. asst. to dep. under sec. state, 1965-67; asso. dean Fgn. Service Inst., 1967-68; cons. Dept. State, 1968-72. Host: radio show Passport, WAMU, 1972—; author, narrator radio show, NBC-TV show, Venice, My Love, 1972; pub. broadcasting The Social Responsibility of Business; radio shows My Beloved Italy; star radio shows, CBS-TV show, The Empty Frame, 1973; appeared in films The Last Detail, 1974, Airport, 1975, Three Days of the Condor, 1975, Franklin and Eleanor, The Other Side of Midnight, Company, The Seduction of Joe Tynan, Justice for All, First Monday in October, BBC's Double Image; author: Petty Destiny, 2004. U.S. del. Conf. of African States on Devel. of Edn. in Africa, 1961. Served to lt. (j.g.) USNR, 1943-46, PTO. Decorated cavaliere ufficiale Order of Merit of Italian Republic. Mem. Screen Actors Guild, AFTRA, Actors Equity, Phi Delta Phi, Phi Kappa Sigma. Espicopalian. Lodge: Masons (Washington).

ADAMS, ELIZABETH HERRINGTON, banker; b. Tulsa, May 25, 1947; d. James Dillon and Helen (Allderdice) Herrington; m. Phillip Hollis Hackney, Mar. 5, 1977 (dec. Jan. 1990); m. Keith R. Adams, Sept. 4, 1993. Student, No. Ariz. U., 1965-67, 68-69. With Coldwater (Kans.) Nat. Bank, summers 1964-67, The Ariz. Bank, Phoenix, 1969, Flagstaff, 1970-71; asst. cashier The Wilmore (Kans.) State Bank, 1972—2001, The Coldwater Nat. Bank, 1974-83, cashier, ops. officer, 1984—; v.p. The Coldwater (Kans.) Nat. Bank, 1998—2002, sr. v.p., 2002—04, exec. v.p., 2005—. Bd. dirs. The Coldwater Nat. Bank., 1972-. Bd. dirs. Pioneer Lodge Nursing Home, Coldwater, 1984-89; mem. sch. site coun., 1993-94; life mem. Girl Scouts, chmn. Neighborhood Cookie Drive, 1991-95; bd. dirs., mem. strategic planning com. Wheatbelt Area Girl Scout Coun., 1994-96—; elder 1st Presbyn. Ch., Coldwater; Kans. Lung Assn. Vol. Spkrs. Bur., 1998—; mem. Ch. Session Bd., Coldwater, 1994-2000. Mem. Fin. Women Internat., Cmty. Bankers Assn. Kans. (membership com. 1991-94, INPAC com. 1992-93), Kans. Ind. Bankers (gen. svcs. com. 1986-87), PEO, Alpha Omicron Pi, Lake Coldwater Archtl. Rev. Bd. Republican. Avocation: music (pianist). Office: Coldwater Nat Bank PO Box 726 Coldwater KS 67029-0726

ADAMS, EULA L., data storage executive; BS in Acctg., Morris Brown U.; MBA, Harvard Bus. Sch. bd. dirs. MasterCard Internat. Former ptnr. Deloitte and Touche; CEO Western Union, exec. v.p. and gen. mgr. Telesvcs. First Data Corp., Atlanta, 1991-98, pres. First Data Resources and Teleservices, 2000—03, exec. v.p., pres. First Data Merchant Svcs. subs., 1998—2003; v.p. global services Storage Technology Corp., Louisville, Colo., 2004—. Bd. dirs. Solidus Networks, Inc, NetBank, Inc. Named one of 50 Most Powerful Black Executives, Fortune mag., 2002. Office: 1 StorageTek Dr Louisville CO 80028 Office Phone: 303-673-5151.

ADAMS, F. GERARD, economist, educator; b. Apr. 28, 1929; s. Walter and Margot Adams; m. Heidi Vernon; children: Leslie, Colin, Loren, Mark. BA, U. Mich., 1949, MA, 1951, PhD, 1956. Instr. dept. econs. U. Mich., Ann Arbor, 1952—56; economist Calif. Tex. Oil Corp., NYC, 1956—59; cons. economist, mgr. gen. econs. dept. Compagnie Française des Pétroles, NYC and Paris, 1959—61; mem. faculty U. Pa., Phila., 1961—98, prof. econs. and fin.; McDonald prof. Northeastern U., Boston, 1998—; Freeman prof. Johns Hopkins U., Balt., 2002. Dir. Econs. Research Unit, 1961-98, chmn. Faculty Senate, 1987-88; chmn. profl. bd. WEFA Group, Phila., 1969-91. Author: (with others) An Econometric Analysis of International Trade, 1969, (with J.R. Behrman) Econometric Models of World Agricultural Commodity Markets, 1976, Commodity Exports and Economic Development, 1982, (with L.R. Klein) Industrial Policies for Growth and Competitiveness, 1983, The Business Forecasting Revolution, 1986; editor: (with S.A. Klein) Stabilizing World Commodity Markets - Analysis, Practice and Policy, 1978, The Macroeconomic Dimensions of Arm Reduction, 1992, Economic Activity, Trade and Industry in the U.S.-Japan-World Economy, 1993, East Asian Development: Will the Miracle Survive?, 1998; Public Policies in East Asian Development: Facing New Challenges, 1999, Macroeconomics for Business and Society, 2002, The E-Business Revolution and the New Economy, 2003, East Asia, Globalization, and the New Economy, 2006. Home: 39 Stafford Rd Newton Center MA 02459-1818 E-mail: adams@ssc.upenn.edu.

ADAMS, FORREST H., retired pediatrician; b. Mpls., Sept. 20, 1919; s. Edward Forrest Adams and Helen Lea Anderson; m. Joan Bloch, Apr. 28, 1969; children: Judd, Scott, Mark, Gregg, Eric, Brent, Kurt, Lynn. Student, Johns Hopkins U., Balt., 1937—38; BA, U. Minn., Mpls., 1941, MB, 1943, MD, 1944, MS, 1949. Diplomate Am. Bd. Pediats., 1948. Intern pediats. U. Minn. Hosp., Mpls., 1943—44, resident pediats., 1944—46; fellow pediats. U. Minn. Nat. Rsch. Coun., Mpls., 1948—49; instr. pediats. U. Minn., Mpls., 1948—49, asst. prof. pediats., 1949—52, dir. pediat. heart clinic, 1951—52; asst. dir. Crippled Children's Program, St. Paul, 1949—50; physician-in-charge Sister Elizabeth Kenny Inst., Mpls., 1949—50; assoc. physician pediats. Mpls. Gen. Hosp., 1949—50, chief. pediats., 1950—52; assoc. prof. pediats. UCLA, 1952—58, acting chmn. dept. pediats., 1958—59, 1964—65, vice-chmn. dept. pediats., 1962—64, head divsn. cardiology, 1958—76, prof. pediats, 1958—78, emeritus prof. pediats., 1978—. Cons. cardiology State Bd. Pub. Health, Calif., 1963—78; cons. office surgeon gen. USPHS, 1965—69; mem. med. appraisal team Vietnam Pres. Lyndon Johnson, 1967; acad. senate UCLA, 1968—70; dir. rsch. and edn. Pediat. Caridology Med. Group Inc., San Diego, 1983—84; dir. rsch. Children's Hosp. and Health Ctr., San Diego, 1984—85; staff mem. Scripps Clinic and Rsch. Found., La Jolla, Calif., 1984—85; cons. North County Health Svcs., San Diego, 1992—99; lectr. in field. Goodwill amb. US State Dept. Cultural Exchange Program, 1964—71; mem. adv. com. Pub. Employees Retirement Sys. Calif., 1984—91, chmn., 1989—91; mem. bd. dirs. Fairbanks Ranch Cmty Svcs. Dist., 1992—96. Lt. med. corp USN, 1946—48. Recipient Career Rsch. award, US Pub. Health Svc., 1962—67, Vol. Svc. award, North County Health Svcs., San Diego, 1996. Master: Am. Coll. Cardiology (chmn. sci. program 1966, mem. credentials com. 1966—70, trustee 1966—75, v.p. 1968—69, pres.-elect 1970—71, pres. 1971—72, Founder's award 2000); fellow: Philippine Coll. Cardiology (hon.), Am. Heart Assn. (hon.; mem. exec. com. coun. rheumatic fever and congenital heart disease 1961—64, mem. adult and pediat. cardiology rsch. study com. 1967—69, coun. clin. cardiology); mem.: Assn. European Pediat. Cardiologists, Calif. Soc. Pediat. Cardiology, Am. Pediat. Soc., Spanish Soc. Cardiology (hon.), Venezuelan Soc. Cardiology (hon.), Peruvian Soc. Cardiology (hon.), Western Soc. Pediat. Rsch. (sec. 1953—54, coun. mem. 1954—57, v.p. 1961—62, pres. 1962—63), Soc. Pediat. Rsch. (coun. mem. 1960—62), Am. Acad. Pediats. (chmn. com. residency fellows 1961—63, coun. mem. section cardiology 1961—63).

ADAMS, FRANCES GRANT, II, lawyer; b. Wheeling, W.Va., Nov. 30, 1955; d. Jack Richard and Frances Irene (Grant) A. BA, W.Va. U., 1976, JD, 1979; MA, Webster U., 1983. Bar: W.Va. 1979, U.S. Dist. Ct. (so. dist.) W.Va. 1979, U.S. Ct. Mil. Appeals 1979, U.S. Supreme Ct. 1988, D.C. 1989. Asst. staff judge advocate armament divsn. USAF, Eglin AFB, Fla., 1979-82, dep. staff judge advocate Keflavik, Iceland, 1982-83, staff judge advocate 71st Air Base Group Vance AFB, Okla., 1984-86, chief gen. torts sect. claims and tort litig. staff hdqrs. Washington, 1986-88, chief mgmt. and analysis br. claims and tort litig. divsn. Legal Svcs. Agy., 1988-92, sr. tort atty. tort claims and litig. divsn. Legal Svcs. Agy., 1992-97, chief internat. torts br., 1997—2005; atty. environ. law and litig. divsn., Legal Svcs. Agy. USAFR, USAF, Washington, 1992—99; atty. advisor Office of Gen. Counsel, Dept. Homeland Security, Washington, 2005—. Program chmn. Pentagon chpt. Fed. Bar Assn., 1989-90. Mem. DAR (chmn. procedures manual W.Va. chpt. 1989-92), Magna Carta Dames, Ancient and Honorable Arty. Co., Air Force Assn. (life), Ret. Officers Assn. (life). Avocations: photography, travel, farming, gardening. Office: Dept Homeland Security Office Gen Counsel Washington DC 20528

ADAMS, GEORGE BELL, lawyer; b. NYC, Sept. 16, 1930; s. George Bell and Mary Josephine (Smith) Adams; m. Lucy Elizabeth Ahearn, Sept. 10, 1952; children: Lucy S., Marea F., George B. Adams Jr., Alison E. BA, Yale U., 1952; LLB cum laude, Harvard U., 1957. Bar: N.Y. 1957, U.S. Dist. Ct. (so. and ea. dists.) N.Y. 1965, U.S. Ct. Appeals (2d cir.) 1973. Assoc. Debevoise, Plimpton, Lyons & Gates, NYC, 1957-65; ptnr. Debevoise & Plimpton, NYC, 1966-97, chmn. corp. dept., 1988-93, mng. ptnr. London, 1993-96, of counsel NYC, 1998—. Arbitrator China Internat. Econ. & Trade Arbitration Commn. Trustee Sarah Lawrence Coll., Bronxville, NY, 1977—, chmn. bd. trustees, 1987—91, vice chmn., chmn. exec. com., 1981—87; bd. dirs., exec. com. United Way of NYC, 1982—95, chmn. nominating com., 1985—93; fellow Pierpont Morgan Libr., NYC, 1977—, coun. of fellows, 1983—87, Yale U. Coun., 1983—90, chmn. alumni publs., 1979—83; trustee, mem. exec. com. Am. Trust for Brit. Libr., 1998—; bd. visitors CUNY Law Sch., 2003—; trustee Am. Assn. Internat. Com. of Jurists, 1998—; bd. dirs. New Amsterdam Singers, 1997—. Lawyers Alliance for World Security, 1989—98, Greater NY Fund, NYC, 1977—84, pres., 1981—84. 1st lt. US Army, 1952—54. Fellow, Davenport Coll., Yale U., 1983—90. Fellow: Am. Bar Found., Royal Soc. for Arts; mem.: ABA, Assn. Bar City NY, Century Assn., Pilgrim Soc., Racquet and Tennis Club, Cosmos Club. Office: Debevoise & Plimpton 919 3rd Ave Fl 44 New York NY 10022-3904 Business E-Mail: gbadams@debevoise.com.

ADAMS, GERALD DWAYNE, medical technician; b. Knoxville, Tenn., Sept. 13, 1963; s. Barney No Middle Name and Wanda Lynn Adams. BS in Ch. Edn., Tenn. Temple U., Chattanooga, 1992—93; grad. diploma in theology, Pacific Coast Bapt. Bible Coll., San Dimas, Calif., 1989—92; MEd in TESOL, Regent U., Va. Beach, 2002—05. Psychiat. technician Lakeshore Mental Health Inst., Knoxville, 1995—. Choir mem., visitation ministry Midway Bapt. Ch., San Diego, 1987—89; singer mens' chorus Calvary Bapt. Ch., San Dimas, Calif., 1989—92; ministry to homeless people Pacific Coast Bapt. Bible Coll., San Dimas, 1989—92; Sunday sch. tchr. Liberty Bapt. Ch., Long Beach, Calif., 1991—92; group care leader Highland Pk. Bapt. Ch., Chattanooga, 1992—93; prayer ministry intercessor W. Pk. Bapt. Ch., Knoxville, 1993—2006. E-4 USN, 1981—89, US, Italy, e-6 USN, 1990—96. Decorated Cert. Merit Divsn. Officer, Sea Svc. award USN, Good Conduct, Nat. Def. award, Naval Res. Meritorious Svc. award; recipient Cert. Appreciation, US Dept. Energy, 1988, Letter Appreciation, USN, 1988, Officer-in-Charge, Tenn., 1995, Lakeshore Mental Health Inst., 1996, Five & Ten-Years Svc. award, 2000, Nursing Dept. Cert. Appreciation, 2005, Five & Ten-Years Svc. award, 2005. Mem.: Tenn. State Employees Assn. (assoc.), Tenn. TESOL (assoc.), Tchrs. English Speakers Other Langs. (assoc. Cert. for attending TESOL conf. 2006), USS Constellation Assn. (assoc.), USS Orion Veterans Hist. Orgn. (assoc.), Am. Legion (assoc.). Bapt. Avocations: reading, horseback riding, walking, travel, sightseeing. Home: 824 Wooddale Church Rd Knoxville TN 37924 Office: Lakeshore Mental Health Inst 5908 Lyons View Pike Knoxville TN 37919 Home Phone: 865-933-3092. Personal E-mail: jumpingjackrussell@msn.com.

ADAMS, HAROLD LYNN, architect; b. Palmer, Tex., May 15, 1939; s. Charles Roy and Lola (Beck) A.; m. Janice Lindhurst, Aug. 29, 1963; children: Harold Lynn, Abigail, Ashley, Sam. BS in Architecture, Tex. A&M U., 1962. Registered architect 44 states and U.K.; 1st class registered architect Japan. Draftsman Pratt Box Henderson, Dallas, 1960; intern William B. Tabler & Assocs., NYC, 1961—62; architect John Carl Warnecke & Assocs., Washington, 1962—66; pres. RTKL Assocs., Inc., Balt., 1967—87, chmn. bd., 1987—2003, chmn. emeritus, 2003—. Regent Am. Archtl. Found., 1989—, chmn., 2000—; cons. Nat. Caital Planning Commn., 1992; dir. Lincoln Elec. Corp., 2001—. Legg Mason, 1987—, Renaissance Weekend, 1996—, Comml. Metals Corp., 2003-. Contbg. author: Current Techniques in Architectural Practice, Representative Am. Speeches, 1987-88, Technology: Trap or Triumph. Chmn. archtl. divsn. United Fund Drive, 1972; mem. task force on econ. devl. Balt. C. of C., 1975; pres. Econ. Devel. Coun. of Balt.; exec. com. Mt. Washington Country Sch. for Boys, 1976-77; bd. mgrs. Black Rock YMCA, 1971; vice chmn. GBC Found.; mem. Greater Balt. Com. on Edn., 1977-80, Com. on Planning, 1980-82; bd. dirs. Greater Balt. Com., 1983-90; mem. devel. coun. Tex. A&M U., 1982-90; mem. vis. com. Dept. Architecture U. Md., 1985-87; trustee Md. Inst. Coll. Art, Balt., 1984—, Maryvale Prep. Sch., Brooklandville, Md., 1985-89, Peale Mus., Balt., 1985-92, Balt. City Life Mus., 1985-92; regent Morgan State U., Balt., 1985-87; regent Am. Architecture Found., 1989-98, chmn., 2000—; trustee Balt. Fgn. Rels. Coun., 1987-93, Walter Gallery Art, 1987—; Balt. Metro. YMCA, 1987-90; chmn. World Trade Ctr. Inst., Md., 1990-99; mem. svcs. policy adv. com. U.S. Trade Rep., 1990—; bd. dirs. Internat. Visitors Ctr., 1990-92; mem. U.S.-China Bus. Coun., U.S.-Korea Bus. Coun.; adv. bd. Korea Econ. Inst. of Am.; chmn. Downtown Partnership Balt.; commr. Md. Econ. Devel. Comm.; chair Nat. Bldg. Mus., 1998—. Recipient Featherlite Design award Tex. A&M U., 1962; recipient Davidson Design award Tex. A&M U., 1962, Alpha Rho Chi medal, 1962, Tau Sigma Delta Gold medal Assn. Collegiate Schs. Architecture, 1993, Gov.'s award World Trade Ctr. Md., 1996, Outstanding Alumni award Tex. A&M U., 1998. Fellow AIA (pres. Balt. chpt. 1973-74, chmn. large firm roundtable 1984—, chancellor Coll. of Fellows 1997-98, nat. dir. 1999—, Kemper medal 1997); mem. Urban Land Inst., Am. Inst. Architects (chmn. large firm roundtable 1984—), Soc. Am. Mil. Engrs. (Urban medal 1997), Bursar Coll. of Fellows (vice chancellor), Royal Inst. Brit. Architects, Japan Inst. Architects, Center Club (Balt.), Met. Club (Washington), Cosmos Club, The Athenaeum (London). Democrat. Baptist. Home: 1601 The Terraces Baltimore MD 21209-3636

ADAMS, HAZARD SIMEON, retired language educator, writer; b. Cleve., Feb. 15, 1926; s. Robert Simeon and Mary (Thurness) A.; m. Diana White, Sept. 17, 1949; children: Charles Simeon, Perry White. AB, Princeton, 1948; MA, U. Wash., 1949, PhD, 1953. Instr. English Cornell U., 1952-56; asst. prof. U. Tex., 1956-59; vis. assoc. prof. Washington U., St. Louis, 1959; from assoc. prof. to prof. Mich. State U., 1959-64; Fulbright lectr. U. Dublin, 1962-63; prof. U. Calif.-Irvine, 1964-77, founding chmn. English dept., 1964-69; dean Sch. Humanities, 1970-72, vice chancellor acad. affairs, 1972-74; co-founder, co-dir. Sch. Criticism and Theory, 1975—77; sr. fellow, 1975-88; hon. sr. fellow, 1988—; prof. English and comparative lit. U. Wash., Seattle, 1977-97, Byron W. and Alice L. Lockwood prof. humanities, 1988-97, prof. emeritus, 1997—. Prof. English U. Calif., Irvine, 1990-94. Author: Poems by Robert Simeon Adams, 1952, Blake and Yeats: The Contrary Vision, 1955, 2d edit., 1969, The Contexts of Poetry, 1963, William Blake: A Reading of the Shorter Poems, 1963, Poetry: An Introductory Anthology, 1968, The Horses of Instruction, 1968, Fiction as Process, 1968, The Interests of Criticism, 1969, William Blake: Jerusalem, Selected Poems and Prose, 1970, The Truth About Dragons, 1971, Critical Theory Since Plato, 1971, 3d edit., 2004, Lady Gregory, 1973, The Academic Tribes, 1976, 2d edit., 1988, Philosophy of the Literary Symbolic, 1983, Joyce Cary's Trilogies, 1983, Critical Theory Since 1965, 1986, The Book okf Yeats's Poems, 1991,

Antithetical Essays, 1991, Critical Essays on William Blake, 1991, The Book of Yeats's Vision, 1995, The Farm at Richwood and Other Poems, 1997, Many Pretty Toys, 1999, Four Lectures on the History of Criticism in the West, 2000, Home, 2001, The Offense of Poetry, 2007; mem. editl. bd. Epoch, 1954—56, Tex. Studies Lit. and Lang., 1957—68, Studies in Romanticism, 1966—, Blake Studies, 1969—89, Modern Lang. Quar., 1977—84. Served to 1st lt. USMC, 1943-45, 51. Guggenheim fellow, 1974-75 Mem. Internat. Assn. Univ. Profs. English, Am. Conf. for Irish Studies, Phi Beta Kappa. Home: 3930 NE 157th Pl Lake Forest Park WA 98155-6730 Personal E-mail: HAdams3048@aol.com.

ADAMS, HENRY, art educator; b. Boston, May 12, 1949; s. Thomas Boylston and Ramelle (Cochrane) A.; m. Marianne Berardi, Apr. 12, 1989. BA, Harvard U., 1971; MA, Yale U., 1977, PhD, 1980. Asst. prof. U. Ill., Champaign, 1981-82; curator fine arts Carnegie Mus., Pitts., 1982-84; Samuel Sosland curator Am. Art Nelson-Atkins Mus. Art, Kansas City, Mo., 1984-93; dir. Cummer Mus. Art, Jacksonville, Fla., 1994—95; interim dir. Kemper Mus. Art, Kansas City, Mo., 1996; curator, Am. Art Cleve. Mus. Art, 1996; prof., Am. Art Case Western Reserve Univ., Cleve., 1997—. Adj. prof. U. Kans., U. Mo., Kans. Author: Thomas Hart Benton: An American Original, 1989, Thomas Hart Benton: Drawing from Life, 1990, Andrew Wyeth: Master Drawings, 1996, Albert Bloch: The American Blue Rider, 1997, Eakins Revealed: The Secret Life of an American Artist, 2005, American Da Vinci: Viktor Schreckengost and Modern Design, 2006, (with others) John La Farge, 1989; contbr. articles to jours. in field. Recipient Arthur Kingsley Porter prize Coll. Art Assn., 1985, William F. Yates Disting. Svc. medal William Jewell Coll., 1989, Frances Blanshard prize Yale U., Inst. of Mus. Svcs. Nat. Mus. Svc. award for Cummer Mus., 1994. Office: Mather House Case Western Reserve Univ 11201 Euclid Ave Cleveland OH 44106-7110 Office Phone: 216-368-4119. E-mail: henry.adams@case.edu.

ADAMS, HERBERT RYAN, management consultant, retired minister, mediator; b. Phila., Apr. 19, 1932; s. Leander Hampton and Helen Marguerite (Richards) Adams; m. Carol Anne Levine, Aug. 27, 1956 (div.); children: Ashley Pozefsky, Joshua, Lee, Rachel; m. Mary Ryan, Aug. 20, 1977. AB, Colby Coll., 1954; student, Harvard Div. Sch., 1955-56, Kent State U., 1957, Boston U., 1963; EdD, Harvard U., 1972. Ordained to ministry Congregationalist Ch., 1952, Unitarian Universalist, 1968. Minister Fairfield and Pine Point, Maine, 1950-56, Chelsea, Mass., 1962-66, Lexington, Mass., 1967-75, Winnetka, Ill., 1978-87, South Paris, Maine, 1988-94, West Paris, Maine, 1991-94; iterim Ithaca, NY, 1997-98, Santa Fe, 1998-99, Port Charlotte, Fla., 2001-02; editor Allyn and Bacon, Boston, 1959-62; sr. editor Ginn & Co., Boston, 1962-68; v.p. mktg. Visual Learning Corp., Cambridge, Mass., 1968-71; dir. Sci. Rsch. Assocs. divsn. IBM, Chgo., 1975-83; v.p. Laidlaw Bros., River Forest, Ill., 1983-84, pres., CEO, 1984-87; pres. Ryan-Adams Cons. Svcs., Center Lovell, Maine, 1994—. Author: Poetry on Film, 1970, Listening Your Way to Management Success, 1983; contbr. articles to profl. jours. Tchr. Greenville (Pa.) HS, 1956—58, Euclid (Ohio) HS, 1958—59, Lexington (Mass.) HS, 1968—69, Harvard Gradh. Sch. Edn., 1971—72, Oxford Hills (Maine) HS, 1987—88; prin. Oxford Hills Jr. HS, 1989—91. Recipient Coe Found. award, DePauw U., 1958, cert. of Merit, VFW, 1989, Disting. Pres. award, Norway-Paris Kiwanis, 1996. Mem.: Lovell Hist. Soc., Mediators Maine, Lovell Land Trust, Unitarian Universalist Ret. Mins. Assn., Oxford Hills Ret. Tchrs. Assn., Girard Coll. Alumni Assn. (life). Home: 252 Brentwood Dr Lake Placid FL 33852 Personal E-mail: herbadams32@hotmail.com.

ADAMS, HUNTER (PATCH ADAMS), internist, health facility administrator; b. Washington, May 28, 1945; Student, Sewanee U.; BA, George Washington U., 1967; MD, Med. Coll. Va., 1971. Resident pediat. Georgetown U. Hosp., Washignton, 1971; founder, dir. Gesundheit Inst., Arlington, Va., 1971—92. Author: House Calls: How We Can All Heal the World One Visit at a Time, 1998; co-author: Gesundheit!: Bringing Good Health to You, the Medical System, and Society through Physician Service, Complementary Therapies, Humor, and Joy, 1998. Recipient Inst. of Noetic Sci. award for Creative Altruism, 1994. Office: Gesundheit Institute PO Box 50125 Arlington VA 22205 also: Gesundheit PO Box 3134 Hagerstown MD 21741-3134

ADAMS, J. PHILLIP, oil industry executive; BA in Fin. and Acctg., Utah State U., 1978. With Brown and Davis, CPAs, 1978—80, Flying J. Airlines, Inc., Brigham City, Utah, 1980—, CEO, 1992—. Office: Flying J Inc PO Box 150310 Ogden UT 84415-0310*

ADAMS, JAMES CHARLES, lawyer; b. Cleve., June 20, 1949; s. Charles Otterbein and Loraine Ida (Bagnoli) Adams; m. Donna Elaine Roe, Aug. 7, 1971 (dec. 1983); 1 child, Heather Anne; m. Naz D. Edwards, Aug. 29, 1998. BA, Mich. State U., 1971; JD, U. Mich., 1974. Bar: Mich. 1974, U.S. Dist. Ct. (ea. dist.) Mich. 1974. Assoc. Honigman Miller Schwartz, Detroit, 1974—75, Dykema Gossett, PLLC, Detroit, 1975—82, ptnr., 1982—86, Simpson & Moran, Birmingham, Mich., 1986—87; prin. James C. Adams, Traverse City, Mich., 1987—93, Adams & Assocs., Traverse City, 1993—95; ptnr. Running, Wise, Ford & Phillips, Traverse City, 1995—98; mem. Dykema Gossett PLLC, Detroit, 1998—2006; shareholder Ufer & Spaniola, 2006, Butzel Long, Detroit, 2007—. Mem.: ABA, Detroit Bar Assn., Phi Kappa Phi, Order of the Coif. Office: Butzel Long Stoneridge West 4100 Woodward Ave Bloomfield Hills MI 48304 Office Phone: 248-258-2901. Personal E-mail: jcmcadam@comcast.net. Business E-Mail: adamsj@butzel.com.

ADAMS, JAMES FREDERICK, psychologist, academic administrator, educator; b. Andong, Korea, Dec. 27, 1927; s. Benjamin Nyce and Phyllis Irene (Taylor) A.; m. Carol Ann Wagner, Jan. 17, 1980; children— James Edward, Dorothy Lee Adams Vanderhorst, Robert Benjamin. BA In Psychology, U. Calif.-Berkeley, 1950; Ed.M. in Counseling and Psychology, Temple U., 1951; PhD in Exptl. Psychology, Wash. State U., 1959. Cert. psychologist, Wash., Pa.; lic. psychologist, Pa. Psychometrician Measurement and Research Ctr., Temple U., Phila., 1951-52; asst. prof. psychology Whitworth Coll., Spokane, Wash., 1952-55; teaching and research asst. State U. Wash., 1955-57; research assoc. Miami U., Oxford, Ohio, 1957-59; asst. prof. psychology Coll. Liberal Arts, Temple U., 1959-62, assoc. prof., 1962-66, prof., 1966-80, chmn. dept. counseling psychology, 1969-72; vis. prof. psychology Coll. Soc. Scis., U. P.R., Rio Piedras, 1963-64, Coll. Scis., Cath. U., Ponce, PR, 1971-72; chmn. dept. counseling psychology Coll. Edn., Temple U., 1973-77, coord. divsn. ednl. psychology, 1974-76; grad. dean, prof. psychology Grad. Coll., U. Nev., Las Vegas, 1980-85; acad. (sr.) v.p. Longwood Coll., Farmville, Va., 1985-86. Author: Problems in Counseling: A Case Study Approach, 1962, Instructors Manual for Understanding Adolescence, 1969; (exhbn. catalogue with J. D. Selig) Colonial Spanish Art of the Americas, 1976; (comml. pamphlet with C. L. Davis) The Use of the Vu-graph as an Instructional Aid, 1960; editor: Counseling and Guidance: A Summary View, 1965, Understanding Adolescence: Current Developments in Adolescent Psychology, 1968, 4th edit., 1980, Human Behavior in a Changing Society, 1973, Songs that had to be Sung (by B. N. Adams), 1979; contbr. chpts., articles, tests and book revs. to profl. publs. Donor James F. Adams Endowment Wash. State U., Pullman, 2003. Served to cpl. USMC, 1945—46. Recipient Alexander Meiklejohn award AAUP, 1984; James McKean Cattell Rsch. Fund grantee Miami U., Oxford, Ohio, 1958, Bolton Fund Rsch. grant Temple U., 1960, 62, Faculty Rsch. grant Temple U., 1961, 63, Commonwealth of Pa. Rsch. grant Temple U., 1969-72, Summer Rsch. fellow Temple U., 1979; U. Munich scholar, 1955; named James F. Adams scholarship U. Nev., Las Vegas. Fellow Am. Psychol. Assn. (divs. 26, 17); mem. Eastern Psychol. Assn., Western Psychol. Assn., Interam. Soc. Psychology, Sigma Xi, Psi Chi Avocation: Art collecting and restoring. Home: 130 Palacio Rd Corrales NM 87048-9648

ADAMS, JAMES THOMAS, surgeon; b. Rochester, NY, Mar. 28, 1930; s. Thomas and Sarah A.; m. Jacqueline K. Stemmler, July 7, 1952; children— Pamela, Mark, Sari Lynn. AB, Washington U., St. Louis, 1951, MD, 1955. Intern, then resident in surgery Barnes Hosp., St. Louis, 1955-60; mem. faculty U. Rochester Med. Sch., 1962—, prof. surgery, 1977—. Author papers in field, chpts. in books. Served as officer M.C. USAR, 1960-62. Mem. Am. Surg. Assn., Soc. Internat. de Chirurgie, Soc. U. Surgeons, Central Surg. Assn., Soc. Vascular Surgery, Am. Gastroenterol. Assn., Soc. Surgery Alimentary Tract, Am. Assn. Surgery Trauma, Phi Beta Kappa, Sigma Xi, Alpha Omega Alpha. Clubs: Oak Hill Country (Rochester). Achievements include co-designing inferior vena cava clip. Office Phone: 585-275-2726. Personal E-mail: jadams06@rochester.rr.com.

ADAMS, JANELLE R., mathematics educator, gifted and talented educator; d. James R. and Judy K. Adams. BA in Math. Edn., Hastings Coll., Nebr., 1999; MA in Spl. Edn., Edn. of the Gifted and Talented, U. No. Colo., Greeley, 2004. Math. tchr. Pine Creek HS, Colorado Springs, 1999—, talented and gifted coord., 2005—. Named Tchr. of Week, KYGO, 2004. Mem.: Colo. Edn. Assn., Mensa, Pi Lambda Theta. Avocations: dance, travel, mentoring students, choreography, musical theater. Office: Pine Creek HS 10750 Thunder Mountain Ave Colorado Springs CO 80908 Home Phone: 719-596-8738; Office Phone: 719-234-2600. Personal E-mail: adamsjanelle@yahoo.com. Business E-Mail: jadams@asd20.org.

ADAMS, JEAN MARIE, biology professor; d. Walter R. and Frances R. Adams; life ptnr. Carolyn E. Woodard. BS in Biol. Sci., Auburn U., Ala., 1979; MEd in Sci. Edn., Ga. State U., Atlanta, Ga., 1985; MS in Zoology, U. South Fla., Tampa, Fla., 1991. Tchr. sci. Griffin (Ga.) Spalding Jr. H.S., 1980, Griffin (Ga.) Spalding Sr. H.S., 1980—89; tchg. asst. U. South Fla., Tampa, Fla., 1989—91; biol. specialist Dept. Natural Resources, St. Petersburg, Fla., 1991—92; prof. biology Pasco-Hernando C.C., New Port Richey, Fla., 1992—. Senator faculty Pasco-Hernando C.C., 2002—06, co-chmn. faculty divsn. sacs study, mem. sci. course design, 2005—06, tech. com., 1999—2006, dept. chmn., 2007; instr. biology Hillsborough C.C., Tampa, 1991—92. Contbr. photographs to mags.; set designer, asst. on art design: MAD Theater Tampa, 2005—06; actor: Plant City (Fla.) Entertainment Inc., 2003—05. Team leader coastal cleanup Pasco-Hernando C.C., 1994—2002; driver Big Ride Across Am. Am. Lung Assn., 1998. Named one of Young Women of Am., 1987; recipient Cast Choice award, Plant City (Fla.) Entertainment Inc., 2005, Tech. Contbn. award, 2005. Avocations: birdwatching, kayaking, scuba diving, fishing. Home: 24219 Painter Drive Land O Lakes FL 34639 Office: Pasco-Hernando Community College 10230 Ridge Rd New Port Richey FL 34654-5129 Home Phone: 813-948-2756; Office Phone: 727-816-3245. Business E-Mail: adamsj@phcc.edu.

ADAMS, JEFFREY, mathematics professor; married; children: Rachel, Joshua Robert. PhD, Yale Univ., 1981. Prof., math dept. Univ. Md., College Park, policy coord. for info. tech. The project leader of 18 top mathematicians and computer scientists (Atlas of Lie Groups Project) from the US to successfully map E8, one of the largest and most complicated structures in mathematics. Office: Math Dept Univ Md Room 2310 Math Building College Park MD 20742 Office Phone: 301-405-5493. Business E-Mail: jda@math.umd.edu.*

ADAMS, JENNIFER, medical products executive; MBA, Northwestern Univ. Kellogg Sch. Mgmt., 1998. Office supplies sales; with Deerfield Med. Supplies, Chgo., Baxter Internat. Inc., Chgo., 1994—, v.p. sales, transfusion therapies, 2002—. Named one of 40 Under Forty, Crain's Bus. Chgo., 2005. Avocations: running sprint triathlons, running marathons.*

ADAMS, JIMMIE VICK, communications systems company executive, retired military officer; b. Prichard, Ala., May 1, 1936; s. Anthony J. and Verlie (Adams) Antonidis; m. Ouida Bumpers, Dec. 27, 1955; children: Vickie, Lisa Floyd. BS in Mech. Engring., Auburn U., Ala., 1957; MME, U. Tex., 1963; grad., Squadron Officer Sch., 1964, Indsl. Coll. Armed Forces, 1978, Joint Flag Officer Warfighting Course, 1987. Advanced through ranks to gen. USAF, 1957, commd., 1958, various flying and staff positions, 1958-85, dep. chief of staff Requirements HQTAC Langley AFB, Va., 1985-87, comdr. 1st Air Force, 1987-88, vice comdr. Tactical Air Command, 1988-89, dep. chief of staff Plans and Ops. Washington, 1989, comdr. in chief Pacific Air Forces Hickam AFB, Hawaii, 1993; positions up to v.p., officer Loral Corp., 1993—96; v.p. Washington ops. for C3I and Systems Integration Sector Lockheed Martin; sr. v.p. Washington ops. L-3 Comm. Holdings, Inc. Mem. AF Assn., Daedalians. Avocations: golf, fishing. Office: L-3 Comm Holdings Inc 1215 S Clark St Ste 1205 Arlington VA 22202 Office Phone: 703-412-7190.*

ADAMS, JO-ANN MARIE, lawyer; b. LA, May 27, 1949; d. Joseph John and Georgia S. (Wein) A. AA, Pasadena C.C., 1968; BA, Pomona Coll., 1970; MA, Calif. State U., LA, 1971; MBA, Pacific Luth. U., 1983; JD, Santa Clara U., 1996. Cert. in telecom. and info. resource mgmt. Secondary tchr. South Pasadena Unified Schs., 1970-71; appraiser Riverside County Assessor's Office, 1972-74; systems and procedures analyst Riverside County Data Processing Dept., 1974-76, supr. systems analyst, 1976-79; systems analyst computer Boeing Computer Svcs. Co., Seattle, 1979-81; sr. systems analyst Thurston County Ctrl. Svcs., Olympia, Wash., 1981-83, data processing systems mgr., 1983-84; data processing systems engr. IBM Corp., 1984-87; realtor assoc. Dower Realty, 1987-92; corp. sales rep. UniGlobe Met. Travel, 1988-89; project mgr. Servco Pacific, 1989-90, Scott Software Systems, 1990-91; systems analyst Dept. Atty. Gen., 1991-93; pvt. practice Honolulu, 1996—; with Bervar & Jones, 2002—03. Cons. in field, 1993—; corp. counsel RightWorks Corp., 2000-01, Law Offices Thomas R. Hogan, 1999; instr. Riverside City Coll., 1977-79; adj. prof. Santa Clara U., 1997-2000. Actor: films and TV shows. Chair legis. task force Riverside, San Bernardino chpt. NOW, 1975-76, chpt. co-chair, 1978; mem. ethics com. Calif. NOW, Inc., 1978; alt. del. Calif. Dem. Caucus, 1978; del. Hawaii Dem. Caucus, 2002; mem. Gay, Lesbian, Bisexual and Transgender Caucus of Hawaii Dem. Party, chair, 2006-07; mem. Hawaii Dem. State Ctrl. Com., Waikiki Neighborhood Bd., 2005—. Mem. Pomona Coll. Alumni Assn., Santa Clara U. Alumni Assn. Home: 411 Hobron Ln # 801 Honolulu HI 96815-1210 Office: Seven Waterfront Plz 500 Ala Moana Blvd Ste 400 Honolulu HI 96813-4920 Office Phone: 808-528-2100. Personal E-mail: jadamsesq@aol.com.

ADAMS, JOANNE NELSON, special education educator; b. Memphis, Jan. 20, 1946; d. William Anthony and Evelyn Mary Nelson; m. Jeffrey Lee Adams, July 27, 2002; children: Bryon McAllister, Erin James stepchildren: Kellie, Chris. BA in English, Georgian Ct. Coll., Lakewood, NJ, 1968; MS in Varying Exceptionalities, Barry U., Miami Shores, 1999. English, drama coach St. Veronica Sch., Howell, NJ, 1976—78, 1983—95; English tchr. Freehold Regional Sys., NJ, 1978—83; resource, English tchr. Epiphany Cathedral Sch., Venice, Fla., 1995—2002; spl. edn. tchr. Bell St. Mid. Sch., Clinton, SC, 2002—03, 2003—04, 2006—07, Clinton Elem. Sch., 2004—05, 2005—06. Participant, presenter SCIRA, Clinton. Named Tchr. Yr., Laurens County Dist. 56, 2005—06; recipient Nat. Tchr. Excellence award, Nat. Cath. Edn. Assn., 1992, 2000, Disney Tchr. Excellence award, Walt Disney, 1999. Mem.: Coun. Exceptional Children, Nat. Coun. Tchrs. English, Nat. Autism Soc. Independent. Lutheran. Avocations: gardening, reading, walking, travel. Home: 202 Bellmont Stakes Clinton SC 29325 Mailing: PO Box 438 Clinton SC 29325 Office Phone: 864-833-0807.

ADAMS, JODY, chef, restaurant owner; m. Ken Rivard; children: Oliver Rivard, Roxanne Rivard. Student, Brown U. Apprentice, class asst. Nancy Verde Barr; chef Seasons restaurant, Boston, 1983—86; sous chef Hamersley's Bistro, Boston, 1986—90; exec. chef Michela's, Boston, 1990—94; ptnr., chef Rialto, Cambridge, 1994—; ptnr. Sapphire Restaurant Group, Cambridge, 1994—, blu, Boston, 2001—, Noik, Cambridge, Mass., 2002—. Author: (cookbooks) In the Hands of a Chef: Cooking with Jody Adams of Rialto Restaurant, 2002 (One of Best Cookbooks of Season, NY Times, 2002). Named Best Chef, Boston Mag., 1997, Culinary Profl. of Yr., Sante Mag., 2006; named one of Five Rising Stars, Restaurant Hospitality, 1992, Am.'s Best Young Chef's to Keep Your Eye On, Esquire mag., 1992, Am.'s Ten Best new Chefs, Food and Wine mag., 1993; named to Fine Dining Hall of Fame, Nation's Restaurant News, 2000; recipient Perrier-Jouet Best Chef award N.E., James Beard Found., 1997, Life Achievement award, Great Boston Concierge Assn., 2006, Women Chefs & Restaurateurs Golden Whisk award, 2006. Office: Sapphire Restaurant Grp 20 Univ Rd Cambridge MA 02138*

ADAMS, JOHN BRETT, investment banker, pharmaceutical executive; b. Eng., Dec. 6, 1940; arrived in U.S., 1972; s. Harold Coates and Mildred B. (Jones) Adams; m. Laura Marie Schneider, July 24, 1970; children: Alexa, Caroline. BA, Oxford U., Eng., 1962; MBA, Stanford U., 1964. Exec. dir. S.G. Warburg & Co., Ltd., London, 1964—72; dir. Singer & Friedlander, Ltd., London, 1972—74; sr. v.p. White, Weld & Co., Inc., NYC, 1974—78; mng. dir. Merrill Lynch Capital Markets, NYC, 1978—85; ptnr. M.J.H. Nightingale & Co., NYC, 1986—89; v.p. corp. devel. Wyeth (formerly Am. Home Products Corp.), 1991—2002. Dir. Am. Swiss Assn., NYC; mem. internat. com. Securities Industry Assn., NYC. Mem. bd. advisers Godwin-Ternbach Mus., Queens, NY; bd. dirs. Am. Friends of the Warburg Inst., The Actors Co. Theatre, NYC, Brit. Schs. and Univs. Found., Inc., NYC, 1982—98. Mem.: Devon Yacht Club, Maidstone Club, Racquet and Tennis Club. Avocations: golf, art, theater. Home: 224 E 68th St New York NY 10021-6001 E-mail: adamsjb2003@yahoo.com.

ADAMS, JOHN CARTER, JR., retired insurance executive; b. Williston, Fla., June 13, 1936; s. John Carter and Katharine Anna (Beall) A.; m. Leila Nora Johnson, Nov. 28, 1958; children: Julia Katharine, Ruth Anne. BSBA, U. Fla., 1958. Agt. Pan Am Ins. Co., 1958-59; acct. exec. Guy B. Odum & Co., Inc., 1959-63, v.p., 1963-66, exec. v.p., 1966-71, pres., 1971-76, Jay Adams & Assocs., Inc., Daytona Beach, Fla., 1976-85, Hilb Rogal & Hamilton Co., Daytona Beach, Fla., 1986-89, CEO, 1986-92, chmn., 1986-98, mem. oper. com. Richmond, Va., 1988-95, chmn. oper. com., 1987-93, sr. v.p. ops., 1989-90, exec. v.p. sales and mktg., 1991-93, exec. v.p., COO, 1993-94, exec. v.p. ops., 1994-99; exec. v.p. Brown & Brown Inc., Daytona Beach, 1999—2006, mem. leadership coun., 1999—2006; ret., 2006. Bd. dirs. Consol. Tomoka Land Co., chmn. compensation com., 1990- , mem. audit com., 2004—, mem. exec. com.; chmn. adv. bd. Daytona Beach region Am. Pioneer Savs. Bank005, Orlando, Fla., 1986-90. Mem. bd. visitors Embry-Riddle Aero. U., Daytona Beach, 1967-69, trustee, 1969—, mem. exec. com., 1972—, vice chmn. bd. 1981—, chmn. exec. com, 1983—2006, devel. coun. chmn. fund drive Hunt Meml. Libr. Embry-Riddle Aero U., 1985; chmn. Commitment 2000 Fund Drive Embry-Riddle Aero U.; campaign chmn. Easter Seal Soc., 1969, trustee, 1970-73, pres., 1972-73; bd. dirs. YMCA, Daytona Beach, 1968-76, 78—, treas., 1970, v.p., 1971-82, pres., 1983; mem. Metro Bd. Daytona Beach YMCA, 1992-2001, trustee, 2002—; dir. Futures, Inc., 1985-93, pres., 1987; dir. Nat. Intercollegiate Sports Festival, 1985-87; gen. campaign chmn. United Way of Volusia County, Fla., 1977, pres., 1979, dir., 1976-82, trustee, 1985—; chmn. Civic League of Halifax Area, 1983-84, exec. com., 1977-92; chmn. Fla. Internat. Festivals, Inc., 1990-91, bd. dirs. 1987—, exec. com., 1991—, chmn. Lively Arts Ctr. Inc., 1997-2002, chmn. emeritus, 2003-; mem. Tourist Devel. Coun. Volusia County 1983-85, Halifax Advt. Authority, 1985; bd. dirs. Volusia County Bus. Devel. Coun., 1984-92, Daytona Beach Cmty. Found., 1984-87, Fla. State C. of C., 1985-86; mem. bd. trustees St. James Episc. Day Sch., 2005—. Served with USNR, 1953-61. Recipient Disting. Svc. award Bd. visitors Embry-Riddle Aero. U., 1975, Champion Higher Ind. Edn. in Fla. award Ind. Colls. and Univs. of Fla., 1973, 1st Ann. Herbert M. Davidson Cmty. Svc. award United Way of Volusia County, 1992, J. Saxton Lloyd Outstanding Cmty. Svc. award Civic League of the Halifax Area, 2003; named Citizen of Yr., Boys and Girls Club of Volusia-Flagler Counties, 2000, Ctrl. Fla. Coun. Boy Scouts Am., 2001; established John C. Adams Cmty. Svc. award Embry-Riddle Aero U., 1990. Mem. Daytona Beach C. of C. (bd. govs. 1968-70, v.p. bus. and govt. 1970, pres. 1975, gen. campaign chmn. devel. fund drive 1984, Louis Fuchs Man of Yr. award 1985), Volusia County Insurors Assn. (pres. 1971-72), Fla. Assn. Ins. Agts. (bd. dirs. 1978-81), Coun. Ins. Agts. and Brokers (bd. dirs. 1989—, co-chmn. exec. liasion com., mem. fin. and audit com. 1993-94, sec. 1994-95, treas. 1995-96, vice chmn. 1996-97, chmn. 1997-98, co-chmn. nominating com. 1998-99), Rotary (bd. dirs. 1989-91). Republican. Episcopalian.

ADAMS, JOHN COOLIDGE, composer, conductor; b. Worcester, Mass., Feb. 15, 1947; s. Carl John and Elinore Mary (Coolidge) A. Studied with Leon Kirchner, Earl Kim, Roger Sessions, Harvard U., AB magna cum laude, 1969, MA, 1971. Former composer-in-residence, condr. San Francisco Symphony Orch., 1979—85. Artistic advisor, San Francisco Symphony Orch., from 1978, former composer-in-residence, San Francisco Symphony Orch.; dir., New Music Ensemble, from 1972-81; faculty mem., San Francisco Conservatory, 1972-83; composer-in-residence, Marlboro Festival, 1970, Richard & Barbara Debs composer, Carnegie Hall, 2003-07; musical compositions include Electric Wake, 1968, Heavy Metal, 1971, American Standard, 1973, Kataadn, 1973, Onyx, 1976, Phrygian Gates, 1977, Shaker Loops, 1978; Onyx, Grounding, Sermon, Common Tones, 1979, Harmonium, 1980, Grand Pianola Music, 1982, Harmonielehre, 1985, Nixon in China, 1987 (Grammy for best contemporary composition, 1989), The Death of Klinghoffer, 1991, Chamber Symphony, 1993 (Royal Philharmonic Soc. Music award, 1994), Violin Concerto (Grawemeyer award for music, 1995), Naive and Sentimental Music, 1999, On The Transmigration of Souls, 2002 (Pulitzer prize for music, 2003), My Father Knew Charles Ives, 2003, Doctor Atomic, 2003, The Dharma at Big Sur, 2004, A Flowering Tree, 2006. Named to rank of Chevalier dans I'Ordre des Artes et des Lettres, French Ministry of Culture; recipient Cyril Magnin Awd. for Outstanding Achievement in the Arts, Calif. Gov.'s. Awd. for Lifetime Achievement in the Arts, Centennial medal, Harvard U. Grad. Sch. Arts & Sciences, 2004, Nemmers prize in Music Composition, Northwestern U., 2004, Disting. Composer award, Am. Composers Orch., 2007. Office: Boosey & Hawkes 24 E 21st St New York NY 10010 also: California Artists Mgt 41 Sutter St # 420 San Francisco CA 94104-4903

ADAMS, JOHN HAMILTON, lawyer; b. NYC, Feb. 15, 1936; s. John and Barbara (Johnston) A.; m. Patricia Brandon Smith, Sept. 30, 1963; children: Katherine L., John H., Ramsay W. BA, Mich. State U., 1959; LL.B., Duke U., 1962. Bar: NY 1963. Assoc. Cadwalader, Wickersham & Taft, NYC, 1962-65; asst. US atty. So. Dist. NY, NYC, 1965-69; co-founder and exec. dir. Nat. Resources Def. Coun., Inc., NYC, 1970-98, pres., 1998—2006, founding dir., 2006—. Chmn. Open Space Inst., N.Y.C., 1979—. Bd. dirs. Catskill Ctr. for Conservation, Arkville, N.Y., 1974—, Hudson River Found. Sci. and Environ. Rsch., Inc., 1981—, Winston Found. World Peace, 1984—, World Resources Inst., 1987—. Recipient As They Grow award Parents mag., 1989, Frances K. Hutchinson award Garden Club Am., 1990, Disting. Alumni award Duke U., 1991. Mem. Am. Conservation Assn. (bd. dirs. 1985—), Century Assn. Office: Natural Resources Def Coun Inc 40 W 20th St New York NY 10011-4211 Office Phone: 212-727-4535. E-mail: jcoifman@nrdc.org.*

ADAMS, JOHN HURST, bishop; b. Columbia, SC, Nov. 27, 1929; s. Eugene Avery and Charity A. (Nash) A.; m. Dolly Desselle, Aug. 25, 1956; children: Gaye Desselle, Jann Hurst; 1 child, Madelyn Rose. AB, Johnson C. Smith Coll., 1948; STB, Boston U., 1951, STM, 1953; DD, Wilberforce U., 1956, Paul Quinn Coll., 1972. Ordained deacon A.M.E. Ch., 1948, elder A.M.E. Ch., 1952, bishop A.M.E. Ch., 1972. Pastor Bethel A.M.E. Ch., Lynn, Mass., 1950—52; prof. Wilberforce (Ohio) U., 1952—56; pres. Paul Quinn Coll., Waco, Tex., 1956—62, chmn. bd., 1972—; pastor 1st A.M.E. Ch., Seattle, 1962—68, Grant A.M.E. ch., LA, 1968—72; 87th A.M.E. bishop 10th Dist. Tex. councils chs., 1972—; bishop 2d Dist., 1986—89; sr. bishop Atlanta, 1989—92, 7th Episcopal Dist., Columbia, SC, 1992—. Author: Ethnic Education in Black Church, 1970. Bd. dirs. Nat. Coun. Chs., Nat. Conf. Black Churchmen, Nat. Bd. Black United Funds, People United to Save Humanity (PUSH), Tex. Coun. Chs. Named Man of Yr., B'nai B'rith, 1964, Urban League, Seattle, 1965. Mem.: Boulé, Alpha Phi Alpha. Office: 110 Pisgah Church Rd Columbia SC 29203-9351

ADAMS, JOHN LEWIS, transportation executive; BBA in Fin, U. Tex., 1966, JD, 1969. Joined Tex. Commerce Bank, Houston, 1973, pres., 1983—87, chmn., CEO Dallas - Fort Worth, 1987—88; vice chmn. Tex. Commerce Bank NA, 1988—97; chmn., pres., CEO Chase Bank of Tex., 1997—98; exec. v.p. Trinity Industries, Dallas, 1999—; bd. dir. Group 1 Automotive, Houston, 1999—, non-exec. chmn., 2005—. Office: Trinity Industries 2525 Stemmons Freeway Dallas TX 75207-2401*

ADAMS, JOHN M., library director; b. Chgo., June 10, 1950; s. Merlin J. and Esther (Bohn) A.; m. Nancy Ileen Coultas, June 12, 1970; 1 child, Arwen Lee BA in English, U. Ill., 1972, MLS, 1973. Grad. asst. U. Ill. Libr., Urbana, 1972-73; libr. reference Sherman Oaks Libr., LA, 1973-75; libr. philosophy dept. LA Pub. Libr., 1975-77, head gen. reading svc., 1977-78; dir. Moline Pub. Libr., Ill., 1978-83, Tampa-Hillsborough County Pub. Libr. Sys., Fla., 1983-91; dir., county libr. Orange County Pub. Libr., Calif., 1991—2007, dir. emeritus Calif., 2007—. Dir. Tampa Bay Libr. Consortium, Fla., 1983-91, Santiago Libr. Sys., 1991—2007, chmn., 1999; mem. adv. com. on pub. librs. Online Computer Libr. Ctr., 1992-95; bd. govs. Am. Rsch. Ctr. in Egypt, 2003-06. Contbr. articles to profl. jours. Pres. Orange County chpt. Am. Rsch. Ctr. in Egypt, 2002—07; bd. dirs. Planned Parenthood Tampa, 1984. Recipient Frontier award ALA Mag., 1981; named Outstanding Young Man, Moline Jaycees, 1983. Mem. ALA (J.C. Dana award 1982, 93, 2004), Calif. Libr. Assn. (named Literacy Libr. of Yr. 2006), Calif. County Librs. Assn., Orange County C. of C. Avocations: music, tennis. Office: Orange County Pub Libr 1501 E Saint Andrew Pl Santa Ana CA 92705-4930 Office Phone: 714-566-3040. E-mail: jadams@irtc.net.

ADAMS, JOHN MARSHALL, lawyer; b. Columbus, Ohio, Dec. 6, 1930; s. H.F. and Ada Margaret (Gregg) A.; m. Janet Hawk, June 28, 1952; children: John Marshall, Susan Lynn, William Alfred. BA, Ohio State U., 1952; JD summa cum laude, 1954. Bar: Ohio 1954. Mem. Cowan & Adams, Columbus, 1954—55; asst. city atty. City of Columbus, 1955—56; mem. Knepper, White, Richards & Miller, 1956-63; practiced in Columbus, 1963—74; ptnr. Porter, Wright, Morris & Arthur, Columbus, 1975—91, of counsel, 1992—. Vice chmn. Ohio Bar Liability Ins. Co., 1990-93, chmn., 1994-2002, chair emeritus, 2002—; trustee Ohio Legal Ctr. Inst., 1976-81, Ohio Lawpac, 1980-89. Fellow Am. Coll. Trial Lawyers, Am. Bar Found., Ohio Bar Found. (trustee 1975-84); mem. ABA, Ohio State Bar Assn. (exec. com. 1975-80, pres. 1978-79, Ohio Bar medal 1994), Columbus Bar Assn. (bd. govs. 1970-76, pres. 1974-75), Lawyers Club (pres. 1968-69), 6th Cir. Jud. Conf. (life), Am. Contract Bridge League (life master), Order of Coif, Grey Oaks Country Club (Naples, Fla.), Scioto Country Club, Delta Upsilon, Phi Delta Phi. Republican. Home: 1566 A Oyster Catcher Point Naples FL 34105

ADAMS, JOHN S., insurance company executive; V.p., corp. fin. and svcs. Old Republic Internat. Corp., Chgo., sr. v.p., chief fin. officer, 2001—04, v.p., fin., 2004—. Office: Old Rep Internat Corp 307 N Michigan Ave Chicago IL 60601 Office Phone: 312-346-8100 ext. 205. Office Fax: 312-726-0309.

ADAMS, JOHN STEPHEN, geography educator; b. Mpls., Sept. 7, 1938; s. Edward Francis and Ellen Cecilia (Cullen) A.; m. Judith Estelle Nielsen, Sept. 1, 1962; children: John D., Ellen Anastasia, Martin Francis, David Joseph Cullen. BA, U. St. Thomas, 1960; MA, U. Minn., 1962, PhD, 1966. Rsch. asst., rsch. fellow Upper Midwest Econ. Study, Mpls., 1960-64; teaching asst. dept. geography U. Minn., Mpls., 1964-66, from assoc. prof. to prof. emeritus geography, 1970—2007, prof. emeritus geography, 2007—, assoc. dean H.H. Humphrey Inst. Pub. Affairs, 2007—; asst. prof. geography Pa. State U., State College, 1966-70. Rsch. asst. N. Star Rsch. and Devel., Inc., Mpls., 1964; Fulbright prof. geog. Econ. U. Vienna, Austria, 1975-76; vis. prof. geography U. Wash., Seattle, 1979; vis. prof. geography and environ. engring. U.S. Mil. Acad., West Point, N.Y., 1990-91; vis. prof. geography and earth scis. Marie Curie-Sklodowska U., Lublin, Poland, 1997; mem. nat. adv. com. H.H. Humphrey N.-S. Fellowship Program, Inst. Internat. Edn., N.Y.C., 1979-81, coord. at U. Minn., 1981-87, 89-90; econ. geographer in residence Bank of Am., San Francisco, 1980-81; mem. exec. com. Nat. Com. Rsch. on 1980 census Social Sci. Rsch. Coun., N.Y.C., 1981-88; bd. dirs. Consortium of Social Sci. Assns., Washington, 1983-85, FVB Energy Inc.; mem. geography panel Coun. for Internat. Exchange of Scholars, Washington, 1983-85, chair, 1986, mem. Soviet-Eastern European panel, 1990-93; mem. geography div. adv. com. U.S. Bur. Census, Washington, 1985; Bush sabbatical fellow, 1987-88, Fulbright prof. geography Moscow State U., 1988. Author: (with R. Abler and P. Gould) Spatial Organization, 1971, (with Abler and K. Lee) A Comparative Atlas of America's Great Cities, 1976 (Geog. Soc. Chgo. award 1977), Housing America in the 1980s, 1987); editor: Contemporary Metropolitan America, 4 vols., 1976, Urban Policy Making and Metropolitan Dynamics, 1976, (with B. Van Drasek) Minneapolis-St. Paul People, Place and Public Life, 1993; mem. editl. bd. Geographia Polonica, Govt. and Policy, Urban Geography, Eurasian Geography and Economics. Bd. dirs. Newman Ctr., Mpls., 1983—88, 1994—2002. Sr. Scientist Rsch. fellow NSF, Berkeley, Calif., 1980-81. Mem. Assn. Am. Geographers (nat. sec. 1975-78, v.p. 1981-82, pres. 1982-83, honors award 1988), Nat. Coun. Geog. Edn., Mpls. Com. Fgn. Rels. Democrat. Roman Catholic. Avocations: photography, coin collecting/numismatics, gardening. Home: 2611 W 49th St Minneapolis MN 55410-1902 Office: U Minn Dept Geography 267 19th Ave S Minneapolis MN 55455-0499 Home Phone: 612-925-1340; Office Phone: 612-625-0571. Business E-Mail: adams004@umn.edu.

ADAMS, JOSEPH ANDREW, internist, health facility administrator, educator; b. Tarrytown, NY, Jan. 21, 1956; s. Elijah Adams and Blanche Macoff; m. Linda Freda Barr, Aug. 11, 1984; children: Zachary Elijah, Jackson Barney. BA, U. Pa., 1978; MD, U. Md., 1984. Diplomate Am. Bd. Internal Medicine (added qualification in geriatric medicine). Pvt. practice internal medicine, Towson, Md., 1988—; med. dir. Blakehurst Life Care Cmty., Towson, 1995—. Clin. asst. prof. U. Md. Sch. Medicine, Balt., 1999—. Contbr. articles to profl. jours. Pres. Smoke Free Md. Coalition, Balt., 1997—97, Md. Childrens Initiative Edn. Fund, Inc., Balt., 1998—99; sec. Smoke Free Balt. County Coalition, Towson, 1999—2002; bd. dirs. Balt. County Med. Assn., Towson, 1998—2002; bd. dirs. Md. & DC chpts. Asthma and Allergy Found. of Am., Balt., 2000—02. Recipient Physician Recognition award for Continuing Med. Edn., AMA, 1991, Best Article of 1995 award, Md. Med. Jour., 1995, Disting. Svc. award, Am. Lung Assn. Md., 1996, 2001, Physician's Disting. Svc. award, Balt. County Med. Assn., 1997; grantee, Md. Dept. Health and Mental Hygiene, 2000. Fellow: ACP, Am. Soc. Internal Medicine (life); mem.: APHA, Am. Soc. Addiction Medicine. Liberal. Jewish. Avocations: jogging, cooking. Home: 1405 Berwick Rd Towson MD 21204 Office: 6701 N Charles St Ste 4104 Towson MD 21204

ADAMS, JOSEPH KEITH, lawyer; b. Provo, Utah, Apr. 3, 1949; s. Joseph S. and Marian (Bellows) A.; m. Myrle June Overly, Sept. 2, 1971; children: Derek J., Bret K., Stephanie, Julie K., Scott J., Laura. BA summa cum laude, Brigham Young U., 1973; JD, Harvard U., 1976. Bar: Utah 1976, U.S. Dist. Ct. Utah 1976, U.S. Tax Ct. 1983. Assoc. Van Cott, Bagley, Cornwall & McCarthy, Salt Lake City, 1976-82, shareholder, 1982-98; also bd. dirs. Van Cott, Bagley, et al, Salt Lake City, 1993-97, chmn. tax and estate planning sect., 1995-98; ptnr. Stoel, Rives, LLP, Salt Lake City, 1998—. Adj. faculty Brigham Young U. Law Sch., Provo, 1993. Co-author: Practical Estate Planning Techniques, 1990. Planned giving com. Restoration Cathedral Madeleine, Salt Lake City, 1991-93; pres. Utah Planned Giving Roundtable, Salt Lake City, 1994, Salt Lake City Estate Planning Coun.; planned giving com. U. Utah Hosp. Found., 1994; bd. dirs. Salt Lake C.C. Found., 1982-98; chair Salt Lake profl. adv. group LDS Philanthropies, mem. nat. planned giving coun.; past stake pres. LDS Ch. David O. Mackay scholar Brigham Young U., 1967-73. Fellow Am. Coll. Trust and Estate Counsel; mem. ABA (real property, probate and trust sect.), Utah State Bar (past exec. com., past chmn. estate planning probate sect.), Harvard Alumni Assn. Utah (chair bd. dirs. 1980-90), Harvard Law Sch. Assn. Utah (vice chair). Republican. Mem. Lds Ch. Avocations: skiing, reading, golf. Office: Stoel Rives LLP 201 S Main St Ste 1100 Salt Lake City UT 84111-4904 Home Phone: 801-942-8534; Office Phone: 801-328-3131. Business E-Mail: jkadams@stoel.com.

ADAMS, JULIAN TIMOTHY, psychologist; s. Julian and Bertha Ozella Adams; m. Sharlene Frances Bunge, Nov. 15, 1992; m. Martha Jo House, Mar. 22, 1975 (div. July 0, 1990); children: Julian Mclane, Thomas Daniel, Timothy James, Pamela Rose Bunge, Todd Bunge. BS, Columbus Coll., Ga., 1974—76; MA, U. W. Fla., Pensacola, 1983—84; PsyD, Forest Inst. Profl. Psychology, Springfield, Mo., 1987—91. Diplomate Am. Bd. Psychol. Specialties; lic. clin. psychologist Va., 1995, Ariz., 1991. Clin. psychologist U.S. Army, 1989—94; CEO Psychol. Assessments, Interventions and Resources, Inc., Annandale, Va., 1994—2002; clin. psychologist Ednl. and Devel. Intervention Services, U. S. Army Hosp., Heidelberg, Germany, 2002—; rehab. psychologist Veterans Adminstrn., Washington, 2002. Adv. bd. mem. Am. Bd. Psychol. Specialties, 1996—99. Auxillary police officer Fairfax County Police Dept., Va., 1996—99; rape crisis counselor Lakeview Ctr. Inc., Pensacola, Fla., 1983—86, helpline counselor, 1983—86. Fellow: Nat. Bd. Certified Clin. Hypnotherapists, Am. Coll. Forensic Examiners, Washington D.C. Area Geriatric Edn. Consortium. Home: CMR 442 Box 214 AE APO 09042 Germany Home Phone: 06205 30 7456. Personal E-mail: dr.juliantadams@mindspring.com.

ADAMS, KEITH ROBERT, military officer; b. Mount Holly, NJ, May 30, 1960; s. Robert Marshall and Shirley (Dunfee) Adams; m. Lucy T. Tamn, Apr. 17, 1982; children: Andrew Michael Dunfee, Geoffrey Robert Forte. Cert. fire officer, incident mgr. Internat. Fire Svc. Accreditation Coun., 2000, fire officer U.S. Dept. Def. Fire Svc. Qualification Bd. Fire chief Lebanon Lakes Fire Co., Woodland Twp., NJ, 1978—79, Pemberton Fire and Rescue, NJ, 1980—82; firefighter USN, Lakehurst, NJ, 1982—89; asst. chief ops., logistics and readiness U.S. Army, Fort Dix, NJ, 1989—. Pres. Pemberton Borough Bd. of Edn., 1997—2004; chmn. sch. leadership coun. Helen A. Fort Mid. Sch., Pemberton, 2004—06; mem. No Child Left Behind adv. coun. N.J. State Dept. Edn., Trenton, 2006—; vestryman Grace Episcopal Ch., Pemberton, 1982—84. Decorated Spl. Act medal USN, U.S. Army, Cold Warrior cert. U.S. Dept. Def., commendation for Operation Desert Storm/Shield U.S. Army, Meritorious Achievement commendation; named Fire Officer of Yr., VFW, 2002. Mem.: Am. Fedn. Labor and Congress of Indsl. Orgn., Internat. Assn. Fire Fighters (local pres. 1988—89, 1991—96, dist. rep. 1992—96), Internat. Assn. Fire Chiefs. Democrat. Mem. Anglican Ch. Office: US Army Fire and Emergency Services 6049 Eighth St Fort Dix NJ 08640 Home Phone: 609-894-9531; Office Phone: 609-562-3822. Office Fax: 609-562-3338. Business E-Mail: keith.adams@us.army.mil.

ADAMS, KENNETH FRANCIS, automotive executive; b. Danbury, Conn., Feb. 4, 1946; s. Donald and Evelyn Trocola (Mulvihill) Adams; m. Annette Talarico, Sept. 28, 1968; children: Amy, Ella Louise, Elizabeth. Student, Mt. St. Mary's Coll., 1964—68. C.P.A., Conn. Mgr. Price Waterhouse & Co., Bridgeport, Conn., 1968—74; v.p. fin. and adminstrn., dir. Saab Cars USA, Inc., Norcross, Ga., 1974—2005; dir. Telzuit Inc., 2006—. With USAR, 1968—74. Mem.: AICPA, Inst. Mgmt. Accts., Fin. Exec. Inst., Conn. Soc. CPAs. Roman Cath. Office: 9565 Red Bird Ln Alpharetta GA 30022 Home Phone: 770-410-0593.

ADAMS, KENNETH STANLEY, JR., (BUD), energy executive, professional sports team executive; b. Bartlesville, OK, Jan. 3, 1923; s. Kenneth Stanley and Blanch (Keeler) Adams; m. Nancy Neville, Oct. 26, 1946. Student, Menlo Coll., 1940—41, U. Kans., 1941—44. Chmn. bd. Adams Resources & Energy, Inc., Houston, Travel House of Houston; owner Bud Adams Ranches, KSA Industries, Inc.; owner, pres. Houston Oilers, 1946—97, Tenn. Titans, Nashville, 1997—; owner Southwest Lincoln-Mercury, Inc. Mem. exec. bd. Sam Houston Area Coun. Boy Scouts Am.; trustee Profl. Football Hall of Fame. With USNR, 1943—46. Named Houston Salesman of Yr., 1960, Mr. Sportsman of 1961, Westerner of Yr., 1969. Mem.: Houston Geol. Soc., Houston Assn. Petroleum Landmen, Ind. Petroleum Assn. Am., Tex. Ind. Producers and Royalty Owners Assn., 100 Club of Houston (dir.), River Oaks Country Club, Petroleum Club, Houston Club, Sigma Chi (named Significant Sig 1963). Office: care Tenn Titans Baptist Sports Park 460 Great Circle Rd Nashville TN 37228-1404*

ADAMS, KEVIN, lighting designer; Lighting designer (Broadway plays) Getting and Spending, 1998, A Class Act, 2001, Hedda Gabler, 2001, Sexaholix, 2001, An Almost Holy Picture, 2002, Take Me Out, 2003, The Good Body, 2004, Latinologues, 2005, Spring Awakening, 2006 (Lucille Lortel award outstanding lighting design, 2007, Tony award best lighting design of a musical, 2007), (plays) Tea at Five, The Mysteries, Mr. Marmalade, Spatter Pattern, Hedwig and the Angry Inch, The Mineola Twins (Lucille Lortel award outstanding lighting design, 1999), The Mines of Sulfur, Mary Rose, 2007, Some Men, 2007, Passing Strange, 2007, (films) Without You I'm Nothing. Recipient OBIE award for sustain excellence in lighting design, Village Voice, 2001.*

ADAMS, KEVIN MACGREGOR, military officer, educator; b. New Brunswick, NJ, Dec. 7, 1952; s. Frank George Adams and Lisbeth Ann Yates; m. Sherry Ann Bressette, Dec. 29, 2000; m. Claire Elaine Gagnon, Mar. 18, 1954 (div. May 28, 1998); children: Jennifer Lee, Brian Allen, Kristen Lisbeth. BS in Ceramic Engring., Rutgers U., New Brunswick, NJ, 1981; MS in Naval Arch. and Marine Engring., MIT, Cambridge, 1986, MS in Materials Engring., 1986; PhD in Engring. Mgmt. and Sys. Engring., Old Dominion U., Norfolk, Va., 2007. EIT NJ, 1981. Asst. prof. U. Md. U. Coll., Adelphi, Md., 1999—. Va. Wesleyan Coll., Norfolk, Va., 2002—. Sr. engring. scientist CACI, Norfolk, 2002—; prin. cons. PriceWaterhouse Coopers, Fairfax, Va., 1999—2002; dir., navy and marine corps bus. unit Computer Scis. Corp., Falls Church, Va., 1997—99; group mgr. Q.E.D. Sys., Virginia Beach, 1996—97; machinist's mate USN, Washington, 1971—81, naval officer, 1981—96. Decorated Navy Achievement medal with two gold stars USN, Meritorious Svc. medal, Navy Commendation medal with 2 gold stars, Def. Superior Svc. medal, Def. Meritorious Svc. medal. Mem.: IEEE, US Naval Inst., Am. Soc. Naval Engrs. (Acad. scholar 1978, 1979, 1980, Pres. award 1990), Am. Soc. of Naval Engineers, Boy Scouts of Am. (jr. asst. scoutmaster 1969—70, Eagle Scout award 1968), Epsilon Mu Eta, Phi Kappa Phi, Keramos, Tau Beta Pi. Libertarian. Anglican. Avocations: sailing, rowing, ncaa lacrosse official. Home: 7006 Gardner Dr Norfolk VA 23518-4906 Office: Old Dominion U Norfolk VA 23529 Home Phone: 757-855-1954; Office Phone: 757-683-4558. Personal E-mail: kmacgadams@alum.mit.edu. Business E-Mail: kadams@vwc.edu.

ADAMS, LAVONNE MARILYN BECK, critical care nurse, educator; b. Bridgeport, Conn., Feb. 22, 1965; d. Adolf and Hazel B. (Henderson) Beck. ASN, Kettering Coll. Med. Arts, 1985; BSN, Wright State U., 1988; MSN, Andrews U., 1992, PhD, 2003. CCRN. Staff nurse Kettering Med. Ctr., Ohio, 1985-89, resource staff nurse, 1989-95, instr. in nursing, 1989-92; asst. prof. nursing Kettering Coll. Med. Arts, 1992—99, Southwestern Adventist U., Keene, Tex., 1999—2003, assoc. prof., 2003—04; asst. prof. nursing Harris Coll. Nursing and Health Scis. Tex. Christian U., Ft. Worth, 2004—; PRN staff nurse Huguley Mem. Hosp., 2002—. Vol. Adventist Comty. Svcs.Disaster Response, 2004—, ARC, 2005—; active Southwestern Sem. Oratorio Chorus, 1999—. Mem.: Am. Assn. Critical Care Nurses, Pi Lambda Theta, Sigma Theta Tau, Phi Kappa Phi. Avocations: music, travel. Home: 7000 Welch Ct Fort Worth TX 76133-6726 Office: Tex Christian U Harris Coll Nursing and Health Scis TCU Box 298620 Fort Worth TX 76129

ADAMS, LEE TOWNE, lawyer; b. Chatham, Ont., Can., July 12, 1922; arrived in U.S., 1923; s. Lee Eugene and Josephine Towne A.; m. Muriel Kathryn Stang, June 29, 1946; children: Nancy Louise, Carol Josephine, Jane Bertha. BA, U. Rochester, 1943; JD, Yale U., 1949. Atty. pvt. practice, Forestville, NY, 1949-72; mcpl. atty. various towns and villages, 1955-72; judge State of N.Y., Chautauqua County, 1972-93; retired, 1993—. Trustee Presbytery of Western N.Y., 1970-76; dir., vice chmn. Presbyn. Homes Western N.Y., 1984-90. Lt. USN, 1943-46. Mem. VFW, Am. legion, Submarine Vets. WWII, Masons, Jamestown Consistory, Ismaila Temple, Phi Beta Kappa. Republican. Avocations: gardening, reading. Home: 21 Pearl St PO Box 306 Forestville NY 14062-0306

ADAMS, LEOCADIA DONAT, secondary school educator, writer; b. Clinton, Mass., Oct. 9, 1947; d. Leokadia Marianna Donat; children: Erik Paul, Keith David. BS in Edn. and Vocat. Home Econs., Ctrl. Mo. State U., 1972, MA in Edn., Spl. Edn., Learning Disabilities, Emotionally Disturbed, 1987. Pre-sch. dir. La Petite Acad., Overland Park, Kans., 1973—74; vocat. home econ. instr. Martin Luther King Jr. HS, Kansas City, Mo., 1974—75, Longfellow Elem., Kansas City, Mo., 1975—76; instr. needle arts, head dept. St. Teresa's Acad., Kansas City, Mo., 1976—83; owner The Light Ho., Kansas City, 1983—84; learning disabilities specialist. itinernant tchr. Kans. City Sch. Dist., 1985—86; learning disabilities specialist Westport Mid. Sch., Kansas City, 1986—89, SW HS, Kansas City, 1989—90, Satchel Paige Elem. Sch., Kansas City, 1990—96, Chester R. Anderson Alternative Mid. Sch., Kansas City, 1997—99, Ctrl. Mid. Sch., 1999—2000; learning disabilities specialist, mentor tchr. Van Horn HS, Independence, Mo., 2000—. Presenter in field. Author: (text book) Beginning to Advanced Sewing, (cookbook) Drink's On Me, 1994; prodr.: Poland's History and Culture, 1988—95; columnist: Clinton Item, guest columnist: Post Eagle; contbr. columns in newspapers. Zone coord., block capt. 49/63 Neighborhood Coalition, Kansas City, 1974—79, co-chmn. edn. com., 1974—75, chmn. govt. com., 1977; campaign mgr. Jim Dolan for State Rep., Kansas City, 1977—78; vol. Elect Ed Growney, Kansas City, 1978—88. Named to Wall of Freedom, Southern Poverty Law Ctr., Birmingham, Ala., Outstanding Am. Tchrs., 2005—06. Mem.: AAUW, ASCD. Roman Catholic. Avocations: reading, classical music, gourmet cooking, Polish studies, sewing. Personal E-mail: lodgia@sbcglobal.net.

ADAMS, LILIANA OSSES, music performer, harpist; b. Poznan, Poland, May 16, 1939; came to U.S., 1978, naturalized, 1990; d. Sylwester and Helena (Koswenda) O.; m. Edmund Pietryk, Sept. 4, 1965 (div. Aug. 1970); m. Bruce Meredith Adams, Feb. 3, 1978. MA, Music Acad. Poznan, Poland, 1971. Prin. harpist Philharm. Orch. of Szczecin, Poland, 1964-72, Imperial Opera and Ballet Orch., Tehran, Iran, 1972-78; pvt. music tchr. Riyadh, Saudi Arabia, 1979-81; soloist Austrian Radio, 1981-86; solo harpist, pvt. tchr. harp and piano Antioch, Calif., 1986—. Music cons. Schs. and Librs., Calif., 1991—. Contbr. articles to profl. jours. Mem. Am. Fedn. of Musicians, Am. Harp Soc., Music Tchrs. Assn. Calif., Internat. Soc. of Harpers, U.K. Harp Assn., Internat. Harp Ctr. (Switzerland). Home: PO Box 233 Antioch CA 94509-0023 E-mail: harpliliana@comcast.net.

ADAMS, LISA, lawyer; BS in Chemistry, Tex. State U., 1996; JD, New England Sch. Law, 1999. Bar: Mass. 1999, US Patent and Trademark Office, US Dist. Ct. (Dist. Mass.). Assoc. intellectual property practice group and life sciences practice group Nutter, McClennen & Fish LLP, Boston. Pro bono atty. Volunteer Lawyers for Arts Mass. Mem.: ABA, Am. Intellectual Property Law Assn., Boston Patent Law Assn. (sec. bd. governors, former chair pro bono com., activities com. and young lawyers com.). Office: Nutter McClennen & Fish LLP World Trade Center West 155 Seaport Blvd Boston MA 02210 Office Phone: 617-439-2550. Office Fax: 617-310-9550. E-mail: ladams@nutter.com.

ADAMS, LORETTA, marketing executive; b. Panama; BS in Internat. Mktg., Am. U., 1962; postgrad. in Econs., U. Panama, 1963-64. Mgmt. trainee Sears Roebuck & Co., Panama City, 1962-63, mgmt. pers., 1963-65; supr. internat. advertising projects Kenyon & Eckhardt Advertising, Inc., NYC, 1965-68; asst. rsch. dir. divsn. L.Am. and Far E. Richardson-Vicks Internat., Mexico City and Wilton, Conn., 1968-69, rsch. dir. divsn. Mex. and L.Am., 1969-75, mem. top mgmt. strategic planning team, 1975-78; founder, pres. Mkt. Devel., Inc., San Diego, 1978—. Contbr. articles to profl. jours. Mem. Am. Mktg. Assn., European Soc. for Opinion & Market Rsch., Advt. Rsch. Found., Coun. Am. Survey Rsch. Orgns., Market Rsch. Assn. Office: Market Devel Inc 600 B St Ste 1600 San Diego CA 92101-4584

ADAMS, MARC ANTHONY, medical statistician, researcher; b. Oak Park, Ill., Mar. 14, 1975; s. Jacob K. and Christine G. Adams. BA in Psychology, San Diego State U., 2001; MPH, 2003; PhD in Pub. Health - Health Behavior Sci., San Diego State U. and U. of Calif., 2005. Automotive svc. excellence Ill. Rsch. assoc. Ctr. for Behavioral Epidemiology and Cmty. Health, San Diego State U., 1998—; trainee Pubic Health Inst., Sacramento, 2002—03; asst. statistician Physician-based Assessment and Counseling for Exercise - PACE Project, U. of Calif. - San Diego, La Jolla, 2005—. Contbr. articles and abstracts to profl. jours. Recipient Cornelius Hopper Diversity award, Calif.'s Tobacco-Related Disease Rsch. Program, 2004—05. Mem.: Assn. for Behavior Analysis, Cambridge Ctr. for Behavioral Studies, Soc. for Behavioral Medicine. Independent. Avocations: sailing, cooking, travel, exercise. Home: #305 6416 Friars Rd San Diego CA 92108 Office: U Calif - San Diego Ste B-122 8950 Villa La Jolla Dr La Jolla CA 92037 Home Phone: 619-220-0048; Office Phone: 858-457-7280 236. E-mail: m1adams@ucsd.edu.

ADAMS, MARGARET BERNICE, retired museum official; b. Toronto, Ont., Can., Apr. 29, 1936; arrived in U.S., 1948, naturalized, 1952; d. Robert Russell and Kathleen Olive (Buffin) A.; m. Alberto Enrique Sánchez-Quiñonez, Nov. 30, 1956 (div. 1960). AA, Monterey Peninsula Coll., 1969; BA, San Jose State U., 1971; MA, U. Utah, 1972. Curator ethnic arts Civic Art Gallery, San Jose, Calif., 1971; staff asst. Utah Mus. Fine Arts, Salt Lake City, 1972; lectr., curator Coll. Seven, U. Calif., Santa

Cruz, 1972-74; part-time educator Cabrillo Coll., Aptos, Calif., 1973, Monterey Peninsula Coll., 1973-84; dir. U.S. Army Mus., Presidio of Monterey, 1974-83; chief. mus. br. Ft. Ord Mil. Complex, 1983-88; ret., 1988. Guest curator Am. Indian arts Monterey Peninsula Mus. Art, 1975-88. Author: Indian Tribes of North America and Chronology of World Events in Prehistoric Pueblo Times, 1975, Historic Old Monterey, 1976; contbg. editor Indian Am., Writing on the Wall, WWII Patriotic Posters, 1987; contbr. articles to jours. Mem. Native Am. adv. panel AAAS, Washington, 1972-78; mem. rev. and adv. com. Project Media, Nat. Indian Edn. Assn., Mpls., 1973-78; working mem. Program for Tng. Am. Indian Counsellors in Alcoholism Counselling and Rehab. Programs, 1972-74; mem. hist. adv. com. Monterey County Bd. Suprs., 1987-89. Grad. fellow, dean's scholar U. Utah, 1972; dean's scholar Monterey Peninsula Coll., 1969, San Jose State U., 1971. Mem. Am. Anthrop. Assn., Am. Assn. Museums, Soc. Am. Archeology, Nat., Calif., Indian Edn. Assns.

ADAMS, MARK KILDEE, lawyer; b. Des Moines, Oct. 8, 1938; s. Walter Bunting and Regina (Kildee) A.; m. Helen von Bachmayr Larsen, May 22, 1982; 1 child, Kirsten. AB, Harvard U., 1960, JD, 1966. Bar: N.Mex. 1966, U.S. Dist. Ct. N.Mex. 1966, U.S. Ct. Appeals (10th cir.) 1970, U.S. Claims Ct., Zuni Pueblo Tribal Ct. Assoc. Rodey, Dickason, Sloan, Akin & Robb, Santa Fe, 1966-70, ptnr., 1970—, dir. Santa Fe office. Co-author: N. Mex. Environ. Law Handbook; author: Unitization of Solid Mineral Properties, 1982, Minimum Work Clauses in Mining Leases, 1976. Capt. U.S. Army, 1960-62. Mem. ABA, Albuquerque Bar Assn. (bd. dirs. 1976-78), Lawyers Club (officer 1980-84). Republican. Office: Rodey Dickason Sloan Akin & Robb PA 315 Paseo de Peralta Santa Fe NM 87501 Office Phone: 505-954-3903. Office Fax: 505-954-3942. Business E-Mail: mkadams@rodey.com.

ADAMS, MARTY E., diversified financial services company executive; BS, West Liberty State U. Pres., CEO Citizens Bancshares, Inc., 1987—98; pres., COO Sky Fin. Group, Inc., 1998—99, pres., CEO, 1999—2000, chmn., pres., CEO, 2000—07; pres., COO Huntington Bancshares Inc., Columbus, Ohio, 2007—. Office: Huntington Bancshares Inc 41 S High St Columbus OH 43287*

ADAMS, MICHAEL FRED, academic administrator, political scientist, educator; b. Montgomery, Ala., Mar. 25, 1948; s. Hubert W. and Jean (Taylor) A.; m. Mary Lynn Ethridge, June 7, 1969; children: David Winston, Stephen Taylor. BA, Lipscomb U., 1970; MA, Ohio State U., 1971, PhD, 1973. Asst. prof. Ohio State U., 1973-74; chief of staff for Sen. Howard Baker, Washington, 1975-79; advisor to gov. State of Tenn., Nashville, 1981-82; v.p. Pepperdine U., Malibu, Calif., 1982-88; pres. Centre Coll., Danville, Ky., 1988-97, U. Ga., Athens, 1997—. Chmn. Nat. Assn. Ind. Colls. and Univs., 1995-96, Assoc. Colls. of South; mem. coun. for advancement and support of edn. NCAA Pres. Commn., 1992-94; chmn. Commn. on Colls. of So. Assn. Colls. and Schs.; vice chmn. task force that founded Coun. for Higher Edn. Accreditation; chair Am. Coun. on Edn., 2000. Author: Rhetorical Strategies of Howard Baker, 1973; contbr. articles to various publs. Pres. Circle K Internat., Chgo., 1970; nominee for U.S. Congress, Nashville, 1980; mem. site host com. 1984 Olympiad, L.A.; elder Christian Ch. Recipient Bronze Quill award Internat. Assn. Bus. Communicators, 1986, Excellence award Nat. Sch. Pub. Relations Soc., 1985; Ohio State U. grad. fellow, 1970-73 Mem. Young Pres. Orgn., Speech Comm. Assn., Ctr. for Study of Presidency, Univ. Club (N.Y.C.), Coun. Fgn. Relations. Republican. Avocations: golf, reading, travel. Office: Pres Office U Ga Adminstrn Bldg Athens GA 30602 Office Phone: 706-542-1214. E-mail: presuga@uga.edu.

ADAMS, NANCY R., nurse, retired military officer; b. Rochester, NY, Apr. 20, 1945; BSN, Cornell U., 1968; MSN, Cath. U. Am., 1974; grad., U.S. Army War Coll., 1986. Advanced through grades to maj. gen. U.S. Army, 1991; comdr. William Beaumont Army Med. Ctr., S.W. Regional Med. Command; chief Army Nurse Corps; asst. surgeon gen. for pers. and comdr. U.S. Army Ctr. for Health Promotion and Preventive Medicine; lead agt. TRICARE Region VII U.S. Army; chief nurse Frankfurt Army Regional Med. Ctr., 1987—89; staff asst. profl. affairs and quality assurance Office of Asst. Sec. of Def., asst. inspector gen., dir. intensive care nursing course; nursing cons. Army Surgeon Gen., 1989—91; commd. Nurse Corps U.S. Army, 1991—95; commdg. gen. Tripler Army Med. Ctr., Hawaii, 1998—2002; sr. advisor to the dir. TRICARE Mgmt. Activity, 2002—04, north region dir., 2004—05. Decorated Legion of Merit, Meritorious Svc. medal; recipient DSM, Defense Superior Svc. medal. Fellow: Am. Acad. Nursing; mem.: ANA, Am. Orgn. of Nurse Execs., Assn. of Mil. Surgeons of the U.S., Sigma Theta Tau. Home: 1920 S Ocean Dr Apt 1611 Fort Lauderdale FL 33316-3730 Personal E-mail: nradams2@aol.com.

ADAMS, PETER DAVID, physicist, writer, editor; b. Cardiff, Wales, U.K., Nov. 18, 1937; came to US, 1964; s. Frederick George and Rose Ellen (Fidoe) A.; m. June Mary Tatchell, Dec. 27, 1960; children: Joanne Louise, Lindsay Stuart. BS, U. Wales, Aberystwyth, 1959; PhD, Imperial Coll., London, 1964. Physicist Brookhaven Nat. Lab., Upton, NY, 1964-69; editor Am. Phys. Soc., Ridge, NY, 1969—, dep. mng. editor, 1980, dep. editor-in-chief, 1980-89, editorial office mgr., 1980-89. Cons. EPA study Brookhaven Nat. Lab., 1973-74; advisor to coun. Am. Phys. Soc., 1980-89. Editor: Properties of Liquid Metals, 1966; editor Phys. Rev. Jour., 1969—; chmn. publs. bd. Am. Inst. Physics, 1972-74, 95-97; editorial bd. Jour. Phys. and Chem. Ref. Data, 1974-77; contbr. rsch. articles to various publs. Fellow Am. Phys. Soc. (rep. to info., computing and communication sect. of AAAS 1980-91), Inst. Physics England; mem. AAAS (chmn. pubs. sect. Coun. Engring. and Scientific Soc. Execs. 2004—, editor-in-chief 2004—). Office: Am Phys Soc PO Box 9000 Ridge NY 11961-0701

ADAMS, PHYLLIS YEWELL, foreign language educator; Student, George Peabody Coll. for Tchrs., Nashville, 1964—66; BA in Spanish and Sociology, Murray State U., Ky., 1969, MA in Spanish, 1972. Cert. Spanish preK-12 Va. Dept. Edn., sociology Va. Dept. Edn. Tchr. Christian County Sch., Hopkinsville, Ky., 1969, Marshall County Sch., Benton, Ky., 1969—70, Murray Ind. Sch., 1970—72; Spanish tchr. Va. Beach City Pub. Sch., 1972—75, 1996—; tchr. Dept. Def. Sch., Naples, Italy, 1975—76. Author: Literatura-Una Experiencia Personal, 1972. Mem.: NEA, Va. Beach Edn. Assn., Va. Assn. of Am. Tchrs. of Spanish and Portugese, Va. Edn. Assn., Foreign Lang. Assn. Va., Am. Coun. Tchrs. of Foreign Langs., Am. Assn. of Tchrs. of Spanish and Portuguese, Zeta Upsilon, Sigma Delta Pi. Avocations: gardening, swimming, cooking, travel.

ADAMS, R. SCOTT, lawyer; b. Altus, Okla., Aug. 17, 1963; BBA, U. Ctrl. Okla., 1986; JD, Okla City U., 1989. Bar: Okla. 1989, U.S. Dist. Ct. Okla. (We. Dist.) 1989, U.S. Dist. Ct. (Ea. Dist.) 1990. Ptnr. Adams & Assocs PC, Okla. City. Mem.: Okla. Bar Assn., Nat. Assn. Criminal Def. Lawyers (life), Alpha Chi. Office: Adams & Assocs PC City Place Bldg 204 N Robinson 25th Fl Oklahoma City OK 73102 Office Phone: 405-232-9100. Office Fax: 405-232-9114.

ADAMS, RANALD TREVOR, JR., retired air force officer; b. Ft. Sill, Okla., Mar. 7, 1925; s. Ranald Trevor and Mary (King) A.; m. Jeannette Malloy Chichester, May 3, 1947; children: Ranald T. III, Mary M., Jeannette M. Student, Va. Poly. Inst., 1941-43; BS, U.S. Mil. Acad., 1946; MS, George Washington U., 1966. Commd. 2d lt. USAF, 1946, advanced through grades to lt. gen., 1978; served in Korean conflict, 1950-51; served in Vietnam, 1968—69; comdr. 408 Fighter Group, 1969-71; asst. dep. chief staff ops. N.Am. Air Def. Command, 1971-73; comdr. 26 N.Am. Air Def. Command Region/Air Div. Luke AFB, Ariz., 1973-74; dep. insp. gen. inspection and safety Norton AFB, Calif., 1974-77; dir. InterAm. Def. Coll., Ft. McNair, D.C., 1977-78; chmn. Interam. Def. Bd., Washington, 1978-81, ret., 1981; cons., 1981-91. Decorated Legion of Merit, Meritorious Service medal, D.S.M., D.F.C., Air medal. Mem. Air Force Assn., Order Daedalians (flight capt. 1973) Home and Office: 1002 Emerald Dr Alexandria VA 22308-2626

ADAMS, REID, physician; MS, U. Va., Charlottesville, 1987. Diplomate Am. Bd. Surgery, 2003. Assoc. prof. surgery U. Va. Health Sys., Charlottesville, 2001—, chief hepatobiliary and pancreatic surgery, 2001—. Office: U Va Dept Surgery HSC Box 800709 Charlottesville VA 22908-0709 Office Phone: 434-924-2839.

ADAMS, REID C., JR., lawyer; b. Kinston, NC, June 26, 1956; married; 2 children. BA cum laude, Wake Forest U., 1978; JD cum laude, Wake Forest Sch. Law, 1981. Bar: NC 1981, admitted to practice: US Dist. Ct. (Middle and Western Districts, NC), Dist. Ct. Appeals (4th & 11th Circuits). Clerk Morris, Rochelle, and Duke, Kinston, NC, 1979, Divsn. Youth Svcs., NC Dept. Human Resources, Raleigh, NC, 1980; assoc. Nichols Caffrey Hill Evans & Murrelle, Greenboro, NC, 1981—85; practice group leader, insurance, govt. & tort litig. sect. Womble Carlyle Sandridge & Rice, PLLC, Winston-Salem, NC, 2001—06, chmn., 2007—. Mem. pro bono com. Womble Carlyle Sandridge & Rice, PLLC. Pres. legal bid State of NC, 2005—07, vice chmn. equal access and justice commn.; pres. bd. dirs. Legal Aid Soc. of NW NC, 1996—2001; bd. dir. Legal Svcs. NC, exec. com. chair, grievance com. Hankins Scholar, Wake Forest U. Mem.: ABA (mem. pro bono adv. com.), NC Bar Assn. (mem. litig. sect.), Forsyth County Bar Assn. (liasion, vol. lawyers program, chair, pro bono com.). Avocations: golf, reading. Home and Office: Womble Carlyle Sandridge & Rice PLLC One West 4th St Winston Salem NC 27101 Office Phone: 336-721-3674. Office Fax: 336-733-8333. Business E-Mail: radams@wcsr.com.

ADAMS, REX, dean; m. Ellen Cates; 3 children. BA in Polit. Sci. magna cum laude, Duke U., 1962. Govt. rels. trainee Mobil Internat., London, 1965-70; dir. employee and govt. rels. Mobil Oil, Libya, 1970-72, pers. dir. European ops. London, 1972-75; mgr. recruitment and placement Mobil Oil Corp., 1975-79, mgr. employee rels. exploration and producing divsn., 1979-84; v.p. employee rels. Mobil Corp., 1984-88; v.p. adminstrn. Mobil Oil Corp. and Mobil Corp., 1988-96; prof. bus. adminstrn., dean Fuqua Sch. Bus. Duke U., 1996-2001, prof. bus. adminstrn., dean emeritus, 2001—. Past chmn. bd. dir. PBS; bd. dir. INVESCO, chmn. 2006-; bd. dir. Vintage Pet., Alleghany Corp., Vera Inst. Justice; trustee Com. for Econ. Devel. and Woods Holes Oceanog. Instn.; former trustee Duke U. and Va. Union U. Rhodes scholar Merton Coll., Oxford U., 1962. Fellow Nat. Acad. Human Resources (disting.); mem. Phi Beta Kappa. Office: 1900 Faucette Mill Rd Hillsborough NC 27278

ADAMS, RICHARD GEORGE, writer; b. Newbury, Berkshire, Eng., May 9, 1920; s. Evelyn George Beadon and Lilian Rosa (Button); m. Elizabeth Acland, Sept. 26, 1949; children: Juliet Vera Lucy, Rosamond Beatrice Elizabeth. MA, Oxford U., 1948. With Brit. Home Higher Civil Svc. Ministry Housing and Local Govt., 1948-74; asst. sec. Dept. Environ., 1968-74. Writer-in-residence U. Fla., 1975, Hollins Coll., 1976. Author: Watership Down, 1972 (Guardian award Children's Lit. 1972, Carnegie Medal 1972), Shardik, 1974, (with Max Hooper) Nature Through the Seasons, 1975, The Tyger Voyage, 1976, The Adventures and Brave Deeds of the Ship's Cat on the Spanish Main: Together with the Most Lamentable Losse of the Alcestis and Triumphant Firing of the Port of Chagres, 1977, The Plague Dogs, 1977, (with Max Hooper) Nature Day and Night, 1978, Introduction to Faithful Ruslan, 1979, The Unbroken Web: Stories and Fables, 1980, Voyage Through the Antarctic, 1982, The Girl in a Swing, 1980, Maia, 1985, The Bureaucats, 1985, A Nature Diary, 1985, The Legend of Te Tuna, 1986, Traveller, 1988, The Day Gone By, 1990, Tales from Watership Down, 1996, The Outlandish Knight, 2000, Daniel, 2006; editor, contbr. Occasional Poets, 1986. With Brit. Army, 1940—46. Fellow: Royal Soc. Lit.; mem.: Royal Soc. for Prevention of Cruelty to Animals (former pres.). Mem. Ch. Of Eng. Home: 26 Church St Whitchurch Hampshire England

ADAMS, RICHARD LLOYD, lawyer; b. Cape Girardeau, Mo., Feb. 25, 1951; s. John Alexander and Opal Elizabeth Adams; m. Susan Hefley, Feb. 12, 1983 (div. May 11, 2000); children: Audrey Elizabeth, Adelaide Hefley, Wilson Joseph. BA, S.E. Mo. State U., 1972; JD, U. Mo., 1974. Bar: Mo. 1975, Fla. 1975, Tex. 1978, US Ct. Appeals (8th cir.) 1975, US Ct. Appeals (5th and 11th cirs.) 1981, US Ct. Appeals (10th cir.) 1982, US Ct. Appeals (DC cir.) 1987, US Ct. Appeals (9th cir.) 1992, US Supreme Ct. 1982, (US Ct. Appeals (fed. cir.)) 1997. Assoc. Schafly, Griesedieck Ferrell & Toft, St. Louis, 1975—78; mng. ptnr. Worsham Forsythe Wooldridge LLP, Dallas, 1978—2001; ptnr. Hunton & Williams LLP, Dallas, 2002—. Mem. editl. bd. Missouri Law Rev. Mem. bd. dirs. Beringer Wine Estates, 1996—2000. Named Tex. Super Lawyer, Tex. Monthly Mag., 2007; named one of Best Lawyers in Am., 2007. Mem.: ABA, Mo. Bar, Fla. Bar, State Bar Tex., Dalhousie Golf Club, Country Club Mo., Preston Trail Golf Club. Republican. Methodist. Avocations: golf, travel, wine collecting, art. Home: 7202 Centenary Ave Dallas TX 75225 Office: Hunton & Williams LLP 1445 Ross Ave Ste 3700 Dallas TX 75202 Home Phone: 214-365-0601; Office Phone: 214-979-3040. Business E-Mail: radams@hunton.com.

ADAMS, ROBERT BRERETON, lawyer; AB, Boston Coll., 1961; JD, NYU, 1965. Bar: N.Y. 1965. Dep. county atty. Nassau County, NY, 1965-67; assoc. Cullen & Dykman, 1968-70; v.p., asst. gen. counsel Chase Manhattan Corp., 1971-86, sr. v.p., dep. gen. counsel NYC, 1986-97; ptnr. Kelley, Drye & Warren, NYC, 1998—. Office: Kelley Drye & Warren 101 Park Ave Fl 29 New York NY 10178-0062 Office Phone: 212-808-7710. Business E-Mail: radams@kelleydrye.com.

ADAMS, ROBERT EDWARD, journalist; b. Geneseo, Ill., Apr. 27, 1941; s. Horace Mann and Florence (Beidelman) A. BS, U. Ill., 1963. Reporter Champaign-Urbana Courier, 1962-64; reporter, city staff St. Louis Post-Dispatch, 1966-72, Washington corr., 1972-93, asst. Washington bur. chief, 1981-83, Washington bur. chief, 1983-93. Washington commentator Sta. KMOX, St. Louis, 1984—; founding mem. St. Louis Journalism Rev., 1970 Recipient reporting award Nat. Civil Service League, 1975, Polit. Reporting award Lincoln U., Jefferson City, Mo., 1984, Raymond Clapper Meml. award for Washington Corr., 1987. citation for excellence Overseas Press Club, for series on Soviet Union, 1988; co-recipient Fgn. Corr. award Overseas Press Club Am., 1984, Nat. Headliner award, 1986. Mem. Nat. Press Club, Internat. Platform Assn., Com. to Protect Journalists, Washington Ind. Writers, The Gridiron Club, Sigma Delta Chi (Outstanding Young Reporter award St. Louis chpt. 1969). Roman Catholic. Home: Apt 707 2500 Wisconsin Ave NW Washington DC 20007-4504 Office: 529 14th St NW Washington DC 20045-1000 Office Phone: 202-333-1026. Personal E-mail: lauriebob01@earthlink.net.

ADAMS, ROBERT MCCORMICK, anthropologist, educator; b. Chgo., July 23, 1926; s. Robert McCormick and Janet (Lawrence) Adams; m. Ruth Salzman Skinner, July 24, 1953 (dec.); 1 child, Megan. PhB, U. Chgo., 1947, MA, 1952, PhD, 1956; DSc (hon.), U. Pitts., 1985, Dartmouth Coll., 1989; LHD (hon.), Hunter Coll., CUNY, 1986, Coll. William and Mary, 1989, Brandeis U., 1992; LD (hon.), Harvard U., 1992; PhD (hon.), U. Copenhagen, 2002. Archaeol. field tng. in, Jarmo, Iraq, 1950—51, Yucatan, Mexico, 1953; field studies history irrigation and urban settlement Iraq, 1956—75, Saudi Arabia, 1976—77; reconnaissance and excavation ancient Mayan settlement patterns Chiapas, Mexico, 1958—61; mem. faculty dept. anthropology, Oriental Inst. U. Chgo., 1955—84, assoc. prof. Oriental Inst., 1961—62, prof., 1962—84, dir. Oriental Inst., 1962—68, 1981—83, dean div. social scis., 1970—74, 1979—80, provost, 1982—84; sec. Smithsonian Instn., Washington, 1984—94; Homewood prof. dept. anthropology and near ea. studies Johns Hopkins U., 1984—94. Adj. prof. U. Calif., San Diego, 1993—; fellow Inst. for Advanced Study, Berlin, 1995—96; resident dir. Baghdad Sch., Am. Schs. Oriental Rsch., 1968—69; chmn. assembly behavioral and social scis. NRC, 1972—76, chmn. commn. on behavioral and social scis. and edn., 1987—93. Author: Land behind Baghdad, 1965, The Evolution of Urban Society, 1966; author: (with H.J. Nissen) The Uruk Countryside, 1972; author: Heartland of Cities, 1981, Paths of Fire: An Anthropologist's Inquiry into Western Technology, 1996; editor (with C.H. Kraeling): City Invincible: A Symposium on Urbanization and Cultural Development in the Ancient Near East, 1960; editor: (with C.S. Schelling) Corners of a Foreign Field, 1979; editor: (with N.J. Smelser and D.J. Treiman) Behavioral and Social Science Research: A National Resource, 1982; editor: Trends in American and German Higher Education, 2002. Trustee Nat. Opinion Rsch. Ctr., 1970—94, Nat. Humanities Ctr., 1976—83, Russell Sage Found., 1978—91, Santa Fe Inst., 1984—, Am. U. Beirut, 1989—94, Morehouse Coll., 1989—94, German Am. Acad. Coun., 1993—99. Recipient UCLA medal, 1989, Great Cross of Vasco Nuñez de Balboa, Panama, 1993, Gold medal, Am. Inst. Archaeology, 2002, award of merit, Field Mus., 2003. Fellow: AAAS, Soc. Antiquaries London, Mid. East Studies Assn., Am. Anthrop. Assn., Iraqi Acad. (assoc.), Am. Acad. Arts and Scis.; mem.: NAS, Coun. Fgn. Rels., Am. Philos. Soc., German Archaeol. Inst., Soc. Am. Archaeology (Disting. Svc. award 1996), Sigma Xi. Business E-Mail: rmadams@ucsd.edu.

ADAMS, ROBERT T., lawyer; b. 1954; BA in Economics, Colgate U.; MS in Economics, SUNY, Stonybrook; JD, Pace U., 1986. Bar: NY 1987, Conn. 1987, US Dist. Ct. So. Dist. NY, NY Dist. Ct. Ea. Dist. NY. Ptnr. Wilson, Elser, Moskowitz, Edelman & Dicker LLP, White Plains, NY. Mem.: ABA (entertainment & sports law sect.), NY State Bar Assn. (entertainment & sports law sect.). Office: Wilson Elser Moskowitz Edelman & Dicker LLP 3 Gannett Dr White Plains NY 10604 Office Phone: 914-323-7000 ext. 4201. Office Fax: 914-323-7001. Business E-Mail: adamsr@wemed.com.

ADAMS, ROBERT WAUGH, state agency administrator, economist, educator; b. Johnstown, Pa., Oct. 26, 1936; s. Robert Waugh and Mary Louise (Pyle) A.; m. Karen Day, June 13, 1964; children: Robert W. and Tara Anne Adams Mason. BS in Acctg., Pa. State U., 1958; MBA, U. Louisville, 1967. Acct., comptr., v.p. lending Citizens Fidelity Bank, Louisville, 1959-77; dir. fin., planning, and from dep. exec. dir. to exec. dir. Ky. Housing Corp., Frankfort, 1977-96; owner Adams Consulting Co., Louisville, 1996—2004, ret., 2004. Past pres. Bank Adminstrv. Inst., 1966, Planning Exec. Inst., 1970, Fin. Exec. Inst., 1974. Bd. dirs. Habitat for Humanity, Ctr. for Non Profit Excellence. Capt. U.S. Army Infantry, 1958-62. Mem. Louisville Boat Club (past pres.). Republican. Roman Catholic. Home and Office: 5210 Tamerlane Rd Louisville KY 40207-1160

ADAMS, ROBIN SUE, engineering educator; b. Newport Beach, Calif., Aug. 13, 1963; d. Marge A. and Wendell R. Adams. BS in Mech. Engring., Calif. Poly. State U., San Luis Obispo, 1986; MS in Materials Sci. and Engring., U. Wash., Seattle, 1996, PhD in Edn., 2001. Cert. EIT, Calif., 1988. Sr. designer Olin Interconnect Technologies, Santa Clara, Calif., 1986—91; asst. dir. Ctr. for Engring. Learning and Tchg., Seattle, 2003—05; asst. prof. Purdue U., Coll. Engring., West Lafayette, Ind., 2005—. Lead dir., inst. scholar engring. edn. Ctr. for Advancement for Engring. Edn., 2003—. Grantee, NSF, Purdue Rsch. Found.; Apprentice Faculty grant, ASEE, Ednl. Rsch. and Methods Divsn., 2001. Mem.: Soc. Women Enggrs., Internat. Soc. Learning Sci., Design Rsch. Soc., Am. Ednl. Rsch. Assn., Am. Soc. Engring. Edn. (bd. dir. 2005—07). Achievements include design of cognition and learning; research in interdisciplinarity thinking and working; engineering epistemologies. Office: Purdue Univ 400 Centennial Mall Dr West Lafayette IN 47907-2016 Office Phone: 765-496-3267.

ADAMS, ROGER C., federal official, lawyer; b. 1944; married; 1 child. BA cum laude, Bowdoin Coll., 1966; JD, Boston Coll., 1969. Bar: 1969. With criminal divsn. US Dept. Justice, 1972-93, counsel to dep. atty. gen., 1993-97, acting pardon atty., 1997—98, pardon atty., 1998—. Mem. Maine Bar Assn. Office: US Dept Justice Office Pardon Atty 500 1st St NW Ste 400 Washington DC 20530-0001*

ADAMS, RONALD G., elementary school educator; b. Boston, July 7, 1948; s. Russell Lawrence and Alice Gertrude (LeCorn) A.; m. Patricia Marie Sullivan, Mar. 15, 1950; children: Ronald Patrick, Michael Joseph, Kevin Russell. BS, U. Mass., 1975; MEd, Cambridge Coll., 1992. Cert. tchr. English, reading, adult basic edn., Mass. Tchr. English Quincy (Mass.) Pub. Sch., 1975-81, tchr. grade 7, 1983—; tchr. grade 7/8 Lincoln (Mass.) Pub. Schs., 1981-83. Mem. adv. bd. Mass. Carnegie Coun.: Turning Points, Dept. Edn., Mass., 1991-93; founding mem. Internat. Space Educators Coun., Huntsville, Ala., 1992-93; on-air moderator PBS Annenberg documentary series Primary Sources in Teaching American History, 2001. Prodr. TV documentary Quincy Shipbuilding, 1989 (award Dept. Edn. 1990); co-author: (booklet) Not Me, I Can Handle It, 1985 (Gov.'s award 1986); cons. TV series A Century of Women, TBS, 1994 (A&E Cable award 1992). Founder Winnie the Welder Day, City of Quincy, 1991-93; coach Houghs Neck Women's Softball League, Quincy, 1980-85; vol. Cub Scouts, Weymouth, Mass., 1989-93; mem. edn. steering com. Amnesty Internat., Somerville, Mass., 1989-93; mem. adv. bd. U.S. Naval Shipbldg. Mus., Quincy, 1992-93. Recipient Nat. Ednl. award Cable in Classroom, 1992, George Washington medal Freedoms Found., 1992, Young Prodr.'s award Continental Cablevision, 1992, A World of Difference Tchr. award Anti-Defamation League, 1994, Giraffe award, Reebok Internat. Youth-in-Action Human Rights award, 1995, Minn. Advocates for Human Rights award, 1997, Domestic Partnership award US AID, 1998, Anti-defamation League's Global Activism award 1998, 99, Darryl Williams Human Rights Leadership award Northeastern U., 1999, Bearer of Light award Union of Am. Hebrew Congregations, 1999, Hero Among Us award Boston Celtics, 2000, Global Edn. award The Peace Corps, 2000; named Tchr. of Yr., Mass. Dept. Edn., 1992, Nat. Consumers League Trumpeter award, 1998, Citizen of the Yr. 2000, Quincy Sun Newspaper. Fellow Mass. Acad. Tchrs. (history coord. 1992-93), Boston Writing Project; mem. NEA (Human and Civil Rights award 2000Applegate/Dorros Peace and Global Edn. award 2000), Nat. State Tchrs. of Yr., Nat. Coun. Social Studies, Nat. Coun. Tchrs. English, Mass. Tchrs. Assn. (Human Rights award 1991), Quincy Edn. Assn. (exec. bd. 1980-81). Avocation: football. Office: Broad Meadows Middle Sch 50 Calvin Rd Quincy MA 02169-2516 Home: 85 Homestead Ave Weymouth MA 02188-2125

ADAMS, RUSSELL LEE, neuropsychologist; b. Jefferson, Tex., Mar. 2, 1941; s. Irby Ray and Verda Mae Adams; m. Carolyn Sue Pulley, Aug. 8, 1964; children: David Lee, Scott Russell. BBA, Tex. A&M U., College Station, 1962; PhD, U. Tex., Austin, 1967. Diplomate Am. Bd. Clin. Neuropsychology. Assoc. prof. dept. psychiatry U. Tex. Health Scis. Ctr., San Antonio, 1969—78; assoc. prof. U. Okla. Health Scis. Ctr., Oklahoma City, 1978—82, prof., 1978—, dir. psychology internship program, 1978—, dir. postdoctoral neuropsychology fellowship program, 1982—. Co-author: Neuropsychology In Clinical Practice; mem. editl. bd numerous profl. jours., 1980—2006; contbr. articles to profl. jours. Adminstr. Scott Russell Adams Meml. Scholarship Baylor U., Waco, Tex., 1990—2006. Capt. US Army, 1967—69. Recipient Gordon Deckert award for Sustained

Excellence In Edn., U. Okla. Health Scis. Ctr., 1989, 2002. Fellow: APA (various positions 1980—2006), Nat. Acad. Neuropsychology (com. chair 1980—2006). Baptist. Avocations: travel, reading. Office: U Okla Health Scis Ctr 920 Stanton L Young Blvd Oklahoma City OK 73104 Office Fax: 405-271-8802. Business E-Mail: russell-adams@ouhsc.edu.

ADAMS, RYAN (DAVID RYAN ADAMS), musician; b. Jacksonville, NC, Nov. 5, 1974; Founder The Patty Duke Syndrome, NC; co-founder Whiskeytown, 1994—99; solo career, 2000—. Singer: (albums) Heartbreaker, 2000, Gold, 2001, Demolition, 2002, Rock N Roll, 2003, Love is Hell, 2004, Cold Roses, 2005, Jacksonville City Nights, 2005, 29, 2006, Easy Tiger, 2007. Office: c/o Frank Callari Lost Highway Records 54 Music Sq E Ste 300 Nashville TN 37203 Office Phone: 310-865-5000.*

ADAMS, S.C. (CHASE), lawyer, writer, radio and television commentator, financial consultant; b. Bklyn., July 10, 1934; s. Charles Joseph and Rose (Scala) A.; m. Ann Shepherdson, Aug. 3, 1957 (div. Feb. 1973); children: Mark, Scott, David, Christopher; m. Mary Jo Comstock, Dec. 8, 1990. BSCE, Rensselaer U., 1955; MS, U. Conn., 1961; JD, U. Miami, 1968. Bar: Fla 1968, U.S. Dist. Ct. (so. dist.) Fla. 1969, U.S. Tax Ct. 1990, U.S. Ct. Appeals (11th cir.) 1974, U.S. Supreme Ct., 1974; registered profl. engr., N.Y., Conn. V.p. Motivation Cons., Miami, Fla., 1965-68, Exposition Corp., Miami, 1968-72; gen. counsel City of Pompano Beach, Fla., 1972-76; mcpl. judge Broward County, Fla., 1974-76; corp. counsel Five Star Industries, Hialeah, Fla., 1976-80; vice chmn., COO Atlantic Svcs. Group, Ft. Lauderdale, Fla., 1977-86; prin. Adams & Assocs., Ft. Lauderdale, 1986—. Bd. dir. Good Steward Ministries, The Legacy Found., Minute Man Found., In God We Trust; gen. counsel Planned Giving Found., 1993—, Morgan, Howen & Co., 1993—, Srs. Helping Srs. U.S., 2006—; bd. regents nat. Heritage Found., 2003—. Author: Your Fiscal Fitness; creator radio commentary Your Fiscal Fitness; talk show host The Bus. Round Table; pub. Timely Tax and Money Strategies Newsletter, Fin. Strategies in Estate Planning, Preventing the Second Am. Revolution, One Nation Under God, Living in Paradise, The Repeal of the Income Tax, Preserving the Form of Govt. Established by the Constitution; author, Win-Win Financial Solutions For Lose-Lose Financial Situations, Land Use and Municipal Finance. Bd. dirs., pres. Planned Giving Coun., 1993-96, Fla. Bar Mgmt. Sect.; del. White House Conf. on Small Bus., Washington, 1986; apptd. to joint Presdl.-Congl. Com. by Pres. Reagan, 1984; pres. Broward Planned Giving Coun., 1994-95, Broward Estate Planning Coun., endowment com. Broward Performing Arts Ctr., planned giving com. United Way, 1992—98, fin. com. Honda Classic, 1988-2002; bd. dirs. Minute Man Found., 1995—, In God We Trust Ministries. Recipient Pres.'s award Broward County Bar Assn., 1975. Mem. Nat. Soc. Fundraising Execs. (bd. dirs. 1991-95), North Broward County Bar Assn. (treas., bd. dirs.), Broward County Mcpl. Judges Assn., Nat. Inst. Mcpl. Law Officers (chmn. ethics com.), Rensselaer Alumni Assn. (pres. South Fla. chpt.), Christian Stewardship Assn., Christian Legal Soc. Republican. Avocations: golf, tennis, racquetball, sailing, travel. Office: Adams & Assocs PO Box 30488 Fort Lauderdale FL 33303-0488 Office Phone: 954-566-1793. Personal E-mail: info@adamslaw.org. E-mail: chase99@pobox.com.

ADAMS, SCOTT, cartoonist; b. Windham, NY, June 8, 1957; s. Paul and Virginia Adams; m. Shelly Miles, July 22, 2006; 2 stepchildren. BA in Econs., Hartwick Coll., Oneonta, NY, 1979; MBA, Univ. Calif., Berkeley. Cert. hypnotist. Bank teller, computer programmer Crocker Nat. Bank, 1979—86; engr. Pacific Bell, San Ramon, Calif., 1986—95; cartoonist, Dilbert United Features Syndicate, 1989—. Cartoon, Dilbert, syndicated in 1,550 newspapers in 35 countries; author: The Dilbert Principle: Cubicle's-Eye View of Bosses, Meetings, Management Fads, and Other Workplace Afflictions, 1996, Dogbert's Top Secret Management Handbook, 1996, The Dilbert Future: Thriving on Business Stupidity in the 21st Century, 1997, Random Acts Of Management, 2000, Dilbert and the Way of the Weasel: A Guide to Outwitting Your Boss, Your Coworkers, and the Other Pants-Wearing Ferrets in Your Life, 2002, Words You Don't Want to Hear During Your Annual Review, 2003. Recipient Reuben award, 1997. Office: c/o United Media 200 Madison Ave New York NY 10016-3903*

ADAMS, SHARON BUTLER, minister, philosopher, researcher; b. Chgo., Oct. 30, 1949; d. Lionel Augustus and Clara Bernice Butler; m. Vernon McFadden Jr., June 13, 1968 (div. Oct. 1977); children: Vernon McFadden III, Aleceia Marie McFadden. Ordained min. African-Am. Universal Ministry. Engring. technician Servitron, Baton Rouge, 1976—78; instr. Coml. Bus. Coll, Baton Rouge, 1978—80; project mgr. Minority Engrs. La., Baton Rouge, 1980—86; cleric adminstr. Baton Rouge African-Am. Cath. Cong., 1997—98, cleric adminstr., So. Region Baton Rouge, 1998—99; interim pastor Imani Temple, Baton Rouge, 1998—99; pastor Ch. of the Living God, Baton Rouge, 1999—2002. Advisor Kwanzaa celebration A-A Universal Apostolic Ministry, Baton Rouge, 1999—; dir. Females in Ministry, Baton Rouge, 1999—; spiritual adv. Jazz and Heritage Festival, New Orleans, 2001—; cons. NAACP, New Orleans, 2001; advisor La. Dept. of Environ. Quality, 1990; owner ADHD-Alarm, 2004—. Author to newspapers and jours. Panelist New Orleans Jazz & Heritage Festival, 2002, Jazz Festival, 2003; bd. dirs. Cmty. Devel. Project, Baton Rouge, 1998, La. Dem. Project, Baton Rouge, 2000. Recipient Kwanazz Celebration award, Mayor & Metr. Coun. of Baton Rouge, 2001. Mem.: Internat. Black Environ. & Econ. Justice, Soc. Am. Music. Avocations: reading, sewing, music. Office Phone: 225-383-6479. E-mail: asharon@bellsouth.net.

ADAMS, SUSAN L., art educator; d. Leo Edward and Eleanor Gertrude (Yatko) Adams; 1 child, Adam Joseph Guzik. BA in Art, Wilkes U., Wilkes-Barre, Pa., 1978; MS in Edn. Adminstrn., U. Scranton, Scranton, Pa., 1985; postgrad., Pa. State U., University Park, 1991. Cert. Instrl. II Art, elem. prin., asst. supt. Dist. mgr. Wilkes-Barre Times Leader, Pa., 1978—79; HS art tchr. Williams Valley Sch. Dist., Tower City, Pa., 1980—86, elem. art tchr., 1986—. Bldg. com. Williams Valley Elem., Tower City, Pa., 1990—92; in svc. com. Williams Valley HS, Tower City, Pa., 1982—85; adj. prof. King's Coll., Wilkes Barre, Pa., 1988—96. Reviewer (edn. textbook) In the Classroom an Intro to Education, 1995. Den mother Tiger Cub Pack, Crressona, Pa., 2001—02; base coach Pirates Tee Ball, Crressona, Pa., 2001—02; catechist 2nd grade St. Patrick's ch., Pottsville, Pa., 2001—. Named Crayola Gold Star Tchr., 2006. Mem.: NEA, W.Va. Edn. Assn., Pa. State Edn. Assn., Kappa Delta Pi, Pi Lambda Theta. Democrat. Roman Catholic. Avocations: painting, photography, piano, interior decorating, gardening. Office: Williams Valley Elem 10400 State Rte 209 Tower City PA 17980

ADAMS, THOMAS LAWRENCE, lawyer; b. Jersey City, Apr. 14, 1948; s. Lawrence Ignatius and Dorothy Tekla (Halgas) A. BS, N.J. Inst. Tech., 1969; JD, Seton Hall U., 1975. Bar: N.J. 1975, U.S. Dist. Ct. N.J. 1975, U.S. Patent Office 1975, N.Y. 1976. Sys. engr. Grumman Aerospace, Bethpage, N.Y., 1969-71; sr. engr. Weston Instruments, Newark, 1971-74; mem. patent staff RCA, Princeton, NJ, 1974-75; corp. atty. Otis Elevator, NYC, 1975-77; ptnr. Goebel & Adams, Morristown, NJ, 1978-80, Behr & Adams, Morristown and Edison, NJ, 1981—2000. Mem. Seton Hall Law Rev. Mem. Livingston (N.J.) Twp. Coun., 1985-88, dep. mayor, 1987; mem. Livingston Environ. Commn., 1984-87; chmn. Livingston Rep. County Com., 1992-98. Mem. N.J. Patent Law Assn., Trial Attys. N.J., N.J. Bar Assn. (chmn. patent, trademark, copyright law and unfair competiton 1991), Morris County Bar Assn., KC (grand knight 1980), Tau Beta Pi, Eta Kappa Nu. Office Phone: 973-463-0100. Business E-Mail: adams@newidea.com.

ADAMS, THOMAS LYNCH, JR., lawyer; b. Fayette County, Ky., Nov. 22, 1941; s. Thomas Lynch and Amanda (Keith) A.; m. Anne Randolph, Aug. 13, 1974 (div. 1992); children: Thomas Lynch III, Randolph T., Alexander K., Andrew D. BA in History, U. Va., 1963; JD, Vanderbilt U., 1970. Bar: Ky. 1970, DC 1970, Tenn. 1970. Appellate atty. U.S. Dept. Justice, Washington, 1970-72; minority counsel U.S. Senate Commerce Com., Washington, 1972-75; legal counsel SBA, Washington, 1975; asst. gen. counsel FTC, Washington, 1975-77; govt. rels. Rep. Steel Corp., Washington, 1977-83; dep. gen. counsel U.S. EPA, Washington, 1983-86, asst. adminstr., presdl. appointee, 1986-89; ptnr. Dechert, Price & Rhoads, 1989-93; environ. dir. Internat. Paper, 1993; counsel to pres. America's Clean Water Found., 1994-95; of counsel Perkins Coie, Washington, 1995-2000; pres. Oxygenated Fuels Assn., Washington, 2000—02, sr. advisor dept. energy, asst. sec. environ. mgmt., 2002—04; sr. advisor, dept. energy, asst. sec. energy efficiency, renewables. Lt. (j.g.) USNR, 1963-67. Mem. ABA, Ky. Bar Assn., DC Bar Assn., Met. Club, Beta Theta Pi. Office Phone: 202-586-3179.

ADAMS, THOMAS MERRITT, lawyer; b. St. Louis, Sept. 27, 1935; s. Galen Edward and Chloe (Merritt) A.; m. Sarah McCardell Davis, June 6, 1959; children: Mark Merritt, John Harrison, William Shields, Thomas Bondurant. AB, Washington U., St. Louis, 1956, JD, 1960; postgrad., London Sch. Econs., 1957; LLM, George Washington U., 1966. Bar: Mo. 1960, Calif. 1971. Atty. SEC, Washington, 1964-66; asst. dir., asst. gen. counsel Investment Bankers Assn., Washington, 1966-68; pres. Transamerica Investment Mgmt., 1969-80; ptnr. Lanning Adams & Peterson, 1980—. Author: State and Local Pension Funds, 1968; contbr. articles to profl. jours. Chmn. Salina Cmty. Ambassador program, Kans., 1961. Served to capt. USAF, 1960-63. Decorated Air Force Commendation medal. Mem. Phi Beta Kappa. Episcopalian. Office: Lanning Adams & Peterson 11777 San Vicente Blve #750 Los Angeles CA 90049-5067

ADAMS, THOMAS TILLEY, lawyer; b. Orchard Park, NY, Oct. 9, 1929; s. Floyd Tilley and Clara Elizabeth (Potter) A.; m. Virginia Rives Smith, Sept. 1, 1956; children: Julia, Janet, Claire, Douglas. BA, U. Buffalo, 1951; JD, Cornell U., 1957. Bar: N.Y. 1957, U.S. Ct. Appeals (2d cir.) 1962, U.S. Supreme Ct. 1962, Conn. 1964. Tchr. Lake Shore Cen. Sch., Angola, NY, 1953-54; assoc. Davies, Hardy & Schenck, NYC, 1957-63; prin. Gregory & Adams P.C., Wilton, Conn., 1963—2001, of counsel, 2002—. Lectr. Cornell U. Law Sch., Ithaca, N.Y., 1962-65, emeritus mem. adv. coun., 1990—; adj. assoc. prof. law Fordham U., N.Y.C., 1973-76; adviser Dana Fund Internat. and Comparative Legal Studies, Toledo, 1976-91; assoc. bd. dirs. Union Trust Co., Stamford, Conn., 1982-94; mem. adv. bd. Norwalk Savs. Soc., 1993-97. Town atty. Town of Wilton, 1966-71; pres. Five Town Found., Norwalk, Conn., 1983-85, trustee, 1989-91; chmn. bldg. com. Wilton High Sch., 1966; bd. dirs. Woodcock Nature Ctr., Wilton-Ridgefield, Conn., 1997-99, trustee Norwalk Hosp., 1974, Wilton Library Assn., Inc., 2000-01, Elizabeth Raymond Ambler Trust, 2004—. Capt. USAF, 1951—53, Korea. Recipient Silver Beaver award Boy Scouts Am., 1980, Disting. Alumnus award Cornell Law Sch., 1990. Mem. ABA, Am. Judicature Soc. (dir. 1991-92), Norwalk-Wilton Bar Assn. (pres. 1990), Stamford-Norwalk Regional Bar Assn. (bd. dirs. 1991-93), Conn. Bar Assn. (ethics com. 1970-75, 92-93, mem. coun. bar pres.'s 1988-90), N.Y. Bar Assn., Assn. Bar City of N.Y., Silver Spring Country Club (gov. 1998-2004, asst. sec. 2003-04), Algonquin Roundtable of 21st Century, Cornell Club (N.Y.), Phi Delta Phi. Episcopalian. Office: Gregory & Adams PC 190 Old Ridgefield Rd Wilton CT 06897-4023 Home: 55 Deer Run Rd Wilton CT 06897-1204 also: Rogers Rock Clb Ticonderoga NY 12883 Office Phone: 203-762-9000. Office Fax: 203-834-1628.

ADAMS, THOMAS WALTON, corrections official; b. Midland, Mich., Apr. 15, 1947; s. Lawrence Walton and Elizabeth (Miller) A.; m. Karen Lynn Perry. BS with honors, Mich. State U., 1973, MS, 1987. Probation agt. 75th Dist. Ct., Midland, 1973—2003; cmty. corrections coord. Midland County, 2003—. Mem. Midland County Alcohol Svcs. Bd., 1975-78, Midland-Gladwin County Community Mental Health Bd., 1978-87, chmn. 1980-82; mem. allocation panel Midland County United Way, 2002—; mem. adv. Mt. Pleasant Regional Ctr. for Devel. Disabiities, 1988-89; active Act 511 Bd., 1990-2003; adv. bd. Midland County Jail, 1991-93; bd. dirs. FACE, 1995—; mem. violence/gang task force Midland County, 1998-2004; co-chair Domestic Violence Coordinating Coun., Midland County, 2000—; councilman Midland City Coun., 2005— Named One of Outstanding Young Men Am., 1982; recipient Liberty Bell award, Midland Bar Assn., 1983. Mem.: Am. Correctional Assn., Sigma Chi, Alpha Phi Sigma. Avocations: music, photography. Office: Adult Probation Courthouse Midland MI 48640 Home: 2605 Hearthstone Cir Midland MI 48642 Office Phone: 989-832-6646.

ADAMS, TIMOTHY D., former federal agency administrator; b. 1961; m. Jennifer T. Adams; 3 children. BA, MS, U. Ky. Dep. assoc. dir. Office Policy Devel. Exec. Office of Pres., Washington, 1990—93; co-founder, mgmt. dir. G-7 Group, Washington, 1993—2000; policy dir. Bush-Cheney Presdl. Campaign, Washington, 2004, sr. mem. policy staff, 2000; chief of staff US Dept. Treasury, Washington, 2001—03, under sec. for internat. affairs, 2005—07.*

ADAMS, VELMA M., assistant principal, consultant; b. Balt., Oct. 1, 1945; d. George and Anna Jones; m. Kenneth G. Adams, Jan. 5, 1946; 1 child, Mark. MusB in Edn., Howard U., 1968; MusM, Morgan State U., 1978; Profl. Cert. for Adminstrn. and Supervision, Queens Coll. Cert. bldg. and dist. adminstrn. N.Y., 1996. Choral and gen. music tchr. Balt. City Pub. Schs., 1968—80; vocal and gen. music tchr. Uniondale (N.Y.) Pub. Schs., 1980—99, asst. prin., 2000—; discipline supr. Lawrence Rd. Jr. High, Uniondale, 1999—2000. Second step character edn. trainer. Recipient Jenkins PTA award, PTA of Turtle Hook Mid. Sch., 1998. Mem.: ASCD, The Mid. Sch. Adminstr., Curriculum Audit Mgmt. Ctrs., Inc. (assoc.), Nassau Music Educators Assn. (life; pres.). Democrat. Episcopalian. Achievements include development of peer mediation program. Avocations: avid reader, mediation consultant, curriculum auditor, rehearsal and show pianist, computer enthusiast. Home: 71-24 Sutton Place #2 Fresh Meadows NY 11365 Office: Lawrence Rd Middle School 50 Lawrence Rd Hempstead NY 11550 Office Phone: 516-918-1503. Business E-Mail: vadams@uniondaleschools.org. E-mail: velmaa1@hotmail.com.

ADAMS, WAYNE VERDUN, pediatric psychologist, educator; b. Rhinebeck, NY, Feb. 24, 1945; s. John Joseph and Lorena Pearl (Munroe) A.; m. Nora Lee Swindler, June 12, 1971; children: Jennifer, Elizabeth. BA, Houghton Coll., 1966; MA, Syracuse U., 1969, PhD, 1970; postgrad., U. NC, 1975. Diplomate Am. Bd. Profl. Psychology (hon.); lic. psychologist, NY, Oreg. Asst. prof. Colgate U., Hamilton, NY, 1970-75; chief psychologist Alfred I. DuPont Inst., Wilmington, Del., 1976-86; dir. divsn. psychology, dept. pediat. DuPont Hosp. for Children (formerly Alfred I. DuPont Inst.), Wilmington, 1987-99; mem. Del. Bd. Licensure in Psychology, 1983-86, bd. pres., 1986; assoc. prof. pediat. Thomas Jefferson Coll. Medicine, Phila., 1995-99; prof. psychology George Fox U., Newberg, Oreg., 1999—, chair grad. dept. clin. psychology, 2001—. Grant reviewer NIH, 1999—; vis. prof. Wuhan U., China, 2004, 06. Cons. editor Jour. Pediatric Psychology, 1980-83, guest reviewer, 1984—; co-author 5 nationally used psychol. tests in field; contbr. over 25 articles to profl. jours. Scholar, Fulbright Found., 2006—. Fellow APA, Nat. Acad. Neuropsychology; mem. Soc. Pediatric Psychology, Del. Psychol. Assn. (exec. com. 1979-82, pres. 1981-82), Oreg. Psychol. Assn. Office: George Fox U Grad Dept Clin Psychology Box 6141 414 N Meridian St Newberg OR 97132-2697 Office Phone: 503-554-2761.

ADAMS, WESTON, former diplomat, military officer, lawyer; b. Columbia, SC, Sept. 16, 1938; s. Robert and Helen Hayes (Calhoun) A.; m. Elizabeth Nicholson Nelson, Mar. 2, 1962; children— Robert VI, Weston III, Daniel Wallace, Julian Calhoun II AB in History, U. S.C., 1960, LL.B., 1962. Bar: S.C. 1962. Research dir. S.C. Republican Orgn., Columbia, 1966-67; trust officer S.C. Nat. Bank, Columbia, 1967-70; assoc. counsel Select Com. on Crime, U.S. Ho. of Reps., Washington, 1970-71; solo practice Columbia, 1971-84, 86—; ambassador to Malawi U.S. Dept. of State, Lilongwe, 1984-86. Mem. S.C. House of Reps., 1972-74; presdl. elector U.S. Electoral Coll., S.C., 1980; del. Rep. Nat. Conv., Kansas City, Mo., 1976, New Orleans, 1988, Houston, 1992, alt. del., Detroit, 1980, San Diego, 1996; mem. diplomatic adv. com. and exec. com. bus./industry adv. com. Am. Bicentennial Presdl. Inaugural, 1989; mem. U.S. presdl. del. to inauguration of Pres. of Dominican Republic, 1982; United Nations Day Chmn. for the State of S.C., honoring its 50th Anniversary, 1995; mem. UNESCO, 1982-84. Capt. USAF, 1963—66, with US Air Force Res., 1966—73, maj. Spl. Ops. Adv. Group, 2001—, SC, brig. gen. Spl. Ops. Adv. Group, SC. Recipient Order of Palmetto, Gov. S.C., 1974. Mem. S.C. Bar, Richland County Bar Assn., U. S.C. Alumni Assn., U. South Carolina Hist. Soc., S.C. Soc. of Cincinnati, Order First Families N.C., Magna Charta Barons (Somerset chpt.), St. Andrews Soc., Soc. Colonial Wars, Huguenot Soc. of S.C., Soc. Lower Richland, Jamestowne Soc., Welcome Soc. Pa., The Society of First Families of S.C. 1670-1700, Most Venerable Order Hosp. St. John Jerusalem, Coun. Am. Ambs., Knight Grand Cross, Imperial Order of Holy Trinity (Imperial Ethiopia), Knight Grand Cross, Order of St. Michael of Wing (Portugal-Braganza), Clubs: Palmetto Columbia). Episcopalian.

ADAMS, WILLIAM D., academic administrator; b. Pontiac, Mich., Aug. 18, 1947; s. Waldemar Harmon Adams and Charlotte Elizabeth (Drea) Rising; m. Catherine Spaulding Bruce, Oct. 10, 1993; children: Sean Douglass Vallant, Carmen Milena. BA magna cum laude, The Colo. Coll., 1972; PhD, U. Calif., Santa Cruz, 1982. Vis. asst. prof. polit. sci. U. N.C., Chapel Hill, 1983—84, U. Santa Clara, Calif., 1984—85; instr. great works in western culture program Stanford U., Calif., 1985—86, program coord. great works in western culture program, 1986—88; exec. asst. to pres. Wesleyan U., Middletown, Conn., 1988—93, v.p., sec., 1993—95; pres. Bucknell U., Lewisburg, Pa., 1995—2000, Colby Coll., Waterville, Maine, 2000—. Contbr. articles to profl. jours. 1st lt. US Army, 1966—69. Office: Colby Coll Office of Pres 4601 Mayflower Hl Waterville ME 04901-8846 Home Phone: 207-873-0588; Office Phone: 207-859-4600, 207-859-4603. E-mail: wadams@colby.edu.*

ADAMS, WILLIAM HENSLEY, ecologist, educator; b. Nashville, Aug. 14, 1929; s. William Hensley and Mary Pauline (Vaughn) A.; children: Deska Lee, Norma Dee, Anita Rice, Patricia Lynn; m. Mary Lou Adams, 1999. AB, U. Tenn., 1951; postgrad., U. Okla., 1951, Tulane U., 1953—54; MS, La. State U., 1956; PhD, Auburn U., 1959. Grad. rsch. asst. Auburn U., 1956—59; sr. rsch. biologist Tenn. Game and Fish Commn., 1959—60; chmn. dept. biology, prof. biology Tenn. Wesleyan Coll., 1960—64, dean Coll. Arts and Scis.; prof. biology Tenn. Technol. U., Cookeville, 1964—66; with disnv. pre-coll. edn. in sci. NSF, 1966—68, divsn. undergrad. edn. in sci., 1969—73, divsn. higher edn. in sci., 1973—75, divsn. sci. edn. devel. and rsch., 1975—77, divsn. sci. improvement, 1977—81; cons., 1981—; pres. BIADA Constrn. Devel. Co. and Empire Realty Investment Co., Vienna, Va., 1990—92; broker ERA Real Estate, Hilton Head, SC, 1992—. Mem. NSF Research Participation for Coll. Tchrs. Highlands Biol. Sta., 1961, NSF Summer Inst. Radiation Biology Oak Ridge Inst. Nuclear Studies, 1961, NSF Summer Inst. Comparative Anatomy Harvard, 1962, NSF Summer Inst. Marine Biology Duke Marine Lab., 1963, NSF-Tenn. Acad. Sci. Vis. Scientist Program, 1962-66; dir. NSF Coop. Coll.- Sch. Sci. Program, 1963-65; mem. Commn. Undergrad. Edn. in Biol. Scis. Southeastern Regional Conf., 1965, Advanced Placement Reader in Biology, 1965; Oak Ridge Inst. Nuclear Scis. Radiation Biology Conf., 1965 Mem. Savanah River Site Citizens Adv. Bd. Served to lt. col. Med. Service Corps, USAF, 1951-53, 68-69. Recipient Sigma Xi-Research Engring. Soc. Am. grant-in-aid, 1960-61, Tenn. Wesleyan Coll. Faculty award, 1962, Tenn. Technol. U. faculty research grant, 1966 Fellow Explorers Club; mem. Am. Soc. Mammalogists (honorarium 1959), Am. Ornithologists Union, Cooper Ornithol. Soc., Wilson Ornithol. Soc., Wildlife Soc. Home: 4 Field Sparrow Ct Hilton Head Island SC 29926-1881 Office: 840 Wm Hilton Pkwy Hilton Head Island SC 29928 Business E-Mail: adamshhi@hargray.com. *Increasingly, people in positions of responsibility are abdicating their concomitant role as respected leaders and thereby failing to set good examples for young people to follow, especially at a time when they need high standards for self-emulation. Therefore I challenge young people to set forceful leadership as their highest personal goal in life and remember, as I have, that attainment of this goal will require the stamina necessary to remount their white chargers each time and no matter how often they are unseated.*

ADAMS, WILLIAM JAMES, JR., (WILL.I.AM), rap artist; b. Mar. 15, 1975; Founding mem. band Atban Klann, 1992—95, band Black Eyed Peas, 1998—. Co-founder i.am clothing, 2001—. Singer, prodr. (albums) Behind the Front, 1998, Bridging the Gap, 2000, Elephunk, 2003, Monkey Business, 2005 (Favorite Rap/Hip-Hop Album, Am. Music Awards, 2006); singer: (songs) Joints & Jams, 1998, Fallin' Up, 1998, Where is the Love? (feat. Justin Timberlake), 2003, Shut Up, 2003, Hey Mama, 2004 (MTV Video Music Award), Let's Get It Started, 2004 (Grammy, Best Rap Performance, 2005), Don't Phunk with My Heart, 2005 (Grammy award, Best Rap Group Performance, 2006), Don't Lie, 2005, My Humps, 2005 (MTV Video Music award for Best Hip-Hop Video, 2006, Grammy award, Best Group Pop Vocal Performance, 2007), (with Santana) I Am Somebody, 2005. Co-founder Peapod Found., LA. Recipient MTV Europe award for Best Pop Act (with Black Eyed Peas), 2004, 2005, Favorite Pop Group & Rap Group, Am. Music Awards, 2005, Favorite Soul/Rhythm & Blues Grp., 2006, Favorite Rap/Hip-Hop Grp., 2006. Office: iam clothing PO Box 664 Hollywood CA 90078 Office Phone: 323-469-5181, 323-661-1524. Office Fax: 213-856-2712. E-mail: iamclothing@aol.com.*

ADAMS, YOLANDA YVETTE, singer; b. Houston, Aug. 27, 1962; m. Timothy Crawford, Jr., 1997; 1 child, Taylor Ayanna Crawford. Singer: (albums) Just as I Am, 1988, Through the Storm, 1991, More Than a Melody, 1995, Shakin' the House, 1996, Yolanda Live in Washington, 1996, Battle is the Lord, 1996, Songs from the Heart, 1998, Mountain High.Valley Low, 1999 (Grammy award for Best Contemporary Soul Gospel Album, 1999), Christmas with Yolanda Adams, 2000, The Experience, 2001 (Grammy award for Best Contemporary Soul Gospel Album, 2001), Believe, 2001, Day by Day, 2005, (songs) Be Blessed, 2005 (Grammy award, Best Gospel Song, 2006), Victory, 2005 (Grammy award, Best Gospel Song, 2007). Recipient Image award for Outstanding Gospel Artist, NAACP, 2000—02, 2006, Image award for Outstanding Female Artist, 2001. Office: N-House Mgmt Inc Ste 220 4204 Bellaire Blvd Houston TX 77025 also: Atlantic Records Publicity Dept 1290 Ave of the Americas New York NY 10104 Office Phone: 832-778-6774. E-mail: yolanda@yolandaadams.com.

ADAMSON, GEOFFREY DAVID, endocrinologist, surgeon; b. Ottawa, Ont., Can., Sept. 16, 1946; came to U.S., 1978, naturalized, 1986; s. Geoffrey Peter Adamson and Anne Marian Allan; m. Rosemary C. Oddie, Apr. 28, 1973; children: Stephanie, Rebecca, Eric. BSc with honors, Trinity Coll., Toronto, Can., 1969; MD, U. Toronto, 1973. Diplomate Am. Bd. Ob-Gyn., Am. Bd. Laser Surgery; cert. Bd. Reproductive Endocrinology. Resident in ob-gyn. Toronto Gen. Hosp., 1973-77, fellow in ob-gyn., 1977-78; fellow reproductive endocrinology Stanford (Calif.) U. Med. Ctr., 1978-80; practice medicine specializing in infertility Los Gatos, Calif.,

1980-84; instr. Stanford U. Sch. Medicine, 1980-84, clin. asst. prof. Calif., 1984-92, clin. assoc. prof., 1992-95, clin. prof., 1995—; assoc. clin. prof. Sch. Medicine U. Calif., San Francisco, 1992—; founder, chmn., CEO Advanced Reproductive Care Inc., Palo Alto, Calif., 1997—. Tech. adviser WHO, 2003—. Editor: (textbook) Endoscopic Management of Gynecologic Disease, 1996, Modern Management of Endometriosis, 2005; mem. editl. bd. Can. Doctor mag., 1977—83, Jour. Am. Assn. Gynecol. Laparoscopists, 1996—, Fertility and Sterility, 2000—03, mem. editl. adv. bd. Mid. East Fertility Soc., 2004—, mem. editl. bd. others; assoc. editor: Mid. E. Fertility Soc., 2004—. Recipient Spl. Congl. Recognition cert., US Congress, 2006; fellow, Ont. Ministry of Health, 1977—78. Fellow ACS, Royal Coll. Surgeons Can., Am. Coll. Ob-Gyns.; mem. AAAS, AMA, Am. Assn. Gynecol. Laparoscopists (adv. bd., bd. trustees, sec., treas. 2002-03, v.p. 2003-04, exec. com. 2002—, v.p. 2003-04, pres. 2004-05, past pres. 2005-06), Am. Soc. Reproductive Medicine (com. mem., bd. dirs. 1997-99, 2000-03, exec. com., 2002-04, v.p., 2005-06, pres. elect 2006-), Soc. Reproductive Endocrinologists (charter), Soc. Reproductive Surgeons (charter, bd. dirs., sec., treas., v.p., pres., past pres.), Soc. Assisted Reproductive Tech. (treas., dir., v.p., pres., past pres. bd. dirs. 1991-05), Nat. Coalition Oversight of Assisted Reproductive Technicians (vice-chair 2001-03, chair 2003-05), Internat. Com. Monitoring Assisted Reproductive Techs. (sec.-treas. 2005-), Internat. Fedn. Fertility Socs. (audit com. 2001—, bd. dirs. 2007—), Pacific Coast Reproductive Soc. (dir., sec., v.p., pres., past pres.), Pacific NW Ob-Gyn Soc. (hon. life), Pacific Coast Ob-Gyn. Soc., Soc. Gynecologic Surgeons, San Francisco Gynecol. Soc. (past pres.), Soc. for Gynecologic Investigation, Bay Area Reproductive Endocrinologists Soc. (founding pres., hon. life), Gynecol. Laser Soc., N.Y. Acad. Scis., Shufelt Gynecol. Soc., Peninsula Gynecol. Soc. (past pres.), Calif. Med. Assn., San Mateo County Med. Assn., Santa Clara County Med. Assn. (Outstanding Achievement in Medicine award 2006), Am. Fedn. Clin. Rsch., Nat. Resolve (bd. dirs. 1991-01, sec., treas., Lifetime Svc. award 1999), Can. Assn. Interns and Residents (hon. life, pres. 1977-79, bd. dirs. 1974-79, rep. AMA resident physician sect. 1978-79, rep. Can. Med. Protective Assn. 1975-78, rep. Can. Med. Assn. 1975-78, Disting. Svc. award 1980), Profl. Assn. Interns and Residents Ont. (bd. dirs. 1973-76, v.p. 1974-75, pres. 1975-76), Royal Coll. Physicians and Surgeons Can. (com. exams. 1977-80), Ont. Med. Assn. (sec. interns and residents sect. 1973-74). Avocations: hiking, ice hockey, skiing. Office: 540 University Ave Ste 200 Palo Alto CA 94301-1929

ADAMSON, JEREMY E., library director; BFA, U. Toronto, MA in Art History; PhD in Art History, U. Mich. Collections curator Nat. Gallery Can.; sr. curator Renwick Gallery, Smithsonian Am. Art Mus., 1988—2001; joined Libr. of Congress, Washington, 2001, chief Prints and Photog. Div., 2001—06, dir. collections and svcs., 2006—. Tchr. art history U. Toronto. Office: Libr of Congress 101 Independence Ave, SE Washington DC 20540*

ADAMSON, RICHARD HENRY, pharmacologist; b. Council Bluffs, Iowa, Aug. 9, 1937; s. Holger Nels and Mary Caroline (Dengle) A.; m. Charlene Denham, Oct. 25, 1963; children: Kristin, Kara. BA, Drake U., 1957; MS, U. Iowa, 1959, PhD, 1961; MA, George Washington U., 1968. Fellow U. Iowa Coll. Medicine, Iowa City, 1958-61; commd. officer USPHS, NIH, Bethesda, Md., 1961-63; sr. investigator lab. chem. pharmacology Nat. Cancer Inst., Bethesda, Md., 1963-69, head pharmacology and exptl. therapeutics sec., 1969-73, acting chief lab. chem. pharmacology, 1973-76, chief lab. chem. pharmacology, 1976-81, dir. divsn. cancer etiology, 1981-94; v.p. scientific and tech. affairs to v.p. scientific and regulatory affairs Nat. Soft Drink Assn. (now Am. Beverage Assn.), Washington, 1994—2004; sr. scientific cons. Am. Beverage Assn., Washington, 2004—. Lectr. physiology George Washington U., Washington, 1963-70; Fulbright vis. scientist St. Mary's Hosp. Med. Sch., London, 1965-66; sr. policy analyst Office Sci. and Tech. Policy Exec. Office of Pres., 1979-80 Author: numerous publs. in field; mem. editorial bd.: Cancer Treatment Reports, 1972-75, Xenobiotica, 1971-84, Cancer Research, 1980-87, Jour. Biolchem. Toxicology, 1984—, Regulatory Toxicology and Pharmacology, 1984—, Health and Environment Digest, 1986—, Japanese Jour. Cancer Research (Gann), 1986-96, In Vivo, 1990—, Teratogenesis, Carcinogenesis and Mutagenesis, 1991—. Recipient USPHS Superior Svc. award, 1976, 82, Spl. Achievement award EEO, 1982, Presdl. Meritorious Exec. Rank award, 1989, Toxicology Forum Anderson award, 1990, PHS Spl. Recognition award, 1992, Leadership for Combined Fed. Campaign award NIH, 1993, 94; named hon. mem. Japanese Cancer Assn., 1988. Mem. AAAS, Am. Assn. Cancer Rsch., Biochem. Soc., Am. Soc. Pharmacology and Exptl. Therapeutics, Soc. Toxicology (Lehman award 1989), Internat. Soc. Beverage Technologists, Assn. Food and Drug Ofcls. (tech. forum), Comparative Rsch. Leukemia. Office: Am Beverage Assn 1101 16th St NW Ste 700 Washington DC 20036-4877

ADAMSON, TERRENCE BURDETT, lawyer; b. Floyd County, Ga., Nov. 13, 1946; s. Sollie Burdett and Lois Antoinette (Rogers) A.; m. Ede E. Holiday, June 8, 1985; children: Terrence Morgan, Kathlyn Watson Holiday, Elizabeth Rogers Holiday. BA, Emory U., 1968, JD with distinction, 1973. Bar: Ga. 1973, U.S. Supreme Ct. 1978, D.C. 1981. Reporter Atlanta Constn., 1968-70; law clk. to Hon. Griffin B. Bell U.S. Ct. Appeals (5th cir.), 1973-74; assoc. Hansell & Post, Atlanta, 1974-77; spl. asst. U.S. Atty. Gen., 1977-79; ptnr. Hansell & Post, Atlanta and Washington, 1979-86, Dow, Lohnes & Albertson, Atlanta, 1986-91, Donovan, Leisure, Rogovin & Schiller, Washington, 1991-93, Kaye, Scholer, Fierman, Hays & Handler, LLP, Washington, 1993—98; exec. v.p. Nat. Geographic Soc., 1998—. Henry Luce scholar Ishii Law Office, Tokyo, 1975-76, scholar selector, 2002-; dir. office pub. affairs, chief spokesman U.S. Dept. Justice, Washington, 1978-79; bd. dirs. Nat. Geographic Ventures, 1996—; bd. dirs., mem. exec. com. State Justice Inst., Alexandria, Va., U.S. Presdl. appointment, 1990, 92, 94, Senate confirmed 1990, 92, 95; bd. dirs. Nat. Legal Ctr. for Pub. Interest. Contbr. articles to newspapers, mags. and law revs. Trustee Asia Found., 1984—, vice chmn. 1991-95, chmn. bd. 1995-2000; mem. steering com. Nat. Libel Def. Resource Com., 1987-91, co-chair Biennial Media Seminar, 1987-96; site selection com. 1988 Dem. nat. conv.; mem. U.S. Nat. Com. for Pacific Econ. Coop., 1983—, Leadership Atlanta, 1988-89, bd. trustee, exec. com., bd. councillors, gen. counsel, Carter Presdl. Ctr., Atlanta, 1983—; mem. Coun. for Excellence in Govt., 1991-94; mem. Clinton-Gore transition, 1992-93; mem. adv. com. Presdl. Librs. Nat. Archive; bd. dirs. Nat. Legal Ctr. for Pub. Interest, 2006—. Kennedy fellow Inst. Politics, Harvard U., 1979 Fellow Soc. Values in Edn.; mem. ABA (law and media project, conf. com. on lawyers and media 1987-90, chair defamation and media law com. 1992-93), U.S. Supreme Ct. Hist. Soc., Ga. Bar Assn., D.C. Bar Assn., Order of Coif, Order of Barristers, Omicron Delta Kappa. Democrat. Office: National Geographic Soc 1145 17th St NW Washington DC 20036-4688 Office Phone: 202-857-7449. Business E-Mail: tadamson@ngs.org.

ADAMYAN, TSOVINAR, medical educator; b. Stepanakert, Aremenia, May 8, 1939; d. Ishkahan Adamyan and Piruza Khachatryan; m. Kirakos Manukyan, June 15, 1964; children: Karen Manukyan, Arshar Manukyan. Grad. in Biology, Yerevan State U., Armenia, 1968, PhD, 1980. Rsch. asst. Yerevan State U., 1975—89, rsch. officer, 1990—2000, assoc. prof., 2000—, Med. Inst., Yerevan, 1997—. Mem. biol. faculty, sci. coun. Yerevan State U., 2001—. Author: (book) Human and Animal Physiology, 2006; contbr. articles to profl. jours. Mem.: Armenian Physiol. Assn. Office: Yerevan State Univ Charents 0010 Yerevan Armenia

ADARKAR, ADITYA, humanities educator; PhD, U. Chgo., 2001. Asst. prof., classics and gen. humanities Montclair State U., Upper Montclair, NJ, 2001—. Office: Montclair State Univ Classics and General Humanities Montclair NJ 07043

ADAWI, IBRAHIM HASAN, physics professor; b. Palestine, Apr. 18, 1930; came to U.S., 1951, naturalized, 1961; s. Hasan and Dabella (Miari) A.; children: Omar, Nadia, Yasmin, Rhonda, Tariq. BS in Engring. Physics, Washington U., St. Louis, 1953; PhD in Engring. Physics, Cornell U., 1957. Mem. tech. staff RCA Labs., Princeton, NJ, 1956-60; research cons. Battelle Meml. Inst., Columbus, Ohio, 1960-68; adj. prof. elec. engring. Ohio State U., 1965-68; prof. physics U. Mo., Rolla, 1968-97, emeritus prof. physics, 1997—. Vis. prof. U. Hamburg, W.Ger., winter 1977, Sch. Math. and Physics, U. East Anglia, Norwich, Eng., fall 1982; Fulbright lectr. Rabat, Morocco, 1982; sr. scientist Motorola, Phoenix, summer 1979; rsch. leader Internat. Ctr. Theoretical Physics, Trieste, Italy, summers 1982, 83, 85. Jr. fellow Cornell U., 1953-54; J. McMullen scholar, 1954-55; Sigma Xi fellow, 1955-56 Mem. Am. Phys. Soc Home: 10540 County Road 3010 Rolla MO 65401-7754 Office: U Mo-Rolla Dept Physics Rolla MO 65401 Business E-Mail: adawi@umr.edu. *Goals in science, and perhaps in life, are seldom reached; they are only approached asymptotically. The higher we soar the more dazzling is the panorama, but the wider is the horizon, and the frontiers of knowledge keep expanding.*

ADAWI, NADIA SHARON, energy executive; b. Princeton, NJ, Aug. 29, 1958; d. Ibrahim Hasan and Gerda (Obert) Adawi; m. Patrick John Loll, June 18, 1983. BSEE, U. Mo., 1980; MBA, Yale U., 1997. Electronics engr. FCC, Washington, 1980-81; cons. engr. Washington, 1981-89; asst. dir. advanced cellular tech. Ameritech Mobile Communications, Schaumburg, Ill., 1989-93; regional ops. mgr. Ericsson, Inc., Schaumburg, 1993-95; bus. ethics cons. Arthur Andersen, NYC, 1997-99; dir. ops. The Energy Cooperative, Phila.; pres. Phila. Fry-o-Diesel LLC. Co-chair Sustainable Bus. Network of Greater Phila.; treas. Greater Phila. Clean Cities. Named one of Phila. Bus. Jour. Women of Distinction, 2001. Avocations: music, literature, travel. Home: 329 S 46th St Philadelphia PA 19143-1801 E-mail: nsadawi@aol.com.

ADCOCK, ERIC, application developer; s. Phil G. Adcock and Doris L. Ryan. BS in Computer Sci., MS in Computer Sci., Western Ill. U., Macomb, 1987—93. Cert. solution developer Microsoft, 2000. Programmer, analyst CIBER, Springfield, Bloomington, 1996—2006, Ind. Bankers' Bank, Springfield, 2006—. Mem.: Mensa. Home: 4 Greenview Ct Springfield IL 62074-2145 Office: Ind Bankers Bank 3161 W White Oaks Dr Ste 300 Springfield IL 62704 Home Phone: 217-726-5480.

ADCOCK, MURIEL W., special education educator; b. Chgo. BA, U. Calif. Sonoma State, Rohnert Park, 1979. Cert. spl. edn. tchr., Calif., Montessori spl. edn. tchr. Tchr. The Concordia Sch., Concord, Calif., 1980-85; tchr., cons. Tenderloin Community Children's Ctr., San Francisco, 1985-86; adminstr. Assn. Montessori Internat.-USA, San Francisco, 1988, tchr., advisor, 1989—. Course asst. Montessori Spl. Edn. Inst., San Francisco, 1985-87, tchr. spl. edn., 1990, tchr. cons., 1991—, rschr. 1992—. U.S. mng. editor World Futures: The Jour. of Gen. Evolution, 2000—; contbr. articles to profl. jour. Sec. Internat. Forum World Affairs Coun., San Francisco, 1990-95, program chair, 1993-95, pres./founder Club of Budapest, U.S., 2000—. Mem. ASCD, Am. Orthopsychiat. Assn., Internat. Soc. Sys. Scientists, Internat. Sys. Inst., Assn. Montessori Internat., N.Am. Montessori Tchrs. Assn., Assn. Childhood Edn. Internat., Smithsonian Assocs., N.Y. Acad. Scis., Internat. Sys. Inst. Avocations: general evolutionary systems theory, sustainable development, human capacity building. Office: 4040 Civic Center Dr Ste 200 San Rafael CA 94903

ADCOCK, ROBERT H., JR., (BUNNY), state agency administrator; b. McGehee, Ark. m. Carol Coleman; children: Hillary, Ashton. Dir. European Office of the Gov. Ark. Indsl. Devel. Commn., Brussels, 1976—80; adminstrv. asst. Staff of Gov. Frank White, Ark., 1981—83; exec. v.p. First Nat. Bank Conway, Ark., 1983—96; pres. Ark. Devel. Fin. Authority, 1996—97; co-organizer First State Bank, Conway, 1999, vice chmn.; also coach men and women's golf teams U. Ctrl. Ark., 2000—03, v.p. alumni svcs. and devel., 2003; commr. Ark. State Bank Dept., 2003—. Office: Ark State Bank Dept Ste 100 400 Hardin Rd Little Rock AR 72211 Office Phone: 501-324-9019. Office Fax: 501-324-9028. E-mail: asbd@banking.state.ar.us.

ADCROFT, PATTI (PATRICE GABRIELLA), editor; b. Scranton, Pa., Apr. 15, 1954; d. Joseph Raymond and Patricia Ann (Ryan) Adcroft. BA In Mag. Journalism and Creative Writing, Syracuse U., 1976. Editor-in-chief Carbondale (Pa.) Miner Mid Valley Gazette, 1976—77; staff writer Good Housekeeping Mag., NYC, 1978—80; mng. editor Family Media/Alive and Well, NYC, 1980—81; freelance writer, editor NYC, 1981—82; sr. editor CBS Mags. Family Weekly, NYC, 1982—84, Omni Mag., NYC, 1984—85, exec. editor, 1985—86, editor-in-chief, 1986—90, Seventeen Mag., 1998—2001; exec. editor Marie Claire, 2004—06; spl. projects editor Discover mag., 2006—. Vis. prof. Syracuse U., 1992—93. Editor-in-chief Omni Future Medical Almanac, 1987, NetGuide Mag., 1994—95, deputy editor InStyle Mag., 1995—98; author: (novels) Every Day Doughnuts; contbr. writer Arthur C. Clarke's 2019, 1986, Omni Book of Continuum, 1982. Bd. advisors SCI Ctr. for Advanced Studies in Mgmt. Wharton Sch., U. Pa. Roman Catholic. Office: Discover 90th Fifth Ave New York NY 10011

ADDAI, JOSEPH, professional football player; b. Houston, Tex., May 3, 1983; BA in gen. studies, LSU, 2005. Running back Ind. Colts, 2006—. Achievements include being mem. BCS Nat. Championship team, 2003-2004; holding record for post-season reception and yards by rookie, 2007; leading all rookies in rushing yards, 2006-2007. Office: Ind Colts 7001 W 56th St Indianapolis IN 46254*

ADDERLEY, TERENCE EDWARD, human resources executive; b. 1933; BBA, U. Mich., 1955, MBA, 1956. Fin. analyst Standard Oil Co. NJ, 1956-57; with Kelly Svcs., Inc., Troy, Mich., 1958—61, v.p., 1961-65, exec. v.p., 1965-67, pres., COO, 1967—87, pres., CEO, 1987—98, chmn., CEO, 1998—2006, chmn., 2006—. Mem. vis. com. Ross Sch. Bus., Univ. Mich.; mem. health sys. adv. group Univ. Mich.; bd. mem. Detroit Renaissance Found., Oakland County Bus. Roundtable, Detroit County Day Sch., William Beaumont Hosp., Citizens Rsch. Council Mich., Detroit Econ. Club. Office: Kelly Svcs Inc 999 W Big Beaver Rd Troy MI 48084-4716*

ADDESSO, ANGELA JOYCE, school system administrator; m. Jack Anthony Addesso, Oct. 21, 1973; children: Adam Louis, Jack, Jr. Anthony. BS in Art and Art History, Herbert H. Lehman Coll., Bronx, 1983; MS in Edn., Herbert H. Lehman Coll., 1989; postgrad., Coll. of New Rochelle, NYC, 1995. Cert. sch. adminstrn. and supervision N.Y. State Dept. Edn., 2003, dist. adminstr. N.Y. State Dept. Edn., 1995, art tchr. K-12 N.Y. State Dept. Edn., 1989, reading tchr. N.Y. State Dept. Edn., 1991. Art instr. Longfellow Elem. - Mt. Vernon C.S.D., NY, 1984—85; dist. wide humanities art coord./instr. Dist. Elem. Schools - Mt. Vernon C.S.D., Mount Vernon, NY, 1985—88; art instr. Mt. Vernon C.S.D. - Franko Mid. Sch., NY, 1988—90, Thornton Elem. Sch. - Mt. Vernon C.S.D., NY, 1990—99; adj. prof. - edn. Mercy Coll., Dobbs Ferry, NY, 1998—; dist. adminstr. for the arts Mt. Vernon C.S.D., Mount Vernon, NY, 1999—. Com. chairperson profl. devel. Mt. Vernon C.S.D., NY, 2004—. Exhibitions include Fried Eggs Mixed Media and other untitled works (Third Pl. - Rye Womans Club, RYE, NY, 2001). Adv. bd. Concordia Conservatory; coord. United Way, Mount Vernon, NY, 2004—06. Recipient Mosaic Award for Multi-Cultural Edn., Mt. Vernon C.S.D., 1992. Mem.: Phi Delta Kappa, Westchester Coalition for Arts Leadership Assn., Nat. Art Edn. Assn., N.Y.State Art Tchrs. Assoc. (sec., v.p., pres. 1998—2004, Region 7 Award for Outstanding Leadership 2001). Avocations: painting, museums, theater, exercise, travel. Home: 4 Sutton Pl Katonah NY 10536 Office: Mount Vernon City School District 165 N Columbus Ave Mount Vernon NY 10553 Home Phone: 914-232-5605; Office Phone: 914-665-5181. E-mail: aaddesso@mtvernoncsd.org.

ADDINGTON, DAVID S., federal official, lawyer; b. Washington, Jan. 22, 1957; s. Jerry and Eleanor Addington; m. Linda Werling (div.); m. Cynthia Mary Smith; 3 children. BS in Fgn. Svc., Georgetown U., 1978; JD with honors, Duke U. Sch. Law, 1981. Asst. gen. coun. CIA, Washington, 1981—84; counsel for House Com. on Intelligence and Fgn. Affairs US Ho. Reps., Washington, 1984—87; spl. asst. to pres. The White House, Washington, 1987, dep. asst. to pres., 1988; spl. asst. to sec. & dep. sec. US Dept. Def., Washington, 1989—92, gen. counsel, 1992—93; counsel Baker, Donelson, Bearman & Caldwell LLP; ptnr. Holland & Knight LLP, Washington; sr. v.p., gen. counsel Am. Trucking Assn.; counsel to v.p. The White House, Washington, 2001—05, chief of staff to v.p., 2005—. Office: The White House Rm 268 1600 Pennsylvania Ave NW Washington DC 20500-0005 Office Phone: 202-456-9089. Office Fax: 202-456-6429.*

ADDIS, ILANA BETH, obstetrician; b. 1971; BA, U. Chgo., 1992; MPH, U. Calif., 1996; MD, U. Ariz. Coll. Medicine, 1998. Cert. Obsterics and Gynecology. Assoc. dir. Divsn. Female Pelvic Medicine & Recovery Surgery; asst. prof., Obstetrics & Gynecology U. Ariz. Coll. Medicine. Mem. Planned Parenthood of Southern Ariz., Southern Ariz. Human Soc., Big Brothers/Big Sisters; vol. Shubitz refugee clinic. Named one of 40 Under 40, Tucson Bus. Edge, 2006; fellow Am. Coll. Obstetrics and Gynecology; women's health clinical rsch. fellowship, U. Calif. Mem.: Nat. Physicians Alliance, Am. Urogynecologic Assn. Office: University of Arizona College of Medicine PO Box 245017 1501 N Campbell Ave Tucson AZ 85724

ADDIS, KAY TUCKER, newspaper editor; AB in English, Coll. of William and Mary, 1970. Editor The Virginian-Pilot, Norfolk, 1996—. Office: The Virginian-Pilot 150 W Brambleton Ave Norfolk VA 23510-2075 also: Virginian Pilot P O Box 449 Norfolk VA 23501-0449

ADDIS, LAIRD CLARK, JR., philosopher, educator, musician; b. Bath, NY, Mar. 25, 1937; s. Laird Clark and Dora Ersel (Webber) A.; m. Patricia Karen Peterson, Dec. 20, 1962; children— Kristin, Karin. BA, U. Iowa, 1959, PhD, 1964; MA (Woodrow Wilson fellow), Brown U., 1960. Instr. U. Iowa, Iowa City, 1963-64, asst. prof., 1964-68, asso. prof., 1968-74, prof. philosophy, 1974—2004, chmn. dept. philosophy., 1977-85, emeritus, 2004—. Sr. Fulbright lectr. State U. Groningen, Netherlands, 1970-71 Author: (with Douglas Lewis) Moore and Ryle: Two Ontologists, 1965, The Logic of Society, 1975, Natural Signs, 1989, Of Mind and Music, 1999; contbr. articles to profl. jours. Mem. Am. Philos. Assn., Philosophy of Sci. Assn., Am. Soc. for Aesthetics, Am. Fedn. Musicians, Quad City Symphony Orch. (ret.), Soc. Humanist Philosophers. Home: 20 W Park Rd Iowa City IA 52246-2304 Office: U Iowa Dept Philosophy Iowa City IA 52242 Office Phone: 319-335-0021. Business E-Mail: laird-addis@uiowa.edu.

ADDISON, ANNE SIMONE POMEX, television director, consultant, commentator; b. Antwerp, Belgium, Dec. 2, 1927; d. Eli and Mary Deborah (Rubinstein) Cleeman; m. Joseph B. Pomex, Mar. 6, 1947 (div. Apr. 1954); 1 child, Steven M.; m. John Addison, Sept. 1, 1966. BA, Barnard Coll., 1947; MA, Columbia U., 1952. Instr. Columbia U., NYC, 1947-48; circulation dir. Ford Found., NYC, 1952-58; assoc. dir. radio Broadcasting Found. Am., NYC, 1958-60; dir., v.p. NET-WNET-13 TV, NYC, 1960—, internat. dir., 1960—; cons., producers rep., pres. Communications Internat., NYC. Cons. dept. culture U.S. Dept. of State, Washington, 1961; dir. Coll. Skills, N.Y.C.; bd. dirs. ednl. dept. Internat. Ctr. Photography, 1983, Bezalel Acad. Design and Architecture, 1994. Contbr. articles to profl. jours; producer TV dramas, dance and documentaries. Bd. dirs. Am. Friends of Hermitage, 1994. Recipient awards, medals for fostering understanding and cultural cooperation: Austria, Belgium, Holland, Israel, Italy and Brazil, Woman of Achievement award Broadcasting Industry, 1967; featured in N.Y. Times Mag., others. Mem. Am. Women in Radio and TV (1st v.p. 1972—), Am. Women in Communications, Women's Econ. Forum, NATAS, Lotos Club, Advt. of Am. Club, Paris-Am. Club. Office: 1035 5th Ave New York NY 10028-0135

ADDISON, BRIAN MICHAEL, lawyer; b. Norwalk, Ohio, Mar. 2, 1954; s. William Edward and Betty Mae (Urban) A.; m. Jeanne Lorraine Brown, Jan. 17, 1981; children: Stephen Christian, Andrew Michael, Jeremy Thomas. BA with distinction, Pa. State U., 1976, MBA, 1990; JD cum laude, Dickinson Sch. Law, 1979. Bar: Pa. 1979, U.S. Dist. Ct. (ea. dist.) Pa. 1979, U.S. Dist. Ct. (mid. dist.) Pa. 1982, U.S. Supreme Ct. 1981. Law clk. IRS, Washington, summer 1978; assoc. German, Gallagher & Murtagh, Phila., 1979-82; sr. counsel Hershey (Pa.) Foods Corp., 1982-94; ptnr. McNees, Wallace & Nurick, Harrisburg, Pa., 1994; corp. counsel DENTSPLY Internat. Inc., York, Pa., 1994-97, v.p., sec., gen. counsel, 1998—. Mediator U.S. Dist. Ct. (mid. dist.) Pa. mediation panel. Vice chmn. Conewago Zoning Hearing Bd., 1995, Dauphin County. Mem. ABA (antitrust law sect., vice chair corp. counseling com. 1993-95, editor antitrust compliance handbook, co-editor corp. counseling newsletter, bus. law sect. mem., labor and employment law sect. mem.), Pa. Bar Assn. (chair alt. dispute resolution com. 1990-93, corp., banking and bus. law sect. mem., antitrust com., corp. counsel com., labor rels. law sect. mem.), Dauphin County Bar Assn. (bd. dirs. 1991-93, chair alt. dispute resolution com. 1987-90), York County Bar Assn., York County Bar Found. (bd. dirs. 1998—, treas. 2001—), Am. Corp. Counsel Assn., Pi Sigma Alpha. Avocation: golf. Office: DENTSPLY Internat Inc Susquehanna Commerce Ctr 221 W Philadelphia St York PA 17405-0872 Office Phone: 717-845-7511. Office Fax: 717-849-4753. E-mail: baddison@dentsply.com, bmaesq@aol.com.

ADDISON, FERGUSON LOFTON LIGHTBOURNE, retired bank executive; b. Punta Gorda, Fla., Sept. 10, 1922; s. Locke and Maysoura Lofton (Hall) Addison. BA, Harvard U., 1950. Safety patrol sponsor Coconut Grove Elem. Sch., Miami, Fla., 1952—53. Svc. cons. Dun & Bradstreet, Miami, 1954—57. Feature writer: Dun's Bull. The Gold Coast Story, 1956. Pres. Shaughnessy Club, First Nat. Bank, Palm Beach, 1962. With USNR, 1942—46. Mem.: English Speaking Union, Martin County Hist. Soc., Harvard Club of Palm Beach (organizer 1962, pres. 1964—65). Achievements include receiving approval from the Fla. Dept. of State of the nomination of W.S. Lightbourn as a Great Floridian, 2000 and Frances Langford into Fla. Women's Hall of Fame, 2002. Avocations: genealogy, antiques. Home: 300 Forest Hill Blvd West Palm Beach FL 33405-4614

ADDISON, HERBERT JOHN, consulting editor, writer; b. Berkeley, Calif., Nov. 21, 1932; s. Herbert and Clara Virginia (Mason) A.; m. Geraldyne Elaine Harvey, Aug. 17, 1957; children: Bradley Thomas, Gregory James. BA, U. Calif.-Berkeley, 1958; MA, NYU, 1959. Office-personnel mgr. Thomas Y. Crowell Co., NYC, 1958-65; editor-in-chief coll. dept. Holt, Rinehart & Winston, Inc., NYC, 1965-70; v.p., gen. mgr. coll. dept. Thomas Y. Crowell Co., NYC, 1970-74; exec. editor coll. dept. John Wiley & Sons, Inc., NYC, 1974-78; gen. mgr. coll. dept. Oxford U. Press, Inc., NYC, 1978-82, v.p., exec. editor bus., 1982-2000, cons. editor,

2000—. Adj. lectr. NYU, 1977-83. Co-author: Idealized Design: Creating an Organization's Future, 2006. Trustee Adult Sch. Montclair, N.J., 1976-80; mem. Civic Conf. Com., Glen Ridge, N.J., 1974-77, 2004-07; mem. Glen Ridge Hist. Preservation Commn., 2005—. Served with U.S. Army, 1953-55. Mem. Acad. Mgmt. Home: 46 Sherman Ave Glen Ridge NJ 07028-1441 Personal E-mail: herb.addison@verizon.net.

ADDISON, JAMES W., lawyer; b. Langdale, Ala., Aug. 18, 1946; BA, Clemson U., 1968; JD, U. Va., 1971. Bar: Ga. 1971. Assoc. Hansell, Post, Brandon & Dorsey, 1971—74, Troutman Sanders LLP, Atlanta, 1974—76, ptnr., 1976—, sect. chief, real estate law, mem. exec. com. Named a Super Lawyer, Law & Politics and Atlanta Mag., 2004. Mem. ABA, State Bar Ga., Internat. Bar Assn., Phi Kappa Phi. Office: Troutman Sanders LLP Ste 5200 600 Peachtree St NE Atlanta GA 30308-2216 Office Phone: 404-885-3103. Office Fax: 404-885-3900. Business E-Mail: james.addison@troutmansanders.com.

ADDISON, JASON LAWRENCE, multifamily community development executive; b. Westmount, Que., Can., Aug. 10, 1967; came to U.S., 1995; s. Victor Robert Addison and Erla Marie Daly; m. Diane St. Laurent, July 20, 1991 (div. 1995); m. Marie-Pascale Louise Addison, Nov. 6, 1997; children: Mathieu, Olivia, Maxime, Sebastien. Civil Engring. Technologist, Dawson Coll., Montreal, Can., 1992; B in Commerce, McGill U., Montreal, Can., 1994; MSc in Real Estate Devel., MIT, 1996. Real estate sales rep. Century 21, Hamilton, Ont., Can., 1986-88, Re/Max, Hamilton, 1988-90; land surveyor Daniel Lacroix, Montreal, 1991-94; land planning coord. Intrawest Corp., Mt. Tremblant, Que., Can., 1994-95; sr. assoc. Ocwen Fin. Corp., West Palm Beach, Fla., 1996-97; project devel. mgr. Life Care Svcs. LLC, Des Moines, 1997-2000; sr. devel. dir. AvalonBay Comtys. Inc., LI, 2000—. Mem. Urban Land Inst. Avocations: scuba, alpine skiing, viticulture. Home: 25 Starrs Ridge Rd Redding CT 06896 Office Phone: 631-834-1444.

ADDISON, LINDA LEUCHTER, lawyer, writer, commentator, columnist; b. Allentown, Pa., Nov. 25, 1951; d. Marcus and Sophie Theresa (Tisch) Leuchter; m. Max M. Addison, Sept. 10, 1977; 1 child, Alexandra Leuchter Addison. BA with honors, U. Tex., 1973, JD, 1976. Bar: Tex. 1976, US Dist. Ct. (so. dist.) Tex. 1977, US Ct. Appeals (5th cir.) 1981, US Dist. Ct. (no. dist.) Tex. 2000, US Dist. Ct. (ea. dist.) Tex. 2003, US Ct. Appeals (fed. cir.) 2003, US Supreme Ct. 2003, DC, 2007. Assoc. Fulbright & Jaworski LLP, Houston, 1976—83, ptnr., 1984—, exec. com., tech. ptnr., 2002—. Expert on fed. and Tex. evidence. Author: Texas Practice Guide: Evidence, 2006; mng. editor Tex. Law Rev. 1975-76; contbr. chpt. to book, articles to profl. jours. Trustee U. Tex. Law Sch. Found., 1994-2006; mem. fed. jud. evaluation com. of Senators Hutchison and Cornyn, 1997-; exec. com. chancellor's coun. U. Tex. Sys., 1999-; bd. dirs. Holocaust Mus. Houston, 2001-, Ctr. for Houston's Future, 2007; mem. Commn. of 125, U. Tex., Austin, 2003-04, vice chmn. mission task force centennial commn., 1981-83, mem. U.S. commn. preservation Am.'s heritage abroad U.S., 2006-; bd. visitors U. Tex. M.D. Anderson Cancer Ctr., U. Cancer Found., 2006—. Named a Woman on the Move, Tex. Exec. Women, 2000, Woman to Watch, Jewish Women Internat., 2002, Woman of Yr., United Way Tex. Gulf Coast, 2006; named an Hon. Barrister, U. Tex. Sch. Law Bd. Advs., 2000, Outstanding Young Lawyer of Houston, 1984-85; named one of Am.'s Top 50 Women Litigators, Nat. Law Jour., 2001, 100 Most Influential Lawyers in Am., Nat. Law Jour., 2006, The 50 Most Influential Women Lawyers in Am., Nat. Law Jour., 2007, Tex. Go To Litigators, Tex. Lawyer, 2002, Most Fascinating People in Houston, Friends of Tex. Med. Ctr. Libr., 2001, Best Lawyers in Am., Woodard and White, 2003—, Tex. Super Lawyers, Tex. Monthly, 2003, 04, 05, 06, 07, 500 Leading Litigators in Am., Lawdragon, 2006, 500 Leading litigators in Am., 2006; named to Chambers & Ptnrs. USA, 2004, 05, 06. Fellow: Tex. Bar Found. (life; trustee 2003—), Houston Bar Found. (life), Am. Bar Found. (life); mem.: ABA, Am. Bd. Trial Advs., World Internat. Patent Orgn. (arbitration and mediation ctr. domain name panel 2002—), Am. Intellectual Property Law Assn., Am. Arbitration Assn. (internat. panel 1992—, panel of neutrals, large complex case panel), Houston Young Lawyers Assn. (chmn. cont. legal edn. com. 1977—78, bd. dirs. 1978—81, Outstanding Chmn. award), Tex. Young Lawyers Assn. (bd. dirs. 1981—83), Houston Bar Assn. (chmn. cont. legal edn. com. 1981—82, mem. jud. evalns. com. 1982—83, Pres.'s award for outstanding svc. 1982), State Bar Tex. (chmn. bar jour. com. 1988—90, adminstr. rules evidence com. 1988—90, chmn. bar jour. com. 1991—99), Tex. Law Rev. Ex-Editors Assn. (life), Abbot, Friar Soc., United Way, deTocqueville Soc., Anti-Defamation League (bd. dirs. S.W. Region 1992—94), Omicron Delta Kappa. Office: Fulbright & Jaworski LLP 1301 McKinney St Ste 5100 Houston TX 77010-3095

ADDO, CHARLES KWAME, science educator; s. James and Mary; Student, SUNY Maritime Coll., Bronx, 1977—79; BS, Mercy Coll., Dobbs Ferry, NY, 1996; MBA, L.I. U., 1999; PhD, Walden U., 2006. Cert. merchant marine officer. Shipdeck officer Golotrade Shipping and Chartering, NYC, 1981—90; adj. prof. Mercy Coll., Dobbs Ferry, 1999—. Author: Corporate Mergers and Acquisitions: A Case Study, 2000, Burdens of the Mirage Dream, 2001. Methodist. Avocation: writing.

ADDUCCI, JOSEPH EDWARD, obstetrician, gynecologist; b. Chgo., Dec. 1, 1934; s. Dominee Edward and Harriet Evelyn (Kneppreth) A.; m. Mary Ann Tiertje, 1958; children: Christopher, Gregory, Steven, Jessica, Tobias. BS, U. Ill., 1955; MD, Loyola U., Chgo., 1959. Diplomate Am. Bd. Ob-Gyn., Nat. Bd. Med. Examiners. Intern Cook County Hosp, Chgo., 1959-60; resident in ob-gyn Mt. Carmel Hosp., Detroit, 1960-64; practice medicine specializing in obstetrics and gynecology Williston, ND, 1996—; chmn. dept. ob-gyn. Mercy Hosp., 1994—2004; councillor ND Med. Assn., 2004—. Chief staff, chmn. obstetrics dept, Mercy Hosp., Williston, gov. bd., 1996, chmn. dept. surgery; clin. prof. U. ND Med. Sch., 1973—; gov. bd. Mercy Hosp. Cath. Health Corp.; mem. coun. Accreditation Coun. for Gynecologic Endoscopy, 1999—. Mem. ND Bd. Med. Examiners, 1974—, past chmn.; project dir. Tri County Family Planning Svc.; past pres. Tri County Health Planning Coun.; governing bd. Mercy Hosp., Williston, ND With Med. Corps, AUS, 1964-66. Fellow Am. Soc. Abdominal Surgeons, ACS (regent ND 1990—), Am. Coll. Obstetrics and Gynecologists (sect. chmn. ND), Internat. Coll. Surgeons (regent 1972-74, 88-89), Am. Fertility Soc., Am. Assn. Internat. Lazar Soc., Gynecol. Lataropists, ND Obstetricians and Gynecologists Soc. (pres. 1966, 76); mem. Am. Soc. for Colopscopy and Colpomicroscopy, Am. Soc. Cryosurgery, Am. Soc. Contemporary Medicine and Surgery, Am. Assn. Profl. Ob-Gyn., Pan Am. Med. Assn., ND State Med. Assn. (coun. 2004-05), Kotana Med. Soc. (pres. 2003—), Elks. Home: 1717 Main St Williston ND 58801-4244 Office: Med Ctr Dept Ob-Gyn Williston ND 58801 Office Phone: 701-572-0316. Personal E-mail: jadducci@prodigy.net.

ADDUCCI, STEVEN A., lawyer; b. 1965; BA summa cum laude, U. ND, 1987, JD with honors, 1990. Bar: DC, US Ct. Appeals, DC Cir. Ptnr. Venable LLP, Washington, DC. Mem. bd. dirs. Am. Red Cross, Alexandria, Va. Mem.: ABA, Energy Bar Assn., Fed. Bar Assn. (mem. Adminstrv. Law & Regulatory Practice and Health Law Forum Sects.), DC Bar Assn. (mem. Adminstrv. Law and Agency Practice, Environment, Energy and Natural Resources and Health Law Sects.), Phi Alpha Delta. Office: Venable LLP 575 7th St NW Washington DC 20004 Office Phone: 202-344-4361. Office Fax: 202-344-8300. E-mail: saadducci@venable.com.

ADDY, ALVA LEROY, mechanical engineer; b. Dallas, SD, Mar. 29, 1936; s. Alva Isaac and Nellie Amelia (Brumbaugh) A.; m. Sandra Ruth Turney, June 8, 1958 BS, S.D. Sch. Mines and Tech., 1958; MS, U. Cin., 1960; PhD, U. Ill., 1963. Engr. Gen. Electric Co., Cin., also Lancaster, Calif., 1958-60; prof. mech. engring. U. Ill., Urbana, 1963-98, prof. emeritus, 1998—, dir. mech. engring. lab., 1965-97, assoc. head mech. engring. dept., 1980-87, head, 1987-98. Aerodynamics cons. U.S. Army Missile Command, Redstone Arsenal, Ala., summers 1965-98; cons. U.S. Army Research Office, 1964—; cons. in high-speed fluid dynamics to indsl. firms, 1963—; vis. research prof. U.S. Army, 1976; lectr. Von Karman Inst. Fluid Dynamics, Brussels, 1968, 75, 76 Fellow ASME (hon. fellow award 2006), AIAA (assoc.), Am. Soc. for Engring. Edn. (Ralph Coates Roe award 1990); mem. Sigma Xi, Pi Tau Sigma, Sigma Tau. Home: 726 Elk Run Rd Spearfish SD 57783

ADDY, DAWN EMERSON, adult education educator, consultant; b. LI, NY, July 4, 1949; d. Robert Harold and Gloria Ann Emerson; m. Willard Fredrick Addy, May 7, 1983; children: Alison Christine Emerson Legatt, Dustin Frederick Muller. PhD, U. Minn., Mpls., 1997. Property designer Minnetonka Cmty. Theater, Minn., 1976—80; artist dir. Valley Fair, Savage, Minn., 1977—80; driver Ind. Sch. Dist. 277, Mound, Minn., 1980—87; union officer, rep. Amalgamated Transit Union, Mpls., 1982—87; program coord., faculty U. Minn. Labor Edn. Svc., Mpls., 1987—96; adult educator, coord. Graphic Arts Inst., St. Paul, 1990—96; dir., faculty Fla. Internat. U. Coll. Edn., Ctr. for Labor Rsch., Miami, 1996—. Vice chair Equal Opportunity Bd. Miami-Dade County, 1997—2002; prison programs coord. Miami Alternatives to Violence Project, 1997—; pres. Many Voices: One Cmty., Miami, 1998—; chair Fla. Internat. U. Diversity Initiative, Miami, 1998—2005; commr. Miami-Dade Commn. on Ethics and Pub. Trust, 2002—. Author: (curriculum) Workplace Cultures, 1992, (reference) Entering the Building Trades in Minnesota, 1996, (curriculum) The Diverse Workplace, 1996, (manual) South Florida Workers' Rights Manual, 2003, (monograph) Miami-Dade Mosaic, 2004. Task force mem. Minn. Govs. Literacy Task Force, St. Paul, 1987—89; vice chair Miami-Dade County Equal Opportunity Bd., 1997—2002; commr. Miami-Dade Commn. on Ethics and Pub. Trust, 2002—07; vol. chaplain Fla. State Correctional Facilities, Miami, 1997—2007. Recipient Disting. Svc. award, Minn. AFL-CIO, 1996, Labor Edn. Adv. Bd., 1996, Humanitarian award, Everglades Correctional Instn., 2004, Presdl. Excellence in Svc. award, Fla. Internat. U. Access and Equity, 2005, Excellence in Svc. award, Fla. Internat. U. Faculty Senate, 2005. Mem.: United Labor Edn. Assn. (assoc.; exec. v.p. 2004—07). Avocations: gardening, travel. Home: 14951 SW 157 Terrace Miami FL 33187 Office: Florida International University LC305 University Park Campus Miami FL 33199 Office Phone: 305-348-2615. Personal E-mail: d.addy@fiu.edu. Business E-Mail: addyd@fiu.edu.

ADDY, JO ALISON PHEARS, economist; b. Germany, May 2, 1951; d. William Phears and Paula Hubbard; m. Tralance Obuma Addy, May 25, 1979; children: Mantse, Miishe, Dwetri, Naakai. BA, Smith Coll., 1973; MBA, Adelphi U., 1975; postgrad., Stanford U., 1975—79; MPA, Harvard U., 2006. Econ. analyst Morgan Guaranty, NYC, 1973—75; economist Young Profls. Program, World Bank, Washington, 1979—80; asst. v.p., internat. economist Crocker Bank, San Francisco, 1980—85; asst. v.p., economist for money markets 1st RepublicBank, Dallas, 1985—87; prin. SEGI Internat., Dallas, 1987—91; pres. Unimed Ventures, Inc., 1991—95; mng. dir. Alsweb Bus. Advantage, 2000—; mem. adv. bd. Plebys Internat. LLC, 2003—. Lectr. in field. Docent Bowers Mus.; vice chmn. St. John's Sch. Com.; pres. Saddleback Valley chpt. Nat. Charity League. Office: 8 Palomino Trabuco Canyon CA 92679-4837 Business E-Mail: jo.addy@gmail.com.

ADELBERG, ARNOLD MELVIN, mathematics professor, researcher; b. Bklyn., Mar. 17, 1936; s. David and Evelyn (Brass) A.; m. Harriet Diamond, June 30, 1962; children: Danielle Hamill, Erica. BA, Columbia U., 1956; MA, Princeton U., 1959, PhD, 1996. Instr. Columbia U., NYC, 1959-62; instr., asst. prof., assoc. prof., prof. Grinnell (Iowa) Coll., 1962—, Myra Steele prof. math., 1991—. Chair math. dept., sci. div. several times, chmn. faculty Grinnell Coll., 1974-76. Contbr. articles to profl. jours. Mem. Math. Assn. Am., Am. Math. Soc. Avocations: bridge, chess. Home: 1930 Manor Cir Grinnell IA 50112-1136 Office: Grinnell Coll Math Dept PO Box 805 Grinnell IA 50112-0805 Office Phone: 641-269-4201. Business E-Mail: adelbe@math.grinnell.edu.

ADELI, HOJJAT, engineer, educator, computer scientist; b. Langrood, Iran, June 3, 1950; came to U.S., 1974; s. Jafar and Mokarram (Soofi) A.; m. Nahid Dadmehr, Mar. 1979; children: Amir, Anahita, Mona, Cyrus Dean. MSCE summa cum laude, U. Teheran, Iran, 1973; PhD in Civil Engring. summa cum laude, Stanford U., 1976. Asst. prof. Northwestern U., Evanston, Ill., 1977, U. Teheran, 1978-81, assoc. prof., 1981-82, U. Utah, Salt Lake City, 1982-83, Ohio State U., Columbus, 1983-88, prof., 1988—, chmn. structures faculty, 1988-91, dir. Knowledge Engring. Lab., 1994—, exec. com., dept. civil/environ. engring., geodetic sci., 1994-95. Cons. Atomic Orgn. Iran, Teheran, 1978-79, Iran Ministry Housing, Teheran, 1970-82, U.S. Army Constrn. Engring. Rsch. Lab., 1988; keynote lectrs. in Italy, 1989, Mex., 1989, Japan, 1991, China, 1992, Can., 1992, 96, Portugal, 1992, Germany, 1993, U.S., 1993, 95, 96, Morocco, 1994, Singapore, 1994, 96, Australia, 1995, Bulgaria, 1995, New Zealand, 1995, Bahrain, 1996, Lithuania, 1996, France, 1997, Bahamas, 1997; contbr. to 100 confs. Author: Interactive Microcomputer-Aided Structural Steel Design, 1988; co-author: Expert Systems for Structural Design: A New Gerneration, 1988, Parallel Processing in Structural Engineering, 1993, Machine Learning-Neural Networks, Genetic Algorithms, and Fuzzy Systems, 1995; editor: Expert Systems in Construction and Structural Engineering, 1988, Microcomputer Knowledge-Based Expert Systems in Civil Engineering, 1988, Parallel and Distributed Processing in Structural Engineering, 1988, Knowledge Engineering, vols. 1 & 2, 1990, Supercomputing in Engineering Analysis, 1992, Parallel Processing in Computational Mechanics, 1992, Advances in Design Optimization, 1994; co-editor: Mechanics Computing in the 1990's and Beyond, vols. 1 & 2, 1991; Computing and Information Technology for Architecture, Engineering and Construction, 1996, Intelligent Information Systems, 1997, editor-in-chief, founder Internat. Jour. Computer-Aided Civil & Infrastructure Engring, 1986—, Integrated Computer-Aided Engring., 1993—; editor-in-chief Heuristics: The Jour. of Knowledge Engring., 1991-93; assoc. editor Control Engring. Practice, 1993-96, Jour. Artificial Neural Networks, 1995—; mem. editorial bd., editorial adv. bd. 30 sci. engring. jours. including Neural, Parallel, and Sci. Computations, 1993—, Parallel Algorithms and Applications, 1993—, Nanobiology-Jour. Rsch. Nanoscale Living Systems, 1993, Structural Engring. Review, 1989-91, Heuristic-Jour. Knowledge Engring., 1989-91, Engring. Analysis with Boundary Elements, 1987-92, Jour. of Condition Monitoring and Diagnostic Tech., 1990-92, Knowledge Based Systems, 1988—, ASCE Jour. of Aerospace Engring., 1989—, Internat. Jour. of Computers and Applications, 1990—, Internat. Jour. of Imaging Systems and Tech., 1990—, Mechatronics, 1991—, Advances in Engring Software, 1991-95, Neurocomputing, 1991—, Jour. of Systems Engring., 1991—, Internat. Jour. of Construction Information Tech., 1992—, Chaos, Solitons and Fractals, 1991—, Structural Optimization, 1991—, Computer Applications in Engring. Edn., 1993—, Asian Jour. of Structural Engring., 1995—, Theory and Practice of Object Systems, 1995—, IASTED Control & Computers Jour., 1996—, Internat. Jour. Computational Intelligence and Organization, 1996—, Int. Jour. of Computer Systems Science and Engineering, 1995, Iranian Jour. Sci. and Tech., 1997—, Internat. Jour. Parallel and Distributed Systems and Networks, 1998—; contbr. over 275 publs. Recipient 1st degree medal of Knowledge Iran Ministry Higher Edn., 1973, Rsch. award NSF, USAF Flight Dynamics Lab., Cray Rsch., Inc., Bethlehem Steel Corp., Ohio Dept. Devel. Thomas edison Program, Am. Inst. Steel Constrn., Am. Iron and Steel Inst., U.S. Army Constrn. Engring. Rsch. Lab., Ohio Dept. Transp., Fed. Hwy. Adminstrn. Fellow World Lit. Acad., ASCE (mem. numerous coms. including aerospace structures and materials com. Aerospace divsn. 1986—, real time data acquisition com., 1988—, inelastic behavior com. engring. mechanics divsn. 1987—, com. on metrication, 1991—, advanced composite materials com. 1994—); mem. IEEE Computer Soc. (mem. numerous coms. including computational medicine com. 1988-94, pattern analysis and machine intelligence com. 1988-94, microprocessors and microcomputers com. 1988-95, distributed processing com. 1988-95, data base engring. com. 1993-95, software engring. com. 1993-95, sys. engring. 1993-95, robotics and automation com. 1993-95, design automation com. 1994-95, optical processing and switching com. 1994-95, hon. chrmn. Nat. Com. for the Preservation of Scientific and Academic Information Resources, 1995-96), AAAI, Assn. for Computing Machinery, Earthquake Engring. Rsch. Inst., Internat. Soc. for Structural and Multidisciplinary Optimization, Int. Soc for Mini and Microcomputers (bd. dirs. 1996—). Office: Ohio State U Coll Engring 470 Hitchcock Hall 2070 Neil Ave Columbus OH 43210-1226 Office Phone: 614-292-7929. E-mail: Adeli.1@osu.edu.

ADELL, HIRSCH, lawyer; arrived in US, 1937; s. Nathan and Nachama (Wager) A.; m. Judith Audrey Fuss, Feb. 8, 1963; children— Jeremiah, Nikolas, Balthasar, Valentine. Student, CCNY, 1949—52; BA, UCLA, 1955, LLB, 1963. Bar: Calif. 1963. Adminstrv. asst. to State Senator Richard Richards, 1956-60; ptnr. Warren & Adell, LA, 1963-75, Reich, Adell & Cvitan (and predecessor firm), LA, 1975—. Gen. counsel Ctrl. Valley Trust, 2003—. Served with AUS, 1953-55. Mem. ABA (labor and employment law sect.) Home: 545 S Norton Ave Los Angeles CA 90020-4610 Office: Reich Adell & Cvitan 3550 Wilshire Blvd Ste 2000 Los Angeles CA 90010-2421 Home Phone: 213-384-1295; Office Phone: 213-386-3860. Business E-Mail: hirscha@rac-law.com.

ADELMAN, HOWARD, philosophy educator; b. Toronto, Jan. 7, 1938; s. Harry Adelman and Frances (Duviner) Bromstein; m. Margaret Dorothy Smith, May 31, 1960; children: Jeremy Ian, Shonagh Eva, Rachel Esther, Eric Reuben; m. Nancy Jean Garrett, June 15, 1985; children: Daniel Jacob, Gabriel Benjamin. BA, U. Toronto, 1961, MA, 1963, PhD, 1971. From asst. prof. to assoc. prof. philosophy York U., Toronto, Ont., 1966-80, prof. North York, Ont., 1981-83, acting dean Atkinson Coll., 1973-74, dir. grad. programme in philosophy, 1980-83, 95-96, dir. Ctr. for Refugee Studies, 1986-93, chmn. senate, 1981-82. Lady Davis vis. prof. Hebrew U., 1977-78, Woodrow Wilson Sch. Princeton U., 2004; vis. fellow, Princeton U., 2003—; adj. prof. Griffith U., 2005—, rsch. prof. Key Ctr., 2006—. Author: Beds of Academe, 1970, The Holiversity, 1973, Canada and the Indochinese Refugees, 1982; co-author: Early Warning and Conflict Management: The Genocide in Rwanda, 1996; editor: Refugee Policy: Canada and the United States, 1991, Legitimate and Illegitimate Discrimination: New Issues in Migration, 1993, Immigration Policy and Practice in Canada, 2002; co-editor: African Refugees, 1994, Immigration and Refugee Policy: Australia and Canada Compared, 1994, (with John Simpson) Multiculturalism, Jews and Canandian Identity, 1996, Immigration and Refugee Policy: Canada and Europe, 1998, The Path of a Genocide: The Rwanda Crisis from Uganda to Zaire, 1998, (with Govind Rao) War and Peace in Zaire/Congo, 2004; editor Refuge, 1982-93; co-editor: (with F. Chalk) A Kiss, (with Schabas and Shalton) Encyclopedia of Genocide, Against Humanity; contbr. articles to profl. jours Harvard Harvey Harnick scholar, Queen Elizabeth II scholar, Can. Coun. Writing scholar; Grad. fellow Province of Ont.; grantee Ctrl. Mortgage and Housing Corp., Slater Found., 1980, Social Sci. Humanities Rsch. Coun., 1983, 90-93, Aktinson Coll., 1982-86, Can. Internat. Devel. Agy., 1991, UNESCO, 1991, CAn. Employment and Immigration Commn., 1982, 86-93, Ford Found., 1984, 86-89, Internat. Devel. Rsch. Commn., 1982, 92, Internat. Cath. Migration Commn., 1982, Ditchley Conf., 1983, Orgn. Econ. Coop. and Devel., 1995, Rsch. Travel grant, 1998, Rsch. grant Can. Immigration Commn., 1999, Travel grant YUFA, 2001, Rsch. grant USIP, 2001, others; recipient Gerstein award, 1996, Marvin Gelber award, 1996, European Task Force award, 1996, John Holmes Found. award, 1997, Soc. Sci. Humanities Rsch. Coun., 1997 Home: 64 Wells Hill Ave Toronto ON Canada M5R 3A8 Office: York U Philosophy Dept 4700 Keele St North York ON Canada M3J 1P3 Business E-Mail: hadelman@yorku.ca.

ADELMAN, JONATHAN REUBEN, political science professor; b. Washington, Oct. 30, 1948; s. Benjamin and Kitty (Sandler) A. BA, Columbia U., 1969, MA, 1972, M in Philosophy, 1974, PhD, 1976. Vis. asst. prof. Columbia U., NYC, 1977; vis. asst. prof. U. Ala., Tuscaloosa, 1977-78; asst. prof. Grad. Sch. Internat. Studies U. Denver, 1978-85, assoc. prof., 1985-92, prof. polit. sci., 1992—; sr. rsch. analyst Sci. Applications, Inc., Denver, 1981-87, 96—; hon. prof. People's U., Beijing, 1996—; sr. fellow Found. for the Def. of Democracies, 2001—03; hon. prof. Beijing U., 1996—. Cons., 1988-89, 96—; Lady Davis vis. assoc. prof. Hebrew U., Jerusalem, 1986; vis. fellow Soviet Acad. Scis., 1989, 90, Chinese Inst. Contemporary Internat. Rels., Beijing, 1988, People's U., Beijing, 1990, 94, 96, 97, 98, 99, 2000; vis. prof. Beijing U., 1989, 98, U. Haifa, Israel, 1990, Ctrl. European U., Budapest, 2000; vis. spkr. Soviet Acad. Scis., 1990, Barcelona (Spain) U. and Complutense U., 1990, Cambridge (Eng.) U., 1991, Nat. Taiwan U., 1998, 99; vis. lectr., Japan, India, Hong Kong, Yugoslavia, Spain, 1990, 91, Germany, 1991, Bulgaria, 1991; vis. spkr. Conf. for Study of European Ideas, Aalborg U., Denmark, 1992; vis. prof. People's U., Beijing, 1990, 97, Janus Pannonius U., Pecs, Hungary, 1981. Author: The Revolutionary Armies, 1980, Revolution, Armies and War, 1986, Prelude to the Cold War: Tsarist, Soviet and U.S. Armies in Two World Wars, 1988, Torrents of Spring: Soviet and Post Soviet Politics, 1994; co-author: The Dynamics of Soviet Foreign Policy, 1988; editor: Communist Armies in Politics, 1982, Terror and Communist Politics, 1984, Superpowers and Revolution, 1986; co-editor: Contemporary Soviet Military Affairs: The Legacy World War II, 1989; contbr. numerous articles in fieod to profl. jours. Charles Phelps Taft fellow U. Cin., 1976-77; Am. Philos. Soc. grantee, 1980. Mem. Am. Polit. Sci. Assn., Am. Assn. Advancement Slavic Studies. Democrat. Jewish. Office: U Denver Grad Sch Internat Studies Denver CO 80208-0001 Office Phone: 303-871-2548. Business E-Mail: jadelman@du.edu.

ADELMAN, KENNETH LEE, journalist, former ambassador; b. Chgo., June 9, 1946; s. Harry and Corinne (Unger) A.; m. Carol Craigle, Aug. 29, 1971; children: Jessica Craigle, Jocelyn Craigle. BA, Grinnell Coll., 1968; MA, Georgetown U., 1969, PhD, 1975. With US Dept. Commerce, Washington, 1968-70; asst. to sec. US Dept. Def., Washington, 1976-77; sr. polit. scientist Stanford Research Inst., Arlington, Va., 1977-81; amb., dep. permanent rep. to UN US Dept. State, NYC, 1981-83; dir. Arms Control and Disarmament Agy., Washington, 1983-88; exec. dir. USA for Innovation, Washington; nat. editor Washingtonian mag., 1991—. Vice chmn. Newmyer Assoc.; bd. dirs. IPAC, Newmyer Assoc.; instr. Shakespeare, Georgetown U.; mem., Def. Policy Bd. Author: African Realities, 1981, The Great Universal Embrace, 1989, Getting the Job Done, 1992; co-author (with Norman Augustine) The Defense Revolution, 1990, Shakespeare in Charge: The Bard's Guide to Leading and Succeeding on the Business Stage, 1999; contbr. numerous articles to profl. jours., newspapers and mags. Bd. dirs. IPAC. Jewish. Office: USA for Innovation PO Box 57052 Washington DC 20037*

ADELMAN, MICHAEL SCHWARTZ, lawyer; b. Cambridge, Mass., June 6, 1940; s. Benjamin Taft and Sally Frances (Schwartz) A.; m. Amy Kay, June 15, 1962; children: Robert, Jonathon. Student, Boston U., 1958—59; BA in English with honors, U. Mich., 1962, JD cum laude, 1967. Bar: Mich. 1968, Miss. 1974; cert. for death penalty post-conviction collateral relief cases. Assoc. Zwerdling, Miller, Klimist & Maurer, Detroit, 1968-69; ptnr. Philo, Maki, Ravitz, Glotta, Adelman, Cockrel & Robb, Detroit, 1969-70, Glotta, Adelman & Dinges, Detroit, 1970-74, Andalman, Adelman & Steiner P.A., Hattiesburg, Miss., 1974-86, Adelman & Steiner

P.A., Hattiesburg, 1986—2005, Michael Adelman, P.A., 2005—. Pres., bd. dirs. Miss. Ctr. Legal Svcs., Hattiesburg. Contbr. short stories: The Deputy, The Detention Center to New Renaissance. Treas. Hattiesburg Area Equal Rights Coun.; mem. Hattiesburg Biracial Adv. Com., 1987-89, chmn., 1988-89; v.p. state bd. dirs. NAMI, 2000—. Recipient Ralph T. Abernathy award Jackson County (Miss.) So. Christian Leadership Conf., 1978. Mem.: ABA, South Ctrl. Miss. Bar Assn. (pres. 2002). Address: 33 Camellia Ct Hattiesburg MS 39402-6112 Home Phone: 601-268-6605; Office Phone: 601-544-8291. E-mail: adelst33@aol.com.

ADELMAN, PAMELA BERNICE KOZOLL, education educator; b. Milw., Dec. 26, 1945; d. Harry and Rebecca (Sharp) Kozoll; m. Steven H. Adelman, June 30, 1968; children: David, Robert. BS, U. Wis., Madison, 1967; MA, Northwestern U., Evanston, Ill., 1972, PhD, 1982. Cert. tchr., Ill. Chair edn. dept. Barat Coll., Lake Forest, Ill., 1986-97; tchr. Peckham Jr. High Sch., Milw., 1967-68, Fairview Sch., Skokie, Ill., 1968-70; learning disabilities specialist Sch. Dist 28, Northbrook, Ill., 1971-77; instr., rsch. asst. Northwestern U., Evanston, Ill., 1977-80; lectr., asst. prof., then assoc. prof. Barat Coll., Lake Forest, Ill., 1977-90, prof. edn., 1990-99, dir. learning opportunities program, 1985-99, chmn. edn. dept., 1986-97, grad. dean, 1997-99, chmn. edn. dept., 1986-97; founding exec. dir. Hyde Park Day Sch., 1999—, Hyde Park Day Sch. North, Chgo., 2004—. Cons. Deerfield Pub. Schs., Ill., 1986-90; proposal reviewer State of NJ, Trenton, 1986-87; mem. Pres.'s Com. on Hiring of Disabled, 1990; higher edn. adv. coun. State of Ill.; mem. Coun. Chgo. Area Deans of Edn., 1992-99, chair, 1998-99; comprehensive sys. of pers. devel. adv. com. Ill. State Bd. Edn.; presenter in field. Co-author: Learning Disabilities, Graduate School, and Careers, 1990; co-editor: Success for College Students with Learning Disabilities, 1993; consulting editor Learning Disabilities Focus, 1989-92, Jour. Developmental Edn., 1990-98, Jour. of Postsecondary Edn. and Disabilities, 1991-95; contbr. articles to ednl. publs. Chair Sch. Dist. 107 Caucus, Highland Park, Ill., 1982; bd. dirs. Jewish Children's Bur., Chgo., 1985—, pres., 1994-96; co-author brochure for Ill. Dept. Human Rights, Chgo., 1986; bd. dirs. Jewish Fedn. Met. Chgo., 1996. Paul A. Witty fellow Northwestern U., 1978-80; grantee Lloyd A. Fry Found., 1985-86, McDonald's Corp., Chgo., 1986, Kraft Corp., Chgo., 1989, Thorn River Found., 1990—. Fellow Internat. Acad. for Rsch. in Learning Disabilities; mem. Internat. Dyslexia Assn. (bd. dirs. Ill. br. 2000—), Coun. Exceptional Children, Learning Disabilities Assn. Am., Coun. Learning Disabilities. Avocations: reading, walking, music, swimming. Office: Hyde Park Day Sch 1375 E 60th St Chicago IL 60637-2856 Office Phone: 773-834-5080. Business E-Mail: pbadelma@uchicago.edu.

ADELMAN, RICK (RICHARD LEONARD ADELMAN), professional basketball coach; b. Lynwood, Calif., June 16, 1946; m. Mary Kay Adelman; children: Kathryn Mary, Laura, R.J., David, M, Loyola Marymount U. Profl. basketball player San Diego Rockets, 1968-70, Portland Trail Blazers, Oreg., 1970-73, asst. coach, 1983-89, head coach, 1989-94; profl. basketball player Chgo. Bulls, 1973—75, New Orleans Jazz, 1975, Kans. City-Omaha Kings, 1975; head coach Chemeketa CC, Salem, Oreg., 1975-83, Golden State Warriors, Oakland, Calif., 1995-97, Sacramento Kings, 1998—2006, Houston Rockets, 2007—. Office: Houston Rockets 1510 Polk St Houston TX 77002*

ADELMAN, ROBERT PAUL, retired construction executive, lawyer; b. NYC, Dec. 7, 1930; s. Saul and Eva (Ochs) A.; m. Renee Gratum, June 7, 1953 (dec. Apr. 1998); children: Michael, Susan, John; m. Judith A. Turner, Jan. 9, 1999. BA, Columbia U., 1952, JD, 1954. Bar: N.Y. 1954, U.S. Supreme Ct. 1960. Assoc. Winthrop, Stimson, Putnam & Roberts, NYC, 1956-64; with Celanese Corp., NYC, 1964-71; v.p., treas., gen. counsel Calina Industries, Inc., NYC, 1971-73; chief fin. officer Rockefeller Group, Inc., NYC, 1975-84; chmn., chief exec. officer, pres. Rogers Group, Inc., Nashville, 1984-88, chmn., 1988-92, vice chmn., 1992—2001, cons. to the pres. and CEO, 2001—04. Mem. Fin. Execs. Inst., 1973-84, Conf. Bd. Exec. Coun., 1985-90; trustee No. European Oil Royalty Trust, 1987—, chmn. audit com., 1995-2006, mng. trustee, 2006—; bd. dirs. CPRC Group LLC, 2004-. Treas. and chief fin. officer NY State Urban Devel. Corp., 1973-75; trustee The Jackson Lab., 1981—. Served with US Army, 1954-56, instr. Corps of Cadets US Mil. Acad., West Point, NY. Mem. University Club (N.Y.C.), Amelia Island Club. Avocations: sailing, golf. Home: 9 Fox Tail Rd Amelia Island FL 32034-6610

ADELMAN, STANLEY JOSEPH, lawyer; b. Devils Lake, ND, May 20, 1942; s. Isadore Russell Adelman and Eva Claire (Robins) Stoller; m. Mary Beth Petchaft, Jan. 30, 1972; children: Laura E., Sarah A. BS, U. Wis., 1964, JD, 1967. Bar: Ill. 1967, U.S. Dist. Ct. (no. dist.) Ill. 1967, Wis. 1968, U.S. Ct. Appeals (7th cir.), U.S. Dist. Ct. (ea. dist.) Wis. 1979, U.S. Supreme Ct. 1982, U.S. Ct. Appeals (10th cir.) 1984, U.S. Ct. Appeals (fed. cir.) 1987. Assoc. Sonnenchein, Carlin, Nath & Rosenthal, Chgo., 1967-75, ptnr., 1975-85, DLA Piper US LLP, Chgo., 1985—, co-chmn. litigation dept., 1985-91, 96-97, profl. responsibility ptnr., 1992-94, mem. mgmt. com., 1985-97, co-chmn. complex litigation practice group, 1997-98, pro bono ptnr., 2003—. Bd. dirs. Legal Assistance Found., Chgo., 1982—83. Fellow Nat. Inst. Trial Advocacy; mem. Chgo. Bar Assn., Chgo. Coun. Lawyers, Am. Inns of Ct. (pres. Markey/Wigmore chpt. 1998-99), Lawyers Club Chgo., Order of Coif. Jewish. Home: 115 Crescent Dr Glencoe IL 60022-1303 Office: DLA Piper US LLP 203 N La Salle St Ste 1900 Chicago IL 60601-1210 Home Phone: 847-835-1343; Office Phone: 312-368-4095. Business E-Mail: stanley.adelman@dlapiper.com.

ADELMAN, STEVEN ALLEN, chemist, educator; b. Chgo., July 4, 1945; s. Hyman and Sarah Adelman; m. Barbara Stolberg, May 13, 1974 BS, Ill. Inst. Tech., 1967; PhD, Harvard U., 1972. Postdoctoral fellow MIT, Cambridge, 1972-73; postdoctoral fellow U. Chgo., 1973-74; asst. prof. chemistry Purdue U., West Lafayette, Ind., 1975-77, assoc. prof., 1977-82, prof., 1982—. Cons. Exxon Rsch. Co., Los Alamos Nat. Lab.; vis. prof. U. Paris, 1985; nominator 1994 Nobel Prize in Chemistry, Royal Swedish Acad. Scis.; Renaissance Weekend Participant, 2003. Contbr. articles to profl. jours.and chapters to books. Vol. U.S. Peace Corp., Ankara, Turkey, 1969-70. Fellow Alfred P. Sloan Found., 1976-78, Guggenheim Found., 1982-83; NSF grantee, 1976—; named Outstanding Sr. in Chemistry, Am. Inst. Chemistry, 1967. Fellow Am. Phys. Soc.; mem. AAAS, Am. Chem. Soc., Am. Statis. Assn., Math. Assn. Am., Sigma Xi. Achievements include creating the mathematical and physical foundation for studying chemical reaction dynamics on solid surfaces and in liquid solution; developing the theory of fast variable/slow bath irreversible motion; making basic contributions to the theory of friction on molecules and to the theory of liquid phase vibrational energy relaxation. Avocations: long-distance running, strength training, turkish language and literature. Home: 3037 Courthouse Dr W Apt 2C West Lafayette IN 47906-1035 Office: Purdue U Dept Chemistry 560 Oval Dr West Lafayette IN 47907-2084 Office Phone: 765-494-5277. Business E-Mail: saa@purdue.edu.

ADELMAN, STEVEN HERBERT, lawyer; b. Dec. 21, 1945; s. Irving and Sylvia (Cohen) A.; m. Pamela Bernice Kozoll, June 30, 1968; children: David, Robert. BS, U. Wis., Madison, 1967; JD, DePaul U., 1970. Bar: Ill. 1970, U.S. Dist. Ct. (no. dist.) Ill. 1970, U.S. Ct. Appeals (7th cir.) 1975. Ptnr. Keck, Mahin & Cate, Chgo., 1970-93, Lord, Bissell & Brook, Chgo., 1993—. Bd. dirs. Bur. Jewish Employment Problems, Chgo., 1983—, pres. 1991, 92; employment relations com. Chgo. Assn. Commerce and Industry, 1982-90. Contbr. chpts. to books, articles to profl. jours. Bd. dirs. Victory Gardens Theater, 2004—. Named one of leading labor and employment lawyers in Ill., Leading Lawyers Network; recipient, Leading Atty. Network. Fellow Coll. Labor and Employment Lawyers; mem. ABA (Silver key award 1969), Chgo. Bar Assn. (chmn. labor and employment law com. 1988-89), Ill. State Bar Assn., Chgo. Coun. Lawyers, Decalogue Soc. Office: Lord Bissell & Brook 111 S Wacker Dr Chicago IL 60606 E-mail: sadelman@lordbissell.com.

ADELMAN, WILLIAM J., JR., biophysicist; b. Mt. Vernon, NY, Jan. 29, 1928; s. William Joseph Adelman and Helen Emma Carlock; m. Jean Alma Mayo, Sept. 3, 1951; children: Everett M., John W., Willa J. BS, Fordham U., 1950; MS, U. Vt., 1952; PhD, U. Rochester, 1955. Aviation physiologist Sch. Aviation Medicine, Randolph AFB, 1955—56; instr. U. Buffalo (N.Y.) Sch. Medicine, 1956—57, asst. prof. physiology, 1957—59; neurophysiologist Lab. Biophysics Nat. Inst. Neurol. Diseases and Blindness, NIH, Bethesda, Md., 1959—62; prof. physiology dept. physiology U. Md. Sch. Medicine., Balt., 1962—72; chief lab. biophysics Nat. Inst. Neurol., Communicative Disorders, and Stroke, NIH, Bethesda, 1972—89. Treas. Soc. Gen. Physiology; trustee Marine Biol. Lab., Woods Hole, Mass. Editor: Biophysics and Physiology Excitable Membranes, 1971; contbr. articles to profl. jours.; newspaper art critic:. Recipient Spl. Recognition award, USPHS, 1985; fellow, AAAS, 1965; grantee in field; spl. fellow, NIH, 1969. Avocation: fine art. Home: 160 Locust St Falmouth MA 02540-2674

ADELMAN, WILLIAM JOHN, retired academic administrator, industrial relations specialist; b. Chgo., July 26, 1932; s. William Sidney and Annie Teresa (Goan) A.; m. Nora Jill Walters, June 26, 1952; children: Michelle, Marguerite, Marc, Michael, Jessica. Student, Lafayette Coll., 1952; BA, Elmhurst Coll., 1956; MA, U. Chgo., 1964. Tchr. Whitecross Sch., Hereford, Eng., 1956-57, Jefferson Sch., Berwyn, Ill., 1957-60, Morton High Sch., Berwyn, 1960-66; mem. faculty dept. labor and indsl. relations U. Ill., Chgo., 1966-91, prof., 1978-91, prof. emeritus, 1991—; coordinator Chgo. Labor Edn. Program, 1981-87. Lectr. Road Scholar Program, Ill. Humanities Coun., 1997. Author: Touring Pullman, 1972, Haymarket Revisited, 1976, Pilsen and the West Side, 1981; writer: film Packingtown U.S.A., 1968; narrator: Palace Cars and Paradise: Pullman's Model Town, 1983' appeared on PBS Am. Experience, City of the Century, 2003, PBS History Detective, 2007. Bd. dirs. Chgo. Regional Blood Program, 1977-80; mem. Ill. State Employment Security Adv. Bd., 1974-75; Democratic candidate U.S. Ho. of Reps. from 14th dist. Ill., 1970; organizer Haymarket Centennial Events, 1986; chmn. adv. bd. Jane Addams' Hull House, 1991-99; mem. adv. bd. Maxwell St. Mus., 2001—; mem. Haymarket Monument Adv. Panel, 2002-04. Ill. Humanities Council grantee, 1977; German Marshall Fund U.S. grantee, 1977; recipient Tradition of Excellence award Oak Park/River Forest H.S., 1993, Eugene V. Debs award Midwest Labor Press assn., 1995. Mem. Ill. Labor History Soc. (founding mem., v.p., Union Hall of Honor 1993), Am. Fedn. Tchrs., Doris Humphrey Soc. (v.p. 1990—). Unitarian Universalist. Home and Office: 613 S Highland Ave Oak Park IL 60304-1524

ADELSBERG, HARVEY, hospital administrator; b. Bronx, NY, Aug. 5, 1931; s. Joseph and Becky (Rindner) Adelsberg; m. Miriam Levine, June 20, 1964; children: Jonathan, Risa, Seth. BA, NYU, 1953, MPA, 1960, postgrad., 1960—65. Adminstrv. resident Beth David Hosp., NYC, 1953—54; adminstrv. asst. Met. Jewish Geriatric Center, Bklyn., 1954—58; asst. dir. Kingsbrook Jewish Med. Center, Bklyn., 1958—61, Hosp. for Joint Diseases, NYC, 1961—64; exec. dir. Theresa Grotta Center for Restorative Svcs., Caldwell, NJ, 1964—70; asst. dir. Mt. Sinai Hosp., NYC, 1970—72; cons. med. care and svcs. to aged Fedn. Jewish Philanthropies, NYC, 1972—74; exec. dir. Daus. of Miriam Center for Aged, Clifton, NJ, 1974—76, exec. v.p., 1977—95, exec. v.p. emeritus, 1996; adj. prof. MBA health sys. mgmt. program Fairleigh Dickinson U., Coll. of Bus., 2002—. Adj. asst. prof. health care adminstrn. Bernard M. Baruch Coll., Mt. Sinai Sch. Medicine, CUNY, 1973—, U. Medicine and Dentistry, N.J., 1995; mem. adv. com. Rutgers U., 1969—; mem. adj. prof. N.J. Grad. Sch. Pub. Health, 1995; cons. Consulting Svcs. Inst., 1995; mem. N.J. Licensing Bd. for Nursing Home Adminstrs., 1969—, vice chmn., 1969—77; mem. Adv. Council on Aging, Livington, NJ, 1977—; sr. exec. fellow long term care studies MBA Health Sys. Mgmt. Program Fairleigh Dickinson U., 2002; sr. exec. fellow long term care studies. V.p. Solomon Schechter Day Sch. of Essex and Union, 1980—; trustee Synagogue of Suburban Torah Center, Livingston, 1978—; v.p. Temple Beth Shalom, Livingston, 1970—71, 1973, trustee, 1968—70, 1975—; mem. governing com. Camp Ramah, Wingdale, NY, 1979—; exec. bd. Jewish Communal Svc. Assn., 1993—; trustee Hosp. and Council Met. N.J., 1967—70, Health and Hosp. Council So. N.Y., 1972—74, N.J. Assn. Non-Profit Homes for Aging, 1976—, Jewish Cmty. Housing Corp. , Paterson, NJ, 1975—; trustee tng. Dist. 1199J, 1990; bd. govs. Greater N.Y. Hosp. Assn., 1972—74; agt. Daus. of Miriam Found., 1984. Fellow: Am. Geriatric Soc., Am. Coll. Nursing Home Adminstrs., Am. Coll. Hosp. Adminstrs.; mem.: APHA, Am., N.J. hosp. assns., B'nai B'rith (v.p. 1960—64), Hosp. Exec. Club. Home and Office: 27 Tuxedo Dr Livingston NJ 07039-2452 Office Phone: 973-992-0498. Personal E-mail: harveyadelsberg@aol.com.

ADELSMAN, JEAN (HARRIETTE ADELSMAN), newspaper editor; b. Indpls., Oct. 21, 1944; d. Joe and Beatrice Irene (Samuel) A. BS in Journalism, Northwestern U., 1966, MS in Journalism, 1967. Copy editor Chgo. Sun-Times, 1967-75, fin. news editor, 1975-77, entertainment editor, 1977-80, asst. mng. editor features, 1980-84; now mng. editor Daily Breeze, Torrance, Calif. Office: Daily Breeze 5215 Torrance Blvd Torrance CA 90503-4077

ADELSON, EDWARD, physicist, educator, musician; b. Bklyn., Aug. 19, 1934; s. Barnet and Sarah (Strongin) A.; m. Juliane A.W. Riedel, Aug. 5, 1961 (div. June 1982). BA, NYU, 1956; postgrad. (Woodrow Wilson fellow), Eastman Sch. Music, 1956-57; MS, Ohio State U., 1965, PhD, 1974. Prin. physicist Battelle Mem. Inst., Columbus, Ohio, 1957-71; lectr. Ohio State U., Columbus, 1974-88, acad. program specialist, 1988—. Cons. in field. Author: Student Companion for Reese's University Physics, vol. 2, 2001; editor test books; contbr. articles to profl. jours. Organist, choirmaster emeritus St. Alban's Episcopal Ch., Bexley, Ohio. Mem.: AAAS, Am. Guild Organists, Am. Assn. Physics Tchrs., Am. Phys. Soc., Chrichton Club, Sigma Pi Sigma, Phi Beta Kappa. Home: 6384 Falkirk Pl Columbus OH 43229-2045 Office: Ohio State U Smith Lab Columbus OH 43210

ADELSON, EDWARD H., vision science educator; BA in Physics and Philos., Yale U., New Haven, 1974; PhD in Exptl. Psych., U. Mich., 1979. Postdoctoral fellow NYU, 1979—81; staff scientist RCA Labs., 1981—86; assoc. prof. vision sci. Media Lab. MIT, Cambridge, Mass., 1987—94, assoc. prof. vision sci. dept. brain and cognitive scis., 1994—97, prof., 1997—. Contbr. articles to sci. jours. Recipient Marquis award, U. Mich., 1980, Adolph Lomb medal, Optical Soc. Am., 1984, Rank prize in opto-electronics, 1992, Longuet-Higgins award for outstanding contbns. to computer vision that have withstood the test of time, IEEE, 2005. Mem.: NAS. Office: Dept Brain and Cognitive Scis MIT 43 Vassar St Bldg 46-4115 Cambridge MA 02139

ADELSON, JAY, Internet company executive; b. Sept. 7, 1970; BS in Comm., Boston Univ. Head, network ops. Netcom, 1993—96; founder Equinix; co-founder, ops. mgr., Palo Alto Internet Exchange Digital Equipment Corp., 1996—2003; co-founder, CEO Digg, 2004—; co-founder, chmn. Revision3 Corp., 2005—. Named one of 50 Who Matter Now, Business 2.0, 2007. Office: Digg Inc 3rd Fl 135 Mississippi St San Francisco CA 94107 Office Phone: 415-436-9638.*

ADELSON, KENNETH I., sports association executive; m. Lauren Adelson; children: Richard, Michael. BS in Broadcasting, U. Fla., Gainesville. Sportscaster, sports dir. WECT-TV, Wilmington, NC, 1982; sports anchor, prodr. WVIT-TV, Hartford, Conn., KTVK-TV, Phoenix, KTVX-TV, Salt Lake City; prodr. NBA Entertainment, Secaucus, NJ, 1990, sr. prodr., dir. prodn. sales, mktg. and PSA grp., sr. v.p. prodn., mng. dir., sr. v.p. prodn. ops. and planning. Office: NBA Entertainment Olympic Tower 645 5th Ave Fl 10 New York NY 10022-5986*

ADELSON, LAWRENCE SETH, electronics executive, lawyer; b. San Francisco, Mar. 28, 1950; s. Joseph Bernard Adelson and Edna Sylvia (Kamener) Fraiberg; m. Pamela Joan Williams, Dec. 1, 1984; 1 child, Emily. BA, U. Mich., 1972; JD, Harvard U., 1975. Bar: Ill. 1977, U.S. Dist. Ct. (no. dist.) Ill. 1977, U.S. Ct. Appeals (7th cir.) 1980. Law clk. to judge U.S. Ct. Appeals for 9th Cir., Honolulu, 1975-76; assoc. Isham Lincoln & Beale, Chgo., 1976-85; gen. counsel CMC Real Estate Corp., Chgo., 1985-90, v.p., 1987-90, v.p., gen. counsel, 1988-90, CMC Heartland Ptnrs., Chgo., 1990—. V.p. and gen. counsel Chgo.-Milw. Corp., 1988—, Heartland Tech., Inc., 1998—; chmn., CEO Heartland Tech., Inc., 2002—; CEO Heartland Ptnrs., 2002—. Editor Harvard Law Rev., 1973-75. Pres., bd. dirs. Gus Giordano Jazz Dance; pres. West Ctrl. Assn., 1997-2000. Mem. Chgo. Bar Assn. (chmn. law week subcom. 1982, neighborhood outreach project 1983-84, membership com. 1987-88), Lawyers Club. Jewish. Office: Heartland Tech Inc 303 N Jefferson Ct, Ste 305 Chicago IL 60661

ADELSON, P. DAVID, pediatric neurosurgeon; b. Queens, NY, Aug. 27, 1960; m. Barbara, May 2, 1994. BA, Columbia U., 1982, MD, 1986. Cert. Am. Bd. Neurol. Surgeons, Am. Bd. Pediatric Neurol. Surgery. Resident UCLA, 1986-93; fellow Boston Children's Hosp., 1993-94; asst. prof. then A. Leland Albright Prof. of Neurol. Surgery Dept. Neurol. Surgery, U. Pitts., 1994—, vice-chmn. Rsch., dir. Walter Copeland Neurosurgical Rsch. Lab.; dir. Surgical Epilepsy Ctr. U. Pitts.; dir. Brachial Plexus and Peripheral Nerve Ctr. and Clinic Children's Hospital of Pitts.; dir. Pediatric Neurotrauma Children's Hospital Pitts. V.p. Congress of Neurol. Surgeons; chair AANS/CNS Sect. on Neurotrauma and Critical Care; co-chair AANS/CNS Jt. Guidelines Com.; mem. exec. com. Think First Found.; editl. bd. Neurosurgery News, Self-Assessment in Neurol. Surgery (SANS), Neurosurgery, CNS Website; ad hoc reviewer Brain Research, Child's Nervous System, Epilepsia, Journal of Neurocritical Care, Journal of Neurotrauma, Pediatric Neurosurgery. Named one of The Best Doctors in Am.; recipient Young Investigators Award, Brain Injury Assn., Clinical Investigation Award, Congress of Neurol. Surgeons, Outstanding Physician Award. Mem. Am. Assn. Neurol. Surgeons, Interant. Neurotrauma Soc., Soc. Neurosci., Congress Neurol. Surgeons, Epilepsy Found. Western Pa., Allegheny County Med. Soc., Am. Acad. Pediatrics, Am. Coll. Surgeons, Am. Epilepsy Soc., Am. Soc. Pediatric Neurosurgeons, Hydrocephalus Assn., Internat. Soc. Pediatric Neurosurgery, Jt. Sect. on Pediatric Neurosurgery, Jt. Sect. on Neurotrauma and Critical Care, Nat. Neurotrauma Soc., Pa. Med. Soc., Sect. on Injury, Violence and Poisoning Prevention, Soc. of U. Neurosurgeons, Spina Bifida Assn. of Greater Pitts., U. Pitts. Epilepsy Ctr. Office: Children's Hosp Pitts 3705 5th Ave Pittsburgh PA 15213-2524 Office Phone: 412-692-6347. Business E-Mail: david.adelson@chp.edu.*

ADELSON, SHELDON GARY, hotel and gaming company executive; b. Dorchester, Mass., Aug. 4, 1933; m. Miriam Ochshorn, 1991; children: Adam Arthur, Matan Sarel. Student, CCNY. Paperboy; mortgage broker; investment adv.; fin. cons.; chmn., CEO Interface Group Inc., Needham, Mass., 1974; chmn., CEO, treas. Las Vegas Sands, Inc., 1989—; chmn., CEO Las Vegas Sands Corp., 2004—; founder COMDEX Trade Shows, 1991—95, Sands Expo & Convention Ctr., 1990—. Venetian Resort-Hotel-Casino, 1991—, Sands Macau, 2004—. Guest spkr. U. New Haven, Harvard Bus. Sch., Columbia Bus. Sch., Tel Aviv U., Babson Coll. Mem., US Holocaust Meml. Coun. US Holocaust Meml. Mus., Washington. Named one of Forbes Richest Americans, 2006, Forbes World's Richest People, 2005, 2007. Jewish. Office: Venetian Resort Hotel Casino 3355 Las Vegas Blvd S Las Vegas NV 89109 Office Phone: 702-414-1000. Office Fax: 702-414-4884.*

ADELSPERGER, JENNIFER, forensic scientist; d. James and Jody Adelsperger. BS in Biology, Temple U., Phila., 2003; postgrad. in forensic molecular biology, George Washington U., Washington, 2007. Tech. rsch. asst. Brigham and Women's Hosp., Boston, 2003—05; forensic scientist I Armed Forces DNA Identification Lab., Rockville, Md., 2006—. Contbr. articles to profl. jours. Mem.: Am. Acad. Forensic Scis. Office: Armed Forces DNA Identification Lab 1413 Research Blvd Rockville MD 20850 Home Phone: 610-653-4878; Office Phone: 301-319-0255. Business E-Mail: jen.adelsperger@us.army.mil.

ADELSTEIN, JONATHAN STEVEN, commissioner; b. Rapid City, SD, 1962; m. Karen Adelstein; children: Adam, Lexi. BA with distinction, Stanford U., MA; attended, Harvard U. Tchg. fellow Harvard U.; tchg. asst. Stanford U., comm. cons. grad. sch. bus.; staff mem. US Senate, sr. legis. aide to Senator Tom Daschle, 1995—2002; commr. FCC, 2002—. Mem.: Nat. Acad. Social Ins., Pi Sigma Alpha, Phi Kappa Phi. Office: FCC 445 12th St SW Rm 8-A302 Washington DC 20554 Office Phone: 202-418-2300.

ADELSTEIN, S(TANLEY) JAMES, radiologist, educator; b. NYC, Jan. 24, 1928; s. George and Belle (Schild) Adelstein; m. Mary Charlesworth Taylor, Sept. 20, 1957; children: Joseph Burrows, Elizabeth Dunster. BS, MS, MIT, Cambridge, 1949, PhD in Biophysics, 1957; MD, Harvard U., Cambridge, 1953. Med. house officer Peter Bent Brigham Hosp., Boston, 1953-54, sr. asst. resident physician, 1957-58, chief resident, 1959-60; fellow Howard Hughes Med. Inst., 1957-58, Henry A. and Camilus Christian fellow, 1959-60; Moseley travel fellow Harvard U. Med. Sch., Boston, 1958-59, instr. anatomy, then asst. prof., 1961-68, assoc prof. radiology, 1968-72, prof., 1972-89, Paul C. Cabot prof. med. biophysics, 1989-97, prof. pathology, Daniel S. Tosteson univ. prof., 1997—2003, Paul C. Cabot disting. prof. med. biophysics, 2003—, dean for acad. program, 1978-97. Dir. Nat. Coun. for Radiation Protection Measurements, 1980—2002, v.p., 1982—2002, hon. v.p., 2002—; cons. Med. Found. fellow, 1960—63; Walter Dandy lectr. Johns Hopkins U., 1996; John Cameron lectr. U. Wis., 1998; Laurensten Taylor lectr. Nat. Coun. for Radiatide Photection, 2000; radiation rsch. bd. NAS, 1999—2002, chair, 2002—05, nuc. and radiol. studies bd., vice chair, 2005—; biol. and environ. rsch. adv. com. Dept. Energy, 2001—; L. Taylor lectr. Nat. Coun. for Radiation Protection, 2000; rsch. coll. adv. bd. U. Tasmania, 2003—. Mem. editl. bd.: Investigative Radiology, 1972—80, Postgrad. Radiology, Radiology Rsch., 1990—94; editor (assoc. editor): Jour. Nuc. Medicine, 1975—81; contbr. articles to profl. jours. Trustee Am. Bd. Nuc. Medicine, 1972—78; mem. fellowship adv. com. Whitaker Found. , 1991—97. Recipient Career Devel. award, NIH, 1965—68; fellow Nat. Found., MIT, 1953—57, Fogarty Sr. Internat., 1976. Fellow: AAAS, Am. Coll. Nuc. Physicians; mem.: Inst. Medicine, Boylston Med. Soc., Soc. Nuc. Medicine (trustee 1970—74, Blumgart award 1983, Aebersold award 1986, Dr. Hevesy award 1999), Radiation Rsch. Soc. (councillor 1975—78), Assn. Radiation Rsch., Biophys. Soc., Am. Chem. Soc., Alpha Omega Alpha, Tau Beta Pi, Sigma Xi. Office: Harvard Med Sch 25 Shattuck St Boston MA 02115-6027

ADELSTEIN, STEVEN PAUL, lawyer; b. Bellingham, Wash., June 28, 1949; s. Melvin S. and Shirley A. Adelstein; m. Deborah F. Sawyer, Jan. 15, 1972; children: Aaron B., Rena L. JD, Gonzaga U., Spokane, Wash., 1974. Bar: Wash. 1974. Ptnr. Adelstein, Sharpe & Serka LLP, Bellingham, 1974—. Del. Downtown Devel., Bellingham; chair Citizen's Adv. Com.

Sch. Dist. 501, Bellingham, 1990; former dir. and pres. Whatcom Vol. Ctr., Bellingham, 1998—2000; dir. Mt. Baker Theater, Bellingham, 1999; dir. and pres. Interfaith Coalition, Bellingham; trustee Whatcom CC, 2006—; dir. St. Luke's Found., Bellingham, 2006—, We. Wash. U. Found., Bellingham. Mem.: Whatcom County Bar Assn. (pres. 1991), Wash. State Bar Assn., Wash. State Trial Lawyers, Am. Trial Lawyers Assn., Rotary (dir. 2007—). Avocations: tennis, skiing. Office: Adelstein Sharpe & Serka LLP 400 N Commercial Bellingham WA 98225 Office Phone: 360-671-6565. Office Fax: 360-647-8148; Home Fax: 360-647-8148. Business E-Mail: sadelstein@adelstein.com.

ADERHOLT, ROBERT B., congressman, lawyer; b. Haleyville, Ala., July 22, 1965; m. Caroline McDonald; children: Mary Elliot, Robert Hayes. BA, Birmingham Southern U., 1987; JD, Samford U. Cumberland School of Law, 1990. City judge, Haleyville, Ala., 1992—96; asst. legal advisor to Al. gov., 1995—96; mem. U.S. Congress from 4th Ala. dist., 1997—, mem. appropriations com., vice chmn. military quality of life subcom., mem. transp., treasury subcom., housing and urban develop. subcom. & interior and environ. subcom. Mem. Helsinki Commn. on Security and Cooperation in Europe. Republican. Office: US Ho of Reps 1433 Longworth Bldg Washington DC 20515-0104 also: Dist Office 247 Carl Elliott Bldg 1710 Alabama Ave Jasper AL 35501*

ADERMAN, OSCAR DARRELL, retired music educator; s. Oscar Dearl and Anna Marie Aderman; m. Billie Marion Wilma Hope, Aug. 25, 1951; children: Sheila Aderman Squires, Carmala Jean, Tamara Hope Aderman Smith, Mark Allan. MusB, U. Wis., Madison, 1954, MS in Music Edn., 1971. Music supr. Shell Lake Pub. Schs., Wis., 1954—72; founder, dir. Indianhead Arts and Edn. Ctr. U. Wis., Shell Lake, 1968—95, regional arts dir. Extension, 1973—90, dir. Extension Rhinelander (Wis.) Sch. Arts, 1981—82, prof. Madison, Wis., 1982—95, prof. emeritus, 1995—. String adv. bd. mem. Wis. Sch. Music Assn., Madison, 1977, state chmn., continuing edn., Shell Lake, 1989—93, Madison, 1989—93; exec. bd. mem. Wis. Alliance Arts Edn., Madison, 1973—76; state pres. Nat. Assn. Jazz Educators, Madison, 1978—80; music adv. panel mem. Wis. Arts Bd., Madison, 1973—75. Course designer Bi-Lingual/Bi-Cultural Tribal Workshop; contbg. editor: Foreward Freemasonry, 1995. Mem. Shell Lake C. of C., 1955; adv. Shell Lake Devel. Corp., 1967; mem. Shell Lake Econ. Devel. Corp., 1985, Wis. Alliance for Arts Edn., 1972—78; founder U. Wis., Extension Indianhead Arts & Edn. Ctr.; Grand Master Wis. Masonic Lodge, Wis., 1984—85; coun. mem. Salem Luth. Ch., Shell Lake, Wis., 1957—79, com. chair, SHOUT Team, 1998; past master and adv. Shell Lake-Spooner Masonic Lodge #221, 1963. Recipient Citizen of Yr., Shell Lake C. of C., 1984, Order of Purple Cross, Western Wis. Masonic York Rite Coll. #85, 1993, 33rd Degree, Masonic Scottish Rite, 1995, U. Wis. award of Excellence, U. Wis., Extension, 1996, Internat. Recognition, U. Wis., Extension Indianhead Arts & Edn. Ctr., 1996, Disting. Svc. award, Wis. Music Educators Assn., 1997, Meritorious Svc. award, Grand Lodge of Wis., 1997, Spring Scottish Class Name O. Darrell Aderman 33rd Degree, Scottish Rite Valley Eau Claire, 2003, Disting. Svc. award, Internat. Assn. Jazz Educators, 2003. Mem.: NRA, Music Educators Nat. Conf., Wis. Sch. Music Assn., Internat. Assn. Jazz Educators, Music Edn. Nat. Conf., U. Wis. Alumni Assn. (pres. N.W. Wis. 1955, 1971), Ducks Unlimited, Masonic Philalathes Soc., Wis. Masonic Lodge Rsch., Masonic Red Cross Constantine (past soverign 1990), Masonic Lodge, F&AM (grand master 1984—85), Masonic Societas Rosicruciana In Civitatibus Foederatis (chief adept 2001), Epsilon Sigma Phi, Coop. Ext. Frat., Phi Beta Mu, Nat. Bandmasters Frat. Luth. Avocations: hunting, woodworking, fishing, music. Home and Office: 522 W Lake Dr Shell Lake WI 54871 Personal E-mail: opaoma@charter.net.

ADERSON, SANFORD M., lawyer; b. Pitts., July 15, 1949; s. Sanford C. and Marjorie S. (Stern) A.; m. Leslie S. Sertner, Aug. 12, 1972; children: Benjamin, Jonathan. BSBA, Boston U., 1971, JD, 1974. Bar: Pa. 1974, U.S. Dist. Ct. (we. dist.) Pa. 1974, U.S. Tax Ct. 1978, U.S. Ct. Appeals (3d cir.) 1986. Law clk. to judge Ct. of Common Pleas, Pitts., 1974-83; with Aderson, Frank, Steiner & Blechman, Pitts., 1976-2001; of counsel Strassburger, McKenna, Gutnick & Potter, Pitts., 2000—; pres. Luttner Fin. Group, Pitts., 2001—. Bd. dirs. Jewish Cmty. Ctr. of Pitts., 1993-98; chmn. bd. Make-A-Wish, 2004-05—; mem. bus. com. Pitts. Cultural Trust, 2001—. Mem.: ABA, Allegheny County Bar Assn. (bankruptcy sect. mem. of coun. 1993—98), Pa. Bar Assn., Westmoreland Country Club (bd. dirs. 1987—, pres. 2002—03). Office: Strassburger McKenna Gutnik & Potter 4 Gateway Ctr 15th Fl Pittsburgh PA 15222 Office Phone: 412-391-6700. Business E-Mail: saderson@smgpdan.com.

ADESIDA, ILESANMI, engineering educator, researcher, dean; BS, U. Calif., Berkeley, MS in Elec. Engring., PhD in Elec. Engring., 1979. Prof. Dept. Elec. and Computer Engring. U. Ill., Urbana-Champaign, Donald Biggar Willett prof. engring., dir. Ctr. for Nanoscale Sci. and Tech., dir. Micro and Nanotechnology Lab., interim dean Coll. Engring., 2005—. Rschr. Beckman Inst. for Advanced Sci. and Tech. Fellow: AAAS, IEEE; mem.: NAE, Optical Soc. Am., Am. Vacuum Soc., Bohmische Soc. Office: U Ill at Urbana-Champaign 127 Micro and Nanotechnology Lab 208 N Wright St Urbana IL 61801 Office Phone: 217-333-3097. E-mail: iadesida@uiuc.edu.*

ADETUNJI, BABATUNDE ABAYOMI, forensic psychiatrist; s. Babajide Aderogba and Florence Oluyemi Adetunji; m. Oluyemisi Hannah Quadri, Sept. 20, 1990; children: Oluwadamilola Temidayo, Opeposi Abimbola, Oluwanifemi Aderonke. BSc with honors in health sci., Obafemi Awolowo U., Nigeria, 1980—84; M in human ecology, Vrije U., 1990—93; MSc, U. London, 1995—97. Medical Doctor Obafemi Awolowo U., 1987, diplomate Royal Coll. Physicians and Surgeons Ireland, 2000, Conjoint Bd. of Guys Hosp. and U. of Bahrain, 1999, bd. cert. Am. Bd. Psychiatrists and Neurology Inc. Staff forensic psychiatrist Redford Lodge Hosp., London, 1998—2001; cons. psychiatrist and dir. Medikhelp Cons. Ltd., London, 2001—02; attending psychiatrist Kirby Forensic Psychiat. Ctr., Manhattan, NY, 2004—05, MHM-Correctional Services, Phila., 2005—. Dir. Medikhelp Cons. Ltd., London, 2001—; locum cons. in forensic psychiatry Broadmoor Hosp., Crowthorne, England, 2001—02, Three Bridges Medium Secure Unit, Ealing, England, 2001—02; medicolegal cons. Bajikijaye Solicitors, Toronto, Canada, 2001—04; locum cons. in geriatric psychiatry Princess Alexandra Hosp., Harlow, England, 2004, Lincolnshire Cmty. NHS Trust, Lincoln, England, 2004—04; locum cons. psychiatrist Oxleas NHS Trust, Sidcup, England. Book reviewer Royal Society of Medicine Press; contbr. articles to profl. jours. Recipient Internat. Cert. in Human Ecology, UNESCO, 1993; Belgian Govt. schorlaship (ABOS), Belgian Govt., 1990—93. Fellow: Royal Acad. of Medicine of Ireland, Am. Soc. Addiction Medicine; mem.: Am. Coll. of Forensic Examiners Internat., Assn. of European Psychiatrists, Am. Acad. of Psychiatry and the Law, Brit. Acad. of Forensic Sciences, Internat. Acad. of Law and Mental Health, Soc. of Expert Witnesses, NY Acad. of Sciences, Brit. Assn. of Med. Managers, Acad. of Experts. Achievements include design of information package on HIV-AIDS in 3 Nigerian languages; risk monitoring inventory for mental health multidisciplinary team (RMI-MDT); research in assessment of the effectiveness of day hospitals using preadmission and 6-months intra-admission questionnaire scores; perception of mental health professionals with regards to issue of racism in psychiatry; community hypertension survey; AIDS awareness survey. Office: MHM-Correctional Services Mod Ii 8001 State Rd Philadelphia PA 19136 Home Phone: 856-753-7615; Office Phone: 267-918-9672. Office Fax: 215-685-7166. Personal E-mail: medikhelp@yahoo.com.

ADHIKARI, DHARMA NANDA, journalist, writer, educator; b. India, Jan. 1, 1969; s. Bishnu Prasad and Chandra Wati; m. Kabita Khanal Adhikari; children: Astitwa, Aaditi, Aadarsha. BA in English and Philosophy, Tribhuvan U., Kathmandu, 1989, M in English Lit., 1992; Diploma in Journalism, Nepal Press Inst., 1991; M in Journalism, Mo. Sch. Journalism, Columbia, 2000, PhD in Journalism, 2004. Reporter, editor, translator and freelance journalist, Nepal, 1986—98; lectr. in media studies and Am. Lit. Tribhuvan U. at Kathmandu, 1995—97; taught courses in journalism and mass media Mo. Sch. Journalism at Columbia, 2001—03; journalism program coord., asst. prof. Ga. So. U. Contbr. to newspapers and magazines in Asia, N.Am. and Europe; founder, editor Newslook.org, Nepalmonitor.com. Recipient Mahendra Vidhya Bhusan Gold medal, King of Nepal, 1990, South Asian Journalism award in Am. for Outstanding Editorial.op-ed/commentary for The Reversal of Democracy in Nepal, 2006; ICFJ-ASNE Internat. Journalism Exchange Fellow, 1996, Fulbright Scholar, Mo. Sch. Journalism at Columbia, 1998—2000. Mem.: South Asian Journalists Assn., Internat. Comm. Assn., Assn. Edn. Journalism and Mass Comm. Avocations: writing, swimming, movies, browsing the Internet. Office: Ga So U 1034 Communications Arts PO Box 8091 Statesboro GA 30460-8091 Office Phone: 912-681-5369.

ADIZES, ICHAK, management consultant, writer; PhD, Columbia U. Prof. Hebrew U., Jerusalem, Tel Aviv U., Stanford (Calif.) U., Columbia U., NYC, UCLA; founder, profl. dir. Adizes Inst., Santa Barbara, Calif., 1975—; acad. dean Adizes Grad. Sch. for Study of Change and Leadership, Santa Barbara, Calif. Lectr. in field. Author: Self-Management, 1975, How to Solve the Mismanagement Crisis, 1979, Corporate Lifecycles: How and Why Corporations Grow and Die and What to Do About It, 1988, Mastering Change: The power of Mutual Trust and Respect in Personal Life, Business and Society, 1992, The Pursuit of Prime, 1996, Managing Corporate Life Cycles, 1999, The Ideal Executive: Why You Cannot Be One and What to Do About It, 2004, Management/Mismanagement Styles: How to Identify A Style and What to Do About It, 2004, Leading the Leaders: How to Enrich Your Style of Management and Handle People Whose Style Is Different From Yours, 2004; contbr. articles to profl. jours., newspapers. Office: Adizes Inst 6404 Via Real Carpinteria CA 93013-1611 Office Phone: 805-565-2901. Fax: (805) 565-0741. E-mail: ichak@adizes.com.

ADJARIAN, MAUDE MADELEINE, literature educator, researcher; b. Santa Monica, Calif., Oct. 10, 1965; BA Comparative Lit., U. of Calif., Berkeley, 1987; PhD Comparative Lit., U.of Mich., Ann Arbor, 1994. Adj. instr., women's studies/program in personal devel. UC Berkeley Ext., San Francisco, 1995—97; instr., English Skyline HS, Oakland, Calif., 1997—2000; assoc. rschr. U. of Ariz., Dept. Women's Studies, Tucson, 2000—; adj. instr., English Pima CC, Tucson, 2000—. Reader English lit. exam. Ednl. Testing Services, Princeton, NJ, 2000—01; referee Coll. Lit., West Chester, Pa.; adj. lectr. women's studies U. Ariz., 2003—; reviewer Choice, 2004—. Contbr. articles literary criticism and revs. to various jours.; editor: Michigan Feminist Studies, 1993—94; author: Allegories of Desire: Body Nation and Empire in Modern Caribbean Literature by Women, 2004. Vol.literacy tutor Berkeley Pub. Libr., Mich., 1995—97. Grantee U. of Mich. Departmental Fellowship, Program in Comparative Lit., 1988—89, Rackham Discretionary Grant, Rackham Grad. Coll., U. of Mich., 1990, Program in Comparative Lit., Departmental Block Grant, U. of Mich., 1990. Mem.: MLA, Phi Beta Kappa. Office: Univ Ariz Dept Womens Studies 1443 E 1st St PO Box 210403 Tucson AZ 85721 Home Phone: 520-790-4149. Business E-Mail: adjarian@u.arizona.edu.

ADKERSON, RICHARD C., mining executive; BA with honors, Miss. State U., 1969, MBA, 1970. Prof. acctg. fellow SEC, Washington, 1976-78; ptnr., mng. dir., head worldwide oil and gas practice Arthur Anderson & Co.; fin. mgmt. positions with Freeport-McMoRan Copper & Gold, New Orleans, 1989—92, CFO, 1992—97, pres., COO, CFO, 1997—2000, pres., CFO, 2000—03, pres., CEO, 2003—; co-chmn. McMoRan Exploration Co. Trustee Nat. D-Day Mus.; v.p., bd. dir., mem. exec. com. Miss. State Univ. Found.; mem. adv. bd. Coll. Bus. & Ind. & Agribus. Inst., Miss. State Univ.; mem. Bus. Council New Orleans & River Region; mem. develop. bd. Fellowship Christian Athletes New Orleans; mem. exec. bd. adv. Ourso Coll., La. State Univ.; mem. Pres. Council Xavier Univ.; mem. bd. vis. M.D. Anderson Cancer Ctr.; mem. adv. bd. Crosby Arboretum. Office: Freeport McMoRan Copper & Gold Inc 1 N Ctrl Ave Phoenix AZ 85004*

ADKINS, ELIZABETH W., archivist; b. Port Chester, NY, Mar. 22, 1957; d. Herbert Arthur and Carol (Magnusson) Woodger; m. Fred D. Adkins Jr., Nov. 12, 1983. BA in History, SUNY, Binghamton, 1979; MA in History, Carnegie-Mellon U., 1980. Cert. archivist. Project archivist Matthew G. Norton Co., Seattle, 1981-83; archives dir. Laird Norton Co., Seattle, 1983-86; archives specialist Kraft, Inc., Glenview, Ill., 1986-87, archives mgr., 1987-89, Kraft Foods, Inc., Glenview, 1989—96; mgr. archives services Ford Motor Co., Dearborn, Mich., 1996, dir. global info. mgmt., 1996—2001, 2001—. Mem. Ill. State Archives adv. com., 1992—. Mem. Soc. Am. Archivists (steering com. acquisitions and appraisal sect. 1986-88, chair 1988-89, program com. 1989-90, chair bus. archives sect. 1991-92, com. on pub. info. 1990, treas. 2000-03, fellow 2002-, v.p., 2005-2006, pres. 2006-07), Acad. Cert. Archivists (charter, mem. fin. com. 1990-92, v.p. 1992-1995, pres., 1995-1996), Midwest Archives Conf., Mich. Archive Assn., Internat. Coun. on Archives (mem. steering com. bus. and labour archives sect.) Office: Ford Motor Co Archives Schaefer Ct III Ste 180 14441 Rotunda Dr Dearborn MI 48120 Office Phone: 313-845-0556. Office Fax: 313-248-4921.

ADKINS, JEANNE M., state agency administrator; b. North Platte, Nebr., May 2, 1949; BA, U. Nebr. Journalist; mem. Colo. Ho. of Reps., 1988—99, chairwoman judiciary com., vice-chairwoman legal svcs. com., mem. fin. com., regional air quality control coun., state edn. accountability commn.; dir. policy and planning Colo. Dept. Edn.; dir. Colo. Student Loan Program, 2002—. Founding sec. Douglas County Econ. Devel. Coun., bd. dirs., 1988. Fellow Vanderbilt U. Govt., Gates fellow JFK Sch. Govt. State/Local Program, Toll fellow. Mem. Am. Soc. Newspaper Editors, Soc. Profl. Journalists, Suburban Newspaper Assn. Republican. Baptist. Office: CSLP 999 18th St Ste 425 Denver CO 80202

ADKINS, RODNEY, computer company executive; Joined IBM, 1981, various positions as an engr. with prod. devel., bus. operations and gen. mgmt., 1981—2001, gen. mgr. pervasive computing White Plains, NY, 2001—03, v.p., systems group devel., 2003—. Bd. govs. IBM Academy Tech.; co-chmn., multi-cultural people in tech. IBM; co-chmn. Nat. Black Family Tech. Awareness; bd. dirs. Peopleclick, Inc. Pres. advisory coun. Ga. Tech; bd. trustees Ga. Tech Rsch. Corp. Mem.: NAE, Exec. Leadership Coun., Nat. Society Black Engineers. Office: IBM 1133 Westchester Ave White Plains NY 10604

ADKINS, THOMAS SAMUEL, library director; b. Portsmouth, Ohio, Oct. 24, 1965; s. Millard Elwood and Ruth Caroline (Shultz) A. BS, Ohio U., 1988; MLS, Kent State U., Ohio, 1993. Tchr. Cmty. Action Agy., Portsmouth, Ohio, 1988, Scioto County Schs., Portsmouth, 1988-89; ext. svcs. coord. Portsmouth Pub. Libr., 1989-95; dir. G.A. Wilson Pub. Libr., Waverly, Ohio, 1996—. Chairperson Libr. Adv. Coun., Wellston, Ohio, 1997. Author: Lucasville Cemeteries, 1988; editor: A Backward Glance, vol. 1, 1987, vol. 2, 1990. Mem. Cmty. Svcs. Coun., Waverly, Ohio, 1996—; treas. Lucasville (Ohio) Hist. Soc., 1986—; mem. Valley Alumni Scholarship Com., Lucasville, 1990—; govt. rels. com. Ohio Libr. Coun., 1998—, treas. bd. dirs., 2000-2002, pres. 2004; participant Libr. Leadership Inst., Snowbird, Utah, 1999. Recipient Diana Vescelius Meml. award, 1998. Mem. ALA (Emerging Leaders 2000), Pike County C. of C. (bd. dirs.). Avocations: book collecting, local history, movies, travel.

ADKINSON, BRIAN LEE, manufacturing executive; b. Lebanon, Ind., July 10, 1959; s. Marion Leroy and Edith Marie (Shonkwiler) A.; children: Katherin Elizabeth, Anna Mary Josephine. BS in Fin., Ind. U., 1982; postgrad., Keller Sch. Mgmt., 1992—93. Asst. bank examiner FDIC, Chgo., 1980-81; acctg. assoc. battery prodn. Union Carbide Co., Bennington, Vt., 1982-83; sr. ptnr. AC Sales Assocs., Murfreesboro, Tenn., 1983-89; spl. mkts. mgr. Chgo. Cutlery Housewares, div. Gen. Housewares Corp., Terre Haute, Ind., 1989-90; nat. sales mgr. Gerber Legendary Blades, a Fiskers Co., Portland, Oreg., 1990-91, Fiskers Inc, Wausau, Wis., 1992-94; mktg. mgr. Fiskars Inc., Wausau, Wis., 1994-98, dir. mktg., 1998-99; group dir. sales/mktg. Recreation Group, 1999-2000; gen. mgr. Fiskars Outdoor Leisure Products, 2000; mng. dir. Fiskar U.K. Ltd., 2000—02; v.p. Jensen Co., Racine, Wis., 2002—03; v.p. sales and mktg. Walnut Hollow INc., Dodgeville, Wis., 2003—. Spl. examiner-in-charge Union Carbide Credit Union, Bennington, 1982-83, acctg. adv. co. store, 1982-83; mem. industry stds. com. Hobby Industries Assn. Patentee in field. Vol. Zionsville (Ind.) Christian Ch., 1975-82, Ctrl. Christian Ch., Murfreesboro, 1983-87; mem. edn. com. Trinity United Meth. Ch., Murfreesboro, 1987-89, chmn. fin. com., 1989-89, adminstrv. bd., 1988-89; bd. dirs. Wesley Found., Mid. Tenn. State U., Murfreesboro, 1989; mem. Rutherford County Humane Soc., Beasley, 1987-89. Mem. Am. Mgmt. Assn., Am. Mktg. Assn., Ind. U. Alumni Membership Assn. (Nashville chpt.), Sigma Pi (mem. alumni assn., Hobby & Craft Industry of Am., Am. Hardware Manufacturer's Assn Republican. Methodist. Avocations: investments, reading, sports, computer science. Office Phone: 608-574-1496. Personal E-mail: alegandron@yahoo.com.

ADKINSON, THEODORE H., lawyer; b. Newport Beach, Calif., Apr. 2, 1968; BA, Colgate Univ., 1990; JD cum laude, Pepperdine Univ., 1993. Bar: Calif. 1993. Assoc., bus. environ. & marine litigation Keesal, Young & Logan, Long Beach, Calif., 2000—. Named a Rising Star, So. Calif. Super Lawyers, 2006. Mem.: LA County Bar Assn. (mem. exec. bd., internat. sect.), Long Beach Maritime Bar Assn. Office: Keesal Young & Logan PO Box 1730 400 Oceangate Long Beach CA 90801-1730 Office Phone: 562-436-2000. Office Fax: 562-436-7416. Business E-Mail: ted.adkinson@kyl.com.

ADKISON, DAVID PAUL, orthopedic surgeon; b. July 30, 1952; BS in Math., U. Ala., Birmingham; MD, U. South Ala. Coll. Medicine, Mobile. Cert. Am. Bd. Orthop. Surgery, Nat. Bd. Med. Examiners. Intern, surgery Nat. Naval Med. Ctr., resident, orthop. surgery; fellow, knee, Shoulder & Sports Medicine Orthop. Specialty Hosp., Salt Lake City; chmn., dept. orthop. Bethesda Naval Hosp.; attending orthop. surgeon White House Med. Unit, US Capital Physician's Office; staff orthop. St. Vincent's Orthopedics, PC, Birmingham, Ala. Operation Restore Hope, 1st Marine Divsn., Mogadishu, Somalia, gen. med. officer, 3rd Marine Divsn., Fleet Marine Force, Okinawa, hosp. corpsman USN. Fellow: Am. Acad. Orthop. Surgery; mem.: Arthroscopy Assn. N.Am., Am. Orthop. Soc. for Sports Medicine (Excellence in Rsch. award 1997), Soc. Mil. Orthop. Surgeons. Office: St Vincents Orthop PC 2700 10th Ave S Birmingham AL 35205 Office Phone: 205-933-7838. Office Fax: 205-933-0951.*

ADKISON, RON, lawyer; b. Nacogdoches, Tex., Jan. 8, 1955; s. Robert Edward and Doris Ozelle (Pollard) A.; m. Tanya Regina Williamson, June 2, 1979 (div. Dec. 1984); 1 child, Veronica Alexis Adkison; m. Donna Elaine Dennis, Apr. 1, 1990 (divorced); 1 child, Alexander Aron; m. Tamra Bryan, July 4, 2001. BA, Stephen F. Austin U., 1976; JD, Baylor U., 1978. Bar: Tex. 1979, U.S. Dist. Ct. (ea., we., so. and no. dists.) Tex., U.S. Ct. Appeals (5th cir.), U.S. Supreme Ct. Atty. Wellborn & Houston, Henderson, Tex., 1979; ptnr. Wellborn, Houston, Adkison, et al., Henderson, Tex., 1980—. Regent Stephen F. Austin State U., Nacogdoches, 1993-99; chair bd. regents, 1995-96. Fellow Am. Bd. Trial Advs., Tex. Inst. for Legal Ethics and Professionalism; mem. Coll. State Bar Tex. (Disciplinary Rev. com., Adminstrn. Rules Civil Evidence com.), Tex. Trial Lawyers Assn. (dir., chair Toxic Torts com.), Henderson Country Club (pres. 1989-94). Avocations: golf, aviation. Office: Wellborn Houston Adkison et al 300 W Main St Henderson TX 75652-3109 Home Phone: 903-657-4600; Office Phone: 903-657-8544. Personal E-mail: t-adkison@msn.com.

ADKISSON, HUBERT KEITH, military officer; b. Lincoln, Nebr., Sept. 21, 1924; s. Hubert Julius and Gladys Marie Adkisson; m. Loa Janice Pauley, Feb. 10, 1946 (dec. 1992); children: Steven M., Rebecca S., Richard K.; m. Hazel Mae Chambers, Sept. 11, 1999; stepchildren: Theresa Rickman, Lisa Howarth, Christopher Chambers, Denise Chambers. Student, U. Nebr., 1942—43, Doane Coll., 1943—44, Columbia U., 1944, Harvard U., 1945, U. Colo., 1945, U. Md., 1949. Commd. ensign USN, 1944, advanced through grades to capt., 1945—75, ret., 1975; program mgr. MRJ, Inc., Fairfax, Va., 1975—86; ret., 1986. Vol. Rep. Party, Fla., 2004. Decorated Commendation medal USN, Jt. Svcs. Commendation medal Dept. Def. Mem.: Mil. Officers Assn. Am., Navy Cryptologic Vets. Assn., US Navy League, Assn. Former Intelligence Officers. Republican. Methodist. Avocations: travel, reading, swimming, exercise, golf. Home: 3740 Ocean Beach Blvd #707 Cocoa Beach FL 32931 Personal E-mail: hkadkisson1@aol.com.

ADKISSON, PERRY LEE, university system chancellor; b. Hickman, Ark., Mar. 11, 1929; s. Robert Louis and Imogene (Perry) A.; m. Frances Rozelle, Dec. 29, 1956 (dec. 1995); m. Gloria Ray, May 16, 1998; 1 dau., Jean Amanda. BS, U. Ark., 1950, MS, 1954; PhD in Entomology, Kans. State U., 1956; DS (hon.), U. Ark., 1997; DHL, Tex. A&M U., 2001. Asst. prof. entomology U. Mo., 1956-58; assoc. prof. Tex. A&M U., 1958-63, prof., 1963-67, Disting. prof. entomology, 1967—, head dept. entomology, 1967-78, v.p. for agr. and renewable resources, 1978-80, dep. chancellor for agr., 1980-83, dep. chancellor, 1983-86, chancellor, 1986-91, regent's prof., 1991-95. Cons. Internat. AEC, Vienna, 1969-74; chmn. sci. adv. panel Gov. Tex. on Agrl. Chems., 1970-72; chmn. Tex. Pesticide Adv. Com., 1972; mem. panel experts on integrated pest control UN/FAO, Rome, 1971-78, chmn., 1992-96; mem. Structural Pest Control Bd., Tex., 1972-78, NRC World Food and Nutrition Study Team, 1977; chmn. com. biology pest species NRC, 1974; mem. environ. studies bd., study group problems pest control NAS-NRC, 1973-75; mem. U.S. directorate UNESCO Man and the Biosphere Program, 1975-77; mem. bd. on agr. NRC, 1985-87, mem. Nat. Sci. Bd., 1985-96; mem. governing bd. Internat. Crops Rsch. Inst. for Semi-Arid Tropics, 1982-88; mem. rsch. adv. com. Agr. for Internat. Devel., 1986; mem. com. on life scis. NRC, 1985-85; mem. Tex. Sci. and Tech. Coun., 1986-88; mem. Standing Com. for Internat. Plant Protection Congresses, 1984—, adv. dir. Export-Import Bank U.S., 1987. Mem. editorial com. Ann. Rev. Entomology, 1973-78; contbr. articles to profl. jours. Exec. dir. G.H.W. Bush Presdl. Libr. Ctr. and Bush Libr. Found., 1991-93. With M.C., U.S. Army, 1951-53. Recipient Faculty Disting. Achievement award for rsch. Tex. A&M U., 1965, Alexander Von Humboldt award, 1980; Disting. Svc. award Am. Registry Prof. Entomology, 1979, Disting. Scientist of Yr. award Tex. Acad. Scis., 1982, Disting. Alumnus Svc. award Kans. State U., 1980, Disting. Svc. award Am. Inst. Biol. Sci., 1987, Nat. 4-H Alumni award, 1988, Outstanding Alumnus award Coll. of Agr. and Home Econs., U. Ark., 1990, Disting. Alumni award U. Ark., 1990, Disting. Svc. award Am. Agrl. Editors Assn., 1992, Wolfe prize in agr., Wolf Found., Israel, 1994-95, World Food prize, 1997, medallion alumni award Kans. State U., 1999; USPHS postdoctoral fellow Harvard U., 1963-64; Tex. Heritage Hall of Honor, 1998. Fellow AAAS, Entomol. Soc. Am. (governing bd. 1971-75, pres. 1974, Bussart Meml. award 1967, Founders Meml. lectr. 1985); mem. Am. Acad. Arts and Scis., Kans. Entomol. Soc., Internat. Orgn. Biol. Control, Am. Registry Profl. Entomologists (governing council 1976-78, pres. 1977), Nat. Acad. Scis., Phi Kappa Phi, Sigma Xi. Office: Tex A&M U Dept Entomology College Station TX 77843-0001

ADLEMAN, LEONARD M., computer scientist, educator; b. San Francisco, Dec. 31, 1945; m. Lori Bruce, 1983; 3 children. BS, U. Calif., Berkeley, 1968; PhD in Computer Sci., U. Calif., 1976. Instr. math. MIT, Cambridge, 1976—77, asst. prof. math., 1977—79, assoc. prof. math., 1979—80; assoc. prof. U. So. Calif., LA, 1980—83, prof., 1983—85, Henry Salvatori prof. computer sci., 1985—. Asst. prof. math. RSA Data Security, 1983—. Recipient Koji Kobayashi Computers and Comm. award, IEEE, 2000, ACM Turing award, 2003, ACM Paris Kanallakis award, 1996, Alexander von Humboldt Fellowship and Disting. Alumnus award, 1995. Mem. NAE, NAS; fellow Am. Acad. Arts & Sciences Office: U So Calif Dept Computer Sci 941 West 37th Place Los Angeles CA 90089-0781 E-mail: adleman@usc.edu.

ADLER, CHARLES SPENCER, psychiatrist; b. NYC, Nov. 27, 1941; s. Benjamin H. and Anne (Greenfield) A.; m. Sheila Noel Morrissey, Oct. 8, 1966 (dec.); m. Peggy Dolan Bean, Feb. 23, 1991 BA, Cornell U., 1962; MD, Duke U., 1966. Diplomate Nat. Bd. Med. Examiners, Am. Bd. Psychiatry and Neurology. Intern Tucson Hosps. Med. Edn. Program, 1966-67; psychiat. resident U. Colo. Med. Sch., Denver, 1967-70; pvt. practice medicine specializing in psychiatry and psychosomatic medicine Denver, 1970—. Chief divsn. psychiatry Rose Med. Ctr, 1982-87; co-founder Applied Biofeedback Inst., Denver, 1972-75; prof. pro tempore Cleve. Clinic, 1977; asst. clin. prof. psychiatry U. Colo. Med. Ctr., 1986—, chief psychiatry and psychophysiology Colo. Neurology and Headache Ctr., 1988-95; med. dir. Colo. Ctr. for Biobehavioral Health, Boulder, 1994—. Author: (with Gene Stanford and Sheila M. Adler) We Are But a Moment's Sunlight, 1976, (with Sheila M. Adler and Russell Packard) Psychiatric Aspects of Headache, 1987; contbr. (with S. Adler) sect. biofeedback med. and health ann. Ency. Britannica, 1986; chpts. to books, articles to profl. jours.; mem. editorial bd. Cephalalgia: an Internat. Jour. of Headache, Headache Quar. Emeritus mem. Citizen's Adv Bd. Duke U. Ctr. Aging and Human Devel. Recipient Award of Recognition, Nat. Migraine Found., 1981; N.Y. State regents scholar, 1958-62 Fellow Am. Psychiat. Assn.; mem. AAAS (rep. of AAPB to med. sect. com.), Am. Assn. Study Headache, Internat. Headache Soc. (chmn. subcom. on classifying psychiat. headaches), Am. Acad. Psychoanalysis (sci. assoc.), Biofeedback Soc. Colo. (pres. 1977-78), Assn. for Applied Psychophysiology and Biofeedback (rep. to AAAS, chmn. ethics com. 1983-87, bd. dirs. 1990-93, Sheila M. Adler cert. honor 1988). Jewish. Office: 955 Eudora St Apt 1605 Denver CO 80220-4341 Office Phone: 303-333-0505.

ADLER, CHRISTOPHER ALAN, composer, educator; b. Mountain View, Calif., Sept. 27, 1972; s. Gordon Alan and Pamela Adler; m. Supeena Insee Adler, Nov. 21, 2003. BS in Math., MIT, Cambridge, 1994, BS in Music, 1994; PhD in Music Composition, Duke U., Durham, NC, 1999. Assoc. prof. of music U. of San Diego, 1999—, dir. of music program, 2002—05. Pianist and composer-in-residence NOISE, San Diego, 2003—; pianist Christopher Adler Trio, San Diego, 2000—; editor San Diego New Music newsletter, 2003—05. Composer: (compact disc) Epilogue for a Dark Day, Tzadik Records TZ 8004; musician: Transcontinental, the Christopher Adler Trio (9 Winds Records), (mini-compact disc) Christopher Adler, khaen, ArtShip Recordings, (compact disc) Nathan Hubbard, Skeleton Key Orchestra (Circumvention Records). Mem.: ASCAP, Am. Music Ctr., Soc. for Ethnomusicology. Office: University of San Diego Music Program 5998 Alcala Pk San Diego CA 92110 Home Phone: 619-298-8203; Office Phone: 619-260-7502.

ADLER, DALE STEVEN, internist, cardiologist; b. Cleve., July 31, 1953; m. Nancy Feins, Oct. 1985. AB in Biochemistry (magna cum laude), Harvard Coll., 1975; MD, Weill Med. Coll., Cornell U., 1979. Diplomate in internal medicine and cardiovascular diseases Am. Bd. Internal Medicine. Intern, medicine Brigham and Women's Hosp., Boston, 1979-80, jr. asst. resident, internal medicine, 1980—81, sr. asst. resident, internal medicine, 1981—82, clin. fellow, divsn. cardiology, 1982—83, clin. and rsch. fellow, divsn. cardiology, 1983—85, Henry J. Kaiser Rsch. Fellow, gen. internal medicine and clin. epidemiology, Harvard Med. Sch., 1983—85, Percutaneous Transluminal Coronary Angioplasty Fellow, divsn. cardiology, 1984—85, assoc. physician, 1984—85, vice chair medicine for network develop. and strategic planning, 2006—; head, invasive cardiology Mt. Sinai Med. Ctr., Cleve., 1985, co-chief cardiology, acting co-chief, divsn. cardiology, 1987, co-chief, divsn. cardiology, 1988—97; chief, divsn. cardiology U. Hosps. Cleve., 1997; asst. prof. medicine Case Western Res. U., Cleve., 1985—99, assoc. prof. medicine, 1999—2003, prof. medicine, 2003, chief, divsn. cardiology, 1996—2004, vice-chair for clin. affairs, dept. medicine, 2004—06. Contbr. articles to profl. jours., chapters to books. Named Best Doctors-Cleve. Ohio, Cleve. Mag., 1987, 1988, 2002, Top Docs, Northeast Ohio Live Mag., 2000, 2001, Hon. co-chair of gala, Am. Heart Assn., Northeastern Ohio, 2004. Mem. Am. Heart Assn. (mem. clin. cardiology coun., 1986-), Am. Profs. Cardiology, Alpha Omega Alpha, Phi Beta Kappa Office: Brigham and Women's Hosp Brigham Med Specialties 45 Francis St Boston MA 02115 Office Phone: 617-732-4837. Office Fax: 617-566-4092.*

ADLER, DAVID NEIL, lawyer; b. Bklyn., Apr. 11, 1955; s. Leonard Howard and Elaine (Holder) A. Student, Colgate U., 1973-75; BA, NYU, 1977; JD, St. John's U., 1980. Bar: N.Y. 1981, U.S. Dist. Ct. (ea. and so. dists.) N.Y. 1986, U.S. Tax Ct. 1989. Pvt. practice, Kew Gardens, NY, 1982—. Contbr. articles to profl. jours. Mem. Queens County Bar Assn. (com. chmn. 1983—, co-editor Queens Bar Bull. 1987—, bd. mgrs. 1989—, officer 1993—, pres. 1998), N.Y. State Bar Assn. (exec. com. trusts and estates). Office: 12510 Queens Blvd Kew Gardens NY 11415-1519 Office Phone: 718-263-0677.

ADLER, EDWARD I., media and entertainment company executive; b. NYC, Jan. 12, 1954; s. Walter S. and Justine (Rosenberg) P.; m. Shari Goldman; children: Alexander Justin, Jillian Haly. BA, Vassar Coll., 1976; MA in Journalism, NYU, 1979. Reporter Time Mag. (subs. Time Inc), NYC, 1976-79; sports programming exec. HBO Inc. (subs. Time Inc.), NYC, 1979-81; news editor TV-Cable Week Mag. (subs. Time Inc.), NYC, 1981-83; sr. assoc. corp. pub. affairs Time Inc., NYC, 1983-88; mgr. media rels. corp. comm. Time Warner Inc., NYC, 1989-93, dir. media rels. corp. comm., 1993-97, v.p. corp. comm., 1997-2000, sr. v.p. corp. comm., 2000—04, exec. v.p. corp. comm., 2004—. Bd. dirs. NY Cares, Big Apple Circus. Bd. dirs. City Pks. Found. Mem.: Internat. Radio and TV Soc. Office: Time Warner Inc One Time Warner Ctr New York NY 10019 Home Phone: 212-288-7200. Business E-Mail: edward.adler@timewarner.com.*

ADLER, ERWIN ELLERY, lawyer; b. Flint, Mich., July 22, 1941; s. Ben and Helen M. (Schwartz) A.; m. Stephanie Ruskin, June 8, 1967; children: Lauren, Michael, Jonathan BA, U. Mich., 1963, LL.M., 1967; JD, Harvard U., 1966. Bar: Mich. 1966, Calif. 1967. Assoc. Pillsbury, Madison & Sutro, San Francisco, 1967-73; assoc. Lawler, Felix & Hall, LA, 1973-76, ptnr., 1977-80, Rogers & Wells, LA, 1981-83, Richards, Watson & Gershon, LA, 1983—. Bd. dirs. Hollywood Civic Opera Assn., 1975-76, Children's Scholarships Inc., 1979-80 Mem. ABA (vice chmn. appellate advocacy com. 1982-87), Calif. Bar Assn., Phi Beta Kappa, Phi Kappa Phi. Jewish. Office: Adler Law Group 350 S Figueroa St Ste 557 Los Angeles CA 90071

ADLER, FRED PETER, retired electronics company executive; b. Vienna, Mar. 29, 1925; came to U.S., 1942, naturalized, 1947; s. Michael and Ellida (Bronner) A.; m. Alicia Gulkis, 1950; children; Michael Steven, Andrew David; m. Adrienne Wilcox, 1991. BSEE with honors, U. Calif., Berkeley, 1945; MSEE (Charles A. Coffin fellow), Calif. Inst. Tech., 1948, PhD magna cum laude, 1950. Elec. engr. GE Rsch. and Cons. Labs., 1945-47; project engr. Jet Propulsion Lab., 1950; with Hughes Aircraft Co., 1950-70, sr. staff physicist, dept. mgr., 1954-57, mgr. advanced planning, 1957-59, dir. advanced projects labs., 1959-61, v.p., mgr. space systems div., 1961-66, v.p., asst. group exec. Aerospace Group, 1966-70; pres. Nadgeco Ltd., 1970—73, chmn. bd., 1973-77; v.p., group exec. aerospace groups Hughes Aircraft Co., 1973-81, sr. v.p., pres. electro-optical and data sys. group, 1981-87; dir. Jefferson Ctr. for Character Edn., Monrovia, Calif., 1973-99, chmn. bd., 1988-99; ret., 1999. Co-author: text Guided Missile Engineering, 1959; also articles tech. jours. Fellow AIAA; mem. N.Y. Acad. Scis., Sigma Xi, Tau Beta Pi. Home: 10795 Woodbine St Apt 208 Los Angeles CA 90034 Personal E-mail: fredad690@cs.com.

ADLER, FREDA SCHAFFER (MRS. G. O. W. MUELLER), criminologist, educator; b. Phila., Nov. 21, 1934; d. David and Lucia G. (de Wolfson) Schaffer; children by previous marriage: Mark, Jill, Nancy. BA, U. Pa., 1956, MA, 1968, PhD (fellow), 1971. Instr. dept. psychiatry Temple U., Phila., 1971; rsch. coord. Addiction Scis. Ctr., 1971—72; rsch. dir. sect. on drug and alcohol abuse Med. Coll. Pa., 1972—74, asst. prof. psychiatry, 1972—74; assoc. prof. criminal justice Rutgers U., Newark, 1974—79, prof., 1979—82, disting. prof., 1982—, acting dean grad. sch. criminal justice, 1986—87. Bd. dirs. Internat. Sci. and Profl. Adv. Coun. UN Programs in Crime Prevention and Criminal Justice; vis. fellow Yale U., 1976; cons. to Nat. Commn. on Marijuana and Drug Abuse, 1972-73, NYU Sch. Law, 1972-74; mem. faculty Nat. Jud. Coll., U. Nev., 1973—, Nat. Coll. Criminal Def. Lawyers and Pub. Defenders U. Houston, 1975; mem. adv. com. Gen. Fedn. Women's Clubs, 1975-77; UN rep. Internat. Prisoner Aid Assn., 1973-75, Centro Nat. di Prevenzione e Difesa Sociale, 1989—, Internat. Soc. Social Def., regional sec. gen., 1991—, bd. dirs.; sec. bd. dirs. Inst. for Continuous Study of Man, 1974-77, v.p., 1977—; adv. bd. Internat. Jour. Comparative and Applied Criminal Justice, 2005— Author: Sisters in Crime, 1975, The Incidence of Female Criminality in the Contemporary World, 1981, Nations Note Obsessed with Crime, 1983; co-author: A Systems Approach to Drug Treatment, 1975, Medical Lollypop, Junkie Insuline or what?, 1974, Criminology of Deviant Women, 1978, Outlaws of the Ocean, 1985, Criminology, 1991, 6th edit., 2007, Criminal Justice, 1993, 4th edit., 2006, Criminology and the Criminal Justice System, 1995, 5th edit., 2007, Criminal Justice: The Core, 1996, Kriminologia, 2000, Criminology and the Criminal Justice System: United States and Georgia, 2003; editor: Advances in Criminological Theory, 1987—; mem. editl. bd.: Criminology, 1971—73, Jour. Criminal Law and Criminology, 1982—, The American Sociologist, 1999—, Feminist Criminology, 2006—; co-editor: Politics, Crime and the International Scene, 1972, Revue Internationale de Droit Penal, 1974, European Jour. Criminology, 2003—; assoc. editor: LAE Jour., 1977—85, cons. editor: Jour. Criminal Law and Criminology, mem. adv. bd.: Internat. Jour. Comparative and Applied Criminal Justice, 2005—; contbr. numerous articles on criminology and psychiatry to profl. jours. Bd. dirs. U. Pa. Alumnae Assn., 1974—77, The Police Found., 1996—2002. Named Cecil H. and Ida Green Honors Prof., Tex. Christian U., 1998, Ind. U. Disting. Scholar of Crime, Law and Justice, 1999; recipient (with G.O.W. Mueller) Beccaria medal in Gold, Deutsche Krimiologische Gesellschaft, 1979, Excellence award minorities and women's sect., Acad. Criminal Justice Scis., 2001, 1st Disting. Criminology award, U. Pa., 2006, Alumni award established in her honor, Rutgers U. Sch. Criminal Justice, 2006, Lifetime Achievement award, Northeastern Assn. Criminal Justice Scis., 2006, Founder's award, Acad. Criminal Justice Scis., 2007; fellow, Max Planck Inst. Fgn. and Internat. Law and Criminology, 1984, Am. Soc. Criminology, 1994, Northeastern Criminal Justice Assn., 2002. Fellow: Am. Soc.Criminology (pres. 1994—95, Herbert Bloch award 1972, Lifetime Achievement award divsn. internat. criminology 2006); mem.: Internat. Assn. Penal Law, Am. Sociol. Assn., U. Pa. Alumnae Assn. (bd. dirs. 1974—77), Chi Omega. Home: 30 Waterside Plz Apt 37J New York NY 10010-2628 Office: Rutgers U Sch Criminal Justice 123 Washington St Newark NJ 07102-3094 Office Phone: 858-350-8908. Personal E-mail: freadler@nyc.rr.com, f-adler@cox.net.

ADLER, FREDERICK RICHARD, lawyer, corporate financial executive; b. NYC, Apr. 4, 1926; s. Samuel and Rose (Axelrod) A.; m. Catherine R. George, Apr. 25, 1986; Christopher Wells, Frederick George Richard; children by previous marriage: Barbara Ilene, James Richard, Susan Ruth Chapman, Elizabeth Anne Wertheimer. BA, Bklyn. Coll., 1948; JD magna cum laude, Harvard U., 1951; Doctorate (hon.), Technion-Israel Inst. Tech., 1998. Bar: N.Y. 1952. Assoc. Reavis & McGrath, NYC, 1951-58, ptnr., 1959-89, Fulbright, Jaworski, Reavis & McGrath, NYC, 1989-91; ret. sr. ptnr. Fulbright & Jaworski, NYC, 1991-95, of counsel, 1996—; dir., chmn. exec. com. Data Gen. Corp., Westbo, Mass., 1968-99; mng. ptnr. VENAD Assocs., Adler & Co. Bd. dirs. Sentigen Holding Corp., Colo., SIT Investment Assocs., Minn. Trustee Tchrs. Ins. and Annuity Assn., 1977-95; bd. mgrs./overseers Meml. Sloan-Kettering Cancer Ctr.; mem. dean's adv. bd. Harvard Law Sch; trustee Horace Mann School; With U.S. Army, 1943-45. Mem. Harvard Club, Met. Club, Univ. Club (N.Y.), Atlantic Golf Club (Southampton, N.Y.), Old Oaks Country Club (Purchase, N.Y.), Palm Beach Country Club (Palm Beach, Fla.), N.Y. Athletic Club. Office: 220 Sunrise Ave Palm Beach FL 33480-3869

ADLER, HOWARD BRUCE, lawyer; b. NYC, Apr. 29, 1951; s. Mandel and Dora (Rosenblatt) A.; m. Tanya Jean Potter; 1 child, Alexandra. BA, Johns Hopkins U., 1972; JD, NYU, 1975. Bar: N.Y. 1976, U.S. Dist. Ct. (ea. and so. dists.) N.Y. 1976, D.C. 1979, U.S. Dist. Ct. D.C., 1979, U.S. Ct. Appeals (D.C. cir.) 1979. Assoc. Shearman & Sterling, NYC, 1975-79, Arnold & Porter, Washington, 1979-82; mng. counsel Mellon Bank N.A., Pitts., 1982-84; exec. v.p., gen. counsel The Riggs Nat. Bank of Wash. D.C., Riggs Nat. Corp., 1984-87; ptnr. Gibson, Dunn & Crutcher LLP, Washington, 1987; co-head Corp. Transactions Practice Group. Contbr. articles to profl. jours. Finalist Top Washington Lawyers corp./fin., Washington Bus. Jour., 2004; named one of Tier 1 Leading Lawyers corp./comml., Chambers USA, 2005—06, Law Dragon 1000, 2006. Mem. ABA (banking law com.), Fed. Bar Assn. (exec. coun. banking law com. 1990-98), D.C. Bar (treas. 1996-97, steering com. corp., fin. and securities law sect., 1991-96, chmn. 1994-95, vice chmn. 1993-94, budget com. 1996-97, chmn. task force of lawyers for econ. redevel. of D.C. 1997-99), Archdiocesan Legal Network of Washington (adv. bd. 1995-2002), Congl. Country Club, Met. Club, Knights of Malta. Avocation: civil war history. Home: 11103 Cripplegate Rd Potomac MD 20854 Office: Gibson Dunn & Crutcher LLP 1050 Connecticut Ave NW Ste 900 Washington DC 20036-5306 Office Phone: 202-955-8589. Business E-Mail: hadler@gibsondunn.com.

ADLER, IRA JAY, lawyer; b. NYC, Jan. 1, 1942; s. Ralph and Beatrice (Rosenblum) A.; m. Laraine Sheila Garfinkel, July 4, 1965; children: Jodi, Michael. BA, NYU, 1963, JD, 1966. Bar: N.Y. 1966. Ptnr. Certilman, Balin, Adler & Hyman, LLP, East Meadow, NY, 1973—. Contbr. to profl. publs. Mem. N.Y. State Bar Assn., Nassau County Bar Assn., L.I. Builders Inst. (bd. dirs. 1985—), Real Estate Inst. C.W. Post (bd. dirs. 1986—), N.Y. State Builders Assn. (bd. dirs. 1988—) Office: Certilman Balin Adler & Hyman LLP 90 Merrick Ave East Meadow NY 11554-1571

ADLER, IRVING, mathematician; b. NYC, Apr. 27, 1913; s. Marcus and Celia (Kress) A.; m. Ruth Relis, June 2, 1935 (dec. 1968); children: Stephen L., Peggy A.; m. Joyce Lifshutz, Sept. 16, 1968 (dec. 1999). BS, CCNY, 1931, DHL (hon.), 2002; MA, Columbia U., 1938, PhD, 1961; DSc (hon.), St. Michael's Coll., 1990. Tchr. pub. high schs., NYC, 1932-46; chmn. dept. math. Textile High Sch., NYC, 1946-52; instr. math. Columbia U., NYC, 1957-60, Bennington Coll., North Bennington, Vt., 1961, So. Vt. Coll., Bennington, 1983; researcher in math. biology North Bennington, 1972—. Lectr. in field. Author 49 books; co-author 34 books; contbr. articles to profl. jours.; contbg. editor Sci. and Society, 1981—; mem. editl. bd. Sci. and Nature, 1978-89. Recipient awards for outstanding sci. books for children Children's Book Coun. and Nat. Sci. Tchrs. Assn., 1972, 75, 80, 90, Townsend Harris medal for outstanding achievement CCNY Alumni Assn., 1993. Fellow AAAS, Vt. Acad. Arts and Sci.; mem. Am. Math. Soc., Math. Assn. Am., Nat. Council Tchrs. Math., Soc. for Indsl. and Applied Math., Authors League, Townsend Harris Hall of Fame, 1996, Phi Beta Kappa, Sigma Xi. Democrat. Jewish. Avocation: gardening. Home: 297 Cold Spring Rd North Bennington VT 05257-9767 Personal E-mail: iadler@sover.net.

ADLER, JACK SAUL, retired accountant; b. Pabianice, Poland, Feb. 1, 1929; arrived in US, 1946; s. Cemach Eli and Ruchel Fay Adler; children: Elliott Cary, Paula Fay Shapiro. BS, Walton Sch. Commerce, Chgo., 1955. Cost and tax acct. various orgns., Chgo., 1955—72; pvt. practice cost and tax acct. Miami, Fla., 1972—79, Ft. Lauderdale, Fla., 1979—92; vol. lectr. Denver, 1992—. Receiver Cir. Ct. Broward County, Ft. Lauderdale, 1976—77. With US Army, 1950—52. Recipient award, USN, USMC, 1950, US Army, 2001, award, USAF, 2002, 2003. Mem.: Am. Legion.

ADLER, JAMES BARRON, publishing executive; b. NYC, Mar. 8, 1932; s. George G. and Mollie (Barron) A.; m. Esthy Lehmann, June 26, 1956; children: Laura Frances, Eric Stephen. AB magna cum laude, Harvard U., 1953. With NBC, NYC, 1956-57, R.R. Bowker Co., NYC, 1957-61, Random House, Inc., NYC, 1961-64, G.P. Putnam's Sons, NYC, 1964-67; founder James B. Adler, Inc., 1967; founder, pres., chmn. Congressional Info. Service, Inc., Washington, 1969-81; mng. partner Adler Assos., 1981—; pres. Adler & Adler Pubs., 1983—. Chmn. Greenwood Press, Inc., 1976-79; mem. U.S. Nat. Advisory Commn. Internat. Documentation Fedn., 1972-73 Served with U.S. Army, 1954-55. Recipient Profl. award Spl. Libraries Assn., 1972; Product of Yr. award Info. Industry Assn., 1971, 76 Mem. ALA, Am. Soc. Info. Sci. Clubs: Cosmos, Nat. Press. Home: 5630 Wisconsin Ave Apt 1205 Chevy Chase MD 20815-4457 Office: 5530 Wisconsin Ave Chevy Chase MD 20815-4404

ADLER, JEFFREY D., media consultant, management consultant; b. Cleve., July 10, 1952; s. Bennett and Edythe Joy (Eisner) A.; m. Colleen Ann Bentley, May 29, 1983 (div. 2006). BS in Journalism, Northwestern U., 1975. Porter, waiter, bartender Amtrak, Chgo., 1975-76; reporter Enterprise-Courier, Oregon City, Oreg., 1977, Las Vegas Sun, 1977-80, O.C. Daily Pilot, Costa Mesa, Calif., 1982-85; v.p. pub. affairs Englander Comm., Newport Beach, Calif., 1985-86; pres. Adler Wilson Campaign Svcs., Laguna Hills, Calif., 1990-95, Adler Pub. Affairs, Long Beach, Calif., 1987—. Chair bd. dirs. Pacific Pub. Radio (KKJZ-FM), Long Beach, 2002—06. Mem. Am. Assn. Polit. Cons. Democrat. Jewish. Office: Adler Pub Affairs 200 Pine Ave Ste 300 Long Beach CA 90802-3038 Home: 1995 Molino Ave #202 Signal Hill CA 90755 Office Phone: 562-435-5551. Business E-Mail: jeffadler@adlerpa.com.

ADLER, JERRY, journalist, writer; BA, Yale U., 1970. Reporter Jour. Commerce, 1970—72, NY Daily News, 1972—79; assoc. editor Newsweek, 1979—80, gen. editor, 1980, sr. writer, 1981—93, sr. editor, 1993—. Author (with Allen Gerson): (book) The Price of Terror: The History-Making Struggle for Justice After Pan Am 103, 2001. Finalist Spl. Interest award, Nat. Mag., 1993; recipient Sidney Hillman award, 1987, First Prize award, NY Bar Assn., 1988, 2d Pl. Nat. Headliner award. Office: Newsweek 251 W 57th St New York NY 10019-1894 Office Phone: 212-445-4000.

ADLER, JULIUS, biochemist, educator, biologist; b. Edelfingen, Germany, Apr. 30, 1930; came to U.S., 1938, naturalized, 1943; s. Adolf and Irma (Stern) A.; m. Hildegard Wohl, Oct. 15, 1963; children: David Paul, Jean Susan. AB, Harvard U., 1952; MS, U. Wis., 1954, PhD, 1957; postdoctoral fellow, Washington U., St. Louis, 1957-59, Stanford U., 1959-60; doctorate (hon.), U. Tübingen, Germany, 1987, U. Regensburg, 1995. Asst. prof. biochemistry and genetics U. Wis., Madison, 1960-63, assoc. prof., 1963-66, prof., 1966-96; prof. emeritus U.Wis., Madison, 1996—; Edwin Bret Hart prof. biochemistry and genetics U. Wis., Madison, 1972, Steenbock prof. microbiol. scis., 1982-92. Recipient hon. symposium on behavior and signaling in microorganisms, 1995. Research, publs. in field. Recipient Otto-Warburg medal German Soc. Biol. Chemistry, 1986, R.H. Wright award Simon Fraser U., 1988, Hilldale award U. Wis., 1988, Abbott-Am. Soc. Microbiology Lifetime Achievment award, 1995, William C. Rose award Am. Soc. Biochemistry and Molecular Biology, 1996. Mem. NAS (Selman A. Waksman Microbiology award 1980), Am. Acad. Arts and Scis., Am. Philos. Soc., Wis. Acad. Scis., Arts and Letters. Home: 1234 Wellesley Rd Madison WI 53705-2232 Office: U Wis Dept Biochemistry Madison WI 53706 Business E-Mail: adler@biochem.wisc.edu.

ADLER, KARL PAUL, academic administrator, medical educator; b. Paterson, NJ, July 9, 1939; Grad., Seton Hall U.; MD, Georgetown U., 1966. Diplomate Am. Bd. Internal Medicine. Intern 2d med. div. Bell Hosp., Cornell U., 1966-67, jr. asst. resident 2d med. div., 1967-68; jr. asst. resident Meml. Hosp., 1967-68; sr. asst. resident Cornell Cooperating Hosps., 1968-69, chief resident in medicine, 1969-70; sr. asst. resident North Shore Hosp., Manhasset, NY, 1968-69, chief resident in medicine, 1969-70, assoc. dir. dept. medicine, 1972-74, chief nephrology, 1972-74; med. dir. dept. emergency services Kings County Hosp. Ctr., Bklyn., 1974-77, med. dir. dept. medicine, 1974-77; asst. prof. medicine Cornell U., 1971-74, SUNY Med. Sch., Bklyn., 1974-76, assoc. prof. clin. medicine, 1976-77; chief dept. medicine Ellis Hosp., 1977-81; vice chmn. at Albany Med., 1977-81, assoc. prof. med., 1977-81; chief dept. medicine Met. Hosp. Ctr., 1981-87; dean NY Med. Coll., Valhalla, 1987-94, prof. medicine, 1981—, v.p. for med. affairs, 1990-94, pres., 2007—; pres., CEO St. Vincent's Hosp. and Med. Ctr., NYC, 1994-2000. Pres. Assoc. Med. Schs. NY, 1991—93; Archbishop's delegate Health Care in Archdiocese of NY; chmn. bd. Cath. Health Care Sys. Mem. ACP, Am. Assn. Med. Colls., Alpha Omega Alpha. Office: NY Med Coll Adminstrn Bldg 40 Sunshine Cottage Rd Valhalla NY 10595 Office Fax: 914-594-4600.*

ADLER, KENNETH R., oncologist; b. Bklyn., Sept. 22, 1947; BS, U. Pitts., 1968; MD, Albany Med. Coll., NY, 1973. Diplomate Am. Bd. Internal Medicine, Am. Bd. Hematology. Intern Albany Med. Ctr. Hosp., 1973—74, resident in internal medicine, 1974—76, resident in hematology and oncology, 1976—78; oncologist Carol G. Simon Cancer Ctr., Morristown (N.J.) Meml. Hosp. Clin. asst. prof. medicine N.J. Med. Sch. Named one of Top Drs. in N.Y. Met. Area, Castle Connolly, Top Drs. 2003, N.J. Monthly Mag., Top Drs. 2006. Office: Carol G Simon Cancer Ctr Morristown Meml Hosp 100 Madison Ave Morristown NJ 07960 Home Phone: 973-984-2692; Office Phone: 973-538-5210. Business E-Mail: kenneth.adler@ahsys.org.

ADLER, LEWIS GERARD, lawyer; b. NYC, Sept. 13, 1960; s. Sherman and Esther (Weiss) A.; m. Kim Adler, Sept. 5, 1988; children: Craig, Stephanie, Katie, Samantha. AS, Vanderbilt U., 1981; JD, Rutgers U., 1985. Bar: NJ. 1986, Pa. 1985, U.S. Dist. Ct. N.J. 1986, U.S. Dist. Ct. Pa. 1990, U.S. Supreme Ct. 1990, U.S. Tax Ct. 2000, U.S. Ct. Appeals (3d cir.) 2000. Solicitor Gloucester County Constrn. Bd. Appeals, Woodbury, N.J.,

1987-88; atty. Gloucester County Sr. Citizen Will Program, Woodbury, 1987-88; pvt. practice Woodbury, N.J., 1989—; spl. counsel Gloucester County, 1990—. Pub. defender Deptford Township, 1996, zoning bd. solicitor, 1997-2000. Designer computer software. Pres. Haddonfield Plays & Players, 2002—. Mem. ABA, N.J. Bar Assn., Gloucester County Bar Assn., Phila. Trial Lawyers, Pa. Bar Assn. Democrat. Avocations: water and snow skiing, spelunking, chess, bicycling, rappelling. Home: 215 Douglass Ave Haddonfield NJ 08033-1626 Office: 26 Newton Ave Woodbury NJ 08096-4633 Office Phone: 856-845-1968. Personal E-mail: lewisadler@verizon.net.

ADLER, MARGOT SUSANNA, journalist, radio producer, correspondent, writer; b. Little Rock, Apr. 16, 1946; d. Kurt Alfred and Freyda (Nacque) A. BA, U. Calif., Berkeley, 1968; MS, Columbia U., 1970. Newscaster Sta. WBAI-FM, NYC, 1968-71, host talk show, 1972-90; chief Washington bur. Pacifica News Svc. Network; corr., prodr. All Things Considered, Morning Edit., Nat. Pub. Radio, NYC, 1978—, host Justice Talking, 1999—. Instr. radio comms. Goddard Coll., Plainfield, Vt., 1977; instr. religion and ecology Inst. for Social Ecology, Vt., 1986-93. Author: Drawing Down the Moon, 1979, Heretic's Heart, 1997; co-prodr., dir. (radio drama) War Day, 1985; contbr. articles to prof. jours. Nieman fellow Harvard U., 1982. Mem. Phi Beta Kappa. Avocations: swimming, bird watching, science fiction. Home: 333 Central Park W New York NY 10025-7145 Office: Nat Pub Radio 11 W 42d St 19th Fl New York NY 10036 Home Phone: 212-222-6298; Office Phone: 212-880-3435. Business E-Mail: madler@npr.org.

ADLER, MARTIN WILLIAM, neuropharmacologist; b. Phila., Oct. 30, 1929; s. Jack and Sonia (Coopersmith) A.; m. Toby Wisotsky, June 28, 1953; children: Charles Howard, Eve Robin. BA, NYU, 1949; BS, Bklyn. Coll. Pharmacy, 1953; MS, Columbia U., 1957; PhD, Albert Einstein Coll. Medicine, 1960. From instr. to assoc. prof. Temple U. Sch. Medicine, Phila., 1960-73, prof., 1973—; Laura H. Carnell prof. pharmacology, 1999—. Chmn. rsch. rev. coms. NIH, 1980-2000; exec. officer Coll. on Problems of Drug Dependence, Phila., 1986—; dir. Ctr. for Substance Abuse Rsch., 1998—. Author: 5 book chpts., 6 major revs.; editor: Factors Affecting Action of Narcotic Drugs, 1976, Testing of Drugs of Abuse, 1990; contbr. more than 200 articles to profl. jours. Sgt. U.S. Army, 1953-55, Korea. Grantee Nat. Inst. on Drug Abuse, 1973—, Dir. Tng. grant, 1989-2002; recipient Nathan B. Eddy award Coll. on Problems of Drug Dependence, Jos. Wybran Award, Soc. Neuroimmune Pharmacology. Fellow AAAS, Coll. on Problems of Drug Dependence, Am. Coll. Neuropsychopharmacology; mem. Am. Soc. Pharmacology and Exptl. Therapeutics. Jewish. Achievements include patent for drug combination to produce profound hypothermia; discoveries that endogenous opioid system has a role in analgesia, thermoregulation, and brain excitability, that opioids produce marked oscillations in size of pupil, that recovery from brain damage is accompanied by supersensitivity, that opioids are involved in immunoregulation and in the actions of cytokines and chemokines in the brain; proposed theory that chemokine system in brain neurons are involved in neuronal communcation, similar to neuropeptides and neurotransmitters. Office: Temple U Sch Medicine 3420 N Broad St Philadelphia PA 19140-5104

ADLER, MICHAEL I., lawyer; b. San Francisco, May 10, 1949; BA in Polit. Sci. summa cum laude, UCLA, 1971, JD, 1976; MA, Columbia U., 1973. Bar: Calif. 1977. Extern to Hon. Matthew O. Tobriner Calif. Supreme Ct., 1975; law clerk to Hon. William B. Enright U.S. Dist. Ct. (so. dist.) Calif., 1976-77; mem. mitzlell Solberbery & Knubb, LA, 1977—97; ptnr. Lichter, Grossman, Nichols & Adler, Inc., LA, 1997—. Mem. entertainment law symposium com. UCLA, 1979—; instr. UCLA Extension, 1980. Woodrow Wilson fellow, 1972; Columbia U. Presdl. fellow, 1973. Mem. ABA, State Bar Calif., L.A. County Bar Assn., Beverly Hills Bar Assn., Phi Beta Kappa, Phi Eta Sigma. Office: Lichter Grossman Nichols & Adler Inc 9200 W Sunset Blvd Ph 1200 Los Angeles CA 90069-3607 E-mail: madler@lgna.com.

ADLER, NORMAN TENNER, psychology educator, dean; b. Chgo., June 7, 1941; BA, Harvard U., 1962; MA in Endocronology, U. Calif., 1967. Prof. U. Pa., 1968—93; rsch. prof. dept. elec. engring. Drexel U., 1985-93; prof. psychology in psychiatry sch. medicine U. Pa., 1988-93, assoc. dean coll. Sch. Arts and Scis., 1989-93; vice provost rsch. Northeastern U., 1993-95; prof. psychology Yeshiva U., NYC, 1995—2005, dean, 1995—2005, u. prof., 2005—. Organizer, Roundtable on Liberal Learning in Rsch. Univs. Am. Assn. Colls., 1994—. Recipient Charles A. Dana Found. Prize, 1988; grantee John Simon Guggenheim Fellow, 1985—86, Harry Frank Guggenheim Fellow, 1985—86. Mem.: AAAS, Endocrine Soc., Am. Soc. of Zoologists, Society for Neuroscience, Soc. for Neuroethology, Internat. Soc. for Devel. Psychobiology, Animal Behavior Soc., Am. Psychol. Assn. (chair, Sci. Awards Com. 1993—95). Office: Office VP Acad Affairs Yeshiva U 500 W 185th St New York NY 10033 Office Phone: 212-960-5217. Office Fax: 212-960-0060. Business E-Mail: adler@yu.edu.

ADLER, PEGGY ANN, writer, illustrator, consultant, protective services official; b. NYC, Feb. 10, 1942; d. Irving and Ruth Adler; children: Tenney Whedon Walsh, Avery Denison Walsh (Mrs. Adam I. Lapidus). Student, Bennington Coll., Vt., 1959—60, Columbia U., NYC, 1962. Illustrator, author children's books, 1958—; logistics and ticket sales and mgmt. the world premiere "Butch Cassidy and Sundance Kid", 1969; agt. Jan J. Agy., Inc., NYC, 1981-82; freelance talent scout Cuzzins Mgmt., NYC, 1982-83; personal mgmt. and pub. rels. cons. Madison, Conn., 1983-93. Rsch. assoc. Steve Fredericksen, Pvt. Investigator, Conn. and NY, 1990—96; investigative rschr., writer, lit. cons., 1986—; asst. investigator Ho. of Reps. October Surprise Task Force, Washington, 1992; pvt. investigator; child care provider, 1998—. Author (illustrator): The Adler Book of Puzzles and Riddles, 1962, The 2nd Adler Book of Puzzles and Riddles, 1963, Metric Puzzles, 1977, Math Puzzles, 1978, Geography Puzzles, 1979; author: Hakim's Connection, 1988; co-author: Skull and Bones: The Skeleton in Bush's Closet?, 1988; contbr. illustrator numerous books including Hot and Cold, 1959, Numbers New and Old, 1960, Reading Fundamentals for Teen-Agers, 1973, Do a Zoomdo, 1975, Pet Care, 1974, Caring for Your Cat, 1974; graphic designer: various book covers, posters, and logos; pub. rels. Sweetie, Baby, Cookie, Honey (Freddie Gershon), 1986, rschr. Passion and Prejudice: A Family Memoir (Sallie Bingham), 1989, The Village Voice, 1991, 1992, numerous others; contbr. The President's Private Eye: The Journey of Detective Tony U. from N.Y.P.D. to the Nixon White Ho., 1990; cons., rschr.: Bush's Boys Club: Skull and Bones, 1990; cons. Spy Saga (Philip H. Melanson), 1990; contbr. Lies of Our Times; licensee/story cons. 60 Minutes, 1991; cons., rschr.: London Sunday Times, 1991; contbr. The Independent London, 1994, 1995; rsch. assoc. for Ron Rosenbaum, I Stole the Head of Prescott Bush! More Scary Skull and Bones Tales, NY Observer, 2000, rsch. assoc. Inside Skull and Bones' Secret Initiation Ritual, 2001, cons. BBC Current Affairs, 2004. Founder Shoreline Youth Theatre, Inc., 1979, bd. dirs., 1979—81, adv. bd., 1981—86; bd. dirs. Greens Condominium Assn. Branford, Conn., 1975—78, Arts Coun. Greater New Haven, 1971—73, Planned Parenthood Greater New Haven, 1972—73, Assassination Archives and Rsch. Ctr., Washington, 1990—96; v.p., bd. dirs. Pub. Info. Rsch., Washington, 1989; hon. mem. Forgotten Families; chmn. majority subcom. study com. 10 Killingworth Turnpike bldg., mem. charter revision commn. Town of Clinton, 1997—98, 2003—04, author, charter revisions, legal notice and ballot questions, 1998, 2004, mem. design adv. bd., 2000—07, chmn. design adv. bd., 2003—06, vice chmn., 2005—06, chmn., 2006—07, mem. Clinton Landing study com.; vol. Clinton Pub. Schs.; project dir. Clinton Village/Main St. Hist. Enhancement Project Phase I; asst. softball coach Clinton Park and Recreation Commn., 2007—; mem. hist. dist. commn. Town of Clinton, 2001—06, vice chmn., 2005—06, constable, 2001—05, police commr., 2005—. Mem.: Police Commr.'s Assn. Conn., Conn. Soc. Genealogists Inc., Assn. Former Intelligence Officers (program coord. 1997—2004, bd. dirs. 1997—, pres. New Eng. chpt. 2001—03, ex officio 2004—, Gen. Richard G. Stilwell Chmn.'s award 2001), Rotary (mem. cancer relief fund com. Clinton chpt. 2006—), Duck Island Yacht Club (membership com. 1997—2000, social com. 1997—2004, Duck Stop 1997—2004, Don Dyson Corinthian award 1998). Home and Office: 5 Liberty St Clinton CT 06413

ADLER, RAPHAEL, retired humanities educator, speech pathology/audiology services professional; b. NYC, Feb. 21, 1922; s. Marcus and Celia (Kress) A.; m. Minna Adler, Sept. 23, 1948; children: Ava Dee, Roxanne, Margo Celeste. BA, Wayne State U., 1953, M in Edn., 1962; PhD, Walden U., 1981. Cert. tchr. secondary schs., Mich.; cert. speech pathologist Am. Speech and Hearing Assn. Tchr. dept. English/speech Berkley (Mich.) Sch. Dist., 1954-68; prof. Oakland C.C., Union Lake, Mich., 1968-92, prof. emeritus, 1992—2002; pres. P.W. Mulligan Enterprises, LLC. Dir. speech and hearing St. Joseph Mercy Hosp., Pontiac, Mich.,1965-84; owner, dir., pres. Speech Pathology Svcs., Southfield, Mich., 1972-86; cons. hosps., nursing homes, VNA, S. Oakland County Health Dept.; bd. dirs. Motion Picture Inst. Mich. Author: The Magical Adventures of Pee Wee Mulligan, 2001. Com. mem. Am. Heart Assn. of Mich., past chmn.; chmn., bd. trustees State of Mich. Stroke Com. Recipient many speaking citations and awards, 1953-62, Toastmasters Internat. 1971, Mrs. Horace Elgin Dodge award Am. Heart Assn. Mich., 1989, 92, 95. Avocations: reading, gardening, writing, poetry.

ADLER, RICHARD, composer, lyricist; b. NYC, Aug. 3, 1921; s. Clarence and Elsa (Richard) A.; children by previous marriage: Andrew H., Christopher E. (dec.); children: Katherine J.S.; 1 stepson, Charles A. Shipman. AB, U. NC, 1943; D in Music and Theatre, Wagner Coll., 2003. Mem. advt. dept. Celanese Corp. Am., 1946-50; White House cons. on the arts, 1965-69. Cons. on arts gov. N.C. Adv. bd. Inst. Outdoor Drama, 1968-83, N.C. School arts, 1963—; commd. by Harvard U. to write a march for 50th Anniversary of Neiman Found. Journalist Soc., 1989. Collaborator (with Jerry Ross): on music and lyrics for musicals John Murray Anderson's Almanac, 1953, Pajama Game, 1954, Damn Yankees, 1955; composer, lyricist Kwamina, 1961, TV prodns. Little Women, 1959, Gift of the Magi, 1959; produced and staged White House Press Corrs. and Photographers show for Pres. Kennedy and Prime Minister MacMillan, 1962, N.Y.'s Birthday Salute for Pres. Kennedy, 1962, Inaugural Anniversity Salute to Pres. Kennedy, 1963, Salutes to Pres. Johnson, 1964, Inaugural Gala for Pres. Lyndon Johnson, 1965; producer, composer, lyricist: ABC-TV Stage 67 Musical Olympus 7-0000, fall 1966; composer, lyricist: A Mother's Kisses, 1968; producer: revival Pajama Game, 1973; producer: Rex, 1976; co-producer-composer: Music Is, 1976, Yellowstone Overture (Pulitizer prize nomination); commd. by Dept. of Interior to write Wilderness Suite (Pulitzer prize nomination), 1983, recorded by Utah Symphony; commd. by Statue of Liberty/Ellis Island Found. to write The Lady Remembers (Pulitzer prize nomination), recorded by Detroit Symphony, Retrospectrum (Pulitizer prize nomination); commd. by Chgo. City Ballet to write Eight by Adler, 1984 (Emmy award for TV version 1985); commd. by City of Chgo. to write (ballet) Chicago for sesquicentennial, 1987; commd. by Olympic Com. to write fanfare and overture for U.S. Olympic Festival, 1987, commd. by U. N.C. to write suite to commemorate bi-centennial, 1993, recorded by London Symphony Orch.; author: (autobiography) You Gotta Have Heart, 1990; collaborator lyrics, composer: Off Key, 1995; composer The House of Bernarda Alba, 1998, Wilderness Suite Ballet, 2001, Notes on My Life, 2002. Trustee John F. Kennedy Ctr. for Performing Arts, 1964-77, exec. com., 1975-77; bd. dirs. Southampton Cultural Com. Lt. (j.g.) USNR, 1943-46. Recipient Antoinette Perry award, Donaldson award, Variety Critics Poll for Pajama Game 1954, Damn Yankees 1955, Antoinette Perry nomination Kwamina 1962, Pulitzer Prize nomination Retrospectrum 1980, Yellowstone Overture 1981, Playmaker Life Time Achievement award dept. dramatic art U. N.C., 1999, Richard Rodgers award ASCAP Found., 2002, U. N.C. Lifetime Achievement award, 2005; Pulitzer prize nominee for rec. The Statue of Liberty Suite; named to Songwriters Hall of Fame, 1984; Hon. Park Ranger award Nat. Park Service, 1984. Mem. Dramatists Guild (exec. coun. 1958-68), Songwriters Guild Am. (bd. dirs., exec. com., exec. v.p. 1985—), New Dramatists (bd. dirs. 1974-2001), Nat. Hypertension Assn. (bd. dirs. 1978—). Address: 8 E 83d St New York NY 10028-0418 E-mail: reldar2@aol.com.

ADLER, RICHARD MELVIN, architect, planner; b. NYC, Mar. 25, 1928; s. Jacob William and Betty (Uffer) A.; children: Robin Sheryl, Joy Lois; m. Marie Fusco, 1986. BArch, Pratt Inst., Bklyn., 1948. Registered architect, N.Y., others. Airport architect Port Auth. N.Y., 1952-58; ptnr. Brodsky Hoff & Adler, NYC, 1959-71; pres. BHA Architects & Engrs., NYC, 1971-75, Brodsky & Adler, NYC, 1975-80, R.M. Adler & Assocs., Peterborough, N.H., 1993—. Pres. Adler, Goodman A Kolab For Architects & Engrs., Great Neck, 1993—; chmn. bd. Geller Termotto & Adler, Teaneck, N.J., 1982— , Clendening Adler, Arlington, Tex., 1983—. Elected to budget com., Peterborough, 1998—; chmn. capital improvement com. Town of Peterborough, 1996—. Served to 1st lt., N.Y. Nat. Guard, 1948-63. Recipient Disting. Svc. award Engrs. News Record, 1974, Creative Design award ASCE, 1973. Mem. AIA (emeritus; Merit award 1977, bd. dirs. L.I. chpt. 1988), N.Y. Soc. Architects, Peterborough C. of C. Republican. Jewish. E-mail: rmaaia@pobox.com.

ADLER, ROBERT L., lawyer; b. NYC, Nov. 14, 1947; m. Sara M. Adler; 2 children. AB magna cum laude, Harvard U., 1969, JD cum laude, 1973. Bar: Calif. 1974. Exec. asst. Orange County Bd. Suprs., 1970-71; legis. asst. to mem. congress, 1973-74; pres., CEO Ray Wilson Co., 1985; mem. Munger, Tolles & Olson, LA, ptnr., 1978—. Articles editor Harvard Law Rev., 1972-73. Mem. ABA, State Bar Calif., L.A. County Bar Assn., Phi Beta Kappa. Office: Munger Tolles & Olson 355 S Grand Ave 35th Fl Los Angeles CA 90071-1560 Office Phone: 213-683-9129. Office Fax: 213-683-5129. Business E-Mail: robert.adler@mto.com.

ADLER, ROBERT MARTIN, lawyer; b. Toledo, Oct. 2, 1943; s. Charles J. and Barbara (Sechback) A.; m. Andrea Rosenberg, June 12, 1966; children: Rebecca J., David C. BA, Oberlin Coll., 1965; JD, U. Mich., 1968. Bar: D.C. 1969. Trial atty. tax divsn. U.S. Dept. Justice, Washington, 1968-74; ptnr. Stiller, Adler & Schwartz, Washington, 1974-81; pvt. practice Law Offices Robert M. Adler, Washington, 1981-91; sr. ptnr. Drinker Biddle & Reath, Washington, 1991-96; ptnr. O'Connor & Hannon, L.L.P., Washington, 1996—. Chmn. Stiller Meml. Found., Washington, 1979-91. Avocation: sailing. Office: O'Connor & Hannan LLP 1666 K St NW Ste 500 Washington DC 20006-1217

ADLER, SAMUEL HANS, retired conductor, composer; b. Mannheim, Germany, Mar. 4, 1928; came to U.S., 1939, naturalized, 1945; s. Hugo Chaim and Selma (Rothschild) A.; m. Carol Ellen Stalker, Feb. 14, 1960 (div. 1989); children: Deborah Ruth, Naomi Leah; m. Emily Freeman Brown, June 8, 1991. MusB, Boston U., 1948; MA, Harvard U., 1950; MusD (hon.), So. Methodist U., 1969; DFA (hon.), Wake Forest U.; D.F.A. (hon.), St. Mary's Coll., Ind., 1986; DMus (hon.), St. Louis Conservatory, 1986. Music dir. Temple Emanu-El, Dallas, 1953-66; prof. composition North Tex. State U., Denton, 1957-66; Eastern regional dir. contemporary music project Ford Found., 1966-70; prof. composition Eastman Sch. Music, U. Rochester, NY, 1966-94; hon. prof. U. Wales, Cardiff, 1984-89; ret., 1994; tchr. Julliard Sch. Music, NYC. Lectr., condr. throughout world Condr. Dallas Chorale, 1954—57, Dallas Lyric Theatre, 1955—59; composer: 6 symphonies, 4 operas, 8 string quartets, sonatas for piano, violin (4), cello, flute, viola, guitar, oboe, clarinet, organ, saxophone, concertos for piano (3), violin, horn, cello, flute, saxophone quartet, organ, woodwind quintet, guitar, viola, also for orch. and band, chamber and choral works, songs; author: Choral Conducting, 1971, 2d revised edit., 1985, Sight Singing, 1979, 2d revised edit., 1996, The Study of Orchestration, 1982, 3d edit., 2002. Served with AUS, 1950-52. Grantee Nat. Endowment Arts, Ford Found., Rockefeller Found.; recipient 6 1st prizes Tex. Composers Contest, Charles Ives award, 1965, Lillian Fairchild award, 1968, Deems Taylor award, 1983, Am. Acad. and Inst. Arts and Letters award, 1990; Guggenheim fellow, 1984-85; named Composer of the Yr. Music Teachers' Nat. Assn. 1986, 87, Composer of the Yr. Am. Guild of Organists, 1989, 91. Mem.: ASCAP (awards 1960—), Music Tchrs. Nat. Assn., Music Educators Nat. Conf., Phi Beta Kappa, Phi Mu Alpha Sinfonia, Am. Acad. Arts and Letters. Jewish. E-mail: sadlercomp@yahoo.com.

ADLER, SARA, arbitrator, mediator; b. Chgo., Jan. 26, 1942; d. Matthew Michael and Mildred Paula (Eckhaus) Lewison; m. James N. Adler, Aug. 19, 1967; children: Michael, Philip, Matthew. AB, U. Chgo., 1961; JD, UCLA, 1969. Bar: Calif. Cons. Inst. Criminal Justice Adminstrn. U. Calif., Davis, 1969-71; assoc. Law Office of Sara Radin, LA, 1971-72; assoc. dir. Paralegal Tng. Inst. U. So. Calif., LA, 1972-74; assoc. Wyman, Bautzer, et al, LA, 1974-78; arbitrator, mediator Dispute Resolution Svcs., LA, 1978—. Fellow: Coll. Labor and Employment Lawyers; mem.: ABA (neutral co-chair ADR in Labor/employment Law 1995—98, neutral mem. coun. Labor & Employment sect.), Labor and Employment Rsch. Assn. (nat. bd. dirs. 2005—), L.A. County Bar Assn. (chmn. labor and employment sect. 1997—98), Labor Employee Rsch. Assn. (pres. so. Calif. 1991—92, exec. bd. mem. 2005—07, nat. exec. bd. mem. 2005—), Nat. Acad. Arbitrators (regional chair 1994—96, bd. govs. 2000—03, v.p. 2005—, chpt. pres. 2007), Am. Arbitration Assn. (bd. dirs., exec. com., labor mgmt. law task force, employment ADR steering com.). Avocations: travel, theater, bridge. Office: Dispute Resolution Svcs 1034 Selby Ave Los Angeles CA 90024-3106 Home Phone: 310-470-3360; Office Phone: 310-474-5170. Personal E-mail: sadlerarb@earthlink.net.

ADLER, SEYMOUR JACK, social services administrator; b. Chgo., Oct. 22, 1930; s. Michael L. and Sarah (Pasnick) A.; m. Barbara Fingold, Mar. 24, 1958; children: Susan Lynn Adler, Karen Sandra Adler-Marder, Michelle Lauren Adler-Morrison. BS, Northwestern U., 1952; MA, U. Chgo., 1958. Caseworker Cook County Dept. Pub. Aid, Chgo., 1955; juvenile officer Cook County Sheriff's Office, 1955—56; U.S. probation-parole officer U.S. Dist. Ct., Chgo., 1958—68; exec. dir. Youth Guidance, Chgo., 1968—73; dir. court svcs. Juvenile Ct. Cook County, Chgo., 1973—75; exec. dir. Meth. Youth Svcs., Chgo., 1975—85; program mgr. Dept. Social Svcs., Kenosha, Wis., 1985—91, dir., 1992—95, Dept. Human Svcs., Kenosha, 1996—99, coord. Kenosha Yes, Juvenile Justice Project, 1999—2002; cmty. liaison Wis. Coun. on Children and Families, 2002—. Mem. Ill. Law Enforcement Commn., 1969—72; instr. corrections program Chgo. State U., 1972—75; instr. Harper Coll., 1977, St. Joseph's Coll., 1978; case developer Nat. Ctr. on Instns. and Alternatives, 1985—86; mem. soc. sci. adv. com. Carthage Coll., 1997—. Chair adminstrn. com. Joint Youth Devel. Program, 1973—75; bd. dirs. Kenosha Area Family and Aging Svcs., Inc., 2003—, Child Care Assn. Ill., 1979—84; exec. bd. Kenosha br. NAACP, 1998—, v.p., 2004—, W-2 steering com., 1998—99; chair ethics bd. Village Twin Lakes, 2003—, mem. election bd., 2007—; mem. Gov's Juvenile Justice Commn., 2005—, SE Wis. Area Adv. Com. Aging, 2005—, Wis. State Aging Adv. Coun., 2006—07; mem. Kenosha mental health com. Comprehensive Cmty. Svcs. Bd., Kenosha Schs. Pre-K Planning Group; mem. Kenosha Coalition on Homeless, Holiday House, Concerned Citizens' Coalition and Healthy Cmty. and Healthy Youth. 1st lt. USMCR, 1952—55. Recipient Meritorious Svc. award Chgo. City Colls., 1968, Appreciation award NAACP, 1999, Svc. award, 2003, award Kenosha County Foster Parents Assn., 2000. Mem. NASW (del. Assembly 1977, 1979, 1981, 1984, 1987, chmn. Chgo. dist. 1978-80, com. inquiry Wis. chpt. 1990—, leadership ID com. 2002-05, chair 2006—), Ill. Acad. Criminology (pres. 1972, Morris J. Wexler award 1975, Pres.'s award 1997, Svc. award 2004), Alpha Kappa Delta, Tau Delta Phi. Home: 232 Grandview Ln Twin Lakes WI 53181-9572 Office: Kenosha Dept Human Svcs 8600 Sheridan Rd Kenosha WI 53143 Office Phone: 262-605-6521. Business E-Mail: sadler@co.kenosha.wi.us.

ADLER, STEPHEN J., editor-in-chief; b. NYC; m. Lisa Grunwald; children: Elizabeth, Jonathan. BA, Harvard Coll., 1977; JD, Harvard Law Sch., 1983. Reporter Tampa Times, Tallahassee Democrat; editor The American Lawyer, 1983—88; legal editor The Wall Street Journal, 1988—94, spl. projects editor Page One, 1994—97, dep. Page One editor, 1997—99, dep. mng. editor, 1999—2005; editor-in-chief BusinessWeek Mag., NYC, 2005—. Author: The Jury: Trial and Error in the American Courtroom (ABA Silver Gavel Award, 1995); editor: Letters of the Century, 1999. Bd. dir. Goddard-Riverside Cmty. Ctr. Recipient Nat. Magazine award for Best Interactive Svc. for B-School Ch. on Business-Week.com, Am. Soc. Mag. Editors, 2007. Office: BusinessWeek 43rd Fl McGraw-Hill Bldg 1221 Ave of Americas New York NY 10020-1093 Office Phone: 212-512-2511.*

ADLER, STEPHEN LOUIS, physicist; b. NYC, Nov. 30, 1939; s. Irving and Ruth Adler; children: Jessica Wendy, Victoria Stephanie, Anthony Curtis; m. Sarah C. Brett-Smith, 1995. AB summa cum laude, Harvard U., 1961; PhD, Princeton U., 1964. Jr. fellow Soc. Fellows Harvard U., 1964—66; rsch. assoc. Calif. Inst. Tech., 1966; mem. Inst. for Advanced Study, Princeton, NJ, 1966—69, prof. Sch. Natural Scis., 1969—, N.J. Albert Einstein prof. Sch. Natural Scis., 1979—2003. Vis. lectr. dept. physics Princeton U., 1969—. Author: (with R.F. Dashen) Current Algebras, 1968, Quaternionic Quantum Mechanics and Quantum Fields, 1995, Quantum Theory as an Emergent Phenomenon, 2004, Adventures in Theoretical Physics, 2006; contbr. articles to profl. jours. Recipient J.J. Sakurai prize Am. Phys. Soc., 1988, Dirac medal Internat. Ctr. Theoretical Physics, Trieste, Italy, 1998. Fellow Am. Acad. Arts and Scis., AAAS, Am. Phys. Soc.; mem. Nat. Acad. Scis., Phi Beta Kappa, Sigma Xi. Home: 287A Nassau St Princeton NJ 08540-4618 Office: Sch Natural Scis Inst Advanced Study Einstein Dr Princeton NJ 08540 Office Phone: 609-734-8051.

ADLER, TRACY L., curator; b. NYC; BA in Art History, Skidmore Coll., Saratoga Springs, NY, 1990; MA in Art History, Hunter Coll., NYC, 1996. Asst. curatorial dept. prints and photographs Met. Mus. of Art, NYC, 1991—92; adminstrv. asst. BlumHelman Gallery, NYC, 1992—93; asst. office mgr. James Mansour Design, Ltd., NYC, 1993—94; studio mgr./dir. Shonna Valeska Photography, NYC, 1994—97; exhbn. asst. curatorial dept. The Jewish Mus., NYC, 1997—98; curator Hunter Coll. Art Galleries, NYC, 1998—. Cons. Adler Arts, NYC, 2005—. Author: numerous exhbn. catalogue essays. Mem.: Am. Assn. Museums, New Leadership Assoc. Office: Hunter Coll Art Galleries 695 Park Ave New York NY 10021 Office Phone: 212-772-4991.

ADLERSBERG, JAY BEN, internist; b. Pitts., Nov. 25, 1944; s. Herman and Mathilda (Marshall) A.; 1 child, Zoe. BS magna cum laude, U. Pitts., 1965; MD, U. Pa., 1969. Diplomate Am. Bd. Internal Medicine, Nat. Bd. Med. Examiners. Intern in internal medicine NYU Med. Ctr., NYC, 1969-70, jr. asst. resident, asst. resident medicine Bellevue Hosp., 1970-72, NIH fellow in rheumatology/immunology, 1972-74; asst. prof. medicine divsn. rheumatic diseases/immunology Albert Einsteon Coll. Medicine, Bronx, 1974-80; assoc. attending physician Bronx (N.Y.) Mcpl. Hosp. Ctr., 1976-80; attending physician Beth Israel Med. Ctr., NYC, 1980—, Lenox Hill Hosp., NYC, 1986—; asst. prof. medicine Mt. Sinai Sch. Medicine,

NYC, 1980—. Assoc. attending physician Hosp. for Joint Diseases/Orthopaedic Inst., N.Y.C., 1980—; attending physician Hosp. Albert Einstein Coll. Medicine, 1974-80, Montefiore Hosp. Med. Ctr., Bronx, 1974-76; teaching asst. in medicine NYU Med. Ctr., 1972-74; teaching fellow in rheumatology Bellevue Hosp., 1972-74; keynote speaker Jonas Salk Scholarship Awards CUNY, 1993. Contbg. corr. ABC News Now, 1992—; weekly med. corr. The Health Show, ABC News, 1987-90; med. reporter Eyewitness News, WABC-TV, NY, 1983—; co-host Arthritis Telethon, WOR-TV, NYC, 1982-86; guest host Healthline, WNYU-AM Radio, NYC, 1980;host Healthy Life, 2007; contbr. weekly health column Bridgehampton Sun, NY,1980-81. Master of ceremonies gala Cystic Fibrosis Found., 1990, S.I. Hospice Assn., 1990, Town Hall Arthritis Found., NYC, 2007, Catle Connelly Best Doctors Pubs., Awards for Achievement in Clin. Medicine, NYC, 2007; mem. med. and sci. com. NY chpt. Arthritis Found., 1985-88, bd. dirs., 2005-; elected dir. of bd. Arthritis Found., NY Chpt., 2005. Named One of Best Drs. in NY NY Mag., 1998, 05; included in How to Find the Best Doctors, New York, 1998, 99, 00, 01, 02, 03, 04, George Foster Peabody award Excellence Journalism, 2001; citation NY City Coun., 2003; Am. Cancer Soc. grantee, 1977-79. Fellow Am. Coll. Rheumatology; mem. AMA, N.Y. Acad. Scis., Am. Rheumatism Assn., N.Y. Rheumatism Assn., Med. Soc. County of N.Y., Med. Soc. State of N.Y., Phi Beta Kappa. Avocations: road bicycling, skiing, tennis, reading. Office: 220 E 69th St New York NY 10021-5737 Home Phone: 212-362-3888; Office Phone: 212-570-1800. Business E-Mail: drjay@medasso.com.

ADLERSHTEYN, LEON, retired marine architect, retired engineering educator and researcher; b. St. Petersburg, Russia, Oct. 28, 1925; arrived in U.S., 1994, naturalized, 2000; s. Tsalim and Judith (Shusterovich) Adlershteyn; m. Irina Bereznaya, Feb. 24, 1962. MS in Shipbuilding, Shipbuilding Inst., St. Petersburg, 1951; ScD in Engring., Ctr. Rsch. Inst. Shipbuilding Tech., St. Petersburg, 1970. Foreman, dep. chief of the hull shop Baltic Shipyard, St. Petersburg, 1951-63; chief technologist Ctrl. Rsch. Inst. Shipbuilding Tech., St. Petersburg, 1963-65, team leader, 1965-74, chief rschr., 1993-94; head dept. Acad. Shipbuilding, St. Petersburg, 1974-88, prof., 1988-94; ret., 1994. Coun. mem. Ctrl. Rsch. Inst. Shipbuilding Tech., St. Petersburg, 1963—94, Acad. Shipbuilding, St. Petersburg, 1974—94; chmn. state exam. commn. State Marine Tech. U., St. Petersburg, 1989—94. Co-author: Accuracy in Ship Hull Manufacturing, Mechanization and Automation of Ship Manufacturing, Modular Ship Building, Ship Examiner; contbr. articles to profl. jours. Bd. dirs. Union Scientists and Engrs., St. Petersburg, 1990—94, chmn. coun. sect., 1992—94. With Russian Army, 1943—45, ETO. Decorated 14 mil. and 3 non-mil. medals Pres. of USSR Supreme Soviet and Pres. of Russian Fedn., 4 mil. awards Am. Legion and Am. Assn. Invalids and Vets. WWII, Order of Patriotic War 1st Class Pres. of USSR Supreme Soviet; recipient 5 medals, Russian Nat. Indsl. Exhbn., 1955—2005. Fellow: Inst. Marine Engring., Sci. and Tech. (U.K.); mem.: Russian Soc. Shipbuilders (various prizes 1955—93), Union Scientists and Engrs., Soc. Naval-Archs. and Marine Engrs., Am. Assn. Invalids and Vets WWII. Achievements include patents in field; research in accuracy in ship hull manufacturing; development of mechanized means for ship manufacturing. Home: 72 Montgomery St Apt 1510 Jersey City NJ 07302-3827 Personal E-mail: bereznaya@gmail.com.

ADNET, JACQUES JIM PIERRE, astronautical and electrical engineer, consultant; b. Sermaize-les-Bains, Marne, France, Dec. 12, 1929; arrived in U.S., 1947; s. Julien Charles and Aline Georgette (Klein) A.; m. Mildred Ann Pruet, June 8, 1952 (div. Apr. 1982); children: Denise E., Lisa A., Paul A.; m. Helen Ilene Milam, Nov. 3, 1990. BA with honors, U. Fla., 1951, BEE with honors, 1960; MS in Astronautics, AF Inst. Tech., 1965; grad., Indsl. Coll. Armed Forces, 1972. Interpreter (civilian) U.S. Army, France, 1945—46; enlisted USAF, 1951, commd. 2d lt., 1952, advanced through grades to lt. col., 1968, elec. warfare officer Wiesbaden, Germany, 1954—57; with Radar Evaluation Flight Air Def. Command, Griffiss AFB, NY, 1957—58; flight test engr. USAF Sys. Command, Hanscom Field, Mass., 1960—61, subsys. devel. engr., 1961—63, site implementation engr. France, Belgium, Italy, 1968; chief space sys. divsn. USAF Fgn. Tech. Divsn., Dayton, Ohio, 1968—71; R&D dir. aero. sys. divsn. USAF Sys. Command, Dayton, 1971—73, ret., 1973; instr., course dir. Air Force Acad., Colorado Springs, Colo., 1974—81; tech. cons. and tech. translator Adnetech, Colorado Springs, 1973—. Dir. Dept. Def. Protocol Office Paris Internat. Air and Space Show, 1969, 71, 73, 75, 77; translator for U.S. Army in France, 1945—46; recognized as expert translator fed. and city cts. Author: When I See a " Forty and Eight"., 2001; contbr. articles to profl. jours. Dir. of protocol 1986 World Cycling Championships, Colorado Springs, 1985-86; active Tri-Lakes (Colo.) Comprehensive Plan Com., Tri-Lakes Land Use Com.; co-founder Am. Air Mus. Britain; active Air Force Acad. Environ. Coun., 1999—. Decorated Air Force Meritorious Svc. medal; recipient Ordre Nat. Du Mérite French Govt., Paris, 1982, French Legion of Honor, 2004; named hon. citizen of Sermaize les Bains, France; Groupe Scolaire Jacques Adnet named in his honor, 2001. Mem.: VFW, AIAA (sr.), Planetary Soc., Nat. Space Soc., USAF Acad. Environ. Coun., Air Force Acad. Assn. of Grads. (assoc.), Air and Airways Comm. Svc. Alumni Assn., Nat. Air Intelligence Ctr. Alumni Assn., Ret. Officers' Assn., USAF Acad. École de l'Air Exch. Assn. (hon.; exec. sec.), USAF Acad. Assn. Grads. (assoc.), Am. Legion, Air Force Assn., U. Fla. Alumni Assn., Am. Soc. French Legion of Honor. Roman Catholic. Achievements include design of modifications and conceptual design of electronic warfare equipment, unique passively heated solar homes; research in analysis of foreign space systems and equipment. Home and Office: Adnetech 4360 Diamondback Dr Colorado Springs CO 80921-2364 Office Phone: 719-481-2887. Personal E-mail: adnet@adnetech.net.

ADOLPH, KATHRYN ANN, passenger service employee; b. Hartington, Nebr., Dec. 20, 1945; d. Edmund Leonard and Elizabeth Claire Arens; m. Lester Leroy Adolph, Jan. 2, 1965 (div. July 1998); children: Leslie Marie, Edmund Glenn. BS in Adult and Occupation Edn., Kans. State U., 1981. Passenger svc. employee TWA, Kansas City, Mo., 1978—2001, Am. Airlines, Kansas City, 2001—. Industry expert (TV appearance) CNN. Avocations: writing, photography.

ADOUR, COLLEEN MCNULTY, artist, educator; BFA in Studio Arts, cum laude, Syracuse U., 1980, postgrad. in Studio Arts, 1980—84; grad. level ceramics, Alfred U., 1994; MFA in Art History, magna cum laude, SUNY, Binghamton, 2002. Daytime supr., art and music libr. Bartle Libr., SUNY, Binghamton, 2000—02; art tchr., lectr. Broome CC, SUNY, 2003—. Pub. info. mgr. Everson Mus. Art, Syracuse, NY, 1982—84. Notary pub. Dept. State, Divsn. Licensing Svcs., Albany, NY, 1998—; insp. of elections Broome County Bd. Elections, Binghamton, 1998—. Mem.: Binghamton U. Medieval and Renaissance Group (assoc.; v.p., treas. 2000—02). Office: Adour Art & Pottery PO Box 1196 Vestal NY 13850-1196

ADREANI, MICHAEL B., lawyer; b. Nashua, NH, Nov. 23, 1969; BA, Univ. Calif., Berkeley, 1993; JD, Northeastern Univ., 1997. Bar: Calif. 1998, US Dist. Ct. Ctrl., No., Ea., So. Calif. Assoc. to ptnr., bus. & comml. litigation Roxborough, Pomerance & Nye LLP, Woodland Hills, Calif., 1997—. Contbr. articles to profl. jours. Named a Rising Star, So. Calif. Super Lawyers, 2006. Mem.: ABA, LA County Bar Assn., Italian-Am. Bar Assn., Risk & Ins. Mgmt. Soc. Office: Roxborough Pomerance & Nye Ste 250 5820 Canoga Ave Woodland Hills CA 91367 Office Phone: 818-992-9999. Office Fax: 818-992-9991. Business E-Mail: mba@rpnlaw.com.

ADRIAAN, SAINT CLAIRE MARLIN, elementary school educator; b. Port Elizabeth, South Africa, Sept. 10, 1966; arrived in US, 1999; d. Neville Anthony and Brenda Una Adriaan. Diploma in elem. edn., Dower Coll. Edn., 1987; BA in Secondary Edn., U. Port Elizabeth, 1993, MA with honors, 1994, MEd, 1995; diploma, Rhodes U., Grahamstown, South Africa, 1997. Cert. tchr. Calif. Tchr. Rep. Primary, Port Elizabeth, 1997—98, Kagisanong Coll., Bloemfontein, South Africa, 1998—99, Jack Britt HS, Fayetteville, NC, 1999—2002, Noble St. Charter, Chgo., 2002—04, Kipp Adelante, San Diego, 2004—, also bd. dirs. Staff developer Kipp Nat., San Francisco, 2004—. Sponsor Nat. Honor Soc. Noble St., Chgo., 2002—04; sponsor Jr. Beta Club, San Diego, 2004—. Recipient NC Tchr. of the Yr., Wal-Mart, 2002, NC Cultural Educator of the Yr., Vis. Internat. Faculty, 2002, Tchr. Who Made a Difference award, U. Ky., 2006, Dream Classroom award, San Diego CW5, 2006. Avocations: travel, reading. Home: 1657 Guy St San Diego CA 92103 Office: Kipp Adelante Prep Acad 1465 6th Ave 2d San Diego CA 92101

ADRIAENS, PETER, environmental engineer, consultant; m. Iris Dinah Albrecht, Apr. 9, 1994; children: Sven Albrecht, Noelle Irene. PhD, U. Calif., Riverside, Calif., 1989. Registered profl. engr., Belgium, 1986. Prof. U. Mich., Ann Arbor, Mich., 1992—; prin., owner Consultancy, Brighton, Mich., 2002—. Adj. prof. U. Tuebingen, Belgium, 1999—2005. Editor profl. jours. Mem.: Assn. Environ. Engring. and Sci. Profls. Achievements include patents pending for genomic analysis technologies. Office: University of Michigan 1351 Beal Ave Ann Arbor MI 48109 Home Phone: 586-344-8490; Office Phone: 734-763-8032. Business E-Mail: adriaens@umich.edu.

ADRIAN, BARBARA (MRS. FRANKLIN C. TRAMUTOLA), artist; b. NYC, July 25, 1931; d. Allen Isaac and Mildred (Brown) A.; m. Franklin C. Tramutola, July 26, 1972. Student, Art Students League, 1947-54, Hunter Coll., NYC, 1951, Columbia Sch. Gen. Study, 1952-54. Art cons. Doyle-Dane-Bernbach, advt. agy., 1960, A.H. Macy, NYC, 1960-61, Saks Fifth Avenue, 1960, Black, Starr & Gorham, 1960; instr. art workshop Jamaica, NY, 1958-59; pvt. tchr. art, 1960—; instr. Art Students League, NY. One man shows, G. Gallery, 1957, San Juan, P.R., 1951, Grippi Gallery, NYC, 1963, Banfer Gallery, NYC, 1966, Eileen Kuhlik Gallery, 1973, Century Assn., NYC, 1998, 2007, Nat. Acad. Design, 2007; exhibited in group shows, G. Gallery, 1955-59, City Center Gallery, NYC, 1954, NYC Festival, 1957, Portland Mus., Maine, 1958, Workshop Gallery, NYC, 1959, Grippi Gallery, 1960-63, Lane Gallery, Calif., 1962-63, Mus. Gallery, Lubbock, Tex., 1962-63, The Gallery, Norwalk, Ohio, 1962, Gallery 777, Plainview, LI, NY, 1963, NAD, 1963, 81, Butler Art Inst., Youngstown, Ohio, 1963, Gallery Modern Art, NYC, 1969, Child Hassam Fund Purchase Exhbn., NYC, 1968, Orr's Gallery, San Diego, 1968, Pa. Acad. Fine Arts, Phila., 1980, Art Students League, NYC, 1982, Norman A. Eppink Art Gallery, Emporia State U., Kans., 1983, Assn. of Bar of City of NY, 1986, Loyola Law Sch., L.A., 1986, Blanden Meml. Art Mus., Ft. Dodge, Iowa, 1986-87, Minn. Mus. Art, St. Paul, 1987, Sunrise Art Mus., Charleston, W.Va., 1987, Capricorn Gallery, Washington, Kenmore Gallery, Phila., Whitney Mus. Am. Art, Albrecht Art Mus., Minn. Mus. Art, St. Paul, Nat. Acad. Design, NYC, 1991, 2003-04, Century Assn., NYC, 2001-07, Nat. Acad. Design, NYC, 2004-07, Babcock Gallery, NYC, 2006—; represented in permanent collections, Grippi Gallery, Summer Found., Butler Inst., McMay Mus., U. So. Ill., San Antonio, Corcoran Gallery, Washington, Assn. of Bar of City of NY, Loyola U. Law Sch., LA, Blanden Meml. Art Mus., Ft. Dodge, Iowa, Minn. Mus. of Art, St. Paul, Sunrise Art Mus., Charleston, W.Va., Ark. Arts Ctr., Little Rock. Recipient Dorothy Lapham Ferriss award, 1983, Walker award, 1985, Spring Oil Exhbn. Forbes Inc. award, 1990, Elizabeth Morse Genius award, 1992. Mem. NAD (academician), Century Assn. Address: 420 E 64th St New York NY 10021-7853 Office Phone: 212-371-3598. *I want to paint the magic of man, and that magic, both real and phantasmagorical, by which he lives and feels. Art to me is more than a profession, it is the expression of all life.*

ADRIAN, RONALD JOHN, science educator; b. Mpls., June 16, 1945; BME, U. Minn., 1967, MS in Mech. Engring., 1969; PhD in Physics, U. Cambridge, 1972; D honoris causa, Inst. Superior Tecnico, Lisbon, Portugal, 1996. Asst. prof. U. Ill., Urbana, 1972-77, assoc. prof., 1977-81, prof., 1981—2005, Leonard C. and Mary Lou Hoeft chair in engring., 1997—2005, Leonard C. and Mary Lou Hoeft chair in engring. emeritus, 2005—; Ira A. Fulton prof. mech. and aerospace engring. Ariz. State U., Tempe, 2005—. Vis. prof. mech. engring. Stanford (Calif.) U., 1982; vis. rsch. scientist Nat. Supercomputer Applications, Urbana, Ill., 1989-90. Co-editor: Applications Laser Techniques to Fluid Mechanics Vols. I-VIII, 1996, Springer Series in Experimental Fluid Mechanics, 1994—; editor Expts. Fluids, 1990-96; assoc. editor Jour. Fluid Mechanics, 1996-2007; co-founder, editor, eFluids.com; contbr. over 150 articles to profl. jours. Recipient Colwell Merit award, Soc. Automotive Engineers, 1990, 1991, US Churchill Found. award, 1994, Inst. Physics Best Paper, 1995, Asanuma award, 2002. Fellow AIAA (hon., Measurement Tech. award, 2002, FLuid Dynamics award 2007), ASME (Nusselt-Reynolds prize, 2001), Am. Phys. Soc. (Fluid Dynamics prize, 2005), Am. Acad. Mechanics, World Innovation Found.; mem. NAE, Laser Inst. Am. (sr.). Office: Ariz State U Mech & Aerospace Engring Office ERC 342 PO Box 876106 Tempe AZ 85287-6106 Office Phone: 480-965-6469. Office Fax: 480-965-1384. Business E-Mail: rjadrian@asu.edu.

ADRIANOPOLI, BARBARA CATHERINE, librarian; b. Fort Dodge, Iowa, Jan. 27, 1943; d. Daniel Joseph and Mary Dolores (Coleman) Hogan; m. Carl David Adrianopoli, June 28, 1969; children: Carlin, Laurie. BS, Mundeline Coll., 1966; MLS, Rosary Coll., 1975; postgrad., Ozark Rsch. Inst., 1999—2000. Cert. in Pranic Healing and Dowsing Ozark Rsch. Inst. Dir. br. and extension svcs. Schaumburg Twp. (Ill.) Dist. Libr., 1979—. Mem. commn. Hoffman Estates History Mus., 2004, Ill. Libr. Assn. Cultural and Racial Diverstiy; co-chair Dorothy Brown Clk. of Cook County Cts. Adv. Com. on Women's Issues, 2002. Columnist local newspaper, 1995—, Sr. Connection, 2000—; contbr. articles to profl. jours. Mem. com. Schaumburg Twp. Disabled, 1981-95; historian Village of Hoffman Estates, 1986-99; adv. com. Hoffman Estates Sister Cities, 1996-98, Hoffman Estates History Mus., 2004—; mem. Hoffman Estates 50th Ann. Com., 2007—; asst. coach St. Viator H.S., 1999-2003; mem. adv. bd. Cmty. Nutrition Network, 1994—; organizer, mem. Northwest Corridor-St. Patrick's Day Parade com., 1986-2003; trainer A World of Difference Anti-Defamation League, 1994; mem. Com. For Choices For Success-Seminars For Young Women, 1996-2002; mem. Hoffman Estates Sr. and Disabled Commn., 2001; apptd. 8th Dist. State Dem. Com. Women, 2002-06; appt. to cultural and racial diversity com. Ill. Libr. Assns, 2006—. Recipient Hoffman Estates Citizen of Yr. award, VFW, 1995, Studs Terkel Humanitarian Svc.award, Ill. Humanities Coun., 2006, Vol. Yr. award, Disables Svcs. Schaumburg Twp., 2007. Mem.: ALA, Ill. Libr. Assn. (mem. com. cultural and racial diversity 2006—). Home: 1105 Kingsdale Rd Hoffman Estates IL 60194-2378 Office: Schaumburg Twp Pub Libr 130 S Rosedale Rd Schaumburg IL 60193 Personal E-mail: cadriano@sbcglobal.net.

ADRINE-ROBINSON, KENYETTE, writer, educator, poet, artist, photographer; b. Cleve., May 14, 1951; d. James Leroy Adrine and Beatrice (Jones) Johnson; (div. Aug. 1980); 1 child, Jua. BA, Kent State U., Ohio, 1976, MEd, 1980, M in Edn., 1985. Cert. spl. edn., developmentally handicapped, behavior disorders and learning disabilities tchr., Ohio, Mich. Pub. info. specialist morale support activities U.S. Army, Wiesbaden, Fed. Republic of Germany, 1981-83, writer, editor pub. info. office Mainz, Fed. Republic of Germany, 1983-84; tchr. intern Positive Edn. Program, Cleve., 1984-85; tutor Glenville Presbyn. Ch., Cleve., 1985-86; mem. residential team, case mgmt. therapist Murtis H. Taylor Multi Svcs. Ctr., Cleve., 1985-86; resident photographer, tchr. Ann Arbor (Mich.) Art Assn., 1986; tchr. Cleve. Mcpl. Schs., 1986—, Juvenile Detention Ctr. Sch., Cleve. Bd. of Edn., 1987-91; instr. dept. Pan-African studies Kent State U., 1978—93; tchr. Child Mgmt. Program, Cleve., 1991. Pres. Kenyette Prodns., Cleve., 1976—; mem. Karamu Ho., Inc., Cleve., 1988—99, New Day Press, Inc., Cleve., 1989—99, trustee, 1991—99; mem. artists in edn. program Ohio Arts Coun., Columbus, 1989—, Poets' and Writers' League Greater Cleve., 1989—2007, trustee, 1991—2006; instr. Cleve. State Univs. First Coll., 1990; cons. NE Women's Pre-Release Ctr., Cleve., 1991. Author: Thru Kenyette Eyes, 1978, Be My Shoo-Gar, 1987; editor: Black Image Makers, 1988, Love is a Child, 1992, The Ghetto in Me, 1994; author poems. Trustee Cmty. Christian Ch., Euclid, Ohio, 2001-05. With U.S. Army, 1969-71. Recipient Fela Sowande award Inst. for African Am. Affairs, 1976, Cert. of Recognition, Cuyahoga Spl. Edn. Svc. Ctr., 1988. Mem. Am. Fedn. Tchrs., Internat. Assn. Ind. Pubs., Verse Writers Guild Ohio (hon. mention 1988), Internat. Black Writers and Artists Assn., Urban Lit. Arts Workshop (treas. Cleve. chpt. 1988, pres. 1989-91), Kent State U. Alumni Assn. (life). Avocations: travel, music, photography, drumming, meeting with other artists. Home: 20131 Champ Dr Euclid OH 44117-2208 Office Phone: 216-671-0272. Personal E-mail: k_adrine@yahoo.com.

ADRION, WILLIAM RICHARDS, academic administrator, computer and information sciences educator, writer; b. Nov. 2, 1943; s. Vernon Richards and Mary Leone (Carlock) A.; m. Jacqueline Cotner, July 3, 1971; children: Carrie Buchanan, Emily Richards. BEE, Cornell U., Ithaca, NY, 1966, MEE, 1967; PhD in Elec. Engring., U. Tex., Austin, 1971. Computer engr. Honeywell EDP, Waltham, Mass., 1969—70; asst. prof. U. Tex., Austin, 1971—72; area chmn., asst. prof. Oreg. State U., Corvallis, 1972—78; program dir. NSF, Washington, 1976—78, 1980—85, dep. divsn. dir., 1985—86, chief scientist computer rsch., 1986, divsn. dir., 2000—02, sr. advisor, 2002—03; group mgr. Nat. Bur. Stds., 1978—80; prof. U. Mass., Amherst, 1986—, chmn. computer scis., 1986—94, dir. Ctr. Realtime Intelligent Complex Computing Sys., 1988—99; dir. RIPPLES Group, 1996—; co-dir. Commonwealth Info. Tech. Initiative, 2004—; dir. Commonwealth Alliance for Info. Tech. Edn., 2007—. Cons. Applied Theory Assocs., Corvallis, 1973-78; cons. Tektronix, Portland, Oreg., 1974-76; prof., lectr. Am. U., Washington, 1978; cons. Radio Free Europe/Radio Liberty, Munich, 1981-82; vis. prof. U. Calif., Berkeley, 1984-85; cons. Lawrence Livermore (Calif.) Labs., 1985-88; adj. rsch. prof. Georgetown U., 1985-86; chmn. bd. dirs., pres. Applied Computing Sys. Inst. of Mass., Inc., 1989-99, Applied Computing Sys. Inst. of Mass., Inc. Labs., 1990-99; founder, editor-in-chief, ACM Transactions on Software Engineering and Methodology, 1989-95; chair-elect, chair, AAAS Section T: Info. and Computing Sci., 1998-2001; vis. prof., U. Paris-Sud, 1992—1993; bd. dirs, Computing Rsch. Assn. 1987-96; mem. NSF/CISE adv. com., 1995-98; Ex-Officio mem. bd. dir. Nat. Libr. Medicine 2000-02; tech. cons., adv. coun., Nat. Inst. Neurological Disorders and Stroke, 2001-02; gen. chair ACM SIGSOFT Symposium on Found. Software Engring., 1994; gen. chair 19th Internat. Conf. Software Engring., 1997; steering comm. co-chair, 1st MA Tech. Conf. Telecommunications, 1994; organizer, NSF/CRA Workshop Rsch. Infrastructure, 1991; Program Chair, ACM/CRB Conf. on Strategic Directions in Computing, 1989. Contbr. articles to profl. jours. DOW/ASEE Outstanding Young Prof., 1974; NSF Spl. Achievement award, 1986, NSF Outstanding Performance award, 1985, NSF Merit award, 1980, 1981, 1982, 1983, 1984, NSF Sustained Superior Performance award, 1978; U. Mass. Advancement award, 1996; ACM/SIGSOFT Disting. Svc. award, 1996; Fellow, Assn. for Computing Machinery, 1997; U. Mass. Coll. NSM Outstanding Faculty award, 2001 Fellow AAAS, Assn. Computing Machinery (editor-in-chief Trans. on Software Engring. and Methodology 1989-95); mem. IEEE, Soc. Indsl. and Applied Math., N.Y. Acad. Scis., Computer Rsch. Assn. (bd. dirs. 1988-96, chmn. govt. ops. 1990-94), CSNET (exec. com. 1986-89), Sigma Xi, Phi Kappa Phi. Home: 104 Wildflower Dr Amherst MA 01002-3447 Office: U Mass Amherst Dept Computer Sci 140 Governors Dr #310 Amherst MA 01003-4610

ADROGUE, HORACIO ESTEBAN, nephrologist, educator; b. Jan. 10, 1969; MD, Tex. Tech. U., Lubbock, 1997. Lic. transplant nephrologist, bd. cert. internal medicine and nephrology. Resident in internal medicine and pediats., Mpls., 1997—2001; fellow in adult nephrology, 2001—03; asst. prof. medicine Baylor Coll. Medicine, Houston, 2003—. Primary physician pancreatic islet transplant program Meth. Hosp., Houston, 2003—. Mem.: Am. Soc. Nephrology, Am. Soc. Transplantation. Achievements include research in clinical transplantation. Office: 1709 Dryden Ste 900 Houston TX 77030 Office Phone: 713-798-8350.

ADROGUÉ, SOFIA, lawyer; b. Buenos Aires, Apr. 9, 1967; arrived in US, 1975; d. Horacio J. and Sara J. Adrogué; m. Sten L. Gustafson, Sept. 19, 1992; children: Sloane Adrogué Gustafson, Schuyler Adrogué Gustafson, Stefan Adrogué Gustafson. BA magna cum laude, Rice U., Houston, 1988; JD magna cum laude, U. Houston Law Ctr., 1991. Bar: Tex. 1992, DC 1993, US Dist. Ct. (so. dist.) Tex. 1996, US Ct. Appeals (5th cir.) 1996. Jud. clerk to Hon. Jerre S. Williams US Ct. Appeals (5th cir.), 1991—92; assoc. Shea & Gardner, Washington, 1992—93, Susman Godfrey LLP, 1993—97, of counsel, 1997—99, Solar & Fernandes, LLP, 1999—2000; sr. counsel Diamond McCarthy Taylor Finley Bryant & Lee, LLP, 2000—04; ptnr. Epstein Becker Green Wickliff & Hall, P.C., 2004—06; mem. firm Looper Reed & McGraw, PC, Houston, 2006—. Pres. Brown Coll., 1987—88; adj. law prof. mass tort litig. U. Houston Law Ctr., 1995. Ofcl. reporter Bus. Torts The Fifth Cir. Reporter, chief articles editor, mem. exec. bd. Houston Law Rev., 1990—91;, author over 60 profl. articles in legal jours. or law rev. pubs., over 100 legal or civic speeches. Bd. dirs. United Way of Tex. Gulf Coast, 2007—, RICE-TMS, CHRISTUS Health Gulf Coast, Meml. Hermann Found., Theatre Under Stars, Mus. Fine Arts, Houston; adv. bd. dirs. Girls Inc. Greater Houston, bd. chair, former pres., bd. chair; adv. bd. dirs. Chinquapin Sch. Named one of Houston's Lawyers are Houston's Leaders, Houston Lawyer, 2001, Tex.'s Top 40 under 40, Tex. Lawyer, 2001, 5 Outstanding Young Houstonians, Tex. Jaycees, 2002, 5 Outstanding Young Texans, 2002, Inaugural Barbara Jordan Legacy award, Barbara Jordan Houston Sect., Nat. Coun. Negro Women, 2004, Women of Distinction, ABC Channel 13, 2005, Houston's Top Lawyers, H Tex. Mag., 2005, Houston's Profl. on the Fast Track, 2005, Tex. Rising Stars, Tex. Monthly Mag., 2005, 10 Outstanding Young Ams., U.S. Jaycees, 2005, YMCA's Woman of Achievement, 2005, Neuhaus Edn. Ctr. Icons, 2005; recipient Houston's Top Lawyers, H Tex. Mag., 2006; James H. Durbin scholar, Rice U., 1985—88, Bd. Gov.'s scholar, 1985—88, Dean scholar, U. Houston Law Ctr., 1988—91, Harold Sellers scholarship, 1989. Fellow: Tex. Bar Found., Houston Bar Found. (life), Am. Leadership Forum (bd. dirs. Houston Gulf Coast Chpt.), Leadership Tex.; mem.: ABA (ofcl. reporter litig. sect. 5th cir., mem. litig. sect. task force on judiciary), Houston Law Rev. Alumni Assn. (former pres., bd. mem.), Leadership Houston, U. Houston Law Alumni Assn. (bd. dirs.), Alumni Assn. Rice U. (bd. dirs.), Order of Barons, Order of Coif, Phi Beta Kappa. Office: Looper Reed & McGraw PC 1300 Post Oak Blvd Ste 2000 Houston TX 77056 Home Phone: 713-819-7618; Office Phone: 713-986-7110. Business E-Mail: sadrogue@lrmlaw.com.

ADROUNIE, V. HARRY, retired military medical service officer, science educator, environmentalist; b. Battle Creek, Mich., Apr. 29, 1915; s. Haroutune Asadour and Dorthy (Kalaidjian) A.; m. Emalea Riley, June, 1943 (div. Jan. 1980); children: Harry Michael, Vee Patrick; m. Agnes M. Slone, June 26, 1981. BS, St. Ambrose U., 1940, BA, 1959; MS in Environ. Health, PhD in Environ. Health, We. States U. Profl. Studies, 1984, PhD in Pub. Health, 1984. Diplomate Am. Bd. Indsl. Hygiene, Am. Acad. Sanitarians; registered sanitarian Calif., Mich., Pa. Enlisted staff sgt. U.S. Army, 1941, commd. 2d. lt., 1943; advanced through grades to lt. col. USAF, ret., 1968; founder, tech. dir. ARA Environ. Svcs., 1968—72; dir. environ. health div. Chester County Health Dept., Pa., 1972—75, Berrien

County Health Dept., Berrien County, Mich., 1975—78; prof. environ. health Sch. Pub. Health U. Hawaii, Manoa, 1978—80; dean, prof. Sch. Pub. Health, We. States U. Profl. Studies, Mo., 1980—83; vis. prof. environ. and pub. health Am. U., Armenia, 1995. USAF rep. U.S. Interdepartmental Com. on Nutrition for Nat. Def., 1959—61; cons. Health Mobilization Program USPHS Surgeon Gen., 1957—61; mem. USAF Surgeon Gen.'s med. goodwill tour all S. Am. countries, 1960; chmn., vis. assoc. prof. dept. environ. health, faculty med. scis. Am. U. Beirut, 1963—66, chmn. dept. environ. health, 1964—66; mem. pub. health exam. bd., cons. Mid. East UN Welfare Relief Agy., 1963—66; founder, coord. 1st and 2nd Environ. Health Symposium of Mid. East, 1965—66; mem. Mich. Hazardous Waste Policy Com., 1990—91; fin. policy bd. Mich. Underground Storage Tank, 1994—2001; adv. com. environ. health Ferris State Coll., Big Rapids, 1974—75, adj. instr. environ. health, 1977—78. Contbr. articles to profl. jours. Chmn. Barry County Solid Waste Planning and Oversight com., 1981—; mem. Barry County Dept. Human Svcs., 1996—, vice-chmn., 1998—, chmn., 2003—; vice-chmn. Hastings City Planning Commn., 1984—; mem., vice chmn., co-founder sci. adv. and policy bd. Mich. Ground Water Survey, Inc., 1983—90, chmn., 1988—91; chmn. adv. coun. South Ctrl. Mich. Commn. on Aging, 1981—91; charter mem. UL Underwriters adv. coun. environ. and pub. health, 1996—2005, emeritus mem., 2005—; appointed mem. Vision 2020 Com. St. Ambrose U., 2000—01; past adult leader Boy Scouts Am., chmn. com. negative aspects environ. health on children, tchrs., and tng. manual, 2003—05; co-founder, co-chmn. med. coord. coun. Barry County, 2004—; mem. policy com. home health care Pennock Hosp., Hastings, Mich., 2004, mem. home health care adv. bd., 2005—. Decorated Legion of Merit, USAF, 1966; named Alumnus of Yr., Hastings H.S., 1961; recipient Walter S. Mangold award Nat. Environ. Health Assn., 1963, spl. recognition Mich. Environ. Health Assn., 1992, Safety Person of World Safety Orgn., 1991, State of Mich. White Pine award, 1998; congl. act named after him, Mich., 2004, Liberty Bell award, Barry County Bar Assn., 2006. Mem.: APHA (charter, emeritus conf. pres. 1995—97, task force on aging 2002—), NRA (life; cert. rifle marksmanship instr.), VFW (life), Indonesian Environ. Health Assn. (co-founder 1979), World Safety Orgn. (bd. dirs. 1986—95, cert. bd. 1987—2000, editl. bd. 1988—2000), Global Health Assn., Internat. Pub. Health Soc. (charter-emeritus), Mich. Assn. Local Environ. Health Adminstrs. (pres., founder 1976, V. Harry Adrounie award named in his honor 2001), Mich. Environ. Health Assn. (life; pres. 1991—92), Assn. Mil. Surgeons (life), Nat. Environ. Health Assn. (life; pres. 1961—62), Am. Legion (comdr. post 45 1989—90), Air Force Assn., Mil. Officers Assn. Am. (life), Disabled Vets. Assn. (life), Kiwanis (pres. Hastings chpt. 1985—86), Moose, Elks (life). Home: 1905 N Broadway Hastings MI 49058-1086 Personal E-mail: vee1@voyager.net.

ADSIT, RUSSELL ALLAN, landscape architect; b. Syracuse, June 11, 1952; B of Landscape Arch., U. Ga., 1975; M of Agribus. Mgmt., Miss. State U., 1997. Registered landscape arch., Ala., Ark., Ga., Miss., Tenn. Landscape designer Landscape Svcs., Birmingham, Ala., 1975-76; pres., owner, gen. mgr. Adsit Landscape and Design Firm, Inc., Memphis, 1976-94; owner Natural Design Solutions, Memphis, 1995-98; prin. Fisher & Arnold, Inc., Memphis, 1998—2005; landscape architect Michael Hatcher & Assocs., Memphis, 2005—. Instr. Toro U., 1990-91, Tenn. Fedn. Garden Clubs, 1990-92; instr. Miss. State U., 1995-98, asst. prof., 1995-98; spkr. Hinds C.C., Jackson, Miss. Mem. Intern Program at Cobelskill Program, 1991-92, Co-op Program at Miss. State U., 1980-92, Econs. Amenities Task Force, 1982; mem. finance com. Asbury Meth. Ch., 1991-92. Named Outstanding Small Bus. of Yr., Memphis Bus. Jour., 1981, Outstanding Bus. Vol., Memphis Bot. Garden Found., 1988. Fellow Am. Soc. Landscape Archs. (chmn. membership application rev. com. 1978-80, water mgmt. ednl. seminar 1979, pres. Tenn. chpt. 1980-81, 84-85, chmn. nat. coun. chpt. pres. 1981, judges panel Miss. ann. awards 1981, spkr. nat. conv. Cin. 1985, Tenn. trustee 1987-93, judges facilitator Okla. ann. awards 1987, mem. ann. conf. organizing com. Tenn. chpt. 1989, chpt. membership com. 1989-91, publs. bd. 1991-92, fin. and adminstrn. com. 1991-92, v.p. 1999-2000, merit award 1979, 80, honor award 1981); mem. Assn. Turf and Ornamental Mgrs. (charter, pres. 1986), Assoc. Landscape Contractors Am. (distinction award 1990, 92, 93, merit award 1991), So. Nurserymen's Assn., Memphis Bot. Garden Found. (bd. dirs. 1984-92, chmn. master plan selection com. 1987, 2d v.p. 1989-90), West Tenn. Nursery and Landscape Assn., Tenn. Nursery Assn., Memphis Hort. Soc., Memphis Assn. Bldg. Owners and Mgrs., Memphis C. of C. (small bus. coun., chmn. small bus. connection 1992). Office: 5466 Hacks Cross Rd Memphis TN 38125 Office Phone: 901-755-3207.

ADSUMILLI, CHOWDARY B., research scientist; s. Raja Rao Adsumilli. BTech, JNT U., Hyderabad, India, 1999; MS in Elec. and Computer Engring., U. Wis., Madison, 2001; PhD in Elec. and Computer Engring., U. Calif., Santa Barbara, 2005. Rschr. Navigational Electronics Rsch. & Tng. Unit, Hyderabad, 1999, Auburn U., Ala., 1999—2000; engring. optimization specialist Sprint PCS, Santa Clara, Calif., 2000; rsch. assoc. U. Wis., 2000—02; sr. tech. design early identification GE Med. Sys., Milw., 2001; rsch. assoc. U. Calif., 2002—05; rsch. internship Philips Rsch. Labs., Eindhoven, Netherlands, 2003; rsch. scientist Citrix Online, LLC, Santa Barbara, 2006—. Electronic equipment trainee ARM Pvt. Ltd., Hyderabad, Andhra Pradesh, India, 1997—97. Author: (books) Watermark Based Error Concealment Algorithm for Low Bitrate Video Communications, 2005; contbr. articles to profl. jours. Recipient Best Paper award, Computer Soc. India, 1996, Excellence in Math. award, All India Math. Olympaid, 1991—93; grantee MICRO grant, U. Calif., 2002—03, NSF, 2002—05, Rsch. grant, Microsoft, 2003. Fellow: Vlsi - Dsp (hon.); mem.: IEEE (Best Paper award 1998), SPIE (corr.), Inst. Electronics and Comm. Engrs. (assoc. Best Paper award 1998). Achievements include patents pending for a set of low complexity error concealment methods for video communications over wireless channels; invention of watermark-based error concealment for wireless video communications; research in undisclosed research and development work in image and video processing at Citrix Online. Office Phone: 805-690-2980. Business E-Mail: chowdary.adsumilli@citrix.com.

ADU, FREDDY, professional soccer player; b. Tema, Ghana, June 2, 1989; Professional soccer player D.C. United, Washington, 2004—. Mem. U.S. under 17 Nat. Soccer Team, 2002—03. Named Chevy Young Male Athlete of the Year, U.S. Soccer, 2003; named to MLS All-Star Team, 2004. Achievements include being one of the youngest atheletes to ever compete in a major professional sport; graduated High School in an accelerated program; member of MLS Cup Champion D.C. United, 2004.

ADUBATO, RICHARD ADAM (RICHIE ADUBATO), former professional basketball coach; b. Irvington, NJ, Nov. 23, 1937; m. Carol Begerow, July 25, 1989; children: Beth, Scott, Adam. Grad., William Paterson Coll., Wayne, NJ, 1959, grad. degree. Head coach Our Lady of the Valley HS, Orange, NJ; asst. coach Upsala Coll., East Orange, NJ, 1969-72, head coach, 1972-78; asst. coach NBA Detroit Pistons, 1978-79, head coach, 1979-80; scout NBA Atlanta Hawks, 1980-82; asst. coach NBA NY Knicks, 1982-86, NBA Dallas Mavericks, 1986-89, head coach, 1989-93; asst. coach NBA Cleve. Cavaliers, 1993-96; head coach NBA Orlando Magic, 1996-97, WNBA NY Liberty, 1999—2004, WNBA Washington Mystics, 2005—07; spl. cons. NBA Boston Celtics, 1997—98. Head coach WNBA Ea. Conf. All-Star Team, 2000, 01, 03. Named to William Paterson Ahtletic Hall of Fame, 1991; recipient Profl. Basketball Coach of Yr. award, NJ Sports Writers Assn., 2000.*

ADUEN, JAVIER FRANCISCO, physician, researcher; b. Ovejas, Colombia, Mar. 28, 1959; s. Reginaldo Aduen and Bray Hellen; m. Diana Mattos, 1985; 1 child, Paula Andrea. Physician (hon.), Universidad del Norte, Colombia, 1983; Internal Medicine Residency (hon.), Universidad Nacional De Colombia, 1988, Critical Care Medicine Clin. fellowship (hon.), 1989; Critical Care Medicine Clin. Fellowship, Johns Hopkins U. Sch. of Medicine, Balt., 1994; Internal Medicine Residency, Maimonides Med. Ctr., Bklyn., 1997; Critical Care Medicine Fellowship, Mayo Clinic, Minn., 1999; Pulmonary Fellowship, Mayo Clinic, Jacksonville, 2001. Cert. Am. Bd. Internal Medicine, 1997, Critical Care Medicine Am. Bd. Internal Medicine, 1999, Pulmonary Am. Bd. Internal Medicine, 2002. Mandatory med. svc. Hosp. Monte Carmelo, El Carmen de Bolivar, Colombia, 1983—84; physician-in-chief ICU, Hosp. Universitario de Barranquilla, Barranquilla, Colombia, 1989—91, ICU, Clinica del Caribe, Barranquilla, Colombia, 1994—95; assoc. cons. Critical Care Medicine, Mayo Clinic, Jacksonville, 1999; asst. prof. medicine Divsn. of Pulmonary Medicine, Dept. Critical Care Medicine, Mayo Clinic, Jacksonville, 2001—, sr. assoc. cons., 2001—. Author: (book chpt.) Magnesium and calcium: Two keys to unlocking the dilemmas of cardiovascular diseases. In: Critical Care State of the Art. Society of Critical Carte Medicine, 1993, Adrenal disease in the critically ill patient. In: Critical Care Medicine, Principles of Diagnosis and Management, 1995, Lactic acidosis. In: Critical Care State of the Art. Society of Critical Care Medicine, 1995. Recipient Invited Prof., Universidad del Norte. Barranquilla, Colombia, 1990—, Best Resident of Yr. Internal Medicine Residency Program, Maimonides Med. Ctr., Bklyn., 1997, Am's. Top Physician award, Consumer's Rsch. Coun. of Am., 2003. Achievements include research in Predictive Biological Markers of Acute Lung Injury After Liver Transplantation; Predictive Biological Markers of Ischemia-Reperfusion-Induced Lung Injury After Lung Transplantation; Etiology of Leukocytosis in the Early Postoperative Period After Lung Transplantation; Lung Allograft Rejection Gene Expresion Observational (Largo) Study; The Impact of Standardizing Initial Sepsis Management in the Four Mayo Clinic Hospitals: A Quality Improvement Intervention. Avocations: soccer, movies. Office Phone: 904-953-2282.

ADU-GYAMFI, R. SIISI, multi-industry company executive; BS in Mgmt., MIT, Cambridge, BS in Mech. Engring., MS in Mech. Engring., MIT, Cambridge; MBA, Harvard Bus. Sch. Various gen. mgmt. and mktg. positions Digital Equipment Corp.; v.p. strategic planning and devel. Carrier divsn. United Techs.; corp. v.p. mktg. Power Generation, gen. mgr. Generator Drive Cummins, Inc.; corp. v.p. mktg. Eaton Corp.; sr. v.p. internat. & mktg. Textron, Inc., Providence, 2007—. Office: Textron Inc 40 Westminster St Providence RI 02903 Office Phone: 401-421-2800.*

ADVANI, DEEPAK, computer company executive; b. India; BS in Computer Sci., Mich. State U., 1986; MS in Computer Engring., Wright State U.; MBA, U. of Pa. Dir. Scalable Parallel (SP) system software devel. orgn. IBM, v.p. worldwide Linux strategy, head High End Intel Server bus., v.p. mktg. strategy personal computing divsn., mem. global mktg. bd., mem. sr. leadership team; sr. v.p., chief mktg. officer Lenovo, 2005—. Mem. advisory bd. Mich. State U. Achievements include part of the team that built a $1 billion supercomputer business in four years at IBM. Office: Lenovo 3039 Cornwallis Rd Research Triangle Park NC 27709

ADZICK, NICK SCOTT, surgeon, educator; b. Omaha, May 14, 1953; MD, Harvard Coll., 1975; postgrad., 1979. Resident gen. surgery Mass. Gen. Hosp., 1979-83, 85-86; resident surg. rsch. U. Calif., San Francisco, 1983-85; resident pediat. surgery Boston Children's Hosp., 1986-88; faculty U. Calif., San Francisco, 1988—; surgeon-in-chief The Children's Hosp., Phila.; C. Everett Koop prof. pediat. surgery U. Pa. Sch. Medicine, 1995—; pediat. surgery tng. program dir., dir. Ctr. for Fetal Diagnosis and Treatment. Fellow: ACS; mem.: AMA, Am. Acad. Pediat. (surg. sect.), Am. Coll. Physician Execs., Am. Pediat. Surg. Assn., Am. Surg. Assn., Assn. Acad. Surgery, Soc. Univ. Surgeons, Nat. Inst. Medicine, Internat. Fetal Medicine and Surgery Soc., Brit. Assn. Pediat. Surgery, Pacific Assn. Pediat. Surgeons, Wound Healing Soc, Coll. Physicians Phila., John Morgan Soc., Ravdin-Rhoads Surg. Soc. E-mail: adzick@email.chop.edu.

AEHLERT, BARBARA JUNE, health facility administrator; b. San Antonio, June 17, 1956; d. Bobby Ray and Ronella Su (Light) Mahoney; m. Dean A. Aehlert, Sept. 6, 1980; children: Andrea, Sherri. AA in Nursing, Glendale CC, Ariz., 1976; BS in Profl. Arts, St. Joseph's Coll., Windham, Maine, 1997. Cert. ACLS instr., BLS and PALS instr., emergency med. tng./paramedic instr. Gen. mgr. Hosp. Ambulance Svc., Phoenix, 1982-83; critical care nurse Samaritan Health Svcs., Phoenix, 1978-80, coord. patient transp., 1980-82, mgr. clin. programs, 1983-92; dir. emergency med. svcs. edn. EMS Edn. and Rsch., 1992-97; pres. S.W. EMS Edn. Inc., Glendale, Ariz., 1997—2006; dir. field tng. S.W. Ambulance, Mesa, Ariz., 2006—. EMS coord., City of Mesa Fire Dept., 2001-04. Author: ACLS Study Guide, 3d edit., 2007, ACLS Quick Review Slide Set, 1994, ACLS Quick Review Study Cards, 2003, PALS Study Guide, 3d edit., 2006, ECGs Made Easy, 3d edit., 2006, ECGs Made Easy Lesson Plans, 1996, Mosby's Computerized Paramedic Test Generator, 1996, Aehlert's EMT Basic Study Guide, 1997, ECGs Made Easy Study Cards, 2003, Mosby's Comprehensive Pediatric Emergency Care, 2005. Republican.

AELION, C. MARJORIE, science educator; BS summa cum laude, U. Mass., 1980; MSCE, MIT, 1983; PhD, U. N.C., 1988. Park ranger Nat. Park Svc., Cape Cod Nat. Seashore, South Wellfleet, Mass., 1976-78; biologist, resource assessment divsn. Nat. Marine Fisheries, Woods Hole, Mass., 1978-84; rsch. asst. MIT, Cambridge, Mass., 1981-83, U. Mass.-Amherst, Amherst, Peru, 1983-84, U. N.C., Chapel Hill, 1986-88, tchg. asst., 1987; hydrologist U.S. Geol. Survey, Water Resources Divsn., Columbia, SC, 1988-91, faculty mem., 1991-97; asst. prof. dept. environ. health scis. U. S.C., Columbia, 1991-97, assoc. prof., 1997-2001, prof., 2001—. Presenter in field. Contbr. articles to profl. jours. Fulbright-Hayes scholar, 1980-81; Bd. Govs.' fellow U. N.C., 1984-86, Dissertation fellow, 1988, NSF fellow in engring., 1993; grantee U.S. EPA, 1991-93, Hazardous Waste Mgmt. Rsch. Fund, 1991-94, 99-2002, Nat. Geographic Soc., 1992, S.C. Dept. Health and Environ. Control and Hazardous Waste Mgmt. Rsch. Fund, 1991-94, U. S.C., 1993-94, NSF, 1993-00, 99—, NIEHS, 2005—; Fulbright scholar, 2002; grad. student travel grantee award U. N.C., 1988; Rsch. fellow Internat. Agrl. Ctr., The Netherlands, 2002. Mem. Am. Chem. Soc., Am. Soc. Microbiology, Assn. for Women in Sci. (sec. S.C. chpt. 1996-97, pres. S.C. chpt. 1997-98), Soc. Women Engrs., Soc. Environ. Toxicology and Chemistry, Phi Kappa Phi, Delta Omega. Office: U SC Environ Health Scis Dept Columbia SC 29208-0001

AFFELDT, JOHN ELLSWORTH, retired physician; b. Lansing, Mich., May 26, 1918; s. John Ferdin and Pearl Heald (Gardner) Affeldt; m. Nancy Faye Spomer, Sept. 2, 1942; children: John C., Elizabeth Affeldt Westberg, Cindy L. BS, Andrews U., Berrien Springs, Mich., 1939; MD, Loma Linda U., Calif., 1944. Intern Detroit Gen. Hosp., 1943—44; resident in internal medicine White Meml. Hosp., Los Angeles, 1946—49; fellow in pulmonary physiology Harvard Sch. Pub. Health, 1949—51; med. dir. Rancho Los Amigos Hosp., Downey, Calif., 1956—64, Los Angeles County Dept. Hosps., 1964—72, Los Angeles County Dept. Health Services, 1972—77; pres. Joint Commn. Accreditation Hosps., Chgo., 1977—86; med. advisor Beverly Enterprises, Fort Smith, Ark., 1986—97. With US Army, 1944—47. Mem.: ACP, AMA, Calif. Assn. Med. Dirs. (pres. 1993—94), Los Angeles County Med. Assn., We. Soc. Clin. Rsch., Ins. Medicine NAS, Am. Congress Rehab. Medicine. Home: 5140 Bareback Sq PO Box 8432 Rancho Santa Fe CA 92067-8432

AFFLECK, BEN, actor; b. Berkeley, Calif., Aug. 15, 1972; s. Tim and Chris Affleck; m. Jennifer Garner, June 29, 2005; 1 child, Violet Anne. Actor: (films) School Ties, 1992, Dazed and Confused, 1993, Mallrats, 1995, Going All the Way, 1997, Chasing Amy, 1997, Armageddon, 1998 (Favorite Supporting Actor in Sci. Fiction Blockbuster Entertainment award, 1999), Phantoms, 1998, Reindeer Games, 1999, Forces of Nature, 1999 (Favorite Actor in Comedy/Romance Blockbuster Entertainment award, 2000), Dogma, 1999, 200 Cigarettes, 1999, Daddy and Them, 1999, Boiler Room, 1999, Bounce, 2000 (Favorite Actor in Drama/Romance Blockbuster Entertainment award, 2001), Jay and Silent Bob Strike Back, 2001, Pearl Harbor, 2001, The Sum of All Fears, 2002, Changing Lanes, 2002, The Third Wheel, 2002, Daredevil, 2003, Gigli, 2003, Paycheck, 2003, Jersey Girl, 2004, Surviving Christmas, 2004, Man About Town, 2006, Clerks II, 2006, Hollywoodland, 2006 (Hollywood Best Supporting Actor award Hollywood Awards, 2006), Smokin' Aces, 2006; actor, writer (films) Good Will Hunting, 1997 (Acad. award for Best Orginial Screenplay, 3d pl. Boston Soc. Film Critics award Best Screenplay, Broadcast Film Critics Assn. award Best Screenplay-Motion Picture, Golden Satellite award Best Motion Picture Screenplay-Original, London Critics Cir. award Screenwriter of Yr., others); prodr.: (films) Stolen Summer, 2002; exec. prodr.: Crossing Cords, 2001, Speakeasy, 2002, The Battle of Shaker Heights, 2003; (TV series) Project Greenlight, 2001, Project Greenlight 2, 2003, Project Greenlight 3, 2005, Push, Nevada, 2002. Office: c/o Creative Artists Agy 9380 Wilshire Blvd Beverly Hills CA 90212*

AFFLECK, IAN KEITH, physics educator; b. Vancouver, BC, Can., July 2, 1952; s. William Burchill and Evelyn Mary (Carter) A.; m. Glenda Ruth Harman, July 2, 1977; children: Geoffrey Roger, Ingrid Katherine. BSc, Trent U., Peterborough, Ont., 1975; AM, Harvard U., 1976, PhD, 1979. Asst. prof. physics Princeton U., NJ, 1981-87; rsch. scientist Centre d'Etudes Nucléaire, Saclay, France, 1984-85; prof. physics U. BC, Vancouver, 1987—. Contbr. articles on physics to profl. jours. Recipient Gov. General's medal, 1975, Steacie prize Nat. Rsch. Coun. Can., 1988, Hertzberg medal Can. Assn. Physicists, 1990, Rutherford medal, 1991, Theoretical and Math Physics prize, CAP/CRM, 1997, BC Sci. & Tech. prize, 1998. Fellow Royal Soc. Can. (Rutherford medal 1991), Can. Inst. for Advanced Rsch., Harvard Soc. Fellows (jr.). Achievements include research in interface between elementary particle theory and condensed matter theory. Office: U BC Dept Physics & Astronomy Vancouver Hennings 406 2329 W Mall Vancouver BC Canada V6T 1Z4 Office Phone: 604-822-2137.

AFFLECK, MARILYN, retired sociology educator; b. Logan, Utah, July 1, 1932; d. Clark B. and Velda (Bryson) A.; children: Michelle Alisa, Kimberly Kay, Lacey Dawn. BA, U. Okla., 1954; MA, Brigham Young U., 1957; PhD, UCLA, 1966. Instr. Ctrl. State Coll., Edmond, Okla., 1958—60; asst. prof. Fla. State U., Tallahassee, 1966—68; asst. prof. sociology U. Okla., Norman, 1968—70, assoc. prof., 1971—90, interim dean Grad. Coll., 1978—79, asst. dean, 1976—82. Editor Free Inquiry in Creative Sociology Jour., 1984-90. Recipient AMOCO Good Tchg. award U. Okla., 1974 Mem. Okla. Sociol. Assn. (pres. 1974-75), South Ctrl. Women's Studies Assn. (treas. 1979-83), Phi Beta Kappa. Democrat. Mem. Lds Ch. Home: 6395 Corky Dr NE Norman OK 73026-3135

AFFLICK, GILBERT LESLIE, editor, journalist; b. Lucea, Jamaica, Apr. 18, 1931; arrived in US, 1979; s. Jack Gilbert and Hattie Laura (Kennedy) Afflick; m. Pearly Brown Dickens, Dec. 26, 1991 (dec. Nov. 1997); m. Shirley Veronica Goldsmith (div.); 1 child, Gregory Julian; m. Velrose Maureen Wiggan, Jan. 24, 2006. Cert. in journalism, U. West Indies, 1960. Acctg. clk. Jamaica Pub. Works Dept., Kingston, 1949—53; sports reporter Daily Gleaner, Kingston, 1953—58; copy editor Daily Gleaner and Star, Kingston, 1959—68; sports editor, features editor, night editor Jamaica Daily News, Kingston, 1973—79; editor Merrill Lynch IBK, NYC, 1982—2001. Author: The Farmer and the Thief, 2004; contbr. articles to profl. jours. Active Orphans Internat., NY, 2000; assoc. mem. Nat. Trust Historic Preservation, 1999. Fellow, Commonwealth Press Union, 1962. Independent. Avocations: reading, theater, photography, travel, dance. Home and Office: 13 Flanders Ln Palm Coast FL 32137

AFFONSO, DYANNE D., dean; BSN, U. Hawaii, 1966; MN in Nursing, U. Wash., 1967; MA in Clin. Psychology, U. Ariz., 1980, PhD in Clin. Psychology, 1982. Asst. prof. sch. nursing U. Miss., 1967-68; OB staff nurse, night charge nurse Kinchloe AFB Hosp., Mich., 1968-70; instr. sch. nursing U. Hawaii, 1970-73; asst. prof. coll. nursing U. Ariz., 1974-77, assoc. prof. coll. nursing, 1978, coord. psychiatric mental health nursing coll. nursing, 1982-84, joint appointment in psychology dept. psychology, 1983; assoc. prof. sch. nursing U. Calif., San Francisco, 1984-87, prof. sch. nursing, 1988; prof., dean sch. nursing Emory U., Atlanta, 1993-98, assoc. prof. women's & children's divsn. sch. pub. health, 1993—. Prof. sch. nursing Emory U., Atlanta, 1998—. Contbr. articles to profl. jours.; presenter in field. Mem. NAS (mem. inst. medicine 1994), NIH (mem. adv. coun. nat. inst. child health & human devel. 1979-83, mem. agenda com. nat. inst. child health & human devel. 1982, mem. scientific rev. com. nat. ctr. nursing rsch. 1986, mem. adv. coun. nat. ctr. nursing rsch. 1986-88, mem. steering com. rsch. patient outcomes nat. ctr. nursing rsch. 1991, sec.'s conf. 1993, charter mem. adcv. coun. office rsch. on women's health 1995). Office: Emory U Sch Nursing 531 Asbury Cir Atlanta GA 30322-0001

AFFRONTI, LEWIS FRANCIS, SR., microbiologist, educator; b. Rochester, NY, Aug. 12, 1928; s. John and Mary (Least) A.; m. Aileen Ledford, June 2, 1956; children: John, Lewis, Mary Louise, Eileen. BA, U. Buffalo, 1950, MA, 1951; PhD, Duke U., 1958. Rsch. assoc. Buffalo VA Hosp., 1951-52, Roswell Meml. Cancer Inst., 1954, TB Henry Phipps Inst. U. Pa., 1957-58; asst. prof. Sch. Medicine, George Washington U., Washington, 1962-65, assoc. prof., 1965-72, prof. microbiology, 1972-93, prof. emeritus, 1994—, chmn. dept. microbiology, 1973-93. Cons. AVCO Rsch. Corp., VA Hosp., Martinsburg, W.Va., VA Hosp. Ctr., Wilmington, Del.; U.S. rep. WHO Conf. on Skin Test Antigens and Vaccines, Geneva, 1966; mem. med. adv. bd. VA, Wilmington. Mem. editl. bd. Infection and Immunity, 1972-78. Bd. dirs. Lynchburg (Va.) unit Am. Cancer Soc., 1996. Commd. officer USPHS (CDC), 1958-62; with USAF, 1952-54. NIH Spl. fellow, 1969; Nat. Tb fellow for Internat. Conf. on Tb Moscow, 1971; Nat. Tb fellow for Internat. Conf. on Tb Tokyo, 1973; Washington Acad. Sci. fellow; Recipient WHO Exch. Rsch. Workers award, 1970, Scientist Emeritus award Soc. Expl. Biology and Medicine, Washington, 1994; interacad. exch. program award NAS, 1980. Fellow Am. Acad. Microbiology, Assn. Med. Sch. Microbiology Chmn. (sec.-treas. 1976-86, bd. dirs. 1976-86), Washington Acad. Sci.; mem. AAAS (life), Am. Soc. Microbiology, Am. Assn. Immunologists, Reticuloendothelial Soc., Am. Thoracic Soc., Assembly on Microbiologists and Immunologists (sec. 1971-72), The Protein Soc., Toastmasters Internat. (Atlanta), Mil. Order World Wars, KC, Sigma Xi (local pres. 1986-87). Office: George Washington U Med Ctr Dept Microbiology 2300 I St NW Washington DC 20037-2336

AFIELD, WALTER EDWARD, psychiatrist, educator, health facility administrator; b. NYC, Dec. 28, 1935; s. Walter Edward and Mollie Evelyn (MCGovern) A.; m. Nancy Browning, Dec. 27, 1973; children: Walter Edward, Neva Browning. AB, U. Pa., Phila., 1956; MD, Johns Hopkins U., Balt., 1960. Intern Grady Meml. Hosp., Atlanta, 1960-61; fellow in psychiatry Harvard U., Cambridge, Mass., 1961-64, 66-67; asst. prof. psychiatry Johns Hopkins U., Balt., 1967-70, dir. dept. child psychiatry, 1967-70; prof. U. South Fla. Coll. Medicine, 1970-74, chmn. dept. psychiatry, 1970-74; exec. dir. Tampa Bay Neuropsychiat. Inst., Tampa, Fla., 1970—; chmn., chief exec. officer The Mental Health Programs Corp., Tampa, 1985-92. Author: The Children of Resurrection City, 1970; contbr. articles to profl. jours. Pres. Fla. Lyric Opera, 1976—. Capt. USAF, 1964-66. Fellow Am. Coll. Psychiatrists; mem. AMA, Am. Acad. Neurology, Univ. Club, Tampa Yacht Club. Republican. Roman Catholic. Home:

4619 W Bay To Bay Blvd Tampa FL 33629-7610 Office: 5820 W Cypress St Ste B Tampa FL 33607-1785 Office Phone: 813-636-8811. Personal E-mail: hogheavn@tampabay.rr.com.

AFIFI, ALAA YOUSSEF, cardiothoracic surgeon; b. Cairo, Jan. 19, 1965; arrived in U.S., 1972; s. Youssef S. Afifi and Samia A. Salem. BS in Biology magna cum laude, Siena Coll., 1985; MD magna cum laude, Albany Med. Coll., 1989. Diplomate Nat. Bd. Med. Examiners, Am. Bd. Surgery, Am. Bd. Thoracic Surgery. Intern Wilford Hall USAF Med. Ctr., Lackland AFB, 1989-90, resident, 1990-91, Keesler USAF Med. Ctr., Keesler AFB, Miss., 1991-93, chief resident, instr. surgery, 1993-94, chief cardiothoracic surgery, dir. surg. ICU, 1999-2000; jr. fellow, instr. cardiothoracic surgery U. Rochester Med. Ctr., NY, 1994-95, chief fellow, instr., 1995-96; asst. prof. surgery Uniformed Svcs. U. Health Scis., Bethesda, Md., 1999—; attending cardiothoracic surgeon Biloxi VA Med. Ctr., Miss., 1996-2000, Meml. Hosp. Gulfport, Miss., 1998-2000, Ellis Hosp., Albany Med. Ctr., St. Peter's Hosp., Albany, NY, 2000—04, Anaheim Meml. Hosp., 2004—, Fountain Valley Hosp., 2004—, Irvine Regional Med. Ctr., 2004—, Western Med. Ctr., Anaheim, Santa Ana, 2004—, Saddleback Med. Ctr., 2004—, West Anaheim Hosp., 2004—, West Med. Ctr., Anaheim, 2004—, Santa Ana, Calif., 2004—, Hoag Hosp., Newport Beach, Calif., 2006—. Presenter in field. Contbr. articles to profl. jours. Recipient Ralph D. Alley award Cardiothoracic Surgery, 1989, award, Soc. Laparoendoscopic Surgeons, 1994; Presdl. scholar, 1981—85. Fellow: ACS, So. Thoracic Surgeons Assn., Soc. Thoracic Surgeons, Am. Coll. Cardiology, Am. Coll. Chest Physicians; mem.: AMA, Soc. Air Force Clin. Surgeons, Monroe County Med. Soc., Med. Soc. State N.Y., Am. Heart Assn.; Sigma Xi, Alpha Omega Alpha, Delta Epsilon Sigma, Alpha Kappa Alpha. Avocations: travel, sports, landscaping, photography. Home: 10 Sable Sands Newport Coast CA 92657 Office: 999 N Tustin Ave #103 Santa Ana CA 92705 Home Phone: 949-856-3080; Office Phone: 714-973-9903. Personal E-mail: alaaafifi@msn.com.

AFRASIABI, PETER R., lawyer; BA magna cum laude, UCLA; JD, Univ. So. Calif. Bar: Calif. Law clk. Judge Alicemarie Stotler, US Dist. Ct. Ctrl. Calif., Judge Ferdinand F. Fernandez, US Ct. Appeals Ninth Cir.; atty. O'Melveny & Myers LLP; ptnr., comml. litigation practice Turner, Green, Afrasiabi & Arledge LLP, Costa Mesa, Calif. Adj. prof. Chapman Univ. Sch. Law, 2001—; bd. dir. Legal Aid Soc. Orange County, 2001—05. Contbr. articles to profl. jours.; editor (articles): Univ. So. Calif. Law Rev. Mem. human rels. com. City of Costa Mesa, Calif., 2000—01. Named a Rising Star, So. Calif. Super Lawyers, 2006; recipient Public Counsel Advocate of the Year award, 2002, USC Paul Davis Meml. award, Public Interest Legal Found., 2006. Mem.: Fed Bar Assn. Orange County (bd. dir. 2004), Order of the Coif. Office: Turner Green Afrasiabi & Arledge Ste 850 535 Anton Blvd Costa Mesa CA 92626 Office Phone: 714-434-8743. Office Fax: 714-434-8756. Business E-Mail: pafrasiabi@turnergreen.com.

AFRICA, COLBY TAIT, information technology executive, poet; b. Santa Fe, Sept. 23, 1974; s. Deirdre Africa. Sr. software engr. Critical Path Tech. Svcs., Inc., Redmond, Wash., 1995—97; product mgr. Microsoft Corp., Redmond, 1997—99; software devel. mgr. Pacific Edge Software, Inc., Kirkland, Wash., 1999—2000, chief software arch., 2000—01; pres. PM Blvd., LLC, Alexandria, Va., 2001—; chief tech. officer Robbins-Gioia, LLC, Alexandria, 2004—. Chairperson Project Mgmt. XML Working Group, Kirkland, 1999—2001. Author: (poetry) Strands of Sanity (Editors Choice award Poetry.com, 2003). Mem.: IEEE (assoc.). E-mail: colbyafrica@hotmail.com.

AFSARY, CYRUS, artist; b. Oct. 18, 1940; s. Mehraban Afsary and Mehrbanoo Jamasbi; children: Bonnie, Jacqui-Mitra. BA in Art, U. Mid. East, 1962, BA in Interior Design, 1971. Resident artist Grand Gallery, Las Vegas, Nev., 1975-80; freelance artist Las Vegas, 1980-88, Scottsdale, Ariz., 1988—. Art tchr., Mid. East, 1967-68; participant Artists of Am., 1988, 92. Works featured in Southwest Art, 1987, Midwest Art, 1988, Arts of the West, 1988, 99, Am. Artist, 2002. Recipient Exceptional award Pastel Soc. Am., 1986; named Best of Show, C.M. Russell Show, 1985, Best Oil, Amarillo Rotary Club Art Show, 1991, chosen Ofcl. Poster Artist, 1991. Mem. Nat. Acad. Western Art (gold medal 1987, Robert Lougheed gold medal 1988, silver medal 1989), N.W. Rendezvous Art (merit award 1987). Avocations: photography, reading, music (new age). Studio: PO Box 3217 Scottsdale AZ 85271-3217 Office Phone: 480-481-9000. Personal E-mail: cyrus@cyrusafsary.com. Business E-Mail: ca@cyrusafsary.com.

AFSHARI, NATALIE ADEL, ophthalmologist, surgeon, educator; d. Roy Adel and Safa (Farhad) Afshari. MD, Stanford U., Calif., 1995. Intern Harvard U./Brigham and Women Hosp., Boston, 1995—96; resident in internal medicine Harvard Med. Sch./Mass. Eye and Ear Infirmary, Boston, 1996—99; fellow Harvard Med. Sch., Boston, 1999—2001; asst. prof. Duke U. Med. Ctr., Durham, NC, 2001, assoc. prof. ophthalmology, 2006—. Dir. cornea and refractive surgery fellowship program Duke U. Med. Ctr., Durham, NC, 2005—; assoc. examiner Am. Bd. Ophthalmology. Assoc. editor: Eyenet Jour. Named Tchr. of Yr., Duke U. Eye Ctr., 2001—02; named one of Best Doctors in Am., Best Doctors, Inc., 2003—06, Best Doctors in NC, Bus. NC, 2004—06; recipient Deans Rsch. award, Stanford U., 1995; fellow, HEED Found., 1999—2000; scholar, Stanford U., 1993—94. Fellow: Am. Acad. Ophthalmology (councilor); mem.: Assn. for Rsch. in Vision and Ophthalmology, Am. Soc. Cataract and Refractive Surgery. Office: Duke Univ Med Ctr Duke Univ Eye Ctr Box 3802 Durham NC 27710 Home Phone: 919-619-5406; Office Phone: 919-684-3799. Office Fax: 919-681-7661; Home Fax: 919-681-7661.

AFTERMAN, ALLAN B., accountant, educator, financial consultant, researcher; b. LA, Jan. 25, 1944; s. Joseph and Ruth Gertrude (Jacobson) Afterman; m. Joan Elaine Hoffman, Apr. 30, 1974; children: Debra, Lori, Julie, Robin. BBA, Roosevelt U., 1964; PhD, U. Birmingham, Eng., 1989. CPA Calif. Asst. dir. securities exchange com. practices Alexander Grant & Co., Chgo., 1967—70; nat. staff mgr. Touche Ross & Co., Chgo., 1970—73; nat. tech. dir. Practice Devel. Inst., Chgo., 1977—82; acctg. prof. U. Ill., Chgo., 1983—88, dir. exec. edn.; mem. faculty grad. sch. bus. U. Chgo., 1992—99. Cons. to govts. Author: Accounting and Auditing Disclosure Manual, 1982, Compilation and Review, 1983, Accounting and Auditing Update, 1984, SEC Accounting and Auditing Update, 1985, GAAP Practice Manual, 1985 (Best Loosleaf Bus. Reference award Profl. and Scholastic Divsn. Assn. Am. Pubs., 1985), Accounting and Tax Highlights, 1986, Handbook of SEC Accounting and Disclosure, 1987, Credit Analyst's Report, 1988, Financial Reporting and Disclosure Manual in the United Kingdom, 1989, Public Accounting Practice Manual, 1990, Governmental Accounting & Auditing Disclosure Manual, 1991, Nonprofit Accounting and Auditing Disclosure Manual, 1992, Auditing Standards and Practices in Poland, 1993, SEC Regulation of Public Companies, 1994, International Financial Accounting, Reporting & Analysis, 1994, U.S. Securities Regulation of Foreign Issuers, 1996, Charities Accounting and Auditing Disclosure Manual in the United Kingdom, 1996, Audit Committee Governance Report, 2000, Guide to Preparing Management's Discussion and Analysis, 2005, Guide to Preparing Proxy and Information Statements, 2005. Mem.: AICPA, N.Y. Soc. CPAs, Practicing Law Inst., Am. Acctg. Assn. Jewish. Home: 3900 Mission Hills Rd Apt 302 Northbrook IL 60062-5721 Office: 600 Central Ave STE 322 Highland Park IL 60035-3257 Office Phone: 847-433-6222. Business E-Mail: allan@allanafterman.com.

AFTERMAN, JEAN, professional sports team executive; BA in History of Art, U. Calif., Berkeley, 1979; JD, U. San Francisco, 1991. Aide Don Nomura, 1994—99; pvt. practice, 1999—2001; asst. gen. mgr. N.Y. Yankees, Bronx, 2001—, v.p., 2003—. Office: NY Yankees Yankee Stadium E 161 St & River Ave Bronx NY 10451*

AGAH, MASOUD, electrical engineer, educator; arrived in US, 2000; m. Leyla Nazhandali. BEE, Sharif U. Tech., Iran, 1996, MEE, 1998; PhD, U. Mich., Ann Arbor, Mich., 2005. Rsch. asst. U. Mich., Ann Arbor, 2001—05; asst. prof. Va. Tech, Blacksburg, Va., 2005—. Recipient The First Iranian Student Sci. Olympiad on Elec. Engring. award, Iran's Ministry Sci., Rsch., and Tech., 1996, Iranian Exemplary Grad. Student award, Pres. Iran, 1998, 2nd Pl. award, Design Automation Conf., 2003; grantee, NSF, 2006. Mem.: IEEE, Am. Chem. Soc. Achievements include patents for separation microcolumn assembly for a microgas chromatograph and the like. Office: Virginia Tech 469 Whittemore Hall Blacksburg VA 24061 Home Phone: 540-250-7682; Office Phone: 540-231-2653. Office Fax: 540-231-3362.

AGAJANIAN, GILDA, pianist; d. Oganes and Azatuhi A. BA, U. So. Calif., 1973, Grad. Study, 1974-76; Diploma, Am. Coll. of Musicians, Austin, Tex., 1981, Artist Diploma, 1984. Russian educator, Calif., 1976-81; music educator Gilda Agajanian Piano Studio, La Habra Heights, Calif., 1987—; profl. classical pianist Calif., 1985—; entrepreneur, ptnr. Aggie's Restaurants, Calif., 1981-89. Mem. Westshore Musicians Club (pres. 1992-95), Music Tchrs. Nat. Assn., Calif. Assn. Profl. Music Tchrs. (chmn. recitals 1992—), Dominant Club (sec. 1994-96), Nat. Guild of Piano Tchrs. Avocations: Slavic language and literature, exotic birds, horticulture, cats, dogs. Office: Gilda Agajanian Piano Studio 2039 N Cypress St La Habra Heights CA 90631

AGALLIANOS, DENNIS DIONYSIOS, psychiatrist; b. Galati, Romania, Jan. 1, 1923; arrived in U.S., 1957; s. Dionysios Nicholas and Eleni (Craciun) Agallianos; m. Georgia-Lee Virginia Foden, June 20, 1964 (dec. 2004); 1 child, Helen Penelope. BA, Classical Gymnasium, Galati, Romania, 1941; MD, Victor Babes Med. Sch., Cluj, Romania, 1948. Diplomate Am. Bd. Psychiatry and Neurology. Pvt. practice, Romania, 1948-49; preparator urol. dept. Victor Babes Med. Sch., 1949-51; intern. urol. dept. U. Athens Med. Sch., Greece, 1951-54; asst. prof. urology Med. Sch. U. Athens, Greece, 1956-57; staff physician Polikliniki Athinon, Athens, 1954-56; intern, resident French Hosp., NYC, 1957-58; resident in psychiatry Brattleboro Retreat, 1958-60; resident, staff psychiatrist Spring Grove State Hosp., Balt., 1960-64, chief of divsn., 1965-68; staff psychiatrist Brattleboro (Vt.) Retreat, 1969-76, chief of profl. svc., 1976-80, dir. older adult program, 1980-92; asst. prof. psychiatry Dartmouth Med. Sch., Hanover, 1978—95; pvt. practice, 1992—2000; locum tenens staff psychiatrist, 2000—. Adj. asst. prof. clin. psychiatry Dartmouth Med. Sch. , Hanover, 1995—2000. Contbr. articles to profl. jours. Pres. Parish Coun. St. George Greek Orthodox Ch., Keene, NH, 1985—86; sustaining mem. Greek Orthodox Archdiocese N. and S.Am., 1966—; founding father United Greek Orthodox Charities, 1967. Recipient Exemplary Psychiatrist award, Nat. Alliance Mentally Ill, 1994; grantee, NIMH. Fellow: Am. Psychiat. Assn. (life Disting. life fellow); mem.: AMA, Vt. State Med. Soc., Vt. Psychiat. Assn. Home: PO Box 759 Brattleboro VT 05302-0759 E-mail: dagallia@sover.net.

AGANI, FATON HILMI, anatomist, educator; b. Gjakova, Kosovo, Oct. 4, 1956; arrived in U.S., 1992; s. Hilmi and Mukades Agani. MD, U. Prishtina, Kosovo, 1980; MS, U. Zagreb, Croatia, 1987; PhD, U. Prishtina, 1990. Cert. MD Yugoslavia. Rsch. fellow Brookhaven Nat. Lab., Upton, L.I., NY, 1985; postdoctoral rschr. Case Western Res. U., Cleve., 1992—95, Johns Hopkins U., Balt., 1995—98; instr. Case Western Res. U., 1998—99, asst. prof. anatomy, 2000—. Achievements include discovery of basic mechanisms of cell response to hypoxia; effects of insulin-like growth factor (IGF-1), nitric oxide (NO), role of mitochondria on regulation of transcription factor hypoxia-inducible factor 1 (HIF-1). Avocations: painting, running, reading. Office: Case Western Res U Euclid Ave 10900 Cleveland OH 44106 E-mail: fxa5@po.cwru.edu.

AGARD, DAVID A., biochemistry and biophysics educator; BS in Molecular Biology and Biochemistry, Yale U., New Haven, 1975; PhD in Chem. Biology, Calif. Inst. Tech., Pasadena, 1980. Postdoctoral rschr. dept. biochemistry and biophysics U. Calif., San Francisco, 1980, asst. prof., 1983—89, assoc. prof., 1989—92, prof. biochemistry and biophysics and pharm. chemistry, 1992—; postdoctoral rschr. Med. Rsch. Coun. Lab. of Med. Biology, Cambridge, England, 1981—82; asst. investigator structural biology Howard Hughes Med. Inst., 1986—89, assoc. investigator, 1989—92, investigator, 1993—. Mem. Comprehensive Cancer Ctr. U. Calif., San Francisco, chair grad. group biophysics, 1995—, dir. Inst. Bioengineering, Biotechnology and Quantitative Biomedical Rsch., San Francisco, Berkeley and Santa Cruz, 2001—02, sci. dir. Inst. Bioengineering, Biotechnology and Quantitative Biomedical Rsch., 2002—. Contbr. articles to sci. jours. Recipient Presdl. Young Investigator award, NSF, 1983—91, Sidhu Award for Outstanding Contbns. Crystallography, 1986. Mem.: NAS. Office: Dept Biochemistry & Biophysics U Calif San Francisco 600 16th St San Francisco CA 94143-2240 Office Phone: 415-476-2521. Office Fax: 415-476-1902. E-mail: agard@msg.ucsf.edu.

AGARWAL, BANKE, gastroenterologist, educator; b. New Delhi, Aug. 3, 1965; s. Nathmal and Vijaya Agarwal. MBBS, Jawaharlal Inst. for Med. Edn. and Rsch., India, 1989, MD, 1992. Diplomate in gastroenterology Am. Bd. Internal Medicine. Residency in internal medicine Columbia U., NYC, 1993—96, fellowship training in gastroenterology, 1996—99; fellowship in advanced gastrointestinal endoscopy Harvard Med. Sch., Boston, 1999—2000, instr. in medicine, 1999—2000; asst. prof. medicine MD Anderson Cancer Ctr., Houston, 2000—02, St. Louis U. Sch. Medicine, 2002—, dir. advanced gastrointestinal endoscopy, assoc. prof. medicine divsn. gastroenterology and hepatology, 2006—. Course dir. Ann. Symposia on Gastrointestinal Cancers, St. Louis, 2002—. Named one of Best Drs. in Am., 2005, 2006, Am. Top Physicians, 2006—; recipient Charles Flood Rsch. prize, Columbia U. Coll. P&S, 1999, REGAL award (Rsch. Excellence in Gastrointestinal and Liver Disease), 2005. Mem.: Am. Assn. for Cancer Rsch., Am. Soc. Gastrointestinal Endoscopy, Am. Gastroenterology Assn. (Young Clinician award 1998). Hindu. Achievements include Conceived and developed the annual symposium on Gastrointestinal Cancers to promote their multidisciplinary management; development of one of nation's largest referral clinical practice specializing in diagnosis and staging of gastrointestinal cancers. Avocations: reading, running, tennis. Office: Saint Louis U Sch Medicine 3635 Vista Ave Saint Louis MO 63105 Home Phone: 314-721-4117; Office Phone: 314-577-8764. Office Fax: 314-577-8757. Personal E-mail: agarwalb@slu.edu.

AGARWAL, RAMESH KUMAR, aeronautical scientist, researcher, educator; b. Mainpuri, India, Jan. 4, 1947; came to U.S., 1968; s. Radhakishan and Parkashvati (Goel) A.; m. Sugita Goel, Oct. 26, 1976; children: Vivek, Gautam. BS, U. Allahabad, 1965; BTech, Indian Inst. Tech., 1968; MS, U. Minn., 1969; PhD, Stanford U., Calif., 1975. Rsch. assoc. NASA Ames Rsch. Ctr., Moffett Field, Calif., 1976-78; McDonnell Douglas fellow, program dir. McDonnell Douglas Aerospace, St. Louis, 1978-94; Bloomfield disting. prof., chair aerospace engring. Wichita State U., 1994-96, Bloomfield disting prof., exec. dir. Nat. Inst. Aviatn Rsch., 1997—2001; William Palm prof. engring., dir. Aerospace Rsch. and Edn. Ctr. Washington U., St. Louis, 2001—. Affiliate prof. Washington U., St. Louis, 1986-95. Contbr. more than 200 articles to profl. jours. Fellow AIAA, AAAS, ASME, SME, IEEE, Soc. Automotive Engring., Royal Aero. Soc., Am. Phys. Soc.; mem. Am. Helicopter Soc., World Innovation Found., Tau Beta Pi, Sigma Gamma Tau, Pi Tau Sigma. Office: Washington U Dept Mech Engring Saint Louis MO 63130 Office Phone: 314-935-6091. Business E-Mail: rka@me.wustl.edu.

AGARWAL, SANJIV, nutritionist, researcher; m. Anita Agarwal; 1 child, Ankita. PhD in Sci., Calcutta U., India, 1987. Sr. nutrition scientist Unilever, Englewood Cliffs, NJ, 2000—03; sr. nutritionist ConAgra Foods, Inc., Omaha, 2003—. Recipient Shakuntala Amirchand prize, Indian Coun. Med. Rsch., 1990. Fellow: Am. Coll. Nutrition; mem.: Am. Soc. Nutrition. Home Phone: 402-884-5435. Personal E-mail: agarwal47@yahoo.com.

AGARWAL, SHASHI KANT, cardiologist; b. Jullundur, Punjab, India, June 15, 1952; arrived in US, 1975; s. Vadhika Ram and Raj Aggarwal; children: Neil, Ayna. Bd. cert. internal medicine and cardiovascular diseases 1979, bd. cert. cardiovascular diseases 1981, bd. cert. managed care medicine and disability analysts 1999, isntr. fundamental critical care support Soc. Critical Care Medicine, 2000, bd. cert. disability analysts 2002, bd. cert. holistic medicine 2004, cert. hosp. physicians 2005, geriatrics 2005, ethical physicians 2005, diplomate anti-aging medicine 2006. Attending cardiologist Orange Meml. Hosp., NJ, 1985—97; pvt. practice Orange. Tchr. U. N.Mex., Albuquerque, St. Michael's Med. Ctr., Newark, 1979-81, asst. to chief of cardiology, 1980-81; dir. divsn. cardiology South Amboy Meml. Hosp., 1991; ofcl. physician India Festival Com.; lectr. in field. Author, editor: (monthly newsletter) Good Health Long Life; reviewer: Catheterization and Cardiovasc. Diagnosis; appeared on weekly TV show To Your Health, 1995-96; contbr. over 500 articles to profl. publs. Del. citizen amb. program People to People Internat., Med. Writers Del. to Russia and Estonia, 1997; gen. sec. Overseas Indian Congress, 1993-95; v.p. Asian Am. Heritage Coun., 1994-97; mem. nat. fin. com. Nat. Rep. Party, 1995-96; mem. Rep. Senatorial Trust, Nat. Rep. Congl. Com., Rep. Presdl. Legion of Merit; life mem. Rep. Presdl. Task Force; mem. steering com. Vedic Cultural Ctr. Project NY; pres. Asian Music Acad., 1997-98, Asian Am. Heritage Coun., 1997-99, chmn., 2000-01, Pragya Mission USA Inc; chmn. internat. adv. com. Physicians Panel of Sarvodaya Health Charitable Found., exec. dir. Sarvodaya Health Found., USA; judge MIss India Worldwide, Mumbai, India, 2004, 06, Miss Indian Can. Worldwide, Toronto, 2005, Miss India USA, Tampa, Fla., 2005, Miss Phillipine USA, Secaucus, NJ, 2005, Miss India UK, Leicester, 2005, several other beauty contests. Recipient Physician's Recognition award AMA, 1992-95, 95-98, 98-01, Rep. Presdl. award, 1994, Rep. Senatorial Medal of Freedom, 1994, News India Times Contbr.'s award, 1994, Rep. Presdl. Legion of Merit medal 1995, Key to West Orange, NJ, 1996, 98, Internat. Cultural Diploma of Honor, 1997, Med. Medal of Honor for Treatment of the Indigent, 1997, Chmn.'s Spl. award Asian Am. Heritage Coun., 1997, Hind Rattan award (Gem of India award) Indian Prime Minister Hon. I.K. Gural, 1998-2001. Fellow Am. Coll. Cardiology (cert.), Am. Coll. Chest Physicians, Am. Coll. Internat. Physicians, Internat. Coll. Physicians, Royal Soc. Medicine UK, Internat. Coun. Integrative Medicine Australia, Coll. Geriatric Cardiology, Acad. Medicine NJ; mem. ACP, Internat. Coll. Physicians (founder NJ chpt.), Am. Soc. Spiritual Medicine (founder), Am. Assn. Cardiologists of Indian Origin (life), Am. Assn. Physicians from India (patron), Am. Coll. Nuclear Physicians, Am. Sleep Disorders Assn., Am. Inst. Ultrasound Medicine, Am. Coll. Physician Execs., Soc. Critical Care Medicine, Heart Friends Around the World, Am. Acad. Family Physicians (supporting), Am. Philatelic Soc., Asian Am. Polit. Coalition (life), Mensa. Republican. Hindu. Avocations: flying, boating, singing, music. Office: 85 S Harrison St Ste 104 East Orange NJ 07018 Home Phone: 732-205-1848; Office Phone: 973-676-1234. Office Fax: 973-676-0009. Personal E-mail: skagarwal@pol.net.

AGARWAL, SUMAN KUMAR, editor; b. Bolpur, India, Jan. 21, 1945; came to U.S., 1980; s. Hari Prasad and Rukmini (Modi) A.; children: Tripti, Samantha Rani. BSc with honors, Visva-Bharati, Santiniketan, India, 1966; MSc, Delhi U., India, 1971; PhD, U. Paris, 1975, DSc, 1979. Rsch. scholar Atomic Energy Commn. of France, Saclay, 1976-80; rsch. assoc. Purdue U., West Lafayette, Ind., 1980-82; sr. sci. info. analyst Chem. Abstracts Svc., Columbus, Ohio, 1982—; pres. Commodities Internat. Ltd. Inc., Columbus, Ohio, 1992—2002, Concrete Machines, Inc., Hilliard, Ohio, 2006—. Contbr. articles to profl. jours. Vol. Columbus Schs., 1984-85, Ohio State U. TV, Columbus, 1986-88. Scholar Govt. of France, 1973-76. Mem. Am. Chem. Soc. Avocations: bridge, photography, tennis. Personal E-mail: suman_agarwal33@yahoo.com.

AGASSI, ANDRE KIRK, retired professional tennis player; b. Las Vegas, Nev., Apr. 29, 1970; s. Mike and Elizabeth Agassi; m. Brooke Shields, Apr. 19, 1997 (div. 1999); m. Steffi Graf, Oct. 22, 2001; children: Jaden Gil, Jaz Elle. Profl. Tennis player ATP Tour, 1986—2006. Mem. U.S. Davis Cup Team, 1988—, U.S. Olympic Tennis Team, Atlanta, 1996. Founder, Andre Agassi Charitable Foundation, 1994, Andre Agassi Boys & Girls Club, 1997, Andre Agassi College Prep Academy, 2001 Named Most Improved Player of the Year, ATP, 1998, Player of the Year, 1999, Most Caring Athlete, USA Today, 1996, 2001, Champion of Champions, L'Equipe, 1999; named one of Barbara Walters-10 Most Fascinating People of 2006, 2006; recipient Arthur Ashe Humanitarian Award, ATP, 1995, 2001, Outstanding Men's Tennis Performer, ESPY Awards, 2000. Achievements include being oldest player to be ranked no. 1 in the ATP entry system, 2003; winning Wimbledon, 1992, US Open, 1994, 1999, Australian Open, 1995, 2000, 2001, 2003, Roland Garros, 1999; winning gold medal, US Men's Singles, Atlanta Olympic Games, 1996; member of US Davis Cup Championship Teams, 1990, 1992, 1995; winner of 60 career singles titles, 1 doubles title, ATP Tour. Address: International Mgmt Group 1 Erieview Plz Ste 1300 Cleveland OH 44114-1715 Office: ATP Tour Internat 201 ATP Tour Blvd Ponte Vedra Beach FL 32082*

AGASSOUNON, WILLIAM B. G., engineer, researcher, scientist; s. Bertin Agassounon and Bernadette Tossa. MSEE, Calif. Inst. Tech., 1999; Diplome d'Ingenieur, Ecole Superieure d'Ingenieurs Electronique Electrotechnique, Paris, 1999; PhD in Elec. Engring., Calif. Inst. Tech., 2003. Rsch. asst. Calif. Inst. Tech., Pasadena, 1998—2003; prin. scientist Phys. Scis. Inc., Andover, Mass., 2003—. Minority outreach program and initiation h.s. students sci. rsch. Jisan Rsch. Inst., Pasadena, Calif., 2003—03; adviser and jury mem. rsch. competition Caltech Summer Undergraduates Rsch. Fellowship Program, 2001. Recipient Small Bus. Innovative Rsch. award, US Army, 2006; fellow, Ctr. Neuromorphic Sys. Engring., 1999—2003; grantee, Northrop Grumman, 2001—03. Mem.: IEEE (tech. program com. 2005—07), AAAS, Swarm Intelligence Symposium (tech. program com. 2005—06), Nat. Soc. Black Engrs. Achievements include research in Swarm Intelligence and Collective Robotics; development of Biomimetic Image Processing; research in Fly Inspired Autonomous Navigation. Office: Physical Scis Inc 20 New England Bus Ctr Andover MA 01810 Home Phone: 781-526-4780; Office Phone: 978-689-0003. Office Fax: 978-689-3232; Home Fax: 978-689-3232. E-mail: agassounon@psicorp.com.

AGATA, BURTON C., lawyer, educator; b. NYC, Feb. 7, 1928; s. Max and Augusta (Steger) A.; m. Dale Granirer, Dec. 24, 1955; children: Seth Hugh, Abby Fran. AB, U. Mich., 1947, JD, 1950; LLM in Trade Regulation, NYU, 1951. Bar: NY 1951. Counsel divsn. NY State Banking Dept., 1955-59; ptnr. firm Burstein & Agata, Mineola and NYC, 1959-61; prof. Mont U., 1961-62, N.Mex. U., 1962-63, Houston U., 1963-69; counsel Nat. Commn. on Reform Fed. Criminal Laws, 1968-70; prof. law Hofstra U., 1970-2001, Max Schmertz disting. prof. law, 1982-2001, disting. prof. emeritus, 2001—, interim dean, 1989; mem. faculty Nat. Inst. Trial Advocacy, 1977-81; dir. N.E. Regional Program, 1981-84. Spl. counsel NYC Charter Revision Commn., 1987-89, NY State Senate

Minority, 1982-87; cons. Fed. Jud. Ctr., 1972, Inst. Jud. Adminstrn., 1973, HEW, 1971, White House Spl. Action Office Drug Abuse Prevention, 1973, NY State Temp. Com. on Constl. Revision, 1993-95; chmn. NY State Task Force, Std. and Go als for Prosecution and Def., 1977-79; cons. Adv. Com. on Qualifications of Counsel, 2d Ct., 1977; bd. dirs. Nassau Economic Opportunity Commn., 1972-73; reporter-cons. action unit on criminal justice system NY State Bar Assn., 1986-90. Author: (with B.S. Meyer and Seth H. Agata) The History of the New York Court of Appeals, 1932-2003, 2006; contbr. articles to law jours. With JAGC US Army, 1951—54. Food Law fellow NYU, 1951, fellow U. Wis., 1963. Fellow Am. Bar Found. (life); mem. Am. Law Inst. (life), ABA (state antitrust law commn. 1980-2001, vice chair com. on professionalism sr. lawyers divsn. 1996-2000), NY State Bar Assn. (exec. com. criminal justice sect., chmn. com. rev. of criminal law 1987-2003, spl. com. on pre-sentence reports 1989-2001, Donnelly Act com. 1990-2001), Assn. Bar City of NY (criminal cts. com. 1970-73, penology com. 1973-76, criminal justice coun. 1983-85, antitrust com. 1986-89), Fed. Jud. Coun., Assn. Am. Law Schs. (chmn. criminal law sect. 1973). Office: 209 Mt Merino Rd Hudson NY 12534 Personal E-mail: vze2vnja@verizon.net.

AGAZZI, SIVIERO, neurosurgeon; s. Evandro and Lucia Agazzi. MD, U. of Geneva Sch. of Medicine, 1991—96. Swiss Neurosurgery Board Certification FMH, Swiss Med. Fedn., Switzerland, 2003. Resident Dept. Neurosurgery Ul. Lousanne, Switzerland, 1996—2002; faculty U. of Lausanne Dept. of Neurosurgery, Lausanne, Switzerland, 2002—03; skull base and cerebrovascular surgery fellow U. of South Fla. Dept. of Neurosurgery, Tampa, Fla., 2003—05, faculty, 2005—. Sci. reviewer for grant applications Nat. Med. Rsch. Coun., Singapore. Contbr. articles to profl. jours. Mem.: AMA, Am. Assn. of Neurol. Surgeons, Swiss soc. of Neruosurgery, Swiss Med. Fedn. Office: Univ of South Fla Dept Neurosurgery 4 Columbia Dri Ste 730 Tampa FL 33606 Office Phone: 813-259-0901. E-mail: sagazzi@hsc.usf.edu.

AGBEH, ANTHONY ODEY, education educator, consultant; arrived in US, 1979; s. Jonas Offum and Rosemary Agbede Agbeh; m. Elizabeth Adeshi Agbeh, Dec. 9, 1991; children: Antonia, Rosemary, Samuel, Patricia. BS, Fla. Internat. U., 1982, MS, 1983. Dir. Wiley Coll., Marshall, Tex.; dept. chmn. Morris Brown Coll., Atlanta; prof. Ferris State U., Big Rapids, Mich.; assoc. prof. Northampton Coll., Bethlehem, Pa. Mgr. Victoria Sta., Miami, Fla. Sec. Conv. and Vis. Bur., Big Rapids, 1994—2002, bd. dirs., 2002—04. Fellow: Am. Hotel and Lodging Assn. (bd. trustees 1996—2002, hospitality educators com. 2002); mem.: KC, Lehigh Valley Realtors. Office: Northampton Coll Bethlehem PA 18020 Home: 5020 Derby Lane Bethlehem PA 18020 Office Phone: 610-861-4114. Personal E-mail: aagbeh@yahoo.com.

AGBEMABIESE, PADMORE ENYONAM, educator; b. Abor, Volta Region, Ghana, Jan. 12, 1965; s. Leo and Anna Ablavi Agbemabiese. BA in English and Drama, U. Ghana, Legon, 1996; M, Ohio State U., Columbus, 1998, PhD, 2006. Lectr. Ohio State U., 1997—. Author of poems. Recipient Gwen Kagey award High Acad. Achievement, Ohio State U., 1998, Disting. Diversity Enhancement award, Ohio State U., Coll. Edn., 2005; Howard Seely scholar, 2003. Roman Catholic. Achievements include research in a comparative studies of Ghana and US educational reforms. Home: 7669 Swindon St Blacklick OH 43004 Office: Ohio State University 486 University Hall 230 Noval Mall Columbus OH 43210 Home Phone: 614-563-2087; Office Phone: 614-292-3700.

AGBETSIAFA, DOUGLAS KOFI, academic administrator, financial and management consultant; b. Anloga, Volta, Ghana; arrived in U.S., 1976; s. Benjamin K. Agbetsiafa and Rebecca Afafa Agbakpe; m. Patricia Ann Williams. BS, U. Ghana, 1971, MS, 1975; MA, Western Ontario, 1976; PhD, U. Notre Dame, 1980. Secondary sch. tchr. Mininstry Edn., Accra, Ghana, 1966-68; instr. U. Western Ontario, London, 1973-75, U. Notre Dame, 1976-80; prof. econs., acad. senate pres., spl. asst. to chancellor Ind. U., South Bend, pres. Smith Bend Faculty and Staff Coun., 2006—. Contbr. articles to profl. jours. Sec.-treas. United Way St. Joseph's County, bd. dirs., 1987—; trustee Urban League, South Bend, 1988; bd. dirs., trustee Urban Leauge South Bend and St. Joseph's County, 1996—. Mem.: Assn. Global Bus. (program dir. 1993—94, v.p. program dir. 1995—), Bus. Assn. Latin Am. Studies, Ind. Acad. Soc. Sci., Midsouth Acad. Econs. and Fin. (bd. dirs.), Midwest Econ. Assn., Western Econ. Internat., Internat. Bus. Assn., Am. Statis. Assn., Am. Econ. Assn. Am., Am. Math. Soc., Math. Assn. Am., U. Notre Dame Alumni Assn., South Bend-Mishawaka C. of C. (bd. dirs., mem. minority bus. devel. task force). Avocations: raquetball, reading poetry, gardening, travel. Home: 224 N Sunnyside Ave South Bend IN 46617-3332 Office: Ind U 1700 Mishawaka Ave South Bend IN 46615-1400 Office Phone: 574-520-4208. Business E-Mail: dagbetsi@iusb.edu.

AGEE, BOB R., academic administrator, educator, minister; b. Brownsville, Tenn., Sept. 30, 1938; s. Edwin L. and Katie L. (Stewart) A.; m. Nelle Rose; children— Nancy Denise, Robyn Janelle BA, Union U., Tenn., 1960; M.Div., So. Bapt. Theol. Sem., 1964, D.Min., 1974; PhD, Vanderbilt U., 1986. Ordained to ministry Baptist Ch. Pastor Shively Heights Bapt. Ch., Louisville, 1964-70, Ardmore Bapt. Ch., Memphis, 1970-75; dean, v.p. religious affairs Union U., Jackson, Tenn., 1975-82, dir. Master's program in Christian Studies, prof. ednl. leadership, 2005—; pres. Okla. Bapt. U., Shawnee, 1982-98, pres. emeritus, 1998—. Mem. edn. commn. So. Bapt. Conv., 1985-93, chmn., 1987-90; bd. dirs. Co-op Svcs. Internat. Edn. Consortium, chmn., 1988-90; cons. evaluator North Ctrl. Assn. Colls. and Univs., 1987—; bd. dirs. Nat. Assn. Ind. Colls. and Univs., 1986-90, 93—. Author Bibl. study materials and articles Mem. human relations com. Memphis Bd. Edn., 1972-74; mem. Memphis Mayor's Crime Commn., 1973-75; mem. Okla. Ind. Coll. Found., 1982-98, chmn., 1985-87. Inducted into Okla. Higher Edn. Hall of Fame, 1999. Mem. Soc. Coll. and Univ. Planning, Shawnee C. of C. (bd. dirs. 1983-98), So. Bapt. Theol. Sem. Alumni Assn. (nat. pres. 1985-86), AAUP, Am. Assn. Univ. Adminstrs., Nat. Assn. Ind. Colls. and Univs. (bd. dirs. 1988-97), Coun. for Christian Colls. and Univs. (bd. dirs. 1997-2003), Assn. So. Bapt. Colls. and Schs. (exec. dir. 1998—, exec. dir. consortium global edn. 1998-2002). Republican. Avocations: racquetball, golf, fishing, writing. Office: PO Box 11655 Jackson TN 38308-0127

AGEE, G. STEVEN, state supreme court justice; b. Roanoke, Va., Nov. 12, 1952; BA, Bridgewater Coll.; JD, U. Va.; LLM in Taxation, NYU. Mem. 7th dist. Va. Ho. of Dels., 1982—94; judge Va. Ct. Appeals, Richmond, 2001—03; justice Va. Supreme Ct., Richmond, 2003—. Former mem. Va. Criminal Sentencing Commn. Trustee Bridgewater Coll. Served in Judge Advocate General Corps USAR, 1985—97. Mem.: Roanoke County-Salem Bar Assn. (former pres.), Va. Bar Assn., DC Bar Assn. Office: Supreme Ct Va PO Box 1315 Richmond VA 23219*

AGGARWAL, SHUSHMA, anesthesiologist, educator; b. India, Nov. 2, 1949; BS in Biology, Agra U., India, 1968; B Medicine B Surgery, Lucknow U., India, 1971. Diplomate Am. Bd. Anesthesiology. Resident in anesthesiology King George's Med. Coll., Lucknow U., 1973—75, rotating intern, 1972; resident in anesthesiology Western Pa. Hosp., Pitts., 1979—81, fellow anesthesia burn unit, ICU, neuro, 1981; fellow anesthesia ICU U. Health Ctr. Pitts., VA Med. Ctr., 1981, fellow neuro-anesthesia, 1981; asst. prof. dept. anesthesiology U. Pitts. Sch. Medicine, Pitts., 1982—92, assoc. prof., 1992—. Staff anesthesiologist King George's Med. Ctr., Lucknow, 1975—77, Presbyn. U. Hosp., Pitts., 1982—; rschr., lectr. in field; dir. symposia in field. Contbr. articles, papers, conf. procs. to profl. publs., chapters to books. Mem. Pa. Gov.'s Sch. for Health Care Shadow Day, Pitts., 1999—2001; vol. clinic Healing for Children, Dominican Republic, 2003, 2005, Guatemala, 2004. Grantee, Dept. Anesthesiology/CCM, 1986, 1987, 1991. Mem.: Liver Intensive Care Group Europe, Internat. Liver Transplantation Soc. (mem. organizing and sci. com. for 5th congress 1999), Western Pa. Soc. Anesthesiologists, Internat. Anesthesia Rsch. Soc., Am. Soc. Anesthesiologists. Home: 2512 Lindenwood Dr Wexford PA 15090 Office: U Pitts Dept Anesthesiology 200 Lothrop St Pittsburgh PA 15213 Business E-Mail: aggarwals@anes.upmc.edu.

AGGARWAL, VANEET, research scientist; PhD, Mich. State U., East Lansing, 2005. Asst. prof. Punjab Agrl. U., Ludhiana, Punjab, India, 1994—2000; vis. rsch. assoc. Mich. State U., East Lansing, 2005—. Mem.: Assn. Agrl. Scientists Indian Origin (sec., treas. 2006—), Am. Chem. Soc., Soil Sci. Soc. Am., Indian Soc. Soil Sci. (life). Office: Michigan State University Dept of Crop & Soil Sciences PSSB East Lansing MI 48824 Home Phone: 517-347-3728; Office Phone: 517-355-0271 ext. 1245.

AGGARWAL, VINOD K., political science professor; b. Seattle, Wash. BA in Polit. Sci., U. Mich., 1975; MA in Polit. Sci., Stanford U., 1977, PhD in Polit. Sci., 1981. Special adviser on trade Nnegotiations United Conference on Trade and Develop., Geneva, 1989; prof. polic. sci. U. Calif., Berkeley, Calif., 1980—, prof. Haas Sch. of Bus., 1992—, dir. APEC Study Ctr., 1996—. Bd. mem. Calif. Council for Internat. Trade; mem. Council on Foreign Relations, 1987—92; charter mem. Pacific Council on Internat. Economic Policy; editor in chief Bus. and Politics; chair Polit. Economy of Industrial Societies, 1991—94; rsch. fellow and guest scholar Brookings Inst.; fellow Woodrow Wilson Internat. Ctr. for Scholars; consultant Mexican Govt., US Dept. of Commerce, WTO, OECD, Group of Thirty, IFAD, World Bank. Author: Liberal Protectionism: The International Politics of Organized Textile Trade, 1985, International Debt Threat: Bargaining Among Creditors and Debtors in the 1980s, 1987, Debt Games: Strategic Interaction in International Debt Rescheduling, 1996. Grantee Rockefeller Internat. Relations Fellowship, 1984—85, Council on Foreign Relations Internat. Affairs Fellowship, 1987. Mem.: Am. Polit. Sci. Assn. (chair internat. polit. economy div. 1994), Am. Economic Assn. Office: U Calif BASC 802 Barrows Hall 1970 Berkeley CA 94720-1970

AGGREY, ORISON RUDOLPH, former ambassador, consultant, academic administrator; b. Salisbury, NC, July 24, 1926; s. J.E. Kwegyir and Rose Rudolph (Douglass) A.; m. Francoise Fratacci, Nov. 5, 1966; 1 dau., Roxane Rose. BS, Hampton Inst., 1946; MS, Syracuse U., 1948; fellow Ctr. for Internat. Affairs, Harvard U., 1964-65; LLD, Livingstone Coll., 1977. Publicity asst. United Negro Coll. Fund, 1947, 50; reporter Cleve. Call and Post, 1948-49; corr. Chgo. Defender, 1949; publicity dir. Bennett Coll., 1950; info. officer, vice consul Am. Consulate Gen., Lagos, Nigeria, 1951-53; asst. dir. USIS, Lille, France, 1953-54; asst. cultural affairs officer Am. embassy, Paris, 1954-57; dir. USIS Cultural Ctr., Paris, 1957-60; dep. pub. affairs adviser for Africa Dept. State, 1961-64; acting chief French br. Voice of Am., 1965; 1st sec., dep. pub. affairs officer Am. embassy, Kinshasa, Democratic Republic of Congo, 1966-68; program mgr. Motion Picture and TV Service, USIA, 1968-70; dir. West African affairs Dept. State, 1970-73; ambassador to The Gambia and Senegal, 1973-77; ambassador to Romania, 1977-81; career min. info., 1979; career min., 1981; Dept. State fgn. affairs sr. fellow, rsch. prof. diplomacy Georgetown U., Washington, 1981-83; spl. asst. Office Analysis Soviet Union and Eastern Europe Dept. State, Washington, 1983-84; internat. rels. cons., 1984-87, 94—; dir. Patricia Roberts Harris pub. affairs program Howard U., 1987-90; acting dir. Howard U. Press, 1988-90, dir., 1990-94. Mem. adv. coun. Joint Ctr. for Polit. and Econ. Studies. Decorated grand officer Senegalese Nat. Order of Lion, 1977; recipient Meritorious Svc. award USIA, 1955, Superior Svc. award, 1960; Hampton Inst. Alumni award, 1961, Meritorious Svc. award Pres. of U.S., 1984, Chancellor's medal Syracuse U., 1984, Meritorious Achievement award Fla. A&M U., 1985, Disting. Achievement award Dillard U., 1987. Mem. Soc. Prodigal Sons State of N.C., Acad. Jazz Paris (hon.), Assn. Black Am. Ambassadors, Assn. Diplomatic Study and Tng. (bd. dirs.), Am. Acad. Diplomacy (former trustee Phelps Stokes Fund, exec. com. Atlantic Coun.), Fed. City Club, Alpha Phi Alpha, Sigma Delta Chi, Alpha Kappa Mu, Sigma Pi Phi. Home: 320 Twenty-Third St SApt 726 Arlington VA 22202

AGHAZADEH, SEYED-MAHMOUD, finance educator; b. Tehran, Iran, Jan. 21, 1950; s. Davood Aghazadeh and Fatemeh Hajghafour; m. Lily Salahy, July 22, 1990; children: Shirin, Shiva, Rana. BS, Nat. U. Iran, Tehran, 1971; MS, Iowa State U., Ames, 1977; PhD, U. Nebr., Lincoln, 1983. Asst. prof. SUNY, Fredonia, 1983—89, assoc. prof., 1989—98, prof., 1998—. Academic grievance officer United Univ. Professions, Fredonia; mem. various coms. SUNY, Fredonia. Guest editor: Internat. Jour. Svcs. Tech. and Mgmt.; contbr. over 60 to profl. jours.; reviewer: Computers & Indsl. Engring., Jour. Orgnl. and End User Computing, Am. Soc. Bus. and Behavioral Scis., others. Vol. cmty. improvement project poor and elderly Iowa State U. Recipient Merit award, SUNY, Fredonia, 1985—90, 1996—2006, Excellence Tchg. award, U. Nebr., Lincoln, 1982—83. Avocations: jogging, ping pong/table tennis, reading. Office: SUNY E350 Thomson Hall Fredonia NY 14063 Office Phone: 716-673-3504. Business E-Mail: aghazade@fredonia.edu.

AGHDASHLOO, SHOHREH, actress; b. Tehran, Iran, May 11, 1952; m. Houshang Touzie, 1985; 1 child, Tara; m. Aydin Aghdashloo, 1972 (div. 1980). BA in Internat. Rels., 1984. Actor: (films) Shatranje bad, 1976, Gozaresh (The Report), 1977, Sootah Delaan, 1978, Guests of Hotel Astoria, 1989, Twenty Bucks, 1993, Maryam, 2000, Surviving Paradise, 2000, America So Beautiful, 2001, House of Sand and Fog, 2003 (best supporting actress award L.A. Film Critics Assn., 2003, best supporting actress award N.Y. Film Critics Cir., 2003, Ind. Spirit award for best supporting female, 2004, Acad. award nomination for best supporting actress, 2004), The Exorcism of Emily Rose, 2005, American Dreamz, 2006, X-Men: The Last Stand, 2006, The Lake House, 2006, The Nativity Story, 2006, (guest appearances): (TV series) Martin, 1993, "24", 2005.

AGIDIUS, MICHAEL GREGORY, music educator; b. Portland, Oreg., Sept. 19, 1965; s. Donald V. and Adele Agidius; m. Virginia Merrit Hunt, Aug. 15, 1987; children: Marcus M., Alexander G. B Music Edn., Willamette U., Salem, Oreg., 1987; MA in Tchg., Lewis & Clark Coll., Portland, 1991. Cert. tchr. Oreg. Musical instrument repair technician, 1983—; music tchr., band dir. Milton-Freewater (Oreg.) Sch. Dist., 1987—. Adj. prof. music Walla Walla Coll., dir. jazz ensemble. Named Laughlin HS Tchr. of Yr., Masons, Milton-Freewater, 1994; recipient Crystal Apple Excellence in Edn. award, Umatilla Elem. Sch. Dist., Pendleton, Oreg., 2001. Mem.: NEA, Nat. Assn. Profl. Band Instrument Repair Technicians (cert.), Milton-Freewater Edn. Assn. (treas. 2005—06), Oreg. Music Educators Assn. (dist. pres. 2001—02). Avocations: musical performance, hunting, fishing, hiking. Home: 390 Triangle K Rd Walla Walla WA 99362 Office: McLaughlin HS 120 S Main Milton Freewater OR 97862

AGISIM, PHILIP, advertising and marketing executive; b. Newark, Jan. 12, 1919; s. Isidore and Jennie (Socket) A.; m. Blanche Tedlow, June 14, 1942; children: Leslie Wayne, Elliot Steven. BS, Rutgers U., 1941; MBA, N.Y. U., 1949. Asst. market research dir. Crowell-Collier Pub. Co., NYC, 1945-49; asso. market research dir. Cowles Pub. Co., NYC, 1949-54; research and planning dir. J.B. Williams Co., NYC, 1954-59, v.p., advt. dir., 1970-71; research dir. Parkson Advt. Agy., NYC, 1959-63, v.p., 1963-69, exec. v.p., 1971-72, vice chmn., 1972-77, pres., 1978—, chief exec. officer, 1980-84, also bd. dirs. Vice chmn. Ohlmeyer Advt., 1984; pres. Product Opportunities Unltd., Inc., 1985-92; sr. acct. mgr. Granite Securities, LLC, 2005-; ptnr. Ron Meyer and Assocs.; bd. dirs. Trevor, Cole, Reid & Monroe Inc., TCRM Comml. Corp., Residential Fin. Svcs. Inc. Contbr. articles in field to profl. jours. Mem. Nat. Acad. TV Arts and Scis., Am. Mktg. Assn., Friars Club. Jewish. Home: 650 Park Ave New York NY 10021-6115 Office: Trevor Cole Reid & Monroe 515 Madison Ave New York NY 10022-5403 Office Phone: 212-371-3933.

AGLER, RICHARD DEAN, rabbi; b. NYC, May 11, 1952; s. Eugene and Sylvia (Spieler) A.; m. Mindy Steinberg, June 19, 1976; children: Jesse Allen, Talia Faith, Sarah Suzan. BA in Polit. Sci., NYU, 1973; MA in Hebrew Lit., Hebrew Union Coll.-Jewish Inst. Religion, 1976; DDiv (hon.), Hebrew U., 2003. Ordained rabbi, 1978. Rabbi Stephen Wise Free Synagogue, NYC, 1978-80, Temple Beth Shalom, Vero Beach, Fla., 1980-82, Temple Beth El, Boca Raton, Fla., 1982-84; founding rabbi Congregation Bnai Israel, Boca Raton, 1984—. Bd. dir. Anti Defamation League, Palm Beach County; mem. pres.'s rabbinic coun., Hebrew Union Coll., Jewish Inst. Religion, 2005. V.p. Handgun Control of Palm Beach County, Fla., Fla., 1983—93; co-founder Boca Raton Black-Jewish Fellowship, 1984—; founder Ctr. Justice, Boca Raton, 1989, Save Darfur Coalition South Palm Beach County, 2004. Named Outstanding Young Man Am., 1989. Mem. Ctr. Conf. Am. Rabbis, South Palm Beach County Rabbinical Assn. (pres. 1991-93), S.E. Assn. Ctrl. Conf. Am. Rabbis (spirituality chair 1984-2002), Assn. Reform Zionists of Am. (life, bd. dirs.), Palm Beach County Bd. Rabbis. Jewish. Avocations: literature, athletics, sailing. Office: Congregation Bnai Israel 2200 Yamato Rd Boca Raton FL 33431-4325

AGNEW, CHARLIE MARTIN, art educator, artist; b. Nassawadox, Va., Sept. 26, 1973; s. George Thurman and Janice Adams Agnew; m. Jackie Lynn Jerrolds, May 28, 2004; 1 child, Timothy Josiah. BA, Bluefield Coll., Va., 1995; MFA, U. Memphis, 1999. Grad. asst., instr. art U. Memphis, 1996—99, part-time instr., 1999—2001, instr. art continuing edn., 2000—03; part-time instr. art Union U., Jackson, Tenn., 2002, vis. instr. art, 2002—04; asst. prof. art Middle Ga. Coll., Cochran, 2004—. Studio/gallery mgr. Second Street Studio, Memphis, 1999—2001. Mem. Compassion Internat., Colorado Springs, Colo., 2004—; usher Cmty. Bible Ch., Memphis, 2003—04; head usher My Father's House Ch., Cochran, 2005—. Named Best in Show, Lynwood Artists, Martinsville, Va., 1999; recipient 1st Pl. Oil/Acrylic Divsn., Crittendon Arts Coun., West Memphis, Ark., 2002, award of distinction, Lynwood Artists, Martinsville, 2003. Mem.: Cochran-Bleckley Arts Alliance (adv. bd. 2005—), Christians in the Virtual Arts, Coll. Art Assn. Independent. Avocations: art, camping, canoeing, hiking, collecting. Home: 122 N 6th St Cochran GA 31014 Office: Middle Ga Coll Humanities Divsn 1100 Second St SE Cochran GA 31014 Office Phone: 478-934-3043.

AGNEW, CHRISTOPHER MACK, minister, historian; b. Santa Barbara, Calif., Aug. 7, 1944; s. Jack and Agnes Emma (Mack) A.; m. Suzanne Marie Souder, June 1, 1974 (div.); m. Elizabeth Lewis Lyddane, Apr. 25, 1998. AB, Bucknell U., Lewisburg, Pa., 1967; MA, U. Del., Newark, 1975, PhD, 1980; STM, Gen. Theol. Sem., NYC, 1991. Ordained to ministry as deacon Episcopal Ch., 1991, as priest Episcopal Ch., 1992. Reference libr. Dover (Del.) Pub. Libr., 1969—72; tchg. asst. dept. history U. Del., Newark, 1972—76; manuscript libr. Hist. Soc. Del., 1979—81; asst. prof. history and Can. studies SUNY, Plattsburgh, 1981—84; registrar Diocese of Del., Wilmington, 1985—89; assoc. ecumenical officer Episcopal Ch., NYC, 1989—94; standing commn. on ecumenical rels., 1989—94; deacon St. Thomas' Ch., Newark, 1991—92; priest-in-charge St. Marks, Teaneck, NJ, 1992; priest assoc. All Angels Ch., NYC, 1992—95; interim rector St. Martin's, Maywood, NJ, 1994—95, All Hallows, Wyncote, Pa., 1995, St. Michael's, Litchfield, Conn., 1995—97, Ch. of the Ascension, Norfolk, Va., 1997, St. Peter's in Great Valley, Paoli, Pa., 1997—99; priest in charge St. Paul's, Owens, Va., 2000—02; interim rector Vauter's Ch., Loretto, Va., 2002—, St. Paul's, Nomini Grove, Va., 2002—. Exec. bd. Episcopal Diocesan Ecumenical Officers, 1989—94, 2007—; mem. Episcopal-Reformed Episcopal Dialogue, 1989—94, mem. standing com. ecumenical rels., 1989—94; mem. NCC Christian-Muslim Rels. Commn., 1989—91, NCC Christian-Jewish Rels. Commn., 1989—99, Anglican-Roman Cath. Consultation, U.S.A., 1989—94, NCC Interfaith Working Group, 1990—95; mem. planning com. Nat. Workshop on Christian Unity, 1990—94, 2007—; mem. Faith and Order Commn., 1991—95; chmn. NCC Christian-Jewish Rels. Commn., 1991—99; mem. Parliament of the Worlds Religions, 1993, Interfaith Rels. Commn., 1996—99, Episcopal-Reformed Episcopal-Anglican Province of Am. Dialogue, 2003—, Episc. Russian Orthodox Joint Coordinating Com., 1990—94. Editor: The Ecumenical Bull., 1989-94, Anglican Statements on the Church: Selected Documentary Sources for a Study of Anglican Ecclesiology, 1994; author: God With Us, 1986; contbr. articles to profl. jours. Mem. Ecumenical Interfaith Commn. Diocese of Va., 2000—, co-chmn., 2004—; mem. faith and order workgroup Va. Coun. Chs., 2002—, chmn. workgroup, 2004—, chair, 2004—, mem. coord. cabinet, 2003—. Mem. Nat. Episc. Historians Assn. (mem. exec. bd. 1995-99, 2006—), Hist. Soc. Episc. Ch. (bd. dirs. 2005—), Order Crown Charlemagne U.S. (asst. chaplain 1997-2005, chaplain 2005—), Assn. for Preservation Va. Antiquities (trustee No. Neck br. 2004-05), Orgn. Am. Historians, Am. Hist. Assn., N.Am. Acad. Ecumenists (mem. exec. bd. 2004—), Can. Hist. Assn., Assn. Can. Studies in U.S., Interim Ministry Network, Mil. Order of Loyal Legion of U.S. (chaplain-in-chief 1995—), Mil. Order of Stars and Bars, Soc. Colonial Wars, N.Am. Guild of Change Ringers. Home: 12433 Richards Ride King George VA 22485

AGNEW, GARY, professional hockey coach; b. Niagara Falls, Ont., Can., May 24, 1960; m. Barbara Agnew; children: Brett, Lindsay. Grad., U. NB, 1982; M in Coaching, U. We. Ont. Asst. coach U. New Brunswick Hockey Team, 1985—87; head coach London Knights (Ont. Hockey League), 1990—94, 1997—2000, Kingston Frontenacs, 1994—97, Syracuse Crunch (Am. Hockey League), 2000—06; asst. coach Columbus Blue Jackets, 2006—, interim head coach, 2006. Recipient Matt Leyden Trophy as Coach of Yr., Ont. Hockey League, 1993, 1998. Office: Columbus Blue Jackets Nationwide Arena 200 W Nationwide Blvd, Ste Level Columbus OH 43215*

AGNEW, HAROLD MELVIN, physicist; b. Denver, Mar. 28, 1921; s. Sam E. and Augusta Agnew; m. Beverly Jackson, May 2, 1942; children: Nancy E. Agnew Owens, John S. AB, U. Denver, 1942; MS, U. Chgo., 1948, PhD, 1949; PhD (hon.), Coll. Santa Fe, 1980, U. Denver, 1992. With Los Alamos Sci. Lab., 1943-46, alt. div. leader, 1949-61, leader weapons div., 1964-70, dir., 1970-79; pres. Gen. Atomics, San Diego, 1979-85, also bd. dirs., 1985—. Sci. adviser Supreme Allied Comdr. in Europe, Paris, 1961-64; chmn. Army Sci. Adv. Panel, 1965-70, San Diego County adv. bd.; mem. aircraft panel President's Sci. Adv. Com., 1965-73; mem. USAF Sci. Adv. Bd., 1957-69, Def. Sci. Bd., 1965-70, Gov. of N.Mex.'s Radiation Adv. Coun., 1959-61; sec. N.Mex. Health and Social Svcs., 1971-73; chmn. gen. adv. com. ACDA, 1974-77, mem., 1977-81; mem. aerospace safety adv. panel NASA, 1964-70; mem. U.S. Army Sci. Bd., 1978-80, White House Sci. Coun., 1982-89; adj. prof. U. Calif., San Diego, 1988—. Mem. council engring. NRC, 1978-82; mem. Los Alamos Bd. Ednl. Trustees, 1950-55, pres., 1955; trustee San Diego Mus. Art, 1983-87; mem. Woodrow Wilson Nat. Fellowship Found., 1973-80; N.Mex. State senator, 1955-61; sec. N.Mex. Legis. Council, 1957-61; chmn. N.Mex. Senate Corp. Commn., 1957-61; mem. Fed. Emergency Agy., 1982-88; bd. dirs. Fedn. Rocky Mountain States, Inc., 1975-77, Charles Lee Powell Found., 1993—; chmn. U. Calif. San Diego Chancellors Assocs., 1998-2000. Recipient Ernest Orlando Lawrence award AEC, 1966; Enrico Fermi award Dept. Energy, 1978; Pres's. medal, U. of Calif., 2003. Fellow Am. Phys.

Soc., AAAS; mem. Nat. Acad. Scis., Nat. Acad. Engring., Council on Fgn. Relations, Phi Beta Kappa, Sigma Xi, Omicron Delta Kappa. Home: 322 Punta Baja Dr Solana Beach CA 92075-1720

AGNEW, JOHN A., science educator; b. Millom, Cumbria, England, Aug. 29, 1949; arrived in U.S., 1971; s. Herbert and Anne (MacPherson) A.; children: Katherine, Christine. BA, Exeter U., Eng., 1970; Cert. Edn., Liverpool U., Eng., 1971; MA, Ohio State U., 1973, PhD, 1976. From asst. prof. to prof. Syracuse (NY) U., 1975—96; prof. UCLA, 1996—, chair dept. geography, 1998—2002, chair global studies program, 2007—. Dir. social sci. program Syracuse U., 1981—88; vis. prof. U. Chgo., 1992, U. Cambridge, England, 1992, U. Iowa, 1995, Univ. Coll., London, 1996, U. Durham, 2003, Queen's U., Belfast, 2003, Emmanuel Coll., Cambridge, 2004; Hettner lectr. U. Heidelberg, 2000; Guggenheim fellow UCLA, 2003—04. Author: Place and Politics, 1987, The U.S. in World Economy, 1987, Rome, 1995, Geopolitics: Re-Visioning World Politics, 1998, 2d edit., 2003, Place and Politics in Modern Italy, 2002, Making Political Geography, 2002, Hegemony, The New Shape of Global Power, 2005 (Outstanding Academic Title, 2005); co-author: Mastering Space, 1995, The Geography of World Economy, 1989, 4th edit., 2003, Berlusconi's Italy, 2007; editor: The City in Cultural Context, 1984, The Power of Place, 1989, Human Geography: An Essential Anthology, 1996, Political Geography: A Reader, 1997, American Space/American Place, 2002, Companion to Political Geography, 2002, The Marshall Plan Today: Model and Metaphor, 2004; co-editor Geopolitics, 1999—; mem. editl. bd. Polit. Geography, Nat. Identities, Global Networks, Scottish Geog. Jour., European Jour. Internat. Rels., Progress in Human Geography, Irish Geography, Internat. Polit. Sociology. Recipient Disting. scholarship award, Assn. Am. Geographers, 2006. Fellow: AAAS, Royal Geog. Soc.; mem.: N.Y Acad. Sci., Am. Polit. Sci. Assn., Coun. European Studies, Am. Assn. Geographers (v.p. 2007—08). Office: UCLA 1255 Bunche Hl Los Angeles CA 90095-1524 Office Phone: 310-825-1713. Business E-Mail: jagnew@geog.ucla.edu.

AGNEW, PETER TOMLIN, employee benefit consultant; b. Orange, NJ, Nov. 20, 1948; s. William Harold and Janet Elisabeth (Gittinger) A.; m. Linda W. Seyffarth; children: Jonathan, Stephen, Douglas, Karen; 1 step child, Kristin Seyffarth. BA in English cum laude, Amherst Coll., 1971; MBA in Fin., NYU, 1976. CLU. Asst. investment officer Mutual Benefit Life, Newark, 1971—78; exec. v.p., bd. dir., prin. Post & Kurtz, Inc., NYC, 1978—85, exec. v.p., prin., 1993—2006, also bd. dirs., pres., 1998—2006; sr. regional dir. Minet, NYC, 1985—92; pres. Post & Kurtz, Inc. divsn. HUB Internat. NE, NYC, 2006—. Pres. P. Tomlin Agnew Assocs., Glen Ridge, N.J., 1982—. Contbr. articles to profl. jours. Capt. United Way, Newark, 1978; assoc. class agt. Amherst Coll. Alumni Fund, 1980—, class agt., 1993—; exec. bd. Rep. Congl. Leadership Coun., 1988-92; vice chair Civic Conf. Com. of Glen Ridge, 1998-99; asst. treas. Glen Ridge Congl. Ch., 1996-2006; parents coun. Hamilton Coll., 1997-2001, Skidmore Coll., 2002-03; mem. Glen Ridge Bd. Edn., 2005—. Fellow Life Mgmt. Inst.; mem. Soc. CLU (com. chmn. NY chpt. 1984), Nat. Assn. Securities Dealers, Yale Ins. Group (chmn. 1988-90), Glen Ridge Country Club, Downtown Assn. Avocations: swimming, bridge, skiing, music, golf. Home: 75 Glen Ridge Pky Glen Ridge NJ 07028-1821 Personal E-mail: pagnew236@aol.com.

AGNO, JOHN G., management consultant; b. Gloversville, NY, Dec. 8, 1940; s. John G. and Margretta (Luff) Anagnostopulos; m. Karen Clark Mikus, June 29, 1985 (div. Nov. 2002). BBA, U. Fla., 1962. Mktg. specialist Eastman Kodak Co., Rochester, NY, 1965-73; gen. mgr. sanitation appliance divsn. Thetford Corp., Ann Arbor, Mich., 1973-80; v.p. mktg. and adminstrn. Stirling Power Systems Corp. divsn. McDonnell Douglas Corp., Ann Arbor, 1980-87; pres. Signature, Inc., Ann Arbor, 1983—. Deacon First Presbyn. Ch., Ann Arbor; bd. dirs. Washtenaw United Way, 1991-95; bd. dirs. YMCA, 1995-2000. 1st lt. U.S. Army, 1963-65. Mem. Recreational Vehicle Industry Assn. (chmn. mktg. commn. 1978-82, bd. dirs. 1981-83), Turnaround Mgmt. Assn., Ann Arbor Country Club, Rotary. Republican. Home: 4701 Midway Dr Ann Arbor MI 48103-9427 Office: Signature Inc PO Box 2086 Ann Arbor MI 48106-2086 Office Phone: 734-426-2000. Business E-Mail: johnagno@signatureseries.com.

AGOGINO, ALICE MERNER, computer scientist, mechanical engineer, educator; b. Albuerque, N.Mex., Dec. 1, 1952; married; 2 children. BS in Mech. Engring., U. N.Mex., 1975; MS in Mech. Engring., U. Calif. Berkeley, 1978; PhD in Engring. Econ. Systems, Stanford U., 1984. Registered Profl. Mech. Engr., Calif., 1978. Project engr. Dow Chem., Freeport, Tex., 1972-73; mech. engr. GE, San Jose and Sunnyvale, Calif., 1975-78, commercial specialist San Jose, Calif., 1978-79; systems analyst SRI Internat., Menlo Park, Calif., 1980; dir. Women-in-Engring. program U. Santa Clara, Calif., 1980-81; prin., engring. and mgmt. cons. firm Agogino Engring., 1979—; asst. prof., mech. engring. U. Calif., Berkeley, 1984—88, assoc. prof., mech. engring., 1988—92, dir., curriculum reform, synthesis coalition, 1990—94, prof. mech. engring., 1992—, co-chair, instructional tech. com. of the campus computing and communication policy bd., 1993—97, dir., synthesis coalition, 1994—97, assoc. dean spl. programs Coll. Engring., 1995—99, assoc. dean, instructional tech./distance learning, coll. engring., 1996—99, chair, instructional tech. com. of the campus computing and communication policy bd., 1997—2001, dir., Instructional Tech. Program, 1999—2001, faculty asst. to Exec. Vice Chancellor and Provost Carol Christ in Educational and Develop. Tech., 1999—2000, faculty asst. to Exec. Vice Chancellor and Provost Paul Gray, 2000—01, vice-chair, Faculty Academic Senate, Berkeley Divsn., 2004—05, chair, faculty academic senate, Berkeley Divsn., 2005—06, Roscoe and Elizabeth Hughes prof. mech. engring, 1998—. Spkr. in field; proposed reviewer NSF, U. Calif. Microelectronics Innovation and Computer Rsch. Opportunities (MICRO), Electric Power Rsch. Inst. (EPRI), Australian Science Fund, Canadian Nat. Sci. and Engring. Rsch. Coun. and Swedish Coun. Higher Edn.; mem. exec. com. Digital Media Innovation Initiative, U. Calif. Sys., 2000—02; mem. adv. bd. Nat. Digitial Libr. for Technological Literacy project, 2001—02, Jet Propulsion Lab, 2002—04; mem. Radcliffe Inst. for Advanced Study, MIT Corp. vis. com. in mech. engring.; mem. mfg. engring. lab. Nat. Inst. of Standards & Tech., 2004—05; mem. Women in Academic Sci. Engring. Com. of the Nat. Academies Com. on Sci., Engring., and Pub. Policy, 2005—06, Nat. Academies Bd. on Sci. Edn., 2005—; pres., Assn. of Academic Women U. Calif., Berkeley, 2001—03, chair, Studies in Engring. , Sci., and Math. Edn., 2003—04, co-chair, working group, Berkeley Diversity Rsch. Intiative, 2005, co-chair, steering com., Berkeley Diversity Rsch. Initiative, 06, co-chair, U. Athletics Bd., 2005—06; and several others. Reviewer for: ASME Transactions, Journal of Optimization Theory and Applications, IEEE Transactions, IEEE Computer, AI in Engineering, Design, Analysis and Manufacturing, Research in Engineering Design, Journal of Intelligent Computing, ASEE Journal of Engineering Education, Engineering with Computers, and Advances in Engineering Software, and numerous technical confs.; mem. editl. review bd., Journal of Engineering Education, mem. editl. bd., Concurrent Engineering: Research and Applications, Research in Engineering Design; assoc. editor Artificial Intelligence in Engineering, Design, Analysis and Manufacturing. Chancellor's Hon. Fellow in Mech. Engring., U. Calif. Berkeley, 1977; recipient IBM Faculty Develop. award, 1985-86, Presdl. Young Investigator award NSF, 1985, Ralph R. Teetor Educator award Soc. Automotive Engrs., 1987, Young Mfg. Engr. Yr., Soc. Mfg. Engrs., 1987-88, Most Outstanding Alummnus, Dept. Mech. Engring., U. New Mexico, 1992, NSF Director's award for Disting. Tchg. Scholars, 2004; co-recipient Best Paper at the Conf. on AI Apllications, 1992, Best Paper award , Artificial Intelligence in Design Conf., 1996, John Wiley & Sons Premier Courseware award for Virtual Disk Drive Design Studio, 1997 Fellow AAAS (mem. electronics nominating com., sect. engring., 1994-95, chair, 1995, mem.-at-large engring. sect. 1996-2000, mem. com. on opportunities in sci., 1997-2003, chair sect. engring., 2001-02, retiring chair, 2002-03), Assn. for the Advancement of Women; mem. NSF (mem. proposal review adv. team, 1996-97, mem. adv. com. for engring., engring. doctorate, 1991-96, co-chair, 1996-97), ASME (chair Santa Clara Valley sect. 1981-82, dir. 1983-84, mem. program com. design for manufacture conf., 1997, bd. dir. Ctr. for Edn., 2004-06, co-recipeint, Xerox Best Paper award, 2004), IEEE(recipient Helen Plants award for Best Non-Traditional Session at Frontiers in Edn., 1998, co-recipient Robotics & Automation Soc. Best Paper award, 2005, NAE(mem. academic adv. bd., 1998-99, mem. com. on tech. literacy standards, 1997-2000, mem. com. engring. edn., 1999-2002, mem. Bernard M. Gordon prize for Innovation in Engring. and Tech. Edn. com., 2001-02, co-chair planning com. on engring. edn. for the yr. 2020, 1999-2000, vice-chair mech. engring. peer com., 2004-05, chair 2005-06), Am. Soc. Elec. Engrs.(mem. Fred Merryfield Design award com., 1993-96, mem. Wickenden award com., 1997-98, mem. women and minorities task force, 2001-02, co-recipient Best Paper award, 1997, Best Overall Paper award, 1998), European Acad. Sciences, Am. Assn. Artificial Intelligence, Assn. Computing Machinery, Soc. Women Engrs. (v.p. San Francisco Bay Area, 1979-80), Pi Tau Sigma (Academic Honor award, 1973, award for Excellence in Tchg., 1986), Tau Beta Pi, Phi Kappa Phi. Avocations: guitar, gardening, hiking, exploring. Office: U Calif 5136 Etcheverry Hall Mail Stop 1740 Berkeley CA 94720-1740 Office Phone: 510-642-6450. Office Fax: 510-643-5599. Business E-Mail: agogino@berkeley.edu, agogino@socrates.berkeley.edu.

AGOORA, LAMMIA HASSON, mathematics educator; arrived in U.S., 1972; d. Hasson Ali Agoora and Fathia Mohamed Yousuf. BA, We. Conn. State U., Danbury, 1985, MA in History, 1988; post grad., U. Bridgeport, Conn., 1989, EdD, 1997. Substitute tchr. Danbury Bd. Edn., Conn., 1986—92, tchr. math, 1992—; coord. EXCEL program Western Conn. State U., 1999—. Patricipant St. Jude Children's Hosp. Math-a-Thon, 1997—2000; mentor program Danbury Bd. Edn., Conn., 1997—, mentoring tchr., 2006—, mem. supt. adv. com., mem.prin. adv. com.; participant Delta Adminstrv. Aspirants Program. Mem.: NEA, Conn. Edn. Assn. Democrat. Avocation: running. Office: 2 Whitney Ave Danbury CT 06810-6209 Home: 11 Hoyt Ave Bethel CT 06801

AGOSTA, VITO, mechanical and aerospace engineering educator; b. NYC, July 26, 1923; s. John and Elizabeth (Alvares) A.; m. Mary Frago, Aug. 9, 1952; children: John, Diana, Charles. MS in Engring., U. Mich., 1949; PhD, Columbia, 1959. Registered profl. engr., NY. Thermodynamicist DeLaval Steam Turbine Co., 1946—47; mem. faculty Poly. Inst. NY, Bklyn., 1950—, prof. mech. and aerospace engring., 1962—, prof. emeritus, 1986—; Fulbright prof. Queen Mary Coll., London U., 1966—67; pres. Propulsion Scis., Inc., Huntington, NY, 1966—75, Fuels Systems Design Corp., Huntington, NY, 1975—94, Propulsion Scis. Co., Huntington, 1989—; adj. prof. U.S. Merchant Marine Acad., 2004—. Cons. in field in fluid dynamics in transportation sys., energy sys., boilers, engines & alternate fuels. With AUS, 1943—45. Recipient Alexander Hamilton award, Grand Army Rep., 1943; grantee, Fulbright Found., 1966—67. Mem.: ASME, Tau Beta Pi, Sigma Xi. Democrat. Roman Catholic. Achievements include invention of non-miscible liquid emulsifier; modulating oil burner; design of and mfr. of modulating fuel emulsifier systems for engines and boilers; research in combustion instability in rocket motors; supersonic combustion of two phase systems; air and thermal pollution; heat transfer analysis in reacting fuels; ventilation in Boston and New York City automobile tunnels; air movement studies in train stations; use of ammonia as a hydrogen carrier and an alternative fuel additive in engines and burners; patents for the process of hydrodynamic emulsification; hydrodynamic proportionate mixing of liquids; chemical mixing and metering apparatus. Avocation: photography. Home: 42 Cherry Ln Huntington NY 11743-2945 Office: Propulsion Scis Co 300 Broadway Huntington Station NY 11746-1405 Office Phone: 631-219-0708. Personal E-mail: vagosta@optonline.net.

AGOSTA, WILLIAM CARLETON, chemist, educator; b. Dallas, Jan. 1, 1933; s. Angelo N. and Helen Carleton (Jones) A.; m. Karin Solveig Engstrom, July 2, 1958; children— Jennifer Ellen, Christopher William. BA, Rice Inst., 1954; AM, Harvard U., Cambridge, Mass., 1955, PhD, 1957. NRC postdoctoral fellow Oxford U., England, 1957-58; Pfizer postdoctoral fellow U. Ill., Urbana, 1958-59; asst. prof. U. Calif., Berkeley, 1959-61; liaison scientist US Navy, Frankfurt, Germany, 1961-63; asst. prof. chemistry Rockefeller U., NYC, 1963-67, assoc. prof., 1967-74, prof., 1974-98, prof. emeritus, 1998—. Vis. prof. U. Innsbruck, 1995, Princeton U., 1996; cons. in field; officer Chiron Press, Inc., 1977-85; mem. NRC Associateship Programs Chem. Scis. Panel, 1997-2005. Author: Chemical Communication, 1992, Bombardier Beetles and Fever Trees, 1996, Thieves, Deceivers, and Killers, 2001; mem. editl. adv. bd. Jour. Organic Chemistry, 1984-88; contbr. articles to profl. jours. Bd. dirs. San Juan Cmty. Home Trust, 2003—06, pres., 2004—06; bd. visitors U. Wash. Sch. Medicine, Wash., 2006—, mem. scholarship com. Wash., 2006—; mem. Noxious Weed Control Bd., San Juan County, Wash., 2002—, Housing Bank Commn., San Juan County, 2006—. John Angus Erskine fellow U. Canterbury, New Zealand, 1981 Fellow AAAS; mem. Chem. Soc. London, Am. Chem. Soc., Interam. Photochem. Soc., European Photochemistry Assn., Am. Soc. Photobiology, Internat. Soc. for Chem. Ecology, Phi Beta Kappa, Sigma Xi. Home: PO Box 1547 Friday Harbor WA 98250-1547 Office Phone: 360-378-0816. E-mail: agosta@u.washington.edu.

AGOSTI, DEBORAH ANN, retired senior justice; BA cum laude, U. Toledo, 1973, JD, 1976. Bar: Nev., U.S. Supreme Ct. Dep. pub. defender Montgomery County, Ohio, 1977; sr. staff atty. Sr. Citizens Legal Assistance Program, Washoe County, 1977—79; dep. dist. atty., 1979—82; justice of the peace Reno Twp., Nev., 1982—85; dist. judge 2d Jud. Dist., Reno, 1985—99; justice Nev. Supreme Court, Carson City, 1999—2004, sr. justice, 2005—. Trustee Nat. Jud. Coll., 2001—, Pretrial Svcs. Resource Ctr., 1999—; co-chmn. jury improvement commn. Supreme Ct. of Nev., 2001—; mem., dean's adv. bd. U. Toledo Coll. Law. Chmn. Task Force to Revitalize Interest in Attendance at Washoe County Bar Meetings, 2001—. Named Outstanding Young Woman for State of Nev., 1983, One of Am.'s 100 Young Women of Promise, Good Housekeeping mag., 1985, Reno's Outstanding Woman for 1986, One of Three Outstanding Young Nevadans, Reno Jaycees, 1986, Outstanding Women Lawyer, No. Nev. Women Lawyer's Assn., 1993, Judge of Yr., Nev. Dist. Judge's Assn., 1989, Woman of Achievement, Nev. Women's Fund, 1998, Woman of Distinction, Nat. Assn. Women Bus. Owners-So. Nev. Chpt., 2004, One of Nev.'s First One Hundred Women Attys., Woman of Distinction, Soroptimists of Reno, 2005. Master: Bruce Thompson Inn of Ct.; mem.: No. Nev. Women Lawyers Assn., Nat. Assn. Women Judges, Soroptimists Internat. of Truckee Meadows (life mem., Woman of Distinction 2001). Office: Supreme Ct Nev 201 S Carson St Carson City NV 89701-4702 Home Phone: 775-851-3360; Office Phone: 775-684-1600. E-mail: dagosti@nvcourts.state.nv.us.

AGOSTINELLI, ROBERT FRANCESCO, investment banker; b. Rochester, NY, May 21, 1953; BA, St. John Fisher Coll., 1976; MBA, Columbia U., 1981. Assoc. Jacob Rothschild, London, 1981-82; v.p. investment banking Goldman, Sachs & Co., NYC and London, 1982-87; sr. mng. dir. investment banking Lazard Frères & Co. LLC, NYC, 1987-96; bd. dirs. Rhone Group/Rhone Capital, NYC, 1996—. Mem. Coun. Fgn. Rels.; former vice-chmn. Coun. US and Italy, European Inst., Am.-Italian Cancer Found.; bd. dirs., mem. exec. com. Almatis B.V.; non-resident fellow; bd. dirs. ISB, Marco Polo. Office: Rhone Group 630 5th Ave Ste 2710 New York NY 10111-0100

ÁGOSTON, GÁBOR, history professor; s. Gábor Ágoston and Ilona Kovács; m. Aliz Gebula; 1 child, Márk Gábor. MA, Eötvös Loránd U., Budapest, Hungary, 1984, D, 1986; PhD, Hungarian Acad. Scis., Budapest, 1994. Asst., assoc. prof. Eötvös Loránd U., 1987—98; assoc. prof. U. Pécs, 1995—98; asst. prof. Georgetown U., Washington, 1998—2004, assoc. prof., 2004—. Prof. U. Wien, Vienna, 2003; assoc. rschr. U. Istanbul, 2006—. Office: Georgetown University Dept of History 37th & O Streets Washington DC 20057 Office Phone: 202-687-7758. Office Fax: 202-687-7245. E-mail: agostong@georgetown.edu.

AGRANOFF, BERNARD WILLIAM, biochemist, educator; b. Detroit, June 26, 1926; s. William and Phyllis (Pelavin) A.; m. Raquel Betty Schwartz, Sept. 1, 1957; children: William, Adam. MD, Wayne State U., 1950; BS, U. Mich., 1954. Intern Robert Packer Hosp., Sayre, Pa., 1950-51; commd. surgeon USPHS, 1954-60; biochemist Nat. Inst. Neurol. Diseases and Blindness, NIH, Bethesda, Md., 1954-60; mem. faculty U. Mich., Ann Arbor, 1960—, prof. biochemistry, 1965—; R.W. Gerard prof. of neurosci. in psychiatry, 1991. Rsch. biochemist Mental Health Rsch. Inst., 1960—, assoc. dir., 1977-83, dir. 1983-95, dir. neurosci. lab., 1983-2000; vis. scientist Max Planck Inst. Zellchemie, Munich, 1957-58, Nat. Inst. Med. Rsch., Mill Hill, Eng., 1974-75; Henry Russel lectr. U. Mich., 1987; cons. pharm. industry, govt. Contbr. articles to profl. jours. Fogarty scholar-in-residence NIH, Bethesda, Md., 1989-95; named Mich. Scientist of Yr. Mus. of Sci., Lansing, 1992. Fellow AAAS, Am. Acad. Arts and Scis., N.Y. Acad. Sci., Am. Coll. Neuropsychopharmacology; mem. Am. Soc. Biochemistry and Molecular Biology, Am. Chem. Soc., Inst. Medicine of NAS, Internat. Soc. Neurochemistry (treas. 1985-89, chmn. 1989-91), Am. Soc. Neurochemistry (pres. 1973-75). Achievements include research in brain lipids, biochem. basis of learning, memory and regeneration in the nervous system, human brain imaging. Office: U Mich Molecular and Behavior Rsch Inst 205 Zina Pitcher Pl Ann Arbor MI 48109-5720 Personal E-mail: agranoff@umich.edu.

AGRANOFF, GERALD NEAL, lawyer; b. Detroit, Nov. 24, 1946; s. Carl and Frances (Solomon) A.; children: Lindsay Sara, Dana Jill, Charley Elisabeth. BS, Wayne State U., 1969, JD, 1972; LLM, NYU, 1973. Bar: Mich. 1973, N.Y. 1975, U.S. Tax Ct. 1974, U.S. Ct. Claims 1974. Atty.-advisor U.S. Tax Ct., Washington, 1973—75; assoc. Baker & McKenzie, NYC, 1975—79, Baer Marks & Upham, NYC, 1979—80; counsel Pryor, Cashman et al, NYC, 1980—82; gen. counsel Arbitrage Securities Co., Plaza Securities Co., NYC, 1982—2003; gen. ptnr. Edelman Securities Co., NYC, 1984—2003; counsel Kupferman & Kupferman LLP, NYC, 2003—. Mem. Inveraray Capital Mgmt. LLC, 2002—, Crosshaven Capital LLC, 2002—; bd. dirs. Triple Crown Media, Inc., Petrosearch Corp.; adj. instr. NYU Inst. Fed. Taxation, 1980-81. Bd. dirs. Soho Repertory Theatre, NYC, 1982. Office: 1251 Ave of Americas Ste 810 New York NY 10020 Home: PO Box 641 North Salem NY 10560 Office Phone: 212-575-1557. Business E-Mail: agranoffg@aol.com.

AGRAST, MARK DAVID, lawyer; b. Cleve., Mar. 31, 1956; s. Harold and Charlotte Agrast; life ptnr. David Michael Hollis. BA summa cum laude, Case Western Res. U., 1978; postgraduate Rhodes Scholar, Oxford Univ., 1978—81; JD, Yale U., 1985. Bar: Ohio 1986, D.C. 1988, U.S. Supreme Ct. Atty. Jones Day Reavis & Pogue, Washington, 1985—91; sr. legis. asst. Hon. Gerry E. Studds, U.S. Ho. of Reps., Washington, 1992—97; counsel and legis. dir. Hon. William D. Delahunt, U.S. Ho. of Reps., Washington, 1997—2003; sr. v.p. for domestic policy Ctr. for Am. Progress, Washington, 2003—05, sr. fellow, 2005—. Rhodes scholar, Oxford U., 1978—81. Fellow: Am. Bar Found.; mem.: ABA (chair sect. individual rights and responsibilities 2002—03, bd. govs. 2004—, exec. com. 2006—). Office: Center American Progress 10th Fl 1333 H St NW Washington DC 20005

AGRAWAL, DHARMA PRAKASH, engineering educator; b. Balod, India, Apr. 12, 1945; arrived in US, 1976; s. Saryoo Prasad and Chandra K. Agrawal; m. Purnima Agrawal, June 7, 1971; children: Sonali, Braj. BE, Ravishankar U., Raipur, India, 1966; ME with honors, Roorkee U., India, 1968; DSc, Fed. Inst. Tech., Lausanne, Switzerland, 1975. Lectr. M.N.R. Engring. Coll., Allahabad, India, 1968-72, Roorkee U., 1972-73; asst. Fed. Inst. Tech., Lausanne, 1973-75; instr., postdoctoral work So. Meth. U., Dallas, 1976-77; asst. prof., then assoc. prof. Wayne State U., Detroit, 1977-82; assoc. prof. N.C. State U., Raleigh, 1982-84, prof., 1984-98; OBR Disting. prof. U. Cin., 1998—. Gen. co-chair Advanced Computing Conf., 1997—2000; Fulbright sr. specialist, 2002—; keynote spkr. Internat. Conf. on Parallel and Distributed Sys., 1997; presenter in field. Co-author: Introduction to Wireless and Mobile Systems, 2003, Ad Hoc and Sesor Networks, 2006; editor: Advanced Computer Architecture, 1986, Advances in Distributed System Reliability, 1990, Distributed Computing Network Reliability, 1990; editor: Jour. Parallel and Distg. Computing, 1984, Computer mag., 1986-91. Fellow AAAS, IEEE (chair tech. com. on computer architecture, IEEE Computer Soc. 1991-94, chair McDowell Award and Harry Grode Award coms. 1991-99, chair Eckerdt Mauchley award in computer architecture, program chair internat. conf. on parallel processing 1994, chair disting. visitor program, workshop chair internat. conf. on parallel processing 1995, gen. chair 4th internat. workshop on modeling analysis and simulation of computer and telecom. sys. 1996, 2001, editor jour. 1992-96), Assn. Computing Machinery, World Innovation Found.; mem. AIM, Internat. Conf. on Mobile Adhoc Sensor Sys. (gen. chair), Sigma Xi. Office: U Cin CS Dept PO Box 210030 Cincinnati OH 45221-0030 Business E-Mail: dpa@ececs.uc.edu.

AGRAWAL, KRISHNA CHANDRA, pharmacology educator; b. Calcutta, India, Mar. 15, 1937; naturalized; s. Prasadi Lal and Asarfi Devi (Agrawal) A.; m. Mani Agrawal, Dec. 2, 1960; children— Sunil, Lina, Nira BS in Pharmacy, Andhra U., Waltair, India, 1959, MS, 1960; PhD, U. Fla., 1965. Cert. in pharm. chemistry. Research assoc. dept. pharmacology Yale U. Sch. Medicine, New Haven, 1966-69, instr., 1969-70, asst. prof., 1970-76, assoc. prof., 1976; assoc. prof. dept. pharmacology Tulane U. Sch. Medicine, New Orleans, 1976-81, prof., 1981—, interim chmn., 1996-99, regents prof., chmn., 1999—. Cons. mem. Southeastern Cancer Study Group, 1980—85; mem. adv. com. on instnl. grants Am. Cancer Soc., 1980—85; mem. AIDS and Related Rsch. Rev. Group NIH, 1989—94, 1999—2002; mem. oncology merit rev. com. Vets. Adminstrn., 2002—04; exptl. therapeutics NIH, 2002—05. Conbr. articles to profl. jours.; patentee radiosensitizers for hypoxic tumor cells and compositions; novel AZT analogs. Grantee Nat. Cancer Inst., 1976-89, WHO, 1979-82, La. Bd. Regents, 1981-82, Nat. Inst. Allergy and Infectious Diseases, 1987—, Dept. Def., 1994-96, Nat. Heart Lung and Blood Inst., 1997—. Fellow Am. Inst. Chemists; mem. Am. Chem. Soc., Am. Assn. Cancer Rsch., Internat. Soc. Antiviral Rsch., Radiation Rsch. Soc., Am. Soc. Pharmacology and Exptl. Therapeutics, Am. Soc. Hematology, Sigma Xi. Home: 26 Olympic Ct New Orleans LA 70131-8614 Office: Tulane U Sch Medicine Dept Pharmacology New Orleans LA 70112 Office Phone: 504-988-5444. Business E-Mail: agrawal@tulane.edu.

AGRAWAL, PIYUSH C., school system administrator; b. Khairagarh, Agra, India, June 26, 1936; arrived in U.S., 1976; s. Ram C. and Chameli (Kiran) Agrawal; m. Sudha Sita Bansal, May 18, 1963; children: Seema, Sukrit, Akhil. BSc, Agra U., India, 1955, MSc, 1963; BEd, Delhi U., 1958; MS, SUNY, Albany, 1972, EdS, 1978, EdD, 1979. Tchr., dept. head Delhi Adminstrn., 1958-68; expert UNESCO, Liberia, 1971—76, Tanzania,

1968—70; dir. metric edn. Regional Planning Ctr., Albany, 1977-79; supr. math. Dade County Pub. Sch., Miami, Fla., 1979-94; assoc. supt. Piscataway Bd. Edn., 1992-94, dep. supt., 1994-97, acting supt., 1997-98; chmn. & CEO APS Tech., Inc., 2000. Cons. in field; Fla. state coord. nat. math. competition Am. Jr. HS Math. Exam., 1989—92; rev. panelist Am. 2000 proposals New Am. Schs. Devel. Corp., 1992; tchr. enhancement program NSF, 1992; mem. nat. adv. panel Md. Pub. TV, 1993—95; mem. nat. adv. coun. South Asian affairs, 1994—, vice chair, 1998—. Author: numerous books and booklets. Chair closing the gap adv. com. Reducing the Health Disparities-Fla., 2005—; mem. U.S. Census 2000 Adv. Com. on Asian and Pacific Islander Populations, 1994—, chair, 1995, 1997, 1999, 2000, 2001; mem. Fla. House Spkr.'s Task Force on Math., Sci., and Computer Edn., 1982—83; nat. selection com. mem. Presdl. Awards for Excellence in Sci. and Math. Tchg., 1990, state selection com. mem., 1987, 1990, 1991; chmn. Secondary math. Fla. State Textbook Adoption Coun., 1984; bd. dirs. Fla. Fund for Minority Tchrs., 2004—. Mem.: Asian-Am. Fed. of Fla. (pres. 2003—), Asian Am. Cmty. Forum (founding Chair 2002), Asian Am. Found. (chair 2001—), Asian Am. Alliance (founding mem. 2001—, chair 2002—), Mid. States Assn. Colls. and Schs. (task force 1993—95), Fla. Leadership Alliance for Improving Math. Edn. (founder 1991), Dade County Sch. Adminstrs. Assn. (v.p. 1985—86), Fla. Assn. Instrnl. Supr. and Adminstrs. (bd. dirs. 1985—86), UNESCO Staff Assn. (pres. 1971—76), Fla. Assn. Math. Supr. (pres. 1986—87), Fla. Coun. Tchrs. Math. (pres. 1990—92), U.S. Metric Assn. (ann. conf. chmn. 1982), Assn. Indians in Am. (nat. v.p. 1984—88, 1992—94, trustee 1997—, nat. pres. 2000—04). Home: 1625 Eagle Bnd Weston FL 33327-1615 Office: APS Technologies 630 W 84th St Hialeah FL 33014-4418 E-mail: sudhapca@aol.com.

AGRAWAL, PRATHIMA, engineering educator; PhD, Univ. So. Calif., LA, 1977. Head dept. Bell Labs, Murray Hill, NJ, 1978—98; asst. vp Telcordia Technologies, Morristown, NJ, 1998—2004; Samuel Ginn disting. prof. Auburn U., Ala., 2004—. Fellow: IEEE (chmn. fellow com. 1998—99). Achievements include 48 US patents in wireless networking. Office: Auburn Univ 200 Broun Hall ECE Dept Auburn AL 36849 Office Phone: 334-844-8208.

AGRAWAL, SHRUTI, researcher; d. Kunjabiharilal and Kanak Agrawal. BS in Pharmacy, Amravati U., India, 1998; MS in Pharmacy, Nat. Inst. Pharm. Edn. Rsch., India, 1999, PhD, 2003; postdoctoral assoc. degree, Rutgers U. Postdoc. fellow Dr. Reddy's Labs., Hyderabad, India, 2003—04; postdoc. assoc. Ernest Mario Sch. of Pharmacy, Piscataway, NJ, 2004—06; rsch. investigator Bristol-Myers & Squibb Comp., Princeton, NJ, 2006—. Author/co-author: over 35 rsch. papers, reviews and commentaries in peer reviewed jours.; scientic presentor (over 30 oral or poster presentations in internat. confs.), com. mem. PPDM open forum at AAPS NBC Conf., 2006, reviewer (scientific publs.) Jour. of Pharmaceutical Sciences, Internat. Jour. Tuberculosis and Lung Disease, Jour. Pharmaceutical and Biomedical Analysis, Analyica Chemica Acta. Vol. in polio eradication program, India. Recipient Medley Gold medal, Medley Pharmaceuticals, India, 1998, U. Gold medal, Amravati U., India, 1998, G.P. Nair award, Indian Drug Manufacturers Assn., 1999, award, Maharashtra State Pharmacy Coun., 2000; Pre-doctoral Fellowship, Nat. Inst. of Pharm. Edn. and Rsch., India, 2000—03, Post-doctoral fellowship, Ernest Mario Sch. of Pharmacy, 2004—06. Mem.: Am. Assn. for Cancer Rsch., Indian Pharm. Assn., Internat. Soc. for the Study of Xenobiotics, Americal Assn. of Pharm. Scientists. Achievements include research in biopharmaceutics, pharmokinetics and drug metabolism in new drug development, bioavailability and bioequivalence tials, Novel dosage form delivery systems. Home: 33 Marvin Ln Piscataway NJ 08854 Office: Bristol Myers & Squibb Comp Princeton NJ Home Phone: 732-485-9966; Office Phone: 732-485-9966, 609-252-7121. Personal E-mail: skagrawal02@yahoo.com.

AGRE, JAMES COURTLAND, physiatrist; b. Northfield, Minn., May 2, 1950; s. Courtland Leverne and Ellen Violet (Swedberg) A.; m. Patti Dee Soderberg, Aug. 6, 1982. MD, U. Minn., 1976, PhD, 1985. Cert. diplomate Nat. Bd. Med. Examiners, bd. cert. Am. Bd. Phys. Medicine and Rehab. Rsch. fellow dept. phys. medicine and rehab. U. Minn., Mpls., 1979-80, instr. dept. phys. medicine and rehab., 1980-84; asst. prof. dept. phys. medicine and rehab. U. Wis., Madison, 1984-90, assoc. prof. dept. rehab. medicine, 1990-93, chmn. dept. rehab. medicine, 1991-97, prof. dept. rehab. medicine, 1993-97; practitioner in svc. Ministry Health Care, Rhinelander and Eagle River, Wis., 1997—. Mem. editorial bd. and contbr. articles to Archives of Phys. Medicine and Rehab., 1988-2000. Ski coord. Wis. Ski for Light, Madison, 1985-95. Fellow Am. Acad. Phys. Medicine and Rehab. (Elizabeth and Sidney Licht award 1989, Excellence in Sci. Writing award 1990), Am. Coll. Sports Medicine (New Investigator award 1991). Office: Ministry Health Care 930 E Wall St Eagle River WI 54521 Office Phone: 715-477-3000. Business E-Mail: jagre@shsmh.org.

AGRE, PETER COURTLAND, medical educator; b. Northfield, Minn., Jan. 30, 1949; BA in Chemistry with honors, Augsburg Coll., 1970. Postdoctoral fellow dept. pharmacology Johns Hopkins, 1974—75; from intern to resident Case Western Res. U., 1975—78; postdoctoral fellow dept. medicine, hematology/oncology divsn. U. NC, Chapel Hill, 1978—80, clin. asst. prof. medicine, 1980—81; sr. clinical rsch. scientist Wellcome Labs., Research Triangle Park, NC, 1980—81; from rsch. assoc. to instr. dept. cell biology/anatomy and medicine Johns Hopkins Sch. Medicine, 1981—83, asst. prof. dept. medicine and cell biology/anatomy, 1984—88, assoc. prof., 1988—93; sabbatical dept. embryology Stephen L. McKnight lab. Carnegie Inst., Washington, 1988—89; co-dir. office of rsch. planning dept. medicine, 1990—94; dir. grad. program in cellular and molecular medicine Johns Hopkins, 1996—99, chair adv. bd. grad. program in cellular and molecular medicine, 1999—2005; vice chancellor sci. and tech., prof. cell biology Duke Univ. Med. Ctr., Durham, NC, 2005—. Recipient Clin. Investigator award, Nat. Heart, Lung and Blood Inst., 1981—85, Basil O'Connor award, March of Dimes Birth Defects Found., 1986—88, Established Investigator award, Am. Heart Assn., 1987—92, Young Investigator award, Am. Fedn. Clin. Rsch., 1991, Disting. Alumnus award, Augsburg Coll., 1995, Nobel prize for chemistry, 2003, Golden Plate award, Acad. Achievement, 2004. Mem.: AAAS, NAS, Inst. Medicine, Am. Soc. Nephrology (Homer Smith award 1999), Am. Soc. for Biochemistry and Molecular Biology, Am. Physiol. Soc., Am. Soc. for Clinical Investigation, Am. Soc. for Cell Biology, Interurban Clinical Club (hon.). Office: Vice Chancellor Sci Tech Duke Univ Med Ctr Box 3701 Durham NC 27710

AGRESS, HARRY, JR., radiologist, nuclear medicine physician; s. Harry and June W. Agress. BA in Math., Tufts U., 1968, MD, 1972. Diplomate Am. Bd. Radiology, Am. Bd. Nuclear Medicine, Nat. Bd. Med. Examiners. Intern Mt. Sinai Med. Ctr., NYC, 1972—73; fellow NIH, Bethesda, Md., 1973—75; resident in diagnostic radiology Columbia-Presbyn. Med. Ctr., NYC, 1975—78; dir. divsn. nuc. medicine Hackensack U. Med. Ctr., NJ, 1978—; from asst. to attending physician Hackensack (NJ) U. Med. Ctr., 1980—96; asst. clin. prof. Columbia U. Coll. Physicians and Surgeons, NYC, 1980—88, assoc. clin. prof. radiology, 1988—2001; sr. attending radiologist Hackensack (NJ) U. Med. Ctr., 1996—; dir. Positron Emission Tomography Ctr., 1999—; clin. prof. Columbia U. Coll. Physicians and Surgeons, NYC, 2002—; chmn. dept. radiology Hackensack (NJ) U. Med. Ctr., 2005—. Bd. dirs. PET/CT, GE Med. Sys., Milw.; oral exam examiner Am. Bd. Radiology, Tucson, 1999—; lectr., spkr., presenter in field. Contbr. chapters to books, articles to profl. jours. Bd. vis. Mary Inst. St. Louis Country Day Sch., 2003—. Lt. comdr. USPHS, 1973—75. Mem.: AMA, Radiol. Soc. NJ, NJ Med. Soc., Acad. Molecular Imaging, Radiol. Soc. N.Am., Soc. Nuclear Medicine, Am. Coll. Radiology. Achievements include research in positron emission tomography detection of unexpected asymptomatic cancers. Avocations: piano, photography, golf. Office: Hackensack Univ Med Ctr Dept Radiology 30 Prospect Ave Hackensack NJ 07601 Office Phone: 201-996-2196.

AGRESTI, ALAN, statistics educator; b. Syracuse, NY, Feb. 6, 1947; m. Jacalyn Levine. BA, U. Rochester, 1968; PhD, U. Wis., 1972; doctorate (hon.), De Montfort U., 1999. Prof. U. Fla., Gainesville, 1972—. Author: Categorical Data Analysis, 2002, Statistical Methods for the Social Sciences, 1997, Analysis of Ordinal Categorical Data, 1984, Introduction to Categorical Data Analysis, 1996, Statistics: The Art and Science of Learning From Data, 2006. Fellow Am. Statis. Assn.; mem. Royal Statis. Soc., Biometric Soc., Inst. Math. Stats. Office: U Fla Griffin-Floyd Hall Gainesville FL 32611

AGRESTI, MIRIAM MONELL, psychologist; b. NYC, Mar. 23, 1926; d. James McCloud and Marion Henrietta (Zippel) Monell; children: Robert, Carol. BS, Queens Coll., 1947; MA in Sci. Edn., Columbia U., 1949; PhD in Clin. Psychology, Yeshiva U., 1976; postgrad., Ackerman Inst. Family Therapy, 1977-81, L.I. Jewish Hosp. Human Sexualality Ctr. Lic. psychologist, N.Y. Diplomate Am. Bd. Family Psychology (fellow, pres. 1984-85). Psychology intern Creedmoor Psychiat. Ctr., Queens, N.Y., 1963-64, family therapist, 1964-69; psychologist Northeast Nassau Psychiat. Ctr., Kings Park, N.Y., 1969-72; adminstrv. dir. Friendship House Day Hosp., Glen Cove, N.Y., 1972-74; psychologist and team leader Ctrl. Islip (N.Y.) Psychiatr. Ctr., 1974-75; tchr., coord. family therapy program Pilgrim Psychiat. Ctr., West Brentwood, N.Y., 1976-80; pvt. practice psychotherapy, 1977—. With Nassau County Med. Ctr., 1990-95; co-dir. L.I. Family Inst., 1976-79; cons. family therapy Cath. Charities, 1979, St. Vincent's Hall, 1979, Nassau County Mental Health Assn., 1980; adj. faculty Sch. Edn., C.W. Post Coll., L.I. U., 1972, CUNY, 1978-80, St. John's U., 1983, Hofstra U., 1985-88. Exec. dir. movie/videotape Beware the Gaps in Medical Care for Older People (1st prize Am. Film Festival). Fellow Am. Orthopsychiat. Assn.; mem. APA, N.Y. State Psychol. Assn., Nassau County Psychol. Assn., Am. Assn. for Marriage and Family Therapy (pres. L.I. chpt. 1981-83, sec. N.Y. state divsn. 1996-98), Pi Lambda Theta. Unitarian Universalist. Address: 1110 Dee Ln Woodbury NY 11797 Office Phone: 516-921-3924.

AGUAYO, ALBERTO JUAN, neuroscientist; b. Argentina, July 16, 1934; MD, U. Cordoba, Argentina, 1959; Dr. Honoris Causa, U. Lund, Sweden. Cert. specialist in neurology, Que., cert. EEG specialist, Que. Intern Port Arthur Gen. Hosp., 1960-61; resident in neurology Toronto Gen. Hosp., 1961-62, resident in medicine, 1962-63; resident in neurology Montreal Gen. Hosp., 1964-65; prof. neurology and physiology McGill U., 1977—; prof. medicine McGill U. and Montreal Gen. Hosp. Rsch. Inst., 1976—, asst. dept. physiology, 1981—, dir. Ctr. for Rsch. in Neurosci., 1985—; sec.-gen. Internat. Brain Rsch. Org., 2001. Mem. sci. adv. bds. and coms. including Med. Rsch. Can., Howard Hughes Med. Inst., Am. Paraplegic Assn., Ipsen Found., Max Planck Inst., Munich, Germany, Friedrich Miescher-Inst., Basle, Switzerland. Co-editor Current Opinion in Neurobiology; mem. editorial bd. European Jour. Neurosci., Experimental Brain Rsch., Brain Rsch., Synapse, Jour. of Neural Transplantation, Jour. Neurobiology; mem. adv. bd. Neuroscis. Rsch.; mem. internat. adv. bd. NeuroReport. Decorated Order of Can.; recipient Gairdner Found. Internat. award, Ipsen award on Neural Plasticity, WH Helmerich III award for Outstanding Achievement in retina rsch., Leo Parizeau Prize in Biology Assn. Canadienne-Française pour l'Avancement des Sciences, 1993, Killam prize for health scis. Can. Coun. for Arts, 1999, recognition award for outstanding contbns. in field of visual rsch. Alcon Labs., 1998, Prix du Que.-Wilder Penfield award, 1994, prize Ameritec Found., 1993, Christopher Reeve Rsch. medal, 1999; rsch. fellow Banting Inst., U. Toronto, 1963-64, Montreal Gen. Hosp., 1965-66, traveling fellow McLaughlin Found., 1966-67, Reeve medal, 2000. Fellow Royal Soc. Can., AAAS; mem. Inst. Medicine of the NAS (U.S), N-Am. Soc. for Neurosci. (pres.), Can. Neurol. Soc. (pres.), Can. Assn. of Neuroscientists (pres.), Third World Congress of the Internat. Brain Rsch. Orgn. (pres.), Can. Neurosci. Found. (v.p., bd. dirs.), Soc. Neurosci. (pres. 1987-88), Internat. Brain Rsch. Orgn. (sec.-gen. 2001). Office: McGill U Gen Hosp Rsch Inst 1650 Cedar Ave Montreal PQ Canada H3G 1A4 E-mail: mcio@musica.m.gill.ca.

AGUDO, MERCEDES ENGRACIA, psychiatrist; arrived in U.S., 1990; d. Isidoro Reyes and Pura Engracia Agudo. MD, U. Santo Tomas, Manila, Philippines, 1989; degree in psychiatry, Howard U. Hosp., Washington, 1996; degree in child and adolescent psychiatry, Med. Coll. Va., Richmond, 1998. Child, adolescent & adult psychiatrist pvt. solo. practice, Iligan City, Philippines, 1998—2002; faculty Mindanao State U., Iligan City, 1999—2002; child & adolescent psychiatrist Philhaven, Mt. Gretna, Pa., 2002—. Officer Rotary Club Maria Cristina, Iligan City, Philippines, 1998—2002; aux. mem. Legion of Mary, Hershey, Pa., 2003—; extraordinary eucharistic minister St. Joan of Arc Ch., Hershey, Pa., 2005—. Fellow: Am. Coll. Ethical Physicians, Am. Bd. Hosp. Physicians; mem.: APA. Roman Catholic. Avocations: piano, drawing, cooking, travel. Office: Philhaven 283 S Butler Rd Mount Gretna PA 17064 Personal E-mail: meagudo1@comcast.net.

AGUERO, JOSEPH EDWARD, psychologist, educator; b. Havana, Cuba, July 14, 1946; s. Enrique and Maria Teresa (Carillo) Aguero; m. Sonia Dionisia Socorro, Dec. 4, 1964 (div. Mar. 6, 1970); children: Diane Carol(dec.), Joseph Edward Jr., Thomas Arthur, Wendy Marie. BA, Ind. U. NW, Gary, 1974; MS, Purdue U., 1977, PhD, 1982. Vis. instr. St. Mary's Coll. Md., St. Mary's City, Md., 1980—81; asst. prof. psychology Midwest Univs. Consortium for Internat. Affairs/Inst. Teknologic MARA, Shah Allam, Selangor, Malaysia, 1986—88, U. Wis. Ctr., Menasha, 1981—88; prof. psychology U. PR at Mayaguez, 1988—. Author (in Spanish): (text book) The Psychology of Human Sexuality: A Social-Psychological and Humanist Perspective, 2004; contbr. chapters to books. External evaluator Hogar Portal de Amor, San German, PR, 2002—05. Mem.: APA (assoc.). Roman Catholic. Avocations: computer games, music, gardening. Home: PO Box 5733 Mayaguez PR 00681 Office: U PR at Mayaguez Dept Social Scis PO Box 9266 Mayaguez PR 00681 Home Phone: 787-553-0488; Office Phone: 787-265-3839. Personal E-mail: jaguero@lycos.com. E-mail: joseph@uprm.edu.

AGUIAR, ADAM MARTIN, chemist, educator; b. Newark, Aug. 11, 1929; s. Joaquim Ramahlo and Emilea Andrada (Nunes) A.; m. Laura E. Brand, Sept. 2, 1980; children: Justine Diane, David Laurence, Adam Albert, Erick Arthur, Aaron Benjamin, Evan Joaquim. BS, Fairleigh Dickinson U., 1955; MA, Columbia U., 1957, PhD, 1960. Chemist Otto B. May, Newark, 1948-55; asst. prof. Fairleigh Dickinson U., Rutherford, NJ, 1959-63; asst. prof. chemistry Tulane U., New Orleans, 1963-65, assoc. prof., 1965-67, prof., 1967-72, head dept. chemistry Newcomb Coll. divsn., 1970; dean grad. and research programs William Paterson Coll., Wayne, NJ, 1972-73; rsch. prof. Rutgers U., Newark, 1973-75; prof. chemistry Fairleigh Dickinson U., Madison, NJ, 1975-93, chmn. dept. chemistry/geol. scis., 1984-89; pres. Seltox Corp., NJ, 1980—. Adj. prof. chemistry Monmouth U., West Long Branch, N.J., 1993—; adj. prof. humanities Ocean County Coll. ext. Fairleigh Dickinson U., 2004; cons. chem. firms in La. and N.J. Contbr. articles to profl. jours. Union Carbide fellow, 1957; NIH fellow, 1959; recipient other grants. Mem. AAUP, Am. Chem. Soc., AASS, N.Y. Acad. Sci., Ctr. for Profl. Advancement, Sigma Xi, Phi Lambda Epsilon, Phi Omega Epsilon. Home and Office: 37 Wyncrest Ln Neptune NJ 07753-7421 Office Phone: 732-922-3031. Personal E-mail: a.aguiar@att.net, aaguiar37@comcast.net. Business E-Mail: amaguiar@fdu.edu.

AGUIGUI, IGNACIO CRUZ, lawyer; b. Agana Heights, Guam, Dec. 3, 1970; s. Joaquin Tyquiengco and Teresita Cruz Aguigui. BA magna cum laude, Yale U., 1991; JD with honors, Columbia Law Sch., 1997. Bar: Calif. 1997, US Ct. Appeals (9th cir.) 1997, US Dist. Ct. (no. dist.) Calif. 1997, Guam 1999, US Dist. Ct. Guam 1999, US Dist. Ct. (ctrl. dist.) Calif. 2001. Spl. asst. to the gov. Office of Gov. of Guam, Hagatna, 1993—94; extern law clk. US Dist Ct. (so. dist.) NY Hon. Barrington D. Parker, Jr., NYC, 1995; atty. Morrison & Foerster LLP, San Francisco, 1997—98; atty. Superior Ct. Guam Chambers of Hon. Katherine A. Maraman, Hagatna, 1998—99; atty. Calvo and Clark, LLP, Tamuning, Guam, 1999—2002; legal counsel Camacho/Moylan Gubernatorial Transition Com., Hagatna, 2002; ptnr. Lujan, Aguigui & Perez LLP, Hagatna, 2003—; counsel to gov. Office Gov. Guam, Hagatna, 2003. V.p., bd. dirs. Guam Legal Svcs. Corp., Hagatna, 2000—03. Mem. Rep. Party of Guam, Hagatna, Guam Election Commn., Hagatna, 2002—04, Guam Pub. Libr., Hagatna, 1991—92. Recipient Centennial Scholar award, NIH, 1987, US Congl. award, Office of Guam's Del. to the US Ho. of Reps., 1987, Prin.'s award, Inarajan HS, Inarajan, Guam, 1987, Valedictorian award, 1987, Robin Berlin Meml. prize, Yale U., 1989; fellow Pub. Svc. fellow, Columbia Law Sch., 1994; Profl./Tech. scholar, Govt. of Guam, 1994-1997, Harlan Fiske Stone scholar, Columbia Law Sch., 1996, Merit scholar, Govt. of Guam, 1987-1991, Summer Rsch. fellow, U. Calif., Berkeley, 1989, U. Calif., San Francisco, 1990. Mem.: ABA (assoc.). R-Liberal. Roman Catholic. Avocations: travel, music, French language and culture. Home: 275-G Farenholt Ave #20 Tamuning GU 96913 Office Phone: 671-727-2881. E-mail: iaguigui@aya.yale.edu.

AGUILAR, DARLA J., adult education educator; d. Leonard and Betty Begger; m. Mario B. Aguilar, Feb. 16, 1985. MA in TTE, U. Ariz., Tucson, 1994. Faculty Pima CC, Tucson, 1993—. Mem.: NADE. Office: Pima CC 5901 S Calle Santa Cruz Tucson AZ 85709 Home Phone: 520-206-5160; Office Phone: 520-206-5160.

AGUILAR, SHELLEY KEZER, biology professor, research scientist; d. Dearrel and Willie Mae Kezer; life ptnr. David Aguilera Aguilar, Feb. 14, 1981; children: David Dearrel, Heather Diane. AA, San Bernardino Valley Coll., Calif., 1975; BA, U. Calif., Riverside, 1977; MS, Calif. State U., San Bernardino, 1982; D of Edn., U. La Verne, Calif., 2004. Cert. clin. lab. scientist Calif. State Dept Health Svcs., 1980, med. technologist Am. Soc. Clin. Pathologists, 1980. Clin. lab. scientist St. Bernardine Med. Ctr., San Bernardino, Calif., 1980—; assoc. prof. Mt San Jacinto Coll., Menifee, Calif., 1998—. Mem.: Am. Soc. Microbiology. Democrat. Baptist. Avocations: travel, reading. Office: Mt San Jacinto College 28237 La Piedra Rd Menifee CA 92584 Home Phone: 951-657-2939; Office Phone: 951-639-5732. Business E-Mail: saguilar@msjc.edu.

AGUILAR, VALENTIN G., II, lawyer; BS, U. Calif., Riverside, 1991; JD, U. So. Calif., 1996. Bar: Calif. 1996, NJ 2001. Ptnr., comml. real estate practice Manatt, Phelps & Phillips LLP, LA. Named a Rising Star, So. Calif. Super Lawyers, 2006. Mem.: State Bar Calif., Philippine Am. Bar Assn. (bd. dir.), LA County Bar Assn. Office: Manatt Phelps & Phillips Ea Tower Trident Ctr 11355 W Olympic Blvd Los Angeles CA 90064 Office Phone: 310-312-4313. Office Fax: 310-312-4224. Business E-Mail: vaguilar@manatt.com.

AGUILAR-ALVAREZ, GUILLERMO, lawyer; b. Cuernavaca, Mex., 1958; Grad., U. Nat. Autonoma of Mex. Counsel, gen. counsel ICC Internat. Ct. Arbitration, Paris, 1984—90; chief legal counsel Govt. of Mex. for NAFTA, 1990—94; ptnr. SAI Abogados, Mex. City, Weil, Gotshal & Manges, NYC, 2006—. Vis. lectr. Yale Law Sch., 2005—06. Named to Chambers USA. Achievements include fluency in Eng., Spanish, and French. Office: Weil Gotshal & Manges 767 5th Ave New York NY 10153 Office Phone: 212-310-8981. Office Fax: 212-310-8007. E-mail: guillermo.aguilar-alvarez@weil.com.

AGUILAR-BRYAN, LYDIA, medical educator, researcher; b. Mexico City, Feb. 25, 1951; m. Joseph Bryan; 1 child. MD, U. Nacional Autonoma de Mex., 1975; PhD in Population Studies, U. Tex., 1985. Rsch. assoc. Inst. Biomed. Rsch., U. Nacional Autonoma de Mex., Mexico City, 1985—86, Baylor Coll. of Medicine, Dept. of Medicine, Divsn. of Endocrinology, Houston, 1987—88, postdoctoral fellow, 1988—90, instr., 1990—91, asst. prof., 1991—; prof. M.D. Anderson Cancer Ctr. U. Tex. Contbr. articles to profl. jours. Recipient postdoctoral fellowship, Juvenile Diabetes Found., 1988—90. Mem.: AAAS, Endocrine Soc., Biophys. Soc., Am. Diabetes Assn. (Rsch. grantee 1995—).

AGUILERA, A. ERIC, lawyer; b. May 14, 1972; BA, Univ. Calif., Berkeley, 1994; JD, UCLA, 1997. Bar: Calif. 1997, US Dist. Ct. Ctrl., So., Ea. & No. Calif., US Ct. Appeals Ninth Cir. Assoc. Wood, Bohm & Francis LLP; ptnr., bus. litigation & employment law practice Bohm, Matsen, Kegel & Aguilera, Costa Mesa, Calif. Named a Rising Star, So. Calif. Super Lawyers, 2005—06. Mem.: ABA, Fed. Bar Assn., State Bar Calif., Orange County Bar Assn. Office: Bohm Matsen Kegel & Aguilera Ste 700 Park Tower 695 Town Ctr Dr Costa Mesa CA 92626 Office Phone: 714-384-6500. Office Fax: 714-384-6501.

AGUILERA, CHRISTINA, singer; b. Staten Island, NY, Dec. 18, 1980; d. Fausto Agilera and Shelly Kearns; m. Jordan Bratman, Nov. 19, 2005. Vocalist New Mickey Mouse Club, 1994-96; vocalist theme song for Disney animated film Mulan, 1998); (Albums) Christina Aguilera, 1999 (Grammy award, Best New Artist, 2000), My Kind of Christmas, 2000, Mi Reflejo, 2000, Just be Free, 2001, Stripped, 2002 (Grammy award, Best Female Pop Vocal Performance for song "Beautiful", 2003), Back to Basics, 2006; singles: What A Girl Wants, 1999, Come on Over Baby (All I Want Is You), 1999, Genie in a Bottle, 1999, The Christmas Song, 1999, (with Lil'Kim, Pink, Mya) Lady Marmalade, 2001 (Grammy award for Best Pop Collaboration with Vocals, 2002), Beautiful, 2003, Dirty, 2003, Ain't No Other Man, 2006(Best Female Pop Vocal Performance, Grammy Awards, 2007); video: The Genie Gets Her Wish, 1999. Recipient ALMA award, best new artist, 1999, Best Female award, MTV Europe Music Awards, 2006.*

AGUINSKY, RICHARD DANIEL, electrical engineer, engineering executive; b. Buenos Aires, Dec. 26, 1958; arrived in U.S., 1986; s. Elias Lorenzo and Rosa Isabel Aguinsky; m. Adriana Faiman; 1 child, Marina Sasha. BSEE, U. Técnica Nacional, Avellaneda, Buenos Aires, 1984; MSEE, San Jose State U., Calif., 1991. Serial prodn. technician Norman S.A., Buenos Aires, 1978-80; prof. asst. U. Técnologica Nacional, Buenos Aires, 1980-84; sr. design engr., mgr. Nortel Networks, 1983-2000; sr. engr., project leader Jetstream Comms., 2000-01; hardware mgr. Vpacket Comms., Milpitas, Calif., 2001—03; pres., CEO Cinensis, Inc., 2003; hardware mgr. Riverbed Tech., 2003—. Mentor adelante program San Jose City Coll. Contbr. articles to profl. jours. Avocations: travel, sailing, flying. Office Phone: 415-247-7347. E-mail: richard@riverbed.com.

AGUIRRE, EDUARDO, JR., ambassador, former federal agency administrator; b. Cuba; m. Tere Aguirre; 2 children. BS, La. State U.; D (hon.), U. Tecnologica Santiago, Dominican Republic, U. Conn., U. Houston. With Tex. Commerce Bank, 1969, Bank of Am., 1978—2000, pres., 1999—2000; vice chmn., 1st v.p. Export-Import Bank of US, Washington, 2001—02; dir. bur. citizenship and immigration svcs. US Dept. Homeland Security, Washington, 2003—05; US amb. to Spain and Andorra US Dept. State, Madrid, 2005—. Hon. prof. Beijing Poly. U., Ctrl. U. Nationalities, Beijing; former chmn. bd. trustees Tex. Bar Found.; founding chmn. bd. dirs. Houston Livestock Show and Rodeo; former chmn. bd. dirs. Tex.

Children's Hosp.; regent U. Houston Sys. Bd. Regents, 1995—2001, chmn., 1996—98. Recipient Order of José Matías Delgado, Grade of Grand Officer, Republic of El Salvador, Order of Christopher Columbus, Grade of Grand Officer, Dominican Republic, Americanism medal, Daughters of the Am. Revolution, 2004. Office: DOS Amb 8500 Madrid Pl Washington DC 20521*

AGUIRRE, FERNANDO, food products executive; b. Mex. BSBA, So. Ill. U. With Procter & Gamble, 1980—2004, pres., gen. mgr. P&G Brazil, 1992—96, pres. P&G Mex., 1996—99, v.p. global and U.S. snacks and food products, 1999—2000, pres. global feminine care, 2000—04; chmn., pres., CEO Chiquita Brands Internat., Inc., Cin., 2004—. Bd. dirs. Univision Comm., Inc.; chmn. emeritus corp. adv. bd. Marshall Sch. Bus. U. So. Calif. Office: Chiquita Brands Internat 250 E 5th St Cincinnati OH 45202*

AGUIRRE, MICHAEL JULES, lawyer; b. San Diego, Sept. 12, 1949; s. Jules and Margaret Aguirre; m. Kathleen Jones, Jan. 16, 1982; children: Arthur Michael, Emilie Kathleen. BS, Ariz. State U., 1971; JD, U. Calif., Berkeley, 1974. Bar: Calif. 1974, U.S. Dist. Ct. (so. dist.) Calif. 1975, U.S. Ct. Appeals (9th cir.) 1975. Asst. U.S. atty. State of Calif., San Diego; dep. legal counsel Calif. State Legislature, San Diego; asst. counsel U.S. Subcom. Investigation, Washington; assoc. Phleger & Harrison, Los Angeles, Silverberg, Rosco et al, Los Angeles; ptnr. Law Offices of Aguirre & Meyer APC, San Diego, 1980—2004; city atty. City of San Diego, 2004—. Adj. prof. history U. So. Calif., San Diego, chmn. conf. Kennedy, conf. organized crime. Contbg. editor Golden Hills Newspaper. Founding officer San Diego Crime Commn., 1982; mem. San Diego Speaker's Program on Ethical Practices, 1982; candidate U.S. Congress, 1982, 8th dist. San Diego City Council, 1986. Mem. Calif. Bar Assn., San Diego Bar Assn., LaRaza Lawyers Assn., San Diego County Urban League, World Affairs Counsel Assn., Bus. Practices Assn., Calif. Trial Lawyers Assn. Clubs: City (San Diego). Democrat. Roman Catholic. Office: Office of City Atty Civic Ctr Plaza Ste 1620 1200 Third Ave San Diego CA 92101 E-mail: cityattorney@sandiego.gov.

AGUIRRE, SARAH K., lawyer; BA, Tex. A&M U., 1997; JD, U. Houston Law Ctr., 2001. Bar: Tex. 2001. Intern Tex. Dept. Commerce, Mexico City; jud. intern Staff of US Magistrate Marcia Crone, US Dist. Ct., So. Dist. Tex.; assoc. Baker Hostetler, Houston. Named a Rising Star, Tex. Super Lawyers mag., 2006. Mem.: Orgn. Women in Internat. Trade, Tex.-Mex. Bar Assn. Office: Baker Hostetler 1000 Louisiana Ste 2000 Houston TX 77002-5009 Office Phone: 713-646-1330. Office Fax: 713-751-1717. E-mail: saguirre@bakerlaw.com.*

AGUIRRE BATTY, MERCEDES, Spanish, English and literature educator; b. Cd Juarez, Mex., Dec. 20, 1952; arrived in US, 1957; d. Alejandro M. and Mercedes (Peón) Aguirre; m. Hugh K. Batty, Mar. 17, 1979; 1 child, Henry B BA, U. Tex., El Paso, 1974, MA, 1977; PhD in edn., Capella U., 2005. Cert. online tchr., Calif. Instr. ESL Paso del Norte- Prep Sch., Cd Juarez, 1973-74; tchg. asst. ESL and English U. Tex., El Paso, 1974-77; instr. ESL English Lang. Svcs., Bridgeport, Conn., 1977-80; instr. Spanish and English, coord. modern lang. Sheridan (Wyo.) Coll., 1980—, pres. faculty senate, 1989-90; pres. faculty senate, chair dist. coun. No. Wyo. C.C. Dist., 1995-96. Planning com. No. Wyo. C.C. Dist., 1996-97; advanced placement faculty Spanish cons. Coll. Bd. Ednl. Testing Svc., 1996-99; adj. prof. Spanish, U. Autonoma Cd Juarez, 1975; adj. prof. Spanish and English, Sacred Heart U., Fairfield, Conn., 1977-80; spkr. in field Bd. dirs. Wyo. Coun. for the Humanities, 1988-92; translator county and dist. cts., Sheridan; vol. Wmen's Ctr.; translator Sheridan County Meml. Hosp.; del. Citizen Ambassador Program, People to People-India, 1996. NEH fellow, 1991-92; Wyo. State Dept. Edn. grant, 1991. Mem. MLA (del. assembly 1998-2000, 2004-), Wyo. Fgn. Lang. Tchrs. Assn. (pres. 1990-92), Am. Assn. Tchrs. Spanish and Portuguese (founder, 1st pres. Wyo. chpt. 1987-90), TESOL, Sigma Delta Mu (v.p. 1992-99, pres. 2000—), Sigma Delta Pi (Alpha Iota chpt. pres. 1974-75). Avocations: travel, reading, archaeology, languages, geography. Office: Sheridan Coll NWCCD 3059 Coffeen Ave Sheridan WY 82801-9133

AGUIRRE-SACASA, FRANCISCO XAVIER, international banker, diplomat; b. Managua, Nicaragua, Sept. 4, 1944; s. Francisco and Gladys (Sacasa) A.; m. Maria de los Angeles, Oct. 6, 1968; children: Rafael Ignacio, Roberto Francisco, Georgiana Eugenia. BS in Fgn. Svc., Georgetown U., 1966; JD, Harvard U., 1969. Contributing writer Christian Sci. Monitor, Boston Herald Traveler, Boston Globe, Wall Street Jour., Fin. Times, Wash. Post, Wash. Times, La Prensa (Nicaragua), Diario Las Americas, 1968—; young profl. and loan officer The World Bank, Washington, 1969-76, div. chief, 1977-86, asst. dir., 1986-87, sr. ops. advisor, 1987-88, dir., external affairs, 1988-90, dir. Africa region, 1990-95, dir. ops. evalutation dept., 1995-97; ambassador to U.S., Canada govt. Nicaragua, Washington, 1997—. Named one of Nicaragua's Citizen of the Century, 2000; OAS scholar Harvard U., 1966-68. Mem. Nat. Press Club, Nicaraguan Acad. Geography and History, Am.-Nicaraguan Found. (treas.), U. Mobile Latin Am. Campus (adv. bd.), Zamorano Agrl. Sch. (internat. adv. bd.), Congl. Country Club (Bethesda, Md.), Harvard Club of Washington, Univ. Club (Wash.), Hist. Georgetown Club (Wash.). Roman Catholic. Avocations: carpentry, golf, farming. also: Valhalla Farm 11302 Obannons Mill Rd Boston VA 22713-4132 Office: Embassy Of Nicaragua 2655 S Le Jeune Rd Ste 714 Miami FL 33134-5815

AGVANIAN, YOURI, mathematician, educator, physicist; b. Yerevan, Armenia, Sept. 22, 1950; s. Martiros and Eranuhe Agvanian; m. Anahit Hovhanesyan; children: Zara, Elina. BS, Yerevan State U., Armenia, 1972; MS, Moscow U., 1980, PhD, 1990. Prof. physics, dean Yerevan Poly. U., 1973—92; prof. math. Pasadena City Coll., Calif., 1998—2000, L.A. Mission Coll., Sylmar, Calif., 1998—, Moor Park Coll., Calif., 1998—; prof. physics, astronomy Calif. State U., LA, 1999—2001; prof. math. Calif. State Poly. U., Pomona, 2000—, Mt. San Antonio Coll., Calif., 2004—. Author: Transforamtion of Drops in NonHomogenious Temperature and Concentration Binary Vescous Environments, 1978, The Theory of Diffusive Magnetism of "Flying" High Heat Transferring Spherical Drops, 1978, The Theory of Thermal Magnetism of Spherical Drops in a Binary Liquid, 1979; contbr. articles to profl. jours. Mem.: Math. Assn. Am., N.Y. Acad. Sci. (Nat. Counsel of Scientific and Technol. Soc. Competition award 1980), Am. Math. Soc., Am. Phys. Soc. Office: Calif State Polytechnic U 3801 West Temple Ave Pomona CA 91768 Home Phone: 626-795-5777; Office Phone: 909-869-6743. E-mail: agvaniz@edu.com.

AGWU, IDIKA UME, chemist, educator, reading specialist; m. Ugo Idika Agwu, July 25, 2001; children: Adanna Brittany, Bessy Anele, Ume Brian. BS in Chemistry Edn., U. Lagos, 1990; MEd in Curriculum & Instrn., Loyola Coll., Balt., 2001; MEd in Reading, Bowie State U., 2002; post masters cert. in adminstrn. and supervision, Coppin State U., Balt., 2005. Advanced Profl. Cert. in Chemistry Md. State Dept. of Edn., 2001, Advanced Profl. Cert. in Reading Md. State Dept of Edn., 2002, adminstr. I cert. Md. State Dept. Edn., 2005. Chemistry educator Abia State Sch. Mgmt. Bd., Aba, Nigeria, 1992—98; sci. tchr. Parkdale HS, Riverdale, Md., 1999—2000, Suitland HS, Forestville, Md., 2000—02; reading specialist Dodge Pk. Elem. Sch., Landover, 2002—04, Adelphi Elem. Sch., Md., 2004—, sch. test coord., 2004—; math. tchr. Adult Basic Edn., Suitland HS, Forestville, 2003—05; tchr. writing enrichment Crossland Saturday Sch., Temple Hills, 2004—05. Ind. contractor Porter Edn. & Comm., Landover, Md., 2003—; site supr. Am. Reads, Adelphi Elem. Sch., 2004—; coord. Ptnrs. in Print, Adelphi Elem. Sch., 2004—; sch. test coord. Adelphi Elem. Sch., 2004—; adj. prof. Trinity Washington U., Washington. Chair sch. planning & mgmt. team Adelphi Elem. Sch., 2004—; mem. sch. planning & mgmt. team Dodge Pk. Elem. Sch., Landover, 2002—04, coord. spelling bee, 2002—04, chair book fair, 2002—04, mem. prin. selection, 2004; mem. Adelphi Elem. Sch. PTA, 2004—; mem. sch. improvement team, multidisciplinary team, curriculum and assessment com., tech. com. and staff devel. com. Adelphi Elem. Sch., 2004—; chair reading com. Dodge Pk. Elem. Sch., 2002—04; mem. Dodge Pk. Elem. Sch. PTA, 2002—04; mem. interim chief Exec. Officer's Tchrs. Adv. Group, 2005. Recipient cert. of Appreciation, Suitland H.S., 2001—02, Dodge Pk. Elem. Sch., 2003—04. Mem.: ASCD, NEA, Sci. Tchrs. Assn. Nigeria, Geol. Assn. Am., Prince George's County Educators Assn., Md. State Tchrs. Assn., Internat. Reading Assn. Mem. Lds Ch. Achievements include presenting workshops to teachers on four square writing, balanced literacy workshop, reciprocal teaching, reading centers, cooperative learning, writing objectives, and running records; presenting workshops to teachers on directed reading assessment and test security and administration. Avocations: soccer, reading, writing, music, movies, ping pong/table tennis. Office: Adelphi Elem Sch 8820 Riggs Rd Adelphi MD 20783 Home: 4010 Ethan Thomas Dr Clinton MD 20735 Home Phone: 301-234-0197; Office Phone: 301-906-9133. Personal E-mail: iagwu@yahoo.com.

AHARONOV, YAKIR, physicist, researcher; b. Haifa, Israel, July 28, 1932; BS, Technion U., 1956, Dr, 1992; PhD, Bristol U., 1960; DSc, U. S.C., 1993. Rsch. assoc. Brandeis U., 1960-61; from asst. prof. to prof. Yesiva U., 1964-73; Miller prof. U. Calif., Berkeley, 1988-90; prof. Tel Aviv U., 1967—; disting. prof. U. S.C., 1973—; Disting. Professor of Quantum Information Science Center for Quantum Studies, George Mason U., 2006—. Vis. prof. Boston U., 1991-92. Recipient Weizmann prize, 1984, Rothschild prize, 1984, Nat. Physics prize, Israel, 1989, Elliot Cresson Medal, 1991, Disting. Scientists Gov. award, State of SC, 1993, Hewlett-Packard Europhysics prize, 1995, Wolf prize in physics, Wolf Found., Israel, 1998. Fellow Am. Physics Soc.; mem. Nat. Acad. Sci., Nat. Acad. Sci. Israel. Office: George Mason U 4400 University Dr Fairfax VA 22030*

AHEARN, ARTHUR MASON, orthopedist, surgeon, consultant; b. NYC, Nov. 5, 1936; s. Arthur John and Ella Highbie (Mason) Ahearn; m. Rita Claire Grubbs, June 5, 1982; m. Betty Jean Cheek, Apr. 4, 1964 (div. Nov. 20, 1981); children: John Mason, Ella Lea Ahearn Whelan, Peter Cheek, Susan Elizabeth, Noel Mason, Briggs Mason. AB, U. Rochester, NY, 1958; MD, Weill Cornell U., NYC, 1962. Diplomate Am. Bd. Orthop. Surgeons, 1972. Surgeon US Army, Ft. Bragg, NC, 1963, c team surgeon 5th spl. forces group, 1964—65; dep. surgeon USA JFK Spl. Warfare Ctr., Ft. Bragg, 1966—67; pvt. practice Georgetown and Murrells Inlet, SC, 1981—; chief dept. surgery Georgetown Meml. Hosp., SC, 1990—92, chief med. staff, 1994—95, Waccamaw Cmty. Hosp., Murrells Inlet, SC, 2002—03. Active USNG, 1995—96. Comdr. USAR, 1990—91. Decorated Bronze Star for Valor USN, Bronze Star Merit US Army, Order of Mil. Med. Merit, Legion of Merit; recipient Order of Palmetto award, Gov. of SC, 1996. Fellow: ACS, Am. Acad. Orthop. Surgeons; mem.: AMA, Soc. Med. Cons. to the Armed Forces (pres. 2007—, John R. Seal award 2004), SC Med. Assn., Assn. Mil. Surgeons of the US (life), Soc. Mil. Orthop. Surgeons, US Army Spl. Forces Assn. (life). Home: 752 Collins Meadow Dr Georgetown SC 29440 Office: Bay Orthop Assoc PO Box 1777 1001 N Fraser St Georgetown SC 29442 Home Phone: 843-546-4811; Office Phone: 843-527-4447. Personal E-mail: amahearn2@yahoo.com.

AHEARN, ELIZABETH LOWE, performing arts educator; b. Oklahoma City, Oct. 8, 1963; d. James Benjamin and Linda Ann Lowe; m. Thomas Joseph Ahearn, May 27, 1989; children: Alexandra Nicole, Brandon Thomas. BFA, N.Y. U., NYC, 1988, MFA, 1989. Asst. prof. Goucher Coll., Balt., 1990—91, 1993—2007, U. Wash., Seattle, 1991—93; instr. Carver Ctr. for Arts and Tech., 1994—2006. Dir. Pilates Ctr. Curator, performer Eleanor King Centennial Concert, Balt., 2005; featured artist Art of the Solo, Balt., 2006; Exhibited in group shows at Balt. Mus. Art, 2006; choreographer Inside Out, Balt., 2004, Conversio, 2006; contbr. articles to profl. jours. Mem. Jr. League, Balt., 1990—2004. Mem.: Corps de Ballet Internat., World Dance Americas, Pilates Method Alliance, Am. Coll. Dance Festival Assn. (bd. dis. 2005—). Home: 12845 Stone Eagle Rd Phoenix MD 21131 Office: Goucher Coll 1021 Dulaney Valley Rd Towson MD 21204 Office Phone: 410-337-6399. Office Fax: 410-337-6433. Business E-Mail: eahearn@goucher.edu.

AHEARN, GERALDINE, medical/surgical nurse, writer, poet; b. Bklyn., Aug. 14, 1950; d. Louis Principessa and Patricia Donato; m. James J. Ahearn, Aug. 13, 1972 (div. June 4, 2001); children: Alicia Danielle, Katherine Ann. AA, Suffolk County CC, Selden, NY, 1971; diploma in nursing, Ctrl. Islip State Hosp. Sch. Nursing, 1974. LPN, NY, Ariz., RN NY, Ariz., cert. CCRN, Am. Heart Assn., EKG technician, Am. Heart Assn., med. claims and billing, med. coding. RN Bayshore Hosp., NY, 1970—83, Farmingville Clinic, NY, 1986—87, Sachem Schs., Farmingville, 1988—93; hosp. CCRN cardiac care NY, 1978—83; hosp. CCRN severely disabled children NY, 1989—90; freelance writer Mesa, Ariz., 1993—. Instr. CPR ARC, Coram, NY, 1986—90, instr. first aid, 1986—90, instr. CPR, Bohemia, NY, 1986—90. Author: (book) Inspirations, 2001, Words to Live By, 2001, Life's Poetic Journey, 2002, (series) The Nurse in the Purse, Vol. 1, 2001, (book) From America's Future Leaders, 2005; contbr. poetry to anthologies. Leader Girl Scouts U.S., Farmingville, 1988—91; cmty. leader Am. Online, 2001—04; catechist Farmingville Ch., 1985—87. Recipient Internat. Peace Prize, United Cultural Convention, 2006; vis. scholar Poet fellow, Noble House, 2006. Mem.: ARC, Am. Heart Assn. Republican. Roman Catholic. Avocations: gardening, reading, walking, writing. Home and Office: 1015 S Val Vista Dr Apt 81 Mesa AZ 85204 Personal E-mail: hrt4angel@aol.com.

AHEARN, JAMES, columnist; b. South Bend, Ind., Dec. 26, 1931; s. Francis T. and Loretto (Lorden) A.; m. Mary Ann Boesch, June 7, 1954; children— Michael James, Mary Elizabeth, Sarah Katharine, Margaret Ann. BA, Amherst Coll., 1953; Nieman fellow, Harvard U., 1970-71. Reporter UPI, Boston, Newark and Trenton, NJ, 1957-61; state house corr. The Record, Hackensack, NJ, 1961-65, editorial writer, then editor editorial page, 1965-77, mng. editor, 1977-87, assoc. editor, 1987-91, contbg. editor, 1993—. Served with USNR, 1953-57. Office: 150 River St Hackensack NJ 07601-7110

AHEARNE, JOHN FRANCIS, science foundation director, researcher; b. New Britain, Conn., June 14, 1934; s. Daniel Paul and Balbena Marian (Baloski) A.; m. Barbara Helen Drezek, June 19, 1956; children: Thomas, Paul, Mary Ann, Robert, Patricia. B of Engring. Physics, Cornell U., 1957, MS in Physics, 1958; MA, Princeton U., 1963, PhD, 1966. Nuc. weapons analyst USAF, 1959-61; assoc. prof. physics USAF Acad., 1964-69; from analyst to dir. tactical air Office Asst. Sec. Def. for Systems Analysis, 1969-72; dep. asst. sec. def. for gen. purpose programs, 1972-74; prin. dep. sec. def. manpower and res. affairs, 1974-76; staff White House Energy Office, 1977; dep. asst. sec. Dept. Energy, 1978; commr. U.S. Nuc. Regulatory Commn., 1978-83, chmn., 1980-81; mgmt. cons. Comptr. Gen of U.S., 1983-84; v.p., sr. fellow Resources for the Future, 1984-89; exec. dir. Sigma Xi, The Sci. Rsch. Soc., Research Triangle Park, NC, 1989-96; dir. Sigma Xi Ctr., 1995-99; dir. ethics program Sigma Xi, 1999—2007, exec. dir. emeritus, 2007—; lectr. pub. policy Duke U., Durham, NC, 1995—2006. Adj. fellow Resources for Future, 1992—; adj. prof. civil and environ. engring. Duke U., 1996-2002; adj. prof. U. Colo., 1966-69; adj. fellow Resources for the Future, 1992—; vice-chmn. Nat. Rsch. Coun. Bd. on Radioactive Waste Mgmt., 1997-99, chmn., 2000—04; chmn. adv. com. on nuc. facility safety U.S. Dept. Energy, 1988-91, environ. mgmt. adv. bd., 1994-2002, co-chmn. adv. com. on external regulation, 1995-96, nuc. energy rsch. adv. com., 1998—, vice chmn., 2002—; chmn. risk perception and comm. com. NAS, 1987-89, chmn. future nuc. power com., 1990-93, com. on tech. bases for Yucca Mountain Stds., 1993-96, com. on risk characterization, 1994-97, dual use techs. and export controls com., electrometallurg. tech. com., co-chmn. burning plasma experiment assessment com., 2002-04, co-chmn. forum on the environment, 1995-97, vice-chmn. com. risk assessment and mgmt. marine sys., 1996-98, com. on battlefield radiation exposure, 1996-99, chmn. com. to rev. rsch. under EPACT, 1997-99, co-chmn. com. on end points of U.S. and Russian nuc. waste, 2001—03, com. on indigenization of programs to prevent leakage, jt. acad. com. on counterterrorism challenges for Russia and the US, 2002—, chmn. com. on earth penetrator nuc. weapons, 2004-06; co-chair, joint NAS/RAS com. internat. fuel cycle, 2006-, chair, 2007-, chair com. Opportunities US-Russian Coop. Combating Radiological Terrorism, 2004-; mem. pres.'s coun. for nat. labs. U. Calif., 199-2007; vice-chmn. U.S. Commn. for IIASA, 1992-93, chmn., 1994-98; adv. com. Princeton Plasma Physics Nat. Lab., 1993-98; co-chmn. panel on opportunities in plasma sci. tech. NAS, 1992-96, reactor panel for disposition of weapons plutonium, 1992-96; bd. dirs. Wis. Energy Corp.; lectr. Colo. Coll., 1966-69; pres. com. adv. S&T Energy R&D panel, 1997-98; USGAO exec. coun. Info. Mgmt. and Tech., 1997-2004; mem. adv. coun. Jet Propulsion Lab., 2004—05. Bd. dirs. Woodstock Theol. Ctr., chmn., 1980-85. Gen. Electric Coffin fellow, 1957-58; recipient Dept. Def. Disting. Civilian Svc. medal and bronze palm, Sec. Def. Meritorious Svc. medal; named Boss of Year D.C. chpt. Nat. Secs. Assn., 1976. Fellow AAAS, Am. Phys. Soc. (chmn. forum on physics and soc. 1996-97, chair panel on pub. affairs 2003—04), Am. Acad. Arts and Scis., Soc. Risk Analysis; mem. NAE, Nat. Acads. (nat. assoc.), Nat. Coun. for Radiation Protection and Measurement, Am. Nuc. Soc., Soc. for Risk Analysis (past pres.), Sigma Xi. Democrat. Roman Catholic. Office Phone: 919-547-5213. Business E-Mail: ahearne@sigmaxi.org.

AHERN, GEOFFREY LAWRENCE, behavioral neurologist; b. NYC, Feb. 20, 1954; BA, SUNY, Purchase, 1976; MS, Yale U., 1978, PhD in Psychology, 1981, MD, 1984. Med. intern Waterbury (Conn.) Hosp., 1984-85; resident in neurology Boston U., 1985-88; fellow in behavioral neurology Beth Israel Hosp., Boston, 1988-90; instr. neurology Harvard Med. Sch., Boston, 1988-90; asst. prof. neurology and psychology U. Ariz., Tucson, 1990-96, assoc. prof. neurology and psychology, 1996-99, assoc. prof. neurology, psychology and psychiatry, 1999—2002, prof. neurology, psychology and psychiatry U. Med. Ctr., 2002—. Contbr. articles to profl. jours., chapters to books. Mem.: Am. Neurol. Assn., Am. Acad. Neurology. Office: U Ariz U Med Ctr Dept Neurology 1501 N Campbell Ave Tucson AZ 85724-5023

AHERN, MICHAEL JAMES, lawyer; b. Red Wing, Minn., Aug. 20, 1951; s. Andrew Alyosious and Cecelia Mame (Ackerman) A.; m. Sharon Marie Kaufman, June 21, 1975; children: Ryan Michael, Emily Treise. BA, U. Minn., 1973; JD, William Mitchell Coll. Law, 1977. Bar: Minn. 1977, U.S. Dist. Ct. Minn. 1977, U.S. Ct. Appeals (8th cir.) 1992. Law clk. Van Valkenburg, Comaford, Moss, Fassett, Flaherty & Clarkson, Mpls., 1976-77; atty. Moss & Barnett, P.A., Mpls., 1977-80, shareholder, atty., 1980-98, also bd. dirs.; ptnr., co-chmn., legis. practice group Dorsey & Whitney LLP, Mpls., 1999—. Contbr. chpt. to book Minnesota Administrative Procedure. Bd. dirs., chmn. Group Health Plan, Inc., St. Paul, 1978-88; vice chmn. Midwest Assurance Co., Inc., St. Paul, 1990-93; bd. dirs. Group Health Inc. Adminstrs. and Medcenters Managed Care Inc., 1993-95. Mem. ABA, Minn. State Bar Assn. (exec. com. 1980-93, chair adminstrv. law sect. 1991-92), Hennepin County Bar Assn. (chair environ. law sect. 1986-87), Minn. Govtl. Rels. Coun. (pres. 1989). Office: Dorsey & Whitney LLP 50 S Sixth St Minneapolis MN 55402-1498 Office Phone: 612-340-2881. Office Fax: 612-340-2868. Business E-Mail: ahern.michael@dorsey.com.

AHLEM, LLOYD HAROLD, psychologist; b. Moose Lake, Minn., Nov. 7, 1929; s. Harold Edward and Agnes (Carlson) A.; m. Anne T. Jensen, Dec. 29, 1952; children: Ted, Dan, Mary Jo, Carol, Aileen. AA, North Park Coll., 1948; AB, San Jose State Coll., 1952, MA, 1955; Ed.D., U. So. Calif., 1962. Tchr. retarded children Fresno County (Calif.) Pub. Schs., 1953-54; psychologist Baldwin Park (Calif.) Sch. Dist., 1955-62; prof. psychology Calif. State U., Stanislaus (formerly Stanislaus State Coll.), Turlock, Calif., 1962-70; pres. North Park U., Chgo., 1970-79, dir., 1966-70; exec. dir. Covenant Village Retirement Center, Turlock, 1979-89; dir. spl. projects Covenant Retirement Communities, Chgo., 1989-93; dir. Emanuel Med. Ctr., Turlock, Calif., 1984-99, Merced Mut. Ins. Co., Atwater, Calif., 1993—2005; chmn. Capital Corp. of West, Merced, Calif., 1995—2002; ret. Author: Do I Have To Be Me, 1974, How to Cope: Managing Change, Crisis and Conflict, 1978, Help for the Families of the Mentally Ill, 1983, Living and Growing in Later Years, 1992; columnist Covenant Companion, 1972-90. Decorated comdr. Order of Polar Star Sweden. Mem. Assn. Colls. Ill. (vice chmn. 1975-79) Mem. Covenant Ch. Club: Rotary (Paul Harris fellow 1987). Home: 2125 N Olive C-11 Turlock CA 95382

AHLERS, GLEN-PETER, SR., law library director, educator, consultant; b. NYC, Mar. 15, 1955; s. LeGrande Jacob and Joan (Stoltz) A.; m. Sondra Sue Wadley, May 17, 1987; children: Glen-Peter II, Sandia Marie, Gavin Patrick, Sierra Le Ann Rose, Stacia Camille, Sienna Catherine. BS, U. N.Mex., Albuquerque, 1979; MA, U. of South Fla., 1983; JD, Washburn U., 1987. Bar: Kans. 1987, U.S. Dist. Ct. Kans. 1987, U.S. Ct. Mil. Appeals 1988, D.C. 1990. Reference asst. U. N.Mex. Sch. Law, Albuquerque, 1979-83; asst. dir. Washburn Sch. Law Libr., Topeka, 1983-87; assoc. libr. dir. Wake Forest U., Winston-Salem, N.C., 1987-90; libr. dir., assoc. prof. D.C. Sch. Law, Washington, 1990-92, U. Ark., Fayetteville, 1992-2000, prof., 2001—02; assoc. dean info. services Barry U. Dwayne O. Andreas Sch. of Law, Orlando, Fla. Computer and libr. cons. Ctr. for R&D in Law-Related Edn., Winston-Salem, 1987-90; adj. prof. Sch. of Law Wake Forest U., Winston-Salem, N.C., 1987-90; Mid-Am. Law Sch. Libr. Consortium, 1992-2002, bd. dirs. Consortium of Southestern Law Librs., 1988-90, pres. 2000-02. Author: History of Law School Libraries in the United States, 2002, Election Laws of the United States, 1995; co-author: Notary Law and Practice, 1997; editor The Maall Newsletter, 1984-87, The Scrivener, 1992—2004; tech. editor Washburn Law Jour., 1985-86; contbr. articles to profl. jours. Mediator N.C. Neighborhood Justice Ctr., Winston-Salem, 1989-90. Mem. ABA, ALA, Fla. Bar Assn., Am. Assn. Law Librs., Southwestern Assn. Law Librs. (pres. 1995-97), Southeastern Assn. of Law Librs., Mid Am. Assn. Law Librs. (pres. 1999-2000), Scribes (exec. dir. 1997—), Phi Kappa Phi, Kappa Delta Pi, Beta Phi Mu. Avocation: writing. Home: 1069 Winding Waters Cir Winter Springs FL 32708-6326 Office: Barry U Dwayne O Andreas Sch of Law 6441 E Colonial Dr Orlando FL 32807-3650 Office Phone: 321-206-5701. Business E-Mail: gahlers@mail.barry.edu.

AHLERS, GUENTER, physicist, researcher; b. Bremen, Germany, Mar. 28, 1934; came to U.S., 1951; s. William Carl and Ida Pauline (Cornelson) A.; m. June Bly, Aug. 24, 1964 BS in Chemistry, U. Calif., Riverside, 1959; PhD in Physical Chemistry, U. Calif., Berkeley, 1963. Mem. tech. staff Bell Labs., Murray Hill, NJ, 1963—78; prof. physics U. Calif., Santa Barbara, 1979—. Chair fundamental physics discipline working group NASA, 1998—99. Contbr. over 260 articles to profl. jours. Recipient Tenth Fritz London Memorial award, 1978, Alexander von Humboldt Senior U.S. Scientist award, 1989—90, Fluid Dynamics prize, Am. Phys. Soc., 2007. Fellow AAAS, Am. Phys. Soc. (Fluid Dynamics prize, 2007), Am. Acad. Arts & Sci.; mem. NAS. Office: U Calif Dept Physics Santa Barbara CA 93106 Home: 1051B Senda Verde Santa Barbara CA 93105 Business E-Mail: guenter@physics.ucsb.edu.

AHLERS, LINDA L., retail executive; BA, U. Wisc. Buyer, Target Stores Dayton Hudson Corp., 1977-83, divsn. mdse. mgr., Target Stores, 1983-85, dir. mdse. planning and control, 1985-88, v.p. mdse. planning and control, 1988, sr. v.p. Target Stores, 1988-95, exec. v.p. merchandising, dept. store divsn., 1995-96; pres., dept. store divsn. Dayton Hudson Corp. (now Marshall Field's), 1996—; bd. dirs. Dayton Hudson Corp., 1997—. Dir. Guthrie Theatre; mem. Com. of 200, Detroit Renaissance Bd., Minn. Women's Econ. Roundtable. Office: Target Corp 1000 Nicollet Mall Minneapolis MN 55403-2467

AHLERS, ROLF WILLI, philosopher, theologian; b. Hamburg, Germany, June 22, 1936; arrived in US, 1966; s. Arthur W. and Ilse F. (Freund) A.; m. Luise Kuse, July 1965; children: Christoph Matthias, Marcus Andreas. BA, Drew U., 1958; MDiv, Princeton Theol. Sem., 1961; Dr. Theol., U. Hamburg, 1966. Wissenschaftlicher Assoc. Seminar Für Systematische Theologie und Sozialethik, U. Hamburg, Germany, 1962-66; asst. prof. religion Ill. Coll., Jacksonville, 1966-72; Reynolds prof. philosophy and religion Russell Sage Coll., Troy, 1973—. Author: The Barmen Declaration of 1934: Archeology of a Confessional Text, 1986, The Community of Freedom: Karl Barth and Presuppositionless Theology, 1989; author, editor: System and Context/System und Kontext: Early Romantic and Early Idealistic Constellations, New Athenaeum/Neues Athenaeum, vol. VII, 2004. NEH grantee, 1972-73; Soc. for Health and Human Values grantee, 1975. Mem.: Hegel Soc. Am., Am. Acad. Religion, Am. Philos. Soc, Internationale Hegel Vereinigung, Internationale Fichte Gesellschaft, Fichte Soc. N.Am. Presbyterian. Home: 3 Academy Rd Albany NY 12208-3102 Office: Russell Sage Coll Philosophy Dept Troy NY 12180 Office Phone: 518-244-2322. *The cunning of history, pure grace and keen sense of self made me the person who I am.*

AHLGREN, JAMES DAVID, oncologist; b. Washington, Feb. 17, 1934; s. Charles David and Dorothy Elizabeth (Webb) A.; m. Barbara Elizabeth Donelko, Sept. 7, 1957 (div. Mar. 1978); children: Gillian Webb, Nils William; m. Alice Duong, Sept. 1978; 1 child, Mats Erik. BSEE, MIT, 1955; MD, Georgetown U., 1977. Diplomate Am. Bd. Internal Medicine, Am. Bd. Med. Oncology. Chief engr. McIntosh Electronics, Binghamton, N.Y., 1955-56; chief circuit design Reed Rsch., Washington, 1956-58; rsch. engr., asst. dir. R&D Page Comm. Engrs., Washington, 1958-63; v.p., acting pres. Telcom, Inc., McLean, Va., 1963-73; intern Georgetown U. Med. Ctr., Washington, 1977-78, resident in internal medicine, 1979-80, from instr. to assoc. prof., 1980-88; assoc. prof. George Washington U. Med. Ctr., Washington, 1988-94, prof. medicine, pharmacology, 1994—. Chmn. Mid-Atlantic Oncology Program, Silver Spring, Md., 1983-95, bd. dir. Ptnr. for Surgery. Author: Gastrointestinal Oncology, 1992. Chmn. Mid-Atlantic Cancer Rsch. Found., Silver Spring, 1989—. Recipient Edward B. Bunn award Georgetown U., Washington, 1977, Dept. Medicine award, 1977, Jonathan M. Wainwright award Moses Taylor Hosp., 1993, Elaine Snyder Cancer Rsch. award George Washington U., 1994. Mem. ACP, IEEE (sr. mem.), Am. Soc. Clin. Oncology, Am. Geophys. Union, Am. Meteorol. Soc. Republican. Lutheran. Avocations: amateur radio, piano, cooking. Office: George Washington U Med Ctr 2150 Pennsylvania Ave NW Washington DC 20037-3201 E-mail: jahlgren@mfa.gwu.edu.*

AHLQUIST, JOHN B., application developer; b. Springfield, Mass., June 29, 1959; s. John B. and Donna Jo Ahlquist; m. Karen Lynn Bowles, July 8, 1978; children: Elizabeth Lynn Lamb, Curtis Andrew, Nicholas Ryan. BA in Computer Sci., U. Minn., Mpls., 1982. Sr. mem., tech. staff Tex. Instruments, Dallas, 1982—89; prin. engr. Macromedia, Dallas, 1989—2001, Electronic Arts, LA, 2001—05, Trilogy Studios, Santa Monica, Calif., 2005—06; propr. Ahlquist Software, Orange, Calif., 2006—. Author: Video Game Essentials: Game Artificial Intelligence. Mem.: IEEE, Internat. Game Developers Assn. Methodist. Achievements include patents in field. Avocation: Tae Kwon Do. Office: Ahlquist Software 8502 E Chapman Ave 342 Orange CA 92869 Home Phone: 714-771-7714; Office Phone: 714-633-4853. Business E-Mail: info@ahlquistsoftware.com.

AHLSTROM, MICHAEL JOSEPH, lawyer; b. NYC, June 1, 1953; s. Albert Warren and Bernadette Patricia (Flynn) A.; m. Mary Lou Donnelly, Apr. 19, 1980; 1 child, Courtney Leigh. BS, St. Francis Coll., 1975; JD, U. San Francisco, 1978. Bar: N.Y. 1980, U.S. Dist. Ct. (so. and ea. dists.) N.Y. 1980, Ga. 1982, U.S. Dist. Ct. (no. dist.) Ga. 1983, U.S. Ct. Appeals (11th cir.) 1984, U.S. Supreme Ct. 1987; registered neutral, arbitration, domestic mediation and early case evaluator, Ga. Counsel Gear Design, Inc., NYC, 1979—80; ptnr. Ahlstrom & Ahlstrom, NYC, 1981-83; gen. counsel Network Rental, Inc., Atlanta, 1984—87; assoc. John Marshall and Assocs., P.C., Atlanta, 1997; ptnr. Marshall & Ahlstrom, P.C., Atlanta, 1987—88; mng. atty. UAW-GM-Ford Chrysler Legal Plan Ga., Atlanta, 1993—96; pvt. practice Marietta, Ga., 1988—92, 1996—. Arbitrator Nat Assn. Securities Dealers, Superior Ct. Fulton County, Ga., 1987—, Ga. Lemon Law, 1991—; panel atty. Cobb County Circuit Defender; spl. master Cobb County Superior Ct., mediator, 1966-1996; mediator domestic cases Fulton County Superior Ct., 1998—, mediator juvenile cases; guardian ad litem Cobb County Superior Ct. Mem. N.Y. Bar Assn., Ga. Bar Assn. (pub. rels. com. 1989-91), Cobb County Bar Assn., Am. Corp.Counsel Assn. (program chmn. 1986-87), Am. Arbitration Assn. (comml. panel 1987—), St. Thomas Moore Soc., KC, Phi Delta Phi, Alpha Kappa Psi. Republican. Roman Catholic. Avocations: fishing, hunting, tennis, golf, croquet. Home: 613 Fairway Ct Marietta GA 30068-4159 Office Phone: 770-565-0622.

AHLSTROM, RONALD GUSTIN, artist; b. Chgo., Jan. 17, 1922; s. Frederick Karl and Gertrude (Gustin) A.; m. Nancy Costa; 1 son, Arn Gustin. Student, U. Chgo., Art Inst. Chgo.; B.F.A., 1955. Asst. dir. McCormick Pl. Gallery, 1960-63; dir. Tacoma Art Mus., 1963—. One-man shows include Barat Coll., Lake Forest, Ill., 1958, Blackhawk Restaurant, Chgo., 1961, collages at Main St. Galleries, Chgo., 1969, J. Faulkner Galleries, Chgo., 1970, 71, Spiesberger Gallery, Skokie, Ill., 1975, Zriny-Hayes Gallery, Chgo., 1978; group shows include Chgo. and vicinity ann., Art Inst. Chgo., 1955, 56, 59, 61, 62, 64, other shows at Art Inst., 1957, 58, Inst. Jewish Studies, 1956, 1020 Art Ctr., 1957, Navy Pier, 1957, 58, Old Town Art Center, 1959, B.C. Holland Gallery, 1961, McCormick Pl. Art Gallery, 1961, 62, 63, Hyde Park Art Ctr., 1963, Studio 22, 1970, all Chgo., C. McNider Mus., Mason City, Iowa, 1971, Touchstone Gallery, N.Y.C., 1973; exhibited in Chgo. Artists European Tour Exhibit, USIA, 1957-59, Festival of Fine Arts, Lake Forest, 1958, Soc. of Four Arts Exhibit, West Palm Beach, Fla., 1959, E. Mich. Coll. at Ypsilanti, 1960, Corcoran Gallery Art, Washington, 1961, Tacoma Art Mus., 1963, 5 Abstractionists, Main St. Galleries, 1968, Corbett Js. Dempsey Gallery, Chgo., 2007; represented in permanent collections Tacoma Art Mus., Barat Coll. Gallery, Gutenberg Mus., Mainz, Germany, Art Inst. Chgo., Blue Cross, Chgo., Atlantic-Richfield, Chgo., Ill. Bell Telephone, Container Corp. Am., Chgo., also in numerous pvt. collections; work represented in book Collage and Foundation Art (Meilach and Ten Hoor), 1964, Collage and Assemblage, Trend and Techniques (Meilach and Ten Hoor), 1973. Served with U.S. Army, 1942-46. Recipient Clyde M. Carr prize for painting, 1955, Alumni of Sch. Art Inst. prize, 1959, Jane Broadus Clark prize, 1958; Singer & Sons prize, Navy Pier; Abel Fagan prize Festival Fine Arts, Lake Forest, 1958; Ford Found. purchase prize Seattle Art Mus., 1964 Achievements include being represented in The Art of Collage (Gerald F. Brommer Davis) 1978, Collage and Found Art, MEilach & Tenhoor, Collage and Assemblage, Meilach & Tenhoor. Home: 121 W Park Dr Lombard IL 60148-3320 E-mail: nahlstrom@msn.com.

AHLVERS, STEVEN J., athletic trainer; b. Edina, Minn., Nov. 2, 1974; s. James M. and Deveny J. Ahlvers; m. Pamela J. Stierlen, June 19, 1999; 1 child, Tyler J. BS in Athletic Tng., Minn. State U., Mankato, 1998; MA in Edn., Hamline U., St. Paul, 2002. Cert. athletic trainer Bd. Cert. Athletic Trainers, 1998. Athletic trainer, intern Minn. Vikings Football Club, Eden Prairie, Minn., 1993—94; athletic trainer Orthop. and Fracture Clinic, Mankato, 1998—99; adj. staff Augsburg Coll., Mpls., 1999—2000; athletic trainer Hamline U., St. Paul, 1999—2001; educator Ind., Mendota Heights, Minn., 2001—02; athletic trainer Ind. Sch. Dist. 197, Mendota Heights, 2001—02, Augsburg Coll. Inst. Athletic Medicine, Mpls., 1999—2004; athletic trainer, indsl. rehab. HealthSouth, St. Paul, 2004—. Contbr. policy and procedure manual. Hockey ofcl. US Hockey, Lakeville, Minn., 2001—. Mem.: Leukemia and Lymphoma Soc. (honors and awards com. 2001—), Minn. Athletic Trainers Assn. (exec. bd. mem., sec. 2000—04, sec. 2000—04, clin., indsl. and corp. com. 2004—), Gt. Lakes Athletic Trainers Assn., Nat. Athletic Trainers Assn. Independent. Methodist. Office: Select Med 60 E Marie Ste 111 Saint Paul MN 55118 Home Phone: 952-469-8889; Office Phone: 651-210-8696. Personal E-mail: steve.ahlvers@gmail.com. Business E-Mail: steve.ahlvers@healthsouth.com.

AHMAD, ARIF, surgeon; b. Calcutta, India, July 9, 1959; s. Maqbool and Khashia Ahmad; m. Seema Arif Khan, Dec. 17, 1987; children: Zeba, Zoha. MD, Calcutta Med. Coll., 1983; CM, U. Calcutta, 1988. Diplomate Am. Bd. Surgery. Registrar in surgery Princess Margaret Hosp., Swindon, England, 1989—90; surg. registrar Macclesfield Gen. Hosp., Macclesfield, Cheshire, England, United Kingdom, 1990—92, Whiston Gen. Hosp., Merseyside, United Kingdom, 1992—93; clin. fellow in surgery Harvard Med. Sch. (Deaconess Hosp.), Boston, 1994—95; surg. resident U. of Conneticut Health Ctr./Hartford Hosp., Hartford, Conn., 1995—2000; clin. instr. of surgery U. of Va., Charlottesville, Va., 2000—01; dir. laporascopic surgery, asst. prof. surgery Stony Brook (NY) U. Sch. Medicine, 2001—04, clin. asst. prof. surgery, 2000—; attending surgeon John T. Mather /St. Charles Hosp., Port Jefferson, NY, 2004—, dir. bariatric surgery, 2004—. Contbr. articles to med. jours. Fellow: Royal Coll. Surgeons England, Royal Coll. Surgeons Edinburgh; mem.: ACS, Soc. Am. Gastrointestinal Surgeons, Am. Soc. Bariatric Surgery. Achievements include design of new technique of enteroenterostomy surgical technique; test for completeness of vagotomy. Home: 7 Captains Walk Setauket NY 11733 Office: LI Laparoscopic Surgery PLLC 625 Belle Terre Rd Ste 202 Port Jefferson NY 11777 Home Phone: 631-689-8582; Office Phone: 631-689-0220. Office Fax: 631-686-7626. Personal E-mail: aahmadmd@netscape.net.

AHMAD, FARRUKH, environmental engineer, chemist; arrived in US, 1987; s. Islam and Surayia Ahmad; m. Alya Ahmad, May 30, 1971; children: Ayesha Fatima, Jamil Saadi. BA, U. Tex., Austin, 1991; MS, U. Houston, 1994; PhD, Rice U., 2001. Environ. engr. SAIC, San Antonio, 1994—96; sr. cons. Booz-Allen & Hamilton, Inc., San Antonio, 1996—98; sr. environ. engr. Universe Techs., San Antonio, 1998—99; rsch. assoc. Rice U., 1998—2001; sr. environ. engr., chemist Groundwater Svcs., Inc., Houston, 2001—. Adj. prof. U. Houston, 2006—. Contbr. articles to profl. jours., chapters to books. Vol. relief effort hurricane Katrina victims City of Houston, 2005; organizer track event Tex. Spl. Olympics, San Antonio, 1998. Grantee, DOD, 2004, 2007. Mem.: Nat. Groundwater Assn., Geophys. Union, Am. Soc. Microbiology, Am. Chem. Soc. Avocations: literature, filmmaking. Home: 5317 Val Verde St Houston TX 77056 Office: Groundwater Svcs Inc 2211 Norfolk St Houston TX 77098-4096

AHMAD, JAMEEL, civil engineer, researcher, educator; b. Lahore, Punjab, Pakistan, May 22, 1941; came to U.S. 1962; s. Naseer and Iftikhar (Dean) Bakhsh; m. Rosalba Quiroz, March 31, 1983; children Monica, Sidney. BSc, Punjab U., Lahore, 1962; MS, U. Hawaii, 1964; PhD, U. Pa., 1967. East-west ctr. fellow U. Hawaii, Honolulu, 1962-65; rsch. fellow U. Pa., Phila., 1965-67; asst. prof. Widener U., Chester, Pa., 1967-68, Cooper Union, NYC, 1968-71, assoc. prof., 1971-80, prof. civil engring., 1979—, chmn. civil engring., 1980—; dir. rsch. Cooper Union Rsch. Found., NYC, 1983—2007; sr. advisor Verdant Power LLC, Arlington, Va., 2003—; dir. Cooper Union Ctr. for Urban Infrastructure, NYC, 2005—, Cooper Union Inst. for Urban Security, 2005—. Dir. High Techs., Inc., N.Y.C., 1986—; bd. dirs. Consortium of N.Y.C. Engring. Colls. and Univs., Mayor's Office of Constrn., 1994—, fellow Rsch. Inst. for the Study of Man, 2002. V.p. Vilmanor Cmty. Assn., N.Y.C., 1992, West Side Cmty. Assn., N.Y.C., 1976. Mem. ASCE (life, Outstanding Svc. award 1985), ASME, Am. Soc. Engring. Edn., Am. Inst. Steel Constrn., Structural Engring. Inst., Pakistan League Am. (bd. dirs., Abdus Salam medal disting. rsch. engring. scis. 1993), Chi Epsilon, Phi Kappa Phi. Achievements include patents for fleximech reinforcement sys., asphalt reinforcement sys., blast-mitigation protective structure and protective sys. Office: Cooper Union Coll 51 Astor Pl New York NY 10003-7132 Home Phone: 718-275-0851; Office Phone: 212-353-4294. Business E-Mail: ahmad@cooper.edu. *My philosophy of life is best exemplified by the great 19th century industrialist/philanthropist Peter Cooper - concentrate on giving something back to society. As the founder of the only tuition-free private college in America, his legacyhas benefited generations of young people since 1849.*

AHMAD, MOGHISUDDIN, chemist, researcher; b. Dhanbad, India, July 1, 1950; arrived in U.S., 1979; s. Moinuddin Ahmad and Zaibun Nesa; m. Athar Bano Hussain, Mar. 23, 1985; children: Waseem, Raees. BS with honors, Aligarh Muslim U., India, 1971, MS, 1973, MPhil., 1975, PhD, 1978. Postdoctoral fellow Aligarh Muslim U., 1978-79; rsch. assoc. dept. biochemistry and biophysics Tex. A&M U., College Station, 1979-81; rsch. assoc. dept. food sci. Oregon State U., Corvallis, 1981-88; chemist Lipids dept. Sigma Chem. Co., St. Louis, 1988—95, chemist II bio-organics dept., 1995—2001; assoc. dir. lipid chemistry NeoPharm, Inc., Waukegan, Ill., 2001—02; dir. lipid chemistry NeoPharm, Inc. R&D, Waukegan, Ill., 2002—03; v.p. Lipid Chemistry, 2003—06; v.p. chem. technology and mfg. Jina Pharms. Inc., Libertyville, Ill., 2006—. Contbr. articles to profl. jours. Mem.: Internat. Lecithin and Phospholipid Soc. (sec. 2005—; mem. exec. com. 2005—), Am. Chem. Soc., Am. Oil Chemists Soc. (bd. dirs. phospholipid divsn. 2005—). Avocations: reading, writing. Home: 3050 N Forrest Hills Ct Wadsworth IL 60083 Home Phone: 847-662-9504; Office Phone: 847-573-0707. E-mail: moghis@jinapharma.com.

AHMAD, SHAMOON, hematologist, oncologist, consultant; b. Pakistan; arrived in U.S., 1988; MB, BChir, Dow Med. Coll., Karachi, Pakistan, 1987; law student, U. Nev., 2004—. Diplomate Am. Bd. Hosp. Physicians, Am. Bd. Hematology, Am. Bd. Oncology, Am. Bd. Internal Medicine, lic. physician Pa., Ala., N.Y., Nev. Resident in internal medicine Seton Hall U., NJ, 1989—92; fellow in hematology Mt. Sinai Sch. Medicine, NYC, 1992—93, 1995—96, fellow in neoplastic diseases, 1996—97, fellow in bone marrow transplant, 1997—98; dir. blood and marrow transplant program Comprehensive Cancer Ctrs. of Nev., Las Vegas, 1998—. Asst. med. dir. Jackson County (Ala.) Rural Health Project, Scottsboro, 1993—95; chair cancer com., sect. chief hematology/oncology Sunrise Hosp. and Med. Ctr., Las Vegas, 2001—02; part-time med. dir. therapeutic apheresis program United Blood Svcs., Las Vegas, 2002—; chair pain com. Sunrise Hosp. and Med. Ctr., 2002—, vice chmn. instnl. rev. bd., 2002—03; mem. gov.'s task force on prostate cancer State of Nev., 2004—; pres. Physician & Legal Consultants, Inc., 2004; lectr., presenter in field. Contbr. articles to profl. jours. Named to Who's Who in So. Nev., In Bus. Las Vegas mag., 2003; recipient Physician's Recognition award, AMA, 1992—2000, Curtsey Las Vegas award, C. of C., Las Vegas, 2002. Fellow: ACP, Am. Bd. Hosp. Physicians; mem.: Am. Coll. Legal Medicine, Am. Coll. Physician Execs., Am. Soc. Blood and Marrow Transplantation, Clark County Med. Soc. (bylaws, policies and procedures com., profl. stds. coun. 2002—), Nev. State Med. Assn. (coun. on pub. health 2002—), Assn. Cmty. Cancer Ctrs. (ho. dels. 2003—), Am. Soc. Clin. Oncology (clin. practice com. 2003—), Nev. Oncology Soc. (pres. 2003—). Office: PO Box 60327 Las Vegas NV 89160 Office Phone: 702-363-2020. Fax: 702-458-2436. E-mail: shamoonahmad@yahoo.com.

AHMAD, SYEDA SULTANA, physician; b. Pakistan; d. Syed Wakil and Syeda (Begum) A. B in Medicine and Surgery, Punjab U., Lahore, Pakistan, 1977; MD, Ednl. Commn. Fgn. Med. Grads., Phila., 1982. Resident pediatrics Narain Das Mool Chand Children Hosp., Lahore, 1978; resident ob-gyn. U. Punjab, Sir Ganga Ram Hosp., Lahore, 1978-79; med. officer ob-gyn. Fertility Svcs. and Tng. Ctr., Dhaka, Bangladesh, 1980; clin. attachment staff S. Georgia Med. Ctr., Amarillo, Tex., 1983-84, Pvt. Clinic, Bedford, Tex., 1985-89; rschr. U. Tex. South Western Med. Ctr., Dallas, 1989; resident pathology U. Okla., Oklahoma City, 1989-90; resident pediatrics U. Tenn., Le Bonheur Childrens Med. Ctr., Memphis, 1990-92; resident in pediats. Tex. A&M U. and Scott and White Hosp., Temple, 1992-94, Scott and White Hosp., 1992-94. Avocations: travel, reading, bicycling. Office Phone: 972-509-1153.

AHMADI, MOJTABA, engineering educator, consultant; BSc, Sharif U., Tehran, 1988; MSc, Tehran U., 1992; PhD, McGill U., Montreal, Can., 1998. Postdoctoral fellow Ecole Polytecnique de Montreal, 1998—2000; mgr. advanced robotics and controls group Opal-RT Technologies Inc., Montreal, 2000; sr. servo engr. Maxtor and Qunatum Corps., Milpitas, Calif., 2001; rschr. NRC, Ottawa, Canada, 2002—05; prof. mech. and aero. dept. Carleton U., Ottawa, 2005—. Rsch. cons. Inst. for Aerospace Rsch., NRC, Ottawa, 2005—. Contbr. chapters to books, articles to profl. jours. Grantee, Ont. Ctrs. Excellence, 2006, 2006. Mem.: IEEE, IEEE Robotics and Automation Soc. Achievements include development of dontrolled passive dynamic running strategy for efficient locomotion of legged robots; ARL Monopod II robot with compliant knee and hip. The robot set the efficiency record at its time for actively controlled legged robots; performed the robotic analysis and contributed to the design of a Captive Trajectory Simulation System (CTS): A redundant robotic arm used in supersonic tunnels. Office: Mech&Aero Dept Carleton University 1125 Colonel By Dr Ottawa ON Canada K1S 5B6 Home Phone: 613-823-6588; Office Phone: 613-520-2600 x.4057.

AHMADY, ALI, lab administrator, director; arrived in US, 2006; s. Mahmoud Ahmady and Zinat Molla-Ahmady; m. Nikoo Afifiyan; children: Kimia, Donya. BSc, Tehran U., Iran, 1988; MSc, Nat. U. Singapore, 1995, PhD, 1998. Cert. high complexity clin. lab. dir. Am. Bd. Bioanalysis, Mo., 2004, lab. dir. in andrology and endocrinology NY State Dept. Health. Chief embryologist human reproduction ctr. Yazd Med. U., Iran, 1988—92, lab. dir., 2005; rsch. fellow Nat. U. Singapore, 1998—2000; post-doctoral rsch. fellow Samuel Lunenfield rsch. inst. Mt. Sinai Hosp., Toronto, Ont., Canada, 2000—01; dir. lab. Nustar Fertility Ctr., Mississauga, Ont., Canada, 2001—04, Astra Fertility Ctr., Mississauga, 2004—06, U. Fertility Ctr., Torrance, Calif., 2006—; sci. dir. Ctr. Reproductive Health and Gynecology, Beverly Hills, Calif., 2006—. Vis. scientist UCLA, 2007; dir. Isatis Sci., Rancho Palos Verda, 2007; lectr. in field. Contbr. articles to profl. jours. Recipient Infertility Rsch. Award, Royan Internat., 2000; scholar, Nat. U. Singapore, 1995—98. Achievements include produced the first live-birth from ICSI-derived embryos in the mouse; performed the first systematic study in fertilising ability of dead sperm; produced healthy baby using non-viable frozen testicular sperm and oocyte activation; development of hamster-ICSI assay as a test for fertilizing ability of severe male factor sperm prior to clinical ICSI; single sperm curling (SSC) test for selection of viable sperm in ICSI procedure. Mailing: PO Box 5245 Palos Verdes Peninsula CA 90274 Office Phone: 310-378-7445. Personal E-mail: ali_ahmady@yahoo.com.

AHMAN, ARNOLD J., pediatrician; b. Balt., Dec. 23, 1939; s. Frank and Sophie (Goldberg) Altman; m. Cheryl Toby Steinberg, Dec. 28, 1969; children: David, Joseph. AB, Johns Hopkins U., Balt., 1961, MD, 1965. Intern pediats. Yale U., New Haven, 1965—66; asst. pres. pediats. Boston Children's Hosp., Boston, 1968—70, fellow pediats., 1970—72; asst. prof. pediats. Ind. U. Med. Ctr., Indpls., 1972—74; chief divsn. pediats., hematology and oncology U. Conn., Farmington, 1974—96; chief divsn. hematology and oncology Conn. Children's Med. Ctr., Hartford, Conn., 1996—. Author: (book) Malignant Diseases of Infancy, Childhood and Adolescence, 1978; editor: Supportive Care of Children With Cancer, 2004. Adv. bd. U. Conn. Children's Cancer Fund, Farmington, 1980—96. Lt. comdr., 1968. Mem.: Children's Oncology Group, Am. Soc. Clin. Oncology, Am. Soc. Hematology. Office: Conn Childrens Med Ctr 282 Washington St Hartford CT 06106

AHMANN, JOHN STANLEY, retired psychologist; b. Struble, Iowa, Oct. 17, 1921; s. Henry Francis and Philomine (Wictor) Ahmann; children: Sandi Ann, Sheri Kay, Gregory Steven, Shelly Joan. BA, Trinity Coll., 1943; BS, Iowa State U., Ames, 1947, MS, 1949, PhD, 1951. Instr. profl. studies Iowa State U., 1949-51, prof. edn. and psychology Ames, 1975—, disting. prof. edn., 1981—, chmn. dept. profl. studies, 1975-84; asst. prof. div. ednl. psychology and psychol. measurement Cornell U., 1951-54, asso. prof., 1954-58, prof., 1958-60; prof. psychology Colo. State U., 1960-75; assoc. dir. Human Factors Rsch. Lab., 1969-71, asst. to pres., 1961-64, head dept. psychology, 1962-64, acad. v.p., 1964-69; retired. Adj. prof. psychology and edn. U. Denver, 1971—76; vis. prof. Colo. State U., 1951, Wash. State U., 1960, Western Wash. U., 1970; cons. rsch. programs U.S. Dept. Edn.; cons. evaluation ednl. programs, Colo., NY, La., Tex., Ark., Hawaii, Ga., Ariz., Ohio, Minn., Iowa; project dir. Nat. Assessment Ednl. Progress, 1971—75; dir. various fed. and state sponsored rsch. projects; hon. lectr. Mid-Am. State U. Assn., 1976—77. Author: (book) Statistical Methods in Educational and Psychological Research, 1954, Evaluating Student Progress, 6th edit., 1981, Evaluating Elementary School Pupils, 1960, Testing Student Achievement and Aptitudes, 1962, Measuring and Evaluating Educational Achievement, 2d edit., 1975, How Much Are Our Young People Learning?, 1976, Needs Assessment for Program Planning in Vocational Education, 1979, Academic Achievements of Young Americans, 1983; assoc. editor: Ednl. Studies, 1975—79. With USNR, 1943—46, PTO. Recipient Laureate award, Iowa State U., 1975. Fellow: APA, AAAS; mem.: Nat. Coun. Measurement Edn., Am. Ednl. Rsch. Assn., Psi Chi, Alpha Chi Sigma, Phi Lambda Upsilon, Phi Delta Kappa, Phi Kappa Phi, Sigma Xi. Home: 5055 S Lemay Ave Unit I 201 Fort Collins CO 80525-9401

AHMANSON, HOWARD, JR., Philanthropist; b. 1950; s. Howard Fieldstead Ahmanson; m. Roberta Green Ahmanson, 1986; 1 child. BA Econ., Occidental Coll.; MA Linguistics, U. of Texas, Arlington. Head, personal philanthropic orgn. Fieldstead Inst.; provides funds for Fullhart-Carnegie Museum Trust, Drew U., Discovery Inst., Claremont Inst., St. James Episcopal Church, Calvin Coll., American Anglican Coun., Chalcedon Report, United States Republican Party and many others. Author multiple articles appearing in The Los Angeles Times, Philanthropy, Religion and Liberty, and other publ. Mem. Republican state ctr. com.; chmn. California Ind. Bus. Pol. Action Com. (PAC). Named one of 25 Most Influential Evangelicals in America, TIME Magazine, 2005. Mem.: Coun. for Nat. Policy (Bd. of Gov. 1996—98), Claremont Inst., John M. Perkins Found. Office: The Ahmanson Found 9215 Wilshire Blvd Beverly Hills CA 90210 Office Phone: 310-278-0770.*

AHMANSON, ROBERTA, Philanthropist; b. Perry, Iowa, 1949; d. Earl and Virginia Green; m. Howard Ahmanson, 1986; 1 child. BA, Calvin Coll., Grand Rapids, MI, 1972; MA English, U. of Michigan, Ann Arbor, MI. Religion reporter The Orange County Register; bd. of advisors Claremont Inst.; bd. of dir. Inst. on Religion and Democracy; head, personal philanthropic orgn. Fieldstead Inst. Author: (novels) They Got It All Wrong. Named one of 25 Most Influential Evangelicals in America, Time Magazine. Anglican/Episcopalian. Office: The Ahmanson Found 9215 Wilshire Blvd Beverly Hills CA 90210 Office Phone: 310-278-0770. E-mail: info@theahmansonfoundation.org.*

AHMED, AKBAR S., religious studies educator; BA, Punjab U., 1964; PhD, London U., 1978; MA, Cambridge U., 1994. Various positions including additional sec. home tribal affairs Register Coop. Societies, pres. N.W. Frontier Province, Pakistan, 1966—88; polit. agent South Waziristan Agy. Govt. N.W. Frontier Province, 1978—80; commr. of three divsns. Baluchistan, 1982—88; founder, dir.-gen. Nat. Ctr. Rural Devel., 1982—88; high commr. for Islamic Rep. of Pakistan to UK and Ireland, 1999—2000; Ibn Khaldun Chair of Islamic Studies, prof. internat. rels. Am. U., Washington, 2001—. With Inst. Advanced Study, Princeton; vis. prof. dept. anthropology Harvard U., 1981—82; affiliate prof. dept. anthropology U. Washington, Seattle, 1982—2000; vis. prof. dept. anthropology Princeton U., 2000—01, Stewart fellow humanities coun., 2000—01; sr. fellow Case Foundation, Washington; vis. fellow Brookings Instn. Author: Religion and Politics in Muslim Society, 1983, Resistance and Control in Pakistan, 1991, Pakistan Society: Islam, Predicament and Promise, 1992, Postmodernism and Islam: Predicament and Promise, 1992, Islam, Globalization and Postmodernity, 1994, The Future of Anthropology: Ist Relevance to the Contemporary World, 1995, Jinnah, Pakistan and the Islamic Identity: The Search for Saladin, 1997, Islam Today: A Short Introduction to the Muslim World, 2002, others. Co-recipient Purpose Prize, Civic Ventures, 2006; fellow Ford Found., London U., 1977—78, Selwyn Coll., Cambridge U., 1988—93; Iqbal Fellow, 1988—93. Office: Am U 4400 Massachusetts Ave NW Washington DC 20016-8071 E-mail: akbar@american.edu.

AHMED, ATIF ALI, pathologist; b. Khartoum, Sudan, Mar. 7, 1965; arrived in US, 1994; s. Ali Ahmed Hussein and Habiba F Aljarrari; m. Susan J Veit, Apr. 5, 2004; 1 child, Sarra. MBBS, U. Khartoum, Sudan, 1988. Diplomate Am. Bd. of Pathology, 2003, cert. in pediat. pathology Am. Bd. of Pathology, 2005. Tchg. asst., resident in pathology and microbiology U. Khartoum, 1991—94; med. intern Mt. Vernon Hosp., NY, 1995—96; resident in pathology Columbia U., NY, 1996—98, U. Okla., 1998—2000; post-residency fellowship in pediat. pathology NYU, 2000; clin. fellow Nat. Cancer Inst., NIH, Bethesda, Md., 2003—04; attending pathologist Children's Nat. Med. Ctr., Washington, 2004—. Enhanced profl. info. pathologist Nat. Cancer Inst., NIH, Bethesda, Md., 2003—04. Contbr. articles various profl. jours. Tchg. Albert-Einstein Coll. of Medicine, Bronx, NY, 2002—03. Fellow Advanced subspecialty in Pediatric Pathology, U. South Fla., 2002. Fellow: Assn. of Clin. Scientists, Coll. of Am. Pathologist; mem.: Soc. Pediat. Pathology. Achievements include research in expression of C-kit in Ewing family of tumors in intestitial cells of cajal in children, and complete hydatidiform mole; Fryns syndrome-like phenotype with mosaic chromosomal translocation; placenta membranacea; solid tumors on children. Office: Childrens Nat Med Ctr 111 Mich Ave NW Washington DC 20009 Home Phone: 301-929-8882; Office Phone: 202-884-2175. Office Fax: 202-884-4030. Personal E-mail: atifaahmed@yahoo.com.

AHMED, IQBAL, psychiatrist, consultant; b. Tumkur, Karnataka, India, Aug. 23, 1951; arrived in US, 1976, naturalized, 1982; s. Rahimuddin Ahmed and Arifa (Banu) Rahimuddin; m. Lisa Suzanne Rose, Oct. 9, 1983; children: Yasmin, Jihan. BS, MB, St. John's Med. Coll., 1975. Diplomate in gen. psychiatry, geriatric psychiatry and psychosomatic medicine Am. Bd. Psychiatry and Neurology. Intern St. Martha's Hosp., Bangalore, India, 1974-75; resident in psychiatry U. Nebr. Med. Ctr., Omaha, 1976-79; fellowship in consultation Boston U. Sch. Medicine, 1979-81; staff psychiatrist in consultation liaison psychiatry Boston City Hosp., 1981-87, staff psychiatrist, geriatric psychiatry, 1983-85, dir. geriatric neuropsychiatry unit, 1985-87, dir. geriatric psychiatry, 1988-92; assoc. dir. consultation liaison psychiatry New England Med. Ctr., Boston, 1989-92. Asst. prof. psychiatry Boston U. Sch. Medicine, 1981—87, Tufts U. Sch. Medicine, Boston, 1987—92; dir. med. student edn. in psychiatry Boston City Hosp., 1981—87; chief spl. svcs. Hawaii State Hosp., 1991—94, pres. med. staff, 1994—95, chief geriatric psychiatry, 1994—97; assoc. prof. dept. psychiatry U. Hawaii John A. Burns Sch. Medicine, 1992—97, prof. dept. psychiatry, 1997—; vice chmn. dept. psychiatry U. Hawaii, 1999—2001; cons. Triple Army Med. Ctr., 1997—; program dir. gen. and geriatric psychiatry residency programs U. Hawaii, 1998—2004; dir. pyschopharm. Adult Dept. Mental Health State of Hawaii, Honolulu, 2003—; cons. geriatric psychiatry Queens Med. Ctr., Honolulu, 2003—, vice chmn. edn., dept. psychiatry, 1999—2004. Author, co-editor: Spectrum of Psychotic Disorders-Neurobiology, Etology amd Pathogenesis, 2007; contbr. articles to profl. jours., chapters to books. Mem. Mass. State Dem. Party Minority Caucus, Boston, 1983. Finalist Parker Palmer Courage to Teach award, Accreditation Council Grad. Med. Edn., 2004; recipient Irma Bland award, APA, 2005. Fellow: Royal Coll. Psychiatrists; mem.: Am. Psychiatric Assn. (mem. ethnic minority elderly com.), Acad. Psychosomatic Medicine, Am. Acad. Psychosomatic Medicine, Am. Coll. Psychiatrists, Internat. Coll. Geriatric Psychoneuropharmacology (founding mem.), Am. Assn. Geriatric Psychiatry (chair tchg. and training com.), Am. Neuropsychiat. Assn., Alpha Omega Alpha (hon. elected hon. faculty mem. 2007). Democrat. Avocations: web surfing, snorkeling. Office: 1356 Lusitana St Fl 4 Honolulu HI 96813-2421 Business E-Mail: ahmedi@dop.hawaii.edu.

AHMED, RAMADAN, engineering educator, educator; s. Mohammed Ahmed and Kadija Yusuf; m. Rehana A. Sherif, 2004; children: Eman R., Sabrin R. PhD, Norwegian U. Sci. and Tech., Trondhiem, 2001. Rsch. assoc. U. Tulsa, Okla., 2003—. Mem.: SPE. Office: Univ Tulsa 2450 E Marshall Tulsa OK 74110

AHMED, S. BASHEER, research and development company executive, educator; b. Kurnool, Andhra, India, Jan. 1, 1934; arrived in US, 1961, naturalized; s. S. M. and K.A. (Bee) Hussain; m. Alice Cordelia Pearce; 1 child, Ivy Amina. BA, Osmania Coll., Kurnool, 1955; MA, Osmania U., Hyderabad, India, 1957; MS, Tex. A&M U., 1963, PhD, 1966. Asst. prof. Tenn. Tech. U., Cookeville, 1966-68, Ohio U., Athens, 1968-70; vis. fellow Princeton U., NJ, 1977-78; prof. Western Ky. U., Bowling Green, 1970-80; prof. Mgmt. Scis. Lubin Grad. Sch. Bus., dir. doctoral program Pace U., NYC, 1982-92, prof. emeritus, 1993—2003; pres. Princeton Econ. Rsch., Inc., 1980-99, Pearce Cons. Svcs., 2000—. Cons. Oak Ridge (Tenn.) Nat. Lab., 1969-77, Inst. for Energy Analysis, Oak Ridge, 1975, Honeywell Corp., Mpls., 1985. Author: Quantitative Methods for Business, 1974, Nuclear Fuel and Energy Policy, 1979; author, editor: Technology, International Stability, and Growth, 1984. Mem. cirs. bd. The Kennedy Ctr., 1997-2000. Recipient Achievement award Oak Ridge Nat. Lab., 1977, IEEE Centennial Medal, 1983, Millennium medal, 2000. Fellow AAAS, Systems, Man, and Cybernetics Soc. (pres. 1980-82). Home: 817 Albemarle Dr Bowling Green KY 42103 Office Phone: 703-797-3052.

AHMED, SALEEM, management consultant, educator; b. Agra, India, Mar. 16, 1945; came to U.S., 1969; s. Mohammed Wasi and Iqbal Begum Uddin; m. Joumana Chebbani; children: Nadeem Saleem, Asmahan Saleem, Nabeel Saleem, Heba Saleem Ahmed. AEPT in Power Tech., Karachi Polytech Inst., Pakistan, 1965; BA in Math, U. Karachi, Pakistan, 1965; BSME, Detroit Inst. Tech., 1971; MBA in Systems Approach, Baldwin Walace Coll., 1980; PhD in Mktg. and Mgmt., Calif. Coast U., Santa Ana, 1985. Cert. mfg. engr. Project engr. Union Carbide Corp., Westlake, Ohio, 1977—85; mgmt. cons. Saleem & Assocs., Detroit, 1986—89; pres. Mich. Ctr. For Excellence, Inc., Dearborn, Mich., 1990—, Soc. for Profl. Advancement, Inc., Dearborn, Mich., 1991—. Author: Project Management Systems Approach for Plastics Engineers, 1990, The Excellence in Sales for Executives, 1991, Multi-Level Marketing, 1991, The Psychology of Winning, 1992, The Job Connection, 1992, How to Close Sale Every Time, 1992, Systems Approach Application for Engineers, 2000, Systems Approach Application for Every One, 2000, How to Achieve Zero Defects, 2000, How to Conduct Self Internal Audit, 2001, How to Conduct Tool Tryout, Process and Production Capabilities, 2001, How to Design Tools from Setup and Production Point of Views, 2001, Financially Focused Advanced Product Quality Planning, 2007. Avocations: wood working, photography. Home: 2024 N Silvery Ln Dearborn MI 48128-1021 Office: Soc Profls Advancement Inc PO Box 5116 Dearborn MI 48128-8727 Home Phone: 313-277-0920; Office Phone: 313-277-1434. Personal E-mail: saleemheba@aol.com.

AHMED, SHABBIR, chemical engineer; s. A.Z.M. Abdul Ala and Taiyaba Begum; m. Ismat Jahan, Dec. 25, 1985; 1 child, Shayan. BSc, Bangladesh U. Engring. and Tech., Dhaka, 1982, MS, 1983; PhD, U. Nebr., Lincoln, 1988. Chem. engr. group leader Argonne Nat. Lab., Ill., 1988—. Presenter in field. Contbr. numerous articles to profl. jours. Recipient Gold medal, Partnership for a New Generation of Vehicles, 1998. Achievements include 10 patents related to fuel processing for fuel cells and autothermal reforming of fuels for hydrogen production for fuel cells. Office: Argonne Nat Lab 9700 S Cass Ave Argonne IL 60439 Office Phone: 630-252-4553.

AHMED, SYED Z., anthropologist; b. Meerut, India, Aug. 19, 1923; s. Syed Riazuddin and Shah Jehan Begum; m. Susan Ahmed, Feb. 20, 1944; 1 child, Suraiya. PhD, Eng. Leader Sahara Recon Expdn., North Africa; prodr. 40 scientific documentary films for TV, Europe; pres., exec. prodr. Xploration Internat. Rschr., traveler numerous expdns. worldwide. Author: Twilight of an Empire in India, Twilight of an Empire in China, Twilight on the Silk Road, Ruwenzori: A Land Journey Through Europe to Central Africa, Twilight on Caucausus, Incredible Journeys Around the World, Tales of Imperial China and Asia, 1997, Travel in Shangri-La, 1998, East of Tien Shan, 1998, An Imperial Affair, 1999, I Was a Geisha, 1999, A Daring Escape, 2002, Manchukou, 2004, Chaghatai, 2004, Bambuti: Life of Primaties of Rain Forest of Congo, 2005, Zenith of an Empire, 2006, Imperial Turkey, 2007. Islamic.

AHMED, WALID KHAIRY MOHAMED, electrical engineer; b. Cairo, Dec. 5, 1968; arrived in Canada, 1992, arrived in US, 1997; s. Khairy Mohamed Sulaiman and Rafia Zaki Ahmed; m. Nevin El-Sayed Ali Sultan, 1995; children: Maryam, Marwa, Omar. BSc with honors in electrical engring., commn. and electronics engring., Ain Shams U., Egypt, 1991; PhD in electrical and computer engring., Queen's U. at Kingston, Canada, 1997. Registered electrical engr. Syndicate of Engrs. of Egypt, 1991, cert. green belt six sigma 2005. Rsch. asst. Wireless Commn. Lab., Dept. Electrical and computer engring., Queen's U. at Kingston, Ontario, Canada, 1992—97; DSP engr. Radio DSP Dept., Nortel Tech., Ottawa, Canada, 1997; tech. staff, design supr. Bell Labs., Wireless Organ. Consumer Products Organ., Lucent Tech., Holmdel, NJ, 1997—98; tech. staff Bell Labs., Performance Analysis Dept. Bell Labs Advanced Commn. Tech. Ctr., Lucent Tech., Holmdel, NJ, 1998—2001; tech. lead, prin. engr. Tyco Electronics, Sys. Engring, M/A-COM, NJ, 2001—03, sr. prin. engr., tech. lead mgr., 2003—; tchr., lab. asst. Benha Higher Inst. of Tech., Dept. Electrical Engring., Egypt, 1991; tchr., lab asst. Sin Shams U., Ept. of Electronics and Commn. Engring., Faculty of Engring., Egypt, 1992—97; adj. prof. Wesley J. Howe Sch. Tech. Mgmt., Stevens Inst. of Tech., NJ, 2002—. Reviewer various profl. jours. and papers. Pres. student assn. Queen's U. at Kingston, Ontario, Canada, 1994—95. Named Sr. Prin. Engr., Tyco Electronics; recipient Sr. mem. of IEEE award, IEEE, 2000, Commn. Soc. Cert. of Appreciation, 2001, Impact award, M/A-COM Tyco Electronics, 2002, 2003, Key Contbr. award, 2004, 2005; scholarship, Canadian Internat. Devel. Agency, 1992—94, Grad. scholarship, Gov. of Ontario, 1995—96. Mem.: IEEE (sr. mem. 2000—). Achievements include many patents and original research publications on wireless communications networks and systems, signal processing, and wireless transeiver design. Avocations: Karate, reading, music. E-mail: walidmail@yahoo.com.

AHMOSE, NEFERTARI A., journalism educator; b. Kingston, Jamaica, Oct. 3, 1951; arrived in U.S., 75; d. Cecil Alexander Rose and Florence Rhodian Daley. Student, L.A. Valley Coll., 1975. Journalist Jamaica Daily News, 1974—80; pub. African Expression, Bronx, NY, 1982—91; founder Royal Wafrakan Stock Exch., 1982—, Royal Wafrakan U. in West, Bklyn., 1996—, Royal Wafrakan Ins. Co., 1990—, Kiafrakan Corp. Leader Empress Afrikan Diasporan Nation, Queendom of Wafrakan. Author: Black Sovereign-The Black Alternative, 1992, Harmonization, Unification and Standardization in Wafrakan Tribal Vernaculars into Kiafrakan Language-Dictionary and Grammar, 1996, Ki-Afrakan-English Exercise, 1997, Ki-Afrakan Grammar, 1996, Ki-Afrakan Dictionary, 1996, Incorp. Afrakan Standard Language, 1994, Sex Education for Youngsters, 1994, Kemet Calendar, 2000. Founder Royal Bank Wafrakan, Merkhutu Currency, Kiafrafan Lang., Kemet-Kush (now Royal Wafrakan Polit. Party), NY, 2000—. Mailing: PO Box 971 Bronx NY 10472 Home Phone: 718-904-0787; Office Phone: 718-601-9419. Personal E-mail: nefertari@kiafrakan.com, nefertari023@aol.com.

AHN, DAE UP, polymer engineer, researcher; b. Seoul, Republic Of Korea, Dec. 11, 1971; arrived in US, 2003; s. Tae Sun Ahn and Kyoung Jha Lee; m. So Young Park. MS, Seoul Nat. U., 2000; PhD, U. Akron, Ohio, 2007. Rschr. Rsch. Inst. Advanced Materials, Seoul Nat. U., 2000—01, U. Akron, 2003—. Author: (book) Polymer Surface Modification: Relevance to Adhesion Vol. 4; contbr. articles to profl. jours. Grad. scholar, Seoul Nat. U. Achievements include patents for dentritic polyetherketone and heat-resistant blend of PVC. Office: U Akron Dept Polymer Engring Akron OH 44325-0301 Home Phone: 330-633-4585; Office Phone: 330-633-4585. Personal E-mail: duahn@dreamwiz.com. Business E-Mail: dua1@uakron.edu.

AHN, JUNG HWAN, physiatrist, educator; b. Korea; MD, Cath. U. Med. Coll., Seoul, 1970. Cert. Am. Bd. Phys. Medicine and Rehab., Am. Bd. Spinal Cord Injury Medicine. Clin. prof. NYU Sch. Medicine, NYC. Assoc. clin. dir. Rusk Inst., NYC; med. dir. Rusk Inpatient Svcs., NYC. Recipient Appreciatin award, Korean- Am. Assn. Queens, 1998, Spl. Recognition award, Paralyzed Vets. Am., 1999, Svc. citation, NYU, 2005. Mem.: Am. Spinal Injury Assn., Am. Acad. Phys. Medicine and Rehab. Office: Phys Medicine and Rehab NYU Med Ctr 400 E 34 St New York NY 10016 Office Phone: 212-263-6122.

AHN, SHI HYUN, professional golfer; b. Inchon, Korea, Sept. 15, 1984; Winner three events Apache Dream Tour, 2002; winner CJ Nine Bridges Classic, 2003. Mem. Korean Nat. Team, 2000—01. Recipient Louise Suggs Rolex Rookie of Yr., LPGA, 2004. Achievements include being the youngest internat. winner in LPGA history and sixth youngest winner in LPGA history. Avocation: quilting. Office: c/o LPGA 100 International Dr Daytona Beach FL 32124-1092

AHN, SOHYUN, neuroscientist, researcher; BS, Seoul Nat. U., South Korea, 1992, MS, 1994; PhD, Johns Hopkins U. Sch. Medicine, Balt., 2000. Postdoctoral fellow Joyner Lab. NYU, 2000—05; investigator unit of devel. neurogenetics Lab. of Mammalian Genes and Devel. NIH Nat. Inst. Child Health & Human Devel., Bethesda, Md., 2005—. Contbr. articles to profl. jours. Recipient Presdl. Early Career award for Scientist and Engrs., Pres. George W. Bush, 2005—. Office: Lab of Mammalian Genetics and Devel Nat Inst Child Health & Human Devel 6 Center Dr Rm 2B222 MSC 2790 Bethesda MD 20892-2790 Office Phone: 301-402-2426. E-mail: ahnsohyun@mail.nih.gov.*

AHN, STEVEN, finance company executive, educator; MBA, Wharton U. Pa., 1996—98. Lic. series 7 & 63 NASD. Fin. Internat. Paper Co., Purchase, NY, 1991—94, Ga. Pacific Corp.; investment banker Schroder & Co., JP Morgan & Co.; corp. fin. adv. H&R Block; ptnr. AbacusTD, LLC. Prof. dept. fin. Pepperdine U., Malibu, Calif.; prof. sch. mgmt. Mercer U., Atlanta, U. Tex., Dallas; prof. dept. banking & fin. U. Ga., Athens. Author: (book) Modern Global Cash Management; mng. editor The Wharton Jour., book reviewer Graziadio Bus. Mag., editl. reviewer (textbooks), McGraw-Hill. Vol. MADD; bd. mem. Atlanta Goizueta Grp., Atlanta, 2006—, Spruill Entrepreneurs Grp., Alpharetta, Ga., 2006—. Master: Assn. Fin. Profs. & Practioners; mem.: Am. Fin. Assn., Beta Gamma Sigma. Office: Univ Ga 1000 University Center Ln A-1113 Lawrenceville GA 30043 Personal E-mail: admin@abacustd.com. Business E-Mail: steveahn@uga.edu.

AHO, MELISSA KAY, librarian, educator, writer; b. Mpls., Apr. 5, 1972; d. Terrence Michael and Carole Kay Aho. AA, Anoka-Ramsey C.C., Coon Rapids, Minn., 1992, AS in Geog. Info. Sys. and Cartography, 2005; BA in Anthropology and History, St. Cloud State U., Minn., 1994; MS in Anthropology, U. Wis., Milw., 1998; BA in Art History, U. Minn., Mpls., 1999; M in Libr. and Info. Sci., Dominican U., River Forest, Ill., 2001; AAS in Bus. Adminstrn., Minn. Sch. Bus., Brooklyn Center, 2005. Cert. in geog. info. systems and cartography Anoka-Ramsey C.C., 2005. Libr. intern James J. Hill Reference Libr., St. Paul, 1999; rsch. libr. St. Paul Pioneer Press, 2000—01; libr. intern Cambridge C.C., Minn., 2000—01, Utne Reader Mag., Mpls., 2002; libr. Textile Ctr. Minn., Mpls., 2002, Mazapan Sch. (Dole/Std. Fruit Corp.), La Ceiba, Honduras, 2002—03; campus acquisitions and bus. resources libr. Minn. Sch. Bus., Brooklyn Center, Minn., 2003—; map libr. intern East View Cartographic, Mpls., 2005. Adj. faculty online Nat. Am. U., Rapid City, SD, 2004—. Acad. Coll., Bloomington, Minn., 2006; weekend reference libr. Met. State U., St. Paul, 2006—. Author book revs. and articles. GIS scholar, Anoka-Ramsey C.C., 2005. Mem.: ALA, Assn. Art Historians, Coll. Art Assn., Career Coll. Librs. Minn., Spl. Librs. Assn. Avocations: reading, travel. Home Phone: 763-780-2200.

AHO, SANDRA CHRISTINE, textile conservator; b. Willimantic, Conn., Mar. 12, 1958; d. Aaro Adolph Aho and Frances Viola Laivo. BS in Textile and Apparel Mktg., SUNY, NYC, 1981, Fashion Inst. Tech.; postgrad. in Textiles, Fashion Merchandising and Design, U. RI, Kingston, 2000—. Mktg. adminstr. Gimbels East, NYC, 1981—83; devel. adminstr. Hartford Region Y.W.C.A., Conn., 1983—89; arts exhbn. adminstr. Wadsworth Atheneum Mus. Art, Hartford, Conn., 1989—93; account relationship adminstr. Fleet Nat. Bank, Hartford, Conn., 1993—2000; costume and textile conservator Coventry, Conn., 1998—; textile conservation lab. mgr. U. R.I., Kingston, 2001—03; Andrew W. Mellon fellow Am. Textile History Mus., Lowell, Mass., 2004. Costume and textile cons. Wadsworth Atheneum Mus. Art, Hartford, Conn., 1995—. Mem., vol. 4-H Clubs Conn., Vernon, 1965—76, Wadsworth Atheneum Mus. Art, Hartford, Conn., 1985—, Prince of Peach Luth. Ch., Coventry, Conn., 1963—. Mem.: Am. Inst. for Conservation of Hist. and Artistic Works. Democrat. Lutheran. Achievements include costume and textile conservation internship with Museum of Fine Arts, Boston, 2001; Conn. 4-H clothing del. to nat. 4-H Conf., Chgo., 1976; winner of Vogue Patterns "Vintage Vogue Pattern Search"-appeared in Sept. 2000 Vogue Patterns Mag. Avocations: hand sewing, needle arts, garment design and construction, collecting vintage clothing, fitness and nutrition enthusiast. Home: 2880 South St Coventry CT 06238 E-mail: sathreads@aol.com.

AHOY, CHRISTOPHER KEEN, educational association administrator, architect; b. Kalimpong, India, May 29, 1939; came to US, 1964; s. King Nam (Lai) and Chun Oi (Tham) A.; m. Breena E. D'Silva (div.); m. E. Ruth Lynn, Nov. 6, 1981; stepchildren: Gregorio, Deborah, Claudette Altomirono. Student, St. Xavier's Coll., Calcutta, India, 1959; BArch, Indian Inst. Tech., Kharagpur, India, 1964; MArch, U. Calif., Berkeley, 1965; postgraduate student, U. So. Calif. Registered arch., Calif., Alaska. Arch. Joseph Esherick & Assocs., San Francisco, 1965—73; project mgr. M. Arthur Gensler & Assocs., San Francisco, 1973; chief arch., mgr. Natkin and Weber, San Francisco, 1973—74; assoc. arch. to asst. dir. design svcs. U. Calif., Berkeley, 1974—77, campus arch., sr. mgr. tech. svcs. dept. facilities mgmt., 1977—81; dir. statewide office facilities planning and constrn. U. Alaska, 1981—87; pres., CEO Comprehensive Facilities Mgmt., Berkeley, 1987—94; asst. v.p. bus. and fin., dir. facilities planning and mgmt. U. Nebr. sys., Lincoln, 1994—97; assoc. v.p. facilities Iowa State U., Ames, 1997—. Conductor seminars; spkr. in field. Author: Manual for Selection Consultants, 1988. Commr. Urban Beautification Commn., Fairbanks, Alaska, 1982-85, chmn. 1983-85. Mem. AIA (Cert. of Appreciation, 1974), Assn. Univ. Architects (Resolution Appreciation award, 1987, bd. regents U. Alaska 1987), Soc. Coll. Univ. Planners, Am. Planning Assn., Assn. Phys. Plant Adminstrs., Nat. Assn. Coll. Univ. Bus. Officers, Internat. Facility Mgmt. Assn., MIT Office of Facilities Mgmt. Systems (mem. bd. tech. adv. group), Assn. Higher Edn. Facilities Officers (pres.), Toastmasters, Rotary. Office: Facilities Planning and Mgmt Iowa State U Gen Serv Rm 108 Ames IA 50011-4001 Office Phone: 515-294-8079. Office Fax: 515-294-4593. E-mail: ckahoy@iastate.edu.*

AHRARI, EHSAN M., political science professor, dean; b. Hyderabad, India, Nov. 24, 1945; came to U.S. 1968; s. Mohammed Hashmatullah and Sayyeda Ahrari; m. Sharon Leyland Ahrari. BA, Ea. Ill. U., 1971, MA, 1972; PhD, So. Ill. U., 1976. Grants specialist Jackson County Housing, Murpheesboro, Ill., 1977; vis. asst. prof. Ea. Ill. U., Charleston, 1977-79, Kean Coll. N.J., Union, 1980; asst. prof. polit. sci. Eastern Carolina U., Greenville, 1980-86; assoc. prof. polit. sci. Miss. State U., 1986-90; prof. Middle East and Southwestern Asian Studies Air War Coll., Maxwell AFB, Ala., 1990-94; prof. nat. security and strategy joint and combined warfighting sch. Joint Forces Staff Coll., Nat. Def. U., Norfolk, Va., 1994—2005, assoc. dean of joint and combined warfighting sch., 1995—96; prof. counterterrorism Asia-Pacific Ctr. for Security Studies, Honolulu, 2007—. Sr. rsch. fellow Ctr. for Internat. Security and Strategic Studies, Miss. State U. Author: The Dynamics of Oil Diplomacy, 1980, OPEC-The Failing Giant, 1986, Ethnic Groups and U.S. Foreign Policy, 1987, The Gulf and International Security: The 1980's and Beyond, 1989, the Persian Gulf After the Cold War, 1993, The Middle East in Transition, 1994, Change in the Continuity in the Middle East, 1996, The New Great Game in Central Asia, 1996; contbr. book revs. and articles to profl. jours. NEH fellow, 1979, 84-85. Mem. Am. Polit. Sci. Assn., Am. Soc. Pub. Adminstrn. (bd. dirs. Ea. N.C. chpt. 1985-86, pres. Ea. N.C. chpt. 1985-86, editl. bd. Internat. Jour. Pub. Adminstrn.), Pi Sigma Alpha, Pi Alpha Alpha. Democrat. Muslim. Avocations: photography, tennis, travel. Home: 1717 Ala Wai Blvd # 2203 Honolulu HI 96815-1523 Personal E-mail: eahrari@earthlink.net.

AHRENDTS, ANGELA J., apparel executive; b. New Palestine, Ind., June 7, 1960; d. Richard and Jean Ahrendts; m. Greg Couch; children: Jennings, Summer, Angelina. Degree (hon.), Ball State U., 1993. Account exec. Damon Creations, 1981—83, Warnaco, Inc., 1983—85, nat. sales mgr., 1985—87, v.p. sales Geoffrey Beene knitware, pres. Pringle of Scotland divsn., sr. v.p. Valentino intimate apparel & Ungaro intimate apparel; v.p. mktg. & sales Carmelo Pomodoro Ltd., 1989—90, pres., 1990—91; v.p. merchandising Donna Karen Co., 1992, pres. Donna Karen Collection, 1992—96; v.p. gen. mdse. mgr. Henri Bendel, 1996—98; v.p.

corp. merchandising and design Liz Claiborne, Inc., NYC, 1998—2000, sr. v.p. corp. merchandising, grp. pres., 2000—02, exec. v.p., 2002—06; CEO Burberry Grp. plc, London, 2006—. Bd. dirs. Burberry Grp. plc, 2006—. Named one of 50 Women to Watch, Wall St. Jour., 2005, 2006, 100 Most Powerful Women, Forbes mag., 2006; recipient Alumni Achievement award, Ball State U., 2003. Achievements include being featured in Time Magazine Style and Design Women in Fashion Power List, 2004. Office: Burberry Group plc 18-22 Haymarket SW1 4DQ England*

AHRENS, FRANKLIN ALFRED, veterinary pharmacology educator; b. Leigh, Nebr., Apr. 27, 1936; s. Alfred Henry and Agnes Elizabeth (Higgins) A.; m. Katherine Aldene Henning, May 8, 1960; children— Jeffrey, Gregory, Matthew, Kristin D.V.M., Kans. State U., 1959; MS, Cornell U., 1965, PhD, 1968. Instr. U. Minn.-St. Paul, 1959-60; asst. prof. pharmacology Coll. Vet. Medicine, Iowa State U., Ames, 1968-70, assoc. prof. pharmacology, 1970-75, prof. pharmacology, 1975—2001, chmn. dept. vet. physiology and pharmacology, 1982-90; prof. emeritus Coll. Vet. Medicine Iowa State U., 2001—. Served as capt. USAF, 1960-63, lt. col. Air N.G., 1971-91. Recipient Norden Disting. Tchr. award Iowa State U., 1981; NIH spl. research fellow Cornell U., 1967-68 Mem. AVMA, N.Y. Acad. Scis., Assn. Mil. Surgeons U.S., Sigma Xi Democrat. Lutheran.

AHRENS, KENT, museum director, art historian; b. Martinsburg, W.Va. s. Fred E. and Mary C. (Routzahn) A. AB, Dartmouth Coll., 1961; MA, U. Md., 1966; PhD, U. Del., 1972. Mem. faculty Fla. State U., Tallahassee, 1971-74, Randolph-Macon Woman's Coll., Lynchburg, Va., 1974-77; mem. curatorial staff Wadsworth Atheneum, Hartford, Conn., 1977-78; mem. faculty Georgetown U., Washington, 1979-82; dir. Everhart Mus., Scranton, Pa., 1982-90, Rockwell Mus., Corning, NY, 1990-95, Civic Fine Arts Ctr., Sioux Falls, SD, 1996-97, Kennedy Mus. of Art, Ohio U., Athens, 1997—2000; mus. cons., 2000—; dir. devel. Cmty. Action, Athens, 2002—06. Mem. task force on art activities Lynchburg Bicentennial Commn., 1975-76; project evaluator Md. Com. Humanities, 1980-82; adv. panel Lucan Ctr., Scranton, Pa., 1983-84; mus. adv. com. Pa. Hist. and Mus. Commn., 1984-86; trustee Williamstown (Mass.) Regional Art Conservation Lab., Inc., 1984-92; art mus. adv. panel Pa. Coun. on Arts, 1984-87; adv. panel Pa. Fedn. Mus. and Hist. Orgns., 1989-90; adv. com. on exhbns. at Pa. Gov.'s residence, 1987-90; juror Regional Art '89, Marywood Coll. Art Galleries, Scranton, 1989, Regional 1991, Arnot Art Mus., Elmira, 1991, Cmty. Cultural Ctr., Brookings, SD, 1996; juror Fiber and Textile Exhibn. Civic Fine Arts Ctr., Sioux Falls, SD, 1996, Wilbur Stilwell Student Awards Exhibn., U. SD, Vermillion, 1997, Zanesville (Ohio) Art Ctr., 2000; adj. prof. Sch. Art, Ohio U., Athens, 1997-2000, percent for art com., 1997-99. Author: (with others) Rembrandt in the National Gallery of Art, 1969; author: The Drawings and Watercolors by Truman Seymour (1824-1891), Everhart Mus. 1986; co-author: Frederic C. Knight (1898-1979), Everhart Mus., 1987; author: The Oils and Watercolors by Edward D. Boit (1840-1915), Everhart Mus., 1990, Cyrus E. Dallin: His Small Bronzes and Plasters, Rockwell Mus., 1995, others; contbg. author: American Paintings and Sculpture: Illustrated Catalogue, Nat. Gallery of Art, 1970, Wadsworth Atheneum Paintings: The Netherlands and German-speaking Countries, 1978, Dictionary of Women Artists, 1997, Allgemeines Künsterlexikon, 1999—; author: Currier & Ives: Selection from the Nationwide Collection, Kennedy Mus. Art, 2000; Small Bronzes by Harriet W. Frishmuth, Kennedy Mus. of Art, 2001. Vol. Bosnia-Herzegovina Heritage Rescue, London, 1995-2001; trustee, bd. dirs. Bosnia-Herzegovina Heritage Rescue, Inc., USA, 2001-03; trustee Cmty. Shares of Mid Ohio, 2004-2005, v.p., 2005. 1st lt. US Army, 1962—64. Recipient grant-in-aid Am. Philos. Soc., 1975; Samuel H. Kress fellow Nat. Gallery of Art, 1968-69; Chester Dale fellow Nat. Gallery Art, 1970-71; NEH fellow, 1973-74, Mus. Mgmt. Inst., J. Paul Getty Trust, 1991, award for superior vol. svc. Am. Assn. Mus., 1999, award The Fund Raising Sch., Ctr. on Philanthropy, Ind. U., Indpls., 2004. Mem. Coll. Art Assn., Am. Assn. Mus. (on-site surveyor mus. assessment program 1984-89, 92—, accreditation com. 1986, 90—), Mus. Assn. Pa. (chmn. 1984-90), Mid-Atlantic Assn. Mus., Ohio Assn. Non-profit Orgns.(peer rev., standards on excellence, 2005-06), Am. Vets., Rotary, Elks. Business E-Mail: kenta@frognet.net.

AHRENS, LYNN, lyricist; b. NY, Oct. 1, 1948; m. Neil Costa. BA in Comms., Syracuse U., 1970. Author book, lyricist: Once On This Island, 1995 (Olivier award best musical, Tony nominations for best book and score, NAACP award for best playwright), Lucky Stiff, 1988 (Helen Hayes award for best musical), lyricist: My Favorite Year (Lincoln Ctr. Theatre), 1993, Ragtime, 1998 (Grammy nomination, Tony award, Drama Desk award, Outer Critics Cir. award), Anastasia, 1997 (2 Acad. award nominations, 2 Golden Globe nominations), Bartok the Magnificent, 1999, With Voices Raised (Boston Pops), 1999, Seussical, 2000 (Grammy nomination), A Man of No Importance, 2002 (Outer Crix Cir. award for best musical, 2003), The Glorious Ones, 2007, co-author, lyricist: A Christmas Carol (Madison Sq. Garden), 1994—2004, Schoolhouse Rock, 1973—85 (Emmy award, 4 Emmy nominations), 1992—98. Mem.: NARAS, ASCAP, Dramatists Guild Coun., Acad. Motion Picture Arts and Scis. Office: c/o William Morris Attn Peter Franklin 1325 Avenue Of The Americas New York NY 10019-6026*

AHRENS, MARY ELIZABETH, lawyer; b. Smithtown, NY, Jan. 24, 1975; d. Helen Ann and Ralph Charles Ahrens. BA, U. NC, Chapel Hill, 1997; JD, UCLA, Los Angeles, 2003. Atty. Morrison & Foerster LLP, LA, 2003—, Seyfarth Shaw LLP, LA. Office: Seyfarth Shaw LLP 2029 Century Pk E Los Angeles CA 90067 Office Phone: 310-201-1512. Business E-Mail: mahrens@seyfarth.com.

AHRENS, THOMAS H., communications executive; b. NYC, Oct. 25, 1919; BA magna cum laude, U. Buffalo, 1938; JD, Harvard U., 1941; certificate in Culinary Arts, N.Y.C. Tech. Coll., 1953. Bar: N.Y. 1944. Dir. Edward F. Gallaher Prodns., 1946—; lectr. wines and beverages N.Y.C. Tech. Coll., 1953-55, prof. hotel and restaurant mgmt., 1971—; dir. rsch., security analyst Templeton, Dobbrow and Vance, 1962-64; pres. Chef Phillip, Inc., 1956-69. Author radio and TV scripts on wines, gastronomy and music, 1946—. Mem. chmn.'s coun. Lincoln Ctr. for Performing Arts. 2d lt. AUS, 1942-45. Decorated officer Chaine des Rotisseurs; Confrerie Saint Etienne d'Alsace; Chevaliers du Tastevin; Commanderie des Cordons Bleus de France; Medaille de la Ville de Paris, 1976 Mem. ABA, N.Y. Soc. Security Analysts, Phi Beta Kappa. Clubs: Harvard, Paris-American, Met., Met. Opera (all N.Y.C.); Travellers, Cercle de l'Union Interalliée (Paris).

AHRENS, WILLIAM HENRY, architect; b. NYC, May 12, 1925; s. John Karl and Sophie (Hashage) A.; m. Joyce Nolan, Mar. 27, 1951; m. Katherine Bledsoe, July 5, 2006. Student, R.I. Sch. Design, 1946; AB in Architecture, Princeton U., 1950, M.F.A. in Arch. and Urban Planning, 1953; postgrad., Tehran U., 1960. Chief architect Litchfield, Whiting, Bowne, Iran, 1958-61, Rome, 1961-64; dir. internat. ops. Whiting Assos., Rome, 1964-67; architect William H. Ahrens, AIA, Rome, 1968—95. Chmn. John's Island Archtl. Review com., 1997—. Prin. archtl. works include ITT Sheraton Hotels, Tunisia and Iraq, Marriott Hotels, Egypt and Iran, Esso Hotels, Bologna, Italy and Bordeaux, France, Holiday Inn at Salalah Oman, Univ. of Dallas Rome Campus, various projects for NATO, Pontifical N.Am. Coll., Vatican City State. Trustee John Cabot U.; adv. bd. U. Dallas, U. Rome; bd. regents Marymount Internat. Sch., Rome; councilman Indian River Shores, Fla., 2003—. With USAAF, WWII, PTO. Recipient Pub. Svc. award Tehran Lions Club, 1961, Rector's award Pontifical N.Am. Coll., Rome, 1994. Mem. AIA (award 1953), Princeton Club (NYC), John's Island Club, Circolo del Golf Club (Rome), Knight of Malta, Knight of St. Gregory, Met. Club (NYC). Home: John's Island 250 Ocean Rd Vero Beach FL 32963-3281

AHRENSFELD, THOMAS FREDERICK, retired lawyer; b. Bklyn., June 30, 1923; s. Frederick Herman and Madeline Florence (Moffett) A.; m. Joan Ann McGowan, Mar. 17, 1944; 1 child, Thomas Frederick. AB, Bklyn. Coll., 1948; LL.B., Columbia U., 1948. Bar: N.Y. 1948. Assoc., then ptnr. Conboy, Hewitt, O'Brien & Boardman, NYC, 1948-58; sec., assoc. gen. counsel Philip Morris Inc., NYC, 1959-70, v.p., gen. counsel, 1970-76, sr. v.p., gen. counsel, 1976-85, Philip Morris Cos., Inc., NYC, 1985-88. Trustee Trinity-Pawling Sch. Corp., 1976-98; elder Presbyn. Ch. 1st lt. USAAF, 1942-45. Decorated D.F.C., Air medal with oak leaf clusters. Mem. ABA, N.Y.C. Bar Assn., N.Y. Athletic Club, Mt. Kisco (N.Y.) Country Club, Johns Island (Fla.) Club. Home: 450 Beach Rd Vero Beach FL 32963

AH-TYE, KIRK THOMAS, lawyer; b. LA, Mar. 31, 1951; s. Thomas and Ruth Elizabeth (Liu) Ah-T.; m. Deborah Ann Wells, Jan. 31, 1981; 1 child, Torrey Ann. BA, U. Calif., Santa Barbara, 1973; JD, Boston Coll., 1976. Bar: Calif. 1977, U.S. Dist. Ct. (ctrl. dist.) Calif. 1978, U.S. Dist. Ct. (ea. dist.) Calif. 1994, U.S. Ct. Appeals (9th cir.) 1978, U.S. Supreme Ct. 1981. Co-exec. dir., mng. atty. Channel Counties Legal Svcs. Assn., Santa Barbara, Calif., 1977—2001; directing atty. Calif. Rural Legal Assistance, Inc. Expert witness Assembly Com. on Edn., Calif. Legis., Sacramento; panelist Ctr. for the Study of Dem. Instns., Santa Barbara; panelist, instr. CLE approved classes; past legal cons. Santa Barbara chpt. calif. Assn. Bilingual Educators; inaugural prodr., moderator Santa Barbara Law, Sta. KTMS-AM, 1994—. Editor (bar newsletter) Santa Barbara Lawyer, 1992-93, (monthly legal series) Santa Barbara News-Press; contbr. articles to profl. jours. Trustee Montessori Ctr. Sch., Santa Barbara, 1991-93; bd. dirs., v.p. Santa Barbara Internat. Film Festival, 1991-93; chair adv. bd. Santa Barbara Regional Health Authority, 1985; mem. blue-ribbon com. County Bd. Suprs., Santa Barbara, 1988; chair Santa Barbara County Affirmative Action Commn., 1987-88; mem. grant-making com. Fund for Santa Barbara, 1988-92; mock trial coach San Marcos H.S., Santa Barbara, Calif. Recipient Local Hero award Santa Barbara Ind., 1988. Master Santa Barbara Am. Inns of Ct.; mem. State Bar Calif. (state resolutions com. to state bar conf. of dels. 1994-96, exec. com. to conf. dels. 1997, ann. legal svcs. achievement award for so. Calif. 1997, Achievement award for legal svc. 1997), Santa Barbara County Bar Assn. (jud. svc. award com. 1992, chmn. pro bono com. 1993, bd. dirs., sec., CFO 1992—, pres. 1997-98), Lawyer Referral Svc. Santa Barbara (bd. dirs., pres. 1992). Avocations: sports, films, literature, weights, tennis. Office: Calif Rural Legal Asstance Inc 324 E Carrillo St Ste B Santa Barbara CA 93101-7438 E-mail: Kirk.cclsa@gte.net.

AHUJA, JAGDISH CHAND, mathematics professor; b. Rawalpindi, West Pakistan, Dec. 24, 1927; came to U.S., 1966, naturalized 1972; s. Nihal Chand and Ishwardai (Chhabra) A.; m. Sudarshan Sachdeva, May 18, 1955; children— Naina, Anita BA, Banaras U., 1953, MA, 1955; PhD, U. B.C., 1963. Sr. math. tchr. D.A.V. High Sch., Nairobi, Kenya, 1955-56; tchr. math. Tanzania, 1956-58; teaching asst. U. B.C., 1958-61, teaching fellow, 1961-63, stats. lab. instr., 1959-61, lectr. stats., 1961-63; asst. prof. math. U. Calgary, Can., 1963-66; assoc. prof. math. Portland State U., Oreg., 1966-69, prof. math. Oreg., 1969—. Contbr. articles to profl. jours.; referee profl. jours., reviewer profl. jours. Mem. Inst. Math. Stats. Home: 4016 Orchard Dr Lake Oswego OR 97035-2406 Office: Portland State U Dept Math PO Box 751 Portland OR 97207-0751 Office Phone: 503-725-3627. Business E-Mail: ahujaj@pdx.edu.

AIBEL, HOWARD JAMES, arbitrator, mediator; b. NYC, Mar. 24, 1929; m. Katherine Webster, June 6, 1952 (dec. Feb. 22, 2006); children: David Webster, Daniel Walter, Jonathan Brown. AB magna cum laude, 1950; JD cum laude, Harvard U., 1951. Bar: N.Y. 1952. Assoc. White & Case, NYC, 1952-57; trade regulation counsel GE, 1957-60, spl. litigation counsel elec. equipment antitrust cases, 1960-64; antitrust counsel ITT Corp., NYC, 1964-66, v.p., assoc. gen. counsel, 1966-68, sr. v.p., gen. counsel, 1968-87, exec. v.p., gen. counsel, 1987-92, exec. v.p., chief legal officer, 1992-94; ptnr. LeBoeuf Lamb Greene & MacRae, NYC, 1994-99, of counsel, 1999-2001. Vice chmn. Fund for Modern Cts., 1985-95; mem. AAA/ABA/AMA Com. Health Care Dispute Resolution, 1997-2000, trustee, Sacred Heart U. Fairfield, CT, 2003—; dir. Farrel Corp., 1994-2005. Mem. vis. com. Northwestern U. Law Sch., 1984—90; mem. adv. com. Corp. Counsel Ctr., chmn., 1986—87; trustee Lawyers Com. for Civil Rights, 1991—95, U. Bridgeport, 1989—91, chmn. adv. com. Sch. Law, 1987—92; cons. trustee Westport Nature Ctr. for Environ. Activities; mem. dean's adv. com. Harvard Law Sch., 2004—; commr. Conservation Commn., Weston, Conn., 2004—; trustee Westport Country Playhouse, 2005—; bd. dirs. Alliance of Resident Theatres, NY, 1986—, chmn. NY, 1989—2002, chmn. emeritus NY, 2002—; bd. dirs., 1st v.p. Westport Arts Ctr., 1993—96. Ret. lt. comdr. USNR, 1946—66. Fellow Am. Bar Found. (life); mem. ABA (bus. law sect. corp. governance 1994-98), Am. Law Inst. (elected mem.), Am. Arbitration Assn. (chmn. exec. com. 1992-95, chmn. bd. dirs. 1995-98), Assn. Gen. Counsel, pres. Harvard Law Sch. Assn. NY, 1992-94, v.p. Harvard Law Sch. Assn., 1994-2002, Am. Judicature Soc. (bd. dirs. 1994-2001, exec. com. 1996-2001), Harvard Club NYC. Democrat. Unitarian Universalist. Home and Office: 183 Steep Hill Rd Weston CT 06883-1924 Home Phone: 203-227-0738. Personal E-mail: howardaibel@sbcglobal.net. Business E-Mail: hjaibel@post.harvard.edu.

AIDINOFF, M(ERTON) BERNARD, retired lawyer; b. Newport, RI, Feb. 2, 1929; s. Simon and Esther (Miller) A.; m. Celia Spiro, May 30, 1956 (dec. June 28, 1984); children: Seth G., Gail M.; m. Elsie V. Newburg, Nov. 29, 1996. BA, U. Mich., 1950; LLB magna cum laude, Harvard U., 1953. Bar: D.C. 1953, N.Y. 1954. Law clk. to Judge Learned Hand, U.S. Ct. of Appeals, NYC, 1955-56; with Sullivan & Cromwell, NYC, 1956-63, ptnr., 1963-96, sr. counsel, 1997—. Bd. dirs. Am. Internat. Group Inc., 1984-06, Goldman Sachs Philanthropy Fund; mem. adv. com. to IRS commr., 1979-80, 85-86. Editor in chief The Tax Lawyer, 1974-77. Trustee Spence Sch., 1971-79; mem. adv. com. Gibbs Bros. Found., 1965-94; mem. vis. com. Harvard U. Law Sch., 1976-82, 99-05; adv. dir. Met. Opera Assn., 1989-02; chmn. bd. dirs. St. Luke's Chamber Ensemble, 1988-01, chmn. emeritus, 2001—; pres. Soc. Friends of Touro Synagogue, 2002-03; chair Touro Synagogue Found., 2003-06. 1st lt. JAGC, AUS, 1953-55. Recipient Judge Learned Hand award Am. Jewish Com., 1997. Mem.: ABA (vice chmn. sect. taxation 1974—77, chmn.-elect 1981—82, chmn. 1982—83, chmn. commn. taxpayer compliance 1983—88, Ho. of Dels. 1988—91, sect. taxation Disting. Svc. award 2003), Am. Law Inst. (chmn. tax program com. 1988—, John Minor Wisdom award 1995), Assn. Bar City of N.Y. (exec. com. 1974—78, chmn. exec. com. 1977—78, v.p. 1978—79, chmn. taxation com. 1979—81, chmn. govt. ethics com. 1988—90), NY State Bar Assn., The Parks Coun. (bd. dirs. 1995—97), Human Rights First (bd. dirs. 1986—, treas. 1997—2002), Coun. Fgn. Rels., East Hampton Hist. Soc. (trustee 1983—89, 1990—95), Found. for a Civil Soc. (bd. dirs. 1994—, vice chmn. 1997—98, chmn. 1999—2006), Guild Hall (trustee 1989—94, treas. 1993—94, 1995—2002, trustee 1995—2003), Met. Club, Century Assn., India Ho., Phi Beta Kappa. Home: 980 5th Ave New York NY 10021 Office: Sullivan & Cromwell 125 Broad St New York NY 10004-2498 Office Phone: 212-558-3708. E-mail: aidinoffmb@sullcrom.com.

AIELLO, GENNARO C., insurance company executive; b. Ridgway, Pa., Dec. 16, 1953; s. Victor C. and Victoria I. (Bevacqua) A.; m. Cynthia K. Medvid, Sept. 20, 1975; children: Erin M., Kathryn T. BS, Gannon U., 1975; postgrad., Pa. State U. 1974—78. Lic. ins. agt., real estate agt. Sales rep. Met. Ins. Co., DuBois, Pa., 1975—80; owner, agt. Ins. Mktg. Assocs., Ridgway, 1980—86; acct. exec. Pa. Mfrs. Assn. Group, Ridgway, 1986—94; acct. mgr. EBI Cos., Erie, Pa., 1994—98; comml. account mgr., pres. Anderson and Kime Ins., Inc., Ridgway, 1998—. Gen. mgr. Wolf Run Marina, Warren, Pa., 1978-79; contr. U.S. Coal, Inc., Ridgway, 1981-83; realtor Anderson and Kime, St. Marys, Pa., 1983—; bd. dirs. Cmty. Nurses, Inc. Bd. dirs., v.p. Ridgway Action for Cmty. Enhancement, 1986-88, W.R.C. Cmty. Health Svcs., 2000—; chmn. St. Leo's Home and Sch. Assn., Ridgway, 1989-91; bd. dirs. St. Leo's Parish Coun., 1986-90, 2000, pres. sports assn., 1988-91; pres. Elk County Coun. Arts, 1991-92, v.p., 1990-91, pres., 1991-92; pres. Ridgway Independence Festival Inc., 1990-94; v.p., bd. dirs. Outdoor Companions Inc., 1991, Citizens Against Phys., Sexual and Emotional Abuse, 1992-93; treas. Ridgway Cmty. Nurses, 2000-05; bd. dirs. Ridgway Heritage Coun.; bd. dirs., treas. Ridgway Ambulance Corp., 2000—; chmn. Cmty. Nurses Homehealth Support Svcs., 2002—; dir., treas. Elk County Freshwater Assn., 2006—. Mem. Johnsonburg C. of C. (bd. dirs., pres. 1989—), Ridgway-Elk County C. of C. (dir. 2007-), Elk-Cameron Bd. Realtors, Jaycees (pres. local chpt. 1986-87), Ducks Unltd. (spons. chmn. 1987-88), Elk County Country Club (bd. dirs. 1991-95, v.p. 1992-93, pres. 1993-95), Rotary (pres. Johnsonburg lodge 1980-81), KC (3d degree). Avocations: hunting, fishing, archery, boating, golf. Home: 220 Montmorenci Ave Ridgway PA 15853-1615 Office: Anderson and Kime Ins 212 Main St Ridgway PA 15853-0507 Home Phone: 814-776-1199.

AIELLO, MICHAEL BENJAMIN, secondary school educator; b. San Francisco, May 1, 1947; s. Benjamin Richardo and Mary Alice Aiello; m. Florence Grace Simmons, Nov. 28, 1968; children: Jonathan Michael, Thomas Benjamin. BA in Zoology, U. Calif., Santa Barbara, 1969, MA in Cellular and Organismal Biology, 1970. Cert. tchr. Calif. Classroom tchr. San Luis Obispo (Calif.) HS, 1970—. Mem. Calif. Commn. for Establishment of Content and Performance Stds., Calif. State Dept. Edn., Sacramento, 1997—98, mem. Commn. for Establishment of Performance Stds. for the Pub. Sch. Sys., 1998—99; mem. Commn. for Establishment of Content and Performance Stds. for Tchr. Edn. Programs, Calif. State Dept. of Edn., 1999—2001. Founder Troop 104 Boy Scouts Am., Atascadero, Calif., 1984—89. Named Outsatnding Secondary Sci. Tchr., Sigma Xi, 1981—83, Calif. State Tchr. of Yr., 1997; recipient cert. of recognition and commendation, Calif. State Dept. Edn., 1988—89, Ctrl. Coast Outstanding Educator award, AIAA, Vandenburg AFB, 1993—94, Nat. Educator award, Milken Family Found., 1997. Mem.: Am. Assn. Physics Tchrs. (licentiate). Home: 7435 Sonora Ave Atascadero CA 93422 Office: San Luis Obispo HS 1499 San Luis Dr San Luis Obispo CA 93401 Office Phone: 805-596-4040. E-mail: morfaiello@charter.net.

AIGLER, WILLIAM FRANK, lawyer; b. Bellewe, Ohio, July 20, 1916; s. Allan Garfield and Magdalene Louise Aigler; m. Nancy B. Aigler (dec.); children: Mark, Thomas; m. Marjorie B. Aigler, Apr. 8, 1989. BA, U. Mich., Ann Arbor, 1938, JD, 1943; HLLD (hon.), Heidelberg Coll., Tiffin, Ohio, 1994. Bar: Ohio 1943. Atty. Garfield, Baldwin, Cleve., 1943—52, Aigler Law Office, Bellevue, Ohio, 1952—. Mem. bd. trustees Heidelberg Coll., 1972—96, emeritus trustee, 1996—, vice chair bd., 1979—89, chair bd., 1989—94. Bd. dirs. homeland ministry United Ch. of Christ, vice chmn. bd. homeland ministry, 1977—87, chmn. bd. homeland ministry, 1985—87. Mem.: ABA, Ohio State Bar Assn. Republican. Avocation: sailing. Office: Aigler Law Office PO Box 157 202 W Main St Bellevue OH 44811 Office Phone: 419-483-0867.

AIGNER, DENNIS JOHN, economics professor, consultant; b. LA, Sept. 27, 1937; s. Herbert Lewis and Della Geraldine (Balasek) A.; m. Vernita Lynne White, Dec. 21, 1957 (div. May 1977); children: Mitchell A., Annette N., Anita L., Angela D.; m. Gretchen Camille Bertolet, Dec. 22, 1992. BS, U. Calif.-Berkeley, 1959, MA, 1962, PhD, 1963. Asst. prof. econs. U. Ill., Urbana, 1962-67; from assoc. prof. to prof. U. Wis., Madison, 1967-76; prof., chmn. dept. econs. U. So. Calif., LA, 1976-88; dean grad. sch. mgmt. U. Calif., Irvine, 1988-97, prof. grad. sch. mgmt., 1988—2007, prof. emeritus, 2007—, assoc. dean sch. environ. sci. and mgmt. Santa Barbara, 1998-2000, acting dean, 2000-01, dean, 2001—05, adj. prof., 2005—07. Pres. Dennis Aigner Inc., L.A., 1978—; dir. Analysis Group Econs. Author: Introduction to Statistical Decision Making, 1968, Basic Econometrics, 1971; editor: Latent Variables in Socio-Economic Models, 1977; co-editor: Jour. Econometrics, 1972-91. Fulbright fellow Belgium, 1970, Israel, 1983, Bren fellow U. Calif. Santa Barbara, 1998-2005; NSF grantee, 1968-70, 70-72, 73-76, 79-81, 84-86. Fellow Econometric Soc.; mem. Am. Statis. Assn., Am. Econ. Assn. Office: Merage Sch Business Univ California Irvine CA 92697 Office Phone: 949-824-6229. Business E-Mail: djaigner@uci.edu.

AIGNER-CLARK, JULIE, consumer products company executive; m. William Clark; 2 children. Attended, Mich. State U. Former English and Art tchr.; founder The Baby Einstein Co. (acquired by Walt Disney Co.), 1997—2001; founder, CEO Aigner Clark Creative, The Safe Side (affiliated co.), 2002—. Cons. with husband Walt Disney Co., 2001—; started with John Walsh The Safe Side; created Memory Lane. Recipient Entrepreneur of the Yr. award, Ernst & Young, Entrepreneur of the Yr. award: Most Philanthropic Co., Most Innovative Bus. and Best Small Co., Working Mother's, Disting. Alumni award, Mich. State U., 2003. Achievements include appearances on The Oprah Winfrey Show, Entertainment Tonight, Live! With Regis and Kelly, The View and The John Walsh Show; feature articles in USA Today, The New York Times, The Washington Post, The Wall Street Journal, Los Angeles Times, Time Magazine, People Magazine, Redbook, Elle, Entrepreneur, Parenting Magazine, Child Magazine, Baby Talk and Working Mother; The Baby Einstein Company and its products have won several awards from family/retail magazines and educational foundations; The Safe Side produces videos that teaches young kids about avoiding dangerous situations, like abduction and abuse; Memory Lane creates videos and CD's that entertain people who suffer from memory loss diseases like Alzheimer's and dementia. Office: The Safe Side 9285 Teddy Ln Ste 215 Littleton CO 80163 Office Phone: 303-649-9374, 866-723-3022. Office Fax: 303-706-9799. Business E-Mail: aignerclark@mac.com.*

AIKAWA, JERRY KAZUO, internist, educator; b. Stockton, Calif., Aug. 24, 1921; s. Genmatsu and Shizuko (Yamamoto) A.; m. Chitose Aihara, Sept. 20, 1944; 1 son, Ronald K. AB, U. Calif., 1942; MD, Wake Forest Coll., 1945. Intern, asst. resident N.C. Baptist Hosp., 1945-47; NRC fellow in med. scis. U. Calif. Med. Sch., 1947-48; NRC, AEC postdoctoral fellow in med. scis. Bowman Gray Sch. Medicine, 1948-50, instr. internal medicine, 1950-53, asst. prof., 1953; established investigator Am. Heart Assn., 1952-58; exec. officer lab. service Univ. Hosps., 1958-61, dir. lab. services, 1961-83, dir. allied health program, 1969—, assoc. dean allied health program, 1983—, pres. med. bd.; assoc. dean clin. affairs asst. prof. U. Colo. Sch. Medicine, 1953- 60, asso. prof. medicine, 1960-67, prof., 1967—, prof. biometrics, 1974—, assoc. dean clin. affairs, 1974—. Pres. Med. bd. Univ. Hosps. Fellow ACP, Am. Coll. Nutrition; mem. Western Soc. Clin. Research, So. Soc. Clin. Research, Soc. Exptl. Biology and Medicine, Am. Fedn. Clin. Research, AAAS, Central Soc. Clin. Research, AMA, Assn. Am. Med. Colls., Phi Beta Kappa, Sigma Xi, Alpha Omega Alpha Home: 501 E Ironwood DR Phoenix AZ 85020-1044 Office: Univ Of Colo Hsc Ob Gyn 12303 NE 130th Ln Ste 230 Kirkland WA 98034-3041

AIKEN, CLAY (CLAYTON HOLMES AIKEN), singer; b. Raleigh, NC, Nov. 30, 1978; s. Vernon Grissom and Faye (Parker) Aiken. Student, U. NC at Charlotte. Founder Bubel/Aiken Found. for children. Singer: (single) This is the Night, 2003, (albums) Measure of a Man, 2003 (triple platinum), Merry Christmas with Love, 2004, A Thousand Different Ways, 2006; singer: (with various artists) American Idol Season 2: All Time, 2003; singer, runner up (TV series) American Idol: The Search for a Superstar, 2003; performer: Miss America Pageant, 2003, An American

Idol Christmas, 2003, The Nick at Nite Holiday Special, 2003, Fromage, 2003; co-author (with Allison Glock): (books) Learning to Sing: Hearing the Music in Your Life, 2004. Apptd. mem. President's Com. for People with Intellectual Disabilities. Address: Clay Aiken Official Fan Club PO Box 90217 Raleigh NC 27675 Office: Bubel/Aiken Found PO Box 90307 Raleigh NC 27675 Address: c/o The Firm Mgmt Agy Jacobson & Colfin PC 19 W 21st St New York NY 10010

AIKEN, MICHAEL THOMAS, former academic administrator; b. El Dorado, Ark., Aug. 20, 1932; s. William Floyd and Mary (Gibbs) Aiken; m. Catherine Comet, Mar. 28, 1969; 1 child, Caroline R. BA, U. Miss., 1954; MA, U. Mich., 1955, PhD, 1964. Asst. prof. U. Wis., Madison, 1963—67, assoc. prof., 1967—70, prof., 1970—84, assoc. dean coll. arts and scis., 1980—82; prof. U. Pa., Phila., 1984—93, dean sch. arts and scis., 1985—87, provost, 1987—93; chancellor U. Ill., Urbana, 1993—2001, Champaign/Urbana, 1993—2001. Co-author: The Dynamics of Idealism, 1971, Economic Failure, Alienation, and Extremism, 1968; co-editor: Complex Organizations: Critical Perspectives, 1981, The Structures of Community Power, 1970. Mem.: Am. Sociol. Assn. (sec. 1986—89). Office Phone: 307-587-7506. E-mail: windymt22@aol.com.

AIKEN, PETER HAYNES, systems engineer, educator, architect, consultant, data engineer; b. Washington, Jan. 17, 1959; s. Benjamin Hayes and Susan (Benck) Aiken. BS, Va. Commonwealth U., Richmond, 1981, MS, 1984; PhD, George Mason U., Fairfax, Va., 1989. Sr. engr. Va. Commonwealth U., Richmond, 1980-85, asst. prof. info. systems Sch. Bus., 1992-98, assoc. prof. infosys., dir. Inst. for Data Rsch., 1998—; rsch. asst. George Mason U., 1985-89, vis. asst. prof., 1989-93, dir. Hypermedia Tech. Lab., 1989—93; computer scientist Ctr. for Info. Mgmt. US Dept. Def., Vienna, Va., 1992—97; CEO Data Blueprint, 1999—. Cons. many leading internat. orgns. including Carnegie-Mellon U., Deutsche Bank, Eli Lilly & Co., Hoffman La Roche Inc., Mattel, Time Life, Inc. Office Sec. Def., numerous others. Author: Data Reverse Engineering, 1995; author: (with W. C. Fikelstein) Building Corporate Portals Using XML, 1999; author: (with David Allen) XML for Data Managers, 2004, 2d edit., 2006. Finalist IT Builders award, Greater Richmond Tech. Coun., 2006; recipient Internat. Achievement award, Data Mgmt. Assn. Internat., 2001, Cmty. award, 2005; scholar George Mason Inst., 1985—88. Mem.: IEEE (sr.), Assn. Computing Machinery. Avocations: electric bass, horseback riding. Office: School of Bus Dept of ISY 1015 Floyd Ave Richmond VA 23284-4000 Home: 13155 Country Garden Ln Montpelier VA 23192-3028 Office Phone: 804-521-4056. Office Fax: 804-828-8884. Business E-Mail: paiken@acm.org.

AIKEN, VERNOY FRED, government agency administrator; b. Atlanta, Jan. 30, 1938; s. Vernoy Grady and Anne Whitehead Aiken; m. Sue Carol Camp, Aug. 1, 1959; 1 child, Susan Leigh Aiken Grier. Student, U. Ga., 1960; LLB, Atlanta Law Sch., 1965; banking cert., La. State U., 1969. V.p. Cobb Bank and Trust, Smyrna, Ga., 1973—79; owner Alfredo's Restaurant, Dallas, Ga., 1975—89; state rep. Ga. State Ho. Reps., Atlanta, 1980—92; dist. rep. U.S. Congressman Newt Gingrich, 1992—97; dist. dir., sr. dist. rep. U.S. Congressman Bob Barr, Marietta, Ga., 1997—2003; econ. devel. and devel. gov. rels. specialist Ga. Dept. Labor, Atlanta, 2003—. Bd. mem. SafePath Child Advocacy Ctr.; active No. Ga. Svcs. for Blind and IOW Vision, Cancer Crusade, March of Dimes; past pres. Smyrna Rotary, Marietta-Metro Rotary. Sgt. Ga. Air Nat. Guard. Named Outstanding Legislator, Ga. Mcpl. Assn., 1980. Mem.: Cobb County C. of C. (pres. 1976), Jaycees. Republican. Avocations: reading, golf, watching College football, Nascar auto racing. Home: 4020 Pineview Dr Smyrna GA 30080 Office: Ga Dept Labor Ste 650 148 International Blvd Atlanta GA 30303-1751 Office Phone: 404-232-3789.

AIKENS, MARTHA BRUNETTE, park service administrator; b. Jayess, Miss., Aug. 23, 1949; d. Walter and Elnora La Doris (Bridges) A. BS in Social Sci., Alcorn State U., 1971; postgrad., George Williams Coll., 1974, Fla. Internat. U., 1977, George Washington U., 1979, Pa. State U., 1979, U. So. Calif., DC Ext., 1980. Social worker Pearl River County Devel. Corp., Picayune, Miss., 1971—72; environ. ednl. specialist Nat. Park Svc., Homestead, Fla., 1973—75, environ. ednl. coord., 1973—75, comm. specialist, 1976—78; park mgr. Bklyn., 1978—79, Dept. Interior's Mgmt. Program, 1979—80, St. Augustine, Fla., 1979—83, Washington, 1983—88; dir. tng. and employee development Nat. Park Svc., 2002—. Instr., cons. Coll. African Wildlife Mgmt., Tanzania, 1980. Fed. Law Enforcement Tng. Ctr., Glynco, Ga., 1983—, Stephen T. Mather Employee Devel. Ctr., Harper's Ferry, W.Va., 1988—91; supt. Independence Nat. Hist. Pk., Phila., 1991—2002; chair Nat. Pk. Svc. Women's Conf., New Orleans, 1991. Author: tchrs. guides on Everglades Nat. Park, 1973—76, park brochure, 1977; contbr. chapters to books chpts. to books. Active Dept. Interior's Partnership in Edn. Commn., Washington, 1983—, Fed. Interagy Commn. on Edn., Washington, 1983—, Nat. Park Svc. Employee Rels. Task Force, Washington, 1983—, 21st Century Task Force, 1988—, Salt River Bay Nat. Hist. Pk. and Ecol. Preserve Adv. Commn., 1993—, Strategic Planning Task Force, Atlanta, 1981—83, S.E. Regional Equal Opportunity Commn., Atlanta, 1982—83; bd. trustees Walnut St. Theatre, Phila., 1993—; bd. dirs. Peopling of Phila., 1993—; mem. Leading by Example, 1992—. Recipient Star 104.5 Woman of Yr. award, 1993, Image award, YWCA. Office: Dept Training & Employee Devel Nat Park Svc 1849 C St NW Washington DC 20240

AIKINS, CANDACE SUE, music educator, consultant; b. Pitts., Feb. 7, 1973; d. Ronald Leason and Bonnie Graham Aikins. MusB, Grove City Coll., Pa., 1995; MusM, Carnegie Mellon U., Pitts., 1997. Ch. organist Vandergrift Presbyn. Ch., Pa., 1988—94; ch. organist, choir dir. Natrona Heights Presbyn. Ch., Pa., 1994—; tchr. music Ambridge HS, 1998, Moniteau Jr./Sr. HS, West Sunbury, 1999—2001, Valley HS, New Kensington, 2001—02, Highlands Sch. Dist., Natrona Heights, 2002—04; cons. music Mmacmillan/McGraw Hill, NYC, 2004—. Fellow, Carnegie Mellon U., 1995. Mem.: Am. Guild Organists, Pa. Music Educators Assn., Music Educators Nat. Conf., Kappa Delta Pi. Republican. Presbyterian. Home: 127 E Adams Ave Vandergrift PA 15690

AIKMAN, ALBERT EDWARD, lawyer; b. Norman, Okla., Mar. 11, 1922; s. Albert Edwin and Thelma Annette (Brooke) A.; m. Shirley Barnes, June 24, 1944; children: Anita Gayle, Priscilla June, Rebecca Brooke. BS, Tex. A&M U., 1947; JD cum laude, So. Meth. U., 1948, LLM, 1954. Bar: Tex. (no. dist.) 1948, U.S. Supreme Ct. 1956, U.S. Ct. Appeals (5th dist.), U.S. Tax Ct. Tax ct. staff atty. Phillips Petroleum Co., Amarillo, Tex., 1948-49; sole practice pvt. practice, Amarillo, Tex., 1949-53; tax counsel Magnolia Petroleum Co. (Mobil), Dallas, 1953-56; ptnr. Locke, Purnell, Boren, Laney & Neely, Dallas, 1973-81; of counsel Pickens Energy Corp., Dallas, 1981-96, Ptnrs. in Exploration, Dallas, 1997—; couns. Ptnrs. in Exploration, LLC, Dallas, 1997—. Contbr. articles to profl. jours. Served in inf. U.S. Army, 1943-45. Mem. ABA, Tex. Bar Assn., Dallas Bar Assn. Methodist. Personal E-mail: aikmanae@aol.com.

AIKMAN, TROY, sportscaster, retired professional football player; b. West Covina, Calif., Nov. 21, 1966; Student, U. Okla., Norman, UCLA. Quarterback Dallas Cowboys, 1989—2000; color commentator Fox, 2001, mem. lead announcing crew, 2002—. Mem. Super Bowl Championship Team, 1992, 93, 95. Co-host (with Brad Sham) weekly radio show, 1989—2000, co-host (with Pat Summerall) TV program, co-host (with Bruce Murray) Troy Aikman Football Show, Sporting News Radio, 2003. Founder The Troy Aikman Found., 1992—. Named Super Bowl MVP, 1992, TV's Top Newcomer, Sports Illus., 2001; named to Sporting News Coll. All-Am. team, 1988, Pro Bowl team, 1991, 1992, 1993, 1994, 1996, Sporting News NFL All-Pro team, 1993, NFL Hall of Fame, 2006. Mailing: The Troy Aikman Found PO Box 3427 Coppell TX 75019 also: SPRINGboard Agency PO Box 581 Grapevine TX 76099*

AILEEN-DONOHEW, PHYLLIS AUGUSTA, educational consultant; b. Cin., Aug. 27, 1948; d. Earl John and Mary Roth (Groh) Wilson; m. Robert Lewis Donohew, Oct. 19, 1998; children: Kimberly Aileen Braun, Kelly Augusta Chin-Yee, Kristopher Adam Braun stepchildren: Robert Lewis Donohew Jr., Susan Kerry Schneider, John Patrick Donohew. AA with high distinction, Somerset CC, Ky., 1993; BS in Comm. summa cum laude, U. Ky., Lexington, 1995, MA in Comm., 1995, PhD in Higher Edn., 2003. Gen. office acctg. Bendix Corp., Cin., 1966—71; ind. cons. pub. rels., devel., seminars Cin., 1971—95; comml./indsl. chem. specialist, ter. sales mgr. Phillips Supply Co., Cin., 1974—82; corp. exec., dist. sales mgr. Owens, Mpls., 1982—86; realtor, v.p., owner R and L Realtors, Inc., Sarasota, Fla., 1986—90; grant adminstr. fed. part B, Kera at-risk programming, family literacy programming, parent and child edn. Pulaski County Schs., Somerset, 1990—93; pvt. practice Mt. Sterling, Ky., 1995—. Cons. devel. and fund raising U. Ky. Coll. of Comm., Lexington, 1993—95; rsch. asst., devel., pub. rels. U. Ky. Appalachian Ctr., Lexington, 1993—95; adj. faculty orgnl. comms., cons. bus. and curriculum devel. Midway (Ky.) Coll., 1995—96; field interviewer U. Ky. Survey Rsch. Ctr., Lexington, 1995; rsch. asst. to dir. grad. studies U. Ky. Coll. of Edn., Lexington, 1996—99; prodr. conf. presentation The Charism of the Carmelite Cloistered; presenter in field. Contbr. chapters to books. Founding team mem. Archdiocese of Cin., 1977—78; retreat coord., educator Incarnation Parish, Sarasota, 1977—82; adv. bd. mem. Montgomery County Arts Coun., Mt. Sterling, 2004—05; adviser, spkr. Transitional Support for Displaced Homemakers, Somerset, 1991—94; coach, judge Nat. Forensic League, Sarasota, 1963—85. Recipient Lyman T. Johnson Grad. fellowship, U. Ky. Fellowship Bd., 1996—99, Commonwealth scholarship, U. Ky. Merit Bd., 1995, full acad. scholarship, Somerset C.C. Fin. Aid Bd., 1991—93, Disting. Svc. award, Mirror Student Newspaper Faculty Advisor, 1991—93. Fellow: U. of Ky. Fellows Soc. (life); mem.: Mt. Notre Dame H.S. (assoc.), U. of Ky. Alumni Assn. (assoc.), Ky. Comm. Assn. (assoc.; editl. bd. 1994—98), Ky. Vineyard Assn. (assoc.). Democrat. Roman Catholic. Avocations: reading, walking, cross stitch. Home: 1428 Lemon Bay Dr Englewood FL 34223 Office: 5488 Howards Mill Rd Mount Sterling KY 40353 Home Phone: 941-473-4023; Office Phone: 859-585-3673. Office Fax: 859-498-7496. Business E-Mail: aileen@uky.edu.

AILES, ROGER EUGENE, broadcast executive; b. Warren, Ohio, May 15, 1940; s. Robert Eugene and Donna Marie (Cunningham) Ailes; m. Elizabeth Tilson, Feb. 14, 1998; 1 child. B.F.A., Ohio U., 1962, D in Communications (hon.), 1989. Assoc. dir. Sta. KYW-TV, Cleve., 1962-63, prodr., dir., 1963-65; prodr. Mike Douglas Show Westinghouse Broadcasting Corp., Phila., 1965-67, exec. prodr., 1967-68; exec. prodr. TV for Richard M. Nixon, 1968; chmn. Ailes Comm., Inc., NYC, 1969—92; exec. v.p. TV News Inc., NYC, 1975-76; pres. CNBC, NYC, 1993-96, America's Talking, NYC, 1993; chmn., CEO, Fox News, NYC, 1996—; exec. editor FOXNews.com, 2000—; chmn. Fox Television Stations, 2005—. Former cons. WCBS-TV; communications cons. to polit. and bus. leaders; v.p. Conf. Personal Mgrs. Author: You Are the Message: Secrets of the Master Communicators, 1987; producer: Broadway mus. Mother Earth, 1972, (play) Hot-L Baltimore, 1973-76 (4 Obie awards, 1973); exec. producer, dir.: (TV spl.) The Last Frontier, 1974, Television and the Presidency, 1984 (Emmy award); producer, dir.: (TV spl.) Fellini: Wizards, Clowns and Honest Liars (Emmy nominee 1977); exec. producer: Tomorrow: Coast to Coast, 1981, The Rush Limbaugh Show, 1992-96, A Current Affair, The Maury Povich Show, The Leeza Show; co-exec. prodr.: An All-Star Salute to Our Troops, 1991. Polit. cons. Reagan '84, Bush '88. Recipient 2 Emmy awards for The Mike Douglas Show, 1967, 68, award for Shakespeare prodn., Fine Arts Mag., 1964, Liberty Bell award, Advt. Alliance Phila., 1971, Commendation award for contbn. comm., Ohio U., 1972, Silver Cir. award, Nat. Acad. TV Arts and Scis., 1999. Mem. AFTRA, Dirs. Guild Am., Radio and TV News Dirs. Assn. Office: Fox News 1211 Ave of Americas New York NY 10036

AILLONI-CHARAS, DAN, marketing executive; b. Ploiesti, Romania, May 22, 1930; came to U.S., 1950, naturalized, 1960; s. Max and Felicia (Lupescu) Charas; m. Miriam C. Taytelbaum, Oct. 8, 1957; children: Ethan Benjamin, Orrin, Adam. AB with honors, U. Calif., Berkeley, 1952, MA, 1953; PhD, NYU, 1968. Mem. editl. staff San Francisco Call Bull., 1953-54; exec. sec. TAHAL, 1955-56; project dir. Marplan divsn. Interpub., NYC, 1958-60; supr. advt. studies NBC, NYC, 1960-62; dir. consumer and comm. rsch. Forbes Rsch., Inc., NYC, 1962-63; mgr. market rsch. Chesebrough-Pond's, Inc., NYC, 1963-64, new products mgr., 1964-68, mgr. internat. mktg. services dept., 1968-69; pres. Stratmar Sys., Inc., Port Chester, NY, 1969-91, CEO, 1991—2001, chmn., 2001—; asst., then prof. mktg. Pace U., 1963-85. Mem. adv. bd. Premium Incentive Show, 1986-92, Nat. Premium Incentive Show, 1987-92; lectr. Israel Inst. Tech., 1956-58, dir. extension divsn. no. region, 1956-58. Author: Promotion: A Guide to Effective Promotional Planning, Strategies and Execution, 1984; editor: Mktg. Rev., 1960-63, Proc. 1st Ann. Conf. on Rsch. Design, 1964, New Directions in Research Design, 2d Conf., 1965, Planning, 1968-71; bd. editors Jour. Consumer Mktg., 1982—, Jour. of Brand and Product Mgmt., 1991—, Jour. Svc. Mktg., 1992—; contbr. to Brandweek, Mktg. News, Chain Drug Rev., MMR, New Product News. Trustee Inst. Advanced Mktg. Studies, 1965-66, Philharmonic Symphony of Westchester, 1977-80; bd. dirs. Young Men's Bd. Trade, 1960-63, state dir., N.Y. StatJr. C. of C., 1962-63; bd. advisers Ad Expo, 1978; 1st v.p. Student World Affairs Coun. Northern Calif., 1953-54, chmn. Asilomar World Affairs conf., 1954; founder Israel Assn. Grads. Social Scis. & Humanities, 1955; pres. Haifa Jr. C. of C., 1956-57. Coro Found. fellow, 1953; Univ. honors scholar NYU, 1968. Mem. Am. Mktg. Assn. (pres. N.Y. chpt. 1965-66, nat. v.p. 1970-71), Promotion Mktg. Assn. Am. (bd. dirs. 1978-98, chmn. edn. com. 1979-81, 82-91, chmn. premium show com. 1982-91, exec. com. 1986-87, 89-93, 94-95, 96-97, 99-2000, chmn. nat. conf. 1988, 96, v.p. 1989-93, 94-95, chmn. retailers and mfrs. conf. 1992, 93, chmn. in-store mktg. coun. 1993-94), N.Am. Soc. Corp. Planning (bd. dirs. 1970-72), Nat. Assn. Chain Drug Stores (nat. industry adv. bd. 1992—2003), Am. Friends of the Coll. Mgmt. (chmn. 1999-2004), Soc. Profl. Journalists, Nat. Press Club, Coro Alumni Assn. (nat. bd. dirs. 1989-95), Sigma Delta Chi, Phi Sigma Alpha. Office: Stratmar Bldg 109 Willett Ave Port Chester NY 10573-4287 Business E-Mail: dailloni@stratmar.com.

AILMAN, CHRISTOPHER J., investment company executive; b. 1958; m. Robin Ailman; 3 children. BA in Bus. Econs., U. Calif., Santa Barbara, 1980. Chief investment officer Sacramento Employees Retirement Sys. and County of Sacramento; mgr. Wash. State Investment Bd.; chief investment officer Calif. State Tchrs. Retirement Sys. (CalSTRS), Sacramento, 2000—. Named Chief Investment Officer of Yr., Inst. Fiduciary Edn., 2000; recipient Richard L Stoddard Award, 2003, IFE Leadership Award. Office: CalSTRS PO Box 15275 Sacramento CA 95851-0275 Office Phone: 800-228-5453. Office Fax: 916-229-3879.*

AIN, SANFORD KING, lawyer; b. Glen Cove, NY, July 24, 1947; s. Herbert and Victoria (Ben Susan) A.; m. Miriam Luskin, July 12, 1980; children: David Lloyd, Daniel Jason. BA cum laude, U. Wis., 1969; JD, Georgetown U., 1972. Bar: Va. 1972, DC 1973, Md. 1982. Ptnr. Sherman, Meehan, Curtin & Ain P.C., Washington, 1972—2003, Ain & Bank, P.C., Washington, 2003—. Mem. faculty continuing legal edn. program State Bar Va., D.C. Bar, Md. Bar. Named one of 75 Best Lawyers, Washingtonian mag., 2002. Fellow: Am. Coll. Family Trial Lawyers, Am. Acad. Matrimonial Lawyers (pres. D.C. chpt. 1991—94, counsel 1999—2000, pres. D.C. chpt. 2002—06, bd. govs. 2003—05, counsel 2005—06); mem.: Am. Coll. Trial Lawyers, Md. Bar Assn., Va. Trial Lawyers Assn. (diplomate). Office: Ain & Bank PC 1900 M St NW Ste 600 Washington DC 20036-3519 Office Phone: 202-530-3330.

AINBINDER, BRUCE, lawyer; b. Bklyn., Nov. 17, 1961; BS, U. Fla., 1984; MBA, Adelphi U., 1990; JD cum laude, St. John's U., 1993. Bar: NY 1994, US Dist. Ct. Ea., So., No. & We. Districts NY 1994. Ptnr. Wilson, Elser, Moskowitz, Edelman & Dicker LLP, NYC. Mem.: ABA, NY Bar Assn. Office: Wilson Elser Moskowitz Edelman & Sicker LLP 23rd Fl 150 E 42nd St New York NY 10017-5639 Office Phone: 212-490-3000 ext. 2136. Office Fax: 212-490-3038. Business E-Mail: ainbinderb@wemed.com.

AINGE, DANNY RAY, professional sports team executive, retired professional basketball player; b. Eugene, Oreg., Mar. 17, 1959; m. Michele Ainge; children: Ashlee, Austin, Tanner, Taylor, Cooper, Crew. Grad., Brigham Young U., 1981. Player Boston Celtics, 1981—89, Sacramento Kings, 1989—90, Portland Trail Blazers, 1990—92, Phoenix Suns, 1992—95, asst. coach, 1996, head coach, 1996—99; color analyst TNT, 1995—96, 1999; exec. dir. basketball ops. Boston Celtics, 2003—. Player Celebrity Golf Assn. Tour. Active Children's Miracle Network, Spl. Olympics. Named to Oreg. State Sports Hall of Fame, 1999; recipient John Wooden award, 1981, Eastman award, 1981, Silver Anniversary award, NCAA, 2006. Achievements include holding record for most 3-pointers attempted and made in the NBA playoffs; one of 4 players in NBA history to make 1,000 or more career 3-pointers; won NBA Championships as a member of the Celtics, 1984, 86. Avocation: golf. Office: Boston Celtics Fourth Fl 226 Causeway St Boston MA 02114-4714*

AINLAY, STEPHEN CHARLES, academic administrator, educator; b. South Bend, Ind., July 30, 1951; s. Charles William and Dorothy Marie A.; m. Judy Renee Gardner, Aug. 16, 1975; children: Jesse Gardner, Jonathan Charles. BA in Sociology, Goshen Coll., Ind., 1973; MA in Sociology, Rutgers U., 1977, PhD in Sociology, 1981. Asst. prof. Coll. of the Holy Cross, Worcester, Mass., 1982-87, assoc. prof., 1987-93, prof. sociology and anthropology, 1993—, dir. Ctr. for Interdisciplinary and Spl. Studies, 1993—, v.p. for acad. affairs, dean of the Coll., 1996—2006; pres. Union Coll., Schenectady, NY, 2006—. Cons. Am. Found. for the Blind, N.Y.C., 1980-81; vis. scholar St. Edmunds Coll., Cambridge U., Eng., 1987. Author: Day Brought Back My Night, 1989; co-author: Mennonite Entrepreneur, 1995; editor: The Dilemma of Difference, 1986, Making Sense of Modern Times, 1986. Mem. adv. bd. Mass. Assn. for Blind, Worcester, Audio Jour., Worcester, 1992-94; mem. Coun. on Aging, Holden, Mass., 1992-94; mem. exec. com. Colls. of Worcester Consortium, 2002-04. Princeton U. postdoctoral fellow, 1981-82. Mem. Soc. for Sci. Study of Religion, Am. Conf. Acad. Deans. Office: Union Coll Office of the President 807 Union St Schenectady NY 12308-3107 Business E-Mail: ainlays@union.edu.

AINSLEY, P. STEVEN (STEVE AINSLEY), publishing executive; BA, NYU, 1976; grad. Advanced Mgmt. Program, Emory U., 1986. Publ. newspapers Ala., Fla. Maine NY Times Co., 1982—93, publ. The Santa Barbara News-Press, 1993—99, sr. v.p. Regional Newspaper Group, 1999—2003, pres., COO Regional Newspaper Group, 2003—06, publ. Boston Globe, 2006—, head New England Media Group, 2006—. Mem.: So. Newspaper Publishers Assn. (dir. 2004—), Ala. Press Assn. (past. dir.), New England Press Assn. (past. dir.). Office: Boston Globe PO Box 55819 Boston MA B2205*

AINSLIE, GEORGE WILLIAM, psychiatrist; b. Ithaca, NY, Sept. 19, 1944; s. George William and Elizabeth Lee Ainslie; m. Elizabeth Boyd Keeney, June 25, 1966; children: Matthew Forrest, Roger Scott, Eleanor Ruth. BA, Yale Coll., 1965; MD, Harvard Med. Sch., 1969. Diplomate Am. Bd. Psychiatry and Neurology; cert. adult psychiatry. Intern Mary Imogene Bassett Hosp., Cooperstown, NY, 1969-70; resident in psychiatry Mass. Mental Health Ctr., Boston, 1970-71, 73-75; fellow Harvard U. Health Svcs., Cambridge, Mass., 1975-76; asst. clin. dir. Mass. Mental Health Ctr., Boston, 1976-79; psychiatrist VA Med. Ctr., Coatesville, Pa., 1979-90, chief psychiatrist, 1990—. Asst. prof. Jefferson Med. Coll., Phila., 1979-85, assoc. prof., 1985-92; clin. prof. Temple U. Med. Coll., Phila., 1992—; rsch. assoc. Harvard Lab. Exptl. Psychology, Cambridge, Mass., 1967-78. Author: Picoeconomics: The Strategic Interaction of Successive Motivational States Within The Person, 1992, Breakdown of Will, 2001; contbr. articles on motivational conflict to profl. jours. Surgeon, USPHS, 1971-73. Mem. Players Club Swarthmore (stage dir.), Phi Beta Kappa. Avocation: theater. Office: Dept Psychiatry VA Med Ctr 116A Coatesville PA 19320 Home Phone: 610-328-5436; Office Phone: 610-383-0260. Business E-Mail: Ainslie@Coatesville.va.gov, George.Ainslie@va.gov.

AINSWORTH, LOUIS LYNDE, lawyer, manufacturing executive; b. Moline, Ill., Aug. 31, 1947; s. Calvin and Elizabeth (Carney) A.; m. Susan H. Hopper, Mar. 22, 1969; children: Katherine E., Lucy A. BA summa cum laude, Seattle U., 1972; JD cum laude, William Mitchell Coll., St. Paul, 1977. Bar: Minn. 1977, U.S. Dist. Ct. Minn. 1977, U.S. Ct. Appeals (8th cir.) 1981. Assoc., ptnr. Wiese & Cox Ltd., Mpls., 1977-84; ptnr. Henson & Efron, P.A., Mpls., 1984-97; sr. v.p. and gen. counsel Pentair, Inc., St. Paul, 1997—, sec., 2002—. Office: Pentair Inc 5500 Wayzata Blvd Golden Valley MN 55416-1259*

AIONA, JAMES R., JR., lieutenant governor; b. Honolulu, June 8, 1955; m. Vivian Welsh; children: Makana, Ohulani, Kulia, Kaimilani. BA in Polit. Sci., U. of the Pacific; JD, U. Hawaii. Law clk. hon. Wendell K. Huddy Cir. Ct. Judge First Cir. Hawaii, 1981—82; dep. pros. atty. City and County Honolulu, 1982—85, dep. corp. counsel City Attys. Office, 1985—87, chief litigator, 1987—90; family ct. judge 1st Cir. State Hawaii, 1990—93, cir. ct. judge 1st divsn., 1993—96; adminstrv. judge Drug Ct. Program, 1996—98; ret., 1998; pvt. practice, 1997—2002; part-time family dist. ct. judge, 1999—2002; lt. gov. State of Hawaii, Honolulu, 2002—. Asst. basketball coach varsity boys St. Louis H.S.; vol. soccer coach AYSO; vol. youth baseball coach Makakilo-Kapolei; vol. judge H.S. mock trials competition State of Hawaii; bd. mem. The Salvation Army, Reid J.K. Richards Found., Youth At Risk Adv. Coun., Maryknoll Schs., 1995—98. Republican. Office: Ofice Lt Governor Executive Chambers Hawaii State Capitol Honolulu HI 96813 Office Phone: 808-586-0255. Office Fax: 808-586-0231. E-mail: ltgov@hawaii.gov.

AIOSA, CHARLOTTE NELSON, music educator; b. Detroit, Dec. 21, 1949; d. Theron Seth and Vera Charlotte Nelson; m. Angelo Aiosa, Dec. 18, 1993. BS in Music Edn., U. Md., 1972, MusM in Voice Performance, 1977; D in Musical Arts in Voice Performance, U. Mich., 1987. Prof. music Shenandoah Conservatory Music, Shenandoah U., Winchester, Va., 1979—. Chmn. voice divsn. Shenandoah Conservatory Music, Winchester, 1988—98. Recipient Wilkens Faculty Appreciation award, Shenandoah Conservatory Music, 1992; grantee Grad. Assistantship, U. Md., 1977, U. Mich., 1985—86; Regents fellow, Rackham Grad. Sch., U. Mich., 1984—86, Opera scholar Aspen Opera Program, Aspen Music Festival, 1985. Mem.: Nat. Assn. Tchrs. Singing (v.p. Va. chpt. 2001—03, pres. Va. chpt. 2003—05, pres. emeritus Va. chpt. 2005—), Pi Kappa Lamda, Sigma Alpha Iota (life; pres. 1971—72, Svc. award 1972). Office: Shenandoah University 1460 University Dr Winchester VA 22601 Office Phone: 540-665-4580. Office Fax: 540-665-5402. Business E-Mail: caiosa@su.edu.

AIRHART, DOUGLAS L., horticulturist, educator; BS in Renewable Natural Resources, U. Calif., Davis, 1970; MS in Water Resources Mgmt., U. Wis., Madison, 1972; PhD in Plant Sci., U. Ga., Athens, 1977. Cert. arborist Internat. Soc. Arboriculture, 1997. Asst. prof. plant and soil scis. U. Mass., Amherst; mem. faculty to prof. horticulture Tenn. Technol. U., Cookeville, 1984—. Mem. Tenn. Urban Forestry Coun.; mem. bd. trustees Cheekwood Botanic Garden and Fine Arts Ctr., Nashville, 1988—91; charter mem., treas. Cookeville Tree Bd., Tenn., 1988—91. Recipient Rhea McCandliss Profl. Svc. award, Am. Hort. Therapy Assn., 1992. Office: Sch Agr Tenn Technol U PO Box 5034 Cookeville TN 38505 E-mail: dairhart@tntech.edu.

AISEN, ARI, economist, researcher; b. Sao Paulo, Brazil, June 30, 1971; s. Julinho and Miriam Aisen; m. Marina Bassi, Sept. 18, 2005; 1 child, Benjamin. BA in Econs., U. Sao Paulo, 1992; MA in Econs., Hebrew U., Jerusalem, 1997; PhD, U. Calif., LA, 2003. Lectr. U. Calif., LA, 1999—2003; economist Internat. Monetary Fund, Washington, 2003—. Pres. grad. econs. assn. UCLA, 1999—2000; tourist guide Hebrew U., 1995—97; cons. Wong Metals Co., Singapore, 1993—98; economist Banco do Brasil, Sao Paulo, 1992—93. Contbr. articles to profl. jours. Donations asst. Chabad Isreali Ctr., Rockville, Md., 2005—07. Recipient Golda Meir award, Hebrew U. Jerusalem, 1995; fellow, U. Calif., LA, 2003. Mem.: Am. Econs. Assn. Home Phone: 301-279-2196.

AISEN, PAUL S., neurologist, researcher, educator; b. Sept. 1954; MD, Columbia U., 1979. Vice chair, prof. neurology and medicine Georgetown U. Sch. Medicine, dir. Memory Disorders Program; assoc. dir. Alzheimer's Disease Cooperative Study (ADCS) Group. Mem. Neuro-Hitech Affiliated Sci. Adv. Bd., 2006—. Contbr. articles to profl. jours. Office: Divsn Clin Pharmacology Georgetown U Med Ctr, 202B 3900 Reservoir Rd NW Washington DC 20057 Office Phone: 202-687-7337. E-mail: psa@georgetown.edu.*

AISENBERG, IRWIN MORTON, retired lawyer; b. Worcester, Mass., Aug. 8, 1925; s. William and Esther (Lewis) A.; m. Lois P., Sept. 4, 1955 (div. Apr. 1986); children: Karen Sue Portner, Sondra Lee, David Craig, Steven Bennett; m. Hana Jane Barton, June 19, 1999. BS in Chem Engring., Carnegie Mellon U., 1946; JD, Georgetown U., 1957. Bar: DC 1958, US Ct. of Customs and Patent Appeals 1958, US Ct. Appeals (DC cir.) 1958, US Supreme Ct. 1964, NJ 1965, Va. 1969, US Ct. Appeals (fed. cir.) 1982; registered profl. engr., Mass. Patent examiner US Patent Trademark Office, Washington, 1954-57; assoc. atty. Wenderoth, Lind & Ponack, Washington, 1957-63; chief patent counsel Sandoz, Inc., Hanover, NJ, 1963-67; pvt. practice Washington, 1967-75; ptnr. Berman, Aisenberg & Platt, Washington, 1975-91, mng. ptnr., 1980-85; ptnr. Jacobson Holman PLLC, Washington, 1991—2005; ret. Lectr. Franklin Pierce Law Sch., Concord, NH, 1980-88; mem. appeal bd. Nat. Register Health Svc. Providers Psychology, 1987-89. Mem. editl. bd. IDEA, Jour. of Law and Tech., 1981-95, Patent Strategy and Management; author: Attorney's Dictionary of Patent Claims, 1985, with yearly supplements, Patent Law Precedent, 1991, 2d edit., 1992, Modern Patent Law Precedent, 3d edit., 1997, 8th edit., 2007; contbr. articles to profl. jours. Vol. Literacy Coun. Montgomery County, Md., Inc., bd. dirs., 2006—; vol. Housing Opportunities Commn. Montgomery County; rep. payee Mental Health Assn. Served to cpl. US Army, 1950-52. Mem. ABA, Internat. Assn. Protection Indsl. Property, Am. Intellectual Property Law Assn., Am. Arbitration Assn. (mem. panel arbitrators). Clubs: Kenwood Golf Country, Am. Contract Bridge League (life master). Jewish. Achievements include patents in field. Home: 9707 Old Georgetown Rd Bethesda MD 20814-1763 Personal E-mail: iwa25@comcast.net.

AISNER, JOSEPH, oncologist, medical educator; b. Munich, Jan. 5, 1944; came to U.S., 1948; s. Philip and Faye Aisner; m. Seena Feldman, Aug. 31, 1969; children: Dara Lianna, Leon Andrew. BS in Chemistry, Wayne State U., 1965, MD, 1970. Intern Sinai Hosp. Detroit, 1970-71; resident Georgetown U. Hosp., Washington, 1971-72; commd. med. officer USPHS, 1972, advanced through grades to rank 05; clin. assoc. Nat. Cancer Inst., Balt., 1972-75, sr. investigator, 1975-78, chief med. oncology, 1978-81; resigned USPHS, 1982; chief med. oncology U. Md. Cancer Ctr., Balt., 1981-92, dep. dir. clin. affairs, 1982-88, ctr. dir., 1988-93; prof. medicine U. Medicine and Dentistry of N.J., New Brunswick, 1995—, prof. environ. and cmty. medicine, 1996—; assoc. dir. clin. svcs. Cancer Inst. NJ, New Brunswick. Prof. medicine U. Md., 1982-95, prof. oncology, 1982-95, prof. pharmacology, 1985-95, prof. clin. pharmacy, 1987-95, prof. epidemiology preventive medicine, 1993-95; mem. N.J. Legis. Commn. Pain Mgmt., 1998-2000, N.J. Com. to improve outcomes on cancer patients, 1999—. Editor books; contbr. numerous chpts. to books and articles and abstracts to profl. jours. Bd. dirs. Md. Chpt. Am. Cancer Soc., 1988-94, Am. Assn. Cancer Edn., 1990; exec. com. Md. Cancer Consortium, chmn. breast cancer sect., 1992-93, chmn., 1993-95,; mem. Gov.'s Coun. Cancer Prevention, 1991, exec. com., 1991-95; bd. dirs. Md. Children's Cancer Found., 1991-95. Nat. Cancer Inst. grantee, 1982-95, 2000-; named a Top Doctor, NY mag., 2007. Fellow ACP; mem. Am. Fedn. Clin. Rsch., Am. Soc. Clin. Oncology (dir. edn. program 1985-86, bd. dirs. 1991-94), Am. Assn. Cancer Rsch., Cancer Leukemia Group B (bd. dirs. 1982-95, vice chair breast sect. 1980-86), Am. Radium Soc. (sci. program com. 1993-94), Ea. Cooperation Oncology Group (prin. investigator com. 1996—, data audit com. 1999—, sci. adv. com. 2000—, exec. com. 2003-, fin. oversight com. 2005—). Office: Cancer Inst NJ 195 Little Albany St New Brunswick NJ 08903-2681 Office Phone: 732-235-2465. Personal E-mail: aisnerjo@verizon.net. Business E-Mail: aisnerjo@umdnj.edu.*

AITKEN, ANDREW C., lawyer; b. Washington, May 24, 1961; BS, Loyola Coll., Md., 1983; JD, Cath. U. of Am., 1988. Bar: Md. 1988, US Dist. Ct., Dist. of Md. 1989, US Ct. Appeals, Fed. Cir. 1991, US Patent and Trademark Office 2000. Law clk. to Hon. L. Leonard Ruben Cir. Ct. of Montgomery County, Md., 1988—89; ptnr. Intellectual Property Litig. and Patent Prosecution Depts. Venable LLP, Washington, DC. Bd. mem. CYO. Mem.: ABA, Patent Lawyers' Club of Washington, DC, Am. Intellectual Property Law Assn., Md. State Bar Assn. Office: Venable LLP 575 7th St NW Washington DC 20004 Office Phone: 202-344-8165. Office Fax: 202-344-8300. E-mail: acaitken@venable.com.

AITKEN, ASHLEIGH E., lawyer; BA cum laude, Boston Coll., 1997; JD, Univ. So. Calif., 2002. Bar: Calif. Assoc., bus. litigation Morrison & Foerster, Irvine, Calif., 2005—. Commr. Cmty. Services Bd., Anaheim, Calif. Named Rising Star, So. Calif. Super Lawyers, 2005—06; Scholar, State Bar Calif. Leadership Acad., 2005. Mem.: Assn. Bus. Trial Lawyers, Celtic Bar Assn. (bd. dir.), State Bar Calif., Orange County Bar Assn. (bd. dir.), Hispanic Bar Assn. (sec.), Orange County Women Lawyers. Office: Morrison & Foerster 12th Fl 19900 MacArthur Blvd Irvine CA 92612 Office Phone: 949-251-6833. Office Fax: 949-251-0900. Business E-Mail: aaitken@mofo.com.

AITKEN, CHRISTOPHER CHARLES, investment consultant; b. Phila., July 19, 1957; s. Charles Walter and Mary (Brumitt) A.; children: Tracy, Shelby. BS in Acctg., U. Md., 1983. Cert. investment mgmt. analyst. Sr. acct. Price Waterhouse, Washington, 1983-86; sr. v.p. Smith Barney, Balt., 1986—. Named one of Top 100 Fin. Advisors, Barron's Mag. Mem. Assn. Investment Profls., Investment Mgmt. Cons. Assn. Office: Smith Barney 2330 W Joppa Rd Ste 255 Lutherville MD 21093-4600*

AITKEN, CHRISTOPHER R., lawyer; b. Orange, Calif., May 10, 1969; married; 3 children. BA, UCLA, 1992; JD, Univ. So. Calif., LA, 1996. Bar: Calif. 1997. Ptnr., civil trial practice Aitken Aitken & Cohn, Santa Ana, Calif. Bd. chmn. Laura's House. Named a Rising Star, So. Calif. Super Lawyers, 2006. Mem.: William P. Gray Inn of Ct., Assn. Bus. Trial Lawyers, Consumer Attorneys Calif., Orange County Trial Lawyers Assn., Hispanic Bar Assn., State Bar Calif., Orange County Bar Assn. Office: Aitken Aitken & Cohn 3 Imperial Promenade Ste 800 PO Box 2555 Santa Ana CA 92707-0555 Office Phone: 714-434-1424. Office Fax: 714-434-3600. Business E-Mail: chris@aitkenlaw.com.

AITKEN, DOUG, artist; Student, Marymount Coll., Palos Verdes, Calif., 1986—87; BFA, Art Ctr. Coll. Design, Pasadena, Calif., 1991. One-man shows include ACl Project Room, N.Y.C., 1993, 303 Gallery, 1994, 1997, 1998, Pasco Art Ctr., Holiday, Fla., 1994, Taka Ishil Gallery, Tokyo, 1996, 1998, Gallery Side Two, 1998, Jiri Svestka Gallery, Prague, 1998, Doug Lawing Gallery, Houston, 1999, Victoria Miro Gallery, London, 1999, Dallas Mus. Art, 1999, Pitti Discovery Series, Florence, Italy, 1999, Galerie Eva Presenhuber, Zurich, 2005, exhibited in group shows at AC Project Room, N.Y.C., 1991, 1993, 1998, Stux Gallery, 1992, New Mus. Contemporary Art, 1992, Christopher Middendorf Gallery, Washington, 1992, Rushmore Estate, 1993, 303 Gallery, 1993, Santa Monica Mus. Art, 1994, Ma'nes Space, Prague, 1994, Espace Montjoie, Paris, 1994, Flash Art Mus., Trevi, Italy, 1994, Lisson Gallery, London, 1994, Mus. Lab. Art Contemporanea, Rome, 1995, Musee Art Ville Paris, 1995, Elga Wimmer Gallery, N.Y.C., 1996, Lauren Wittles Gallery, 1996, Basilico Fine Arts, 1996, Bard Ctr. Curatorial Studies, Annandale-on-Hudson, 1996, Kunsthalle N.Y., 1996, Kunstraum Vienna, 1996, Galleria Civica Art Modern Contemporanes Turin, Italy, 1996, Bonnefanten Mus., Maastricht, The Netherlands, 1996, Modern Gallery, Ljubljiana, 1997, Tivoli Gallery, 1997, San Casciano Dei Bagni, Italy, 1997, Taka Ishii Gallery, Tokyo, 1997, Galleri Index, Stockholm, 1997, Cubitt Gallery, 1997, Whitney Mus. Am. Art, N.Y.C., 1997, Photographer's Gallery, 1998, Mus. Ludwig, Cologne, Germany, 1998, Walker Art Ctr., 1998, Long Beach (Calif.) Mus. Art, 1998, Galerie Peter Kilchmann, Zurich, 1998. Office: c/o 303 Gallery 525 W 22nd St New York NY 10011-1100

AITKEN, PAUL ARTHUR, composer, conductor; b. Listowel, Ontario, Canada, Nov. 10, 1970; s. Donald Arthur and Elke Aitken; m. Stephanie Michelle Sharp, July 15, 2000; children: Michael Charles, Wilson Arthur. MusB in Edn, U. Western Ont., London, Canada, 1989—93; MusM, So. Ill. U., 1996; DMA, U. Okla., 2006. Lectr. So. Ill. U., Carbondale, Ill., 1996—97; dir. of music ministries Cathedral of Rockies, Boise, Idaho, 2002. Pres. www.FlandersPublications.com, 2006—. Composer: (choral composition) Flanders Fields (Raymond W. Brock Meml. Student Composition Competition, 1999), (choral arrangement) Huron Carol. Mem.: Am. Guild Organists, Am. Choral Dirs. Assn. (regional chair 2003—06, nat. chair 2006). Office: Cathedral of Rockies 717 N 11th St Boise ID 83702 Home Phone: 208-447-8641. Business E-Mail: paitken@boisefumc.org.

AITKEN, WYLIE A., lawyer; b. Detroit, Jan. 4, 1942; AA, Santa Ana Coll., Calif. State Coll.Fullerton; LLB, Marquette U., 1965. Bar: Calif. 1966, U.S. Dist. Ct. (Ctrl. dist. Calif.). Founding ptnr. Aitken Aitken Cohn, Santa Ana, Calif. Assoc. editor: Marquette Law Review, 1963—65; contbr. articles to profl. jours. Named So. Calif. Super Lawyer, OC Bus. Jour., 2004, Atty. of Year, 2006; named one of Top 100 Influential Lawyers, Calif., 1998—2003; named to 500 Leading Lawyers in Am., Lawdragon, 2005; recipient Jurisprudence award, Anti Defamation League, 2003, OCTLA Top Gun award. Mem.: Robert A. Banyard Am. Inns of Ct., Am. Bd. Trial Advocates (trustee, Plaintiff Trial Lawyer of Yr. 1998), Nat. Bd. Trial Advocacy, Assn. Trial Lawyers Am. (mem. bd. govs. 1977—), Calif. Trial Lawyers Assn. (mem. state bd. 1970—73, chmn. consumer protection com. 1972, v.p. 1973—75, pres. 1977), Orange County Trial Lawyers Assn. (Bus. Trial Lawyer of Yr.), State Bar Calif., Celtic Bar Assn. Orange County (founding mem.), Orange County Bar Assn. Office: Aitken Aitken Cohn 3 Imperial Promenade Ste 800 Santa Ana CA 92707 Office Phone: 866-434-1424. E-mail: wylie@aitkenlaw.com.

AIT-SAHALIA, YACINE, finance educator; BS, Ecole Polytechnique, France, 1987; MS in Econs., Ecole Nationale de la Statistique et de Admnistration Economique, France, 1989; PhD, MIT, 1993. Prof. fin. U. Chgo., 1993—98; Otto A. Hack prof. Princeton U., NJ, 1998—. Dir. Bendheim Ctr. Fin. Princeton U., 1998; rschr. in field. Dir. Western Fin. Assn. Office: Princeton Univ Bendheim Ctr Fin 26 Prospect Ave Princeton NJ 08540 Office Phone: 609-258-4015.

AIUTO, RUSSELL, science education consultant; b. Monroe, Mich., July 13, 1934; s. Crispino and Maria (d'Aiuto) A.; m. Nancy Jane Obenauf, Dec. 17, 1955 (dec. 1980); children: Mary T. Carroll, Susan M. Summa; m. Beverly Bradley, Jan. 3, 1981 BA, Ea. Mich. U., 1958, U. Mich., 1995; MA, U. N.C., 1963, PhD, 1971. Tchr. speech, drama Monroe High Sch., Mich., 1958-61; prof. biology Albion Coll., Mich., 1966-82, provost Mich., 1982-85; pres. Hiram Coll., Ohio, 1985-88; div. dir. tchr. preparation and enhancement NSF, Washington, 1988-90; program mgr. Nat. Sci. Tchrs. Assn., Washington, 1990-93, Coun. Ind. Colls., 1993-95. Cons. Gygi Found., Dundee, Mich., 1984—2001; adj. prof. Montgomery Coll., Md., 2005—. Author: Mencken and Sara, 1980, Ring Lardner's America, 1984, Dorothy Parker, 1986; co-author: Science Interactions, 3 vols., 1993; contbr. articles to profl. jours. Vice chmn. Albion Improvement Com., 1983-85; v.p. Patton Ridge Homeowners Corp., 2001-. NSF grantee, 1968 Mem. Sigma Xi, Omicron Delta. Episcopalian. Avocation: collecting books. Home: 9631 Duffer Way Gaithersburg MD 20886-1309

AIZENMAN, MICHAEL, mathematics and physics professor, researcher; b. Aug. 28, 1945; m. Marta Beatriz Gershanik; children: Nurith Celina, Ya'ir Gideon. BS, Hebrew U., Jerusalem, Israel, 1969; PhD, Yeshiva U., 1975. Postdoctoral vis. mem. Courant Inst. Math. Scis. Courant Inst. Math. Scis. NYU, 1974-75, prof., 1987-90; postdoctoral position to asst. prof. physics Princeton (N.J.) U., 1975-82, prof. math. and physics, 1990—; from assoc. prof. to prof. math. and physics Rutgers U., New Brunswick, N.J., 1982-87. Vis. prof. Institut des Hautes Etudes Scientifiques, Bures-sur-Yvette, U. Paris, 1984-85, Inst. Advanced Study, 1991. Mem. Nat. Acad. Scis., 1997. Sloan fellow, 1981-84, Guggenheim fellow, 1984-85; Fairchild scholar, 1992; recipient Giudo Stampacchia prize Scuola Normale Superior di Pisa, 1982, Excellence in Rsch. award Rutger U. Bd. Trustees, 1987, Norbert Wiener award Am. Math. Soc. and Soc. Indsl. and Applied Math., 1990. Achievements include rsch. in physics and math. with focus on math. analysis of issues arrising in statis. mechanics, theory of Schrödinger operators and disorder effects, random fields and stochastic geometry. Office: Princeton U 347 Jadwin Hall Washington Rd Princeton NJ 08544-0708

AIZMAN, ALEXANDER, ophthalmologist; m. Natalie Tabachuk. MD, NYU, 2000. Diplomate Am. Bd. Ophthalmology, 2006. With Kellogg eye ctr. U. Mich., 2000—04, lectr., 2004—06; physician retina svc, NY Eye and Ear Infirmary, NYC, 2006—, mem. trauma svc., 2006—. Lectr. in field. Achievements include research in novel treatment approaches to age-related macular degeneration. Avocations: running, martial arts, reading. Home: 1820 Ave N Apt 3D Brooklyn NY 11230 Business E-Mail: aaizman@umich.edu.

AJA-HERRERA, MANUEL ANGEL, art educator; b. Santiago de Compostela, Galicia, Spain, May 2, 1955; s. Antonio Aja and Bibiana Herrera; m. Marie C. Swiejkowski, Oct. 24, 1981. BFA in Painting with honors, U. Ctrl. Eng., Birmingham, 1978; MA in Design Studies, London Inst., 1992; MFA, Manchester Metro. U., Eng., 1979. Dir. Herrera Ltd. Design, 1982—95; prof. Southbank U., South Thames Coll., 1993—97; prof. found. studies Savannah Coll. Art and Design, 1997—. Lectr. U. Derbyshire, 1980—81, U. Essex, Southend Coll. Tech., 1981—86, Ealing U. (formerly Ealing Poly.), 1982—84, U. Hertfordshire, 1983—92, Kent Inst., England, 1988—97, Am. U., London, 1989—93, West Hertis Coll., 1991—93, London Inst. Coll. Fashion, 1996—97; freelance cons. in field. Exhibited in group shows at Dudley Mus., Eng., 1976, Air Gallery, London, 1989, 1990, Royal Acad., 1991, 1992, Imperial Coll. Gallery, 1993, Birmingham Mus., 1994, Bergen Hall Gallery, Savannah, Ga., 1998, 1999, Alexander Hall Gallery, Savannah, 2000, one-man shows include Midlands Art Ctr., Birmingham, 1976, Dudley Mus., 1977, Spanish Inst. London, 1978, Oval Arts Ctr., London, 1979, Spanish Inst., 1980, 1981, 1982, Wooldands Art Gallery, 1987, Represented in permanent collections Air Gallery, one-man shows include Mercury Gallery, 1995, 2002, Galleria Taurr, Barcelona, Spain, 1996, Hamilton Gallery, London, 1997, Stowells Art Gallery, 1998. Recipient Fine Art Printmaking prize, Birmingham City Coun., Eng., 1976, Stowells Trophy award, Royal Acad., London, 1977, Fine Art award, Whitworth Wallis Found., 1978; scholar, Cracow U., Poland, 1979.

AJA-HERRERA, MARIE, fashion designer, educator; b. Bedford, Eng., Mar. 19, 1955; d. Henry and Ariadne Swiejkowski; m. Manny Anjel Aja-Herrera, Oct. 24, 1981. BA in Fashion, U. Ctrl. England, 1977; MA in Fashion and Textiles, Lodz U./Krakow U., Poland, 1980; MA in Design Studies, Ctrl. St. Martins, England, 1995; postgrad. cert. in Edn., U. London, 1981; D in Fashion (hon.), NYU, 2006, PhD (hon.), 2006. Head fashion dept. Southend Coll. Essex U., 1981—84; head womenswear design (Byblos) Ghirombelli/Pacanina Modas/Santini S.A., Barcelona, Milan, London, 1984—88; head womenswear design Jefferson Internat. PLC, Hong Kong, 1988—89; sales exec., design & edn. coord. Lectra Sys., 1989; chair fashion design, chair fashion merchandising Am. Coll. in London, 1989—92; design dir. CAD, knitwear, textiles Jacques Vert PLC, 1992—95; dean faculty of art and design Am. U. Dubai, United Arab Emirates, 1995—96; head of design Twins/NIKE Enterprise PLC, 1996—97; chair fashion design Savannah Coll. Art & Design, Ga., 1997—. Cons. Herrera UK Ltd., 1982—95. Fellow: Soc. Artists & Designers (lic.); mem.: Textile Inst., Polish Union Artists, The Fashion Group Internat., Clothing & Footwear Inst. Avocations: horse riding, skiing, collecting antiques, travel. Office: Savannah Coll Art and Design HR-Clinard Hall Drayton St Savannah GA 31401-5644 Office Phone: 912-525-6661. Business E-Mail: mcajaher@scad.edu.

AJALAT, SOL PETER, lawyer; b. Chgo., July 12, 1932; s. Peter S. and Tesbina (Shahadie) Ajalat; m. Lily Mary Roum, Aug. 21, 1960; children: Stephen, Gregory, Denise, Lawrence. BS, UCLA, 1958, JD, 1962. Bar: Calif. 1963, U.S. Dist. Ct. (no., cen., ea. and so. dists.) Calif. 1963, U.S. Claims Ct. 1990. Pvt. practice, LA, 1965—. Referee Calif. State Bar Ct., 1984-90; chmn. sr. lawyers com. State Bar Calif., 2006. Pres. bd. dirs. St. Nicholas Orthodox Cath. Ch., L.A., 1976-78; pres. Toluca Lake Elem. Adv. Coun., L.A., 1979, L.A. Unified Sch. Dist. Area I Adv. Coun., 1980, Providence High Sch. Adv. Coun., L.A., 1985; bd. dirs. Med. Ctr. North Hollywood, 1991-98, Angels of the Yr. Awards, 1996-2003, Life Svcs., Inc., 1997-2001, Hollywood Cmty. Hosp., 2004—; mem. improvement adv. com. Burbank City media dist., 1997-2000; chmn. Toluca Lake Neighborhood Coun., 2002-04. Mem. Calif. Bar Assn., L.A. County Bar Assn. (mem. L.A. Superior Ct. bench and bar com. 1987-96, chmn. mcpl. ct. com. 1985-86, trustee 1987-88), Calif. Trial Lawyers Assn., Conf. Bar Dels. (del. 1985—), L.A. Trial Lawyers Assn., Lawyers Club L.A. County (pres. 1985-86), Toluca Lake C. of C. (pres. 1997), Wm. A. Neima Rep. Club (pres. 1978-79), Masons, Shriners, Kiwanis (pres. North Hollywood chpt. 2002-03). Eastern Orthodox. Avocation: physical fitness. Office: Ste 850 5200 Lankershim Blvd Ste 850 North Hollywood CA 91601 Office Phone: 818-506-1500.

AJAMI, FOUAD, professor of middle eastern studies; b. Arnoun, Lebanon, Sept. 19, 1945; arrived in US, 1963, naturalized; m. Michelle Ajami. Ed., Eastern Org. Coll.; PhD in Internat. Relations and World Govt., U. Washington. Rsch. fellow The Lehrman Inst.; fellow Ctr. Internat. Studies Princeton U., prof. Dept. Politics, 1973; dir. Middle East Studies Program Johns Hopkins U. Paul H. Nitze Sch. Advanced Internat. Studies, Washington, 1980, Majid Khadduri prof., 1980—. Contbg. editor US New & World Report; contbr. on Middle Eastern issues and contemporary internat. history NY Times Book Rev., Fgn. Affairs, The New Republic, Wall Street Jour.; mem. edit. bd. Middle East Quarterly; bd. adv. Fgn. Affairs jour.; bd. dirs. Coun. Fgn. Relations. Author: The Arab Predicament: Arab Political Thought and Practice Since 1967, 1981, The Vanished Imam: Musa Al-Sadr and the Shia of Lebanon, 1986, Beirut: City of Regrets, 1988, The Dream Palace of the Arabs: A Generation's Odyssey, 1998, The Foreigner's Gift: The Americans, The Arabs and the Iraqis in Iraq, 2006. Recipient Nat. Humanities Medal, NEH, 2006; MacArthur Prize fellowship arts and sciences, 1982—87. Office: SAIS Johns Hopkins Univ Nitze 504 1740 Massachusetts Ave Washington DC 20036 Office Phone: 202-663-5677.*

AJAMIL, LUIS, civil engineer; b. Havana, Cuba, Sept. 17, 1950; came to U.S., 1962; s. Oscar Vicente and Maria Teresa (Anrrich) A.; m. Sofia L. Lorie, 1974 (div. 1978); m. Robyn Marjorie Bennett; children: Brook, Mark, Loren, Trevor. BCE, U. Fla., 1972. Registered profl. engr., Fla. Exec. v.p. Post, Buckley, Schuh & Jernigan, Inc., Miami, Fla., 1974-92; ptnr. to principal in charge Bermello, Ajamil & Ptnrs., Inc., Miami, Fla., 1992—. Contbr. articles to profl. jours. Chmn. Lake Okeechabbee Tech. Coun., West Palm Beach, Fla., 1990-92; pres. Dade Pub. Edn. Fund, Miami, 1990-92; bd. dirs. Greater Miami Free Zone Corp., 1988—, Greater Miami Progress Found., 1988—, Bapt. Hosp. of Miami, 1992—; mem. exec. com. World Trade Ctr., Miami, 1992—, Beacon Coun., 1989—. Recipient Consulting Engineer of the Year award, Am. Inst. Architects, Miami Chapter, 2005. Mem. ASCE, Fla. Engring. Soc. (Prin. of Yr. 1988), Greater Miami C. of C. (vice chmn. 1989—, Bill Colson Leadership award 1991). Roman Catholic. Office: Bermello Ajamil & Ptnrs Inc 2601 S Bayshore Dr Fl 10 Miami FL 33133-5417

AJEMIAN, MARIANNE, lawyer; b. 1956; BA in Polit. Sci. with honors, Wellesley Coll., Mass., 1978; JD, Boston U., 1982. Bar: Mass. 1982, US Dist. Ct. (dist. Mass.) 1983. Ptnr. real estate and fin., mem. exec. com. Nutter, McClennen & Fish, L.L.P., Boston. Bd. dirs. HomeStart, Inc., Boston. Named a Mass. Super Lawyer, 2004—05. Mem.: Boston Bar Assn., Greater Boston C. of C. (bd. dirs., Pinnacle Award for Achievement in the Professions 2006), Comml. Real Estate Women Network (bd. dirs., pres.-elect), New Eng. Women in Real Estate (past. pres.), Mass. Assisted Living Facilities Assn., Real Estate Fin. Assn., Mass. Bar Assn. (mem. real property and probate and bus. sects.). Office: Nutter McClennen & Fish LLP World Trade Ctr West 155 Seaport Blvd Boston MA 02210-2604 Office Fax: 617-439-2891, 617-310-9891. E-mail: majemian@nutter.com.*

AJLOUNI, RAED FAKHRY, dentist, educator; b. Mafraq, Jordan; s. Fakhry Mohammad Ajlouni and Naifeh Ali Shehabat. DDS, Jordan U. Sci. and Tech., Irbid, 1995; MS, U. Iowa, Iowa City, 2002. Diplomate Am. Acad. Operative Dentistry, 2003. Asst. prof. Baylor Coll. Dentistry, Tex. A&M U. Sys. Health Sci. Ctr., Dallas, 2003—06; pres. DaVinci Dentistry, PA, Southlake, Tex., 2005—; assoc. prof. Baylor Coll. Dentistry, Tex. A&M U. Sys. Health Sci. Ctr., 2006—; v.p. Biomedical Ingenuity Inc., Southlake, Tex., 2006—. Mem. editl. bd.: Operative Dentistry Jour. Recipient Jordan Nat. Writing Contest award, Ministry Edn., 1987, Jordan Nat. Sci. Achievement award, 1989; scholar, Ministry Higher Edn., 1990—95, Jordan U. Sci. and Tech., 1999—2002. Mem.: Am. Bd. Operative Dentistry, Am. Acad. Operative Dentistry, Omicron Kappa Upsilon. Achievements include research in clinical, laboratory and translational research on dental and biomedical materials, devices and technologies. Office: Baylor Coll Dentistry 3302 Gaston Ave Dallas TX 75246 Office Phone: 214-828-8274. Office Fax: 214-828-8952. E-mail: rajlouni@bcd.tamhsc.edu.

AJZENBERG-SELOVE, FAY, physicist, researcher; b. Berlin, Feb. 13, 1926; came to U.S., 1940, naturalized, 1946; d. Mojzesz A. and Olga (Naiditch) A.; m. Walter Selove, Dec. 18, 1955. BS in Engring., U. Mich., 1946; MS, U. Wis., 1949, PhD, 1952; DSc (hon.), Smith Coll., 1995, Mich. State U., 1997, Haverford Coll., 1999—. Rsch. fellow Calif. Inst. Tech., 1952, 54; lectr. Smith Coll., 1952-53; cons., fellow MIT, Cambridge, 1952-53; from asst. prof. to rsch. assoc. prof. Boston U., 1953-57; mem. faculty Haverford Coll., 1957-70, prof. physics, 1962-70, acting chmn. dept. physics, 1967-69; rsch. prof. U. Pa., Phila., 1970-73, prof. physics, 1973—2005, prof. emeritus, 2005—, assoc. chmn., 1989-93. Vis. asst. prof. Columbia, summer 1955, Nat. U. Mexico, summer 1955; lectr. U. Pa., 1957; cons. in field, 1962-63; vis. assoc. Calif. Inst. Tech., 1973-74; Exec. sec. com. physics faculties in colls. Am. Inst. Physics, 1962-65, mem. adv. com. manpower, 1963-68, adv. com. vis. scientists program, 1963-67; commr. Commn. on Coll. Physics, 1968-71; exec. sec. ad hoc panel on nuclear data compilations NAS-NRC, 1971-75; mem. Commn. on Nuclear Physics, Internat. Union Pure and Applied Physics, 1972-78, chairperson. 1978-81; mem. U.S. del. low energy nuclear physics to USSR, AEC, 1966; mem. Distinguished Faculty Awards Commn. Commonwealth of Pa., 1976; mem. nuclear sci. adv. com. Dept Energy-NSF, 1977-80; mem. numerical data adv. bd., assembly math. and phys. scis. NRC, 1977-79; lectr. U. Minn., 1994 Author: A Matter of Choice, Memoirs of a Female Physicist, 1994; editor: Nuclear Spectroscopy, vol. A and B, 1960; bd. editors Phys. Rev. C., 1981-83. Mem. Bower awards com. Franklin Nat. Meml., 1993. Recipient Christian R. and Mary F. Lindback award for disting. teaching, 1991, Nicholson medal for humanitarian svc. Am. Phys. Soc., 1999, 1st Disting. Alumni fellow in Physics, U. Wis., 2001; Smith-Mundt fellow, 1955; Guggenheim fellow, 1965-66. Fellow AAAS (mem. governing coun. 1974-80, mem. com. on coun. affairs 1977, 78), Am. Phys. Soc. (chairperson divsn. nuclear physics 1973-74); mem. AAUP, NRC (mem. phys. scis. panel, associateship program 1988-91), Am. Inst. Physics (mem. com. on pub. edn. and info. 1980-83), Phi Beta Kappa, Sigma Xi (nat. lectr. 1973-74). Home: 118 Cherry Ln Wynnewood PA 19096-1209 Office: U Pa Philadelphia PA 19104-6396 Business E-Mail: fay@pobox.upenn.edu.

AKAIKE, HIROKO, music educator, conductor; arrived in U.S., 1997; d. Hiroshi and Etsuko Akaike. BMus in Edn., Kunitachi Coll. Music, Tokyo, 1995; MS in Music Performance, Shenandoah U., 1999, MS in Music, 2003. Lic. tchg. Va. Tutor, accompanist Shenandoah U., Winchester, Va., 1998—2003; substitute tchr. Winchester Pub. Sch., 2002—03; band, choir dir. Highland County Pub. Sch., Monterey, Va., 2003—06; choir dir. Charles City Pub. Schs., 2006—07; band and choir dir. Mathews County Pub. Schs., Va., 2007—. Pvt. piano, vocal instr., 1997—; pianist Wesleyan Fellowship Ch., Winchester, 1998—2003; asst. music dir., conductor Mary Washington Coll., Fredericksburg, Va., 1999; music dir. Highland County Arts Coun., Monterey, 2004—06. Contbr. articles to newspaper. Musician West Minster Canterbury Nursing Home, Winchester, 1999—2003. Named Employee of Month, Highland County Pub. Schs., 2003; fellow, Shenandoah U., 1999—2003; scholar, Ikueikai, 1991—95, Kunitachi Coll. Music, 1991—95. Mem.: Conductors Guild, Va. Edn. Assn., Nat. Assn. Music Educators. Avocations: dance, reading. Office: Mathews County High Sch PO Box 38 Mathews VA 23109 Home Phone: 804-725-7617; Office Phone: 804-715-3702. Personal E-mail: hakaike@yahoo.com.

AKAKA, DANIEL KAHIKINA, senator; b. Honolulu, Sept. 11, 1924; s. Kahikina and Annie (Kahoa) A.; m. Mary Mildred Chong, May 22, 1948; children: Millannie, Daniel, Gerard, Alan, Nicholas. BEdn, U. Hawaii, 1952, MEdn, 1966. Tchr., Hawaii, 1953-60; vice prin., then prin. Ewa Beach Elem. Sch., Honolulu, 1960-64; prin. Pohakea Elem. Sch., 1964-65, Kaneohe Elem. Sch., 1965-68; program specialist Hawaii Compensatory Edn., 1978-79, from 1985; dir. Office Economic Opportunity, Hawaii, 1971-74; spl. asst. human resources Office Gov. Hawaii, 1975-76; mem. US Ho. of Reps. from 2d Dist., Hawaii, 1977-90; US Senator from Hawaii, 1990—. Chmn. Hawaii Principals' Conf.; mem.com. armed svc. US Senate, com. energy and natural resources, com. homeland security and govtl. affairs, com. Indian affairs, com. veteran affairs. Bd. dirs. Hanahauoli Sch., Honolulu; mem. Act 4 Ednl. Adv. Council, Library Adv. Council.; Trustee Kawaiahao Congl. Ch. Served with US Army, 1945—47, Asia Pacific, World War II. Named Friend of Nat. Parks, Nat. Parks Conservation Assn., 2005; recipient Lifetime Achievement award, U. Hawaii Founders Alumni Assn., 1999, Stan Suyat Meml. Leadership award, Asian Govt. Exec. Network, 2003, Stephen L. Jackstadt award, Hawaii Coun. Econ. Edn., 2003, Congressional Am. Spirit Medallion, Nat. D-Day Mus., 2004, George "Buck" Gillispie Congressional award meritorious svc., Blinded Am. Veteran Assn., 2004, Adam Smith award for excellence in econ. edu., Nat. Council on Econ. Edu., 2005. Mem. NEA, Musicians Assn. Hawaii. Democrat. Congregationalist. Office: US Senate 141 Hart Senate Office Bldg Washington DC 20510-0001 also: Prince Kuhio Fed Bldg 300 Ala Moana Blvd Rm 3-106 PO Box 50144 Honolulu HI 96850-4977 Office Phone: 202-224-6361, 808-522-8970. Office Fax: 202-224-2126, 808-545-4683.*

AKASE, MASAKO, humanities educator; b. Tokyo, Nov. 25, 1933; d. Tashiro and Haru (Mori) A. BA, Waseda U., 1957, MA, 1959; diploma of phonetics, Paris U., 1962. Lectr. Momoyama Gakuin U., Osaka, Japan, 1968-70, assoc. prof., 1970-74, prof., 1974—, prof. grad. course, 1993—2004, prof. emeritus, 2004—. Guest prof. U. Paris VII, 1984, 97, 2002. Author: Kafu Nagai and French Literature, 1976, Development of Comparative Studies, 1983, Kafu Nagai-Comparative Study, 1986, Comparative Literature Comparative Culture, 1995, Kafu Nagai and French Culture, 1998; author, editor: Kafu Nagai-Bibliographical Study, 1990, Ryunosuke-Akutagawa Bibliographical Study, 2004. Recipient Mozume Sakuin prize, 1990. Mem. Japanese Comparative Lit. Assn. (coun. mem.), France-Japanese Hist. Studies Assn. (trustee), Pen Club, French Lang. and Lit. Assn., Japanese MLA. Avocations: ballroom dance, Latin dance, yoga, kiko. Office: Momoyama Gakuin U 1-1 Manabino Izumishi Osaka 5941198 Japan Home: 5-29-13-406 Hongo Bunkyoku Tokyo 1130033 Japan Office Phone: 0725 54 3131. Personal E-mail: masako-akase@andrew.ac.jp. Business E-Mail: m-akase@andrew.ac.jp.

AKEEL, HADI ABU, robotics executive; b. Cairo, Apr. 9, 1938; came to U.S., 1961; s. Kobaisi Aly Abu-Akeel and Zeinab Makhlouf; children: Shereef, Nezar; m. Naglaa Mostafa. BS in Mech. Engring., Cairo U., 1959; MS in Applied Mechanics, UCLA, 1963; PhD in Mech. Engring., U. Calif., Berkeley, 1966. Cert. mfg. engr. Acting instr. U. Calif., Berkeley, 1963-66; analytical specialist Bendix Corp., South Bend, Ind., 1966-69; assoc. prof. Ain Shams U., Cairo, 1969-74; sr. staff engr. GM Mfg., Warren, Mich., 1974-76; program mgr. GM Corp., Warren, 1976-78; dept. head mfg. staff GM, Warren, 1978-80, chief engr. flexible automation systems, 1980-82; v.p., chief engr. GMFanuc Robotics Corp., Auburn Hills, Mich., 1982-92; sr. v.p. Fanuc U.S.A., 1992-96, also bd. dirs., vice chmn., 1992-98; gen. mgr. Berkeley Lab. Fanuc Am. Corp., Union City, Calif., 1992—2001; sr. v.p. Fanuc Robotics Am., Inc., 1996—99. Tech. advisor FANUC Ltd., Japan, 1992—; advisor Mgmt. of Tech. Program U. Calif., Berkeley, 1988-92; chmn. bd. dirs. Robotics Internat. of SME, Dearborn, Mich., 1992-93; pres. Amteng Corp., 1996—. Author: Machine Design, 1972; contbr. articles to profl. jours.; holds over 60 U.S. and fgn. patents. Soccer coach Am. Youth Soccer Orgn.; mem. bd. advisors Sch. Engring., U. Mich., Dearborn, 1991-2006; chmn. bd. visitors Sch. Engring., Oakland U., 1991-92. Recipient Joseph F. Engleberger award Robotic Industries Assn., 1989, Mich. Sci. Trailblazer award State Mich., 1989. Fellow ASME, Soc. Mfg. Engrs. (internat. dir. 1998-2003); mem. IEEE, Nat. Acad. Engring. Independent. Muslim. Avocations: tennis, swimming, camping, travel, machine shop. Office: Fanuc Robotics Corp 3900 W Hamlin Rd Rochester Hills MI 48309-3253 Home: 20660 Sutherlin Pl Sterling VA 20165-8500 Personal E-mail: majestícct-who@yahoo.com.

AKEHURST, WALLACE EDWARD, marketing professional, consultant; b. Balt., Oct. 6, 1965; adopted s. David Elmer and Margaret Lois Akehurst; m. Jami Lyn Meyer, June 19, 1990 (div. Dec. 15, 1993); children: David Edward, Helen Frances; m. Adele Margaret Shilko, Oct. 6, 1995. Cert. life health property casualty Md. Ins. Bd., 1988; series 7 securities SEC, 1989, contractor Md. MHIC, 1994. Owner HydroClean Enterprises, Elkton, Md., 1985—90; founder Ctr. Citizen's Rights, Balt., 1990—2004; CEO Fin. Workshop Enterprises, Monkton, Md., 1998—2004; gen. mgr. Oak Thorn Wellness Group, Wapakoneta, Ohio, 2006—; mgr. Storm Import/Export, Balt., 2006. Cons. FFA Seminars, Ltd., San Diego, 1999—2004. Author: (novels) Taro Danmet, (book) Non-Salesman's Guide to Direct Sales, (textbook) Practical Modern Applications of Monetary Theory; patent electrical ionization of automotive pollutants. Treas. Libertarian Ctrl. Com., Hunt Valley, Md., 1995—98; rschr., dir. Ctr. Non-Dual Studies, Balt., 2005—07; bd. dirs. Firefox Endowment, Balt., 2004—07. Mem.: Hist. Rsch. Soc. (bd. dirs. 1995—, Rsch. Fellow Achievement award 1996). Non-Dualist. Avocations: Kung Fu, motorcycling, chess, travel, spirituality. Home: 11509 Cedar Ln Kingsville MD 21087 Home Phone: 443-992-5004. Home Fax: 410-510-1121. Personal E-mail: edakehurst@edakehurst.com. Business E-Mail: healthyspray@yahoo.com.

AKELEY, KURT BARTON, computer graphics company executive, engineer; b. Wilmington, Del., June 8, 1958; s. David Francis and Marcy Claire (McCullough) A. BSEE, U. Del., 1980; MSEE, Stanford U., 1982. Mem. tech. staff, co-founder Silicon Graphics, Inc., Mountain View, Calif., 1982-87, prin. engr., 1987-89, chief engr., 1989-90, v.p., chief engr., 1990; sr. rschr. Microsoft Rsch. Asia, Beijing, 2004—. Mem. Coll. Engring. Adv. Coun., U. Del., 1993—. Patentee, inventor in field; contbr. articles to profl. publs. Named Disting. Alumnus, Dept. Elec. Engring., Coll. Engring., U. Del., 1993. Mem. NAE, Assn. Computing Machinery. Avocation: woodworking motorcycle riding. Office: Microsoft Rsch Asia 5/F, Beijing Sigma Ctr No 49, Zhichun Rd, Hai Dian Dist Beijing 100080 China

AKENSON, DONALD HARMAN, historian, educator; b. Mpls., May 22, 1941; s. Donald Nels and Fern L. (Harman) A. BA, Yale U., 1962; PhD, Harvard U., 1967; LittD (hon.), McMaster U., 1995; HHD (hon.), U. Lethbridge, 1996; LittD (hon.), Guelph U., 2000; DLaws (hon.), Regina U., 2002. Allston Burr sr. tutor Dunster House, Harvard U., 1966-67; asst. prof. history, asst. dean Yale Coll., 1967-70; assoc. prof. history Queens U., Kingston, Ont., Canada, 1970-74, prof., 1974—2003, Douglas chair Canadian and colonial hist., 2003—; hon. prof. U. Aberdeen, 2002—; Beamish rsch. prof. migration studies U. Liverpool, England, 1997—2002; sr. editor McGill-Queens Univ. Press, 1982—. Hon. rsch. fellow Queens U., Belfast, 1976-77, sr. rsch. fellow, 1995-96; hon. prof. edn. Trinity Coll., Dublin, 1976-77; hon. lectr. Australian Nat. U., 1985; Cecil H. Green disting. vis. prof. Green Coll., U. B.C., 1995; guest artist Yaddo Colony, 1985; writer-in-residence Bellagio Ctr., Lake Como, Italy, 1993; hon. rsch. prof. Irish and Scottish studies U. Aberdeen, Scotland, 2002-06; Freilich Found. lectr. Australian Nat. U., 2003; vis. prof. U. Liverpool, Eng., 2006-. Author: The Irish Education Experiment: The National System of Education in the Nineteenth Century, 1970, The Church of Ireland: Ecclesiastical Reform and Revolution 1800-1885, 1971, Education and Enmity: The Control of Schooling in Northern Ireland 1920-50, 1973, The United States and Ireland, 1973, A Mirror to Kathleen's Face: Education in Independent Ireland 1922-60, 1975, Local Poets and Social History: James Orr, Bard of Ballycarry, 1977, Between Two Revolutions: Islandmagee, County Antrim, 1798-1920, 1979, The Lazar House Notebooks, 1981, A Protestant in Purgatory: Richard Whately, Archbishop of Dublin, 1981, The Irish in Ontario, 1984, Brotherhood Week in Belfast, 1984, Being Had: Historians, Evidence, and the Irish in North America, 1985, The Orangeman: The Life and Times of Ogle Gowan, 1986, The Edgerston Audit, 1987, Small Differences: Irish Catholics and Irish Protestants, 1815-1922, 1988, Half the World from Home; Perspectives on the Irish in New Zealand, 1990, At Face Value: The Life and Times of Eliza McCormack/John White, 1990 Occasional Papers on the Irish in South Africa, 1991, God's Peoples: Covenant and Land in South Africa, Israel and Ulster, 1992, The Irish Diaspora A Primer, 1993, Conor: A Biography of Conor Cruise O'Brien, 1994, If the Irish Ruled thr World: Montserrat 1630-1730, 1997, Surpassing Wonder. The Invention of the Bible and the Talmuds, 1998, Saint Saul: A Skeleton Key to the Historical Jesus, 2000, Intolerance. The E. Coli of the Human Mind, 2004, An Irish History of Civilization, 2 vols., 2005; editor: Canadian Papers in Rural History, 1978-96; sr. editor McGill-Queen's U. Press, 1982—. Recipient rsch. award Can. Coun., 1974-83, 91-94, Am. Coun. Learned Socs., 1976-77, Chalmers prize, 1985, Landon prize, 1987, Grawemeyer award for improving world order, 1993, Biography medal U. B.C., 1994, Trillium prize, 1995, Molson Laureate, 1996; Guggenheim fellow, 1981-85, John David Stout rsch. fellow Victoria U., 1988-89, Univ. fellow Rhodes U., 1990. Fellow Royal Soc. Can., Royal Hist. Soc. (U.K.); mem. Am. Conf. Irish Studies, Phi Beta Kappa. Office: Queens U Dept History Kingston ON Canada K7L 3N6

AKER, DUNCAN DANFORTH, JR., minister, educator; b. Texas City, Tex., Oct. 19, 1951; s. Duncan Danforth Aker and Dolores Doreen Mazzantini; m. Catherine Marie Dowling-Aker, Nov. 19, 1984; 1 child, Jamie Cimar Aker-Morris. AA in Edn., Coll. of the Mainland, Texas City, 1978. Ordained Christian Ch., 1998. With Christian Ch. Children's Homes, 1985—99; pastor various chs., 1998—; sr. pastor Vanceburg Christian Ch., Ky., 2004—. Mem. ethics bd. City of Vanceburg, 2006—; bd. dirs. Vanceburg Renaissance, 2005—. Served with US Army, 1972—75. Recipient Timothy award, Arcadia Christian Ch., 1994, Direct Svc. award, State of Tenn. Assn. Child Care, 1998, Arthur H. Diebold Cmty. Involvement award, Christian Endeavor Assn., 1970. Mem.: Ministerial Assn. Vanceburg, 50's Unlimited Auto Club Tex. (co-founder 1978). Avocations: genealogy, gardening, restoring old toys. Home: 412 Front St Vanceburg KY 41179 Office Phone: 606-796-2431. Personal E-mail: duncanakerjr@yahoo.com.

AKER, SUSAN K., elementary school educator, assistant principal; b. Bklyn., Aug. 4, 1951; d. Mike and Rose Kriegsman; m. David Aker, Sept. 1, 1974; children: Michael, Jessica. BA, CUNY, 1973, MS, 1975, LI U., Brookville, NY, 1976, MS, 1991, Coll. New Rochelle, NY, 1998. Cert. early childhood edn., elem. edn., spl. edn., libr. sci., sch. adminstrn. and supervision. Tchr. 4th grade Yeshiva Crown Heights, Bklyn., 1974-75; tchr. 6th grade Hebrew Acad. Nassau County, Bethpage, NY, 1975-76; libr. Jericho (NY) Jewish Ctr., 1978-81, Half-Hollow Hills Pub. Libr., Dix Hills, NY, 1978-81; libr. media specialist Uniondale (NY) Free Sch. Dist., 1989-90, Hempstead (NY) Union Free Sch. Dist., 1990-92; tchr. 105 NYC Bd. Edn., Bronx, 1993—2004; adj. prof. Mercy Coll., Yorktown; mentor NYC Dept. Edn., Region 2, Bronx, 2004—05; asst. prin. NYC Dept. Edn., Bronx, NY, 2006—. Internal geography cons. NYC Bd. Edn., 1996—, staff devel. workshop presenter, 1996—. Contbr. articles to TeacherLink. Grantee United Fedn. Tchrs., 1997, NY Geographic Alliance, 1998, 99, McDonald's Corp., 2001. Mem.: ASCD, N.Y. Reading Assn., Assn. Early Childhood Internat., N.Y. Geog. Alliance, Phi Delta Kappa. Home: 23 Southern Rd Hartsdale NY 10530-2128 Office Phone: 914-645-8100.

AKER, SUZANNE DEVERSE, physical movement educator; b. Kansas City, Mo., Sept. 19, 1926; d. Earnest Hillborn and Clara Maude Scruggs; m. Meredith Eugene Aker, Jan. 28, 1960 (div. Feb. 1977); children: alan Morrow, Jan Ameen, John Bettis, Elizabeth Aker, Laura Greer. Student, Ballet Theater Sch., 1953; BA, Tulsa U., 1962. Cert. profl. dance tchr. Profl. dancer Burchmann Dancers, Hollywood, N.Y., 1944-45; tchr. Tulsa U., 1959-62; chmn. dept. dance Tex. Tech. U., Lubbock, 1962-69; founding artistic dir., choreographer, tchr. Ballett Lubbock, 1969-2000; phys. movement tchr. Covenant Health Sys., Lubbock, 2000—. Choreographer Tex. Tech. U., 1963-85, Lubbock Theater Ctr., 1965-76, Lubbock Christian U., 1981-90; choreographer, tchr. Wayland Bapt. U., Plainview, Tex., 1979-83. Assoc. Cmty. of Holy Spirit Episcopal Convent, 1985—. Nat. Endowment for Arts grantee, 1980; recipient Pathfinder's award Lubbock C. of C., 1987. Mem. Chi Omega (v.p. 1946), Alpha Psi Omega (hon.), Delta Psi Kappa (hon.). Avocations: icon painting, dance related artwork. Home: 5016 27th St Lubbock TX 79407 Office Phone: 806-725-6579.

AKERLOF, CARL WILLIAM, physics professor; b. New Haven, Mar. 5, 1938; s. Gosta Carl and Rosalie Clara (Hirschfelder) A.; m. Carol Irene Ruska, Sept. 4, 1965; children— Karen Louise, William Gustav BA, Yale U., 1960; PhD, Cornell U., 1967. Research assoc. U. Mich., Ann Arbor, 1966-68, asst. prof., 1968-72, assoc. prof., 1972-78, prof. physics, 1978—. Contbr. articles to profl. jours. Incorporator Ann Arbor Hands-On Mus. Fellow Am. Phys. Soc.; mem. Am. Astron. Soc. Office: U Mich Randall Lab Physics Dept Physics Ann Arbor MI 48109 Home Phone: 734-973-9579.

AKERLOF, GEORGE ARTHUR, economics professor; b. New Haven, June 17, 1940; s. Gosta Carl and Rosalie C. Akerlof; m. Janet Louise Yellen, July 7, 1978; 1 child, Robert. BA, Yale U., 1962; PhD, MIT, 1966; D Econs. (hon.), U. Zurich, Switzerland, 2000. Cassell prof. of money and banking London Sch. Econs., 1978-80; assist. prof. U. Calif., Berkeley, 1966—70, assoc. prof., 1970—77, prof., 1977—78, 1980—; sr. fellow Brookings Instn., Washington, 1994—. Bd. dirs. Nat. Bur. Econ. Rsch., 1997—; mem. bd. editors Quar. Jour. Econs., 1983—, Am. Econ. Rev., 1983-90.; sr. advisor Bookings Panel Econ. Activity Author: An Economic Theorist's Book of Tales, 1984; co-author: Efficiency Wage Theories of Unemployment, 1988; co-editor Jour. Econs. and Politics, 1990—; contbr. articles to profl. jours. Recipient Woodrow Wilson fellow, 1962—63, Cooperative fellow NSF, 1963—66, Fulbright fellow, 1967—68, Nobel Prize in Economics, 2001. Fellow Am. Acad. Arts and Scis.; mem. Am. Econ. Assn. (mem. exec. com. 1988-91, v.p. 1995), Can. Inst. Advanced Rsch. (assoc.), Russell Sage Round Table on Behavioral Econs. Office: U Calif Dept Econs 549 Evans Hall # 3880 Berkeley CA 94720-3880

AKEROYD, RICHARD G., JR., library director; BA, U. Conn.; MLS, U. Pitts., 1969. With U. Conn. Libr., Nat. Commn. Libr. & Info. Sci., Denver Pub. Libr.; state libr. Conn. State Libr., Hartford, 1986—97; dir. libr. programs Bill & Melinda Gates Libr. Found., 1997—2003; state libr. N.Mex State Libr., Santa Fe, 2004. Mem.: ALA, Western Coun. State Libraries, Coalition for Networked Info., Am. Soc. Info. Sci. Office: NMex State Libr 1209 Camino Carlos Rey Santa Fe NM 87507 Office Phone: 505-476-9762. Office Fax: 505-476-9761. E-mail: richard.akeroyd@state.nm.us.*

AKERS, SAUNDRA RUTH, retired disability rights advocate; b. Urbana, Ohio, July 21, 1943; d. Henry Albert and Clara Velma (Stultz) Crum; m. Larry Roger Akers, Mar. 1, 1964 (div. Feb. 1986); children: Crystal Annette Castle, H. Roger, Noel Justin, Pride A. Cert. paralegal, Am. Inst. Paralegal Practice. Mgr. Marathon Sta., Columbus, Ohio, 1972—73; nursing assoc., mental health tech., mental health tech. supr. Columbus Devel. Ctr., residential area program planner, vocat. habilitation specialist; disability rights advocate Ohio Legal Rights, Columbus; ret., 2005. Liaison Gov.'s Coun. People with Disabilities, 1997—, Ohio Devel. Disability Coun., 1994—97. Author: Curious Concepts, 2005, Fear Treads the Mountain, 2006, Tempest Rider, Spooked. Sec. Citizen's Com., Hilliard, Ohio, 1973; mem. Lifetime Learning Columiba State U. Mem.: Toastmasters Internat. Avocations: public speaking, creative writing, genealogy. Home: 3260 Colony Hill Ln Columbus OH 43204

AKERS, WILLIAM WALTER, chemical engineering educator; b. Panola County, Tex., Dec. 31, 1922; s. Oscar Walter and Lela (Malone) A.; m. Nancy Tressel, Mar. 1, 1947; children— Susan Elaine, Carol Lorraine. BS, Tex. Tech Coll., 1943; MS, U. Tex., 1944; PhD, U. Mich., 1951. With Atlantic Refining Co., 1947; mem. faculty Rice U., 1947-93, prof. chem. engring., 1956—93, prof. emeritus, 1993—, chmn. dept., 1955-66; dir. Bio-Med. Engring., Lab., 1963-69, asst. to pres. univ., 1973-74, dir. univ. relations, 1974, v.p. for external affairs, 1975-80, v.p. adminstrn., 1980-89. Cons. chem. industries, 1947-65; mem. coun. Oak Ridge Inst. Nuclear Studies, 1958-63, vice chmn., 1962, bd. dirs., 1963-69; tech. adviser to Yugoslavia, 1962; mem. U.S.-Afghanistan Ednl. Consortium, 1963-70; rshc. project dir. Baylor Coll. Medicine, 1965-70; mem. biomed. engring. fellowship com. NIH, 1967-70; mem. Sec.'s Adv. Coun. for Coal Mine Health Rsch., 1970-71; mem. adv. coun. Nat. Inst. Occupational Safety and Health, 1971-73; mem. adv. com. on nuclear energy Tex. Energy and Natural Resources Adv. Coun., 1980-88. Author papers in field. Trustee St. Luke's Hosp., Houston, 1975-79; bd. dirs. South Main Center Assn., 1976-87, Houston Symphony Soc., 1983-85; mem. adv. bd. Salvation Army, 1998—. Served with C.E., AUS, 1941-43. Recipient Disting. Engring. Alumnus award Tex. Tech U., 1967, Disting. Alumnus award, 1968 Mem. AAAS, Am. Chem. Soc., Am. Inst. Chem. Engrs. (Best Fundamental Paper award 1967, Distinguished lectr. 1969), Am. Soc. Artificial Organs, Council on Fgn. Relations, Houston Philos. Soc., Sigma Xi, Tau Beta Pi. Episcopalian. Home: 4718 Hallmark Dr Apt 1001 Houston TX 77056 E-mail: wwakers@rice.edu, w.akers@sbcglobal.net.

AKHAVAN-HEIDARI, MEHDI, cardiothoracic surgeon; b. Tehran, Iran, Feb. 21, 1971; s. Reza Akhavan-Heidari and Sakineh Najmabadi; m. Naghmeh Khodabandeh Lou, Aug. 19, 1998; 1 child, Imaan. MD, U. Vienna, Austria, 1999—. Cert. Ednl. Commn. Fgn. Med. Grads., 2000. Resident family medicine Landeskrankenhaus Rohrbach, Oberoesterreich, Austria, 1999—2001; resident physician gen. surgery W.Va. U., Charleston, 2001—02; resident gen. surgery Marshall U., Huntington, W.Va., 2002—06; fellow cardiothoracic surgery Loyola U. Med. Ctr., Chgo., 2006—. Instr. med. software evaluation and med. tchg., faculty medicine U. Vienna, 1993—99; rep. acad. med. educators Marshall U., Huntington, W.Va., 2004—05, bd. mem., 2004—05, rep. internal resident affairs com., 2005—06; rep. Pediatric ICU Collaborative Practice Com., Huntington, 2005—06. Scholar, Vienna Med. Sch., 1993—99; Tchg. Resident scholar, Marshall U. Acad. Med. Educators, 2005. Fellow: ACS; mem.: Soc. Thoracic Surgeons, Am. Coll. Chest Physicians, So. Med. Assn., Am. Med. Assn., Austrian Coll. Surgeons. Office: Loyola Univ Med Ctr 2160 S 1st Ave Bldg 110 Rm 6243 Maywood IL 60153 Home Phone: 304-208-5836; Office Phone: 708-327-2487. Personal E-mail: pmuko@yahoo.com.

AKHONDI, HOSSEIN, internist, researcher; b. Tehran, Iran, Nov. 16, 1968; s. Mahmood Akhondi and Parvaneh Espahbodi. MD, Iran U., Tehran, 1995. Diplomate Am. Bd. Internal Medicine. Instr. anatomy and neuroanatomy Iran U. Med. Scis., Tehran, 1990—95; hospitalist physician Police Hosp., Tehran, 1995—97; emergency room physician Day Gen. Hosp., Tehran, 1997—99; rsch. asst. Mercer U., Savannah, Ga., 1999—2001, internal medicine resident, 2001—. Mem. rsch. com. Mercer U. Meml. Hosp., Savannah, 2000—, mem. quality mgmt. resident liaison com., 2000—; presenter in field. Contbr. articles to profl. jours. Mem. nat. screening team for rheumatic heart diseases Ministry Health, Tehran, 1993—94. Recipient Continued Med. Edn. course prize, MAYO Clinic, 2000. Fellow: Iranian Med. Coun. (licentiate; young physicians 1995—97); mem.: AMA, Ga. Chpt. Physicians, ACP - Am. Soc. Internal Medicine (assoc. Second place for best original rsch. presentation 2002, Second place for an oral presentation award 2001), So. Med. Assn. (mem. resident adv. com. 2002—, First place for oral presentation 2002). Achievements include research in tongue piercing with infective endocarditis; role of positive pressure ventilation in treating patients with diastolic heart failure; role of illicit drug use in spinal cord infarct; ESR in Alzheimer and non-Alzheimer dementia; physicians using evidence based medicine in atrial fibrilation; discovery of the correlation of SPECT brain scan, Tau and Beta-42 protein with Alzheimer disease; development of antibody coated bacteria in UTI differentiation; presented first case of subclavian vein thrombosis after weigh lifting. Avocations: movies, reading, chess, tennis. Office: Suburban Hosp 8600 Old Georgetown Rd Bethesda MD 20814 Office Phone: 301-896-3100. Personal E-mail: h68akhond@hotmail.com.

AKIBA, LORRAINE HIROKO, lawyer; b. Honolulu, Dec. 28, 1956; d. Lawrence H. and Florence K. (Iwasa) Katsuyama. BS with honors, U. Calif., Berkeley, 1977; JD, U. Calif., San Francisco, 1981. Bar: Hawaii 1981, US Dist. Ct. Hawaii 1981, US Ct. Appeals (9th cir.) 1981, US Supreme Ct. 1986. Dir. State of Hawaii Dept. Labor and Indsl. Rels., 1995—2000; ptnr. Cades, Schutte, Fleming & Wright, Honolulu, 1981—94, McCorriston Miller Mukai and MacKinnon LLP, Honolulu, 2000—. Lawyer rep. 9th Cir. Jud. Conf., 1991-94; mem., past treas. Hawaii Inst. for CLE, Honolulu, 1987—. Chairperson attys. divsn. Aloha United Way, Honolulu, 1991, 04, statewide chairperson, 1995; mem. State of Hawaii Environ. Coun., Honolulu, 1990-94, chair, 1992; mem. city and county Honolulu Transp. Commn., 2005-. Named one of Outstanding Young Women Am., 1985, Hawaii's Best Bus. Lawyers, 2007; named Lawyer of Yr., Hawaii Women Lawyers', 1990. Mem. ABA, Hawaii Bar Assn., Hawaii Women Lawyers Assn., Hawaii Women Lawyers Found. (pres. 1988-92), Honolulu Club, Phi Beta Kappa. Office: McCorriston Miller Mukai MacKinnon LLP PO Box 2800 Honolulu HI 96803-2800 Office Phone: 808-529-7300. Business E-Mail: akiba@m4law.com.

AKIL, HUDA, neuroscientist, educator, researcher; b. Damascus, Syria, May 19, 1945; came to U.S., 1968; d. Fakher and Widad (Al-Imam) A.; m. Stanley Jack Watson Jr., Dec. 21, 1972; children: Brendon Omar, Kathleen Tamara. BA, Am. U., Beirut, Lebanon, 1966, MA, 1968; PhD, UCLA, 1972. Postdoctoral fellow Stanford U., Palo Alto, Calif., 1974-78; from asst. prof. to prof. psychiatry and neuroscience U. Mich., Ann Arbor, 1979—, co-dir., sr. rsch. scientist Mental Health Rsch. Inst. Mem. adv. bd. Neurex Corp., Menlo Park, Calif., 1986—, Neurobiol. Techs., Inc., 1994-97; sec. Internat. Narcotics Rsch. Conf., 1990-94. Editor: (jour.) Pain and Headache: Neurochemistry of Pain, 1990; contbr. articles over 300 articles to profl. jours., 1971—2001. Recipient Pacesetter award Nat. Inst. Drug Abuse, 1993, Pasarow award Pasarow Found., 1994, Bristol-Myers Squibb award, 1998, Edward Sachar award Columbia U., 1998; Rockefeller scholar, Beirut, 1963-66; Alfred P. Sloan fellow, Stanford, Calif., 1974-78; grantee Nat. Inst. Drug Abuse, Washington, 1978—, NIMH, Washington, 1980—, Markey Found., U. Mich., 1988-97. Fellow Am. Acad. Arts & Scis., Am. Coll. Neuropsychopharmacology (pres. 1997-98), U. Mich. Soc. Fellows; mem. Inst. Medicine (coun. mem. 2006), NAS, Soc.for Neuroscience (pres. 2002-03). Achievements include first to produce physiological evidence for existence of naturally occurring opiate-like substances (endorphins) in brain; described phenomenon of stress-induced analgesia; described functions and regulation of endorphins in brain and pituitary gland; contributed to understanding of biological mechanisms of morphine tolerance and physical dependence; (with colleagues) cloned two main types of opiate receptors, described critical brain circuits relevant to stress and depression. Office: Univ Michigan Neuroscience Dept 4137 Undergraduate Research Bldg 204 Washtenaw Ave Box 2215 Ann Arbor MI 48109 Office Phone: 734-763-3770. E-mail: akil@umich.edu.*

AKIMOTO, MARTIN WAYNE, mental health services professional; b. Chgo., July 24, 1949; s. Ned E. and Emmy (Tsujimoto) Akimoto; m. Barbara Wendley, June 11, 1983; children: Emily, Ellen. BS in Psychology, U. Utah, 1972, MSW, 1974. Lic. social worker; cert. suicide intervention trainer Calif. Social worker Protective Svc. Davis County, Div. Family Svc., Utah, 1974; pvt. practice Simi Psychotherapy Group, Simi Valley, Calif., 1979-87; field work supr. U. So. Calif., 1983-85; sr. psychiat. social worker Simi Valley Mental Health, Ventura County Mental Health Dept, 1975-76, Conejo Valley Mental Health, 1976-87; coord. outpatient children's svc. Ventura County Mental Health, Thousand Oaks, 1987-88; regional supr. children's svcs. Ventura County Mental Health Dept., 1988-92, program supr. options program, 1992-2000; program mgr. Butte County Dept. Behavioral Health, Chico, 2000—04, sr. program mgr., 2004—06; pvt. practice cons. Chico, 2007—. Vol. lectr., rap session leader Planned Parenthood Utah, 1972—73. Office: 2571 Calif Park Dr Ste 210 Chico CA 95928 Home Phone: 530-893-2764; Office Phone: 530-395-4600. Business E-Mail: maelstrim57@comcast.com. E-mail: makimoto@buttecounty.net.

AKIN, BILAL, electrical engineer; s. Kadir and Zeynep Akin. PhD (hon.), Tex. A&M U., 2007. Rsch. assc Tex. A&M U., College Station, 2003—07; r&d engr. Toshiba, Houston. Fellow EPPEI, Tex. A&M U., 2005—07. Mem.: IEEE (assoc.). Achievements include patents for system fault diagnostics. Home: 1602 Barak Ln Bryan TX 77802 Office: Tex A&M Univ Elec Engring Depart College Station TX 77843 Home Phone: 979-739-6374; Office Phone: 979-862-7463. Personal E-mail: bilalakin@ieee.org.

AKIN, CEM, internist, allergist, medical researcher; b. Istanbul, Turkey, Nov. 25, 1964; came to U.S., 1989; s. Rifat and Ozden Akin. MD, Istanbul U., 1988; PhD, U. Louisville, 1995. Diplomate Am. Bd. Internal Medicine, Am. Bd. Allergy and Immunology. Intern, then resident U. Louisville Hosps., 1993-96; fellow in allergy and immunology NIH Clin. Ctr., 1996—; clin. assoc. NIH, Bethesda, Md., 1996—99, staff clinician, 2000—04; asst. prof. U. Mich., 2004—. Advisor European Competence Network on Mastocytosis, 2004—; med. adv. bd. Mastocytosis Soc., 2004—. Contbr. articles to profl. jours., chpts. to books. U. Louisville fellow, 1989-93. Mem. Am. Acad. Allergy, Am. Coll. Allergy Asthma and Immunology, Am. Soc. Hematology. Avocations: travel, photography, music. Office: U Mich 1150 W Med Ctr Dr 5520B MSRB1 Ann Arbor MI 48109 Business E-Mail: cemakin@umich.edu.

AKIN, STEVEN PAUL, finance company executive; b. Hackensack, NJ, Apr. 6, 1945; s. Richard Ernest and Lucille F. (Mosher) A.; m. Jane Goddard, Nov. 24, 1973; children: Kyla, Sus. BA in Econs., Ohio Wesleyan U., 1969; postgrad., Columbia U., Harriman, NY, 1986. Lic. series 7 and 24, NASD, NYSE. Mgmt. trainee customer svc. mgmt. N.Y. Telephone, 1969-78; asst. v.p. customer svc. United Tel. Co. Ohio, Mansfield, 1978-85; v.p. ops. United Tel. Co. Ind., Warsaw, 1985-86, United Tel. Co. Midwest, Overland Park, Kans., 1986-87; sr. v.p., then pres. US Sprint, Kansas City, Mo., 1987-92; pres. Fidelity Retail Investor Svcs., Boston, 1992-95, Fidelity Brokerage Svcs., Inc., Boston, 1995-97, Fidelity Retail Customer Svcs., Boston, 1995-96; pres., chief info. officer Fidelity Investments Sys. Co., Boston, 1997-99; pres. Fidelity Capital, 1999—2002; pres., CEO Colt Telecomms., London, 2002—04; exec. v.p. corp. svcs. Fidelity, 2004—05, exec. v.p. distbn., 2005—. Pres. Mansfield Symphony, 1985—86, Lyric Opera, Kansas City, Kans., 1991—92; trustee Kents Hill Sch., Kents Hill, Maine, 2002—; trustee, vice-chmn. Boston Lyric Opera, 2002—03, vice chmn., 2005—. Office: EVP Fidelity 82 Devonshire St F5E Boston MA 02109 Home: PO Box 186 Belmont MA 02478-0002 Business E-Mail: steve.akin@fmu.com.

AKIN, TODD (WILLIAM TODD AKIN), congressman, former state legislator; b. NYC, July 5, 1947; m. Lulli Boe, 1971; 6 children. BS in Mgmt. Engring., Worcester Poly. Inst., Mass., 1971; MDiv, Covenant Theol. Sem., St. Louis, 1984. Mktg. mgr. IBM Computer Systems, 1973—77; corp. mgr. Laclede Steel Co., 1977—82; internat. mktg. educator, 1985—92; mem. Mo. State Ho. Reps. from Dist. 86, 1988—2001, US Congress from 2nd Mo. dist., 2001—. Mem. armed svcs. com. US Congress, mem. small bus. com., mem. sci. and tech. com., ranking mem. oversight & investigations subcommittee. Bd. dirs. Mission Gate Prison Ministry. Officer to 2nd lt. Army Combat Engrs. US Army, 1971—80. Recipient Award, Mfg. Legis. Excellence, NAM, 2003, Lawmaker award, Independent Elec. Contractors, Inc., 2004, Taxpayers' Friend award, Nat. Taxpayers Union, Hero of the Taxpayer award, Ams. for Tax Reform. Republican. Office: US House Reps 117 Cannon Ho Office Bldg Washington DC 20515-2502 Office Phone: 202-225-2561. Office Fax: 202-225-2563.*

AKIN, WANDA M., lawyer, literary and sports agent; BA, U. Louisville, 1979; JD, Seton Hall U. Sch. Law, 1982. Bar: NJ 1982, US Dist. Ct. (dist. NJ) 1982, US Supreme Ct. 1995, US Ct. Appeals (3rd cir.) 1998. Law clk. to Hon. Robert A. Matthews NJ Superior Ct. (appellate divsn.), 1982—83; assoc. Shanley & Fisher, P.C., 1983—86; ptnr., mng. atty. Scanlon & Akin (house counsel law firm for The Chubb Grp. of Ins. Cos.), 1986—94; sr. trial atty. Podvey, Sachs, Meanor, Catenacci, Hildner & Cocoziello, 1994—96, of counsel, 1997—98; sole practice atty. Newark; founding agt. Akin & Randolph Agy. Trustee Trial Attys. NJ, 1990—2004; guest faculty mem. intensive trial advocacy prog. Yeshiva U. Benjamin N. Cardozo Sch. Law, NYC, 1997—2002, 2005; adj. prof. law Cairo Prog. Seton Hall U. Sch. Law, 1998—2000; adj. prof. Seton Hall U. John C. Whitehead Sch. Diplomacy and Internat. Rels., 2000—05; mem. com. on rules of evidence NJ Supreme Ct., 2002—; adj. prof. law Seton Hall U. Sch. Law, 2004, 05. Mem. coun. Seton Hall U. Sch. Law Alumni Assn., 1989—, treas., 1994—95, sec., 1995—96, 2nd v.p., 1996—97, 1st v.p., 1997—98, pres., 1998—99. Recipient Outstanding Young Woman of Am. award, 1985, Bus. Woman of Yr. award, Nat. Assn. Negro Bus. and Profl. Women's Clubs, Inc. (North Jersey unit), 2005. Mem.: NJ State Bar Assn. (mem. com. jud. adminstrn. 1993—96), Nat. Bar Assn., Assn. Black Women Lawyers NJ, ABA (mem. task force on the pub. perception of the justice sys. 1998—), Assn. Criminal Def. Lawyers NJ, Nat. Assn. Criminal Def. Lawyers (mem. continuing legal edn. com. 1998—99), Garden State Bar Assn. Office: 1 Gateway Ctr Ste 2600 Newark NJ 07102 Office Phone: 973-623-6834. Office Fax: 973-353-8417. E-mail: wakin@akinandrandolph.com.*

AKINAKA, ASA MASAYOSHI, lawyer; b. Honolulu, Jan. 19, 1938; s. Arthur Yoshinori and Misako (Miyoshi) A.; m. Betsy Yoshie Kurata, Oct. 7, 1967; children— David Asa Yoshio, Sarah Elizabeth Sachie. BA magna cum laude, Yale U., 1959; postgrad. (Rotary Found. fellow), Trinity Coll., Oxford U., 1959-60, Yale Law Sch., 1960-61; LL.B., Stanford Law Sch., 1964. Bar: Hawaii 1964. Research asst. U.S. Senator Oren Long, Washington, 1961-62; pvt. practice law Honolulu, 1964—. Bd. visitors Stanford Law Sch., 1971-74. Mem. Am. Bar Assn., Hawaii State Bar Assn. (pres. 1977), Nat. Conf. Bar Presidents, Pacific Club, YMCA (bd. dirs., v.p. 1970-81). Democrat. Episcopalian. Office: PO Box 1035 Honolulu HI 96808-1035

AKINDEMOWO, OLUJOKE ENIOLA, law educator, researcher; d. Oluwunmi Enoch and Remilekun Solape Longe; m. Olanrewaju Michael Akindemowo, Dec. 26, 1996; children: Oluwadamilola Oluwatoni, Mojoyinoluwa Oluwafunmilola. LLB, Obafemi Awolowo U., Nigeria, 1984; LLM in Comml. Law, U. London, 1988, PhD in Info. Tech. Law, 1992; Grad. Cert. in Higher Edn. Tchg., Monash U., 2004. Barrister at law: Nigerian Law Sch. 1985. Legal practitioner Messr J.B Majiyagbe (Sr. Advocate of Nigeria) and Co., Kano, Kano State, Nigeria, 1985—86, Messrs Abayomi Sogbesan (Sr. Advocate of Nigeria) and Co., Lagos, Lagos State, 1986—87; tutor U. East London, Dagenham, Essex, England, 1990—91; lectr., tutor Middlesex U., The Burroughs, Hendon, 1990—91; lectr., sr. lectr. U. Western Sydney Faculty Law, Australia, 1993—2001; sr. lectr. Monash U. Faculty Law, Melbourne, Victoria, Australia, 2001—06; prof. Thomas Jefferson Sch. Law, San Diego, 2006—. Conf. spkr. acad. and profl. confs.; nat. mem. Australian Transaction Reports & Analysis Ctr./Office Strategic Crime Assessments Electronic Commerce Task Force, Sydney, 1996—97; cons. IIR Legal Confs., 1999—2002; assoc. dir. Ctr. Law Digital Economy, Melbourne, 2001—04. Contbr. articles to profl. jours. Australian internat. del. Internat. Fedn. Info. Processing, 2000—; convenor law and tech. group Brain Drain Brain Gain Assn., Sydney, 2000—02; mem. mgmt. com. Liverpool Migrant Resource Ctr. NSW, 2001—02. Nat. Tchg. Devel. grant, Dept. Employment, Edn., Tng. and Youth Affairs, 1997, Rsch. grant, U. Wollongong, 1997. Mem.: ABA (assoc.), Am. Soc. Internat. Law, Assn. Am. Law Schs., Australian Law Tchrs. Assn., Internat. Assn. Lawyers, Nigerian Bar Assn., Internat. Bar Assn., Banking and Fin. Svcs. Law Assn., Info. Tech. Law Assn. Home Phone: 858-703-4887. Personal E-mail: eniolaloh@yahoo.com.

AKINNUOYE-AGBAJE, ADEWALE, actor; b. London, Aug. 22, 1967; LLM, U. London. Actor: (films) Congo, 1995, Ace Ventura: When Nature Calls, 1995, Legionnaire, 1998, Red Shoe Diaries 12: Girl on a Bike, 2000, The Mummy Returns, 2001, Lip Service, 2001, The Bourne Identity, 2002, Unstoppable, 2004, Mistress of Spices, 2005, On the One, 2005, Get Rich or Die Tryin', 2005; (TV films) Deadly Voyage, 1996, 20,000 Leagues Under the Sea, 1997, Enslavement: The True Story of Fanny Kemble, 2000; (TV series) Oz, 1997—2000, Linc's, 1998, Lost, 2005—06 (Outstanding Performance by an Ensemble in a Drama Series, Screen Actors Guild award, 2006).*

AKINS, CARY WILLARD, surgeon, educator; b. July 13, 1944; AB, Harvard Coll., 1966; MD, Harvard U., 1970. Diplomate Am. Bd. Thoracic Surgery. Resident in gen. surgery Mass. Gen. Hosp., Boston, 1970—74, fellow in cardiac surgery, 1975, clin. prof. surgery, dir. clin. cardiac rsch./end results cardiac surgery; fellow in cardiac surgery Southampton Western Hosp., Eng., 1974. Office: Mass Gen Hosp Cox 648 55 Fruit St Boston MA 02114-2696 Office Phone: 617-726-8218.

AKINS, NICHOLAS K., electric power industry executive; B in Elec. Engring., La. Tech U., Ruston, 1982, M in Elec. Engring., 1986. Registered profl. engr., Tex. Various dir. and mgr. positions including CSWS dir. restructuring readiness, CSWS dir. mergers and acquisitions, CSWS dir. solid fuels, WTU dir. fuels Ctrl. and South West Corp.; v.p. industry restructuring Am. Electric Power Svc. Corp., v.p. energy mktg. svcs., pres., COO Southwestern Electric Power Co., 2004, exec. v.p. generation. Mem.: NSPE, Tex. Soc. Profl. Engrs., Eta Kappa Nu, Tau Beta Pi. Office: Am Electric Power Svc Corp 1 Riverside Plz Columbus OH 43215-2373 Office Phone: 614-716-1000.*

AKINS, VAUGHN EDWARD, retired engineering company executive; b. Gowanda, NY, Sept. 28, 1934; s. Elsworth D. and Alice (Carlton) A.; m. Muriel M. Hoglund, May 15, 1960 (dec. 1992); children: Sonja L., Coleen R., Joseph E.; m. Lois B. Monroe, June 10, 2006. Student, U.S. Naval Schs., 1956-57, IBM Engring. Sch., 1961-65. Lab. specialist IBM, Poughkeepsie, NY, Boulder, Colo., East Fishkill, NY, 1959—69; test mgr. Semi, Phoenix, 1969-74; mgr. computer-aided mfg. and test engring. semicondr. R&D Motorola Corp., Mesa, Ariz., 1974-84; applications mgr. (SIM) Motorola Corp. New Enterprises Group, Mesa, 1984-86; mgr. computer integrated mfg. semicondr. products sector Motorola Corp., Phoenix, 1986-87; with start-up team SEMATECH, Inc., Austin, Tex., 1988-93, dir. internat. standards programs, 1989-93, mgr. incubator programs, 1992; mgr. strategic integration Motorola Ctr. Advanced Computer Products, Austin, 1993-96; ret. Motorola Wireless Sys. Ctr., Austin, 1996-98; cons. in field, 2000—. Personal and bus. coach. Precinct committeeman N.Y. State Conservative Party, 1963; instr. first aid ARC, 1971-78; chair U.S. exec. com. S.E.M.I., Inc., mem. exec. std. com. internat. standard program, 1987-1993. With USNR, 1953-59. Mem. IEEE (sr.), NRA, Electrochem. Soc. (cons. to exec. bd., co-chmn. founding com. Automation in Mfg. chpt., exec. com. electronics divsn. 1985-92), World Future Soc Fundamentalist. Home: 6511 Abilene Trail Austin TX 78749 Office Phone: 512-217-9312. Personal E-mail: vaughn@akinsolan.com. Business E-Mail: vakins@ieee.org.

AKINS, ZANE VERNON, agricultural products executive; b. Bethel, Kans., Apr. 13, 1940; s. Gerald Vernon and Vesta Jean (Rutherford) A.; m. Kay Ellen Cowan, Aug. 17, 1963; children: Michael Scott, Deborah Lynn, Christine Sue. BS in Agr., U. Mo., 1962. Farmer, 1962-64; svc. technician No. Ohio Breeders Assn., Tiffin, 1964-66; program dir. Holstein Assn. Am., Brattleboro, Vt., 1966-73, mgr. sire devel. svc., 1973-77, adminstrv. asst., 1977-78, CEO, 1978-90; exec. v.p. Holstein-Friesian Svcs., Inc., Brattleboro, 1978-90; pres. Zane Akins and Assocs., West Brattleboro, 1991—. Pres., chmn. bd. dirs. Nat. Integrated Techs. Inc., 1996—; bd. dirs. Earthwide Assocs., Inc., pres. 1994—; pres. A&S Assocs., Ltd., 1995—; bd. dirs. Vt. Nat. Bank, 1987-2000, Earthwide Sys. Inc., v.p., 1995—; v.p. Earthwide Products Corp., 1996—; bd. dirs. Vt. Fin. Svcs., 1987-2000, chmn. exec. com., 1995-96, chmn. audit com., 1996-97, chmn. loan com., 1997-98; regional leader Primerica Fin. Svcs., 1991-2006; chmn. bd. dirs. Anitech Internat. Inc., Boulder, Colo., 1991-92; trustee N.E. Delta/Vt. Dental Soc., Inc., 1990-99, chmn., 1995-99; chmn. bd. NEDA, 1999-2004; pres. Vt. Natural Food Products Inc., 2001—; real estate agt., 2004—; ptnr. Akins Fin. Group, 2005—. Bd. dirs. Windham County United Way, 1980-84; corporator Brattleboro Meml. Hosp., 1980—, chmn. pub. rels. com., 1982-83, bd. dirs., 1983-86; pres. Windham County Humane Soc., 1992-93; bd. dirs. Brattleboro Area Boys & Girls Club, 1998-2002, treas., 1999-2002. Sears & Roebuck scholar, Freshman Curators scholar, Borden's scholar, U. Mo., 1958-59, Sophomore Curators scholar, Campus Chest scholar, 1958-60; recognized as Man of the Yr. Tri-State Breeders Coop., 1984; recipient Citation of Merit U. Mo., 1986. Mem. Purebred Dairy Cattle Assn. (bd. dirs. 1978-90, Recognition award 1991), Nat. Soc. Livestock Records Assn. (v.p. 1982-84), Nat. Pedigree Livestock Coun. (pres. 1984-86, sec., treas. 1989—, Disting. Svc. award 1993), Nat. Coop. Dairy Herd Improvement Programs (policy bd. 1980-90), Geonomics Inst., Boston Dist. Export Coun., Brattleboro C. of C. (bd. dirs. 1979-81), Alpha Zeta (Centennial Honor Roll 1997), Alpha Gamma Rho (regional v.p. 1980-84, bd. dirs. 1984-90, grand pres. 1986-89, Man of Yr. award Chgo. Alumni chpt. 1991, Bro. of the Century 2004, inductee Hall of Fame 2006). Congregationalist. Home and Office: 177 Palermo Pl Lady Lake FL 32159-0094

AKINTIMOYE, AKINDELE D., lawyer, consultant; b. Sept. 3, 1968; s. Moses Oyenusi and Victoria Okunade Akintimoye; m. Elizabeth Olabisi Garuba, Dec. 27, 1997; children: Deborah, Daniel, Grace. LLB, U. Benin, Edo State, 1992; Barrister at Law, Nigerian Lw Sch., Lagos, 1993. Bar: Calif. 2003. Intern Oluyede & Onwuagbo, Lagos, Nigeria, 1992; assoc. A. Babalola & Co. Barristers & Solicitors, Lagos, Nigeria, 1993—94; prin. lawyer Dele Akintimoye & Co. Barristers & Solicitors, Lagos, Nigeria, 1994—2001; fgn. legal cons. Law Offices A. Sam Akintimoye, Ontario, Calif., 2001—03; prin. atty. Law Offices David Akintimoye, Inc., Riverside, Calif., 2004—. Contbr. articles to profl. jours. Recipient Nat. Leadership award, Nat. Rep. Congl. Com., 2006. Mem.: ABA, Assn. Trial Lawyers Am. Office: Law Offices David Akintimoye 5900 Magnolia Ave Riverside CA 92506 Office Phone: 951-369-0259. Office Fax: 951-369-0028. Business E-Mail: deleakintimoye@yahoo.com.

AKISKAL, HAGOP SOUREN, psychiatric researcher, educator; b. Beirut, Jan. 16, 1944; U.S., 1969; s. Stephen Jacques and Vehanoushe Dickran (Bedrossian) A. MD, Am. U., Beirut, 1969; Dr honoris causa, U. Lisbon, 2003; Dr honoris causa (hon.), Aristotle U., Greece, 2005. Instr. U. Tenn., Memphis, 1972-73, asst. prof., 1973-77, assoc. prof., 1977-80, prof. psychiatry, dir. sect. affective disorders program, 1975—, dir. med. student edn., 1974-78. Co-dir. Sleep Disorders Ctr., Bapt. Meml. Hosp., Memphis, 1983—; Eli Robins lectr. Washington U., 1980; sr. sci. advisor Nat. Inst. Mental Health, 1990-94; prof. psychiatry, dir. Internat. Mood Ctr., Divsn. Internat. Health and Cross-Cultural Medicine, U. Calif. San Diego, 1994—. Editor (editor-in-chief): Jour. of Affective Disorders, 1996—. Recipient Anna Monika prize, 1999, Affective Disorders prize, NARSAD, 2001, Jean Delay prize, World Psychiat. Assn., 2002, Ellis Island medal of honor, 2003, Aristotle Gold medal, Brain & Behavior Soc., Greece, 2006. Fellow Am. Psychiat. Assn. (disting.), Soc. Biol. Psychiatry (Gold medal 1995), Am. Coll. Psychiatrists, Internat. Coll. Neuropsychopharmacology, Royal Coll. Psychiatrists (hon.), French Nat. Academy Medicine (fgn. mem., Paris), Armenian Nat. Acad. Scis. (hon). Office: Univ Calif Psychiatary 0603 9500 Gilman Dr La Jolla CA 92093-5004 Office Phone: 858-552-8585. Business E-Mail: hakiskal@ucsd.edu.

AKIYAMA, CAROL LYNN, motion picture industry executive; BA magna cum laude, U. So. Calif., JD. Bar: Calif. Atty. NLRB, LA, ABC-TV, Hollywood, Calif., So. Calif. Edison, Rosemead; asst. gen. atty. CBS Inc., LA; sr. v.p. Alliance Motion Picture and TV Producers, Sherman Oaks, Calif., 1982-88; ind. producer and writer TV, motion pictures and multimedia/new techs., Woodland Hills, Calif., 1988—. Cons. entertainment industry; founding ptnr. Bierstedt, Akiyama and Assocs., Woodland Hills, 1988—. Mem.: Phi Beta Kappa, Phi Kappa Phi. Office Phone: 818-713-9987. E-mail: carol@bierstedt.com.

AKIYAMA, CLIFF, forensic science educator, criminologist, researcher, consultant; b. LA, May 9, 1973; s. Drew and Helen (Handa) A. BA in Philosophy, U. Va., 1998; MA in Criminology with distinction, U. Pa., 2004, student, 2005—. Cert. in cmty. partnership program FBI, Phila., 2006. Vis. rsch. student S.W. divsn., gang detail unit and N.E. divsn., sci. investigation divsn. LA Police Dept., 1995—97; rsch. assoc. in spinal surgery Calif. Med. Ctr. Minimally Invasive Spine Surgery and Conejo Multi-Splty. Med. Group, Thousand Oaks, Calif., 1995—97; dep. sheriff res. forces bur. LA County Sheriff's Dept., 1999—2001; therapeutic staff support Devereux Found., Devereux Cmty. Svcs. Phila., 2002—06, instr., 2003—06; behavioral specialist cons. Cmty. Orgn. Mental Health and Retardation, Inc., Phila., 2006—. Presenter in field, 1995—; interviewee in field, 1997, 2003; instr. youth st. gangs Ctrl. Shenandoah Criminal Justice Tng. Ctr., Police Acad. Commonwealth Va., Waynesboro, 1997; spl. cons. in youth violence Sch. Medicine, Sch. Nursing, Ctr. Study of Mind and Human Interaction, Inst. Quality Health, U. Va. Health Scis. Ctr., Charlottesville, Va., 1997—98; workshop conf. moderator in field, 1998—2003; guest lectr. in field, 1998—; instr. Asian Am. youth and pub. health Summer Pub. Health Rsch. Inst. and Videoconference Minority Health, U. NC, Chapel Hill, 2002; co-instr. law enforcement topics U. Pa., Phila., 2002; grad. rsch. asst. in legal studies Carol and Lawrence Zicklin Ctr. Bus. Ethics Rsch., Wharton Sch., U. Pa, Phila., 2003—04; instr. Commonwealth Pa., Dept. Health, Emergency Med. Svcs. Office, Harrisburg, Pa., 2003—; grad. tchg. asst. victimology, forensic mental health, forensic sci. Sch. Nursing, U. Pa., Phila., 2004—05; lectr. in forensic sci. Sch. Nursing, Divsn. Family and Cmty. Health, U. Pa., Phila., 2005—. Contbr. articles to profl. jours., abstracts, book chpts. and revs. in field. Social co-chmn. Grad. Assn. Asian Am. Students and Studies, Phila., 2002-03, com. chmn. Asian Pacific Islander Am. Heritage Week, 2003-04; com. mem. Interpersonal Violence Against Asian Communities Task Force, Women Organized Against Rape, 2006-, v.p. Gold Congl. Alumni Assn., Congl. Award Found., 2007-. Recipient Disting. Cmty. Svc. award Gardena Valley Chpt., Kiwanis Club Internat., 1990, Fellowship award LA Pediatric Soc., 1991, Cert. of Recognition Calif. State Senate, 1996, Proclamation of Commendation County of LA, 1996, 97, Cert. Outstanding Svc. City of Torrance,

1996, Cert. of Recognition LA City Coun., 1996, Proclamation of Commendation City of LA, 1996, 97, Cert. of Recognition Calif. State Assembly, 1996, Cert. of Commendation Nat. award, Pres.'s Youth Svc. awards, Office Nat. Svc., Am. Inst. Pub. Svc. Commn. Nat. and Cmty. Svc., 1996, US Senate, Gold Congl. award US Congress, 1996, Silver Congl. award, 1998, Clin. Investigator Scholarship award D. Ralph Millard MD Plastic Surg. Soc. and Found., 1996, Mayor's Cert. of Commendation City of LA, 1997, Pres.'s Youth Svc. awards, Office Nat. Svc., Am. Inst. Pub. Svc. Commn. Nat. and Cmty. Svc., 1997, Cert. of Appreciation, Devereux Cmty. Svcs. Phila., 2003; Nisaburo Aibara Meml. scholarship Japanese Am. Citizens League, 2005. Mem.: APHA (immediate past recipient mem. selection com. 1998, com. mem. task force assn. improvement and reorganization 2002—05, com. mem. task force universal health care 2002—05, abstract reviewer 2003—, Jay S. Drotman Meml. award 1997), Congl. Award Alumni Assn., Japanese Am. Citizens League (bd. dirs. Phila. chpt. 2006—), Nat. Eagle Scout Assn. (life named Eagle Scout with 66 merit badges and 6 palms 1989, Cert. of Recognition for Eagle Scout Rank 1990, Merit award 1990, Cert. of Commendation 1990, Resolution of Commendation 1990, named Robert O. Anderson Outstanding Eagle Scout of Yr. 1993), Boy Scouts Am. (named William "Bill" Hillcourt Outstanding Eagle of Yr. 1993), Phi Eta Sigma. Methodist. Avocations: golf, Judo, autograph collecting, hiking, running. Office: U Pa Sch Nursing 420 Guardian Dr Rm 402 Philadelphia PA 19104-6096 Personal E-mail: cliffakiyama@yahoo.com. Business E-Mail: cakiyama@nursing.upenn.edu.

AKIYAMA, TOSHIO, cardiologist, educator, researcher, director; b. Shimizu, Japan, Mar. 10, 1941; came to U.S., 1968; m. Akiko Okamura Akyama; children: Naoko, Sachiko. MD, Kyoto Prefectural U. Med., 1966. Cert. in internal medicine, specialty in cardiovasc. disease. Rotating intern U.S. Naval Hosp., Yokosuka, Japan, 1966—67; med. resident, 3d internal medicine dept. Kyoto Prefectural U. Medicine, 1967; staff physician Atomic Bomb Casualty Commn., Hiroshima, Japan, 1967—68; intern Rochester Gen. Hosp., 1968-69, resident in medicine, 1969-70, Strong Meml. Hosp.-U. Rochester, 1970-71, resident in cardiology, 1972-73; fellow in cardiology Emory U., Atlanta, 1971-72, U. Chgo., 1973-75; dir. heart sta. Strong Meml. Hosp., Rochester; prof. medicine with unltd. tenure U. Rochester Sch. Medicine, 1993—2006; co-dir. cardiovasc. scis. Covance, Reno, 2006—. Reviewer NIH study sect. Biomed. Tech. Spl. Emphasis Panel; cons. Exec. com. for Japanese Med. Specialist Joint commn. Mem. editl. bd. Jour. Electrocardiology, Jour. Arrhythmia, Japanese Circulation Jour., Jour. Arrhythmia, Acta Medica Mem. Biologica; contbr. over 160 articles to profl. jours Chmn. Rochester Hamamatsu Sister City Com., chmn., 1998-2000. Fellow Am. Coll. Cardiology; mem. Am. Heart Assn., N.Am. Soc. of Pacing and Electrophysiology, Japanese Med. Soc. (exec. com. joint commn. med. specialist sys.), Japanese Clin. Cardiology Soc. Office: Covance Cardiac Safety Svcs 9390 Gateway Dr Reno NV 89521 Personal E-mail: takiyama1558@charter.net. Business E-Mail: toshio.akiyama@covance.com.

AKIYOSHI, TOSHIKO, jazz composer, pianist; b. Ryoyo, Manchuria, Dec. 12, 1929; arrived in USA, 1956; d. Tatsuro and Shigeko (Hiraike) A.; m. Charlie Mariano, 1959 (div. 1967); m. Lewis Tabackin, Nov. 3, 1969; 1 child, Michiru Mariano Grad., Berklee Coll. Music, Boston. Founder, pianist, trio, 1953-70; appeared throughout U.S., Europe, Japan, founder, leader, composer-arranger, Toshiko Akiyoshi/Lew Tabackin Big Band, 1972-83, ToshikoAkiyoshi Jazz Orchestra, 1983—; albums include Long Yellow Road, 1976 (named Best Jazz Album of Yr., Stereo Rev.), Insights, 1978, Notorious Tourist from the East, 1978, Farewell to Mingus, 1980, European Memoirs, 1984, Top of the Gate, 1986, Finesse, 1987, Interlude, 1987, Remembering Bud, 1990, Wishing Peace, 1991, The Toshiko Akiyoshi/Lew Tabackin Big Band, 1991; Live at Birdland 1960-61, with The Charlie Mariano Quintet, 1992, Live at Carnegie Hall, 1992, Hiroshima: Rising from the Abyss, 2001, Last Live in Blue Note Tokyo, 2003; appears in (documentaries): Toshiko Akiyoshi: Jazz is My Native Language, 1984; author: Life With Jazz, 1996. Named Best Arranger, Best Band by Downbeat Poll, 1978, 79, Best Arranger, 1989; recipient Ellis Island Medal of Honor, National Ethnic Coalition of Organizations, 1986, Liberty award, 1986. first Japanese jazz artist to be recorded by a US record label (1953), to release an LP in the US (1954), to attend what was then-called Berklee Sch. Music. in Boston (1956), and to perform in the US, both as a leader and with such jazz artists as Miles Davis, Max Roach and Charles Mingus (1956-62); first to introduce Japanese element with straight-ahead jazz in big band composition (1972-2003).

AKKARA, JOSEPH AUGUSTINE, chemist, educator; arrived in US, 1964, naturalized, 1980; s. Augustine Aippu Akkara and Theresa Anthony Kolapran; m. Mary Ann Malaickel, Aug. 18, 1969; children: Augustine Viju, Jeena Theresa. PhD in Biochemistry, U. Mo., 1969. Med. rschr. Med. Coll. Trivandrum, Kerala, India, 1959-61; tech. asst. Ctrl. Food Technol. Rsch. Inst., Mysore, India, 1961-64; grad. asst., rsch. assoc. Sch. Medicine U. Mo., Columbia, 1964-69; rsch. assoc. Rockefeller U., NYC, 1969-71, Brookdale Hosp. Med. Ctr., Bklyn., 1971-73, chief radioassay, 1973-80; sr. scientist Med. Rsch. Inst., Worcester, Mass., 1980-81; biochemist stat. Toxicology Svc. Boston, 1981-84; rsch. chemist U.S. Army Natick Rsch. and Engring. Ctr., 1984-99; program dir. NSF, 1999—. Adj. faculty Framingham State Coll., 1996-99; mem. biotechnology adv. bd. Mass. Bay Coll.; advisor NRC; bd. dirs. Invention Evaluation. Recipient R&D award U.S. Army, 1992, 96, Inventor of Yr. award U.S. Army Soldier Sys. commd., 1998. Mem. Materials Rsch. Soc., Am. Chem. Soc., N.Y. Acad. Scis., Kerala Assn. New Eng. (pres. 1986-87), Indian Assn. Greater Boston (sec. 1986-88, 1st v.p. 1988-89), Lions Club, Rotary (pres. Falls Church Club 2006—), Sigma Xi (pres. Natick chpt. 1998-99). Roman Catholic. Achievements include patents and publications in synthesis, modification, characterization, and applications of polymers and materials for electro-optic and high performance multifunctional applications; enzymology, nutrition, endocrinology, analytical chemistry, and research program management. Home: 7520 Walnut Hill Ln Falls Church VA 22042-3539 E-mail: jakkara@nsf.gov, jaakkara@aol.com.

AKKER, ARLENE F., social sciences educator; d. Herman C. and Marjorie K. Dekker; m. William J. Akker, July 23, 1976; children: Scott E., Kathryn J. AA in English and Social Sci., Muskegon C.C., Mich., 1973; BA in English, Social Sci. and Secondary Edn., Hope Coll., Holland, Mich., 1975; MA in Reading, Western Mich. U., Kalamazoo, 1994. Cert. continuing secondary edn. Mich., social studies tchr. Mich. Tchr. part-time Asst. Adult Edn. Programs, Muskegon, 1975—81; supr. environ. svcs. Hackley Hosp., Muskegon, 1981—87; tchr. Muskegon Pub. Schs., 1987—; founds. dir. Jordan Coll., Grand Rapids, 1992—95. Advisor Nat. Honor Soc. Muskegon Pub. Schs.; coord. activities/social work asst. Christian Convalescent Home, Muskegon, 1978—81. Mem.: Nat. Coun. English Tchrs., Nat. Coun. Social Studies. Mem. Reformed Ch. In Am. Achievements include development of Strategic Reading as a "double-dip" English credit for students entering ninth grade with reading levels below eighth grade. Avocations: travel, reading, web development. Office: Muskegon HS 80 W Southern Muskegon MI 49441 Business E-Mail: aakker@mpsk12.net.

AKKOR, GUNDOGDU, retired architectural firm executive, engineering executive, foundation administrator; b. Ankara, Turkey, Apr. 3, 1936; s. Omer Faruk and Servet Akkor; m. Inci Ayse Benler, Oct. 11, 1962; children: Gunin, Gun. Architect, Istanbul Tech. U., 1955, Engr. MS, 1961. Chief hosp. planning group Hacettepe Sci. Ctr. Archtl. Office, Ankara, 1961-70; mgr. bldg. design group, dir. SISAG Co. Ltd., Ankara, 1970-76; mgr. archtl. and engring. svcs. group, dir. TEKSIS Co. Ltd., Ankara, 1976-81; dir. 2 Hacettepe Found. Cos. and UCME Archtl. and Engring. Co. Ltd., 1981—. Instr. Middle East Tech. U., 1971; bd. dirs. Bilkent Holding Inc.; cons. to Turkish State Planning Orgn., 1965, 70. Archtl. works include Gen. Tchg. Hosp., Hacettepe U., Ankara, 1963, Children's Hosp., Hacettepe U., 1967, Turkish Gen. Hosp., Nicosia, Cyprus, 1971, Gen. Tchg. Hosp., Istanbul U., Edirne, Turkey, 1975, also 10 other tchg. hosps. in Turkey, 1975-85. V.p. bd. trustees Bilkent U. Served to 2d lt. Armoured Divsns., Turkish Armed Forces, 1972-74. WHO fellow, 1963. Mem. Union Chamber Turkish Engrs. and Architects.

AKO, HARRY, engineering educator, researcher; b. Honolulu, Mar. 16, 1945; s. Lawrence and Margaret Ako; m. Joan Arakaki; children: Christopher Joel, Michelle Stewart. AB, U. Calif., Berkeley, 1967; PhD, Wash State U., Pullman, 1972. Prof. dept. molecular bioscis. U. Hawaii, Honolulu, 2000, chmn. dept. molecular bioscis. and bioengring., 2005—. Chmn. Ctr. Tropical and Subtropical Aquaculture, Honolulu, 1994—. Contbr. articles to profl. jours. Recipient Tchg. award, N.Am. Colls. Tchrs. Agr., 1988. Achievements include research in omega-3 fatty acids. Home: 1114 Wilder Ave #708 Honolulu HI 96822 Office: Univ Hawaii 1955 East West Rd #218 Honolulu HI 96822 Home Phone: 808-956-2012; Office Phone: 808-956-2012. Office Fax: 808-956-3542; Home Fax: 808-956-3542. Business E-Mail: hako@hawaii.edu.

AKON, (ALIAUNE THIAM), singer; b. St. Louis, Apr. 30, 1973; s. Mor Thiam. Founder Kon Live Distbn., 2006, Konvict Clothing, 2007. Singer: (albums) Trouble, 2004, Konvicted, 2006, In My Ghetto, 2007, (songs) Locked Up, 2004, I Wanna Love You, 2006, Smack That, 2006, (with Gwen Stefani) The Sweet Escape, 2006. Founder Konfidence Found. Recipient Best African Act award, Music of Black Origins (MOBO) Awards, 2005, Male Breakout Artist award, Teen Choice Awards, 2007. Office: Konvict Online Ste 807 307 W 38th St New York NY 10018 also: c/o Universal Records 825 8th Ave New York NY 10019*

AKOS, FRANCIS, retired violinist, conductor; b. Budapest, Hungary, Mar. 30, 1922; came to U.S., 1954; s. Karoly and Rose (Reti) Weinberg; m. Phyllis Malvin Sommers, June 7, 1981; children from previous marriage: Katherine Elizabeth, Judith Margaret. Baccalaureate, Budapest, 1941; MA, Franz Liszt Acad. Music, Budapest, 1940, PhD, 1941. Concertmaster, Budapest Symphony Orch., 1945-46, Royal Opera and Philharmonic Soc., Budapest, 1947-48, Gothenburg (Sweden) Symphony Orch., 1948-50, Municipal Opera (now Deutsche Oper), West Berlin, Ger., 1950-54, Mpls. Symphony Orch., 1954, asst. concertmaster, Chgo. Symphony Orch., 1955—, ret., 2003, concertmaster emeritus, 1997-, also performed as soloist; performed at Salzburg Festival, 1948, Scandinavian Festival, Helsinki, Finland, 1950, Berlin Festival, 1951, Prades Festival, 1953, Bergen Festival, 1962, Vienna Festival, 1962, founder, condr., Chgo. Strings, chamber orch., 1961, condr., Fox River Valley Symphony, Aurora, Ill., 1965-73, Chicago Heights Symphony, Ill., 1975-79, Highland Park Strings, 1979—. Prizewinner Hubay competition, Budapest, 1939, Remenyi competition, Budapest, 1939 Personal E-mail: violak1310@yahoo.com.

AKOURIS, DIANNE, elementary school educator; d. Sylvester X. and Marcella H. Hefter; m. John Akouris, June 19, 1976. BS in Edn., Alverno Coll., Milw., 1969; MA in Reading, Northeastern Ill. U., Chgo., 1988. Cert. advanced study of supr. Nat. Louis U., 1992, elem. and secondary tchg. Ill. Tchr. Parochial Archdioceses of Chgo., 1959—64, 1966—85, St. Mary's Sch., Holly Springs, Miss., 1964—66, Cook County, Chgo., 1985; tchrs. aide Westnorthfield Elem. Sch., Glenview, Ill., 1985—86; comm. tchr. Waukegan Pub. Sch., Ill., 1986—87; tchr. Fremont Sch. Dist., Fremont, Ill., 1987—88, Waukegan Pub. Sch., Waukegan, Ill., 1988—2000, summer bridges coord., 2000; facilitator Waukegan Tchrs. Acad., 2000—06, lead tchr., curriculum specialist, 2006—. Coop. tchr. Barat Coll., Lake Forest, Ill., 1995, Lake Forest, 97, Nat. Louis U., Evanston, Ill., 1999; presenter in field. Moderator League of Women Voters, Libertyville, Ill., 1993, WKRS Radio Station, Waukegan, Ill., 1993. Nominee Golden Apple award, Golden Apple Found., 2000; recipient First Grant award, First Bank of Am., 1995, Excellence in Tchg. award, Classic Cheverlot of Waukegan, 2000. Mem.: ASCD, Suburban Coun. Ill. Reading Assn., Ill. Reading Coun., Internat. Reading Assn., Ill. Principals Assn. Avocations: gardening, reading, choir. Home: 2004 Sunset Ct Zion IL 60099 Office: Curriculum Dept Lincoln Ctr 1201 N Sheridan Rd Waukegan IL 60085

AKSELRAD, HAL (HAROLD EATON), broadcast executive, lawyer; b. Bklyn., Sept. 19, 1953; s. Ralph and Rachel (Albert) A. BA, NYU, 1974, JD, 1977. Bar: NY 1978, US Dist. Ct. (so. & ea. dists.) NY. Law asst. appellate div. 2d jud. dept. NY State Supreme Ct., Bklyn., 1978-80; assoc. litig. Cravath, Swaine & Moore, NYC, 1980-83; assoc. counsel litig. HBO Inc., NYC, 1983—84, counsel litig., 1984—85, chief counsel litig., 1985—86, v.p. & chief counsel litig., 1986—89, sr. v.p. bus. affairs, 1989—99, exec. v.p. bus. affairs, 1999—2002, gen. counsel & exec. v.p. legal, bus. affairs & film programming, 2002—07, gen. counsel & co-pres., 2007—. Mem. Assn. of Bar of City of NY (sec. trade regulation com. 1982-83). Office: HBO 1 Time Warner Ctr New York NY 10019-8016*

AKSEN, GERALD, arbitrator, mediator, lawyer; b. NYC, Feb. 16, 1930; AB, CCNY, 1951; MA, Columbia U., 1952; LLB, NYU, 1958. Bar: N.Y. 1959, U.S. Dist. Ct. (so. and ea. dist.) N.Y. 1961, U.S. Supreme Ct. 1964. Assoc. Flood & Purvin, NYC, 1958—61; assoc. gen. counsel Am. Arbitration Assn., NYC, 1962—63, gen. counsel, 1964—80; ptnr. Reid & Priest LLP, NYC, 1981—98, Thelen Reid & Priest LLP, NYC, 1998—2002; ret. ptnr. Thelen Reid Brown Raysman & Steiner LLP (formerly Thelen Reid & Priest LLP), NYC, 2003—. Adj. prof. NYU, N.Y.C., 1968-2001; mem. First Dept. Jud. Screening Com., 1983-93; bd. dirs. U.S. Coun. Internat. Bus., 1982—; ICC Inst. World Bus. Law, 1992—; vice chmn. ICC Internat. Ct. Arbitration, 2000-02; pres. Coll. Coml. Arbitrators, 2002-03. Bd. dirs. Nat. Inst. Consumer Justice, 1971-72, World Arbitration Inst. 1984-2000; mem. adv. bd. Inst. for Internat. and Comparative Law, 1988—; pvt. adjudications com. Ctr. for Pub. Resources, 1988-2002. 1st lt. U.S. Army, 1952-55. Fellow Am. Bar Found; mem. ABA (ho. of dels. 1985-87, chmn. sect. internat. law and practice 1982-83), N.Y. State Bar Assn., Assn. Bar City of N.Y. (chmn. adv. com. on ADR 1992-93), London Ct. Internat. Arbitration, Am. Arbitration Assn. (bd. dirs. 1982-95), Citizens Union (bd. dirs. 1983-86), Am. Soc. Internat. Law. Office: Thelen Reid Brown Raysman & Steiner LLP 875 Third Ave 10th Fl New York NY 10022 Office Phone: 212-603-2174. Business E-Mail: gaksen@thelen.com.

AKSOY, HAKAN, mechanical engineer; s. Mehmet and Nevin Aksoy; m. Elvan Ozlu, July 26, 1989; children: Kaan, Selin. Degree, Bogazici U., Istanbul, Turkey, 1986; PhD, Ariz. State U., Tempe, 1995. Prin. engr. Honeywell Internat., Phoenix, Ariz., 1996—. Recipient The Lewis F. Moody Award for Best Paper in Mech. Engring. Practice, ASME, 1996. Mem.: AIAA, ASME (session chair 2006—). Achievements include patents in field. Home: 443 West Courtney Ln Tempe AZ 85284 Office: Honeywell Engines Sys & Svcs MS 101-113 111 S 34th St Phoenix AZ 85072 Office Phone: 602-231-1588. Office Fax: 602-231-3811. Business E-Mail: hakan.aksoy@honeywell.com.

AKUKWE, CHINUA, public health physician, health service executive; b. Aug. 7, 1962; MD, U. Nigeria, Enugu, 1985; M in Pub. Health, Hebrew U., Jerusalem, Israel, 1991; cert. in Exec. Pub. Health Mgmt., Johns Hopkins U., 1998. Sci. coord. NIH, D.C. Initiative, Washington, 1993-97; sr. policy and planning advisor to dir. D.C Dept Health, Washington, 1997-98; assoc. prof. U. Md., College Park, 1997—, George Washington U. Sch. Pub. Health, Washington, 1998—, U. D.C., Washington, 1998—. Coord. Global Health Seminars George Washington U. Med. Ctr., Washington, 1997—98; vice chmn. Nat. Coun. Internat. Health, Washington, 1997—98; workshop expert minority health Dept. Health, Columbia, SC, 1998; mem. tech. rev. panels for maternal and child health and health stats. U.S. Dept. HHS, 1995—; mem. com. on faculty support and profl. devel. George Washington U. Hosp. Ctr., 1999—2004, mem. exec. com., faculty senate, 2004—05, chair tech. adv. com., Africa Ctr. for Health and Security, 2005—; bd. dirs. Constituency for Africa, Washington; mem. expert com. HIV/AIDS in Africa and governance UN Econ. Commn. Africa; tech. advisor Howard U., Washington, coord. global health com., 2004; chmn. bd. dirs. Africa Ctr. Epidemiology and Econ. Rsch., Abuja, Nigeria, 2006—; spkr. in field. Author: Healthcare in Africa, 2006, Development Issues in Africa, 2006; co-author: AIDS Orphans in Africa and Their Grandparents, 2006; editor-in-chief Jour. Pub. Health, Biotech. and Pharm. Products; editor: (spl. edit.) Africa Renaissance Jour. on Health Care Delivery in Africa, 2006; mem. editl. bd. Am. Jour. Pub. Health, 1999—2003, author, co-author 46 tech. monographs on various health issues; contbr. more than 100 articles on HIV/AIDSand health issues in Africa. Bd. dirs. Christian Connections for Internat. Health, 1994—96, Peace Corps Nigeria Alumni Found., Washington, 2002—. Fellow: Am. Coll. Epidemiology, Royal Soc. Medicine London, Royal Soc. Health (Eng.); mem.: N.Y. Acad. Scis., Am. Pub. Health Assn. (co-chair 125th Ann. Conf. 1997). Achievements include development of the Communicable Diseases Guidelines for Africa Development Bank, 2003-04; HIV/AIDS, TB and Malaria Continental Implementation Plan for African Union, 2006-07. Avocations: current affairs, soccer, reading biographies, health books. Office: George Washington Univ Dept Global Health 2175 K St NW Ste 810 Washington DC 20037 Business E-Mail: cakukwe@gwu.edu.

AKURA, JUNSUKE, ophthalmologist, researcher; b. Kurashiki, Japan, Dec. 2, 1954; s. Yasushi and Sachiko Akura; m. Kaori Akura, Apr. 5, 1998; children: Erika, Madoka. MD, Tottori U., Japan, 1980, PhD, 1987. Asst. prof. Faculty of Medicine, Tottori U., 1987—88; hosp. dir. Kushimoto (Japan) Rehab. Ctr., 1991—. Author: Letters from Birganj, 1991; patentee in field. Bd. dirs. Assn. for Ophthalmic Cooperation to Asia, Osaka, Japan, 1988—2002, chmn., 2002—. Recipient Film Festival award, Am. Soc. Cataract and Refractive Surgery, 1996, prize, Atsuhito Nakata Meml. Found. Charitable Trust, Japan, 1997, Prabal Gorkhadachhinbahu medal, King of Nepal, 2001. Achievements include development of new surgical methods of astigmatic keratotomy (FDAK); manual small incision cataract surgery (claw-vectis technique, quarter extraction); pterygium surgery (mini-flap technique); glaucoma surgery (Uveal shunt). Avocation: tennis. Office: Kushimoto Rehab Ctr 259-6 Kushimoto Kushimoto 649-3503 Japan Home: 1222-11 Kujinokawa Kushimoto 649-3511 Japan Home Phone: 81-735-62-0958; Office Phone: 81 735 62 3600. Office Fax: 81 735 62 3694.

ALABI, KEHINDE, research scientist, mechanical engineer; s. Augustine and Rachel Alabi; m. Malgorzata Anna Kroliczewska, Mar. 14, 2004; 1 child, Olivia Tolulope. BSc in Engring., Obafemi Awolowo U., Ife, Nigeria, 1992; MCAE, U. Strathclyde, Scotland, 1994; PhD, SUNY, NYC, 2003. Cons. Andersen Consulting, Lagos, 1995—97; campus-wide tchg. asst. coord. SUNY, Stony Brook, 2001—02, adj. instr., 2003; sr. rsch. scientist, engr. TTC Techs. Inc., Centereach, NY, 2003—. Dir. Tutor Ctrl. Inc., Rocky Point, NY, 2005—07. Named one of LI Top Twenty Young Tech. Profls., LISTnet - LI Software and Tech. Network, 2003; Shell Petroleum Devel. Corp. scholar, 1988—92, Commonwealth Overseas Devel. Student scholar, Brit. Coun., 1993—94. Mem.: ASME, AIAA, Am. Phys. Soc., CFD Gen. Notation Sys. (com. mem. 2006—07). Achievements include patents pending for system and method for managing the presentation and customization of web applications and web pages; generation, documentation and presentation of mathematical equations and symbolic scientific expressions using Pure HTML, CSS, and JavaScript; system and method for generating mathematical equations and symbolic scientific expressions in HTML and CSS; calendar-based and services-oriented bidding process for tutoring request and fulfillment; development of NETVIOS Web Platform and Internet Operating System. Office: TTC Technologies Inc 2100 Middle Country Rd Centereach NY 11720 Home Phone: 631-849-5064; Office Phone: 631-285-7128. E-mail: kenny@datalomtech.net.

ALAÏA, AZZEDINE, fashion designer; b. Tunis; arrived in France, 1957:; Student, Ecole des Beaux Arts, Tunis; student of sculpture, student of dressmaking. With Christian Dior, Paris, Guy Laroche, Paris; founder dressmaking bus. Paris, 1960s; founder atelier in Faubourg St. Germain, 1965-84; opened Azzedine Alaïa boutique, Beverly Hills, Calif., 1983, Marais dist. Paris, 1984. Exhibited in retrospective at Mus. Modern Art, Bordeaux, 1985; definative retrospective Groninger Mus., Groningen, The Netherlands, 1997; work represented in book entitled Alaïa, 1998. Named Designer of Yr., French Ministry of Culture, 1985. Office: 18 rue de la Verrerie 75004 Paris France

ALAIMO, TERRY M., financial consultant; b. Orange, NJ, Dec. 3, 1955; d. Louis Joseph and Julia Clara (Carlin) Mazziotto; m. Salvatore Alaimo, June 5, 1972 (div. Mar. 1975); 1 child, Roxanne. Student, William Patterson Coll., 1974-78. Organizer 1199 Nat. Union Health and Human Svc., NYC, 1984-88; organizing coord. Pub. Employers Fedn., NYC, 1988-89; organizer 1199 Nat. Union, NYC, 1989-92, v.p., 1992-96; cons. S.I. (N.Y.) Amalgamated Transit Union, 1996-97, Svc. Employers Internat. Union, Washington, 1997, 1199 N.W., Seattle, 1997-99; fin. advisor Prudential Securities, 1999-2000, Montauk Securities, Paramus, N.J., 2000—. Coord. Dinkins for Mayor, S.I., 1990, 94, Albanese for Congress, S.I., 1992. Mem. Nat. Abortion Rights Action League. Democrat. Avocations: painting, writing, travel.

AL-AKASH, SAMHAR I., pediatrician, nephrologist; MD, U. Jordan, Amman, 1991. Diplomate Am. Bd. Pediat., 1996, Subboard Nephrology Am. Bd. Pediat., 1999. Pediat. resident Children's Hosp. Mich. Wayne State U.; assoc. dir. pediat. kidney transplant program Mattel Children's Hosp., UCLA Sch. Medicine, 1999—2001; cons. pediatric nephrologist King Faisal Specialist Hosp. and Rsch. Ctr., Riyadh, Saudi Arabia, 2001—, dep. dir. kidney transplant program, 2001—; med. dir. renal transplant program Driscoll Children's Hosp. Contbr. articles to profl. jours. Fellowship grantee, Nat. Kidney Found., 1996. Mem.: Internat. Pediatric Nephrology Assn. (corr.), Internat. Pediatric Transplant Assn. (corr.), Am. Soc. Transplantation (corr.). Achievements include research in immunosuppressive therapies in pediatric kidney transplantation. Office: Driscoll Children's Hospital 3533 S Alameda St Corpus Christi TX 78411 Office Phone: 361-694-5179. Business E-Mail: salakash@hotmail.com.

ALAM, A.N.M. MAHBUB UL, engineer, educator; b. Dhaka, Bangladesh, Aug. 26, 1940; naturalized, US, 1993; s. Abdul Mannan Mirdha and Ambia Khatun; m. Saleha Khatun, June 11, 1967; children: M. Nayeem Ul, Shuvo Mayeem Ul. BS Agrl. Engring., Am. U. Beirut, 1961, MS Irrigation Engring., 1978; PhD, Colo. State U., Ft. Collins, 1985. Chief exec. officer Epwapda, Bwdb, Kushtia, Dhaka, Bangladesh; prin. sci. officer Bangladesh Agrl. Rsch. Coun., Dhaka, 1978—80; rsch. assoc. Colo. State U. and USDA-ARS, Fort Collins, 1985—88; ext. irrigation specialist Colo. State U., Fort Collins, 1988—95; asst. prof. Kans. State U., Garden City, 1996—2000, assoc. prof., ext. specialist irrigation, 2000—06, prof., 2006—. Reviewer: Applied Engring. in Agr.; contbr. articles to profl. jours. Organizer youth program on water and natural resources Childrens Water Festival, River Festival, and Earth Awareness Rschrs. for Tomorrows Habitat, Delta (CO), Garden City ,Wichita, 1990; pres. Kushtia Shahitya Parishad (Kushtia Lit. Coun.), Bangladesh; founder Tarun Krishak (orgn.

for rural farm youth), Kushtia, Bangladesh, 1965—70. Sr. Fulbright scholar, J. William Fulbright Fgn. Scholarship Bd., 2003—04, Rsch. grant, Kans. Corn Commn., 1997—2004, Rsch. grants, Kans. Dept. Health and Environ., 1998—, Rsch. and demonstration grant, Kans. Water Office, 1999—2004. Mem.: Am. Water Resources Assn., Am. Soc. Agrl. Bioengrs. (Kans. sect. chair 2002—07, Blue Ribbon 1998), Irrigation Assn. (life), Epsilon Sigma Phi. Avocations: travel, international programs. Office: Kans State Univ SWREC 4500 E Mary St Garden City KS 67846 Office Phone: 620-275-9164. Business E-Mail: malam@ksu.edu.

ALAPONT, JOSÉ MARIA, automotive executive; b. Spain; Degree in Indsl. Engring., Tech. Sch. Valencia, Spain; degree in Philology, U. Valencia, Spain. With Ford Motor Corp., 1974—90; ops. dir. through group v.p. Valeo Group, 1990—97; exec. dir., through pres. internat. ops. Delphi Automotive Sys., 1997—2003; CEO, dir. IVECO S.p.A., Torino, Italy, 2003—05; chmn., pres., CEO Federal Mogul Corp., Southfield, Mich., 2005—. Office: Federal Mogul Corp 26555 Northwestern Hwy Southfield MI 48034*

ALARCÓN, ARTHUR LAWRENCE, federal judge; b. LA, Aug. 14, 1925; s. Lorenzo Marques and Margaret (Sais) A.; m. Sandra D. Paterson, Sept. 1, 1979; children— Jan Marie, Gregory, Lance BA in Polit. Sci., U. So. Calif., 1949, LLB, 1951. Bar: Calif. 1952. Dep. dist. atty. L.A. County, 1952—61; legal adv. to gov. State of Calif., Sacramento, 1961—62, exec. asst. to Gov. Pat Brown, 1962—64; chmn. Calif. parole bd., 1964; judge L.A. Superior Ct., 1964—78; assoc. justice Calif. Ct. Appeals, LA, 1978—79; judge US Ct. Appeals (9th cir.), LA, 1979—92, sr. judge, 1992—. Adj. prof. Southwestern U. sch. of law, LA, 1985—2004, Loyola Marymount sch. of law, 1993—94. Editor: U. So. Calif. Law Rev. With US Army, 1943—46, ETO. Decorated Bronze Star, Purple Heart; recipient Infantry badge, Expert Rifleman medal, Four Battle Stars, ETO Ribbon. Mem.: ABA, LA Bar Assn. Office: US Ct Appeals 9th Cir 1607 US Courthouse 312 N Spring St Los Angeles CA 90012-4701 also: US Ct Appeals 95 Seventh St San Francisco CA 94103 Office Phone: 213-894-2693.*

ALARCON, CESAR L, electrical engineer; m. Lydia Alarcon; children: Faber M., Julio C. Elec. Engr., U. of Camaguey, 1981; D (hon.), Internat. Iberoamerican Congress, Uruguay, 2005. Pres. Movimiento Cubano Unidad Democratica, Balt., 2003—. Coord. internat. and nat. activities Movimiento Cubano Unidad Democratica, Balt., 2001. Avocations: fishing, philosophy. Office: Movimiento Cubano Unidad Democratica Baltimore MD Home Phone: 443-653-5347. E-mail: info@cubamcud.org.

ALARCON, ROGELIO ALFONSO, retired internist, retired researcher; b. Yungay, Nuble, Chile, Feb. 14, 1926; arrived in U.S., 1954; s. Alfredo and Carmen Rosa (Carrasco) A. BS, U. Chile, Concepcion, 1943; MD, U. Chile, Santiago, 1950. Staff physician internal medicine U. Chile Hosp. Salvador, Santiago, 1951-52, Hosp. Gonzalez Cortez, Santiago, 1952-54; resident medicine Meml. Ctr. Cancer and Allied Diseases, NYC, 1955—56; fellow internal medicine George Washington U. Hosp. George Washington Sch. Medicine, Washington, 1956—57; resident internal medicine Lemuel Shattuck Hosp., Boston, 1957-58; rsch. fellow pathology Children's Cancer Rsch. Found., Children's Hosp. Med. Ctr., Boston, 1958-60; rsch. assoc. Children's Cancer Rsch. Found., Boston, 1960-74, Harvard Med. Sch., Boston, 1962-76, Cancer Rsch. Inst., New Eng. Deaconess Hosp., Boston, 1974-76; staff physician Boston Children's Hosp. Med. Ctr., Wrentham, Mass., 1977-79, VA Med. Ctr., Phila., 1979-80, Bedford, Mass., 1980—2002; ret., 2002. Contbr. articles to profl. jours. Mem. Am. Chem. Soc., N.Y. Acad. Scis. Roman Catholic. Achievements include discovery of the enzymatic generation of acrolein, a highly cytotoxic aldehyde, from biogenic polyamines; development of a fluorometric method to measure minimal amounts of acrolein; research in the growth inhibitory effects of oxidized spermine on mammalian cells, research involving acrolein in cell growth regulation, and identification of acrolein as a metabolite of cyclophosphamide and related chemotherapeutic agents. Home: 33 Pond Ave Apt B-915 Brookline MA 02445-7163

AL-ASAAD, HUSSAIN, electrical engineer, educator; s. Said Al-Asaad and Wasfie Dayfallah; m. Darin Dayfallah, Apr. 4, 1999; 1 child, Yusuf. B of Engring., Am. U. Beirut, Lebanon, 1991; MS, Northeastern U., 1993; PhD, U. Mich., 1998. Asst. prof. U. Calif., Davis, 1998—. Recipient Career award, NSF, 2001—06. Mem.: IEEE. Achievements include research in design validation and test. Office: U Calif One Shields Ave Davis CA 95616-5294 Office Phone: 530-752-5545. Business E-Mail: halasaad@ece.ucdavis.edu.

ALATIS, JAMES EFSTATHIOS, university dean emeritus; b. Weirton, W.Va., July 13, 1926; s. Efstathios and Vasiliki (Galanoudis) A.; m. Penelope Mastorides, Dec. 30, 1951; children: William, Stephen, Anthony. BA, W.Va. U., 1948; MA, Ohio State U., 1953; PhD, 1966. Fulbright lectr. English U., Athens, 1955-57; English testing and teaching specialist Dept. State, 1959-61; specialist for lang. research U.S. Office Edn., 1961-65, chief lang. sect., 1965-66; asso. dean Sch. Langs. and Linguistics, Georgetown U., Washington, 1966-73, dean, 1973-94; dean emeritus Georgetown U., Washington, 1994—, sr. advisor to exec. v.p. internat. lang. programs and rsch., 1994-96, sr. advisor to Dean of Georgetown Coll. for internat. langs. programs and rsch., 1996—; assoc. prof. linguistics Sch. Langs. and Linguistics, Georgetown U., Washington, 1966-75; disting. prof. linguistics and modern Greek Georgetown U., Washington, 1994—. Exec. sec. TESOL, 1966-87, exec. dir. emeritus, 1987—; pres. Joint Nat. Com. for Langs., 1980-88, bd. dirs. 1998—, TESOL Internat. Rsch. Found., 1999—; mem. Greek Orthodox Archbishop's commn., 1999; bd. advisors U.S. Dept. Agriculture Grad. Sch. Author: (with Peter Lowenberg) The Three Circles of English: A Conference in honor of Braj B. Kachru, 2002; editor: Studies in Honor of Albert H. Marckwardt, 1972, (with Kristie Twaddell) English as a Second Language in Bilingual Education, 1976, (with Ruth Crymes) Human Factors in ESL, 1977, (with Gerli and Brod) Language in American Life, 1978, Internat. Dimensions of Bilingual Education, 1978, (with G. R. Tucker) Language in Public Life, 1979, Current Issues in Bilingual Education, 1980, (with others) The Second Language Classroom: Directions for the 1980s, 1981, Applied Linguistics and the Preparation of Second Language Teachers: Toward a Rationale, 1983, (with John J. Staczek) Perspectives on Bilingualism and Bilingual Education, 1985, (with Deborah Tannen) Language and Linguistics: The Interdependence of Theory, Data, and Application, 1986, Language Teaching, Testing, and Technology: Lessons from the Past with a View Toward the Future, 1989, Linguistics, Language Teaching and Language Acquisition: The Interdependence of Theory, Practice, and Research, 1990, Quest for Quality: The First 21 Years of TESOL, 1991, Linguistics and Language Pedagogy: The State of the Art, 1991, Language, Communication and Social Meaning, 1993, Strategic Interaction and Language Acquisition: Theory, Practice and Research, 1993, Educational Linguistics, Cross-Cultural Communication, and Global Interdependence, 1994, (with others) Linguistics and the Education of Language Teachers: Ethnolinguistic, Psycholinguistic, and Sociolinguistic Aspects, 1995, (with others) Linguistics, Language Acquisition and Language Variation: Current Trends and Future Prospects, 1996, (with others) Aspects of Sociolinguistics in Greece, 1997, (with others) Language in Our Time: Bilingual Education and Official English, Ebonics and Standard English, Immigration and the Unz Initiative, 1999, (with others) Linguistics, Language, and the Professions: Education, Journalism, Law, Medicine and Technology, Georgetown Univ. Round table on Languages and Linguistics, 2000, Linguistics, Language, and the Real World: Discourse and Beyond, Georgetown Univ. Round Table on Languages and Linguistics, 2001 (with Deborah Tannen) Georgetown University Round Table on Language and Linguistics, 2001; mem. editl. bd. World Englishes, English Today. Served with USNR, 1944-46. Recipient N.E. Conf. award, 1985, Pres.'s award Nat. Assn. for Bilingual Edn., 1987. Mem. MLA, Am. Coun. on Teaching Fgn. Langs., Linguistic Soc. Am (del. 1966-69), Nat. Assn. Fgn. Student Affairs (dir. 1965-66), Def. Lang. Inst. (bd. visitors), Phi Beta Kappa. Home: 5108 Sutton Pl Alexandria VA 22304-2704 Office: Georgetown U Int'l Langs Prog & Rsch 37th & 0 St Washington DC 20057-0001 Home Phone: 703-370-3745; Office Phone: 202-687-5659. Business E-Mail: alatisj@georgetown.edu.

ALATZAS, GEORGE, delivery service company executive; b. Salonika, Greece, Sept. 30, 1940; came to US, 1954; s. Gus Alatzas and Georgia Karayanidou; m. Ida Elizabeth Feldman, Sept. 26, 1965; children: Dennis, Ari. AA in Liberal Arts, Middlesex CC, 1979; student, Rutgers U. Dept. mgr. Bamberger's NJ div. Macy's Dept. Store, Newark, 1959-61, 63-65; buyer Koos Bros., Rahway, NJ, 1965-67; sales rep. Bassett Furniture, Va., 1967-69; store mgr. W&J Sloane, Union, NJ, 1969-72, Steinbach & Co., Freehold, NJ, 1972-78; owner, pres. Lawyers & Corp. Messenger Svc., Bridgewater, NJ, 1978-84; pres., chief exec. officer Pegasus Delivery Systems, Inc., Somerville, NJ, 1984—; pres. It's All About the Flag, Inc., Alatzas Group LLC Investments, Denton, Tex., 2006—. Pres. Just In Time Inc. fin. mgmt. and support svcs., It's All About the Flag Inc.; bd. dirs. Alternarives Inc. Instr. swimming Am. Legion Children's Camp, Newburgh, NY, 1957-58; instr. marksmanship reservation Boy Scouts Am., Yards Creek, and Blairstown, NJ, 1980-83; pres. Office Condominium Assn. Ctr. at Raritan. With US Army, 1961—63, Command Sgt. Major USAR, 1973—75. Recipient Somerset County Businessman of Yr. award, 1999; Paul Harris fellow. Mem. Assn. US Army, Nat. Alliance Businessmen, 78th Divsn. NCO Assn., 78th Divsn. Vets. Assn., NJ Bus. and Industry Coun., Rotary, Denton C. of C., Denton Rotary (dir.), Somerset County C. of C. (bd. dirs.) Greek Orthodox. Avocations: tennis, golf, walking. Home: 10312 Countryside Dr Denton TX 76207-6610 Personal E-mail: gapegasus@aol.com.

ALAUPOVIC, ALEXANDRA VRBANIC, artist, educator; b. Slatina, Yugoslavia, Dec. 21, 1921; d. Joseph and Elizabeta (Papp) Vrbanic; m. Peter Alaupovic, Mar. 22, 1947; 1 child, Betsy. Student Bus. Sch., Zagreb, Yugoslavia, 1940-41, Acad. Visual Arts, Zagreb, Yugoslavia, 1944-48; postgrad. Acad. Visual Arts, Prague, Czechoslovakia, 1949, Art Sch., U. Ill., 1959-60; MFA, U. Okla., 1966; came to U.S., 1958. Sec., Arko Liquer & Yeast Factory and Distillery, Zagreb, 1941-44; instr. U. Okla., Norman, 1964-66; instr. three dimensional design sculpture Oklahoma City U., 1969-77, Okla. Sci. Found., Oklahoma City, 1969-75; one-woman shows at Okla. Art Ctr., Oklahoma City, U. Okla. Mus. Art, Norman, La Mandragore Internat. Galerie d'Art, Paris, 1984; exhibited art in group shows retrospective 50 yrs. Struggle, Growth and Whimsy, 1987-88, Okla. Art Ctr., Springfield (Mo.) Art Mus., Okla. U. Mus., Norman, 7th Ann. Temple Emanuel Brotherhood Arts Festival, Dallas, Salon des Nation, Paris, 1983; since statehood twevle Okla. artists Art. Mus., Okla. 1996; represented in permanent collections Okla. U. Art Mus., Okla. State Art Collection, Okla. Art Ctr., Mercy Health Ctr. Recipient Jacobson award U. Okla., 1964; hon. mention in sculpture Philbrook Art Ctr., Tulsa, 1967; 1st sculpture award Philbrook Art Ctr., Tulsa, 1970; biography included in Virginia Watson Jones' Contemporary American Women Sculptors, 1986, Jules and Nancy Heller's North American Women Artists of 20th Century, 1995; State of Okla. Art commemdation, 1996. Mem. Internat. Sculpture Center, Lausanne, Suisse, Prestige de la Peinture et de la Sculpture d'Aujourd'hui dans le Monde, 1992, Paris, 1995. Home and Office: 11908 N Bryant Ave Oklahoma City OK 73131-4823

ALAUPOVIC, PETAR, biochemist, educator; b. Prague, Czechoslovakia, Aug. 3, 1923; arrived in US, 1957; married, 1947; 1 child. ChemE, U. Zagreb, 1948, PhD in Chemistry, 1956; DHC (hon.), U. Lille, France, 1987, U. Buenos Aires, 1994, U. Goteborg, 1999. Rschr. pharms. rsch. lab. Chem Corp, Prague, 1948-49; rschr. organic lab. Inst. Indsl. Rsch., Yugoslavia, 1949-50; asst. agrl. faculty U. Zagreb, 1951-54, asst. chem. inst. med. faculty, 1954-56; rsch. biochemist U. Ill., 1957-60; with cardiovascular sect. Okla. Med. Rsch. Found., Oklahoma City, 1960—, head lipoprotein lab., 1972-92, also head Lipid and Lipoprotein Lab. Prof. rsch. biochemistry, sch. med. U. Okla., 1960—. Assoc. editor Lipids, 1974-78. Named Disting. Career Scientist Okla. Med. Rsch. Fund, 1990; NIH grantee, 1961-95. Mem. AAAS, Am. Soc. Biol. Chemists, Am. Chem. Soc., Am. Heart Assn. (Spl. Recognition award 1994), Am. Oil Chemistry Soc. Achievements include research in chemistry of naturally occuring macromolecular lipid compounds such as serum and tissue lipoproteins and bacterial endotoxins, biochemistry of red cell membranes isolation and characterization of tissue lipases. Office: Okla Med Rsch Found Lipid and Lipoprotein Lab 825 NE 13th St Oklahoma City OK 73104-5005 Office Phone: 405-271-7703. Business E-Mail: alaupovicp@omrf.org.

ALAV, FARAMARZ, cardiologist, internist; b. Akstafa, Azerbaijan, Jan. 26, 1958; s. Ahmed Alav and Ashraf Abulmulla; m. Kristina Jalilova, Nov. 7, 2000; children: Leila, Emin children: Emil. MD, Azerbaijan State Med. Inst., Baku, Azerbaijan, 1974—80. Intern Rsch. Inst. Cardiology, Baku, Absheron, Azerbaijan, 1980—81; emergency unit physician Ctrl. Hosp. Emergency Unit, Baku, Azerbaijan, 1981—86; fellow Inst. Advanced Med. Studies, Baku, Azerbaijan, 1986—88; cardiologist Diagnostic Ctr., Baku, Azerbaijan, 1988—93; internist Bonab Ctrl. Hosp., Bonab, Iran, 1993—94; telemetry technician St. Joseph Hosp., Orange, 1995—98; resident in internal medicine Wayne State U. Sinai-Grace Hosp., Detroit, 1988—2001; physician in internal medicine United Family Care, Fontana, Calif., 2001—. Contbr. articles to profl. jours. Recipient award for Outstanding Performance and Svc. to the Cmty., State Bd., 1995. Mem.: Am. Soc. Internal Medicine, Am. Coll. Physicians. Office: PO Box 610 Rialto CA 92377-0610 Office Phone: 909-874-2371. Personal E-mail: falav@hotmail.com.

ALBA, JESSICA, actress; b. Pomona, Calif., Apr. 28, 1981; Actor: (films) Camp Nowhere, 1994, Venus Rising, 1995, P.U.N.K.S., 1999, Never Been Kissed, 1999, Idle Hands, 1999, Paranoid, 2000, The Sleeping Dictionary, 2003, Honey, 2003, Sin City, 2005 (Sexiest Performance, MTV Movie awards, 2006), Fantastic Four, 2005, Into the Blue, 2005, The Ten, 2007, Fantastic Four: Rise of the Silver Surfer, 2007; (TV films) Too Soon for Jeff, 1996; (TV series) Flipper, 1995—96, Dark Angel, 2000—02, (guest appearance) The Secret World of Alex Mack, 1994, Chicago Hope, 1996, Beverly Hills 90210, 1998, The Love Boat: The Next Wave, 1998, Entourage, 2004. Recipient Choice Hottie-Female, Teen Choice Awards, 2006, Choice Red Carpet Fashion Icon (Female), 2006.*

ALBA, LOIS, singer, educator; b. Houston; d. Albert and Opal Plummer; m. Arthur Wachter, May 16, 1976; 1 child, Jeri Woishnis; m. Herbert H. Townsend (div.); children: Debbi D. Carlisle, Jeff Townsend, Shelley D. Townsend. At, Mannes Music Sch., NYC, 1945—48, Julliard Sch. Music, 1946—47; student in bel canto, Rosa Poselle, Villa Pace, Md., 1953. Appeared in opera, 1961—71, Liceu, Barcelona, Teatro Verdi, Trieste, Italy, La Fenice, Venice, Teatro Bellini, Catania, Italy, France, Germany, Yugoslavia; coached with Alberta Masiello Met. Opera, NYC, 1973; pvt. practice, 1973—; tchr. master class ILLAR, Chiari, Italy, 1992; prodr. and dir. Opera Rediviva, Houston, 1993—95, Black Tie Opera Ensembles, Houston, 1993—95; co-founder, artistic dir. Opera in the Heights, Houston, 1996—98. Student of bel canto with Rosa Poselle, Stevenson, Md., 1953; student Maria Castelazzi, Germaine Lubin, Paris, 1959—61, Luisa Pallazini, Alfredo Strano, Milan, 1961, Elena Nikolaidi, Houston, 1983; founder SOMA Internat. Found., NYC, 1978—83, Houston, 2006. Singer: Houston Symphony with Leopold Stokowski, 1956, 1957, Der Rosenkavalier, 1958, 1959; prodr.: Les Boreades, 1978; prodr.: Saffo, 1983; performer: (one-woman show) The Odyssey of Opera, 1988; author: Diary of a Woman's Life, 2001, Vocal Rescue: Rediscover, 2005, (recordings) The Beauty, Power and Freedom in Your Singing. Host Inaugural Lois Alba Aria Competition Soma Internat. Found., Inc., Houston, 2006. Recipient 1st pl. Southwest Regional Auditions, Met. Opera, 1956, Outstanding Svc. award, Fedn. Italian-Am. Orgns. Greater Houston, 1989. Mem.: Nat. Singing Tchrs. Assn. Avocation: writing.

ALBAIN, KATHY S., oncologist; b. Monroe, Mich., June 4, 1952; d. James Jay and Elizabeth G. (Jakscy) A. BS in Chemistry summa cum laude, Wheaton Coll., 1974; MD, U. Mich., 1978. Diplomate Am. Bd. Internal Medicine, Am. Bd. Oncology. Instr. physical diagnosis U. Mich. Med. Sch., 1978; intern U. Ill. Med. Ctr., Chgo., 1978-79, resident in internal medicine, 1979-81, clin. instr. medicine, 1980-81; instr. in medicine U. Ill. Hosps. and Clinics, 1980-81; fellow dept. medicine sect. hematology/oncology U. Chgo. Med. Ctr./U. Chgo. Hosps. and Clinics, 1981-84; asst. prof. medicine Loyola U. Chgo. Strich Sch. Medicine, 1984-91, assoc. prof. medicine divsn. hematology/oncology, prof. medicine, hematology/oncology; attending physician Hines (Ill.) VA Hosp., 1984—, Loyola U. Chgo. Foster G. McGaw Hosp., 1994—. Co-investigator multidisciplinary lung cancer staging and rsch. group U. Chgo. and Michael Reese Hosp. Med. Ctrs., 1982-84; coord. ann. breast cancer screening program Sr. Ctr. LaGrange, Ill., 1985-91; mem. med. adv. bd. Y-Me Nat. Breast Cancer Orgn., 1987—; co-dir. Multidisciplinary Breast Care Ctr. Loyola U. Med. Ctr., 1991—, dir. Multidisciplinary Lung Cancer Evaluation Ctr., 1994—; mem. oncology med. adv. bd. Eli Lilly and Co., 1993—; co-investigator nat. surg. adjuvant breast and bowel project U. Chgo., 1982-84; mem. breast cancer com., breast cancer working group, lung cancer com., lung cancer working group S.W. Oncology Group, 1986—, mem. gynecol. cancer com. and working group, 1989—, sarcoma and brain coms., 1990—, chair com. on women's health, 1992—; mem. intergroup lung cancer working cadre Nat. Cancer Inst., 1993—, mem. breast cancer intergroup com. on correlative scis. Nat. Cancer Inst., 1995, mem. breast cancer intergroup chairs com., 1994—; clin. trials co-chair Sec. of HHS Nat. Breast Cancer Action Plan, 1993-94; mem. adv. panel State of Ill. Breast and Cervical Cancer Rsch. Fund, 1994—; charter mem. adv. com. on rsch. in women's health NIH, 1995—; mem. Early Breast Cancer Trialists' Collaborative Group, 1995—; mem. clin. trials working group Sec. of Health Nat. Breast Cancer Action Plan, 1995—; mem. adv. bd. cancerandcareers.org; rschr., lectr., presenter in field. Reviewer jours. Cytometry, Breast Cancer Rsch. and Treatment, Cancer Rsch., Jour. Clin. Oncology, Cancer, Chest; contbr. articles to profl. publs. Mem. sr. choir Grace Luth. Ch., River Forest, Ill. Nat. Cancer Inst. fellowship tng. grantee, 1981-84, grantee Bristol-Myers, 1988-93, Squibb Mark Co., 1989, UpJohn Co., 1990, 92, Office Rsch. on Women's Health/Nat. Cancer Inst., 1992, 93-95, Nat. Cancer Inst., 1993—. Mem. ACP, Am. Assn. Cancer Rsch., Am. Fedn. Clin. Rsch., Am. Soc. Clin. Oncology, Internat. Assn. for Study of Lung Cancer, Christian Med. and Dental Soc. Avocations: classical music, travel, bicycling, reading, hiking, singing, exercise, pipe organ. Office: Loyola U Med Ctr Divsn Hematology/Oncology 2160 S 1st Ave Maywood IL 60153-3304*

ALBAINY-JENEI, STEPHEN R., lawyer; b. Ohio; BS, U. Dayton, Ohio; MS in Physiology, U. Dayton; JD, postgrad. in pharmacology and cellular biology, U. Cin. Bar: Ohio 1995, US Patent and Trademark Office, US Dist. Ct. (so. dist.) Ohio. Asst. gen. counsel, asst. dir. intellectual property U. Cin., 1995—2000; mem. Frost Brown Todd LLC, Cin., 2000—. Editor: Patent Baristas blog. Mem. leadership coun. CincyTechUSA, Cin.; mem. presenters' com. Greater Cin. Venture Assn. Recipient America's Leading Bus. Lawyer in Intellectual Property, Chambers & Partners, 2004, Rising Star, SuperLawyers, 2005. Mem.: ABA, Am. Intellectual Property Law Assn. (life. scis. group), U. Cin. Coll. of Law Alumni Assn. (life). Office: Frost Brown Todd LLC 2200 PNC Ctr 201 E 5th St Cincinnati OH 45202-4182 Office Phone: 513-651-6839. Office Fax: 513-651-6981. Business E-Mail: salbainyjenei@fbtlaw.com.

ALBALA, A. ARI, medical educator, director, psychiatrist; b. Coronel, Chile, Mar. 2, 1947; s. Americo and Juanita Albala; m. Barbara Pimstein, Oct. 20, 1970; children: Johanna E., Keren, David E. MD, U. Chile, Santiago, 1970, U. Tel-Aviv, Israel, 1975. Lic. Gen. Psychiatry Am. Bd. Psychiatry and Neurology, 1982, Geriatric Psychiatry Am. Bd. Psychiatry and Neurology, 1992. Resident in psychiatry U. Mich., Ann Arbor, 1975—78, clin. rsch. fellow, 1978—80, asst. prof. psychiatry, 1981—84; clin. prof. psychiatry U. Calif., San Diego, 1984—; med. dir. Psychiat. Ctrs., San Diego, 1988—; exec. med. dir. Behavioral Health Svcs., Paradise Valley Hosp., National City, Calif., 1997—; sr. prin. investigator PCSD-Feighner Rsch., San Diego, 1999—. Cons. psychiatrist Washtenaw County Cmty. Mental Health Ctr., Ann Arbor, 1976—81, San Ysidro Mental Health Ctr., San Ysidro, Calif., 1986—87; clin. dir., Hispanic program Southwood Psychiat. Ctr., Chula Vista, Calif., 1989—90; med. dir. Southwood Psychiat. Hosp., Chula Vista, 1991—94; med. dir. mood disorders program Charter Hosp. North, San Diego, 1995—97. Author: (profl. textbook) The Therapist's Guide To Psychopharmacology. Named one of Top Drs. in San Diego, San Diego Med. Soc. and San Diego Mag., 2002, 2003, 2004, 2006; recipient, 2005. Fellow: Am. Psychiat. Assn. (hon. Disting. Fellow 1995); mem.: San Diego Psychiat. Soc. (pres. 2004—05, Edn. award 2006), Am. Assn. for Geriatric Psychiatry, Soc. Biol. Psychiatry, Chilean Soc. Neurology, Psychiatry, and Neurosurgery (hon.), Harley-Davidson Owners Group. Avocations: golf, motorcycling, reading, history, classical music. Office: Psychiatric Ctrs 765 Third Ave Ste 301 Chula Vista CA 91910 Home Phone: 619-498-5454; Office Phone: 619-498-5454.

ALBALA, DAVID MOIS, urologist, educator; b. Chgo., Dec. 25, 1955; m. Francene Ann Salerno, Oct. 23, 1999; 1 child, Jack. BA in Geology, Lafayette Coll., Easton, Pa., 1978; MD, Mich. State U., 1983. Prof. urology Loyola U. Med. Ctr., Maywood, Ill., 1990—2000, Duke U. Med. Ctr., Durham, NC, 2000—. Mem. editl. bd.: Jour. Endourology, Urology Index and Revs. Fellow, White House, 1995—96. Mem.: Am. Urol. Assn. Office: Duke Univ Medical Center Rm 1112 DUMC #3457 Durham NC 27710 Home Phone: 919-942-9415; Office Phone: 919-668-6401. Office Fax: 919-681-7423. Personal E-mail: albal002@mc.duke.edu.

ALBANESE, THOMAS, entrepreneur; b. Passaic, NJ, June 27, 1930; s. Charles and Viola (Gueritey) A.; m. Theresa Mary Perez, Aug. 8, 1953; children: Thomas II, John, Theresa Lynn, Richard Charles, Michael Quintin. Grad. Garfield (NJ) H.S. Pres. Thomas Albanese Inc., Clifton, NJ, 1958-60; founder, pres. Albanese Products Inc., Las Vegas, Nev., 1960—; exec. cons. The Norlen Co., Las Vegas, 1971—; exec. dir. The Las Vegas Chili Co., 1982—; owner The Chef Tomal Co., Las Vegas, 1995—. Creator Gourmet Chili Meals and Desserts-La Chilafesta, 1982, Mr. B's Hang All Kit, 1971; patentee plumbing sys. Founder Double TT Rancho, dir., 1986—. With USAF, 1951-55. Mem. United Assn. Plumbers and Pipefitters, Plumbers and Pipefitters Local 525. Avocations: designing, inventing.

ALBANI, THOMAS J., investor; b. Hartford, Conn., May 3, 1942; s. Charles A. and Marie F. Albani; m. Suzanne Beardsley, Sept. 3, 1966; children: Karin, Steven. BA, Amherst Coll., 1964; MBA, Wharton Sch. U. Pa., 1967. Asst. product mgr. Gen. Mills, Inc., Mpls., 1967-69; dir. mktg. Am. Can Co., Greenwich, Conn., 1969-73; mgmt. cons. McKinsey and Co., Inc., NYC, 1973-78; gen. mgr. GE, Bridgeport, Conn., 1978-84; group v.p. Black & Decker, Inc., Bridgeport, 1984; pres. Sunbeam No. Am. Appliance Div. Allegheny Internat., Oak Brook, Ill., 1984-86; pres. appliance bus. Allegheny Internat. Inc., Pitts., 1986, exec. v.p., COO, 1986-89; prin. New Eng. Cons. Group, Westport, Conn., 1990-91; pres., CEO Electrolux Corp., Atlanta, 1991-98; pres. Canopache Cons., Siasconset, Mass., 1999—. Bd. dir. Select Comfort Corp., Igloo Products Corp. Home: 31 Island Pl Orchid FL 32963-9505 Office: Canopache Cons PO Box 855 Siasconset MA 02564-0855 Personal E-mail: tjalbani@aol.com.

ALBANO, ANDRES, JR., real estate developer, real estate broker; b. Honolulu, Apr. 16, 1941; s. Andres Pacis and Florence (Paglinawan) A.; m. Sandra Kam Mee Ymas, Nov. 29, 1961; children: Cheryl Ann, Denise Lynn. BEE, U. Hawaii, 1965, MBA, 1972. Engr. nuclear power USN, 1965—67; elec. engr. FAA, Honolulu, 1967—69, Honolulu Bd. Water Supply, 1969—79; exec. v.p. MidPac Devel. Ltd., 1979—84; pres. Albano & Assocs., 1984—; prin. broker Gen. Growth Mgmt. of Hawaii, Inc., 1993—96; ptnr., sr. v.p., dir. devel., cons. CB Richard Ellis Hawaii, Inc., 1998—. Vice chmn. bd. regents U. Hawaii, chmn. pub./pvt. partnership task group, chmn. standing com. on fin. and facilities, chmn. rsch. corp. com. on fin. and personel; vice-chmn. U. Hawaii Rsch. Corp. Mem. NSPE, Hawaii Soc. Profl. Engrs. (pres. 1979-80), Devel. Assn. Hawaii (pres. 1992-93), Hawaii Developers Coun. (pres. 1995-96, 99-00), Rotary, Beta Gamma Sigma. Roman Catholic. Avocations: tennis, Karate, weightlifting. Home: 748 Kokomo Pl Honolulu HI 96825-1603 Office: CB Richard Ellis Inc 1001 Bishop St Ste 1800 Honolulu HI 96813 Office Phone: 808-521-1200. Business E-Mail: andres.albano@cbre.com.

ALBANO, CHRISTINE GRACE, lawyer; BA, So. Meth. U., Dallas, 1993; JD, U. Mo., Kansas City, 1996. Bar: Tex. 1997. Assoc. Loughmiller & DePlaza, Dallas, 1997—98; staff atty. Legal Svcs. of North Tex., McKinney, 1998—2003; pvt. practice law McKinney, 2003—. Contbr. articles to profl. jours. Mem. Collin County Dems., McKinney, 2004—05, Planned Parenthood of North Tex., Plano, 2004—05. Named a Rising Star, Tex. Super Lawyers mag., 2006. Fellow: Am. Bar Found.; mem.: ABA (family law sect., gen. practice, solo and small firm sect.), State Bar of Tex. (family law and women and the law sects. 1997—), Grayson County Bar Assn., Frisco Bar Assn., Plano Bar Assn., Tex. Young Lawyers Assn. (dir. 2004—06, sec. 2006—, Presdl. award of merit for exemplary svc. to the bar and pub. 2003—05, Outstanding Dir. of Yr. 2005—06), Collin County Bench Bar Found. (bd. dirs. 2001—02, treas. 2002—04, trustee 2002—06), Collin County Bar Assn. (mem. family law sect. 1999—, liaison to Collin County Young Lawyers Assn. 2003—05, Svc. Star award 1998—2001, Golden Chalice award 2004—05), Collin County Young Lawyers Assn. (bd. dirs. 2000—01, sec. 2001—02, treas. 2002—03, pres. 2006—, Outstanding Young Lawyer of Collin County 2001—02), Attys. Serving the Cmty., Phi Delta Phi, Chi Omega. Office: Law Office of Christine G Albano 201-1/2 E Virginia Ste 5 Mc Kinney TX 75069 Office Phone: 972-562-5884. E-mail: calbano@albanolaw.com.

ALBANO, DAVID WARREN, financial executive, business analyst; b. Orange, NJ, Mar. 16, 1959; s. Nicholas Henry Jr. and Anne (Warren) A. BA, U. Pa., 1982; MBA, NYU, 1990. Gen. sales mgr. Sta. WZIP, South Daytona, Fla., 1985-88; fin. analyst Motion Picture Assn. Am., NYC, 1990-93; sr. fin. analyst Children's TV Workshop, NYC, 1994-96, fin. dir., 1996-2000; asst. v.p. internat. fin. Sesame Workshop, NYC, 2000—03; v.p. fin. and acctg. Global Consumer Licensing, NYC, 2003—. Home: 32 West 40th St Apt 11A New York NY 10018

ALBANO, MICHAEL SANTO JOHN, lawyer; b. Bklyn., Jan. 13, 1944; s. Alexander Joseph and Josephine (Giannetto) A.; m. Grace Alma Hoelzel, Mar. 14, 1944; children: Christine Grace, Sarah Michelle. BA, U. Mo., Kansas City, 1965, JD, 1968. Bar: Mo. 1968, U.S. Dist. Ct. (we. dist.) Mo. 1968. From assoc. to shareholder Welch, Martin & Albano LLC, Independence, Mo., 1968—. Contbr. articles to profl. jours. Recipient Practitioner of Yr. award U. Mo. Kansas City Law Alumni, 2001, Presdl. Alumni Svc. citation U. Mo., Kansas City, 2003, Best Friend award U. Mo. Law Sch., Kansas City, 2006; scholar Tchrs. Assn., 1963-64, U. Mo., Kansas City, 1963-66. Mem. ABA (chmn. family law sect. 1984-85), Am. Acad. Matrimonial Lawyers (pres. 1993-94), Mo. Bar Assn.(Practitioner of Yr. 2004), Kansas City Bar Assn., Am. Coll. Family Trial Lawyers (diplomate, exec. com. 1994-2007), U. Mo. Kansas City All Alumni Assn. (pres. 2001-03), Phi Delta Phi. Democrat. Lutheran. Office: 311 W Kansas Ave Independence MO 64050-3715 Office Phone: 816-836-8000. E-mail: mjalbano@wmamlaw.com.

ALBANO, PASQUALE CHARLES, finance educator, management consultant; b. Bayonne, NJ, Dec. 3, 1941; s. Armando and Marie (Fasulo) A.; m. Norma Agnes Eichholz, July 16, 1960; children: Donna, Nancy, Susan, Carol BS Edn.-Social Sci. cum laude, Monmouth U., 1967; postgrad., Rutgers U., 1969; MA Mgmt. magna cum laude, Pepperdine U., 1976; cert. orgnl. cons., U.S. Army Tng. Ctr., 1979; EdD Leadership and Policy summa cum laude, Temple U., 1987. Cert. tchr. social scis., N.J.; orgn. devel. cons. Pers.-employee devel. specialist Hdqs. Army Comm.-Electronics Command, Ft. Monmouth, NJ, 1967—69; chmn. mgmt. devel. dept. army edn. ctr. Hdqs. Army Comm. Command, Ft. Monmouth, 1969—75, dir. northea. U.S. regional tng. ctr., 1975—78, orgnl. effectiveness officer R & D ctr., 1978—81, chief orgnl. effectiveness office, 1981—85, chief leadership rsch. office, 1985—87, chief orgnl. consulting office, 1987—94; pvt. practice cons., 1999—. Tchr. U.S. Army Pers. Mgmt. Program, Ga., Wash., Pa., NJ, Ala., Ariz., Va., NY, Okla., SC, Panama, 1976—78, Internat. Assn. Quality Cirs., Internat. Pers. Mgmt. Assn., Info. Resource Mgmt. Assn., USAR, 1981—91, Am. Mgmt. Assn., 1995—, Ctr. for Bus. and Inds., Monmouth and Ocean Counties, 1995; adj. prof. mgmt. and social psychology small bus. mgmt. Kean Coll., Union, NJ, 1981—96, Brookdale C.C., NJ, 1975—93, Pepperdine U., LA, 1977—81, Temple U., Phila., 1987—88, grad. sch. bus. Fairleigh Dickinson U., 1990—; adj. prof. tchr. mgmt. and orgnl. psychology in MBA and spl. corp. onsite edn. programs Rutgers U., 1997—, adj. prof. M of Adminstrv. Sci. program, Jewish and Israeli fgn. student program, 2002; tchr. interpersonal rels. Ocean County Coll., 1971—73; creative thinking Brookdale C.C., 1972—73; mem. small bus. adv. coun., 1996; cons. Mut. UFO Network, 1998; global CEO Inst. Chartered Fin. Analysts, India, 2002—; adj. prof. global mgmt., internat. bus., strategic planning, organ. theory and planning N.J. City U., Jersey City, 2003—; adj. prof. human behavior, orgnl. behavior, introductory mgmt., mgmt. of innovation St. Peter's Coll., Jersey City, 2003—; reviewer coll. textbooks Prentice-Hall Pubs., 2003—; presenter Bayonne Hist. Soc., 2003; program instr. Brookdale Coll. Communiversity, Camp Evans, Belmar, NJ, 2003; presenter Nuc. Regulatory Comm. Hearing, NJ, 2004; adj. prof. by invitation U. Can.-West, 2005; submitted testimony to N.J. Legis. Hearing on Nuc. Security/Pub. Safety, 2005. Author: Transactional Analysis on the Job, 1974, Retention of Engineers and Scientists, 1983, The Effects of an Experimental Training Program on the Creative Thinking Abilities of Adults, 1987, Value-Adding Leadership, 1988, Tapping the Potential to Contribute, 1998, One Summer, A Thousand Days, 2001, The Cloud Shaman, 2001, Fires Burning Deep Inside, 2001, Turn the Sandglass Over, 2001, Skyline Drive: A Poetic Journey Through Business Life, 2001; contbr. poetry anthologies Anagram: Art and Literature of Asian Americans, 1998, Snow and Barn, The Golden Wings, Bytes of Poetry, 2001—02, Taj Mahal Rev., India, 2002, developer mgmt. tng. curriculum for Monmouth and Ocean County Adult Edn. Commn., 1996, also instnl. materials for tng. tel. crisis hotline ctr. workers Contact USA, ednl. programs for lab. software engrs. and orgnl. surveys of U.S. Army, 1995, merger, mgmt. and original design tng. programs, 1996—, internet-based orgnl. assessments, orgnl. learning disabilities, 1997—, orgnl. learning disabilities, motivation and productivity change mgmt., bus. ethics assessment, 2003; contbg. editor: workingmanaging.com (U.K.), 2004; contbr.: strategic planning, thinking, adaptive leadership and self-mastery arts Russia Jour. Bus., Globiz internat. bus. jour., 2004—; contbr. materials for use in tng. sr. officers, fgn. mil. officers U.S. Army and Command Gen. Staff Coll., articles various other profl. jours. Tchr. human rels. ednl. assns. Monmouth and Ocean Counties, 1970-74, Fed. Women's Program, 1980, ESL Cmty. and Family Svcs., Monmouth, 1990-93; pvt. tutor English Citizenship; vol. Habitat for Humanity Internat., 1995-96, Contact USA, 1995-96, Presbyn. Youth Program, 1965; mem. NAACP, 1963-64; mem. Small Bus. Adv. Coun., Ocean County Coll., 1996; vol. Sierra Club, Wilderness Soc., Save the Planet, Nat. Resources Def. Coun., Nat. Wildlife Fedn., Nat. Environ. Trust, True Majority, Oceans Conservancy, League Conservation Voters, Consumers Union, Am. Fedn. Tchrs., Move On.org, Common Cause, 2002—, NJ Pub. Interest Rsch. Group, 2004—, Ctr. Constitutional Rights, 2003—, Amnesty Internat., 2006—, Vets. Common Sense, 2006—, Bill of Rights Def. Com., 2006. With U.S. Army, 1958-60 Recipient Bernard Watson award William Penn Found., 1987, Quality Circle Devel. commendation U.S. Army, 1981, Devel. Sci. Pers. commendation, 1983, Creative Edn. Techniques commendation, 1988, ESL Textbooks commendation U.S. Army Materiel Command, 1992, Mgmt. Devel. Curriculum commendation, 1992, numerous World Wide Net awards for creative writing, 1998 Mem. ASTD, ACLU, Am. Mgmt. Assn., Creative Edn. Found., Internat. Transactional Analysis Assn., Adult Edn. Assn., Nat. Assn. Ret. Fed. Employees, Nat. Speleol. Soc., Archaeol. Inst. Am., Soc. Advancement Mgmt., Acad. Mgmt., World Future Soc., Assn. U.S. Army, Internat. Platform Assn. (elected), Union Concerned Scientists, Jersey Shore Quality Coun., Nat. Space Soc., Inst. Noetic Scis., Acad. Am. Poets, Planetary Soc. (cons. mut. UFO network 1998), Search for Extraterrestrial Intelligence Inst., Mensa, Phi Alpha Theta, Phi Delta Kappa Avocations: investigating mysteries, exploring caves and ancient ruins, digging fossils, inventing, poetry. Personal E-mail: charlesalbano@webtv.net. *There is a continuity in life that comes of one's core identity, the whispered voice of youth. When heeded, it unfailingly provides motivation, persistence, satisfaction and direction. Life's purpose is not given; it is self-determined. Compounded of breaks, burdens, chance, successes, failures, myths and realities, we are nevertheless, self-made. Living well means respecting life, living to one's potential, adding value, and reducing pain and suffering of others. Success must be measured against how well one has met his/her own standards and purposes in living.*

ALBARADO, REBECCA HILL, elementary school educator; b. Langdale, Ala., Oct. 17, 1952; d. Benjamin Harvey and Annie Ruth (Taylor) Hill; m. Edward Joseph Albarado, July 1, 1990 (dec.); m. Madison Grover Blackwell (div.); 1 child, Adam. BS in Elem. Edn., U. West Ga., 1985, MEd, 1987. Payroll clk. Milliken, LaGrange, 1979—83; tchr. Troup County, LaGrange, Ga., 1985—91; historian Ctr. for Environ. Health, Charleston, SC, 1991—94; tchr. Troup County, West Pt., Ga., 1994—. Author: (book) A Story Worth Telling, 2005. Mem.: Profl. Assn. of Ga. Educators, Chattahoochee Hist. Soc. Avocations: reading, gardening, painting. Home: 86 Highland Dr West Point GA 31833 Business E-Mail: rhalba@knology.net.

AL-BATAINEH, OSAMA MOHAMMAD, biomedical engineer; b. Zarqa, Jordan, Apr. 22, 1971; s. Mohammad Theeb Albataineh and Turkieh Radwan Mahmoud; m. Malak Sami Bataineh, Dec. 19, 2000; children: Sarah Osama Albataineh, Reem Osama Albataineh. MS in Bioengring., Pa. State U., State College, 2002; PhD in Bioengring., Pa. State U., 2005. Computer engr. Irbid Nat. U., Irbid, Jordan, 1995—97, Yarmouk U., Irbid, 1997—98; computer programmer, analyst Jeraisy Co., Riyadh, Saudi Arabia, 1998—2000; rsch., tchg. asst. Pa. State U., State College, 2000—05; asst. prof. Hashemite U., Zarqa, Jordan, 2005—. Scholar, Hashemite U., 2000—05. Achievements include invention of medical applications of high-frequency piezoelectric ceramic hollow spheres as high power hydrophones and tumor ablation. Office: Hashemite Univ PO Box 150459 2044 Engring Blding Zarqa 13115 Jordan Home Phone: 962-776865363; Office Phone: 962-776865363. Office Fax: 962-53826348. Business E-Mail: omabio@hu.edu.jo.

ALBATINEH, AHMED NAJEEB, statistician, researcher; s. Najeeb Khalaf Albatineh and Alia Rasheed Keewan; m. Rola M. Alkhatib, Aug. 5, 2001; 1 child, Hatoon A. BS in Math., Yarmouk U., Irbid, Jordan, 1988; MS, We. Mich. U., Kalamazoo, 1996, MS, 1998, PhD, 2004. Asst. prof. stats. Nova Southeastern U., Ft. Lauderdale, Fla., 2004—. Contbr. articles to profl. jours. Scholar, We. Mich. U., 1998—2004. Mem.: Am. Statis. Assn. (assoc.), Classification Soc. N.Am. (assoc.). Office: Nova Southeastern Univy 3301 College Ave Fort Lauderdale FL 33314 Office Phone: 954-262-8344. Business E-Mail: albatine@nova.edu.

ALBAUGH, JAMES F., aerospace transportation executive; b. May 31, 1950; BA in Math. and Physics, Willamette U.; MCE, Columbia U. Joined Boeing co., Hanford, Wash., 1975, mgr. process engring., plant mgr. El Paso, Tex., v.p. ops. autonetics electronic sys. divsn.; pres. Rocketdyne Propulsion & Power; sr. v.p., pres. space and comm. Boeing Space Transp., 1998—2002, pres., CEO integrated defense systems, 2002—. Mem. Nat. Security Telecom. Adv. Com., 2003—. Mem. corp. adv. com. Harvey Mudd Coll.; bd. dirs. St. Joseph Ballet. Mem. AIAA (sr.), Nat. Mgmt. Assn. (gold knight, silver knight), Interant. Cad. Astronautics, Nat. Def. Industrial Assoc. (Bob Hope Dist. Citizen award, 2001), Air Force Assoc., Am. Astronautical Soc. Office: Boeing Integrated Def Sys PO Box 516 Saint Louis MO 63166 Office Phone: 314-232-0232.*

ALBEE, ARDEN LEROY, geologist, educator; b. Port Huron, Mich., May 28, 1928; s. Emery A. and Mildred (Tool) A.; m. Charleen H. Ettenheim, 1978; children: Janet, Margaret, Carol, Kathy, James, Ginger, Mary, George. BA, Harvard U., 1950, MA, 1951, PhD, 1957. Geologist U.S. Geol. Survey, 1950-59; prof. geology Calif. Inst. Tech., 1959—2002, prof. emeritus, 2002—; chief scientist Jet Propulsion Lab., 1978-84, dean grad. studies, 1984—2001, project scientist Mars Observer and Global Surveyor Missions, 1984—. Cons. in field, 1950; chmn. lunar sci. rev. panel NASA, 1972-77, mem. space sci. adv. com., 1976-84; mem. exam. bd. T.O.E.F.L. (Test of English as a Foreign Lang.), 1995-97; mem. Grad. Record Exam. Bd., 1995-98; mem. exec. com. Assn. Grad. Schs., 1995-97. Assoc. editor Jour. Geophys. Rsch., 1976-82, Ann. Rev. Earth Space Scis., 1978—; contbr. numerous articles to profl. jours. Bd. regents L.A. Chiropractic Coll., 1990-98. Recipient Exceptional Sci. Achievement medal NASA, 1976 Fellow Mineral Soc. Am. (assoc. editor Am. Mineralogist 1972-76), Geol. Soc. Am. (assoc. editor bull. 1972-89, councilor 1989-92), Am. Geophys. Union. Office: Calif Inst Tech Mail Code 150-21 Pasadena CA 91125-0001 E-mail: aalbee@gps.caltech.edu.

ALBEE, EDWARD FRANKLIN, playwright, writer; b. Mar. 12, 1928; s. Reed A. and Frances (Cotter) Albee. Student, Trinity Coll., 1946-47. Disting. prof. U. Houston, 1988—. Author: (plays) The Zoo Story, 1958, The Death of Bessie Smith, The Sandbox, 1959, The American Dream, 1960, Who's Afraid of Virginia Woolf?, 1962 (Tony award best play, 1963), The Ballad of the Sad Cafe (adaption of Carson McCullers' novella), 1963 (Tony nom. best play, 1964), Tiny Alice, 1964 (Tony nom. best play, 1965), Malcolm, 1966, A Delicate Balance, 1966 (Pulitzer Prize for drama, 1967, Tony nom. best play, 1967), Everything in the Garden, 1968, Box and Quotations from Chairman Mao, 1970, All Over, 1971, Seascape, 1975 (Pulitzer prize for drama, 1975, Tony nom. best play, 1975), Counting the Ways, 1976, Listening, 1977, The Lady from Dubuque, 1979, adaptation of Lolita (Nabokov), 1980, The Man Who Had Three Arms, 1981, Finding the Sun, 1982, Marriage Play, 1987, Three Tall Women, 1991 (Pulitzer Prize for drama, 1994), Fragments, 1993, About the Baby, 1996, Occupant, 2001, The Goat, Or Who is Sylvia?, 2002 (Tony award best play, 2002, LA Drama Critics Cir. award for writing, 2005), Peter and Jerry, 2004, Me, Myself and I, 2007, (essays collection) Stretching My Mind, 2005; dir.: (plays) Happy Days, 1993, Alley Theatre, 1991. Pres. Edward F. Albee Found. Named to Theater Hall of Fame, 1985; recipient gold medal in drama Am. Acad. and Inst. Arts and Letters, 1980, Nat. Medal of Arts, 1996, Kennedy Ctr. honoree, 1996, Spl. Tony award for Lifetime Achievement in Theatre, 2005, Golden Plate award, Acad. Achievement, 2005. Mem.: Nat. Inst. Arts and Letters, Dramatists Guild Coun. Address: 14 Harrison St New York NY 10013-2842

ALBEE, GLORIA, playwright; b. Brockton, Mass., Apr. 26, 1931; d. Earl Fredric and Rita Marie (Walls) Albee; m. Leonard Goodman, Jan. 13, 1961 (div.); 1 child, Anna Albee Goodman. Student, Boston U., 1948-49, U. Wash., 1972-74, Sarah Lawrence Coll., 1975-76, Hunter Coll., 1986-92. Playwright: Medea, 1975, Helen of Sparta, 1991; plays produced include Medea, Nothing Personal, The Yellow Wallpaper. Recipient John Golden Theatre award Hunter Coll., 1986, Mary M. Fay award in poetry Hunter Coll., 1990, Honorable Mention award Jane Chambers Playwriting Award, 1994; Rockefeller Bros. Found. grantee; Nat. Arts Club Lit. scholar, 1990. Mem. Dramatists Guild. Home: 828 Blackwood Clementon Rd # 73 Pine Hill NJ 08021

ALBER, JOHN I., lawyer; AB, Ind. U., Bloomington, 1974; JD, So. Ill. U., Edwardsville, 1979. Bar: Ill. 1979, Mo. 1979, US Dist. Ct., Ea. Dist. Mo. 1981. Assoc. to ptnr. Bryan Cave LLP, St. Louis, 1980—88, tech. ptnr., 1999—; CEO database, software company, 1988—99. Named one of Top 25 Chief Tech. Officers, InfoWorld mag., 2007. Office: Bryan Cave LLP One Metropolitan Square 211 North Broadway, Ste 3600 Saint Louis MO 63102 Office Phone: 314-259-2144. E-mail: jialber@bryancave.com.*

ALBER, ORO LINDA, healthcare educator, consultant; b. Barranquilla, Colombia, Colombia, June 27, 1952; arrived in US, 1971; d. Cevastian Alcala and Ana Mendez; m. Charles Alber, Aug. 10, 1974; 1 child, jonathan. BA, St. Thomas U., Miami, 1986. Cert. HIV/AIDS. Tchr. spl. assignment Sch. Bd. Broward County, Ft. Lauderdale, Fla., 1981—91; sr. health educator Broward County Health Dept., Ft. Lauderdale, Fla., 1991—97, Vista Health Plans, Sunrise, Fla., 1999—2003; health educator Total Edn., Inc., Hollywood, Fla., 2003—. World refugee program adv. Sheridan Tech. Ctr., Hollywood, Fla., 2003—04; founder, dir. Total Edn., Inc., Hollywood, Fla., 2003—; health cons. Broward Career Inst., Pembroke Pines, Fla., 2003—06; lead ctr. field officer FEMA, West Palm Beach, Fla., 2005—. Prodr.: HIV/AIDS Edn., 1997. Nat. trainer Parent-Tchr. Assn, Chgo., 2005—; pres. Latin Am. Democrats, Broward County, Fla., 2000—. Recipient Employee of Year, Broward County Health Dept., 1995, Outstanding Adv. Mem. award, Broward County, 2005. Mem.: Hispanic Am. Alliance (bd. adv. 2002—). Democrat. Roman Catholic. Avocations: angels, wrist watches. Home: 141 NW 73rd Ave Pembroke Pines FL 33024 Personal E-mail: lindaalber@bellsouth.net.

ALBER, PHILLIP GEORGE, lawyer; b. Lansing, Mich., Dec. 10, 1948; s. Phillip Karl and Audrey Irene (Putnam) A.; m. Shari Thornton; children: Emily Nicole, Phillip George, Elisabeth Whitney, Christian Thornton. BA magna cum laude, U. Mich., 1971; JD cum laude, Wayne State U., 1974. Bar: Mich. 1975, U.S. Dist. Ct. (ea. dist.) Mich. 1975, U.S. Ct. Appeals (6th cir.) 1978, U.S. Dist. Ct. (we. dist.) Mich. 1982. Assoc. Harvey, Kruse, Westen & Milan, Detroit, 1975-79, ptnr., 1979-85, Mager, Mercer and Alber, Detroit, 1985-2000, Alber Crafton, PSC, Troy, Mich., 2001—. Lectr. Ill. Inst. Continuing Edn., Chgo., 1980. Mem. ABA (torts ins. practice sect., vice chair fidelity and surety law com.), Detroit Bar Assn. (pub. adv. com. 1979—, cir. ct. com. 1978—), Mich. Bar Assn. (rep. assembly 1970-80), Internat. Assn. Def. Counsel (fidelity and surety com. 1984—), Surety Claims Inst., Nat. Bd. Claim Assn. (pres. 1992-94, program chair 1990—), Assn. Def. Trial Counsel, Detroit Athletic Club, Hundred Club, Goodfellows Old Newsboys Club (Detroit). Republican. Roman Catholic. Home: 673 Washington Rd Grosse Pointe MI 48230-1253 Office: Alber Crafton PSC Ste 300 2301 W Big Beaver Rd Troy MI 48084-4906 Home Phone: 313-382-4091; Office Phone: 248-822-6190. Business E-Mail: palber@albercrafton.com.

ALBER, RICHARD LAWRENCE, quality assurance professional; b. Troy, NY, Aug. 5, 1947; s. Norman Lawrence and Jane Frances (Procak) A.; m. Janet Carol Pakatar, Oct. 28, 1967; children: Michael, David. AS, Hudson Valley C.C., Troy, 1975; grad. mgmt. devel., Rensselaer Polytechnic Inst., 1992. Cert. lead quality auditor. Machinist Watervliet (N.Y.) Arsenal, 1966-72; intern quality assurance specialist Dept. Army, Washington, 1972-75; quality assurance specialist Watervliet Arsenal, 1975-86, supr. quality assurance specialist, 1986—. Mem. Am. Soc. for Quality (cert.), U.S. Water Polo (referee), Mt. Zion Free and Accepted Masons Lodge #311 (master 1992-93). Avocations: swimming, biking, travel, greek language, computers. Home: 42 Whiteview Rd Wynantskill NY 12198-7832 Office: SIOWV-ODP-M Watervliet Arsenal Watervliet NY 12189 Office Phone: 518-266-5936. Personal E-mail: autoplak@yahoo.com.

ALBERG, JAMES L., lawyer; b. NYC, July 11, 1952; BA cum laude, Union Coll., 1974; JD, Boston Univ., 1977. Bar: NY 1978, DC 1979, Mass. 1986, Ga. 1994, US Dist. Ct. (DC, ea. dist. Mass.), UK (registered fgn. lawyer). Atty. Gen. Electric Corp., Citibank; sr. v.p. & gen. counsel Dun & Bradstreet Software, 1989—96; ptnr., chmn. global sourcing group Pillsbury Winthrop Shaw Pittman, Washington, 1996—. Contbr. articles to profl. jours. Mem.: ABA, DC Bar Assn., Computer Law Assn. Office: Pillsbury Winthrop Shaw Pittman 2300 N St NW Washington DC 20037-1128 Office Phone: 202-663-9123. Office Fax: 202-663-9120. Business E-Mail: james.alberg@pillsburylaw.com.

ALBERG, TOM AUSTIN, investment company executive, lawyer; b. San Francisco, Feb. 12, 1940; s. Thomas A. and Miriam A. (Twitchell) A.; m. Mary Ann Johnke, June 8, 1963 (div. July 1989); children: Robert, Katherine, John; m. Judith Beck, Aug. 8, 1989; children: Carson, Jessica. AB cum laude, Harvard Coll., 1962; JD, Columbia U., 1965. Bar: N.Y. 1965, Wash. 1967. Assoc. Cravath, Swaine & Moore, NYC, 1965-67, Perkins, Cole, Stone, Olsen & Williams, Seattle, 1967-71, ptnr., 1971-90, chmn. exec. com., 1986-90; exec. v.p. legal and corp. affairs McCaw Cellular Comm. Inc., Kirkland, Wash., 1990-95; pres., CEO, dir. Personal Connect Comm. Corp., Kirkland, 1995—; prin. Madrona Investment Group, 1996—. Pres., COO, dir. Lin Broadcasting Inc., Kirkland, 1991-95; bd. dirs. Active Voice Corp., VISIO Corp., Emeritus Corp., Amazon Com., Inc.; pres. Seattle Legal Svcs., 1973-74; lectr. on securities and fin. law. Editor Law Rev., Columbia U. Contbr. articles to profl. jours. Pres. Intiman Theatre, Seattle, 1981-83, Pacific Sci. Ctr. Found., Seattle, 1982-84; chmn. Discovery Inst., 1991—, Seattle Commons, 1991-94; trustee Children's Hosp. Found., 1992-95, Pacific Sci. Ctr., 1994—, U. Puget Sound, 1994—, Sta. KING-FM, 1994—. Stone scholar Columbia U., 1963-65. Mem. ABA, Wash. State Bar Assn. (chmn. corp. sect. 1975-76, securities com. 1974-75), Univ. Club, Seattle Yacht Club. Office: Madrona Investment Group LLC 1000 2nd Ave Ste 3700 Seattle WA 98104-1053 Office Phone: 206-674-3000. E-mail: tom@madrona.com.

ALBERGER, WILLIAM RELPH, lawyer, former legislative staff, government official; b. Portland, Oreg., Oct. 11, 1945; s. Relph Griffin (dec.) and Ferne (Ahlstrom) A. (dec.); children: Eric Griffin, Blake Eugene. BA, Willamette U., 1967; MBA, U. Iowa, 1971; JD, Georgetown U., 1973. Bar: DC 1974. Spl. asst. to US Senator Bob Packwood, 1969-71; legis. asst. US Rep. Al Ullman, Washington, 1972-75, adminstrv. asst., 1975-77, House Com. on Ways and Means, 1977; vice-chmn. US Internat. Trade Commn., Washington, 1978-80, chmn., 1980-82; pvt. practice Washington, 1982—. Mem. ABA (chmn. standing com. customs law 1983-85), DC Bar Assn., Internat. Bar Assn. Democrat. Avocations: softball, tennis, fantasy sports. Office Phone: 703-461-3791. E-mail: bill.alberger@comcast.net.

ALBERS, CHARLES EDGAR, retired investment company executive; b. Flushing, NY, Nov. 30, 1940; s. Edwin M. and Olive F. (Van Dyke) A.; m. Judy Mae Hite, Dec. 18, 1961 (dec. June 1998); children: Robert, Karin, Laura. AB in Econ., cum laude, Kenyon Coll., Gambier, Ohio, 1962; MBA, Columbia U., NYC, 1967. CFA. Portfolio mgr. Guardian Park Ave. Fund, Inc., NYC, 1972—98; sr. v.p. Oppenheimer Funds, NYC, 1998—2003; portfolio mgr. Oppenheimer Main St. Fund, NYC, 1998—2003; ret., 2003. Supporter Cato Inst., Atlas Econ. Rsch. Found., Bill of Rights Inst., Club for Growth, Appalachian Mountain Club, mem. adv. bd. Woodrow Wilson Fellow in Econ., 1962-1963. Named to Forbes Mag.'s Mutual Funds Honor Roll 9 times. Variable Annuity Mgr. of Yr. Morningstar, 1996 Mem.: Short Hills Club, Columbia Club. Unitarian Universalist. Avocations: reading, hiking. Personal E-mail: chuckalbers@aol.com.

ALBERS, DOLORES M., secondary school educator; b. Lander, Wyo., June 2, 1949; AA, Casper Coll., 1969; BS, U. No. Colo., 1972; postgrad., U. N.C., U. Wyo., Chadron State. Lic. massage therapist Utah. Physical edn. instr. for grades K-12, 6th and 8th grade sci. tchr. Bent County Sch. Dist. 2, McClave, Colo., 1972-75; physical edn./health instr. Sweetwater County Sch. Dist. # 2, Green River, Wyo., 1972—. Mem. phys. edn. coun. Mid. and Secondary Schs., 1999—2003, chmn. phys. edn. coun., 2002—03. Mem., chmn. Green River Parks and Recreation Bd.; coord. Hoops for Heart; co-chmn. United Way Sweetwater County, 1999-2001. Named Tchr. of Yr., Ctrl. Dist., 1994—95, Nat. Assn. Sport and Phys. Edn., 1995. Mem. AAHPERD, AALR, ASCD/NFOIA, NEA, Wyo. Edn. Assn., Wyo. Assn. Health, Phys. Edn., Recreation and Dance (Tchr. of Yr. award 1994-95), Green River Edn. Assn., Nat. Assn. for Sport and Phys. Edn., Mid. and Secondary Sch. Phys. Edn. Coun. (chmn. 2002-03). Roman Catholic. Avocations: snowboarding, backpacking, woodworking, crewel, cross country skiing. Home: 1745 Massachusetts Ct Green River WY 82935-6229 Office: Green River HS 1615 Hitching Post Dr Green River WY 82935-5771 Office Phone: 307-872-4747.

ALBERS, JAN MARIA, historian, museum director; b. Northfield, Minn., Sept. 29, 1952; d. Lowell Archibald Albers and Helen Verna Anderson; m. Paul Kleber Monod, Aug. 11, 1984; 1 child, Evan Kleber Albers Monod. BA, Carleton Coll., 1978; MA, Yale U., 1981, MPhil, 1983, PhD, 1988. Dir. Chellis Ho. Women's Ctr. Middlebury (Vt.) Coll., 1995—97; writer, lectr. Orton Family Found., Rutland, Vt., 1997—2004; exec. dir. Henry Sheldon Mus. Vt. History, Middlebury, Vt., 2005—. Author: Hands on the Land: A History of the Vermont Landscape, 2000 (named Book of the Yr., Soc. Preservation New Eng. Antiquities, 2002). Chmn. Weybridge (Vt.) Planning Commn., 2003—06; rep. regional planning commn. Addison County, Middlebury, 2001—06; bd. dirs. Rokeby Mus., Ferrisburgh, Vt., 2000—05. Avocations: travel, reading. Office: Henry Sheldon Museum of Vermont History 1 Park St Middlebury VT 05753 Office Phone: 802-388-2117.

ALBERS, LUCIA BERTA, land developer; b. Guatemala, Feb. 10, 1943; d. Jose Luis De Leon Polanco and Maria Marta (Vasquez) De Leon; m. Ray Cisneros, Nov. 2, 1968 (div. 1972); 1 child, Elizabeth Ann Albers Cisneros; m. Monte Dean Albers, June 12, 1974; 1 child, Monte Roberto. Grad. in Acctg., Sacred Heart, Guatemala, 1963; student in Econs., San Carlos, Guatemala, 1964; student, Diablo Valley Coll., 1975-76. Chief acct. Discovery Bay, Byron, Calif., 1971-76; asst. fin. dir. City of Pittsburg, Calif., 1976-78; corporate contr. Conco Cement, Concord, Calif., 1981-90; land developer Contra Costa County, Calif., 1990—. Mem. adv. coun. City of Byron, Calif., 1991-94; dir. Ctr. for New Ams., Concord, 1994—. Mem. Nat. Assn. Accts., Nat. Assn. Exec. Women, Nat. Assn. Women, Mex.-Am. Polit. Assn. Home: PO Box 458 Brentwood CA 94513-0458 Personal E-mail: albers9601@aol.com.

ALBERS, MARK W., oil industry executive; b. Calgary, Alta., Canada; B engring., Tex. A&M Univ. Mgmt. positions Exxon Mobil Corp., 1979—91; tech. mgr., ops. mgr. Esso Australia, Melbourne, 1991; Alaska interests mgr. Exxon Mobil Corp., prod. mgr. we. U.S.; v.p. Africa, Chad/Nigeria Exxon Mobil Develop. Co., Houston, 2001; exec. asst. to chmn. & pres. Exxon Mobil Corp.; pres. Exxon Mobil Develop. Co., Houston, 2004—07; sr. v.p., mem. mgmt. com. Exxon Mobil Corp., Irving, Tex., 2007—. Mem. engring. adv. council Tex. A&M Univ. Mem.: CEO Forum, Inst. Engineers Australia, Soc. Petroleum Engineers. Office: Exxon Mobil Corp 5959 Las Colinas Blvd Irving TX 75039*

ALBERS, SHERYL KAY, state legislator; b. Sauk County, Wis., Sept. 9, 1954; d. Marcus J. and Norma Gumz; 1 child, Joel Albert. BA, Ripon Coll., 1976; JD, U. Wis., 2004. Mem. children and families com. Wis. State Assembly, chmn. property rights/land mgmt. com. Assembly Rep. Caucus Wis., 1987-91; mem. Local Emergency Planning Com. Juneau County; mem. Joint Com. on Fin., 1996-2000; mem. Sauey Foun. Scholarship Com. Recipient Campbell award Sauk County Rep. Com., 1981, 90, Top 10 County award Wis. State Rep. Party, 1982, Pacesetter award Wis. Forage Coun., 1983, Bovay award Rep. Party Wis., 1990; named one of Outstanding Farmers Sauk County Farm Bur., 1982. Mem. Sauk County Farm Bur. (dir., treas. 1977-82), Sauk County Hist. Soc., Agrl. Bus. Coun. Wis., Kiwanis. Republican. Office: Hazelbaker and Assoc SC 3240 University Ave Ste 3 Madison WI 53704 Office Phone: 608-266-8531. Business E-Mail: Rep.Albers@legis.state.wi.us.

ALBERT, ALAN DALE, lawyer; b. Christiansburg, Va., Feb. 6, 1956; s. Horace Wendell and Alma Juanita (Morris) A.; m. Charlotte Lynne Anders, Sept., 27, 2003; children: Amber Lynne Reed, Alexander, Caroline. AB magna cum laude, Harvard Coll., 1979; MPhil, Oxford U., 1981; JD cum laude, Harvard U., 1985. Bar: Va. 1985, US Dist. Ct. (ea. dist.) Va. 1989, US Ct. Appeals (4th cir.) 1989, US Bankruptcy Ct. (ea. dist.) Va. 1991, US Ct. Appeals (fed. cir.) 2003 US Supreme Ct. 2005. Instr. in legal methods, teaching fellow in fed. litigation Harvard Law Sch., 1983-85; teaching fellow faculty arts and scis. Harvard U., 1984-85; law clk. Office of the Legal Adviser U.S. Dept. State, 1984; rsch. dir., speech writer Baliles for Gov., Richmond, Va., 1985; dir. policy devel. Gov.'s Transition Office Commonwealth of Va., Richmond, 1985-86, spl. asst. to Gov. of Va., 1986-89; assoc. Mays & Valentine, Norfolk and Richmond, 1989-93, ptnr., 1994—2000, Troutman Sanders LLP, Norfolk and Richmond, Va., 2001—04; shareholder, v.p. LeClair Ryan PC, 2004—. Mem. Va. Bd. Conservation and Recreation, Richmond, 2002—, chmn., 2002—06. Author books on environ. law, real estate and land use law, freedom of info. and pub. records access; editor Harvard Law Rev., 1983-85; contbr. articles to profl. jours. Vol. Dem. nat., state and local polit. campaigns and com. activities, 1976—; exec. dir. Va. Dems., 1988; bd. dir. Va. Opera, 1990—, pres., 1998-00; trustee Va. Symphony, 2004—; co-founder, gen. coun. Commonwealth Theatre Co.; mem. Leadership Metro Richmond, 1987-88. Harvard Nat. scholar, 1974-79, George C. Marshall scholar, 1979-82, European Consortium Polit. Rsch. scholar, 1982, Pres.'s Disting. Svc. award Treas. Assn. of Va., 1995, 2003. Mem. ABA, Fed. Bar Assn., Am. Intellectual Property Law Assn., Va. Bar Assn. (sect. bd. govs. 1991-94), Va. State Bar, Tidewater Legal Aid Soc. (bd. dir. 1990-93), Norfolk-Portsmouth Bar, Virginia Beach Bar, Owl Club, Phi Beta Kappa. Office: 999 Waterside Dr Ste 2525 Norfolk VA 23510 Address: 951 E Byrd St Richmond VA 23219 Office Phone: 757-441-8914. Business E-Mail: alan.albert@leclairryan.com.

ALBERT, DANIEL MYRON, ophthalmologist, educator; b. Newark, Dec. 19, 1936; s. Maurice I. and Flora Albert; m. Eleanor Kagle, June 26, 1960; children: B. Steven, Michael. BS, Franklin and Marshall Coll., Lancaster, Pa., 1958; MD, U. Pa., 1962; MA (hon.), Harvard U., Cambridge, Mass., 1976; D honoris causa, Louis Pasteur U., Strasbourg, 1992; MS, U. Wis., Madison, 1997. Diplomate Am. Bd. Ophthalmology. Intern Hosp. U. Pa., 1962-63, resident, 1963-66; surgeon USPHS, 1966-68; NIH spl. fellow in ophthalmic pathology Armed Forces Inst. Pathology, 1968-69; asst. prof. ophthalmology Yale U. Sch. Medicine, 1969-70, assoc. prof., 1970-75, prof., 1975-76; practice medicine specializing in ophthalmology; assoc. surgeon Mass. Eye and Ear Infirmary, 1976-86, surgeon, 1986-92, dir. David G. Cogan eye pathology lab., 1979-92; prof. ophthalmic pathology Harvard U. Med. Sch., 1976-84, David G. Cogan prof. ophthalmology, 1984-92; Frederick Allison Davis prof., dept. ophthalmology U. Wis., Madison, 1992—, chmn. dept. ophthalmology, 1992—2002, emeritus chmn., 2002—, Lorenz E. Zimmerman prof. dept. ophthalmology emeritus chmn., 1999—, dir. Eye Rsch. Inst., 2002—. Author: (with Scheie) A History of Ophthalmology at the University of Pennsylvania, 1965, Textbook of Ophthalmology, 8th edit. 1969, 9th edit. 1977; co-author: Jaeger's Atlas of Ophthalmology, 1972, (with Puliafito) Foundations of Ophthalmology, 1979, Men of Vision, 1993, (with Jakobiec) Atlas of Clinical Ophthalmology, 1996; editor: Archives of Ophthalmology, 1994—, (with Edwards) The History of Ophthalmology, 1996, John Jeffres' Lectures on the Diseases of the Eye, 1998, Ophthalmic Surgery: Principles and Techniques, 1998, A Physician's Guide to Health Care Management, 2002, (with Polans) Ocular Oncology, 2003, (with Lucarelli) Clinical Atlas of Procedures in Ophthalic Surgery, 2003; co-editor (with Jakobiec) Principles and Practice of Ophthalmology, 1994, 2d edit., 1999, A Physician's Guide to Healthcare Management, 2002, Dates in Ophthalmology, 2002, (with Lucarelli) Clinical Atlas of Procedures in Ophthalmic Surgery, 2003, (with Polans) Ocular Oncology, 2003, (with Miller, Azar, and Blodi) Albert & Jakobiec's Principles and Practice of Ophthalmology, 3rd edit., 2007; contbr. articles to profl. jours. Recipient Oliver Meml. medal, U. Pa., 1962, Friedenwald award, Assn. for Rsch. in Vision and Opthamology, 1981, Von Sallmann award in vision and ophthalmology, Internat. Conf. for Eye Rsch., 1988, award, Humboldt Found., 1991, MacKenzie medal, Scottish Ophthal. Soc., 1992, Lighthouse Pisart Vision award, The Lighthouse Inc., 1997, Lorenz E. Zimmerman (WARF) professorship, 1999, Disting. Alumni award, U. Pa. Sch. Medicine, 2001, Weisenfeld award, Fight for Sight, 2003; William and Mary Greve scholar, 1978—79, Alcon Rsch. Inst. scholar, 1984—85. Fellow ACS; mem. Am. Assn. Ophthalmic Pathology (Zimmerman medal 1993), Am. Acad. Ophthalmology (Jackson Meml. lectr. 1996), Am. Bd. Ophthalmology (dir. 1997-2005), Macula Soc. (W. Richard Green award 2003), Fight for Sight, New Eng. Ophthal. Soc. (Taylor Smith Gold medal 2004), Midwest Glaucoma Soc. (Albert C. Muse award 2006), Am. Ophthalmological Soc. (Howe medal 2007). Jewish. Home: 1106 Wellesley Rd Madison WI 53705-2230 Office: Univ Wis Sch Medicine and Pub Health Dept Ophthalmology K6/412 CSC 600 Highland Ave Madison WI 53792-4673 Office Phone: 608-263-9798.

ALBERT, ELIZABETH FRANZ (MRS. HENRY B. ALBERT), investor, artist, conservationist; b. Chgo., Nov. 9, 1923; d. Herbert George and Louise Anders Franz; m. Henry Burton Albert, Oct. 24, 1964 (dec. July 1980). Student, Chevy Chase Jr. Coll., 1942. Investor stock market, real estate. Breeder several champion Miniature Poodles. Exhibitions include portraits, still life (various painting awards); contbr. biology textbook; editor: biology textbook. Former mem. Landmarks Preservation Coun. Chgo. Mem.: Am. Farmland Trust, Nat. Trust Hist. Preservation, Cousteau Soc. (founding mem.), Natural Resources Def. Coun., Environ. Def. Fund (Osprey Soc.), Nat. Mus. Women in the Arts (charter mem.), Chgo. Symphony Orch. Soc., Art Inst. Chgo. (life). Republican. Episcopalian. Achievements include design of a house in college within the architectural field; conservationist who campaigned against the herbicide Dacthal which causes lymphoma and Parkinson's Disease and is used by lawn care companies, home owners, farmers, and golf course greens keepers. Avocations: music, renovating houses, antiques, gardening, reading. Home: 316 Courtland Ave Park Ridge IL 60068

ALBERT, GARETT J., lawyer; b. Sept. 7, 1943; m. Eleanor Lanier Culbertson, Oct. 2, 1971. BA cum laude, Columbia U., 1965; postgrad., Harvard U. Bus. Sch., 1967-68; JD, Harvard U., 1968. Bar: D.C. 1969, N.Y. 1970. Atty. U.S. Atomic Energy Commn., 1968; assoc. Hughes Hubbard & Reed, NYC, 1969-77; ptnr. Hughes Hubbard & Reed, LLP, NYC, 1977—. Contbr. articles to various publs. including James Joyce Quar. Bd. dirs., pres. Perlman Music Program; bd. dirs. Mannes Coll. Music, Nat. Acad. Design, Nat. Corp. Fund for Dance, Paul Taylor Dance Found. Winner U.S. Nat. Powerlifting Championship, Nat. Physique com., Tournament of Champions, 1996, Mr. USA, 1996, Kevin Levrone Bodybuilding Classic, 1995, others Mem. Union Club, Quogue (N.Y.) Field Club. Office: Hughes Hubbard & Reed LLP 1 Battery Park Plz Fl 12 New York NY 10004-1482

ALBERT, GERALD, clinical psychologist; b. NYC, Nov. 13, 1917; s. Andrew I. and Eleanor (Walder) A.; divorced; m. Norma Holm Haskell, 1983 (dec. 2004); children: Jay Harvey, Laurie Ellen Albert Moxham. BA, CCNY, 1938; MA, New Sch. for Social Research, 1958; EdD, Columbia U., 1964; Cert. psychoanalytic tng. program, L.I. Inst. Mental Health, Queens, NY, 1964. Editor Vulcan and Creston Pubs., NYC, 1939-45; nat. dir. advt., pub. relations Universal Pictures, div. ednl. films, NYC, 1945-50; exec. dir. Advt. Enterprises and Continental Research Inst., Queens, NY, 1951-64; asst. to full prof. LIU, 1964-85, prof. Emeritus, 1985—; dir. L.I.U. C.W. Post Counseling Ctr., 1964-70. Psychologist, supervising psychologist, clin. dir. L.I. Consultation Ctr., 1966-86, clin. cons., 1986-95; pvt. practice marriage and individual therapy, 1958—. Author: (cassette) How To Choose and Keep a Marriage Partner, 1980, The Wonderful Magic of No-Fault Living, 1990, Japanese edit., 1996, (feature series for website) Making Your Marriage Work Better, 2001-02; editor-in-chief Jour. Contemporary Psychotherapy, 1985-87; contbr. articles to profl. jours. Recipient 1st prize Most Effective Comms./Newsletters Cmty. Agys. Pub. Rels. Assn., 1983. Fellow Am. Assn. for Marriage and Family Therapy (L.I. Family Therapist of Yr. 1993, founder L.I. recorded telephone series "Helpful Hints for Happier Marriage" 1995, contbr. to webpage, 2001); mem. APA, Am. Soc. for Psychical Rsch., Nat. Coun. Family Rels., Soc. Clin. and Exptl. Hypnosis, Soc. Sci. Exploration, Internat. Soc. for Study of Subtle Energy and Energy Medicine, Inst. Noetic Scis. Office: 1900 Hempstead Tpke East Meadow NY 11554-1724 Office Phone: 516-794-6848.

ALBERT, JANYCE LOUISE, human resources specialist, retired business educator, banker, consultant; b. Toledo, July 27, 1932; d. Howard C. And Glenola Mae (Masters) Blessing; m. John R. Albert, Aug. 7, 1954; children: John R., James H. Student, Ohio Wesleyan U., 1949-51; BA, Mich. State U., 1953; MS, Iowa State U., 1980. Asst. pers. mgr./tng. sup. Sears, Roebuck & Co., Toledo, 1953-56; tchr. adult edn. Tenafly Pub. Schs. (N.J.), 1966-70; pers. officer, tng. officer, tng. and edn. mgr. Iowa Dept. Transp., Ames, 1974-77; coll. recruiting coord. Rockwell Internat., Cedar Rapids, Iowa, 1977-79, engring. adminstrn. mgr., 1979-80; employee rels. and job evaluation analyst, recruiter Phillips Petroleum Co., Bartlesville, Okla., 1980-81; v.p., dir. pers. Rep. Bancorp, Tulsa, 1981-83; sr. v.p. and dir. human resources First Nat. Bank, Rockford, Ill., 1983-94; dir. bus. divsn. Rock Valley Coll., Rockford, Ill., 1994-99, ret., 1999; human resources cons. Furst Group, Rockford, 2000—04. Advisor to Nat. Profl. Secs. Assn.; mem. adv. com. Zion Devel. Corp., 1999-2002. Bd. dirs. Rocvale Children's Home, 1986-97, 99-2001, pres. 1991-94; bd. dirs. United Way of Ames, 1976-77; mem. employee svc. comm., Rockford Pub. Schs., 1988-92; acct. exec. United Way Rockford, 1993-98, acct. sec. head, 1996, allocations com., 2000-01; bd. dirs. Rockford Human Resources Cmty. Action Program; chair legis. com. Rockford Human Svcs. Dept., 1989-92; chair Rockford State of Ill. Job Svcs. Employers Coun., 1990-97; publicity chmn. Tenafly, NJ 300th Ann. Celebration, 1969; task force Rockford Bd. Edn., 1993-94; gala com. Janet Wattles Mental Health Ctr., 1990; deacon Collegiate Presbyn. Ch., Ames, 1972-75; adv. coun. Rockford YWCA, 1986, fund drive task force, 1998-99, co-chair YWCA Leader Luncheon, 1986-87; advisor Rockford chpt. ARC, 1991-04; mem. Mayor's Task Force for Rockford Project Self-Sufficiency, 1986-89, chmn. adv. coun., 1991; chair info. and referral com., bd. dirs. Contact, 1994-03; bd. dirs. Rockford Symphony Orch., 1992-95, sec. 1994-95; bd. dirs. Rockford Leadership Found., 1994-96; chair pers. com. Rockford Ctrl. Area Commn., 1997-99, v.p., bd. dirs.; fund drive taskforce Blackhawk Day Nursery, 1998-99; bd. dirs. Rock Valley Coll. Found., 2000-03, co-chmn. governance com., 2001-03; mem. session 1st Presbyn. Ch., Rockford, 2000-01, chair mktg. task force, 2003, mem. space allocation task force, 2004; ctrl. steering com. Ctr. for Learning in Retirement, 2000-01; bd. dirs., mem. strategic planning com. Mendelssohn Ctr. Performing Arts, 2005-; co-chair pub. fund dr. Burpee Mus. Connecting Our Future and Discovery Ctr., 2006—; bd. mem., chair resource deevel. com., mem. strategic planning com. Mendelssohn Performing Arts Ctr.; co-chair pub. campaign com., mem. campaign steering com. Discovery Ctr. and Burpee Mus. Connecting Our Future. Pres.'s scholar Mich. State U., 1951-53; recipient YWCA Kate O'Connor award for Women in Labor Force, 1984, Bus. Leadership award, 1985; named Bd. Mem. of Yr. Rockford Human Resources Community Action Program, 1992. Mem.: Ill. Consortium Internat. Travel (mentor The Netherlands 1997), Employee Benefits Assn. No. Ill. (mem. chmn.), Am. Soc. Pers. Adminstrn., Crusader Clin. Found. (bd. dirs. 1997—2003, v.p., bd. dirs. 2000, chmn. 2001—02, pres. bd. 2001—02), Rockford Pers. Assn. (adv. coun. 1983—91, co-chmn. programs 1985—86), Rockford C. of C. (leadership program 1989, Athena event com. 1990—2005, chmn. Rockford Athena chpt. 1991, pres. coun. 1991—94, internat. bus. coun. 1993—99, transp. com., human resources com., Nat. Athena Found. award for Rockford 1991, Woman of Yr.), Rockford Network (past chair 1985—86, awards com. 1995—97), World Trade Coun. (bd. dirs. 1994—97), Womenspace (bd. dirs. 1993—95, mktg. com. 1993—99, awards com. 1995—98, adv. bd. 1996—2005), Rockford Panhellenic Coun. (sec. 1992—93, treas. 1993—94, v.p. 1994—95, pres. 1995—96, Woman of Yr. award 1994, Rockford Lifescape Sr. of Yr. award 1999), PEO, Rockford Rotary Internat. (mem. com. 1999—2003, chair steering com. 2000—01, co-chair mem. com. 2001—03, Svc. Above Self com. 2004—, bd. dirs. 2004—06, co-chair Rockford Acad. Event), Phi Kappa Phi, Alpha Gamma Delta, Sigma Epsilon. Home and Office: 5587 Thunderidge Dr Rockford IL 61107-1756 Office Phone: 815-877-8364. Fax: 815-282-8248. E-mail: janycealbert@hotmail.com.

ALBERT, JEFFREY B., lawyer; b. Phila., Sept. 12, 1946; s. Arthur A. and Ida (Gindin) A.; m. Karen Malamed, July 18, 1971; children: Barbara, Eric. BS in Polit. Sci. cum laude, U. Pa., 1968; JD, Harvard U., 1971. Bar: Pa. 1971, U.S. Dist. Ct. (ea. dist.) Pa. 1971, U.S. Ct. Appeals (3d cir.) 1974, U.S. Supreme Ct. 1978. Assoc. Goodis, Greenfield, Henry, Shaiman & Levin, Phila., 1971-74, Mann & Ungar, Phila., 1974-76, Fox Rothschild O'Brien & Frankel, Phila., 1976-80, ptnr., 1980-96; shareholder McKissock & Hoffman, P.C., Phila., 1996—. Contbr. articles to legal jours., author Recent Developments in Pennsylvania's Attorney Malpractice Law published by Pa. Bar Inst., co-author survey of attorney malpractice law published in Temple Law Rev. 1988. Pres. Dreshertown Road Civic Assn., Dresher, Pa., 1990—; commr. Abington Twp., Pa., 1986-89; chmn. Upper Dublin Dem. Com., 1991—; mem. Montgomery County Fiscal Waste Commn., 1992—. Recipient Best Lawyers in Am., 1998, Super Lawyers, Phila. Mag., 2004—05. Mem. Pa. Bar Assn. (profl. liability ins. com. 1989—, vice chmn. 1991-93, chmn. 1993-96, co-chmn. 1998—, tech. law office mgmt. task force), Pa. Def. Inst. (chmn. atty. liability com. 1988-93), Harvard Law Sch. Assn. Greater Phila. (pres. 1989-90), ABA, Phila. Bar Assn. Office: Mckissock Hoffman PC 1818 Market St Fl 13 Philadelphia PA 19103-3608 Office Phone: 215-246-2100. Office Fax: 215-246-2144. Business E-Mail: jalbert@mckhof.com.

ALBERT, MARTIN LAWRENCE, behavioral neurologist, writer, educator, researcher; b. Lawrence, Mass., Jan. 7, 1939; s. Benjamin and Alice (Kaminsky) A.; m. Phyllis Gloria Cohen, Dec. 25, 1960; children: David, Michael, Rachel. MD, Tufts U., 1963; PhD, U. Paris, France, 1971. Diplomate Am. Bd. Psychiatry and Neurology. Intern Maimonides Med. Ctr., Bklyn., 1963-64; resident in neurology Boston U. Med. Sch./Boston VA Hosp., 1966-69; fellow in behavioral neurology Boston U. Med. Sch., 1969-71, Laboratoire de Neuropsychologie, Hopital Ste-Anne, Paris, 1969-71; chief, clin. neurology Boston VA Med. Ctr., 1978-83; clin. dir., co-prin. investigator Aphasia Rsch. Ctr. Boston U., 1979-96, prof. neurology Sch. Medicine, 1980—, dir. behavioral neuroscis., dept. neurology, 1983-92, dir. Aphasia Rsch. Ctr., 1996—; dir. med. rsch. svc. Dept. of Veterans Affairs, Washington, 1992-95. Cons. in behavioral neurosci. WHO, Geneva, Switzerland, 1981—; cons. to Pres.' Office of Sci. and Tech. Policy, Washington, 1993-95; Sackler scholar Inst. Advanced Studies Tel Aviv U., 1996; vis. prof. neurology Hebrew U. Med. Sch., Jerusalem, 1993, Hosp. de la Salpetriere, Paris, France, 2001-02; nat. adv. coun. Program in Bioethics Dept. VA, Washington, 1995—; nat. adv. coun. Nat. Inst. Gen. Med. Scis. NIH, 1992-93. Author: Human Neuropsychology, 1978, The Bilingual Brain, 1978, Clinical Aspects of Aphasia, 1981, Language in the Aging Brain, 1981, Manual of Aphasia Therapy, 1991, Clinical Neurology of Aging, 1984, 2d edit., 1994, Manual of Aphasia and Aphasia Therapy, 2004; contbr. over 200 articles to profl. jours. Mem. adv. bd. program in med. ethics Hebrew Coll., Boston, 1987; mem. adv. bd. U.S. Israel Mental Health Fedn., Worcester, Mass., 1991. Capt. U.S. Army, 1965-66. Grantee NIH, 1970—. Fellow Am. Acad. Neurology (co-founder, chmn. sect. geriatric neurology 1989-91); mem. Acad. Aphasia (bd. govs. 1986-88), Am. Neurol. Assn., Nat. Aphasia Assn. (v.p. 1988-2007). Jewish. Achievements include introduction of the concept subcortical dementia; development new treatment approaches for aphasia, including melodic intonation therapy and pharmacotherapy for aphasia; development of the field of language in aging and dementia, created popular diagnostic tests in behavioral neuroscience. Office: VA Boston Healthcare Sys 12A 150 S Huntington Ave Boston MA 02130-4817 Business E-Mail: malbert@bu.edu.

ALBERT, MARV, sportscaster, program director; b. NYC, June 12, 1944; s. Max and Alida (Kahn) A.; children: Kenny, Jackie, Denise, Brian. Student, Syracuse U., NY, 1960-63; BS in Journalism, NYU, 1964. Announcer Sta. WOLF, Syracuse, NY, 1961-64, NY Knicks basketball team, 1967—2004, NY Rangers hockey team, 1967—2004; sports dir. Sta. WHN, NYC, 1967-73, Sta. WNBC-TV, NYC, 1974-88; basketball, football and boxing announcer, host baseball pre-game show NBC Sports Network, 1977—97; announcer NBA games TNT, 1999—; sportscaster Westwood One/CBS Radio Sports, 2002—. Author: Yes--A Guide to Sportscasting, 1981, Marv Albert's Quiz Book, 1976, Krazy About the Knicks, 1970, I'd Love To But I Have a Game, 1993. Recipient Global Ace award for Play-by-Play, 1990, Emmy award, 1990, 93, Curt Gowdy Media Award, Naismith Memorial Basketball Hall of Fame, 1997, Cable Ace award Play-by-Play sportscasting, 1989, 1991-95; named Sports Personality of Yr., Spl. Olympics, NYC, 1983. Mem. Nat. Sportscaster and Sportswriters Assn. (Sportscaster of Yr. 1971-90), Internat. Boxing Writers Assn. Office: Turner Sports One CNN Ctr 13 South Tower Atlanta GA 30303*

ALBERT, ROBERT HAMILTON, lawyer; b. Columbus, Ohio, May 25, 1931; s. Raymond Joseph Albert and Kathryn Mary (Hildebrand) Lett; m. Patricia A. Smith, June 23, 1962; children: Julie Ann Certain, Karen Marie Groeber, Robert H. Jr. BSBA, Ohio State U., 1953; LLB, Franklin U., 1960; JD, Capitol U., 1966. Bar: Ohio, 1960, U.S. Tax Ct. 1961, U.S. Dist. Ct. (so. dist.) Ohio, 1962, U.S. Ct. Appeals (6th cir.) 1966, U.S. Ct. Claims 1971, U.S. Supreme Ct. 1971. Indsl. engr. Fairmont Foods Co., Columbus, 1951-52; acct. E.C. Redman CPA, Columbus, 1953-54; acct., contract adminstr. N.Am. Aviation, Columbus, 1956-60; ptnr. Kagay, Albert Diehl & Groeber, Columbus, 1961—. Mem. Rep. Nat. Com. Capt. USAF, 1954-56, Korea. Fellow Columbus Bar Found., Legal Advisory Comm. of the Columbus Found.; mem. Ohio State Bar Assn., Columbus Bar Assn., Am. Legion, Order of Curia, Beta Gamma Sigma, Beta Alpha Psi. Roman Catholic. Office: Kagay Albert Diehl & Groeber 6877 N High St Ste 300 Worthington OH 43085-2411 Office Phone: 614-433-9612. Business E-Mail: albert@kadglaw.com.

ALBERT, ROSS ALAN, lawyer; b. Boston, Nov. 22, 1958; s. Richmond G. and Mary (Day) A.; m. Nancy Ada Christian, July 16, 1983. AB, Harvard U., 1982, postgrad., 1985—86; JD, U. Calif., Berkeley, 1986. Bar: Mass. 1986, DC 1988, Ga. 2002, U.S. Dist. Ct. Md. 1987, U.S. Dist. Ct. (no. dist.) Ga. 2005, U.S. Ct. Appeals (4th cir.) 1987, U.S. Ct. Appeals (5th cir.) 1993, U.S. Ct. Appeals (DC cir.) 1994, U.S. Ct. Appeals (2d cir.) 1994, U.S. Ct. Appeals (6th cir.) 1994, U.S. Ct. Appeals (9th cir.) 1994, U.S. Ct. Appeals (11th cir.) 1994, U.S. Supreme Ct. 1994, U.S. Ct. Appeal (8th cir.) 1995. Jud. law clk. U.S. Dist. Ct. Md., Balt., 1986-88; assoc. Wilmer, Cutler & Pickering, Washington, 1988-93; spl. counsel Office of Gen. Counsel-appellate group U.S. SEC, Washington, 1993-97, counsel to commr. Norman S. Johnson, 1997-2000, sr. spl. counsel Divsn. of Enforcement, 2000-01; ptnr. Morris, Manning & Martin LLP, Atlanta, 2001—. Assoc. editor Calif. Law Rev., 1985-86; contbr. chpts. to books. Alumni Assn. Securities & Exchange Commn.; mem. reunion com. Boalt Hall Class 1986; mem. scholarship com. U. Calif.-Berkley Club, Ga., v.p., pres.-elect Ga., 2006, Ga., 2007; mem. sch. and scholarship com. Harvard Club, Ga. Mem.: ABA, Atlanta Bar Assn., Ga. Bar Assn. Office: Morris Manning & Martin LLP 1600 Atlanta Fin Ctr 3343 Peachtree Rd Atlanta GA 30326 Office Phone: 404-504-7768. Personal E-mail: ra81@post.harvard.edu. Business E-Mail: raa@mmmlaw.com. *Notable cases include: U.S. vs. Lincoln, U.S. Dist. Ct. N.D. Ga. & U.S. Ct. App. 11th Cir., assisted at trial and served as lead appellate counsel for largest securities fraud prosecution in Georgia history; Vail vs. SEC, U.S. Ct. App. 5th Cir., successfully argued novel disciplinary case arising from broker's theft of funds from a political group; SEC vs. Midwest Investments, Inc., U.S. Ct. App. 6th Cir., drafted brief and successfully argued case of first impression, a jurisdictional challenge to the SEC's ability to regulate interstate securities fraud; SEC vs. Grossman, U.S. Ct. App. 2d Cir., drafted brief and successfully argued case involving challenge to misappropriation theory of insider-trading.*

ALBERT, SUSAN WITTIG, writer; b. Maywood, Ill., Jan. 2, 1940; d. John H. and A. Lucille (Franklin) Webber; m. William Albert, 1986; children by previous marriage: Robert, Robin, Michael. BA, U. Ill., 1967; PhD, U. Calif.-Berkeley, 1972. Instr. U. San Francisco, 1969—71; asst. prof. to assoc. prof. U. Tex., Austin, 1971—79; assoc. dean Grad. Sch., U. Tex., Austin, 1977—79; dean Sophie Newcomb Coll., New Orleans, 1979—81; dean of faculty. grad. dean S.W. Tex. State U., San Marcos, 1981—82, v.p. acad. affairs, 1982—86, prof. English, 1981—87. Founder Story Circle Network, Inc., 1997. Author: Work of Her Own, 1992, Writing From Life, 1996; author: (China Bayles novels) Thyme of Death, 1992, Witch's Bane, 1993, Hangman's Root, 1994, Rosemary Remembered, 1995, Rueful Death, 1996, Love Lies Bleeding, 1997, Chile Death, 1998, Lavender Lies, 1999, Mistletoe Man, 2000, Bloodroot, 2001, Indigo Dying, 2003, An Unthymely Death, 2003, A Dilly of a Death, 2004; author: Dead Man's Bones, 2005, Bleeding Hearts, 2006, The China Bayles Herbal Book of Days, 2006, Spanish Dagger, 2007; author: (as Robin Paige with Bill Albert) Death at Bishop's Keep, 1994, Death at Gallows Green, 1995, Death at Daisy's Folly, 1997, Death at Devil's Bridge, 1998, Death at Rottingdean, 1999, Death at Whitechapel, 2000, Death at Epsom Downs, 2001, Death at Dartmoor, 2002, Death at Glamis Castle, 2003, Death in Hyde Park, 2004, Death at Blenheim Palace, 2005, Death on the Lizard, 2006; author: (Cottage Tales of Beatrix Potter novels) The Tale of Hill Top Farm, 2004, The Tale of Holly How, 2005, The Tale of Cuckoo Brow Wood, 2006, The Tale of Hawthorn House, 2007; editor: With Courage and Common Sense: Memoirs from the Older Women's Legacy Circles, 2003, What Wildness is This, 2007; contbr. articles to profl. jours. Danforth grad. fellow, 1967—72. Home and Office: PO Box 1616 Bertram TX 78605 Personal E-mail: china@tstar.net.

ALBERTI-CHAPPELL, ROXANA DEARING, psychologist; b. LA, June 8, 1945; d. George Arthur and Ollie (McMurtrey) Dearing; m. Robert Brian Chappell, Mar. 23, 1998; children: Anthony Wyatt Alberti, Luke Alexander Enrique Alberti. BA in English, Calif. State U., 1967, MA in Ednl. Psychology, 1972; PhD in Counseling Psychology, U. So. Calif., 1996. Standard lifetime tchg. Calif., 1972, cert. pupil pers. svcs. Calif., 1987, bilingual cert. competence Calif., 1990. Sch. tchr. LA Unified Sch. Dist., 1967—87, bilingual sch. psychologist, 1987—. Sabbath sch. tchr Seventh Day Adventist Ch., Northridge, Calif., 1980—87, sec. bd., 1984—87. Avocations: bicycling, hiking, dance. Home Phone: 818-755-1502.

ALBERTS, BARRY S., lawyer; b. Chgo., Feb. 2, 1946; s. Irving and Evelyn Alberts; m. Susan Weinstein, Apr. 28, 1974; 1 child, Jaime Eliana. BA cum laude, Miami U., 1968; JD, U. Chgo., 1971. Bar: Ill. 1971, US Dist. Ct. (no. dist.) Ill. 1971, US Ct. Appeals (7th cir.) 1989, US Ct. Appeals (6th cir.) 1996, US Ct. Appeals (2d cir.) 1997. Ptnr. Schiff Hardin LLP, Chgo. Adj. prof. law Northwestern U. Law Sch., Chgo., 1991—98, Chgo., 2003; lectr. law U. Chgo. Law Sch., 1995—2007. Contbr. articles to profl. jours. Mem. bd. dirs. Chgo. Children's Choir, 2002—07. Mem. Am. Law Inst. (hon.), ABA (co-chair ethics and professionalism sect. litig. 1998-2002, trial evidence com., 1995-98, task force ethical guidelines settlement negotiations 2001-2002), Acad. Laureates Ill. Lawyers (hon., bd. regents), Ill. State Bar Assn. (hon.), Chgo. Bar Assn., Chgo. Coun. Lawyers, Lincoln-Am. Inn of Ct., Phi Beta Kappa. Office: Schiff Hardin LLP 6600 Sears Tower Chicago IL 60606-6473 Home: 200 Dempster St Evanston IL 60202-1406 Office Phone: 312-258-5611. Business E-Mail: balberts@schiffhardin.com.

ALBERTS, BRUCE MICHAEL, cell biologist, former foundation administrator; b. Chgo., Apr. 14, 1938; s. Harry C. and Lillian (Surasky) A.; m. Betty Neary, June 14, 1960; children: Beth L., Jonathan B., Michael B. AB in Biochemical Scis. summa cum laude, Harvard Coll., 1960; PhD in Biophysics, Harvard U., 1965. Postdoctoral fellow NSF Institut de Biologie Moleculaire, Geneva, 1965-66; asst. prof. dept. chemistry Princeton U., NJ, 1966-73, assoc. prof. dept. biochemical scis. NJ, 1971-73, Damon Pfeiffer prof. life scis. NJ, 1973-76; prof., vice chmn. dept. biochemistry and biophysics U. Calif., San Francisco, 1976-81, Am. Cancer Soc. Rsch. prof., 1981-85, prof., chmn., 1985-90, Am. Cancer Soc. Rsch. prof. of biochemistry, 1990-93; pres. NAS, Washington, 1993—2005; former chmn. NRC, Washington; prof., biochem. and biophysics dept. U. Calif., San Francisco, 2005—. Trustee Cold Spring Harbor Lab., 1972-75; adv. panel human cell biology NSF, 1974-76; adv. coun. dept. biochemical scis. and molecular biology Princeton U., 1979-85; chmn. vis. com. dept. biochemistry and molecular biology Harvard Coll., 1983-86; chmn. mapping and sequencing the human genome Nat. Rsch. Coun. Com., 1986-88; bd. sci. couns. divsn. arthritis and metabolic diseases NIH, 1974-78, molecular cytology study sect. 1982-86, chmn. 1984-86; program adv. com. NIH Human Genome Project, 1988-91; sci. adv. bd. Jane Coffin Childs Meml. Fund for Med. Rsch., 1978-85, Markey Found., 1984—, Fred Hutchinson Cancer Rsch. Ctr., Seattle, 1988—; com. mem. corp. vis. dept. biology MIT, 1978—, dept. embryology Carnegie Inst., Washington, 1983—; faculty rsch. lectr. U. Calif., San Francisco, 1985; sci. adv. com. Marine Biological Lab., Woods Hole, Mass., 1988—; bd. dirs. Genentech Rsch. Found., Fed. Am. Socs. for Experimental Biology; adv. bd. Bethesda Rsch. Labs. Life Tech. Inc., Nat. Sci. Resources Ctr., Smithsonian Inst., 1990—; com. mem. adolescence and young adulthood/sci. standards, Nat. Bd. Profl. Teaching Standards, 1991—; co-chair InterAcademy Council, Amsterdam, 2000. Co-author: The Molecular Biology of the Cell, 1989; editor: Mechanistic Studies of DNA Replication and Genetic Recombination, 1980; editorial bd. Jour. Biological Chemistry, 1976-82, Jour. Cell Biology, 1984-87; assoc. editor Annual Reviews Cell Biology, 1984—; essay editor Molecular Biology of the Cell, 1991—; contbr. numerous articles to profl. jours. including Saunders Sci. Publ., Current Sci., Ltd. Trustee Gordon & Betty Moore Found., Carnegie Corp. Fellow NSF, 1960-65; recipient Eli Lilly award in biological chemistry Am. Chemical Soc., 1972, Baxter award for Disting. Rsch. in Biomedical Scis. Assn. Am. Med. Colls., 1992; named Lifetime Rsch. Prof. Am. Cancer Soc., 1980, Outstanding Vol. Coord. Calif. Sch. Vol. Partnership, 1993. Gairdner Found. Internat. award, 1995. Fellow AAAS; mem. NAS (commn. life scis. Nat. Rsch. Coun. 1988—, chmn. 1988-93, adv. bd. Nat. Sci. Resources Ctr. 1990—, Nat. Com. Sci. Edn. Standards and Assessment 1992—, com. mem. Nat. Edn. Support System for Tchrs. and Schs. 1992—, U.S. Steel Found. award 1975), Am. Chemical Soc., Am. Soc. for Cell Biology (pres.-elect), Am. Soc. for Microbiology, Genetics Soc. Am., Am. Soc. Biochemistry and Molecular Biology (councilor 1984—), Am. Philos. Soc., European Molecular Biology Orgn. (assoc.), Phi Beta Kappa. Office: UC San Francisco Dept Biochem & Biophysics 600 16th St San Francisco CA 94143

ALBERTS, DAVID SAMUEL, physician, pharmacologist, educator; b. Milw., Dec. 30, 1939; m. Heather Alberts; children: Tim, Sabrina. BS, Trinity Coll., Hartford, Conn., 1962; MD, U. Va., 1966. Dir. clin. pharmacology Ariz. Cancer Ctr., Tucson, 1975—, prof. medicine and pharmacology, 1982—99, dir. cancer prevention and control, 1988—2005, dep. dir., 1989-96, assoc. dean rsch. Coll. Medicine, 1996—2002, acting chief hematology and oncology, 1998-99, Regent's prof. medicine, pharmacology and pub. health, 2004—, dir., 2005—; v.p. bus. devel. AMPLIMED, Tucson, 2003—. External advisor U. Chgo. Cancer Ctr., 1993-98, Tulane U. Cancer Ctr., New Orleans, 1993-96, M.D. Anderson Cancer Ctr., Houston, 1994—2004, Norris Cotton Cancer Ctr., Hanover, 1995-2000, Lee Moffit Cancer Ctr., Tampa, 2003—; mem. bd. sci. counselors divsn. Cancer Prevention and Control, Nat. Cancer Inst., NIH, 1990-94, chmn. chemoprevention external com. divsn. cancer prevention, 1997-2001; chmn. gynecologic cancer com. S.W. Oncology Group, 1977-2001; mem. monitoring and adv. panel Nat. Prostate Lung-Colon-Ovary Cancer Study, NCI-NIH, 1994—; mem. oversight com. NCI Nat. Lung Cancer Screening Trial, 2002—; chmn. cancer prevention com. Gynecologic Oncology Group, 1995—; chmn. oncologic adv. com. U.S. FDA, 1982-84, spl. cons., 1984-86; mem. bd. sci. adv., Nat. Cancer Inst., NIH, 1999—; bd. dirs., Cancer Rsch. and Prevention Found., 1992—. Co-editor-in-chief Cancer Epidemiology, Biomarkers and Prevention, 2002—; assoc. editor Cancer Rsch., 1989-2002, Cancer Chemother. and Pharmacol., 1992—, Clin. Cancer Rsch., 1994-96, Neoplasia, 1998—; editor Fundamentals of Cancer Prevention, 2005; contbr. articles to over 500 to profl. jours., 90 book chpts.; inventor azamitosene and anthracene anticancer agts., tumorimeter, hypodermic needle with automatic retracting point; tropical DFMO; two step carcinogen/HIV chemical deactivation system; method and composition for deactivating HIV infected blood and anticancer drugs; amifostine reversal of platinum-induced neuropathy; measurement of lesion progression via mapping of chromatin texture features along progression curve. Grantee Nat. Cancer Inst., NIH, 1975—. Mem. Am. Soc. Clin. Pharmacology and Therapeutics, Am. Soc. Clin. Oncology (ACS Prevention award 1999), Am. Cancer Soc. Cancer Prevention, Am. Soc. Preventive Oncology (Disting. Achievement award 2004), Am. Assn. Cancer Rsch. (Jos. Burchenal clin. rsch. award 2003, Excellence in Cancer Prevention award 2004), Soc. Gynecologic Oncologists. Achievements include Listed by Sci. June 15, 2001 as 3rd highest NIH peer reviewed funded clin. rschr. in U.S. Office: Ariz Cancer Ctr 1501 N Campbell Ave Tucson AZ 85724-0001

ALBERTS, MARION EDWARD, retired physician; b. Hastings, Nebr., Mar. 14, 1923; s. Eddie and Mary Margaret (Hilbers) A.; m. Jeannette McDaniel, Dec. 25, 1944 (dec. Dec. 2006); children: Kathryn (dec.), Brian, Deborah, Timothy BA, U. Nebr., 1944, MD, 1948. Diplomate Am. Bd. Pediatrics. Intern Iowa Meth. Hosp., Des Moines, 1948-49; resident in pediatrics Raymond Blank Hosp. Children, Des Moines, 1949-50, 52-53; practice medicine specializing in pediatrics Des Moines, 1953-88; ret., 1988. Chief pediatrics Mercy Hosp., 1953-69, 74-78, chief med. staff, 1966; mem. med. staff Iowa Luth. Hosp., 1953-88, Iowa Meth. Hosp., 1953-88, Broadlawns Polk County Hosp., 1983-88; instr. clin. pediatrics Coll. Osteo. Medicine and Surgery, 1970-82. Author: History of the Polk County Medical Society 1951-2001, 2003; sci. editor Iowa Medicine, 1971—97; contbr. articles to profl. jours. Pres. Polk County Tb and Respiratory Diseases Assn., 1965, 66, 70. Comdr. USNR, 1943-45, 50-52 (ret.) 1983. Recipient Whitaker Interstate Teaching award Interstate Postgrad. Med. Assn., 1980; Service award Sisters of Mercy, 1978 Fellow Am. Acad. Pediatrics, AMA (recognition awards 1969—), Iowa Med. Soc.; mem. Masons, Kiwanis. Presbyterian (elder). Home: 5991 Pommel Cir West Des Moines IA 50266-6324

ALBERTS, RENÉE MILLER, counselor, alcohol/drug abuse services professional; b. NYC, Oct. 17, 1930; d. Julius and Bertha (Brookner) Miller; m. Henry Celler Alberts, Jan 13, 1950; children: Jo Alberts Lord, Nina Alberts Charnley, Hope Alberts Megonical, Jody Alberts Naleppa. BA, Queens Coll., 1950; MA, U. Va., 1979; postgrad., Va. Poly. U.; cert. in cmty. alcohol edn., Howard U., 1973. Cert. substance abuse counselor, Va.; lic. profl. counselor, Va. Substance abuse counselor, asst. dir., then acting dir. Fairfax Alcohol Safety Action Program, Va., 1972—89; substance abuse coord. Mt. Vernon Ctr. Cmty. Mental Health, Alexandria, Va., 1989—2001; overseer mental health, mental retardation and alcohol and drug svcs. Fairfax, Falls Church Cmty. Svcs. Bd., 2001—, chair mental health com., 2003—, vice chair and acting chair, 2005—06. V.p. Va. Coalition on Women, Alcohol and Drugs, Fairfax, 1985-96; mem. dual diagnosis subcom. Met. Washington Coun. Govts., 1990-2001; bd. apptd. Woman's Collaborative on HIV/AIDS, 1995-2001. Personal E-mail: ralber@erols.com.

ALBERTSON, CHRISTOPHER ADAM, librarian; b. Oak Park, Ill., Dec. 10, 1951; Student, U. New Orleans, 1969—70; BA with high honors, U. Tex.-Arlington, 1972; MLS, U. N. Tex., 1973. Cataloger Orange (Tex.) Pub. Libr., 1974-75, asst. libr., 1975-79, city libr., 1979-81, Tyler (Tex.) Libr., 1981—. Contbr. articles to profl. jours. Mem. ALA, ASPA, Am. Mgmt. Assn., Am. Soc. Info. Sci., Tex. Libr. Assn., Rotary. Presbyterian. Home: 3100 Pounds Ave Tyler TX 75701-8034 Office: Tyler Pub Library 201 S College Ave Tyler TX 75702-7381 Office Phone: 903-593-7323. Business E-Mail: citylibn@tylertexas.com.

ALBERTSON, MARTY P., music company executive; Salesperson Guitar Ctr. Inc., 1979—85, v.p. corp. devel., 1985—87, v.p. sales & mktg., 1987—90, exec. v.p. & CEO, 1990—99, pres. & co-CEO, 1999—2004, chmn. & CEO, 2004—; pres. Music & Arts Ctr., 2005—. Bd. mem. NAMM - Internat. Music Products Assn., 1999—; bd. dirs. Mr. Holland's Opus Found. Co-founder Music Rising initiative, 2005. Office: Guitar Ctr Inc 5795 Lindero Canyon Rd Thousand Oaks CA 91362*

ALBERTY, ROBERT ARNOLD, chemistry professor; b. Winfield, Kans., June 21, 1921; s. Luman Harvey and Mattie (Arnold) Alberty; m. Lillian Jane Wind, May 22, 1944; children: Nancy Lou, Steven Charles, Catherine Ann. BS, U. Nebr., 1943, MS, 1944; PhD, U. Wis., 1947; DSc (hon.), U. Nebr., 1967, Lawrence U., 1967. Engaged in rsch. blood plasma fractionation for U.S. Govt., 1944—46; mem. faculty U. Wis., 1946—67, prof. chemistry, 1955—67, assoc. dean letters and sci., 1961—63, dean Grad. Sch., 1963—67; prof. chemistry MIT, 1967—91, dean Sch. Sci., 1967—82, prof. emeritus, 1991—. Cons. NSF, 1958—83, NIH, 1962—72; chmn. commn. on human resources NRC, 1974—77; dir. Colt Industries, 1978—88, Inst. for Def. Analysis, 1980—86; pres. phys. chemistry divsn. Internat. Union Pure and Applied Chemistry, 1991—93. Co-author: Experimental Physical Chemistry, 1970, Thermodynamics of Biochemical Reactions, 2003, Physical Chemistry, 2005. Recipient Eli Lilly award biol. chemistry, 1955; fellow Guggenheim, Calif. Inst. Tech., 1950—51. Fellow: AAAS; mem.: NAS, Am. Acad. Arts and Scis. (coun. 1991—94, 2003—), Am. Chem. Soc. (chmn. com. on chemistry and pub. affairs 1978—80), Inst. Medicine, Sigma Xi, Phi Beta Kappa. Home: 931 Massachusetts Ave Cambridge MA 02139-3171 Office: MIT 77 Massachusetts Ave Rm 6-215 Cambridge MA 02139-4307 Business E-Mail: alberty@mit.edu.

ALBIN, BARRY G., lawyer, rabbi; b. Wichita, Kans., Sept. 6, 1948; s. Frederick Eugene Albin and Eloise Nelda Riley; m. Marianne Kay Olish, Aug. 8, 1970 (div. Feb. 1997); children: Thomas C., Michael A., Benjamin J., Joshua S. BA, U. Kans., 1970, JD, 1973; cert. in data processing, Kansas City C.C., 1981. Bar; Kans. 1973, U.S. Dist. Ct. Kans. 1973. Staff counsel Wyandotte Legal Aid Soc., Kansas City, Kans., 1974-76; pvt. practice Kansas City, 1976-83, 85—; gen. mgr. Chameleon Dental Products, Kansas City, 1983-85; grand hierophant, CEO Modern Rite of Memphis, Inc., 2002. Lectr. bus. law Maple Woods C.C., Kansas City, Mo., 1978; staff counsel Kans. State Dept. Social and Rehab. Svcs., Kansas City, 1986-91; legal counsel Mid. Am. Gay Ecumenical Found., Kansas City, Mo., 1975-80, Phylaxis Soc., 1999-2005, N.E. Kans. Valley, AASR, 1995-2005, Chi Rho Fraternity, Grand Tribune, 2001-05; steering com. Kans. City Downtown Shareholders, 2003-06; pres. Bus. of Strawberry Hill, Inc., 2002-06; energetic healer and exorcist. Author: Climbing Jacob's Ladder, 1981, Believers Commentary on Mark, 1985, Believers Commentary on Barnabas, 1986, Catechism of Nasorean Church, 1995, Commentary on the Nasorean Letters, 2006. Mebbaker rabbi Nasorean Orthodox Qahal, Kansas City, 1985—; rabbi Congregation B'nai Or; state treas. Green Party, 2000—02; bd. dirs. Wyandotte Interfaith Sponsoring Coun., 2004—05. Mem. Internat. Soc. Study of Subtle Energies and Energy Medicine, Common Cause (state sec. 1978, state v.p. 1978-79), Inst. Noetic Sci., Masons (various offices 1989—), Dist. Dep. Grand Master of 4th Dist. Kans., Scottish Rite (33d degree), York Rite (Knight York Cross of Honor), Masonic Brotherhood of Blue Forget-Me-Not, Blue Lodge, Adept Coll. Consistory. Democrat. Avocations: computers, reading, hiking, teaching, scripture. Office Phone: 913-269-0343. Personal E-mail: balbin@kc.rr.com.

ALBIN, BARRY TODD, state supreme court justice; b. Bklyn., July 7, 1952; m. Inna Albin; 2 children. BA with high honors, Rutgers U., 1973; JD, Cornell U., 1976. Bar: N.J. 1976, U.S. Supreme Ct. 1984, U.S. Ct. Appeals (3d cir.) 1985. Dep. atty. gen. N.J. Div. Criminal Justice, Trenton, 1976-78; asst. prosecutor Passaic County, Paterson, NJ, 1978-79, Middlesex County, New Brunswick, NJ, 1979-82; assoc. Wilentz, Goldman & Spitzer, Woodbridge, NJ, 1982—86, ptnr., 1986—2002; justice NJ Supreme Ct., 2002—. Mem. NJ Supreme Ct. Criminal Practice Com., 1987—92. Trustee Nat. Conf. of Christians and Jews, Edison, N.J., 1986. Mem. N.J. Bar Assn., Middlesex County Bar Assn., NJ Assn. Criminal Def. Lawyers (pres. 1999-2000). Office: 50 Division St Ste 201 Somerville NJ 08876 Office Phone: 908-704-8109.*

ALBIN, LESLIE OWENS, biology professor; b. Spur, Tex., Jan. 8, 1940; s. John Leslie and Ottie Maude (Lassetter) A.; m. Monta Kay Gragg, Sept. 3, 1961; children: Leslie Susan Albin Gann, Kimberly Ann Albin. BA, McMurry Coll., Abilene, 1962; MA, N. Tex. State U., 1969. Instr. biology E. Cen. State U., Ada, Okla., 1969-71; rsch. assoc. M.D. Andrson Hosp. & Tumor Inst., Houston, 1971; asst. prof. biology Western Tex. Coll., Snyder, 1971-74, assoc. prof. biology, 1974-77; prof. Austin C.C., Tex., 1977—, chmn. divsn. natural scis. Tex., 1978-95, head dept. biology Tex., 1977-97. NDEA fellow, 1968. Mem. Am. Inst. Biol. Scis., Faculty Assn. Western Tex. Coll. (pres. 1973-74), Faculty Assn. Austin C.C. (pres. 1987-88), Faculty Senate Austin C.C., Tex. C.C. Tchrs. Assn., Tex. Acad. Sci., Am. Soc. for Microbiology, Alpha Chi. Office: Austin Community Coll Cypress Creek Campus 1555 Cypress Creek Rd Cedar Park TX 78613-3607 Business E-Mail: lesalbin@austincc.edu.

ALBINO, JUDITH ELAINE NEWSOM, university president; b. Jackson, Tenn. m. Salvatore Albino; children: Austin, Adrian. BJ, U. Tex., 1967, PhD, 1973. V.p. acad. affairs and rsch, dean system grad. sch. U. Colo., Boulder, 1990-91; mem. faculty sch. dental medicine SUNY, Buffalo, 1972-90, assoc. provost, 1984-87, dean sch. arch. and planning, 1987-89, dean grad. sch., 1989-90; pres. U. Colo., Boulder, 1991-95, pres. emerita, prof. psychiatry, 1995-97; pres. Calif. Sch. Profl. Psychology Alliant Internat. U., San Francisco, 1997—2004; cons. Health Sci. Ctr., Univ. Colo., Denver, 2004—. Contbr. articles to profl. jours. Acad. Adminstrn. fellow Am. Coun. on Edn., 1983; grantee NIH. Fellow APA (treas., bd. dirs.); mem. Behavioral Scientists in Dental Rsch. (past pres.), Am. Assn. Dental Rsch. (bd. dirs.), Psychologists in Mgmt. (pres.). Mailing: Health Sciences Ctr Campus Box 8120 4200 E 9th Ave Denver CO 80262 Personal E-mail: judithalbino@comcast.net.

ALBOM, MITCH DAVID, sports columnist; b. Passaic, NJ, May 23, 1958; s. Ira and Rhoda Albom. BA in Sociology, Brandeis U., 1979; M in Journalism, Columbia U., 1981, M in Bus. Adminstrn., 1982. Sportswriter, Ft. Lauderdale News and Sun-Sentinel, Florida, Panelist, ESPN's Sports Reporters, feature reporter, ESPN-TV, contributing commentator, ESPN radio, WLLZ-FM, Detroit, sports director, 1985-, sports columnist, Detroit Free Press, 1985-, Sunday Sports Albom, co-host, 1988-, WDIV-TV, Detroit, broadcaster and commentator, 1987. Author: (book) The Live Album, 1988, The Live Albom II, 1990, The Live Albom III, 1992, Tuesdays With Morrie, 1997, The Five People You Meet In Heaven, 2003, For One More Day, 2006; co-author Bo: The Bo Schembecher Story, 1989; playwright: And The Winner Is, (Purple Rose Theatre, Chelsea, Mich.), 2005. Chmn. Hospice Mich. Fundraising, 1987—; speaker, vol. Heart Assn. Mich., 1985—, Am. Cancer Soc. Mich. Pub. Broadcasting, 1985—. Named #1 Sports Columnist in U.S.A. AP Sports Editors, 1987, 88, 89, #1 Sports Columnist in Mich. AP and UPI, 1985, 86, 87, 88, #1 Sports News Story in U.S.A., 1985, #1 Sports Columnist in Mich. United Press Internat., 1986, 87, 88, #1 Sports Columnist in Mich. Nat. Assn. Sportswriters and Broadcasters, 1988, 89, #2 Outstanding Writer Nat. Headliners award, 1989. Mem. Baseball Writers Am., Football Writers Am., Tennis Writers Am. Avocation: former musician. Office: Detroit Free Press Inc 600 W 4th St Detroit MI 48226*

ALBRECHT, KAREN ELIZABETH, voice educator, theater director; d. Albrecht; m. John Thomas Chatmas, Jan. 1, 1995. PhD in Voice Pedagogy, U. North Tex., Denton, Texas, 1991. Cert. all-level choral music tchr. Tex. Singer, actress Augburg Opera, Ft. Worth Opera, Dallas Lyric Stage, Waco Lyric Opera, various locations, 1981—; voice instr., music theater dir. McLennan Coll., Waco, Tex.; music dir. mus. theater Brookhaven Theatre, Granbury Theatre, Waco Summer Musicals, others, various locations, Tex. Performer opera, music theatre, concerts. Singer: (various mus. performances) A Little Night Music, Sweeney Todd, Madama Butterfly, Acis and Galatea, Cosi fan tutti; dir.(music dir.): (music theater prodns.) State Fair, Seven Brides for Seven Brothers, Cabaret, Kiss Me Kate, others; actor: (TV and industrial films). Bd. dirs. Waco Summer Musicals, Tex., 1996—2000, Waco Civic Theatre, 1995—99. Named regional finalist, Met. Opera, finalist, Shreveport Opera; recipient Meistersinger Finalist, Am. Inst. of Musical Studies. Mem.: Tex. Music Edn. Assn. (coll. vocal chairperson 1993—98), Music Tchrs. Nat. Assn., Music Educators Nat.

Conf., Nat. Assn. of Tchrs. of Singing (bd. dirs.), Phi Kappa Lamda, Mu Phi Epsilon. Democrat. Achievements include research in Voice Teaching Techniques; patents pending for Voice teaching visual aid. Avocations: travel, gourmet cooking, music collecting, hiking, snorkeling. Office: McLennan Coll 1400 College Drive Waco TX 76708 Home Phone: 254-756-7762; Office Phone: 254-299-8284. Office Fax: 254-299-8242. Business E-Mail: kalbrecht@mclennan.edu.

ALBRECHT, KATHE HICKS, art historian, visual resources manager; b. Ann Arbor, Mich., Aug. 21, 1952; d. Richard Brian and Mafalda (Brasile) Hicks; m. Mark Jennings Albrecht, July 20, 1973; children: Nicole, Alexander, Olivia. BA in Art History, UCLA, 1975; MA in Art History, Am. U., 1989. Slide libr. asst. Am. U., Washington, 1986—88, visual resources curator, 1991—; pres.-elect Visual Resources Assn., 2003, pres., 2004—06. Co-coord. Mus. Ednl. Site Licensing Project (Nat. Initiative Getty), 1994; mem. Conf. on Fair Use (Dept. of Commerce) VRA rep. to Digital Future Coalition, 1996—; mem. Nat. Initiative for a Networked Cultural Heritage, 1996-2003. Vol. Fairfax County Pub. Sch. Sys., 1980-2000; re-election com. Rep. Nat. Com., Washington, 1984; Rep. precinct worker Mason dist., 1980s. Grantee Am. U. (image processing, database devel.), 1995, 2003. Mem.: Visual Resources Assn. (pres. Mid-Atlantic region 1995—96, chair nat. membership com. 1995—97, chair intellectual property rights com. 1996—2000, pres. Mid-Atlantic region 2000—02, pres.-elect 2003—04, pres. 2004—06), Southeastern Coll. Art Conf., Am. Assn. Mus., Coll. Art Assn. Presbyterian. Avocation: antiques. Office: Am Univ 4400 Massachusetts Ave NW Washington DC 20016-8001 Home Phone: 703-255-3264; Office Phone: 202-885-1675. E-mail: kalbrec@american.edu.

ALBRECHT, RALPH P., lawyer; b. Watertown, NY; BSEE, Va. Polytechnic Inst. and State Univ., Blacksburg, 1989; JD, George Mason U., Arlington, Va., 1997. Bar: DC 1997, Ct. Appeals for Fed. Cir. 1999, US Patent and Trademark Office. Rschr., mktg. and sales cons. IBM Corp., 1985—97; assoc. Sterne, Kessler, Goldstein & Fox, 1997—99, Lane, Aitken & McCann LLP, 1999—2000; ptnr. Venable LLP, Washington, 2000—05, co-chair Patent Prosecution Practice Group, mem. Patent Prosecution and Intellectual Property Litig. Dept., ptnr. Vienna, Va., 2006—. Contbr. articles tp profl. jours. Mem.: ABA, Bar Assn. DC (treas.-elect 2006—07, sec. 2005—06, patent, trademark and copyright sect. chair 2003—04, exec. coun. mem., newsletter editor, Outstanding Svcs. award 1990, 2000, 2002), Capital Telecom. Profls., Am. Intellectual Property Law Assn. Avocations: golf, tennis. Office: Venable LLP 575 7th St NW Washington DC 20004 Office Phone: 703-760-1681. Office Fax: 202-344-8300. Business E-Mail: rpalbrecht@venable.com.

ALBRECHT, REBEKAH S., mathematician, educator; b. Scranton, Pa. m. Thomas C. Albrecht; children: Thomas, Matthew, Stephen, Elizabeth, Mark, Andrew, Peter. BA in Math. and Secondary Edn., Marywood U., Scranton, Pa., 1975; MA in Math., West Chester U., Pa., 1978. Cert. in bibl. counseling Christian Counseling and Edn. Found., 2005. Tchr. East H.S., West Chester, 1978—79; faculty Broward County C.C., Ft. Lauderdale, Fla., 1979—80; adj. faculty Northeastern Christian Jr. Coll., Villanova, Pa., 1992, Delaware County C.C., Media, Pa., 2000—. Mem. Rep. Com. of Chester County, 1996—2002. Mem.: Christian Motorcyclists Assn. Presbyterian.

ALBRECHT, RONALD FRANK, anesthesiologist; b. Chgo., Apr. 17, 1937; s. Frank William and Mabel Dorothy (Cassens) A.; children: Ronald Frank II, Mark Burchfield, Meredith Ann. AB, U. Ill., 1958, BS, 1959, MD, 1961. Diplomate Am. Bd. Anesthesiology. Intern U. Cin. Hosp., 1961-62; resident in anesthesiology U. Ill. Hosp., Chgo., 1962-64, attending physician, 1966-73, 89—, chief dept. anesthesiology, 1989—, pres. med. staff, 1999-2001; clin. assoc. NIH, Bethesda, Md., 1964-66; practice medicine specializing in anesthesiology Chgo., 1966—; asst. prof. anesthesiology U. Ill., Chgo., 1966-70, clin. assoc. prof., 1970-73, prof. anesthesiology, 1989—, head dept. Coll. Medicine, 1989—2007, chief dept. anesthesiology, 1989—2007. Chmn. dept. anesthesiology Michael Reese Med. Ctr., Chgo., 1971-2005; prof. anesthesiology U. Chgo., 1973-89. Contbr. articles to profl. jours. Served to lt. comdr. USPHS, 1964-66. Fellow Am. Coll. Anesthesiologists; mem. AMA, Internat. Anesthesia Rsch. Soc., Am. Soc. Anesthesiologists, Assn. Anesthesists Gt. Britain and Ireland, Am. Physiol. Soc., Soc. Acad. Anesthesiology Chairs, Assn. Anesthesiology Program Dirs. (pres. 1991-93), Ill. Soc. Anesthesiologists (pres. 1980-81), Ill. State Med. Soc., Chgo. Med. Soc., Chgo. Soc. Anesthesiologists (pres. 1986-90), Assn. Univ. Anesthesiologists. Presbyterian. Home: 1020 Chestnut Ave Wilmette IL 60091-1732 Office: U Ill Chgo Coll Medicine Dept Anesthesiology MC/515 1740 W Taylor St Ste 3200 Chicago IL 60612-7239 Home Phone: 847-256-1955; Office Phone: 312-996-4020. Business E-Mail: ralbrech@uic.edu.

ALBRECHT, STAN LEROY, academic administrator, sociologist, educator; b. Fremont, Utah, July 13, 1942; s. Rex LeRoy and Alta (Taylor) A.; m. Joyce Van Wagoner; children: Sheri, Michael, Bryant, Rachelle, Stacia. BS, Brigham Young U., 1966; MA, Wash. State U., 1968, PhD, 1970. Asst. prof. Utah State U., Logan, 1970-74, exec. v.p., provost, 2000—05, pres., 2005—; assoc. prof. Brigham Young U., Provo, Utah, 1974-78, prof., 1978—, dean, 1988-89, acad. v.p., 1989. Vis. asst. prof. SUNY, Albany, 1973. Author: Social Psychology, 1981, 87, Divorce and Remarriage, 1980, Research Methods, 1984. Mem. Am. Sociol. Assn., Rural Sociol. Soc. (v.p. 1986). Democrat. Mem. Lds Ch. Avocations: hiking, fishing. Office: Utah State U 1420 Old Main Hill Logan UT 84322-1420 Home: 818 E Summit Dr Smithfield UT 84335*

ALBRECHT, THOMAS CHARLES, III, computer technician; b. Bryn Mawr, Pa., July 14, 1977; s. Thomas Charles and Rebekah Sue Albrecht; m. Sarah Joy Phenicie, Aug. 27, 1999; children: Thomas Charles, Tabitha Joy, Aiden Matthew, Micah Stephen, Leah Grace. BS in Computer Sci., W.Chester U., Pa., 1996—2001. Cert. informatics sys. security profl. Internat. Info. Sys. Security Cert. Consortium, 2005. Computer programmer SCS Automation, Norristown, Pa., 2001—03; sys. integrator Lockheed Martin IS&S, King of Prussia, Pa., 2003—. Mem.: Am. Mensa. R-Consevative. Presbyn. Home: 1010 Stirling St Coatesville PA 19320 Home Phone: 610-466-0171. Personal E-mail: talbrech@speakeasy.net, talbrech@glamdring.com.

ALBRECHT, WILLIAM PRICE, economist, educator, government official; b. Pitts., Jan. 7, 1935; s. William Price and Jane Lanier (Moses) A.; m. Alice Annette Cooper, June 14, 1956 (div. Nov. 1975); children—William, Alison, Jonathan, Jeffrey; m. Fran Jaecques, July 4, 1976 AB, Princeton U., 1956; MA, U. S.C., 1962, Yale U., 1963, PhD, 1965. Asst. prof. U. Iowa, Iowa City, 1965-70, assoc. prof., 1970-82, prof. econs., 1982-88, assoc. dean Coll. Bus. Adminstrn., 1984-88; self-employed antitrust cons., 1978-88; commr. Commodity Futures Trading Commn., Washington, 1988-93; prof. econs. U. Iowa, Iowa City, 1993—, dir. Inst. for Internat. Bus., 1998—2003, Justice prof. Internat. Bus., 2000—. TV fin. advisor. Author: Economics, 1974, 4th edit., 1986, Black Employment, 1970, Microeconomic Principles, 1979, Macroeconomic Principles, 1979 Candidate U.S. Ho. of Reps., 1970; legis. asst. U.S. Senator Dick Clark, 1974; mem. nat. adv. coun. US Small Bus. Adminstrn., 2003—. Served to lt. USN, 1956-61. Mem. Am. Econ. Assn., Midwest Econ. Assn. (v.p. 1981-82). Avocations: tennis, farming. Home: 5770 NE Morse Rd Solon IA 52333-8806 Office: U Iowa Dept Econs Iowa City IA 52242 Office Phone: 319-335-3125. Business E-Mail: william-albrecht@uiowa.edu.

ALBRETHSEN, ADRIAN EDYSEL, metallurgist, consultant; b. Carey, Idaho, June 20, 1929; s. Norman Carl and Dollie Gustina (Brown) A.; m. Joan Alice Phelan, July 8, 1961; children: Thomas, Eric, Carl. BS in Mining Engring., U. Idaho, 1952, MSMetE, 1958; PhD in Mineral Engring., MIT, 1963. Analytical chemist Bunker Hill Co., Kellogg, Idaho, 1954-55; mining engr. Anaconda Co., Butte, Mont., 1955-57; rsch. asst. MIT, Cambridge, 1958-63; sr. engr. GE, Richland, Wash., 1963-65; sr. rsch. engr. Battelle Meml. Inst., Richland, Wash., 1965-66, ASARCO, Inc., South Plainfield, NJ, 1966-86; plant metallurgist Nord Ilmenite Corp., Jackson, NJ, 1989-92; cons. pvt. practice, Bridgewater, NJ, 1986—2005; ret., 2005. 1st lt. USAF, 1952-54, Korea. Mem. ASM Internat., Soc. Mining Engrs., Sigma Xi. Avocation: gardening. Home: 485 Vicki Dr Bridgewater NJ 08807-1941

ALBRIGHT, CHRIS, professional soccer player; b. Phila., Jan. 14, 1979; m. Leah Albright. Attended, Univ. Va. Midfielder DC United, 1999—2002, LA Galaxy, 2002—. 20 caps, 2 goals U.S. Nat. Soccer team, 1999—; mem. U.S. World Cup team, 2006. Named to All-Am. team, 1999, All-Star team, Major League Soccer, 2005. Mailing: US Soccer Fedn 1801 S Prairie Ave Chicago IL 60616

ALBRIGHT, ERIC D., medical librarian, director; b. Seattle, Aug. 21, 1964; s. David Karl and B. Ann (Wyant) A.; m. Karin E. Zitzewitz, Aug. 4, 1990; 2 children, Hannah C.M. and Paul C. AB in History of Sci., U. Chgo., 1986, AM in Libr. Sci., 1990. Head circulation Crerar Libr. U. Chgo., 1988-90; reference libr. Galter Libr., Northwestern U., Chgo., 1990-94, collection devel./spl. collections libr., 1994-97; head info. & edn. svcs. Duke U. Med. Ctr. Libr., Durham, NC, 1997-98, head pub. svcs., asst. dir., 1998—2002; dir. Hirsh Health Scis. Libr. Tufts U., Boston, 2002—. Book reviewer Libr. Jour., 1990—; jour. reviewer Jour. AMA, 1994—. Mem. exec. bd. Luth. Campus Ministry Met. Chgo., 1991-95. Mem. ALA, Med. Libr Assn. (NAHSL chpt.), Acad. Health Info. Profls. (disting. mem.), ASBE. Lutheran. Avocations: reading, knitting, gaming, Web surfing. Office: Tufts Univ Hirsh Health Sci Libr 145 Harrison Ave Boston MA 02111 Office Phone: 617-636-2481.

ALBRIGHT, GIFFORD HARRY, retired architectural engineering educator, consultant; b. Pottsville, Pa., Feb. 14, 1931; s. Harry Clayton and Grace Reinhart Albright. BArch in Engring., Pa. State U., 1953; MS, MIT, 1955. Rsch. projects dir. U.S. Naval Civil Engrs. Corps, Washington, 1956—58; prof. archtl. engring. Pa. State U., University Park, 1958—91, dept. head archtl. engring., 1962—83; program dir. NSF, Washington, 1983—88; prof. ermeritus archtl. engring. Pa. State U., 1991—. Bldg. rsch. cons. G. H. Albright Assocs., State College, 1958—. Author: (technical publication) Planning Atomic Shelters- A Handbook. Chair, bldg. code appeals bd. Borough of State Colege, State College, Pa., 1965—68; councilman Triangle Nat. Frat., Plainfield, Ind., 1982—86; pres. PS Alumni Chpt., Triangle Frat., 1965—69. Lt. j.g. USNR. Mem.: Am. Soc. Testing Materials, Am. Concrete Inst., Earthquake Engring. Rsch. Inst., Am. Soc. Heating, Ventilation and Refrigeration Engrs., Constrn. Specification Inst. (advisor 2004—), Pa. State Ret. Faculty Staff Club (pres. 2004—05), Am. Inst. Archs. (assoc.), Pa. State Faculty Staff Club (pres. 1998—99). Home: P O Box 196 State College PA 16804-0196 Business E-Mail: gha1@psu.edu.

ALBRIGHT, JOSEPH P., state supreme court justice; b. Parkersburg, W.Va., Nov. 8, 1938; s. M.P. and Catherine (Rathbone) A.; m. Patricia Ann Deem, 1958 (dec. 1993); children: Terri Albright Cavi, Lettie Albright Muckley, Joseph P. Jr., John Patrick (dec.); m. Nancie Gensert Divvens, 1995; stepchildren: Susan Divvens Bowman, Debbie Divvens Rake, Sandy Divvens Fox. BBA cum laude, U. Notre Dame, JD, 1962. Bar: W.Va. 1962, U.S. Dist. Ct. W.Va. 1962. Pvt. practice, Parkersburg, 1964-95; asst. prosecuting atty. Wood County, 1965-68; city atty. City of Parkersburg, W.Va., 1968; justice W.Va. Supreme Ct. of Appeals, Charleston, 1995—96; pvt. practice Parkersburg and Charleston, 1997—2000; justice W.Va. Supreme Ct. of Appeals, Charleston, 2001—, chief justice, 2005. Former mem. W.Va. State Ethics Commn.; bd. dirs. Albrights of Belpre (Ohio), Inc. Former clk. Charter Bd. of Parkerburg; mem. W.Va. Ho. of Dels., 1970-72, 74-86, mem. jud. com., chmn. com. on edn., 1977-78, chmn. com. on judiciary, 1979-84, 52d spkr. of Ho. of Dels., 1985-86; mem., former chmn. Blennerhassett Hist. Park Commn.; former co-chmn. Blennerhassett Hist. Commn.; mem. St. Francis Xavier Ch., Parkersburg, past pres. parish adv. coun. Named Freshman Legislator of Yr., Charleston Gazette, 1971. Democrat. Roman Catholic. Office: WVa Supreme Ct Appeals State Capitol Complex Bldg 1 Room E308 1900 Kanawha Boulevard E Charleston WV 25305 Office Phone: 304-558-2605.

ALBRIGHT, JOSEPH WILLIAM, civilian military employee; b. Chillicothe, Ohio, Feb. 3, 1954; s. Herman LeRoy and Catherine Regina (Rieder) A.; children: Andrea Lyn, Jason Michael. BME, U. Dayton, 1976; M in Strategic Studies, U.S. Army War Coll., 2000; MS in Indsl. Engring., U. Tenn., 2001. Commd. 2nd lt. Ordnance br. U.S. Army, 1976; advanced through grades to col. Ordnance br. U.S. Army, 1999; accountable officer 9th ordnance co. 9th Ordnance Co., Germany, 1977-79, ops. officer, 1979-80; rsch. engr., chief integrated logistic support office large caliber weapon sys. lab., 1980-82; material officer 3rd ordnance bn. 59th ordnance brigade 3d Ordnance Bn., 59th Ordnance Brigade, 1982-85; Dept. of Army coord. for ammunition logistics Dept. of Army, 1985-87; asst. exec. officer to dep. commanding gen. Material Readiness Army Material Commd., 1987-88; commdr. 96th ordnance co. 96th Ordnance Co., 1988-90; inspector gen. Tech. Insp. divsn. Army Material Command Tech. Insp. divsn. Army Materiel Command, 1990-93, chief program mgmt. divsn., 1993-94; comdr. Milan Army Ammunition Plant Milan Army Ammunition Plant, Tenn., 1994-96; dep. support ops. officer 3rd corps support command V U.S. Army Corps, 1996-98; depot maintenance project chief Hdqrs., Dept. of Army, 1998-99, indsl. ops. project chief, office dep. chief staff logistics, 2000—02; sr. logistics analyst Office of Dep. Undersec. of Army, Washington, 2002—04; ret., 2004. Sr logistician Office of Sec. Army, Washington, 2004—05; dir. situational awareness Office Deputy Under Sec. Army For Bus. Transformation., 2005—. Decorated Legion of Merit, Meritorious Svc. medal 6 awards, Army Commendation medal 2 awards, Army Achievement medal; named Disting. Mil. Grad., 1976, Disting. Grad. Ordnance Officer Advanced Course, 1980. Mem. ASME, SAR, US Army Ordance Corps Assn. (life), Pi Sigma Tau. Home: 22 Norva Ave Frederick MD 21701 Office Phone: 703-695-7612. Business E-Mail: joseph.albright@us.army.mil.

ALBRIGHT, LYLE FREDERICK, chemical engineering educator; b. Bay City, Mich., May 3, 1921; s. William Edward and Isabella (Sidebotham) A.; m. Jeanette Van Belle, Mar. 4, 1950; children: Christine, Diane. BS in Chem. Engring, U. Mich., 1943, MS in Chem. Engring, 1944, PhD in Chem. Engring, 1950. Lab. technician Dow Chem. Co., Midland, Mich., 1939-41; chem. engr. Manhattan Project E.I. duPont de Nemours & Co., Hanford, Wash., 1944-46; research chem. engr. Colgate-Palmolive Co., Jersey City, 1950-51; asst. prof. U. Okla., Norman, 1951-54, assoc. prof., 1954-55, Purdue U., West Lafayette, Ind., 1955-58, prof. chem. engring., 1958—. Cons. to numerous chem. petroleum cos., 1960—Author: Industrial and Laboratory Pyrolyses, 1976, Industrial and Laboratory Alkylations, 1977, Coke Formation on Metals, 1982, Pyrolysis: Theory and Industrial Practice, 1983, Processes for Major Addition Type Plastics and Their Monomers, 2d edit., 1985, Novel Production Methods for Ethylene, Light Hydrocarbons, and Aromatics, 1992, Nitrations: Recent Laboratory and Industrial Developments, 1996. Recipient Shreve prize Purdue U., 1960, 70, 88, Potter award for best instr. Schs. of Engring. Purdue U., 1988. Fellow AIChE (dir. 1982-84, Van Antwerpen award 2003); mem. Am. Chem. Soc., Internat. Brotherhood Magicians, Sigma Xi, Tau Beta Pi. Methodist. Home: 4750N N 250 W West Lafayette IN 47906-5525 Office: Purdue Univ Sch Chem Engring West Lafayette IN 47907 Home Phone: 765-463-1660; Office Phone: 765-494-4087. E-mail: albright@ecn.purdue.edu.

ALBRIGHT, MADELEINE KORBEL, former secretary of state; b. Prague, Czechoslovakia, May 15, 1937; arrived in Am., 1950, naturalized, 1957; d. Josef and Anna (Speeglova) Korbel; m. Joseph Medill Patterson Albright, June 11, 1959 (div. 1983); children: Anne Korbel, Alice Patterson, Katharine Medill. BA with honors in Polit. Sci., Wellesley Coll., 1959; student, John's Hopkins U.; MA, Columbia U., 1968, cert.Russian Inst., 1968, PhD, 1976. Washington coord. Maine for Muskie, 1975-76; chief legis. asst. to Senator Edmund S. Muskie US Senate, 1976-78; mem. staff NSC, 1978-81, The White House, 1978-81; sr. fellow in Soviet and Eastern European Affairs Ctr. for Strategic and Internat. Studies, Ctr. for Strategic and Internat. Studies, 1981; fellow Woodrow Wilson Internat. Ctr. for Scholars, Washington, 1981-82; research prof. internat. affairs, dir. women in fgn. service Sch. Fgn. Service Georgetown U., 1982-93; pres. Ctr. for Nat. Policy, 1985-93; fgn. policy coord. Mondale for Pres. campaign, 1984, to Geraldine A. Ferraro, 1984; vice chmn. Nat. Dem. Inst. for Internat. Affairs, Washington, 1984-93; perm. rep. of the U.S. UN, NYC, 1993-97; sec. US Dept. State, Washington, 1997-2001; founder & prin. The Albright Group LLC, Washington, 2001—; chair Nat. Dem. Inst., Washington, 2001—; Michael and Virginia Mortara Endowed prof. in practice of diplomacy Georgetown Sch. Fgn. Svc.; Disting. scholar William Davidson Inst., U. Mich. Bus. Sch. Sr. fgn. policy advisor Dukakis for Pres. Campaign, 1988 Author: Poland: The Role of the Press in Political Change, 1983, Madam Secretary: A Memoir, 2003; Co-author: (with Bill Woodward) The Mighty and the Almighty: Reflections on America, God, and World Affairs, 2006; contbr. articles to profl. jours., chpts. to books; (TV appearances) The Gilmore Girls, 2005 Bd. dirs. Beauvoir Sch., Washington, 1968-76, chmn., 1978-83; trustee Black Student Fund, 1969-78, 82-93, Dem. Forum, 1976-78, Williams Coll., 1978-82, Wellesley Coll., 1983-89; mem. exec. com. D.C. Citizens for Better Pub. Edn., 1975-76; bd. dirs. Washington Urban League, 1982-84, Atlantic Coun., 1984-93, Ctr. for Nat. Policy, 1985-93, Chatham House Fedn., 1986-88. Mem. Council Fgn. Relations, Am. Polit. Sci. Assn., Czechoslovak Soc. Arts and Scis. Am., Atlantic Council U.S. (dir.), Am. Assn. for Advancement Slavic Studies. Democrat. Office: The Albright Group LLC 901 15th St NW Ste 1000 Washington DC 20005 Office Phone: 202-842-7222. Office Fax: 202-354-3888.

ALBRIGHT, MICHAEL, construction executive; BS in Acctg., Miss. State U., MBA. CPA. Audit mgr. Arthur Andersen; group v.p. Rollins, Inc., Atlanta; sr. v.p. Carlisle Property Co., Dallas; contr. Centex Corp., Dallas, 1987—89, v.p., 1989, sr. v.p. adminstrn., 1999—; pres. Tex. Trust Savings Bank, FSB, 1994; chmn., CEO Centex Life Solutions, 1996—99. Mem.: AICPA, Tex. Soc. CPAs. Office: Centex Corp PO Box 199000 Dallas TX 75219-9000*

ALBRIGHT, RAYMOND JACOB, federal official; b. Reading, Pa., Apr. 7, 1929; s. Raymond Wolf and Mary Catherine (Sherr) A.; m. Ruthmarie Reich, Sept. 13, 1952; children: Raymond Jacob, David Reich. BA, Yale, 1951; Fulbright scholar, U. Vienna, Austria, 1951-52; MA, Harvard, 1954, PhD; in Polit. Sci., 1961. Fgn. affairs officer (Nat. Security Council affairs and policy planning) Office Asst. Sec. Def. (Internat. Security Affairs), 1954-61; with Office Asst. Sec. State (European affairs), 1961-62; nat. security affairs adviser Treasury Dept., 1962-67; asst. to sec. treasury (Nat. Security Affairs) Office Sec. Treasury, 1967-69; counselor for econ. affairs Am. embassy, Belgrade, Yugoslavia, 1969-72; fgn. service res. officer Dept. State, 1969-73; v.p. Export-Import Bank U.S., 1973-92, sr. v.p., 1992-95; mng. dir. AM Global Fin. LLC. Lectr. Yale, 1959, George Washington U., 1960, George Mason U., 2005; cons. Asea Brown Boveri, 1995-2004. Author (with others): Forging a New Sword, 1958. Pres. Fgn. Policy Discussion Group, Washington. Mem.: Yale Club (Washington) (bd. dirs., chmn. Yale and govt. com. 1966-69). Home: 3609 Dunlop St Chevy Chase MD 20815-5926 Office Phone: 202-429-2720. E-mail: rj.albright2@verizon.net.

ALBRIGHT, TERRILL D., lawyer; b. Lebanon, Ind., June 23, 1938; s. David Henry and Georgia Pauline (Doty) A.; m. Judith Ann Stoelting, June 2, 1962; children: Robert T., Elizabeth A. AB, Ind. U., 1960, JD, 1965. Bar: Ind. 1965, US Dist. Ct. (so. dist.) Ind. 1965, US Dist. Ct. (no. dist.) Ind. 1980, US Ct. Appeals (7th cir.) 1981, US Ct. Appeals (3d and DC cirs.) 1982, US Supreme Ct. 1972; cert. arbitrator for large complex cse program constrn. and internat. comml. cases; cert. mediator; on constrn. master arbitrator roster, Am. Arbitration Assn. Assoc. Baker and Daniels Law Firm, Indpls., 1965-72, ptnr., 1972—. Mem. panel of disting. neutrals. nat. panel for constrn. and regional comml. panel CPR Inst. for Dispute Resolution, NYC. Pres. Christamore House, Indpls., 1979-86; bd. dirs. Greater Indpls. YMCA, 1980-82; chmn. Jordan YMCA, Indpls., 1982; pres. Community Ctrs. Indpls., 1987-90. 1st lt. US Army, 1960—62. Named Disting. Ind. Lawyer, 2006. Fellow: Acad. Law Alumni, Ind. U. Sch. of Law (bd. dirs. 1974—80, pres. 1979—80), Am. Coll. Trial Lawyers, Ind. Bar Found, Indpls. Bar Found., Am. Bar Found.; mem.: Am. Arbitration Assn., Ind. State Bar Assn. (chmn. young lawyers sect. 1971—72, rep. 11th dist. 1983—85, bd. dirs., v.p. 1991—92, pres.-elect 1992—93, pres. 1993—94), Nat. Conf. Bar. Pres. (exec. coun. 1995—98). Democrat. Office: Baker & Daniels 300 N Meridian St Ste 2700 Indianapolis IN 46204-1782 Office Phone: 317-237-1262. Business E-Mail: terry.albright@bakerd.com.

ALBRIGHT, TOWNSEND SHAUL, brokerage house executive, consultant; b. Anderson, Ind., May 1, 1942; s. Townsend S. and Maxine Aree (Zimmerman) A.; m. Eileen Therese Argent, Aug. 30, 1968; children: Megan Eileen, Alexandra Michele. BA, Wabash Coll., 1964; MBA, U. Mich., 1966. With Mead Corp., Cin. and Chgo., 1966-69; mcpl. bond underwriter No. Trust Co., Chgo., 1969-71; v.p. Channer Newman Securities Co., Chgo., 1971-80; v.p., treas., dir. Croake Roberts, Inc., Chgo., 1980-86; v.p. instl. sales John Nuveen & Co., Chgo., 1986-90; with Fin. Forum, 1991—; sr. funding mgr. Ill. Fin. Authority, Chgo., 2004—; faculty mem. Loyola U., 1990—. Bd. dirs. Urban Gateways, Chgo., 1976—; dean Mcpl. Bond Sch. Chgo.; with Inst. Entrepreneurial Studies U. Ill., Chgo. Served with USAR, 1966-72. Mem. Chgo. Assn. Wabash Men, U. Mich. Alumni Assn., Mcpl. Bond Club Chgo., Econ. Club Chgo., Phi Gamma Delta (Chgo. grad. chpt., former bd. dirs., Econ. Club. Presbyterian. Home: 2019 Beechwood Ave Wilmette IL 60091-1503 Office Phone: 312-651-1338. Business E-Mail: talbright@il-fa.com.

ALBRINK, MARGARET JORALEMON, medical educator; b. Warren, Ariz., Jan. 6, 1920; d. Ira Beaman and Dorothy (Rieber) Joralemon; m. Wilhelm Stockman Albrink, Sept. 16, 1944 (dec. July 1991); children: Frederick Henry, Jonathan Wilhelm, Peter Varick (dec. March 2003). BA in Psychology cum laude, Radcliffe Coll., 1941; MS in Physiol. Chemistry, Yale U., 1943, MD, 1946, MPH, 1951. Cert. Diplomate Am. Bd. Med. Examiners, Diplomate Am. Bd. Nutrition, Diplomate Am. Bd. Physician Nutrition Specialists. Intern New Haven (Conn.) Hosp., 1946—47; NIH postdoctoral fellow Yale U., New Haven, 1947—49, fellow pub. health, 1950—51, instr. medicine, 1952—58, asst. prof. medicine, 1958—61; assoc. prof. W.Va. U., Morgantown, 1961—66, prof. medicine, 1966—90, prof. emerita, 1990—, mem. grad. faculty, 1977—92; mem. med. and dental staff W.Va. U. Hosp., Morgantown, 1961—2000. Vis. scientist Donner Lab., U. Calif., Berkeley, 1993—; assoc. physician Grace-New Haven Cmty. Hosp., 1952-61; cons. nutrition study sect. NIH; vis. scholar U. Calif., Berkeley, 1977-78; established investigator Am. Heart Assn., 1958-63. Guest editor: Clinics in Endocrinology and Metabolism, 1976;

guest editor Am. Jour. Clin. Nutrition, 1968, mem. editorial bd., 1963-68; mem. editorial adv. bd. Jour. Am. Coll. Nutrition, 1988-89; reviewer jours.; contbr. articles, chpts. and abstracts to profl. jours. Recipient Rsch. Career award Nat. Heart, Lung and Blood Inst., 1963-90. Fellow: ACP, Am. Coll. Nutrition, Am. Heart Assn. (emeritus, fellow arteriosclerosis coun., fellow coun. epidemiology); mem.: LWV, ACLU, Am. Diabetes Assn. (epidemiology coun.), Am. Soc. Clin. Nutrition, Am. Soc. Clin. Investigation, Am. Fedn. Clin. Rsch., Phi Beta Kappa, Sigma Xi, Alpha Omega Alpha. Democrat. Avocations: music, archaeology, computers, nature conservation. Home: 817 Augusta Ave Morgantown WV 26501-6237 Office: WVa U Dept Medicine PO Box 9159 Morgantown WV 26506-9159 E-mail: mjalbrink@aol.com.

ALBRITTON, ARTHUR DALLAS, lawyer; b. Jacksonville, Fla., June 16, 1928; s. Arthur Dallas and Grace Elizabeth (Pratt) Albritton; m. Frances Gail Kelley, Dec. 21, 1951; m. Ann Elizabeth Hill, Dec. 27, 1968; m. Grace Lovelace, Jan. 26, 1991; children: Gary Callan, Andrew Brian, Laura Elizabeth, Rachel Ann, Jacoba Lehane. BS, Fla. State U., 1950, MS, 1951; JD, Yale U., 1956. Bar: Fla. 1956, U.S. Dist. Ct. (so. dist.) Fla. 1956, U.S. Dist. Ct. (mid. dist.) Fla. 1959, U.S. Ct. Appeals (5th cir.) 1959, U.S. Supreme Ct. 1966, U.S. Ct. Appeals (11th cir.) 1981. Ptnr. Hardee & Ott, Tampa, Fla., 1956—60; sr. ptnr. Albritton & Sessums, Tampa, 1961—82; pres. Albritton & Lunsford, P.A., Tampa, 1982—. Counsel Fla. Bd. Bar Examiners, 1958—68; asst. county solicitor Hillsborough County, 1960, asst. state atty., 1961—62; chmn., mem. Jud. Nominating Commn., 1972—79; pres. Albritton and Lunsford Lawyers, 2006—; arbitrator; lectr.; participant various seminars. Contbr. articles to legal publs. Sec.-treas., mem. Tampa Sports Authority, 1966—70; chmn. Mayor's Mgmt. Analysis Team, City of Tampa, 1962—66; pres. Agape Evangelistic Mission, 1980—. 1st lt. USAF, 1951—53. Recipient various awards of recognition for profl. svc. activities. Mem.: Fla. Acad.Trial Lawyers, Hillsborough County Bar Assn. (pres. 1965, Outstanding Trial Lawyer award 2000), Fla. Bar, Univ. Club, Bay Area Yale Club. Democrat. Office: 100 E Madison St Ste 302 Tampa FL 33602-4703

ALBRITTON, WILLIAM HAROLD, III, federal judge; b. Andalusia, Ala., Dec. 19, 1936; s. Robert Bynum and Carrie (Veal) A.; m. Jane Rollins Howard, June 2, 1958; children: William Harold IV, Benjamin Howard, Thomas Bynum. AB, U. Ala., 1959, JD, 1960. Bar: Ala. 1960. Assoc. firm Albrittons & Rankin, Andalusia, 1962-66, ptnr., 1966-76; ptnr. firm Albrittons & Givhan, Andalusia, 1976-86; ptnr. Albrittons, Givhan & Clifton, Andalusia, 1986-91; judge U.S. Dist. Ct. (mid. dist.) Ala., Montgomery, 1991-97, chief judge, 1998—2004, sr. judge, 2004—. Mem. 11th Circuit Jud. Coun., 1998—2004, com. on ct. adminstrn. and case mgmt. US Jud. Conf., 1999-2004. Pres. Ala. Law Sch. Found., 1988-91 Fellow Am. Coll. Trial Lawyers, Am. Bar Found.; mem. Fed. Judges Assn. (bd. dirs. 1999-2002), Ala. State Bar (commr. 1981-89, disciplinary commn. 1981-84, v.p. 1985-86, pres.-elect 1989-90, pres. 1990-91), Am. Judicature Soc., Am. Inns of Ct., Bluewater Bay Sailing Club, Bluewater Bay Country Club, Phi Beta Kappa, Phi Delta Phi, Omicron Delta Kappa, Alpha Tau Omega.

ALBRITTON, WILLIAM HAROLD, IV, lawyer; b. Tuscaloosa, Ala., Mar. 21, 1960; s. William Harold III and Jane Rollins (Howard) A.; m. Lucille Smith, July 23, 1983; 1 child, Elizabeth Rollins. BA, U. Ala., Tuscaloosa, 1982, JD, 1985. Ptnr. Albrittons, Clifton, Alverson, Bowden, Moody P.C., Andalusia, Ala., 1985-2001, Bradley, Arant, Rose & White, Birmingham, Ala., 2001—. Bd. dirs. The Bank, Andalusia; judge Mcpl. Ct. Andalusia, 1989-2000. Bd. dirs. Covington County Arts Coun., Andalusia, 1986-90, Andalusia City Schs. Found., 1991-2001, Andalusia Area C. of C., 1986-89; elder 1st Presbyn. Ch., Andalusia, 1990—. Mem. ABA, Ala. Bar Assn. (sec. pres.'s adv. task force 1986-88, chmn. com. on local bar activities 1990, task force on minority opportunity 1990-96, character and fitness com. 1991-96, chmn. 1993-96, chmn. com. solo practitioners & small firms 1997-99), Ala. Def. Lawyers Assn. (bd. dirs. young lawyers sect. 1991-96, amicus curiae com. 1992-2002), Internat. Assn. Def. Counsel, Am. Inns of Ct., Kiwanis. Avocations: scuba diving, music, photography, sailing, motorcycling. Office: One Federal Pl 1819 Fifth Ave N Birmingham AL 35203 Office Phone: 205-521-8740. E-mail: halbritton@bradleyarant.com.

ALBUM, JERALD LEWIS, lawyer; b. Monroe, La., Oct. 18, 1947; s. Natt B. and Rose Marie (Pickens) A.; m. Joan Abbey Lurie, July 30, 1983; children: Nicole, Jeffrey. BS, Tulane U., 1969, JD, 1973. Bar: La. 1973, Colo. 1990, Tex. 1992, U.S. Dist. Ct. (ea. dist.) La. 1975, U.S. Dist. Ct. (mid. dist.) La. 1980, U.S. Dist. Ct. (we. dist.) La. 1983, U.S. Ct. Appeals (5th cir.) 1976. Assoc. Mmahat, Gagliano, Duffy & Giordano, Metairie, La., 1973-79; assoc. to ptnr. Lemle, Kelleher, Hunley, Moss & Frilot, New Orleans, 1980-85; shareholder Abbott Simses, Album & Knister, New Orleans, 1985-96; ptnr. Album, Stovall, Radecker & Giordano, New Orleans, Reich, Album & Plunkett, Metairie, La., 2001—. Mem. La. Assn. of Def. Counsel, New Orleans Bar Assn., La. State Bar Assn. Avocations: golf, volleyball, gardening. Home: 4637 Southshore Dr Metairie LA 70002-1430 Office: Reich Album & Plunkett 3850 N Causeway Blvd Ste 1000 Metairie LA 70002-7247

ALBYN, RICHARD KEITH, retired architect; b. Detroit, Apr. 8, 1927; s. Walter Harris and Corrine Henrietta (Miller) A.; m. Nancy Jane Cosby; children: Keith Cosby, Lisa Benton Albyn Drummond. Student, U. Ill., 1945-49. Registered architect, Mich., Ohio, Fla., Md., W.Va., N.C. Prin. dir. Linn Smith Assocs., Inc., Birmingham, Mich., 1962-64, TMP Assocs., Inc., Bloomfield Hills, Mich., 1964-82, HEPY Assocs., Inc., Southfield, Mich., 1982-86; ret., 1986. Co-author: Buildings of Michigan, 1987; also articles in profl. jours. and hist. publs.; illustrator: A Handbook for the Amateur Archaeologist, 1967, The Archaeologists Coloring Book, 1964. Mem. Preservation N.C., Transylvania Cmty. Arts Coun., Asheville Art Mus.; bd. dirs. Asheville Pub. Radio Sta. WCQS, 2003—. Recipient citation Am. Assn. Sch. Adminstrs., 1964, 70, 1st pl. award Ch. Architects Guild, 1965, others. Fellow: AIA (lectr. 1961—65, treas. 1968, sec. 1969, pres. Detroit chpt. 1971, pres. Detroit archtl. found. 1971, host chpt. com. nat. conv. 1971, mem. past pres com. 1971—86, mem. vocat.-tech. edn. svc. study com. 1976, honor award 1964, 1971, award of merit 1971, honor award 1977, 1st pl award Focus on Art Exhibit 1997, Viewer's Choice award 1997, Merchant's award 1998, Merit award 1999, Patrons award 2000, Hon. Men. 2001, 2002, Merit award 2003, 1st pl award Focus on Art Exhibit 2004, Bonus award 2005); mem.: Brevard Music Ctr. Assn. (pres. 2001—02), Preservation N.C. (bd. advisors 1999—), Archaeol. Soc. N.C., Transylvania County Joint Hist. PreservationCommn. (chmn. 1993—96), Transylvania County Hist. Soc. (bd. dirs. 1919—94, bd. visitors 1999—), AIA N.C. Presbyterian. Avocations: painting, archaeology, genealogy, photography, writing. Home: 425 Kentwood Ln Pisgah Forest NC 28768-9511

ALCALAY, ALBERT S., artist, design educator; b. Paris, Aug. 11, 1917; came to U.S., 1951, naturalized, 1956; s. Samuel and Lepa (Afar) A.; m. Vera Eskenazi, Nov. 11, 1950; children: Leor, Ammiel. Student in Paris, Rome. Lectr. design Carpenter Center, Harvard U., 1960—. One man shows, De Cordova and Dana Mus., Lincoln, Mass., 1968, Swetzoff Gallery, Pucker-Safrai Gallery, Pace Gallery, others; retrospective, Carpenter Ctr., Harvard U., 1982; group shows, Inst. Contemporary Art, Boston, 1960, Venice (Italy) Biennale, Mus. Modern Art., 1955, Whitney Mus. Am. Art, 1956, 58, 60, U. Ill., Urbana, Pa. Acad. Fine Arts, 1960; represented in permanent collections, Mus. Modern Art, N.Y.C., Boston Mus. Fine Arts, Fogg Art Mus., DeCordova and Dana Mus., Phillips Acad., Mus. Am. Art, Brandeis U. Rose Art Mus., U. Mass. Mus., Wellesley Coll. Mus., Colby Coll. Mus., Smith Coll., Rome Mus. Modern Art, U. Rome, Brockton Art Mus., Tufts U., Medford, Mass., Boston Pub. Library, Smithsonian Inst. Archives of Am. Artists; documentary fmil A.A. Self-Portraits. Guggenheim fellow, 1959-60; recipient prize Boston Arts Festival, 1960 Home: 66 Powell St Brookline MA 02446-3929 Office: Harvard U Carpenter Ctr Cambridge MA 01238

ALCALAY, EUGENE CHRISTIAN, pianist; b. Bucharest, Romania, Oct. 13, 1966; arrived in U.S., 1984; s. Alexander and Gina Alcalay; m. Ruth Elisabeth Mayers, July 19, 2003. Diploma, The Curtis Inst. Music, 1990; MusB, Ind. U., 1988; MusD, The Juilliard Sch., 1998. Asst. prof. piano Geneva Coll., Beaver Falls, Pa., 1999—2005; instr. piano 6th Internat. Music Festival and Sch., Bogota, Colombia, 2000; Fulbright scholar, instr. U. Nacional de Colombia, Bogota, Colombia, 2003; Fulbright sr. specialist Fundacion U. Juan N. Corpas, Bogota, Colombia, 2004; mem. faculty piano and chamber music Masterworks Internat. Festival and Sch., London, 2004; Steinway artist, 2005; asst. prof. piano U. Wis., Platteville, 2005—. Adjudicator young artist competitions Duquesne U., 2000; adjudicator concerto competitions U. Nacional de Colombia, 2003; adjudicator Steinway Soc. We. Pa., 2005; judge in field; mem. jury Ibla Grand Prize Internat. Piano Competition, Ragusa-Ibla, Italy, 2006. Musician: (debut) Carnegie Hall, 1998. Recipient award, Pro-Piano Recital Series, N.Y., 1997, winner, Pitts. Concert Soc. Maj. Auditions, 2001; scholar, Fulbright Found., 2003, Steinway Artist, 2005; The Leonard Bernstein Personal scholar, 1982—91. Mem.: Madison Area Piano Tchrs. Assn., Wis. Music Tchrs. Assn., Pitts. Piano Tchrs. Assn., Pa. Music Tchrs. Assn., Music Tchrs. Nat. Assn., Mortar Bd., Pi Kappa Lambda (life). Home: 940 St James Cir Platteville WI 53818 Office: U Wis Platteville Dept Fine Arts 1 University Plz 175C Doudna Hall Platteville WI 53818 Office Phone: 608-342-1292. Personal E-mail: ecalcalay@yahoo.com. Business E-Mail: alcalaye@uwplatt.edu.

ALCALDE, HECTOR, public relations executive; b. NYC; BA, U. Tampa; MA, Peabody Coll. Former educator, Fla.; chief of staff to former chmn. of ways and means com. U.S. Ho. of Reps., Washington, 1962—74; founder, chmn. Alcalde & Fay, Arlington, Va., 1973—. Bd. dirs. SAFLink, Inc. Fomer trustee Fairfax County Pub. Schs. Edn. Found. Office: Alcalde & Fay 2111 Wilson Blvd 8th Fl Arlington VA 22201 also: 400 N Capitol St NW Ste 475 Washington DC 20001 Office Phone: 202-783-6669, 703-841-0626.

ALCANTARA, ANITA LUISA, community arts administrator; b. May 30, 1942; d. Francisco B. and Eleanor E. (Locke) A. AA, Wright City Coll., Chgo, 1962; BEd, Northeastern Ill. U., Chgo., 1964; cert. cmty. svc. mgmt., Roosevelt U., Chgo., 1989; postgrad., Garrett Evang. Theol. Sem, Evanston, Ill. Tchr. 5th grade Chgo. Pub. Schs., 1964—65; libr. technician at main libr. Chgo. Pub. Libr., 1967—71; field dir., ednl. svcs. dir. Girl Scouts of Chgo., 1971-79; nat. tng. coord. Girl Scouts U.S.A., NYC, 1979-84; mgmt. devel. cons. Equitable Corp., NYC, 1984; adminstr. United Ch. of Rogers Park, Chgo., 1985-86, min. of cmty. life, 1986—2000; dir. adminstrv. svcs. and cmty. life United C.h. of Rogers Park, 2000—03; older adult program, adminstrv. asst. Insight Arts, 2003—. Cons. Contact Chgo., 1985—86, Yule Connection mgr., 1985—86; adminstrv. support United Ch. Rogers Park, Chgo., 2007—. Author: You Make the Difference, Leaders' Guide: Council Guide, 1980. Leadership Let's Get Started print/video tng. program, 1981; coun. guide Daisy Girl Scouts Coun., 1983; exec. dir. Insight Arts, 1993-96; collaborator exhibn. Out of the Loop: Neighborhood Voices, Chgo. Hist. Soc., 2001; active Chgo. Hist. Soc.; mem. Parliament, World's Religion Project in Rogers Park; bd. mem. Rogers Park Cmty. Action Network, Chgo. Northwestern Dist., No. Ill. Conf.; superintendency com. mem. United Meth. Ch. Recipient Chgo. Youth award Mayor's Commn. Youth Welfare, 1968, Chgo. Pub. Libr. award, 1970, Thanks Badge award, Girl Scouts Chgo., 1975; named Vol. of Yr. Chgo. Area Project, 1993 Office: 1545 W Morse Ave Chicago IL 60626-3306 Office Phone: 773-973-1521. Personal E-mail: rochafan@aol.com. Business E-Mail: anita_a@insightartsliberation.org.

ALCH, MARK LEE, finance educator, researcher, real estate investor; b. Mpls., Oct. 21, 1945; s. Harry Brown and Dora Alch; m. Sharlene Rivi Eigen, June 22, 1969; children: Matthew Cary, Nikkie Shana. BA, U. Minn., 1967, MA, 1970; PhD, UCLA, 1977, C.Phil, 1973. cert. tchr., Calif., Calif. C.C. supr. credential, instr. credential; lic. real estate sales, Calif. Asst. mgr. Eagle Cleaners & Launderers, Mpls., 1961-72; grad. asst. U. Minn., Mpls., 1969-70; program coord., tchg. asst. UCLA, 1972-76, asst. to vice chancellor for student and campus affairs, 1976—77; tng. mgr. So. Calif. divsn. Fluor-Daniel, Irvine, 1977-80, project adminstr. advanced tech. divsn., 1980-81; v.p. Drake Beam Morin, Inc., Irvine, 1981—84, sr. v.p., mng. dir., offices in Orange County, San Diego, Phoenix, Tucson, Las Vegas, Riverside and San Bernardino, Calif., 1985-95; CEO, v.p. edn., tng. and devel. Uniben, Inc., Pasadena, Calif., 1996-99; instr. extension divsn. bus. mgmt. program U. Calif., Irvine, 1997—; nat. dir. edn. Am. Youth Soccer Orgn., Hawthorne, Calif., 2000—01, Kuykendall and Alch Real Estate Investments, 2000—; realtor Team Gage Realtors, 2002; dir., exec. v.p. Hall Career Svcs., 2003—, Ryness Co., San Diego, 2003—04. Adj. prof. Occidental Coll., Eagle Rock, Calif., 1977; instr. U.C. Irvine; cons. Mark Alch & Assocs., Irvine, 1996-2000; adj. Temps Plus, 2003-2004, Ryness Co., 2004; presenter in field Author: A Diplomatic Study of Anglo-German NavalTensions 1904-08, Including Kaiser Wilhelm's Year of Indiscretions, 1970, Germany's Naval Resurgence, British Appeasement, and the Anglo-German Naval Agreement of 1935, 1977, A Financial Aid and College Planning System for Parents of High School Students, 1996, How to Become a Millionaire: A Straightforward Approach to Achieving Wealth, 1999, Coaching for the New Century, 2004, others; contbr. over 50 articles to profl. jours., internet and online broadcasts. Exec. com. Irvine, Newport Beach and Costa Mesa YMCA, 1992-93, fedn. chief, 1992-93; co-chmn. econ. devel. com. City of Irvine and Irvine C. of C., 1992-95; active Am. Youth Soccer Orgn., 1991—, referee com. region 213, Irvine, 1994—, area referee, 1995, sect. referee, 1996, referee assessor, 1996-, dir. referee instrn. region 213, 1997-98, sect. referee instr., trainer regional, referee intermediate and advanced, 2000—, others; beadkeeper Indian Guides, YMCA, 1989-90, asst. chief, 1990-91, chief, 1991-92, fedn. chief, 1992-93, mem. exec. com. YMCA, 1992-94, nation elder, 1999-93. Mem. ASTD (membership com. Orange County chpt. 1995-96), Assn. Profl. Cons., Med. Mktg. Assn., Profl. Coach and Mentors Assn. (dir. evaluations nat. conf. 2003), Nat. Human Resources Assn., Life Sci. Industry Coun., Nat. Assn. Realtors, Calif. Assn. Realtors, Orange County Assn. Realtors, Inland Empire (sales mktg. coun.), Orange County Indsl. League, Orange County Venture Network (sales and mktg. coun.), UCLA Alumni Assn. (life), Orange County Mustang Assn., Am. Youth Soccer Orgn. (advanced referee, instr.), US Soccer Fedn., So. Calif. Soccer Referee Assn., Orange County Soccer Referee Assn., Orange County Soccer Ofcls. Assn., Orange County Mustang Club, Cobra Owners Club, Shelby Am. Automobile Club, U. Minn. Alumni Assn. Democrat. Jewish. Avocations: jogging, travel, high performance and muscle car restoration, music, public speaking. Office: 25 W Lucero Irvine CA 92620 Office Phone: 949-413-9511. E-mail: markalch@cox.net.

AL-CHALABI, SUHAIL ABDUL-JABBAR, transport economist, consultant; b. Baghdad, Iraq, July 14, 1940; arrived in U.S., 1965; s. Abdul Jabbar and Wajeeha al-Chalabi; m. Margery Lee Pupach, Mar. 9, 1965. BArch, MIT, 1962; MSc, Athens Tech. Inst., Greece, 1965. Planner, arch. Doxiadis Assocs., Athens, 1963-65, Skidmore Owings & Merrill, Chgo., 1965-67; rsch. dir. Northeastern Ill. Planning Commn., Chgo., 1967-74; exec. dep. dir. Chgo. Area Transp. Study, 1974-81; spl. advisor to mayor City of Chgo., 1981-82, commr. dept. econ. devel., 1982-83; exec. v.p., CFO The al Chalabi Group, Ltd., Chgo., 1983—. Mem. 3d airport planning team, Chgo., 1986—2006; adapted hwy. planning models for use in planning airports, commuter rail and interurban bus; initiated build/no-build analyses EIS; project mgr. numerous transp. projects: rail, toll road, airport sys., bridges. Mem. rsch. and forecast adv. com. Northeastern Ill. Planning Commn., Chgo., 1992—. Mem.: Am. Assn. Airport Execs. (corp.), World Soc. Ekistics, Chgo. Southland C. of C., Lambda Alpha. Achievements include securing financing, overseeing restoration, operation of Chicago Theater, 1984-95. Home: 718 Wilson Ave Beverly Shores IN 46301-0232 also: Apt 2708 330 W Diversey Pkwy Chicago IL 60657 Office: al-Chalabi Group Ltd Ste 1403 330 W Diversey Pkwy Chicago IL 60657-6206 E-mail: acgtran@aol.com, suhailaj@aol.com.

ALCHIN, JOHN REGINALD, cable tv company executive; b. Springsure, QLD, Australia, May 21, 1948; arrived in US, 1980; s. William R. and Jean M. (Sowden) Alchin. BA, U. Toronto, Ont., Can., 1977, MBA, 1979. Mng. dir. Toronto Dominion Bank, NYC, 1980-90; sr. v.p., treas. Comcast Corp., Phila., 1990—2002; exec. v.p., treas. Comcast Holdings, Phila., 2000—02; exec. v.p., treas., co-CFO Comcast Corp., Phila., 2002—. Bd. dir. BNY Hamilton Funds, Big Brothers Big Sisters of Southeastern Pa.; adv. bd. Met. AIDS Neighborhood Nutrition Alliance (MANNA); corp. exec. bd. dir. Phila. Mus. of Art. Co-recipient CFO of Yr. award, Broadcast Cable Fin. Mgmt. Assn., 2004; named one of America's Best CFOs, Instl. Investor mag., 2004. Office: Comcast Corp 1500 Market St Philadelphia PA 19107-3721 Office Phone: 215-981-7503. Office Fax: 215-981-7790.*

ALCINDOR, LEWIS FERDINAND See ABDUL-JABBAR, KAREEM

ALCOCK, CHARLES ROGER, science educator; b. Windsor, Eng., June 15, 1951; arrived in US, 1973; BS in Physics and Math., U. Auckland, 1972; PhD in Astronomy and Physics, Calif. Inst. Tech., 1977. Long-term mem. Inst. for Advanced Study, Princeton, NJ, 1977-81; assoc. prof. dept. physics MIT, Cambridge, 1981-86; head Astrophysics Ctr., Inst. Geophysics & Planetary Physics Lawrence Livermore (Calif.) Nat. Lab., 1986-97, head Inst. Geophysics and Planetary Physics, 1994-98, dep. assoc. dir. for sci. in the physics directorate, 1998-2000; Reese W. Flower prof. astronomy and astrophysics Univ. Pa., 2000—04; dir. Harvard-Smithsonian Ctr. for Astrophysics, Smithsonian Astrophysical Observatory, Harvard Coll. Observatory, Cambridge, Mass., 2004—. Vis. prof. Niels Bohr Inst., Copenhagen, 1979; vis. fellow Australian Nat. U. , Canberra, 1983; adj. prof. dept. astronomy U. Calif., Berkeley. Recipient R&D 100 award, 1993, E.O. Lawrence award, 1996, Beatrice M. Tinsley prize, Am. Astron. Soc., 2000; fellow Earle C. Anthony, Caltech. U., 1973—79, Alfred P. Sloan rsch., MIT, 1983—86. Fellow: Am. Acad. Arts and Sciences; mem.: NAS. Office: Harvard Smithsonian Ctr for Astrophysics Director's Office 60 Garden St Cambridge MA 02138

ALCOCK, GEORGE LEWIS, JR., (PETER), investor, business strategist; b. Boston, Feb. 26, 1940; s. George Lewis and Louise Hall Alcock; m. Louise Stewart Bachelder, Sept. 29, 1984; children: Peter L., Caroline S. BS, Northeastern U., Boston, 1962. Prodn. supr. J.H. Winn, Winchester, Mass., 1963-65; sales staff Liberty Mutual Ins., Boston, 1966-68; fin. staff Nat. Med. Leasing, Cambridge, Mass., 1968-69; cons. Innovative Mgmt., Cambridge, Mass., 1970-73; treas. Devel. Mgmt. Consultants, Boston, 1973-80; chmn. M.B. Claff & Sons Inc., Brockton, Mass., 1980-2001; corp. fin. staff Alcock Investments, Watertown, Mass., 1980-87; pres., CEO U.S. Repeating Arms Co., New Haven, Conn., 1987-90; gen. ptnr. Alcock Ltd. Ptnrs., Weston, Mass., 1991—. Pres. Beckwood Svcs., Inc., Pliastow, N.H., 2001—. Dir. The Nat. Coun. Northeastern U., Boston, 1989—; trustee Fitchburg (Mass.) State Coll., 1999—, chmn. bd. trustees, 2001—; bd. mem. Mass. Bd. Higher Edn., 2003—; bd. dirs. Mass. State Coll. Bldg. Authority. Mem.: Assn. Corp. Growth. Avocation: outdoor sports. Office: Alcock Ltd Ptnrs 105 Cherry Brook Rd Weston MA 02493-1347 Home Phone: 781-894-9469; Office Phone: 781-894-4947. Personal E-mail: palcock@comcast.net.

ALCON, SONJA L., retired medical social worker; b. Orange City, Iowa, Aug. 2, 1937; d. Albert Lee Gerard and Clarice Victoria (Brown) deBey; m. Richard J. Gebhardt, June 6, 1959; children: Russell Gebhardt, Cheryl Gebhardt, Kurt Gebhardt; m. George W. Ryan, Dec. 28, 1968; 1 child, Alanna Ryan (dec.); m. David E. Alcon, July 20, 1985. BA, Western Md. Coll./McDaniel Coll., 1959; MSW, U. Md., 1973. Caseworker Springfield State Hosp., Sykesville, Md., 1959-61; dir. social work dept. Hanover (Pa.) Gen. Hosp., 1966-96; ret., 1996. Staff Matthews Hallmark Store, Hanover, 1997—99, Hanover, 2002; sales assoc. BONTON Dept. Store, Hanover, 2003—05; field instr. Western Md. Coll., 1967—96, social work adv. coun., 1979—81, 1984—86; clin. assoc. prof. Sch. Social Work and Social Planning U. Md., 1987—92; cons. Golden Age Nursing Home, Hanover, 1973—76, Carlisle (Pa.) Hosp., 1974—78, Hanover Vis. Nurse Assn., 1977—83; emergency svcs. Mental Health Clinic, 1972; chmn. profl. adv. com. Vis. Nurses Assn. Hanover and Spring Grove, 1986—89; ind. beauty cons. Mary Kay, 1999—2000. Bd. dirs. Hospice of York, 1980—82, Hanover chpt. ARC, 1976—79, Adams-Hanover Mental Health, 1973—76; pres. Human Svcs. Orgn., 1980, v.p., 1985—86; adv. coun. Hanover Hospice, 1982—85; treas. Hanover Cmty. Progress Com., 1976—80; mem. Adams-Hanover Sheltered Workshop Com., 1968—70; bd. dirs. Hanover Cmty. Players, 1974—77, sec., 1982; organizer local chpt. Make Today County and Peemie Parent Support Group, 1979; initiator, co-trustee Children's Cardiac Fund, 1979—82; adv. bd. United Cerebral Palsy S. Ctrl. Pa., 1989—90; active YWCA, 1979—84, 1996—98; co-organizer Adams-Hanover chpt. Compassionate Friends, 1983; adminstr. Hanover Gen. Hosp. Spl. Needs Fund, 1986—96; mem. cmty. adv. com. Healthsouth Rehab. York, 1995—96; co-facilitator I Can Cope classes Am. Cancer Soc., 1989—92; active Cmty. Needs Coalition, 1990—96, S. Ctrl. Pa. Coalition Organ/Tissue Donation, 1994—98; mem. Case Mgmt. Network S. Ctrl. Pa., 1994—96; vol. Hanover Hosp.; adv. group Inst. Pastoral Care, 1976—77; adv. coun. Parents Anonymous, 1976—79, 1985—92; mem. vestry All Sts. Episcopal Ch., 1973—74, 1976—79, 1983—86, 1997, vestry sec., 1975, diocesan del. Ctrl. Pa., 1978, 1980—86, altar guild, 1968—86, 1992—93, treas. ch. women, 1979—83, ch. choir, soloist, 1975—; vol. Hanover Area Coun. Chs.; bd. dirs. Episcopal Home Shippensburg, 1979—85, Ea. Star Home, Warminster, Pa., Grand Ct. of Pa., 1995—98. Finalist YWCA Salute to Women, 1986, 1987; recipient York Daily Record Exceptional Citizen award, 1979, Recognition cert., Col. Richard McAllister chpt. DAR, 1980, Companion of the Temple award, Grand Encampment Knights Templar, 1999. Mem.: NASW, Acad. Cert. Social Workers, Hanover Hosp. Aux. (life), Pa. White Shrine Club (pres. 2002—03), Md. Alumni Assn. (bd. dirs. 1983), Hanover Hosp. Auxiliary (life), Hanover Gen. Hosp. Aux. (life), Westminster Assembly, Social Order of Beauceant (worthy pres. 1999, supreme worthy preceptress 2003—04, supreme worthy 2d v.p. 2004—05, supreme worthy 1st v.p. 2005—06, worthy pres. 2006, supreme worthy pres. 2006—07), Order of White Shrine of Jerusalem (life; worthy high priestess 1994—95, watchman of shepherds 1999—2000, supreme worthy herald 1999—2000), Order of Amaranth (life; royal patron 1988—89, royal matron 1995—96, grand historian 1998—99, royal matron 1999—2000, grand standard bearer 2001—02, royal patron 2001—02, grand rep. to Eng. 2002—03, grand rep. Iowa 2005—06), Order Eastern Star (life; worthy matron 1985—86). Home: 6918 Seneca Ridge Dr York PA 17403

ALCORN, WALLACE ARTHUR, minister, writer; b. Milw., Aug. 29, 1930; s. William Keith and Dora Mildred (Brazee) Alcorn; m. Ann Margaret Carmichael, June 5, 1958; children: John Mark, Allison Alcorn-Oppedahl, Stephen, Paul. Student, Marquette U., 1950; AB, Wheaton Coll., 1952; MDiv, Grand Rapids Bapt. Theol. Sem., 1959; AM, Wheaton Grad. Sch. Theology, 1959; postgrad., Mich. State U., 1959-60, U. Mich., 1960-61; ThM, Princeton Theol. Sem., 1965; PhD, NYU, 1974; cert. in clin. pastoral edn., Fitzsimons Army Med. Ctr., 1975; postgrad., U. Minn., 1980-81. Ordained to ministry Gen. Assn. Regular Bapt. Chs., 1957; cert. advanced mediator Am. Arbit. Assn. Program sec. Wis. Heart Assn., 1954—55; field program rep. Chgo. Heart Assn., 1955—56; pastor Caddy Vista Bapt. Ch., Caldonia, Wis., 1955-57; tchr. Wyoming (Mich.) Schs., 1958-60; pastor Bloomfield Hills (Mich.) Bapt. Ch., 1960-61; English tchr. Waterford-Kettering H.S., Drayton Plaines, Mich., 1961-62; pastor Cmty. Bapt. Ch. Shark River Hills, Neptune, NJ, 1962-67, 1st Bapt. Ch., Austin, Minn., 1976-83; prof. bible Moody Bible Inst., Chgo., 1967-73; assoc. prof. N.T. N.W. Bapt. Sem., Tacoma, 1974-76; clin. pastoral care specialist Madigan Army Med. Ctr., Tacoma, 1974-76; police chaplain Tacoma, 1974-76, Austin, 1976-90; pres. Faith Acad., Mpls., 1986; prin. Wallace Alcorn Assocs., Austin, 1983—; pastoral counselor New Life Family Svcs., Rochester, Minn., 1987-92. Cons. NJ Dept. Edn., 1964—67, US Dept. Edn., 1953—54; radio tchr. Moody Radio Network, 1968—74; chmn. Minn. Assn. Regular Bapt. Chs., 1980—83; radio commentator Sta. KTIS and Northwestern Coll. Network, 1987—98; syndicated newspaper columnist, 1993—; adj. faculty Riverland CC, 1994—99; lectr. Seminario Batista do Carini, Brazil, 2006—07. Author: (book) The Bible as Literature, 1965, Elijah, Prophet of God, 1972, The Life of Christ Visualized, 1973, Knowing and Using the Bible, 1975, Momentum, 1986; nat. editor: Christian Life, 1956—60, Mil. Life, 1983—86, Ampersand, 1995—99, Living Bible Commentary, 1974—76, The Book We Love, 1994, Como a Biblia Chegou a Ser a Biblia, 2006; contbr. Wycliffe Bible Ency., 1974, Tyndale Family Bible Ency., 1976, New Commentary on the Whole Bible, 1990, Stones of Remembrance, 1995, Austin Remembers, 2006, Ency. of Activism and Social Justice, 2007, articles to profl. jours. Mem. citizen's adv. coun. Neptune Bd. Edn., 1965—67; chair Austin Human Rights Commn., 1989—98; mem. profl. adv. coun. Pub. Edn. Religion Studies Ctr., Wright State U., 1972—76; pub. mem. 10th Jud. Dist. Ethics Com., 1993—99; dir. Good News Hour, Austin, 1976—83, Minn. Human Rights Commn., 1990—98, Coop. Solutions Mediation Ctr., Austin, 1995—99. With USNR, 1947—52, with US Army, 1952—54, with USAR, 1954—57, chaplain, col. USAR, 1957—90. Recipient Amy Writing award, Amy Found., 1988, Baptist Heritage award, 2003, 2004. Mem.: AAUP, Soc. Biblical Lit., Organ. Am. Historians, Am. History Assn., Am. Assn. for History of Medicine, Am. Acad. Religion, Am. Pub. Health Assn., Hist. Soc. Minn., Hist. Soc. S.C., Hist. Soc. Ohio, Hist. Soc. Wis., Mil. Chaplains Assn. (pres. Chgo. chpt. 1970—74), Assn. Former Intelligence Officers, Soc. Profl. Journalists, Nat. Religious Broadcasters, Evang. Press Assn., Evang. Theol. Soc., Soc. Mil. History. Office: 500 J Oakland Place NE Austin MN 55912

ALCOTT, MARK HOWARD, lawyer; b. NYC, Aug. 11, 1939; s. Harvey and Rose (Eigerman) A.; m. Susan M. (Bell), Sept. 3, 1961; children: Jill, Laura, Daniel, Elizabeth. AB, Harvard U., 1961, LLB, 1964. Bar: N.Y. 1965, U.S. Dist. Ct. (so. and ea. dists.) N.Y. 1966, U.S. Ct. Appeals (2d cir.) 1966, U.S. Ct. Appeals (9th and 10th cirs.) 1980, U.S. Ct. Internat. Trade 1980, U.S. Supreme Ct. 1982, U.S. Ct. Appeals (D.C. cir.) 1983, D.C. 1984, U.S. Tax Ct. 1985; U.S. Ct. Appeals (1st. cir.),2000; U.S. Ct. Appeals (11th. cir.), 2003, U.S. Ct. Appeals (7th cir.) 2004. Assoc. Paul, Weiss, Rifkind, Wharton, and Garrison LLP, NYC, 1964-73, ptnr., 1973—. Mediator Mandatory Mediation Program, U.S Dist. Ct. (so. dist.) N.Y.; spl. master, mediator commercial divsn. N.Y. Supreme Ct.; Spl. Master Appellate Divsn. first dept. Mem. Community Planning Bd., Riverdale, N.Y., 1970-72; comr. Larchmont, N.Y. Planning Commn., 1982-94; bd. dir. Mosholu-Montefiore Community Ctr., Bronx, N.Y., 1966-77. Fellow: Am. Bar Found., N.Y. Bar Found., Am. Coll. Trial Lawyers (chmn. downstate N.Y. com., 1994-1996, chmn. internat. com., 1998-2002); mem.: ABA (litig. sect. internat. litig. com.), Fed. Bar Coun., Internat. Bar Assn. (bus. law sect., internat. litigation com.), Assn. Bar: City of N.Y. (fed. legis. com. 1970—73, commn. campaign fin. reform 1997—99), N.Y. State Bar Assn. (chmn. internat. litig. com. comml. and fed. litig. sect. 1989—92, sec. exec. com., sect. exec. vice chmn. 1992—93, sect. chmn.-elect 1993—94, sect. chmn. 1994—95, chmn. spl. commn. on continuing legal edn. 1996—98, chmn. spl. commn. on admin. adjudication 1998—2001, exec. com., v.p. 2001—05, pres. elect 2005—06, pres. 2006—, chmn. ho. of dels. 2005—06). Avocation: sailing. Office: Paul Weiss Rifkind Wharton & Garrison LLP 1285 Ave Americas New York NY 10019-6064

ALDA, ALAN, actor, film director, scriptwriter; b. NYC, Jan. 28, 1936; s. Robert and Joan (Browne) A.; m. Arlene Weiss; children: Eve, Elizabeth, Beatrice. BS, Fordham U., 1956, degree (hon.), 1978, Drew U., 1979, Columbia U., 1979, Conn. Coll., 1980, Kenyon Coll., 1982. Ind. actor stage, screen, TV, 1956—. Tchr. Compass Sch. Improvisation. Actor: (Broadway plays) including The Apple Tree (nominated Tony award), The Owl and the Pussycat, Purlie Victorious, Fair Game for Lovers, Jakes Women (Tony award nominee), Art, (films) including Gone Are the Days, 1963, The Moonshine War, Paper Lion, 1968, The Extraordinary Seaman, 1968, Jenny, 1970, The Mephisto Waltz, 1971, To Kill a Clown, 1972, California Suite, 1978, Same Time, Next Year, 1978, The Seduction of Joe Tynan, 1979, Crimes and Misdemeanors, 1989 (D.W. Griffith award, N.Y. Film Critics award), Whispers in the Dark, 1992, Manhattan Murder Mystery, 1993, Canadian Bacon, 1995, Flirting With Disaster, 1996, Everyone Says I Love You, 1996, Murder at 1600, 1997, Mad City, 1997, The Object of My Affection, 1998, What Women Want, 2000, The Aviator, 2004, Resurrecting the Champ, 2007; (TV movies) include The Glass House, 1972, Marlo Thomas and Friends in Free to be.You and Me, 1974, 6 Rms Riv Vu, 1974, Kill Me If You Can, And The Band Played On, 1993 (Emmy nomination, Supporting Actor - Special, 1994), White Mile, 1994, Club Land, 2001, The Killing Yard, 2001, (TV series) M*A*S*H, 1972-83 (also writer of 17 episodes, dir. 30 episodes, recipient 5 Emmy awards, 5 Golden Globe awards, Humanitas award for writing), The West Wing, 2004-06 (Emmy award for Outstanding Supporting Actor in a Drama Series, 2006); creator: (TV series) We'll Get By, 1975, The Four Seasons; writer, narrator Scientific American Frontiers, 1993—; actor, writer, dir.: (films) The Four Seasons, 1981, Sweet Liberty, 1986, A New Life, 1987, Betsy's Wedding, 1990; TV guest appearances include Route 66, 1963, The Nurses, 1963, The Carol Burnet Show, 1974, ER, 1999.; author: Never Have Your Dog Stuffed - and Other Things I've Learned, 2005. Presdl. appointee Nat. Commn. for Observance of Internat. Women's Yr., 1976; co-chair Nat. ERA Countdown Campaign, 1982; trustee Mus. of TV and Radio, 1985, Rockefeller Found., 1989. Recipient Theatre World award for Fair Game for Lovers, 7 People's Choice awards; elected to TV Acad. Hall of Fame, 1994. Mem. AFTRA, Dirs. Guild Am. (awards 1977, 82), Writers Guild Am. (award 1977), Screen Actors Guild, Actors Equity Assn.; fellow Am. Acad. Arts & Sciences Mailing: Author Mail Random House 1745 Broadway New York NY 10019*

ALDAG, RAMON JOHN, management and organization educator; b. Beccles, Suffolk, Eng., Feb. 11, 1945; came to U.S., 1947; s. Melvin Frederick and Joyce Evelyn (Butcher) A.; children: Elizabeth, Katherine BS, Mich. State U., 1966, MBA, 1968, PhD, 1974. Thermal engr. Bendix Aerospace divsn., Ann Arbor, Mich., 1968—70; tchg. asst., instr. Mich. State U., East Lansing, 1968—73; asst. prof. mgmt. U. Wis., Madison, 1973—78, assoc. prof., 1978—82, prof. mgmt. and orgn., 1982—, chmn. dept. mgmt., 1986—88, assoc. dir. Indsl. Rels. Rsch. Inst., 1977—83, co-dir. Ctr. for Study of Orgnl. Performance, 1982—, faculty senator, 1980—84, Pyle Bascom prof. leadership, 1982—, student advisor, 1979—, Glen A. Skillrud Family chair in bus., 2001—, chmn. dept. mgmt. and human resources Sch. Bus., 1995—, co-dir. Weinert Ctr. for Entrepreneurship, 2000—, exec. dir. Weinert Ctr. Entrepreneurship, 2002—. Mgmt. cons. various businesses and industries, 1973- Author: Task Design and Employee Motivation, 1979, Managing Organizational Behavior, 1981, Introduction to Business, 1984, (now titled Business in a Changing World), 3d edit., 1993, 4th edit., 1996, Management, 1987, 2d edit., 1991, Leadership and Vision, 2000, Organizational Behavior and Management, 2002, Mastering Management Skills, 2005; contbr. articles to profl. jours.; cons. editor for mgmt. South-Western Pub. Co., 1987—; assoc. editor Jour. Bus. Rsch., 1988—, Decision Scis., 2002-; essays co-editor Jour. Mgmt. Inquiry. Bd. dirs. Family Enhancement Program, Madison Grantee U. Wis., HEW, 1975-85; recipient Adminstrv. Rsch. Inst. award, 1976, Jerred Disting. Svc. award, 1993, NSF, 2000—; U. Wis. faculty rsch. fellow, 1985-88 Fellow. Acad. of Mgmt. (divsn. chmn. 1971—, bd. govs. 1986—, v.p. and program chair 1989—, pres. elect 1990, pres. 1991, past pres. 1992—, dep. dean 2003-05, dean 2005—, recipient Disting Svc. award, 1995); mem. Midwest Acad. Mgmt. (pres. 1973-), Decision Scis. Inst. (track chmn. 1975-), Indsl. Rels. Rsch. Assn. (elections commn. 1980—), Found. Adminstrn. Rsch. (pres. 1992—), Pi Tau Sigma, Tau Beta Pi, Sigma Iota Epsilon, Beta Gamma Sigma, Alpha Iota Delta Avocations: bicycling, gardening, reading, fishing. Office: U Wis 3112 Grainger Hall 975 University Ave Madison WI 53706-1323 Home: 19 Halite Way Madison WI 53711 Office Phone: 608-263-3771. Business E-Mail: raldag@bus.wisc.edu.

ALDANA, PHILIPP ROQUE, neurosurgeon; b. Cebu, Philippines, July 3, 1966; s. Benigno Salcedo Aldana, Jr. and Estelita Roque Aldana; m. Carmina Montesa, Oct. 19, 1969; children: Carissa, Katrina. BS in zoology cum laude, U. Philippines, 1987; MD in rsch. with distinction magna cum laude, St. Louis U., 1994. Diplomate Am. Bd. Neurol. Surgery, 2005. Resident dept. surgery U. Miami, Fla., 1994—95; resident dept. neurosurgery U. Miami/Jackson Meml. Hosp., 1995—2001; pediatric neurosurgery fellow U. Utah, Primary Children's Hosp., Salt Lake City, 2001—02; asst. dir. divsn. neurosurgery, dir. comprehensive traumatic brain injury program Akron Children's Hosp., Ohio, 2002—06; clin. asst. prof. neurosurgery U. Fla., Jacksonville, 2006—; dir. clin. svcs. Pediatric Neurosurgery Ctr., Wolfson Children's Hosp., Jacksonville, 2006—. Clin. asst. prof. neurosurgery Northeastern Ohio U. Coll. Medicine, Akron, 2002—06, U. Fla., Jacksonville, 2006—. Contbr. chapters to books, articles to profl. jours. Recipient Mo. State Med. Assn. award, St. Louis U., 1994, Resident Day Rsch. award, U. Miami Dept. Neurosurgery, 2001; grantee Instl. grantee brain tumor rsch., Miami Children's Hosp., 1999; Akron Children's Hosp. Found. grantee for brain injury rsch., 2004. Fellow: Am. Acad. Pediat.; mem.: Children's Oncology Group, Congress Neurol. Surgeons, Am. Assn. Neurol. Surgeons, Alpha Sigma Nu, Alpha Omega Alpha. Office: Lucy Gooding Pediatric Neurosurgery Ctr 836 Prudential Dr Ste 1005 Jacksonville FL 32207 Office Phone: 904-633-0780. Business E-Mail: philipp.aldana@jax.ufl.edu.

ALDAVE, BARBARA BADER, lawyer, educator; b. Tacoma, Dec. 28, 1938; d. Fred A. and Patricia W. (Burns) Bader; m. Rafael Aldave, Apr. 2, 1966; children: Anna Marie Alkin, Anthony John. BS, Stanford U., 1960; JD, U. Calif., Berkeley, 1966. Bar: Oreg. 1966, Tex. 1982. Assoc. law firm, Eugene, Oreg., 1967-70; asst. prof. U. Oreg., 1970-73, prof. Eugene, 2000—; vis. prof. U. Calif., Berkeley, 1973-74; from vis. prof. to prof. U. Tex., Austin, 1974-89, co-holder James R. Dougherty chair for faculty excellence, 1981-82, Piper prof., 1982, Joe A. Worsham centennial prof., 1984-89, Liddell, Sapp, Zivley, Hill and LaBoon prof. banking fin. and comml. law, 1989; dean Sch. Law, prof. St. Mary's U., San Antonio, 1989-98, Ernest W. Clemens prof. corp. law, 1996-98; Loran L. Stewart prof. corp. law, dir., Ctr. for Law and Entrepreneurship U. Oreg. Sch. Law, 2000—. Vis. prof. Northeastern U., 1985-88, 98, Boston Coll. 1999-2000, Cornell U., 2002; ABA rep. to Coun. Inter-ABA, 1995-99; NAFTA chpt. 19 panelist, 1994-96. Pres. NETWORK, 1985-89; chair Gender Bias Task Force of Supreme Ct. Tex., 1991-94; bd. dirs. Tex. Alliance Children's Rights, Lawyer's Com. for Civil Rights Under Law of Tex., 1995-2000; nat. chair Gray Panthers, 1999-2003; pres. Portia Project, 2003—; vice chair Mex. Am. Cultured Ctr., 2003—. Recipient Tchg. Excellence award U. Tex. Student Bar Assn., 1976, Appreciation awards Thurgood Marshall Legal Soc. of U. Tex., 1979, 81, 85, 87, Tchg. Excellence award Chicano Law Students Assn. of U. Tex., 1984, Hermine Tobolowsky award Women's Law Caucus of U. Tex., 1985, Ethics award Kugle, Stewart, Dent & Frederick, 1988, Leadership award Women's Law Assn. St. Mary's U., 1989, Ann. Inspirational award Women's Advocacy Project, 1989, Appreciation award San Antonio Black Lawyers Assn., 1990, Spl. Recognition award Nat. Conv. Nat. Lawyers Guild, 1990, Spirit of the Am. Woman award J. C. Penney Co., 1992, Sarah T. Hughes award Women and the Law sect. State Bar Tex., 1994, Ann. Tchg. award Soc. Am. Law Tchrs., 1996, Legal Svcs. award Mexican-Am. Legal Def. and Ednl. Fund, 1996, Woman of Justice award NETWORK, 1997, Ann. Peacemaker award Camino a la Paz, 1997, Outstanding Profl. in the Cmty. award Dept. Pub. Justice, St. Mary's U., 1997, Charles Hamilton Houston award Black Allied Law Students Assn. St. Mary's U., 1998, Woman of Yr. award Tex. Women's Polit. Caucus, 1998, award Clin. Legal Edn. Assn., 1998, Lifetime Achievement award Jour. Law and Religion, 1998, Harriet Tubman award African-Am. Reflections, 2002. Mem.: ABA (com. on corp. laws, sect. banking and bus. law 1982—88, Latin Am. law initiative coun. 2004—06), US-Mex. Bar Assn. (U.S. chair legal edn. com. 2005—), Inter-Am. Bar Assn., Am. Bar Found. (life), Tex. Bar Found. (life), Stanford U. Alumni Assn., Order of Coif, Delta Theta Phi (Outstanding Law Prof award St. Mary's U. chpt. 1990, 1991), Omicron Delta Kappa, Iota Sigma Pi, Phi Delta Phi. Roman Catholic. Home: 86399 N Modesto Dr Eugene OR 97402-9031 Office: U Oreg Sch Law Eugene OR 97403-1221 Home Phone: 541-344-0555; Office Phone: 541-346-3985. Personal E-mail: balaw98@aol.com. Business E-Mail: aldave@uoregon.edu.

ALDAY, PAUL STACKHOUSE, JR., retired mechanical engineer; b. Camden, NJ, May 31, 1930; s. Paul Stackhouse and Amanda (Knocke) A.; m. Ethel Humes O'Connor, Nov. 29, 1952; children: Amy Jane, Paul Stackhouse III, Sarah Jean. BS in ME, Drexel U., 1953, MS in ME, 1957. Registered profl. engr., N.J. Engr. Naval Shipyard/Burroughs Corp., Phila., 1953-56; rsch. engr. Franklin Rsch. Labs., Phila., 1956-57, Univac, Phila., 1957-59; sr. engr. RCA Corp., Camden, 1959-68; sr. design engr. Univac/Burroughs/Control Data, southeastern Pa., 1968-74; project engr. Campbell Soup Co., Camden, 1974-90; cons. Budd Co., Phila., 1990-91; mail processing equipment U.S. Post Office, Phila., 1991-98; ret., 1998. Drexel U. scholar, 1948. Mem. Sigma Xi, Tau Kappa Epsilon Frat. Achievements include stress analysis, supports and preliminary bearing test on design of Enrico Fermi Nuclear Reactor; mechanical concept and design of digital data recorder for Gemini Spacecraft; concepts and designs of video recorder mechanisms used in surveillance satelites, digital computer input/output and memory devices, single position mail sorting machine for the U.S. Post Office. Home: 5759 Rogers Ave Pennsauken NJ 08109-2374

ALDEA, PATRICIA, architect; b. Bucharest, Romania, Mar. 18, 1947; came to U.S., 1976; d. Dan Jasmin Negreanu and Sonia (Friedgant) Philip-Negreanu; m. Val O. Aldea, Feb. 17, 1971; 1 child, Donna-Dana. March, Ion Mincu, Bucharest, 1970. Registered architect, N.Y. Architect, project. mgr. The Landmark Preservation Inst., Bucharest, 1971-76; architect Edward Durell Stone Assn., NYC, 1977-79; sr. assoc. architect, project mgr. Alan Lapidus P.C., NYC, 1980-2001; assoc. project arch., mgr. HLW, NYC, 2001—02; chief plan examiner DOB, NYC, 2003—. Columnist Contemporanul art jour., 1969-73. Hist. landmarks study fellow Internationes Fed. Republic of Germany, 1974. Office: DOB 120-55 Queens Blvd Kew Gardens NY 11424

ALDEN, INGEMAR BENGT, pharmaceutical executive; b. Stockholm, Feb. 23, 1943; s. Bengt Erik and Agnes (Eriksson) A.; m. Estelle Cuni Skrabanek, June 18, 1977; children: Lars, Sonja, Ingela. M in Social and Bus. Sci., Stockholm U., 1969. Field supr. Astra Lakemedel Sweden, Sodertalje, 1970-71, nat. sales mgr., 1971-72, mgr. mktg. and sales, 1973-74; internat. mktg. mgr. Astra Pharms., Sodertalje, 1975-76; dir. pharm. div. Astra Ltd., Watford, Eng., 1977-78; mng. dir. Merck Sharp & Dohme, Sweden, 1979-89; chief exec. officer Aldenco AB, 1989-91; dir. Pharma/Agro/Vet div. Svenska Hoechst AB, 1991-95; gen. mgr. Hoechst Marion Roussel AB, Stockholm, 1996; CEO Aldenco AB, Huddinge, Sweden, 1997—; chmn. Aldenco AB, Axelar AB, IsiFer AB, Aprea AB, LipoPeptide AB, SoftCure Pharms. AB., Moberg Derma AB., Recopharma AB. Mem. Rotary, RVC Club. Office Phone: 46 8 774 2011. E-mail: ingemar.alden@aldenco.se.

ALDEN, JOHN W., lawyer; BS, Stanford U., 1955, MS, 1956, JD, 1959. Bar: Calif. 1960. Assoc. Pillsbury, Madison & Sutro, 1959-67; assoc. gen. counsel Occidental Petroleum Corp., LA, 1967—2004; ret., 2004. Office: Occidental Petroleum Corp 10889 Wilshire Blvd Ste 1500 Los Angeles CA 90024-4216 E-mail: john_w_alden@oxy.com.

ALDEN, STEVEN MICHAEL, lawyer; b. LA, May 19, 1945; s. Herbert and Sylvia Zina (Hochman) A.; m. Evelyn Mae Subotky, Dec. 31, 1977; children: Carissa Louise, Bramley Marshall, Darym Alexander. AB, UCLA, 1967; JD, U. Calif., Berkeley, 1970. Bar: Calif. 1971, NY 1971. Assoc. Debevoise & Plimpton LLP, NYC, 1971-78, ptnr., 1979—, head Real Estate Dept. Lectr., seminar panelist Practising Law Inst., NYC, 1981—; panelist, lectr. NY State Bar, Albany, 1984. Contbr. articles to profl. jours. Chmn. bd. Symphony Space, Inc., NYC. Mem. ABA (real estate fin. com.), Assn. of Bar of City of NY (com. real property law), Am. Land Title Assn. (assoc. lender's counsel group), Am. Coll. Real Estate Lawyers, Am. Coll. Mortgage Attys., Order of Coif, Phi Beta Kappa, Sky Club (N.Y.C.). Republican. Office: Debevoise & Plimpton LLP 919 3rd Ave Fl 42 New York NY 10022 Office Phone: 212-909-6481. Office Fax: 212-909-6836. Business E-Mail: smalden@debevoise.com.

ALDEN, VERNON ROGER, academic administrator; b. Chgo., Apr. 7, 1923; s. Arvid W. and Hildur Pauline (Johnson) A.; m. Marion Frances Parson, Aug. 18, 1951 (dec. Aug. 1999); children: Robert Parson, Anne Elizabeth, James Malcolm, David Douglas. AB magna cum laude, Brown U., Providence, RI, 1945; LLD (hon.), Brown U., Providence, 1964; MBA, Harvard U., Cambridge, Mass., 1950; LLD (hon.), Emerson Coll., Boston, 1957, Ohio Wesleyan U., Delaware, 1964, RI Coll., 1965, William Jewell Coll., Liberty, Mo., 1965, Loyola U., 1966, Wilberforce U., Ohio, 1970, Ottawa U., 1970, Babson Coll., Babson Park, Mass., 1972; LHD (hon.), North Park Coll., 1965; LittD, Ohio U., 1969; DPS, Bowling Green U., 1969; LittD (hon.), Bethany Coll., 1970. Admission officer Brown U., 1946-48; asst. dir. admissions Northwestern U., 1950-51; dir. fin. aid Harvard Grad. Sch. Bus. Adminstrn., assoc. dean, faculty, 1951-61; ednl. dir. U. Hawaii Advanced Mgmt. Program, summer 1960, Keio U. Advanced Mgmt. Program, Tokyo, summers 1960-61; pres. Ohio U., Athens, 1961—69; chmn. bd., chmn. exec. com. Boston Co. and subsidiary Boston Safe Deposit & Trust Co., 1969-78. Bd. dirs. Colgate-Palmolive Co., Digital Equipment Corp., Mead Corp., McGraw Hill, Sonesta Internat. Hotels Corp., Tax-Free Trust Funds Hawaii, Oreg. and Rhode Island, ML-Lee Fund, Ind. Gen. Ptnrs.; hon. consul-gen. Kingdom of Thailand. Chmn. Pres.' Task Force Job Corps Program, com. Future of U. Mass, 1971, chmn. Mass. Coun. Arts/Humanities, 1972-84, Mass. Bus. Devel. Coun./Fgn. Bus. Coun., 1978-83; life trustee Boston Symphony Orch., Mus. Sci., Boston; chmn. arts facilities com. MIT; fellow emeritus Brown U.; life trustee French Libr., Boston; adv. com. Harvard Program Japan-U.S. Rels. Lt. USNR, 1943-46 Recipient Gov.'s award State Ohio, 1969; Founder's citation Ohio U., 1969; Bus. Statesman award Harvard Grad. Sch. Bus., 1975; named Hon. Consul-Gen. Kingdom of Thailand; decorated Order Rising Sun, Star (Japan), Most Noble Order of the Crown of Thailand, Disting. Civilian Svc. medal U.S. Army, Most Exalted Order of the White Elephant (Thailand). Mem. Nat. Assn. Japan-Am. Socs. (chmn.), Japan Soc. of Boston (chmn.), Somerset Club (Boston), Edgartown Yacht Club (Martha's Vineyard), Country Club (Brookline), Farm Neck Golf Club (Martha's Vineyard), Phi Beta Kappa, Phi Kappa Phi, Phi Delta Theta, Beta Gamma Sigma. Episcopalian. Avocations: golf, tennis, reading. Home: 37 Warren St Brookline MA 02445-5925 Office: 20 Park Plz Ste 414 Boston MA 02116-4308 Office Phone: 617-948-2185.

ALDER, BERNI JULIAN, physicist, researcher; b. Duisburg, Germany, Sept. 9, 1925; came to U.S., 1941, naturalized, 1944; s. Ludwig and Ottilie (Gottschalk) A.; m. Esther Berger, Dec. 28, 1956; children: Kenneth, Daniel, Janet. BS, U. Calif., Berkeley, 1947, MS, 1948; PhD, Calif. Inst. Tech., 1951. Instr. chemistry U. Calif., Berkeley, 1951-54; theoretical physicist Lawrence Livermore Lab., Livermore, Calif., 1955-93; prof. dept. applied sci. U. Calif., Davis, 1987-93, prof. emeritus, 1993; van der Waals prof. U. Amsterdam, Netherlands, 1971; prof. associé U. Paris, 1972. G.N. Lewis lectr. U. Calif., Berkeley, 1984, Hinshelwood prof., Oxford, 1986, Lorentz prof., Leiden, 1990, Kistiakowsky lectr. Harvard U., 1990, Royal Soc. lectr., 1991. Author: Methods of Computational Physics, 1963; editor: Jour. Computational Physics, 1966-91. Served with USN, 1944-46. Recipient Boltzmann medal Internat. Union Pure and Applied Physics, 2001; Guggenheim fellow, 1954-55; NSF sr. postdoctoral fellow, 1963-64, Japanese Promotion of Sci. fellow, 1989; Berni J. Alder prize established by European Phys. Soc., 1999. Fellow: Am. Phys. Soc.; mem.: Rare Gas Dynamics Soc. (Grad lectr. 2000), Am. Chem. Soc. (Hildebrand award 1985), Nat. Acad. Scis. Republican. Jewish. Office: Lawrence Livermore Lab PO Box 808 Livermore CA 94551-0808 Office Phone: 925-422-4384. Business E-Mail: alder1@llnl.gov.

ALDER, DONNA BORDELON, biologist, educator; b. Baton Rouge, July 7, 1946; d. Chalmette Edward and Roma Janet (Boldt) Bordelon; m. John Edward Alder, Dec. 27, 1966; children: Kerri Alder Todd, Cameron, Lorien Alder Urban. BS Biology, Bethany Nazarene Coll., Okla., 1967; MS Biology, postgrad., U. Rochester, NYC, 1972. Tchr. Southeast Jr. H.S., Kansas City, Mo., 1967—69, Roberts Wesleyan Coll., Rochester, 1983—. Contbr. articles to profl. jours. Bd. trustees, acad. chair Ea. Nazarene Coll., Quincy, Mass., 1994—2006, Nazarene Bible Coll., Colorado Springs, 2001—; guest pres. Africa Nazarene U., Nairobi, Kenya, 2006; bd. trustees Southeast Cmty. Ctr., Kansas City, 1969—71; bd. dirs. Crossroads Youth Ctr., Rochester, 1995—98; aux. dir. children Upstate N.Y. Dist., 1983—86; tchr. Sun. sch. Grace Ch. Nazarene, Rochester, 1980. Named to Who's Who Am. Tchrs.; grant Rsch. water quality, Roberts Wesleyan Coll., grant computer studies. Mem.: Assn. Biology Lab. Edn., Human Anatomy Phys. Soc. Avocations: painting, gardening. Office: Roberts Wesleyan Coll 2301 Westside Dr Rochester NY 14624

ALDERFER, CLAYTON PAUL, organizational consultant, writer; b. Sellersville, Pa., Sept. 1, 1940; s. Joseph Paul and Ruth Althea (Buck) A.; m. Charleen Judith Frankenfield, July 14, 1962; children: Kate, Benjamin. BS with high honors, Yale U., 1962, PhD, 1966. Cert. Am. Bd. Profl. Psychology. Asst. prof. Cornell U., Ithaca, NY, 1966-68, Yale U., New Haven, 1968-70, assoc. prof., 1970-78, prof. Sch. Orgn. Mgmt., 1978-92, assoc. dean Sch. Orgn. Mgmt., 1982-84; prof. II Grad. Sch. Applied and Profl. Psychology Rutgers U., 1992—2006, dir. Orgnl. Psychology program, 1992—2004; prin. Alderfer and Assocs., 2006—. Author: Existence, Relatedness and Growth, 1972, Learning from Changing, 1975; mem. editl. bd. Jour. Applied Behavioral Sci., 1978-89, editor, 1990-2003; mem. editl. bd. Family Bus. Rev., 1987-2006, Jour. Orgnl. Behavior, 1988-92; editor: Advances in Experiential Social Processes, vol. 1, 1979, vol. 2, 1980; contbr. articles to profl. jours. Bd. dirs. NTL Inst., Arlington, Va., 1975-78, DATA, New Haven, 1989-92. Grantee Office Naval Rsch., 1970-74, 79-80, 82-86; recipient Cattell award, 1972, McGregor award, 1979, Levinson award, 1997, Helms award, 1999. Fellow Am. Psychol. Assn., Soc. Applied Anthropology, Am. Psychol. Soc.; mem. Sigma Xi, Tau Beta Pi. Independent. Lutheran. Office Phone: 908-281-6548. E-mail: claygray@aol.com.

ALDERMAN, ELIZABETH, pediatrician, educator; m. Eric Alderman, Aug. 7, 1988. MD, SUNY, Stony Brook, 1987. Clin. prof. pediat. Albert Einstein Coll. Medicine, Bronx, 2004—06. Office: 111 East 210 St Division of Adolescent Medicine Bronx NY 10467 Office Phone: 718-920-6614.

ALDERMAN, MARLENE H., law librarian, educator; BS cum laude, SUNY, Buffalo; MLS, U. Md.; JD with honors, George Washington U. Asst. law libr. Judges Libr., US Ct. Appeals, DC Cir., Washington, 1976—78; rsch. assoc., writer Herner and Co., Nat. Ctr. on Child Abuse and Neglect, 1979—80; asst. dir. Office of Libr. and Legal Rsch. Svcs., Adminstrv. Office of US Cts., Washington, 1980—83; lectr. law Rsch. and Writing Prog. Boston U. Sch. Law, 1984—85, lectr. advanced legal rsch., 1992—; reference libr. Pappas Law Libr., 1983—85, assoc. dir., head pub. svcs, 1985—, acting dir., 2006—. Mem.: New England Law Librs. Consortium, Assn. Boston Law Librs., Law Librs. New England, Am. Assn. Law Librs. Office: Boston U Sch Law Pappas Law Libr 765 Commonwealth Ave Boston MA 02215 Office Phone: 617-353-8870. E-mail: alderman@bu.edu.*

ALDERMAN, MINNIS AMELIA, psychologist, educator, small business owner; b. Douglas, Ga., Oct. 14, 1928; d. Louis Cleveland Sr. and Minnis Amelia (Wooten) A. AB in Music, Speech and Drama, Ga. State Coll., Milledgeville, 1949; MA in Supervision/Counseling Psychology, Murray State U., Ky., 1960; postgrad., Columbia Pacific U., L.A., 1987. Tchr. music Lake County Sch. Dist., Umatilla, Fla., 1949—50; instr. vocal/instrumental music, dir. band, orch., choral Fulton County Sch. Dist., Atlanta, 1950—54; instr. English, speech, debate, vocal and instrumental music Elko County Sch. Dist., Wells, Nev., 1954—59, dir. drama, band, choral and orchestra, 1954—59; tchr. English and social studies Christian County Sch. Dist., Hopkinsville, Ky., 1960; instr. psychology, counselor critic prof. Murray State U., Ky., 1961—63, U. Nev., Reno, 1963—67; owner Minisizer Exercising Salon, Ely, Nev., 1969—71, Knit Knook, Ely, 1969—, Minimimeo, Ely, 1969—, Gift Gamut, Ely, 1977—; prof. dept. fine arts Wassuk Coll., Ely, 1986—91, assoc. dean, 1986—87, dean, 1987—90; counselor White Pine County Sch. Dist., Ely, 1960—68; dir. Child and Family Ctr. Ely Indian Tribe, 1988—93. Supr. testing Ednl. Testing Svc., Princeton, NJ, 1960-68, Am. Coll. Testing Program, Iowa, 1960-68, U. Nev., Reno, 1960-68; chmn. bd. White Pine Sch. Dist. Employees Fed. Credit Union, Ely, 1961-69; psychologist mental hygiene divsn. Nev. Pers., Ely, 1969-75, dept. employment secrity, 1975-80; sec.-treas. bd. dirs. Gt. Basin Enterprises, Ely, 1969-71; rep. Ely/East Ely Bus. Coun., 1997—; mem. Econ. Devel. Bd., 1998—; prof. Great Basin C.C., 1999—, pvt. instructor piano, violin, voice and organ, Ely, 1981—; spkr., presenter in field. Contbr. articles to profl. jours. Dir. Family Resource Ctr. (Great Basin Rural Nev. Youth Cabinet), 1996—; bd. dir. band Sacred Heart Sch., Ely, 1982-99; active Gov.'s Mental Health State Commn., 1963-65, Nev. Hwy. Safety Leaders Bd., 1979-82, Ely Shoshone Tribal Youth Camp, 1991-92, Elys Shoshone Tribal Unity Conf., 1991-92, Tribal Parenting Skills Coord., 1991, White Pine Overall Econ. Devel. Plan Coun., 1992-2005; bd. dir. White Pine County Sch. Employees Fed. Credit Union, 1961-68, pres., 1963-68; 2d v.p. White Pine Cmty. Concert Assn., 1965-67, pres., 1967, 85—, treas., 1975-79, dr. chmn., 1981-85; chmn. bd., 1984; bd. dir. United Way, 1970-76, White Pine chpt. ARC, 1978-82; mem. Gov.'s Commn. on Status Women, 1968-74, Gov.'s Nevada State Juvenile Justice Adv. Commn., 1992-94; dir. White Pine Cmty. Choir, 1962—, Ret. Sr. Vol. Program, 1973-74, White Pine Legis. Coalition, 2002—; sec.-treas. White Pine Rehab. Tng. Ctr. for Retarded Persons, 1973-75, White Pine County Juvenile Problems Cabinet, 1994—, Gt. Basin chpt. Nev. Employees Assn., 1970-76; chmn. adv. coun. White Pine Sr. Ctr., 2005—; mem. Gov.'s Commn. on Hwy. Safety, 1979-81, Gov's. Juvenile Justice Program; vice-chmn. Gt. Basin Health Coun., 1973-75, Home Ext. adv. Bd., 1977-80; vice-chmn. White Pine Coun. on Alcoholism and Drug Abuse, 1975-76, chmn., 1976-77, White Pine County Bus. Coun., 1998—; dir. White Pine Coalition; grants author 3 yrs. Indian Child Welfare Act, State Hist. Preservation, Fair and Recreation Bd. Centennial Fine Arts Ctr.; originator Cmty. Tng. Ctr. Retarded People, 1972, Ret. Sr. Vol. Program, 1973-74, Nutrition Program Sr. Citizens, 1974, Sr. Citizens Ctr., 1974, Home Repairs Sr. Citizens, 1974, Sr. Citizens Crafters Assns., 1976, Inst. Current World Affairs, 1989, Victims of Crime, 1990-92, grants author Family Resource Ctr., 1995; bd. dirs. Family coalition, 1990-92, Sacred Heart Parochial Sch., dir. band, 1982-2000; candidate diaconal ministry, 1982-93; invited performer Branson Jubilee Nat. Ch. Choir Festival, Mo., Ely Meth. Ch. Choir, 1960-84; choir dir., organist Sacred Heart Ch., 1984—; Precinct reporter ABC News, 1966; bd. dir. White Pine Juvenile Cabinet, 1993—, Ely/East Ely Bus. Coun., 1997—, Econ. Devel. Bd., 1998—; chmn. adv. coun. White Pine Sr. Ctr., 2005—; bd. White Pine C. of C., 2000—; bd. dirs. Whtie Pine Mus., 2006—; pres. White Pine Sr. Adv. Coun., 2005—. Named scholar, Nat. Trust for Hist. Preservation, 2000; recipient Recognition rose, Alpha Chi State Delta Kappa Gamma, 1994, Recognition Rose, 2002, Perserving America's Treasures in the 21st Century, 2001; grantee, Nat. Trust for Historic Preservation, LA, 2000. Fellow Am. Coll. Musicians, Nat. Guild Piano Tchrs.; mem. NEA (life), UDC, DAR, Nat. Fedn. Ind. Bus. (dist. chair 1971-85, nat. guardian coun. 1985—, state guardian coun. 1987—), AAUW (pres. Wells br. 1957-58, pres. White Pine br. 1965-66, 86-87, 89-91, 93—, bd. dir. 1965-87, rep. edn. 1965-67, implementation chair 1967-69, area advisor 1969-73, 89-91), Nat. Fedn. Bus. and Profl. Women (1st v.p. Ely chpt. 1965-66, pres. Ely chpt. 1966-68, 74-76, 85—, bd. dir. Nev. chpt., 1st v.p. Nev. Fedn. 1970-71, pres. Nev. chpt. 1972-73, nat. bd. dir. 1972-73), White Pine County Mental Health Assn. (pres. 1960-63, 78—), Mensa (supr. testing 1965—), White Pine C. of C. (bd. dirs. 2000—), White Pine Nuc. Waste Assn., Lincoln Hwy. Assn. (bd. dirs., 2004—), Bus. Area Network Group, Delta Kappa Gamma (br. pres. 1968-72, 94-99, state bd. 1967—, chpt. parliamentarian 1974-78, 99—, state 1st v.p. 1967-69, state pres. 1969-71, nat. bd. 1969-71, state parliamentarian 1971-73, 95—, chmn. state nominating com. 1995-97, chmn. bylaws com. 2003—, workshop presenter aging, itelligence and learning, San Francisco, 1995), White Pine Knife and Fork Club (1st v.p. 1969-70, pres. 1970-71, bd. dirs.), Soc. Descs. Knights Most Noble Order of Garter, Nat. Soc. Magna Charta Dames, Delta Kappa Gamma (SW regional conf. workshop presenter 1995). Office: 1280 E Aultman St Ely NV 89301 Office Phone: 775-289-2116. *My mission in this life: To use to the fullest good, the talents and abilities that have been given to me in order to productively help whenever and wherever the opportunity arises.*

ALDERMAN, WILLIAM FIELDS, lawyer; b. Hamilton, Ohio, 1945; AB summa cum laude, Miami U., 1967; JD, Yale U., 1970. Bar: Calif. 1971. Ptnr. Orrick, Herrington & Sutcliffe, San Francisco, 1976—. Ct. apptd. arbitrator, mediator, evaluator, 1988—. Contbr. articles to profl. jours. Dir. Lawyers Com. Civil Rights San Francisco Bay Area, 1985—95, St. Thomas More Soc. San Francisco, 1987—94, pres., 1993; dir. Bay Area Legal Aid, 1995—. Recipient Jr. Pro Bono award, Lawyers Com., 1996. Mem.: ABA, State Bar Calif., Bar Assn. San Francisco (chair audit com. 2002—04), Phi Beta Kappa. Office: Orrick Herrington Sutcliffe 405 Howard St Fl 7 San Francisco CA 94105-2680 Office Phone: 415-773-5700. Business E-Mail: walderman@orrick.com.

ALDERSON, PHILIP OTIS, radiologist, educator; b. San Francisco, Aug. 11, 1944; s. Lloyd I. and Helen A. (Boekemeier); m. Marjorie Jean Hawkins, June 13, 1970; children: Kelly Suzanne, Lisa Joanne. AB in Zoology, Washington U., St. Louis, 1966, MD, 1970. Cert. Diplomate Am. Bd. Nuclear Medicine, Am. Bd. Radiology (Diagnosis). Intern Jewish Hosp., Washington U. Med. Sch., St. Louis, 1970-71, resident in radiology and nuclear medicine, 1971-74; instr. in radiology Mallinckrodt Inst., Washington U. Med. Sch., St. Louis, 1974-75; from asst. to assoc. prof. dept. radiology Johns Hopkins Med. Inst., Balt., 1977-80; prof. radiology Columbia-Presbyn. Med. Ctr., NYC, 1980—, James Picker prof., chmn. dept. radiology, 1990—. Trustee Am. Bd. Nuc. Medicine, 1989—95, Am. Bd. Radiology, 1998—, sec.-treas., 2002—04, pres.-elect, 2004—06, pres., 2006—; trustee NY Presbyn. Hosp., 2004—06, pres. med. bd., 2005—06. Author 4 books; contbr. articles to profl. jours. Maj. USAF, 1975—77. Recipient Alumni Achievement award, Washington U. Med. Sch., 1995; grantee, NIH, 1974—2001. Fellow: AAAS, Am. Inst. Med. and Biol. Engrs., N.Y. Acad. Medicine, Am. Coll. Radiology (bd. chancellors 1993—2000, v.p. 1999—2000), Am. Coll. Nuclear Physicians; mem.: Soc. Chmn. Acad. Radiology Depts. (rep. Coun. Acad. Socs. of Am. Assn. Med. Colls. 1990—95, pres. 1994—95), Acad. Radiology Rsch. (sec. 1998—99, v.p. 1999—2001, pres. 2001—03), Am. Roentgen Ray Soc. (chmn. exec. coun. 1997—98, v.p 2004—05, pres.-elect 2005—06, pres. 2006—07), Assn. Residency Program Dirs. in Radiology (sec.-treas. 1996—97, pres. 1998—99), Assn. Univ. Radiologists (sec.-treas. 1994—95, pres. 1996—97), Soc. Nuclear Medicine (v.p. 1984—85, chmn. sci. program com. 1984—86), N.Y. State Radiol. Soc. (sec.-treas. 1991—93, pres. 1993—94), N.Y. City Roentgen Soc. (v.p. 1989—90, pres. 1991—92), Fleischner Soc. (sec. 1989—92, treas. 1996—99, pres. 2000—01), Omicron Delta Kappa. Office: Columbia-Presbyn Med Ctr Dept Radiology 630 W 168th St New York NY 10032-3702 Business E-Mail: poa1@columbia.edu.

ALDERSON, SANDY (RICHARD LYNN ALDERSON), major league baseball executive; b. Seattle, Nov. 22, 1947; s. John Lester and Gwenny (Parry) A.; m. Linda Lee Huff, Dec. 20, 1969; children: Catrin Gwennan, Bryn Garreth. BA, Dartmouth Coll., 1969; JD, Harvard U., 1976. Assoc. Farella, Braun & Martel, San Francisco, 1976-81; gen. counsel Oakland Athletics, Calif., 1981-83, v.p. baseball ops. Calif., 1983-93, pres., gen. mgr. Calif., 1993—95, Calif., 1997—98; exec. v.p., baseball ops. Major League Baseball, 1998—2005; CEO San Diego Padres, 2005—. Dir. Major League Scouting Bur., Newport Beach, Calif. Served to lt. USMC, 1969-73, Vietnam

ALDERSON, VANESSA, administrative assistant; b. Columbia, Tenn., Feb. 15, 1961; d. Lilburn English and Bettie English-Handley. AS in Data Processing, Columbia State CC, 1981; BBA, Mid. Tenn. State U., 1994. Sr. adminstrv. asst. Meharry Med. Coll., Nashville, 2001—04; adminstrn. asst./ophthalmology rsch. adminstrn. Vanderbilt U., Nashville, 2004—. Dir. Miss Image Pagent; choreographer, cheerleader dance team coach; dir. youth ministry program Yes to the King. Named Miss Black Mid. Tenn. State U., Mid. Tenn. State U., 1982; recipient Outstanding Achievement award, Alpha Phi Alpha, 1983, Outstanding Young Women in Am. Achievement award, Outstanding Young Women, 1998, Outstanding Young Achiever award, Nat. Bus. and Profl. Women's, 1998, Team work of Excellence award, Meharry Med. Coll. Office Profl., 2003. Mem.: Nat. Coun. U. Rsch. Adminstrs. (assoc.), Order of the Eastern Star. Office Fax: 615-936-6410. Business E-Mail: vanessa.alderson@vanderbilt.edu.

AL-DHAHIR, NAOFAL, engineering educator; BSc, Kuwait U., 1989; MSEE, Stanford U., Calif., 1990, PhD, 1994. Sr. mem. tech. staff Gen. Electric R&D Ctr., Schenectady, NY, 1994—99; prin. mem. tech. staff AT&T Shannon Lab., Florham Park, NJ, 1999—2003; prof. elec. engring. U. Tex., Dallas, 2003. Named Innovator, AT&T Shannon Lab., 2001; recipient R&D Mgmt. award, GE, 1995, 1996, 1999, Vehicular Tech. Conf. Best Paper award, IEEE, 2005, Young Author Best Paper award, 2005, Donald G. Fink Best Paper award, 2006. Achievements include 19 US Patents. Office: U Texas 2601 N Floyd Rd MS EC 33 Richardson TX 75083

ALDINGER, WILLIAM F., III, diversified financial services company executive; b. 1947; BA, CUNY, 1969. With U.S. Trust Co., NYC, 1969-75, Citibank Corp., NYC, 1975-76; exec. v.p. Wells Fargo Bank NA, San Francisco, 1986-98; CEO HSBC N. Am. Inc. (Formerly Household Internat., Inc.), Prospect Heights, Ill., 1994—, chmn. bd. dirs., 1996—. Office: HSBC N America Inc 2700 Sanders Rd Prospect Heights IL 60070-2701

ALDISERT, RUGGERO JOHN, federal judge; b. Carnegie, Pa., Nov. 10, 1919; s. John S. and Elizabeth (Magnacca) Aldisert; m. Agatha Maria DeLacio, Oct. 4, 1952; children: Lisa Maria, Robert, Gregory. BA, U. Pitts., 1941, JD, 1947. Bar: Pa. 1947. Gen. practice law, Pitts., 1947—61; judge Ct. Common Pleas, Allegheny County, 1961—68, U.S. Ct. Appeals (3d cir.), Pitts., 1968—84, chief judge, 1984—87, sr. judge Pitts., Santa Barbara, Calif., 1987—. Adj. prof. law U. Pitts. Sch. Law, 1964—87; faculty Appellate Judges Seminar, NYU, 1971—85, assoc. dir., 1979—85; chmn. Fed. Appellate Judges Seminar, 1972—78; mem. Pa. Civil Procedural Rules Com., 1965—84, Jud. Conf. Com. on Adminstrn. Criminal Law, 1971—77; chmn. adv. com. on bankruptcy rules Jud. Conf. U.S., 1979—84; vis. prof. univs. in U.S. and abroad, 1965—99; intensive lectures at univs in , Italy, Germany, France, Poland, Croatia and Serbia. Author: Il Ritorno al Paese, 1966—67, The Judicial Process, Readings, Materials and Cases, 1996, 2d edit., 1996, Logic for Lawyers: A Guide to Clear Legal Thinking, 1997, 3d edit., 1997, Opinion Writing, 1990, Winning on Appeal, 2003, Road to the Robes: A Federal Judge Recollects Young Years and Early Times, 2005; contbr. over 50 articles to profl. publs. Allegheny dist. chmn. Multiple Sclerosis Soc., 1961—68; pres. ISDA, Cultural Heritage Found., 1965—68; trustee U. Pitts., 1968—; mem. bd. visitors Pitts. Sch. Law, 1968—, chmn., 1969—99. Maj. USMC, 1942—46, with USMC, 1946—51. Recipient Outstanding Merit award, Allegheny County Acad. Trial Lawyers, 1964, Disting. Appellate Jurist award, 2005, Disting. Citizen of Carnegia Borough award, 2005. Mem.: Am. Law Inst., Italian Sons and Daus. Am. Fraternal Assn. (nat. pres. 1954—68), Omicron Delta Kappa, Phi Alpha Delta, Phi Beta Kappa. Democrat. Roman Catholic. Office: US Ct Appeals 120 Cremona Dr Ste D Santa Barbara CA 93117-5511*

ALDOCK, JOHN DOUGLAS, lawyer; b. Washington, Jan. 20, 1942; s. Sam I. and Myrtle C. (Cohen) Aldock; m. Judy Robichek, May 18, 1969; children: Jessica Lauren, Stephanie Lisa. BS with honors, Northwestern U., Evanston, Ill., 1964; LLB cum laude, U. Pa., 1967. Bar: D.C. 1968, Md. 1973, U.S. Supreme Ct. 1972. Law clk., Hon. Luther W. Youngdahl U.S. Dist. Ct. D.C., 1967-68; asst. U.S. atty. Dept. of Justice, Washington, 1968-71; ptnr., chair, Wash. off. Shea & Gardner (now Goodwin Procter LLP), Washington, 1971—, and mem. exec. com. Chmn. Adv. Com. on Rules to U.S. Dist. Ct. for D.C., 1987—; ind. counsel Meese investigation Adminstrv. Office of U.S. Cts., Washington, 1984; mem. Dist. Ct. Civil Adv. Com., 1991—; mem. panel disting. neutrals CPR Internat. Inst. for Conflict Prevention and Resolution, Washington. Mem. ABA, Jud. Conf. for D.C. Cir., Am. Law Inst., D.C. Bar Assn., Asst. U.S. Attys. Assn. (pres. 1975); fellow, Am. Coll. Trial Lawyers, Am. Bar Found. Office: Goodwin Procter LLP 901 New York Ave NW Washington DC 20001 Office Phone: 202-346-4240. Office Fax: 202-346-4444. Business E-Mail: jaldock@goodwinprocter.com.

ALDONAS, GRANT D., lawyer, former federal agency administrator; b. Mpls. m. Pam Olson; children: Nicole, Kirsten, Noah. BA in Internat. Rels., U. Minn., 1975, JD, 1979. Spl. asst. Under Sec. of State for Econ. Affairs; dir. South Am. and Caribbean Affairs Office of the U.S. Trade Rep.; ptnr. Miller & Chevalier, Washington; chief internat. trade counsel Chmn. of the Senate Fin. Com.; under sec. for internat. trade US Dept. Commerce, Washington, 2001—05; ptnr. Akin Gump Strauss Hauer & Feld LLP, Washington, 2005—. Adj. prof. law Georgetown U. Law Ctr.; counsel Bipartisan Commn. on Entitlement and Tax Reform; adviser Commn. on U.S.-Pacific Trade and Investment. Mem.: ABA (chair task force on multilateral investment agreements, vice chair com. on trade and fgn. investment sect. internal law and pr). Office: Akin Gump Strauss Hauer & Feld LLP Robert S Strauss Bldg 1333 New Hampshire Ave NW Washington DC 20036

ALDOUS, CHARLA G., lawyer; b. Sherman, Tex., Jan. 4, 1960; 4 children. BA in Polit. Sci. and Hist., Austin Coll., 1982; JD, So. Meth. U. Sch. Law, 1985. Bar: Tex. 1985, US Dist. Ct. (ea. and no. dists. Tex.) 1985. Ptnr., co-founder Aldous & McDougal, L.L.P., Dallas; spl. counsel Baron & Budd, P.C., Dallas, 2005—06. Named a Tex. Super Lawyer, 2003, 2004, 2005; named one of Best Lawyers in Dallas, D Magazine, 2001, 2003, 2005, Best Lawyers in Am., 2003—04, 2005—06, Top 10 Trial Lawyers in Am., Nat. Law Jour., 2005, Top 100 Dallas/Ft. Worth Super Lawyers, Top 50 Female Tex. Super Lawyers. Mem.: Tex. Trial Lawyers Assn., Tex. Bar Found., State Bar Tex., Dallas Trial Lawyers Assn., Dallas Bar Assn. (mem. ethics com.), Assn. Trial Lawyers Am., Am. Bd. Trial Advs. (exec. com., Dallas Chpt.), ABA.*

ALDREDGE, THEONI VACHLIOTIS, costume designer; b. Athens, Greece, Aug. 22, 1932; d. Gen. Athanasios and Meropi (Gregoriades) Vachliotis; m. Thomas E. Aldredge, Dec. 10, 1953. Student, Am. Sch., Athens, 1949—53, Goodman Theatre, Chgo.; LHD, De Paul U., 1985. Mem. design staff Goodman Theatre, 1951-53; head designer NY Shakespeare Festival, 1962—91. Designer numerous Broadway and off Broadway shows, ballet, opera, TV spls.; films include Girl of the Night, You're a Big Boy Now, No Way to Treat a Lady, Uptight, Last Summer, I Never Sang for My Father, Promise at Dawn, The Great Gatsby (Brit. Motion Picture Acad. award 1976), Network, The Cheap Detective, The Fury, The Eyes of Laura Mars (Acad. Sci. Fiction Films award), The Champ, Semi-Tough, The Rose, Monsignor, Annie, Ghostbusters, Moonstruck, We're No Angels, Stanley and Iris, Other People's Money, Night and the City, Addams Family Values, Milk Money, Mrs. Winterbourne, The Mirror Has Two Faces, The First Wives Club; over 100 Broadway shows include A Chorus Line (Theatre World award 1976), Annie (Tony award 1977), Barnum (Tony award 1979), Dream Girls, Woman of the Year, Onward Victoria, La Cage Aux Folles (Tony award 1984), 42d Street, A Little Family Business, Merlin, Private Lives, The Corn Is Green, The Rink, Blithe Spirit, Chess, Gypsy (1989 revival), Oh, Kay, The Secret Garden, Nick and Nora, High Rollers, Putting It Together, Annie Warbucks, The Flowering Peach, School for Scandal, Taking Sides, The Three Sisters, St. Louis Woman, The Best Man, "EFX" MGM Grand, Follies 2001 Revival, A Chorus Line 2006 Revival. Recipient Obie award for Disting. Svc. to Off-Broadway Theatre Village Voice, Maharam award for Peer Gynt, N.Y.C. Liberty medal, 1986, Career Achievement award Costume Designers Guild, 2000, DePaul U., 1999, TDF Irene Sharaff Lifetime Achievement award, 2002, numerous Drama Desk and Critic awards; inducted into Theatre Hall of Fame. Mem. United Scenic Artists, Costume Designers Guild, Acad. Motion Picture Arts Scis. (Oscar award Great Gatsby 1975).

ALDRICH, ANN, judge; b. Providence, June 28, 1927; d. Allie C. and Ethel M. (Carrier) A.; m. Chester Aldrich, 1960 (dec.); children: Martin, William; children by previous marriage: James, Allen; m. John H. McAllister III, 1986. BA cum laude, Columbia U., 1948; LLB cum laude, NYU, 1950, LLM, 1964, JSD, 1967. Bar: DC, NY 1952, Conn. 1966, Ohio 1973, US Supreme Ct. 1956. Rsch. asst. to mem. faculty NYU Sch. Law; atty. IBRD, 1952; atty., rsch. asst. Samuel Nakasian, Esq., Washington, 1952—53; gen. counsel's staff FCC, Washington, 1953—60; US del. to Internat. Radio Conf., Geneva, 1959; practicing atty. Darien, Conn., 1961—68; assoc. prof. law Cleve. State U., 1968—71, prof., 1971—80; judge US Dist. Ct. (no. dist.) Ohio, Cleve., 1980—. Instrn. com. Sixth Cir. Pattern Criminal Jury, 1986—. Mem. Fed. Bar Assn., Nat. Assn. of Women Judges, Fed. Communications Bar Assn., Fed. Judge Assn. Episcopalian. Office: US District Court Ste 17B 801 W Superior Ave Cleveland OH 44113-1829 Home Phone: 216-761-1112; Office Phone: 216-357-7200. Business E-Mail: ann_aldrich@ohnd.uscourts.gov.

ALDRICH, DAVID ALAN, accountant, consultant; b. West Haven, Conn., Jan. 14, 1958; s. Harold and Janet (Candia) A. BS in Fin. Acctg., U. New Haven, 1980; BS in Profl. Acctg., Tampa Coll., 1990. CPA, Fla.; cert. bus. mgr. Assn. Profls. in Bus. Mgmt., 2002; cert. real estate sales assoc., Fla. Acct. State Nat. Bank of Conn., Bridgeport, 1981-82, Coordinated Benefit Plans Inc., Tampa, Fla., 1984-85, N.Am. Telephone, Tampa, 1986; acctg. mgr. Coordinated Benefit Plans Inc., Tampa, 1987-90; sr. acct. EPIX, Inc. (formerly Payroll Transfers, Inc.), Tampa, 1991—2001; cons. in acctg. to clients in employee leasing industry, 2002. Tax acct. Dougherty & Assoc., LLC, Spring Hill, Fla., 2003, DeBoer Tax Adv. Group, 2004; acctg. instr. Webster Coll., Holiday, Fla., 2006—; ind. acct., bus. cons., 2005—. Mem. AICPA, Fla. Inst. CPAs.

ALDRICH, FRANK NATHAN, banker; b. Jackson, Mich., June 8, 1923; s. Frank Nathan and Marion (Butterfield) A.; m. Edna Dora DeJan, Nov. 21, 1956; children: Marion Dolores, Clinton Pershing. Student, U. Md., College Park, 1943; AB in Govt., Dartmouth Coll., Hanover, NH, 1948; postgrad., Harvard U., Cambridge, Mass., 1948. Sub-mgr. First Nat. Bank of Boston, Havana, Cuba, 1949—60, Rio de Janeiro, 1961—62, Sao Paulo, Brazil, 1963—64, mgr., 1965, exec. mgr. Rio de Janeiro, 1966, v.p. Brazilian brs., 1966—69, v.p. overseas ops. Boston, 1969—70; v.p. Latin Am.-Asia-Africa-Middle East div., Boston, 1970—73; sr. v.p. Latin Am. div., Boston, 1973—88; pres., CEO McLaughlin Bank N.V., Netherlands Antilles, 1989; CEO Amicorp N.V., Netherlands Antilles, 1996—. Dir. Paradigm Fin. Svcs., Netherlands Antilles; prin. Mitan Capital Corp., N.Y.C. Trustee Pan Am. Devel. Found., Washington. With USAAF, 1943-46. Decorated Air medal with 4 oak leaf clusters, D.F.C. U.S.; Medalha Marechal Candido Mariano da Silva Rondon (Brazil); Ordem Nacional do Cruzeiro do Sul (Brazil). Fellow Brit. Interplanetary Soc.; mem. Air Force Assn., Res. Officers Assn., Confederate Air Force, Inst. Navigation, Royal Astron. Soc. Can., Soc. of the Cin., Sphinx Soc., Vets of Battle of the Bulge, Squadron A Assn. of N.Y., Disting. Flying Cross Soc., Harvard Club (Boston), Dartmouth Coll. Club, Yale Club (N.Y.C.), Army and Navy Club (Washington), Wellesley (Mass.), Country Club, Wellesley Coll. Club, Masons, Shriners., Beta Theta Pi. Home: 3 Indian Spring Rd Dover MA 02030-2331 Business E-Mail: amicorp@amicorp.com.

ALDRICH, FRANKLIN DALTON, medical researcher, consultant; b. Detroit, Jan. 25, 1929; s. George Franklin and Ruth Markham (Dalton) A.; m. Margaret Joan Pearson, Mar. 22, 1952; children: Allison R., Janet D., George P.; m. Gertrude Suydam Melsom, Mar. 24, 1984. BS, Mich. State U., 1950; MA, Oreg. State U., 1953, PhD, 1954; MD, Case Western Res. U., 1962. Diplomate Am. Bd. Med. Toxicology. Intern U. Iowa Hosps., Iowa City, 1962-63; fellow in medicine U. Colo., Denver, 1964-65; resident and chief resident Lemuel Shattuck Hosp., Boston, 1969-71; physician Colo. Dept. Pub. Health, Denver, 1966-69; asst. med. dir. MIT, Cambridge, 1971-76; med. dir. Climax (Colo.) Molybdenum Co., 1976-77; health effects research mgr. IBM, Boulder, Colo., 1977-92, ret., 1992; cons. Boulder, 1992—. Mem. com. mil. environ. rsch. Nat. Acad. Scis., 1976-80; mem. toxicology adv. com. U.S. Consumer Product Safety Com., 1982-85; clin. assoc. prof. medicine U. Colo. Health Scis. Ctr., Denver. Contbr. articles to profl. jours. Served with AUS, 1954-56. Case Meml. scholar, Mich. State U., 1948. Fellow ACP (Mead Johnson resident scholar 1970), Am. Acad. Clin. Toxicology (pres. 1980-82). Avocations: fishing, amateur radio. Personal E-mail: w1fa@hotmail.com.

ALDRICH, GARY O., singer, educator; b. Gloversville, NY, Apr. 12, 1947; s. Orville Bert and Maretta Hill Aldrich; life ptnr. Ronald J. Miller. MA, SUNY, Albany, 1970. Cert. permanent secondary English, drama and music N.Y. State Dept Edn., 1971. Founder and dir. Gary Aldrich Vocal Studios, Albany, NY, 1971—2000; asst. music dir. Empire State Inst.

Performing Arts, 1978—79; teacher-artist The Theatre Inst., Troy, 1979—90; founder and artistic dir. N.Y. Concert Artists, Albany, 1996—2000, Lyric Opera Theatre, Reno, 2000—04; founder and dir. Gary Aldrich Vocal Studios, 2000—; vocal music faculty U. Nev., 2000—. Dir. Sierra Lyric Opera Studio, Reno, 2004—. Prodr.: (musical) M4M; composer: (songs) One Common Heartbeat; performer: Amahl and the Night Visitors, Kennedy Ctr., 1991, (Am. premiere) 60th Parallel, Berkeley Symphony, 1995, (soloist) Nat. Chorale, Lincoln Ctr., 1995—2007, (title role) Die Fleidermaus, 2004. Mem.: Nat. Assn. Tchrs. Singing (assoc.), Am. Guild Musical Artists (assoc.), Actor's Equity Assn. (assoc.), Phi Mu Alpha Sinfonia (assoc.). Avocations: gardening, travel. Office: Univ Nev 3565 Balboa Dr Reno NV 89557

ALDRICH, GEORGE HOOVER, judge, arbitrator; b. St. Louis, Feb. 25, 1932; s. Emmett Porter and Hettie Barbara (Hoover) A.; m. Rosemary Margaret Balmforth Aldrich, June 6, 1959; children: Edward, Stephen, Robert. BA, DePauw U., 1954; LLB, Harvard Law Sch., 1957, LLM, 1958; LLD (hon.), DePauw U., 2006. Bar: Ind., 1958. Atty. Dept. Navy, Washington, 1959-60, Dept. Def., Washington, 1960-63; legal adv. U.S. Delegation to NATO, Paris, 1963-65; asst. legal adv. Dept. State, Washington, 1965-69, deputy legal adv., 1969-77, amb., deputy spl. rep. to pres., 1977-81; judge Iran-U.S. Claims Tribunal, The Hague, The Netherlands, 1981—; commr. Eritrea-Ethiopia Claims Commn, The Hague, The Netherlands, 2001—. U.S. amb. for Laws of War Negotiations, Geneva, Switzerland, 1974-77; mem. UN Internat. Law Commn., Geneva, Switzerland, 1981; bd. editors Am. Jour. Internat. Law, 1987—; prof. Leiden U., The Netherlands, 1990-97; comr. Eritrea-Ethiopia Claims Commn., The Hague, The Netherlands, 2001—. Author: The Jurisprudence of the Iran-United States Claims Tribunal, 1996; author, negotiator: The Protocols to the 1973 Vietnam Peace Agreement.; contbr. articles to profl. jours. Pres. Exec. com. of Am. Sch. of The hague, 1987-88. Named Disting. Sr. Exec. President Carter, 1980. Mem. Coun. on Fgn. Rels., Am. Soc. Internat. Law, Internat. Inst. Humanitarian Law. Avocations: tennis, sailing. Office: Iran-US Claims Trib Parkweg 13 2585 JH The Hague Netherlands Home Phone: 31 70 324 2108; Office Phone: 31 70 352 0064. E-mail: GAldrich@compuserve.com.

ALDRICH, JOHN HERBERT, political science professor; b. Pitts., Sept. 24, 1947; s. Herbert Canon and Ruth Eleanor (Taggart) A.; m. Cynthia Kay Aldrich, June 13, 1970; 1 child, David Shawn BA, Allegheny Coll., 1969; MA, U. Rochester, 1971, PhD, 1975. Asst. prof. polit. sci. Mich. State U., East Lansing, 1974-78, assoc. prof., 1978-81; assoc. prof. polit. sci. U. Minn., Mpls., 1981-83, prof., 1983-87, Duke U., Durham, NC, 1987—, chmn. dept. polit. sci., 1992—96, 1999—2000, Pfizer-Pratt univ. prof., 1997—. Vis. prof. Harvard U., 1996-97. Author: Before the Convention, 1980, Why Parties?, 1995; co-author: Change and Continuity in the 1980 Elections, 1982, rev. edit., 1983, Change and Continuity in the 1984 Elections, 1986, rev. edit., 1987, Change and Continuity in the 1988 elections, 1990, rev. edit., 1991, Change and Continuity in the 1992 Elections, 1994, rev. edit., 1995, Change and Continuing in the 1996 Elections, 1997, Change and Continuity in the 1996 and 1998 Elections, 1999, Change and Continuity in the 2000 and 2002 Elections; Change and Continuity in the 2004 Elections, 2006, Change and Continuity in the 2004 and 2006 Elections, 2007; co-editor: A Positive Change in Political Sic., 2007; co-editor: Am. Jour. Polit. Sci., 1985-87; contbr. articles to profl. jours. Served with U.S. Army, 1970-72, Vietnam Ctr. for Advanced Study in Behavioral Scis. fellow, 1989-90; NSF rsch. grantee, 1977-79, 81-87; NEH teaching grantee, 1977-79; resident fellow Rockefeller Found., 2002. Fellow: Am. Acad. Arts and Scis.; mem.: Midwest Polit. Sci. Assn. (pres. 2004—05), So. Polit. Sci. Assn. (rec. sec. 1992—93, v.p. 1995—96, pres. 1998—99, Pi Sigma Alpha award 1997), Am. Polit. Sci. Assn. (sec. 1993—94, Eulau prize 1990, Kammerer prize 1996, CQ Press award 1996). Office: Duke U Dept Polit Sci Durham NC 27708 Business E-Mail: aldrich@duke.edu.

ALDRICH, MICHAEL RAY, library curator, health educator; b. Vermillion, SD, Feb. 7, 1942; s. Ray J. and Lucile W. (Hamm) A.; m. Michelle Cauble, Dec. 26, 1977. AB, Princeton U., 1964; MA, U. S.D., 1965; PhD, SUNY, 1970. Fulbright tutor Govt. Arts and Commerce Coll., Indore, India, 1965-66; founder Lemar Internat., 1966-71; mem. faculty Sch. Critical Studies Calif. Inst. Arts, Valencia, 1970-72; co-founder Amorphia The Cannabis Co-op, Mill Valley, Calif., 1969—74; curator Fitz Hugh Ludlow Meml. Libr., San Francisco, 1974—2003, curator Aldrich Archives, 1974—. Cons. Commn. of Inquiry into Non-Med Use of Drugs, Ottawa, Ont., 1973; rsch. aide select com. on control marijuana Calif. Senate, 1974; mem. Princeton working group Future of Drug Policy, 1990—93; asst. dir. Nat. Inst. on Drug Abuse AIDS Project Menu, Youth Environment Study, San Francisco, 1987—88; project adminstr. YES Tng. Ctr., 1989; program. coord. Calif. AIDS Intervention Tng. Ctr. Inst. for Cmty. Health Outreach, 1990—2001; bd. dirs. Exotic Dancers Alliance, San Francisco, 1997—, Calif. Helping Alleviate Med. Problems (CHAMP), 1997, exec. dir., 2001—02; cons. on drug rsch.; freelance writer, photographer; lectr. in field. Author: The Dope Chronicles 1850-1950, 1979, Coricancha, The Golden Enclosure, 1983; co-author: High Times Ency. of Recreational Drugs, 1978, Fiscal Costs of California Marijuana Law Enforcement, 1986, YES Tng. Manual, 1989, Methods of Estimating Needle Users at Risk for AIDS, 1990; editor: Marijuana Rev., 1968-74, Ludlow Libr. Newsletter, 1974-81; contbg. author: Cocaine Handbook, 1981, 2d edit., 1987, Cannabis in Medical Practice, 1997; mem. editl. rev. bd. Jour. Psychoactive Drugs, 1981—, marijuana theme issue editor, 1988; rsch. photographer Life mag., 1984; contbg. editor High Times, 1979-85; contbr. articles to prfl. publs. Office: PO Box 640346 San Francisco CA 94164-0346

ALDRICH, PATRICIA ANNE RICHARDSON, retired magazine editor; b. St. Paul, Apr. 6, 1926; d. James Calvin and Anna Catherine (Eskra) Richardson; m. Edwin Chauncey Aldrich, July 31, 1948; 1 son, Mason Calvin. Student, Stout Inst., 1944-45; BS in Journalism; scholar, Northwestern U., 1948. Editor Child's World News, The Child's World, Inc., Chgo., 1952-57; assoc. editor Home Life mag. Advt. Div., Inc., Chgo., 1957-71, editor, 1971-90, ret., 1990; pres. Aldrich Enterprises, Inc., Chgo. Mem. steering com., publicity chmn. Evanston Urban League, 1961-64. Democrat.

ALDRICH, RICHARD KINGSLEY, lawyer; b. Denver, Dec. 31, 1943; s. Harold Eugene and Mary Frances (Kingsley) A.; m. Katherine Ann Kirwan, Sept. 26, 1970; children: Amy Marie Aldrich McAffee, Lori Ann Aldrich Selwyn, Sara Kathleen. Student, Tex. Tech. U., 1962-64; BA in History, U. Mont., 1966, JD, 1969. Bar: Mont. 1969, U.S. Dist. Ct. Mont. 1969, U.S. Supreme Ct. 2004. Staff atty. Office of Field Solicitor, Dept. of Interior, Billings, Mont., 1969-85, field solicitor, supervising atty., 1985; spl. counsel to sec. Indian Water Rights Office, 2004. Bd. dirs. Billings Pub. Edn. Found., 1992-97, Mont. State U. Parent Assn., Bozeman, 1993-96, Billings Sr. Bronc Booster Club; bd. dirs., pres. Billings Sr. High Parent Adv., 1991-95. Recipient cert. of appreciation, U.S. Dept. Justice, Nat. Park Svc. and U.S. Fish and Wildlife Svc., 1994, 96, Dept. of Interior Meritorious award, 1998. Mem. ABA (spkr. panel presentation 1997, 2001, natural resources sect., environment and energy law sect., Indian law sect., sr. lawyers divsn., alternate dispute resolution sect.), Mont. State Bar, Yellowstone County Bar, Phi Delta Phi, Sigma Nu. Avocations: long distance running, skiing, fly fishing, hiking, reading. Office: Dept of Interior Office of Field Solicitor 316 N 26th St Ste 3005 Billings MT 59101-1373

ALDRICH, ROBERT ADAMS, agricultural engineer, consultant; b. Veteran Twp., NY, Apr. 25, 1924; s. Luman Woodbridge and Mabel Hastings (Gibbs) A.; m. Roberta Ann Bowlby, Aug. 27, 1946; children—Susan Carol, Gail Jessica, Kathleen Lois, Margaret Louise. BS in Agrl. Engring, Wash. State U., 1950, MS, 1952; PhD, Mich. State U., 1958. Instr., then asso. prof. agrl. engring. Wash. State U., 1951-58; asso. prof. U. Ky., 1958-59, Mich. State U., 1959-62; asso. prof., then prof. Pa. State U., 1962-79; prof. agrl. engring., head dept. U. Conn., Storrs, 1979-88, prof. dept. nat. rsch., mgmt. and engring., 1988-89, ret., 1989; prin. Aldrich Engring. Author papers in field. Served with C.E. AUS, 1942-46. Mem. NSPE, Am. Soc. Agrl. Engrs. Home: 72 Tressler Blvd Lewisburg PA 17837-1033

ALDRICH, THOMAS ALBERT, former brewing executive, consultant; b. Rosebud, Tex., Nov. 30, 1923; s. John Albert and Georgia Opal (Hilliard) A.; m. Virginia Elaine Peterson, Mar. 1, 1944; children: Sharon Aldrich Lingis, Pamela Aldrich Williams, Thomas Charles. Student, Tex. A&M U., 1942-43, U. Chgo., 1943-44; BA in Math., George Washington U., 1961, MS in Bus. Adminstrn., 1968; student, Air War Coll., 1960-61. Commd. 2d lt. USAF, 1944, advanced through grades to maj. gen., 1974, pilot, meteorologist, 1943-57; dep. dir. air ops. Air Weather Svc., Washington, 1957-60; comdr. 57th Weather Reconnaissance Squadron, Melbourne, Australia, 1962-65; chief mil. employment div. Air Command and Staff Coll., 1965-68; dir. war plans Hdqrs. Mil. Airlift Command, Scott AFB, Ill., 1968-69; comdr. 9th Weather Reconnaissance Wing, McClellan AFB, Calif., 1969-70; vice comdr. USAF Air Weather Svc., Scott AFB, Ill., 1970-71, comdr., 1973-74, U.S. Forces Azores, Portugal, 1971-73; dep. chief of staff plans Hdqrs. Mil. Airlift Command, 1974-75; comdr. 22d Air Force, Travis AFB, Calif., 1975-78; ret., 1978; v.p., corp. rep. Anheuser-Busch Cos., Inc., Sacramento, 1978-94, ret., 1994. Decorated D.S.M., Legion of Merit with oak leaf cluster, Meritorious Service medal. Mem. Nat. Honor Soc., Brewers Inst., Calif. Mfrs. Assn. (chmn.), Calif. C. of C. (bd. dirs.), Air Force Acad. Falcon Found. (bd. dirs.), No. Calif. Ret. Officers Cmty. (vice chmn.), Phi Theta Kappa. Republican. Presbyterian. Home: 659 Lake Wilhaggin Dr Sacramento CA 95864-7226 Personal E-mail: tomginnya@aol.com.

ALDRIDGE, ADRIENNE YINGLING, accountant, financial analyst, writer; b. Hershey, Pa., June 10, 1959; d. Richard Terry Yingling and Dolores Jean (Ott) Brown. BA in Acctg. summa cum laude, N.C. State U., 1989. CPA; FLMI. Asst. mgr. Fast Fare, Raleigh, 1979—80; statis. analyst S.P.A.R., Elmsford, NY, 1980-81; relocation dir., sales assoc. Realty World, Cary, NC, 1981-83; product mgr. Southeastern Electronics, Raleigh, 1983-84; results acct. No. Telecom, Rsch. Triangle Park, NC, 1984-88; sr. auditor Deloitte & Touche, 1989-93; group contr. SPAR Mktg., Bloomington, Minn., 1994; pvt. practice, 1995; acctg. mgr. U. NC Physicians & Assocs., Chapel Hill, 1996-97, Progress Energy Svc. Co., Raleigh, NC, 1998—2007. Mem.: NCACPA, AICPA, Omicron Delta Epsilon, Phi Kappa Phi. Avocations: photography, writing, physical fitness, travel, music. Office Phone: 919-546-2311. Personal E-mail: yofreespirit@gmail.com.

ALDRIDGE, CHRISTOPHER D., biotechnology executive, consultant; b. Oklahoma City; B of Bus. Adminstrn., U. Ctrl. Okla., Edmond. Facility mgr. Cumbre Inc., Dallas, 2001—05; v.p. ops. Precision Facility Svcs., LLC, Dallas, 2005—. E4 USN, 1986—90, Newport, RI. Mem.: IFMA (assoc.). Conservative. Home Phone: 817-692-4192; Office Phone: 817-692-4192.

ALDRIDGE, DONALD O'NEAL, military officer; b. Solo., Mo., July 22, 1932; BA in History, U. Nebr., Omaha, 1974; postgrad., Creighton U., 1975. Commd. 2d lt. USAF, 1958, advanced through grades to lt. gen., 1988, asst. dir. plans Washington, 1978-79; spl. asst. to dir. Joinr Chiefs of Staff, Washington, 1979-80; dep. dir. Def. Mapping Agy., Washington, 1980-81; dep. U.S. rep. NATO Mil. Com., Brussels, 1981-83; rep. Joint Chiefs of Staff, Geneva, 1983-86; comdr. 1st Strat. Aerospace Divsn. USAF, Vanderberg AFB, Calif., 1986-88, vice-CINC Strategic Air Command Offutt AFB, Nebr., 1988—91; mgmt. cons. Sacramento, 1991—. Chmn. bd. dir. Octus, Inc., 1995—98, Ceracon, Inc., 1996—2005. Home Phone: 402-293-0543; Office Phone: 402-293-0543. Personal E-mail: daldridge@cox.net.

ALDRIDGE, EDWARD CLEVELAND, JR., (PETE ALDRIDGE), former federal agency administrator; b. Houston, Aug. 18, 1938; BS, Tex. A&M U., 1960; MS in Aero. Engring., Ga. Inst. Tech., 1962. Mgr. missile and space divsn. Douglas Aircraft Co., Santa Monica, Calif., 1962-67, Washington, 1962-67; dir. strategic def. divsn. US Dept. Def., 1967-72, dep. asst. sec. for strategic progs., 1974-76, dir. planning and evaluation Office of Sec., 1976-77, under sec. acquisition, tech. and logistics Washington, 2001—03; sr. mgr. LTV Aerospace Corp., Dallas, 1972-73; sr. mgmt. assoc. Office Mgmt. & Budget, Washington, 1973-74; v.p. Strategic Systems Grp. System Planning Corp., Arlington, Va., 1977-81; under sec. USAF, 1981-86, sec., 1986-88; pres. McDonnell Douglas Electronic Systems Co., McLean, Va., 1988-92; pres., CEO Aerospace Corp., El Segundo, Calif., 1992—2001. Dir. emeritus US Space Found.; bd. dirs. Alion Sci. & Tech., Lockheed Martin Corp., 2003—, Global Crossing; mem. Nat. Space Coun. Space Policy Bd.; chair Pres. Commn. on the Implementation of the US Space Exploration Vision, 2004—. Recipient George M. Low Space Transp. award, AIAA, 1990, Disting. Pub. Svc. award, Dept. Def., James Hill Lifetime Space Achievement award, Rotary Nat. Award for Space Achievement, Robert H. Goddard Meml. Trophy, Nat. Space Club, Bob Hope Disting. Citizen award, Nat. Def. Indsl. Assn., Harry S. Truman award, Nat. Guard Assn., Engring. Hall of Fame award, Ga. Inst. Tech. Fellow: AIAA (hon.); mem.: NAE, Air Force Assn. (life W. Stuart Symington award, Max Kriendler award, Gen. Bernard Schriever award, Disting. Am. award), Air Force Thunderbirds (hon.), Sigma Xi, Sigma Gamma Tau, Tau Beta Pi. Mailing: Bd Directors Lockheed Martin Corp 6801 Rockledge Dr Bethesda MD 20817*

ALDRIDGE, JOHN, lawyer; b. Durham, NC, Jan. 31, 1943; BA, Duke U., 1965; JD with honors, U. N.C., 1968. Bar: Ga. 1968, D.C. 1969. Mem. Long, Aldridge & Norman (now called McKenna Long & Aldridge LLP), Atlanta, 2006—. Assoc. editor N.C. Law Rev., 1967-68. Mem. ABA, State Bar Ga., D.C. Bar, Atlanta Bar Assn., Lawyers Club Atlanta, Order of Coif. Office: McKenna Long & Aldridge LLP One Peachtree Ctr 303 Peachtree St NE Ste 5300 Atlanta GA 30308-3264 Office Phone: 404-527-4000. Business E-Mail: jaldridge@mckennalong.com.

ALDRIDGE, LAMARCUS NURAE, professional basketball player; b. Dallas, July 19, 1985; s. Georgia Aldridge. Student in Corp. Comm., U. Tex., Austin, 2004—06. Draft pick Chgo. Bulls, 2006; forward Portland Trail Blazers, Oreg., 2006—. Named Big 12 Defensive Player of Yr., 2006; named to First-Team All-Big 12, 2006, NBA All-Rookie First Team, 2007. Mailing: Portland Trail Blazers Rose Quarter One Center Ct Ste 200 Portland OR 97227*

ALDRIDGE, MELVIN DAYNE, engineering educator; b. Crab Orchard, W.Va., July 20, 1941; s. William Bert and Gladys Revelle A.; m. Nancy L. Dickinson, June 6, 1963; children: Kenrick Lee, Randal Jay. BSEE with high honors, W.Va. U., 1963; MEE, U. Va., 1965, D of Elec. Engring., 1968. Registered profl. engr., W.Va. Electronic engr. NASA, 1963-68; from asst. prof. to assoc. prof. elec. engring. W.Va. U., Morgantown, 1968-76, prof., 1976-84; dir. Energy Rsch. Ctr., 1978-84; asst. dean for rsch. Auburn (Ala.) U., 1984-87, dir. engring. expt. sta., 1984-89, prof. elec. engring., 1984-89, acting dean coll. engring., 1987-88, assoc. dean for rsch., 1988-90, assoc. dean for cross-disciplinary programs, 1989-99, dir. ctr. for tech. mgmt., 1989-99; dean, prof. Mercer U., Macon, Ga., 1999—, Kaolin chair engring., 2004—. Chmn., officer Engring. Accreditation Commn.; cons. tp pvt. and govtl. orgns. Contbr. articles to profl. publs. Thomas Walter Eminent scholar Auburn U., 1994-99; recipient Rufus A. West award, 1963; named Outstanding Young Engr. W.Va., 1977-78. Fellow IEEE (sr.), ASEE, Accreditation Bd. for Engring. and Tech. (officer); mem. Indsl. Applications Soc. of IEEE (officer). Baptist. Home: 669 River North Blvd Macon GA 31211-6333 Office: Macon U 1400 Coleman Ave Macon GA 31207-0001

ALDRIDGE, SANDRA, civic volunteer; b. Iowa, Apr. 22, 1939; d. Maurice D. and Maureen M. (Bennett) Anderson; m. Guy E. Seymour, Jan. 8, 1960 (div. Oct. 1966); m. Victor E. Aldridge, Jr., Nov. 11, 1970 (dec. May 1995); 1 child, Victor E. III. Student, Millikin U., Decatur, Ill., 1957—58. Pres. Crawford Sch. PTA, 1976-78, Terre Haute Lawyers Aux., 1979; pres., dir. Wabash Valley Assn. for Gifted and Talented Children, 1981-83, Vigo County Task Force for Alcohol and Drug Abuse, 1983-84; treas., dir. Union Hosp. Svc. League; bd. dirs. YWCA Terre Haute, Inc., 1987-89; v.p., fin. chair, mem. exec. coun. Wabash Valley coun. Boy Scouts Am., Inc.; active Vigo County Tax Adjustment Bd., 1986-88, Class IX Leadership Terre Haute, 1985; bd. trustees Vigo County Sch. Corp., Terre Haute, 1985-97, v.p., 1992-93, 96; sec. Ernie Pyle Chpt., Ret. Officers Assn., 1998-2006; active Children's Theatre, United Way Wabash Valley Mem. Ind. Assn. Gifted Children, Swope Art Gallery, Vigo County Hist. Soc., Women's Dept. Club, Arts Illiana, Elks Women's Golf League Episcopalian. Home: 2929 Winthrop Rd Terre Haute IN 47802-3443

ALDRIN, BUZZ, retired astronaut; b. Montclair, NJ, Jan. 20, 1930; s. Edwin Eugene and Marion (Moon) Aldrin; m. Lois Driggs Cannon, Feb. 14, 1988; children from previous marriage: James Michael, Janice Ross, Andrew John. BS, U.S. Mil. Acad., 1951; ScD in Astronautics, MIT, 1963; ScD (hon.), Gustavus Adolphus Coll., 1967, Clark U., 1969, U. Portland, 1970, St. Peter's Coll., 1970; LittD (hon.), Montclair State Coll., 1969; HHD (hon.), Seton Hall U., 1970. Commd. officer USAF, 1951, advanced through grades to col.; served as fighter pilot in Korea, 1953; pilot Gemini XII orbital rendezvous space flight, Nov. 11-15, 1966; lunar module pilot on first manned lunar landing Apollo XI; comdr. Aerospace Rsch. Pilots Sch., Edwards AFB, Calif., 1971-72; ret. USAF, 1972; with Ctr. for Aerospace Scis. U. N.D., Grand Forks, 1989. Sci. cons. Beverly Hills Oil Co., Inforex Computer Co., Laser Video Corp., Mut. of Omaha Ins.; founder Starcraft Enterprises (Starcraft Boosters, Inc.), 1988-; created ShareSpace Found. to promote affordable space tourism for all people; lectr. in field; bd. dir. Neah Power Systems, 2007-. Author: Return to Earth, 1973, Men From Earth, 1989, Encounter with Tiber, 1996, The Return, 2000, (children's book) Reaching for the Moon, 2005. Decorated D.S.M., Legion of Merit, D.F.C. with oak leaf cluster, Air medal with 2 oak leaf clusters; recipient Horatio Alger award, 2005, numerous other awards including Presdl. medal of Freedom, 1969. Fellow AIAA; mem. Nat. Space Soc. (chmn.), Soc. Exptl. Test Pilots, Royal Aero. Soc. (hon.), Sea Space Symposium; charter Internat. Acad. Astronautics (corr.), Sigma Xi, Tau Beta Pi. Clubs: Masons (33 degree). Shot down two MiG-15s during 66 combat mission in the Korean War; In November, 1966, established record over 7 hours and 52 minutes outside spacecraft in extra-vehicular activity on the Gemini XII orbital flight mission; On July 20, 1969, walked on moon along with Neil Armstrong during Apollo XI Mission, becoming the first two humans to set foot on another world. This heroic endeavor was witnessed by the largest worldwide television audience in history; In 1993, received US patent for permanent space station he designed. Legally changed name from Edwin E. Aldrin Jr.*

ALDROW-LIPUT, PRISCILLA REESE, retired elementary school educator; b. Kingston, Pa., Apr. 10, 1951; d. Thomas Edward and Martha Mae (Hadsall) Reese; children: Colin Michael, Justin John; m. Willard C. Aldrow. BS, Bloomsburg U., 1973; MS, Walden U., 2007. Cert. instructional II. Tchr. grade 5 Dallas Sch. Dist., Pa., 1973—2001, ret., 2001. Homebound tchr. Rockingham Country Pub. Schs., Va., 2001—07. Mem. NEA, Pa. State Edn. Assn., Dallas Edn. Assn. Home Phone: 540-433-1117; Office Phone: 540-383-5038. Personal E-mail: praldrow@quixnet.net.

ALEALI, SEYED HOSSAIN, internist; b. Pahlavi, Iran, Jan. 18, 1938; MD, U. Tehran, 1964. Intern internal medicine Uniontown Hosp., 1971; resident hematology Med. Coll. Ohio, Toledo, 1972—74; fellow Yale Affiliate Hosp., New Haven, 1974—76; attending physician St. Vincent Med. Ctr., Bridgeport, Conn.; instr. NY Med. Coll., Valhalla, NY; clin. asst. prof. Columbia U. Recipient Leadership award (Internat. med. Grad. Physician), AMA Found, 2006. Mem.: Conn. State Med. Soc. (pres. 2004). Office: Ste 204 4699 Main St Bridgeport CT 06606 Office Phone: 203-371-5228. Office Fax: 203-374-4920.

ALEINIKOFF, THOMAS ALEXANDER, dean, law educator; b. 1952; BA, Swarthmore Coll., 1974; JD, Yale U., 1977. Bar: NY 1978, Mich. 1983. Law clk. to Judge Edward Weinfeld, 1977-78; atty., advisor Office Legal Counsel Dept. Justice, 1978-80; trail atty. wildlife sect. Land & Nat. Resources Dept. Justice, 1981; asst. prof. law U. Mich., 1981-84, assoc. prof., 1984-86, prof., 1984-86, 1986—94; gen. counsel US Dept. Justice Immigration and Naturalization Svc., 1994—95, exec. assoc. commr. for programs, 1995—97; prof. law Georgetown U. Law Ctr., 1997—, assoc. dean rsch., 2003—04, dean, 2004—; exec. v.p. law ctr. affairs Georgetown U., 2004—. Past rschr. in Internat. Migration Policy Carnegie Endowment for Internat. Peace. Co-author (with J. Garvey): Modern Constitutional Theory: A Reader, 1994; co-author: (with D. Martin and H. Motomura) Immigration: Process and Policy, 1995. Office: Georgetown U Law Ctr 600 NJ Ave NW Washington DC 20001 Office Phone: 202-662-9031.*

ALEMÁN, MARTHANNE PAYNE, environmental scientist, consultant; b. Houston, Dec. 3, 1938; d. Charles Franklin and Evelyn Inez (Dudley) Payne; m. Samuel Garza Alemán, July 5, 1968. BS in Landscape Arch. magna cum laude, Tex. A&M U., 1988; MS in Interdisciplinary Studies, Tex. Tech. U., 1989; PhD in Urban and Regional Sci., Tex. A&M U., 1995. Engring. aide City of Austin, 1966-69, Bryant-Curington Engrs., Austin, 1969-72; entrepreneur Rio Verde Farm, San Benito, Tex., 1972-83; rsch. asst. Tex. Tech. U., Lubbock, 1988-91, Tex. A&M U., College Station, 1993-94; cons. Rio Verde Land & Investment Corp., Calvert, Tex., 1995—. Sec./treas., bd. dirs. Tex. Avocado Growers Assn., Weslaco, 1979-83. Author: Soil Salinity in the Texas Lower Rio Grande Valley: Cause for Concern, 1987, Export-Driven Development of Soil and Water Resources: Barrier to Sustainable Development and Inducement to Desertification, 1995. Mem. and active participant Robertson County Hist. Commn., Calvert, 1980-83. Smithsonian Instn. intern, Washington, 1987, Presdl. scholar U.S. Fed. Register, 1993; recipient Nat. Collegiate Archtl. and Design award, U.S. Achievement Acad., Lexington, Ky., 1989. Mem. Am. Planning Assn., Soil and Water Conservation Soc. of Am. (vol. Heart of Tex. chpt., Waco, Tex.). Avocation: dog breeding. Office: Rio Verde Land and Investment Corp 201 E Browning Calvert TX 77837 Office Phone: 979-364-2631.

ALEMANY, ELLEN R., bank executive; b. Dec. 27, 1955; 3 children. MBA, Fordham U., 1980. With ops., structured trade, media & electronics depts. Chase Manhattan Bank, 1977—87; various positions including sr. lender media and electronics dept., head N.Y. Leveraged Capital Group, sr. credit officer, customer group exec. N.Am. Citibank, 1987—; chmn., CEO Citibank Internat. PLC, exec. v.p. Comml. Bus. Group; pres., CEO CitiCapital, 2001—06; CEO, Global Transactions Services Citigroup Corp. & Investment Banking, NYC, 2006—07; CEO The Royal Bank of Scotland (RBS) Am., NYC, 2007—. Bd. dirs. Citicorp USA Inc., Citicorp N. Am. Inc., Equipment Leasing Assn. Bd. dirs. March of Dimes, NYC, 2005—. Named one of 25 Most Powerful Women in Banking, US Banker mag., 2005, 2006. Mem.: Equipment Leasing and Fin. Found. (bd. mem., treas. 2004). Avocation: jogging. Office: The Royal Bank of Scotland 101 Park Ave 10th Fl New York NY 10178*

ALEMNEH, DANIEL GELAW, information technology manager, educator; b. Addis Ababa, Shewa, Ethiopia, Dec. 28, 1972; s. Gelaw Alemneh and Birtukan Derbe; m. Selamawit Pantaleo, Feb. 21, 1998; children: John K. Daniel, Hannah M. Daniel, Lia A. Daniel. B of Libr. and Info. Sci. (hon.), Addis Ababa U., Ethiopia, 1994; M of Libr. & Info. Mgmt., U. Sheffield, England, 1997; postgrad., U. North Tex., 2000—. Head faculty law libr. Addis Ababa U., Ethiopia, 1997—99; digital projects mgr. and metadata specialist U. North Tex., Denton, 2005—. Cons. UN Econ. Commn. Africa, Addis Ababa, 1998—99; adj. instr. Addis Ababa U., 1998—99, U. North Tex., 2004—. Contbr. articles to profl. jours. Asst. soccer coach US Youth Soccer, Denton Soccer Assn., 2006. Fellow, U. North Tex., 1999, 2000, U. Ill., Urbana-Champaign., 2003; grantee, Addis Ababa U., 1998, Addis Ababa U., Ethiopia, 1999, U. North Tex., 2001, 2003, 2005; scholar, Addis Ababa U., 1996—97, U. North Tex., 2000, 2001, 2002. Mem.: ALA, Tex. Libr. Assn., Visual Resources Assn., Am. Soc. Info. Sci. and Tech. (Eugene Garfield scholar 2003), Assn. Libr. and Info. Sci. Edn., Ethiopian Libr. and Info. Profls.Assn. (corr.), Pan-African Students Assn., Addis Ababa U. Alumni Assn. (life), U. Sheffield Alumni Assn. (life).

ALEMU, FITSUM ACHAMYELEH, lawyer, researcher; b. Addis Ababa, Ethiopia, July 13, 1968; s. Achamyeleh Alemu and Nigatua Tessemma. JD, Eötvös U., Budapest, 1996; MA, Budapest Econ. U., 1999; LLM, Am. U., 2000. Bar: Supreme Ct. Va., U.S. Ct. Appeals (4th cir.), Va., U.S. Dist. Ct. eastern dist. Va. Staff atty. NEKI (Legal Def. Bur. Ethnic Minorities), Budapest, 1996—2000; rsch. asst. Wash. Coll. Law, 2000; cons. HACTIN, Wash., 2001; freelance cons. Alexandria, Va., 2001—03; assoc. Law Offices of Fitsum Alemu, Arlington, 2003—04, private atty., 2004—. Editor: Litigation Manual for Hungarian Lawyers, 2000; contbr. articles to profl. jours. Chmn. Ethiopian Student Free Union in Hungary, Budapest, 1991—94, 1995—96; bd. mem. Martin Luther King Orgn., Budapest, 1998—2000. Mem.: Am. Immigration Lawyers Assn., ABA, Va. Bar Assn. Orthodox Christian. Avocations: jogging, exercise, reading, music. Office Phone: 703-522-8900. Office Fax: 703-522-4314. Personal E-mail: fitsumka@aol.com.

ALESCH, DANIEL JAMES, social sciences educator, researcher; b. Appleton, Wis., Apr. 21, 1939; s. Roman William Alesch and Margaret Ella Danielsen; children: Kirsten Ann Muth, Greta Jane Liddell. BS, U. Wis., 1962, MS, 1964; MA, U. Calif., 1969, PhD, 1970. Post grad. fellow Inst. Pub. Adminstrn., NYC, 1964—65; planner Exec. Chamber, Albany, NY, 1965—67; sr. rschr. U. So. Calif., LA, 1967—68; prof. U. Wis., Green Bay, 1976—2001, prof. emeritus, 2001—; sr. social scientist The RAND Corp., Santa Monica, Calif., 1968—79. Bd. dirs., v.p. Fox-Wolf Basin 2000, Green Bay, 1992—97; commr., pres. Green Bay (Wis.) Met. Sewerage Dist., 1992; bd. dirs. Brown County Planning Commn., Green Bay, Wis., 1980—87; chmn. bd. dirs. Housing Allowance Office of Brown County, Inc., Green Bay, 1973—95. Home: 909 Forest Hill Drive Green Bay WI 54311 Home Phone: 920-468-0132. Personal E-mail: dalesch@new.rr.com.

ALESCHUS, JUSTINE LAWRENCE, retired real estate broker; b. New Brunswick, NJ, Aug. 13, 1925; d. Walter and Mildred Lawrence; m. John Aleschus, Jan. 23, 1949; children: Verdene Jan, Janine Kimberley, Joanna Lauren. Student, Rutgers U., New Brunswick, NJ. Dept. sec. Am. Bapt. Home Mission Soc., NYC, 1947-49; claims examiner Republic Ins. Co., Dallas, 1950-52; broker Damon Homes, LI, 1960-72; pres. Justine Aleschus Real Estate, Smithtown, NY, 1975—2002; ret. Exclusive broker estate of Kenneth H. Leeds, L.I., N.Y., 1980-90; past pres. S.C. Real Estate Bd. Past pres. Nassau-Suffolk Coun. of Hosp. Aux, 1981-82; hon. mem. aux. St. Catherine of Siena, Smithtown, N.Y., past pres., hosp. adv. bd.; past pres. L.I. Coalition for Sensible Growth, Inc.; past v.p. Suffolk County Boy Scouts Am.; grad. S.C. Citizen Police Acad., Jacksonville Beach Police Res. Mem. Sky Island Club (gov.), Jacksonville Beach City Police Acad. (res.). Republican. Lutheran. Address: 2261 The Woods Dr East Jacksonville FL 32246 Personal E-mail: landauntjay@aol.com.

ALESHIRE, JOAN ALLAN, poet, creative writing educator; b. Balt., Mar. 18, 1938; d. Warde Baunton and Angelica Peale (Iglehart) Allan; 1 child from previous marriage, Anne Aleshira. AB, Radcliffe Coll., Cambridge, Mass., 1960; MFA, Goddard Coll., Plainfield, Vt., 1980. Faculty mem. Warren Wilson Coll., 1983—. Founder, pres. Shrewsbury Libr., Cuttingsville, Vt., 1975—; interim dir. Warren Wilson Coll., Swannano, NC, 1952—84, 1987, 93; lectr., scholar Vt. Coun. On Humanities, Hyde Park, 1978—95. Author: (books) Cloud Train, 1982, This Far, 1987, The Yellow Transparents, 1997, Litany of Thanks, 2003. Mem. Amnesty Internat., 1976—; trustee, libr. Shrewsbury Libr., Cuttingsville, 1975—; bd. mem. Hayes Found., Wallingford, Vt., 1980—. Personal E-mail: joanaleshire@vermontel.net.

ALESINA, ALBERTO, economist, educator; b. Broni, Italy, Apr. 29, 1957; arrived in U.S., 1982; s. Giancarlo Alesina, Piera Bolognesi; m. Susan Adler. Laurea, U. Bocconi, Milan Italy, 1982; PhD, Harvard U., 1986. Asst. prof. econs. Carnegie Mellon U., Pitts., 1986—88; asst. prof. economics Harvard U., 1988—93, Nathaniel Ropes prof. polit. economy Cambridge, Mass., 1993—. Author: (book) Partisan Politics Divided Government and the Economy, 1995, Political Cycles and the Macroeconomy, 1997, The Size of Nations, 2003, Fighting Poverty in U.S. and Europe, 2004, The Future of Europe: Reform or Decline, 2006; contbr. articles to profl. jours. Fellow, Sloan Found.; grantee, NSF, 1988—. Fellow: Am. Acad. Arts & Scis.; mem.: Ctr. for Econ. Policy Rsch. (assoc.), Nat. Bureau of Econ. Rsch. (assoc.). Office: Harvard U Littauer Ctr Cambridge MA 02138 Office Phone: 617-495-8388. Business E-Mail: aalesina@harvard.edu.

ALESIO, STEVEN W., financial services company executive; BS, St. Francis Coll., Pa.; MBA, U. Pa., 1981. Joined Am. Express Co., 1981, various mktg. positions in comml. bus. units, named sr. v.p. and gen. mgr. consumer travel bus., 1989, exec. v.p. and gen. mgr. small bus. services group, 1993, divsn. pres. small bus. services, tax and acctg. services, and consumer travel network, 1996, most recently pres. and gen. mgr. bus. services group; sr. v.p. The Dun & Bradstreet Corp., Short Hills, NJ, 2001—02, pres., COO, 2002—05, CEO, 2005—, chmn., 2005—. Bd. trustees Liberty Sci. Ctr., Jersey City; chmn. NJ All Stars Project. Office: The Dun & Bradstreet Corp 103 JFK Pkwy Short Hills NJ 07078*

ALESSI, DAVID MICHAEL, surgeon; children from previous marriage: David Jr., Machenzie, Dominique. BS, Mich. State U., Lansing, 1979; MD, Wayne State U., Detroit, 1983. Surgeon pvt. practice, Beverly Hills, Calif., 1989—. CEO Alpha Health Care, LA, 1998. Mem.: LA Tennis Club. Office: 8670 Wilshire #200 Beverly Hills CA 90211

ALESSI, ROBERT JOSEPH, lawyer, real estate developer, pharmacist; b. Rome, NY, Aug. 22, 1958; s. William John and Mary Jean A.; m. Ellen Mary (Paczkowski), May 21, 1988; children: Laura C., and Grace E. BS in Pharmacy, Union Univ., 1982; JD cum laude, Albany Law Sch., 1985. Bar: N.Y. 1986; U.S. Dist. Ct. (no. dist.) N.Y. 1986; U.S. Dist. Ct. (we. dist.) N.Y. 1986; U.S. Dist. Ct. (ea. dist.) N.Y. 1993; U.S. Dist. Ct. (so. dist.) N.Y. 1993; U.S. Ct. Appeals (2d cir.) 1995; U.S. Supreme Ct. 1996; registered NY State Pharmacist. Assoc. Nixon, Hargrave, Devans, and Doyle, Albany, NY, 1985-90, LeBoeuf, Lamb, Greene, & MacRae LLP, Albany, NY, 1990-93, ptnr., 1994—, mng. ptnr., hiring ptnr. Albany office, 1999—; mng. dir. Hudson Heritage LLC, 1999—2005. Ad., prof. law Albany Law Sch., 1989—94; town atty. Bethlehem, NY, 2001—03. Co-author: Yr. 2000 Deskbook, 1998. Mem. master plan com. Town of Bethlehem, Delmar, N.Y., 1989-89; mem. planning bd. counsel, 1990-94. Mem. N.Y. State Bar Assn., Albany Law Sch., Environ. Alumni Group, Rockefeller Found., advisor Pocantico roundtable consensus on brownfields. Avocations: tennis, reading, exercise. Office: LeBoeuf Lamb Greene & MacRae LLP One Commerce Plz Ste 2020 99 Washington Ave Albany NY 12210 Office Phone: 518-626-9000. Office Fax: 518-626-9010. Business E-Mail: ralessi@llgm.com.

ALEWINE, BETTY, retired telecommunications executive; V.p. sales and marketing Comsat Internat., v.p. & gen. mgr., pres.; CEO, pres. Comsat (merged with Lockheed Martin), Bethesda, Md., 1996—2000; ret., 2000. Bd. dirs. Rockwell Internat. Corp., 2000. Dir. The Nat. Symphony Orchestra, The Brink's Co., NY Life Ins. Co., Rockwell Automation, 2000—. Mailing: The Brink's Co PO Box 18100 Richmond VA 23226-8100

ALEX, JOANNE DEFILIPP, elementary school educator; m. Joseph Alex; children: Jessica, Joel, Julianna. BA in Art and Edn., Colby Coll., 1976; grad./cert., Montessori Methods, 1982; MEd, U. Maine, 2001. Tchr., kindergarten, Montessori schs., various cities, 1979-83; founder, tchr. Montessori Sch., Stillwater, Maine, 1983—; instr. elem. sci. methods U. Maine, 2003. AMS Montessori intern supr., Univ. student tchr. placements (supr. tchr.); presenter numerous workshops and confs.; trained facilitator of Systematic Tng. for Effective Parenting; instr. parenting courses; ednl. cons.; facilitator Project Learning Tree, Project Wild, Project Aquatic, Project Wet workshops; coord 1st Maine Tchrs. Forum, 1998; tchr. cons., Nat. Geographic Soc., 1993-; pub. engagement coord. Nat. Geographic My Wonderful World Campaign, Maine, 2006-07. Co-author: I Wonder What's Out There? A Vision of the Universe for Primary Classrooms, 2002. Selected to attend Nat. Geographic Soc. Summer Inst., 1993, Nat. Geographic Soc. Alliance Leadership Acad., 1999; named State Coord. Maine, Nat. Geographic Soc. Action 2003!, Outstanding Environ. Educator of Yr. (nat.), Am. Tree Found., 1994, Tchr. of Yr., Maine Audubon Soc., 1995, Maine Tchr. of Yr., 1998; recipient award for outstanding contbns. to child-care in Maine, 1996, Rudie Memmel Chpt. Vol. award Children's Internat. Summer Village, 2005; state finalist Presdl. Award for Excellence in Elem. Sci. Tchg., 2002, 04. Mem. Am. Montessori Soc. (cert. tchr.), Maine Montessori Assn. (treas.), Maine Geog. Alliance, Roots and Shoots Jane Goodall Inst., Maine Audubon Soc., Maine Tchr. of Yr. Assn., Nat. Coun. Geog. Edn. Avocations: biking, hiking, wild flowers, children's books, children's resources. Office: Stillwater Montessori Sch 1024 Stillwater Ave Unit 1 Old Town ME 04468-5112 Office Phone: 207-827-2404. E-mail: jalex1@adelphia.net.

ALEX, PAULA ANN, foundation administrator; b. New Haven, May 1, 1945; d. Ralph P. and Louise A. (Pesanelli) A. Student, Conn. Coll., 1962-64; diploma, U. Paris, Sorbonne, 1966; BA, Am. U., 1967; cert. bus. mgmt., NYU, 1978. Exec. asst. Olin Corp., Stamford, 1968-72, Wheelabrator-Frye, NYC, 1973-75; account exec. SSC & B: Lintas, NYC, 1976-82; account supr. Lawrence Charles Free & Lawson, NYC, 1982—84; v.p. Advt. Ednl. Found., NYC, 1985-88, exec. v.p., 1989—, mng. dir., bd. dirs., 1992—, CEO, 2003—. Mem. exec. com. Murray Hill Aux. Lenox Hill Hosp., N.Y.C. Mem. Am. Acad. Advt., Am. Advt. Fedn. Bd., Advt. Women N.Y. Avocations: southeast asian art, opera, riding. Office: Advt Ednl Found 220 E 42d St Ste 3300 New York NY 10017-5806 Office Phone: 212-986-8060. E-mail: pa@aef.com.

ALEXANDER, ADRIAN W., library director, dean; BA, Tex. Tech. U., 1972; MLS, U. North Tex., 1976. Asst. humanities libr. U. North Tex., Denton, 1976—77, adminstrv. svcs. libr., 1977—81; sales rep. Libr. Bur., Inc., Dallas, 1981—85; sales mgr. western region Faxon Co., Inc., Westwood, Mass., 1985—96, dir. strategic develop., 1996—98; sales mgr. western region Swets Subscription Svcs., Inc., Exton, Pa., 1996; exec. dir., COO Greater Western Libr. Alliance, Kansas City, Mo., 1998—2007; R.M. and Ida McFarlin dean libr. U. Tulsa, Okla., 2007—. Dir. BioOne Inc., 2000—. Editl. bd. Libr. Acquisitions: Practice & Theory, 1991—96, Serials Review, 1997—99, Libr. Consortium Mgmt., 1999—2001; contbr. articles to profl. jours. Mem.: ALA, Tex. Libr. Assn., North American Serials Interest Group, Libr. Info. and Tech. Assn., Assn. Libr. Collections and Tech. Svcs., Am. Fedn. of Radio and TV Artists. Office: McFarlin Libr U Tulsa 2933 E Sixth St Tulsa OK 74101 Office Phone: 918-631-2356. E-mail: adrian-alexander@utulsa.edu.*

ALEXANDER, ALONZO, III, music educator, composer; b. Cin., Sept. 4, 1956; s. Alonzo Alexander Jr. and Mamie (Comer) Alexander. MusB, U. Cin., Coll. Conservatory of Music, 1978, MusM, 1982, MusD, 1997. Music dir. St. Mark Cath. Ch., Cin., 1980—84, 1990—99; instr. Pasadena Conservatory of Music, Pasadena, Calif., 1985—90; adj. instr. Coll. Conservatory of Music, Cin., 1996—99, Antioch U., Yellow Springs, Ohio, 1996—97; asst. prof. music Morris Brown Coll., Atlanta, 1999—2003, Spelman Coll., Atlanta, 2004—. Accompanist Americolor Opera Alliance, Atlanta, 2000—05. Recipient Cert. of Honor award, Pi Kappa Lambda (Pi Chpt.), 1977, Recognition award, Phi Mu Alpha Sinfonia, 2004. Mem.: Phi Mu Alpha Sinfonia (faculty adv. 2001—04). Democrat. Cath. Avocations: poetry, singing, Greek mythology. Home: 1406Graham St SW # A Atlanta GA 30310-4328 Office Phone: 404-270-5494. E-mail: alonzoafricano@aol.com.

ALEXANDER, ANTHONY J., electric power industry executive; m. Becky Alexander; 4 children. BS, U. Akron, 1972, JD, 1975. Bar: Ohio 1976. Sr. tax acct. Ohio Edison Co., Akron, 1972-76, atty., 1976-83, sr. atty., 1984-87, assoc. gen. counsel, 1987-89, sr. v.p., gen. counsel, 1898-91; exec. v.p., gen. counsel Ohio Edison Co. (merged with Centerior Energy to form FirstEnergy), Akron, 1996—97, FirstEnergy Corp., Akron, 1997—2000, pres., 2000—, COO, 2001—04, CEO, 2004—. Bd. dir. Ohio Electric Utility Inst., Assn. of Edison Illuminating Companies, Inc; bd. dir., mem. exec. com. Nuclear Energy Inst. Bd. trustees Akron Gen. Health System, The NEOUCOM Found., Playhouse Square Found., Green Schools Found., U. Akron Found.; vice chmn. Greater Akron Chamber. Recipient Dr. Frank L. Simonetti Dist. Bus. Alumni award, U. Akron. Mem.: Nat. Assn. of Manufacturers (dir.-at-large). Office: FirstEnergy Corp 76 S Main St 18th Fl Akron OH 44308-1812*

ALEXANDER, ARTHUR JACOB, economist; b. Carbondale, Pa., Oct. 6, 1936; s. Howard R. and Sylvia (Eisner) A.; m. Elaine Averich, Aug. 25, 1963; children: Sarah, Jonathan. BS, Mass. Inst. Tech., 1958; MSc, London Sch. Econs., 1966; PhD, Johns Hopkins U., 1969. Sys. analyst IBM, Poughkeepsie, NY, 1960-63; rsch. economist Rand Corp., Santa Monica, Calif., 1968-90; pres. Japan Econ. Inst., Washington, 1990—2001. Vis. prof. UCLA, 1988-90, George Mason U., 1998-2000, Georgetown U., 2000—, Johns Hopkins U., 2006—; mem. U.S. Army Sci. Bd., Washington, 1978-82; rsch. assoc. Internat. Inst. Strategic Studies, London, 1976-77. With U.S. Army, 1959-60. Avocations: photographica collections, running. Office: Japan Econ Inst 3517 Raymond St Chevy Chase MD 20815-3227 Office Phone: 301-652-4574. Personal E-mail: arthur.alexander@att.net.

ALEXANDER, ASCENCION (CENCY) H., school psychologist, educator; b. Flagstaff, Ariz., Aug. 14, 1955; d. Paul Ruiz and Carmen Mayorga Lopez; m. Philip Mark Alexander, Oct. 10, 1987; children: Freddy, Danny. BS in Elem. Edn., No. Ariz. U., 1978, MA in Tchg. English as a Second Lang., 1986, MA in Sch. Psychology, 1994. Sch. Psychologist Ariz. Bd. Edn., 1994, Elem. Edn. Ariz. Bd. Edn., 1978, Bilingual Endorsement Ariz. Bd. Edn., 1978. 3rd, 4th grade tchr. Tucson Unified Sch. Dist. #1, 1978—79; 4th grade tchr. Roosevelt Sch. Dist., Phoenix, 1979—80, Kyrene Sch. Dist., Tempe, Ariz., 1980—81; substitute tchr. Flagstaff Unified Sch. Dist., Ariz., 1982—83; esl adult edn. tchr. Mesa Cmty. Schs., Mesa, Ariz., 1983—84; esl transitional lab tchr. Mesa Sch. Dist., Ariz., 1983—85; 4th grade tchr. Flagstaff Unified Sch. Dist., 1986—95; esl immersion program tchr. Mesa CC, Mesa, Ariz., 1984—84; grad. asst. No. Ariz. U., 1985—86; bilingual edn. safety svcs. coord. and instr. Coconino County, 1985—88; sch. psychologist intern Cartwright Sch. Dist., Phoenix, 1994—95; sch. psychologist Flagstaff Unified Sch. Dist., Flagstaff, 1995—96; bilingual sch. psychologist Phoenix Elem. Sch. Dist., 1996—97; dist. wide bilingual sch. psychologist Flagstaff Unified Sch. Dist., 1997—2000; contracting cons. bilingual sch. psychologist Self-Employed, Greater Phoenix Area, Ariz., 2000—. Beautification commn. mem. Beautification Commn., Flagstaff, Ariz., 1994—99; mem. Ministry of Mothers Sharing, Chandler, Ariz., 2004—05, Coconino Ctr. for the Arts, Flagstaff, Ariz., 1990—92. Raymond Found. scholar, Raymond Found., 1978-79. Mem.: NASP (life), Ariz. Assn. of Sch. Psychologists (life). Roman Catholic. Avocations: reading, estate sale shopping, decorating, walking, crafts. Home Phone: 480-802-2929; Office Phone: 480-802-2929.

ALEXANDER, BARBARA LEAH SHAPIRO, clinical social worker; b. St. Louis, May 6, 1943; d. Harold Albert and Dorothy Miriam (Leifer) Shapiro; m. Richard E. Alexander. B in Music Edn., Washington U., St. Louis, 1964; postgrad., U. Ill., 1964-66; MSW, Smith Coll., 1970; postgrad., Inst. Psychoanalysis, Chgo., 1971-73, grad., child therapy program, 1976-80; cert. therapist Sex Dysfunction Clinic, Loyola U., Chgo., 1975. Diplomate in Clin. Social Work. Rsch. asst., NIMH grantee Smith Coll., 1968-70; probation officer Juvenile Ct. Cook County, Chgo., 1966-68, 70; therapist Madden Mental Health Ctr., Hines, Ill., 1970-72; supr., therapist, field instr. U. Chgo., U. Ill. Grad. Schs. Social Work; therapist Pritzker Children's Hosp., Chgo., 1972-82; therapist, cons., also pvt. practice, 1973—; pres. On Good Authority, 1992—; intern Divorce Conciliation Svc., Circuit Ct. Cook County, 1976-77. Contbr. articles to profl. jours. Bd. dirs., Grant Park Concerts Soc.; sec. Art Resources in Teaching. Recipient Sterling Achievement award Mu Phi Epsilon, 1964. Mem. Nat. Fed. Soc. for Clin. Social Work (chmn. 20th ann. conf., exec. bd.), Ill. Soc. Clin. Social Work (pres. 1986-90, bd. dirs., chmn. svcs. to mems. com., dir. pvt. practitioners' referral service), Assn. Child Psychotherapists, Amateur Chamber Music Players Assn., Jewish Geneal. Soc., Smith Coll. Alumni Assn. (bd. dirs., v.p. 1992-94). Home and Office: 6 Horizon Ln Galena IL 61036-9258

ALEXANDER, BARBARA TOLL, financial consultant; b. Little Rock, Dec. 18, 1948; d. Lawrence Jesser and Geraldine Best (Proctor) Toll; m. Lawrence Allen Alexander, Jan. 25, 1969 (div. 1980); m. Thomas Beveridge Stiles, II, Mar. 7, 1981; stepchildren: Thomas B. Stiles III, Jonathan E. Stiles. BS, U. Ark., 1969, MS, 1970. Asst. v.p. Wachovia Bank & Trust Co., Winston-Salem, NC, 1972—77; security analyst Investors Diversified Services, Mpls., 1977—78; 1st v.p. Smith Barney Inc., NYC, 1978—84; mng. dir. Salomon Bros., NYC, 1984—91, Dillon Read & Co., 1992—97, UBS Securities, 1997—99, sr. advisor, 1999—2004. Bd. dirs. Centex Corp., mem. nominating and governance com.; bd. dirs. Harrah's Entertainment, Inc., chmn. audit com., chmn. fin. com.; bd. dirs. Freddie Mac, mem. fin. and capital deployment com., chmn. mission, sourcing and tech. com.; mem. governance, nominating, and risk oversight com. QUALCOMM Inc., bd. dirs., mem. audit com.; mem. governance com. Harvard U., former chmn. policy adv. bd. Joint Ctr. Housing Studies, exec. fellow; bd. dirs. Home Aid Am. Presbyterian. E-mail: barbara.alexander@cox.net.

ALEXANDER, BRUCE DONALD, real estate executive, educator; b. Hartford, Conn., May 11, 1943; BA, Yale U., 1965, MA (hon.), 1998; JD, Duke U., 1968. With Rouse Co., Balt., 1969-96, sr. v.p., dir. comml. devel. divsn., 1978-93, sr. v.p., dir. new bus., 1993-96; dir. Balt. Equitable Ins., 1987-89, Enterprise Social Investment Corp., 1995-2000, Balt. Devel. Corp., 1996-98; v.p., dir. New Haven and State Affairs Yale U., New Haven, 1998—, v.p. New Haven and state affairs and campus devel., 2006—; adj. prof. real estate Yale Sch. Mgmt., New Haven, 1998—2005. Trustee Goucher Coll., Balt., 1984-2001, chmn., 1991-96; trustee Columbia (Md.) Found., 1981-86, pres., 1983-85; trustee Balt. Ednl. Scholarship Trust, 1990-93, Conn. Pub. Broadcasting, 2002-06; co-chair eastern region Yale U. Campaign, 1991-97; bd. dirs. Balt. Symphony Orch., 1986-91, Cmty. Found. Greater New Haven, 2003-. Recipient John Franklin Goucher medal. Office: Yale Univ 433 Temple St New Haven CT 06511-6803 Business E-Mail: bruce.alexander@yale.edu.

ALEXANDER, BUZZ (WILLIAM), literature and language professor; BA, Harvard U., PhD, 1967; BA, U. Cambridge. Prof. English and lit. U. Mich., Ann Arbor, 1971—, Arthur F. Thurnau prof., 2003—, founder Prison Creative Arts Project. Contbr. articles to profl. jours. Recipient US Professors of Yr. Award for Outstanding Doctoral and Rsch. Universities Prof., Carnegie Found. for Advancement of Tchg. and Coun. for Advancement and Support of Edn., 2005. Office: U Mich Dept English 435 S State St 3187 Angell Hall Ann Arbor MI 48109-1003 Office Phone: 734-764-2393. E-mail: alexi@umich.edu.*

ALEXANDER, CARL ALBERT, materials engineer, engineering educator; b. Chillicothe, Ohio, Nov. 22, 1928; s. Carl B. and Helen E. Alexander; m. Dolores J. Hertenstein, Sept. 4, 1954; children: Carla C., David A. BS, Ohio U., 1953, MS, 1956; PhD, Ohio State U., 1961. Mem. staff Battelle Columbus Labs., 1956—, rsch. leader, 1974—, mgr. physico-chem. systems, 1976—; mem. faculty Ohio State U., 1963—, prof. ceramic and nuc. engring., 1977—. Sr. rsch. leader, chmn. tech. coun. of Biol. and Chem. Scis. Directorate, 1987—, chief scientist, 1987; prof. materials sci. and engring., 1988—. Author; patentee in field. Served to lt. (j.g.) USNR, 1951-54. Recipient Merit award NASA, 1971, IR-100 award, 1987, R & D-100 award, 1988; citations Dept. Energy, citations AEC, citations ERDA. Mem. Am. Soc. Mass Spectrometry, Keramos, Sigma Xi Home: 4249 Haughn Rd Grove City OH 43123-3216 Office: 505 King Ave Columbus OH 43201-2696 Home Phone: 614-209-3240; Office Phone: 614-424-5233. Business E-Mail: alexandc@battelle.org.

ALEXANDER, CECIL ABRAHAM, academic administrator, consultant, retired architect; b. Atlanta, Mar. 14, 1918; s. Cecil Abraham and Julia (Moses) A.; m. Hermione Weil, Jan. 20, 1943 (dec. 1983); children: Therese, Judith, Douglas; m. Helen Eisemann, 1985. Student, Ga. Inst. Tech., 1936; AB, Yale, 1940; student, Mass. Inst. Tech., 1941; M. Arch., Harvard, 1947. Partner Alexander & Rothschild (architects), Atlanta, 1949-58; chmn. bd. Finch, Alexander, Barnes, Rothschild & Paschal, Architects and Engrs., Inc., Atlanta, 1958-86; archtl. cons. Atlanta, 1986-90; coord. continuing edn. Ga. Inst. Tech. Coll. Architecture, Atlanta, 1994-96; prin.-in-charge Leo A. Daley Archtl. Engrs., Atlanta, 1996-97; ptnr. Alexander-Weiner Baker Architects, Atlanta, 1997—, Alexander Weiner Architects, 00—. Coord., chmn. bd. A.S.D. Inc., interior design svc.; chmn. Atlanta Citizens Adv. Com. Urban Renewal, 1958-60; vice chmn. Atlanta Met. Planning Commn., 1962—; past chmn. Ga. Fgn. Trade Zone Corp. Prin. works include Ga. Power Bldg., Atlanta, 1st Nat. Bank, Atlanta, Cin. Riverfront Stadium, Coca-Cola Internat. Hdqs., Sci. Atlanta Hdqs., U.S. Pavilion Expo '82, So. Bell. Hdqs.; designer new Ga. flag, 2001. Past vice chmn. Cmty. Coun., Atlanta; mem. Mayor's Adv. Com. Race Rels., Nat. Citizens Com. Cmty. Rels.; chmn. Atlanta chpt. Am. Jewish Com., 1963; chmn. housing resources com. City of Atlanta; past chmn. coun. Yale Sch. Architecture; pres., founder Resurgens Atlanta; past v.p. Atlanta Symphony Orch.; mem. Yale Nat. Alumni Bd., 1963; bd. dirs. Atlanta U.; bd. dirs. emeritus Clark Atlanta U.; past bd. dirs. Marist High

Sch., Atlanta; chmn. Com. to Combat Drugged and Drunken Driving; past pres. Atlanta's Clifton Corridor Biomed. Rsch. Coun. Served to lt. col. USMCR, World War II. Decorated Air medal, D.F.C.; (2) Recipient Brotherhood award NCCJ, 1973; Archdiocesan medal of St. Paul, 1980, Yale medal, 1980. Fellow AIA (pres. Ga. 1957, Ivan Allen award, Bernard B. Rothschild award, Ga. chpt.); mem. Atlanta C. of C. (dir., Whitney Young award, Nat Am. Inst. Architects). Home: 2677 Rivers Rd NW Atlanta GA 30305-3549 Office Phone: 404-261-9230. E-mail: cecilalexander@comcast.net.

ALEXANDER, CHRISTINA ANAMARIA, translator, performing company executive; b. Bucuresti, Romania, June 30; naturalized U.S. citizen, 1975. d. Peter Vladimir and Maria Nicolae (Suciu) A. BA, Old Dominion U., 1990, MA, 1992; PhD in Religion (hon.), Pacific Universal Life Ch., 1996; acctg. degree, Sch. Acctg. and Bookkeeping, Atlanta, 2000. Cert. natural health cons. Translator, interpreter Word for Word, Inc., Norfolk, Va., 1990—; exec. dir. KultureKastle, Virginia Beach, Va., 1996—. Instr. lang. Prague (Czech Republic) Lang. Sch., 1990-91; adj. faculty Old Dominion U., Norfolk, 1993; prof. humanities St. Petersburg Coll., Fla., 2006—; cons. pub. rels. High Frequency Wavelengths, N.Y.C., 1995-96; cons. V.A.C.A., Richmond, Va., 1995-96; internat. star Oriental Dance Festival of Finland, 2002; artist in residence Beaux Arts Gallery and Mus., St. Petersburg, Fla., 2004. Performing artist MARA Agy., Vienna, Austria, 1994, Joy Fund Theater, Norfolk, 1996-97, Boys and Girls Club, Inc., Newport News, Va., 1997, M.E. Cox Ctr., Virginia Beach, 1997, Waterfront Arts Festival, Virginia Beach, 1997, Cox Comm., 1997, Pepsi Island Music Festival, 1999, Frequencia Latina Network Peru, 1999, Multicultural Alliance Va. World Bazaar, 2000, Opsail 2000, Norfolk, Va., MTV Sink or Swim Talent Show, 2001, City of Clearwater Players, 2004, Pinellas Opera League, 2005; internat. star dancer Oriental Dance Festival of Finland, 2001; creator, dancer, choreographer Secret of the Lost Treasure, 1997 (award 1997); dancer Mantra, 1997; guest star Frequencia Latina Network; cons. Va. Ballet Theater, 2000. Bd. dirs., rec. sec. Bay West Condominiums, 2001—02. Named Ms. Petite Va. Beach, 1996. Mem. Hampton Roads Cultural Alliance, Multicultural Alliance of Va., Virgina Beach C. of C. Avocations: skiing, travel, costume design, nutrition. Office: 2525 W Bay Dr Apt A23 Belleair Bluffs FL 33770-1986 Personal E-mail: christalx@juno.com.

ALEXANDER, CLIFFORD JOSEPH, lawyer; b. New Orleans, Oct. 2, 1943; s. Charles Ernest and Lois Primus (Boley) A.; m. Elizabeth McAnany, June 11, 1966; children: Brian, Heather, Rachel. AB, Rockhurst Coll., 1966; JD, Georgetown U., Washington, DC, 1969. Bar: Mass. 1970, DC 1977. Mem. staff SEC, Washington, 1967-70; assoc. Gaston Snow & Ely Bartlett, Boston, 1970-75; mem. staff U.S. Senate Banking Com., Washington, 1975-77; mem. Kirkpatrick & Lockhart Preston Gates Ellis LLP, Wash., 1977—. Co-editor: Money Managers Compliance Manual. Mem. ABA (corp., banking and bus. law sect.), Boston Bar Assn., Fed. Bar Assn. (securities and banking law sects.), DC Bar Assn., Mass. Bar Assn., US Supreme Ct. Bar. Home: 8721 Bluedale St Alexandria VA 22308-2307 Office: Kirckpatrick & Lockhart Preston Geater Ellis LLP 1601 St NW Washington DC 20006-1600 Office Phone: 202-778-9068. Business E-Mail: calexander@klng.com.

ALEXANDER, CYNTHIA LOUISE, psychologist, educator; d. Glenn Elting and Flora Louise Alexander. BS in Psychology, summa cum laude, Tex. Christian U., 1994; MS in Clin. Psychology, Nova Southeastern U., 1995, D in Psychology, 1999. Intern Nova, Broward Gen. Hosp., Ft. Lauderdale, Fla.; clin. cons. U. Pavilion Hosp., Tamarac, Fla., coord. social svcs., 1999—2004; adj. prof. psychology Nova Southeastern U., Ft. Lauderdale, Fla., 2002—06; psychologist 17th Cir. Ct. Fla., Ft. Lauderdale, 2003—, Cleveland Clinic Fla., Weston, 2004—. Mem. editl. bd.: Bariatric Times, 2003—07; author: The Emotional First Aid Kit-A Guide to Life After Bariatric Surgery. Mem.: APA, Am. Soc. Bariatric and Metabolic Surgery, Psi Chi. Avocations: running, kayaking, travel. Office: Cleveland Clinic Fla 2950 Cleveland Clinic Blvd Weston FL 33331 Office Phone: 954-659-5267. Office Fax: 954-659-5256. E-mail: alexanc@ccf.org.

ALEXANDER, DONALD CRICHTON, lawyer; b. Pine Bluff, Ark., May 22, 1921; s. William Crichton and Ella Temple (Fox) A.; m. Margaret Louise Savage, Oct. 9, 1946; children: Robert C., James M. BA with honors, Yale U., 1942; LLB magna cum laude, Harvard U., 1948; LLD (hon.), St. Thomas Inst., 1975, Capital U., 1989. Bar: D.C. 1949, Ohio 1954, N.Y. 1978. Assoc. Covington & Burling, Washington, 1948-54, Taft, Stettinius & Hollister, Cin., 1954-56, ptnr., 1956-66, Dinsmore, Shohl, Coates & Deupree, Cin., 1966-73; commr. IRS, 1973-77; mem. Commn. on Fed. Paperwork, 1975-77; ptnr. Olwine, Connelly, Chase, O'Donnell & Weyher, NYC, Washington, 1977-79, Morgan, Lewis & Bockius, NYC and Washington, 1979-85, Cadwalader, Wickersham & Taft, Washington, 1985-93; ptnr., tax. practice group Akin, Gump, Strauss, Hauer & Feld, Washington, 1993—. Mem. adv. bd. NYU Tax Inst., 1969-73, 77-87, Tax Mgmt., Inc., 1968-73, 77—; mem. adv. Treas. Dept., 1970-72; mem. adv. group to commr. IRS, 1969-70, chmn. exempt orgns. adv. group, 1987-89; mem. adv. bd. Mertens, 1986-2002, Maxwell Macmillan fed. Taxes 2d, 1989-92; commr. Martin Luther King, Jr. Fed. Holiday Commn., 1993-96; mem. Harvard Bd. Overseers' vis. com. to law sch., 1999-2005; mem. com. on univ. resources Harvard U., 2002—; mem. interior dept. commn. on coal leasing, 1983-84. Author: The Arkansas Plantation, 1943; editor Harvard Law Rev., 1947-48; contbr. more than 50 articles on fed. taxation. Co-chmn. bd. advisors NYU/IRS Continuing Profl. Edn. Program, 1982-85; dir. Treasury Hist. Assn., 1996-2006. Served to maj. AUS, 1942-45. Decorated Silver Star, Bronze Star; re. Mem. ABA (vice chmn. taxation sect. 1967-68), Am. Law Inst. (tax adv. group), U.S. C. of C. (taxation com. 1981-91, bd. dirs. 1984-89, health and employee benefit com. 1989-94, regulatory affairs com. 1993-98), Chevy Chase Club (Md.), Met. Club, Nantucket Yacht Club (Mass.), Mill Reef Club (Antigua, B.W.I.), Yale Club N.Y. Office: Akin Gump Strauss Hauer & Feld Robert S Strauss Bldg 1333 New Hampshire Ave NW Washington DC 20036-1564 Office Phone: 202-887-4064. Office Fax: 202-887-4288. E-mail: dalexander@akingump.com.

ALEXANDER, DONALD G., state supreme court justice; Grad., Bowdoin Coll.; JD, U. Chgo. Bar: Maine 1972, U.S. Supreme Ct. 1973. Former legislative counsel Nat. League of Cities; former mem. Sen. Edmund Muskie's staff; asst. Maine atty. gen., 1974-76; dep. atty. gen.; judge Dist. Ct., 1979, Maine Superior Ct., 1980-98; justice Maine Supreme Ct., 1998—. Ct. liaison Advisory Com. on Maine Rules of Civil Procedur, State Ct. Library Com., Maine State Bar Assn. Continuing Legal Education Com. Author: (books) The Maine Jury Instruction Manual, 2003, Maine Appellate Practice, 2003; editor: The Maine Rules of Civil Procedure with Advisory Committee Notes from 1981, Commentary and Recent Case Citations, 2003. Office: Cumberland County Courthouse 142 Federal St PO Box 368 Portland ME 04112-0368*

ALEXANDER, DRURY BLAKELEY, retired architecture educator; b. Paris, Tex., Feb. 4, 1924; s. Drury Blakeley and Katherine (Stone) Alexander. B.Arch., U. Tex., 1950, BS in Art, 1951; MA, Columbia U., 1953. Instr. Kans. State U., Manhattan, 1953-55; asst. prof. architecture U. Tex., Austin, 1955-60, assoc. prof., 1960-67, prof., 1967-84, Meadows Found. prof. architecture, 1984-94, emeritus prof., 1994—; ret., 1994. Eugene McDermott lectr. U. Tex., 1983—85. Author: Texas Homes of the 19th Century, 1966, Sources of Classicism, 1978. Chmn. Hist. Landmark Commn., Austin, 1975—85. With US Army, ETO. Decorated Bronze Star medal; named a Arch. Archive in his name, The Arch. Libr. The U. Tex., Austin, 2002; recipient Tchg. Excellence award, U. Tex. Student's Assn., 1958, Disting. Svc. award, City of Austin, 1976, Svc. award for hist. preservation, Heritage Soc. Austin, 1976, Tex. Hist. Preservation award, Tex. Hist. Commn., 1986, Nat. Preservation Honor award, Nat. Trust for Hist. Preservation, 1991, Disting. Achievement award in archtl. edn., Tex. Soc. Architects, 1994, Disting. Prof. award, Assn. Collegiate Schs. of Arch., 1995, D.B. Alexander Lifetime Achievement award named in his honor, Heritage Soc. Austin, 2001. Mem.: Victorian Soc. Am., Assn. Preservation Technologists, Soc. Archtl. Historians (bd. dirs. 1979—82). Democrat. Presbyterian. Avocations: book collecting, travel. Home: 4100 Jackson Ave 115 Austin TX 78731-6029 Office: U Tex Sch Architecture Austin TX 78712 Office Phone: 512-454-3364.

ALEXANDER, DUANE FREDERICK, federal agency administrator, pediatrician, researcher; b. Balt., Aug. 11, 1940; s. Fred Lucas and Christiana H. (Showacre) A.; m. Marianne Ellis, June 23, 1963; children: Keith Duane, Kristin Marianne. BS, Pa. State U., 1962; MD, Johns Hopkins U., 1966. Diplomate: Am. Bd. Pediatrics. Intern Johns Hopkins Hosp., Balt., 1966—67, resident, 1967—68, fellow, 1970—71; commd. officer USPHS, 1968—2000, ret. rear adm.; clin. assoc. Nat. Inst. Child Health and Human Devel., NIH, Bethesda, Md., 1968—70, asst. to sci. dir., 1971—74, asst. to dir., 1978—82, dep. dir., 1982—86, dir., 1986—; staff pediatrician Nat. Commn. for Protection of Human Subjects of Research, 1974—78. Contbr. articles to profl. jours. Recipient Commendation medal USPHS, 1970, Meritorious Svc. medal USPHS, 1985, Spl. Recognition medal USPHS, 1985, Surgeon Gen.'s Exemplary Svc. medal, 1990, Irving B. Harris Lectureship award Soc. Behavioral Pediatrics, 1991, Pub. Svc. award Am. Coll. Ob-Gyn., 1992, Surgeon Gen.'s Medallion, 1993, Disting. Pub. Svc. award Am. Acad. Phys. Medicine and Rehab., 1993, Presdl. Citation, APA, 1992, Sec.'s Disting. Svc. award HHS, 1997, 98, Disting Alumnus award Pa. State U., 1999, Nathan Davis award AMA, 2004; alumni fellow Pa. State U. Alumni Assn, 1993. Fellow Am. Acad. Pediatrics (Excellence Pub. Svc. award 1998), Soc. Devel. Pediatrics, Am. Pediatric Soc., Assn. for Retarded Citizens. Methodist. Office: Nat Inst Child Health-Human Devel 31 Center Dr Msc 2425 Bldg 31 Bethesda MD 20892-0001 Business E-Mail: da43w@nih.gov, nichddir@mail.nih.gov.

ALEXANDER, ERIKA, actress; b. Winslow, Ariz., Nov. 19, 1969; m. Tony Puryear, Sept. 27, 1997. Student, NYU. Prin. prodn. co. Cimarron Entertainment; mgr. Shawana Kemp. Actor: (TV series) The Cosby Show, 1990-92, Going to Extremes, 1992-93, Living Single, 1993—97 (NAACP Image award 1996), (TV miniseries) George Washington II: The Forging of a Nation, 1986, The Mahabaharta, 1989, (TV films) The Last Best Year of My Life, 1990, Common Ground, 1990, Override, 1994, Mama Flora's Family, 1998; (films) The Long Walk Home, 1990, He Said, She Said, 1991, Fathers & Sons, 1992, 54, 1998, 30 Years to Life, 2001, Love Liza, 2002, Full Frontal, 2002, Tricks, 2004, Deja Vu, 2006; stage appearances include The Forbidden City, N.Y.C., 1989, Mahabaharta, N.Y.C., 1987. also: York & Harper 7364 1/2 Melrose Ave Los Angeles CA 90046-7527*

ALEXANDER, F. KING, academic administrator; b. Ky. BA in Polit. Sci., St. Lawrence U.; MS in Comparative Edn. Policy, Oxford U.; PhD in Higher Edn. Adminstrn., U. Wis., Madison. Mgr. Liberty Nat. Bank, Louisville; postdoctoral rschr., office of the provost U. Wis., Madison, vice chancellor for acad. affairs, lectr. ednl. adminstrn.; adminstr., mem. faculty U. Ill., Urbana-Champaign; pres. Murray State U., 2001—05, Calif. State U., Long Beach, 2006—. Found. fellow U. Oxford; faculty affiliate Cornell Higher Edn. Rsch. Inst., Inst. Govt. and Pub. Affairs. Contbr. articles to profl. jours. and publs. Office: Calif State U Long Beach BH 300 1250 N Bellflower Blvd Long Beach CA 90840-0006

ALEXANDER, FAITH DOROTHY, retired training services executive; b. NYC, Aug. 1, 1933; d. Howard Phillip and Ruth Dorothy Rubinow; m. Fred John Dunne (dec.); children: John Dunne, Robert Dunne, Laurie Martin, Bonnie Hunter; m. Daniel Lee Alexander, Apr. 27, 2000. BA, MA, Columbia U. Sales promotion mgr. Aseptic Thermo Indicator Co., N. Hollywood, Calif., 1956—57; v.p. Dunne, Rogers, Dunne Advt. and Pub. Rels., LA, 1958—79, NYC, 1958—79; records supr., training officer Newport Beach Police Dept., Calif., 1980—86; records, info. svcs. command Riverside County Calif. Sheriff Dept., Calif., 1987—2000; cert. instr. Ben Clark Training Acad., 0187—1990; instr. Regional Training Ctr., San Diego, 1996—2003, Calif. Peace Officer Assn., Sacramento, 1996—2003; ret., 2000. Author: Early Childhood Education, Coast Guard Prodecures, 2003; co-editor: Calif. Police Recorder Mag. Pres. Barrance Elem. Sch. PTA, Covina, Calif., 1972—74; sec. Covina Valley PTA, 1974—75; pres. Sierra Vista Intermediate Sch. PTA, 1974—75; mem. Lake Elsinore Grand Prix Races, Calif., 1986; vol. Helmet Images, Riverside, Calif., 1988—2005; sec., mem. exec. bd. Urban League Formation Com., 1989—90; bd. dirs. Greater Riverside Area Urban League, 1990—93; commr. Riverside County Commn. Women, 1995—97; mem. vol. Homeland Security Dept., 2003—; mem. LA Rep. Ctrl. Com., 1974, Rep. Presdl. Task Force, 1981, 1989, 2003; chair Larry Smith for Sheriff of Riverside County, 1993, co-chair, 1998; chair Del Norte County Bush/Cheny Campaign, 2003; mem. vol. Del Norte County Elections Bd., 2003; life mem. Nat. Rep. Senatorial Com., 2006—; registrar of voters Del Norte County, 2006; vol. Faith EV Luth. Ch., Medford, Oreg., 2004—05; hon. chair House Majority Trust, 2006. Recipient 2000 Women of Achievement award, 1961, 1971, Wall of Tolerance award, 2003, Riverside Calif. Pub. Svc. award, 1999, Nat. Rep. Party Gold medal, 1992, 2004, Rep. Yr., 2003. Mem.: Crescent city Coast Guard Aux., Del Norte County Rep. Women, Calif. Dept. Edn. Task Force, Campfire Girls (bd. mem., vice chair 1972—74), Nat. PTA (Hon. Svc. 1961), Am. Records Mgmt. Assn., Calif. Peace Officer's Assn., Calif. Law Enforcement Assn. of Record Suprs. (life; state conf. chair 1978, pres. So. Chpt. 1988—90, state conf. dir. 1989, founder, pres. Inland chpt. 1992—95, state exec. bd. 1992—95, Hon. Svc. award 1991, 1996), Nat. Rep. Senatorial Com. (life). Republican. Avocations: theater, music, art, writing, travel. Personal E-mail: faithanddan@earthlink.net.

ALEXANDER, FRED CALVIN, JR., lawyer; b. Abingdon, Va., Nov. 4, 1931; s. Fred C. and Mary F. (White) A.; m. Betsy Jones, May 17, 1957 (div.); children— Mitchell, Mary, Marjorie, Margaret; m. Janet Lee Hammond, Jan. 2, 1982 Student, Davidson Coll., 1950-52; BA, U. Va., 1954, LLB, 1959. Bar: Va. 1959, U.S. Dist. Ct. (ea. dist.) Va. 1959, U.S. Ct. Appeals (4th cir.) 1960. Assoc. Boothe, Prichard & Dudley, Alexandria, Va., 1959-64; ptnr. McGuire, Woods, Battle & Boothe LLP and predecessor firms, Alexandria, Va., 1964-97, ret. McLean, Va., 1997. Mem. jud. conf. U.S. Ct. Appeals (4th cir.), 1964-99; lectr. legal edn. Va. State Bar, 1970, 75-77, 89; chmn. adv. com. rules of ct. Supreme Ct. of Va., 1984-98; bd. dirs. Thomas Rutherford, Inc. Past bd. dirs. counsel to Alexandria Hosp., St. Stephens Sch. 1st lt. U.S. Army, 1954-56. Nominee Rhodes scholar U. Va., 1954. Fellow: Am. Coll. Trial Lawyers (chmn. Va. com. 1994—96), Va. Law Found.; mem.: Alexandria Bar Assn. (pres. 1969—70), Va. Bar Assn. (chmn. civil litigation sect. 1989—92), Va. Assn. Def. Attys., Va. Trial Lawyers Assn., Nat. Assn. R.R. Trial Counsel, Def. Rsch. Inst. (chmn. railroad law com. 1989—92), Belle Haven Country Club (bd. dirs. 1997—2000, 2001—04), Wyndemere Country Club. Episcopalian. Home: 1313 Gatewood Dr Alexandria VA 22307-2033 Office: McGuire Woods LLP 1750 Tysons Blvd Ste 1800 Mc Lean VA 22102-4231

ALEXANDER, GARY R., lawyer, state legislator, lobbyist; b. Washington, Nov. 16, 1942; s. Orville I. and Ann Z. Alexander; m. Anita G. Alexander; children: Jennifer Paige, Cory Brooke. BA, U. Va., 1964; LLB, George Washington U., 1967. Pvt. practice, Washington, Md. and Va., 1967-69; ptnr. Giordano, Alexander, Haas, Mahoney & Bush, Oxen Hill, Md., 1970-78, Haas & Alexander, Md., 1978-82; prin. ptnr. Alexander & Cleaver, P.A., Ft. Washington, Md., 1982—. Bd. dirs., chmn. Prince George County bar legis. com., 1972-79; bd. vis. U. Md. Sch. Pub. Policy, 2002—. Del. Md. Ho. of Dels., 1983-94, spkr. pro tem, 1993-94; chmn. Dem. Cen. Com., Prince George County, 1978-86; people's counsel Md. Pub. Svc. Commn., 1974-78; apptd. Gov.'s Task Force to Study Gambling, Md., 1993; taxation com. Md. C. of C., 1995; bd. trustees U. Md. Found., 2002—. Recipient Outstanding Svc. award Md. Senate, 1976, Outstanding Svc. citation, 1976, Pub. Svc. cert. Prince George County Exec. and County Coun., 1976, Local Employer of Yr. award Bus. and Profl. Woman's Club, 1993, Outstanding Atty. award Washington mag., 1997. Mem. ABA (chmn. automobile law com. 1975-77, chmn. automobile ins. legis. com. 1977-80), Nat. Conf. State Legislatures, Md. Bar Assn. (chmn. fed. laws com. 1973-79), D.C. Bar Assn., Va. Bar Assn., Md. Govt. Rels. Assn. Jewish. Avocations: history, gardening, golf, cooking. Office: Alexander & Cleaver PA 11414 Livingston Rd Fort Washington MD 20744-5145 also: Alexander & Cleaver PA 54 State Cir Annapolis MD 21401-1906 Office Phone: 410-974-9000. Business E-Mail: galexander@alexander-cleaver.com.

ALEXANDER, GEORGE JONATHON, lawyer, educator, dean; b. Berlin, Mar. 8, 1931; s. Walter and Sylvia (Grill) A.; m. Katharine Violet Sziklai, Sept. 6, 1958; children: Susan Katina, George Jonathon II. AB with maj. honors, U. Pa., 1953, JD cum laude, 1969; LLM, Yale U., 1965, JSD, 1969. Bar: Ill. 1960, NY 1961, Calif. 1974. Instr. law, Bigelow fellow U. Chgo., 1959-60; instr. internat. relations Naval Res. Officers Sch., Forrest Park, Ill., 1959-60; prof. law Syracuse U. Coll. Law, 1960-70, assoc. dean, 1968-69; prof. law U. Santa Clara Law Sch., Calif., 1970—, dir. Inst. Internat. and Comparative Law Calif., 1986—2004, disting. univ. prof. Calif., 1994-95, Elizabeth H. and John A. Sutro prof. law Calif., 1995—2005, pres. faculty senate Calif., 1996-97, dir. grad. programs, 1998-2001, co-dir., 2002; dean Santa Clara U., Calif., 1970—85, dean emeritus Calif., 2005—; pvt. practice, 2004—. Dir. summer programs at Oxford, Geneva, Strasbourg, Budapest, Tokyo, Hong Kong, Beijing, Shanghai, Ho Chi Minh City, Singapore, Bangkok, Kuala Lumpur, Seoul, Munich, Sydney, 1986-2004; vis. prof. law U. So. Calif., 1963; vis. scholar Stanford (Calif.) U. Law Sch., 1985-86, 92; cons. in field. Author: Civil Rights, U.S.A., Public Schools, 1963, Honesty and Competition, 1967, Jury Instructing on Medical Issues, 1966, Cases and Materials on Space Law, 1971, The Aged and the Need for Surrogate Management, 1972, Commercial Torts, 1973, 2d edit. 1988, U.S. Antitrust Laws, 1980, Writing A Living Will: Using a Durable Power of Attorney, 1988, (with Scheflin) Law and Mental Disabilities, 1998; author, editor: International Perspectives on Aging, 1992; also articles, chpts. in books, one film. Dir. Domestic and Internat. Bus. Problems Honors Clinic, Syracuse U., 1966-69, Regulations in Space Project, 1968-70; ednl. cons. Comptroller Gen. US, 1977-2002; mem. Nat. Sr. Citizens Law Ctr., 1983-90, pres., 1986-90. With USN, 1953-56. US Navy scholar U. Pa., 1949-52; Law Bds. scholar, 1956-59; Sterling fellow Yale, 1964-65; recipient Ralph E. Kharas Civil Liberties award, Syracuse U. Sch. Law, 1970, Owens award as Lawyer of Yr., 1984, Disting. prof. Santa Clara Univ. Faculty Senate, 1994-95, 2000 award for outstanding contbns. to cause of civil liberties Freedom of Thought Found.; named Disting. Vis. Prof. Krems Danube U., Vienna, 2001. Mem. Internat. Acad. Law Mental Health (mem. sci. com. 1997-99), Calif. Bar Assn. (first chmn. com. legal problems of aging), Assn. Am. Law Schs., Soc. Am. Law Tchrs. (dir. 1979-2004, pres. 1979-80, Visionary Activist for Equality, Access and Diversity Throughout Law and Soc. award 2000), AAUP (chpt. pres. 1962), NY Civil Liberties Union (chpt. pres. 1965, dir., v.p. 1966-70), Am. Acad. Polit. and Social Sci., Order of Coif (chpt. pres. 2004-), Justinian Honor Soc., Phi Alpha Delta (chpt. faculty adviser 1967-70) Achievements include having the university law clinic renamed the Katharine and George Alexander Law Center in 2004. *I think a primary purpose of law is the protection of individual rights. That requires disproportionate attention to the interests of groups not in the mainstream of our society.*

ALEXANDER, GERRY L., state supreme court justice; b. Aberdeen, Wash., Apr. 28, 1936; BA, U. Wash., 1958, JD, 1964; LLD (hon.), Gonzaga U., 2005. Bar: Wash. 1964, U.S. Supreme Ct. 2000. Pvt. practice, Olympia, Wash., 1964—73; judge Wash. Superior Ct., Olympia, 1973—85, Wash. Ct. Appeals Divsn. II, Tacoma, 1985—95; justice Wash. Supreme Ct., Olympia, 1995—2000, chief justice, 2000—. Lt. US Army, 1958—61. Named Disting. Alumnus, U. Wash., 2000. Mem.: ABA, Statute Law Com., Washington Cts. Hist. Soc., Bench-Bar-Press (chair), Puget Sound Inn of Ct. (pres. 1996), Thurston-Mason County Assn. (pres. 1973), Wash. State Bar Assn., Am. Judges Assn. Office: Temple of Justice PO Box 40929 Olympia WA 98504-0929 Office Phone: 360-357-2029. E-mail: j_g.alexander@courts.wa.gov.

ALEXANDER, GREGORY STEWART, law educator; b. Chgo., 1948; BA, Ill. U., 1970; JD, Northwestern U., 1973; postgrad., U. Chgo., 1974-75. Law clk. to chief judge U.S. Ct. Appeals, 1972-74; asst. prof. law U. Ga., 1975-78, assoc. prof., 1978-84; prof. Cornell U., Ithaca, NY, 1984—, A. Robert Noll prof. law, 2000—. Vis. prof. Harvard Law Sch., 1997—. Bigelow fellow U. Chgo., 1974-75; fellow Max-Planck Inst. (Germany), 1995-96, Ctr. for Advanced Study in Behavioral Scis., Palo Alto, Calif., 2003-2004, Inst. for Advanced Study, Stellenbosch, South Africa. Fellow Ctr. Advanced Study in Behavioral Scis., Stellenbosch, South Africa, 2004; mem. Am. Soc. Politics and Legal Philosophy, Am. Soc. Legal History. Office: Cornell U Law Sch Myron Taylor Hall Ithaca NY 14853 Home Phone: 607-277-3567; Office Phone: 607-255-3504. Business E-Mail: gsa9@cornell.edu.

ALEXANDER, HERBERT E., political scientist; b. Waterbury, Conn., Dec. 21, 1927; s. Nathan and Pearl (Shub) A.; m. Nancy Frances Greenfield, Dec. 5, 1953 (dec.); children: Michael David, Andrew Steven, Kenneth Bruce. BA, U. N.C., 1949; MA, U. Conn., 1951; PhD, Yale U., 1958. Asso. dir. adminstrn. officer money in politics research project U. N.C. at Chapel Hill, 1954-55; instr. Princeton U., 1956-58; dir. Citizens' Rsch. Found., Princeton, 1958-78, LA, 1978-98, dir. emeritus, 1998—; prof. polit. sci. U. So. Calif., 1978—, prof. emeritus, 1998—. Exec. dir. Pres.'s Com. on Campaign Costs, Washington, 1961-62; study commn. Gen. Assembly, State of Md., 2000, 04; cons. in field. Author: Money in Politics, 1972, Financing the 1976 Election, 1979, Financing the 1980 Election, 1983, Financing Politics, 1976, 2d edit., 1980, 3d edit., 1984 4th edit., 1992, Campaign Money, 1976; (with Brian A. Haggerty) Financing the 1984 Election, 1987; editor: Studies in Money in Politics, vol. 1, 1965, vol. 2, 1970, vol. 3, 1974, Comparative Political Finance in the 1980s, 1989, (with Rei Shiratori) Comparative Political Finance Among the Democracies, 1994, (with Monica Bauer) Financing the 1988 Election, 1991, Reform and Reality: The Financing of State and Local Campaigns, 1991, (with Anthony Corrado) Financing the 1992 Election, 1995, Spending in the 1996 Elections, 1999, Financing the 1996 Election, 1999 Served with AUS, 1946-47. Mem. Am. Polit. Sci. Assn., Study Commn. on Lobbyist Ethics, Maryland, 2000, Study Commn. on Public Financing of Campaigns, Maryland, 2004, Nat. Mcpl. League, Pi Sigma Alpha. Home: Unit 314 2904 N Leisure World Blvd Silver Spring MD 20906

ALEXANDER, JACQUELINE PETERSON, retired librarian; b. NYC, Aug. 28, 1928; d. Stephen Edgar and Anna (Boehm) Peterson; m. Lewis McElwain Alexander, Dec. 30, 1950; children: Louise, Lance. AB, Hunter Coll., 1949; MLS, U. R.I., 1972. Asst. editor Law of the Sea Inst. Procs., 1966—71; reference libr. U. R.I., Kingston, 1971; rsch. libr. Internat. Ctr. Marine Resource Devel., 1973—79, 1988—92; tech. libr., head books, periodicals divsn. Naval Underwater Sys. Ctr., Newport, RI, 1971—72; regional libr. U.S. Naval Edn. and Tng. Support Ctr., Groton, Conn., 1979—81; asst. chief acquisitions sect. Dept. Transp., 1983—84; libr. Edwards & Angell, Providence, 1984—88; pres. Offshore Cons., Inc., Wakefield, RI, 1992—96; ret., 1992. Pres. South County Sr. Citizens

Housing, 1974—82; active South Kingstown Citizens Adv. Bd., 1965—71; vol. AARP; vol. for tax aide, 1997—2003; vol. libr. Vis. Nurse Assn., 1992—95; bd. dirs., sec. South County Housing Improvement Found., 1966—83; bd. dirs. Washington County Vis. Nurse Assn., 1968—71. Mem.: R.I. Libr. Assn., Law Librs. New Eng., Internat. Assn. Marine Sci. Librs. and Info. Ctrs., Am. Assn. Law Librs., Beta Phi Mu. Home: 66 Beech Hill Rd Wakefield RI 02879-2524

ALEXANDER, JAMES H., industrial designer; b. Livermore, Calif., May 31, 1945; s. James and Erin Estelle (Livingston) Alexander; m. Pauline Ann Rosile, Oct. 10, 1970 (div. June 1985); m. Jeanne Marie Montgomery, Aug. 31, 2001; children: James Blake, John Harvey. AA in Liberal Arts, Valley Forge Mil. Jr. Coll., 1965; BA in Psychology, Case Western Res. U., Cleve., 1969; BFA in Indsl. Design, Cleve. Inst. of Art, 1976; Grad. in Indsl. Design, U. Mich., 1977. Tchr. Youngstown Bd of Edn., Ohio, 1969—72; auto. stylist Chrysler Corp., Highland Park, Mich., 1976—77; designer Richardson Smith Inc., Worthington, Ohio, 1977—78, Edward J. DeBartolo Corp., Youngstown, 1979—84; owner Alexander & Co., Hubbard, Ohio, 1984; co-owner, mgr. Lex Pub. Co., Hubbard, 1999—. Editor: Making Money, 1999. Recipient Cover Illustration award, Metal Progress Mag., 1976. Mem.: Union Pacific Hist. Soc., Indsl. Designers Soc. of Am., SAR. Achievements include design of first postal drive-through fac. Avocations: reading, railroad historian, landscaping, photography, sculpting.

ALEXANDER, JAMES PATRICK, lawyer, educator; b. Glendale, Calif., Oct. 14, 1944; s. Victor Elwin and Thelma Elizabeth (O'Donnell) A.; m. Jeanne Elizabeth Bannerman, June 10, 1967; children: Rene Leigh, Amy Lynne. AB, Duke U., 1966, JD, 1969. Bar: Ala. 1969. Assoc. Bradley, Arant, Rose & White, Birmingham, Ala., 1969-75, ptnr., 1975—. Adj. lectr. employment discrimination law U. Ala. Sch. Law, 1981-2003; exec. adv. com. spl. studies program U. Ala., Birmingham, 1991-93; mem. local rules adv. com. U.S. Dist. Ct. (no. dist.) Ala., 1997—. Trustee Ala. chpt. Nat. Multiple Sclerosis Soc. (vice-chmn. 1987-89, chmn. 1990-91); bd. dirs. Birmingham Civil Right Inst. 1998-2004. Fellow Coll. Labor and Employment Lawyers; mem. Birmingham Bar Assn., Ala. State Bar., ABA, Am. Arbitration Assn. (comml. arbitrator, employment disputes arbitrator), Labor Employment Rels. Assn. (Ala. chpt.), Sigma Nu, Duke Law Alumni Assn. (pres. Ala. chpt. 1989-90). Home: 4309 Altamont Rd Birmingham AL 35213-2407 Office: Bradley Arant Rose & White LLP 1819 5th Ave N Birmingham AL 35203 Office Phone: 205-521-8348. Business E-Mail: jalexander@bradleyarant.com.

ALEXANDER, JAMES WESLEY, surgeon, educator; b. El Dorado, Kans., May 23, 1934; s. Rossiter Wells and Merle Lydia Alexander; m. Maureen L. Strohofer; children: Joseph, Judith, Elizabeth, Randolph, John Charles, Lori, Molly. Student, Tex. Technol. Coll., 1951-53; MD, U. Tex., 1957; ScD, U. Cin., 1958-64; postgrad., U. Minn., 1966-67. Diplomate Am. Bd. Surgery, Am. Bd. Thoracic Surgery, lic. physician Ohio. Intern Cin. Gen. Hosp., 1957-58; resident U. Cin.-Cin. Gen. Hosp., 1958-64; mem. faculty Coll. Medicine, U. Cin., 1962-64, 66—, prof. surgery, 1975—, dir. transplantation div., dept. surgery, 1967-99, dir. surg. immunology lab., 1967—2000; dir. research Shriners Burns Inst., 1979-90; practice medicine and surgery Cin., 1966—; dir. Ctr. for Surg. Weight Loss, 2001—. Mem. staff U. Cin. Hosp., Bethesda Hosp., Christ Hosp., Good Samaritan Hosp., Jewish Hosp.; mem. study sect. NIH, 1983—87, 1989—93, chmn, 1990—93, mem. ad hoc com., 1990—. Author (with R.A. Good): Fundamentals of Clinical Immunology, 1977; mem. editl. bd. Annals of Surgery, 1975—, Jour. Burn Care and Rehab., 1979—99, Burns, Including Thermal Injury, 1985—98, Graft, 1998—, Jour. Parenteral and Enteral Nutrition, 1991—99, Nutrition, 1991—2000, Transplantation Sci., 1991—94, Jour. Trauma, 1998—2005; contbr. more than 670 articles to sci. jours. Capt. M.C. US Army, 1964—66. Mem.: ACS, AAAS, Am. Soc. Bariatric Surgeons, Mont Reid Surg. Soc., Shock Soc., Transplantation Soc., Surg. Infection Soc. (sec. 1981—84, pres.-elect 1985—86, pres. 1986—87), Soc. Univ. Surgeons, Ohio State Med. Assn., St. Paul Surg. Soc., Internat. Soc. Surgery, Halsted Soc., Am. Surg. Assn., Am. Soc. Parenteral and Enteral Nutrition, Am. Soc. Transplant Surgeons (sec. 1985—87, pres.-elect 1987—88, pres. 1988—89), Am. Burn Assn. (pres.-elect 1983—84, pres. 1984—85), Am. Assn. for Surgery of Trauma, Peruvian Acad. Surgery (hon.), Colombian Coll. Surgeons (hon.), Surg. Biology Club, Phi Eta Sigma, Alpha Epsilon Delta, Alpha Chi, Alpha Omega Alpha. Home: 757 Riverwatch Dr Crescent Springs KY 41017-4480 Office: 2123 Auburn Ave Ste 315 Cincinnati OH 45219 Office Phone: 513-558-6006, 513-585-2434. Business E-Mail: jwesley.alexander@uc.edu.

ALEXANDER, JANE (JANE QUIGLEY), actress, theater educator, writer; b. Boston, Oct. 28, 1939; d. Thomas Bartlett and Ruth (Pearson) Quigley; m. Robert Alexander, July 23, 1962 (div. 1969); 1 child, Jason; m. Edwin Sherin, Mar. 29, 1975. Student, Sarah Lawrence Coll., 1957—59, PhD (hon.), 1998; student, U. Edinburgh, 1959—60; LHD, Wilson Coll., 1984; LHD (hon.), Coll. Santa Fe, 1997; PhD (hon.), U. Pa., 1995, Duke U., Durham, NC, 1996; DFA (hon.), Julliard Sch., 1994, NC Sch. Arts, 1994, The New Sch. Social Rsch., 1996, Smith Coll., 1999, Pa. State U., 2000. Ind. TV, film and theatrical actress, 1962—; chmn. Nat. Endowment for Arts, Washington, 1993-97. Guest artist in residence Okla. Arts Inst., 1982, tchr. adult theatre workshop, 1984, 91, tchr. master class, 1990, Francis Eppes prof. Fla. State U., 2002-2004; bd. trustees Wildlife Conservation Soc., 1997—, Am. Bird Conservancy, 1995-98, The MacDowell Colony, 1997—, Arts Internat., 2000-2004. Author: (with Greta Jacobs) The Bluefish Cookbook, 7 edits., 1979-95; translator: (with Sam Engelstad) The Master Builder (Henrik Ibsen), 1978; Command Performance, An Actress in the Theater of Politics, 2000; appeared in prodns.: Charles Playhouse Boston, 1964-65, Arena Stage, Washington, 1965-68, 70—, Am. Shakespeare Festival; plays include Major Barbara, Mourning Becomes Electra, Merry Wives of Windsor, Stratford, Conn., summers 1971-72; Broadway prodns. include The Great White Hope, 1968-69 (Tony award 1969, Drama Desk award, Theatre World award), 6 Rms Riv Vu, 1972-73 (Tony nomination), Find Your Way Home, 1974 (Tony nomination), Hamlet, 1975, The Heiress, 1976, First Monday in October, 1978 (Tony nomination), Goodbye Fidel, 1980, Monday After the Miracle, 1982, Night of the Iguana, 1988, Shadowlands, 1990-91, The Visit, 1992 (Tony nomination), The Sisters Rosensweig, 1993 (Drama Desk award 1992-93, Tony award nomination, Obie award 1993), Honour (Tony nomination), 1998; also appeared in plays The Time of Your Life, Present Laughter, 1975, The Master Builder, 1977, Losing Time, 1980, Antony and Cleopatra, 1981, Hedda Gabler, 1981, Old Times, 1984, Approaching Zanzibar, 1989, Mystery of the Rose Bouquet, 1989, The Cherry Orchard, 2000, Mourning Becomes Electra, 2002, Rose and Walsh, 2003, Ghosts, 2003, What of the Night, 2005; appeared in films The Great White Hope, 1970 (Acad. award nomination), A Gunfight, 1970, The New Centurions, 1972, All the President's Men, 1976 (Acad. award nomination), The Betsy, 1978, Kramer vs. Kramer, 1979 (Acad. award nomination), Brubaker, 1980, Night Crossing, 1981, Testament, 1983 (Acad. award nomination), City Heat, 1984, Sweet Country, 1986, Square Dance, 1987, Glory, 1989, The Cider House Rules, 1999, Sunshine State, 2001, The Ring, 2002, Carry Me Home, 2003, Fur, 2006, Feast of Love, 2007; appeared in TV films Welcome Home Johnny Bristol, 1971, Miracle on 34th Street, 1973, Death Be Not Proud, 1974, This Was the West That Was, 1974, Eleanor and Franklin, 1976 (Emmy nomination), Eleanor and Franklin: The White House Years, 1977 (Emmy nomination, TV Critics Circle award), Lovey, 1977, A Question of Love, 1978, Playing for Time, 1980 (Emmy award 1980), Calamity Jane: The Diary of a Frontier Woman, 1981, Dear Liar, 1981, Kennedy's Children, 1981, In the Custody of Strangers, 1982, When She Says No, 1983, Mountainview, 1989, Daughter of the Streets, 1990, A Marriage: Georgia O'Keeffe and Alfred Stieglitz, 1991; appeared in TV spls. A Circle of Children, 1977, Blood and Orchids, 1986, Calamity Jane, 1984 (Emmy nomination), Malice in Wonderland, 1985 (Emmy nomination), In Love and War, 1987, Open Admissions, 1988, A Friendship in Vienna, 1988, Stay the Night, 1992, The Jenifer Estess Story, 2001; appeared in TV series: Law and Order/Spl. Victims Unit, 2000, (Emmy nomination); Intimate Portrait, Lifetime TV Biography, 1998, Warm Springs (TV), 2005 (Emmy award, outstanding supporting actress in a mini series or movie, 2005), Tell Me You Love Me, 2007. Recipient Achievement in Dramatic Arts award St. Botolph Club, 1979, Israel Cultural award, 1982, Western Heritage Wrangler award, 1985, Helen Caldicott Leadership award, 1984, Living Legacy award Women's Internat. Ctr., San Diego, 1988, Environ. Leadership award Eco-Expo, 1991, Muse award N.Y. Women in Film, 1993, Torch of Hope award, 1992, Lectureship award NIH, 1994, Houseman award The Acting Co., 1994, medal UCLA, 1994, Outer Critics Circle award Disting. Voice in Theatre, 1994, Helen Hayes award Am. Express Tribute, 1994, Women of Achievement award Anti-Defamation League, 1994, Margo Jones award, 1995, Mass. Soc. award, 1995, N.Am. Mont Blanc de la Culture award, 1995, Common Wealth award, 1995, Creative Coalition: Christopher Reeve First Amendment award, 1998, Outstanding Leadership for Advancement in Arts, People for Am. Way, 1998, Lifetime Achievement award Americans for Arts and U.S. Conf. Mayors, 1999, Harry S. Truman award for pub. svc., Independence, Md., 1999; Woman of Achievement Award, San Antonio, 2000, Dirs. Guild Am. award, 2002, Web of Life award High Falls Film Festival, 2005; named to Theatre Hall of Fame, 1993. Mem. AFTRA, SAG, Actors Equity Assn., Acad. Motion Picture Arts and Scis., Acad. Arts and Scis., Actors Fund. Avocation: birdwatching. Office: William Morris Agy c/o Samuel Liff 1325 Avenue of Americas New York NY 10019

ALEXANDER, JANET COOPER, law educator; b. 1946; BA in English Lit. with distinction, Swarthmore Coll., 1968; MA in English, Stanford U., 1973; JD, U. Calif., Berkeley, 1978. Bar: Calif. 1978, DC 1980, US Dist. Ct. Ctrl. Dist. Calif. 1978, US Dist. Ct. No. Dist. Calif. 1982, US Dist. Ct. Ea. Dist. Calif. 1985, US Supreme Ct. 1987. Jud. clk. to Hon. Shirley M. Hufstedler US Ct. Appeals 9th Cir., 1978—79; jud. clk. to Hon. Thurgood Marshall US Supreme Ct., 1979—80; assoc. Califano, Ross & Heineman, Washington, 1980—82, Morrison & Foerster, San Francisco, 1982—84, ptnr., 1984—87; assoc. prof. law Stanford Law Sch., Calif., 1987—94, prof. Calif., 1994—2002, Frederick I. Richman prof. Calif., 2002—, Justin M. Roach, Jr. faculty scholar Calif., 1998—2002; prin. investigator Stanford Ctr. on Conflict and Negotiation, 1994—2002. Vis. prof. Toin U. of Yokohama, Japan, 1998. Alumni coun. Swarthmore Coll., 2001—, exec. com., 2003—, co-chair coll. advisory and support com., 2003—, acting chair, 2003; leadership coun. Castilleja Sch., Palo Alto, Calif., 2002—, athletic coun., 2002—, sch. assn. bd., 2002—03, co-chair parent edn., 2002—03, lead parent rep., 2002—03. Mem.: Am. Assn. Law Schools (sections on civil procedure, fed. courts, women and the law). Office: Stanford Law Sch Crown Quadrangle 559 Nathan Abbott Way Stanford CA 94305-8610 Office Phone: 650-723-2892. Business E-Mail: jca@stanford.edu.

ALEXANDER, JASON (JAY SCOTT GREENSPAN), actor; b. Newark, Sept. 23, 1959; s. Alexander and Ruth Minnie (Simon) Greenspan; m. Daena E. Title, May 31, 1982;1 child, Gabriel. Student, Boston U., 1977-80. Artistic dir. Reprise!, N.Y.C. stage debut in Merrily We Roll along, Alvin Theatre, 1981; other theater appearances include America Kicks Up Its Heels, 1982, On Hold With Music, 1982, Fragments, 1982, Forbidden Broadway, 1983, The Rink, 1984, D, 1985, Personals, 1985-86 season, Broadway Bound, 1986-87 season, Jerome Robbins' Broadway, 1989 (Tony award for best performance by a leading actor in a musical), Accomplice, 1990, Light Up The Sky, 1990, Give 'Em Hell, Harry, 1993 (Drama-Loge award), The Producers (Los Angeles), 2003; stage dir., The God of Hell, 2006; film debut in The Burning, 1979; other film appearances include The Mosquito Coast, 1986, Brighton Beach Memoirs, 1986, Pretty Woman, 1989, Jacobs Ladder, 1989, White Palace, 1989, I Don't Buy Kisses Anymore, 1991, Coneheads, 1993, Sexual Healing, 1993, North, 1994, The Paper, 1994, Blankman, 1994; The Last Supper, 1995, Love! Valour! Compassion!, 1996, the Hunchback of Notre Dame, 1996, For Better or Worse, 1996, Dunston Checks In, 1996, Denial, 1998, Adventures of Rocky & Bullwinkle, 1999, On Edge, 2001, Shallow Hal, 2001, How to Go Out on a Date in Queens, 2003; TV films include Senior Trip, 1981, Rockabye, 1986, Favorite Son, 1988, Bye Bye Birdie, 1995, Cinderella, 1998, Love & Action in Chicago, 1998,; TV series: E/R, 1984-85, Everything's Relative, 1987, Seinfeld, 1990-98 (Emmy nomination, Supporting Actor - Comedy, 1993, 94), Duckman (voice only), 1994—97, Bob Patterson, 2001, Listen Up, 2004; guest appearances include Dream On, 1993 (Emmy nomination, Guest Actor - Comedy Series, 1994), Star Trek, Voyager, 1999, actor, dir. For Better or Worse, 1995.

ALEXANDER, JEREMIAH ROY, molecular biologist, researcher; BS in microbial, cellular, molecular biology, Ea. Ky. U., Richmond, 2007. Cert. air traffic contr. FAA/USAF, 1997. Air traffic contr. USAF, Minot AFB, ND, 1995—99, Prince Sultan AFB, Saudi Arabia, 1999. Sr. airman USAF, 1995—99. Decorated Ky. Svc. Ribbon Ky. Army N.G., Nat. Def. Svc. medal USAF, Armed Forces Expeditionary medal; recipient Poster award, Ky. Acad. Scis., 2006; grantee Lafuze scholar, Ea. U. Ky., 2006. Mem.: AAAS, Hon. Order Ky. Cols., Phi Sigma. Democrat. Achievements include research in genetic discoveries in environmental effects on heredity and health; molecular genetic assessment of the effects of urbanization on salamander populations in the greater Charlotte, North Carolina area. Avocations: weightlifting, running, reading, politics.

ALEXANDER, JESSICA ARONOW, anesthesiologist; b. Beaumont, Tex., May 19, 1957; MD, U. Tex. Health Sci. Ctr., 1984. Diplomate Am. Bd. Anesthesiology. Resident in anesthesiology Med. U. S.C., Charleston, 1984-87, fellow in obstet. anesthesiology, pain mgmt., 1987-88; staff anesthesiologist Cape Fear Valley Med. Ctr., Fayetteville, NC, 1989-98, Highsmith-Rainey Meml. Hosp., Fayetteville, 1988-98; pvt. practice Valley Anesthesia, P.A., Fayetteville, 1988-90; founding ptnr., sec. bd. dirs. Cumberland Anesthesia Assocs., P.A., Fayetteville, 1990-98; asst. prof. anesthesiology U. N.C., Chapel Hill, 1989-94; assoc. prof. divsn. anesthesia, symptom control and palliative care U. Tex. M.D. Anderson Cancer Ctr., Houston, 1998—2003; clin. prof. anesthesiology U. Tex. Health Sci. Ctr., San Antonio, 2003—. Lectr., author on dangers of nutraceuticals and on physician stress; owner art studio Alexander Studios. Contbr. articles to profl. jours.; exhibited art work in one-woman show, 2004. Active Fayetteville Area C. of C., 1988-98, Fayetteville Area Econ. Devel. Corp., 1996-98. Recipient 1st prize award Am. Soc. Anesthesiologists Art Exhbn., 1999, 2000. Mem. AMA, Am. Soc. Anesthesiologists, So. Med. Assn., N.C. Med. Soc., N.C. Soc. Anesthesiology (past pres.), Tex. Soc. Anesthesiologists, Tex. Med. Assn. (comms. com., legis. affairs com.). E-mail: jleak@houston.rr.com.

ALEXANDER, JIM R., social sciences educator; b. Gainesville, Tex., Aug. 16, 1946; s. Gordon Lee and Esther Ruby Alexander; m. Mona Sue Beeler, June 7, 1968; 1 child, Jason Fields. AA, North Ctrl. Tex. Coll., Gainesville, 1966; BA in Govt. and Bus. Adminstrn., East Tex. State U., Commerce, 1968, MA in Govt. and Bus. Adminstrn., 1969; PhD in Govt. and Pub. Adminstrn., Am. U., Washington, 1974. Prof., chair, dept. of history and govt. Tex. Woman's U., Denton, Tex., 1984—, chair dept. history and govt., 1984—, dir. Law Enforcement Mgmt. Inst. Tex., 1989—, spl. asst. to pres., 1995—2000. Elected city coun. mem. Denton City Coun., 1986—92; mem. exec. bd. North Ctrl. Tex. Coun. Govts., Arlington, 1989—93, pres. exec. bd., 1991—92; mem., bd. of trustees Denton Ind. Sch. Dist., Denton, Tex., 1993—, pres. bd. trustees, 1999—2000. Contbr. chapters to books, articles to profl. jours. Nat. del. Dem. Nat. Conv., NYC, 1980; conv. del. Tex. Dem. Party, 1974—84; apptd. mem. Governor's Criminal Justice Adv. Bd., Austin, Tex., 1981—83. Recipient Leadership award, Tex. Assn. Sch. Bds., 2004; fellow, Tex. Higher Edn. Coordinating Bd., 1986; Nat. Def. Edn. Act fellow, Am. U., 1969—72, Malone fellow, Coun. on U.S.-Arab Rels., 2006. Mem.: Leadership Summit Adv. Bd. (exec. com. 2007—), World Future Soc., Am. Soc. Pub. Adminstrn., Soc. Police Futurists Internat., Assn. Tex. Law Enforcement Educators (pres. 1978—79), Southwestern Assn. Criminal Justice Educators (pres. 1981—82), Acad. Criminal Justice Sci. (life; bd. dirs. 1982—85), Rotary (Paul Harris Fellow award 1988, 2002). Office: Dept History and Govt Texas Woman's Univ Denton TX 76204 Office Phone: 940-898-2133.

ALEXANDER, JOHN CHARLES, pharmaceutical executive, preventive medicine physician; b. Perth Amboy, NJ, Dec. 28, 1943; s. Charles John and Agnes (Maloney) A.; m. Margaret Ann Kohler, July 19, 1969; children: Laurel, Jennifer, Anna. BS, St. Francis Coll., Loretto, Pa., 1965; MD, St. Louis U., 1970; MPH, Johns Hopkins U., Balt., 1972. Intern Barnes Hosp./Washington U., St. Louis, 1970-71; resident in gen. preventive medicine State of Va./Med. Coll. Va., Richmond, 1974-76; clin. rsch. dir. Squibb Inst. Med. Rsch., Princeton, NJ, 1976—82, v.p. cardiovascular clin. rsch., 1982-86, sr. v.p. med. affairs, 1986-90; v.p. rsch. Bristol-Myers-Squibb Pharm. Rsch. Inst., Princeton, 1990-91; sr. v.p. med. rsch. Searle, Skokie, Ill., 1991-93, exec. v.p. med. rsch., 1993-99; pres. Daiichi Sankyo Pharma Devel., Edison, NJ, 1999—; chmn. bd. Daiichi Sankyo Inc., Parsippany, NJ; global head R&D Sankyo Co. Ltd., Tokyo, 2003—; also. bd. dirs. Chmn. bd. Daiichi Sankyo, Inc., Parsippany, NJ. Patentee in field. Lt. comdr. USN, 1972-74. Mem. Drug Info. Assn. (pres., bd. dirs.), Alpha Omega Alpha. Home: 86 Beech Hollow Ln Princeton NJ 08540-1235 Office: Daiichi Sankyo Pharma Inc 399 Thornall St Edison NJ 08837-2236 Home Phone: 609-924-9758; Office Phone: 732-590-5000. Business E-Mail: jalexander@daiichisankyo-us.com.

ALEXANDER, JOHN DAVID, JR., college administrator; b. Springfield, Tenn., Oct. 18, 1932; s. John David and Mary Agnes (McKinnon) A.; m. Catharine Coleman, Aug. 26, 1956; children: Catharine McKinnon, John David III, Julia Mary. BA, Southwestern at Memphis, 1953; student, Louisville Presbyn. Theol. Sem., 1953—54; PhD, Oxford U., Eng., 1957; LLD, U. So. Calif., Occidental Coll., 1970, Centre Coll. of Ky., 1971, Pepperdine U., 1991, Albertson Coll. Idaho, 1992; LHD, Loyola Marymount U., 1983; LittD, Rhodes Coll., 1986, Pomona Coll., 1996. Assoc. prof. San Francisco Theol. Sem., 1957-65; pres. Southwestern at Memphis, 1965-69, Pomona Coll., Claremont, Calif., 1969-91. Am. sec. Rhodes Scholarship Trust, 1981—98; mem. commn. liberal learning Assn. Am. Colls., 1966—69, mem. commn. instl. affairs, 1971—74; mem. commn. colls. So. Assn. Colls. and Schs., 1966—69; mem. Nat. Commn. Acad. Tenure, 1971—72; bd. dirs. Children's Hosp., LA, 1994—2000, Wenner-Gren Found. for Anthrop. Rsch., 1995—2007; trustee Tchrs. Inst. and Annuity Assn., 1970—2002, Woodrow Wilson Nat. Fellowship Found., 1978—99, Webbs Schs., Calif., 1995—2004, Seaver Inst., 1992—, Fellows of Soc. Phi Beta Kappa, 1993—, v.p., 1998—; trustee Emeriti Retirement Health Care Inc., 2004—; bd. dirs. Webb Schs. Calif.; bd. overseers Huntington Libr., 1991—. Editor: The American Oxonian, 1997-2000, History of the American Rhodes Scholarships in History of Rhodes Trust, The Goddess Pomona. Pres. Am. Friends of Nat. Portrait Gallery (London) Found., 2004—. Decorated comdr. Order Brit. Empire; named Disting. Friend of Oxford U., 2000; Rhodes scholar, Oxford U., 1955—57. Fellow AAAS; mem. Soc. Bib. Lit., Soc. Religion in Higher Edn., Phi Beta Kappa Alumni in So. Calif. (pres. 1974-76), Century Club, Calif. Club, Bohemian Club, Athenaeum (London) Phi Beta Kappa, Omicron Delta Kappa, Sigma Nu. Office: Pomona Coll 333 N College Way Claremont CA 91711-4429 Personal E-mail: a.cadalex@verizon.net.

ALEXANDER, JOHN KURT, history professor; b. Vancouver, Wash., Oct. 25, 1941; s. Eugene Victor and Marta T. Alexander; m. June Granatir, Dec. 29, 1973. BS in Edn. with honors, Western Oreg. U., Monmouth, 1964; MA in History, U. Chgo., 1965, PhD in History, 1973. From asst. prof. to prof. history U. Cin., 1969—81, Disting. tchg. prof., 2003—. Mem. U.S. Mint Citizens Coinage Adv. Com., 2005—. Author: Render Them Submissive, 1980, The Selling of the Constitutional Convention, 1990, Samuel Adams, 2002; assoc. editor Am. Nat. Biography, Oxford U. Press, 1989-99; contbr. articles to profl. jours. Appointed to US Mint's Citizens Coinage Adv. Com., 2005. Mem. Orgn. Am. Historians, Hist. Soc. Pa., Pa. Hist. Soc., Ohio Acad. History (Outstanding Tchr. award 2002), Soc. for Historians of Early Am. Republic. Home: 3410 Bishop St Cincinnati OH 45220-1831 Office: Univ Cin Dept History Ml 0373 Cincinnati OH 45221-0373 Office Phone: 513-556-2137. Business E-Mail: John.K.Alexander@uc.edu.

ALEXANDER, JOHN MACMILLAN, JR., chemistry professor; b. Columbia, Mo., Aug. 17, 1931; s. John Macmillan and Victoria (Holladay) A.; m. Betty Jo Linton, Aug. 1, 1953; children: Mary Jo, John Macmillan III, Frank Linton, James Holladay. BS, Davidson Coll., 1953; PhD, MIT, 1956. Research assoc. MIT, 1956-57; research chemist Lawrence Radiation Lab., Berkeley, Calif., 1957-63; assoc. prof. chemistry SUNY at Stony Brook, 1963-67, prof., 1968—96, leading prof., 1996—2007, rsch. prof., 2007—. Rscher. AEC-ARDA Dept. Energy, 1964—; rsch. collaborator Brookhaven Nat. Lab., 1964—, program adv. com. tandem Van De Graaff accelerator, 1977—83, rsch. collaborator E895 and PHENIX, 1997—; chmn. Gordon Rsch. Conf. on Nuc. Chemistry, 1966; chmn. exec. com. faculty senate SUNY at Stony Brook, 1969, chmn. dept. chemistry, 1970—72; mem. exec. com. Berkeley Superhilac Accelerator, 1975—78, 1985—87; vis. scientist Centre d'Etudes Nucléaires, Bordeaux, France, 1974; vis. prof. Centre d'Etudes Nucléaires-Gradignan et Institut de Physique Nucléaire, Orsay, France, 1978; program adv. com. Heavy Ion Rsch. Facility Oak Ridge Nat. Lab., 1986—87, SARA accelerator Institut des Sciences Nucléaires, Grenoble, France, 1988. Assoc. editor: Am. Chem. Soc. Monographs, 1968-69; contbr. articles to profl. jours. Recipient Great Amer. Home award Nat. Trust for Historic Preservation, 1993; Dupont teaching fellow, 1955-56, Sloan fellow, 1964-67, Guggenheim fellow Laboratoire de Chimie Nucléaire, Orsay, France, 1969-70. Fellow Am. Phys. Soc.; mem. Am. Chem. Soc. (chmn. divsn. nuclear chemistry and tech. 1988, vice chmn. 1987, nuclear chemistry award 1991), Phi Beta Kappa. Democrat. Achievements include research on radioactivity, high-energy nuclear reactions: fission, spallation and fragmentation; heavy ion reactions: elastic scattering, complete and incomplete fusion and reaction cross sections; splintering central collisions; energy thermalization mechanisms from low to relativistic energies; hot nuclei; energy and spin dissipation, evaporative deexcitation; fragmentation; emission lifetimes; nuclear equation of state; statistical and dynamical models; hadron correlations driven by collective flow, source size, emission times and jet physics. Office: SUNY Dept Chemistry Stony Brook NY 11794-3400 Home: 2 Linda Ln East Setauket NY 11733 Office Phone: 631-632-7904.

ALEXANDER, JOHN THORNDIKE, historian, educator; b. Cooperstown, NY, Jan. 18, 1940; s. Edward Porter and Alice Wagner (Bolton) A.; m. Maria Kovalak Hreha, June 13, 1964; children— Michal Porter, Darya Ann BA, Wesleyan U., Middletown, Conn., 1961; cert. regional specialization Russian Inst., Ind. U., 1963, MA, 1963, PhD, 1966. Asst. prof. U. Kans., Lawrence, 1966-70, assoc. prof., 1970-74, prof. history, 1974—. Fellow Inter-Univ. Com. on Travel Grants, 1964-65, Internat. Research and Exchanges Bd., 1971, 75, 96. Author: Autocratic Politics, 1969, Emperor of the Cossacks, 1973, Bubonic Plague in Russia, 1980, 2003, Catherine the Great, 1989 (Byron Caldwell Smith award for best book by a Kans. author pub. in 1987-88), reissued luxury edit., 1999; translator, editor: Platonov, Time of Troubles, 1970, Anisimov, Reforms of Peter the Great, 1993,

Anisimov, Empress Elisabeth, 1995. Recipient Balfour Jeffrey Higuchi Endowment Rsch. Achievement award, 1992. Mem. Am. Assn. for Advancement Slavic Studies, Brit. Study Group on 18th Century Russia, So. Conf. on Slavic Studies (ann. sr. scholar award 2001). Democrat. Roman Catholic. Avocation: sports. Home: 2216 Orchard Ln Lawrence KS 66049-2706 Office: U Kans Dept History Wescoe Hall Rm 3001 1445 Jayhawk Blvd Lawrence KS 66045-7590 E-mail: jatalex@ku.edu.

ALEXANDER, JON M., contractor, consultant; BA in Environ. Studies, U. Wash., Seattle, 1977. Pres. Sunshine Constrn., Seattle, 1983—. Green bldg. cons., Seattle, 1993—. Recipient Innovation in Conservation award, Built Green Pioneer award. Mem.: Built Green King and Snohomish Counties (mem. exec. bd. 2001—), NW EcoBuilding Guild (founder, treas. 1992—99). Home Phone: 206-782-4619; Office Phone: 206-782-4619. Home Fax: 206-782-4102. Personal E-mail: jonalex315@aol.com.

ALEXANDER, JONATHAN, cardiologist, consultant; b. NYC, Nov. 29, 1947; s. Josef and Hannah (Margolis) A.; m. Karen Deborah Einhorn, Aug. 8, 1971; children: Jessica Beth, Daniel Lewis, Benjamin Joel. BA, Harvard U., Cambridge, Mass., 1968; MD, Albert Einstein Coll. Medicine, 1973. MD. Intern, resident Yale-New Haven Hosp., 1973-76; fellow dept. cardiology Sch. Medicine Yale U., New Haven, 1976-78, asst. clin. prof. medicine, 1978-83, assoc. clin. prof., 1983-95, clin. prof., 1995—; attending physician West Haven Vets. Hosp., Conn., 1978—, New Milford Hosp., Conn., 1980, Danbury Hosp., Conn., 1978—, dir. cardiac rehab. unit and nuclear cardiology Conn., 1978—. Recipient Samuel Kushlan award Yale-New Haven Hosp., 1974, Revlon award 11th Internat. Congress Chemotherapy, 1983. Fellow: ACP, Found. for Cmty. Health Care, Conn. Hosp. Assn., Conn. chpt. Am. Coll. Cardiology (pres. 1993—96), Am. Coll. Cardiology (gov. Conn. 1993—96); mem.: Yale Cardiovascular Network. Jewish. Office Phone: 203-797-7155. Personal E-mail: jaheart1@aol.com.

ALEXANDER, JOSEPH KUNKLE, JR., physicist; b. Staunton, Va., Jan. 9, 1940; s. Joseph Kunkle and Charlotte (Harper) A.; m. Diana Lenore Titolo, Sept. 22, 1962; children: Kathryn, Stephen, David. BS in Physics, Coll. William and Mary, 1960, MA in Physics, 1962. Physicist Nat. Bur. Standards, 1960; research asst. Coll. William and Mary, Williamsburg, Va., 1960-62; physicist Goddard Space Flight Ctr., NASA, Greenbelt, Md., 1962-85, head planetary magnetospheres br., 1976-84; dep. chief scientist NASA, Washington, 1985-87, asst. assoc. adminstr. space sci. and applications, 1987-93; assoc. dir. space scis. Goddard Space Flight Ctr., NASA, Greenbelt, Md., 1993-94; dep. asst. adminstr. R&D EPA, Washington, 1994-98; dir. space studies bd. NAS/NRC, Washington, 1998—2005, sr. program officer, 2005—. Vis. scientist U. Colo., 1973-74; sr. policy analyst White House Office Sci. and Tech. Policy, Washington, 1984-85; assoc. chief Lab. Extraterrestrial Physics, 1985, acting dir. life scis. NASA, Washington, 1992-93; acting chief Lab. Extraterrestrial Physics, Goddard Space Flight Ctr., NASA, Greenbelt, Md., 1994. Contbr. articles to profl. jours. Mem. Am. Geophys. Union, Am. Astron. Soc., Internat. Astron. Union. Office: Nat Acad of Scis 500 Fifth St Washington DC 20001 Home Phone: 301-490-8783. Business E-Mail: jalexander@nas.edu.

ALEXANDER, JUDD HARRIS, retired paper company executive; b. Owatonna, Minn., Mar. 23, 1925; s. Mark Hastings and Veta Enola (Harris) A.; m. Theo Mary Paltzer, May 19, 1956; children: Morah Lee, Duncan McIndoe, Todd Stewart. BA, Carleton Coll., 1949, PhD (hon.), 2001; postgrad., Harvard U., 1967. Co-founder Nu-Bilt Co., Owatonna, dir., 1942-71; sec. in pres.'s office, salesman Marathon Corp., Rothschild, Wis., 1949-57; with Am. Can Co., Greenwich, Conn., 1957-82, v.p., gen. mgr. spl. products packaging, 1972-73, sr. v.p. group exec. packaging, 1974-75, sr. v.p. office of chmn., 1975-81, exec. v.p. paper sector, 1981-82; exec. v.p. James River Corp., Norwalk, Conn., 1982-89, ret., 1989; chmn. Paperboard Packaging Council, 1976-78, Can Mfrs. Inst., 1978-80, Solid Waste Coun. of Paper Industry, 1977-88. Adj. prof. environ. sci. SUNY, Syracuse, 1979-84. Author: In Defense of Garbage, 1993; contbr. articles to profl. and bus. jours., including Wall Street Jour., N.Y. Times, Industry Week. Trustee Carleton Coll., 1973-2000, Am. Shakespeare Theater, 1980-82; bd. dirs. New Eng. Legal Found., 1979-82, Norwalk (Conn.) Hosp., 1985-88, Ctr. for Advanced Studies U. Va., 1988—; chmn. bd. trustees Keep Am. Beautiful (bd. dirs. 1979-90), 1986-88. Decorated Bronze Star medal; Woodrow Wilson vis. fellow, 1975-82 Mem. Conn. Bus. Industry Assn. (bd. dirs. 1976-80, 85-89). Republican. Congregationalist.

ALEXANDER, JUDY LYNNE, investor; d. Richard M. and Ursula J. Scott; 1 child, Darbi Lynne Gilbert. CFO Calculated Industries, Inc., Carson City, Nev., 1978—; pres. Aspen Chelsea, Inc., Colo., 1998—; v.p. Believe Productions, Inc., Denver, 2000—. Real estate investor, 1976—. Pres. Fred and Judy Alexander Found., Lake Tahoe, Nev., 1992—2006; mem. nat. coun. JazzAspen, 2002—06. Named Citizen of Yr., Vail Valley Found., 1999. Mem.: Vail Valley Found. Friends of Vail (assoc.), Game Creek Club Vail (assoc.), Aspen Mountain Club (assoc.), PGA West Golf Club (assoc.). Republican. Avocations: skiing, golf, hiking. Office: Calculated Industries Inc 4840 Hytech Dr Carson City NV 89706 Home Phone: 775-588-2155; Office Phone: 775-885-4900.

ALEXANDER, KAREN, museum staff member; m. Walter Alexander. Vice chmn. bd. trustees Art Inst. Chgo., vol. Dept. European Decorative Arts and Sculpture and Ancient Art. Office: Art Inst Chgo 111 S Michigan Ave Chicago IL 60603

ALEXANDER, KATHARINE VIOLET, lawyer; b. NYC, Nov. 19, 1934; d. George Clifford and Violet (Jambor) Sziklai; m. George Jonathon Alexander, Sept. 6, 1958; children: Susan Katina, George J. II. Student, Smith Coll., Geneva, 1954-55; BA, Goucher Coll., Balt., 1956; JD, U. Pa., 1959; student specialized courses, U. Santa Clara, 1974-76. Bar: Calif. 1974, U.S. Dist. Ct. (no. dist.) Calif. 1974, U.S. Ct. Appeals (9th cir.) 1974; cert. criminal lawyer Calif. State Bar Bd. Legal Specialization. Research dir., adminstr. Am. Bar Found., Chgo., 1959-60; lectr. law San Jose (Calif.) State U., 1972-74; sr. atty. Santa Clara County, San Jose, 1974—2000, ret., 2000. Editor: Mentally Disabled and the Law, 1961; contbg. author: The Aged and the Need for Surrogate Management, 1969-70, Jury Instructions on Medical Issues, 1965-67. Community rep. Office Econ. Opportunity Com., Syracuse, N.Y., 1969-70. Mem. AAUW, Food and Wine Inst., Calif. Bar Assn., Santa Clara County Bar Assn. (trustee 1981-82), Calif. Attys. for Criminal Justice (bd. govs. 1988-92), Jr. League, Anthropology and Stanford Museum of Arts. Presbyterian. Achievements include having Santa Clara Law School's Center named the Katharine and George Alexander Law Center. Avocations: stock market, gourmet, travel. Home and Office: 1030 The Alameda San Jose CA 95126 Personal E-mail: Katharine_Alexander@mail.com.

ALEXANDER, KEITH B., federal agency administrator, career military officer; b. Syracuse, NY; BS, U.S. Mil. Acad., 1974; MBA, Boston U.; MS in Physics and Electronic Warfare, Naval Post Grad. Sch.; grad., U.S. Army Command Staff Coll., Nat. War Coll. Commd. 2d lt. U.S. Army, 1974, advanced through grades to lt. gen., 2003; platoon leader, B Co., 2nd Bn. 81st Armor, 1st Armored Divsn. U.S. Army Europe & 7th Army, Germany, 1975—76, asst. S-4 (logistics), later S-4, 511th mil. intelligence bn. 66th mil. intelligence group, 1976—77, comdr. field office, 511th mil. intelligence bn. 66th mil. intelligence group, 1977—78; electronic warfare staff officer 525th mil. intelligence group U.S. Army, Ft. Bragg, NC, 1979, comdr. 336th Amy Security Agy. Co., 319th mil. intelligence bn. (corps electronic warfare intelligence) 52th mil. intelligence group, 1979—81, asst. S-3 (ops.) 525th mil. intelligence group, 1981; ops. officer, later chief intelligence electronics warfare systems task force, later chief concepts & studies divsn. US Army Intelligence Ctr & Sch., Ft. Huachuca, Ariz., 1983—85; dep. dir. intelligence & electronics warfare master plan spl. task force, intelligence staff officer, Office Dep. Chief of Staff for Intelligence U.S. Army, Washington, 1986—88, S-3 ops. later exec. officer, 522nd mil. intelligence bn. 2nd armored divsn. Ft. Hood, Tex., 1988—90; asst. chief of staff, G-2 (intelligence), 1st armored divsn. US Army Europe & Seventh Army & Operation DESERT SHIELD/STORM Saudi Arabia, 1990—91; comdr. 204th mil. intelligence bn. US Army Europe & Seventh Army, Germany, 1991—93; chief, army intelligence initiative, Office of the Dep. Chief of Staff for Intelligence U.S. Army, Washington, 1994—95, exec. officer 522d mil. intelligence brigade Ft. Bragg, NC, 1995—97; dep. dir. for intelligence The Joint Staff, Washington, 1997—98; dir. intelligence (J-2) U.S. Ctrl. Command, MacDill AFB, Fla., 1998—2001; comdr. US Army Intelligence & Security Command U.S. Army, Ft. Belvoir, Va., 2001—03, dep. chief of staff (G-2) Washington, 2003—05; dir. Nat. Security Agy./Ctrl. Security Svc., Ft. George E. Meade, Md., 2005—. Decorated Disting. Svc. medal, Def. Superior Svc. medal with oak leaf cluster, Legion of Merit with four oak leaf clusters, bronze star, Meritorious Svc. medal with 4 oak leaf clusters, Air medal, Army Commendation medal, Army Achievement medal,. Office: Nat Security Agy 9800 Savage Rd Fort George G Meade MD 20755

ALEXANDER, KENT B., lawyer; b. Atlanta, Nov. 7, 1958; BA in Polit. Sci. magna cum laude, Tufts U., 1980; JD, U. Va., 1983. Bar: Ga. 1983. Assoc. Long & Alridge, Atlanta, 1983-85; asst. U.S. atty. for no. dist. Ga., U.S. Dept. Justice, Atlanta, 1985-92, U.S. atty., 1994-97; of counsel, ptnr. King & Spalding, Atlanta, 1992-94, ptnr., 1997-99; sr. v.p., gen. counsel Emory Univ., 2000—. Co-founder Hands On Atlanta; pres. Am. Jewish Com., Atlanta. Office: Emory Univ 401 Administration Bldg Atlanta GA 30322-0001

ALEXANDER, KURT See BIG BOY

ALEXANDER, (ANDREW) LAMAR, senator, former secretary of education, governor; b. Maryville, Tenn., July 3, 1940; s. Andrew Lamar and Geneva Floreine (Rankin) A.; m. Leslee Kathryn Buhler, Jan. 4, 1969; children: Andrew, Leslee, Kathryn, Will. BA in Latin Am. Hist., Vanderbilt U., 1962; JD, NYU, 1965. Bar: Tenn. 1965. Law clk. to Hon. John Wisdom U.S. Ct. Appeals (5th cir.), New Orleans; assoc. Fowler, Rountree, Fowler & Robertson, Knoxville, 1965; legis. asst. to Senator Howard Baker, 1967-68; exec. asst. to Bryce Harlow, White House Congl. Liaison Office, 1969-70; ptnr. Dearborn and Ewing, Nashville, 1970-76; gov. State of Tenn., Nashville, 1979-87; chmn. Leadership Inst. Belmont Coll., Nashville, 1987-88; pres. U. Tenn., 1988-91; sec. US Dept. Edn., Washington, 1991-93; counsel Baker, Donelson, Bearman & Caldwell, Nashville, 1993-98; pvt. practice Nashville, 1999—2001; US Senator from Tenn., 2003—. Mem. Pres.'s Task Force on Federalism; chmn. Nat. Govs. Assn., 1985-86, Pres.'s Commn. on Ams. Outdoors, 1985-87; co-director Empower Am., 1994-95; Goodman vis. prof. practice of pub. svc. Harvard U., 2001-02; mem. com. budget, US Senate, com. energy and natural resources, com. fgn. affairs, com. health, edn., labor and pensions, spl. com. aging. Author: Steps Along the Way, 1986, Six Months Off, 1988, We Know What To Do, 1995; co-editor: The New Promise of American Life, 1995, Friends, Japanese and Tennesseans: A Model of U.S.-Japan Cooperation, 1986, Lamar Alexander's Little Plaid Book, 1998. Mgr. Winfield Dunn for Gov. Campaign, 1970, chief transition, 1970-71; Rep. nominee for Gov. of Tenn., 1974; chmn. Rep. Exch. Satellite Network, 1993-95; Rep. Presdl. candidate, 1995-96. Recipient Nat. Disting. Svc. to Edn. award Burger King, 1988, James B. Conant award Edn. Commn. of the States, 1988, Disting. State Leadership award Am. Assn. State Colls. and Univs., 1989, Teddy Roosevelt award Nat. Coll. Athletic Assn., 1993, Conservationist of Yr. Tenn. Conservation League, Disting. Congressional award Nat. League Cities, 2003, Krieble Freedom and Democracy award Free Congress Found., 2004; NYU Law Sch. Root-Tilden scholar. Fellow (sr.) Hudson Inst.; mem. Phi Beta Kappa. Republican. Presbyn. Office: US Senate 302 Hart Senate Ofc Bldg Washington DC 20510 Office Phone: 202-224-4944, 615-736-5129. Office Fax: 202-228-3398, 615-269-4803.*

ALEXANDER, LESLIE LEE, professional sports team owner; b. NYC, June 30, 1943; m. Nanci Alexander (div. 2002); 1 child, Jodi. BS, NYU, 1965; JD, Western State Coll., 1977. With Lawrence Kotkin Assocs.; owner, pres. Houston Rockets, 1993—; owner Women's NBA Houston Comets, 1996—; former owner Arena Football League Houston Thunder-Bears. Bd. dirs. First Marblehead Corp., 1995—. Bd. dirs. Humane Soc. US; founder City Clutch Found., Houston, 1995—. Named one of Forbes Richest Ams., 2006. Mem.: Calif. State Bar Assn. Office: Houston Rockets 1510 Polk St Houston TX 77002*

ALEXANDER, LEWIS MCELWAIN, retired geographer, educator; b. Summit, NJ, June 15, 1921; s. Harry Louis and Laura (Stryker) A.; m. Jacqueline Peterson, Dec. 30, 1950; children: Louise Anne, Lance Stryker. AB, Middlebury Coll., Vt., 1942; MA, Clark U., 1948, PhD, 1949. Instr. geography Hunter Coll., 1949-50; asst. prof. geography Harpur Coll., SUNY, 1950-57, asso. prof., 1957-60; prof. geography U. RI, Kingston, 1960-80, 83-91, prof. emeritus, 1991—, chmn. dept., 1960-80, dir. marine affairs program, 1968-80, dir. Ctr. for Ocean Mgmt. Studies, 1983-89; cons. State Dept., 1963-80; dir. Office of Geographer, 1980-83. Exec. dir. Law of Sea Inst., 1965-73, mem. exec. bd., 1973-82, 85-91; mem. ocean affairs adv. com. Dept. State, 1973-80; dep. dir. Pres.'s Commn. on Marine Sci., Engring. and Resources, 1967-68; cons. Nat. Coun. for Marine Resources and Engring. Devel., 1969-70; mem. adv. com. on law of sea Interagy. Law of Sea Task Force, 1973-80; mem. ocean policy com., ocean affairs bd. NRC, 1973-76; maritime boundary cons. Equatorial Guinea, 1977, Guinea, 1984-85, N.S. Province (Can.), 1994-2000, Govt. of Bahrain, 1998-2001, Govt. of Thailand, 2001-05. Author: World Political Patterns, 2d edit, 1963, Offshore Geography of Northwestern Europe, 2d edit, 1966, The Northeastern United States, 2d edit., 1976, Regional Cooperation in Marine Science, 1979, Navigational Restrictions within the New Los Context: Geographical Implications for the United States, 1986; mem. editl. bd. Ocean Devel. and Internat. Law Jour., 1973-99, Ocean Mgmt., 1973-87, Marine Policy, 1976-98; editor: (with J. Charney) International Maritime Boundaries, 3d edit., 1998. With USAAF, 1942—46. Recipient Ann. award Sea Grant Assn., 1979; Office Naval Rsch. grantee, 1958, 62, 66, 76. Mem. Assn. Am. Geographers (Honors award 1980), Am. Geog. Soc., Am. Soc. Internat. Law, Marine Tech. Soc., Cosmos Club. Home: 66 Beech Hill Rd Peace Dale RI 02879-2524 Office: U RI Washburn Hall Kingston RI 02881

ALEXANDER, LORA KAY, writer, composer; b. Campton, Ky. d. Dewey Raymond and Ada Ann (Bankenship) Tyra; m. James Kenneth Alexander; children: Kristi Eve, Eva Wynne, James Kenneth Jr. Student in video/films, Writers Digest Sch., Anacontes, Wash., 1985. Spl. writer Wolfe County News, Campton, Ky., The Times, Kettering, Oakwood; adminstrv. asst. Shawnee Kitchens, Centerville, Ohio; staff writer Blue Mountain Arts; owner Gift Shop, Roses in the Rain, 2001; prodr. and owner Country Unplugged, TV show; pres. Roses in the Rain Music Pub., Nashville; teller, sales Front Sill Nat. Bank, Gallatin, Tenn., 2007—. (films, ednl.) White Tigers, 1985; Wobbles World, 1985; Deer Daniel, 1985; author: (novels) By Appointment Only, 1985 (commonwealth publication, 1992), Until We're Free, 1986 (commonwealth publication, 1992), Roses In The Rain, 1987 (commonwealth publication, 1992), Until We're Free, 2005, (booklet) Strength of the Towers (award Pres. Bush); composer: (songs) Our People are Free (letter and award from Pres. Carter for song.), (video) She Won't Come Close/Trailblazer, 1992 (Video, 1992), (CD) Roses In the Rain (with Reba McEntire's band). Achievements include design of the greeting card line named Lovelines; development of 1000 songs; recorded and sang with Reba McIntire's band; two music videos; 10-45rpm records; CD sales. Avocations: cooking, running, psychology. E-mail: lorakay10@juno.com.

ALEXANDER, LYNN See MARGULIS, LYNN

ALEXANDER, MARJORIE ANNE, artist, consultant; b. Chgo., Apr. 16, 1928; d. Alexander and Nancy Rebecca (Cordrey) Roberts; m. Harold Harman Alexander, June 13, 1948; children: Jeffrey C., Cassandra J., Peter B., Timothy C., Patrick J. Student, Wilson Jr. Coll., 1945-47; MFA in Painting, U. Ill., 1968, MA in Art Edn., 1972. cert. tchr. K-12, Ill., Minn. Graphic artist Barry Martin Studio, Rumson, NJ, 1963-65; instr. painting, drawing U. YMCA, Champaign, Ill., 1968-72; teaching asst. U. Ill., Urbana, 1968-72, rsch. assoc., 1972-76; instr. art Champaign High Sch., 1973-75, Urbana High Sch., 1976-80, Concordia Acad., St. Paul, 1982-84, U. Minn., Mpls., 1984-87, design, housing and apparel artist in residence St. Paul, 1984-88; craft cons. and educator tech. asstance program USAID, OAS, U. Minn., Kingtson, Jamaica, 1986—. Design cons. J.A.M. Corp., Mpls., 1988—; tech. cons. OAS, Kingston, 1990-91, Blandin Found. grantee, Minn., 1989—; rsch. and product devel. agrl. unilization rsch. inst., 1992-95; tech. cons. Zabbaleen Paper Project, Assn. for the Protection of the Environment, Cairo, 1993—, St. Lucia Paper project Weyerhauser Found., 1994—, paper project YMCA, Jamaica, W.I., 1997—; co-curator Paper Trivia and Treasure exhibit Goldstein Mus. Design/U. Minn., St. Paul, 2000; guest lectr. Chonbuk Nat. U. Republic of Korea, 2005-06, Chonbok Nat. U., 2006; invited artist Oesterreiches Papierniagher Mus. Austria, 2006, Mus. Der Stadt, Deggendorf, Germany, 2007. Exhibits include Leopold-Hoesch Mus., Doren, Germany, 1999, Mus. Santa Maria Della Scala, Siena, Italy, 2003, Augsburg Coll. Mpls., 2003, Hist. Mus. Jeongju, South Korea, 2004, Palos Verdes Art Ctr., Calif., 2007, others; traveling exhibit, Bavaria, Germany, Geneva; work chosen for inclusion 1996 Internat. Calendar Papierfabak Schfufelen Lenningen, Germany; invited guest profl. designer Fashion Fair, Joenju, Korea, 2006-07; represented in permanent collections Imadate, Fukui, Japan, U. Ill., Weisman Art Mus., U. Minn., So. Cross U., NSW, Australia, Montclair Art Mus., NJ, Am. U, Cairo, Sori Arts Ctr., Jeonju, Mus. Louvre It or Leavie It, Mpls., others; co-author: Selected Papers, 1994, Handcrafted paper and Paper Products Made from Indigenous Plant Fibers, 1997; contbr. articles to profl. jours, columns to newspaper Vestry mem. St. John's Episcopal Ch., Champaign, 1975-78, St. Matthew's Episcopal Ch., St. Paul, 1989—. Recipient Celebrity award, Minn. State Fair, 1984, book First award, 1986, Honorable mention, 3d On/Off Paper Nat., Wis., 1984, 1st prize cmty. fine art exhibit, St. Paul, Minn., 2002, 2003; grantee, Blandin Found., U. Minn., 1989—90, OAS, 1990—91, Agrl. Utilization Rsch. Inst., 1992—95, Weyerhauser Found., 1997, Minn. Arts Bd., 1999. Mem.: Internat. Assn. Hand Papermakers and Paper Artists (pres. 2003—05), Nat. League Am. Penwomen (state v.p. 1994—96, Minn. art chair 2002—), Friends of Dard Hunter Paper Mus. (com. chair 1990—95, adv. bd. 2001—). Episcopalian. Avocations: swimming, cooking, theater, travel.

ALEXANDER, MARK A., energy executive; BBA, Univ. Notre Dame. Positions through sr. v.p. corp. develop. Hanson Industries, 1989—96; exec. vice-chmn., CEO Suburban Propane Partners LP, Whippany, NJ, 1996, pres., CEO, 1996—2005, CEO, 2005—. Mem. exec. com. Nat. Propane Gas Assn.; pres. Coalition for Fair Competition; chmn. rsch. & develop. adv. com. Propane Edn. & Rsch. Council. Office: Suburban Propane 1 Suburban Plz 240 Rt 10 W Whippany NJ 07981-0206*

ALEXANDER, MARK C., law educator, policy advisor; b. Aug. 5, 1964; m. Amy Alexander; 3 children. BA, Yale U., 1986, JD, 1992. Bar: Calif., NJ, DC, US Supreme Ct. Legis. asst. to Senator Howard M. Metzenbaum, 1986—88; issues dir. Com. to Re-elect Senator Edward M. Kennedy, 1988, Bill Bradley for Pres., 1999—2000, Senator Barack Obama for Pres., Washington, 2007—; law clk. to Chief Judge Thelton E. Henderson No. Dist. Calif., 1992—93; litig. assoc. Gibson, Dunn & Crutcher, San Francisco, 1993—95; asst. prof. Seton Hall U. Sch. Law, Newark, 1996—98, assoc. prof., 1998—2003, prof., 2003—. Lectr. West Bar Review, 1997; vis. scholar Yale Law Sch., New Haven, 2003; delegate US-Japan Leadership Program, 2005—06, fellow, 2006—; mem. selection com. Leadership NJ, 2005, 07; lectr. in field. Contbr. articles to law jours. Bd. dirs. Shoot for the Stars, Inc., 1994—96, St. James Pre-Sch., Montclair, NJ, 1999; v.p. Yale Law Sch. Exec. Com., 2005—. Named Student Bar Assn. Prof. of Yr., 1996—97; grantee Fulbright Scholar, Universidad Carlos III, Madrid, 2003—04. Mem.: Black Law Students Assn. Office: Seton Hall U Sch Law One Newark Ctr Newark NJ 07102 Office Phone: 973-642-8523. Office Fax: 973-642-8194. E-mail: alexanma@shu.edu.*

ALEXANDER, MARTIN, microbiologist, educator; b. Newark, Feb. 4, 1930; s. Meyer and Sarah (Rubinstein) A.; m. Renee Rafaela Wulf, Aug. 26, 1951; children: Miriam H., Stanley W. BS, Rutgers U., 1951; MS, U. Wis., 1953, PhD, 1955. Asst. prof. Cornell U., Ithaca, NY, from 1955, now L.H. Bailey prof. Advisor agys. fed. govt., Washington, 1965—, UN agys., Kenya, France, Italy, 1963—; mem. coms. Nat. Acad. Sci., Washington, 1971—; cons. Author: Microbial Ecology, 1971, Introduction to Soil Microbiology, 1977, Biodegradation and Bioremediation, 1994; editor: Advances in Microbial Ecology, 5 vols., 1977-81. Recipient Indsl. Research 100 award, 1968, Fisher award Am. Soc. Microbiology, 1980, Superior Svc. award USDA, 1989. Fellow Am. Acad. Microbiology, AAAS, Internat. Inst. Biotechnology, Am. Soc. Agronomy (Soil Sci. award 1964) Home: 301 Winthrop Dr Ithaca NY 14850-1736 E-mail: ma59@cornell.edu.

ALEXANDER, MICHAEL ALLEN, pediatrician, educator; b. Riverside, Calif., Aug. 12, 1947; s. Alvin Wesley and Mabel Bernice Alexander; m. Michele Y. Yermack, Aug. 14, 1971; children: Alexia Michele, Aaron Michael, Adam Mikael. MD, U. Va., Charllotesville, 1969—72. Lic. pediatrics Am. Bd. Pediat., 1977, cert. pediatric rehab. medicine Am. Bd. Phys. Medicine & Rehab., 2003. Resident Ohio State U., Columbus, 1972—76, asst. prof. pediat. & phys. medicine, 1976—79; med. dir. D.T. Watson Rehab. Hosp. for Children, Sewickley, Pa., 1979—86; chief rehab. Alfred I du Pont Hosp. for Children, Wilmington, Del., 1986; prof. pediat. and phys. medicine and rehab. Thomas Jefferson U., Phila., 1987—. Editor: (textbook) Pediatric Rehabilitation Medicine. Dir. Nat. Patient Safety Found., DC, 2001—05; mem., asst. pres. Med. Soc. Del., Wilmington, 1995—2001. Recipient Rosenberg award for tech. in dissabled children, United Cerebral Palsy Found., 2003. Fellow: Am. Acad. Cerebral Palsy (assoc.; trustee, pres. 1989—94). Roman Cath. Office: Alfred I du Pont Hosp Children 1600 Rockland Rd Wilmington DE 19808 Home Phone: 302-239-9752.

ALEXANDER, MILES JORDAN, lawyer; b. Reading, Pa., Nov. 20, 1931; s. Abe Alexander and Sarah (Gold) Fidlow; m. Elaine Eve Barron, May 29, 1955; children: Kent, David, Michael, Paige. BA in Polit. Sci. with honors, Emory U., Atlanta, 1952; LLB cum laude, Harvard U., Cambridge, Mass., 1955. Bar: Ga. 1955, DC 1977. Assoc. Kilpatrick & Stockton, Atlanta, summers 1954-55; tchg. fellow Harvard U., Cambridge, Mass., 1957-58; assoc. Kilpatrick Stockton LLP, Atlanta, 1958-63; chmn. Kilpatrick & Stockton LLP, Atlanta, 1996—. Lectr. P.L.I., Internat. Trademark Assn., Am. Law Inst., ABA Internat. Franchise Assn., other seminars on trademarks and unfair competition, antitrust, franchising, dispute resolutions and litig. tactics; guest lectr. on trademark law NYU, U.Ga., Ga. State Law Sch., also bd. visitors; bd. visitors Emory U.; chmn. US trademark pub. adv. com. Emory U., 2000-03. Editor-in-chief: The Trademark Reporter, 1978-80; contbr. numerous articles to jours. in trademark field. Mem. City of Atlanta Ethics Bd., chmn., vice-chmn., 1980-92, Emory U. and Harvard Law Sch. Alumni Funds; legal counsel to Mayor Maynard

Jackson, 1974-82, 89-93; chmn. City of Atlanta Lic. Rev. Bd., 1976-79; former pres. Am. Jewish Com.; mem. Friends of Morehouse Coll.; adv. bd. Family Outreach Ctr.; mem. adv. coun. J. Thomas McCarthy Inst. Intellectual Property and Tech. Law, 2001--. Capt. USAF, 1955-57. Recipient Human Rels. award Anti-Defamation League, 1997, Disting. Alumni award Emory U., 2000, ADL Lifetime Achievement award, 2006, Justice Robert Benham Lifetime Achievement Cmty. Svc. award, 2007, State Bar Ga., 2007. Fellow Am. Bar Found., Am. Coll. Trial Lawyers; mem. ABA, Internat. Trademark Assn. (counsel 1997-2000, chmn. trademark pub. com.), Ga. Bar Assn. (1st recipient Intellectual Property Sect. Lifetime Achievement award 2006), Ga. State Bar Assn. (former chmn. antitrust sect., advisor to legal counsel 1997—), Atlanta Bar Assn., Lawyers Club Atlanta, Internat. Trademark Assn. (lectr., bd. dirs. 1980-82, rev. commn. 1986, legal counsel 1987-2000, Pres.'s Lifetime Achievement award 2003), Am. Law Inst. (adv. com. restatement of law of unfair competition 1986-95), 191 Club (bd. dirs.), Atlanta City Club (chmn. bd.), Commerce Club, Standard Club, Old War Horse Lawyers Club , Phi Beta Kappa. Avocations: reading, sports. Office: Kilpatrick Stockton LLP 1100 Peachtree St NE Ste 2800 Atlanta GA 30309-4530 Office Phone: 404-815-6410. Business E-Mail: malexander@kilpatrickstockton.com.

ALEXANDER, NANCY A., information technology manager, consultant; b. Kansas City, Kans., Mar. 31, 1957; d. Carl Glenn and Norma Louise Hanks; m. Steven Dale Alexander, May 20, 1981; 1 child, Anne Louise. AS in Computer Info. Systems summa cum laude, Kansas City C.C., 1989; BS in Computer Info. Systems with highest honors, Friends U., Wichita, Kans., 1999, MS in Mgmt. Info. Systems, 2001. Sec., a/c schedule control Trans World Airlines, Inc., Kansas City, Mo., 1976—79, coord. scheduling and planning group, 1979—80, planner, facilities and equipment engring., 1980—81, master planner, facilities and equipment programs, 1981—82, mgr., facilities and equipment programs, 1982—83; office mgr., info. tech. dir. Steven D. Alexander, Chtd., Overland Park, Kans., 1983—2004. Faculty adv. bd. Kansas City (Kans.) C.C., 1988—90; cons. Profl. Support, Shawnee, Kans., 1983—; real estate investor, 1978—; real estate agent, cons., 2002—. Software developer Legal Billing and Analysis System, 1989; author: Think of Your Future, 1992. Troop leader Girl Scouts Am., Shawnee, 1988—92; county coun. rep., project leader 4-H, Olathe, Kans., 1994—97, judge, 1995—97; youth group leader Master's Cmty. Ch., Kansas City, Kans., 1999—2001. Avocations: travel, racquetball, swimming, painting.

ALEXANDER, PATRICK BYRON, hospital administrator; b. Texas City, Tex., May 11, 1950; s. Alvin Wesley and Mabel Bernice Alexander; m. Linda Graham, May 7, 1975. BA in Econs., George Mason Coll., U. Va., 1972; MLA, Oklahoma City U., 2006. Publs. dir. George Mason U., Fairfax, Va., 1973-75, U. Okla. Health Scis. Ctr., Oklahoma City, 1975-78, Presbyn. Hosp. Inc., Oklahoma City, 1978-79; mng. dir. Okla. Symphony Orch., Oklahoma City, 1979-88; exec. dir. Allied Arts Found., 1988-92, Okla. Zool. Soc., 1992—2001; exec. dir. advancement Oklahoma City U., 2001—03; planned giving dir. The Children's Ctr., 2003—. Bd. dirs. Okla. Philharm. Found. Recipient Gov.'s award for excellence in arts, 1987, Okla. Fundraiser of Yr. award, 1991; Kerr Found. fellow, 1981. Mem.: English Speaking Union, Rotary Club, Econ. Club of Oklahoma City. Home: 1515 Glenwood Ave Oklahoma City OK 73116-5206 Office: The Childrens Ctr 6800 NW 39th Expy Bethany OK 73008 E-mail: palexander@tccokc.org.

ALEXANDER, PAUL RICHARD, illustrator; b. Richmond, Ind., Sept. 3, 1937; s. Fred and Olive (Phillips) A. BFA, Wittenberg U., 1959; BFA in Illustration, Art Ctr. Coll. Design, 1967. Archtl. delineator Forest Studios, Chgo., 1961-64; advt. illustrator Pitt Studios, Cleve., 1967-70; freelance illustrator Chgo., 1970-76, Mendola Artist's Rep., NYC, 1976—. Contbg. artist: (anthologies) Tomorrow and Beyond, 1970s, Infinite Worlds—The Fantastic Visions of Science Fiction Art, 1997, Spectrum Sci. Ficton Annual, Vol. 1-4, 1990. With USAR, 1960-66. Mem. Mensa. Episcopalian. Avocations: art, architecture, classical music, railfan. Home and Office: 1380 Oaktree Dr Greenville OH 45331-2730 Office Phone: 937-547-9568.

ALEXANDER, PETER HOUSTON, artist; b. LA, Feb. 27, 1939; s. Richard Henry and Marion Celeste (Pluard) A.; m. Clytie Patricia Moore, June 8, 1964; children: Clytie Hope, Julia Pebrina. One man shows: Nicholas Wilder Gallery, L.A., 1970, Robert Elkon Gallery, N.Y.C., 1970, Art in Progress, Munich, 1973, U. Calif., Irvine, 1975, Calif. State U., Long Beach, 1976, Rico Mizuno, L.A., 1980, James Corcoran, L.A., 1981, Charles Cowles Gallery, N.Y.C., 1982, Arco Ctr., L.A., 1983, L.A. Mcpl. Art Gallery, 1983, Cirrus Gallery, L.A., 1983, Fuller Goldeen Gallery, San Francisco, 1984, James Corcoran Gallery, Santa Monica, Calif., 2989, Barbara Mathes Gallery, N.Y.C., 1994, Stremmel Gallery, Reno, 1997, Franklin Parrasch Gallery, N.Y.C., 2004, others; group shows include Seattle Art Mus., 1968, Mus. Modern Art, N.Y.C., 1969, 83, 84, Walker Art Ctr., Milw., 1969, Whitney Mus. Am. Art, N.Y.C., 1969, Mus. Contemporary Art, Chgo., 1970, Locksley/Shea Gallery, L.A., 1971, Calif. State U., Long Beach, 1975, 78, San Francisco Mus. Modern Art, 1976, La Jolla (Calif.) Mus. Contemporary Art, 1981, Art Ctr. Coll. Design, Pasadena, Calif., 1981, Bklyn. Mus., 1983. Centre Pompidou, Paris, 2006; retrospective exhbn. Orange County Mus. Art, Newport Beach, Calif., 1999; represented in permanent collections: Walker Art Ctr., Mpls., Mus. Modern Art, N.Y.C., La Jolla Art Mus., Vancouver (Can.) Mus. Art, Los Angeles County Mus. Art, Corcoran Gallery Art, Washington, Ft. Worth Art Mus., San Francisco Mus. Modern Art, Bklyn. Mus., Newport Harbor Art Mus., Walker Art Ctr., Fogg Mus., Harvard U., others. Served with USMC, 1961-66. Nat. Endowment for Arts artist fellow. Address: 1811 16th St Santa Monica CA 90404-4403 Business E-Mail: peter@peteralexander.com.

ALEXANDER, RALPH WILLIAM, JR., physics professor; b. Phila., May 17, 1941; s. Ralph William and Gladys (Robin) A.; m. Janet Erdien Bradley, Sept. 4, 1965; children: Ralph III, Margaret. BA, Wesleyan U., Middletown, Conn., 1963; PhD, Cornell U., Ithaca, NY, 1968; postdoctoral study, U. of Freiburg, Fed. Republic Germany, 1968-70. From asst. to assoc. prof. physics U. Mo., Rolla, 1970-80, prof., 1980—, chmn. dept., 1983-92. Contbr. articles to profl. jours. Mem. Am. Phys. Soc., Assn. Am. Physics Tchrs. Office: U Mo Dept Physics Rolla MO 65409-0640 Home Phone: 573-364-1512; Office Phone: 573-341-4796. Business E-Mail: ralexand@umr.edu.

ALEXANDER, RICHARD ELMONT, lawyer; b. Yellow Springs, Ohio, Dec. 14, 1924; s. Joseph Arthur and Charlotte (Gunckel) Alexander. Student, U. Dayton, 1942—43, Carnegie Inst. Tech., 1943—44, student, 1946—47; JD, U. Chgo., 1950. Bar: Ohio 1951, U.S. Ct. Customs and Patent Appeals 1955, Ill. 1956, U.S. Dist. Ct. (no. dist.) Ill. 1958, U.S. Patent Office 1958, U.S. Dist. Ct. (ea. dist.) Calif. 1968, U.S. Supreme Ct. 1971, U.S. Ct. Appeals (4th, 7th and 9th cirs.) 1975, U.S. Ct. Appeals (2d cir.) 1977, U.S. Ct. Appeals (1st cir.) 1980, U.S. Ct. Appeals (D.C. cir.) 1982. Patent atty. Gen. Motors Corp., Washington, 1953—55; assoc. Wilkinson, Huxley, Byron & Hume, Chgo., 1955—58; ptnr. Alexander & Slater, Chgo., 1958—59, Dawson, Tilton, Fallon, Lungmus & Alexander, Chgo., 1959—67, Alexander & Speckman, Chgo., 1967—74; prin. Richard E. Alexander, Chgo., 1975—81; ptnr. Alexander & Zalewa, Chgo., 1981—84, Alexander, Unikel, Bloom, Zalewa & Tenenbaum, Ltd., 1984—89, Alexander, Zalewa, Liss & Orloff, Ltd., 1989—91, Dickinson, Wright, Moon, Van Dusen & Freeman, 1991—. Editor: Meditions of Andrew Morehouse, 1952. Chmn. Inst. Clin. Social Work, Chgo., 1981—84; trustee Episc. Charities, Chgo., 1982—88, v.p., 1984—88, Jo Daviess County Bd., 2002—03; bd. dirs. Great Books Found., 1960, St. Leonard's House, Chgo., 1979—87, v.p., 1980—82. With US Army, 1944—46. Decorated Purple Heart. Mem.: ABA, Chgo. Bar Assn., U.S. Trademark Assn. (editl. bd. 1965—77), Chgo. Patent Law Assn., Sigma Alpha Epsilon. Episcopalian.

ALEXANDER, ROBERT GARDNER, lawyer; b. Madison, Wis., May 19, 1949; s. Charles Kohl and Jean (Gardner) A.; m. Karen Lynn Kaminski, Sept. 30, 1989; children: Elizabeth Jean, Sarah Lynn, Rebecca Ann. BA, U. Wis., 1971, JD, 1976; ML in Taxation, DePaul U., 1984. Bar: Wis. 1976, U.S. Dist. Ct. (we. dist.) Wis. 1976, U.S. Dist. Ct. (ea. dist.) Wis. 1978, U.S. Tax Ct. 1982, U.S. Ct. Appeals (7th cir.) 1983. Rsch. atty. U. Wis., Madison, 1976-77; atty. McLario Law Offices, Menomonee Falls, Wis., 1978-87, Alexander & Klemmon, S.C., Wauwatosa, Wis., 1987—. Mem. ABA, Nat. Acad. Elder Law Attys., Wis. State Bar, Milw. Estate Planning Coun., Nat. Assn. Estate Planning Couns. (bd. dirs., accredited estate planner, estate planning law specialist), Ea. Wis. Planning Giving Counsel, Phi Kappa Phi. Republican. Avocations: music, art, sports, philosophy. Office: Alexander & Klemmer SC Ste 304 2675 N Mayfair Rd Wauwatosa WI 53226-1305 Office Phone: 414-476-5020. E-mail: bob@alexander-klemmon.com.

ALEXANDER, ROBERT JACKSON, economist, educator; b. Canton, Ohio, Nov. 26, 1918; s. Ralph S. and Ruth (Jackson) A.; m. Joan O. Powell, Mar. 26, 1949; children: Anthony, Margaret. BA, Columbia U., NYC, 1940, MA, 1941, PhD, 1950. Asst. economist Bd. Econ. Warfare, 1942, Office Inter-Am. Affairs, 1945—46; mem. faculty Rutgers U., 1947—, prof. econs., 1961—89, prof. emeritus, 1989—. Mem. Pres.-elect Kennedy's Latin Am. Task Force, 1960-61 Author 46 books including Juan Domingo Peron: A History, 1979, Romulo Betancourt and the Transformation of Venezuela, 1982, Bolivia: Past, Present and Future of Its Politics, 1982, Biographical Dictionary of Latin American and Caribbean Politics, 1988, Juscelino Kubitschek and the Development of Brazil, 1991, International Trotskyism 1929-85, 1991, The ABC Presidents, 1992, The Bolivarian Presidents, 1994, The Presidents of Central America, Mexico, Cuba and Hispaniola, 1995, Presidents, Prime Ministers and Governors of the English Speaking West Indies and Puerto Rico, 1997, The Anarchists in the Spanish Civil War, 1999, International Maoism in the Developing World, 1999, Hava de la Torre Man of the Millennium: His Life, Ideas and Continuing Relevance, 2001, A History of Organized Labor in Cuba, 2002, History of Organized Labor in Brazil, 2003, History of Organized Labor in Argentina in English Speaking West Indies, 2003, History of Organized Labor in Uruguay and Paraguay 2005 Nat. bd. League Indsl. Democracy, 1955—; nat. exec. com. Socialist Party-Social Dem. Fedn., 1957-66; bd. dirs. Rand Sch. Social Sci., 1951-56; exec. com. Open Door Student Exch., 1970-94. Decorated officer Order Condor of the Andes Bolivia Mem. Am. Econ. Assn., Latin Am. Studies Assn., Mid. Atlantic Coun. Latin Am. Studies (v.p. 1986-87, pres. 1987-88), Coun. Fgn. Rels., Interam. Assn. Democracy and Freedom (chmn. N.Am. com. 1970-87), Phi Gamma Delta. Home: 944 River Rd Piscataway NJ 08854-5504 Office: Rutgers U Dept Econs New Brunswick NJ 08903 *I have sought to extend the bounds of knowledge through research and writing, and to pass on to my children and students not only what I have learned, but also, hopefully, some idea of how to behave in a civilized manner.*

ALEXANDER, RODNEY M., congressman; b. Jonesboro, La., Dec. 5, 1946; m. Nancy Sutton; children: Ginger, Rod, Lisa. Attended, La. Tech. U., 1965. Ins. agent; mem. La. Ho. Reps., 1987—2002, US Congress from 5th La. dist., 2003—. Mem. Jackson Parish, La. Police Jury, 1970—85, pres., 1978—85. With USAF, 1965—71. Named Legis. of Yr., La. Rural Health Assn., 1997. Republican. Baptist. Office: US Ho Reps 316 Cannon Ho Office Bldg Washington DC 20515-1805 Mailing: Monroe Dist Office Ste B 1900 Stubbs Ave Monroe LA 71201 Office Phone: 202-225-8490, 318-322-3500. Office Fax: 318-322-3577, 202-225-5639.*

ALEXANDER, ROY, public relations executive, writer; b. Asheville, NC, Feb. 3, 1928; s. William Roy and Ruth (Upshaw) A. PhB, Northwestern U., 1954. Mng. editor Daily Northwestern, 1951-52; assoc. editor Food Retailing, 1951-55; dir. pub. relations Mid-States Corp., 1952-53; editor Splty. Salesman, 1953-56, Mobile Homes mag., 1953-54; account exec. Philip Lesly Co., 1956-58, sr. v.p. NYC, 1958—62; pres. Alexander Co., NYC, 1962—2004, Taggart & Alexander, NYC, 1993—. Mgr. N.Y. product publicity for Wurlitzer Co.; pub. relations counsel to Grad. Sch. Sales Mgmt. and Mktg., Lincoln Logs Ltd., Maleck Group, Barter Advantage, Inc., Mantis Mfg. Co., Huntingdon Valley, Pa.; Z-Flex, Manchester, N.H., Sales and Mktg. Mgmt., Sturm, Ruger & Co., Southport, Conn. Writer, exec. producer: (motion picture) The Greening of Augusta; dir.: (pub. edn. program) Iron Mountain Stoneware; creator: (pub. edn. program) W.Va. Coal Assn.; designer, creator (communications and promotion program) Nat. Pest Control Assn; author: Direct Salesman's Handbook, 1958, Mehdi: Story of Metlife's Top Salesman, 1977, Duke Medical Center's Ricer's Guide, 1984, Climbing the Corporate Matterhorn, 1985, Power Speech: Your Quickest Route to Success, 1986, Taking Your Company Public, 1990, Commonsense Time Management, 1992, More Mehdi: Everything Is Possible, 2000, Secrets of Closing Sales, 7th edit., 2004; editor Mktg. Times, 1970-80. Served with AUS, 1946-49; feature editor Armed Forces Press Service, 1948-49. Address: 430 E 20th St Ste 5C New York NY 10009-8203 Office Fax: 212-420-7768. Personal E-mail: 113streetman@msn.com. *My guiding principles: (1) Do something even if it's wrong - percentages favor the activist. (2) Don't waste words or time; both are in finite supply. (3) All generalizations are false, including these. (4) Assume most people will fail their responsibilities and plan accordingly. (5) Avoid all medication; solve health problem with diet and exercise. (6) Work is a chance to find yourself. (7) Never forget: The market economy makes it all possible.*

ALEXANDER, SETH, investment company executive; m. Cristina Alexander. Grad., Yale U., 1995. Dir. Yale U. Investment Office, New Haven; pres. MIT Investment Mgmt. Co., Cambridge, 2006—. Office: MIT Investment Co E48-200 77 Massachusetts Ave Cambridge MA 02139-4307 Office Phone: 617-253-6083. E-mail: seth.alexander@mit.edu.

ALEXANDER, SHAUN, professional football player; b. Florence, Ky., Aug. 30, 1977; m. Valerie Alexander, May 18, 2002; 1 child, Heaven. BS in Mktg., U. Ala., 1999. Running back Seattle Seahawks, 2000—. Co-author (with Cecil Murphey): Touchdown Alexander: My Story of Faith, Football, and Pursuing the Dreams, 2006. Founder The Shaun Alexander Found., 2000—. Named Offensive Player of Yr., AP, 2005, Best NFL Player, ESPY award, 2006; named to Nat. Football Conf. Pro Bowl Team, 2003—05, NFL All-Pro Team, 2005; recipient NFL MVP award, AP, 2005, Best Record Breaking Performance (38 Yards), ESPY award, 2006. Office: Seattle Seahawks 11220 NE 53rd St Kirkland WA 98033

ALEXANDER, SHELDON, psychology educator; b. NYC, July 16, 1930; s. Saul and Sylvia Alexander; m. Donna Delores Rudig, Aug. 13, 1960; children: Joanne, Janice, Steven. BA, CUNY, 1952; PhD, U. Rochester, 1958. Grad. asst. U. Rochester, NY, 1952—57, instr. NY, 1955—57; USPHS postdoctoral rsch. fellow U. Ill., Champaign-Urbana, 1957—59, asst. prof., 1959—60; assoc. prof. So. Ill. U., Carbondale, 1960—67; health scientist adminstr. NIH, Bethesda, Md., 1967—73; dept. chmn. Wayne State U., Detroit, 1973—83, prof. psychology, 1973—2006, prof. emeritus, 2006—. Mem. exec. bd. Ctr. for Peace and Conflict Studies, Detroit, 1989—; mem. adv. bd. Fraser Ctr. for Workplace Issues, Detroit, 1999—. Co-author: (book chpts.) Altruism, Narcissism, Comity, 1999, Changing Employment Relations, 1995. Mem.: APA, SPSSI, SPSP, Mid-western Psychol. Soc., Sigma Xi, Phi Beta Kappa. Office: Wayne State U Psychology Dept 5057 Woodward Detroit MI 48202 Office Phone: 313-577-5247. E-mail: sheldon.alexander@wayne.edu.

ALEXANDER, SUE, writer; b. 1933; Student, Drake U., Des Moines, Iowa, 1950—52, Northwestern U., Evanston, Ill., 1952—53. Writer. Author: Small Plays for You and a Friend, 1973, Nadir of the Streets, 1975, Peacocks Are Very Special, 1976, Witch, Goblin and Sometimes Ghost, 1976, Small Plays for Special Days, 1977, Marc the Magnificent, 1978, More Witch, Goblin and Ghost Stories, 1978, Seymour the Prince, 1979, Finding Your First Job, 1980, Whatever Happened to Uncle Albert? and Other Puzzling Plays, 1980, Witch, Goblin and Ghost in the Haunted Woods, 1981, Witch, Goblin and Ghost's Book of Things to Do, 1982, Nadia the Willful, 1983, Dear Phoebe, 1984, World Famous Muriel, 1984, Witch, Goblin and Ghost Are Back, 1985, World Famous Muriel and the Scary Dragon, 1985, Lila on the Landing, 1987, There's More-Much More, 1987, America's Own Holidays, 1988, World Famous Muriel and the Magic Mystery, 1990, Who Goes Out on Halloween?, 1990, Sara's City, 1995, What's Wrong Now, Millicent?, 1996, One More Time, Mama, 1999, Behold the Trees, 2001. Home and Office: 6846 McLaren Ave West Hills CA 91307-2525 E-mail: sue@sue-alexander.com.

ALEXANDER, SUSAN H., lawyer, pharmaceutical executive; BA, Wellesley Coll., Mass.; JD, Boston U. Ptnr. Hinckley, Allen & Snyder and Fine & Ambrogne; counsel Cabot Corp., 1995—2001; gen. counsel IONA Technologies, 2001—03; sr. v.p., gen. counsel, corp. sec. PAREXEL Internat. Corp., 2003—06; exec. v.p., gen. counsel, corp. sec. Biogen Idec Inc., Cambridge, Mass., 2006—. Office: Biogen Idec Inc 14 Cambridge Ctr Cambridge MA 02142

ALEXANDER, WILLIAM HERBERT, business educator, former construction executive; b. Harrisburg, Pa., Apr. 17, 1941; s. Wallace Hale and Jeannette Kauffman (Hackenberger) A.; m. Marion Elizabeth Carey, Nov. 30, 1963; children: Charles, Elizabeth, Robert, Kathryn. BS, U.S. Mil. Acad., 1963; MBA, U. Pitts., 1969; D of Pub. Svc. (hon.), Harrisburg C.C., Pa., 1992. Registered profl. engr., Pa. Commd. 2d lt. U.S. Army, 1963, advanced through grades to capt., 1968; platoon leader, co. comdr. Kitzingen, Germany, 1963-66; capt., co. comdr. Officer Candidate Regiment, Ft. Belvoir, Va., 1966-67; staff officer, engr. constrn. battalion Cu Chi, Vietnam, 1968; resigned, 1968; project mgr. H.B. Alexander & Son, Inc., Harrisburg, 1970-77, chmn., 1977-94; dir. Pa. Blue Shield, Mchts. & Businessmen's Mut. Ins. Co., 1985—97; dir. family bus. programs Wharton Sch. U. Pa., 1988-94, mng. dir. Sol. C. Snider Entrepreneurial Ctr. Wharton Sch., 1994-98; chair Wharton Family Controlled Corp. Program, 1998—2002; dir. Gelsinger Health Sys., Danville, 1997—. Pres. Capital Region Econ. Devel. Corp., 1987—88; chmn. Hershey Trust Co., 1997—98; lectr. Mgmt. Dept. Wharton Sch. U. Pa., Phila., 1998—; vis. lectr. Stanford U., 2005. Bd. dirs. AAA Ctrl. Penn Auto Club (chmn. 1991-93); pres. Tri County United Way, 1979-80, Ams. for Competitive Enterprise System, 1981-82; bd. dirs. Milton Hershey Sch., 1989-2002, chmn., 1997-98; chmn. Harrisburg Area C.C. Found., 1981-92. Decorated Bronze Star; recipient Whitney award for tchg. excellence undergrad. divsn., Wharton Sch., U. Pa., 2005. Mem. ASCE, Pa. Soc. Profl. Engrs. (Engr. of Yr. in Ctrl. Pa. 1986), Harrisburg C. of C. (bd. dirs., chmn. 1982-83), Harrisburg Rotary (pres. 1981-82), Beta Gamma Sigma, Delta Mu Delta. Presbyterian (elder). Home: 16 Wagner St Hummelstown PA 17036-9113 Office: 428 Vance Hall 3733 Spruce St Philadelphia PA 19104-6301 Business E-Mail: alexwh@wharton.upenn.edu.

ALEXANDER, WILLIAM WOODWARD, JR., military officer; b. Charlottesville, Va., Aug. 17, 1946; s. William Woodward and Elizabeth Dunavant Alexander; m. Hannelore Brigitte Keller, Feb. 20, 1986. Grad., Fishburne Mil. Sch., East Tenn. State U., 1968; M in Mid. East Studies, U. Kans. Pres. Fishburne Mil. Sch., Va. Sec. Assn. Mil. Colls. and Schs. of US; bd. dirs. Artisan Ctr. Va. Decorated Disting. Svc. medal US Army, Silver Star medal, Bronze Star medal with V device, Meritorious Svc. medal with oak leaf cluster, Joint Svc. Commendation medal, Army Commendation medal. Avocations: travel, shooting sports. Office: Fishburne Mil Sch 225 S Wayne Ave Waynesboro VA 22980

ALEXANDRA, ALLISON MELISSA, artist, writer, educator; BA with honors, U. Calif.-Berkeley, 1987; student, Acad. Art U., 2005—. Cert. acupressure practitioner Acupressure Inst., 1996, hypnotherapist Inner Quest Awareness Ctr., 1996. Graphic asst. LA Parent Mag., 1988, East Bay Express, Oakland, Calif., 1988; art tchr. for emotionally challenged teens Berkeley Acad., Calif., 1990; freelance graphic artist Berkeley, 1995—96, Oakland, 1995—96; instr. Kaplan Ednl. Ctrs., El Paso, Tex., 1998—99; counselor Life Healing Ctr., Sante Fe, 2000; art tchr., asst. mgr. Santa Fe Children's Mus., 2000—01; freelance illustrator, designer, writer Tuscon, Ariz., 2004—. Freelance graphic artist. Exhibitions include Annual Cmty. Art Exhibit, Oakland, 1994—95, Las Cruces, 1999, one-woman shows include Oakland, 1996, exhibited in group shows at Artists So. N.Mex., Las Cruces, 1998, We. Nat. Parks Assn. Bldg., Tuscon, Ariz., 2004, Joel D. Valdez Main Pub. Libr., Tucson, Ariz., 2004, Academy Art U., San Francisco, 2006, Rose Portrait, 1996, digital illustration, Reflections, 2003; contbr. illustrations to Sierra Club Canyon Echo; editor: Mandana Newsletter, 1996. Vol. tutor San Fernando Valley Child Guidance Clinic, Northridge, Calif., 1982—83; vol. art/natural sci. floors Oakland Mus., 1998; vol. graphic designer Santa Fe (N.Mex.) Vipassan Sangha, 2000, Our Town, Tuscon, 2003; vol. Santa Fe Children's Mus., 2000—01. Co-recipient Courtyard Design Illustration award, Southwestern Grad. Coll., 1996. Mem.: Portrait Soc. Am., Graphic Artists Guild, Soc. Children's Books, Writers & Illustrators, Phi Theta Kappa. Avocations: cooking, music, hiking, travel. Office Phone: 925-324-9335. Home Fax: 925-932-6053. Personal E-mail: allisonalexandra@msn.com.

ALEXANDRATOS, SPIRO DIONISIOS, chemistry professor, dean; b. NYC, Dec. 11, 1951; m. Olga Pantos; 1 child, Jonathan. BS, Manhattan Coll., 1973; PhD, U. Calif., Berkeley, 1977. Sr. rsch. chemist Rohm and Haas Co., Phila., 1977-81; from asst. prof. to assoc. prof. U. Tenn., Knoxville, 1981-92, prof. chemistry, 1993-2000, Paul and Wilma Ziegler prof. chemistry, 2000-01; univ. dean for rsch. CUNY, 2001—03, prof. chemistry Hunter Coll., 2001—. Collaborating scientist U. Tenn./Oak Ridge Nat. Lab., 1998-2001. Holder 12 patents in field; mem. editorial adv. bd. Reactive and Functional Polymers, Separation Science and Technology, Solvent Extraction and Ion Exchange. Recipient Hoechst-Celanese Rsch. award, 1993, R&D 100 award R&D Mag., 1994, 2004, Tech. Achievement award Lockheed-Martin, 1999. Mem. Am. Chem. Soc. (chmn. divsn. indsl. engring. chemistry 1993-94, chmn. subdivsn. separation sci. 1991-92, councilor 2005—, assoc. editor Jour. of Indsl. and Engring. Chemistry Rsch.), Gordon Rsch. Conf. Reactive Polymer (chmn. 1995-97), Sigma Xi, Phi Beta Kappa (cert. merit 1993). Personal E-mail: alexsd1@gmail.com.

ALEXANDRE, KRISTIN KUHNS, public relations executive, writer; b. Dayton, Ohio, July 15, 1948; d. James Edward and Faith (Colgan) Kuhns; m. DeWitt Loomis Alexandre, 1988; children: James Andrew, Cynthia Lenox Banks. BA, Sweet Briar, 1968. Editor C.I.T. Finance Corp., NYC, 1970-73; newscaster Channel 5 News, NYC, 1973-74, Channel 13 News, NYC, 1974-75; editor Champion Internat., NYC, 1975-76; copy editor House Beautiful, NYC, 1975-76; pub. rels. officer Economic Devel. Adminstrn. Puerto Rico, NYC, 1976-80; pres. Kristin Alexandre Pub. Rels., NYC, 1980—. Prodr., host www.thenewgentleman.com. Author: The Perfect Gentleman. The Secrets Rich Girls Use to Choose the Classiest Guys. Trustee Friends Clarence Dillo Libr. Mem. New York Jr. League. Home: PO Box 367 Far Hills NJ 07931-0367 Home Phone: 908-295-8092. Personal E-mail: cowshorses@aol.com.

ALEXANDRIDIS, PASCHALIS, chemical engineer, educator; arrived in US, 1989; Degree in Chem. Engring., Nat. Tech. U., Athens, Greece, 1989; PhD, MIT, Cambridge, Mass., 1994. Cert. profl. engr., Greece, 1990. Rsch. fellow Lund U., Sweden, 1994—96; from asst. prof. to prof. SUNY, Buffalo, 1997—2003, prof., 2003—. Vis. assoc. prof. Tokyo U. Sci., 2001. Editor: (book) Mesoscale Phenomena in Fluid Systems, 2003, Amphiphilic Block Copolymers: Self-Assembly and Applications, 2000; contbr. chapters to books, over 150 articles to profl. jours. Recipient Career award, NSF, 1999, Inst. Lectr. award, Japan Rsch. Inst. Material Tech., 2001, Exceptional Scholar award, SUNY, 2002, Chancellor's Excellence in Tchg. award, 2006, Applied Sci. prize, Bodossaki Found., 2005. Mem.: AIChE (chair Area 1C interfacial phenomena 2004—07), Am. Soc. Engring. Edn. (Dow Outstanding New Faculty award 1999), Soc. Plastics Engrs., Am. Chem. Soc., Tau Beta Pi (named Eminent Eng. 2004), Sigma Xi (Young Investigator award 2002). Achievements include 10 patents in field. Office: Univ Buffalo SUNY Dept Chem and Biol Engring Buffalo NY 14260-4200 Office Phone: 716-645-2911 2210. Business E-Mail: palexand@eng.buffalo.edu.

ALEXANDRIN, JULIE RICHMOND, special education educator, consultant; d. John Andrew and Jane Anderson; life ptnr. Ilana Lyn Schreiber, June 26, 2005; children: Lucia Ross, Elsa Josephine. PhD, U. Conn., Storrs, 2001. Asst. prof. Ea. Conn. State U., Windham, Conn., 1999—2001; spl. edn. program dir., asst. prof. St. Joseph Coll., West Hartford, Conn., 2001—. Self-employmed edn. cons., Storrs, 1995—. Author: (text) Study Guide For Gargiulo's For Special Education in Contemporary Society, (ednl. manual) Schooling Without Walls: A Curriculum For Transitioning To Adulthood; contbr. articles to profl. jours., chapters to books. Mem. planning bd. Conn. Multicultural Conf., 2002—06; chpt. pres. Nat. Assn. Multicultural Edn., Conn., 2003—; adv. bd. LifeChoice Donor Svcs., Conn.; vol. Mansfield Pub. Schs., Mansfield, 2000—; scout leader Girl Scouts Am., Mansfield, Conn., 2001—; bd. mem. Conn. Chpt. Coun. Exceptional Children, Conn., 2004—05; bd. dirs. Educators with Disabilities Caucus, 2002—04. Grantee, Hartford Consortium Higher Edn., 2004—05, Conn. Dept. Edn., 2005—06. Mem.: Coun. Exceptional Children, Nat. Assn. Multicultural Edn. Office: St Joseph Coll 1678 Asylum Ave West Hartford CT 06268 Office Phone: 860-231-5362. Business E-Mail: jalexandrin@sjc.edu.

ALEXANIAN, RAYMOND, hematologist; b. NYC, June 8, 1932; s. Hagop and Eleeza (Bynderian) A.; m. Lois Abbott, Jan. 16, 1960; 1 dau., Jane. BA with highest honors, Dartmouth Coll., 1952; MD, Harvard U., 1955. Diplomate: Am. Bd. Internal Medicine. Intern King County Hosp., Seattle, 1955-56; successively asst. resident in medicine, research fellow in hematology, instr. medicine U. Wash. Med. Sch., 1958-64; mem. faculty U. Tex. M.D. Anderson Hosp., Houston, 1964—, prof. medicine, 1975—. Contbr. numerous articles on myeloma and related disorders to med. jours. Served as capt. M.C. AUS, 1956-58. Mem. Am. Soc. Hematology, AMA, Tex. Med. Assn. (Waldenstrom award 1997). Home: 4082 Breakwood Dr Houston TX 77025-4033 Office: MD Anderson Hosp Dept Lymphoma-Myeloma 1515 Holcombe Blvd Houston TX 77030-4009 Office Phone: 713-792-2850.

ALEXEEV, DMITRI KONSTANTINOVICH, pianist; b. Moscow, Aug. 10, 1947; s. Konstantin and Gertrude (Bolotina) A.; m. Tatiana Sarkisova, 1970; 1 child. Studied with Dmitri Bashkirov, Moscow Conservatoire. Pianist performing USSR, U.K., Europe, U.S., touring Australia, Japan, Hong Kong, others; pianist London Philharm. Orch., Berlin Philharm., Berlin Radio Symphony Orchs., Chgo. Symphony Orch., Phila. Orch., London Symphony Orch., St. Petersburg Philharm. Orch., Royal Concertgebouw of Amsterdam, Munich Bavarian Radio Orch., Orchestre de Paris, City of Birmingham Symphony Orch., Royal Philharm. Orch., Hallé Orch., Balt. (Md.) Symphony Orch., Royal Flanders Philharm. Orch., Israel Philharm.; recordings include concertos by Schumann, Grieg, Rachmaninov, Prokofiev, Shostakovich, Scriabin, Medtner and solo works by Brahms, Rachmaninov, Schumann, Chopin, Liszt; performed at recitals in Munich, Florence, Rome, London, St. Petersburg, and Helsinki among others; worked with conductors such as Ashkenazy, Boulez, Dorati, Giulini, Muti, Rozhdestvensky, Tennstedt, Temirkanov, Tilson Tomas, and Jansons, among others. Recipient top honours Marguerite Long Competition, Paris, 1969, George Enescu Competition, Bucharest, 1970, Tchaikovsky Competition, Moscow, 1974, first prize 5th Leeds Internat. Piano Competition, Eng., 1975, Edison award The Netherlands, 1994. Office: IMG Artists/Lovell House 616 Chiswick High St London W4 5RX England Office Phone: 44-20-8-2335832. E-mail: cdyer@imgartistsworld.com.

ALEXEFF, IGOR, retired electrical engineering educator; b. Pitts., Jan. 5, 1931; s. Alexander and Tamara (Tchirkow) A.; m. Anne I. Fabina, Feb. 4, 1954; children: Alexander, Helen. BA with honors, Harvard U., 1952; MS, U. Wis., 1955, PhD, 1959. Registered profl. engr., Tenn. Research engr. Westinghouse Corp., Pitts., 1952-53; NSF postdoctoral fellow U. Zurich, Switzerland, 1959-60; group leader controlled thermonuclear fusion Oak Ridge Nat. Lab., 1960-71; prof. elec. engring. U. Tenn., 1971-96, prof. emeritus, 1996—; chief scientist Haleakala R&D Corp., Del., 2004—. Vis. prof. Inst. Plasma Physics, Nagoya, Japan, 1973, Phys. Rsch. Lab., Ahmedabad, India, 1975, physics dept. U. Natal, Durban, South Africa, 1976, U. Fed. Fluminense Niteroi, Brazil, 1978, Birla Inst. Tech., Ranchi, India, 1991; organizer Plasma Physics Workshop, U.S. and India, 1976; chmn. Gordon Rsch. Conf. on Plasma Physics, 1974; pres. So. Appalachian Sci. and Engring. Far, 1985-86. Co-author: High Power Microwave Sources, 1987; contbr. articles to profl. jours. Chancellor's rsch. scholar U. Tenn., 1984; recipient Advanced Tech. award Internat. Hall of Fame, 1989, 91, (with others) R&D 100 award R&D Mag., 1989, 91; named Most Outstanding Tchr. of Yr., U. Tenn. Elec. Engring. Dept., 1992. Fellow IEEE (assoc. editor Trans. on Plasma Sci., organizer 1st Internat. Conf. on Plasma Sci. 1974, former pres. Oak Ridge sect., Centennial medal 1987, Outstanding Engr. in S.E. award 1987), Am. Phys. Soc. (past sec.-treas. div. plasma physics); mem. ASI (co-founder), Tech. Corp., Tenn. Inventors Assn. (founding pres., Inventor of Yr. award 1988), Nuclear and Plasma Scis. Soc. of IEEE (chmn. plasma sect. 1983-84, v.p. 1998, pres. 1999-2000, Shea award for outstanding svc., Plasma Scis. and Applications award 2002). Achievements include patents in field. Home: 2790 Turnpike Oak Ridge TN 37830 Office: U Tenn Ferris 315 Knoxville TN 37996-2100 Office Phone: 865-974-5467. Personal E-mail: ialexeff@comcast.net. Business E-Mail: alexeff@utk.edu.

ALEXIADES-ARMENAKAS, MACRENE RENEE, dermatologist, scientist, researcher, educator, consultant; d. Gregory and Sophia Alexiades; m. Noel Anthony Armenakas, Oct. 26, 1996; children: Sophia Stella Armenakas, Anthony Emmanuel Armenakas. BA, Harvard U., 1989; MD, Harvard Med. Sch., 1997; PhD, Harvard U., 1997. Cert. MD, PhD, lic. medicine & surgery N.Y., 1998, medicine and surgery Conn., 2004, Greece, 2004, credentialed in medicine and surgery European Union, 2004, diplomate Am. Bd. Dermatology, 2002. Rschr. Harvard U., Cambridge, 1984—91, tutor supr., 1985—89, tchg. asst., 1990—97, doctorate rschr. Boston, 1991—97; intern medicine Lenox Hill Hosp., NYC, 1997—98; Fulbright scholar U. Heraklion, Crete, Greece, 1989—90; resident dermatology NYU Sch. Medicine, NYC, 1998—2000, chief resident dermatology, 2000—01; dir. rsch. & laser dermatology Laser & Skin Surgery Ctr. N.Y., 2001—03; attending physician Lenox Hill Hosp., NYC, 2001—; pres., dir. dermatology & laser surgery Macrene Alexiades-Armenakas, MD, PhD, PC, 2003—; asst. clin. prof. Yale U. Sch. Medicine, 2003—; attending physician Yale/New Haven Hosp. Tutor supr. Harvard Bur. Study Coun., 1985—89; mem. MD/PhD program steering com. Harvard Med. Sch., 1993—94, mem. MD/PhD program retreat com., 1992—94, mem. minority recruitment com., 1992—95, mem. advanced biomed. scis. com., 1993—95, admissions interviewer com., 2002—; cons. dermatologist L'Oreal, Paris, 2005—; sci. advisor Archdiocese of N.Am., 2006—. Editor: (jour.) Dermatologic Surgery, 2004—, The Harvard Polit. Rev., 1985—89; editor: (writer) The Biology Rev., 1986—89; mem. editl. bd.: The Harvard Crimson, 1985—89, columnist, editor: Jour. Drugs in Dermatology, 2005—, staff reviewer: Dermatologic Surgery, 2004—, Lasers in Medicine and Surgery, 2005—; author: abstracts, jour. articles, book chpts. Counselor rape crisis Response, Cambridge, 1988-89; counselor Harvard Med. Sch. peer counseling, 1990-92; yoga instr. Vanderbilt Hall Athletic Facility, Boston, 1990-92; vol. St. Francis House Soup Kitchen, 1990-94; solicitation coord. fundraising com. William Woodward Nursery Sch., 2001-02, chairperson, 2004-, bd. trustees, 2004-; mem. art com. The Chapin Sch., 2004-05, sci. and rsch. advisor, 2006—; mem. Parents Assn., 2004-05; bd. mem. Cathedral Sch., chair afternoon sch. Recipient Husik prize, 2001, First Pl. award, Jour. Drugs in Dermatology Rsch. Competition, 2004; grantee, Nat. Eye Inst., 1995; scholar, Fulbright Found., 1989—90; Paul Dudley White scholar, Harvard U., 1991. Fellow: Hellenic Med. Soc.; mem.: Women's Dermatologic Soc., Am. Soc. Laser Medicine and Surgery, Dermatology Found., Am. Acad. Dermatology, Harvard Hellenic Soc. (founder), Mass. Med. Soc., Am. Soc. Dermatologic Surgery (chmn. rsch. com. 2004—, councilman edn. and rsch. com. 2004—, editor, columnist jour. 2005), Harvard Greek Club. Greek Orthodox Christian. Achievements include numerous scientific discoveries, inventions, and patents. Avocations: portraiture, sculpting, drawing, painting, skiing, yoga, photography. Office Phone: 212-570-2067. Office Fax: 212-861-7964. Business E-Mail: dralexiades@nyderm.org.

ALEXIEV, BORISLAV ALEXANDROV, pathologist; b. Sofia, Bulgaria, Aug. 26, 1958; s. Alexander Borislavov and Violetta Borisova (Delova) A.; m. Anna Petrova Vasileva, Aug. 4, 1984; children: Alexander, Julia. MD, Med. Faculty of Sofia, 1984, PhD in Pathology, 1993. Medical diplomate. Pathologist Alexandrov Hosp./Med. Faculty, Sofia, 1985-94, head of rsch. lab., dept. pathology, 1994—. Mem. Union of Dem. Forces, 1995. Recipient award for Outstanding Work in Cancer Rsch., Clin. Digest Series J. Mem. Bulgarian Soc. Pathology, N.Y. Acad. Scis. Avocation: bodybuilding. Office: Alexandrov Hosp/Dept Pathology Med Faculty Sofia Zdrave 2 1431 Sofia Bulgaria

ALEXIS, ANDREW F., dermatologist; s. Nicholas and Mercy Alexis; m. Ama Gyekye, Sept. 21, 2002. MD, MPH, Columbia U., 1999. Diplomate Am. Bd. Dermatology. Resident in dermatology NY Presbyn. Hosp., Cornell U., NYC, 2003; rsch. fellow in dermatopharmacology, dept. dermatology NYU, NYC, 2003—04; assoc. dir. Skin of Color Ctr., St. Luke's-Roosevelt Hosp., NYC, 2004—05, dir., 2005—. Asst. clin. prof. dermatology Columbia U., NYC, 2004—. Contbr. articles to profl. jours. and book chpts. in field. Recipient Disting. Housetaff award, Weill Med. Coll., Cornell U., 2003; fellow Stanley scholar, Stanley Found. Rsch. Fund, 1996; Rudin scholar, Louis and Rachel Rudin Found., 1997, 1998. Fellow: Am. Acad. Dermatology; mem.: AMA, Skin of Color Soc., Soc. Investigative Dermatology, Nat. Med. Assn. Achievements include research in Psoriasis, Alopecia Areata. Office: Skin of Color Ctr 1090 Amsterdam Ave 11B New York NY 10025 Home Phone: 212-397-7879; Office Phone: 212-523-3816. Personal E-mail: andrew.alexis@columbia.edu.

ALEXIS, GERALDINE M., lawyer; b. NYC, Nov. 3, 1948; d. William J. and Margaret Daly; m. Marcus Alexis, June 15, 1969; children: Marcus L., Hilary I., Sean C. BA, U. Rochester, 1971; MBA, JD, Northwestern U., 1976. Bar: Ill. 1976, Calif. 2001, U.S. Dist. Ct. (no. dist.) Calif. 1976, U.S. Dist. Ct. (no. dist.) Ill. 1976, U.S. Trial Bar 1985, U.S. Ct. Appeals (7th cir.) 1986, U.S. Ct. Appeals (5th cir.) 1996, U.S. Ct. Appeals (9th cir.) 2002. Law clk. to Hon. John F. Grady, justice U.S. Dist. Ct. (no. dist.) Ill., Chgo., 1976-77; assoc. Sidley & Austin, Chgo., 1977-79, 81-83, ptnr., 1983-2000; advisor U.S. Dept. Justice Office Legal Counsel, Washington, 1979-81; ptnr. McCutchen, Doyle, Brown & Enersen (now Bingham McCutchen LLP), San Francisco, 2001—. Mem.: ABA (co-chair fin. svcs. com. antitrust sect.). Democrat. Office: Bingham McCutchen LLP 3 Embarcadero Ctr San Francisco CA 94111

ALEXIS, TRACY L., project manager, project specialist, information technology manager, small business owner; b. Atlanta, Oct. 15, 1955; d. William Emanual and Hazel Harcourt Alexis; children: Karrie Crystallyn Mayes, Ryan Andrew McClelland. AA with high honors, Ga. Perimeter Coll., South Campus, 1981; BA magna cum laude, U. N.Mex, Albuquerque, 2003. Cert. Micropigmentation SofTap, Las Vegas Nev., 2005, permanent cosmetic technician SofTap, Las Vegas Nev., 2005. Exec. event coord./mgr. Global Player Events, Albuquerque, 1999—2006; strategic project mgr. Strategic & Learning Svcs., Inc., Albuquerque, 2005—. Author: Birth Announcement, 1979. Vol. Habitat for Humanity, Albuquerque, 1996—2003. Pell grantee, U. N.Mex, 2001-2003, Amigo Transfer scholar, 1999, Native scholar High Honors, Native Am. Scholarship and Rsch. Coun., 2000. Mem.: Phi Theta Kappa, Golden Key Internat., Psi Chi, Mortar Bd. Alumni (assoc.). Achievements include patents for Automatic Faucet Drip. Avocations: hiking, travel, fine dining, reading, gardening. Office: Strategic & Learning Svcs Inc 6100 Seagull Ln NE Ste B200 Albuquerque NM 87109 Office Phone: 866-827-3500. Personal E-mail: gpexecutive@att.net. Business E-Mail: talexis@slsinc.com.

ALEXOPOULOS, NICOLAOS GEORGE, electrical engineering educator, dean; b. Athens, Greece, Apr. 14, 1942; arrived in US, 1959; s. Yeoryeos A. and Efstathia (Yiannopoulou) A.; m. Sue B. Bunting, June 25, 1966; children: Efstathia Nicole, Christina Ariadne, Theodore Andrew. BSEE, U. Mich., 1965, MSEE, 1967, PhD in Elec. Engring., 1968. Asst. prof. elec. engring. UCLA, 1969-75, assoc. prof., 1975-81, prof., 1981—96, assoc. dean faculty affairs, 1986-87, chmn. dept., 1987—92; dean The Henry Samueli Sch. Engring. U. Calif., Irvine, 1997—, prof. elec. engring. and computer sci., 1997—. Pres. Phraxos R & D Corp., Santa Monica, Calif., 1986—; cons. aerospace industry, 1970—. Contbr. articles to profl. jours. NSF rsch. grantee, 1979—. Fellow: IEEE (S.E. Schelkunoff Prize, Best Paper award 1985, 1998, Orange County Sec. Engr. of Yr. 2001); mem.: NAE. Office: U Calif Irvine 305 Rockwell Engring Ctr Box 2700 Irvine CA 92697-2700 Office Phone: 949-824-6002. Office Fax: 949-824-7966. E-mail: alfios@uci.edu.*

ALF, MARTHA JOANNE, artist; b. Berkeley, Calif., Aug. 13, 1930; d. Foster Wise and Julia Vivian (Kane) Powell; m. Edward Franklin Alf, Mar. 17, 1951; 1 child, Richard Franklin. BA with distinction, San Diego State U., 1953, MA in Painting, 1963, jr. coll. teaching credential, 1969; MFA in Pictorial Arts, UCLA, 1970. Rsch. asst. Health and Welfare Assn., Seattle, 1956; tchg. asst. in drawing, instr. design San Diego State U., 1963; instr. drawing L.A. Valley Coll., 1970-73, El Camino Coll., Hawthorne, Calif., 1971; instr. drawing and painting L.A. Harbor Coll., Wilmington, Calif., 1971-75; instr. art UCLA Extension, 1971-79. Instr. contemporary art Brand Library Art Ctr., Glendale, Calif., 1973; vis. artist Calif. State Coll., Bakersfield, 1980; freelance art critic Artweek, Oakland, Calif., 1974-77; guest curator Lang Art Gallery, Scripps Coll., Claremont, Calif., 1974. Retrospective exhbn. Fellows Contemporary Art, LA Mcpl. Art Gallery, San Francisco Art Inst., 1984; exhibited in group shows at San Diego Mus. Art, 1964, 67-68, 70-71, 77-78, 83, Whitney Mus. Contemporary Art Biennial, 1975, Newport Harbor Art Mus., 1975, Marion Koogler McNay Art Inst., San Antonio, 1976, Long Beach Mus. Art, 1972, 82, 86, Am. Acad. Arts and Letters, NY, 1985, 96, Henry Art Gallery, U. Wash., Seattle, 1985, LA County Mus. Art, 1979, 82 (Kay Neilson award 1979), Womens Mus., Wash., 1994, Bakersfield Mus. Art, 1999, Santa Barbara Mus. Art, 2001, Calif. State U., LA, 2001, Laguna Beach Art Mus., 2001, San Jose Mus. Art, 2003-04, Pasadena Mus. Calif. Art, 2004, Contemporary Arts Ctr., New Orleans, 2004, Norton Mus. Art, West Palm Beach, Fla., 2004, Hudson River Mus., Yonkers, NY, 2004, Arcadiana Ctr. Arts, Lafayette, La., 2005, McDonough Mus. Arts, Youngstown State U., Ohio, 2005, Tucson Mus. Art, 2006; one-woman shows include John Berggruen Gallery, San Francisco, 1977, Forth Worth Art Mus., 1988, Susan Caldwell Gallery, NY, 1980, Dorothy Rosenthal Gallery, Chgo., 1982, Eloise Pickard Smith Gallery, Cowell Coll., U. Calif., Santa Cruz, 1983, Newspace Gallery, LA, 1976-85, 90-2004, Henry Gardiner Gallery, Palm Beach, 1986, Tortue Gallery, Santa Monica, 1986, Jan Baum Gallery, LA, 1988, Trabia Gallery, NY, 1990, 871 Fine Arts, San Francisco, 1991, Art Inst. So. Calif., Laguna Beach, Calif., 1991, Fresno Art Mus., 1992, Mt. San Antonio Coll., Walnut, Calif., 1993; represented in permanent collections LA County Mus. Art, Chem. Bank NY, Ga. Mus. Art., Israel Mus. Art, Jerusalem, LA County Mus. Art, McCrory Corp., NY, Metromedic Inc., LA, NY, San Diego Mus. Art, San Jose Mus., Santa Barbara Mus. Art, Southland Corp., Dallas, Spencer Mus. Art, U. Kans., Lawrence, Met. Mus. Art., NY, Phoenix Art Mus., Fresno Art Mus., Grand Rapids Art Mus., Orange County Mus. Art, Newport Beach, Calif., Palm Springs Desert Mus., Laguna Art Mus., U. Calif. Santa Barbara Art Gallery, Eli Broad Collection, Santa Monica, U. Va. Bayley Art Mus., Charlottesville. Nat. Endowment for Arts grantee, 1979, 89; recipient Richard Florsheim Art Fund award, 1996, Calif. Heritage Mus. print commn., 1998. Avocations: body building, walking, reading, bird study and videos. Home: 103 Brooks Ave Venice CA 90291-3254 Home Phone: 310-396-3031; Office Phone: 310-396-3031. Personal E-mail: alf1@earthlink.net.

ALFANO, CHARLES THOMAS, SR., lawyer; b. Suffield, Conn., June 21, 1920; s. Dominick and Rosina (Dimartino) A.; m. Mary Ann Sinatro, Nov. 13, 1954; children: Diane Elizabeth, Andrea Rose, Charles Thomas Jr., Susan Marie. Student, Ill. Coll., 1939-40; BA cum laude, U. Conn., 1943; LL.B., JD, U. Mich., 1948. Bar: Conn. 1948. Since practiced in, Hartford; partner firm Alfano Halloran & Flynn; judge Town Ct. of Suffield, 1949-51, 55-59; mem. Conn. Senate, 1959-77, asst. majority leader, 1966, pres. pro tem, 1967-73, minority leader, 1973-75, v.p. pro tem, 1975-77; corp. counsel Town of Suffield, 1977-83. Dir., chmn. bd. Suffield Savs. Bank; dir. Conn. Water Co. Bd. dirs. Conn. Pub. TV. Served with USNR, 1942-47, PTO. Mem. ABA, ATLA, Conn. Bar Assn., Hartford County Bar Assn., Conn. Trial Lawyers Assn. (bd. dirs.), Hartford Club, Mystic Yacht Club, Mason's Island Yacht Club, N.Y. Athletic Club, KC, Sigma Nu. Home: 50 Marbern Dr Suffield CT 06078-1533 Office: 93 Oak St Hartford CT 06106-1515 also: 53 Mountain Rd Suffield CT 06078-2041 Office Phone: 860-668-0221.

ALFANO, MICHAEL CHARLES, university administrator; b. Newark, Aug. 8, 1947; s. Michael Ferdinand and Anne Marie (Barrington) A.; m. JoAnn Mary Coletta, Mar. 30, 1969; children: Michael Anthony, Kristin Lynn. Student, Rutgers U., 1965-67; DMD, U. Medicine and Dentistry of N.J., 1971; postgrad. in periodontics, Harvard U., 1971-74; PhD, MIT, 1975. Asst. prof. dentistry Fairleigh Dickinson U., Hackensack, NJ, 1974-77, assoc. prof., 1977-80, prof. with tenure, 1980-82, dir. Oral Health Rsch. Ctr., 1977-82, asst. dean grad. affairs and rsch., 1981-82; v.p. dental rsch. Block Drug Co., Inc., Jersey City, 1982-84, sr. v.p. R&D, 1987-98, bd. dirs., 1988-98, pres. dental products divsn., 1985-88, cons. office of chief exec., 1990-98; dean Coll. Dentistry NYU, 1998—2006, prof. basic scis. & periodontology Coll. Dentistry, 1998—2006, exec. v.p., 2006—. Cons. Nat. Inst. Dental Rsch., Bethesda, Md., 1976-82; apptd. nat. adv. dental rsch. coun. NIH, Bethesda, 1994-98; apptd. vis. prof. Nat. Dairy Coun., Chgo., 1981; vis. sr. scientist Fairleigh Dickinson U., 1982-88; adj. prof. U. Medicine and Dentistry of N.J., Newark, 1985-2003; mem. sci. adv. coun. Office of Gov., State of N.J., 1981-84; bd. dirs. Dentsply, Inc. Editor: Symposium on Nutrition, 1976; contbr. articles to profl. jours. and chpts. to books; patentee in field. Trustee Found. of U. Medicine and Dentistry of N.J., 1988-98, N.Y. State Dental Found., 2004-06; mem. adv. bd. Columbia U. Sch. Dental and Oral Surgery, 1990-98; mem. program com. Am. Fund for Dental Health, 1991-93; bd. overseers Forsyth Dental Ctr., Boston, 1992-99, U. Pa. Coll. Dental Medicine, 1992-2004; trustee Santa Fe Group, 1998—; founding dir. Friends of Nat. Inst. Dental Rsch., 1998-2006; dir. Dentsply Internat., 2001—. Recipient Leadership citation Newark YMCA, 1966, Disting. Alumnus award U. Medicine and Dentistry of N.J., 1986, Harvard U. Sch. Dental Medicine, 1998; NIH rsch. grantee, 1974-82; NIH postdoctoral fellow, 1971-74. Fellow Am. Coll. Dentists, Am. Coll. of Prosthodontists (hon. fellow), Internat. Congress Oral Implantologists (hon. life 2002-); mem. Am. Acad. Oral Med. (hon. mem., 2003), ADA (cons., Future of Dentistry Commn. 1999-2001, bd. govs. student clinicians 2000—, Nat. Achievement award 1978), Internat. Assn. for Dental Rsch., Am. Assn. for Dental Rsch. (pres. N.J. chpt. 1985, Hein Pub. Svc. award 2004, Shils award 2004), Am. Inst. Nutrition. Independent. Roman Catholic. Achievements include 8 patents; discovery of role of Vitamin C in mucous membrane barrier function. Home: 29 Washington Sq W Apt 5C New York NY 10011-9132 Office: NYU 70 Washington Square South New York NY 10010 Office Fax: 212-995-4789. Business E-Mail: mca1@nyu.edu.

ALFANO, ROBERT R., science and engineering educator; BS, Fairleigh Dickinson U., Teaneck, NJ, 1963, MS, 1964; PhD, NYU, NYC, 1972. Rschr. GTE, NYC, 1964-72; from asst. prof. to prof. CUNY, NYC, 1972-88, disting. prof. sci., 1988—; dir. N.Y. State Ctr. for Adv. Tech. in Ultrafast Photonics, 1992—; pres., CEO Alfanix Tech. Ltd., 1997—; co-dir. NASA Ctr. for Optical Sensing and Imaging, 2003—; dir. DOD Ctr. for Nanoscale Photonic Emitters and Sensors, 2003—. Dir. Ctr. on Laser in Medicine, Dept. Energy, 1998-2002. Editor: Biological Events Probed by Ultrafast Laser Spectroscopy, 1982, Semiconductors Probed by Ultrafast Laser Spectroscopy, 1985, The Supercontinuum Laser Source, 1989, 2d edit., 2006, Photonics: Nonlinear Optics and Ultrafast Phenomena, 1990; contbr. 700 articles to profl. jours.; 94 patents in field. A.P. Sloan fellow, OSA fellow, APS fellow. Fellow: IEEE. Office Phone: 212-650-5531. Business E-Mail: Alfano@alfanix.com.

ALFERINK, LARRY ALLEN, psychology professor; b. Holland, Mich., May 26, 1948; s. Benjamin and Dorothy (DeVisser) A.; m. Laura Rae Lawrence, Aug. 29, 1970; children: Kristine Jennifer Mertens, Paul Raymond. BA, Western Mich. U., Kalamazoo, 1970; MS, Utah State U., 1973, PhD, 1975. Instr. psychology Drake U., Des Moines, 1974, asst. prof., 1975-79, assoc. prof., 1979-83, chair dept., 1981-83, assoc. prof., 1983—93; prof. Psychology Ill. State U., Normal, 1993—, chair dept. psychology, 1983-98, acting assoc. dean grad. studies, 1998-2000, asst. to the assoc. v.p. for undergrad. studies, 2000—03, interim dir. honors program, 2002—04. Chmn. exec. com. Coun. Applied Masters Programs in Psychology, exec. com. Coun. Grad. Depts. in Psychology, 1991-96; mem. Ill. Consortium Ednl. Opportunity Programs Adv. Bd., 1998-2004, chmn., 1999-2001. Fellow APA (sec.-treas. divsn. 25 1995-2004, chair Master's Edn. Working Group, mem. coalition for Psychology in the schs. and edn. 2002—, pres.-elect divsn. 25 2005, pres. 2006, past pres. 2007); mem. AAAS, Assn. Behavior Analysis, Mid-Am. Assn. Behavior Analysis (treas. 2001-2003, pres. 2003-2004). Office: Ill State U PO Box 4620 Normal IL 61790-4620 E-mail: alferink@ilstu.edu.

ALFIDI, RALPH JOSEPH, retired radiologist, educator, researcher; b. Rome, Apr. 20, 1932; s. Luca and Angeline (Panella) A.; m. Rose Esther Senesac, Sept. 3, 1956 (div. 1991); children: Suzanne, Lisa, Christine, Katherine, Mary, John; m. Mariella Boller, Aug. 29, 1992. AB, Ripon Coll., Wis., 1955; MD, Marquette U., Milw., 1959. Intern Oakwood Hosp., Dearborn, Mich., 1959-60; resident, chief resident, A.C.S. fellow U. Va., 1960-63; practice medicine, specializing in radiology Cleve., 1965-2000; staff mem. Cleve. Clinic, 1965-78, head dept. hosp. radiology, 1968-78; dir. dept. radiology Univ. Hosps., Cleve., 1978-92; prof. radiology U. N.Mex.,

Albuquerque, 2000—03. Cons. VA Hosp., Cleve.; chmn. dept. radiology Case Western Res. U. Sch. Medicine, 1978-92; chmn. staff Cleve. Clinic Found., 1975-76; co-founder Steris Corp. Author: Complications and Legal Implications of Special Procedures, 1972, Computed Tomography of the Human Body: An Atlas of Normal Anatomy, 1977; editor: Whole Body Computed Tomography, 1977; contbr. articles to radiology jours. Served to capt., M.C. U.S. Army Res., 1963-65 Picker Found. grantee, 1969-70; NRC grantee, 1969-70 Mem. Radiol. Soc. N. Am., Am. Roentgen Ray Soc., Am. Heart Assn., Soc. Cardiovascular Radiology, Soc. Gastrointestinal Radiology, Soc. Computed Body Tomography (pres. 1977-78), Eastern Radiol. Soc., Cleve. Radiol. Soc. (pres. 1976-77), Las Campanas Club. Roman Catholic. Achievements include discovery of renal splanchnic steal syndrome: aka Alfidi's Syndrome; patents for nitinol. Home: 81 Calle Ventoso W Santa Fe NM 87506-0141

ALFIERI, VINCENT, lawyer; BA, Fordham U., 1975; JD, NY Law Sch., 1980. Bar: NY, US Dist. Ct., So. and Ea. Dists. NY 1981, US Ct. Appeals, Second Cir. 1982, US Dist. Ct., No. Dist. NY. Ptnr., group leader Labor and Employment Bryan Cave LLP, NYC. Office: Bryan Cave LLP 1290 Ave of the Americas New York NY 10104 Office Phone: 212-541-2270. E-mail: valfieri@bryancave.com.

ALFINI, JAMES JOSEPH, dean, educator, lawyer; b. Yonkers, NY, Oct. 12, 1943; s. James Joseph and Olga (Genish) Alfini; m. Carol Miller, Dec. 23, 1966; children: David James, Michael Steven. AB, Columbia U., 1965; JD, Northwestern U., 1972. Bar: N.Y. 1973, Ill. 1976, U.S. Dist. Ct. (no. dist.) Ill. 1976, U.S. Supreme Ct. 1977, U.S. Ct. Appeals (7th cir.) 1982, Tex. 2005. Reginald Heber Smith cmty. lawyer Monroe County Legal Assistance Corp., Rochester, NY, 1972—73; asst. dir. rsch. Am. Judicature Soc., Chgo., 1973—77, dir. rsch., 1977—80, asst. exec. dir. programs, 1980—85; adj. prof. law IIT Chgo.-Kent Sch. Law, 1978—85; assoc. prof. law Fla. State U., Tallahassee, 1985—90, prof. law, 1990—91; dean, prof. No. Ill. U. Coll. Law, 1991—97, prof., 1997—2003; pres., dean South Tex. Coll. Law, Houston, 2003—. Co-author: (book) Making Jury Instructions Understandable, 1982, Judicial Conduct and Ethics, 1990, Judicial Conduct and Ethics, 2d edit., 1995, Judicial Conduct and Ethics, 3d edit., 2000, Mediation Theory and Practice, 2000; bd. editors: jour. Ohio State Jour. Dispute Resolution, 1994—98. Mem. governing bd. Cook County Legal Assistance Found., 1981—83; chmn. coord. coun. Nat. Ct. Orgns., 1982—83; arbitration and mediation rules com. Fla. Supreme Ct., 1988—91; mem. Ill. Jud. Ethics com., 1993—97; bd. govs. Chgo. Coun. Lawyers. 1st lt. US Army, 1965—69. Decorated Commendation medal U.S. Army. Mem.: ACLU, ABA (sect. dispute resolution, chmn., mem. ho. dels. 2002—, mem. joint commn. evaluate model code jud. conduct 2003—), Law and Soc. Assn., Am. Law Inst. Democrat. Home: 3928 Southwestern Houston TX 77005 Office Phone: 713-646-1819.

ALFOND, THEODORE B., retired shoe company executive; b. Maine; s. Harold and Dorothy Alfond; m. Barbara Alfond; 1 child, John Lawrence; children: Jennifer Grace, Katharine Brooke. BA in bus., Rollins Coll., Fla., 1968. Exec. v.p. Dexter Shoe Co. (merged with Berkshire Hathaway Group, 1993), 1969—99. Trustee Rollins Coll., Fla., Holderness Sch., NH, Kents Hill Sch., Maine, 1979—, US Ski & Snowboard Team Found., 2003—; limited ptnr. Boston Red Sox, 1980—. Named one of Top 200 Collectors, ARTnews, 2006. Home: 1 Chestnut St Weston MA 02493-1525 Office: Rollins Coll 1000 Holt Ave Winter Park FL 32789-4499

ALFONSO, ANTONIO ESCOLAR, surgeon; b. Manila, Nov. 25, 1943; came to U.S., 1968, naturalized, 1978; s. Ricardo Lagdameo and Marita (Escolar) Alfonso; m. Teresita Nazareno, Apr. 25, 1970; children: Margaretta, Roberto. AB cum laude, Ateneo U., 1963; MD cum laude, U. Philippines, 1968. Diplomate: Am. Bd. Surgery. Intern U. Philippines-Philippine Gen. Hosp., 1968; instr. surgery Temple U., Phila., 1968-72; sr. fellow surg. oncology Meml. Sloan-Kettering Cancer Ctr., NYC, 1972-74; dir. head and neck surgery svc. SUNY Downstate Med. Ctr., Bklyn., 1974—, assoc. dir. divsn. surg. oncology, 1974—, asst. prof. surgery, 1974-77, assoc. prof., 1977-82, prof., 1982—, vice-chmn. dept. surgery, 1988—. Chmn. dept. surgery Bklyn. Hosp., 1982-88; chmn. Dept. Surgery LI Coll. Hosp., 1988—; cons. head and neck surgery Bklyn. VA Hosp., 1974— Author: Principles of Surgery Oncology; contbr. articles to profl. med. jours., chpts. in med. books. Recipient rsch. essay prize NY Colon and Rectal Surg. Soc., 1973; grantee Am. Cancer Soc., 1978 Mem. ACS (bd. govs. Bklyn.-LI chpt., gov. 1998—), Assn. Acad. Surgeons, Am. Soc. Clin. Oncology, Am. Assn. Cancer Edn., Soc. Head and Neck Surgeons, NY Surg. Soc. (treas. 1994, v.p. 1998, pres. 1999), Bklyn. Surg. Soc. (pres. 1986-87), NY Cancer Soc. (v.p. 1986-87, pres.-elect 1987-88, pres. 1988-89), Soc. Surg. Oncology, NY Head and Neck Soc. (sec. 1993-97, pres. 1998), NY Soc. Colon and Rectal Surgeons, Triboro Dirs. of Surgery Assn. (pres. 1989—), Phi Kappa Phi. Roman Catholic. Home: 50 Olive Pl Flushing NY 11375-5938 Office: LI Coll Hosp Dept Surgery 340 Henry St Brooklyn NY 11201-5514 Office Phone: 718-875-3244.

ALFONSO, FRANK A., lawyer; b. LA, May 1, 1970; BS, Calif. State Univ., LA, 1994; JD, Southwestern Univ., 1998. Bar: Calif. 1998. Assoc. Law Offices of C. Michael Alder, Beverly Hills, Calif. Contbr. articles to profl. jours. Named a Rising Star, So. Calif. Super Lawyers, 2006. Office: Law Offices of C Michael Alder 9308 Civic Ctr Dr Beverly Hills CA 90210

ALFONSO-BICA, KRISTY LYNN, elementary school educator; b. Port Jefferson, NY, Jan. 6, 1979; d. Oswaldo and Patricia Alfonso; m. Giuseppe Bica, June 26, 2004. BA in Edn. with honors, SUNY, Geneseo, 2001; MA in Reading Edn. with honors, Dowling Coll., Oakdale, NY, 2005. Tchr. Pub. Sch. 171, Astoria, NY, 2001—02, Clayton Huey Elem. Sch., Center Moriches, NY, 2002—03, Fairview Sch., Corona, NY, 2003—. Religious educator St. Gerards Ch., Terryville, NY, 1997—2001. Recipient Gold award, Girl Scouts USA, 1997, Hon. award, United Fedn. Tchrs., 2002. Roman Catholic. Avocations: swimming, travel, horsebackriding, reading, writing. Personal E-mail: elmo7979@aol.com.

ALFORD, BOBBY RAY, otolaryngologist, educator, academic administrator; b. Dallas, May 30, 1932; s. Bryant J. and Edith M. (Garrett) A.; m. Othelia Jerry Dorn, Aug. 28, 1953; children: Bradley Keith, Raye Lynn, Alan Scott. AS, Tyler Jr. Coll., 1951; postgrad., U. Tex., 1951-52; MD, Baylor U., 1956. Diplomate Am. Bd. Otolaryngology (dir. 1972-90, pres. 1985-86, exec. v.p. 1986-90). Intern Jefferson Davis Hosp., Houston, 1956-57; resident Baylor U. Coll. Medicine Affiliated Hosps. Program, 1957-60; mem. faculty Baylor U. Coll. Medicine, 1962—, prof. otolaryngology, 1966—, chmn. dept., 1967-95, 96—, v.p. and dean acad. and clin. affairs, 1984-88, disting. service prof., 1985—, interim chmn. dept. surgery, 1983—84, exec. v.p., dean medicine, 1988—2004, chancellor, 2004—; pres., CEO BaylorMedCare, Houston, 1994-96; chmn., CEO Nat. Space Biomed. Rsch. Inst., 1997—. Rev. panel surgeon gen. on neurol. and sensory disease USPHS, 1965-67; cons. Nat. Inst. Neurol. Disease and Stroke, 1970-74; cons. to surgeon gen. U.S. Army, 1963-73; nat. adv. coun. Neurol. and Communicative Disorders and Stroke, NIH, 1977-80, Deafness and Other Communicative Disorders, 1991-95, NASA, 1992-95, chmn. aerospace medicine adv. com., 1993-94, chmn. life microgravity scis. and applications adv. com., 1993-95. Author: Neurological Aspects of Auditory and Vestibular Disorders, 1964, Electrophysiologic Evaluation in Otolaryngology, 1997; chief editor: A.M.A. Archives of Otolaryngology, 1970-79. Bd. dirs. Houston Acad. Medicine Tex. Med. Ctr. Libr., 1983-94. Recipient Herman Johnson award Baylor U. Coll. Medicine, 1956, NASA Disting. Pub. Svc. award, 1992, 95, Jeffries Aerospace Medicine and Life Scis. Rsch. award Am. Inst. Aeronautics and Astronautics, 2003, Bobby Alford award for Academic Clin. Professionalism Ben and Margaret Love Found., 2005; spl. NIH fellow Johns Hopkins Hosp., 1961-62. Fellow ACS (bd. govs. 1977-82); mem. AIAA (Jeffries Aerospace Medicine and Life Scis. Rsch. award 2003), NAS Inst. Medicine, Am. Laryngol. Assn., Soc. Univ. Otolaryngologists-Head and Neck Surgeons (sec. 1965-69), Am. Otol. Soc., Assn. Acad. Dept. Otolaryngology-Head and Neck Surgery, Am. Laryngol., Rhinol. and Otol. Soc., Am. Soc. Head and Neck Surgery (councillor 1978-80) Am. Acad. Otolaryngology-Head and Neck Surgery (pres. 1981), Am. Coun. Otolaryngology-Head and Neck Surgery (pres. 1980-81), Am. Bronchoesophagological Assn., Soc. Head and Neck Surgeons, Acoustical Soc. Am., Collegium Oto-Rhino-Laryngologicum Amicitiae Sacrum, Johns Hopkins U. Soc. Scholars, Univ. Space Rsch. Assn. (bd. dirs. 1991-95), Tex. Corinthian Yacht Club (bd. dirs. 1978-80, 94-95), Doctors Club (bd. govs. 1967-70, 91-93), Petroleum Club, Alpha Omega Alpha. Office: 6501 Fannin Ste NA102 Houston TX 77030 Office Phone: 713-798-5906. Business E-Mail: balford@bcm.tmc.edu.

ALFORD, KATHERINE, food products executive; b. NYC; Attended, Pomona Coll., Calif., NY Restaurant School, NYC, La Varenne, France. Dir. instrn. Inst. of Culinary Edn., NYC; sous chef Quilted Giraffe, NYC; dir. Food Network Test Kitchen. Co-author: Union Square Cafe Cookbook, 1994; author: Caviar, Truffles and Foie Gras, 2001. Office: Home of Food Network 75 9th Ave New York NY 10011

ALFORD, LARRY P., university librarian; BA, MLS, U. NC. Dep. univ. libr. U. NC, Chapel Hill, interim univ. libr.; vice provost librs., univ. libr. Temple U., Phila., 2005—. Mem. S.E. Libr. Network, 1992—96; trustee Online Computer Libr. Ctr.; mem. steering com. Scholarly Pub. and Academic Resources Coalition. Contbr. articles to profl. jours. Mem.: ALA, Assn. Rsch. Librs. Fin. Com., Assn. for Libr. Collections and Tech. Svcs. Office: Samuel L Paley Libr 1210 W Berks St Philadelphia PA 19122 Office Phone: 215-204-8231. Office Fax: 215-204-5201. E-mail: larry.alford@temple.edu.*

ALFORD, MARGIE SEARCY, lawyer, writer; b. Tuscaloosa, Ala., Dec. 20, 1949; d. Joseph Alexander and Margaret Tyler (Zehmer) Searcy; m. Andrew Ray Alford, Sept. 4, 1992. BS, U. Ala., 1967-69, 70-71; student, U. Ams., Mexico City, 1969, Emory U., Atlanta, 1970; JD, U. Ala., 1974. Bar: Ala. 1974; U.S. Dist. Ct. (no. dist.) Ala. 1975. Assoc. univ. counsel U. Ala., Tuscaloosa, 1974-75; pvt. practice Tuscaloosa, 1975-92, Birmingham, Ala., 1992—. Editor-in-chief, prin. author: Matthew Bender's A Guide to Toxic Torts, 4 vols., 1986; contbg. author: Matthew Bender's Drug Product Liability, 4 vols.; contbr. numerous articles to legal jours., freelance writer for numerous publs. Group leader Ea. Area Diabetes Support Group, 1997—; mem. Trussville Area C. of C. Named Most Outstanding Young Career Woman in Ala. Ala. Bus. and Profl. Women, 1986. Mem. ATLA (twice nat. chair environ. and toxic tort law sect., twice nat. chair of women trial lawyers caucus), Nat. Assn. Women Bus. Owners, Bus. and Profl. Women, Ala. State Bar, Ala. Media Profls. Presbyterian. Avocations: collecting antique furniture and paintings, chow chow dog breeder, gardening, travel. Office: PO Box 610781 Birmingham AL 35261-0781 Fax: (205) 520-5083. E-mail: margialfor@aol.com.

ALFORD, RENEE MARIE, speech pathology/audiology services professional, educator; d. James, Jr. and Claudia Mae Alford, Aloysius (Stepfather) and Emily Patricia Chisley (Stepmother). BS in Speech and Lang. Pathology, U. DC, 1986, MS in Speech and Lang. Pathology, 1993. Cert. speech-lang. pathology Va., lic. speech/lang. disorders PreK-12 Va.; cert. early/primary edn. PreK-3 Va., devel. reading assessment Fairfax County Pub. Schs. Tchr. Fairfax County Pub. Schs., Alexandria, Va., 1990—, speech and lang. pathologist, 1990—2000, Chesapeake Ctr., Inc., Springfield, Va., 1998. Presenter mentoring program Fairfax County Pub. Schs., Alexandria, 2001—; presenter troops tchrs. program Old Dominion U., Ft. Belvior, Va., 2002—. Clinic team coord. Mid-Atlantic Pom and Dance Assn.; team coord. Mid Atlantic Poand Dance Assn. Named Outstanding Young Women of Am., 1988; scholar, U. DC, 1982, 1983; Dept. of Edn. Minority Tng. grantee, 1988—90. Mem.: Mid-Altantic Pomand Dance Assn. (team coord.), Am. Speech-Lang. Hearing Assn. (life cert. clin. competence in speech-lang. pathology), Nat. Allied Health Honor Soc., Delta Sigma Theta (life scholar 1984), Phi Delta Kappa (life). Avocations: dance choreography, pom pon coach. Personal E-mail: teachernva2000@aol.com.

ALFORD, STEVE (STEVEN TODD ALFORD), men's college basketball coach; b. New Castle, Ind., Nov. 23, 1964; m. Tanya Frost: children: Kory, Bryce, Kayla. BS, Ind. U. Mem. gold-medal U.S. basketball team Olympic Games, LA, 1984; professional basketball player Dallas Mavericks, Golden St. Warriors; head coach Manchester (Ind.) Coll., 1992-95, U. Iowa Hawkeyes, 1999—2007, U. New Mexico, 2007—. Named Ind. Collegiate Conf. Coach of Yr., 1993, 94, 95. Office: U New Mexico Athletic Dept Albuquerque NM 87131*

ALFRED, STEPHEN JAY, retired lawyer; b. NYC, Aug. 15, 1934; s. George J. Alfred and Janet (Brenner) Miller; m. Nora Richman, June 24, 1956 (div. 1980); children: Deborah Susan, Lynda Beth, Bruce David, Julianne Richman; m. Lynne Belofsky Durchslag, Jan. 10, 1981 (div. 1992); m. Rita G. Hungate, Aug. 23, 1997. AB, Princeton U., 1956; JD, Harvard U., 1959. Bar: Ohio 1959. From assoc. to ptnr. Squire, Sanders & Dempsey, Cleve., 1959—97; councilman City of Shaker Heights, Ohio, 1972—79, 1981, mayor, 1984—91; exec. dir. Common Cause/Ga., 1998—2001; ret., 2001. Gen. chmn. Cleve. Tax Inst., 1981. Contbr. articles to profl. jours. Trustee Citizens League of Cleve., 1976-83, Com. for Sandy Springs, Atlanta, 1998-2001, vice-chair, 1999-2000; trustee Beech Brook Children's Home, Orange, Ohio, 1968-84, pres., 1971-72, treas., 1979-81; pres. Lomond Assn., Shaker Heights, 1965-67, Harvard Law Sch. Assn. of Cleve., 1982; active Peoria County Govt. Study Commn., Peoria, 2000-01; govt. vision task force Peoria Area C. of C., 2001-02; bd. dirs. Ill. Campaign for Polit. Reform, Chgo., 2000—, v.p., 2002—; bd. dirs. Mayors Vision 2020, Peoria, 2002-06, Counseling and Family Svcs., Peoria, 2002—, v.p., 2003-04, pres. 2004-05; exec. dir. Ctrl. Ill. Biomed. Rsch. Group, 2000-02, vice-chmn., 2001-02; assoc. bd. dirs. WCBU, Peoria, 2001-07, v.p., 2003-05, pres., 2005-07. Democrat. Jewish. Personal E-mail: sjalfred@aol.com.

ALFREY, MARIAN ANTOINETTE, retired education educator; b. Crab Orchard, Nebr., Dec. 5, 1925; d. Rollin Milton and Emma Antoinette (Schultz) S.; m. David Homer, Aug. 10, 1947; children: Gary David, Judith Ann. BS, U. Nebr., Lincoln, 1968; MA, U. No. Iowa, Cedar Falls, 1972. Permanent Profl. Cert. Tchr. Louisville (Nebr.) Schs., 1945-46, Tecumseh (Nebr.) Schs., 1946-47, North Loup (Nebr.) Schs., 1949-51, Malvern (Iowa) Schs., 1951-52, Beatrice Schs., 1967-68, Waterloo (Iowa) Community Schs., 1968-89. Active Waterloo Cmty. Schs., 1973-88. Mem. Covenant Hosp. Aux., 1989—, pres.; diplomat Waterloo C. of C., 1995, sec. Recipient Mayors' Vol. award, Mayors of Black Hawk County, 2000, Vol. Performance award, Cedar Valley Mayors, 2000. Mem. NEA, Nebr. Congress PTA (hon. life). Republican. Methodist. Home: 1925 Westchester Rd Apt 220 Waterloo IA 50701-4522

ALFRIEND, KYLE TERRY, aerospace engineer; b. Macon, Ga., Aug. 17, 1940; s. Kyle Terry Sr. and Esther Alfriend; m. Bonnie Gray Chattin; children: Kyle, Kim. BS, Va. Poly. Inst. & State U., 1962; PhD, Stanford U., Calif., 1967, MS, 1964. Asst. prof. Cornell U., Ithaca, N.Y., 1967-74; head advanced systems br. Naval Rsch. Lab., Washington, 1974-85; dir. Washington br. Gen. Rsch. Corp., Vienna, Va., 1985-93; editor-in-chief AIAA Jour. Guidance, Control and Dynamics, 1992—; Navy TENCAP space chair prof. Naval Postgrad. Sch., Monterey, Calif., 1994—; prof., head aerospace engring. Tex. A&M U., College Station, 1997—, inaugural holder of the Royce E. Wisenbaker '39 Chair in Engineering, 2001. Editor-in-chief AAS Jour. Astronaut. Scis., 1985-87; contbr. numerous articles to profl. jours. Co-recipient 2005 AAAS Internat. Scientific Cooperation award, 2006. Fellow AIAA (chmn. Astrodynamics Tech. Com.), Am. Astronaut. Soc. (Dirk Brouwer award 1990), mem. NAE.

ALGEO, JOHN THOMAS, association executive, retired educator; b. St. Louis, Nov. 12, 1930; s. Thomas George and Julia Winifred (Wathen) A.; m. Adele Marie Silbereisen, Sept. 6, 1958; children: Thomas John, Catherine Marie. EdB cum laude, U. Miami, Coral Gables, 1955; MA, U. Fla., Gainesville, 1957, PhD, 1960. Instr. Fla. State U., Tallahassee, 1959-61; from asst. to full prof. U. Fla., Gainesville, 1961-71, asst. dean grad. sch., 1969-71, dir. program in linguistics, 1969-71; prof. U. Ga., Athens, 1971-88, dir. program in linguistics, 1974-79, head dept. English, 1975-79, alumni found. disting. prof., 1988-94; nat. pres. Theosophical Soc. in Am., Wheaton, Ill., 1993—2002; internat. v.p. Theosophical Soc., Adyar, India, 2002—. Mem. gen. coun. Theosophical Soc., Adyar, India, 1993—; dir. Manor Found. Ltd., Sydney, Australia, 1995—; accreditation cons. So. Assn. Colls. and Schs., Atlanta, 1967-90; cons. NEH, Washington, 1974-94; dir. Commn. on the English Lang., Nat. Coun. Tchrs. of English, Urbana, Ill., 1976-82; del. Am. Coun. Learned Socs., NYC, 1984-87; cons. in lang. and lexicography Cambridge Univ. Press, NYC, 1987-93; cons. in Am. usage Kenkyusha Ltd., Tokyo, 1991-99; cons. Webster's New World Dictionary, 4th edit., Cleve., 1993-95. Author: Problems in the Origins and Development of the English Language, 1966, 5th edit., 2004, On Defining the Proper Name, 1973, Exercises in Contemporary English, 1974, Reincarnation Explored, 1987, Reincarnatie in Kaart gebracht, 1990, Fifty Years "Among the New Words": A Dictionary of Neologisms, 1941-91, 1991, Eigo no kigen to hattatsu, 1991, Reinkarnation: Evolution der Seele, 1991, 96, Reinkarnation i ny belysning, 1994, Investigando a reencarnacao, 1996, Unlocking the Door: Studies in The Key to Theosophy, 2001, British or American English? A Handbook of Word and Grammar Patterns, 2006; co-author: English: An Introduction to Language, 1970, Spelling: Sound to Letter, 1971, The Origins and Development of the English Language, 1982, 5th edit., 2004, Elements of Literature, Sixth Course: Literature of Britain, 1989, The Power of Thought, 2001, Pensamento: O que e e como usar, 2003, British or American English?, 2006; editor: American Speech, 1972-81, Thomas Pyles: Selected Essays on English Usage, 1979, Among the New Words, American Speech, 1987-97, Cambridge History of the English Language, vol. 6, English in North America, 2001, 02, The Quest, 1997-03, The Letters of H.P. Blavatsky, vol. 1, 2003, Echoes From the Gnosis, 2006; assoc. editor: The Oxford Companion to the English Language, 1992; mem. editl. bd. Jour. of English Linguistics, 1970—, Internat. Jour. Lexicography, 1990-93, World Englishes, 1996—, Names, 1997—, Language Problems Language Planning, 1997-99, Studies in English Language, 1987—. Sgt. US Army, 1951-54, Korea. Fellow Guggenheim Found., London, 1986-87; Fulbright scholar U. Coll. London, Eng., 1986-87. Mem. Am. Dialect Soc. (pres. 1979), Am. Name Soc. (pres. 1984), Internat. Assn. Univ. Profs. English, Internat. Linguistic Assn., Ea. Order Internat. Co-Freemasonry, Internat. Phonetic Assn., Linguistic Assn. of the U.S. and Can., Linguistic Soc. Am., Modern Lang. Assn. Am., Philological Soc., Southeastern Conf. on Linguistics (pres. 1970-71), Dictionary Soc. N.Am. (pres. 1995-97), Theosophical Soc. (nat. pres. 1993-2002, internat. v.p. 2002-), Ea. Order Internat. Co-Freemasonry (adminstr. 2002—). Democrat. Home: PO Box 80206 Athens GA 30608-0206 Personal E-mail: jalgeo@jalgeo.com.

ALGER, CHADWICK FAIRFAX, political scientist, educator; b. Chambersburg, Pa., Oct. 9, 1924; s. Herbert and Thelma (Drawbaugh) A.; m. Elinor Reynolds, Aug. 28, 1948; children: Mark, Scott, Laura, Craig. BA, Ursinus Coll., 1949, LLD, 1979; MA, Johns Hopkins U., 1950; PhD, Princeton, 1958. Internat. relations specialist Dept. Navy, 1950-54; instr. Swarthmore Coll., 1957; faculty Northwestern U., Evanston, Ill., 1958-71, prof. polit. sci., 1966-71, dir. internat. relations program, 1967-71; Mershon prof. polit. sci. and pub. policy Ohio State U., 1971-95, emeritus prof., 1995—, dir. transnat. intellectual cooperation program, 1971-80, dir. world affairs program, Mershon Ctr., 1980-88, coord. working group on global rels. and peace studies, 1988-95, acting dir. univ. ctr. for internat. studies, 1990-91. Vis. prof. UN affairs NYU, 1962-63 Author: Internationalization from Local Areas: Beyond Interstate Relations, 1987, Perceiving, Understanding and Coping with World Relations in Everyday Life, 1993, The United Nations System: Potential for the Twenty-First Century, 1998, The United Nations System: A Reference Handbook, 2006; co-author: Simulation in International Relations, 1963, You and Your Community in the World, 1978, Conflicts and Crisis of International Order: New Tasks for Peace Research, 1985, A Just Peace Through Transformation: Cultural, Economic and Political Foundations for Change, 1988, The United Nations System: The Policies of Member States, 1995; contbr. articles to profl. jours. Mem. Trade Coun., State of Ohio, 1984-87; adv. com. Global Issues Ctr. Cuyahoga C.C., 2005—; mem. adv. coun. Ams. for UNESCO, 2006—. Served with USNR, 1943-46. Recipient Disting. Scholar award Internat. Soc. for Ednl., Cultural and Sci. Interchanges, 1980, Golden Apple award Am. Forum for Global Edn., 1993. Mem. Am. Polit. Sci. Assn. (coun. 1970-72), Internat. Polit. Sci. Assn., Internat. Studies Assn. (pres. 1978-79), Internat. Studies Assn. Midwest (Quincy Wright disting. scholar award 2000), Internat. Peace Rsch. Assn. (coun. 1971-77, sec.-gen. 1983-87), Internat. Peace Rsch. Assn. Found. (v.p. 1998—), Midwest Conf. Polit. Scis. (recipient prize 1966), Consortium on Peace Rsch., Edn. and Devel. (exec. com. 1971-77, chmn. 1976-77), Hunger and Devel. Coalition of Cen. Ohio (bd. dirs. 1983-90), Columbus Coun. on World Affairs (bd. dirs. 1974-88), UN Assn. (pres. Columbus chpt. 1991-93). Home: 2674 Westmont Blvd Columbus OH 43221-3354 Office: Ohio State U Mershon Ctr 1501 Neil Ave Columbus OH 43201-2602 E-mail: Alger1@osu.edu.

ALGIERE, DENNIS LEE, state legislator; b. Westerly, RI, July 30, 1960; s. Joseph L. and Ida R. (Vacca) A.; m. Leigh A. Williams, Nov. 7, 1992. BA, Providence Coll., 1982; MS, Northea. U., 1984; JD, So. New England Sch. Law, 1991. Town councilor Town of Westerly, RI, 1990-92; mem. RI Senate, Dist. 38, 1993—; minority leader R.I. Senate, 1997—. Sr. v.p. Washington Trust Co. Dir. adv. com. for the arts John F. Kennedy Ctr. Performing Arts, 2002—; bd. dirs. Chorus of Westerly, 2005—. Mem. Lions. Republican. Roman Catholic. Home: 6 Elm St Westerly RI 02891-2126 Office: RI Senate State House Rm 120 Providence RI 02908

ALHADEFF, DAVID ALBERT, economics professor; b. Seattle, Mar. 22, 1923; s. Albert David and Pearl (Taranto) A.; m. Charlotte Pechman, Aug. 1, 1948. BA, U. Wash., 1944; MA, Harvard U., 1948, PhD, 1950. Faculty U. Calif.-Berkeley, 1949-87, prof. bus. adminstrn., 1959-87, prof. emeritus, 1987—, assoc. dean Sch. Bus. Adminstrn., 1980-82, 85-86. Author: Monopoly and Competition in Banking, 1954, Competition and Controls in Banking, 1968, Microeconomics and Human Behavior, 1982; Contbr. articles to profl. jours., chpts. to books. Served with AUS, 1943-46. Recipient The Berkeley Citation U. Calif.-Berkeley, 1987. Home: 2101 Shoreline Dr Apt 456 Alameda CA 94501-6249 Office: Haas Sch Bus Berkeley CA 94720-0001

AL-HAFEEZ, HUMZA, minister, editor; b. NYC, Feb. 28, 1931; s. Asa Moss and Rosa May Danielson-Weir; children: Jacqueline, Yuhanna, Rasul, Bismillah, Habib, Wardi, Larry, Don, Mariama. Student, Food Trades Vocat. Sch., 1947-48. Patrolman N.Y.C. Police Dept., from 1959; chmn. Temple of Islam, Inc. Founder Nat. Soc. Afro-Am. Policemen Inc.; also past pres.; cons. community relations to chief insp. N.Y.C. Police Dept., to; U.S. Dept. Justice; investigator of corruption among N.Y.C. police officers Knapp Commn.; undercover narcotic officer, investigator Manhattan office Dist. Atty.; investigator Office of 1st Dep. Policy Commr.;

undercover investigator U.S. Dept. Justice.; insp. N.Y. State Athletic Commn.; Lectr. Princeton U., Mich. State U., N.Y. State U., Pace Coll., Bklyn. Coll., U. Chgo., NYU, Satellite Acad., N.Y.C., Kinlock Mission for Blind, City N.Y. Police Acad., Nassau Community Coll.; others Appeared on radio and TV; editor-in-chief: Your Muhammad Speaks newspaper; author: The Slanderer, 1987, Some Things to Think About, 2003. Pastoral bd. Interfaith Hosp.; chaplain Frackville (Pa.) Correctional Facility, 1995—. Recipient Father of Yr. award Kinlock Freedom Found. for the Blind, 1973; Community Service award United Council of Chs., 1975; named Person of Yr. Nat. Assn. Black Policemen, 1982. Mem. Internat. Platform Assn. Mem. Nation of Islam; minister Muhammad's Temple of Islam, Bklyn. Home: 361 Clinton Ave Apt 12C Brooklyn NY 11238-1145 Office: 1211 Atlantic Ave Brooklyn NY 11216-2709 Office Phone: 718-789-7747. Personal E-mail: humzahafeez@msn.com. *To expect all of the people to cooperate is something that should be given some thought. Change comes through the efforts of a person, or a small group of people, not all of the people. However, all of the people may benefit, or suffer, from the action of a person, or a small group. History will bear me witness.*

AL-HAJJ, MUHAMMAD, biologist; BSc, Am. U. Beirut, 1992; PhD, Wayne State U., Detroit, 1999. Rsch. fellow U. Mich., Ann Arbor, 1999—2004; rsch. investigator Novartis, Cambridge, Mass., 2004—06, group leader San Diego, 2006—. Vol. sci. instr. various schs., Cambridge. Achievements include discovery of identification of the first solid tumor stem cell (breast). E-mail: selfrenew@gmail.com.

ALI, ARSHAD, medical researcher; m. Shamsa A Maqbool, Jan. 16, 2000. MBBS, Rawalpindi Med. Coll., Pakistan, 1983. Diplomate Am. Bd. Internal Medicine, 1994, with subspeciality in cardiovascular disease Am. Bd. Internal Medicine, 1998, with subspeciality in interventional cardiology ABIM, 2002. Dir. cardiology rsch. St John Hosp., Detroit, 1998—2003. Scholar, Govt. of Pakistan, 1977—83. Fellow: Am. Coll. Cardiology (licentiate); mem.: Royal Coll. Physicians. Independent. Muslim. Achievements include research in thrombectomy in AMI. Office: Guthrie Clinic 1 Guthrie Sq Sayre PA 18840 Office Phone: 570-882-2279. Office Fax: 570-882-3507. E-mail: mdali1992@aol.com.

ALI, ASHRAF, psychiatrist; b. Dhaka, Bangladesh, June 7, 1951; s. Wazed Ali and Noorjahan Khatoon; m. Shada Ali, Oct. 19, 1984; children: Sanah, Amir, Omar. MD, Rajshahi Med. Coll., Bangladesh, 1974; diploma in Child Health, Nat. U. Ireland, Dublin, 1988. Diplomate Am. Bd. Psychiatry and Neurology, Am. Bd. Adolescent Psychiatry. Resident in psychiatry Brookdale U. Hosp., Bklyn., 1993—96; fellow in child and adolescent psychiatry SUNY, Bklyn., 1996—98; area dir. Camino Real Cmty. Mental Health Mental Retardation Ctr., Eagle Pass, Tex., 1998—2001; med. dir. Border Region Cmty. Ctr., Laredo, Tex., 2001—05; lead med. dir. Cigna Behavioral Health, Irving, Tex., 2005—. Fellow: Royal Soc. Health London; mem.: Am. Med. Soc. Vienna, Am. Soc. Addiction Medicine, Am. Soc. Clin. Psychopharmacology, Am. Psychiat. Assn. Muslim. Avocations: travel, fishing. Home: 2608 Elmbrook Dr Carrollton TX 75010 Office: Cigna Behavioral Health 6600 E Campus Circle Dr Ste 110 Irving TX 75063 Office Phone: 972-465-7027. Personal E-mail: ashrafali80@hotmail.com.

ALI, JEFFER, lawyer; b. Buffalo, Mar. 17, 1966; PharmD, U. Mich., 1990; JD cum laude, U. Minn., 1994. Bar: Minn. 1994, US Dist. Ct. (dist. Minn.) 1995. Hiring ptnr. Merchant & Gould, P.C., Mpls. Adj. prof. U. Minn. Law Sch. Intellectual Property Moot Ct. Named a Rising Star, Minn. Super Lawyers mag., 2006; recipient Pro Bono Atty. of Yr. award, Vol. Lawyers Network, 2000. Mem.: Minn. State Bar Assn., Minn. Intellectual Property Law Assn., Am. Intellectual Property Law Assn. Office: Merchant & Gould PC 3200 IDS Ctr 80 S 8th St Minneapolis MN 55402 Office Phone: 612-371-5351. E-mail: jali@merchant-gould.com.*

ALI, MIR MASOOM, retired statistician, educator; b. Bangladesh, Feb. 1, 1937; arrived in U.S., 1969; s. Mir Muazzam and Azifa Khatoon (Chowdhury) Ali; m. Firoza Chowdhury, June 25, 1959; children: Naheed, Fahima, Farah, Mir Ishtiaque. BSc, U. Dhaka, 1956, MSc, 1957, U. Toronto, 1967, PhD, 1969. Rsch. officer, Ministry of Food and Agr., Ministry of Commerce, Ctrl. Pub. Svc. Commn. Govt. of Pakistan, 1958—66; tchg. asst. U. Toronto, Ont., Canada, 1966—69; asst. prof. math. scis. Ball State U., Muncie, Ind., 1969—74, assoc. prof., 1974—78, prof., 1978—2000, George and Frances Ball disting. prof. stats., 2000—07, George and Frances Ball Disting. Prof. Emeritus of Stats., 2007. Vis. prof. U. Windsor, Canada, 1972—73, U. Dhaka, 1983—84, Purdue U., 1978, Jahangirnagar U., 1991, Indian Stats. Inst., Calcutta, 1991, Yeungnam U., Republic of Korea, 1993, King Saud U., 1999. Assoc. editor Jour. Statis. Rsch., Aligarh Jour. Stats., Pakistan Jour. Stats., Jour. Statis Mgmt. Systems, overseas exec. editor Jour. Statis. Studies; contbr. articles to profl. jours. Named Sagamore of the Wabash, State of Ind., 2002; recipient Q.M. Husain Gold medal, Bangladesh Stats. Assn., 1990. Fellow: Bangladesh Acad. Sci., Inst. Statisticians, Royal Statis. Soc., Am. Statis. Assn. (Meritorious Svc. award biopharm. sect. 1987, 1997, 2002); mem.: Islamic Statis. Soc., Inst. Math. Stats., Internat. Statis. Inst. (Gold medal 2005). Muslim. Home: 5200 W Deerbrook Dr Muncie IN 47304-3475 Office: Ball State U Dept Math Scis Muncie IN 47306-0490 Office Phone: 765-285-8670. Business E-Mail: mali@bsu.edu.

ALI, MOHAMMED ZAMSHED, information technology executive, researcher; b. Gaibandha, Bangladesh; s. Md Abdur and Jarina Rahman; m. Shamima Afroze Ali; children: Mihir, Maimun. BSEE, Bangladesh U. Engring. and Tech., Dhaka, 1991; MSEE, U. Tex., Arlington, 1994; PhD in Elec. Engring., U. Tex., Dallas, 2005. Networks systems engr. MCI, Richardson, 1994—95; mem. sci. staff Nortel, 1995—97; requirements and systems design engr. Alcatel, Plano, 1997—2002; co-founder, CEO Flex-Solv, Richardson, 2002—; cons. mem. tech. staff Verizon, Irving, 2002—06. Adj. faculty dept. elec. engring. U. Tex. Contbr. more than ten publs. in telecommunication jours. and conf. procs. Scholar, U. Tex., Dept. Elec. Engring., 1994. Mem.: Am. Assn. Bangladeshi Engrs., Archs. and Tech. Profls. (pres. North Tex.). Achievements include patents for focused overload detection in telecommunication networks; patents pending for IS-41 application location register routing in telecommunications networks; web based automatic call distribution and computer telephony integration. Office Phone: 214-893-5556. Personal E-mail: zamshed@yahoo.com.

ALI, MUHAMMAD (CASSIUS MARCELLUS CLAY), retired boxer; b. Louisville, Jan. 17, 1942; s. Marcellus and Odessa (Grady) Clay; m. Sonji Roi, August 14, 1964 (div. Jan. 10, 1966); m. Kalilah Tolona (Belinda Boyd), Apr. 17, 1967 (div. 1977) children: Rasheeda, Jamilla, Maryum, Muhammed Jr.; m. Veronica Porshe, June 19, 1977 (div. 1986), children: Hana, Laila; m. Yolanda Williams, Nov. 19, 1986, 1 child, Asaad; two other children Miya, Khalilah. D Pub. Svc. (hon.), Northeastern U., 1994; LHD (hon.), Ky. State U., 2003; HHD (hon.), Princeton U., 2007. Profl. boxer, 1960—79, 1980—81; ret., 1981. Film appearances: The Greatest, 1976, Freedom Road (TV), 1978; author: The Greatest: My Own Story, 1975, (with Thomas Hauser) Healing, 1996, (with Hana Ali) More Than a Hero, 2000, (with Hana Ali and Hana Yasmeen Ali) The Soul of a Butterfly: Reflections on Life's Journey, 2004. Named the greatest heavyweight champion of all time, Ring Mag., 1987, Muhammad Ali Mus., Louisville Galleria opened, 1995; named to U.S. Olympic Hall of Fame, 1983, World Boxing Hall of Fame, 1986, Internat. Boxing Hall of Fame, 1990, Sport in Soc. Hall of Fame, 1994; recipient 6 Kentucky Golden Gloves titles, Olympic gold medal in boxing, 1960, Nat. Golden Gloves titles, 1959—60, Jim Thorpe Pro Sports award, lifetime achievement, 1992, Essence award, 1997, Presdl. Medal of Freedom, The White House, 2005, Council of 100 Leaders Award, World Economic Forum, 2006. Mem. World Community Islam. Achievements include being a light heavyweight champion AAU, 1959, 60; light heavyweight champion Golden Gloves, 1959, heavyweight champion, 1960; light heavy weight champion Olympic Games, 1960, world heavyweight champion, 1964-67, 74-78, 78-79.*

ALI, OMAR H., history professor; b. Lima, Peru, Feb. 10, 1971; BSc in Social Anthropology, London Sch. Econs. and Polit. Sci., 1992; PhD in History, Columbia U., 2003. Vis. scholar Ctr. Study of Am. South U. NC, Chapel Hill, 2002; lectr. Inst. Rsch. in African Am. Studies Columbia U., NYC, 2003—04; asst. prof. history Towson (Md.) U., 2004—. Hist. commentator PBS program Transforming America: US History since 1877, 2005. Editor: Souls: A Critical Jour. of Black Politics, Culture and Society, 2005, Jour. Colonialism and Colonial History, 2007; author: In the Balance of Power: Independent Black Politics and Third Party Movements in the United States. Program dir. Clemente course in humanities Bard Coll., NJ; dir. rsch. and edn. Com. for Unified Ind. Party, NYC. Recipient Rsch. and Lecture award, Fulbright Scholar, Bogota, Colombia, 2006; grantee, Inst. So. Studies, U. SC, 2006; Libr. scholar, Harvard U., 2007. Office: Towson U Dept History 8000 York Rd Towson MD 21252-0001 Office Phone: 410-704-2914. Business E-Mail: oali@towson.edu.

ALIANO, JOY CARYL, retired elementary school educator; b. NYC, Mar. 13, 1944; d. Irving and Iris (Plavnick) Cofsky; m. John Anthony Aliano, Aug. 20, 1966; children: Catherine, Kelly. BS, CCNY, 1964; MA, NYU, NYC, 1969. Cert. elem., reading tchr. N.Y. Salesperson Macy's, NYC, 1960—61; proof reader, editor Plenum Pub., NYC, 1964—66; tchr. N.Y.C. Bd. Edn., 1967—79; ret., 1979. Mem.: Phi Beta Kappa. Home: 790 Mervin Ct Baldwin NY 11510-4038

ALIBER, ROBERT Z., economist, educator; b. Keene, NH, Sept. 19, 1930; s. Norman H. and Sophie (Becker) A.; m. Deborah Baltzly, Sept. 9, 1955; children: Jennifer, Rachel, Michael. BA, Williams Coll., Williamstown, Mass., 1952, Cambridge U., 1954, MA, 1957; PhD, Yale U., New Haven, Conn., 1962. Staff economist Commn. Money and Credit, NYC, 1959-61, Com. on Econ. Devel., Washington, 1961-64; sr. econ. advisor AID, Dept. State, Washington, 1964-65; assoc. prof., then prof. internat. econs. and fin. U. Chgo., 1965—2004; pres. Dorchester Capital Mgmt., 1990—2007. Vis. prof. Brandeis U., 1987-93; vis. Bundesbank prof. Free U. Berlin, 1999; Houblon-Norman fellow, Bank of Eng., 1996, J.P. Morgan Internat. prize fellow, Am. Academy in Berlin, 2002. Author: The International Money Game, 1973, 76, 79, 83, 87, 2001, Exchange Risk and Corporate International Finance, 1978, Your Money and Your Life, 1982; co-author: Money, Banking, and the Economy, 1981, 84, 87, 90, 93, The Multinational Paradigm, 1993; co-author Manias, Panics, and Crashes, 2005; editor: National Monetary Policies and the International Financial System, 1974, The Political Economy of Monetary Reform, 1976, The Reconstruction of International Monetary Arrangements, 1987, The Handbook of International Financial Management, 1989; co-editor Global Portfolios, 1991, Readings in International Business: A Decision Approach, 1993. With US Army, 1954—56. Fulbright fellow, 1952-54. Fellow Woodrow Wilson Internat. Ctr. Scholars, 2004-05; mem. Am. Econs. Assn., Acad. Internat. Bus., Quadrangle Club, Williams Club of NY, Post Mills Soaring Club. Office Phone: 603-643-0107. Business E-Mail: rza@chicagogsb.edu.

ALI G, See BARON COHEN, SACHA

ALIKHANI, ZOUBIN, internist, molecular biologist, researcher; m. Arezou Khosroshahi. MD, Tehran U. Med. Scis., Iran, 2000. Cert. of Proficiency In English U. Cambridge, 1999. Med. dir. Pouya Day Clinic, Tehran, 2000—02; postdoctoral rsch. fellow Boston U. Med. Ctr., 2002—04; medicine housestaff Columbia U. at St.Luke's-Roosevelt Hosp. Ctr., NYC, 2004—, Meml. Sloan Ketteing Cancer Ctr., 2004—; fellow in cardiovasc. medicine Tufts U. Med. Sch./St. Elizabeth Med. Ctr., Boston, 2007—. Rsch. vol. Tehran U. Med. Scis., Imam Khomeini Hosp., Dept. of Cardiology, Tehran, 1994—96; rsch. asst. Tehran U. Med. Scis., Dept. of pharmacology, 1996—97, Tehran U. Med. Scis., Dept. of Allergy and Immunology, 1997—98, Imam Khomeini Hosp., Dept. of Neurosurgery, 1998—2000, Imam Khomeini Hosp., Dept. of Endocrinology, 1999—2000; spkr. and presenter in field. Contbr. scientific papers to profl. jours. Mem.: ACP, AMA, NY State Med. Soc. Avocations: poetry, running, tennis, swimming, fishing. Office: St Lukes Roosevelt Hosp Ctr Dept Medicine 1000 Amsterdam Ave New York NY 10019 Home Phone: 646-649-2355; Office Phone: 917-757-8889. E-mail: za2115@columbia.edu.

ALINDER, MARY STREET, writer, educator; b. Bowling Green, Ohio, Sept. 23, 1946; d. Scott Winfield and McDonna Street; m. James Gilbert Alinder, Dec. 17, 1965; children: Jasmine, Jesse, Zachary. Student, U. Mich., 1964-65, U. N.Mex., 1966-68; BA, U. Nebr., 1976. Mgr. The Weston Gallery, Carmel, Calif., 1978-79; chief asst. Ansel Adams, Carmel, 1979-84; exec. editor, bus. mgr. The Ansel Adams Pub. Rights Trust, Carmel, 1984-87; freelance writer, lectr., curator, Gualala, Calif., 1989—; selector and writer biographies Focal Press Ency., 3d edit., 1993; ptnr. The Alinder Gallery, Gualala, 1990—; cultural expert U.S. State Dept., Guadalajara, Mexico, 2003. Curator Ansel Adams Centenial Celebration, 2002, Ansel Adams: 80th Birthday Retrospective, Friends of Photography, Carmel, Acad. Sci., San Francisco, Denver Mus. Natural History, Ansel Adams and the West, Calif. State Capitol, Sacto., 2001; co-curator One With Beauty, M.H. deYoung Meml. Mus., 1987, Ansel Adams: American Artist, The Ansel Adams Ctr., San Francisco; lectr. Nat. Gallery Art, Barbican Ctr., M.H. deYoung Meml. Mus., Stanford U., LA County Mus., U. Mich.; vis. artist and lectr. Nebr. Art Assn., 1997; Wallace Stegner meml. lectr. Peninsula Open Space Inst., Mountainview, Calif., 1998, Assn. Internat. Photographic Art Dealers, NYC, 1999, Cin. Art Mus., 2000, Eiteljorg Mus., Indpls., 2001, Internat. Wildlife Mus., Jackson Hole, 2003, Telluride Mountain Film Festival, Nev. Mus. Art, Reno, 2004, U. Tex., Austin, 2005, Manzanar Hist. Monument, 2006; Sierra Club Golden Keynote spkr.; faculty Stanford U., 2000. Author: Picturing Yosemite (Places), 1990, The Limits of Reality: Ansel Adams and Group f/64 (Seeing Straight), 1992, Ansel Adams, A Biography (Henry Holt), 1996, Mabel Dodge Luhan, 1997 (ViewCamera), Ansel Adams: Milestone, 2002; (with others) the Scribner Encyclopedia of American Lives, 1998; co-author: Ansel Adams: An Autobiography, 1985; co-editor: Ansel Adams: Letters and Images, 1988; columnist Coast and Valley Mag., 1993-98, Ansel Adams: Political Landscape, Focal Ency. Photography, 1993; political landscape (Civilization), 1999; contbr. articles to profl. jours., popular mags. Business E-Mail: alinders@mcn.org.

ALIOTO, ANGELA MIA, lawyer; b. San Francisco, Oct. 20, 1949; m. Adolfo Veronese (dec. Sept. 1990); children: Angela Veronese, Adolfo Veronese, Joseph Veronese, Gian-Paolo Veronese. BA, Lone Mountain Coll., 1971; JD, U. San Francisco, 1983. Lawyer Alioto and Alioto, San Francisco, 1980—; mem. bd. supr. City and County of San Francisco, 1989—97, pres. bd. supr., 1993—95. Candidate for mayor City of San Francisco, 1991, 2003; first vice-chair Calif. State Dem. Party, 1991—93; co-chair Calif. del. Dem. Nat. Conv., 1992; mem. Golden Gate Bridge Dist., Outer-Continental Shelf Bd. Control; vice-chair San Francisco County Transp. Authority; mem. San Francisco Mental Health Bd. Author: Straight to the Heart. Chair bd. dir. Nat. Shrine St. Francis Assisi. Mem.: Soc. Profl. Journalists, Am. Trial Lawyers Assn., Bar Assn. San Francisco, NAACP (life), Dante Soc. Am. Democrat. Roman Catholic. Office: Alioto & Alioto 700 Montgomery St San Francisco CA 94111

ALISETTI, EDWIN LUIS, engineer, corporate financial executive; b. Caracas, Venezuela, Aug. 10, 1969; s. Gualtiero Alisetti and Rina Esther Pacillo. BSCE, U. Catolica Andres Bello, Caracas, Venezuela, 1995; MSME, U. Miami, 1998, MBA, 2001. Pres. Casa Bella, Caracas, Venezuela, 1992-95; apt. adminstr. Miami, 1996-98; data analyst U. Miami Sch. Architecture, Coral Gables, Fla., 2000—; jr. analyst M&A dept. Royal Bank of Can., 2001; bus./fin. intern Merrill Lynch, Miami, 2001; eCommerce Latin Am. intern Fed. Express, Miami, 2000; cons. The Fin. Group, Fort Lauderdale, Fla., 2002—. Tutor econs. and fin. U. Miami Sch. Bus., 2000—; pres. KateMi Group Inc. Contbr. articles to sci. and tech. jours. Mem.: ASME. Avocations: martial arts, soccer, rugby. Home: 1217 NW 107th Terr Plantation FL 33322 Personal E-mail: ealisett@hotmail.com.

ALITO, SAMUEL ANTHONY, JR., United States supreme court justice; b. Trenton, NJ, Apr. 1, 1950; s. Samuel and Rose (Fradusco) Alito; m. Martha-Ann Bomgardner, 1985; children: Philip, Laura. JD, Yale U., 1975. Bar: NJ 1975, NY 1970. Law clk. to Hon. Leonard I. Garth US Ct. Appeals (3rd Cir.), Newark, 1976—77; asst. US atty. NJ US Dept. Justice, Newark, 1977—81, US atty., 1987—90, asst. to solicitor gen. Office of Solicitor Gen. Rex E. Lee Washington, 1981—85, dep. asst. to atty. gen. Edwin Meese, Office of Legal Counsel, 1985—87; judge US Ct. Appeals (3rd Cir.), Newark, 1990—2006; assoc. justice US Supreme Ct., Washington, 2006—. Editor Yale Law Jour., 1974—75; adj. prof. Seton Hall U. Capt. USAR, 1972—80. Recipient St. Thomas More award, Diocese of Trenton, St. Thomas More Soc., 2006. Fellow: Am. Bar Found.; mem.: Essex County Bar Assn., Am. Judicature Soc., Federalist Soc. for Law & Pub. Policy Studies, Assn. Fed. Bar NJ, Am. Law Inst., Advisory Com. on Appellate Rules. Office: US Supreme Ct One First St NE Washington DC 20543

ALIVISATOS, ARMAND PAUL, chemist, educator; b. Chgo., Nov. 12, 1959; BA in Chemistry, U. Chgo., 1981; PhD in Chem. Physics, U. Calif., Berkeley, 1986. Postdoctoral fellow AT&T Bell Labs., 1986-88; asst. prof. to assoc. prof. U. Calif., Berkeley, 1988-95, prof. chemistry, 1995—, vice chmn. dept. chemistry, 1995-98, Chancellor's prof., 1998—2001, prof. materials sci. and mineral engring., 1999—; dir. materials sci. divsn. Lawrence Berkeley Nat. Lab., 2002—. Head Molecular Foundry Lawrence Berkeley Nat. Lab., 2001-05. Editor Am. Chem. Soc. Jour., Nano Letters; mem. editl. bd. Jour. Phys. Chem., Chem. Physics, Jour. Chem. Physics, Advanced Materials Jour. Recipient Outstanding Sci. Accomplishment in Materials Chemistry award Dept. Energy, 1994, Coblentz award, 1994, Colloid and Surface Chemistry ACS award, 2004; co-recipient Ernest Orlando Lawrence award for Materials Rsch. Dept. Energy, 2007. Fellow Am. Phys. Soc., Am. Acad. Arts & Scis., AAAS; mem. Am. Chem. Soc.(Colloid and Surface Chemistry award, 2004), Materials Rsch. Soc. (Outstanding Young Investigator award 1995), NAS. Office: Dept Chemistry U Calif Alivisatos Grp Box 101 Berkeley CA 94720 Business E-Mail: alivis@berkeley.edu.

ALIZADEH, KAVEH, plastic surgeon, educator; b. Tehran, Iran; s. Hossein and Mina Alizadeh. BA, Cornell U., 1988, MD, 1993; MS, Columbia U., 2000; postgrad., Harvard U., 2006. Am. Bd. Plastic Surgery, 2001. Vice chmn. plastic surgery Winthrop U., Mineola, NY, 2003; chmn. microsurgery Winthrop U., Mineola, 2002—; ptnr. L.I. Plastic Surgery, Garden City, NY, 2001—; program dir., plastic surgery Nassau U. Med. Ctr., 2001—. Chief med. officer Advance Aesthetic Inst. Contbr. articles to jours. Recipient Disting. Alumni award, Dwight Englewood Sch., 2004; fellow, Meml. Sloan Kettering Cancer Ctr., 2000; Edn. grant, Smile Train. Fellow: Am. Coll. Surgeons; mem.: Assn. Acad. Chmn. Plastic Surgery, Am. Soc. Aesthetic Plastic Surgery, Am. Soc. Plastic Surgeons. Office: 501 Madison Ave New York NY 10020 Office Phone: 516-742-3404. Business E-Mail: ka89@cornell.edu.

ALKADRY, MOHAMAD G., public administration educator; s. Ghazi M. Alkadry and Nahla Khoayer; m. Rania Salem, July 16, 2000; children: Kenda M., Jad M. BA with honors, Carleton U., Ottawa, Ont., 1994; M of Pub. Policy and Pub. Adminstrn., Concordia U., Montreal, Can., 1996; PhD, Fla. Atlantic U., Boca Raton, 2000. Sr. counsellor III Total Comm. Environment, Nepean, Ont., 1990—94; auditor Office of Auditor Gen. Can., Ottawa, Ont., 1994—96; instr. Fla. Atlantic U., Boca Raton, 1996—99, sr. rsch. assoc. Ft. Lauderdale, 1998—2000; assoc. prof. pub. adminstrn. W.Va. U., Morgantown, 2000—. Dir. masters pub. adminstrn. program W.Va. U., Morgantown, 2006—; forum editor Adminstrv. Theory and Praxis, Omaha, 2002—06; dir. Local Govt. Leadership Acad., Morgantown, W.Va., 2000—04. Author: (book) Compensation Survey, 2003, These Things Happen: Stories from the Public Sector; contbr. articles to profl. jours., chapters to books. V.p. Grad. Student Assn., Fla. Atlantic U., 1996—99, Grad. Students Assn., Concordia U., Montreal, Quebec, Canada, 1994—95; mem. adv. bd. Nova Inst. Pub. Deliberation, Morgantown, W.Va., 2005—07. Recipient Alumni of Yr. award, Fla. Atlantic U., 2006. Mem.: Am. Soc. Pub. Adminstrn. (chpt. pres. 2002—04). Office: WVa U 217 Knapp Hall Morgantown WV 26508 Home Phone: 304-291-3532. Business E-Mail: malkadry@wvu.edu.

ALKALAY, ARIE L., pediatrician; b. July 23, 1946; MD, Hadassah Sch. Medicine, Jerusalem, 1971. Intern Belinson Med. Ctr./Kaplan Hosp., Israel, 1971-72, Cedars Sinai Med. Ctr., LA, 1984-85; resident in pediat. Kaplan Hosp., Israel, 1975-80, fellow in neonatal-perinatal medicine, 1980-82, Cedars Sinai Med. Ctr., LA, 1982-84; assoc. dir. neonatology Cedars-Sinai Med. Ctr., LA, 1992-97, dir. Well Baby Nursery, 1993-99, 2004—; prof. pediat. UCLA, 1997—. Contbr. over 50 articles to profl. jours. Recipient the Morris Press Humanism award Cedars-Sinai Med. Ctr., 1989. Office: 8700 Beverly Blvd Los Angeles CA 90048-1804 Office Phone: 310-423-2157. Business E-Mail: arie.alkalay@cshs.org.

ALKANA, LINDA KELLY, history professor; b. Calgary, Alta., Can., Nov. 9, 1946; arrived in U.S., 1963; d. Bernard Joseph and Lorna Lucille (Sutherland) Kelly; m. Ronald Lee Alkana, Sept. 12, 1970; children: Alexander Philippe, Lorna Jane. BA, UCLA, 1969; MA, U. Calif., Irvine, 1975, PhD, 1985. Lectr. humanities U. Calif., Irvine, 1985-93; lectr. history Calif. State U., Long Beach, 1981—, lectr. internat. studies, 2000—. Affiliate scholar Ctr. Study Women UCLA, 1987—89. Assoc. editor: The History Teacher, 1987—; contbr. articles to profl. jours. Mem.: Popular Culture Assn., Western Assn. Women Historians, Am. Hist. Assn. Office: Calif State U Long Beach Dept History 1250 N Bellflower Blvd Long Beach CA 90840-0006 Office Phone: 562-985-4429. Business E-Mail: lalk@csulb.edu.

ALKASSAB, FIRAS, rheumatologist; b. Damascus, Syria, Apr. 23, 1976; s. Mounir Alkassab and Huda Kazziha; m. Alia Nassri, May 25, 2002; 1 child, Jad F. MD, U. Damascus, 2000. Cert. Ednl. Commn. for Fgn. Med. Grads., 2002, Am. Bd. Internal Medicine, 2005. Rsch. fellow Mass. Gen. Hosp., Boston, 2001—02; resident dept. internal medicine U. Tex., Houston, 2002—05, clin. fellow divsn. rheumatology, 2005—07; asst. prof. medicine divsn. rheumatology U. Mass. Meml. Med. Ctr., Worcester, 2007—. Peer reviewer Arthritis and Rheumatism and Rheumatology Jour., 2006—. Mem.: Am. Soc. Internal Medicine (assoc.), ACP (assoc. Cert. Achievement, Cert. Appreciation), Am. Coll. Rheumatology (assoc. Fellows Recognition 2006). Islam. Achievements include research in allograft inflammatory factor association in systemic sclerosis scleroderma. Avocations: travel, piano. Office: Univ Mass Meml 119 Belmont St Worcester MA 01605 Office Phone: 508-334-6273.

ALKIRE, JOHN D., lawyer, arbitrator, mediator; b. Seattle, Nov. 15, 1948; s. Durwood Lee and Dorys (Maryon) A.; m. Karen A. Heerensperger, May 6, 1994; children: Lauren M., Kevin G. Student, U. Calif., Berkeley, 1967-68; BA, Principia Coll., Elsah, Ill., 1970; JD, U. Wash., 1975. Bar: Wash. 1975, Washington 1977, U.S. Dist. Ct. (we. dist.) Wash., U.S. Ct. Appeals (4th, 9th and D.C. cirs.), U.S. Supreme Ct. Budget analyst Office Mgmt. and Budget, Seattle, 1970-72; law clk 9th cir. Honorable Eugene A. Wright, Seattle, 1975-76; assoc. Jones, Grey & Bayley, Seattle, 1976-77, Steptoe & Johnson, Washington, 1977-80, Perkins Coie, Seattle, 1980-85, ptnr., 1985—. Mem. ABA, Wash. State Bar Assn. Avocations: sports, baseball, travel, meditation. Office: Perkins Coie 1201 3rd Ave Fl 40 Seattle WA 98101-3029

ALKIRE, MICHAEL T., anesthesiologist, researcher; s. Lloyd Gordon and Lydia Ann Alkire; m. Monica L. Brown; children: Erik, Claire. BS, U. Oreg., 1984; MD, UCLA, 1990. Diplomate Am. Bd. Anesthesiology. Asst. clin. prof. U. Calif., Irvine, 1995—99, asst. prof. residence, 1999—2006, assoc. prof., 2006—. Assoc. fellow ctr. neurobiology learning and memory U. Calif., 2004—. Grantee, NIH, 2002—. Mem.: Am. Soc. Anesthesiologists. Achievements include first to use PET-Fluoro-Deoxy-glucose brain imaging in volunteers for anesthesia research; discovery of role played by the amygdala in mediating anesthetic involved amnesia; role played by the thalamus in mediating anesthetic induced unconsciousness. Office: U Calif 101 City Dr S Orange CA 92868 Office Phone: 714-456-5501. Office Fax: 714-456-7702.

ALKON, ELLEN SKILLEN, physician; b. LA, Apr. 10, 1936; d. Emil Bogen and Jane (Skillen) Bogen Rost; m. Paul Kent Alkon, Aug. 30, 1957; children: Katherine Ellen, Cynthia Jane, Margaret Elaine. BA, Stanford U., 1955; MD, U. Chgo., 1961; MPH, U. Calif., Berkeley, 1968. Diplomate Nat. Bd. Med. Examiners, Am. Bd. Pediat., Am. Bd. Preventive Medicine in Pub. Health. Chief sch. health Anne Arundel County Health Dept., Annapolis, Md., 1970-71; practice medicine specializing in pediat. Mpls. Health Dept., 1971-73, dir. MCH, 1973-75, commr. health, 1975-80; chief preventive and pub. health Coastal Region of Los Angeles County Dept. Health Svcs., 1980-81; chief pub. health West Area Los Angeles County Dept. Health Svcs., 1981-85; acting med. dir. pub. health Los Angeles County Dept. Health, 1986-87, med. dir. pub. health, 1987-93; med. dir. Coastal Cluster Health Ctrs. L.A. County Dept. Pub. Health Svcs., 1993-96, CEO, 1996-98, med. dir., 1998-2000; dir. Pub. Health Edn. in Medicine, 2000—. Adj. prof. UCLA Sch. Pub. Health, 1981—; adminstr. vis. nurses svc., Mpls., 1975-80. Fellow Am. Coll. Preventive Medicine, Am. Acad. Pediat.; mem. So. Calif. Pub. Health Assn. (pres. 1985-86, 04), Minn. Pub. Health Assn. (pres. 1978-79), Am. Pub. Health Assn., Calif. Conf. Local Health Officers (pres. 1990-91), Calif. Ctr. for Pub. Health Advocacy (pres. 2002-03), Calif. Acad. Preventive Medicine (pres. 1988-92, 2003-05), Delta Omega. Office: Los Angeles County DHS 241 N Figueroa St Rm 151 Los Angeles CA 90012 Office Phone: 213-250-8623. Business E-Mail: ealkon@ph.lacounty.gov.

ALKON, PAUL KENT, language educator; Grad., Phillips Acad., 1953; AB, Harvard U., 1957; PhD in English Lit., U. Chgo., 1962. Instr., asst. prof. English lit. U. Calif.-Berkeley, 1962-70; assoc. prof. U. Md., 1970-71; assoc. prof. English U. Minn., Mpls., 1971-73, prof., 1973-80; Leo S. Bing prof. English emeritus U. So. Calif., L.A., 2007—. Vis. prof. English, Ben Gurion U. of Negev, Israel, 1977-78 Author: Samuel Johnson and Moral Discipline, 1967, Defoe and Fictional Time, 1979, Origins of Futuristic Fiction, 1987, Science Fiction Before 1900, 1994, Winston Churchill's Imagination, 2006. Mem. Am. Soc. 18th Century Studies (pres. 1989-90), Sociètè française d'Etude du 18ème Siècle, Churchill Ctr. (bd. acad. advisers). Home: 17 Masongate Dr Palos Verdes Peninsula CA 90274-1560

ALLABY, STANLEY REYNOLDS, clergyman; b. Providence, Dec. 28, 1931; s. Edwin T. and Hope (Swift) A.; m. Marion Arlene Johnson, Dec. 18, 1954; children— Norman R., Darlene R., Kimberly A., Stephen R. AB, Gordon Coll., 1953; M.Div., Gordon Conwell Sem., 1956; D.D., Barrington Coll., RI, 1977; D.Min., Westminster Theol. Sem., 1978. Ordained to ministry, 1956; pastor Black Rock Conglist. Ch., Fairfield, Conn., 1956-97; dir. Sudan Interior Mission, NC, 1970—2006, chmn. bd., 1985—2005, vice chmn. internat. bd. govs., 1985-90; vice chmn. Billy Graham New Haven Crusade, 1982; exec. com. Billy Graham Hartford Crusade, 1985; prof. practical theology Bethel Sem. of the East, 1999—; Ockenga lectr. Gordon-Conwell Sem., 1983; sr. cons. Wilson Ctr. for Missions, Gordon-Conwell Sem., 2001—. Guest lectr. Tyndale Theol. Sem., Amsterdam, 1996. Bd. dirs. United Neighbors for Self Devel., Bridgeport, Conn., 1963-64, Christian Freedom Found., 1960-70, Operation Hope, Fairfield, 1986-89; trustee Gordon Div. Sch., 1965-69. Recipient George Washington honor medal Freedoms Found., 1968, 69; Alumnus-of-Year award Gordon Coll., 1976 Mem. Gordon Coll. Alumni Assn. (past pres.), Nat. Assn. Evangelicals (dir. 1974-95, exec. com. 1980-82, nat. conv. coordinator 1981-82, (chmn. resolutions com. 1982-83), Bridgeport Pastors Assn. (past pres.), Greater Bridgeport Fellowship Evangelicals (past pres.) Home: 123 Lyon Rd Woodstock Valley CT 06282-2612 E-mail: stanreynolds6@juno.com.

ALLAIN, LOUIS, literature educator; b. Brest, France, June 28, 1933; s. Louis and Louise (Nicolas) A.; m. Annie Luc, May 21, 1964; children: Andree-Lise, Juliette, Laurence, Alexandre. B Degree, Ecole Normale Superieure, Paris, 1958, Agregation, 1957; Doctorate, Sorbonne, Paris, 1979. Sch. tchr. Lycee Lakanal, Paris, 1961; asst. lectr. Sorbonne, 1961-63, sr. lectr., 1963-69; mng. lectr. Univ. Lille, 1969-81, prof., head dept. Slavic langs., 1981-98, prof emeritus, 1998—. Contbr. Acad. Sci., Hungary, 1988, Russia, 1988, 90, 94, 96, 2000, Israel, 1994, Poland, 1995, 96, 97, 98, 2000, Montenegro, 1996, U. Houston, 1989, Cornell U., 1994, Columbia U., 1998, Dostoevsky Symposium, Cerisy-la-Salle, 1983, Ljubljana, 1989, Oslo, 1992, Kartause Gaming, 1995, N.Y. 1998, Gumilev Symposium I & II, Glasgow, 1986, St. Petersburg, 1996, Chekhov Symposium I & II, Badenweiler, 1985, 94, From Dissidence to Democracy, Paris, 1996., Jerusalem in Slavic cultures and religious traditions, 1996, others. Author: Dostoievski et Dieu, 1981, Dostoievski et l'Autre, 1984, Etiudy o russkoi literature, 1989, Dostoevsky i Bog, 1993, F.M. Dostoevsky: Poetika, mirooshchushchenie, bogoiskatel'stvo, 1996, Skvoz' prizmu vekov, 1998, Shtrikhi k portretu F.M. Dostoevskogo, 1998; editor: B. Poplavsky, I&II, 1993, N. Otsup, 1993-95, G. Adamovich, 1993, G. Ivanov, 1993, V. Vishnjak, 1993, V.V. Rozanov, (study), 1993, A. Remizov, 1994, N. Plevitskaya, 1994, N. Fedorova, 1994, V. Gippius, 1994, V. Zen'kovsky, 1994, I. Napelbaum, 1995, M. Voloshin (study), 1996, F. M. Dostoevsky: Poetika, mirooshchushchenie, bogoiskatel'stvo, 1996, Skvoz' Prizmu Vekov, 1998, Shtrikhi k portretu F.M. Dostoevskogo, 1998, D. Granin, Tajny znak Peterburga, 2000; co-editor: Jews and Slavs, vol. 2, 1994; contbr. articles to profl. jours. Lt. French Navy, 1958-61, France. Comdr. of Acad. Palms, French Ministry of Edn., 1990, medal City of Lille, 1994, Melanges offerts au Professeur Louis Allain, Lille, 1996, Am. Order of Excellence, 2000. Mem. Alumni Ecole Normale Superieure, Intra-Marine/France, Internat. Dostoevsky Soc., Inst. Slavic Studies, Paris. Avocations: cooking, gardening. Home: Rue Jules Guesde 408 Villeneuve d'Ascq 59650 France Office: Charles de Gaulle Univ BP 149 Villeneuve d'Ascq Cedex 59653 France

ALLAIRE, GASTON GEORGE, music educator, researcher; b. Berlin, NH, June 18, 1916; s. Francis Xavier Allaire and Mary Laura Pellerin; m. Fleurette Carmen Turcotte, July 1, 1963; children: Anne, Claud. MusB, U. Montreal, 1947; MA, U. Conn., 1956; PhD, Boston U., 1960. Organist, choirmaster Our Lady's, Holyoke, Mass., 1950—54, St. Joseph's, Belmont, Mass., 1954—56, Paulist Ctr., Boston, 1956—60; prof. music Loyola Coll., Montreal, Canada, 1962—67, U. Moncton, New Brunswick, 1967—84, prof. emeritus, 1984—. Mem. rsch. coun. U. Moncton, 1968; cons. Can. Coun. Arts, Ottawa, Canada, 1970—79. Editor: CFMS Newsletter, 1969—71; author: The Theory of Hexachords, 1972; contbr. articles to profl. jours. Nat. pres. Can. Folk Music Soc., 1968—71. Finalist, Can. Coun. Arts, 1961; fellow, Fulbright Found., 1962; grantee, Ministry Cultural Affairs, Quebec, Can., 1965. Mem.: Am. Musicological Soc. Avocations: swimming, walking, piano, music, reading. Home: 82 Markham E Deerfield Beach FL 33442-2757

ALLAIRE, JEREMY, Internet company executive; Co-founder, chief tech. officer Allaire Corp., 1995; chief tech. officer Macromedia; technologist, entrepreneur-in-residence Gen. Catalyst, Cambridge, Mass.; founder, CEO Brightcove, 2004—. Named one of 50 Who Matter Now, CNNMoney.com Bus. 2.0, 2006. Office: Brightcove Inc 1 Cambridge Ctr Cambridge MA 02142*

ALLAM, HANNAH, journalist; b. 1978; Grad., U. Okla., 1999. Reporter St. Paul Pioneer Press, Minn., 1999—2003; bur. chief Knight Ridder, Baghdad, Iraq, 2003—05, Cairo, 2006—. Co-recipient Hal Boyle award, Overseas Press Club, 2006; recipient Journalist of Yr. award, Nat. Assn. Black Journalists, 2004, Journalism Excellence award, Knight Ridder, 2004. Office: Knight Ridder Washington Bur Ste 1000 700 12th St NW Washington DC 20005-3994 Office Phone: 202-383-6000. E-mail: hallam@krwashington.com.

ALLAMON, KAREN HENN, minister; b. Jackson, Mich., Aug. 1, 1958; d. Richard Leonard and Lujean Lirones Henn; m. Randall M. Allamon, Nov. 26, 1983; children: Matthew B., Lucas A. BFA, Webster U., 1992; MDiv, Princeton Theol. Sem., 1994—96, post grad, 2002—. Crisis Counselor Life Crisis Services - St. Louis, 1992. Pastor Barre Ctr. Presbyn. Ch., Albion, NY, 1996—; interim spiritual care coord. Hospice of Orleans County, Albion, NY, 1998—99; critical incident stress debriefer COVA, Albion, NY, 1998—; instr., worship, sacraments, preaching Presbytery of Genesee Valley, Rochester, NY, 2001—04. Presbyn. worship coord. Presbyn. of Genessee Valley, Rochester, NY, 2001—04. Cmty. leadership participant Albion Sch. Sys., NY, 1996—; mem. Ministirial Alliance, Albion, NY, 1996—; Legacy of Love endowment com. ARC of Orleans County, Albion, 2003—05; with Rural Opportunities Bd., 2005—. Recipient One of the Fastest Growing Congregations in the US: US Congl. Study, Eli Lilly Found., 2002, Excellence in Evangelism, Synod of the NE, Presbyn. Ch. (USA), 1998—99, Preaching prize, Princeton Theol. Sem., 1996, Bibl. Theology; Hebrew, Eden Theol. Sem., 1994; Synod Mission Partnership Grant: Leadership Devel., Synod of the NE, 2003. Mem.: Albion Area Ministirium (treas. 2002, v.p. 2003). Achievements include development of family systems leadership group for pastors. Office: Barre Center Presbyterian Church 4706 Oak Orchard Albion NY 14411 Personal E-mail: pastorkaren96@yahoo.com.

ALLAMONG, BETTY DAVIS, retired academic administrator, biology professor; b. Morgantown, W.Va., Apr. 8, 1935; d. Lonnie R. and Jessie R. (Hoffman) Davis; m. Joseph K. Allamong, Sept. 12, 1954; 1 child, John Bradley. BS, W.Va. U., Morgantown, 1961, MA, 1964, PhD, 1971; student Inst. Ednl. Mgmt. program, Harvard U., Cambridge, Mass., 1984. Instr. biology Morgantown HS, 1961-67; instr. edn. W.Va. U., Morgantown, 1965-67, instr. biology, 1967-72; from asst. prof. to prof. Ball State U., Muncie, Ind., 1972-87, assoc. dean scis. and humanities, 1981-86, dean scis. and humanities, 1986-87; provost, v.p. acad. affairs Bloomsburg U., Pa., 1987-92; ret., 1992. Mem. Ind. Corp. Sci. & Tech., 1983—87. Co-author: Energy for Life, 1976; author: numerous lab. manuals; contbr. articles to profl. jours. Recipient Women of Achievement Edn. award, Women in Comm. Inc., 1981. Fellow: Ind. Acad. Sci. Home: 253 Pixler Hill Rd Morgantown WV 26508-9541

ALLAN, ALEXANDER R.C. (SANDY ALLAN), food products executive; Joined The Coca-Cola Co., 1968, internal auditor, 1968, mem. Home Office traveling audit team, 1971, fin. controller So. Africa Divsn., 1978, asst. divsn. mgr. and fin. mgr. So. and Cent. Africa Divsn., mng. dir. NATBEV, 1987, pres. Middle East Divsn. (renamed Middle East and N. Africa Divsn. 1998), 1993, pres. Asia Pacific Group, 1999—2000, pres., COO Asia Group, exec. v.p., pres., COO Europe, Eurasia, and Middle East, 2001—. Office: The Coca-Cola Co PO Box 1734 Atlanta GA 30301

ALLAN, BARRY DAVID, research chemist, government official; b. Steubenville, Ohio, Jan. 20, 1935; s. John Young and Frances Lucy (Halbrunner) A.; m. Inge Elisabeth Bergeler, Aug. 5, 1961; children—Barbara Diane, Stephen Barry. BS, Ariz. State U., Tempe, 1956; MS, U. Ala., 1964, PhD, 1968. Chemist White Sands Missile Range, N.Mex., 1956; aero. fuels research chemist Army Missile Command, Redstone Arsenal, Ala., 1958-62, research chemist-phys., 1962-96, research chemist, 1968-95; prof. J.C. Calhoun Coll., Decatur, Ala., 1969-73, Athens Coll., Ala., 1970-73, U. Ala., Huntsville, 1974-76; rsch. cons. Allan Cons., Huntsville, 1996—. Cons., 1965—; reviewer Nat. Sci. Found., 1973—. Publs. in field. Active Huntsville Civic Assn., 1961—. Served to capt. AUS, 1956-58. Recipient Army Research And Devel. Achievement award, 1962, Navy commendation, 1968, Army commendation, 1971, 72 Mem. Am. Chem. Soc. (treas. 1969-73, pres. 1974-76), Combustion Inst., Pasteur Soc., Assn. U.S. Army, N.Y. Acad. Scis., Joint Army, Navy, NASA, Air Force Propellant Characterization Group on Fluids and Materials, Sigma Xi, Gamma Sigma Epsilon, Theta Chi. Office: Barry D Allan Cons 7803 Michael Cir SW Huntsville AL 35802-2900 Office Phone: 256-881-4088. Office Fax: 256-881-4101. E-mail: ballan@hiwaay.net.

ALLAN, BRENT RUSSOTTO, public health service officer; b. LA, Jan. 26, 1953; s. Milton Yale and June Clara Russotto; m. Debbie Britton Allan, Mar. 31, 1985; children: Brittany Mica, Corey Frances, Lawrence Jake. BS, UCLA, 1975; MPH, Tulane U., New Orleans, 1976; DO, Mich. State U., East Lansing, 1982. Intern Phoenix Gen. Hosp., 1982—83; CEO, family physician Desert Health Assocs., Scottsdale, Ariz., 1983—95; assoc. med. dir., family physician Scottsdale Family Practice, 1995—97; pres., med. dir. Med. Weight Loss Specialists, Scottsdale, 1997—2006, Infinity Health Scis., Scottsdale, 2004—06; exec. dir. global safety AMGEN, Thousand Oaks, Calif., 2006—. Cons. in field. Contbr. articles to profl. jours. Fellow: Am. Acad. Family Physicians, Royal Soc. Tropical Medicine & Hygiene; mem.: Delta Omega, Sigma Sigma Phi. Avocations: gourmet cooking, fly fishing, tennis, baseball. Office: AMGEN 1 AMGEN Ctr Dr Thousand Oaks CA 91320

ALLAN, COL, editor-in-chief; m. Sharon Bowditch; children: Michael, Tom, Mathew, Kate. NY corr. for Australian papers News Corp., 1978—80, London corr. for Australian papers, 1981—82; chief of staff Brisbane Sun, Australia, 1982—85; news editor The Australian, 1985—88; dep. editor Daily Telegraph, 1988—92, editor, 1992—99; editor-in-chief Daily Telegraph and Sunday Telegraph, Sydney, 1999—2001, NY Post, 2001—. Office: Editor in Chief New York Post 1211 Ave of Americas New York NY 10036*

ALLAN, JANET D., dean; BSN, Skidmore Coll., 1964; MS in Cmty. Health Nursing, U. Calif.-San Francisco, 1968; PhD in Med. Anthropology. Cert. adult nurse practitioner ANA. Former dean Health Sci. Ctr. U. Tex., San Antonio; dean Univ. of Maryland Sch. of Nursing, Baltimore, Md., 2001—. Recipient 2001 Distinguished Researcher Award. Mem.: Am. Assn. Colls. of Nursing (mem. Healthy People Curriculum Task Force 2004—). Office: U Md Sch Nursing Ste 505D 655 West Lombard St Baltimore MD 21201-1579

ALLAN, JONATHAN DAVID, autograph dealer, pop culture historian; b. Grasmere, NH, July 23, 1948; s. David Nisbet and Natalie Mary (Chandler) A.; m. Barbara Lauderbach, 1966 (div.); 1 child, Jonathan David II; m. Nancy Page, 1982. BA magna cum laude, U. N.H., 1972. Registered dealer. Bookseller, book buyer, columnist, book reviewer, freelance writer, 1972-81; co-owner, pres. Elmer's Nostalgia, Inc., Sanford, Maine, 1981—. Author: The Rock Trivia Book, 1976; columnist; mem. adv. bd. Autograph Collector Mag., 1986-92. N.H. chmn. Nat. Com. to Reopen the Rosenberg Case, 1973-77; vol. York County Shelters, Alfred, Maine, 1993—. Served with USNR, 1966-67. Mem. ACLU, NAACP, Ams. United for Separation Ch. and State, Universal Autograph Collectors Club (Outstanding Autograph Dealer award 1998), Am. Polit. Items Collectors, Maine People's Alliance, Planned Parenthood, People for the Am. Way, So. Poverty Law Ctr., Amnesty Internat., McFarlane Clan Soc., Phi Beta Kappa. Mem. Green Party of Maine. Avocations: collecting autographs and historical ephemera, painting, gardening, doing historical research. Office: Elmer's Nostalgia Inc 3 Putnam St Sanford ME 04073-2024 Office Phone: 207-324-2166. E-mail: jon@elmers.net.

ALLAN, LARRY See BOERSMA, LAWRENCE

ALLAN, LIONEL M., director for-profit and non-profit companies, educator; b. Aug. 3, 1943; AB cum laude, U. Mich., 1965; JD, Stanford U., 1968; student, U. Paris. Bar: Calif. 1969, US Supreme Ct. 1972. Law clk. US Dist. Ct. (no. dist.) Calif., 1969—70; pres. Allan Advisors, Inc., bd. governance and legal cons. firm. Spkr. and writer in field of corp. and bd. governance law; sec. adv. com. San Jose Fed. Ct., 1969-85; mem. bd. visitors Stanford Law Sch., 1985-88; mem. com. comml. code State Bar Calif., 1974-77, corps. com., 1983-86; elected to Am. Law Inst., 1989; spkr. Stanford Dir. Coll., 2004-. Co-author: How to Structure the Classic Venture Capital Deal, 1983, Equity Incentives for Start-up Companies, 1985, Master Limited Partnerships, 1987. Bd. dirs. San Jose Mus. Art, 1983-87; trustee KTEH-TV Channel 54 Found., 1987-2002, chair, 1992-94; dir. NCCJ, 1995-2001, Harker Sch., 1998—, chair 2002-; dir. Villa Montalvo Arts Ctr., 1986-2000, chair, 1989-93. Served to capt. JAGC USAR, 1974. Mem. ABA (com. on small bus., chmn. internat. bus. subcom. 1985-88, chmn. small bus. com. 1989-93), Santa Clara Bar Assn. (chmn. fed. ct. sect. 1971, 77), Internat. Bar Assn., Nat. Assn. Corp. Dirs. (chair Silicon Valley Calif. chpt. 2004-06, CEO 2006-), San Jose/Silicon Valley C. of C. (dir.), Pi Sigma Alpha, Phi Sigma Iota, Phi Delta Phi. Office: NACD Silicon Valley Chpt PO Box 562 Los Gatos CA 95031-0562 Office Phone: 408-354-8854. Business E-Mail: lonallan@comcast.net.

ALLAN, RICHMOND FREDERICK, lawyer; b. Billings, Mont., Apr. 22, 1930; s. Roy F. and Edith (Prater) A.; m. Dorothy Frost, Aug. 9, 1954; children: Richmond P., David F., Michael R. BA, U. Mont., 1954, JD, 1957; postgrad., London Sch. of Econs., 1957-58. Bar: Mont. 1957, U.S. Supreme Ct. 1961, D.C. 1965. Law clk. U.S. Ct. Appeals (9th cir.), San Francisco, 1958-59; ptnr. Kurth, Conner, Jones & Allan, Billings, 1959-61; chief asst. U.S. atty. U.S. Dept. of Justice, Billings, 1961-64; assoc. solicitor U.S. Dept. of Interior, Washington, 1965-67, dep. solicitor, 1968-69; ptnr. Weissbrodt & Weissbrodt, Washington, 1969-77, Casey, Lane & Mittendorf, Washington, 1977-78, Duncan, Weinberg, Miller & Pembroke, P.C., Washington, 1979—. Fulbright Commn. scholar, 1957. Mem. Fed. Bar Assn. (pres. Mont. chpt. 1963-65). Avocation: trap and skeet shooting. Office: Duncan Weinberg Genzer & Pembroke PC 1615 M St NW Ste 800 Washington DC 20036-3219 Home Phone: 301-340-8338. E-mail: rfa@dwgp.com.

ALLAN, RONALD GAGE, academic research coordinator; b. Cin., May 9, 1941; s. Robert Gage Allan, William Herbert (Stepfather) and Gladys (Mosier) Anderson; life ptnr. Miriam Scholar Clinton. BS in Indsl. Mgmt., U. Cin., 1966, MBA, 1968; PhD, George Washington U., 1977; MS in Taxation, Georgetown U., 1993. Rsch. economist US Dept. Commerce, Bur. Econ. Analysis, Washington, 1972-79; tax analyst Congl. Budget Office, Washington, 1979-81; planning dir. and analyst Vanguard Techs., Fairfax, Va., 1982-88; rsch. coord. Georgetown U., Washington, 1988—. Mem. rsch. com. Nat. Assn. Student Fin. Aid Adminstrs. Contbr. articles to profl. jours. Mem. Nat. Economists Club, Data Warehousing Inst., Am. Taxation Assn., Assn. Instnl. Rsch., Omicron Delta Epsilon. Episcopalian. Home: Apt 406 7401 Eastmoreland Rd Annandale VA 22003 Office: Georgetown U Office of Student Fin Svcs Washington DC 20057 Office Phone: 202-687-8967. Business E-Mail: allanr@georgetown.edu.

ALLAN, WALTER ROBERT, lawyer; b. Detroit, Aug. 1, 1937; s. Walter Francis and Henrietta (Fairchild) A. AB, U. Mich., 1959, JD, 1962. Bar: Calif. 1964, U.S. Ct. Appeals (9th Cir.) 1964, U.S. Supreme Ct. 1972, U.S. Ct. Appeals (D.C. cir.) 1973, U.S. Ct. Appeals (5th cir.) 1977, U.S. Ct. Appeals (3d cir.) 1988. From assoc. to ptnr. Pillsbury, Madison & Sutro, San Francisco, 1963—98; sole practitioner Tiburon, Calif., 1998—. Office: PO Box 771 Belvedere Tiburon CA 94920-0771 Office Phone: 415-889-4048. Business E-Mail: walterallan@mac.com.

ALLAN, WILLIAM GEORGE, artist, educator; b. Everett, Wash., Mar. 28, 1936; BFA, San Francisco Art Inst., 1958. Instr. painting U. Calif., Davis, 1965-67, Berkeley, 1969; prof. art Calif State U., Sacramento, 1968—99, prof. art emeritus, 1999—. Exhibited in group shows at Carnegie Internat. Exhbn., Pitts., 1975, Continuing Surrealism, La. Jolla (Calif.) Mus. Art, 1971, Whitney Painting Ann., NYC, 1972, 70th Ann. Exhbn. Art Inst. Chgo., 1972, Indpls. Mus. Art Exhbn., 1972, Whitney Mus. Am. Art, NYC, 1973-74, Painting and Sculpture in Calif.: The Modern Era, San Francisco Mus. Modern Art, 1976, Chgo. Arts Club, 1978; represented in permanent collections at Dallas Mus. Art, San Francisco Mus. Art, Phila. Mus. Art, Whitney Mus. Am. Art, Mus. Modern Art, NYC. Named Academician, NAD, 1997. Office: Calif State U Sacramento Dept Art 6000 J St Sacramento CA 95819-2605

ALLARD, CATHERINE, music educator, musician; b. Watertown, NY, Nov. 13, 1950; d. Joseph Ambrose and Sally (Phillips) Allard. BS in Music Edn., SUNY Coll.-Potsdam, 1972, MusM, 1974; D of Musical Arts, Peabody Conservatory Johns Hopkins U., 1991. Profl. singer, condr.; choral music tchr. Binghamton City Schs., 1974—78; condr. Binghamton Symphony Chorus, 1978—83; music dir. Summer Savoyards, Binghamton, 1976—87; prof. music Troy U., Ala., 1989—, prodr. Lyceum Series; condr. Ala. Jubilee Chorus, Troy, Ala., 2004—. Singer Opern Aachen, Germany, 1984—85; cons. SPEBSQSA, Troy, Ala., 1998—. Singer: (opera) From Winter Darkness (World Premiere Performance), Galileo Galilei (World Premiere), Requiem for the Victims of AIDS (World Premiere); prodr.(host): (TV series) Opus 3, 2000—. Pres. Pilot Club of Troy, Ala., 1994—95, 2003—04. Fellow Chancellor's Fellowship, Troy U., 2004; grantee Performance Enhancement grant, Ala. State Arts Coun., 1999, 2000, Summer Musical, Troy Arts Coun., 1996, 1997, 1998, 2000, 2001, 2002, Amahl and the Night Visitors, 2003, 2004. Mem.: Am. Musicological Soc., Music Educators Nat. Assn., Am. Choral Dirs. Assn., Nat. Assn. Tchrs. of Singing, Sigma Alpha Iota. Liberal. Office: 202 Smith Hall University Ave Troy AL 36082 Office Fax: 334-670-3858. E-mail: callard@troy.edu.

ALLARD, DEAN CONRAD, historian, retired historical center director; b. Kansas City, Mo., Oct. 19, 1933; s. Dean Conrad Sr. and Elizabeth Donaldson (Graves) A.; m. Constance Lynne Morgan, June 17, 1955; children: Scott, Hunt, Elizabeth. AB, Dartmouth Coll., 1955; MA, Georgetown U., 1959; PhD, George Washington U., 1967. Head Naval Operational Archives, Washington, 1958-82; sr. historian Naval Hist. Ctr., Washington, 1982-89; dir. naval history USN, Washington, 1989-95. Adj.

prof. George Washington U., 1979-89, v.p. Internat. Commn. Mil. History, 2000—05. Author: The United States Navy and the Vietnam Conflict, Vol. I, 1976, Spencer Fullerton Baird: A Study in the History of American Science, 1978; also articles on naval and maritime history; editor: U.S. Naval History Sources in the United States, 1979. Chmn. Hist. Commn., Arlington, Va., 1978-80; pres. Arlington Hist. Soc., 1974-75; mem. coun. Woodlawn Plantation, Fairfax, Va., 1976-84; mem. French-U.S. Sci. Com. on CSS, Ala., 1991-95. Lt. (j.g.) USN, 1955-58. Recipient Superior Civil Svc. award U.S. Govt., 1995, Samuel Eliot Morison award for Disting. Svc., USS Constn. Mus. Found., Boston, 1995. Mem.: Internat. Commn. Mil. History (v.p. 2000—05), Internat. Commn. Maritime History (mem. exec. coun. 1990—2002), U.S. Commn. Mil. History (pres. 1995—99), World War II Studies Assn. (bd. dirs.), Soc. for Mil. History (v.p. 1983—86), N.Am. Soc. for Oceanic History (pres. 1985—89), Cosmos Club (Washington), Phi Beta Kappa. Avocations: gardening, hiking. Home: 2701 N Quincy St Arlington VA 22207-5046 E-mail: allard@prodigy.net.

ALLARD, J., computer scientist; b. Glens Falls, NY, Jan. 12, 1969; m. Rebecca Norlander. BA in Computer Sci., Boston U. Computer scientist Microsoft Corp., Redmond, Wash., 1991—, corp. v.p., chief XNA arch., v.p., design and develop. entertainment and devices divsn., corp. v.p., design and develop., entertainment and devices divsn., corp. v.p., entertainment bus. group, 2007—. Mem. World Econ. Forum Young Global Leader program. Named Disting. Alumnus, Boston Univ., 2003, Baby Bill, Business 2.0; named one of Top 35 Entertainment Execs Under 35, Hollywood Reporter, Most Powerful Men Under 38, Details. Avocation: bicycling. Office: Microsoft Corp 1 Microsoft Way Redmond WA 98052-6399*

ALLARD, JUDITH LOUISE, retired secondary school educator; b. Rutland, Vt., Feb. 21, 1945; d. William Edward and Orilla Marion (Trombley) A. BA, U. Vt., 1967, MS, 1969. Nat. bd. cert. tchr. in adolescent and young adulthood sci., 1999. Tchr. math., sci. Edmunds Jr. H.S., Burlington, Vt., 1969-73, biology tchr., 1973-78, sci. dept. chair, 1975-78; biology tchr. Burlington (Vt.) H.S., 1978—2001, lead sci. tchr., 2001—05. Bd. dirs. Vt. Creative Imagination, Inc.; instr. U. Vt., Burlington, 1988-89, lectr., 2002—, St. Michaels Coll., Winooski, Vt., 2001-02; adviser Nat. Honor Soc., 1986—; mentor No. New Eng. Comentoring Network, 2002—05; leader Vt. Profl. Devel. Network, 2004—. Co-author Favorite Labs of Outstanding Tchrs., 1991. Active Amnesty Internat., 1985—; mem. Lake Champlain Com., Burlington, 1987—, Vt. Goals 2000 Panel, 1995—99, Vt. State Licensing Commn., 1995—96, Vt. Stds. Bd. for Profl. Educators, 1996—2002, co-vice chair, 2000—01, chmn., 2001—02; state bd. dirs. Odyssey of the Mind, 1986—98. Named Outstanding Vt. Educator, U. Vt., 1983, Outstanding Vt. Sci. Tchr., Sigma Xi Soc., 1984, Vt. Tchr. Yr., 1998, Outstanding Vt. Sci. Tchr., Vt. Acad. Sci. and Engring., 2000, Tandy Tech. scholar, 1990, Genentech Access Excellence fellow, 1995, 1996, Access Excellence Retro fellow, 1996, Tchr. of Yr., Biol. Scis. Curriculum Study, 2001; recipient Presdl. Sci. Tchg. award, NSF, 1983, Tech. award, Tandy, 1998, Siemens award for Advanced Placement, 2000. Mem. NEA (bd. dirs. Vt. chpt., 1990-98), Vt. Sci. Tchrs. Assn. (bd. dirs. 1980-92, treas. 1985-92), Burlington Profl. Stds. Bd. (chair 1991-2001), Parents and Friends of Edn. (trustee), Nat. Assn. Biology Tchrs. (dir. Vt. Outstanding Biology Tchr. award program 1977—, Outstanding Biology Tchr. award 1975), Assn. Presdl. Awardees in Sci., Phi Delta Kappa. Roman Catholic. Avocations: needlecrafts, fishing, music. Home: 221 Woodlawn Rd Burlington VT 05401-5722 Home Phone: 802-864-6446; Office Phone: 802-864-8411. Business E-Mail: jallard@bsdvt.org.

ALLARD, LINDA MARIE, fashion designer; b. Akron, Ohio, May 27, 1940; d. Carroll Preston and Zella Viola (Indoe) A. BFA, Kent State U., 1962, LHD (hon.), 1992. Dir. design Ellen Tracy, NYC, 1962—. Design critic Fashion Inst. Tech., N.Y.C.; vis. prof. Internat. Acad. Merchandising and Design, Chgo. Author: Absolutely Delicious cookbook, 1994. Bd. dirs. N. Y. adv. bd. Kent State U.; bd. dirs. Kent State U. Found. Bd. Recipient Dallas Fashion award Dallas Apparel Mart, 1986, 87, 94. Mem. Fashion Group Internat., Inc. (past bd. dirs.), Coun. Fashion Designers Am. Avocations: cooking, gardening, painting. Office: Ellen Tracy 575 7th Ave Fl 11 New York NY 10018-2095

ALLARD, NICHOLAS W., lawyer; b. Suffern, NY, Oct. 4, 1952; BA with honors, Princeton U., 1974; MA, Oxford U., 1976; JD, Yale U., 1979. Bar: NY, DC, 1981, US Ct. of Appeals (fed.cir.), US Ct. Internat. Trade, US Cts. (no., so., ea.& we. dists.) NY, US Ct. (no. dist.) Calif. Law clk. to cheif judge Robert F. Peckham US dist., San Francisco; hon. Robert P. Peckham US Dist. Ct. (no. dist.), Calif., 1979—80; law clk. to judge Patricia M. Wald US Ct. of Appeals (DC cir.), Wash., 1980—81; chair govt. rels. practice group Latham & Watkins, ptnr. Wash., Patton Boggs LLP, Wash., DC. Mem. minority staff counsel Senate Com. 1984-1986, prin. legal counsel to Sen. Edward Kennedy, Senate Com. on Judiciary, 1983-86; liaison Nat. Assn. State Attys. Gen.; adminstrv. asst., chief of staff to Sen. Patrick Moynihan, 1986-87; spkr. on health and comms. issues, adj. prof. George Mason U. Law Sch., Georgetown U., nat. adv. bd. Ctr. Nat. Policy Wash. DC 1994, adv. bd. Hastings U. Comm. and Entertainment Law Jour. 1994, adv. bd. & Founding mem. Ctr. Tech.Law George Mason U. 1998, dir. Assn. of Am. Rhodes Scholars 1998, exec. adv. bd. U. Wash. Sch. Law, 2003, adv. bd. Clean Energy Systems Inc. 2005, Mem. Compass Grp. Health Care Policy and Risk Mgmt. 2005, spkr. in feilds. Mem. editl. bd.; contbr. Spectrum, Pvt. Cable and Wireless Cable Mag., others; contbr. articles to profl. jours. Rhodes scholar Oxford U. 1976, Disting. Svc. award Fed. Bar Assn 1985, John W. Bader Princeton Class Svc. award 1974-2004, President's award Wireless Comms. Assn. Internat 1992-1993, Wireless Atty. of the Yr. Nat. Satellite Pub. Inc. 1995, Top 40 Health Lawyers US 1997, Alumni Coun. award 1999. Office: Patton Boggs LLP 2550 M St NW Washington DC 20037 Office Phone: 202-457-6465. Office Fax: 202-457-6315. Business E-Mail: nallard@pattonboggs.com.

ALLARD, (ALAN) WAYNE, senator, veterinarian; b. Ft. Collins, Colo., Dec. 12, 1943; m. Joan Malcolm, Mar. 23, 1967; children: Christie, Cheryl. DVM, Colo. State U., 1968. Veterinarian, dir. Allard Animal Hosp.; mem. Colo. State Senate, 1983-90, US Ho. of Reps., Washington, 1991-96; US Senator from Colo., 1997—; deputy maj. whip U.S. Senate, 2003—. Chmn. health, environment and instn. com., chmn. senate majority caucus; mem. 102nd-104th Congresses from 4th dist., Colo., 1991-96; mem. agrl. com., 1991-92, 93-94, 95-96, mem. small bus. com., 1991-92, mem. interior and insular affairs com., 1991-92, mem. com. on coms., 1991-92, 93-94, mem. budget com., 1993-94, 95-96, mem. natural resources com., 1993-94, 95-96, mem. joint com. on reorganization of Congress, 1993-94, 95-96, chmn. subcom. of agr. conservation, forest and water, 1995-96; senator 105th Congress, 1997—, mem. banking, urban affairs com., 1997—, environment and pub. works com., 1997—, intelligence select com., 1997—, Senate armed svcs. com., banking, housing and urban affairs com., select com. on intelligence; mem. select com. on intelligence, armed svcs. com., chmn. pers. subcom., banking, housing and urban affairs com., chmn. subcom. on housing and transp. 106th Congress; health officer, Loveland, Colo.; mem. regional adv. coun. on vet. medicine Western Interstate Commn. Higher Edn.; mem. Colo. Low-Level Radioactive Waste Adv. Com. Chmn. United Way; active 4-H Found. Recipient Charles A. Lory Public Svc. award, Colo. State U., 1999, Outstanding Legis. award, Home Care Assn. of Colo., Humane Legis. of Yr. award, Am. Humane Assn., 2001, Champion of Wheat award, Nat. Assn. Wheat Growers, 2003, Friend of Home Care, Home Care Assn. Colo., 2003. Mem. Am. Veterinary Med. Assn., Colo. Vet. Medicine Assn., Larimer County Vet. Medicine Assn. (past pres.), Bd. Vet. Practitioners (charter mem.), Am. Animal Hosp. Assn., Nat. Conf. State Legislatures (vice-chmn. human resources com. 1987—, healthcare cost containment com.), Loveland C. of C., Republican. Office: US Senate 521 Dirksen Senate Office Bldg Washington DC 20510-0001 also: District Office Ste 203 5401 Stone Creek Cir Loveland CO 80538-6155 Office Phone: 202-224-5941, 970-461-3530. Office Fax: 202-224-6471, 970-461-3658.*

ALLASTER, STACEY, sports association executive; V.p. Tennis Canada, 1990—; tournament dir. Rogers Cup Women's and Men's Championships; pres. Sony Ericsson WTA Tour, 2006—. Bd. mem., Tournament Coun. Sony Ericsson WTA Tour, 2001—, Tournament Class rep., 2002—. Named Can. Sports Exec. of Yr., 2002, 2006 Exec. of Yr., Sports Media Can.; named one of Top 25 leaders in Can. Sport, Globe & Mail, 2003, 2005. Achievements include becoming first woman ever to win prestigious Can. sports bus. award., 2006. Office: WTA Corp Hdqs One Progress Plz Ste 1500 Saint Petersburg FL 33701*

ALLBRITTON, CLIFF, personal and organizational consultant; b. Aransas Pass, Tex., Aug. 19, 1931; BS, Okla. State U.; MDiv, Southwestern Sem.; MA, Baylor U.; PhD, Columbia Pacific U., 1994. Editor family ministry dept. Lifeway Christian Resources, Nashville, 1979-91; pres. Cliff Allbritton Rsch. Ctr., Nashville, 1991-96. V.p. Corp. Pers. Cons., Dallas, 1972-79; acct. exec. Beaver Assocs. Advt., Akron, Ohio, 1971-72. Author: How to Get Married and Stay That Way, 1982, Dare to Win-How to Live the American Dream, 1992, Personal Riches for Today's Singles, 1992, The Psychology of Grace, 1994; co-author: Solo Flight, 1981, Single Adult Ministry in Your Church, 1985. Min. 8 congregations, Tex., N.Mex., Ohio, Va., 1954-71. Recipient Presdl. Legion of Merit, 2003. Mem. Am. Assn. Christian Counselors, Am. Assn. Family Counselors, Internat. Platform Assn., Natural Resources Def. Coun., Omicron Delta Kappa, Alpha Zeta, Kappa Tau Pi. Home: 865 Bellevue Rd U21 Nashville TN 37221-2794

ALLCOCK, HARRY R., chemistry professor; b. Loughborough, Eng., Apr. 8, 1932; naturalized U.S. citizen; s. Claud Leonard and Nora (Clarke) A.; m. Noreen Raworth, Nov. 14, 1959. BSc, U. London, 1953, PhD, 1956; DSc (hon.), Loughborough U., 2006. Cert. chemist. Postdoctoral fellow Purdue U., West Lafayette, Ind., 1956-58, Can. Nat. Rsch. Coun., Ottawa, Ont., 1958-60; rsch. scientist Cen. Rsch. Labs. Am. Cyanamid Co., Stamford, Conn., 1961-66; assoc. prof. chem. Pa. State U., University Park, 1966-70, prof. chem., 1970-85, Evan Pugh Prof. Chem., 1985—. Author: (books) Heteroatom Ring Systems and Polymers, 1967, Phosphorus-Nitrogen Compounds, 1972, (monograph) Chemistry and Applications of Polyphosphazenes, 2003; author: (with F.W. Lampe) (books) Contemporary Polymer Chemistry, 1981; author: (with F.W. Lampe and J.E. Mark), 2003; author: (with M. Zeldin & K.J. Wynne) Inorganic and Organometallic Polymers, 1988; author: (with P. Wisian-Neilson and K.J. Wynne) Inorganic and Organometallic Polymers II, 1994, editor Inorganic Syntheses Vol. XXV, (jours.) Phosphorous, 1973—77, Macromolecules, 1974—79, Chem. Revs., 1974—79, Biomaterials, 1980—82, Jour. of Polymer Sci., 1987—, Inorganic Chem., 1988—91, Chem. of Materials, 1988—, Heteroatom Chem., 1988—93, Jour. Inorganic and Organometallic Polymers, 1990—. Guggenheim fellow 1986-87. Fellow Am. Inst. Chemists (Chem. Pioneer award 1989); mem. Am. Chem. Soc. (Nat. Polymer Chemistry award 1984, Nat. Chemistry Materials award 1992, Herman Mark Polymer Chemistry award 1994, Nat. Applied Polymer Sci. award 2007), Royal Soc. Chemistry (various coms.), Corp. Inorganic Syntheses. Office: Pa State U Dept Chemistry 104 Chemistry Bldg University Park PA 16802-4615

ALLDAY, MARTIN LEWIS, JR., retired lawyer; b. El Dorado, Ark., May 30, 1926; s. Martin L. Sr. and Bess (Kavanaugh) A.; m. Patricia Pryor, May 1, 1954; children: Katherine, Elizabeth, Martin III. JD, U. Tex., Austin, 1951. Bar: Tex. 1951. Examiner oil and gas div. R.R. Commn. of Tex., Austin, 1951-53; legal dept. Superior Oil Co., Midland, Tex., 1953-57, Houston, 1957-59; ptnr. Lynch, Chappell, Allday and Alsup, Midland, Austin & Dallas, 1959-89; past solicitor Dept. of Interior, Washington, 1989; chmn. Fed. Energy Regulatory Commn., Washington, 1989-93; of counsel Scott, Douglass and McConnico, Austin, Tex., 1993—2006; pvt. practice, 2006—07; ret., 2007. Past pres. Midland Jaycees, C. of C., Indsl. Found.; past trustee Midland Meml. Hosp.; trustee Petroleum Mus. Hall of Fame; presiding officer Tex. State Cemetery Commn., Austin, 1998-04; pres. Friends of the Cemetery, 2004-. With Inf. U.S. Army, 1944-46. Decorated Purple Heart, Bronze Star, Combat Infantry badge, 96th Presdl. Citation award; recipient Disting. Alumni award Schreiner U., 2004; named Pioneer, Tex. R.R. Commn., 2003; named one of top 50 Oil and Gas Attys. Tex. Monthly Mag. Mem. ABA, Tex. Bar Assn. (chmn. oil, gas and mineral sect. 1970), Tex. Bar Found., Midland County Bar Assn. (pres. 1972-73), Ind. Prodrs. Assn. Am. (Hard Hat award 1992), Midland Country Club (pres.), Petroleum Club (bd. dirs.), Tex. Ind. Prodr. and Royalty Orgn. (Hats Off award 1992). Republican. Episcopalian. Avocations: fishing, hunting, golf. Personal E-mail: martin.allday@yahoo.com.

ALLDREDGE, NOREEN S., librarian; b. Sacramento, Apr. 8, 1939; d. Harold and Cecelia (Doherty) Sunderland. BA, Mount St. Mary's Coll., LA, 1961; MS, Columbia U., 1965; MA, Tex. A&M U., 1980. Film librarian N.Y. Pub. Library, NYC, 1964-65; reference librarian U. Nev., Reno, 1965-66, librarian Desert Rsch. Inst., 1966-70, circulation librarian, 1970-74, collection devel. librarian, 1974-76; asst. dir. Tex. A&M U., College Station, 1976-81; dean libraries Mont. State U., Bozeman, 1981—93; libr. Calif. State U., Hayward, 1993—2001. Accreditation visitor ALA, 1982-90, N.W. Assn. Schs. and Colls., 1985-02. Vol. Am. Hiking Soc., 1985-88; sr. assoc. U.S. Dept. Edn., 1990. Mem. ALA, Women Acad. Library Dirs., Am. Assn. Higher Edn. Home: 2203 Pinehurst Ct El Cerrito CA 94530-1881

ALLECTA, JULIE, lawyer; b. Worcester, Mass., Oct. 28, 1946; BA magna cum laude, U. N. Mex., 1973, MBA magna cum laude, 1977, JD, 1977. Bar: M. Mex. 1978, D.C. 1984, Calif. 1985, U.S. Supreme Ct., U.S. Ct. Appeals, fifth & tenth cir. Office gen. counsel SEC, Washington, 1977—81; ptnr. Paul, Hastings, Janofsky & Walker LLP, San Francisco. Editl. bd. Arlen Mutual Fund Handbook, Bd. IQ. Mem.: Am. Law Inst. ABA Com. Continuing Profl. Edn. (faculty mem.), Mutual Fund Dir. Forum (adv. dir.), ABA-Bus. Law Sect. (com. fed. regulation securities, sub. com. investment co. & investment advisers). Office: Paul Hastings Janofsky & Walker LLP 55 Second St 24th Floor San Francisco CA 94105 Office Phone: 415-856-7000. Office Fax: 415-856-7106. Business E-Mail: julieallecta@paulhastings.com.

ALLEGRA, FRANCIS M., federal judge, retired federal official; b. Cleve., Oct. 14, 1957; m. Regina Lynne Esposito. Student, Case Western Res. U.; BA magna cum laude, Borromeo Coll. Ohio, 1978; JD magna cum laude, Cleve. State U., 1981. Bar: DC, Ohio, Ct. Fed. Claims, US Ct. Appeals, US Supreme Ct. Jud. clk. Chief Trial Judge Philip R. Miller, 1981-82; assoc. Squire, Sanders & Dempsey, Cleve., 1982-84; line atty., appellate sect. US Dept. Justice, 1984-88, counselor to the asst. atty gen. Tax Divsn., 1994, dep. assoc. atty. gen. Washington, 1996-98, counselor to the assoc. atty. gen., 1994-96; judge US Ct. Fed. Claims, Washington, 1998—. Contbr. articles to profl. jours. Mem. Coun. 1000 Nat. Italian Am. Found., Sons of Italy of Am. Office: US Court of Federal Claims 717 Madison Pl NW Washington DC 20439-0002*

ALLEGRUCCI, DONALD LEE, state supreme court justice; b. Pittsburg, Kans., Sept. 19, 1936; s. Nello and Josephine Marie (Funaro) A.; m. Joyce Ann Thompson, Nov. 30, 1963; children: Scott David, Bowen Jay. AB, Pittsburg State U., 1959; JD, Washburn U., 1963. Bar: Kans. 1963. Asst. county atty. Butler County, El Dorado, Kans., 1963-67; state senator Kans. Legislature, Topeka, 1976-80; mem. Kans. Pub. Relations Bd., 1981-82; dist. judge Kans. 11th Jud. Dist., Pittsburg, 1982-87, adminstrv. judge, 1983-87; justice Kans. Supreme Ct., Topeka, 1987—. Instr. Pittsburg State U., 1969-72; exec. dir. Mid-Kans. Community Action Program, Inc.; mem. exec. com. Kansas Dist. Judges Assn., 1982-87; chmn. KDJA Legislative Coordinating Com., 1982-86; mem. Judicial Council Ct. Unification Advisory Com., 1984-85. Mem. Dem. State Com., 1974-80; candidate 5th Congl. Dist., 1978; past pres. Heart Assn.; bd. dirs. YMCA. Served in USAF, 1959—66. Mem. Kans. Bar Assn.; former mem. Crawford County Bar Assn. (past pres.), Butler County Bar Assn. (past pres.). Democrat. Office: Kansas Supreme Court 374 Kansas Judicial Ctr 301 SW 10th Ave Fl 3 Topeka KS 66612-1507*

ALLEMANG, ARNOLD A., chemicals executive; B in Chemistry, Sam Houston State U. Unit mgr. Dow Chem. Co., 1981—84, prodn. mgr. Terneuzen, Netherlands, 1984—88, mgr. hydrocarbon prodn. Freeport, Tex., 1988—89, dir. tech. ctrs. Midland, Mich., 1989—92, mfg. gen. mgr. Dow Benelux, 1992—93, regional v.p. mfg. and adminstrn. Dow Benelux, 1993, v.p. mfg. ops. Dow Europe, 1993—95, VP ops. Midland, 1995—, exec. v.p., 2000—04, bd. dir., sr. advisor, 2004—. Bd. dirs. Dow Corning Corp., Liana Ltd., Dorinco Reinsurance Co., Mems. Com. of Dupont Dow Elastomers LLC, Cargill Dow, LLC. Adv. bd. President's Cir. of Sam Houston State. U.; adv. bd. Coll. Engring. Kans. State U. Mem.: Nat. Assn. Mfrs. (bd. dirs.), Am. Chem. Soc., Ctr. Chem. Process Safety (advisory bd.).

ALLEN, A. WILLIAM, III, (BILL), food service executive; CEO la Madeleine French Bakery and Cafe; pres. West Coast Concepts, 2004—05; CEO Outback Steakhouse (OSI Restaurant Partners), 2005—. Office: Outback Steakhouse Company 10001 E Pinnacle Rd Scottsdale AZ 85255*

ALLEN, ALICE, communications and marketing executive; b. NYC, May 31, 1943; d. C. Edmonds and Helen (McCreery) A.; 1 child, Helen. Student, Conn. Coll., 1961. Pres. Alice Allen, Inc., NYC, 1970—83; sr. v.p. Robert Marston, NYC, 1983—84, Cunningham & Walsh, NYC, 1984—86, Carl Byoir (acquired by Hill & Knowlton), NYC, 1986; sr. v.p., dir. comms. and corp. mktg. Hill & Knowlton, NYC, 1986—88; pres., owner Allen Comms. Group, Inc., NYC, 1988—95, Alice Allen Comms., 1995—2003. Bd. dirs. Family Dymanics, N.Y.C., 1976-78, Veritas, 1980-85; v.p. Jr. League, N.Y.C., 1975-76; mem. adv. bd. Enterprise Found., 1992-2001. Mem. Pub. Rels. Soc. Am., Pub. Publicity Assn. (pres. 1969-71), Women's Media Group, Comm. Network. Office: Alice Allen Comms 320 E 72nd St New York NY 10021-4769

ALLEN, ANNETTE, minister; b. Helena, Ga., Apr. 27, 1962; d. Raymond and Nonie Mae Allen; m. Tigen R. Griffith (div.); children: Erick Raphael Griffith, Leah Charisse Griffith. Student, Medgar Evers Coll., Bklyn., 1983—85; cert., Inst. Biblical Studies, Lynchburg, Va., 2000; diploma, Liberty U., Lynchburg, 2004; DD, World Christianship Ministry, Fresno, Calif., 2004; diploma, Stratford Inst. Sexuality and Drug Counseling, 2005, Light U., Va. Biblical Counseling, 2006. Cert. biblical counselor 2007. Program asst. Nat. Coun. Ch. World Svc., NYC, 1981—90; cmty. activist Clergy Inc., Bklyn., 1990—92; office mgr. United Ch. of Christ, NYC, 1992—93; freelance writer Bklyn., 1993—96; metaphysician Lady Solomon, McRae, Ga., 1997—; min. New Hope Deliverance Ctr., McRae. Motivational spkr., Ga., 2000—. Author: War Between Two Minds, 2003. Founder New Hope HIV/AIDS Outreach Ctr., 2005. Republican. Home: Rte 1 Box 26C Mc Rae GA 31055 Office Phone: 229-315-9614. Home Fax: 229-868-5886. Personal E-mail: ladysolomon@planttel.net. E-mail: drallen@msn.com.

ALLEN, BEATRICE, music educator, pianist; b. NYC, June 30, 1917; d. Samuel and Rose (Krell) Hyman; m. Eugene Murray Allen, Jan. 23, 1937; children: Marlene Allen Galzin, Julian Lewis. Student, NYU, 1933—36; diploma (scholar), Inst. Musical Arts, NYC, 1939, postgrad. (scholar), 1939—40; diploma, Juilliard Grad. Sch., NYC, 1943; BA magna cum laude, Cedar Crest Coll., 1980. Mem. faculty prep. div. Juilliard Sch. Music, NYC, 1957—69, Moravian Coll., 1967—68, Northampton County Area CC, 1968—70, Manhattan Sch. Music, NYC, 1969—89. Mem. founding faculty Cmty. Music Sch., Allentown, Pa., 1982—; artist-in-residence, condr. Tchrs. Workshop, Antioch Coll., Yellow Springs, Ohio, 1966; Bach lectr., recitals various univs.; concert appearances Town Hall, NYC, Chautauqua, NY, others. Named Winner, NJ Artists contest, 1936. Mem.: Pa. Music Tchrs. Assn., Music Tchrs. Nat. Assn. (program chmn. Lehigh Valley chpt. 1981—82). Address: 580 Morningstar Lane Bethlehem PA 18018-6347

ALLEN, BELLE, management consulting firm and communications executive; b. Chgo. d. Isaac and Clara (Friedman) Allen., U. Chgo. Cert. conf. mgr. Internat. Inst. Conf. Planning and Mgmt., 1989. Reporter, spl. corr. The Leader Newspapers, Chgo., Washington, 1960—64; cons., v.p., treas., dir. William Karp Cons. Co. Inc., Chgo., 1961—79, chmn. bd., pres., treas., 1979—; pres. Belle Allen Comm., Chgo., 1961—; nat. corr. CCA Press, 1990—. Apptd. pub. mem., com. on judicial evaluation Chgo. Bar Assn., 1998—; v.p., treas., bd. dirs. Cultural Arts Survey Inc., Chgo., 1965-79; cons., bd. dirs. Am. Diversified Rsch. Corp., Chgo., 1967-70; v.p., sec., bd. dirs. Mgmt. Performance Sys. Inc., 1976-77; cons. City Club Chgo., 1962-65, Ill. Commn. on Tech. Progress, 1965-67; hearing mem. Ill. Gov.'s Grievance Panel for State Employees, 1979—; hearing mem. grievance panel Ill. Dept. Transp., 1985—; mem. adv. governing bd. Ill. Coalition on Employment of Women, 1980-88; advisor, spl. program The President's Project Partnership, Washington, DC, 1980-88; bd. govs. fed. res. com., nominee consumer adv. coun. FRS, 1979-82; reporter CCA Press, 1990—; panel mem. Free Press vs. Fair Trial Nat. Ctr. Freedom of Info. Studies Loyola U. Law Sch., 1993, mem. planning com. Freedom of Info. awards, 1993; conf. chair The Swedish Inst. Press Ethics: How to Handle, 1993. Editor: Operations Research and the Management of Mental Health Systems, 1968; contbr. articles to profl. jours. Mem. campaign staff Adlai E. Stevenson II, 1952, 56, John F. Kennedy, 1960; founding mem. women's bd. United Cerebral Palsy Assn., Chgo., 1954, bd. dirs., 1954-58; pres. Dem. Fedn. Ill., 1958-61; pres. conf. staff Eleanor Roosevelt, 1960; mem. Welfare Pub. Rels. Forum, 1960-61; bd. dirs., mem. exec. com., chmn. pub. rels. com. Regional Ballet Ensemble, Chgo., 1961-63; bd. dirs. Soc. Chgo. Strings, 1963-64; mem. Ind. Dem. Coalition, 1968-69; bd. dirs. Citizens for Polit. Change, 1969; campaign mgr. aldermanic election 42d ward Chgo. City Coun., 1969; mem. selection com. Robert Aragon Scholarship, 1991; mem. planning com. mem. Hutchins Era reunion U. Chgo., 1995, 2000. Recipient Outstanding Svc. award United Cerebral Palsy Assn., Chgo., 1954, 55, Chgo. Lighthouse for Blind, 1986, Spl. Comms. award The White House, 1961, cert. of appreciation Ill. Dept. Human Rights, 1985, Internat. Assn. Ofcl. Human Rights Agys., 1985; selected as reference source Am. Bicentennial Rsch. Inst. Libr. Human Resources, 1973; named Hon. Citizen, City of Alexandria, Va., 1985; selected to be photographed by Bachrach nat. exhibit for Faces of Chicago, 1990. Mem. AAAS, NOW, AAAU, Affirmative Action Assn. (bd. dirs. 1981-85, chmn. mem. and programs com. 1981-85, pres. 1983—), Fashion Group (bd. dirs. 1981-83, chmn. Retrospective View of an Hist. Decade 1960-70, editor The Bull. 1981), Indsl. Rels. Rsch. Assn. (bd. dirs., chmn. pers. placement com. 1960-61), Sarah Siddons Soc., Soc. Pers. Adminstrs., Women's Equity Action League, Nat. Assn. Inter-Group Rels. Ofcls. (nat. conf. program 1959), Publicity Club Chgo. (chmn. inter-city rels. com. 1960-61, Disting. Svc. award 1968), Ill. C. of C. (cmty. rels. com., alt. mem. labor rels. com. 1971-74), Chgo. C. of C. and Industry (merit employment com. 1961-63), Internat. Press Club Chgo. (charter 1992—, bd. dirs. 1992—), Chgo. Press Club (chmn. women's activities 1969-71), U. Chgo. Club of Met. Chgo. (program com. 1993—, chair summer quarter programs 1994), Soc. Profl. Journalists (Chgo. Headline Club 1992—, regional conf. planning com. 1993, co-chair Peter Lisagor awards 1993, program com. 1992—), Assn. Women Journalists, Nat. Trust for Historic Preservation. Office: 111 E Chestnut St Ste 29J Chicago IL 60611

ALLEN, BENJAMIN J., academic administrator; b. Jan. 5, 1947; BS in Bus. Econs., Ind. U., 1969; MA in Econs., U. Ill., 1973, PhD in Econs., 1974. Asst. prof. Wash. State U., 1974—79, mem. grad. faculty, 1976—79, Iowa State U., 1979—90, Iowa, 1991—, acting head transp. and logistics area, 1982—83, prof., 1984—88, Iowa, 1991—, dir. Midwest Transp. Ctr., 1988—90, dean Coll. Bus. Iowa, 1994—2001, interim v.p. external affairs Iowa, 2001—02, provost Iowa, 2002—; prof. U. Ark., 1990—91, mem. grad. faculty, 1990—91. Bd. dirs. Heartland Express, INc.; pres. Midwest Bus. Deans Assn., 1998—99. Mem. editl. rev. bd.: Jour. Bus. Logistics, 1986—94, Transp. Jour., 1988—, Jour. Advanced Transp., 1990—92, Transport Logistics, 1995—, Jour. Transp. Rsch. Forum, 1996—; contbr. articles to profl. jours. Bd. dirs. Ames (Iowa) C. of C., 1995—2000, pres.-elect bd. dirs., 1996, pres. bd. dirs., 1998; mem. exec. com., bd. dirs. Greater DesMoines C. of C. Fedn., 1998. Recipient Disting. Transp. Rsch. award, Transp. Rsch. Forum, 1996; NSF fellow, U. Ill., 1969—70, Univ. fellow, 1972—73, Brookings Econ. Policy fellow, 1976—77, Twin City Barge fellow in transp., 1980—81. Mem.: Transp. and Pub. Utilities Group, Am. Soc. Transp. and Logistics, Am. Econ. Assn., Golden Key Nat. Honor Soc., Phi Kappa Phi. Office: Iowa State Univ Office of the Provost 1550 Beardshear Hall Ames IA 50011-2021*

ALLEN, BENNIE CARNEL, employee relations specialist; b. Detroit, Feb. 3, 1947; s. John Wilson and Rosella (Griffin) Allen; m. Janet Smith, 2005; children: Daron K., Kevin D. BA in Hist., Wayne State U., 1968; Grad. Studies, Wayne State U., Detroit Mich., 1972—78, Hampton U., 1991. Employee relations spec. U.S. Army Tank-Automotive Command, Warren, Mich., 1982—2002; supr. pers. staff. spec. IRS, Detroit, 1979; pers. staff. spec. US. Vet. Admin., 1975—79. Adj. course mgr. instr. US Army Ctr. for Civil. Human Resource Mgmt., Lancaster, Pa., 1993—2002. Editor: (Regulations) Supr. Pers. Mgmt. Manual, 1987; author: (policy) Family Leave Update, 2000. Bd. mem. Detroit Fed. Exec. Bd., Detroit, 1975—79. Sgt. (E-5) USMC, 1968—71. Mem.: Detroit Instit. of Arts, Detroit Pub. Television, Marine Corps. League. Independent. Avocation: reading. E-mail: bcallendet@yahoo.com.

ALLEN, BETTY (MRS. RITTEN EDWARD LEE III), mezzo-soprano; b. Campbell, Ohio, Mar. 17, 1930; d. James Corr and Dora Catherine (Mitchell) Allen; m. Ritten Edward Lee, III, Oct. 17, 1953; children: Anthony Edward, Juliana Catherine. Student, Wilberforce U., 1944-46; certificate, Hartford Sch. Music, 1953; pupil voice, Sarah Peck More, Zinka Milanov, Paul Ulanowsky, Carolina Segrera Holden; LHD (hon.), Wittenberg U., 1971; MusD (hon.), Union Coll., 1981; DFA (hon.), Adelphi U., 1990, Bklyn. Coll., 1991; LittD (hon.), Clark U., 1993; MusD (hon.), New Sch. Social Rsch., 1994. Mem. voice faculty Manhattan Sch. Music, 1969—; mem. faculty NC Sch. Arts, 1978-87, Phila. Mus. Acad., 1979, Curtis Inst. Music; mem. faculty to pres. emeritus Harlem Sch. Arts. Tchr. master classes Inst. Teatro Colon, 1985-86, Curtis Inst. Music, 1987—; exec. dir. Harlem Sch. Arts, 1979; vis. faculty Sibelius Akademie, Helsinki, Finland, 1976; mem. adv. bd. music panel Amherst Coll.; mem. music panel NY State Coun. of the Arts, Dept. State Office Cultural Presentations, Nat. Endowment Arts.; bd. dirs. Arts Alliance, Karl Weigl Found., Diller-Quaile Sch. Music, US Com. for UNICEF, Manhattan Sch. Music, Theatre Devel. Fund, Children's Storefront; mem. adv. bd. Bloomingdale House of Music; bd. vis. artists Boston U.; bd. dirs., mem. exec. com. Carnegie Hall, Nat. Found. for Advancement in the Arts; bd. dirs. Chamber Music Soc. of Lincoln Ctr., NYC Housing Authority Orch., Ind. Sch. Orch., NYC Opera Co., Joy in Singing, Arts & Bus. Coun.; mem. Mayor's adv. commn. Cultural Affairs. Appeared as soloist: Leonard Bernstein's Jeremiah Symphony, Tanglewood, 1951, Virgil Thomson's Four Saints in Three Acts, NYC and Paris, 1952, NYC Light Opera Co., 1954; recitalist, also soloist with major symphonies on tours including ANTA-State Dept. tours, Europe, North Africa, Caribbean, Can., US, S.Am., Far East, 1954-, S.Am. tour, 1968, Bellas Artes Opera, Mexico City, 1970; recital debut, Town Hall, NYC, 1958, ofcl. debuts, London, Berlin, 1958, formal opera debut, Teatro Colon, Buenos Aires, Argentina, 1964; US opera debut San Francisco Opera, 1966; NYC opera debut, 1973, Mini-Met. debut, 1973; Broadway debut in Treemonisha, 1975; opened new civic theaters in San Jose, Calif., and Regina, Sask., Can., concert hall, Lyndon Baines Johnson Libr., Austin, Tex., 1971; artist-in-residence, Phila. Opera Co.; appeared with Caramoor Music Festival, summer 1965, 71, Cin. May Festival, 1972, Santa Fe Opera, 1972, 75, Can. Opera Co., Winnipeg, Man., 1972, 77, Washington Opera Co., 1971, Tanglewood Festival, 1951, 52, 53, 67, 74, Oslo, The Hague, Montreal, Kansas City, Houston and Santa Fe operas, 1975, Saratoga Festival, 1975, Casals Festival, 1967, 68, 69, 76, Helsinki Festival, 1976, Marlboro Festival, 1967-74, numerous radio and TV performances, US, Can., Mex., Eng., Germany, Scandinavia; rec. artist, London, Vox, Capitol, Odeon-Pathe, Decca, Deutsche Grammophon, Columbia Records, RCA Victor records; represented US in Cultural Olympics, Mexico City, 1968. Recipient Marian Anderson award, 1953-54, Nat. Music League Mgmt. award, 1953, 52 St Am. Festival Duke Ellington Meml. award, 1989, Bowery award Bowery Bank, 1989, Harlem Sch. Arts award Harlem Sch. and Isaac Stern, 1990, Womans Day Celebration award St. Thomas Episcopal Ch., 1990, St. Thomas Ch. award St. Thomas Cath. Ch., 1990, Men's Day Celebration award St. Paul's Ch., 1990, Martell House of Segram award Avery Fisher Hall, 1990; named Best Singer of Season Critics' Circle, Argentina and Chile, 1959, Best Singer of Season Critics' Circle, Uruguay, 1961; Martha Baird Rockefeller Aid to Music grantee, 1953, 58; John Hay Whitney fellow, 1953-54; Ford Found. concert soloist grantee, 1963-64 Mem. NAACP, Urban League, Hartford Mus. Club (life), Am. Guild Mus. Artists, Actors Equity, AFTRA, Silvermine Guild Artists, Jeunesses Musicales, Gioventu Musicale, Student Sangverein Trondheim, Unitarian-Universalist Women's Fedn., Nat. Negro Musicians Assn. (life), Concert Artists Guild, Met. Opera Guild, Amherst Glee Club (hon. life), Union Coll. Glee Club (hon. life), Met. Mus. Art, Mus. Modern Art, Am. Mus. Natural Hist., Century Assn., Sigma Alpha Iota (hon.) Unitarian-Universalist. Clubs: Cosmopolitan, Second. Office: Harlem Sch Arts 645 St Nicholas Ave New York NY 10030-1098 *To be able to combine childhood fantasies of self-expression, to travel and roam the world, to meet again and make new friends, to serve the demanding, yet fulfilling art of music - these are some of the wonderful joys of being a singer. I have been free to be me.*

ALLEN, BETTY NOLDON, education educator, consultant; b. Jerome, Ark., Jan. 29, 1940; d. Roscoe and Polly Noldon; m. Irving M. Allen, June 12, 1965; children: Donia Elizabeth, David Merrill. MEd, Lesley U., Cambridge, Mass., 1990. Cert. tchr. of young children with spl. needs Mass., 1988. Tchr. various preschools, Brookline, Newton, Mass., 1978—89; spl. needs resource tchr. Eliot-Pearson Children's Sch., Medford, Mass., 1999—2007. Cons. Tufts U., Medford, Mass., 1994—. Contbr. chapters to books, articles to profl. jours. Trustee Conservatory Lab Charter Sch., Boston, 2003—07. Mem.: Nat. Orgn. for the Edn. of Young Children. Independent. Avocations: travel, reading. Home Phone: 617-731-4735; Office Phone: 617-627-2592.

ALLEN, BEVERLY E., medical librarian; B. U. Mo.; MSLS, Syracuse U. Joined Morehouse Sch. Medicine, Atlanta, 1976, dir. Multi-Media Ctr., ret., 2004. Mem. Nat. Mus. and Libr. Svcs. Bd., Washington, 2004—; past regent Nat. Libr. Medicine. Mem.: ALA, AAMC Group for Info. Resources, Am. Assn. Health Scis. Librs., Med. Libr. Assn. Avocations: travel, reading, classical music. Office: Inst Mus and Libr Svcs 1100 Pennsylvania NW Washington DC 20506

ALLEN, BLAIR HAMILTON, writer, poet, artist, editor, photographer; b. LA, July 2, 1933; s. Wendall Boyd and Ethel Rose Allen; m. Juanita Aguilar Raya, Jan. 27, 1968; children: Theresa, Geoffrey. AA in Social Studies, San Diego Jr. Coll., 1964; student, U. Wash., 1965—66; BA in Graphic Arts, San Diego State U., 1970. Book reviewer LA Times, 1977—78; assoc. editor, advisor Cerulean Press and Kent Publs., Northridge, Calif., 1982—. Author: Televisual Po-ums for Bloodshot Eyeballs, 1973, Malice in Blunderland, 1974, N/Z, 1979, The Atlantis Trilogy, 1982, Dreamwish of the Magician, 1983, Right Through the Silver Lined 1984 Looking Glass, 1984, Trapped in a Cold War Travelogue, 1991, May Burning into August, 1992, The Subway Poems, 1993, When the Ghost of Cassandra Whispers in my Ears, 1996, Ashes Ashes All Fall Down, 1997, Around the World in 56 Days, 1998, Jabberbunglemerkletoy, 1999, Thunderclouds from the Door, 1999, The Athens Cafe, 2000, The Day of the Jamberee Call, 2001, Assembled I Stand, 2002, Wine of Starlight, 2002, Hour of Iced Wheels, 2003, Trek Into Yellowstone's Cascade Corner Wilderness, 2003, Light in the Crossroads, 2004, Shot Doves, 2005, What Time Does: One Man Show, 2006, Moon Hiding in The Orange Tree, 2007; editor: The Magical World of David Cole, 1984, Snow Summits in the Sun, 1988, 3 poetry anthologies; one-man shows include The Unicorn Gallery, LaJolla, Calif., 1970, Chatterton's Bookstore Gallery, LA, 1974, What Time Does, 2006. Sgt. USMC, 1953—59. Nominee Pushcart prize for poetry, 1982, Pushcart prize; recipient 1st prize poetry, Pacificus Found., LA, 1992, Lifetime Achievement in Poetry and Story Writing Literary prize, 2003. Mem.: Poets and Writers, Am. Acad. Poets. Democrat. Roman Catholic. Avocation: travel. Mailing: PO Box 162 Colton CA 92324

ALLEN, BRUCE, physicist; b. Boston, May 11, 1959; s. Steven and Malwina (Gerson) A.; m. Sylvie Debaisieux, Aug. 26, 1986 (div. 1992); m. Marialessandra Papa, Apr. 1, 2000; children: Daniel, Martin. BS in Physics, MIT, 1980; PhD in Gravitation/Cosmology, Cambridge U., Eng., 1984. Rsch. assoc. U. Calif., Santa Barbara, 1983-85, Tufts U., Medford, Mass., 1985-86, rsch. asst. prof., 1987-89; Chercheur Associe CNRS, Paris, 1986-87; asst. prof. physics U. Wis., Milw., 1989-92, assoc. prof. physics, 1992—97, prof. physics, 1997—2006, adj. prof. physics, 2007—. Vis. Isaac Newton Mat. Inst., 1994, Albert Einstein Inst., Berlin, 2000—05; vis. assoc. Calif. Inst. Tech., 1995—97; dir. Einstein@home project, 2005—, Max Planck Inst. Gravitational Physics, Hannover, Germany. Mem. editl. bd. Classical and Quantum Gravity, 2001—; contbr. more than 70 articles to profl. jours. Recipient Knight prize Cambridge U., 1981, first prize Gravity Rsch. Found., 1990, Bessel prize Alexander Von Humboldt Found., 2003; named Marshall scholar, 1980-83; NSF rsch. grantee, 1987—. Fellow Inst. Physics, Am. Phys. Soc.; mem. IEEE, Phi Beta Kappa. Avocations: swimming, French and Italian language and culture. Office: Albert Einstein Inst Callinstrasse 38 Hannover 30167 Germany Home Phone: 414-962-0516; Office Phone: 414-229-6439. E-mail: ballen@uwm.edu.

ALLEN, BRUCE TEMPLETON, retired economics professor; b. Oak Park, Ill., Jan. 27, 1938; s. William Hendry and Harriet (Iverson) A.; m. Virginia Elizabeth Peterson, June 16, 1962; children: Elizabeth Rachel, Catherine Grace. AB, De Pauw U., 1960; MBA, U. Chgo., 1961; PhD, Cornell U., 1965. Asst. prof. econs. Mich. State U., East Lansing, 1965-75, assoc. prof., 1975-80, prof., 1980—2003; ret., 2003. Mem. Am. Econ. Assn., Indsl. Orgn. Soc. Avocations: railroads, choral singing. Personal E-mail: allenb@msu.edu.

ALLEN, CAROL E., retired elementary school educator; b. Anthony, Kans., Feb. 2, 1950; d. Hubert Lawrence and Alta Clarissa Hoel; m. Terry F. Allen, Aug. 21, 1970; children: Jeffrey L., Stephanie L. Halsey. BS, Northwestern Okla. State U., Alva, 1972, MS, 1977. 4th grade tchr. Unified Sch. Dist. #361, Harper, 1972—92, 5th grade tchr., 1993—2005; ret., 2005. Pres. Harper County, Nat. Edn. Assn., Harper, Kans., 2000—03, sec., 1996—2000. Sec. Bus. and Profl. Women, Anthony, 1990—92, pres., 1992—94. Christian. Avocations: reading, gardening.

ALLEN, CHARLES E., federal agency administrator; B, U. NC, Chapel Hill; grad., USAF Air War Coll. With CIA, Washington, 1958—2005, overseas intelligence liaison, 1974—77, directorate intelligence, 1977—80, mgr. major classified program, 1980—82; with US Dept. Def., Washington, 1982—85; nat. intelligence officer for warning CIA, Washington, 1988—94, asst. dir. for collection, 1998—2005; chief intelligence officer US Dept. Homeland Security, Washington, 2005—. Recipient Nat. Intelligence medal for Achievement, CIA, 1983, President's award for Disting. Fed. Civilian Svc., The White House, 1986, CIA Commendation medal, 1991, Disting. Intelligence medal, CIA, 2005, Nat. Intelligence Disting. Svc. medal, 2005.

ALLEN, CHARLES EUGENE, university administrator, agriculturist, educator; b. Burley, Idaho, Jan. 25, 1939; s. Charles W. and Elsie P. (Fowler) A.; m. Connie J. Block, June 19, 1960; children: Kerry J., Tamara S. BS, U. Idaho, 1961; MS, U. Wis., 1963, PhD, 1965. NSF postdoctoral fellow, Sydney, Australia, 1966-67; asst. prof. agr. U. Minn., St. Paul, 1967-69, assoc. prof., 1969-72, prof., 1972—, dean Coll. Agr., assoc. dir. Agrl. Expt. Sta., 1984-88, acting v.p., 1988-90, v.p. agriculture, forestry and home econs., dir. Minn. Agr. Expt. Sta., 1990-95, provost profl. studies, dir. Minn. Agr. Expt. Sta., 1995-97, dir. global outreach, 1997-98, exec. dir. internat. programs, 1998—2004, assoc. v.p. for internat. programs, 2004—06. Vis. prof. Pa. State U., 1978; cons. to industry; C. Glen King lectr. Wash. State U., 1981; Univ. lectr. U. Wyo., Laramie, 1984; adj. prof. Hassan II U., Rabat, Morocco, 1984. Recipient Horace T. Morse-Amoco Found. award U. Minn., 1984, Disting. Tchr. award U. Minn. Coll. Agr., 1984, Disting. Alumni award U. Idaho, 1989. Fellow AAAS, Inst. Food Tech.; mem. Am. Meat Sci. Assn. (bd. dirs. 1970-72, Rsch. award 1980, Signal Svc. award, 1985), Am. Soc. Animal Sci. (Exceptional Rsch. Achievement award 1972, Rsch. award 1977). Avocations: photography, reading, outdoor sports, golf. Business E-Mail: ceallen@umn.edu.

ALLEN, CHARLES FRANKLIN, music educator; b. Kingsport, Tenn., Mar. 1, 1964; s. Clarance Allen and Barbara Charlene Messick. MusB Edn., Union U., 1986. Cert. elem. tchr. Tenn, Orff-Schulwerk Level One. Elem. music tchr. McDowell County Schs., Welch, W.Va., 1989—96, Sarasota County Pub. Schs., Sarasota, Fla., 1996—; vocal instr. Venice (Fla.) Little Theatre, 2003—, musical theatre instr., 2004—. Dir. choral music competition Music USA Choral Festival, Universal Studios; dir. choral performance ABC 7 Sunrise Morning News program, Sarasota County Fair, W.Va. State Capital Showcase of Music Edn.; tupperware cons. Author: (musical) Rappin' Romantic, 1992, (book) Teaching Tolerance: A Handbook for Teachers, 1992, (play) It's the Chance You Take, 1995; composer: (opera) The Magical Friendship, 1997; musician: (PBS gulf coast TV show feature) Venice Little Theatre's Theatre Fest, 2002. Tech. staff vol. Player's Theatre, Sarasota, 2002—03; rep. W.Va. Edn. Assn., Charleston, 1992—95, state educator trainer, 1992—96, mem. minority affairs com., 1995—96; pres. McDowell County Music Edn. Assn., Welch, W.Va., 1995—96; sec. Polit. Com. of the Sarasota County Classified Teachers Assn., Sarasota, Fla., 2004—05, First Congl. United Ch. of Christ Bd. of Music and Fine Arts, Sarasota, Fla., 2005—05. Named Tchr. of the Yr., Panther Elem. Sch., 1993, Wal-Mart, 1999; recipient Outstanding Sch. Project award, Partnerships and Alliances Linking Schs., 1999. Mem.: Sarasota Classified Teachers Assn. (faculty representive 2002—05), Sarasota Assn. Music Edn. (pres. 2000—03, sec. polit. com. 2004—05, Music Tchr. of Yr. 2002), Fla. Elem. Music Educators Assn., Fla. Music Educators Assn., Phi Mu Alpha Sinfonia (life; v.p. 1984—85). Democrat. Mem. United Ch. Of Christ. Avocations: cooking, paranormal investigations, dog shows, reading. Home: 2713 Wells Ave Sarasota FL 34232 Office: Wilkinson Elem Sch 3400 Wilkinson Rd Sarasota FL 34232 Home Phone: 941-343-0245; Office Phone: 941-361-6477. Personal E-mail: defyinggravity2713@comcast.net.

ALLEN, CHARLES NORMAN, television, film and video producer; b. Miami, July 13, 1944; s. Claude Braswell and Virginia Lucille (Gravitt) A.; m. Susan Carole Dorn, May 1, 1970; children: Jennifer, Brian. BS, U. Miami, 1967. V.p. Tel-Air Interests Inc., Miami, 1967-79; pres. Cinema East Corp., Miami, 1979—, World Studios Corp., Atlanta, 1987—, ADR Internat., Miami, 1991—2001. Bd. dirs. World Studios Corp. Representer prodns. U.S. internat. film events CINE-Washington, 1974, 75, 80, 81, 87, 88, 89, 92. Trustee Dade County Pub. Health Trust; commr. Biscayne Park, Fla., 1974-76; active Dade County Dem. Exec. Commn., 1976-80, Dade Dem. Treas., 1976-79; mem. Gov.'s Fla. Motion Picture and TV Adv. Coun., 1978-80. Mem.: Greater Miami C. of C., Advt. Miami, Greater Miami Advt. Fedn., Nat. Advt. Fraternity, Internat. Cinematographers Guild (dir. photography), Assn. Ind. Comml. Producers, S. Fla. Film and Tape Producers Assn., Am. Advt. Fedn., Iron Arrow Hon. Soc., Alpha Delta Sigma, Sigma Chi. Democrat. Methodist. Office: Cinema East Corp 5859 Biscayne Blvd Miami FL 33137-2690 Home Phone: 305-756-5859; Office Phone: 305-757-5859. E-mail: callen@cinemaeast.com.

ALLEN, CHARLES WILLIAM, mechanical engineer, educator; b. Newbury, Eng., July 24, 1932; s. Isaac William and Emily (Butler) A.; m. Rita Joyce Pembroke, Dec. 28, 1957; children: Malcolm Charles, Verity Simone. BS, U. London, 1957; MS, Case Inst. Tech., 1962; PhD, U. Calif., Davis, 1966. Design engr. Lear Siegler, Cleve., 1957-62; group leader Aerojet Gen., Sacramento, 1962-63; assoc. engring. U. Calif., Davis, 1965-66; assoc. prof. Calif. State U., Chico, 1966-71, prof. engring., 1971-88, prof. emeritus, 1988—, head mech. engring., 1976-79, 82-84. Vis. fellow U. Leicester, Eng., 1974; vis. lectr., rschr. U. Guadalajara, Mex., 1986, guest prof., 1997. Contbr. articles to profl. jours. Fellow NASA, 1967, 68, 69 Mem. ASME. Home: 1691 Filbert Ave Chico CA 95926-1777 Office: Calif State U Dept Mech Engring Chico CA 95629 Personal E-mail: charleswilliamallen@yahoo.com.

ALLEN, CHARLOTTE, secondary school educator; m. Ricky Allen. BS in Edn., Athens State Coll. Teacher aide Falkville H.S.; tchr. sci. East Lawrence H.S., Trinity, Ala., 1988—95; tchr. sci. and physical edn. Lacey Spring. Cheerleading coach Decatur H.S., East Lawrence H.S.; judge World Cheerleading Competition. Named Outstanding Sci. Tchr., 1992. Mem. Nat. Assn. Geology Tchrs., Nat. Cheerleading Assn. (camp dir.) Avocations: church activities, hiking.

ALLEN, CHRISTOPHER C., publishing executive; V.p., pub. Cooking Light mag., Birmingham, Ala., 1987—. Office: Cooking Light 2100 Lakeshore Dr Birmingham AL 35209 Office Phone: 205-445-6000.*

ALLEN, CLARENCE RODERIC, geologist, educator; b. Palo Alto, Calif., Feb. 15, 1925; s. Hollis Partridge and Delight (Wright) A. BA, Reed Coll., 1949; MS, Cal. Inst Tech., 1951, PhD, 1954. Asst. prof. geology U. Minn., 1954-55; mem. faculty Calif. Inst. Tech., 1955—, prof. geology and geophysics, 1964-91, prof. emeritus, 1991—; interim dir. Seismological Lab., 1965-67, acting chmn. division of geological scis., 1967-68. Phi Beta Kappa Disting. lectr., 1978; chmn. cons. bd. earthquake analysis Calif. Dept. Water Resources, 1965-74; chmn. geol. hazards adv. com. for program Cal. Resources Agy., 1965-66; mem. earth scis. adv. panel NSF, 1965-68, chmn., 1967-68, mem. adv. com. environmental scis., 1970-72; mem. U.S. Geol. Survey adv. panel to Nat. Center Earthquake Research, Calif. Cal. Mining and Geology Bd., 1969-75, chmn., 1975; mem. task force on earthquake hazard reduction Office Sci. and Tech., 1970-71; mem. Can. Earthquake Prediction Evaluation Council, 1983-88; vice-chmn. Nat. Acad. Sci. Com. on Advanced Study in china, 1981-85; chmn. geology sect. Nat. Acad. Sci., 1982-85, Com. on Scholarly Communication with People's Republic China, 1984-89, chmn., 1987-89; mem. Nat. Acad. Sci. Commn. on Phys. Scis., Math. and Resources; mem. Pres.'s Nuclear Waste Tech. Rev. Bd., 1989-97. Served to 1st lt. USAAF, 1943-46. Recipient G.K. Gilbert award seismic geology Carnegie Instn., 1960. Fellow Am. Geophys. Union, Geol. Soc. Am. (counselor 1968-70, pres. 1973-74), Am. Acad. Arts Scis.; mem. Nat. Acad. Scis., Earthquake Engring. Research Inst. (bd. dirs. 1985-88, Housner medal 2001), Seismological Soc. Am. (dir. 1970-76, pres. 1975-76, medal 1995), Nat. Acad. Engring., Phi Beta Kappa. Office: Calif Inst Tech Dept Geology Pasadena CA 91125-0001 Office Phone: 626-395-6904. Business E-Mail: allen@gps.caltech.edu.

ALLEN, CLAUDE ALEXANDER, former federal official; b. Phila., Oct. 11, 1960; m. Jannese Mitchell; children: Claude Alexander III, Lila-Cjoan, Christian Isaiah. BA in Polit. and Sci. and Linguistics, U. NC, 1982; JD, Duke U., 1990. Bar: Pa. 1991, DC 1992, Va. 1995. Law clerk to Hon. David B. Sentelle U.S. Ct. Appeals (D.C. cir.), 1990—91; atty. Baker & Botts, L.L.P., Washington, 1991—95; counsel to atty. gen. Office of the Atty. Gen., Commonwealth of Va., 1995—97, dep. atty. gen. for civil litigation divsn. Va., 1997—98; sec. health and human resources Commonwealth of Va., 1998—2001; dep. sec. US Dept. Health & Human Svcs., Washington, 2001—05; asst. to the Pres. for domestic policy The White House, Washington, 2005—06, dir. domestic policy coun., 2005—06.

ALLEN, CLAXTON EDMONDS, III, investment banker; b. NYC, Aug. 27, 1944; s. C. Edmonds and Helen (McCreery) A. BA, Washington and Lee U., 1964, JD, 1967. Bar: N.Y. 1969. Assoc. Simpson Thacher & Bartlett, NYC, 1967-70; assoc. gen. counsel GE Credit Corp., NYC, 1970-71; investment banker Merrill Lynch, Pierce, Fenner & Smith, Inc., NYC, 1971-72; pres. Gloucester Internat. Ltd., NYC, 1972-82, Comanche Exploration Corp., NYC, 1981-86, Compass Internat. Corp., NYC, 1982—, Horizon Coal Corp., Mineral Res. Corp., NYC, 1982-85, Compass Coal Corp., NYC, 1986-91, Overseas & Fgn. Investors, Inc., NYC, 1990—. Bd. dirs. Purbrook Ltd., Cranbrook Investments Ltd., Lupton Estates Ltd., Morehead State U. Found., Inc., L&H Internat. Ltd. Mem. Met. Club. Home: 405 E 54th St New York NY 10022-5123 Office: 123 E 54th St 8th Fl New York NY 10022-4506 Office Phone: 212-308-0606. Business E-Mail: ceallen@compass1.com.

ALLEN, CRAIG ADAMS, lawyer, director; b. Ironton, Ohio, June 30, 1941; s. Enoch Stanely and Margaret (Adams) Allen; m. Carol Linda Brewster, Aug. 15, 1964; children: Laura, Kathy. BA cum laude, Denison U., 1963; JD, Ohio State U., 1966. Bar: Ohio 1966. Ptnr. Edwards, Klien, Compton & Allen, Ironton, Ohio, 1966—76; sole practice Ironton, 1976—77; ptnr. Allen & Anderson, Ironton, 1977—78, Allen, Anderson & Anderson, Ironton, 1978—82, Allen & Stillpass, Ironton, 1983—84, Allen & Payne, Ironton, 1985—; sole practice, 1985—. Served Ohio Nat. Guard, 1966—72. Mem.: Hosp. Atty. Assn., Lawrence County Bar Assn., Ironton C. of C., Lawrence County Democratic Ctrl Com., So. Ohio AAA, Elks, Lions. Episcopalian. Office: 311 S 3rd St Ironton OH 45638-1630 Office Phone: 740-533-1700. Business E-Mail: alcaa@bright.net.

ALLEN, DAVID, systems engineer; b. York, Maine, May 15, 1942; s. Pliny Arunah and Tillie (MacQuinn) A.; m. JoAnn Moeckly, 1968 (div. 1975); children: Torrie, Heather; m. Robin Lee Perry, Mar. 11, 1983 (div. 2004); children: Rebecca, Patrick. BA, Lake Forest Coll., 1965; MA, U. Ariz., 1967, PhD, 1968. Asst. prof. dept. psychology S.D. State U., Brookings, 1968-71; rsch. psychologist CIA, Washington, 1971-78, chief rsch. br., 1978-85, dep. chief psychol. svcs. divsn., 1985-87, chief rsch. and info. systems divsn. Washington, 1987-90, trustee investment plan, 1988-92, investigator Office of Insp. Gen., 1990-92, chief info. systems Latin Am. divsn., 1992-95; chief electronic messaging divsn., program dir.

Enterprise Messaging Svcs., Office of Comm. CIA, Washington, 1995-97; dir. program devel./mktg. for Ctr. for Sci. and Tech. Mitretek Sys., Inc., 1998—2000; program dir. SRS Technologies, 2002—07; sr. program mgr. Jasmah Cons., 2007—. Contbr. articles to profl. jours. Rsch. fellow USPHS, 1967-68; Rsch. grantee NSF, 1970-71; recipient U.S. Govt. Career Intelligence medal, CIA, 1997. Republican. Avocations: choral singing, amateur radio, cosmology, mathematics, information technology. Home: 905 N Emerson St Arlington VA 22205-2562 Office: INSA 901 N Stuart St Ste 205 Arlington VA 22203 Personal E-mail: davidalle1@aol.com.

ALLEN, DAVID JAMES, lawyer; b. East Chicago, Ind. BS, Ind. U., 1957, MA, 1959, JD, 1965. Bar: Ind. 1965, U.S. Dist. Ct. (so. dist.) Ind. 1965, U.S. Ct. Appeals 1965, U.S. Tax Ct. 1965, U.S. Supreme Ct. 1965, U.S. Ct. Appeals (fed. and 7th cirs.) 1983. Of counsel Hagemier, Allen and Smith, Indpls., 1975—. Adminstrv. asst. Gov. of Ind. Mathew E. Welsh, 1961—65; counsel Ind. Gov. Roger D. Branigin, 1965—69; asst. to Gov. Edgar D. Whitcomb, 1969; univ. counsel Ind. State U., Terre Haute, 1969—70; legis. counsel Ind. Gov. Evan Bayh, 1989—90; spl. counsel Gov. Frank O'Bannon State of Ind., 1999—2002; mem. Spl. Commn. on Ind. Exec. Reorgn., 1967—69; commr. Ind. Utility Regulatory Commn., 1970—75; mem. Ind. Law Enforcement Acad. Bd. and Adv. Coun., 1968—85, Ind. State Police Bd., 1968—; commr. for revision Ind. Commn. Recommend Changes Ind. Legis. Process, 1990—2002; commr. Ind. Criminal Code Revision Study Commn., 1998—2002; nat. judge adv. Acacia Frat., 1980—86, 1992—2002, internat. pres., 2002—; chief counsel Ind. Ho. Reps., 1975—76, spl. counsel, 1979—89, Ind. Senate, 1990—97; adj. prof. pub. law Sch. Pub. and Environ. Affairs, Ind. U., Bloomington, 1976—. Author: (book) New Governor in Indiana: Transition of Executive Power, 1965. Mem.: ABA, Indpls. Bar Assn., Ind. State Bar Assn. (criminal justice law exec. com. 1966—72, mem. adminstrv. law com. 1968—77, chmn. adminstrv. law com. 1973—76, mem. law sch. liaison com. 1977—78). Office: Hagemier Allen & Smith 1170 Market Tower 10 W Market St Ste 1170 Indianapolis IN 46204-5924

ALLEN, DAVID MARK, psychiatrist, educator, director; b. Glendale, Calif., Apr. 26, 1949; s. Emmanuel and Ann Allen; m. Harriet Allen, Dec. 24, 1972; children: Angela, Paula. BA, UCLA, 1970; MD, U. Calif., San Francisco, 1974. Diplomate Am. Bd. Psychiatry and Neurology. Resident in psychiatry U. So. Calif. Med. Ctr., LA, 1977; mem. staff Gateways Hosp., LA, 1977-79; pvt. practice Burbank, Calif., 1979-91; dir. psychiat. residency tng., asst. prof. dept. psychiatry U. Tenn., Memphis, 1992—2004, prof., 2004—. Author: Unifying Individual and Family Therapies, 1988, Deciphering Motivation in Psychotherapy, 1991, Psychotherapy with Borderline Patients - An Integrated Approach, 2003. Mem.: Internat. Soc. Study of Personality Disorders, Soc. Psychotherapy Rsch., Tenn. Psychiat. Assn., Soc. Exploration Psychotherapy Integration, Am. Psychiat. Assn. Office: U Tenn Dept Psychiatry 135 N Pauline St # 6 Memphis TN 38105-4619 Business E-Mail: dmallen@utenn.edu.

ALLEN, DAVID RATCLIFF, management consultant, writer; b. Jonesboro, La., Dec. 28, 1945; s. Gordon Emmet Allen and Miriam Allen (Foster) Drummond; m. Kathryn Allen. BA, New Coll., Sarasota, Fla., 1968. Gen. mgr. Natural Landscape Co., LA, 1977-80; pres. Allen Assocs., LA, 1980-83; v.p. Insight Consulting Grp., Santa Monica, Calif., 1983; founder, pres. David Allen Co., Ojai, Calif., 1996—. Contbr. articles to profl. publs.; author: Getting Things Done: The Art of Stress-Free Productivity, 2001, Ready for Anything: 52 Productivity Principles for Work and Life, 2003. Named one of 50 Who Matter Now, CNNMoney.com Bus. 2.0, 2006. Avocations: Karate, music. Office: David Allen Co 1674 McNell Rd Ojai CA 93023*

ALLEN, DONALD VAIL, investment company executive, pianist; b. South Bend, Ind., Aug. 1, 1928; s. Frank Eugene and Vera Irene (Vail) A.; m. Betty Dunn, Nov. 17, 1956. BA magna cum laude, UCLA, 1972, MA, 1973. Pres., chmn. bd. dirs. Cambridge Investment Corp.; music editor and critic Times-Herald, Washington; music critic L.A. Times. Transl. works of Ezra Pound from Italian into English; author of papers on the musical motifs in the writings of James Joyce; specialist in works of Beethoven, Chopin, Debussy, Liszt, and Scriabin; premiere performances of contemporary piano music; represented by William Matthews Concert Agy., NYC; selected by William Steinway and Sascha Greiner of Steinway Piano Co. as an exclusive Steinway concert artist. Pres. Funds for Needy Children, 1974-76; mem. Am. Guild Organists. Mem. Ctr. for Study of Presidency, Am. Mgmt. Assn., Internat. Platform Assn., Nat. Assn. Securities Dealers, Chamber Music Soc., Am. Mus. Natural History. Avocations: languages, music, travel, writing, financial market.

ALLEN, DOROTHEA, secondary school educator; b. Rockaway, NJ, Apr. 30, 1919; d. Harrison Engleman and Caroline (Tierney) Allen. AB, Montclair U., 1941, MA, 1949. Cert. secondary, sci., math. tchr., counselor, supr., prin. N.J. Tchr. sci. and math. Denville (N.J.) Jr. High Sch., 1942-46; tchr. sci. Boonton (N.J.) High Sch., 1946-94, supr. sci. dept., 1978-94. Lab. technician Drew Chem. Corp., Boonton, 1942—47; tech. asst. Bell Telecom. Lab., Whippany, NJ, 1956; rsch. scientist Warner Lambert Rsch. Inst., Morris Plains, NJ, 1959—62; tchr. sci. enrichment Boonton Summer Sch., 1963—85; curriculum developer Morris County Vocat.-Tech. Sch., Denville, 1987; project evaluator Mid. States Assn., 1973, 79; facilitator Ptnrs. in Edn. Program; promoter Media Ctr. Open House; cons., reviewer Am. Biol. Tchr. Mag., 1975—; com. mem. Sch. Articulation Program Boonton Schs., 1991—94; media ctr. spkr. Meet the Author; sponsor Student Showcase of Excellence in Sci., 1990—94; faculty sponsor, mentor h.s. students, 1966—94; mentor Alt. Rt. Program Tchrs. N.J. Organizer Am. Dental Health Clinic, Boonton, 1968—72; presenter, spkr. in field. Author: Research Projects for High School Biology, 1971, Biology Teacher's Desk Book, 1979, Science Activities for Every Month of the School Year, 1981, Science Demonstrations for Elementary Classrooms, 1988, Hands-on Science, 1991; contbg. mem.: Family Edn. Network divsn. Pearson Edn.; contbr. articles to profl. jours. including Am. Biology Tchr., The Sci. Tchr. Mem. career com. N.J. divsn. Theobald Smith Soc., 1975—76, mentoring program, 1992—; fundraiser Am. Hemophilia Found., Rockaway, NJ, 1985—, Am. Heart Assn., 1995—, Nat. Children's Cancer Soc., 1996—; mothers march vol. March of Dimes, 1990—; cons. Cmty. Mid. Sch. Planning Com., Boonton, 1988—90; bd. advisors ABI Rsch., 1995—; contbg. mem. Family Edn. Network. Named Outstanding Biology Tchr., Nat. Assn. Biology Tchrs., 1972, Outstanding Sci. Tchr., Rsch. Assn. N.Am., 1980, Woman of the Yr., 1993—98; named to Sci. Edn. Hall of Fame, 1994—98, Boonton H.S. Wall of Fame, 1996, 1997, 1998; recipient Disting. Citizen's award, Town of Rockaway, 1984, Gov.'s and Edn. award, N.J. Dept. Edn., 1984, Morris County Tchr. of the Yr. award, 1990, Presdl. award, NSF, 1984, Cert. of Honor, State of N.J., 1985, World Lifetime Achievement award, 1994, Internat. Order of Merit, 1994, Spotlight award, Boonton Bd. Edn., 1980—86, Tchr. of Yr., 1984, 1990, Women's Inner Cir. of Achievement award, 1995. Mem.: NSTA, ASCD, NEA, NEA Ret., Morris Area Sci. Alliance, N.J. Dept. Edn. Exec. Acad., N.J. Dept. Edn. Exec. Acad., N.J. Alliance for Math. and Sci., N.J. Prins. And Suprs. Assn., N.J. Edn. Assn., Assn. Presdl. Award Winners in Sci. Tchg., Nat. Assn. Secondary Sch. Prins., Morris County Ret. Educators Assn. Avocations: reading, propagating plants, collecting gold coins. Home: 115 Jackson Ave Rockaway NJ 07866-3039

ALLEN, DWAYNE LEROY, information systems specialist; b. Sumter, SC, Aug. 13, 1961; s. LeRoy and Charity (White) A.; m. Jennifer Marie Jackson, Nov. 28, 1992. BA in Comms., U. Va., 1984; postgrad., Yale U., 1993; MBA, George Washington U., 1996. Mgr. info. systems Roy Rogers divsn. Restaurant Ops. group Marriott Internat., Inc., dir. corp. systems devel. info. systems and tech. divsn. reengring. Washington, dir. Marriott Yr. 2000 Project; v.p. info. tech. First Union Corp., Charlotte, NC; chief tech. advisor Hill Ventures, Detroit. Mem. adv. bd. Am. Visions, Washington. Deacon, mem. pastoral search com. Heritage United Ch. of Christ, Reston; mem., cons. Greater Washington Cultural Alliance; vol. mentor Fairfax County Juvenile and Domestic Ct. Sys. Mem. Washington D.C. Electronic Data Interchange Users Group, Alpha Phi Alpha. Avocations: travel, sports, art, theater, basketball, golf. Office: First Union Corp 1 Marriott Dr Washington DC 20058-0001

ALLEN, ELIZABETH FRATER, artist; b. Sparta, Tenn. d. Homer Byron Frater and Notie Snodgrass Fancher; m. Robert Earl Allen, Feb. 25, 1944 (dec.); children: Robert Lester, Byron Frater, Marshall Trigg. AA, Montgomery Coll., Rockville, Md., 1968; postgrad., Corcoran Sch. Art, Washington, 1968—69. Organizing chmn. Fire Hall Gallery, Charles Town, W.Va. One-woman shows include Rockville Civic Ctr. Gallery, Founders Room, Old Opera House, Charles Town, Boarman Arts Ctr., Martinsburg, W.Va., exhibitions include Montgomery County Art Assn., White Oak, Md., 1973, Arts & Crafts Gallery, Portales, N.Mex., 1974, Fairfax County Coun. of the Arts, No. Va. C.C., 1977, Montgomery County Arts Coun., Bethesda, Md., 1977, Nat. League Am. Penwomen, Chevy Chase Br., Washington, 1977, Montgomery Coll., Rockville, 1980, Cultural Ctr., Charleston, 1984, Theatre Project Gallery, Balt., 1985, Boarman Arts Ctr., Martinsburg, 1988, 1990, 1991, 1993, 1994, Youth Mus. So. W.Va., Beckley, 1990, others, Represented in permanent collections Howard U. Hosp., Washington, NY Cmty. Coll. Libr., Annandale. Mem. gallery com. Boarman Arts Ctr., Martinsburg, 1983—99. Mem.: Arts and Humanities Alliance Jefferson County (sec.), Nat. League Am. Penwoman. Home: Osage Studio Box 141 Bakerton WV 25410

ALLEN, ERNIE (ERNEST EUGENE ALLEN), non-profit organization executive, lawyer; b. Louisville, Jan. 6, 1946; s. William Ernest and Mary Alice (McIntyre) A.; m. Linda S. Broadus, June 10, 1985. BA, U. Louisville, 1968, JD, 1972. Bar: Ky. 1972. Exec. dir. Crime Commn., Louisville, 1973-83; dir. safety City of Louisville, 1983-85; chief adminstrv. officer Jefferson County, Louisville, 1985-89; pres., CEO, Nat. Ctr. for Missing and Exploited Children, Arlington, Va., 1989—. Chmn. Nat. Ctr. Missing and Exploited Children, Washington, 1984-88, Nat. Assn. Criminal Justice Planners, Washington, 1977-79, Am. Soc. Assn. Execs. TF on Philanthropic Orgn., Washington, 1991-92. Contbr. articles to profl. jours. Chmn. Ky. Alliance Against Rape, Louisville, 1979-89, Nat. Multiple Sclerosis Soc, Louisville, 1984-86; v.p. Ky. Horseman's Benevolent and Protection Assn., Louisville, 1987-89; sec., treas. Ky. Racing Health & Welfare Fund, Louisville, 1987-89. Sgt. Ky. Nat. Guard, 1969-75. Recipient Outstanding Alumnus award U. Louisville Coll. Arts and Scis., 1984, Order of Merit award U. Louisville, 1990, Disting. Alumnus award U. Louisville Sch. Law, 1991, Ellis Island Honor medal Nat. Ethnic Coalition of Orgns., 1993. Mem. Am. Soc. Assn. Execs., Ky. Bar Assn. Office: Nat Ctr Missing & Exploited Children Charles B Wang Internat CHildren's Bldg 699 Prince St Alexandria VA 22314*

ALLEN, FRANCES ELIZABETH, computer scientist; b. Peru, NY, Aug. 4, 1932; d. John Abram and Ruth Genevieve (Downs) A. BS in Math., Albany State Teachers Coll. (now SUNY), Albany, 1954; MA in Math., U. Mich., 1957; DSc (hon.), U. Alta., 1991, Pace U., 1999, U. Ill., Urbana-Champaign, 2004. With IBM Thomas J. Watson Rsch. Ctr., Yorktown Heights, NY, 1957—2002, sr. tech. advisor to rsch. v.p. for solutions, applications, and services. Adj. assoc. prof. N.Y.U., 1970-73; mem. computer and info. sci. and engring. sci. adv. bd. NSF, 1972-75, cons., 1975-78; lectr. Chinese Acad. Scis., 1973, 77; IEEE disting. visitor, 1973-74; cons. prof. Stanford U., 1977-78; founder Parallel TRANslation Group (PTRAN); chancellor's disting. vis. lectr. and Mackay lectr., U. Calif., Berkeley, 1988-89; Regents lectr., U. Calif. San Diego, 1997; mem. Stretch/HARVEST project.; pres. IBM Acad. Tech., 1995; mem. bd. Computer Sci. and Telecommunications. Author: (papers) Program Optimization, 1966, Control Flow Analysis, 1970, A Basis for Program Optimization, 1970; co-author (with John Cocke): A Catalog of Optimizing Transformations, 1971. IBM Corp. fellow (first women to be named this highest technical honor), 1989, Fellow Emerita, 2002-; recipient fellow award Computer History Mus., 2000, Frances E. Allen Women in Tech. Mentoring award (first recipient-named in honor of), 2000, Grace Hopper Celebration of Women in Computing award, 2002, Augusta Ada Lovelace award, 2002, Anita Borg Technical Leadership award, 2004; named to Women In Tech. Internat. Hall of Fame, 1997. Fellow IEEE, Am. Acad. Arts and Scis., Assn. Computing Machinery (nat. lectr. 1972-73, mem. job migration task force, mem. Spl. Interest Group on Programming Language (SIGPLAN), mem. editl. bd., SIGPLAN's Programming Languages Achievement award, 2006 A.M. Turing award (first women to receive honor); mem. NAE Programming Sys. and Langs. (Paper award 1976), Computing Rsch. Assn. (bd. mem.), Am. Philosophical Soc., Am. Alpine Club, Alpine Club Can. Achievements include being the pioneer in the field of optimizing compilers. Avocation: hiking.

ALLEN, FRANCES L. (BRITCHFORD), marketing executive; b. 1962; Dir. internat. advt. Frito-Lay PepsiCo Inc., v.p. innovation N.Am.; v.p. mktg. Sony Ericsson Mobile Comms., 2005—07; brand mktg. officer Dunkin Doughnuts Dunkin Brands, Inc., 2007—. Office: Dunkin Doughnuts 130 Royall St Canton MA 02021

ALLEN, FRANCES MICHAEL, publisher; b. Charlotte, NC, Apr. 7, 1939; d. Thomas Wilcox and Lola Frances (Horne) A.; m. Joseph Taylor Lisenbee, Feb. 24, 1955 (div. 1957); 1 child, Leslie Autice. Abilene Christian U., Tex., 1954-56, Chico State U., Calif, 1957-59. Art dir. B&E Publs., LA, 1963-65, editor, 1969-70; art dir. Tiburon Corp., Chgo., 1970-75; founder, editor Boxers, Internat., LA, 1970-76; editor The Hound's Tale, 1974, Saints, Incorp., 1974-76; founder, editor Setters, Incorp., Costa Mesa, Calif., 1975-85; founder, owner Michael Enterprises, Midway City, Calif., 1976—; editor Am. Cocker Rev., Midway City, 1980-81; editor, pub. Am. Cocker Mag., 1981-99; editor, co-pub. Sporting Life, 1991; editor, pub. The Royal Spaniels, 1995—. Author: The American Cocker Book, 1989; editor, pub. The Royal Spaniels, 1995— (Dogs Writer's Assn. awards 1995, 96, 99); illustrator: The First Five Years, 1970, The Aftercare of the Ear, 1975, The Shenn Simplicity Collection, 1976, The Miniature Pinscher, 1967; prin. works include mag. and book covers for USA, most widely published show dog artist world wide, past 30 yrs. Recipient Dog World Award Top Producer, 5 times, 1966-88, 10-time winner and nominee Dog Writers Assn. Am., winner best breed publ. World Congress Pet Publs., Ukraine, 1995, winner Kirk Paper Co. award of excellence. Mem. Dog Writers Assn. Am. (life), Am. Spaniel Club (life). Republican. Mem. Ch. of Christ. Avocations: dog exhibiting, ballooning, photography, art. Home and Office: 14531 Jefferson St Midway City CA 92655-1030 Office Phone: 714-893-0053. E-mail: baliwck@socal.rr.com.

ALLEN, FRANK CLINTON, JR., lawyer, chemical engineer; b. New Orleans, Apr. 14, 1934; s. Frank Clinton and Lucy Charlotte (Walters) A.; m. Cynthia Ann Church, June 7, 1958; children: Frank C. III, Thomas Church, C. Ann. BSChemE, Tulane U., 1955, LLB, 1964. Registered profl. engr., La.; bar: La. 1964, Miss. 1977, Tex. 1991, U.S. Supreme Ct. 1972. Process engr. Am. Oil Co., New Orleans, 1955-60, Chevron Oil Co., New Orleans, 1960-64; atty. Jones, Walker, Waechter, New Orleans, 1964-78; v.p., gen. counsel, corp. sec. McDermott Internat., Inc., New Orleans, 1978-99; atty. Jones, Walker, Waechter, Poitevent, Carrere, Denegre, New Orleans, 1999—2002; of counsel Killen & Assocs., P.C., Houston, 2002—. Mem. AIChE, ABA, La. Bar Assn., Miss. Bar Assn., Tex. Bar Assn. Avocation: sailing. Office: Killen & Assocs PC 8 Greenway Plz Ste 614 Houston TX 77046 also: Graham Arceneaux And Allen Llc 601 Poydras St Ste 1871 New Orleans LA 70130-6018 Home Phone: 228-452-2251; Office Phone: 504-522-8256, 228-806-7100. Personal E-mail: fallen@datasync.net. Business E-Mail: fca@gra-arc.com. E-mail: frankcallen@yahoo.com, fallen@cableone.net.

ALLEN, GARLAND EDWARD, biologist, professor, writer; b. Louisville, Feb. 13, 1936; s. Garland Edward and Virginia (Blandford) A.; children: Tania Leigh, Carin Tove. AB, U. Louisville, 1957; AMT, Harvard U., 1958, AM, 1963, PhD, 1966. Programmer, announcer WFPL-WFPK, Louisville, 1956—58; tchr. Mt. Hermon (Mass.) Sch., 1958—61; Allston-Burr sr. tutor, instr. history of sci. Harvard, 1965—67; asst. prof. biology Washington U., St. Louis, 1967—72, assoc. prof., 1972—80, prof., 1980—. Cons. Ednl. Rsch. Corp., Cleve., 1967-85; commr. Commn. Undergrad. Edn. in Biol. Scis., 1967-70; mem. NSF Panel for Social Scis., 1968-71; mem. ELSI rev. panel NIH, 2002; trustee Marine Biol. Lab., Woods Hole, Mass., 1985-93; Sigma Xi nat. lectr., 1973-74, bicentennial lectr., 1974-77; Watkins vis. prof. Wichita State U., 1984; vis. prof. dept. history of sci. Harvard U., 1989-91, Sarton Award Lecture, AAAS, 1998. Author: Life Sciences in the Twentieth Century, 1975, 1978, T.H. Morgan: The Man and His Science, 1978; author: (with J.J.W. Baker) Matter, Energy and Life, 1965, 1970, 1975, 1981; author: The Study of Biology, 1967, The Study of Biology, 4th edit., 1982, Hypothesis, Prediction and Implication, 1969, The Process of Biology, 1970, Biology: Scientific Process and Social Issues, 2001; co-editor: Mendel Newsletter, 1989—92, Jour. History of Biology, 1996—2006; mem. editl. bd.: San Josè Studies, —, Jour. History of Biology, 1968—91, Folia Mendeliana, History and Philosophy of the Life Scis., 1993—; co-editor: Science, History, and Social Activism: A Tribute to Everett Mendelsohn, 2002, Centennial History of the Carnegie Institution of Washington's Department of Embryology, 2005. Adv. bd. Holocaust Meml. Mus., 2000—01, Human Genome Sequencing Ctr. Outreach Washington U., 2003—06, Beach Ctr. for Disability U. Kans., 2003—07. Fellow Charles Warren Ctr. for Studies in Am. History, Harvard U., 1981-82; sr. fellow Dibner Inst. for the History of Sci. and Tech., MIT, 2002. Mem. AAAS (coun., sect. L exec. com. 1975, Sarton award lectr. 1998), History Sci. Soc. (chmn. Schumann Prize com. 1972, Pfizer prize com. 1977, 80, 91-94, HSS coun. 1994-96, nominating com. 2006—, vis. lectr. program 1985-87), Internat. Soc. for the History, Philosophy and Social Studies of Biology (pres.-elect 2003-05, pres. 05-07), Sigma Xi. Home: 1526 Mississippi Ave Saint Louis MO 63104-2512 Office: Washington U Biology Dept Saint Louis MO 63130 Office Phone: 314-935-6808. Business E-Mail: allen@biology2.wustl.edu.

ALLEN, GEORGE FELIX, JR., former senator, governor; b. Whittier, Calif., Mar. 8, 1952; s. George H. and Henrietta Lumbroso A.; m. Susan M. Brown; children: Tyler, Forrest, Brooke. BA in History, cum laude, U. Va., 1974, JD, 1977. Bar: Va., DC. Atty., Charlottesville, Va., 1983—91; mem. Va. Ho. of Dels., Richmond, 1982—91, US Congress from 7th Dist. Va., 1991-93; gov. State of Va., 1994-98; ptnr. McGuire Woods Battle & Boothe, LLP, Richmond, 1998-2001; US Senator from Va., 2001—07. Mem. com. commerce, sci. and transp. US Senate, com. energy and natural resources, com. fgn. relations, com. small bus. and entrepreneurship. Bd. dirs. United Way; chmn. Chesapeake Bay Exec. Coun., 1995—96, So. Gov.'s Assn., 1996—97; adv. bd. Jr. League, 1987—88; bd. dirs. Atlantic Rural Exposition Bd., Commonwealth Biotechnologies, Inc., Richmond Historic Riverfront Found., Richmond Sports Backers, Va. Coun. Econ. Edn., Va.-Israel Adv. Bd., Xybernaut Corp. Recipient Founders Cir. award, TechNet, 2002, Champion Sci. award, The Sci. Coalition, 2003, Congressional Leadership award, Semiconductor Industry Assn., 2003. Republican. Presbyn.*

ALLEN, GEORGE SEWELL, neurosurgery educator; b. St. Louis, Jan. 10, 1942; BA in Chemistry, Wesleyan U., 1963; MD, Washington U., St. Louis, 1967; PhD, U. Minn., 1975. Diplomate Am. Bd. Neurol. Surgeons. Intern Duke U., Durham, NC, 1967-68; rsch. assoc. Nat. Inst. Neurol. Disease and Stroke, NIH, 1968-70; resident dept. neurol. surgery U. Minn., Mpls., 1970-75; asst. prof. neurol. surgery Johns Hopkins U. and Hosp., Balt., 1975-79, assoc. prof., 1979-83, prof., 1983-84; prof. neurol. surgery, chmn. dept. Vanderbilt U. Med. Ctr., Nashville, 1984—. Mem. med. staff Vanderbilt U. Hosp., Met. Nashville Gen. Hosp., VA Hosp., Nashville, St. Thomas Hosp., Nashville, all 1984—; A.W. Rogers lectr. Milw. Acad. Medicine, 1988, J. Jay Keegan Meml. lectr. U. Nebr. Med. Ctr., Omaha, 1988, J. Cochran lectr. Med. Assn. Ala., Montgomery, 1988, A.B. Baker lectr. U. Minn., Mpls., 1988. Contbr. articles to profl. jours. Comdr. USPHS, 1968-70. Mem. ACS, Am. Assn. Neurol. Surgeons, Congress of Neurol. Surgeons, Brain Surgery Soc., Soc. Neurol. Surgeons, H. William Scott, Jr. Soc., Soc. Neurosurg. Anesthesia and Neurologic Supportive Care Office: Vanderbilt U Med Ctr N Dept Neurosurgery Rm T 4224 Nashville TN 37232-2380 E-mail: george.allen@vanderbilt.edu.

ALLEN (IRVIN M.N.), GEORGIANNE LYDIA CHRISTIAN, writer, poet; b. Chgo., Apr. 30, 1943; d. George Aaron Irvin and Madeline Anandabai (Sobrian M.N.) Irvin Gordon, Earl Ovington Gordon (Stepfather); m. Ernest James Allen, Feb. 29, 1992; m. Hillard Roland Phillips, July 1, 1960 (div. June 16, 1977); children: Kellie Annette Phillips Mortley, Madeline Charlotte Phillips Kimmich, Matthew Roland Phillips. Secretarial cert., Chgo. Coll. Commerce, 1963; AA in Psychology, Southwestern Coll., Chula Vista, Calif., 1974; AS in Nursing, Mo. So. State Coll., Joplin, 1977; BSN, Pittsburg State U., Kans., 1979; clin. pastoral edn., St. Paul Sch. Theology and Ossawatomie State Hosp., Kans., 1984; MDiv, MRE, St. Paul Sch. of Theology, Kansas City, Mo., 1985; postgrad., Ga. State U., 2005. RN Mo., Ga., 1977; ordained to ministry Mo. West Conf., 1980; lic. practitioner Nambudripad Allergy Ellimination. Bd. dirs. United Meth. Ch. Black Meth. for Ch. Renewal, 1981—82; pastor Pitts Chapel United Meth. Ch., Springfield, Mo., 1984—85; founder, chairperson Matthew 25 Collaboration, Atlanta, 1998—99; pastor, CEO Ch. of the Creator Incarnate, Coverings, Creative Theol. Ministries, Stone Mountain, Ga., 1994—; nursing instr. Pacific Coast Coll., Chula Vista, Calif., 1990—91; mem. adv. bd. Nambudripad's Allergy Rsch. Found. Author: How to Study and Pass Tests (on line at Virtual University, www.vu.com), I Will Trust Him, Poetry of Faith, (book of poetry) Today (appeared in Poetry's Elite the Best Poets of 2000, 2000); composer: (songs) Atlanta, God Will See You Through, On this Our Wedding Day, The Gospel in Calypso, When I See a Rainbow et al.; prodr.: (radio broadcast) Creative Christian Living; prodr.: (motivational/relaxation cassette) How to Release Worry Anxiety and Stress; web site designer www.coverings.org;, author of poems. Participant Atlanta Taskforce for the Homeless, 1994—98; lectr. leadership classes Dekalb Hist. Soc., Decatur, Ga., 1999—2001; newsletter editor and organizer Stone Mountain Estates Cmty. Orgn., Ga., 2002—03; bd. dirs. Black Methodists for Ch. Renewal, 1981—82; chairperson Matthew 25 Collaboration, Atlanta, 1998—99; treas. Conf. Youth Coun. of Rock River Conf. of Meth. Episcopal Ch., 1959—60; designer, coord. Project Hope. Nominee Ga. Author Yr., Ga. Writers Assn., 2000; recipient Instr.'s Appreciation plaque, Nursing Students Pacific Coast Coll., 1991, Appreciation Cert., Bd. Dirs. Coverings Ministry, 1997, Internat. Poet of Merit award, Internat. Soc. Poets, 2000 - 2003; Betty Stephens Scholarship award for religious edn., St. Paul Sch. of Theology, 1980—81. Mem.: Sigma Theta Tau. Achievements include research in basis for harmonius race relations (100+ yrs) between residents of the Village of Stone Mountain, GA, former home of the Grand Imperial Wizard of the Ku Klux Klan, site of USAs largest Klan rallies; first African Am. woman to enter and grad. from both Mo. So. State Coll.'s Nursing Program and St. Paul Sch. of Theology. Avocations: travel, music (writing, playing and listening), sewing, writing, history. Home: 4965 Dantel Way Stone Mountain GA 30083 Office Phone: 770-469-6611.

ALLEN, HENRY SERMONES, JR., lawyer; b. Bronxville, NY, Aug. 26, 1947; s. Henry S. and Cecelia Marie (Chartrand) A.; m. Patricia Stromberger, Nov. 26, 1988; children: David Beckman, Amy Louise, Jeffrey Roy. AB magna cum laude, Washington U., St. Louis, 1969; MPA, Cornell U., 1973, JD, 1974. Adminstrv. resident Montefiore Hosp. and Med. Ctr., Bronx, NY, 1971; rsch. trainee Nat. Ctr. Health Svcs. Rsch. HEW, 1974—75; assoc. Vedder, Price, Kaufman & Kammholz, Chgo., 1975—79; pvt. practice Springfield, 1979—81; ptnr. Allen & Reed, Chgo., 1981—86, McBride, Baker & Coles, 1986—2002, Holland & Knight LLC, Chgo., 2002—. Adj. asst. prof. hosp. law Ithaca (NY) Coll., 1974-75; adj. prof. Cornell U., 1995—, Northwestern U. Sch. Law, 2003—, Northwestern U. Kellogg Sch. Mgmt., 2003—. HUD fellow, 1969-71. Mem. Am. Health Lawyers Assn., Ill. Soc. Hosp. Attys., Nat. Health Lawyers Assn., Cornell U. Club Chgo., Phi Beta Kappa, Omicron Delta Epsilon Office: Holland and Knight LLC 131 S Dearborn St Chicago IL 60603-5506 Business E-Mail: henry.allen@hklaw.com.

ALLEN, HENRY SOUTHWORTH, journalist, critic; b. Summit, NJ, May 23, 1941; s. Henry Southworth and Mary Darmour (Williams) A.; m. Deborah Etta Mandel, Mar. 25, 1972; children: Hannah Rose, Peter Griffith, Nicholas Isaac DeWolf. BA, Hamilton Coll., 1967. Copy editor New Haven (Conn.) Register, 1966; reporter N.Y. News, NYC, 1967-70; reporter, editor, critic The Washington Post, 1970—. Tchr. in culture and meaning U. Md. Honors Program. Author: Glare, 1991, Fool's Mercy, 1982, Going Too Far Enough, 1994, What It Felt Like B Living in the American Century, 2000; writer (articles) New York Review of Books, New Yorker, Forbes, Paris Review, Smithsonian, Vogue, Wilson Quarterly. Cpl. USMC, 1963-66, Vietnam. Recipient Am. Soc. Newspaper Editors award for commentary, 1992, Am. Soc. of Sunday and Feature Editors prize for creative writing, finalist Pulitzer prize , 1994, Pulitzer prize Journalism for Criticism, 2000, Sherwood Media award, Blinded Americans Veterans Found., 2000; NEH fellowship for journalists, U. Mich., 1975-76. Mem. Marine Corps Hist. Assn. Avocations: art, bicycling. Office: The Washington Post 1150 15th St NW Washington DC 20071-0002 E-mail: hsallen4@yahoo.com.

ALLEN, HENRY WESLEY, biomedical researcher, consultant; b. Louisville, Oct. 16, 1927; s. John Turk and Irene Victoria (Slater) A.; m. Evelyn Chen, Dec. 29, 1968 (div. Dec. 1988); children: Lillian Chen, Rosaniline Chen, Dianne Chen. Student, U. Louisville, 1945-46, U. Chgo., 1946-47, U. So. Calif., 1960-61. Rschr. Loma Linda (Calif.) U., 1962-77, Am. Biologics, Chula Vista, Calif., 1977—. Author: International Protocols in Cancer Management, 1983, The Study of Reactive Oxygen Toxic Species and Their Metabolism, 1985, 2d edit., 1997, The Biochemistry of Live Cell Therapy, 1986, Fibromyalgia, 2001; contbr. articles to Jour. of Theoretical Biology, Analytical Biochemistry, Nature, others. Achievements include patents in field. Office: Am Biologics 1180 Walnut Ave Chula Vista CA 91911-2622 Office Phone: 619-429-8200. Business E-Mail: ambio@ix.netcom.com.

ALLEN, H(ENRY) WILLIAM, lawyer; b. Nevada, Mo., Apr. 7, 1944; s. Henry W. and Betty Jeane (Grover) A.; m. Kay Willis, Sept. 22, 1944; children— West, Farrell, Lindsay BA, Rhodes Coll., 1966; JD, Washington U., St. Louis, 1969. Bar: Ark. 1969, Ill. 1969, Mo. 1969. Asst. U.S. atty., Chgo., 1969-70; spl. asst. to pres. ABA, 1970-71; assoc. Wright Lindsey & Jenninger, 1971-76, ptnr., 1976-80; spl. chief just. Ark. Supreme Ct., 1980; sr. ptnr. Allen Cabe & Lester, Little Rock, 1980-86; mng. ptnr. Allen Law Firm, P.C., Little Rock, 1986—. Mem. ABA (ho. of dels. 1991-00, chmn. com. on ethics and profl. responsibility 1978-84, bd. gov. 1975-78, 2002-05), Am. Bar. Found. (pres., bd. dirs.), Am. Judicature Soc. (bd. dirs. 1981-85); Pulaski County Bar Assn (pres. 1984-85, Outstanding Lawyer award, 1991); Ark. Bar Assn. (chmn. Commn. Ethics 1989-92); Am. Law Inst. Office: Allen Law Firm 9th Floor 212 Center St Little Rock AR 72201-2425 Office Phone: 501-374-7100.

ALLEN, HERBERT ANTHONY, JR., investment company executive; 4 children. Grad., Williams Coll. Mng. dir. Allen & Co. LLC, 2002—03; pres., CEO, dir. Allen & Co. Inc. Chmn. bd. Columbia Pictures Industries, Inc.; bd. dirs. Coca-Cola Co., 1982—, Convera Corp., Global Edn. Network. Trustee Am. Film Inst., Rochester U. Named one of 400 Richest Ams., Forbes mag., 2006. Office: Allen & Co Inc 711 5th Ave Fl 9 New York NY 10022

ALLEN, HERBERT ELLIS, environmental chemistry educator; b. Sharon, Pa., July 19, 1939; s. Jacob Samuel and Florence (Safier) A.; m. Deena Wilner, 1962 (dec. 1983); children: Francine Joy, Julie Michelle; m. Ronnie Magil, 1984 BS in Chemistry, U. Mich., 1962; MS, Wayne State U., 1967; PhD, U. Mich., 1974. Chemist U.S. Bur. Comml. Fisheries, Ann Arbor, Mich., 1962-70; lectr. U. Mich., Ann Arbor, 1970-74; asst. prof. Ill. Inst. Tech., Chgo., 1974-76, assoc. prof., 1976-80, prof. environ. engring., 1980-83; dir. Environ. Studies Inst., Drexel U., Phila., also prof. chemistry, 1983-89; prof. civil engring. U. Del., Newark, 1990—, dir. Ctr. for Study of Metals in the Environment, 2002—; dir. Del. Waste Reduction Assistance Program, 1991-95. Vis. prof. Water Rsch. Ctr., Medmenham, Eng., 1980-81, Nankai U., Tianjin, People's Republic of China, 1993—; cons. WHO, U.S. EPA. Editor: Nutrients in Natural Waters, 1972, Analysis and Effects of Metal Speciation, Applications to Water, Waste, Soil, 1988, Metals in Groundwater, 1993, Metal Speciation and Contamination of Soil, 1994, Metal Contaminated Aquatic Sediments, 1995, Metals in Surface Water, 1998, Bioavailability of Metals in Terestrial Ecosystems, 2002, Solid Waste, 2004. Fellow, WHO, 1981. Mem. Am. Chem. Soc. (chmn. divsn. environ. chemistry 1972-75), Water Environment Fedn., Soc. for Environ. Toxicology and Chemistry, Internat. Water Assn. Home: 21 E Levering Mill Rd Bala Cynwyd PA 19004-2251 Office: Univ Delaware Dept Civil & Environ Enging Newark DE 19716 Office Phone: 302-831-8449. Business E-Mail: allen@ce.udel.edu.

ALLEN, HOWARD NORMAN, cardiologist, educator; b. Chgo., Nov. 19, 1936; s. Herman and Ida Gertrude (Weinstein) Allen; children: Michael Daniel, Jeffrey Scott. BS, U. Ill., Chgo., 1958, MD, 1960. Diplomate Am. Bd. Internal Medicine, Am. Bd. Cardiovasc. Disease, Nat. Bd. Med. Examiners. Intern Los Angeles County Gen. Hosp., LA, 1960—61; resident in internal medicine Wadsworth VA Med. Ctr., LA, 1961, 1964—66; fellow in cardiology Cedars-Sinai Med. Ctr., LA, 1966—67, dir. cardiac care unit Cedars of Lebanon Hosp. div., 1968—74, dir. Pacemaker Evaluation Ctr., 1968—89, dir. Cardiac Noninvasive Lab., 1972—88; Markus Found. fellow in cardiology St. George's Hosp., London, 1967—68; attending physician cardiology svc. Sepulveda (Calif.) VA Med. Ctr., 1972—86; pvt. practice Beverly Hills, Calif., 1988—. Asst. prof. medicine UCLA, 1970—76, assoc. prof., 1976—84, adj. prof., 1984—88, clin. prof., 1988—; cons. Sutherland Learning Assocs., Inc., LA, 1970—75; cardiology cons. Occidental Life Ins. Co., LA, 1972—86. Contbr. articles to profl. jours., chapters to books. Commr. L.A. County Emergency Med. Svcs., 1989—91. Capt. M.C. US Army, 1962—63, Korea. Recipient Lou Liay Spirit award, U. Ill. Alumni Assn. at Chgo., 2005; fellow, NSF, 1958, NIH, 1966—67. Fellow: ACP, Am. Coll. Cardiology (Calif. chpt. dist. councilor 1999—2003); mem.: Shakespeare Globe 1000 Club, Am. Heart Assn. (bd. dirs. 1979—94, fellow coun. clin. cardiology, pres. Greater L.A. affiliate 1987—88, Disting. Svc. award 1988, Heart of Gold award 1994), U. Ill. Alumni Assn. (life; Loyalty award 1996, Lou Liay Spirit award 2005), Cedars-Sinai Alumni Assn. (exec. bd. 1999—, sec., treas. 2000, pres. 2001—02), Big Ten Club So. Calif. (bd. dirs.), Pi Kappa Epsilon, Alpha Omega Alpha. Office: 414 N Camden Dr Ste 1100 Beverly Hills CA 90210-4532 Office Phone: 310-278-3400. Business E-Mail: allen@cvmg.com.

ALLEN, IRMA M., adult education educator; d. Henry Lemons and Mattie Robinson-Lemons; m. Ulysses Allen, Sept. 24, 1950; children: Wanda, Ulysses Jr., Walter, Richard, Eric, Janet Anderson. BS in Criminal Justice, San Jose State U., 1973. Cert. tchr. Calif. Substitute tchr. Monterey (Calif.) Unified Sch. Dist., 1972—73; correctional officer Fed. Correctional Instn., Dublin, Calif., 1975—77, GED tchr., 1977—95; adult edn. tchr. Milpitas (Calif.) Unified Sch. Dist., 1995—. Mem. St. James. A.M.E. Ch., San Jose, 1975—; chairperson St. James Outreach and Prison Ministry. Recipient cert. of appreciation, Fed. Correctional Instn., Dublin, 1976—2004, A.M.E. Ch., Oakland, 1999, Skyline Convalescent Hosp., San Jose, 2003—04. Mem.: Josephine Young Women's Missionary Soc. (v.p.), Southbay Mins., Wives and Widows (devotion dir., co-chairperson). Democrat. Methodist. Office: Milpitas Unified Sch Dist 1331 E Calaveras Milpitas St Milpitas CA 95035 Office Phone: 408-945-2341. Office Fax: 408-224-4257.

ALLEN, JANE FOLGER, psychologist; b. San Francisco, July 23, 1925; d. James Athearn and Jane (Carrigan) Folger; m. James Carrigan, Nov. 4, 1944 (div. 1964); 1 child, Andrew; m. Thomas B. Allen, Jan. 14, 1967. BA, Stanford U., 1948; PhD, Cath. U. Am., 1971. Lic. psychologist, Md., Washington, W.Va. Dir. exptl. counseling program Family Svcs. Montgomery County, Rockville, Md., 1964-65; counselor Pastoral Counseling Svcs., Washington, 1965-66; staff psychologist Pastoral Counseling Consultation Ctrs., Washington, 1966-76; pvt. practice Washington, 1966-76, Montgomery County, Md., 1976-83, Washington, 1983-91. Co-founder, dir. In-the-Swim, Montgomery County, 1967-70; pres. Folger Found., San Francisco, 1980-96. Mem. APA, D.C. Psychol. Assn. (sec. 1975-78), Am. Acad. Psychotherapists. Democrat. Avocation: computer programming. Personal E-mail: jfa72714@cs.com.

ALLEN, JANET LEE, special education educator; d. James Monroe and Clara Faye (Greiner) Crowder; m. Thomas Scott Allen, Aug. 11, 1973; children: Brian Alexander, Timothy Michael. BS in Edn., Emporia State U., 1974. Cert. tchr. Kans. From stenographer to trainmaster, various clk. positions Atchison, Topeka & Santa Fe Rlwy. Co., Kansas City, Kans., 1971—76; paraprofessional Shawnee Mission (Kans.) Sch. Dist., 1986—88, 2001—, ESL aide, 1997—2000. Cub scout leader Boy Scouts Am., Shawnee, 1985—89; vol. Project Finish Johnson County Libr., Merriam and Olathe, Kans., 1988; Sunday sch. tchr. St. Paul's United Meth., Lenexa, Kans., 1983—94. Named Outstanding Employee of Yr., Shawnee Mission Sch. Dist., 2002. Avocations: languages, reading, theater, travel. Office: Nieman Elem Sch 10917 W 67th St Shawnee Mission KS 66203 Personal E-mail: jallen7779@hotmail.com.

ALLEN, JEFFERSON F., oil industry executive; Pres., CEO, chmn. bd. dirs. Comfed Bancorp, Inc., Lowell, Mass.; exec. v.p., CFO Tosco Corp., Stamford, Conn., pres., 1997—, pres., CFO. Office: Tosco Corp # 500 1700 E Putnam Ave Old Greenwich CT 06870-1321

ALLEN, JEFFREY MICHAEL, lawyer; b. Chgo., Dec. 13, 1948; s. Albert A. and Miriam (Feldman) A.; m. Anne Marie Guaraglia, Aug. 9, 1975; children: Jason M., Sara M. BA in Polit. Sci. with great distinction and distinction in honors, U. Calif., Berkeley, 1970, JD, 1973. Bar: Calif. 1973, U.S. Dist. Ct. (no. and so. dists.) Calif. 1973, U.S. Ct. Appeals (9th cir.) 1973, U.S. Dist. Ct. (ea. dist.) Calif. 1974, U.S. Dist. Ct. (cen. dist.) Calif. 1977, U.S. Dist. Ct. (so. dist.) Calif., U.S. Supreme Ct.; solicitor Supreme Ct. Eng. and Wales; lic. real estate broker. Prin. Graves & Allen, Oakland, Calif., 1973—; solicitor Supreme Ct. Eng. and Wales. Tchg. asst. dept. polit. sci. U. Calif., Berkeley, 1970-73; lectr. St. Mary's Coll., Moraga, Calif., 1976-90; bd. dirs. Family Svcs. of East Bay, 1987-92, 1st v.p., 1988, pres., 1988-91; mem. faculty Oakland Coll. Law, 1996-98, 2004-; mem. panel arbitrators Ala. County Superior Ct.; arbitrator comml. arbitration panel Am. Arbitration Assn.; assoc. prof. U. Phoneix, 2004-, Calif. State U., East Bay, 2005-; solicitor Supreme Ct. Eng. and Wales, 2006. Mem. editorial bd. U. Calif. Law Rev., 1971-73, project editor, 1972-73; mem. Ecology Law Quar., 1971-72; contbr. articles to profl. jours. Mem. U.S. Youth Soccer Constl. Commn., 1997—98, U.S. Youth Soccer Bylaws Com., 1998—; mem. region 4 regional coun. U.S. Youth Soccer, 1996—99, chmn. mediation and dispute resolution com., 1999—2000; bd. dirs. U.S. Futsal Fedn., 2000—; treas. Hillcrest Elem. Sch. PTA, 1984—86, pres., 1986—88; past mem. GATE adv. com., strategic planning com. on fin. and budget, dist. budget adv. com., instructional strategy counsel Oakland Unified Sch. Dist., 1986—91; mem. Oakland Met. Forum, 1987—91, Oakland Strategic Planning Com., 1988—90; mem. adv. com. St. Mary's Coll. Paralegal Prog.; commr. Bay Oaks Youth Soccer, 1988—94; asst. dist. commr. dist. 4 Calif. Youth Soccer Assn., 1990—92, also bd. dirs., pres. dist. 4 competitive league, 1990—93, sec. bd. dirs., 1993—96, chmn. bd. dirs., 1996—99; chmn. U.S. Soccer dateabase mktg. com. Calif. Soccer Assn., 1997—99; bd. dirs. Montera Sports Complex, 1988—89, Jack London Youth Soccer League, 1988—94, Calif. Soccer Assn., 1996—99. Mem.: Law Soc. Eng. and Wales, Rotary (bd. dirs. Oakland 1992—94), Oakland C. of C., Assn. Conflict Resolution, Calif. North Referee Assn. (referee adminstr. dist. 4 1992—96, state bd. dirs. 1996—2000), U.S. Soccer Fedn. (nat. C lic. coach and state referee, state referee instr. and state referee assessor), Calif. Scholarship Fedn., U.S. Soccer Assn. (database mktg. com., constl. commn.), Alameda County Bar Assn. (past vice chmn. com. continuing edn., exec. com. alternative dispute resolution programs, panel mediator, arbitrator), Calif. Bar Assn. (mem. ADR com. 2001—04), ABA (chmn. subcom. on use of computers in real estate trans. 1985—86, chmn. real property com. gen. practice sect. 1987—91, mem. programs com. 1991—93, adv. coord. 1993—96, sect. coun. 1994—98, mktg. bd. 1996—98, mem. 1998—99, editor, columnist Tech. and Practice Guide 1998—, editl. bd. GP Solo 1999—, editor, columnist Tech. e Report 2002—, advisor to nat. counsel commrs. of uniform state laws, online form state laws drafting com. for electronic discovery). Avocations: reading, computers, photography, skiing, baseball. Office: Graves & Allen 436 14th St Ste 1400 Oakland CA 94612-2716 Office Phone: 510-839-8777. Personal E-mail: jallenlaw@aol.com. Business E-Mail: jallenlaw@gravesallen.com.

ALLEN, JEFFREY RODGERS, lawyer; b. West Point, NY, Aug. 15, 1953; s. James R. and Kathryn (Lewis) A.; m. Cynthia Lynn Colyer, Aug. 10, 1975; children: Emily Rodgers, Elizabeth Colyer, Richard Byrd. BA in History, U. Va., 1975; JD, U. Richmond, 1978. Bar: Va. 1978, U.S. Ct. Mil. Appeals 1981, U.S. Ct. Appeals (4th cir.) 1982, U.S. Supreme Ct. 1982. Trial atty. Michie, Hamlett, Donato & Lowry, Charlottesville, Va., 1982-86; chief counsel Va. Dept. Mil. Affairs, Blackstone, Va., 1986-2000; US property and fiscal officer Va. Blackstone, 2001—07. Atty., advisor U.S. Army Mobile Air Surg. Transport Team, Savannah, Ga., 1980-82; steering com. X-Car Litigation Group, 1983-85; lectr., organizer Law Everyone Should Know series Piedmont (Va.) C.C., Charlottesville, 1984-86; trial atty., of counsel Thorsen, Marchant & Scher, L.L.P., Richmond, 1986-98; mem. legal adv. com. Va. Gov.'s Mil. Adv. Commn., 1987-00, judge advocate adv. coun. N.G. Bur., 1993-96, TJAG Air N.G. judge advocate adv. coun., 1997-, coord. strategic planning com.; US property and fiscal officer Coun. Futures Com., 2002—, chmn. coun. edn. com., 2004-07. Pres. Regency Woods Condominium Assn., Richmond, 1976-78, Ashcroft Neighborhood Assn., Charlottesville, 1983-86; treas. Va. N.G. Found., 1986-02, mem. strategic planning coun. US Planning and Fin. Officer Coun., 2002—. Capt. U.S. Army, 1978-82, lt. col. JAGC, Va. Air N.G., 1982-00, col. USAF, 2001-07. Mem. Assn. Trial Lawyers Am., Va. Trial Lawyers Assn., Richmond Bar Assn. Avocations: jogging, mountain climbing, photography, fishing, swimming. Home: 2700 Cottage Cove Dr Richmond VA 23233-3318 Office Phone: 434-298-6161. Business E-Mail: jeff.allen1@us.army.mil.

ALLEN, JESSE OWEN, III, organizational behavior specialist; b. Albany, Ga., Apr. 7, 1938; s. Jesse Owen Jr. and Erma Hazel (Pearson) A.; children by previous marriage: Charlotte Renee, Garrett Owen, Cheryl Hazel; m. Barbara Joanna Smith Ozment, May 23, 1987; 1 stepchild, Pamela Ozment Cartee. LLB, LaSalle Law Sch., 1967; AS, U. State N.Y., Albany, 1978, BS in History, Lit. and Bus., 1986; MA in Philosophy, Calif. State U., 1987; PhD in Organizational Behavior, The Union Grad. Sch., 1991; postgrad., Oxford U., England, 1997. Founder, pres. Specific Action Corp., Greensboro, N.C., 1971—; pres. Inst. for Christian Studies, Inc., Greensboro, N.C., 1987—. Bd. dirs. ECA Internat.; pres. Worldwide Travel, Greensboro, NC, 1994—; lectr., cons. in field. Author: Weatherization Production Control, 1978, Personal Profile Labs, 1980, Management Power: The Specific Action Way, 1985, Personality Power: The Specific Action Way, 1988, Master of Personal Excellence Program, 1994; contbr. articles to profl. jours., Specific Action Management System, 1996, Specific Action Personality System, 1996, Specific Action Team System, 1997; patentee Allen valve, 1967. Named to Hon. Order of Ky. Cols., Commonwealth of Ky., 1978, Hon. Adm. State of Nebr., 1978. Mem. Am. Soc. Tng. and Devel. (pres. 1976, Best Chpt. award 1976), Nat. Speakers Assn. (cert. speaking profl. 1988), Greensboro City Club, Inst. Mgmt. Cons. (cert. 1989). Republican. Home: 520 Lindley Rd Greensboro NC 27410-4933 Office: Specific Action Corp PO Box 19125 Greensboro NC 27419-9125 Office Phone: 336-854-9494.

ALLEN, JOAN, actress; b. Rochelle, Ill., Aug. 20, 1956; m. Peter Friedman, Jan. 1, 1990; 1 child. Student, Ea. Ill. U., No. Ill. U. Founding mem. Steppenwolf Theatre Co., Chgo.; theater appearances include (debut) And A Nightingale Sang, N.Y.C. (Clarence Derwent award, Drama Desk award, Outer Critics Circle award 1984), Steppenwolf Theatre Co., also Hartford, 1983, The Marriage of Bette and Boo, N.Y. Shakespeare Festival, 1986, Burn This! (Tony awrd for Best Actress 1989) Mark Taper Forum, L.A., also NYC, 1987, The Heidi Chronicles, N.Y.C., 1988, 89; film appearances include Compromising Positions, 1985, Peggy Sue Got Married, 1986, Manhunter, 1986, Tucker: The Man and His Dream, 1988, In Country, 1989, Ethan Frome, 1993, Searching for Bobbie Fischer, 1993, Josh and S.A.M., 1993, Nixon, 1995 (Acad. award nominee for best supporting actress 1996), Mad Love, 1995, The Crucible, 1996, Ice Storm, 1997, Face/Off, 1997, Pleasantville, 1998, Veronica Guerin, 1999, All the Rage, 1999, When the Sky Falls, 2000, The Contender, 2000, Off the Map, 2003, The Notebook, 2004, The Bourne Supremacy, 2004, Yes, 2004, The Upside of Anger, 2005, The Bourne Ultimatum, 2007; TV appearances include The Twilight Zone, 1987, Am. Playhouse, PBS, 1987, Robert Frost, Voices and Visions, PBS, 1988, Fraiser, 1996, TV films All My Sons, 1986, The Room Upstairs, 1987, Without Warning: The James Brady Story, 1991, Say Goodnight, Gracie, PBS, TV miniseries Evergreen, 1985, The Mists of Avalon, 2001. Office: ICM care Brian Mann 8942 Wilshire Blvd Beverly Hills CA 90211-1934*

ALLEN, JOHN LOGAN, geographer, department chairman; b. Laramie, Wyo., Dec. 27, 1941; s. John Milton and Nancy Elizabeth (Logan) Allen; m. Anne Evelyn Gilroy, Aug. 9, 1964; children: Traci Kathleen, Jennifer Lynne. BA, U. Wyo., 1963, MA, 1964; PhD (univ. grad. fellow 1964-67), Clark U., Worcester, Mass., 1969. Mem. faculty U. Conn., Storrs, 1967—2000, prof. geography, 1979—2000, head dept., 1976—94, dir. grad. program in geography, 1992—2000, mem. nat. exec. com. Faculty Athletic Rep. Assn., 1987—96; parliamentarian Faculty Athletic Rep. Assn., 1996—; prof., chair dept. geography U. Wyo., Laramie, 2000—. Non-resident fellow Ctr. Great Plains Studies; scholar-in-residence Nat. Lewis and Clark Trail Interpretive Ctr. Author: Passage Through the Garden: Lewis and Clark and the Geog. Lore of the Am. N.W., 1975, Jedediah Smith and the Mountain Men of the Am. West, 1991, Lewis and Clark and the Images of the Am. N.W., 1991, Student Atlas of World Politics, 1991, 8th edit., 2007, Atlas of Economic Development, 1997, Atlas of Environmental Issues, 1997, Student Atlas of World Geography, 1998, 5th edit., 2007, Student Atlas of Anthropology, 2003; editor (ann. edits.): Environment, 1982—, Reshaping Traditions, 1994—; mem. editl. bd.: Jour. Hist. Geography, —, project dir., gen. editor: North Am. Exploration: A Comprehensive History, 3 vols., 1997—; contbr. articles articles to profl. jours., chapters to books. Pres. Mansfield Mid. Sch. Assn., Conn., 1979—80; active Mansfield Conservation Commn., Mansfield Planning and Zoning Commn.; vice chmn. Mansfield Zoning Bd. Appeals; mem. adv. bd. Nat. Lewis and Clark Bicentennial Commn., Nat. Lewis and Clark Interpretive Ctr. Recipient Meritorious Achievement award, Lewis and Clark Trail Heritage Found., 1976, Excellence in Tchg. award, U. Conn. Alumni Assn., 1987, Outstanding Contbn. award, U. Conn. Club, 1993, Oustandint Alumnus award, U. Wyo. Coll. Arts and Scis., 1999, Spl. Recognition award, U. Conn., 2000; GMC scholar, 1957—63, NSF Postdoctoral fellow, 1970—71. Fellow: Royal Geog. Soc., Am. Geog. Assn.; mem.: AAAS, Soc. History Discovery (nat. councilor), Western History Assn. (hon.), Soc. Historians Early Am. Republic, Assn. Am. Geographers, Masons, Elks, Phi Beta Kappa, Omicron Delta Kappa, Phi Kappa Phi. Democrat. Congregationalist. Home: 2703 Leslie Ct Laramie WY 82072-2979 Office: Univ of Wyoming Dept Geography PO Box 3371 Laramie WY 82071-3371 Office Phone: 307-766-2836. Business E-Mail: jlallen@uwyo.edu. *As a scientist and educator, I have tried to abide by the principle that learning is necessary for the public good and that academicians should make their skills and knowledge available to society at large. Service to others is as important an educational function as the more frequently recognized components of teaching and research.*

ALLEN, JOSE R., lawyer; b. Panama, Sept. 8, 1951; arrived in US, 1956; s. Joseph R. and Grace A. (Osborne) A.; m. Irvenia E. Waters, July 20, 1986; 1 child, Jeffrey Richard Allen. BA, Yale U., 1973; JD, Boston Coll., 1976. Bar: Mass. 1977, Calif. 1986. Asst. atty. gen. Mass. Atty. Gen. Office, Boston, 1976-79; trial atty. US Dept. Justice, Washington, 1979-80, asst. sect. chief, 1980-82, sect. chief, 1982-85, chief, environ. def. sect., land, and natural resources divsn., 1981—84, chief, gen. litigation sect., land, and nat. resources divsn., 1984—85; of counsel Orrick, Herrington & Sutcliffe, San Francisco, 1985-88; ptnr., environment practice area Skadden, Arps, Slate, Meagher & Flom LLP, San Francisco, 1988—. Mem. adv. com. on environ. Practising Law Inst., NYC, 1992—; spkr. in the field. Contbr. articles in profl. jours. Bd. dirs. San Francisco Bay Area Lawyers' Com. Urban Affairs, 1990, Legal Aid Soc. San Francisco, 1993. Mem. ABA (mem. sect. on natural resources, energy and environ. law and lit. sect.), Bar Assn. San Francisco, Charles Houston Bar Assn., State Bar Calif. (mem. environ. law sect.). Office: Skadden Arps Slate Meagher & Flom LLP Four Embarcadero Ctr San Francisco CA 94111 Office Phone: 415-984-6442. Office Fax: 888-329-1260. Business E-Mail: jrallen@skadden.com.

ALLEN, JOSEPH HENRY, retired publishing company executive; b. Evanston, Ill., Nov. 9, 1916; s. Joseph Henry and Ann Eugenia (Jansen) A.; m. Eleanor Clark, June 14, 1941; children— David, Elisabeth Allen Adams, Melinda Allen Beardsley. BA, Kenyon Coll., 1938; advanced mgmt. program, Stanford Grad. Sch. Bus., 1953. Joined McGraw-Hill Inc., 1938, regional editor and advt. salesman, 1938-42, established S.W. office Dallas, also mgr., 1948, div. mgr. Los Angeles, 1951-55, v.p., dir. mktg. NYC, 1955-63, v.p. ops., 1963-66; pres. McGraw-Hill Publs. Co., 1966-70; group pres. McGraw-Hill, Inc., 1970-74, dir., 1966-75; sr. v.p. United Techs. Corp., Hartford, Conn., 1974-77; asst. dean U. Conn. Sch. Bus. Adminstrn., Storrs, Conn., 1978—85. Bd. dirs. Ronin Corp. Served as lt. USNR, 1942-45. Mem. Wee Burn Country Club. Home: 213 Park St New Canaan CT 06840-5711

ALLEN, JULIAN LEWIS, medical educator, researcher; b. Elizabeth, NJ, Oct. 7, 1952; s. Eugene Murray and Beatrice (Hyman) A.; m. Debra Lynne Stoll, June 4, 1978; children: Eli, Jeremy. BA, Columbia U., 1974, MD, 1978. Diplomate in pediat. and pediatric pulmonology Am. Bd. Pediat. Pediatric intern Columbia-Presbyn. Med. Ctr., NYC, 1978-79, resident in pediatrics, 1979-81; fellow in pediatric pulmonology Boston Children's Hosp., 1981-84; instr. pediatrics Harvard Med. Sch., Boston, 1984-86; asst. prof. pediatrics Temple U. Sch. Medicine, Phila., 1986-90, assoc. prof., 1990-95, prof., 1995-97; prof. pediat. Hahnemann Med. Sch. Allegheny (Pa.) U. Health Scis., 1997-98; prof. pediat., Robert Gerard Morse chair in pulmonary medicine U. Pa. Sch. Medicine, 1998—; attending physician in pulmonary disease The Children's Hosp., Boston, 1984-86, St. Christopher's Hosp. for Children, Phila., 1986—98, dir. pulmonary function lab., 1986—94, sect. chief pediatric pulmonary medicine, 1994-98; attending physician, acting chief divsn. pulmonary medicine/cystic fibrosis ctr. Children's Hosp. Phila., 1998-99, chief, 1999—. Sub-bd. pediatric pulmonology Am. Bd. Pediat., 2001—, chmn., 2005—. Author: The Children's Hospital of Philadelphia Guide to Asthma, 2004; mem. editl. bd. Pediat. Pulmonology, 2002—; contbr. chapters to books; reviewer (profl. jours.); contbr. articles to profl. jours., chpts. in books. Recipient 1st award NIH, 1988-94, Investigator award, 1993—; Parker B. Francis Found. fellow, 1982-86, Sandoz award Coll. Phys.&Surg., N.Y.C., 1978; named Top Doc for Kids, Phila. Mag., 2002, Best Drs. in Am., 2005-06. Fellow: Am. Acad. Pediats.; mem.: Pediat. Pulmonary Tng. Dirs. Assn., Soc. for Pediat. Rsch., European Respiratory Soc. (joint com. on infant respiratory physiology 1990—, co-chmn. 1996), Am. Thoracic Soc. (program com. 1991—93, long range planning com. 1993—, chmn. 1996—98, pediat. assembly chmn. 1999—2001, bd. dirs. 1999—2001, rsch. advocacy com. 2000—02). Achievements include research in lung and chest wall development in infants; pulmonary insults in childhood, pulmonary complications of sickle cell disease and respiratory function. Avocation: violin. Office: Childrens Hosp Phila Divsn Pulmonary Medicine 34th St and Civic Ctr Blvd Philadelphia PA 19104 Home Phone: 610-664-8919; Office Phone: 215-590-3749. Business E-Mail: allenj@email.chop.edu.

ALLEN, KATHERINE SPICER, writer, former chemist; b. Plainfield, NJ, Apr. 29, 1919; d. Arthur Joseph and Linda Varner (Morrison) Spicer; m. Carl Holley Allen, Sept. 24, 1943; children: Carl Holley, Jr., David Randolph, Katherine Allen Fehn, Linda Ruth Allen Taylor. BA, U. Del., 1942. Ordained deacon Presbyn. Ch., 2000. Libr. asst. State Libr., Dover, Del., summers 1936-41; typist U. Del., Newark, 1940-42; chemist Esso Rsch. Divsn., Bayway, Elizabeth, NJ, 1942-46; analyst Azoplate Corp., Murray Hill, NJ, 1963-67; enumerator U.S. Census Bur., Somerset County, NJ, 1980, 90; contbg. writer Bernardsville (N.J.) News, 1982—. Co-author: A History of the Presbyterian Church of Liberty Corner, 1837-1987, 1987, (booklet) Christian Education Goals and Objectives, 1991 (with others) Past and Present Lives of New Jersey Women, 1990. Mem. Bernards Twp. Local Assistance Bd., 1972-96, sec., 1974-89, chmn., 1990; mem. Bernards Twp. Mcpl. Alliance, 1992-96; mem. Somerset County Rep. Com., 1972-93; mem. personnel com. Mcpls. Com. Bernards Twp., 1990-93, mem. comm. com. am. Cancer Soc., 1990-94, vol. Reach to Recovery, 1985—, Somerset County coord. programs, 1987-89; ordained elder Presbyn. Ch. U.S.A., 1980, ordained deacon, 2000; mem. justice for women com. Elizabeth Presbytery, 1988-2000, mem. comm. com., 1992-1995, commr. to Synod of N.E., 1991, 92-93, mem. media com. 1988-90, mem. nominating com. 1987-92, vice chairperson 1990-92, mem. search com. for assoc. exec. 1993; pres. Liberty Corner Presbyn. Ch. Women's Assn., 1973, 74, 84, ch. sch. tchr., 1952-81, ruling elder, 1980-82; mission chair United Presbyn. Ch., Plainfield, 1995-97; dir. Ch. Women United Somerset County, 1979-81; state chmn. Ecumenical Action, 1982-83; mem. Somerset County Breast Cancer Awareness Task Force, 1996-97—; mem. Plainfield Area Mission Group, 1998-01. Named Somerset County Reach to Recovery Vol. of Yr., Am. Cancer Soc., 1991; recipient svc. pins. Mem. N.J. Press Women (various awards for articles written in Bernardsville News). Avocations: cooking, computers, travel, reading, crosswords. Home: 6301 Monroe Vlg Monroe Township NJ 08831-1926 Home Phone: 732-521-6971. Personal E-mail: kinsmere@msn.com.

ALLEN, LAYMAN EDWARD, law educator, research scientist; b. Turtle Creek, Pa., June 9, 1927; s. Layman Grant and Viola Iris (Williams) A.; m. Christine R. Patmore, Mar. 29, 1950 (dec.); children: Layman G., Patricia R.; m. Emily C. Hall, Oct. 3, 1981 (div. 1992); children: Phyllip A. Hall, Kelly C. Hairston; m. Leslie A. Olsen, June 10, 1995. Student, Washington and Jefferson Coll., 1945-46; AB, Princeton U., 1951; MPA, Harvard U., 1952; LLB, Yale U., 1956. Bar: Conn. 1956. Fellow Ctr. for Advanced Study in Behavioral Scis., 1961-62; sr. fellow Yale Law Sch., 1956-57, lectr., 1957-58, instr., 1958-59, asst. prof., 1959-63, assoc. prof., 1963-66; assoc. prof. law U. Mich. Law Sch., Ann Arbor, 1966-71, prof., 1971—2006, prof. emeritus, 2006; disting. vis prof. Detroit Mercy Law Sch., 2006—. Chmn. bd. trustees Accelerated Learning Found., 1998—; sr. rsch. scientist Mental Health Rsch. Inst., U. Mich., 1966-99; cons. legal drafting Nat. Life Ins. Co., Mich. Blue Cross & Blue Shield (various law firms); mem. electronic data retrieval com. Am. Bar Assn.; ops. rsch. analyst McKinsey & Co.; orgn. and methods analyst Office of Sec. Air Force.; trustee Ctr. for Study of Responsive Law. Founding editor: Jurimetrics Jour.; editor: Games and Simulations, Artificial Intelligence and Law Jour., Theoria, Simulation/Gaming/News, Jour. Legal Edn., Jour. of Conflict Resolutiion; author: WFF 'N Proof: The Game of Modern Logic, 1961, rev. edit., 1990, (with Robin B.S. Brooks, Patricia A. James) Automatic Retrieval of Legal Literature: Why and How, 1962, WFF: The Beginner's Game of Modern Logic, 1962, rev. edit., 1973, Equations: The Game of Creative Mathematics, 1963, rev. edit., 1994, (with Mary E. Caldwell) Reflections of the Communications Sciences and Law: The Jurimetrics Conference, 1965, (with J. Ross and P. Kugel) Queries 'N Theories: The Game of Science and Language, 1970, rev. edit., 1973, (with F. Goodman, D. Humphrey and J. Ross), On-Words: The Game of Word Structures, 1971, rev. edit., 1973; contbr. articles to profl. jours.; co-author/designer: (with J. Ross and C. Stratton) DIG (Diagnostic Instrnl. Gaming) Math; (with Charles Saxon) Normalizer Clear Legal Drafting Program, 1986, MINT System for Generating Dynamically Multiple-Interpretation Legal Decision-Assistance Systems, 1991, The Legal Argument Game of Legal Relations, 1997, (with Sandra Bartlett) LawToe: the Game to Learn the Game Rules of The Legal Argument Game of Legal Relations, 2003, (with Sandra Bartlett) The New Legal Argument Game of Legal Relations, 2003, (with Adam Trury) New MINT System for Dynamically Generating Multiple Interpretation Legal Analysis Systems, 2004, (with Sandra Bartlett) A Learning Program for the Legal Relations Language. With USNR, 1945—46. Mem. ABA (coun. sect. sci. and tech.), AAAS, ACLU, Assn. Symbolic Logic, Nat. Coun. Tchrs. Math. Democrat. Unitarian Universalist. Home: 5353 Red Fox Run Ann Arbor MI 48105 Office: U Mich Sch Law 808 Legal Rsch Ann Arbor MI 48109-1215 Office Phone: 734-764-9339. Business E-Mail: laymanal@umich.edu.

ALLEN, LEE NORCROSS, historian, educator; b. Shawmut, Ala., Apr. 16, 1926; s. Leland Norcross and Dorothy (Whitaker) A.; m. Catherine Ann Bryant, Aug. 24, 1963; children— Leland Norcross, Leslie Catherine. BS, Auburn U., 1948, MS, 1949; PhD, U. Pa., 1955. From instr. to prof. history Ea. Bapt. Coll., St. Davids, Pa., 1952-61; prof. history Samford U., Birmingham, Ala., 1961-2001, grad. dean, 1965-86; dean Howard Coll. Arts and Scis., 1975-90, rsch. prof., 2001—. Author: (with Mrs. E.S. Bee) History of Ruhama, 1969, The First One Hundred Fifty Years: First Baptist Church of Montgomery, 1979, Born for Missions, 1984; Southside Baptist Church: A Centennial History, 1985, Woodlawn Baptist Church: The First Century, 1886-1986, 1986; (with Catherine B. Allen) Courage to Care, 1988; Expanding the Dream, Montgomery Baptist Hospital, 1988, Notable Past, Bright Future: First Baptist Church 1893-1993, 1993, Born for Missions, 16th Decade, 1993, Outward Focus: Mountain Brook Baptist Church, The First Fifty Years, 1994, The First 150 Years Supplement: 1980-1995, 1996, (with Catherine B. Allen) Christ Is Our Salvation: Paul Piper, 1998, (with Catherine B. Allen) The Boaz Heritage: A Centennial History, Boaz, Alabama, 1897-1997, 1999, Ralph W. Beeson: A Biography, 2005. Served with AUS, 1944-46. Recipient Commendation cert. Am. Assn. State and Local History, Thomas Jefferson award, 1985, disting. svc. award Ala. Baptist Hist. Commn., 1996; Auburn U. rsch. fellow, 1948-49; Harrison fellow U. Pa., 1949-52. Mem. Am. Hist. Assn., Am. Bapt. Hist. Assn. (editor The Ala. Bapt. Historian 1989—), So. Bapt. Hist. Assn. (pres. 1987-88), So. Hist. Assn., Ala. Hist. Assn. (editor newsletter 1989-2001, pres. 1994-95), Rotary (pres. Shades Valley chpt. 1969-70), Omicron Delta Kappa, Phi Alpha Theta, Phi Kappa Phi, Pi Gamma Mu. Baptist. Home: 5025 Wendover Dr Birmingham AL 35223-1631

ALLEN, LEON ARTHUR, JR., lawyer; b. Springfield, Mass., July 15, 1933; s. Leon Arthur, Sr. and Elsie (Shoemaker) Allen; m. Patricia Mellion, June 23, 1961; 1 child, Christopher. BEE, Cornell U., 1955; LLB, NYU, 1964. Bar: N.Y. 1964, U.S. Dist. Ct. (so. and ea. dists.) N.Y. 1965. Tech. editor McGraw Hill Pub. Co., NYC, 1958-62; constrn. engr. Gilbert Assocs., NYC, 1962-64; assoc. LeBoeuf, Lamb, Leiby & MacRae, NYC, 1964-70; ptnr. LeBoeuf, Lamb, Leiby & MacRae (name changed to LeBoeuf, Lamb, Greene & MacRae), NYC, 1971—. With US Army, 1956—58. Mem.: ABA, Assn. Bar City of N.Y. (chmn. adminstrv. law com. 1972—74), Tuxedo Club (Tuxedo Park, N.Y.), Union Club (N.Y.C.), Racquet & Tennis Club (N.Y.C.). Home: 530 E 86th St New York NY 10028-7535 Office: LeBoeuf Lamb Greene MacRae 125 W 55th St New York NY 10019-5369 Business E-Mail: laallen@llgm.com.

ALLEN, LOIS ARLENE HEIGHT, musician; b. Kenton, Ohio, Sept. 2, 1932; d. Robert Harold and Frances (Sims) Height; m. James Pierpont Allen, June 14, 1953; children: Daniel Pierpont, Carole Elizabeth. BS, Ohio State U., 1954, MA, 1958. Tchr. jr. and sr. high music Upper Arlington H.S., Columbus, Ohio, 1954-56; h.s. music supr. Westerville, Ohio, 1956-57; tchr. music Ohio State U. Sch., 1957-59; pvt. tchr. music Columbus, 1960—. Exec. dir. Battelle Scholars Program Trust Fund, 1983-86; ch. organist, choir dir. Mountview Bapt. Ch., Upper Arlington, Ohio, 1960-77, moderator, 1996-97; ednl. radio interviewer WOSU, 1970, 71, 72. Mem. Project Hope, Ctrl. Ohio, 1967-73; mem. sustaining bd. Maryhaven House for Alcoholic Women, 1969-73, 1st v.p.; mem. women's bd. Columbus Symphony, 1965-79, 91—, bd. trustees edn. com., 1992-07, co-chair edn. com. women's assn., 1992-07, charter mem. trustee's cir., 2000-07, bd. dirs., chmn. youth coun., 1965-68, pres.-elect women's assn., 1973, chmn. edn. com., 1991—, pres., 1974-76; pres. vol. coun. Am. Symphony Orch. League, 1987-89; organist, choir master The Ch. of St. Edwards, 1990-92; chmn. juried art competition Cen. Ohio Arts Festival, 1969, 70, chmn. fine and applied arts, 1971, gen. chmn. of festival, 1972; area chmn. United Appeals Franklin County, 1966-68, Heart dr., 1968-85; pres. Ohio State U. Soc. Friends Sch. Music, 1977-78; trustee Columbus Symphony Orch., 1973-81, Opera/Columbus, 1981-85; v.p. women's guild Opera/Columbus, 1986-94, pres., 1987-88; mem. vol. coun. Am. Symphny Orch. League, 1981—, v.p., 1983-84, mem. exec. com., 1986-88, mem. artistic affairs com., 1987-89, pres., 1987-88; organist, choir dir. North Congregational Ch., 1979-85; area leader Rep. Party, 1966-68; mem. Mayor's Award Coun. Com., 1981-84; active Connexions, Columbus Literacy Coun.; bd. dirs., pres. Ohio Theatre Shop, 1995-96, publicity dir. 1996—; bd. dirs., pres. Women's Bd. Columbus Mus. Art, 1991—; organist Glen Echo Presbyn. Ch., 2002-04. Recipient Columbus Symphony Advocate award, 2002, Music Educator award, Columbus Symphony Orch., 2005. Mem. Am. Guild Organists, Choristers Guild Am., Fedn. Am. Bapt. Musicians, Ctr. Sci. and Industry, Ohio State Hist. Soc., Ohio Orgn. Orchs. (treas. 1976-79, sec. 1979-82), Nat. Trust U.S.A., Mountview Bapt. Ch. (moderator 1996—), Rotary Club (Women of Yr. Upper Arlington Ohio 1995), Order Ea. Star, White Shrine of Jerusalem, Ohio State U. Alumnae of Franklin County Club (pres. 1962-64, 71-72), Tau Beta Sigma, Delta Omicron, Kappa Delta (Cen. Ohio Woman of Yr. 1970). Home: 3355 Somerford Rd Columbus OH 43221-1436 Personal E-mail: jallen6@columbus.rr.com.

ALLEN, LOUIS ALEXANDER, management consultant; b. Glace Bay, NS, Oct. 8, 1917; s. Israel Nathan and Emma (Greenberg) A.; m. Ruth Graham, Aug. 24, 1946; children: Michael, Steven, Ace, Terry Allen Beck, Deborah Allen. BS cum laude, Wash. State U., 1941. Cert. mgmt. cons. Asst. to dean of men Wash. State U., Pullman, 1940-42; tng. supr. Aluminum Co. Am., Pitts., 1946-49; mgr. pers. adminstrn. Koppers Co. Inc., Pitts., 1949-53; dir. rsch. projects The Conf. Bd., NYC, 1953-56; dir. orgnl. planning Booz, Allen & Hamilton, Chgo., 1956-58; founder Louis Allen Assocs., Inc., Los Altos, Calif., 1958-92; ind. rschr., 1992-95. Lectr. on bus. mgmt. Stanford U., U. Chgo., NYU, Japan, China, Australia, Africa and Europe. Author: Improving Staff and Line Relationships, 1956, Preparing the Company Organization Manual, 1957, Organization of Staff Functions, 1958, Management and Organization, 1958, The Management Profession, 1964, Professional Management: New Concepts and Proven Practices, 1973, Time before Morning: Art and Myth of the Australian Aborigines, 1975, Making Managerial Planning More Effective, 1982, The Allen Guide for Management Leaders, 1989, Common Vocabulary for Management Leaders, 1989, The Louis Allen Leader's Handbook, 1995, The New Leadership, 1996; (mus. catalog) Australian Aboriginal Art, 1972; translated into Japanese, German, French, Finnish, Swedish, Dutch, Spanish, Portuguese, Bahasa; contbr. numerous articles and monographs to profl. jours. on mgmt., primitive art; exhibitor primitive art major mus. worldwide, 1969—. Maj. USAF, 1942-55, PTO. Decorated Legion of Merit; recipient McKinsey award Acad. Mgmt. Mem. Inst. Mgmt. Cons. (sr. assoc., regional pres. 1985). Achievements include first to fully classify human work into categories, a typology which facilities diagnosis and correction of organizational problems. Personal E-mail: laglaceby@aol.com.

ALLEN, LYLE WALLACE, lawyer; b. Chillicothe, Ill., June 17, 1924; s. Donald M. and Mary Ellen (McEvoy) A.; m. Helen Kolar, Aug. 16, 1947; children: Mary Elizabeth Watkins, Bryan James. Student, N.C. State Coll., 1943-44; BS, Northwestern U., 1947; postgrad., Columbia Law Sch., 1947-48; JD, U. Wis., 1950. Bar: Ill. 1950, Wis. 1950. Of counsel Heyl Royster Voelker & Allen, Peoria, Ill., 1951—. Served with 87th Inf. Div. U.S. Army, World War II. Decorated Purple Heart, Bronze star, Combat Infantry badge, Presdl. Unit Citation. Mem. ABA, Ill. State Bar Assn. (pres. 1972-73), Assn. of Ins. Attys. (pres. 1965-66), Illinois Valley Yacht Club. Democrat. Presbyterian. Office: 124 SW Adams St Ste 600 Peoria IL 61602-1392 Office Phone: 309-676-0400.

ALLEN, MARC KEVIN, emergency physician, educator; b. Bedford, Ind., Sept. 2, 1956; s. Robert Edward and Edna Ruth (Little) A.; m. Marita Ann Volk, May 13, 1995. AB, Washington U., St. Louis, 1978; MD, Wright State U., 1982. Diplomate Am. Bd. Emergency Medicine. Intern Mt. Sinai Med. Ctr., Cleve., 1982-83, chief resident in emergency medicine, 1984-85, rsch. dir. emergency med. residency, 1986-96; attending physician Worcester (Mass.) City Hosp., 1985-86; flight physician Metro Lifeflight, Cleve., 1984—; attending physician Summa Health Sys., Akron, Ohio, 1999—, Lake County Hosp., Willoughby, Ohio, 2005—. Co-author: A Practical Approach Emergency Medicine, 1987. Co-chmn. Washington U. YWCA-YMCA, 1977—78; med. dir. Ohio Assn. EMS, 2004—, Aurora (Ohio) Fire Dept., 1997—, Six Flags Worlds of Adventure, 2001—03. Fellow Am. Coll. Emergency Physicians (councillor 1996-98, Star of Life Ohio chpt. 2005); mem. Assn. Air Med. Svcs., Assn. Air Med. Physicians, N.E. Soc. Emergency Med. (bd. dirs. 1992-99), Ohio Assn. Emergency Med. Svcs. (med. dirs. 2004—), South Ea. Area Law Enforcement (med. dir. 2004-05), Phi Rho Sigma. Avocations: skiing, golf, cooking. Home: 485 Club Dr Aurora OH 44202-8564 Office: Summa Health Sys Akron City Hosp 525 E Market St Akron OH 44304-1619 Personal E-mail: ermarc@aol.com.

ALLEN, MARILYN MYERS POOL, theater director, video specialist; b. Fresno, Calif., Nov. 2, 1934; d. Laurence B. and Asa (Griggs) Myers; m. Joseph Harold Pool, Dec. 28, 1955; children: Pamela Elizabeth, Victoria Anne, Catherine Marcia; m. Neal R. Allen, Apr. 1982. BA, Stanford U., 1955, postgrad., 1955—56, U. Tex., 1957—60, West Tex. State U., 1962—63, Odessa Coll., 1987—88. Free-lance radio and TV actress; adj. prof. theatre Midland Coll., 1997—98; dir. Globe Theater, Odessa, 1998, 2002; asst. mng. dir. Amarillo Little Theatre, 1964—66, mng. dir., 1966—68, Horseshoe Players, touring profl. theater, 1969—73; actress multi-media prodn. Palo Duro Canyon, 1971; dir. touring children's theatre, 1978—79; guest actress in Medea at Amarillo Coll., 1981; guest reciter Amarillo Symphony, 1972, Midland-Odessa Symphony, 1984. Pres. Tex. Non-Profit Theatres, 1972-74, 75-77, bd. dirs., 1988-91; 1st v.p. High Plains Ctr. for Performing Arts, 1969-73; adv. dept. fine arts Amarillo Coll., 1980-82; adv. Tex. Constnl. Revision Commn., 1973-75; adv. coun. U. Tex. Coll. Fine Arts, 1969-72; cmty. adv. com. for women Amarillo Coll., 1975-79; conv. program com. Am. Theatre Assn., 1978, program participant, 1978-80, bd. dirs., 1980-83; bd. dirs. Amarillo Found. Health and Sci. Edn., 1976-82, program v.p., 1979-81; bd. dirs. Domestic Violence Coun., 1979-82, March of Dimes, 1979-81, Tex. Panhandle Heritage Found., 1964-82, Friends of Fine Arts, West Tex. State U. (now West Tex. A&M U.), 1980-82, Amarillo Pub. Libr., 1980-82, Amarillo Symphony, 1981-82; publicity chmn. Midland Cmty. Theatre, 1984-87, bd. govs., 1986-92, sec., 1987-88, v.p., 1988-92; bd. dirs. Globe of the Great S.W., Odessa, 1998-2005, v.p. media, 2000-02, v.p. vols., 2002-05; active Mus. of S.W., Midland Arts Assembly; bd. dirs. Midland County Rep. Women, Ways and Means Ch., 1991, 1st v.p., 1992, publicity chair, 1994; mem. Midland County Redistricting com., 1991; cultural exch. del. from Midland, Tex., to Dong Ying, China, 1993; Tex. UIL one act play adjudicator, 1974-99; mem. N.W. Tex. Diocesan Mission Com., 2003-05; co-chmn. Companion Diocese Com., Spain, 2003-06. Recipient cert. of appreciation Woman of Yr., Amarillo Bus. and Profl. Women's Club, 1966, Best Actress award for Hedda Gabler role Amarillo Little Theatre, 1965, Best Dir. award for Rashomon, 1967, 1st Pl. award for video spl. Tex. Press Conf., 1988, 1st Pl. award for news Tex. Press Conf., 1989, Disting. Svc. award Tex. Non-Profit Theatres, 1992; named Amarillo Woman of Yr., Beta Sigma Phi, 1980, Broadcaster of the Yr., Rocky Mountain Press Conf., 1988, Hamhock of Yr., Midland Cmty. Theatre, 1992, Outstanding Svc. award Midland Arts Assembly, 1992; Travel fellow AAUW, 1973, 78. Fellow Am. Assn. Cmty. Theatre (dir. 1969-72, 82-84, v.p. planning and devel. 1985-87, co-chair AACT/Fest '95), Internat. Amateur Theatre Assn. 23d World Congress (del. Monaco 1997, mem. festival com. 2006); mem. USTA (sr. women's team sect. winner 1993, 94), S.W. Theatre Conf. (dir. 1973-76, 82-84, exec. com. 1982-84, Disting. Svc. award 1985), Tex. Theatre Coun. (dir. 1974-78, exec. com., pres. 1975-76), AAUW (br. pres. 1973-75, state chmn. cultural interests 1975-77, 86-88, state program v.p. 1977-79, state bd. dirs. 1984-88, program v.p. Midland 1988-89), Episc. Ch. Women (program v.p. Midland 1988-89), outreach chair 1996, 2005, program v.p., pres.-elect 1997-98, pres. 1999-00), N.W. Tex. Deanery Ch., 2005-, Holy Trinity Vestry, 2006-, DAR (chpt. chaplain 1971-75, historian 1975-77), C. of C. (fine arts coun.), U.S. Tennis Assn. (sr. mixed doubles sect. winner 1999), U.S. Judo Assn., Symphony Guild, Amarillo Art Assn., Midland Symphony Guild (arrangements chmn. 1983-84), Act IX, Amarillo Law Wives Club (pres. 1976-77), Hamhocks (hon. life mem. 1985-86).

ALLEN, MARYON PITTMAN, former senator, clothing designer, journalist; b. Meridian, Miss., Nov. 30, 1925; d. John D. and Tellie (Chism) Pittman; m. Joshua Sanford Mullins, Jr., Oct. 17, 1946 (div. Jan. 1959); children: Joshua Sanford III, John Pittman, Maryon Foster; m. James Browning Allen, Aug. 7, 1964 (dec. June 1978). Student, U. Ala., 1944—47, Internat. Inst. Interior Design, 1970. Office mgr. for Dr. Alston Callahan, Birmingham, Ala., 1959-60; bus. mgr. psychiat. clinic U. Ala. Med. Center, Birmingham, 1960-61; life underwriter Protective Life Ins. Co., Birmingham, 1961-62; women's editor Sun Newspapers, Birmingham, 1962-64; v.p., ptnr. Pittman family cos., J.D. Pittman Partnership Co., J.D. Pittman Tractor Co., Emerald Valley Corp., Mountain Lake Farms, Inc., Birmingham; mem. U.S. Senate (succeeding late husband James B. Allen), 1978; dir. pub. rels. and advt. C.G. Sloan & Co. Auction House, Washington, 1981; feature writer Birmingham News, 1964; writer syndicated column Reflections of a News Hen, Washington, 1969—78; feature writer, columnist Maryon Allen's Washington, Washington Post, 1979—81; columnist McCall's Needlework Mag., 1993—. Owner The Maryon Allen Co. (Restoration/Design), Birmingham, 1982—. Contbg. editor: So. Accents Mag., 1976—78. Mem. Ladies of U.S. Senate unit ARC, Former Mems. of Congress, Ala. Hist. Commn., Blair House Fine Arts Commn.; charter mem. Birmingham Com. of 100 for Women; mem. steering com. Ala. Gov.'s Mansion; trustee Children's Fresh Air Farm; trustee, deacon, elder Ind. Presbyn. Ch., Birmingham; Dem. Presdl. elector, Ala., 1968. Recipient 1st place award for best original column Ala. Press Assn., 1962, 63, also various press state and nat. awards for typography, fashion writing, food pages, also several awards during Senate service; sponsor, U.S. Navy Nuclear submarine, U.S.S. Birmingham, S.S.N. 695, launched Newport News, Va., 1977, commissioned 1978. Mem.: Nat. Press Club, 1925 F St. Club, 91st Congress Club, Congl. Club, Birmingham Country Club. Home and Office: Creekstone Cottage 1551 Creekstone Cir Birmingham AL 35243 Office Phone: 205-822-9266. Personal E-mail: maryonallenco@aol.com. *You have to believe in yourself, your talents and the premise that you were put here to contribute of yourself.not always to take.*

ALLEN, MATTHEW ARNOLD, physicist; b. Edinburgh, Apr. 27, 1930; came to U.S., 1955; s. William Wolff and Clara (Bloch) A.; m. Marcia Harriet Katzman, Sept. 15, 1957; children: Bruce William, Peter Jonathan, David Michael. BSc in Physics, U. Edinburgh, 1951; PhD in Physics, Stanford U., 1959. Rsch. assoc. Hansen Labs., Stanford (Calif.) U., 1959-61; rsch. mgr. tube div. Microwave Assocs., Burlington, Mass., 1961-65; radio frequency group leader Stanford Linear Accelerator Ctr., 1965-82, head accelerator physics dept., 1982-84, head klystron microwave dept., 1984-90, asst. dir. for elec. and electronic systems, 1989-90, assoc. dir. lab., 1990—2003, emeritus, 2003—. Cons. Microwave Assocs. Inc., 1965-71, Aerojet Gen., Azusa, Calif., 1959-62, Bechtel Corp., San Francisco, 1965-67; mem. tech. rev. com. Synchotron Radiation Rsch. Ctr., Taipei, Taiwan, 1985-98; chmn. U.S.A. Particle Accelerator Conf., 1991. Contbr. articles to profl. jours.; patentee in field. Commr. Environ. Planning Commn., Mountain View, Calif., 1971-74; councilman Mountain View City Coun., 1974-82; mayor City of Mountain View, 1977, 81; pres. Mountain View Community TV, 1989. Lt. British Army, 1953-55. Fellow IEEE, Am. Phys. Soc.; mem. IEEE Nuclear and Plasma Scis. Soc. (adminstrv. com. 1978-84, 98-2001), Dem. Club (bd. dirs. 1980-84), Sigma Xi. Democrat. Avocations: skiing, running, tv producing. Home: 620 Sand Hill Rd # 318D Palo Alto CA 94304 Office: Stanford Linear Accelerator Ctr 2575 Sand Hill Rd Menlo Park CA 94025 Business E-Mail: mattmar@pacbell.net.

ALLEN, MERRILL JAMES, marine biologist; b. Brady, Tex., July 16, 1945; s. Clarence Francis and Sara Barbara (Finlay) A. BA, U. Calif., Santa Barbara, 1967; MA, UCLA, 1970; PhD, U. Calif., San Diego, 1982. Cert. jr. coll. tchr., Calif. Asst. environ. specialist So. Calif. Coastal Water Rsch. Project, El Segundo, 1971-77; postdoctoral assoc. Nat. Rsch. Coun., Seattle, 1982-84; oceanographer Nat. Marine Fisheries Svc., Seattle, 1984-86; sr. scientist MBC Applied Environ. Scis., Costa Mesa, Calif.,

1986-93; prin. scientist So. Calif. Coastal Water Rsch. Project, Long Beach and Westminster, Calif., 1993—. Tech. adv. com. Santa Monica Bay Restoration Project/Commn., L.A., 1989-; steering com. So. Calif. Bight Pilot Project, 1993-98, So. Calif. Bight 1998, 2003, Regional Marine Surveys, 1998-; affiliate asst. prof. sch. fisheries U. Wash., Seattle, 1985-89; mem. sci. rev. panel for marine ecol. reserves rsch. program Calif. Sea Grant Coll., 1996-97; adj. prof. dept. biology Calif. State U., Long Beach, 1996—. Mem. Calif. Marine Life Mgmt. Act Evaluation Com., 2000—. Fellow Am. Inst. Fisheries Rsch. Biologists (dir. So. Calif. dist. 1991-93); mem. AAAS, Am. Fisheries Soc., Am. Soc. Ichthyologists and Herpetologists, So. Calif. Acad. Sci. (bd. dirs. 2000—). Achievements include development of most comprehensive atlas of marine fishes from Bering Sea to Mexico; description of state of contamination of Santa Monica Bay. Office: 3535 Harbor Blvd Ste 110 Costa Mesa CA 92626-1437 Business E-Mail: jima@sccwrp.org.

ALLEN, MICHAEL JOHN BRIDGMAN, language educator; b. Lewes, Eng., Apr. 1, 1941; came to U.S., 1966; m. Elena Hirshberg; children: William, Benjamin. BA, Oxford U., Eng., 1964, MA, 1966, DLitt, 1987; PhD, U. Mich., 1970. Asst. prof. UCLA, 1970-74, assoc. prof., 1974-79, prof. English, 1979—, disting. prof., 1994, assoc. dir. Ctr. for Medieval and Renaissance Studies, 1978-88, dir., 1988—93, 2003—04; v.p. Renaissance Soc. Am., 2004—06, pres., 2006—. Editor Renaissance Quar., 1993—2001; faculty rsch. lectr. UCLA, 1998. Author: Marsilio Ficino: The Philebus Commentary, 1975, Marsilio Ficino and the Phaedran Charioteer, 1981, The Platonism of Marsilio Ficino, 1984, Icastes: Marsilio Ficino's Interpretation of Plato's "Sophist," 1989, Nuptial Arithmetic, 1994, Plato's Third Eye: Studies in Marsilio Ficino's Metaphysics and Its Sources, 1995, Synoptic Art: Marsilio Ficino on the History of Platonic Interpretation, 1998; co-author: Sources and Analogues of Old English Poetry, 1976, Marsilio Ficino: Platonic Theology, Vol. I, Books I-IV, 2001, Vol. 2, Books V-VIII, 2002, Vol. 3, Books IX-XI, 2003, Vol. 4, Books XII-XIV, 2004, Vol. 5, Books XV-XVI, 2005, Vol. 6, Books XVII-XVIII, 2006; co-editor: First Images of America, 1976, Shakespeare's Plays in Quarto, 1984, Sir Philip Sidney's Achievements, 1990, Marsilio Ficino: His Theology, His Philosophy, His Legacy, 2002. Recipient Eby award for disting. tchg. UCLA, 1977; Guggenheim fellow, 1977; disting. vis. scholar Ctr. for Reformation and Renaissance Studies, U. Toronto, 1997, Ludwig Maximilians U., Munich, 1999, Ariz. Ctr. for Medieval and Renaissance Studies, 2002. Office: UCLA 149 Humanities Bldg 405 Hilgard Ave Los Angeles CA 90095-1530 Business E-Mail: mjballen@humnet.ucla.edu.

ALLEN, NANCY H., dean, library director; BA, U. Ill., Urbana, 1972, MLS, 1973. Reserve book libr. Univ. Libr. U. Ill., Urbana, 1974—76, asst. undergrad. libr., 1978—84, comm. libr., 1978—84, acting asst. dir. Dept. Libr. Svcs. for Social Scis., 1983—84; asst. dir. pub. svcs. Wayne State U. Librs., Detroit, 1984—86, asst. dir. svcs., 1986—88; asst. dir. pub. svcs. Colo. State U. Librs., Fort Collins, 1988—92; dean, dir. Penrose Libr. U. Denver, 1992—, interim exec. dir. Collaborative Digitization Program, 2003—04. Bd. mem. Ctr. for Rsch. Librs., 2005—07. Contbr. articles to profl. jours. Mem.: Assn. Coll. and Rsch. Librs. Office: U Denver Penrose Libr 2150 E Evans Ave Denver CO 80208 Office Phone: 303-871-2007. E-mail: nallen@du.edu.*

ALLEN, NEWTON PERKINS, lawyer; b. Memphis, Jan. 3, 1922; s. James Seddon and Sarah (Perkins) Allen; m. Malinda Lobdell Nobles, Oct. 4, 1947 (dec. Nov. 1986); children: John Lobdell, Malinda Nobles, Newton Perkins, Cannon Fairfax; m. Malinda Lobdell Crutchfield, June 23, 1990. AB, Princeton U., 1943; JD, U. Va., 1948. Bar: Tenn. 1947, NC 1990. Assoc. Armstrong, Allen, Prewitt, Gentry, Johnston & Holmes, Memphis, 1948, ptnr., 1950-95; assoc. Dann & Allen, 1996—2001; pvt. practice Memphis, 2001—. Contbr. articles to profl. jours. Mem exec bd Boy Scouts Am., 1961—69; trustee LeBonheur Children's Hosp., Memphis, 1964—72, vice chmn. bd., 1965; mem. alumni coun. Princeton U., 1954—64, 1990—93; chmn. Greater Memphis Coun. Crime and Delinquency, 1976—80; pres. bd. trustees St. Mary's Episcopal Sch., 1966—67, v.p., 1972—73; co-chmn. Memphis Conf. Faith at Work, 1975, bd. dirs., 1976—79; mem Chickasaw coun. Boy Scouts Am., 1958—60; bd. dirs. Memphis Orch. Soc., pres., 1979—81. Mem.: ABA (edn. bd. sr. lawyers divsn. 1990, pub. com. chair 1993—95, coun. mem. 1994—95, chair travel and leisure com. 1995—96, vice chair 1996—97, chair-elect 1997—98, chair 1998—99), Princeton Alumni Assn. Memphis (pres. 1992), NC Bar Assn., Tenn. Def. Lawyers Assn., Memphis Bar Assn., Tenn. Bar Assn., Am. Coll. Trust and Estate Coun., Memphis Lions (pres. 1956). Office: 840 Valleybrook Dr Memphis TN 38120 Office Phone: 901-682-0555. Personal E-mail: lawmemphis@aol.com.

ALLEN, NORMA ANN, librarian, educator; b. Balt., Jan. 22, 1951; d. James Crawley and Thelma Agusta (Keaton) Ghee; children: Lamont Ricardo Ghee, Alissa S. Allen, Avery O. Allen. BA in Adminstrn. Mgmt., Sojourner Douglass Coll., Balt., 1987; MS in Instrnl. Tech., Towson State U., 1999. Instr. data processing PSI Inst., Balt., 1987-88; acquisition technician Social Security Adminstrn., Balt., 1987-89, reference librarian, 1989-91, acquisitions librarian, 1991—; librarian United Bapt. Membership Conv., Balt., 2002—. Instrnl. developer Computer Asst. Instrn., Towson U., 1995—; bus. computer tech. instr. Balt. City C.C., 2000—; freelance floral designer/arranger, freelance instr. basic writing skills and computer literacy; instr. bus. computer tech. Balt. City C.C., 2000—. Sec., bd. dirs. New Image Child Care Facility, Balt., 1992, chmn. bd. dirs., 2001-02; instr. active reading literacy program Enoch Pratt Libr., Balt., 1992; instr. United Missionary Bapt. Conv., 1997, libr., 2003. Multicultural scholar Towson U., 1995-96. Mem. ALA, Spl. Librs. Assn., Horizon User Group. E-mail: norma.allen@ssa.gov.

ALLEN, OLIVER E., writer; b. Cambridge, Mass., June 29, 1922; s. Frederick Lewis and Dorothy Cobb Allen; m. Deborah Hutchison, May 8, 1948; children: Stephen(dec.) , Frederick, Henry, Letitia, Jennie. AB, Harvard Coll., 1943. Writer, editor Life Mag., NYC, 1947—60; editor Life World Libr. Time-Life Books, 1960—65, editor Time-Life Libr. Am., 1965—68, dir. editl. planning, 1968—76; freelance writer, 1976—. Author: Wildflower Gardening, 1977, Decorating With Plants, 1978, Pruning and Grafting, 1978, The Windjammers, 1978, Shade Gardens, 1979, Winter Gardens, 1979, The Pacific Navigators, 1980, The Airline Builders, 1981, Building Sound Bones and Muscles, 1981, Secrets of Good Digestion, 1982, The Atmosphere, 1983, The Vegetable Gardeners' Journal, 1985, Gardening With the New Small Plants, 1987, New York, New York, 1991, The Tiger, 1993, Tales of Old Tribeca, 1999. 1st lt. US Army, 1943—46. Mem.: Century Club. Democrat. Home: 42 Hudson St New York NY 10013

ALLEN, P. BLAKE, lawyer; s. Robert Dee and Mary Latimer Allen; m. Ginger Renee James, Sept. 9, 1995. BA, Vanderbilt U., 1986; JD, MBA, U. Okla., 1990. Bar: Okla. 1990, Okla. (U.S. Dist. Ct. (we. dist.)) 1990, (U.S. Dist. Ct. (10th cir.)) 1990, Calif. 1992, Nev. (U.S. Dist. Ct.) 1992, Colo. 1994, (U.S. Ct. Appeals (9th cir.)) 1994. Law clk. to Chief Judge William J. Holloway, Jr. U.S. Ct. Appeals 10th cir., Oklahoma City, 1990—92; assoc. atty. Vargas & Bartlett/Kummer Kaempfer Bonner & Renshaw, Las Vegas, 1993—96; assoc. Conner & Winters, Oklahoma City, 1996—97, ptnr., 1997—2001; spl. counsel Luce, Forward, Hamilton & Scripps, San Diego, 2001—02, ptnr., 2002—04, Duane Morris LLP, San Diego, 2004—. Contbr. articles to profl. jours. Rsch. Fellow, Southwestern Legal Found. Mem.: Calif. Bar Assn., Okla. Bar Assn., State Bar Nev. (mem. exec. coun. young lawyers divsn. 1995—96), Nev. Bar. Assn., ABA (mem. com. fed. regulation of securities 1998—, mem. com. negotiated acquisitions 2001—, aquisitions of pub. co. task force 2001—, subcom. on annual review of Fed. Securities Regulation), Assn. Corp. Growth (bd. dirs. 2005—), Sigma Alpha Epsilon. Avocations: travel, tennis, golf, sailing. Home: 6875 Paseo Laredo La Jolla CA 92037 Office: Duane Morris LLP 101 W Broadway Ste 900 San Diego CA 92101 Home Phone: 858-459-0301; Office Phone: 619-744-2200. E-mail: ballen@duanemorris.com.

ALLEN, PAMELA SMITH, retired psychologist, writer; b. Marianna, Fla., Dec. 19, 1943; d. Milton Clark Smith and Dora Bernadette Gordy; m. William Thomas Lassiter, Aug. 8, 1964 (div. 1972); 1 child, Kerry Lassiter Arnsten; m. George Young, 1974 (div. 1977); m. William Kelly, Feb. 11, 1979 (div. 1992); m. Lawrence Allen, Feb. 14, 2000 (div. Feb. 5, 2004); life ptnr. Lawrence Allen, 2005. BA, U. Fla., Gainesville, 1964; MEd, U. Fla., 1967, EdS, 1968; PhD, US Internat. U., San Diego, 1989. Lic. psychologist (inactive) Calif., marriage and family therapist (inactive) Calif., cert. pupil pers. svcs. plus psychology Calif., gen. elem. tchr. Calif. Spl. edn. tchr. Alachua County Schs., Gainesville, 1964—68, Duval County Schs., Jacksonville, Fla., 1969—70, sch. psychologist, 1970—72, spl. edn. tchr., 1972—73, Daniel Meml. Home, Jacksonville, 1973—74; 1st grade tchr. Valley Ctr. Schs., Valley Center, Calif., 1976—78; spl. edn. tchr. San Diego City Schs., 1978—79, sch. psychologist, 1979—2005; pvt. practice psychotherapist Escondido, Calif., 1990—92, Carlsbad, Calif., 1992—94. Adj. prof. US Internat. U., 1991—94; tchr. Camelrock Yoga Ctr., Valley Center, 2002—04; Tai Chi Chuan instr. Am. Universalist Temple of Divine Wisdom, Valley Center, 2005—, workshop presenter, 2004—05. Author: Enhancing Children's Creativity and Self Perceptions Through the Arts, 1989, Awakening to the Spirit Within: Eight Paths, 2004, (poetry) Unfolding, 1987; prodr.(with Barbara Morse): (game) Squnch Journey, 1993. Mem.: Inst. Noetic Scis., Assn. Rsch. and Enlightenment, Assn. Ret. Persons. Home Phone: 760-643-1492. Personal E-mail: pmsmallen@yahoo.com.

ALLEN, PATRICIA J., retired library director; b. McLean County, Ky., Nov. 10, 1941; d. Richard Louis and Helen (Hancock) Jones; m. Jerry M. Mize, Mar. 19, 1960 (div. 1978); children: Martin P., Elizabeth M. Atherton; m. Lawrence A. Allen, Nov. 24, 1983 (div. 1985). Student, Murray State U., Ky., 1959-60; BA, Ky. Wesleyan Coll., 1962; MA, Western Ky. U., 1974; MLS, U. Ky., 1982; postgrad., U. N.C., 1983-84. Libr. pub. elem. schs., Daviess County, Ky., 1963-70; media specialist pub. elem., mid. and high schs. McLean County, Ky., 1970-78; head pub. svcs., assoc. prof. libr. sci. Ky. Wesleyan Coll., Owensboro, 1978-83; asst. dir. Evansville (Ind.) Vanderburgh County Pub. Libr., 1985-89; dir. Carmel (Ind.) Clay Pub. Libr., 1989-91, Sanibel (Fla.) Pub. Libr., 1991—2007; ret., 2007. Mem. adj. faculty Western Ky. U., Bowling Green, 1977-78, Ind. U., Bloomington, 1988; workshop presenter Nursing Home Activities Dirs. Assn., Owensboro, Ky., 1981; cons. Ky. Dept. Librs. and Archives, Frankfort, 1982, Purchase (Ky.) Regional Libr. Sys., Murray, 1983, Henderson (Ky.) C.C. Libr., 1988. Editor: Emergency Handbook, 1987, Circulation Policies and Procedures, 1988, Sanibel Public Library Building Program Statement, 1992; contbr. article to profl. jours. Pres. Ret. Sr. Vol. Program Adv. Coun., Evansville, 1986-88; bd. dirs. Evansville Goodwill Industries, 1987-89. Named Outstanding Citizen of the Yr., Sanibel-Captiva Islands C. of C., 1995; Caroline M. Hewins scholar U. Ky., 1982, Margaret Ellen Kalp scholar U. N.C., 1983-84; hon. Ky. Col., 1981. Mem. Ky. Libr. Assn., Beta Phi Mu. Democrat. Baptist. Avocations: travel, walking, swimming, needlecrafts, reading.

ALLEN, PAUL GARDNER, professional sports team and computer company executive; b. Seattle, Wash., Jan. 21, 1953; s. Kenneth and Faye Allen. Student, Wash. State U., 1971—73. Co-founder Traf-O-Data Co., Seattle, 1972—73; progammer Honeywell Internat. Inc., Waltham, 1974—75; co-founder Microsoft Corp. (formerly Micro-Soft), Albuquerque, 1975; gen. ptnr. Microsoft Corp., 1975—77, v.p., 1977—81, exec. v.p. rsch. & new product devel., 1981—83, sr. strategy adv., 2000—; founder Asymetrix Corp., Bellevue, Wash., 1985, Starwave Corp., Bellevue, 1992; co-founder Interval Rsch. Corp., Palo Alto, Calif., 1992; founder Vulcan Prodns.; founder, chmn. Vulcan Inc., Seattle; CEO Vulcan Ventures, Bellevue, 1987—; owner, chmn. bd. Portland Trail Blazers, 1988—; owner, chmn. Seattle Seahawks, 1997—; chmn. Charter Comm. Inc., 1998—, Charter Investment, Inc., 1998—; owner TechTV; sponsor, funder SpaceShipOne Venture, Mojave, Calif., 2003; founder Allen Telescope Array, SETI Inst. U. Calif. Berkeley, 2004. Bd. dirs. Egghead Discount Software, Microsoft Corp., 1983—2000, Darwin Molecular, Inc.; founder Allen Inst. Brain Sci., 2003—, Allen Brain Atlas Initiative, Experience Music Project, Seattle, Sci. Fiction Mus. and Hall of Fame, Seattle, 2004—; ptnr. DreamWorks SKG. Exec. prodr.: (film series) The Blues. Founder Paul G. Allen Family Found. Co-recipient with Burt Rutan, Smithsonian's Nat. Air and Space Mus. Trophy, 2005, Rave award-Science, WIRED Mag., 2007; named one of Top 15 Philanthropists in Am., Top 200 Collectors, Artnews mag., 2004—06, World's Richest People, Forbes mag., 1999—2007, Forbes' Richest Ams., 2006, The World's Most Influential People, TIME mag., 2007; named to Computer Mus. Hall of Fame. Mem.: NAE. Achievements include sponsoring and funding the record flights for SpaceShipOne, which won the Ansari X prize on Oct. 4, 2004; SpaceShipOne donated to Smithsonian Instn. on October 6, 2005. Avocation: Collecting impressionism, Old Masters, pop art, tribal art. Office: Vulcan Inc 505 5th Ave S Ste 900 Seattle WA 98104 also: Seattle Seahawks 11220 NE 53rd St Kirkland WA 98033-7505 Office Phone: 425-453-1940, 206-342-2000. Office Fax: 206-342-3000.*

ALLEN, PHILIP, artist; b. NYC, Jan. 15, 1952; s. Abraham and Ruth Allen; m. Laura Hartheimer; 1 child, Daniel Rembrandt. Ed., Art Students' League, NY, Franconia Coll., SUNY, Purchase, NY Studio Sch. Painting, Drawing and Sculpture. Faculty mem. Fine Arts Dept. Boston Mus. Sch., 1992, Parsons Sch. Design, 1994—2003; vis. artist, RISD vis. artist Fordham U.; vis. artist Mass. Coll. Art. One-man shows include Rosa Esman Gallery, 1985, Sorkin Gallery, NY, 1990, Eli Marsh Gallery, Amherst Coll., 1992, exhibited in group shows at CAPS Painters 79-80, Rennselaer Polytechnic Inst., 1980, Young Painters 1980, Bronx Mus. Art, 1980, Five from NY, Washington Project for Arts, 1982, New Talent, AM Sachs Gallery, NY, 1982, Paintings, SUNY, Purchase, 1982, NY to Bennington: Paintings, Susanne Lemberg Usdan Gallery, Bennington Coll., 1983, AVA II, DeCordova and Dana Mus. and Park, Lincoln, Mass., 1983, Mus. Contemporary Art Chgo., 1983, NYC Painters, Fabian Carlsson Gallery, London, 1985, New Response: Contemporary Painters of the Hudson River, Albany Inst. History and Art, 1986, More than Meets the Eye: 9 Painters from NYC, Galleria Carini, Florence, Italy, 1986, The Legacy of the Abstract Expressionists, Gallery at Hastings on Hudson, 1990, Gallery Artists, German Van Eck Gallery, NY, 1992, Maine Coast Artists, Rockport, Main, 1997, Nat. Acad. Design Exhbn., 2006, Represented in permanent collections First Nat. Bank Chgo., Equitable Life Co., NY, Walter Hopps, Houston, Tex. Recipient Award in Visual Arts, Charlotte, NC, 1983; CAPS fellow, NY, 1980, NEA fellow, Washington, DC, 1982, Louis Comfort Tiffany fellow, Louis Comfort Tiffany Found., 1986. Business E-Mail: cadredmed@gmail.com.

ALLEN, PINNEY L., lawyer; b. Marshalltown, Iowa, Jan. 26, 1953; d. Walker Woodrow and Doris (Pinney) A.; m. Charles C. Miller, III, Aug. 20, 1977; children: Linden, Doria. AB summa cum laude, Harvard U., 1976; JD cum laude, Harvard Law Sch., 1979. Bar: Ga., 1976; U.S. Tax Ct. 1984. Assoc. Alston & Bird, Atlanta, 1979-86; ptnr., co-chair, tax practice group Alston & Bird LLP, Atlanta, 1986—. Contbr. articles to profl. jours., 1981—. Mem. ABA, Nat. Soc. Accts. for Coops., Ga. Bar Assn., Atlanta Bar Assn., Atlant Tax Forum. Office: Alston & Bird 1 Atlantic Ctr 1201 W Peachtree St NW Atlanta GA 30309-3424 Office Phone: 404-881-7485. Office Fax: 404-881-7777. Business E-Mail: pallen@alston.com.

ALLEN, RACHEL LOREY, lawyer; b. Pitts., Oct. 23, 1964; d. Phillip Joseph and Patricia Grace (Mullen) L. BS, Allegheny Coll., Meadville, Pa., 1986; JD, U. Va., Charlottesville, 1989. Bar: Pa. 1989. Assoc. atty. Kirkpatrick & Lockhart, Pitts., 1989-96, Jones, Day, Reavis & Pogue, Pitts., 1996-99; v.p. DQE Enterprises, Pitts., 1999—2001; ptnr. Jones Day, Pitts., 2001—. Dir. Program for Female Offenders, Inc., Pitts., 1991-2005, Arc Washington County (Pa.), Inc., 1991-99 Bd. dirs. Women's Ctr. and Shelter Greater Pitts., 2000—; dir. Alpha Chi Omega Found., 2004-06, Brothers Brother Found., 2004—. Mem. ABA, Allegheny County Bar Assn., Order of the Coif, Phi Beta Kappa. Office: Jones Day 31st Fl 500 Grant St Pittsburgh PA 15219 Home Phone: 412-276-2329; Office Phone: 412-391-3939. Business E-Mail: rlallen@jonesday.com.

ALLEN, RALPH CARNELL, retired assistant principal; b. Alto, Tex., Jan. 5, 1921; s. Jame Porter and Cashie Carrie Allen; m. Theressa McDonald (div.); 1 child, William Lafayette. AB, Tex. Coll., Tyler, 1943; MEd, Tex. So. U., Houston, 1957. Tchr., coach Dunbar H.S., Temple, Tex., 1945—48, E. J. Campbell H.S., Nacogdocher, Tex., 1948—59, Lincoln H.S., LaMarque, Tex., 1959—65, asst. prin., 1965—66, prin., 1966—70; asst. prin. LaMarque H.S., 1970—83; ret. Treas. St. Vincent Ho., Galveston, Tex., 1983—90; vestry mem. St. Michael's Episc. Ch., LaMarque, 2003—06. Mem.: LaMarque Tex. Ret. Tchrs. Assn. (pres. 1983—85), Omega Psi Phi. Democrat. Episcopalian.

ALLEN, RANDALL L., lawyer; b. Tullahoma, Tenn., Sept. 10, 1956; BA, Ga. State Univ., 1982, JD cum laude, 1986. Bar: Ga. 1986. Ptnr., co-chmn, litig. and trial practice group Alston & Bird LLP, Atlanta. Bd. visitors Ga. State Univ. Coll. of Law; bd. dir, gen. counsel Ronald McDonald Children's Charities. Mem.: ABA. Office: Alston & Bird LLP One Atlantic Ctr 1201 W Peachtree St NW Atlanta GA 30309-3424 Office Phone: 404-881-7196. Office Fax: 404-881-7777. Business E-Mail: rallen@alston.com.

ALLEN, RAY (WALTER RAY ALLEN), professional basketball player; b. Merced, Calif., July 20, 1975; Student, U. Conn., 1996. Shooting guard Milw. Bucks, 1996—2003, Seattle SuperSonics, 2003—07, Boston Celtics, 2007—. Actor: (films) He Got Game, 1998. Founder Ray of Hope Found. Co-recipient Gold medal, Summer Olympics, 2000; named to Ea. Conf. All-Star Team, NBA, 2000, 2001, 2002, Western Conf. All-Star Team, 2004, 2005, 2006, 2007; recipient Joe Dumars Sportsmanship award, 2003. Achievements include holding the NBA record for most seasons leading the league in three-point field goals made with 3. Office: Boston Celtics 226 Causeway St 4th Fl Boston MA 02114*

ALLEN, REX WHITAKER, retired architect; b. San Francisco, Dec. 21, 1914; s. Lewis Whitaker and Maude Rex (Allen) A.; m. Elizabeth Johnson, Oct. 11, 1941 (div. 1949); children: Alexandra A., Frances Lambert (Mrs. Andrew Dunn); m. Ruth Batchelor, Apr. 1, 1949 (div. 1971); children: Mark B., Susan Moore (Mrs. Kofy Lechner); m. Bettie J. Crossfield, Nov. 6, 1971. AB, Harvard U., 1936, MArch, 1939; student, Columbia U. Archtl. Sch., 1936—37. With Rsch. and Planning Assocs., NYC, 1939-42, Camloc Fastener Corp., NYC, 1942-45, Isadore Rosenfield (arch.), NYC, 1945-48, Blanchard and Maher (archs.), San Francisco, 1949-52; established pvt. practice San Francisco, 1953; pres. Rex Whitaker Allen & Assocs., San Francisco, 1961-71, Archtl. Prodns., Inc., 1971-76; prin. Hugh Stubbins/Rex Allen Partnership, 1968, Rex Allen Partnership, 1971-76; pres. Rex Allen-Drever-Lechowski, Archs., 1976-85, Rex Allen/Mark Lechowski & Assocs., 1985-87; cons. arch., health facility planner, 1987—. Mem. Calif. Bldg. Safety Bd., 1973-93. Author: (with Ilona von Karolyi) Hospital Planning Handbook, 1976; contbr. articles to profl. jours.; prin. works include French Hosp., San Francisco, Mercy Hosp., Sacramento, Roseville (Calif.) Dist. Hosp., Highland Hosp., Oakland, St. Francis Hosp., San Francisco, Dominican Hosp., Santa Cruz, Alta Bates Hosp., Berkeley, Calif., Boston City Hosp., Out-Patient bldg. Woodland (Calif.) Meml. Hosp., Stanislaus Meml. Hosp., Modesto, Calif., Madera (Calif.) Cmty. Hosp., Sacred Heart Hosp., Eugene, Oreg., St. Joseph Hosp., Mt. Clemens, Mich., Commonwealth Health Ctr., Saipan, Guam Meml. Hosp. and Nursing Facility. Chmn. Mill Valley Adv. Edn. Coun., 1956; mem. Blue Ribbon com. Sonoma Valley Unified Sch. Dist., 1997-2002. Fellow AIA (nat. pres. 1969-70, v.p. No. Calif. chpt. 1964, bd. dirs. Calif. coun. 1955-56, 1962-64), Royal Archtl. Inst. Can. (hon.), Am. Coll. Healthcare Archs. (Lifetime Achievement award 2003, Gold medal 2003); mem. Constrn. Specification Inst. (pres. San Francisco chpt. 1961), San Francisco Zool. Soc. (bd. dirs. 1974-86, 88-95, exhibits com. 1988—, chmn. design stds. com. Assn. Western Hosps., chmn. arch. sect. 1957-58), Calif. Hosp. Assn., Am. Hosp. Assn., Internat. Hosp. Fedn., Am. Assn. Hosp. Planning (pres. 1971-72), Union Internat. des Architectes Pub. Health Work Group (dir. 1979-80), La Sociedad de Arquitectos Mexicanos (hon. mem.), Federaciñn Panamericana de Asociaciones de Arquitectos (v.p. 1980-84), San Francisco Planning and Urban Renewal Assn., San Francisco Mus. Modern Art, Japanese Garden Soc. of Oreg., Portland Classical Chinese Garden, Asian Art Coun., Portland Art Mus., Sierra Club. Home and Office: 9946 SW 61st Ave Portland OR 97219 Office Phone: 503-977-2770. Business E-Mail: rethmore@comcast.com.

ALLEN, RICHARD CUTLER, surgeon, researcher; b. St. Louis, June 16, 1965; s. John Fingal Allen, III and Anne Scholz Allen; m. Melissa Susan Gaido, Dec. 22, 1993; children: Augustus Sellards, Astrid Sophia. BS in Chemistry, Duke U., Durham, NC, 1987; PhD in Molecular Genetics, Baylor U., Houston, 1993, MD, 1995. Lic. Am. Bd. Ophthalmology, Pa., 2002, Am. Soc. Ophthalmic Plastic & Reconstructive Surgery, Fla., 2006. Intern U. N.Mex Sch. Medicine, Albuquerque, 1995—96, asst. prof., 2002—04, 2006—; resident ophthalmology U. Iowa, Iowa City, 1997—2000, fellow ophthalmology, 2004—06; asst. prof. Baylor Coll. Medicine, 2000—02. Office: Eye Assocs NMex 5757 Harper Dr NE Albuquerque NM 87109 Office Phone: 505-888-5757. Personal E-mail: richardcutlerallen@hotmail.com. Business E-Mail: rcallen@eyenm.com.

ALLEN, RICHARD GARRETT, healthcare educator; b. St. Paul, July 8, 1923; s. John and Margaretta (Taggart) A.; m. Ida Elizabeth Vernon, July 5, 1944; children: Richard Garrett, Barbara Elizabeth, Julie Frances (dec.). BS cum laude, Trinity U., 1954; MHA, Baylor U., 1957; postgrad., Indsl. Coll. of Armed Forces, 1962, USAF Command and Staff Coll., 1962. Commd. 2d lt. Med. Svc. Corps USAF, 1948, advanced through grades to maj., 1961; served in U.S., Pacific, Germany; ret., 1964; asst. adminstr. U. Ala. Hosp. and Clinics; dir. Ctr. for Hosp. Continuing Edn., Sch. for Health Svcs., U. Ala., Birmingham, 1965-68; dir. edn. New Eng. Hosp. Assembly, Inc., New Eng. Ctr. for Continuing Edn., U. N.H., Durham, 1968-74; dir. Office Health Care Edn., 1970-74; exec. v.p. Edn. and Rsch. Found., San Francisco, 1974-77, Assn. West Hosps., 1974-77. V.p. health affairs M G & M Comm., Foster City, Calif.; pres. Calif. Coll. Podiatric Medicine; CEO Calif. Podiatry Hosp. and Outpatient Clinic, San Francisco, 1977-81; prof. health care adminstrn. St. Mary's Coll. of Calif., Moraga, 1982-85; cons. health care and edn., 1985—; owner Sleepy Hollow Books, 1985—; mem. Nat. Adv. Coun. on Vocat. Edn., 1969-71; also cons.; cons. Booz, Allen & Hamilton, Washington, Ops. Rsch., Inc., Silver Spring, Md., Republic of Korea Air Force Med. Svcs., Seoul, Bio-Dynamics, Inc., Cambridge, Mass., HEALTHSAT-Appalachia Cmty. Svcs. Network, Washington, 1980—. Pub.: Hosp. Forum, San Francisco, 1974-77; contbr. articles to profl. jours. Decorated Air Force Commendation medal with oak leaf cluster. Fellow Am. Coll. Hosp. Adminstrs.; mem. Am. Soc. for Health Manpower Edn. and Tng., Am. Hosp. Assn., AAUP, Am. Soc. Hosp. Edn. and Tng. (pres. 1972), Am. Assn. Colls. Podiatric Medicine (pres. 1979-81), Sherlock Holmes Soc. London, Masons. Episcopalian. Home and Office: Sleepy Hollow Books 1455 Camino Peral Moraga CA 94556-2018 E-mail: dick78@earthlink.net. *Uncertainty is a fact of life; there is no* *progress free of the risk of change. Sharpen your sense of timing and know when it is time to let go and when to hang on. Trials and defeats are inevitable elements of the committed life; welcome these conflicts for it is your principles that are involved. Appreciate the past, but focus on today's tasks— while realizing that tomorrow will be nothing like you expect it to be. Cultivate a cheerful acceptance of your own mortality, and its attendant limitations and blessings.*

ALLEN, RICHARD S., engineering company executive; BS in Chem. Engring., Tex. A&M U., Coll. Station, 1978; MS in Petroleum Engring., U. Houston, 1983. V.p. global power industry sales Intergraph Corp., Madison, Ala., 2006—. Achievements include patents in field.

ALLEN, RICHARD STANLEY (DICK ALLEN), literature and language professor, writer; b. Troy, NY, Aug. 8, 1939; s. Richard Sanders and Doris (Bishop) A.; m. Loretta Mary Negridge, Aug. 13, 1960; children: Richard Negridge, Tanya Angell. AB, Syracuse U., NYC, 1961; MA, Brown U., 1963. Teaching assoc. Brown U., 1962-64; instr. English Wright State U., Dayton, Ohio, 1964-68; mem. faculty U. Bridgeport, Conn., 1968—, prof. English, 1976-79, Charles A. Dana prof. English, 1979—2001, also dir. creative writing, Dana prof. emeritus English, 2001—. Author: Anon and Various Time Machine Poems, 1971, Overnight in the Guest House of the Mystic, 1984, Regions with No Proper Names, 1975, Flight and Pursuit, 1987, Ode to the Cold War: Poems New and Selected, 1997, The Day Before: New Poems, 2003; also poems, articles, revs.; editor, poetry editor: Mad River Rev., 1964-68; co-editor: Detective Fiction: Crime and Compromise, 1974, Looking Ahead: The Vision of Science Fiction, 1975; book reviewer: Poetry, Hudson Rev., Am. Book Rev.; editor: Science Fiction: The Future, 1982, Crosscurrents Expansive Poetry: The New Formalism and the New Narrative, 1989. Recipient poetry prize Union Arts and Civic League, 1971, Disting. Tchg. award MLA-Assn. Depts. English, 1971, San Jose poetry prize, 1976, poetry prize Nassau Rev., 1995, Poetry award L.A. (Calif.) Times, 2004; Hart Crane Meml. poetry fellow, 1966, Robert Frost poetry fellow, 1972, Mellon rsch. fellow, 1981, poetry writing fellow Ingram Merrill Found., 1986; poetry writing grantee Nat. Endowment Arts, 1984, Nat. Millennium Survey Project, 2000; finalist Winship/PEN Am. award, W. Carlos Williams PSA 1st Finalist award, NBCC Poetry Book award, Conn. Poetry Book award, 2004, Sheila Motion Poetry prize, 2004, Pushcart prize, 2005. Mem. Associated Writers Programs, Poets and Writers, PEN, Poetry Soc. Am. (Carolyn Davies Meml. Poetry award 1986), Modern Poetry Soc. Republican. Unitarian Universalist. Home: 74 Fern Cir Trumbull CT 06611-4910 Personal E-mail: rallen285@earthlink.net.

ALLEN, RICHARD VINCENT, international business consultant, former national security advisor; b. Collingswood, NJ, Jan. 1, 1936; s. Charles Carroll and Magdalen (Buchman) A.; m. Patricia Ann Mason, Dec. 28,1957; children: Michael, Kristin, Mark, Karen, Kathryn, Kevin, Kimberly. BA, U. Notre Dame, 1957, MA, 1958; postgrad., U. Munich, W. Ger., 1958-61; doctorate (hon.), Hanover Coll., Korea U., Pepperdine U. Instr. U. Md. Overseas Div., 1959-61; asst. prof. polit. sci. Ga. Inst. Tech., 1961-62; sr. staff mem. Center for Strategic and Internat. Studies, Georgetown U., 1962-66, Hoover Instn. on War, Revolution and Peace, Stanford U., 1966-69; fgn. policy coord. Richard Nixon Presdl. campaign, 1967-68; sr. staff mem. NSC, 1969; dep. asst. to Pres. The White House, Washington, 1971-72; pres. Potomac Internat. Corp., Washington, 1972-80; sr. fgn. policy adv. to Pres. The White House, Washington, 1978-80; asst. to Pres. for nat. security affairs NSC, Washington, 1981-82; pres. Richard V. Allen Co., Washington, 1982-90, chmn., 1991—2003. Disting. fellow, chmn. Asian Studies Ctr. Heritage Found., 1982-98; sr. counselor for fgn. policy and nat. security Rep. Nat. Com., 1982-88; sr. fellow Hoover Instn., 1983—; vice chmn. Internat. Dem. Union, 1983-88; chmn. German-Am. Tricentennial Found., 1983; mem. Pres.'s Task Force on U.S. Govt. Internat. Broadcasting, 1991-92; mem. adv. bd. Cath. Campaign for Am., 1993-96; mem. Rep. Congl. Policy Adv. Bd., 1998-2001; mem. U.S. Def. Policy Bd., 2001—. Author: Peace or Peaceful Coexistence, 1966, (with others) Communism and Democracy: Theory and Action, 1967; editor: (with David M. Abshire) National Security: Political, Military and Economic Strategies in the Decade Ahead, 1963, Yearbook on International Communist Affairs, 1969. Chmn. com. on intelligence Republican Nat. Com., 1977-80; trustee St. Francis Prep. Sch., Spring Grove, Pa. Named Patriot of Yr. SAR, 1981; H.B. Earhart fellow Relm Found., 1958-61; decorated Order of Diplomatic Merit Republic of Korea, 1982, Knight Comdr.'s Cross Fed. Republic of Germany, 1983, Badge and Star of Order of Merit Fed. Republic of Germany, 1983, Order of Brilliant Star, Republic of China, 1986, Sovereign Mil. Order of Knights of Malta, 1987. Mem. Am. Polit. Sci. Assn., Coun. on Fgn. Rels., Intercollegiate Studies Inst. (trustee), Com. on Present Danger (dir. 1976-90), Univ. Club, Farmington Country Club (Charlottesville, Va.), Burning Tree Club (Bethesda, Md.), Met. Club, Cordillera Club (Colo.). E-mail: rvallen@aol.com.

ALLEN, ROBERT DEE, lawyer; b. Tulsa, Oct. 13, 1928; s. Harve and Olive Jean (Brown) A.; m. Mary Latimer Conner, May 18, 1957; children: Scott, Randy, Blake. Grad. with honors, ROTC, 1951; BA, U. Okla., 1951, LLB, 1955, JD, 1970. Bar: Okla. 1955, Ill. 1979, U.S. Dist. Ct. (we., no. and ea. dists.) Okla. 1955, U.S. Dist. Ct. (no. dist.) Ill. 1979, U.S. Ct. Appeals (10th cir.) 1956, U.S. Ct. Appeals (7th cir.) 1980, U.S. Supreme Ct. 1985. Assoc. Abernathy & Abernathy, Shawnee, Okla., 1955; law clk. to judge 10th U.S. Ct. Appeals, Denver, 1956; to judge Western Dist. Okla., 1956-57; asst. ins. commr., gen. counsel Okla. Ins. Dept., 1957-63; ptnr. firm Quinlan, Allen & Batchelor, Oklahoma City, 1963-65, DeBois & Allen, 1965-66; counsel AT&T, Washington, 1966-67; gen. atty. Southwestern Bell Telephone Co., Okla., 1967-79; v.p., gen. counsel Ill. Bell Telephone Co., Chgo., 1979-83; solo practice law Chgo. and Oklahoma City, 1983—; mcpl. counselor Oklahoma City, 1984-89; of counsel Hartzog, Conger & Cason, 1983-90, Kimball, Wilson, Walker and Ferguson, 1990-93, Berry & Durland, 1993-94, Durland & Durland, 1994-96, White, Coffey, Galt & Fite, P.C., 1996-97, Phillips, McFall, McCaffrey, McVay & Murrah, P.C., 1997-2000; asst. gen. counsel Okla. Corp. Commn. Pub. Utilities Divsn., 2000—04, Roberrt D. Allen PC, 2004—; ret., 2004. Spl. counsel Okla. Mcpl. Power Authority, 1990-94, City of Altus, Okla., 1990-95; mem. Gov.'s Ad Valorem Tax Structure and Sch. Fin. Commn., 1972; bd. dirs. Taxpayers Fedn. Ill., 1980-83; adv. bd. dirs. Ctr. Am. and Internat. Law., 1985—; rsch. fellow Ctr. Am. and Internat. Law, 1994—; adj. prof. ins. law Oklahoma City U. Coll. Law, 1985—. agy. and partnership law, U. Okla. Coll. Law, 1989—; Okla. State chmn. Nat. Inst. Mcpl. Law Officers, 1984-89; apptd. mem. Legis Task Force on Okla. Adminstrv. Code, 1987; founding mem. U. Okla. Assocs., 1980. Bd. dirs. Oklahoma County Legal Aid Soc., 1973—; trustee Oklahoma City Riverfront Redevel. Authority, 1997-2003; dir. Okla. City Town Hall, 2006-. With U.S. Army, 1946-48, 1st lt., 51-53; lt. col. USAR. Fellow Am. Bar Found., Okla. Bar Found. (charter benefactor); mem. ABA, Fed. Bar Assn. (v.p. Okla. chpt. 1977—), Okla. Bar Assn., Okla. County Bar Assn., Am. Judicature Soc., Okla. Assn. Mcpl. Attys. (bd. dirs. 1984-89), English Speaking Union (dir. 2001—), Order of Coif, Chgo. Club, Lions Club of Oklahoma City (Melvin Jones fellow), The Econs. Club of Okla., Men's Dinner Club, Oklahoma City Golf and Country Club, Phi Delta Phi, Sigma Phi Epsilon (dir.) Presbyterian. Home and Office: 8101 Glenwood Ave Oklahoma City OK 73114-1107 Personal E-mail: rdeeallen@sbcglobal.net.

ALLEN, ROBERT EUGENE BARTON, lawyer; b. Bloomington, Ind., Mar. 16, 1940; s. Robert Eugene Barton and Berth R. A.; m. Cecelia Ward Dooley, Sept. 23, 1960 (div. 1971); children: Victoria, Elizabeth, Robert, Charles, Suzanne, William; m. Judith Elaine Hecht, May 27, 1979 (div. 1984); m. Suzanne Nickolson, Nov. 18, 1995. BS, Columbia U., 1962; LLB, Harvard U., 1965. Bar: Ariz. 1965, U.S. Dist. Ct. Ariz. 1965, U.S. Tax Ct., 1965, U.S. Supreme Ct. 1970, U.S. Ct. Customs and Patent Appeals 1971, U.S. Dist. Ct. D.C. 1972, U.S. Ct. Appeals (9th cir.) 1974, U.S. Ct. Appeals (10th and D.C. cirs.) 1984, U.S. Dist. Ct. N.Mex., U.S. Dist. Ct. (no. dist.) Calif., U.S. Dist. Ct. (no. dist.) Tex. 1991, U.S. Ct. Appeals (fed. cir.) 1992, U.S. Dist. Ct. (ea. dist.) Wis. 1995. Spl. asst. atty. gen., 1978; judge pro-tem Ariz. Ct. Appeals, 1984, 92, 99; Ptnr., dir. Allen, Price & Padden, Phoenix, 2000—. Nat. pres. Young Dems. Clubs Am., 1971-73; mem. exec. com. Dem. Nat. Com., 1972-73, Ariz. Gov.'s Kitchen Cabinet working on a wide range of state projects; bd. dirs. Phoenix Bapt. Hosp., 1981-83, Phoenix and Valley of the Sun Conv. and Visitors Bur., United Cerebral Palsy Ariz., 1984-89, Planned Parenthood of Ctrl. and No. Ariz., 1984-87, Ariz. Heart Found., 1998—, Cordell Hull Found. for Internat. Edn., 1996—; trustee Environ. Health Found., 1994-97, Friends of Walnut Canyon, 1991-94; bd. dirs. Ariz. Aviation Futures Task Force, chmn. Ariz. Airport Devel. Criteria Subcom.; Am. rep. exec. bd. Atlantic Alliance of Young Polit. Leaders, 1973-77, 77-80; trustee Am. Counsel of Young Polit. Leaders, 1971-76, 81-85; mem. Am. delegations to Germany, 1971, 72, 76, 79, USSR, 1971, 76, 88, France, 1974, 79, Belgium, 1974, 77, Can., 1974, Eng., 1975, 79, Norway, 1975, Denmark, 1976, Yugoslavia and Hungary, 1985; Am. observer European Parlimentary elections, Eng., France, Germany, Belgium, 1979, Moscow Congressional, Journalist delegation, 1989, NAFTA Trade Conf., Mexico City, 1993, Atlantic Assembly, Copenhagen, 1993. Contbr. articles on comml. litig. to profl. jours. Mem. ABA, Ariz. Bar Assn., Maricopa County Bar Assn., N.Mex. State Bar, D.C. Bar Assn., Am. Judicature Soc., Fed. Bar Assn., Am. Arbitration Assn., Phi Beta Kappa, Harvard Club. Democrat. Episcopalian. Home: 4610 North Borgatello Phoenix AZ 85018 Office Phone: 602-478-9933. Personal E-mail: allenfamily5330@yahoo.com.

ALLEN, ROBERT JOHNSON, plastic surgeon; b. Florence, Mar. 19, 1951; s. James and Lucta Johnson Allen; m. Linda Truluck Perry Allen, June 5, 1976; children: Julia Marshall, Robert Johnson, James Perry, Celeste Blackwell. BS, Wofford Coll., Spartanburg, SC, 1972; MD, Med. U. S.C., Charleston, 1976; post grad. gen. and plastic surgery, La. State U. Med. Ctr., 1976—82. Cert. Am. Bd. Surgery, 1983, Am. Bd.Plastic Surgery, 1985. Microsurgery fellow N.Y. U. Med. Ctr., NYC, 1982—83; clin. instr. dept. surgery La. State U., New Orleans, 1983—88; clin. asst. prof. La. State U. Med. Ctr., 1988—97; program dir. plastic surgery La. State U. Health Sci. Ctr., 1988—98, clin. assoc. prof., 1997—2005, chief plastic surgery, 1998—, clin. prof. surg., 2005—; staff Ctr. Microsurgical Breast Reconstruction, New Orleans, Charleston, NYC. Editl. bd. Jour. Reconstructive Microsurgery, NYC, 1998—, Breast Diseases; A Yearbook Quarterly, Houston, 1999—, Annals Plastic Surgery, NYC, 2000—. Editor: Seminars in Plastic Surgery, 2002; contbr. articles to profl. jours.; editl. bd. Annals of Plastic Surgery, 2004. Vol. celebrity waiter La. Breast Cancer Task Force, New Orleans, 2005. Recipient Spirit award, Am. Cancer Soc., 2003. Mem.: Am. Soc. Reconstructive Microsurgery (edn. com. 1998—99), Southeastern Soc. Plastic Reconstructive Surgeons (bd. dir. 1998—2001), Am. Assn. Plastic Surgeons, Internat. Course on Perforator Flaps (sec. gen. 1998, faculty), World Soc. Reconstructive Microsurgery (sec. gen. 2003—06, founding mem., coun. mem. 2001—03). Achievements include design of deep inferior episcastric perforator flap; superficial inferior episcastric artery flap; glutal artery perforator flap; first to complete breast reconstruction transplant in identical twins. Avocations: pottery, tennis, running, literature. Office: Ctr Microsurg Breast Reconstruction 125 Doughty St # 480 Charleston SC 29403 also: Ctr Microsurg Breast Reconstruction 2820 Napoleon Ave New Orleans LA 70115 also: Ctr Microsurg Breast Reconstruction 1776 Broadway Ste 1200 New York NY 10019 Office Phone: 888-890-3437. E-mail: boballen@diepflap.com.*

ALLEN, ROBERTA, writer, photographer, conceptual artist; b. NYC, Oct. 6, 1945; d. Sol and Jeanette (Waldner) A. Student, Inst. Bellas Artes, Mex., 1971. Lectr. Corcoran Sch. Art, Washington, 1975, Kutztown State Coll., 1979, C.W. Post Coll., 1979. Instr. creative writing Parsons Sch. Design, NYC, 1986; instr. The Writer's Voice, 1992—97, The New Sch., 1993—, Dept. Continuing Edn., NYU, 1993—99; Tennessee Williams fellow, writer-in-residence U. of the South, Sewanee, Tenn., 1998; adj. asst. prof. Columbia U. Sch. of the Arts, 1998—99, Eugene Lang. Coll., 2000. Author: Partially Trapped Lines, 1975, Pointless Arrows, 1976, Pointless Acts, 1977, Everything in The World There Is To Know Is Known By Somebody, But Not By the Same Knower, 1981, Amazon Dream, 1993; author: (fiction) The Daughter, 1992, The Dreaming Girl, 2000, The Traveling Woman, 1986, Certain People, 1997; author: (writing guide) Fast Fiction, 1997, The Playful Way to Serious Writing, 2002, (Personal Growth) The Playful Way to Knowing Yourself, 2003; one-woman shows include Galerie 845, Amsterdam, Netherlands, 1967, John Weber Gallery, N.Y.C., 1974—75, 1977, 1979, Inst. for Art and Urban Resources, 1977, 1980, Galerie Maier-Hahn, Dusseldorf, Germany, 1977, MTL Galerie, Brussels, 1978, C.W. Post Coll., Glenvale, N.Y., 1978, Galerie Walter Storms, Munich, 1981, Kunstforum, Stadt. Galerie in Lenbachhaus, 1981, Galeria Primo Piano, Rome, 1981, Perth Inst. Contemporary Arts, 1989, Art Resources Transfer, Inc., 2001, SUNY, Binghamton, 2001. Fellow, Va. Ctr. Creative Arts, 1985, 1994, 2005; McDowell Colony fellow, 1971—72, Yaddo fellow, 1983, 1987, 1993, LINE grantee, 1985. E-mail: robertaallen@mac.com.

ALLEN, RONALD CARL, commissioner, artist, consultant, former state senator, computer company executive; b. Salt Lake City, Mar. 25, 1953; s. Carl Franklin and Mary Jean (Benson) A.; m. Delia Ann Fordham, Nov. 15, 1974; children: Lisa, Cindy, Jeffrey. BS in Acctg., U. Utah, 1980, MA in Art History, 2004. Owner, bus. mgr. Alinco Mfg., Salt Lake City, 1977-79; owner, pres. Comics Utah Bookstores, Salt Lake City, 1984-86; adminstrv. supr. Am. Stores, Salt Lake City, 1978-89; pres. Cons. Svcs., Salt Lake City, 1989—2003; fire chief No. Tooele County Fire Dept., 1987-96; mem. Utah Senate, Salt Lake City, 1998—2005, Dem. whip, 2001—05. Adj. instr. Utah State U. Chmn., chief North Tooele County (Utah) Fire Dept., 1987—95; mem. adv. bd. USUTE Found., Mus. Utah Art and History. Recipient over 40 awards for visual arts, 1981—. Mem., Tooele County Chamber of Commerce. Mem. Lds Ch. Avocations: photography, sailing, golf. Office: 160 E 300 S Salt Lake City UT 84111 Office Phone: 801-530-6716. Personal E-mail: rallen@vonallen.com.

ALLEN, RONALD JAY, law educator; b. Chgo., July 14, 1948; s. J. Matteson and Carolyn L. (Latchum) A.; m. Debra Jane Livingston, May 25, 1974 (div. 1982); children: Sarah, Adrienne; m. Julie O'Donnell, Sept. 2, 1984; children: Michael, Conor. BS, Marshall U., 1970; JD, U. Mich., 1973. Bar: Nebr. 1974, Iowa 1979, US Ct. Appeals (8th cir.) 1980, US Supreme Ct. 1981, Ill. 1986. Prof. law SUNY, Buffalo, 1974-79, U. Iowa, Iowa City, 1979-82, 83-84, Duke U., Durham, NC, 1982-83, Northwestern U., Chgo., 1984—, John Henry Wigmore prof., 1992—. Pres. faculty senate U. Iowa, 1980-81. Author: Constitutional Criminal Procedure, 1985, 3rd edit., 1995, An Analytical Approach to Evidence, 1989, Evidence: Text, Cases and Problems, 1997, Arthritis of the Hip and Knee: The Active Person's Guide to Taking Charge, 1998, Comprehensive Criminal Procedure, 2d edit., 2005, Evidence: Text, Problems, Cases, 2002, 4th edit., 2006, Criminal Procedure: Investigation and Right to Counsel, 2005; contbr. articles to profl. jours. Bd. dirs. Constnl. Rights Found., 1992—, Joffrey Ballet, 2003. Mem. ABA (rules com. criminal justice sect.), Am. Law Inst. Office: Northwestern U Sch Law 357 E Chicago Ave Chicago IL 60611-3059 Office Phone: 312-503-8372.

ALLEN, RONALD JOHN, astrophysics educator, researcher; b. Prince Albert, Sask., Can., Nov. 12, 1940; s. Arthur and Lillian May (Brown) A.; m. Janice Ruth Nielsen, Jan. 7, 1967; children: Melanie Ruth, Matthew John, Stefan Ronald. BA in Physics with honors, U. Sask., 1962; PhD in Physics, MIT, Boston, 1967. Postdoctoral fellow NRC Can., Paris, 1967-68; rsch. assoc. Kapteyn Astron. Inst., U. Groningen, The Netherlands, 1969-70, rsch. supr., 1971, lectr. in radio astronomy, 1972-80, prof. radio astronomy, 1980-85, chmn., 1982-85; prof. astronomy U. Ill., Urbana, 1985-90, head dept. astronomy, 1985-88; astronomer Space Telescope Sci. Inst., Balt., 1989—, head sci. computing divsn., 1989-95, head rsch. programs office, 1995-99, mgr. dirs. discretionary rsch. fund, 1995—2006, head Hubble fellowship program, 2006—; mission scientist NASA/JPL Space Interferometry Mission, 2000—. Vis. lectr. Cavendish Lab., Cambridge, Eng., 1971; mem. acad. council Ministry Edn. and Sci., The Netherlands, 1982-85; mem. vis. com. Nat. Radio Astronomy Obs., Charlottesville, Va., 1986-89; sr. scientist NATO, U.S., 1975-76; vis. prof. Kapteyn Astron. Inst., 1985-95; adjunct prof. Johns Hopkins U., 1991—; advisor NSF, NASA, Can. Nat. Sci. Engring. Rsch. Coun., Swedish Nat. Rsch. Bd., French Conseil Nat. Rsch. Sci., European Space Agy., U.K. Sci. Rsch. Coun., Academia Sinica Taiwan. Co-editor: Image Processing in Astronomy, 1979, The Milky Way Galaxy, 1985, The Restoration of HST Images and Spectra, 1991; contbr. numerous articles to sci. jours. Fellow Inst. des Hautes Etudes Scientifiques, Bures-sur-Yvette, France, 1974. Mem. Internat. Astron. Union, Am. Astron. Soc.; Internat. Radio Sci. Union. Office: Space Telescope Sci Inst 3700 San Martin Dr Baltimore MD 21218-2464

ALLEN, RONDALL E., pharmacist, educator; s. Remus C. and Sarah L. Allen; m. Adrienne M. Brentzel, Nov. 13, 1999; 1 child, Jordyn A. BS in Pharmacy, Fla. Agrl. and Mech. U., Tallahassee, 1989; PharmD, Xavier U. La., New Orleans, 1993. Chief pharmacist K-mart Corp., Orlando, Fla., 1989—91; staff pharmacist Eckerd Drug Co., Perry, Fla., 1992—95; clin. pharmacist Bapt. Meml. Hosp., Memphis, 1995—96; asst. prof. Fla. Agrl. and Mech. U. Coll. Pharmacy, Tampa, 1996—98; med. sci. mgr. Bristol-Myers Squibb Co., New Orleans, 1998—2002; dir. profl. experience program Xavier U. La. Coll. Pharmacy, New Orleans, 2003—05, asst. dean program assessment, 2006—. Contbr. chapters to books. Sunday sch. tchr. Mem.: Am. Soc. Health Sys. Pharmacists, Am. Assn. Coll. Pharmacy. Baptist. Avocations: reading, music. Office: Xavier U La 1 Drexel Dr New Orleans LA 70125 Home Phone: 504-340-7734; Office Phone: 504-520-5365. Office Fax: 504-520-7971. Business E-Mail: reallen@xula.edu.

ALLEN, ROSEMARY M., lawyer; b. 1948; BA, Ind. U., 1970; MEd, Boston U., 1979; JD, Northeastern U., 1986. Bar: Mass. 1987, RI 1995, US Ct. Appeals (1st Cir.). Law clk. to Hon. Bruce M. Selya US Ct. Appeals (1st Cir.), 1987; ptnr. Mintz, Levin, Cohn, Ferris, Glovsky & Popeo PC, Boston, coord., Intellectual Property Sect. Mem.: ABA, RI Bar Assn., Mass. Bar Assn., Boston Bar Assn. Office: Mintz Levin Cohn Ferris Glovsky & Popeo PC One Financial Center Boston MA 02111 Office Phone: 617-348-1601. Office Fax: 617-542-2241. Business E-Mail: rallen@mintz.com.

ALLEN, RUSSELL G., lawyer; b. Ottumwa, Iowa, Nov. 7, 1946; BA, Grinnell Coll., 1968; JD, Stanford U., 1971. Bar: Calif. 1971. Ptnr. O'Melveny & Myers LLP, Newport Beach, Calif., 1975-2001; wealth advisor J.P. Morgan Chase & Co., Newport Beach, Calif., 2001—04. Trustee Grinnell Coll. Capt. JAGC, USAF, 1971-75. Fellow Am. Coll. Trust and Estate Counsel; mem. ABA (real property, probate and trust law and taxation sects.), Orange County Bar Assn. (estate planning, probate and trust sects.) Office: 2101 East Coast Hwy Ste 215 Corona Del Mar CA 92625 Office Phone: 949-760-4090. E-mail: Russ@russallenlaw.com.

ALLEN, SCOTT D., architect; BA in Environ. Design, U. Wash., 1980; MArch, U. Pa., 1982. Cert. Nat. Coun. Archtl. Registration Bds. With Raleigh Design Group, 1982—84, Ibsen Nelsen & Assocs., Seattle, 1984—85, Olson Sundberg Archs., Seattle, 1985—94; prin. Olson Sundberg Kundig Allen Archs., Seattle, 1994—. Prin. works include Overlake Pk. Presbyn. Ch. (Citation award, Seattle AIA Chpt., 1990), Cliff House, Gig Harbor, Wash., Hesterberg Residence, Hong Kong, Calkins Point Residence, Mercer Island, Wash., Gig Harbor Heritage Ctr., Seattle U. Sch. Law (Merit award, Seattle AIA Chpt., 2001), Pratt Fine Arts Ctr., Seattle, NW Family Retreat (NW Design awards, 2006). Mem.: AIA. Office: Olson Sundberg Kundig Allen Archs 159 S Jackson St Ste 600 Seattle WA 98104 Office Phone: 206-624-5670. Office Fax: 206-624-3730.*

ALLEN, SHARON, accounting firm executive; B in Acctg., U. Idaho, 1973, Ph.D (hon.) in Adminstrv. Sci., 2004. Mng. ptnr. Pacific Southwest practice Deloitte & Touche USA LLP, LA, 2003—, chmn. bd., 2003—. Mem. bd. United Way Greater LA; bd. mem. YMCA Met. LA; co-chair Nat. Campaign Com. Campaign for Idaho; bd. dirs. Malcolm Baldridge Found., Harvard U., John F. Kennedy Sch. Govt. Women's Leadership Coun.; chmn. bd. dirs. Independent Coll. So. Calif. (ICSC), 2003—; adv. bd. Coll. Bus. and Econ. Named Woman of the Yr., Fin. Woman's Assn., 2006; named one of Top 100 Most Influential People in 2003, Acctg. Today mag., 100 Most Powerful Women, Forbes Mag., 2006. Mem.: LA Area C. of C. (bd. mem.). Office: Deloitte & Touche USA LLP Two Calif Plz 350 S Grand Ave Ste 200 Los Angeles CA 90071-3492 Office Phone: 213-688-0800. Office Fax: 213-688-0100.*

ALLEN, STACEY R., forensic specialist; d. Douglas L. and Margie L. Allen. MS, John Carroll U., Univ. Heights, Ohio, 1997—2000. Cert. DNA analyst Office Forensic Scis., NJ, 2005, secondary biology tchr. Ohio Bd. Edn., 2000. Rsch. asst. III CWRU, Cleve., 1994—97; account mgr. Kelly Sci. Resources, Wyomissing, Pa., 2000—03; pharm. sales rep. Quintiles/McNeil, Pottstown, Pa., 2003; DNA analyst NJ State Police OFS, Hamilton, NJ, 2003—. Contbr. articles to profl. jours. Grantee Rsch. fellowship, Howard Hughes Med. Inst., 1992. Mem.: N.Ea. Assn. Forensic Scientists (assoc.), NJ Assn. Forensic Scientists (assoc.), Am. Acad. Forensic Scientists (assoc.). Office: N J State Police OFS 1200 Negron Rd Hamilton NJ 08691 Home Phone: 609-298-4540. Business E-Mail: lppalles@gw.njsp.org.

ALLEN, STACY DALE, historian, parks director; b. Independence, Kans., Apr. 23, 1958; s. Charles Bradley and Etta JoAnn Allen; m. Diane Elizabeth Woodford, July 14, 1992; children: Jennifer Elizabeth Harrison, Jonathan C. Morton. B in Anthropology, U. of Kans., 1983. Fed. Law Enforcement Commn. Fed. Law Enforcement Tng. Ctr., 1987, Ranger Skills Nat. Pk. Svc. Albright Tng. Ctr., 1989. Pk. ranger Nat. Pk. Svc. Vicksburg (Miss.) Nat. Mil. Pk., 1984—89; lead pk. ranger Nat. Pk. Svc. Shiloh (Tenn.) Nat. Mil. Pk., 1989—92, historian, 1992—2002; supervisory pk. ranger Shiloh (Tenn.) Nat. Mil. Pk. Nat. Pk. Svc., 2002—. Agy. Ea. Nat. coord. Ea. Nat. Bookstore Shiloh Nat. Mil. Pk., 1992—; historian, subject matter advisor Miss. Civil War Battlefield Commn., 2000—; historian NPS Core Study Team, Corinth Spl. Resource Study, Corinth, Miss., 2000—04, NPS Core Study Team: Vicksburg Campaign Trail Spl. Resource Study, Shiloh, 2000—04; historian, subject matter advisor Siege and Battle of Corinth (Miss.) Commn., 1992—; historian Lower Miss. Civil War Task Force, Shiloh, 1995—97; historian, site investigator Civil War Sites Adv. Commn., Shiloh, 1992—93. Author: (Blue & Gray Magazine) Corinth: Crossroads of the Western Confederacy, 2002, (audio cassette, CD tape tour) Battle of Shiloh (Nat. Silver Microphone award, 2001), (guidebook) Blue & Gray Magazine: Shiloh! A Visitor's Guide, 2001, (publn.) Blue & Gray Magazine: Shiloh! Campaign and First Day of Battle; Second Days Battle and Aftermath, 1997, (tour guide) A Guide to the Corinth Campaign of 1862, 1998, (publn.) The Tennessee Conservationist: Hell on the Hatchie, 1998; contbr. Atlas of the Civil War, James A. McPherson, ed.,1994, The Civil War Battlefield Guide, Francis Kennedy, Ed., 1998, Steven E. Woodworth, Ed., 2001. Recipient drama scholarship, Coffeyville C.C., Kans., 1976, Outstanding Achievement in Theater award, Field Kindley Meml. H.S., 1975. Mem.: The Civil War Fortification Study Group (assoc.; editor 1993—, pres. 1999—), Shiloh Battlefield Employees Assn. (assoc.; pres. 1990—2000, treas. 2000—02), NPS Employee and

Alumni Assn. (assoc.), U. of Kans. Alumni Assn. (assoc.), Civil War Historians of the Western Theater (assoc.), Orgn. of Am. Historians (assoc.). Conservative. Achievements include research in Corinth/Battery Robinett Archaeological Investigations; Shiloh National Military Park Archaeological Investigations; Battlefield Investigations: Civil War Sites Advisory Commission; National Park Service, Corinth Special Resource Study; National Park Service, Vicksburg Campaign Trail Special Resource Study. Avocations: hunting, travel, drawing and painting, retriever training, reading. Home: 290 Residence Cir Shiloh TN 38376 Office: Shiloh Nat Mil Pk 1055 Pittsburg Landing Rd Shiloh TN 38376 Office Phone: 731-689-5275 x32. Business E-Mail: stacy_allen@nps.gov.

ALLEN, STANLEY T., architect, dean, educator; BA, Brown U.; BArch, Cooper Union Sch. Arch.; MArch, Princeton U. Dean, prof. Sch. Arch. Princeton U.; arch., prin. Field Ops. Recipient fellowship in arch., N.Y. Found. for Arts, 1986, fellowship in design arts, NEA, 1990, Graham Found. fellowship, 1993. Office: Princeton Univ School of Architecture Princeton NJ 08544

ALLEN, STEPHEN D. (STEPHEN DEAN ALLEN), pathologist, microbiologist; b. Linton, Ind., Sept. 8, 1943; s. Wilburn and Betty Allen; m. Vally C. Autrey, June 17, 1964; children: Christopher D., Amy C. BA, Ind. U., 1965, MA, 1967; MD, Ind. U., Indpls., 1970. Diplomate Am. Bd. Pathology Anatomic and Clin. Pathology and Med. Microbiology. Intern in pathology Vanderbilt U. Hosp., Nashville, 1970-71, resident in pathology, 1971-74; clin. asst. prof. pathology Emory U., Atlanta, 1974-77; asst. prof. clin. pathology Ind. U., Indpls., 1977-79, asst. prof. pathology, 1979-81, assoc. prof. pathology, 1981-86, prof. pathology, 1986-92, prof. pathology and lab. medicine, 1992—, James Warren Smith prof. clin. microbiology, 2006—, assoc. dir. div. clin. microbiology, dept. pathology, 1977-92, dir. grad. progam pathology, 1986—, sr. assoc. chmn. dept. pathology, 1990-91, dir. divsn. clin. microbiology dept. pathology/lab. medicine, 1992-98, assoc. chair dept. pathology and lab. medicine & dir. labs., 1996-99; dir. disease control lab. divsn. Ind. State Dept. Health, Indpls., 1994—2004; dir. divsn. clin. microbiology dept. pathology/lab. medicine Clarian-Meth.-Ind U.-Riley Hosps., 1998—. Mem. residency rev. com. for pathology Accreditation Coun. for Grad. Med. Edn., 1996—2004, mem. residency rev. com. for molecular genetic pathology, 1999—2004, vice chmn., 2003—04, mem. molecular genetic pathology policy com., 1999—; trustee Am. Bd. Pathology, 1995—2006, life trustee, 2007—, chmn. microbiology test devel. and adv. com., 1995—2006, sec. bd., 2001—02, v.p., 2002, pres., 03, immediate past pres., 04. Co-author: Introduction to Diagnostic Microbiology, 1994, Color Atlas and Textbook of Diagnostic Microbiology, 1997, 2006, Direct Smear Atlas, A Monograph of Gram-Stained Smear Preparations of Clinical Specimens, 2001, (CD-ROM) Direct Smear Atlas, 1998, Parasitology Image Atlas, 2003, Mycology Image Atlas, 2004, Bacteriology I Image Atlas, 2005; contbr. With USPHS, 1974—77. Fellow: Binford-Dammin Soc. Infectious Disease Pathologists, Infectious Diseases Soc. Am., Am. Acad. Microbiology, Coll. Am. Pathologists; mem.: Anaerobe Soc. Ams. (mem. coun. 1994—2002, pres. 2002—04), Am. Soc. Clin. Pathologists (coun. microbiology 1983—89), Masons (32d deg.), Shriners, Sigma Xi. Avocations: musicial instruments, fly fishing. Office: Ind U Sch Medicine Clarian Pathology Bldg Rm 6027 350 West 11th St Rm 6027 Indianapolis IN 46202

ALLEN, STEVEN GLEN, economics and business professor; b. Louisville, Mar. 17, 1952; s. Charles Freeman and Lois (Crask) A.; m. Linda L. Pattison, May 19, 1978. BA in Math., Mich. State U., 1973, MA in Econs., 1974; PhD in Econs., Harvard U., 1978. Asst. prof. econs. and bus. N.C. State U., Raleigh, 1978—83, assoc. prof., 1983—87, prof., 1987—, dir. MS mgmt. program, 1993—2002, dir. MBA program, 2002—, assoc. dean grad. programs and rsch., 2003—. Rsch. economist Nat. Bur. Econ. Rsch., Cambridge, Mass., 1983-86, rsch. assoc., 1986—; mem. bd. reviewers Indls. Rels., Berkeley, Calif., 1989—. Contbr. articles to profl. jours. Recipient Allyn Young award Harvard Coll., 1975, 76, Disting. Rsch. and Lit. Publ. award Sch. Humanities and Social Scis., N.C. State U., 1986, Outstanding Rsch. award Coll. Mgmt., 1993; NSF grantee, 1984-86, 87-92, five-time U.S. Dept. Labor grantee; Fulbright scholar, 1991, 93. Mem. Am. Econ. Assn., Soc. Labor Economists. Office: NC State U PO Box 7229 Raleigh NC 27695-7229 Office Phone: 919-515-5584. Business E-Mail: steve_allen@ncsu.edu.

ALLEN, STEVEN JEFFREY, anesthesiologist, educator; b. Abilene, Tex., 1952; MD, U. Tex. Med. Br., Galveston, 1977. Diplomate Am. Bd. Anesthesiology, Am. Bd. Critical Care Medicine. Intern U. Utah Med. Ctr., Salt Lake City, 1977-78; resident in anesthesiology U. Wash., Seattle, 1980-82; fellow in critical care medicine U. Tex. Med. Sch., Houston, 1982-83, prof. anesthesiology, 1983—; med. staff Hermann Hosp., Houston, 1983—; med. dir. Meml. Hermann Hosp., 1996—. Mem. AMA, Am. Soc. Anesthesiologists, Soc. Critical Care Medicine. Office: U Tex HSC Anesthesiology 6431 Fannin MSMB 5 020 Houston TX 77030-1501

ALLEN (SUP), STUART, film and television company executive; b. NYC, July 24, 1943; s. Rudolph and Rita Geraldine (Tellez) Sup; m. Carol Ann Terminelli, June 30, 1982. AA in Engring., NYU, 1961; BA in Commn., Pace U., 1963. Free-lance photographer, photojournalist, NYC, 1963—; producer, dir. Stuart Allen Assocs., Iselin, NJ, 1967-76; pres., chief exec. officer Internat. Media Svcs., Inc., Plainfield, NJ, 1976—; pres., gen. mgr. The Legal Svcs. Group, Plainfield, NJ, 1976—. Mem. adj. faculty roundtable group IEEE. Spl. producer ABC-TV Evil Knievel Snake River Canyon Jump, 1974; author, producer Counterattack, 1978 (One to One Media award 1979), producer, dir. Eagle in the Wind, 1980 (Best Film award 1984); producer 2d unit The Girl Next Door, CBS TV Movie of the Week. Chmn. Plainfield (N.J.) Cultural and Heritage Commn., 1982-96; mcpl. liaison Union County (N.J.) Cultural and Heritage Adv. Bd., 1982-92; trustee Drake House Mus., Plainfield Hist. Soc., 1982-92; dir. Plainfield Econ. Devel. Corp., 1984—; trustee DeCret Sch. of Arts, 1990—; vice chmn. Plainfield City Coun. Budget Adv. Com., 1992-94; mem. Ctrl. Jersey C. of C. N.J. State Council Arts grantee, 1979, 86. Mem. Indsl. Photographers Assn. N.J. (pres. 1976-77, award of Excellence), Internat. TV Assn., Am. Film Inst., Internat. Platform Assn., Am. Coll. Forensic Examiners, Am. Bd. Recorded Evidence, Soc. Motion Picture and TV Engrs., Marco Polo Club (Chgo.). Avocations: travel, exploration, fishing. Home and Office: 718 Sherman Ave Plainfield NJ 07060-2232 Home Phone: 908-756-4060; Office Phone: 908-756-4060. E-mail: stuartallen@intlmediasvc.com.

ALLEN, SUSAN DIANE, educator; b. Ithaca, NY, Jan. 5, 1954; d. Bruce Richard and Judith Diane Schueler; m. Terrence Paul Allen, Aug. 6, 1977; children: Christopher Kirk, Justin Thomas. BS in Edn., SUNY, Fredonia, 1976; MS in Edn., SUNY, Buffalo, 1979; cert. in coaching, Batavia, 2006. Cert. permanent tchg. Dept. Edn. N.Y., 1979. Adminstrv. asst. Empire State Coll., Buffalo, 1977—78; tchr. Attica Ctrl. Sch., NY, 1978—. Advisor student coun. Attica Ctrl. Sch., 1978—, soccer coach, 1979—81, advisor yearbook, 1988—, varsity soccer coach, jr. varsity coach, modified coach, 1997—; coord. United Schools In Action, Attica, 2001—. Bd. dirs. Attica Youth Athletics, Attica, 1990—97, Angel Action, Perry, NY, 2000—. Named Educator of Week, Channel 2, Buffalo, 2006, Citizen of Yr., Lion's Club, 2006; recipient Adult Vol. award, Wyo. County Youth Bd., 2002, 2004, Outstanding Orgn. for Youth award, 2004. Mem.: Delta Kappa Gamma. Avocations: racquetball, reading, bicycling. Home: 3043 Dunbar Rd Attica NY 14011 Office: Attica Ctrl Sch 3338 E Main St Attica NY 14011 Office Phone: 585-591-0400 ext. 1164. Business E-Mail: sallen@atticacsd.org.

ALLEN, SUZANNE, financial planning executive, insurance agent, writer, educator; b. Santa Monica, Calif., May 31, 1963; d. Raymond A. and Ethel Allen; m. Steve Milstein Roth, Dec. 27, 1992, (div. 2000). BA, U. Calif., Santa Cruz, 1986; MA in Edn., Calif. State U., LA, 1990. Cert. tchr., Calif.; lic. real estate agt., Calif. Interviewer LA Times Newspaper, 1986-88; educator LA Unified Sch. Dist., 1987-90, Burbank Unified Sch. Dist., Calif., 1990-94, 1994—2000; ptnr. fin. svc. Roth & Assoc./NY Life, LA, 1993-2000; educator Pasadena Unified Sch. Dist., 2001—02; ptnr. fin. svc. Pacific Life Ins. Co.; v.p. Jarvis & Mandell LLC Estate Planning Svc., Mass. Mut. Ins. Co., 2001—; agt. Mass. Mut. Ins., Beverly Hills, Calif. Ptnr. Retirement Educators Fin. Svc.; agt.-cons. Frasier Fin. Group, 2001—02; bilingual program coord. Amadeo Spanish Lang. Enrichment Sch., 2004—. Model, actor:, 1998—; author: End of Days, 2001—, numerous poems, Gospel in the Air, 2005 (named Best Poems and Poets, Libr. Cong., 2005), (albums) Sound of Poetry, 2005. Mem. PTA, United Tchr. Pasadena, Civil War Trust; vol. SPCA/Humane Soc., 1999—; mem. Nat. Trust Hist. Preservation, Honor Roll mem.; bd. mem. Bungalow Heaven Neighborhood Assn.; hon. mem. Top Bus. Rep. Party for Sen. Tom Delany. Recipient 4 Silver Cups, Internat. Poet of Merit, 8 Bronze medals, Internat. Poets Soc., Piece of the Roof award, N.Y. Life Ins. Co. for Roth & Assocs., 1994, Nat. Leadership award, Nat. Rep. Congl. Com., 2003, Silver trophy Outstanding Achievement in Poetry, 2003, 2004, 2005, 2006. Mem.: NEA, Libr. of Congress, Nat. Soc. for Hist. Preservation, Burbank Tchrs. Union, U. Calif. Santa Cruz Alumni Assn., Internat. High IQ Soc., Abraham Lincoln Assn., Internat. Soc. Poets (hon.). Avocations: painting, jewelry designing, writing, weight training, quilting. Office: Michael's Agy Mass Mut Beverly Hills Office 1875 Century Park E # 1550 Los Angeles CA 90067 also: Jarvis And Mandell Llc 2321 Rosecrans Ave Ste 1280 El Segundo CA 90245-4933 Office Phone: 626-296-8479.

ALLEN, TED, television personality; b. 1965; life ptnr. Barry Rice. Co-author: Things a Man Should Know About Marriage: A Groom's Guide to the Wedding and Beyond, 1999, Things a Man Should Know About Style, 1999, Things a Man Should Know About Sex, 2001, Things a Man Should Know About Handshakes, White Lies and Which Fork Goes Where, 2001, Queer Eye for the Straight Guy: The Fab 5's Guide to Looking Better, Cooking Better, Dressing Better, Behaving Better, and Living Better, 2004, (cookbooks) The Food You Want to Eat: 100 Smart, Simple Recipes, 2005; co-author and contbg. editor: Things a Man Should Know column Esquire mag., contbg. author: Conde Nast Traveler, Travel & Leisure, GQ, Nat. Geog. Adventure, Self, Men's Jour., Women.Com, Chgo. Sun-Times; sr. editor and restaurant critic Chgo. mag., food and wine specialist (TV series) Queer Eye for the Straight Guy, 2003—, judge Top Chef, Bravo, 2007. Office: William Morris Agy One William Morris Pl Beverly Hills CA 90212

ALLEN, TERRENCE R., lawyer; b. Phila., 1967; BA cum laude, BS cum laude, Univ. So. Calif., 1989; JD, Univ. So. Calif., 1993. Bar: Calif. 1993. Ptnr., corp. law practice O'Melveny & Myers LLP, Newport Beach, Calif. Named a Rising Star, So. Calif. Super Lawyers, 2004—06. Office: O'Melveny & Myers LLP 17th Fl 610 Newport Ctr Dr Newport Beach CA 92660 Office Phone: 949-823-6930. Office Fax: 949-823-6994. Business E-Mail: tallen@omm.com.

ALLEN, THAD WILLIAM, career military officer; b. Tucson, Jan. 16, 1949; s. Clyde and Wilma Allen; m. Pamela A. Hess; children: Amanda, Meghan, Lucas. Grad., USCG Acad., 1971; MPA, George Washington U.; MS, Sloan Sch. Mgmt., MIT. Advanced through ranks to admiral USCG, 2006, previous flag assignments include commdg. the Seventh Coast Guard Dist., previous flag assignments include directing all Coast Guard ops. in SC, Ga., Fla., and the Caribbean, dir. resources, comdr. Coast Guard Atlantic Area, Fifth Coast Guard Dist., operational comdr. US Maritime Def. Zone, Atlantic Portsmouth, Va., chief of staff Washington, 2002—06, commdg. officer Coast Guard Hdqs., 2002—06, comdt., 2006—; chmn. Joints Requirement Coun. US Dept. Homeland Security, 2003—06, prin. fed. ofcl. Hurricanes Katrina & Rita, 2005—06, comdr. Hurricane Katrina Relief Effort, 2005—06. Specialist for Coast Guard cutters ANDROSCOGGIN, GALLATIN, CITRUS; coastal ops. assignments include Capt. of the Port Group Long Island Sound, Conn., Group Atlantic City, NJ, and LORAN Sta., Thailand; search and rescue controller Greater Antilles Sect., San Juan; intelligence watch officer DEA/INS El Paso Intelligence Ctr., Tex.; chief budget officer Maintenance and Logistics Command, Atlantic, Governors Island, NY; dep. project mgr. Fleet Modernization and Rehabilitation (FRAM) Project; asst. divsn. chief, programs divsn., Office Chief of Staff Coast Guard Hdqs. Recipient Alumni Achievement award, George Washington U., 2006. Fellow: Nat. Acad. Pub. Adminstrn. Office: USCG Hdqs 2100 Second St SW Washington DC 20593*

ALLEN, THOMAS DRAPER, lawyer; b. Detroit, June 25, 1926; s. Draper and Florence (Jones) A.; m. Joyce M. Johnson, July 18, 1953; children— Nancy A. Bowser, Robert D., Rebecca A. Hubbard. BS, Northwestern U., 1949; JD, U. Mich., 1952. Bar: Ill. 1952, U.S. Supreme Ct. 1971. Assoc. Kirkland & Ellis, Chgo., 1952-60, ptnr., 1961-67, Wildman, Harrold, Allen & Dixon, Chgo., 1967-96, of counsel, 1997—. Chmn. Community Caucus, Hinsdale, Ill., 1960-61; mem. Hinsdale Bd. Edn., 1965-71, pres., 1970-71; pres. West Suburban coun. Boy Scouts Am., 1980-82, mem. nat. exec. bd., 1986-2006, chmn. internat. com., 1995-99, chmn. resolutions com., 1995-2006, mem. world program com., 1983-93, mem. nat. adv. coun. 2006—; moderator Union Ch., Hinsdale, 1983-84; trustee Chgo. Theol. Sem., 1988-97, chair, 1990-96, life trustee, 1997—. With USN, 1944-46. Recipient Silver Beaver award Boy Scouts Am., 1964, Silver Buffalo award, 1997, Bronze Wolf award World Scout Orgn., 1993. Fellow Am. Coll. Trial Lawyers (state chair 1984-85, chair internat. com. 1997-99); mem. ABA, Ill. Bar Assn., Chgo. Bar Assn. (bd. of mgrs 1989-91), Law Club of Chgo., Legal Club of Chgo., Jaycees Internat. (senator, 1965), Internat. Bar Assn., Hinsdale Golf Club. Mem. United Ch. of Christ. Home: 505 N Lake Shore Dr Chicago IL 60611-3427 Office: Wildman Harrold Allen & Dixon 225 W Wacker Dr Chicago IL 60606-1224 Office Phone: 312-201-2630. Business E-Mail: allen@wildman.com.

ALLEN, THOMAS E., obstetrician, gynecologist; b. Bairdford, Pa., July 2, 1919; s. Emerson Ray and Lillie Mabel (McIntyre) A.; m. Ruth Jenkins, 1943 (dec. 1991); m. Judi Cannava, 1995; children: Catherine, Christine, Cynthia, Carolyn, Thomas J., Candace. BS, U. Pitts., 1940, MD, 1943. Diplomate Am. Bd. Ob-Gyn. Rotating intern U. Pitts., 1944, assoc. clin. prof. ob-gyn. Sch. Medicine; resident in gynegology Magee Hosp., Pitts., 1944-45, resident in ob-gyn., 1948-51; gen. practice medicine Oakmont, Pa., 1947-48; practice medicine specializing in ob-gyn. Pitts., 1951—. Med. dir., co-founder Women's Health Service, Inc., Pitts., 1973-94, cons., 1994—; cons. ob-gyn Russelton Med. Group, New Kensington, Pa., 1953-73. Pres. Oakmont Sch. Bd., 1962-71; pres. bd. dirs. Am. Waterways Wind Orch., Pitts., 1970-93, chmn. bd. dirs., 1993—; bd. dirs. ACLU, Pitts., 1972-90. Served to capt. U.S. Army, 1945-47. Am. Legion and Buhl scholar, 1937. Fellow ACS, Am. Coll. Obstetricians and Gynecologists, Pan Pacific Surg. Assn., Pitts. Ob-gyn. Soc.; mem. AMA, county and state med. assns. Democrat. Avocations: cooking, music, reading, golf. Home: 301 Halket St Pittsburgh PA 15213-3104 Office: Planned Parenthood 933 Liberty Ave Pittsburgh PA 15222-3783 Office Phone: 412-687-5785. E-mail: tomjud@verizon.net, ccann19601@aol.com.

ALLEN, THOMAS H., congressman, lawyer; b. Portland, Maine, Apr. 16, 1945; s. Charles and Genevieve A.; m. Diana Bell; children: Gwen, Kate. BA, Bowdoin Coll., 1967; BPhil, Oxford U., 1970; JD, Harvard U., 1971. Atty. Drummond, Woodsum, Plimpton and MacMahon, Maine, 1974—94; mem. Portland (Maine) City Coun., 1989-95; mayor City of Portland, 1991-92; mem. U.S. Congress from 1st Maine dist., 1997—, armed svcs. com., energy & commerce com., dep. whip-at-large, former mem. govt. reform and oversight com., co-chair, affordable medicines task force & bipartisan house oceans caucus. Dem. candidate for Gov., State of Maine, 1994; chair Clinton/Gore campaign, Maine, 1992; mem. Pres. Clinton's Agrl. Transition Team; bd. overseers Bowdoin Coll.; bd. dirs. Shalom House, United Way; chair Gov. Joseph Brennan Task Force on Foster Care for Children; pres. Portland Stage Co.; mem. exec. and legis. policy coms. Maine Mcpl. Assn. Rhodes scholar Oxford U. Mem.: Phi Beta Kappa. Democrat. Office: US Ho Reps 1127 Longworth Ho Office Bldg Washington DC 20515-1901 also: Portland Dist Off Ste 302 57 Exchange St Portland ME 04101 Business E-Mail: rep.tomallen@mail.house.gov.*

ALLEN, THOMAS JOHN, business educator; b. Newark, Aug. 20, 1931; s. Thomas John and Margaret Ann (Conley) A.; m. Joan Marie Gilmartin, Jan. 28, 1961; children: Thomas John, Susan Marie, Máirín. BS, Upsala Coll., East Orange, NJ, 1954; postgrad., U. Wash., 1957-58; SM, MIT, 1963, PhD, 1966; PhD (hon.), Ramon Llull U., Spain, 2003; D Mgmt. (hon.), Rijkuniversiteit Gent, Belgium, 1990; DSc (hon.), Chalmers U. Tech., Gothenburg, Sweden, 1992; D in Engring. (hon.), Linkoping U., Sweden, 1998. Design engr. Tung-Sol Electric Co., Bloomfield, NJ, 1956-57; research engr. Boeing Co., Seattle, 1957-64; research assoc. MIT, Cambridge, 1963-66, assoc. chmn. faculty, 1983-85, MacVicar faculty fellow Cambridge, 1993—; dep. dean, Howard W. Johnson prof. mgmt. Sloan Sch. Mgmt., 1993—98; co-dir. Leader for Mfg. program, system design mgmt. program MIT, 2003—. Disting. vis. prof. U. Coll. Dublin, Ireland, 1993; hon. mem. of faculty Chalmers U. of Tech., Gothenburg, Sweden, 1992—. Author: Managing the Flow of Technology, 1977; co-author (with M.S. Scott Morton) Information Technology and the Corporation of the 1990s, 1993, Lean Enterprise Value: Insights from MIT's Lean Aerospace Initiative, 2002 (Engring. Sci. Book award Internat. Acad. Astronautics 2003), (with G.W. Henn) The Organization and Architecture of Innovation, 2006. Chmn. Cath.-Jewish Com., Boston, 1977-79; chmn. bd. Rosary Acad., Watertown, Mass., 1976-79; trustee Mt. St. Joseph Acad., Boston, 1992-98, 99-04. Served USMC, 1954—56. Hon. sr. rsch. fellow U. Manchester, 1970—; Macvicar Faculty fellow, MIT, 1993—; named disting. vis. prof. U. Coll. Dublin, Ireland, 1993. Fellow AAAS; mem. IEEE, Am. Psychol. Assn., Irish Am. Cultural Assn., Sigma Xi Office: Mass Inst Tech 77 Massachusetts Ave E52-536 Cambridge MA 02142-1347 Home Phone: 781-639-1732. Business E-Mail: tallen@mit.edu.

ALLEN, TIM (TIMOTHY ALLEN DICK), actor, comedian; b. Denver, June 13, 1953; s. Gerald and Martha Dick; m. Laura Diebel, Apr. 7, 1984 (div. Mar. 2003); 1 child, Kady; m. Jane Hajduk, Oct. 7, 2006. Grad., Western Mich. U., 1975. Appeared in numerous Showtime spls.; actor: (TV series) Home Improvement, 1991-99 (Emmy award nomination, Lead actor - comedy 1993), exec. prodr., 1996-99, also writer; (films) The Santa Clause, 1994; (voice) Toy Story, 1995, Meet Wally Sparks, 1997, Jungle 2 Jungle, 1997, For Richer or Poorer, 1997, (voice) Toy Story 2, 1999, Galaxy Quest, 1999, Who is Cletis Tout, 2001, Joe Somebody, 2001, Big Trouble, 2002, The Santa Clause 2, 2002, Christmas with the Kranks, 2004, The Shaggy Dog, 2006, Zoom, 2006, The Santa Clause 3: The Escape Clause, 2006, Wild Hogs, 2007; (TV films) (voice) Jimmy Neutron: You Bet Your Life Form, 2004, (TV spls.) Comedy's Dirtiest Dozen, 1988, exec. prodr. Men Are Pigs, 1991; author: I'm Not Really Here, 1996, Don't Stand Too Close to a Naked Man, 1994; TV guest appearances The Flying Doctors, 1985, The Drew Carey Show, 1995, The Front, 1996, Soul Man, 1997, The Larry Sanders Show, 1992, Spin City, 1996, (voice) The Adventures of Jimmy Neutron: Boy Genius, 2004; exec. com. TV series Home Improvement, 1991. Recipient Golden Globe, 1995, Favorite Comedy Actor People's Choice award, 1995,97, 98, 99, TV Guide award 1999; nominated for Golden Globe awards 1993, 94, 96, 97, Blockbuster Entertainment award 1998. Office: William Morris Agy 151 El Camino Dr Beverly Hills CA 90212 Address: care Messina Baker 955 S Carillo Dr Ste 100 Los Angeles CA 90048*

ALLEN, TONI K., lawyer; b. NYC, Aug. 6, 1940; d. Irving M. and Mary (Sackler) Schoolman; m. Robert W. Clark III, July 22, 1985. AB, Wellesley Coll., 1960; LLB, NYU, 1964. Bar: NY 1964, DC 1972. Atty. Office of Irving M. Wall, Esquire, NYC, 1964-68; gen. counsel, asst. to pres. Nat. Econ. Rsch. Assocs., NYC, 1968-71; atty., advisor Postal Rate Commn., Washington, 1971-72; assoc. Wald, Harkrader & Ross, Washington, 1972-73, ptnr., 1974-85, Piper & Marbury LLP, Washington, 1986-98, chmn. environ. dept., 1991-94, mem. policy and mgmt. com., 1992-94, ptnr. emeritus, 1999—. Adj. fellow Hudson Inst., 2001—. Trustee Levine Sch. Music, Washington, 1981—2004, pres., 1991-96; co-chair exec. bd. Environ. Lawyer, 1994-96, Leadership Washington, 1996-97; bd. dirs., 2003—, vice chair United Way of the Nat. Capital Area, 2003—05, treas. 2005-06. Fellow Am. Bar Found.; mem. Order of Coif. Democrat. Avocations: sports, music, travel, cooking. E-mail: tka5640@aol.com.

ALLEN, TONY, professional basketball player; b. Jan. 11, 1982; Attended, Okla. State. Basketball player Boston Celtics, 2004—. Office: The Boston Celtics 100 Legends Way Boston MA 02114

ALLEN, WALTER RECHARDE, sociology educator; b. Kansas City, Mo., Feb. 3, 1949; s. Grady Lee and Freddie Mae (Clayton) Allen; m. Wilma Jean Sharber, Sept. 26, 1970 (dec.); children: Rena Marie, Binti Tamarra, Bryan Recharde. BA, Beloit Coll., Wis., 1971; MA, U. Chgo., 1973, PhD, 1975. Asst. prof. sociology U. NC, Chapel Hill, 1974-79; asst. prof. sociology, Afro-Am. and African studies U. Mich., Ann Arbor, 1979-84, assoc. prof. sociology, Afro-Am. and African studies, 1985-88, assoc. dir. Cen. for Afro-Am. Studies, 1987-89, dir. Nat. Study Black Coll. Students, 1979-89, prof. sociology Afro-Am. and African studies, 1989-91; prof. sociology UCLA, 1989, assoc. dir. Robert Wood Johnson clin. scholars program, Sch. Medicine, 1992—97, prof. grad. sch. edn. & info. studies, 2004—. Co-author: The Colorline and the Quality of Life, 1987, African American Education: Race Community, Inequality and Achievement-A Tribute to Edgar G. Epps, 2006, Higher Education in a Global Society: Achieving Diversity, Equity, and Excellence, 2006,; co-editor: (book) Beginnings: Development of Black Children, 1985, College in Black and White, 1991; (bibliography) Black Families, 1965-80, 1986. Recipient distinguished leadership award United Negro Coll. Fund, 1985; Rockefeller Found. fellow, 1982-83, Fulbright scholar, 1984, 86-87; named Allerton Lectr. U. Ill., 1988. Mem. Internat. Sociol. Assn., Am. Sociol. Assn. (coun. 1991-94), Am. Edml. Rsch. Assn. (disting. scholar 1987, rsch. excellence award, 1993), Assn. Black Sociologists (pres. 1992, disting. career award 1995), Assn. Study Higher Edn. (spl. merit award 2002), Sociol. Rsch. Assn., Phi Delta Kappa. Baptist. Avocations: reading, travel, swimming, gardening. Office: UCLA Dept grad sch edn & info studies 405 Hilgard Ave Los Angeles CA 90095-1521 Office Phone: 310-206-7107. Personal E-mail: walterrallen@yahoo.com. Business E-Mail: wallen@ucla.edu.

ALLEN, WILLIAM HAYES, lawyer, educator; b. Palo Alto, Calif., Oct. 19, 1926; s. Ben Shannon and Victoria Rose (French) Allen; m. Joan Webster Emmett, July 16, 1950 (dec. Oct. 2005); children: Edwin Hayes, Neal French, William Kent. Student, Deep Springs Coll., 1942—44; BA with gt. distinction, Stanford U., 1948, LLB, 1956. Bar: D.C. 1958. Corr. AP, Fresno, Calif., 1948—49, newsman Sacramento, 1950—53; law clk. to Chief Justice Earl Warren U.S. Supreme Ct., Washington, 1956—57; assoc. Covington & Burling, Washington, 1957—64, ptnr., 1964—92; ret., 1993. Acting. prof. Stanford U. Law Sch., 1979; adj. prof. Howard U. Law Sch., 1981—83; lectr. George Mason U. Law Sch., 1983—86; practitioner-in-residence Cornell U. Law Sch., 1992; vis. prof. Deep Springs Coll., 1973,

96, 2007; chmn. jud. rev. com. Adminstrv. Conf. U.S., 1972—82, sr. conf. fellow, 1982—95; mem. steering com. Nat. Prison Project, 1975—93. Pres. Stanford Law Rev., vol. 8, 1955-56; contbr. articles to legal jours. Trustee Deep Springs Coll., 1984-92, chmn. bd. trustees, 1992; mem. Fair Housing Bd., Arlington County, Va., 1974-79. With U.S. Army, 1945-47. Mem. ABA (mem. coun. adminstrv. law sect. 1969-72, 79-81, chmn. 1982-83), D.C. Bar (chmn. legal ethics com. 1976-78); Am. Law Inst., Am. Acad. of Appellate Lawyers, Order of Coif, Cosmos Club. Democrat. Mem. United Ch. Of Christ. Office Phone: 202-662-5420. Personal E-mail: billthedog2001@comcast.net.

ALLEN, WILLIAM JERE, minister; b. Greenville, Miss., Apr. 23, 1934; s. Marion Goodman and Gradie Lee (Yates) A.; m. Lorena Faye Franklin, June 24, 1960; children: Lorena Lynn Brickson, Jennifer Dawn Moradi, William Jere Allen Jr. B of Bldg. Constrn., Auburn U., 1956; BDiv, So. Bapt. Theol. Sem., 1963; DMin, Union Theol. Sem., 1973. Ordained to ministry First Bapt. Ch., 1960. Pastor 45th Street Mission, Ashland, Ky., 1959-60, Rose Hill Bapt. Ch., Ashland, 1960-62, Colonial Ave. Bapt. Ch., Roanoke, Va., 1962-67, Bainbridge St. Bapt. Ch., Richmond, Va., 1967-71, Bainbridge Southampton Bapt. Ch., Richmond, 1972-75; cons., dir. spl. missions dept. Ala. Bapt. State Conv., Montgomery, 1975-79; assoc. then dir. met. mission dept. Home Mission Bd., So. Bapt. Conv., Atlanta, 1979-91; exec. dir., min. D.C. Bapt. Conv., Washington, 1992-2000; interim pastor Calvary Bapt. Ch., Washington, 2001—03, Broadview Bapt. Ch., Chesapeake Beach, Md., 2004—05, Washington Plz. Bapt. Ch., Reston, Va., 2006—. Mega focus cities cons. Home Mission Bd., So. Bapt. Conv., Atlanta, 1982—2002. Co-author: Shaping a Future for Church in Changing Community, 1981, Church and Community Diagnostic Workbook, 1986; author: (with others) Shooting the Rapids: Efective Ministry in a Changing World, 1990, Faith and Social Ministry: Ten Christian Perspectives, 1990. Capt. USAF, 1956—62. Baptist. Avocations: jogging, reading, golf. Home: 3041 Chestnut St NW Washington DC 20015-1407

ALLEN, WILLIAM RICHARD, retired economist; b. Eldorado, Ill., Apr. 3, 1924; s. Oliver Boyd and Justa Lee (Wingo) A.; m. Frances Lorraine Swoboda, Aug. 15, 1948 (dec.); children: Janet Elizabeth, Sandra Lee. AB, Cornell Coll., Iowa, 1948; PhD, Duke U., 1953. Faculty, Washington U., St. Louis, 1951-52; faculty UCLA, 1952—, prof., 1963-91, prof. emeritus, 1991—. Vis. prof. Northwestern U., 1952, U. Wis., 1964, U. Mich., 1965, So. Ill. U., 1969, Tex. A&M, 1971-73; cons. Dept. Commerce, 1962; v.p. Found. Rsch. in Econs. and Edn., 1971-73; pres. Internat. Inst. Econ. Rsch., 1974-86; v.p. Inst. for Contemporary Studies, 1986-90; assoc. Reason Found., 1990-92; econs. corr. Calif. Polit. Rev., 1992-2002; newspaper, mag. columnist; nationally syndicated radio commentator, 1979-92. Author: (with others) Foreign Trade and Finance, 1959, Essays in Economic Thought, 1960, University Economics, 3d edit., 1972, Exchange and Production, 3d edit., 1983, International Trade Theory, 1965, Midnight Economist, 1981, vol. 2, 1989, vol. 3, 1997; mem. adv. bd.: History of Polit. Economy, 1969-84, Social Sci. Quar., 1975-2003; contbr. articles to profl. jours. Served with USAAF, 1943-46. Social Sci. Research Council grantee, 1950-51, 62; Ford Found. grantee, 1958-59, 72-74; NSF grantee, 1965-66; Earhart Found. grantee, 1972, 74-75 Mem. Western Econ. Soc. (pres. 1970-71), So. Econ. Assn. (v.p. 1978-79), History of Econs. Soc. (v.p. 1974-75), Phi Beta Kappa. Home: 11809 Allaseba Dr Los Angeles CA 90066-1112 Office Phone: 310-825-1011. Personal E-mail: midnightecon@mac.com. Business E-Mail: allen@econ.ucla.edu.

ALLEN, WILLIAM SHERIDAN, retired social sciences educator; b. Evanston, Ill., Oct. 5, 1932; s. William S. and Rose (Brahm) Allen; m. Karen Miller, Jan. 9, 1982; children: Caitilyn, Jefferson, Rebecca, Claire. AB, U. Mich., 1955; MA, U. Conn., 1956; PhD, U. Minn., 1962. Instr. history Bay City (Mich.) Jr. Coll., 1957-58; instr. humanities MIT, Cambridge, Mass., 1960-61; asst. prof. history U. Mo., Columbia, 1961-65, assoc. prof., 1966-67, Wayne State U., Detroit, 1967-70; prof. SUNY, Buffalo, 1970-2001, chmn. history dept., 1987-90. Vis. prof. U. Mich., Ann Arbor, 1967; cons. Time-Life Books, Alexandria, Va., 1988—89. Author: (book) The Nazi Seizure of Power, 1984; editor, translator: book The Infancy of Nazism, 1976; contbr. articles to profl. jours. V.p. Holocaust Resources Ctr., Buffalo, 1985—90; publicity chmn. Buffalo Group Amnesty Internat., 1985—87; dir. Parkside Fed. Credit Union, Buffalo, 1986—87. Fellow, Alexander von Humboldt Found., 1965—66, NEH, 1979. Mem.: United Univ. Profs. (pres. Buffalo chpt. 1978—81), N.Y. State Assn. European Historians (pres. 1983—84), Am. Conf. Irish Studies. Avocations: sailing, gardening.

ALLEN, WILLIAM THOMAS, law educator; b. Phila., July 17, 1944; s. E. William and Mary E. (Graef) Allen. BS, NYU, 1969; JD, U. Tex., 1972; LLD (hon.), Dickinson Law Sch., Pa. State U. Law clk. to Hon. Walter King Stapleton US Dist. Ct. Dist. Del., Wilmington, 1972-74; assoc. Morris, Nichols, Arsht & Tunnell, Wilmington, 1974-79, partner, 1979-85; chancellor Ct. Chancery, State of Del., Wilmington, 1985-97; Nusbaum prof. law & bus. NYU Sch. Law & Stern Sch. Bus., NYC, dir. Ctr. for Law and Bus., 1997—; of counsel Wachtell, Lipton, Rosen & Katz, NYC, 1997—. Flegler vis. prof. Stanford Law Sch., 1989, 93; adj. prof. law U. Pa. Law Sch., 1991-93, 95; Raben lectr. Yale Law Sch., 1996. Trustee U. Del., Newark, 1997—2003. Recipient Chief Justice Award for Jud. Svc., Del. Supreme Ct., 1997. Fellow Am. Acad. Arts & Sciences; mem. AICPA (chmn. Independence Standards Bd. 1997-2000), ABA, Am. Law Inst., Am. Economics Assn. Office: NYU Stern Sch Bus Kaufman Mgmt Ctr 44 W 4th St New York NY 10012-1126 also: NYU Sch Law Vanderbilt Hall Rm 336B 40 Washington Sq S New York NY 10012-1099 Office Phone: 212-403-1261. Business E-Mail: WTA1@nyu.edu.

ALLEN, WOODY (ALLEN STEWART KONIGSBERG), director, actor, writer; b. NYC, Dec. 1, 1935; s. Martin and Nettie (Cherry) Konigsberg; m. Harlene Rosen, Mar. 15, 1956 (div. 1962); m. Louise Lasser, Feb. 2, 1966 (div. 1969); ptnr. Mia Farrow; 1 child , Satchel; adopted children: Moses, Dylan; m. Soon-Yi Previn, Dec. 22, 1997; adopted children: Bechet, Manzie Tio Student, NYU, 1953, CCNY, 1953. Writer TV comedy for Sid Caesar, 1957, Art Carney, 1958-59, Herb Shriner, 1953; appeared in numerous nightclubs, TV shows, from 1961; actor: (films) What's New Pussycat?, 1964, The Front, 1976, King Lear, 1988, Scenes From a Mall, 1990, Cannes.les 400 coups, 1997, Waiting for Woody, 1998, Impostors, 1998, (voice only) Antz, 1998, Wild Man Blues, 1998, Stuck on You, 1998, Company Man, 1999 Picking Up the Pieces, 1999; actor, dir., writer: (films) Take the Money and Run, 1969, Bananas, 1971, What's Up Tiger Lily?, 1966, Everything You Always Wanted to Know About Sex But Were Afraid to Ask, 1972, Sleeper, 1973, Love and Death, 1975, Manhattan, 1979 (Brit. Acad. award 1979, N.Y. Film Critics award), Stardust Memories, 1980; actor, dir., prodr., writer: (films) Annie Hall, 1977 (N.Y. Film Critics Circle award for Best Dir. and Best Screenplay 1977, Acad. Awards for Best Picture, Best Director, Nat. Soc. Film Critics Screenwriting award), Zelig, 1983, Broadway Danny Rose, 1984, Hannah and Her Sisters, 1986 (Acad. Award for Best Screenplay, D.W. Griffith award for Best Dir., Nat. Bd. Rev. Motion Pictures), New York Stories (Oedipus Wrecks segment), 1989, Mighty Aphrodite, 1995, Everyone Says I Love You, 1996, Deconstructing Harry, 1997, Count Mercury Goes to the Suburbs, 1997, Sweet and Lowdown, 1999, Small Town Crooks, 2000, The Curse of the Jade Scorpion, 2001, Hollywood Ending, 2002, Anytyhing Else, 2003, Scoop, 2006; writer, dir.: (films) Radio Days, 1987; dir., writer: (films) Interiors, 1978, Purple Rose of Cairo, 1985, A Midsummer Night's Sex Comedy, 1982, September, 1987, Another Woman, 1988, Crimes and Misdemeanors, 1989, Alice, 1990, Shadows and Fog, 1992, Husbands and Wives, 1992, Manhattan Murder Mystery, 1993, Bullets Over Broadway, 1994, Celebrity, 1998, Melinda and Melinda, 2004, Match Point, 2005; author play: Don't Drink the Water, 1966 (actor, dir. of TV movie, 1994), The Floating Lightbulb, 1981, (one act) Death Defying Acts, 1995, Sounds from a Town I Love (TV movie), 2001; play, screenplay Play It Again, Sam, 1969, film, 1972; author: Getting Even, 1971, Without Feathers, 1975, Side Effects, 1980, Mere Anarchy, 2007; (TV appearances) Just Shoot Me; writer, director (off broadway play) A Second Hand Memory, 2004 Recipient Sylvania award, 1957; Spl. award Berlin Film Festival, 1975 Democrat.

ALLENDER, JOHN ROLAND, lawyer; b. Boone, Iowa, Oct. 22, 1950; s. John S. and C. Corinne (Hayes) A.; m. Patti Allender; children: Susan A., Andrew J. BS, Iowa State U., 1972; JD, U. San Diego, 1975; LLM in Taxation, NYU, 1976. Bar: Calif. 1976, Tex. 1977, US Ct. Claims 1977, US Tax. Ct. 1977, US Dist. Ct. (so. dist.) Tex. 1977. Assoc. Fulbright & Jaworski LLP, Houston, 1976-83, ptnr., 1983—, and head, tax dept. Mem. adv. commn. Tex. Bd. Legal Specialization, 1986-2000. Bd. dirs. Ronald McDonald House, Houston, 1991—, pres. 2003-05, Cath. Charities, Houston/Galveston; trustee S.W. Rsch. Inst. Mem. State Bar of Tex. (chmn. sect. taxation 1990), Houston Bar Assn. (chmn. sect. taxation 1979). Office: Fulbright & Jaworski Ste 5100 1301 McKinney St Houston TX 77010-3031 Office Phone: 713-651-5151. Office Fax: 713-651-5246. Business E-Mail: jallender@fulbright.com.

ALLENDER, JULIE ANN, psychologist; b. Elmhurst, Ill., Feb. 27, 1950; d. Frank and Edith (Gluklick) A.; m. Louis Zivic, May 18, 1980 (div.); 1 child, Jonathan Ephriam Allender-Zivic. BS in Psychology, U. Ill., 1973; MEd in Psychoednl. Processes, Temple U., 1974, EdD in Psychoednl. Processes, 1978. Lic. psychologist, Pa., Mass.; cert. sch. psychologist, Pa. Asst. prin. Beth Or Congregation Religious Sch., Spring House, Pa., 1977-78; dir. Homebased Businesswomen's Network, Lebanon, Pa., 1983-88; pvt. practice psychologist Lebanon, 1980—; staff cons. Good Samaritan Hosp., 1989—, Ctrl. Montgomery Med. Ctr., 2004—. Former adj. faculty Community Coll. Phila., Temple U., Phila., Phila. Coll. Textile & Scis., Thomas Jefferson U. Med. Sch., Phila., Wheelock Coll., Boston, Pa. State U., Hershey, Reading; cons. med. staff Good Samaritan Hosp.; pvt. practice therapy, consultation and testing Pa. Coll. Optometry, Phila., Headstart, Chgo., Peabody (Mass.) Pub. Schs., Lynn (Mass.) Hist. Soc., Mich. Edn. Assn., Lansing, Dept. Agr. Extension Program, Lebanon, Pa., Lebanon Valley Coll., Annville, Pa., other orgns. Author: End of My Rope: Gender Cooperation Model, 1996, Chronic Illnes: Helping the Wounded Heart, 1999, (ednl. program) Kids Concern, 1996; contbr. articles to profl. jours. and newspapers, chpts. to books; participant media programs Sta. WRKO, Boston, 1983, Sta. WVLV, Lebanon, 1983-84, Sta. WAHT, Lebanon, 1988-90. Active Potential Reentry Opportunities in Bus. and Edn., 1986—, Homebased Businesswomen's Network of the Lebanon Valley, 1983-88; mem. women in bus. com. Lebanon C. of C., 1985-87; bd. dirs. Assn. for Humanistic Edn., 1983-87; mem. women's pavilion adv. bd. Lebanon Valley Gen. Hosp., 1986-90; bd. dirs. Interagency Mental Health Coun., Inc., 1995-99. Mem. APA, ASTD, Pa. Psychol. Assn., Lancaster-Lebanon Psychol. Assn. (treas. 1990-2000. pres. 1999-2000), Orthopsychiat. Assn., Assn. for Humanistic Psychology. Jewish. Home Phone: 215-799-2222; Office Phone: 215-799-2220. Personal E-mail: jaallenoer@comcast.net.

ALLEN-MEARES, PAULA G., social work educator, dean; b. Buffalo, Feb. 29, 1948; d. Joe N. and Mary T. (Hienz) Allen; married; children: Tracey, Nikki, Shannon BS, SUNY, Buffalo, 1969; MSW Child Welfare, U. Ill., Urbana-Champaign, 1971, PhD Social Work and Ednl. Adminstrn., 1975; cert. mgmt., Harvard U., 1990; cert. mgmt. of mgrs., U. Mich., 1993. Lic. cert. social worker, Ill.; lic. clin. social worker, Ill. Rsch. asst. SUNY, Buffalo, 1966—69; child welfare worker Dept. Children and Family Svcs., Champaign, Ill., 1970—71; sch. social worker Urbana Sch. Dist. 116, Urbana, 1971—78; supt. Sch. Social Work U. Ill., Urbana-Champaign, 1973—78, asst. prof. Sch. Social Work, 1978—83, chair Sch. Social Work Specialization, 1978—84, dir. doctoral program Sch. Social Work, 1985—88, 1989, assoc. prof. Sch. Social Work Urbana-Champaign, 1983—89, acting dean Sch. Social Work, 1989—90, prof. Sch. Social Work, 1989—93, dean, prof. Sch. Social Work, 1990—93, U. Mich., Ann Arbor, 1993—. Scholars forum vis. lectr. U. Tex., Austin, 1992; vis. scholar Sch. Social Work, U. S.C., 1994, U. Ga., Athens, 1997; manuscript and book reviewer; reviewer Social Casework, summers 1988-90; Children & Youth Svcs. Rev., 1988-90, Jour. Ethnic and Multicultural Concerns in Social Work, 1990, among others; cons. Ill. Office Edn., Pupil Pers. Svc. Unit, Springfield, 1977, Detroit Pub. Schs., 1979, Decatur (Ill.) Pub. Schs., 1979, Family Svcs. Champaign County, 1979, Dept. Pub. Instrn., State of N.C., 1979, Urbana Sch. Dist. 116, 1978-80, Ill. State Bd. Edn., 1979-81, Chgo. Pub. Schs., 1981, Champaign Pub. Schs., 1981, Vermillion County Spl. Edn. Coop., Danville, 1982, Pembroke Sch. Dist., Kankakee, Ill., 1982, Champaign Pub. Schs., 1982, Defferin-Pell Sch. Dist., Mississauga, Ont., Can., 1982, Mid-State Spl. Edn., 1983, Wis. Office Edn., Milw., 1983, D.C. Sch. Social Work, 1984, Ind. Office Edn. Pupil Pers. Divsn., Indpls., 1984, Glenbrook (Ill.) Sch. Dist., 1984-86, Kankakee Spl. Edn. Coop., 1985, N.J. State Dept. Edn. Office Cert., Trenton, 1985, Pub. Sch. Disvn., Mississauga, 1985, Budapest, Hungary, 1990, Dept. Def., 1991, Cath. Social Svcs., Indpls., 1991, Bd. Sch. Commrs., Indpls. Pub. Schs., 1991, Brown U. and Lilly Endowment, Indpls., 1992; external reviewer U. Mo., 1995, Columbia U., 2001, Wayne State U., 2002, U. Calif. Berkeley, 1995, Hunter U., 2006; keynote spkr. N.Mex., Ga., Mo. 1997; cons. in field. Author: Intervention with Children & Adolescents, 1995, (with others) Social Work Services in Schools, 1986, Controversial Issues in Social Work Research, 1995, Handbook of Social Work Direct Practice; co-editor: Methods and Issues-Evaluating Social Services in Education Settings, 1988, Adolescent Sexuality-An Overview and Principles of Intervention, 1986, Conducting Research: A Handbook For Schook Social Workers, 1988, The School Services Source Book: A Guide For School Based Professionals, 2006; mem. editl. bd. Jour. of Women in Social Work, 1990-93, Arete, 1989—, Sch. Jour. Social Work, 1986—, Ednl. and Psychol. Rsch., 1983-89, Jour. Social Svc. Rsch., 1993—, Children and Youth Svcs. Rev., 1991—, Jour. Tchg. Social Work, 1990—; cons. editor Social Work in Edn., 1978-84; editor-in-chief Social Work in Edn., 1989-93, Jour. of Social Work Edn., 1997—; tech. adv. com. Social Work in Edn. spl. edit., 1996—; mem. editl. adv. bd. Families in Contemporary Soc., 1991—; contbr. articles to profl. jours Human rels. dir. Urbana Edn., 1973-75; mem. regional adv. bd. Gifted, 1977-78; mem. planning com. Ill. March of Dimes, 1978; bd. dirs. Vol. Action Ctr. Champaign County, 1978-80, chair nomination com., ad hoc com. on bd. policy; mem. program com. Girls Club Champaign, 1978-81; mem. adv. bd. Ambulatory Care Ctr., Mercy Hosp., 1981-82; bd. dirs. devel. svcs. Champaign County, 1973-75; moderator black adoptions Children's Home and Aid Soc. Ill. and Dept. Children and Family Svcs., 1984; mem. policy com. Regional Ill. Children's Home and Aid Soc., 1980-84; bd. dirs. Family Svc. Champaign County, 1988-89; mem. Champaign county child placement rev. com. Champaign County Cir. Ct., 1985-93; trustee WT Grant Found., chair nomination com., 2004-2007. Recipient scholarship SUNY, 1966, Alumni of Yr. U. Ill., 1993, Human Rels. award Ill. Edn. Assn., 1975; fellow U. Ill., 1969-71; grantee Urban Sch. Dist. 116, 1976, Dept. Children and Family Svcs., 1983, Workshops on Prevention of Teenage Pregnancy, 1985, Dept. Edn., 1986, 89, U. Ill., 1986—, Mich. Dept. Social Svcs., 1994 Mem. NASW (chair comm. com. 1993—, comm. bd. dirs., coun. editors bd. 1990—, cert., editor-in-chief Social Work in Edn. 1990—,jour. editl. bd. 1984-88, grantee 1988-92, Social Worker of Yr. Illini dist. 1992), Nat. Assn. Black Social Workers, Nat. Assn. Deans and Dirs. (v.p. 1993-95, v.p. 1993—, bd. dirs. 1991-93), Coun. on Social Work Edn. (treas. 1992—, bd. dirs. 1989-91, del. assembly 1988-89), Soc. Social Work Edn. and Rsch. (pres.-elect, 2001-2002, pres, 2002-2004, Padgett early career achievement award com.), NY Acad. Medicine (mem. steering com., chair, nat. adv. panel, social work leadership pub. policy com.), Nat. Acads. Inst. Medicine (vice chair section X, mem. com., mem. health disparities interest group, com. future health care workforce older Ams.), Rotary, Phi Delta Kappa, Delta Mu, Delta Kappa Gamma (Xi chpt.) Avocations: jogging, aerobics. Office: U Mich Sch Social Work 1080 South U Ann Arbor MI 48109-1106

ALLER, WAYNE KENDALL, psychologist, educator, computer company executive, property manager; b. Slyvia, Kans., Feb. 20, 1933; s. Alvin Ray and Florence Dorothy (Snowbarger) A.; m. Sharon Cecelia Forray, Aug. 21, 1962 (div.); children: Jay Ramzi, Joyce Amal; m. Sonia Y. Konialian, Apr. 8, 1969 BA in Physics, N.W. Nazarene Coll., Nampa, Idaho, 1955; MS in Psychology, U. Wash., 1960, PhD in Psychology, 1964. Asst. prof. psychology Pacific Lutheran U., 1962-64; asst. prof., chmn. divsn. behavioral scis. Beirut Coll. for Women, 1964-67; assoc. prof. Mankato State Coll., Minn., 1967-68, Ind. State U., Terre Haute, 1968—85, prof., 1985—, acting chair, psychology dept., 2001—02; pres. Learning Unlimited, 1983—, CompuLearn, 1983-87. Adj. prof. psychology Calif. State U., Northridge, 1984-2003; sr. rsch. adv. Ctr. Ednl. R&D, Ministry Planning, Republic Lebanon, Beirut, 1974-75; sr. rsch. assoc. Ctr. Behavioral Rsch., Am. U. of Beirut, 1974-75; vis. scholar dept. psychology UCLA, 1982-83; cons. English as fgn. lang. Vietnamese Affairs Ctr., Terre Haute, 1976-78. Author: Readings and Experiments in General Psychology, 1970, rev. edit., 1971 Pres. Knollwood Property Owners Assn., 2002—; sec. City of LA Sunshine Canyon Landfill Citizens Advisory Com., 2002—, mem., 2002—, mem. tech. adv. com., 2002—; mem. adv. bd. United Campus Ministries, Calif. State U., Northridge, 2005—, Knollwood United Meth. Ch., 2004, chmn. bd. trustees, 2006, chmn. ch. coun., 2007; bd. dirs. Granada Hills North Neighborhood Coun., 2002—; mem. adv. bd. Cmty. Integration Svcs., 2007. Recipient Outstanding Cmty. Svc. by Sr. Citizen award LA Pearl, 2007; grantee Ford Found., 1974-75. Mem. Western Psychol. Assn., N.Y. Acad. Scis., Soc. Computers in Psychology, Computer Users Speech and Hearing, Wabash Valley Apple Byters Club (Terre Haute)(pres. 1981-82), LA Astronomical Soc., Sigma Xi, Psi Chi, Sigma Phi Iota. Methodist. Home: 12045 Susan Dr Granada Hills CA 91344-2642 Personal E-mail: waynealler07@hotmail.com.

ALLERHAND, JOSEPH S., lawyer; b. Bklyn., Aug. 10, 1953; BA, Columbia U., 1975; JD, Georgetown U. Law Ctr., 1978. Bar: NY 1979, US Dist. Ct. (Ea. and So. Districts NY) 1979, US Ct. Appeals (8th Cir.) 1984, US Ct. Appeals (2nd Cir.) 1985, US Ct. Appeals (3rd Cir.) 1986, US Ct. Appeals (6th Cir.) 1992. Law clerk ti Hon. David N. Edelstein, 1978—80; ptnr., co-head bus. and securities litigation dept. Weil, Gotshal & Manges LLP, NYC. Lectr. in field. Mem. Georgetown Jour., 1977—78; contbr. articles to profl. jours. Bd. dir. NY Legal Assistance Corp., Big Brother/Big Sisters NY, UJA Fedn. NY; pres. UJA Fedn. NY Lawyer's Divsn.; founder, bd. dir. Solomon Schechter Sch. Manhattan. Mem.: Fed. Bar Coun., ABA. Office: Weil, Gotshal & Manges LLP 767 Fifth Ave New York NY 10153 Office Phone: 212-310-8725. Office Fax: 212-310-8007. Business E-Mail: joseph.allerhand@weil.com.

ALLEY, KIRSTIE, actress; b. Wichita, Kans., Jan. 12, 1951; m. Parker Stevenson Dec. 22, 1983 (div. Dec. 1997); children: William True, Lillie. Student, U. Kans., Kans. State U. Actress: (stage prodns.) Cat on a Hot Tin Roof, Answers; (feature films) Star Trek II: The Wrath of Khan, 1982, Blind Date, 1984, Champions, 1984, Runaway, 1984, Summer School, 1987, Shoot to Kill, 1988, Look Who's Talking, 1989, Daddy's Home, 1989, One More Chance, 1990, Madhouse, 1990, Sibling Rivalry, 1990, Look Who's Talking Too, 1990, Look Who's Talking Now, 1993, Village of the Damned, 1995, It Takes Two, 1995, Sticks and Stones, 1996, For Richer of Poorer, 1997 (People's Choice award 1997), Deconstructing Harry, 1997 (People's Choice award 1997), Toothless, 1997, Drop Dead Gorgeous, 1999, The Mao Game, 1999, Back by Midnight, 2002; (TV mini-series) North and South Book I, 1985, North and South, Book II, 1986, The Last Don, 1997, The Last Don Part II, 1998 (Emmy nomination), Blonde, 2001, Salem Witch Trials, 2002; (TV movies) Sins of the Past, 1984, A Bunny's Tale, 1984, The Prince of Bel Air, 1985, Stark: Mirror Image, 1986, Infidelity, 1987, David's Mother, 1994 (Emmy award, Lead Actress - Special, 1994), Radiant City, 1996, Family Sins, 2004; (TV series) Masquerade, 1984-85, Cheers, 1987-1993 (Emmy award as Outstanding Lead Actress in a Comedy Series 1991); actress, exec. prodr.: Suddenly, 1996, Profoundly Normal, 2003; actress, co-prodr.: Nevada, 1997; prodr., actress: Veronica's Closet, 1997-2000; actress, writer, exec. prodr.: Fat Actress, 2005; TV appearances include The Match Game PM, 1979, The Hitchhiker, 1985, 87, Wings, 1993, Ink, 1997, Dharma & Greg, 2001, Without a Trace, 2004; spokesperson for Jenny Craig. Spokesperson for Narcanon Drug Rehab.; founder Ch. of Scientology, Mission of Wichita; involved with Fight for Kids. Recipient People's Choice award, 1998. Mem.: Gamma Phi Beta.

ALLEY, MARY LOU VANDE WOUDE, retired medical/surgical nurse; b. Sioux Center, Iowa, Mar. 23, 1942; d. Bert John Van Maanen and Gertrude Winters; m. Dallas Glen Alley, June 29, 2003; children: Michelle, Michael, Mark. RN, Meth. Hosp., Sioux City, 1963. Staff nurse Orange City (Iowa) Mcpl. Hosp., 1963—64, Hartley (Iowa) Cmty. Hosp., 1964—67, Mercy Hosp., Council Bluffs, Iowa, 1972—74, Jennie Edmunson Hosp., Council Bluffs, 1974—75; staff nurse, unit dir. Nebr. Med. Ctr., Omaha, 1975—2004; ret., 2004. Leader bible study United Meth. Ch., Council Bluffs. Methodis. Avocations: Bible study, golf, reading, travel. Home: #9 Virginia Hills Rd Council Bluffs IA 51503 Personal E-mail: mvande5257@cox.net.

ALLEYNE, SIR GEORGE A.O., public health administrator, educator; b. St. Philip, Barbados, Oct. 7, 1932; m. Sylvan I. Chen; 3 children. MB, U. London, 1957, MD, 1965; DSc (hon.), U. W.I., McGill U., Montreal, Can., Queens U., Ont., Can., 2001. Researcher Univ. W.I., West Indies, 1962—72, prof. medicine, 1972—76, chmn. Dept. Medicine, 1976—81; chief of rsch. promotion & coordination Pan Am. Health Org., 1981—85, Dir., 1995—2003, dir. emeritus, 2003—; chancellor Univ. W.I., West Indies, 2003—. Spl. envoy of UN Sec.-Gen. for HIV/AIDS in the Caribbean region, 2003—. Named Knight Bachelor, 1990; recipient Order of the Caribbean Community (O.C.C.), 2001. Office: Pan Am Health Org Regional Office WHO 525 TwentyThird St NW Washington DC 20037

ALLGEIER, PETER FREDERICK, ambassador; b. Orange, NJ; m. Marsha Uehara; 2 children. AB in Internat. Rels., Brown U.; MA in Internat. Rels., Johns Hopkins U.; PhD in Internat. Economics, U. N.C. Internat. economist USAID, Washington; internat. economist Asia US Trade Reps., 1980—81, dir. Japanese affairs, 1981, dep. asst. US Trade Rep. Asia and the Pacific, 1981—85, asst. US Trade Rep. for Asia & the Pacific, 1985—89, asst. US Trade Rep. Europe & the Mediterranean, 1989—95, assoc. US Trade Rep. for western hemisphere Washington, 1995—2001; sr. dir. internat. econ. affairs Nat. Econ. Coun., Washington, 2001; dep. US Trade Rep. Exec. Office of the Pres., Washington, 2001—, acting US Trade Rep., 2005, amb., perm. rep. to WTO Geneva, 2005—. Vis. instr. econ. Duke U. Recipient Presdl. Disting. Rank award, 1988. Office: US Trade Rep 600 17th St NW Washington DC 20508-4801

ALLINSON, DEBORAH LOUISE, economist; b. Providence, Oct. 30, 1950; d. Wayne Clinton and Barbara (Pearson) A.; m. Thomas J. Lamb, Apr. 27, 1973; children: Andrew Allinson Lamb, Michael Allinson Lamb, Peter Allinson Lamb, Emily Allinson Lamb. BA in Econs. cum laude, Tufts U., 1972. Rsch. asst. Wellington Mgmt., Boston, 1972-75, asst. v.p., 1975-78, v.p., 1978-89, sr. v.p., 1990-91, ptnr., 1991—2005; pvt. investor counselor Hingham, Mass., 2005—. Bd. dirs. Wellington Trust Co., South Shore Conservatory of Music; investment com. Wheeler Sch., Providence, 2006—; planning, devel. com. Tabor Acad., Marion, Mass. Active Alexis de Tocqueville Coun. United Way; mem. investment com. Wheeler Sch.,

2006—; mem. adv. com. Town of Hingham, Mass., 2006—. Mem. Nat. Assn. Bus. Economists, Boston Assn. Bus. Economists, Boston Econ. Club (pres. 1995, mem. exec. com.), Washington Nat. Econ. Club. Office: Wellington Mgmt 75 State St Boston MA 02109-1700 Home: 17 Martins Cove Rd Hingham MA 02043-1042 Office Phone: 617-951-5226. Personal E-mail: dlallinson@comcast.com.

ALLIS, DAMIAN GREGORY, chemist, technologist, consultant; b. Syracuse, NY, July 2, 1976; s. John George and Maria Magdalene Allis. BS, Syracuse U., NY, 1998, PhD, 2004. Sr. scientist, sci. adv. bd. mem. Nanorex, Inc., Bloomfield Hills, Mich., 2004—; theorist-in-residence Syracuse U., 2004—; rsch. fellow Intelligence Cmty. Post-doctoral Rsch. Fellowship Program, 2005—. Webmaster somewhereville.com, Syracuse, 1997—; cons., computational pharm. design Molecular Insight, Inc., Cambridge, Mass., 2003—; working group mem. Tech. Roadmap for Productive Nanosys., Palo Alto, Calif., 2005—; rsch. fellow Molecular Engrng. Rsch. Inst., Palo Alto, 2005—; reviewer Inorganic Chemistry Comms., Chem. Physics Letters; lectr. in field. Contbg. author: CRC Handbook of Nanoscience, Engineering and Technology, 2007; designer (web exhibit, image gallery) Structural Motifs of Advanced Molecular Manufacturing, 2004—; contbr. over 20 to profl. sci. jours.; musician: (albums) Tjaden: Tjaden, 1998, Jolie Rickman: Sublime Detonation, 1998, Excelsior Cornet Band: Cheer, Boys, Cheer!, 2005. Grantee, CIA. Mem.: AAAS, Tech. Alliance Ctrl. NY, Internat. Soc. Nanoscale Sci., Computation and Engring., Am. Chem. Soc., Syracuse Astronomical Soc. (pres. 2007—), Foresight Inst., Planetary Soc., Phi Eta Sigma, Golden Key Nat. Honor Soc., Phi Beta Kappa. Independent. Greek Orthodox. Achievements include patents for the design and fabrication of molecular nanostructures from polyhedral-based molecular synthetic subunits and new classes of high linear and nonlinear response compunds; active in the design and analyses of nanosystems and research fields related to advanced molecular manufacturing. Avocations: auto racing, photography, computers, bicycling, percussion. Home: 313 E Willow St Apt 501 Syracuse NY 13203 Office: Syracuse Univ 1-014 CST 111 College Pl Syracuse NY 13244 Home Phone: 315-559-4737; Office Phone: 315-443-2067. Office Fax: 315-443-4070. Home Fax: 314-443-4070. Business E-Mail: marquis@somewhereville.com.

ALLIS, DAVID C., biologist, educator; BS in Biology, U. Cin., 1973; MS, Ind. U., PhD in Biology, 1978. Postdoctoral fellow Rochester U., 1978—81; faculty mem. Baylor Coll. Medicine, 1981—90, Syracuse U., 1990—95, U. Rochester, 1995—98, Marie Curran Wilson & Joseph Chamberlain Wilson prof. biology, 1997—98; Harry F. Byrd Jr. prof. biochemistry and molecular genetics U. Va. Health Sci. Ctr., 1998—2003, prof. microbiology, mem. Ctr. for Cell Signaling; Joy and Jack Fishman prof. Rockefeller U., 2003—, head Lab of Chromatin Biology and Epigenetics, 2003—. Recipient Wiley prize biomedical sciences, The Wiley Found., 2004, Gairdner Internat. award, 2007. Mem.: Am. Acad. Arts and Sciences, NAS. Office: The Allis Lab Rockefeller Univ Box 78 1230 York Ave New York NY 10021 E-mail: alliscd@ockefeller.edu.

ALLISON, ANDREW MARVIN, church administrator; b. Long Beach, Calif., May 21, 1949; s. Howard C. and Wilma A. (Franks) A.; m. Kathleen L. Anderson, May 28, 1971; children: Rebecca, Nathan, Joanna, Spencer, Jacob, Camilla. AA, Glendale CC, Ariz., 1972; BA in History, Brigham Young U., Provo, Utah, 1974; PhD of Polit. Sci., Coral Ridge U., Jacksonville, Fla., 1993. Cert. secondary tchr., Ariz., Utah. Adminstrv. staff, editor Brigham Young U., Provo, Utah, 1972-74; adminstrv. asst. LDS Ch., Salt Lake City, 1977-79; prin., tchr. LDS Seminaries, Ariz.,Utah, 1974-77, 79-80; assoc. editor, art dir. Bookcraft Publs., Salt Lake City, 1983-85; dir. rsch. and publs. Nat. Ctr. for Constl. Studies, Salt Lake City, 1980-83, 85-91, chmn., pres. West Jordan, Utah, 1991-95; product devel. editor Deseret Book Co., Salt Lake City, 1995-96; supr. confidential applications LDS Ch., Salt Lake City, 1996-99, mgr. confidential records, 1999—2006, product mgr., mem. and statis. records, 2006—. Adj. prof. polit. sci. George Wythe Coll., Cedar City, Utah, 1993—2006. Author: The Real Thomas Jefferson, 1982, The Real Benjamin Franklin, 1983, The Real George Washington, 1991; contbr. articles to profl. jours. Mem. West Jordan City Coun., Utah, 2000—03, mayor pro-tem, 2001. Mem.: Phi Kappa Phi.

ALLISON, ANNE MARIE, retired librarian; b. Oak Park, Ill., Oct. 3, 1931; d. Gerald Patrick and Anna Evelyn (Beam) Myers; m. James Dixon Alison, Aug. 28, 1954; children: Mark, Mary, Clare, Ruth, Edward. BA in French, St. Mary of the Woods Coll., 1951; postgrad., U. Fribourg, 1952-53; MLS, Rosary Coll., 1968. Asst. libr. Triton Coll., River Grove, Ill., 1967-68; asst. libr. tech. svcs. Moraine Valley Community Coll., Palos Hills, Ill., 1968-69; dir. learning resources, head libr. Coll. Lake County, Grayslake, Ill., 1969-71; asst. head catalog dept. Kent (Ohio) State U. Librs., 1971-73, head processing dept., 1973-79, asst. dir. libr. svcs., 1979-81; acting dir. Fla. Atlantic U. Libr., Boca Raton, 1980-81; asst. dir., head tech. svcs. Wayne State U. Librs., Detroit, 1981-83; dir. librs. U. Cen. Fla., Orlando, 1983-97, ret., 1997. Past chair, bd. dirs. Fla. Extension Libr., Tampa; bd. dirs. Ctr. for Libr. Automation, Gainesville, Fla., Cen. Fla. Holocaust Meml. Resource Ctr., Orlando; adj. prof. Libr. and Info. Sci., U. S. Fla., Tampa. Editor: OCLC: A National Library Network, 1979; contbr. articles to profl. jours. Arbitrator alternative dispute resolution program Better Bus. Bur. Cen. Fla., Maitland, 1985—; active Friends Winter Park Pub. Libr., Friends of Orlando Pub. Libr. Recognized for Outstanding Leadership in Edn. Cen. Fla. Ednl. Consortium for Women, 1990. Mem. ALA (chair profl. ethics com.), Fla. Libr. Assn., Fla. Assn. Coll. and Rsch. Librs. (pres. bd. dirs.). Avocations: fruit farming, collecting china. Office: U Cen Fla PO Box 25000 Orlando FL 32816-0001

ALLISON, DWIGHT LEONARD, JR., investor; b. Boston, Oct. 27, 1929; s. Dwight Leonard and Stella (DeGrasse) A.; m. Lyona G. Strohacker, June 19, 1954; children: Dwight Leonard III, Barbara Lynn, Laurie. AB, Dartmouth Coll., 1951, MBA, 1952; LLB, Harvard U., 1956; DCS (hon.), Suffolk U., 1989. Bar: Mass. 1956. Pvt.practice, Boston, 1956—66; assoc. Goodwin, Procter & Hoar, 1956-64, ptnr., 1965-66; v.p., dir. Gardner Assocs., Inc., Boston, 1966-68; chmn. fin. com. C.H. Sprague & Son Co., 1968-69; chmn. bd. Sprague Assoc., Inc., Boston, 1969-71; gen. ptnr. Sprague & Co., 1971-80; pvt. investor, 1973-77; pres. and CEO Boston Co., 1977-81, chmn. bd., 1981-83, vice chmn., 1983-86; pvt. investor, 1986—. 1st lt. USAF, 1952—53. Address: 4228 Pine Cone Ln Boynton Beach FL 33436-3017 Home (Summer): 32641 Sea Island Dr Dana Point CA 92629 Personal E-mail: DA1296@aol.com.

ALLISON, FRED, JR., internist, retired medical educator; b. Abingdon, Va., Sept. 8, 1922; s. Fred and Elizabeth Harriet (Kelly) A.; m. Clara Knox, Oct. 14, 1949; children: Rebecca Allison Parsley, Martha Allison Brown, Fred III, Robert Gardiner. BS, Ala. Poly. Inst., 1944; MD, Vanderbilt U., 1946. Diplomate: Am. Bd. Internal Medicine. Intern Vanderbilt Hosp., Nashville, 1946-47; resident Peter Bent Brigham Hosp., Boston, 1949-50; practice medicine specializing in internal medicine, 1946—; asst. prof. medicine Washington U., St. Louis, 1955; prof. medicine, head infectious disease divsn. U. Miss., Jackson, 1955—68; vis. scientist Rockefeller U., NYC, 1966-67; Edgar Hull prof. medicine, head dept. medicine La. State U., New Orleans, 1968-87; chief medicine La. State U. div. Charity Hosp., 1968—87; prof. medicine emeritus La. State U., 1987—; prof. medicine Vanderbilt U., Nashville, 1987-96, prof. medicine emeritus, 1996—, med. cons. Zerfoss Student Health Svc., 1996-99; physician-in-chief Met. Nashville Gen. Hosp., 1987-93; chief, divsn. gen. internal medicine Vanderbilt U., 1993-96. Bd. dirs. La. State U. Health Network, 1995-01; vice chmn. bd. trustees Hosp. Authority of Metro. Nashville and Davidson County, 1999—. With US Army, 1943-46, 47-49. Home: 418 Fairfax Ave Nashville TN 37212-4009

ALLISON, GRAHAM TILLETT, JR., political science professor, former federal agency administrator; b. Charlotte, NC, Mar. 23, 1940; s. Graham Tillett and Virginia (Wright) A.; m. Elisabeth Kovacs Smith, Aug. 23, 1968. AB, Harvard U., 1962, PhD, 1968; BA, MA, Hertford Coll., Oxford U., Eng., 1964. Asst. prof. John F. Kennedy Sch. Govt., Harvard U., Cambridge, Mass., 1968-70, assoc. prof., 1970-72, profl., 1972—, assoc. dean, 1975-77, dean, 1977-89, Douglas Dillon prof. govt., 1989—, dir., Belfer Ctr. for Science & Internat. Affairs; spl. adviser to sec. US Dept. Def., Washington, 1985-87, asst. sec. for policy and plans, 1993—94; dir. Project on Strengthening Dem. Institutions, 1990-93. Fellow Ctr. for Advanced Studies, Stanford, Palo Alto, Calif., 1973-74; mem. Sec. Def.'s Policy Bd., 1985—; cons. Rand Corp., U.S. Dept. Def., others; mem. numerous NAS panels; mem. Trilateral Commn., 1974-84, Coun. on Fgn. Rels.; mem. Fgn. Affairs Task Force Dem. Adv. Com., 1974-80; mem. vis. com. on fgn. policy studies Brookings Instn., 1972-77. Author: Essence of Decision: Explaining the Cuban Missile Crisis, 1971, Remaking Foreign Policy: The Organizational Connection, 1976, Sharing International Responsibility Among the Trilateral Countries, 1983, Nuclear Terrorism: The Ultimate Preventable Catastrophe, 2004; co-author: (with Carnesale and Nye) Hawks, Doves and Owls: An Agenda for Avoiding Nuclear War, 1985, Fateful Visions: Avoiding Nuclear Catastrophe, 1988, (with W. Ury) Windows of Opportunity: From Cold War to Peaceful Competition, 1989, (with Grigory Yavlinsky) Window of Opportunity: The Grand Bargain for Democracy in the Soviet Union, 1991, (with Greg Treverton) Rethinking America's Security, 1992, (with Konstantin Sarkisov and Hiroshi Kimura) Beyond the Cold War to Trilateral Cooperation in the Asia-Pacific Region, 1992, (with Sammantha Power) Realizing Human Rights: Moving From Inspiration to Impact, 2000; contbr. articles to profl. jours. Democrat. Office: Belfer Ctr for Science & Internat Affairs John F Kennedy Sch Govt Littauer 368 79 JFK St Cambridge MA 02138 E-mail: graham_allison@harvard.edu.*

ALLISON, HERBERT MONROE, JR., investment company executive; b. Pitts., Aug. 24, 1943; s. Herbert M. Sr. and Mary B. (Boardman) A.; m. Simin N. Nazemi, May 9, 1974; children: John, Andrew. BA, Yale U., 1965; MBA, Stanford U., 1971. With Merrill Lynch & Co., Inc., NYC, Paris, London and Tehran, Iran, 1971-78, asst. to pres. NYC, 1978-80, mgr. market planning, 1980-83, treas., 1983-86, sr. v.p., dir. human resources, from 1986, CFO, pres., COO until 1999; pres., CEO AllLearn.org; chmn., pres., CEO Teachers Ins. & Annuity Found. Coll. Retirement Equities Fund (TIAA-CREF), NYC, 2002—. Bd. dirs. NY Stock Exch., 2003—05, NY Infirmary-Beekman Downtown Hosp. Served in USN, 1965—69. Mem. Wall Street Personnel Mgmt. Assn. Office: TIAA-CREF 730 Third Ave New York NY 10017*

ALLISON, JEFFERY CLAY, pharmacist, educator; b. Altoona, Pa., Sept. 27, 1948; s. John Wilmer and Charlotte Lorraine Allison; m. Nancy Wood Wood, Dec. 18, 1971; children: Scott Jeffery, Sharon Louise Gibson. BS in Pharmacy, Ohio No. U., Ada, 1971, PharmD, 1995. Registered pharmacist Ohio, 1971, Fla., 1986. Clin. pharmacist St. Rita's Med. Ctr., Lima, Ohio, 1973—88; pharmacist Gardners Drug Store, Ada, 1973—2000; prof. pharmacy practice Ohio No. U., 1995—. Cons. Blue Ridge Paper Co., Olmsted Falls, Ohio, 2003—07. Contbr. articles to profl. jours. Advisor Habitat for Humanity, Ada, 1996. Grantee, PSA3 Agy. Aging, 2002—07. Mem.: Ohio Pharmacists Assn. (mem. bylaws com. 2004—07), Am. Pharmacy Assn., Am. Assn. Health-Systems Pharmacists, NW Ohio Pharmacists Assn. (pres. 1992), Am. Assn. Colls. Pharmacy, Phi Kappa Phi, Phi Lambda Sigma, Omicron Delta Kappa. Methodist. Avocations: swimming, travel. Office: Ohio No U Coll Pharmacy 525 S Main St Ada OH 45810 Home Phone: 419-772-1488; Office Phone: 419-772-1488. Business E-Mail: j-allison@onu.edu.

ALLISON, JOAN KELLY, music educator, pianist; b. Denison, Iowa, Jan. 25, 1935; d. Ivan Martin and Esther Cecelia (Newborg) K.; m. Guy Hendrick Allison, July 25, 1954 (div. Apr. 1973); children: David, Dana, Douglas, Diane. MusB, St. Louis Inst. of Music, 1955; MusM, So. Meth. U., 1976. Korrepetitor Corpus Christi (Tex.) Symphony, 1963-85; staff pianist Am. Inst. Mus. Studies, Graz, Austria, 1974-89; prof. Del Mar Coll., Corpus Christi, 1976—2002. Adj. prof. Del Mar Coll., 1959-75, 06-07, Corpus Christi State U., 1978-93, Tex. A&M U., Corpus Christi, 1993-04; program dir. Corpus Christi Chamber Music Soc., 1986—; piano chmn. Corpus Christi Internat. Competition for Piano and Strings, 1987—; chmn. Del Mar Coll. Student Programs Com., 1986-88, 91-92, 94-95, 01-02; chmn. radio com., S.Tex. Pub. Broadcasting Svc., Corpus Christi, 1987-88; asst. mus. dir. Little Theater, Corpus Christi, 1970-74; judge, Houston Symphony Auditions, 1988, S.C. Young Artist Competition, Columbia, 1990; freelance accompanist, 1955—, adjudicator, 1960—; v.p. united faculty Del Mar Coll., 1986-88; pianist with Del Mar Trio, 1965-95, Young Audiences, Inc., 1975-83; recital tours in US, Mex., Austria, 1954-88. Piano soloist, St. Louis Symphony, 1956, 57, Bach Festival Orch., St. Louis, 1955, Corpus Christi Symphony; recipient Artist Presentation award, Artist Presentation Soc., St. Louis, 1956; contbr. articles to profl. jours., including Internat. Piano Quar. Co-chmn. Mayor's Com. on Recycling, Corpus Christi, 1989-91; bd. dirs. Corpus Christi Symphony; adv. bd. Corpus Christi Concert Ballet; mem. steering com. cultural devel. plan City of Corpus Christi, 1995-96. Recipient Women in Careers award YWCA, 1985. Mem. Corpus Christi Music Tchrs. Assn., Liszt Soc. (contbr. to jour.). Avocations: foreign travel, water-skiing, hiking, acting in community theatre. Home: 4709 Curtis Clark Dr Corpus Christi TX 78411-4801 Personal E-mail: Jallison@the-i.net.

ALLISON, JOHN ANDREW, IV, bank executive; b. Charlotte, NC, Aug. 14, 1948; s. John Andrew III and Anne Allison; m. Elizabeth Mc Donald, Aug. 19, 1973; children: Eric, William, Sarah. BBA, U. N.C., 1971; M in Mgmt., Duke U., 1974; grad. Stonier Sch. Banking, Rutgers U., 1981. Chmn., CEO BB&T Corp.; mgr. fin. analysis Br. Banking & Trust Co., Wilson, NC, 1971-72, mgr. loan officer devel. program, 1972-73, regional loan adminstr., 1973-80, mgr. bus. loan adminstrn., 1980-81, mgr. banking div. (now Br. Banking Group), 1981—, pres., 1987—, also bd. dirs.; vice chmn. BB&T Fin. Corp., Wilson, 1987—; chmn., CEO So. Nat. Corp., Winston-Salem, NC, 1996—, BB&T & Branch Banking & Trust Co., Winston-Salem, NC. Bd. dirs., chmn. capital campaign Children's Svcs. Ea. N.C., Greenville, 1985—; bd. dirs. Diversified Opportunities, Inc., Wilson, l980-87; mem. exec. com. state fin. com. Com. to Reelect Gov. Martin, Raleigh, N.C., 1988; mem. N.C. bus. adv. bd. Fuqua Sch. Bus., Duke U.; bd. dirs. Med. Found. East Carolina U., Brody Found.; mem. communications, agy. and pub. rels. subcom. United Way Wilson County, Inc., 1989—; mem. So. Growth Policies Bd. Mem. Am. Bankers Assn., N.C. Bankers Assn., Robert Morris Assocs. (past bd. dirs. Carolinas-Va. chpt.), N.C. Citizens for Bus. and Industry, Phi Beta Kappa. Office: BB&T Corp 200 W 2nd St Winston Salem NC 27101-4019*

ALLISON, JOHN LANGSDALE, naval architect, marine engineer; b. Sutton Coldfield, Eng., Aug. 10, 1930; arrived in US, 1966; s. Herbert Mandall and Eva May (Langsdale) A.; m. Eunice Quick, Apr. 7, 1956; children: Christopher John, Nigel Mark, Katherine Sarah. BSc in Engring., U. Nottingham, Eng., 1954, postgrad.; aero. engring. cert., Royal Naval Engrng. Coll., Plymouth, Eng., 1955; profl. mgmt. cert., U. Aston, Birmingham, Eng., 1959. Chartered engr., UK. Sr. rsch. engr. Birmingham Small Arms Co./Daimler Group Rsch. Ctr., 1956-58; lectr. in engring. Bromsgrove Coll. of Further Edn., Worcestshire, Eng., 1958-66; sr. rsch. engr. Bell Aerospace Textron, Buffalo, 1966-71; chief engr. ship tech. Textron Marine Sys. Inc. divsn. Bell Aerospace Textron, New Orleans, 1971-87; chief engr. Band, Lavis & Assocs., Inc., Severna Park, Md., 1987—2002, CDI Marine Sys. Design & Devel. (formerly Band, Lavis & Assocs., Inc.), Severna Park, Md., 2002—07. Student advisor George Washington U., Washington, 1991-92; cons. Outboard Motor Corp., Waukegan, Ill., 1994-97; presenter, cons. marine waterjet propulsion Inst. for Maritime Dynamics and Meml. U., St. Johns, Nfld., Can., 1995; cons. ACV lift fans Kvaerner Mandal (Norway) A.S., 1995-99, UMOE, Mandal, Norway, 1999—; advisor H.S. students Hi-Frontiers Hovercraft Competition; presenter in field. Contbr. articles to profl. jours., chapters to books. Sub-lt. Royal Navy, 1954-56. Recipient Maritech award U.S. Govt./Advanced Rsch. Projects Agy., 1995. Fellow Inst. Mech. Engrs., Royal Instn. Naval Architects; mem. Am. Soc. Naval Engrs. Ret., Soc. Naval Architects and Marine Engrs. (Vice Adm. Cochrane award 1993), Navy League, US Naval Inst. (ret.). Republican. Presbyterian. Achievements include patents for waterjet steering and reversal for large ships, and design of heavy lift air cushion vehicle; inventor of low-profile thrusters for naval hovercraft. Home: 4119 Hummingbird Ct Lebanon OH 45036 Office: CDI Marine / Sys Design & Devel 900 Ritchie Hwy Severna Park MD 21146-4142 Office Phone: 513-696-8054. Personal E-mail: jaeqallison@aol.com.

ALLISON, JOHN ROBERT, lawyer; b. San Antonio, Feb. 9, 1945; s. Lyle (stepfather) and Beatrice (Kaliner) Forehand; m. Rebecca M. Picard; 1 child, Katharine. BS, Stanford U., 1966; JD, U. Wash., 1969. Bar: Wash. 1969, DC 1973, Minn. 1994, US Supreme Ct. 1973. Assoc. Garvey, Schubert & Barer, Seattle, 1969-73; ptnr., 1973-86; prin. Betts, Patterson & Mines, P.S., 1986-94; sr. counsel 3M Co., 1994-2000, asst. gen. counsel, 2000—. Bd. dirs. So. Minn. Regional Legal Svcs.; pres. Jewish Family Svc., St. Paul, 2005-07; lectr. bus. law Seattle U., 1970, U. Wash., 1970-73; judge pro tem, King County Superior Ct., 1983-94 Mem. ABA (vice chmn. toxic and hazardous substances and environ. law com. 1986-91, chair elect 1991-92, chair 1992-93), Minn. Bar Assn., Seattle-King County Bar Assn. (chmn. jud. evaln. polling com. 1982-83), Wash. State Bar Assn. (bd. bar examiners 1984-94), DC Bar Assn., Nat. Inst. Pollution Liability (co-chmn. 1988), Order of the Coif. Office: 3M Co 3 M Ctr Saint Paul MN 55144-1000 Office Phone: 651-736-3993. Business E-Mail: jrallison@mmm.com.

ALLISON, JOHN S., state agency administrator; b. Olive Branch, Miss., 1948; m. Jan Garner; 2 children. BBA in Banking and Fin., U. Miss.; postgraduate student, Sch. Banking of South, La. State U. Various positions Dept. Banking and Consumer Fin., Jackson, Miss., 1972—94, dep. commr., 1994—2000, acting commr., 1996—97, commr., 2000—. Mem. Conf. State Bank Suprs., bd. dirs., chmn. dist. III, sec., 2002—03, chmn.-elect, 2003—04, chmn., 2005; mem. state liaison com. Fed. Fin. Insts. Exam. Coun., 2002—06. Served in US Army, Vietnam. Decorated Bronze Star medal. Office: Miss Dept Banking and Consumer Fin PO Drawer 23729 Jackson MS 39225-3729 Office Phone: 601-359-1031. Office Fax: 601-359-3557. E-mail: jallison@dbcf.state.ms.us.

ALLISON, JON B., lawyer; b. Dayton, Ohio, Oct. 25, 1970; BA, U. Mich., 1994; JD, U. Cin. Coll. of Law, 2001. Bar: Ohio 2001, Ct. of Appeals, Sixth Cir., Ct. of Appeals, Eleventh Cir., USDC Southern Dist. Ohio, USDC Eastern Dist. Wis., USDC Southern Dist. Ind. Assoc. Dinsmore & Shohl LLP, Cin. Named one of Ohio's Rising Stars, Super Lawyers, 2006. Mem.: Cin. Bar Assn., Ohio State Bar Assn. Office: Dinsmore & Shohl LLP 255 E 5th St Ste 1900 Cincinnati OH 45202 Office Phone: 513-977-8410. Office Fax: 513-977-8141.

ALLISON, JONATHAN MACKINNON, university professor, researcher; b. Belfast, Northern Ireland, May 8, 1958; s. Victor James Frederick and Anne Mackinnon Allison; m. Anna Ruth Bosch, July 17, 1999; children: Victor Paul Mackinnon, Andrew Philip Mackinnon. BA with honors, The Queen's U. of Belfast, Northern Ireland, 1980, Postgrad. cert. of Edn., 1981; MA, U. Mich., Ann Arbor, 1983, PhD, 1988. Tchr. Dunmurry H.S., Northern Ireland, 1982; tchg. asst. U. Mich., Ann Arbor, 1983—85; tutor English lit. U. Coll. London, 1985—87; editl. asst. London Rev. of Books, 1987—87; asst. prof. U. Ky., Lexington, 1988—94, assoc. prof., 1994—. Guest Ky. Ednl. TV, Lexington, 1998—2003; dir. W.B. Yeats Internat. Summer Sch., Sligo, Ireland, 2003—. Contbr. articles to profl. jours. Fellow, U. Edinburgh, 1996, 2003. Mem.: MLA (corr.), Yeats Soc. (corr.), Am. Conf. for Irish Studies (corr.). Presbyterian. Avocations: swimming, tennis, travel, reading, book collecting. Office: Univ Ky Dept English 1215 Patterson Tower S Limestone Lexington KY 40506-0027 Home Phone: 859-269-5024; Office Phone: 859-257-2901. Office Fax: 859-323-1072. E-mail: jalliso@uky.edu.

ALLISON, KIMBERLY HELLER, pathologist, educator; b. Washington, Oct. 28, 1974; d. Robert and Emily Heller; m. Ryan Allison, June 4, 2001; children: Madeline, Henry. BA, Princeton U., NJ, 1997; MD, NY Med. Coll., Valhalla, 2001. Lic. in medicine Wash., diplomate in anatomic and clin. pathology Am. Bd. Pathology, 2006. Resident dept. pathology U. Wash., Seattle, 2001—06, acting instr. dept. pathology, 2006—. Office: Univ Washington 1959 NE Pacific Box 356100 Seattle WA 98195 Office Phone: 206-598-2918.

ALLISON, MARY ANN, consulting company executive, writer, speaker; b. Sept. 27, 1949; d. David S. and Mary (McNaughton) Burnet; m. Eric William Allison, July 17, 1971. BA, Shimer Coll., 1971; MBA, L.I. U., 1977; PhD, NYU, 2005. Various positions Avis Rent-a-Car, Garden City, NY, 1971-80; v.p. Citicorp, NYC, 1980-96; pres. Human Ordered Tech. LLC., 1996-97; prin. The Allison Group, LLC, 1996—, Allison-LoBue Group, LLC, 1999-2000. N.Y.C. artist in residence; asst. prof. Hofstra U. Co-author: Through the Valley of Death, 1983, Managing Up, Managing Down, 1984, The Complexity Advantage: How the Science of Complexity Can Help Your Business Achieve Peak Performance, 1999; contbr. articles to profl. publs. and nat. mags. Bd. advisors Leadership Forum, N.Y.C. Artist in Residence. Mem. OD Network, Soc. Orgnl. Learning (rsch. mem.), Authors Guild. Episcopalian. Office: The Allison Group 100 Freeman St Ste F2 Brooklyn NY 11222-5899 E-mail: maa@allisongroup.com.

ALLISON, MICHAEL DAVID, space scientist, educator; b. Salem, Ill., Oct. 11, 1951; s. James M. and Claudine K. A.; m. Siri Wannamaker, Feb. 4, 1984; children: Hilary Kirstyn, Christopher Caleb. AB in Physics and English, Wittenberg U., 1973; SM in Physics, U. Chgo., 1976; PhD in Space Physics and Astronomy, Rice U., 1982. Resident rsch. assoc. Nat. Rsch. Coun. NASA/Goddard Inst for Space Studies, NYC, 1981-83, space scientist, 1984—2005, emeritus, 2006—. Guest lectr. Am. Mus. Natural History, Hayden Planetarium, N.Y.C., 1984-88, 94-2003; mem. joint sci. working group for the NASA/ESA assessment study of the Cassini mission to Saturn and Titan, 1984-89; adj. prof. astronomy Columbia U., N.Y.C.-1987—; co-investigator Huygens, Titan Doppler Wind Expt., U. Bonn., Germany, 1990—, scientist Mars Observer and Surveyor, 1998, team mem. Cassini Radar investigation, NASA, 2000—; rsch. assoc. Am. Mus. Dept. Astronomy, 1997-99; co-investigator Juno Mission, 2005—. Co-editor: (conf. proceedings) The Jovian Atmospheres, 1986; contbr. articles to profl. jours. including Science, Icarus, Jour. of Atmospheric Scis., Geophys. Rsch. Letters, Planetary and Space Sci. Mem. Am. Astron. Soc. (divsn. for planetary scis.), Am. Meteorol. Soc., Internat. Astronomical Union, Brit. Interplanetary Soc. Achievements include research in planetary atmospheric dynamics and meteorology, application of potential vorticity homogenization to planetary zonal circulation studies, first identification of Saturn's polar hexagon as a planetary Rossby wave, inference of a probable super-solar abundance of water on Jupiter based on the diagnostic analysis of equatorial waves, development of efficient planetocentric solar timing algorithms for Mars and other planets. Home: 56 Gillis Hill Ln Salem NY 12865 Office: NASA/Goddard Inst Space Studies 2880 Broadway New York NY 10025-7848 Business E-Mail: michael.d.allison@nasa.gov.

ALLISON, RICHARD CLARK, judge; b. NYC, July 10, 1924; s. Albert Fay and Anice (Clark) A.; m. Anne Elizabeth Johnston, Oct. 28, 1950; children: Anne Sidney, William Scott, Richard Clark. BA, U. Va., 1944, LLB, 1948. Bar: N.Y. 1948. Assoc. Satterlee, Warfield & Stephens, NYC, 1948—52, 1954—55; with CIA, 1952—54; assoc., ptnr. Reid & Priest, 1956—87; mem. Iran-U.S. Claims Tribunal, The Hague, 1988—. Lt. (j.g.) USNR, 1945—46. Fellow Am. Bar Found.(life), Ctr. for Am. and Internat. Law; mem. ABA (chmn. com. Latin Am. Law 1964-68, chmn. Internat. Law Sect. 1977, chmn. Nat. Inst. on Doing Bus. in Far East 1972, chmn. internat. legal exch. program 1981-85), Internat. Bar Assn. (chmn. 1986 Conf., ethics com. 1986-89), Société Internat. des Avocats, Inter-Am. Bar Assn., Am. Arbitration Assn. (internat. panel), Am. Soc. Internat. Law, Coun. on Fgn. Rels., Assn. Bar City N.Y., Raven Soc., SAR, St. Andrew's Soc. N.Y., Manhasset Bay Yacht Club, Phi Beta Kappa, Omicron Delta Kappa, Pi Kappa Alpha, Phi Delta Phi. Republican. Congregationalist. Home: 224 Circle Dr Manhasset NY 11030-1123 Office: c/o Iran-US Claims Tribunal Parkweg 13 2585 JH The Hague Netherlands

ALLISON, STUART ANTHONY, chemistry professor, researcher; b. Kalispell, Mont., Mar. 26, 1951; s. Bruce and Arretta Allison; m. Lenong Wang. BA Chemistry, U. Mont., 1973; MS Phys. Chemistry, U. Calif., Berkeley, 1975; PhD Phys. Chemistry, U. Wash., 1980. Postdoctoral fellow U. Oreg., Eugene, 1980—82, U. Houston, Houston, 1982—84; asst. prof. chemistry Ga. State U., Atlanta, 1984—90, assoc. prof. chemistry, 1990—2000, prof. chemistry, 2000—. Contbr. articles to profl. jours. Recipient Presdl. Young Investigator award, NSF, 1985. Mem.: Am. Biophysical Soc. Roman Catholic. Achievements include development of numerical methods for computing transport properties of complex model systems. Avocations: hiking, coin collecting/numismatics, stamp collecting/philately. Home: 978 Biltmore Dr Atlanta GA 30329 Home Phone: 404-982-9401; Office Phone: 404-651-1986. Business E-Mail: sallison@gsu.edu.

ALLITON, VAUGHN, brokerage executive; b. Owosso, Mich., Apr. 16, 1966; s. Marjorie Anne (Jones) Sutliff; life ptnr. Ian Au. BA in Econs., U. Mich., 1988; MBA in Internat. Fin., Nova U., 1992; postgrad. in tech. mgmt, Pace U., NYC, 2001—. Pers. asst. U. Mich., Ann Arbor, 1986—88; pers. generalist Vision-Ease, Ft. Lauderdale, Fla., 1988—89; human resources generalist World Omni Fin. Corp., Deerfield Beach, Fla., 1989—92; cons. IES, Tokyo, 1992; dir. Asia ops. NSU Japan Ltd., 1993—94; mktg. mgr. PTS, Tokyo, 1994—95; adminstrv. mgr. Merrill Lynch Japan, Tokyo, 1995—97, bus. mgr., 1997—98; v.p. Asia project office Merrill Lynch, Hong Kong, 1998—99, v.p. global regions project office, 1999—2000, dir. internat. pvt. client, global expansion project NYC, 2000—01; chief adminstrv. officer Internat. Pvt. Client Tech., NYC, 2002—03, Global Banking Tech., 2003—05; v.p. co. IT Morgan Stanley Dean Witter, NYC, 2005—. Cons. Greater Orlando Auto Action, Fla., 1991-92; adv. bd. Born & Born Med. Personnel, West Palm Beach, Fla., 1992-93; dir. Nova U., Tokyo, 1992-94; adj. prof. Lubin Sch. Bus., Pace U., 2003-06. Author: (manuals) AIDS Sensitivity Education, 1992, Self-Directed Work Teams, 1992, A Model for the Regulation of Technology Innovation, 2005. Recipient IT Leadership award, Morgan Stanley & Co., 2005. Office: Morgan Stanley 195 Broadway New York NY 10007 Personal E-mail: valliton@nyc.rr.com.

ALLITT, PATRICK NICHOLAS, history professor, writer; b. Birmingham, Warwickshire, Eng., Aug. 26, 1956; s. Sidney Eric and Sylvia Allitt; m. Toni Marie Albertson, Sept. 16, 1984; 1 child, Frances Catherine. MA with honors, Oxford U., Eng., 1977; PhD, U. Calif., Berkeley, 1986. Henry luce postdoctoral fellow Harvard U. Div. Sch., Cambridge, Mass., 1985—88; postdoctoral fellow Princeton U., NJ, 1992—93; prof. Emory U., Atlanta, 1988—, dir. Ctr. Tchg. and Curriculum. Author: Catholic Intellectuals and Conservative Politics in America: 1950-1985, 1993, Catholic Converts: British and American Intellectuals Turn to Rome, 1996, Major Problems in American Religious History, 2000, Religion in America Since 1945: A History, 2003, I'm the Teacher, You're the Student, 2004. Recipient Tchg. award, Emory Coll., 1999. Ch. Eng. Avocations: public speaking on history and education, travel, golf. Office: Emory U History Dept 561 S Kilgo Cir Atlanta GA 30322 Office Phone: 404-727-4471. Office Fax: 404-727-4959. Business E-Mail: pallitt@emory.edu.

ALLMAN, MARGARET ANN LOWRANCE, counseling administrator; b. Carmel, Calif., June 2, 1938; d. Edward Walton and Rhoda Elizabeth (Patton) Lowrance; m. Jackie Howard Hamilton, Dec. 21, 1959 (div. May 1976); children: John Scott Hamilton, David Lee Hamilton, Dennis Lynn Hamilton; m. Jack Fredrick Allman, Dec. 22, 1977; stepchildren: John Frederick(dec.) , James Paul, Jeffrey Lee. AA, Christian Coll., 1958; BA in Spanish, U. Mo., 1960, MEd, 1971, EdD, 1994. Tchr. Spanish Neosho (Mo.) HS, 1961-62, asst. prin., 1974-77; florist Wallflower Shop and Greenhouse, Joplin, Mo., 1962-69; dean girls Joplin Sr. HS, 1967-69; florist, bookkeeper Mueller's Garden Ctr., Columbia, Mo., 1969-71; instr. edn., asst. dean of students Columbia Coll., 1971-74; dir. guidance Am. Cmty. Sch., Buenos Aires, 1978-81; tchr. Spanish, psychology Ava (Mo.) HS, 1982-84; tchr. Spanish, social studies McDonald County HS, Anderson, Mo., 1984-88; counselor, acad. advisor Mo. So. State U., Joplin, 1988—2003. Cons. Mo. So. State Univ., 1990—; mem. internat. task force Mo. So. State Coll., 1994—96; mem. adv. bd. Adult Basic Edn., Joplin, 1992—2003; presenter Ctr. Applications Psychol. Type Internat. Conf., 1996. Elder First Christian Ch., Neosho, Mo. Named to Outstanding Young Women Am., 1972; recipient William D. Phillips Music award, 1st Christian Ch., Columbia, 1956. Mem.: Southwest Mo. Sch. Counselor Assn. (sec. 1994—97, v.p. 1992—94, 1999—2001, mem. governing bd., chmn. publs. and rsch. com. 1997—99), Mo. Sch. Counselor Assn., Phi Theta Kappa, Sigma Delta Pi, Phi Sigma Iota (romance lang., pres. 1959—60), Delta Eta Chi, Sigma Phi Gamma, Kappa Delta Pi. Avocations: music, photographer, sketch artist, needlecrafts, jewelry crafts. Home: 1214 Circle Dr Neosho MO 64850-1301 Office Phone: 417-451-7633. Personal E-mail: jfallman@sbcglobal.net.

ALLMAN, MARGO HUTZ, sculptor, painter; b. NYC, Feb. 23, 1933; d. Werner H. and Avis (Newcomb) Hutz; m. William B. Allman, Feb. 19, 1954; children: Avis Louise, David Drue. Student, Smith Coll., 1950-51, Moore Coll. Art, 1952-55, Hans Hofmann Sch. Art, 1953, U. Del., 1967-70. Artist-in-residence Canakkale Seramik, Turkey, 1995. One-woman shows include Wallingford (Pa.) Art Ctr., 1964, Windham Coll., 1974, Bloomsburg State Coll., 1976—77, Moore Coll. Art and Design, 1979, Marian Locks Gallery, Phila., 1984, McKinney Gallery West Chester U., Pa., 1994, Gomez Gallery, Balt., 2002, Garrubbo Bazan Gallery, West Chester, 2005, exhibited in group shows at Phila. Art Alliance, 1954, Del. Art Mus., Wilmington, 1958, 1965, 1967, 1993, 2000, Print Club, Phila., 1959, U. Del., 1977, Del. State Arts Coun., Wilmington, 1981, C. Grimaldis Gallery, Balt., 1983, Art in Form Gallery, Karlsruhe, Germany, 1984, Contemporary Women Artists Phila., 1986—87, Del. Ctr. Contemporary Arts, Wilmington, 1995, 2002, 2005, Long Beach Island Found. Arts and Scis., Loveladies, N.J., 1995, Cecil County Arts Coun., Elkton, Md., 1998—99, Chester County Art Assn., West Chester, 1999—2001, 2003, Regional Ctr. Women Arts, 2001, 2003, Garrubbo Bazan Gallery, 2005, Moore Coll. Art and Design, 2005, Art Trust, West Chester, 2005, Art Scene, 2006, Represented in permanent collections Del. Mus., Phila. Mus., Tidewater Pub. Co., Centerville, Md., Hercules, Inc., Wilmington, Connolly Bove Lodge & Hutz LLP. Bd. dirs. Robert Small Dance Co., NYC, 1979—80. Recipient Mildred Boericke prize, Print Club, 1958, Landscape prize, Wilmington Trust Bank, 1969, Disting. Alumnae award, Moore Coll. Art Design, 1998. Mem.: Phila. Mus. Art, Nat. Mus. Women Arts (charter), Del. Art Mus., Del. Ctr. Contemporary Arts, Moore Coll. Art and Design Alumnae Assn. Home: 202 State Rd West Grove PA 19390-8906

ALLMAN, WILLIAM BERTHOLD, musician, engineer, consultant; b. Phila., Feb. 16, 1927; s. Drue Nunez and Blanche (Oppenheimer) A.; m. Margo Hutz, Feb. 19, 1954; children: Avis Louise, David Drue. BSEE, Drexel U., 1949; MBA, U. Pa., 1951. Registered profl. engr., Pa. Contract engr. Atlantic Refining, Phila., 1951-55, E.I. DuPont de Nemours & Co., Inc., Wilmington, Del., 1955-58; constrn. engr. Niagra Falls, NY, 1958-59; cons. engr. Wilmington, 1959-82, Allman Assocs., West Grove, Pa., 1982—. Owner, mgr. Allman Bldgs., Phila., 1965-87. Contbr. numerous articles on plastic pipe to profl. mags.; drummer, washboard player with The Melton Bros. and Washboard Bill Allman band; performed with various musicians including Lionel Hampton, Brownie McGhee, Mississippi Fred McDowell, Sonny Terry. Mem. Bi-racial com. City of Newark, Del., 1963-71, chmn. 1965, London Grove Township Mcpl. Authority, Chester County, Pa., 1985-89, chmn. 1986; Dem. committeeman, Del., 1964-71, chmn., 1968; candidate Mayor City of Newark, 1970; adv. coun. Neighborhood Svcs. Ctr., Oxford, Pa., 1989—. With USNR, 1945-46. ETO. Mem. Am. Assn. Individual Investors, Del. Ctr. Contemporary Arts, Del. Art Mus., Phila. Mus. Art, Nature Conservancy. Avocations: painting, music, gardening, travel, reading. Home and Office: 202 State Rd West Grove PA 19390-8906

ALLMON, CHARLES W., investment advisor; b. East Liverpool, Ohio, Feb. 9, 1921; s. E. Floyd Allmon and Josephine T. Tate; m. Gwen D. Allmon, Apr. 15, 1954; children: Kathy Allmon Goodrich, Jane Allmon Heath. BS, Purdue U., 1941, PhD, 1994. With rsch. dept. United Fruit Co., Honduras, 1941-42; supt. divsn. Firestone Rubber Co., Liberia, 1943-46; freelance photographer, writer various mags., 1947-53; asst. editor illustrations Nat. Geographic Mag., Washington, 1953-69; pres., editor Growth Stock Outlook, Inc., Bethesda, Md., 1965—. Speaker in field. Interviewee over 1600 radio and T.V. programs, 1975—. Mem. citizen's com. North Chevy Chase, Md., 1962-65; trustee Alexander Graham Bell Assn. Deaf, Washington, 1972-98. Mem. Explorers Club N.Y., Masons. Presbyterian. Avocations: photography, international travel. Office: Growth Stock Outlook Inc 4405 E West Hwy Bethesda MD 20814-4522

ALLMON, MICHAEL BRYAN, accountant, financial consultant; b. Oceanside, Calif., July 14, 1951; s. William Bryan and Cecelia Audrey (Wright) A.; m. Monika Ann Arth, Sept. 15, 1979; children: Stefanie Michele, Danika Audrey. BBA, U. Tex., 1975; MBT, U. So. Calif., 1986. CPA, Calif., 1978; registered pvt. trusee, Calif. Dept. Justice, 2005. Acct. Alexander Grant & Co., LA, 1976—77, Laventhol & Horwath, CPAs, LA, 1977—85; dir. tax, fin. planning svcs. Zusman, Cameron and Allmon, CPAs, 1985-88; CEO, dir. Essential Profl. Svcs., Inc., 1985-86; ptnr. Michael B. Allmon & Assocs. LLP, CPAs, Manhattan Beach, Calif., 1988—; pres. MBA Group, Inc., Marina Del Rey, 1991—2004. Chmn., MBA Advisors, Inc., Manhattan Beach, 1999—; exec. bd. dirs. estate and gift com. of taxation sect. State Bar Calif, 2001—. Contbr. articles to profl. jours. Mem. AICPAs (fed. tax divsn.), Calif. Soc. CPAs (fin. planning com., tax com., v.p., bd. dirs. LA chpt. 1992-99, statewide bd. dirs. 1995-97, 2000-2003, chmn. LA estate planning com. 1992—, founding chair statewide estate planning com. 2000-2003, com. mem. 2000—, chmn. LA mentoring com. 2007—), Am. Assn. Profl. Fin. Planners (pres. LA chpt.), Wall-Nuts Track Club (LA, pres. team), Manhattan Beach Country Club (Calif.). Office: 1230 Rosecrans Ave Ste 102 Manhattan Beach CA 90266

ALLNUTT, ROBERT FREDERICK, management consultant, lawyer; b. Richmond, Va., June 15, 1935; s. Robert Carhart and Evelyn Rosalie (Brooks) A.; m. Jan Latven, July 17, 1938; children: Robert David, Thomas Frederick. BS in Indsl. Engring, Va. Poly. Inst., 1957; JD with distinction, George Washington U., 1960, LLM, 1962. Bar: D.C. 1960, Va. 1960. Patent examiner U.S. Patent Office, 1957-60; with NASA, 1960-70, 78-83, asst. adminstr. legis. affairs, 1967-70, assoc. dep. adminstr., 1978-81, assoc. adminstr. external rels., dep. gen. counsel, 1981-83; legal counsel, corp. sec. U.S. Com. Energy Awareness, 1983-84; v.p. Communication Satellite Corp., 1984-85; exec. v.p. Pharm. Mfrs. Assn., 1985-95; sr. counselor APCO Worldwide, Washington, 1995—. Assoc. gen. counsel Commn. on Govt. Procurement, 1970-73; staff dir. com. aero. and space scis. U.S. Senate, 1973-75; dep. asst. adminstr. ERDA, 1975-78; lectr. law Am. U. Law Sch., 1964; bd. dirs. Cortex Pharms., Inc., Irvine, Calif. Trustee Air and Space Heritage Coun.; bd. dirs. Nat. Health Coun., 1987-98, Nat. Coun. on Aging, 1990-98; mem. Com. of 100, Va. Poly. Inst., 1991—; mem. program coun. Internat. Ctr. for Sci. Lit., Chgo. Acad. Scis.; bd. dirs. Nat. Medals Sci. and Tech. Found., 1997-2005, Partnership for Caring, 1998-2001; vice chair Am. Hospice Found., 2003—. Recipient Superior Performance award U.S. Patent Office, 1959, Apollo Achievement award NASA, 1969, Meritorious Svc. medal ERDA, 1976, Exceptional Svc. medal NASA, 1981, Disting. Svc. medal NASA, 1983; named Meritorious Fed. Exec. with Presdl. Rank Office of Pres., 1981. Mem. Legal Aid Soc. D.C. (bd. dirs.), Nat. Space Soc. (bd. govs.), NASA Alumni League (v.p.), Edgemoor Tennis Club (Bethesda, Md., pres. 1987-89), Order of Coif. Home: 5415 Moorland Ln Bethesda MD 20814-1335

ALLOTT, ANTHONY J., packaging industry executive; BS, Boston Univ. CPA. CPA Deloitte & Touche, 1986—92; corp. contr., dir. fin. reporting Ground Round Restaurants, 1992—94; v.p., treas. Applied Extrusion Technologies Inc., 1994—96, sr. v.p., CFO, 1996—2002; exec. v.p., CFO Silgan Holdings Inc., Stamford, Conn., 2002—04, pres., 2004—05, pres., COO, 2005—06, pres., CEO, 2006—. Office: Silgan Holdings Inc Ste 400 4 Landmark Sq Stamford CT 06901*

ALLRED, ALBERT LOUIS, chemistry professor; b. Mount Airy, NC, Sept. 19, 1931; s. Caleb Haynes and Bessie (Brown) A.; m. Nancy Jean Willis, Aug. 30, 1958; children— Kevin Scott, Gregg Warren, Sarah Elaine. BS in Chemistry, U. N.C., 1953; A.M., Harvard, 1955, PhD, 1956. Chemist E.I. du Pont de Nemours Co., Wilmington, Del., 1952, 55, Mallinckrodt Chem. Works, St. Louis, 1954, Argonne (Ill.) Nat. Lab., 1958, 76; mem. faculty Northwestern U., 1956—, prof., 1969-91, prof. emeritus, 1991—, assoc. dean Coll. Arts and Scis., 1970-74, chmn. dept. chemistry, 1980-86, acting dean Coll. Arts and Scis., 1987-88, acting v.p. for rsch. and dean Grad. Sch., 1992, acting provost, 1995. Vis. scholar Cambridge (Eng.) U., 1987. Alfred P. Sloan fellow, 1963-65; postdoctoral fellow U. Rome, Italy, 1967; hon. research asso. Univ. Coll., London (Eng.), 1965 Mem. AAUP (pres. Northwestern U. 1968-69), , Am. Chem. Soc., Chem. Soc. (London), Coun. Chem. Rsch. (gov. bd. 1985-88), Rotary Internat., Phi Beta Kappa, Phi Lambda Upsilon, Sigma Xi, Alpha Chi Sigma. Home: 820 Milburn St Evanston IL 60201-2450

ALLRED, C. STEPHEN, federal agency administrator; b. Idaho; m. Sally Allred; 2 children. BS, U. Idaho, MS, 1967. Various positions including civil engr., dir. Idaho Dept. Water Resources, Calif., 1967—81; with Morrison-Knudson Corp., 1981—98; adminstr. Idaho Dept. Environ. Quality, 1999—2004, dir., 2000—04; ret., 2004; owner, mng. mem. Allred Consultants, LLC, 2004—; asst. sec., land minerals mgmt. U.S. Dept. Interior, 2006—. Mem. dean's adv. bd. U. Idaho; mem. biol. and agrl. engring. bd.; mem. Idaho Rsch. Found., Inc. Office: US Dept Interior 1849 C St NW Rm 6615 Washington DC 20240 Office Phone: 202-208-6734. Office Fax: 202-208-3619.*

ALLRED, DAWN PETERMAN, adult education educator; b. Roscrea, Ireland, Aug. 15, 1952; arrived in U.S., 1958, naturalized; d. Eugene Vincent and Ruth Kavanaugh Peterman; children: Anne Kavanaugh, Brendan, James. BA in Speech and Comm., U. Mo., Columbia, 1973; MEd in Spl. Edn., U. Mo., St. Louis, 2000, PhD, 2005. Cert. tchr. Mo. Rschr. comm. divsn. Marshall Field & Co., Chgo., 1979; tchr. ESL Parkway Sch. Dist., Creve Coeur, Mo., 1977—78; tchr. grade 3, primary grade coord. Annunziata Sch., St. Louis, 1974—77; tchr. grades 4, 5, 6, 7 St. Justin the Martyr Sch., St. Louis, 1979—82; grad. tchg. fellow U. Mo., 2000—, instr. Coll. Edn., 2001—04, student tchr. supr., 2004. Mem. com. Qualitative Rsch. Conf., St. Louis, 2001—. Pres. PTA The Miriam Sch., Webster Groves, Mo., 1993—95; mem. govt. rels. com. Parkway Sch. Dist., Chesterfield, Mo., 2000—05; bd. dirs. Spl. Edn. Transition Adv. Bd., St. Louis, 2001—. Recipient Meritorious Svc. commendation, U. Mo., 2004, 2005, 2006. Mem.: Mo. Assn. on Higher Edn. and Disability, Learning Disabilities Assn. Mo., Assn. for Study Higher Edn., Equestrian Order of the Holy Sepulchre of Jerusalem, Kappa Delta Phi, Phi Kappa Phi. Roman Catholic. Avocations: travel, Irish history and culture, hiking. Business E-Mail: allredd@umsl.edu.

ALLRED, GLORIA RACHEL, lawyer; b. Phila., July 3, 1941; d. Morris and Stella Bloom; m. Peyton Bray; 1 child, Lisa; m. William Allred (div. Oct. 1987). BA, U. Pa., 1963; MA, NYU, 1966; JD, Loyola U., LA, 1974; JD (hon.), U. West LA, 1981. Bar: Calif. 1975, U.S. Dist. Ct. (ctrl. dist.) Calif. 1975, U.S. Ct. Appeals (9th cir.) 1976, U.S. Supreme Ct. 1979. Ptnr. Allred, Maroko, Goldberg & Ribakoff (now Allred, Maroko & Goldberg), LA, 1976—. Former host KABC TalkRadio, Los Angeles. Co-author: (with Deborah Caulfield Rybak) Fight Back and Win: My Thirty-year Fight Against Injustice--and How You Can Win Your Own Battles, 2006; Contbr. articles to profl. jours. Pres. Women's Equal Rights Legal Def. and Edn. Fund, LA, 1978—, Women's Movement Inc., LA. Recipient Commendation award City of LA, 1986, Mayor of LA, 1986, Pub. Svc. award Nat. Assn. Fed. Investigators, 1986, Vol. Action award Pres. of U.S., 1986, Women of Distinction award Nat. Coun. on Aging, 1994, The Judy Jarvis Meml. award, 2001; Named to Millennium Hall of Fame, Nat. Assoc. Women Bus. Owners, LA Chapter, 2000. Mem. ABA, Calif. Bar Assn., Nat. Assn. Women Lawyers, Calif. Women Lawyers Assn., Women Lawyers L.A. Assn., Friars Club (N.Y.C.), Magic Castle Club (Hollywood, Calif.) Office: Allred Maroko & Goldberg 6300 Wilshire Blvd Ste 1500 Los Angeles CA 90048-5217 Office Phone: 323-653-6530.

ALLRED, SUSAN G., school system administrator; b. Greensboro, NC, Aug. 6, 1949; d. Hoyle and Dorothy Allred. BS in History, U. NC, 1971; MA in Edn., Gardner Webb U., 1982; cert. edni. specialist, Appalachian State U., 1989. Tchr., prin., supt. NC. Tchr. Gaston County Schools, Gastonia, NC, 1971—90; sch. and dist. adminstr. Ft. Mill (NC) Sch. Dist., 1990—99; dir. K-12 curriculum Transylvania County Schs., Brevard, NC, 1999—2004; dir. elem. edn. Iredell-Statesville (NC) Schs., 2003—05, chief academic officer, 2004. Mem. Iredell County Partnership for Young Children, Statesville, 2003, Jr. Achievement, Mooresville, NC, 2003; co-chmn. Transylvania County Arts Coun., Brevard, 1999—2003. Named Tchr. of Yr., Gaston County Schools, 1979, Ashbrook H.S., 1989; recipient Barbara James award for Vocat. Edn., SC Dept. Edn., 1999. Mem.: ASCD (assoc.), NCAFE (licentiate; examiner), Malcolm Baldrige Bd. of Examiners (licentiate; examiners 2005—06), PDK (assoc.), Am. Soc. Quality (assoc.). Democrat. Baptist. Office: Iredell-Statesville Schs 410 Garfield St Statesville NC 28677 Home Phone: 704-658-9103; Office Phone: 704-832-2521.

ALLSBROOK, OGDEN OLMSTEAD, JR., retired economics professor; b. Wilmington, NC, July 1, 1940; s. Ogden Olmstead Sr. and Elizabeth Barringer (Warren) A. BA, Wake Forest U., 1962; PhD, U. Va., 1966. Ops. rsch. analyst Dep. Def., Washington, 1966-68; asst. prof. econs. U. Ga., Athens, 1968-73, dir. grad. studies econs., 1971-81, assoc. prof., 1974-96, ret., 1996. Author: Utilization of Military Resources, 1969; contbr. articles to profl. jours. Capt. U.S. Army, 1966-68. Mem. AAUP, Nat. Soc. SAR (pres. Athens chpt. 1992-94), Cape Fear Club, So. Econ. Assn. Lutheran. Avocations: motor sports, stamp collecting/philately, turned wood objects, coin collecting/numismatics, Japanese cloisonne. Home: 115 Tillman Ln Athens GA 30606-4115 E-mail: ooalls1@wmconnect.com.

ALLSHOUSE, MERLE FREDERICK, educational organization administrator; b. Pitts., Apr. 26, 1935; s. Merle Lawrence and Helen (Frederick) A.; m. Myrna Mansfield, Apr. 1, 1956; children: Frederick Scott, Kimberly Dawn. BA (Rector fellow), DePauw U., 1957; MA (Rockefeller Theol. fellow), Yale, 1959, PhD (Rockefeller fellow 1959-61, Kent fellow 1961), 1965; DCL (hon.), Farleigh Dickinson U., 1986; EdD (hon.), Bloomfield Coll., 1986. Instr. philosophy Dickinson Coll., 1963-65, asst. prof., 1965-68, assoc. dean of coll., assoc. prof. philosophy, 1968—70; dean of coll., prof. philosophy Bloomfield (N.J.) Coll., 1970-71, pres., 1971-86, Myron Stratton Home Found., Colorado Springs, Colo., 1986-88; prof. publ adminstr. Grad. Sch. Pub. Affairs, U. Colo., 1988; v.p. U. Colo. Found., 1989-94; exec. dir. Acad. Sr. Profls., Eckerd Coll., St. Petersburg, Fla., 1994—2002; fellow U. South Fla., St. Petersburg, 2004—. Adv. bd. U. South Fla. Sch. Bus.; mem. NJ Student Assistance Bd. Co-editor (with George Allen): Nature, Truth and Value, 2005; co-author (with Robert Diamond): Utilizing America's Most Wasted Resource-Inside Higher Ed, 2007. Bd. dirs. Presbyn. Career and Counseling Ctr., N.J. Coll. Fund, Inc., Colo. Children's Campaign-The Goodwill of Colorado Springs, The Colorado Springs Symphony Orch., Coun. Ind. Colls., N.E. region Boy Scouts Am., Colorado Springs Symphony Orch., The Broadmoor Improvement Soc.; pres., Beth El Coll. Nursing, Goodwill of Colorado Springs; moderator Broadmoor Community Ch.; div. chmn. United Way; mem. Da Vinci Quartet; trustee Montclair Kimberley Acad.; pres. Presbyn. Coll. Union. Named one of 100 Most Effective Coll. and U. Pres. in Nat. Exxon Edn. Found., 1977; HEW fellow, 1979-80 Mem. Metaphys. Soc. Am. (chair 2004), Am. Philos. Assn., Am. Acad. Religion, Assn. Ind. Colls. and Univs. in N.J. (dir., chmn. bd.), Nat. Assn. Ind. Colls. and Univs. (chmn. secretariat 1983-86, bd. dirs.), Council Ind. Colls. (bd. dirs.), St. Petersburg Rotary. Home: Marina Bay 15 Crescent Pl S Saint Petersburg FL 33711-5118 Home Phone: 727-866-7291. Personal E-mail: allshouse@ureach.com.

ALLSTON, CHARITA CAPERS, music educator; d. Lloyd Sterling and Viretta Thomas Bond; children: Paul Capers Jr., Wayne Capers. AS in Music Edn., Essex County Coll.; BS in Voice, William Paterson Univ. Cert. tchg. cert. State of N.J. K-12. Acctg. tech. U.S. Postal Svc., Newark, 1973—91; choral instr. Orange Bd. of Edn., Orange, NJ, 1991—93, Elizabeth (N.J.) Bd. of Edn., 1993—99, Newark (N.J.) Newark Bd. of Edn., 1999—. Choir mem. R.P. Means Gospel Choir, 1975—99, M.A. Zimmerman Youth Choir, 1975—79, M.D. Birt AME Choir, 1977—92, Polyphonics Com. Ens., 1975—90; choir dir. Henry Tucker Male Chorus, 1977—84, rainbow Children's Choir, 1989—91, Chancellor Choir, 1989—91, St. Matthews Children's Choir, 1988—92, Angels of Zion Youth Choir, 1993—95, Allston/Shepard Gospel Music Works, 1991—2003, Park Ave. Christian Ch. Inspirational Choir and Crusaders For Christ, 1993—. Contbr. (vocals and piano for record album by Buddy Terry) Lean on Him; cinematographer: (organ and vocals for nat. TV) Dr. Albert Lewis Gospel Hour - Gospel Explosion; contbr. (organ and vocals for nat. TV) Bobby Jones Gospel Show: Black History Month Mass Concert; contbr. over 100 concerts and major events; contbr. US. Tennis Opening with Queen Latifah, 2000, in Going Home Celebration (Funeral) Lionel Hampton, 2002, Jubilation Choir N.J. Performing Arts, 2000, 02, Ray Charles Celebrates Christmas with the Voices of Jubilation, 2002, (CD) Launching Out Into the Deep, 2005. Recipient Charita C. Allston Resolution, City of Newark N.J., 1997, R.P. Means Adult Gospel Choir, 1997, Charita C. Allston Resolution for N.J. Performing Arts, City of Newark, N.J., 2003. Mem.: N.J. Music Edn. Assn., Newark Teachers Union, Nat. Assn. for Music Edn., Am. Fedn. of Musicians of US and Can. (Local 16). Personal E-mail: satindollcca@comcast.net.

ALLSUP, ROXANE CUELLAR, curriculum and instruction educator; b. Laredo, Tex., Feb. 26, 1968; d. Angel Arturo and Rosa Ramirez Cuellar; m. Christopher Bryan Allsup, July 28, 2001; children: Isabella Rose, Christopher Andrew. BS, Tex. A&M U., College Station, 1990, MEd, 1993, PhD, 2000. Cert. elem. edn. tchr., bilingual/ESL tchr., supr. Tex. Bilingual 2d grade tchr. Bryan Sch. Dist., Tex., 1991—94, bilingual resource specialist, 1995—96, 1997—98; asst. lectr., tchg. asst. Tex. A&M U., College Station, 1994—2000; vis. asst. prof. U. Houston, 2000—01; asst. prof. Tex. State U., San Marcos, 2001—. Cons., literacy coach Round Rock Sch. Dist., Tex., 2003—06; co-dir. bilingual edn. grant Tex. State U., San Marcos, 2005—06. Contbr. articles to profl. jours. Asst. chairperson multicultural awareness com. Bryan Sch. Dist., 1997—98; mem. San Marcos Sch. Dist., 2005—06. Bilingual Edn. fellowship, Tex. A&M U., 1994—97. Mem.: Tex. Assn. Bilingual Edn., Nat. Assn. Hispanic and Latino Studies, Nat. Assn. for Bilingual Edn., Phi Kappa Phi, Kappa Delta Pi. Roman Catholic. Avocation: spending time with my children. Office: Tex State Univ 601 University Dr San Marcos TX 78666 E-mail: rcuellar@txstate.edu.

ALLVIN, PAUL G., communications educator; b. 1970; B in Journalism, U. Ariz., 1993. Exec. dir. Ariz. Students Assn.; dir. Comm. Gov. Janet Napolitano; interim v.p., External Rels. U. Ariz., assoc. v.p., Comm. Mem. U. Ariz. Commn. on Status of Women. Dir. Comm. Make-A-Wish-Found.; mem. Phoenix Day and Family Learning Ctr., Valley of the Sun Chpt. Named one of 40 Under 40, Tucson Bus. Edge, 2006. Mem.: Pub. Rels. Soc. of Am., Ariz. Students Assn. Office: University of Arizona Administration Rm 116 PO Box 210066 Tucson AZ 85721 Office Phone: 520-621-4608. Office Fax: 520-621-6259. Business E-Mail: pallvin@email.arizona.edu.

ALM, JOHN RICHARD, beverage company executive; b. Jamestown, NY, Feb. 25, 1946; s. Carl Raymond and Erma Grace (Williams) A.; m. Cheryl D. Van Marter; Apr. 26, 1969; children: Lara, Richard. BS in Acctg., SUNY, Buffalo, 1972. Sr. auditor Price Waterhouse, NYC and Los Angeles, 1974-77; sr. v.p. fin., controller Johnston Coca-Cola Bottling Group, Inc., 1977—, v.p., CFO Atlanta, pres., COO; pres., CEO Coca-Cola Enterprises Inc., Atlanta, 2004—05. CPA, Minn. Served with USAF, 1969-72. Mem. Fin. Execs. Inst., Am. Inst. CPA's, Minn. Soc. CPA's.

ALMAGUER, FRANK, ambassador; m. Antoinette Gallegos, 1970; children: Francisco Daniel, Nina Suzanne. BA in Polit. Sci., U. Fla., 1967; MS in Govt. and Bus. Adminstrn., George Washington U., 1974. Vol. Peace Corps, Orange Walk Town, Belize, 1967-69; mgmt. analyst Office of Auditor Gen., USAID; mgmt. analyst for health affairs Office of Econ. Opportunity; assoc. country dir. U.S. Peace Corps, Belize City, 1974-76, country dir. Tegucigalpa, Honduras, 1976-79; dep. mission dir. USAID, Panama City, 1979-83, dir. Office of S.Am. and Mex. Affairs Washington, 1983-86, mission dir. Quito, Ecuador, 1986-90; mem. Sr. Seminar Fgn. Svc. Inst., 1990-91; regional mission dir. Eastern Europe USAID, Washington, 1991-93, acting asst. adminstrn. Bur. for Europe, 1993, dep. asst. adminstr. human resources Bur. of Mgmt., 1993-96, mission dir. La Paz, Bolivia, 1996-99; amb. Republic of Honduras Dept. State, Tegucigalpa, 1999—2002; internat. cons. and lectr. on L.Am. and social and econ. devel. issues, 2003—. U.S. del. UN Commn. on Human Rights, 2004; sr. advisor Pan Am. Devel. Found., 2004—05; asst. sec. adminstrn. and fin. OAS, 2005—. Recipient Meritorious award U.S. Peace Corps, 1979, Disting. svc. award USAID, 1989, Spl. Act award, 1992, Presdl. Meritorious awards, 1988, 99, Roger W. Jones Exec. Leadership award, 1996, State Dept. Superior Honor award, 1999, Sec. of State's Career Achievement award, 2002, AID Adminstr.'s Disting. Career award, 2002. Home: 1503 Dulcimer Ct Vienna VA 22182-1607 Office: 1889 F Street NW Washington DC 20006 Office Phone: 202-458-3436. Personal E-mail: falmaguer@oas.org.

AL MALIK, AMIR ISA, entrepreneur, consultant, musician; b. Shreveport, La., Apr. 2, 1951; s. Samuel Leroy and Evelyn Cynthia (Jones) K.; m. Sannah N. Parkies. AA Arts and Humanities, Laney Coll., 1981, AA Social Sci., 1983, AA Language Arts, 1985, AA Theater Arts, 1989, AA in Music, 1995; student, Columbia Sch. Broadcasting, Radio & T.V. Announcing, 1986; male modeling student, Barbizon Sch. Modeling, 1994; cert., Founds. of Faith Theology, 1994. Assoc. The Heritage Group, Walnut Creek, Calif., 1974—; pres., CEO Magnetic Phi Artists, Oakland, Calif., 1988—; supr. Loomis Armored Inc., Oakland, Calif., 1991—; coach San Francisco Generals; coord.-backfields and lineman Am. Athletic League; coach Alameda County Knights. Musician, poet free-lance, Oakland, 1970—; model, actor, Laney Coll., Yosson Enterprises, Oakland, San Francisco, 1981—; actor, dir. The Mahdi Theater, Oakland, 1989—; rschr., dir., The Oil Bandana, Oakland, 1989—. Author: (book of poetry) Africa Sweet Africa Me Africa Me, 1991, (short story) Three Coins for the Fisherman, 1990; composer: Tally of the Leaves, 1994, Clown Cloud, 1999; musician: Ben Oni Orch. Min. Imam Nation of Islam, San Francisco, 1975—; min.-in-tng. Allen Temple Bapt. Ch., 1981; fruit of Islam, Nation of Islam Mosque 26; asst. coach Peralta Coll. Dist., Oakland, 1986-87; active spl. svcs. Rainbow Coalition Calif., 1984; del. Students for Jesse Jackson Campaign, Calaif., 1989; candidate for mayor City of Oakland, 1994. With U.S. Army, 1975-76. Named Citizen of Yr., recipient Ambassador award Principality of the Hutt River Province, Queensland, Australia. Mem. Internat. Platform Assn., Pre-Paid Legal Svcs. (assoc., license), The Fed. Bear Sports Club (diploma), Nirvana Found. for Psychic Rsch. (life), Am. Legion (life), Smithsonian Inst., Knight of the Realm (ambassador, Citizen of Yr. 1995, Principality of Hutt River Province Australia), Phi Beta Lambda, Epsilon Alpha Phi (past pres., past v.p. state chpt.). Republican. Muslim. Avocations: martial arts, weightlifting, yoga, wrestling. Home and Office: 3600 Dimond Ave Apt 304 Oakland CA 94602-2207 E-mail: amir6.2@netzero.net.

ALMEIDA, RICHARD JOSEPH, finance company administrator; b. NYC, Apr. 29, 1942; s. Caetano Escudero and Grace (Maya) A.; m. Jill Farris, Mar. 17, 1979; 1 child, Alexis Farris. BA in Internat. Affairs, George Washington U., 1963; MA in Internat. Adminstrn., Maxwell Sch. Syracuse U., 1965. Comml. and internat. banker Citibank, NY, S.Am., 1966; area head comml. and internat. banking Citicorp/Citibank, Chgo., 1976, LA, 1978-84, dep. strategic planning NYC, 1984; head fin. inst. and investment banking origination Citicorp Investment Bank, 1985-87; CFO Heller Fin., Inc., Chgo., 1987—2002, chmn., CEO, 1995—2002. Bd. dirs. Corn Products Internat., E-funds Corp., United Airlines, Care-USA, Marmon Group. With USCG, 1966—72. Mem.: Chgo. Coun. Fgn. Rels., Comml. Club Chgo, Econ. Club. Chgo, Racquet Club, Casino, Chgo. Club. Roman Catholic. Office Phone: 312-214-3969.

ALMEN, LOWELL GORDON, church official; b. Grafton, ND, Sept. 25, 1941; s. Paul Orville and Helen Eunice (Johnson) A.; m. Sally Arlyn Clark, Aug. 14, 1965; children: Paul Simon, Cassandra Gabrielle. BA, Concordia Coll., Moorhead, Minn., 1963; MDiv, Luther Theol. Sem., St. Paul, 1967; LittD (hon.), Capital U., 1981; DD (hon.), Carthage Coll., 1989, Concordia Coll., 1994. Ordained to ministry Luth. Ch., 1967. Pastor St. Peter's Luth. Ch., Dresser, Wis., 1967-69; asso. campus pastor, dir. communications Concordia Coll., Moorhead, Minn., 1969-74; mng. editor Luth. Standard ofcl. publ. Am. Luth. Ch., Mpls., 1974-78; editor Luth. Standard, 1979-87; sec., officer Evangelical Luth. Ch. Am., Chgo., 1987—. Author: Old Songs for a New Journey, 1990, One Great Cloud of Witnesses, 1997, author, co-editor: The Many Faces of Pastoral Ministry, 1989; editor: World Religions and Christian Mission, 1967, Our Neighbor's Faith, 1968. Recipient Disting. Alumnus award Concordia Coll., 1982; Bush Found. grantee, 1972 Lutheran. Office: Evang Luth Ch 8765 W Higgins Rd Chicago IL 60631-4101

ALMERS, WOLFHARD, physiology and biophysics educator; b. Helmstedt, W.Ger., May 29, 1943; came to U.S., 1966; s. Eberhard and Ute (Plathner) A.; m. Hilary M. Turnbull, May 17, 1967; children: Mattias, Lucy. Student, Free U. Berlin, 1963-66, Duke U., 1966-69; PhD in Physiology, U. Rochester, 1971. Postdoctoral fellow physiology Cambridge U., 1971-74; tutor Churchill Coll., Cambridge U., Eng., 1972-73; asst. prof. physiology biophysics U. Wash., Seattle, 1974-78, assoc. prof., 1978—84, prof., 1984—92; dir. dept. molecular and cellular rsch. Max-Planck Inst., Heidelberg, Germany, 1992—95; prof. biology U. Heidelberg, 1995—99; sr. scientist Vollum Institute, Portland, Oreg., 1999—; prof. biochemistry and molecular biology Oreg. Health and Sci. U., Portland, 1999—. Contbr. articles to sci. jours.; mem. editorial bd.: Jour. Physiology, 1981—, Am. Jour. Physiology, 1981—. NIH grantee, 1974—; Muscular Dystrophy Assn. grantee, 1981-84; Alexander von Humboldt award for sr. U.S. scientists, 1984; Guggenheim fellow, 1984; recipient Merit award NIH, 1986. Mem. Soc. for Neurosci, Biophys. Soc., Physiol. Soc. Gt. Brit., NAS. Office: The Vollum Inst Oregon Health and Sci U 3181 SW Sam Jackson Park Rd Portland OR 97239-3098

ALMES, JUNE, retired education educator, librarian; b. Pitts., Feb. 14, 1934; d. Donald John Rowbottom and Marie Catherine (Linz) Douglas; widowed; children: Lawrence John, Douglas Alan. BS in Edn., Ind. U. of Pa., 1955; MLS, U. Pitts., 1969. Tchr. Shippensburg (Pa.) Area High Sch., 1964-68; assoc. prof. Lock Haven (Pa.) U., 1971-94; ret., 1990. Instr. Changsha U. Electric Power, Hunan, China, 1989-90, 95. Co-author: A Survey of the United Kingdom and the United States of America, 2004. Trustee Ross Pub. Libr., Lock Haven, 1975-88, community story programs, 1973-86; tutor Clinton City Literacy Found., Lock Haven, 1979; pres. Ea. Clinton Co. Democratic Women's Club, 2003—. Mem. Am. Assn. Sch. Librs., Pa. Assn. Sch. Librs., ACLU, Phi Kappa Phi, Phi Delta Kappa. Democrat. Avocations: bridge, reading, travel. Home: 228 East Hillside Dr Lock Haven PA 17745-1733 Personal E-mail: jalmes@lhup.edu.

ALMODOVAR, EDNA, pharmacist, educator; b. Yauco, PR, July 9, 1965; d. Rafael Almodovar and Gladys Caraballo; m. Armando Silva, Dec. 27, 1987; children: Armando Silva, Diego Silva, Rafael Arturo Silva. BS in Pharmacy, U. PR, 1989; PharmD, U. Kans., 1997. Registered pharmacist PR, 1992. Staff pharmacist VA Consol. Mail Outpatient Pharmacy, Leavenworth, Kans., 1996—98, Dwight D. Eisenhower VA Med. Ctr., Leavenworth, 1998—99; primary care pharmacy practice resident UAMC, San Juan, 2002; asst. prof. sch. pharmacy U. PR, San Juan, 2002—. Clin. pharmacist, preceptor home based primary care San Juan VA Med. Ctr., 2002—06. Vol. Antilles HS, San Juan, 2006—07. Recipient Team Recognition award, San Juan VA Med. Ctr., 2004. Mem.: Am. Coll. Clin. Pharmacy, Am. Soc. Cons. Pharmacists, Am. Assn. Colls. Pharmacy, Rho Chi (life). Achievements include development of home based primary care pharmacy practice model. Office: Univ Puerto Rico Sch Pharmacy Gpo Box 365067 San Juan PR 00936-5067 Home Phone: 787-293-0946; Office Phone: 787-758-2525 5310. Office Fax: 787-754-6995. Business E-Mail: ealmodovar@rcm.upr.edu.

ALMODOVAR, PEDRO, filmmaker; b. Calzada de Calatrava, Spain, Sept. 25, 1949; s. Francisca Caballero. Co-founder El Deseo S.A. prodn. co., 1987. Theater group actor: Los Goliardos; short films include: Salome, 1978-83; films: Pepi, Luci, Bom y otras chicas del monton, 1980, Laberinto de pasiones, 1980, Dark Habits, 1983, What Have I Done to Deserve This?, 1985, Matador, 1986, Law of Desire, 1987, Women on the Verge of a Nervous Breakdown, 1988 (Felix award 1988), Tie Me Up, Tie Me Down, 1990, High Heels, 1991, Kika, 1993, The Flower of My Secret, 1995, Live Flesh, 1997, All About My Mother, 1999 (Best Dir., Cannes Film Festival, 1999, Best Fgn. Lang. Film, Acad. Awards 2000), Talk To Her, 2002 (Best Original Screenplay Academy award, 2003, Best Screenplay-Original, British Acad. Film Award (BAFTA), 2003), Bad Education, 2004; pub. Fuego en las entrañas, 1982, Patty Diphusa and Other Stories, 1992. Recipient Prince of Asturias prize, 2006.

ALMON, LORIE, lawyer; b. NYC, Feb. 19, 1969; d. William Scott and Margaret Elise (Erickson) A. BA, U. Vt., 1991; JD, U. Va., 1994. Bar: N.Y. 1995, Conn., U.S. Dist. Ct. (so., ea. no. and we. dists.) NY, US Ct. of Appeals (2 and 3d cirs.). Asst. Corp. Counsel Office Corp. Counsel, NYC, 1994—98; co-mng. ptnr. Seyfarth Shaw, LLP, NYC, 1998—. Mem. regional bd. advisors Jumpstart. Named one of Top 40 Under 40 Lawyers, Nat. Law Jour., 2005, Litigation's Rising Stars, The Am. Lawyer, 2007. Mem. ABA, NYC Bar Assn., Soc. Human Resource Mgmt. Office: Seyfarth Shaw LLP 1270 Avenue Of The Americas Ste 2500 New York NY 10020-1801 Office Phone: 212-218-5517. Office Fax: 212-218-5526.*

ALMOND, CARL HERMAN, surgeon, physician, educator; b. Latour, Mo., Apr. 1, 1926; s. Hugh Herman and Sylvia (Morrison) A.; m. Nancy Ginn, June 18, 1964 (div. 1990); children: Carrie, Callie, Carl, Christopher. BS, Washington U., St. Louis, 1949, MD, 1953. Diplomate Am. Bd. Surgery, Am. Bd. Thoracic Surgery. Rotating intern Los Angeles County Gen. Hosp., 1953-54; resident surgery U. Mich., Ann Arbor, 1954-56, jr. clin. instr. surgery, 1956-57, sr. clin. instr., 1957-58; fellow surg. pathology Barnes Hosp.-Washington U., St. Louis, 1956; sr. surg. resident in urology Baylor U. Affiliated Hosps., 1958-59; resident thoracic surgery U. So. Calif., Los Angeles, 1959, fellow thoracic surgery, 1962-63; staff surgeon Univ. Hosp., Columbia, Mo., 1959-78, dir. thoracic and cardiovascular surgery, 1968-77, VA Hosp., Columbia; fellow Brompton Hosp., London, Eng., 1961; asst. prof. surgery U. Mo. Sch. Medicine, Columbia, 1959-64, asso. prof., 1964-69, prof., chief thoracic and cardiovascular surgery, from 1969; prof. and chmn. dept. surgery Sch. Medicine, U. S.C., Columbia, 1978-85, dir. gen. surgery residency program, 1979-85, assoc. dean clin. research and devel., 1986-90. Vis. prof. U. Geneva, Switzerland, 1972—73; mem. med. adv. panel FAA, 1970—75; mem. U.S. Commn. on UNESCO, 1983. Contbr. articles to profl. jours. With USNR, 1944—52. Fellow ACS; mem. AMA, Boone County Med. Soc., Columbia Med. Soc., S.C. Med. Assn., S.C. Thoracic Soc., Am. Assn. Med. Colls., Frederick H. Coller Surg. Soc., St. Louis Surg. Soc., Am. Coll. Cardiology, Am., S.C. heart assns., Am. Soc. Artificial Internal Organs, Soc. Med. Cons. to Armed Forces, Am. Coll. Chest Physicians, So. Thoracic Surg. Assn., Central Surg. Soc., Am. Assn. Thoracic Surgery, So. Surg. Assn., S.C. Surg. Soc., Chest Club, Soc. Surg. Chairmen, Marion S. DeWeese Surg. Soc., Southeastern Surg. Soc., So. Surg. Soc., Internat. Cardiovascular Soc., Soc. Thoracic Surgeons, Sigma Xi, Nu Sigma Nu, Sigma Chi. Home: 1829 Senate St 4E Columbia SC 29201 Office: U SC Sch Medicine Dept Surgery Two Medical Park Ste 402 Columbia SC 29203 Office Phone: 803-254-4158.

ALMOND, PAUL, film director, film producer, scriptwriter, writer; b. Montreal, Que., Can., Apr. 26, 1931; s. Eric and Irene Clarice Almond; m. Joan Elkins, Sept. 11, 1976; 1 child, Matthew James. Student, McGill U., Montreal, 1948—49; BA, Balliol Coll., Oxford, 1952, MA, 1954. TV producer-dir. CBC, Toronto, also in Los Angeles, NYC, London, 1954-67; pres. Quest Films, Montreal, 1967—2002. Writer, producer, dir.: (films) Isabel, 1968 (DGA nomination Best Feature Dir); Act of the Heart, 1970 (Genie for Best Feature Dir., 1970); Journey, 1972; Ups & Downs, 1982; The Dance Goes On, 1991; dir.: Captive Hearts, 1984; author: La Vengeance des Dieux, 1999; author: (with M Ballantyne) High Hopes, 1999. Decorated officer Order of Can.; recipient Liberty All Can. TV award for best drama dir., 1958, Spec Diploma of Merit, Prague for Seven Up, 1963, Genie for Best Can TV Drama Dir, 1980, Lifetime Achievement award, Directors Guild Can., 2007. Mem.: Writers Union of Can., Royal Can. Acad. Arts, Dirs. Guild Am., Dirs. Guild Can. (hon.). Anglican. Home: 54 Malibu Colony Malibu CA 90265-4637 Business E-Mail: paul@paulalmond.com.

ALMONY, ROBERT ALLEN, JR., librarian; b. Charleston, W.Va., Oct. 14, 1945; s. Robert Allen and Margaret Elizabeth A.; m. Carol A. Krzeminski, May 6, 1972; children— Rob, Michael, Chandra, Rachel. AA, Grossmont Coll., 1965; BA, San Diego State U., 1968; M.L.S., U. Calif.-Berkeley, 1977. Sr. div. clk. San Diego State U. Library, 1965-68; acct. Calif. Tchrs. Fin. Services, Orange County, 1968-70, v.p., gen. mgr., 1971-76; research asst. library sch. U. Calif.-Berkeley, 1976-77; reference librarian Oberlin Coll. Library, Ohio, 1977-79; asst. dir. libraries U. Mo., Columbia, 1980—; owner Almony & Assocs. Tax and Fin. Planning, Columbia, 1980—; distbr. USA Today, Columbia, 1984-88. Guest lectr. libr. budgeting, personal fin. planning; spkr. on fin. planning, U. Mo. HR seminars, 1999—; cons. libr. copy svcs.; faculty coun. exec. bd., 1994-2000, recorder Mo. U., 1994-98, chair fiscal affairs, 1998-2000, learning strategies tchr., 1986—, adj. faculty Libr. Sch., 1997—. Contbr. articles to profl. jours. Treas. Bahai's of Columbia, 1982-86, 95-97, 2003-, sec., 1987-89, 93-95, 1998-2001, 2001-2002, chmn., 1989-93; coach Columbia Youth Soccer League, 1981-92; cubmaster Boy Scouts Am., Columbia, 1983-85; asst. scoutmaster, 1985-91; hon. warrior Mic-O-Say, 1986-, treas. Mo. U. Soccer Boosters, 1996—2003; mem. Daniel Boone Regional Libr. Devel. Bd., 1999-2000. Mem. ALA, Mo. Libr. Assn. (treas. 1996-97, 98-99), Assn. Coll. and Rsch. Librs. (exec. com. 1983-86), Libr. Adminstrn. and Mgmt. Assn. (chmn. mem. 1991-93, 2000-01, Outstanding Svc. award 1994, B & F Officers Group Libr. Adminstrn. and Mgmt. (chmn. 1987-91), Nat. Commn. on Ednl. Stats. Integrated Post-Secondary Edn. Data Sys. Acad. Librs. (coord. Mo. 1992-, Mo. Assn. Coll. and Rsch. Librs. (vice chmn., chmn. 1982-84), Hickman Athletic Boosters (pres. 1991-94), Maplewood Barn Theater (bd. dirs. 1993-00, sec., treas. 1998-00), COE Coll. Parents (bd. dirs. 1993-95). Home: 301 Rothwell Dr Columbia MO 65203-0257 Office: U Mo 104 Ellis Libr Columbia MO 65201-5149 Office Phone: 573-882-4701. Personal E-mail: ralmony@aol.com. Business E-Mail: almonyr@missouri.edu. *Be of service to others in everything you do. Become a person of value to others.*

ALMORE-RANDLE, ALLIE LOUISE, special education educator, academic administrator; b. Jackson, Miss., Apr. 20; d. Thomas Carl and Theressa Ruth (Garrett) Almore; m. Olton Charles Randle, Aug. 3, 1974. BA, Tougaloo Coll., 1951; MS in Edn., U. So. Calif., LA, 1971; EdD, Nova Southeastern U., 1997. Recreation leader Pasadena Dept. Recreation, Calif., 1954—58; demonstration tchr. Pasadena Unified Sch., 1956—63; cons. spl. edn. Temple City Sch. Dist., Calif., 1967; supr. tchr. edn. U. Calif., Riverside, 1971; tchr. spl. edn. Pasadena Unified Sch. Dist., 1955—70, dept. chair spl. edn. Pasadena H.S., 1972—98, adminstrv. asst. Pasadena H.S., 1993—98; ind. rep. Am. Comm. Network, Inc., 1997—. Supr. Evelyn Frieden Ctr., U. So. Calif., LA, 1970; mem. Coun. Exceptional Children, 1993—; ednl. cons. Shelby Renee Ednl. Ctr., Gardena, Calif., 2000—. Organizer Northwest Project, Camp Fire Girls, Pasadena, 1963; leader Big Sister Program, YWCA, Pasadena, 1966; organizer, dir. March on The Boys' Club, the Portrait of a Boy, 1966; organized Dr. Allie's Book Mobile Project, 2002; pub. souvenir jours. Women's Missionary Soc., Meth. Ch., State of Wash. to Mo.; mem. Ch. Women United, Afro-Am. Quilters L.A.;, established Dr. Allie Louise Almore-Randle Scholarship Award, Pasadena H.S., 1998, Tougaloo Coll., 2005, First Meth. Ch., Pasadena, 2005, developer Econ. Devel. Fund, Inc., developer award; co-established Theressa Garrett Almore Music Scholarsip award Jackson State U., Jackson, Miss., 1989; charter mem. Cmty. Women of San Gabriel Valley, 1998, Women of Pasadena, 2002. Recipient Cert. of Merit, Pasadena City Coll., 1963, Outstanding Achievement award Nat. Coun. Negro Women, Pasadena, 1965, Earnest Thompson Seton award Campfire Girls, Pasadena, 1968, Spl. Recognition, Outstanding Cmty. Svc. award Tuesday Morning Club, 1967, Dedicated Svc. award AME Ch., 1983, Educator of Excellence award Rotary Club of Pasadena, 1993, Edn. award Altadena NAACP, 1994; named Tchr. of Yr., Pasadena Masonic Bodies, 1967, Woman of the Yr. Zeta Phi Beta, 1992, Commendation, City of Pasadena, 1998, Outstanding Educator, Phi Delta Kappa, 1998; Grad. fellow U. So. Calif., LA, 1970, recognition Uniformly Excellent Work and Exceptional Commitment and Dedication to Altadena/Pasadena Communities, Pasadena African Amer. Sch. Administr., 1998, Cert. Achievment award First AME Ch., 1998, Fran Cook Salute Great Inspiring Educator Award, United Tchr. of Pasadena, 1998; named Dr. Allie Louise Almore-Randle scholar in her honor Tougaloo Coll., Miss., 2005, First AME Ch., Pasadena, Calif., 2005. Mem. NAACP (life; bd. dirs., chmn. ch. workers com. 1955-63, Fight for Freedom award West Coast region 1957, Edn. award Altadena, Calif. chpt. 1994), ASCD, Calif. Tchrs. Assn., Calif. African Am. Geneal. Soc., Nat. Coun. Negro Women, African Pan Am. Doctoral Scholars, L.A. World Affairs Coun., Phi Delta Gamma (hospitality chair 1971—), U. So. Calif. Alumni Assn. (life), Tougaloo Coll. Nat. Alumni Assn. (life), Phi Delta Kappa, Alpha Kappa Alpha (life, membership com.), Phi Delta Phi (founder, organizer 1961), Phi Gamma Sigma. Democrat. Avocations: photography, gardening, genealogy, scrapbooks, church and family historian. Personal E-mail: akainger@sbcglobal.net.

ALMQUIST, DON, illustrator, artist; b. Hartford, Conn., July 21, 1929; s. Nils Herbert and Jeannette Theresa (Perrow) A.; m. Kerstin Rigmor Jesslen, May 21, 1955; children: Kristina, Jan Christian BFA, RI Sch. of Design, 1951. Staff artist Esquire, Inc., NYC, 1951; creative dir. Ahlen & Akerlund, Stockholm, 1963-66; adj. prof. Paier Coll. of Art, Hamden, Conn., 1979-84; graphic advisor U.S. Dept. of Fish and Wildlife, Washington, 1981-83. Illustrator: Christmas With Ed Sullivan, 1960, Doomed Road of Empire, 1962, What Did I See?, 1961, Loudmouse, 1962, (new illustrations) 1967, (new edit./illustrations) 1982, Spring is Like the Morning, 1964, Summer is a Very Busy Day, 1967, Dolls from Cheyenne, 1968, Some Animals Are Very Small, 1968, When Grandmother was Young, 1970, When Great Grandmother was Young, 1971, Getting to Know New York State, 1971, Den Förtrollade Lådan, 1967, It Never Is Dark, 1967, Not Very Much of a House, 1967, Cathy Uncovers a Secret, 1969, Ginnie and the Mystery Light, 1973, Libby Shadows a Lady, 1974, Season at the Point, 1991, The Little Red Hen, 1991, Dragged Aboard, 1998; one-man shows include Askersund, Sweden, 1993, Miriam Schiell Fine Arts, Toronto, 1994, Gallery M2, Stockholm, 1995, Gallery Vättern Askersund, Sweden, 1996, Montchanin Arts, Del., 1996, New Castle Arts, 1998, Galleri Cafe Lucas, Stockholm, 1999, Galleri Z, Ystad, Sweden, 2000, Carolynn Roberts Gallery, Hockessin, Del., 2002, 05, Rosenfield Gallery, Phila., 2003, 06, Am. Swedish Hist. Mus., Phila., 2004, Agilent Tech., 2006, Carspecken Scott Gallery, Wilmington, Del., 2007; exhibited in group shows at New Castle Arts Gallery, Ltd., Del., 1991, Springfield Art Mus., 1993, Miss. Watercolor Soc., Miss. Mus. Art, Hoyt Inst. Fine Arts, 1993, Nat. Art Show, New Castle, Pa., La. Art & Artists Guild and River Show, 1993, Soc. Devel. en Arts Contemporains, Montreal, 1994, Aqueous '95 Show, Louisville (Grumbacher Gold medal), Charlotte County Art Guild, Punta Gorda, 1997-98, New Castle Hist. Soc., Kent. Watercolor Soc., 1997, Pleiades Gallery, NYC, 2002, Md. Fedn. Art Am. Landscapes, Annapolis, Md., 2002, Rosenfeld Gallery, Phila., 2003, 06, Pleiades Gallery, NYC, 2003. Served as sgt. U.S. Army, 1951-53, Korea. Recipient awards of merit Soc. of Illustrators, NYC., 1953-84, Silver medal Phila. Art Dirs., 1955, Gold medal Milw. Art Dirs., 1963, Gold medal Grumbacher, 1997, awards of merit NY Art Dirs., NYC. Episcopalian. Avocation: horticulture. Home and Office: 103 The Strand New Castle DE 19720-4827 Office Phone: 302-322-1609. E-mail: almquistart@verizon.net, don@almquistart.com.

ALMQUIST, KATHERINE J., federal agency administrator; b. 1972; BA in Internat. Rels., Johns Hopkins U., Balt., Md.; MA in Internat. Rels., Johns Hopkins U. Paul H. Nitze Sch. Advanced Internat. Studies, Wash., DC. Chief of staff to sr. v.p., assoc. dir. public policy and govt. rels., internat. liaison officer World Vision, 1992—99; chief of staff Mass. Turnpike Auth., 1999—2001; chief of staff, adminstrn. and fin. Commonwealth of Mass., 1999—2001; spl. asst., sr. policy adv., dir. Sudan task force US Agy. Internat. Devel., 2001—04, dep. asst. adminstr. for Africa,

2004—07, US rep. to assessment and evaluation commn., 2005—, asst. adminstr. for Africa, 2007—. Office: US Agy Internat Devel 1300 Pennsylvania Ave NW Washington DC 20523*

ALMQVIST, PELLE, singer; With band The Hives, 1995—. Music tchr., Skinnskatteberg, Sweden. Singer: (albums) Barely There, 1997, A.K.A. I-D-I-O-T, 1998, Veni Vidi Vicious, 2000, Your Favorite New Band, 2002, Tyrannosaurus Hives, 2004. Co-recipient Best Nordic Act, MTV Europe awards, 2004. Mailing: Interscope Records 2220 Colorado Ave Santa Monica CA 90404

ALMSTEAD, SHEILA LOUISE, art gallery owner; b. Albuquerque, Apr. 8, 1955; d. Laurence and Ida Seif Bair; m. Arlington J. Almstead (div.); children: Stacy Lynne Fusilier, Michael Laurence, Christopher James, Jason Andrew. BSW summa cum laude, Our Lady of the Lake U., San Antonio, 1991; MSW, Our Lady of the Lake U., 1992. Case mgr. III San Antonio State HOsp. & Bexar County Mental Health, 1991—97; dir. health care svcs. Brighton Gardens, San Antonio; owner Zingaro Home Accents, Glendale, Ariz., 2002—. Mem. select Edn. Reform Com., San Antonio, 1991; mental health cons. Monarch Apts., San Antonio, 1995; med. social worker Morningside Home Health, San Antonio, 1996—97; juror Am. Art Trade Web Site, 2006—07; juror 1st ann. trade show Am. Craft Retailers Expo, 2007. Vol. ct. adv. Ct. Apptd. Spl. Advs., San Antonio, 1989—91. Mem.: Alpha Chi, Phi Theta Kappa. Democrat. Agnostic. Avocations: theater, travel, music, reading, art. Office: Zingáro Home Accents 5746 W Glendale Ave Glendale AZ 85301 Business E-Mail: shopzingaro@hotmail.com.

AL-NASSER, NASSIR ABDULAZIZ, ambassador; b. Sept. 1952; Grad. in Law, Beirut Arab U. Attache Qatar Fgn. Svc., Beirut, 1972—74, with embassy Pakistan, 1975, gen. counselor Dubai, India, 1975—81, with Ministry Fgn. Affairs Doha, 1981—85, min. to Permanent Mission to UN NYC, 1986—93, amb. to Jordan, 1993—98, amb., permanent rep. to UN NYC, 1998—. Chmn. Group of 77 UN, 2004, pres. security coun. Named Grand Comdr. of the Order of Makarios III, Republic of Cyprus, 2007. Office: Permanent Mission of Qatar to UN 809 United Nations 4th Fl New York NY 10017 Office Phone: 212-486-9335. Office Fax: 212-758-5630. E-mail: nassir@qatarmission.org.

ALNESS, MAE CHRISTINE, retired medical/surgical nurse; b. Granite Falls, Minn., Apr. 12, 1929; d. John N. Reese and Genevieve Mae Seim; m. Inghart Merdell Allness, Dec. 29, 1951; children: Cynthia Alness Boily, Mark, Mary Alness Jauss, Carol Alness Soine, Jon, John O'Connor. BSN, Deaconess Sch. Nursing, Mpls., 1950. RN Minn. Nurse Upper Sioux Cmty., Granite Falls; head nurse Renville County Hosp., Oliiva, Minn., G. F. Mcpl. Hosp., Granite Falls; rehab. nurse Project Turnabout, Granite Falls. Named Mother of the Yr., State of Minn., 1988. Democrat. Lutheran. Avocations: reading, cooking, walking, knitting. Home: 1175 Prentice St Granite Falls MN 56241

ALO, ADENIYI, pharmacist, federal agency administrator; b. Lagos, Nigeria, Dec. 31, 1973; arrived in US, 2002; s. Adedeji Alo and Olufunmilayo Ogundipe. B in Pharmacy, U. Lagos, Idi-Araba, Nigeria, 1999; MPH, U. Ariz., Tucson, 2004; PharmD, ND State U., Fargo, 2006. Registered pharmacist Ariz. State Bd. Pharmacy, 2007. Supr. poverty alleviation program Fed. Govt Nigeria, Bali, Nigeria, 2000—01; dist. coord. nat. immunization days WHO, Kiagama, Nigeria, 2000—01; pharmacist Nat. Youth Svc. Corp, Bali, Nigeria, 2000—01; regulatory officer, pharmacist Nat. Agy. Food and Drug Adminstrn. and Control, Ikoyi, Nigeria, 2001—02; intern pharmacist Thrifty White Pharmacy, Fargo, ND, 2005—07, Workforce Safety and Ins., Fargo, 2006; pharmacist Walgreen, Tucson, 2007—. Recipient Commendation cert., Taraba State, Nigeria, 2001, Patient Care award, Glaxo Smith Kline Beecham Pharm., 2007; scholar, U. Ariz. Alumni, 2003, Semi-Conductor Environ. Safety Health Assn., 2003, Rite Aid Corp., 2006, Walgreen, 2007; Charles R. Walgreen Jr. scholarship, 2006. Mem.: Am. Pharmacists Assn., Am. Soc. Health Sys. Pharmacist. Avocations: travel, reading, hiking. Office: Walgreen 2560 South Kolb Rd Tucson AZ 85710 Personal E-mail: aloadeniyi@yahoo.co.uk.

ALOE, PAUL HUBSCHMAN, lawyer; b. Phila., Feb. 2, 1957; s. Paul Edward and Mary (Hubschman) Aloe; children: Jessica, Ryan. BA with distinction, George Washington U., 1980; JD with distinction, Hofstra U., 1983. Bar: N.J. 1983, U.S. Dist. Ct. N.J. 1983, N.Y. 1984, U.S. Dist. Ct. so. and ea. dists.) N.Y. 1985, U.S. Ct. Appeals (2d cir.) 1990, U.S. Supreme Ct. 1991, U.S. Ct. Appeals (3d cir.) 1991, Pa. 1991, U.S. Dist. Ct. (no. dist.) N.Y. 1992; U.S. Dist. Ct. (ea. dist.) Pa. 1993. Law clk. N.Y. State Third Dept., Albany, 1983-84; ptnr. RubinBaum LLP, NYC, 1984—2003, Kudman Trachten Aloe LLP, NYC, 2003—. Contbr. articles to profl. publs. Mem. ABA, N.Y. State Bar Assn. (chair com. on civil practice law and rules 1993-99), Assn. Bar City N.Y. Mem. Office: 350 5th Ave New York NY 10020 Home Phone: 516-883-2203; Office Phone: 212-868-1010. Business E-Mail: paloe@kudmorlaw.com.

ALOFF, MINDY, writer; b. Phila., Dec. 20, 1947; d. Jacob and Selma (Album) A.; m. Martin Steven Cohen, June 16, 1968 (div. June 2000); 1 child, Ariel Nikiya. AB in English, Vassar Coll., 1969; MA in English, SUNY, Buffalo, 1972. Asst. prof. English U. Portland, Oreg., 1973-75; editor Encore Mag. of the Arts, Portland, 1977-80, Vassar Quar., Poughkeepsie, NY, 1980-88; dance critic New Republic, Bklyn., 1993—2001; cons. The George Balanchine Found., 2000—; editor Dance Critics Assn. Newsletter, 2003—06. Coord. Portland Poetry Festival, 1974—75; adj. assoc. prof. Barnard Coll., 2000—; lectr. Eugene Lang Coll., 2005—06. Author: (poems) Night Lights, 1979, (anthology) Dance Anecdotes, 2006; author essays and revs. theatrical dancing and lit. for NY Times Weekend, Book Rev. and Arts & Leisure, New Republic mag., Nation mag., Threepenny Rev., Dance mag., New Yorker mag., ann. Ency. Britannica, others. Recipient Whiting Writers award Mrs. Giles Whiting Found., N.Y.C., 1987; Woodrow Wilson Found. fellow, 1969, Woodburn fellow SUNY-Buffalo, 1972, Am. Dance Festival Dance Critics Inst. fellow, New London, Conn., 1977, John Simon Guggenheim Meml. Found. fellow, 1990. Mem. PEN Am. Ctr., Nat. Book Critics Circle (bd. dirs. 1988-91), Authors Guild, Aus. Guild, Phi Beta Kappa. Personal E-mail: MindyAloff@aol.com.

ALOFSIN, ANTHONY, architect, art historian, writer, educator; b. Memphis, June 22, 1949; s. Frederick Benjamin and Eleanor (Brodsky) A.; m. Patricia Tierney, June 5, 1993. AB magna cum laude, Harvard U., 1971, MArch with distinction, 1981; MPhil, Columbia U., 1983, PhD, 1987. Assoc. chmn. divsn. hist. preservation Columbia U., NYC, 1983-84, adminstrv. dir., founder Ctr. Preservation Rsch., 1984-85, asst. prof. architecture, 1984-86; scholar-in-residence The Frank Lloyd Wright Found., 1984-85; from assoc. prof. to prof. architecture U. Tex., Austin, 1987—99, prof. art and art history, Roland Roessner Centennial prof., 1999—. Rsch. dir. A Tense Alliance: Arch. Cen. Europe, Internat. Travelling Exhbn., 1993-96; consulting curator: Frank Lloyd Wright, Arch., Mus. Modern Art, 1994; guest curator Prairie Skycraper, 2005; dir. MS in archtl. studies, history and theory program and PhD program, U. Tex., Austin, 1987-97 2005-06; cons., lectr., spkr. in field. Author: Frank Lloyd Wright: Lost Years 1910-1922, 1993, The Struggle for Modernism: Architecture Landscape Architecture and City Planning At Harvard, 2002, Prairie Skyscraper: Frank Lloyd Wright's Price Tower, 2005, When Buildings Speak: Architecture as Language in the Habsburg Empire and Its Aftermath, 1867-1933, 2006; editor: Frank Lloyd Wright: An Index to the Taliesin Correspondence, 1988, Frank Lloyd Wright: Europe and Beyond, 1999, Prairie Skyscraper, 2005; contbr. articles to lit. and profl. jours. Recipient Vasari award Dallas Mus. Art, 1989; Graham Found. Advanced Studies grantee, 1993 96, 97, 05; Santa Fe Workshop Contemporary Art scholar, 1971; fellow Fulbright prof. Acad. Fine Arts, Vienna, Austria, 1989-90, Internationales Forschungzentrum Kulterwissenschaften, Vienna, 1995, Ailsa Mellon Bruce Sr. fellow CASVA Nat. Gallery Art, Washington, 2003-04, MacDowell Colony, 2006; Bogliasco fellow Liguria Study Ctr. for the Arts and Humanities, 2007. Mem. AIA, Soc. Archtl. Historianss, (nat. bd. dirs. 2005—), Coll. Art Assn., Harvard Grad. Sch. Design Alumni Coun., Fulbright Assn., US Internat. Coun. Monuments and Sites, Phi Kappa Phi. Avocation: gardening. Office: U Tex Sch Arch 1 University Sta B7500 Austin TX 78712-0222 Home: 1801 Lavaca #10A Austin TX 78701 Office Phone: 512-471-8156. Business E-Mail: alofsin@mail.utexas.edu. E-mail: anthony@alofsin.com.

ALOI, MICHAEL JOHN, lawyer; b. Apr. 1958; BA, W.Va. Wesleyan Coll.; JD, W.Va. U. Bar: W.Va. 1983. Pntr. Manchin & Aloi, PLLC, Fairmont, W.Va. Mem.: W.Va. State Bar (pres. 2002). Address: Manchin & Aloi Ste 203 1543 Fairmont Ave Fairmont WV 26554 Office Phone: 304-367-1862. E-mail: maloi@manchin-aloi.com.

ALONEFTIS, ANDREAS, business executive; b. Nicosia, Cyprus, Aug. 24, 1945; BA, Sch. Accountancy and Bus. Studies, Glasgow, Scotland, 1973; MBA, So. Meth. U., 1978; postgrad., N.Y. Inst. Fin., 1982, Henley Mgmt. Coll., UK, 1996—2000, Middlesex U., 2002. Acct. Cyprus Devel. Bank, Nicosia, 1966—72, chief acct., 1972—76, mgr. fin., 1976—78, sr. mgr. investments, 1978—82; gen. mgr., chief executive officer Cyprus Investment and Securities Corp., Nicosia, 1982—88; minister of def. Republic of Cyprus, 1988—93; chief exec. Am. Life Ins. Co., Nicosia, Cyprus, 1993—95; mng. dir. CypriaLife Ins., Nicosia, Cyprus, 1995—99, group gen. mgr. ins., 1999—2000; mng. dir., CEO Lambousa Venture Capital and Olympos Investments, Nicosia, 2000—01; exec. chmn. Allied Capital, 2001—; exec. vice chmn. Alliance Internat. Reinsurance, 2001; chmn. Cyprus Broadcasting Corp., 2003—06. Contbr. articles to profl. jours. and newspapers. 2nd lt. Cyprus N.G., 1964-66. Fulbright Found. grantee, 1977-78; So. Meth. U. fellow, 1977-78, Salzburg Seminaz fellow, 1984. Fellow Assn. Internat. Accts. (vice chmn.), Rotary. Greek Orthodox. Avocations: music, reading, cinema, jogging. Home: 10 Kastellorizo St Nicosia 2108 Cyprus Office: Allied Capital Ltd PO Box 14131 Nicosia 2154 Cyprus Home Phone: 357-22817970. E-mail: alonefan@cytanet.com.cy, andreas.aloneftis@alliancereinsurance.com.

ALONSO, CARIDAD, elementary school educator; BSBA in Anthropology, Fgn. Languages, Lit., Univ. Del., 1991, MEd, 1996. Tchr., 1996—; now Spanish reading specialist William C. Lewis Dual Lang. Elem. Sch., Wilmington, Del. Named Del. Tchr. of Yr., 2007. Office: William C Lewis Dual Lang Elem Sch 920 North Van Buren St Wilmington DE 19806 Business E-Mail: caridad.alonso@redclay.k12.de.us.*

ALONZO, MARTIN VINCENT, mining and aluminum company executive, investor, financial consultant; b. NYC, Apr. 8, 1931; s. Mariano and Mary (Traina) A.; m. Sabina Gallucci, June 7, 1952; children: Martin Vincent, Marlene, Sabrina. BBA in Acctg. cum laude, Baruch Coll., CUNY, 1952, MBA in Fin. and Investments, 1971. CPA, N.Y. Acct. Eisner and Lubin CPAs, NYC, 1952-57; treas., contr. Credit-Am. Corp., NYC, 1957-60; asst. v.p. indsl. time sales, financing and leasing A.J. Armstrong Co., Inc., NYC, 1960-65; treas., sec. So. Nitrogen Co., Savannah, Ga., 1965-67; asst. to v.p. fin. AMAX Inc., Greenwich, Conn., 1967-68, mgr. fin. planning, 1968-69, asst. contr., 1969, contr., 1970, v.p. and contr., 1973-78, sr. v.p. controls and adminstrn., 1978-80, sr. v.p. and pres. indsl. minerals div., 1981-82, exec. v.p. and pres. splty. and light metals ops., 1982-83, exec. v.p., chief fin. officer, 1983-87; pres. MVA Fin. Corp., 1987—; chmn., pres., CEO Chase Industries, Inc., 1990—2001; ptnr. Tri-Artisan Capital Ptnrs., LLC, Mcht, Bankers, 2002—. Mem. Am. Copper Coun.; bd. dirs. Copper & Brass Fabricators Coun., Inc., Copper Devel. Assn.; mem. pres.'s coun. MAPI, 1993; mem. Internat. Wrought Copper Coun., 1999-2002; trustee IPO Plus After Market Fund, 1997-2005. Bd. dirs. Greenwich Health Assn., 1978-90, Am. Found., 1993-95; active Greenwich Bd. Health, 1982-92, U.S. Nat. Com. Pacific Econ. Cooperation, 1993-99; trustee Baruch Coll. Fund, 2004. Recipient Freedom of the Human Spirit award, Internat. Ctr. for the Disabled, 1999, Alumni Achievement award, Bernard M. Baruch Coll., 2002. Mem. Nat. Assn. Accts. (chmn. mgmt. acctg. practices com. 1976-79), Conf. Bd., Coun. Fin. Execs., Fin. Adv. Coun. (exec. com. 1984-87), Extractive Industries Luncheon Group (chmn. 1978-79), Am. Mining Congress (chmn. acctg. com. 1980-82, mem. pension com. 1978-82), Internat. Magnesium Assn. (bd. dirs. 1983-84), AICPA, Fin. Execs. Inst., AIME, Phosphate Rock Export Assn. (dir. 1982-83), Mining Club N.Y.C. (dir.), Econ. Club N.Y., Westchester Country Club, Sky Club, Roundtable of Greenwich, Yale Club, The Union League Club, Beta Alpha Psi, Beta Gamma Sigma, Am. Assn. Sovereign Mil. Order of Malta, Legatus Republican. Office: 2 Sound View Dr Ste 100 Greenwich CT 06830 Office Phone: 203-622-1340. Personal E-mail: mvalonzo1@aol.com.

ALOU, FELIPE ROJAS, former professional baseball team manager; b. Santo Domingo, Dominican Republic, May 12, 1935; Player San Francisco Giants, 1958-62, Milw. Braves, 1964-65, Atlanta Braves, 1966-69, Oakland Athletics, 1970-71, N.Y. Yankees, 1971-73, Montreal Expos, 1973, Milw. Brewers, 1974; coach Montreal Expos, 1979-80, 84, mgr., 1992—2001; bench coach Detroit Tigers, 2002; mgr., S.F. Giants, 2002—. Named to Nat. League All-Star team Sporting News, 1966; named Nat. League Mgr. of Yr. Sporting News, 1994, Baseball Writers' Assn. Am., 1994.

ALOU, MOISES, professional baseball player; b. Atlanta, July 3, 1966; s. Felipe Alou. Outfielder Pitts. Pirates, 1990, Montreal Expos, 1990, 1992—96, Fla. Marlins, 1997, Houston Astros, 1998—2001, Chgo. Cubs, 2002—04, San Francisco Giants, 2005—06, NY Mets, 2006—. Named to Nat. League All-Star Team, 1994, 1997, 1998, 2001, 2004; recipient Buck Canel award for Top L. Am. Player, 1994. Achievements include being a member of World Series Champion Florida Marlins, 1997. Office: New York Mets 123-01 Roosevelt Ave Flushing NY 11369-1699*

ALOZIE, EMMANUEL C., writer, educator; s. Boniface Nwalozie-Amah and Agatha (Okere) Alozie; m. Caroline E. Nwaiwu; children: Eberechukwu E., Uchechukwu I., Emmanuel N., Nnanna T., Amechi-Anthony Chikwadolam. BA, Rust Coll., Holly Springs, 1985; MS, Ark. State U., Jonesboro, 1987; PhD, U. So. Miss., Hattiesburg, 1999. Banking accts., pub. rels. United Bank for Africa, Lagos, Nigeria, 1980—83; prof. Edward Waters Coll., Jacksonville, Fla., 1987—90, Lincoln U., Jefferson City, Mo., 1991—97, Shaw U., Raleigh, NC, 1999—2000; mktg., pub. rels. outreach coord. St. Marys Health Ctr., Jefferson City, Mo., 1999—2000; prof. Governors State U., University Park, Ill., 2000—. Reporter Topeka-Capital Jour., 1993, Asbury Park Press, NJ, 1995, Kansas City Star, Mo., 1995; cons. Village of Matteson, Ill., 2001—06; reporter Columbus Ledger-Inquirer, Ga., 2002, AP, Chgo., 2006, Oakland Tribune, Oakland, Calif., 1992—92. Editor: Toward the Common Good: Perspectives in International Public Relations; author: Cultural Reflections and the Role of Advertising in the Socio-economic and National Development of Nigeria; contbr. articles to profl. jours. Recipient Top Faculty Paper award, Global Fusion 2000 at So. Ill. U., 2000, Profl. Devel. award, Governors State U. Alumni Assn., 2002, Excellence award in rsch., Governors State U., 2006, Top Faculty Paper award, Internat. Divsn. of the Assn. for Edn. Journalism and Mass Comm., 2006; fellow, Freedom Forum, 1992, Am. Press Inst., 1993, Inland Press Assn., 1993, Cap-Cities/Am. Broadcasting Co. Fellow, 1994; Rsch. grant, Governors State U., 2004—05, 2007, Journalism Excellence fellow, Am. Soc. Newspaper Editors, 2002, 2006. Mem.: Union for Dem. Comm., Am. Acad. Advt. (internat. advt. divsn. 2004—07), Assn. for Edn. Journalism and Mass Comm. Home: 7044 W Gabreski Ln Monee IL 60449 Office: Governors State Univ One University Pkwy University Park IL 60466 Home Phone: 708-746-5200; Office Phone: 708-534-4057. Office Fax: 708-534-7894; Home Fax: 708-746-5200. Personal E-mail: alozieemmanuel@hotmail.com. Business E-Mail: e-alzoie@govst.edu.

ALPEN, EDWARD LEWIS, biophysicist, educator; b. San Francisco, May 14, 1922; s. Edward Lawrence and Margaret Catherine (Shipley) A.; m. Wynella June Dosh, Jan. 6, 1945; children: Angela Marie, Jeannette Elise BS, U. Calif., Berkeley, 1946, PhD, 1950. Br. chief, then dir. biol. and med. scis. Naval Radiol. Def. Lab., San Francisco, 1952—68; mgr. environ. and life scis. Battelle Meml. Inst., Richland, Wash., 1968—69, assoc. dir., then dir. Pacific N.W. divsn., 1969—75; dir. Donner Lab., U. Calif., Berkeley; also assoc. dir. Lawrence Berkeley Lab., 1975—87; prof. biophysics emeritus U. Calif., Berkeley, 1975—, prof. radiology emeritus San Francisco, 1976—, dir. U. Calif. Study Ctr. London, 1988—90; councillor, dir. Nat. Coun. Radiol. Protection, 1969—92; exec. v.p., tech. dir. Neutron Tech. Corp., Berkeley, 1990—93. Mem. Gov. Wash. Coun. Econ. Devel., 1973-75; bd. dirs. Wash. Bd. Trade, 1973-76 Author books, papers, abstracts in field Served to capt. USN, 1942-64 Recipient Navy Sci. medal, 1962, Disting. Svc. medal Dept. Def., 1963, Sustaining Members medal Assn. Mil. Surgeons, 1971; fellow Guggenheim Found., 1960-61; sr. fellow NSF, 1958-59 Fellow: Calif. Acad. Scis.; mem.: Biophys. Soc., Radiation Rsch. Soc., Am. Philat. Soc., Bioelectromagnetics Soc. (pres. 1979—80), Sigma Xi (nat. lectr. 1994—96). Episcopalian. Home Phone: 510-232-3520. Personal E-mail: e.alpen@comcast.net.

ALPER, ANDREW MICHAEL, former investment banker; b. Feb. 21, 1958; s. Jerome Milton Alper; m. Sharon Sadow, Sept. 22, 1985. BA, U. Chgo., 1980, MBA, 1981. Assoc., Corp. Fin. Dept. Goldman, Sachs & Co., 1981, v.p., 1985—90, ptnr., mng. dir., 1990—2002, co-head Fin. Institutions Group, 1993—96, COO, Investment Banking Divsn., 1996—2002; pres. NYC Econ. Devel. Corp., 2002—06. Vice chmn bd. trustees U. Chgo.; v.p. bd. govs. U. Chgo. Alumni Assn., 1996—98; chmn. The Chgo. Intiative, 2005—. Recipient Young Alumni Svc. Citation, U. Chgo. Grad. Sch. Bus., 1993, Disting. Pub. Svc./Pub. Sector Alumni award, 2004.

ALPER, HOWARD, chemistry professor; b. Montreal, Oct. 17, 1941; s. Max and Frema (Weinstein) A.; m. Anne Elizabeth Fairhurst, June 4, 1966; children: Lara, Ruth. BS, Sir George Williams U., Montreal, 1963; PhD, McGill U., 1967. From asst. prof. to assoc. prof. SUNY, Binghamton, 1968-74; assoc. prof. U. Ottawa, Canada, 1975-77, prof., 1977—, disting. univ. prof., 2006—. Chmn. dept. chemistry U. Ottawa, 1982-85, 88-94, asst. v.p. rsch., 1995-96, v.p. rsch., 1997-2006; co-chair InterAmerican Network of Acads. of Scis., 2004-07, co-chair interacad. panel, 2006—; chair Govt. Can. Sci., Tech. and Innovation Coun., 2007—; vis. exec. Internat. Devel. Rsch. Ctr. Contbr. articles to profl. jours. Mem. adv. coun. Order of Can., 2001—03. Decorated officer Nat. Order of Merit (France); recipient Alfred Bader award in organic chemistry, 1990, Commemorative medal for significant contbns. to Can. , 125th Anniversary of Can., 1992, E.W.R. Steacie award for disting. contbns. to chemistry, Can. Soc. for Chemistry, 1993, Urgel-Archambault prize in phys. scis., math. and engring., 1996, Bell Can. Forum award, 1998, Gerhard Herzberg Gold medal, 2000, Nat. Merit award, Life Scis. Coun., 2001, Le Seuer meml. award, Soc. Chem. Industry, 2002, Montreal medal, Can. Soc. Chemistry, 2003; fellow, NATO, 1967—68, Killam Found., 1986—88; Steacie fellow, Nat. Sci. Engring. Rsch. Coun., 1980—82, Guggenheim fellow, 1985—86. Fellow: Acad. of Sci. (v.p. 1995—98, pres. 1999—2003, co-chmn. interam. network 2004—, chair partnership group sci. and engring. 1995-99), Royal Soc. Can. (former pres.), Chem. Rsch. Soc. India (hon.), 3d World Acad. Scis. (assoc.), Chem. Inst. Can. (hon.); mem.: Coun. Can. Acads. (chair bd. govs. 2005—), Order of Can. (officer 1999), European Acad. Arts Sci. Humanities (titular mem.), Chem. Inst. Can. (Alcan award 1980, Catalysis award 1984, CIC medal 1997 , Montreal medal 2003), Royal Soc. Chemistry (London), Am. Chem. Soc., Natural Scis. and Engring. Rsch. Coun. Can. (group chmn. chemistry 1987-90). Jewish. Achievements include patents in field. Office: U Ottawa Dept Chemistry 10 Marie Curie Ottawa ON Canada K1N 6N5 Home Phone: 613-241-7382; Office Phone: 613-562-5189. Business E-Mail: howard.alper@uottawa.ca.

ALPER, MERLIN LIONEL, corporate financial executive; b. Bklyn., May 25, 1932; s. James B. and Rose (Mellis) Alper; m. Elaine R. Honig, Dec. 21, 1957; children: Jerome Eric, Alyssa Ellen. BBA, Adelphi U., 1955. CPA N.Y. With Arthur Andersen & Co., NYC, 1955-68, comml. audit mgr., 1963-68; dir. fin. controls ITT, NYC, 1968-73, asst. comptr., 1973-93, corp. v.p., 1979; v.p., contr. ITT Europe, Inc., 1978-84; corp. v.p., comptr., dir. ITT Telecom. Corp., 1984-85; v.p., dep. contr. ITT Corp., NYC, 1993-95; exec. v.p., CFO Madison Sq. Garden, NYC, 1995-98; mng. dir. Ind. Coll. Fund N.Y., 1999—, also chmn. bd. dirs., 2003—07. Mem. emerging issues task force Fin. Acctg. Stds. Bd., 1990—95. With Chem. Corps US Army, 1956—58. Named to Acad. of Distinction, Adelphi U. Alumni, 1984. Mem.: AICPA, Fin. Execs. Internat. (mem. com. on corp. reporting), Inst. Mgmt. Accts. (dir. NY chpt. 1965—66), N.Y. State Soc. CPAs. Personal E-mail: malper@prodigy.net.

ALPERIN, RICHARD MARTIN, social worker, psychoanalyst; b. Mt. Vernon, NY, Oct. 16, 1946; s. Israel and Sara A.; children: Heather Nicole, Alexander Scott. BBA, We. Mich. U., Kalamazoo, 1968; MSW, Fordham U., Bronx, NY, 1974; DSW, Columbia U., NYC, 1982; postdoctoral diploma in psychotherapy and psychoanalysis, Adelphi U., Garden City, NY, 1988. Lic. clin. social worker, NY, NJ; diplomate Am. Bd. Examiners in Clin. Social Work; cert. group psychotherapist Nat. Registry Cert. Group Psychotherapists. Cons. Mt. Vernon Youth Bd., 1972-76; adj. faculty Marymount Manhattan Coll., NYC, 1974-76; psychotherapist Riverdale Mental Health Clinic, Bronx, 1974-77; psychol. counselor, psychotherapist Ctr. Counseling and Psychol. Svcs. Ramapo Coll. of NJ, 1976-81, adj. faculty, 1977-86, moderator evening forums, 1978, 80; counselor, psychotherapist Ctr. Counseling and Psychol. Svcs. SUNY, Purchase, 1981-82, 84-85, acting dir., 1982-84; clin. cons. Westside Ctr. for Family Svcs., NYC, 1985-87; pvt. practice psychotherapy and psychoanalysis Riverdale, NY, 1977—, Teaneck, NJ, 1980—, NYC, 1984—. Lectr. Cabrini Med. Ctr., 1979; guest lectr. grand rounds dept. psychiatry, Brookdale Hosp. Med. Ctr., 1996; field instr. Grad. Sch. Social Work-Columbia U., 1983-85; adj. assoc. prof. Grad. Sch. Social Svc.-Fordham U., 1985-98; adj. asst. prof. Grad. Sch. Social Work-NYU, 1989-91; faculty, dean curriculum Rockland Inst. for Psychoanalysis and Psychotherapy, 1990-95; faculty Advanced Inst. Analytic Psychotherapy, 1992-95, Object Rel. Inst. Psychoanalysis and Psychotherapy, 1992—, Psychoanalytic Psychotherapy Study Ctr., 1994—, NJ Inst. for Tng. in Psychoanalysis, 1994—. Co-editor: The Impact of Managed Care on the Practice of Psychotherapy: Innovation, Implementation, and Controversy, 1996; contbr. articles to profl. jours.; rsch. on psychotherapy, suicide and provision of preventive svcs. Nat. Jewish Welfare Bd. fellow Fordham U., 1972-74. Trainee NIMH Columbia U., 1978. Mem.: NASW, Nat. Acads. Practice (disting. practitioner), NJ Coalition Mental Health Profls. and Consumers (mem. adv. bd.), Nat. Study Group on Social Work and Psychoanalysis, Alliance for Universal Access to Psychotherapy (founder, membership chair, mem. steering com. 1994-96), Nat. Membership Com. Psychoanalysis Clin. Social Work (treas. 1991—93, chair NY-NJ area 1992—94), Nat. Fedn. Soc. Clin. Social Work, Acad. Cert. Social Workers (cert.), Ea. Group Psychotherapy Soc., Am. Group Psychotherapy Assn., Adelphi Soc. Psychoanalysis and Psychotherapy, NY State Soc. Clin. Social Work (chair com. on psychoanalysis 1991—96, diplomate). Office: 175 Cedar Ln Teaneck NJ 07666-4315 Office Phone: 201-836-5050. Business E-Mail: ralperin@aol.com.

ALPERIN, STANLEY I., writer, editor, consultant; b. Boston, Jan. 3, 1931; s. Herman and Esther (Gorovitz) A.; m. Sondra Price, Sept. 8, 1957; children: Lisa Alperin Rose, Marlene Alperin Hochman, Hillary Baker. Pub., pres. U.S. Directory Service, Miami, Fla., 1966-91; pres. Unicol, Inc., Miami, 1991—. Cons. U.S. Directory Svc., Macmillan Pub., Reed Reference Pub. Author: Careers in the Health Care Field, Careers in Nursing, U.S. Medical Directory, Directory Medical Schools Worldwide, The Hospital Phone Book, The Federal Hospital Phone Book, Insurance Phone Book & Directory, Hospital Telephone Directory, University & College Phonebook, Discover America Directory; editor, researcher numerous medical directories. Home: 8821 SW 103rd St Miami FL 33176-3053 Office: UNICOL Inc PO Box 1690 655 NW 128th St Miami FL 33168-2735

ALPERIN, STUART N., lawyer; b. Bklyn., 1953; BA, SUNY, Binghamton, 1973; JD, Syracuse U., 1976; LLM in Taxation, NYU, 1980. Bar: NY 1977. Assoc. Skadden, Arps, Slate, Meagher & Flom LLP, NYC. Survey editor Survey of NY Law, 1975; contbr. articles to profl. jours. Mem. Order of Coif, Phi Beta Kappa, NY Bar Assn. (co-chair, Committee on Employee Benefits, Tax Section, 1990, Committee on Qualified Plans, Tax Section, 1991-96). Office: Skadden Arps Slate Meagher & Flom LLP 4 Times Sq New York NY 10036 Office Phone: 212-735-3920. Office Fax: 917-777-3920. Business E-Mail: salperin@skadden.com.

ALPERN, ANDREW, lawyer, architect, historian; b. NYC, Nov. 1, 1938; s. Dwight K. and Grace M. (Michelman) Alpern. BArch, Columbia U., 1964; DSc, London Coll. Applied Sci., 1971; JD magna cum laude, Benjamin N. Cardozo Sch. Law, 1992. Registered arch., N.Y.; bar: N.Y. 1993, U.S. Dist. Ct. (so. and ea. dists.) N.Y. 1994. With Haines Lundberg Waehler, archs., NYC, 1962—67; project dir. Saphier, Lerner, Schindler, Environetics, NYC, 1968—72; v.p., dir. arch. Environ. R&D, Inc., Space Planning & Design, NYC, 1972—75; dir. rsch. Corp. Planners & Coord., NYC, 1973—75; project mgr. Hellmuth, Obata & Kassabaum, P.C., NYC, 1977—78; mgr. real estate and facilities planning Coopers & Lybrand, NYC, 1978—88; cons. arch., hist. arch. NYC, 1988—. Mem. adv. bd. Inst. Applied Psychotherapy, 1969—72; nat. panel arbitrators Am. Arbitration Assn., 1971—86; cons. lawyer, 1993; spl. counsel Hughes Hubbard & Reed LLP, 1994—2002; exec. v.p., counsel, chief compliance officer Peter Kimmelman Asset Mgmt. LLC, 2002—; lectr. CUNY, Inst. Architecture and Urban Studies, Grolier Club, Mcpl. Art Soc., Sotheby's Art Inst. Author: Apartments for the Affluent: A Historical Survey of Buildings in New York, 1975, Garret Ellis Winants: 1813-1890, 1976, Alpern's Architectural Aphorisms, 1979, Handbook of Specialty Elements in Architecture, 1981, In the Manor Housed, 1982, Holdouts!, 1983, Fifth Avenue, 1986, New York's Fabulous Luxury Apartments, 1987, Statutes of Repose and the Cons. Industry: A Proposal for New York, 1991, Luxury Apt. Houses of Manhattan: An Illus. History, 1993, Hist. Manhattan Apt. Houses, 1996, New York's Arch. Holdouts, 1997, 101 Questions About Copyright Law, 1999, The New York Apartment Houses of Rosario Candela and James Carpenter, 2001; editor-in-chief: Legal Briefs for the Cons. Industry, 1978—92, pub.: F.M.R.A. (Edward Gorey), 1980; contbg. editor: NY Habitat, 1985—92; mem. bd. adv. Profl. Office Design Mag., 1986—89; contbg. columnist: Avenue Mag., 2000—02. Recipient Presdl. citation, N.Y. State Assn. Archs., 1991, Restoration award, Friends of Upper East Side Historic Dist., 2005. Mem.: AIA, NY Genealogical and Biographical Soc., Friends Cast Iron Architecture, Mcpl. Art Soc., NY Hist. Soc., Bklyn. Hist. Soc., Soc. Archtl. Historians.

ALPERN, ROBERT J., dean, medical educator; b. Nov. 3, 1950; m. Patricia Ann Preisig; chilren: Rachelle, Kyle. BA in Chemistry with honors and highest distinction, Northwestern U., 1972; MD with honors, U. Chgo., 1976. Diplomate Am. Bd. Internal Medicine; bd. cert in nephrology. Intern in internal medicine Columbia U., NYC, 1976-77, resident in internal medicine, 1977-79; fellow in nephrology and renal physiology U. Calif. Cardiovascular Rsch. Inst., San Francisco, 1979-82, asst. prof. medicine divsn. nephrology, 1982-87; assoc. prof. medicine U. Tex. Southwestern Med. Ctr., Dallas, 1987-90, chief nephrology, 1987-98, prof. medicine, 1990—2004, Ruth W. and Milton P. Levy, Sr. chair in molecular nephrology, 1994—2004, dean, 1998—2004, Atticus James Gill M.C. Chair in Med. Sci., 2000—04; dean Yale U. Sch. Medicine, New Haven, 2004—. Max Martin Salick vis. prof., UCLA Sch. Medicine, 1994; mem. Med. Sch. Admissions com. U. Calif. San Francisco, 1985-87, general clin. rsch. ctr. adv. com. U. Tex. Southwestern Med. Ctr., 1987-91, search com. for chief of cardiology, 1989, search com. for chmn. urology, 1993, search com. for chief of hematology/oncology, 1997, Med. Sch. Admissions com., 1994-96, chmn. 1996-98; chmn. general clin. rsch. ctr. adv. com. U. Tex. Southwestern Med. Ctr., 1988-90, search com. for chief of infectious diseases U. Tex. Southwestern Med. Ctr., 1994-96; adv. coun. Nat. Inst. Diabetes and Digestive and Kidney Diseases; presenter, lectr. in field. Editl. bd: Kidney Internat., 1989-90, Renal Physiology and Biochemistry, 1989-95, Am. Jour. Physiology, 1992-94, Internat. Yearbook of Nephrology, 1989-92, Seminars in Nephrology, 1990—, Am. Jour. Kidney Diseases, 1991-96, Kidney and Blood Pressure Research, 1996—, Am. Jour. Med. Scis., 1996—, Am. Jour. Medicine, 1997—; cons. editor: Jour. Clin. Investigation, 1993-99, Kidney Internat., 1990—; editl. com. Jour. Clin. Investigation, 1988-93; assoc. editor Am. Jour. Physiology, 1989-92, Hospital Practice: Physiology in Medicine, 1991-94; section editor: Annual Review of Physiology, 1993-97, Current Opinion in Nephrology and Hypertension, 1997-99; contbr. papers, chaps., articles to profl. pubs. Recipient NSF award for rsch. in developmental biology, 1971, NIH Merit award, 1996-2003. Mem. Am. Soc. Nephrology (mem. coun. 1995-2002, pres.-elect 2000, pres. 2001), Internat. Soc. Nephrology, Am. Physiological Soc., Am. Heart Assn., Am. Soc. Clin. Investigation, Assn. Am. Physicians, Alpha Omega Alpha, Sigma Xi, Phi Beta Kappa. Office: Yale U Sch Medicine Physicians Bldg 800 Howard Ave New Haven CT 06520 Office Phone: 203-785-4672. Business E-Mail: robert.alpern@yale.edu.

ALPEROVITZ, GAR, author, educator; b. Racine, Wis., May 5, 1936; s. Julius and Emily (Bensman) A.; m. Sharon Sosnick, Aug. 29, 1976; children by previous marriage: Kari Fai, David Joseph. BS in History, U. Wis., 1958; MA in Econs, U. Cal. at Berkeley, 1960; PhD in Polit. Economy, U. Cambridge, Eng., 1964. Congl. legis. asst., 1961-62; Senate legis. dir. U.S. Senate staff, 1964-65; spl. asst. Dept. State, 1965-66; fellow Kings's Coll., Cambridge (Eng.) U., 1964-68, Inst. Politics Harvard, 1965-68, Brookings Instn., 1966, Inst. Policy Studies, 1968-69, 89-99; co-dir. Cambridge (Mass.) Inst., 1968-71; dir. Exploratory Project Econ. Alternatives, 1973—; pres. Nat. Center Econ. and Security Alternatives, 1978—. Guest prof. Notre Dame U., 1982-83; sr. rsch. scientist, dept. govt. and politics U. Md., College Park, 1993-96, Harrison rsch. prof. dept. govt. and politics, 1996-99, Lionel R. Bauman prof. polit. economy, 1999—. Author: Atomic Diplomacy: Hiroshima and Potsdam, 1965, rev., 1985, 1994, Cold War Essays, 1970, Strategy and Program, 1973, Rebuilding America, 1984, American Economic Policy, 1985, The Decision to Use the Atomic Bomb, 1995, Making a Place for Community, 2002, America Beyond Capitalism, 2004; also articles. Home: 2317 Ashmead Pl NW Washington DC 20009-1413 also: Univ Md 3140 Tydings Hall College Park MD 20742-7215

ALPERS, DAVID HERSHEL, gastroenterologist, educator; b. Phila., May 9, 1935; s. Bernard Jacob and Lillian (Sher) A.; m. Melanie Goldman, Aug. 12, 1977; children: Ann, Ruth, Barbara. BA, Harvard U., 1956, MD, 1960. Cert. Am. Bd. Internal Medicine, 1967. Intern Mass. Gen. Hosp., Boston, 1960-61, resident in internal medicine, 1961-62; instr. medicine Harvard U., 1965-67, assoc. in medicine, 1967-68, asst. prof., 1968-69; asst. prof. medicine Washington U., St. Louis, 1969-72, assoc. prof., 1972-73, prof., 1973—, William B. Kountz prof., 1997—, dir. gastrointestinal divsn., 1969-97, asst. dir. clin. nutrition rsch. unit, 1999—; sr. cons. R&D GlaxoSmithKline, 1999—. Author: (with others) Manual of Nutritional Therapeutics, 4th edit., 2002; assoc. editor: Textbook of Gastroenterology, 4th edit., 2003, Physiology of the Gastrointestinal Tract, 4th edit., 1997; assoc. editor Jour. Clin. Investigation, 1977-82, Encyclopedia of Gastroenterology, 2003; editor: Am. Jour. Physiology, Gastrointestinal and Liver Physiology, 1991-97; mem. editl. bd.: Jour. Biol. Chemistry, 1998-2003; editor, Curr Opin Gastroenterol, sect. Small Intestine and Nutrition, 1995-; contbr. articles and revs. to profl. jours., chpts. to books. With USPHS, 1962—64. Fellow, Am. Soc. Nutritional Scis., 2003; David H. Alpers Ann. lectureship, Wash. U., Sch. Medicine, 1999. Fellow Am. Soc. Nutritional Scis.; mem. Am. Soc. Clin. Investigation, Assn. Am. Physicians, Am. Gastroent. Assn. (chmn. tng. and edn. com. 1974-78, dir. undergrad. tchg. project 1974-99, pres. 1990-91, Julius Friedenwald medal 1997), Am. Soc. Biochem. Molecular Biology (editl. bd. 1998-2003), Am. Fedn. Clin. Rsch., Am. Soc. Clin. Nutrition, Am. Psychol. Assn. (mem. gastrointestinal sect. steering com. 1991-97, Disting. Gastrointestinal Physiology Rsch. award 1998, mem. pubs. com. 1999-2001). Avocation: music. Office: Washington U Med Sch Dept Internal Medicine PO Box 8031 Saint Louis MO 63110-1010 Office Phone: 314-362-8943. Business E-Mail: dalpers@im.wustl.edu.

ALPERS, EDWARD ALTER, history professor; b. Phila., Apr. 23, 1941; s. Bernard Jacob and Lillian (Sher) A.; m. Ann Adele Dixon, June 14, 1963; children: Joel Dixon, Leila Sher. AB magna cum laude, Harvard U., 1963; PhD, U. London, 1966. Lectr. history Univ. Coll., Dar es Salaam, Tanzania, 1966-68; from asst. prof. to prof. history UCLA, 1968—, dean divsn. honors Coll. Letters and Sci., 1985-87, dean honors and undergrad. programs, 1987-96, chair dept history, 2005—. Author: Ivory and Slaves in East Central Africa, 1975; editor: Walter Rodney: Revolutionary and Scholar, 1982, History, Memory and Identity, 2001, Africa and the West, 2001, Sidis and Scholars: Essays on African Indians, 2004, Slavery and Resistance in Africa and Asia, 2005, Slave Routes and Oral Tradition in Southeastern Africa, 2005, Resisting Bondage in Indian Ocean Africa and Asia, 2006, Cross Currents and Community Networks: Excapsulating the History of the Indian Ocean, 2007; (newsletter) Assn. Concerned Africa Scholars, 1983-85; contbg. editor: Comparative Studies of South Asia, Africa and the Middle East, 1997—; bd. editors The American Historical Rev., 2002-05; contbr. articles to profl. jours. Fellow Ford Found., 1972-73, NEH, 1978-79, Fulbright Found., 1980; Conf. fellow Humanities Rsch. Ctr., Nat. Australia U., Canberra, 1998; Fundacao Calouste Gulbenkian grantee, Lisbon, Portugal, 1975. Mem. Am. Hist. Assn. (mem. com. Joan Kelly Meml. prize 1998-99, chair 2000), Africa Studies Assn. (bd. dirs. 1985-88, v.p. 1992-93, pres. 1993-94), Assn. Concerned Africa Scholars (bd. dirs. 1983-93), Alliance for Undergrad. Edn. (UCLA rep. 1987-95, co-chair 1989-92), Hist. Abstracts (adv. bd. 1994—). Office: UCLA Dept History Los Angeles CA 90095-1473 Home Phone: 310-454-3239; Office Phone: 310-825-1883. Business E-Mail: alpers@history.ucla.edu.

ALPERT, BARRY MARK, insurance company and banking executive; b. Chgo., Apr. 17, 1941; s. Isadore Daniel and Betty Shane A.; m. Judith Rae Schwartz, Dec. 24, 1969; children: Daniel Ian, Jason Bradley, Stephanie Ann. Student, Ind. U., 1958-60; BBA, Roosevelt U., 1961; MBA in Banking, U. Wis., 1965. V.p. Exch. Nat. Bank, Chgo., 1961-72; pres., CEO Belleair Bluffs Corp., Largo, Fla., 1973-77; chmn., CEO Orange State Life and Health Ins. Co., Largo, 1977-87, Home Life Fin. Assurance Corp., 1982-88; pres., CEO United Ins. Cos., Inc., Largo, 1988-89; pres. Pioneer Western Corp., Largo, 1989-91; vice chmn. Western Res. Life Assurance Co. of Ohio, Largo, 1989-91, Colony Savs. Bank, Clearwater, 1989-92. Chmn. bd., CEO Alpert Fin. Group Inc., 1988; sr. v.p. Robert W. Baird & Co., Inc., Tampa, Fla., 1991-97; chmn. bd., founder Life Savs. and Loan Assn., Clearwater, Vla., 1979-83; asst. prof. fin. Roosevelt U., Chgo., 1965-69; host radio program Ask a Banker, Sta. WBBM/CBS, Chgo., 1966-67; mng. dir. Raymond James, 1997—. Founding dir., chmn. Ruth Eckerd Hall-Pact Inc., Clearwater, 1980-86, Fla. Holocaust Mus., 1995—; founder North Suncoast Symphony Guild, Clearwater, 1974; bd. dirs. Fla. Orch., Clearwater, 1974-80, St. Petersburg (Fla.) chpt. United Way, 1975; trustee Fla. House Washington, 1984—, Tampa Bay Rsch. Inst., 1993—. Served with USAFR, 1961-65. Home and Office: Alpert Fin Group Inc 239 Bath Club Blvd N Redington Beach FL 33708 Home Phone: 727-393-7642; Office Phone: 727-567-5029. Business E-Mail: barry.alpert@raymondjames.com.

ALPERT, DANIEL, broadcast executive; b. Chgo., June 20, 1952; s. Herbert and Miriam Florence (Nemiroff) A.; m. Doreen Marie Podolski, Apr. 30, 1976; children: Hilary Marie, Neil Andrew. BA, Mich. State U., 1973, postgrad., 1974-76. News reporter, disk jockey Sta. WITL-AM-FM, Lansing, Mich., 1973; audio producer Instructional Media Ctr. Mich. State U., East Lansing, 1973-74; dir. pub. info. Sta. WKAR-TV, East Lansing, 1974-76; v.p., dir. pub. info. Sta. WTVS Detroit Pub. TV, 1976-82, sr. v.p., acting gen. mgr., 1983, sr. v.p., asst. gen. mgr., 1983-96, sr. v.p. sta. mgr., 1996-2000, COO, Sta. mgr., 2000—, interim gen. mgr., 2007—. Contbr. articles on travel and sci. local newspapers. Trustee Karmanos Cancer Inst., Detroit, 1984-2004. Recipient Devel. award Corp. for Pub. Broadcasting, 1976, Promotion award Broadcast Promotion Assn., 1978, Pub. Broadcasting Svc., 1981, Govt. Rels. awards Nat. Assn. Pub. TV Stas., 1989, 96, ACE award Mich. Assn. Broadcasters, 1991. Mem. NATAS (gov. Detroit chpt. 1980-97, Silver Circle award Mich. chpt. 2000), Mich. Assn. Broadcasters, Mich. Pub. Broadcasters (exec. com. 1995—). Office: Sta WTVS 7441 2nd Ave Detroit MI 48202-2796 Business E-Mail: alpert@dptv.org.

ALPERT, HERB, composer, recording artist, producer, painter; b. LA, Mar. 31, 1935; s. Louis and Tillie (Goldberg) A.; m. Sharon Mae Lubin, Aug. 5, 1956 (div.); children: Dore, Eden; m. Lani Hall. Co-owner, founder A&M Record Co., 1962-94, Rondor Music Internat., 1994—. Band leader, trumpeter, arranger producer music group Herb Alpert & The Tijuana Brass, 34 recs. including The Lonely Bull, Whipped Cream & Other Delights, Going Places, Rise, Under A Spanish Moon, Colors, 1999 (14 Platinum recs., 15 gold recs., 7 Grammy awards); prodr. Broadway shows, including Angels in America, Jelly's Last Jam, Seven Guitars. Founder Herb Alpert Found. Recipient Lifetime Achievement award, Rock and Roll Hall of Fame, 2006. Mem.: Calif. Horse Racing Bd. Office: c/o No Bull Inc 1414 6th St Santa Monica CA 90401-2510

ALPERT, HOLLIS, writer; b. Herkimer, NY, Sept. 24; s. Abram and Myra (Carroll) A.; m. Joan O'Leary (dec.). Student, New Sch. Social Research, 1947-49. Book reviewer Sat. Rev., N.Y. Times, others, 1947-59; film critic Sat. Review, after 1950, Woman's Day, 1953-60; assoc. fiction editor New Yorker, 1950-56; contbg. editor Woman's Day, 1956-69; mng. editor World Mag., after 1972, film editor, lively arts editor, after 1973; editor in chief Am. Film Mag., Washington, 1975-80; Algur Meadows Disting. vis. prof. So. Meth. U., 1982; freelance author, 1980—. Past dir. Edward MacDowell Assn.; vis. lectr. Yale U., 1972; lectr. film and writing Philharm. Ctr., Naples, Fla., 1995—. Author: The Summer Lovers, 1958, Some Other Time, 1960, The Dreams and the Dreamers, 1962, For Immediate Release, 1963, The Barrymores, 1964, The Claimant, 1968, The People Eaters, 1971, Smash, 1973, (under name Robert Carroll) A Disappearance, 1974, The Life and Times of Porgy and Bess, 1990, Broadway! 125 Years of Musical Theatre, 1991; editor: The Actors Life—Journals, Charlton Heston, 1978, Burton, 1986, Fellini, 1986; contbr. numerous short stories to mags. including Harper's Bazaar, The New Yorker. Served to 1st lt. AUS, 1942-46, ETO. Recipient Critic's award Screen Dirs.' Guild Am., 1957. Mem. Nat. Soc. Film Critics (chmn. 1972-73) Home: 6935 Carlisle Ct C-148 Naples FL 34109 Personal E-mail: halpert109@aol.com.

ALPERT, JOEL JACOBS, pediatrician, educator; b. New Haven, May 9, 1930; s. Herman Harold and Alice (Jacobs) A.; m. Barbara Ellen Wasserstrom, July 13, 1957; children: Norman, Mark, Deborah. AB, Yale U., 1952; MD, Harvard U., 1956. Diplomate Am. Bd. Pediatrics. Intern in medicine Children's Hosp. Med. Ctr., Boston, 1956-57, jr. asst. resident in medicine, 1957-58, chief resident for ambulatory svcs., fellow in medicine, 1961-62, from asst. to sr. assoc., 1962-72; exch. registrar St. Mary's Hosp. Med. Sch., London, 1958-59; from instr. to assoc. prof. Med. Sch., Harvard U., Boston, 1962-72, lectr., 1972; pediatrician in chief Boston City Hosp., 1972-92; prof. pediatrics and pub. health Boston U. Sch. Medicine, 2002—02, chmn. dept. pediatrics, 1972-93, also prof. sociomed. scis. and pub. health law, 1980—2002, prof. emeritus pediats. cmty. medicine and sociomed. scis., chmn. pediats., 2002—, prof. emeritus pub. health and health law, 2002—. Dozer vis. prof. Ben. Gurion Sch. Medicine, Beersheva, Israel, 1979; Raine Found. vis. prof. U. Western Australia, Perth, 1983; James and Jean Davis Prestige visitor U. Otago, Dunedin, New Zealand, 1995; cons. USPHS, 1972—, Children's Hosp., Boston, 1972; spl. cons. pres. N.Y.C. Health and Hosps. Corp., 1989; vis. prof. pediatrics Columbia Coll. Phys. and Surg., NYU Sch. Medicine; mem. med. adv. com. N.Y.C. Health and Hosps. Corp., 1989—; courtesy prof. U. Fla., Gainesville, 2007—. Author books, including: The Education of Physicians For Primary Care, 1974; also numerous papers Mem. Town Meeting, Winchester, Mass., 1970-72; mem. exec. com. Mass. Com. for Children and Youth, Boston, 1975-82; chmn. adv. com. Mass. Poison Info. System, Boston, 1980-92; bd. dirs. Med. Found., Boston, 1992—; cons. Commonwealth Fund and MEM Assocs., 1996—. Capt. U.S. Army, 1959-61. Recipient lifetime achievement award Mass. Poison Info. System, 1992, Hon. Mention Pub. Health Svc. award Pew Found., 1999, Pew Found. award for Achievement in Primary Care Edn.; numerous grants, 1965—; spl. fellow Nat. Ctr. Health Svcs. Rsch., London, 1971. Fellow: Royal Coll. Pediat. and Child Health (hon. 2000, U.K.), Am. Acad. Pediat. (v.p. 1997—98, pres. 1998—99, Job Lewis Smith award 1992); mem.: Mass. Assn. Pediat. Dept. Chmn. (chmn. 1976—78, 1981—93), Ambulatory Pediat. Assn. (pres. 1969, George Armstrong medal 1989, Lifetime Career Achievement award 2000, Pub. Policy and Advocacy award 2002), Philippine Ambulatory Pediat. Assn. (hon.), Soc. Pediat. Rsch., Am. Pediat. Soc., Inst. Medicine NAS (mem. governing coun. 1993—95, mem. bd. families and children 1993—95, mem. task force on future of primary care 1994—96), St. Botolph Club, Aescalapian Club, Harvard Club, Yale Club, Lancet Club, Alpha Omega Alpha. Jewish. Office: Boston U Sch Medicine Boston Med Ctr 91 E Concord St Boston MA 02118-2335 Home: 152 Orchid Lay Dr Palm Beach Gardens FL 33418

ALPERT, JON, television producer, director, reporter; b. Port Chester, NY; m. Keiko Tsuno; 1 child. BA, Colgate U., 1970. Taxi driver, NYC, 1970—72; co-founder Downtown Cmty. TV Ctr., 1972; contbr. NBC, 1979; co-founder, co-dir., video prodr. & reporter DCTV. Co-prodr.: (documentaries) Cuba: The People, Chinatown: Immigrants in America, 1976 (Alfred I. duPont-Columbia U. award, 1976, Christopher award, 1976), Vietnam: Picking Up the Pieces, 1977; dir., prodr. (documentaries) One Year in a Life of Crime, 1989, Lock-Up: The Prisoners of Rikers Island, 1994, Life of Crime 2, 1998, Latin Kings: A Street Gang Story, 2003, Independent Lens: The Last Cowboy, 2005, Baghdad ER, 2006 (3 Emmy awards, 2006, Alfred I. duPont-Columbia U. award, 2007), Wide Angle: Turkey's Tigers, 2006; dir.: (documentaries) Afghanistan: From Ground Zero to Ground Zero, 2002, Wide Angle: To Have & Have Not, 2002, Wide Angle: Coca & the Congressman, 2003; exec. prodr.: Dope Sick Love, 2005, Venezuela: Revolution in Progress, 2005, Off to War, 2005; prodr.: (TV miniseries) Animal Minds, 1999. Recipient 15 Emmy awards, 3 Alfred I. du-Pont-Columbia U. awards, Carl Spielvogel award, Overseas Press Club Am., 2007. Achievements include first Am. TV crew to film in Vietnam after the war; first Am. TV reporter to enter Cambodia after the end of the Vietnam war; only reporter to enter S. Vietnamese "re-education" camps; only Am. TV reporter to remain in Nicaragua during the Sandinista takeover; only non-Cuban allowed access to Fidel Castro during his visit to the UN. Office: DCTV 87 Lafayette St New York NY 10013 Office Phone: 212-966-4510. Office Fax: 212-226-3053. E-mail: jonny@dctvny.org.*

ALPERT, JOSEPH STEPHEN, cardiologist, educator; b. New Haven, Feb. 1, 1942; s. Zelly Charles and Beatrice Ann (Kopsofsky) A.; m. Helle Mathiasen, Aug. 6, 1965; children: Eva Elisabeth, Niels David. BA magna cum laude, Yale U., 1963; MD cum laude, Harvard U., 1969. Diplomate internal medicine and cardiovasc. disease Am. Bd. Internal Medicine. Successively intern, resident in internal medicine, fellow in cardiovascular disease Peter Bent Brigham Hosp.-Harvard U. Med. Sch., Boston, 1969-74, dir. Samuel A. Levine cardiac unit, asst. prof. medicine, 1976-78; prof., dir. divsn. cardiovascular medicine U. Mass. Med. Sch., Worcester, 1978-92, vice-chm. dept. medicine, 1990—, Edward Budnitz prof. of cardiovascular medicine, 1988-92; Robert W. and Irene P. Flinn prof. U. Ariz., 1992—, chmn. dept. medicine, 1992—2006, asst. to the dean Coll. Medicine, 2006—. Cons. West Roxbury VA Hosp., Boston, VA Med. Ctr., Tucson; sec., treas. med. staff U. Mass. Med. Ctr., 1979-81, pres. med. staff, 1981-82; bd. dirs. Am. Bd. Internal Medicine. Author: The Heart Attack Handbook, 1978, 3d edit., 1993, Cardiovascular Physiopathology, 1984; co-author: Manual of Coronary Care, 1977, 1980, 1984, 1987, 1993, 2000, Manual of Cardiovascular Diagnosis and Therapy, 1980, 1984, 1988, 1996, 2003, Valvular Heart Disease, 1981, 1987, 2000, Intensive Care Medicine, 1985, 2d edit., 1991, The Clinician's Companion, 1986, Modern Coronary Care, 1990, 2d edit., 1996, Diagnostic Atlas of the Heart, 1994, Cardiology for the Primary Care Physician, 1996, 3d edit., 2000, Primary Care of Native American Patients, 1999, American Heart Association's Clinical Cardiology Consult, 2001, 2006; editor-in-chief Current Cardiology Reports, 2001—05, Am. Jour. Medicine, 2005—; editor: Cardiology in Rev., 2001—05; assoc. editor Jour. History of Medicine and Allied Scis., 1977—80, editl. cons. Little, Brown & Co., Appleton-Century Crofts, mem. editl. bd. Am. Jour. Cardiology, 1985—, Archives Internal Medicine, 1987—, Heart and Lung, 1987—90, Geriatric Cardiovascular Medicine, 1988—89, Am. Jour. Noninvasive Cardiology, 1987—95, Am. Heart Jour., 1992—97, Internat. Jour. Cardiology, 1992—, European Heart Jour., 1995—, Heart Disease, 1999—2004, Cardiology, 1985—, assoc. editor, 1987—, editor-in-chief, 1991—2005, Am. Jour. Medicine, 2005—; contbr. articles to profl. jours. Lt. comdr. USNR, 1974—76. Recipient Gold medal U. Copenhagen, 1968, Edward Rhodes Stitt award San Diego Naval Hosp., 1976, George W. Thorn award Peter Bent Bingham Hosp., 1977, Outstanding Tchr. award U. Mass. Med. Sch., 1981, 86, 87, 90, U. Ariz. Med. Sch., 1995, 97-2002, 06; Fulbright scholar Copenhagen, 1963-64; USPHS-Mass. Heart Assn. fellow, 1971-72, NIH spl. rsch. fellow, 1972-73 Fellow ACP, Am. Coll. Cardiology (jour. editl. bd. 1983-86, chmn. tng. dirs. com. 1991—, trustee 1996-2001, Gifted Tchr. award 2004), Am. Coll. Chest Physicians (gov. for Mass. 1983-85); mem. AAAS, Am. Heart Assn. (fellow coun. clin. cardiology, vice chmn. 1991-92, chmn. 1993-95, exec. com. 1986—, Disting. Achievement award 2001), Am. Assn. History of Medicine, Am. Fedn. Clin. Rsch., Assn. Univ. Cardiologists, New Eng. Cardiovascular Club, Assn. Profs. of Medicine, Danish Cardiology Assn. (hon.), Argentine Heart Assn. (fgn. corr.), Israeli Heart Soc. (hon.), Am. Clin. and Climatological Assn., Aesculapian Club, Phi Beta Kappa, Sigma Xi, Alpha Omega Alpha. Office: U Az Coll Medicine 1501 N Campbell Ave Tucson AZ 85724-5017 Office Phone: 520-626-6118. Business E-Mail: jalpert@email.arizona.edu. *I have lived my life following 3 rules: (1) maintain enthusiasm for living and learning; (2) love family and friends; and (3) work hard.*

ALPERT, MARK IRA, marketing educator; b. Duluth, Minn., Nov. 6, 1942; s. Isadore L. and Lillian Alpert; m. Judith Itzkovits, Sept. 3, 1967; 1 child, Nicole Deborah. BS, MIT, 1964; MBA, U. So. Calif., 1965, MS,

1967, D of Bus. Adminstrn., 1968. Asst. prof. mktg. Calif. State U., Long Beach, 1967-68, U. Tex., Austin, 1968-72, assoc. prof., 1972-76, prof., 1976—, La Quinta Motor Inns Centennial prof. bus., 1982-87, Foley's Federated prof. in retailing, 1987—. Vis. prof. bus. U. Pitts., 1978; cons. Zenith Mgmt. Co., Duluth, 1980—. Author: Pricing Decisions, 1971; co-author: Managerial Analysis Marketing, 1970; also articles in profl. jours.; mem. editl. rev. bd. Jour. of Mktg., 1979—, Jour. of Retailing, 1979—, Jour. Mktg. Rsch., 1985-91, Jour. of Bus. Rsch., 1988—95. Mem. exec. com. Congregation Agudas Achm, Austin, 1977, 78, bd. dirs., 1977-79, 85-88; bd. dirs. B'nai Brith Hillel, Austin, 1980-85; adv. coun. Shattuck-St. Mary's Sch., 2004— Mem. Am. Mktg. Assn. (track chmn. 1976, 87), Assn. for Consumer Research, Am. Psychol. Assn. Avocations: tennis, golf, water-skiing, music. Office: U Tex Austin McCombs Sch Business, Dept Mktg 1 Univ Sta B6700 Austin TX 78712-0218 Home Phone: 512-453-5365; Office Phone: 512-471-5417.

ALPERT, MARTIN JEFFREY, chiropractic physician; b. NYC, Apr. 22, 1951; s. Sheldon Lee and Beatrice (Ostrager) Alpert; m. Gilberta Joachim, May 4, 2000; children: Chad, Mitchell, Eva. BA, Syracuse U., NY, 1972; DC, NY Chiropractic Coll., Seneca Falls, 1976; MS, U. Bridgeport, Conn., 1979. Diplomate Am. Bd. Disability Analysts, Am. Acad. Pain Mgmt., Am. Bd. Profl. Disability Cons., Am. Acad. Experts Traumatic Stress, Am. Assn. Integrative Medicine, Coll. Pain Mgmt. Pvt. practice, Yonkers, NY, 1977-84, Hollywood, Fla., 1985, Coconut Creek, Fla., 1987-92, Miami, Fla., 1992-95, Ft. Lauderdale, Fla., 1985—, Orlando, Fla., 1994—. Adj. faculty US Army Command and Gen. Staff Col., Ft. Leavenworth, Kans., 1998—. Lt. col. ret. USAR, 1970—2005. Decorated Meritorious Svc. medal with oak leaf cluster, Army Commendation medal with Five Oak Leaf Cluster, Army Achievement medal, Nat. Defense Svc. medal, Army Reserve Component Achievement medal, Armed Forces Reserve medal, Army Svc. Ribbon, Humanitarian Svc. Medal. Fellow: Am. Acad. Experts in Traumatic Stress, Am. Assn. Integrative Medicine (diplomate), Am. Back Soc., Internat. Biog. Assn.; mem.: U.S. Sports Chiropractic Fedn., Fla. Chiropractic Assn., Fla. Chiropractic Soc., Am. Acad. Spine Physicians, Am. Acad. Chiropractic Physicians, Internat. Fedn. Sports Chiropractic, World Fedn. Chiropractic, Am. Pub. Health Assn., N.Y. Acad. Scis., Am. Coll. Sports Medicine, Internat. Chiropractors Assn., Am. Chiropractic Assn., Signal Corps Regimental Assn., Army Hist. Found., Mil. Officers Assn. Am., Res. Officers Assn. U.S., Assn. U.S. Army. Democrat. Avocations: jogging, chess, basketball, piano. Home: 19674 Black Olive Ln Boca Raton FL 33498 Office: Third Ave Chiropractic Ctr Inc 300 W Sunrise Blvd Ste 7 Fort Lauderdale FL 33311-6200 also: Colonial Chiropractic Ctr 1310 W Colonial Dr Ste 21 Orlando FL 32804 Office Phone: 954-524-1416. Business E-Mail: doctorofchiropractic@hotmail.com.

ALPERT, NORMAN, chemical company executive; b. Phila., May 5, 1921; s. Barnet and Celia A.; m. Adeline Edna Gushman, Apr. 9, 1948; children: Rosalind Alice, Barbara Naomi. AB in Chemistry, Temple U., 1942, MA, 1947; PhD (AEC research fellow 1948-49), Purdue U., 1949. Devel. engr. Publicker Industries, Phila., 1942-45; group head Texaco, Inc., Beacon, N.Y., 1949-59; div. mgr. Exxon Research, Linden, N.J., 1959-79; v.p., dir. research Hooker Chem. Co., Grand Island, N.Y., 1979-82; v.p. spl. environ. projects Occidental Chem. Corp., Niagara Falls, N.Y., 1982-84, v.p. corp. environ. affairs, 1984-86. Environ. cons. Author; patentee in field. Mgr. Career Explorer Post local Boy Scouts Am., 1981. Mem. Am. Chem. Soc., Soc. Automotive Engrs., Niagara Frontier Assn. Research and Devel. Dirs. Home: 4060 Lower River Rd Youngstown NY 14174-9739 Personal E-mail: naalp@aol.com.

ALPERT, REVELL JUDITH, retired data processing executive; b. Bayonne, NJ, July 24, 1941; d. Charles and Belle (Laks) Motin; m. Norman W. Alpert, May 2, 2004; stepchildren: Joshua, Benjamin;children from previous marriage: Laura D. Mantell, Deborah P. Mantell. BS in Psychology cum laude, Bklyn. Coll. CUNY, 1969. Systems analyst Univac div. Sperry Corp., NYC, 1961-66; programmer, analyst J.C. Penney Co., NYC, 1966-67; systems and programming cons. Automated Concepts, Inc., NYC, 1968-72; ind. systems and programming cons. NYC, 1972-76; mgr. systems and programming Citibank, NA, NYC, 1976-83; v.p. data processing Columbia Bank, Fair Lawn, NJ, 1983-96; ret., 1996. Mem. Fin. Mgrs. Soc., Mensa. Jewish. Home: 43 Riverside Ave Haverstraw NY 10927-2009 E-mail: revnorm@aol.com.

ALPERT, SEYMOUR, anesthesiologist, educator; b. NYC, Apr. 20, 1918; s. Louis and Ida (Freedman) Alpert; m. Cecile Bernadine Cohen, Sept. 7, 1941. AB, Columbia U., NYC, 1939; MD, SUNY, Bklyn., 1943; LLD (hon.), George Wash. U., DC, 1984. Diplomate Am. Bd. Anesthesiology. Intern Beth Israel Hosp., NYC, 1943-44; resident in anesthesiology Gallinger Mcpl. Hosp., Washington, 1946-47; mem. faculty dept. anesthesiology George Wash. U. Sch. Medicine and Hosp., Washington, 1948—, prof., 1961-83, prof. emeritus, 1983—; v.p. for devel. George Wash. U., 1969-83, v.p. emeritus for devel., 1983—. Cons. in anesthesiology Walter Reed Army Hosp., Washington, 1948-83, VA Hosp., Washington, 1948-70, DC Gen. Hosp., 1948-69, Mead Dental Hosp., 1949-69; dir. Jefferson Fed. Savs. and Loan Assn., 1979-82; adv. bd. Washington Fed. Savs. & Loan, 1982-89. Contbr. articles to med. jours. Bd. govs. Hebrew U., Jerusalem, 1968-; bd. govs. State of Israel Bonds, 1964—, nat. chmn. med. divsn., 1969-86; bd. dirs. Israel Investors Corp., 1965-82, exec. com., 1974-82; bd. dirs. Am. Friends of Hebrew U., 1966—, chmn. med. divsn., 1969-86, v.p., 1969-90, hon. v.p. 1990—; examining physician Met. Police Boys Clubs, 1952-76; pres. United Jewish Appeal Greater Washington, 1966-67, exec. com., 1955—; bd. dirs. United Givers Fund, 1972-74; exec. com. Jewish Community Council, 1958-75; bd. mgrs. Adas Israel Congregation, 1963—; bd. dirs. Kaufmann Camp for Boys and Girls, 1964-78, Council Jewish Fedn. and Welfare Funds, 1966-73, Jewish Cmty. Found., 1966—, v.p., 1968-69; trustee United Jewish Endowment Fund D.C. 1984-98, trustee emeritus, 1998—, vice chmn., 1984-98, 1984-86, pres. 1986-88; found. com. Jewish Fedn. Palm Bch., Fla., 1990—. Capt. AUS, 1944-46. Recipient Man of Yr. award State of Israel Bonds, 1964; Freedom award, 1970; Disting. Svc. award Phi Delta Epsilon, 1971, 73; Torch of Learning award Am. Friends of Hebrew U., 1975; Med. award United Jewish Appeal, 1980; Achievement award Profl. Fraternity Assn., 1995; State of Israel Bonds Salvador Dali Menorah award, 2001. Fellow Am. Coll. Anesthesiology; mem. Am. Soc. Anesthesiologists (dir. 1963-66, trustee Wood Lib. Mus. Anesthesiology 1968-74, v.p. 1970-74), Md.-DC Soc. Anesthesiologists (pres. 1968-69), AMA, Med. Soc. D.C. (mem. numerous coms.), Jacobi Med. Soc., Pan Am. Med. Soc. (pres. 1967), Assn. Am. Med. Colls. (co-dir. nat. med. lib. study 1965-66), Assn. Univ. Anesthetists, Phi Delta Epsilon (nat. pres. 1961-62, exec. com. 1961—, exec. sec. 1963-72, v.p. bd. trustees 1972-73, pres. bd. trustees 1973-74), Cosmos Club (Washington), Woodmont Country Club (Rockville, Md.). Home: Brighton Gardens 5555 Friendship Blvd Apt 424 Chevy Chase MD 20815

ALPERT, WILLIAM HAROLD (BILL ALPERT), artist, painter; b. Bronx, Dec. 21, 1934; s. Jacob Joseph and Fannie (Leff) Alperovicz. PharmD, U. So. Calif., 1958; BA, UCLA, 1963, MA, 1965. Adj. prof. painting Cooper Union Sch. Art, N.Y.C., 1979-82; adj. instr. drawing Parsons Sch. Design, N.Y.C., 1981-82, Pratt Inst. Summer Program, 1981; prof. painting, drawing and watercolor Sch. Visual Arts, 1989—; guest lectr. and studio visitor Yunnan Art Inst., Kunming, China, 1993, Ctrl. Acad. Fine Arts, Bejing, China, 1993, The Green Horse Coll. Art, Ulaanbaatar, Mongolia, 1998. Exhbns. include Constructs Orgn. Ind. Artists, Bleecker Renaissance, NY, 1978, OIA: 6 Artists View Devel., N.Y. Acad. Sci., Orgn. Ind. Artists Postcard Show, Bologna Art Fair, Italy, 1978, Indpls. Mus. Art, 1978, Albright-Knox Mus., 1978, Joe & Emily Lowe Art Gallery, Syracuse U., 1980, W. Paterson Collection of NJ, 1981, Coll. Charleston (S.C.), 1987, 89, The N.Y. Bot. Garden, Bronx, 1993, Yunnan Art Inst., Kunming, China, 1993, The Dactyl Found. Arts and Humanities, NYC, 2005; pub. collections include Power Gallery Contemporary Art, Sydney, Australia, contbr. to NY Art Yearbook, 1975-76, The Sciences, NYAS, 1978, Art Informa, 1981. Avocations: pharmacy, photography, travel. Home: 64 Grand St # 5 New York NY 10013-2267 Office Phone: 212-966-1715.

ALPHER, RALPH ASHER, physicist, educator; b. Washington, Feb. 3, 1921; s. Samuel and Rose (Maleson) Alpher; m. Louise Ellen Simons, Jan. 28, 1942; children: Harriet Alpher Lebetkin, Victor. BS, George Washington U, 1943, MS, 1945, PhD, 1948; ScD (hon.), Union Coll., 1992, Renssalaer Poly. Inst., 1993. Physicist Bur. Ordnance and Naval Ordnance Lab., USN, Washington, 1940-44, Applied Physics Lab., Johns Hopkins U., Silver Spring, Md., 1944-55, GE R&D Ctr., Schenectady, NY, 1955-86; disting. rsch. prof. physics Union Coll., Schenectady, 1986—2004, prof. emeritus, 2004—07. Adj. prof. aero engring. Renselaer Poly. Inst., 1958—63, adj. prof. physics, 1986—92. Contbr. chapters to books, articles to profl. jours. Bd. dirs. Mohawk-Hudson Coun. Ednl. TV, 1974—80, 1982—87, chmn., 1978—80, 1986—87; bd. dirs. Dudley Obs., Union U., Albany, NY, 1968—72, 1980—86, v.p., 1983—86, adminstr., disting. sr. scientist, from 1987. Recipient Magellanic Premium, Am. Philos. Soc., 1975, Georges Vanderlinden prize, Belgian Royal Acad. Scis., Letters and Fine Arts, 1975, John Price Wetherill medal, Franklin Inst., 1980, Phys. and Math. Scis. prize, NY Acad. Scis., 1981, Disting. Alumnus award, George Washington U., 1987, Henry Draper medal, NY Acad. Scis., 1993, 2005 Nat. Medal Sci., NSF, 2007. Fellow: AAAS (sect. B physics steering com. 1982—86), Am. Acad. Arts & Scis., Am. Phys. Soc. (councillor-at-large 1979—82, mem. exec. com. 1980—81); mem.: Internat. Astron. Union, Am. Astron. Soc., Fedn. Am. Scientists, Internat. Torch Club, Sigma Xi. Home: Austin, Tex. Died Aug. 12, 2007.

ALPHER, VICTOR SETH, clinical psychologist, consultant; b. Washington, Oct. 20, 1954; s. Ralph Asher and Louise Ellen (Simons) A. BA, U. Pa., Phila., 1976; PhD, Vanderbilt U., Nashville, Tenn., 1985. Diplomate in clin. psychology Am. Bd. Profl. Psychology. Grad. fellow Vanderbilt U., Nashville, 1981-85; asst. prof. U. Tex. Health Sci. Ctr., Houston, 1986-88, clin. asst. prof., 1989-96; ret., 1996. Cons. Rsch. Inst. on Addictions, Buffalo, 1990—, Meml. Geriatric Evaluation and Resource Ctr., Houston, 1991-95; bd. cons. Fla. Inst. Psychology, 1994—. Cons. reviewer Jour. Cons. and Clin. Psychology, 1996; contbr. articles to profl. jours., including Jour. Cons. and Clin. Psychology, Jour. Personality Assessment, Jour. Psychopathology and Behavioral Assessment, Psychotherapy, and Jour. Applied Physiology. Fellow Am. Acad. Clin. Psychology; mem. Sigma Xi. Personal E-mail: Victor.S.Alpher.85@alumini.vanderbilt.edu, valpher@aol.com.

ALPHIN, J. STEELE, bank executive; b. Windsor, Va. BS in Mil. Hist., U. NC, Chapel Hill. With consumer bank Bank of Am., Chapel Hill, NC, 1977—80, compensation analyst pers. Charlotte, NC, 1980—84, regional personnel mgr. Tampa, Fla., 1984—85, pers. dir. Fla. bank, 1985—88, corp. pers. divsn. exec. Charlotte, NC, 1988—92, Atlanta, 1992—94, pers. exec. consumer & comml. bank and wealth mgmt. Charlotte, NC, 1994—99, corp. pers. exec., 1999—, chief adminstrv. officer. Bd. mem. Bank Adminstrn. Inst.; mem. bd. visitors Class of 2006 U. NC. Bd. trustees Thompson Child & Family Focus. Office: Bank of America Corp 100 N Tryon St Charlotte NC 28255*

AL-RABADI, ANAS NASER ESSA, electrical and computer engineer; b. Ajloun, Jordan, Apr. 14, 1973; arrived in US, 1996; BS in Electronics Sys. Design and Comm. Electronics and Comms. Sys. Design, Jordan U. Sci. and Tech., 1995; MS in Elec. and Computer Engring., Portland State U., Oreg., 1998, PhD in Elec. and Computer Engring. Design, 2002. Tv engr. LG Electronics, Amman, Jordan, 1996; computer and mainframe engr. Unisys, Amman, 1995—96; from rsch. and tchg. asst. to fellow, adj. prof. Portland (Oreg.) State U., 1997—2002, post-doctoral rsch. fellow, 2002—, adj. prof., 2002—; electronics instr. Heald Coll., Portland, Oreg., 1999. Author: (textbook) Reversible Logic Synthesis: From Fundamentals to Quantum Computing, 2003; contbr. some 60 articles to profl. jours. Vol. mentor of mid. sch. students Future Scientists and Engineers of Am., Milwakie, Oreg., 2003; bd. planning policies for student housing Coll. Housing North West, Portland, 1999; student rep. student union. Jordan U. Sci. and Tech., Irbid, Jordan, 1995. Fellow, Portland State U., 2003—04; scholar, Jordan U. of Sci. and Tech., 1990—95. Mem.: IEEE (corr.), Am. Phys. Soc. (corr.), Optical Soc. Am. (corr.), Soc. Indsl. and Applied Math. (corr.), Internat. Neural Network Soc. (corr.), Assn. for Computing Machinery. (corr.), Am. Soc. Engring. Edn. (corr.), Internat. Soc. for Optical Engring. (corr.), Eta Kappa Nu (life), Tau Beta Pi (life), Sigma Xi (life). Achievements include invention of new types of functional and circuit decompositions for electrical circuits design; new types of set-theoretic reconstructability analysis as new decomposition for the design of circuits and systems; Carbon Nano Tube (CNT) Multiplexers for binary and multiple-valued logic circuit designs; Optical Gates using Linear Optics to synthesize logic circuits; discovery of new technologies in quantum computing; new methods for reversible logic synthesis; computer-aided design algorithms; patents pending for carbon nano tube (CNT) multiplexers, circuits and actuartors. Avocations: swimming, cooking, basketball, european football. Home: SW Clay Street Post Office Box 85 Portland OR 97207-0085 Office: Portland State University 1604 SW 10th Avenue Portland OR 97201 Personal E-mail: alrabadi@yahoo.com.

ALRED, GERALD JAMES, literature and language professor; b. Dayton, Ohio, Feb. 24, 1943; s. Edgar James and Leona Jane (Evans) Alred; m. Janice Ruth Moody, Aug. 17, 1974; children: Elaine, Jeanette. BA, U. Dayton, 1965, MA, 1968; postgrad., Miami U., Oxford, Ohio, 1971—74. Instr. Sinclair Coll., Dayton, 1968—71; prof. English U. Wis., Milw., 1974—. Guest prof. Justos Liebig U., Giessen, Germany, 1994, Giessen, 98, Giessen, 2004. Author: Practical Writing: Composition for the Business and Technical World, 1973, Business and Technical Writing: An Annotated Bibliography of Books, 1880-1980, 1981, The Professional Writer: A Guide for Advanced Technical Writing, 1991, The St. Martin's Bibliography of Business and Technical Communication, 1997, The Technical Writer's Companion, 3rd edit., 2002, The Business Writer's Companion, 4th edit., 2005, Handbook of Technical Writing, 8th edit., 2006, The Business Writer's Handbook, 8th edit., 2006, Writing That Works, 9th edit., 2007; mem. editl. bd.: Jour. Bus. and Tech. Comm., 1987—, Jour. Bus. Comm., 2005—; contbr. articles to profl. jours. Recipient Jay R. Gould award, Soc. for Tech. Comm., Washington, 2004. Mem.: Assn. Tchrs. Tech. Writing, Nat. Coun. for Tchrs. English, Assn. for Bus. Comm. Avocations: running, yoga. Office: Univ Wis 3243 N Downer Ave Milwaukee WI 53211 Business E-Mail: alred@uwm.edu.

ALSAUD, PRINCE ALWALEED BIN TALAL BIN ABDULAZIZ, investment company executive, investor, entrepreneur; b. Riyadh, Saudi Arabia, Mar. 1955; s. Prince Talal Bin AbdulAziz Alsaud and Princess Mona El-Solh; divorced; children: Khalid, Reem; m. Princess Kholood Alsaud (div.); m. Princess Ameera Alsaud. BSc magna cum laude, Menlo Coll., 1979; MA with honors, Syracuse U., 1985; DHL (hon.), U. New Haven, 1992; D in bus. adminstrn. (hon.), Kyungwon U., 1998; LLD (hon.), Syracuse U., 1999, Exeter U., 2002, Am. U., Cairo, 2002. Chmn. Kingdom Holding Co., Saudi Arabia, Azizia Commercial Investment Co., Rotana Video and Audio Visual Co.; pvt. entrepreneur; investor Four Seasons Hotel and Resorts, Fairmount Hotels and Resorts, Mövenpick Hotels and Resorts, US, Middle East, and Africa, Citigroup, 1991—, News Corp, Time Warner, Motorola, Apple Computers, Ballast Nedam, Canary Wharf, Disneyland Paris, Saks Inc., Kingdom Ctr. Named one of World's Richest People, Forbes Mag., 2005—; recipient Presdl. medal, U. New Haven, 1999, Arab Bankers Assn. of Am. Lifetime Achievement award, 2000. Avocations: exercise, reading. Office: Kingdom Holding Co PO Box 2 Riyadh 11321 Saudi Arabia

ALSBORG, THOMAS C., electronics executive; BS acctg., Oral Roberts Univ.; MBA, Univ. Santa Clara. CPA. Mgmt. positions McDonald's Corp.; CPA Ernst & Young; fin. mgmt. positions Solectron Corp., 1995—2002; v.p., CFO Solectron Global Services, 2002—05; CFO SYNNEX Corp., Fremont, Calif., 2007—. Office: SYNNEX Corp 44201 Nobel Dr Fremont CA 94538-3178*

ALSCHULER, AL, freelance/self-employed writer; b. Gary, Ind., Jan. 27, 1934; s. Harold Morris and Sarah N. Alschuler; m. Joy Van Wye, June 28, 1956 (div. 1986); children: Mari Lynn, David Van, Mark Jonathan; m. Jacqulyn Yde, Oct. 7, 2000. BA in Journalism with honors, U. Okla., 1955. Exec. v.p. Vanleigh Furniture Showrooms, NYC, 1958-71, Miami, Fla., 1971-79; advt. and pub. rels. cons., Miami Beach, Fla., 1979-82; mng. editor Fla. Designer Quar., Miami, 1982-84, Design South, Miami Beach, 1984-87; freelance writer, pub. rels. counsel Miami, 1987—. Cons. interior design adv. bd. Fla. Internat. U., Miami, 1988—, Art Inst. Ft. Lauderdale, 1991—. Editor: I.D.E.A.S., 1994—95; contbg. editor: South Fla., 1996—97, Gables Living mags., 2004—, Miami Monthly mag., 2005—; guest expert on design WFOR-TV; contbr.: publs. including articles U.S. Architecture, Casa and Estilo Internat.; contbr. articles to profl. jours. Founding chmn. Players State Theatre Conservatory, Coconut Grove, Fla., 1975; mem. Metro Dade Performing Arts Dist. Commn., 1976—77, Miami Com. Beautification, 1977; trustee Miami Design Preservation League, 1988—98, Interior Design Guild Found., 1999—; bd. dirs. Skyline Theatre Co.; committeeman East Rockaway (N.Y.) Dem. Com., 1968—69; bd. dirs. City Theatre, 1999—2006. Recipient Rachline Comm. award, 1996. Fellow: Interior Design Guild (past pres., Comm. award 1996); mem.: Miami Internat. Press Club (pres. 1994), Soc. Profl. Journalists, Mensa, Phi Beta Kappa. Avocations: theater, travel. Home and Office: 2430 Brickell Ave Apt 104A Miami FL 33129-2455 Office Phone: 305-860-0730. E-mail: alal34@aol.com.

ALSCHULER, STEVEN, public relations executive, writer, consultant; b. NYC, Feb. 12, 1958; s. Robert and Caroline (Benjamin) A. BA, Queens Coll., CUNY, 1979. Press sec. State Senator Roy Goodman, NYC, 1979-86, NY State Senate Com. Investigations, Taxation and Govt. Ops., NYC, 1979-86; sr. v.p. Howard Rubenstein Assoc., Inc., NYC, 1986-93; pres. Linden Alschuler & Kaplan, Inc., NYC, 1993—. Mem. spl. com. cultural affairs, NY State Senate, 1979-86; cons. in field. Co-author: Lethal Medicine, 1993. Pub. rels. advisor N.Y. Rep. County Com., 1981-86. Mem. Pub. Rels. Soc. of Am. Office: Linden Alschuler & Kaplan Inc 1251 Ave of the Americas New York NY 10020 Office Phone: 212-575-4545. Business E-Mail: salschuler@lakpr.com.

ALSDORF, ROBERT HERMANN, lawyer; b. Ashland, Ohio, Mar. 5, 1946; s. Howard Alton and Henrietta (Bulleit) A.; m. Sarah Jane Schlick, Nov. 27, 1970; children: Matthew William, Paul August. B.A. magna cum laude, Carleton Coll., 1967; M.A. in U.S. History, Yale U., 1973, J.D., 1973. Bar: D.C. 1973, Wash. 1975, U.S. Dist. Ct. (we. dist.) Wash. 1975, U.S. Ct. Appeals (9th cir.) 1975, U.S. Dist. Ct. (ea. dist.) Wash. 1981, U.S. Supreme Ct. 1984. Trial atty. Dept. Justice, Washington, 1973-75; assoc. Culp, Dwyer, Guterson & Grader, Seattle, 1975-79; ptnr. Armstrong, Alsdorf, Bradbury & Maier P.C. and predecessor Armstrong & Alsdorf, Seattle, 1979-84, pres., 1984—90; trial judge Wash. Superior Ct. 1990-2004; ptnr. Davis Wright Tremaine LLP, Seattle, 2004-; speaker continuing legal edn. seminars; pvt. arbitrator of disputes. Author continuing legal edn. materials. Bd. dirs. Stevens Neighborhood Housing Improvement Program, Seattle, 1979-82, pres., 1980-81. Mem. ABA, Am.Judicature Soc., ADR Roundtable, Am. Law Inst., Inns of Ct. Seattle chapter, Superior Ct. Judges Assn., Fed. Bar Assn., Wash. State Bar Assn., King County Bar Assn., Phi Beta Kappa. Office: Davis Wright Tremaine LLP 2600 Century Sq 1501 Fourth Ave Seattle WA 98101-1688

ALSENTZER, WILLIAM JAMES, JR., lawyer; b. Ravenna, Ohio, Mar. 15, 1942; s. William J. Alsentzer and Vivian (Guy) Soash; children: Lesley Joan, Michelle Guy. AB, Duke U., 1964, JD, 1966. Bar: Del. 1966, U.S. Dist. Ct. Del. 1967, Ariz. 1980, U.S. Dist. Ct. Ariz. 1980. Assoc. Wilson & Lynam, Wilmington, Del., 1967-70; ptnr. Bayard, Brill & Handelman, Wilmington, 1970-79; v.p., gen. counsel Bapt. Hosps. and Health Systems, Phoenix, 1979-2000; legal counsel BHHS Legacy Found., Phoenix, 2000—. Mem. Maricopa County Bar Assn., Am. Health Lawyers Assn., Fedn. Def. and Corp. Counsel. Office: 2999 N 44th St Ste 530 Phoenix AZ 85018

ALSHARE, KHALED A., information systems educator; b. Ramtha, Jordan, Dec. 22, 1965; s. Abdel Kareem Mohammad and Fatima H. Alshare; m. Muna R. Alabdullat, Aug. 22, 1996; children: Mohammad, Islam, Ahmad, Salam. BSCE, Jordan U. Sci. and Tech., Irbid, 1989; MS in Internat. Bus., Grambling State U., La., 1993; PhD in Bus. Adminstrn., U. Tex., Arlington, 1998. Grad. tchg. asst. Grambling State U., 1991—93, asst. prof., 1997—2001; grad. tchg. assoc. U. Tex., Arlington, 1994—97; assoc. prof. Emporia State U., Kans., 2001—. Conf. program co-chair Oluolu Inst., La., 2003—; paper rev. chair Conf. for Computing Sci. in Coll., 2004—. Contbr. articles to profl. jours. Mem. Timmerman Elem. Sch. PTO, Emporia, 2005—; pres. Islamic Ctr. of Emporia, 2003—04, chmn. bd., 2004—, treas., 2002—03. Recipient Faculty Recognition award Intellectual Contributions, Emporia State U., 2003—04, Faculty Recognition award for svc., 2004—05; grantee Rsch. grantee, 2002—05. Mem.: Assn. Computing Machinery Decision Sci. Inst., Assn. for Info. Tech. Profls., Consortium for Computing Sci. in Coll., Assn. of Info. Systems. Avocations: reading, sports. Office: Emporia State University 1200 Commercial St Emporia KS 66801

AL-SHAWWA, BAHAUDDIN A., pediatrician, medical educator; Pediatrician Ottumwa Regional Health Ctr., Iowa, 2000—05; pediatric pulmonary instr., fellow Med. Coll. Wis., Milwa., 2005—. Adj. clin. asst. prof. U. Iowa Hosps. and Clins., Iowa City, 2003—05. Fellow: Am. Acad. Pediats.

ALSOBROOK, DAVID ERNEST, library director, archivist, historian; b. Eufaula, Ala., Sept. 17, 1946; s. Thomas Neville and Frances Joy (Starnes) Alsobrook; m. Ellen Meredith Lester, May 22, 1976; children: Adam, Meredith A. Hobin. BS in Edn., Auburn U., Ala., 1968; PhD in History, Auburn U., 1983; MA in History, W. Va. U., Morgantown, 1972. Tchr. Eufaula HS, 1968—69, Theodore HS, Mobile County, 1969—72; civil archivist Ala. Dept. Archives & History, Montgomery, 1975—76; supr. archivist Jimmy Carter Libr. and Mus., Atlanta, 1981—91; dir. George Bush Presdl. Libr. and Mus., Coll. Sta., Tex., 1993—2000, William J. Clinton Presdl. Libr. & Mus., Little Rock, 2000—. Adj. prof. Dekalb CC, Clarkston, Ga., 1984—91; adv. bd. mem. Ala. Ctr. for the Book, Auburn, 2001—. Contbr. articles to profl. jour. (Milo B. Howard award, 2004). Recipient Milo B. Howard award, 2004. Mem.: Ala. Hist. Assn., Phi Alpha Theta. Avocations: gardening, renovating old houses, history. Office: William J Clinton Presdl Libr 1200 Pres Clinton Ave Little Rock AR 72201*

ALSOBROOK, HENRY BERNIS, JR., lawyer; b. New Orleans, Nov. 9, 1930; s. Henry Bernis and Ethel (Smith) A.; m. Carey Turner Mackie; children: Eugenie Alsobrook Burglass, John Gleason, Emily Alsobrook Kayton BA, Tulane U., 1952, JD, 1957. Bar: La. 1957. Since practiced in, New Orleans; sr. partner firm Adams & Reese. Past mem. faculty Tulane U.

Law Sch.; bd. dirs. Def. Research Inst., 1978-81, 85-88, chmn. med.-legal com., 1967-72; lectr. in field. Author articles in field;; editorial bds. legal jours. Chmn. dean's coun. Tulane U., 1983-88; elder St. Charles Ave. Presbyn. Ch., New Orleans; 1st pres. Les Compagnons du Barreau de La Louisiane, 1985—; treas., bd. dirs. La. State Mus.; bd. dirs. New Orleans Symphony Soc., New Orleans Opera.; mem. La. Gov.'s Commn. on Med. Malpractice, 1989—; mem. Audubon Inst. Aquarium Capital Campaign Commn. With USNR, 1953. Fellow Am. Bar Found., Am. Coll. Trial Lawyers (state chmn.); mem. ABA (past chmn. standing com. commerce, ho. of dels. 1984-89), La. Bar Assn. (pres. 1982-83), New Orleans Bar Assn., Internat. Assn. Def. Counsel (exec. com. 1982-88, pres. 1986-87), Fedn. Ins. Counsel, New Orleans Assn. Def. Counsel (pres.), La. Assn. Def. Counsel (gov. 1965), La. Law Inst. (council 1984-89), Soc. Med. Assn. Counsel (charter), Soc. Hosp. Attys. (charter), AMA (hon.), Confrerie des Chevaliers du Tastevin (grand cellerier 1990-2001), New Orleans Country Club, Avoca Duck Club, Lakeshore Club, Pickwick Club, La. Club. Office: Adams & Reese 4500 One Shell Sq New Orleans LA 70139-4501 Office Phone: 504-585-0211. Business E-Mail: alsobrookhb@arlaw.com.

ALSOP, DONALD DOUGLAS, federal judge; b. Duluth, Minn., Aug. 28, 1927; s. Robert Alvin and Mathilda (Aaseng) A.; m. Jean Lois Tweeten, Aug. 16, 1952; children: David, Marcia, Robert. BS, U. Minn., 1950, LLB, 1952. Bar: Minn. 1952. Pvt. practice, New Ulm, Minn.; ptnr. Gislason, Alsop, Dosland & Hunter, 1954-75; judge U.S. Dist. Ct. Minn., St. Paul, 1975—, chief dist. judge, 1985-92, sr. dist. judge, 1992—. Mem. 8th cir. jud. coun., 1987-92, Jud. Conf. Com. to Implement Criminal Justice Act, 1979-87; mem. exec. com. Nat. Conf. Fed. Trial Judges, 1990-94. Chmn. Brown County (Minn.) Republican Com., 1960-64, 2d Congl. Dist. Rep. Com., 1968-72, Brown County chpt. ARC, 1968-74. Served with AUS, 1945-46. Mem. 8th Cir. Dist. Judges Assn. (pres. 1982-84), New Ulm C. of C. (pres. 1974-75), Order of Coif. Office: US Dist Ct 754 Fed Bldg 316 Robert St N Saint Paul MN 55101-1495

ALSOP, MARIN, conductor, violinist, music director; b. NYC, Oct. 16, 1956; d. LaMar and Ruth A. Attended, Yale Univ., 1973—75; MusB, Julliard Sch., 1977, MusM, 1978. Debut with Symphony Space, NYC, 1984; founder, artistic dir. Concordia Chamber Orchestra, NYC, 1984; asst. condr. Richmond Symphony, Va., 1987; music dir. Eugene Symphony Orchestra, Oreg., 1989—96, Long Island Philharmonic, 1989—96, Cabrillo Music Festival, 1991, Colorado Symphony Orchestra, Denver, 1993—; prin. guest condr. City of London Sinfonia, 1999—; prin. condr. Bournemouth Symphony Orch., Poole, England, 2001—07; musical dir. Balt. Symphony Orch., 2007—. Guest condr. San Francisco Symphony Orchestra, Boston Pops, Los Angeles Philharmonic Orchestra, 1991, City Ballet Orchestra, 1992; dir. Cabrillo Music Festival, Calif., 1991—; concertmaster Northeastern Pennsylvania Philharmonic, Scranton; founder, mem. String Fever (swing band), 1980—. Recipient Koussevitzky Conducting prize, Tanglewood Music Ctr., 1988, ASCAP award, CSO's Contemporary Music Festival, 2002—03, Conductor's award, Royal Philharmonic Soc., Artist of Yr., Gramophone, Classical Brit award, best female artist, 2005; MacArthur Fellow, John D. and Catherine T. MacArthur Found., 2005. Office: Balt Symphony Orch Meyeroff Symphony Hall 1212 Cathedral St Baltimore MD 21201-5545*

ALSPACH, PHILIP HALLIDAY, manufacturing executive; b. Buffalo, Apr. 19, 1923; s. Walter L. and Jean E. (Halliday) A.; m. Jean Edwards, Dec. 20, 1947 (dec.); children: Philip Clough, Bruce Edwards (dec.), David Christopher; m. Loretta M. Hildebrand, Aug. 1982. B in Mech. Engring., Tulane U., 1944. Registered profl. engr., Mass., Wis., La. With GE, 1945-64, mgr. indsl. electronics divsn. planning, 1961-64; v.p., gen. mgr. constrn. machinery divsn. Allis Chalmers Mfg. Co., Milw., 1964-68; exec. v.p., dir., mem. exec. com. Jeffrey Galion, Inc., 1968-69; v.p. I.T.E. Imperial Corp., Springhouse, Pa., 1969-75; pres. E.W. Bliss divsn. Gulf & Western Mfg. Co., Southfield, Mich., 1975-79; group v.p. Katy Industries, Inc., Elgin, Ill., 1979-85; pres. Intercon Inc., Irvine, Calif., 1985—, also bd. dirs.; pres. Intercon Publ., Irvine, 1991—. Bd. dirs. Fortifiber Corp.; adv. bd. Diamond Stainless, Inc. Author: Swiss-Bernese Oberland, 1992, 3d edit., 2004; contbr. articles to profl. jours. Mem. pres.'s coun. Tulane U., 1982-90. Mem. IEEE, Soc. Automotive Engrs. (sr.), Soc. Mfg. Engrs., Internat. Forum Corp. Dirs., Inst. Dirs. (U.K.), Am. Mgmt. Assn., Chaîne des Rotisseurs (officier). Home: 23 Alejo Irvine CA 92612-2913 Office: Intercon Inc 2500 Michelson Dr Ste #125 Irvine CA 92612-1529 Office Phone: 949-955-2344.

ALSTADT, LYNN JEFFERY, lawyer; b. Erie, Pa., Dec. 27, 1951; s. Willis Harry and Norma Margaret (Linn) A.; m. Nancy Ann Welz, Apr. 16, 1977. BS, BA, U. Pitts., 1973, JD, 1976. Bar: Pa. 1976, U.S. Dist. Ct. (we. dist.) Pa. 1976, U.S. Patent and Trademark Office 1979, U.S. Ct. Appeals (3d cir.) 1980, U.S. Ct. Appeals (6th and Fed. cirs.)1983, U.S. Supreme Ct. 1982, U.S. Ct. Internat. Trade 1983. Assoc. Blenko, Buell, Ziesenheim & Beck, Pitts., 1976-79; ptnr. Buell, Blenko, Ziesenheim & Beck, Pitts., 1979-84, Buell, Ziesenheim, Beck & Alstadt, Pitts., 1984-88, Buchanan Ingersoll & Rooney, Pitts., 1988—. Adj. prof. U. Pitts. Sch. Law, 1988—, Duquesne U. Sch. Law, 1995—; dir. Internat. Congress on Tech., Pitts., 1983-84. Contbr. articles to legal jours. Treas. Moon Twp. Planning Agy., 1984; mem. Moon Twp. Vol. Fire Dept., 1981—. Recipient Samuel G. Wagner prize U. Pitts. Law Sch., 1976. Mem. ABA, Pa. Bar Assn., Allegheny County Bar Assn., Pitts. Intellectual Property Law Assn. (chmn. pub. rels. 1982-83, 2005-06, treas. 1993, chmn. ethics grievences and membership coms. 1994-95, bd. dirs. 2000-01, 03-04, v.p. 2001-02, pres. 2002-03), Rivers Club, Phi Alpha Delta. Republican. Home: 1918 Franklin Pl Moon Township PA 15108-3531 Office Phone: 412-562-1632. E-mail: alstadtlj@bipc.com.

ALSTON, ALYCE C., publishing executive, former diamond company executive; b. June 12, 1964; married; 2 children. BA, So. Meth. Univ., Dallas; MBA, Pepperdine Univ., Calif. Writer to West Coast mgr. TV Guide Mag.; assoc. pub. Allure Mag.; pub. YM/Young & Modern/Gruner & Jahr, USA Pub., NYC, O, The Oprah Mag., 2000, W Mag., Fairchild Pubs., 2000—05; CEO De Beers LV USA, 2005—07; pres. home & garden and health & wellness Reader's Digest Assn., Inc., Pleasantville, NY, 2007—. Office: The Reader's Digest Assn Inc Reader's Digest Rd Pleasantville NY 10570

ALSTON, JAMETTA O., lawyer; 1 child. Grad., Temple U.; JD, Howard U. Bar: D.C., RI 1987, Fed., Dist. and Cir. Cts. Asst. atty. gen. civil divsn., RI, 1993—2002; city solicitor Cranston, RI, 2002—. Mem. jud. nom. com., RI, 2003—; mem. exec. com. Edinburgh U.; gov. attys. com. women and minority involvement McGeorge U., 1985; spkr. in field. West Elmwood devel. Supreme Ct. com., 2003—; city solicitor Providence Shelter for Colored Children. Recipient Pro Bono award, Edinburgh, Scotland, 1989. Mem.: RI Bar Assn. (pres.-elect 2003, pres. 2004—05). Office: 869 Park Ave Cranston RI 02910 Office Phone: 401-780-3133. Office Fax: 401-780-3179. E-mail: jalston@cranstonri.org.*

ALSTON, WILLIAM PAYNE, philosophy educator; b. Shreveport, La., Nov. 29, 1921; s. William Payne and Eunice (Schoolfield) A.; m. Mary Frances Collins, Aug. 15, 1943 (div.); 1 dau., Frances Ellen; m. Valerie Tibbetts Barnes, July 3, 1963. MusB, Centenary Coll., Shreveport, La., 1942; PhD, U. Chgo., 1951; LHD (honoris causa), Ch. Div. Sch. Pacific, 1988. Instr. philosophy U. Mich., 1949-52, asst. prof., then asso. prof., 1952-61, prof., 1961-71, acting chmn. dept., 1961-64; prof. philosophy Rutgers U., 1971-76, U. Ill., Champaign, 1976-80, chmn. dept., 1977-80; prof. philosophy Syracuse (N.Y.) U., 1980-99, prof. emeritus, 1999. Vis. asst. prof. UCLA, 1952-53; Austin Fagothey vis. prof. philosophy Santa Clara U., 1991; vis. lectr. Harvard U., 1955-56; fellow Ctr. for Advanced Study in the Behavioral Scis., 1965-66; dir. summer seminars for coll. tchrs. NEH, 1978-79, NEH Summer Inst. in Philosophy of Religion, 1986, NEH Fellowship for Univ. Tchrs., 1988-89, Vatican Obs. Project on Divine Action in the Light of Contemporary Sci., Symposium of Chinese-Am. Philosophy and Religious Studies, 1994; dir. Calvin Coll. Summer Seminar in Christian Scholarship, 1999; Nathaniel Taylor lectr. Yale Div. Sch., 2005. Author: Religious Belief and Philosophical Thought, 1963, (with G. Nakhnikian) Readings in Twentieth Century Philosophy, 1963, Philosophy of Language, 1964, (with R.B. Brandt) The Problems of Philosophy: Introductory Readings, 1967, 3d edit., 1978; Divine Nature and Human Language, 1989, Epistemic Justification, 1989, Perceiving God, 1991, The Reliability of Sense Perception, 1993, A Realist Conception of Truth, 1996, Illocutionary Acts and Sentence Meaning, 2000, A Sensible Metaphysical Realism, 2001, Realism and Antirealism, 2002, Beyond "Justification," 2005; editor: Philos. Rsch. Archives, 1974-77, Faith and Philosophy, 1982-90, Cornell Studies in Philosophy of Religion, 1987-2005; contbr. articles to profl. jours., chpts. in books. Served with AUS, 1942-46. Recipient Chancellor's Exceptional Acad. Achievement award Syracuse U., 1990. Fellow Am. Acad. Arts and Scis.; mem. Am. Philos. Assn. (pres. Western divsn. 1978-79), Soc. Christian Philosophers (pres. 1978-81), Scholarly Engagement Anglican Doctrine, Am. Theol. Soc., Soc. for Philosophy Religion (pres. 2001-02). Democrat. Episcopalian. Avocation: reading. Home: 1301 Nottingham Rd #A224 Jamesville NY 13078 Office: Syracuse U Dept Philosophy Syracuse NY 13244-1170 Business E-Mail: wpalston@syr.edu.

ALSTOTT, MICHAEL JOSEPH (MIKE ALSTOTT), professional football player; b. Joliet, Ill., Dec. 21, 1973; Student, Purdue U. Fullback Tampa Bay Buccaneers, 1996—. Office: Tampa Bay Buccaneers 1 Buccaneer Pl Tampa FL 33607-5797

ALSTROM-BEANS, GAIL, Native American tribal leader; d. William and Hilda Alstrom; m. David Beans; children: Angelia, Ayden, Ronald, Madison, David II. BA in psychology, Stanford U., 1994. YKHC ops. mgr. St. Mary's Subregional Clinic; pres. Yupiit of Andreafski Tribe. Office: Yupiit of Andreafski PO Box 88 Westdahl St Saint Marys AK 99658-0088 Office Phone: 907-438-2312. Office Fax: 907-438-2512.

ALT, CAROL A., actress, model, entrepreneur, writer; d. Anthony Ted and Muriel B. Alt; m. Ronald John Greschner, Nov. 21, 1983 (div. Mar. 12, 2001). Student, Hofstra U., LI, NY. Model Ford Models, NYC; actress Moress Nanas Hart Enterprises, LA; spokesperson QVC, Westchester, Pa. Reporter Fox News, 2002. Author: Eating In the Raw, 2004. Vol. Tribeca Performing Arts Ctr., NYC, MS, NYC, Am. Cancer Soc., NYC, Cerebral Palsy. With US Army, 1978—79. Recipient Model Woman of Yr., CFDA, 1981, Female Model of Yr., 1986, Oscar Moda New Actress of Yr., Moda Mag., 1986, European Emmy, Berlosconi Group, 1987, Cert. of the Arts, European Artistic Cmty., 1988, European Emmy, Berlosconi Group, 1990, Mont Blanc award, 1991, Golden Box Office Ticket, Fedn. of European Theater Owners, 1993, European Emmy, Berlosconi Group, 1994. Avocations: amateur race car driver, interior decorating, marketing. Office: Just Simplicity c/o Assante 280 Park Ave New York NY 10010 Home Phone: 917-301-1217; Office Phone: 818-342-9800. Personal E-mail: altie1A@aol.com.

ALT, JAMES EDWARD, political science professor; b. NYC, Aug. 16, 1946; s. Franz Leopold and Alice (Modern) A.; m. Elaine Fiore, June 26, 1968; children: Rachel, Adam. AB, Columbia U., 1968; MSc in Econs., London Sch. Econs., 1970; PhD, Essex U., Eng., 1978. Lectr. U. Essex, Wivenhoe Park, Eng., 1971-79; assoc. prof. Washington U., St. Louis, 1978-82, prof., 1982-86, Harvard U., Cambridge, Mass., 1986—; dir. Ctr. for Basic Rsch. in Social Sci., 1998—2004. Author: Politics of Economic Decline, 1979, (with K. Chrystal) Political Economics, 1983; editor: (with K. Shepsle) Perspectives on Positive Political Economy, 1990, (with M. Levi and E. Ostrom) Competition and Cooperation, 1999; contbr. articles to profl. jours. Rsch. grantee, NSF, 1980, 1985, 1991, 1993, 2001, 2002, Guggenheim fellow, 1997—98. Fellow Am. Acad. Arts and Scis.; mem. Brit. Politics Group (pres. 1983-85), Am. Polit. Sci. Assn. (coun. 1996-97), Midwest Polit. Sci. Assn. (exec. coun. 1985-88). Office: Harvard U Dept Govt Cambridge MA 02138 Business E-Mail: james_alt@harvard.edu.

ALTABEF, PETER ANTHONY, lawyer; b. NYC, June 13, 1959; s. Isaac and Dolores (Cristiani) A.; m. Jennifer Leigh Burr, Aug. 10, 1985; 2 children, Hayley, Will. BA, SUNY, Binghamton, 1980; JD cum laude, U. Chgo., 1983. Bar: Tex. 1985. Law clk. U.S. Ct. Appeals, Dallas, 1983-84; assoc. Simpson, Thacher & Barlett, NYC, 1984-85, Hughes & Luce, Dallas, 1985-90, ptnr., 1991-93; assoc. gen. counsel Perot Systems Corp., Dallas, 1993-94, v.p., gen. counsel, secy., 1994—2004, pres., CEO, 2004—. Mem. ABA, Dallas Bar Assn., Tex. Bar Assn. Office: Perot Systems Corp 2300 W Plano Pkwy Plano TX 75075 Office Phone: 972-577-6692. E-mail: peter.altabef@ps.net.*

ALTAFULLAH, IRFAN M., neurologist; b. Nov. 14, 1958; s. Mohammed and Shamim Altafullah; m. Tabinda Husain; children: Ikram, Aman, Salman. MBBS, Govt. Med. Coll., Nagpur, India, 1980. Diplomate Am. Bd. Psychiatry and Neurology, 1991, clin. neurophysicology Am. Bd. Psychiatry and Neurology, 1997, vascular neurology Am. Bd. Psychiatry and Neurology, 2006. Instr. to asst. prof. medicine, neurology Aga Khan U., Karachi, Pakistan, 1198—1991; neurologist Mpls. Clin. Neuroology, 1991—. Adj. asst. prof. neurology U. Minn., Mpls., 1997—2003; dir. stoke ctr. North Meml. Health Care, Mpls., 1997—, chief, 2005, mem. bd. trustees, 2005—06, chief med. info. officer, 2006—; adj. assoc. prof. neurology U. Minn., 2003—. Founding mem. Al Shifa Clinic, Minn., 1997. Mem.: Am. Stroke Assn., Am Acad. Neurology, Am. Heart Assn. (greater Mpls. bd. dirs. 2000—02). Avocations: photography, travel, music. Office: Mpls Clinic Neurology 4225 Golden Valley Rd Golden Valley MN 55422

ALTAN, M(USTAFA) CENGIZ, mechanical engineering educator; b. Ankara, Turkey, Dec. 26, 1963; s. A. Rifki and Nursel Altan; m. Betul S. Marmara, July 4, 1992. BSME, Mid. East Tech. U., Ankara, 1985; PhD in Mech. Engring., U. Del., 1989. Tchg. asst. U. Del., Newark, 1985-86, rsch. asst., 1986-89; asst. prof. mech. engring. U. Okla., Norman, 1989-95, assoc. prof., 1995—2004, prof., 2004—06, Presdl. prof., 2006—. Editor: (conf. procs.) Developments in Non-Newtonian Fluid Mechanics, 1993, Intelligent Manufacturing and Material Processing, 1995, Processing and Design of Multicomponent Materials, 2000; contbr. articles to profl. jours. Recipient Rsch. Initiation award Soc. Mfg. Engrs., 1990, Regents' award for superior tchg. U. Okla., 1998; rsch. grantee Okla. Ctr. for Advancement Sci. and Tech., 1991, NASA, 1996, Seagate Tech., 1996, Hawthorne York Internat., 1999, SIAC Corp., 2001, All Tech Inc., 2002, TMI Inc., 2003, USAF, 2003, NSF, 2004, TGV Rockets, Inc., 2006, Anautics Inc., 2006, TSM Corp., 2007. Mem. ASME (assoc., chmn. materials processing com. materials divsn. 1994-97), Soc. Rheology, Internat. Polymer Processing Soc. (treas. 2005—), Am. Soc. Engring. Edn., Am. Phys. Soc., Am. Soc. for Composites, Pi Tau Sigma (hon., Most Outstanding Prof. award for U. Okla. 1997, 2007). Achievements include patents for computer-controlled curing of composite materials. Office: U Okla Sch Aero-Mech Eng 865 Asp Ave Rm 212 Norman OK 73019-1029 Business E-Mail: altan@ou.edu.

ALTAN, TAYLAN, engineering educator, director; b. Trabzon, Turkey, Feb. 12, 1938; arrived in US, 1962; s. Seref and Sadife (Baysal) Kadioglu; m. Susan Borah, July 18, 1964; children: Peri Michele, Aylin Elisabeth Diploma in engring., Tech. U., Hannover, Fed. Republic Germany, 1962; MS in Mech. Engring., U. Calif.-Berkeley, 1964, PhD in Mech. Engring., 1966. Rsch. engr. DuPont Co., Wilmington, Del., 1966-68; rsch. scientist Battelle Columbus Labs., Ohio, 1968-72, rsch. fellow Ohio, 1972-75, sr. rsch. leader Ohio, 1975-86; prof. mech. engring., dir. engring. rsch. ctr. Ohio State U., Columbus, 1985—. Chmn. sci. com. N.Am. Mfg. Rsch. Inst. Soc. Mfg. Engrs., Detroit, 1982-86, pres., 1987; dir. Ctr. for Net Shape Mfg. Co-author: Forging Equipment, 1973, Metal Forming, 1983, Metal Forming and the Finite Element Method, 1989, Cold, Warm and Hot Forging, 2004; contbr. more than 400 tech. articles to profl. jours. Fellow: ASME, Am. Soc. Metals (chmn. forging com. 1978—87), Soc. Mfg. Engrs. (Gold medal 1985). Avocations: languages, travel. Office: Ohio State U 210 Baker Bldg 1971 Neil Ave Columbus OH 43210-1210 Office Phone: 614-292-5063. Business E-Mail: altan.1@osu.edu.

ALTBACH, PHILIP, director, educator; b. Chgo., May 3, 1941; s. Milton and Josephine (Huebsch) A.; m. Edith Hoshino, June 16, 1962; children: Eric, Frederick Gabriel. BA, U. Chgo., 1962, MA, 1964, PhD, 1966. Lectr. Harvard U., Cambridge, Mass., 1967-68; from asst. prof. to assoc. prof. U. Wis., Madison, 1968-75; prof., chmn. dept. ednl. orgn., adminstrn. and policy SUNY, Buffalo, 1976-80, 86-92, dir. Comparative Edn. Ctr., 1978-94; prof. sch. edn. Boston Coll., 1994—, dir. Ctr. Internat. Higher Edn., 1995—, J. Donald Monan SJ prof. higher edn., 1996—. Fulbright rsch. prof. U. Bombay, 1968; cons. Regional Inst. Higher Edn., Singapore, 1979, 81, 82, Carnegie Found. Advancement Tchg., 1990-94, Rockefeller Found., 1991—; vis. prof. Moscow State U., 1981, Stanford U., 1989; Fulbright cons. U. Singapore, 1982; sr. assoc. Carnegie Found. Advancement Tchg., 1992-96; sec.-gen. Bellagio Publ. Network, 1992-98; guest prof. Peking U.; leader New Century Scholars, Fulbright Inst. Program, 2005. Author: Student Politics in America, 1975, rev., 1997, Higher Education in Third World, 1982, Knowledge Context, 1987, International Higher Education: An Encyclopedia, 1991, Publishing and Development in the Third World, 1994, Higher Education in the 21st Century, 1999, rev. edit., 2005, Private Prometheus: Private Higher Education and Development, 2000, Comparative Higher Education, 2000, In Defense of American Higher Education, 2001, The Decline of the Guru, 2003, Asian Universities, 2004, International Handbook of Higher Education 2 vols., 2006, others; editor: Comparative Edn. Rev., 1979—89, Rev. of Higher Edn., 1996—2004, Ednl. Policy, 1989—2004, Internat. Higher Edn., various newsletters and publs. Mem. capital budget rev. com. City of Buffalo, 1980. Grantee, NEH, 1976, Exxon Edn. Found., 1982, 1984, NSF, 1987, Rockefeller Found., 1993, 1994, 1995, Ford Found., 1998, 2001—04, MacArthur Found., 2003, Toyota Found., 2003, Carnegie Corp. N.Y., 2003; scholar, Fulbright Found. Mem. Comparative Edn. Soc. (editor jour. 1980-89), Assn. Study Higher Edn. (editor jour. 1996-2004). Office: Boston Coll 207 Campion Hall Chestnut Hill MA 02467 Office Phone: 617-552-4236. E-mail: altbach@bc.edu.

ALTCHEK, DAVID WILSON, orthopedist, surgeon; b. NYC, Dec. 27, 1956; MD, Cornell U. Cert. Am. Bd. Orthopaedic Surgeons. Resident gen. surgery NY Presbyn. Hosp., NYC; resident Hosp. Spl. Surgery, NYC, 1983—87, fellowship Sports Medicine and Shoulder Svc., 1987—88, attending orthopaedic surgeon. Team physician NY Mets, now med. dir.; N.Am. med. dir. Assn. Tennis Profls. (ATP); team physician US Davis Cup tennis team; assoc. prof. orthopaedic surgery Weill Medical Coll., Cornell U. Contbr. articles to med. jours. Recipient T. Campbell Thompson Award, Ea. Orthopaedic Assn. Fellowship Award, John Jay Award, Charles S. Neer Award, Am. Shoulder & Elbow Surgeons. Office: Hosp Spl Surgery 535 E 70th St New York NY 10021 Office Phone: 212-606-1909. Office Fax: 212-879-6526.*

ALTEKRUSE, JOAN MORRISSEY, retired preventive medicine physician; b. Cohoes, NY, Nov. 15, 1928; d. William T. Dee and Agnes Kay (Fitzgerald) Morrissey; m. Ernest B. Altekruse, Dec. 17, 1950; children—Michael, Philip, Clifford, Lisa, Janice, Charles, Sean, Lowell, Patrick, E. Caitlin. AB, Vassar Coll., NYC, 1949; MD, Stanford U., Calif., 1960; MPH, Harvard U., Cambridge, 1965; DPH, U. Calif., Berkeley, 1973; MPS, Loyola U., New Orleans, 1999. Cons., program dir. Calif. State Health Dept., 1966-69; vis. mem. faculty U. Heidelberg, Germany, 1970-72; med. dir. regional office Fla. State Health Dept., 1972-75; prof., dir. health adminstrn. Sch. Pub. Health, U. S.C., Columbia, 1975-77; prof. preventive medicine Univ. S.C. Sch. of Medicine, Columbia, 1975-94, chmn. dept., 1979-89, disting. prof. emerita, 1994—. Fellow, assoc. dir. Irish Peace Inst., U. Limerick, Ireland, 1990; vis. scholar Ctr. for Rsch. in Disease Prevention, Stanford U., 1992; women in medicine liaison officer Assn. Am. Med. Colls., 1980-94; mem. editl. bd. Aspen Publs. Mem. editl. bd. Family and Cmty. Health Jour., Jour. Cmty. Health; editl. adv. bd. VA Practitioner. Sr. docent chair, vol. bd. mem. Hunter Mus. Am. Art, Chattanooga, 1996—2002; activist in social justice, peace and health advocacy orgns. Lt. USMC, 1949—51, sr. surgeon USPHS, 1960—64, capt. USPHS. Recipient Adminstrn. award Women in Higher Edn., 1989, Achievement award S.C. Comm. on Women, 1990, Ann. award, 1991, Life Achievement award Emma Willard Sch., 1996; WHO travel fellow, Eng., 1974; grantee NIH, NCI, Ctr. for Disease Control, pvt. founds; recipient Alumni award of merit Harvard Sch. Pub. Health, 1997. Fellow: APHA (mem. emerita), Assn. Tchrs. Preventive Medicine (pres. 1986, Spl. Recognition award 1995), Am. Coll. Preventive Medicine; mem.: Nat. Bd. Med. Examiners (comprehensive test com. 1986—92), Am. Heart Assn. (SC affiliate pres. 1986, mem. nat. agenda planning com. 1987—89, women and minorities leadership com. 1989—92, Lifetime Achievement award 1992), Am. Bd. Med. Specialties, Am. Bd. Preventive Medicine (trustee 1983—92), Emma Willard Sch. Alumni Assn. (coun. mem. 2003—), Am. Womens Med. Assn., Harvard Sch. Pub. Health Alumni Assn. (pres. 1999—2001, leadership coun. 2003—06), Harvard Alumni Assn. (bd. dirs. 2001—03). Democrat. Roman Catholic. Personal E-mail: jaltekruse@yahoo.com.

ALTENBURG, JOHN D., JR., lawyer, retired military officer; b. Phila., June 10, 1944; m. Diane Sedler, 1970. BA, Wayne State Univ., 1966; JD, Univ. Cincinnati, 1973; M Mil. Art & Sci., US Army Command & Staff Coll.; graduate, Nat. War Coll. Bar: Ohio, DC, US Army Ct. Criminal Appeals, US Ct. Appeals Armed Forces, US Supreme Ct. Advanced through grades to maj. gen. US Army, 2001, 1st lt., 1973, dep. judge advocate gen. Pentagon, Va., 1997—2001; cons. Office of Pres., World Bank Group, 2002; of counsel Greenberg Traurig LLP, Washington, 2002—03, 2007—; appointing authority US Office of Military Commissions for military tribunals at Guantanamo Bay, Cuba, Washington, 2003—06. Mem. bd. govs. Judge Advocates Assn. Contbr. articles to profl. jour. V.p. & mem. bd. dir. Nat. Coalition for Homeless Vets.; pres. & mem. bd. gov. VII Corps Desert Storm Vet. Assn.; US rep., experts panel Internat. Inst. Humanitarian Law; trustee Joseph House Homeless Vets. Decorated DSM, Legion of Merit (2), Bronze Star (2); recipient Disting. Alumnus award, Univ. Cincinnati Coll. Law, 2003. Office: Greenberg Traurig LLP Suite 500 800 Connecticut Ave NW Washington DC 20006 Office Phone: 202-331-3136.*

ALTENBURGER, KARL MARION, allergist; b. Coral Gables, Fla., Nov. 13, 1949; s. Karl and Carol Altenburger; m. Carol Bauer, May 25, 1974; children: Laura Alyson, Ashley Carolyn, Elizabeth Ann, Allison Nicole. BA in Zoology, U. South Fla., 1971, MD, 1974. Diplomate Am. Bd. Pediatrics, Am. Bd. Allergy and Immunology, Nat. Bd. Med. Examiners. Intern in pediatrics U. Colo. Med. Ctr., Denver, 1975-76, resident, 1976-78, fellow in allergy and immunology, 1978-81, Nat. Jewish Hosp. and Rsch. Ctr.-Nat. Asthma Ctr., Denver, 1978-81; pvt. practice, Ocala, Fla., 1981—2006. Instr. dept. pediatrics U. Colo. Sch. Medicine, 1980-81; pres. Fla. Med. Polit. Action Com., 1998-2001 Contbr. articles to profl. jours. Trustee Am. Lung Assn. Ctrl. Fla., 1985—93. Fellow Am. Acad. Allergy, Asthma and Immunology, Am. Coll. Allergy Asthma and Immunology; mem. AMA, Fla. Med. Assn. (bd. dirs. 2002-, v.p. 2004-06, pres.-elect 2006-07, pres. 2007-), Southeastern Allergy Assn., Fla. Med. Assn. (Marion County del. 1990—), Fla. Allergy Asthma and Immunology Soc. (exec. com. 1990-96, pres. 1993-94), Marion County Med. Soc. (bd. dirs. 1983-88, pres. 1985-86, editor Bull. 1986-89), U. South Fla. Coll. Medicine Alumni Assn. (pres. 1983-87), Alpha Omega Alpha. Roman Catholic. Avocations: history, books. Office: 1800 SE 17th St Ste 300 Ocala FL 34471-4173 Personal E-mail: altenburge@aol.com.

ALTENKIRCH, ROBERT A., academic administrator; b. St. Louis; m. Beth Harsch Altenkirch; 2 children. BS in Mech. Engring., Purdue U., 1970; MS, U. Calif., Berkeley, 1971; PhD, Purdue U., 1975. Grad. instr. rsch. Sch. Mech. Engring. Purdue U., West Lafayette, Ind., 1971—75; asst. prof. mech. engring. U. Ky., Lexington, 1975—80, assoc. prof. mech. engring., 1980—85, prof. mech. engring., 1985—88, chmn. mech. engring., 1985—88; prof. mech. engring., dean Coll. Engring. Miss. State U., Mississippi State, 1988—95, v.p. for rsch., prof. mech. engring., 1998—2002; prof. mech. and materials engring., dean Coll. Engring. and Arch. Wash. State U., Pullman, 1995—98; pres. NJ Inst. Tech., Newark, 2002—, disting. prof. mech. engring., 2002—. Mem. NASA Microgravity Combustion Discipline Working Group, 1992; mem. com. on microgravity rsch. Space Studies Bd. NRC Commn. on Phys. Scis., Math. and Applications, 1995—99, mem. bd. assessment Nat. Inst. Stds. and Tech., 2000—04; vice-chair governing coun. Partnership for Natural Disaster Relief, 1998—2002; mem. rev., planning and implementation steering com. Govs. Commn. on Health Sci., Edn. and Tng., NJ, 2002—03; trustee Prosperity N.J., 2002; mem. Govs. Commn. on Job Growth and Econ. Devel., NJ, 2003—04, Govs. Blue Ribbon Commn. on Transp., NJ, 2003, NJ Amistad Commn., 2004—, Mayor's Blue (Newark) Ribbon Commn. on downtown core redevelopment, 2004; bd. dirs. Golden Triangle Enterprise Ctr., EPSCoR Found., R&D Coun. N.J. Recipient Ralph R. Teetor award, Soc. Automotive Engrs., 1979, Outstanding Mech. Engr. Alumnus award, Purdue U. Sch. Mech. Engring., 2001. Fellow: ASME (bd. govs. task force on electronic networking 1993—96, member-at-large coun. on edn. 1993—97, Gustus L. Larson Meml. award 1984); mem.: NSPE, Miss. Engring. Soc., Am. Soc. for Engring. Edn., Combustion Inst., Phi Kappa Phi, Sigma Xi, Tau Beta Pi, Pi Tau Sigma, Phi Eta Sigma. Office: NJ Inst Tech University Heights 310 Fenster Hall Newark NJ 07102

ALTER, EDWARD T., treasurer; b. Glen Ridge, NJ, July 26, 1941; s. E. Irving and Norma (Fisher) A.; m. Patricia R. Olsen, 1975; children: Christina Lyn, Ashly Ann, Darci Lee. BA, U. Utah., 1966; MBA, U. Utah, 1967. CPA Calif., Utah. Sr. acct. Touche Ross & Co., LA, 1967—72; asst. treas. U. Utah, Salt Lake City, 1972-80; treas. State of Utah, Salt Lake City, 1981—. Mem. Anthony Com. on Pub. Fin., 1988—92, Utah State Rep. Ctrl. Com., 1981—; bd. dirs. Utah Housing Corp., Utah State Retirement Bd., pres., 1984—93, 2003—04; mem. NASDAQ Bd. Nominating Com. Sgt. USAR, 1958—66. Named to All-pro Govt. Team, City and State Mag., 1988; recipient Adminstr. of Yr. award Romney Inst. Pub. Mgmt., Brigham Young U., 2003. Mem. AICPA, Nat. Assn. State Treas. (past sr. v.p., pres. 1987-88, Harlan E. Boyles Disting. Svc. award 2003, Jesse M. Uhruh award svc. to state treas. 1989), Utah Assn. CPAs (Outstanding CPA 2000), Utah Bond Club (pres. 1981-82), Delta Sigma Pi, Delta Phi Kappa. Republican. Office: State Capitol E215 State Capitol Bldg PO Box 142315 Salt Lake City UT 84114-2315 Office Phone: 801-538-1042. Business E-Mail: ealter@utah.gov.

ALTER, ELEANOR BREITEL, lawyer; b. NYC, Nov. 10, 1938; d. Charles David and Jeanne (Hollander) Breitel; children: Richard B. Zabel, David B. Zabel. BA with honors, U. Mich., 1960; postgrad., Harvard U., 1960-61; LLB, Columbia U., 1964. Bar: N.Y. 1965. Atty., office of gen. counsel, ins. dept. State of N.Y., 1964-66; assoc. Miller & Carlson, NYC, 1966-68, Marshall, Bratter, Greene, Allison & Tucker, NYC, 1968-74, mem. firm, 1974-82, Rosenman & Colin, 1982-97, Kasowitz, Benson, Torres & Friedman, NYC, 1997—. Fellow U. Chgo. Law Sch., 1988; adj. prof. law NYU Sch. Law, 1983-87; vis. prof. law U. Chgo., 1990-91, 93; lectr. in field. Mem. editl. bd. N.Y. Law Jour.; contbr. articles to profl. jours. Trustee Lawyers' Fund for Client Protection of the State of N.Y., 1983—, chmn., 1985—; bd. visitors U. Chgo. Law Sch., 1984-87. Mem. Am. Law Inst., Am. Coll. Family Trial Lawyers, N.Y. State Bar Assn., Assn. of Bar of City of N.Y. (libr. com. 1978-80, com. on matrimonial law 1977-81, 87-88, 2002-05, judiciary com. 1981-84, 94, 95, 96, exec. com. 1988-92), Am. Acad. Matrimonial Lawyers, Internat. Acad. Matrimonial Lawyers. Office: Kasowitz Benson Et Al 1633 Broadway New York NY 10019 Office Phone: 212-506-1760. Business E-Mail: ealter@kasowitz.com.

ALTER, GARY, plastic and reconstructive surgeon, urologist; Attended, U. Calif., Berkeley; MD, UCLA, 1973. Cert. Plastic Surgery, Urology, lic. Calif., NY. Resident, general surgery UCLA, 1973—75; urology tng. Baylor Coll. Medicine, Houston, 1975—79; practiced urology, 1979—89; resident, plastic surgery Mayo Clinic, Rochester, Minn., 1989—92; fellowship, genital plastic reconstructive surgery Eastern Va. Grad. Sch. Medicine, Norfolk, Va., 1992; asst. clin. prof., plastic surgery UCLA; private practice, plastic, reconstructive surgery Beverly Hills, Calif., 1993—, Manhattan, NY, 1993—. Asst. clin. prof., plastic surgery UCLA Sch. Medicine; presenter in field. Co-editor: (med. textbook) Reconstructive and Plastic Surgery of the External Genitalia; contbr. scientific papers articles to profl. jours.; featured on Dr. 90210, E-TV, occasional host (radio show) Loveline. Recipient Best Reconstruction Paper at Plastic Surgery Sr. Resident's Conf., Montreal, 1992. Mem.: Soc. Genitourinary Reconstructive Surgeons, Am. Urological Assn. (mem. Western sect.), Am. Assn. Plastic Surgeons, Am. Soc. Plastic Surgeons. Achievements include being a recognized leader in female genital surgery, labiaplasty or labia minora surgery, penis/scrotal surgery, penis enhancement, and transsexual surgery. Office: 416 N Bedford Dr Ste 400 Beverly Hills CA 90210 also: 461 Park Ave S 7th Fl Ste New York NY 10016 Office Phone: 310-275-5566. Office Fax: 310-271-0521. Business E-Mail: altermd@earthlink.com.*

ALTER, HARVEY J., hematologist, educator; b. NYC; BA, U. Rochester, MD, 1960. Internship, first-yr. resident Strong Meml. Hosp., Rochester, NY, 1960—61; clin. assoc. NIH, Bethesda, Md., 1961—63; second-yr. resident U. Wash. Hosp. Sys., Seattle, 1964—65; hematology fellow Georgetown U. Hosp., Wash., DC, 1965—66; instr. medicine Georgetown U. Sch. Medicine, Wash., 1966—68; dir. hematology rsch. Georgetown U. Hosp., Wash., 1966—69; asst. prof. medicine Georgetown U. Sch. Medicine, Wash., 1968—69, clin. asst. prof. medicine, 1969—71, clin. assoc. prof. medicine, 1969—71; sr. investigator NIH, Bethesda, Md., 1969—, chief infectious disease sect. clin. ctr., 1972—, assoc. dir. rsch. clin. ctr. dept. transfusion medicine, faculty clin. rsch., 1988—; clin. prof. medicine Georgetown U. Hosp., Wash., 1988—. Adj. prof. S.W. Found. Biomed. Rsch., San Antonio, 1986—. Contbr. articles to profl. jours. Recipient DSM, U.S. Pub. Health Svc., 1977, Karl Lansteiner award, Am. Assn. Blood Banks, 1992, Lab. Pub. Svc. Nat. Leadership award, 1999, World Health Day award, Am. Assn. World Health, 2000, Albert Lasker award Clin. Med. Rsch., 2000. Master: ACP; fellow: Am. Soc. Internal Medicine; mem.: Nat. Acad. Scis., Inst. Medicine, Am. Bd. Pathology. Achievements include first to conduct work leading to the discovery of the virus that causes hepatitis C; development of screening methods that reduced the risk of blood transfusion-associated hepatitis in the U.S. from 30% in 1970 to virtually zero. Office: NIH Warren G Magunson Clin Ctr Dept Transfusion Medicine 10/1C711 10 Center Dr MSC-1184 Bldg 10 Room 1C711 Bethesda MD 20892

ALTER, JONATHAN HAMMERMAN, journalist; b. Chgo., Oct. 6, 1957; s. James M. and Joanne (Hammerman) A.; m. Emily Lazar, Oct. 18, 1986; children: Charlotte Helen, Thomas Beck, Molly Cecelia. AB in History cum laude, Harvard U., 1979. Mem. staff speech writing office The White House, 1978; editor The Washington Monthly, 1981-82; sr. editor, columnist, media critic Newsweek, NYC, 1983—; on-air analyst, corr. NBC News, 1996—. Ferris vis. prof. Princeton U., 1997, Minow vis. prof., Northwestern U., 2003. Author: The Defining Moment: FDR's Hundred Days and the Triumph of Hope, 2006; co-author: Selecting A President, 1980; editor: (with Charles Peters) Inside the System. 5th edit., 1984. Bd. dirs. Donors Choose, 2003—, The Blue Card, 1999—, Bone Marrow Found., 2006—. Recipient Gerald Loeb award 1987, Lowell Mellett award for Improving Journalism, 1987, Clarion award, 1994, N.Y. Press Club award, 2001, ABA Silver Gavel award, 2001, John Bartlow Martin award Northwestern U., 2001; fellow U.S.-Japan Leadership program, 1992-93, Nat. Headliners Best Column award, 1997, 2001, Mentoring USA award, 1999, SPJ Pub. Svc. award, 2006; named 1 of Top 10 Media Critics in U.S., Columbia U., 1991. Office: care Newsweek Magazine 251 W 57th St New York NY 10019-1802 Business E-Mail: jalter@newsweek.com.

ALTER, MILTON, retired neurologist; b. Buffalo, Nov. 11, 1929; s. Samuel and Rose (Schaffer) Alter; m. Reina Rolnick, Aug. 31, 1952; children: David S., Daniel M., Michael A., Naomi T., Joel A. BA, U. Buffalo, 1951, MD, 1955; PhD, U. Minn., 1966. Diplomate Am. Bd. Psychiatry and Neurology. Intern U. Minn., Mpls., 1955-56; sr. surgeon USPHS, Bethesda, Md., 1956-62; fellow Med. Coll. S.C., Charleston, 1956-57, Dalhousie U., Halifax, 1957, Columbia U. Coll. Physicians and Surgeons, NYC, 1957-58, Hebrew U., Jerusalem, 1960-62; mem. faculty, chief neurology svc. U. Minn., Mpls., 1962—67, Mpls. VA Hosp., 1967-76; chmn. dept. neurology Temple U., Phila., 1976-87, prof. neurology, 1987—89; prof., dir. residency tng. Med. Coll. Pa., Phila., 1989-91; clin. prof. Drexel U., 1995—. Mem. sci. adv. bd. Nat. Multiple Sclerosis Soc., NYC, Dystonia Med. Rsch. Found., Alzheimer Disease Assn.; peer reviewer Epidemiology and Disease Control 1 and 2 NIH, Bethesda, Md.; adj. prof. Ctr. Clin. Epidemiology and Biostats. U. Pa., 1995—2004; adj. prof. Thomas Jefferson U., 1999. Guest editor: numerous profl. jours., editor-in-chief: Neuroepidemiology, 1989—96; editor emeritus Neuroepidemiology; contbr. articles to profl. jours., chapters to books. Capt. USPHS, 1962. Grantee, NIH, Multiple Sclerosis Soc. Mem.: AMA, World Fedn. Neurology (chair rsch. group epidemiology 1998—2001), Am. Epidemiology Soc., Am. Neurol. Assn., Am. Acad. Neurology. Democrat. Jewish. Home: 236 Indian Creek Rd Wynnewood PA 19096-3404 also: Prof Lankenau Med Rsch Ctr 100 E Lancaster Ave Wynnewood PA 19096-3404 Office Phone: 610-649-2095. Personal E-mail: malter5280@aol.com.

ALTER, NELSON TOBIAS, retail executive, wholesale distribution executive; b. San Antonio, July 14, 1926; s. William and Celia (Tobias) A.; m. Shirley Ann Jacobs, June 12, 1949; children: Dennis Ira, Keith Alan, Brian Reid, Wendy Ilene. BBA in Acctg., U. Tex., 1948, JD, 1950. Mgr. 9 coin-operated washeterias, 1960-67; mgr. Sta. KOGT radio, Orange, Tex., 1950-65; ptnr. Calder Properties, 1977—; mng. ptnr. Crow Road Devel. Co., Beaumont, Tex., 1976-77, Normandy Townhomes, Beaumont, 1978—, Griffing Devel. Co., Beaumont, 1978—; Griffing Realty Joint Venture, Beaumont, 1983—; comptroller Gem Jewelry Cos., Beaumont, 1950-58; pres. Gem Jewelry Co. of Beaumont, Inc., 1958—, chmn. of bd., 1991—; mng. ptnr. Gem Distbg. Co. Wholesale Jewelry, Beaumont, 1958—; gen. ptnr. Alter's Gem Jewelry, Ltd. (formerly Gem Jewelry Corp.), Beaumont. Also pres., chmn. of bd. Gem Jewelry Co. of Port Artur, Inc., 1991—, Gem Jewelry C. of Orange, Inc., 1991—, Gem. Jewelry C. of Alexandria (La.), Inc., 1991—, Gem. Jewelry C. of Rapides (La.) Inc., 1991, Gem Jewelry Distbg. Co. Inc., 1991—; U.S. rep. Tex. region Habsbourg-Feldman Fine Art Auctioneers, Geneva, 1986, 87, 88, 89; real estate developer Normandy Townhomes, Griffing Devel. Co., Joint Venture, Griffing Realty Joint Venture, Partner Calder Properties. Past pres. Downtown Beaumont Unltd.; co-chmn. Beaumont Urban Renewal; drive chmn. United Jewish Appeal, Beaumont, 1954, 67; pres. Temple Emanuel, 1974-75, pres., 1981; mem. Beaumont Heritage Soc., Beaumont Music Commn., Beaumont Symphony Soc., Am. Cancer Soc.; co-founder, mem. BBB S.E. Tex.; bd. dirs. A.W. Schlesinger Geriatric Ctr., 1996-2003. Recipient Paul Harris Fellow, Rotary Internat. Found., 2002. Mem. Tex. Retail Jewelers Assn. (v.p. 1974-75), Jefferson County Bar Assn., Tex. Bar Assn. (50 Yr. Mem. award), Edna Gladney Aux., Beaumont Jewish Fedn., Buckner Benevolences, Tower Club, Masons, Masonic Lodge (50 Yr. membership award), B'nai Brith, Phi Eta Sigma, Beta Gamma Sigma, Phi Alpha Delta, Sigma Alpha Mu. Jewish. Avocations: art collecting, swimming, golf. Office: Alter's Gem Jewelry Ltd 3155 Dowlen Rd Beaumont TX 77706 Office Phone: 409-861-3005.

ALTER, PAUL R., lawyer; b. NYC, June 22, 1941; AB, Columbia Univ., 1962; JD, Cornell Univ., 1965. Bar: NY 1965. Shareholder, real estate, bd. dir. Greenberg Traurig LLP, NYC. Mem.: ABA, NY State Bar Assn., Assn. Bar NYC, NY Assn. New Americans (dir., past pres.), UJA Fedn. NY (chair, real estate lawyers divsn.). Office: Greenberg Traurig LLP MetLife Bldg 200 Park Ave New York NY 10166 Office Phone: 212-801-9292. Office Fax: 212-801-6400. Business E-Mail: alterp@gtlaw.com.

ALTER, ROBERT BERNARD, literature educator, critic; b. NYC, Apr. 2, 1935; s. Harry and Tillie (Zimmmerman) A.; m. Judith Berkenbilt, June 4, 1961 (div. 1973); children: Miriam, Dan; m. Carol Cosman, June 17, 1973; children: Gabriel, Micha. BA, Columbia U., 1957; MA, Harvard U., 1958, PhD, 1962; LHD (hon.), Hebrew Union Coll., 1985. Instr., then asst. prof. English Columbia U., 1962-66; mem. faculty U. Calif.-Berkeley, 1967—, prof. Hebrew and comparative lit., 1969—, chmn. dept. comparative lit., 1970-73, 88-89, class of 1937 prof., 1989—; columnist Commentary mag., 1965-73, contbg. editor, 1973-86. Author: Rogue's Progress: Studies in the Picaresque Novel, 1964, Fielding and the Nature of the Novel, 1968, After the Tradition, 1969, Partial Magic: The Novel as a Self-Conscious Genre, 1975, Defenses of the Immagination, 1977, A Lion for Love, 1979, The Art of Biblical Narrative, 1981, Motives for Fiction, 1984, The Art of Biblical Poetry, 1985; co-editor: The Literary Guide to the Bible, 1987, The Invention of Hebrew Prose, 1988, The Pleasures of Reading in an Ideological Age, 1989, Necessary Angels, 1991, The World of Biblical Literature, 1992, Hebrew and Modernity, 1994, Genesis: Translation and Commentary, 1996, The David Story: A Translation with Commentary of 1 and 2 Samuel, 1999, Canon and Creativity, 2000, The Five Books of Muses: A Translation with Commentary, 2004, Imagined Cities, 2005, The Book of Psalms: A Translator with Commentary, 2007; contbg. editor: Tri Quarterly mag., 1975—. Recipient essay prize English Inst., 1965, Nat. Jewish Book award for Jewish thought, 1982, Present Tense award for Jewish thought, 1986, Bay Area Book Reviewers Transl. award, 1997, Koret Book award, 2005, PEN-USA Transl. award, 2005; Guggenheim fellow, 1966-67, 78-79, sr. fellow NEH, 1972-73, fellow Inst. for Advanced Studies, Jerusalem, 1982-83; scholar Nat. Found. for Jewish Culture, 1995. Fellow Am. Acad. Arts and Scis., Am. Philosoph. Soc.; mem. Council of Scholars of Library of Congress, Assn. Lit. Scholars and Critics (pres. 1996-97). Jewish. Home: 1475 Le Roy Ave Berkeley CA 94708-1911 Office: U Calif Dept Comp Lit 4408 Dwinelle Hall Berkeley CA 94720-2510 Business E-Mail: altcos@berkeley.edu.

ALTERMAN, DANIEL L., lawyer; b. NYC, May 11, 1944; BA, State U. NY, 1966; JD, NYU, 1969, LLM, 1971. Bar: NY 1969, U.S. Supreme Ct., Fla. 1972, U.S. Dist. Ct. (so. dist.) Fla., U.S. Dist. Ct. (so. and ea. dist.) NY 1972, U.S. Ct. Appeals (2d cir.) 1973, Vt. 1979, U.S. Dist. Ct. Vt. 1979, Wis. 1986, U.S. Dist. Ct. (we. dist.) Wis. 1986. Mem. Alterman & Boop LLP, NYC. Adj. prof. NY Law Sch., 1995—2000; mem. Bd. Cooperative Attys., Ctr. Constl. Rights, 1971—. Fellow: Coll. Labor and Employment Lawyers Inc.; mem.: Nat. Employment Lawyers Assn., Nat. Lawyers Guild (past pres. NYC chpt.), Am. Civil Liberties Union, NY Civil Liberties Union, NY State Trial Lawyers Assn., NY State Bar Assn., Assn. of the Bar City of NY. Office: Alterman & Boop LLP 35 Worth St New York NY 10013 Office Phone: 212-226-2800. Office Fax: 212-431-3614.*

ALTERMAN, IRWIN MICHAEL, lawyer; b. Vineland, NJ, Mar. 4, 1941; s. Joseph and Rose A.; m. Susan Simon, Aug. 6, 1972 (dec. Apr. 1997); 1 son, Owen. AB, Princeton U., 1962; LLB, Columbia U., 1965. Bar: N.Y. 1966, Mich. 1967. Law clk. to chief judge Theodore Levin U.S. Dist. Ct. (ea. dist.) Mich., 1965-67; assoc. Kaye Scholer, NYC, 1967—70, Hyman, Gurwin, Nachman, Friedman & Winkelman, Southfield, Mich., 1970-74, ptnr., 1974—88, Kaufman and Payton, Farmington Hills, 1988—89, Kemp Klein, Troy, 1989—. Author: Plain and Accurate Style in Court Papers, 1987; founding editor: Mich. Antitrust, 1975—92; editor: Mich. Antitrust Digest, 3d edit., 2001; contbr. articles to profl. jours. Bd. gov. Jewish Fedn. Detroit, 1990—; nat. young leadership cabinet United Jewish Appeal, 1978-79, nat. exec. com., 1980; past pres. Adat Shalom Synagogue, Farmington Hills, Mich., Jewish Cmty. Ctr., West Bloomfield, Mich. Mem. ABA, Am. Law Inst., State Bar Mich. (past chmn. com. on plain English, past. chmn. antitrust sect.), Princeton Club (past pres. Mich.). Office: Kemp Klein Ste 600 201 W Big Beaver Rd Troy MI 48084-4136 Office Phone: 248-528-1111. Business E-Mail: irwin.alterman@kkue.com.

ALTERMAN, MICHAIL A., biochemist, researcher; b. Moscow, Apr. 29, 1951; s. Aron and Blyuma Alterman; m. Marina V Shegai, Dec. 26, 1983; children: Julia M, Elina M, Jonathan Aron. MS in bioorganic chemistry, Lomonosov Moscow State Acad. of Fine Chem. Tech., Russia, 1974; PhD in biol. scis., Russian State Med. U., Moscow. Sr. rschr. dept. of biochemistry Russian State Med. U. (formerly 2nd Moscow Med. Inst.), Moscow, 1976—90; asst. rsch. prof. dept. of vet. anatomy and pub. health Tex. A&M U. Coll. of Vet. Medicine, Coll. Sta., 1991—93; lab. dir. and sr. scientist U. of Kans., Lawrence, 1994—. Courtesy prof. pharm. toxicology Sch. Pharmacy. Contbr. articles to profl. jours. Sr. lt. Russian Army, 1974—76. Grantee, NIH, 1989, U. Kans., Russian Acad. of Scis. Independent. Jewish. Achievements include patents for membrane-associated methane monooxygenase from methylococcus capsulatus. Avocations: reading, travel. Office: U Kans 1251 Wescoe Hall Dr Lawrence KS 66045 E-mail: malterman@ku.edu.

ALTERS, JEREMY W., lawyer; b. Chgo., Jan. 15, 1971; m. Rachel; children: Logan, Dawson, Cameron. BA, U. Mass., Amherst, 1994; JD, U. Miami Sch. Law, 1996. Bar: Fla. 1997. Ptnr. Alters, Boldt, Brown, Rash & Culmo, PA, Miami-Dade, Broward, Palm Beach County, Fla. Founding shareholder Ratzan & Alters PA, 2001, Alters, Boldt, Brown, Rash & Culmo, PA, 2007. Sec. Miami-Dade Justice Assn. Bd., 2001—02, treas., 2002—03, pres.-elect, 2003—04, orgn. pres., 2004—05. Fellow: ABA; mem.: AAJ (bd. dirs., nat. fin. com., membership com., F. Scott Baldwin award 2004), Spellman-Hoeveler Am. Inn of Ct., Miami-Dade County Bar Assn., Fla. Justice Assn. (bd. dirs., Miami-Dade County Legislative Task Force). Achievements include has settled and/or achieved verdicts totaling over 175 million dollars; achieved single largest settlement in Florida history for one plaintiff. Avocations: surfing, training and racing in triathlons, snowboarding.

ALTFEST, LEWIS JAY, financial planner; b. NYC, Oct. 14, 1940; s. Sam and Ruth (Zwang) A.; m. Karen Caplan, Dec. 25, 1966; children: Ellen Wendy, Andrew Gamer. BBA with honors, CCNY, 1962; MBA, NYU, 1970; PhD, CUNY, 1978. CPA NY; CFA, CFP, cert. personal fin. specialist. Sr. investment analyst Wertheim and Co., NYC, 1969-75, Lehman Bros., 1975-76; dir. rsch., gen. ptnr. Lord Abbett and Co., 1976-82; pres. L.J. Altfest and Co., Inc., 1982—; assoc. prof. fin. Pace U. Grad. Sch. Bus., 1984—; dir. fin. planning and investments program New Sch. for Social Rsch., 1988—2005. Arbitrator Nat. Assn. Securities Dealers, Am. Arbitration Assn., 1985-88; bd. dirs. Consumer Fin. Edn. Found., 1994-95. Author: (with others) Introduction to Business, 1978, Capital Budgeting Handbook, 1986, Personal Financial Planning, 2006; author: Lew Altfest Answers Almost All Your Questions About Money, 1992, rev. edit., 1994; contbr. articles to profl. jours. Pres. 240 E. 79th Coop. Bd., NYC, 1983-86; bd. dirs. Consumer Fin. Edn. Found., 1993-97. With U.S. Army, 1962-63. Named One of Best Fin. Planners in U.S., Money Mag., 1987, One of Best Fin. Advisors, Worth Mag., 1996, 97, 98, One of Best Advisers for Physicians, Med. Econs., 1998, 2000, 02, 04, 06, One of 100 Gt. Fin. Planners, Mut. Funds Mag., 2001, One of Top Wealth Mgrs. (Bloomberg), firm L.J. Altfest & Co., 2003, 04, 05, 06, Firm Lead Registered Investment Advisors Fin. Advisor Mag., 2006; recipient Disting. Alumni award PhD Alumni Assn. CUNY, 1992, Career Achievement award Bus. and Econs. Alumni Soc., CCNY, 2006. Mem. Nat. Assn. Personal Fin. Advisors (bd. dirs. 1985-89, Outstanding Leadership award 1989), AICPA, Internat. Assn. for Fin. Planning (bd. dirs. NY chpt. 1987-93), Inst. Chartered Fin. Analysts, Am. Fin. Assn., Fin. Analysts Fedn., Fin. Mgmt. Assn., NY Soc. Security Analysts, Registry Fin. Planning Practitioners, CCNY Bus. Alumni Assn. (bd. dirs. 1983-87), Acad. Fin. Svcs. Office: LJ Altfest & Co Inc 425 Park Ave 24th Fl New York NY 10022 Office Phone: 212-406-0850. Business E-Mail: lja@altfest.com.

ALTHAUS, SCOTT L., political science professor; m. Ellen Wang Althaus. AB in Rhetoric, U. Calif., Berkeley, 1991; MA in Polit. Sci., PhD in Polit. Sci., Northwestern U., Evanston, Ill., 1996. Asst. prof., speech comm. U. Ill., Urbana-Champaign, 1996—2003, asst. prof., polit. sci., 1996—2003, assoc. prof., polit. sci., 2003—, assoc. prof., speech comm., 2003—. Author: Collective Preferences in Democratic Politics (co-winner Goldsmith prize, Harvard U., 2004, David Easton award Am. Polit. Sci. Assn., 2004). With US Army, 1984—87. Named Helen Corley Petit scholar of Liberal Arts and Scis., Coll. Liberal Arts and Scis. U. Ill. Urbana-Champaign, 2003—04; fellow Beckman Assoc., Ctr. for Advanced Studies, U. Ill. Urbana-Champaign, 2004—05. Mem.: Am. Assn. Pub. Opinion Rsch., Am. Polit. Sci. Assn., Internat. Comm. Assn., Christians in Polit. Sci., Phi Beta Kappa. Office: Dept Political Science UIUC 702 South Wright St Rm 361 Urbana IL 61801 Office Phone: 217-333-8968.

ALTHAVER, LAMBERT EWING, manufacturing executive; b. Kansas City, Mo., May 18, 1931; s. Edward William and Dorothy Lambert (Ewing) A.; m. Holly Elizabeth Walpole, Feb. 28, 1953; children: Brian, Lauren BA, Principia Coll, 1952; LLD honoris causa, Northwood U., 2003. Account exec. Walbro Corp., Cass City, Mich., 1954-58, asst. to pres., 1958-65, v.p. fin., 1965-70, exec. v.p., 1970-77, pres., chief ops. officer, 1977-82, pres., CEO, 1982-87, chmn., pres., CEO, 1987-96, also bd. dirs., chmn., CEO, 1996-98, chmn. emeritus, 1998-2000. Councilman Village of Cass City, 1963—65, pres., 1965—84, 1987—2000, 2004—; mem. Tuscola County Planning Commn., Caro, Mich., 1966—94; chmn. Cass City Econ. Devel. Corp., 1983—96, Tuscola Area Airport Authority, 1994—2004; co-founder, v.p. Village Bach Festival, 1979—; mem. Mich. Jobs Commn., 1996—99; bd. dirs. Tuscola Econ. Devel. Corp., 1985—2004; vice-chmn., sec., dir. Artrain, Inc., 1975—96, chmn., 1996—2003; v.p., bd. dirs. Lake Huron area Boy Scouts Am., 1988—94; dir. Am. Bus. Conf. Found., Washington, 1998—, Mich. Mcpl. League Found., Ann Arbor, 1999—2002; trustee Jordan Coll., 1990—95, Northwood U., 2000—, Hills & Dales Hosp., Cass City, 1998—. With US Army, 1952—54. Named Citizen of Yr., Case City C. of C., 1978, Outstanding Bus. Leader, Northwood U., 1997; recipient Silver Beaver award, Boy Scouts Am., 1995, Disting. Eagle Scout award, 1989; Paul Harris fellow, Rotary Internat., Evanston, Ill., 1979, 1994, 1999, 2002, 2004, 2005, 2006. Mem.: Mich. C. of C. (bd. dirs. 1986—92), Cass City C. of C. (bd. dirs. 1985—2004), Detroit Athletic Club, Rotary. Avocation: golf. Office: PO Box 27 Cass City MI 48726-0027 Office Phone: 989-872-8183. E-mail: althaver@tband.net.

ALTHEIMER, BRIAN P. See TUTASHINDA, KWELI

ALTIERE, LAUREN M., music educator, consultant; d. Charles and Jane McAlister; m. Michael P. Altiere, June 10, 1968 (dec. May 5, 1992); 1 child, Tamara Rae Miller. BA in Voice, Allegheny Coll., Meadville, Pa., 1968; ESL Certification, U. Phoenix, Ariz., 1998; M in Music Edn., Ctrl. Mo. State U., Warrensburg, 1978. Music specialist St. Joseph's Elem. Sch., Wichita, Kans., 1969—97, Yamaha Music Sch., Wichita, 1970—74, Carlton Jr. H.S., Derby, Kans., 1973—74, Windsor Pub. Sch., Mo., 1974—78, Massillon City Schs., Ohio, 1978—80, Shreveport City Schs., La., 1980—84, Dodge Elem. Sch., Wichita, 1985—95, Payne Elem. Sch., Wichita, 1995—97, Wilson Sch. Dist., Phoenix, 1997—. Music edn. cons. Yamaha Corp. Am., Buena Park, Calif., 1987—; chorus dir. Young Women in Harmony, Phoenix, 1990—. Avocation: singing with sweet adelines. Office: Wilson School District 415 N 30th St Phoenix AZ 85008 Home Phone: 602-569-9802; Office Phone: 602-683-2500.

ALTIERI, JAMES M., lawyer; b. Dumont, NJ, 1949; BS magna cum laude, Univ. Md., Balt., 1971; JD, Fordham Univ., 1975. Bar: NJ 1975, NY 1976, Ariz. 1987. Atty. Simpson Thacher & Bartlett, NYC; joined Drinker Biddle & Reath LLP, 1985, mng. ptnr., head, insurance practice group Florham Park, NJ. Mem.: ABA, Assn. Bar City NY, Assn. Fed. Bar, NJ Bar Assn. Office: Drinker Biddle & Leath LLP 500 Campus Dr Florham Park NJ 07932-1047 Office Phone: 973-549-7060. Office Fax: 973-360-9831. Business E-Mail: james.altieri@dbr.com.

ALTIERI, PETER LOUIS, lawyer; b. Norwalk, Conn., Dec. 7, 1955; s. John L. and Eileen Mary (Rudden) A.; m. Sandra Shelton White, Sept. 3, 1983; children: Brianna Burr, John Shelton. AB, Georgetown U., 1977; JD, Fordham Sch. Law, 1980. Bar: N.Y. 1981, U.S. Dist. Ct. (so. and ea. dists.) N.Y. 1981, U.S. Dist. Ct. (no. and we. dists) N.Y. 1983, U.S. Dist. Ct. Conn. 1983, U.S. Supreme Ct. 1984, U.S. Ct. Appeals (2d cir.) 1986, Conn. 1987, U.S. Ct. Appeals (6th cir.) 2001. Law clk. to judge U.S. Dist. Ct., 1978; intern U.S. Attys. Office, NYC, 1978; assoc. Law Firm Malcolm A. Hoffmann, NYC, 1980-87; ptnr. Epstein, Becker & Green, NYC, 1987—. Mem. ABA, Conn. Bar Assn. (exec. com. antitrust sect. 1988—), Assn. Bar City N.Y. (com. uniform state laws 1985-88, com. on inter-Am. affairs 1997-99), The Patterson Club Conn., Union League Club N.Y.C. Home: 140 Burr St Fairfield CT 06824-7105 Office: Epstein Becker & Green 250 Park Ave Ste 1201 New York NY 10177-0001 Home Phone: 203-255-9755; Office Phone: 212-351-4592. Business E-Mail: paltieri@ebglaw.com.

ALTISENT, MARTA, humanities educator; b. Barcelona, July 20, 1950; arrived in US, 1975; d. Antonio and Maria Rosa (Serra) Altisent; m. Iain Johnstone. BA, U. Barcelona, 1974; MA, U. Ill., Urbana, 1976, PhD, 1980. Asst. prof. Washington U., St. Louis, 1980—83, U. Calif., Davis, 1984—2007, prof., 2007—. Vis. prof. U. Calif., Berkeley, 2001—02; presenter in field. Contbr. articles to profl. jours., chapters to books. Mem.: MLAa, Assn. Lit. Hispanic Women, Inst. Cervantes, Inst. Lit. Hispanic Culture, Assn. Internat. Hispanistas, N.Am. Catalan Soc. Office: Univ Calif Dept Spanish and Classics 711 Sproul Hall Davis CA 95616 Business E-Mail: mealtisent@ucdavis.edu.

ALTMAN, BERNIE, retired secondary school educator, editor; b. NYC, May 9, 1924; s. George and Esther Altman; m. Marcia Helen Beyer, May 25, 1947; children: Rosalie Olds, Hillery. BS in Edn., NYU, NYC, 1946, MA in Edn., 1948. Tchr. Comertown Pub. Sch., Mont., 1946—48, Kelso Pub. Schs., Wash., 1948—76; editor Sr. News Cmty. Action Program, Longview, Wash., 1983—96; editor supplement The Daily News, Longview, 1997—. Mem.: AARP (sec. Lower Columbia 2004—, Andrus award 2005), Nat. Alliance for the Mentally Ill (pres. 1983—2004), Long-term Care Ombudsman (treas. 1985—). Avocations: pickle-ball, gardening. Home: 1000 North 20 Ave Kelso WA 98626 Office: The Daily News 770 11 Ave Longview WA 98632 Office Phone: 360-577-7827. Business E-Mail: secondhalf@tdn.com.

ALTMAN, BRIAN DAVID, pediatric ophthalmologist; b. Temple, Tex., Feb. 29, 1944; s. Harold and Alice A. BA, Adelphi U., 1965; MD, Yale Med. Sch., 1969. Diplomate Am. Bd. Pediatrics, Am. Bd. Opthalmologists. Pediatric ophthalmologist pvt. practice, Huntington Valley, Pa., 1976-98, Plymouth, Pa., 1976-98, Ocean City, NJ, 1992—, Cape May Courthouse, 1992—. Cons. in pediatric ophthalomogy several hosps. in Pa. and N.J., 1977—. Co-author: (with others) Medications in Pediatric Ophthalmology, 1975. Lt. cmmdr. USPHS, 1970-72. Fellow Am. Acad. Opthalmology, Am. Acad. Pediatrics, Am. Assn. Pediatric Ophthalmologists. Office: 315 Rt 9 S Cape May Court House NJ 08210 Home and Office: PO Box 1259 Ocean City NJ 08226-7259 Office Phone: 609-398-1100.

ALTMAN, DREW E., foundation executive; b. Boston, Mar. 21, 1951; s. George and Harriet A.; m. Pamela Koch; children: Daniel, Jessica. BA magna cum laude, Brandeis U., 1973; MA, Brown U., 1974; PhD in Polit. Sci., MIT, 1983. Postdoctoral fellow, rsch. assoc. Harvard U. Sch. Pub. Health, Boston, 1975-76, 78-80; prin. rsch. assoc. Codman Rsch. Group, Boston, 1976-80; spl. asst. office of adminstr. Health Care Fin. Adminstrn. Dept. HHS, Washington, 1979-81; v.p. Robert Wood Johnson Found., Princeton, NJ, 1981-86; commr. N.J. Dept. Human Svcs., Trenton, 1986-89; program dir. health and human svcs. The Pew Charitable Trusts, Phila., 1989-90; pres., CEO Henry J. Kaiser Family Found., Menlo Park, Calif., 1990—. Contbr. articles to profl. jours. Mem. Inst. of Medicine, Nat. Acad. of Soc. Ins., Assn. for Health Svcs. Rsch. Office: Henry J Kaiser Family Found 2400 Sand Hill Rd Menlo Park CA 94025-6941

ALTMAN, IRWIN, psychologist, educator; BA, NYU, 1951; MA, U. Md., 1954, PhD, 1957. Asst. prof. psychology Am. U., Washington, 1957-58, sr. rsch. scientist, assoc. prof., 1960-62, adj. prof., 1962-69; rsch. scientist in human scis. Arlington, Va., 1958-60; rsch. psychologist Naval Med. Rsch. Inst., Bethesda, Md., 1962-69; adj. prof. U. Md., 1968-69; prof. U. Utah, Salt Lake City, 1969-79, chmn. dept. psychology, 1969-76, dean Coll. Social and Behavioral Sci., 1979-83, v.p. for acad. affairs, 1983-87, disting. prof., 1987—2005, disting. prof. emeritus, 2005—. Author: (with J.E. McGrath) Small Groups, 1966, (with D.A. Taylor) Social Penetration, 1973, Environment and Social Behavior, 1975; (with M. Chemers) Culture and Environment, 1980; (with J. Wohlwill) Human Behavior and Environment: Vol. I, 1976, Vol. II, 1977, Vol. III, 1978, Vol. IV, 1980, Vol. V, 1981, Vol. VI, 1983, Vol. VII, 1984, (with C. Werner) Vol. VIII, 1985, (with A. Wandersman) Vol. IX, 1987, (with E. Zube) Vol. X, 1989, (with K. Christensen) Vol. XI, 1990, (with S. Low) Vol. XII, 1992, (with A. Churchman) Women and the Environment, Vol. XIII, 1994; (with D. Stokols) Handbook of Environmental Psychology, Vols I and II, 1987; (with J. Ginat) Polygamous Families in Contemporary Society, 1996; mem. editl. bds.: Small Groups, 1970-79, Man-Environment Systems, 1969-73, Jour. Applied Social Psychology, 1973-85, Sociometry, 1973-76, Environment and Behavior, 1975, Jour. Personality and Social Psychology, 1974-83, Contemporary Psychology, 1975-86, Environ. Psychology and Nonverbal Behavior, Psychology, 1976-90, Am. Jour. Cmty. Psychology, 1978-81, Population and Environment, 1979, Jour. Environ. Psychology, 1982, Computers and Human Behavior, 1985, Internat. Jour. Applied Social Psychology, 1984, Communication Monographs, 1992-95; assoc. editor Am. Jour. Cmty. Psychology, 1988-92; co-editor Jour. Environ. Psychology, 1990-98; contbr. articles to profl. jours. 1st lt. Adj. Gen. Corps, AUS, 1954-56. Mem. APA (pres. divsn. population and environment), AAAS, Soc. Exptl. Social Psychology, Soc. Psychol. Study of Issues, Soc. Personality and Social Psychology (pres.), Environ. Design Rsch. Assn., Am. Psychol. Soc. Office Phone: 801-581-7109. Business E-Mail: irwin.altman@m.cc.utah.edu.

ALTMAN, LAWRENCE KIMBALL, physician, journalist; b. Quincy, Mass., June 19, 1937; s. William S. and Esther (Kimball) A. AB cum laude, Harvard U., 1958; MD, Tufts U., 1962. Diplomate: Am. Vet. Epidemiology Soc. Intern Mt. Zion Hosp., San Francisco, 1962-63; USPHS epidemic intelligence service officer CDC, Atlanta, 1963-66; med. resident, fellow U. Wash. Hosp., Seattle, 1966-69; med. corr., columnist The Doctors World NY Times, 1969—; clin. prof. medicine NYU, 1970—. Vis. physician Serafimer Hosp., Karolinska Inst., Stockholm, Sweden, 1973; vis. scientist U. Wash., 1971; Chancellor's Disting. Lecture for Pub. Understanding of Sci., U. Calif., San Francisco, 1989; Ida Beam Disting. vis. prof. U. Iowa, 2000. Author: Science of The Times, 1981, Who Goes First? The Story of Self-Experimentation in Medicine, 1987, 98; contbr. chpts. to books, articles to profl. jours.; contbr. Ency. Brit., 1979, Grolier Ency., 1972-87. Recipient Claude Bernard award, Nat. Soc. Med. Rsch., 1971, 1974, Pub. Svc. award, Nat. Kidney Found., 1977, Walter C. Alvarez award, Am. Med. Writers Assn., 1980, journalism award, Am. Acad. Pediat., 1982, Pub. Svc. award, Nat. Kidney Found., 1983, Howard W. Blakeslee award, Am. Heart Assn., 1982—83, 1994, Journalism award, Coll. Am. Pathologists, 1985, George Polk award, 1986, Vincent Downing award, 1988, Med. Media Excellence award, Friends Nat. Libr. Medicine, 1993, Victor Cohn prize, Coun. for the Advancement of Sci. Writing, 2000, Howard Lewis Career award, Am. Heart Assn., 2001, medal, U. Calif., San Francisco, 2004, Walsh McDermott award, Associated Med. Schs. NY, 2004. Master ACP; fellow Am. Coll. Epidemiology, NY Acad. Medicine; mem. Inst. Medicine, NAS, Am. Soc. Tropical Medicine and Hygiene, Soc. Epidemiology, Am. Bd. Med. Spltys. (pub. 1986-88), Alpha Omega Alpha, Century Club (NYC), Harvard Club (NYC). Home: 140 W End Ave New York NY 10023-6131 Office: New York Times 620 Eighth Ave New York NY 10018-1405 Business E-Mail: altman@nytimes.com.

ALTMAN, LOUIS, lawyer, author, educator; b. NYC, Aug. 6, 1933; s. Benjamin and Jean (Zimmerman) A.; m. Sally J. Schlesinger, Dec. 26, 1955 (dec.); 1 child: Andrew; m. Eleanor Silver, Oct. 30, 1966; 1 child: Robert. AB, Cornell U., 1955; LLB, Harvard U., 1958. Bar: N.Y. 1959, Conn. 1970, Ill. 1973. Assoc. Amster & Levy, NYC, 1958-60; patent atty. Sperry Rand, NYC, 1960-63; chief patent counsel Gen. Time Corp., NYC, 1963-67; ptnr. Altman & Reens, Stamford, Conn., 1967-72; chief patent counsel Baxter Labs, Deerfield, Ill., 1972-76; assoc. prof. John Marshall Law Sch., 1976-79, adj. prof., 1979-96, Loyola Law Sch., 1996-97; of counsel Gerlach, O'Brien & Kleinke, Chgo., 1981-83; ptnr. Laff, Whitesel & Saret, Chgo., 1983-2001; of counsel Michael Best & Friedrich, Chgo., 2001—06; dir. Congregation Humanistic Jidaism, Sarasota, Fla., 2006—. Author: Callmann on Unfair Competition, Trademarks & Monopolies, 4th edit., 1981, Business Competition Law Adviser, 1983; contbr. Construction Law, 1986, Legal Compliance Checkups, 1985, articles to legal jours. Recipient Gerald Rose Meml. award John Marshall Law Sch., 1988. Mem.: Soc. Humanistic Judaism (pres. 2006—), Humanists Fla. Assn. (dir. 2007—). Home Phone: 847-530-2104. Personal E-mail: laltman@louisaltman.com.

ALTMAN, ROBERT, lawyer; b. St. Paul, Feb. 21, 1949; s. Milton and Helen (Horwitz) A.; m. Margo Geller, Mar. 28, 1998; children by previous marriage: Jesse, David, Aaron. BA, U. Calif., Berkeley, 1970; JD, U. Minn., 1973. Bar: Minn. 1975, Ga. 1978, U.S. Ct. Appeals (5th cir.) 1978, U.S. Ct. Appeals (11th cir.) 1981, U.S. Supreme Ct. 1981; registered mediator and arbitrator Ga. Supreme Ct., 2003—. Atty. Team Def. Project, Atlanta, 1976-77; assoc. dir. So. Prisoners Def. Com., New Orleans, 1978-79; exec. dir. Fed. Defender Program, Inc., 1980-84; pvt. practice Atlanta, 1984—; judge Mcpl. Ct. City of Atlanta, 1988-96; mediator/arbitrator JAMS, Atlanta. Pres. Fed. Defender Program, Inc., 1990-91; instr. Nat. Inst. Trial Advocacy, Emory U., Atlanta, 1983-2000; com. to rev. the criminal justice act U.S. Jud. Conf., 1991-93. Contbr. articles to profl. jours. Bd. dirs. votehealthcare.org, 2007—. Mem. ATLA, Ga. Bar Assn., Atlanta Bar Assn. (Blue Ribbon commn.), Ga. Trial Lawyers Assn. (chair bad faith ins. litigation group, mem. exec. com. 1999-2004), Ga. Assn. Criminal Def. Laywers, Phi Beta Kappa. Office: Hughes & Altman LLP 1842 Independence Sq Atlanta GA 30338 also: Jams 1100 Peachtree St NE Ste 640 Atlanta GA 30309-4516 Office Phone: 404-892-8766. Personal E-mail: altlaw@mindspring.com.

ALTMAN, ROBERT ALAN, lawyer; b. Washington, Feb. 23, 1947; s. Norman S. and Sophie B. (Robinson) A.; m. Lynda J. Carter, Jan. 29, 1984; children: James Clifford, Jessica Carter. BA, U. Wis., 1968; JD, George Washington U., 1971. Bar: D.C. 1971. Ptnr. Clifford & Warnke, Washington, 1971—91; chmn., CEO ZeniMax Media, Inc., Washington, 1999—. Pres. 1st Am. Corp., Washington, 1982-91; bd. dirs. 1st Am. Bankshares Inc., Washington, 1st Am. Bank N.Y., N.Y.C. Avocations: tennis, skiing.

ALTMAN, ROY PETER, pediatric surgeon; b. NYC, Apr. 13, 1934; s. Charles and Sue (Solomon) A.; m. Hanna Diamond, Aug. 22, 1964; children: James David, Robert Ross. AB, Colgate U., 1955; MS, U. Rochester Sch. Medicine, 1957; MD, NY Med. Coll., 1961. Diplomate Am. Bd. Surgery, Am. Bd. Thoracic Surgery, Am. Bd. Pediatric Surgery. Intern Mount Sinai Hosp., NYC, 1961-62; surg. resident Tufts-New Eng. Med. Ctr, Boston, 1962-66, chief resident, 1966-67; postdoctoral fellow NIH, Dept. Surgery Tufts-New Eng. Med. Ct., 1964-65; chief resident in thoracic surgery George Washington U. Hosp., Washington, 1967—68; chief resident in pediatric surgery Children's Hosp. Nat. Med. Ctr., Washington, 1967-69; spl. fellow clin./rsch. surgery (transplantation) U. Colo. Health Scis. Ctr., Denver, 1974; prof. surgery in surgery and pediatrics Coll. Physicians and Surgeons, Columbia U., NYC, 1980—; surgeon in chief Morgan Stanley Children's Hosp. of NY-Presbyn., 1980—; v.p. med. affairs, physician in chief Children's Health System, 1998. Prof. surgery and child health George Washington Sch. Medicine, 1977-80; sr. attending surgeon Children's Hosp., Nat. Med. Ctr., Washington, 1973-80, dir. surg. rsch., 1975-80, surg. dir. clin. rsch. ctr., 1975-80, dir. organ transplantation, 1975-80; cons. surgeon Walter Reed Army Hosp., 1974-80, Dewitt Army Hosp., Ft. Belvoir, Va., 1973-80, The Hosp. for Sick Children, Washington, 1974-80; asst. prof.surgery and child health George Washington U. Sch. Medicine, 1970-73, Tufts U. Sch. Medicine. Editl. cons. Pediat. Surgery Internat., 1985—; editl. adv. bd. Surgery Ann., 1986—, Surgery, 1992-98, Jour. Pediat. Surgery, 1996. Bd. dirs. Ronald McDonald House and Found. Children's Oncology Soc., N.Y. C.V. Mosby Scholar, N.Y. Med. Coll., 1961. Fellow: ACS, Am. Acad. Pediats.; mem.: Am. Pediat. Surg. Assn. (gov. 1996, bd. govs. 1996—99, pres. 2002—, bd. govs. 2003, pres. elect 2002, pres. 2003, bd. govs. 2004), Internat. Coll. Surgery, Soc. Univ. Surgeons, Am. Surg. Assn., Alpha Omega Alpha. Avocations: skiing, golf, tennis, music. Home: 15 W 81st St New York NY 10024-6022 Office: Morgan Stanley Children's Hosp of NY Presbyn Columbia Univ Med Ctr 3959 Broadway 116 Ctrl New York NY 10032-1590 Home Phone: 212-787-7869. Business E-Mail: rpa1@columbia.edu.

ALTMAN, SAMUEL PINOVER, mechanical engineer, research consultant; b. Atlantic City, Apr. 15, 1921; s. Ben and Beatrix (Pinover) A.; m. Francine Danish, Oct. 5, 1943; children: Ellen Beatrix, Sharon Anita. BSME, CCNY, 1942. System engr. USAF, Lear, Lockheed, Bendix, various, 1943-58; prin. engr. Martin Co., Waterton, Colo., 1958-61; supr. space scis. United Aircraft Systems Ctr., Farmington, Conn., 1961-63; cons. engr. GE, Missile & Space Div., King of Prussia, Pa., 1963-69; sr. staff engr. System Devel. Corp., Santa Monica, Calif., 1969-72; dir. space mechanics Can. Govt., Dept. Communications, Ottawa, Ont., Can., 1972-85; rsch. cons. Ottawa, 1985—. Author: Orbital Hodograph Analysis, 1965. Capt. USAF, 1943-53. Mem. IEEE, Am. Astronautical Soc. Achievements include 3 patents on aircraft inertial instruments; development of math. methods for selection/optimization of orbital parameters for 2-impulse orbital transfer, of algebraic transformations of orbital parameters between position, velocity and acceleration states, of alternative hodographic formulations for orbit analysis, based upon orbital hodograph parameters. Home and Office: 465 Richmond Rd 2107 Ottawa ON Canada K2A 1Z1 Business E-Mail: samuel.altman021@sympatico.ca.

ALTMAN, SCOTT, law educator, dean; b. 1962; BA, Univ. Wis., Madison, 1983; JD cum laude, Harvard Univ., 1987. Law clerk U.S. Ct. Appeals 9th cir., 1987—88; asst. prof. Univ. So. Calif. Law Sch., 1988—90, assoc. prof., 1990—93, prof., 1993—97, assoc. dean, 1995—, Virginia S. & Fred H. Bice prof., 1997—. Contbr. articles prof. law jour. Mem.: Phi Beta Kappa. Office: The Law Sch Univ So Calif Los Angeles CA 90089

ALTMAN, SIDNEY, biology professor; b. Montreal, Que., Can., May 7, 1939; s. Victor Altman and Ray Arlin; m. Ann Korner, 1972; children: Daniel, Leah. BS, MIT, 1960; PhD in Biophys., U. Colo., 1967; DSc (hon.), McGill U., Montreal, 1991, York U., U. Colo., U. Montreal, U. B.C. Teaching asst. Columbia U., 1960—62; Damon Runyon Meml. Fund cancer rsch. fellow in molecular biology Harvard U., 1967—69; Anna Fuller Fund fellow, then Med. Rsch. Coun. fellow Med. Rsch. Coun. Lab. Molecular Biology, 1969—71; from asst. to assoc. prof. Yale U., New Haven, 1971—80, prof. molecular cellular and devel. biology, 1980—, Sterling prof. biology, 1990—, prof. biophysical chemistry, 1994—, chmn. dept., 1983—85; dean Yale Coll., 1985—90. Tutor Radcliffe Coll., 1968—69. Author: Transfer RNA, 1978. Recipient Nobel Prize in Chemistry, 1989, Merit Award, Nat. Inst. Health, 1989, Yale Sci. and Engring. Assn. Award, 1990. Fellow: AAAS; mem.: Am. Philos. Soc. (Rosenstiel award 1989), Nat. Acad. Scis., Genetics Soc. Am., Am. Soc. Biol. Chemists. Achievements include research in on effects of acridines on T4 DNA replication, mutants, precursors of tRNA processing by catalytic RNA and ribonuclease function. Office: Yale U Kline Biology Tower 402 New Haven CT 06520-8103

ALTMAN, STEVEN, financial consulting company executive, academic administrator; b. Jacksonville, Fla., Oct. 24, 1945; s. Harold and Estelle (Avchin) A.; m. Judy Ellen Ovadenko, Feb. 8, 1969. BA, UCLA, 1967; MBA, U. So. Calif., 1969, DBA, 1975. Asst. dean Sch. Bus. U. So. Calif., LA, 1969-72; asst. prof. div. mgmt. Fla. Internat. U., Miami, 1972-76, chmn. divsn. mgmt., 1972-77, assoc. prof. divsn. mgmt., 1976-84, prof. divsn. mgmt., 1984-85, asst. v.p. acad. affairs, 1977-78, assoc. v.p. acad. affairs, 1978-80; v.p. acad. affairs Fla. Internat U., 1981-85; univ. provost Fla. Internat. U., 1982-85; pres. Tex. A&M U., Kingsville, 1985-89, prof. mgmt., 1985-89; pres., prof. mgmt. U. Cen. Fla., Orlando, 1989-91; pres. SynerCo, Inc., Pasadena, Calif., 1992—94, Lynx Worldwide, Inc., LA, 1995—96, Med. Telecomms. Assocs., Inc., LA, 1994—2002; v.p. Lido Capital, Irvine, Calif., 2002—05, Anthem Capital Ptnrs., LLC, LA, 2005—; pres. New Sch. Architecture and Design, San Diego, 2006—. Spl. master Fla. Pub. Employees Relations Commn., 1976-85; mem. 4th quadennial evaluation com. Ala. Commn. for Higher Edn., 1986-87; bd. dirs. Internat. Ctr. of Fla., Miami, 1982-85; cons. in field Author: Organizational Behavior, 1979, 84, Readings in Organizational Behavior, 1979, Organizational Behavior, 1985, Profit Basics, 1977, Home Health Telecommunications, 1999; editor: Organization Development: Progress and Perspectives, 1982; co-author: Home Health Telecommunications, 1999. Mem. adv. bd. Assn. for Retarded Citizens, Miami, 1978-85; vice chmn. Internat. Health Com., 1984-85; exec. com. Metro-Miami Action Plan, 1983-85; bd. dirs. Found. Excellence in Pub. Edn., 1984-85, Kingsville Econ. Devel. Coun., 1986-89; mem. planning com. Spohn Kleberg Hosp., 1986-89; dir. Orange County Pub. Schs. Found., 1989-91; bd. dirs. Heart of Fla. United Way, 1989-91, Orlando/Orange County Compact, 1989-91, Orlando Ctr. for Humanities, 1989-91, Jr. Achievement Ctrl. Fla., 1989-91, Ctrl. Fla. coun. Boy Scouts Am., 1989-91; trustee WMFE/90.7 Pub. TV, Orlando, 1990-91. With USAR, 1968-74. Recipient Gold medal for econs. edn. Freedom Found., 1971, Excellence in Tchg. award Sch. Bus. Adminstrn., U. So. Calif., 1972, Labor Edn. award, 1982, Tree of Life award Nat. Jewish Found., Orlando, 1991; named Outstanding Faculty Mem. Coll. Bus. Adminstrn. Fla. Internat. U., 1975. Mem. Am. Arbitration Assn. (arbitrator 1977—), Hispanic Assn. Colls. and Univs. (founder, v.p. 1986-89), South Miami-Kendall Area C. of C. (bd. dirs. 1982-85, pres. 1983-85), Kingsville C. of C. (bd. dirs. 1985-89, pres. 1986-87), Greater Orlando C. of C. (bd. dirs. 1989-91), Winter Park C. of C. (bd. dirs. 1989-91), BGeta Gamma Sigma, Phi Kappa Phi, Phi Theta Kappa, Omicron Delta Kappa. Home: 850 Beech St #1605 San Diego CA 92101 Business E-Mail: steve@stevenaltman.com.

ALTMAN, STEVEN R., telecommunications executive; BS magna cum laude, No. Ariz. Univ., 1983; JD cum laude, U. San Diego, 1986. Atty. Gray, Cary, Ware & Freidenreich, San Diego; corp. counsel Qualcomm, San Diego, 1989—92, v.p., gen. counsel, 1992—95, gen mgr. tech. licensing, 1995—96, sr. v.p., 1996—98, exec. v.p., 1998—2000, pres. tech. licensing, 2000—05, pres., 2005—. Bd. mem. Salk Inst.; mem. Amylin Pharms. Office: 5775 Morehouse Dr San Diego CA 92121-1714*

ALTMAN, STUART HAROLD, economist, educator; b. NYC, Aug. 8, 1937; s. Sidney and Florence A.; m. Diane Kleinberg, June 7, 1959; children: Beth, Renee, Heather. BBA, CCNY; MA in Econs; PhD, UCLA. Asso. prof. econs. Brown U., 1966-71; dep. asst. sec. health and planning HEW, 1971-76; dep. dir. for health (Cost of Living Council), 1973-74; dean Florence Heller Grad. Sch., Brandeis U., Waltham, Mass., 1977-92; Sol C. Chaikin prof. Nat. Health Policy, 1992—. Chmn. bd. Univ. Health Policy Consortium; chmn. U.S. Prospective Payment Assessment Commn.; mem. Inst. Medicine, Nat. Acad. Scis., 1978— Author, editor govt. publs., reports. Bd. dirs. Beth Israel Hosp., Brookline, Mass., 1979—. Mem. Am. Public Health Assn. Office: Inst for Health Policy Heller Grad Sch PO Box 9110 Waltham MA 02454-9110

ALTMAN, WILLIAM CARL, health facility administrator, industrial relations specialist, investment company executive, consultant; b. La Grange, Tex., Nov. 11, 1957; s. Lester Arthur and Goldie Bertha (Kretzschmar) A.; m. Danguole Julia Spakevicius, Sept. 2, 1989; children: Darius, Indre, Ilona, Isabella. BS, Tex. A&M U., 1979; BA, MA, Oxford U., Eng., 1982; MBA, Harvard U., 1984. Project dir. Trammell Crow Co., Houston, 1984-85; cons. McKinsey & Co., Inc., Houston, NYC, 1985-89; v.p. Capital Guidance Corp., Houston, 1989-93, sr. v.p., 1993-94; COO Obstet. and Gynecol. Assocs., PA, Houston, 1994-97; exec. v.p. acquistions FemPartners, Inc., Houston, 1997—, also bd. dirs.; mng. dir. Interlaken Ventures, Inc., 2000—; sr. client ptnr. Korn Ferry, Internat., 2005—. Pres. Tredex Tile Corp., Houston, 1993—94. Devel. bd. dirs. Tex. A&M U. Coll. Liberal Arts, College Station, 1987—; bd. dirs. U.S.-Baltic Found., Washington, 1990—, chmn., 1993-96, 2001—; mem. N.Y. coun. on Fgn. Rels., 2000—; mem. Houston com. Coun. on Fgn. Rels., 1990—; co-chair Houston com. Campaign for Oxford, 1990-91; mem. Tex. Rhodes Scholarship Selection com., 1990-91. Recipient Rhodes scholarship Rhodes Scholarship Trustees, Oxford, Eng., 1980. Mem. Harvard Bus. Sch. Club. Republican. Avocations: scouting, politics. Office: Interlaken Ventures Inc 4030 Case St Houston TX 77005-3606

ALTMAN, WILLIAM KEAN, lawyer; b. San Antonio, Feb. 18, 1944; s. Marion K. and Ruth (Nunnelee) A.; m. Doris E. Johnson, May 29, 1964; children: Brian, Brad, Blake. BBA, Tex. A&M U., 1965, MBA, 1967; JD, U. Tex., 1979. Bar: Tex. 1970, Okla. 1993, U.S. Dist. Ct. (no. and ea. dists.) Tex., U.S. Ct. Appeals (5th and 11th cirs.), U.S. Supreme Ct. Pres. Altman

& Nix, Wichita Falls, Tex., 1970—. Mem. Wichita Falls City Coun., 1998-2002; mayor of Wichita Falls, 2002-05. Mem. ABA, Tex. Bar Assn., Assn. Trial Lawyers Am. (life) (bd. of govs. 1980-83, active coms. and sects.), Tex. Trial Lawyers Assn. (assoc. bd. dirs. 1977-78, bd. dirs. 1978—, active various coms. and sect.). Democrat. Baptist. Office: Atlman & Nix Ste 500 2525 Kell Blvd Wichita Falls TX 76308-1061

ALTMANN, STUART ALLEN, biologist, educator; b. St. Louis, June 8, 1930; s. Maurice Walter and Deborah (Freedman) A.; m. Jeanne Glaser, June 20, 1959; children: Michael Alexander, Rachel Ann. BA in Zoology, UCLA, 1953, MA, 1954; PhD in Biology, Harvard U., 1960. Asst. prof. zoology U. Alta., Can., 1960-65, assoc. prof., 1965; sociobiologist Yerkes Regional Primate Rsch. Ctr., 1965-70; prof. anatomy U. Chgo., 1970-80, prof. biology, 1970-88, prof. ecology and evolution, 1988-95, prof. human nutrition and nutritional biology, 1985—95, prof. emeritus, 1995—; lectr., prof. ecology and evolutionary biology Princeton (N.J.) U., 1998—. Hon. rsch. assoc. Haile Sellaissie I U., Ethiopia, 1971; exptl. psychology sci. adv. panel NIMH, 1969-73; primate conservation com. NAS-NRC, 1970-72; grant reviewer NSF, NIH, NIMH, Spencer Found., Nat. Geog. Soc., Smithsonian Instn., others Mem. editl. bd. Behavioral Ecology and Sociobiology, 1976-79, Am. Naturalist, 1977-79, Animal Behavior, 1978-79, Ethology, Ecology and Evolution, 1989—; mem. bd. editl. commentators The Behavioral and Brain Scis., 1977-82 Fellow AAAS, Am. Acad. Arts and Scis., Animal Behavior Soc. (pres. 1977, exec. com. 1975-78); mem. Comparative Nutrition Soc., Internat. Primatol. Soc. Avocations: making pottery, orchard farming. Office: Princeton U Dept Ecology Evol Biology Princeton NJ 08544-1003 Home Phone: 609-279-0403; Office Phone: 609-258-4520. E-mail: salt@princeton.edu.

ALTMIRE, JASON, congressman; b. Lower Burrell, Pa., Mar. 7, 1968; m. Kelly Altmire; 2 children. BS in Polit. Sci., Fla. State U., 1990; M in Health Adminstrn., George Washington U., 1998. Legis. asst. to US Rep. Pete Peterson US Congress, Washington, 1991—96; asst. v.p. Fedn. Am. Hospitals, 1996—98; with U. Pitts. Med. Ctr., 1998—2005, acting v.p. govt. relations & cmty. health services, 2005; mem. US Congress from 4th Pa. dist., 2007—, mem. edn. & labor com., small bus. com., transp. & infrastructure com., chmn. investigations and oversight subcommittee. Mem. health sys. adv. bd. Am. Hosp. Assn.; govt. relations rep. Assn. Am. Med. Collleges; adv. bd. Nat. Ctr. Early Defibrillation; legis. com. Allegheny Valley C. of C., Northern Allegheny C. of C.; mem. selection com. Good Govt. Award League of Women Voters Greater Pitts., co-chair 2003 clean campaign com.; pres. Northern Allegheny Lions Club, McCandless Rotary Club; resource faculty mem. U. Pitts. Grad. Sch. Health Policy and Mgmt. Named one of Pitts. 40 Under 40; recipient Arcadia award, Northern Allegheny C. of C., 2005. Democrat. Office: 1419 Longworth House Office Bldg Washington DC 20515 also: 2124 Freeport Rd Natrona Heights PA 15065 Office Phone: 724-226-1304. Office Fax: 724-226-1308.*

ALTOMARA, RITA ECKE, library director, writer; b. Englewood, NJ, June 27, 1950; d. Russell and Rita (Walsh) Ecke; m. Gary John Altomara, Dec. 14, 1969; 1 child, Ginevra Marie. BA, Barnard Coll., NYC, 1972; MS, Columbia U., NYC, 1975. Jr. libr. Ft. Lee Pub. Libr., N.J., 1974-77, sr. libr., 1977-80, prin. libr., 1980-82, asst. dir., 1982-84, dir., 1984—. Coord. Women's Info and Referral Svc., Ft. Lee, 1975—. Author: Hollywood on the Palisades, 1983; contbg. author: Encyclopedia of New Jersey, 2004. Mem. exec. bd. Ft. Lee Hist. Soc., 1982—; liaison Bergen County Office Hist. and Cultural Affairs, Hackensack, NJ, 1978—. Mem.: ALA, N.J. Libr. Assn. Roman Catholic. Home: 121 Engle St Cresskill NJ 07626-2246 Office: Ft Lee Pub Library 320 Main St Fort Lee NJ 07024-4706

ALTON, ANN LESLIE, judge, lawyer, educator; b. Pipestone, Minn., Sept. 10, 1945; d. Howard Robert, Jr. and Camilla Ann (DeMong) A.; m. Gerald Russell Freeman Sr. (dec. 2004); children: Brady Michael Alton Freeman, Matthew Alton Freeman (dec.). BA, Smith Coll., 1967; JD, U. Minn., 1970; postgrad., Nat. Jud. Coll., U. Nev., 1989. Bar: Minn. 1970, U.S. Dist. Ct. Minn. 1972, U.S. Supreme Ct. 1981. Apptd. gen. jurisdiction state trial ct. judge civil and criminal jurisdiction Dist. Ct., 4th Jud. Dist., Hennepin County, Minn., 1989—, elected, 1990—96, 2002—, mem. exec. com. Hennepin County, 1995—98, chair psychol. svcs. com., 1996, vice chair adminstrv. com., 1989-94, asst. county atty. Mpls., 1970-89, felony prosecutor, criminal divsn., 1970-75, acting chief citizen protection divsn., 1975-76, chief citizen protection/econ. crime divsn., 1976-79, chief econ. crime unit, 1979-85, sr. atty. civil divsn. handling labor and employment law, 1989-89, mem. civil com., 1989—, presiding judge probate/mental health div., 1995-98, mem. exec. com., 1995-98, chair psychol. svcs. to ct. com., 1997-2000, 2002. Adj. prof. law Hamline U. Law Sch., St. Paul, 1973-77, 2004—; adj. prof. law William Mitchell Coll. Law, St. Paul, 1977—; adj. prof. U. Minn. Law Sch., 1978-82; dir. Trial Advocacy, U. St. Thomas Sch. Law., 2005-; lectr. in field, 1970—; sr. faculty Minn. Advocacy Inst., Minn. CLE, 1988—; mem. faculty Nat. Inst. Trial Advocacy, U. Notre Dame Law Sch., 1989—, asst. team leader North Ctrl. Regional Jury Trial Advocacy Course, 1991—; sr. critiquing judge Jud. Trial Skills Tng. Program Minn. Supreme Ct. Continuing Edn. Program for State Cts., 1993—; mem. faculty intensive trial advocacy program Widener U. Sch. of Law, Wilmington, Del., 1993-96; bd. dirs. Pan-O-Gold Realty Co., 1986-89, Alton Realty Co., 1986-89, Alton Found., 1999—. Author articles, pamphlet, manual. Vice-chmn. bd. dirs. Minn. Program on Victims of Sexual Assault, 1974-76; bd. dirs. Physician's Health Plan (now Allina), Health Maintenance Orgn., 1976-80, exec. com., 1977-80; mem. legal drug abuse subcom. Gov. Minn. Adv. Com. Drug Abuse, 1972-74; bd. visitors U. Minn. Law Sch., 1979-85; mem. child abuse project coordinating com. Hennepin County Med. Soc., 1982-83, chmn. corp., labor, ins. subcom., 1982; commr. corrections task force sex offenders, 1999-2001. Recipient Honorable Mention Roscoe Pound award for Excellence in Tchg. Trial Advocacy, Roscoe Pound Inst., Washington, 2000. Mem. ABA (jud. adminstrn. divsn.), Minn. Bar Assn. (criminal law, labor and employment law, civil litigation sects.), Hennepin County Bar Assn. (ethics com. 1973-76, criminal law com. 1973—, vice chmn. 1979-80, 83-84, unauthorized practice law com. 1977-78, individual rights and responsibilities com. 1977-78, labor and employment law com. 1985—, civil litigation com. 1985—), Minn. Dist. Judges Assn. (benefits com. 1991—, mem. program and edn. com. 1993—, mem. worker compensation risk mgmt. com. 1995-97), U. Minn. Law Sch. Alumni Assn. (bd. dirs. 1979-85), Nat. Women Judges, Douglas K. Amdahl Inn of Ct. (master, exec. bd. 2003-). Achievements include being the first woman supervisory attorney in Hennepin county; being first woman to prosecute felony trials for Hennepin county; being part of changing state-wide systems for sexual assault victims, child abuse victims and battered women. Office: 1251-C Hennepin County Govt Ctr 300 S 6th St Minneapolis MN 55487 Office Phone: 612-348-8105. E-mail: ann.alton@courts.state.mn.us. *The greatest joy and biggest challenge of my life has been the privilege of loving, nurturing and guiding my son. Motherhood is my most rewarding accomplishment. The most important lesson I've learned is that one person with vision, perseverance, and energy can cause significant changes in government, in an organization, in society. My great-grandmother told me, "You can do anything you want to do if you're willing to work hard for it, and don't let anyone tell you otherwise". She was right.*

ALTON, GREGG H., lawyer; BA, U. Calif., Berkeley, 1989; JD, Stanford U., 1993. Atty. Cooley Godward Kronish LLP; assoc. gen. counsel Gilead Scis., Inc., Foster City, Calif., 1999—2001, v.p., gen. counsel, 2001—05, sr. v.p., gen. counsel, 2005—. Mem. BIO's Gen. Counsel Com.; bd. dir. Phytogen Life Scis., BayBio. Co-author: Potential Securities Law Liabilities in the Sale of a Privately Held Business, California Business Law Practitioner. Chair bd. dirs. Bay Area Bioscience Ctr. Mem.: AIDS Healthcare Found. (bd. dirs., treas.), ABA (mem. com. on negotiated acquisitions, sect. of bus. law). Office: Gilead Scis Inc 333 Lakeside Dr Foster City CA 94404 Office Phone: 650-574-3000. Office Fax: 650-578-9264.*

ALTON, HOWARD ROBERT, JR., lawyer, food company executive, real estate executive; b. Pipestone, Minn., May 12, 1927; s. Howard Robert Sr. and Vera Edna (Boehmke) A.; m. Camilla Ann DeMong; children: Ann, Jeanine, Howard R. III, Patricia, Michelle. BBA, U. Minn., 1950; JD cum laude, Hamline U., 1975. Bar: Minn., 1975, U.S. Ct. Appeals (8th cir.) 1975, U.S. Dist. Ct. Minn. 1976. Founder Hamline Sch. Law, 1972-74, Alton, Severson & Sovis, Apple Valley, Minn., 1978-86; CEO, Pan-O-Gold Baking Co., Wayzata and St. Cloud, Minn., now vice chmn., treas., chief investment officer. With U.S. Marines, 1945-46. Mem. World Pres.' Orgn. (Palm Beach chpt.), Minn. Young Pres.' Orgn. (past chmn.), The Mpls. Club, Old Port Cove Yacht Club, North Palm Beach City Club, Gt. Lakes Cruising Club, Wayzata Country Club, Ocean Reef Club, Madaline Island Yacht Club (LaPointe, Fla.), Madaline Island Golf Club, Govs. Club Palm Beach. Avocations: conservation, wildlife preservation, power boating. Home and Office: 338 S Ocean Blvd Palm Beach FL 33480

ALTON, LLOYDE LOREN, retired defender; b. Tacoma, Apr. 4, 1932; s. Lloyde Loren and Edna Georke Alton; m. Carmen Cayanan, Dec. 29, 1962; children: Christopher Clifford, Kenneth Kendal. BS in CE, U. Wash., Seattle, 1955; JD, U. Puget Sound, Tacoma, 1978. Bar: Wash. 1979. Pub. defender Dept. Assigned Counsel, Tacoma, 1981—98; ret., 1998. Mem. death penalty com. Washington Assn. Criminal Def. Lawyers, Wash. Maj. USAF, 1955—75. Decorated Air Force Commendation medal USAF; recipient Outstanding Def. Atty., Pierce County Prosecuting Attys., 1995, 1997. Unitarian-Universalist. Avocations: photography, golf. Home: HCR 2 Box 6219 Keaau HI 96749 Home Phone: 808-982-6693. Personal E-mail: lloydealton@hotmail.com.

ALTSCHAEFFL, ADOLPH GEORGE, retired civil engineering educator; b. Passaic, NJ, July 20, 1930; s. Ludwig and Crescenz (Liebl) A.; m. Martha Anne Filiatreau, Aug. 6, 1966. BSC.E., Purdue U., 1952, MSC.E., 1955; PhD, 1960. Instr. civil engring. Purdue U., West Lafayette, Ind., 1952-60, asst. prof. civil engring., 1960-64, assoc. prof., 1964-74, prof., 1974-2000, asst. head dept., 1983-91, head geotech. engring., 1994-2000; with Waterways Expt. Sta., C.E., Vicksburg, Miss., 1955, U.S. Geol. Survey, Indpls., 1956; ret., 2000. Cons. civil engring. with various architect and contractor firms. Contbr. articles to profl. jours. Trustee, v.p. West Lafayette Pub. Libr., Ind., 2005—, v.p. bd. trustees, 2007—. With USAR, 1950—61. Mem.: NSPE, ASCE, Am. Soc. Engring. Edn. Personal E-mail: altsch@ecn.purdue.edu.

ALTSCHUL, ALFRED SAMUEL, airline executive; b. Chgo., Oct. 16, 1939; s. Herman and Lillian (Ginsburg) A.; m. Lynn Silverman, Sept. 8, 1968; children: Howard, Steven, Mark. BS, U. Wis., 1961; MBA, U. Chgo., 1963. CPA Ill. With G.A.T.X. Corp., Chgo., 1965-69, asst. treas., 1967-70, treas., 1970-81; v.p. fin., chief fin. officer Midway Airlines, Chgo., 1981-90, sr. v.p., chief fin. officer, 1990-92; CFO Sage Enterprises, Des Plaines, Ill., 1993-95; exec. v.p., CFO A. Epstein and Sons Internat., 1995-96; v.p., CFO Amtrak, 1996-99, Airlines Reporting Corp., 1999—. Lectr. in field. With AUS, 1963—69. Mem. AICPA, Fin. Execs. Inst., Alpha Epsilon Pi. Clubs: Standard (Chgo.). Jewish. Home: 3909 Highwood Court NW Washington DC 20007-2268 Office Phone: 703-816-8150. Personal E-mail: bigchiefal@aol.com.

ALTSCHUL, B. J., public relations counselor; b. Jan. 28, 1948; d. Lemuel and Sylva (Behr) A. Student, Goucher Coll., 1965-67; BA, U. South Fla., 1970; MA, U. Md., 1995. Reporter St. Petersburg (Fla.) Times, 1973—74; dir. pub. rels. Valkyrie Press, Inc., St. Petersburg, 1974—77; founding editor Bay Life, Clearwater, Fla., 1977—79, Tampa Bay Monthly, Clearwater, 1977—79; mng. editor Fla. Tourist News, Tampa and Orlando, 1981; founder Capital Comms. of Tampa, 1981; owner, prin. b j Altschul & Assocs. (formerly Capital Comms. of Tampa), 1985—. Mgr. editl. and info. svcs. Va. Pt. Authority, Norfolk, 1985-88; dir. pub. rels. Va. Dept. Agr. and Consumer Svcs., Richmond, 1988-93; adj. faculty Old Dominion U., Norfolk, 1986-88, U. Richmond, 1990, 94, Washington Ctr. Internships, 1995-96; mgr. pub. rels. U. Md. Biotech. Inst., 1997-99; lectr. dept. comm. U. Md., 1999-01; asst. prof. Am. U., 2001-06; adj. prof. U. Md., 2006-. Author: Cracker Cookin' & Other Favorites, 1984; contbg. author: Virginia: A Commonwealth Comes of Age, 1988. Bd. dirs. Pinellas County Big Bros.-Big Sisters, 1980-82, Fla. Folklore Soc., 1984-85. Mem. Fla. Motion Picture and TV Assn. (treas. 1976-78), Hampton Rds. C. of C. (co-chmn. pub. rels. Internat. Azalea Festival 1986, chmn. publs. 1987), Va. Conf. on World Trade (chmn. pub. rels. com.), Downtown Norfolk Devel. Corp. (chmn. urban living com.), Pub. Rels. Soc. Am. (chmn. Mid.-Atlantic Dist. 1988, chmn. govt. sect. 1989, bd. dirs., chmn. chpt. accreditation, chmn. Univ. Rels. Nat. Capital chpt. 2002-), Va. State Agy. Pub. Affairs Assn. (pres. 1990), Internat. Assn. Bus. Communicators (v.p. mem. svcs. Richmond chpt. 1996), Nat. Assn. Sci. Writers, D.C. Sci. Writers Assn. (bd. dirs. 2004—), Forum Agr. and Consumer Topics (founder, chmn. 1992), Sierra Club (mem. Montgomery County environ. edn. com. 2004—). Avocations: piano, sailing, music, traditional Irish set dancing, dogs. Office: b j Altschul & Assocs 14100 Beechvue Ln Silver Spring MD 20906 Personal E-mail: sunrises111@gmail.com.

ALTSCHUL, DAVID EDWIN, record company executive, lawyer; b. NYC, Apr. 8, 1947; s. Norbert and Grace (Aderer) A.; m. Margaret Berne, July 4, 1969; children: Jonathan, Jared, Eric, Emily. BA summa cum laude, Amherst Coll., 1969; JD, Yale U., 1974. Bar: Calif. 1974. Law clerk U.S. Dist. Ct. Conn., Hartford, 1974-75; assoc. Tuttle & Taylor, Los Angeles, 1975-76, Pryor, Cashman, Sherman & Flynn, Beverly Hills, Calif., 1976-77, Hardee, Barovick, Konecky & Braun, Beverly Hills, 1977-79; prin. Rosenfeld, Kassoy & Kraus, Beverly Hills, 1979-80; dir. bus. affairs Warner Bros. Records, Inc., Burbank, Calif., 1980-83, v.p. bus. and legal affairs, 1983-88, sr. v.p. bus. and legal affairs, 1988-93, gen. counsel and sr. v.p. bus. affairs, 1993-95, vice chmn., gen. counsel, 1995—; co-chair, ptnr. Altschul & Olin LLP, Encino. Bd. dirs. Rec. Industry Assn. Am., Reprise! Broadway's Best in Concert, 1998-99, L.A. Jewish Fedn. Music Industry Divsn.; mem. Millenium Coun., Save Ams. Treasures, 1998—. Bd. dirs. Los Encinos Sch., Encinos, Calif., 1986-93, treas., 1986-87, pres., 1987-92; bd. dirs. People for the Am. Way, 1991—, vice chmn., 1996-97, chmn., 1998—; bd. dirs. People for the Am. Way Found., 1991—, bd. dirs. exec. com., 1993—; bd. dirs. San Fernando Valley Neighborhood Legal Svcs., Inc., 1989-90, Rock the Vote, 1997-98. Mem. Phi Beta Kappa. Democrat. Jewish. Avocations: photography, reading. Office: Altschul & Olin LLP 16133 Ventura Blvd Suite 1270 Encino CA 91436-2408 Office Phone: 818-990-1800. Office Fax: 818-990-1429. Business E-Mail: daltschul@altolinlaw.com.

ALTSCHULER, BRUCE ROBERT, research dentist; b. Bklyn., Feb. 17, 1947; s. Frank Philip and Sarah Gertrude (Cloder) A.; m. Ruth Phyllis Gass, Oct. 27, 1974; children: Joan Ellen, Wendy Karen, Cheryl Miriam. BA, Bklyn. Coll., 1967; DDS, Temple U., Phila., 1971. Lic. dentist Md., Pa., Conn., Maine, N.Y. Commd. capt. USAF, 1971, advanced through grades to col., 1986; project scientist dental holography Dental Scis. Br., Brooks AFB, Tex., 1971-74, chief dental consultation, 1975-76; chief dental laser holography USAF Dental Investigation Svc., Brooks AFB, Tex., 1976-80; chief dental computer/laser tech. USAF Aerospace Medicine, Brooks AFB, Tex., 1980-82; chief avionics advanced systems rsch. group Info. Processing Br., Wright-Patterson AFB, Ohio, 1982-84; dep. optical processing Systems Avionics Div., Wright-Patterson AFB, 1985; dental resident Advanced Clin. Dentistry Residence Program, Eglin AFB, Fla., 1985-86; Air Force rsch. liaison, chief laser imaging U.S. Army Inst. Dental Rsch., Ft. Meade, Md., 1986-94; chief imaging robotics lab. Walter Reed Army Inst. Rsch. Dental Rsch. Detachment, Ft. Meade, Md., 1995-97; dir. rsch. devel. Cobalt Rsch. LLC, 1997—2003, CEO, 2004—. Clin. asst. prof. dept. diagnosis/roentgenology U. Tex. Health Sci. Ctr., San Antonio, 1976-80, dept. dental diagnostic svc., 1980-82; mem. dental x-ray subcom. 26 Am. Nat. Standards Inst., Washington, 1980-85; reviewer NIH Computer Aided Dentistry, Washington, 1987; chmn. SPIE Robotics and Machine Perception Tech. Group, 2006. Editor 3-D Machine Perception; patentee in field. Bd. dirs. Am. Cancer Soc., Bexar County, Tex., 1980-82, mem. pub. edn. com., 1980-82; campaign coord. Avionics Lab. Combined Fed. Campaign, Dayton, Ohio 1984; spl. award judge Alamo Regional Sci. Fair, San Antonio, 1980-82. Mem. ADA, Internat. Assn. Dental Rsch., Soc. Photo Optical Instrumentation Engrs. (chmn. robotics and machine perception tech. group 2006), Air Force Assn., Armed Forces Communications, Electronics Assn., Nat. Def. Indsl. Assn., Md. State Dental Assn., Tex. Dental Assn., Am. Mensa. Republican. Jewish. Avocations: photography, electronics, computers. Home: PO Box 458 Simpsonville MD 21150-0458 Office: Cobalt Rsch LLC PO Box 458 Simpsonville MD 21150-0458 Office Phone: 410-309-6085. E-mail: cobalt-research@starpower.net.

ALTSCHULER, STEVEN M., health facility executive, pediatrician, gastroenterologist; m. Robin L. Altschuler. degree, MD, Case Western. Bd. cert. pediatrician, gastroenterologist. Pediat. residency tng. Children's Hosp., Boston; subspecialty tng., pediat. gastroenterology and nutrition Children's Hosp. Phila.; prof. pediat. U. Penn. Sch. Med., chmn. pediat. dept., 1997; fellow Children's Hosp. Phila., 1982, joined, 1985, physician-in-chief, chmn. dept. pediat., 1997, pres. & CEO, 2000—. Faculty mem. Harvard Med. Sch.; Leonard and Madlyn Abramson endowed chair, pediat. med. Children's Hosp. Phila., chmn. exec. com. Joseph Stokes Jr. Rsch. Inst.; spkr. in pediat. healthcare, gastroenterology, and rsch. Contbr. articles to med. jours., chapters to books. Recipient Janssen award, Janssen Pharmaceutica, 1999. Mem.: No. Am. Soc. Pediat. Gastroenterology, Am. Gastroent. Assn. Sect. on Motility and Nerve/Gut Interaction. Office: Children's Hosp Phila 34th St and Civic Ctr Blvd Philadelphia PA 19104-4399

ALTSHULER, DAVID MATTHEW, geneticist, endocrinologist; b. Ithaca, NY, Aug. 27, 1964; s. Alan Anthony and Julie Maller Altshuler; m. Jill Dara Suttenberg, Aug. 5, 1990; children: Zachary Miles, Jason Leonard. BS, MIT, 1986; PhD in Genetics, Harvard U., 1993; MD, Harvard Med. Sch., 1994. Diplomate in internal medicine Am. Bd. of Internal Medicine, in endocrinology, diabetes and metabolism Am. Bd. of Internal Medicine, 2000. Intern Mass. Gen. Hosp., Boston, 1994—95, resident in internal medicine, 1995—96, fellow in diabetes, endocrinology and metabolism, 1996—99, attending physician, diabetes unit; asst. prof. genetics and medicine Harvard Med. Sch. and Mass. Gen. Hosp., Boston, 2000—; dir. program in med. and population genetics, Whitehead Inst./MIT Ctr. for Genome Rsch. MIT, Cambridge, Mass., 2000—. Chmn. personalized medicine sci. adv. bd. Marshfield (Wis.) Clinic, 2001; mem. clin. genomics adv. bd. Merck Rsch. Labs, West Point, Pa., 2001—; mem. sci. adv. bd. Genomics Collaborative, Inc, Cambridge, 2000—, Reify Corp., Cambridge, 2002—; co-chair Analysis, Intetnational Haplotype Map Project; mem. exec. com, Whitehead Ctr. for Genome Rsch. MIT, 2000—; founding mem. The Broad Inst. of Harvard and MIT, 2003—. Contbr. articles to profl. jours.; mem. bd. reviewing editors Science. Trustee The Commonwealth Sch., Boston, 2002. Recipient Steven Krane award, Mass. Gen. Hosp., 2002; scholar, Burroughs Welcome Fund, 2002—, Charles E. Culpeper scholar, Rockefeller Bros. Fund, 2002—. Mem.: Am. Soc. Clin. Investigation. Office: Mass Gen Hosp Richard B Simches Rsch Ctr 185 Cambridge St Rm 6806 Boston MA 02114 Office Phone: 617-726-5940. Office Fax: 617-726-5937. Business E-Mail: altshuler@molbio.mgh.harvard.edu.*

ALTSHULER, EDWARD ELIHU, physicist, researcher; b. Boston, Jan. 10, 1931; s. Maurice and Aida B. Altshuler; m. Ruth Muriel Liberfarb, June 25, 1978; m. Sheila Glazer, Aug. 30, 1958 (dec. Mar. 25, 1977); children: Robert Charles, Robin Lee McDonough, Michael Eric, David Steven. BS, Northeastern U., Boston, 1953; MS, Tufts U., Medford, Mass., 1954; PhD, Harvard U., Cambridge, Mass., 1960. Antenna engr. Sylvania Electric, Waltham, Mass., 1954—57; rsch. asst. Harvard U., Cambridge, Mass., 1958—60; physicist Air Force Cambridge Rsch. Labs., Hanscom Air Force Base, Mass., 1960—61; dir. engring. Gabriel Elecs., Millis, Mass., 1961—63; supervisory physicist Air Force Cambridge Rsch. Labs., 1963—2007. Fellow: IEEE (life; chmn. Boston sect. 1995—96, Boston Sect. award Continuous and Meritorious Svc. 2004, Harry Diamond Meml. award 1997, IEEE Millennium medal 2000), Air Force Rsch. Lab. (sci. adv. bd. 1973—75); mem.: Sigma Xi, Sigma Pi Sigma. Independent. Achievements include patents for double folded monopole; a process for the design of antennas using genetic algorithms. Avocations: tennis, gardening. Home: 55 Montrose St Newton MA 02458 Office: Air Force Rsch Lab 80 Scott Dr Hanscom Afb MA 01731-2909 Home Phone: 617-332-2071; Office Phone: 781-377-4662. Personal E-mail: rml@massmed.org. E-mail: edward.altshuler@hanscom.af.mil.

ALTSHULER, KENNETH Z., psychiatrist, educator; b. Paterson, NJ, Apr. 11, 1929; s. Jacob and Altie (Freedman) A.; m. Gloria Seigel, June 14, 1952 (div. 1981); children: Steven, Lori, Dara; m. Ruth Collins Sharp, Dec. 5, 1987. BA, Cornell U., 1948; MD, U. Buffalo, 1952; DSc (hon.), Gallaudet Coll., 1972. Intern Kings County Hosp., Bklyn., 1952-53; resident NY State Psychiat. Inst., NYC, 1955-58; asst. in psychiatry Columbia U., 1958-59, instr., 1959-63, rsch. assoc., 1963-67, asst. clin. prof., 1967-71, assoc. clin. prof., 1971-75, prof., 1975-77; tng. analyst Columbia U. Psychoanalytic Clinic for Tng. and Rsch., 1969-77; project dir. Essential Aspects of Deafness, 1972-76, Trauma and Sleep Physiology, 1975-77; Stanton Sharp prof., chmn. psychiatry U. Tex.-Southwestern Med. Sch., Dallas, 1977-2000, Stanton Sharp prof. psychiatry, 2000—; tng. analyst New Orleans Psychoanalytic Inst., 1979-86, Dallas Psychoanalytic Inst., 1986—. Chief of deafness unit Rockland State Hosp., Orangeburg, NY, 1966-77; cons. to NIH; dir. Am. Bd. Psychiatry and Neurology, 1990-97, pres., 1996; mem. Nat. Bd. Med. Examiners, 1986-89, chmn. Part II psychiatry com., 1988-89; dir. bd. Tex. Dept. Mental Health and Mental Retardation, 1999-2004; mem. Am. Assn. Chmn. Depts. Psychiatry, 1977-2000, pres. 1990-91. Co-author: Managing Sleep Complaints, 1982; co-editor: Family and Mental Health Problems in a Deaf Population, 1963, Comprehensive Mental Health Svc. for the Deaf, 1966, Psychiatry and the Deaf, 1968, Expanded Mental Health Care for the Deaf, 1970, Depression: Mechanisms, Diagnosis and Treatment, 1986; others.; Contbr. articles to profl. jour. Mem. governing bd. Tex. Sch. for the Deaf, 1986-90; bd. dir. Tex. Dept. Mental Health and Mental Retardation, 1999-2004. Served with USNR, 1953-55. Recipient Wilson award in genetics and preventive medicine, 1961, Disting. Cmty. Svc. award Dallas County Mental Health Assn., 1986, Prism award, 1992, Disting. Alumnus award SUNY, Buffalo, 1993, 1st Trailblazer award named in his honor, Dallas County Mental Health and Retardation Ctr., 1996, Tex. Star award for Outstanding Cmty. Svc. Tex. Mental Health Assn., 1997; named Outstanding Psychiatrist, Tex. Soc. Psychiat. Physicians, 1996, Alumnus of the 1960s Decade Columbia U., 1996; Kenneth Z. Altshuler Clinic named in honor by Dallas County Mental Health & Mental Retardation Ctr., 1997, Medical Leadership award Turtle Creek Manor, 2003; Cert. of Achievement Bd. of Hosp. Psychiatry, Cert. of Significant Achievement for Deafness Program, NY State, 1976, Cert. of Significant Achievement for Mental Health Connections Program, 1995. Fellow Am. Psychiat. Assn., Am. Coll. Psychiatrists, Am. Coll. Psychoanalysts; mem. AMA, Am. Psychoanalytic Assn., Assn. for Psychoanalytic Medicine (Merit award 1965), Tex. Med. Soc., Dallas County

Med. Soc., Am. Psychopathol. Assn., Assn. Dir. Med. Student Edn. in Psychiatry (founder, v.p. 1976-77), So. Assn. Rsch. Psychiatry (pres. 1993-94). Office Phone: 214-648-5588. Business E-Mail: kenneth.altshuler@utsouthwestern.edu.

ALTSULER, KENT, lawyer; b. Houston, July 26, 1970; s. Arnold and Joan Altsuler; m. Kimberly Gorel. BA, Duke U., 1993; JD, U. Tex. Sch. Law, 1997. Bar: Tex. Atty. Jackson Walker LLP, Fulbright & Jaworski LLP, Houston, Connelly Baker Maston Wotring Jackson LLP, Houston. Fulbright scholar, Korea, 1994; named a Rising Star, Tex. Super Lawyers mag., 2006.

ALTURA, BELLA T., physiologist, educator; b. Solingen, Germany; came to U.S., 1948; d. Sol and Rosa (Brandstetter) Tabak; m. Burton M. Altura, Dec. 27, 1961; 1 child, Rachel Allison. BA, Hunter Coll., 1953, MA, 1962; PhD, CUNY, 1968. Instr. exptl. anesthesiology Albert Einstein Coll. Medicine, Bronx, 1970-74; asst. prof. physiology SUNY Health Sci Ctr., Bklyn., 1974-82, assoc. prof. physiology, 1982-97, rsch. prof. physiology, 1997—, rsch. prof. pharmacology, 1998—. Vis. prof. Beijing Coll. of Traditional Chinese Medicine, 1988, Jiangxi (China) Med. Coll., 1988, Tokyo U. Med. Sch., 1993, U. Brussels Esramé Hosp., 1995, Humboldt U.-Charité Hosp., 1995, Kagoshima U., Japan, 1995, U. Birmingham, England, 1996, Self Med. Def. Coll. Japan, 1996, Nat. Def. Med. Sch., Japan, 1996, Albert Szent Gyorgi Med. U., Szeged, Hungary, 1997; mem. Nat. Coun. on Magnesium and Cardiovascular Disease, 1991—; cons. NOVA Biomedical, 1989—; Niche pharm. cons. Protina GmbH, Munich, 1992—96, Otsuka Pharm. Co., Japan, 1995—97, Roberts Pharm. Co., 1999—2000; v.p. for rsch. and diagnostics Bio-Def. Sys., Inc., 2005—; co-prin. investigator NIH, Nat. Heart, Lung and Blood Inst., NIMH, Nat. Inst. on Alcoholism and Alcohol Abuse. Contbr. over 700 articles to profl. jours. Fellowship NASA, 1966-67, CUNY, 1968; co-recipient Gold-Silver medal French Nat. Acad. Medicine, 1984, Silver medal Mayor of Paris, 1984, Seelig award for lifetime rsch. on magnesium, Am. Coll. Nutrition, 2002, Outstanding Inventor of Yr., SUNY, 2002, Seelig award for lifetime rsch. Gordon Rsch. Conf. on Magnesium, 2005. Mem. Am. Physiol. Soc., Am. Soc. Pharmacology and Exptl. Therapeutics, Am. Soc. for Magnesium Rsch. (founder, treas. 1984—), Hungarian Soc. Electrochemistry (hon. co-pres. 1995-96), Nat. Heart, Lung and Blood Inst., Nat. Inst. on Alcohol Abuse and Alcoholism, Phi Beta Kappa, Sigma Xi. Achievements include first measurement ionized magnesium with ion selective electrode in blood, serum and plasma in health and disease states; demonstration that substances of abuse can cause cerebrovasospasm and stroke. Office: SUNY Health Sci Ctr Box 31 450 Clarkson Ave Brooklyn NY 11203-2056 Office Phone: 718-270-2205. Business E-Mail: baltura@downstate.edu.

ALTURA, BURTON MYRON, physiologist, educator; b. NYC, Apr. 9, 1936; s. Barney and Frances (Dorfman) A.; m. Bella Tabak, Dec. 27, 1961; 1 child, Rachel Allison. BA, Hofstra U., 1957; MS, NYU, 1961, PhD, 1964. Diplomate Am. Bd. Forensic Med., Am. Coll. Forensic Medicine, Am. Bd. Forensic Examiners, Coll. Pharm. and Apothecary Scis., Am. Assn. Integrative Medicine. Tchg. fellow in biology NYU, 1960—61, instr. exptl. anesthesiology Sch. Medicine, 1964—65, asst. prof. Sch. Medicine, 1965—66; rsch. fellow Bronx Mcpl. Hosp. Ctr., 1967—76; asst. prof. physiology and anesthesiology Albert Einstein Coll. Medicine, NYC, 1967—70, assoc. prof., 1970—74, vis. prof., 1974—78; prof. physiology SUNY Health Sci Ctr., Bklyn., 1974—, prof. medicine, 1992—; mem. Ctr. Cardiovasc. and Muscle Rsch., 1995—; prof. pharmacology SUNY Health Sci. Ctr., Bklyn., 1998—. Spl. study sect. on toxicology Nat. Inst. Environ. Health Scis., 1977—78, 2001; Alcohol Biomed. Rsch. Rev. Com. Nat. Inst. Alcohol Abuse and Alcoholism, 1978—83, spl. study sect. medications, 2002; panel CNF bd. Inst. Med., NAS, 1996—97; adj. prof. biology Queens Coll., CUNY, 1983—84; pres. (hon.) Internat. Symposium on Interactions of Magnesium and Potassium on Cardiac and Vascular Muscle, Montbazon, France, 1984; pres. (hon.), lectr. (hon.) Hungarian Soc. Electrochemistry, Budapest, 1995; organizer, condr. symposia; condr., chmn. Gordon Rsch. Conf. on Magnesium in Biochem. Processes and Medicine, 1984; v.p. Internat. Symposium on Magnesium, Blacksburg, 1985; adv. coun. Nat. Found. Addictive Drugs, 1986—; vis. prof. Yamaguchi U., Japan, 1988, 93, Beijing Coll. Traditional Chinese Medicine, China, 1988, Harvard U. Med. Sch., 1988, U. Tokyo, 1979, 93, 96, Kyoto U. Sch. Medicine, 1979, 93, Kumamoto U., 1993, U. Copenhagen, 1994, U. Florence, 1994, Humboldt Univ., Berlin, 1995, U. Birmingham, England, 1996, Self Med. Def. Coll., Japan, 1996, U. Calif., Riverside, 1998, Fla. Atlantic U., 1998, Inst. Water, Soil and Air Hygiene, Fed. Health Inst., Berlin, 1991, Max Planck Inst., Dortmund, Germany, 1992, 94, British Min. Defense, Porton Down, Salisbury, England, 2004, Naval Med. Rsch. Ctr., Walter Reed Med. Ctr., Silver Spring, Md., 2004, U.S. Def. Threat Reduction Agy., Ft. Belvoir, Va., 2005; vis. prof., lectr. Navy Med. Rsch. Ctr., Silver Spring Med. Ctr., 2004, Def. Threat Reduction Agy., Ft. Belvoir, Va., 2005; founder, CEO, chmn. and chief sci. officer Bio-Defense Sys., Inc., Rockville Center, NY; cons. NSF, panel grad. fellows, 2004—07; cons. Nat. Heart, Lung, and Blood Inst., Nat. Inst. Drug Abuse; guest lectr., vis. prof. Nat. Inst. Allergy and Infectious Diseases, 2006. Author: Microcirculation, 3 vols., 1977—80, Vascular Endothelium and Basement Membranes, 1980, Pathophysiology of the Reticuloendothelial System, 1981, Ionic Regulation of the Microcirculation, 1982, Handbook of Shock and Trauma, Vol. 1: Basic Science, 1983, Magnesium and the Cardiovascular System, 1985, Cardiovascular Actions of Anesthetic Agents and Drugs Used in Anesthesia, vol. I, 1986, vol. II, 1987, Magnesium, Stress and the Cardiovascular System, 1986, Magnesium in Biochemical Processes and Medicine, 1987, Magnesium in Clinical Medicine and Therapeutics, 1992, Unique Magnesium-Sensitive Ion Selective Electrodes, 1994; editor-in-chief: Physiology and Patho-physiology Series, 1976—81, Microcirculation, 1980—84, Magnesium: Exptl. and Clin. Rsch., 1981—89, Microcirculation, Endothelium and Lymphatics, 1984—, Magnesium and Trace Elements, 1990—, mem. editl. bd.: Jour. Circulatory Shock, 1973—85, Advances in Microcirculation, 1976—92, Jour. Cardiovasc. Pharmacology, 1977—84, Prostaglandins, Leukotrienes and Fatty Acids, 1978—2001, Substance and Alcohol Actions/Misuse, 1979—84, Alcoholism: Clin. and Exptl. Rsch., 1982—87, assoc. editor: Jour. Artery, 1974—, Microvasc. Rsch., 1978—85, Agts. and Actions, 1981—88, Biogenic Amines, 1985—88, Jour. Am. Coll. Nutrition, 1982—94, Frontiers in Biosci., 1996—, Internat. Jour. Cardiovasc. Medicine, Surgery and Biomechanics, 1997—; contbr. over 900 articles to profl. jours.; patentee in field. Recipient Rsch. Career Devel. award USPHS, 1968-72, Silver medal furthering French-U.S. sci. rels. Mayor of Paris, 1984, Medaille Vermeille, French Nat. Acad. Medicine, 1984, Travel awards NIH, 1968, Am. Soc. Pharm. and Exptl. Therapeutics, 1969, First Golden Hippocrates award, Haifa, Israel, 2002, Chancellor's Outstanding Inventor of Yr. award SUNY, 2002, medal Lifetime of Basic Med. Rsch. and Tchg., Haifa, Israel, 2002, Seelig award for lifetime of rsach. on magnesium in biochemistry and health processes Gordon Rsch. Conf. on Magnesium, 2005; grantee NIH, 1968—, NIMH, 1974-78, Nat. Heart Lung Blood Inst., 1974-86, Nat. Inst. Drug Abuse, 1979-83, Nat. Inst. Alcohol Abuse and Alcoholism, 1990-, US Naval Med. Rsch. Ctr., 2005—; Eminent fellow Wisdom Hall of Fame, 1999, Winston Churchill fellow Wisdom Hall of Fame, 2000. Fellow: AAAS, Molecular Medicine Soc., Royal Australian Chem. Inst., Am. Soc. Angiology, Nat. Acad. Clin. Biochemistry, Am. Heart Assn. (coun. basic sci. 1969—, coun. on thrombosis 1971—, coun. on stroke 1973—, cardiovasc. A study sect. 1978—81, coun. on circulation 1978—, coun. on high blood pressure 1978—, coun. on cardiopulmonary circulation 1987—, coun. on arteriosclerosis, thrombosis, and vascular biology 1997—, coun. on cardiovascular basic scis. 2001—, fellow coun. on high blood pressure rsch. 2002, rsch. grants rev. com. N.E. 2004—), Am. Coll. Angiology (hon. lectr.), Am. Bd. Forensic Examiners (life), Am. Soc. Integrative Medicine (life; hon. lectr.), Am. Coll. Forensic Examiners (life), Internat. Coll. Angiology, Am. Inst. Chemists (hon. lectr.), Am. Coll. Nutrition (Seelig award 2002, hon. lectr.), Assn. Clin. Scientists, Am. Physiol. Soc. (circulation group 1971—, pub. info. com. 1980—84), Anglo-Am. Acad. (hon. 1980); mem.: NSF, AAUP, APHA, Internat. Soc. Interferon and Cytokine Rsch., AHA NE Study Section, AM Physiol. Soc., Internat. Soc. Free Radical Rsch., Am. Soc. Biochemistry and Molecular Biology, Am. Inst. Biol. Sci., Internat. Soc. Police Surgeons, Am. Med. Writers Assn., Nat. Coun. Magnesium and Cardiovasc. Disease, Am. Assn. Pharm. Scis., Inter-Am. Soc. Hypertension, Am. Soc. Hypertension (founder), Internat. Soc. Hypertension, Internat. Anesthesia Soc., Coun. Biology Editors, NY Soc. Electron Microscopy, NY Heart Assn., NY Acad. Scis. (com. mem.), Am. Soc. Magnesium Rsch. (exec. dir. 1984—, founder, symposium chmn. and organizer, pres.), Am. Soc. Bone and Mineral Rsch., Am. Soc. Cell Biology, The Oxygen Soc., Am. Soc. Zoologists, Am. Microscopical Soc., Am. Assn. Lab. Animal Sci., Soc. Xenobiotics, Internat. Platform Assn., Soc. Scholarly Pub., Soc. Nutrition Edn., Soc. Parenteral and Enteral Nutrition, Liposome Soc., Internat. Soc. Exposure Analysis, Reticuloendothelial Soc. (hon. lectr., hon. lectr.), Soc. Cardiovasc. Pathology, Soc. Environ. Geochemistry and Health (hon lectr. and symposium organizer), Soc. Leukocyte Biology, Internat. Soc. Biorheology, Biomed. Optics Soc., Internat. Soc. Biomed. Rsch. on Alcoholism (founder), Am. Soc. Microbiology, Am. Inst. Nutrition (symposium chmn., organizer, hon. lectr.), Fedn. Am. Soc. Exptl. Biology (pub. info. com. and symposium organizer 1981—86), Internat. Anesthesia Rsch. Soc., Neurotrauma Soc., European Conf. Microcirculation (symposium organizer and hon. lectr.), Microscopy Soc. Am., Am. Fedn. Clin. Rsch., Shock Soc. (founder, symposium organizer, hon. lectr.), Soc. Neurosci., Am. Thoracic Soc., Soc. Critical Care Medicine, Am. Oil Chemists Soc., Rsch. Soc. on Alcoholism (hon lectr., symposium organizer), Am. Coll. Toxicology, Harvey Soc., Endocrine Soc., Am. Soc. Nutritional Scis., Am. Soc. Pharm. and Exptl. Therapeutics (symposium organizer), Am. Chem. Soc., Am. Soc. Headache, Am. Assn. Clin. Chemistry (hon. lectr.), Soc. Exptl. Biology and Medicine (editl. bd. 1976—83), Microcirculatory Soc. (nominating com. 1973—74, past exec. coun., hon. lectr.), Am. Soc. Investigative Pathology (lectr.), Soc. Magnetic Resonance, Sigma Xi. Office: 450 Clarkson Ave Brooklyn NY 11203-2056 Office Phone: 718-270-2194. Business E-Mail: baltura@downstate.edu.

ALUMBAUGH, JOANN MCCALLA, magazine editor; b. Ann Arbor, Mich., Sept. 16, 1952; d. William Samuel and Jean Arliss (Guy) McCalla; m. Lyle Ray Alumbaugh, Apr. 27, 1974; children: Brent William, Brandon Jess, Brooke Louise. BA, Ea. Mich. U., 1974. Cert. elem. tch., Mich. Assoc. editor Chester White Swine Record Assn., Rochester, Ind., 1974-77; prodn. editor United Duroc Swine Registry, Peoria, Ill., 1977-79; dir., pres. Nat. Assn. Swine Records, Macomb, Ill., 1979-82; free-lance writer, artist Ill. and Nat. Specific Pathogen Free Assn., Ind. producers, Good Hope, Emden, Ill., 1982-85; editor The Hog Producer Farm Progress Publs., Urbandale, Iowa, 1985-99; exec. editor Nebr. Farmer, Kans. Farmer, Mo. Ruralist, We. Beef Prodr., Beef Prodr., Farm & Fireside, 1999—2003; dir. comms. Farms.Com, 2003—. Family Living Program, Farm Progress Show, 1985-2004, Master Farm Homemaker Program, 1989-99; mem. U.S. Agrl. Export Devel. Coun., Washington, 1979-82, apptd. mem. Blue Ribbon Com. on Agr., 1980-81. Contbr. numerous articles to profl. jours. Precinct chmn. Rep. Party, Linden, Iowa, 1988; mem. Keep Improving Dist. Schs., Panora, Iowa, 1990-91; v.p. Sunday sch. com. Sunset Circle, United Meth. Ch., Linden, 1990-91; pres. PTA, Panorama Schs., Panora, 1993-94; coach Odyssey of Mind Program World Competition, 1994—. Mem.: Iowa Master Farm Homemakers (chair nat. farm homemakers planning com. 2005—06), Guthrie County Prok Prodrs., McDonough County and Ill. Porkettes (county pres. 1978—79, Belleringer award 1979), Nat. Pork Prodrs. Coun., Iowa Pork Prodrs. Assn. (legis. com. 1990—95, hon. master pork prodr.), U.S. Animal Health Assn., Am. Agrl. Editors Assn. (chmn. dist. svc. com. 1991, master writer 1997, pres.-elect 1998, pres. 1999, chmn. adv. coun. 1999—2002, trustee 2002—, chmn. internat. com. 2005—, co-chmn. comm. clinic, chmn. comms. clinic, chmn. agrl. media summit, chmn. steering com., World of Difference award 1995, Oscar in Agr. 1999), Internat. Platform Assn. Avocations: reading, painting, gardening. Home: 2644 Amarillo Ave Linden IA 50146-8029 Office: PigChamp Aspen Business Park 426 S 17th Ames IA 50010 Office Phone: 641-744-2114. Business E-Mail: joann.alumbaugh@farms.com.

ALUTHGE, ARIYADASA, mathematics professor, researcher; arrived in U.S., 2003; s. Siyadoris Aluthge and Gimarahami Vidanepallattarage; m. Amara Mangalika Aluthge; 1 child, Dilum Priyanka. BS, U. Kelaniya, Sri Lanka, 1977—81; MS, U. Ottawa, Canada, 1983—85; PhD, Vanderbilt U., Nashville, 1985—90. Asst. lectr. U. Ruhuna, Matara, Sri Lanka, 1981—83; tchg. asst. U. Ottawa, 1983—85, Vanderbilt U., 1985—90; prof. math. Marshall U., Huntington, W.Va., 1990—. Vol. Boy Scouts Am., Huntington, W.Va., 2002—. Achievements include discovery of aluthge operator transform, a technique introduced that became very popular among researchers in the field of operator theory. Office: Marshall Univ 1 John Marshall Way Huntington WV 25755

ALUTTO, JOSEPH ANTHONY, academic administrator, former dean, management educator; b. Bronx, NY, June 3, 1941; s. Anthony and Concetta (Del Prete) Alutto; m. Carol Newcomb, Sept. 9, 1948; children: Patricia, Christina, Kerrie, Heather. BBA, Manhattan Coll., Riverdale, NY, 1962; MA in Indsl. Relations, U. Ill., 1965; PhD in Orgnl. Behavior, Cornell U., 1968. Asst. prof. orgnl. behavior SUNY, Buffalo, 1966-72, assoc. prof., 1972-75, prof., 1975-91, dean Sch. Mgmt., 1976-91, Clarence S. Marsh chair mgmt., 1991; dean Max M. Fisher Coll. of Bus. Ohio State U., Columbus, 1991—2007, exec. dean for profl. colleges, 1998—2007, John W. Berry sr. chmn. bus., 1999—2007, interim pres., 2007, interim exec. v.p. and provost, 2007—. Bd. dirs. United Retail Group, Inc., Nationwide Fin. Svcs.; pres., bd. dirs. M/I Homes. Author: (with others) Theory Testing in Organizational Behavior: The Varient Approach, 1983; contbr. 65 articles to profl. jours. United Way, Buffalo, 1982—91; pres. Amherst Cen. Sch. Bd., 1982—86. Mem. APA, AAAS, Acad. Mgmt. (pres. Ea. divsn. 1980-81), Am. Sociol. Assn., Am. Assembly of Collegiate Schools Bus. - Internat. Assn. Mgmt. Edn. (pres. 1996-98), Capital Club, Athletic Club. Business E-Mail: alutto.1@osu.edu.*

ALVARADO, JORGE A., ophthalmologist, researcher; m. Jean C. Afendorf, July 7, 1962; children: Maria, Julie Rosenfeld, Amy. MD, U. Calif., San Francisco, 1973. Physicians and surgeons cert. Med. Bd. Calif., 1975, lic. Am. Bd. Ophthalmology, Calif., 1979, cert. DEA Calif., 1977. Prof. ophthalmology U. Calif., San Francisco, 1977—. Recipient Kimura Excellence Tchg. award, 1987, AAO, Honor Award, 1988, Alcon Rsch. award, 1993, Sr. Sci. Investigator award, 1993, Sr. Honor award, AAO, 1999; grantee Zaffaroni Glaucoma Rsch. award, 1994. Mem.: Am. Ophthal. Soc., Americal Glaucoma Soc., Pan-Am. Assn. Ophthalmology, Frederick C. Cordes Eye Soc., ARVO, Amerian Ophthal. Soc. Achievements include patents for macrophages. Office: Univ Calif 10 Koret Way San Francisco CA 94143-0730 Home Phone: 415-461-5128; Office Phone: 415-476-3944. Office Fax: 415-476-0336. Business E-Mail: alvaradoj@vision.ucsf.edu.

ALVARADO, PABLO, day laborer organizer, immigrant rights activist; b. El Salvador; married; 2 children. High Sch. teaching credential, Universidad de El Salvador, 1989. Prog. coord. Inst. of Popular Edn. of So. Calif., 1991—95; lead coord., day labor project Coalition for Humane Immigrant Rights, LA, 1995—2002; nat. coord. Nat. Day Laborer Organizing Network, LA, 2002—. Named one of 25 Most Influential Hispanics, Time Mag., 2005; recipient Leadership for a Changing World award, 2004. Office: National Day Laborer Organizing Network Ste 101 2533 W Third St Los Angeles CA 90057

ALVARADO, SERAFIN, wine connoisseur; m. Soyoung Alvarado; 3 children. Grad. in Chemistry, U. Puerto Rico. Master sommelier 2005. Room svc. waiter Hilton Hotels, PR; head wine sch. Cadierno Corp., PR, 1994; wine steward Charlie Trotter's, Chgo., 2001—05; dir. wine edn. So. Wine & Spirits of Ill., 2005—. Wine columnist El Nuevo Dia, PR. Named one of Top 40 Under 40, Crain's Chgo. Bus., 2006; recipient Bill Rice Disting. Sommelier of Yr. award, 2005. Mem.: Ct. Master Sommeliers. Achievements include being the first Puerto Rican named a master sommelier. Avocation: jazz. Mailing: Southern Wine & Spirits of Ill 300 E Crossroads Pky Bolingbrook IL 60440*

ALVARE, CHARLES DAGUERRE, financial advisor, educator; s. Carlos J. and Mary J. H. Erskine Alvare; m. Carrie Rudolf, Oct. 10, 1999. BA, Columbia Coll., 1979; MPhil, Cambridge U., 2003. Network TV supr. Young & Rubicam, NYC, 1979—81; mktg. dir. Praxis Film Works, North Hollywood, Calif., 1983—86; exec. prodr. EUE/Screen Gems, Burbank, Calif., 1986—88; ind. prodr. LA., NYC, London, 1989—99; pres. Sanctuary Media, Hollywood, 2000—02; fin. advisor Merrill Lynch, Beverly Hills, Calif., 2005—. Lectr. LA City Coll., 2004—05, Santa Monica Coll., Calif., 2005—. Mem.: ATAS (Emmy Awards) (judge), Delta Psi. E-mail: sanctuarymedia@hotmail.com.

ALVAREZ, AIDA M., former federal agency administrator; b. Aguadilla, PR, July 22, 1949; BA cum laude, Harvard U., 1971; LLD (hon.), Iona Coll., 1985. News reporter, anchor Metromedia TV, NYC; reporter N.Y. Post, NYC; mem. N.Y.C. Charter Revision Commn.; v.p. N.Y.C. Health and Hosps. Corp., 1984—85; investment banker 1st Boston Corp., NYC, San Francisco, 1986-93; dir. Office Fed. Housing Enterprise Oversight, Washington, 1993-97; adminstr. Small Bus. Adminstrn., 1997-2001. Bd. dirs. Pacific Healthcare Systems, 2003—05, UnionBanCal Corp., 2004—, Wal-Mart Stores Inc., 2006—; diversity advisory bd. Deloitte & Touche LLP. Former mem. bd. dirs. Nat. Hispanic Leadership Agenda, N.Y. Cmty. Trust, Nat. civic League; former chmn. bd. Mcpl. Assistance Corp./Victim Svcs. Agy., N.Y.C.; N.Y. State chmn. Gore Presdl. Campaign, 1988; nat. co-chmn. women's com. Clinton Presdl. Campaign, 1992; mem. President's Econ. Transition Team, 1992. Recipient Front Page award, award for excellence AP, 1982, Emmy nomination for reporting guerrilla activities in El Salvador. Democrat.

ALVAREZ, CESAR L., lawyer; b. Havana, Cuba, June 17, 1947; arrived in US, 1960; m. Kathleen Alvarez; children: Elizabeth, Christopher, Kathryn, Colleen. AA, Miami-Dade CC; BS, U. Fla., 1969, MBA, 1970, JD with high honors, 1972. Bar: Fla. 1973. Joined Greenberg Traurig LLP (Greenberg Traurig Hoffman Lipoff Rosen & Quentel until 1998), Miami, Fla., 1973, pres., CEO, 1997—; exec. v.p. Air Fla., 1981—82. Mem. U. Fla. Legal Aid and Defender Clinic, 1971-72. Editor U. Fla. Law Rev., 1972. Participant Guardian Ad Litem Program, Miami; trustee Vizcaya Found., Our Kids Inc., Nat. Found. for Advancement in the Arts, Miami Art Mus., Manhattanville Coll., NY, Fla. Internat. U. Found., John S. and James L. Knight Found., 2000—; mem. exec. com. New World Symphony; bd. dirs. Holocaust Documentation and Edn. Ctr. Inc.; chair adv. bd. Fla. Internat U. Law Sch.; chmn. bd. dirs. United Way of Miami-Dade, 2003—04. Named a Top Managing Partner, Fla. Trend Mag., 2005, 2006; named one of 100 Most Influential Hispanics, Hispanic Bus., 1996, 1998, 100 Most Influential Lawyers in Am., Nat. Law Jour., 1997, 2000, 2006, 100 Most Powerful People in Miami, Miami Bus. Mag., 2001, 100 Most Powerful People in So. Fla., So. Fla. CEO Mag., 2002, 50 Most Powerful People in So. Fla., Poder Mag., 2003, 2004, 100 Most Powerful Latinos, 2003, 2004, 2004 Legal Elite, Fla. Trend Mag., 2005 Legal Elite, Top Lawyers in So. Fla., So. Fla. Legal Guide, 2004; named to Miami-Dade CC Hall of Fame, 2003; recipient Humanitarian of Yr. Award, Women's Internat. Zionist Orgn., 1997, Atty. of Yr. Award, Hispanic Nat. Bar Assn., 2001, Golden Castanets Award, Ballet Hispanico, 2002, Silver Medallion for Svc. to Humanity Award, Nat. Conf. for Cmty. and Justice, 2003, New Am. Award, Archdiocese of Miami, Inc., 2003, Diversity Works! Advocate-Individual Award, So. Fla. Bus. Jour., 2004, FIU Medallion, Fla. Internat. U., 2005, CEO of the Year Award, MultiCultural Law Mag., 2006. Mem.: Miami Bus. Forum, Fla. Coun. of 100, Dade County Bar Assn., Fla. Bar, Cuban-Am. Bar Assn. (Pro-Bono Award), ABA, Cuba Study Group, Order of Coif. Office: Greenberg Traurig LLP 1221 Brickell Ave Miami FL 33131*

ALVAREZ, JULIA, writer; b. NYC, 1950; m. Bill Eichner. Attended, Conn. Coll., Bread Loaf Sch. English, Middelbury Coll.; BA summa cum laude, Middlebury Coll., 1971; MFA, Syracuse U., 1975; LHD honoris causa (hon.), CUNY John Jay Coll., 1996; D (hon.), Union Coll., Schenectady, NY, 2004. Poet-in-the-schools, Ky., 1975—78, Del., 1975—78, NC, 1975—78; prof. creative writing and English Phillips Andover Acad., Mass., 1979—81, U. Vt., 1981—83, U. Ill., 1985—88; prof. English Middlebury (Vt.) Coll., 1988—98, writer-in-residence, 1998—; co-owner Café Alta Gracia fair trade organic coffee co., Dominican Republic; co-creator Fundación Alta Gracia Sch., Dominican Republic. Jenny McKean Moore vis. writer George Wash. U., 1984; nat. mem. coun. PEN Am. Ctr., 1997—99. Author: (novels) How the Garcia Girls Lost Their Accents, 1991 (selected as notable book Am. Libr. Assn., 1992, Pen Oakland/Josephine Miles award for multicultural viewpoint, 1991, one of 21 classics for 21st century NY Librarians, 1999), In the Time of Butterflies, 1994 (selected as notable book Am. Libr. Assn., 1994, finalist Nat. Book Critics Cir. award in fiction, 1995, one of Best Books for Young Adults YA Libr. Svcs. Assn., Am. Libr. Assn., 1995), The Other Side, 1995, YO!, 1997, Something to Declare, 1998, In the Name of Salomé, 2000 (One of top 10 books Latino.com, 2000), The Secret Footprints, 2000, How Tia Lola Came to Stay, 2001 (Parent's Guide to Children's Media Inc. outstanding book, 2001, Child Mag. Best Children's Book, 2001), A Cafecito Story, 2001 (Nebr. Book award for fiction, 2002), Before We Were Free, 2002 (Am. Libr. Assn. notable book, 2002, Am. Libr. Assn. Best Book for Young Adults, 2002, Américas award for Children's and Young Adult Lit. Consortium Latin Am. Studies Programs, 2002), Saving the World, 2006, (poetry) The Woman I Kept to Myself, Homecoming: New and Collected Poems. Named Woman of Yr., Latina Mag., 2000; recipient Benjamin T. Marshall Poetry Prize, Conn. Coll., 1968, 1969, prize, Acad. Am. Poetry, 1974, poetry award, La Reina Press, 1982, Third Woman Press award, first prize in narrative, 1986, award for younger writers, Gen. Elec. Found., 1986, syndicated fiction prize for "Snow" grant from Ingram Merrill Found., PEN, 1990, Josephine Miles award, PEN Oakland, 1991, Lit. Leadership award, Dominico-Am. Soc. of Queens, Inc., 1998, Fray Anton de Montesinos award, Alumni Assn. Univ. Santo Domingo, 2002, Sor Juana award, Mexican Fine Arts Mus., Chgo., 2002, Hispanic Heritage award in lit., Kennedy Ctr., Washington, 2002; grantee, Nat. Endowment Arts, 1987—88; creative writing fellow, Syracuse U., 1974—75, Robert Frost Poetry fellowship, Bread Loaf Writers' Conf., 1986, Kenan grant, Phillips Andover Acad., 1980, exhbn. grant, Vt. Arts Coun., 1984—85. Mem.: Latin Am. Writers' Inst., Poets & Writers, Associated Writing Programs, Acad. Am. Poets, Phi Beta Kappa, Sigma Tau Delta (hon.). Mailing: Susan Berghol Literary Svcs 17 W 10th St 5B New York NY 10011 Home: Weybridge VT Address: care Algonquin Books of Chapel Hill PO Box 2225 Chapel Hill NC 27515-2225

ALVAREZ, MANUEL, hospital executive, medical educator, medical news correspondent; married; 3 children. MD. Cert. Am. Bd. Obstetrics and Gynecology, with subspecialty Bd. Fetal Medicine. Resident, obstetrics/gynecology and anesthesiology St. Joseph Hosp. and Med. Ctr., Paterson, NJ; fellow in maternal fetal medicine and critical care medicine Mt. Sinai Hosp., NYC; assoc. prof. Mt. Sinai Sch. Medicine; vice-chmn., Dept. Obstetrics and Gynecology and Reproductive Sci. Mt. Sinai Med. Ctr., NYC; chmn., Dept. Obstetrics and Gynecology and Reproductive Sci.

Hackensack Univ. Med. Ctr., NJ, 1996—. Adj. prof. obstetrics and gynecology NYU Sch. Medicine; examiner Am. Bd. Obstetrics and Gynecology; spkr. in field. Former health sci. reportor Telemundo, developer (nightly news segment) A Dose of Health, med. contbr. FOX News Channel, including shows FOX & Friends and Dayside; contbr. articles to numerous publs. Mem. Celia Cruz Found.; bd. dir. Life Opportunities Unlimted. Named Man of Yr., NJ SEEDS, 2004. Mem.: Assn. Professors Gynecology and Obstetrics, Soc. Maternal Fetal Medicine, Am. Coll. Obstetrics and Gynecology, Am. Soc. for Blood and Marrow Trnsplantation, Am. Inst. Ultrasound and Medicine, Soc. Prenatal Care. Office: Hackensak Univ Med Ctr Dept Obstetrics and Gynocology 30 Prospect Ave Hackensack NJ 07601 Address: Hackensak Univ Med Ctr 20 Prospect Ave Ste 601 Hackensack NJ 07601 Home Phone: 201-227-0108; Office Phone: 201-996-2765. E-mail: m.alvarez@humed.com.

ALVAREZ, MARIANNE, artist, photographer, educator; b. Miami, Nov. 27, 1930; d. Walter Knox and Irma Margaret (Rempe) Payne; m. Jack Alvarez, Dec. 19, 1969. B in Art Edn., U. Fla., 1959; MA, U. South Fla., 1967; postgrad., S.E. Ctr. for Photographic Studies, Daytona Beach, 2001. Adminstrv. sec. Walter Reed Army Med. Ctr., Washington, 1952-58; art tchr. Sligh Jr. H.S., Tampa, 1959-60, Tyrone Jr. H.S., St. Petersburg, 1960-61, Dunedin (Fla.)-Highland Jr. H.S., 1961-66; media specialist Volusia County Secondary Schs., Daytona Beach, Fla., 1967-90. One-woman shows include The Capitol, Tallahassee, 1997, two-person show, Art League of Daytona Beach, 2002, exhibited in group shows at Art League Daytona Beach, 1986—, exhibitions include Carnegie Mus. Natural History, Pitts., 1992, 1994, 1996, Cork Gallery, Lincoln Ctr., N.Y.C., 1994, U. Mobile, Ala., 1995, Charles Summer Sch. Mus., Washington, 1995, Mobile Mus. Art, 1996, Walter Greer Gallery, Hilton Head, S.C., 1997, Cen. Arts Collective, Tucson, 1998, S.E. Mus. Photography, Daytona Beach, Fla., 1999, Harris House, New Smyrna Beach, Fla., 1999, William Benton Mus. Art, U. Conn., Storrs, 2000, Ormond Meml. Art Mus., 2002, Represented in permanent collections Fla. Art in State Bldgs. program, Fla. State Capitol, William Benton Mus. Art, U. Conn., Storrs, S.E. Mus. Photography, Daytona Beach, Fla., Halifax Collection, ArtHaus Found., Port Orange, Fla., work on display, Nassau County Health Dept., Fernandina Beach, Yulee, also pvt. collections. Mem. Jr. League Daytona Beach. Recipient Grumbacher Gold Medallion award, 1995, numerous others. Mem. Nat. League Am. Pen Women (pres. 2000-02), Fla. Ret. Educators Assn., Volusia County Ret. Educators Assn., Beaux Arts Volusia, Ormond Meml. Art Mus., Ormond Beach, Daytona Beach, Mus. Arts and Scis., Art League of Daytona Beach, Delta Kappa Gamma Soc. Internat., Alpha Delta Pi Alumnus. Democrat. Roman Catholic. Home and Studio: 2727 N Atlantic Ave Apt 611 Daytona Beach FL 32118-3047 Personal E-mail: jamaimages@aol.com.

ALVAREZ, RALPH, food products executive; b. Cuba; BBA cum laude, U. Miami, 1976. Various pos., including mng. dir. Burger King Spain, pres. Burger King Can., regional v.p. Fla. region Burger King Corp., 1977—89; divsn. v.p.-Fla. to corp. v.p. Wendy's Internat. Inc., 1990—94; dir. devel. for No. Calif. McDonald's Corp., 1994, regional v.p., Sacramento region, regional dir., Chipotle Mex. Grill, 1999—2000, pres. McDonald's Mex., 2000—01, pres., ctrl. divsn., McDonald's USA, 2001—03; COO, exec. v.p. McDonald's USA, Oak Brook, Ill., 2003—04, pres., 2004—05, McDonald's N. Am., 2005—06; pres., COO McDonald's Corp., 2006—. Named one of 50 Most Important Hispanics in Tech. & Bus., Hispanic Engr. & Info. Tech. mag., 2005. Office: McDonald's Corp 1 McDonald's Plz 2915 Jorie Blvd Oak Brook IL 60523*

ÁLVAREZ, RODOLFO, sociology educator, consultant; b. San Antonio, Oct. 23, 1936; s. Ramon and Laura (Lobo) A.; m. Edna Rosemary (Simons), June 25, 1960 (div. 1984); children: Ánica, Amira. Cert. European Studies, Inst. Am. Univ., Aix en Provence, France, 1960; BA, San Francisco State U., 1961; MA, U. Wash., 1964, PhD, 1966. Tchg. fellow U. Wash., Seattle, 1963—64; asst. prof. Yale U., New Haven, 1966—72; dir. Chicano Studies Rsch. Ctr. Univ. Calif. at Los Angeles, 1972—74, assoc. prof. sociology, 1972—80, prof., 1980, chair under grad. coun., 1995—97. Vis. lectr. Wesleyan Univ., Middletown, Conn., 1970; founding dir. Spanish Speaking Mental Health Rsch. Ctr., 1973-75. Author: Discrimination in Organizations: Using Social Indicators to Manage Social Change, 1979; Racism, Elitism, Professionalism: Barriers to Cmty. Mental Health, 1976; mem. editorial bd. Social Sci. Quar., 1971-86. Pres. ACLU So. Calif., 1980-81, sec., treas. 1999, pres. Westwood Dem. Club, Calif., 1977-78, v.p. 2003-2005; trustee Inst. for Am. Univ., Aix en Provence, France, 1968—; bd. dir. Mex. Am. Legal Def. and Ednl. Fund, 1975-79, 88-92; mem. adv. commn. on housing 1984 Olympic Organizing Com., 1982-84; chmn. bd. dir. Narcotics Prevention Assn., L.A., 1974-77; mem. bilingual adv. com. Children's TV Workshop, N.Y.C., 1979-82; candidate rep. Nat. Dem. Platform Com., Washington, 1976; alt. del. Nat. Dem. Conv., N.Y.C., 1976; bd. dir. Univ. Credit Union, 1985-92, chmn. strategic plan com., 1987-92. Sgt. USMC, 1954-57. Pres. Mgmt. Fellow U. Calif., 1994-95; recipient citation meritorious svc. for devel. of Nat. Fed. Offenders Rehab. and Rsch. Program, State of Wash., 1967. Mem.: Pacific Sociol. Assn. (mem. coun. 1979—83, 1987—89, v.p. 1991—93, pres. 1996—97), Soc. Study of Social Problems (bd. dir. 1982—87, pres. 1985—86), Am. Sociol. Assn. (mem. coun. 1982—85, chair person sect. racial and ethnic minorities 1989—90, assoc. editor Am. Sociol. Rev. 1989—91), Internat. Sociol. Honor Soc. (pres. 1976—79), Archtl. Rev. Bd. City of Santa Monica, Calif., Marines Meml. Club, Rotary Internat. (dist. 5280, exec. aide 2005—06), Westwood Village Rotary Club (pres. 2004—05). Office: UCLA Dept Sociology 405 Hilgard Ave Los Angeles CA 90095-1551 Office Phone: 310-392-5125. Business E-Mail: alvarez@soc.ucla.edu.

ALVAREZ, SCOTT G., lawyer; b. 1955; BA in Econ., Princeton U., 1977; JD cum laude, Georgetown U., 1981. Bar: 1981. Joined bd. as staff attorney Fed. Res. Sys., Washington, 1981—85, bd. sr. attorney, 1985, asst. gen. counsel, 1989—91, assoc. gen. counsel, 1991—2004, legal divsn./gen. counsel, 2004—. Office: Fed Res Sys Legal Divsn Rm 1046A 20th & C Sts NW Office Washington DC 20551-0001 Office Phone: 202-452-3000. Office Fax: 202-452-3101. Business E-Mail: scott.alvarez@frb.gov.*

ALVAREZ, TIRSO REYES, JR., engineer; b. San Antonio, Dec. 26, 1948; s. Tirso and Casimira (Reyes) A.; m. Melinda Marie Jaurequi, May 12, 1975 (div. Feb. 1998); children: Sonya Marie, Tirso Adrian. Student in Automotive Mechanics, Internat. Correspondence Sch. Edn. Svc. Ctr., Scranton, Pa., 1990. With electro-motive divsn. GM, Commerce, Calif., 1970-82, 92-97; electronic motors technician A/R Delco, Signal Hill, Calif., 2000—; with G.M.C./U.A.W. Nat. Employee Placement Ctr. Svs. Parts Ops., Rancho Cucamonga, Calif., 2003—. Democrat. Roman Catholic. Avocations: fishing, automotive repairs, hiking, boating. Home: 2599 Walnut Ave Unit 229 Signal Hill CA 90755-3672 Mailing: PMB 337 2201 E Willow St Ste D Signal Hill CA 90755-2148 Office: GMC/UAW Nat Employee Placement Ctr Svc Parts Ops 9150 Hermosa Ave Rancho Cucamonga CA 91730 Office Phone: 909-477-5804, 909-477-5800. Personal E-mail: solmerito@aol.com, tralvarezjr@aol.com.

ALVAREZ-BUYLLA, ARTURO, neurobiologist, researcher; b. Mexico City, Mar. 16, 1958; came to U.S., 1983; s. Ramon and Elena (Roces) A.-B. Degree in biomedicine, U. Nat. Autonoma de Mex., 1983; PhD, Rockefeller U., 1988. Assoc. prof. Rockefeller U., NYC, 1989-91, asst. prof., head of lab., 1991—. Cons. Genentech Inc., San Francisco, 1993-94. Contbr. articles to profl. jours. including Sci., Nature, and Jour. Neurosci., among others; inventor of device for mounting tissue sections on histological slides, design of a digital stereotaxic apparatus for mice and song birds, and computer-based mapping system for tissue sections. NIH grantee. Mem. Soc. for Neurosci., Internat. Brain Rsch. Orgn., Soc. for Biochemistry. Achievements include research in showing long-range neuronal migration in the brain of adult birds and mammals; demonstrating the birth and differentiation of long projection neurons in adult birds, A new form of neuromal migration called chain migration, A network of pathway for chain migrationin adult brain. Office: Dept of NeurolSurgery UCSF Sch of Medicine 513 Parnassus Ave HSW 1201 San Francisco CA 94143

ALVAREZ-CORONA, MARTI, school psychologist, educator; b. Phoenix, Jan. 14, 1949; BA, Calif. State U., LA, 1984; MA, Western N.Mex. U., 1992. Nat. cert. counselor. ESL adult educator LA Unified Sch. Dist.; trilingual elem. edn. tchr. Glendale Sch. Dist., Ariz.; behavioral counselor St. Lukes Behavioral Ctr., Phoenix; cert. sch. psychologist Isaac Sch. Dist., Phoenix, 1994—. Recipient Silver Apple award Dial Corp, News Channel 3; featured in Phoenix mag., 1992, Ariz. Republic. Mem. APA, Am. Counseling Assn., Nat. Assn. Sch. Psychologists, Ariz. Assn. Sch. Psychology, Nat. Assn. Masters in Psychology.

ALVERO, RUBEN J., medical educator; b. Miami, Fla., Jan. 14, 1958; s. Elesvan and Sarah Cristina Alvero; m. Karen Ann Koski, June 22, 1985; children: Erika Noel, Alicia Megan, William Carlos. BA, Harvard U., Cambridge, Mass., 1980; MD, Uniformed Svcs. U. of Health Scis., Bethesda, Md., 1986. Lic. reproductive endocrinology Am. Bd. Ob-Gyn., ob-gyn Am. Bd. Ob-Gyn. Divsn. dir. Walter Reed Army Med. Ctr., Washington, 1998—2001; assoc. prof. U. Colo., Aurora, 2002—. Editor: (textbook) Reproductive Endocrinology -The Requisites. Lt. col. US Army, 1982—2001. Recipient Nat. Faculty award, Com. on Resident Edn. in Ob-Gyn., 1998, 2006. Home: 7875 S Wabash Ct Centennial CO 80112 Office: U Colo Mail Stop F701 PO Box 6510 Aurora CO 80045 Office Phone: 720-848-1760. Office Fax: 720-848-1662; Home Fax: 720-848-1662. Business E-Mail: ruben.alvero@uchsc.edu.

ALVERSON, WILLIAM H., lawyer; b. Rockford, Ill., July 23, 1933; AB, Princeton U., 1955; LL.B., U. Wis., 1960. Bar: Wis. 1960. Currently mem. firm Godfrey & Kahn. Pres. Milw. Profl. Sports and Services, 1972-76; chmn. Houston Rockets basketball team, 1977-79; chmn. bd. govs. Nat. Basketball Assn., 1975-76. Mem. Milw., Am. bar assns., State Bar Wis., Phi Delta Phi. Office: 780 N Water St Milwaukee WI 53202-3512

ALVES, FLAVIO P., researcher, director; b. Rio De Janeiro, Brazil, Nov. 30, 1969; arrived in U.S., 1995; s. Joao Teodoro Alves and Marli Eugenia Pimenta. BA, Columbia U., NYC, 2006. Founder, dir. Asylum Rsch., NYC, 1996—. Guest lectr. Law Sch. Fordham U., 2003; presenter in field. Author: Toque de Silencio, 1997. Intern Amnesty Internat., 2003, Congressman Anthony Weiner, Sen. Hillary Clinton, 2004. Mem.: Oral History Assn., Human Rights Campaign, Stonewall Dem. Club. Avocations: photography, reading, travel. Office: Asylum Rsch 110-20 73rd Rd Ste 2F Forest Hills NY 11375

ALVES, KYRIN JEAN, cultural organization administrator, educator; b. Milw., Sept. 5, 1949; d. Donald Eugene Bailey and Lila Anna Monday; m. David Vierra Alves, Dec. 9, 1967 (div. 1973); children: Sean David, Kyle Vierra. AS in Bus. Adminstrn., Pima CC, 1977, AAS in Computers, 1987; BA in Philosophy and Classics, U. Ariz., 1980; MEd, Northern Ariz. U., 1997. Cert. CC tchr. Ariz. Project controls adminstrn. Hughes Aircraft Co., Tucson, 1973-79; prin., co-owner Computers for People, Tucson, 1983-84; sr. budget rsch. analyst Pima County Govt., Tucson, 1981-82, 85-88, info. sys. mgr., 1989-94; prof. Kazakh State Acad. Arch. and Construction, Almaty, Kazakhstan, 1994; pres., CEO Rebuilding Together Tucson, 1994—; owner, pres. Kritter Kisses, Inc., 2006—. Instr. Pima CC, 1987—96. Mem. Met. Housing Commn., Tucson, 1994—96, Almaty Sister City Com., Tucson, 1993—95; dir. Vets. Transitional Housing Project, 1993—95; mem. adv. bd. Homeless Mgmt. Info. Sys. Project, 2004—06. Recipient Women on the Move award, YWCA, Tucson, 1995, Exemplary Mgmt. award, Booz Allen Hamilton, Washington, 1999, Dynamic Duo award, Compass Health Care, Tucson, 1999, Best of Pima award, Pima Coll., Tucson, 1992, 2002, Outstanding Svc. award, Old Pueblo Rotary, Tucson, 2003. Mem.: Housing Rehab. Collaborative (co-chair 1999), Southern Ariz. Home Bldrs. Assn. (remodelors coun., sec. 1995—2001). Democrat. Avocations: travel, reading, learning. Business E-Mail: k_alves@cox.net.

ALVEY, BRIAN, blogger; Chief tech. officer Rising Tide Studios; co-founder, pres. Weblogs, Inc. (purchased by America On Line in 2005), 2003—; chief architect Netscape Comm. (Netscape.com); co-founder, chmn. ComicMix.com (subs. Comic Mix, LLC), 2006—. Designer (website) TV Guide, 1995, sr. tech. mem. BusinessWeek, 1995, designer, developer (websites) Intel, J.D. Edwards, Deloitte & Touche, & McGraw-Hill Companies, blogger (website) brianalvey.com, invented and launched Blogstakes, creator, host (series of talk shows-style events) Meet the Makers conf., art dir. for print magazines, developer Venture Reporter Network (for Rising Tide Studios), (web design mag.) A List Apart, (website) Kansas City Chiefs. Office: Comic Mix LLC 304 Main Ave Ste 194 Norwalk CT 06851 Business E-Mail: brian.alvey@comicmix.com.*

ALVINE, ROBERT, industrialist, entrepreneur, world business leader, philanthropist, business owner; b. Newark, Aug. 25, 1938; s. James C. and Marie Alvine; m. Diane C. Marzulli, May 6, 1961 (div. 1995); children: Robert James, Laurie Anne. BA, Rutgers U., 1960; postgrad., Syracuse U., 1968-69; grad. PMD, Harvard Bus. Sch., 1972; DHL (hon.), U. New Haven, 2000. With Celanese Corp., 1960-77; bus.gen. mgr. nylon products Celanese Plastics Co., Newark, 1967-69, bus. gen. mgr. polyolefin products, 1969-72; sr. dir. mktg. and ops. and gen. mgmt. Celanese Piping Systems and Fabricated Products Co., Hilliard, Ohio, 1972—74, Univroyal Corp., 1977—87; pres., CEO Uniroyal Merchandising Co., 1974—77, Uniroyal Devel. and Rsch. Co., 1980—82; v.p gen. mgr. Uniroyal Tire Co. Worldwide, 1977—82; v.p., gen. mgr. comml. Celanese Polymer Spltys. Co., Louisville, 1974—77; CEO, pres., COO Uniroyal Engineered Products & Svcs., Worldwide, 1982-87; sr. v.p. strategic planning, corp. devel. mktg., mergers and acquisitions and capital planning Uniroyal, Inc. Worldwide, 1987—; founder, chmn., CEO I-Ten Mgmt. Corp., Woodbridge, Conn., 1987—; founder, chmn., CEO, I-Ten Capital Corp., Woodbridge, 1987, Aim Capital Group, Woodbridge, 1987—; entrepreneur, prin., sr. oper. ptnr. and bus. leader Charterhouse Group Internat., Inc., NYC, 1988—96; chmn., CEO, prin. shareholder Charter Power Sys. (now C&D Techs. Inc.), Blue Bell, Pa., 1988—95; chmn., prin. investor, chmn. bd. Wedge Computer, 1987—91; vice-chmn., CEO, major shareholder AP Parts Mfg. Co., Toledo, 1989—96; prin., dir., chmn. Internat. Automobile Products Holdings Corp., NYC, 1990—96; prin. owner, chmn. Premier Subaru, Branford, Conn., 1999—, Premier Realty LLC, 2000—, Global Automotive Reins., Ltd., 2005—. Prin. Uniroyal Holdings, Waterbury, Conn., 1985—; trustee Uniroyal Liquidating Trust, 1985-95; sr. oper. ptnr., investment com. Desai Capital Pvt. Equity Investors, 1999—; chmn. compensation com., strategic com., exec. com., chmn. spl. com., chmn. pension com., audit com., fin. com., governance com., bd. EDO Corp., 1994-; trustee Jackson Labs., Bar Harbor, Maine, 1995-; chmn. Jax Resource Sys., 2003-06; mem. compensation and pers. com., fin. com. bd. dirs. Kaman Corp., 2005—; chmn. bd. trustees, Jackson Lab, 2006-, chmn. exec. com., 2006-; exec. com. capital campaign, devel. com., 1998—; adv. bd. and investment com. Polaris Fund, NYC, 1996-2000; bd. govs. U. New Haven, 1998-, chmn. audit com., chmn. exec. com., chmn. commn. on future of U. New Haven, 1998-2006, bd. govs., 2000, chmn. exec. com., 2000-06, chmn. bd. govs., 2000-06, chair univ. presdl. search com., 2003,; prin. designer and founder Henry Lee Inst. Forensic Scis., 1997, chmn. bd. dirs., 1998-; bd. dirs. Kaman Corp., Bloomfield, Conn., 2005-, personel and compensation com., 2006-, fin. com., 2006-;. Bd. dirs. Nat. Theater of the Deaf, Chester, Conn., 1993—98, trustee, 1994—98, chmn. bd. dirs., 1995—98, hon. chmn., 1998—; bd. dirs. Wildlife Conservation Soc., NY, 1994—2003; trustee Long Wharf Theatre, New Haven, 1993—, exec. fin. com., chmn. bus. devel. com., strategy com.; mem. adv. bd. Arts Scis. Coun., Rutgers U., NJ; mem. Navy War Coll. Found., The Naval Inst., Assn. Governing Bds. of Univs. and Colls.; mem. sch. bus. adv. bd. U. New Haven; state chmn. United Way Campaign, 1975; hon. trustee Parent's TV Coun., 2001—; sustaining mem. Boy Scouts Am., 1975; charter mem. Bloomfield HS Edn. Found., 2005; chmn. bd. gov. trustees The Jackson Lab., Bar Harbor, Maine, 2006—; mem. Rep. Presdl. Task Force, Pres.'s Roundtable, Citizens Against Govt. Waste, Presdl. Legion of Merit; Conn. state chmn. Congl. Bus. Adv. Coun., 2002; mem. bd. dirs. Kaman Corp., 2005—. With US Army, 1961—68, active duty Cuban Missile Crisis, 1962—63. Recipient Disting. Leadership award proclaimed by Congl. Bus. Adv. Coun., 2002, Man of Yr. for Outstanding Accomplishments, 1991, Disting. Bus. Achievement and Svcs. to the Nation award, 1984, Presdl. Legion Merit, Honor grad. Southeastern Signal Sch., 1962, Proclamation for Supreme Achievement Within the Internat. Cmty., 1986; named Ky. Col., Gov. Ky., 1976; Yale fellow Morse Coll., 2005—. Mem.: VFW, Jackson Lab. Discovery Soc., Nat. Paint and Coatings Assn, Soc. Chemie Industriale, Mfg. Chemists Assn, Soc. Plastics Engrs. (past dir.), Battery Coun. Internat., Rubber Mfrs. Assn., Nat. Assn. Corp. Growth, Nat. Planning Inst., World Affairs Coun.-Conn., Am. Inst. Mgmt., Assn. Governing Bd. of Univ. and Coll., Nat. Adv. Coun., Pres.'s Assn., Nat. Assn. Corp. Dirs. (charter mem.), Soc. Plastics Industry (sr.; past dir., Industry Legend Honor for plastic milk, juice and water bottles 1971), Concerns for Police Survivors (founding mem.), Coun. of Ams., Nat. Maritime Hist. Soc., Nat. Trust for Hist. Preservation, New Haven Colony Hist. Soc., So. Conn. Ellis Island Found. (charter mem.), U.S. Navy Meml. Found. (charter founding mem.), U.S. Senatorial Inner Circle, WWII Meml. Found. (charter founding mem., founder Nat. Law Enforcement Officers Meml., charter mem. U.S. Army Meml.), Commanders Club, Newcomen Soc. Am. (chmn. Conn. com., state chmn.), US Vets Assn., Marine Corp. Heritage Found., Nat. Mus. US Army (founding mem.), U.S. Naval Inst., Nat. Campaign for Tolerance and Wall of Tolerance (founding mem.), World Trade Ctr. Meml. Found., Col. Rutgers Legacy Soc., Harvard Bus. Sch. Club Conn., Harvard Bus. Sch. Club Greater N.Y., Harvard Bus. Sch. Alumni Assn., U. New Haven Legacy Soc., Columbus House, Rutgers Alumni Assn., Oaklane Country Club, Renaissance Club, Am. Legion, Chi Phi. Achievements include invention of and market creator of plastic non retunable milk, water and juice bottle to a leader in the worldwide market; created & developed largest single application for high densely poly. worldwide while also being the single most important factor to turn Celanese to a leader in the entire industry from 1968 to 1974; leading corporate officer for world's largest management led leveraged buyout of Uniroyal Inc. in 1985; centrally instrumental and recognized for the strategy and board institutional leadership to create and implement a complete transformation of the University of New Haven, from 1999 to 2006; significant leadership for the worldwide turnaround restructuring and re-engineering of Uniroyal Inc; recognized board leader and chair for the restructuring, transformation and growth positioning of Jackson Laboratory resources and mouse modals and services critical to worldwide bio-medical research; chair of the board of governing trustees for an 80-year historically monumental governance and institutional restructuring; repositioning and establishing a new platform for achieving a new vision to advance the cures for worldwide disease research. Home: 55 N Racebrook Rd Woodbridge CT 06525-1407 Office Phone: 203-387-1550. Office Fax: 203-389-5153.

ALVING, BARBARA, federal agency administrator, hematologist; BS with highest distinction, Purdue U., 1967; MD cum laude, Georgetown U., 1972. Intern in internal medicine Georgetown U.; resident in internal medicine Johns Hopkins U. Hosp., fellow in hematology; rsch. investigator Divsn. Blood and Blood Products FDA; joined dept. hematology and vascular biology Walter Reed Army Inst. Rsch., 1980, chief dept. hematology and vascular biology, 1992—96; dir. med. oncology/hematology sect. Washington Hosp. Ctr., 1996—99; dir. extramural Divsn. Blood Diseases and Resources Nat. Heart, Lung, and Blood Inst., NIH, Bethesda, Md., 1999—2001, dep. dir., 2001—03, acting dir., 2003—05, dir. Women's Health Initiative, 2002—; acting dir. Nat. Ctr. Rsch. Resources, NIH, 2005—. Prof. medicine Uniformed Services U. Health Services, Bethesda. Master: ACP. Achievements include patents in field. Office: Nat Ctr Rsch Resources Democracy Plz One 9th Fl 6701 Democracy Blvd MSC 4874 Bethesda MD 20892-4872 also: Women's Health Initiative Program Office 2 Rockledge Ctr Ste 8093 6701 Rockledge Dr MS 7935 Bethesda MD 20892-7935 Office Phone: 301-496-5793. Office Fax: 301-402-0006. E-mail: alvingb@mail.nih.gov.

ALVIS, JOEL LAWRENCE, JR., minister; b. Memphis, Nov. 12, 1955; s. Joel Lawrence Sr. and Martha Jean (Lowe) A.; m. Vicki Lynn Welch, Aug. 12, 1978; children: Joel Lawrence III, Mark Thomas. BA, Samford U., 1977; MA, U. Miss., 1980; PhD, Auburn U., 1985; MDiv, Louisville Presbyn. Theol. Sem., 1989. Ordained to ministry Presbyn. Ch. (U.S.A.), 1989. Local ch. history and records adminstr. Presbyn. Hist. Found., Montreat, N.C., 1982-86; rsch. assoc. Louisville Presbyn. Sem., 1986-89; pastor St. Pauls (N.C.) Presbyn. Ch., 1989-97; assoc. pastor St. Luke's Presbyn. Ch., Dunwoody, Ga., 1998—2003, interim ministry spec., 2003—. Mem. com. on ministry Coastal Carolina Presbytery, 1990-93, moderator of Presbytery, 1997. Author: (with others) Diversity of Discipleship, 1991, Religion and Race: Southern Presbyterians, 1946-1983, 1994. Mem. congl. ministry team Greater Altanta Presbyn. Ch., com. preparation of ministry, 2005—. Recipient Nelson R. Burr prize Hist. Soc. of Episcopal Ch., 1981, Book award N.C. Presbyn. Hist. Soc., 1995; Univ. fellow U. Miss., 1977-78, Anderson fellow Louisville Presbyn. Theol. Sem., 1991.

ALVORD, CHASE, lawyer; b. 1968; BA, Furman Univ., 1990; JD, Willamette Univ. Coll. Law, 1996. Bar: Wash. 1996. Counsel State Commodity Commn. First Amendment; atty., media and first amendment rights Tousley Brian Stephens PLLC. Contbr. articles to numerous profl. jours. Named Wash. Rising Star, SuperLawyers Mag., 2006. Office: Tousley Brain Stephens Ste 2200 1700 Seventh Ave Seattle WA 98101-1332

ALWARD, RUTH ROSENDALL, nursing consultant; d. Henry Rosendall and Freda Jonkman; m. Samuel Alward, Jan. 17, 1976. RN, Butterworth Hosp. Sch. Nursing, Grand Rapids, Mich.; BSN summa cum laude, Hunter Coll./CUNY, NYC, 1980; MA Tchrs. Coll., Columbia U., 1982, EdM, 1983, EdD, 1986. Sr. clin. nurse Wadsworth VA Hosp., LA, 1966-68; exec. dir. nursing Care Corp, Grand Rapids, Mich., 1968-71; nursing cons. Humana Inc., Louisville, 1972-76; asst. prof., dir. nursing adminstrn. grad. prog. Hunter Coll., CUNY, NYC, 1986-90; pres. Nurse Exec. Assocs., Inc., Washington, 1990—; series editor Delmar Pubs. Inc., Albany, 1993-96. Co-author: The Nurse's Shift Work Handbook, 1993, The Nurse's Guide to Marketing, 1991; contbr. articles to profl. jours.; mem. editorial adv. bd. Jour. of Nursing Adminstrn. Bd. dirs., past pres. James Lenox House Assn.; bd. dirs. IONA Sr. Svcs., 1998-2004. Mem. Nat. League Nursing (treas. D.C. chpt.), Am. Orgn. Nurse Execs., Sigma Theta Tau. Home and Office: 2011 N St NW Washington DC 20036-2301 Home Phone: 202-728-2956; Office Phone: 202-728-2956. E-mail: ruthalward@aol.com.

ALWORTH, CHARLES WESLEY, lawyer, engineer; b. Buenos Aires, Aug. 23, 1943; s. Cecil Dwight and Kathleen Mary (Whitaker) A.; m. Sally Ann Wells, Dec. 21, 1967 (div. Nov. 1981); m. Madeline E. Wilson, Feb. 14, 1983; children: Cecil Dwight II, Barbara Diane. BSEE, U. Okla., 1965, M in Elec. Engring., 1967, PhD, 1969; JD, U. Tulsa, 1992. Bar: U.S. Patent Bar Office 1989, Tex. 1993, U.S. Dist. Ct. (ea. dist.) Tex. 1993, U.S. Dist. Ct. (no. dist.) Tex. 1997, U.S. Ct. Appeals (fed. cir.) 2001, U.S. Supreme

Ct. 2003; registered profl. engr., La., Tex. Tchg. asst. elec. engring. U. Okla., Norman, 1965, grad. asst. elec. engring., 1965-67, spl. instr. elec. engring., 1967-68; asst. prof. elec. engring. Tex. A&M U., College Station, Tex., 1968-74; chief, prin. cons. Conoco, Inc., Ponca City, Okla., 1974-90; rsch. assoc. profl. engr. U. Tulsa, Okla., 1990—; chief engr. Alworth Cons., Tyler, Tex., 1990—; of counsel Sefrna & Assocs., Tyler, 1993-95; prin. Charles W. Alworth Engr. & Atty. at Law; assoc. prof. and head elec. engring. U. Tex., Tyler, 1997-98. Patentee in field; contbr. articles to profl. jours. City councilman dist. 6 City of Tyler, Tex., 2004—. Mem. Phi Delta Phi, Tau Beta Pi, Eta Kappa Nu, Sigma Xi. Reformed Episcopalian. Avocations: aviation, woodworking, gardening. Home: 505 Cumberland Rd Tyler TX 75703-9325 Office Phone: 903-534-0477. Personal E-mail: calworth@alworth.com.

ALYKOVA, VALENTINA, musician, music educator; b. Moscow, June 22, 1949; arrived in U.S., 1991; d. Trifon Alykov and Zoya Alykova; m. Vladimir Binevitch, Jan. 19, 1991. M in Musical Arts, Moscow Conservatory, 1973; postgrad., Gnessin Musical Pedagogical Inst., Moscow, 1980. Violin instr. Music Sch. for Gifted Children, Moscow, 1973—77; asst. prof. Gnessin Musical Pedagogical Inst., Moscow, 1978—82; violinist Moscow String Quartet, 1973—96; artist-in-residence Lamont Sch. Music, Denver U., 1991—96; violin instr. Forte Acad. Music, Littleton, Colo., 1997—. Recipient Second prize, Internat. Quartet Competition, Budapest, Hungry, 1978, Grand Prix and First prize, Internat. Quartet Competition, Evian, France, 1979; grantee, Colo. Coun. on the Arts, Denver, 1999, 2000. Mem.: Music Tchrs. Nat. Assn. Russian Orthodox. Avocations: reading, travel, mahjong. Home: 14299 E Arizona Ave Aurora CO 80012 Office: Forte Acad Music Ste 15 10143 W Chatfield Ave Littleton CO 80127-4245 Personal E-mail: walter2B@aol.com.

AL-ZUBAIDI, AMER AZIZ, physicist, researcher; b. Najaf, Iraq, June 10, 1945; came to U.S., 1974; s. Aziz Allawi and Shahai Ali (Al Fartousi) A.; m. Haifa M. Al-Zubaidi, Aug. 24, 1972; children: Samer, Akrum. BS in Physics, U. Baghdad, Iraq, 1966; MS in Physics, Pa. State U., 1976, postgrad., 1977-81, Va. Poly. Inst. and State U., 1977-82. bd. dirs. KCIK. Hs tchr. Inst. for Tchrs., Riyadh, Saudi Arabia, 1966-68; hs tchr. physics, math., and related scis. Saudi Ministry of Edn., Riyadh, 1966-68; hs tchr. physics, math., mem. phys. lab. supplies and equipments com. Agrl. Vocat. Sch., Iraqi Ministry Edn., Baghdad, 1968-74; grad. tchg. asst. Va. Poly. Inst. and State U., Blacksburg, 1976-82, rsch. sci. nuclear physics, 1982—; owner Al's Internat. Editor-in-chief Al-Kufa, 1994. Chmn. bd. dirs. Kufa Ctr. of Islamic Knowledge, editor-in-chief newsletter; min. Mem. Union of Concerned Scientists, Sigma Xi. Home: 2319 10th St NW Roanoke VA 24012-3929 Office Phone: 540-563-8471. Personal E-mail: amer@aalzubaidi.com.

AMABILE, CELENE, pharmacist; d. Joseph and Barbara Amabile. BA, U. Va., Charlottesville; PharmD, Va. Commonwealth U., Richmond, 2001. Asst. prof., clin. pharmacist Midwestern U., Glendale, Ariz.; pharmacy resident Med. U. SC, Charleston; clin. coord., residency program dir. Gaston Meml. Hosp., Gastonia, NC, 2004—. Mem.: Am. Soc. Health-Systems Pharmacists, Am. Coll. Clin. Pharmacy (cert. pharmacotherapy specialist).

AMABILE, JOHN LOUIS, lawyer; b. NYC, Oct. 13, 1934; s. John A. and Rose (Singer) A.; m. Christina M. Leary, Nov. 23, 1963; children: Tracy Ann, John Christopher. BS cum laude, Coll. Holy Cross, Worcester, Mass., 1956; LLB, St. John's Sch. Law, 1959. Bar: NY 1959, US Dist. Ct. (so. and ea. dists.) NY 1961, US Supreme Ct. 1964, US Ct. Claims 1964, US Ct. Appeals (2d cir.) 1970, US Tax Ct. 1984, US Ct. Appeals (9th cir.) 1984. Assoc. Law Office of Allen Taylor, NYC, 1959-62; assoc. Schwartz & Frohlich, NYC, 1963-69, ptnr., 1969, Summit, Solomon & Feldesman (and predecessor firms), NYC, 1971-93, Putney, Twombly Hall & Hirson, NYC, 1993-2000, of counsel, 2001—04. Faculty mem. ann. seminar Practising Law Inst., 1987-91; mediator so. dist. U.S. Dist. Ct. N.Y., comml. divsn. Supreme Ct., N.Y.; arbitrator ea. dist. U.S. Dist. Ct., Bklyn.; panel chair appellate divsn. Disciplinary Com., 1980-85, 87-92; lectr. in field. Author: Responses to Complaints: Commercial Litigation in New York State Courts, 1995, 2d edit., 2005, Warranties: Business and Commercial Litigation in Federal Courts, 1998, 2d edit., 2005, The City of New York as a Major Institutional Litigant: A Follow-up on the Price Waterhouse Study, The Record of the Association of the Bar of the City of New York, vol. 54, no. 5, 1999; editor St. John Law Rev. 1958-59. Regional commr. Am. Youth Soccer Orgn., Chappaqua, NY, 1975-84; mem. New Castle Recreation and Parks Commn., 1984-90, chair, 1987-89; bd. dirs. Aiken Area Coun. on Aging, 2003—, vice chair, 2006. Mem. ABA, N.Y. State Bar Assn., Assn. Bar City N.Y. (mem. com. on state legis. 1971-74, chair 1975-78, com. on grievances 1979-80, com. on women in cts. 1988-94, com. on judiciary 1989-92, interim mem. 1992, 93, 94, 96, 97, 98, 99, 2000, chair com. on gender bias in fed. cts. 1991-93, coun. judicial adminstrn. 1996-2001, com. on symposium 1997-2000, chair 1998-2000), Fed. Bar Coun., Practising Law Inst. (chair winning strategies for depositions in corp. litigation 1991-92, co-chair seminars on art of taking and defending depositions in corp. litigation 1982-85). Democrat. Roman Catholic. Personal E-mail: jlamabile@bellsouth.net.

AMACHER, ARTHUR LOREN, neurosurgeon; b. Saskatoon, Sask., Can., Oct. 22, 1938; came to U.S., 1983; s. Arthur Melvin and Johanna Martha (Niebergall) A.; m. Jane Elizabeth Tomlinson, Sept. 20, 1961; children: Scott, Jon, Marc. MD, U. Western Ont., London, Can., 1962. Intern Victoria Hosp., London, Ont., 1962-63, resident (jr.) surgery, 1963-64, resident neurosurgery, 1965-67, chief resident neurosurgery, 1969-70; fellow anatomy and neuroanatomy U. Western Ont., 1964-65; resident (sr.) surgery Vets. Hosp., London, 1965; fellow neuropathology U. Toronto, 1967; resident neurosurgery Childrens Hosp. Med. Ctr. and Peter Bent Brigham Harvard U., 1968, chief resident, teaching fellow surgery, 1969; from lectr. to assoc. prof. clin. neuro-sci., surgery U. Western Ont., London, Can., 1970-83; prof. neurosurgery U. Conn., Farmington, 1983-87; neurosurgeon Geisinger Med. Ctr., Danville, Pa., 1987-95, chief, 1995—2003; neurosurgeon Evangelical Med. Svcs. Found., 2003—. Cons. treatment alogitm USN, Washington, 1989, Via Cyometrics, Bel Air, Md. Author: Patient Care in Neurosurgery, 1990, Pediatric Head Injuries, 1988; contbr. over 130 articles to profl. jours., chpts. to books. Chorister Susquahanna Valley Chorale, Lewisburg, 1989—. Recipient Harriman award, Bucknell U., 1994, Svc. Cmty. and Univ. Backcourt award, Bison Club, Bucknell U., 2005. Fellow ACS, Royal Coll. Surgeons of Can.; mem. N.Y. Acad. Sci., Pa. Neurosurg. Soc. (pres. 1997), Acad. Am. Poets. Avocations: poetry, writing, reading, fishing, sailing. Home Phone: 510-523-8686; Office Phone: 570-522-5033. E-mail: aljamach@ptd.net.

AMACHER, RICHARD EARL, retired literature educator; b. Ridgway, Pa., Dec. 13, 1917; s. Albert and Emma (Luchs) Amacher; m. Cordelia Anne Ward, Aug. 26, 1953; 1 child, Alice Marie. AB, Ohio U., 1939; postgrad., U. Chgo., 1939-42; PhD, U. Pitts., 1947. Instr. English Yale U., New Haven, 1944-45; instr. Rutgers U., New Brunswick, NJ, 1945-47, asst. prof., 1947-53, lectr., 1953-54; chmn. English dept. Henderson State Tchrs. Coll., Arkadelphia, Ark., 1954-57; assoc. prof. Auburn (Ala.) U., 1957-65, prof., 1965-78, Hargis prof. Am. Lit., 1978-84, prof. emeritus, 1984—. Fulbright prof., Wurzburg, Germany, 1961—62, Konstanz, Germany, 1969—70. Author: Franklin's Wit and Folly, 1953, Practical Criticism, 1956, Benjamin Franklin, 1962, Edward Albee, 1969, rev. edit., 1982, American Political Writers, 1588-1800, 1979; author: (with Margaret Rule) Edward Albee at Home and Abroad, 1973; author: (with Victor Lange) New Perspectives in German Literary Criticism, 1979; editor (with G. Polhermus): J. G. Baldwin's The Flush Times of California, 1966. Chmn. Auburn Chamber Music Soc., 1980—82, 1985—86, 1988—89; elder Presbyn. Ch. Am. Coun. Learned Socs. grantee, 1972. Mem.: Nat. Soc. Lit. and Arts, Société Historique d'Auteuil et de Passy, Am. Studies Assn. (pres. southeastern sec. 1977—79). Democrat. Home: 515 Auburn Dr Auburn AL 36830-5547 E-mail: amacher@mailstation.com.

AMADA, GERALD, retired psychotherapist; b. Newark, Aug. 13, 1938; s. Samuel and Rose Amada; m. Marcia Rae Hirshberg, Aug. 9, 1962; children: Robin, Naomi, Laurie, Eric. BA, Rutgers U., Newark, 1960; MSW, Rutgers U., 1962; PhD, Wright Inst., Berkeley, Calif., 1977. Psychotherapist Mercer County Mental Health Clinic, Trenton, NJ, 1962—64, Dept. Mental Hygiene, Modesto, Calif., 1964—66, Homewood Terrace, San Francisco, 1966—68; staff devel. supr. Solano County Dept. Social Svcs., Vallejo, Calif., 1968—70; dir. Mental Health Program, City Coll. of San Francisco, 1970—2000; psychotherapist Mill Valley, Calif., 1980—2003; cons. colls. and univs., 1980—. Cons. KPIX-TV, San Francisco, 1980—82, Mass. Mutual Life Ins. Co., San Francisco, 1980—83. Author: Mental Health on the Community College Campus, 1977, Mental Health and Authoritarianism on the College Campus, 1978, A Guide to Psychotherapy, 1995, Coping with the Disruptive College Student, 1994, The Mystified Fortune and Other Tales from Psychotherapy, 1998, Coping with Misconduct in the College Classroom, 1999, The Power of Negative Thinking, 1999, Mental Health and Student Conduct Issues, 2001, Anker's Plight, 2006; reviewer Am. Jour. Psychotherapy, 1983—, contbr., reviewer Jour. Coll. Student Psychotherapy, 1988—; author: Mushu: A True Story, 2006; contbr. articles to profl. jours. Commr. Marin County Human Rights Commn.; facilitator Alzheimer's Orgn., San Rafael, Calif., 1998—2003. Recipient Award of Excellence, Nat. Assn. of Vocat. Edn. Spl. Needs Pers., 1984. Mem.: Am. Fedn. Tchrs., NASW, Freedom for Individual Rights in Edn. Avocations: tennis, writing, reading, travel, classical music. Mailing: 185 Mount Lassen Dr San Rafael CA 94903 Office Phone: 415-479-8889. Business E-Mail: mgamada@earthlink.net.

AMADO, HONEY KESSLER, lawyer; b. Bklyn., July 20, 1949; d. Bernard and Mildred Kessler; m. Ralph Albert Amado, Oct. 24, 1976; children: Jessica Reina, Micah Solomon, Gabrielle Beth. BA in Polit. Sci., Calif. State Coll., Long Beach, 1971; JD, Western State U., Fullerton, Calif., 1976. Bar: Calif. 1977, US Dist. Ct. (ctrl. dist.) Calif. 1981, US Ct. Appeals (9th cir.) 1981, US Supreme Ct. 1994. Pvt. practice, Beverly Hills, Calif., 1978—. Mem. family law exec. com. Calif. State Bar, 1987—91; lectr. in field. Contbr. articles to profl. jours.; mem. editl. bd. LA Lawyer mag., 1996—, articles coord., 1999—2000, chair, 2000—01. Nat. v.p. Jewish Nat. Fund, 1995—97, bd. dirs., 2002—; mem. Com. Concerned Lawyers Soviet Jewry, 1979—90; bd. dirs. Jewish Nat. Fund LA, 1990—98, 2002—, Women's Alliance Israel; sec. LA region, bd. dirs. Jewish Feminist Ctr., co-chair steering com., 1994—96; mem. pres.'s coun. Am. Jewish Com. Nat. Coun., LA, 2002—, bd. dirs., 2002—; sec. LA region, bd. dirs. Am. Jewish Com., 1991—94, Am. Jewish Congress, co-chair internat. rels. com. LA region, 2002—04, chair internat. com., 2004—; mem. Commn. Soviet Jewry Jewish Fedn. Coun. Greater LA, 1977—83, chmn., 1979—81, commn. edn., 1982—83, mem. cmty. rels. com., 1979—83. Named Superlawyer Southern Calif., 2005, 2006, 2007. Mem.: Calif. Ct. Appeal, Calif. State Bar, LA County Bar Assn. (family law sect., appellate cts. com. 1987—, chmn. subcom. to examine reorgn. Calif. Supreme Ct. 1990—94, judge pro tem panel 1985—95, appellate jud. evaluations com. 1989—, Dist. 2 settlement program 1996—), Beverly Hills Bar Assn. (family law mediators panel 1985—94), Calif. Women Lawyers (bd. govs. 1988—90, 1st v.p. 1989—90, jud. evaluations co-chair 1988—90). Democrat. Jewish. Office: 261 S Wetherly Dr Beverly Hills CA 90211-2515 Office Phone: 310-550-8214. Business E-Mail: hkaatty@earthlink.net.

AMADOR, JOSÉ JORGE, computer engineer, researcher; b. Miami, Fla., July 4, 1967; s. José Maria Amador and Rosa Gil Figueroa; m. Karen Lynn Jones, May 18, 1991; children: Angelica Lynnette, Antonio Javier, Andres Bryan, Adrian Cordero. BS in Computer Engring., Fla. Inst. Tech., 1990, MS in Computer Engring., 1994, PhD in Computer Engring., 2001. Computer engr. Checkout Sys. Br. NASA, Kennedy Space Center, Fla., 1990—96, computer engr., rschr. software developer, 1996—. Contbr. articles to profl. jours. Recipient Group Achievement award, Spacelab Experiment Integration Control Room Reconfiguration, 1989, Dir.'s Performance Recognition award, John F. Kennedy Space Ctr., 1993, Performance awards, 1993—2005, Cert. of Recognition, Biphase Bus. Monitor Design, 1994, Cache Memory Design Analysis Software, 1997, Group Achievement award, Payload Canister/Transporter Instrumentation and Communication Subsystem (I&CS) Design and Implementation Team, 1996, High Rate Data Equipment Controller Upgrade Project Team, 1996, Cert. of Recognition, Hypothesis Support Mechanism for Mid-Lvel Visual Pattern Recognition, 2004, Hypothesis Support Mechanism for Mid-Level Visual Pattern Recognition, 2005, Software award, NASA Adminstr., 2005, Silver Quality Dollar award, 2006. Achievements include patents for biphase bus monitor. Avocations: surfing, reading, racquetball, home improvement. Office: NASA John F Kennedy Space Center Kennedy Space Center FL 32899 Home Phone: 321-636-2291; Office Phone: 321-853-9551. Business E-Mail: jose.j.amador@nasa.gov.

AMAECHI, JOHN, retired professional basketball player; b. Nov. 26, 1970; Student, Pa. State Coll. Center Cleve. Cavaliers, 1995—96, Orlando Magic, Fla., 1999—2001, Utah Jazz, 2001—03. Author: (memoir) Man in The Middle, 2007. Named to NBA All-Interview First Team, 1999-2000. Office: Utah Jazz Delta Center 301 West South Temple Salt Lake City UT 84101 Office Phone: 407 89M AGIC.*

AMAKER, TOMMY, men's college basketball coach; b. Falls Church, Va., June 6, 1965; m. Stephanie Pinder-Amaker. BA, Duke U., 1987. Asst. coach Duke U., 1988—97; head basketball coach Seton Hall U., 1998—2001, U. Mich., 2002—07, Harvard U., 2007—. Recipient Henry Iba Corinthian Nat. Defensive Player Yr., 1986. Achievements include playing on Gold Medal Winning Team, FIBA Championships, 1986. Office: Harvard U Dept Athletics Murr Ctr 65 No Harvard St Boston MA 02163*

AMALSAD, MEHER DADABHOY, writer, speaker, seminar leader; b. Karachi, Pakistan, Sept. 12, 1958; s. Dadabhoy and Nancy A.; m. Katayoon Amalsad; 1 child, Anahita Meher. BS in Engring., Nadirshaw Edulgee Dinshaw Engring. Univ., Karachi, Pakistan, 1982; MS in Engring., Northrop Univ., 1987. Program mgr. Hughes Aircraft Co., Rancho Santa, Calif., 1988-95; dist. mgr. ICM, Garden Grove, Calif., 1995-97; pres., CEO Starmasters, Garden Grove, Calif., 1997—. Mem. acad. svcs. com. The Pegasus Sch., Huntington Beach, Calif., 1991-98. Author: Gifts That Lift, Shift and Uplift, 1996, Bread for the Head, 1997, In Search of Your Quest, How to Be Your Best, 1995, Love Grows and Shows Only When it Flows, 1995; co-author: (with Shahriar Shahriari) SOUL (Success Out-of Understanding Love), 1998, Bread for the Parents' Head, 1997; inventor. Chairperson First World Zoroastrian Youth Congress, 1993, First North Am. Zoroastrian Youth Congress, 1987, Helping Hands Com. of Fedn. of Zoroastrian Assns. N.Am., 1987-93; pres. Hughes Toastmasters, 1995. Mem. Profl. Speakers Network, Relationship Building Network (sponsor), Leads Club. Avocations: music, writing, dance, speaking, inventing, creative cooking. Home: 15842 Villanova Cir Westminster CA 92683-7616

AMAN, ALFRED CHARLES, JR., law educator; b. Rochester, NY, July 7, 1945; s. Alfred Charles Sr. and Jeannette Mary (Czebatul) Aman; m. Carol Jane Greenhouse, Sept. 23, 1976. AB, U. Rochester, 1967; JD, U. Chgo., 1970. Bar: (D.C.) 1971, Ga. 1972, N.Y. 1980. Law clk. U.S. Ct. Appeals, Atlanta, 1970—72; assoc. Sutherland, Asbill & Brennan, Atlanta, 1972—75, Washington, 1975—77; assoc. prof. Sch. Law, Cornell U., Ithaca, NY, 1977—82, prof. law, 1983—91, exec. dir. Internat. Legal Studies Program, 1988—90; dean Sch. Law, Ind. U., Bloomington, 1991—2002, prof. law, 1991—, Roscoe C. O'Byrne chair in law, 1999—, disting. Fulbright chair in comparative constitutional law, 1998; vis. prof. law U. Paris II, 1998; vis. fellow law and pub. affairs program Princeton U., 2002—03. Cons. U.S. Adminstrv. Conf., Washington, 1978—80, Washington, 1986—; trustee U. Rochester, 1980—; vis. fellow Wolfson Coll., Cambridge U., 1983—84, 1990—91. Author: Energy and Natural Resources, 1983, Administrative Law in a Global Era, 1992, Administrative Law Treatise, 1992, 2d edit., 2001. Chmn. Ithaca Bd. Zoning Appeals, 1980—82. Mem.: ABA, N.Y. State Bar Assn., Ga. Bar Assn., D.C. Bar Assn., Am. Assn. Law Schs., Phi Beta Kappa. Avocations: music, piano. Office: Ind U Sch Law 211 S Indiana Ave Bloomington IN 47405-7001

AMAN, GEORGE MATTHIAS, III, lawyer; b. Wayne, Pa., Mar. 2, 1930; s. George Matthias and Emily (Kalbach) A.; m. Ellen McMillan, June 20, 1959; children: James E., Catherine E., Peter T. AB, Princeton U., 1952; LL.B., Harvard U., 1957. Bar: Pa. 1958. Assoc. Townsend Elliot & Munson, Phila., 1960-65; ptnr. Morgan Lewis & Bockius, Phila., 1965-93; of counsel High, Swartz, Roberts & Seidel, Norristown, Pa., 1993—. Commr. Radnor Twp., Pa., 1976-80, 86-92, planning commr., 1981-86; pres. bd. trustees Wayne Presbyn. Ch., Pa., 1981-84. Served to 1st lt. U.S. Army, 1952-54. Mem. ABA, Pa. Mcpl. Authorities Assn., Nat. Assn. Bond Lawyers, Pa. Assn. Bond Lawyers; Clubs: Merion Cricket (Haverford, Pa.); Princeton (Phila.) (dir 1977-79, treas. 1985-86). Republican. Home: 246 Upland Way Wayne PA 19087-4859 Office: High Swartz Roberts Seidel 40 E Airy St Norristown PA 19401-4803 Office Phone: 610-275-0700. Personal E-mail: george.aman@verizon.net. Business E-Mail: gaman@highswartz.com.

AMAN, KALLEY R., lawyer; BS, Portland State Univ., 1995, MS, 1997; JD, Lewis & Clark Sch. Law, 2000. Bar: Calif. 2001, Oreg. 2001, US Dist. Ct., Ctrl. Calif. Oreg. Assoc. Buchalter Nemer PC, LA. Editor: Jour. Small & Emerging Bus. Law; contbr. articles to profl. jours. Named a Rising Star, So. Calif. Super Lawyers, 2006. Office: Buchalter Nemer PC Ste 1500 1000 Wilshire Blvd Los Angeles CA 90017-2457 Office Phone: 213-891-0700. Office Fax: 213-896-0400. Business E-Mail: kaman@buchalter.com.

AMAN, MOHAMMED MOHAMMED, dean, library and information science professor; b. Alexandria, Egypt, Jan. 3, 1940; came to U.S., 1963, naturalized, 1975; s. Mohammed Aman and Fathia Ali (al-Maghrabi) Mohammed; m. Mary Jo Parker, Sept. 15, 1972; 1 son, David. BA, Cairo U., 1961; MS, Columbia U., 1965; PhD, U. Pitts., 1968. Libr. Egyptian Nat. Libr., 1961-63, Duquesne U., Pitts., 1966-68; asst. prof. libr. sci. Pratt Inst., NYC, 1968-69; from asst. prof. to assoc. prof. St. John's U., Jamaica, NY, 1969-73, prof., dir. divsn. libr. and info. sci., 1973-76; prof. libr. sci., dean Palmer Grad. Libr. Sch., C.W. Post Ctr., L.I. U., 1976-79; dean Sch. Info. Studies U. Wis., 1979—2003, prof., dean, interim dean Sch. Edn. Milw., 2001—02, dean emeritus, prof. Sch. Info. Scis., 2003—. Cons. UNESCO, U.S., AID and UNIDO; USIA acad. specialist, Germany, 1989; Fulbright lectr. Cairo U., 1990-91; USIA-sponsored lectr. Mohamed V. Univ., Rabat, Morocco, 1997. Author: Librarianship and the Third World, 1976, Cataloging and Classifications of Non-Western Library Material: Issues, Trends and Practices, 1980, Arab Serials and Periodicals: A Subject Bibliography, 1979, Online Access to Databases, 1983, On Developing Computer-Based Library Systems (Arabic), 1984, Information Services (Arabic), 1985, Trends in Urban Library Management, 1989, The Bibliotheca Alexandrina: A Link in the Chain of Cultural Continuity, 1991, Information Technology Use in Libraries (Arabic), 1998, Internet Use in Libraries, 2000, The Gulf War in World Literature, 2002; editor-in-chief: Digest of Middle East Studies, 1991-. Chmn. Black Faculty Coun., U. Wis., Milw.; mktg. com. Milw. Art Mus.; bd. dirs. Clara Mohammed Sch., 2001-. Recipient Outstanding Achievement award, Egyptian Libr. Assn., 1997. Mem. NAACP, ALA (chmn. internat. rels. com. 1984-86, standing com. on libr. edn., internat. subcom. 1990-91, chmn. 1991-93, internat. rels. Round Table 1993-94, John Ames Humphry/Online Computer Libr. Ctr. Outstanding Contbn. award 1989, Leadership award black caucus 1994, Excellence award black caucus 1995), Assn. Libr. and Sci. (Svc. award 1988), Am. Soc. for Info. Sci. (chmn. spl. interest group in internat. info. issues, internat. rels. com.), Egyptian Libr. Assn. (life, Outstanding Achievement award 1997), Arab/Jewish Dialogue, Egyptian-Am. Scholars Assn., Assn. for Libr. and Info. Sci. Edn. (chmn. internat. rels. com. 1983-85), Wis. Libr. Assn. (Svc. award 1992, P.N. Kaula Internat. award and medal 1996, Wis. Libr. of Yr. 1998), Libr. Svcs. and Constrn. Act. (adv. com. 1986-89), Internat. Archtl. Jury for Bibliotheca Alexandrina, Internat. Fedn. Libr. Assns. and Insts. (sec. on edn. and tng. 1983-92), Coun. on Egyptian Am. Rels., The Gamaliel Chair (bd. dirs. 1995-97), Leaders Forum (bd. dirs. 1995—), America's Black Holocaust Mus. (bd. dirs. 1999—), Islamic Social Family Svcs. (bd. dirs. 1999—), Milw. Tchr.'s Edn. Ctr. (bd. dirs.). Democrat. Muslim. Office: U Wis-Milw Sch Info Studies PO Box 413 Milwaukee WI 53201-0413 Home Phone: 262-242-9031; Office Phone: 414-229-3315. Business E-Mail: aman@sois.uwn.edu.

AMAN, REINHOLD ALBERT, philologist, writer; b. Fuerstenzell, Bavaria, Apr. 8, 1936; came to U.S., 1959, naturalized, 1963; s. Ludwig and Anna Margarete (Waindinger) A.; m. Shirley Ann Beischel, Apr. 9, 1960 (div. 1990); 1 child, Susan. Student, Chem. Engring. Inst., Augsburg, Germany, 1953—54; BS with high honors, U. Wis., 1965; PhD, U. Tex., 1968. Chem. engr., Munich and Frankfurt, Germany, 1954-57; petroleum chemist Shell Oil Co., Montreal, Que., Canada, 1957-59; chem. analyst A. O. Smith Corp., Milw., 1959-62; prof. German U. Wis., Milw., 1968-74; editor, pub. Maledicta Jour., Maledicta Press Publs., Santa Rosa, Calif., 1976—; pres. Maledicta Press, Santa Rosa, 1976—. Dir. Internat. Maledicta Archives, Santa Rosa, 1975— Author: Der Kampf in Wolframs Parzival, 1968, Bayrisch-oesterreichisches Schimpfwoerterbuch, 1973, 86, 96, 2005, Talking Dirty, 1993, Opus Maledictorum, 1996, Hillary Clinton's Pen Pal, 1996; gen. editor Mammoth Cod (Mark Twain), 1976, Dictionary of International Slurs (A. Roback), 1979, Graffiti (A. Read), 1977; editor Maledicta: The Internat. Jour. Verbal Aggression, 1977—, Maledicta Monitor, 1990-92; contbr. articles to profl. jours. U. Wis. scholar, 1963-65; U. Wis. research grantee, 1973, 74; NDEA Title IV fellow, 1965-68 Mem. Internat. Maledicta Soc. (pres.), Am. Dialect Soc., Am. Name Soc., Dictionary Soc. N.Am. Home and Office; PO Box 14123 Santa Rosa CA 95402-6123 Home Phone: 707-795-8178; Office Phone: 707-795-8178. E-mail: aman@sonic.net.

AMANN, CHARLES ALBERT, mechanical engineer, researcher; b. Thief River Falls, Minn., Apr. 21, 1926; s. Charles Alois and Bertha Ann (Oetting) Amann; m. Marilynn Ann Reis, Aug. 26, 1950; children: Richard, Barbara, Nancy, Julie. BS, U. Minn., 1946, MSME, 1948. Instr. U. Minn., Mpls., 1946-49; rsch. engr. GM Rsch. Labs., Detroit, 1949-54, supervisory rsch. engr. Warren, Mich., 1954-71, asst. dept. head, 1971-73, dept. head, 1973-89, rsch. fellow, 1989-91; prin. engr. KAB Engring., 1991—. Spl. instr. Wayne State U., Detroit, 1952—55; guest lectr. Mich. State U., 1980—; outside prof. U. Ariz., 1983; mem. adv. com. Gas Rsch. Inst., 1992—98, Oak Ridge Nat. Lab., 1996—98; invited lectr. Inst. Advanced Engring., Seoul, Republic of Korea, 1994. Author (with others): Automotive Engine Alternatives, 1986, Advanced Diesel Engineering and Operations, 1988, Marks' Standard Handbook for Mechanical Engineers, 2007; co-editor: Combustion Modeling in Reciprocating Engines, 1980. Lt. (j.g.) USNR, 1944—46. Recipient James Clayton prize, Inst. Mech. Engrs., 1975, Outstanding Achievement award, U. Minn., 1991. Fellow: Soc. Automotive Engrs. (Arch T. Colwell merit award 1972, Disting. Spkr. award 1981, Arch T. Colwell merit award 1984, Disting. Spkr. award 1991, Forest R. McFarland award 2001); mem.: ASME (Richard S. Woodbury award 1989, Soichiro Honda lectr. 1992, Spkr. award Internal Combustion

Engine Divsn. 1997, Internal Combustion Engine award 2000, Disting. lectr. 2002—04), NAE, Tau Beta Pi, Tau Omega, Sigma Xi. Presbyterian. Achievements include patents in field. Avocation: music. Home Phone: 248-646-0198. E-mail: mcamann@juno.com.

AMANN, LESLIE KIEFER, lawyer, educator; b. Pensacola, Fla., Dec. 21, 1955; d. Robert C. and Marilyn Joan (Franklin) K.; children: Augustus Kiefer, Nicholas Jacob. BMEd, S.W. Tex. State U., 1976; JD, U. Houston, 1987. Bar: Tex. 1987, U.S. Dist. Ct. (so. dist.) Tex. 1988, U.S. Ct. Appeals (5th cir.), 1991, U.S. Dist. Ct. (no. dist.) Tex. 1992. Legis. aide to Lindon Williams Tex. State Senate, Austin, 1977-81; tchr. The Lincoln Sch., Guadalajara, Mex., 1979-82; legal asst. Koons Rasor Fuller & McCurley, Dallas, 1983-84; clk., assoc., participating assoc. Reynolds, Allen, Cook, Reynolds & Cunningham, Houston, 1984-93; shareholder Cunningham & Amann, Houston, 1993-94; asst. gen. counsel Charter Bank, Houston, 1995-96; sr. v.p., fiduciary counsel, market trust exec. Bank of America, Houston, 1996—2006; sr. v.p., lead fiduciary officer Sentinel Trust Co., 2006—. Adj. faculty Law Sch., U. Houston, 1988-2000; faculty Tex. Bankers Assn. Trust Sch., 1998-2007, Am. Bankers Assn. Nat. Grad Trust Sch., 2005-06; bd. dirs. U. Houston Law Alumni Assn., Houston Bus. and Estate Planning Coun., pres. exec. bd.; mem. planned giving adv. bd. U. St. Thomas, Houston Estate and Fin. Forum. Contbr. articles to profl. jours. Mem. adv. bd. Probate and Trust Law Inst., South Tex. Coll. Law, Houston, 1998-2000; vol. Annunciation Orthodox Sch., Houston, 1996-2007; vol. Greater Houston Partnership Tex. Scholars, 2000-05, St. Thomas H.S. Recipient Adj. Faculty award U. Houston Law Sch., 1999, U. Houston Law Alumni Gala award, 2005. Fellow Tex. Bar Found. (life); mem. Tex. Bankers Assn. (mem. adv. bd. wealth mgmt. and trust divsn., adv. coun. 2004-07), Houston Bar Assn. (vol. lawyers in pub. schs. 1998), Tex. State Bar. (real estate, probate and trust law sect.), Attys. in Tax and Probate, Houston Bus. and Estate Planning Coun., Houston Estate and Fin. Forum, U. Houston Law Alumni Assn. (bd. dirs. 2003—, sec. 2005-06, chair 2008 Gala). Republican. Methodist. Avocations: writing, reading, book collecting, music. Office: Sentinel Trust Co 2001 Kirby Dr Ste 1200 Houston TX 77019 Office Phone: 713-630-9614. Business E-Mail: lamann@sentineltrust.com.

AMANPOUR, CHRISTIANE, news correspondent; b. London, Jan. 12, 1958; m. James Rubin, 1998; 1 child, Darius John Rubin. BA in Journalism, summa cum laude, Rhode Island U. Reporter, anchor, prodr. WBRU-Radio, Providence, 1981—82; asst. internat. assignment desk CNN, Atlanta, 1983, correspondent Frankfurt, West Germany, 1989, Kuwait, 1990; contbr. 60 Minutes CBS News, 1996—. Named Woman of Yr., Women in Cable and Telecommunications, NY Chpt., 1994; named one of 100 Most Powerful Women, Forbes mag., 2005—06; recipient News & Documentary Emmy, George Foster Peabody award, 1994, 1997, Courage in Journalism award, Worldfest-Houston Internat. Film Festival Gold award, Livingston award for young journalists, Breakthrough award, Women, Men and Media, 1991, Sigma Chi award, Edward R. Murrow award for disting. achievement in broadcast journalism, 2002. Fellow: Soc. of Profl. Journalists. Fluent in English and Farsi (Persian). Mailing: CNN One CNN Center Atlanta GA 30303

AMAR, AKHIL REED, law educator; b. Ann Arbor, Mich., Sept. 6, 1958; s. Arjan D. and Kamla (Chabra) A.; m. Vinita Parkash, Sept. 3, 1989. BA summa cum laude, Yale U., 1980, JD, 1984; LLD (hon.), Suffolk U., 1997. From asst. prof. to assoc. prof. Yale Law Sch., New Haven, Conn., 1985-90, prof. law, 1990-93, Southmayd prof. law, 1993—. Samuel Rubin vis. prof. law Columbia Law Sch., NYC, 1993; vis. prof. Stanford U., 2001. Author: The Constitution and Criminal Procedure, 1997, The Bill of Rights, 1998, Processes of Constitutional Decisionmaking, 2000; co-author: For the People, 1998; contrib. articles to law jours. Recipient Paul M. Bator award Federalist Soc., 1993; named 36th Ann. Coen lectr. U. Colo., 1992, Dillard lectr. U. Va., 1994, 7th ann. Barrett lectr. U. Calif., Davis, 1994, 57th Cleveland-Marshall lectr., 1994, Rutgers-Camden U., 1995, Suffolk U., 1996, Tuft lectr. U. Cin., 1998, Seegers lectr. Valparasio, 1998; DePaul Coll. Law Disting. scholar, 1991. Fellow, Am. Acad. Arts & Scis. Mem. United Ch. of Christ. E-mail: akhil.amar@yale.edu.*

AMARA, LUCINE, vocalist; b. Hartford, Conn., Mar. 1, 1925; d. George and Adrine (Kazanjian) Armaganian; married, Jan. 7, 1961 (div. June 1964). Student, Music Acad. of West, 1947, U. So. Calif., 1949-50. Artistic dir. N.J. Assn. Verismo Opera, Ft. Lee. Tchr. master classes U.S., Mex., Can., Australia. Appeared at Hollywood Bowl, 1948, soloist, San Francisco Symphony, 1949-50; career includes over 1000 operatic performances; with Met. Opera, N.Y.C., from 1950, sang 800 performances, 9 new prodns., 5 opening nights, 57 radio broadcasts, 4 telecasts including appeared on Met. Opera: In Performance, 1982, 83, 84, 85, 86, 87, 88, 90, 91; recorded Pagliacci, 1951, 60; singer with New Orleans, Hartford, Pitts., Central City operas, 1952-54, appeared Glyndebourne Opera, 1954, 55, 57, 58, Edinburgh Festival, 1954, Aida, Terme Di Caracalla, Rome, 1954, also Stockholm Opera, N.Y. Philharm., St. Louis Civic Light Opera, 1955-56; has appeared in leading or title roles in several operas including: Tosca, Aida, Amelia in Un Ballo in Maschera, Turandot, Riverside Opera Assn., 1986, others; appeared with St. Petersburg (Fla.) Opera, Venezuela Philharm. Orch., 1988, 93; opera and concert tour, USSR, 1965, 91, Manila, 1968, Paris, Mex., 1966, Hong Kong and China, 1983, Yugoslavia, 1988; rec. artist, Columbia, RCA, Victor, Angel records, Met. Opera Record Club; albums include: Beethoven's Symphony No. 9, Leoncavallo's, I Pagliacci, Puccini's La Bohème, Verdi Requiem. Recipient 1st prize Atwater-Kent Radio Auditions, 1948; inducted to Acad. Vocal Arts Hall Fame, 1989. E-mail: lamara@nyc.rr.com. *My life has been filled with new experiences. I have been most fortunate to have achieved a career that has introduced me to so many wonderful people. Some have become close friends; others, because of time and distance, have become warm acquaintances. I am humbly grateful for all God's blessings.*

AMARA, SUSAN, neuroscientist; BS, Stanford U.; PhD in Physiology and Pharmacology, U. Calif., San Diego, 1983. Sr. scientist Vollum Inst.; investigator Howard Hughes Med. Inst.; prof. Oreg. Health Sci. U.; Thomas Detre prof., chair, dept. neurobiology Pitts. Sch. Medicine, U. Pitts., 2003—. Mem.: Dana Alliance Brain Initiatives, Soc. Neurosci., NAS. Office: Univ Pitts Dept Neurobiology E1440 Biomedical Sci Tower 3500 Terrace Pittsburgh PA 15261 Business E-Mail: amaras@pitt.edu.

AMARAL, ANDRE RENATO SALES, education educator, researcher; b. Vitoria, Espirito Santo, Brazil, Mar. 22, 1969; s. Arides and Terezinha Sales Amaral. BSc in Elec. Engring., Fed.U. Espirito Santo, Brazil, 1990, MSc in Elec. Engring., 1993; PhD in Mgmt. Sci., Lancaster U., England, 1999. Prof. U. Fed. Espirito Santo, Vitoria, 2000—06; rschr. Rutgers U., Piscataway, NJ, 2006—. Grantee, Brazil Rsch. Coun., 2000—02, 2003—06. Achievements include research in polyhedral approach to linear arrangement problems; analysis of upper bounds for the pallet loading problem; development of system for allocation of ships in a port in Brazil; efficient algorithms for a number of graph optimization problems. Office: Rutgers Univ 640 Bartholomew Rd Piscataway NJ 08854-8003 Business E-Mail: amaral@rutcor.rutgers.edu.

AMARAL, JOSEPH FERREIRA, surgeon; b. Pawtucket, RI, Aug. 9, 1955; s. Joseph and Rosa (Ferreira) A.; m. Linda Watson, June 6, 1981; children: Courtney, Ashley, Gregory. BS in Biology summa cum laude, Providence Coll., 1977; MD, Brown U., 1981. Diplomate Am. Bd. Surgery, Am. Bd. Med. Examiners. Intern R.I. Hosp., Providence, 1981-82, resident, 1982-83; surg. rsch. fellow Brown U./R.I. Hosp., Providence, 1983-86; sr. surg. resident R.I. Hosp., Providence, 1986-88, adminstrv. chief surg. resident, 1988-89, coord. surg. residency, asst. surgeon, asst. prof. Brown U., 1989-91, coord. surg. residencey, dir. laparoscopic surgery, 1991-92, dir. laparoscopic surgery, asst. surgeon, asst. prof., 1991-93, assoc. prof., surgeon, 1993-98, prof., 1998—, pres., CEO, 2000—. Treas. R.I. Hosp. Staff Assn., 1991-93; sec. R.I. Hosp. Surg. Found., 1992—; bd. dirs. R.I. Hosp. PHO; vis. surgeon hosps. in Australia, Argentina, Portugal, Austria, Rome, Singapore and Brazil. Contbr. articles to numerous profl. jours.; numerous internat., nat. and regional presentations; various scientific exhibits. Recipient Merck Clin. Achievement award, 1981, Haffenraffer Surg. Rsch. fellowship, 1983-85, 16th ACS scholarship, 1984-86, Young Investigators award Shock Soc., 1986, Residents Rsch. award Surg. Infection Soc., 1986. Fellow ACS, Internat. Coll. Surgeons; mem. AMA, AAAS, R.I. Med. Soc., Providence Surg. Soc., New Eng. Surg. Soc., Soc. Laproendoscopic Surgeons, Assn. Surg. Edn., Ctrl. N.Y. Surg. Soc. (hon.), Soc. Minimally Invasive Therapy, Am. Soc. Gastrointestinal Endoscopy, Am. Biatric Soc., Surg. Infection Soc., N.Y. Acad. Scis., Wound Healing Soc., Am. Soc. Eternal and Parenteral Nutrition, Shock Soc., Assn. Acad. Surgeons, Brown Med. Alumni Assn., Sigma Xi, Phi Sigma Tau, Sigma Pi Sigma. Office: Univ Surg Assn Ste 470 2 Dudley St Providence RI 02905-3236 Business E-Mail: jfamaral@lifespan.org.

AMARELO, MONICA A., public relations executive, writer; BS, Syracuse U., NY, 1995. Comm. assoc., editor Portuguese Am. Leadership Coun. US, Washington, 1995—98; comm. mgr. Nat. Assn. Home Builders, Washington, 1998—2001; sr. comm. mgr. AAAS, Washington, 2001—04; dir. of comm. Fedn. Am. Scientists, Washington, 2005; founder and owner MAACOMM, Washington, 2004—. Mem.: DC Sci. Writers Assn. (bd. dirs. 2007). Office: Fedn Am Scientists 1717 K Street NW Washington DC 20036 Home Phone: 202-425-8776; Office Phone: 202-454-4680. Office Fax: 202-675-1010. Personal E-mail: monica_amarelo@yahoo.com. Business E-Mail: mamarelo@fas.org.

AMASINO, RICHARD M., plant physiologist; b. Pitts., May 11, 1956; s. Richard L. and Lucille H. (Patrick) A. BS, Pa. State U., 1977; PhD, Ind. U., 1982. Postdoctoral rschr. U. Wash., Seattle, 1982; faculty then prof. biochemistry U. Wis. Madison, 1985—. Mem. N.Am. arabidopsis steering com., 1996—99; editl. bd. Plant Physiology, 1997; bd. dirs. internat. soc. plant molecular biology, 1997—2000; editl. bd. Plant, Cell Environment, 1999; adv. bd. Plant Jour., 2001; prof. Howard Hughes Med. Inst., 2006—. Contbr. articles to profl. jours. Recipient Presdl. Young Investigator award, Nat. Sci. Found., 1989—94, Alexander von Humboldt Found. award, 1999. Mem. AAAS, Am. Soc. Plant Physiology, Am. Soc. Plant Biologists, NAS. Office: 215B Biochemistry Addition 433 Babcock Dr Madison WI 53706-1544

AMATO, DEBORAH DOUGLASS, aerospace engineer; b. Mo. d. Clyde and Wilma Douglass; m. Michael Amato, 1996. BS, MIT, 1994; MS, U. Md., 1998. Programmer Orbital Scis. Corp., Va., 1993; aerospace engr. NASA-Goddard Space Flight Ctr., Greenbelt, Md., 1993—. Mem.: AIAA. Avocations: music, swimming. Office: NASA Goddard Space Flight Ctr Greenbelt MD 20771-0001

AMATO, VINCENT VITO, marketing and business consultant; b. Bklyn., Oct. 14, 1929; s. Anthony and Josephine (Maniscalco) A.; m. Marie Dioguardi, Apr. 24, 1955; children— Stephanie, Janine, Anthony, Christopher. BBA, CCNY, 1951, MBA, 1958. Liaison to div. contr. Allied Chem. Corp., NYC, 1951-59; acctg. systems rep. Olivetti-Underwood, NYC, 1958-61; v.p. planning, contr., acquisitions exec. Ingredient Tech. SuCrest Corp., NYC, 1961-72, v.p. planning, treas., 1972-73, pres. splty. products, 1973-78; pres., owner Market Makers Inc., Woodbridge, NJ, 1978-97; owner Animated Computer Engring. Inc., Woodbridge, NJ, 1991-97; founder imadeadifference.com. Adj. asst. prof. NYU; presenter seminars Am. Mgmt. Assn.; mem. food sci. adv. bd. Rutgers U., 1988—, also adv. bd. Cook Coll. Rutgers U. Pres. Lakeridges Civic Assn. Mem. Fin. Execs. Inst., Assn. for Corp. Growth, Am. Mgmt. Assn. (tech. adviser) Home and Office: Vincent V Amato Mktg Consulting 7 Alder Ct Matawan NJ 07747-3717 Home Phone: 732-583-2599; Office Phone: 732-583-2599. Personal E-mail: vincemarie@aol.com.

AMATO CHIARAMONTE BORDONARO, BARON CARLO CAMILLO, ambassador, consultant; s. Giuseppe Michele Amato and Fernanda Giannini Paolini; m. Lorraine Manville-Dresselhouse, Feb. 22, 1959 (dec. June 1998); m. Irela Fabiola Lopez Fonseca, Nov. 16, 2003. Diploma Archaeology, Mex. U., U. Barcelona, Spain. Appraiser Assn. of Am., N.Y., 1978. Pres., founder Old World Internat., Canada, 1968—; asst. prof. biology Ga. State U., Athens, 1971—81; amb. Sovereign Mil. Order of Malta, Saint Vincent and the Grenadines, 1983—; pres., founder Old World Galleries, NYC, 1977—84; editor-at-large Conde.Nast Publs., Milan and Paris, 1984—91; dir. fgn. rels. Gesfid, Lugano, Switzerland, 1984—98, fin. mgr., 1984—94; mng. dir. Canouan Resort Devel. Co. Ltd, Saint Vincent and the Grenadines, 1994—98; min. plenipotentiary at large Republic of San Marino, 1983—2000. Author: (book) The Wild Boar: History Husbandry The Hunt; editor: (mag.) Artequia Internat., Harper-Bazaar. Named Man of Yr., World Inst. for Sci. Humanism, Fordham U., 1982; recipient Cert. of Appreciation, City of N.Y., 1977, Order of the Trinity, Imperial Ho. of Ethiopia, 1997, Knight of Real Cuerpo de la Nobleza de Madrid, Nobility of Castilla, 1998, Knight Comdr. of St. Maurice and Lazarus, The Savoy Order, 1999, Knight of Grace and Devotion of the Sacred Mil. Order of Malta, 2000. Fellow: Explorer Club; mem.: Knickerbocker Club. Roman Catholic. Avocations: landscaping, ecological research, cooking, gardening, enology.

AMATULI, ROBERT ALEXANDER, architect; b. NYC, May 30, 1957; s. A. James and Catherine Amatuli; m. Jeanne Marie Amatuli, Apr. 19, 1985; children: Robert Alexander II, Nicholas Brandon. BS in Archtl. Tech., NY Inst. Tech., 1979. Registered architect N.Y., Conn.; registered interior design, Conn. Dir. archtl. dept. United Artists Comm., Dallas, 1979—85, dir. east coast constrn. NYC, 1982; assoc., asst. office mgr. Page Southerland Page, Ft. Worth, 1985—87, assoc., prodn. coord. Dallas, 1987—95; v.p., dir. healthcare Gideon Toal Inc., Ft. Worth, 1995—99; sr. v.p., dir. ops., telecomm. Gideon Toal Fulwiler Oates, Ft. Worth, 1997—99; assoc., unit mgr. Carter & Burgess Inc., Hartford, Conn., 1999—2001; dir. health care design Tecton Archs., PC, Hartford, 2001—. Cons. JPS Archtl. Cons., Ft. Worth, 1996—. Recipient craftsmenship award Knights of Pythius, N.Y.C., 1972. Mem. AIA (design award Ft. Worth 1999). Avocations: golf, auto racing, hockey, basketball, ambulist. Office: Tecton Architects pc One Hartford Sq W Hartford CT 06106

AMBACH, DWIGHT RUSSELL, retired foreign service officer; b. Highland Park, Ill., Jan. 9, 1931; s. Russell William and Ethel (Repass) A.; m. Betsy Hunter, Aug. 27, 1955; children: Hunter MacKay, Nancy Cole, James Gordon. AB, Brown U., 1952; MA, Fletcher Sch., 1953; postgrad., MIT, 1963-64. Dep. dir. Office Regional Econ. Policy, Bur. Inter-Am. Affairs Dept. State, Washington, 1971-74; exec. asst. to chmn. Export-Import Bank, Washington, 1974-76, 84-86; counselor for econ. and comml. affairs Am. Embassy, Vienna, 1976-80; dean Fgn. Service Inst., Washington, 1980-84; office dir. Bur. Adminstrn. and Info. Services, 1986-88; cons., 1988-96; mem. Fgn. Svc. Res. Corps, 1995—2001. Pres. Montgomery County chpt. Md. Mcpl. League; bd. dirs. Mathews County Cmty. Found. Recipient Superior Honor award Dept. State, 1973; Disting. Service award Export-Import Bank, 1985 Mem. Am. Fgn. Service Assn., Am. Econ. Assn., Phi Beta Kappa Home: Aldendale PO Box 26 Susan VA 23163-0026

AMBACH, GORDON MAC KAY, educational association executive; b. Providence, Nov. 10, 1934; s. Russell W. and Ethel (Repass) A.; m. Lucy DeWitt Emory, Mar. 9, 1963; children: Kenneth Emory, Alison Repass, Douglas Mac Kay. BA, Yale U., 1956; MA, Harvard U. Grad. Sch. Edn., 1957, cert. advanced study, 1966. Tchr. social studies 7th and 8th grades East Williston Sch. Dist., LI, NY, 1958-61; asst. program planning officer US Office Edn., Washington, 1961-62, asst. legis. specialist, 1962-63, exec. sec. Higher Edn. Facilities Act Task Force, 1963-64; adminstrv. asst. to mem. Boston Sch. Com., 1964-65; mgr. staff seminar on Coleman study, 1965—66; mem. staff Harvard U. Grad. Sch. Edn., Cambridge, Mass., 1966—67; spl. asst. to commr. for long range planning NY State Edn. Dept., Albany, 1967-69, asst. commr. for long range planning, 1969-70, exec. dep. commr., 1970-77; commr. edn. and pres. U. of the State of NY, 1977-87; exec. dir. Coun. Chief State Sch. Officers, Washington, 1987—2001; ret., 2001. Del., chmn. resolutions com. The White House Conf. on Librs. and Info. Scis., 1991; mem. Nat. Coun. on Edn. Stds. and Testing, 1993; mem. edn. com. Nat. Alliance for Bus., 1994-2001; mem. Nat. Bd. Internat. Comparative Studies in Edn., US rep. to Internat. Assn. for Evaluation of Edn. Achievement, mem. standing com., 1990-2001; bd. dirs. Wallace Found., Newspaper Assn. Am. Found., Ctr. for Naval Analysis Corp.; mem. edn. bd. NAS. With USAR, 1957-63. Mem. Acad. Polit. Scis., Am. Assn. Sch. Adminstrs., PEW Forum on Edn. Reform, Phi Delta Kappa.

AMBADY, NALINI, social psychologist, educator, researcher; b. Calcutta, India; came to U.S., 1983; d. Shanker and Viji Ambady; m. Raj Marphatia, June 8, 1988; children: Maya Mallika, Leena Anupama. PhD, Harvard U., 1991. Asst. prof. Holy Cross Coll., Worcester, Mass., 1993-94, Harvard U., Cambridge, Mass., 1994-99, Ruth and John Hazel assoc. prof. social sci., 1999—2004; prof., social psychology Tufts U., Medford, Mass., 2004—. Recipient, Behavioral Sci. Rsch. prize AAAS, 1993, Presdl. Early Career award U.S. Govt., 1998, Excellence in Mentoring Award, Harvard U., 2000. Office: Tufts U The Psychology Bldg 490 Boston Ave Medford MA 02155 E-mail: naliniambady@tufts.edu.

AMBALAVANAN, SIVA, nephrologist, educator; b. Madras, India, Nov. 26, 1962; arrived in U.S., 1993; d. A. and Sundari Sivasankaran; m. Geetha Ambalavanan, Aug. 22, 1991; children: Anita, Manoj. MB, BS, Madras Med. Coll., 1985. Cert. nephrology, internal medicine, Fed. Lic. Exam., Ednl. Commn. Fgn. Med. Grads. Tutor in medicine U. Aberdeen, Scotland, 1990—92; fellow Stanford U. Med. Ctr., 1993—95; physician VA Med. Ctr., Salt Lake City, 1996—97; resident Med. Ctr. U. Utah, Salt Lake City, 1996—97, asst. prof. medicine, cons. nephrologist Sch. Medicine, 1996—98. asst. prof. medicine Wright State U., Dayton, Ohio, 1998—; adj. prof. U. Utah; mem. transfusion com. Fransiscan Med. Ctr., 1999—2000; mem. transplant com. Miami Valley Hosp. Contbr. articles to profl. jours. Active Hindu Cmty. Orgn., Dayton, Ohio, 1999. Recipient Trainee Investigator award for excellence in sci. rsch., Clin. Rsch. Meeting, 1995; grantee, Allan Evan. Fellow: Royal Coll. Physicians; mem.: AMA, ACP. Avocations: golf, travel, cooking, music. Office: Renal Physician Inc 1427 Business Ctr Dayton OH 45410 Office Phone: 937-254-0161.

AMBER, DOUGLAS GEORGE, lawyer; b. East Chicago, Ind., Apr. 15, 1956; s. George and Margaret (Watson) A. BA in Polit. Sci., Ind. U., 1978; JD, U. Miami, 1985. Bar: Fla. 1985, US. Ct. Claims 1986, U.S. Ct. Internat. Trade 1986, U.S. Tax Ct. 1986, U.S. Ct. Appeals (11th cir.) 1986, U.S. Dist. Ct. (mid. and so. dists.) Fla. 1987, U.S. Ct. Mil. Appeals 1987, U.S. Ct. Appeals (fed. cir.) 1987, Ind. 1988, U.S. Dist. Ct. (no. and so. dists.) Ind. 1988, U.S. Ct. Appeals (7th cir.) 1989, U.S. Supreme Ct. 1989; Ind. Registered Civil Mediator. Dep. prosecutor 31st Jud. Cir. Ind., Crown Point, 1988-93; pvt. practice Munster, 1993—. Adj. prof. polit. sci. Purdue U., 1997—. Mem. exec. bd. dirs. Calumet coun. Boy Scouts Am., 1994-96; apptd. Ind. State Pub. Defenders Coun., 2001—. Mem. Ind. State Bar Assn., Lake County Bar Assn. (bd. dirs. 1990-96), Mensa, Delta Theta Phi. Avocations: bicycling, weight training. Office: Amber Golding & Hofstetter 9250 Columbia Ave Ste E-2 Munster IN 46321-3530 Office Phone: 219-836-8530. E-mail: amber@calumet.purdue.edu.

AMBER, LAURIE KAUFMAN, lawyer; b. NYC, Apr. 15, 1954; d. Martin and Barbara (Schiffman) Kaufman; m. Henry Michael Amber, June 18, 1977; children: Ian, Kyle. BS, Cornell U., 1974, MBA, 1975; JD, U. Miami, 1978. Bar: Fla. 1978, U.S. Dist. Ct. (so. dist.) Fla. 1978, U.S. Tax Ct. 1978, U.S. Ct. Appeals (5th cir.) 1979, U.S. Ct. Customs and Patent Appeals 1979, U.S. Customs Ct. 1979, U.S. Ct. Appeals (11th cir.) 1981, U.S. Ct. Internat. Trade 1981, U.S. Supreme Ct. 1982, U.S. Claims Ct. 1985; cert. civil circuit mediator Supreme Ct. Fla.; cert. family mediator Supreme Ct. Fla. Staff mgr. Proctor & Gamble Mfg. Co., Staten Island, N.Y., 1975; adj. asst. prof. Nova U., Fort Lauderdale, Fla., 1976-77; atty., labor arbitrator Amber & Amber, P.A., South Miami, Fla., 1978—. Arbitrator nat. labor panel Am. Arbitration Assn., Miami, 1982—, Grievance Arbitration Panel of Fla. PERC, Tallahassee, 1979—; hearing examiner pers. appeals County of Dade, Miami, 1985-91, 2000—; bd. dirs. Kids That Care Pediat. Cancer Fund, Fla. Lawyers' Legal Ins. Corp. Pres. Office Village Condominium Assn., South Miami, 1994, Children's Cancer Fund, 1996-2000; bd. dirs. Jackson Meml. Found., 1996-2000, Kids That Care Pediatric and Cancer Fund, 2000—. Named Woman of Yr. ABWA, 1983. Mem. ABA, Zonta (bd. dirs. Coral Gables, Fla. club 1988). Office: Amber & Amber PA 7731 SW 62nd Ave Ste 202 Miami FL 33143-4908 Office Phone: 305-661-5629.

AMBERG, THOMAS L., public relations executive; b. Glen Cove, NY, Apr. 13, 1948; s. Richard Hiller Amberg and Janet Law Volkman; m. Tauna Urban, June 19, 1971 (div. Jan. 1980); children: Edward, Robert; m. Kathy Stewart, Oct. 9, 1982; 1 child, Thomas Jr. BA, Colgate U., 1971; MBA, U. Mo., St. Louis, 1980. Reporter, editor St. Louis Globe-Democrat, 1971-83; pres., coo Aaron D. Cushman and Assocs., Chgo., 1991—; pres. Cushman Amberg Comms., Chgo. Mem. adv. bd. Salvation Army, St. Louis, 1986-91, Chgo., 1992—, pres., 1995-2003; bd. dirs. Wishing Well Found., St. Louis, 1985-91, Hope Ctr., St. Louis, 1985-91; bd. trustees St. Patrick's Sch., Chgo., 1994-2001. Recipient Disting. Achievement award Inland Daily Press Assn., 1978, 82, Frank Kelly Meml. award, 1980, Gavel award ABA, 1983, Unity awards in Media Lincoln U., 1984. Mem. Mental Health Assn. St. Louis (pres. 1987-88), Pub. Rels. Soc. Am., Press Club Met. St. Louis (pres. 1981-83), Internat. Assn. Bus. Communicators, Soc. Am. Travel Writers. Presbyterian. Home: 1783 Bowling Green Dr Lake Forest IL 60045-3559 Office: Cushman Amberg Comms 180 N Michigan Ave Ste 1600 Chicago IL 60601-7478

AMBERSOUND, ROCHELLE LILLIAN, retired social worker; d. Theodore Miller and Bernice Piltch-Miller, adopted d. Samuel Goldstein and Marien Mae Balikov; children: Aaron P. Lieberman, Jacob M. Lieberman. BA cum laude, UCLA, 1967. Social worker in child abuse LA Dept. Pub. Social Svcs., 1967—79, Orange County Social Svcs. Agy., Calif., 1979—2000, social svcs. supr., 2000—05; ret. Mem. representing LA County Dept. Pub. Social Svcs. West Area Cmty. Action Coun., US OEO, Venice, Calif., 1968—70; mem. steering com. Family Addictions Crisis Terminal, 1969—71; mem. youth adv. com. Alcoholism Coun. San Fernando Valley, Calif., 1970—75; rsch. asst. U. Calif., San Diego, prof., 1970—72, cross-trainer Law Sch. Clin. Legal Program, LA, 1972—74; child abuse multidisiplinary symposia presenter, crosstrainer, 1976—79; instr., foster parent educator ABC Unified Sch. Dist., Norwalk, Calif., 1976—77, foster parent educator, 1976—77; mem. forms revision com. Orange County Social Svcs. Agy., Orange, 1982—85, mem. quality assurance com., 1984—86, mem. contracts proposal evaluation com., 1987, 93, 98, mem. caseload mgmt. forum, 1989—2000, mem. foster care coordination coun., 2000—03, mem. foster parent utilization rev. com., 2000—03, apty. liaison to human svcs., 2003—05, chair biligual social worker language-fluency qualifying exam. standardization com., 2003—05, spkrs. bur. coord., 2003—05; vice-chair, inter-agency case mgmt. rev. team Tustin Acts for Families and Youth, Tustin, 1996—2000, mem. exec. com., 1997—2000. Mem. Ad Hoc Com. for Day Care in Irvine, Calif., 1978—80; course developer Osher Lifelong Learning Inst., U. Calif, Irvine, Ext. Divsn., 2006—, mem. arts and humanities curriculum devel. com., 2006—, vol. course facilitator, 2006—; mem. intergroup rels. com. Anti-Defamation League Orange County and Long Beach, Costa Mesa, Calif.; mem. ann. cmty. Jewish art show planning com. Shir Ha-Ma'alot Synagogue, Newport Beach, Calif., 1985—87; vol. art tchr. Purim camp Bur. Jewish Edn., Costa Mesa, Calif., 1986; vol. tchr./spl. project developer Shir Ha-Ma'alot Synagogue, Newport Beach, 1988—89; mem. Kol HaNeshemah Synagogue, Irvine, Calif.; mem. congregation Shir Ha-Maalot, 2007; cmty. alternative dispute mediator Cmty. Services Program, Irvine, 1998—; vol. tchr. ESL for fgn.-born adults South Coast Literacy Coun., Capistrano Beach, Calif., 1999—2004; mem. Jewish-Latino Roundtable Anti-Defamation League of Orange County and Long Beach, Costa Mesa, Calif., 2006—. Finalist Gamoran Curriculum award, Nat. Assn. Temple Educators, Union for Reform Judaism, 1989. Mem.: Irvine Multi-Cultural Assn., Lifelong Learning Inst., South Coast Literacy Coun., Congregation Kol HaNeshemah, Pi Gamma Mu. Jewish. Avocations: designing and crafting character dolls, travel, creative writing, reading, theater.

AMBIZAS, EMILY MARGUERITE, pharmacist, educator; b. Jamaica, NY, Aug. 20, 1977; d. Joseph Henry and Chieko Arweiler; m. Alberto Harry Ambizas, Oct. 11, 2003; 1 child, Athena Marie. BS in Pharmacy, St. John's U., Queens, NY, 2000, PharmD, 2002. Asst. clin. prof. St. John's U., Queens, 2003—. Mem.: NY State Coun. Health Sys. Pharmacists, Pharmacist Soc. State NY, Am. Assn. Colls. Pharmacy, Am. Pharmacists Assn., Am. Coll. Allergy, Asthma and Immunology, Acad. Allergy, Asthma and Immunology. Office: St Johns Univ 8000 Utopia Pky Jamaica NY 11439 Home Phone: 516-679-1477; Office Phone: 718-990-2753. Office Fax: 718-990-1986. Personal E-mail: arweilem@aol.com. Business E-Mail: arweilee@stjohns.edu.

AMBOIAN, JOHN PETER, JR., investment company executive; b. 1961; m. Ann Amboian; 3 children. BS in Econs., U. Chgo., 1983, MBA, 1984. Various fin. positions Philip Morris Cos., Kraft Foods, Inc.; CFO, sr. v.p. fin., strategy & sys. Miller Brewing Co.; exec. v.p., CFO Nuveen Investments, Inc., Chgo., 1995—98, pres., 1999—2007, CEO, 2007—. Mem. fin. com. Chgo. Humanities Festival, bd. governance and mem. nominating com.; bd. dirs. Boys and Girls Clubs Chgo., N. Shore Country Day Sch., Children's Meml. Hosp. Office: Nuveen Investments Inc 333 W Wacker Dr Chicago IL 60606*

AMBORSKI, LEONARD EDWARD, retired chemist; b. Buffalo, Aug. 23, 1921; s. Nicholas Leon and Angeline (Laskowska) A.; m. Irene Kazmierczak, Oct. 3, 1944; children: Donna Marie, David Paul. BS, Canisius Coll., 1943; MA, SUNY, Buffalo, 1949, PhD, 1951. Cert. indsl. hygienist Am. Bd. Indsl. Hygiene; cert. EPA instr. in lead abatement and hazardous materials worker tng. Instr. physics Canisius Coll., 1943-44; physicist Carnegie Mellon Inst., Washington, 1944-45; with E.I. DuPont de Nemours & Co., Buffalo, 1945-90, staff scientist, 1973-90, environ. health cons., 1973-90; cons. in environ. health, 1990—. Rsch. assoc. Toxicoloty Rsch. Ctr., SUNY, Buffalo. Patentee in field. Bd. dirs. Am. Lung Assn. of N.Y. State, Buffalo, 1985—; chmn. Tonawanda (N.Y.) Citizen Pre-Treatment Program, 1985-86, Tonawanda Hazardous Materials Adv. Com., Buffalo, 1985-88; chmn. local emergency planning commn. Buffalo and Erie County, N.Y., 1988—; mem. citizens adv. com. Remedial Action Plan for Niagara River Recipient Indsl. and Hazardous Waste award N.Y. State Water Pollution Control Assn., 1989. Mem. Air Pollution Control Assn. (chmn. 1983-84, Svc. award 1984), Am. Chem. Soc., Am. Indsl. Hygiene Assn., Am. Bd. Indsl. Hygiene, Am. Pub. Health Assn., Am. Soc. Safety Engrs., Water Pollution Control Fedn. Republican. Roman Catholic. Avocations: photography, swimming, bicycling. Home: 62 Wedgewood Dr Buffalo NY 14221-1469 E-mail: lamborski@webtv.net.

AMBRIZ, LORELY, library and information scientist; b. Mexico; MS in Libr. and Info. Sci., U. Tex., Austin, 2004. Health reporter, editor, prodr. Univision TV; libr. Info. & Knowledge Mgmt. Ctr. Pan Am. Health Orgn. Named one of the Movers & Shakers, Libr. Jour., 2007. Mem.: Tex. Libr. Assn. (mem. pub. relations com.). Mailing: Librarian Documentation Ctr Pan American Health Orgn 5400 Suncrest C-4 El Paso TX 79912 Office Phone: 915-845-5950. Office Fax: 915-845-4361. E-mail: ambrizlo@feb.paho.org.

AMBRO, THOMAS L., federal judge; b. Cambridge, Ohio, Dec. 27, 1949; BA, Georgetown U., 1971, JD, 1975. Bar: Del. 1976. Clk. Hon. Daniel L. Herrmann Del. Supreme Ct., 1975—76; assoc. Richards, Layton and Finger, 1976—82, ptnr., 1982—2000; judge US Ct. Appeals (3d cir.), 2000—. Mem. NY TriBar Opinion Com., 1988—. Author: Third Party Legal Opinions in Asset Based Financing: A Transactional Guide, 1990; contbr. articles to profl. jours. Mem.: ABA (vice-chair com. on programs 1987—90, chair com. on meetings 1988—90, participant Silverado Conf. on Legal Opinions 1989, mem. drafting subcom. third-party legal opinion report 1989—91, chair subcom. on opinion letters 1989—95, mem. com. on comml. fin. svcs. 1989—95, chair com. on meetings 1990—94, chair or co-chair com. on publs. 1994—97, chair com. on legal opinions 1994—98, mem. coun. sect. bus. law 1994—98, editl. bd. The Bus. Lawyer 1998—99, editor The Bus. Lawyer 1999—2000, vice-chair sect. bus. law 1999—2000, chair elect bus. law 2000—01, chair sec. bus. law 2001—02, sec. sect. bus. law 1998-99, immediate past chmn. 2002—03, mem. com. on uniform comml. code, mem. com. on negotiated acquisitions, mem. bus. bankruptcy com.), Am. Law Inst., Am. Coll. Comml. Fin. Lawyers, Am. Coll. Bankruptcy, Del. State Bar Assn. (chmn. 1979—82, vice-chmn. 1982—83, comml. law sect., chair subcom. on uniform comml. code 1983—2003), Phi Beta Kappa. Office: J Caleb Boggs Federal Courthouse 844 N King St Wilmington DE 19801 E-mail: judge.thomas.ambro@ca3.uscourts.gov.*

AMBROS, VICTOR R., geneticist, educator; SB in Biology, MIT, Cambridge, 1975, PhD in Biology, 1979. Postdoctoral fellow MIT, 1979—83; faculty mem. dept. cellular and devel. biology Harvard U., 1984—92; faculty mem. to prof. genetics Dartmouth Med. Sch., Hanover, NH, 1992—. Contbr. articles to sci. jours. Co-recipient Newcomb Cleve. prize, AAAS, 2002; recipient Lewis S. Rosenstiel award for Disting. Work in Basic Med. Rsch., Brandeis U., 2005, Genetics Soc. Am. medal, 2006. Mem.: NAS. Office: Dept Genetics Dartmouth Med Sch HB 7400 Hanover NH 03755 Office Phone: 603-650-1939. Office Fax: 603-650-1188. E-mail: Victor.R.Ambros@Dartmouth.EDU.

AMBROSE, DANIEL MICHAEL, publishing executive; b. Salem, Oreg., Nov. 1, 1955; s. Franklin Burnell and Jean Marie (Crakes) A.; m. Cynthia Barbara Friedman, Mar. 26, 1983; children: Robert Grant, Michael Bruce. BS in Polit. Sci., Lewis and Clark Coll., 1977. Mktg. mgr. Washington Monthly, 1978-79; advt. promotion mgr. Am. Film Mag., Washington, 1979-80, advt. mgr., 1980-81, advt. dir., 1981-83, Backpacker Mag., NYC, 1983-84; advt. salesman House Beautiful, Hearst Mag., NYC, 1984-85; corp. advt. dir. mag. div. Hearst Pub. Corp., NYC, 1985-87; pub. Fathers Mag., NYC, 1987-89; advt. dir. Cahners Pub. Co., NYC, 1989-92; pub. Child Mag. Network Women's Mag. div. N.Y. Times Co., NYC, 1992-94; mng. dir. ambro.com., NYC, 1994—, DeSilva & Phillips Media Investment Bankers, NYC, 1998—2003. Media cons., investments and sales, N.Y.C., 1994—; presenter Mag. Pubs. Am.; bd. mem. Guard Pub. Co., 2005—; bd. dirs. Kaboose, Inc. Contbr. articles on mag. mgmt. to Folio mag. Chmn. bd. Kidsports, 2002—03. Avocations: book collecting, skiing, triathlons.

AMBROSE, DONETTA W., federal judge; b. New Kensington, Nov. 5, 1945; m. J. Raymond Ambrose Jr., Aug. 19, 1972; 1 child. BA, Duquesne U., 1963-67, JD cum laude, 1967-70. Law clerk to Hon. Louis L. Manderino Commonwealth Ct. Pa., 1970-71, Supreme Ct. Pa., 1972; asst. atty. gen. Pa. Dept. Justice, 1972-74; pvt. practice atty. Ambrose & Ambrose, Kensington, Pa., 1974-81; asst. dist. atty. Westmoreland County, Pa., 1977-81; judge Ct. Common Pleas Westmoreland County, 1982-93, US Dist. Ct. (We. Dist.) Pa., Pitts., 1994—, chief judge. Resident advisor Duquesne U., 1967-70. Scholar Pa. Conf. State Trial Judges, 1992, State Justice Inst., 1993. Mem. ABA, Nat. Assn. Women Judges, Am. Judicature Soc., Pa. Bar Assn., Women's Bar Assn. Western Pa., Pa. Conf. State Trial Judges (sec. 1992-93), Westmoreland County Bar Assn., Italian Sons and Daus. Am., William Penn Fraternal Assn., New Kensington Women's Club, Delta Kappa Gamma. Office: US Courthouse Office 700 Grant St Rm 307 Pittsburgh PA 15219-1906

AMBROSE, JUDITH ANN, retired wedding and floral designer; b. San Jose, Calif., Oct. 22, 1940; d. Howard Linse and Beula May (Russell) Shannon; m. James Paul Ambrose, Apr. 17, 1965; children: Sheryl Ann Beckey, James Paul Jr. BS, Salem Coll., Winston-Salem, NC, 1962; postgrad., Purdue U., 1963—64. Lic. home econs. tchr. Fla., NC. Home econs. tchr. Broward County, Ft. Lauderdale, Fla., 1962—67; owner Decorative Accents, Ft. Lauderdale, 1984—99; wedding coord. Christ Ch. United Meth., Ft. Lauderdale, 1990—2004; ret., 2004. Home econs. curriculum dir. Broward County Schs., Ft. Lauderdale, 1965—66. Pres. Parent Tchr. Fellowship Westminster Acad., 1982—83; mem. resource group Children's Diagnostic and Treatment Ctr., Ft. Lauderdale, 1997—2003, bd. dirs., 2001—, sec. bd. dirs., 2003—07, interim co-chair Sunflower Cir. of Friends, 2004; founder Friends of Jack & Jill Nursery, Ft. Lauderdale; organizer shoe fund for children in cmty. Christ Meth. Ch., 1992—; mem. Pres's Coun. Ft. Lauderdale, 1989; bd. dirs. Jack & Jill Nursery Sch., Ft. Lauderdale, 1974—2000; mem. Beaux Arts, 1986—90. Recipient Outstanding Cmty. Svc. award, Jr. League of Ft. Lauderdale, 1989, Golden Rule award, J C Penney, Ft. Lauderdale, 1995, Heart of the Cmty. Vol. of Yr. award, Children's Diagnostic and Treatment Ctr., Broward, Fla., 2002, 2005. Mem.: AAUW, Charity Guild (chmn. fall function 1992, publicity chmn. 1993—96, chmn. fall function 1997, pres. 1998—99, bd. dirs. 2001—03, rep. to Kids in Distress), Coral Ridge Jr. Women's Club (hon.; past pres., Clubwoman of Yr. 1975—76). Republican. Methodist. Avocations: growing orchids, volunteer work. Home: 4720 NE 25th Ave Fort Lauderdale FL 33308-4811

AMBROSE, LAUREN (LAUREN ANNE D'AMBRUOSO), actress; b. New Haven, Conn., Nov. 16, 1978; d. Frank and Annie Ambrose; m. Sam Handel, 2001; 1 child, Orson. Attended, Conn. Ednl. Ctr. Arts, Tanglewood Inst., Boston U., Yale U.; classically trained opera singer. Actor(guest appearances): (TV series) Law & Order, 1992—98, Party of Five, 1999, Saving Graces, 1999, Six Feet Under, 2001—05 (Emmy nom. Supporting Actress Drama, 2003); (plays, off-Broadway) Soulful Scream of a Chosen Son, 1992; (plays, Nat. Theatre) Buried Child, 2004; (Broadway plays) Awake and Sing!, 2006; (films) In & Out, 1997, Can't Hardly Wait, 1998, Summertime's Calling Me, 1998, Psycho Beach Party, 2000, Swimming, 2000. Office: c/o United Talent Agency 9560 Wilshire Blvd Ste 500 Beverly Hills CA 90212

AMBROSE, MYLES JOSEPH, lawyer; b. NYC, July 21, 1926; s Arthur P. and Ann (Campbell) A.; m. Elaine Miller, June 26, 1948 (dec. Sept. 1975); children: Myles Joseph, Kathleen Anne, Kevin Arthur, Elise Mary, Nora Jeanne, Christopher Miller; m. Lorraine Genovese, June 3, 1994. Grad., New Hampton Sch., NH, 1944; BBA, Manhattan Coll., 1948, LLD (hon.), 1972; JD, NY Law Sch., 1952. Bar: NY 1952, US Supreme Ct. 1969, DC 1973, US Ct. Appeals (fed. cir.) 1970, US Ct. Internat. Trade 1970, DC Ct. Appeals 1973. Pers. mgr. Devenco, Inc., 1948-49, 51-54; adminstrv. asst. US atty. So. dist., NY, 1954-57; instr. econs. and indsl. rels. Manhattan Coll., 1955-57; asst. to sec. US Treasury, 1957-60; exec. dir. Waterfront Commn. of N.Y. Harbor, 1960-63; pvt. practice law NYC, 1963-69; chief counsel NY State Joint Legislative Com. for Study Alcoholic Beverage Control Law, 1963-65; U.S. commr. customs Washington, 1969-72; spl. cons. to Pres., spl. asst. atty. gen., 1972-73; ptnr. Spear & Hill, 1973-75, Ambrose & Casselman, P.C., 1975—78, O'Connor & Hannan, Washington, 1978—88, Ross and Hardies, Washington, 1988—98; of counsel Arter & Hadden, Washington, 1998—2002; currently sr. advisor Sandler Travis Trade Adv. Svc. US observer 13th session UN Commn. on Narcotics, Geneva, Switzerland, 1958; chmn. US del. 27th Gen. Assembly, Internat. Criminal Police Orgn., London, 1958, 28th Extraordinary Gen. Assembly, Paris, 1959; US observer 29th Gen. Assembly, Washington, 1960; mem. US del., Mexico City, 1969, Brussels, 1970, Ottawa, 1971, Frankfurt, 1972; chmn. US-Mexico Conf. on Narcotics, Washington, 1960, mem. confs., Washington and; Mexico City, 1969, 70, 71, 72; chmn. US-Canadian-Mexican Conf. on Customs Procedures, San Clemente, Calif., 1970; chmn. US del. Customs Cooperation Coun., Brussels, 1970; chmn., Vienna, 1971, US-European Customs Conf. Narcotics, Paris and; Vienna, 1971; organized Drug Enforcement Adminstrn. (DEA), 1973; hon. consul Principality of Monaco, Washington, 1973-98; mem. adv. com. on customs comml. ops. US Treasury Dept., 1988-91; past chmn. ABA standing com. on customs law. Author: Primer on Customs Law. Bd. dirs. U. Coll. of Dublin-Grad. Bus. Sch., 1996-2001; bd. mem. Daytop Village, 1973—; vice-chmn. Reagan-Bush Inaugural Com., 1980; mem. adv. bd. Eisenhower Inst. of World Affairs. Decorated chevalier Order of Grimaldi (Monaco), knight comdr. Order of Merit Italian Republic, Knight of the Holy Sepulchre; recipient Presdl. Mgmt. Improvement cert. Pres. Nixon, 1970, Sec. Treasury Exceptional Svc. award, 1970, Disting. Alumnus award NY Law Sch., 1973, Alumni award for pub. svc. Manhattan Coll., 1972 Fellow Am. Bar Found.; mem. Friendly Sons of St. Patrick, Univ. Club (DC), Alpha Sigma Beta, Phi Alpha Delta (hon.) Republican. Roman Catholic. Home: #912 19375 Cypress Ridge Ter Leesburg VA 20176-5182 Office: Sandler Travis Trade Adv Svc 1300 Penn Ave Washington DC 20004-9307 Personal E-mail: ballyeagna@aol.com.

AMBROSE, THOMAS WILLIAM, retired broadcast executive; b. Mpls., Feb. 11, 1946; s. Leo Joseph and Mary (Girling) A.; m. Kathryn Marie Murphy, June 28, 1969; 1 child, Timothy Thomas. BA, U. Minn., 1969. Announcer Sta. WCCO-TV, Mpls., 1969-73; program mgr. Sta. WCCO-FM, Mpls., 1973-82; ops. mgr. Sta. WAYL-FM, Mpls., 1982-84, Sta. KSSS, Mpls., 1982-84; v.p. MNN Radio Networks Inc, St. Paul, 1984-93; pres., COO, vice-chmn. bd. dirs. SportsAmerica Radio Network, Mpls., 1993—; ret., 2004. Mem. alumni bd. dirs. St. John's U., Collegeville, Minn., 1985--. Mem. Nat. Assn. State Radio Networks, AFTRA, Advt. Fedn. (bd. dirs. Mpls. 1984--), Alpha Epsilon Rho, Psi Upsilon. Republican. Roman Catholic. Home: 3657 W Broadway Ave Minneapolis MN 55422-2333 Office Phone: 612-296-7845.

AMBROSE, TOMMY W., chemical engineer, engineering executive; b. Jerome, Idaho, Oct. 14, 1926; s. Fines M. and Avice (Barnes) A.; m. Shirley Ann Ball, June 23, 1951; children: Leslie Ann, Julie Lynn, Pamela Lee. BS, U. Idaho, 1950, MS, 1951, PhD (hon.), 1981; PhD, Oreg. State U., 1957. Registered profl. engr., Wash., Ohio, Idaho. Engr. GE, Richland, Wash., 1951-54, 57-60, supr. reactor fuels, 1960-63, mgr. process and reactor devel., 1963-65, mgr. rsch. and engring., 1965; mgr. for rsch. and engring. Douglas United Nuclear Co., Richland, 1969-71; asst. dir. Battelle Seattle Rsch. Ctr., 1969-71, exec. dir., 1971-75; dir. Battelle Pacific N.W. Labs., Richland, 1975-79; corp. dir. multicomponent ops. Battelle Meml. Inst., Columbus, Ohio, 1979-88, dir. Battelle Edn. and Tng. Bus., 1988-90, v.p., 1975-90; liaison officer Lawrence Livermore (Calif.) Nat. Lab., 1990-91; spl. asst. lab. affairs U. Calif., Oakland, 1992-96. Adj. prof. grad. level Idaho State U. Coll. Engring., 1998—. Mem. adv. bd. Coll. Engring., U. Idaho, Moscow, 1974-83, 85-91, chmn. adv. bd., 1988-91, 96—; mem. vis. com. Coll. Engring., U. Wash., 1974-83; adj. prof. grad. level Idaho State U. Coll. Engring., 1998-, mem. adv. coun., 1999—; mem. gov.'s adv. coun. Dept. Commerce and Econ. Devel., 1975-79; mem. Wash. State Coun. Postsecondary Edn., 1977-79; chmn. bd. trustees Columbia Basin Coll., 1967-69; bd. dirs. N.W.Coll., U. Assn. for Sci., 1976-79; v.p., trustee, mem. exec. com. Pacific Sci. Ctr. Found.; trustee, mem. exec. com. Columbus Symphony Orch., 1980-84; trustee Ohio Wesleyan U., 1987-91; bd. dirs. Idaho State Civic Symphony, 1999—, pres., 2000-01; mem. Gov.'s Sci. and Tech. Coun. for Idaho, 1999—; mem. adv. bd. Natural Heritage Ctr., 1998—2002; bd. dirs. U. Idaho Found., 1996-2002; chmn. Mayor's Sci. Adv. Coun., Pocatello, Idaho. Recipient Profl. Achievement award Idaho State U. Coll. Engring., 2000; inductee Oreg. State U. Coll. Engring. Hall of Fame, 2001. Fellow AICE (chmn. comms. com. mgmt. divsn. 1981-87, program evaluator and mem. Accreditation Bd. for Engring. and Tech. engring. accreditation commn. 1989-96); mem. Am. Nuclear Soc., Ohio Acad. Sci., Sigma Xi (George Bigalow award), Pi Lambda Upsilon. Methodist. Home: 2500 Spider Creek Inkom ID 83245-1740

AMBROSE, WILLIAM WRIGHT, JR., dean, educator, academic administrator; b. Norfolk, Va., Oct. 13, 1947; s. William Wright and Charlotte Gertrude (Williamson) Ambrose; m. Marcelia A. Conerly, Aug. 7, 1971 (div. Dec. 1986); children: William Wright III, Xandrea M., Mark S., Ariana R., LaConda G. Fanning; m. Jacqueline D. Woodard, Dec. 28, 1998. BSBA, Norfolk State U., 1974; MBA, Pepperdine U., postgrad. in EdD program. Enrolled agt. IRS; lic. ins. broker, notary pub., cmty. coll. teaching credential, Calif.; cert. tax profl. Quality assurance mgr. mfg. Corning (N.Y.) Glass Co., 1974-78; contr., plant mgr. Phillip Morris, Auburn, NY, 1978-79; sr. exec. mgr. Kerr Glass Corp., LA, 1979-84; instr. Nat. Edn. Corp., Anaheim, Calif., 1985-87; assoc. prof., chmn. dept. acctg. and bus., dean, regional dean so. Calif. DeVry U., Calif., 1987—, prof. bus., 1994—, dean of bus., 1998—. CEO Global Bus. Agents, Inc. , 2000; cons. Protrans , Santa Ana, Calif., 1985—, Castillo Electronics, Los Alamitos, Calif., 1986. Co-patentee polarized contaminate viewer. Sgt. Army Security Agy., U.S. Army, 1967-71, Vietnam. Mem.: Calif. Soc. CPA's, Nat. Soc. Tax Profls., Am. Prodn. and Inventory Control Soc., Am. Mgmt. Assn., Am. Acctg. Assn., Nat. Bus. Edn. Assn., Inst. Mgmt. Accts., Nat. Assn. Acad. Affairs Adminstrs., Am. Assn. Higher Edn., Sigma Beta Delta, Phi Delta Kappa. Avocations: computer programming, golf, writing, international consulting, ebusiness. Home: 795 S Pampas Ave Rialto CA 92376-2102 Office: DeVry U 901 Corporate Center Dr Pomona CA 91768-2642 E-mail: bambrose@socal.devry.edu.

AMBROSINI, ARMAND ANTHONY, music educator; b. New Haven, Ct., Sept. 11, 1949; s. Armand and Dina Ambrosini. BFA, Calif. Inst. of Arts, 1972, MFA, 1974; MusM, Yale Sch. of Music, 1976; MusD, SUNY, 1995. Vis. asst. prof. U. Nebr., Lincoln, Nebr., 1989—90; lectr. Humboldt State U., Arcata, Calif., 1990—93; vis. asst. prof. U. Okla., Norman, Okla., 1993—. Performing artist, coach Sequoia Chamber Music Workshop, Arcata, Calif., 1992—; artist, coach Ashland Chamber Music Workshop, Ashland, Oreg.; 1995—, Humbolt Chamber Music Workship, Arcata, 2004—; performing artist, coach Chamber Music Conf., Composer's Forum of East, Bennington, Vt., 2001—. Author, recording artist: book and cd Ned Rorem's Song Cycle Areil: A Musical Dramatization of Five Poems by Sylvia Plath, 2001; co-author: Introduction To Western Concert Music, 2003, rev. edit., 2005. Treas. Chamber Musicians' Alliance of Greater New Haven, New Haven, 1979—80; bus. mgr. Cordier Ensemble, 1974—. Mem.: Coll. Music Soc., Alpha Lambda Chpt. of Pi Kappa Lambda Nat. Music Honor Society. Achievements include founding mem. Cordier Ensemble. Avocations: sailing, hiking, camping. Home: 709 S Flood Ave Norman OK 73069 Office: U Okla 500 W Boyd St Rm 138 Norman OK 73019-3130 Office Phone: 405-325-0434. E-mail: aambrosini@ou.edu.

AMBROSINO, RALPH THOMAS, JR., retired telecommunications executive; b. Gloversville, NY, Aug. 5, 1940; s. Ralph Thomas and Mary Agnes (Peters) A.; m. Roberta Joy Goldman, Nov. 1, 1970; children: Robin, Jill. BS in Acctg., U. Buffalo, 1961. With Gen. Telephone Co., 1968-74; gen. comml. mgr. Upstate N.Y., Johnstown, 1968-70, gen. service office mgr., 1970-74; regulatory matters mgr. GTE Service Corp., Stamford, Conn., 1974-76, revenues and earnings mgr., 1976-78; dir. regulatory affairs Gen. Telephone Co. of Calif., Santa Monica, 1979-81; dir. regulatory matters GTE Service Corp., Stamford, 1981-84, v.p. investor relations, 1984-87, v.p. external affairs, 1987. Mem. Investor Relations Assn. Home: 154 Southport Woods Dr Southport CT 06890

AMBROSIO, ANTHONY G., broadcast executive; married; 2 children. BA in Econs. and Polit. Sci., U. Pitts., 1982; MBA, NYU, 1991. Cert. employee benefits specialist U. Pa. Wharton Sch., 1993, compensation profl. Am. Compensation Assn., 1993. Position in recruitment and placement CBS Corp., NYC, 1985, various human resources positions in compensation, policy, HRIS and benefits functions, dir. pers., 1995, v.p. benefits, 1995—99, v.p. corp. human resources, 1999—2000, sr. v.p. human resources and adminstrn. CBS, Infinity Broadcasting and Viacom Outdoor, 2000—05, co-exec. v.p. human resources Viacom, 2005—06, exec. v.p. human resources and adminstrn., 2006—. Bd. dirs. Am. Benefits Coun. Office: CBS Corp 51 W 52nd St New York NY 10019-6188 Office Phone: 212-975-4321.*

AMBROZIC, ALOYSIUS CARDINAL (HIS EMINENCE ALOYSIUS CARDINAL AMBROZIC), archbishop emeritus; b. Gabrje, Slovenia, Jan. 27, 1930; s. Aloysius and Helen (Pecar) Ambrozic. Student, St. Augustine Sem., 1955; STL, U. San Tommaso, Rome, 1958, Sacrae Scripturae Licentiatus, Biblicum, Rome, 1960; ThD, U. Wurzburg, 1970. Ordained priest Roman Cath. Ch., 1955. Ordained aux. bishop of Roman Cath. Ch., Toronto, 1976; appointed coadjutor archbishop of Toronto, 1986; archbishop of Toronto, 1990—2006; archbishop emeritus, 2006—; created cardinal, 1998. Faculty St. Augustines Sem., Scarborough, Ont., Canada, 1956—76, dean studies, 1971—76; rep. Synod on the Formation of Priests, Rome, 1990, Synod on Religious Life, Rome, 1994; prof. N.T. exegesis Toronto Sch. Theology, 1970—76; apptd. to Pontifical Coun. for Pastoral Care of Migrants and Itinerant People, 1990, Vatican Congregation for Clergy, 1991, Pontifical Coun. for Culture, 1993, Vatican Congregation for Divine Worship and Discipline of Sacraments, 1999, Congregation for Oriental Chs., 1999, Coun. Cardinals for Study Orgnl. and Econ. Problems of Holy See, 2004—06. Author: The Hidden Kingdom: A Redaction-Critical Study of the References to the Kingdom of God in Mark's Gospel, 1972, Remarks on the Canadian Catechism, 1974; past columnist: Cath. Register. Roman Catholic.

AMBRUS, CLARA MARIA, physician; b. Rome, Dec. 28, 1924; arrived in U.S., 1949, naturalized, 1955; d. Anthony and Charlotte (Schneider) Bayer; m. Julian Lawrence Ambrus, Feb. 17, 1945; children: Madeline Ambrus Lillie, Peter, Julian, Linda Ambrus-Broenniman, Steven, Katherine Ambrus-Cheney, Charles. Student, U. Budapest, Hungary, 1943—47; MD, U. Zurich, Switzerland, 1949; postgrad., U. Paris, 1949; PhD, Jefferson Med. Coll., 1955. Diplomate Am. Bd. Clin. Chemists. Research asst. Inst. Histology, Embryology and Biology U. Budapest, 1943-45; demonstrator in pharmacology U. Budapest Med. Sch., 1946-47; asst. dept. pharmacology U. Zurich Med. Sch., 1947-49; asst. dept. therapeutic chemistry and virology Inst. Pasteur, Paris, 1949; asst. prof. pharmacology Phila. Coll. Pharmacy and Sci., 1950-52, assoc. prof., 1952-55; research assoc. Roswell Park Meml. Inst., Buffalo, 1955-58, sr. cancer research scientist, 1958-64, assoc. scientist, 1964-69, prin. cancer research scientist, 1969-85; prof. pharmacology State U. N.Y., Buffalo Med. and Grad. Schs., 1955—, assoc. prof. pediatrics, 1955-76, prof. pediatrics, 1976, research prof. ob-gyn, 1983—; chmn., founder, chief of

R&D Hemex Inc., 1984—. Contbr. articles to med. and sci. jours. Trustee Nichols Sch., Buffalo, Cmty. Music Sch. Decorated lady comdr. Equestrian Order of the Holy Sepulchre of Jerusalem; named Outstanding Woman of Western N.Y., Cmty. Adv. Coun., SUNY, Buffalo, 1980, Med. Woman of Yr., Buffalo Gen. Hosp., 2000; recipient award for excellence in clin. care, d'Youville Coll., 2004, George F. Koepf, MD award, Hauptman-Woodward Med. Rsch. Inst., Buffalo, 1997. Fellow: ACP, Internat. Soc. Hematology; mem.: Hungarian Acad. Sci. (fgn. mem.), Am. Med. Women's Assn., Buffalo Acad. Medicine, Am. Soc. Hematology, Am. Physiol. Soc., Am. Fedn. Clin. Rsch., Am. Soc. Cancer Rsch., Am. Soc. Pharmacology and Exptl. Therapeutics, Saturn Club, Clarksburg Country Club, Garrett Club, Sigma Xi. Home: 143 Windsor Ave Buffalo NY 14209-1020 also: West Hill Farm Boston NY 14025 Office: Buffalo Gen Hosp 100 High St Buffalo NY 14203-1154 Office Phone: 716-859-1399. Office Fax: 716-859-3659. Personal E-mail: jlambrus@netscape.net.

AMBRUS, JULIAN L., physician, educator; b. Budapest, Hungary, Nov. 29, 1924; arrived in U.S., 1949, naturalized, 1955; s. Alexander and Elizabeth Ambrus; m. Clara M. Bayer, Feb. 18, 1945; children: Madeline Lillie, Peter, Julian, Linda Broenniman, Steven, Katherine Cheney, Charles. Student, U. Budapest, 1942—47; MD, U. Zurich, 1949; postgrad., Sorbonne U., 1949—50; PhD in Med. Sci, Jefferson Med. Coll., 1954; ScD (hon.), Niagara U., 1984. Diplomate Am. Bd. Clin. Chemistry, Am. Acad. Pain Mgmt. Rsch. asst., instr. histology and med. biology U. Budapest, 1943-45, demonstrator pharmacology, 1946-47; asst. pharmacology U. Zurich, 1947-49; asst. dept. therapeutic chemistry, virology and tropical medicine Inst. Pasteur, Paris, 1949; asst. prof., assoc. prof., prof. Phila. Coll. Pharmacology and Sci., 1950-55; prin. cancer rsch. scientist Roswell Park Meml. Cancer Inst. and Hosp., 1955-65; asst. to dir. Roswell Park Meml. Inst. and Hosp., 1961-65; dir. Springville Labs., 1965-75, dir. cancer rsch., head dept. pathophysiology, 1975-89, mem. dept. medicine, 1989-92; asst. prof. pharmacology U. Buffalo Med. Sch., 1955-61, assoc. prof. pharmacology, 1961-65, prof., 1965-72; chmn. Roswell Park divsn. exec. com. Grad. Sch., 1955-65; assoc. in internal medicine SUNY, Buffalo, 1961-64, asst. prof. internal medicine, 1964-66, prof. biochem. pharmacology, 1964-80, assoc. prof. internal medicine, 1966-71, prof., 1971—, prof., chmn. dept. exptl. pathology Grad. Sch., 1972-92, prof. emeritus, 1992—. Attending physician Roswell Park Meml. Cancer Hosp., 1955-92, prof. emeritus Roswell Park Cancer Inst., 1992—; attending physician Buffalo Gen. Hosp., Erie County Med. Ctr., Children's Hosp. Buffalo, 1983—; cons. Millard Fillmore Hosp., Sisters of Charity Hosp., Buffalo, 1983—; dir. Instnl. Cancer Tng. Program, USPHS, 1956-65; mem. com. Thrombolytic agts. USPHS-NIH, 1960-66; cons. adv. com. on thrombosis AMA Coun. Drugs; Blood Coagulation Components, Protein Found., Cambridge, Mass.; Bur. Drugs FDA, WHO, Geneva; commr. Lake Erie chpt. U.S. Pony Clubs, mem. intercollegiate polo com. Editor-in-chief: Revs. of Hematology Jour. Medicine; contbr. articles to profl. jours. Trustee Calasanctius Prep. Sch. for Academically Gifted, 1964-92; bd. trustees Elmwood Franklin Sch., 1967-79, v.p., 1978-79. Decorated Order of Alexander the Great (France), knight comdr. Equestrian Order Holy Sepulcher of Jerusalem; recipient first prize med. student paper Hungarian Med. Sch., 1947, 1st prize surgery U. Budapest, 1947, Nelson lectureship and medal U. Calif. Davis, 1972, George F. Koepf award in biomed. rsch. Hauptman-Woodward Med. Rsch. Inst., 1997, Heart and Hand award EUA, 1997, Louis A. and Ruth Siegel award SUNY Buffalo Sch. Medicine, 1997, Achievement award in health care D'Youville Coll., 2004; named Disting. Alumnus Thomas Jefferson U., 1990. Fellow ACP, AAAS, Am. Coll. Nuc. Physicians, Am. Coll. Angiology, Royal Soc. Medicine, Am. Coll. Pharmacology and Chemotherapy, Coun. on Clin. Cardiology, Am. Heart Assn., Internat. Coll. Angiology, Am. Geriat. Soc., NY Acad. Sci., Internat. Soc. Hematology; mem. NAS (fgn. mem. Hungary), Am. Soc. Hematology, Am. Soc. Pathologists, Am. Soc. Nuc. Medicine, Am. Soc. Pharmacology and Exptl. Therapeutics, Am. Soc. Physiology, Am. Assn. Cancer Rsch., Am. Soc. Clin. Oncology, Fedn. Clin. Rsch., Soc. Exptl. Biology and Medicine, Assn. Am. Med. Colls., Cath. Physicians Guild (pres. 1985-86, 93-96), Sigma Xi, Rho Chi, Physiol. Soc. Phila., Radiation Rsch. Soc., Buffalo Zool. Soc. (chmn. sci. com. 1965-66), Buffalo Acad. Medicine (pres. 1976-77). Home: 143 Windsor Ave Buffalo NY 14209-1020 also: West Hill Farm Emmerling Rd Boston NY 14025 Office: Buffalo Gen Hosp Kaleida Health Sys SUNY/B 100 High St Buffalo NY 14203-1154 Office Phone: 716-859-1399. Fax: 716-859-1491. Personal E-mail: jlambrus@netscape.net.

AMDAHL, DOUGLAS KENNETH, retired state supreme court justice; b. Mabel, Minn., Jan. 23, 1919; BBA, U. Minn., 1945; JD summa cum laude, William Mitchell Coll. Law, 1951, L.L.D. (hon.), 1987. Bar: Minn. 1951, Fed. Dist. Ct. 1952. Ptnr. Amdahl & Scott, Mpls., 1951-55; asst. county atty. Hennepin County, Minn., 1955-61; judge Mcpl. Ct., Mpls., 1961-62, Dist. Ct. 4th Dist., Minn., 1962-80, chief judge, 1973-75; assoc. justice Minn. Supreme Ct., 1980-81, chief justice, 1981-89; of counsel Rider, Bennett, Egan & Arundel, Mpls., 1989-99; ret. Asst. registrar, then registrar Mpls. Coll. Law, 1951-65; moot ct. instr. U. Minn.; faculty mem. and advisor Nat. Coll. State Judiciary; mem. Nat. Bd. Trial Advocacy; chmn. Nat. Ctr. for State Cts. Delay Reduction Adv. Com., 1986-88, Nat. Ctr. for State Cts. Coordinating Coun. on Life-Sustaining Decisionmaking by the Cts., 1989-93. Mem. ABA (chmn. com. on stds. of jud. adminstrn. 1987-96), Minn. Bar Assn., Hennepin County Bar Assn., Internat. Acad. Trial Judges, State Dist. Ct. Judges Assn. (pres. 1976-77), Conf. of Chief Judges (bd. dirs. 1987-88), Delta Theta Phi (assoc. justice supreme ct.). Home: 6600 Lyndale Ave S 905 Richfield MN 55423 Personal E-mail: dougamdahl@aol.com.

AMDUR, ARTHUR R., lawyer; b. Houston, Jan. 19, 1946; s. Paul S. and Florence Amdur; m. Dora B. Amdur; children: Josh, Jonny. BA, 1967, JD, 1970, LLM, 1974. Bar: Tex. 1970, D.C. 1974, cert.: Tex. Bd. Legal Specialization (in immigration law) 1988. Pvt. practice, Houston, 1970—76, Washington, 1970—76; asst. U.S. atty. Houston, 1976—82; pvt. practice, 1982—. Adj. prof. law S. Tex. Coll. Law, Houston; lectr. on immigration law. Spl. asst. to gen. counsel Republican Nat. Com., Washington, 1974; bd. dirs. YMCA Internat. Refugee Ctr., 1985—. Named Adj. Prof. Yr., S. Tex. Coll. Law, 1983. Mem.: Immigration Law Examiner, Am. Immigration Lawyers Assn., Tex. State Bar Assn. (bd. legal specialization 1997—2001), Fed. Bar Assn., Georgetown U. Alumni (pres., Houston chpt. 1984). Jewish. Office: Amdur Law Office 6161 Savoy Dr Ste 450 Houston TX 77036-3379 also: Amdur Law Office PO Box 770699 Houston TX 77215-0699 Office Phone: 713-268-1000. Business E-Mail: visas@amdurlaw.com.

AMDUR, MARTIN BENNETT, lawyer; b. NYC, Aug. 19, 1942; s. Charles and Helen (Freedman) A.; m. Shirley Bell, May 25, 1975; children: Richard J., Stephen B. AB, Cornell U., 1964; LLB, Yale U., 1967; LLM in Taxation, NYU, 1968. Bar: N.Y. 1968, U.S. Tax Ct. 1970, U.S. Dist. Ct. (so. and ea. dists.) N.Y. 1971. Assoc. Weil, Gotshal & Manges LLP, NYC, 1968-75, ptnr., 1975—. Lectr. various tax insts. Contbr. articles to legal jours. Mem. ABA, Am. Coll. Tax Counsel, N.Y. State Bar Assn., Assn. Bar City N.Y. Home: 983 Park Ave Apt 6B New York NY 10028-0808 Office: Weil Gotshal & Manges LLP 767 Fifth Ave New York NY 10153-0119 Office Phone: 212-310-8224. Business E-Mail: Martin.Amdur@Weil.com.

AMELAN, BJORN G., sculptor, set designer; Ptnr. Fashion Designer Patrick Kelly, 1983—90; creative dir. Bill T. Jones/Arnie Zane Dance Co., NYC, 1993—. Office: Bill T Jones/Arnie Zane Dance Co Found for Dance Promotion 27 W 120th St #1 New York NY 10027 Office Phone: 212-426-6655. Business E-Mail: info@billtjones.org.

AMELAR, RICHARD DANIEL, urologist; b. NYC, July 9, 1927; m. Alice Zinman, 1952; children: Jessica, Sarah, Susanna. BA, NYU, 1946, MD, 1950. Intern in urology French Hosp., 1950-51, resident in urology, 1951-54, attending urologist, 1956—68, dir. urology, 1968—77; pvt. practice urology, NYC, 1956-96; mem. faculty NYU, 1956—, prof. clin. urology, 1977—; dir. Male Infertility Clinic, Bellevue Hosp., 1958-72, dir. Free Vasectomy Clinic, 1970-72, attending urologist, 1972—96; expert urol. cons. NY State Dept. Health, Office Profl. Med. Conduct, 2001—. Dir. male infertility svcs. Margaret Sanger Rsch. Bur., 1959-68; cons. WHO, Nat. Inst. Child Health and Human Devel., drug evaluation sect. AMA, NSF. Cons. editor Urology; assoc. editor Internat. Jour. Fertility; editl. bds. Fertility and Sterility, Jour. Andrology Internat. Jour. Nephrology, Urology, Andrology. Capt. M.C., USAF, 1954-56. Grantee Irene Heinz Given and John La Porte Given Found. and N.Y. Found., 1970; recipient Disting. Andrologist award Am. Soc. Andrology, 1999; recipient Disting. Svc. award Am. Soc. Reproductive Medicine, 2002. Fellow ACS; mem. Am. Soc. Andrology, Soc. Sci. Study Sex (pres. 1970-71), Soc. Reproductive Surgeons, Am. Soc. for Study of Male Reprodn., Am. Urol. Assn., Am. Fertility Soc., Endocrine Soc., Pacific Coast Fertility Soc., NYU Sch. Medicine Alumni Assn. (pres. 1984-85, named Disting. Alumnus 2005), Alpha Omega Alpha. Home: 526 Bull Mill Rd Chester NY 10918-4706 Home Phone: 845-783-1741; Office Phone: 845-783-6768. Personal E-mail: ramelar@frontiernet.net.

AMELIO, BILL (WILLIAM J.), computer company executive; b. Nov. 25, 1957; BSChemE, Lehigh U., 1979; MS in Mgmt., Stanford U., 1989. With IBM, 1979—97; named pres. Turbocharging Systems AlliedSignal Inc., 1997; (AlliedSignal Inc. merges with Honeywell Internat. Inc., 1999); pres., CEO transp. and power systems divsn. Honeywell Internat. Inc.; exec. v.p., COO retail and fin. group NCR Corp., 2000—01; sr. v.p. relationship group Dell Inc., Round Rock, Tex., 2001, sr. v.p. Asia-Pacific/Japan Singapore, 2001—05; pres., CEO Lenovo Group Ltd., Purchase, NY, 2005—. Patentee in field. Office: Lenovo Group Ltd One Manhattanville Rd Ste PH Purchase NY 10577-2100

AMEMIYA, KOICHI, motor vehicle company executive; Pres. Am. Honda Motor Co., Torrance, Calif., 1989—; COO, Automobile Operations/N. Am. Honda Motor Co., 1992—94, exec. v.p. Office: Am Honda Motor Co 1919 Torrance Blvd Torrance CA 90501-2722

AMEN, ROBERT M., manufacturing and retired paper company executive; b. NYC, 1949; BA, Boston Coll., 1971; MBA, Columbia U., 1973. From v.p., contr. to v.p. Bleached Bd., Folding Carton and Label, 1988—94; v.p. Consumer Packaging, 1994—96; pres. Internat. Paper-Europe, Brussels, 1996—2000; exec. v.p. Internat. Paper Co, Stamford, Conn., 2000—03, pres., 2003—06; chmn., CEO Internat. Flavors & Fragrances, NYC, 2006—. Office: Internat Flavors & Fragrances 521 W 57th St New York NY 10019-2960*

AMEND, BILL, cartoonist; b. Northampton, Mass., Sept. 20, 1962; married; 2 children. BA, Amherst Coll., Mass., 1984, LHD (hon.), 2000. Syndicated by Universal Press Syndicate, 1987—. Author & artist (comic strips) FoxTrot, 1988—, (FoxTrot books), Pass the Loot, Black Bart Says Draw, Eight Yards, Down & Out, Bury My Heart at Fun-Fun Mountain, Say Hello to Cactus Flats, May the Force Be With Us, Please, Take Us to Your Mall, The Return of the Lone Iguana, At Least This Place Sells T-Shirts, Come Closer, Roger, There's a Mosquito On Your Nose, Welcome to Jasorassic Park, I'm Flying, Jack.I Mean, Roger, Think iFruity, Death By Field Trip, Encyclopedias Brown & White, His Code Name Was The Fox, Your Momma Thinks Square Roots are Vegetables, Who's Up for Some Bonding?, Am I a Mutant, or What!, Orlando Bloom Has Ruined Everything, My Hot Dog Went Out, Can I Have Another?, How Come I'm Always Luigi?. Mem.: Nat. Cartoonists Soc. (2nd v.p. 2007—09, Reuben award for Outstanding Cartoonist of Yr. 2006). Office: c/o Universal Press Syndicate 4520 Main St Kansas City MO 64111-7701 E-mail: billamend@mac.com.

AMEND, WILLIAM JOHN CONRAD, JR., physician, educator; b. Wilmington, Del., Sept. 17, 1941; s. William John Conrad and Catherine (Broad) A.; m. Constance Roberts, Feb. 3, 1962; children— William, Richard, Nicole, Mark BA, Amherst Coll., 1963; MD, Cornell U., 1967. Diplomate Am. Bd. Internal Medicine. Asst. clin. prof. U. Calif. Med. Ctr., San Francisco, 1974-76, assoc. clin. prof., 1977-82, prof. clin. medicine and surgery, 1982—2005, prof. emeritus medicine, 2005—; chief divsn. nephrology U. Calif., San Francisco, 1998—2003; physician Falmouth Med. Assocs. Contbr. articles to med. jours. Chmn. med. adv. com. No. Calif. Kidney Found., 1987-88; mem. stewardship com. 1st Presbyn. Ch., Burlingame, Calif., 1983, 84, elder, 1982-85, 93-96. Maj. U.S. Army, 1969-71. Simpson fellow, 1963; recipient Gift of Life award No. Calif. Kidney Found., 1993 Fellow: ACP; mem.: Amherst Coll. Alumni Fund (class agt. 1973-83, reunion chmn. 2003, class pres. 2003—). Avocations: golf, gardening, hiking. Home: 2860 Summit Dr Burlingame CA 94010-6257 Office: U Calif Med Ctr 3rd & Parnassus San Francisco CA 94143-0001

AMENDOLA, SAL JOHN, artist, educator, writer; b. Fiumefreddo, Calabria, Italy, Mar. 8, 1948; came to U.S., 1948; s. Joseph and Mary (Amendola) A. 3-yr. cert., Sch. Visual Arts, 1966—69, BFA, 2004, MFA Illustration, 2006. Illustator, writer DC Comics, Archie Comics, Marvel, NYC, 1969—86; asst. editor, prodn. DC Comics, NYC, 1970; talent coord., editor DC Comics, Warner Comm., NYC, 1983—86; instr. illustration Sch. Visual Arts, Fashion Inst., NYC, 1974—; founder SRV plus 1, 1990. Lectr., cons., instr. seminars at librs., mus., schs., U.S., Can., 1983-86; freelance illustrator, 1987—. Writer, illustrator: (comic book) Batman Night of the Stalker, 1972 (Best Story Nominee 1973); editor: (comic books) Elvira's House of Mystery, Talent Showcase, 1984-86; co-artist: (movie adaptation) Superman III, 1983, (comic book) Star Trek, 1984; author, artist: (book) Perspective for Artists, 1984, (book) Other Intelligences/A Sociopolitical View, 1990; artist: (comic book) Archie, 1987 (Best Artist nominee 1988); creator young adult books The Yoomee Adventures; designer toys and games; book illustrator, designer, illustrator book jackets; portrait painter. Mem. Nat. Cartoonist Soc. (profl. com. 1987), Soc. Illustrators. Liberal Democrat. Avocations: science, politics, languages. Home: 1028 67th St Brooklyn NY 11219-5923 Personal E-mail: SRVplus1@aol.com.

AMENOFF, GREGORY, artist, educator; b. St. Charles, Ill., 1948; BA, Beloit Coll., 1970; DFA (hon.), Mass. Coll. Arts, 1994. Pres. Nat. Acad. Mus. & Sch. Fine Arts, NYC, 2001—05; Eve and Herman Gelman prof. visual arts Columbia U., NYC. One-man shows include Galerie Marie-Louise Wirth, Zurich, 1990, Hirchl & Adler Modern, NYC, 1990, Kirchgemeinde Aussershihl, Kohn, Germany, 1991, Gerald Peters Gallery, Santa Fe, 1991, Galerie Bernard Vidal, Paris, 1991, Victoria Munroe Gallery, NYC, 1992, Nielsen Gallery, Boston, 1992, Tampa Mus. Art, Tampa, Fla., 1993, Norton Gallery Art, West Palm Beach, Fla., 1993, Galerie Vidal-Saint-Phalle, Paris, 1994, Oestreicher Fine Arts, New Orleans, 1994, Betsy Senior Gallery, NYC, 1995, Stephen Wirtz Gallery, San Francisco, 1995, Allen Priebe Gallery U. Wis., Oshkosh, Wis., 1996, Schick Art Gallery Skidmore Coll., NY, 1997, U. Tenn., 1997, Calif. Ctr. for Arts, Escondido, Calif., 1997, Maier Art Mus., Lynchburg, Va., 1998, Lowe Art Mus., Coral Gables, Fla., 1998, Silvermine Guild Arts Ctr., New Cannan, Conn., 1999, others, exhibited in group shows at Atkins Mus. Art, Kans. City, Mo., 1990, Dalsheimer Gallery, Balt., 1990, Whitney Mus. Am. Art, NY, 1991, Adair Margo Gallery, El Paso, Tex., 1991, L.A. County Mus. Art, L.A., 1992, Pratt Manhattan Gallery, NYC, 1992, Cute-des-Neiges, Montreal, 1993, Centre Culturel Pierrefonds, France, 1993, Elvehjem Mus. Art, Madison, Wis., 1994, Gallery Camino Real, Boca Raton, Fla., 1994, Fletcher/Priest Gallery, Worcester, Mass., 1995, Columbia U., NYC, 1995, Boston U. Art Gallery, 1996, Ark. Arts Ctr., Little Rock, 1996, Newhouse Ctr. Contemporary Art, Staten Island, NY, 1997, Calif. Mus. Art, 1997, Butler Inst. Am. Art, Youngstown, Ohio, 1998, Cleve. Mus. Art, Ohio, 1998, Philbrook Mus. Art, Tulsa, 1999, U. Colo. art Galleris, Boulder, 1999, Represented in permanent collections Mus. Fine Arts, Boston, Bklyn. Mus. Art, NY, Mpls. Inst. Art, Minn., Whitney Mus. Am. Art, NYC, San Francisco Mus. Art, Phoenix Art Mus., NY Pub. Libr., Nat. Mus. Am. Art, Washington, Mus. Modern Art, NYC, Albright-Knox Art Gallery, Buffalo, NY, Francis and Sidney Lewis Found., Richmond, Va., Phoenix Art Mus., others; author (with Donald Kuspit and William Corbett): Sky Below: 18 Paintings by Gregory Amenoff, 1997; exhibitions include Salander O'Reilly Gallery, N.Y., —, exhibited in group shows at Whitney Biennials, 1981—85. Recipient Purchase award, AAAL, 1993, 1995, 1996. Office: Columbia U Sch of the Arts 305 Dodge Hall Mail Code 1808 2960 Broadway New York NY 10027 Office Fax: 212-426-1711.

AMENT, KYLE TYLER, director; b. Warrensburg, Mo., Nov. 12, 1968; s. Larry P. and Carolyn J. Ament; m. Cynthia J. Bennett, May 11, 2001; m. Sherrie J. Strong (div.); 1 child, Madeline O. BS, Mo. State U., Springfield, 1991; MPA, U. Mo., Columbia, 2003. Deputy juvenile officer Platte County Juvenile Ct., Mo.; case mgr. Dept. Mental Health Springfield Rig Ctr., Mo.; spl. investigator Dept. Mental Health State Mo., Jefferson City, Mo., asst. to investigations dir., 2000—04; program dir. Cole County Residential Svcs., Inc., Jefferson City, 2004. Contbr. articles to profl. jours. Membership com. mem. YMCA, Jefferson City, 2006—. Avocations: weightlifting, winemaking, martial arts.

AMENTA, PETER SEBASTIAN, pathologist; b. Middletown, Conn., Feb. 21, 1953; s. Sebastian Peter and Mary Veronica (Branciforte) Am. m. Edna A. Salvo, Aug. 26, 1978; children: Peter S., Katherine D. BS, Trinity Coll., 1975; MS, MD, Hahnemann U., 1980, PhD, 1984. Cert. anatomic and clin. pathologist. Asst. prof. pathology Hahnemann U., Phila., 1984-89, Robert Wood Johnson U. Hosp., New Brunswick, NJ, 1989-93, assoc. prof. clin. pathology, 1993, dir. residency program, 1994—2001, 2003—05, chief pathology svc., 1999—, dir. assoc. residency program, 2001—03, chmn. pathology and lab. medicine, 2002—, interim chief of staff, 2002—05, interim sr. v.p. med. affairs, chief staff, 2002—05, chief of staff, 2005—, assoc. program. dir., 2005—, sr. v.p. med. affairs, chief staff, 2005—06; interim dean U. Medicine and Dentistry NJ, Robert Wood Johnson Med. Sch., 2006. Mem. Am. Soc. Cell Biology, US Can. Assn. Pathology, Can. Assn. Pathology, Hahnemann Club, Alpha Omega Alpha. Achievements include research in extracellular matrix pathobiology. Home: 2 Cartwright Dr Princeton Junction NJ 08550-1928 Home Phone: 609-275-8373; Office Phone: 732-235-8120. E-mail: amenta@umdnj.edu.

AMENU, GEREMEW GURMESSA, engineering educator, researcher; b. Wellega, Oromia, Ethiopia, May 10, 1974; s. Gurmessa Amenu and Likitu Benti (Yadeta) Angere; m. Kulani Dejene Fite, July 28, 2001; 1 child, Natiiol Geremew Gurmessa. BS in Water Resources Engring., Arba-Minch Water Tech. Inst., Ethiopia, 1996; MS in Hydropower Engring. with honors, Norwegian U., Trondheim, 2000; PhD in Civil Engring. with honors, U. Ill., Urbana, 2007. Asst. lectr. Arba-Minch Water Tech. Inst., 1997—98, lectr., 2000—01; tchg. asst. U. Alta., Edmonton, Alberta, Canada, 2001; rschr. Ill. State Water Ctr., Champaign, 2002—03, U. Ill., Urbana, 2004—. Recipient Gold medal, Arba-Minch Water Tech. Inst., 1996, Best Student Poster award, Ill. Water Resources Ctr., 2004; scholar, Norwegian U. Sci. and Tech., 1998; ICSC - World Lab. fellow, U. Ariz., 2002. Mem.: ASCE, Oromo Studies Assn., Nat. Soc. Black Engrs., Internat. Water Resources Assn., Am. Water Resources Assn., Am. Geophys. Union. Office: Univ Ill 205 N Mathews Ave MC-250 Urbana IL 61801 Home Phone: 217-344-3401; Office Phone: 217-244-1796. Business E-Mail: amenu@uiuc.edu.

AMES, ADELBERT, III, neuroscientist, educator; b. Boston, Feb. 25, 1921; MD, Harvard U., 1945. Intern, then resident in internal medicine Presbyn. Hosp., 1945-52; rsch. assoc. Med. Sch. Harvard U., Boston, 1955-69, prof. physiology, dept. surgery, 1969-91, Charles Anthony Pappas prof. neurosci. Med. Sch., 1983-91, prof. emeritus, 1991—; neurophysiologist in neurosurgery Mass. Gen. Hosp., Boston, 1983—. Recipient Rsch. Scientist award NIMH, 1968-80. Mem. Am. Physiol. Soc., Am. Soc. Neurochemistry, Soc. Neurosci., Internat. Soc. Neurochemistry. Home: 84 Jenckes Rd Brattleboro VT 05301-9258 E-mail: delames@sover.net.

AMES, BRUCE NATHAN, biochemistry and molecular biology professor, department chairman; b. NYC, Dec. 16, 1928; s. Maurice U. and Dorothy (Andres) A.; m. Giovanna Ferro-Luzzi, Aug. 26, 1960; children: Sofia, Matteo. BA, Cornell U., 1950; PhD, Calif. Inst. Tech., 1953. Chief sect. NIH, Bethesda, Md., 1962-67; prof. biochemistry and molecular biology U. Calif., Berkeley, 1968—, chmn. biochemistry dept., 1983-89. Mem. Nat. Cancer Adv. Bd., 1976-82. Research, publs. on bacterial molecular biology, histidine biosynthesis and its control, aging, mutagenesis, detection of environ. mutagens and carcinogens, genetic toxicology, oxygen radicals and disease. Recipient Flemming award, 1966, Rosensteil award, 1976, Felix Wankel award, 1978, John Scott medal, 1979, Corson medal, 1980, Mott prize GM Cancer Rsch. Found., 1983, Gairdner award, 1983, Tyler prize for environ. achievement, 1985, gold medal Am. Inst. Chemists, 1991, Glenn Found. Gerontology award, 1992, Roentgen prize Nat. Acad. Lincei, 1993, Lovelace award for excellence in environ. health rsch., 1995, Honda prize, 1997, Kehoe award, 1997, The U.S. Nat. Medal of Sci., 1998, Medal City of Paris, 1998, The Linus Pauling Inst. prize for health rsch., 2001, Lifetime Achievement award Abbott-ASM, 2001. Fellow Acad. Toxicol. Scis., Am. Acad. Microbiology, Gerontol. Soc. Am.; mem. NAS, Am. Soc. Biol. Chemists, Am. Soc. Microbiology (N.B. lectr. 1980, Abbott Lifetime Achievement award 2001), Environ. Mutagen Soc. (award 1977), Genetics Soc., Am. Assn. Cancer Rsch., Soc. Toxicology (Gustavus John Esselen award 1992), Am. Chem. Soc. (Eli Lilly award 1964), Royal Swedish Acad. Scis., Am. Acad. Arts and Scis. Office: Children's Hosp Oakland Rsch Inst 5700 Martin Luther King Jr Way Oakland CA 94609 Office Phone: 510-450-7625. E-mail: bnames@berkeley.edu.

AMES, DONALD PAUL, retired air research director; b. Brandon, Man., Canada, Sept. 13, 1922; came to U.S., 1932; s. Paul M. and Della Johanna (Hebel) A.; m. Doris Elizabeth Ubbelohde, Dec. 30, 1949; children: Elizabeth Carol Ames Herbert, Barbara Louise Ames Jones. BS in Chemistry, U. Wis., 1944, PhD in Phys. Chemistry, 1949; LLD (hon.), U. Mo., St. Louis, 1978. AEC postdoctoral fellow, 1949—50; staff chemist Los Alamos Sci. Lab., 1950—52; asst. prof. phys. chemistry U. Ky., Lexington, 1952—54; staff chemist DuPont Co., Aiken, SC, 1954—56; sr. rsch. chemist, scientist/fellow Monsanto, St. Louis, 1956—61; from scientist to sr. scientist rsch. div. McDonnell Aircraft Co., St. Louis, 1961—68; from dep. dir. rsch. to dir. rsch. McDonnell Douglas Rsch. Labs., St. Louis, 1968—71, dir., 1971—76, staff v.p., 1976—86, staff v.p., gen. mgr., disting. fellow, 1986—89, cons., 1989—; pres. Fluotech Inc., 1991—. Adj. prof. physics U. Mo., St. Louis, 1989—2000, Washington U., St. Louis, 1989-99; mem. vis. com. dept. mech. engring. Lehigh U., 1984-90; mem. adv. bd. Coll. Engring., U. Ill., Urbana, 1986-89; mem. spl. com. U. Chgo. 7 GeV Synchrotron Light Source, 1984-89; adv. com. U. Mo. Rsch. Reactor, Columbia, 1985-92; mem. indsl. adv. coun. dept. chemistry U. Mo., St. Louis, 1985-95; mem. subcom. on materials sci. and engring. needs and opportunities in aerospace industry NAS, 1985-86; bd. dirs. St. Louis Tech. Ctr., 1983-95; participant Manhattan Project U.S. Army, 1944-46. Contbr. articles to profl. jours.; patentee in field. Special engr. detachment US Army, 1944—46. Recipient Civic award St. Louis sect. AIAA, 1985, James B. Eads award Acad. Sci. St. Louis, 2003; Wis.

Alumni Rsch. fellow, 1946-48, AEC fellow, 1948-49, Monsanto fellow, 1959-61, McDonnell Douglas Disting. fellow, 1986-89. Fellow Acad. Sci. St. Louis; mem. Am. Phys. Soc., Am. Chem. Soc., Soc. Engring Sci., Combustion Inst., Mo. Acad. Sci.; Phi Beta Kappa, Sigma Xi, Phi Eta Sigma, Phi Kappa Phi, Phi Lambda Upsilon, Gamma Alpha, Alpha Chi Sigma. Office Phone: 314-984-8846. E-mail: ames922@sbcglobal.net.

AMES, FRANK ANTHONY, musician, film producer; b. Wheeling, W.Va., Oct. 12, 1942; s. Louis Higgins and Camille (O'Brien) A.; m. Susan Whalley, June 14, 1966 (div. 1971); 1 child, Kristan; m. Annette Ruth Beck, 1980; 1 child, Angharad Elisabeth. MusB, Eastman Sch. Music, Rochester, NY, 1964; MFA, Carnegie Mellon U., 1966. Percussionist Pitts. Symphony, 1964-66, Balt. Symphony, 1966-68; prin. percussionist Nat. Symphony, Washington, 1968—; exec. dir. 20th Century Consort, Washington, 1975-83, Millennium Inc., Washington, 1979—; pres. Potomac Prodns., Washington, 1982—; ind. film producer Washington, 1982—; assoc. prof. percussion U. Md. Sch. Music, 2004—. Assoc. faculty Sch. Music U. Md., 2002—. Producer, performer various recs., producer (film) Music of the 12th Century, 1986 (1st prize Houston Film Frestival 1986), (music) Arrangements for children's musical Red Shoes, 1993, showcased in Arlington, Va., 1993, Wheeling, W.Va., 1994; author; (script) Petrushka, 1987. Founder, dir. Nat. Symphony outreach program In Your Neighborhood, 1992-94. Recipient Mayor's Achievement award, Washington, 1982. Mem. Chamber Music Am., Cosmos Club Washington. Avocations: sailing, squash. Home and Office: 1235 Potomac St NW Washington DC 20007-3230 Personal E-mail: faames@gmail.com.

AMES, KATHRYN S., library director; b. Pontiac, Ill., Oct. 2, 1946; d. John W. and Marjorie I. (Williams) Sandford; m. Glenn C.W. Ames; children: A. Michael, Thomas, Allison. BA, No. Ill. U., 1968; MLS, U. Tenn., 1970; postgrad., U. Ga. Libr. City Sch. Dist., Rochester, N.Y., 1968-69, Cocke County Sch. Dist., Newport, Tenn., 1971-72, Am. Sch. Bangalore, India, 1972-73; asst. dir. Athens Regional Libr. Sys., Ga., 1973-86, dir. Ga., 1986—. Bldg. cons. various programs, 1976—. Co-author: (jours.) Visit with a Private Ukrainian Farmers, 1994, Republic of Georgia: Choices, 1993, Georgia Librarian, 1994. Mem. Leadership Athens, 1988; bd. dirs., chair com. Athens YWCO, 1989—. Recipient Cmty. Cultural award Clarke County Govt., 1987, Gov.'s Humanities award Ga. Endowment of Humanities, 1990, Excellence in Pub. Libr. Svcs. award State Dept. of Edn., 1989. Mem. ALA, Pub. Libr. Assn. (Nat. Achievement citation 1992, Highsmith Libr. Innovation award for Familia a Familia program, 2007), Southeastern Libr. Assn. (com. chair 1973—), Ga. Libr. Assn. (com. chair 1973—), Ga. Coun. Pub. Librs. (chair constn. com. 1992—). Office: Athens Regional Libr Sys 2025 Baxter St Athens GA 30606-6331 E-mail: kames@gcpl.net.

AMES, LOIS WINSLOW SISSON, social worker, educator, writer; b. Boston, Jan. 21, 1931; d. Winslow Chase and Lois (Barton) Sisson; m. Robert Webb Ames, Dec. 15, 1956 (div. Aug. 1969); children: Elisabeth Harriett Winslow, Adam Barton. AB, Smith Coll., 1952; AM in Psychiat. Social Work, U. Chgo., 1958. Lic. social worker Mass., cert. Acad. Cert. Social Workers, bd. cert. diplomate Nat. Registry Health Care Providers in Clin. Social Work, bd. cert. diplomate clin. social work Am. Bd. Examiners Clin. Social Work, lic. ind. clin. social worker. Caseworker children's divsn. City of Chgo. Pub. Welfare Dept., 1953—56; intern Family Svc. Salvation Army, Chgo., 1956—57, Ill. Neuropsychiat. Inst., Chgo., 1957—58; child care worker Inst. for Juvenile Rsch., William Healy Residential Treatment Ctr., Chgo., 1957; psychiat. social worker Lake County Mental Health Clinic, Gary, Ind., 1958—59; pvt. clin. practice, 1958—; counselor Hyde Park Unitarian Cooperative Nursery Sch., Chgo., 1964—68; lower and middle sch. counselor U. Chgo. Lab. Schs., 1966—69; lectr. Northeastern U., Boston, 1969—77, asst. prof. Coll. Criminal Justice, 1970—77, coord. social welfare and social work practice curriculum, 1970—77, asst. dir. The Weekend Coll., 1969—70, dir. The Weekend Coll., 1970—72; lectr. psychiatry dept. psychiatry Harvard Med. Sch., Cambridge (Mass.) Hosp., 1982—; asst. editor Women's Page Tucson (Ariz.) Daily Citizen, 1952—53. Dir. The Cmty. Svc. Practicum, Boston, 1972—77; vis. lectr. Sch. Social Work Smith Coll., Northampton, Mass., 1975; mem. adv. com. career edn. Lincoln Sudbury (Mass.) Regional H.S., Sudbury, Mass., 1975—77; mem. adv. bd. Mass. Correctional Instn., Concord, Mass., 1977—82; pvt. psychotherapy cons., Cambridge and Sudbury, Mass.; lectr. psychiatry Harvard Med. Sch., Cambridge Hosp., Mass., 1982—. Editor (with L. Gray Sexton): Anne Sexton: A Self Portrait in Letters, 1977; mem. editl. bd.: Suicide and Life Threatening Behavior; contbr. chapters to books;, author poems and essays. Bd. mem. adv. bd. Franklin Pierce Coll., NH, 1982—85. Recipient Alumni Gold medal citation, U. Chgo., Sch. Social Svcs. Adminstrn., 1974, Affirmative Action cert appreciation, Northeastern U., 1976; rsch. fellow, State Ill. Mental Health Grant, 1956—57, Nat. Inst. Mental Health Grant, 1957—58, Ella Lyman Cabot Trust Grant, 1966, Ill. Arts Coun., 1967, U. Chgo. Lab. Schs., 1967. Mem.: NASW (registered social worker, diplomate in clin. social work), New Eng. Poetry Club (bd. mem. 1987—92). Home: 285 Marlborough Rd Sudbury MA 01776 Office Phone: 978-443-2601.

AMES, MARC L., retired lawyer; b. Bklyn., Mar. 14, 1943; s. Arthur L. and Ray (Sardas) Ames; m. Eileen Moll, July 12, 1970 (div. Mar. 2000); children: Adam, Kimberly. JD, Bklyn. Law Sch., 1967; LLM, NYU, 1968. Bar: N.Y. 1967, U.S. Dist. Ct. (ea. and so. dist.) N.Y. 1973, U.S. Ct. Appeals (2nd cir.) 1973, U.S. Supreme Ct. 1973, U.S. Ct. Appeals (3d cir.) 1982, Pa. 1988; lic. radio amateur. Mem. faculty L.I. U., 1968-69, N.Y.C. Community Coll., 1969-70; pvt. practice, 1967—97; ret. Arbitrator U.S. Dist. Ct. (ea. dist.) N.Y. 1985, small claims divsn. N.Y.C. Civil Ct., N.Y.C. Civil Ct.; cons. disability retirement and pensions; arbitrator Am. Arbitration Assn.; bd. dirs. Internat. Comms. Concepts, Inc. Contbr. articles to profl. jours. Recipient cert. appreciation N.Y. State Trial Lawyers, commendation for disting. svc. as arbitrator. Mem. N.Y. State Trial Lawyers Assn., N.Y. County Lawyers, N.Y. State Bar Assn., Electronic Technol. Soc. N.J. Inc. Achievements include patents in field.

AMES, MATTHEW B., lawyer; b. Feb. 6, 1973; BA with hon., Univ. Fla., 1995, JD with hon., 1997. Bar: Ga. St. Cts. With Balch & Bingham, LLP, Atlanta, 1998—, ptnr., 2005—. Contbr. articles to numerous profl. jours. Named Ga. Rising Star, Atlanta Mag., 2005. Mem.: ABA, Atlanta Bar Assn. Office: Balch and Bingham 30 Allen Plz Ste 700 30 Ivan Allen Jr Blvd NW Atlanta GA 30308 Office Phone: 404-261-6020.

AMES, RICHARD POLLARD, physician, educator, lecturer; b. Northampton, Mass., Aug. 4, 1932; s. Harold Leslie and Effie Melissa (Crowley) A.; m. Janet Ann Shaw, Oct. 7, 1961; children: Patricia Jean, Brian Shaw. BA cum laude, Williams Coll., 1954; MD, Columbia U., 1958. Diplomate Am. Bd. Internal Medicine, Am. Bd. Nephrology, Am. Bd. Med. Oncology, Am. Bd. Hematology, Am. Soc. of Hypertension Specialist in Clin. Hypertension. Intern Boston City Hosp., 1958-59, resident, 1959-61; fellow N.Y. Heart Assn. Presbyn. Hosp., NYC, 1961-63; clin. assoc. Nat. Cancer Inst., Bethesda, Md., 1963-65; investigator Nat. Inst. Arthritis Metab., Paris, 1965-66, Whitehall Found., NYC, 1967-70; nephrologist St. Luke's Roosevelt Hosp., NYC, 1970—, chief hypertension clinic, 1973-94, dir. phys. diagnosis, 1981-94, assoc. dir. nephrology, 1990-93; chief nephrology St. Clare's Hosp., NYC, 1998-2000. Dir. hypertension Am. Health Found., N.Y.C., 1972-82; clin. prof. Columbia U., N.Y.C., 1989—. Contbg. author: Topics in Hypertension, 1980, Frontiers in Hypertension Res., 1981, Clinical Cardiovascular Therapeutics, 1989, Hypertension, 1995, Messerli's Cardiovascular Drug Therapy, 1996; co-editor: Medical Symposium Drugs, 1988. Asst. surgeon USPHS, 1963-65. Fellow ACP, AHA (mem. Coun. For High Blood Pressure Rsch., Kidney Coun.); mem. Am. Soc. Hypertension (charter), Phi Beta Kappa. Office: 1886 Broadway New York NY 10023- Office Phone: 917-224-4270.

AMES, ROBERT G., lawyer; b. Buffalo, Feb. 24, 1949; BBA, Temple U., 1970; JD with honors, George Washington U., 1973. Bar: Ga. 1973, DC 1976, Md. 1980. Ptnr. Labor & Employment Dept. Venable LLP, Washington, DC. Mem.: ABA (mem. Labor Law Sect.), State Bar Ga., DC Bar, Fed. Bar Assn., Md. State Bar Assn., Bar Assn. of Balt. City, Order of the Coif. Office: Venable LLP 575 7th St NW Washington DC 20004 Office Phone: 202-344-4840. Office Fax: 202-344-8300. E-mail: rgames@venable.com.

AMES, ROGER, recording industry executive; b. Trinidad, West Indies; With EMI UK, 1975—79; with A&R dept., then head London Records PolyGram UK, 1979—93, chmn., CEO, 1993—96; pres. PolyGram Music Group, 1996—99, Warner Music Internat., 1999; chmn., CEO Warner Music Group, 1999—2004; cons. EMI, 2006—07, head EMI Music North America, 2007—. Office: EMI North America 1290 Ave of the Americas 38th Fl New York NY 10104*

AMES, SANDRA CUTLER, secondary school educator; b. Putnam, Conn., Nov. 3, 1935; d. Loid C. and Sophie M. (Kowal) Cutler; m. David Crouse Ames, Oct. 28, 1955; children: Deborah Lee, Susan Lynn. BS, U. Conn., 1957, MS, 1959; postgrad., Ea. Conn. State U., 1965. Cert. elem. tchr., Conn. Tchr. elem. Killingly Ctrl. Sch., Dayville, Conn., 1959-88, tchr. K-4 resource math., testing coord., 1988—97; ret., 1997; substitute tchr., 1997—. Presenter math. workshops, Dayville, 1981—; co-chair Invention Conv., Dayville, 1987-90. Recipient Presdl. award in math. Fed. & State Bds. Edn., 1990, 93. Mem. Delta Kappa Gamma. Avocations: crafts, crocheting, knitting, decorating. Home: 235 Chase Rd Putnam CT 06260-2810 Office Phone: 860-974-1130.

AMES, SANDRA PATIENCE, sales executive; b. Quincy, Calif., May 23, 1947; d. Bruce Ray Richards and Margaret Elizabeth (Steiner) Richards Johnson; m. Thomas William Ames, Nov. 28, 1975. Student, Yuba City Jr. Coll., 1965-66. Sales corr. Nat. Can Corp. (now Am. Nat. Can Co.), Seattle, 1974-76, Lehigh Valley, Pa., 1976-79, nat. acct. sales corr. Chgo., 1979-81, dist. sales office mgr., 1981-82, sales analyst I Oakbrook, Ill., 1982-84, regional sales office mgr., 1984-86, mgr. regional sales office, 1987-89, mgr. ctrl. sales adminstrn., 1989-93, inside sales assoc., 1993-95, Silgan Containers, Rosemont, Ill., 1995-98, office adminstr., 1998—; ret., 2004. Office: Silgan Containers Mfg Corp 1140 31st St Downers Grove IL 60515-4736 Personal E-mail: sames@wavecable.com.

AMES, STEPHEN MICHAEL, professional golfer; b. San Fernando, Trinidad and Tobego, Apr. 28, 1964; m. Jodi Ames. Profl. golfer PGA, 1987—. Mem. Trinidad and Tobago team WGC World Cup, 2000, 02, 03, 06. Achievements include winning the Trinidad and Tobago Open, 1989, Ben Hogan Pensacola Open, 1991, Open V33, 1994, Benson and Hedges Internat. Open, 1996, Cialis Western Open, 2004, Can. Skins Game, 2005, The Players Championship at Sawgrass, 2006 (tied largest margin of victory at event), Skins Game, 2006.*

AMES, STEVEN, management consultant; m. Sharon Ames (div.); m. Ann Ames. Former ptnr. Oppenheimer; pres. Steven Ames & Assoc. Adv. bd. Gugenheim Mus.; trustee Whitney Mus. Am. Art. Mailing: BCE Place 181 Bay St Heritage Bldg Fl 2R Toronto ON M5J 2T3 Canada also: c/o Whitney Mus Am Art 945 Madison Ave New York NY 10021 E-mail: stevenames@shaw.ca.

AMES, STEVEN REEDE, financial planner; b. Washington, Aug. 15, 1951; s. Reede Maughan and Mary (Soderberg) Ames; m. Marsha M. Ames, Sept. 1994. BSBA, U. Md., 1973; MPA, Am. U., 1976; MS, Coll. Fin. Planning, 1994. Cert. fin. planner, registered investment advisor, enrolled agt. IRS. Specialist bus. financing Gov.'s Office State Del., Dover, 1978-83; exec. v.p. Econ. and Bus. Devel. Corp. Montgomery County, Rockville, Md., 1983-85; owner, operator Scarborough Ames and Assocs., Annapolis, Md., 1986-92; owner, prin. Ames Fee-Only Fin. Planning, Annapolis, 1993—. Instr. Anne Arundel CC, Annapolis, 1987—98. Bd. dirs. Md. Hall Creative Arts; mem. charitable gift planning adv. com. Anne Arundel Med. Ctr.; mem. fin. and asset mgmt. com. Chesapeake Cmty. Found. Named among best fin. advisors, Worth Mag., 1996—2002; named one of 100 Gt. Fin. Planners, Mut. Funds Mag., 2001, 2002. Mem.: Md. Soc. Accts., Nat. Assn. Securities Dealers (bd. arbitrators 1996—), Nat. Assn. Personal Fin. Advisors (regional chmn. bd.), Annapolis C. of C. (bd. dirs., Mem. of the Yr. 1990), Kiwanis (bd. dirs. Annapolis club 1986—97, pres. 1989—90). Avocations: sports, travel, reading. Home: 503 Fifth St Annapolis MD 21403 Home Phone: 410-703-9999; Office Phone: 410-280-2390. Personal E-mail: steve.ames@comcast.net.

AMES, TED, environmental scientist; MS in Biochemistry, U. Maine, Orono, 1971. Pres., lab. dir. Alden/Ames Lab.; marine resources dir. Island Inst.; exec. dir. Maine Gillnetters Assn.; independent rschr., comml. fisherman. Chmn. Penobscot East Resource Ctr.; bd. dirs. Northwest Atlantic Marine Alliance; advisor New England Fisheries Mgmt. Coun. Named MacArthur fellow, John D. and Catherine T. MacArthur Found., 2005. Mem.: Stonington Fisheries Alliance (founding mem.). Achievements include research in spawning, habitat and fishing patterns to develop new strategies for marine management in the Gulf of Maine. Office: Northwest Atlantic Marine Alliance 200 Main St Ste A Saco ME 04072

AMES, WILLIAM FRANCIS, mathematician, educator; b. Brandon, Man., Can., Dec. 8, 1926; s. Paul Main and Della Johanna (Hebel) A.; m. Theresa Danielson, May 29, 1951; children: Karen Anne, Susan Lynn, Pamela Margaret. MS, U. Wis., 1950. Instr. U. Wis., Racine, 1953-55; sr. engr. DuPont Co., Wilmington, Del., 1955-59; prof. U. Del., Newark, 1959-67, U. Iowa, Iowa City, 1967-75, Ga. Inst. Tech., Atlanta, 1975—, Regents prof., 1980-91, prof. emeritus, 1991—, dir., 1981-87; research prof. U. Ga., Athens, 1977-79. Cons. in field. Author: Nonlinear Partial Differential Equations in Engineering, Vol. I, 1965, Vol. II, 1972, Nonlinear Ordinary Differential Equations in Transport Processes, 1968, Numerical Methods for Partial Differential Equations, 1970, 77, 92, Nonlinear Boundary Value Problems in Science and Engineering, 1989; book and jour. editor for Academic Press; editor 9 books.; contbr. articles to profl. jours. Served with USNR, 1944-46, 51-52. NSF faculty fellow, 1963-64, NATO sr. fellow, 1972-73; grantee, 1964-67, 76-79, 79-81, 83-85, 89-91, 92-95, NBS grantee, 1967-71, USPHS grantee, 1961-63, EPA grantee, 1978-81, U.S. Army grantee, 1968-75, 81-87; Humboldt sr. scientist, 1974-75. Home: 125 Tamarisk Dr NE Atlanta GA 30342-1421 Office: Ga Inst Tech Sch Math Atlanta GA 30332-0001 Personal E-mail: williamames@hotmail.com.

AMESTOY, JEFFREY LEE, former state supreme court chief justice, educator; b. Rutland, Vt., July 24, 1946; s. William Joseph and Diana (Wood) Amestoy; m. Susan Claire Lonergan, May 24, 1980; children: Katherine Leigh, Christina Elizabeth, Nancy Claire. BA, Hobart Coll., 1968; JD, U. Calif., San Francisco, 1972; MPA, Harvard U., 1982; D of Pub. Adminstrn. (hon.), Norwich U., 1994; LLD (hon.), Vermont Law Sch., 2002. Bar: Vt. 1973, U.S. Dist. Ct. Vt. 1973. Assoc. Mahady & Klevana, Windsor, Vt., 1973—74; legal counsel Gov.'s Justice Commn., Montpelier, Vt., 1974—77; asst. atty. gen., chief of Medicaid fraud div. State of Vt., Montpelier, 1978—81, commr. labor and industry, 1982—84, atty. gen., 1985—97; chief justice Supreme Ct. Vt., 1997—2004; fellow John F. Kennedy Sch. of Govt. Harvard U., 2004—. Pres. Nat. Assn. of Attys. Gen., 1992—93. Trustee Thomas Waterman Wood Gallery, Montpelier, 1986—92. With USAR, 1968—74. Mem.: Conf. Chief Justices, Vt. Bar Assn., Kennedy Sch. Govt. Harvard U. Alumni Exec. Coun. Republican. Congregationalist.

AMEZCUA, ESTHER HERNANDEZ, elementary school educator; b. Guadalajara, Jalisco, Mexico, Nov. 9, 1949; came to the U.S., 1961; d. Rodolfo (stepfather) and Guillermina (Hernandez) Sanchez; m. Juan Elizondo Amezcua, June 23, 1973; children: Juanguillermo Gabriel, Jaime Jose Vicente. BA, U. Calif., Davis, 1972. Life tchg. credential, Calif.; multicultural and bilingual credential. With Sacramento City Unified Sch., 1973—; intermediate tchr. William Land Elem., 1973-81, 83-93, primary tchr., 1981-83, 2002—; intermediate tchr., head tchr. Oak Ridge Elem., 1993-97, Caroline Wenzel Elem., 1997—2002. Head tchr. William Land Sch., Sacramento, 1976-83, 89-93, Oak Ridge Elem., Sacramento, 1993-94; mentor tchr. Sacramento Unified Sch. Dist., 1991-93. Vol. Short Term Emergency Assistance Ctr., Davis, Calif., 1990—; dance instr. ballet folklorico, Sacramento, 1990—; vol. tutor, Sacramento, 1993—. Named Educator of Yr. Yolo County, Mexican-Am. Concilio of Woodland, 1997. Mem. Hispanic Educators Sacramento, Calif. Tchrs. Assn., Sacramento City Tchrs. Assn. Democrat. Roman Catholic. Avocations: reading, crocheting, sightseeing, dance, family activities. Home: 3207 Monte Vista Pl Davis CA 95616-4932 Office: William Land Sch 2120 12th St Sacramento CA 95818 Office Phone: 916-264-4166. Personal E-mail: amezcua20@yahoo.com.

AMHOWITZ, HARRIS J., lawyer, educator; b. NYC, Mar. 19, 1934; s. Samuel and Ruth Amhowitz; m. Melanie Leigh Gale; children: Jennifer Ann, Joshua Seth. AB, Brown U., 1955; LLB, Harvard U., 1961. Bar: N.Y. 1961, U.S. Supreme Ct. 1967. Law clk. to judge U.S. Dist. Ct. N.Y., 1961-63; assoc. Hughes Hubbard & Reed, NYC, 1963-69; gen. counsel Coopers & Lybrand, NYC, 1970-96, dep. chmn., 1991-95, mem. internat. exec. com., 1991-95; of counsel Hughes Hubbard & Reed, 1996—2003. Adj. prof. NYU Sch. Law, 1975-83; receiver, spl. master U.S. Dist. Ct., 1963-70; pres. bd. dirs. Prosher Group, Ltd., 1970-71; trustee Citizens Budget Commn., Inc., 1983-97. Lt. comdr. USN, 1955—58. Mem. Assn. Bar City N.Y. (spl. com. on lawyers' role in securities transactions 1975-77, com. profl. and jud. ethics 1983-86, com. profl. discipline 1987-91), Harmonie Club. Home: 5150 N Windsong Canyon Dr Tucson AZ 85749

AMICHETTI, DENNIS JOSEPH, advertising and marketing executive; b. Phila., Apr. 24, 1946; s. Frank and Margret H. (Ziegler) A.; m. Elizabeth Keefe, June 27, 1970; children: Christine, Karen. BS, Drexel U., 1969, MBA, 1973. Mfg. engr. GE, Phila., 1969-70; mgr. mktg. devel. ESB, Inc., Phila., 1970-74; asst. v.p., dir. mktg. Phila. Sav. Fund Soc., 1974-78; v.p. SE Nat. Bank, Malvern, Pa., 1978-79; sr. v.p. Mel Richman Inc., Bala Cynwyd, Pa., 1979-83; v.p. Beneficial Corp., Wilmington, Del., 1983-86; pres. Amichetti, Lewis & Assocs., Wayne, Pa., 1987—. Planning commn. East Goshen Twp., Pa., 1977-83, Cath. Philopatrian Lit. Inst., bd. dirs. Recipient Gold Effie award for fin. advt. Mem. Am. Mktg. Assn., Acad. for Health Svcs. Mktg., Direct Mktg. Assn., Beta Gamma Sigma. Republican. Roman Catholic. Avocations: music, theater, golf. Home: 814 Wetherill Ln Wayne PA 19087-2072 Office: Amichetti Lewis & Assocs Inc PO Box 1977 Southeastern PA 19899-1977 Office Phone: 610-341-9545. E-mail: ala300@aol.com.

AMICK, STEVEN HAMMOND, state legislator, lawyer; b. Ithaca, NY, May 13, 1947; s. Arthur Hammond and Marolyn Dee (Hollingshead) A.; m. Helen Louise Masten, Aug. 9, 1969. BA, Washington Coll., 1969; JD, Dickinson Sch. Law, 1972. Bar: Del. 1972, US Dist. Ct. Del. 1973. Assoc. Daley & Lewis, Wilmington, Del., 1972-74; atty. E.I. Dupont De Nemours and Co., Wilmington, 1974-85, counsel, 1986-96; mem. Del. Ho. of Reps., Dover, 1986-94; spl. counsel Cooch and Taylor, 1996—2002; mem. Del. Senate, Dover, 1994—, minority leader, 1998—2002. Pres. Com. of 39, Wilmington, 1978, Civic League for New Castle County, Wilmington, 1984-86. Mem. Del. Bar Assn. Republican. Presbyterian. Avocation: antique cars. Home: 449 W Chestnut Hill Rd Newark DE 19713-1132 Office: Legislature Hall PO Box 1401 Dover DE 19901 Office Phone: 302-744-4138.

AMICK, WILLIAM WALKER, golf course architect; b. Scipio, Ind., June 16, 1932; s. George Ellsworth Sr. and Myrtle (Walker) A.; m. Sara Dell Rogers, Apr. 6, 1957; 1 child, David Walker. BA, Ohio Wesleyan U., 1954. Golf course archtl. asst. William H. Diddel, GCA, Carmel, Ind., 1954-55, Charles Adams, GCA, Atlanta, 1957-58; golf course architect Daytona Beach, Fla., 1959—. Capt. USAF, 1955-57. Fellow Am. Soc. Golf Course Architects; mem. Am. Soc. of Golf Course Architects (treas., v.p., pres. 1975-77). Avocation: low handicap golf. Office: PO Box 1984 Daytona Beach FL 32115-1984 Office Phone: 386-767-1449. E-mail: amick@iag.net.

AMIDON, PAUL CHARLES, publishing executive; b. St. Paul, July 23, 1932; s. Paul Samuel and Eleanor Ruth (Simons) A.; m. Patricia Jean Winjum, May 7, 1960; children: Karen, Michael, Susan. BA, U. Minn., 1954. Bus. mgr. Paul S. Amidon & Assocs., Inc., St. Paul, 1956-66, pres., 1966—. Served with AUS, 1954-56. Home: 1582 Hillcrest Ave Saint Paul MN 55116-2147 Office: 1966 Benson Ave Saint Paul MN 55116-3214 Business E-mail: paul@amidongraphics.com.

AMIDON, ROGER LYMAN, public health service officer, educator; b. Burlington, Vt., Apr. 8, 1938; s. Ellsworth L. and Mae (Liddle) A.; m. JoAnn Reiland, Aug. 1, 1968. BA, U. Vt., 1960; MA in Hosp. and Health Adminstrn., U. Iowa, 1965, PhD (USPHS trainee), 1968. Asst. prof. hosp. and health adminstrn. U. Iowa, 1968-73, asso. prof., 1973-77; prof., chmn. dept. health adminstrn. U. Okla., 1977-81; prof., chmn. dept. health svcs. policy and mgmt. U. S.C., 1981-88, on sabbatical, 1988-89, prof., grad. dir., 1989—2002, disting. prof. emeritus, 2002—. Exec. sec. Nat. Ctr. Health Svcs. Rsch., 1975-76; dir. Am. Indian Grad. Program in Health Adminstrn., U. Okla., 1977-81; cons. China Med. U. Hosp., 1999—, vis. scholar, Nat. Def. Med. Ctr., Taiwan, 2003. Contbr. articles to profl. jours. Chair S.C. Ctr. for Gerontology, 1999-01. Lt., M.S.C. US Army, 1961—62, exec. officer and platoon leader, 418 Med. Co. (Ambulance), XVIII Airborne Hdqs. Mem. APHA (emeritus), AARP (exec. coun. 2004—), Am. Coll. Healthcare Execs., Am. Hosp. Assn. (life), Vermont Soc. Colonial Wars (gov. 2006). Home: 234 Saluda Ave Columbia SC 29205-3031 Office: Arnold SPH U SC Health Svcs Policy and Mgmt Columbia SC 29208-0001 Personal E-mail: uvmer1@aol.com.

AMIEL, HOWARD, ophthalmologist, corneal surgeon; s. Barry and Batya Amiel. BS, U. Iowa, 1994; MS, Chgo. Med. Sch., 1997; MD, U. Ill. Coll. Medicine, Chgo., 2001. Bd. cert. medicine RI, 2002, Colo., 2002. Instr. Brown U., Providence, 2005—; corneal fellow Royal Victorian Eye and Ear Hosp., Melbourne, Victoria, Australia, 2006—. Contbr. articles to profl. jours., scientific papers. Anterior Segment fellowship, Koch Eye Assocs., 2005—06, Corneal fellowship, Royal Victoria Eye and Ear Hosp., 2006—. Mem.: Internat. Soc. Refractive Surgery, Am. Soc. Cataract and Refractive Surgery, Am. Acad. Ophthalmology, Psi Chi. Avocations: swimming, travel, painting, running, bicycling. Home Phone: 303-947-3262; Office Phone: 03-9929-8666. Personal E-mail: howard_amiel@brown.edu.

AMIN, ALPESH N., internist; s. Navin and Harshila Amin; m. Sonali Amin; 1 child, Aanya. MD, Northwestern U., Chgo., 1994; MBA, U. Calif., Irvine, 2000. Physician U. Calif., Irvine Med. Ctr., Orange, 1997. Office: U Calif Irvine Med Ctr 101 The City Drive S Bldg 58 Rm 110 Orange CA 92868 Office Phone: 714-456-3785. Office Fax: 714-456-7182. E-mail: anamin@uci.edu.

AMIN, IRAN ARBABI, language educator; d. Hadi Arbabi and Poorandokht Kaveh; m. Mahmoud Arbabi, July 17, 1967; 1 child, Said. PhD, Sorbonne U., Paris, 1981. Cert. K-12 Tchr. Md., 1984. 6th grade immersion tchr. Oakview Elem. Sch., Silver Spring, Md., 1984—89; fgn. lang. tchr. Ea. Mid. Sch., Silver Spring, 1989—96, Bethesda-Chevy Chase HS, 1996—98; fgn. lang. resource tchr. Silver Spring Internat. Mid. Sch., Silver Spring, 1998—2000; fgn. lang. immersion specialist Montgomery County Pub. Schs., Rockville, Md., 2000—. Pres., founder Iran Cultural and Ednl. Ctr., Potomac, Md., 1989—2006. Rsch. Fellowship, Rockefeller Found., 1989, Fellowship, French Govt., 1996. Mem.: NE Conf. on Tchg. Fgn. Langs., Am. Coun. on Tchg. Fgn. Langs. Home Phone: 301-545-0817; Office Phone: 301-279-3380.

AMIN, ISAM ELDIN, science educator, researcher; s. Amin Ali Amin and Nafisa Hassan Arabi; m. Ragaa Gouda, Apr. 5, 2002; children: Amin Isam, Mohamed Isam, Zena Isam, Fatima Isam. BSc in Geology with honors, U. Khartoum, Sudan, 1977; MS in Hydrogeology, N. Mex Inst. of Mining and Tech., Socorro, New Mex., 1983; PhD in Hydrogeology, U. Nevada-Reno, 1987. Lectr. U. Khartoum, Sudan, 1987—90; sr. hydrogeologist Remediation Technologies, Chapel Hill, NC, 1990—93; asst. prof. Calif. State U., Long Beach, 1993—98, Am. U. of Beirut, 1998—2000; assoc. prof. Youngstown State U., Youngstown, Ohio. Dir. environ. studies Youngstown State U.; presenter in field. Co-author: (book) Tracer Hydrology, 1992, Groundwater in the Urban Environment, 1997, Gambling with Groundwater - Physical, Chemical, and Biological Aspects of Aquifer-Stream Relations, 1998, Coastal Aquifers Intrusion Technology: Mediterranean Countries, 2003; contbr. articles to profl. jours. Mem. Africana studies bd. Youngstown State U., Ohio; hydrogeology rep. UNESCO Nat. Com. of Sudan, Khartoum, Sudan, 1988—90. Recipient U. Khartoum prize, U. Khartoum, Sudan, 1977, Rsch. professorship, Youngstown State U., 2002—03; grant, Youngstown State U., Ohio, 2003—06. Mem.: Am. Geophys. Union, Geol. Soc. of Am., Internat. Assn. of Hydrological Sciences. Office: Youngstown State U One University Plaza Youngstown OH 44555 Home Phone: 330-533-1808.

AMIN, MOHAMMAD, urology educator; b. Sargodha, Pakistan, Jan. 1, 1942; came to U.S., 1964; s. Mohammad and Gulzar (Begum) Nawaz; m. Elizabeth Anne Howarth, May 25, 1973; children: Daniel, Omar. MB, BS, King Edward Coll., Lahore, Pakistan, 1963. Diplomate Am. Bd. of Urology. Intern Muhlenberg Hosp., Plainfield, NJ, 1964-65; resident in surgery Norton Hosp., Louisville, 1965-66; asst. prof. urology U. Louisville, 1971-74, assoc. prof., 1974-80, prof. urology, 1980—, resident in urology, 1966-69; med. officer Social Security, Pakistan, 1969-70; house officer urology Southmede Hosp., Bristol, England, 1970-71. Contbr. articles and book chpts. to profl. jours. Recipient Health Advancement award Nat. Kidney Found., 1981. Mem.: ACS, Soc. Internat. d'Urologie, Am. Urol. Assn. Democrat. Islamic. Address: VA Med Ctr 800 Zorn Ave Louisville KY 40206 Office Phone: 502-287-4000. Personal E-mail: maminlouky@yahoo.com.

AMINIAN BAGHAI, ARASH, lawyer; b. Tehran, Iran, Sept. 6, 1973; s. Shahideh Baghai and Rezvanollah Aminian. B in Comm., U. Toronto, Can., 1995; MBA, Ariz. State U., 1998; JD, U. Calif. Hastings Coll. Law, 2001. Bar: (7th dist.) Calif. 2001. Assoc. Dewey Ballantine LLP, Los Angeles, 2001—. Recipient Order of the Coif, Nat. Order of the Coif, 2001, award, Thurston Soc., 2001. Office: Dewey Ballantine LLP 333 S Grand Ave 26th Fl Los Angeles CA 90071 Home Phone: 323-229-5364.

AMIR, MICHAEL M., lawyer; BA, Univ. Calif., Santa Barbara, 1995; JD, Univ. Calif., Hastings, 1999. Atty. Gibson, Dunn & Crutcher LLP, LA, O'Brien, Zarian LLP, LA; co-founder, ptnr., bus. litigation, intellectual property practice Doll, Amir & Eley LLP, LA. Editor (sr. exec. project): Hastings Constitutional Law Quarterly. Named a Rising Star, So. Calif. Super Lawyers, 2005—06. Mem.: State Bar Calif., Assn. Bus Trial Lawyers. Office: Doll Amir & Eley LLP Ste 1106 1888 Century Park E Los Angeles CA 90067 Office Phone: 310-557-9100. Office Fax: 310-557-9101. Business E-Mail: mamir@dollamir.com.

AMIS, EDWARD STEPHEN, JR., radiologist, retired military officer; b. Baton Rouge, June 23, 1941; s. Edward Stephen and Annie Velma (Birdwhistell) Amis; m. Anne Schneider, Sept. 2, 1984. Student, U. Rochester, 1959-61; BS, U. Ark., 1963; MD, Northwestern U., 1967. Diplomate Am. Bd. Urology, Am. Bd. Radiology. Commd. ensign USN, 1966, advanced through grades to capt., 1980; resident in urology Naval Hosp., San Diego, 1968-72, resident in radiology, 1975-78, staff radiologist, 1978-80, 81-82, staff urologist Great Lakes, Ill., 1972-75; radiology fellow Mass. Gen. Hosp., Boston, 1980-81; chmn. radiology Naval Hosp., Bethesda, Md., 1982-84, exec. officer, 1984-85, comdg. officer, 1985-87; head sect. uroradiology dept. radiology Columbia U., NYC, 1987-91, vice chmn. dept. radiology, 1990-91; chmn. dept. radiology Albert Enstein Coll. Medicine and Montefiore Med. Ctr., Bronx, NY, 1991—. Co-author: Essentials of Uroradiology, 1990, Textbook of Uroradiology, 2000; contbr. chapters to textbooks. Leadership council Montgomery County Heart Assn., Bethesda, 1986-87. Bausch and Lomb scholar, 1959. Mem.: Am. Coll. Radiology (bd. chancellors 1995—, vice chair 2000—02, chair 2002—04, pres. 2004—05, Gold medal 2007), Am. Roentgen Ray Soc., Soc. Uroradiology, Assn. Univ. Radiologists, Radiol. Soc. N.Am. Republican. Avocations: stamp collecting/philately, art. Business E-Mail: amis@aecom.yu.edu.

AMISANO, JOSEPH, architect; b. NYC, Jan. 10, 1917; s. Ernest and Mary (Farrais) A.; m. Dorothy Baxter, June 10, 1946; m. Rosellen Goodrich, July 12, 1958; children— Paul, Tina, Lisa B.Arch., Pratt Inst., 1941. Registered architect, 14 states including Ga. Designer Walter Sanders, NYC, 1940-41, Harrison & Fouihoux, NYC, 1941-42, Harrison & Abramovitz, NYC, 1942-44; structural engr. Pan Am. Airport, NYC, 1944-45; designer Ketchum, Gina & Sharp, NYC, 1946-49; pres. Toombs, Amisano & Wells Architects, Atlanta, 1955—. Guest lectr. Washington U., St. Louis, 1963, Cornell U., 1964, Ga. Inst. Tech., 1985; cons. Carlson Group Mem. placement com. Regional Office Dept. Edn., Washington, 1961; bd. dirs. Northside Sch. Performing Arts; mem. local com. Nat. Assn. Real Estate Execs., Miami, Atlanta Art Inst., 1981 Recipient various regional and nat. awards AIA, 1946-83; Academician, NAD, 1994. Fellow AIA; mem. NAD, Am. Acad. Rome (Prix de Rome 1952), Internat. Council Shopping Centers, Am. Inst. Planners Democrat. Roman Catholic.

AMLING, FREDERICK, economist, educator, investment advisor; b. Cleve., Dec. 23, 1926; s. Gustav and Elsie (Fischer) Amling; m. Gwendolyn Stewart, Feb. 17, 1951; children: Jeffrey, Scott, Terrance. BA, Baldwin Wallace Coll., 1948; MBA, Miami U., Oxford, Ohio, 1949; PhD, U. Pa., 1957. Instr. U. Maine, 1948-50, U. Pa., 1950- 52, U. Conn., 1952—; prof. finance and investment chmn. dept. Miami U., Oxford, 1955-66; prof. finance U. R.I., Kingston, 1966-69, dean Coll. Bus. Adminstrn., 1966-69; prof. fin. Grad. Sch. Bus. and Pub. Mgmt. George Washington U., 1970-2000, prof. emeritus, 2000—; pres. Frederick Amling & Assocs., computer models, Amling & Co. Investment Advisers. Cons. fin. and investment, 1959—; cons. Riggs Nat. Bank, 1970—90, Am. Psychiat. Assn., 1975—91; bd. advisers Rsch. Ctr. Credito Emiliano, Milan, 1991—93. Author: (book) Investments: An Introduction to Analysis and Management, 1963, Investments: An Introduction to Analysis and Management, 7th edit., 2000, Plaid on Investments, 1983, Dow Jones Irwin Guide to Personal Financial Planning and Personal Financial Management, 1986; author: (with Bill Droms) Investment Fundamentals, 1994; editor, contbr.: articles on fin. to profl. jours., newspapers and mags. Chmn. local Cancer Crusade, 1964; trustee Georgetown Prebyn. Ch., 1977—79; elder Presbyn. Ch., 1962—. With USNR, World War II, lt. (j.g.) USNR, 1955. Recipient Alumni Merit award, Baldwin Wallace Coll., 1973, Sch. Bus. and Pub. Mgmt. George Washington U., 1982. Mem.: Eastern Fin. Assn. (v.p. 1979), Am. Fin. Assn. (membership chmn. 1973—90), Fin. Mgmt. Assn., Washington Soc. Fin. Analysts (treas.), Colett Club, Cosmos Club, Turks Head Club (Providence), Univ. Club (Miami U., Oxford), George Washington U. Club, Congl. Country Club, Lambda Chi Alpha, Delta Sigma Pi, Beta Gamma Sigma (pres. George Washington U. chpt. 1985). Office Phone: 301-299-3935. E-mail: tigerfred@aol.com. *To work for family and society with God's help.*

AMMAN, E(LIZABETH) JEAN, academic administrator; b. Hoyleton, Ill., July 13, 1941; d. James Kerr and Marie Fern (Schnake) White; m. Douglas Dorrance Amman, Aug. 12, 1962; children: Mark, Kirk, Jill, Drew, Gwen, Joyce. BA in English, Ill. Wesleyan U., 1963; MA in English, U. Cin., 1975. Cert. tchr., Ill. Tchr. lang. arts John Greer Jr. High Sch., Hoopeston, Ill., 1963-64, Pleasant Hill Sch., East Peoria, Ill., 1966-67; tchr. English, chmn. Am. studies Anderson Sr. High Sch., Cin., 1967-69; instr. English, No. Mich. U., Marquette, 1976-82, Ball State U., Muncie, Ind., 1982-86, adminstrv. intern, 1983-84, asst. to chmn. dept., 1984-86, adminstrv. asst., 1986, asst. to provost, coord. provost's lecture series, 1986—, exec. sec. student and campus life coun., 1986—2002. Editor: Provost's Lecture Series: Perspectives on Culture and Society, Vol. I, 1988, Vol. II, 1991, The Associator, 1983-86; flutist Muncie Westminster Orch., 1989-2004, Am.'s Hometown Band, 1991—, Baroque Consort, 1998—, East Ctrl. Ind. Chamber Orch., 2004— Mem. choir College Ave. Meth. Ch., Muncie, 1989—; fundraiser Delaware County Coalition for Literacy, 1989, 90; v.p. Cornerstone Ctr. Arts, 2005— Recipient recognition Black Student Assn., Ball State U., 1988, cert. of svc. for minority student devel., 1990, 91, 92. Mem. AAUW (pres. Muncie br. 1997-98, Ind. dir. programs 1999-2003, pres. elect Ind. chpt. 2003-04, pres. Ind. chpt. 2004—), Ind. Coll. English Assn. (editor 1983-85, exec. bd. 1983-86), P.E.O. (pres. Muncie 1985-87), Sigma Alpha Iota (v.p. 1994-97, pres. 1999-2000, Sword of Honor 1995), Kappa Delta (Ind. Kappa Delta of Yr. 1994, advisor 1992-95, collegiate province pres. 1995-98), Phi Kappa Phi. Democrat. Avocations: travel, reading, music. Home: 4305 Castleton Ct Muncie IN 47304-2476 Office: Ball State U 2000 W University Ave Muncie IN 47306-0002 Home Phone: 765-282-2188; Office Phone: 765-285-1333. Business E-Mail: jamman@bsu.edu.

AMMANN, JEAN-CHRISTOPHE, art director; b. Berlin, Jan. 14, 1939; PhD, U. Fribourg, Switzerland, 1966. Asst. Kunsthalle Bern, Switzerland, 1967-68; dir. Kunstmuseum, Lucerne, Switzerland, 1968-77, Kunsthalle, Basle, Switzerland, 1978-88, Mus. für Moderne Kunst, Frankfurt, Germany, 1989—2001, prof., 1998—. Commr. German Pavillion of Biennial of Venice, Italy, 1995; lectr. U. Frankfurt/M. and Giessen, 1992—, U. Heidelberg, 2001—02. Author: Rèmy Zaugg—Discussion with Jean-Christophe Ammann, 1994, (with Harald Szeemann) Von Hodler zur Antiform, 1968, Louis Moilliet: Das Gesamtwerk, 1972, Bewegung im Kopf. Vom Umgang mit der Kunst, 1993, Kulturfinanzierung, 1995, Annäherung. Über die Notwendigkeit von Kunst, 1996, Remy Zaugg-Conversation with Jean Christophe Ammann, French edit., 1990, German edit., 1994, Das Glück Zu Sehen, 1998, (with Corinna Thierolf) In the Beginning the Word.About Language in Contemporary Art, 2006; co-organizer of documenta 5, Kassel, 1972; curator: 9th Triennial small sculptures, Fellbach-Stuttgart, Germany, van Gogh bis Beuys at Aussenstellungshalle, Bonn, 2005; organizer (with Natalie De Ligt): Ninth Triennial of Small Sculptures, Fellbach-Stuttgart, 2004. Decorated Officier Des Arts et Des Lettres, Goethe-medal City of Frankfurt, Germany; recipient Culture award, Wormland Found., 2001, Dr. Herbert Zapp award for cultural excellence, 2006. Office: Klettenbergstrasse 11 60322 Frankfurt Germany Home Phone: 0049/69/5963 160.

AMMANN, LILLIAN ANN NICHOLSON, writer, editor, small business owner; b. Pearsall, Tex., June 20, 1946; d. Harvey Franklin and Annie Laura (Matthews) Nicholson; m. Jack Jordan Ammann Jr., May 31, 1967; 1 child, William Erik. BA magna cum laude, Southwestern U., 1968. Mgr. inventory Kelly AFB, San Antonio, 1967-70; employment counselor Tex. Employment Commn., San Antonio, 1970-75; owner, operator Lillie's Lovely Little Gardens, San Antonio, 1975-77, Lillie's Interior Landscapes, San Antonio, 1980-82, pres., 1983-96; sec. Jack Ammann Inc., 1983-87; pres. Lillie's & Sherry's Plants & Pottery, San Antonio, 1977-80; pub., editor-in-chief Our Mail Network, LLC, 2000—. Author: Lillie's Lovely Gardening Book, 1976, Look Beyond Tomorrow: The Carola Spencer Story, 1998, Stroke of Luck, 1999, How to Get Started in Network Marketing from Home, 2001; editor: A Bouquet of Recipes from the Diocese of the Southwest of the Anglican Church in America; author: Dream or Destiny, 2007. Vol. All Saints Anglican Ch. Mem.: San Antonio Writers Guild (past pres.), Electronically Published Internet Connection. Home and Office: 603 Mauze Dr San Antonio TX 78216-3711 Home Phone: 210-344-5554. Home Fax: 210-344-1958. Personal E-mail: lillie@lillieammann.com.

AMMAR, ALIA N., neuropsychologist, educator; b. Chgo., Nov. 8, 1968; d. Buthaynah A. Ammar and Paul A. Asad (Stepfather); m. M. Shaik Hussain, 1991 (div. Nov. 4, 2004); children: Nazir S. Hussain, Asim S. Hussain. PhD, Loyola U., Chgo., 2003. Lic. Clinical Psychologist Ill., 2006. Lectr., adj. prof. Loyola U. Chgo., 1998—; neuropsychologist Neuropsychological Svcs., PC, Arlington Heights, Ill., 2006—. Fellow Fellowship, Ill. Consortium for Ednl. Opportunities Program, 1996—2000. Mem.: APA, Internat. Neuropsychological Soc. Independent. Islam. Achievements include research in elucidating cognitive effects of electrical injury and PTSD. Office: 3375 Arlington Heights Rd Arlington Heights IL 60004 Home Phone: 847-309-9121; Office Phone: 847-309-9121.

AMMAR, RAYMOND GEORGE, physicist, researcher; b. Kingston, Jamaica, July 15, 1932; arrived in US, 1950, naturalized, 1965; s. Elias George and Nellie (Khaleel) A.; m. Carroll Ikerd, June 17, 1961 (dec. 2004); children: Elizabeth, Robert (dec.), David. AB, Harvard U., 1953; PhD, U. Chgo., 1959. Rsch. assoc. Enrico Fermi Inst., U. Chgo., 1959-60; asst. prof. physics Northwestern U., Evanston, Ill., 1960-64, assoc. prof., 1964-69; prof. physics U. Kans., Lawrence, 1969—, chmn. dept. physics and astronomy, 1989—2003; (on sabbatical leave Fermilab and Deutsches Elektronen Synchrotron, 1984-85). Cons. Argonne (Ill.) Nat. Lab., 1965-69, vis. scientist, 1971-72; vis. scientist Fermilab, Batavia, Ill., summers 1976-81, Deutsches Elektronen Synchroton, Hamburg, Germany, summers 1982-88, lab. of nuclear studies Cornell U., summers 1989-98; project dir. NSF grant for rsch. in high energy physics, 1962-2001. Contbr. articles to sci. jours. Fellow Am. Phys. Soc.; mem. AAUP. Home: 1651 Hillcrest Rd Lawrence KS 66044-4525 Office: U Kans Dept Physics And Astronomy Lawrence KS 66045-7582 Home Phone: 785-842-4285; Office Phone: 785-864-4626. Business E-Mail: ammar@ku.edu.

AMMERMAN, ALBERT JAY, archaeologist, humanities educator; s. Albert Merlin Ammerman and Ruth Lennox; m. Rebecca Lynne Miller, July 16, 1983; children: Richard Albert, Dora Q. BA, U Mich., Ann Arbor, 1964; PhD, U. London, 1972. Sr. rsch. assoc. Stanford U., Palo Alto, Calif., 1972—77; asst. prof. SUNY, Birmingham, NY, 1978—83; vis. prof. U. Parma, Italy, 1982—92, U. Trent, Italy, 1994—99; sr. rsch. assoc. Colgate U., Hamilton, NY, 1986—2003, O'Connor prof. humanities, 2006—. Dir. Venice Study Group Colgate U., Hamilton, NY, 1999; dir. Archaeology Sch. Am. Acad. Rome, 2001. Author: The Neolithic Transition and., 1984, The Acconia Survey, 1985; editor: The Widening Harvest, 2003. Recipient Writing awards, U. Mich., 1964; grantee, Nat. Geog. Soc., 1985—2002, Delmas Found., 1990—2001. Mem.: Am. Sch. Classical Studies (mng. com. 1990—), Archaeol. Inst. Am. (sci. com. 1992—98). Avocations: winemaking, rowing. Home: 81 Hamilton St Hamilton NY 13346

AMMON, GARY D., lawyer; b. Frederick, Md., 1947; BA, Allegheny Coll., 1969; JD, Duquesne U., 1977; LLM in Taxation, Temple U., 1992. Bar: Pa. 1977. Law clerk, Judge Aldisert Ct. of Appeals (3d cir.); assoc., employee benefits group Drinker Biddle & Reath LLP, Phila., 1981—88, ptnr., employee benefits and exec. compensation group, 1988—, chair, employee benefits and exec. compensation group, 1996—2007. Office: Drinker Biddle & Reath LLP One Logan Sq 18th & Cherry Sts Philadelphia PA 19103-6996 Office Phone: 215-988-2981. Office Fax: 215-988-2757. Business E-Mail: gary.ammon@dbr.com.

AMMON, JOHN RICHARD, anesthesiologist; b. NYC, 1948; MD, U. Pa., 1974. Cert. in anesthesiology. Intern Crozer Chester Med. Ctr., 1974—75; resident in anesthesiology Mass. Gen. Hosp., Boston, 1975—77; fellow in cardiac anesthesiology Stanford (Calif.) Med. Ctr., 1977—78; dir., v.p. Am. Bd. Anesthesiology, Phoenix, 1988—99; pvt. practice Valley Anesthesiology Ltd., Phoenix, 1999—. Mem.: Am. Soc. Anesthesiology, Alpha Omega Alpha. also: Am Bd Anesthesiology 4101 Lake Boone Trl Ste 510 Raleigh NC 27607-7506 Office: Valley Anesthesiology Consultants 2901 N Central Ave Ste 500 Phoenix AZ 85012-2700

AMOLSCH, ARTHUR LEWIS, publishing executive; b. LA, Nov. 28, 1939; s. Arthur Bruce Amolsch and Mildred Vivian (Guyott) Fry; m. Judith Ann Marolda, Aug. 27, 1963 (div. 1982); children: Christopher Bryan, Kira Leigh; m. Imelda Marie Moore Madden, Mar. 27, 1983. BS, Ea. Mich. U., 1963. Tchr. Edmondson Jr. High Sch., Ypsilanti, Mich., 1963-66; fgn. svc. officer Dept. State, Washington, 1971-72; head speech writer Com. for Re-election of the Pres., Washington, 1972; dep. dir., press rels. Presdl. Inaugural Com., Washington, 1973; dir. pub. info. FTC, Washington, 1973-76; pres., pub. Washington Regulatory Reporting Assocs., 1976—. Capt. USAF, 1967-71. Home: PO Box 356 Basye VA 22810-0356 Office Phone: 202-639-0581. E-mail: ftcwatch@usa.net.

AMON, CAROL BAGLEY, federal judge; b. 1946; BS, Coll. William and Mary, 1968; JD, U. Va., 1971. Bar: Va. 1971, D.C. 1972, N.Y. 1980. Staff atty. Communications Satellite Corp., Washington, 1971-73; trial atty. U.S. Dept. Justice, Washington, 1973-74; asst. U.S. atty. Ea. Dist. N.Y., 1974-86, U.S. magistrate, 1986-90, dist. ct. judge, 1990—. Recipient John Marshall award U.S. Dept. Justice, 1983. Mem. ABA (joint commn. evaluate model code judicial conduct 2004-05), Va. State Bar Assn., D.C. Bar Assn. (chair codes of conduct com. of jud. conf. 1998-2001), Fed. Bar Coun. Inn of Ct. (pres. 2007—). Office: US District Court 225 Cadman Plz E Brooklyn NY 11201-1818 Office Phone: 718-613-2410.

AMON, CRISTINA HORTENSIA, mechanical engineering educator, researcher; b. Oct. 12, 1956; m. Carmelo Parisi, Dec. 6, 1980; children: Andreina, Gabriel. Degree in mech. engrng. summa cum laude, U. Simon Bolivar, Caracas, Venezuela, 1981; MS, MIT, 1985, PhD, 1988. Instr., researcher U. Simon Bolivar, Caracas, 1981-83; asst. prof. Carnegie-Mellon U., Pitts., 1988-93, assoc. prof., 1993-97, prof., 1997-2000, dir. Inst. Complex Engineered Sys., 1999—, Raymond J. Lane disting. prof. mech. engrng., 2001—06; dean Faculty Engrng. U. Toronto, Canada, 2006—. Bd. dirs. MKS Instruments, Inc., 2007—. Contbr. articles to profl. jours. Recipient Rsch. Initiation award NSF, 1989, G.T. Ladd award CIT, 1991, Ednl. award Ladd, 1998. Fellow AIAA (assoc.), ASME (Pitts. Engr. of Yr. 1999, Gustus L. Larson Meml. award 2000, assoc. editor Jour. Heat Transfer); mem. IEEE (sr., assoc. editor CPMT), NAE, Soc. Automotive Engrng. (R. Teetor Ednl. award 1994), Sci. Rsch. Soc., Am. Soc. Engrng. Edn. (North Ctrl. Sect. Outstanding Tchr. award 1995, Best Campus Rep. award 1996, George Westinghouse award 1997, Teare award 1998), Soc. Women Engrs. (Distig. Educator award 1999), Soc. Hispanic Profl. Engrs., Sigma Xi. Office: Carnegie Mellon U 1201 Hamburg Hall 5000 Forbes Ave Pittsburgh PA 15213 Office Phone: 412-268-3651. E-mail: camon@cmu.edu.*

AMONETTE, REX. A., physician; b. Ozan, Ark., June 17, 1939; MD, U. Ark., 1966. Intern Ark. Bapt. Med. Ctr., Little Rock, 1966-67; resident U. Tenn., Memphis, 1969-71; physician Balt. Meml. Hosp., Memphis, 1974—. Mem. AMA, Am. Dermatology Assn. Office: Memphis Dermatology Clinic 1455 Union Ave Memphis TN 38104-6727 Office Phone: 901-726-6655.

AMONTE, TONY (ANTHONY LEWIS AMONTE), professional hockey player; b. Weymouth, Mass., Aug. 2, 1970; Attended, Boston U., 1989—91. Profl. hockey player NY Rangers, 1988—94, Chgo. Blackhawks, 1994—2002, Phoenix Coyotes, 2002—03, Phila. Flyers, 2003—05, Calgary Flames, 2005—. Mem. Team USA, World Cup of Hockey, 1996, USA Olympic Hockey Team, Salt Lake City, 2002. Named NCAA All-Tournament Team, 1990—91; named to NHL All-Rookie Team, 1992, NHL All-Star Team, 1997—2001. Achievements include being a member of World Cup Champion Team USA, 1996; being a member of silver medal winning USA Hockey Team, Salt Lake City Olympics, 2002. Office: c/o Calgary Flames PO Box 1540 Stn M T2P 3B9 Calgary Al Canada

AMORE, SHIRLEY C., library director; Dir. Sarasota County Libr. Sys., Fla., 1997—2000; exec. dir. cmty. svcs. Sarasota County, 2000—06; city libr. Denver Pub. Libr., 2006—. Mem. legis. com. Colo. Assn. Librs. Co-author: The Librarian's Guide to Partnerships, 1999. Office: Denver Pub Libr 10 W Fourteenth Ave Pky Denver CO 80204 Office Phone: 720-865-1711. Office Fax: 720-865-1785. E-mail: samore@denverlibrary.org.

AMORELLO, MATTHEW JOHN, former state agency administrator, state senator; b. Worcester, Mass., Mar. 15, 1958; s. Edward Vincent and Eunice Colleen (Byrnes) Amorello; m. Charlotte Amorello; 1 child, Mayo. BA, Assumption Coll., 1980; MPA, Am. U., 1983; JD, Suffolk Law Sch., 1990. Budget analyst U.S. EPA, Washington, 1983-86, program analyst Boston, 1986-87; state senator State of Mass., Boston, 1991-99; commr. Hwy. Commn., Boston, 1999—2002; chmn. Mass. Turnpike Authority, 2002—06. Sec., commr. Blackstone River Valley Nat. Heritage Corridor, Woonsocket, R.I., 1991—; chmn. Ctrl. Mass. Legis. Caucus, 1992-93, Rep. Senate Caucus, Boston, 1992-94, Grafton (Mass.) GOP Com., 1990—. Named Outstanding Young Leader Worcester Jaycees, 1992, Legislator of Yr. Worcester County Bar Assn., 1993, First Joseph Moakly award Public Service, 2006, Disting. Leadership award, Artery Bus. Com., Frank Sargent Clean Harbor award. Mem.: Internat. Bridge, Tunnel and Turnpike Assn. (bd. dirs.). Republican.

AMOROSO, FRANK, retired communication system engineer, consultant; b. Providence, July 31, 1935; s. Michele and Angela Maria Barbara (D'Uva) A. BSEE, MSEE, MIT, 1958; postgrad., Purdue U., 1958—60, U. Turin, 1964—65. Registered profl. engr., Calif. Instr. elec. engring. Purdue U., West Lafayette, Ind., 1958—60; rsch. engr. Melpar Inc., Roxbury, Mass., 1959, MIT Instrumentation Lab., Cambridge, Mass., 1960, Litton Sys. Advanced Devel. Lab., Waltham, Mass., 1960—61; engr. Melpar Applied Sci. Divsn., Watertown, Mass., 1961; mem. tech. staff RCA Labs. David Sarnoff Rsch. Ctr., Princeton, NJ, 1962—64, Mitre Corp., Bedford,

Mass., 1966—67; sr. applied mathematician Collins Radio Co., Newport Beach, 1967—68; comm. sys. engr. N.Am. Rockwell Corp., El Segundo, Calif., 1968—71, Northrop Electronics Divsn., Palos Verdes Peninsula, 1971—72; comm. sys. engr., sr. staff engr. Hughes Aircraft Co., Fullerton, 1972—89; ret., 1989; cons., developer, presenter ednl. seminars, 1989—; profl. mentor to writers, 2005—. Cons. Lincom, Inc., LA, 1994—96, Omnipoint Corp., Price Comms., 2004—; cons. client Sklar Comm. Engring., 1996—, Mascarell Microones, S.L., Tarragona, Spain; instr. continuing engring. edn. program George Washington U., San Diego, 1993; instr. ext. short courses UCLA, 1987—89, 1998—; cons. Mobile Elec. Tracking Sys., Boca Raton, Fla., 1992, Word Works, Newport Beach, Calif., 2003—. Co-author: (book) Power Amplifier Design, 2002. 1st lt. U.S. Signal Corps, 1961-62. Recipient Outstanding Achievement award RCA Labs., 1964; grad. study scholar Italian Govt., 1964-66. Mem. IEEE (sr., life, session organizer, reviewer sci. paper submissions, chmn. conf. on mil. com., presenter). Achievements include patents in field. Home and Office: Digital Data Modulation Studies 271 W Alton Ave Apt D Santa Ana CA 92707-4171 Office Phone: 714-557-1061.

AMOROSO, RICHARD LOUIS, psychologist, educator; b. Medford, Mass., Apr. 24, 1946; s. Louis Raymond and Marjorie Lou (McCathie) Amoroso; m. Juliette Noble Sherer, Oct. 1982 (div. 1986); 1 child, Juliette Rachael. BS in Psychology, U. Mass., 1972; postgrad., Stanford U., 1972—74, Harvard U., 1980—82; PhD in Cosmology, Internat. Noetic U., 1992; MA in Consciousness Studies, J.F.K. U., 1994. Computer engr. Harvard Smithsonian Astrophys. Obs., Cambridge, Mass., 1980-82; instr. Peralta Coll., Oakland, Calif., 1987-88; dir. Mus. Robotics, Berkeley, Calif., 1989—, Noetic Advanced Studies Inst., Orinda, Calif., 1992—; pres. Cereroscopic Sys., Inc., Provo, Utah; CFO Elec. Corp., Oakland, 1992-94; prof. philosophy of mind Internat. Noetic U., Oakland, 1995—. Founding editor: Noetic Jour., 1997—; editor: Science and the Primary of Consciousness, 1998, The Scientific Origins of Sexual Preference, 2000, Gravitation and Cosmology: From the Hubble Radius to the Planck Scale, 2001, The Complementarity of Mind and Body, 2003, What is Conciousness? Introducing the Cosmology of Being, 2003, Shifting the Medical Paradigm, 2004, A Revolucao da Consciencia, 2005, Extending the Standard Model: The Search for Unity in Physics, 2005, Unified Theories, 2007, Rendezvous at The Temple of Love, 2007, Metatheory, 2007. Mem.: AAAS, N.Y. Acad. Sci., Romanian Acad. Sci. (hon.). Republican. Mem. Lds Ch. Achievements include having the 1st comprehensive theory of dualism in history. Avocations: meditation, scuba diving, robotic sculpture, reading, sailing. Personal E-mail: noeticj@mindspring.com.

AMORUSO, LEONARD J., lawyer; b. 1965; BBA in Banking, Fin. and Investment, Hofstra Univ., JD. Bar: NJ 1989. Dep. dir. & chief counsel NASD Dist. Office 10, NYC; asst. gen. counsel & chief compliance officer Knight Securities, 1999—2003; chief compliance officer Knight Trading Group, 2003—, co-head office of gen. counsel, 2005—. Office: Knight Trading Group 545 Washington Blvd Fl 1 Jersey City NJ 07310-1607

AMOS, BETTY GILES, food service executive, accountant; b. Lebanon, Mo., July 18, 1941; d. Clarence Edgar and Clara Mae (Gann) Giles; m. E.L. Amos, Sept. 18, 1959 (div. Oct. 1965); 1 child, Jeffrey Lee; m. Thomas R. Righetti, Jan. 2, 1983 (dec. Sept. 18, 2002). BBA magna cum laude, U. Miami, Coral Gables, Fla., 1973, MBA, 1976; D of Bus. Adminstrn. honoris causa, Johnson & Wales U., 1990. CPA, Fla. Sec. City of Lebanon, 1959-63; dept. head Empire Gas Co., Lebanon, 1963-68; fin. analyst asst. Biscayne Assocs., Ltd., Miami, Fla., 1968-73; investment mgr. Universal Restaurants Inc., Miami, 1973-77; pvt. practice acct., investment mgr. Miami, 1977-83; pres. The Abkey Cos., Miami, 1983—. Founder Mega Bank, Miami, 1983-94; mem. adv. com. Fuddruckers, Inc., Boston, 1986-2002. Trustee Miami Project, 1986-89, United Fund of Dade County, 1992—; pres. Humane Soc. Greater Miami, 1994-2000, bd. dirs., 1993-2000; mem. pres. coun. U. Miami, 1994—, mem. founder's soc., 1994—, bd. trustees, 1997—; mem. presdl. search com. U. Miami, 2000; mem. Orange Bowl Com., 2002—; dir. Wings Over Miami Aviation Mus., treas., 2002-03, pres., 2004—; bd. dirs. IVAX Corp., 2003—; mem. audit com. Miami-Dade County Sch. Bd., 2004—. Recipient Philip J. Romano Founders award, 1988. Mem. AICPA, Fla. Inst. CPAs, Am. Women's Soc. CPAs, Coconut Grove C. of C. (trustee 1988-2001), Nat. Assn. Women Bus. Owners (Outstanding Woman Bus. award 1993), U. Miami Alumni Assn. (nat. pres. 1999-2001), Iron Arrow, Internat. Women's Forum (bd. dirs. 2006—), Women of Tomorrow (bd. dirs. 2006—), Women's Exec. Leadership (adv. bd. 2005—). Republican. Avocations: skiing, waterskiing, scuba diving, tennis. Office: The Abkey Cos 9275 Coral Reef Dr Ste 107 Miami FL 33157 Home: 8206 SW 171 Ter Palmetto Bay FL 33157 Home Phone: 305-232-1313; Office Phone: 305-278-4422. Business E-Mail: bgamos@bellsouth.net.

AMOS, DANIEL PAUL, insurance company executive; b. Pensacola, Fla., Aug. 13, 1951; s. Paul Shelby and Mary Jean (Roberts) A.; m. Mary Shannon Landing, Sept. 12, 1972; children: Paul Shelby, Lauren Alyse. BS in Risk and Ins. Mgmt., U. Ga., Athens, 1973. Co-state mgr. Aflac (Am. Family Life Assurance Co.), Columbus, Ga., 1973-78, state mgr., 1978-83, pres., 1983-96, COO, 1987—90, CEO Columbus, Ga., 1990—, chmn., 2001—; dep. CEO Am. Family Corp., Columbus, Ga., 1996. Dir. Columbus Bank & Trust Co., Synovus Fin. Corp., So. Co. Bd. trustees Children's Healthcare of Atlanta, House of Mercy of Columbus. Recipient Dr. Martin Luther King Jr. Unity award, Torch of Liberty award, Anti-Defamation League. Methodist. Avocation: bridge. Office: Aflac Inc 1932 Wynnton Rd Columbus GA 31999 Office Phone: 706-323-3431.*

AMOS, DEBORAH SUSAN, foreign correspondent; b. Glen Ridge, NJ, May 18, 1950; d. John and Regina (Conner) A.; m. Ronald Charles Davis, Sept. 7, 1991. BS in Broadcasting, U. Fla., 1972. Nieman fellow Harvard U., Cambridge, Mass., 1991-92; documentary prodr. Nat. Pub. Radio, Washington, 1979-85, Mid. East corr. London and Amman, Jordan, 1985-89, roving corr. London, 1989-91, bur. chief, 1992—93, Iraq war corr., 2003—; corr. ABC News, 1993—. Author: Lines in the Sand, 1992; contbr. articles to popular publs. Recipient Prix Italia for coverage of last days of Jonestown, 1982, Alfred I. duPont-Columbia award for Gulf War coverage, 1992, for coverage of Iraq, 2007. Mem. Coun. on Fgn. Rels. Office: NPR 635 Massachusetts Ave NW Washington DC 20001 also: ABC News 7 W 66th St New York NY 10023*

AMOS, JAMES LYSLE, photographer; b. Kalamazoo, Jan. 25, 1929; s. George Elsworth and Lois Hazel (Noffsinger) A.; m. Martha Imogene (Holbrook), Sept. 1975. Student, U. Idaho, 1947-49; AAS, Rochester Inst. Tech., 1951. Trainee Eastman Kodak Co., 1951-53, salesman Des Moines, 1956, tech. sales rep. Balt., 1957-67. Free lance photographer, 1967-69, 93—; staff photographer, Nat. Geog. Soc., Washington, 1969-89, contract photographer, 1989-93; prin. photographer (books) on Hawaii and America's Inland Waterway. Served with AUS, 1953-55. Named Mag. Photographer of Yr., Nat. Press Photographers Assn., 1969, 70. Mem. N.Am. Nature Photography Assn., Internat. Assn. Panoramic Photographers. Home: PO Box 807 Chestertown MD 21620-0607 *To achieve success we must love what we are doing, be willing to take risks and trust our instincts.*

AMOS, LINDA K., academic administrator; b. Findlay, Ohio, Sept. 7, 1940; d. Blond G. and Dorotha (Brinkman) A. BS, Ohio State U., 1962, MS, 1964; EdD, Boston U., 1977. Asst. dean of baccalaureate affairs Boston U. Coll. Nursing, 1971-74, dean, prof., 1975-80, U. Utah Coll. Nursing, Salt Lake City, 1980—2000, dean, prof. emerita, 2006—; assoc. v.p. for health scis. U. Utah, Salt Lake City, 1998—2006, Dorthie & Keith Barnes presdl. chair, prof. nursing, prof. emerita, dean emerita Coll. Nursing, 2006—. Cons. Social Sci. Rsch. Inst., Boston; chmn. Commn. on Collegiate Nursing Edn., 1998-2000; bd. dirs. Univ. Health Network. Contbr. articles to profl. jours. Chmn. Presdl. Commn. on Status of Women, U. Utah, 1995—99; bd. dirs. Utah Heart Assn.; trustee U. Utah Hosp. Served as cons. with USPHS. Named for Outstanding Contbns. to the Nursing Profession, Utah Citizen's League for Nursing, 1989, Linda K. Amos Atrium, U. Utah, 2005; recipient VA Chief Nurse award for promoting unity between edn. and practice, Lawrence and Delores Weaver Coll. Pharmacy Recognition award, 2002, Disting. Woman prize Salt Lake Jr. Assistance League, 2004, Client Achievement award, Utah AIA, 2005, Utah Owner of Yr. award Am. Gen. Contractors Utah, 2006; named Atrium in her honor, U. Utah, 2006. Fellow Am. Acad. Nursing (governing coun. 1986-90, selection com. 1995—98); mem. ANA, Am. Assn. Colls. of Nursing (pres. 1984-86, Sister Bernadette Armiger award 2000), Nat. Adv. Coun. on Nurse Tng., Utah Women's Forum, Internat. Women's Forum, Salt Lake City Rotary, Sigma Theta Tau (internat. nominating com. 1995-97, Mary Tolle Wright award for excellence in leadership 1991).

AMOS, PAUL SHELBY, II, insurance company executive; B in Econs., Duke U., Durham, NC; MBA, Emory U., Atlanta; JD, Tulane U., New Orleans. With corp. legal divsn. Skadden, Arps, Slate, Meagher and Flom, Washington; state sales coord. Ga.-North AFLAC, 2002, exec. v.p. US Ops., 2005, pres. Aflac, COO Aflac US, 2006—. Office: AFLAC 1932 Wynnton Rd Columbus GA 31999 Office Phone: 706-323-3431.*

AMOS, REED C., lawyer; b. Richmond, Va., Sept. 1973; BA, Brigham Young Univ., 1997; JD, Catholic Univ, 2000. Bar: Calif. 2001. Law clk. Office Internat. Affairs, Criminal Div., US Dept. Justice; assoc., criminal defense practice Sherman & Sherman plc, Santa Monica, Calif. Atty. Angel de la Communidad Fundacion, LA. Named a Rising Star, So. Calif. Super Lawyers, 2006. Mem.: Am. Soc. Internat. Law, Nat. Coalition Concerned Legal Professionals. Office: Sherman & Sherman PLC 2115 Main St Santa Monica CA 90405 Office Phone: 310-399-3259. Office Fax: 310-392-9029.

AMOS, TORI, musician, singer; b. NC; d. Edison and Mary Ellen A. Student, Peabody Conservatory. Albums: Y Kant Tori Read, 1988, Little Earthquakes, 1992, Under the Pink, 1994 (Grammy nomination, Best Alternative Music Performance, 1995), Boys for Pele, 1996, From the Choirgirl Hotel, 1998, To Venus and Back, 1999, Strange Little Girls, 2001, Scarlet's Walk, 2002, Tales of a Librarian: Tori Amos Collection, 2003, The Beekeeper, 2005, A Piano: The Collection, 2006, American Doll Posse, 2007; author: (with Ann Powers) Tori Amos: Piece By Piece, 2005. Office: Atlantic Records 1290 Avenue Of The Americas New York NY 10104-0184*

AMOS, WALLY (FAMOUS AMOS), entrepreneur; b. Tallahassee, July 1, 1936; s. Wallace Sr. and Ruby Amos; m. Maria LaForey (div.); children: Michael, Gregory; m. Shirlee Ellis (div.); 1 child, Shawn; m. Christine Amos, 1979; 1 child, Sarah. Stockroom clk. Saks Fifth Ave., NYC, 1957-58, stockroom supr., 1958-61; mail room clk. William Morris Agy., NYC, 1961, sec., 1961-62, asst. agt., 1962; talent agt., 1962-67; ind personal mgr. LA, 1967-75; founder Famous Amos Chocolate Chip Cookie Corp., Hollywood, Calif., 1975-89, Wally Amos Presents: Chip and Cookie, Kailua, Hawaii, 1991—, UNCLE Nonamé Cookie Co., 1992—; chmn. Uncle Wally Cookie Co. Author: The Famous Amos Story: The Face That Launched a Thousand Chips, 1983, The Power In You: Ten Secret Ingredients for Inner Strength, 1988, Man with No Name: Turn Lemons Into Lemonade, 1994. Nat. spokesman Literacy Vols. of Am., 1979-. Served with USAF, 1953—57. Recipient Pres.' award for Entrepreneurial Excellence, 1986, Horatio Alger award 1987, Nat. Literacy Honors award 1990.*

AMOSS, WALTER JAMES, III, (JIM), editor; b. New Orleans, Oct. 22, 1947; s. Walter James Jr. and Berthe Lathrop (Marks) A.; m. Nancy Brooks Monroe, Apr. 5, 1975; children: Adam Brooks, Sophia Philomene. BA magna cum laude, Yale U., 1969. Reporter The States-Item, New Orleans, 1974-79, The Times-Picayune, New Orleans, 1980-82, city editor, 1982-83, met. editor, 1983-88, assoc. editor, 1988-90, editor, 1990—. Bd. vis. La. State U. Manship Sch. Mass. Comms.; trustee Trinity Episcopal Sch.; mem. Pulitzer Prize bd., 2003-, juror, 1994-95, 1999-2000. Mem. La. Com. of Selection for Rhodes Scholarships, 1982—. Rhodes scholar Oxford (Eng.) U., 1970-71; Journalistes en Europe grantee, 1979-80; named Nat. Press Found.'s Editor of Yr., 1997, named Editor & Publisher's Editor of Yr., 2006. Mem. Am. Soc. Newspaper Editors, AP Mng. Editors, Phi Beta Kappa. Roman Catholic. Office: The Times-Picayune 3800 Howard Ave New Orleans LA 70125-1429

AMPARADO, KEITH D., communications company executive; b. Bklyn., Oct. 5, 1952; m. Arcadeo and Sadie J. (Browne) A. BS, SUNY, Empire State Coll. Supr. data processing Franklin Nat. Bank/European Am. Bank, 1974-78; mgr. Ctr. for Computing Activity Columbia U., NYC, 1978-80; systems analyst Morgan Guaranty Trust Co., 1980-81; programmer, analyst European Am. Bank, 1981-83; sr. tech editor Mfrs. Hanover Trust, 1983-85; founder, pres. KDA Comm, Bklyn., 1985—. Cons. Siloam Presbyn. Ch., Bklyn., 1988—. Mem. Soc. for Tech. Communication (sr.), Am. Mgmt. Assn., Am. Mktg. Assn., Mktg. Rsch. Assn., Nat. Assn. Desktop Pubs., Qualitative Rsch. Cons. Assn., Internat. Assn. of Bus. Communicators.

AMPY, FRANKLIN ROOSEVELT, zoologist; b. Dinwiddie, Va., June 22, 1936; s. Preston and Beatrice Tucker A.; B.S., Va. State Coll., 1958; M.S., Oreg. State U., 1960, Ph.D., 1962. Asst. prof. Am. U. Beirut, 1962-68; NIH fellow U. Calif., Davis, 1968-71; assoc. prof. zoology Howard U., Washington, 1971—90 , prof. biology, 1990-, acting chmn. dept. zoology, 1973-75, 84-86, 90-92, now acting chmn. dept., dir. undergrad. edn., dept. biology, 2003-; geneticist Lebanese del. to World Poultry Conf., 1966; cons. NIH, 1981, 83. NASA-Ames faculty fellow, 1976; dir. undergraduate edn. biology, 2003-04; NIH grantee, 1978—; NSF grantee, 1978,95. Mem. Bd. dirs., Project 30, Am. Genetic Assn., Am. Soc. Genetics, Environ. Mutagenesis Soc., Am. Soc. Cell Biologists, Smithsonian Assocs., Sigma Xi (pres. Howard U. cptr., 1993-94), Beta Kappa Xi, Alpha Phi Alpha. Democrat. Episcopalian. Home: PO Box 91886 Washington DC 20090-1886 Office: Dept Biology Howard Univ 415 College St Washington DC 20001

AMRHEIN, JOE, artist; Owner, dir. Pierogi 2000, 1994—. One-man shows include Fiona Whitney Gallery, LA, 1985, Ivory/Kimpton Gallery, San Francisco, 1986, Turske & Whitney Gallery, LA, 1987, Turske & Whitney Gallery, Zurich, 1989, Earl MaGrath Gallery, NYC, 1996, Leytonstone Ctr. Contemporary Art, Leytonstone, Eng., 2001, Roebling Hall, Bklyn., 2001, Galerie Bernard Jordan, Paris, 2002, exhibited in group shows at The Design Ctr., LA, 1984, Mitzi Landau Gallery, LA, 1984, Pepper Art Gallery, Redlands, Calif., 1986, LA County Mus. Art, 1986, David Zwirner Gallery, NY, 1993, Postmasters Gallery, NYC, 1995, Williamsburg Art & Hist. Ctr., NYC, 1997, Staatsgalerie Stuttgart, Germany, 2000, Cynthia Broan Gallery, NYC, 2001, Wythe Studio, Bklyn., 2002, others. Office: 175 N 9th St Brooklyn NY 11211 Office Phone: 718-599-2144. E-mail: joe@pierogi2000.com.

AMRON, CORY M., lawyer; b. NYC; BA, U. Rochester, 1974; JD, Harvard U., 1977. Ptnr. Vorys, Sater, Seymour and Pease, LLP. Mem.: Commercial Real Estate Women Fellows of the Am. Bar Found. (state chair 2001—), Women's Bar Assn. DC (tres. 1982—83, mem., bd. dirs. 1994—97, Woman Lawyer Yr. 2004), Am. Bar Assn. (mem., Task Force Law Schools and Profession: Narrowing the Gap 1988—92, chair, Commn. Women Profession 1991—94, mem., Commn. Domestic Violence 1998—2002), Bar Assn. DC (chair, Young Lawyers Sect. 1983—84, mem., bd. dirs. 1985—87, mem., Out of Box Com., Sect. Legal Edn. 2001—), DC Bar (editor, DC Practical Manual 1985—87, chair, Commerical Real Estate Com. 1986—89, mem., Steering Com., Real Estate Housing and Land Use Sect. 1989—94, mem., Reproductive Cancer Task Force 1994—96). Office: Vorys Sater Seymour and Pease LLP 11th Fl 1828 L St NW Washington DC 20036-5109 Business E-Mail: cmamron@vssp.com.

AMSDEN, TED THOMAS, lawyer; b. Cleve., Dec. 11, 1950; s. Richard Thomas and Mary Agnes (Hendricks) A.; m. Ruth Anna Rydstedt, May 1, 1982; children: Jennifer Rydstedt, Matthew Lars, Alexis Linnea. BA in econs., Wayne State U., 1972; JD, Harvard U., 1975; Grad. in orgn. devel., Ea. Mich. U. Bar: Mich. 1975, U.S. Dist. Ct. (ea. dist.) Mich. 1975, U.S. Ct. Appeals (6th cir.) 1975, U.S. Supreme Ct. 1979. Assoc. Dykema Gossett PLLC, Detroit, 1975—, ptnr.; sr. cons. Leadership Grp., Grosse Pointe Shores, Mich. Chmn. Baha'i Justice Soc., 1986-88, corr. sec., 1988-92, bd. dirs., 1986-93, 95—; bd. dirs. Internat. Inst., Detroit, 1989-97, 99—, v.p. legal affairs, 1991-94, v.p., 1994-95, pres.-elect 1995-96, pres., 1996-97, co-chair Ethnic Summit '96; bd. dirs. Racial Justice Ctr., Grosse Pointe, Mich., 1992-94, Greater Detroit Interfaith Roundtable, 1994—, bd. dirs. Model of Racial Unity, Inc., 1995-97, treas., 1997—, chmn., 1998—, vice chmn.; mem. Mich. Bar Rep. Assembly, 1988-94. Recipient Detroit Principles award of Race Relations Coun. of Metropolitan Detroit, 1993, Spirit of Detroit award City of Detroit Common Coun., 1996, 97, Diversity Champion award Birmingham-Bloomfield Task Force on Race Rels., 2002. Mem. ABA, Mich. Bar Assn., Wolverine Bar Assn., Detroit Bar Assn., Detroit Bar Assn. Found. (bd. dirs. 1992-98, sec., 1993-95, pres. 1995-97), Macomb County Bar Assn., Assn. Def. Counsel, Civic Searchlight (Macomb County steering com., jud. com. 1990-91, Wayne County jud. com. 1992-95). Office: Leadership Grp 987 Lake Shore Rd Grosse Pointe MI 48236 Office Phone: 313-506-2550. Office Fax: 313-885-3777. Business E-Mail: amsdener@yahoo.com.*

AMSEL, ERIC DAVID, psychology professor; b. Can. s. Arthur Amsel; m. Judith Gundersheimer Suben, May 28, 1989; 2 children. BA, McGill U., Montreal, Que., Can., 1979; MEd, Harvard U., Cambridge, 1980; PhD, Columbia U., NYC, 1986. Postdoctoral fellow Yale U., New Haven, 1985—87; asst. prof. U. Sask., Saskatoon, Canada, 1987—89, Vassar Coll., Poughkeepsie, NY, 1989—96, Weber State U., Ogden, Utah, 1996—98, assoc. prof., 1998—2003, prof. psychology, 2003—, chair dept. psychology, 2006—. Vis. prof. Clark U., Worcester, Mass., 2002—03. Contbr. articles to profl. jours., chapters to books; co-author: The Development of Scientific Thinking Skills, 1988; co-editor: Change and Development: Issues of Theory, Method and Application, 1997, Language, Literacy and Cognitive Development: The Development and Consequences of Symbolic Communication, 2002; assoc. editor: New Ideas in Psychology, 2005—. Bd. dirs. Treehouse Children's Mus., Ogden, 1997—, vice chair, 2000—03. Recipient US Prof. of Yr. award, Carnegie Found. for Advancement of Tchg. and Coun. for Advancement and Support of Edn., 2006. Mem.: Soc. Rsch. in Child Devel., Rocky Mountain Psychol. Assn., Jean Piaget Soc. (bd. dirs. 1991—94, 2003—06), Internat. Soc. for Study of Behavioral Devel., Cognitive Devel. Soc., Am. Psychol. Soc., Am. Ednl. Rsch. Assn., Phi Kappa Phi (pres. 2001—02). Avocations: golf, skiing. Office: Dept Psychology Weber State U Ogden Campus 1202 University Cir Ogden UT 84408-1202 Office Phone: 801-626-6658. Office Fax: 801-626-6275. E-mail: Eamsel@weber.edu.*

AMSTER, LINDA EVELYN, newspaper executive, consultant; b. NYC, May 21, 1938; d. Abraham and Belle Shirley (Levine) Meyerson; m. Robert L. Amster, Feb. 18, 1961 (dec. Feb. 1974). BA, U. Mich., 1960; M.L.S., Columbia U., 1968. Tchr. English Stamford High Sch., Conn., 1961-63; research librarian The Detroit News, 1965-67, The N.Y. Times, NYC, 1967-69, supr. news research, 1969-74, news research mgr., 1974—2004, dir. news research, 2004—05; pvt. practice cons. NYC, 2005—. Bd. dirs. Council for Career Planning, N.Y.C., 1982— Editor: The New York Times Passover Cookbook, 1999, Kill Duck Before Serving, 2002, The New York Times Jewish Cookbook, 2003, The New York Times Chicken Cookbook, 2005, The New York Times Country Weekend Cookbook, 2007; contbr. articles to books, N.Y. Times and other publs. Mem. adv. com. N.Y.C. 100 Greater N.Y. Centennial Celebration. Mem.: NY Women's Culinary Alliance, Spl. Librs. Assn., Coffee House. Home: 336 Central Park W New York NY 10025-7111 Business E-Mail: liamst@nytimes.com.

AMSTERDAM, ANTHONY GUY, law educator; b. Phila., Sept. 12, 1935; s. Gustave G. and Valla (Abel) A.; m. Lois P. Sheinfeld, Aug. 29, 1968. AB, Haverford Coll., Pa., 1957, LLD (hon.), 1993; LLB, U. Pa., Phila., 1960; LLD (hon.), John Jay Coll. Criminal Justice, NYC, 1987. Bar: DC 1960. Law clk. to US Supreme Ct. Justice Felix Frankfurter, 1960-61; asst. U.S. atty., 1961-62; prof. law U. Pa., 1962-69, Stanford U., 1969-81, Montgomery prof. clin. legal edn., 1980-81; prof. law, dir. clin. programs and trial advocacy NYU, 1981—2001, univ. prof., 2001—. Cons. litigating atty. numerous civil rights groups; cons. govt. commns.; mem. Commn. to Study Disturbances at Columbia, 1968; trustee Death Penalty Info. Ctr., Lawyers Constl. Def. Com., NAACP Legal Def. Fund, Nat. Coalition to abolish the Death Penalty, So. Poverty Law Ctr., mem. Calif. Fed. Jud. Selection Com., 1976-80; mem. coord. coun. on lawyer competence Conf. of Chief Justices; gen. counsel NY Civil Liberties Union; adv. counsel Civil Liberties Union No. Calif.; mem. ABA task force. Author: The Defensive Transfer of Civil Rights Litigation From State to Federal Courts, 1964, Trial Manual for Defense of Criminal Cases, 5th edit., 1989, (with Hertz and Guggenheim) Trial Manual for Defense Attorneys in Juvenile Court, 1991, 2d edit., 2007, (with Bruner) Minding the Law, 2000; editor-in-chief: U. Pa. Law Rev., 1959-60; contbr. articles to profl. jours. Named Outstanding Young Man of Year Phila. and Pa. Jaycees, 1967; recipient First Disting. Service award U. Pa. Law Sch., 1968; Haverford award Haverford Coll., 1970; Arthur V. Briesen award Nat. Legal Aid and Defender Assn., 1972, 76; named Lawyer of Year Calif. Trial Lawyers Assn., 1973; recipient 1st Earl Warren Civil Liberties award No. Calif. chpt. ACLU, 1973, Citizen of Merit award Sun Reporter, 1974, Walter J. Gores award Stanford U., 1977, William O. Douglas award Pub. Counsel, 1977, 2d ann. award Calif. Attys. Criminal Justice, 1978, award for enhancement human dignity Durfee Found., 1982, Francis Rawle award ALI-ABA, 1984, 3d ann. Civil Liberties award Pa. ACLU, 1985, clinical legal edn. award AALS Sect. on Clinical Legal Edn., 1986, August Vollmer award Am. Soc. Criminology, 1986, Disting. Tchr. award NYU, 1988, award N.Y. Criminal Bar Assn., 1989, Tchg. Achievement award Soc. Am. Law Tchrs., 1999, Kutak award ABA, 2002, Outstanding Scholar award Am. Bar Found., 2006; named MacArthur fellow, 1989; hon. fellow for pub. interest svc. U. Pa. Law Sch., 2001. Fellow Am. Acad. Arts and Scis. Home: 68 Middle Line Hwy Southampton NY 11968-1645 Office: NYU Sch Law Clinical Ctr 245 Sullivan St 5th Fl New York NY 10012 Business E-Mail: aa1@nyu.edu.

AMSTERDAM, MARK LEMLE, lawyer; b. NYC, June 10, 1944; s. Leonard M. and Erica (Lemle) A.; children: Lauren, Matthew. AB, Columbia U., 1966; JD cum laude, Columbia Law Sch., 1969. Bar: N.Y. 1969, U.S. Dist. Ct. (so., ea.) N.Y. 1972, U.S. Supreme Ct. 1973. Assoc. Fried, Frank, Harris, NYC, 1969-70; staff atty. Ctr. Constl. Rights, NYC, 1970-75; atty. pvt. practice, NYC, 1975-76, 81—; ptnr. Rubin Hanley & Amsterdam, NYC, Amsterdam & Lewinter LLP, NYC, 1990—. Instr. N.Y. Law Sch., 1982-83. Contbr. articles to profl. jours. Fellow: NY State Bar Found.; mem.: Columbia Coll. Alumni Assn. (bd. dirs.), Columbia U. Club (pres.), Gardiners Bay Country Club. Home: 1220 Park Ave New York NY 10128-1733 Office: 9 E 40th St New York NY 10016-0402

AMSTUTZ, CURTIS J., music educator; s. Joseph and Charlene Amstutz; m. Kemper D. Shoemaker; children: Benjamin children: Gabrielle, Joshua. BS, Ball State U., Muncie, Ind., 1991, MA, 1999. Band dir. Woodland CUSD #5, Streator, Ill., 1991—92; band dir., music dept. chair South Adams Schools, Berne, Ind., 1992—. Mem.: Music Educators Nat. Conf. Home Phone: 260-589-3681; Office Phone: 260-589-3131.

AMSTUTZ, DANIEL GORDON, agricultural products executive, consultant, retired federal agency administrator, grain company executive; b. Cleve., Nov. 8, 1932; s. Gordon M. and Elizabeth (Kiss) Amstutz. BS, Ohio State U., 1954. Trainee Cargill, Inc., Mpls., 1954-55, grain mcht. Ft. Worth, 1959, sr. grain mcht. Mpls., 1960-72; grain mcht. Tradax Can., Ltd., Montreal, Que., 1955-56, Tradax Geneva S.A., 1956-57; mgr. Deutsche Tradax GMBH, Hamburg, Germany, 1957-58; pres. Cargill Investor Svcs., Inc., Chgo., 1972—78; ptnr. Goldman, Sachs & Co., NYC, 1978-82; undersec. Dept. Agr., Washington, 1983-87; pres. Cmty. Credit Corp., Washington, 1983-87; amb., chief trade negotiator for agr. USDA, Washington, 1987-89; exec. dir. Internat. Wheat Coun., London, 1992-95; pres., CEO N.Am. Export Grain Assn., Inc., Washington, 1995-2000; pres. Amstutz & Co., Washington, 2000—; sr. ministry adv. agrl. Iraq, 2003—04. Mem. U.S. Agrl. Policy Adv. Com., 1998—2003, U.S.-Russian Joint Commn. Econ. and Tech. Coop., 1996—2000; bd. dirs. U.S. Feed Grains Coun., 1967—72. Mem.: Nat. Grain and Feed Assn. (bd. dirs. 1973—82), Ohio State U. Found. (bd. dirs. 1998—), Ohio State U. Alumni Assn. (v.p. 1989, co-chair fund raising campaign 1990—99). Business E-Mail: dan@amstutzandcompany.com.

AMSTUTZ, HAROLD EMERSON, veterinarian, educator; b. Barrs Mill, Ohio, June 21, 1919; s. Nelson David and Viola Emma (Schnitzer) A.; m. Mabelle Josephine Bower, June 26, 1949; children: Suzanne Marie, Cynthia Lou, Patricia Lynn, David Bruce. BS in Agr., Ohio State U., 1942, DVM, 1945. Diplomate Am. Coll. Vet. Internal Medicine (pres. 1972-73, chmn. bd. regents 1973-74); hon. diplomate Am. Coll. Theriogenology. Pvt. practice vet. medicine, Orrville, Ohio, 1946-47; instr. vet. medicine Ohio State U., 1947-52, asst. prof., 1952-54, asso. prof., 1954-56, prof., 1957-61, prof., head dept. vet. medicine, 1956-61; head dept. vet. clinics Purdue U., West Lafayette, Ind., 1961-75, prof. large animal clinics, 1975-89, prof. emeritus, 1989—. Editor: Bovine Medicine and Surgery Book, 1979; contbg. editor: Modern Veterinary Practice, 1979-84; mem. editorial bd. The Merck Vet. Manual, 6th, 7th and 8th edits.; contbr. to books on diseases of large domestic animals. Mem. exec. bd. Ind.-Ky. synod Luth. Ch. Am., 1986-88; pres. World Assn. for Buiatrics, 1972-84. Served with U.S. Army, 1945-46. Recipient Borden award for outstanding research in diseases of dairy cattle, 1978; named Disting. Alumnus Ohio State U. Coll. Vet. Medicine, 1974; recipient Alumni Faculty award Sch. Vet. Medicine, Purdue U., 1989, Sagamore of the Wabash Ind. Gov., 1990, Ark. Traveler award Ark. Gov., 1969, Gustav Rosenberger Meml. award Dutch Veterinary Assn., 1992, Alumni Recognition award Vet. Medicine Alumni Soc. Ohio State U., 1998. Mem. AVMA (12th Internat. Congress prize for contributing to internat. understanding of vet. medicine 1995), Am. Assn. Vet. Clinicians (pres. 1972), Am. Assn. Bovine Practitioners (exec. sec. 1971-89, exec. v.p. 1989-93, hon. mem. 1993), World Assn. Buiatrics (pres. 1972-84), Am. Coll. of Theriogenologists (hon. diplomate 1993), Sigma Xi, Phi Zeta, Gamma Sigma Delta (award of merit), Omega Tau Sigma (nat. Gamma award). Republican. Avocations: tennis, gardening. Office: Purdue Univ Dept Veterinary Sci West Lafayette IN 47907 Office Phone: 765-494-8560. Business E-Mail: amstutzh@purdue.edu.

AMTOFT, TORBEN, adult education educator, researcher; b. Copenhagen, June 6, 1963; s. Henning Hansen and Tove Amtoft. PhD, U. Aarhus, Denmark, 1993. Rsch. assoc. U. of Aarhus, 1992—98, Boston U., 1999—2002, Heriot-Watt U., Edinburgh, Scotland, 2002—02; asst. prof. Kans. State U., 2002—. Avocations: reading, theology, travel. Office: Kansas State U 234 Nichols Hall Manhattan KS 66506

AMTOWER, DEBRA LYNN, nursing consultant; b. Florence, Ariz., Sept. 19, 1965; d. M. L. and Catherine Louise Wisehart; m. Phil M. Amtower, June 11, 1993; children: Jessica Erin, Mark Allen, Christopher James. Degree in Nursing, St. John's U., 1994. Cert. EMT Mo., 1989. Nurse, EMT Cox Med. Ctrs., Springfield, 1989—97; correctional officer Dept. Justice Fed. Med. Ctr. Men, Springfield, 1997—98; coord. sr. svcs. Oxford Healthcare, Springfield, 1998—2001; RN Intelistaff Healthcare, Springfield, 2001—04; legal nurse cons. Strong Law Firm, Springfield, 2004—. Vol. emergency mgmt. EMA; firefighter Med. Tng. Office Vol. Fire Dept., EMT. Recipient Citizenship award, City Ozark, Mo., 1993. Mem.: Am. Assn. Legal Nurse Cons. Office: Strong Law Firm 901 E Battlefield Springfield MO 65807 Home Phone: 417-743-2266. Office Fax: 417-887-4385; Home Fax: 417-743-2908. Personal E-mail: dlamtower@aol.com. Business E-Mail: dlamtower@stronglaw.com.

AMUNDSON, BEVERLY CARDEN, artist; b. Kansas City, Kans., Dec. 31, 1937; d. Linton Franklin and Arlene Rose Carden; m. Jerry Warren Amundson; children: Sherry Camargo, Cynthia Harmison, Eric. Student, Kansas City Art Inst., 1955—58; studied with, Robert Byerley, Harry Fredman, Daniel Greene, Burton Silverman, Albert Handell and Anita Louise West. Freelance illustrator, designer, Kansas City, Mo., 1958—64; founding ptnr., dir. Amundson & Assoc. Art Studio, DBA The Amundson Group, Kansas City, Mo., 1964—2003, AGI Inc., Kansas City, Kans., 1994—, Taipei, 1994—, Hong Kong, 1994—, AGI Packaging Svcs. Ltd., Taipei, 1994—, Kansas City, Kans., 1999—, Hong Kong, 1999—. Lectr., cons. in field; pvt. lessons and workshops, Merriam, Kans. Work exhibited in shows and galleries nationwide. Com. worker Rep. Party, Merriam. Recipient numerous art awards; scholar Scholarship, Kansas City Art Inst., 1955—58. Master: Mid-Am. Pastel Soc.; mem.: Conn. Pastel Soc., Degas Pastel Soc., Kansas City Artist Coalition, Am. Soc. Classical Realism, Portrait Soc. Am. (charter), Nat. Pastel Soc. Am. (signature). Covenant Ch. Avocations: travel, textile weaving. Studio: 9903 West 70th Terrace Merriam KS 66203 Office: AGI Inc & AGI Packaging Svcs Home Offices 8008 Floyd Overland Park KS 66204

AMUNDSON, JOHN KAY, electrical engineer; b. Glasgow, Mont., Aug. 28, 1925; s. Fred K. Amundson and Grace Ethel Westerman; m. Catherine M. Sutherland, June 12, 1951; children: Lynn M., Michael K. BS in electrical engring., Mont. State U., 1951. Sr. engr. IBM, San Jose, Calif., 1951—84; ret., 1984. With Conflict Resolution Program, Santa Cruz, Calif., 1985—90; special advocate Silver Haired Legislature, 1999—2002; founder, mem. Kiwanis Key Club Douglas HS, 2000—05; with Purple Ribbon Coalition Abused Adults & Children; ct. apptd. spl. advocate for children (CASA), 1994—2005. With USN, 1943—50, Hawaii. Mem.: TRIAD (sec. 2000—05), Partnership of Cmty. Resources (pres., v.p., treas. 2003—05), Douglas County Sheriffs Dept. (Citizen of Yr. 2003), Elks Club (Citizen of Yr. 2001), Carson Valley Kiwanis Club (Kiwanis Dist. Svc. award 2000). Avocations: car restoration, photography, travel. Personal E-mail: jkcma@charter.net.

AMUSSEN, SUSAN DWYER, history professor; b. NYC, Aug. 24, 1954; d. Robert Martin and Diane (Duke) Amussen. AB, Princeton U., 1976; MA, Brown U., 1977, PhD, 1982. Mellon postdoctoral fellow Cornell U., Ithaca, NY, 1982—83; asst. prof. history Conn. Coll., New London, 1984—91; prof., interdiciplinary studies The Union Inst. and U., 1990—. Author: An Ordered Society: Gender and Class in Early Modern England, 1988, Caribbean Exchanges: Slavery and the Transformation of English Society, 1640-1700, 2007; contbr. articles to profl. jours. Fellow Shelby Cullom Ctr. Hist. Studies, Princeton U., 1988—91, The Huntington Libr., 2002—03, Yale Ctr. for Brit. Art, 2004; Alice Freeman Palmer fellow, Wellesley Coll., 1981—82. Mem.: Berkshire Conf. Women Historians (co-chair book prize com., chair article prize com., program chair), N.Am. Conf. on Brit. Studies (regional co-program chmn., regional pres, chair fellowship com.), Women in Hist. Profession (mem. coordinating com.), Am. Hist. Assn. Business E-Mail: susan.amussen@tui.edu.

AMWEG, ERIC PAUL, music educator; b. Elkhart Lake, Wis., Sept. 13, 1963; s. George Fredrick and Inez Clarine Amweg; m. Denise Fern DeZwarte, July 5, 1985; 1 child, Dexter Jonathan. BA in Music Edn., Lakeland Coll., Sheboygan, Wis., 1987; MS in Edn. Adminstrn., U. Wis., Platteville, 2005. Sch. bus. driver Johnson Transp., Plymouth, Wis., 1987—88; instrumental music tchr. Iowa-Grant H.S., Livingston, Wis., 1988—2006; instrumental music educator Southwestern Sch. Dist., Hazel Green, Wis., 2006—. Artistic dir. Wis. Youth Symphony Orch., Madison, 2004—. Dir. Mineral Point City Band, Wis., 1991—, United Meth. Ch. Choir, Livingston, 1989—2006. Recipient Excellence in Tchg. award, Milw. Sch. Engring., 2001, Outstanding Tchg. award, U. Wis. Oshkosh, 2002. Home: 12111 Stockyard Rd Montfort WI 53569 Office: Southwestern Cmty Sch Dist 1415 Fairplay Rd Hazel Green WI 53811

AN, CHUNGMING, telecommunications industry executive; s. Charles and Nancy An; m. Linda Huang, Sept. 28, 1942; children: Charlene H., Angela H. BA in Math., Nat. Taiwan U., Taipei, 1964; PhD in Math., U. Pa., 1969; MS in Computer Sci., Rutgers U., 1978. Asst. prof. Johns Hopkins U., Balti., 1969—72; assoc. prof. Seton Hall U., So Orange, 1972—78; dir., supr., engr. Bell Lab., Holmdel, 1978—98; pres. Mobitai Comm., Taichung, Taiwan, 1998—2002; CEO Asia Pacific Broadband Wireless, Taipei, 2002—06; v.p. CDMA Devel. Group, Calif., 2006—. Mem. tech. adv. bd. Ministry of Telecomm., Taipei. Named Noble Knight, Study Group XI, Internat. Telecomm. Union, Internat. Telephone and Telegraph Consultative Com., 1987; recipient Golden Peak award, Econ. R&D Acad., Taipei, 2000; Rsch. grant, NSF, 1970. Mem.: IEEE. Achievements include patents for shared flexible rating of telecom calls. Home Phone: 886-980-200-888; Office Phone: 510-759-3327. Personal E-mail: cman41@gmail.com.

AN, DOROTHY, lawyer; BA, Harvard U.; JD, Stanford U., 1990. With Cooley Godward (now Cooley Godward Kronish), Fenwick & West, 1994—96; lead atty. for Asia-Pacific region, Latina Am., Can. Cisco Sys. Inc., 1996—99; gen. counsel PlanetRx.com Inc., 1999—2000, Ishoni Networks, 2001, Centillium Comm. Inc.; gen. counsel, v.p. Internap Network Svcs. Corp., 2005—. Office: Internap Network Svcs Corp 250 Williams St Atlanta GA 30303

AN, HONG, engineer; arrived in U.S., 1989; s. Yimin An and Xiulan Huang; m. Xiangwei Zhang, Oct. 22, 1988; children: Isabella Emma children: Miranda Bonnie. B in Engring., Tsinghua U., Beijing, 1982; MS, U. Iowa, 1991, Wayne State U., 1993; PhD, Columbia U., 1999. Engr. Chongqing (China) Inst. Steel, 1982—85, Sichuan Inst. Antibiotics, Chengdu, China, 1985—87; rschr. Tsinghua U., Beijing, 1987—89; engr. Millipore, Bedford, Mass., 1999—2003; co-founder Galaxy Inst., Acton, Mass., 2003—. Grad. student adv. coun. mem. Columbia U. Grad. Sch., NYC, 1996—97; mem. Scienceboard.net, 2002. Internat. com. mem. AIChE, NYC, 1995—2000; press marshal Atlanta Olympics Com., 1996; active Hist. Dist. Com. Recipient Atlanta Olympics Vols. Recognition award, Internat. Olympic Com., Juan A. Samaranch, 1996, Fellowship award, Am. Soc. Artificial Internal Organs, 1997. Mem.: Am. Chem. Soc., Internat. Soc. for Pharm. Engring., Sigma Xi. Achievements include patents for protein aggregates removal; research in mathematical analysis of a flame front inside a combustion chamber; cell deformation in an asymmetric thin liquid film. Avocations: swimming, painting, golf. Home: 5 Reeve St Acton MA 01720 Office: Galaxy Inst PO Box 2862 Acton MA 01720 Personal E-mail: ha13@columbia.edu.

ANAGNOSTOPOULOS, CONSTANTINE EMMANUEL, venture capitalist, former company executive; b. Athens, Greece, Nov. 1, 1922; came to U.S., 1946; s. Emmanuel Constantine A. and Helen (Michaelides) Kefalas; m. Maria Tsagarakis, July 10, 1949; 1 son, Paul Constantine. Sc.B. in Chemistry, Brown U., 1949; MS in Chemistry, Harvard U., 1950, PhD in Chemistry, 1952; postgrad. in bus. adminstrn., Columbia U., 1964. Dir. research and devel. organic div. Monsanto Co., St. Louis, 1962-67, research scientist, 1952-61, bus. dir., 1967-71, gen. mgr. New Enterprise div., 1971-75, gen. mgr. rubber chem. div., 1975-80; v.p. mng. dir. Monsanto Europe-Africa, Brussels, 1980-82; corp. v.p., vice chmn. corp. devel. and growth com. Monsanto Co., St. Louis, 1982-85; cons., 1986-87; mng. gen. ptnr. Gateway Venture Ptnrs., L.P., St. Louis, 1987—. Bd. dirs. Advent Capital Ltd., London, U.S.A., Advent Internat. Corp., Genzyme Corp., Biotage Corp., CytoMed, Inc., Virus Rsch. Inst., Inc.; chmn. bd. Monsanto Europe S.A., Brussels, 1980-82; mem. com. on patent system Nat. Acad. Engring., 1971; mem. nat. inventors coun. Dept. Commerce, 1964-72. Patentee in organic and polymer chemistry, 1953-67; contbr. articles to profl. jours. Bd. dirs. Am. C. of C., Brussels, 1981-82; mem. European Govt. Bus. Coun., Strasbourgh, France, 1981-82; pres. United Fund Belgium, 1982; mem. presdl. com. prizes for innovation, Washington, 1972, U.S.-USSR Trade and Econ. Coun., 1980-82; chmn. bd. St. Louis Tech. Ctr. Served to capt. Brit. Army, 1944-46. Recipient chemistry prize Brown U., 1949, teaching award Harvard U., 1950, 51, 52, St. Louis Tech. award Regional Comml. and Growth Assn., 1987. Mem. Rsch. Soc. Am., Comml. Devel. Assn., Am. Chem. Soc., St. Louis Art Mus. Clubs: Bellerive Country (St. Louis). Republican. Episcopalian. Office: Gateway Assocs LP 8000 Maryland Ave Ste 1190 Saint Louis MO 63105-3910 Home: 213 N Bemiston Ave Clayton MO 63105-3827

ANAND, JAIDEEP, management educator, consultant; b. Delhi, India, Aug. 13, 1966; arrived in U.S., 1998; s. Krishan Kumar and Nirmal Anand; m. Seema Monga, Feb. 26, 1997; children: Alvin Shiv, Audrey Nirmal. BS in Tech., Indian Inst. of Tech., 1987; PhD, U. Pa., 1994. Asst. prof. Ivey Bus. Sch. U. Western Ont., London, Ontario, Canada, 1994—98; asst. prof. Bus. Sch. U. Mich., Ann Arbor, Mich., 1998—2004; assoc. prof. Fisher Coll. of Bus. Ohio State U., Columbus, Ohio, 2004—. Contbr. articles to profl. jours. Recipient Cert. Excellence in Rsch. award, ANBAR, 1997; Alliance Edge Rsch. fellowship, Queen's U., 2003. Mem.: Strategic Mgmt. Soc. (Booz, Allen and Hamilton fellowship 2001), Acad. Mgmt. (Outstanding Rev. award 2000, Best Paper award 2001). Office: Ohio State Univ 2100 Neil Avenue Columbus OH 43210-1144 Home Phone: 614-339-3034. Business E-Mail: anand.18@osu.edu.

ANAND, RAJEN S., physiologist, educator; b. Kohat, India, June 8, 1937; came to U.S., 1963; s. Dial Singh and Daya Kaur (Kohli) A.; m. Asha Angela Bawa, Oct. 29, 1969; children: Sunjay, Shabeen. BS, Meerut U., 1956; DVM, M.P. Vet. Coll., 1960; PhD in Physiology, Biochem. & Nutrition, U. Calif., 1969. Demonstrator M.P. Vet. Coll., Mhow, India, 1960-63; research asst. U. Calif., Davis, 1963-68, P.G. research physiologist, 1968-69; prof. physiology Calif. State U., Long Beach, 1970—, chmn. dept. anatomy and physiology, 1970-95, chmn. dept. communicative disorders, 1990-92; exec. dir. Ctr. for Nutrition Policy & Promotion USDA, Washington, 1995—2001; prof. emeritus Calif. State U., Long Beach, Calif., 2002—. Freelance journalist; apptd. to Nat. Com. on Accreditation Fgn. Med. Schs., 1994—. Contbr. articles to profl. jours. Mem. state Dem. ctrl. com., 1982-97; vice chmn. Coun. Asian and Pacific Am. Dems., 1988-91, del. to Dem. Nat. Conv., 1988, 92; mem. exec. bd. Calif. Dem. Party, chair Asian and Pacific caucus, 1991-93. Named Outstanding Prof., Calif. State U., Long Beach, 1983, Outstanding Student, U. Calif., Davis, 1967, 68; recipient Hertzendorf prize in physiology, 1969; postdoctoral fellow UCLA Harbor Med. Ctr., Torrence, 1977-78, Meritorious Performance and Profl. Promise award Calif. State U., Long Beach, 1986, 88. Mem. Am. Physiol. Soc., AAAS, Sigma Xi, Fedn. Indian Assns. (sec. 1981-84, pres. 1984-86, chmn. 1986-88), Nat. Fedn. Indian-Am. Assns. (exec. dir. 1990-92, sec. 1996—), Indo-Am. Polit. Assn. (chair 1986—). Avocations: writing, hiking. Home: 6912 Winter Ln Annandale VA 22003-6162 Office: Ctr for Nutrition Policy & Promotion #200 North Lobby 1120 20th St NW Washington DC 20036-3406

ANAND, SANJAY, training services executive, consultant, entrepreneur, educator; s. Ram Dhan and Sudarshan Anand; m. Jennifer Tran, Mar. 22, 2003. MSc in Tech., Birla Inst. Tech. and Sci., Pilani, India, 1990, MSc in Computers, 0192; MBA summa cum laude, Boston Coll., 1995, MS in Fin., 2002. Instr. cert. profl. J.D. Edwards, 1998, cert. webmMaster profl. NJ. Inst. Tech., 2001; export mgmt. cert. Nat. Export Programmes, 1993. Software engr. Ctr. Devel. Advanced Computing, Pune, Maharashtra, India, 1991—92; software designer Yojana Sys., Pune, Maharashtra, India, 1992—93; sr. cons. J.D. Edwards, Rutherford, NJ, 1995—98, global enterprise mgr. Denver, 1998—2001; v.p., internat. bus. devel. HyperSpace Comm., Denver, 2001—02; founder, chmn., pres., CEO The CLA Group of Cos., Clifton, NJ, 2002—. Tech. cons. InterPrint, CALS, SAC, DCM, New Delhi, 1986—90; adj. faculty Maharashtra Inst. of Tech., Pune, Maharashtra, 1992—93; rschr. ops. and strategic mgmt. Boston Coll., Chestnut Hill, Mass., 1993—95, cons. small bus. devel. ctr., 1994—95; dir. CLA Solutions Assurance Systems, New Delhi, 2003, ASPL, Pune, 2002—03. Contbr. articles to profl. jours. Vol. cons. UN Assn. Greater Boston, Boston, 1994—95; young leader United Way of Essex and West Hudson, Newark, 2000—03; team leader Nat. Multiple Sclerosis Soc., Jersey City, 2000—01; founder Career Path Work Team, Woodcliff Lake, NJ, 2002. Recipient Ann. Gold medal, Birla Inst. of Tech. and Sci., 1992. Fellow: Inst. Electronics and Telecom. Engrs. (life Elected Fellow 1999); mem.: Fast Co.-Co. of Friends. Achievements include patents for Watch with Therapeutic Metal Strap; design of standard Point-to-Point Protocol network; development of X.25 wide area network; iterative network based logic emulator. Avocations: motorcycling, music, poetry, swimming, travel. Home Phone: 973-680-1419. Personal E-mail: sanjay@anands.com.

ANAND, SURESH CHANDRA, physician; b. Mathura, India, Sept. 13, 1931; arrived in U.S., 1957, naturalized, 1971; s. Satchit and Sumaran Bai Anand; m. Wiltrud Anand, Jan. 29, 1966; children: Miriam, Michael. MB, BS, King George's Coll., U. Lucknow, India, 1954; MS in Medicine, U. Colo., 1962. Diplomate Am. Bd. Allergy and Immunology. Fellow pulmonary diseases Nat. Jewish Hosp., Denver, 1957-58, resident in chest medicine, 1958-59, chief resident allergy-asthma, 1960-62; intern Mt. Sinai Hosp., Toronto, Ont., Can., 1962-63, resident in medicine, 1963-64, chief resident, 1964-65, demonstrator clin. technique, 1963-64, U. Toronto fellow in medicine, 1964-65; rsch. assoc. asthma-allergy Nat. Jewish Hosp., Denver, 1967-69; clin. instr. medicine U. Colo., Denver, 1967-69; internist Ft. Logan Mental Health Ctr., Denver, 1968-69; pres. Allergy Assocs. & Lab., Ltd., Phoenix, 1974—. Mem. staff Bapt. Hosp., chmn. med. records com., 1987; mem. staff St. Joseph's Hosp., St. Luke's Hosp., Human Hosp., John C. Lincoln Hosp., Good Samaritan Hosp., Phoenix Children's Hosp., Tempe St. Luke Hosp., Desert Samaritan Hosp., Mesa Luth. Hosp., Scottsdale Meml. Hosp., Chandler Regional Hosp., Ariz., Valley Luth. Hosp., Mesa, Ariz.; mem. staff. Phoenix Meml. Hosp., mem. med. com.; pres. NJH Fed. Credit Union, 1967—68; adj. assoc. prof. medicine Midwestern U., 2004—. Contbr. articles to profl. jours. Mem. citizens adv. bd. Camelback Hosp. Mental Health Ctr., Scottsdale, Ariz., 1974—80; mem. Phoenix Symphony Coun., 1973—90, Ariz. Opera co., Boyce Thompson Southwestern Arboretum, Ariz. Hist. Soc., Phoenix Arts Mus., Smithsonian Inst. Fellow: ACP, Am. Coll. Allergy and Immunology (pub. edn. com. 1991—94, aerobiology com., internat. com.), Am. Assn. Cert. Allergists, Am. Coll. Chest Physicians (crit. care. com.), Am. Acad. Allergy (pub. edn. com.); mem.: AMA, AAAS, European Acad. Allergology and Clin. Immunology, Ariz. Thoracic Soc., Assn. Care of Asthma, Internat. Assn. Asthmology, World Med. Assn., NY Acad. Soc., Greater Phoenix Allergy Soc. (v.p. 1984—86, pres. 1986—88, med. adv. team sports medicine Ariz. State U.), West Coast Soc. Allergy and Immunology, Maricopa County Med. Soc. (bd. dirs. 1996—98, exec. com. 1996—98, pres.-elect 2002, pres. 2003, chmn. bd. census 2006), Ariz. Allergy Soc. (v.p. 1988—90, pres. 1990—91), Ariz. Med. Assn. (ctrl. dist. dir. 2006—), Internat. Assn. Allergy and Clin. Immunology, Scottsdalians Toastmasters, Phoenix Zoo, Nat. Geog. Soc., Ariz. Wild Life Assn., Village Tennis Club. Office: 1006 E Guadalupe Rd Tempe AZ 85283-3047 also: 4901 N 44th St Phoenix AZ 85018 also: 6553 E Baywood Ave Ste 201 Mesa AZ 85206-1754 also: 2248 N Alma School Rd Chandler AZ 85224-2488 Home Phone: 602-840-0924; Office Phone: 480-838-4296. Personal E-mail: sanand1@aol.com.

ANANI, TARIG, lawyer; b. Riyadh, Saudi Arabia, Jan. 22, 1965; s. Faisal Anani and Diane Katherine Hill. BA cum laude, Univ. Houston, 1988, JD, 1991; MBA, Rice Univ., 1992; MS of Jurisprudence, Stanford U., 1994. Bar: Tex. 1991, Calif. 1993, D.C. 2002, U.S. Supreme Ct. 1995. Corp. assoc. Curtis, Mallet-Prevost, Colt & Mosle, Manhattan, NY, 1994-97; gen. counsel SAP Arabia, Dubai, United Arab Emirates, 1998—2002; pres. internat. chief legal officer Tristone Energy Svcs./P2 Energy Solutions, Houston, 2002—07; pres. P2ES Holdings, Inc., Houston, 2007—, P2 Energy Solutions, Inc., Houston, 2007—. Bd. dirs. Mail2World, Inc., Century City, Tristone Energy Svcs., Inc., Denver, P2 Energy Solutions, Inc., Houston. Recipient Best Enterprise Resource Planning Solution in the Mid. East, v.p. Al Gore, 2002. Home: 1300 Woodhollow Dr Apt 23202 Houston TX 77057 Office: P2 Energy Solutions 4 Houston Ctr 1221 Lamar Ste 1300 Houston TX 77010 Office Phone: 713-481-2003. E-mail: tarig.anani@stanfordalumni.org, tanani@p2es.com.

ANANIAS, JOSÉ, retired school system administrator; b. NYC, Aug. 17, 1929; s. Jose A. and Inez Beatrice Johnson; m. Mamie Seymour, Dec. 30, 1953 (div. Feb. 1978) children: Jose III, Antonio, Ersell; m. Wilhemina Wright, June 17, 1978 (dec. June 1992); m. Ivanete do Nascimento Pena Lins, May 24, 1994. BA, Morehouse Coll., 1951; postgrad., NYU, 1957-59; MEd, CUNY, 1968. Cert. sch. adminstr. and supr., attendance tchr., English tchr., phys. edn. and recreation tchr., subst. attendance tchr. Social investigator St. Nicholas Welfare Ctr. NYC Dept. Welfare, 1955-60; attendance tchr. NYC Bd. Edn., 1965-67; adminstrv. asst. to supr. recreation Cmty. Sch. Dist. # 7, Bronx, 1969-75; supr. Office of High Sch. SPARK program Drug Abuse Prevention Citywide, Bronx, 1971-77; borough supr., asst. coord. Office of HS SPARK program, Bklyn., 1971-77; tchr. English HS Redirection, Bklyn., 1977-78, asst. prin., 1978-79; dist. supervising attendance officer Chancellor's Task Force on Attendance, Bklyn., 1978-79; dist. supervising attendance officer Evander Childs HS Bronx HS Attendance Dist., 1979; dist. supervising attendance officer office of dir. pupil personnel svcs., 1979-84; ret., 1984. Mem. Borough Pres. Sutton's Adopt a Child com., edn. com.; mem. bd. mgr. Harlem br. YMCA, 1974-96, mem. adv. com., editor, compiler brochure; founder Dist. 7 Scholarship Awards Fund, 1971-78; Dem. county committeeman 71st A.D.; edn. chmn. Com. to Rebuild Harlem, 1978; mem. parish coun. St. Charles Borromeo Cath. Ch., 1979; mem. PTA John F. Kennedy HS, DeWitt Clinton HS; svc. officer VFW Post 1753, Las Vegas, 2000-06; mem. Our Lady of Las Vegas Ch.; served as US amb., world forum del., St. Catherine's Coll., Oxford U., Eng., 2006. Served with USN, 1951-55, Korea. Recipient Citation, Gov. Mario Cuomo, 1984, Citation, Mayor Edward I. Koch, 1984, Cert. Recognition Sec. of Def., Cert. Appreciation, Harlem Bd. Mgrs., 1996, Lifetime Achievement award World Congress of Arts, Scis. and Comm., Cambridge, Eng., 2005; named Vol. of Yr., YMCA Greater NY, 1995; José Ananias Day proclaimed in his honor. Mem. VFW (Cmmdr.'s Spl. Merit award 2003), Assn. Black Educators NY, Am.

Legion, USN Meml., Holy Name Soc. St. Charles Borromeo Cath. Ch., So. Nev. Alumni Chpt. CCNY, Kappa Alpha Psi. Democrat. Roman Catholic. Home: El Parque Condominium 1800 Edmond St A-164 Las Vegas NV 89146 Office Phone: 202-258-8679.

ANASTACIA, (ANASTACIA LYN NEWKIRK), singer; b. Chgo., Ill., Sept. 17, 1973; Grad., Profl. Children's Sch. Of Manhattan. Former dancer Club MTV. Singer: (songs-single) I'm Outta Love, 2000, Not That Kind, 2000, One Day In Your Life, 2002, Left Outside Alone, 2004 (nominated for best song, MTV Europe Music Awards, 2004), (albums) Not That Kind, 2001, Freak of Nature, 2002, Anastacia, 2004; singer, performer (DVD Video) The Video Collection, 2002, One Day In Your Life, 2003, (DVD Video (single), 2002; singer: (TV) Party in the Park 2001, 2001, Double Bill, 2003, (films) Coyote Ugly, 2000, Chicago, 2002, (TV series) Um Anjo Caiu do Céu, 2001; composer, performer (TV) VH1 Divas Las Vegas, 2002, guest singer Elton John: One Night Only-Greatest Hits Live, 2001; performer: (TV) Pavarotti & Friends for Afghanistan, 2001, Nobel Peace Prize Concert, 2001, Danish Music Awards, 2001, Brit Awards, 2002, Royal Variety Performance, 2002, 95.8 Capital FM's Party in the Park for the Prince's Trust, 2004; presenter (TV) MTV Europe Music Awards, 2002, special guest appearences I Love the 80's, Tops of the Pops, 2000, 2001, 2004, Ally McBeal, 2001, Wetten, dass.?, 2002, 2004, and several others. Her trademark: rose-colored glasses. Address: Club Anastacia PO Box 7149 San Francisco CA 94120-7149

ANASTASI, WILLIAM JOSEPH, artist; b. Aug. 11, 1933; s. Joseph Anthony and Jeanette (Corona) A.; m. Irene Ierardi, Aug. 15, 1951 (div. 1964); children: William, Lawrence, Jean. Student, U. Pa., 1953-61. Tchr. painting Sch. Visual Arts, NYC, 1971-86; co-artistic advisor Merce Cunningham Dance Co., NYC, 1984—. Artist in residence Sirius Art Ctr., Ireland, 2000, Statens Vaerksteder for Kunst, Copenhagen, 2000, Deutscher Akademischer Austauschdienst, Berlin, 2002; presenter in field. One-man shows include Dwan Gallery, NYC, 1966—67, 1970, Witherspoon Gallery U. NC, Greensboro, 1965, Washington Sq. Gallery, N.Y.C, 1964, PS 1 Mus., L.I., N.Y., 1977, Hetzler and Keller Gallery, Stuttgart, Germany, 1979, Whitney Mus. Am. Art, N.Y.C., 1979, 1981, Kuntsmuseum Dusseldorf, Fed. Republic Germany, 1979, Bess Culter Gallery, NYC, 1987—88, The New Mus., N.Y.C., Stalke Gallery, Copenhagen, Denmark, 1988, 1996, 1999, 2004—05, Scott Hanson Gallery, 1989, Ball State U., Muncie, Ind., 1990, Sandra Gering Gallery, N.Y.C., 1991, 1993—95, Krister Fahl Gallery, Stockholm, 1994, The Sorbonne, Paris, 1994, Rosenbach Mus. & Libr., Phila., 1995, Brown U., Providence, R.I., 1995, Pier Gallery, Orkney, Stromness, Scotland, 1995, Moore Coll. Art and Design, Phila., 1995, Anders Tornberg Gallery, Lund, Sweden, 1996, Hubert Winter Gallery, Vienna, Austria, 1998, 2001, The Mus. of Judaica, Phila., 1998, Specta Gallery, Copenhagen, 1999, Galerij S6, Aalst, Belgium, 1999, Gary Tatintsian Gallery, N.Y.C., 1999, 2003, Art Agents Gallery, Hamburg, Germany, 2000, 2004, Niels Borch Jensen Gallery, Berlin, 2000, Nikolaj Comtemporary Art Ctr., Copenhagen, 2001, Thomas Rehbein Gallery, Cologne, 2002, 2004—05, The Annex, N.Y.C., 2003, Quadrum Gallery, Lisbon, Portugal, 2003, Slought Found., Phila., 2004, Solway Gallery, L.A., Reykjavik Art Mus., 2004, Bayly Mus., U. Va., 2005, Stefanie Hering Gallery, Berlin, 2005, Art Agts. Gallery, Hamburg, 2005, Baumgartner Gallery, N.Y.C., 2006, Bjorn Ressle Gallery, 2006, White Box, NYC, 2006—07, Birmingham Mus. Art, 2007, Drawing Ctr., NYC, 2007, Orangegroup Gallery, LA, 2007, others, Represented in permanent collections Neuberger Mus., Purchase, N.Y., Met. Mus. Art, N.Y.C., Bklyn. Mus. Art, Phila., Mus. Art, Phoenix Mus. Art, Ga. Mus. Art, Walker Art Ctr., The Getty Ctr., Santa Monica, Calif., The Mus. Contemporary Art, L.A., Davison Art Ctr., Wesleyan U., Middletown, Conn., Des Moines Art Ctr., Mus. Modern Art, N.Y.C., Art Inst. of Chgo., Nat. Gallery Art, Washington, Fogg Art Mus., Harvard Univ. Art Mus., Cambridge, Mass., Contemporary Mus., Honolulu, Musee Moderne, Stockholm, Sweden, Whitney Mus. Am. Art, Denver Art Mus., Chrysler Mus., Norfolk, Va., J.B. Speed Art Mus., Louisville, Ky., Le Witt Collection, Chester, Conn., Jewish Mus., N.Y.C., Statensmuseum for Kunst, Copenhagen, Rooseum, Ctr. Contemporary Art, Malmo, Sweden, Phila., Mus. Jewish Art, Guggenheim Mus., N.Y.C., Ark. Art Ctr., Okla. City Art Mus., Milw. Art Mus., Museet for Samtidskunst, Roskilde, Denmark, Contemporary Arts Mus., Houston, Balt. Mus. Art, Md., Mus. Ludwig Koln, Cologne, Wadsworth Athenaeum, Hartford, Conn., Rubin Mus. Art, N.Y.C., Birmingham Mus. Art, Ala., U. Va. Art Mus., others, Progressive Contemporary Collection, Cleve., Harold Fulekenberg Collection, Hamberg, Germany; author: William Anastasi's Pataphysical Society: Jarry, Joyce, Dechamp and Cage, 2005. Home: 924 W End Ave New York NY 10025-3534 Personal E-mail: wanastasi@nyc.rr.com.

ANASTASIO, MICHAEL R., science foundation director; m. Ann Anastasio; children: Alison, Alexandra. B in Physics, Johns Hopkins U.; MA in Theoretical Nuclear Physics, PhD in Theoretical Nuclear Physics, SUNY, Stony Brook. Physicist, B-Divsn. Lawrence Livermore Nat. Lab., Calif., 1980, assoc. dir. def. and nuclear techs., dep. dir. strategic ops., dir., 2001—. Sci. advisor Dept. of Energy; chair Coun. for Nat. Security, Coun. for Strategic Ops. Recipient Weapons Recognition of Excellence award, Dept. of Energy, 1990. Mem.: Sigma Pi Sigma. Avocations: sports, cello. Office: Lawrence Livermore Nat Lab 7000 East Ave Livermore CA 94550-9234

ANASTASIOU, HARRY, international peace and conflict studies professor; arrived in US, 2002; s. Stasis and Maroulla Anastasiou; m. Theodora Fantousi, June 2, 1972; children: Anastsis, Michaelangelo. BA in Polit. Sci., Geneva Coll., Beaver Falls, Pa., 1975; MPhil in Philosophy Sci. and Tech., ICS Toronto, Can., 1977; MA in Social Sci., U. Toronto, Can., 1979; D in Social Sci. and Philosophy, Free U. Amsterdam, The Netherlands, 1982; PhD in Internat. Peace and Conflict Studies, Union Inst. and U., Cin., 2002. Head humanities Am. Acad., Larnaca, Cyprus, 1981—96; lectr. Higher Technol. Inst., Nicosia, Cyprus, 1981—96; sr. rschr, curriculum developer Cyprus Neuroscience & Tech. Inst., Nicosia, 1996—98; acad. auditor social sci. Intercollege, Nicosia, 1998—2002, mem. bd. govs., 1980—; prof. conflict resolution & internat. studies Portland State U., 2002—. Exec. dir. eastern Mediterranean br. Inst. World Affairs, Washington, 1997—2002; co-dir. Peace Initiative Project Portland State U., 2002—; sr. rschr., dir. curriculum devel. Cyber Kids, 1996—98. Article reviewer, evaluator Jour. Peace Rsch., 2002—; author: The Broken Olive Branch: Nationalism, Ethnic Conflict and the Quest for Peace in Cyprus, 2007; contbr. articles to profl. jours. Core leader Cyprus Peace Movement, 1990—2002; mem. nat. exec. coun. Movement Free Dems., Nicosia, 1995—98, pres. dist. exec. coun. Larnaca, 1995—98, mem. parliament candidate, 1996; bd. dirs. Future Worlds Ctr., Nicosia, 2006—, Intercollege, Cyprus, 1980—, Future Worlds Ctr., 2006—. Named to Cir. of Scholars, Union Inst. and U., 2001; recipient Internat. Grand priz Leader, Prestige and Quality, 1996, 1st prize for Innovation award, Employers and Industrialists Fedn. Cyprus, 1998; grantee, AMIDEAST, 1998, UN Office Project Svcs., 2002. Mem.: Am. Hellenic Ednl. Prog. Assn., Internat. Studies Assn. Avocations: poetry, painting, films, sports. Office: Portland State U PO Box 715 Portland OR 97207-0751 Office Phone: 503-725-9711. Business E-Mail: harrya@pdx.edu.

ANAWALT, PATRICIA RIEFF, anthropologist, researcher; b. Ripon, Calif., Mar. 10, 1924; d. Edmund Lee and Anita Esto (Capps) Rieff; m. Richard Lee Anawalt, June 8, 1945; children: David, Katherine Anawalt Arnoldi, Harmon Fred. BA in Anthropology, UCLA, 1957, MA in Anthropology, 1971, PhD in Anthropology, 1975. Cons. curator costumes and textiles Mus. Cultural History UCLA, 1975-90, dir. Ctr. for Study Regional Dress, Fowler Mus. Cultural History, 1990—; trustee S.W. Mus., LA, 1978-92; rsch. assoc. The San Diego Mus. Man, 1980—, UCLA Inst. Archaeology, 1994—. Trustee Archaeol. Inst. Am., U.S., Can., 1983-95, 98—; traveling lectr., 1975-86, 1994-2000, Pres.'s Lectureship, 1993-94, Charles E. Norton lectureship, 1996-97; cons. Nat. Geog. Soc., 1980-82, Denver Mus. Natural History, 1992-93; apptd. by U.S. Pres. to Cultural Property Adv. Com., Washington, 1984-93; fieldwork Guatemala, 1961, 70, 72, Spain, 1975, Sierra Norte de Puebla, Mex., 1983, 85, 88, 89, 91. Author: Indian Clothing Before Cortés: Mesoamerican Costumes from the Codices, 1981, paperback edit., 1990; co-author: The Codex Mendoza, 4 vols., 1992 (winner Archaeol. Inst. Am. 1994 James Wiseman Book award), The Essential Codex Mendoza, 1996; mem. editl. bd. Ancient Mesoamerica; contbr. articles to profl. jours. Adv. com Textile Mus., Washington, 1983-87. Grantee NEH, 1990, 96, J. Paul Getty Found. 1990, Nat. Geog. Soc., 1983, 85, 88, 89, 91, Ahmanson Found., 1996; Guggenheim fellow, 1988. Fellow Am. Anthrop. Assn.; mem. Centre Internat. D'Etude Des Textiles Anciens, Am. Ethnol. Soc., Soc. Am. Archaeology, Soc. Women Geographers (Outstanding Achievement award 1993), Textile Soc. Am. (bd. dirs. 1992-96, co-coord. 1994 biennial symposium), Soc. Antiquaries, London. Avocations: ballet, reading, hiking. Office: Fowler Mus Cultural History Ctr Study Of Regional Dress Los Angeles CA 90095-0001 Business E-Mail: panawalt@arts.ucla.edu.

ANAYA, RICHARD ALFRED, JR., financial consultant; b. NYC, Dec. 19, 1932; s. Ricardo Martinez and Clara (Chamarro) A.; m. Ninette Calandra, Sept. 8, 1957; children: Suzanne, Richard J. BBA, CCNY, 1958. CPA, N.Y. Tax acct. C.I.T. Fin. Corp., NYC, 1964-67; asst. treas. Mut. Broadcasting System, Inc., NYC, 1967-72; treas. Host Internat., Inc. (N.Y.S.E.), Santa Monica, Calif., 1972-85; dir. fin. Windsor Fin. Corp, Encino, Calif., 1985; ind. cons. mergers and acquisitions A&I Investments, Inc, Century City, Calif., 1986-87, Anaya Assocs., Century City, Calif., 1987-90, CPA cons. mergers and acquisitions Woodlands Hills, Calif., 1990—. Founder retail store chain, Clear Connect Comms., LLC, 1995. Served with U.S. Navy, 1952-54. Mem. AICPA, Calif. State Soc. CPAs, N.Y. State Soc. CPAs. Roman Catholic. Home Phone: 818-222-2747; Office Phone: 818-222-2747. E-mail: anayaassociates@pacbell.net.

ANAYA, RUDOLFO, writer, educator; b. Pastura, N.Mex., Oct. 30, 1937; s. Martin and Rafaelita (Mares) A.; m. Patricia Lawless, July 23, 1966. BA, U. N.Mex., Albuquerque, 1963, MA, 1968; PhD (hon.), U. Albuquerque, 1982; PhD, Mary Crest Coll., 1984; LLD (hon.), U. N.Mex., 1996. Prof. U. N.Mex., Albuquerque, 1974—. Author: (novels) Bless Me Ultima, 1972 (Premio Quinto sol) Heart of Aztlan, 1976, Tortuga, 1979 (Before Columbus Found. award), Alburquerque, 1992 (Pen West award for fiction), Zia Summer, 1995, The Farolitos of Christmas, 1995, Jalamanta, 1996, Rio Grande Fall, 1996, Jemez Spring, 2005, Curse of The Chupacabra, 2006, (children's picture book) Maya's Children, 1997, Shaman Winter, 1999, Roadrunner's Dance, 2000, Elegy for Cesar Chavez, 2000, Farolitos for Abuelo, 2000, The Santero's Miracle, 2004, The First Tortilla, 2007, (young adult) Serafina's Stories, 2004; (short stories) The Man Who Could Fly, 2006. NEA fellow, Nat. Medal of Arts (lit.), 2001. Home: 5324 Canada Vista Pl NW Albuquerque NM 87120-2412 Office: U NMex English Dept Albuquerque NM 87131-0001

ANBAR, MICHAEL, biophysics professor; b. Danzig, June 29, 1927; came to U.S., 1967, naturalized, 1973; s. Joshua and Chava A.; m. Ada Komet, Aug. 11, 1953; children: Ran D., Ariel D. MSc, Hebrew U., Jerusalem, 1950, PhD, 1953. Instr. chemistry U. Chgo., 1953-55; sr. scientist Weizmann Inst. Sci., 1955-67; prof. Frienberg Grad. Sch., Rehovoth, Israel, 1960-67; sr. rsch. assoc. NASA Ames Rsch. Ctr., 1967-68; dir. phys. sci. SRI Internat., Menlo Park, Calif., 1968-72, dir. mass spectrometry research ctr., 1972-77; prof. biophysical sci., chmn. dept. Sch. Medicine, SUNY, Buffalo, 1977-90, rsch. prof. dental materials, rsch. prof. ophthalmology, 1990—, exec. dir. Health Instrument and Device Inst., 1983-85, assoc. dean applied research, 1983-85; v.p. R&D AMARA Inc, Amherst, NY, 1992—; rsch. prof. surgery Sch. Medicine, SUNY, 1998—. Author: The Hydrated Electron, 1970, The Machine of the Bedside: Strategies for Using Technology in Parient Care, 1984, Clinical Biophysics, 1985, Computers in Medicine, 1986, Quantitative Dynamic Telethermometry in Medical Diagnosis and Management, 1994; editor-in-chief: Thermology, 1993; contbr. articles to profl. jours. With Israeli Air Force, 1947-49. Fellow, AIMBE, 2001; grantee in field. Fellow Am. Inst. Biomed. Engrs.; mem. IEEE, AAAS, IEEE Computer Soc., IEEE Engring. in Biology and Medicine Soc., Assn. Am. Med. Colls., Am. Inst. Physics, Am. Chem. Soc., Am. Inst. Ultrasound in Medicine, Am. Assn. Clin. Chemistry, Am. Assn. Dental Rsch., Am. Assn. Mass Spectrometry, Am. Acad. Thermology, Am. Assn. Med. Systems Informatics, N.Y. Acad. Scis., Internat. Assn. Dental Rsch., Radiation Rsch. Soc., Internat. Med. Informatics Assn., Internat. Soc. Optical Engring., Radiol. Soc. N.Am., Am. Soc. Clin. Oncology. *Any scientist should first try to understand nature and then to utilize knowledge for the betterment of the quality of life. Even a single modest contribution to medicine can help thousands, making it a worthwhile cause for any scientist. My research and teaching focus, therefore, is on the application of the physical sciences to medicine.*

ANBINDER, PAUL, publishing executive, consultant; b. Bklyn., Apr. 19, 1940; s. Tulea Herzel and Gussie (Dandeshane) A.; m. Helen Rabinowitz, Feb. 16, 1964; children: Mark Harris, Jeffrey Todd. BA, Cornell U., 1960; postgrad., Columbia U., 1960—61. Editor Dover Publs., NYC, 1961-64; editor-in-chief Shorewood Pubs., NYC, 1964-69; with Harry N. Abrams, Inc., NYC, 1969-71, sr. v.p., 1972-73, pres., 1974-75; v.p., editor trade paperbacks Ballantine Books, 1975-78; dir. spl. projects Random House/Alfred A. Knopf, NYC, 1975-78; pres., pub. Hudson Hills Press, NYC, 1978—2002, chmn., founding pub., 2002—, cons. art book pub., 2007—. Bd. dirs. Friends of the Neuberger Mus. of Art, Purchase, N.Y., 1986-96; vol. Westchester Med. Ctr., 2003—. Mem. Assn. Am. Pubs. (bd. dirs. N.Y.C. and Washington chpts. 1987-91), Century Assn. Democrat. Jewish. Avocations: opera, collecting art, travel. Office: 144 Southlawn Ave Dobbs Ferry NY 10522 Home Phone: 914-693-0589. Personal E-mail: panbinder@14850.com.

ANCELL, ROBERT MANNING, leadership organization executive; b. Phoenix, Oct. 16, 1942; s. Robert Manning and Alice (Lovett) A.; m. Janet Claire Neuber, Dec. 21, 1966 (div. Oct. 1984); children: Kevin Robert, Kristin Deann; m. Christine M. Miller, Mar. 30, 1995. BA, U. N.Mex., 1971. Lic. pvt. pilot. Reporter KOB Radio and TV, Albuquerque, 1966-72; sr. sales rep. Xerox Corp., Albuquerque, 1972-78; pub. Colo. Bus. mag., Denver, 1978-83; publ. mgr. Denver Bus. mag., 1983-84; pub. Endless Vacation mag., Indpls., 1985-88; mktg. mgr. World Pub. Co., Evanston, Ill., 1989-92; writer, 1962—; founder, exec. dir. Soc. for 4-Star Leadership, Alexandria, Va., 1998—. Cons. Cowles Mags., Harrisburg, Pa., 1994-95, Exec. Books, Mechanicsburg, Pa., 1996-98. Author: The Biographical Dictionary of World War II Generals and Flag Officers, 1997; co-author: Who Will Lead?, 1996, Four-Star Leadership for Leaders, 1997, Vol. I and II, 1999. Lt. comdr. USNR, 1971-93. Recipient 1st pl. TV Documentary award N.Mex. Broadcasters Assn., Albuquerque, 1968, UPI, Albuquerque, 1968, Washington Ind. Writers. Mem. Naval Order of U.S. (v.p. pub. affairs 1997-99), Am. Soc. Journalists and Authors, Soc. for Mil. History, U.S. Naval Inst., Ret. Officers Assn., Assn. of U.S. Army, Air Force Assn., Am. Turkish Soc. Republican. Presbyterian. Avocations: flying, photography, outdoors activities. Home: 11419 South Lakes Dr Reston VA 20191 Personal E-mail: rmancell@comcast.net.

ANCES, BEAU M., neurologist; b. Balt., Md., Feb. 24, 1972; s. I.G. and Marlene Ances; m. Elizabeth Z. Wheeler, May 22, 2004. MSc, London Sch. of Economics, 1993—94; PhD, U. of Pa., 1994—2000, MD, 1994—2001, BA, 1989—93. Neurologist Hosp. of U. of Pa., 2001—. Editor Neurology. Achievements include research in Neuroimaging and NeuroAIDS. Office: Hosp of the Univ of Pennsylvan 3400 Spruce St Philadelphia PA 19103-4283 Home Phone: 215-568-7938; Office Phone: 215-662-2700. Personal E-mail: beau.ances@uphs.upenn.edu.

ANCES, I. G(EORGE), obstetrician, gynecologist; b. Balt., July 3, 1935; s. Harry and Fanny A.; m. Marlene Roth, Oct. 23, 1966; 1 son, Beau Mark. BS, U. Md., 1956, MD, 1959. Diplomate Am. Bd. Ob-Gyn. Intern Ohio State U. Hosp., 1959-60; resident in ob-gyn. Univ. Hosp., Balt., 1960-61, 63-65; faculty U. Md. Med. Sch., Balt., 1966—, prof. ob-gyn., 1975-83, dir. labs. obstetrics and gynecol. rsch. and clin. labs., 1967-83, dir. divsn. adolescent ob-gyn. and family planning, 1981-83; prof. ob-gyn., chmn. dept. Rutgers U. Sch. Medicine, Camden, NJ, 1983—. Contbr. chpts. to books, articles to profl. jours. Capt. sustaining fund drive Balt. Symphony Orch., Opera Co. Phila.; med. adv. com. Fire Dept. Balt. City. With USAF, 1961-63. Recipient of Outstanding Tchg. and Edn. award Robert-Wood Johnson Sch. of Medicine-Cooper Hosp., 1989, 92, 96, 2000, 01, 02, o4, Appreciation Coverage award, 1999, 2000, 02, 04, Nat. Faculty award for excellence in resident edn., 1996. Fellow Am. Coll. Obstetrics and Gynecology; mem. Endocrine Soc., Soc. Gynecol. Investigation, Soc. Study Reprodn. (charter), Internat. Soc. Rsch. in Biology Reprodn. (charter), Md. Obstetrics and Gynecol. Soc. (sec. 1978-81, dir. 1979—), Med. and Chirurgical Soc. Md., Soc. Adolescent Medicine, Douglas Obstet. and Gynecol. Soc. (pres. 1984—), N.J. State Med. Soc. (chmn. neo-natal coop. So. Jersey 1986—), Phila. Ob-Gyn. Soc., English Speaking Union, Cooper Found., N.J. Conservation Coun., Harbour League Club, Md. Club, Towson Golf and Country Club, Sigma Xi. Clubs: Maryland, Towson Golf and Country. Home: 1 Lane Of Acres Haddonfield NJ 08033-3504 Office: Rutgers U Sch Medicine Dept Ob-Gyn 3 Cooper Plz Camden NJ 08103-1438

ANCIER, GARTH RICHARD, broadcast executive; b. Perth Amboy, NJ, Sept. 3, 1957; s. Sherman and Jean Ancier. BA, Princeton U., 1979. Exec. prodr. syndicated program Am. Focus, 1975—79; v.p. comedy programs NBC Entertainment, NYC and Burbank, Calif., 1979—86; pres. entertainment Fox TV Network, LA, 1986—89; pres. network TV shows Walt Disney Studios, Burbank, 1989—90; corp. officer, prodr. Fox, Inc., LA, 1991—92; pres. The Warner Bros. TV Network, 1994—99, NBC Entertainment, Burbank, Calif., 1999—2000; exec. v.p. programming Turner Networks, 2001—03; co-chmn. The Warner Bros. TV Network, 2003—04, chmn., CEO, 2004—06; pres. BBC Worldwide Am., 2007—. TV cons. Dem. Nat. Com., Washington, 1991—92; trustee Nat. Coun. Families and TV, 1991—; creator, exec. prodr. (TV show) Ricki Lake The Garth Ancier Co., 1992—97, exec. cons., 1997—. Mem.: Hollywood TV and Radio Soc. (trustee 1996—99). Democrat. Office: BBC Worldwide Am Inc 747 3rd Ave Fl 7 New York NY 10017*

ANCKER-JOHNSON, BETSY, physicist, engineer, retired automotive executive; b. St. Louis, Apr. 29, 1927; d. Clinton James and Fern (Lalan) Ancker; m. Harold Hunt Johnson, Mar. 15, 1958; children: Ruth P. Johnson, David H. Johnson, Paul A. Johnson (dec.), Marti H. Johnson. BA in Physics with high honors (Pendleton scholar), Wellesley Coll., Mass., 1949; PhD in Exptl. Physics magna cum laude, U. Tuebingen, Germany, 1954; DSc (hon.), Poly. Inst. NY, 1979, Trinity Coll., Northbrook, Ill., 1981, U. So. Calif., LA, 1984, Alverno Coll., Milw., 1984; LL.D. (hon.), Bates Coll., Lewiston, Maine, 1980. Instr., jr. research physicist U. Calif., Berkeley, 1953-54; physicist Sylvania Microwave Physics Lab., 1956-58; mem. tech. staff RCA Labs., 1958-61; rsch. specialist Boeing Co., 1961-70, exec., 1970-73; asst. sec. U.S. Dept. Commerce for Sci. and Tech., 1973-77; dir. phys. rsch. Argonne Nat. Lab., Ill., 1977-79; v.p. for environ. activities GM, Warren, Mich., 1979-92. Affiliate prof. elec. engring. U. Wash., 1961-73; mem. US Dept. Energy Rsch. Adv. Bd., 1983-87, adv. com. on inertial confinement fusion Dept. Energy, 1992-94, US Antarctic Safety Rev. Panel NSF, 1987-88; cons. Inland Steel Inc., 1991-96; adv. com. Rowan Sch. Engring., 1993-96; Regents vis. prof. U. Calif., Berkeley, 1988-89; founding dir. Acad. Medicine, Engring. and Sci. Tex., 2004-07. Contbr. articles to profl. jours. Mem. staff Inter-Varsity Christian Fellowship, 1954-56; mem. vis. com. elec. and computer divsn. MIT, U.S. Dept. Def. Sci. Bd.; mem. adv. bd. Stanford U. Sch. Engring., Fla. State U., Fla. A&M U., Congl. Caucus for Sci. and Tech.; trustee Wellesley Coll., 1971-77; chair bd. dirs. World Environ. Ctr., 1988-93, dir. 1988-99; founding trustee Johnson Scholarship Found., 1991-2001; founding dir. Work Place Influence, 1997-2006, dir. adv. bd. Coll. Engring. Enterprise Devel. Internat., 1992—; mem. U. Tex., 1998—; bd. dirs. Tex. Environ. Forum, 2000-01. Named one of Top Ten World Master Swimmers, 2006; recipient Chmn's. award Am. Assn. Engring. Socs., 1986, Award of Honor, Licensing Execs. Soc.; AAUW fellow, 1950-51, Horton Hollowell fellow, 1951-52; NSF grantee, 1967-72. Fellow AAAS, IEEE, Am. Phys. Soc. (councillor-at-large 1973-76); mem. NRC (bd. engring. edn. 1991-95, com. on women in sci. and engring. 1990-96, office sci. and engring. pers. adv. com. 1993-96), Nat. Acad. Engring. (councillor 1995-2001), Air Pollution Control Assn., Soc. Automotive Engrs. (bd. dirs. 1979-81); Phi Beta Kappa, Sigma Xi Achievements include patents in field. Business E-Mail: bancker-johnson@alum.wellesley.edu.

ANCONA, GEORGE EFRAIN, photographer, author; b. NYC, Dec. 4, 1929; s. Ephraim Jose and Emma Graziana (Diaz) A.; m. Helga Von Sydow, July 20, 1968; children: Lisa, Gina, Tomas, Isabel, Marina, Pablo. Student, Academia de San Carlos, Mexico, 1949, Art Students League, 1950, Cooper Union Sch. Design, 1950. Art dir. Esquire Inc., NYC, 1951-53, Seventeen mag., NYC, 1953-54, Grey Advt. Agy., NYC, 1954-58, Daniel & Charles Advt. Agy., NYC, 1958-60; free lance photographer, film producer NYC, 1960—. Lectr. graphic design, photography Rockland Community Coll., 1973— , Parsons Sch. Design, 1974— , Sch. Visual Arts, 1978— Author-illustrator: Handtalk, 1974, Monsters on Wheels, 1974, What Do You Do?, 1976, I Feel, 1977, Growing Older, 1978, It's a Baby!, 1979, Dancing Is, 1981, Bananas, from Manolo to Margie, Team Work, 1983, Monster Movers, Sheepdog, Helping Out, Freighters, 1985, Handtalk Birthday, 1986 (NY Times 10 Best Illustrated Children's Books of Yr.), Turtle Watch, 1987, Handtalk Zoo, 1989, Riverkeeper, 1990, Handtalk School, 1991, The Aquarium Book, 1991, Man and Mustang, 1992, Pow Wow, 1992, My Camera, 1992, Pablo Remembers, 1993, The Pinatamaker, 1994, The Golden Lion Tamarin Comes Home, 1994, Fiesta U.S.A., 1995, Cutters, Carvers & the Cathedral, 1995, Earth Daughter, 1995, Mayeros, 1997, Fiesta Fireworks, 1998, Barrio, 1998, Let's Dance, 1998, Charro, The Mexican Cowboy, 1999, Carnaval, 1999, Cuban Kids, 2000, Harvest, 2001, Viva Mexico, the Food, The Fiestas, The Folk Arts, The People, The Past, 2001, Murals: Walls That Sing, 2002, Somos Latinos: Mi Casa-My House, 2004, Mis Amigos-My Friends, 2004, Mi Escuela-My School, 2004, Mi Barrio-My Neighborhood, 2004, Mi Familia-My Family, 2004, Mis Bailes-My Dances, 2004, Mis Fiestas-My Festivals, 2005, Mis Quehaceros-My Chores, 2005, Mi Musica-My Music, Mis Comidas-My Foods, Mis Juegas-My Games, Mis Abuelos-My Grandparents, Self-Portrait, 2006; author-illustrator Capoeira-a dance, a game, a martial art. Office Phone: 505-471-8755. E-mail: geoancona@cybermesa.com. *Curiosity is the biggest element in my work. Watching people and making contact through my photographs have given me a sense of myself. My work keeps me in touch with the world around me. Whether a person bakes, builds, sings, or drives, people reach one another in their own way. Mine is taking pictures. Reaching out to others.I think that's what living is all about.*

ANCU, EDWARD FLORIN, veterinarian; b. Galati, Romania, Oct. 14, 1969; s. Vasile and Haiganush Ancu-Gheorghiu; m. Jennifer Ann Marvel, Aug. 2, 2003; children: Evan Theodore-Joseph, Elise Agavni. BA in Biology, U. Calif. San Diego-Revelle, 1991; DVM, U. Wis., Madison, 1996. Intern small animal surgery and medicine Calif. Animal Hosp., LA,

1996—97; relief Dr. self-employed, 1997—2000; pvt. practice Big Tujunga Vet. Hosp., Calif., 2000—. Mem.: Lions Club (Tujunga chpt.). Avocations: travel, reading. Office: Big Tujunga Vet Hosp 6934 Foothill Blvd Tujunga CA 91042 Office Phone: 818-352-6085.

ANDELBRADT, MARK, chef; Studied, Kendall Coll. Chef Morimoto, Phila.; chef de cuisine Tru, Chgo.; sous chef Daniel, NYC; exec. chef Compass, NYC, 2003—04, Morimoto, NYC, 2006—. Named one of NYC's Rising Stars, StarChefs.com, 2006. Office: Morimoto 88 10th Ave New York NY 10011 Office Phone: 888-354-8842.*

ANDERBERG, ROY A., journalist; b. Camden, NJ, Mar. 30, 1921; s. Arthur R. and Mary V. (McHugh) A.; m. Louise M. Brooks, Feb. 5, 1953; children: Roy, Mary. AA, Diablo Valley Coll., 1975. Enlisted USN, 1942, commd. officer, 1960, ret., 1970; waterfront columnist Pacific Daily News, Agana, Guam, 1966-67; pub. rels. officer Naval Forces, Mariana Islands, 1967; travel editor Contra Costa Times, 1968-69; entertainment and restaurant editor Concord Transcript, 1971-75; entertainment editor Contra Costa Advertiser, 1975-76; dining editor Rossmoor News, Walnut Creek, Calif., 1977-78; free-lance non-fiction journalist, 1976—. Recipient Best Feature Story award Guam Press Assoc., 1966. Mem. VFW, DAV, U.S. Power Squadron, Ret. Officers Assn., Am. Legion, U.S. Submarine Vets. WWII (state comdr., regional dir., nat. 2d v.p.), Naval Submarine League (XO), Martinez Yacht Club (charter), Rossmoor Yacht Club (commodore 1995), Toastmasters. Democrat.

ANDEREGG, KAREN KLOK, business executive; b. Council Bluffs, Iowa; d. George J. and Hazel E. Klok; m. George F. Anderegg Jr., Aug. 27, 1970 (div. Dec. 1993); m. William Drake Rutherford, Jan. 2, 1994. BA, Stanford U., 1963. Copywriter Vogue Mag., NYC, 1963-72; copy editor Mademoiselle Mag., NYC, 1972-77, mng. editor, 1977-80; assoc. editor Vogue Mag., NYC, 1980-85; editor-in-chief Elle Mag., NYC, 1985-87; pres. Clinique USA, 1987-92; bus. cons. Portland, Oreg., 1993—. Bd. dirs. Oreg. Dental Svcs. Health Plans, EthicsPoint, Inc., NW Dentists Ins. Co.

ANDERER, JOSEPH HENRY, textile company executive; b. Phila., Oct. 12, 1924; s. Joseph L. and Catherine (Fleck) A.; m. E. T'Lene Brinson, Apr. 4, 1948; children: Joseph D., Mark H., Nancy T. B.M.E., Ga. Inst. Tech., 1947, B.I.E., 1948. Chem. engr. Atlantic Richfield Corp., 1947-55; asst. prof. mech. engring. Drexel Inst., Phila., 1949-56; fiber rsch. mgr., textile devel. lab. mgr. Am. Viscose Corp., 1955-62; with Celanese Corp., 1962—68, exec. v.p. textile mktg., 1967-68; pres. cosmetic and fragrance div., also dir. Revlon, NYC, 1968—72; pres., chief operating officer dir. M. Lowenstein, 1972-77; dir. Aloe Creme Labs., Ft. Lauderdale, Fla., 1974-78, Fairfax Mills, NYC, 1977-78; chmn. bd., chief exec. officer Warren Corp., Stafford Springs, Conn., 1978-89, Grendel Corp., Greenwood, SC, 1979-88; v.p., dir. Trivest Corp., Sarasota, Fla., 1989-92. Trustee Lincoln Savs. Bank, N.Y.C., 1973-86, N.Y. Ocean Sci. Lab., Montauk, 1973-80, Mus. Am. Textile History, 1986-93; bd. dirs. U.S. Shoe Corp., Cin., 1980-95, Cleyn & Tinker Ltd., St. Laurent, Que., Can., 1990-94, Soundwaters, Stamford, Conn., 1990-93, Gen. Clutch Corp., Stamford, 1991-95, Storage Sol'ns, Inc., Stamford, 1993-95; chmn. nat. adv. bd. Ga. Inst. Tech., 1976-82; chmn. Emergency Med. Svcs., New Canaan, Conn., 1991-94. Patentee fiber technology. Asst. dist. mgr. SBA, Score, Conn., 1992-93, dist. mgr., 1993-94; bd. dirs. S.W. Heritage Found., 2003-; dir. Precious Cargo Acad., 2004-. Served to lt. USMCR, 1943-47. Named to Hall of Fame Ga. Tech. Coll. of Engring., 1997. Mem. Wool Mfg. Council (exec. com.), No. Textile Assn. (dir., v.p. 1986-88, chmn. 1988-90), Lugano Condominium Assn. (pres. 1997-98), N.Y. Yacht Club, Stamford Yacht Club (dir., comdr.), N.Am. Sta of Royal Scandinavian Yacht Clubs, Tau Beta Pi, Pi Tau Sigma. Congregationalist. Personal E-mail: Wolfeboro@juno.com.

ANDERHALTER, OLIVER FRANK, educational organization executive; b. Trenton, Ill., Feb. 14, 1922; s. Oliver Valentine and Catherine (Vollet) A.; m. Elizabeth Fritz, Apr. 30, 1945; children: Sharon, Stephen, Dennis. B.Ed., Eastern Ill. State Tchrs. Coll., 1943, Ped.D. (hon.), 1956; A.M., St. Louis U., 1947, PhD, 1949. Mem. faculty St. Louis U., 1947—, prof. edn., 1957—; dir. Bur. Instl. Research, 1949-65, 1949-65, Univ. Computer Center, 1961-69, chmn. research methodology dept., 1968-76; v.p. Scholastic Testing Service, Chgo., 1951-89; pres. Scholastic Testing Svc., Chgo. and St. Louis, 1989—. Chmn. finance com. Greater St. Louis Campfire Girls Orgn., 1958-59 Author, editor standardized tests. Served as pilot USNR, 1943-46. Mem. Am. Ednl. Research Assn., Nat. Council Measurement, Am. Statis. Assn., N.E.A. Home: 12756 Whispering Hills Ln Saint Louis MO 63146-4449 Office: Scholastic Testing Svc 4320 Green Ash Dr Earth City MO 63045-1208 Office Phone: 314-739-3650. E-mail: budbetty@sbcglobal.net.

ANDERMANN, MARY ANNETTE, application developer, consultant; b. Santa Fe, May 23, 1972; d. Robert James Andermann and Mary Angelica (Chavez) Rivera. BA in Biology, Benedictine Coll., Atchison, Kans., 1994; postgrad., Concord Law Sch. Quality control microbiologist Pfizer Inc., Lee's Summit, Mo., 1994-95; quality assurance chemist Cargill Inc., Blair, Nebr., 1995-98; software quality cons. Spherion Tech., Oak Brook, Ill., 1998-99, The Systems House, Des Plaines, Ill., 1999—, AVNET, Inc., Phoenix, 2000—01, Cardsystems Solutions, Inc., Tucson, 2002—, SW Airlines, 2002, Scottsdale Ins., 2002—03, JPMChase, 2006—. Mem. safety com. Cargill, Blair, 1995-97. Mem. Sigma Xi (assoc.). Democrat. Roman Catholic. Achievements include research in micro and ultrafiltration applications for chemical and enzyme recovery; elimination of oxalate residue from processing equipment. Avocations: skiing, writing, reading. Office: Scottsdale Ins 8877 N Gainey Ctr Dr Scottsdale AZ 85258 Home: 16432 S 3rd St Phoenix AZ 85048-2023 Personal E-mail: maandermann@msn.com.

ANDERS, DAVID BRIAN, prosecutor; b. NYC, 1969; AB, Dartmouth Coll., 1991; JD cum laude, Fordham U., 1994. Assoc. Simpson, Thacher & Bartlett, 1994—95; law clerk US Dist. Ct., 1995—96; assoc. Davis Polk & Wardwell, 1996—98; asst. US atty. (So. dist.) NY US Dept. Justice, NYC, 1998—. Named one of Top 40 Lawyers Under 40, Nat. Law Jour., 2005. Mem.: Order of Coif. Office: US Attys Office So Dist NY One St Andrews Plz Rm 619 New York NY 10007 Office Phone: 212-637-2200. Office Fax: 212-637-2239.

ANDERS, GEORGE CHARLES, journalist, writer; b. Chgo., Nov. 12, 1957; s. Edward and Joan Elizabeth (Fleming) Anders; m. Elizabeth Anne Corcoran, Aug. 27, 1988. BA in Econs., Stanford U., 1978. Nat. copyreader Wall St. Jour., NYC, 1978—81, Heard on the St. columnist, 1981—82, London bur. chief European edit., 1982—85, news editor, 1985—89, sr. spl. writer, 1988—2000; sr. editor Fast Company Mag., 2000—03; news editor Wall St. Jour., 2003—. Contbg. editor: SmartMoney mag., 1992—95; author: Merchants of Debt, 1992, Health Against Wealth, 1996, Perfect Enough, 2003. Co-recipient Pulitzer Prize for nat. reporting, 1997; recipient Janus award, Am. Mortgage Bankers Assn., 1987.

ANDERS, HARLEY DILLON, SR., retired federal agency administrator; b. Clarita, Okla., Nov. 9, 1918; s. Harley Anders and Malsey Fay Simmons; m. Eleanor J. Fitzwater, July 17, 1941 (div. Nov. 12, 1963); children: Harley, Vicki. Enlisted U.S. Army, 1939; advanced through grade to 2d lt. U. S. Army, 1942; claims examiner U.S. Dept. VA, Muskogee, 1944—66, chief claims svc. Juneau, Alaska, 1966—72, dir. Alaska region, 1972—74; ret., 1974. Cons. comprehensive health State of Alaska, Juneau, 1972—74. Author: (genealogy) The Ancestors and Descendants of Elias M. Anders of Missouri, 1985; editor: (book) Genealogical Gleanings in Southeast United States, 1997; author: The Life and Times of John Turnbull, Indian Trader, 1997. Avocations: genealogy, archaeology. Home: 17543 102nd Ave NE #224 Bothell WA 98011 Personal E-mail: Handers101@aol.com.

ANDERS, JERROLD P., lawyer; b. Wilkes-Barre, Pa., Sept. 21, 1953; m. Joan Anders, June 28, 1975; children: Jessica, Douglas. AB magna cum laude, Franklin & Marshall Coll., 1975; JD cum laude, U. Pitts., 1978. Jud. law clk. to Hon. Martin J. Coyne Lehigh County Ct. of Common Pleas, 1978-79; ptnr. White and Williams, LLP, Phila., 1979—. Mem. Phi Beta Kappa, Order of Coif. Office: White and Williams LLP 1 Liberty Pl 1650 Market St Ste 1800 Philadelphia PA 19103-7304 E-mail: andersj@whiteandwilliams.com.

ANDERSEN, BURTON ROBERT, immunologist, educator, medical historian; b. Chgo., Aug. 27, 1932; s. Burton R. and Alice C. (Mara) A.; children: Ellen C., Julia A., Brian E. Student, Northwestern U., Evanston, Ill., 1950—51; BS, U. Ill., Chgo., 1953, MS, MD, U. Ill., Chgo., 1957. Intern Mpls. Gen. Hosp., 1957-58; resident and fellow U. Ill. Hosp., 1958-61; clin. assoc. NIH, Bethesda, Md., 1961-64; asst. prof. U. Rochester, NY, 1964-67; assoc. prof. Northwestern U., 1967-70; prof. medicine and microbiology U. Ill., Chgo., 1970—, chief infectious diseases, 1986-99, West Side VA Med. Ctr., 1970-90. Contbr. sci. rsch. articles to profl. jours. Served as sr. surgeon USPHS, 1961-63. Grantee Rsch. grantee, NEH, 2000—03. Fellow ACP; mem. Am. Assn. Immunologists, Am. Soc. for Clin. Investigation, Ctrl. Soc. for Clin. Rsch. Achievements include research in infectious diseases, white blood cells and ancient Mesopotamian medicine. Office: U Ill Sect Infectious Diseases 808 S Wood St Chicago IL 60612-7300 Business E-Mail: branders@uic.edu.

ANDERSEN, ERIK M., lawyer; b. Anaheim, Calif., July 26, 1972; BA, UCLA, 1998; JD summa cum laude, Boston Coll., 2001. Bar: Calif. 2002, US Dist. Ct. Ctrl. Calif., US Ct. Appeals Fourth & Ninth Cir. Law clk. Judge Lourdes G. Baird US Dist Ct. Ctrl. Calif., Judge Robert R. Beezer US Ct. Appeals Ninth Cir.; assoc. Paul, Hastings, Janofsky & Walker LLP; assoc., bus. litigation Payne & Fears LLP, Irvine, Calif. Editor (solicitations): Boston Coll. Law Rev. Named Rising Star, So. Calif. Super Lawyers, 2006. Mem.: ABA, State Bar Calif., Order of the Coif. Office: Payne & Fears LLP Ste 1100 4 Park Plz Irvine CA 92614 Office Phone: 949-851-1100. Office Fax: 949-851-1212. Business E-Mail: ema@paynefears.com.

ANDERSEN, IB, performing company executive; b. Copenhagen, 1954; Prin. dancer NYC Ballet, 1980—90; tchr. various companies in Belgium, Norway, Japan, Can. and U.S., 1990—2000; artistic dir., leader artistic team Ballet Ariz., 2000—. Avocations: cooking, painting, music, poetry, literature. Office: Ballet Arizona 3645 E Indian Sch Rd Phoenix AZ 85018 E-mail: ib@balletaz.org.*

ANDERSEN, JAMES A., retired state supreme court justice; b. Auburn, Wash., Sept. 21, 1924; s. James A. and Margaret Cecelia (Norgaard) A.; m. Billiette B. Andersen; children: James Blair, Tia Louise. BA, U. Wash., 1949, JD, 1951. Bar: Wash. 1952, U.S. Dist. Ct. (we. dist.) Wash. 1957, U.S. Ct. Appeals 1957. Dep. pros. atty. King County, Seattle, 1953-57; assoc. Lycette, Diamond & Sylvester, Seattle, 1957-61; ptnr. Clinton, Andersen, Fleck & Glein, Seattle, 1961-75; judge Wash. State Ct. of Appeals, Seattle, 1975-84; justice Wash. State Supreme Ct., Olympia, 1984-92, chief justice, 1992-95; ret., 1995. Mem. Wash. State Ho. of Reps., 1958-67, Wash. State Senate, 1967-72. Served with U.S. Army, 1943-45, ETO. Decorated Purple Heart; recipient Disting. Alumnus award U. Wash. Sch. of Law, 1995. Mem. ABA, Wash. State Bar Assn. Home: 3008 98th Ave NE Bellevue WA 98004-1817

ANDERSEN, K(ENT) TUCKER, investment executive; b. Manchester, Conn., June 5, 1942; s. Alfred Hans and Dorothy Emily (Ray) A.; m. Karen Ann Kirchofer, Oct. 11, 1963; children: Heather Michele, Kristen Eileen. Student, Phillips Exeter Acad., NH, 1957-59; BA, Wesleyan U., 1963. Chartered fin. analyst. Actuarial student Travelers Ins. Co., Hartford, Conn., 1963-66; security analyst Smith Barney & Co., NYC, 1968-69; ptnr. Rudman Assocs., NYC, 1969-72, Cumberland Assocs. LLC, NYC, 1972—99, mng. ptnr., 1982-96, chief investment strategist, 1997—99; founder Above All Advisors, 2000—. Bd. dirs. Cato Inst., Washington, 1987—, exec. com., 1992—; trustee YWCA of Montclair, North Essex, N.J., 1980-1996, 1st United Meth. Ch., Montclair, 1976-94, Martin Luther King Scholarship Fund Montclair, 1989-94, Phillips Exeter Acad., 1989-99, chmn. investment com., 1989—, chmn, 1992-99, bd. v.p. and chmn. exec. com., 1993-1999, trustee Warren Congl. Ch., Conn, 2005-; admissions rep. N.J. area, 1983-93; exec. com. GOPAC, 1993—, bd. dirs., 1995—, Internat. Found. Rsch. Exptl. Econ., 2001-, exec. com., 2005-; dir. Questech Corp., 2005-; Chmn. Artificial Cell Tech. 2006-. With USPHS, 1966-68. Recipient Disting. Alumnus award, Wesleyan U., 1988, Founder's Day award, Phillips Exeter Acad., 2007. Mem. Soc. Actuaries, N.Y. Soc. Security Analysts, Inst. Chartered Fin. Analysts, Polit. Club for Growth (mem. exec. com. 1984-94), Kappa Nu Kappa (pres. 1963). Republican. Avocation: marathon running. Office: Above All Advisors 38th Fl 1114 Avenue Of The Americas New York NY 10036-7703

ANDERSEN, KURT BYARS, writer; b. Omaha, Aug. 22, 1954; s. Robert and Jean (Swarr) A.; m. Anne (Kreamer), May 9, 1981; children: Katherine, and Lucy. AB magna cum laude, Harvard U., 1976. Writer NBC-TV, NYC, 1976-80, Time Mag., NYC, 1981-84, arch. critic, 1984-93, columnist, 1993-94; co-founder, co-editor Spy Mag., NYC, 1986-93; editor-in-chief New York Mag., NYC, 1994-96; columnist The New Yorker, NYC, 1996-99; co-founder, co-chmn. Inside, NYC, 1999—; ptnr. Very Short List Daily Email Svc, 2006—. Author: The Real Thing, 1980; Turn of the Century, 1999, Heyday, 2007; co-author: Tools of Power, 1980; (off-Broadway revue and book) Loose Lips, 1994-95, 98; exec. prodr. TV pilots After Hours, 1987; Zero Hour; 1991, Pranks, 1992; exec. prodr., co-writer TV spl. How To Be Famous, 1990; The Hit List, 1992; host TV spl. Comedy Spotlight, 1996; radio show Studio 360, 2000—. Recipient journalism award ABA, 1983; Page One Award Newspaper Guild N.Y., 1984. Mem.: bd. of trustees Pratt Inst.*

ANDERSEN, LEONARD CHRISTIAN, former state legislator, real estate investor; b. Waukegan, Ill., May 30, 1911; s. Lauritz Frederick and Meta Marie (Jacobsen) A.; m. Charlotte O. Ritland, June 30, 1937; children: Karen Schneider, Paul R., Charlene Olsson, Mark Luther. BA, Huron Coll., SD, 1933; MA, U. S.D., 1937. Tchr. Onida H.S., SD, 1934—35; dir. bus. tng. Waldorf Coll., Forest City, Iowa, 1935—39; ins. salesman, 1939—41; tchrs. econs., current history Morningside Coll., Sioux City, Iowa, 1941—43; ins., real estate investor Sioux City, 1943—76. Mem. Iowa Ho. of Reps., Woodbury County, 1961-64, 66-71; mem. Iowa Senate, 26th Dist., 1972-76, chmn. rules and adminstrn. com.; former mem. Iowa Commn. on Aging; former mem. investment adv. bd. IPERS; former mem. ctrl. com. Woodbury County Reps., del. county, dist. and state convs., 1998, 2000; former mem. Simpco Projects Rev. Com.; former pres., chmn. bd. Siouxland Rental Assn.; past mem. Sioux City Housing Appeals Bd., Siouxland Com. on Alcoholism; bd. regents Augustana Coll., Sioux Falls, S.D., mem. Augustana Fellows, 2003—; mem. fin. com. Morningside Luth. Ch., co-chair call com. 2003—; bd. dirs. Human Rights Commn., Sioux City, 1997-2003 Del. Evang. Luth. Ch. Conv., 1999, 2000, 01, 02, promoter Wordalone movement; apptd. anti-violence com. Siouxland Area; mem. fin. com. Morningside Luth. Ch., 2006—. Mem. Lions. Home: 3112 Nebraska St Apt 2 Sioux City IA 51104-3948

ANDERSEN, MARGO K., federal agency administrator; BA, Gettysburg Coll.; M in Mgmt., George Washington U. Program mgr. for arts programs Nat. Endowment for the Arts, Am. Correctional Assn.; dir. Office Fin. Mgmt. and Performance Measurement, Office Innovation and Improvement U.S. Dept. Edn., Washington. Office: US Dept Edn IES Rm 500F 555 New Jersey Ave NW Washington DC 20208

ANDERSEN, MARK, musician; m. Lynn Rowley, July 5, 2002. PhD, Paris Conservatory, 1971. Concert organist, composer Internat. Artists Records, 1971—; host, performer Crescendo TV Program, Oneonta, NY, 2003—. Composer: (music composition and performance) Fantasie Francais. Recipient Internat. Composer's award, Fedn. of World Music, 1976, 1999. Fellow: Am. Guild of Organists. Episcopalian. Achievements include design of Digital Pipe Organ Voices; development of Pipe Organ Control System; Hospital Data Management Program; Over 200 Classical Compositions Published. Office: Internat Artists 350 5th Ave New York NY 10019 Home Phone: 212-699-0996; Office Phone: 607-847-9496. Personal E-mail: emarka@mac.com. E-mail: internationalartists@mac.com.

ANDERSEN, MORTEN, professional football player; b. Copenhagen, Aug. 19, 1960; s. Erik and Hanne A. Student comms. Field goal kicker Mich. State U., Atlanta Falcons, 1995—2000, 2005—, NY Giants, 2001, Kans. City Chiefs, 2002—03, Minn. Twins, 2004. Analyst TV 3 ScanSat, 1997. Actor dinner theater play, 1985. Active Kick for Kids program, New Orleans. Named Outstanding Sports Citizen of Yr. New Orleans Sports Found., 1990, AFC-NFC Pro Bowl, 1984, 85, 86, 87, 88, 90, 92, 95; All-NFC Football News, AP All-Pro, All-Pro Coll. and Pro Football Newsweekly, All-Pro Football Digest, Pro Football Weekly/PFWA, Sporting News, Sports Illustrated, USA Today, UPI All-NFC, Kicker of the Yr. Pro Football, NFL Alumni, 1989, 95, NFC Spl. Times Player of Mo., NFC Spl. Times Player of Week, 1993, 94, 95 (3 times), Player of the Week Miller Lite; broke Jim Breech's mark of 186, 1995. holding NFL record for most points scored, 2006. Office: Atlanta Falcons 1 Georgia Dome Dr NW Atlanta GA 30313-1504*

ANDERSEN, NIELS HJORTH, chemistry professor, biophysicist, consultant, researcher; b. Copenhagen, Oct. 9, 1943; came to U.S. 1949; s. Orla and Inger (Larsen) A.; m. Sidnee Lee (div. 1986); children: Marin Christine, Beth Arkady; m. Susan Howell, July 21, 1987. BA, U. Minn., 1963; PhD, Northwestern U., 1967. Rsch. assoc and fellow Harvard U., Cambridge, Mass., 1966-68; asst. prof. U. Wash., Seattle, 1968-72, assoc. prof., 1972-76, prof., 1976—; prin. scientist ALZA Corp., Palo Alto, Calif., 1970-75. Cons. Genetic Systems, Seattle, 1984-86, Bristol-Myer Squibb, Princeton, N.J., 1984-95, Amylin Pharmaceutics, San Diego, 1992-2001 Receptron Corp., Mountain View, Calif., 1995—2001, Chiron, Seattle, 1997—2003. Mem. adv. bd. Biopolymers; contbr. articles to profl. jours. Recipient Teacher-Scholar award Dreyfus Found., 1974-79, Career Devel. award NIH, 1975-80. Mem. AAAS, Am. Chem. Soc., Am. Peptide Soc., Protein Soc. Democrat. Avocations: music, dulcimer playing. Office: U Wash Dept Chem PO Box 351700 Seattle WA 98195-1700 Office Phone: 206-543-7099. E-mail: andersen@chem.washington.edu.

ANDERSEN, RICHARD ALAN, physiologist; b. New Kensington, Pa., Oct. 27, 1950; s. John Nikoli and Norma Enid Andersen; m. Carol Louise Ahern, Sept. 11, 1979; children: Michael Blake, Kristen Nicole. BS, U. Calif., Davis, 1974; PhD, U. Calif., San Francisco, 1979. Postdoctoral fellow Johns Hopkins U. Med. Sch., Balt., 1981; asst. prof. Salk Inst., La Jolla, Calif., 1981—86, assoc. prof., 1986—87; adj. asst. prof. dept. neurosci. U. Calif., San Diego, 1982—; assoc. prof. dept. brain and cognitive scis. MIT, Cambridge, Mass., 1987—90, prof., 1990—94; James G. Boswell prof. neuroscience, Biology Divsn. Calif. Tech. Inst., Pasadena, 1994—, dir. Sloan-Swartz Ctr. Theoretical Neurobiology, 1994—2004; vis. prof. Coll. de France, 2005. Contbr. articles to profl. jours. Recipient Scholars award, McKnight Found., 1983—86, McKnight Tech. Innovation in Neuroscience award, 2000—02; fellow, Sloan Found., 1982—86; Abraham Rosenberg fellow, U. Calif., San Francisco, 1973, Regents' fellow, 1974—76. Mem.: AAAS, NAS, Assn. Rsch. in Vision and Ophthalmology, Soc. Neurosci, Helmholtz Club. Office: The Andersen Lab Calif Tech Inst Divsn Biology 216-76 Pasadena CA 91125

ANDERSEN, RICHARD ESTEN, lawyer; b. NYC, Oct. 26, 1957; s. Arnold and Marianne (Singer) A.; m. Patricia Anne Woods, May 9, 1987; children: Benjamin Singer, David Woods. BA, Columbia U., 1978, JD, 1981; LLM, NYU, 1987. Bar: N.Y. 1982, U.S. Tax Ct. 1982. Ptnr. Arnold & Porter LLP, NYC. Mem. bd. advisors Jour. Internat. Taxation, Internat. Tax Jour., World Trade Exec., Tax Mgmt., Inc.; adj. prof. law grad. tax LLM program NYU. Author: Foreign Tax Credits, 1996, US Income Tax Withholding (Fgn. Persons), 1997, Income Tax Treaties of the United States, revised edit., 2002. Mem.: ABA, U.S. Coun. Internat. Bus. (tax com.), Internat. Tax Assn. (pres. 2000—02), Internat. Fiscal Assn. (mem. USA br. coun., N.Y. exec. com.), NY State Bar Assn., French-Am. C. of C. (coun. mem.). Office: Arnold & Porter LLP 399 Park Ave New York NY 10022 Office Phone: 212-715-1095. E-mail: richard_andersen@aporter.com.

ANDERSEN, ROBERT ALLEN, retired federal official; b. Denver, Aug. 27, 1936; s. Emmett Christian and Margaret Irene (Maupin) A.; m. Jane Eng (dec.), May 13, 1967. AB in Polit Sci., U. S.C., 1958, MA in Polit Sci., 1961; postgrad. in law, U. Colo., 1958-59; PhD in Internat. Relations, Am. U., 1973. Area coordinator for econ. devel. Area Redevel. Adminstrn., Commerce Dept., 1962-64; acting dir. urban projects div., program officer, chief Project Adminstrn. VISTA (OEO), Washington, 1964-66; implementation programming, planning and budgeting system Office Program Planning and Evaluation, Office Edn., 1966-67; staff asst. to dep. postmaster gen. Postal Service, 1967-72, sr. planning officer, 1972-74; dir. evaluation Immigration and Naturalization Service, Washington, 1974-86, dir. Office of Program Inpection, 1986-88; dir. mgmt., planning and review Office Inspector Gen., Dept. Justice, Washington, 1988-90, dir. quality assurance rev., 1990-97; ret., 1997. Past pres. bd. dirs. D.C. Assn. Retarded Citizens; past. sec. The Arc. Episcopalian. Home: 5701 Nebraska Ave NW Washington DC 20015-1221

ANDERSEN, RONALD MAX, health services researcher, educator; b. Omaha, 1939; s. Max Adolph and Evangeline Dorothy (Wobbe) Andersen; m. Diane Borella, June 19, 1965; 1 child, Rachel. BS, U. Santa Clara, 1960; MS, Purdue U., 1962, PhD, 1968. Rsch. assoc. Purdue U., West Lafayette, Ind., 1962—63; assoc. study dir. Nat. Opinion Rsch. Ctr., Chgo., 1963—66; rsch. assoc. U. Chgo., 1963—77, from assoc. prof. to prof. Grad. Sch. Bus., 1974—90, dir. Program in Health Adminstrn. and Ctr. for Health Adminstrn. Studies, 1980—90; Wasserman prof. dept. health svcs. and sociology UCLA, 1991—, prof. emeritus, 2004—, chmn. dept. health svcs., 1993—96, 2000—03. Com. mem. Agy. for Health Care Policy and Rsch., Rockville, Md., 1970—. Mem. editl. bd.: Health Adminstrn. Press, 1980—83, 1988—98, Med. Care Rsch. & Rev., 1994—; author: A Decade of Health Services, 1967, Two Decades of Health Service, 1976, Total Survey Error, 1979, Health Services in the U.S., 1980, Ambulatory Care and Insurance Coverage in an Era of Constraint, 1987, Training Physicians, 1994, Changing the U.S. Health Care System, 1996, 2001. Fellow, NIH, 1960—62; grantee, Agy. for Health Care Policy and Rsch, 1982, Robert Wood Johnson Found., 1983, Kaiser Family Found., 1983, WHO, 1990. Mem.: APHA, Assn. for Health Svcs. Rsch. (dir. 1981—83, 1997—99, Disting. Career award 1996), Assoc. Univ. Program in Health Adminstrn. (Baxter Allegiance prize 1999), Inst. Medicine NAS, Am. Sociol. Assn. (chmn. med. sociology sect. 1980—81, Disting. Med. Sociologist 1994).

Roman Catholic. Home: 10724 Wilshire Blvd Apt 312 Los Angeles CA 90024-4453 Office: UCLA Sch Pub Health Los Angeles CA 90024 Office Phone: 310-206-1810. Business E-Mail: randevse@ucla.edu.

ANDERSEN, TORBEN BRENDER, optical researcher, astronomer, software engineer; b. Naestved, Denmark, May 17, 1954; came to U.S., 1983; U.S. citizen, 1994; s. Bjarne and Anna Margrethe (Brender) Andersen; m. Olga Pedina, June 2004; children: Iris, Erik, Maxim. PhD, Copenhagen U., Denmark, 1979. Rsch. fellow Copenhagen U., 1980-82, sr. rsch. fellow, 1982-85; optical cons. Nordic Optical Telescope Assn., Roskilde, Denmark, 1985; optical systems analyst Telos Corp., Santa Clara, Calif., 1985-88; rsch. scientist Lockheed Martin Missiles and Space, Palo Alto, Calif., 1988-93, staff scientist, 1993-95, sr. staff scientist, 1995-96, sr. staff software engr., 1996—. Vis. scholar Optical Scis. Ctr., U. Ariz., Tucson, 1983-85. Editor: Astronomical Papers Dedicated to Bengt Strömgren, 1978; contbr. articles to Jour. Quantitative Spectroscopy Radiation Transfer, Applied Optics, Astronomische Nachrichten. Mem. Optical Soc. Am., Internat. Astron. Union, Soc. Photo-Optical Instrumentation Engrs. Achievements include development of method for computing optical aberration coefficients to arbitrarily high orders; discovery of set of differential equations for the Voigt function; contributing to optical design software. Office: Lockheed Martin Advanced Tech Ctr O/ABDS 3251 Hanover St # B201 Palo Alto CA 94304-1121 Home Phone: 408-736-9568; Office Phone: 650-424-3305. Business E-Mail: torben.andersen@lmco.com.

ANDERSLAND, ORLANDO BALDWIN, retired engineering educator; b. Albert Lea, Minn., Aug. 15, 1929; s. Ole Larsen and Brita Kristine (Okland) A.; m. Phyllis Elaine Burgess, Aug. 15, 1958; children: Mark, John, Ruth BCE, U. Minn., 1952; MSCE, Purdue U., 1956, PhD, 1960. Registered profl. engr., Minn., Mich. Staff engr. NAS, Am. Assn. State Hwy. Ofcls. Road Test, Ottawa, Ill., 1956-57; rsch. engr. Purdue U., West Lafayette, Ind., 1957-59; mem. faculty Mich. State U., East Lansing, 1960—, prof. civil engring., 1968—, prof. emeritus, 1994—. Co-author: Geotechnical Software for the IBM, PC, 1987, Geotechnical Engineering and Soil Testing, 1992, An Introduction to Frozen Ground Engineering, 1994, 2d edit., 2004; sr. editor: Geotechnical Engineering for Cold Regions, 1978; contbr. chpt. Ground Engineer's Handbook, 1987; contbr. articles to profl. jours.; patentee in field. 1st lt. C.E., U.S. Army, 1952-55. Decorated Nat. Def. Svc. medal; UN Svc. medal; Korean Svc. medal; recipient Best Paper award Assn. Asphalt Paving Technologists, 1956; postdoctoral fellow Norwegian Geotech. Inst., 1966; grantee NSF, EPA, Dept. of Energy. Fellow ASCE (best paper award Cold Regions Engring. Jour. 1991); mem. ASTM (sr.), Internat. Soc. Soil Mechanics and Found. Engring., Am. Soc. Engring. Edn. (life), Sigma Xi, Chi Epsilon, Tau Beta Pi. Lutheran. Office: Mich State U Dept Civil/Environ Engring East Lansing MI 48824

ANDERSON, AL H., JR., communications executive; b. Winston Salem, NC, May 4, 1942; s. Al H. Sr. and Gladys (Harris) A.; m. Jeanette R., Nov. 25, 1971; children: April, Albert III. BS, Morehouse Coll., 1964; MBA, Rutgers U., 1970; MS (hon.), Ga. State U., 1972. Mgmt. trainee Allstate Ins. Co., Atlanta, 1968-70; loan officer C&S Bank, Atlanta, 1970-72; v.p. Citizens Trust Bank, Atlanta, 1972-73; pres. Triangle Assocs., Atlanta, 1972-75; chmn., founder Anderson Communications Media, Atlanta, 1975—; pres. The Shiloh Inst., Atlanta, 1979—. Cons. Small Bus. Adminstrn., Atlanta, 1978-85. Dir. Sickle Cell Found. of Ga., Atlanta, 1984, United Way of atlanta, 1987; pres. Cascade Youth Orgn., Atlanta, 1986. Mem. Black Pub. Relations Soc. (v.p. 1986—), Atlanta Bus. League, Atlanta Advt. Club, Pub. Relations Soc. of Am. Democrat. Avocations: classic cars, grand prix racing. Office: Anderson Communications Media 2245 Godby Rd Atlanta GA 30349-5012 Home Phone: 770-719-9044; Office Phone: 404-766-8000.

ANDERSON, ALAN REINOLD, real estate company and computer security firm executive, consultant; b. Danbury, Conn., Nov. 14, 1949; s. Charles Reinold and Lila Mae (Truesdale) A.; children: Sherry, Erick. AA, U.S. Naval Acad., 1972; BBA, Western Conn. State U., 1975, postgrad., 1977-82, Boeing 727 Flight Engr. Sch., Aviation Tng. Ctr., 1979, Lockheed P-3 Orion Schs., Naval Counterinsurgency Sch., Spl. Warfare Sch. Competitor modified and grand nat. divsns. NASCAR, 1971-79; researcher, clk. Law Offices of Gemza & Daly, Danbury, Conn., 1972-77; prin. Anderson-Ricards & Co., Danbury, 1981-86, A.R. Anderson & Co., Danbury, Conn., 1977—. Conn. liaison Courageous Challenge 1987 America's Cup, 1985-87; town coord. steering and fin. com. Bush/Quayle 88, 1992; adv. com. George Bush for Pres., Conn., co-chmn. Stamford dinner com., 1987; alt. Conn., Rep. Nat. Conv., New Orleans, 1988; town coord. Weicker Gov., Conn., 1991; vice chmn. Environ. Impact Commn., Danbury, 1985-88; del. GOP State Conv., 1982; ward chmn. Town Com., 1978-84; asst. football coach Immaculate HS, 1988; town coord. Prescot Bush for U.S. Senate; town and state coord. Labriola for Gov., 1982, 86; rep. Presdl. Legion Merit; active Rep. Presdl. Task Force, Am. Bicentennial Presdl. Inaugural Ball, Washington, 1989; advisor Forbes for Pres., 1996; sponsor U.S. Navy Meml., Washington; charter mem. U.S. Holocaust Meml. Mus.; active USS Saratoga Mus., Marine Corps Heritage Found. With USN, 1967-73, Vietnam. Decorated Air medals, DFC, Navy Commendation with Combat V, Vietnam Gallantry Cross, Vietnam Campaign with Silver Star, Navy Unit citation, Meritorious Unit citation. Mem.: Marine Corps Heritage Found., Blue and Gold, Naval Helicopter Assn., Am. Scandinavian Found., Naval Acad. Alumni Assn. (life), Tailhook Assn. (life), Assn. Naval Aviation (life), U.S. Naval Acad. Athletic Assn./Navy Blue and Gold (life; commodore), N.Y. Sports Clubs, Yale Club (Greater Danbury), Milford Yacht Club. Congregationalist. Avocations: yacht racing, autoracing, weight training, football, golf. Home: 60 Miry Brook Rd Danbury CT 06810-7411 Personal E-mail: flynavyl@att.net.

ANDERSON, ALEXIS, minister; b. St. Louis, Mo. d. William and Martha Crump; children: Marquetta, Michael, Beverly, CeNeisha, Quentin, Anastasia. BA, Rockhurst Coll., Kansas City, 1981; MA, Webster U., St. Louis, 1985. Exec. dir. P.R.E.A.C.H., Baton Rouge; family self sufficiency Coord. Tacoma Housing Authority, Tacoma, 2000—02; pastor Bethel AME Ch., Yakima, Wash., 2002—03, Hannah Chapel AME, Kinder, La., 2003—; cmty. devel. mgr. LA DO ID FCU, Baton Rouge, 2004—06; mng. dir. Earn Found., Baton Rouge, 2006—. Bd. mem. Women Outreaching Women, Denham Springs, La., 2005—, Baton Rouge Black Chamber, Baton Rouge, 2006—. Mem.: Capital City Rotary, Am. Hearts Assn. (bd. mem. 2004—). Office: LA DOTD FCU 1620 S Range Ave Denham Springs LA 70726 Business E-Mail: aanderson@ladotdfcu.org.

ANDERSON, ALFRED OLIVER, mathematician, consultant; b. Marmon, ND, May 18, 1928; s. Frederick Gustav and Minnie Petrine (Jensen) Anderson. BS, Oreg. State U., 1953. Sys. programmer U.S. Army Ballistics Rsch. Lab., Aberdeen, Md., 1953-83; cons. Aberdeen, 1983—. Investment specialist, Palermo, Maine, 1983—. Mem.: Mensa, Pi Mu Epsilon. Democrat. Lutheran. Avocations: wood working, investment analysis. Home and Office: 107 Banton Rd Palermo ME 04354-6521 Office Phone: 207-993-2042.

ANDERSON, ALLAMAY EUDORIS, retired health educator, home economist; b. NYC, July 18, 1933; d. John Samuel and Charlotte Jane (Harrigan) Richardson; m. Edgar Leopold Anderson, Jr., Apr. 14, 1957 (div. Apr. 14, 1963); 1 child, David Lancelot; m. Diane Kay Swartz, July 19, 2003. BA, Queens Coll., CUNY, 1975; MS in Edn., Fordham U., 1984. Profl. mgmt. cert. Adelphi U., 1978. Staff sch. food svc. dietitian Bd. Edn., NYC, 1968-88; tchr. home and career skills Louis Armstrong Mid. Sch., 1988; spl. edn. tchr. Manhattan HS, NYC, 1989-95, coord AIDS resource, 1995, ret. 1995. Profl. devel. cons., NYC, 1978—; ptnr. Masiba Bldg. Corp., Corona, NY, 1975-82; adj. lectr. home econs. Queens Coll., 1987; owner AEA Devel. Svc., 1987-97; exec. bd. Sch. Edn. Alumni Assn., Fordham U., 1997-2006. Sch. coord. League for Better Cmty. Life, Inc., 1977, treas. exec. bd., 1970-76; officer NYC Cmty. Devel. Agy., 1980-83; mem. Kwanzaa Adv. Com. Urban Coalition, PR, 1983, LI # 28 Episcopal Cursillo, 1991; vestry mem. youth ministries Grace Episcopal Ch., 1982-85, vestry mem., 1996-99; asst. presiding ptnr. Dynamic Investors Club, 1996-2007; Bridges chair Srs. of Dorie Miller, 2003-06, Clergy award, 1996, 2006. Recipient Elmcor Cmty. Svc. award Elmcor Youth and Adult Activities, Inc., 1989, Alumni Achievement award Fordham U. Sch. Edn., 2000, Cmty. Svc. award NY State United Tchrs., 2001, Concourse Village Br. Positive Image award Key Women Am., Inc., 2005, Salutatorium, Inst. for Sr. Action, 2005, Appreciation cert. Langston Hughes Libr., 2006. Mem. NAACP (silver life mem., local Women's History Month honoree 1996), Assn. Fundraising Profls. (Greater NY chpt.), Nat. Assn. Investment Clubs (award 2004), Langston Hughes Libr. Action Com. (bd. dirs. 1987—, treas. 1989, Kwanza chair 1994-97, Appreciation cert. 2006), Queens Coll. Home Econs. Alumni Assn. (v.p., chmn. bylaws com. 1982), United Fedn. Tchrs. (Ret. Tchrs. chpt.), Negro Bus. and Profl. Women's Clubs (Profl. award 1998), Joint Pub. Affairs Com. for Older Adults (life), Dynamic Investors Club (v.p. 1996-2007), Phi Delta Kappa. Personal E-mail: nosredna@gis.net.

ANDERSON, ANITA A., secondary school educator; b. Winston-Salem, NC, Sept. 13, 1938; d. Birden Dixon and Lovie Josephine McCoy; m. Clarence B. Crumpton (dec.); children: Clarence B., Victoria E.; m. William Webb (dec.); 1 child, William R.; m. William Wallace Parker, Sept. 8, 1992 (dec. June 1998); m. William G. Anderson, Mar. 27, 1999. BS in English and Social Studies, U. Detroit Mercy, Mich., 1973; MEd, Marygrove Coll., Detroit, 1974, cert. secondary adminstrn., 1994; computerized office cert., Acock Computerized Ctr., Athens, Ga., 1986; postgrad., Oakland U., Rochester, Mich., 1996—. Tchr., dept. head Western H.S., Las Vegas, Nev., 1974-76; tchr. reading, dir. learning ctr. Ecorse (Mich.) H.S., 1976-81; tchr., coord. reading Winston-Salem-Forsyth County Schs., 1981-87; tchr. math. Holt (Ala.) H.S., 1987-88; tchr. algebra and sci. Pontiac (Mich.) Pub. Schs., 1988—, self-esteem, self-awareness and peer rels. grant writr, 1989—. Self-esteem facilitator, substance abuse specialist Washington Mid. Sch., Pontiac, 1991—. Author: (tng. manual) Surving Societal Stressors, 1990. Bd. dirs. Fedn. Youth Svcs., Detroit, 1991—. Recipient Tech. of Yr. award N.C. Bd. Edn., 1994; grantee 1st of Am. Bank, Inc., 1994-95. Mem. AAUW, Internat. Reading Assn., Am. Bus. Women Assn., NAACP (life, bd. dirs. Detroit 1990—), Lions (bd. dirs. Detroit 1992—, sec.-editor 1993-95, Melvin Jones fellow 1997), Order Ea. Star (worthy matron 1996—), Daus. of Isis (dir. team I 1996-97), Gamma Phi Delta (life, internat. Greek queen 1979). Avocations: horticulture, travel, reading, drama, surfing the internet. Office: Washington Middle Sch 701 Menominee Rd Pontiac MI 48341-1544

ANDERSON, ANITA L., psychology professor; d. Wilson Anderson and Frankie Lavallis-Anderson; m. Ernest E. Haffner, Aug. 21, 1984; 1 child, Edwin C. Haffner. BA, U. Tex., San Antonio, 1985; MA, St. Mary's U., San Antonio, 1988; PhD, U. Wis., Milw., 1996. Grad. intern inpatient psychiatry Wilson Hall USAF Med. Ctr., San Antonio, 1987; grad. intern neuropsychol. assessment svcs. Brooke Army Med. Ctr., Fort Sam Houston, Tex., 1988; asst. to clinic coord. U. Wis., Milw., 1991—92; psychometric asst. Milw. Pub. Schs., 1993—94; pre-doctoral fellow clin. psychology Yale U. Sch. Medicine, New Haven, 1994—95; asst. prof. psychology U. Incarnate Word, San Antonio, 1998—, chairperson psychology dept., 2000—02. Mem.: APA, Nat. Social Sci. Assn., Assn. Black Psychologists, Phi Kappa Phi, Sigma Xi. Office: Univ Incarnate Word CPO 102 4301 Broadway San Antonio TX 78209 Office Phone: 210-829-3992. Office Fax: 210-829-3880.

ANDERSON, ARTHUR ALLAN, management consultant; b. Grand Rapids, Mich., Apr. 16, 1939; s. Alvin Alexander and Mildred Jane (Grice) A. AB in History, ScB in Chemistry, Brown U., 1962; LLB, Yale U., 1965. Bar: N.Y. 1966. Assoc. Fish & Neave, NYC, 1965-69; co-founder, pres. Source Securities Corp., 1970-72; gen. counsel Teleprompter Corp., NYC, 1973-74; ptnr. Anderson & Rubin, NYC, 1975-82, Choate, Moore, Hahn & McGarry, NYC, 1982-85; sole practice NYC, 1985-87; prin., bd. dirs. Morgan, AndersonConsulting, NYC, 1988—. Co-chair Woodstock Artists' Assn. Mus.; mem. exec. bd. Samuel Dorsky Mus. of Art, SUNY, New Paltz. Chair adv. coun. Woodstock Byrdcliffe Guild. Mem.: Yale Club NY, Explorers Club. Office: Morgan Anderson Cons 4 Park Ave 22d Flr New York NY 10016 Business E-Mail: office@morgananderson.com.

ANDERSON, ARTHUR OSMUND, pathologist, immunologist, bioethicist, military officer; b. NYC, Mar. 12, 1945; s. Arthur Edmund and Florence Ranveig (Osmundsen) A.; m. Julane Kay Pynn, Oct. 4, 1969; 1 child, Phoebe MacDonald Anderson. BS, Wagner Coll., 1966; MD, U. Md., 1970; PhD (hon.), Wagner Coll., 2003. Diplomate Am. Bd. Pathology. Intern in pathology Johns Hopkins Hosp., Balt., 1970-71, fellow in exptl. pathology, 1970-74, resident in pathology, 1971-73; commd. 2d lt. U.S. Army, 1974, advanced through grades to col., 1988; asst. prof. biology and pathology U. Pa., Phila., 1980-83; prin. investigator pathology div. U.S. Army Med. Rsch. Inst. Infectious Diseases, Ft. Detrick, Md., 1974-80, chief respiratory immunity, 1983—, chmn. human institutional rev. bd., 1976-80, 84—. Appeared in (History Channel) Suicide Missions: Human Guinea Pigs, 2000, (ABC News) A Closer Look Operation Whitecoat, 2001; contbr. numerous articles to profl. jours., chpts. to immunology text books and websites. Advanced through ranks to Col. med. rsch. and material command US Army, 1977—2007. Decorated Meritorious Svc. medal; N.Y. State Regents scholar, 1962-66; recipient Order of Mil. Med. Merit award, 2002. Mem. Found. for Advanced Edn. in Scis., Am. Assn. Immunologists, Am. Assn. Pathologists, Applied Rsch. Ethics Nat. Assn. (treas. 2000-04), Kiwanis (pres. Frederick 1988-89), Beta Beta Beta, Omicron Delta Kappa. Democrat. Episcopalian. Achievements include first documented role of endothelium in immunity; first showed evidence in vivo that lymphocytes adhered to endothelial cells in lymph nodes, first showed that adjuvants could enhance mucosal secretion of IgA; first identified chemokine and antigen transmission function of Fibroblastic Reticular Cell Conduit in lymphatic tissues; contributed to medical ethics as chronicled in the book Undue Risk: Secret State Experiments on Humans, 1999. Office: US Army Med Rsch Inst Infectious Diseases Fort Detrick Frederick MD 21702 Office Phone: 301-619-4723. Personal E-mail: artnscience@yahoo.com. Business E-Mail: art.anderson@us.army.mil.

ANDERSON, AUSTIN GOTHARD, lawyer, consultant, academic administrator; b. Calumet, Minn., June 30, 1931; s. Hugo Gothard and Turna Marie (Johnson) A.; m. Catherine Antoinette Spellacy, Jan. 2. 1954; children: Todd, Susan, Timothy, Linda, Mark. BA, U. Minn., Mpls., 1954, JD, 1958. Bar: Minn. 1958, Ill. 1962, Mich. 1974. Assoc. Spellacy, Spellacy, Lano & Anderson, Marble, Minn., 1958-62; dir. Ill. Inst. Continuing Legal Edn., Springfield, 1962-64; dir. dept. continuing legal edn. U. Minn., Mpls., 1964-70, assoc. dean gen. extension divsn., 1968-70; ptnr. Dorsey, Marquart, Windhorst, West & Halladay, Mpls., 1970-73; assoc. dir. Nat. Ctr. State Cts., St. Paul, 1973-74; dir. Inst. CLE U. Mich., Ann Arbor, 1973-92; dir. Inst. on Law Firm Mgmt., 1992-95; prin. Anderson Boyer Group, Ann Arbor, 1995—; pres. Network of Leading Law Firms, 1995—. Adj. faculty U. Minn., 1974, Wayne State U., 1974-75; mem. adv. bd. Ctr. for Law Firm Mgmt. Nottingham Trent U., Eng.; draftsman ABA Guidelines for Approval of Legal Asst. Programs, 1973, Model Guidelines for Minimum CLE, 1988; chair law practice mgmt. sect. State Bar Mich., 2000-01; mem. Task Force on Court Filing, State Bar of Mich., 2000—; mem. Com. on Quality of Life, 2000-01; cons. in field. Author 3 books 1971; co-editor, contbg. author: Lawyer's Handbook, 1975, co-editor 3d edit., 1992; author: A Plan for Lawyer Development, 1986, Marketing Your Practice: A Practical Guide to Client Development, 1986; cons. editor, contbg. author: Webster's Legal Secretaries Handbook, 1981; cons. editor Merriam Webster's Legal Secretarial Handbook, 2d edit., 1996; co-author: The Effective Associate Training Program-Improving Firm Performance, Profits and Prospective Partners, 2000, Associate Retention: Keeping Our Best and Brightest, 2002; author, co-editor: The Effective Training and Development Program, 2005; contbr. chpt. to book and articles to profl. jours. Chmn. City of Bloomington Park and Recreation Adv. Commn., Minn., 1967-72; chmn. Ann Arbor Citizens Recreation Adv. Com., 1981-89, Ann Arbor Parks Adv. Com., 1983-92, chair, 1991-92; rep. Class of '58 U. Minn. Law Sch., 1996-2004. Recipient Excellence award CLE sect. Assn. of Am. Law Schs., 1992. Fellow Am. Bar Found. (Mich. chmn. 2002—), State Bar Mich. Found.; mem. ABA (vice chmn. CLE com. sect. legal edn. and admission to bar 1988-93, standing com. continuing edn. of bar 1984-90, 00—, chmn. law practice mgmt. sect. 1981-82, Am. Law Inst.-ABA com. on continuing profl. edn. 1993-96, Am. Law Inst.-ABA com. on continuing profl. edn. 1999-02, spl. com. on rsch. on future of legal profession 1998-2000, sec. Coll. of Law Practice Mgmt. 1993-97, house of dels. 1993-99, commn. on lawyer advt. 1994-97, mem. task force Lawyer Ctr. on pers. legal svcs. and client devel. 2002-03, spl. advisor to standing com. on continuing edn. of the bar 2002—, chair cmty. on econ. of law practices, 2002-04, torts, trial and ins. practice sect., mem. sr. lawyers sect. 2005—07, instr. ABA/CLE and bus. devel. workshops, Bahrain 2006), Internat. Bar Assn., Mich. Bar Assn., Ill. Bar Assn., State Bar of Mich. (chair law practice mgmt. sect. 2000-01, disting. lawyer com. 2005—, mem. e-filing task force), Minn. Bar Assn., Internat. Bar Assn., Assn. Continuing Legal Edn. Adminstrs. (pres. 1969-70), Laurel Gardens Condominium Assn. (pres. 2004-07). Home: 4660 Bayberry Cir Ann Arbor MI 48105-9762 Office: AndersonBoyer Group 3135 S State St Ste 360 H Ann Arbor MI 48108 Office Phone: 734-929-6943. Business E-Mail: aga@andersonboyer.com.

ANDERSON, BARBARA JEAN, biology professor; b. Evergreen Park, Ill., June 24, 1950; d. William Albert and Margery Jean Kleist; m. John Donald Anderson, Mar. 14, 1950; 1 child, Megan. BS of Edn. in Biology, Western Ill. U., Macomb, 1972, MS in Botany, 1977. Tchr. sci. Oak Lawn H.S., Ill., 1973—79; prof. biology Coll. DuPage, Glen Ellyn, 1980—. Co-chair Nat. Sci. Ctr., Glen Ellyn, 1983—2007, chair biology faculty, 2004—06, biology liaison to dean, 2004—06. Vol. Eisenhower Jr. High Band Boosters, Darien, Ill., 1993—98, Fairview Sch. Recycling, 1989—93; product chmn. Girl Scouts Am., 1990—2002. Named Outstanding Faculty in Natural and Applied Scis. Divsn., Nat. Sci. Ctr., 2005—06. Mem.: Ill. State Acad. Sci., Nat. Assn. Biology Tchrs., Nat. Sci. Tchrs. Assn. Presbyterian. Avocations: skiing, camping, gardening, bicycling. Office: Coll DuPage 425 Fawell Blvd Glen Ellyn IL 60137 Office Phone: 630-942-2347.

ANDERSON, BARBARA MCCOMAS, lawyer; d. Ben C. Jr. and Elsa A. McComas; m. Roy Ryden Anderson Jr., Dec. 11, 1982; 1 child, Ryden McComas Anderson. BA, Trinity U., San Antonio, 1972; JD, U. Tex., 1978. Bar: Tex. 1978; cert. in estate planning and probate Tex. Bd. Legal Specialization. From assoc. to ptnr. Locke Purnell Rain Harrell, Dallas, 1978-97; of counsel Locke Liddell & Sapp, LLP, Dallas, 1997—2003; pvt. practice Dallas, 1997—. Fellow: Coll. of State Bar of Tex., Tex. Bar. Found., Am. Coll. Trusts and Estates Counsel; mem.: Tex. Acad. Probate and Trust Lawyers (charter, v.p., bd. dirs.), Dallas Bar Assn. (chair probate, trusts and estates sects. 1987—88), Tex. Bar Assn. (chair real estate, probate and trust law sect. 2003—04). Avocations: reading, gardening. Office: PO Box 181147 Dallas TX 75218-8147

ANDERSON, BERNARD E., economist; b. Phila. s. William and Dorothy (Gideon) Anderson; children: Melinda D., Bernard E. II. BA with highest honors, Livingstone Coll., 1959; MA, Mich. State U., 1961; PhD, U. Pa., 1969; LHD (hon.), Shaw U., 1984, Livingstone Coll., 1995; LLD (hon.), Benedict Coll., 2002, Tuskegee U., 2005. Economist U.S. Bur. Labor Stats., Washington, 1963-65; successively asst. prof., assoc. prof., prof. Wharton Sch. U. Pa., Phila., 1969-79; dir. social sci. Rockefeller Found., NYC, 1979-86; mng. ptnr. Urban Affairs Partnership, Phila., 1987-91; pres. Anderson Group, Phila., 1991-93; asst. sec. U.S. Dept. Labor, 1994-2001; chmn. Pa. Intergovernmental Cooperation Authority, Phila., 1991-93; Whitney M. Young prof. mgmt. Wharton Sch., U. Pa., Phila., 2001—. Vice chmn. Manpower Demonstration Rsch. Co., NYC, 1977—93, Pa. Econ. Devel. Partnership, Harrisburg, Provident Mut. Life Ins. Co., 1988—2002; vis. fellow Woodrow Wilson Sch., Princeton (N.J.) U., 1985; bd. dirs. United Bank Phila., Greater Phila. Urban Affairs Coalition. Author: Youth Employment and Public Policy, 1980; co-author: Impact of Government Training and Employment Programs, 1975, Black Managers in American Business, 1978, Soul in Management, 1996; mem. editl. bd. Rev. Black Polit. Economy, 1977—89. Mem. Pres.'s Commn. Employment/Unemployment Stats., Washington, 1979, Com. Fgn. Rels., Phila., 1983—94; trustee Livingstone Coll., Salisbury, NC, 1980—94, 2005—, Tuskegee U., 2006—; chmn. bd. trustees Lincoln U., Oxford, Pa., 1987—93; bd. dirs. Franklin Inst., Phila., 2002—05, Opportunities Industrialization Ctrs. Am., 2001—, Leon H. Sullivan Found., 2002—, Phila. Orch., 2004—, Internat. Found. for Edn. and Self Help, 2001—. With US Army, 1961—63. Recipient Disting. Educator award, Citizens Urbanism, 1987, Cmty. Svc. award, Delaware Valley Housing Assn., 1989, Disting. Svc. award, A. Philip Randolph Inst., 1990, Bayard Rustin Humanitarianism award, 1996. Mem.: Nat. Econ. Assn. (pres. 1982, Samuel Z. Westerfield award 2003), Indsl. Rels. Rsch. Assn. (mem. exec. com. 1979—82), Am. Econ. Assn., Union League, U. Pa. Faculty Club. Democrat. A.M.E. Zion.

ANDERSON, BETTE (BONNIE) FERGUSON, music educator; b. June 28, 1948; d. Richard Allen and Bettie Parsons Ferguson; m. Michael Ratcliff Anderson, June 19, 1971; children: Bettie Michelle Anderson-Haigler(dec.) , Richard Ratcliff. BME, Longwood U., Va., 1970. Cert. tchr. Va. Music tchr. Henrico Co. Schs., Richmond, Va., 1970—74; studio piano, pre-school music Richmond, Va., 1974—84; music tchr. The Steward Sch., Richmond, Va., 1984—. Home: 4115 Roundtree Rd Richmond VA 23294-5620 Business E-Mail: Bonnie.Anderson@stewardschool.org.

ANDERSON, BRADBURY H., retail executive; b. Sheridan, Wyo., 1949; m. Janet Anderson; 2 children. AA, Waldorf Coll., 1969; BA, U. Denver, 1971. Salesman Sound of Music, 1973—81, store mgr., 1981—86; exec. v.p. Best Buy Co., Inc., Richfield, Minn., 1986—91, pres., COO, 1991—2002, vice chmn., 2001—, CEO, 2002—. Bd. dirs. Best Buy Co., 1986—, Minn. Public Radio, Am. Film Inst., Best Buy Children's Found., Internat. Mass Retail Assn., Waldorf Coll. Bd. Regents. Bd. dirs. Am. Film Inst., Best Buy Children's Found., Internat. Mass Retail Assn.; bd. regents Waldorf Coll. Recipient Alumni Disting. Svc. award, Waldorf Coll., 1997, Retail Exec. of the Yr., Retail Merchandiser mag., 2002. Office: Best Buy Co Inc 7601 Penn Ave S Richfield MN 55423-3645*

ANDERSON, BROOKS DORAN, II, geologist, consultant; b. Auburn, NY, June 18, 1941; s. Brooks Doran and Violet (Risley) Anderson; m. Maria de Los Angeles Antuna, Aug. 16, 1963; 1 child, Loani. BSc Geology, Bowling Green State U., 1963; MA Geology, Tex. U., 1965; PhD Ocean and Environ. Affairs, Heed U., 1977. Geologist Geolabs, Inc., Honolulu, 1972—74; project geologist Dames & Moore, Inc., Honolulu, 1974—76; pvt. practice Honolulu, 1976—77; prof. geology U. Baja Calif., Ensenada, Mexico, 1977—78; pvt. practice Saltillo, Mexico, 1982—86, 1991—2001; info. officer Securitas, San Antonio, 2001—03. Cons. in field. Contbr.

articles to profl. jours. Capt. US Army, 1968—70. Grantee, U. Nuevo Leon, Guatemala, 1986; Australian Commonwealth scholar, Australian Fed. Govt., 1971. Achievements include development of grain size analysis method for nuclear craters costing 1% of previous methods; conceptual model of Hawaiian coral cmty. structure; conceptual model of faults for finding groundwater in impermeable shale in Northeastern Mexico. Avocation: writing. Home: Colonia Doctores 204 Dr Miguel Farias 25250 Saltillo Mexico also: 91-1084 Kauiki St Ewa Beach HI 96707 Home Phone: 808-561-7544. Personal E-mail: risleyanderson@yahoo.com.

ANDERSON, CARL ALBERT, fraternal organization administrator, lawyer, dean; b. Torrington, Conn., Feb. 27, 1951; s. Carl August and Louise Joanna (Giorcelli) A.; m. Dorian Jean Lounsbury Anderson, Aug. 19, 1972; children: Carl, Matthew, Teresa, Katherine, Clare. BA in Philosophy, Seattle U., 1972; JD, U. Denver, 1975. Bar: D.C. 1979. Vis. prof. family law Ponfitical Lateran Univ., Rome, 1983—88; v.p., faculty mem. John Paul II Inst. for Studies on Marriage and Family, Cath. Univ., Washington, 1988—; asst. supreme sec., supreme sec. Knights of Columbus, New Haven, supreme knight (corp. chmn. & CEO), 2000—. Legis. asst. U.S. Senate, Washington, 1976-81; counsellor to the Undersec. U.S. Dept. Health and Human Svcs., Washington, 1981-83; staff mem. White House Office of Policy Devel., Washington, 1983-85; spl. asst. to the Pres., 1985-87; acting dir. White House Office of Pub. Liaison, 1987; commr. U.S. Commn. on Civil Rights, Washington, 1990-2000; mem. internat. sci. coun. Studium Generale Marcianum of Venice. Contbr. articles to profl. jours. Mem. transition team Office of the Pres.-Elect, Washington, 1980, 88; trustee Cath. U. Am., 2002—; consultor Pontifical Coun. for the Family, Pontifical Coun. Justice and Peace, Pontifical Coun. for Social Comms., 2006; cons. pro-life com. U.S. Conf. Cath. Bishops. Recipient Thomas Linacre award Nat. Fedn. Cath. Physicians' Guilds, 1992; Knight of the Equestrian Order of the Holy Sepulchre of Jerusalem, Knight of St. Gregory the Great, Pontifical Acad. for Life, Pontifical Coun. for the Laity, consultor Pontifical Coun. for the Family, and Pontifical Coun. for Justice and Peace. Mem. D.C. Bar Assn., KC (v.p. pub. policy 1987-97, state dep. for D.C. 1995-97, asst. supreme sec. 1997-98, supreme sec. 1998-2000), Nat. Cath. Edn. Assn. (trustee). Roman Catholic. Address: KC One Columbus Plz New Haven CT 06510-3326 Business E-Mail: carl.anderson@kofc.org.

ANDERSON, CARLEN JOSEPH, city agency administrator; b. Jamaica, NY, July 3, 1961; s. Clinton Isadore and Althea Elizabeth Anderson. BA in Polit. Sci., York Coll., Jamaica, 1984; MA in Polit Sci., Bklyn. Coll., 2006. Child protective mgr. Adminstrn. Children's Svcs., NYC, 1984—. Mem. NYC City Opera; columnist On Right Side Black Reign Cmty. Newspaper, 1996—2004; mem. Brownstone Rep. Club, Bklyn., 2003—, Nat. Rep. Com., Washington, 2004—; candidate Rep. party NY State Assembly 29A Dist., 1984. Recipient News Commentary award, NY Assn. Black Journalists, 2001. Mem.: Nat. Rifle Assn., Acad. Polit. Sci. Republican. Avocations: writing, opera, films.

ANDERSON, CAROL LYNN, social worker, educator; b. LaPorte, Ind., Apr. 22, 1958; d. Paul Lewis and Marilee Anderson. BS summa cum laude, Ball State U., Muncie, Ind., 1983, BS, 1985; MSW, Ind. U., Indpls., 1986; D of Ministry, U. of Creation Spirituality/Wisdom U., Oakland, Calif., 2004. Cert. addictions counselor, social worker Acad. of Cert. Social Workers, lic. masters of social work. Counselor Adult and Child Mental Health Ctr., Indpls., 1986—88; counselor, program coord. Anderson Ctr. for Chem. Dependency, Ind., 1989—91; pvt. practice therapist Profl. Counseling Ctr. Ind., Anderson, 1990—91; chem. dependency counselor Phoenix Hall, Traverse City, Mich., 1991—95; clin. therapist, dual disorders specialist Great Lakes Cmty. Mental Health, Traverse City, Mich., 1995—2002; expert witness State of Mich., Dept. Consumer and Industry Svcs., Lansing, 2002—05; therapist, cons. Sarah's Cir., LLC, Traverse City, Mich., 1999—; counselor in behavioral health Murson Med. Ctr., Traverse City, Mich., 2002—; instr. social work Ferris State U., Big Rapids, Mich., 2005—. Founder, facilitator Dual Disorders Task Force, Traverse City, Mich., 1995—; guest spkr. Sarah's Cir., LLC, Traverse City, Mich., 1999—. Author: Where All Our Journeys End: Searching for the Beloved in Everyday Life, 2006. Commr. Traverse City Human Rights Commn., 1995—98; spokesperson, mem. com. Traverse City Campaign Against Discrimination, 2000—02; sex edn. adv. com. Traverse City Area Pub. Schs., 2005—. Mem.: Acad. of Cert. Social Workers, NASW. Democrat. Avocations: reading, sports, gardening, writing, drawing. Home: 2016 Chippewa St Traverse City MI 49686 Office: Sarah's Cir LLC PO Box 3052 Traverse City MI 49685 Office Phone: 231-632-5072. E-mail: sarahscirclellc@yahoo.com.

ANDERSON, CATHY C., lawyer; BA, U. Mich.; JD, Loyola U. Dir. comml. law svcs. The Nutrasweet Co., 1986—92, dep. gen. counsel, asst. sec., 1992—95; exec. v.p., gen. counsel, sec. Alliant Foodservice, Inc., Deerfield, Ill., 1995—2003; sr. v.p., gen. counsel, sec. True Value Co. (formerly TruServ Corp.), Chgo., 2003—. Affiliated with Georgetown U. Corp. Coun. Inst. Bd. dirs. Evanston-Northwestern Healthcare. Mem.: ABA, Chgo. Bar Assn. Office: True Value Co 8600 W Bryn Mawr Ave Chicago IL 60631-3505 Office Phone: 773-695-5000.

ANDERSON, CHARLES ANTHONY, lawyer; b. Ashtabula, Ohio, Nov. 21, 1945; s. Charles Lindley and Teresa (Silva) A.; m. Martha M. Bodnar, June 18, 1974; children: Charles Joshua, Kristin, Megan, Caitlin, Justin. BA, Bowling Green State U., 1967; postgrad., U. So. Calif., 1971-72; JD, U. San Francisco, 1975. Bar: Calif. 1976, Va. 1977, U.S. Ct. Appeals (D.C. cir.) 1977, U.S. Dist. Ct. (ea. dist.) Va. 1978. Staff rschr. Commn. on Fed Paperwork, Washington, 1976; com. atty. U.S. Ho. of Reps., Washington, 1977; pvt. practice Reston, Va., 1977-83; ptnr. Ralston, Redick, Norwitch, O'Connor, Craig, Anderson, Reston, 1983-88; trial atty., pvt. practice Charles A. Anderson, P.C., Reston, 1988-2000; mng. ptnr. Grenadier, Anderson, Simpson and Duffett, P.C., Reston, 2000—. Lt. USN, 1968-72. Mem. Va. Trial Lawyers' Assn. (family law exec. bd. 1990-96), KC (trustee 1993-97, Grand Knight 1994). Avocations: poker, reading, world war ii history. Home: 2657 Unicorn Ct Herndon VA 20171-2425 Office: Grenadier Anderson Simpson Starace Duf 12359 Sunrise Valley Dr Ste 230 Reston VA 20191-3493 E-mail: bxqx61a@aol.com.

ANDERSON, CHARLES ARTHUR, retired science administrator; b. Columbus, Ohio, Nov. 14, 1917; s. Arthur E. and Huldah (Peterson) A.; m. Elizabeth Rushforth, Oct. 27, 1942; children: Peter C., Stephen E., Julia E. AB, U. Calif., Berkeley, 1938; MBA, Grad. Sch. Bus. Adminstrn., Harvard U., 1940; LHD, Colby Coll., 1975. Asst. prof. Grad. Sch. Bus. Adminstrn., Harvard U., Boston, 1945-48; v.p. Magna Power Tool Corp., Menlo Park, Calif., 1948-58; prof., asso. dean Stanford Grad. Sch. Bus., 1959-61; v.p. Kern County Land Co., San Francisco, 1961-64; pres. Walker Mfg. Co., Racine, Wis., 1964-66, J.I. Case Co., Racine, 1966-68; pres., chief exec. officer SRI Internat., Menlo Park, 1968-79. Bd. dirs. KRI Internat., Japan, Eaton Corp., Conoco, Owens-Corning Fiberglas, NCR, Boise Cascade, Saga; mem. adv. council Bus. Sch., Stanford, 1966-72, 74-79; mem. industry adv. council Dept. Def., 1971-73 Author (with Anthony) The New Corporate Director. Mem. Menlo Park Planning Commn. and City Coun., 1955-61, Govs. Commn. on Reorgn. Wis. State Govt., 1965-67; bd. dirs. Calif. State C. of C., 1972-77, Internat. House, U. Calif., Berkeley, 1979-90; bd. dirs. Lucile Salter Packard Children's Hosp., Stanford, 1979-95, chmn., 1992-94. With USNR, 1941-45. Recipient Exceptional Service award USAF, 1965 Mem. Palo Alto Club, Pacific-Union Club, Menlo Country Club. Presbyterian. Office: 555 Byron St Apt 207 Palo Alto CA 94301-2037 Personal E-mail: caacaa@pacbell.com.

ANDERSON, CHARLES HILL, lawyer; s. Ray N. and Lois M. Anderson; (div.); children: Eric S., Alicia L., Burton H. JD, U. Tenn., 1953. Bar: Tenn. 1953, U.S. Dist. Ct. Tenn. 1953, U.S. Ct. Appeals (6th cir.) 1956, U.S. Supreme Ct. 1956, U.S. Ct. Mil. 1964. Pvt. practice, Chattanooga, 1953—59, 2001—04, Nashville, 1977—79, 1987—2004, Columbia, SC, 2005—; assoc. gen. counsel Life & Casualty Ins. Co. Tenn., Nashville, 1960-69; dist. atty. US Dept. Justice, Nashville, 1969-77; asst. adj. gen. State of Tenn., Nashville, 1979-87. Mem. U.S. Atty. Gen. Adv. Com., Washington, 1973-77; del. Tenn. Constl. Conv., Nashville, 1965-66; dir. Nashville Pub. TV Coun., 1994-99; chmn. Met. Bd. of Equalization, 1998-2001. Brig. gen. AUS, ret., 1987. Mem. ABA, Tenn. Bar Assn., Nashville Bar Assn., Fed. Bar Assn. (pres. Nashville chpt. 1972), Assn. Life Ins. Counsel, Cumberland Club (pres. 1981-82), The Federalist Soc. Presbyterian. Home: 1515 Woodbine Ct Columbia SC 29206-4403

ANDERSON, CHARLES ROSS, civil engineer; b. NYC, Oct. 4, 1937; s. Biard Eclare and Melva (Smith) A.; m. Susan Breinholt, Aug. 29, 1961; children: Loralee, Brian, Craig, Thomas, David. BSCE, U. Utah, Salt Lake City, 1961; MBA, Harvard U., Cambridge, Mass., 1963. Registered profl. engr. Owner, operator AAA Engring. and Drafting, Inc., Salt Lake City, 1960—. Acad. adv. com. U. Utah, 1990-91, chmn. civil engring. adv. bd., 1995—, U. Utah nat. engring. adv. coun., 2001—. Mayoral appointee Housing Devel. Com., Salt Lake City, 1981-86; bd. dirs., vice chmn. Met. Water Dist., Salt Lake City, 1985-99; bd. dirs., pres., v.p., sec. bd. Utah Mus. Natural History, Salt Lake City, 1980-92; asst. dist. commr. Sunrise dist. Boy Scouts Am., Salt Lake City, 1985-86; fundraising coord. architects and engrs. United Fund; mem. Sunstone Nat. Adv. Bd., 1980-88; bd. dirs. Provo River Water Users Assn., 1986—, Salt Lake Convention & Visitor Bur., 2001-03; mgmt. bd. U. Utah Hosp. and Clinic, 2000—. Recipient Hamilton Watch award U. Utah Nat. Adv. Coun., 2001-, Merit of Honor award U. Utah Alumni Assn., 2001; fellow Am. Gen. Contractors, Salt Lake City, 1960. Mem.: ASCE, Harvard U. Bus. Sch. Club (pres. 1970—72), U. Utah Alumni Assn. (bd. dirs. 1989—92), U. Utah Crimson Club (bd. dirs. 1996—99), The Country Club (bd. dirs., v.p. 1998-2001), Rotary (pres. 1998—99, v.p. Club 24 1990-91, chmn. election com. 1980-81, vice chmn. and chmn. membership com. 1988-90, Salt Lake Rotary Club Found. bd. dirs. 2000-05, 1st v.p. 1997-98), Tau Beta Pi, Chi Epsilon, Phi Eta Sigma, Pi Kappa Alpha (internat. pres. 1972-74, trustee endowment fund 1974-80, Outstanding Alumnus 1967, 72, mem. Hall of Fame 1995). Avocations: fly fishing, golf, foreign travel. Home: 2689 Comanche Dr Salt Lake City UT 84108-2846 Office: AAA Engring & Drafting Inc PO Box 58171 Salt Lake City UT 84158-0171 Office Phone: 801-583-0311. E-mail: cross@sisna.com.

ANDERSON, CHRIS W., editor-in-chief; b. 1961; 4 children. BS in physics, George Washington U.; grad. Quantum Mechanics and Science Journalism, U. California Berkely. Rsch. Los Alamos Nat. Lab. meson physics facility; several editorial positions Nature, Science; editor The Economist, 1994—2001; editor-in-chief Wired mag., 2001—; rsch. asst. Chief Scientist of the Dept. of Transp. Officer Young Presidents' Assn.; regular spkr., participant World Econ. Forum, Davos, Switzerland. Author: (novels) The Long Tail: Why the Future of Bus. Is Selling Less of More, 2006. Named one of The World's Most Influential People, TIME Mag., 2007; recipient Nat. Mag. award for Gen. Excellence in magazines with 500,000-1,000,000 circulation, Am. Soc. Newspaper Editors, 2007. Office: WIRED Ste 305 520 3rd St San Francisco CA 94107 Fax: 415-276-5150. E-mail: canderson@wiredmag.com.*

ANDERSON, CHRISTINE MARLENE, software engineer; b. Washington, Nov. 19, 1947; 2 children. BS in Math., U. Md., 1969. Mathematician Naval Oceanographic Office, Suitland, Md., 1969-71; sr. analyst, fgn. tech. divsn. Planning Rsch. Corp., Ohio, 1971-72; computer scientist USAF Avionics Lab., Wright-Patterson Air Force Base, Dayton, Ohio, 1971-74; sr. analyst USAF C3 Ctr., Cheyenne Mountain, Colorado Springs, Colo., 1974-76; chief computer tech. section USAF Wright Lab./Armament Directorate, Eglin Air Force Base, Fla., 1982-92; ADA 9X project mgr. Office Sec. Defense, 1987-94; chief software tech. br. Phillips Lab., Kirtland Air Force Base, N.Mex., 1992-93, chief, space soperations and simulation divsn.oftware rsch. ctr. N.Mex., 1993-96, dir. space and missiles tech. directorate N.Mex., 1996; mem. sr. exec. svcs., dir. space vehicles directorate Phillips Lab., Kirtland Air Force Base, Air Force Rsch. Lab., N.Mex., 1996—. Co-chmn. on Ada computer programming lang. Am. Nat. Standards Inst., 1989—; editor Ada standard Internat. Standards Orgn., 1991—. Co-author: Aerospace Software Engineering, 1991; contbr. articles to profl. jours. Recipient Engr. of the Year USAF Armament Lab., 1989, Software Engring. award Am. Inst. Aeronautics, 1991, Program Mgr. of the Year award USAF Armament Lab., 1992, Sec. of Defense medal for Meritorious Civilian Svc., 1996. Fellow AIAA (chair software systems tech. com. 1987-89, bd. dirs. 1989—, Aerospace Software Engring. award 1991).

ANDERSON, CHRISTOPHER JAMES, lawyer; b. Chgo., Nov. 26, 1950; s. James M. and Margaret E. (Anderson) A.; m. Lyn R. Buckley, Jan. 3, 1976; children: Vaughn Buckley, Weston Buckley. BA, Grinnell Coll., 1972; JD with highest distinction, U. Iowa, 1975. Bar: Mo. 1975. From assoc. to ptnr. Armstrong Teasdale LLP, Kansas City, Mo., 1975—. Mem. ABA, Mo. Bar Assn., Kans. City Bar Assn., Lawyers Assn. Kansas City, Estate Planning Soc. Office: Armstrong Teasdale, et al 2345 Grand Blvd Ste 2000 Kansas City MO 64108-2617 Office Phone: 816-221-3420. E-mail: canderso@armstrongteasdale.com.

ANDERSON, CLAIRE W., gifted and talented educator; b. Albuquerque, May 22, 1930; d. Wentworth Henry and Clara Lea (Magruder) Corley; m. William James Young (div.); children: Gayle L. Mirkin, D. Young, Sherry B. Butler; m. Wallace L. Anderson. Student in Engring., U. Miss., 1946; BA, Rice U., 1951, postgrad., 1993; MEd, U. Houston, 1962, postgrad., 1963, Carnegie Mellon U., Tex. A&M, 1992. Cert. elem. and secondary tchr., early childhood, exceptional children tchr., Tex. Tchr. Golfcrest Elem. Shc., Houston, 1959-60, Montrose, Poe Elem. Sch., Houston, 1960-62, St. Mark's Private Sch., Houston, 1962-63; substitute teaching Spring Branch Ind. Sch. Dist., Houston, 1965-68; tchr. Meml. Hall, Houston, 1968-73; instr. English, math. Internat. Hispanic U., Houston, 1971-74; tchr. Dogan Elem. Sch., Houston, 1971-74, Lanier Mid. Sch., Houston, 1974-79, High Sch. Health Profl., Houston, 1979-90, Clifton Mid. Sch., Houston, 1990-91, Jesse H. Jones Sr. High Sch., Houston, 1992—. Adj. tutoring David Livingston and Assoc., Houston, 1960-65; instr. Internat. Hispanic U., Houston, 1971-74, Houston C.C., 1984—, Internat. Ednl. Comm. Ctr., High Point, N.C., 1990, Houston C.C. Sys., 1991; invited judge Kiev, Ukraine Math. and Sci. Competitions, 1989; facilitator Tex. Coun. of Women Sch. Execs. Summer Conf., 1994—; active The Rice/HISD Sch. Writing Project; acad. sponsor secondary edn. svc. and sci. clubs. Pres. bd. dirs. Women for Justice, 1990-94; active Houston Photography Ctr., Mus. Fine Arts, Houston Health Objectives 2000, Children's Mus.; coord. study and enrichment tutoring program, 1994. Recipient Tex. award for Excellence in Tchg. and Outstanding Svc. to the Cmty., 1994; scholar Precalculus Design Team, Dow Jones scholar Pa. State, Advance Placement scholar Tex. A&M, Woodrow Wilson; grantee NSF, Impact II. Mem. IEEE, Nat. Coun. Tchrs. Math., Nat. Coun. Tchrs. English, Am. Acoustic Soc., Assn. Calculating Machinery, Assn. for Early Childhood Edn. (internat. chairperson), Tex. Assn. Edn. Tech., Tex. Computers Educators Assn., N.Y. Acad. Sci., Internat. Coun. Computers in Edn., Phi Delta Kappa. Office: 7414 Saint Lo Rd Houston TX 77033-2732

ANDERSON, CLAYTON C., astronaut; b. Omaha, Nebr., Feb. 23, 1959; s. John T. and Alice J. Anderson; m. Susan Jane Harreld; children: Clayton "Cole", Sutton Marie. BS in Physics, Hastings Coll., 1981; MS in Aerospace Engring., Iowa State U., 1983; PhD (hon.), Hastings Coll., 2004. Mem. mission planning and analysis divsn. NASA, Johnson Space Ctr., Houston, 1983—88, flight design mgr. mission ops. directorate, 1988—89, supr. ascent flight design sect., 1989—93, chief flight design br., 1993—96, mgr. emergency ops. ctr., 1996—98, astronaut, mission specialist candidate, 1998—. Lead, Enhanced Caution and Warning Sys. Develop. effort within Space Shuttle Cockpit Avionics Upgrade Project; crew support astronaut Internat. Space Station Expedition 4; served as Internat. Space Station Capsule Communicator; astronaut office crew rep. Internat. Space Station Electrical Power Sys.; back-up flight engr. Expeditions 12, 13 and 14 missions to the Internat. Space Station; crew mem. Expedition 15-launch to the Internat. Space Station aboard Shuttle Atlantis with crew of STS-117 and will return to Earth aboard Shuttle Discovery on mission STS-120, 2007. Named a NCAA Nat. Christian Coll. Basketball Championships Ofcl., 1997, 1998; named Outstanding Young Man Am., 1981, 1985, 1987; recipient Johnson Space Ctr. Cert. Commendation, 1993, NASA Quality and Safety Achievement Recognition award, 1998. Mem.: Johnson Space Ctr. Employee Activities Assn., Aircraft Owners and Pilots Assn., Tex./N.Mex. Jr. Coll. Athletic Conf., Lone Star Conf., So. Collegiate Athletic Conf., Men's Coll. Basketball Ofcls., S.W. Basketball Ofcls. Assn., Red River Athletic Conf., Heart of Tex. Conf., Clear Lake Optimist Club (past. pres., past v.p.), Alpha Chi (Disting. Alumnus award, Nat. Coun. Alpha Chi 2001). Avocations: officiating basketball games, flying, reading, writing music, piano/organ playing and vocal performance. Office: Astronaut Office/CB NASA Johnson Space Ctr Houston TX 77058*

ANDERSON, CLIFTON EINAR, writer, corporate communications specialist; b. Frederic, Wis., Dec. 17, 1923; s. Andrew John and Ida Louise (Johnson) A.; m. Phyllis Mary Nolan, Oct. 5, 1943; children: Kristine, Craig. BS, U. Wis., 1947; MA, U. Calif., Berkeley, 1954. News editor Chgo. Daily Drover's Jour., 1943-45; asst. editor The Progressive, Madison, Wis., 1946-47; dir. publs. Am. Press, Beirut, 1948-53; mgr. rural programs Houston C. of C., 1957-62; faculty Tex. A&M U., College Station, 1962-65; rsch. fellow U. Tex., Austin, 1965-68; faculty Southwestern Okla. U., Weatherford, 1968-72; extension editor U. Idaho, Moscow, 1972-97, prof. emeritus, 1997—. Spkr. John Macmurray Centennial Conf. Marquette U., 1991, Nat. Conf. on Peacemaking and Conflict Resolution, 1993, moderator the UN at 50 seminar, 1995; moderator Korea Today and Tomorrow Symposium Wash. State U., 1995; spkr. in field. Editor: The Horse Interlude, 1976; author: History of the College of Agriculture at the University of Idaho, 1998; (with others) Ways Out: The Book of Changes for Peace, 1988, The Future: Opportunity Not Destiny, 1989, The Years Ahead: Perils, Problems and Promises, 1993, Eating Agendas: Food and Nutrition as Social Problems, 1995, Futurevision: Ideas, Insights, and Strategies, 1996, Frontiers of the 21st Century: Prelude to the New Millenium, 1999, Foresight, Innovation and Strategy: Toward a Wiser Future, 2005; contbr. articles to profl. jours. and mags. Writer campaign staff Senator R.M. La Follette, Jr., Madison, Wis., 1946; on senatorial campaign staff of Hubert H. Humphrey, Mpls., 1948; chmn. Borah Found. for Outlawry of War, U. Idaho, 1986-87 Recipient Rsch. award Fund for Adult Edn., 1954-55, U.S. Office Edn., 1965-68, 1st prize in newswriting competition Assn. Am. Agrl. Coll. Editors, 1976, merit award Agrl. Rels. Coun., 1995, Nat. Svc. award Washington Times Found., 1996. Fellow Martin Inst. Peace Studies and Conflict Resolution; mem. World Future Soc., Assn. for Religion and Intellectual Life, Profs. World Peace Acad., Internat. Forum on Globalization. Democrat. Avocations: gardening, photography, poetry. Home: 234 N Washington St Moscow ID 83843-2757 Personal E-mail: clifa@verizon.net.

ANDERSON, COKIE GASTON, computer educator, humanities educator; b. Athens, Ga., Feb. 21, 1961; d. William David Avera and Martha Cora Gaston. AA, Stephens Coll., Columbia, Mo., 1978; BSBA, U. Tulsa, 1980; MLIS, U. Okla., Norman, 1998. Law libr. Fellers, Snider, Blankenship, Bailey & Tippens, Oklahoma City, 1992—2000; assoc. prof. Okla. State U., Stillwater, 2000—. Adv. coun. Amigos Libr. Svcs., Dallas, 2003—. Co-author Starting a Digitization Center, 2004; author: Ethical Decision Making for Digital Libraries, 2006; contbr. articles to profl. jours. Bd. dirs. Ballet Okla., Okla. City, 1992—93. Recipient Profl. Devel. Fellowship, Amigos Libr. Svcs., 2002; grantee Digitization Project Warrior to Saint, Okla. Humanities Coun., 2005. Mem.: Assn. Computing and Humanities, Mountain Plains Libr. Assn., Okla. Libr. Assn. (chair univ. and coll. divsn. 2006—07), Beta Phi Mu (treas. lambda chpt. 2003—04). D-Liberal. Episcopalian. Avocations: reading, travel, photography. Office: Okla State U 216 Library Stillwater OK 74078 Home Phone: 405-570-6168; Office Phone: 405-744-6316. Office Fax: 405-744-5519. Business E-Mail: cokie.anderson@okstate.edu.

ANDERSON, CRAIG ALLEN, retired art educator, artist; b. Chgo., July 28, 1947; s. Elmer Albert and Roseanne Marie (Werner) A.; m. Mary Susan Scarnato, Apr. 23, 1971. BFA, Bradley U., 1970; MA in Art Edn., U. Ill., 1972; MFA, No. Ill. U., 1978. Cert. art specialist Ill. State Bd. Certification. Tchr., rsch. asst. U. Ill., Champaign, 1970—72; tchr. art Oliver W. Holmes Jr. H.S., Wheeling, Ill., 1972; instr. art Countryside Art Ctr., Arlington Heights, Ill., 1972—74, Harper Coll., Palatine, Ill., 1975—80; tchr. art Palatine H.S., 1972—2003, chmn. dept. art, 1996—2003, chair dist. art, 2000—03. Cons. Ill. Art Coun., Harvey, Ill., 1990; guest lectr. U. Ill. Commencement, Champaign, 1993, Temple U., 1985; mem. adv. bd. Masters program Sch. Art Inst. Chgo., 2000; mem. steering com. Chgo. Artists' Month, Chgo. Cultural ctr., 2001-03; mem. steering com. iTalk@Ispace Gallery, 2004—; dir. Nablab, Chgo., 2004—. One-man shows include Gilman Galleries, Chgo., 1978-85, Heuser Art Ctr., 1989, 100 Paintings/100 Drawings Project, Chgo., 2004-05; exhibited in group shows at Abstract Chgo., 1993, Klein Art Gallery, 1993, 98, New Sch., NYC, 2000, Bridge Art Fair, Chgo., 2007. Co-dir. NAB Gallery, Chgo., 1977—; guest curator Gallery 400, Chgo., 1994, Wooden Gallery, Chgo., 1989; cultural exch. NAB Gallery Palais des Expo, Nice, France, 1987, NAB Gallery Diewand Gallery, Hamburg, Germany, 1983. Recipient Binney & Smith Inc. Tchrs. Portfolio award Nat. Scholastic Art awards, Washington, 1995, Art in Architecture award State of Ill., 1982, 88, Outstanding Art Tchr. award Nat. Scholastic Art, 2003, Outstanding Tchr. award U. Chgo., 1996; Pougialis fellow Columbia Coll., 1990; named Ill. Painter, Ill. Arts Coun., 1980. Mem. Nat. Art Edn. Assn., Ill. Art Edn. Assn. (disting., HS Art Tchr. of Yr. 1994, 2000), Palatine/Inverness Arts Coun. (pres. 2001-04), Chgo. Artists Coalition, Soc. Aesthetics, Soc. Rsch. in Art Edn., Internat. Assn. Emirical Aesthetics. Avocation: volunteering for arts advocacy organizations. Home: 108 N Oak St Palatine IL 60067-5229 Office: 1117 W Lake St Chicago IL 60607 Office Phone: 312-738-1620. Business E-Mail: craig@craigaanderson.com.

ANDERSON, CURTIS THORWALD, II, military officer; b. Ft. Bragg, NC, Jan. 11, 1969; s. Curtis Thorwald, Sr. and Wanda Lee Anderson; m. Faye Renee Ide, Aug. 7, 2004. BA in Polit. Sci., Bemidji State U., 1991. Advanced through grade to maj. U.S. Army, 1992; platoon leader C & B Batteries, 3-4 Air Def. Arty. Bn., 82nd Airborne Divsn., Ft. Bragg, 1992—94; battery exec. officer D Battery, 3-4 Air Def. Arty. Bn., 82nd Airborne Divsn., Ft. Bragg, 1994—95; asst. divsn. air def. officer 3-4 Air Def. Arty. Bn., 82nd Airborne Divsn., Ft. Bragg, 1995—96; bn. intelligence officer 5-5 Air Def. Arty. Bn., 2nd Inf. Divsn., Camp Stanley, Republic of Korea, 1996—97; co. comdr. Hdqs. Svc. Co., 313th M.I. Bn., 82nd Airborne Divsn., Ft. Bragg, 1998—2000; civil affairs team leader Joint Spl. Ops. Task Force North (Task Force Dagger), Herat, Afghanistan, 2001—02, C Co., 96th Civil Affairs Bn., Ft. Bragg, NC, 2002, theater ops. officer, 2002—03; civil affairs officer Joint Spl. Ops. Task Force West, Jordan, 2003; civil mil. ops. officer Coalition Land Component Command, Camp Doha, Kuwait, 2003—04, Mulit-National Forces Iraq, Baghdad, Iraq, 2004; detachment comdr. co. comdr. E Company 96th Civil Affairs

Battalion (Airborne), 2004—06; battalion exec. officer 97th Civil Affairs Bn. (Airborne), 2006—. Decorated Army Commendation medal with 2 oak leaf clusters, Master Parachutist badge, Can. Jump Wings, Meritorious Svc. medal, Bronze Star with 1 oak leaf cluster, Joint Svc. Commendation medal, Combat Action badge. Mem.: NRA (life), VFW (life), Internat. War Vets. Alliance (life), Harley Owners Group, Res. Officers Assn. (life), Assn. U.S. Army (life), 82nd Airborne Divsn. Assn. (life), Civil Affairs Assn. (life), Am. Motorcycle Assn., Future Farmers Am. Alumni (life), Am. Legion (life). Presbyterian. Avocations: hunting, softball. Office: HHC 97th Civil Affairs Bn Fort Bragg NC 28310 Home Phone: 910-822-2842; Office Phone: 910-432-1571. Personal E-mail: curtis.anderson@us.army.mil. Business E-Mail: anderscu@soc.mil.

ANDERSON, DALE C., state agency professional, travel consultant; b. Grinnell, Iowa, Sept. 13, 1953; s. Clifford Simon and Wilma Grace (Grunhaupt) A. AAS in Indsl. Mktg., Des Moines Area C.C., Ankeny, Iowa, 1973; BA in Comm. and Theatre, Cen. Coll., 1978. Asst. buyer Ardan Wholesaler, Des Moines, 1979; office mgr. Moingona Girl Scout Coun., Des Moines, 1979-82, dir. adminstrv. svcs., 1982-88, property/purchasing dir., 1988-96; travel cons. Al Travel, Des Moines, 1989-90, First Tours, Des Moines, 1990-95; clk. typist Iowa State Dept. Transp., Des Moines, 1996-97; acctg. clk. II Iowa Dept. Revenue and Fin., Des Moines, 1997-98; acct./auditor 1 Iowa Dept. Corrections, Des Moines, 1998—2003, acct. 2, 2003—. Chmn. Des Moines Purchasing Agts., 2004—06; camp visitor for camp accreditation State of Iowa, 1990—99. Campaign co-chmn. Kellogg (Iowa) Cmty. Chest, 1983-85, pub. rels. chmn., 1982; leader local club Jasper County 4-H, Kellogg, 1971-76, state leadership conf. del., 1971, nat. citizenship del., Washington, 1971, instr. county officers tng. sch. Jasper County, 1970-71, Jasper County v.p., 1970, state conv. del., Ames, Iowa, 1970, state counselor Des Moines Area 4-H, Madrid, Iowa, 1970; local club pres. Kellogg Club 4-H, 1970-71. Recipient State Leadership award Jasper County 4-H, 1970, named Outstanding 4-H'er of Yr., 1971; named Kellogg's Outstanding Citizen, 1983. Mem. Am. Camping Assn. (stds. chair for camp accreditation Iowa chpt. 1992-95, state of Iowa sec. 1996), Am. Camping Assn. (stds. camp accreditation com. Iowa chpt. 1996-99), Iowa State Grange (lectr. 1983-85, 91-93, state youth com. 1981-82, Iowa state youth rep. 1976), Richland Grange (state del. 1980, 83, sec. 1980-84, steward 1970-73, 77-79, overseer 1973-77, youth chmn. 1973, 75-76). United Methodist. Avocations: collecting horse figures, gardening, travel. Office: 686 Hwy 224 S Kellogg IA 50135-8579

ANDERSON, DARLA K., animated film producer; Mem. Pixar Animation Studios, 1992—. Prodr.: (films) A Bug's Life, 1998, Monsters, Inc., 2001, Cars, 2006 (Prodr. of Yr. award in animated theatrical motion pictures, Producers Guild of Am., 2007); exec. prodr.: (films) It's Tough to Be a Bug, 1998; visual effects (films) Toy Story, 1995. Office: c/o Pixar Animation Studios 1200 Park Ave Emeryville CA 94608*

ANDERSON, DARRELL EDWARD, psychologist, educator; b. Coleridge, Nebr., May 2, 1932; s. Roy Blenton and Ruby Grace (Cisney) A.; m. Violeta Salazar, Sept. 3, 1951; children: Robert, James, Timothy. AB, York Coll., 1953; PhD, U. Nebr., 1958. Counselor, asst. prof. U. Nebr., Lincoln, 1957-59; asst. prof. psychology Wittenberg U., Springfield, Ohio, 1959-61; chief psychologist Weld County Mental Health Ctr., Greeley, Colo., 1961-62; asst. prof. U. No. Colo., Greeley, 1962-66, assoc. prof., 1966-70, prof., 1970-77, chmn. dept. psychology, 1972-77; prof. counselor edn. U. N.Mex., Albuquerque, 1977-87, chmn. dept., 1977-85, prof. counseling and family studies, 1987-92, prof. emeritus, 1992—. Cons. psychologist Dulce (N.Mex.) Pub. Schs., 1984-85. Contbr. articles to profl. jours. Mem. APA, N.Mex. Psychol. Assn. Democrat. Avocation: golf. Home: 4 Latir Ct Santa Fe NM 87508

ANDERSON, D(ARRYL) KENT, bank executive; b. Lake Charles, La., Apr. 18, 1941; s. Byrum Lavelle and Doris Marie (Goodman) A.; m. Linda Clarke, Aug. 23, 1969; children— Whitney Paige, Huntley Clarke, Clarke Kent. BA, Rice U., 1962; MBA, U. Va., 1964. Pres. Rivercrest Investment Corp., Houston, 1965-71; v.p. Underwood Neuhaus & Co., Houston, 1971-78; sr. v.p. Allied Bank of Tex., Houston, 1978-81, exec. v.p., 1981-84; pres. Allied Bancshares, Houston, 1984-88; pres., chief exec. officer First Interstate Bank Tex. N.A., Houston, 1988, chmn., chief exec. officer, 1988-91; chmn. bd., CEO Post Oak Bank, Houston, 1991—2000. Vice chmn. Tex. High Speed Rail Authority; bd. dirs. Joint Civilian Orientation Conf., 2005, Pulte Homes, Inc., Sam Houston Race Park, Ltd. Bd. dirs. Houston Symphony, Houston Ballet, Greater Houston Partnership, Duchesne Acad., Houston, Childrens Mus. Houston; bd. trustees Rice U., chmn. assocs.; adv. coun. Energy Ctr., Okla. U.; trustee Mus. Fine Arts, Houston, Rice U.; chmn. regional mobility com. Greater Houston Partnership, 1992. With U.S. Air N.G., 1964-70; bd. chmn. Houston Endowment, 2000-. Named Outstanding Mil. Grad., Citizens Com. Army and Air Force, San Antonio, 1964; recipient Am. Spirit of Honor medal, Citizens Com. for Army, Navy and Air Force, Gold medal award Rice U., 1999. Mem. Tex. Bankers Assn., Coronado Club, Houston Country Club, Lakeside Country Club, Coronado Club (bd. dirs., pres.). Presbyterian. Office: Houston Endowment 600 Travis Ste 6400 Houston TX 77002

ANDERSON, DAVID ALLEN, military officer, educator; b. Springfield, Minn., Aug. 24, 1960; s. Allen John and Donna Marie Anderson; m. Julia Anne Campbell, Feb. 23, 1984; children: Jennifer Blair children: David Allen, Ashley Elizabeth, Lauren Kate. BS in Geography, U. Wis., River Falls, 1983; MA in Bus. Adminstrn and Mgmt., Webster U., St. Louis, 1987; DBA, Alliant Internat. U., San Diego, 1993. Commd. 2d. lt., 1983; advanced through grades to lt. col., 2000; commdg. officer, combat svc. support detachment-21 Marine Corps Air Sta., Cherry Point, NC, 1995—98; econs. prof. US Naval Acad., Annapolis, Md., 1998—2001; head logistics, strategic force planning Supreme Hdqs. Allied Powers Europe, NATO, Mons, Belgium, 2001—04; logistics, ops. and plans officer II Marine Expeditionary Force, USMC, Camp Lejeune, NC, 2004—05; assoc. prof. Dept. Jt. Multinational Ops., Army Command and Gen. Staff Coll., Fort Leavenworth, Kans., 2005—. Adj. prof. bus. Campbell U., Buies Creek, NC, 1994—98; adj. prof. bus., mgmt. Pk. U., Parkville, Mo., 1995—98; adj. prof. bus. Webster U., St. Louis, 1998. Contbr. articles marine and naval pubs. Conductor fin. planning seminars USMC, 1987—2005; vol. coord. Adopt a Sch. Program, NC, Havelock, 1995—98; tchg. vol. West Annapolis Elem., 1998—2001; coach, track and field boys and girls secondary sch. teams Supreme Hdqs. Allied Powers Europe, Am. H.S., Mons, 2004; officer rep. men's track and field team U.S. Naval Acad., Annapolis, 1998—2001. Decorated Naval Commendation medal USMC, Meritorious Svc. medal (Gold Star in Lieu of fourth award), Def. Meritorious Svc. medal Supreme Hdqs. Allied Powers Europe, NATO; recipient tchg. and rsch. excellence award, U.S. Naval Acad., 2001. Mem.: Mil. Officers Assn. of Am., Marine Corps Assn. Republican. Roman Catholic. Avocations: fishing, running, antique stained glass restoration, softball, writing. Office: US Army Command and Gen Staff Coll Dept Jt and Multinat Ops Fort Leavenworth KS 66027 Home Phone: 913-250-0342; Office Phone: 913-684-4665. Personal E-mail: profusmc@hotmail.com. Business E-Mail: dave.anderson4@leavenworth.army.mil.

ANDERSON, DAVID ARNOLD, law educator; b. 1939; AB, Harvard U., 1962; JD, U. Tex., 1971. Bar: Tex. 1972. Reporter, bur. chief United Press Internat., Austin, Tex., 1963-69; chief counsel Tex. Civil Jud. Coun., Austin, 1972; asst. prof. law U. Tex., Austin, 1972-75, prof., 1975-78, Thompson and Knight Centennial prof., 1987—2003, Fred and Emily Wulff Centennial chair in law, 2005—. Vis. Lee prof. William and Mary U., 1983, Queen Mary Coll. U. London, 1988, 92; vis. scholar Trinity Coll. Cambridge U., 1988; vis. prof. U. New South Wales, 1998, Univ. Coll. London, 2003. Fellow Gannett Ctr. Media Studies. Mem. Assn. Am. Law Schs. (mass communications law sect.), Order of Coif, Phi Delta Phi. Office: U Tex Sch Law 727 Dean Keeton St Austin TX 78705-3224

ANDERSON, DAVID BOWEN, lawyer; b. Seattle, Sept. 19, 1948; s. Gordon Browne and Elizabeth Josephine (Bowen) A.; m. Laura Ann Jorgensen, May 23, 1975; children: Elizabeth Christine, Christina Louise. BA with great distinction, Stanford U., 1970; JD, U. Mich., 1974; MBA, Western Wash. U., 1982. Bar: Wash. 1974, Alaska 2000, Oreg. 2002, U.S. Dist. Ct. (we. dist.) Wash. 1974. Clk. Ctr. for Law and Social Policy, Washington, 1973; assoc. Bogle & Gates, Seattle, 1974-77; ptnr. Anderson, Connell & Carey, Bellingham, Wash., 1977—; pres. San Juan Tug & Barge Co., 1979-85. Arbitrator Whatcom County, Am. Arbitration Assn.; instr. Pacific N.W. Admiralty Law Inst., Seattle, 1983, Nat. Fishery Law Symposium, Seattle, 1984; lectr. constnl. law Western Wash. U., 1996. Mem. adv. com. Bellingham Sch. Bd., 1981-82, Bellingham Vocat. Tech. Inst., 1986; mem. Bellingham Pub. Sch. Found. Bd., 1992, pres., 1992-93; bd. dirs. Interfaith Coalition, 1999-2002; mem. exec. com. Primorsky-Washington Russian Rule of Law Partnership. Mem. ATLA, ABA, Wash. State Bar Assn. (spl. dist. counsel, rules of profl. practice com.), Alaska Bar Assn., Oreg. State Bar, Whatcom County Bar Assn. (pres. 1986), Maritime Law Assn. U.S. (proctor), Wash. Atheltic Club (Seattle). Presbyterian. Home: 500 16th St Bellingham WA 98225-6315 Office: Anderson Connell & Carey 1501 Eldridge Ave Bellingham WA 98225-2801 E-mail: boatlaw@boatlaw.com.

ANDERSON, DAVID BOYD, lawyer, metal products executive; b. Moorhead, Minn., Mar. 10, 1942; children: Kimberly, Erik, Jonathan, Caroline J. BA, U. Minn., 1964, JD, 1967; LLM, DePaul U., 1983. Bar: Minn. 1967, Ill. 1978. Labor rels. supr. Continental Can Co., NYC, 1970—72; asst. gen. counsel Am. Hosp. Supply Co., Evanston, Ill., 1972—83; v.p. planning and gen. counsel Inland Steel Industries, Inc., Chgo., 1983—2001; active adv. com. LISC, planning com. Northwestern U. Corp. Counsel Inst. Capt. USAR, 1967—70. Mem.: Minn. Bar Assn., Ill. Bar Assn., ABA. Office: 16th Fl 30 W Monroe St Fl 16 Chicago IL 60603-2495

ANDERSON, DAVID CORYELL, lawyer, automotive executive; b. Seattle, Apr. 7, 1953; s. George Robert and Margaret Louise (Barron) A.; m. Sharon Lee Pfeifer, Feb. 14, 1976; children: Nicholas, Kate, Patrick. AB, Harvard U., 1975; JD, Stanford U., 1979. Bar: Wash. 1979. Assoc. Foster, Pepper & Shefelman, Seattle, 1979-86, ptnr., 1986-93; v.p., corp. sec., gen. counsel Airborne Express Inc., Seattle, 1993; v.p., gen. counsel PACCAR Inc., Bellevue, Wash., 2004—. Mem.: Wash. State Bar Assn. (at-large mem. exec. com. 2006—07). Office: PACCAR Inc Law Dept PO Box 1518 Bellevue WA 98009 Office Phone: 425-468-7499. Office Fax: 425-468-8228. E-mail: dave.anderson@paccar.com.*

ANDERSON, DAVID DANIEL, retired humanities educator, writer, editor; b. Lorain, Ohio, June 8, 1924; s. David and Nora Marie (Foster) A.; m. Patricia Ann Rittenhour, Feb. 1, 1953. BS, Bowling Green State U., 1951, MA, 1952, DLitt (hon.), 2005; PhD, Mich. State U., 1960; DLitt (hon.), Wittenberg U., 1986. From instr. to prof. dept. Am. thought and lang. to univ. disting. prof. Mich. State U., East Lansing, 1957-90; lectr. Am. Mus., Bath, Eng., 1980; editor U. Coll. Quar., 1971-80; Fulbright prof. U. Karachi, Pakistan, 1963-64. Am. del. to Internat. Fedn. Modern Langs. and Lit., 1969-93, Internat. Congress Orientalists, 1971-79, European Am. Studies Assn., 1994. Author: Louis Bromfield, 1964, Critical Studies in American Literature, 1964, Sherwood Anderson's Winesburg, Ohio, 1967, Sherwood Anderson, 1968 (Book Manuscript award, 1961), Brand Whitlock, 1968, Abraham Lincoln, 1970, Suggestions for the Instructor, 1970, Robert Ingersoll, 1972, Woodrow Wilison, 1978, Igantius Donnelly, 1980, William Jennings Bryan, 1981, Route Two, Titus, Ohio, 1993, The Path in the Shadow, 1998, Command Performances, 2003, Ohio in Myth, Memory, and Imagination, 2004, Ohio in Fact and Fiction, 2006; editor: The Black Experience, 1969, The Literary Works of Abraham Lincoln, 1970, Sunshine and Smoke: American Writers and the American Environment, 1971; editor: (with others) The Dark and Tangled Path, 1971; editor: Mid America, 1974—, 27th edit., 2000, Sherwood Anderson: Dimensions of His Literary Art, 1976, Sherwood Anderson: The Writer at His Craft, 1979, Critical Essays on Sherwood Anderson, 1981, Michigan: A State Anthology, 1983, Myth, Memory and the American Earth: The Durability of Raintree County, 1998, Midwestern Miscellany, 1974—, Lieutenant William E. Slight and the 102nd Regiment, U.S. Colored Infantry, in the Civil War, 2003, numerous articles, essays, short stories, poems. Served with USN, 1942-45; with AUS, 1952-53. Decorated Silver Star, Purple Heart; recipient Disting. Alumnus award Bowling Green State U., 1976, Disting. Faculty award Mich. State U., 1974, Disting. Faculty award Mich. Assn. Governing Bds., 1988, Disting Research award Mich. State U., 1988. Mem. ASA, AAUP, MLA, Popular Culture Assn., Soc. Study Midwestern Lit. (founder, exec. sec., Disting. Service award 1982), Assn. Gen. and Liberal Edn. Am. Assn. Advancement Humanities, Internat. Assn. U. Profs. English, Univ. Club. Home: 6555 Lansdown Dr Dimondale MI 48821-9428 Office: Mich State U Dept Am Thought and Lang East Lansing MI 48824

ANDERSON, DAVID J., corporate financial executive; Grad., Ind. U., 1971; MBA, U. Chgo., 1977. Sr. fin. positions Kraft, Inc., Quaker Oats Co.; sr. v.p., chief fin. officer RJR Nabisco, Newport News Shipbuilding, ITT Industries, mem. exec. com.; sr. v.p., CFO Honeywell Internat. Inc., Morristown, NJ, 2003—. Office: Honeywell Inernat Inc 101 Columbia Rd Morristown NJ 07962*

ANDERSON, DAVID J., manufacturing executive; BS in Mech. Engring., Univ. Wis. Various sales, mktg. leadership positions Sauer-Danfoss, Ames, Iowa, 1984—2001, exec. v.p. strategic bus. devel., 2001—02, pres., dir., CEO, 2002—. Office: Sauer-Danfoss Ste 270 250 Parkway Dr Lincolnshire IL 60069 Office Phone: 515-239-6000. Office Fax: 515-239-6318.*

ANDERSON, DAVID J., biology professor; AB in Biochemical Scis., Harvard U., 1978; PhD in Cell Biology, Rockefeller U., 1983. Asst. prof. Calif. Inst. Tech., Pasadena, 1986—92, assoc. prof., 1992—96, prof., 1996—2004, Roger W. Sperry prof. biology, 2004—; asst. investigator Howard Hughes Medical Inst., 1989—92, assoc. investigator, 1992—97, investigator, 1997—. Contbr. articles to sci. jours. Recipient Presdl. Young Investigator award, NSF, Charles Judson Herrick award in Neuroanatomy, Am. Assn. Anatomists, W. Alden Spencer award in Neurobiology, Columbia U. Mem.: NAS, Am. Acad. Arts & Scis. Office: Divsn Biology 216-76 Calif Inst Tech Pasadena CA 91125 Office Phone: 626-395-8374. Office Fax: 626-564-8243. E-mail: mancusog@caltech.edu.

ANDERSON, DAVID LAWRENCE, lawyer; b. Balt., Oct. 29, 1948; s. Robert L. and Ruth (Hahn) A. BS, Towson U., 1970; JD, U. Md., 1973. Bar: Md. 1973, U.S. Dist. Ct. Md. 1976, D.C. 1979, U.S. Dist. Ct. D.C. 1979, U.S. Ct. Appeals (D.C. cir.) 1976. Asst. revisor Gov.'s Commn. to Revise Md. Annotated Code, Annapolis, Md., 1973-74; counsel Gov.'s Task Force on Campaign Financing, Annapolis, Md., 1974-75; atty. Fed. Election Commn., Washington, 1975-77, Federal Energy Adminstrn., Washington, 1977; asst. chief counsel, trial atty. U.S. Dept. Energy, Washington, 1977-85; sr. trial atty., leader litigation team environ. enforcement sect., environment and natural resources div. U.S. Dept. Justice, Washington, 1986-90; lead counsel for Love Canal, Rocky Mountain Arsenal and New Bedford Harbor Superfund cases; sr. assoc. Shea & Gould, Washington, 1990-91, Arent Fox Kintner Plotkin & Kahn, Washington, 1992-93; ptnr. O'Connor & Hannan, Washington, 1993-95; mgr. regulatory and legis. svcs. group Waste Policy Inst., Arlington, 1995-99; sr. environ. counsel, sr. project mgr. Parsons, Fairfax, Va., 1999—. Adj. prof. polit. sci. Towson State U., 1971-73; adj. prof. legal rsch. and writing Am. U., 1985-87, 93-94. Recipient Outstanding Performance award Dept. Energy, 1981, medal and award Dept. Energy, 1983, spl. commendation Dept. Justice, 1989. Mem. ABA (environment, energy and resources law sect.), D.C. Bar Assn., Environ. Law Inst. Home: 25299 Diligence Ct Aldie VA 20105 Office: Parsons 10521 Rosehaven St Fairfax VA 22030-2839 Business E-Mail: david.l.anderson@parsons.com.

ANDERSON, DAVID LOUIS, academic administrator, history professor; b. Pampa, Tex., Aug. 10, 1946; s. Benjamin Louis and Ruby Lucille (Baird) A.; m. Helen Esther Fleischer, June 9, 1973; 1 child, Hope Mindy. BA cum laude, Rice U., Houston, 1968; MA, U. Va., 1971, PhD, 1974. Vis. asst. prof. history U. Mont., Missoula, 1974-75, 76-77, Tex. Tech. U., Lubbock, 1975-76; asst. prof. history Sam Houston State U., Huntsville, Tex., 1977-80; lectr. in history Calif. Poly. State U., San Luis Obispo, 1980-81; asst. prof. history U. Indpls., 1981-84, assoc. prof. history, 1984-90, prof. history, 1990—2004, dept. chair, 1988-2000, assoc. dean arts and scis., 1999—2001, dean arts and scis., 2001—04; dean univ. studies and programs Calif. State U. Monterey Bay, Seaside, 2004—07, prof. history, 2007—. Author: Imperialism and Idealism, 1985, Trapped By Success: The Eisenhower Administration and Vietnam, 1991 (Robert H. Ferrell Book prize Soc. for Historians of American Fgn. Rels. 1992), Shadow on the White House: Presidents and the Vietnam War, 1993, Facing My Lai, 1998, The Human Tradition in the Vietnam Era, 2000, The Columbia Guide to the Vietnam War, 2002 (Best of Best prize Am. Lib. Assn.), The Human Tradition in America Since 1945, 2003, The Vietnam War, 2005, The War That Never Ends: New Perspectives on the Vietnam War, 2007. Bd. dir. Leadership Monterey Peninsula. Sgt. US Army, 1968—70. Decorated Commendation medal US Army, Bronze Star; named Ind. Prof. of the Yr., Coun. for Advancement and Support of Edn., 1991. Mem. Am. Hist. Assn., Orgn. Am. Historians, Soc. for Historians of Am. Fgn. Rels. (coun. mem. 1995-97, 2006-08, v.p. 2004, pres. 2005), Natividad Med. Found. (pres. bd. dirs.), Ft. Ord Alumni Assn. (adv. bd.). Avocation: magic. Office: Calif State U Monterey Bay 100 Campus Ctr Bldg 86C Seaside CA 93955-8001 Office Phone: 831-582-3818. Business E-Mail: david_anderson@csumb.edu.

ANDERSON, DAVID POOLE, sportswriter; b. Troy, NY, May 6, 1929; s. Robert P. and Josephine (David) A.; m. Maureen Ann Young, Oct. 24, 1953; children: Stephen, Mark, Mary Jo, Jean Marie. BA, Holy Cross Coll., 1951. Sports writer Bklyn. Eagle, 1951—55, New York Jour.-Am., 1955—66, New York Times, 1966—. Author: Countdown to Super Bowl, 1969; (with Ray Robinson) Sugar Ray, 1970; (with Larry Csonka and Jim Kiick) Always On The Run, 1973; Pancho Gonzalez, 1974; (with Frank Robinson) Frank: The First Year, 1976; Sports Of Our Times, 1979; The Yankees, 1979; (with John Madden) Hey, Wait a Minute, I Wrote a Book, 1984; The Story of Football, 1985; (with John Madden) One Knee Equals Two Feet, 1986; (with John Madden) One Size Doesn't Fit All, 1988; The Story of Basketball, 1988; In The Corner, 1991; Pennant Races, 1994; The Story of the Olympics, 1996; (with John Madden) All Madden, 1996; The Story of Golf, 1998; editor: The Red Smith Reader, 1981. Named to Nat. Sportscasters and Sportswriters Assn. Hall of Fame, 1990, N.Y. Sports Mus. and Hall of Fame, 1991; recipient Pulitzer prize for disting. commentary, 1981, Red Smith award, 1994, PGA of Am. Lifetime Achievement award in journalism, 1998, McCann Meml. award for disting. pro football reporting, Pro Football Hall of Fame, 1998, William D. Richardson award, Golf Writers Assn. of Am., 2003, Peter Kihss award, Soc. of Silurians, 2003. Office: NY Times 229 W 43rd St New York NY 10036-3959

ANDERSON, DAVID R., insurance company executive; m. Mary Anderson; 5 children. B, M, U. Wis. Budget dir. Am. Family Mut. Ins. Co., Madison, Wis., 1975, fin. planning dir., acctg. dir., v.p. info. svcs., 1996-98, pres., COO, 1998—2006, chmn., CEO, 2007—. Office: Am Family Ins Group 6000 American Pky Madison WI 53783

ANDERSON, DAVID TREVOR, law educator; b. Winnipeg, Man., Can., Oct. 25, 1938; s. David and Mary (Irwin) A. BA, U. Man., 1959; BA in Jurisprudence, Oxford U., Eng., 1961, B in Civil Law, 1962. Asst. prof. law U. Alta., Edmonton, Can., 1962-66, assoc. prof., 1966-69, prof., 1969-71; prof. law U. Man., Winnipeg, 1971—, assoc. dean faculty of law, 1972-77, dean, 1984-89. Bd. dirs. Alta. Inst. Law Rsch. and Reform, Edmonton, 1968-71; mem. Man. Law Reform Commn., Winnipeg, 1981-84, Man. Pub. Utilities Bd., 1988-2000. Named Queen's Counsel, Province of Man., 1985; Rhodes scholar, 1959. Mem. Law Soc. Man. (dir. edn. 1977-80, bencher 1984-89), Can. Bar Assn. Presbyterian. Office: U Man Faculty of Law Robson Hall Winnipeg MB Canada R3T 2N2

ANDERSON, DAVID WAYNE, entrepreneur, former federal agency administrator; b. Chgo. married. MPA, Harvard U., 1986; Ph.D (hon.), Northland Coll., 2004. Chmn., CEO Famous Dave's of Am., Inc., Eden Prairie, Minn., 1994—2003, chmn. emeritus, 2003—; asst. sec. for Indian affairs US Dept. Interior, Washington, 2004—05. Mem. National Task Force on Reservation Gaming, Bur. Indian Affairs, 1983, Am. Indian Edn. Found., 2003; mem. Presdl. Adv. Coun. Tribal Colls. and Univs., 2001; founder LifeSkills Ctr. for Leadership, 2001—. Author: Life Skills for Success, Backroads & Sidestreets. Named Emerging Entrepreneurof Yr., Ernst and Young, NASDAQ, USA Today, Restaurateur of Yr., Mpls.-St. Paul (Minn.) Mag., 1998, Olympic Torch Carrier, 2002. Office: Famous Dave's America Inc 12701 Whitewater Dr Ste 200 Minnetonka MN 55343*

ANDERSON, DAWOLU JABARI, illustrator; BFA, Tex. So. Univ., Houston, Tex., 1995; MFA, 2003. Asst. coord. Project RowHouses, 1995—97; illustrator, 1997—. One-man shows include Birth of a Nation: Yo! Bumrush the Show!, Art League Houston, 2006, exhibited in group shows at Changing Perspective Mus., 1995, Preventions Collective, Project RowHouse and Community Arts, 1996, Breaking Into the Mainstream, Irving Arts Ctr., 1996, Artist Board Chooses, Diverse Works, 1997, Bound Books, Brazos, 1998, Sixth Annual African Am. Advisory Assn., Mus. Fine Arts, 2002, Soul Sonic LustraSilk, Houston Community Coll NE, 2002, Symmetrical Patterns of Def/Collaborative Group Installation, Lawndale Art Ctr., 2004, Who Goliards? Artists at the Turn of the Century, Univ. Mus. Tex. So. Univ., 2004, Whitney Biennial, Whitney Mus. Am. Art, 2006. Recipient First Prize, Houston Area Exhibition at Blaffer Gallery, 1996; grantee Skowhegan Sch. Paint and Sculpture, 2006.

ANDERSON, DAYNA, medical researcher; b. 1979; Rsch. specialist, Immunology Ariz. Respiratory Ctr. Mem. Prosoc philanthropy com. Mem. Susan G. Komen Breast Cancer Found., Catalina Coun. Boy Scouts Am. Spurs and Stars, Southern Ariz. Ctr. Against Sexual Assault. Named one of 40 Under 40, Tucson Bus. Edge, 2006. Achievements include published article in Jour. of Allergy and Clinical Immunology. Office: Arizona Respiratory Center PO Box 245030 1501 N Cambell Ave Ste 2349 Tucson AZ 85724-5030

ANDERSON, DEAN WILLIAM, museum consultant; b. Mpls., Aug. 28, 1946; s. Edward Marvin and Mabel (Gilland) A.; m. Elaine Heumann Gurian; children: Erik Wheeler, Matthew Edward. BA, Macalester Coll., 1968; MA, U. Calif.-Berkeley, 1970. Examiner Office Mgmt. and Budget, Washington, 1970-73; adminstrv. officer Smithsonian Instn., Washington, 1973-84, asst. sec. history and art, 1984-85, under sec., 1985-90; dep. dir. mgmt. and planning Woodrow Wilson Ctr., Washington, 1990—2001, acting dir., 1997-99; ptnr. Interim Mus. Svcs. LLC, 2005—. Vis. lectr., grad. program Goteborg U., Sweden, 2002—. Trustee Interlochen Ctr. for Arts. Recipient Robert Brooks award Smithsonian Instn., 1983; Minn. SPAN Assn. scholar, Israel, 1967; MacPherson Found. scholar, Mpls., 1967. Mem. Interlochen Alumni Orgn. (pres. 1994-98, nat. bd. dirs.), Phi Beta Kappa, Pi Sigma Alpha. Avocation: golf. E-mail: danderson@ix.netcom.com.

ANDERSON, DON LYNN, geophysicist; b. Frederick, Md., Mar. 5, 1933; s. Richard Andrew and Minola (Phares) Anderson; m. Nancy Lois Ruth, Sept. 15, 1956; children: Lynn Ellen, Lee Weston. BS, Rensselaer Poly. Inst., 1955; MS, Calif. Inst. Tech., 1959, PhD, 1962; DSc (hon.), Rensselaer Poly. Inst., 2000. With Chevron Oil Co., Mont., Wyo., Calif., 1955—56; with Air Force Cambridge Research Center, Boston, 1956—58, Arctic Inst. N.Am., Boston, 1958; mem. faculty Calif. Inst. Tech., Pasadena, 1962—, assoc. prof. geophysics, 1964—68, prof., 1968—, dir. seismol. lab., 1967—89, Eleanor and John R. McMillan prof. of geophysics, 1990—. Prin. investigator Viking Mars Seismic Expt.; mem. various coms. NASA; chmn. geophysics rsch. forum NAS; chmn. Arthur L. Day award com. NSF, chmn. Geosci. adv. com., 1994; chmn. adv. bd. for Sch. of Earth Scis. Stanford U., 1995; mem. adv. com. Purdue U., U. Chgo., U. Tex., Stanford U., U. Calif. Berkeley, Carnegie Instn., Washington, U. Paris, Yale U., Rice U.; Consortium for High Pressure Rsch. U. Calif.-Riverside; co-founder Inc. Rsch. Insts. for Seismology. Assoc. editor Jour. Geophys. Rsch., 1965—67, Tectonophysics, 1974—77; editor: Physics of the Earth and Planetary Interiors, 1984—94. Recipient Exceptional Sci. Achievement award, NASA, 1977, Emil Wiechert medal, German Geophys. Soc., 1986, Crafoord prize, Royal Swedish Acad. Scis., 1998, Nat. medal of Sci., 1998; fellow Guggenheim, 1998, Sloan Found., 1965—67. Fellow: AAAS (pres. tectonophysics sect. 1971—72, chmn. Macelwane award com. 1975, mem. Bowie medal com. 1985, pres.-elect 1986—88, pres. 1988—90, chair 1994, James B. Macelwane award 1966, Bowie medal 1990), Geol. Soc. Am. (assoc. editor bull. 1971—, mem. Penrose medal com. 1989, mem. Arthur L. Day medal com. 1989—90, mem. long range planning com. 1990—, Arthur L. Day medal 1987), Am. Geophys. Union; mem.: NAS (chmh. seismology com. 1975, chmn. Geophysics Rsch. Forum 1984—86), Seismol. Soc. Am., Royal Astron. Soc. (Gold medal 1988), Am. Philos. Soc., Sigma Xi. Home: 669 Alameda St Altadena CA 91001-3001 Office: Calif Inst Tech Seismol Lab 252 21 Pasadena CA 91125-0001

ANDERSON, DONALD BERNARD, oil industry executive; b. Chgo., Apr. 6, 1919; s. Hugo August and Hilda (Nelson) A.; m. Patricia Gaylord, 1945 (dec. 1978); m. Sarah Midgette, 1980. BS in Mech. Engring, Purdue U., 1942. Vice pres. Hondo Oil & Gas Co. (formerly Malco Refineries, Inc.), Roswell, N.Mex.; vice pres. Hondo Oil & Gas Co. and subs. corps., Roswell, N.Mex., 1946-63; pres. Anderson Oil Co., Roswell, 1963—, Cotter Corp., 1966-70, chmn. bd., 1966-74; founder, pres. Anderson Drilling Co., Denver, 1974—, pres., chmn. bd., 1977—. Curator fine arts, mem. acquisitions com. Roswell Mus. and Art Center, 1949-56, trustee, 1956-85, pres. bd., 1960-85, 87—, trustee, pres. 1987-90; bd. dirs. Sch. Am. Rsch., Santa Fe, chmn. bd., 1985-88, bd. dirs. 1989—; bd. dirs. Jargon Soc., Penland, N.C.; regent Ea. N.Mex. U., 1966-72; commr. Smithsonian Instn., Nat. Mus. Am. Art, 1980-88. Lt. USNR, 1942-46. Office: PO Box 1 Roswell NM 88202-0001

ANDERSON, DONALD H., energy executive; b. 1948; Grad., U. Colo., Boulder, 1970. Acct. Peat, Marwick, Mitchell Y Co., Denver, 1970—78, Western Crude Oil Inc., Denver, 1978—82; with Lantern Petroleum Corp., Denver, 1983—; chmn, pres., CEO Pan Energy, Houston; pres., vice-chmn. & CEO TransMontaigne Inc., Denver, 2000—06; chmn. TransMontaigne Partners LP, Denver, 2006—. Office: TransMontaigne Partners LP 1670 Broadway Ste 3100 Denver CO 80217-5660

ANDERSON, DONALD MEREDITH, bank executive; b. Milan, Minn., Feb. 19, 1928; s. Meredith A. and Lydia (Helseth) A.; m. Christine Skorupa; 1 child, Karen. Student, St. Olaf Coll., Northfield, Minn., 1946-48; BA, U. Minn., 1948-50; MBA, Harvard U., 1952; postgrad. Grad. Banking Sch., U. Wis.-Madison, 1965-67. Factory rep. Congoleum-Nairn, Inc., 1953-56; stockbroker J.M. Dain & Co., Mpls., 1956-58; v.p. comml. lending and corr. banking Northwestern Nat. Bank of Mpls., 1958-69; v.p. lending Santa Barbara Nat. Bank, Calif., 1969-71; pres. Santa Barbara Bank & Trust, 1971-89, chmn., 1989—. Dir. Gen. Telephone Calif., 1976— , mem. audit com., 1982—; mem. regional adv. com. Comptroller of Currency, 1975-76 Bd. dirs. Blue Cross So. Calif., 1981—; bd. dirs. Mission council Boy Scouts Am., 1977— , v.p. 1977-80, pres. 1985; bd. dirs. Goleta Valley Hosp., 1978— , pres., 1979-80; mem. Industry Edn. Council, 1975— , chmn., 1984—; trustee U. Calif.-Santa Barbara, 1984—; mem. comdr.'s adv. bd. Vandenberg AFB, 1978—; mem. adv. bd. Vis. Nurses Assn., 1983—; past pres. bd. dirs. Trinity Lutheran Ch., United Way; bd. dirs. Santa Barbara Zoo, 1985—. Served to 1st lt. USAF, 1952-53 Mem. Calif. Bankers Assn. (dir. 1982— , chair comml. lending com. 1977), Santa Barbara C. of C. (v.p. 1979, dir. 1972, 78— , Western Ind. Bankers Assn. (pres. 1985, sec. 1983, dir. 1981—), Am. Bankers Assn. (bank investments com. 1976-79) Republican. Home: 485 Via Hierba Santa Barbara CA 93110-2214 Office: Santa Barbara Bank & Trust 1021 Anacapa St Santa Barbara CA 93101-2102

ANDERSON, DONNA KAY, musicologist, educator; b. Underwood, ND, Feb. 16, 1935; d. Freedolph E. and Olga (Mayer) A. PhD, Ind. U., 1966. Instr. piano MacPhail Sch. Music, 1956-59, Summit Sch., 1959-61; asst. prof. music history SUNY, Cortland, 1967-70, assoc. prof., 1970-78, prof., 1978—, chmn. dept. music, 1985-92, 95-97, faculty rsch. fellow, 1967-69, prof. emerita, 1997—. Spkr. in field. Author: Charles T. Griffes: Annotated Bibliography, Discography, 1977, The Works of Charles T. Griffes: A Descriptive Catalogue, 1983, Charles T. Griffes: A Life in Music, 1993; editor: Three Preludes for Piano, 1967, Four Impressions, 1970, Legend for Piano, 1972, De Profundis, 1978, Song of the Dagger, 1983, Seven English Songs, 1986, Rhapsody, 1992, The Pleasure Dome of Kubla Khan, 1993, The War-Song of the Vikings, 1995, Hampelas, 1995, Kinanti, 1995, Djakoan, 1995, Pieces for Children, 1995; editor, translator: Four German Songs, 1970, Nachtlied, 1983, Six German Songs, 1986, Three German Songs, 1995, A Winter Landscape, 1996, Belle Nuit, 2000, Three Japanese Melodies, 2000; contbr. Griffes biography to The Ency. of N.Y. State, 2005. Bd. dirs. YMCA, 1998—, bd. pres., 2006—; mem. Brooks outstanding tchrs. award com. SUNY, 1999—, chair Brooks outstanding tchrs. award com., 2001—. Recipient N.Y. State/United U. Professions Excellence award, 1991; summer grantee, 1972. Mem. Am. Musicol. Soc., Coll. Music Soc., Soc. Am. Music, Music Library Assn., Tri-M, Mu Phi Epsilon, Pi Kappa Lambda, Alpha Psi Omega, Phi Kappa Phi. Office: SUNY Performing Arts Cortland NY 13045 Business E-Mail: andersond@cortland.edu.

ANDERSON, DORIS EHLINGER, lawyer; b. Houston; d. Joseph Otto and Cornelia Louise (Pagel) Ehlinger; m. Wiley Anderson, Jr. (dec.); children: Wiley Newton III, Joe E. BA, Rice U., Houston, 1946; permanent high sch. tchr. cert., U. Houston, 1948; JD, U. Tex., 1950; MLS in Museology, U. Okla., Norman, 1985. Bar: Tex. 1950, U.S. Supreme Ct. Assoc. Ehlinger & Anderson, Houston, 1950-52, ptnr., 1965—; assoc. Price, Guinn, Wheat & Veltmann, Houston, 1952-55, Wheat, Dyche & Thornton, Houston, 1955-65; life mem. Rice Assocs., Houston, 1984—. Hist. lectr., Harvard Negotiation Seminar, 1992 Edn. for Ministry, U of South, 1999. Editor: Houston City of Destiny, 1980; contbr. articles to hist. pubs. and to Bayou Bend. Parliamentarian Harris County Flood Control Task Force, Houston, 1975-2003; dir. Houston Bapt. Mus Am. Architecture and Decorative Arts, 1980-90, curator costume, 1980; apptd. ambassador Inst. Texan Culture U. Tex. San Antonio; past pres. gen. San Jacinto Descendants; docent Bayou Bend Mus. Fine Arts, Houston. Recipient best interpretive exhibit award Tex. Hist. Commn., 1983, Outstanding Woman of Yr. award YWCA, Houston, 1983; named adm. Tex. Navy, 1980. Mem. ABA, UDC (pres. Jefferson Davis chpt.), Assn. Women Attys. Houston, Houston Bar Assn., Daus. Republic Tex. (parliamentarian gen.), Am. Mus. Soc., Harris County Heritage Soc., Kappa Beta Pi (pres. Lamda alumni). Episcopalian. Office: Ehlinger & Anderson 5556 Sturbridge Dr Houston TX 77056-1600

ANDERSON, DOUGLAS DEL, retired music educator, recording industry executive; b. Norfolk, Nebr., Feb. 7, 1940; s. Delwyn C. and Ruth Ann (Talich) Anderson; m. Donna Lee Anderson (div.); children: Kristin L., Kent D.; m. Janet Carolyn Good, Dec. 26, 1982; stepchildren: Rob Jackman, Scott Jackman, Todd Jackman. B in Music Edn., Nebr. Wesleyan U., 1961; MusM, U. Oreg., 1965. Music tchr. Dalton/Gurley (Nebr.) Pub. Schs., 1961—63; vocal music tchr. McMinnville (Oreg.) HS, 1964—94; founder, mgr. Jazz West Workshops, McMinnville, 1974—84; founder, owner, mgr. DJ Records, Trout Lake, Wash., 1982—. Pres. Oreg. Music Educators, 1974—76. Author: Jazz and Showchoir Handbook, 1981, 1993; contbg. author: On Stage, 1980; editor: (sheet music series) Scott Music Publs., 1985. Music chair Trout Lake Art Coun., 2002—; vol. Pacific Crest Trl.; vol. Santa Trout Lake; elder Presbyn. Ch., Trout Lake, 2003—; pres., bd. dirs. Schooner Landing Resort, Newport, Oreg., 1999—; Am. tour sales mgr. The King's Singers, 1986—. Named Oreg. Tchr. of Yr., Oreg. State Dept. Edn., 1977, Music Alum of Yr., Nebr. Wesleyan U., 2005; recipient Outstanding Svc. award, Oreg. Sch. Activities Assn., 2003. Mem.: Internat. Assn. Jazz Educators, Am. Choral Dirs. Assn. (nat. com. chair 1981—86, NW divsn. rep., nat. chair jazz and showchoir com. 1981—86), Music Educators Nat. Conf. (life; state pres. 1974—76, founding nat. chair membership com. 1976—81). Avocations: fly fishing, hiking. Home: PO Box 445 Trout Lake WA 98650 Office: DJ Records PO Box 445 28 Mt Adams Rd Trout Lake WA 98650 Office Phone: 509-395-3611. Fax: 509-395-9308. E-mail: doug@dj-records.com.

ANDERSON, DOUGLAS RICHARD, ophthalmologist, educator, researcher; b. Memphis, Apr. 7, 1938; s. William Arnold Douglas and Hariott Isabel (Gates) A.; m. Wirtley Anne Raine, Nov. 28, 1964; children: John Douglas, Wendy Anne, Michael Allen Scott. AB magna cum laude, U. Miami, Coral Gables, Fla., 1958; MD, Washington U., St. Louis, 1962. Diplomate Am. Bd. Ophthalmology (bd. dirs. 1988-95). Rotating intern U. Hosp. Cleve., 1962-63; staff assoc. Nat. Cancer Inst., Bethesda, Md., 1963-65; resident in ophthalmology U. Calif. Med. Ctr., San Francisco, 1965-68; rsch. fellow Howe lab. Mass. Eye and Ear Infirmary, Boston, 1968-69; asst. prof. U. Miami (Fla.) Sch. Medicine, 1969-75, assoc. prof., 1975-82, prof., 1982—. Mem. nat. eye adv. coun. NIH, Bethesda, 1982-86, visual sci. study sect. A, 1972-76, chmn., 1975-76; bd. govs. Anne Bates Leach Eye Hosp., Miami, 1987-93, 98-2004, outpatient med. dir., 1993-95, compliance dir., 1997-2002., mem./chmn. med. records com., by-laws com., residency curriculum com., outpatient care com., info. sys. task force, quality assessment and improvement com. Author: Testing the Field of Vision, 1982, Perimetry With and Without Automation, 1987, Automated Static Perimetry, 1992, 2d edit., 1999; co-author Clinical Decision in Glaucoma, 1993; contbr. over 200 sci. articles and book chpts.; co-editor: Discussions on Glaucoma, 1977, Automatic Perimetry in Glaucoma, 1985, Encounters in Glaucoma Research I: Receptors, 1994, Optic Nerve in Glaucoma, 1995, How to Ascertain Progression and Outcome, 1996; assoc. editor Am. Jour. Opththalmology, Chgo., 1973-90; editor (glaucoma sect.) Investigative Opthalmology and Visual Sci., 1978-82; mem. editl. bd., editl. adv. com., Opthalmology, 1985-. Mem., active med. staff Jackson Meml. Hosp., 1969--, Anne Bates Leach Eye Hosp., active med. staff, 1976-, v.p., 1983-84, pres., 1984-86. Surgeon USPHS, 1963-65, inactive reserve 1965-80. Recipient William and Mary Greve Internat. Scholars award Rsch. to Prevent Blindness, Inc., 1978, Sr. Sci. Investigator award, 1986, 93, 99, Recognition award Alcon Rsch. Inst., Ft. Worth, 1986, Dean's Career Achievement award, 1999, Georg von Bartisch Medal for contributions to Glaucoma Rsch., 2002, Global Glaucoma Special Recognition Internat. Glaucoma Review, 2002, Hans Goldmann Medal Glaucoma Soc. of Internat. Congress Ophthalmology, 2003, Disting. Faculty Scholar award, 2007; rsch. grantee Nat. Eye Inst., 1969-91, 93-97, Am. Health Assistance Found., 1978-95, Glaucoma Rsch. Found., 1993-94. Fellow Am. Acad. Ophthalmology (councillor 1984-86, Gold medal 1972, Honor awards 1978, 83, Sr. Honor award 1992, Secretariat award 2004); mem. Am. Glaucoma Soc. (v.p. 1988-90, pres. 1990-92), Assn. for Rsch. in Vision and Ophthalmology (trustee 1983-88, pres. 1987, Mildred Weisenfeld award 1997), Am. Ophthal. Soc., Internat. Perimetric Soc. (hon. lectr. 2004), Optometric Glaucoma Soc. (life, hon. lectr. 2004). Home: 11880 SW 63rd Ave Miami FL 33156-4802 Office: Bascom Palmer Eye Inst U Miami Miller Sch Medicine PO Box 016880 Miami FL 33101-6880 Office Fax: 305-326-6385. Business E-Mail: danderson@med.miami.edu.

ANDERSON, E. KARL, lawyer; b. Huntington, W. Va., Mar. 30, 1931; s. Earle Karl and Helen Emrie (Johnson) A.; m. Mary Elizabeth Williams, Nov. 13, 1953; children: Sharon Elizabeth, Charles Wesley. BBA, So. Methodist U., 1953, LLB, 1960. Bar: Tex. 1960, U.S. Dist. Ct. (no. dist.) Tex. 1963, U.S. Supreme Ct. 1971. Field supr. Travelers Ins. Co., Dallas, 1956-57; claim mgr. Allstate Ins. Co., Dallas, 1958-62; practiced in Dallas, 1963—; pntr. Lastelick, Anderson and Arneson, Dallas, 1968—. 1st lt. USAF, 1954—56. Fellow Tex. Bar Found.; mem. Am. Bar Assn., Dallas Assn. Trial Lawyers (dir. 1964-65, 74-75), Tex. Trial Lawyers Assn., Assn. Trial Lawyers Am., Dallas Country Club, Delta Theta Phi, Sigma Iota Epsilon, Sigma Alpha Epsilon. Presbyterian. Home: 3111 Drexel Dr Dallas TX 75205-2910 Office: Univ Twr Bldg S-402 6440 N Central Expy Dallas TX 75206-4123 Home Phone: 214-521-1211; Office Phone: 214-363-0555.

ANDERSON, EDGAR RATCLIFFE, JR., career officer, physician, health facility administrator; b. Baton Rouge, Mar. 13, 1940; m. Sandra Caston; children: Melisa, Edward, Mark. MD, La. State U., 1964; grad., Industrial Coll. Armed Forces, 1972, Air War Coll., 1982. Diplomate Am. Bd. Family Practice, Am. Bd. Dermatology, Am. Bd. Preventive Medicine. Commd. 2d lt. USAF, 1965, advanced through grades to lt. gen., 1994, flight surgeon 464th Troop Carrier Wing Pope AFB, N.C., 1965-68, chief aerospace medicine 33d Tactical Fighter Wing Eglin AFB, Fla., 1968-69, undergrad. pilot tng. Williams AFB, Ariz., 1969-71, completed F-4 combat crew tng. MacDill AFB, Fla., 1971, aircraft comdr. 336th Tactical Fighter Squadron Seymour Johnson AFB, N.C., 1971, asst. ops. officer Ubon Royal Thai AFB, chief aeromed. svcs. USAF Regional Hosp. MacDill AFB, 1973-75, comdr. USAF Hosp. Seymour Johnson AFB, 1975-77, staff dermatologist USAF Med. Ctr. Keesler AFB, Miss., 1980-81, chief flight test ops. USAF-RAF exchange program Royal Air Force Station, Farnborough, Eng., 1981-83, comdr. USAF Regional Hosp. Langley AFB, Va., 1983-84, dir. profl. svcs. Office of Command Surgeon Tactical Air Command, 1984, command surgeon HQ Pacific Air Forces Hickam AFB, Hawaii, 1984-86, command surgeon SAC Offutt AFB, Nebr., 1986-90, comdr. Wilford Hall USAF Med. Ctr. Lackland AFB, Tex., 1990, surgeon general Washington, ret., 1996; CEO Truman Health Sys., Kansas City, Mo., 1996-98. Dean, prof. Sch. Med. U. Mo., Kansas City, 1996-97; exec. v.p., CEO AMA, Chgo., 1998-2001; pres., CEO Anderson Med. Consulting, LLC, 2001-; prof. medicine Loyola U. Med. Ctr., Chgo., 2002-. Decorated D.S.M. with oak leaf cluster, Legion of Merit with oak leaf cluster, D.F.C. with oak leaf cluster, Meritorious Svc. Medal with two oak leaf clusters, Air medal with nine oak leaf clusters, Air Force Commendation Medal.

ANDERSON, EDWARD RILEY, retired state supreme court justice; b. Chattanooga, Aug. 10, 1932; BS, U. Tenn., 1955, JD, 1957. Bar: Tenn. 1958, U.S. Dist. Ct. (ea. dist.) Tenn. 1965, U.S. Ct. Appeals (4th cir.) 1985, U.S. Ct. Appeals (6th cir.), U.S. Supreme Ct. 1988. Assoc. Joyce & Wilson, Oak Ridge, Tenn., 1957—61; ptnr. Joyce, Anderson & Meredith, Oak Ridge, 1961—87; judge Tenn. Ct. Appeals, Knoxville, 1987—90; justice Tenn. Supreme Ct., Knoxville, 1990—2005, chief justice, 1994—2001. Mem. Tenn. Jud. Conf., 1987—; bd. dirs. Conf. of Chief Justices, 1999-2000, vice chair children and the family com., 1998-99; chmn. Tenn. Jud. Coun., 1990-95, Select Senate/House Com. on Ct. Automation,1990-94. Past commr. Oak Ridge City Charter. Recipient Vocat. Svc. award Oak Ridge Rotary Club, 2000; named Judge of Yr. Am. Bd. Trial Advocates, 1998. Fellow Am. Bar Found., Tenn. Bar Found.; mem. ABA, Am. Bd. Trial Advocates (pres. Tenn. chpt. 1987-88), Tenn. Bar Assn. (William M. Leech Jr. Pub. Svc. award 2001), Anderson County Bar Assn. (pres. 1961), Tenn. Def. Lawyers Assn. (pres. 1980-81), Am. Inns of Ct. (pres. Tenn. chpt. 1988-90). Avocations: reading, golf, tennis.

ANDERSON, EDWARD VIRGIL, lawyer; b. San Francisco, Oct. 17, 1953; s. Virgil P and Edna Pauline (Pedersen) A.; m. Kathleen Helen Dunbar, Sept. 3, 1983; children: Elizabeth D., Hilary J. AB in Econs., Stanford U., 1975, JD, 1978. Bar: Calif. 1978. Assoc. Pillsbury Madison & Sutro, San Francisco, 1978—, ptnr., 1987-94; chmn. mng. ptnr., mem. firm mgmt. com. Skjerven Morrill LLP, San Jose, 1994—2003; ptnr. Sidley Austin Brown & Wood, San Francisco, 2003—. Editor IP Litigator, 1995—; mem. bd. editors Antitrust Law Devel., 1983-86. Trustee Lick-Wilmerding H.S., San Francisco, 1980—, pres.; trustee Silicon Valley Law Found., 1995—; trustee, v.p. Hamlin Sch. for Girls, San Francisco, 1998—, v.p. Mem. ABA, Calif. Bar Assn., San Francisco Bar Assn., Santa Clara Bar Assn., City Club San Francisco, Stanford Golf Club, Phi Beta Kappa. Republican. Episcopal. Home: 330 Santa Clara Ave San Francisco CA 94127-2035 Office: Sidley Austin Brown & Wood Ste 5000 555 Calif St San Francisco CA 94104 Home Phone: 415-661-9473; Office Phone: 415-772-7420. E-mail: evanderson@sidley.com.

ANDERSON, ELLIS BERNARD, retired lawyer, pharmaceutical executive; b. Michigan City, Ind., Aug. 30, 1926; s. A.B. and Esther Anderson; m. Adrienne Scotchbrook, Aug. 6, 1955 (dec. Aug. 1991); children: Rebecca J., Katherine V.; m. Jermain Johnson Andrews, May 22, 1993. AB cum laude, Ind. U., 1949, JD, 1952; grad., Advanced Mgmt. Program, Harvard U., 1970. Bar: Ind. 1952. Ptnr. Butt, Bowers & Anderson, Evansville, Ind., 1952-60; with Baxter Labs. Inc., Morton Grove, Ill., 1961-65; sr. v.p., gen. counsel, dir., mem. exec. com. Hoffmann-La Roche Inc., Nutley, NJ, 1965-88. With AUS, World War II. Mem. Nassau Club, Bay Head Yacht Club, Springdale Golf Club, Phi Beta Kappa. Home: 1 Larch Way Princeton NJ 08540-5053

ANDERSON, ERIC C., aerospace transportation executive; b. Denver, 1974; BA in Aerospace Engring. (magna cum laude), U. Va., 1996. Rsch. position NASA; bus. develop. lead Analytical Graphics; exec. v.p., co-founder Starport.com (sold to space.com in 2000); co-founder Space Adventures, Ltd., Va., 1998, pres., CEO Va. Invited spkr. and lectr. in field. Contbr. to tech. papers and articles in the field; author: Space Tourist's Handbook, 2005. Recipient Outstanding Young Engring. Grad. award, U. Va. Engring. Found., 2005. Achievements include being an advocate in commercial space transportation and private space exploration/space tourism. Office: Space Adventures Ltd 8000 Towers Crescent Dr Ste 1000 Vienna VA 22182 Office Phone: 703-524-7172. Office Fax: 703-524-7176.

ANDERSON, ERIC EDWARD, psychologist, consultant, healthcare educator; b. Mpls., Jan. 24, 1951; s. Charles Eric and Elizabeth Blanche (Engstrand) A.; m. Florence Kaye, June 18, 1978; children: Cara Elizabeth, Evan Travis. BA summa cum laude, U. Minn., 1973; MA, Fuller Theol. Sem., 1977, PhD in Clin. Psychology, 1978. Lic. psychologist Minn., Calif., Pa.; cert. community coll. teaching credential in psychology and philosophy Calif. Postdoctoral intern U. Minn., Mpls., 1978-79, asst. prof., coord. tng. in aging, 1979-83; group v.p. Kiel Profl. Svcs., Inc., St. Paul, 1983-84; pres. Primary Mental Health Care, Inc., Bloomington, Minn., 1984-86, Anderson Health Strategies, LLC, 1996-97, pres., CEO, 2001—06; sr. v.p. Treatment Ctrs. Am., Inc., Pasadena, Calif., 1986-88, LifeLink, Inc., Laguna Hills, Calif., 1988-89, chief operating officer, 1989-91; v.p., managed healthcare Columbia Gen., Laguna Hills, 1990-91; sr. v.p. managed health care Coll. Health Enterprises, Huntington Beach, Calif., 1991-94; exec. v.p. Medco. Behavioral Care/Merck Medco., 1994-96; pres., CEO Integra, Inc., 1997—2001; chair health sci. and svcs. Immaculata U., 2006—. Cons. Ebenezer Soc., Mpls., 1979-82, Wilder Found., St. Paul, 1981-84; rsch. advisor Walden U., Mpls., 1982-86; assoc. prof. Sch. Psychology, Fuller Theol. Sem., Pasadena, 1989; assoc. clin. prof. Widener U., 2000-; adj. prof. Chestnut Hill Coll., Phila., 2005-06. Contbr. articles to profl. jours. Mem.: APA (conf. participant 1981), Am. Mgmt. Assn., Soc. Psychologists in Mgmt., Union League, Phi Beta Kappa. Avocations: tennis, gardening, bicycling, photography, golf. Address: 715 S Bryn Mawr Ave Bryn Mawr PA 19010-2005 Office Phone: 610-519-1793. Personal E-mail: eanderh@aol.com.

ANDERSON, ERIC SCOTT, lawyer; b. Grand Forks, ND, Aug. 26, 1949; s. Lyle William and Norma Sylvia (Lundeby) A.; children: Peter Scott, Nathan William. BSChemE, U. Wis., 1971, JD, 1977. Bar: Wis. 1977, Minn. 1977, U.S. Dist. Ct. (we. dist.) Wis. 1977, U.S. Dist. Ct. Minn. 1978. Assoc. Fredrikson & Byron, P.A., Mpls., 1977-83, shareholder, 1983—. Mem. Wis. Bar Assn., Minn. Bar Assn., Hennepin County Bar Assn., Phi Eta Sigma, Tau Beta Pi, Phi Kappa Phi, Order of Coif. Avocations: golf, running, music. Office: Fredrikson & Byron PA 200 S 6th St Ste 4000 Minneapolis MN 55402-1425 Office Phone: 612-492-7030. E-mail: eanderson@fredlaw.com.

ANDERSON, ERIC SEVERIN, lawyer; b. NYC, Dec. 16, 1943; s. Edward Severin and Dorothy Elvira (Ekbloom) A. BA in History summa cum laude, St. Mary's U., San Antonio, 1968; JD cum laude, Harvard U., 1971. Bar: Tex. 1971. From assoc. to of counsel Fulbright & Jaworski, L.L.P., Houston, 1971—. Served with USAF, 1961-65. Mem. ABA, State Bar Tex., Houston Bar Assn. Clubs: Houston Ctr., Houston City. Democrat. Avocations: classical music, theater, sports. Home: 14 E Greenway Plz Unit 21-O Houston TX 77046-1406 Office: Fulbright & Jaworski LLP 1301 Mckinney St Houston TX 77010-3031 Office Phone: 713-651-5265. Business E-Mail: eanderson@fulbright.com.

ANDERSON, EVELYN LOUISE, elementary school educator; b. Abilene, Tex., Apr. 10, 1943; d. Dexter W. and Hattie M. Armstrong; m. E. Wade Anderson, Dec. 22, 1962; children: Cynthia Gail, Tresa Lynet. BA magna cum laude, Sul Ross State U., 1985. Kindergarten tchr. Socorro Ind. Sch. Dist., El Paso, Tex., 1985-86; tchr. kindergarten through 3d grade, resource rm. Ft. Stockton Ind. Sch. Dist., 1986-90; tchr. kindergarten Lydia Rippey Elem. Sch., Aztec, N.Mex., 1990—. Organizer Children's Libr., Ft. Stockton (Tex.) Pub. Libr., 1980-84, pre-school tchr. First Bapt. Ch., Ft. Stockton, Tex., 1979-84. Nominee Disney Tchr. awrd, 2000. Mem.: Coun. Exceptional Children, Kappa Delta Pi. Democrat. Avocations: writing, reading, travel, painting, crocheting. Home: 1709 Winter Ct Farmington NM 87401-2086

ANDERSON, FRANCILE MARY, secondary school educator; b. Poland, Ind., Nov. 10, 1926; d. Matthew Henry and Emma Alvina (Dettinger) Worthman; m. Robert Charles Anderson, Aug. 23, 1953; children: Sally Quick, Sue Wilkinson, Robert Charles, Russell. BA, U. Mich., 1948. Tchr. Pontiac (Mich.) Sch. Dist., 1948-54. Co-organizer Mich. Law Related Edn. Conf., Lansing, 1978; mem. exec. bd. North Ctrl. Assn. Commn. on Schs., Tempe, Ariz., 1996-99. Trustee North Oakland Med. Ctrs., Pontiac, 1994—; campaign chair United Way of Oakland County, 1995. Recipient

Disting. Svc. award Mich. Assn. Secondary Sch. Prins., 1987; named to Mich. Edn. Hall of Fame, 1990. Mem. Oakland County Hosp. Assn. (pres.), Oakland County Bar Law Libr. Found., North Ctrl. Assn. Mich., North Oakland Med. Ctrs. Found. (pres.), Delta Kappa Gamma. Republican. Presbyterian. Home: 2570 Silverside Dr Waterford MI 48328-1760 Personal E-mail: franan1@earthlink.net.

ANDERSON, FRANK J., JR., retired career officer; BA in Bus. Mgmt. and Econ., Chapman Coll., 1972; student, Office Tng. Sch., Lackland AFB, Tex., 1973, Squadron Officer Sch., 1975; M in Mgmt., Ctrl. Mich. U., 1982; student, Air Command and Staff Coll., 1984, Def. Sys. Mgmt. Coll., 1987, Indsl. Coll. Armed Forces, 1992. Cert. lead assessor ISO 9000 quality sys., total quality mgmt. facilitator, program mgmt. level III, contracting level III. Commd. 2d lt. USAF, 1973, advanced through grades to brig. gen., 1997; base contracting officer, chief constrn. br. Washington Area Contracting Ctr., Andrews AFB, Md., 1973-76, chief specialized contracting br., 1973-76; with Edn. With Industry Program Boeing Co., Phila., 1976-77; chief subcontractor mgmt. div. then dep. chief contract adminstrn. divsn. GE Air Force Plant Rep. Office, Phila., 1977-79; stationed at Andrews AFB, Md., 1979-83, 89-91; comdr. Air Force Plant Rep. Office Rockwell Internat., Columbus, Ohio, 1984-87; dir. contracting Electronic Combat and Reconnaissance Sys. Program Office, Wright-Patterson AFB, Ohio, 1987-89; sys. program dir. Sys. Program Office Aero. Sys. Ctr., Eglin AFB, Fla., 1992-94, dir. Weapons, Air Base and Range Product Support Office, 1994-95, mgr. armament product group, 1995-96, dir. contracting Wright-Patterson AFB, 1996-97; dep. asst. sec. contracting Office Asst. Sec. Acquisition, adv. gen. Air Force Competition Hdqs. USAF, Pentagon, Washington, 1997-2000; comdt. Def. Sys. Mgmt. Coll., Ft. Belvoir, Va., 1999—2000; ret., 2001; pres. Def. Acquisition Univ., Va. Decorated Legion of Merit. Recipient Air Force Professionalism in Contracting award, 1988; named Career Broadening Personnel Officer of Yr., Air Force Sys. Command, 1980, Co. Grade Officer of Yr., Air Force Sys. Command, 1982. Office: Def Acquisition Univ 9820 Belvoir Rd Fort Belvoir VA 22060-5565

ANDERSON, FRED D., investment company executive, retired computer company executive; B in Econs., Whittier Coll.; MBA, UCLA. CPA, Calif. Mgr. consulting divsn. Coopers & Lybrand; sr. v.p., CFO MAI Sys. Corp., pres., COO; v.p., CFO Automatic Data Processing, 1992-96; exec. v.p., CFO Apple Computer Inc., Cupertino, Calif., 1996—2004; mng. dir., co-founder Elevation Partners, NYC, 2004—. Bd. dirs. eBay, Inc., 2003—, Move, Inc., E.piphany; audit chair VG Holding Corp. Capt. USAF. Office: Elevation Partners 70 E 55th St 12th Fl New York NY 10022 Office Phone: 212-317-6555. Office Fax: 212-317-6556.

ANDERSON, FRED RICHARD, minister, writer; b. San Bernardino, Calif., Dec. 27, 1941; s. Elmer Duffield and Gladys Lucile (Lawlace) A.; m. Questa Lucile Donnelly, Sept. 4, 1965; children: Larra Anne, Rebecca Lucile; 1 foster child, James Gordon Cushman. BM in Voice, U. Redlands, 1963; MDiv, Princeton Theol. Sem., 1973, D in Ministry, 1981. Pastor Pompton Valley Presbyn. Ch., Pompton Plains, NJ, 1973-78; sr. pastor Pine St. Church, Harrisburg, Pa., 1978-92, Madison Ave. Presbyn. Ch., NYC, 1992—. Bd. dirs. Liturgical Conf., 1990-94; bd. trustees Princeton Theol. Sem., 1992—; chair edn. bd. Reformed Liturgy and Music, 1983-89. Author: Singing Psalms of Joy & Praise, 1986, The Presbyterian Hymnal, 1990; assoc. editor: Book of Common Worship, 1993; contbr. articles to profl. jours.; opera, concert singer, 1963-64. Trustee Harrisburg Hosp., 1990-92, Chilton Meml. Hosp., Pompton Plains, 1976-78; pres. Pequennock (N.J.) Sr. City Housing, 1974-78; v.p. YMCA, Harrisburg, 1987-92, v.p., 1987-92. Capt. USAF, 1964-69. Recipient Fine Arts award Bank Am., 1959. Mem. Appeal Conscience Found. (trustee), N.Am. Acad. Liturgy, Presbyn. Assn. Musicians, Union League Club (N.Y.C.), The Pilgrims. Avocations: jogging, boating, fishing, hymntext writing, hiking the white mountains. Office: Madison Ave Presbyn Ch 921 Madison Ave New York NY 10021-3508

ANDERSON, FREDERICK RANDOLPH, JR., lawyer, educator; b. Rutherfordton, NC, June 28, 1941; s. Frederick Randolph and Ophelia (Meeler) A.; m. Barbara Alison Rose, Nov., 1991; 1 child, Molly Elizabeth. BA with highest honors, U. NC, 1963; BA in Jurisprudence, Oxford U., Eng., 1965; JD, Harvard U., 1968. Bar: DC 1969, US Supreme Ct. 1980, US Ct. Appeals (DC cir.) 1995, US Ct. Appeals (9th cir.) 1999, US Ct. Appeals (3rd cir.) 2002. Teaching fellow Harvard U., Cambridge, Mass.; editor in chief Environ. Law Reporter, Washington, 1970-73; exec. dir. Environ. Law Inst., Washington, 1973-78, pres., 1978-80; prof. law U. Utah Coll. Law, Salt Lake City, 1980-85; dean Washington Coll. Law Am. U., 1985-88, Ann Loeb Bronfman Prof. Law, 1988-91; mem. firm Cadwalader, Wickersham & Taft, Washington, 1991-93, ptnr., 1993—2004, McKenna Long & Aldridge, Washington, 2004—. Mem. congl. study of common law relief for hazardous waste injuries, 1980-82; mem. Adminstrv. Conf. U.S., 1978-80, cons., 1983-84, 89-91; chmn. adv. working group on environ. sanctions U.S. Sentencing Commn., 1992-94; chmn. bd. govs. Inst. Governance and Sustainable Devel., 2005—; bd. visitors inst. environ. U NC, 2007—. Author: NEPA in the Courts, 1973, Environmental Improvement Through Economic Incentives, 1978, Environmental Protection: Law and Policy, 1984, 4th edit., 2003; contbg. author: Federal Environmental Law, 1974, Occupational and Environmental Health, 1982, The Southwest under Stress, 1981. Chmn. bd. dirs. Ctr. for Internat. Environ. Law, 1993—; v.p. Western Network, 1986-89; mem. Harvard Group on Risk Mgmt. Reform, 1994-96; bd. dirs. René Dubos Ctr., 1994—. Morehead scholar, Nat. Merit scholar U. N.C., Marshall scholar Oxford U. Mem. ABA (chmn. standing com. on environ. law 1980-82, chmn. commn. on inter-Am. affairs 1986-88), NAS (mem. Comm. on Life Scis. 1995-2001, bd. environ. studies and toxicology 1988-94, com. on sci., tech. and law 2000—, bd. on atmospheric sci. and climate 2003-07), Am. Law Inst. (life), NatureServe (bd. dirs. 2000-06). Office: McKenna Long & Aldridge LLP 1900 K St NW Washington DC 20006 Business E-Mail: fanderson@mckennalong.com.

ANDERSON, G. BARRY, state supreme court justice; b. Mankato, Minn., Oct. 24, 1954; m. Louise Helleoid, June 30, 1884; 3 children. BA magna cum laude, Gustavus Adolphus Coll., 1976; JD, U. Minn., 1979. Bar: Minn. 1979, U.S. Dist. Ct. Minn. 1979, U.S. Ct. Appeals (8th cir.) 1980; cert. civil trial specialist. Partner Arnold, Anderson & Dove; city atty. City of Hutchinson, Minn., 1987-88; gen. counsel Minn. Rep. Party, 1987-97; chair Minn. Ethical Practices Bd., 1997-98; judge Minn. Ct. Appeals, St. Paul, 1998—2004; justice Minn. Supreme Ct., 2004—. Bd. dirs. Hutchinson Cmty. Video Network, pres., 1984-98. Mem. Alpha Kappa Psi, Rotary (pres. Hutchinson chpt. 1997-98). Lutheran. Avocations: golf, historical and biographical works. Office: Minn Supreme Ct 305 Minn Jud Ctr 25 Rev Dr Martin Luther King Jr Blvd Saint Paul MN 55155*

ANDERSON, GAIL MARIE, retired librarian; b. St. Cloud, Minn., Apr. 26, 1945; d. George Elroy Carpenter and Blanche Doris (Flam) Carpenter Neel; m. Gordon Alexander Anderson, Aug. 24, 1971. B.S., St. Cloud State U., 1969. Cert. Librarian, Minn.; cert. elem. tchr., Minn. Librarian, Cloquet Pub. Sch., Minn., 1969-70; jr. high media ctr. dir. Roseville Pub. Sch., Minn., 1970-78; asst. program dir., group dir. Afton Alps Ski Sch., 1973-82; library asst. U. Minn. Sch. Dentistry, Mpls., 1979-86; sch. librarian Desert Valley Sch., Bullhead City, Ariz., 1986—2006. Sec., Minn. Christian Youth Council, Mpls., 1960-63; mem. Minn. Ednl. Media Orgn. Methodist. Mem. Bullhead City Tchrs. Union (treas. 1987-2006), Jobs Daus. (guardian 1989-2002), Pheasants Forever. Avocations: outdoor sports, hunting, gardening, travel. Home: 9067 Deer Path Ln Breezy Point MN 56472

ANDERSON, GARLAND D., dean, obstetrician, gynecologist, educator; b. Dec. 11, 1944; MD, U. Tenn. Intern Hermann Hosp., Houston, 1970—71; resident U. Tex. Health Sci. Ctr., Houston, 1971—74; fellow maternal fetal medicine U. Louisville, Ky., 1974—76, instr. ob-gyn. Ky., 1974—75, asst. prof. Ky., 1975—77, med. dir. Teen Alternative Parent Program Ky., 1975—77, assoc. prof. Ky.; dir. resident edn., div. chief Maternal and Fetal Medicine, prof. Dept. Obstetrics and Gynecology U. Tenn. Coll. Medicine, 1978—89; prof. ob-gyn. U. Tenn., 1983—89; prof., chmn. Dept. Ob-gyn. U. Tex. Med. Branch Sch. Medicine, Galveston, 1989—, Jennie Sealy Smith disting. chair ob-gyn., dean, 2006—. Steering com. chair Maternal-Fetal Units Network, Nat. Inst. Child Heath and Human Devel., 2003—06. Contbr. articles to profl. jours. Named a Tex. Super Doc, Tex. Monthly; named one of Best Doctor for Women, Good Housekeeping mag.; named to Best Doctors in Am.; recipient Nicholas and Katherine Leone Award for Adminstrn. Excellence. Fellow: Am. Coll. of Obstetricians and Gynecologists (FACOG); mem.: Coun. of Univ. Chairs in Ob-gyn. (pres.), Soc. Maternal and Fetal Medicine (former bd. mem., pres., Award for Rsch. Excellence). Office: Office of Dean of Medicine 301 University Blvd 5 106 Adminstrn Bldg Galveston TX 77555-0133 Office Phone: 409-772-4797. Office Fax: 409-772-9598. E-mail: ganderso@utmb.edu.*

ANDERSON, GEORGE See WEISSMAN, JACK

ANDERSON, GEORGE KENNETH, physician, retired military officer, foundation administrator; b. Providence, Feb. 17, 1946; s. George Raymond and Mildred (Caster) A.; m. Kimberly Kay Baker, May 18, 1968; children: George D., Ginger K. MD, U. Mich., 1971; MPH, Tulane U., 1973; postgrad., Nat. War Coll., Ft. McNair, Va., 1982-83. Diplomate Am. Bd. Preventive Medicine (chmn. 1991-95), Am. Bd. Med. Mgmt. (bd. dirs.). Intern Wilford Hall USAF Med Ctr., 1971-72; resident USAF Sch. Aerospace Medicine, 1973-75; commd. 2d lt. USAF, 1967, advanced through grades to maj. gen., 1993; comdr. USAF Hosp., Kunsan, Republic of Korea, 1975-76, 86th Tactical Hosp., Germany, 1976-79; mem. faculty USAF Sch. Aerospace Medicine, Brooks AFB, Tex., 1979-82; div. chief Office Surgeon Gen., Bolling AFB, Md., 1983-85, dep. dir., 1985-87; command surgeon Air Force Systems Command, Andrews AFB, Md., 1987-88; dir. med. inspection Air Force ISC, Norton AFB, Calif., 1988-90; comdr. Human Systems Ctr., Brooks AFB, 1990-94; dep. asst. sec. def. Health Svcs. Ops. and Readiness, Washington, 1994; ret. USAF, 1996; pres., CEO Koop Found. Inc., Rockville, Md., 1997-98; exec. v.p. Oceania Corp., Falls Church, Va., 1998-99; pres., CEO Oceania, Inc., Redwood City, Calif., 1999—2005; exec. dir. Assn. of Military Surgeons of U.S., Bethesda, Md. Bd. dir. New World Healthcare Solutions, Washington. Decorated Legion of Merit, Disting. Svc. medal; Koop Found. fellow. Fellow Am. Coll. Preventive Medicine (pres.), Am. Coll. Physician Execs. (disting.), Aerospace Med. Assn. (Julian Ward award 1975); mem. AMA, Air Force Assn. (life). Office: AMSUS 9320 Old Georgetown Rd Bethesda MD 20814-1653

ANDERSON, GEORGE ROSS, JR., federal judge; b. Anderson, SC, Jan. 29, 1929; s. George Ross and Eva Mae (Pooler) A.; m. Dorothy M. Downie, Dec. 2, 1951; 1 son, G. Ross. B.Comml. Sci., Southeastern U., 1949; postgrad., George Washington U., 1949-51; LL.B., U. S.C., 1954, LLD (hon.), 1984, Anderson Coll., 1998. Bar: S.C. 1954. Mem. identification div. FBI, Washington, 1945-47; clk. to U.S. Senator Olin D. Johnston, Washington, 1947-51, Columbia, SC, 1953-54; individual practice law Anderson, SC, 1954-79; U.S. dist. judge Dist. Ct. of S.C., Anderson, 1980—. Asst. editor: U. S.C. Law Rev, 1953-54. Bd. dirs. Salvation Army, 1968, YMCA, 1968-79, Anderson Youth Assn., 1978-80. Served with USAF, 1951-52. Recipient War Horse award So. Trial Lawyers Assn., 1990, Dist. Judicial Svc. award The Civil Justice Found., Am. Trial Lawyers Assn., 1997, Ernest F. Hollings Pub. Svc. award, 2002, Order of the Palmetto award, 2002; named for Federal Bldg. Courthouse in Anderson, SC, 2002. Fellow Internat. Acad. Trial Lawyers (dir. 1979-81), Internat. Soc. Barristers; mem. S.C. Bar Assn. (dir. 1977-80, past cir. v.p.), Assn. Trial Lawyers Am. (bd. govs. 1969-71), S.C. Trial Lawyers Assn. (v.p. 1970-71, pres. 1971-72, Outstanding Trial Judge of Yr. 1984), hon. doctor of Laws, U. SC, 1984, bd. dirs.,Federal Judges Assn., 1993-97. Democrat. Baptist. Office: US Dist Ct PO Box 2147 Anderson SC 29622-2147

ANDERSON, GERALD EDWIN, retired utilities executive; b. Boston, Apr. 9, 1931; s. Clarence Gustav and Lela Pauline (Kelley) Anderson; m. Mary Elizabeth Iverson, May 21, 1955; children: Todd K., Timothy J., Kristin E. May. AA, Worthington Jr. Coll., Minn., 1950; BBA, U. Minn., 1952. CPA Minn. Staff accountant, audit mgr. Arthur Andersen & Co., Mpls., 1953-65; asst. comptroller Commonwealth Energy System (formerly New Eng. Gas & Electric Assn.), Cambridge, Mass., 1966, system comptroller, 1967-71, v.p., comptroller, 1971-72, treas. parent co., financial v.p. system, 1972-74, pres., 1974-91, chief exec. officer, 1975-91; ret., 1992. Trustee parent co., 1974—91; bd. dirs. Commonwealth Energy Sys., 1972—91, Liberty Mut. Ins. Co., Liberty Mut. Fire Ins. Co., 1980—2001, Liberty Life Assurance Co. Boston, 1984—95, Liberty Fin. Cos., Inc., 1995—2001. Vice chmn. United Ways Ea. New Eng., 1986; mem. town fin. com. Carlisle, Mass., 1968—73; chmn., 1972—73; dir. Swedish Coun. Am., 1987—2003; mem. Corps. Mass. Gen. Hosp., 1988—95. 1st lt. USAF, 1952—53. Mem.: AICPA, Fin. Execs. Inst., Minn. Soc. CPAs, Comml. Club Boston, Somerset Club, Oyster Harbors Club, Lakes Country Club, Betta Gamma Sigma, Beta Alpha Psi. Episcopalian. Home: 75 Hornbeam Ln Centerville MA 02632-3521 also: 245 Wild Horse Dr Palm Desert CA 92211-3220 Personal E-mail: geralde.anderson@comcast.net.

ANDERSON, GERALD LESLIE, finance company executive; b. Washington, May 24, 1940; s. Paul Hash and Edith (Hathaway) A.; m. Margaret Marie Curley, June 8, 1974; children: Paul Charles, Laura Marie. BS in Indsl. Mgmt., Carnegie Mellon U., 1961, MS in Indsl. Adminstrn., 1962. Econ. analyst Sun Oil Co., Phila., 1962-66; asst. treas. Selas Corp. Am., Dresher, Pa., 1966-74; treas. Midrex Corp., Charlotte, NC, 1974-76; v.p., treas. Georgetown Industries, Inc., Charlotte, 1976-85, v.p. fin., chief fin. officer, 1985-95; prin. Anderson Investments, Charlotte, NC, 1995—2000. Active Ch. at Charlotte Evangelical Free Ch. Republican. Home and Office: 4519 N Parview Dr Charlotte NC 28226-3450

ANDERSON, GERALDINE LOUISE, medical researcher; d. George M. and Viola Julia-Mary (Abel) Havrilla; m. Henry Clifford Anderson, May 21, 1966; children: Bruce Henry, Julie Lynne. BS in Med. Tech., U. Minn., Mpls., 1963. Cert. med. technologist Am. Soc. Clin. Pathology, clin. lab. scientist, clin. rsch. assoc. Med. technologist Swedish Hosp., Mpls., 1963-68; hematology supr. lab. Glenwood Hills Hosp., Golden Valley, Minn., 1968-70; assoc. scientist pediats. U. Minn. Hosps., Mpls., 1970-74; instr. health occupations, med. lab. asst. Suburban Hennepin County Area Vocat. Tech. Ctr., Brooklyn Park, Minn., 1974-81, 92-95, St. Paul Tech. Vocat. Inst., Brooklyn Park, 1978-81; rsch. med. technologist Miller Hosp., St. Paul, 1975-78; rsch. assoc. Children's and United Hosps., St. Paul, 1979-88; sr. lab. analyst Cascade Med. Inc., Eden Prairie, Minn., 1989-90; lab. mgr. VAMC, Mpls., 1990; tech. support scientist INCSTAR Corp., Stillwater, Minn., 1990-94; mem. network staff Clin. Design Group, Chgo., 1992-98; regulatory affairs product analysis coord. Medtronic Neurol., Mpls., 1995; quality assurance documentation coord. Lectec Corp., Minnetonka, Minn., 1995; clin. rsch. monitor Eli Lilly Rsch. Labs., Indpls., 1995-98; sr. clin. rsch. assoc. Covance, Inc., Princeton, NJ, 1998-99. Sr. clin. rsch. assoc. Parexel Internat., Inc., Chgo., 1999—2000; clin. rsch. assoc. AAI Internat., Boston, 2000—01; regional clin. rsch. assoc. Wyeth, Collegeville, Pa., 2001—02; health occupations adv. com. Hennepin Tech. Ctrs., 1975—90, chairperson, 1978—79; mem. hematology slide edn. rev. bd. Am. Soc. Hematology, 1977—96; mem. flow cytometry and clin. chemistry quality controll subcoms. Nat. Com. for Clin. Lab. Stds., 1988—92; cons. FCM Specialists, 1989—99, 2002—, Clin. Design Group, 1992—98; mem. rev. bd. Clin. Lab. Sci., 1990—91, The Learning Laboratorian Series, 1991; presenter in field. Contbr. articles to profl. jours. Charter orgns. rep. Viking coun. Boy Scouts Am., 1988—90; resource person lab. careers Robbinsdale (Minn.) Sch. Dist., 1970—79; active Women Scientists Spkrs. Bur., 1989—92, Helping Hands, 2002—06, Med. Lab. Tech. Polit. Action Com., 1978—99; observer UN 4th World Conf. on Women, Beijing, 1995; del. Crest View Home Assn., 1981—; sci. and math. subcom. Minn. High Tech. Coun., 1983—88; bd. dirs. Big Pine Lake Property Owners, 1996—. Recipient Svc. awards and honors, Omicron Sigma. Mem.: NAFE, AAUW, AAAS, Grad. Women in Sci., Inc., Great Lakes Internat. Flow Cytometry Assn. (charter mem. 1992), Internat. Soc. Analytical Cytology, Am. Soc. Hematology, Minn. Med. Tech. Alumni, Assn. Clin. Rsch. Profls., World Future Soc., Assn. Women in Sci., Twin Cities Hosp. Assn. (spkrs. bur. 1968—70), Am. Soc. Clin. Lab. Sci. (del. to ann. meetings 1972—, chmn. hematology sci. assembly 1977—79, nomination com. 1979—81, bd. dirs. 1986—88), Am. Soc. Profl. and Exec. Women, Minn. Soc. Med. Tech. (sec. 1969—71), Minn. Emerging Med. Orgns., Nat. Assn. Women Cons., Inc., Soc. Tech. Comm., Assn. Clin. Rsch. Profls. (cert. clin. rsch. assoc.), Women in Comm., Inc., Am. Med. Writers Assn., Nat. Ch. Libr. Assn., Alpha Mu Tau, Sigma Delta Epsilon (corr. sec. XI chpt. 1980—82, pres. 1982—84, nat. membership com. 1990—92, nat. nominations chair 1991—92, nat. v.p. 1992—93, nat. pres.-elect 1993—94, nat. pres. 1994—95, bd. dirs. 1996—2001, chmn. bd. dirs. 2000—01). Avocations: photography, travel, reading.

ANDERSON, GERARD FENTON, economist, academic administrator; b. Mariemont, Ohio, June 24, 1951; s. Harry C. and Dorothy C. (Fenton) A.; m. Judith Rae Peres; 1 child, Anna. BA in Econs., Haverford Coll., 1973; PhD in Pub. Policy, U. Pa., 1978. Spl. asst. Cost of Living Coun. Exec. Office of the Pres., Washington, 1972; research analyst Fed. Reserve Bank, Washington, 1973-74; prin. investigator Phila. Health Mgmt. Corp., 1974-78; economist Office of the Sec. HHS, Washington, 1978-83; assoc. dir. Ctr. for Hosp. Fin. and Mgmt. Johns Hopkins U., Balt., 1983-87, dir., 1987—; co-dir. Johns Hopkins Program for Med. Tech. and Practice Assessment, Balt., 1986-94, 1994—. Cons. Blue Cross Greater Phila., 1978, World Bank, Washington, 1988; adj. prof. Grad. Sch. Pub. Adminstrn. Am. U., Washington, 1978-82; presenter to Congl. coms. over 30 times. Author: Health Care Cost Containment, 1990, Providing Hospital Services, 1989; contbr. over 120 articles to profl. jours. Fellow U. Pa., Phila., 1978. Mem. Am. Econ. Assn., Am. Pub. Health Assn., Assn. for Health Svcs. Rsch., Phi Beta Kappa, Delta Omega. Democrat. Mem. Soc. Of Friends. Home: 8022 Glendale Rd Chevy Chase MD 20815-5903 Office: Johns Hopkins U 624 N Broadway # 300 Baltimore MD 21205-1900 Office Phone: 410-955-3241. E-mail: ganderso@jhsph.edu.

ANDERSON, GERARD M., energy executive; b. Toledo, Ohio; BS in Civil Engring., Notre Dame U.; MBA, U. of Mich., M. in Public Policy. Sr. cons. McKinsey & Co., 1988—93; v.p. non-utility bus. Detroit Edison DTE Energy Co., Detroit, 1993, CEO DTE Biomass Energy, exec. v.p., 1997, pres., COO energy resources bus. unit, 1998, pres., 2004—, COO, 2005—. Vice chmn. Nature Conservancy, Mich. Chap., Mich. Greenway Initiative. Office: DTE Energy Co 2000 2d Ave Detroit MI 48226-1279*

ANDERSON, GILLIAN, actress; b. Chgo., Aug. 9, 1968; d. Edward and Rosemary A.; m. Errol Clyde Klotz, Jan. 1, 1994 (div. 1997); 1 child, Piper; m. Julian Ozanne, Dec. 29, 2004 (separated Apr., 2006) BFA, DePaul U., 1990; grad., Goodman Theatre Sch., Chgo. Appeared on TV series, X-Files, 1993-2002 (Emmy award for Outstanding Lead Actress in a Drama Series, 1997, Golden Globe award for Best Actress in a Drama Series, 1997); stage appearance in Absent Friends, Manhattan Theatre Club, 1991 (Theatre World award 1991), The Philanthropist, Along Wharf Theater, 1992, The Vagina Monologues, 1999, 2000, What the Night is For, 2002-03, The Sweetest Swing in Baseball, 2004; appeared in films Three at Once, 1986, A Matter of Choice, 1988, The Turning, 1992, X-Files the Movie, 1998, The Mighty, 1998, Playing By Heart, 1998, Hellcab, 1998, Princess Mononoke, 1999, The House of Mirth, 2000 (British Independent Film award for Best Actress, 2000); TV appearances Class of '96, 1993, Reboot, 1995, The Simpsons, 1997, Frasier, 1999, Harsh Realm, 1999.

ANDERSON, GLORIA BROWN, publishing executive; BA, U. Texas, 1967; MA, U. Wisconsin, 1969. Reporter Associated Press, Madison, Wis., 1968-69, Sioux Falls, SD, 1968-69; reporter, mag. editor Cin. Enquirer, 1970-74; Sunday & features editor Charlotte Observer, 1975-76; mng. editor Knight News Wire, Detroit, 1977, Washington, 1977, Miami News, 1978-81; founding editor, co-pub. Miami Today, 1982-87; editor, pub. Kendall Gazette, Miami, 1988-91; Week in Review editor NY Times, 1992; exec. editor NY Times Syndicate, 1992-93; exec. editor, v.p. NY Times Syndication Sales Corp., 1994-96, pres., editor in chief, 1997—2002; v.p. internat. & editorial devel. NY Times News Svc. & Syndication Sales Corp., 2002—. Adv. coun. Fla. Internat. Univ. Sch. Journalism & Mass Comm., 1984—. Mem. Leadership Miami, 1981, United Way long range planning com., 1987, Performing Arts Ctr. Trust, Miami, 1990—91; bd. dirs. Hispanic Heritage Festival, Miami, 1981—88; founder, co-chmn. Kendall Awareness Week, 1989—92. Named Outstanding Citizen of Yr., S. Miami & Kendall C. of C., 1989; recipient Clarion award, Assn. Women in Comm., 1976, Juror Pulitzer Prize, 1982, 1983, Cmty. Headliner award, 1990, Matrix award, Assn. Women in Comm., 2005. Mem.: World Editors Forum (pres. 2001—03). Avocations: travel, latin american cultures, the arts, swimming, golf. Office: NY Times News Svc & Syndication Sales Corp Fl 14 122 E 42nd St New York NY 10168 also: NY Times News Svcs Div 229 W 43rd St New York NY 10036

ANDERSON, GREGORY SHANE, insurance executive; b. Mpls., Feb. 8, 1947; s. Donald Manfred and Inez Marie (Dickson) A.; m. Joyce Millicent Goetz, June 15, 1968; children: Kaarin Marie, Kirsten Elise, Todd Gregory, Kathryn Joy. BS, U. Minn., 1969. CLU. Fin. rep. Northwestern Mut. Life Ins. Co., St. Paul, 1970—. V.p. Tri-Lakes Improvement Assn., Lake Elmo, Minn., 1990, pres., 1991, 92. Named Man of the Yr., St. Paul Spl. Agts. Assn., 1984, 95-96, St. Paul Gen. Agts. and Mgrs., 1978, 91. Mem. Nat. Assn. Ins. and Fin. Advisors, Minn. Assn. Ins. and Fin. Advisors (pres. 1985-86), St. Paul Ins. and Fin. Advisors Assn. (pres. 1979-80), St. Paul CLU Soc. (pres. 1992-93, nat. com. 2001—), Million Dollar Round Table (Top of the Table 1993-94), 25 Million Dollar Internat. Forum, 1996, Dellwood Hills Golf Club (pres. 1996). Republican. Lutheran. Avocations: golf, racquetball, tennis, biking. Home: 11 Spyglass Rd Dellwood MN 55110-1227 Office: Northwestern Mutual Life 816 Dominion Dr Ste 200 Hudson WI 54016 Office Phone: 715-377-2086. Personal E-mail: gsa2847@aol.com. Business E-Mail: greg.anderson@nmfn.com.

ANDERSON, GREGORY THOMAS, secondary school educator, researcher, historian; s. Ralph Curtis (Stepfather) and Darlene Dolores Miley, Thomas Lyle Anderson; m. Suzanne Marie Anderson, July 30, 1988; 1 child, Kathryn Michelle. BA, Calif. State U., 1999. Secondary Profl. Clear Tchg. Credential Calif. Commn. on Tchr. Credentialing, 1999, cert. State Calif. Commn. Tchr. Credentialing, 2005. Asst. regional mgr. U.S. Dept. of Commerce, Bur. of the Census, San Pedro, Calif., 1988—90; tchr. Redondo Beach Unifed Sch. Dist., Calif., 1991—2000, Torrance Unifed Sch. Dist., Torrance, Calif., 2000—. Author: (book) Index to the Mayors of Redondo Beach, California, 1991; editor: (newsletter) 1812 Overtures, Golden State Patriot. Mem. Gen. Plan Adv. Com., Redondo Beach, Calif., 1989—92, South Bay Union HS Dist. Hist. Com., Redondo Beach, Calif.; state pres. Soc. of the War of 1812 in the State of Calif., 1989—92; state sec. SR in the State of Calif., 1989—92; state dep. gov. Soc. of Mayflower Descendants in the State of Calif., 1989—2003; mem. Redondo Beach Hist. Soc., Calif., 1993—95. Recipient Games of the XXIII Olympiad, LA Olympic Organizing Com., 1984, Ky. Col. Commn., Commonwealth of Ky., 1989, Medal of Distinction, Hon. Order Ky. Cols., 2005. Mem.: Calif. Coun. History Edn., Nat. Coun. History Edn., New Eng. Geneal. Libr., Orgn. of Am. Historians, Sons and Daughters of the Colonial and Antebellum Bench and Bar 1565-1861, Order of the Crown of Charlemange in the U.S., Flagon and Trencher, SAR in the State of Calif., Soc. of the War of 1812 in the State of Calif. (state pres. 1991—92, Pres's. Commendation 1990), Sons the Revolution in the State of Calif. (state sec. 1989—92, Pres's. Commendation 1992), The Soc. of the Descendants of the Colonial Clergy, Soc. of Mayflower Descendants in the State of Calif. (colony gov. 1999—2003). Democrat. Congregationalist. Avocations: genealogy, travel, local politcs. Personal E-mail: grega25721@roadrunner.com.

ANDERSON, HARRISON CLARKE, pathologist, educator, biomedical researcher; b. Louisville, Sept. 2, 1932; married, 1961. BA in Zoology, U. Louisville, 1954, MD, 1958. Diplomate Am. Bd. Pathology. Pathology intern Mass. Gen. Hosp., Boston, 1958-59; NIH rsch. trainee U. Louisville, Ky., 1959-60; resident in pathology Sloan Kettering Meml. Hosp, NYC, 1960-62; postdoctoral fellow Sloan Kettering Inst., Rye, NY, 1962-63; from asst. prof., assoc. prof. to prof. pathology SUNY Downstate Med. Ctr., Bklyn., 1963-78; prof. pathology, chmn. dept. U. Kans. Med. Ctr., Kansas City, Mo., 1978-90, Harrington prof. orthopedic rsch., 1990—; prof. emeritus pathology, 2002. Mem. study sect. NIH, Bethesda, Md., 1977—81, Bethesda, 1999—2005; chmn. Gordon Rsch. Conf. on Bone, Meriden, NH, 1981. Edit. bd. Am. Jour. Pathology, others, 1981—; contbr. articles to profl. jours. Recipient Biol. Mineralization Research award Internat. Assn. Dental Research, 1985, Sr. Faculty Research award U. Kans. Med. Ctr., 1986, Kappa Delta Orthopedic Rsch. award Orthopedic Rsch. Soc., 1982, Higuchi Biomed. Rsch. award U. Kansas, 1991; NIH rsch. fellow Strangeways Lab., Cambridge, Eng., 1971-72, NIH sr. rsch. fellow in cell biology Yale U., New Haven, , 1984-85; grantee NIH, 1967-2007. Mem. Am. Soc. Investigative Pathologists, Assn. Pathology Chmn. (pres. 1988-90), Am. Soc. Cell Biology, Am. Soc. Bone and Mineral Research, Orthopaedic Research Soc. Clubs: Am. Yacht (Rye); Carriage (Kansas City). Avocations: tennis, skiing, sailing. Office: U Kansas Dept Pathology 39th & Rainbow Kansas City KS 66160-0001 Home Phone: 913-262-8203; Office Phone: 913-588-7474. Business E-Mail: handerso@kumc.edu.

ANDERSON, HARRY W. (HUNK), retired food service executive; b. Corning, NY, Oct. 2, 1922; m. Mary Margaret Ransford, 1950. B, Hobart Coll., 1949, LLD (hon.), 1967, Mount St. Scholastica Coll., 1968. Co-founder Saga Corp. food svc., NY, 1948, v.p. NY, 1957—62, v.p., personnel Calif., 1962—68, sr. v.p., vice-chmn. of bd. Calif., 1968—77; ret., 1978. Charter mem., v.p. Coun. Personnel Officers. Co-founder Harry W. and Mary Margaret Anderson Charitable Found., Atherton, Calif.; trustee Mount St. Scholastica Coll., Kans. Named a Remarkable Alum, Hobart and William Smith Coll.; named one of Top 200 Collectors, ARTnews Mag., 2004. Avocation: Collecting NY Sch. contemporary art. Office: Harry W and Mary Margaret Anderson Charitable Found 62 Faxon Rd Atherton CA 94027-4046

ANDERSON, HERBERT HATFIELD, lawyer, farmer; b. Rainier, Oreg., Aug. 2, 1920; s. Odin A. and Mae (Hatfield) A.; m. Barbara Stuart Bastine, June 3, 1949; children: Linda, Catherine, Thomas, Amy, Elizabeth, Kenneth BA in Bus. Adminstrn., U. Oreg., 1940; JD, Yale U., 1949. Exec. trainee U.S. Steel Co., San Francisco, 1940-41; assoc. Koerner, Young, McColloch & Dezendorf, Portland, Oreg., 1949—54; ptnr. Spears, Lubersky, Bledsoe, Anderson, Young & Hilliard, 1954-90, Lane, Powell, Spears & Lubersky, Portland, 1990—. Instr. law Lewis and Clark Coll., Portland, 1950-70. Mem. planning adv. com. Yamhill County, Oreg., 1974-82; bd. dirs. Emanuel Hosp., 1967—; bd. dirs. Flyfisher Found., 1972—, pres., 1972-84; bd. dirs. Multnomah Law Libr., 1958—, sec. 1962-68, 77-94, pres., 1964-74. Served to maj., parachute inf. U.S. Army, 1942-46, ETO. Fellow Am. Bar Found. (chmn. Oreg. chpt. 1988—); mem. ABA (chmn. governing com. forum on health law 1984-89, chmn. standing com. on jud. selection, tenure and compensation 1978-80, Lawyer's Conf., exec. com. 1980-94, chmn. 1989-90, jud. adminstrn. divsn. coun. 1988-94, sr. lawyer's divsn. coun. 1987-89), Am. Judicature Soc. (bd. dirs. 1981-85), Soc. Law and Medicine, Nat. Health Lawyers Assn., Am. Acad. Hosp. Attys., Oreg. Soc. Hosp. Attys. (pres. 1984-85), Multnomah Bar Found. (bd. dirs. 1955—, pres. 1959-64, 87—), Nat. Bankruptcy Conf. (conferee 1964—, exec. com. 1976-79, chmn. farmer insolvency com. 1985-88), Nat. Assn. R.R. Trial Counsel, Oreg. Bar Assn. (del. to ABA 1966-68), Multnomah Bar Assn. (pres. 1955), Western States Bar Conf. (pres. 1967), Oreg. Asian Per Coun. (pres. 1989-91), Multnomah Athletic Club, Michelbook Country Club, Flyfishers Oreg. Club (pres. 1972), Flyfisher Found. (pres. 1957-67), Willamette Amateur Field Trial Club (pres. 1968-72), Amateur Field Trial Clubs of Am. (trustee 2002-), 101st Airborne Divsn. Assn., Masons, Sigma Chi. Democrat. Lutheran. Home: River Meadow Farm 19289 SE Neck Rd Dayton OR 97114-7815 Office Phone: 503-864-3601. Personal E-mail: hhanderson@verizon.net.

ANDERSON, HERSCHEL VINCENT, retired librarian; b. Charlotte, NC, Mar. 14, 1932; s. Paul Kemper and Lillian (Johnson) Anderson. BA, Duke U., 1954; MS, Columbia U., 1959. Library asst. Bklyn. Public Library, 1954-59; asst. bookmobile librarian King County Public Library, Seattle, 1959-62; asst. librarian Longview (Wash.) Public Library, 1962-63; librarian N.C. Mus. Art, Raleigh, 1963-64; audio-visual cons. N.C. State Library, Raleigh, 1964-68; dir. Sandhill Regional Library, Rockingham, NC, 1968-70; asso. state librarian Tenn. State Library and Archives, Nashville, 1970-72; unit dir. Colo. State Library, Denver, 1972-73; state librarian S.D. State Library, Pierre, 1973-80; dir. Mesa (Ariz.) Public Library, 1980-99. Founding mem., chief officers State Libr. Agys., 1973—80, bd. dirs.; dir. Bibliog. Ctr. Rsch., Denver, 1974—80, v.p., 1977; founding mem. Western Coun. St. Librs., 1975—80, v.p., 1978, pres., 79; mem. libr. technician tng. adv. com. Mesa CC, 1982—85, mem. commn. excellence, 1993—2003; chmn. Serials On-Line Ariz. Consortia, 1985—86; mem. Ariz. Libr. Devel. Coun., 1991—93, Ariz. State Libr. Adv. Coun., 1998—, chair, 1999—; mem. Libr. Facilities Adv. Bd., Gilbert, Ariz., 1999—2006. Mem., treas. Maricopa County Libr. Coun., 1981—99, pres., 1983, 1993; mem. hist. preservation com. City of Mesa, 2000—06, chmn., 2005—06; mem. Valley Citizens League, 1991—; sec. Sunridge Homeowners Assn., 1980—90, La Maricpsa Vaillas VI Homeowners Assn., 1990—99, 2001—; jr. warden St. Mark's Episcopal Ch., Mesa, 1985—87, vestryman, 1987—90, 1995—98, sr. warden, 1996—98, archivist, 2000—; del. ann. conv. Episcopal Diocese Ariz., 1989—92, 1994—98, mem. archives com., 1990—97, mem. Diosecan Coun. Episcopal, 1996—98; mem. steering com. N.E. Regional Parish, 1994—2004, chair Native Am. com., 1999—2004; bd. dirs. Sunridge Homeowners Assn., 1980—90, La Maricpsa Vaillas VI Homeowners Assn., 1990—99, 2001—. With US Army, 1955—57. Recipient Emeritus Honors, Ariz. Libr. Friends, 1987. Mem.: ALA, Nat. Cowboy and Western Heritage Mus., Heard Mus., Mesa Hist. Soc., N.C. Literary and Hist. Assn., Nat. Trust for Hist. Preservation, Ariz. Hist. Found., Ariz. Libr. Assn. (mem. exec. com. 1986—87), Mountain Plains Libr. Assn. (pres. 1974, bd. dirs. 1974—77, 1986—87, Intellectual Freedom award 1979), S.D. Libr. Assn. (life Libr. of Yr. award 1977), Kiwanis (bd. dirs. Mesa 1981—86, v.p. 1983, pres. 1985—86), Phi Kappa Psi. Home Phone: 480-898-9441. E-mail: andersonvince@aol.com.

ANDERSON, HUGH GEORGE, bishop; b. LA, Mar. 10, 1932; s. Reuben Leroy and Frances Sophia (Nielsen) A.; m. Synnøve Anna Hella, Nov. 3, 1956 (dec. Apr. 1982); 1 child, Erik; m. Jutta Ilse Fischer, July 2, 1983; children: Lars, Niels; 1 child, Kristi. AB, Yale U., 1953; BD, Luth. Theol. Sem., Phila., 1956, STM, 1958; MA, U. Pa., 1957, PhD, 1962; LittD, Lenoir Rhyne Coll., 1971; DD, Roanoke Coll., 1971, Wagner Coll., 1987, Gen. Theol. Sem., NYC, 1996, Luther Coll., Decorah, Iowa, 1996; LHD, Newberry Coll., 1979, Columbia Coll., SC, 1981. Ordained Luth. min. Tchg. fellow Luth. Theol. Sem., Phila., 1956—58; prof. ch. history Luth. Theol. So. Sem., Columbia, SC, 1958—70, dir. grad. studies, pres., 1970—82, Luther Coll., Decorah, Iowa, 1982—95; presiding bishop Evang. Luth. Ch. Am., Chgo., 1995—2001; ret., 2001. Chair Pub. House of the Evang. Luth. Ch. Am., 1987—93; co-chmn. U.S. Luth.-Roman Cath. Dialogue, 1979—90; mem. Commn. for a New Luth. Ch., 1982—86; v.p. Luth. World Fedn., 1996—. Author: Lutheranism in the Southeastern States, 1969, A Good Time to be the Church, 1997; co-author: Lutherans in North America, 1975; translator: I Believe (H. Thielicke), 1968, Historical Commentary on the Augsburg Confession (W. Maurer), 1986. Bd. dirs. Minn. Pub. Radio, St. Paul, 1983—91. Mem.: Luth. World Fedn. (commn. on studies 1984—90). Lutheran. Avocations: astronomy, sailing.

ANDERSON, J. TRENT, lawyer; b. Indpls., July 22, 1939; s. Robert C. and Charlotte M. (Pfeifer) Anderson; m. Judith J. Zimmerman, Sept. 8, 1962; children: Evan M., Molly K. BS, Purdue U., 1961; LLB, U. Va., 1964. Bar: Ill. 1965, Ind. 1965. Tchg. asst. Law Sch. U. Calif., Berkeley, 1964-65; assoc. Mayer, Brown & Platt, Chgo., 1965-72; ptnr. Mayer, Brown, Rowe & Maw LLP, Chgo., 1972—. Instr. Loyola U. Law Sch., Chgo., 1985. Mem.: Mich. Shores Club, Union League Club, Law Club. Home: 3037 Iroquois Rd Wilmette IL 60091-1106 Office: Mayer Brown Rowe & Maw LLP 71 S Wacker Dr Chicago IL 60606-4637 Office Phone: 312-701-7365. Business E-Mail: janderson@mayerbrown.com.

ANDERSON, JACK ROY, healthcare company executive; b. Mansfield, Ohio, Feb. 14, 1925; s. Roy L. and Katherine (Munson) A.; m. Rose-Marie J. Garcia, June 24, 1950; children: Gail Ellen, Neil Robert, Barbara Ann. BS, Miami U., Oxford, Ohio, 1947; MS, Columbia Bus. Sch., 1949. Acctg. mgr. Time Inc., NYC, 1950-59; asst. to controller W.R. Grace & Co., NYC, 1959-62; v.p., treas. Hartford Publs., Inc., NYC, 1962-65; controller McCall Corp., NYC, 1965-68; v.p. Reliance Group, Inc., NYC, 1968-70; pres., dir. Hosp. Affiliates Internat., Inc., Nashville, 1970-76, chmn. bd., dir., 1977-81; chmn. INA Health Care Group, Dallas, 1978-81; pres. Manor Care, Inc., Silver Spring, Md., 1981-82; chmn. Republic Health Corp., 1981—82, vice chmn, 1982—86; chmn. Horizen Health Corp., 1981—82; pres. Calver Corp., Dallas, 1982—; chmn. TakeCare, Inc., 1988—94, FHP Internat. Corp., 1995—99. Adj. faculty Vanderbilt Owen Grad. Sch. Mgmt., 1978—79. Author: The Road to Recovery, 1976. Trustee Nat. Com. for Quality Health Care, 1979—87, vice chmn., 1979—82; mem. bus. adv. coun. Miami U., 1975—78, chmn., 1978; mem. bd. overseers Hoover Instn. on War, Revolution and Peace, Stanford U.; mem. Pres.'s Cir., NAS, NAE, Inst. Medicine. Lt. (j.g.) USNR, 1943—46. Mem.: Reform Club, Greenwich Country Club, Desert Forest Golf Club, Double Eagle Club, Blind Brook Club, Beta Alpha Psi, Sigma Chi, Beta Gamma Sigma (hon.).

ANDERSON, JACQUELINE ANNETTE, information technology specialist; b. Balt., Jan. 20, 1962; d. Edward Anderson and Beatrice Ward. AA in Bus. Adminstrn., cert. in Office Skills, C.C. of Balt., 1984; BA in Mgmt. sci., Coppin State Univ., 2001. Sec. Social Security Adminstrn., Balt., 1982—86, computer asst., 1986—99, computer specialist, 2005—. Anointed networking specialist, 1999—. Election judge voting polls Bd. Election, Balt., 1996—99; chmn. Penal Com., 1980—; interviewer Senatorial Scholarship Com., Balt., 1996—2000. Mem.: Black Affairs Adv. Coun., Toastmasters Club (v.p. #7046 1999—2000, treas. #7046 2000—, Trophy 2000). Avocations: sewing, movies, reading, tennis. Personal E-mail: jcdarius@aol.com.

ANDERSON, JAMES ALFRED, cognitive science professor; b. Detroit, July 31, 1940; s. Courtney Alfred and Catherine (Bullock) A.; m. Diana De Vincenzi, Nov. 1, 1969; 1 child, Eric David. BS, MIT, 1962, PhD, 1967. Postdoctoral fellow UCLA, 1967-71; research assoc. Rockefeller U., NYC, 1971-73; asst. prof. cognitive and linguistic scis. Brown U., Providence, 1973—78, assoc. prof., 1978-85, prof., 1985—, chmn. dept. cognitive and linguistic scis., 1993—2002. Chmn. cognitive functional neurosci. rev. panel NIMH, 1992-94; mem. adv. bd. Social, Behavioral and Econ. Scis. Directorate, NSF, 1996-99; founder Artemis Assocs., Inc., 1989-2004. Editor: (with G. Hinton) Parallel Models of Associative Memory, 1981, (with S. Lehmkuhle and W. Levy) Synaptic Modification, Neuron Selectivity and Nervous System Organization, 1985, (with E. Rosenfeld) Neurocomputing: Some Important Papers, 1988, (with E. Rosenfeld and A. Pellionisz) Neurocomputing 2, 1990, An Introduction to Neural Networks, 1995; (with E. Rosenfeld) Talking Nets, 1998. Recipient Info. Sci. award, Joint Conf. on Info. Sci., 2002; grantee, NSF, 1979, 1985, 1991, 1997, Office Naval Rsch., 1986, 1991, 1996, Def. Advanced Rsch. Projects Agy., 2002. Mem. Cognitive Sci. Soc., Psychonomic Soc., Soc. for Neurosci., Soc. for Math. Psychology, Internat. Neural Network Soc. (governing bd. 1987-95), Sigma Xi. Avocation: amateur radio. Home: 1 Mathewson Rd Barrington RI 02806-4414 Office: Brown U Dept Cognitive & Linguistic Scis 190 Thayer St Providence RI 02912-9067 Home Phone: 401-245-8803; Office Phone: 401-863-2195. Business E-Mail: James_Anderson@Brown.edu.

ANDERSON, JAMES E., lawyer; b. Jan. 31, 1965; BA, Univ. Utah, 1988; JD magna cum laude, Brigham Young Univ., 1992. Bar: Utah 1992, DC 1995. Staff atty. Office of Investment Co. Regulation SEC; ptnr., co-chmn. Investment Mgmt. group Wilmer Cutler Pickering Hale & Dorr, Washington, 1994—. Co-author: Investment Advisers: Law & Compliance; author (contbr.): Mutual Fund Regulation. Office: Wilmer Cutler Pickering Hale & Dorr 1875 Pennsylvania Ave NW Washington DC 20006-3642 Office Phone: 202-663-6180. Office Fax: 202-663-6363. Business E-Mail: james.anderson@wilmerhale.com.

ANDERSON, JAMES FRANCIS, lawyer; b. Glen Ridge, NJ, June 13, 1965; BA, Seton Hall U., 1987, JD, 1990. Bar: N.J. 1991, U.S. Supreme Ct. 1995. Pvt. practice, Spring Lake, NJ, 1991—2001; staff atty. Ocean-Monmouth Legal Svcs., Freehold, NJ, 2001—. Pro bono atty. Ocean-Monmouth Legal Svcs., Freehold, N.J., 1991-2001; mentor Manasquan (NJ) HS, 1994. Personal E-mail: janderson@monmouth.com.

ANDERSON, JAMES FREDERICK, clergyman; b. Elizabeth, NJ, Aug. 23, 1927; s. Fred and Hazel Minerva (Brown) A.; m. Bette Dillensnyder, Sept. 8, 1951; children: Judith (Mrs. Wayne Westbury) (dec.), James Frederick, Mark, Rebecca (Mrs. Patrick Williams). BA, Princeton U., 1948; BD, Princeton Theol. Sem., 1952; DD, Alma Coll., 1974. Ordained to ministry Presbyn. Ch., 1952; chaplain Hun Sch. for Boys, Princeton, 1953; instr. religion Lafayette Coll., Easton, Pa., 1954-55; pastor Presbyn. chs., Catasauqua, Pa., 1956-61, Narberth, Pa., 1961-66, Second Presbyn. Ch., Richmond, Va., 1966-72, Kirk in the Hills, Bloomfield Hills, Mich., 1972-94, pastor emeritus, 1994—. Trustee emeritus Alma (Mich.) Coll. With USNR, 1945-46. Home: 3808 Haylor's Beach Way Glen Allen VA 23060-7232

ANDERSON, JAMES GEORGE, sociologist, educator, communications educator; b. Balt., July 24, 1936; s. Clair Sherrill and Kathryn Ann (Plovanich) A.; m. Marilyn Anderson, 1984; children: Robin Marie, James Brian, Melissa Lee, Derek Clair. B in Engring. Scis. in Chem. Engring, Johns Hopkins U., 1957, MSE in Ops. Rsch. and Indsl. Engring., 1959, MAT in Chemistry and Math., 1960, PhD in Edn. and Sociology, 1964. Adminstrv. asst. to dean Eve. Coll., Johns Hopkins U., 1964-65, dir. divsn. engring., 1965-66; rsch. prof. ednl. adminstrn. N.Mex. State U., 1966-70; mem. faculty Purdue U., Lafayette, Ind., 1970—, prof. sociology, 1974—, prof. com., 2004—; asst. dean for analytical studies Sch. Humanities, Social Sci. and Edn., Lafayette, Ind., 1975-78. Assoc. dir. AIDS Rsch. Ctr., Purdue U., 1991—, co-dir. Rural Ctr. for AIDS/STD Prevention, 1993-2006; adj. prof. med. sociology grad. med. edn. program Meth. Hosp. Ind., 1991—; dir. Social Rsch. Inst., Purdue U., 1995-98; cons. in field. Guest editor spl. issue on simulation in health sci.; spl. issues on modeling epidemics: spl. issue on simulation in med. informatics, Jour. the Am. Med. Informatics Assn., 2002, issue on simulation in health care mgmt., Health Care Mgmt. Sci., 2002, 07, issue on performance modeling and simulation in healthcare information systems, Simulation, 2007. Mem. Am. Assn. for Med. Systems and Informatics Del. to the Peoples Republic of China, 1985; mem., citizens amb. People to People Med. Informatics Del. to Hungary and Russia, 1993. USPHS grant; recipient award for outstanding paper Am. Assn. Med. Sys. and Informatics, 1983, Gov. award State of Ind., 1987, T. Hale New Investigators award Assn. Am. Med. Coll., 1988, Wyeth-Ayerst/William Campbell Felch, MD award Alliance for Continuing Med. Edn., 1995, Seeds of Excellence award, Purdue U., 2005. Fellow: Am. Coll. Med. Informatics; mem.: APHA, AAUP, AAAS (rep. soc. for computer simulation biol. scis. sect. 1992—99), Social Sci. Computing Assn. (chair life scis. 1991—), Am. Sociol. Assn. (chair sect. sociology and computers 2000—01), Internat. Soc. Sys. Sci. in Health Care, Internat. Network for Social Network Analysis (chair life scis. 1997—), Soc. Modeling and Computer Simulation (sr.; assoc. v.p. simulation in health care 1992—), Am. Med. Informatics Assn. (internat. affairs com. 1993—96, chmn. sect. ethical, legal and social issues 1997—2000, sci. program com. ann. conf. 1999, mem. editl. bd. 2000—, chmn. sect. on quality improvement 2002—04, guest editor 2002, Best Theoretical Paper award 1997), Am. Ednl. Rsch. Assn. (treas. spl. interest group 1969—71), Am. Sociol. Assn., Assn. for Computing Machinery. Business E-Mail: andersonj@purdue.edu.

ANDERSON, JAMES GILBERT, chemistry professor; BS in Physics, U. Wash., Seattle, 1966; PhD in Physics and Astrogeophysics, U. Colo., Boulder, 1970. Prof. Harvard U., Cambridge, Mass., 1978—, now Philip S. Weld prof. atmospheric chemistry, chmn. dept. chemistry and chem. biology. Recipient Am. Chem. Soc. award, 1989, Gustavus John Esselen award, 1993, Earth Day Internat. award UN, 1992, Arts and Scis. Disting. Alumnus Achievement award U. Wash., 1993, E.O. Lawrence award in environ. sci. and tech., 1993. Fellow Am. Geophysical Union, Am. Assn. for the Advancement of Sci., Am. Acad. of Arts and Sci.; mem. NAS (Arthur Lay prize and lectureship 1996). Achievements include research in stratospheric physics and chemistry central to the understanding of atmospheric ozone and the ozone hole above the Antarctic. Office: Harvard U Dept of Chem & Chem Biology 12 Oxford St Cambridge MA 02138-2902

ANDERSON, JAMES M., pathologist; BS in Chemistry, U. Wis., Eau Claire; PhD in Chemistry, Oreg. State U. Prof. pathology, macromolecular sci. and biomed. engring. Inst. of Pathology, Case Western Res. U., Cleve. Cons. NIH, FDA. Contbr. over 300 articles to profl. jours.; editor: Jour. of Biomed. Materials Rsch. Mem.: Soc. for Biomaterials (past pres.), Controlled Release Soc. (pres.), Inst. of Medicine, 2004 (life). Office: Case Western Reserve Univ Dept Pathology 2103 Cornell Rd Cleveland OH 44106 Business E-Mail: jma6@case.edu.

ANDERSON, JAMES MILTON, lawyer, hospital administrator; b. Chgo., Dec. 29, 1941; s. Milton H. and Eunice (Carlson) A.; m. Marjorie Henry Caldwell, Jan. 22, 1966; children: James Milton, Joseph H., Hilding F., Marjorie II. BA, Yale U., New Haven, Conn., 1963; JD, Vanderbilt U., Nashville, 1966. Bar: Ohio 1967. Assoc. rifm Taft, Stettinius & Hollister, Cin., 1966-75, ptnr., 1975-77, 82-96, mem. exec. com., 1975-77, 91-96; pres. US ops., dir. Xomox Corp., Cin., 1977-81; sec. Access Corp., 1984-96; asst. sec. Carlisle Cos., 1985-90; bd. dirs. Nat. Stock Exch., 1978—, chmn., 1980-89. Bd. dirs. Command Sys. Inc., 1986—2002; trustee, chmn. Monarch Found., 1988—; assoc. sr. v.p. med. affairs U. Cin., 1997—; bd. adminstrs. Coun. Tchg. Hosps., 2000—04; dir. Nat. Assn. Children's Hosps. and Related Instns., 2002—; bd. dirs. 3CDC Inc., 2003—, Uptown Consortium, 2004—, Union Ctrl. Life Ins. Co., 2002—06; chmn. bd. dirs. Cin. br. Fed. Res. Bank Cleve., 2005—; mem. US Medicaid Commn., 2005—06; bd. dirs. UNIFI Mutual Holding Co., 2006—, Inst. for Healthcare Improvement, 2007—. Mem. Indian Hill Coun., 1981-89, vice-mayor, 1985-87, mayor, 1987-89; mem. Hamilton County Airport Authority, 1980-85; trustee Children's Hosp. Med. Ctr., Cin., 1979—, chmn. bd. trustees, 1991-96, pres., CEO, 1996—; trustee The Children's Hosp. Found., 1990—, chmn. bd. trustees, 1990-93; trustee Cin. Ctr. for Devel. Disorders, 1969—, pres., 1974-80; trustee Dan Beard coun. Boy Scouts Am., 1982—, chmn., 1984-87, area pres. Ea. Ctrl. Region, 1989-91; trustee Cin. Mus. Natural History, 1984-87, Coll. Mt. St. Joseph, 1990-98; trustee Joy Outdoor Edn. Ctr., 1984-2000, pres., 1991-93, chmn., 1993-95. Capt. AUS, 1966-68. Decorated Bronze Star with two oak leaf clusters, Air medal. Mem. ABA, Ohio Bar Assn., Cin. Bar Assn., Valve Mfrs. Assn., Young Pres. Orgn., Camargo Club, Queen City Club, Commonwealth Club, Yale Club of N.Y., Cin. Yale Club, Order of Coif, Comml. Club. Avocation: sailing. Office: 3333 Burnet Ave Cincinnati OH 45229-3026

ANDERSON, JAMES WINGO, physician; b. Hinton, W.Va., Aug. 6, 1936; s. Fred Wingo and Georgia Lee (Whittaker) A.; m. Gay Veree Gilbert, June 7, 1957; children: Katherine, Steven. BS, W.Va. U., 1957; MD, Northwestern U., 1961; MS, Mayo Clinic, 1965. Intern Presbyn. Med. Ctr., Denver; resident, fellow Mayo Clinic, Rochester, Minn.; asst. prof. medicine U. Calif., San Francisco, 1968-73; prof. medicine, clin. nutrition U. Ky. Coll. Medicine, Lexington, 1973—; pres., founder HCF Nutrition Found., Lexington, 1979—. Author: Diabetes-A Practical Guide to Healthy Living, 1981, Dr. Anderson's High Fiber Fitness Plan, 1994, Dr. Anderson;s Antioxidant Antiaging, 1996. Trustee Georgetown (Ky.) Coll., 1988—, chmn. bd. trustees, 1994-96. Capt. U.S. Army, 1965-68. Fellow Am. Coll. Physicians. Republican. Baptist. Home: 913 Taborlake Ct Lexington KY 40502-3032 Office: MN 524 UK Med Ctr Lexington KY 40532-0298 Home Phone: 895-269-6642; Office Phone: 859-323-5822.

ANDERSON, J.C., oil and gas industry executive, rancher; b. Oakland, Nebr. Student, Midland Coll., Fremont, Nebr., 1949-51; BSc in Petroleum Engring., U. Tex., 1954. With Amoco Prodn. Co., various locations; chief engr. Amoco Can., Calgary, Alta., Canada, 1966-68; founder, chmn. bd., CEO Anderson Exploration Ltd., Calgary, 1968—2001; rancher Anderson Ranch; pvt. practice. With Counter-Intelligence Corps, U.S. Army, 1954-56. Mem. Assn. Profl. Engrs., Geologists and Geophysicists of Alta., Soc. Petroleum Engrs., Can. Soc. Petroleum Geologists. Office: Ste 239 132-250 Shawville Blvd SE Calgary AB Canada T2Y 2Z7 Office Phone: 403-256-7550. E-mail: husker@telus.net.

ANDERSON, JEFFREY ELTON, history professor; b. Mansfield, Ohio, Oct. 5, 1974; s. William Edward and Reba Loisetta Anderson; m. Nancy Lynn Sillavan, June 28, 1997; children: Michael Lee, David Arthur. BA, Samford U., 1997; MA, U. Fla., 1999, PhD, 2002. Asst. prof. Middle Ga. Coll., Cochran, Ga., 2003—07, U. La., Monroe, 2007—. Presenter in field. Author: Conjure in African American Society, 2005. Tutor First Bapt. Ch., Gainesville, Fla., 1999—2000, tchr. Sunday Sch. Cochran, Ga., 2005—. Recipient Melvin E. Bradford Dissertation prize, St. George Tucker Soc., 2003. Mem.: Ala. Assn. Historians, Ala. Hist. Assn., So. Hist. Assn. So. Bapt. Avocations: travel, reading, board games.

ANDERSON, JEFFREY LEE, physician, anesthesiologist, consultant; b. Fontana, Calif., Feb. 3, 1959; s. Earle R. and Joyce E. Anderson; m. Crystal

G. Anderson, Dec. 18, 1987; children: Kimberly, Kristin. BS, USAF Acad., 1981; MD, Loma Linda U., 1985. Cert. in anesthesiology. Resident in anesthesiology Loma Linda U. Med. Ctr., Calif., 1985-89; chief anesthesiologist USAF Hosp., Mather AFB, Calif., 1989-93; staff anesthesiologist Mercy Hosp. of Folsom, Calif., 1990—, Mercy Gen. Hosp., Sacramento, 1992—, Mercy San Juan Hosp., Carmichael, Calif., 1997—, Creekside Surgery Ctr., Folsom, Calif., 2005—; chief anesthesiologist Folsom Surgery Ctr., 2001—. Medicolegal cons. Med. Bd. Calif., Sacramento, 1995—; clin. faculty U. Calif. Davis Sch. Medicine, 1993-96; anesthesia cons. Blue Shield of Calif., 1998—. Co-author: (textbook) Manual of Postanesthesia Care, 1993. Instr., course dir. ACLS, Am. Heart Assn., Sacramento, 1992—; physician Mercy White Rock Free Clin., 1994—. Mem. Am. Soc. Anesthesiologists, Calif. Soc. Anesthesiologists, C. of C. Office: 1650 Creekside Dr Folsom CA 95630-3400 Office Phone: 916-983-7490. Personal E-mail: folsomlakeortho@aol.com.

ANDERSON, JERRY MAYNARD, retired speech educator; b. Deronda, Wis., Sept. 16, 1933; s. Jens B. and Mamie P. (Hanson) A.; m. Betty Lou Schultz, Feb. 7, 1959; children: Gregory J., Timothy B. BS, Wis. State U. at River Falls, 1958; MS, No. Ill. U., 1959; PhD, Mich. State U., 1964; postgrad., U. Minn., 1987, U. Ariz., 1997. Instr. speech U. Maine, 1959-61; asst. prof. speech, dir. forensics Mich. State U., 1961-68; prof., chmn. dept. speech and dramatic arts Central Mich. U., Mt. Pleasant, 1968-72, vice provost, 1972—73; provost, v.p. acad. affairs and prof. speech Western Wash. U., 1973-75; vice chancellor, prof. speech U. Wis., Oshkosh, 1975-79; pres., prof. speech Ball State U., Muncie, Ind., 1979-81; sr. cons. Am. Assn. State Colls. and Univs., Washington, 1981-82; rsch. adminstr. U. Wis., Stout, 1982—85; v.p. devel. Concordia Coll., Minn., 1985-88, prof. speech comm. Minn., 1988-99, prof. emeritus Minn., 2000—; pres. Anderson and Assoc. Cons., 2000—. Author: Handbook for Forensic Students, 1963, Readings in Argumentation, 1968, Essays in Forensics, 1970, Case Studies in Public Relations: The 1994 U.S. West Crisis in Fargo, 1998; contbr. articles to profl. jours., chapters to books. Trustee Lake Wapogasset Assn.; bd. dirs. Radio Sta. WPCA. With USN, 1952—54. Recipient 1st Sr. Disting. Professionalism award Central Mich. U., 1971; Research fellow Harry S Truman Found., 1965; fellow Am. Council on Edn. Acad. Adminstrn. Internship Program, 1971-72; Recipient Disting. Alumnus award Delta Sigma Rho-Tau Kappa Alpha, 1980; Sagamore of Wabash Public Service award Gov. of Ind., 1980 Mem. Ctrl. States Speech Assn. (pres. 1973, Outstanding Young Tchr. award 1966), Mich. Speech Assn. (pres. 1967-68), Am. Forensic Assn. (pres. 1972-74, Disting. Svc. award 1994), Midwest Forensic Assn. (pres. 1969-72), Speech Comm. Assn. (legis. coun. 1967, legis. assembly 1975), Kiwanis, Rotary. Office Phone: 715-268-8494. Personal E-mail: jandbander@amerytel.net. *During my adult years the aphorism attributed to the late Senator Robert M. laFollette, Sr., has guided my work with others: "Give the people the facts and freedom to discuss and all will go well."*.

ANDERSON, JERRY WILLIAM, JR., diversified financial services company executive, educator; b. Stow, Mass., Jan. 14, 1926; s. Jerry William and Heda Charlotte (Petersen) A.; m. Joan Hukill Balyeat, Sept. 13, 1947; children: Katheleen, Diane. BS in Physics, U. Cin., 1949, PhD in Econs., 1976; MBA, Xavier U., 1959. Rsch. and test project engr. Wright-Patterson AFB, Ohio, 1949-53; project engr., electronics divsn. AVCO Corp., Cin., 1953-70, program mgr., 1970-73; program dir. Cin. Electronics Corp., 1973-78; pres. Anderson Industries Unltd., 1978—. Chmn. dept. mgmt. and mgmt. info. svcs. Xavier U., 1980-89, prof. mgmt., 1989-94, prof. emeritus, 1994—; lectr. No. Ky. U., 1977-78; tech. adviser Cin. Tech. Coll., 1971-80; co-founder, exec. v.p. Loving God Complete Bible Christian Ministries, 1988—. Contbr. articles on radars, lasers, infrared detection equipment, air pollution to govt. pubs. and prof. jours.; author: 3 books in field; reviewer, referee: Internat. Jour. Energy Sys., 1985—86. Mem. Madeira City Planning Commn., Ohio, 1962-80; founder, pres. Grassroots, Inc., 1964; active United Appeal, Heart Fund, Multiple Sclerosis Fund. With USNR, 1943-46. Named Man of Yr., City of Madeira, 1964. Mem. MADD, VFW (life), Am. Mgmt. Assn., Assn. Energy Engrs. (charter), Internat. Acad. Mgmt. and Mktg., Nat. Right to Life, Assn. Cogeneration Engrs. (charter), Assn. Environ. Engrs. (charter), Am. Legion (past comdr.), Acad. Mgmt., Madeira Civic Assn. (past v.p.), Cin. Art Mus., Cin. Zoo, Colonial Williamsburg Found., Omicron Delta Epsilon. Republican. Home and Office: 7208 Sycamorehill Ln Cincinnati OH 45243-2101 Office Phone: 513-561-7685.

ANDERSON, JOAN BALYEAT, theology studies educator, minister; b. Cin., Apr. 14, 1926; d. Hal Donal and Myrtle (Skinner) Hukill Balyeat; m. Jerry William Anderson, Jr., Sept. 13, 1947; children: Katheleen, Diane. AA, Stephens Coll., 1946. Ordained Christian minister Ohio, 1988. Christian ch. bible tchr., Cin., 1944—; Christian counselor, advisor, 1964—; founder, pres., dir., ruling elder, and pastor Loving God Complete Bible Christian Ministries and First Ch., Cin., 1988—. Christian Bible tchr., preacher, pastor daily and Sunday radio throughout the east and midwest, 1988—, world wide internet, 2006—. Mem. Am. Conservative Cause, 1998—2001, Capitol His. Soc., 2000—; legacy leader supporter George Washington's Mt. Vernon, 2001—; coord., collector Heart Fund, T.B., 1948—90; civic assn. officer, rep. edn. com. to all Madeira Schs., 1960—62; co-founder, officer Grassroots, Inc., Cin., 1962—65; mem. Cin. Art Mus., 1972—, Cin. Zoo, 1974—, Colonial Williamsburg Found., 1979—, Nat. Right to Life, 1980—, MADD, 1985—, Heritage Found., 1996—, Am. Conservative Union, 1998, Ronald Reagan Presdl. Found., 1998—, Parents TV Coun., 1998—2001, Am. Policy Ctr., 1998—2001, US Justice Found., 1998—, Nat. Right to Work Legal Def. Found., 1998—, Nat. Security Ctr., 1998—, US Intelligence Ctr., 1998—, Jud. Watch, 1999—, Young Ams. Found., 2000—; supporter The Liberty Com., 2001—; lifelong activist for preservation of US Constn. and Bill of Rights; mem. US Rep. Senatorial Adv. Com., Washington and Cin., 1987—88, Rep. Senatorial Commn., Washington & Cin., 1996—2000, Am. Prayer Network, 1998—. Master: Blue Book of Cin. Avocation: travel. Home: 7208 Sycamorehill Ln Cincinnati OH 45243-2101 Office: Loving God Complete Bible Christian Mins/1st Ch PO Box 43404 Cincinnati OH 45243-2101

ANDERSON, JOAN R., secondary school educator; b. Logan, Utah, Apr. 19, 1952; d. Eleroy and Fae Rasmuson; m. Craig Weilenmann Anderson; children: Paul, Brian. BA, Utah State U., 1974; MA, U. Utah, 1980. Adj. prof. U. Utah, Salt Lake City, 1980—82, Westminster Coll., Salt Lake City, 1992—94; work-based learning coord. Murray (Utah) HS, 1999—. Mem. Utah Symphony and Opera Guild, Salt Lake City, 2000—02. Mem.: UWBLA (membership chair 2003—04, pres.-elect 2004—05, pres. 2005—), Murray C. of C. (bd. dirs., chair 2003—05). Mem. Lds Ch. Avocations: reading, tennis, quilting. E-mail: joanderson@murrayschools.org.

ANDERSON, JOHN ALBERT, physician; b. Ashtabula, Ohio, Jan. 25, 1935; s. Albert Gunnard Anderson and Martha Anetta (Bieshline) White; m. Nicole Jeanne Anderson, July 10, 1963; children: Carole, John-Marc, Christopher B. BS, U. Ill., 1958, MD, 1960. Diplomate Am. Bd. Pediat., Am. Bd. Allergy and Immunology. Intern U. Ill., 1960-61, resident in pediat. Chgo., 1961-62, U.S. Naval Hosp., Bethesda, Md., 1964-65; fellow in allergy and immunology Children's Hosp., Washington, 1967-69; mem. sr. staff Henry Ford Hosp., Detroit, 1969-99, dir. pediat. allergy fellowship program, 1969-77, dir. allergy and immunology program, 1977-99, head divsn. allergy and immunology, dept. pediatrics, 1977-99, chmn. dept. pediatrics, 1982-90; physician Vivra Asthma and Allergy, Tucson, 1999-2000; with Vivra Asthma and Allergy, Inc., 2000—02; physician Allergy and Asthma Ctr. Ariz., Tucson, 2001—03, Aspen Med. Ctr., Fort Collins, Colo., 2003—05, Allergy and Asthma Care Ariz. PLLC, Yuma, 2006—. Clin. prof. U. Mich., Ann Arbor, 1985—94; prof. pediat. Case Western Res. U., 1994—99; dir. Am. Bd. Allergy and Immunology, 1990—96, sec., 1995—96. Contbr. articles Contbr. more than 60 articles to profl. jours. Lt. comdr. USN, 1962-66. Fellow Am. Acad. Allergy, Asthma and Immunology (pres. 1990-91), Am. Acad. Pediat. (chmn. allergy sect. 1979-82), Am. Coll. Allergy, Asthma & Immunology, Mich. Allergy Soc. (pres. 1978-79); mem. Asthma and Allergy Found. Am. (dir. 1992-99, v.p. med. affairs 1992-95, v.p. rsch. 1995-99), Coun. Med. Splty. Socs. (bd. dirs. 1992-94), Am. Bd. Med. Specialists, Sci. Advisors Internat. Life Scis. (allergy sect. 1990-2003). Home: 1609 S 42d Ave Yuma AZ 85365 Office: Allergy and Asthma Care Ariz PLLC 2451 S Ave A Ste 22 Yuma AZ 85364 Office Phone: 928-344-2300.

ANDERSON, JOHN DAVID, architect; b. New Haven, Dec. 24, 1926; s. William Edward and Norma Vere (Carson) A.; m. Florence A. Van Dyke, Aug. 26, 1950; children— Robert Stewart, David Carson. AB cum laude, Harvard U., 1949, MArch, 1952; LHD (hon.), U. Colo., 2006. Draftsman John K. Monroe, Architect, Denver, 1952-54; draftsman, designer, assoc. Wheeler & Lewis, Architects, Denver, 1954-60; pvt. practice Denver, 1960-64; ptnr. Anderson, Barker Rinker, Architects, Denver, 1965-69, A-B-R Partnership, Architects, Denver, 1970-75; prin., CEO Anderson Mason Dale P.C., Denver, 1975-96, sr. v.p., 1997—. Vis. lectr. U. Colo., U. N.Mex., U. Nebr., U. Cape Town, Colo. State U., Plymouth Polytech., Eng.; chmn. Colo. Gov.'s Task Force on Removal of Archtl. Barriers, 1972-74; vice chmn. Colo. Bd. Non-Residential Energy Conservation Stds., 1978-80. Prin. works include: Front Range Community Coll., Westminster, 1977, Solar Energy Rsch. Inst., Golden, 1980 (award winning solar heated structures). Served with USNR, 1944-46. Fellow AIA (pres. Colo. chpt. 1967, Western Mountain region dir. 1995-97, Silver medal, 1984, Firm of Yr. award 1986 Western Mountain region); mem. AIA (Arch. of Yr. award 1987, pres. 1971, nat. v.p. 1999, 1st v.p. 2000, pres. 2001), Internat. Solar Energy Soc., Coun. Edn!. Facility Planners (internat. chmn. energy com. 1980). Democrat. Congregationalist. Home: 57 S Rainbow Trail Golden CO 80401-8341 Office: Anderson Mason Dale Architects 1615 17th St Denver CO 80202-1293 Business E-Mail: janderson@amdarchitects.com.

ANDERSON, JOHN DAVID, JR., aerospace engineer; b. Lancaster, Pa., Oct. 1, 1937; s. John David and Esther Pearl (Stoneback) A.; m. Sarah Allen West, Sept. 11; children: Katherine Josephine, Elizabeth Esther. B.Aero. Engring. with honors (Gen. Motors scholar, J. Hillis Meml. scholar), U. Fla., 1959; PhD in Aero. Engring., Ohio State U. Chief hypersonics group Naval Ordnance Lab., White Oak, Md., 1966-73; prof., chmn. dept. aerospace engring. U. Md., College Park, 1973-99; prof. emeritus U. Md., College Park, 1999—; Charles Lindbergh prof. Nat. Air Space Mus. Smithsonian Instn., 1986-87; curator for aerodynamics Nat. Air Space Mus., Smithsonian Instn., 1998—. Author: Gasdynamic Lasers: An Introduction, 1976, Introduction to Flight: Its Engineering and History, 1978, 5th edit., 2000, Modern Compressible Flow: with Historical Perspective, 1982, 3d edit., 2003, Fundamentals of Aerodynamics, 1984, 4th edit., 2007, Hypersonic and High Temperature Gasynamics, 1989, Computational Fluid Dynamics, 1995; History of Aerodynamics, and Its Impact on Flying Machines, 1997, Aircraft Performance and Design, 1999, The Airplane: A History of Its Technology, 2003, Inventing Flight, 2004; contbr. articles to profl. jours. Served with USAF, 1959-62. Named Disting. scholar/tchr. U. Md., 1981-82; NSF fellow, NASA fellow Ohio State U., 1966; recipient Meritorious Civilian Svc. award Naval Ordnance Lab., 1972 Fellow Washington Acad. Scis. (Engring. Sci. award 1975), AIAA, Royal Aeronaut. Soc.; mem. Am. Soc. Engring. Edn., Am. Phys. Soc., Sigma Xi, Tau Beta Pi, Sigma Tau, Phi Kappa Phi, Phi Eta Sigma. Roman Catholic. Office: U Md Dept Aerospace Engring College Park MD 20742-0001 also: Aeronautics Dept Nat Air and Space Mus Smithsonian Inst Washington DC 20560-0312 Office Phone: 202-633-2632. Business E-Mail: andersonja@si.edu. *A prescription for success in professional life involves a proper balance of hard work, long hours, awareness and clear thinking, with a goal-oriented philosophy and outright love of one's profession. In addition, one must have the desire, abilities and opportunities to accomplish his goals.*

ANDERSON, JOHN EDWARD, mechanical engineering educator; b. Chgo., May 15, 1927; s. Claus Oscar and Ruth Melvina (Engstrom) A.; m. Cynthia Louise Howard, May 24, 1975; children: Candice, James, Stanley. BME, Iowa State U., 1949; MSME, U. Minn., 1955; PhD, MIT, 1962. Registered profl. engr., Minn., Ill. Aero. research scientist Nat. Adv. Com. for Aeros., Langley Field, Va., 1949-51; devel. engr. Honeywell, Inc., Mpls., 1951-53, research engr., 1953-55, prin. research engr., 1955-58, research project engr., 1954-58, sr. staff engr., 1958-62, mgr. space systems, 1963; mem. faculty U. Minn., Mpls., 1963-86, prof. mech. engring., 1971-86, Boston U., 1986-94. Cons. Colo. Regional Transp. Dist., 1974-75, Raytheon Co., 1975-76, Mannesmann Demag, 1978-79, Arthr D. Little, Inc., 1981, Indpls. Transit Commn., 1979-81, Davy McKee Corp., 1984-85; founder, pres., CEO Taxi 2000 Corp. (formerly ATS Inc.), 1983-2004, PRT Internat., LLC, 2005-. Author: Magnetohydrodynamic Shock Waves, Magnetogasdynamics of Thermal Plasma, Transit Systems Theory; editor: Personal Rapid Transit II. With USN, 1945-46. Recipient Outstanding Inventor in Am. award Intellectual Property Owners Found., 1989; Convair fellow. NAS, 1967-68 Fellow: AAAS; mem.: ASME, Soc. Automotive Engrs., Union Concerned Scientists, Citizens for Global Solutions. Unitarian Universalist. Home: 5164 Ranier Pass NE Minneapolis MN 55421-1338 Office Phone: 612-720-5551.

ANDERSON, JOHN EDWARD, diversified holding company executive, lawyer; b. Mpls., Sept. 12, 1917; s. William Charles and Myrtle (Grosvenor) A.; m. Margaret Stewart, Sept. 14, 1942 (dec.); children: Margaret Susan, Judith Grosvenor, John Edward, Deborah Lee (dec.), William Stewart; m. Marion Redding, Mar. 3, 1967. BS cum laude, UCLA, 1940; MBA with distinction (Baker scholar), Harvard U., 1942; JD cum laude, Loyola U., 1950. Bar: Calif. 1950; CPA, Calif. Acct. Arthur Andersen & Co., Los Angeles, 1945-48; since practiced in Los Angeles, Irvine; ptnr. Kindel & Anderson, 1953-85; CEO Topa Equities, Los Angeles, Calif. Dir. Mellon 1st Bus. Bank, Summit Health Ltd., Topa Equities, Ltd., Topa Mgmt. Co., Jas. D. Easton, Inc., Indsl. Tools, Inc., Topa Ins. Co. Trustee Claremont McKenna Coll.; trustee St. John's Hosp. and Health Center Found.; bd. dirs. YMCA Met., Los Angeles. Served to lt. USNR, 1942-45. Named one of Forbes Richest Americans, 2006. Mem. AICPA, ABA, State Bar Calif., Calif. Soc. CPAs, L.A. Country Club, Calif. Club, Eldorado Country Club (Palm Desert, Calif.), Outrigger Canoe Club (Honolulu). Presbyterian (elder). Office: Topa Equities Ste 1400 1800 Avenue Of The Stars Los Angeles CA 90067-4216 Office Phone: 310-203-9199. Business E-Mail: tcurtis@topa.com.

ANDERSON, JOHN FIRTH, retired religious organization administrator, retired librarian; b. Saginaw, Mich., Oct. 5, 1928; s. Harlan Firth and Irene Martha (Bowser) Anderson; m. Patricia Ann Goble, June 18, 1950 (dec. Oct. 1995); children: Douglas Firth, Elizabeth Ann; m. Barbara Peterson Smith, May 18, 1996. BA, Mich. State U., 1949; MS in L.S, U. Ill., 1950. Young people's librarian Enoch Pratt Free Library, Balt., 1950-52; with Baltimore County Pub. Libr., 1952-58, supr. adult work, 1955- 56, asst. county libr., 1956-58; dir. Knoxville Pub. Libr. Sys., 1958-62, Tucson Pub. Libr., 1962-68, 73-82; city libr. San Francisco Pub. Libr., 1968-73; exec. presbyter, stated clk. Presbytery of Santa Barbara, Calif., 1982-91; ret., 1991; interim exec. presbyter Presbytery de Cristo, 1993, stated clk., 1993-2000. Mem. Presbyn. Churchwide Adminstr. Coordinating Cabinet, 1987—89; cons. libr. bldgs., devel. and mgmt. Contbr. articles to profl. publs. Mem. Ariz. Libr. Adv. Coun., 1975—81; bd. dirs. Amigos Bibliographic Coun., 1977—81, vice-chmn., 1977—79, sec., 1980—81; charter mem. Freedom to Read Found.; bd. dirs. Ariz. Theatre Co., 1978—82. Recipient Disting. Citizen award, U. Ariz., 1981. Mem.: ALA (mem. at large coun. 1961—65, bd. dirs. pub. libr. assn. 1961—65, bd. dirs. libr. adminstrn. divsn. 1964—65, chmn. libr. orgn. and mgmt. sect. 1964—65, mem. at large coun. 1966—70, pres. libr. adminstrn. divsn. 1968—69), Ariz. Assn. County Librs. (pres. 1979—80), Ariz. Libr. Assn. (pres. pub. librs. divsn. 1964—65, pres. 1967—68, Libr. of the Yr. 1968, Rosenzweig award 1981), Southwestern Libr. Assn. (pres. 1976—78), Calif. Libr. Assn. (coun. 1970—71), World Alliance Reformed Chs. (mem. Caribbean and N.Am. area coun. 1991—93, rec. clk. 1992—93), Ariz. China Coun. (pres. 1979—80), Beta Phi Mu. Presbyterian.

ANDERSON, JOHN FREDRIC, science administrator, entomologist, researcher; b. Fargo, ND, Feb. 25, 1936; s. Oscar Fredric and Eleanor Birdee (Fiskum) A.; m. Marilynn Joy Robinson, June 30, 1958; children: Linda, John Jr., Kristin. BS, N.D. State U., 1957, MS, 1959; PhD, U. Ill., 1963. NSF postdoctoral fellow Dept. Entomology U. Ill., Urbana, 1963-64; asst. entomologist Conn. Agrl. Expt. Sta., New Haven, 1964-66, assoc. entomologist, 1966-69, chief entomologist, 1969-87, dir., 1987—2004, disting. scientist, 2004—. Mem. Conn. Tree Examining Bd., New Haven, 1969-79. Author: (with others) Biology of Sex, 1967, Diseases Transmitted from Animals to Man, 6th edit., 1975, Perspectives in Forest Entomology, 1976, Preventing Lyme Disease, 1989, Ecology and Environmental Management of Lyme Disease, 1993, The Natural History of Ticks, 2002; editor: Perspectives in Forest Entomology, 1976; contbr. articles to profl. jours. 2d lt. Med. Svc. Corp. U.S. Army, 1959, capt. Res., 1969. Recipient award of Merit Conn. Tree Protective Assn., 1976, Bronze medal Fed. Garden Clubs Conn., 1981, Author Citation award Internat. Soc. Arboriculture, 1983, award of Merit Conn. Nurserymen's Assn., 1994, cert. recognition Conn. Nurserymen's Found., 2000, Environ. Industry Coun. Outstanding Svc. award, 2000, Conn. Friend of Floristry award, 2002, Federated Garden Clubs Conn. presdl. citation, 2004, Conn. Farm Bureau Recognition award, 2004. Mem. AAAS, Entomol. Soc. Am., Am. Mosquito Control Assn., Am. Soc. Microbiology, Am. Soc. Parasitologists, Am. Soc. Tropical Medicine and Hygiene, Soc. Invertebrate Pathology, Conn. Acad. Sci. and Engring., (hon.) Conn. Tree Protective Assn., New Haven, 1976-84, (dir., pres.), Phi Kappa Phi. Office: Conn Agrl Expt Sta 123 Huntington St PO Box 1106 New Haven CT 06504-1106 Office Phone: 203-974-8564. Business E-Mail: John.F.Anderson@PO.state.ct.us.

ANDERSON, JOHN GASTON, electrical engineer, consultant; b. Dante, Va., Aug. 21, 1922; s. Harvey Ellis and Lenora (Ingram) A.; m. Elizabeth Amelia Weller, Sept. 18, 1948 (dec. Mar. 1993); 1 son, David John; m. Avery Emma Weymouth, Sept. 24, 1994. BS with honors in Elec. Engring., Va. Poly. Inst., 1943. Registered profl. engr., Mass. With Gen. Electric Co., 1946-84, mgr. AC transmission studies Schenectady, 1972-74, mgr. high voltage lab. Pittsfield, Mass., 1974-80, cons. engr. transmission systems Schenectady, 1980-84. Sr. cons. Power Techs., Inc., 1984-92; profl. cons. engr., 1992-95; cons., lectr. on high voltage and power transmission; mem. U.S. USSR Tech. Exch. for High Voltage Transmission. Co-author books in field; contbr. articles to profl. publs.; editor: GE Transmission Mag., 1972-74; patentee in field. Active Boy Scouts Am., 1960-79. Served to capt. USAAF, 1943-45. Recipient Nat. prizes for papers Am. Inst. Elec. Engrs., 1957 Fellow IEEE (chmn. transmission and distbn. com. 1980-82, Centennial medal 1984, Halperin award 1991, Excellence Engring. medal 1997, Excellence in Power Distbn. Engring. award 1999, Millennium medal 2000); mem. NAE, Power Engring. Soc. (chmn. nat. pub. affairs subcom. 1979, chmn. tech. coun. 1982-85), Tau Beta Pi, Eta Kappa Nu, Phi Kappa Phi.

ANDERSON, JOHN LEONARD, academic administrator, chemical engineering educator; b. Wilmington, Del., Sept. 29, 1945; m. Patricia Siemen, June 8, 1968; children: Brian Christopher, Lauren Kathleen. B.Ch.E., U. Del., 1967; MS, U. Ill., 1969, PhD, 1971. Asst. prof. chem. engring. Cornell U., Ithaca, NY, 1971-76; assoc. prof. chem. engring. Carnegie-Mellon U., Pitts., 1976-79, prof., 1979—2004, dir. biomed. engring., 1980-85, head dept. chem. engring., 1983-94, dean Coll. Engring., 1996—2004; provost Case Western Reserve U., Cleve., 2004—07; pres. Ill. Inst. Tech., Chgo., 2007—. Holtz lectr. Johns Hopkins U., 1990; 5th ann. Berkeley lectr. chem. engring., 1989; Lacey lectr. Calif. Tech., 1998; vis. prof. MIT, 1982-83; vis. scholar Irish-Am. tech. exch. program dept. chem. engring. Univ. Coll. Dublin, 1983. Assoc. editor Advances in Chem. Engring., Indsl. and Engring. Chem. Research; contbr. articles to profl. jours. 1st lt. U.S. Army, 1972. Predoctoral fellow NIH, 1969-71, grantee, 1981—; Guggenheim fellow, 1982-83. Mem. NAE, AICE (symposium chmn. 1974—, Profl. Progress award, 1989); mem AAAS, Am. Chem. Soc. (symposium chmn. 1974—), Tau Beta Pi, Alpha Tau Omega Office: Ill Inst Tech Office of Pres 3300 S Federal St Chicago IL 60616-3793*

ANDERSON, JOHN MURRAY, operations research specialist, consultant, retired academic administrator; b. Toronto, Ont., Can., Sept. 3, 1926; s. Murray Alexander and Eleanor Montgomery (Valentine) A.; m. Eileen Anne McFaul, Nov. 3, 1951 (dec. Nov. 1983); children: Nancy, Susan, Peter, Katherine; m. Sylvia Richard, May 10, 1986 B.Sc.F., U. Toronto, 1951, PhD, 1958; LL.D., St. Thomas U., 1974, Dalhousie U., 1979; D.Ped., U. Maine, Orono, 1976; DSc, U. N.B., Can., 2001. Asst. prof. U. N.B., Canada, 1958-63; assoc. prof. Carleton U., 1963-67; dir. Fisheries Research Bd. Can. Biol. Sta., St. Andrews, N.B., 1967-72; dir. gen. Canadian Research and Devel., Fisheries and Marine Service, Dept. Environment, Ottawa, Ont., 1972-73; pres. U. N.B., 1973-79, J.M. Anderson Consultants Inc., 1980—; v.p. ops. Atlantic Salmon Fedn., 1984-96. Pres., chmn. bd. dirs. Huntsman Marine Lab., St. Andrews, N.B., 1973-77, bd. dirs., 1985—, chmn. bd. dirs., 1995-99; mem. Huntsman Adv. Bd., 2004—, chmn. adv. bd., 2004-2005; bd. govs. Rothesay (N.B.) Collegiate Sch., 1976, Kenya Tech. Tchrs. Coll., Nairobi, 1977-79; chmn. Assn. Atlantic Univs., 1978-79; v.p. Biol. Coun. Can., 1977-79; mem. Sci. Coun. of Can., 1988-92; sci. advisor Nature Conservancy of Can., 2003—. Contbr. numerous articles on fish physiology to profl. jours. Bd. dirs. Internat. Atlantic Salmon Found., 1979-83, J.R. Bradfield Edn. Fund, Noranda, 1979-86, Aquaculture Assn., N.B., 1981—; pres., chmn. bd. trustees Sunbury Shores Arts and Nature Ctr., Inc., 1982-84; chmn. bd. trustees Mackenzie King Scholarship Trust, 1986—; trustee Nature Trust N.B., Inc., 1987-91; v.p. Atlantic Aquaculture Fair, 1993, pres., 1994; bd. dirs. St. Croix Estuary Program, 1990-2002, vice chmn. sci., 2001-02, bd. dirs. Fundy Cmty. Found., 2004-. Recipient Happy Fraser award Atlantic Salmon Fedn., 2001. Fellow Royal Can. Geographic Soc.; mem. Inst. Can. Bankers (gov. 1974-79), Can. Soc. Zoologists (pres. 1973-74), Aquaculture Assn. Can. (pres. 1984-85), Assn. Univs. and Colls. Can. (dir. 1975-79, chmn. McCain Scholarship Group 1997—), Sigma Chi. Anglican. Office: Atlantic Salmon Fedn Saint Andrews NB Canada E0G 2X0 E-mail: atlsal@nbnet.nb.ca.

ANDERSON, JOHN ROBERT, retired mathematics professor; b. Stromsburg, Nebr., Aug. 1, 1928; s. Norris Merton and Violet Charlotte (Stromberg) A.; m. Bertha Margery Nore, Aug. 27, 1950; children: Eric Jon, Mary Lynn. Student, Midland Coll., 1945-46; AA, Luther Jr. Coll., 1949; BS (Regents scholar), U. Nebr., Lincoln, 1951, MA in Math, 1954; PhD, Purdue U., 1970. Tchr. math., coach Bloomfield (Nebr.) High Sch., 1951-52; control systems analyst, Allison div. Gen. Motors Corp., Indpls., 1954-60; prof. math. Depauw U., Greencastle, Ind., 1960, asst. dean, dir. grad. studies, 1973-76, dir. grad. studies, 1976-84, chmn. math. dept., 1984-90, prof. math., 1990-92, ret., 1992; adj. prof. math. IVTC, Greencastle, 1996—; resident dir. W. European studies program Depauw U., Germany, 1975, resident dir. Mediterranean Studies program Athens, Greece, 1982, 1990; dir. NSF Coop. Coll. Sch., Sci. Inst., 1969-70; instr.

NSF summer inst., 1972; instr. Challenge sci. and math. program U.S. Students in Europe, 1976, 77, 78, 80, 82. Bd. dir. Law Focused Edn., Indpls., 1975-77, Ind. Regional Math. Consortium, 1977-92. Bd. dir. Luth. Brotherhood br. 8746, 1967-2002, pres. Thrivent Luth. chpt. 30903, 2002-06, United Way of Greencastle, Ind., 1992-98, treas., Putnam Co. Food Pantry, 1993-98; officer, elder Peace Evangel. Luth. Ch., 1960—. Served with U.S. Army, 1946-48. Danforth Tchr. fellow, 1963-64; NSF sci. faculty fellow, 1964-65; Lilly Found. edn. grantee, summers 1961-63 Mem. Math. Assn. Am., Nat. Council Tchrs. Math., North Central Assn. (commr. 1974-78), Sigma Xi, Pi Mu Epsilon, Kappa Delta Pi, Beta Sigma Psi. Clubs: Rotary Internat. (sec. 1976-77, v.p. 1977-78, pres. 1978-79, 1998-99). Home: 1560 S Bloomington St Greencastle IN 46135-2212 E-mail: johnanderson@depauw.edu, jranderson28@hotmail.com. *When you work with people, always keep in mind: "If I were in their place, is this the way I would like to be treated by someone in my position?".*

ANDERSON, JOHN THOMAS, lawyer; b. Gary, Ind., July 13, 1930; s. Jack and Dorothy Genevieve (Gustafson) A.; m. Marvel Nancy Filkey, Aug. 15, 1953; children: Kirsten E. Teevens, Katherine L., Eric M. AB, DePauw U., 1952; LLB, Harvard U., 1955. Bar: Ind. 1955, Ill. 1956. Assoc. Lord, Bissell & Brook, Chgo., 1958-66, ptnr., 1966-95, of counsel, 1996-98. Trustee DePauw U., Greencastle, Ind., 1982—; chmn. bd. dirs. Joyce Found., Chgo., 1979—; Lt. USNR, 1955-58. Methodist. Home and Office: 2313 Cassia Ct Naples FL 34109-3370

ANDERSON, JOHN THOMAS, librarian, historian; b. Burlington, Iowa, Feb. 7, 1955; s. Alvin Jay and Margaret Ann (Thomas) A. BA, U. No. Iowa, 1976; MA, Coll. William and Mary, 1979; PhD, U. Va., 1982; M in Info. and Libr. Studies, U. Mich., 1987. Temp. asst. prof. history Chadron (Nebr.) State Coll., 1984; asst. libr. pub. svcs. Mid. Ga. Coll., Cochran, 1989-91; temp. reference libr. U. No. Iowa, Cedar Falls, 1991; reference libr. Palm Beach County Libr. Sys., Boca Raton, Fla., 1992, Salve Regina U., Newport, R.I., 1992-93, catalog libr., 1993-94; media cataloger libr. Tex. A&M U., Commerce, 1997-98; libr. I info. svcs. Abilene (Tex.) Pub. Libr., 1998—2002. Catalog libr. Abilene Christian U., 1999—2002; rare book cataloger UB Found., SUNY, Buffalo, 2002—03; catalog libr. St. Bonaventure (NY) U., 2003—. Exhibits judge Nat. History Day Competition, Chadron, Nebr., 1984. Philip Francis du Pont fellow Coll. William and Mary, 1976; Philip Francis du Pont fellow U. Va., 1977; Virginia Mason Davidge fellow U. Va., 1978, 79. Mem. Soc. Historians Am. Fgn. Rels. Republican. Unitarian Universalist. Avocations: collecting postage stamps and first-edition books, public radio. Office: Tech Svcs Dept St Bonaventure Univ Friedsam Libr Saint Bonaventure NY 14778 Home: 1501 Pleasant St Apt 6D Olean NY 14760-1579 Home Phone: 716-373-8662; Office Phone: 716-375-2340. Business E-Mail: janderso@sbu.edu.

ANDERSON, JON ERIC, lawyer; b. Jacksonville, NC, Feb. 1, 1956; m. Lori Jean Schumacher, June 30, 1979; children: Andrew Jon, Elizabeth Ruth, Margaret Mary. BA, U. Wis., 1978; JD, Marquette U., 1981. Bar: Wis. 1981, U.S. Dist. Ct. (ea. and we. dists.) Wis. 1981, U.S. Ct. Appeals (7th cir.) 1996, U.S. Supreme Ct. 1988. Assoc. Mulcahy & Wherry, S.C., Milw., 1981-84, mng. atty. Sheboygan, Wis., 1984-87, Madison, Wis., 1987-90; shareholder Godfrey & Kahn, S.C., Madison, 1991—. Author: (with others) Comparable Worth-A Negotiator's Guide, 1985; contbg. author Pub. Sector Labor Rels., Wis., 1988. Thomas More Soc. scholar, 1979. Mem.: ABA, Nat. Assn. Coll. and Univ. Attys., Wis. Sch. Attys. Assn. (bd. dirs. 2000—04, pres. 2003—04), Wis. Bar Assn. (bd. dirs. labor law sect. 1988—91, 2007—), Edn. Law Assn., Madison Club, Blackhawk Country Club, Alpha Sigma Nu, Phi Delta Phi. Lutheran. Avocations: woodworking, music. Office Phone: 608-257-3911. Business E-Mail: janderson@gklaw.com.

ANDERSON, JON MAC, lawyer, educator; b. Rio Grande, Ohio, Jan. 10, 1937; s. Harry Rudolph and Carrie Viola (Magee) A.; m. Deborah Melton, June 1, 1961; children: Jon Gordon, Greta. AB, Ohio U., 1958; JD, Harvard Law Sch., 1961. Bar: Ohio 1961. Law clk. Hon. Kingsley A. Taft Ohio Supreme Ct., Columbus, 1961—62; assoc. Wright, Harlor, Morris & Arnold, Columbus, 1962—67, ptnr., 1968—76, Porter, Wright, Morris & Arthur, Columbus, 1977—. Adj. prof. law Ohio State U. Law Sch., Columbus, 1975-83; bar examiner State of Ohio, 1971-76, chmn., 1975-76; lectr. tax and estate planning insts.; bd. dirs. White Castle System, Inc. Trustee Columbus Mus. of Art, 2003—, Berea Coll, Ky., 1976-2000, Pro Musica Chamber Orch., Columbus, 1980-98, Opera Columbus, 1985-88, 1st Congl. Ch., Columbus, 1979-83, Greater Columbus Arts Coun., 1989-99; chmn., 1996-98; mem. adv. coun. The Textile Mus., 1996-2002. Mem. ABA, Ohio State Bar Assn., Columbus Bar Assn., The Columbus Club, Rocky Fork Hunt and Country Club. Democrat. Avocations: music, art, literature, antiques. Office: Porter Wright Morris & Arthur 41 S High St Ste 2800 Columbus OH 43215-6194 Home Phone: 614-235-9526; Office Phone: 614-227-2154. Personal E-mail: jander18@columbus.rr.com. Business E-Mail: janderson@porterwright.com.

ANDERSON, JON STEPHEN, newswriter; b. Montreal, Que., Can., Mar. 13, 1936; arrived in U.S., 1963; s. William Howard and Dorothy Beatrice (Ryan) A.; m. Gail Rutherford, Feb. 20, 1960 (div. 1966); 1 child, Jon Gregory (dec.); m. Abra Prentice, Sept. 14, 1968 (div. 1976); children: Ashley Prentice Norton, Abra Cantrill Williams, Anthony Ryan; m. Pamela Sherrod, Sept. 23, 2001. BA, Mt. Allison U., Sackville, Can., 1955; BCL, McGill U., Montreal, 1959; MAW, U. Iowa, 1991. Reporter Montreal Gazette, 1957-60; chief bur. Time Mag., Montreal, 1960-63, staff corr. Chgo., 1963-66; staff writer Chgo. Sun-Times, 1967-69; columnist Chgo. Daily News, 1969-72; pub. Chicagoan Mag., 1972-74; staff writer Chgo. Tribune, 1978—2006; writing instr. U. Iowa, 1989—2002; freelance writer, 2006—. Author: City Watch: Discovering the Uncommon Chicago, 2000; contbr. articles to Readers Digest, 1977-85, Chgo. Mag., 1977, Clothesline Rev., 1986. Gen. mgr. Second City Ctr. Pub. Arts, 1966-67; bd. dirs. Chgo. Internat. Film Festival, 1975-78 Recipient Stick o' Type award, Newspaper Guild Am., 1969, Studs Terkel Journalism award, 1999. Mem.: Order Ky. Cols. Roman Catholic. Personal E-mail: jonanderson99@aol.com.

ANDERSON, JON TIMOTHY, lawyer; b. Springfield, Vt., Jan. 5, 1953; s. Harold A. and Marjorie (Hinckley) A.; m. Elizabeth Dennis, Mar. 7, 1981; 1 child, Tyler Alan. BS in Chem. Engring., highest distintion, Worcester Poly. Inst., 1975; JD, Yale U., 1978. Bar: Vt. 1980, U.S. Dist. Ct. Vt. 1981. Law clk. hon. Caleb M. Wright US Dist. Ct., Wilmington, Del., 1978-80; assoc. Paterson, Gibson & Noble, Montpelier, Vt., 1980-82; spl. counsel Vt. Dept. Pub. Svc., Montpelier, 1982-85; assoc. Goldstein, Manello & Burak, Burlington, Vt., 1985-89; ptnr. Burak, Anderson & Melloni, 1989—. Interim legal counsel Gov. of Vt., Montpelier, 1990-91; owner operator bed and breakfast, spkr. in fields. Contbr. articles to profl. jours. Chmn. Vt. Blue Ribbon Task Force, Waterbury, 1990-91; mem. Vt. Tech. Adv. Com. on Solid Waste, Waterbury, 1990—; mem. Vt. Bd. Architects, Montpelier 1988, chmn. Montpelier Water Study Com. 1985, dist. chmn. Boy Scouts Am., Waterbury 1992, program dir. Green Mountain Boys' State, Montpelier, 1980—, del. White House Conf. Travel and Tourism, 1995, mem. (bd. trustees) Vt. Arts Coun., bd. mem. Montpelier Downtown Cmty. Assn., Pyralisk Arts Ctr., chmn. Montpelier Travel Information Coun., chmn. com. develop transit ctr.& park downtown Montpelier, pres. Montpelier City Coun., Montpelier Planning Commn., Ctrl. Vt. Regional Planning Commn, Vt. Bd. Architects, counsel Vt. Dept. Pub Svc. Presdl. scholar, 1971, Salisbury award. Mem. Vt. Bar Assn., pres. Cen. Vt. C. of C., (treas. v.p.) Vt. Lodging and Restaurant Assn., Montpelier Kiwanis Club (pres. 1985-86), chmn. Vt. Bar Assns. Environ. Law Com. Democrat. Office: Burak Anderson & Melloni 30 Main St PO Box 787 Burlington VT 05402-0787 Office Fax: 802-862-8176. Business E-Mail: janderson@vtlaw1.com.

ANDERSON, JOSEPH NORMAN, retired food products executive, academic administrator; b. Mpls., May 12, 1926; s. Joseph E. and Helen (Larson) A.; m. Ruth E. Anderson, Sept. 6, 1952; children: Peter, Timothy, Paul, Matthew, Robin, Kathryn, Charles. BBA with distinction, U. Minn., 1947. With Sears, Roebuck & Co., 1947-49, Gamble-Skogmo, Inc., 1950-64; v.p. fin., dir. Nat. Bellas Hess, Inc., 1964-67, pres., chief exec. officer, dir., 1967-69, chmn. bd., pres., chief exec. officer, 1969-75; pres. Jamestown (N.D.) Coll., 1975-83, Dakota Bake-n-Serv, Inc., 1979-86; exec. cons. Gladstone, Mo., 1986-90, Edwardsville, Ill., 1990—. Pres. Mchts. Rsch. Coun., 1961-62. With AUS, 1953-55. Mem. Phi Beta Kappa, Beta Gamma Sigma. Republican. Presbyterian.

ANDERSON, JOSHUA DOUGLAS, military officer; s. Craig Marshall Anderson and Candace Leigh Frey, William Richard Frey (Stepfather) and Bridget Marie Anderson (Stepmother); m. Lisa Ann Newkirk, Mar. 24, 2006. BA in Polit. Sci. summa cum laude, U. Richmond, Va., 1998; grad student, U. Belgrade, Serbia, 2006—. Commd. 2d lt. USMC, advanced through grades to capt., 1998, maintenance mgmt. office combat assault Okinawa, Japan, 1999—2000, exec. officer, hdqs. & svcs. co. 1st transp. support Camp Pendleton, Calif., 2000—01, co. comdr., hdqs. & services co. 1st transp. support, 2001—02; transp. support detachment comdr. 15th Marine Expeditionary Unit, Camp Pendleton, Calif., 2002—03; circuit mgr. Europe & The Balkans Armed Forces Entertainment, Arlington, Va., 2003—04, circuit mgr. SW Asia, 2004—05; Serbo-Croatian lang. student Def. Lang. Inst., Presidio of Monterey, Calif., 2005—06. Decorated Meritorious Svc. medal USAF, Commendation medal Navy & Marine Corps, Achievement medal, USAF; Olmsted scholar, George & Carol Olmsted Found., 2006—. Mem.: Phi Beta Kappa. Presbyterian. Office: A101 Vladimira Popovica 6 Belgrade 11070 Serbia Home Phone: 574-598-4365; Office Phone: 381-63-810-9655. Personal E-mail: joshua.anderson@richmond.edu.

ANDERSON, JOSHUA E., lawyer; BA, Univ. Chgo., 1997; JD, UCLA, 2000. Bar: Calif. 2000, US Dist. Ct. No. & Ctrl. Calif., US Ct. Appeals Ninth Cir. Assoc., bus. litigation practice Sidley Austin LLP, LA, 2000—. Named a Rising Star, So. Calif. Super Lawyers, 2006. Mem.: Phi Beta Kappa, Order of the Coif. Office: Sidley Austin LLP 555 W 5th St Los Angeles CA 90013 Office Phone: 213-896-6687. Office Fax: 213-896-6600.

ANDERSON, JOSHUA M., speech educator; BS in Edn., Emporia State Univ., 1997; MA in Sch. Leadership, Baker Univ., 2001. Lang. arts tchr. Basehor-Linwood H.S., 1997—2003, Olathe (Kans.) Northwest H.S., 2003—. Finalist Nat. Tchr. of Yr., 2007; named Kans. Tchr. of Yr., 2007. Mem.: Internat. Thespian Soc., Nat. Forensics League (Diamond Key Award for Excellence in Edn. 2005), Assn Supervision and Curriculum Devel., E. Kans. Nat. Forensics League, Nat. Cath. Forensics League, Kans. Speech Comm. Assn., Kans. NEA, NEA, ACLU. Office: Olathe Northwest High Sch 21300 College Blvd Olathe KS 66061 Business E-Mail: jandersononw@olatheschools.com.*

ANDERSON, JUDITH HELENA, English language educator; b. Worcester, Mass., Apr. 21, 1940; d. Oscar William and Beatrice Marguerite (Beaudry) A.; m. E. Talbot Donaldson, May 18, 1971 (dec. Apr. 1987). AB magna cum laude, Radcliffe Coll., 1961; MA, Yale U., 1962, PhD, 1965. Instr. English Cornell U., Ithaca, NY, 1964-66, asst. prof. English, 1966-72; vis. lectr. Coll. Seminar Program, Yale U., New Haven, 1973; vis. asst. prof. English U. Mich., Ann Arbor, 1973-74; assoc. prof. Ind. U., Bloomington, 1974-79, prof., 1979—, Chancellor's prof., 1999—, dir. grad. studies, 1986-90, 93, mem. governing bd. univ. Inst. for Advanced Study, 1983-85, 86-88. Morris W. Croll lectr. Gettysburg Coll., 1988, Kathleen Williams lectr., 89, 95; dir. Folger Inst. Sem., 1991; adv. bd. Textbase of Women Writers, Brown U., 1989—2000. Author: The Growth of a Personal Voice, 1976, Biographical Truth, 1984, Words that Matter, 1996, Translating Investments, 2005; editor: (with Elizabeth D. Kirk) Piers Plowman, 1990; (with Donald Cheney and David A. Richardson) Spenser's Life and the Subject of Biography, 1996, (with Christine R. Farris) Integrating Literature and Writing Instruction, 2007; mem. editl. bd. Spenser Ency., 1979-90, Duquesne Studies in Lang. and Lit., 1976-2004, Spenser Studies, 1986—, Medieval and Renaissance Literary Studies, 2004—; contbr. articles to profl. jours. Rsch. grant Huntington Libr., 1978, 97; Woodrow Wilson fellow, 1961-64, NEH summer fellow and sr. rsch. fellow, 1979, 81-82, NEH-Huntington fellow, 1985-86, Mayers Found. fellow, 1990-91, Dulin fellow Folger Libr., 1991, Nat. Humanities Ctr. fellow, 1995-96, NEH-Newberry fellow, 2002-03; recipient Outstanding Scholar award Office of Women's Affairs Ind. U., 1996 Mem. MLA (exec. com. Renaissance divsn. 1973-78, 86-90, del. to assembly 1991-93, publs. com. 1999-2002), AAUP, internat. Spenser Soc. (pres. 1980, 88, Lifetime Achievement award 2004), Renaissance Soc. Am. (rep. for English to coun. 1991-93), Milton Soc., Donne Soc. (exec. com. 2004-06), Shakespeare Assn., Chaucer Soc., Phi Beta Kappa. Home: 2525 E 8th St Bloomington IN 47408-4214 Office: Ind U Dept English Bloomington IN 47405 Office Phone: 812-855-8224. Business E-Mail: anders@indiana.edu.

ANDERSON, KARL See KORS, MICHAEL

ANDERSON, KARL FRANKLIN, systems engineer, researcher; b. Topeka, Nov. 18, 1939; s. Walter Franklin and Volba Linea Anderson; m. Sharyl J. Willows, June 4, 1960; children: Karl Franklin II, Michelle Joy Goodman. BS in Elec. Engring., Kans. State U., Manhattan, 1963, BA in Bus. Adminstrn., 1963. Elecs. engr. Collins Radio Co., Cedar Rapids, Iowa, 1963—64; measurement sys. engr. NASA Dryden Flight Rsch. Ctr., Edwards, Calif., 1966—95; owner Valid Measurements, Lutz, Fla., 1995—. Founder Sensor Tech, Inc., Savannah, Ga., 2004—. Trustee Lancaster Sch. Dist., Calif., 1975—79. 1st lt. US Army, 1964—66. Mem.: IEEE, Western Regional Strain Gage Com. (procs. editor 2000—), Soc. Exptl. Mechanics, Internat. Soc. Automation. Methodist. Achievements include patents for Anderson loop measurement circuit topology; guarding electrical regions having potential gradients. Avocations: amateur radio, philosophy. Home: 5406 Sunflare Way Lutz FL 33558-9010 Office: Valid Measurements 5406 Sunflare Way Lutz FL 33558-9019 Home Phone: 813-926-9516; Office Phone: 813-920-3052. Personal E-mail: karl@v-m.us.

ANDERSON, KARL RICHARD, aerospace engineer, consultant; b. Vinita, Okla., Sept. 27, 1917; s. Axel Richard and Hildred Audrey (Marshall) Anderson; m. Jane Shingeko Hiratsuka, June 20, 1953; 1 child, Karl Richard. BS, Calif. Western U., 1964; MA, 1966; PhD, U.S. Internat. U., 1970. Registered profl. engr., Calif. Engr. personnel subsystems Atlas Missile Program, Gen. Dynamics, San Diego, 1960-63; design engr. Solar divsn. Internat. Harvester, San Diego, 1964-66, sr. design engr., 1967-69, project engr., 1970-74, product safety specialist, 1975-78, aerospace engring. cons., 1979-86; cons. engring. San Diego, 1979—. Lectr. Am. Indian Sci. and Engring. Soc. Served to maj. USAF, 1936—60. Recipient Spl. Commendation award, San Diego Bd. Supr., 1985, Spl Commendation award, City of San Diego, 1994, Grace "Peter" Sargent award, San Diego City Natural Pk., 1994. Home and Office: 5886 Scripps St San Diego CA 92122-3212

ANDERSON, KARL STEPHEN, editor; b. Chgo., Nov. 10, 1933; s. Karl William and Eleanore (Grell) a.; m. Saralee Hegland, Nov. 5, 1977; children by previous marriage: Matthew, Douglas, Eric. BS in Editl. Journalism, U. Ill., 1955. Successively advt. mgr., asst. to pub., plant mgr. Pioneer Press, Oak Park, St. Charles, Ill., 1955-71; asst. to pub., then pub. Crescent Newspapers, Downers Grove, Ill., 1971-73; assoc. pub., editor Chronicle Pub. Co., St. Charles, 1973-80; assoc. pub. Chgo. Daily Law Bull., 1981-88; dir. comm., editor Ill. State Bar Assn., 1988—. Past pres. Chgo. Pub. Rels. Forum. Trustee emeritus Chi Psi Ednl. Trust; trustee Leo Sowerby Found.; bd. dirs. Ill. Press Found., Swedish Am. Hist. Soc., Ill. First Amendment Ctr. Recipient C.V. Amenoff award No. Ill. U. Dept. Journalism, 1976, Bd. Govs. award Ill. State Bar, 1987, Print Media Humanitarian award Coalition Sub Bar Assns., 1987, Robert C. Preble, Jr. award Chi Psi, 1991, Asian-Am. Bar Media Sensitivity award, 1991, Liberty Bell award DuPage County Bar Assn., 1993, Glass Ceiling Busters award DuPage Women Lawyers, 1993, Disting. Svc. award Chgo. Vol. Legal Svcs. Found., 1993, Gratitude award Lawyers Assistance Program, 1993, Outstanding Achievement in Comm. award Justinian Soc., 1994, Communicator of Yr. award, 1999, 3rd prize Nat. Libr. Poetry, 1995, Svc. award Women's Bar Assn. Ill., 1998, Peoria County Bar Assn., 1998 Mem. Nat. Assn. Bar Execs., Baltic Bar Assn., Chgo. Journalists Assn., Ill. Press Assn. (Will Loomis award 1977, 80), Kane County Bar Assn., DuPage Women Lawyers Assn., West Suburban Bar Assn., North Suburban Bar Assn. (Pub. Svc. award 1997), N.W. Suburban Bar Assn. (Svc. award 2005), Bohemian Lawyers Assn. (Liberty award 1999), No. Ill. Newspaper Assn. (past pres.), Pub. Rels. Soc. Ctrl. Ill. (Master Communicator award of achievement 1997), Soc. Profl. Journalists, Headline Club (past pres.), Nordic Law Club, Nellie Fox Soc., Union League Club Chgo., Chgo. Illini Club (bd. dirs.), Chi Psi. Home: 3180 N Lake Shore Dr Apt 14D Chicago IL 60657-4851 Office: Ill State Bar Assn 20 S Clark St Ste 900 Chicago IL 60603-1885 Office Phone: 312-726-8775.

ANDERSON, KATHRYN PARKS, music educator; b. Trenton, Mo., Nov. 30, 1951; d. Carroll Lloyd and Viva Jean (Landes) Parks; m. Leander Albert Anderson, May 31, 1977; children: Lindsay Anderson Guerriere, Kirsten Joy. MusEdB in applied organ, Ctrl. Mo. State U., Warrensburg, 1972, MusM in applied organ, 1974. Cert. Mo. Life Tchg. Cert., Conn. Standard Tchg. Cert. Vocal, instrumental music tchr. Plainville Pub. Schs., Plainville, Conn., 1978—80; dir. music, organist Grace Bapt. Ch., Bristol, Conn., 1977—87; vocal, instrumental music tchr. Archdiocese of Hartford, Sacred Heart Sch., New Britain, Conn., 1986—2001; dir. music, organist Mill Plain Union Ch., Waterbury, Conn., 1987—92, First Bapt. Ch., Meriden, Conn., 1992—2001, Ch. of St. Mary, Newington, Conn., 2001—. Music cons. small Christian cmtys. Archdiocese of Hartford, Bloomfield, Conn., 2003—. Recorded choral and handbell music: various CD's. Mem.: Am. Guild of English Handbell Ringers, Nat. Assn. of Pastoral Musicians, Am. Guild of Organists (registrar Greater Hartford Conn. chpt. 1984—87), Phi Kappa Phi, Pi Kappa Lambda Honor Music Fraternity. Avocations: walking, fitness training, poetry. Home: 112 Butternut Ln Bristol CT 06010-8049 Office: Ch of St Mary 626 Willard Ave Newington CT 06111 Office Phone: 860-666-1858, 860-666-1591. Office Fax: 860-666-5720. E-mail: kathrynparksanderson@hotmail.com.

ANDERSON, KENNETH ALLEN, lawyer, hotel executive; b. Grand Junction, Colo., Sept. 16, 1962; s. Lila Marie and Norling Wayne A. AB in Polit. Sci., U. So. Calif., LA, 1985; JD, Yale U., 1989. Bar: Calif. 1989, U.S. Dist. Ct. (ctrl. dist.) Calif. 1989, U.S. Ct. Appeals (9th cir.) 1989. Assoc. Irell & Manella, LA, 1989-91; sr. assoc. Pettit & Martin, Newport Beach, Calif., 1991-94, O'Melveny & Myers, Newport Beach, 1994—98; v.p., sr. counsel Hilton Hotels Corp., Beverly Hills, Calif., 1998—. Author: White Bird, 1981. Mem. ABA, Beverly Hills Bar Assn., Assn. Corp. Counsel. Avocations: reading, hiking, travel. Home: 24934 Vista Verenda Woodland Hills CA 91367 Office: Hilton Hotels Corp 9336 Civic Ctr Dr Beverly Hills CA 90210 Office Phone: 310-205-4572. E-mail: allen_anderson@hilton.com.

ANDERSON, KENNETH CARL, physician, educator; b. Worcester, Mass., Oct. 3, 1951; s. Kenneth R. and Helen L. Anderson; m. Cynthia Ellen Bird; children: Emily, David, Peter. BA summa cum laude, Boston U., 1973; MD, Johns Hopkins U., 1977. Lic. physician, Md., Mass.; diplomate Am. Bd. Internal Medicine. Intern medicine Johns Hopkins Hosp., Balt., 1977-78, asst. resident medicine, 1978-79, sr. resident, 1979-80, clin. fellow medicine, 1977-80, Harvard Med. Sch., Boston, 1980-83, instr. medicine, 1983-84, asst. prof., 1985-91, assoc. prof., 1992—, Kraft Family Prof. Medicine, 2002—; clin. fellow med. oncology Dana-Farber Cancer Inst., Boston, 1980-83, fellow tumor immunology, 1981-83; clin. fellow medicine Brigham and Women's Hosp., Boston, 1980-83, jr. assoc. physician, 1983—85, attending physician bone marrow transplantation, 1984—88; clin. assoc. med. oncology Dana-Farber Cancer Inst., 1983—85, med. dir. Blood Component Lab., 1984—, attending physician med. oncology, 1984—, attending physician bone marrow transplantation, 1984—, asst. physician, 1985—; dir. Jerome Lipper Multiple Myeloma Ctr. Dana Farber Cancer Inst., med. dir. Kraft Family Donor Ctr.; and a Doris Duke Clin. Rsch. Scientist. Rsch. assoc. Ctr. for Blood Rsch., Boston, 1994—; vis. prof. dept. pathology U. Pa. Sch. Medicine, 1991; Joseph R. Bove transfusion medicine vis. prof. Yale U. Sch. Medicine, 1994; prin. investigator Cancer and Leukemia Group B, 1993—; mem. blood product adv. com. U.S. FDA, 1993—; mem. med. adv. com. ARC Blood Svcs., N.E. Region, 1985—; med. dir. Donor Ctr. Nat. Marrow Donor Program, 1987—; mem. sci. rev. com. Dana Farber Cancer Inst., 1984-90, 92—, clin. exec. com., 1984—, utilization rev. and quality assurance com., 1984—, clin. lab. com., 1984—, chmn. transfusion com., 1984—; mem. sci. adv. bd. Internat. Myeloma Found., 1991—, Multiple Myeloma Rsch. Found.; editorial bd., Transfusion Science, Medical Oncology, American Journal of Hematology, and American Association of Blood Banks Press; assoc. editor, Transfusion and European Journal of Hematology; lectr. various orgns. Reviewer New Eng. Jour. Medicine, Blood, Cancer Rsch., Annals Internal Medicine, Jour. Clin. Oncology, Jour. Immunology, Procs. NAS, Jour. Clin. Investigation, European Jour. Cancer and Clin. Oncology, Transfusion, Procs. Exptl. Biology and Medicine, Transfusion Sci., Intensive Care Medicine, Leukemia, Acta Hematologica; editl. bds. Transfusion Sci., 1990—, Jour. Clin. Oncology, 1990-93, Blood, 1991—, Transfusion, 1994; editor: (with P.M. Ness) Scientific Basis of Transfusion Medicine: Implications for Clinical Practice, 1994; contbr. articles to profl. jours. Bd. dirs. Internat. Myeloma Found., 1993—. Recipient CIBA Cmty. Svc. award, 1975, Jr. Faculty Rsch. award Am. Cancer Soc., 1986-89; Med. Found. fellow, 1984-86, spl. fellow Leukemia Soc. Am., 1986-89, Robert A. Kyle Lifetime Achievement award, Internat. Myeloma Found., 2005. Mem. AMA (Physician's Recognition award), ACP, AAAS, Am. Soc. Hematology (coordinating reviewer in transfusion 1994, reviewer in lymphomas and myelomas 1993), Am. Assn. Blood Banks (chmn. transfusion practice com. 1992-93), Mass. Assn. Blood Banks (Morten Grove-Rasmussen Meml. award 1994), Mass. Med. Soc., Am. Soc. Hemopheresis Specialists, Sigma Xi, Phi Beta Kappa, Alpha Phi Omega. Achievements include research on monoclonal antibodies defining B cell differentiation antigens and B cell malignancies in man, clinical and laboratory aspects of bone marrow transplantation, developing and validating new targeted therapies for myeloma, clinical and laboratory aspects of blood component therapy in patients with malignancy. Office: Dana Farber Cancer Inst 44 Binney St Boston MA 02115-6084*

ANDERSON, KENNETH PAUL, nephrologist, administrator; b. Council Bluffs, Iowa, June 17, 1952; s. Kenneth Paul and and Kathleen Marie (Wyckoff) A.; children: Jennifer, Cassie, Zach. BS with honors, U. Iowa, 1974; DO, Coll. Osteo. Medicine, Des Moines, 1978; MS, U. Wis., 1996; cert., Harvard U., 1993. Diplomate Am. Bd. Family Practice. Resident, chief resident Luth. Hosp.-U. Iowa, Des Moines, 1978-81, Norwalk (Conn.) Hosp.-Yale U., 1981-83; fellow in nephrology, clin. instr. U. So. Calif., LA, 1983-85; med. dir. Mercy Hosp., Iowa Luth. Hosp., Des Moines, 1985-96; clin. instr. Coll. Osteo. Medicine, Des Moines, 1986-96; chief of staff Mercy Hosp. Med. Ctr., Des Moines, 1992-94; sec., bd. officers Iowa Luth. Hosp., Des Moines, 1989-90; chief med. officer Ptnrs. Nat. Health Plans, South Bend, Ind., 1996—2000; v.p. Meml. Hosp., South Bend, 2000—. Chmn., mem. ESRD Network # 12 of HCFA, Kansas City, 1984-95; pres., CEO Nephrology and Internal Medicine Specialists, Des Moines, 1985-96; med. dir. SecureCare of Iowa, Des Moines, 1992-96. Contbr. articles to profl. jours. Bd. dirs. Iowa State Bd. of Health, Des Moines, 1993-96; cons. Nat. Health Policy Adv. Team, Washington, 1989-94, Ind. Perinatal Task Force, 1997-2000; examiner Baldrige Nat. Quality Program, 2003—. Fellow Am. Acad. Family Practice; mem. AMA, Am. Soc. Hypertension, Am. Coll. Physician Execs., Am. Soc. Nephrology, Iowa Osteo. Med. Assn. Democrat. Roman Catholic. Avocations: camping, music, fishing, bicycling, creative writing. Home: 11034 Birch Lake Dr E Granger IN 46530-6013 Office: Meml Hosp and Health System 615 N Michigan St South Bend IN 46601-1033 Office Phone: 574-647-3104. Business E-Mail: kanderson@memorialsb.org.

ANDERSON, KENNETH WARD, investor, consultant; b. Evanston, Ill., Dec. 14, 1931; s. Sydney Cleminson and Grey (Simpson) A.; m. Jean Jensen, Mar. 21, 1953; children: Kenneth Ward, Richard Scott, Wendy Lynn. BSBA, Northwestern U., 1953; postgrad. in fin., UCLA, 1955-56, U. So. Calif., 1956-58. Asst. v.p. United Calif. Bank, LA, 1956-63; v.p. fin., asst. sect. T.I.M.E.-DC, Lubbock, Tex., 1963-70; sr. v.p. fin. Campbell-Taggart, Dallas, 1970-80; sr. v.p., CFO Galveston-Houston Co., Houston, 1980-82; pres., CFO, dir. Cook Data Svcs., Dallas, 1983-85; pres., dir. Blockbuster Entertainment Corp., Dallas, 1985-87; pres., dir., chmn. bd. Amtech Credit Corp., Dallas, 1987-90; chmn. exec. com., dir. Amtech Corp., 1987-92; bd. dirs. Lake Area Health Ctr. Found., 1993—, Fossil, Inc., 1993—, MarketQuiz, Inc., 2000—. Bd. dirs. Ch. at Horseshoe Bay Endowment Fund, 1996—2003; trustee Ch. at Horseshoe Bay, 1999—2002. With US Army, 1953—55, Japan. Mem.: Horseshoe Bay Country Club, Preston Trail Golf Club. Republican. Methodist. Address: PO Box 8189 Horseshoe Bay TX 78657-8189

ANDERSON, KERRII B., food service executive; b. 1957; BS, Elon Coll., 1978; MBA, Duke U., 1987. CPA. With Peat, Marwick, Mitchell & Co., Greensboro, NC, 1978-84, RJ Reynolds Corp., Winston-Salem, NC, 1984-85, Key Co., Greensboro, NC, 1985-87; sec. M/I Schottenstein Homes Inc., Columbus, 1987—94, sr. v.p., CFO, chmn. bd., 1987—2000, asst. sec., 1994—2000; exec. v.p., CFO Wendy's Internat. Inc., Dublin, Ohio, 2000—06, interim CEO, 2006, pres., CEO, 2006—. Bd. dirs. The Lancaster Colony Corp., M/I Schottenstein Homes, Inc., Wendy's Internat. Inc., 2000—. Mem. fin. com. The Columbus Found.; bd. mem. Grant-Riverside Hosp.; mem. dean's adv. com. Fisher Coll. Bus., Ohio State U. Office: Wendys Internat Inc One Dave Thomas Blvd Dublin OH 43017 also: 4288 W Dublin-Granville Rd Dublin OH 43017-0256*

ANDERSON, KEVIN STUART, archivist, librarian; b. Alliance, Nebr., Mar. 25, 1954; s. Allan Earl Anderson and Helen May Faber; m. Cheryl Kay Dusk Newton, Apr. 27, 1989 (div. 1995). AA, Casper Coll., 1974; Cert. of Completion, Western Archives Inst., 1993; BA with honors, U. Wyo., 1997. Cert. Acad. Cert. Archivists. Bookstore mgr. Lange's Book Shop, Casper, Wyo., 1975—82; credit union mgr., treas. Burlington Casper Employees Fed. Credit Union, Casper, 1981—86; loan officer Natrona County Sch. Employees Fed. Credit Union, Casper, 1986—87; cataloging technician Casper Coll. Libr., 1987—89, cataloging, acquisitions technician, automation specialist, 1989—91, Western history tech. specialist, 1992—2007, Western history archivist, 2007—. Mem. task force Wyo. State Hist. Records Adv. Bd., Cheyenne, 1994—95; regional rep. regional coun. Wyo. State Libr., Cheyenne, 1997—2002, mem. interlibrary loan com., 1998—99, mem. Wyo. statewide digitization com., 2004—; bd. dirs., mem. of exhibit design com. Nat. Hist. Trails Interpretive Ctr., Casper, 1999—2003; spkr. in field. Author: Spirit of the Thunderbird: The Growth of Casper College, 1995. Copyright and permissions cons. Nat. Hist. Trails Interpretive Ctr., Casper, 1999—2001; civic, local Western history cons. KCWY TV, Casper, Wyo., 2005—07; civic, local cons. Family History Ctr., Casper, 1975—76, 1982—84, 1999—. Recipient Hon. Lifetime Mem., Friends of the Natrona County Pub. Libr., 1980, Unsung Hero Award, Wyo. Libr. Assn., 1995, Outstanding Historian Award, Regional History Day Coordinators, 2002, Non-Teaching Profl. Leadership Award, Wyo. Assn. of C.C. Trustees, 2004, Arizola Magnenat Award For Encouragement of Writers, Wyo. Writers, Inc., 2005, Outstanding Adminstr. award, Casper Coll., 2007. Mem.: Mountain Plains Libr. Assn. (sec. preservation, archives and spl. collections sect. 1999—2000, chmn. preservation, archives and spl. collections sect. 2004—05), Wyo. Libr. Assn., Acad. Cert. Archivists, Soc. Am. Archivists, Soc. Rocky Mountain Archivists (treas. 1999—2002, v.p. 2002—03, pres. 2003—04), Wyo. State Hist. Soc., Wyo. Assn. Profl. Historians (pres. 2003—04), Ft. Caspar Mus. Assn. (bd. dirs. 2003—06), Oregon-California Trails Assn., Natrona County Geneal. Soc., Friends of the Natrona County Pub. Libr. (life), Natrona County Hist. Soc. (bd. dirs. 1994—96), Phi Kappa Phi. Lutheran. Achievements include development of Huey interlibrary loan database and data transfer system; Pounce MARC record automated data-transfer system. Avocations: creative writing, genealogy. Office: Casper Coll Libr 125 College Drive Casper WY 82601 Office Phone: 307-268-2680. Office Fax: 307-268-2333. Business E-Mail: wyoref@caspercollege.edu.

ANDERSON, KIMBALL RICHARD, lawyer; b. San Antonio, Aug. 20, 1952; s. Richard John and Martha (Bishop) A.; m. Karen Gatsis, Aug. 18, 1974; children: Alexis Katrina, Melissa Martha, Sophia Diane. BA, U. Ill., 1974, JD, 1977. Bar: Ill. 1977, U.S. Ct. Appeals (7th cir.) 1979, U.S. Supreme Ct. 1987; CPA, Ill. 1974. Assoc. Winston & Strawn LLP, Chgo., 1977-84, ptnr., 1984—, chmn. pro bono com., 1984—, mem. exec. com., 1994—, gen. counsel, 2000—. Disting. neutral CPR Inst. for Dispute Resolution; adj. prof. trial advocacy Northwestern U; pres. CBA TV Prodns., Inc., 1989-1991, CBA Ins. Adminstrs., 1993-; spkr. in field. Contbr. articles to profl. jours. V.p. Pub. Interest Law Initiative, 2002—05, pres., 2006—; chmn. bd. AIDS Legal Coun. Chgo.; bd. dirs. De Paul U. Coll. Law Ctr. Justice in Capital Cases, pres., 2003—. Named Person of Yr. 1996 Chgo. Lawyer Mag., laureate Ill. Acad. Lawyers, 2005. Fellow Am. Coll. Trial Lawyers, Am. Bar Found.; mem. ABA (mem. ethics 2000 adv. coun. 1998-, mem. Ctr. Profl. responsibility, Pro Bono Publico award 2003), Ill. Bar Assn., Chgo. Bar Assn. (bd. mgrs. 1990-92), Ill. CPA Soc., Chgo. Bar Found. (2d v.p. 2001-02, 1st v.p. 2003-05, pres. 2005—). Home: 2045 N Seminary Ave Chicago IL 60614-4109 Office: Winston & Strawn 35 W Wacker Dr Ste 4200 Chicago IL 60601-1695 Office Phone: 312-558-5858. Business E-Mail: kanderson@winston.com.

ANDERSON, KRISTINA ELIZABETH, writer; b. Albuquerque, May 31, 1948; d. Sherman Carroll Anderson and Sudie Elizabeth Rumple; 1 child, Pepper Kristofer Fajans. BA, U. N.Mex, Albuquerque, 1970. Writer EasyRead Copywriting, LLC, Albuquerque, 1990—, med. writer, 1996—; program coord. U. Wash., Seattle, 1997—2002. Mem.: Am. Med. Writers Assn. (N. Mex. dir. 2004—07). Office: EasyRead Copywriting LLC PO Box 6146 Albuquerque NM 87197 Home Phone: 505-345-1963; Office Phone: 505-345-3258. Business E-Mail: kristina@easyreadcopywriting.com.

ANDERSON, LAWRENCE KEITH, electrical engineer, consultant; b. Toronto, Ont., Can., Oct. 2, 1935; came to U.S., 1957; s. Wallace Ray and Irene Margaret (Linn) A.; m. Katherine Florence Drechsler, Sept. 21, 1963; children— Susan Barbara, Robert Keith. B. in Engring. Physics, McGill U., 1957; PhDEE, Stanford U., 1962. With Bell Labs., 1961-85, dir. electronic components and Subsystems lab. Allentown, Pa., 1981-85; v.p. component devel. Sandia Nat. Labs., Albuquerque, 1985-88; exec. dir. AT&T Bell Labs. Interconnection and Power Tech. Div., Parsippany, NJ, 1988-89; prof., dir. Alliance for Photonic Tech., Albuquerque, 1990-91; dir. Colo. Inst. Tech. Transfer and Implementation, U. Colo., Colorado Springs, 1991-95. Bd. dirs. Inst. for Lifelong Learning for New Mexicans, 2003—. Fellow IEEE (pres. Electron Devices Soc. 1976-77, bd. dir. 1979-80), Engring. Mgmt. Soc. (bd. govs. 1999-02, v.p. confs. 2001-02). Home: 150 Whitetail Rd NE Albuquerque NM 87122-1921 Personal E-mail: andersnm@aol.com.

ANDERSON, LAWRENCE OHACO, United States magistrate judge, lawyer; b. Phoenix, Sept. 7, 1948; s. Jack M. and Viola (Ohaco) A.; m. Aimee. BS, U. San Francisco, 1971; JD, Ariz. State U., Tempe, 1974. Bar: Ariz. 1975. Prosecutor City of Phoenix, 1973-75; assoc. Jack M. Anderson, Phoenix, 1975-78; sole practice Phoenix, 1978-90; judge Superior Ct. of Ariz., Phoenix, 1990-92, judge, criminal calender, 1992-95, judge, juvenile ct., 1995-98, magistrate judge, 1998—. Natl. Wheelchair Weightlifting Championship, Spokane, Wash., 1974; Victory Achievement Award, State of Ariz., 1990; Outstanding Citizens award, Nat. Counil on Disability, 1992. Mem. ABA, Assn. Trial Lawyers Am., Ariz. Trial Lawyers Assn. (bd. dirs. 1985-90). Republic. Roman Catholic. Avocations: fishing, sports. Office: 401 W Washington SPC11 Phoenix AZ 85003-2120

ANDERSON, LENNART, artist; b. Detroit, Aug. 22, 1928; B.F.A., Art Inst. Chgo., 1950; M.F.A., Cranbrook Acad. Art Mich., 1952. Instr. art Chatham Coll., Pitts., 1961-62, Pratt Inst., NYC, 1962-69, Skowhegan Sch., 1965, 67, Art Students League, NY, Yale U., 1967, Finch Coll., NYC; prof. painting and drawing Bklyn. Coll., 1974—2003. One man shows include Tanager Gallery, NYC, 1962, Graham Gallery, 1963, 67, 69, 70, Davis & Long Co., 1976, Davis & Langdale Co., 1981, 84, 85, 91, 92, William Crapo Gallery, New Bedford, Mass., 1982, Darien Libr., Darien, Conn., 1984, Delaware Art Mus., Wilmington, 1992, Salander-O'Reilly Galleries, 1995, 97, 99, 2002, Rider Univ. Gallery, Lawrenceville, NJ, 2000, others; group shows include March Gallery, NYC, 1957, 58, Palazzo dell'Esposizione, Rome, 1958, 59, 60, Kans. City Art Inst., 1962, Carnegie Internat., Pitts., 1964, 67, Am. Fedn. Arts, NYC, 1965, Yale Univ., 1967, Cleve. Mus. Art, Ohio, 1972, Mus. Fine Arts, Boston, 1975, 1982-83, Art Inst. Chgo., 1976, Harold Reed Gallery, NYC, 1978, Pa. Acad. Fine Arts, Phila., 1981 Robert Schoelkopf Gallery, 1984, 85, Nat. Acad. Design, NYC, 1988, Meml. Art Gallery, Rochester, NY, 1989, Oglethorpe Univ. Art Gallery, Atlanta, 1990, Gerald Peters Gallery, Santa Fe, N.Mex., 1993, Salander-O'Reilly Galleries, Inc., NYC, 1994, 95, Aspen Art Mus., Aspen, Colo., 1996, Art Inst. So. Calif., Laguna Beach, Calif., 1999, Bates Coll. Mus. Art, 2000, Widener Gallery Trinity Coll., Hartford, Conn., 2003, others; represented in permanent collections, Whitney Mus. Am. Art, Bklyn. Mus., Hirschorn Mus., Washington, Mus. Fine Arts, Boston, Cleve., Yale Univ., New Haven, Conn., Delaware Art Mus., Wilmington, Mellon Bank, Pitts., Bklyn. Mus., NY, others. Recipient Prix de Rome, 1958-60; Raymond A. Speiser Meml. prize Pa. Acad. Fine Arts, 1966; Nat. Council on Arts prize, 1966, Academician NAD 1982,Emil & Dines Carlson award NAD, 1988, Benjamin Altman prize, 2005; Mus. Tiffany Found. grantee, 1957, 61, Guggenheim fellow, 1986; grantee Nat. Endowment for Arts, Tiffany Found. Am. Acad. and Inst. Arts and Letters; assoc. Am. Acad. Design. Home: 877 Union St Brooklyn NY 11215-1401

ANDERSON, LESLIE J., lawyer; b. 1953; BA in English Lit. magna cum laude, Allegheny Coll., 1975; MA in English and Comparative Lit., Columbia Univ., 1976, MPhil, 1979; JD cum laude, Univ. Mich., 1983. Bar: Minn. 1983. Assoc. Dorsey & Whitney LLP, Mpls, 1984—91; ptnr., litig. group Dorsey & Whitney, Mpls., 1991, now ptnr., co-chair, employee benefits group. Staff mem. Mich.Yearbook of Internat. Legal Studies, 1981—82, editor-in-chief, 1982—83. Bd. dir. Greater Twin Cities Youth Symphonies, 2003—. Mem.: Minn. Women Lawyers, Minn. Advocates for Human Rights, Phi Beta Kappa. Office: Dorsey & Whitney LLP Ste 1500 50 S Sixth St Minneapolis MN 55402-1498 Office Phone: 612-343-7960. Office Fax: 612-340-2868. Business E-Mail: anderson.leslie@dorsey.com.

ANDERSON, LINDA JEAN, critical care nurse, psychiatric nurse practitioner; b. Louisville, Ky., Mar. 28, 1956; d. James Phillip and Ellabelle Jean (Crowder) Anderson; children: Bradley, Vanessa, Frances, Joseph; m. Donald W. Goodman. BSN, U. Louisville, 1989, MSN, 2000; postgrad. in health care adminstrn., Kennedy Western U., 2005—. ARNP, Ky., Ind. Staff nurse Audubon Regional Med. Ctr., Louisville, 1989-90, Southwest Hosp., 1990-2000, Ctr. for Behavioral Health Bapt. East Hosp., 1996-2000; nurse clinician Vis. Nurses Assn. Louisville, 1990-95; rsch. coord. electrophysiology-cardiology U. Louisville, 1993-94, psychiat. clin. coord. Healthcare U. Hosp., 2000—02; pvt. practice Park View Psychiat. Svc., Jeffersonville, Ind., 2002—05, N.A. Saddiqui & Assocs., Louisville, 2005—07, Frager Assocs., Louisville, 2005—07, Locum Tenens, 2007—. Mem. alumni bd. govs. U. Louisville Sch. Nursing, 1988-97. Mem. ANA, Internat. Soc. Psychiatric Nursing, Kentuckiann Coun. Psychiatric Nursing, Am. Psychiat. Nurses Assn., Sigma Theta Tau. Avocations: watercolor painting, charcoal & pencil sketching, poetry, flute. Office Phone: 502-394-0402.

ANDERSON, LISA, political science professor, researcher, former dean; BA, Sarah Lawrence Coll.; MA in Law and Diplomacy, Tufts U.; PhD in Polit. Sci., Columbia U., certificate in Middle East Studies; LLD (hon.), Monmouth U., 2002. Asst. prof. govt. and social sci. Harvard U.; prof. Middle Eastern and North African studies Columbia U., NYC, 1986, dir. Middle East Inst., 1990—93, chair Polit. Sci. Dept., 1993—97, dean Sch. of Internat. and Pub. Affairs, 1997—2007, James T. Shotwell prof. internat. rels. Chair bd. dirs. Social Sci. Rsch. Coun.; bd. mem. Carnegie Coun. on Ethics in Internat. Affairs; mem. Coun. Fgn. Rels.; bd. mem. emeritus Human Rights Watch. Author: The State and Social Transformation in Tunisia and Libya, 1830-1980, 1986, Pursuing Truth, Exercising Power: Social Science and Public Policy in the Twenty-First Century, 2003; co-editor: The Origins of Arab Nationalism, 1991; editor: Transitions to Democracy, 1999; contbr. articles to profl. jours. Mem.: Am. Polit. Sci. Assn. (coun. mem. 2004—06), Middle East Studies Assn. (past pres.). Office: Columbia U Sch Internat & Pub Affairs 1414 Internat Affairs Bldg, MC 3328 New York NY 10027 Office Phone: 212-854-4604. Office Fax: 212-864-4847. E-mail: la8@columbia.edu.

ANDERSON, LISA D., graphics designer, educator; d. Robert Boston Wilson and Fanny Ruth Dickey. Degree in Mech. Drafting, Mid-Florida Tech. Inst., 1982, Degree in Tech. Illustration, 1983; B in Graphic Design, U. Ctrl. Fla., 1986; MS in Edn., Nova Southeastern U., 1998; PhD, U. South Fla., 2000. Cert. web page design U. South Fla., 2003, web devel. U. South Fla., 2002, Train The Trainer Dvd Sonic, 2002. Mktg. graphic designer east coast Hansen Lind Meyer, Orlando; sr. graphic designer Harris Corp., Orlando, 1991—93; sr. illustrator Westinghouse, Orlando, 1992—95; sr. imager CGS, Tampa, 1995—98; chair advt. and computer graphics IADT, Tampa, 1998—2000, chair graphic design, 1998—2005, pres. interactive group, 2004—. Presenter, rschr. and cons. in field. Named Media Arts Employee Of The Yr., IADT, 2001; recipient Outstanding Contributions To Academic Excellence award, 2003. Mem.: ASCD (assoc.), Soc. For Instrnl. Tech. in Edn. and Tchr. Tng. (assoc.), Internat. Digital Media Assn. (assoc.), Am. Assn. for Computers in Edn. (assoc.), Easter Ednl. Rsch. Assn. (assoc.). Home Phone: 813-431-7424.

ANDERSON, LLOYD LEE, physiologist, educator; b. Nevada, Iowa, Nov. 18, 1933; s. Clarence and Carrie G. (Sampson) A.; m. Janice G. Peterson, Sept. 7, 1958 (dec. Dec. 1966); m. JaNelle R. Hall, June 15, 1970; children: Marc C., James R. *The family cherished 20 years of love and loyal companionship with Cinnamon.* Student, Simpson Coll., 1951-52, Iowa State U., 1952-53, BS in Animal Husbandry, 1957, PhD in Animal Reproduction, 1961; DSc (hon.), Georgian Acad. Scis., Tbilisi, 2003. NIH postdoctoral fellow Iowa State U., Ames, 1961-62, asst. prof., 1961-65, assoc. prof., 1965-71, prof. animal sci., 1971—, Charles F. Curtiss Disting. prof. agr., 1992—, sect. leader animal physiology, 1974—, chmn. com. on coms., faculty senate, 2000—02, prof. biomed. sci., 2002—, sect. leader animal physiology, 1974—. Lalor Found. fellow Sta. Recherches Physiologie Animale, Inst. Nat. Recherche Agronomique, Jouy-en-Josas, France, 1963—64; rschr. physiology of reprodn. and ctrl. nervous sys.-pituitary regulation of growth for increased prodn. efficiency of farm animals; mem. reproductive biology study sect. NIH, 1984—88, NIH Reviewers Res. (NRR), 1988—92; mem. peer rev. panel animal health spl. rsch. grants on beef and dairy cattle reproductive diseases USDA, 1986—88; Honor lectr. representing Iowa State U. Mid-Am. State Univs. Assn., 1989—90; mem. sustainable growth agrl. panel USDA, Agrl. Rsch. Svc., Nat. Program Staff to rev. rsch. projects, 1993; mem. referees panel for sponsored rsch. Kuwait U., 1998—; mem. Janice Peterson Anderson Excellence award and scholarship Coll. of Design Iowa State U., chair com. on coms., Faculty Senate, 2000—02; trustee Asian Inst. Nanobiosci. and Tech., Busan, Republic of Korea, 2002—; mem. selection com. for recipient of George E. Palade Gold Medal and Lecture award Wayne State U. Sch. Medicine, 2003—; hon. mem. sci. coun. Georgian Inst. Physiology, 2003—; mem. competitive grants rev. bd. NSF, 2006—, Georgian NSF, 2006—. Mem. editl. bd. Biology Reprodn., 1968-70, 86-90, Jour. Animal Sci., 1982-87, 98-2001, Animal Reprodn. Sci., 1978—, Inst. for Sci. Info. Atlas of Sci., 1987-90, Domestic Animal Endocrinology, 1992-95, 2004-06, Endocrinology, 1993-97, Jour. Cellular and Molecular Medicine, 2005-; guest editor, Cell Secretion Rev. Series, 2006-; contbr. articles to profl. jours. Mem. 4-H Club. With Constrn. Engrs., U.S. Army, 1953-55, Germany, Signal Corps USAR, 1955-61. Recipient Cert. Recognition, Cold War, 1991, Disting. Achievement award, Iowa State U. Alumni Assn., 2005, Golden Diploma in recognition of 50th anniversary of graduation, 2007, dedication, Little N.Am. Livestock Show, 2006; grantee, USDA, 1978—. Fellow AAAS, Am. Soc. Animal Sci. (hon. Animal Physiology and Endocrinology award 1988, Nat Pork Prodrs. Coun. Innovation award in basic rsch. 1993, Outstanding Achievement in Rsch. award 2001, Animal Growth and Devel. award 2004, F.B. Morrison award 2007); mem. ACLU, NRA, VFW, Endocrine Soc., Am. Physiol. Soc., Iowa Physiol. Soc., Am. Assn. Anatomists, Am. Soc. Cell Biology, Soc. Study of Reprodn., Soc. Exptl. Biology and Medicine (mem. coun. 1980-83), Brit. Soc. for Study of Fertility, Soc. Neurosci., Iowa Acad. Sci., Pituitary Soc., Asian Inst. of Nanobiosci. and Tech., Busan, Korea (trustee 2002—), Am. Legion, Nat. Block and Bridle Club, Osborn Rsch. Club (chair 1994), Sigma Xi, Gamma Sigma Delta (Mission award in rsch. 2002, Alumni Merit award 2004), Alpha Tau Omega (Gold Cir. award 2002). Methodist. Home: 2812 Valley View Rd Ames IA 50014-4506 Office: Iowa State U Dept Animal Sci 2356 Kildee Hl Ames IA 50011-3150 Office Phone: 515-294-5540. Business E-Mail: llanders@iastate.edu.

ANDERSON, LOUIS WILMER, JR., physicist, researcher; b. Houston, Dec. 24, 1933; s. Louis Wilmer and Margaret Quarles (Brockett) A.; m. Marguerite Gillespie, Aug. 30; children— Margaret Mary, Louis Charles, Elizabeth Brockett BA, Rice U., 1956; A.M., Harvard U., 1957, PhD, 1960. Asst. prof. U. Wis.-Madison, 1960-63, assoc. prof., 1963-68, prof. physics, 1968-94, Julian E. Mack prof. physics, 1994—. Cons. U. Calif.-Berkeley Lawrence Lab. Author 2 textbooks. Contbr. articles to profl. jours. Patentee type of N2 laser , collisional pumping ion source. Fellow U. Wis. Tchg. Acad.; co-recipient IEEE Particle Accelerator Conf. Tech. award for invention and devel. of optically pumped polarized H-Ion source, 1993. Fellow Am. Phys. Soc.; mem. Sigma Xi Home: 1818 Chadbourne Ave Madison WI 53726 Office: U Wis Dept Physics Madison WI 53706 Office Phone: 608-262-8962. Business E-Mail: lwanders@wisc.edu.

ANDERSON, LYLE ARTHUR, retired manufacturing executive; b. Jewell, Kans., Dec. 29, 1931; s. Arvid Herman and Clara Vera (Herman) A.; m. Harriet Virginia Robson, June 12, 1953; children— Brian, Karen, Eric. BS, U. Kans., 1953; MS, Butler U., 1961. C.P.A., Mo., Kans. Mgmt. trainee, internal auditor RCA, Camden, N.J. and Indpls., 1955-59; auditor Ernst & Ernst (C.P.A.'s), Kansas City, Mo., 1959-63; v.p. fin. and adminstrn., treas., dir. Affiliated Hosp. Products, Inc., St. Louis, 1963-71; sr. v.p. Sara Lee Corp., Deerfield, Ill., 1971-74; exec. v.p. fin. Consol. Foods Corp., Chgo., 1974-76. Pres. Autotrol Corp., Crystal Lake, Ill. Bd. dirs. Crystal Lake Civic Ctr. Authority. With U.S. Army, 1953-55. Mem. Omicron Delta Kappa. Republican. Methodist. Home: 9804 Partridge Ln Crystal Lake IL 60014-6627

ANDERSON, MARCIE, communications executive; BS in Bus. Mgmt., Bellevue Univ. Broadband installer Nortel Comm.; divsn. team leader Cox Comm., Ariz., project mgr., residential telephone svc. Atlanta, dir. data ops., v.p., bus. devel., 2002—. Fields instr. tech. US Army, 1991. Mem.: Soc. Cable Telecom. Engrs. (Women in Tech. award 2003), Women in Cable TV.

ANDERSON, MARK ROBERT, data processing executive, biochemist; b. Oak Park, Ill., Aug. 11, 1951; s. Robert Hugo and Marilyn Pettee (Johnson) A.; m. Mary Jane Helsell, June 6, 1980; children: Berit Bracken, Evan Robert. BS, Stanford U., 1972; MS, Stanford U., Hopkins Marine Sta., 1973; postgrad., U. Brit. Columbia, Vancouver, 1973. Publisher Potlatch Press, Friday Harbor, Wash., 1974-77; assoc. prof. Western Wash. U., Bellingham, 1977, Harvard U., Boston, 1978; chief scientist Ocean Research & Edn. Soc., Boston, 1978; v.p. Moclips Cetological Soc., Friday Harbor, 1979-81; founder, exec. dir. The Whale Mus., Friday Harbor, 1979-81; pres. The Oikos Co., Friday Harbor, 1980—, San Juan Software, Friday Harbor, 1983-84; pres., bd. dirs. Island Tech. Inc., Friday Harbor, 1984—89; founder, pres. Tech. Alliance Ptnrs., 1989—; pres. SNS Conf. Corp., 2003—. Bd. dirs. Worldesign, PreText, Inc., Wa. Software Assn.; bd. advisors HIT Lab., U. Wash., 1991-95; founder, pres. Strategic News Svc. LLC, 1995—; founder WSA Investment Forum; CEO, bd. dirs. Carrier Wave, Inc., 1996-98; program chair Online Advantage 96; founder, exec. dir. Orca Relief Citizens Alliance, 1998-2001, chmn., 2001-; founder, mgr. The Resonance Fund, 1999—; bd. advisors Smartage, Inc., 1999-2000, E-CHRON, Stockholm, 1999-2001, Ignition Corp., 2000—; dir. Hybrid Vigor Inst., 2001-2003; mem. adv. bd. Merrill Lynch, 1999—; founding chair SNS Project Inkwell, 2003—, The Foresight Found., 2004—. Author: Nineteen Fathers, 1971, (software) The Agent's Advantage, 1983; producer TV film Survivors, 1980; editor, founder Jour. Cetus, 1981; discoverer Resonance Theory, 1980; columnist ABC News.com, 1998-2000, Citywire, UK, 1999-2001, Microsoft Money Central, 2000-2002, Fortune mag., 2003-. Founder San Juan Musicians Guild, 1974-78, Anti-Spray Coalition, 1977, founding chair SNS Future in Rev. Conf., 2003—. Mem. Wash. Software Assn. (bd. dirs. 1988-90, chair pres.'s group 1989-2005. Avocations: theoretical physics, musical composition, skiing. Office Phone: 360-378-3431. Personal E-mail: sns@tapsns.com.

ANDERSON, MARY ANN GRASSO, business executive; b. Rome, NY, Nov. 3, 1952; d. Vincent and Rose Mary (Pupa) Grasso; m. J. Wayne Anderson, Feb. 14, 2004. BA in Art History, U. Calif., Riverside, 1973; MLS, U. Oreg., 1974. Dir. Warner Rsch. Collection, Burbank, Calif., 1975-84; mgr. CBS TV/Docudrama, Hollywood, Calif., 1984-88; v.p., exec. dir. Nat. Assn. Theatre Owners, North Hollywood, Calif., 1988—. Instr. theatre arts UCLA, 1980-85, Am. Film Inst., L.A., 1985-88; founder, CEO Belief Work; pres., CEO An Affair of the Heart. Screen credits: The Scarlet O'Hara Wars, This Year's Blonde, The Silent Lovers, A Bunnies Tale, Embassy. Mem. Burbank Heritage Commn. Named ShoWester of Yr.,

NATO/ShoWest, 2007; recipient Friend award, Tripod Sch., 1999, Stace award, Dolby, 2002, Intersoc. Ken Mason award, 2004, award of commendation, Sci.-Tech. Acad. Motion Pictures Art Scis., 2007. Mem.: Found. of the Motion Picture Pioneers, Acad. Motion Picture Arts and Scis., Retinitis Pigmentosa Internat. (The Vision award 1996), Bus. and Profl. Women's Assn. (Woman of Achievement award 1983), Phi Beta Kappa. Avocations: music, dance. Office: PO Box 371 Taneytown MD 21787 Office Phone: 410-346-6679.

ANDERSON, MARY JANE, music educator; b. St. Louis, Oct. 9, 1954; d. William Edward and Katherine Ruth Anderson. Student, The Juilliard Sch., 1967—72; BFA Piano Performance, Stephens Coll., 1976; MusM Piano Performance, So. Ill. U., Edwardsville, 1991. Mem. piano faculty St. Louis Conservatory and Schs. for Arts, St. Louis, 1977—81, So. Ill. U., Edwardsville, 1984—; pvt. piano instr. St. Louis, 1975—. Adjudicator state and local piano competitions, Mo. and Ill.; soloist St. Louis Symphony, St. Louis Philharmonic; recitalist, orchestral soloist numerous performances throughout Midwest U.S., Pa, N.Y. Recipient 1st pl. Profl. Debut Recital, Artist Presentation Soc., 1975, 1st pl. Dimitri Mitropoulos Nat. Piano Competition, Stephens Coll., 1972; scholar, Dimitri Mitropoulos Piano Competition; Piano scholar, Am. Acad. Arts in Europe, 1975. Mem.: St. Louis Area Music Tchrs. Assn. (pres. 2002—06), Mo. Music Tchrs. Assn., Music Tchrs. Nat. Assn. Avocations: reading, fishing, crossword puzzles. Office: So Ill U Edwardsville Music Dept PO Box 1771 Edwardsville IL 62026-1771 Office Phone: 618-650-2022. Business E-Mail: manders@siue.edu.

ANDERSON, MAURICE ELTON, minister; b. Miami, Fla., Apr. 6, 1958; s. Levi Anderson Sr. and Lois Anderson; m. Marshell Williams Anderson, Apr. 28, 2001; 1 child, Maurice E. Jr. A of Bibl. Studies, Andersonville Theol. Seminary, Camilla, Ga., 1998, B of Theology, 1999, M of Theology, 2001, D of Theology, 2003. Assoc. min. Mt. Olove Primitive Bapt. Ch., Miami, 1990—. Chief petty officer USN, Miami, 1977—2003. Cpo USN, 1977—2003, Miami. Mem.: Am. Postal Workers Union, Chief Petty OFficer Assn. Democrat. Baptist.

ANDERSON, MAXWELL L., museum director; b. NYC, May 1, 1956; AB, Dartmouth Coll., 1977; AM, Harvard U., 1978, PhD, 1981. Asst. curator Met. Mus., 1982-87; dir. Michael C. Carlos Mus., Atlanta, 1987-95, Art Gallery Ont., Toronto, Can., 1995-98, Whitney Mus. Am. Art, NYC, 1998—2003; prin. AEA Consulting; dir. and CEO Indpls. Mus. Art, 2006—. Lectr. Roman art Princeton (N.J.) U., 1985; vis. prof. U. di Roma, 1987; adj. assoc. prof. Emory U., 1989-95. Arranged exhbns. Treasures of the Holy Land, 1986, Roman Portraits in Context, 1988, Souls Grown Deep, 1996, Wired Mus., 1997, 2000 Biennial Exhbn. Mem.: Assn. Art Mus. Dirs. (pres.), Coll. Art Assn., Am. Assn. Mus. Office: Indpls Museum of Art 4000 Michigan Rd Indianapolis IN 46208-3326

ANDERSON, MAYNARD CARLYLE, security firm executive; b. Hesper, Iowa, Aug. 6, 1932; s. Carl Adolph and Mathilda Theodora (Wold) A. BA, Luther Coll., 1954. Mem. spl. ops. group Hqrs. Dept. of Navy, Washington, 1966-68, supervising agt. Naval Investigative Svc. Office Guantanamo Bay, Cuba, 1968-69, asst. head internal security divsn. hqrs. Washington, 1969-73, dir. spl. security and spl. activiites, 1973-78, dir. spl. security, 1978-79; dep. security policy Dept. of Def., Washington, 1979-82, dir. security plans and programs, 1982-88, asst. dep. under sec., 1988-93, acting dep. under sec. def., 1993-94; pres., mng. dir. Arcadia Group Worldwide, Inc., Chantilly, Va., 1994—2006; founder Arcadia Inst., Chantilly, 1997; prin. Strategic Trade Adv. Group, Inc., Washington, 1997—. Dir. Nat. Intellectual Property Law Inst., Washington, 1994; chmn. policy com. Security Affairs Support Assn., Washington, 1988—94; former chmn. adv. com. Dept. of Def. Security Inst., Dept. of Def. Polygraph Inst., Def. Pers. Security Rsch. and Edn. Ctr.; chmn. Nat. Adv. Group/Security Countermeasures; hon. faculty mem. Def. Security Inst.; lectr. Sch. Criminal Justice, Coll. Social Sci. Mich. State U., mem. rsch. task force; lectr. Luther Coll., Decorah, Iowa; del. UN Econ. Commn. for Europe, Com. on Sustained Devel., 1999—; dir. VT Griffin Svcs., Inc., Atlanta, 2002—, mng. dir. multi-sector crisis mgmt. consortium, Arlington, Va., 2003—; dir. Leader Tech., Inc., Columbus, Ohio, 2007—. Author/contbr.: Citizen Espionage: Studies in Trust and Betrayal, 1994; contbr. articles to profl. jours. Mem. pres. coun. Luther Coll., Decorah, Iowa, 1990—. Recipient Meritorious Exec. Presdl. Rank award, Washington, 1985, 92, Disting. Svc. award Luther Coll., Decorah, 1989, Donald B. Woodbridge award of excellence Nat. Classification Mgmt. Soc., Washington, 1990, Def. Disting. Svc. medal, 1992. Lutheran. Avocations: tennis, writing, lecturing, travel. Home: 205 S Yoakum Pky Apt 721 Alexandria VA 22304-3818 Office: The Arcadia Inst Inc PO Box 22030 Alexandria VA 22304 E-mail: arcadiagwi@iopener.net. *Sometimes it seems that significant achievements have been realized by accident. Actually, they have resulted from taking advantage of opportunities.*

ANDERSON, MICHAEL STEVEN, lawyer; b. Mpls., May 25, 1954; s. Wesley James and Lorraine Kathrine (Sword) A.; m. Gail Karin Miller, June 18, 1977; children: Mark, Steven. BA magna cum laude, Cornell U., 1976; JD, Washington U., St. Louis, 1980. Bar: Wis. 1980, U.S. Dist. Ct. (ea. and we. dists.) Wis. 1980, U.S. Ct. Appeals (7th cir.) 1986, U.S. Supreme Ct. 1991. Ptnr. Axley Brynelson, Madison, Wis., 1980—2003, mng. ptnr., 2003—. Bd. dirs. Oakwood Village East Continuing Care Retirement Communities, 2003—, Nehemiah Cmty. Devel. Corp., 2005—, Wis. Equal Justice Fund, Inc., 2005—; chmn. Oakwood Ethics Com., 2005—; chmn. bd. dir. Oakwood Village East Continuing Care Retirement Cmty., 2007—. Editor, author Washington U. Law Quarterly, 1979-80. Bench and Bar Com. State Bar Wis., 2004—; bd. dirs. Blackhawk Ch., 2004—; apptd. mem. local Bd. Attys. Profl. Responsibility, 1993—2001; preliminary rev. com. mem. Office Lawyer Regulation, 2002—, chair preliminary rev. com., 2007—. Mem.: Licensing Execs. Soc., Order of Coif. Mem. Evangelical Free Ch. Office: Axley Brynelson 2 E Mifflin St Madison WI 53703-2889 Office Phone: 608-283-6708. Business E-Mail: manderson@axley.com.

ANDERSON, MICHAEL THOMAS, mathematics professor, researcher, director; b. Boulder, Colo., Nov. 17, 1950; s. Julian Thompson and Elinor Elizabeth (Uhl) A.; m. Myong Hi Kim, Aug. 15, 1986; 1 child, Steven. BA, U. Calif., Santa Barbara, 1975; MA, U. Calif., Berkeley, 1977, PhD, 1981. Rsch. instr. Rice U., Houston, 1981-84; from asst. to assoc. prof. Calif. Inst. Tech., Pasadena, 1984-88; assoc. prof. SUNY, Stony Brook, 1988-91, prof., 1991—, grad. prog. dir., 2004—. Invited spkr. Internat. Congress Maths., Zurich, 1994. Assoc. editor: Duke Math. Jour., 1991—, mem. editl. bd.: Jour. Geometric and Functional Analysis, 1991—2000; contbr. articles to profl. jours. Recipient Annales Henri Poincare prize, 2000; NSF grantee, 1981—; NSF postdoctoral fellow, 1984-86. Mem. Am. Math. Soc. (rsch. fellow 1990-91). Democrat. Office: SUNY Dept Math Stony Brook NY 11794-3651 Home Phone: 631-689-3406; Office Phone: 631-632-8269. E-mail: anderson@math.sunysb.edu.

ANDERSON, MICHELLE J., dean, law educator; m. Gavin P. McCormick, Apr. 2006. BA with honors, U. Calif., Santa Cruz, 1989; JD, Yale U., 1994; LLM, Georgetown U., 1997. Bar: Calif. 1995. Law clerk to Hon. William A. Norris US Ct. of Appeals (9th cir.), 1994—95; supervising atty. Appellate Litig. Clinic Georgetown U. Law Ctr., 1995—97, vis. assoc. prof. Inst. for Pub. Representation, 1997; prof. Villanova U. Sch. Law, 1998—2006; dean CUNY Sch. Law, Flushing, NY, 2006—. Vis. prof. U. Pitts. Sch. Law, 2004; disting. scholar St. John's U. Sch. Law, 2005. Contbr. articles to law jours. Mem.: ABA, Soc. Am. Law Tchrs., Women in Transition, Pa. Coalition against Sexual Assault (bd. dirs.), Nat. Alliance to End Sexual Violence (bd. dirs., policy chair). Office: CUNY Law Sch 65-21 Main St Flushing NY 11367 Office Phone: 718-340-4370. E-mail: academicdeanoffice@mail.law.cuny.edu.

ANDERSON, MO, real estate company executive; b. Okla. m. Richard Anderson; 2 children. BS, U. Okla. Elementary sch. music tchr.; prin., owner office Century 21, Edmond, Okla., 1975—86; dist. v.p. Merrill Lynch Realty Nat., Okla. City, 1986—89; from owner and regional dir. Okla. Region to pres., CEO Keller Williams Realty Internat., Austin, Tex., 1992—95, pres., 1995—2002, CEO, 1995—2005, vice chair. Mem. Okla. Real Estate Commn., 1986, chair. Founder KW Cares, 2003; bd. dirs. Edmond Meml. Hosp., Francis Tuttle Vo-Tech Found., Daily Living Ctr. Named Okla.'s Women in Bus. Advocate of Yr., US Small Bus. Adminstrn.; named one of Real Estate's 25 Most Influential Thought Leaders, Realtor Mag., 2006. Avocation: piano. Office: Keller Williams Realty 1801 S Mo Pac Expressway Austin TX 78746*

ANDERSON, M.T., children's book writer and illustrator; b. 1968; BA, Harvard Univ; MFA, Syracuse Univ. Instr. Vermont Coll., Montpelier, Vt. Illustrator: picture books Handel Who Knew What He Liked, 2002 (Horn Book award, Boston Globe, 2002), Strange Mr. Satie, The Serpent Who Came to Gloucester, Me, all Alone, at the End of the World; author: (children's books) Thirsty, BurgerWuss, Feed, The Game of Sunken Places, Whale on Stilts, The Astonishing Life of Octavian Nothing, Traitor to the Nation, Volume 1, 2006 (Nat. Book award for Children's writing, 2006).*

ANDERSON, N. CHRISTIAN, III, former newspaper publisher; b. Montpelier, Idaho, Aug. 4, 1950; s. Nelson C. and Esther Barbara Anderson; m. Sara Ann Coffenberry, Dec. 11, 1971 (div.); children: Ryan, Erica; m. Aletha Ann Yurewicz, May 3, 1986; children: Paul, Amanda. BA in Liberal Studies with honors, Ore. State U., 1972. From asst. city editor to city editor Albany (Oreg.) Democrat-Herald, 1972—75; mng. editor Walla Walla (Wash.) Union Bulletin, 1975—77; assoc. mng. editor Seattle Times, 1977—80; from editor to exec. v.p., assoc. publisher The Orange County Register, Santa Ana, Calif., 1980—94; pub. Gazette Telegraph, Colorado Springs, 1994—98; pub. & CEO Orange County Register, Santa Ana, 1999—2007; sr. v.p. Freedom Comm., Inc., Irvine, Calif., 1999; pres. & CEO Freedom Orange County Info., 2000—07; pres., metro divsn. Freedom Comm., Inc., Irvine, Calif., 2001—07. Instr. Calif. State U., Fullerton, 1983, Fullerton, 87; Pulitzer Prize juror, 87, 88, 96; exec. editor Freedom Newspapers, Inc., Irvine, Calif., 1990—94; exec. v.p., CEO Golden West Publ., Irvine, 1991—94; mem. adv. bd. Poynter Inst. for Media Studies, St. Petersburg, Fla., 1994—99, also past chmn. adv. bd.; former chmn. bd. dirs. New Directions for News, newspaper think tank; mem. nominating com. AP; bd. dirs. Robert C. Maynard Inst. for Journalism Edn.; editor-in-chief, pub. OC Post, 2006—. Past chmn. Orange County Bus. Com. for Arts; past mem., bd. dirs. Calif. First Amendment Coalition; bd. dirs. Santa Ana Rotary Found., 1984, Colorado Springs Fine Arts Ctr., 1994—98, Colorado Springs Non-Profit Ctr., 1994—98, Colorado Springs Sports Corp., 1994—98, Pike's Peak United Way, 1994—98, South Coast Repertory, Econ. Devel. Corp., Colorado Springs, chmn. bd., 1996; bd. trustees, past pres. South Coast Repertory, 2004—06; bd. trustees Orange County Comm. Found., St. Margaret's Episcopal Sch. Named Nat. Newspaper Editor of Yr., 1989, Calif. Newspaper Exec. of Yr., Calif. Press Assn., 1993, Pub. of Yr., Editor & Pub., 2007; recipient George D. Beveridge award, Nat. Press Found., 1989. Mem.: Calif. Soc. Newspaper Editors (founder, former bd. dirs. and pres.), Soc. Newspaper Design (co-founder), Am. Soc. Newspaper Editors (bd. dirs. 1996, treas. 1996, sec. 1997, v.p. 1998, pres. 1999).*

ANDERSON, NANCY DIXON, librarian; b. Clarkesville, Ga., Oct. 7, 1938; d. Sherman Allen and Willie Mae (Black) Dixon; m. David Morris Anderson, Nov. 23, 1958 (div. June 1978); children: Wendy, Laurie, David Jr. BS in Mid. Grades Edn., Brenau Coll., 1981; MEd in Ednl. Media, U. Ga., 1985. Asst. prof. humanities, libr. Brenau Coll., Gainesville, Ga., 1979-87; also acad. tutor Learning Disability Ctr., 1985-87; dir. libr. Hightower Libr. Gordon Coll., Barnesville, Ga., 1987—, assoc. prof., 1987—. Children's ch. dir. 1st Presbyn. Ch., Gainesville, 1983-87; v.p. Friends of Libr., Barnesville/Lamar County, 1991; pres. Newcomers Club, Gainesville, 1974, Phoenix Soc., Ga. Fedn. Women's Club, Gainesville, 1978; pub. chmn. Barnesville Women's League, 1992-94; pres. Barnesville Garden Club, 1992; mem. Community Svcs. Bd., Barnesville, 1994—; elder Barnesville Presbyn. Ch. Mem. Ga. Libr. Assn., Ctr. Ga. Associated Librs. Consortium (pres. 1992-93). Avocations: gardening, travel, reading. Home: 236 Harrell Cir Barnesville GA 30204-1751 Office: Gordon Coll Hightower Libr 419 College Dr Barnesville GA 30204-1746 Office Phone: 770-358-5078.

ANDERSON, NED, SR., Apache tribal chairman; b. Bylas, Ariz., Jan. 18, 1943; s. Paul and Maggie (Rope) Anderson; m. Delphina Hinton; children: Therese Kay, Linette Mae, Magdalene Gail, Ned, Sean. AA, Ea. Ariz. Coll., 1964, AAS in Computer Sci., 1989; BS, U Ariz., 1967, JD, 1973. Field dir. Nat. Study Indian Edn. dept. anthropology U. Ariz., Tucson, 1968-70, dir. Jojoba Project, Office of Arid Land Studies, 1973-76; tech. asst. Project Head Start Ariz. State U., Tempe, 1970; ethnographer Smithsonian Instn., Washington, 1970-73; with Jojoba devel. project San Carlos Apache Tribe, Ariz., 1976-78, tribal councilman, 1976-78, 93-98, tribal chmn., 1978-86, gen. mgr. spl. housing projects, 1991-99, coord. Ctrl. Ariz. project, 1999—. Contbr. articles to profl. jours. Mem. affirmative action com. City of Tucson, 1975—76; mem. study panel NAS, 1975—76; mem. supervisory bd. Ariz. Justice Planning Commn., 1978; mem. county govt. study commn. State of Ariz., 1981—84; mem. reinvention mgmt. lab. workgroup Nat. Housing Improvement Program, 1995—96; mem. Indian adv. bd. Intergovernmental Pers. Program, 1978; mem. adv. bd. Am. Indian Registry Performing Arts, 1985, San Carlos Fish and Game Commn., 1975, chmn., 1976; pres. Intertribal Coun. Ariz., 1979—85, 1992; pres. bd. dirs. Ft. Thomas HS Unified Dist., 1977, clk., 1987, clk. bd. dirs., 1989; bd. dirs. Southwestern Indian Devel., Inc., 1971, Indian Enterprise Devel. Corp., 1976—78, San Carlos Lake Devel., 1994—98, We. Apache Constrn. Co., 1994—98, Apache Gold Resort Pub. Authority, 1997—99, vice chmn., acting chmn., 2002—03, chmn., 2004—07; mem. adv. bd. Gila Pueblo CC ext. Ea. Ariz. Coll., 1979, Indian Edn., Ariz. State U., Tempe, 1978—86, U. Ariz., Tucson, 1978—86; trustee Bacone Coll.; enterprise bd. chmn. Apache Gold Casino Resort, 2003—07. Recipient Outstanding CC Alumni award, Ariz. CC Bd./Ea. Ariz. Coll., 1982, Outstanding Coop. award, U.S. Secret Svc., 1984, Univ. Rels. award, AT&T, 1989; A. T. Anderson Meml. scholar, 1989. Mem.: Ariz. Acad., Globe C. of C., Nat. Tribal Chmn.'s Assn. (mem. bd. edn., mem. adv. bd. 1978—86), Phi Theta Kappa. Home Phone: 928-475-4205; Office Phone: 928-475-3832.

ANDERSON, NICK, editorial cartoonist; b. Toledo, Ohio; m. Cecilia Anderson; 2 children. Grad in Polit. Sci., Ohio State Univ., 1991. Summer intern Louisville Courier-Journal, Ky., assoc. editl. cartoonist, 1991—95, chief editl. cartoonist, 1995—2006; editl. cartoonist Houston Chronicle, 2006—. Syndicated cartoonist Wash. Post Writers Group, 1996—. Recipient Charles M. Schulz award for best coll. cartoonist in US, Canada, Mexico, 1989, John Fischetti award for editl. cartooning, 1999, Sigma Delta Chi Mark of Excellence award, 2001, Pulitzer Prize for editl. cartooning, 2005. Avocations: kayaking, mountain biking. Office: Editl Cartoonist Houston Chronicle 801 Texas Ave Houston TX 77002 Office Phone: 502-582-4011, 713-362-7171.

ANDERSON, NORMA V., retired state legislator; b. Elyria, Ohio, July 6, 1932; Student, Denver U., Jones Real Estate Coll. Owner, operator KBJ Stables; office mgr. Capitol Solar; supr. Time, Inc.; mem. Colo. Ho. of Reps., Dist. 30, 1986-98, Fin. & State Affairs Coms., Legis. Coun., Colo. Senate, Dist. 22, Denver, 1998—2006, Judiciary, Appropriations Coms., Legis. Coun., State Compensation Bd., Colo. Uninsurable Health Ins. Bd.; majority leader, chair Legis. Audit, Edn., Trans. & Energy Coms.; vice-chair Health, Environ., Welfare & Inst. Com., Legis. Audit Com., Judiciary Com., Assembly on Fed. Issues; chair Minority Caucus, Bus. Affairs & Labor Com.; mem. labor dept. State Adv. Coun.; exec. com., chair Energy & Trans.; co-chair Social Security Task Force, DC. Mem. state adv. coun. labor dept.; bd. dir. state compensation, regional transp. dist., Foothills Found.; mem. West Chamber; mem. numerious senate coms. including most recently jud. com., appropriations com. Vice-chair Health Environ. Welfare Insts.; bd. dirs. Foothills Found.; mem. budget com. R-1 Sch. Dist; exec. com. Nat. Conf. State Legis.; vice-chair Arapahow House; adv. bd. Drug Control Systems Improvement, Com. Corrections; mem. Am. Cancer Soc., Bear Creek Jr. Sports Assn., Great Outdoors Colo. Republican. Office: State Capitol 200 E Colfax Ave Ste 274 Denver CO 80203-1716 Office Phone: 303-866-4859. E-mail: norma.anderson.senate@state.co.us.

ANDERSON, PAMELA DENISE, actress; b. Ladysmith, BC, Can., July 1, 1967; d. Barry and Carol Anderson; m. Tommy Lee, Feb. 19, 1995 (div. Feb. 28, 1998); children: Brandon Thomas Lee, Dylan Jagger Lee; m. Robert James "Kid Rock" Ritchie, July 29, 2006 (separated Nov. 2006). Syndicated columnist Jane, 2002—, Marie Claire, 2002—, Can. Elle, 2002—; launched clothing line "The Pamela Collection", 2003—. Actor: (TV series) Home Improvement, 1991—93, Baywatch, 1992—97; actor, exec. prodr.: (TV series) V.I.P., 1998; actor(voice): Stripperella, 2003, Stacked, 2005—; (TV films) Baywatch: River of No Return, 1992, Come Die with Me: A Mickey Spillane Mike Hammer Mystery, 1994, Baywatch: Forbidden Paradise, 1995, Naked Souls, 1996, Baywatch: Hawaiian Wedding, 2003, (guest appearances): (TV series) Charles in Charge, 1990, Married with Children, 1990, 1991, Top of the Heap, 1991, Days of Our Lives, 1992, The Nanny, 1997, Home Improvement, 1997, Just Shoot Me, 2001, Less Than Perfect, 2002, (guest appearances, voice) Futurama, 1999,: (films) Snapdragon, 1993, Raw Justice, 1994, Naked Souls, 1995, Barb Wire, 1996, Scary Movie 3, 2003, Borat, 2006, (music videos for) Aerosmith, Lit, Cinderella, Vince Neil, Bree Sharp, Methods of Mayhem, Jaz-Z, Kid Rock; author: (novels) Star, 2004. Activist PETA; participant Nat. Conf. Viral Hepatitis, Can. Liver Found.; founder Pamela Anderson Found.; grand marshall S.O.S. ride Am. Liver Found., 2002. Recipient Linda McCartney award for animal rights, 1999. Achievements include has appeared a record twelve times on the cover of Playboy. Office: William Morris Agy 151 El Camino Dr Beverly Hills CA 90212*

ANDERSON, PARKER LYNN, columnist, playwright; b. Wickenburg, Ariz., Apr. 19, 1964; s. Harry Milton and Darla Raejean (Hangartner) A. Mem. prodn. com. Prescott (Ariz.) Fine Arts Assn., 1993-95, 98—, adv. mem., 1987—; columnist, theatre critic The Prescott News, 1995-96; with Cath. Social Svc. of Yavapai, 1983—. Mem. adv. com. The Blue Rose Theatre Co., Prescott, 1994—. Author: (plays) The Startled Cowboys, 1991, Voices From the Past, 1995, The Sleeping Toad, 1997, Virgil Earp, 1998, Until the Last Dog is Hung, 2000, Murder Dismissed, 2001; co-author: (plays) Lady with a Gun (with Jody Drake), 2002, Don't Despise Me (with Gail Mangham), 2006, Another Kind of Miller, 2006. Home: PO Box 1285 Prescott AZ 86302-1285 E-mail: parkerr86302@yahoo.com.

ANDERSON, PAUL HOLDEN, state supreme court justice; b. May 14, 1943; m. Janice M. Anderson; 2 children. BA cum laude, Macalester Coll., 1965; JD, U. Minn., 1968. Atty. Vols. in Svc. to Am., 1968—69; spl. asst. atty. gen. criminal divsn. dept. pub. safety Office Minn. Atty. Gen., 1970—71; assoc., ptnr. LeVander, Gillen & Miller, South St. Paul, Minn., 1971—92; chief judge Minn. Ct. Appeals, 1992—94; assoc. justice Minn. Supreme Ct., 1994—. Mem. PER coms. Ind. Sch. Dist. 199, 1982—84, chmn. cmty. svcs. adv. com., bd. dirs., chmn. bd.; deacon, ruling elder, clk. of session House of Hope Presbyn. Ch., St. Paul. Mem.: Dakota County Bar Assn. (bd. dirs., pres.), South St. Paul/Inver Grove Heights C. of C. (bd. dirs., exec. com.). Avocations: tennis, gourmet cooking, bike riding. Office: 425 Minn Judicial Ctr 25 Rev Dr Martin Luther King Jr Blvd Saint Paul MN 55155-0001 Office Phone: 651-296-3314. Fax: 651-282-5115. Business E-Mail: paul.anderson@courts.state.mn.us.*

ANDERSON, PAUL IRVING, management executive; b. Portland, Oreg., Mar. 23, 1935; s. William F. and Ruth M. (Sundquist) Anderson; m. Lorraine A. Franz, Nov. 21, 1959; children: Todd, Susan, Cheryl, Cynthia. BS, Oreg. State U., 1956. Various positions in mktg., sales and engring. mgmt. 3M Co., St. Paul, Boston, 1956—74, gen. mgr. Brussels, 1974—77, dir. group bus. planning St. Paul, 1977—79; sr. v.p., gen. mgr. Rayovac Corp., Madison, Wis., 1979—82; pres. Anderson Cons. Co., Madison, 1982—83; divsn. v.p. RCA Corp., Indpls., 1983—84; pres. Anderson & Assocs., La Costa, Calif., 1984—87; pres., CEO Electro-Imaging Advisors, Inc., La Jolla, Calif., 1987—93; CEO Strategic Catalysts Inc., La Jolla, 1993—2004. Mem.: Am. Mgmt. Assn., Nakoma Golf Club, Columbia Club (Indpls.), Madison Club, Sigma Tau, Pi Tau Sigma, Tau Beta Pi. Republican. Presbyterian.

ANDERSON, PAUL MAURICE, electrical engineering educator, researcher, consultant; b. Des Moines, Jan. 22, 1926; s. Neil W. and Buena Vista (Thompson) A.; m. Virginia Ann Worswick, July 8, 1950; children: William, Mark, James, Thomas. BSEE, Iowa State U., 1949, MSEE, 1958, PhD, 1961. Registered profl. elec. engr., Ariz., Calif., Iowa, Guam; registered control sys. engr., Calif. Elec. engr. Iowa Pub. Service Co., Sioux City, 1949-55; prof. elec. engring. Iowa State U., Ames, 1955-75; program mgr. Electric Power Research Inst., Palo Alto, Calif., 1975-78; pres., prin. engr. Power Math Assocs. Inc., Palo Alto, Tempe, Del Mar and San Diego, 1978-99; prof. elec. engring. Ariz. State U., Tempe, 1980-84. Schweitzer vis. prof. elec. engring.97 Wash. State U., 1996. Author: Analysis of Faulted Power Systems, 1973; (with others) Power System Control and Stability, 1977, 3d edit., 2003, Subsynchronous Resonance in Power Systems, 1990, Series Compensation of Power Systems, 1996, Power System Protection, 1999; cons. editor: Ency. Sci. and Tech., 1979-92; contbr. articles to profl. jours. NSF faculty fellow, 1960-61; recipient Faculty citation Iowa State U. Alumni Assn., 1973, Profl. Achievement citation Iowa State U., 1981 Fellow IEEE (life mem., chmn. Iowa sect. 1959-60), Conf. Internat. des Grands Reseaux Electriques, Sigma Xi, Phi Kappa Phi, Eta Kappa Nu, Pi Mu Epsilon. Republican. Home: 13335 Roxton Cir San Diego CA 92130-1841 Personal E-mail: p.anderson@ieee.org.

ANDERSON, PAUL MILTON, energy executive; b. Richland, Wash., Apr. 1, 1945; s. Paul Milton and Elfrieda (Blehm) A.; m. Kathleen Sue Kinzel, Feb. 25, 1984; children: Wendy Christine, Heather Colleen. BSME, U. Wash., 1967; MBA, Stanford U., 1969. Mgr. product planning Ford Motor Co., Dearborn, 1969-77; various positions Tex. Eastern Corp., Houston, 1977-85, v.p., 1985-87, sr. v.p., 1987-89; v.p. fin., chief fin. officer Inland Steel Industries, Chgo., 1990-91; exec. v.p. Panhandle Eastern Corp., 1991-94, pres., 1994—, Panhandle Eastern Pipe Line Co., 1991—; pres., CEO Panenergy (named changed Duke Energy), Houston, 1991-97; pres., COO Duke Energy, 1997-99; CEO, mng. prnr. BHP Ltd., Melbourne, Australia, 1998—2002; chmn., CEO Duke Energy, 2003—06; chmn. bd. Spectra Energy Corp., Houston, 2007—. Mem.: Inst. Gas Tech., Interstate Natural Gas Assn. Am. Office: Spectra Energy Corp 5400 Westheimer Ct Houston TX 77056-5310

ANDERSON, PAUL NATHANIEL, oncologist, educator; b. Omaha, May 30, 1937; s. Nels Paul E. and Doris Marie (Chesnut) A.; m. Dee Ann Hipps, June 27, 1965; children: Mary Kathleen, Anne Christen. BA, U.

Colo., 1959, MD, 1963. Diplomate Am. Bd. Internal Medicine, Am. Bd. Med. Mgmt., Am. Bd. Med. Oncology. Intern Johns Hopkins Hosp., Balt., 1963-64, resident in internal medicine, 1964-65, fellow in oncology, 1970-72; rsch. assoc., staff assoc. NIH, Bethesda, Md., 1965-70; asst. prof. medicine, oncology Johns Hopkins U. Sch. Medicine, 1972-76; attending physician Balt. City Hosps., Johns Hopkins Hosp., 1972-76; dir. dept. med. oncology Penrose Cancer Hosp., Colorado Springs, Colo., 1976-86; clin. asst. prof. dept. medicine Colo. Sch. Medicine, 1976-90, clin. assoc. prof., 1990—. Dir. Penrose Cancer Hosp., 1979-86, chief dept. medicine, 1985-86; founding dir. Cancer Ctr. of Colorado Springs, 1986-95, Pikes Peak Forum for Health Care Ethics, 1996—, Rocky Mountain Cancer Ctr., Colorado Springs, 1995—; med. dir. So. Colo. Cancer Program, 1979-86; pres., chmn. bd. dirs. Preferred Physicians, Inc., 1986-92; mem. Colo. Found. for Med. Care Health Stds. Com., 1985, sec., exec. com., 1990, bd. dirs., pres., 1992-93; mem., chmn. treatment com. Colo. Cancer Control and Rsch. Panel, 1980-83; prin. investigator Cancer Info. Svc. of Colo., 1981-87; pres., founder Timberline Med. Assocs., 1986-87, Oncology Mgmt. Network, Inc., 1985-95. Editor Advances in Cancer Control; editl. bd. Jour. Cancer Program Mgmt., 1987-92, Health Care Mgmt. Rev., 1988—; contbr. articles to med. jours. Mem. Colo. Gov.'s Rocky Flats Employee Health Assessment Group, 1983-84; mem. Gov.'s Breast Cancer Control Commn. Colo., 1984-89; founder, dir. So. Colo. AIDS project, 1986-91; mem. adv. bd. Colo. State Bd. Health Tumor Registry, 1984-87; chmn., bd. dirs. Preferred Physicians, Inc., 1986-92; bd. dirs. Share Devel. Co. of Colo. Share Health Plan of Colo., 1986-90, vice chmn., 1989-91; bd. dirs., chmn. Preferred Health Care, Inc., 1991-92; mem. health care stds. com., trustee colo. Found. for Med. Care (PRO); mem. nat. bd. med. dirs. Fox Chase Cancer Ctr. Network, Phila., 1987-89; mem. tech. expert panel Harvard Resource-Based Relative Value Scale Study for Hematology/Oncology, 1991-92. With USPHS, 1965-70. Mem. AMA (mem. practice parameters forum 1989-97, adv. com. to HCFA on uniform clin. data set), AAAS, Am. Coll. Forensic Examiners, Am. Soc. Clin. Oncology (chmn. subcom. on oncology clin. practice stds., mem. clin. practice com., rep. to AMA 1991—, mem. healthcare svcs. rsch. com., chmn. clin. guidelines subcom. 1993—), Am. Assn. Cancer Rsch., Am. Assn. Cancer Insts. (liaison mem. bd. trustees 1980-82), Am. Coll. Physician Execs., Am. Hospice Assn., Am. Soc. Internal Medicine, Nat. Cancer Inst. (com. for cmty. hosp. oncology program evaluation 1982-83), Colo. Soc. Internal Medicine, Assn. Cmty. Cancer Ctrs. (chmn. membership com. 1980, chmn. clin. rsch. com. 1983-85, sec. 1983-84, pres.-elect 1984-85, pres. 1986-87, trustee 1981-88), N.Y. Acad. Scis., Johns Hopkins Med. Soc., Colo. Med. Soc., Am. Mgmt. Assn., Am. Assn. Profl. Cons., Am. Soc. Quality, Am. Acad. Med. Dirs., Am. Coll. Physician Execs., El Paso County Med. Soc., Rocky Mountain Oncology Soc. (chmn. clin. practice com. 1989-94, pres.-elect 1990, pres. 1993-95), Acad. Hospice Physicians, Coalition for Cancer, Colorado Springs Clin. Club, Alpha Omega Alpha. Office: 32 Sanford Rd Colorado Springs CO 80906-4233 Office Phone: 719-577-2555. Business E-Mail: paul-anderson@usoncology.com.

ANDERSON, PAUL WAYNE, assistant principal; b. Cullman, Ala., May 24, 1958; s. Paul Ray Anderson and Edna Faye Carey; m. Kelli Shawn Fox, Mar. 10, 1985; 1 child, Joshua Paul. A in Sci. Music Edn., Wallace State C.C., Hanceville, Ala., 1979; BS in Music Edn., U. North Ala., 1981, MA in Music Edn., 1986; cert. in sch. adminstrn., U. Ala., 1998. Band dir. Lawrence County H.S., Moulton, Ala., 1981—82, Wallace State C.C., Hanceville, Ala., 1982—91, Hanceville H.S., 1991—2004, asst. prin., 2004—, Hanceville Mid. Sch., 1998—2004. Chmn. accrediting com. So. Assn. Colls. and Schs., Hanceville, 1998—99. Mem.: NEA (assoc.), Ala. Music Educators Assn. (assoc.), Music Educators Nat. Conf. (assoc.), Ala. Edn. Assn. (assoc.). Home Phone: 256-338-7124.

ANDERSON, PAULETTE ELIZABETH, real estate developer, entrepreneur, retired elementary school educator; b. LA, 1942; d. J. Paul and Frances L. Ross; m. Kenneth Jerome Anderson, Mar. 27, 1997; children: Melody A. Helland, Edward M. Helland. BA in Elem. Edn., Calif. State U., L.A., 1970; AA, Pasadena City Coll., Calif., 1963; MA in Elem. Edn., Ariz. State U., Tempe, 1976; DD, Christian Internat. Grad. Sch., Pointe Washington, Fla., 1988, D of Ministry, 2001. Cert. tchr. Calif., 1972, elem. tchr. Ariz., 1977. Advisor Wonderful Wonders, Phoenix, 1993—94; kindergarten and first grade tchr. Long Beach Hebrew Acad., Calif., 1969—70; fifth grade tchr. Bullhead City Elem. Sch., Ariz., 1971—72; reading tchr. Florence Mid. Sch., Ariz., 1977—81; first grade tchr. Murphy Sch. Dist. -Sullivan, Phoenix, 1985—87; elem. tchr. grades 2, 5, 8 Roosevelt Sch. Dist.-Valley View, Phoenix, 1993—99, ret., 1999—; owner 42 unit apt. complex. Curriculum guideline's com. mem. Roosevelt Sch. Dist., 1994—98; dist. scheduling com. mem. Rooselvelt Sch. Dist., 1997. Author: (non-fiction) Evidence of Holy Spirit GIven Glossolalia, (children's non-fiction) Polycarp, Martin Luther's Faith and Trust In Jesus. Organizer/pres. Nevitt Neighborhood Assn., Phoenix, 1987—99; organizer VCC Cares for food, 2001—, Rid Neighborhood of Graffiti project, Nevitt; developer Spanish ch. Valley Cmty. Ch., El Monte, Calif., 2004; elected precinct committeeman Rep. Party, Phoenix, 1988—99, chmn. dist. 23, 1994—96; chmn. Christian Coalition, Pasadena, 2000—01; v.p. God Provides Ministry, 2004—. Recipient Cert. of Appreciation, Nat. Rep. Senator Com., 1996, Lincoln Bust Award, Maricopa County Rep. Party, 1993, Vol. of the Yr., Dist. 23, 1998. Republican. Avocations: travel, archaeology. Office Phone: 423-894-6884. Personal E-mail: bebooks@highandliftedup.com. E-mail: melandinvestment@bellsouth.net.

ANDERSON, PEGGY C., retired elementary school educator; d. Thomas Ralph Wilkes and Therese Noreen Higgins; m. Fred E. Anderson, Oct. 28, 1972; children: Tabitha, Glen. BA, Benedictine Coll., Atchison, Kans., 1972; MS, U. Kans., Lawrence, 1975. Tchr. Atchison Cath. Elem. Sch., Kans., 1973—75, Troy Pub. Schs., Kans., 1975—80, Atchison Pub. Schs., 1980—2006; ret., 2006. Instr. Benedictine Coll., Atchison, 2005; presenter in field. Mem. edn. com. Amelia Earhart Festival, Atchison, 1992—2006. Named Tchr. of the Yr., Atchison Elem. Sch., 2002. Mem.: NEA (scholar 1967). Democrat. Roman Catholic. Avocations: English smocking, quilting, sewing. Home: 1943 E Stratford Rd Olathe KS 66062

ANDERSON, PETER JOSEPH, lawyer; b. Camden, NJ, Mar. 15, 1951; s. Lester Ryan and Rose Helen; m. Sheila K.; children: Elizabeth Rose, Hannah Louise. BA, Dickinson Coll., 1972; JD, Dickinson Sch. of Law, 1975. Bar: Pa. 1975, Ga. 1978, U.S. Dist. Ct. (ea. dist.) Pa. 1978, U.S. Dist. Ct. (no. dist.) Ga. 1978, U.S. Ct. Appeals (11th cir.) 1978, U.S. Tax Ct. 1986, U.S. Supreme Ct. 1989. Dep. dist. atty. Dist. Attys. Office, Harrisburg, Pa., 1974-77; ptnr. Peterson, Dillard, Young, Self & Asselin, Atlanta, 1977-92, Sutherland, Asbill & Brennan, Atlanta, 1992—. Bd. dirs. CADEF-Childhood Autism Found., 1986—; chmn. bd. trustees The Paideia Sch., Atlanta, 1997-2000; treas. Serve Haiti, 2005—. Mem. ABA (subcom. securities litigation 1978—), State Bar Ga., Pa. Bar Assn., Atlanta Bar Assn. Republican. Roman Catholic. Home: 1503 Emory Rd NE Atlanta GA 30306-2429 Office: Sutherland Asbill & Brennan 999 Peachtree St NE Ste 2300 Atlanta GA 30309-3996 Office Phone: 404-853-8414. Business E-Mail: peter.anderson@sablaw.com.

ANDERSON, PETER MACARTHUR, retired lawyer; b. New Castle, Ind., July 15, 1937; s. Earl Canute and Catherine Elizabeth (Schultz) A.; m. Ann Warren Gibson, Sept.1, 1962; children: David, Karen. AB, Dartmouth Coll., 1959; LLB, Stanford U., 1962. Bar: Calif. 1963, Wash. 1970. Assoc. O'Melveny & Myers, LA, 1966-70, Bogle & Gates, Seattle, 1970-74, mem., 1974-99; ptnr. Preston Gates & Ellis, Seattle, 1999—2002, sr. counsel, 2003—05; ret. Co-chmn. equal employment law com. ABA, 1983-86. Mem. Ecumenical Commn. for Seattle Archdiocese, St. Petersburg-Seattle Sister Chs. Com. Capt. U.S. Army, 1963-65. Fellow Coll. Labor and Employment Lawyers; mem. Phi Beta Kappa. Roman Catholic. Home: 9200 SE 57th St Mercer Island WA 98040-5005 Home Phone: 206-232-4962.

ANDERSON, PHILIP SIDNEY, lawyer; b. Little Rock, May 9, 1935; s. Philip Sidney and Frances (Walt) Anderson; m. Rosemary Gill Wright, Sept. 26, 1959; children: Sidney Walt Kenyon, Philip Wright, Catherine Gill Askew. BA, LLB, U. Ark., 1959. Bar: Ark. 1960, U.S. Supreme Ct. 1966. Assoc. Wright, Lindsey & Jennings, Little Rock, 1960—65, ptnr., 1965—88, Williams & Anderson PLC, Little Rock, 1988—. Lectr. Ark. Law Sch., 1963—66; mem. com. on jury instrns. Ark. Supreme Ct., 1962—97; mem. panel for 8th cir. U.S. Cir. Judge Nominating Commn., 1978—79; mem. fed. adv. com. U.S. Ct. Appeals 8th cir., 1983—88, co-chmn., 1987—88; bd. dirs. WEHCO Media, Inc., Ark. Dem.-Gazette, Inc. Co-author: Arkansas Model Jury Instructions, 1965, 1974, 1989. Pres. Friends of Little Rock Pub. Libr., 1968—69, Little Rock Unltd. Progress, Inc., 1973—74; trustee Ctrl. Ark. Libr. Sys., 1981—87, pres., 1984; trustee George W. Donaghey Found., 1976—, pres., 1979—80. 2d lt. US Army, 1959—60. Fellow: Ark. Bar Found. (pres. 1973—74), Am. Bar Found.; mem.: ABA (chair ho. of dels. 1992—94, pres. 1998—99), Am. Law Inst. (mem. coun. 1982—), Ark. Bar Assn. (spl. award meritorious svc.), The Grolier Club of the City of N.Y. Episcopalian. Home: 4716 Crestwood Dr Little Rock AR 72207-5436 Office: Williams & Anderson PLC 111 Center St Ste 2200 Little Rock AR 72201-4429

ANDERSON, PHILIP W., physicist; b. Indpls., Dec. 13, 1923; s. Harry W. and Elsie (Osborne) Anderson; m. Joyce Gothwaite, July 31, 1947; 1 child, Susan Osborne. BS, Harvard U., 1943, PhD, 1949; DSc (hon.), U. Ill., 1978, Rutgers U., 1991, Gustavus Adolphus Coll., 1992, Ecole normale Superieure, 1992, Sheffield U., 1995, U. Tokyo, 2002. With Naval Rsch. Lab., Washington DC, 1943—45; vis. fellow Cambridge U., England, 1961—62, prof., 1967—75, fellow Jesus Coll., 1969—75; asst. dir. of physical rsch. lab. Bell Labs., 1974—76; Joseph Henry prof. in physics Princeton U., 1975—97; cons. dir. phys. rsch. lab. Bell Labs., Murray Hill, NJ, 1976—84; prof. emeritus physics Princeton U., 1997—; vice chmn., sci. bd. external prof. Sante Fe Inst., 1985—; with Bell Labs., Murray Hill, NJ, 1949—84. Mem. steering com. Santa Fe Inst., 1989—97. Author: (book) Concepts in Solids, 1963, Basic Notions of Condensed Matter Physics, 1984, A Career in Theoretical Physics, 1994, The Theory of Superconductivity in High-Tc Cuprates, 1997. Chmn. bd. trustees Aspen Ctr. Physics, 1982—87. Recipient Oliver E. Buckley prize, Am. Phys. Soc., 1964, Loeb lectr., Harvard U., 1965, Regents lectr., U. Calif., 1967, Dannie Heinemann prize, Acad. of Sci. at Gottingen, 1975, Centennial medal, Harvard U., 1977, Nobel prize in physics, 1977, Guthrie medal and prize, 1978, London lectr., Duke U., 1980, Abigail and J.H. Van Vleck lectr., U. of Wis., 1983, Nat. medal of sci., 1983, Bethe lectr., 1985, George Eastman prof. of physics, Oxford U., 1993—94, John Bardeen prize; hon. fellow, Jesus Coll., Cambridge U., 1977. Fellow: Inst. of Physics (hon.), Indian Acad. Sci. (hon.; fgn. fellow); mem.: Am. Acad. Arts and Sci., Nat. Acad. Sci. (coun. mem.), Royal Soc. (fgn. mem.), Acad. Lincei (fgn. assoc.), Japan Acad. Sci. (fgn. fellow), Am. Philos. Soc., Russian Acad. Sci. (fgn.mem.), Washington Acad. Sci., N.Y. Acad. Sci. (hon.; life mem. 1992). Office: Dept of Physics Joseph Henry Labs Princeton U 339 Jadwin Hall POB 708 Princeton NJ 08544 Business E-Mail: pwa@princeton.edu.

ANDERSON, PHILLIP VERNE, lawyer; b. Danville, Va., Mar. 22, 1958; s. Verne D. and Joyce (Worley) A.; m. Mary Elizabeth Hankins, Aug. 14, 1982; children: Benjamin, Jordan, William. BA, Hampden-Sydney Coll., 1980; JD, U. Va., 1984. Bar: Va. 1984. Clk. Hon. Jackson L. Kiser U.S. Dist. Ct., Roanoke, Va., 1984-85; ptnr. Gentry Locke Rakes & Moore, Roanoke, Va., 1985—97, Frith, Anderson & Peak, Roanoke, Va., 1997—. Bd. dirs. Jr. Achievement South We. Va.; mem. steering com. Hidden Valley H.S., 2000—02, pres., founding mem. athletic booster club, 2001—02; grad. leadership Roanoke Valley Roanoke Regional C. of C., 1997. Mem. Va. State Bar (8th dist. disciplinary com. 1992-93, standing com. on professionalism 1992—95, professionalism course faculty 1995-98, bd. govs. young lawyers conf., 1989-92, former chmn., sec. 1993-96, mem. lawyer malpractice ins. com. 2000-03, budget and fin. com. 2000-03, mem. exec. com. 2002-, pres.-elect 2004, pres. 2005), Va. Assn. Def. Attys., Def. Rsch. Inst., Va. Trial Lawyers Assn., Roanoke Bar Assn. (sec., treas. 2001-02, pres.-elect 2003). Baptist. Office: Frith Anderson & Peake PC PO Box 1240 Roanoke VA 24006-1240 also: Frith Anderson & Peake PC 29 Franklin Rd SW Roanoke VA 24011*

ANDERSON, PORTER WARREN, JR., retired pediatrics educator; b. Corinth, Miss., Jan. 1, 1937; BA, Emory U., 1958; MA, Harvard U., 1962, PhD, 1967. Rsch. trainee Oak Ridge Nat. Lab., Tenn., 1957; asst. chemist tropical rsch. dept. Uited Fruit Co., Lima, Honduras, 1959-61; faculty mem. dept. chemistry Stillman Coll., Tuscaloosa, Ala., 1966-68; rsch. assoc. infectious diseases The Children's Hosp. Med. Ctr., Boston, 1968-77; asst. prof. microbiology & molecular genetics Harvard U., Cambridge, Mass., 1972-75, assoc. prof., 1975-77; assoc. prof. dept. pediatrics & microbiology U. Rochester (N.Y.) Sch. Medicine & Dentistry, 1977-87, prof., 1987-95, prof. emeritus, 1995-96; ret., 1996. Recipient Albert Lasker Clinical Med. Rsch. award, 1996. Office: U Rochester Sch Medicine & Dentistry Dept Pediatrics 601 Elmwood Ave # 690 Rochester NY 14642-0001

ANDERSON, R. CHRISTIAN, photographer, media consultant, art director; s. Raymond DeArmond (Stepfather) and Lita Santos Bowman. AA in Multimedia, Platt Coll., San Diego, 1997; PhD in Comparative Religion, Am. Coll. Metaphys. Theology, Mpls., 2001. Art dir. Racquet Tech Mag., Del Mar, Calif., 2000—03; sr. art dir. Annenberg Ctr. Health Scis., Rancho Mirage, Calif., 2002—03; creative art dir., CEO R. Christian Anderson Photography, Palm Desert, Calif., 2003—. Fellow, Am. Coll. Metaphys. Theology, 2001. Office: 38-180 Del Webb Blvd - PMB 72 Palm Desert CA 92211 Home Phone: 760-343-7768. Business E-Mail: info@rchristiananderson.com.

ANDERSON, R. JOHN, apparel executive; BCommerce, Univ. New South Wales, 1972. Mgmt. positions Johnson & Johnson, H.J. Heinz Co.; mgmt. positions through v.p. merchandising & product develop. Levi Strauss & Co., San Francisco, 1979—95; gen. mgr. Levi Strauss Canada, 1996—98; pres. Levi Strauss Canada & Latin Am., 1996—98; pres. Asia Pacific Levi Strauss & Co., San Francisco, 1999—2004; interim pres. Levi Strauss Europe, 2003—04; sr. v.p., pres. Asia Pacific & global sourcing Levi Strauss & Co., San Francisco, 2004—06, sr. v.p., COO, 2006, pres., CEO, 2006—. Office: Levi Strauss & Co Levi's Plz 1155 Battery St San Francisco CA 94111*

ANDERSON, RACHAEL KELLER (RACHAEL KELLER), retired library director; b. NYC, Jan. 15, 1938; d. Harry and Sarah Keller; m. Howard D. Goldwyn; children: Rebecca Anderson, Michael Goldwyn, Bryan Goldwyn, David Goldwyn. AB, Barnard Coll., 1959; MS, Columbia U., 1960. Librarian CCNY, 1960-62; librarian Mt. Sinai Med. Ctr., NYC, 1964-73, dir. library, 1973-79; dir. Health Scis Libr. Columbia U., NYC, 1979-91, acting v.p., univ. libr., 1982; dir. Ariz. Health Scis. Libr., U. Ariz., Tucson, 1991-2001; assoc. dir. Ariz. Telemedicine Program, 1996—2001; ret., 2001. Bd. dirs. Med. Libr. Ctr. of N.Y., N.Y.C., 1983-91; mem. biomed. libr. rev. com. Nat. Libr. Medicine, Bethesda, Md., 1984-88, chmn., 1987-88; mem. bd. regents Nat. Libr. Medicine, 1990-94, chmn., 1993-94; pres. Ariz. Health Info. Network, 1995. Contbr. articles to profl. jours. Mem. Med. Libr. Assn. (pres.-elect 1996-97, pres. 1997-98, bd. dirs. 1983-86, 98-99), Assn. Acad. Health Scis. Libr. Dirs. (bd. dirs. 1983-86, 90-93, pres. 1991-92). E-mail: rachaela@ahsl.arizona.edu.

ANDERSON, RACHEL L., healthcare educator, researcher; life ptnr. Alba Nydia Quinones, June 12, 1999; 1 child, Isolina Catherine Quinones Anderson. BA in Psychology, Beloit Coll., Wis., 1987; MA in Human Devel. and Social Policy, Northwestern U., Evanston, Ill., 1995, PhD in Human Devel. and Social Policy, 1997. Post-doctoral fellowship in mental health and policy rsch. Rutgers U., New Brunswick, NJ, 1997—99; asst. prof. Coll. Pub. Health, U. Iowa, Iowa City, 1999—2005, assoc. prof., 2005—, Coll. Nursing, U. Iowa, Iowa City, 2000—; assoc. dir. Nat. Health Law and Policy Resource Ctr., U. Iowa, Iowa City, 2004—; assoc. prof. Coll. Law, U. Iowa, Iowa City, 2005—; dep. dir. Iowa Health and Disability Resource Ctr., Iowa City, 2005—07; dir. Mental Health Svcs. and Policy Collaborative, 2007—. Contbr. chapters to books, articles to profl. jours. Mem. psychiatric epidemiology/biochemistry tng. program steering com. U. Iowa, 2000—02; adv. bd. mem. strengthening cmtys. for youth U. Iowa Ctr. Addiction Rsch./Adolescent Health and Resource Ctr., 2003—06; bd. mem. Women in Sci. and Engring., Iowa City, 2004—06, Johnson County Empowerment Bd., Iowa City, 2005—06. Recipient New Investigator Rsch. award, Coll. Pub. Health and Coll. Medicine, U. Iowa, 2000—01, Coll. Pub. Health Tchg. award, U. Iowa, 2002, Faculty Tchg. award, 2003; fellow Mentoring and Edn. Program in Mental Health Svcs., Nat. Inst. Mental Health, 2001—03; grantee, 2006—, State of Iowa, 2002—, Nat. Inst. on Drug Abuse, 2003—04. Mem.: APA. Avocations: kayaking, wine collection, travel, history. Office: Univ Iowa College Public Health 200 Hawkins Dr E 202 GH Iowa City IA 52242 Office Phone: 319-384-5132. Office Fax: 319-384-7095. Business E-Mail: rachel-anderson@uiowa.edu.

ANDERSON, RALPH ROBERT, endocrinologist, educator; b. Fords, NJ, Nov. 1, 1932; s. Harry Walter and Johanna Katherine (Damgaard) Anderson; m. LaVeta Ann Phillips, Jan. 28, 1961; children: Richard, Laura. BS, Rutgers U., 1953, MS, 1958; PhD, U. Mo., 1961. Rsch. asst. Rutgers U., 1957-58, U. Mo., Columbia, 1958-61, instr. dairy sci. (endocrinology), 1961-62, from asst. prof. to assoc. prof., 1965—72, prof., 1976—97, prof. emeritus, 1997—. Asst. prof. Iowa State U., Ames, 1962—64; rschr. in field. Editor, co-editor: 6 books; contbr. articles to profl. jours., chapters to books. With US Army, 1954—56. Recipient Grad. Tchg. Merit award, U. Mo. chpt. Gamma Sigma Delta, 1982, Rsch. award, 1994, Cook Disting. Alumni award, Rutgers U., 1997; NIH Endocrinology Postdoctoral fellow, 1964—65, Endocrinology fellow, U. Wis., 1964—65, Fulbright-Hays Sr. Rsch. fellow, New Zealand, 1973—74. Mem.: Sigma Xi (sec.-treas. U. Mo. chpt. 1981—83, pres. 1984—85). Presbyterian. Home: 2517 Shepard Blvd Columbia MO 65201-6131 Office: U Mo Animal Sci Rsch Ctr Columbia MO 65211-0001

ANDERSON, RAY C., carpet company executive; b. West Point, Ga., July 28, 1934; BS in Indsl. Engring. with highest honors, Ga. Inst. Tech., 1956; PhD in Pub. Svc. (hon.), Northland Coll.; PhD in Bus. (hon.), LaGrange Coll.; LHD (hon.), NC State Univ., Univ. So. Maine. With Proctor & Gamble, Atlanta, 1956-58; engr. Callaway Mills, La Grange, Ga., 1959-68; with Deering Milliken, Inc., Atlanta, 1958-59; chmn. bd., CEO Interface, Inc., Atlanta, Ga., 1973—. Spkr. in field. Author: The Journey from There to Here - The Eco-Odyssey of a CEO, 1995, Face It, 1996. Mem. Pres. Coun. on Sustainable Devel. (past co-chair during Clinton adminstrn.), Northside Methodist Ch., Atlanta; bd. dir. Natural Step, U.S.A., Ga. Conservancy, Upper Chattahoochee Riverkeeper, Ida Cason Callaway Found., Rocky Mountain Inst., Univ. Tex. Ctr. For Sustainable Develop.; hon. adv., Pres. Peking Univ. Named Internat. Businessman of Yr., Soc. Internat. Bus. Fellows, 1992, Ga., Ga. Conservancy's Conservationist of the Year, 1997, Sr. Fellow and Leading Voice for Green and Sustainable Design, Design Futures Coun., 2003; recipient Entrepreneur of Yr. award Southeast Region, Ernst & Young, 1996, Global Green USA Millennium award, 1996, George and Cynthia Mitchell Internat. prize for Sustainable Develop., 2001, SAM-SPG Sustainability Leadership award, 2001, US Green Bldg. Council's Inaugural Leadership award, 2002, Nat. Wildlife Fedn. Conservation Achievement award for Corporate Leadership, 2002, Star award, Internat. Interior Design Assn.(IIDA), 2003, Assn. Interior Designers(ASID). Presdl. Citation, 2003, Nat. Ethics Advocate award, So. Inst. for Bus. and Profl. Ethics, 2004, Harvard Bus. Sch. Atlanta Alumni Club's Cmty. Leadership award, 2005, Corp. Ally award, Possible Woman Enterprises, 2005. Mem. Am. Archtl. Found. (bd. trustees), Acad. Distinguished Engring. Alumni Ga. Tech. (chmn. adv. bd. 1995-96), LaGrange Coll. (bd. trustees), U. Va. Sch. Architecture (adv. bd.), Bank South Corp. (bd. dirs 1991-96), NationsBank Corp. (bd. dirs.), Royal Ten Cate (bd. dirs.), Bus. Social Responsibility (bd. dirs.), Natural Step (bd. dirs.). His company revolutionized the commercial floorcovering industry by producing America's first free-lay carpet tiles. Currently embarked on a mission to "be the first company that, by its deeds, shows the entire industrial world what sustainability is in all its dimensions: People, process, product, place and profits by 2020 and in doing so, to become restorative through the power of influence. Leading a worldwide effort to pioneer the processes of sustainable development. Office: Interface Inc 2859 Paces Ferry Rd SE Ste 2000 Atlanta GA 30339-6216*

ANDERSON, RAYMOND QUINTUS, diversified company executive; b. Jamestown, NY, Nov. 27, 1930; s. Paul N. and Cecille (Ogren) A.; m. Sondra Rumsey, June 5, 1954; children: Heidi, Kristin, Gerrit, Mitchell, Tracy, Brooks. Grad., Phillips Acad., Andover, Mass., 1949; BS in Engring., Princeton U., 1953; postgrad., Sloane Sch., MIT, MIT. With Dahlstrom Corp., Jamestown, 1957-76, exec. v.p., 1965, pres., 1968-76; founder, pres. Aarque Steel Corp., Jamestown, 1976-78, Aarque Mgmt. Corp., Jamestown, 1978-96; founder, chmn. Aarque Cos., Jamestown, 1980-96, Aarque Capital Corp., 1996—. Bd. dirs. Oneida Ltd., Bus. Coun. N.Y. State, Inc., Cold Metal Products Co., Inc., Aarque Steel Group, Kardex Sys., Inc.; trustee Northwestern Mut. Life Ins. Co. Patentee in field. Chmn. Jamestown United Fund drive, 1964, 74; bd. dirs. N.Y. State Dept. Environ. Conservation; dir. Oneida, Ltd.; trustee Roger Tory Peterson Inst., Chautauqua Found. Inc.; civilian aide to Sec. of the U.S. Army; mem. adv. bd. World Econ. Forum. Served with USNR, 1954-57. Mem. Mfrs. Assn. Jamestown Area (pres. 1967-68), Empire State C. of C. (pres. 1974-76), Royal Round Table of Swedish Coun. Am., U.S. Can. Trade Coun., U.S. Dept. Commerce Ind. Sector Adv. Com., Tau Beta Pi. Clubs: Moon Brook Country (Jamestown); Sportsmen's (Chautaqua, N.Y.); Union League Met. (N.Y.C.). Republican. Episcopalian. Address: 20 W Fairmont Ave Lakewood NY 14750-0109

ANDERSON, REID BRYCE, performing company executive; b. New Westminister, BC, Can., Apr. 1, 1949; s. Warren Nels and Phyllis Jessie Bryce (Purser) Anderson. Student dance, Dolores Kirkwood, Burnaby, B.C., Royal Ballet Sch., 1967-68. Dancer Stuttgart (Fed. Republic Germany) Ballet, 1969-86, prin. dancer, 1975-86, ballet master, 1982-86; artistic dir. Ballet B.C., Vancouver, 1987-89, Nat. Ballet Can., Toronto, Ont., 1989—, Stuttgart Ballet, 1996—. Choreographer numerous works for performing cos. Decorated Order of Fed. Republic Germany; named Best Dir. of Yr., Dance Europe mag., 2006; recipient John Cranko prize for svc. to Art of Classical Ballet and in particular tchg., coaching and maintaining the work of the late John Cranko, 1995, German Dance prize, 2006. Office: The Stuttgart Ballet Obere Schlossgarten 6 70173 Stuttgart Germany

ANDERSON, RICHARD CARL, geophysical exploration company executive; b. Pontiac, Mich., June 6, 1928; s. Earling Adolph and Blenda Maria (Johnson) A.; m. Georgia L. Carnahan, Aug. 14, 1949; children—Laurie Ann, Gary Carl, Curtis Murray, Denise Carla BS in Mining Engring., N.Mex. Inst. Mining & Tech., 1950, MS in Geophysics, 1953. Engr. Allis Chalmers, Milw., 1949-51; geophysicist, v.p. Geophys. Service, Inc., Dallas, 1953-71; v.p., then exec. v.p. Digicon, Houston, 1971-75; sr. v.p., exec. v.p. Seismograph Service Corp., Tulsa, from 1975, pres.,

1981-85; ret., 1985-88; pres. Fairfield Industries, Houston, 1988-91, vice chmn., chief exec. officer, 1991-93; ret., 1993. Mem. Energy Advocates, Tulsa, 1981-93, coordinator, 1983, 86. Served with U.S. Army, 1946-47 Recipient Disting. Achievement award N.Mex. Inst. Mining and Tech., 1984 Mem. Soc. Exploration Geophysicists, Internat. Assn. Geophys. Contractors (hon. life mem., bd. dirs. 1977-85, 89-94, chmn. 1978-79). Home: 1111 Hermann Dr Unit 11F Houston TX 77004-6929

ANDERSON, RICHARD CHARLES, geology educator; b. Moline, Ill., Apr. 22, 1930; s. Edgar Oscar and Sarah Albertina (Olson) A.; m. Ethel Irene Cada, June 27, 1953; children: Eileen Ruth, Elizabeth Sarah, Penelope Cada. AB, Augustana Coll., Rock Island, Ill., 1952; SM, U. Chgo., 1953, PhD, 1955. Geologist Geophoto Svcs., Denver, 1955-57; from asst. prof. to prof. geology Augustana Coll., Rock Island, 1957-96; prof. emeritus, 1996—. Rsch. affiliate Ill. State Geol. Survey, Champaign, 1959—. Editor: Earth Interpreters, 1992; author reports. Recipient Neil Miner award Nat. Assn. Geology Tchrs., 1992. Fellow Geol. Soc. Am. (sect. co-chair 1990). Lutheran. Home: 2012 24th St Rock Island IL 61201-4533 Office: Augustana Coll Dept Geology 639 38th St Rock Island IL 61201-2210 E-mail: glanderson@augustana.edu.

ANDERSON, RICHARD EDMUND, city manager, management consultant; b. Ferndale, Mich., Dec. 23, 1938; s. Richard H. and Carolyn Jeanne (Figg) A.; m. Kay Clarke, Nov. 6, 1961 (div.); children: Pam, Mark, Linda; m. Linda (Hawk)Jenkins, Sept. 11, 1997; stepchildren: Travis, Todd. BA, Mich. State U., 1962; postgrad. in advanced mgmt., Harvard U., 1979. Aide to mgr. City of St. Petersburg, Fla., 1962-64; adminstrv. asst. City of Ft. Lauderdale, Fla., 1964-67, dep. mgr., 1967-75, city mgr., 1975-80; v.p. Fla. Innovation Group, Tampa, 1980-81; pres. Intragrated Systems Assocs., Inc., Ft. Lauderdale, 1981-90; city mgr. City of Florida City, Fla., 1990-94, City of Brooksville, Fla., 1995—. Contbr. articles to profl. jours. Mem. Internat. City Mgmt. Assn. Office: 201 Howell Ave Brooksville FL 34601-2041 Home Phone: 352-796-3734; Office Phone: 352-544-5435. Business E-Mail: reago@tampabay.rr.com.

ANDERSON, RICHARD ERNEST, agricultural engineer, consultant, rancher; b. North Little Rock, Ark., Mar. 8, 1926; s. Victor Ernest and Lillian Josephine (Griffin) A.; m. Mary Ann Fitch, July 18, 1953; children: Vicki Lynn, Lucia Anita. BSCE, U. Ark., 1949; MSE, U. Mich., 1959. Registered profl. engr., Mich., Va. Commd. ensign USN, 1952, advanced through grades to capt., 1968, ret., 1974; v.p. Ocean Resources, Inc., Houston, 1974-77; mgr. maintenance and ops. Holmes & Narver, Inc., Orange, Calif., 1977-78; pres. No. Resources, Inc., Billings, Mont., 1978-81; v.p. Holmes & Narver, Inc., Orange, Calif., 1981-82; owner, operator Anderson Ranch, registered Arabian horses, Pony, Mont., 1982—; pres., dir. Carbon Resources Inc., Butte, Mont., 1983-88, Agri Resources, Inc., Butte, Mont., 1988-95, Anderson Holdings, Inc., Pony, Mont., 1995—. Trustee Lake Barcroft-Virginia Watershed Improvement Dist., 1973-74; pres. Lake Barcroft-Virginia Recreation Center, Inc., 1972-73. With USAAF, 1944-45. Decorated Silver Star, Legion of Merit with Combat V (2), Navy Marine Corps medal, Bronze Star with Combat V, Meritorious Service medal, Purple Heart; Anderson Peninsula in Antarctica named in his honor. Mem.: ASCE. Republican. Methodist. Office: Anderson Holdings Inc PO Box 266 Pony MT 59747-0266

ANDERSON, RICHARD H., air transportation executive; b. Galveston, Tex., 1956; m. Susan Anderson. BS, U. Houston, 1977; JD, South Tex. Coll. Law, 1981. Various positions Harris County Dist. Atty.'s office, Houston, 1978—87; staff v.p., dep. gen. counsel Continental Airlines, 1987—90; v.p., dep. gen. counsel Northwest Airlines Corp., Eagan, Minn., 1990—94, sr. v.p. labor rels., state affairs, law, 1994—96, sr. v.p. tech. ops. and airport affairs, 1997—98, exec. v.p. tech. ops. and airport affairs, 1998, exec. v.p., COO Eagan, Minn., 1998—2001, CEO, 2001—04; exec. v.p., CEO Ingenix subs. UnitedHealth Group, Mpls., 2005—06, exec. v.p., pres. comml. svc. group, 2006—07; CEO Delta Air Lines, Inc., Atlanta, 2007—. Bd. dirs. Mesaba Holdings, Inc., 1999—2003, Northwest Airlines Corp., 2001—05, Medtronic, Inc., 2002—, Xcel Energy, Inc., 2004—06, Cargill, Inc., 2006—, Delta Airlines, Inc., 2007—, Minn. Life Ins. Co., Mpls. Inst. Arts, Mpls. Downtown Coun.; chmn. Min. Bus. Leadership Network. Mailing: Delta Air Lines Inc PO Box 20706 Atlanta GA 30320-6001 Office: Delta Air Lines 1030 Delta Blvd Atlanta GA 30320*

ANDERSON, RICHARD LOUIS, electrical engineer; b. Mpls., Feb. 4, 1927; s. Ben Walter and Anna Elizabeth (Zitcowicz) Anderson; m. Claire Louise Petersen, Sept. 15, 1951; children: Gretchen, Betty Lise, Karl. BS, U. Minn., 1950, MS, 1952; PhD, Syracuse U., 1960; DSc (hon.), U. Sao Paulo, Brazil, 1969. Research asst. U. Minn., 1950-52; research engr. IBM Corp., Poughkeepsie, NY, 1952-60; from. instr. to prof. elec. and computing engring. Syracuse U., 1954-79; prof. elec. engring. U. Vt., Burlington, 1979-95, prof. emeritus elec. engring. and materials sci., 1995—, dir. materials sci. program, 1981-91. Fulbright-Hayes prof. U. Madrid, 1960—61, U. Sao Paulo, 1967—69; cons. in field. Author: 2 textbooks; contbr. articles to profl. jours. With USNR, 1944—47. Recipient 1st Brazilian prize microelectronics, 1980; fellow, Ford Found., 1967—69; grantee, NSF, 1974—85, N.Y. State Sci. and Tech. Found., 1974—75, 1977—78, Dept. Energy, 1979—83. Fellow: IEEE; mem.: AAUP, Am. Phys. Soc., Sigma Xi. Achievements include patents in field. Home: 601 Wake Robin Dr Shelburne VT 05482-7580 Personal E-mail: vze4v7r5@verizon.net.

ANDERSON, RICHARD MCLEMORE, internist; b. Gainesville, Fla., Mar. 3, 1930; s. Montgomery Drummond and Myrtle (McLemore) A.; m. Leewood Shaw, Mar. 21, 1959; children: Richard McLemore Jr., Bruce Dexter. BS, U. Fla., 1951; MD, Emory U., 1958. Diplomate Am. Bd. Internal Medicine. Chief of staff Alachua Gen. Hosp., Gainesville, Fla., 1973-75; internist Gainesville, Fla., 1962—. Chmn. of bd. Santa Fe Health Care, Gainesville, 1984-91, bd. dirs. Pres. Rotary Club of Gainesville, 1980-81. Capt. USAF, 1951-54. Mem. AMA, ACP, Alachua County Med. Soc. (v.p. 1972), Fla. Med. Assn. Presbyterian.

ANDERSON, RICHARD THEODORE, trade association administrator, urban planner; b. Bklyn., Oct. 11, 1940; s. Charles Theodore and Lillian Elizabeth (Holmlin) Anderson; m. Anasta Frank, Oct. 3, 1970; children: Erik Theodore, Leslie Elisabeth. AB, Rutgers U., New Brunswick, NJ, 1962; M in Regional Planning, Cornell U., Ithaca, NY, 1964; postgrad., NYU, NYC, 1964—67. Pres. Regional Plan Assn., NYC, 1964-92; exec. dir. Dallas Plan, 1993-94; pres., CEO NY Bldg. Congress, NYC, 1994—; pres. NY Bldg. Found., NYC, 1998—. Vis. assoc. prof. dept. city and regional planning Pratt Inst., NYC, 1974—92; chmn. Pres.'s Coun. N.Y.C. Planning & Design Orgns., 1982—92. Editl. adv. bd.: Real Estate NY, 2005—. Co-chmn. NY chpt. Rebuild Am. Coalition, 1996—2000; v.p., trustee Big Bros./Big Sisters, NYC, 1969—, Audrey Cohen Coll., 1998—2001; active Times Sq. Adv. Coun., NYC, 1985—89, NYC Partnership, 1994—, NYC and Co., 2001—, Citizens Union, 2002—, Citizens Housing and Planning Coun., 2004—, Hudson River Mus., Nat. Bldg. Mus., Met. Mus. Art, Mus. City NY, Village Planning Bd., Pelham, 1977—80, Whitney Mus. Am. Art, Morgan Libr. and Mus.; mem. Bus. Coun. NY State, 1995—; adv. coun. Cornell U. Coll. Architecture, Art and Planning, 1984—94; bd. dirs. Water Resources Assn. Delaware River Basin, 1977—80, United Way, Pelham, NY, 1977—79, Regional Alliance Small Contractors, 1994—2006, ACE Mentorship Program of Greater N.Y., 1997—, Bklyn. Sports Found., 1998—, Friends of Hudson River Park, 2001—03, Salvadori Ctr., 2002—, ACE Nat. Mentorship Program, 2003—, Picture House Regional Film Ctr., 2005—. Named Pub. Sector Mentor of Yr., ACE Mentorship Program, 2005; recipient Ellis Island medal of honor, 1995, Disting. Svc. award, NY Bldg. Congress, 2004; vis. scholar, NYU, 1992. Fellow: Inst. Urban Design, Am. Inst. Cert. Planners (chmn. Coll. Fellows 2003); mem.: AIA (pub. dir. NY chpt. 2003—05, NY chpt. George S. Lewis award 2001), Nat. Acad. Constrn., Am. Coun. Engring. Cos. (NY chpt.), Soc. Mktg. Profl. Svcs. (N.Y. chpt. Honor award 2004), Archtl. League NY, Gen. Soc. Mechanics and Tradesmen City of NY, Met. Leadership Network, NY Acad. Scis., Urban Land Inst., NY Soc. Assn. Execs., Am. Soc. Planning Ofcls. (bd. dirs. 1977—78), Am. Planning Assn. (dir., treas. 1978—80, pres. 1980—81, Disting. Svc. award 1985), Friends of the Old Croton Aqueduct, Rutgers Alumni Assn. (Loyal Son award 1989), Ellis Island Medal of Honor Soc., Bklyn. C. of C., Nat. Trust Hist. Preservation, Assn. for a Better NY, Empire State Transp. Alliance, Club 101, Sloane Gardens Club. Lutheran. Home: 9 Highview Cir Dobbs Ferry NY 10522 Office: NY Bldg Congress 44 W 28th St New York NY 10001-4212 Office Phone: 212-481-9230.

ANDERSON, ROBERT LANIER, III, federal judge; b. Macon, Ga., Nov. 12, 1936; s. Robert Lanier II and Helen Anderson; m. Nancy Briska, Aug. 18, 1962; 3 children. AB magna cum laude, Yale U., 1958; LLB, Harvard U., 1961. Assoc. Anderson, Walkert, Reichert, Macon, Ga., 1963—79; judge US Ct. Appeals (5th cir.), 1979—81, US Ct. Appeals (reassigned to 11th cir.), 1981—; chief judge US Ct. Appeals (11th cir.), Macon, Ga., 1999—2002. With USAR, 1958—61, capt. US Army, 1961—63. Mem.: ABA, Am. Judicature Soc., State Bar of Ga., Macon Bar Assn., Ga. Bar Assn. Office: US Ct Appeals PO Box 977 Macon GA 31202-0977*

ANDERSON, ROBERT MONTE, lawyer; b. Logan, Utah, Feb. 19, 1938; s. E. LeRoy and Grace (Rasmussen) Anderson; m. Kathleen Hansen, Aug. 12, 1966; children: Jennifer, Katrina, Alexander. AB, Columbia Coll., 1960; LLB, U. Utah, 1963. Bar: Utah 1963, US Ct Appeals (10th cir) 1967, US Supreme Ct 1976. Assoc., shareholder, v.p. Van Cott, Bagley, Cornwall & McCarthy, Salt Lake City, 1963-82; pres., shareholder Berman & Anderson, Salt Lake City, 1982-86; v.p., shareholder Hansen & Anderson, Salt Lake City, 1986-90; pres., shareholder Anderson & Watkins, Salt Lake City, 1990-95; pres. Anderson & Smith, Salt Lake City, 1995-97; lawyer, shareholder, past pres., chmn. Van Cott, Bagley Cornwall & McCarthy, Salt Lake City, 1998—. Bd dirs, mem exec comt Anderson Lumber Co, Ogden, Utah, 1982—2000. Trustee Children's Ctr., Salt Lake City, 1979—84, United Way Salt Lake, 2002—05, Utah Heritage Found., 2003—. Mem.: ABA, Salt Lake County Bar (mem. exec. com. 1967—75, pres. 1973—74), Am Inns Ct, Utah State Bar Asn (cts and judges comt 1991—99), Cottonwood Club, Alta Club, Rotary. Avocations: tennis, skiing. Office: Van Cott Bagley Cornwall & McCarthy 36 State St Ste 1000 Salt Lake City UT 84111 Office Phone: 801-532-3333. Business E-Mail: randerson@vancott.com.

ANDERSON, ROBERT MORRIS, JR., electrical engineer; b. Crookston, Minn., Feb. 15, 1939; s. Robert Morris and Eleanor Elaine (Huotte) A.; m. Janice Ilene Pendell, Sept. 3, 1960; children— Erik Martin, Kristi Lynn. BEE, U. Mich., 1961, MEE, 1963, MS in Physics, 1965, PhD in Elec. Engring, 1967. Asst. research engr. U. Mich., Ann Arbor, 1963-67; research engr. Conductron Corp., Ann Arbor, summer 1967; asst. prof. elec. engring. Purdue U., West Lafayette, Ind., 1967-71, assoc. prof., 1971-79, prof., 1979, engring. coordinator for continuing edn., 1973-79, Ball Bros. prof., 1976-79; mgr. engring. edn. and tng., corp. cons. services GE, Bridgeport, Conn., 1979-82, mgr. tech. edn. operation, corp. engring. and mfg., 1982-88; mgr. tech. edn., corp. mgmt. devel. Gen. Electric Co., Bridgeport, Conn., 1988-90; vice provost, dir. coop. extension Iowa State U., Ames, 1990-95, prof. elec. engring., 1990-2000, prof. emeritus, elec. engring., 2000—. Author: (multi-media learning packagE) Fundamentals of Vacuum Technology, 1973; author: (with others) Divided Loyalties, 1980; contbr. with others articles to profl. jours. Chmn. bd. dirs. Lincoln Way Chapter, Am. Red Cross, 2003—04; bd. trustees Ames Pub. Libr., 2005—. Recipient Dow Outstanding Young Faculty award, 1974, Ky. Col. award, Jullian M. Carroll, Gov., Commonwealth Ky., 1977. Fellow Am. Soc. Engring. Edn. (cert. of merit 1977, Joseph M. Biedenbach Disting. Svc. award 1986), IEEE (Meritorious Achievement award in continuing edn. activities 1987), Rotary Club (pres. 2005-06, Unsung Hero award 2002). Conservative. Lutheran. Office: Iowa State U 2218 Coover Hall Ames IA 50011-0001 Home: 4038 Stone Brook Rd Ames IA 50010-2900 Personal E-mail: bobsoldmr2@aol.com.

ANDERSON, ROBERT ORVILLE, oil and gas company executive; b. Chgo., Apr. 13, 1917; s. Hugo A. and Hilda (Nelson) A.; m. Barbara Phelps, Aug. 25, 1939; children: Katherine, Julia, Maria, Robert Bruce, Barbara Burton, William Phelps, Beverley. BA, U. Chgo., 1939. With Am. Mineral Spirits Co., Chgo., 1939-41; pres. Malco Refineries, Inc., Roswell, N.Mex., 1963-86; with Atlantic Richfield Co., Los Angeles, retired chmn. bd., chief exec. officer. Hon. coun. trustees Aspen Inst.; trustee Calif. Ins. Tech., U. Chgo. Mem. Nat. Petroleum Coun., Am. Petroleum Inst., Century Club (NYC), Calif. (LA), Pacific-Union Club (San Francisco). Office Phone: 505-625-6801.

ANDERSON, ROBERTA JOAN See MITCHELL, JONI

ANDERSON, ROLPH ELY, finance educator; b. Buchanan, Mich., Aug. 27, 1936; s. Eugene Jefferson and Susanna (James) Anderson; m. Sallie Durkee Warner; children: Rachel Elizabeth, Stuart James. BA, Mich. State U., 1958, MBA, 1964; PhD, U. Fla., 1971. Inventory mgr. Shell Oil Co., Detroit, 1958-59; contract adminstr. Westinghouse Elec. Corp., Pitts., 1962-63; mgr. new product devel. Quaker Oats Co., Chgo., 1964-67; prof., chmn. dept. bus. mgmt. Old Dominion U., Norfolk, Va., 1971-75; chmn. dept. mktg. Drexel U., Phila., 1975-97, Royal H. Gibson chair prof. bus. adminstrn., 1991—. Mem. sales com. Fin. Svcs. Advisor mag., 2000—; disting. fellow LeBow Coll. Ctr. for Tchg. Excellence, 2003—. Author: Professional Personal Selling, 1991, Essentials of Personal Selling: The New Professionalism, 1995, Personal Selling: Achieving Customer Satisfaction and Loyalty, 2004; co-author: Introduction to Multivariate Data Analysis, 1974, Multivariate Data Analysis, 1979, 6th edit., 2006, Sales Management, 1983, Professional Sales Management, 3d edit., 1999, Personal Selling: Building Customer Relationships and Partnerships, 2d edit., 2006; translator: Administración De Ventas 2d edit., 1995, 2d edit., 2004, Professionalini Menadzment Prodaje, 1998, Analisis Multivaranada 5th edit., 2004, Análise Multivarianta De Dados 5th edit., 2005. Mem. faculty adv. bd. Fisher Inst. Profl. Selling, 1998—. Served to capt. Supply Corps. USN. Recipient award for best publ. article, Jour. Pers. Selling and Sales Mgmt., 1988, Excellence in Reviewing award, 1996, Rsch. Excellence award, LeBow Coll., 2000—01; fellow, LeBow Coll. Ctr. Tchg. Excellence, 2003—. Mem.: Internat. Am. Mktg. Assn. (Sales Interest Group Inaugural Excellence in Sales Rsch award 1998), N.E. Am. Inst. Decision Scis. (bd. dirs. 1977—78), Acad. Mktg. Sci. (sec., mem. exec. coun. 1984—86), So. Mktg. Assn., Sales and Mktg. Execs. Internat., Am. Mktg. Assn. (internat. conf. co-chmn. 1978, v.p. programming Phila. chpt. 1984—85, bd. dirs. 1986—87, 1992—93), Am. Inst. Decision Scis. (nat. coun. 1977—79), S.E. Am. Inst. Decision Scis. (pres. 1977—78), Res. Officers Assn., Naval Res. Assn., Beta Gamma Sigma. Office: Drexel U LeBow Coll Bus Philadelphia PA 19104 Business E-Mail: andersre@drexel.edu.

ANDERSON, RONALD DELAINE, education educator; b. Poplar, Wis., Aug. 25, 1937; s. Leslie A. and Linnea A. (Bergsten) A.; m. Sandra Jean Wendt, June 1, 1963; children— Debra Jean, Timothy James, Nathan David. BS, U. Wis., 1959, PhD, 1964. Asst. prof. edn. Kans. State U., Manhattan, 1964-65; mem. faculty U. Colo., Boulder, 1965—, prof. edn., 1971—, asso. dean edn., 1972-78. Cons. to numerous edni. agys. Author: Religion and Spirituality in the Public School Curriculum, 2004, Religion and Teaching, 2007; co-author: Developing Children's Thinking Through Science, 1970, Issues of Curriculum Reform, 1994, Local Leadership for Science Education Reform, 1995, Portraits of Productive Schools, 1995, Study of Curriculum Reform, 1996; contbr. articles to profl. jours. Program dir. NSF, 1989—90. Fulbright scholar, 1986-87. Fellow AAAS (chair edn. sect. 1998-99, mem. Assn. Coun. 2002-05); mem. Nat. Assn. Rsch. Sci. Tchg. (pres. 1975-76), Assn. Edn. Tchrs. in Sci. (pres. 1972-73), Nat. Sci. Tchrs. Assn., Phi Delta Kappa. Home: 4800 North Creek Rd Beulah CO 81023-9601 Office: Univ Colo Sch Edn Boulder CO 80309-0001

ANDERSON, RONALD TRENT, artist, educator; b. Madison, Wis., Oct. 10, 1938; s. Delmar LeRoy and Violet (Doering) A.; m. Barbara Groffman, June 9, 1962; 1 child, Brett Erland. BS in Art Edn., U. Wis., 1961, MS in Art, 1962, MFA in Art, 1963. Tchr. Waupun (Wis.) High Sch., 1961; tchg. asst. rural art program U. Wis., Madison, 1961-63; tchr. Bloom Twp. High Sch., Chgo. Heights, Ill., 1963-67; asst. prof. art edn. Nova Scotia Coll. of Art and Design, Halifax, Nova Scotia, 1967-69; tchr. Springfield (Mass.) Pub. Schs., 1969—2000. Represented in permanent collections U. Wis.-Madison, Dalhousie U., Halifax, Westfield Coll., Walter J. Kohler, Jr., family, work reproduced in, Prize-Winning Watercolors Book I, 1963, Prize-Winning Watercolors Book II, 1964, The Art of Written Forms, 1969, one-man shows include Arts Unlimited Gallery, Milw., Wis., 1965, Bradley Gallery, 1967, Burnett Gallery, Amherst, Mass., 2005, retrospective U. Wis.-Madison, 2006, retrospective Westfield Coll., Mass., 2007, exhibited in group shows at Smithsonian Instn., Washington, D.C., 1962, Ill. State Mus., Springfield, Ill., 1965, 1967, Nat. Design Ctr., Chgo., Ill., 1967, Dalhousie U., 1967, Montreal (Can.) Mus. Fine Arts, 1968, Boston Symphony Hall, 1992, Colo. Coll., Colo. Springs, Colo., 1998, Internat. Biennale Contemporary Art, Florence, Italy, 2005, numerous others. Recipient Beacon award for excellence in edn., Springfield Sch. Com., 1992, 25 awards for painting and printmaking in juried art exhbns. U.S. and Can., Mass. Art Educator of Yr. award, Mass. Art Edn. Assn., 1999, Sch. Edn. Alumni Achievement Award, U. Wis. Madison, 2001; fellow Tchr.-Artist Program, The Marie Walsh Sharpe Art Found., 1998. Mem.: NEA, Internat. Platform Assn. (First Prize for Graphics Exhbn. 1995, Best of Show award 2001), Nat. Art Edn. Assn., Salmagundi Club (Rita Duis Meml. award 2003, Gene Magazzini Meml. award traditional oil 2003, Joseph DiMare award 2005, Elizabeth K. Ellis Artists Fellowship award 2006, Gwynne Lennon prize 2007), Phi Delta Kappa. Lutheran. Avocations: studying the arts and humanities, foreign travel, bicycling, photography, fishing. Home: 9 Autumn Ln Amherst MA 01002-3316 Personal E-mail: Ronbarb8@aol.com.

ANDERSON, ROSS BARRETT, healthcare environmental services manager; b. Toronto, Ont., Can., Aug. 25, 1951; arrived in US, 1956; s. John Ross and Constance (Nielson) A.; m. Gladys Jeanette Vincent, Aug. 26, 1972; children: Christopher Matthew, John Ross II, Josiah Dan. Student, Boston U., 1970-73. Housekeeping supr. Parker Hill Med. Ctr., Roxbury, Mass., 1973-76; acct. mgr. Servicemaster Inc., 1973—; housekeeping mgr. Union Hosp., Lynn, Mass., 1976-77, Quincy (Mass.) City Hosp., 1977-78, St. Joseph's Hosp., Lowell, Mass., 1978-79, Waltham Weston Hosp. and Med. Ctr., Waltham, Mass., 1979-86, support services mgr., 1986-90, dir. environ. svcs., 1991-93, chmn. customer svcs. bd., 1992; asst. dir. clin. engring. Good Samaritan Med. Ctr., Stoughton/Brockton, Mass., 1993-95; dir. environ. svcs. Harrington Meml. Hosp., Southbridge, Mass., 1995—. Mem. Boston Latin Sch. Assn., Scots Charitable Soc. Boston, First Congl. Ch., Pomfret, Conn. Avocations: football, softball. Home: 133 Old Town Rd Ashford CT 06278-2020 Office: Harrington Meml Hosp 100 South St Ste 1 Southbridge MA 01550-4047 Business E-Mail: andersonross@aramark.com.

ANDERSON, ROSS CARL, mayor, lawyer; b. Logan, Utah, Sept. 9, 1951; s. E. LeRoy and Grace (Rasmussen) Anderson; 1 child, Lucas Craig Arment. BS in Philosophy magna cum laude, U. Utah, 1973; JD with honors, George Washington U., 1978. Bar: U.S. Dist. Ct. Utah 1978. Assoc. Berman & Giauque, Salt Lake City, 1978-80; v.p., ptnr. Berman & Anderson, Rooker Larsen Kimball & Parr, Salt Lake City, 1980-82; ptnr. Berman & Anderson, Salt Lake City, 1982-85; ptnr., v.p. Hansen & Anderson, Salt Lake City, 1986-89, Anderson & Watkins, Salt Lake City, 1989-92; pres. Anderson & Karrenberg, Salt Lake City, 1992-98, of counsel, 1999; mayor Salt Lake City, 1999—. Columnist: Enterprise, 1997—98, I-15 Mag., 2000—01, Catalyst, 2002—. Pres. bd. dirs. Citizens Penal Reform, 1991—94, Guadalupe Ednl. Programs, Salt Lake City, 1985—96, 1997—99, ACLU Utah, 1980—85; bd. dirs. Common Cause Utah, 1987—89, Planned Parenthood Utah, 1979—83; mem. Salt Lake Com. Fgn. Rels., 1983—95; Dem. candidate for Congress Utah 2d Congl. Dist., 1996. Mem.: Utah State Bar Assn. Avocations: history, skiing. Home: 418 Douglas St Salt Lake City UT 84102-3231 Office: Office Mayor 451 S State St Rm 306 Salt Lake City UT 84111-0005 Home Phone: 801-583-5098; Office Phone: 801-535-7704. Business E-Mail: rocky.anderson@slcgov.com.

ANDERSON, ROXANNA MARION, psychology professor; b. Detroit, Mar. 22, 1945; d. Carlynn Ellen and George Lawrence Anderson; children: Walter Clarence Blenman, Frederick Gerald Ford, Laverne Barbara Ford. BS, NYU, 1968—73, MA, 1973—75, PhD, 1990—97. Dir. support svcs. NYU, 1984—97; assoc. prof. psychology Bennett Coll., Greensboro, NC, 1997—2004, acting chair, 1998—99; asst. prof. N.C. A & T State U., Greensboro, 1998—2005; dean of students Ea. Music Festival, Greensboro, 1998—2000; assoc. prof. psychology Bennett Coll. for Women, Greensboro, 2004—05, William Penn U., Oskaloosa, Iowa, 2005—. Dir. On The Ground Smoking Cessation and Prevention Program, Greensboro, 2004—05; advocacy trainer Crisis Intervention Svcs., Oskaloosa, Iowa, 2005—06. Author: (abstract) APA Women's Health Conference, Psychosocial and Behavioral Factors in Women's Health: Research, Prevention, Treatment, and Service Delivery in Clinical and Community Settings; contbr. articles to profl. pubs. Co-chair Relection Com. for Alma Adams, Ho. of Rep., Greensboro, 2002; mem. Com. to Reelect Ho. Rep. Alma Adams, Greensboro, 2002—04; trainee Episcopal Diocese of N.C., Greensboro, 2004—05; mem. African Am. Atelier, Greensboro, 2002—03, chair, 2003—05. Recipient 2005 Faculty Tchg. Excellence award, Bennett Coll. for Women, 2005; grantee Bush-Hewlett Faculty Develop award, Bennett Coll., 2000. Mem.: APA, Southeastern Psychol. Assn., Assn. Black Psychologist (by-laws com. mem. 2004—06), Am. Psychol. Soc., Pi Gamma Mu. D-Liberal. Episcopalian. Avocations: piano, quilting, travel. Home: 1001 N Market St Oskaloosa IA 52577 Office: William Penn Univ 201 Trueblood Ave Oskaloosa IA 52577 Home Phone: 641-673-1988; Office Phone: 641-673-1073. Office Fax: 641-673-1396. Personal E-mail: roxanna.anderson@gmail.com. Business E-Mail: andersonrm@wmpenn.edu.

ANDERSON, RUSSELL A., state supreme court chief justice; b. Bemidji, Minn., May 28, 1942; m. Kristin Anderson; children: Rebecca, John, Sarah. BA, St. Olaf Coll., 1964; JD, U. Minn., 1968; LLM, George Washington U., 1977. Pvt. practice, 1976-82; county atty. Beltrami County, 1978-82; dist. ct. judge 9th Jud. Dist., 1982-98; assoc. justice Minn. Supreme Ct., 1998—, chief justice, 2006—. Chair Jud. Coun. Lt. comdr. USN, 1968—76. Mem.: Minn. Dist. Judges Assn., Minn. State Bar Assn. Office: Minn Supreme Ct 424 Minn Judicial Ctr 25 Rev Martin Luther King Jr Blvd Saint Paul MN 55155

ANDERSON, RUTH LUCILLE, interior designer, educator, artist, librarian, archivist; b. Cyprus Hills, NY; d. Arthur Albert and Marie Rose (Weston) Buehler; m. Gunnar Bohlin Anderson; children: Anna Kristine Kornblatt, Deborah Val Anderson. Grad., NY Sch. Applied Design Women; Cert., NY Sch. Interior Design; BA, Adelphi U., Garden City, NY, 1979,

MA, 1981; studied life drawing under Terrence Coyle; attended, Nat. Acad. Design; studied dance with Martha Graham; postgrad., NYU, Nat. Acad. Sch. Fine Arts, 1987; MS, C.W. Post Coll./LI U. Cert. pub. libr. N.Y., pub. libr. profl. cert. SUNY Edn. Dept., 2001, archives, qualified interior designer Nat. Coun. Interior Design Qualification. Fabric cons. F. Schumacher & Co., NYC, 1954-60; sr. interior designer W&J Sloane, NYC, 1960-83; adj. assoc. prof. Nassau C.C., 1979—99, Adelphi U., 1980; instr. Hofstra U., Hempstead, NY, 1990; asst. to rsch. libr. Cradle Aviation, Mitchel Air Field, 1998—2003; libr. Planting Fields Libr., Oyster Bay, NY, Arboretum State Historic Park, 2001—. Mem. faculty Parson (New Sch.), 1980-81; lectr. in field. Exhibited at W&J Sloane, Cold Spring Harbor, Oyster Bay Cove, Adelphi U. and 75 Varick St., NYC, Garden City and Cold Spring Harbor Gallery, 1993, Planting Fields, Oyster Bay, NY, 2003, 04; exhibited sculpture Sea Cliff Mus., 2006. Mem. Nat. Trust Historic Preservation, Sea Cliff Village Mus. Recipient Spl. participation award Open Door Program, NYC; named Partner in Edn. NYC Pub. Schs., 1991-92. Mem. Am. Soc. Interior Designers (profl.), LI Early Flyers Club.

ANDERSON, SCOTT RICHARD, geologist, consultant; b. State College, Pa., Dec. 7, 1972; s. Richard Anderson and Marjorie Price, Denny Price (Stepfather) and Sarah Anderson (Stepmother); m. Heidi Renee Sykes, June 17, 1995; children: Megan Rachel, Tyler Ryan, Julie Rosemary, Kelly Rae. BS with honors and high distinction, Pa. State U., 1995. Sr. geologist GeoTrans Inc., Sterling, Va., 1996—2003; earth scientist iii, project geologist Tetra Tech NUS, Inc., Pitts., 2003—. Geology mentor Geol. Soc. of Am., Seattle, 2003—03. Recipient A.P. Honess Geology award, Coll. Earth and Mineral Scis. Pa. State U., 1995, Geosci. Dept. Marshall, Coll. of Earth and Mineral Scis., 1995, Undergraduate Rsch. award, Pa. State U., 1995, Daniel E. Weber Math. award, 1993, Evan Pugh Scholar award, 1994. Mem.: Geol. Soc. Am. (assoc.). Achievements include discovery of soft tissue tongue containing bite mark and multiple insect meals from a 23 million year old tree frog preserved in Dominican Amber; research in frozen insect interactions and behaviors caught in amber; currently compiling and researching scientifically important mid-Cretaceous Burmite (amber from Myanmar) collection (over 800 specimens in 17 insect orders); emphasis is on social insects (evolutionarily primitive ants, termites and wasps). Avocation: golfing. Home: 609 Fieldstone Dr Moon Township PA 15108 Office: Tetra Tech NUS Inc 661 Andersen Dr Foster Plaza #7 Pittsburgh PA 15220-2700 Home Phone: 724-457-7353; Office Phone: 412-921-7090. Office Fax: 412-921-4040. Business E-Mail: scott.anderson@hnus.com.

ANDERSON, SCOTT ROBBINS, hospital administrator; b. Fargo, ND, Mar. 25, 1940; BA, U. N.D., 1962; M Health Adminstrn., U. Iowa, 1964. Adminstrn. res. St. Luke's Methodist Hosp., Veteran's Adminstrn. Med. Ctr., Cedar Rapids, Iowa City, 1963-64; adminstrv. asst. North Meml. Med. Ctr., Robbinsdale, Minn., 1964-65, asst. dir., 1965-69, adminstr., 1969-76, v.p., 1976-81, pres., 1981—; pres., ceo North Meml. Med. Ctr. (now North Meml. Health Care), Robbinsdale, Minn., 1981—. Adj. prof. in field. Office: N Meml Health Care 3300 Oakdale Ave N Robbinsdale MN 55422-2926

ANDERSON, SHAWN RENEE, director; d. Dewayne Paul and Jeanette Sue Neikirk; m. Philip Dale Anderson. BS, Berea Coll., Ky., 1986. Fin. aid dir. Somerset Tech. Coll., Ky., 1992—2003, Somerset C.C., Ky., 2003—. Active Ky. Assn. Student Financial Aid Adminstr., Lexington, Ky., 1992—2006. Home Phone: 606-451-6641; Office Phone: 606-679-8501. Office Fax: 606-679-4369. Business E-Mail: shawn.anderson@kctcs.edu.

ANDERSON, SONYA L., physical therapist, educator; b. Bozeman, Mont., May 18, 1979; d. Charles Dean and Wanda Lou Anderson. BS, SD State U., Brookings, 2001; M in Phys. Therapy, Mayo Sch. Health Scis., Rochester, Minn., 2003. Lic. phys. therapist SD, 2003, Nebr., 2004. Rsch. assoc. U. SD, Vermillion, 2004; staff phys. therapist Madonna Rehab. Hosp., Lincoln, Nebr., 2004—. Adj. faculty SE C.C., Lincoln, 2006—; clin. instr. internat. Creighton U., Santiago, Dominican Republic, 2006, guest lectr., Omaha, 06, U. SD, Vermillion, 2006. Contbr. articles to profl. jours. Vol. track coach Spl. Olympics, Rochester, 2002; vol. Mayo Outreach for Students and Tchrs., Rochester, 2002; vol. sci. judge St. Joseph Sch., Lincoln, 2005. Recipient Youth Svc. award, La Sertoma, 1997; scholar, Treacy Corp., 1997—2001, Marine Corps, Tylenol, 1998—2000, Datatel, 1999—2001, Circle K, 2000—01. Mem.: Nebr. Phys. Therapy Assn., Am. Phys. Therapy Assn. (cardiopulmonary sect.), Mensa Soc., Mayo Clinic Alumni Assn., U. Nebr. Med. Ctr. Jour. Club, Golden Key (grad. scholar 2001), Alpha Lambda, Mortar Bd., Phi Kappa Phi. Avocations: running, exercise, travel, reading. Office: Madonna Rehab Hosp 5401 South St Lincoln NE 68506

ANDERSON, STANFORD OWEN, architect, architectural historian, educator; b. Redwood Falls, Minn., Nov. 13, 1934; s. Carl Alfred and Dora Helena (Paulson) A. BA, U. Minn., 1957; MA in Arch., U. Calif., Berkeley, 1958, postgrad., 1958-59; PhD, Columbia U., 1968. Registered arch., Mass. Tchr. Archtl. Assn., London, 1962-63, 74-78; co-dir. research project Inst. for Architecture and Urban Studies, NYC, 1970-72, fellow, 1971-81; asst. prof. history and architecture MIT, 1963-69, assoc. prof., 1969-72, prof., 1972—, head dept. architecture, 1991—2005. Co-dir. archtl. transl. project Am. Acad. Arts and Scis., 1977-80. Author: Hermann Muthesius: Style-Architecture and Building-Art, 1994, Peter Behrens: A New Architecture for the Twentieth Century, 2000; editor: Planning for Diversity and Choice, 1969, On Streets, 1978, Eladio Dieste: Innovation in Structural Art, 2004. Mem. Boston Landmarks Commn., 1980—87, Massport Designer Selection Panel, 1993—97; bd. dirs. Boston Preservation Alliance, 1989—91, Batuz Found. USA, 1997—, pres., 2000—04; bd. dirs. Fulbright Assn., 1998—2004, Boston Soc. Architects, 1992—2004; mem. Nat. Register Peer Profls., U.S. Gen. Svcs. Adminstrn., 2002—. Named AIA/ACSA Topaz Laureate, 2004, Hon. Citizen, Montevideo, Uruguay, 2004; Fulbright scholar, 1961-62; John Simon Guggenheim fellow, 1969-70; Graham Found. fellow, 1971; ACLS fellow, 1977-78; festschrift pub. in his honor, 1997. Mem. AIA, Assn. Collegiate Schs. Architecture, Boston Soc. Architects, Brit. Soc. for Philosophy of Sci., Coll. Art Assn., Soc. Archtl. Historians (dir. 1969-72, 76-77). Home: 51 Commercial Wharf Boston MA 02110-3814 Office: MIT Dept Architecture 77 Massachusetts Ave Cambridge MA 02139-4307 Office Phone: 617-253-1351. Business E-Mail: soa@mit.edu.

ANDERSON, STANTON DEAN, lawyer; b. Portland, Oreg., Oct. 18, 1940; s. Lloyd T. and Ruth M. (Brunes) A.; children: Stanton D. Jr., Mamie D. BA, Westmont Coll., 1962; JD, Willamette U., 1969. Bar: D.C. 1969. Staff asst. to pres. The White House, Washington, 1971-73; dep. asst. sec. US Dept. State, Washington, 1973-74; assoc. Surrey & Morse, Washington, 1975-76, ptnr., 1977-81, Anderson, Hibey & Blair, Washington, 1981—95; ptnr. to of counsel McDermott, Will & Emery, Washington, 1995—; exec. v.p., chief legal officer US C. of C., Washington, 2003, sr. counsel to the pres. Assoc. editor Willamette U. Law Rev. Mem. D.C. Reps. Cen. Com.; del. Rep. Nat. Conv. 1984. Mem. ABA, D.C. Bar Assn., City Club (Washington), Congl. Country Club (Bethesda, Md.), Robert Trent Jones Golf Club (Lake Manassas, Va.), Bear Lakes Country Club (West Palm Beach, Fla.). Office: McDermott Will & Emery 600 13th St NW Washington DC 20005-3096*

ANDERSON, STEFAN STOLEN, retired banker; b. Madison, Wis., Apr. 15, 1934; s. Theodore M. and Siri (Stolen) A.; m. Joan Timmermann, Sept. 19, 1959; children: Sharon Jill, Theodore Peter. AB magna cum laude, Harvard, 1956; MBA, U. Chgo., 1960; PhD (hon.), Ball State U., 1993. With Am. Nat. Bank & Trust Co. of Chgo., 1960—74, exec. v.p., 1969—74, 1st Mchts. Bank, Muncie, Ind., 1974, pres., 1979—98, chmn. bd. dirs., 1987—2005; pres., dir. First Mchts. Corp., Muncie, 1983—98, chmn. bd. dirs., 1987—2005; dir. Fed. Res. Bank of Chgo., 1991—97; ret., 2003. Bd. dirs. Maxon Corp., 1985-2004, Techpoint Inc., Pub. Radio Capital Fund, 2000-03. Past pres. Delaware County United Way, Muncie Symphony Orch.; trustee Roosevelt U., 1970-74, George Francis Ball Found., Ball State U. Found., BMH Found., Ziegler Found., Ind. State Mus. Found.; trustee, chmn. Minnitrista Cultural Found.; past chair Ind. Nature Conservancy; past pres. Cmty. Found. of Muncie and Delaware County. Mem. Ind. Acad., Skyline Club (Indpls.), Rotary (past pres.), Phi Beta Kappa, Beta Gamma Sigma. Home and Office: 2705 W Twickingham Dr Muncie IN 47304-1050

ANDERSON, STEPHEN HALE, federal judge; b. Salt Lake City, Jan. 12, 1932; m. Shirlee Gehring; 2 children. Student, Eastern Oreg. Coll. Edn., LaGrande, 1951, Brigham Young U., Provo, 1956; LLB, U. Utah, 1960. Bar: Utah 1960, US Claims Ct. 1963, US Tax Ct. 1967, US Ct. Appeals (10th cir.) 1970, U.S. Supreme Ct. 1971, US Ct. Appeals (9th cir.) 1972. Tchr. South H.S., Salt Lake City, 1956—57; trial atty. tax divsn. US Dept. Justice, 1960—64; ptnr. Ray, Quinney & Nebeker, 1964—85; judge US Ct. Appeals (10th cir.), Salt Lake City, 1985—2000, sr. judge, 2000—. Spl. counsel Salt Lake County Grand Jury, 1975; mem. Nat. Jud. Coun. State and Fed. Cts., 1992—96; chmn. fed.-state jurisdiction com. Jud. Conf. U.S., 1995—98; ad hoc. com. on bankruptcy appellate panels 10th Cir. Jud. Coun., 1995—97; com. mem. US Ct. Appeals (10th cir.). Editor (in chief): Utah Law Rev. With US Army, 1953—55. Mem.: Am. Bar Found., Salt Lake County Bar Assn. (pres. 1977—78), Utah State Bar (pres. 1983—84), U. Utah Coll. Law Alumni Assn. (trustee 1979—83, pres. 1982—83), Salt Lake Area C. of C. (bd.govs. 1984), Order of Coif. Office: US Ct Appeals 4201 Fed Bldg 125 S State St Salt Lake City UT 84138-1102*

ANDERSON, STEVEN C., pharmaceutical association executive; BA, Cornell Coll., 1975. Clk. House of Commons UK of Gr. Britain and No. Ireland; Rep. candidate U.S. rep. for 16th dist. Ill., 1980; sr. staff mem. for U.S. rep. John B. Anderson U.S. Ho. of Reps., chmn. Rep. Conf.; pres., CEO Am. Frozen Food Inst.; chmn. Inst. Orgn. Mgmt. U.S. C. of C.; pres., CEO Nat. Restaurant Assn., 1999—2007, Nat. Assn. Chain Drug Stores, 2007—. Vis. lectr. Kellogg Sch. Mgmt. Northwestern U., Wash. Coll. Law Am. U.; Paul E. Wise Exec. in Residence U. Del. Office: Nat Assn Chain Drug Stores 413 N Lee St Alexandria VA 22314-2301 Office Phone: 703-549-3001. Office Fax: 703-836-4869.*

ANDERSON, TERENCE JAMES, law educator; b. Chgo., Feb. 26, 1940; s. James E. and Charlotte (Flatley) A.; m. Carolyn Bugh; children: Michael, Kathleen, Jamie, Andrew. BA, Wabash Coll., 1961; JD, U. Chgo., 1964. Bar: Ill. 1967, D.C. 1973, Fla. 1977. Local cts. commr. Zomba, Malawa, Africa, 1964-66; assoc. Goldberg, Weigle, Mallin & Gitles, Chgo., 1966-69, ptnr., 1970-73; att. prof. Antioch Sch. of Law, Washington, 1973-78, acad. dean, 1975-76; vis. prof. U. Miami Sch. of Law, Coral Gables, Fla., 1976-78, prof., 1978—. Spl. counsel to gen. counsel SEC, Washington, summers 1980-81; dir. Legal Svcs. of Greater Miami, Inc., 1977-83. Author (with William Twining and David Schum): Analysis of Evidence, 1991, 2d edit., 2005; author: The Battles of Hastings: Four Stories in Search of a Meaning, 1996. Bd. dirs. ACLU of South Fla., 1981-85; counsel to former U.S. Judge Alcee L. Hastings and now mem. Ho. of Reps., 1982-93. Netherlands Inst. Advanced Studies fellow, 1994-95. Mem. ABA, Am. Assn. Law Schs. Office: Univ Miami Sch Law PO Box 248087 Miami FL 33124-8087 Office Phone: 305-284-2253.

ANDERSON, THEODORE ROBERT, physicist, small business owner; b. Lodi, Ohio, Jan. 30, 1949; s. Robert Anderson and LaVaughn (Mitchell) Gillotti. BS in Physics, Fla. State U., 1971; postgrad. in math. physics, U. Geneva, 1973, postgrad. in math. physics, 1975; MS in Physics, NYU, 1979, MS in Applied Sci., 1983, PhD in Physics, 1986. Nuc. engr. Gibbs & Hill Inc., NYC, 1980—83; rsch. physicist elec. boat divsn. Gen. Dynamics, Groton, Conn., 1983—88; rsch. physicist Naval Underwater Sys. Ctr., New London, Conn., 1988—; co-founder, CEO Haleakala R & D Inc., Brookfield, Mass., 2002—; prin., owner Smart Band Technologies Inc. Adj. prof. mech. engring., astronomy U. Conn., Storrs, Groton, 1983—; adj. prof. math. Mitchell Coll., New London, 1985, U. Hartford, 1990—; adj. prof. mech. and aero. engring., mgmt. and mech. engring. U. Bridgeport, 1989—; adj. prof. mech. and aero. engring. Hunter Coll.; adj. prof. physics and astronomy CUNY, 1979—83; adj. prof. physics LI U., 1980—83; adj. prof. elec. and mech. engring. Rensselaer Poly. Inst., Hartford, 1986—; adj. prof. mech. engring. and elec. engring. Sch. Bus. U. New Haven, 1983—, adj. prof., 1989—; rsch. prof. Rensselaer Poly. Inst., Troy, NY, Tenn. Elec. Engring. Dept., Knoxville; instr. Cooper Union Sch. Engring., NYC, 1980; prin. investigator ASI Tech. Corp.; founder, CEO, chief tech. officer Haleakala R & D, Inc. Active Met. Opera Guild, NYC, 1986—, Mus. Modern Art, NYC, 1984—, Met. Mus. Art, NYC, 1984—, Am. Mus. Natural History, NYC, 1987—, NY Shakespeare Festival, 1987—, NY Zool. Soc., 1988—, Ea. Nat. Pk. and Monument Assn., 1990—. Recipient Spl. Achievement award, USN, 1989, 1990. Mem.: IEEE, World Powerlifting Alliance, Soc. Rheology, Am. Phys. Soc., Nat. Pks. and Conservation Assn., Nat. Geog. Soc., Electromagnetic Compatibility Soc., Greenpeace, Sierra Club, World Wildlife Fund, Wilderness Soc., Amnesty Internat., Smithsonian Assocs., Nature Conservancy, Adirondack Coun. Achievements include research in fluid dynamics, plasma physics, acoustics and atomic physics, electromagnetic interference, nuclear engineering solar cells; patents for plasma antenna, plasma waveguides and plasma frequency selective surfaces. Home and Office: 7 Martin Rd Brookfield MA 01506 Office Phone: 518-409-1010. Personal E-mail: anderdrted@aol.com. Business E-Mail: tedanderson@haleakala-research.com.

ANDERSON, THEODORE WELLINGTON, portfolio strategist; b. Napa, Calif., Apr. 30, 1941; s. Theodore William and Donna Elorita (Dove) A.; children: Thomas Wellington, Hilary Dove. Student, Princeton U., 1959-60; BA, Stanford U., 1963; MBA, U. Calif., Berkeley, 1966. Portfolio mgr., v.p. John W. Bristol Inc., NYC, 1968-77; assoc. rsch. dir., sr. v.p. Argus Rsch., NYC, 1977-82; portfolio strategist The Ford Found., NYC, 1982—. Mem. Fin. Analysts Fedn., N.Y. Soc. Security Analysts, DeBruce Fly Fishing Club, Angler's Club of N.Y., St. George's Soc. Episcopalian. Avocations: fly fishing, foreign languages and history, tennis, bamboo rod building. Home: PO Box 432 Chappaqua NY 10514-0432 Office: The Ford Found 320 E 43rd St New York NY 10017-4890 Personal E-mail: theodoreand@msn.com. Business E-Mail: t.anderson@fordfound.org.

ANDERSON, THEODORE WILBUR, statistics educator; b. Mpls., June 5, 1918; s. Theodore Wilbur and Evelynn (Johnson) A.; m. Dorothy Fisher, July 8, 1950; children: Robert Lewis, Janet Lynn, Jeanne Elizabeth. BS with highest distinction, Northwestern U., 1939, DSc, 1989; MA, Princeton U., 1942, PhD, 1945; LittD, North Park U., 1988; PhD (honoris causa), U. Oslo, 1997; D (hon.), U. Athens, 1999. Asst. dept. math. Northwestern U., 1939-40; instr. math. Princeton U., 1941-43, rsch. assoc., 1943-45, Cowles Commn., U. Chgo., 1945-46; staff Columbia U., 1946-67, successively instr. math. stats., asst. prof., assoc. prof., 1946-56, prof., 1956-67, chmn. math. stats. dept., 1956-60, 64-65, acting chmn., 1950-51, 63; prof. stats. and econs. Stanford U., 1967-88, prof. stats. and econs. emeritus, 1988—. Dir. project Office Naval Rsch., 1950-82; prin. investigator NSF project, 1969-92, Army Rsch. Office project, 1982-92; vis. prof. math. U. Moscow, 1968; vis. prof. stats. U. Paris, 1968; vis. prof. econs. NYU, 1983-84; acad. visitor math. Imperial Coll. Sci. and Tech., U. London, 1967-68, London Sch. Econs. and Polit. Sci., 1974-75, U. So. Calif., 1989; C.G. Khatri Meml. lectr. Pa. State U., 1992; rsch. visitor Tokyo Inst. Tech., 1977; sabbaticant IBM Systems Rsch. Inst., 1984; rsch. assoc. Naval Postgrad. Sch., 1986-87; cons. RAND Corp., 1949-66; mem. com. on basic rsch. adv. Office Ordnance Rsch., Nat. Acad. Scis.-NRC, 1955-58; mem. panel on applied math. adv. Nat. Bur. Standards, 1964-65; chmn. com. on stats. NRC, 1961-63; mem. exec. com. Conf. Bd. Math. Scis., 1963-64; mem. com. on support rsch. in math. scis. NAS, 1965-68; mem. com. Pres.'s Statis. Socs., 1962-64; sci. dir. NATO Advanced Study Inst. on Discriminant Analysis and Its Applications, 1972. Author: An Introduction to Multivariate Statistical Analysis, 1958, 3d edit., 2003, The Statistical Analysis of Time Series, 1971, (with Somesh Das Gupta and George P.H. Styan) A Bibliography of Multivariate Statistical Analysis, 1972, (with Stanley Sclove) Introductory Statistical Analysis, 1974, An Introduction to the Statistical Analysis of Data, 1986, (with Jeremy D. Finn) The New Statistical Analysis of Data, 1996; editor: (with Krishna B. Athreya and Donald L. Iglehart) Probability, Statistics and Mathematics: Papers in Honor of Samuel Karlin, 1989, (with Kai Tai Fang) Statistical Inference in Elliptically Contoured and Related Distributions, 1990; (with K.T. Fang and I. Olkin) Multivariate Analysis and Its Applications, 1994; editor Anns. of Math. Stats., 1950-52; assoc. editor jour. Time Series Analysis, 1980-88; mem. adv. bd. Econometric Theory, 1985—, Jour. Multivariate Analysis, 1988—; mem. editl. bd. Psychometrika, 1954-72. Recipient R.A. Fisher award Pres.'s Statis. Socs., 1985, Disting. Alumnus award North Park Coll. and Theol. Sem., 1987, Minnehaha Acad., 1992, Award of Merit Northwestern U. Alumni Assn., 1989; named Wesley C. Mitchell Vis. Prof. Columbia U., 1983-84; Guggenheim fellow, 1947-48, fellow Ctr. for Advanced Study in Behavioral Scis., 1957-58; vis. scholar, 1972-73, 80; Sherman Fairchild disting. scholar Calif. Inst. Tech., 1980; vis. disting. prof. Norwegian Coun. Sci. and Indsl. Rsch. U. Oslo; Abraham Wald Meml. lectr., 1982; S.S. Wilks lectr. Princeton U., 1983, P.C. Mahalanobis Meml. lectr., 1985, S.N. Roy Meml. lectr. Calcutta U., 1985, Allen T. Craig lectr. U. Iowa, 1991, C.G. Khatri Meml. lectr. Pa. State U., 1992, George Zyskind Meml. lectr. Iowa State U., 1995. Fellow AAAS (chmn. sect. 1990-91), Am. Statis. Assn. (v.p. 1971-73, Samuel S. Wilks Meml. medal 1988, R.A. Fisher lectr. 1985), Econometric Soc., Royal Statis. Soc., Inst. Math. Stats. (pres. 1963), Am. Acad. Arts and Scis.; mem. NAS, Am. Math. Soc., Internat. Statis. Insts., Bernouilli Soc. for Math. Stats. and Probability, Norwegian Acad. Sci. and Letters (fgn.), Phi Beta Kappa. Achievements include research in multivariate statistical analysis, time series analysis, and econometrics. Home: 746 Santa Ynez St Stanford CA 94305-8441 Office: Stanford U Dept Stats Stanford CA 94305-4065 Home Phone: 650-327-5204; Office Phone: 650-723-4732. Business E-Mail: twa@stanford.edu.

ANDERSON, THERESA ANN, science educator; b. Phila., Aug. 30, 1972; d. Sarah Louise Anderson. B in Chemistry Edn., Fla. A&M U., Tallahassee, 1996; ThD, Z.E. Brown Bible Coll., Tallahassee, Fla., 2003. Cert. 6-12 chemistry tchr. Fla., 2003. Tchr. sci., head dept. sci. Fairview Mid. Sch., Tallahassee, 1998—. Office: Fairview Mid Sch 3415 Zillah Rd Tallahassee FL 32305 Home Phone: 850-222-7764; Office Phone: 850-488-6880. Personal E-mail: resetann@hotmail.com.

ANDERSON, THOMAS CARYL, dean; b. St. Paul, Sept. 3, 1944; s. Willis Cecil and Mary Lou (Kaun) Anderson; m. Catherine Sophia Hofstede, Apr. 20, 1968; children: Nicole, Jennifer, Karilyn. BS, U. Minn., 1966, MS, 1970. Asst. prof. Northeastern U., Boston, 1971—74; lectr. SUNY-Albany, 1974—87, dir. grad. program Sch. Bus., 1976—81, dir. fin. and adminstrv. svcs., 1981—85, exec. officer adminstrn. and fin., 1985—87; dir. adminstrv. svcs. MGH Inst. Health Professions, Boston, 1987—90, v.p. adminstrn. and fin., 1990—93; v.p. fin. and adminstrn. Chatham Coll., Pitts., 1993—96; v.p. finance and adminstrn. Black Hills State U., Spearfish, SD, 1996—2000; assoc. dean, lectr. Wayne State U. Sch. Bus. Adminstrn., Detroit, 2000—02, assoc. dean, chief of staff, 2002—06; assoc. dean, chief adminstv. officer Ill. Inst. Tech. Stuart Sch. Bus., Chgo., 2006—. Cons. various state govt. agys., Albany, 1978—87, Fund Corp. Initiatives, NYC, 1981—, GM, CPC Tarrytown, NY, 1988—89, U. Mass., Lowell, 1990—94, Wang Labs. Inc., Lowell, 1992—93, Wayne State U., 1998—; asst. sec. bd. trustees MGH Inst., Boston, 1987—93. Co-author: Elements of Organizational Behavior, 1972; contbr. articles to profl. jours. Mem. planning bd. Town of Hopedale, Mass., 1990—93; mem. exec. com. Ctrl. Mass. Regional Planning Commn., 1990—93; treas. Black Hills State U. Found. Home: Apt 2701 555 W Madison St Chicago IL 60661 Office: Stuart Sch Bus Ill Inst Tech 565 W Adams St Chicago IL 60661 Business E-Mail: anderson@stuart.iit.edu.

ANDERSON, THOMAS D., prosecutor; b. 1957; married; 3 children. Grad., St. Michael's Coll., 1979; JD, Seton Hall Law Sch., 1984. Atty. Sheehey, Furlong, Rendall & Behm, 1996—2001; asst. US atty. Dist. Vt. US Dept. Justice, Burlington, Vt., 1987—96, 2001—06, US atty., 2006—. Office: US Attys Offiice PO Box 570 Burlington VT 05402*

ANDERSON, TIMOTHY CHRISTOPHER, educational association administrator; b. Hinsdale, Ill., Dec. 27, 1950; s. Paul Eugene and Mary Agnes (Donnell) Anderson. BA in Polit. Sci. with honors, Boston Coll., 1973; MPA, Harvard U., 2000. Rsch. asst. to Rep. Thomas P. O'Neill U.S. Ho. Reps., Washington, 1973; ednl. cons. E. F. Shelly Co., 1973—74; assoc. dir. Boston Zool. Soc., 1974—76, exec. dir. and adminstr. Boston's two zoos, 1976—81; New Eng. regional v.p. Nat. Alliance Bus., 1981—83; pres. Dovetail Cons., Hull, Mass., 1983—2001, Boston Harbor Assocs., 1983—87; ecology coord. Hull Pub. Schs., 1992—93; dir. Hull Environment and Svc. Corps, 1992—94; founder, CEO South Shore Charter Sch., 1994—99, headmaster, 1994—97; founder and pres. World Computer Exch., Hull, 1999—. Bd. dir. VSA Arts Mass., chmn. bd. dir., 1998—2001, 2005—06, vice chmn. bd. dir., 2004—05, treas., 2006—; spl. projects dir. South Shore Edn. Collaborative, 1993—94; cons. NEH, 1977—78; trustee, chmn. bd. dirs. South Shore Charter Sch., 1994—95; chmn. bd. dir. W. Seavey Joyce SJ Award, 1988—; jury mem. Stockholm Challenge, 2005—; e-Granary steering com. U. Iowa, 2005—. Working group on access UN ICT Task Force, 2003—06; steering com. digital libr. U. Iowa, 2005—; Global Digital Divide fask force World Econ. Forum, 2001—03. Named Hon. Prof. Tbilisi Orbeliani, State Pedagogical U., 2002, Hon. Citizen, Kutaisi, Georgia; recipient Cmty. Svc. award, Girl Scouts Greater Boston, 1978, Leadership Commendation award, Nat. Alliance Bus., 1983, Leadership award, Mass. Cultural Alliance, 1986, Pres.'s award, 1986, Leadership award, Franklin Pk. Coalition, 1987, Boston Mgmt. Consortium, 1992, John Ames award, Boston Harbor Assocs., 1987, Mayor's cert. of recognition, 1992, Supts. Leadership award, 1992, Excellence award, South Shore Charter Sch. Students, 1999, badge of honor, Republic of Georgia, 2002. Office: World Computer Exch 936 Nantasket Ave Hull MA 02045-1453 Home Phone: 781-925-8833; Office Phone: 781-925-3078. E-mail: tanderson@worldcomputerexchange.org.

ANDERSON, TIMOTHY J., chemical engineering professor; PhD, U. Calif., Berkeley, 1980. Prof. chem. engring., assoc. dean rsch. and grad. programs U. Fla., Gainsville. Contbr. articles to profl. jours. Recipient Charles M.A. Stine award in Materials Engring. and Sci., Am. Inst. Chem. Engrs., 1994. Mem.: IEEE, AIChE, Electrochemical Soc., Materials Rsch. Soc. Office: U Fla Coll Engring 300 Weil Hall Gainesville FL 32611-6005 Office Phone: 352-392-0946. Office Fax: 352-392-9673. E-mail: tim@ufl.edu.

ANDERSON, TOM, Internet company executive; b. Oct. 13, 1975; BA in English and Rhetoric, U. Calif., Berkeley, 1997; M in Film-Critical Studies, UCLA, 2000. Mem. creative dept. Xdrive Technologies, Inc., asst. mktg. dept.; co-founder ResponseBase Mktg., LLC, 2002; co-founder, pres. MySpace.com, 2003—. Co-recipient with Chris DeWolfe, Breakout of Yr., Webby award, Internat. Acad. Digital Arts and Scis., 2006; named one of 100 Most Influential People, Time mag., 2006, with Chris Dewolfe, 25 Most Influential People in Web Music, Powergeek 25, 2007. Achievements include MySpace.com being the most popular social networking website on the internet.*

ANDERSON, URTON LIGGETT, accounting educator; b. Salem, Ohio, Dec. 10, 1951; s. Urton and Alice (Kenrich) A.; m. Deborah Mary Johnson, June 12, 1973; children: Bryony, Urton. BA in Greek and Philosophy magna cum laude, St. Olaf Coll., 1974; MA in Classics, U. Minn, 1977; PhD in Bus. Adminstrn., U. Minn., 1985. Instr. dept. acctg. U. Tex., Austin, 1984-85, asst. prof. dept. acctg., 1988-89, assoc. prof. dept. acctg., 1989-95, prof. dept. acctg., 1995—, assoc. dir. C. Aubrey Smith Ctr. for Auditing Edn. and Rsch., 1989-92, dir. C. Aubrey Smith Ctr. for Auditing Edn. and Rsch., 1992-93, acting dept. chair, 1996, assoc. dean ubdergrad. programs Coll. Bus., 1997—. Clark W. Thompson Jr. prof. in acctg. edn. U. Tex., Austin, 1997—. Author: Quality Asurance for Internal Auditing, 1983; co-editor: Internal Auditing, 1990—2001;: Implementing the Professional Practices Framework, 2002, 2d edit., 2006, Tha Handbook for Internal Auditors, 2006; contbr. articles to profl. jours. Rsch. fellow KPMG Peat Marwick Found., 1988-89, faculty fellow, 1990-92, Rsch. Opportunities in Auditing grantee, 1991, 94, Ernst & Young faculty fellow, 1988-93, Atlantic Richfield Centennial fellow in acctg., 1993-97. Mem. Inst. Internal Auditors Rsch. Found. (bd. rsch. advisors 1985-94), Inst. Internal Auditors (bd. regents 1994-99, 2003—, chmn. 2003—, internal auditing standards bd. 1999-2003, chair 2002-03, cert. internal auditor, cert. control self-assessment, cert. govt. audit profl). Office: U Tex Austin Dept Acctg CBA 4M 202 Austin TX 78712-1172 Office Phone: 512-471-9481. E-mail: urton@mail.utexas.edu.

ANDERSON, VALERIE B., actress, writer; b. Boston, Jan. 4, 1961; d. Kittridge Anderson and Pamela Evelyn Booth; m. Remington Morris Patrick Murphy, Sept. 26, 1999. Cheerleader Phila. Eagles, 1980; model Reinhard Modelling Agy., Phila., 1980; comml. actress Sears, Phila., 1980; TV spokesperson Arpeggio's Restaurant, Phila., 1980. Subject of articles, radio program; spkr. in field; appearances on TV programs. Musician: (single) My Love Rolls Over, 1982, Dolly is a Swinger, 1984; author: (pen name Christina Alexandra) Five Lost Years: A Personal Exploration of Schizophrenia, 2000; author, illustrator: Reflections on the Word in Black and White, 2002, illustrator: book cover; exhibitions include Main Line Art Ctr., 2004—05. Flute scholar, Jenkintown Music Sch. Mem.: Nat. Alliance of Mentally Ill, Mensa, Am. Assn. People with Disabilities. Avocations: travel, piano. Home: PO Box 12 Abington PA 19001 Personal E-mail: rmurphy483@aol.com.

ANDERSON, VICKI, retired librarian; b. Hazleton, Pa., June 17, 1928; d. Steven and Edith Potochney; m. Richard Anderson. BA, San Diego State Coll., 1961; MLS, U. Calif., Berkeley, 1962; postgrad., U. Pa., 1985—86. Libr. San Diego City Pub. Libr., 1962—64, San Diego City Schs., 1965—90; ret., 1991. Mem. Calif. State Coun. Edn., San Francisco, 1968—71, San Diego Citizen Adv. Com., 1978; spkr. San Diego City Coll., 1965; instr. Grossmont (Calif.) Coll., 1975—80, San Diego State Coll., 1981. Author: Fiction Sequels For readers 10 to16, 1989, 2d edit., 1998, Fiction Index for Readers 10 to 16, 1992, Cultures Outside the Unted States in Fiction, 1994, Sequels in Children's Literature K-6, 1998, Immigrants in the United States in Fiction, 1994, Native Americans in Fiction, 1994; Dime Novel: Its History and Context in Children's Literature, 2005. Chmn. Public Employees Coord. Coun., San Diego, 1978—79; mem. N. Mt. Village Planning Com.; appointed mem. Ariz. State Sch. Redistricting Commn., 2006—07; committeeman North Mountain Precinct Dem. Party, Phoenix, 1995; state com. mem. Dem. Party State Com., Phoenix, 1995; active Legislative Dist. 18, Phoenix, 1994; mem. exec. com. Maricopa County Dem. Party, 2002; chmn. Legis. Dist. 6, 2002; mem. Legis. Dist. 10; pres. Kensington-Talmadge Cmty. Assn., San Diego, 1976—78; adv. coun. mem. Area Agy. on Aging, 2006—. Grantee, Dakota State Coll., 1970. Mem.: AAUW (v.p. fin.), Moon Hills Cmty. Group (chmn.), Ariz. Silver Haired Legislators (elected del.), Ariz. Writers Club. Democrat. Avocations: reading, sewing, weaving. Home: 12833 N Fifteenth Ave Phoenix AZ 85029 Personal E-mail: valjest@aol.com.

ANDERSON, VINTON RANDOLPH, bishop; b. Somerset, Bermuda; came to US, 1947; m. Vivienne Louise Cholmondeley, 1952; children: Vinton Jr., Jeffrey, Carlton, Kenneth. BA, Wilberforce U.; MDiv, Payne Theol. Sem., 1952; MA in Philos., Kans. U., 1962; postgraduate studies, Yale U. Div. Sch.; HHD (hon.), Wilberforce U., 1973; DD (hon.), Paul Quinn Coll., Payne Theol. Sem., Temple Bible Coll., Interdenom. Theol. Sem., Eden Theol. Sem.; LHD (hon.), Morris Brown Coll., ITC Seminary, Eder Theol. Ordained to ministry AME Ch., 1952, bishop, 1972. Pastor various chs. in Kans. and Mo., 1952-72; presiding bishop A.M.E. Ch., Ala., 1972-76; presiding bishop, chief pastor 3rd Episcopal dist. AME Ch., 1976-84, dir. Office of Ecumenical Rels. and Devel., 1984-88, presiding bishop 5th Episcopal dist., 1988-96, presiding bishop 2nd Episcopal dist. Washington, 1996—. Chmn. bd. dirs. Payne Theol. Sem., Xenia, Ohio; preacher, lectr. in Caribbean, Republic of South and West Africa, Mid. East, Europe, South Pacific; del. World Meth. conf., Nairobi, Kenya, 1986; mem. exec. com. World Meth. Coun., 1981—, 1st v.p. N.Am. region; v.p. Consultation on Ch. Union; mem. Gen. Commn. Christian Unity and Interreligious Concern, United Meth. Ch.; pres. World Coun. Chs., 1991—, del. 7th assembly, moderator liaison com. of hist. black chs.; mem. governing bd., faith and order Nat. Coun. Chs.; charter mem., v.p. Congress Nat. Black Chs. Founder, editor Connector, info. publ.; editor A Syllabus for Celebrating the Bicentennial; contbr. articles to profl. jours. Mem. nat. adv. com. on the black population 1990 US Census; mem. Nat. Commn. on Sch./Cmty. Role in Improving Adolescent Health; mem. nat. adv. bd. Schomburg Ctr. for Rsch. in Black Culture; immediate past chairperson bd. trustees Wilberforce U.; chairperson bd. dirs. Payne Theol. Sem. Recipient Ann. Religion award Ebony mag., 1988, Disting. Alumni Honoree award Nat. Assn. for Equal Opportunity in Higher Edn., 1991. Mailing: 2nd Episcopal Dist AME Ch 1134 11th St NW Washington DC 20001

ANDERSON, W. FRENCH (WILLIAM FRENCH ANDERSON), biochemist, physician, educator; b. Tulsa, Dec. 31, 1936; m. Kathryn D. Anderson, June 24, 1961. AB magna cum laude, Harvard U., 1958, MD magna cum laude, 1963; MA, Cambridge U., 1960; LHD (hon.), U. Okla., 1992; DSc (hon.), U. Tulsa, 1996, SUNY, 2002. Diplomate Nat. Bd. Med. Examiners, 1964, lic. DC, 1963. Intern pediatric medicine Children's Hosp. Med. Ctr., Boston, 1963—64; rsch. fellow Harvard Med. Sch., Boston, 1964—65; rsch. assoc. lab. biochem. genetics Nat. Heart, Lung & Blood Inst., 1965-67, rsch. med. officer, 1967-68, head sect. human biochem., 1968-71, head sect. molecular hematology, 1971-73, chief molecular hematology br., 1973-92; cons. in rsch., genetics program George Wash. U., 1975—78; prof. biochemistry and pediatrics, dir. gene therapy labs. U. So. Calif. Norris Cancer Ctr., 1992—, program coord. for gene therapy, 1995—; adj. prof., grad. genetics program George Wash. U., 1978—92; hon. prof. Sun Yat-sen U. Cancer Ctr., Guangzhou, China, 2003, Peking Union Med. Ctr., Beijing, 2003. Rsch. fellow bacteriology and immunology med. sch. Harvard U., 1964—65; prof. lectr. sch. medicine George Washington U., 1967—75; mem. faculty dept. genetics Grad. Program NIH, 1967—92, mem. dept. medicine & physiology, 1981—92, chmn. dept. medicine & physiology, 1984—92, chmn., inter-agy. coord. com. on Cooley's anemia, 1972—77, chmn. inter-agy. coord. com. on Cooley's anemia, HEW, 1975—77, mem. working group human gene therapy, recombinant DNA adv. com., 1984—86, mem. working group on viruses, recombinant DNA adv. com., 1985—86, mem. coord. com. human genome, 1988—92, Mider lectr., 1992, chmn. stem cell RFA Symposium, Md., 2002, 03; mem. heart fellow bd. Nat. Heart & Lung Inst., NIH, 1968—70; mem. task force hemoglobinopathies Nat. Heart, Lung and Blood Inst., NIH, 1972, mem. nat. task group on Cooley's anemia, 1977—78; pres. Assembly of Scientists, Nat. Heart, Lung and Blood Inst., NIH, 1982; mem. exec. com. & bd. dirs. Found. Adv. Educ. in Scis., Inc., nih, 1984—92; hematology program dir. Lab Molecular Hematology, NIH, 1985; mem. sr. exec. sci. svc. Dept. Health and Human Svc., 1980—92; cons. Pres. Commn. Study Ethical Problems Medicine & Biomed. Behavior Rsch., 1981—82, Human Gene Therapy Ctr. for Bioethics, Kennedy Inst. Ethics, Wash., DC, 1982—92, GTI/SyStemix/Novartis, 1992—2003; chmn. sci. adv. bd. Genetic Therapy Inc., Gaithersburg, Md., 1986—87; mem. sci. adv. bd. S/L Health Care Ventures, NYC, 1986—88, NYC, 1993—; cons. human gene therapy St. Jude Childrens Rsch. Hosp., Memphis, 1990—92, U. Pitt., 1990—92, Baylor Coll. Medicine, Houston, 1990—92, M.D. Anderson Hosp., Houston, 1990—92; chmn. scientific adv. com. Children's Nat. Med. Ctr., Wash., DC, 1990—92; mem. sci. adv. coun. Inst. Genomic Rsch. (TIGR), Gaithersburg, Md., 1993—98; Timely Topics lectr. US and Can. Acad. Pathology, 1992; lectr. Am. Fedn. Clin. Rsch., 1992; Myron Karon Meml. lectr. Children's Hosp., LA, 1992; Disting. Sci. lectr. Internat. and Am. Assns. Dental Rsch., 1993; Plenary lectr. 17th Internat. Congress of Genetics, 1993, Am. Acad. Pediat., 1993, Am. Assn. Clin. Chemists, 2001; Martin Meml. lectr. 79th Ann. Clin. Congress, Am. Coll. Surgeons, 1993; Gross Meml. lectr. Am. Pediatric Surgeons Assn., 1994; Alan Gregg Meml. lectr. Assn. Am. Med. Colls., 1994; Frontiers in Biomedicine lectr. George Washington U. Sch. Medicine, 1998; Pres.'s invited lectr. Pacific Coast Surg. Assn., 1999; spl. lectr. Am. Assn. Neurol. Surgeons, 2000; invited lectr. Smithsonian Instn., 2001; lectr. other instns. in field; bd. dirs. various; mem. Inst. Genetic Medicine, U. So. Calif. Sch. Medicine, 1992—; mem. biol. response modifiers adv. com. FDA, 1994—99, mem. biol. response modifiers adv. com., ad hoc voting mem., 2000, chmn. site visit com. intramural rsch. CBER, 1996, mem. external peer rev. com. CBER, 1998—99; mem. adv. bd. Values and Biotech. Program The Hastings Ctr., 1996—2000; sci. cons. movie GATTACA Jersey Films, Inc., 1997; mem. biosafety adv. com. Maxygen, 1997—2001; CEO, pres., bd. dirs. Farmal, Inc., LA, 1999—2001; vis. assoc. in applied physics Calif. Inst. Tech., 2001—; keynote, invited and disting. spkr. in field. Co-editor: Fifth Cooley's Anemia Symposium, 1985; mem. editl. bd. various publs. Mem. med. resources coun. Cooley's Anemia Blood & Rsch. Found. Children, 1974-77; mem. adv. bd. Cooley's Anemia Found., Inc., 1977—; mem. sci. adv. com. Children's Hosp. Rsch. Found., Cin., 1985-88; mem. adv. com. Disting. Scholar Program W.M. Keck Found., 1996-00, mem. sci. adv. com. Disting. Young Scholars med. rsch., 1998-00; mem. hon. com. 10th Anniversary Benefit Gala, Alliance Genetic Support Groups, 1996; mem. internat. bd. advisors. Found. Genetic Medicine, Inc., 1998-00. Commd. officer USPHS, 1965-67. Recipient Thomas B. Cooley award Sci. Achievement Cooley's Anemia Blood & Rsch. Found. for Children, 1977, Mary Ann Liebert Biotherapeutic award, 1991, Pres. Award lectr. Am. Thoracic Soc., 1991, Maude L. Menten award U. Pitts., 1991, Ralph R. Braund award U. Tenn., 1991, Presdl. Meritorious Exec. Rank award HHS, 1991, Fed. Lab. Consortium award for Excellence in Tech. Transfer, 1992, Disting. Svc. award Nat. Ctr. Infectious Diseases, 1993, Dr. Murray Thelin award Nat. Hemophilia Found., 1993, Drew award lectr., 1993, King Faisal ibn Abdul Aziz Internat. Prize for Medicine, 1994, NORD Leadership award Nat. Orgn. Rare Disorders, 1996, Am. Assn. Clin. Chemistry award, 2001, Nat. Biotech. award Oxford BioSci. Ptnrs., 1995, Sheen award Nat. Westminster Bank, 1995, Genesis award Pacific Ctr. Health Policy and Ethics U. So. Calif., 1996, Humanitarian award Nat. Orgn. Rare Disorders, 1996, Treas. of LA award, 2000, Hamdan Internat. award med. excellence, 2002, Coudert Inst. award med. scis., 2003; nominee Time Mag. Man of Yr., 1994; finalist Jefferson award greatest pub. svc. by pvt. citizen Am. Inst. Pub. Svc., 1995; named BioPharm Person of Yr. Biopharm Mag. editl. adv. bd., 1994; named Tribute Symposium in his honor, 1996, Dr. French Anderson Collaborative Lab. Sun Yat-sen U. Cancer Ctr., Guangzhou in his honor., 2003, Outstanding Grad. Student Tchr. of Yr. U So. Calif. Sch. Medicine, 1998, Hon. Prof., Sun Yat-sen U. Cancer Ctr., Guangzhou, China, 2003, Peking Union Med. Ctr., Beijing, 2003; named to Heroes of Medicine Time mag., 1997, Pioneers Molecular Biology Time mag., 2003, Masters of Medicine CBS TV News, 1998, Okla. Hall of Fame, 1998, Profiles in Sci. Nat. Libr. Medicine NIH, 2004. Fellow AAAS (mem. working group ethics and theology project human germ-line interventions 1998-00); mem. Assn. Am. Physicians, Am. Soc. Clin. Investigation, Am. Soc. Hematology, Am. Soc. Human Genetics, Am. Soc. Biol. Chemists, Am. Fedn. Clin. Rsch., Am. Soc. Gene Therapy (mem. adv. bd. 2004-07), Internat. Soc. Stem Cell Rsch., Peripatetic Club. Achievements include research in regulation of RNA and protein synthesis, hemoglobin biosynthesis, thalassemia and hemoglobinopathies, gene expression in mammalian cells, genetic engineering of mammalian cells, human gene therapy; 16 patents in field. Office: U So Calif Keck Sch Medicine Norris Cancer Ctr Rm 6316 1441 Eastlake Ave Los Angeles CA 90033 Office Phone: 323-865-0612. Personal E-mail: wfa64@mindspring.com.

ANDERSON, WALTER ERNEST, church musician; b. Lebanon, Ind., Mar. 6, 1923; s. David Earl and Loudella May Anderson; m. Marjorie Ruth Sherry Anderson, Nov. 24, 1949; children: Kay Kent, Sherry Lynn, Robyn Kay, Scott Edward, Todd Randall. BS, Ind. State U., Terre Haute, 1943, MS, 1948. Ch. musician, India Burma, China, 1943—46, Indpls., 1948—; dir. music Pub. Schs., Hagerstown, Ind., 1948—52, Indpls., 1952—77. Cpl. US Army Air Corp., 1943—46. Republican. Home: 9541 Gemini Dr Indianapolis IN 46229

ANDERSON, WALTER HERMAN, editor, educator; b. Mt. Vernon, NY, Aug. 31, 1944; s. Walter Henry and Ethel Magdalena (Crolly) Anderson; m. Loretta Gritz, Sept. 9, 1967; children: Eric Christian, Melinda Christe. AA, Westchester C.C., 1970; BS summa cum laude, Mercy Coll., 1972; DHL (hon.), St. Ambrose U., 1988, Clemson U., 1990, Mercy Coll., 1989, U. of the Pacific, 1990. Reporter Reporter Dispatch, White Plains, NY, 1967—68, night city editor, 1968—69, editor, gen. mgr., 1975—77; police reporter Westchester Rockland Newspapers, White Plains, NY, 1969—70, help editor for action line, 1970—71, investigative reporter, 1971—72, mng. editor, 1973—74; editor, gen, mgr. Standard Star, New Rochelle, NY, 1974—75; sr. editor Parade mag., NYC, 1977—78, mng. editor, 1978—80, editor-in-chief, 1980—2000, chmn., CEO, 2000—. Author: Courage is a Three-Letter Word, 1986, The Greatest Risk of All, 1988, Read With Me, 1990, The Confidence Course, 1997, Meant to Be, 2003; actor(one-man show): Talkin' Stuff, 1992. Chmn. bd. trustees Mercy Coll, Dobbs Ferry, NY, 1980—88; bd. dirs. St. Vincent Hosp., 1975—80, N.Y. Vietnam Vets. Leadership Program Inc., 1984—89, Dropout Prevention Fund, 1987—, Nat. Ctr. for Family Literacy, 1990—, Very Spl. Arts, 1990—; bd. advisors Naval Postgrad. Sch., 1988—; mem. nat. adv. bd. Lit. Vols., 1990—2002; apptd. to U.S. Commn. on Librs. and Info. Sci., Pres. Clinton, 1995—2001. With USMC, 1961—66. Recipient Frank Tripp Meml. award, Gannett Group, 1971, Tree of Life award, Jewish Nat. Fund, 1988, Spirit of Am. award, 1988, Napoleon Hill Gold award, 1989, Horatio Alger award, 1994, Literacy Vols. of Am. Stars in Literacy cert., 1990, others. Mem.: Soc. Silurians, Overseas Press, Psi Chi, Sigma Delta Chi. Office: Parade Publs Inc 711 3rd Ave New York NY 10017-4014 *I hope a single driving desire remains with me always— that is, to encourage talented people. To share, even in the least of ways, in the growth of a creative talent is the highest goal of an editor, if his career is to matter at all.*

ANDERSON, WARREN RONALD, electrical engineering educator; b. July 31, 1914; s. Wallace Roy and Helen Adelia (Abrahamson) A.; m. Dantza Peinovich, May 28, 1945; children: Richard Godfrey, John Warren, Deborah Annete. AA, Bethel Coll., 1935; BS, U. Minn., 1939; BSEE, La. State U., 1944. Registered profl. engr., Calif. Design engr. Plant Engring. Agy., Phila., 1945-46; circuits engr. Automatic Electric, Chgo., 1946; prof. elec. engring. Calif. Polytech. State U., San Luis Obispo, 1946-76, head elec. engring. dept., 1976-79, prof. emeritus, 1979—. Design engr. GE, Ft. Wayne, Ind., 1951; rsch. analyst Northup Aircraft, Hawthorne, Calif., 1952; sys. engr. Western Gear Corp., Lynwood, Calif., 1955; edn. cons. GE, Schenectady, 1956. Leader Boy Scouts Am., San Luis Obispo, 1958-64. With U.S. Army, 1942-45. Recipient Cert of Appreciation AIEE, 1963. Mem. IEEE, NSPE, Am. Soc. Engring. Edn., Calif. Soc. Profl. Engrs. (dir. 1949-55), Calif. State Employees Assn. (dir. 1955-59), Eta Kappa Nu. Independent. Baptist. Home: 573 Jeffrey Dr San Luis Obispo CA 93405-1003 Office: Calif Poly State Univ Elec Engring Dept San Luis Obispo CA 93407 Personal E-mail: wanderso@sbcglobal.net. Business E-Mail: wanderso@calpoly.edu.

ANDERSON, WAYNE CARL, public information officer, retired corporate financial executive; b. Sheboygan, Wis., May 5, 1935; s. Chester Phillip and Mabel Mary A.; m. Joan Dorothy Staranick, May 18, 1963; children: David Wayne, Steven Michael, Karen Colleen. BS in Bus. Adminstrn., Upsala Coll., 1977. Cert. arbitrator, mediator. Dir. state govt. rels. Nabisco Brands Co., Parsippany, NJ, 1974-78, dir. fed. govt. rels., 1978-79, dir. govt. rels., 1979-81, v.p. govt. rels., 1981-84, v.p. govt. and cmty. rels., 1984-87, v.p. pub. affairs, 1987; non-lawyer exec. Evans Kitchel & Jenckes, P.C., 1988-89; pres., CEO Ariz. C. of C., 1990-95; exec. v.p. Americare, 1996-98; exec. emeritus Thunderbird--The Am. Grad. Sch. Internat. Mgmt., 1999—. Guest lectr. in field. Editl. adv. bd. Pub. Affairs in Rev., 1980; contbr. articles to profl. jours. Mem. Roseland (N.J.) Planning Bd., 1978—79, Roseland Citizens Adv. Com., 1977—78, Gov.'s Adv. Coun. on Quality, 1991—95, Gov.'s Commn. Econ. Devel., 1991—95, Ariz. Space Commn., 1992—2000, commr. emeritus, 1996; trustee State Govt. Rsch. and Edn. Found., 1981—82; bd. dirs. Ariz. Quality Alliance, 1992—95, NCCJ, Fiesta Bowl Com., Ariz. Econ. Forum, Philos. Soc. Ariz., 2001—04; statewide com. chmn. Superbowl XXX, 1995—96; chmn. adv. bd. NYU, Baruch Coll., U. N.Y.; pres. Grace Luth. Ch., Livingston, NJ, 1980—81, chmn. bd. elders, 1981—82, Redeemer Luth. Ch., Scottsdale, Ariz., 1997—98, 2005—, v.p., 1998—; trustee Evang. Luth. Synod, 2003—; pres. State Govtl. Affairs Coun.; bd. dirs. Luth. Schs. Am., 2006—; chmn. bd. Ariz. Investment Coun., 2007. With US Army, 1958—60. Mem. Internat. Jaycees (senator 1989—), U.S. Jaycees (nat. dir. 1964-65), Pub. Affairs Coun. (exec. com. 1986, bd. dirs. 1988—), Nat. Fgn. Trade Coun. (dir. 1986), State Govt. Affairs Coun. (past pres. 1978-79), Ford's Theatre (bd. govs.), Acad. Polit. Sci., Pub. Affairs Profls. Ariz. (founder 1987—), World Affairs Coun. (pres. 1994-95), Thunderbird Am. Grad. Sch. Internat. Mgmt., Thunderbird Global Coun. E-mail: wayneanderson@cox.net.

ANDERSON, WES (WESLEY WALES ANDERSON), film director; b. Houston, May 1, 1969; BA in Philosophy, U. Tex., 1991. Writer, dir.: (films) Bottle Rocket, 1994; writer, prodr., dir. Rushmore, 1998; The Royal Tenenbaums, 2001; The Life Aquatic with Steve Zissou, 2004. Office: UTA 5th Fl 9560 Wilshire Blvd Beverly Hills CA 90212

ANDERSON, WILLIAM (ALBION), JR., management consultant; b. Paris, Ark., July 12, 1939; s. William A. and Maud (Rodgers) A.; m. Patricia P. Puterbaugh, July 5, 1968; stepchildren— Charles L. Kuehn, Cynthia P. Robinson. BSBA, U. Ark., 1961; MBA, Harvard U., 1963. With Blyth Eastman Dillon & Co., Inc., NYC, 1963-75, exec. asst. to chief exec. officer, dir. planning, 1973-74, sr. v.p., 1974-75; sr. v.p., chief fin. officer ENSTAR Corp., Houston, 1975-84; pres. Farmers Oil Co., 1987-96; ltd. ptnr. Weller, Anderson, & Co., Ltd., Houston, 1988—2003. Mng. trustee J. G. Puterbaugh Trust.; cons. Eastman, Dillon Oil & Gas Assocs.; dir. Rancher Energy Corp. Mem. River Oaks Country Club (Houston). Office: 2001 Kirby St Ste 1300 Houston TX 77019 Office Phone: 713-630-9606.

ANDERSON, WILLIAM BANKS, JR., ophthalmology educator; b. Durham, NC, June 14, 1931; s. William Banks and Mildred Ursula (Everett) A.; m. Nancy Eldridge Walker, Sept. 17, 1960; children: Mary Banks, Mark Eldridge, Elizabeth Perry. AB, Princeton U., 1952; MD, Harvard U., 1956. Diplomate: Am. Bd. Ophthalmology (dir. 1986-92). Intern Duke U. Med. Ctr., Durham, NC, 1956-57, resident, 1959-62, asst. prof. ophthalmology, 1962-67, assoc. prof. ophthalmology, 1967-76, prof. ophthalmology, 1976—2007, acting chmn., 1991-92, prof. emeritus, 2007—. Mem. profl. adv. com. N.C. Div. Services to the Blind, Raleigh, 1972-84 Chmn. bd. trustees Durham Acad., 1975-77. Served to capt. M.C. U.S. Army, 1957-59. Fellow ACS; mem. Am. Ophthalmol. Soc. (sec.-treas. 1989-98, v.p. 1998-99, pres. 1999-2000), Am. Acad. Ophthalmology (bd. dirs. 1986-89), Am. Bd. Ophthalmology (bd. dirs. 1986-93). Episcopalian. Home: 2401 Cranford Rd Durham NC 27705-1011 Office: Duke U Eye Ctr Box 3802 Erwin Rd Durham NC 27710

ANDERSON, WILLIAM CARL, civilian military employee, lawyer; b. Syracuse, NY, July 9, 1958; s. Harold Everett and Mildred Dorothy (Weller) A.; m. Deborah L. Harding, Nov. 3, 1990. BA in History, Washington Coll., Chestertown, Md., 1980; JD, Syracuse U., 1983; postgrad., U. Miami, 1993. Bar: Md. 1984, Fla. 1985. Fin. cons. Merrill Lynch, Miami, Fla., 1984-85; tax cons. Arthur Andersen & Co., Miami, 1985-87; sr. tax specialist Ryder System, Inc., Miami, 1987-90; assoc. tax counsel internat. GE Co., Schenectady, NY, 1990-91, tax counsel Plainville, Conn., 1991-93; gen. counsel, dir. environ. and quality programs GE Indsl. Sys. Europe, Gent, Belgium, 1993-96; gen. mgr., sr. counsel environ. health and safety GE Consumer and Indsl., Plainville, Conn., 1996—2005; asst. sec. installations & environ. Dept. Air Force, US Dept. Def., 2005—. Chmn. GE Cmty. Svc. Fund, 1993-94; mem. adv. bd. BNA Environ. Due Diligence Guide, 2003-; advisor/observer Nat. Conf. Commrs. for Uniform State Laws-Environ. Covenants Act, 2002-. Treas. Big Bros./Big Sisters of Broward, Inc., Ft. Lauderdale, Fla., 1988-89, bd. dirs., 1989-90; bd. dirs. Urban League Greater Hartford, 2001—, Middlesex/Ctrl. Conn. chpt. ARC, 2003-. Mem. Md. Bar Assn., Fla. Bar Assn., Jaycees (local v.p., treas. 1984, Fla. legal counsel, 1988-89, 90-91). Republican. Lutheran. Avocations: sailing, rowing, bicycling. Office: USAF 1670 Air Force Pentagon Washington DC 20330

ANDERSON, WILLIAM H., architect; b. Conroe, Tex., July 28, 1933; s. William hartford and Lena Mattie A.; m. Kay W., Sept. 10, 1982; children: Linda, Susan, William, Francis. BArch, Tex. A&M U., 1956. Cert. architect, Tex., S.C. Intern architect George Dahl, Dallas, 1959-60, Caudill Rowlett & Scott, Houston, 1960-61, Howard Barnstone, Houston, 1961-62; architect Houston, 1962-66, Pearlstine Anderson, Columbia, S.C., 1966-74, Anderson Assocs., Columbia, 1975—. Past chmn. SC Bldg. Code Coun., Columbia, 1974—; past mem. Hist. Columbia Found. Properties Co., 1997—. Dir. Architects Bicentennial Com., Columbia, 1976. Served to capt. USAFR, 1956-59. Recipient design & environ. award Army Corps Engrs., 1990. Mem. SC AIA (bldg. and performance regulations com. 1970-94, bd. dirs. SC chpt. 1970, Honor and Merit awards), Nat. Trust Historic Preservation (mem. conservation assessment program 16 mus.). Office: Anderson Assocs Architects PO Box 6203 Columbia SC 29260-6203

ANDERSON, WILLIAM HENRY, psychobiology educator; b. Phila., 1940; s. William Henry Schoen and Elizabeth Winifred (Laverty) A.; m. Catherine Sacchetti, Oct. 7, 1967 (dec. Sept. 1991); 1 child, Jennifer Ann Gist; m. Claudia Winkler, July 25, 2005 BS, MIT, 1962; MA, U. Pa., 1967; MD, Thomas Jefferson U., 1967; MPH, Harvard U., 1977. Diplomate Am. Bd. Psychiatry and Neurology. Intern. Pa. Hosp., Phila., 1967-68; resident in psychiatry Mass. Gen. Hosp., Boston, 1968-71, assoc. psychiatrist dept. psychiatry, 1976-97, sr. psychiatrist, 1998—, dir. postgrad. edn., 1976-81; instr. psychiatry Harvard U., Boston, 1973-75, asst. prof., 1975-81, asst. clin. prof., 1981-82, lectr., 1982—; chmn. psychiatry St. Elizabeths Hosp., Boston, 1981-92. Dir. clinical svcs. Augusta Mental Health Inst., 1993-96;

asst. attending psychiatrist Mclean Hosp., Belmont, Mass.; Cons. Scientists' Inst. Pub. Info.; mem. Carnegie Coun. Ethics and Internat. Affairs. Contbg. editor: The New Physician, 1977-79; editorial bd. Topics in Geriatrics, 1981-87, Jour. Geriatric Psychiatry and Neurology; co-author: (with M.T. McGuire) The U.S. Healthcare Dilemma, 1999. Lt. comdr., M.C. USNR, 1971-73. Fellow Am. Psychiat. Assn., Human Biology coun.; mem. AAAS, Am. Acad. Clin. Psychiatrists, Internat. Soc. Polit. Psychology, Coun. on Fgn. Rels. (lectr. to coms.), Med. Assn. P.R. (hon.), Mass. Med. Soc., Soc. Ethnobiology, U.S. Naval Inst., Boston Athenaeum (proprietor), Harvard Club of Boston, Union Club, Sigma Xi. Office: 34 Coolidge Hill Rd Cambridge MA 02138-5527 Office Phone: 617-492-8090. Business E-Mail: wander@post.harvard.edu.

ANDERSON, WILLIAM HOPPLE, lawyer; b. Cin., Feb. 28, 1926; s. Robert Waters and Anna (Hopple) A.; m. Jean Koop, Feb. 3, 1951; children: Susan Hopple, Nancy, Barbara, William Hopple Jr., Francie. Student, Carleton Coll., 1946; LL.B., U. Cin., 1952. Bar: Ohio bar 1952, U.S. Supreme Ct 1964. Mem. firm Becker, Loeb, & Becker, Cin., 1952-54; asst. pros. atty. Hamilton County, Ohio, 1953-57; of counsel Graydon, Head & Ritchey, Cin.; judge Wyoming (Ohio) Mcpl. Ct., 1960-67. Mem. Ohio Ho. of Reps., 1967-69. With USMC, 1944-46. Republican. Presbyterian. Home: 297 Mount Pleasant Ave Wyoming OH 45215-4212 Office: 511 Walnut St Cincinnati OH 45202-3115

ANDERSON, WILLIAM SCOVIL, classics educator; b. Brookline, Mass., Sept. 16, 1927; s. Edgar Weston and Katrina (Brewster) A.; m. Lorna Candee Bassette, June 12, 1954 (dec. Dec. 1977); children: Judith, Blythe, Heather, Meredith, Keith; m. Deirdre Burt, May 28, 1983. BA, Yale U., New Haven, Conn., 1950, PhD, 1954; AB, Cambridge U., Eng., 1952, MA, 1955. Prix de Rome fellow Am. Acad. in Rome, 1954-55; instr. classics Yale U., 1955-59; resident in Rome, Morse fellow, 1959-60; mem. faculty U. Calif., Berkeley, 1960-94, prof. Latin and comparative lit., 1966-94, prof. charge Intercollegiate Ctr. Classical Studies, 1967-68, chmn. classics, 1970-73. Rsch. prof. U. Melbourne, 1984; Robson lectr. Victoria Coll., Toronto, 1987; Blegen rsch. prof. Vassar Coll., 1989-90, vice chair comparative lit., 1990-93; vis. disting. prof. Fla. State U., spring 1995; Gail Burnett lectr. San Diego State U., 2001; vis. prof. Ohio State U., 2003; vis. Case prof. Ind. U., 2005. Author: The Art of the Aeneid, 1969, Ovid, Metamorphoses, Critical Text, 1977, Essays on Roman Satire, 1982, Barbarian Play: Plautus' Roman Comedy, 1993, Ovid's Metamorphoses 1-5 and 6-10 Text and Commentary, 1972, 2d edit., 1997, Why Horace?, 1998; co-editor (with L.N. Quartarone) Approaches to Teaching Vergil's Aeneid, 2002. With US Army, 1946—48, Korea. Recipient Berkeley citation, 1994; NEH sr. fellow, 1973-74. Mem.: Danforth Assocs., Am. Philol. Assn. (pres. 1977), Soc. Religions. Episcopalian. Office: Univ Calif Dept Classics Berkeley CA 94720 Business E-Mail: wsand@berkeley.edu.

ANDERSON, WILLIAM WALLACE, financial executive; b. Balt., Apr. 8, 1958; s. Joseph Merryman II and Ann Marie (Moran) Anderson; m. Marian A. Gannon, July 24, 1987; children: Ciara Ann, Deirdre Christine. BA in Acctg., U. West Fla., 1980. CPA, Md., Calif. Audit staff to supr. Coopers & Lybrand, Balt., 1980-85, audit mgr. Dublin, 1985-87, Sacramento, 1987—92; dir. acctg. Raley's Supermarkets, Sacramento, 1992—97, v.p., contr., 1992—97, exec. v.p., CFO, 1997—. Bd. dirs., CFO Food for Families, Sacramento, 1990—. Mem. AICPA. Avocations: travel, basketball, tennis. Office: Raleys Supermarkets 500 W Capitol Ave West Sacramento CA 95605

ANDERSON-LEHMAN, RON, air transportation executive; married; 3 children. BS in Computer Sci., Iowa State U., Ames. Computer programmer United Airlines, 1986; with Covia, Galileo Internat.; mng. dir. tech. Continental Airlines, Inc., Houston, 2000—03, staff v.p. tech., 2003, sr. v.p., chief info. officer, 2004—. Bd. dirs. OpenTravel Alliance. Office: Continental Airlines Inc PO Box 4607 Houston TX 77210*

ANDERSON-SPIVY, ALEXANDRA, arts correspondent, editor, critic, writer, historian; b. Boston, May 14, 1942; d. Henry and Marion Ruth (Thompson) Fuller; m. Samuel O.J. Spivy; children: Lafcadio, Genevieve, Oscar. BA, Sarah Lawrence Coll., Bronxville, NY, 1961. Art editor Paris Rev., 1972-76, Village Voice, NYC, 1973-76; features assoc. Vogue mag., NYC, 1976-78; sr. editor Portfolio mag., NYC, 1979-83; editor-in-chief Arts and Antiques mag., NYC, 1983-85; exec. editor Am. Photographer, NYC, 1985-87; arts editor Smart mag., NYC, 1988-90; contbg. arts editor Esquire mag., NYC, 1990-94; NY editor The Argonaut, 1992-96; reviews editor The Art Jour., 1995-2000; editor-in-chief The Craftsman on CD-ROM, 1996—2002; projects editor Interactive Bur., 1996-99; editl. dir. Circle.com, 1999-2001; corr. Bloomberg.com, 2004—06. Bd. govs. Colby Coll. Art Mus.; profl. fellow Morgan Libr. Author: Anderson and Archer's SoHo: The Essential Guide to Art and Life in Lower Manhattan, 1979, Living With Art, 1988, Portraits of Olga, 1992, Keith Haring, Last Works, 1995, Gardens of Earthly Delight: The Art of Robert Kushner, 1997, Foliage: Photographs by Harold Feinstein, 2001; mem. adv. bd. Rev. Mag., 1998-2000. V.p. Mus. Modern Art, Contemporary Arts Coun.; pres., bd. dirs. Exhbns. Internat., 2000-06. Recipient Art Critics' award NEA, 1978; Travel grant Japan Found., 1976. Mem. Internat. Assn. Art Critics (pres. Am. sect. 1997-2001).

ANDERSSON, BO I., automotive executive; b. Oct. 16, 1955; Grad, Sweden's Military Acad.; BBA, Stockholm U.; post grad., Harvard U., 1999. Mgr. Saab, 1987, v.p. purchasing, 1990; exec. dir. worldwide purchasing GM Corp Elec. Commodity Group, 1993; exec. dir. GM Chem. Commodity Group, 1994; v.p. purchasing GM Europe, 1997; exec. worldwide purchasing GM Corp., 1997, v.p. worldwide purchasing, 2001—. Bd. dirs. New United Motors Mfg. Inc. Chmn. bd. dirs. Mich. Minority Bus. Devel. Coun., Mich. With Swedish Army. Mem.: HOPE (adv. bd.), St. Joseph Mercy Oakland Hosp. (bd. trustees).

ANDERSSON, CRAIG REMINGTON, retired chemical company executive; b. Winnipeg, Man., Can., June 16, 1937; came to U.S., 1937; s. Anders Einar and Doris (Pearson) A.; m. Dawn Marie Traver, June 13, 1959; children— Lee Erik, Karin Ingrid, Jon Kristien, Jenni Kate BS in Chem. Engring., U. Minn., 1960; postgrad., U. Del., 1960-66. Rschr. Sun Oil, 1960-67; v.p. ops. Custom Chems., Inc., 1967-68; Engr., supr. U.S. Steel Chems., Haverhill, Ohio, 1968-76, product mgr. Pitts., 1976-80, gen. mgr. Cin., 1980-82, v.p. Pitts., 1982-85, pres., 1985-86; pres., COO Aristech Chem. Corp., Pitts., 1986-93; vice chmn. Aristech Chem. Co., Pitts., 1994-95; ret., 1995. Cons.; bd. dirs. Albemarle Corp., ret., 2002; bd. dirs. RTI Internat. Metals, Inc.; former bd. dirs. Duquesne U. Contbr. articles to profl. jours. Mem. citizen's sponsoring com. Allegheny Conf. Cmty. Devel. Mem. AIChE, Alpha Chi Sigma. Lutheran. Achievements include patents in field. Avocations: golf, hunting, fishing, auto racing.

ANDERTON, JAMES FRANKLIN, IV, real estate company executive; b. Lansing, Mich., Aug. 2, 1943; s. James Franklin III and Florence Ethel (Bear) A.; m. Deborah Anne Garlock, Apr. 2, 1966 (div.); 1 child, James Franklin, V.; m. Denise Marie Thelen, July 6, 1985; 1 child, Sarah Elizabeth. BA, Hobart Coll., Geneva, NY, 1965; MBA, Cornell U, 1967; PhD, Mich. State U., 1997. Controller Summit Steel Processing Corp., Lansing, 1967-69, exec. v.p., 1970, pres., 1971-90, Processed Plastics Co., Ionia, Mich., 1986-90, Universal Steel Co. of Mich., Lansing, 1988-90; chmn., pres., CEO, Summit Holdings Corp., East Lansing, Mich., 1986—2001; pres. Lansing C.C., 1999-2000; mng. gen. ptnr. Summit Holdings Ltd. Partnership, 1996—; mng. mem. Maplegrove Property Mgmt., LLC, 2001—. Pres. Inst. Scrap Recycling Industries, Washington, 1982-83, bd. dirs.; v.p. Bur. Internat. de la Recuperation, Brussels, 1984-85; bd. dirs. Auto-Owners Ins. Co., Lansing; mem. Mich. Resource Recovery Com., 1975-77, Mich. Job Devel. Authority, 1977-79, nat. adv. coun. Mich. State U. Coll. Edn., 1998—; mem. Mich. com. on financing postsecondary edn., 1999-2001; bd. dirs. and chmn. Tchr. Edn. Accreditation Coun. Pres. Lansing Met. Devel. Authority, 1971-72, Delta Twp. Econ. Devel. Authority, 1975-76; campaign chmn. Capital Area United Way, Lansing, 1976; chmn. Lansing Regional C. of C., 1977; chmn. Montessori Children's House, Lansing, 1982-85, St. Lawrence Hosp., Lansing, 1985-86, Capital Region Cmty. Found., Lansing, 1992-93; trustee Hobart and William Smith Colls., Geneva, NY, 1993-98. Staff sgt. USNG, 1968-74 Recipient Am. Spirit Honor medal. Episcopalian. Avocations: reading, hiking, piano, tennis, golf. Home: 1618 Stanlake Dr East Lansing MI 48823-2018

ANDES, LARRY DALE, minister; b. Warrenton, Va., June 7, 1947; s. William Christian and Hilda Elizabeth (Beach) A.; m. Bobbi E. Stephens, July 16, 1966; 1 child, Joshua Dale. BS in Pastoral Studies, North Ctrl. U., 1970; student, U. Richmond, 1991, Bethel Theol. Sem., 1992. Ordained to ministry Assembly of God Ch., 1975, non-denominational, 1987. Assoc. pastor Calvary Assembly of God, Staunton, Va., 1971-72; youth min. Arlington (Va.) Assembly of God, 1972-75; assoc. pastor West End Assembly of God, Richmond, Va., 1975-76; founder, pres., festival dir. Fishnet Ministries Inc., Richmond, Front Royal, Va., 1976—; sr. pastor Fishnet Christian Ctr., Front Royal, 1992—. Named one of Outstanding Young Men of Am., 1984. Office: Fishnet Ministries Inc PO Box 1919 Front Royal VA 22630-1919 Office Phone: 540-636-2961. Personal E-mail: larryandes@hotmail.com. Business E-Mail: fishnet@fishnetministries.org.

ANDJABA, MARTIN, ambassador; Permanent rep. of Republic of Namibia UN, NYC, 1996—; pres. UN Security Council.

ANDO, KUNITAKE, consumer products company executive; Grad., Sch. of Economics, U. Tokyo, 1969. With Sony Corp., 1969—; mng. dir. Sony Life Ins. Co., Ltd. (formerly Sony Prudential Life Ins. Co.), 1979—85, dep. pres., 1985—90; gen. mgr., corp. planning Sony Electronics, Inc. (formerly Sony Corp. of Am.), 1976—79; pres. and COO Sony Engring. and Mfg. of Am. (now part of Sony Electronics Inc.), 1990—94; exec. v.p., sr. gen. mgr., corp. planning, consumer A & V Products Co. Sony Corp., 1994—96, pres., Divisional Info. Tech. Co., 1996—99, pres. and COO, Personal IT Network Co., 1999—2000, pres. and group COO (formerly COO), rep. corp. exec. officer, 2000—05, advisor, 2005—06. Avocations: golf, swimming, tennis.

ANDOLINA, JANET, lawyer; BA magna cum laude, Union Coll., 1990; JD cum laude, U. Chgo. Law Sch., 1994. Bar: NY, Conn. Tax ptnr. King & Spaulding, NYC; ptnr. Goodwin Procter LLP, NYC, 2007—. Office: Goodwin Procter LLP 559 Lexington Ave New York NY 10022 Office Phone: 212-813-8876. E-mail: jandolina@goodwinprocter.com.

ANDOLINO, ROSEMARIE S., airport terminal executive; b. 1967; BS in Mktg., DePaul Univ., Chgo. With City of Chgo., 1990—, with dept. planning and devel., 1999—, first dep. commr. planning devel. dept.; asst. to dir. Mayor of Chgo., 1995—99; exec. dir. O'Hare Modernization Program, 2005—. Named one of 40 Under Forty, Crain's Bus. Chgo., 2005. Office: O'Hare Modernization Project c/o Mayor's Office 121 N LaSalle St Chicago IL 60602*

ANDOLSEN, ALAN ANTHONY, management consultant; b. Cleve., Feb. 19, 1943; s. Lloyd Anthony and Helen Mae (Kozinski) A.; m. Barbara Hilkert, Jan. 20, 1968; children: Daniel, Ruth. AB magna cum laude, Borromeo Coll., 1964; MA, U. Dayton, 1967; postgrad., Vanderbilt U., 1967-69. Cert. mgmt. cons.; cert. records mgr. V.p. Bergamo East, Marcy, NY, 1969-71; dir. Met. Health Dept., Nashville, 1971-76; prin. Naremco Svc., Inc., NYC, 1976-79, v.p., 1979-86, pres., 1986—. Bd. dirs. Assn. Mgmt. Cons. Firms., N.Y.C. Editor: Management Consulting-A Model Course, 1989, 96; contbr. articles to profl. jours. Pres. Inst. Cert. Records Mgrs. Mem. Inst. Mgmt. Cons. (pres.), Assn. Records Mgrs. and Adminstrs., Assn. Image and Info. Mgmt., Am. Mensa Ltd. Roman Catholic. Avocations: music, bicycling, reading. Office: Naremco Svcs Inc 60 E 42nd St New York NY 10165-0006 Office Phone: 212-697-0290.

ANDORKA, FRANK HENRY, lawyer; b. Lorain, Ohio, July 25, 1946; s. Frank Henry and Sue (Parham) A.; m. M. Jean Deliman, Aug. 10, 1968; children: Frank Henry Jr., Claire E. AB, Ohio U., 1968; postgrad., Ind. U., 1968-69; JD, Cornell U., 1975. Bar: Ohio 1975, U.S. Dist. Ct. (no. dist.) Ohio 1975. From assoc. to ptnr. Baker & Hostetler, Cleve., 1975—. Author: A Practical Guide to Copyrights and Trademarks, 1989, What is a Copyright?, 1992. Served to 1st lt. U.S. Army, 1969-72. Mem. ABA (chmn. internat. copyright laws and treaties com. 1984-86, chmn. govt. rels. to copyright com. 1986-88, chmn. broadcasting, sound rec. and performing artists com. 1988-90, chmn. divsn. III copyrights 1990-92, chmn. divsn. IX publs. 1992-93), Ohio Bar Assn., Greater Cleve. Bar Assn. Avocations: bowling, tennis. Home: 31000 Clinton Dr Cleveland OH 44140-1500 Office: Baker & Hostetler 3200 Nat City Ctr 1900 E 9th St Ste 3200 Cleveland OH 44114-3475 E-mail: fandorka@bakerlaw.com.

ANDRADE, ANDRES, vocalist, educator; BA in Vocal Performance, U. So. Fla., 1987; MusM in Vocal Performance, New Eng. Conservatory of Music, 1995. Tchg. asst., vocal music New Eng. Conservatory of Music, Boston, 1993—94; vocal instr., opera theatre dir. LaGuardia Arts HS, NYC, Queens Coll.; pvt. vocal instr. NYC; freelance singer. Prodr.: (Operas) Alcina, 2002, Orfeo ed Euridice, 2003, Dido and Aeneas, 2004, Orpheus in the Underworld, 2005, The Merry Widow, 2006; contbr. articles to profl. jours. Founder Citywide Youth Opera, Inc.; instr. voice and diction. Fellow, New Eng. Conservatory, 1993. Mem.: Nat. Assn. Tchrs. Singing, N.Y. Singing Tchrs. Assn. Home: PO Box 20498 Columbus Circle Sta New York NY 10023 Office Phone: 212-539-3561. Personal E-mail: andradeten@aol.com.

ANDRADE, EDNA, artist, educator; b. Portsmouth, Va. d. Thomas Judson and Ruth (Porter) Wright; m. C. Preston Andrade, Jr., July 12, 1941 (div. 1960). BFA, Pa. Acad. Fine Arts/U. Pa., 1937. Supr. art elem. schs., Norfolk, Va., 1938-39; instr. drawing and painting Newcomb Art Sch., Tulane U., 1939-41; lectr. U. N.Mex., 1971; prof. Phila. Coll. Art, 1957—72, 1973—82, prof. emeritus, 1982—; prof. art Temple U., 1972-73. Adj. prof. art Ariz. State U., 1986—; critic Pa. Acad. Fine Arts, 1988—89. Artist, designer, OSS, 1942-44, free-lance designer, Washington, 1944-46, free-lance painter, designer, muralist, Phila. and, N.Y.C., 1946—, artist-in-residence, Hartford Sch. Art and Tamarind Inst., 1971, U. Sask., Can., 1977, U. Zulia, Maracaibo, Venezuela, 1980, Ariz. State U., Tempe, 1981, 83, Fabric Workshop, Phila., 1984, Hollins Coll., Va., 1985; vis. artist, Skidmore Coll., 1973, 74, one-woman shows, Phila. Art Alliance, 1954, Beaver Coll., 1963, East Hampton Gallery, N.Y.C., 1967, Peale Galleries Pa. Acad., 1967, Rutgers U., 1971, U. Hartford, 1977, Marian Locks Gallery, 1969, 1971,74, 77, 83, 1989, Phila., Hollins Coll., 1985; retrospective Pa. Acad. Fine Arts, 1993-94, Locks Gallery, Phila., 1993, 97, 99, 03, 06, 07, Inst. Contemporary Art, Phila., 2003, Print Ctr., Phila., 2006, Woodmere Art Mus., Phila., 2007; group shows include AAAL, In This Acad., Pa. Acad. Fine Arts, Phila., William Penn Meml. Mus., Harrisburg, Three Centuries Am. Art, Phila. Collects Art Since 1940, Phila. Mus. Art, Bklyn. Mus., Ft. Worth Art Ctr., Des Moines Art Ctr., Philbrook Art Ctr., Tulsa, Contemporary Phila. Artists, 1990, Phila. Mus. Art, Artists Choose Artists, Inst. of Contemporary Art, Phila., 1991, Klein Gallery, Univ. City Sci. Ctr., Phila., 1998, Phila. Mus. Art, 2000, Columbus Mus. Art, 2007, others; represented in permanent collections, Phila. Mus. Art, Pa. Acad. Fine Arts, Print Club, Balt. Mus. Art, Chrysler Mus. Art, Norfold, Va., Addison Gallery Am. Art, McNay Art Inst., San Antonio, Montclair (N.J.) Art Mus., Nat. Collection Fine Arts, Libr. of Congress, USIA, Albright-Knox Art Gallery, Buffalo, Tamarind Collection, U. N.Mex. Mus., Woodmere Art Mus., Phila., Yale Art Gallery, Am. Tel. & Tel. Co., Bell of Pa., Phila., Fed. Res. Bank, Phila., Price-Waterhouse, Phila., Edwin A. Ulrich Mus. Wichita State U., Pepsi-Cola, Leeway Found., Phila., Please Touch Mus., Phila., Va. Mus. Fine Arts, Richmond, Dallas Mus. Art, Mus. Fine Arts, Houston, Del. Art Mus., Wilmington, Del., Columbus Mus. Art. Mem. Mayor's Cultural Adv. Coun., Phila., 1984—85. Recipient 1st and 2d Cresson European Traveling scholarships Pa. Acad., 1936, 37, Eyre medal Phila. Water Color Club, 1968, Mary Smith prize Pa. Acad. Fine Arts, 1968, Childe Hassam Meml. purchases AAAL, 1967, 68, Hazlett Meml. award in arts, 1980, Honor award Women's Caucus for Art, 1983, Hunt award visual arts Phila. Women's Way, 1984, Roland Gallimore Meml. award Interior Design Coun., Phila. Mayor's Arts and Culture award, 1991, Founders award Samuel S. Fleisher Art Meml., 1993, Disting. Daughter Pa. award, 2002 Mem. Coll. Art Assn. (Disting. Tchr. of Art award 1996).

ANDRADE, MANUELA PESTANA, art educator; b. Funchal, Portugal, Oct. 10, 1937; d. Silvestre and Eulalia (Vieira Da Luz) Pestana; m. Manuel Cristao, Jan. 11, 1956 (dec. May 1970); 1 child, Maria Pestana Goldstein; m. Pedro Manuel Rapazote (div. Feb. 1977); 1 child, Antonio Pedro; m. Virgil Sousa Andrade, July 15, 1986. BA, U. Porto, Portugal, 1978-82, MA, 1980-84. Tchr. Externato liceal de Moncao, Portugal, 1971-74, Ministry Edn., Portugal, 1971-87; dept. head Prep. Sch. Ermezinde, Portugal, 1981-82, 83-84, master tchr., 1984-85, 86; tchr. Portuguese United Edn. Sch., 1987—, ednl. dir., 1988—. Author of poems; one-woman shows include Ctr. Internat. D'Art Contemporain, Paris, 1984, Funchal, Madeira, Portugal, 1984, Fall River (Mass.) Art Assn., 1988, Heritage Park, Fall River, 1988, Pilgrim Soc., Plymouth, Mass., 1989, Portuguese Am. Fedn. 25th Anniversary Festival, Bristol, R.I., 1990, Bentley Coll., Waltham, Mass., 1992, Portuguese Am. Women's Assn., Providence, 1998, Newport (R.I.) Art Mus., 1999; represented in permanent collections Nat. Kunsan U., South Korea, Calouste Gulbenkian Found., Portugal. Mem. Portuguese-Am. Bus. Assn., Portuguese-Am. Fedn., Nat. Soc. Fine Arts, Nat. Trust Historic Preservation, Casa da Madeira Norte, Portuguese Tchrs. Assn., Fall River Assn., Home: 27 Alfred St Fall River MA 02721-2620

ANDRASICK, JAMES STEPHEN, transportation executive; b. Passaic, NJ, Mar. 27, 1944; s. Stephen Adam and Emily (Spolnik) A.; children: Christopher J., Gregory O.; m. Ginger Michael Simon, Feb. 22, 1997. BS, USCG Acad., 1965; MS, MIT, 1971. Commd. ensign USCG, 1965, advanced through grades to lt., 1968; assigned to Vietnam, 1967-68; sys. analyst Jamesbury Corp., 1970; corp. fin. and product devel. staffs Ford Motor Co., 1971-74; mgr. corp. devel. IU Internat. Corp., Phila., 1974-78; from v.p. planning, contr. to exec. v.p. C. Brewer & Co., Ltd., Honolulu, 1978-92, pres., 1992-2000; sr. v.p., CFO, treas. Alexander & Baldwin, Inc., Honolulu, 2000—02, exec. v.p., 2002; pres., CEO Matson Navigation Co., 2002—. Chmn. bd., mng. gen. ptnr. ML Macadamia Orchards LP, 1986-88; chmn. bd. HCPC, Olokele Sugar Co., Hawaiian Sugar and Transp. Coop., 1993-96; chmn. Hawaiian Sugar Planters Assn., 1992-93; bd. dirs. Wailuku Agribus. Co., C. Brewer Co., Ltd., Honolulu. Bd. dirs. Aloha United Way, Honolulu, 1983-89, Hawaii Opera Theater, 2001-03; treas., bd. dirs. ARC, Hawaii, 1983-94, 96-2002, chmn., 1989-90; bd. dirs. Hawaii Employers Coun., 1992-98, chmn., 1995-98; trustee UH Found., 1988-94, vice chmn., 1992-93, chmn., 1993-94; trustee Hawaii Maritime Ctr., 1993-98; bd. dirs. Coast Guard Found., 1997—, Honolulu Symphony, 2002-05; trustee Mills Coll., 2004-. Mem.: San Francisco Nat. Maritime Pk. Assn. (bd. dirs.), Standard Club. Office: Matson Navigation Inc 555 12th St Oakland CA 94607 Business E-Mail: jandrasick@matson.com.

ANDRASSY, KYRA E., lawyer; b. Fontana, Calif., Nov. 27, 1972; BA, Univ. Calif., San Diego, 1995; JD, Loyola Law Sch., 1998. Bar: Calif. 2000, US Dist. Ct. No., Ea., Ctrl. & So. Calif. Law clk. Judge John E. Ryan, US Bankruptcy Ct., 1998—2000; assoc., bus. & bankruptcy litigation Weiland, Golden, Smiley, Wang Ekvall & Strok LLP, Costa Mesa, Calif. Editor: Loyola Law Rev., 1997—98. Named a Rising Star, So. Calif. Super Lawyers, 2006. Mem.: Orange County Bar Assn., Orange County Bankruptcy Forum. Office: Weiland Golden Smiley Wang Ekvall & Strok Ste 950 Ctr Tower 650 Town Ctr Dr Costa Mesa CA 92626 Office Phone: 714-966-1000. Office Fax: 714-966-1002.

ANDRE, CARL, sculptor; b. Quincy, Mass., Sept. 16, 1935; s. George Hans and Margaret Andre. Represented in public collections, Tate Gallery, London, Mus. Modern Art, N.Y.C., Rose Art Mus., Brandeis U., Columbus (Ohio) Gallery Fine Arts, Walker Art Center, Mpls., Milw. Art Center, La Jolla (Calif.) Mus. Contemporary Art, Dayton (Ohio) Art Inst., Albright-Knox Art Gallery, Buffalo, Monchengladbach Mus., Germany, Wallraf-Richartz Mus., Cologne, Haus Lange Mus., Krefeld, Germany, Kunstmus. Basel, Switzerland, Hessisches Landesmus., Darmstadt, Germany, Stedelijk Mus., Amsterdam, Van Abbe Mus., Eindhoven, Netherlands, Art Soc. Ghent, Belgium, Art Inst. Chgo., Los Angeles County Mus. Art, Musée Nat. d'Art Moderne, Paris, Carnegie Inst Mus. Art, Pitts., Musèo de Arte Moderno, Bogota, Colombia, Seattle Art Mus., High Mus. Art, Atlanta, Ohio State U. Gallery Fine Art, Bayerischen Staatsgemäldesammlungen, Munich, Kröller-Müller Mus., Otterlo, Netherlands, Detroit Inst. Arts, Guggenheim Mus., N.Y.C., City of Hartford, Conn., Mus. Boymans-van Beuningen, Rotterdam, Netherlands. Address: Konrad Fischer Platanenstr 7 Düsseldorf 40233 Germany

ANDRE, MICHAEL (KENNETH ANDRE), editor-in-chief; b. Halifax, NS, Can., Aug. 31, 1946; s. Kenneth Bailey and Kathleen Mary (Warburton) A.; m. Erika Rothenberg, 1974 (div. 1983); m. Jane Adler (div. 1995); 1 child, Benjamin Eyton. BA, McGill U., 1968; MA, U. Chgo., 1969; PhD, Columbia U., 1973. Lectr. CCNY, NYC, 1973, Baruch Coll., NYC, 1974; editorial assoc. Art News, NYC, 1973-77; treas. SoHo Baroque Opera Co., NYC, 1980—; exec. dir. Unmuzzled Ox, NYC, 1971—. Author: Experiments in Banal Living, 1990, (poetry) Studying the Ground for Holes, 1978, Experiment in Banal Living, 1998, others; edited W.H. Auden libretto for opera produced in spring 2004; opera Orfeo with music by Elodie Lauten produced and released on CD, 2004-05. Grantee Nat. Endowment Arts, Coordinating Coun. Lit. Mags., N.Y. State Coun. on Arts; grad. fellow Can. Coun. Fellow PEN; mem. MLA. Office: Unmuzzled Ox 105 Hudson St New York NY 10013-2331 Office Phone: 212-226-7170. Personal E-mail: MAndre0x@aol.com.

ANDRE, MICHAEL PAUL, physicist, educator; b. Des Moines, Apr. 25, 1951; s. Paul Leo and Pauline (Vermie) A.; m. Janice Joan Hanecak, Mar. 12, 1988. BA, Cen. U. Iowa, 1972; postgrad., U. Ariz., 1972-73; MS, UCLA, 1975, PhD, 1980; cert., Am. Bd. Radiology, 1999. Rsch. assoc. Inst. Atmospheric Physics, Tucson, 1972-73; mem. tech. staff Hughes Aircraft Co., LA, 1973-74; postgrad. researcher UCLA, 1974-77; cons. LA, 1975-84; med. radiologic physicist LACO/UCLA Olive View, LA, 1977-81; sr. radiation physicist Cedars-Sinai Med. Ctr., LA, 1979-84; chief med. physicist Dept. Vet. Affairs, San Diego, 1981—; prof. radiology, chief divsn.Physics and Engring, sch. medicine U. Calif., San Diego, 1981—; chief scientific officer Radco Corp., 1996—; chief med. officer Almen Labs., Inc., 1999—. Qualified expert Calif. Radiol. Health Dept., Berkeley, 1979—; chmn. Nat. Physics Conf., San Diego, 1984-89; mem. U. Calif.-San Diego Cancer Ctr., 2004— Editor: Physics and Biology of Radiology, 1988, Investigative Radiology, 1990—, Acoustical Imaging vol. 28, 2007; guest editor: Internat. Jour. Imaging Sci. & Tech., 1997; contbr. articles to profl. jours. Mountain guide Sierra Club, L.A., 1977-80; dir.

Ariz. PIRG, Tucson, 1973; mountain guide Am. Alpine Inst., Peru, 1987-90. Rsch. grantee U. Calif.-San Diego Found., 1989—, NIH, Nat. Cancer Inst., 1986—, VA, 1989—, U.S. Army, 1994—, Pfeiffer Rsch. Found., 2002—. Mem. Am. Assn. Physicists in Medicine, Am. Inst. Ultrasound in Medicine, San Diego Radiol. Soc., Am. Inst. Physics, Soc. Photo-Optical Inst. Engrs., Am. Coll. Radiology, Soc. of Breast Imaging. Avocations: auto racing, mountain climbing. Office: U Calif Dept Radiology 9114 La Jolla CA 92093 E-mail: mandre@ucsd.edu.

ANDRÉ 3000, See BENJAMIN, ANDRE

ANDREADIS, CONSTANTINE, art educator, therapist; b. NYC; s. George Andreadis and Rita Papatsos; m. Susan Andreadis, June 15, 1990; children: Justin, Zachary. BFA, N.Y. Inst. Tech., 1971; MA, Lehman Coll., 1976; MS, Coll. of New Rochelle, NYC, 1990; EdD, Nova Southea. U., 2000. Program coord. Riverdale (N.Y.) Mental Health Orgn./Riverdale Neighborhood Ho., 1971—76; cmty. worker, tchr. Sch. Dist. 10, Bronx, NY, 1976—80; tchr. Allen-Stevenson Sch., NYC, 1980—87; tchr., coord. Greenburgh Sch. Dist. #7, Hartsdale, NY, 1987—; adj. prof. Westchester C.C., White Plains, NY, 1992—, Fordham U., Tarrytown, NY, 1999—. Program coord. Woodlands Individualized Sr. Experience, Hartsdale, 2000—. Mem.: Am. Art Therapy Assn., Hellenic Am. Educators Assn., Westchester Art Therapy Assn. (bd. dirs. 1995—, past pres., award for significant contbn. to art therapy 1998—99). Avocations: photography, art, writing, web site creation, music. Office: Ctr for Growth and Edn Through the Arts PO Box 406 Dobbs Ferry NY 10522 Office Phone: 914-761-6052 ext 3029. E-mail: arteducator@usa.net, doctorcostas@yahoo.com.

ANDREANO, RALPH LOUIS, economist, educator; b. Waterbury, Conn., Apr. 11, 1928; s. John and Loretta (Creasia) A.; m. Carol Jean Wessbecher, Sept. 5, 1955 (dec. 2003); children: Maria Carol, Nicholas George. AB, Drury Coll., 1952; MA, Washington U., St. Louis, 1955; MA Fulbright scholar, U. Oslo, Norway, 1952-53; PhD, Northwestern U., 1961. Instr. econs. Northwestern U., 1959-60; asst. prof. econs. Earlham Coll., 1961, asso. prof., chmn. dept., 1962-65; asst. prof. bus. adminstrn. Harvard Bus. Sch., 1961-62; Brookings Nat. Research prof., 1964-65; asso. prof. econs., dir. undergrad. program econs. U. Wis., 1965-67, prof., 1967—, dir. Health Econs. Research Ctr., 1969-87, chmn. dept. econs., 1980-83, dir. Ctr. for Devel.; emeritus prof. econs., 1994—. Ofcl. del. Am. Econ. Assn. to Am. Council Learned Socs., 1964-70; adminstr. Div. Health State of Wis., 1976-78; economist WHO, Geneva, 1973-74. Author: (with H.F. Williamson and others) A History of American Petroleum Industry, 2 vols., 1959, 63, No Joy in Mudville: The Dilemma of Major League Baseball, 1965, Student Economists Handbook, 1967, (with B.A. Weisbrod and others) Disease and Economic Development, 1973, (with B.A. Weisbrod) American Health Policy, 1973; editor, author: New Views on American Economic Development, 1965; editor: Economic Impact of the Civil War, 1963, rev., 1967, The New Economic History: Papers on Methodology, 1971, (with J. Siegfried) Economics of Crime, 1981, Essays on International Health, 2001, The International Health Policy Program: An Internal Assessment, 2001; editor, founder: Explorations in Entrepreneurial History, 2d series, 1963-71, Explorations in Economic History 1971-78; editor: Jour. Econ. History, 1974-75; sr. editor (econs.): Social Sci. and Medicine, 1983-87; contbr. articles to profl. jours. Ford Faculty Research fellow, 1968-69 Mem. Inst. Medicine of Nat. Acad. Scis. Democrat. Home: 1815 Vilas Ave Madison WI 53711-2231 E-mail: rlandrea@wisc.edu.

ANDREAS, DAVID LOWELL, retired banker; b. St. Paul, Mar. 1, 1949; s. Lowell Willard and Nadine B. (Hamilton) A.; m. Debra Kelley, June 20, 1985; 2 children. BA, U. Denver, 1971; MA, Mankato State U., 1976. Credit mgmt. trainee United Calif. Bank, Los Angeles, 1976-77; comml. loan officer Nat. City Bank of Mpls., 1977-80; from v.p., sr. vp., to chmn., chief exec. officer to pres. & CEO Nat. City Bancorp., Mpls., 1980—2001. Chmn. ADAPA, Inc., Mpls., 1986-93; chmn. bd. Nat. City Bank, Mpls., 1991-94; pres., CEO Nat. City Bank, Mpls., 1994-2001. Bd. mem. Minn. Ctr. Victims of Torture, Marshall & Ilsley Corp., Milwaukee; mem. exec. com., dir. Children's Heart Link, 1988—, Ctr. Ethical Bus. Cultures, Minn. State U., Mankato Coll. Bus. Adv. Coun., Bus. Adv. Coun.; mem. Minn. State U. Mankato Coll. bus. adv. coun.; mem. Coll. of Social and Behavioral Scis. adv. bd.; trustee Breck Sch., Golden Valley, Minn., 1997, Mpls. Coll. Art and Design. With U.S. Army, 1971-73. Mem.: Golden Valley Golf & Country Club. Avocations: swimming, snowboarding. E-mail: 5033@usinternet.com.

ANDREAS, DWAYNE ORVILLE, agricultural products executive; b. Worthington, Minn., Mar. 4, 1918; s. Reuben P. and Lydia (Stoltz) A.; m. Bertha Benedict, 1938 (div.); 1 dau., Sandra Ann Andreas McMurtie; m. Dorothy Inez Snyder, Dec. 21, 1947; children: TerryLynn, Michael D. Student, Wheaton Coll., Ill., 1935-36; degree (hon.), Barry U. V.p., dir. Honeymead Products Co., Cedar Rapids, Iowa, 1936-46; chmn. bd., chief exec. officer Honeymead Products Co. (now Nat. City Bancorp.), Mankato, Minn., 1952-72; v.p. Cargill, Inc., Mpls., 1946-52; exec. v.p. Farmers Union Grain Terminal Assn., St. Paul, 1960-66; chmn. bd., chief exec. officer Archer-Daniels-Midland Co., Decatur, Ill., 1970-97, chmn. bd., 1997-98, chmn. emeritus, 1999. Mem. Pres.'s Gen. Adv. Commn. of Fgn. Assistance Programs, 1965-68, Pres.'s Adv. Coun. on Mgmt. Improvement, 1969-73; chmn. Pres.'s Task Force on Internat. Pvt. Enterprise. Nat. bd. dirs. Boys' Club Am.; former chmn. U.S.-USSR Trade and Econ. Coun.; former chmn. Exec. Coun. on Fgn. Diplomats; former trustee Hoover Inst. on War, Revolution and Peace; former vice chmn. Woodrow Wilson Internat. Ctr. for Scholars; former mem. Trilateral Commn.; chmn. Found. for Commemoration of the U.S. Constitution, 1986. Mem. Fgn. Policy Assn. N.Y. (dir.), Indian Creek Country Club (Miami Beach, Fla.), Blind Brook Country Club (Purchase, N.Y.), Links, Knickerbocker, Friars (N.Y.C.). Office Phone: 217-424-5515.

ANDREASEN, NANCY COOVER, psychiatrist, educator, neuroscientist; d. John A. Sr. and Pauline G. Coover; children: Robin, Susan. BA summa cum laude, U. Nebr., 1958, PhD, 1963; MA, Radcliffe Coll., 1959; MD, U. Iowa, 1970. Instr. English Nebr. Wesleyan Coll., 1960—61, U. Nebr., Lincoln, 1962—63; asst. prof. English U. Iowa, Iowa City, 1963—66, resident, 1970—73, asst. prof. psychiatry, 1973—77, assoc. prof., 1977—81, prof. psychiatry, 1981—82, Andrew H. Woods prof. psychiatry, 1992—97, Andrew H. Woods chair psychiatry, 1997—. Sr. cons. Northwick Park Hosp., London, 1983; acad. visitor Maudsley Hosp., London, 1986; dir. Mental Health Clin. Rsch. Ctr., 1987—. Author: The Broken Brain, 1984, Introductory Psychiatry Textbook, 1991; editor: Can Schizophrenia be Localized to the Brain?, 1986, Brain Imaging: Applications in Psychiatry, 1988, Brave New Brain: Conquering Mental Illness in the Era of the Genome, 2001, The Creating Brain: The Neuroscience of Genius, 2005, Am. Jour. Psychiat., 1988—, 1989—93; editor-in-chief:, 1993—2005; contbr. articles to profl. jours. Recipient Rhonda and Bernard Sarnat award NAS, 1999, C. Charles Burlingame award, 1999, Arthur P. Noyes award in schizophrenia, 1999, Lieber prize Nat. Alliance for Rsch. on Schizophrenia and Depression, 2000, Pres.'s Nat. Medal Sci., 2000, Interbrew Baillet-Latour Health prize, 2003, William K. Warren award Internat. Schizophrenia Congress, 2005, Vanderbilt prize in Biomedical Sci., Vanderbilt U. Sch. Medicine, 2006; Woodrow Wilson fellow, 1958-59, Fulbright fellow Oxford U., London, 1959-60. Fellow Royal Coll. Physicians Surgeons Can. (hon.), Am. Psychiat. Assn. (Adolf Meyer award 1999, Disting. Svc. award 2004, Judd Marmor award, 2007), Am. Coll. Neuropharmacologists, Royal Soc. Medicine; mem. Am. Acad. Arts and Scis., Am. Psychopathol. Assn. (pres. 1989-90), Inst. Medicine of NAS (coun. 1996—). Office: U Iowa Hosps and Clinics 200 Hawkins Dr Iowa City IA 52242-1057

ANDREASSI, JOHN LAWRENCE, psychologist, educator; b. NYC, Oct. 23, 1934; s. Croce and Agnes Marie Andreassi; m. Gina Maria Andreassi, Mar. 29, 1969; children: John II, Jeanine, Cristina. BA, CCNY, 1956; MA, Fordham U., 1959; PhD, Case Western Res. U., Cleve., 1964. Lic. psychologist, N.Y. Psychologist Dunlap & Assocs., Stamford, Conn., 1958-61; USPHS fellow Case Western Res. U., Cleve., 1961-64; assoc. prof. NYU, NYC, 1967-73; prof. psychology CUNY, 1973—. Author: Psychophysiology, 1980, 5th edit., 2007; editor-in-chief: Internat. Jour. Psychophysiology, 1988—2007. With USN, 1964-67. Disting. Faculty scholar Baruch Coll., CUNY, 1978; Office of Naval Rsch. grantee, 1969-73, Air Force Office of Sci. Rsch. grantee, 1973-85. Mem. APA, Internat. Orgn. Psychophysiology (v.p. 1984-94, bd. govs. 1996—, bd. dirs. 1982-94), Assn. for Applied Psychophysiology and Biofeedback, Sigma Xi. Avocations: tennis, golf, chess. Office: City Univ of New York Baruch Coll Dept Psychology Box B8-215 One Bernard Baruch Way New York NY 10010 Office Phone: 646-312-3790. Business E-Mail: john_andreassi@baruch.cuny.edu.

ANDREASSON, KIM J., writer, consultant; b. Varberg, Sweden, Feb. 17, 1976; s. Kenth and Gullvi Andreasson. BA with honors, NYU, 2000; MIA, Columbia U., 2002. Web editor Goteborgs-Posten, Sweden, 1997—98, asst. editor, 1998—98; forum coord. Fgn. Policy Assn., NYC, 2001—01; assoc. Civic Resource Group, LA, 2003—. Contbr. articles to profl. jours. Mem. Pacific Coun. on Internat. Policy. Recipient, Am.-Scandinavian Found., 2005; scholar, The Marcus Wallenberg Found., 2001. Mem.: Foreign Policy Assn. (John C. Whitehead fellow), Pacific Coun. Internat. Policy, Internat. Inst. Strategic Studies. Personal E-mail: kim@kimandreasson.com.

ANDREE, TIM, advertising executive; BA in Economics, U. Notre Dame. Drafted by Chgo. Bulls, 1983; various sr. level positions Toyota Motor Corp., Canon USA; v.p. corp. comm. BASF Corp., 2001—02, v.p. chief comm. officer, 2005—06; sr. v.p. comm. NBA, 2002—05; CEO Dentsu Am., Inc., 2006—. Office: Dentsu Am Inc 666 5th Ave 9th Fl New York NY 10103 Office Phone: 212-397-3333. Office Fax: 212-261-4286.*

ANDREESSEN, MARC, software company executive, internet innovator; b. Cedar Falls, Iowa, Apr. 26, 1971; m. Laura Arrillaga. BS in Computer Sci., U. Ill., Urbana-Champaign, 1993. With Enterprise Integration Technologies, 1993; co-founder Mosaic Comm. Corp. (now Netscape Comm. Corp.), Mountain View, Calif., 1994; v.p. tech. Netscape Comm. Corp., Mountain View, Calif., 1994-97, exec. v.p., 1997-99; chief tech. officer AOL, 1999; co-founder, chmn. Opsware Inc. (formerly Loudcloud), 1999—; chief tech. officer, co-founder Ning, Inc., 2004—. Bd. dir. Blue Coat Systems; investor, social news website Digg; involved with Ning, 2005. Named one of Top 50 People Under The Age of 40, Time mag., 1994. Achievements include development of Mosaic graphical browser for the World Wide Web. Office: Opsware Inc 599 N Mathilda Ave Sunnyvale CA 94085-3545*

ANDREOFF, CHRISTOPHER ANDON, lawyer; b. Detroit, July 15, 1947; s. Andon Anastas and Mildred Dimitry (Kolinoff) A.; m. Nancy Anne Krochmal, Jan. 12, 1980; children: Alison Brianne, Lauren Kathleen. BA, Wayne State U., 1969; postgrad. in law, Washington U., St. Louis, 1969-70; JD, U. Detroit, 1972. Bar: Mich. 1972, U.S. Dist. Ct. (ea. dist.) Mich. 1972, U.S. Ct. Appeals (6th cir.) 1974, Fla. 1978, U.S. Supreme Ct. 1980. Legal intern Wayne County Prosecutor's Office, Detroit, 1970-72; law clk. Wayne County Cir. Ct., Detroit, 1972-73; asst. U.S. atty. U.S. Dept. Justice, Detroit, 1973-80; asst. chief criminal divsn. U.S. Atty.'s Office, 1977-80; spl. atty. organized crime and racketeering sect. U.S. Dept. Justice, 1980-84, dep. chief Detroit Organized Crime Strike Force, 1982-85, mem. narcotics adv. com., 1979-80; ptnr. Evans & Luptak, Detroit, 1985-93, Jaffe, Raitt, Heuer & Weiss, Detroit, 1995—. Lectr. U.S. Atty. Gen. Advocacy Inst., 1984. Recipient numerous spl. commendations FBI, U.S. Drug Enforcement Adminstrn., U.S. Dept. Justice, U.S. Atty. Gen. Mem. ABA, FBA (spkr. trial adv. and criminal law sect. Detroit 1983—, bd. dirs. 1989-91, chmn. criminal law sect. 1990-91), Mich. Bar Assn., Fla. Bar Assn., Nat. Assn. Criminal Def. Lawyers, Detroit Bar Assn. Greek Orthodox. Home: 4661 Rivers Edge Dr Troy MI 48098-4161 Office: Jaffe Raitt Heuer Weiss 27777 Franklin Rd Ste 2500 Southfield MI 48034-8222 Office Phone: 248-351-3000. Business E-Mail: candreoff@jaffelaw.com.

ANDREOLI, KATHLEEN GAINOR, nurse, educator, dean; b. Albany, NY, Sept. 22, 1935; d. John Edward and Edmunda Elizabeth (Ringlemann) Gainor; children: Paula Kathleen, Thomas Anthony, Karen Marie. BSN, Georgetown U., 1957; MSN, Vanderbilt U., 1959; DSN, U. Ala., Birmingham, 1979. Staff nurse Albany Hosp. Med. Ctr., 1957; instr. St. Thomas Hosp. Sch. Nursing, Nashville, 1958—59, Georgetown U. Sch. Nursing, 1959—60, Duke U. Sch. Nursing, 1960—61, Bon Secours Hosp. Sch. Nursing, Balt., 1962—64; ednl. coordinator, physician asst. program, instr. coronary care unit nursing inservice edn. Duke U. Med. Ctr., Durham, NC, 1965—70; ednl. dir. physician asst. program dept. medicine U. Ala. Med. Ctr., Birmingham, 1970—75, clin. assoc. prof. cardiovasc. nursing Sch. Nursing, 1970—77, asst. prof. nursing dept. medicine, 1971, assoc. prof., 1972—, assoc. prof. nursing Sch. Pub. and Allied Health, 1973—; assoc. dir. Family Nurse Practitioner Program, 1976, assoc. prof. cmty. health nursing Grad. Program, 1977—79, assoc. prof. dept. pub. health, 1978—79; prof. nursing, spl. asst. to pres. for ednl. affairs U. Tex. Health Sci. Ctr., Houston, 1979—82, acting dean Sch. Allied Health Scis., 1981, v.p. for ednl. svcs., interdisciplinary edn., internat. programs, 1983—87; v.p. nursing affairs Rush-Presbyn.-St. Lukes's Med. Ctr., Chgo., 1987—; dean Rush U. Coll. Nursing, 1987—2005, Kellogg emeritus dean, 2005—. Mem. nat. adv. nursing coun. VHA, 1992; adv. bd. Nursing Spectrum, midwest region, 1995—2005; cons. in field. Editor: Heart and Lung, Jour. of Total Care, 1971; editl. bd. Nursing Consult, Elsevier Publs., 2004—05; contbr. articles to profl. jours.; author, editor: Comprehensive Cardiac Care, 1983. Active Internat. Nursing Coalition for Mass Casualty Edn., 2002—; mem. adv. bd. Robert Wood Johnson Clin. Nurse Sch. Program; mem. vis. com. Vanderbilt U. Sch. Nursing; mem. Leadership Ill., 1991; mem. nat. nursing asdv. com. Voluntary Hosp. Am., 1991; mem. governing coun. Inst. for Hosp. Clin. Nursing Edn., Am. Hosp. Assn., 1993; bd. dirs. Ill. League for Nursing, 1994, Lyric Opera Chgo. Guild; bd. dirs., chair rsch. and edn. com. Rehab. Inst. Chgo., 2005—; adv. bd. Hospice Ptnrs. Recipient Founder's award, N.C. Heart Assn., 1970, Disting. Alumni award, Vanderbilt U. Sch. Nursing, 1985, Leadership Tex. award, 1985, Disting. Alumni award, U. Ala. Sch. Nursing, 1991, Henry Betts MD Employment Advocacy award, 2004, Sage Mentor award, Ill. Nursing Leadership Annual Conf., 2005. Fellow: Am. Acad. Nursing; mem.: ACNA, ANA, Internat. Nursing Coalition for Mass Casualty Edn., Inst. Medicine Chgo. (bd. govs. 2004—, sec. bd. 2005—), Nat. Nursing Adv. Coun. Hosps. Am., Am. Heart Assn. Coun. Cardiovasc. Nursing, Coun. Family Nurse Practitioners and Clinicians, Ala. Heart Assn., Nat. League Nursing, Inst. Medicine of NAS, Am. Assn. Colls. Nursing (dean emeritus 2005—), Rotary One Club Chgo., Phi Kappa Phi, Alpha Eta, Sigma Theta Tau (Dreher Outstanding Dean award 2003, Rehab. Inst. of Chgo. Henry Setts Disability Advocacy award 2004, U. Ill. Power Nursing Nursing Mentor award 2005, Sage Membership award Ill. Nursing Leadership Conf. 2005). Roman Catholic. Home: 1212 N Lake Shore Dr Apt 10AN Chicago IL 60610-2359 Office: 1212 N Lake Shore Dr Chicago IL 60610-2359 Office Phone: 312-266-8338. Business E-Mail: kathleen_g_andreoli@rush.edu.

ANDREOLI, THOMAS EUGENE, physician; b. Bronx, Jan. 9, 1935; BA cum laude, St. Vincent Coll., Latrobe, Pa., 1952—56; ScD (hon.), St. Vincent Coll., 1987; MD magna cum laude, Georgetown U., 1956—60; PhD (hon.), Univ. Paris, 1993; MD (hon.), Aristotle U., Thessaloniki, Greece, 2000, Semmelweis U., Budapest, Hungary, 2003. Diplomate: Am. Bd. Internal Medicine and subspecialty in nephrology. Intern, resident in medicine Duke U., Durham, NC, 1960-61, 64-65, assoc. prof. medicine and asst. prof. physiology, 1965-70; prof. medicine and physiology, dir. nephrology research and tng. center U. Ala. Sch. Medicine, Birmingham, 1970-78; prof., chmn. dept. internal medicine U. Tex. Med. Sch., Houston, 1979-87, Edward Randall III prof., chmn. dept. internal medicine, 1986-87; chief medicine Hermann Hosp., Houston, 1979-87; Nolan prof. and chmn. dept. internal medicine U. Ark. Coll. Medicine, Little Rock, 1988—2004, Disting. prof. dept. internal medicine, dept. physiology and biophysics, 2004—. Author: Disturbances in Body Fluid Osmolality, 1977; Physiology of Membrane Disorders, 1978, 86; Cecil Essentials of Medicine, 1986, 90, 93, 97, 2001, 04, 07; Molecular Biology of Membrane Transport Disorders, 1996; Editor Am. Jour. Physiology: Renal, Fluid and Electrolyte Physiology, 1976-83; Kidney Internat., 1984-97; assoc. editor Annual Rev. Physiology, 1977-83; Am. Jour. Medicine, 1979-86; mem. editorial bd. Jour. Clin. Investigation, 1976-81; Mineral and Electrolyte Metabolism, 1977-80, Tex. Health Letter; 1980-88, Seminars in Nephrology; 1980-92, Kidney Internat., 1981-85; Physiol. Revs., 1982-84. Recipient Louis Pasteur medal U. Louis Pasteur Strasbourg, France, 1995, Hume award Nat. Kidney Found., 1997, Making Lives Better award, 2004, Silver Plate award, Hungarian Kidney Found., 2006. Master ACP (Disting. Tchr. award 2000); fellow Royal Coll. Physicians; mem. Assn. Am. Physicians, Assn. Profs. Medicine (Robert H. Williams Disting. Chair of Med. award, 1998), Am. Soc. Clin. Investigation, Am. Physiol. Soc. (Robert W Berliner award for excellence in Renal Physiology, 2000), Am. Soc. Nephrology (coun. 1988-95, pres. 1993-94, Homer W. Smith award 1995), Internat. Soc. Nephrology (hon., exec. com. 1985-2003, v.p. 1995-97, pres.-elect 1997-99, pres. 1999-2001).

ANDREONI, KENNETH A., surgeon; MD, Yale U., New Haven, 1988. Diplomate Am. Bd. Surgery. Resident in gen. surgery Johns Hopkins U., Balt., 1988—95; abdominal transplant fellow Ohio State U., Columbus, 1996—98; assoc. prof. surgery U. NC, Chapel Hill, 2000—. Office: Univ NC 101 Manning Dr 4023 BW 229 Chapel Hill NC Office Phone: 919-966-8008. Office Fax: 919-966-6308.

ANDREOPOULOS, SPYROS GEORGE, writer; b. Athens, Greece, Feb. 12, 1929; came to U.S., 1953, naturalized, 1962; s. George S. and Anne (Levas) A.; m. Christiane Loesch Loriaux, June 6, 1958; 1 child, Sophie. AB, Wichita State U., 1957. Pub. info. specialist USIA, Salonica, Greece, 1951-53; asst. editorial page editor Wichita Beacon, 1955-59; asst. dir. info. svcs., editor The Menninger Quar., The Menninger Found., Topeka, 1959-63; info. officer Stanford U. Med. Ctr., 1963-83; dir. comm., editor Stanford Medicine, 1983-93, dir. emeritus comm., editor emeritus, 1993—. Editor Sun Valley Forum on Nat. Health, Inc. (Idaho), 1972-83, 85-95, editor emeritus, 1995—. Co-author, editor: Medical Cure and Medical Care, 1972, Primary Care: Where Medicine Fails, 1974, National Health Insurance: Can We Learn from Canada? 1975, Heart Beat, 1978, Health Care for an Aging Society, 1989; contbr. articles to newspapers and profl. jours. With Royal Hellenic Air Force, 1949-50. Mem. AAAS, Assn. Am. Med. Colls., Nat. Assn. Sci. Writers, Am. Med. Writers Assn., Am. Hosp. Assn., Am. Soc. Hosp. Mktg. and Pub. Rels., Coun. for Advancement and Support of Edn. Home: 1012 Vernier Pl Stanford CA 94305-1027 Office Phone: 650-725-6911. Business E-Mail: masga@stanford.edu.

ANDREOTTI, LAMBERTO, pharmaceutical executive; B in Engring., U. Rome; MS, MIT. Exec. Farmitalia Carlo Erba, Pharmacia AB; sr. v.p., pres. oncology divsn. Pharmacia & Upjohn; v.p., gen. mgr. Italy and European oncology, Worldwide Medicines Group Bristol-Myers Squibb Co., Paris and Rome, 1998—2002, pres. Europe, Worldwide Medicines Group, 2000—02, sr. v.p. Europe, Asia-Pacific and Africa, pres. Internat., 2002—05, exec. v.p., COO worldwide pharmaceuticals, 2005—. Office: Bristol-Myers Squibb Co 345 Park Ave New York NY 10154-0037 E-mail: lamberto.andreotti@bms.com.*

ANDRES, JOSE, chef; b. Mieres, Spain, 1969; m. Patricia Andres; 3 children. Studied, Escola de Restauracio I Hostalatge de Barcelona, 1990. Chef El Dorado Petit, NYC, 1990—93; exec. chef, ptnr. Jaleo, Washington, 1993—, Bethesda, Md., Crystal City, 2004—, Zaytinya, 2002—, Oyamel, 2004—; exec. chef Café Atlantico. Apprentice El Bulli, 1985—88; founder THINKfoodTANK, 2004—. Contbg. editor Food Arts; featured in Gourmet mag., Sunday Morning News with Chris Wallace, Food Network, USA Today, host, prodr. (TV series) Vamos a Cocinar, Television Española; author: Tapas: A Taste of Spain in America, How to Cook Everything: Bittman Takes on America's Chefs, Los fogones de José Andrés. Named Chef of Yr., Bon Appetit, 2004, Restaurant Assn. of Metro. Washington, 2006; named one of Rising Stars of American Cuisine, Wine Spectator mag., 1999; named to 35 under 35 Tastemakers list, Food and Wine mag., 2004, Saveur 100 list, Saveur mag., 2004; recipient Best Chef of the Mid-Atlantic Region, James Beard Found., 2003. Mem.: D.C. Central Kitchen (chair of bd., Chef/ Ptnr. of Distinction 2001). Office: Jaleo 480 7th St NW Washington DC 20004 Office Phone: 202-628-7949. Office Fax: 202-628-7952.*

ANDRES, KENNETH G., JR., lawyer; b. Trenton, NJ, Nov. 9, 1953; s. Kenneth George and Joan Margaret (Fredericks) A. BA, Swarthmore Coll., 1975; JD, Capital U., 1978. Bar: N.J. 1978, Pa. 1978, U.S. Dist. Ct. N.J. 1978, U.S. Ct. Appeals (3rd cir.) 1981, U.S. Supreme Ct. 1994; cert. civil trial atty., N.J., cert. advocate Am. Bd. Trial Advocates. Ptnr. Andres & Berger PC, Haddonfield, N.J. Adj. prof. law Mercer County C.C., 1983-89, law sch. Rutgers U., Camden, 2006; faculty mem. Am. Trial Lawyers Assn., N.J., 1989—. Contbr. articles to profl. publs. Mem. N.J. Supreme Ct. Dist. III ethics com., 1994-98; mem. N.J. Supreme Ct. Civil Jury Charge Com., 1996-2006. Recipient Civil Trial Bar award Trial Attys. N.J., 2006; named Profl. Lawyer of Yr., N.J. Commn. Professionalism in Law, 1998, Top Civil Trial Lawyer, S.J. Mag., 2004, 06; named one of Top 100 Superlawyers, N.J. Monthly, 2005, 06, 07. Mem. ATLA (nat. gov. 2001—), ABA, Assn. Trial Lawyers Am. (bd. govs. NJ chpt. 1986-90, parliamentarian 1990-91, from asst. sec. to pres. 1990-1999, N.J. Gold Medal award 1999), Pa. State Bar Assn., N.J. State Bar Assn., Burlington County Bar Assn. (chmn. civil bench and bar com. 1992-94, trustee 1993), Trial Attys. NJ (Civil Trial Bar award 2006), Mercer County Bar Assn. (trustee 1982-91). Office: Andres & Berger PC 264 Kings Hwy E Haddonfield NJ 08033-1907 Office Phone: 856-795-1444. Business E-Mail: kandres@andresberger.com.

ANDRETTI, MARIO, retired race car driver; b. Montona, Italy, Feb. 28, 1940; came to U.S., 1955, naturalized, 1964; s. Alvise and Rina (Benvegnu) A.; m. Dee Ann Hoch, Nov. 25, 1961; children: Michael, Jeffrey, Barbra. Began racing career at age 19, Nazareth, Pa.; ret. Champ Car Nat. Champion, 1965, 66, 69, 84; Daytona 500 winner, 1967; 12 Hrs. of Sebring winner, 1967, 70, 72; Indy 500 winner, 1969; Indy 500 pole winner, 1966, 67, 87; USAC Nat. Dirt Track Champion, 1974; Formula One World Champion, 1978; Internat. Race of Champions titlist, 1979; Driver of the Yr., 1967, 78, 84, Driver of the Quarter Century, 1992, Driver of the Century, 1999-00; all-time leader in Champ Car Pole Positions won (67); all-time Champ Car lap leader (7,587); all-time record holder for Champ Car starts (407); oldest race winner in recorded Champ Car history (53 years 34 days, Phoenix, 1993); only driver to win Champ Car races in four decades; had 12 Formula One victories and captured 18 Formula One pole positions.

ANDRETTI, MICHAEL MARIO, racing company executive, retired professional race car driver; b. Bethlehem, Pa., Oct. 5, 1962; s. Mario Andretti and Dee Ann (Hoch); m. Sandra Spinozzi, 1985 (div. 1996); children: Marco, Marissa; m. Leslie Andretti, Dec. 24, 1997 (div.); 1 child,

Lucca; m. Jodi Ann Paterson, Oct. 7, 2006. HS diploma, Nazareth, Pa. Profl. race car driver Bertil Roos, 1980-81, Carl Haas Racing, Arciero Racing, GTC Racing, Garvin Brown Racing, 1982, Ralt Am., Preston Henn Racing, 1983, Kraco Racing, 1983-88, Alfa Romeo, Hendrick Motorsports, Conte Racing, 1987, Newman/Haas Racing, 1989-92, McLaren Internat. Ltd., 1993, Chip Ganassi Racing Teams, 1994, Newman/Haas Racing, 1995-2000, Team Motorola, 2001—03, Andretti Racing, 2003—07; ret., 2007. V.p. Andretti Enterprises Inc., Nazareth, 1986—, Andretti Devel. Co. Inc., Nazareth, 1987—, Andretti/Piazza Sports Cafes, Race Rock Theme Restaurants; owner Andretti Toyota, Andretti Scion, Andretti Ford, Andretti Chrysler-Dodge-Jeep, Andretti Indoor Karting and Games, Andretti Global Devel.; pres. Michael Andretti Powersports, 1999—; CEO Andretti Green Racing, chmn., 2006-. Founder Michael Andretti Found., 2003—. N.E. divsn. Formula Ford champion, 1981; Sports Car Club Am. Pro Rookie of Yr., 1982; Super Vee nat. champion, 1982; Formula Atlantic nat. champion, 1983; Indy 500 Co-Rookie of Yr., 1984; Indy Car nat. champion, 1991; Driver of Yr., 1991. Roman Catholic. Achievements include holding the record for career racing victories with 42; won more races, more poles, and led more laps than any other active Championship Auto Racing Teams Champ car driver; came out of retirement in 2006 to place third at the Indianapolis 500 just behind his son Marco. Office: Andretti Green Racing 7615 Zionsville Rd Indianapolis IN 46268*

ANDREU, HELENE C., dancer, educator; b. NYC, Nov. 8, 1930; d. Gaston Andreu and Clotilde Jaureguibéhére. BA, CUNY, 1953; student, Sch. Am. Ballet, 1948—54; MA in Dance Edn., Columbia U., 1971. Lic. tchr. of dance early childhood, recreational, jr. H.S., H.S. performing arts N.Y.C. Bd. Edn. Singer, dancer, choreographer Am. Savoyards, NYC, 1957—68; dance instr. pvt. dance studios Bklyn., NYC, 1959—92; dance instr., substitute Bd. Edn. After Sch. Ctrs., NYC, 1963—73; singer, dancer, choreographer Ephrata (Pa.) Star Playhouse, 1964—67; part-time adj. lectr. dance CUNY, NYC, 1973—2002; dance instr., choreographer Bd. Edn. Adult Edn., NYC, 1975—92; dance instr. Henry Street Settlement, NYC, 1989—98. Speech/English tutor CUNY, 1989—98. Author, choreographer Jazz Dance: An Adult Beginners Guide, 1983, author, photographer, choreographer Aerobic Razzmatazz, 2000, Jazz Dance Styles and Steps, 2003, Dance, Movement, and Nutrition, 2006. Vol. Bklyn. Pub. Libr. Literacy Program. Mem.: Actors Equity Assn. Avocations: gardening, cats, singing, photography.

ANDREW, DUDLEY, film and comparative literature professor; R. Selden Rose prof. film and comparative lit. Yale U., 2000—, co-chair, dir. grad. studies, 2000—. Published The Major Film Theories, Concepts of Film Theory, Andre Bazin, Film in the Aura of Art, a source book on Mizoguchi, a presentation of Breathless, BFI classic on Mizoguchi's Sansho Dayu, Mists of Regret: Culture and Sensibility in Classic French Film, 1995; co-author (with Steven Ungar): Popular Front Parisand the Poetics of Culture, 2005; edited (anthology) The Image in Dispute, 1997, programmed films Guggenheim Mus., served as film festival judge. Named Chavlier later Officier de l'ordre des arts et des lettres, French Ministry Culture and Communication; recipient of the Guggenheim and several NEH fellowships. Fellow: Am. Acad. Arts & Sciences.

ANDREW, GIACCIA A., lawyer; b. Reading, Pa., Aug. 31, 1959; AB magna cum laude, Georgetown U., 1981, JD, 1984. Bar: Pa. 1984, NJ 1984, DC 1987, US Dist. Ct. (Dist. NJ), US Dist. Ct. (Dist. DC), US Dist. Ct. (Ea. Dist.) Pa., US Ct. Appeals (DC Cir.). Ptnr. Chadbourne & Parke LLP, Washington, chmn. Environ. Practice Group, resident mng. ptnr. Washington Office. Contbr. articles to profl. jour.; spkr. in field. Mem.: DC Bar, ABA, Phi Beta Kappa. Office: Chadbourne & Parke LLP 1200 New Hampshire Ave NW Washington DC 20036 Office Phone: 202-974-5652. Office Fax: 202-974-5602. Business E-Mail: agiaccia@chadbourne.com.

ANDREW, JAMES M., federal agency administrator; BS, U. Ala. Mktg. mgr. Fed. Pacific Elec. Co.; owner BAS, Inc., Waynesboro, Ga., 1978—99, consul., 1999—2005; adminstr., Rural Utilities Svc. USDA, Wasihngton, DC, 2005—. Recipient Disting. Cooperator award, Georgia Coop. Coun., 2004. Office: USDA S Agrl Bldg 1400 Independence Ave SW Rm 5135 Washington DC 20250

ANDREW, JOHN HENRY, lawyer, writer; b. Duluth, Minn., May 23, 1936; s. Frederick William and Florence Elizabeth (Phillips) A.; m. Floretta Claudette Townsend; children: Sean Townsend, Brett Townsend. BA cum laude with distinction, U. Minn., Duluth, 1958; JD, Northwestern U., Evanston, Ill., 1961. Bar: Ill. 1961, Calif. 1975, NY 1980. Assoc. Pattishall, McAuliffe & Hofstetter, Chgo., 1961-71; sr. atty. J.C. Penney Co., Inc., NYC, 1971-74, sr. counsel legis. and regional ops., Western regional coun. LA, Buena Park, Calif., 1974-93, sr. govt. rels. counsel Sacramento, 1993-97, chief counsel govt. rels., 1997. Author: The Hanging of Arthur Hodge: A Caribbean Anti-Slavery Milestone. Chmn. pub. affairs com. Planned Parenthood Assn. Chgo., 1970-71; mem. Calif. State Dem. Cen. Com., 1976-82. Mem.: ABA, Sacramento County Bar Assn. (co-chmn. history com. 2001—02), Calif. State Bar (com. on consumer fin. svcs. 1982—84, 1990—93), Ill. State Bar Assn. (chmn. internat. law sect. 1969—70), Calif. C. of C. (regulatory, consumer and legal affairs com. 1974—86, mem. air and waste mgmt. com. 1994—97), Sullivan County (Pa.) Hist. Soc. (life), Renaissance Soc. Calif. State U. Sacramento (v.p. 2003—05, pres. 2005—07), Cornwall Family History Soc., No. Calif. Pubs. and Authors (Best Gen. Non-Fiction award 2000—01), JCPenney Retirees Club (regional pres. 2003—04). Home: 11359 Mother Lode Cir Gold River CA 95670-3025 Personal E-mail: jandrew523@sbcglobal.net.

ANDREW, JOSEPH JERALD, lawyer; b. Poe, Ind., Mar. 1, 1960; s. Jerald Lee Andrew and Sylvia Huss Hanselmann; m. Anne Slaughter, Sept. 9, 1989. BA, Yale U., 1982, JD, 1985. Bar: Ind. 1986, DC 2002, NY 2002, US Ct. Appeals 7th Cir. 1986, US Dist. Ct. No. & So. Districts Ind. 1986. Law clk to Judge Flaum US Ct. Appeals 7th Cir., Chgo., 1985-86; assoc. Baker & Daniels, Indpls., 1986-89; chief dep. sec. of State of Ind., Indpls., 1989-91; with Bingham, Summers, Welsh & Spilman, Indpls., 1991-95, ptnr., 1992-95; chmn. Ind. Dem. Party, 1995-99; ptnr. Johnson Smith Pence, Indpls., 1997-99; nat. chmn. Dem. Nat. Com., Washington, 1999-2001; ptnr. Cadwalader, Wickersham & Taft, Washington, 2001—03, McDermott, Will & Emery, Washington, 2003—04, Sonnenschein Nath & Rosenthal, LLP, Washington, 2004—. Chmn. adv. bd. New Dem. Network. Author: (book) The Disciples, 1993. Glen Peters Legal Scholar, 1983—85. Democrat. Office: Sonnenschein Nath & Rosenthal LLP Ste 600, E Tower 1301 K St NW Washington DC 20005 Office Phone: 202-408-5210. Office Fax: 202-408-6399. Business E-Mail: jandrew@sonnenschein.com.

ANDREWS, ARCHIE MOULTON, retired federal official; b. Greenwich, Conn., July 29, 1919; s. Archie M. and Eleanor (Underwood) A.; m. Margaret Jane Jones, Mar. 3, 1944 (dec. Sept. 1977); children: Archie Moulton III, Peter Underwood, Duncan Trumbull; m. Nike Smith Middleton, Oct. 3, 1978 (dec. Mar. 1987); m. Dorothy Johnson Conley, Sept. 30, 1989. AB, Princeton U., 1941. Exec. trainee W.R. Grace & Co., 1941-42; econ. analyst State Dept., 1942-43; U.S. rep. blacklist com. Ministry Econ. Warfare, Am. embassy, London, 1943-45; with Dictograph Products, Inc., Danbury, Conn., 1946-63, pres., 1962-63; also dir.; pres. Acousticon-Dictograph Co. Ltd., Can., 1963, dir., 1958-63, Gen. Acoustics Ltd., Eng., 1950-63; dep. dir. Bur. Internat. Commerce, Dept. Commerce, 1964-69; dir. U.S. trade mission to N. Africa, 1966; comml. counsellor Am. embassy, London, 1970-75; dir. bus. services Office Internat. Affairs, HUD, Washington, 1976-77; dir. exporters service Office Export Adminstrn., Dept. Commerce, Washington, 1978-86; sr. policy analyst Office of Tech. and Policy Analysis, 1986-88, ret., 1988. Mem. SAR Clubs: Princeton (Washington and N.Y.C.); Pilgrims; Diplomatic and Consular Officers Ret. Home: 7101 Bay Front Dr #325 Annapolis MD 21403

ANDREWS, BETTY BAUSERMAN, retired secondary school educator, real estate manager; b. Luray, Va, Dec. 29, 1935; d. Raymond Edgar Bauserman and Elizabeth Elaine Houser; m. George Norman Andrews, July 26, 1964 (dec. Apr. 1996). BS, Madison Coll., 1958; postgrad., U. Va., 1964—68, George Mason U., 1969. Cert. coll. profl. cert., Va. Classroom tchr. Clarke County H.S., Berryville, Va., 1958—64, Loudoun Valley H.S., Purcellville, Va., 1964—68; proofreader Missles and Rockets mag., Washington, 1964, Loudoun County H.S., Leesburg, Va., 1968—69; head libr. media specialist Broad Run H.S., Ashburn, Va., 1969—2000. Cons., libr. reorganizer Logetronics Corp., Springfield, Va., 1974; mem. sch. improvement team Broad Run H.S., Ashburn, 1996-2000. Adv. bd. Sterling (Va.) Pub. Libr., 1998—. Mem. NEA, AAUW, James Madison U. Alumni Assn., Va. Edn. Assn. (life), Loudoun Edn. Assn. (life), Loudoun Educators Media Assn. (life), Nat. Soc. DAR, Sparlandria Investment Club, Alpha Gamma Delta. Democrat. Methodist. Avocations: antiques, gardening, sailing, reading. Home: 821 Golden Arrow St Great Falls VA 22066-2517 Personal E-mail: striperstripes@aol.com.

ANDREWS, BILLY FRANKLIN, pediatrician, educator; b. Graham, NC, Sept. 22, 1932; s. Dean Franklin and Arlee (Byers) A.; m. Faye Rich, Dec. 25, 1953; children: Ann Elizabeth Feigenbaum, Billy Franklin Jr., David Ashley. Student, Brevard Coll., NC, 1950, Elon Coll., 1951; BS cum laude, Wake Forest Coll., 1953; MD, Duke U., 1957. Diplomate Am. Bd. Pediat., 1963. Commd. 2d lt. U.S. Army, 1956, advanced through grades to maj., 1962; intern Ft. Benning U.S. Army Hosp., Ga., 1957—58; resident in pediat. Walter Reed Gen. Hosp., Washington, 1958—60; with mil. med. and allied scis. course Walter Reed Army Inst. Rsch., Washington, 1960—61; chief pediat. svc. Rodriguez U.S. Army Hosp., Ft. Brooke, PR, 1961—63; chief pediat. Tropical Med. Rsch. Lab., Ft. Brooke, 1963—64; ret. U.S. Army, 1964; dir. newborn svcs. U. Louisville, 1964—76, from asst. prof. pediat. to chmn., 1964—93, chmn. emeritus, 1993—, dir. neonatology tng. program, 1965—86, dir. doctors' and nurses tng. program and regional tng. programs, 1965—93, co-dir. genetic counseling unit, 1965—68, dir. Comprehensive Health Care Ctr. for High Risk Infants and Children, 1968—98, co-dir. health profls. spl. project grant for preceptorship tng., 1974—77; chief staff Kosair Children's Hosp., Louisville, 1969—93, chief-of-staff emeritus, 1993—. Cons. divsn. adult and child health Ky. Dept. Pub. Health, 1966—2003; lectr. Jour. Pediat. Found., 1972; Staley Disting. Christian scholar Mary Baldwin Coll., Washington and Lee U., Sch. Medicine of U.Va., 1990; vis. scholar in med. history and ethics Green Coll., Oxford (Eng.) U., 1993, vis. fellow med. history, ethics and humanities, 98. Author: Children's Bill of Rights, 1968; editor: Small-for-Date Infants, 1970, The Newborn, Pediatric Clinics of North America, 1977, Aphorisms, Tributes and Tenets of Billy F. Andrews: In Walls, M.E., 1986, Ideals and Inspiration (F.R. Andrews), 1993, Words to Live By (F.R. Andrews), 1993, A Statement on Transplantation and Organ Donors, 1994; contbr. numerous articles to profl. publs.; inventor, poet. Pres. Kornhauser Libr., Health Scis. Ctr., 1981-82, 90-91; mem., tchr., deacon, elder United Ch. of Christ; bd. dirs. Oak Ridge Mil. Acad., 2004-07. Recipient Helen B. Fraser award, 1978, Norton-Children's Hosp. award for leadership in neonatology, 1978, Award of Recognition, XVII Internat. Congress Pediat., Manila, 1983, Wisdom award of honor, eminent fellow The Wisdom Soc., 1991, The Billy F. Andrews, M.D. Endowed Chair in Pediat., U. Louisville, 1993, Winston Churchill medal of Wisdom Soc., Eminent Churchill Fellow of Wisdom Soc., 1993, Disting. Alumnus award Wake Forest U., 1983; Festschrift to Billy F. Andrews, M.D., Jour. of Perinatology, 1995; Billy F. Andrews, MD, scholarship at U. Louisville Sch. Medicine named in his honor, 1986, Billy F. Andrews, MD lectureship in neonatology, U. Louisville, 2002 Fellow ACP, Am. Acad. Pediat., Royal Soc. Medicine (London); mem. AMA, Am. Pediat. Soc., Am. Osler Soc. (pres. 1996-97), Am. Soc. for Bioethics and Humanities, Soc. for Pediat. Rsch., So. Soc. Pediat. Rsch. (founding), Southeastern Perinatal Soc. (founding), Nat. Assn. Children's Hosps. and Related Instns. (founding), Ky. Med. Assn. (faculty Sci. Achievement award 1971, del. 1981-82, Ednl. Achievement award 1997), Jefferson County Med. Soc., Ky. Pediat. Soc., Louisville Pediat. Soc., U. Louisville Sch. Medicine Alumni Assn. (bd. govs. 1972-75), Univ. Pediatric Found. Inc. (pres. 1982-93), Internat. Assn. Bioethics, Am. Soc. Law, Medicine and Ethics, Alpha Omega Alpha. Achievements include invention of infant oxygen hood, iontophoresis sweat induction apparatus, radiant open infant warmer, infant blood warmer, diagnostic and treatment table with warmer and position changes, infant transport incubator, others. Office: Kosair Charities Pediat Ctr 571 S Floyd St Ste 449 Louisville KY 40202-3830 Home Phone: 812-944-8087. Business E-Mail: bfandr01@louisville.edu. *Personal philosophy: "The level of civilization attained by any society will be determined by the attention it has paid to the welfare of its infants and children." Also, "The responsibility of the physician is to prevent, to diagnose, to prognosticate, to treat when and if necessary, and always to keep foremost in mind 'Primum Non Nocere'".*

ANDREWS, BRUCE, automotive executive, lawyer; b. Syracuse, NY; married. BA, Haverford Coll.; JD, Georgetown U. Staff asst. to US Senator Alan Cranston US Senate, Washington; legis. asst. to US Rep. Gus Yatron US Ho. of Reps, Washington, legis. dir. to US Rep. R. Timothy Holden; atty. pub. policy and telecommunications group Arnold & Porter LLP; dir. Quinn Gillespie & Associates, 2000—06; v.p. govt. affairs Ford Motor Co., 2007—. Office: Ford Motor Company Ste 1000 1350 Eye St NW Washington DC 20005 Office Phone: 202-962-5400. Office Fax: 202-336-7228.*

ANDREWS, BYLLIE D'AMATO, retired mathematics professor; b. Denver, Sept. 6, 1943; 1 child, John Robert. BA, Chico State U., Calif., 1967—69; MA, U. San Francisco, 1984—85; PhD, U. Nev., Reno, 1996—2002. Prof. U. Nev., 1996—; adj. prof. Sierran Nev. Coll., Incline Village, Nev., 2001—. Bd. mem. Nev. Women's Lobby, Reno, 2000—06. Recipient Presdl. Excellence award for tchg. math., NSF, 1986. Mem.: AAUW (corr.; pub. policy chair 2002—06, pres. 2006—). D-Liberal. Avocation: political activism. Business E-Mail: byllie@charter.net.

ANDREWS, CAESAR, editor; BA, Grambling State U., La., 1979. Sr. mgr. Florida Today, Melbourne, Fla., The Reporter, Lansdale, Pa., Rockland Jour.-News, West Nyack, NY, Gannett Suburban Newspapers, White Plains, NY; various positions, including dep. mng. editor, spl. sect. and chief states editor USA Today, 1982—86; editor Gannett News Svc., Arlington, Va., 1997—2005; exec. editor Detroit Free Press, 2005—. Lectr. Am. Press Inst. Mem.: Am. Soc. Newspaper Editors, Nat. Assn. Minority Media Exec., Nat. Assn. Black Journalists, AP Mng. Editors (mem. bd., v.p.). Office: Detroit Free Press 600 W Fort St Detroit MI 48226 Office Phone: 313-222-6821. E-mail: candrews@freepress.com.

ANDREWS, C(HARLES) E(LLIOT), (JR.), finance company executive; b. 1952; m. Jean Andrews; 3 children. BA in Acctg.; Va. Tech., 1974. With Arthur Andersen LLP, Chgo., 1974—2002, ptnr., 1984—2002, mng. ptnr. Mid-Atlantic reg., global mng. ptnr. for audit & adv. svcs., 2002; exec. v.p. acctg. & risk mgmt. SLM Corp. (Sallie Mae), Reston, Va., 2003—06, exec. v.p., CFO, 2006—07, CEO, 2007—. Chmn. Sallie Mae Bank, Utah; bd. dirs. Jr. Achievement, Inova Health Systems, The Greater Wash. Bd. Trade; bd. dirs., chair audit com. Six Flags, Inc.; mem. adv. bd. Va. Tech. Acctg. Dept., R.B. Pamplin Coll. Bus. Chmn. Nat. Capital Chapter, ARC, Leadership Washington; bd. overseers Corcoran Gallery of Art; bd. dirs. Boys' Home, Inc, Washington Performing Arts Soc.; mem. Washington/Balt. Regional 2012 Olympics Coalition, Fed. City Coun., Washington. Mem.: VSCPA, AICPA. Office: Sallie Mae 12061 Bluemont Way Reston VA 20190*

ANDREWS, CHARLES ROLLAND, library administrator; b. Scranton, Pa., July 5, 1930; s. Edgar W. and Margaret (Machenry) A.; m. Harriet Williams, Dec. 27, 1954 (dec. 1985); m. Dorothy Kramer, Dec. 10, 1988. BS in Edn., Bloomsburg U., 1954; MA in English Lit., U. Okla., 1959; MS in L.S., Case Western Res. U., 1964, PhD, 1967. Head reference dept. Cleve. Pub. Library, 1966-68, Case Western Res. Univ. Libraries, Cleve., 1968-69, librarian Freiberger Library, 1969-72, asst. dir. pub. services, 1972-74; univ. librarian Southeastern Mass. Univ. Library, North Dartmouth, 1974-76; dean library services Hofstra U. Library, Hempstead, NY, 1976-96, prof. emeritus, 1997—. Lectr. Hofstra U., U. Coll. Continuing Edn., 1997—. Editor: Reference Books for Small and Medium-Sized Libraries, 1973; contbr. articles, revs. to profl. jours. Bd. trustees Unitarian Universalist Congregation, Garden City, NY, 1998—2004, chair art exhibits com., 1999—2002, newsletter editor, 2000—06. Mem. ALA, Assn. Coll. and Rsch. Librs., Archons of Colophon, L.I. Libr. Resources Coun. (chair regional automation com. 1986-92, bd. trustees 1990-94), Am. Express (sr. adv. bd. mem. 1998-99). Democrat. Avocations: calligraphy, word processing, graphics. Home and Office: 305 Hillside Ave Bellmore NY 11710-3519

ANDREWS, DAVID RALPH, lawyer; b. Oakland, Calif., Jan. 4, 1942; m. Rozan McCurdy, July 1, 1962; children: David, Linda. BA, U. Calif., Berkeley, 1968; JD, U. Calif., 1971. Bar: Calif. 1971, D.C. 1986, U.S. Dist. Ct. (no. dist.) Calif. 1971, U.S. Dist. Ct. Hawaii 1991, U.S. Supreme Ct. 1980. Assoc. McCutchen, Doyle, Brown & Enersen, San Francisco, 1971-75; regional counsel Reg. IX US EPA, San Francisco, 1975-77, legal counsel & spl. asst. for policy Washington, 1977-79; dep. gen. counsel US Dept. Health & Human Svcs., Washington, 1980-81; ptnr. McCutchen, Doyle, Brown & Enersen, San Francisco, 1981-97, 2000—02, chmn., 1991-95; legal adv. US Dept. State, Washington, 1997-2000; sr. v.p., govt. affairs, gen. counsel & sec. Pepsi Co. Inc., Purchase, NY, 2002—05. Amb., spl. negotiator U.S./Iran Claims, 2000—; bd. dirs. Union Bank Calif., Kaiser Permanente, NetCel360 Holdings Ltd., PG&E Corp. Trustee San Francisco Mus. of Modern Art, 1988-97; bd. trustees Golden Gate Nat. Park Assn., 1992-95, Marin Cmty. Found., 1996-97; mem. U.S. Agy. for Internat. Devel. Energy Tng. Program Adv. Com. of the Inst. Internat. Edn.; mem. bd. dirs. Union Bank Calif., Kaiser Permanente and NetCel360 Holdings Ltd., 2000—. Fellow Max Planck Inst. of Pub. Internat. Law, Heidelberg, Fed. Republic of Germany, 1974; recipient Lifetime Achievement award, Am. Lawyer mag., 2006 Mem. ABA (natural resources sect.), Calif. Bar Assn.), San Francisco Bar Assn. Avocations: photography, tennis, running.

ANDREWS, DONALD WILFRID KAO, economics professor; BA in Economics with honors, U. British Columbia, Vancouver, Can., 1977; MA in Statistics, U. Calif.-Berkeley, 1980, PhD in Economics, 1982. Asst. prof., dept. economics Yale U., 1982—87, assoc. prof., dept. economics, 1987—88, prof., dept. economics, 1988—98, William K. Lanman Jr., prof. economics, 1998—2005, T.C. Koopmans prof. economics, 2005—. Vis. assoc. prof., divsn. humanities and social sciences Calif. Inst. Tech., 1987; vis. prof., dept. economics U. British Columbia, 1998; lectr. in field. Contbr. articles to profl. jours.; assoc. editor Econometric Theory, 1986—91, Econometrica, 1988—, co-editor Econometric Theory, 1991—2003, fgn. editor Review of Economic Studies, 2005—, referee for several peer-reviewed jours. Recipient Plura Scripsit Econometric Theory award, 1997; recipient of several grants from the NSF, Flood Fellowship in Economics, Dept. Economics, U. Calif. Berkeley, 1978, Imperial Oil Grad. Rsch. Fellowship, 1979, Rsch. Coun. Canada Doctoral Fellowship, 1979—82, Alfred P. Sloan Rsch. Fellowship, 1985—89, Fellow, Jour. Econometrics, 1998. Fellow: Econometric Soc., Am. Acad. Arts & Sciences; mem.: Inst. Mathematical Statistics, Am. Statistical Assn., Am. Economic Assn. Office: Cowles Found PO Box 208281 New Haven CT 06520-8281 Office Phone: 203-432-3698. Business E-Mail: donald.andrews@yale.edu.

ANDREWS, DONNA L., professional golfer; b. Lynchburg, Va., Apr. 12, 1967; d. James Barclay and Helen Louise (Munsey) Andrews. BBA, U. N.C., 1989. Qualified golfer LPGA Tour, Fla., 1990; winner Ping-Cellular One Golf Tounament, Portland, Oreg., 1993, Ping-Welch's Golf Tournament, Tucson, Ariz., 1994, Dinah Shore Major Golf Tournament, Palm Springs, Calif., 1994, Longs Drugs Challenge, Lincoln, CA, 1998. Named to Lynchburg Area Sports Hall of Fame, 2001. Office: LPGA 100 International Golf Dr Daytona Beach FL 32124-1092

ANDREWS, E. WYLLYS, archaeologist, educator; b. Phila., Oct. 10, 1943; s. Edward Wyllys IV and Ann (Wheeler) Andrews; m. Patricia Antell Andrews, June 15, 1965; children: Dwen Hardy Andrews-Cita, Edward Wyllys VI, Ruth Wheeler. AB, Harvard U., 1964; PhD, Tulane U., 1971. Asst. prof. anthropology No. Ill. U., DeKalb, 1970-75; dir. Mid. Am. Rsch. Inst., Program Rsch. in Yucatan Tulane U., New Orleans, 1972-74, dir. Mid. Am. Rsch. Inst., gen. editor publs., 1975—, assoc. prof. anthropology, 1975-80, prof. anthropology, 1980—. Dir. excavations at Quelepa, El Salvador, Tulane U., 1967—69, dir. excavations at Komchen, Yucatan, Mex., 1980—84, dir. excavations Copan Royal Residence, Honduras, 1990—94. Author: The Archaeology of Quelepa, El Salvador, 1976, Excavations at Dzibilchaltun, Yucatan, Mexico, 1980; co-editor: Late Lowland Maya Civilization: Classic to Postclassic, 1986, Five Hundred Years After Columbus, 1994, Copan: The History of an Ancient Maya Kingdom, 2005; mem. editl. bd. Rsch. and Exploration, 1984-95, Latin Am. Antiquity, 1989-95. Grantee NEA, 1978, NSF, 1980, Nat. Geog. Soc., 1992. Mem. Am. Anthrop. Assn., Soc. for Am. Archaeology, Sociedad Mexicana de Antropologia. Avocations: photography, backpacking, cross country skiing, downhill skiing, canoeing. Office: Tulane U Mid Am Rsch Inst New Orleans LA 70118 Office Phone: 504-862-3104. Business E-Mail: wandrews@tulane.edu.

ANDREWS, GAYLEN, public relations executive; Pres. Blitz Media-Direct, Middle Island, NY. Office: Blitz Media-Direct Communications Bldg PO Box 102 Middle Island NY 11953-0102 Office Phone: 631-924-8555. Business E-Mail: blitz4pr@att.net. E-mail: 2gandrews@optonline.net.

ANDREWS, GEORGE EYRE, mathematics professor; b. Dec. 4, 1938; s. Raymond Leslie and Rovena Pearl (Eyre) A.; m. Joy Margaret Brown, Sept. 2, 1960; children: Amy Beth, Katherine Yvonne, Derek George. BS, MA, Oreg. State U., Corvallis, 1960; postgrad., Cambridge U., Eng., 1960—61; PhD, U. Pa., Phila., 1964; Doctorate in Physics (hon.), Parma U., Parma, 1998; DSc (hon.), U. Fla., Gainsvesville, 2002—; DMath (hon.), Waterloo U., Canada, 2004. Asst. prof. math. Pa. State U., University Park, 1964-67, assoc. prof. math., 1967-70, prof. math., 1970-81, Evan Pugh prof. math., 1981—, math. dept. head, 1980-82, 95-97. Hedrick lectr. Math. Assn. Am., 1980, J.S. Frame lectr., 1993, Polya lectr., 2007—; adj. prof. U. Waterloo, Ont., Can., 1982-92, regional conf. lectr., NSF-Conf. Bd. Math. Scis., 1985. Author: Number Theory, 1971, Theory of Partitions, 1976, Partitions: Yesterday and Today, 1979, q-Series, 1986, (with R. Askey and R. Roy) Special Functions, 1998, (with K. Eriksson) Integer Partitions, 2004, (with B. Berndt) Ramanujan's Lost Notebook, Part I, 2005; editor: Collected Papers of P.A. MacMahon, Vol. I, 1978, Vol. II, 1986, Ramanujan Revisited, 1988, The Rademacher Legacy to Mathematics, 1994, (with S. Ahlgren and K. Ono) Topics in Number Theory in Honor of B. Gordon and S. Chowla, 1999. Recipient Disting. Univ. Tchg. award Allegheny

Mountain sect. Math. Assn. Am., 1993, Centennial award U. Pa., 1999; named Polya lectr. Math. Assn. Am., 2007; Guggenheim fellow, 1982-83. Mem.: NAS, Am. Acad. Arts and Scis. Avocation: boogie-woogie piano. Home: 119 Meadow Ln Centre Hall PA 16828-8515 Office: Pa State U Dept Math 306 Mcallister Bldg University Park PA 16802-6404 Office Phone: 814-865-6642. Business E-Mail: andrews@math.psu.edu.

ANDREWS, GERALD BRUCE, SR., business executive; b. Valley, Ala., Sept. 17, 1937; s. Bruce and Sara Andrews; m. Claire Smith; children: Gerald Bruce Jr., Benjamin G., Suzanne Andrews Smith. Diploma in textile mfg., Auburn U., 1956; BS in Mgmt. and Indsl. Engring., Auburn U., 1958; postgrad., Harvard U., 1978—79. Various positions WestPoint Pepperell, Inc., 1954-67, mgr. Opelika (Ala.) Mill, 1967-68, gen. mgr. no. ops. Biddeford, Maine, 1968-70, dir. indsl. engring. West Point, Ga., 1970-72, gen. mgr. towels ops. Valley, 1972-74, v.p. mfg., 1974-80, sr. v.p. merchandising and mktg. NYC, 1980-87; pres. Stores div. N000, West Point, 1987-92; exec. v.p. merchandising WestPoint Pepperell, Inc., NYC, 1992—; pres., COO Johnston Industries Inc., NYC, 1992—, pres., CEO Columbus, Ga., 1995-97, ret., 1997; exec.-in-residence, vis. prof. Auburn U., 1998-99; CEO Accelegrow Techs., Inc., 2006—, also bd. dirs. Chmn. com. to evaluate Sch. Textile Engring., Auburn (Ala.) U., also lay speaker Guest Speakers Bur.; mem. president's adv. com. So. Union Coll.; chmn. Westpoint Pepperell Polit. Action Com., West Point; bd. dirs. Ala. Textile Edn. Found., Johnston Industries Inc., Tapistron Internat., Tech. Textiles U.S.A.; instr. textile mfg. and indsl. engring. Pres. bd. trustees Lanier Meml. Hosp., Valley; chmn. Chattahoochee Valley Health Care Found., Valley; mem. Ala. Gov.'s Adv. Coun., Montgomery; trustee Christian City, Atlanta; chmn. bd. trustees Atlanta Christian Coll., 1995-96; chmn. bd. dirs. Lanier Health Care Found., 2000-01. Named Citizen of Yr., Valley-Lanett C. of C.; recipient President's award Geo. H. Lanier Coun. Boy Scouts Am.; inducted Engring. Hall of Fame, 1995. Fellow Textile Inst. (Manchester, Eng.); mem. Am. Inst. Indsl. Engrs., Am. Textile Mfg. Assn. (dir. 1995, textile leader of yr. in Am. 1995), Ala. Textile Mfg. Assn. (pres.), Harvard Bus. Sch. Assn., Spring Wood Athletic Club (pres.), Rotary (pres. West Point), Harvard Club (N.Y.C.). Avocations: travel, golf, reading, architecture, painting. Home: 111 Highland Dr West Point GA 31833-6100 E-mail: gandrews@knology.net.

ANDREWS, GORDON CLARK, lawyer; b. Boston, Mar. 25, 1941; s. Loring Beal and Flora Spencer (Hinckley) A.; m. Deborah M. Devere, July 9, 1966; children: Christine Leigh, Cynthia Lyn, Carey Loring. BA, Dartmouth Coll., Hanover, NH, 1963; JD, NYU, 1969. Bar: NY 1970, Conn. 1971. Assoc. Morgan Lewis & Bockius (and predecessor), NYC, 1969—72; asst. sec., asst. gen. counsel Howmet Corp., Greenwich, Conn., 1973—75; sec., asst. gen. counsel Beker Industries Corp., Greenwich, 1976—, v.p., 1978—81; gen. counsel M&T Chems., Inc., Woodbridge, NJ, 1982—86, v.p. law dept., 1986—90, sec., 1987—90; v.p., sec. Atochem Inc., Glen Rock, NJ, 1987—; gen. counsel, sec. ESSROC Corp., Bath, Pa., 1990—, sr. v.p., 1993—; ptnr. Epstein, Becker & Green, NYC, 1995—; gen. counsel Troy Corp., Florham Park, NJ, 2000—. Bd. dir. San Juan Cement Co., Inc., Essroc Cement Corp.; chmn. legal counsel com. Portland Cement Assn., 2003—. Mem. exec. com. Cement Kiln Recycling Coalition, 2001—. Lt. USNR, 1963—69. Recipient Am. Law award, 1969. Mem. ABA, N.Y. State Bar Assn., Conn. Bar Assn., Am. Soc. Corp. Secs., Westchester-Fairfield Corp. Counsel Assn., Greenwich Country Club. Republican. Home: 46 Club Rd Riverside CT 06878-2034 Office: Epstein Becker & Green 250 Park Ave Ste 1201 New York NY 10177-0001

ANDREWS, GROVER JENE, retired adult education educator, administrator; b. Batesville, Ark., June 1, 1930; s. Grover Jones and Ruth Burlie (Ruble) A. BA, Vanderbilt U., 1963, MA, 1964; EdD, N.C. State U., 1972. Dir. univ. rels. Baylor U., Waco, Tex., 1955-61; asst. to pres. Peabody Coll. Vanderbilt U., Nashville, 1961-64; asst. prof. English, asst. acad. dean U. Ark., Little Rock, 1964-66; dir. of devel. Meredith Coll., Raleigh, N.C., 1966-67; asst. to dean of extension N.C. State U., Raleigh, 1967-68, assoc. vice chancellor for extension, assoc. prof. adult edn, 1979-89; assoc. exec. dir. commn. on colls. So. Assn. Colls. and Schs., Atlanta, 1968-79; assoc. dir. for instrn. U. Ga. Ctr. for Continuing Edn., 1989—, sr. pub. svc. assoc., chair sr. pub. svc. faculty, 1989—, adj. assoc. prof. adult edn., 1989—, asst. v.p. pub. svc. and outreach, 1998-99, interim dir., 1998—, assoc. v.p. pub. svc. and outreach, 1999—2001; ret., 2001. Bd. dirs. Am. Tech. Inst., Memphis, 1985-98; trustee Coun. for Adult and Exptl. Learning, Chgo., 1985-91; dir. rsch. Internat. Assn. for Continuing Edn. and Tng., Washington, 1987-92, pres., 1992-96. Member Raleigh Lions, 1967-68, 79-89; chair Christmas pageant Waco Jaycees, 1956-60; patron Atlanta Arts Ctr., 1968-79. With USN, 1948-50. Named Educator of the Yr., Fedn. of Women's Clubs, 1966; recipient Nat. Leadership award Assn. for Continuing Higher Edn., 1984, Gruman award N.C. Adult Edn. Assn., 1985, Pinnacle award for outstanding leadership Internat. Assn. for Continuing Edn. and Tng., 1996; named to Internat. Hall of Fame for Adult and Continuing Edn., 1996; Grover J. Andrews Rsch. Endowment established by Internat. Assn., for Continuing Edn. and Tng., 1996. Mem.: So. Assn. Colls. and Schs. (chair accrediting coms. 1980—, Meritorious Svc. award 2003), Ga. Adult Edn. Assn., Nat. Univ. Continuing Edn. Assn. (chair elect rsch. divsn. 1996—97, chair rsch. divsn. 1997—98, 1998—99, M. Nolte award 1995), Pi Kappa Alpha, Sigma Tau Delta, Phi Delta Kappa. Democrat. Baptist. Avocations: gardening, arts, antiques. Home: 243 Ashbrook Dr Athens GA 30605-3956

ANDREWS, HOLDT, investment banker; b. NYC, May 2, 1946; s. William Lloyd and Edna (Faulconer) A.; m. Nina Lawrence, Sept. 16, 1982; 1 child, Kelli. BS, U. Fla., 1968; MBA, Fla. Atlantic U., 1971. Asst. to v.p. mktg. Eltra Corp., Wilmington, Mass., 1972-74; v.p. Bank of Am., NYC, 1974-81; group v.p. Amrobank, NYC, 1981-84; exec. v.p. CenTrust Savs. Bank, Miami, Fla., 1984, KMC Group, Miami, 1985-86; sr. mng. dir. J.W. Charles Capital Corp.-Bush Securities, Boca Raton, Fla., 1986-89; v.p. corp. fin. dept. Internationale Nederlanden Bank N.V., NYC, 1989-94; sr. v.p. S.N. Phelps and Co., Greenwich, Conn., 1994; chief oper. officer VHC, Ltd., West Palm Beach, Fla., 1994-99; sr. exec. mng. dir. The March Group, LLC, Nashville, 1999—2006; exec. mng. dir. Baron Capital Ptnrs., LLC, Boca Raton, Fla., 2006—; prin. Dolan Corp. Svcs. LLC, West Palm Beach, Fla., 2006—. Mem. adv. bd. Tucker State Bank, Jacksonville, Fla., 1987-88; bd. dirs. Qilu-Maul, Shandong, Peoples Republic China, 1997-99. 1st lt. U.S. Army, 1968-70. Mem. Blue Key. Avocations: tennis, sailing, skiing. Office: 13260 Sabal Chase Palm Beach Gardens FL 33418 Office Phone: 570-620-2773. E-mail: haimpact@msn.com.

ANDREWS, J. DAVID, lawyer; b. Decatur, Ill., July 5, 1933; s. Jesse D. and Louise Glenna (Mason) A.; m. Helen Virginia Migely, July 12, 1958; children: Virginia, Robert, Michael, Betsy. BA magna cum laude, U. Ill., 1955, JD with honors, 1960. Bar: Wash. 1961. Ptnr. Perkins Coie, Seattle, 1960-96, sr. counsel, 1997—. Trustee AEF Pension Fund, 1975—79; bd. visitors U. Puget Sound Law Sch., 1976—94, Ill. Coll. Law, 2005—; bd. dirs. Am. Bar Endowment, 1981—94, Endowment for Equal Justice, 2004—; pres. Am. Bar Endowment, 1985—87, Wash. Law Fund, 1997—98; bd. dirs. v.p. Am. Bar Ins. Plans Cons., Inc., 1991—. Contbr. articles to profl. jours Bd. dirs. Leukemia Soc. Wash., 1984-99, pres. 1985-91; nat. bd. dirs. Leukemia Soc. Am., 1992-96. Capt. USAF, 1955-57. Fellow Am. Bar Found. (bd. dirs., former treas.), Am. Coll. Trial Lawyers; mem. ABA (ho. of dels. 1967-69, 75—, asst. treas. 1972-74, treas. 1975-79, bd. govs. 1975-79, fed. judiciary standing com. 1985-90), Wash. Bar Assn. (chmn. pub. rels. com. 1971-73), Seattle-King County Bar Assn., Am. Judicature Soc. (bd. dirs. 1985-89), Phi Beta Kappa, Phi Kappa Phi, Phi Eta Sigma. Home: 9413 SW Quartermaster Dr Vashon WA 98070-7081 Office: Perkins Coie 1201 3rd Ave Ste 4000 Seattle WA 98101-3029 Office Phone: 206-359-8423. Business E-Mail: dandrews@perkinscoie.com.

ANDREWS, JAMES R., orthopedic surgeon; m. Jenelle Andrews; children: Andy, Amy, Archie, Ashley, Amber, Abby. Grad., La. State U., 1963, MD, 1967; LLD, Livingston U.; DSc, Troy State U., La. State U. Orthop. resident Tulane Med. Sch., 1972; surgical fellow in sports medicine U. Va. Med. Sch., 1972, U. Lyon, Lyn, France, 1972; co-founder Ala. Sports Medicine and Orthopedic Ctr., Healthsouth Med. Ctr., Birmingham, Ala.; co-founder, chmn., med. dir. Am. Sports Medicine Inst., Birmingham, Ala.; med. dir. Andrews Inst., Gulf Breeze, Fla. Clin. prof. orthopedic surgery U. Ala. Birmingham Med. Sch., Ala. Med. Sch., U. Va. Sch. Medicine, U. SC Med. Sch., U. Ky. Med. Ctr.; co-medical dir., intercollegiate sports Auburn U.; sr. orthopedic cons., intercollegiate athletics U. Ala.; orthopedic cons. for athletic teams Troy State U., U. West Ala., Tuskegee U., Grambling U.; spl. med. cons., dept. athletics, Ala.; med. dir. Tampa Bay Devil Rays; sr. orthopedic cons. Washington Redskins, Cin. Reds; team physician Birmingham Barons Double A, affiliate Chgo. White Sox; co-med. dir. Sr. PGA Tour; co-medical dir. Ladies Profl. Golf Assn.; mem., sports medicine com. US Olympic Com.; served on NCAA Competitive Safeguards in Medical Aspects of Sports Com.; current mem. med. and safety adv. com. USA Baseball; bd. dirs. Fast Health Corp., Am. Club Sys., Robins Morton Constrn. Co.; nat. med. dir. Benchmark Med. Inc.; lectr. in field. Author numerous sci. articles and books. Mem. bd. trustee Troy State U. Named to Ala. Sports Hall of Fame, La. State U. Alumni Hall of Distinction, 1996; recipient Disting. Sportsman award, Ala. Sports Hall of Fame, 1992. Mem.: Ladies Profl. Golf Assn., Internat. Knee Soc. (bd. dir.), Arthroscopy Assn. N.Am. (bd. dir.), Am. Orthop. Soc. Sports Medicine (bd. dir., sec. bd. dir. 2004—05), Am. Acad. Orthop. Surgeons, Am. Bd. Orthop. Surgery. Widely recognized for his role in advancing the field of shoulder, knee and elbow surgery; mentored over 150 fellows throughout the course of his academic career; considered one of the foremost orthopedic surgeons and sports doctors in the world; and operated on a remarkable number of prominent athletes, including Troy Aikman, Roger Clemens, and Jack Nicklaus. Address: Women's and Children's Ctr 806 Saint Vincents Dr Ste 415 Birmingham AL 35205-1616 Office Phone: 205-939-3000. Office Fax: 205-930-9011.*

ANDREWS, JOHN FRANK, editor, author, educator; b. Carlsbad, N.Mex., Nov. 2, 1942; s. Frank Randolph and Mary Lucille (Wimberley) A.; m. Vicky Roberta Anderson, Aug. 20, 1966 (div. 1983); children: Eric John, Lisa Gail; m. Janet Ann Denton, Oct. 15, 1994. AB, Princeton U., 1965; MAT, Harvard U., 1966; PhD, Vanderbilt U., 1971. Instr. English U. Tenn., Nashville, 1969-70; asst. prof. Fla. State U., Tallahassee, 1970-74, dir. grad. studies in English, 1973-74; dir. acad. programs Folger Shakespeare Library, Washington, 1974-84; chmn. Folger Inst., Washington, 1974-84; exec. editor Folger Books, Washington, 1974-84; dep. dir. div. edn. programs NEH, Washington, 1984-88; editor The Guild Shakespeare, 1988-92; pres. The Shakespeare Guild, 1992—; editor The Everyman Shakespeare, 1993—; exec. dir. Washington br. English-Speaking Union, 2001—. Cons. Time-Life TV, WNET/Thirteen, Corp. for Pub. Broadcasting, Pub. Broadcasting Svc., Nat. Pub. Radio, U.S. Dept. Edn., others; chmn. Nat. Adv. Panel for the Shakespeare Plays, 1979-85; core advisor The Shakespeare Hour, 1985-86; mem. adv. bd. Theatre for a New Audience, Humanities Coun. of Washington, Ctr. for Polit. and Strategic Studies, Ctr. for Renaissance and Baroque Studies, U. Md., others; cons. Shakespeare: The Globe and the World, touring exhbn., 1978-81; adminstr. program grants NEH, Andrew W. Mellon Found., Exxon Corp., Met. Life, Surdna Found., others; founder of the Guild's Gielgud Award for Excellence in the Dramatic Arts, 1994. Asst. editor: Shakespeare Studies, 1972-74; editor: Shakespeare Quar., 1974-85; editor-in-chief, contbr.: William Shakespeare: His World, His Work, His Influence, 1985; editor-in-chief: Shakespeare's World and Work, 2001; contbr. numerous articles to mags. and scholarly jours. Decorated officer Order Brit. Empire; recipient rsch. awards Folger Shakespeare Libr., Fla. State U., NEH. Fellow Royal Soc. Arts; mem. AAUP (sec. chpt. 1972-74), Modern Lang. Assn., Milton Soc. Am., Nat. Council of Tchrs. of English, Renaissance Soc. Am. (mem. council 1975-84), Internat. Shakespeare Conf., Shakespeare Assn. Am. (trustee 1979-82), The Lit. Soc., Cosmos Club. Home and Office: 2141 Wyoming Ave NW Apt 41 Washington DC 20008-3916 Home Phone: 202-483-8646; Office Phone: 202-234-4602. Personal E-mail: shakesgmild@msn.com.

ANDREWS, DAME JULIE (JULIA ELIZABETH WELLS), actress, singer; b. Walton-on-Thames, Eng., Oct. 1, 1935; d. Edward C. and Barbara Wells; m. Tony Walton, May 10, 1959 (div.); 1 child, Emma Walton; m. Blake Edwards, 1969; adopted children: Amy Edwards, Joanna Edwards stepchildren: Jennifer Edwards, Geoffrey Edwards. Studied with pvt. tutors, studied voice with Mme. Stiles-Allen. Debut as singer, Hippodrome, London, 1947; appeared in pantomime Cinderella, London, 1953; appearances include (Broadway prodns.) The Boy Friend, NYC, 1954, (& Conn., 2005), My Fair Lady, 1956-60 (NY Drama Critics award 1956), Camelot, 1960-62, Putting It Together, 1993, Victor/Victoria, 1995 (Tony award nominee Best Actress in a Musical); films include Mary Poppins, 1964 (Acad. award for Best Actress 1964), The Americanization of Emily, 1964, Torn Curtain, 1966, The Sound of Music, 1966, Hawaii, 1966, Thoroughly Modern Millie, 1967, Star!, 1968, Darling Lili, 1970, The Tamarind Seed, 1973, 1979, Little Miss Marker, 1980, S.O.B, 1981, Victor/Victoria, 1982, The Man Who Loved Women, 1983, That's Life!, 1986, Duet For One, 1986, A Fine Romance, 1992, Relative Values, 2000, The Princess Diaries, 2001, Unconditional Love, 2002, Shrek 2 (voice), 2004, The Princess Diaries 2: The Royal Engagement, 2004; TV debut in High Tor, 1956; star TV series The Julie Andrews Hour, 1972-73 (Emmy award for Best Variety Series), Julie, 1992; also spls.; TV movies include Our Sons, 1991, One Special Night, 1999, Eloise at the Plaza, 2003; author: (as Julie Edwards): Mandy, 1971, The Last of the Really Great Whangdoodles, 1974; recs.: The King and I, 1992. Named World Film Favorite (female), 1967; named to 100 Great Britons, 2002; recipient Golden Globe award, Hollywood Fgn. Press Assn., 1964, 1965, Lifetime Achievement award, Kennedy Ctr., 2001, SAG, 2007, Golden Plate award, Acad. Achievement, 2004. Achievements include knighted by Queen Elizabeth, 1999.*

ANDREWS, KAREN LEIGH, language educator; d. Ronald Andrews and Janis Anne. BA, U. Md., Coll. Pk., 2001; MEd, George Washington U., Washington, DC, 2007. Lic. ESOL and Spanish tchr. DC, 2007, ESOL tchr. Md., 2007. Assoc. dir. Hispanic Assn. Colls. and Univs., Washington, 2001—04; ESOL tchr. Montgomery County Pub. Schs., Md., 2004—. Mem.: Hispanic Assn. Colls. and Univs. Alumni Assn. (bd. dirs., mem. at large 2006—). Personal E-mail: kyra2k@yahoo.com.

ANDREWS, MALCOLM JOHN, engineering educator; b. Coventry, Eng., Oct. 4, 1958; came to US, 1986; s. Norman Leslie and Sarah Boyce (Mitchel) Andrews. BA in Math., Oxford U., Eng., 1980, MA in Math., 1984; DIC, PhD in Mech. Engring., Imperial Coll. Sci. & Tech., London, 1986. Registered profl. engr., Tex.; chartered engr., Eng. and Europe. Rsch. asst. UK Atomic Energy Authority, Winfrith, England, 1976-77, 1978; rsch. assoc. Transport and Rd. Rsch. Lab., Crowthorne, England, 1979; project leader, tech. cons. Computer Analysts and Programmers, Inc., London, 1980-83; rsch. fellow Imperial Coll. Sci. & Tech., 1983-86; rsch. staff engine lab. Princeton U., NJ, 1986-91, lectr. mech. engring., 1988-89; asst. prof. mech. engring. Tex. A&M U., College Station, Tex., 1991—96, assoc. prof., 1996—2004, prof., 2004—; nat. security fellow Los Alamos Nat. Lab., N.Mex., 2005—. Cons. in field. Author: Encyclopedia of Fluid Mechanics, vol. 8, 1989; contbr. articles to ASME Jour. Fluids Engring., Internat. Jour. Atomization and Sprays, Physics of Fluids, Jour. Fluid Mechanics. Recipient Mike Ackril award Brit. Heat Transfer Soc., 1986, Engring. Excellence award Tex. Engring. Exptl. Sta., 1991, Ernest Orlando Lawrence award in Nat. Security Dept. Energy, 2007; Dept. Energy fellow, 1994. Mem. AIAA, ASME, Soc. Indsl. and Applied Math., Am. Phys. Soc., Soc. Automotive Engrs. Achievements include patents in field. Office: Los Alamos Nat Lab MS D413 Los Alamos NM 87545 Office Phone: 505-606-1430, 505-606-1430. E-mail: mandrews@tamu.edu.

ANDREWS, MARION E., artist, calligrapher; b. Mar. 6, 1913; Grad., Worcester Art Mus. Sch., Mass., 1933; BS in Edn., Mass. Coll. Art, Boston, 1953, degree in fine arts (hon.), 2006; postgrad., Yale U., New Haven, 1954, Pratt Inst., Art Students League, NY, U. Calif., Santa Criz, 1973, Imperial Coll., London, 1976. Lic. pvt. pilot Teterboro Sch. Aeronautics, 1955. Calligrapher L. G. Balfour Co., Attleboro, Mass., 1936—46; freelance artist Geyer Studio, NYC, 1947—94. Vice chmn. All Woman Transcontinental Air Race Inc., Teterboro, NJ, 1968—77. Represented in permanent collections USN Compat Art Collection, Washington, paintings of Blue Angels, Washington Navy Yard; artist, editors asst.: book The Powder Puff Derby - Awtar, Inc., 1985. Recipient more than 100 awards for juried shows, NY, 1950—. Mem.: Parliamsntarians NY, Soc. Scribes NY, Nat. Assn. Parliamentarians (gov. NY, NJ sect. 1960—62, registered), Audubon Artists, Inc. (aquamedia dir. 1999—, Guilia Palermo award 2004), Artists Fellowship, Inc., Ninety Nines, Inc., Zonta Club, Nat. Arts Club (award for watercolor 2003), Jackson Heights Arts Club (v.p. 1970—76, Best in Show 2003, 1st in watercolor 2004, numerous awards), Salmagundi Club (bd. dirs., Outstanding Achievement award, numerous awards), Pen and Brush Club (pres. 1988—92, solo show award 1963, 2003, numerous awards), Silver Wings Fraternity.

ANDREWS, MARK JOSEPH, lawyer; b. Chgo., July 27, 1944; s. Mark Lewis and Elizabeth (Glendening) A.; m. Martha Jo Shipman, Nov. 29, 1969(div. 2002); children: Eliza, Jonathan. AB, Harvard Coll., 1966; JD, Harvard U., 1969. Bar: U.S. Dist. Ct. D.C. 1970, U.S. Ct. Appeals (D.C. cir.) 1970, U.S. Ct. Appeals (5th and 11th cirs.) 1981, U.S. Ct. Fed. Claims 1983, U.S. Supreme Ct. 1990. From assoc. to ptnr. Verner, Liipfert, Bernhard, McPherson & Hand, Washington, 1969-91; ptnr. Barnes & Thornburg, Washington, 1991—2001, Strasburger & Price, LLP, Washington, 2001—. Co-chmn. federal govt. sponsored task force on regulatory aspects of transp. ins. crisis, 1986-87; vis. lectr. logistics Sturm Coll. Law, U. Denver, 2005, 07. Contbr. articles to profl. jours. Pres. Amadeus Concerts (formerly Gt. Falls Va. Concert Series), 1985-87, bd. dirs., 1984-2000. Mem. ABA (founding mem. internat. transp. com. of sect. internat. law), Transp. Lawyers Assn. (Disting. Svc. 1985, exec. com. 1986-99, 2003-05, pres. 1992-93, Lifetime Achievement award 2005), Assn. Transp. Law Profls., Can. Transport Lawyers Assn., Conf. Claims Counsel, Am. Law Inst. Avocations: photography, hiking, collecting native american artifacts, music. Office: Strasburger & Price LLP 1800 K St NW Ste 301 Washington DC 20006 Home Phone: 703-351-7717; Office Phone: 202-742-8601. Business E-Mail: mark.andrews@strasburger.com.

ANDREWS, MELINDA WILSON, human development researcher; b. NYC, Aug. 12, 1956; d. William Maurice and Natalie Maxine (Amos) Wilson; m. James Robert Andrews, Dec. 3, 1977; children: Christopher Wilson Andrews, William James Andrews. BBA in Mgmt./Mktg., Abilene Christian U., Tex., 1977; MS in Human Devel., U. Tex., Dallas, 1988, postgrad., 1994—. Logics adminstr. Texas Instruments, Dallas, 1977-79, contract adminstr., 1979-81, 82-83; grocery mgr., co-asst. store dir. Tom Thumb, Dallas, 1981-82; teaching asst. U. Tex. at Dallas, Richardson, Tex., 1988-91, rsch. asst., 1991—. Dir. creative presch. coop., Richardson, 2000-02; dir. Waterview Christian Presch., 2002—; validator Nat. Assn. Edn. of Young Children, 2002—06; presenter in field. Contbr. articles to profl. jours. Mem. Richardson Symphony Orch., 1977-79, bd. advs. Canyon Creek Elem. PTA, 2004-06, 5th v.p., 1994-95, libr. rep., 1992-94, Canyon Creek PTA bd., 2004-06; treas. exec. bd. Creative Presch. Coop., 1998-99, sec. ex. bd. 1999-2000, dir., 2000-02; Cub Scout leader, com. chmn., Pack 1001, 2002—06; Girl Scout leader 2004-05; asst. dir. English as second lang. sch. Waterview Ch. of Christ. Mem. Soc. for Rsch. in Child Devel. (co-author paper-poster session 1991, 93 confs.), Southwest Soc. for Rsch. in Child Devel., Psi Chi. Mem. Ch. of Christ. Avocations: music, carpentry. Home and Office: 1089 Edith Circle Richardson TX 75080-2331 Office Phone: 972-238-4725. Personal E-mail: andrewsm1089@tx.rr.net.

ANDREWS, MICHAEL WILLIAM, library and information scientist; b. Rome, NY, Mar. 22, 1948; s. Martin Joseph and Mary (Dublanica) A.; m. Karen Lynn Mauro, July 23, 1982. AB History, Cornell U., 1970; MS Libr. Sci., Syracuse U., 1972. Libr. govt. documents SUNY, Plattsburgh, 1971—76, LI U., Bklyn., 1977—79; rsch. asst. Health Info. Sharing Project, Syracuse U., 1979—80; readers svcs. libr. Elizabethtown Coll., Pa., 1980—85; online data base libr. U. DC, 1986—87; dir. rsch. Korn/Ferry Internat., Washington, 1987—2001; owner Andrews Consulting, Woodbridge, Va., 2001—; libr., selection svcs. Prince William Pub. Libr. Sys., Va., 2001—03, libr., grants and spl. projects, 2003—07, cataloging sup., 2007—. Editor: Proceeding of the Second Annual Government Documents Workshop, 1976. Bd. dirs. Friends Chinn Pk. Regional Libr., 1998-2004. Mem.: ALA, Va. Libr. Assn, Pub. Libr. Assn. Avocations: reading, photography, travel, coaching soccer. Office: PWPLS 13083 Chinn Park Dr Woodbridge VA 22192-5073 Home: 16032 Dancing Leaf Pl Dumfries VA 22025-3609 Home Phone: 703-590-6574. Business E-Mail: mandrews@pwcgov.org.

ANDREWS, MINERVA WILSON, retired lawyer; b. Rock Hill, SC, Feb. 1, 1925; d. York Lowry and Minnie de Foix (Long) Wilson; m. Robert Taylor Andrews, Apr. 15, 1950 (dec. Aug. 2006); children: Susan Allison (Mrs. Robert N. Wiles), Stuart Davidson. AB, U. S.C., 1945; LLB, U. Va., 1948. Bar: Va. 1948. Trial atty. antitrust divsn. U.S. Dept. Justice, Washington, 1949—55; assoc. atty. Bauknight, Prichard, McCandlish & Williams, Fairfax, Va., 1963—72, Boothe, Prichard & Dudley, 1972—80; ptnr. Boothe, Prichard & Dudley, and McGuire, Woods, et al. (merged), McLean, Va., 1980—91; ret., 1992. Author: Carolina-Virginia Recollections, 1999, A Carolina-Virginia Genealogy, vol. 2, 2000. Pres. Nat. Soc. Arts & Letters, 1994—96; bd. dirs. Mclean Citizen Assn., 1968—2000, Fairfax/Falls Ch. United Way, Vienna, Va., 1988—2001; life elder Lewinsville Presbyn. Ch., McLean, 1980—2003; elder Westminster Presbyn. Ch., Charlottesville, Va., 2004—. Named Citizen of the Yr. Fairfax County Fedn. Citizen Assn. and Washington Post, 1997. Mem.: Nat. Soc. Arts and Letters (pres. Wash. chpt. 1973—74), Fairfax Bar Assn. (past chmn. real estate com.), Va. Bar Assn. (chmn. real property com. 1980—82, William B. Spong Jr. Professionalism award 2001), Va. State Bar (past chmn. real property sect.). Republican. Office: Court Square Bldg 310 4th St NE Ste 300 Charlottesville VA 22902-1288 Office Phone: 434-977-2547.

ANDREWS, MITCHELL DEWAYNE, internist, educator, dean; b. Enid, Okla., May 24, 1944; s. Mitchell S. and Truel Eva (Melton) A.; m. Rebecca Ellen Meltzer, Aug. 26, 1984. BS, Baylor U., 1966; MD, U. Okla., 1970. Diplomate Am. Bd. Internal Medicine. Resident internal medicine Johns Hopkins Hosp., Balt., 1970-71, U. Okla. Health Sci. Ctr., Oklahoma City, 1971-72, 74-76; asst. prof., assoc. prof., dir. residency program dept. medicine U. Okla., Oklahoma City, 1976-84, vice chmn., chief gen. internal medicine, prof. dept. medicine, 1986—, assoc. dean grad. med. edn. Coll. Medicine, 1994—2000, sr. assoc. dean, 1996—2002, v.p. health affairs, exec. dean, 2002—; chief of medicine regional med. ctr., vice chmn. dept. medicine U. Tenn. Coll. Medicine, Memphis, 1984-86; chief of staff U. Hosp., Oklahoma City, 1992-94, med. dir., 1994-96. Bd. dirs. Nat. Commn. Certification Physician Assts., 1995—2003. Editor: Jour. Okla. State Med. Assn., 1991—; contbr. numerous articles to profl. jours. Bd. dirs. Chamber Orch. Oklahoma City, 1982-84, Lyric Theatre, Oklahoma City, 1996-2000, Oklahoma City Philharm. Found., 2003—; del. Okla. State Leadership Initiative to Soviet Union, 1988. Surgeon CDC, USPHS, 1972-74. Recipient Stollerman award U. Tenn., 1986, Aesculapian award

U. Okla. Coll. Medicine, 1989; ACP tchg. and rsch. scholar, 1976-79. Master ACP (bd. govs. Okla. 1995-99); mem. AMA, Alpha Omega Alpha. Episcopalian. Avocation: photography. Office: U Okla Coll Medicine RM 357 BMSB PO Box 26901 Oklahoma City OK 73126-0901

ANDREWS, NANCY CATHERINE, dean, pediatrician, hematologist, educator; b. Syracuse, NY, Nov. 29, 1958; d. William Shankland and Virginia Helen (Rogers) A.; m. Bernard Mathey-Prevot, Aug. 10, 1985; children: Camille, Nicolas. BS in Molecular Biophysics and Biochemistry, MS in Molecular Biophysics and Biochemistry, Yale U., 1980; PhD in Biology, MIT, 1985; MD, Harvard Med. Sch., 1987. Intern Children's Hosp., Boston, 1987-88, resident, 1988-89; fellow in pediat. hematology/oncology Children's Hosp. and Dana-Farber Cancer Inst., Boston, 1989-92; instr., pediatrics Harvard Med. Sch., Boston, 1991—93, asst. prof., 1993—98, assoc. prof., 1998—2003, prof., 2003—07, dean, basic scis. and grad. studies, 2006—07; dean Duke U. Sch. Medicine, Durham, NC, 2007—. Assoc. investigator Howard Hughes Med. Inst., Boston, 1993-2006; assoc. faculty dir. Harvard MD-PhD Program, Boston, 1996. Author: (chpt.) Hematology of Infancy and Childhood, 1997; contbr. articles to Nature, others. Merck-AFCR Found. fellow, 1991-94; recipient Rosenthal award 1998. Fellow Molecular Medicine Soc., Am. Acad. Arts & Scis.; mem. Soc. Pediat. Rsch. (Young Investigator award 1994), Am. Soc. Hematology (membership com. 1994—), Am. Soc. Clin. Investigation, Inst. Medicine. Democrat. Achievements include being the first women to be appointed dean of Duke University School of Medicine and becomes the only women to lead one of the nation's top 10 medical schools. Avocations: travel, gardening, cooking. Office: Howard Hughes Med Inst 320 Longwood Ave Boston MA 02115-5746 also: Goldenson Bldg Rm 129 Harvard Med Sch 220 Longwood Ave Boston MA 02115 also: Duke U Sch Medicine Boc 2927 Durham NC 27710 Office Phone: 617-919-2116. Business E-Mail: nancy_andrews@hms.harvard.edu.*

ANDREWS, NAVEEN WILLIAM SIDNEY, actor; b. London, Jan. 17, 1969; children: Jaisal, Joshua. Studied at, Guildhall Sch. of Music and Drama, London. Actor: (films) London Kills Me, 1991, Wild West, 1992, Kama Sutra: A Tale of Love, 1996, The English Patient, 1996, True Love and Chaos, 1997, Bombay Boys, 1998, Mighty Joe Young, 1998, Drowning on Dry Land, 1999, Blessed Art Thou, 2000, Rollerball, 2002, Easy, 2003, Bride & Prejudice, 2004, Provoked: A True Story, 2006, Grindhouse, 2007; (TV films) Double Vision, 1992, The Peacock Spring, 1996, My Own Country, 1998, The Chippendales Murder, 2000, Future Tense, 2003, The Ten Commandments, 2006; (TV miniseries) The Buddha of Suburbia, 1993; (TV series) The Beast, 2001, Lost, 2004— (Outstanding Performance by an Ensemble in a Drama Series, Screen Actors Guild award, 2006).*

ANDREWS, OAKLEY V., lawyer; b. Cleve., Apr. 15, 1940; BA, Yale U., 1962; JD, Western Reserve U., 1965. Bar: Ohio 1965, U.S. Tax Ct. 1968, U.S. Dist. Ct. (no. dist.) Ohio 1968, U.S. Ct. Appeals (6th cir.) 1968. Ptnr. Baker & Hostetler, LLP, Cleve. Fellow Am. Coll. Trust and Estate Coun.; mem. Ohio State Bar Assn., Estate Planning Coun. Cleve. (pres. 1982-83), Cleve. Bar Assn. (chmn. Estate Planning, Probate and Trust law sect. 1984-85), Phi Delta Phi Office: Baker & Hostetler LLP 3200 Nat City Ctr 1900 E 9th St Ste 3200 Cleveland OH 44114-3475 Office Phone: 216-861-7568. E-mail: oandrews@bakerlaw.com.

ANDREWS, PETER JAMES, application developer, writer; b. Mass., 1954; s. George and Clare Andrews; m. Susan Hosford, 1980; children: Carol, Mark. BA, Cath. U. Am., Washington, 1976; MS, U. Va., Charlottesville, 1980. Emerging techs. analyst IBM Global Svcs., Somers, NY, 1998; innovation strategist IBM Exec. Bus. Inst., Palisades, NY, 2002—. Keynote spkr. KMWorld 2006. Author: (online white paper series) Executive Tech Reports; contbr. Worldbook Yearbook, Science and Its Times, Ency. Britannica Sci. and the Future. Mem.: Nat. Assn. Sci. Writers. Achievements include participation in team that created www.ibm.com; first to build the pre-Web prototype for Eureka Alert!, an online resource for science reporters; invention of Future Value technique for evaluating emerging technologies. Avocation: fiction writing. Home: 16 Aimee Ct Mahopac NY 10541 Office: IBM Exec Bus Inst Rt 9W Palisades NY 10964 Office Phone: 845-732-6095. Personal E-mail: andrews845@verizon.net.

ANDREWS, PETER MICHAEL, biology professor; s. Joseph and Sheila Andrews; m. Cheryl Hein, June 17, 1977; children: Ryan Michael, John Paul. PhD, Tulane U., New Orleans, 1971. Assoc. prof. Georgetown U., Washington, 1978—84; prof. Georgetown U. Sch. Medicine, Washington, 1984—, dep. chmn. dept. cell biology, 1984—2005. Grantee, NIH and Pvt. Founds., 1972—. Mem.: Am. Soc. Nephrology, Am. Soc. for Cell Biology, Internat. Soc. Nephrology, Am. Assn. Anatomists. Independent. Achievements include patents for renal preservation solution, adjunct for prostate cancer treatment. Office: Georgetown University 3900 Reservoir Rd NW Washington DC 20007 Home Phone: 703-534-1812; Office Phone: 202-687-1228.

ANDREWS, RICHARD NIGEL LYON, academic administrator, educator; b. Newport, RI, Dec. 6, 1944; s. Nigel Lyon and Constance Doane (Young) A.; m. Hannah Pape Wheeler, June 7, 1969; children: Sarah Huntington, Christopher Page Monteith AB, Yale U., 1966; M in Regional Planning, U. N.C., 1970, PhD, 1972. Vol. U.S. Peace Corps, Bharatpur, Nepal, 1966-68; budget examiner U.S. Office of Mgmt. and Budget, Washington, 1970-72; prof. U. Mich., Ann Arbor, 1972-81; prof. pub. policy U. N.C., Chapel Hill, 1981—, dir. U. N.C. Inst. Environ. Studies, 1981-91, dir. environ. mgmt. and policy program, 1990-94, mem. exec. com. faculty coun., 1994-97, chair of faculty, 1997-00, Thomas Willis Lambeth disting. prof. pub. policy, 2004—, chmn. dept. pub. policy, 2006—. Cons. NSF, Washington, 1982-85, AID, Yaounde, Cameroon, 1983, U.S.-Asia Environ. Partnership, 2000-06, Kenan Inst. Asia, 2000-06; mem. NC Natural Heritage Adv. Com., Raleigh, 1982-87; sr. staff mem. Commn. on Future of N.C., Raleigh, 1982-84; mem. Bd. Environ. Studies and Toxology, NAS, 1986-88; chmn. study com. on opportunities in applied environ. R&D, NAS, 1988-90; mem. risk reduction subcom. Sci. Adv. Bd., EPA, 1989-90, AID, Czech and Slovak Republics, 1991-94; mem. adv. com. Pew Conservation Scholars Program, 1991-94; mem. adv. com. EPA Decisionmaking, Nat. Acad. of Pub. Adminstrn., 1994-95; chmn. adv. panel new approach to environ. regulation Office Tech. Assessment U.S. Congress, Washington, 1993-95; mem. Multi-State Working Group Environ. Mgmt. Systems, 1997—2004; chmn. adv. panel U.S. registration practices for ISO 14001 environ. mgmt. sys. Nat. Acad. Pub. Adminstrn., 2000-01; mem. adv. com. Environ. Stewardship N.C. dept. environ. and natural resources, 2002-06, mem. study com. on environ. decision making, NAS, 2003-2005, mem.com.human dimensions of global change, 2005-. Author: Environmental Policy and Administrative Change, 1976, Managing the Environment, Managing Ourselves: A History of American Environmental Policy, 1999, 2d edit., 2006; editor: Land in America, 1979, Environmental Change and Public Health-The Next Fifty Years, 1990; contbr. articles to profl. jours. Vestry Episcopalian Ch., Chapel Hill, 1986-89. Resources for the Future Inc. fellow, 1971-72, Rockefeller Found. fellow, 1977-78, Fulbright fellow Vienna U. Econs., 1990, Salzburg Seminar faculty fellow, 1990, fellow Nat. Acad. of Pub. Adminstrn., 1996. Fellow AAAS (nominating com. sect. on societal impacts of sci. and engring. 1987-90, chmn. 1989-90, 96-97, ann. meeting program com. 1988-90, com. on sci. engring. and pub. policy 1997-2003, com. sect. social, econ. and polit. scis. 1998-2002); mem. Assn. Pub. Policy and Mgmt. (ann. meeting program com. 2003), Soc. For Policy Scis., Golden Key, Sigma Xi, Delta Omega. Democrat. Avocations: tennis, sailing, camping, photography, squash. Office: U NC Dept Public Policy CB3435 Abernethy Chapel Hill NC 27599-3435 Office Phone: 919-843-5011.

ANDREWS, RICHARD OTIS, museum director; b. LA, Nov. 8, 1949; s. Robert and Theodora (Hammond) A.; m. Colleen Chartier, Jan. 3, 1976; 1 child, Bryce. BA, Occidental Coll., LA, 1971; BFA, U. Wash., 1973, MFA, 1975. Project mgr. Art in Pub. Places, Seattle Arts Commn., 1978-80, coord., 1980-84; dir. visual arts program Nat. Endowment for Arts, Washington, 1985-87; dir. Henry Art Gallery, U. Wash., Seattle, 1987—. Co-curator Art Into Life: Russian Constructivism 1914-1932; curator James Turrell: Knowing Light, 2003, Maya-Lin: Systematic Landscapes, 2006; cons. pub. art program devel., 1982-84; bd. trustees Assn. Art Mus. Dirs., 1997-2000. Author: Insights/On Sites, 1984, James Turrell: Sensing Space, 1992, Maya-Lin: Systematic Landscapes, 2006; editor Artwork/Network, 1984; contbg. editor Going Public, 1988. Mem. Seattle Arts Commn., 2004—. Office: U Wash Henry Art Gallery PO Box 351410 Seattle WA 98195-1410

ANDREWS, RICHARD VINCENT, physiologist, educator; b. Arapahoe, Nebr., Jan. 9, 1932; s. Wilber Vincent and Fern (Clawson) A.; m. Elizabeth Williams, June 1, 1954 (dec. Dec. 1994); children: Thomas, William, Robert, Catherine, James, John; m. Wyoma Upward, Oct. 18, 1997. BS, Creighton U., 1958, MS, 1959; PhD, U. Iowa, 1963. Instr. biology Creighton U., Omaha, 1958-60; instr. physiology U. Iowa, 1960-63; asst. prof. Creighton U., Omaha, 1963-65, assoc. prof., 1965-68, prof. physiology, 1968-97, asst. med. dean, 1972-75, dean grad. studies, 1975-85, dean emeritus, 1995—, prof. emeritus, 1997—. Vis. prof. Naval Arctic Rsch. Lab., 1963-72, U. B.C., 1985-86, U. Tasmania, 1993-94; cons. VA, NSF, NRC, ARS; plenary speaker USSR Symposium on Environment, 1970, Internat. Soc. Biomet., 1972. Contbr. articles to profl. jours. Mem. Gov.'s task force on fatigue State Nebr. Served with M.C. U.S. Army, 1951-54. NSF fellow, 1962-63; NSF-NIH-ONR-AINA grantee, 1963— Fellow Explorers Club, Arctic Inst. N.Am.; mem. Am. Physiol. Soc., Am. Mammal Soc., Endocrine Soc., Soc. Exptl. Biology and Medicine, Internat. Soc. for Biometeorology, Sigma Xi. E-mail: randwandrews@aol.com.

ANDREWS, ROBERT BRUCE, JR., physician, military officer; b. Spokane, Wash., Dec. 14, 1946; s. Robert Bruce and Dorothy Kathryn Andrews; m. Judy Lynn Littell, June 22, 1969; children: Heather N. Gafford, Lili K., Mei Lin, Robert B. III(dec.). BA, Ea. Wash. U., Cheney, 1978; DO, Coll. Osteo. Medicine and Surgery, Des Moines, 1978; MPH, Johns Hopkins U., Balt., 1981. Diplomate Nat. Bd. Examiners Osteo. Physicians and Surgeons. Lt. col., flight surgeon, pvt. pilot US Army, Fort Campbell, Ky., Vietnam, Fort Lewis, Wash., Fort McClellan, Ala., Würzburg, Germany, 1966—2006, chief, divsn. preventive medicine Würzburg, 2004—05; chief, dept. preventive medicine Carl R. Darnall Army Med. Ctr., Fort Hood, Tex., 2005—06; chief med. officer Fort Belknap IHS Hosp., Harlem, Mont., chief med. officer, med. dir., emergency med. svc. Decorated Bronze Star US Army, Vietnam. Mem.: US Army Assn. Flight Surgeons, Aerospace Med. Assn. Republican. Ch. Of Christ. Avocations: woodworking, hunting, fishing. Office: Fort Belknap IHS Hosp RR 1 Box 67 Harlem MT 59526 Office Phone: 406-353-3195.

ANDREWS, ROBERT ERNEST, congressman, lawyer; b. Camden, NJ, Aug. 4, 1957; m. Camille Spinello, Nov. 1993; 2 children. BA summa cum laude in Polit. Sci., Bucknell U., Pa., 1979; JD magna cum laude, Cornell U. Sch. Law, 1982. Bar: NJ 1982. Atty. Archer & Greiner, Haddonfield, NJ, 1982-84, Charles J. Clarke & Assocs., Haddonfield, 1984-85, Kenney & Kenny Assocs., Cherry Hill, NJ, 1985-88; mem. Camden County Bd. Chosen Freeholders, NJ, 1987-90, dir., 1988-90; mem. US Congress from 1st NJ dist., 1990—, mem. armed svcs. com., mem. budget com., mem. edn. and labor com., chmn. subcommittee on health, employment, labor, and pensions. Adj. prof. Rutgers U. Coll. Law. Contbr. Bd. dirs. Camden County March of Dimes; mem. Task Force on Govt. Waste. Mem.: Phi Beta Kappa. Democrat. Episcopalian. Avocation: jogging. Office: US House Reps 2439 Rayburn House Office Bldg Washington DC 20515-3001 Office Phone: 202-225-6501.

ANDREWS, TERRENCE MICHAEL, senior policy advisor; s. Terrence Willard and Ann Bonnie Andrews; m. Lisa Tarsi, Oct. 12, 2002. BS, Morgan State U., Balt., 1992, MA, 1994; JD, Roger Williams U., Bristol, RI, 1997; LLM, George Washington U., 2006. Bar: Ariz. 1997, DC 2001, U.S. Supreme Ct. 2001, Va. 2005. Dep. atty. Pima County Atty., Tucson, 1997—2002; chief prosecutor Pascua Yaqui Tribe, Tucson, 2002—04; spl. asst. U.S. atty. Dept. of Justice, Tucson, 2002—04; sr. policy advisor Dept. of Homeland Security, Washington, 2004—. Firearms instr. Old Pueblo Firearms Acad., Tucson, 2000—04. Soccer referee Ariz. Interscholastic Assn., Tucson, 1998—2004; nat. del. Rep. Party, Tucson, 2004, dist. chmn., 2000—04. Named Govt. Lawyer of Yr., State Bar Ariz., 2004, Animal Prosecutor of Yr., Humane Soc. Ariz., 1999; named to Academic All- Am., Mid Ea. Athletic Conf., 1990, 1991; recipient Pres. Fellowship award, Morgan State U., 1992, Academic All- Am., Mid Ea. Athletic Conf., 1992. Mem.: Masons (life 32nd degree). Republican. Roman Catholic. Avocations: soccer referee, pistol shooting, baseball. Office: Dep Homeland Security Ste 5623 7th and D Washington DC 20045 Home Phone: 202-557-5226; Office Phone: 202-205-9513. Personal E-mail: mandrewsgop@yahoo.com.

ANDREWS, THEODORA ANNE, retired librarian, educator; b. Carroll County, Ind., Oct. 14, 1921; d. Harry Floyd and Margaret Grace (Walter) Ulrey; m. Robert William Andrews, July 18, 1940 (div. 1946); 1 child, Martin Harry. BS with distinction, Purdue U., 1953; MS, U. Ill., 1955. Asst. reference libr. Purdue U., West Lafayette, Ind., 1955—56, pharmacy libr., 1956—79, instr. libr. sci., 1956—60, asst. prof., 1960—65, assoc. prof., 1965—71, prof., 1971—79, 1991—92, prof. libr. sci., pharmacy, nursing and health scis. libr., 1979—90, spl. bibliographer, 1991—92, prof. emeritus libr. sci., 1992—. Del. Ind. Gov.'s Conf. Librs. and Info. Svcs., 1978. Author: A Bibliography of the Socioeconomic Aspects of Medicine, 1975, A Bibliography of Drug Abuse Including Alcohol and Tobacco, 1977, A Bibliography of Drug Abuse, Supplement, 1977-80, 1981, Bibliography on Herbs, Herbal Remedies and Natural Foods, 1982, Substance Abuse Materials for School Libraries, An Annotated Bibliography, 1985, Guide to the Literature of Pharmacy and the Pharmaceutical Sciences, 1986; sect. editor Advances in Alcohol and Substance Abuse, 1981-92; contbr. articles to profl. jours. Mem. Purdue Women's Caucus, 1973—, v.p., 1975-76, pres., 1976-77, Internat. Women's Yr. Regional Planning Com., 1977. Grad. fellow, U. Ill., 1954—55. Mem. ALA, AAUP, Spl. Libr. Assn. (John H. Moriarty award Ind. chpt. 1972), Med. Libr. Assn., Am. Assn. Colls. Pharmacy, Kappa Delta Pi, Delta Rho Kappa. Baptist. Office: Purdue U Sch Pharmacy West Lafayette IN 47907

ANDREWS, WILLIAM COOKE, physician; b. Norfolk, Va., June 7, 1924; s. Charles James and Jean Curry (Cooke) A.; m. Elizabeth Wight Kyle, Nov. 10, 1951; children— Elizabeth Randolph, William Cooke, Jr., Susan Carrington. AA, Princeton U., 1946; MD, Johns Hopkins U., 1947. Diplomate Am. Bd. Ob-Gyn. Intern N.Y. Hosp., 1947, resident in obstetrics and gynecology, 1948-50, 52-53; practice medicine specializing in obstetrics and gynecology Norfolk, Va., 1953-95; asst. in obstetrics and gynecology Cornell U. Med. Sch., 1948-50, 52-53; mem. attending staff Med. Ctr. Hosp.; prof. ob-gyn. Ea. Va. Med. Sch., Norfolk, 1975-95, prof. emeritus, 1995—, pres. faculty senate, 1976-77. Mem. fertility and maternal health drug adv. com. FDA, 1979-83, chmn., 1982-83, cons., 1983-87; mem. sci. adv. bd. Alan Guttmacher Inst., 1992-94; co-chair women's health measurement adv. panel Nat. Com. Quality Assurance, 1996—. Contbr. articles in field to profl. jours. Chmn. Norfolk Bicentennial Commn., 1969-71; mem. Community Facilities Commn., 1971-73, chmn., 1973-79; bd. dirs. Va. League for Planned Parenthood, 1966-68; pres. Norfolk chpt. Planned Parenthood, 1966-68; bd. govs. The Jacobs Inst. Women's Health, 1997-2005. With M.C., USN, 1950-52. Named Hon. Officer of the Most Excellent Order of the Brit. Empire, Queen Elizabeth II, 1967; presented Order of Andres Bello, Pres. Carlos Andres Perez of Venezuela, 1992. Fellow Am. Coll. Obstetricians and Gynecologists (vice chmn. dist. IV 1985-88, chmn. 1988-91, v.p. 1992-93, pres.-elect 1993, pres. 1994-95, exec. bd. 1988-96), Am. Assn. Obstetricians and Gynecologists, Am. Gynecol. and Obstet. Soc., Royal Coll. Obstetricians and Gynecologists (hon.); mem. AMA, Am. Fertility Soc. (bd. dirs. 1970-73, pres. 1977, med. dir. 1986-88, exec. dir. 1988-92), Nat. Osteoporosis Found. (interspecialty med. coun. 1995—), Med. Soc. Va., Norfolk Acad. Medicine, Va. Tidewater Obstetricians and Gynecologists Soc., Continental Gynecol. Soc., South Atlantic Assn. Obs.-Gyns., Norfolk C. of C. (chmn. armed forces com. 1966-68, v.p. 1968-69, pres. 1970), Internat. Fedn. Fertility Socs. (asst. treas. 1974-80, pres. 1983-86, chmn. sci. program com. 1986-89, exec. com. 1974-92), Navy League U.S. (pres. Hampton Roads coun. 1968-70, nat. dir. 1970-74), English Speaking Union U.S. (pres. Norfolk-Portsmouth br. 1964-66), Planned Parenthood Fedn. Am. (cons. nat. med. com. 1975-85, chmn. 1981-83), Norfolk Yacht and Country Club (commodore 1966). Presbyterian.

ANDREWS, WILLIAM DOREY, law educator; b. NYC, Feb. 25, 1931; s. Sidney Warren and Margaret (Dorey) Andrews; m. Shirley May Herrman, Dec. 26, 1953; children: Helen Estelle (Noble), Roy Herrman, John Frederick, Margaret Dorey (Davenport), Susan Louise, Carol Mary (Reid). BA in English, Amherst Coll., 1952; LLD, 1977; LLB, Harvard U., 1955. Bar: Mass. 1959. Practice, Boston, 1959—63; assoc. Ropes & Gray, 1959—63; lectr. Harvard Law Sch., Cambridge, Mass., 1961—63, asst. prof., 1963—65, prof., 1965—, Eli Goldston prof. law, 1984—. Cons. Sullivan & Worcester, 1964—, US Dept. Treasury, 1966—68, 1984. Lt. USNR, 1955—58. Mem.: ABA, Am. Law Inst. Office: Harvard U Law Sch 1545 Massachusetts Ave Cambridge MA 02138-2903 Business E-Mail: andrews@law.harvard.edu.

ANDREWS, WILLIAM FREDERICK, manufacturing executive; b. Easton, Pa., Oct. 7, 1931; s. William Frederick and Lydia Nielson (Cross) Andrews; m. Lin Howard; children: William Frederick III, Whitney, Carter, Clayton, Sloane. BS, U. Md., 1953; MBA, Seton Hall U., 1961. Product mgr. Scovill Mfg. Co., Waterbury, Conn., 1965-68, v.p., gen. mgr. Raleigh, NC, 1968-73, group v.p. Nashville, 1973-79, pres. Waterbury, 1979-81, chmn., pres., CEO, 1981-86, Singer Sewing Machine Co., 1986-89; pres., CEO, chmn. Massey Investment Co., 1989—90; pres., CEO, UNR Industries Inc., 1990—92; CEO, chmn. bd. Amdura Corp., Conn., 1992-94; chmn. bd. Utica Corp., Utica, NY, 1992-94, Schrader Bridgeport, Chgo., 1995—98, Scovill Fasteners, Clarkesville, 1996—2001, Northwestern Steel and Wire Co., Sterling, 1998—2001, Allied Aerospace, Newport News, Va., 2000—06, Corrections Corp. of Am., Nashville, 2000—, Katy Industries, Middlebury, Conn., 2001—, Singer Co., 2004—. Bd. dirs. Corrections Corp., Katy Industries, Black Box, Inc., Trex Industries, O'Charleys' Inc. Capt. USAF, 1953-56. Recipient Silver Beaver award Boys Scouts Am., 1979, Significant Sig award Sigma Chi, 1992. Mem.: The Golf Club of Tenn., Univ. Club (NYC), Chgo. Club, Highfield Country Club (Conn.), Bellemeade Country Club (Nashville). Republican. Episcopalian. Office: Riverstone Farm 1409 Moran Rd Franklin TN 37069-6301 Office Phone: 615-370-0098. Personal E-mail: wmfandrews@aol.com.

ANDREWS, WILLIAM LESTER SELF, chemistry educator; b. Lincolnton, NC, Jan. 31, 1942; s. William Baker and Clara Adele (Self) A.; m. Marjorie Hare, Jan. 30, 1965; children: Scott Hare, Ross Lester. BS in Chem. Engring., Miss. State U., 1963; PhD in Phys. Chem., U. Calif., Berkeley, 1966; D (hon.), U. Paul Sabatier, Toulouse, France, 2004. Asst. prof. chemistry U. Va., Charlottesville, 1966-70, assoc. prof., 1970-76, prof., 1976—. Fellow engring. Miss. State U., 2002. Editor: Chemistry and Physics of Matrix Isolated Species, 1989; mem. editorial bd. Jour. Molecular Structure, 1978. Scoutmaster Boy Scouts Am., Ivy, Va., 1986-89. Recipient Coblentz award, 1978, Lippincott Vibrational Spectroscopy award 2001; A.P. Sloan fellow, 1973-75, Fulbright fellow, 1982-83, 94; grantee NSF, 1968—. Fellow Am. Phys. Soc.; mem. Am. Chem. Soc. Avocations: clarinet, canoeing, camping, backpacking. Office: U Va Chem Dept Mccormick Rd Charlottesville VA 22904-0001 Office Phone: 434-924-6844.

ANDREYCHUK, DAVID, former professional hockey player; b. Hamilton, Ont., Can., Sept. 1963; m. Sue Andreychuk; children, Taylor, Caci. Player Buffalo Sabres, 1982—93, Toronto Maple Leafs, 1993—96, N.J. Devils, Rutherford, 1996—99, Boston Bruins, 1999—2000, Colorado Avalanche, 2000, Buffalo Sabres, 2000—01, Tampa Bay Lightning, 2001—06. Named to NHL All Star Game, 1990, 94. Achievements include being a member of Stanley Cup Champion Tampa Bay Lightning, 2004.

ANDRIANO, KIRK PATRICK, pharmaceutical executive; b. Boise, Idaho, Nov. 10, 1956; s. Donald and Fae Andriano. BS, Utah State U., 1975—79; MS, U. of Utah, 1981—85, PhD, 1985—90. Post-doctoral fellow U. of Utah, 1990—91; nih - fogarty internat. rsch. fellow Tampere U. of Tech., Finland, 1991—92; post-doctoral fellow APS Rsch. Inst., Advanced Polymer Systems, Inc., Redwood City, Calif., 1994—95; vis. rsch. scholar Kyoto U., 1995—97; scientist ii Atrix Laboratories, Inc., Fort Collins, Colo., 1997—99; sr. scientist MacroMed, Inc., Sandy, 1999—2001, exec. dir., preclinical devel., 2002—03; v.p. rsch. & devel. Inion Ltd., Tampere, Finland, 2003—. Indsl. mentor, soc. for biomaterials Johns Hopkins U., Balt. Fogarty Internat. Rsch. fellow, NIH and Acad. of Finland. Master: Nat. Ski Patrol Sys.; mem.: Biomedical Engring. Soc., Soc. for Biomaterials, Controlled Release Soc., ASTM, Am. Assn. of Pharm. Scientists, Tissue Engring. Soc. Home: PMB 31102302 PO Box 311 Mendham NJ 07945-0311 Office: Inion Ltd Loakarinkatu 2 33520 Tampere Finland Home Phone: +358-40-572-8053; Office Phone: +352-3-230-6600. Office Fax: +358-3-230-6602. Personal E-mail: kandriano@aol.com. E-mail: kirk.andriano@inion.com.

ANDRIANO-MOORE, RICHARD COUNT, retired military officer, secondary school educator, elementary school educator; b. Petaluma, Calif., May 25, 1932; s. Norvel and Thelma Elizabeth Koch-Andriano (Cook) Moore; m. Janice Lynn Hironaka, Jan. 10, 1976 (div. Feb. 1990); children: Erika Lynn, Stephen Albert. BA, San Jose State U., 1956; MBA, Pepperdine U., 1977; B in Metaphysical Sci., U. Metaphysics, 1993. Commd. ensign USNR, 1957, advanced through grades to comdr.; 1st lt., gunnery officer USS Jefferson Count LST1068, 1957—60; tchr. 7th grade Oasis Sch., Riverside County, Calif., 1960—63; pers. and legal officer USS Maury AGS-16, 1963—65; commdg. officer Naval & Marine Corps Res. Tng. Ctr., Port Arthur, Tex., 1965—68; ops. officer USS Muliphen LKA 61, 1968—69; ASW & surface program officer 11th Naval Dist., San Diego, 1970—74; commdg. officer Naval Res. Ctr., Hunters Point, Calif., 1974—75, Army, Navy & Marine Corps Res. Ctr., San Bruno, Calif., 1975—79; dir. adminstrn. Nat. Com. Employer, Washington, 1979—82; comdr., recruiting coord. 10 we. states Alameda, Calif., 1982—84; chief staff N. R. Readiness comdr., Treasure Island, Calif., 1984—85; tchr. Shoreline Unified Sch. Dist., Tomales, Calif., 1985—92, 1994—. Editor-in-chief: California Compatriot, 1976—80. Insp. Precinct Bd., Petaluma, 1987—90; scoutmaster Boy Scouts Am., 1989—92, dist. exec., 1992—94; alumni mem. Naval War Coll. Found., Newport, RI, 2002—. Decorated Def. Meritorious Svc. medal Sec. Def., Washington, Ancestral Title and Coat of Arms Counts of Andriano Wappenrolle, Austria, Rome, knight comdr. Order St. John of Jerusalem Knights Hospitaller; recipient knight bachelor, 2005, Disting. Alumni award, San Jose State U., 1991, Scoutmaster award of Merit, Boy Scouts Am., 1992, numerous Best of Show and 1st place ribbons for acrylic paintings, Sonoma-Marin County Fair, 1989—2005. Mem.: Soc. of Colonial Wars, Order of Indian Wars of U.S., Noble Co. of the Rose (lt. magister rosae 1998—), Naval Order U.S., Mil.

Order Loyal Legion U.S. (Calif. comdr. 1982—88), Calif. Soc. SAR (pres. San Francisco chpt. 1976—77, state pres. 1986—87, Silver Good Citizenship medal 1978, Patriot medal 1985, Meritorious Svc. medal 1987, oak leaf cluster 1996, Citation of Merit 2001, oak leaf cluster 2005, Disting. Svc. medal 2007), Augustan Soc. Inc. (v.p. 1995—2004, corp. v.p. 2005—). Avocations: reading, hiking, bicycling, travel, abstract artist. Office: 2920 Carissa Ct Santa Rosa CA 95405 Personal E-mail: cteandriano@netscape.net.

ANDRIAS, RICHARD T., judge; b. NY, 1943; married; 2 children. BA, Bowdoin Coll., 1965; JD, Columbia U., 1970. Bar: N.Y. 1971, U.S. Dist. Ct. (so. and ea. dists.) N.Y., U.S. Ct. Appeals (2d cir.). Assoc. Gilbert, Segall & Young, NYC, 1970-71, Davis & Davis, NYC, 1975-81, Gordon & Shechtman, NYC, 1981-83; lawyer Legal Aid Soc., NYC, 1971-75; judge Criminal Ct. City of N.Y., NYC, 1983-87, Supreme Ct. State of N.Y., NYC, 1988—, assoc. justice appellate divsn. first dept., 1996—. Vis. scholar London Sch. Econs. Law Sch., 1974; adj. prof. trial practice Pace Law Sch., White Plains, NY, 1991—. Contbr. articles to profl. jours. Chair Cmty. Bd. 12, NYC, 1972—76, N.Y. Task Force Civilian Complaints, NYC, 1987—90; bd. dirs., chair Bronx (N.Y.) Legal Svc., 1980—83; bd. dirs. N.Y. Vietnam Vets. Leadership Program, NYC, 1984—97, N.Y.C. Audubon, 2003—; mem. N.Y. State Gov.'s Task Force on Rape and Sexual Violence, 1989—90. 1st lt. US Army, 1965—67. Decorated Bronze Star, Air medal. Fellow: Am. Bar Found.; mem.: ABA (chair AIDS in criminal justice sys. 1987—89, CEELI Russian program 1995—96, victims com. 1995—97), Am. Law Inst., Assn. Bar City of N.Y. (chair victims com. 1992, exec. com. 1998—2002, nominating com. 2004). Office: Appellate Divsn First Dept 27 Madison Ave Rm 305 New York NY 10010-2201 Office Phone: 212-340-0436.

ANDRIL, DAVID T., lawyer; b. Elizabeth, NJ, Aug. 5, 1956; BS, Georgetown U., 1977; JD, U. Va., 1980. Bar: DC 1980. Ptnr., co-head Energy Sect. Vinson & Elkins LLP, Washington, DC. Mem.: Energy Bar Assn. Office: Vinson & Elkins LLP Willard Office Building 1455 Pennsylvania Ave NW, Ste 600 Washington DC 20004 Office Phone: 202-639-6542. E-mail: dandril@velaw.com.

ANDRIOLA, MARY REPOLE, neurologist, pediatrician; b. NYC, Sept. 13, 1942; d. Anthony Francis Repole and Florence Elizabeth Elliott; m. Micheal John Andriola, July 21, 1962 (div. Jan. 1982); children: Margaret Mary Danao, Joseph Anthony, James Michael; m. Jordan I. Levine, Feb. 24, 1990. Student, Vassar Coll., 1958-60; AB, Johns Hopkins U., 1962; MD, Duke U., 1965. Diplomate Am. Bd. Pediatrics, Am. Bd. Psychiatry and Neurology, with spl. competence in child neurology and added qualification in clin. neurophysiology, subspecialty neurodevel. disabilities, 2005. Resident in pediatrs. Duke U. Sch. Medicine, Durham, NC, 1965-66, U. Fla., Gainesville, 1966-67, resident in neurology, 1967-70; asst. prof. neurology and pediats. La. State U. Sch. Medicine, New Orleans, 1970-72; dir. electroencephalography and fellowship program U. Fla. Coll. Medicine, Gainesville, 1975-88, assoc. prof. neurology, 1975-88, assoc. prof. pediats., 1978-88; dir. pediat. neurology All Children's Hosp. U. S. Fla., St. Petersburg; assoc. prof. neurology SUNY, Stony Brook, 1988-98, dir. clin. neurophysiology, 1990-97, dir. divsn. clin. neurophysiology, 1997, prof. neurology and pediats., 1998—, dir. divsn. pediat. neurology, 2001—. Assoc. examiner Am. Bd. Qualification in EEG, 1976-85, Am. Bd. Psychiatry and Neurology, 1983—, Am. Bd. Clin. Neurophysiology, Inc., 1991—; mem. adv. com. Pinellas county Sch. Bd. Health, 1979-88; reviewer Neurology, 1997—; appeared in TV interviews; mem. People to People Women Specialist Med. Exch. to China, 1991; mem. profl. adv. bd. Epilepsy Found L.I., 1991—; mem. team to Russia, Physicians for Social Responsibility, 1992; lectr. in field. Author: Introduction to EEG and Evoked Potentials, 1983; contbr. articles to profl. jours., chpts. to books Grantee Abbott Labs., 1992, 96, Burroughs Wellcome, 1993, NIH, 1993, Parke-Davis, 1994, BECTS, 1995, Hoechst Marion Roussel, 1995, Warner Lambert, 1995, Cyberonics, 1998. Fellow: Am. Clin. Neurophysiology Soc. (program com. 1980—81, practice com. 1980—82, EEG lab. accreditation bd. 1980—90, liaison Child Neurology Soc. 1982—88), Am. Acad. Pediats.; mem.: So. Clin. Neurol. Soc. (bd. dirs.), Suffolk County Pediat. Soc., Tri-State Child Neurology Soc., Ea. Assn. Electroencephalographers, Child Neurology Soc., Am. Epilepsy Soc., So. EEG Soc. (sec.-treas. 1975—78, program chmn. 1979, pres. 1980, edn. chmn. 1981—89), Women's Am. Med. Assn. (sec.-treas. Suffolk County chpt. 1992). Office: SUNY Stony Brook Sch Medicine Dept Neurology Stony Brook NY 11794-0001 Home Phone: 631-751-1356; Office Phone: 631-444-2599. Business E-Mail: mandriol@notes.cc.sunysb.edu.

ANDRIOLA, ROCCO F., lawyer, diversified financial services company executive; b. Astoria, NY, Mar. 24, 1958; s. Pasquale and Lena (Dituri) A.; m. Susan A. Andriola; children: Patrick Nicholas, Mark Vari. BA summa cum laude, Fordham U., 1979; JD, NYU, 1982, LLM (corp. law), 1986. Bar: N.Y. 1983, D.C. 1985, U.S. Dist. Ct. (so., ea., no. and we dists.), U.S. Ct. Appeals (2d cir.) 1983, U.S. Ct. Internat. Trade 1983, U.S. Ct. Claims 1983, U.S. Supreme Ct. 1986; lic. real estate broker. Legal asst. Am. Clerical Svcs., NYC, summers 1978-79; assoc. Ford Marrin Esposito & Witmeyer, NYC, summer 1980, Donovan Leisure Newton & Irvine, NYC, summer 1981, corp. and securities assoc., 1982-86; v.p., assoc. gen. counsel Shearson Lehman Bros., Inc., NYC, 1986-89, 1st v.p. Capital Preservation and Restructuring Group, 1989-91; sr. v.p. diversified asset group Lehman Bros., NYC, 1991-96, mng. dir. diversified asset group, 1996—2004, mng. dir., dir. global corp. svcs., 1998—2004, mng. dir. fixed income divsn., 2004—. Projects editor NYU Moot Ct. Bd., 1981-82. Bd. dirs. Symphony for UN, 1985-89, Playing-to-Win, 1988-94, Monsignor McClancy Meml. HS Alumni, 2000-02, bd. govs., 2007—; bd. dirs. Donate Life Am., 2006-, NY Alliance Donation, 2006—; mem. bd. advisors Fordham U., 1987-97, 2006-, chmn. bd. advisors, 1996-97, 2007—; founder, exec. dir. St. Francis Home Visitors Program, Astoria, 1983-85; v.p. St. Francis Parish Coun., Astoria, 1983-84; mem. Queens Citizens Orgn., 1979-86, Astoria Civic Assn., 1983-86, Residents for a More Beautiful Port Washington, 1992—, Am. Liver Found., bd. dirs. 1993-97, mem. exec. com., 1994-97, acting chmn. bd. dirs. 1995-96, Transplant Recipients Internat. Org., Transplant Living Ctr., Am. Tinnitus Assn., Urban Land Inst.; mem. LI chpt. MADD, 1991—; fellow David Rockefeller Fellowship Program, 1995-96; bd. dirs. United Network for Organ Sharing, 1996, 97, NY Organ Donor Network, 1997—, chmn. governance com., 2000-03, vice-chmn., 2002-03, chmn. bd., 2004-05; mem. fundraising com. St. Peter of Alcantara Parish, 2000; mem. NYC Partnership Borough Devel. Task Force, 2002; mem. nat. spkrs. bur. United Network Organ Sharing, 2006—; adv. com. ednl. assembly Port Wash., 2005—. Recipient George P. Foulk Meml. award, NYU Sch. Law, 1982, Vol. Svc. award, Combined Health Appeal Greater N.Y., 1996, Disting. Grad. award, Nat. Cath. Elem. Sch., 1997, Disting. Cmty. Svc. award, United Hosp. Fund, 2006. Mem. ABA (lt. gov. law student divsn. 1981-82), NY State Bar Assn. (rep. 1980-82), Am. Corp. Counsel Assn. (bd. dirs. 1988-92, v.p. 1989-90, chmn. mergers and acquisitions com. NY chpt. 1987-89), Order of Barristers, Homeowners Assn. Port Washington (pres. gen. coun. 1992-93), Fordham U. Pres. Coun., NYU Sch. Law Alumni Assn. (bd. dirs. 2007-, mem. Weinfeld Program, mem. 25th reunion com., mem. law and bus. mentoring program), Morewood Oaks Homeowners Assn. (pres. 1991-93), Order Sons of Italy in Am. (trustee 1995-97), Am. Israel Pub. Affairs Com., Combined Health Appeal Greater NY (vice chmn., bd. dirs. 1992-95), KC. Roman Catholic. Home: 45 Morewood Oaks Port Washington NY 11050-1603 Office: Lehman Bros Inc 745 7th Ave New York NY 10019-1000 Office Phone: 212-526-3177.

ANDRISANI, JOHN ANTHONY, editor, writer; b. Bayshore, NY, Sept. 24, 1949; s. Pat and Gwendoline Mary (Rose) A. Student, SUNY, Stony Brook, 1968—71. Instr. golf in country club, NY, 1971-78; freelance writer golf mags., 1977—; asst. editor Golf Illus. mag., London, 1980-82; sr. editor instrn. Golf mag., NYC, 1982-98; pres. John Andrisani Assoc. Inc. Co-author: (with Sandy Lyle) Learning Golf: The Lyle Way, 1986, (with Seve Ballesteros) Natural Golf, 1987 (Book of Month Club 1987), (with Chi Chi Rodriguez) 101 Supershots, 1990, (with Robin McMillan) The Golf Doctor, 1990 (Brentanos bestseller 1990), (with Mike Dunaway) Hit It Hard!, 1991, (with Phil Ritson) Golf Your Way, 1992, (with John Daly) Grip It, and Rip It!, 1992, (with Fred Couples) Total Shotmaking, 1994, (with Craig Stadler) I Am The Walrus, 1995, (with Claude "Butch" Harmon Jr.), The Four Cornerstones of Winning Golf, 1996, (with Jim McLean) The X-Factor Swing, 1996, The Tiger Woods Way, 1997, The Short Game Magic of Tiger Woods, 1998, (with Mark Russell) Golf Rules Plain and Simple, 1999, The Hogan Way, 2000, (with John Anselmo) "A-Game" Golf, 2001, The Bobby Jones Way, 2002, Think Like Tiger, 2002, Everything I Learned about People, I Learned From a Round of Golf, 2002, The Nicklaus Way, 2003, Play Like Sergio Garcia, 2004, (with Jim Hardy) The Plane Truth for Golfers, 2005, Tiger's New Swing, 2005, The Michelle Wie Way, 2007, Golf Heaven, 2007, (with Jim Hardy) The Plane Truth Master Class, 2007; contbr. articles to jours. and mags. Mem. Golf Writers Assn. (assn. champion 1985), Ballybunion Golf Club (life, Ireland). Personal E-mail: andrisanik@bellsouth.net.

ANDRITZKY, JOSEPH GEORGE, law educator; b. Milw., Jan. 15, 1947; s. George Joseph and Emma (Schreiner) A. AAS, Milw. Inst. Tech., 1967; BS, Calif. State U., Long Beach, 1971; MPA, U. So. Calif., LA, 1978; PhD, Claremont Grad. Sch., 1984. Vis. prof. criminal law Calif. State U., Long Beach, 1979; adj. prof. criminal law Milw. Area Tech. Coll., 1980—81; instr. law and criminal justice Moraine Park Tech. Coll., Fond du Lac, Wis., 1985—88; asst. prof. criminal law Marquette U., Milw., 1988—89; asst. prof./dir. law enforcement-criminal justice U. Wis., Oshkosh, 1989—90; assoc. prof. criminal law/dir. justice/pub. policy Concordia U. Wis., Milw., 1990—; dir. counterintelligence nat. security law 1st Army Intelligence Sch., Ft. McCoy, Wis., 1988—95; strategic intelligence officer 400th Strategic Intelligence Group, 1995—98, European Command, Ft. Sheridan, Ill., 2000—; chief intelligence G-2 U.S. Army Corps Engrs., Baghdad, Iraq, 2003—04, gen. staff G-2 HQ Washington, 2004—. Sr. instr. mil. law U.S. Army Command and Gen. Staff Coll.; mem. accredited evaluation team Am. Coun. on Edn., N.Y.C., 1992. Author: Civil Rights Law, 1984; editor: Criminal Law, 1990-2001; contbr. articles to profl. jours. Bd. dirs. Waukesha County Law Enforcement Adv. Bd., 1992-2000; elder Trinity Luth. Ch., Milw., 1989-2000; sec. judiciary com. Concordia U. Wis., Milw., 1991—. Lt. col. USAR, 1974—. Mem. ABA (criminal justice assoc.), Res. Officers Assn., Assn. U.S. Army, Nat. Assn. Scholars, Wis. Criminal Justice Edn. Assn. (bd. dirs., pres.), Am. Law Enforcement Trainers Assn. (founder), Pi Sigma Alpha, Alpha Delta Pi. Republican. Lutheran. Avocations: automobile restoration, antique toys and collectables, baseball. Office: Concordia U Wis 12800 N Lake Shore Dr Mequon WI 53097-2418 Home: 401 12th St S Apt 815 Arlington VA 22202 Home Phone: 414-342-2978; Office Phone: 202-761-1259. Personal E-mail: jandritzky@aol.com.

ANDRUK, MARJORIE DEAN, artist, educator; b. Norfolk, Va., Aug. 11, 1922; d. Carl Chadbourne and Bessie Jane (Overman) Dean; m. Richard Andruk, June 5, 1944; children: Richard Dean (dec.), Kenneth Francis. BA, Md. Inst. Coll. Art, 1942; postgrad., Eastman Sch. Photography, Winona Lake, 1943, Inst. Allende, San Miguel de Allende, Guanajuato, Mex., 1968-72; MFA, U. S.C., 1976. 1st woman press photographer Balt. Sun, 1943-45; organizer art dept. Cath. Diocese St. Petersburg, St. Petersburg, Fla., 1957-58; prof. art Gertrude Herbert Art Inst., Augusta, Ga., 1972-76; tchg. assoc. U. S.C., Aiken, 1975-76. Panelist DSAC Grant Rev. Panel, 1984-85; condr. workshops Inst. Allende and Centro cultural El Nigromante. One-woman shows include Coyle & Richardson Gallery, Charleston, W.Va., Learning Founds. Gallery, Athens, Ga., Town and Gown Gallery, Athens, Ga., Mus. Arts and Sci. Mus., Macon, Ga., The Augusta (Ga.)-Richmond County Mus., 1973, 74, Quinlan Art Ctr., Gainesvile, Ga., La Galeria Gaudi, Maracaibo, Venezuela, 1973, Huntington Gallery, U. S.C., 1976, Gertrude Herbert Art Inst., Augusta, 1976, Grande Gallery, Wilmington, Del., 1978, Ware Gallery, Arden, Del., 1979, 81, Casa Carmen Gallery, San Miguel de Allende, 1980, 84, Rodney Square Gallery, Wilmington, Del., 1981, Longwood Gardens Gallery, 1983, The Highland Gallery, Atlanta, 1983, Del. Ctr. for Contemporary Arts, Wilmington, 1983, Evelyn Cobb Gallery, St. Petersburg, Fla., 1994, Lighthouse Gallery, Tequesta, Fla., 1995, St. Petersburg Art Ctr., 1999, many others; group shows include Corcoran Mus., Washington, 1974, Inst. Allende, Russell House Gallery, U. S.C., 1975, Ware Gallery, Rodney Square Gallery, Upham Gallery, St. Petersburg Beach, Fla., 1989, The Arts Ctr., St. Petersburg, Arts on Pk., Lakeland, Fla., 1995, Ridge Art Assn., Winter Haven, Fla., Northwood U., West Palm Beach, 1996, Venice Art Ctr., 1997, Vero Ctr. Arts, 1997, Northwood U., 1997, Southern Coll., Lakeland, Fla., 1999, and many others; permanent collections include Centro Cultural "El Nigromante," San Miguel de Allende, Cathedral Ch. of St. John, Wilmington, Del., Gertrude Herbert Art Inst., Augusta, Augusta-Richmond County Mus., Venice (Fla.) Golf and Country Club., also pvt. collections. Active mem. Suntan Art Ctr., St. Pete Beach, Fla., The Ctr. for the Arts, St. Petersburg, World Art Workshop, Ocean Hills, Calif. Mem. Nat. Assn. Women Artists, Del. State Arts Coun., Fla. Artist Group, Studio 1212. Episcopal. Avocations: world travel, swimming, flower arranging. Studio: 1620 Pelican Creek Xing Saint Petersburg FL 33707-3980

ANDRUS, CECIL DALE, academic administrator; b. Hood River, Oreg., Aug. 25, 1931; s. Hal Stephen and Dorothy (Johnson) A.; m. Carol Mae May, Aug. 27, 1949; children: Tana Lee, Tracy Sue, Kelly Kay. Student, Oreg. State U., 1948-49; LLD (hon.), Gonzaga U., U. Idaho, U. N.Mex., Coll. Idaho, Idaho State U., Whitman Coll. State gen. mgr. Paul Revere Life Ins. Co., 1969-70; gov. State of Idaho, 1971-77, 87-95; sec. of interior, 1977-81; chmn. Andrus Ctr. for Pub. Policy, Boise (Idaho) State U., 1995—. Bd. dirs. Coeur d'Alene Mines; mem. Idaho Senate, 1961-66, 69-70; mem. exec. com. Nat. Gov.'s Conf., 1971-72, chmn., 1976; chmn. Fedn. Rocky Mountain States, 1971-72. Author: Cecil Andrus: Politics Western Style, 1998. Chmn. bd. trustees Coll. of Idaho, 1985-89; bd. dirs. Sch. Forestry, Duke U. With USN, 1951-55. Recipient Disting. Citizen award Oreg. State U., 1980, Collier County Conservancy medal, 1979, Ansel Adams award Wilderness Soc., 1985, Audubon medal, 1985, Statesman of the Yr. award Idaho State U., 1990, Torch of Liberty award B'nai B'rith, 1991, William Penn Mott award, Nat. Parks Conservation Assn., 2000; named Conservationist of Yr. Nat. Wildlife Fedn., 1980, Idaho Wildlife Fedn., 1972, Man of Yr., VFW, 1959. Mem. VFW, Idaho Taxpayers Assn. (bd. dirs. 1964-66). Democrat. Office: Boise State U Andrus Ctr Pub Policy 1910 University Dr Boise ID 83725-0399

ANDRUS, JENNIFER GAIL, otolaryngologist, surgeon, educator, educational consultant; b. Washington, Feb. 15, 1969; d. William Stephen and Gail Witman Andrus; m. Daniel Ernest Ramshaw, May 22, 2004; 1 child, David Ernest Ramshaw. BA cum laude, Bowdoin Coll., Brunswick, Maine, 1990; MD cum laude, Jefferson Med. Coll., Phila., 2001. Ecology intern, advanced studies program St. Paul's Sch., Concord, NH, 1990; resort services adminstrv. asst., spl. events vol. coord., race crew Steamboat Springs Ski & Resort Corp., Colo., 1990—92; sci. instr. Marlborough Sch., LA, 1992—95; outdoor educator Naturalists At Large, Ventura, 1995; sci. coord. St. James' Sch., LA, 1995—97; gen. surgery intern Boston Med. Ctr., 2001—02, resident in otolaryngology, 2002—06; chief resident, clin. fellow laryngology, dept. otolaryngology-head and neck surgery Mass. Eye and Ear Infirmary, 2006—. Resident mem. hosp. ethics com. Boston Med. Ctr., 2001—03; faculty com. admissions, apptd. rep., class of 2001 Jefferson Med. Coll., Phila., 1998—99; grant adminstr. W. Alton Jones found. sci. grant St. James' Sch., 1995—97; children's environ. educator, field guide W. Alton Jones Found. Trustees' Outing, Queen Charlotte Islands, British Columbia, Canada, 1994—94; coord. So. Calif. region Coun. Religion Ind. Schs., LA, 1995—96; presenter in field. Contbr. articles to profl. jours.:, musician solo piano perfomance/competition; dir.(singer): (women's a capella singing group) Arrhythmia (the group's name). Crisis counselor Advocates Against Battering and Abuse, Steamboat Springs, 1991—92; solicitor St. Peter's Episcopal Ch., Phila., 2000—00; youth amb. Soviet Union Wash. Episcopal Diocese, Washington, 1985; com. girls' choral scholars St. Peter's Episcopal Ch., 2000—01, lector, coffee hour host, 1997—2001; mem. Twenties Group, All Saints' Episcopal Parish, Beverly Hills, Calif., 1992—97, pres., 1993—94; stewardship com. mem. All Saints' Episcopal Parish, 1993—95, parish choir mem., 1996—97; tutor math & sci. Colo. Mountain Coll., Steamboat Springs, 1990—92; clin. vol. JEFF Hope, Jefferson Med. Coll., Phila., 1997—2001; student vol., mentor JEFF Moms, Jefferson Med. Coll., 1997—98. Grantee, New Eng. Otolaryn. Soc., 2003, Am. Assn. Otolaryngology - Head & Neck Surgery, 2004—05; scholar, Episcopal Diocese Pa., 1998, 2000, Jefferson Med. Coll., 2000; Copeland scholar, 1997—99, E.K. Van Swearingen scholar, Bowdoin Coll., 1998, Tabas scholar, Jefferson Med. Coll., 1998. Mem.: AMA, ACS, Am. Acad. Otolaryngology, Head & Neck Surgery, Pathology Chairs Assn., Alpha Omega Alpha. Episcopalian. Achievements include development of hands-on thematic science curriculum. Avocations: cooking, hiking, kayaking, travel. Home Phone: 617-270-6717; Office Phone: 617-523-7900.

ANDRUS, ROGER DOUGLAS, lawyer; b. Floral Park, NY, Dec. 3, 1945; s. Winfield and Julia Margaret (Arduino) A.; m. Patricia Ann McDonough, Oct. 4, 1986; children: Justin, Sarah, Michael, David, Molly. AB cum laude, Wagner Coll., 1966; JD, NYU, 1969. Bar: N.Y. 1970, U.S. Dist. Ct. (ea. and so. dists.) 1975, U.S. Ct. Appeals 2d cir.) 1975. Assoc. Cahill Gordon & Reindel, NYC, 1970-78, ptnr., 1978—. Mem. NY State Bar Assn., Canoe Brook Country Club, Grand Harbor Club, Down Town Assn., Omicron Delta Kappa. Office: Cahill Gordon & Reindel 80 Pine St New York NY 10005-1790

ANDRZEJEWSKI, PAT See BENATAR, PAT

ANDSNES, LEIF OVE, concert pianist; b. Karmoy, Norway, Apr. 7, 1970; Student, Bergen Music Conservatory. Concert pianist Oslo Philharm., Edinburgh Festival, 1989, Cleve. Orch. Philharm., Berlin Philharm., London Philharm., Chgo. Symphony, N.Y. Philharm., Boston Philharm., Kirov Orch., London Symphony Orch., Vienna Symphony Orch., L.A. Philharmonic, City of Birmingham Symphony, Brahms Piano Concerto No. 1 with CBSO and Simon Rattle, 1998; records for EMI classics, including Schumann Pianoworks and the Long Long Winter Night (a collection of Norwegian music), 1997, Haydn Piano Sonatas, 1999, Britten Piano Concerto and Shostakovich Concerto for Piano, Trumpet and Strings, 1999, Haydn Piano Concertos, 2000, Liszt Piano Pieces, 2001; recs. Virgin Classics include: Grieg: A minor and Liszt A major, Janacek: Piano Works (Deutschen Schallplaten award), Chopin: Sonatas, Nielsen Piano Works, Grieg Piano Works; maj. tours in Australia, Japan, Europe, U.S. Recipient First prize Hindemith Competition, Frankfurt-am-Main, prizewinner others, Dorothy Chandler award, L.A.; named The 1998 Gilmore Artist by Irving S. Gilmore Internat. Keyboard Festival of Kalamazoo. Home: IMG Artists Lovell House 616 Chiswick High Rd London London W4 2TH England W4 5RX

ANEJA, ALKA, child psychiatrist; b. New Delhi, Feb. 5, 1971; arrived in U.S., 1997; d. K.G. and Parkash Aneja; 1 child, Esha Grewal. B Medicine and Surgery, Maulana Azad Med. Coll., New Delhi, 1995; MA, Western Carolina U., 1999. Resident in adult psychiatry Drexel U., Phila., 2000—02, SUNY Upstate Med. U., Syracuse, NY, 2002—03, 2005—06; fellow in child psychiatry Johns Hopkins U., Balt., 2003—05. Rsch. asst. Western Carolina U., Cullowhee, NC, 1997—99; mem. staff Nat. Eating Disorders Screening Program, Cullowhee, 1998; presenter in field. Contbr. articles to profl. jours. Mem.: Am. Assn. Child and Adolescent Psychiatry, Am. Psychiat. Assn., Sigma Xi. Avocations: playing harmonium, music, art, cooking, meditation. Office: Kennedy Krieger Inst 3901 Greenspring Ave Baltimore MD 21211 Office Phone: 443-923-7620. Business E-Mail: aneja@kennedykrieger.org.

ANEJA, RAJESH, medical educator, pediatrician; b. Pinjore, India, Feb. 21, 1967; s. Charanjit and Krishna Aneja; m. Ruby Varughese, Oct. 12, 2002. MD, Christian Med. Coll., Ludhiana, India, 1990. Cert. Am. Bd. Pediat., 1999. Pediat. resident Winthrop U. Hosp., Mineola, NY, 1997—99; pediatric ICU fellow Children's Hosp., Buffalo, 1999—2002; rsch. fellow Cin. Children's Med. Ctr., 2002—04; asst. prof. Children's Hosp. Recipient Splty. award, Soc. Critical Care Medicine, 2004, 2005. Fellow: Am. Acad. Pediat. Achievements include research in PARP modulates the heat shock response; pediatric sepsis. Office: Children's Hosp Pitts 3705 5th Ave Pittsburgh PA 15213 Office Phone: 412-692-7366. Business E-Mail: rajaneja@pol.net.

ANESH, MARK K., lawyer; b. Bklyn., Sept. 8, 1954; BA, Bklyn. Coll., CUNY, 1975; JD, Rutgers U., Camden, 1978. Bar: NY 1979, US Dist. Ct. So. Dist. NY, US Dist. Ct. Ea. Dist. NY, US Ct. Appeals 2nd Cir. Ptnr. Wilson, Elser, Moskowitz, Edelman & Dicker LLP, NYC. Adj. prof. law Touro Law Sch.; asst. adj. prof. Hofstra Law Sch. Founding pres. Woodbury Jewish Ctr. Mem.: ABA (torts & ins. practice sect., sports & entertainment practice sect.), NY State Bar Assn. (ins. com.), Pine Hollow Country Club (bd. governors). Office: Wilson Elser Moskowitz Edelman & Dicker LLP 23rd Fl 150 E 42nd St New York NY 10017-5639 Office Phone: 212-490-3000 ext. 2517. Office Fax: 212-490-3038. Business E-Mail: aneshm@wemed.com.

ANG, ALFREDO HUA-SING, civil engineering educator; b. Davao, The Philippines, July 4, 1930; came to U.S., 1955; s. Tiong Ang and Khio Tan; m. Myrtle Mae Ang; children: Evelyn, Irene, James. BSCE, Mapua Inst. Tech., Manila, 1954; MS, U. Ill., 1957, Phd, 1959. Registered structural engr., Ill. From asst. prof. to prof. U. Ill., Urbana, 1959-65, prof., 1965-88, U. Calif., Irvine, 1988—. Cons. NRC, Washington, 1979—, Ea. Internat. Engrs., Lafayette, Calif., 1983-90, Internat. Civil Engring Cons., Berkeley, Calif., 1992—; sr. tech. adviser Kajima Corp., Tokyo, 1984—, Tokyo Elec. Power Svcs. Co., 1987—; MCA engr. Mobil Offshore Base. Author: Probability Concepts in Engineering Planning and Design, Vol. I, 1975, Vol. II, 1984; editor Jour. Structural Engring., 1986—; co-editor-in-chief Internat. Jour. Computational Structural Engring., 2000—; mem. editorial bd. Jour. Structural Mechanics, 1971-84, Structural Safety, 1982—, Probabilistic Engring. Mechanics, 1985—, Reliability Engring. and System Safety, 1992—, Internat. Jour. Structural Engring. and Mechanics, 1992—; contbr. numerous articles to profl. jours. Recipient Sr. Rsch. award Am. Soc. Engring. Edn., 1983, Disting. Rsch. award U. Calif.-Irvine Alumni Assn., 1993, Disting. Engring. Alumni award, U. Ill., 2003. Fellow ASME, ASCE (chmn. STD EXCOM, internat. dir. 1998—, rsch. prize 1968, State-of-Art award 1973, Freudenthal medal 1982, Newmark medal 1988, hon. mem. 1991, Ernest Howard award 1996), AIAA (assoc.); mem. NAE, Earthquake Engring. Rsch. Inst., Seismol. Soc. Am., Soc. Naval Architects and Marine Engrs., Internat. Assn. for Structural Safety and Reliability (pres. 1985-89, Rsch. prize 1993). Home: 5311 154th Ave SE Bellevue WA 98006-5151 Office: U Calif Dept Civil Engring Irvine CA 92697-0001 E-mail: ahang2@aol.com.

ANGEL, ARTHUR RONALD, lawyer, consultant; b. Long Beach, Calif., May 10, 1948; s. Morris and Betty Estelle (Unger) A.; 1 child, Jamie Kathryn. BA, U. Calif., Berkeley, 1969; JD, Harvard U., Cambridge, Mass., 1972. Bar: Mass. 1972, DC 1975, Okla. 1979, Calif. 2001, US Dist. Ct. (we. dist.) Okla. 1980, US Dist. Ct. (no. dist.) Okla. 1981, US Dist. Ct. (ctrl. dist.) Calif. 2001, US Supreme Ct. 1983. Atty. FTC, Washington, 1972—78; pvt. practice Oklahoma City, 1978—87; ptnr. Angel & Ikard, Oklahoma City, 1987—93; of counsel Abel, Musser Sokolosky & Assoc., LA, 1994—2000; ptnr. Carrick Law Group, LA, 2001—02; atty. Nagler & Assocs., LA, 2002—04. Mem. adv. panel on cardiovascular devices, Washington, 1979-82; cons. FTC, 1978-79; adminstrv. law judge Okla. Dept. Labor, 1999-2000; spl. mcpl. judge City of Oklahoma City, 1999-2001. Recipient Meritorious Service award FTC, Washington, 1978. Fellow: Inst. Law and Social Scis.; mem.: ATLA, Calif. Bar Assn., DC Bar Assn. Democrat. Jewish. Home: 1305 N Poinsettia Pl Los Angeles CA 90046 Personal E-mail: arthurangel@sbcglobal.net.

ANGEL, AUBIE, endocrinologist, academic administrator; b. Winnipeg, Man., Can., Aug. 28, 1935; m. Esther-Rose Newhouse; children: Jennifer, Jonathan, Suzanne, Steven, Michael. BSc in Medicine, U. Man., 1959, MD, 1959; MSc, McGill U., 1963. Speciality resident in diabetes and endocrinology Montreal Gen. Hosp., 1961-62; postgrad. dept. exptl. medicine McGill U., 1962-63; asst. resident in medicine Royal Victoria Hosp., Montreal, 1963—64; asst. prof. pathology McGill U., Montreal, Que., Canada, 1965-68; staff physician Royal Victoria Hosp., Montreal, 1965-68; sr. physician and staff endocrinologist Toronto Gen. Hosp., 1968-90; asst. prof. medicine U. Toronto, Ont., Canada, 1968-72, assoc. prof., 1972-81, prof. medicine, 1981-90, dir. Inst. Med. Sci. and clin. scis. divsn., 1983-90; prof., head dept. medicine U. Man., Canada, 1991-95, sr. fellow Ctr. for Advancement ofMedicine, 2002—; physician in chief Health Sci. Ctr., Winnipeg, Man., 1991-95. Vis. scientist U. Calif., San Diego, 1977—78, Hammersmith Hosp., London, 1978; founding pres. Diabetes Rsch. and Treatment Ctr., Winnipeg, 1991—; founding pres., chmn. bd. dirs. Friends of CIHR, 1994—; scholar-in-residence MRC, Canada, 1996; pres. 7th Internat. Congress on Obesity, 1994; co-chair Internat. Conf. Diabetes and Cardiovascular Disease, 1999. Editor (with C.H. Hollenberg and D.A.K. Roncari): The Adipocyte and Obesity: Cellular and Molecular Mechanisms, 1983; editor: (with J. Frohlich) Lipoprotein Deficiency Syndromes: Advances in Experimental Medicine and Biology, 1986; editor: (with N. Sakamoto and N. Hotta) New Directions in Research and Clinical Works for Obesity and Diabetes Mellitus, 1991; editor: (with H. Anderson, C. Bouchard, D. Lau, L. Leiter, R. Mendels) Progress in Obesity Research, 1996; editor: (with N. Dhalla, G. Grant, P. Singal) Diabetes and Cardiovascular Disease, 2001. Project dir. Can. Internat. Devel. Agy., Toronto and Costa Rica, 1987-94. Recipient Outstanding Svc. award Heart and Stroke Found. Ont., 1985; U. Toronto Med. Rsch. Coun. scholar, 1965-71; Trinity Coll. fellow, Toronto, 1989—; sr. fellow Massey Coll. U. Toronto, 2005—. Fellow Royal Coll. Physicians and Surgeons Costa Rica (hon.), Royal Coll. Physicians Can., N.Am. Assn. Study Obesity (pres. 1986-87), Can. Soc. Clin. Investigation (councillor 1977-80), Am. Soc. Clin. Investigation, Can. Inst. Acad. Medicine (founding pres. 1990-92), Internat. Assn. Study Obesity (bd. govs. 1986—), Internat. Acad. Cardiovasc. Scis., Juvenile Diabetes Found. Internat. (hon. bd. dirs. 1987-90), Obesity Canada (founding bd. dirs. 1999-2001), Can. Acad. Health Scis. Office: Massey Coll 4 Devonshire Pl Toronto Canada M5S 2E1 Office Phone: 416-506-1597.

ANGEL, CARLOS ALBERTO, pediatric surgeon, urologist; b. Bogota, Colombia, Mar. 16, 1953; arrived in US, 1986; s. Carlos Eduardo and Margarita (De Greiff) A.; m. Claudia Malkun, 1987; children: Santiago, Catalina. BS, Presbyn. Coll., Clinton, SC, 1974; MD, Univ. del Rosario, Bogota, 1980. Resident in gen. surgery U. del Rosario, Bogota, 1983-86; fellow in pediat. surgery U. Tenn., Memphis, 1986-88, chief fellow pediat. surgery, 1988-89, fellow pediat. urology, 1990-91; fellow in pediat. oncologic surgery St. Jude's Children's Rsch. Hosp., Memphis, 1989-90; pediat. surgeon, pediat. urologist U. Tex. Med. Br., Galveston, Tex., 1993—2003; pediat. surgeon, pediat. urologist, assoc. prof. U. Tenn., Knoxville, 2003—. Contbr. articles to profl. jours., chpts. to books. Active vol. colombian Red Cross Surg. Brigades, Chocó, 1985, Meta, 1986. Mem. ACS, Am. Pediat. Surg. Assn., Singleton Surg. Soc., Brit. Assn. Pediat. Surgeons, Internat. Pediat. Endosurgery Group; fellow Am. Coll. Surgeons. Democrat. Roman Catholic. Avocations: tennis, jogging, reading, music, golf. Home Phone: 281-334-0708; Office Phone: 409-772-2308. Business E-Mail: cangel@utmb.edu.

ANGEL, DENNIS, lawyer; b. Bklyn., Feb. 14, 1947; s. Morris and Rosalyn (Sobiloff) A.; m. Linda Marlene Lobel, May 15, 1977; children: Stephanie Lee, Michele Bari, Rebecca Jo. Diplome d'etudes françaises, U. Rouen, France, 1967; BA, St. Lawrence U., 1968; JD, Washington and Lee U., 1972. Cert. pratique de langue française ler Degre U. Rouen, France, 1967; bar: N.Y. 1972, U.S. Dist. Ct. (so. dist.) N.Y. 1977. Assoc. Johnson & Tannenbaum, NYC, 1972-77; sole practice NYC, 1978—. Contbr. articles to profl. jours. With USAR, 1969-75. Mem. ABA (subcommittee chmn. 1977-82), N.Y. State Bar Assn., Copyright Soc. U.S.A., Phi Alpha Delta. Home: 8 High Point Ln Scarsdale NY 10583-3122 Office: 1075 Central Park Ave Ste 306 Scarsdale NY 10583-3232 Office Phone: 914-472-0820. Business E-Mail: dangelesq@aol.com.

ANGEL, JAMES JOSEPH, lawyer; b. Racine, Wis., Apr. 1, 1956; s. William J. and Dorothy P. (Potman) A.; m. Catherine Anne Cowan, Oct. 17, 1981; children: Carter Anne, Riley James, Spenser Catherine. BA, W.Va. Wesleyan Coll., 1977; JD, U. Richmond, 1979. Dep. commonwealth atty. City of Lynchburg (Va.) Commonwealth Atty. Office, 1979-84; ptnr. Smith, Angel & Falcone, P.C., Lynchburg, 1984-87; pvt. practice Lynchburg, 1987—. Former chmn. Boonsboro-Peakland Neighborhood Assn., Lynchburg, 1990—99. Mem. ATLA, Va. Trial Lawyers Assn., Va. Bar Assn., Va. Coll. Criminal Def. Attys., Lynchburg Bar Assn. (past pres. criminal law sect. 1992). Avocations: golf, whitewater rafting. Office: 725 Church St Lynchburg VA 24504-1417 also: Allied Arts Bldg PO Box 1042 Lynchburg VA 24505-1042 Office Phone: 434-845-4551. Office Fax: 434-528-1665. Business E-Mail: james.angel@jjalaw.org.

ANGEL, JAMES ROGER PRIOR, astronomer; b. St. Helens, Eng., Feb. 7, 1941; came to U.S., 1967; s. James Lee and Joan (Prior) A.; m. Ellinor M. Goonan, Aug. 21, 1965; children: Jennifer, James. BA, Oxford U., Eng., 1963, D.Phil., 1967; MS, Calif. Inst. Tech., 1966. From rsch. assoc. to assoc. prof. physics Columbia U., 1967-74; prof. astronomy U. Ariz., 1975—, prof. optical sci., 1984—, Regents prof., 1990—. Sloan fellow, 1970-74; hon. fellow St. Peter's Coll., Oxford U.; MacArthur fellow, 1996. Fellow Royal Soc., Royal Astron. Soc., Am. Acad. Arts and Scis.; mem. NAS, Am. Astron. Soc. (v.p. 1987-90, Pierce prize 1976). Achievements include research on white dwarf stars, quasars, the search for extra-solar planetary systems, astronomical mirrors, telescopes and their instruments, and adaptive optics, concepts to cool the Earth from space and for large scale use of solar energy. Office: Univ Ariz Steward Obs Tucson AZ 85721-0001 Business E-Mail: rangel@as.arizona.edu.

ANGEL, LUIS F., pulmonologist, director; b. Medellin, Antioquia, Colombia, Oct. 7, 1965; s. Emilio Angel and Gloria Amparo Mejia; m. Beatriz E. Escobar, Mar. 12, 1994; children: Sarah Beatriz, Andrea Camila, Carolina Elena. MD, U. Pontificia Boivariana, Colombia, 1986—92. Lic. dr. USMLE, 1994. Dir. lung transplantation uthscsa, San Antonio. Office: Univ Texas Health Sci Ctr 7703 Floyd Curl Dr San Antonio TX 78229 Home Phone: 210-764-0281. Office Fax: 210-567-2877. Business E-Mail: angel@uthscsa.edu.

ANGEL, MARINA, law educator; b. NYC, July 21, 1944; BA, Barnard Coll., NYC, 1965; JD magna cum laude, Columbia U., 1969; LLM, U. Pa., Phila., 1977. Bar: N.Y. 1969, Pa. 1971, U. S. Dist. Ct. (ea. dist.) Pa. 1971, U.S. Dist. Ct. (so. and ea. dists.) N.Y. 1973, U.S. Supreme Ct. 1974. Law clk. NAACP Legal Def. & Edn. Fund; atty. Phila. Voluntary Assn.; assoc. prof. Hofstra U. Law Sch., LI, N.Y., 1971-78; assoc. Gordon & Shectman, PC, NYC, 1973-75; prof. Temple U. Law Sch., Phila., 1979—, assoc. dean grad. legal studies, 1983-84, dir. summer sessions abroad Greece Athens, 1981-83, 85, 87, 89. Vis. prof. Queensland Inst. Tech.and Wollongong U., Australia, 1992, Tel Aviv Univ., 2001, Univ. Puerto Rico, 2002; Stoneman vis. prof. Albany Law Sch., 2006; gen. counsel Modern Greek Studies Assn., 1995—, Greek Am. Women's Network, 1995—; steering com. Temple U. Faculty Senate, 1996-1999. Author of numerous articles in profl. jours.; developed statistics for Pa. Bar Assn. Annual Report Card. Sec. bd. St. George Sr. Housing Corp., Phila., 1980-88; mem. exec. com. Community Legal Svcs., Phila., 1979-88. Named Most Outstanding Prof., Temple Law Sch., Phila., 1989. Mem. ABA (Margaret Brent Women Lawyers of Achievement award 2004), Penn. Bar Assn. (Anne X. Alpern award, 1998, Spl. Achievement award, 2003), Phila. Bar Assn. (Sandra Day O'Connor award 1996, mem Gender Bias Task Force), Assn. of Bar of City of N.Y., Assn. Am. Law Sch. (chair Women in Legal Edn. sect.). Office: Temple U Law Sch 1719 N Broad St Philadelphia PA 19122-6098

ANGEL, STEPHEN F., chemicals executive; b. Sept. 10, 1955; BS Civil Engring., N.C. State U., 1977; MBA, Loyola Coll., Balt., 1989. Engring. & mgmt. positions Gen. Electric, 1979—92, gen. mgr. switchgear bus., 1992—95, gen. mgr. mktg. elec. distribution & control, 1995—96, gen. mgr. mktg. & sales transportation sys., 1996—99, gen. mgr. indsl. sys., 1999—2001; exec. v.p. Praxair Inc., Danbury, Conn., 2001—06, pres., COO, 2006, chmn., pres., CEO, 2007—. Office: Praxair Inc 39 Old Ridgebury Rd Danbury CT 06810*

ANGEL, STEVEN MICHAEL, retired lawyer; b. Frederick, Md., Sept. 19, 1950; s. Charles Robert and Laura Emily (Holland) A.; children: Michael Sean, James Curtis; m. Peggy Whitten, May 4, 1996. BS, U. Md., 1972; MS in Mgmt., U. Md., Lanham, 2007; JD, Okla. City U., 1976; LLM, George Washington U., 1979. Bar: Okla. 1976, Tex. 1979, Tex. 1981. Field atty. NLRB, Balt., 1976-79; supervising trial atty. Fed. Labor Rels. Authority, Dallas, 1979-80; mem. Hughes & Nelson, Oklahoma City and San Antonio, 1980-89; pvt. practice Angel & Assoc., 1984—2003; pres. Human Resources Civil Rights Risk Assessment, LLC, 2003—. Articles editor Oklahoma City U. Law Rev., 1976, 77; contbr. articles to profl. jours. Recipient awards Oklahoma City U., 1975, 76; Spl. Achievement cert. Fed. Labor Rels. Authority, 1980. Mem. ABA, Phi Delta Phi. Democrat. Baptist. Home and Office: 2313 Silverfield Ln Edmond OK 73003-1501 Home Phone: 405-409-0360; Office Phone: 405-285-5101. Personal E-mail: sangel0484@att.net.

ANGELAKIS, MICHAEL J., communications executive; b. Apr. 28, 1964; BS, Babson Coll.; grad., Harvard U. V.p. Mfrs. Hanover Trust Co.; pres., CEO State Cable TV Corp., Aurora Telecomm. LLC; mng. dir. Providence Equity Ptnrs., 1999—2007; dir. Besnan Comm. (Mountain States Cable TV), Metro-Goldwyn-Mayer Inc., Northland Cable Networks, LLC; co-CFO Comcast Corp., 2007—. Office: Comcast Investor Relations 1500 Market St Philadelphia PA 19102*

ANGELES, RODOLFO B., elementary school educator; BS in Elem. Edn., Philippine Normal Coll., 1962, MA, 1966; PhD, U. San Francisco, 1991. Educator Binan Sch. Dist., Laguna, Philippines, 1962-69, Pasadena (Calif.) Unified Sch. Dist., 1969—. Educator Pasadena City Coll., 1980—, Calif. State U., L.A., 1982; adj. faculty Nat. U., L.A., 1998. Author: (children's books) The Enchanted Bird, 1970, Fireflies in the City, 1971. Mem. NEA, Calif. Tchrs. Assn., United Tchrs. Pasadena, Phi Delta Kappa.

ANGELICI, ROBERT J., chemistry educator; b. Rochester, Minn., July 29, 1937; s. Joseph and Alma Marie (Precht) A.; m. Elizabeth Ann Hight, Aug. 13, 1960; children— Scott G., Karen E. BA, St. Olaf Coll., 1959; PhD, Northwestern U., 1962. NSF Postdoctoral fellow U. Munich, 1962-63; instr. chemistry Iowa State U., Ames, 1963-65, asst. prof. chemistry, 1965-68, assoc. prof. chemistry, 1968-71, prof. chemistry, 1971-87, disting. prof. in liberal arts and sciences, 1987—, chair, dept. chemistry, 1977—81. Author: Synthesis and Technique in Inorganic Chemistry, 1977; editor Inorganic Syntheses vol. 28, 1990; contbr. articles to profl. jours. Sloan Found., fellow, Royal Soc. Guest Rsch. Fellow, Eng., 1987; recipient Outstanding Tchr. award Iowa State U., Ames, Gov. of Iowa medal for science teaching, 1989. Mem. Am. Chem. Soc. (chmn. div. inorganic chemistry 1985, award for disting. svc. in the advancement of inorganic chemistry, 2007) Office: Iowa State Univ Dept Chemistry 1605 Gilman Hall Ames IA 50011-3111 Address: 2275 Gilman Hall Ames Lab Iowa State University Ames IA 50011 Office Phone: 515-294-2603. Office Fax: 515-294-0105. Business E-Mail: angelici@iastate.edu.

ANGELILLI, LAWRENCE, construction executive; BA in Econs., Wayne State U., Detroit; MBA, U. Detroit. Fin. analyst City Nat. Bank, Detroit, Am. Natural Resources Corp.; asst. v.p. corp. banking Nat. Bank Detroit, 1981—85; assoc. dir. fin. sales Chrysler Fin. Corp., 1985; asst. treas. Chrysler First Inc.; v.p., treas. NationsCredit Corp. (subs. of NationsBank Corp.), 1994, sr. v.p., treas.; sr. v.p. fin. Centex Corp. Office: Centex Corp PO Box 199000 Dallas TX 75219-9000*

ANGELINI, MARCELLO, performing company executive; b. Naples, Italy, Feb. 11, 1962; Grad., Kiev Inst. Dance, 1980-81. Dancer Maggio Musicale Fiorentino, 1979, soloist, 1981; prin. dancer Deutsche Oper Berlin, 1983-84, No. Ballet Theater, Eng., 1984-87, Ballet West, Salt Lake City, 1988-89, Les Grands Ballets Danadiens, Montreal, 1991-94, Cin. Ballet, 1983-95; artistic dir. Tulsa Ballet, 1995—. Guest prin. dancer San Carlo Opera House, Rome Opera House, the Arena of Verona, Italy, Basler Ballet, Switzerland, English Nat. Ballet, Scottish Ballet, Ballet Ariz., Santiago Teatro Mcpl., Chile. Performer (leading roles in classical repertoire including): Giselle, Sleeping Beauty, Romeo and Juliet, Cinderella; choreographer leading role in Death and the Maiden. Recipient Golden Rose award, Internat. Ballet Competition, Rome, 1982, Leonide Massine Positano prize, 1989, Gov.'s Arts Award, 2002. Office: Tulsa Ballet 4512 S Peoria Ave Tulsa OK 74105-4563*

ANGELINI, MICHAEL P., insurance company executive; BA, Wesleyan U., 1964; JD, Duke U., 1968. Bar: (Mass.) 1968. With Bowditch & Dewey and predecessor firm Bowditch, Gowetz & Lane, 1968—2002, mng. ptnr., 1990—96, chmn., 1997—, Allmerica Fin. Corp., 2002—. Fellow; Am. Coll. Trial Lawyers; mem.: ABA, Worcester County Bar Found., Worcester County Bar Assn. (pres. 1983—84, bd. dirs.). Office: 440 Lincoln St Worcester MA 01653

ANGELINO, MARK E., telecommunications industry executive; BA, Colgate Univ.; MBA, Harvard Univ. Mgmt. positions through v.p. org. transformation IBM, 1979—2001; sr. v.p. ind. sales. & svc. Nextel Communications Inc., 2001—05; pres. bus. solutions Sprint Nextel, Reston, Va., 2005—06, pres. sales & distbn., 2006—. Office: Sprint Nextel 2001 Edmund Halley Dr Reston VA 20191*

ANGELL, KENNETH ANTHONY, bishop; b. Providence, Aug. 3, 1930; s. Henry L. and Mae T. (Cooney) Angell. AB in Philosophy, St. Mary's Sem., Balt., 1952, STB, 1954; STD (hon.), Our Lady of Providence Sem., 1975; JCD (hon.), Providence Coll., 1975; DHL (hon.), St. Michael's Coll., 1999, Salve Regina, 2000. Ordained priest Roman Cath. Ch., 1956, consecrated bishop Roman Cath. Ch., 1974. Vicar St. Mark Ch., Jamestown, RI, 1956; parochial vicar Sacred Heart Ch., Pawtucket, RI, 1956—60; asst. pastor St. Mary Ch., Newport, RI, 1960—68; asst. chancellor and sec. to bishop Diocese of Providence, 1968—72, chancellor, 1972—74, titular bishop Settimunicia, aux. bishop, 1974—92; pastor St. John Ch., Providence, 1975—81; bishop Diocese of Burlington (Vt.), 1992—. Trustee Wadhams Hall Sem. Coll., 1995—2002, Champlain Coll., 1995—98; v.p. Vt. Ecumenical Coun. & Bible Soc., 1997—99, pres., 1999—2000; bd. dirs. Sr. Thea Bowman Black Cath. Ednl. Fund, 1995—99. Mem.: U.S. Cath. Conf., Nat. Conf. Cath. Bishops. Roman Catholic. Office: Diocese of Burlington 351 North Ave PO Box 489 Burlington VT 05402-0526

ANGELL, LOIS LOUISE, writer, actor, comedienne, poet; b. Riceville, Iowa; d. Kenneth Edwin and Marie E. (Dynes) A.; 1 child, Jim Barrett. Student, Am. U., 1959—60, student, 1962—63, U. Alta., 1978. Staff dir. Justice Rehnquist U.S. Supreme Ct., Washington, 1971-80; pub. rels. dir. Better Comm. Found., Silver Spring, Md., 1984; freelance writer and performer Arlington, Va. Numerous appearances on talk and news shows; spkr. Washington's Angell; invited to read poetry under aegis of Dept. of State, Budapest and China. Performer at comedy and supper clubs, radio and TV. Bd. dirs. Accokeck Pub. Libr., Md. Recipient Spl. Achievement award U.S. Dept. Justice, 1971, Outstanding Svc. to the Arts in Comm. award Capitol Hill Arts Workshop, 1984 Mem. NAFE, Washington Ind. Writers, The Capitol Hill Club, Internat. Platform Assn., Capitol Hill Poetry Group (founder), Nat. Conf. Rsch. on Women, Nat. Capitol Spkrs. Assn., Washington Conv. and Visitors Assn., World Affairs Coun., The Cato Inst. Episcopalian. Home: The Georgetown 2512 Q St NW 314 Washington DC 20007-4310 Home Phone: 202-965-5568; Office Phone: 202-965-5568.

ANGELL, MARY FAITH, federal magistrate judge; b. Buffalo, May 7, 1938; d. San S. and Marie B. (Caboni) A.; m. Kenneth F. Carobus, Oct. 27, 1973; children: Andrew M. Carobus, Alexander P. Carobus. AB, Mt. Holyoke Coll.; MSS, Bryn Mawr Coll.; JD, Temple U. Bar: Pa. 1971, U.S. Dist. Ct. (ea. dist) Pa. 1971, U.S. Ct. Appeals (3rd cir.) Pa. 1974, U.S. Supreme Ct. 1979; Acad. Cert. Social Workers. Dir. social work, vol. svcs. Wills Eye Hosp., Phila., 1961-64, 65-69; dir. soc. work dept. juvenile divsn. Defender Assoc., Phila., 1969-71; asst. dist. atty. City of Phila., 1971-72; asst. atty. gen. Commonwealth of Pa., Phila., 1972-74, deputy atty. gen., 1974-78; regional counsel ICC, Phila., 1978-80, regional dir., 1980-88; adminstrv. law judge Social Security Adminstrn., Phila., 1988-90; U.S. magistrate judge U.S. Dist. Ct. (ea. dist.) Pa., Phila., 1990—2004, chief U.S. magistrate judge, 2004—. Adj. prof. Temple U. Law Sch., Phila., 1976-94, clin. instr., 1973-76; co-chmn. Commn. on Gender, 3d Cir. Task Force on Equal Treatment in Cts., 1994—99; mem. com. on racial and gender bias in the justice sys. Supreme Ct. of Pa., 2000-02; bd. adv. Grad. Sch. Social Work and Social Rsch. Bryn Mawr Coll., 2004. Federal trustee Defender Assn. Phila., 1985-90; bd. dirs. Child Welfare Adv. Bd., Phila., 1984-90, Federal Cts. 200 Adv. Bd., Phila., 1987-88, Phila. Woman's Network, 1986-88. Recipient Sr. Exec. Svc. award U.S. Govt., 1980. Mem. NASW, FBA (chair exec. com., pres. 1990-92, recognition 1992), Nat. Assn. Women Judges, Fed. Magistrate Judges Assn. (dist. dir. 1994-98), Phila. Bar Assn. (chmn. com. 1976-77), Temple Am. Inn of Cts. (master 1993-98), Third Circuit Task Force on Equal Treatment in the Courts (co-chair Commn. on Gender 1994-97), Temple Law Alumni Exec. Bd. (Women's Law Caucus Honoree 1996). Office: US District Court 601 Market St 3030 US Courthouse Philadelphia PA 19106 Office Phone: 215-597-6079. Business E-Mail: chambers_of_chief_magistrate_judge_m_faith_angell@paed.uscourts.gov.

ANGELL, ROGER, writer, magazine editor; b. NYC, Sept. 19, 1920; s. Ernest and Katharine Shepley (Sergeant) A.; m. Evelyn Ames Baker, Oct. 1942 (div. 1963); children— Caroline S., Alice; m. Carol Rogge, Oct. 1963; 1 child, John Henry. Grad., Pomfret Sch., 1938; AB, Harvard, 1942. Editor, writer Mag. X, Curtis Pub. Co., 1946-47; sr. editor Holiday mag., 1947-56; fiction editor, gen. contbr. New Yorker mag., N.Y.C., 1956— Author: The Stone Arbor, 1961, A Day in the Life of Roger Angell, 1971, The Summer Game, 1972, Five Seasons, 1977, Late Innings, 1982, Season Ticket, 1988, Once More Around the Park, 1991, A Pitcher's Story: Innings with David Cone, 2001, Game Time, 2003, Let Me Finish, 2006; editor: Nothing But You: Love Stories from the New Yorker, 1997. Served with USAAF, 1942-46, PTO. Recipient George Polk award for commentary, 1981, Authors Guild award for disting. svc. to Am. Letters, 2000. Mem. Authors Guild (nat. council, v.p.), Authors League (nat. council), PEN Clubs: Century Assn., Coffee House; fellow, Am. Acad. Arts & Scis. Office: New Yorker Mag 4 Times Sq New York NY 10036-6561*

ANGELL, STEPHEN W., religious studies educator; s. Stephen LeRoy Angell and Barbara Allee; m. Sandra Ward, May 26, 1984. BA in Math., Boston U., 1974; MA in Quaker Faith and History, Earlham Sch. Religion, Richmond, Ind., 1982; PhD in History of Christianity, Vanderbilt U., Nashville, 1988. Prof. religious studies Fla. A & M U., Tallahassee, 1990—2001; Leatherock prof. Quaker studies Earlham Sch. Religion, Richmond, 2001—. Clk. Southeastern Yearly Meeting Religious Soc. Friends, Melbourne Beach, Fla., 1999—2001; series editor African-Am. religious history U. Press Fla., Gainesville, 2001—; trustee Pendle Hill, Wallingford, Pa., 2006—. Editor: (anthology) The Quaker Bible Reader, Social Protest Thought in the African Methodist Episcopal Church; author: (monograph) Bishop Henry McNeal Turner and African-American Religion in the South. Mem.: Am. Acad. Religion (chair Afro-Am. religious history group 1997—2000, mem. steering com. Afro-Am. religious history group 2005—). Quaker. Avocation: sacred harp singing. Office: Earlham School Religion 228 College Ave Richmond IN 47374 Home Phone: 765-962-0168; Office Phone: 765-983-1496. Business E-Mail: angelst@earlham.edu.

ANGELL, TONY, artist, writer; b. LA, Nov. 15, 1940; s. Frank Angell and Florence Brown; m. Elizabeth Rolfe, June 1, 1991; children: Gavia, Larka;children from previous marriage: Gilia, Bryony. BA, MA, U. Wash., Seattle. Profl. artist at CC and high schs., 1966—; instr. U. Wash., Seattle, 1980—2002. Author, illustrator: Birds of Prey, 1972 (Wash. State Author award Best Book), Ravens, Crows, Magpies and Jays, 1978 (Wash. State Author award Best Book), Blackbirds of the Americas, 1986 (Wash. State Author award Best Book), In the Company of Crows and Ravens, 2005 (Wash. State Best Book award, 2006, Victoria and Albert Mus. Overall Illustration award, 2006); sculpture, Ascending Eagles, Quest Comm., Emmissaries, Sleeping Lady Conf. Ctr., Leavenworth, Prix De West, Oklahoma City No. West Art, 2003. Chmn. visual arts com. King County Arts Commn., Seattle, 1980—86. Named a Master Artist, Leigh Yawkey Woodson Art Mus., 2001; recipient Golden Oakleaf award, Nature Conservatory, 1976, 501 Finestone award, SUNY Stonybrook, 1976, Bloedel fellow award, 1994. Fellow: Nat. Sculpture Soc.; mem.: Nature Conservancy (bd. mem. Wash. state chpt. 1974—2004, chair Wash. state chpt. 1976—78, Golden Acorn award 1976). Independent. Mailing: 18237 40th St NE Lake Forest Park WA 98155-4205

ANGELO, E. JOANNE, child, adolescent and adult psychiatrist; b. Boston, Feb. 11, 1936; d. Gaspar and Eda (Polcari) A. AB, Mt. Holyoke Coll., 1957; MD, Tufts U., 1961. Diplomate Am. Bd. Psychiatry and Neurology, 1972. Med. dir. Canarsie Mental Health Ctr., Bklyn., 1967—69; staff psychiatrist Cmty. Mental Health Svcs., Mass. Mental Health Ctr., Boston, 1969—73; psychiat. dir. Laboure Ctr., South Boston, Mass., 1974—78; pvt. practice Boston, 1969—. Cons. Chandler Sch. for Women, Boston, 1971-72, Kennedy Meml. Hosp., Boston, 1971-72, St. Margaret's Hosp., Boston, 1976-83, North Suffolk Health Ctr., Boston,

1978-79; mem. staff St. Elizabeth's Hosp., Boston, Good Samaritan Hospice Boston, 1985-1990. Mem. editl. bd. (Jour.) Nat. Cath. Bioethics Quar. Mem. Pontifical Acad. for Life (corr.). Office: 403 Commonwealth Ave Boston MA 02215-2326 Office Phone: 617-266-3093. E-mail: joanneangelo@massmed.org.

ANGELOFF, DANN VALENTINO, brokerage house executive; b. Hollywood, Calif., Nov. 15, 1935; m. Jo Jeanne Ahlstrom, Sept. 26, 1964; children: Jennifer J., Dann V., Julie A. BS in Fin., U. So. Calif., 1958, MBA, 1963. Trainee Dean Witter & Co., Inc., LA, 1957-60; v.p. Dempsey-Tegeler & Co., Inc., LA, 1960-70; mng. dir. West Coast corp. fin. dept. Reynolds Securities, Inc., LA, 1970-76; pres., bd. dirs. The Angeloff Co., LA, 1976—. Bd. dirs. Softbrands Inc., Mpls., Bjurman Barry Funds, Inc., Century City, Calif., Electronic Recyclers Internat., Fresno, Calif., Pub. Storage, Glendale, Calif., Nicholas-Applegate Fund, San Diego; chmn. bd. Marshall Ptnrs./U. So. Calif.; bd. dirs. Marshall Bd. Leaders, U. So. Calif. Trustee U. So. Calif., 1979-86, univ. counselor; bd. dirs., chmn. Trojan Bd. Govs., 1990-92. Mem. Bond Club LA, Commerce Assocs. U. So. Calif., Skull and Dagger, Cardinal and Gold, Calif. Club, Pacific Club, Valley Hunt Club, San Marino City Club, Kappa Beta Phi. Office: The Angeloff Co 626 Wilshire Blvd Ste 727 Los Angeles CA 90017

ANGELOS, PETER G., professional sports team executive, lawyer; b. Pitts., July 4, 1929; LLB, U. Balt. Bar: Md. 1961, D.C. 1974, Tenn. 1990, U.S. Dist. Ct. Md. 1964, U.S. Supreme Ct. 1974, U.S. Tax Ct. 1975, U.S. Ct. Appeals 1990. Pvt. practice atty., Balt., 1961—; mng. ptnr. Baltimore Orioles, 1993—; chmn., CEO Balt. Orioles, 1993—. Mem. Balt. City Coun., 1959—63; trustee Loyola Coll., Md. Mem.: Bar Assn. Balt. City, Tenn. Bar Assn., Md. Trial Lawyers Assn., Md. Trial Lawyers Assn., N.Y. State Trial Lawyers Assn., Criminal Def. Lawyers Assn., Assn. Trial Lawyers Am., Am. Judicature Soc. Office: 100 N Charles St # 22D Baltimore MD 21201-3805 also: Baltimore Orioles 333 W Camden St Baltimore MD 21201-2435*

ANGELOU, MAYA (MARGUERITE ANNIE JOHNSON), writer, actress; b. St. Louis, Apr. 4, 1928; d. Bailey and Vivian (Baxter) Johnson; m. Tosh Angelos, 1950, (div. 1952); m. Vusumzi Make, 1960 (div. 1963), m. Paul Du Feu, 1973 (div. 1981), 1 child Guy Johnson. Studied dance with, Pearl Primus, NYC; degrees (hon.), Smith Coll., 1975, Mills Coll., 1975, Lawrence U., 1976, Portland State U., 1973, Occidental Coll., 1979, Atlanta U., 1980, U. Ark., 1980, U. Minn., 1980, Austin Coll., 1980, Wheaton Coll., 1981, Kean Coll., 1982, Spelman Coll., 1983, Boston Coll., 1983, Winston-Salem U, 1984, U. Brunesis, 1984, Howard U., 1985, Tufts U., 1985, Va. Commonwealth U., 1985, Northeastern U., 1992, Academy of Southern Arts & Letters, 1993, Brown U., 1994, U. Durham, UK, 1995, Hope Coll., 2001, Columbia U., 2003, Eastern Conn. U., 2003. Taught modern dance The Rome Opera House and Hambina Theatre, Tel Aviv; writer-in-residence U. Kans., Lawrence, 1970; disting. vis. prof. Wake Forest U., 1974-, Wichita State U., 1974, Calif. State U., Sacramento, 1974; apptd. mem. Am. Revolution Bicentennial Council by Pres. Ford, 1975-76; 1st Reynolds prof. Am. Studies, Wake Forest U, 1981-, a lifetime appointment. Author: I Know Why the Caged Bird Sings, 1970, Just Give Me A Cool Drink of Water 'Fore I Die, 1971, Georgia, Georgia, 1972, Gather Together in My Name, 1974, Oh Pray My Wings are Gonna Fit Me Well, 1975, Singin' and Swingin' and Gettin' Merry Like Christmas, 1976, And Still I Rise, 1978, The Heart of a Woman, 1981, Shaker, Why Don't You Sing?, 1983, All God's Children Need Traveling Shoes, 1986, Now Sheba Sings the Song, 1987, I Shall Not Be Moved, 1990, On the Pulse of Morning: The Inaugural Poem, 1993, Lessons in Living, 1993, Wouldn't Take Nothing for My Journey Now, 1993, My Painted House, My Friendly Chicken, and Me, 1994, The Complete Collected Poems of Maya Angelou, 1994, Phenomenal Women: Four Poems for Women, 1995, A Brave and Startling Truth, 1995, From a Black Woman to a Black Man, 1996, Kofi and His Magic, 1996, Extravagant Spirits, 1997, Making Magic in the World, 1998, Even the Stars Look Lonesome, 1997, A Song Flung Up To Heaven, 2002, Angelina of Italy, 2004, Amazing Peace, 2006 (winner of The Quill award for Poetry, 2006), Celebrations: Rituals of Peace and Prayer (NAACP Image award for poetry, 2007); (cookbooks) Hallelujah! The Welcome Table: A Lifetime of Memories with Recipes, 2004; (plays) Cabaret for Freedom, 1960, The Least of These, 1966, Gettin' Up Stayed On My Mind, 1967, Ajax, 1974, Moon On a Rainbow Shawl, 1988; (screenplays) Georgia, Georgia, 1972, All Day Long, 1974; author/prodr. Three Way Choice, Afro-American in the Arts (Golden Eagle award); wrote and presented Trying to Make it Home, 1988; writer for Oprah Winfrey's Harpo Prodns.; poetry writer for film Poetic Justice, 1993; appeared in plays: Porgy and Bess, 1954-55 (Europe), 1957 (U.S.), Calypso, 1957, The Blacks, 1960, Mother Courage, 1964, Medea, Look Away, 1973, Ajax, 1974, And Still I Rise, 1976, Moon on a Rainbow Shawl, 1988; (films) Porgy and Bess, 1959, Poetic Justice, 1993, How to Make an American Quilt, 1995, The Journey of August King, 1995, Madea's Family Reunion, 2006; dir. (films) Down in the Delta, 1998; (TV minseries) Roots, 1977 (Emmy Nom. best sup. actress), TV appearances include The Richard Pryor Special, Sister, Sisters, 1982, There Are No Children Here, 1993, Touched By An Angel, 1995, Moesha, 1999, Runaway, 2000; spoken word albums include The Poetry of Maya Angelou, 1969, Women in Business, 1981, Been Found, 1996; contbd. articles, short stories, poems to Black Scholar, Chgo. Daily News, Cosmopolitan, Harper's Bazaar, Life Mag., Redbook, Sunday N.Y. Times, Mademoiselle Mag., Essence, Ebony Mag., Calif. Living Mag, Ghanaian Times. Apptd. by Dr. Martin Luther King Jr. No. Coord., SCLC, 1959-60, apptd. by Pres. Ford to Bicentennal Commn., by Pres. Carter to Nat. Commn. on Observance of Internat. Women's Yr., ambassador, Unicef Internat., 1996. Chubb fellowship award Yale U., 1970, named Woman of Yr. in Comm., 1976; Ladies Home Jour. Top 100 Most Influential Women, 1983, The Matrix award, 1983, Living Legacy award, Women's Internat. Ctr., 1986, The North Carolina Award in Lit., 1987, Woman of the Yr. Essence Mag., 1992, Disting. Woman of NC, 1992, Horatio Alger award, 1992, Grammy award best spoken word or non-traditional album, 1994 (for recording of "On the Pulse of the Morning"), Grammy award best spoken or non-traditional album, 1994 (for recording of "Phenomonal Woman"); NAACP Image Award for Outstanding Literary Work for "Even the Stars Look Lonesome", 1997, National Medal of Art, 2001; inducted into the Women's Hall of Fame, 1998; named one of Most Influential Black Americans, Ebony mag., 2006; named to The Ebony Power 150, Ebony mag., 2007. Mem. AFTRA, Dirs. Guild Am., Equity, Harlem Writers Guild, Am. Film Inst. (trustee), Women's Prison Assn., Horatio Alger Assn. Dist. Americans, Nat. Soc. Prevention of Cruelty to Children (Maya Angelou Ctr. opened 1992), W.E.B. duBois Found., Nat. Soc. Collegiate Scholars, Nat. Soc. High School Scholars. Office: c/o Dave La Camera Lordly and Dame Inc 51 Church St Boston MA 02116-5417*

ANGEL-URDINOLA, DIEGO FERNANDO, economist; b. Bogota, Colombia, Dec. 27, 1974; s. Diego Angel-Duran and Luz Maria Urdinola-Mejia; m. Angela Maria Hoyos, June 29, 2001; 1 child, Sebastian Angel. PhD, Georgetown U., Washington, 2003. Economist World Bank, Washington, 1999—2007. Cons. Georgetown U., 2002—03. Contbr. articles to profl. jours.; singer: (concert) Grupo Habana. Candidate Consevative Party, Colombia, 2002; internat. evangelistic team United Ministries, Falls Church, Va., 2007—07. Fellow, Georgetown U., 1999—2003. Mem.: Colombian-Am. C. of C. (pres. 2003—04). Conservative. Home: 42451 Longacre Dr Chantilly VA 20152 Office: The World Bank Group 1818 H Street NW Washington DC 20433 Home Phone: 202-473-4161; Office Phone: 202-473-4161. Office Fax: 202-614-4161; Home Fax: 202-614-4161. Business E-Mail: dangelurdinola@worldbank.org.

ANGER, PAUL, newspaper editor; m. Vickie Dahlman-Anger. Graduate, Univ. Wis., Oshkosh. Sports copy editor, page designer Miami Herald, 1972—77, sports editor, 1977—95, page 1A duty officer, 1989—95, Broward editor Hollywood, Fla., 1995—98, v.p., pub., Broward edition, 1998—2001; v.p., editor Des Moines Register, Iowa, 2002—05; Washington bur. news editor Knight Ridder, 2001; editor Detroit Free Press, 2005—. Office: Detroit Free Press 600 W Fort St Detroit MI 48226 Office Phone: 313-222-6606.*

ANGERS, WINSTON THOMAS, lawyer, publishing executive; b. Franklin, La., June 21, 1952; s. Robert John, Jr. and Geraldine Beaulieu Angers; 1 child, Austen John. BA in Polit. Sci. cum laude, U. La., 1974; JD, La. State U., 1976. Bar: La. 1977. Rsch. asst. Inst. for Civil Law Studies La. State U. Law Ctr., Baton Rouge, 1975—76; law clk. 15th Jud. Dist. Ct., New Iberia, La., 1976—77; pvt. practice Lafayette, La., 1977—; pres. Beau Bayou Pub. Co., Lafayette, 1985—. Author: Cajun Cuisine, 1986; editor: History of the Louisiana Society of the Sons of the American Revolution, 1997; contbr. articles to mags.; co-author: My Wars: Nazis, Mobsters, Gambling and Corruption: Colonel Francis C. Greuemberg Remembers, 2004. Bd. dirs. Coun. Devel. of French in La.; past chmn. bd. zoning adjustments City of Lafayette; pres. Acadiana Arts Coun., Lafayette, 1990—91; co-founder Citizens of S. Lafayette; pres. Attakapas chpt. SAR, 1994; pres. Acadian Civitan Club, Lafayette, 1997—98; del.-attendee Young Rep. Nat. Fedn. Conv., 1971; alt. del. Rep. Nat. Conv., Dallas, 1984, del. Houston, 1992, 7th district elector for pres. La., 2004; past chmn. by laws com. La. Rep. State Ctrl. Com.; chmn. Lafayette Parish Rep. Exec. Com., 1995—96; past chmn. Lafayette Parish Rep. Polit. Action Coun.; del. numerous state convs. La. Rep. Party; chair U. La. at Lafayette Coll. Reps., 1971—72. Recipient Bronze Good Citizenship medal, Attakapas Chpt. SAR, 1992, Oak Leaf Cluster, 1993, Meritorious Svc. medal, 1994, Oak Leaf Cluster, 1995, Oak Leaf Cluster for Meritorious Svc. medal, La. Soc. SAR, 1996. Mem.: La. State Bar Assn. (governing coun. arts, entertainment and sports sect.), Rotary Internat., Phi Eta Sigma, Phi Delta Phi. Republican. Avocation: collecting rare documents and political memorabilia. Home: 116 Teche Dr Lafayette LA 70503 Office: 304 Audubon Blvd Lafayette LA 70503 Office Phone: 337-233-3268. Personal E-mail: tomangers@cox.net.

ANGHELESCU, DORALINA LUCIA, anesthesiologist; b. Bucharest, Romania, Aug. 1, 1961; d. Liviu Veneriu and Aurelia Niculina (Arseni) Gontea; m. Mircea Vladimir Anghelescu, June 6, 1987 (div. July 1991); 1 child, Andrei. MD, Bucharest Sch. Medicine, 1985. Intern Elias Found. Hosp., Bucharest, 1985—87; staff physician in anesthesiology Inst. Endocrinology, Bucharest, 1987—93; resident in anesthesiology U. N.Mex., Albuquerque, 1993—97, fellow in pain mgmt., 1998—99; fellow in pediat. anesthesia Childrens Nat. Med. Ctr., Washington, 1997—98; pediat. anesthesiologist, dir. pain mgmt. svc. St. Jude Children's Rsch. Hosp., Memphis, 1999—. Co-author: The Pain Clinic Manual, 2d edit., 2000; contbr. articles to profl. jours. Grantee, Jenssen Found., 2001. Mem.: Internat. Assn. for the Study Pain, Am. Acad. Pain, Soc. Pediat. Anesthesia, Am. Soc. Anesthesiologists. Office: St Jude Childrens Rsch Hosp 332 N Lauderdale St Memphis TN 38105 Office Phone: 901-495-4034. Business E-Mail: doralina.anghelescu@stjude.org.

ANGIER, NATALIE MARIE, science journalist; b. NYC, Feb. 16, 1958; d. Keith and Adele Bernice (Rosenthal) A.; m. Richard Steven Weiss, July 27, 1991. Student, U. Mich., 1974-76; BA, Barnard Coll., 1978. Staff writer Discover Mag., NYC, 1980-83, Time Mag., NYC, 1984-86; editor Savvy Mag., NYC, 1983-84; journalism educator NYU, NYC, 1987-89; became reporter NY Times, NYC, 1990, now science correspondent Washington. Author: Natural Obsessions, 1988, The Beauty of the Beastly, 1995. Recipient Pulitzer Prize for beat reporting, 1991, Journalism award GM Ind. Bd., 1991, Lewis Thomas award Marine Biol. Labs., 1990, Journalism award AAAS, 1992, Disting. Alumna award Barnard Coll., 1993. Mem. Nat. Assn. Sci. Writers. Avocation: weightlifting. Office: NY Times Washington Bureau 1627 I St NW Fl 7 Washington DC 20006-4007

ANGINO, ERNEST EDWARD, retired geology and engineering educator; b. Winsted, Conn., Feb. 16, 1932; s. Alfred and Filomena Mabel (Serluco) A.; m. Margaret Mary Lachat, June 26, 1954; children— Cheryl Ann, Kimberly Ann. BS in Mining Engring., Lehigh U., Bethlehem, Pa., 1954; MS in Geology, U. Kans., 1958, PhD in Geology, 1961. Instr. geology U. Kans., Lawrence, 1961-62, prof. civil engring., 1971-99, prof. geology, 1972-99, prof. emeritus, 1999—, chmn. dept. geology, 1972-86, dir. water resources ctr., 1990-99; asst. prof. Tex. A&M U., College Station, 1962-65; chief geochemist Kans. Geol. Survey, Lawrence, 1965-70, assoc. state geologist, 1970-72. Cons. on water chemistry and pollution to various cos. and govt. agys. including Dow Chem. Co., Ocean Mining Inc., Envicon, Oak Ridge Lab., Fisheries Rsch. Bd. Can., Midwest Rsch. Inst., Coast and Geodetic Survey, U.S. Geol. Survey. Author: (with G.K. Billings) Atomic Absorption Spectrometry in Geology, 1967; author, editor: (with D.T. Long) Geochemistry of Bismuth, 1979; editor: (with R.K. Hardy) Proc. 3d Forum Geol. Industrial Minerals, 1967, (with G.K. Billings) Geochemistry Subsurface Brines, 1969; contbr. more than 125 articles to sci. and profl. jours. Sec. Geochem. Soc., 1970-76; mem. Lawrence City Police Rels. Commn., 1970-76, Lawrence City Commn., 1983-87, mayor, 1984-85; pres. Soc. Environ. Geochemistry and Health, 1978-79; treas. Internat. Assn. Geochemistry and Cosmochemistry, 1980-94; mem. Lawrence 2020 Planning Commn., 1992-94, Police Adv. Coun., 1994-06, Crimestoppers Bd., 1994-03, Lawrence Tax Abatement Commn., 2001-02, Lawrence-Douglas County Planning Commn. 2002-05, Health Care Access Bd., 1997-02, Lawrence-Douglas County Econ. Devel. Commn., 2006—. With U.S. Army, 1955-57. NSF fellow Oak Ridge Lab., 1963; recipient Antarctic Service medal Dept. Def., 1969; Angino Buttress in Antarctica named in his honor, 1967. Mem. Am. Philatelist Soc., Meter Stamp Soc., Forum Club (Factotum 1978-79), Rotary (pres. 1993-95). Republican. Roman Catholic. Avocations: philately, Western history, Indian lore. Home: 4605 Grove Dr Lawrence KS 66049-3777 Office: U Kans Dept Geology Lindley 120 1475 Jayhawk Blvd Lawrence KS 66045-0001 Personal E-mail: rockdoc@sunflower.com. *Knowledge is what really counts. The world does not owe anyone anything!.*

ANGINO, RICHARD CARMEN, lawyer; b. McKeesport, Pa., May 2, 1940; s. Carmen and Filomena (Lombardi) A.; m. Alice K. Angino, May 2, 1976; children: Elizabeth, Richard, William. BA in English, Franklin and Marshall Coll., Lancaster, Pa., 1958-62; JD, Villanova Law Sch., Pa., 1965. Bar: Pa. 1965, U.S. Supreme Ct. 1968, U.S. Ct. Appeals (3rd cir.) 1975, U.S. Dist. Ct. (ea. and cen. dist.) 1966. Pres., civil litigation specialist Angino & Rovner PC, Harrisburg, Pa., 1965—. Pres. Pa. Trial Lawyers Assn., Pa., 1982-83. Co-author: The Pennsylvania No-Fault Motor Vehicle Insurance Act, 1979, Pennsylvania Personal Injury Evidence, 1990. Pres. Leukemia Soc. Am., Ctrl. Pa., 1989-92; v.p. Am. Horticulture Soc., Alexandria. Va., 1990-92, Friends of Wildwood, Harrisburg, Pa., 1989-96; assoc. trustee Franklin and Marshall, 1979—; bd. cons. Villanova Univ. Sch. Law, 1994—, govs. residence preservation com., 1997-2002. Mem. Internat. Soc. Barristers, Dauphin County Bar Assn., Pa. Bar Assn., Pa. Trial Lawyers Assn., Am. Assn. for Justice. Republican. Roman Catholic. Avocation: horticulture. Home: 2040 Fishing Creek Valley Rd Harrisburg PA 17112-9245 Office: Angino & Rovner PC 4503 N Front St Harrisburg PA 17110-1799 Office Phone: 717-238-6791. Business E-Mail: rca@angino-rovner.com.

ANGIONE, HOWARD FRANCIS, lawyer, retired editor; b. NYC, Aug. 3, 1940; s. Charles Francis Angione and Genevieve Rita (McCarthy) A.; m. Maryann Allgaier, June 24, 1971; children: Charles Francis, Mary Christine, Kathleen Elizabeth. BA in History, Holy Cross Coll., 1962; MA in Internat. Relations, Clark U., 1966; JD cum laude, St. John's U., Jamaica, NY, 1989. Bar: Conn. 1989, N.Y. 1990, D.C. 1991. Reporter, sci. writer Worcester Telegram, Mass., 1961-65; writer, day editor, sci. writer AP, Boston, 1965-69, editor, shift supr. Gen. Desk NYC, 1969-77; tech. editor N.Y. Times, 1977-87; assoc. Weil, Gotshal & Manges, NYC, 1989-93; pvt. practice, 1997—. Pub. N.Y. Region Lawyers Coop. Practice Guides, 1993-96; editor AP Stylebook, 1977; editor-in-chief N.Y. State Bar Jour., 1998—2004. Sec. Class of 1962 Holy Cross Coll., 1966-80. Mem.: NY State Bar Assn. (mem. exec. com. Elder Law sect., mem. exec. com. Trusts and Estates sect.). Roman Catholic. Home and Office: 80-47 192d St Jamaica NY 11423-1042 Office Phone: 718-468-7700. Personal E-mail: angione@att.net. Business E-Mail: angione@nyelderlaw.com.

ANGLAND, JOSEPH, lawyer; b. NYC, Sept. 1, 1949; s. Patrick and Josephine (Woods) A.; m. Ida Wolff, Aug. 4, 1984. BS, MIT, 1972; JD, Harvard U., 1975. Bar: N.Y. 1977, D.C. 1988, U.S. Dist. Ct. (so. and ea. dists.) N.Y. 1978, U.S. Ct. Claims 1983, U.S. Tax Ct. 1985, U.S. Ct. Appeals (2d cir.) 1982, U.S. Ct. Appeals (D.C. cir.) 1988, U.S. Dist. Ct. D.C. 1988, U.S. Ct. Appeals (3d cir.) 1990, U.S. Ct. Appeals (D.C. cir.) 1992, U.S. Ct. Appeals (5th cir.) 1993, U.S. Ct. Appeals (7th cir.) 1993, U.S. Supreme Ct. 1990. Law clk. to presiding justice Calif. Supreme Ct., San Francisco, 1975-76; assoc. Dewey, Ballantine, Bushby, Palmer & Wood, NYC, 1976-83; ptnr. Dewey Ballantine, NYC, 1984—2005; shareholder Heller Ehrman LLP, NYC, 2005—. Bd. dirs. Legal Aid Soc., 1993—2001. Chmn. editl. bd. Antitrust Law Devel. Mem. ABA (chmn. antitrust sect.), NY State Bar Assn., Assn. of Bar of City of NY(com. on antitrust and trade regulation). Home: 292 Stanwich Rd Greenwich CT 06830-3528 Office: Heller Ehrman LLP 7 Times Square New York NY 10036-6524 Office Phone: 212-847-8730. Business E-Mail: joseph.angland@hellerehrman.com.

ANGLE, COLIN, electrical engineer, robotic company executive; BSEE, MIT, MS in Computer Sci. Co-founder ISRobotics (now iRobot Corp.), Burlington, Mass., 1990—; CEO iRobot Corp., Burlington, Mass. Named (with Helen Greiner) Ernst and Young New England Entrpreneur of Yr., 2003; recipient DEMO God award, IDG Exec. Forum, 2001. Achievements include pioneer in the field of mobile robots, designing the behavior-controlled rovers for NASA that led to the Sojourner exploring Mars in 1997. Office: iRobot Corp 63 South Ave Burlington MA 01803 Office Phone: 781-345-0200. Office Fax: 781-345-0201.

ANGLIN, LINDA MCCLUNEY, retired elementary school educator; b. Turrell, Ark., Apr. 20, 1929; d. Denton Sims and Helen Louise (Davis) McCluney; m. Joe Van Anglin, Aug. 30, 1952; children: Van, Cheryl, Dent, George. BA magna cum laude, Millsaps Coll., Jackson, Miss., 1951; MEd, Miss. Coll., Clinton, 1970; Edn. Specialist, Miss. State U., Starkville, 1974. Cert. tchr., Miss. Tchr. St. Andrew's Episcopal. Sch., Jackson, Miss., 1952-53, Carthage Elem. Sch., 1956-57, Jackson Pub. Schs., 1957-94. Founder Miss. Profl. Educators, 1979, pres., 1979-82; dir. Pub. Edn. Forum Miss., Jackson, 1989-93; classroom cons. Scholastic Tchr.; bd. dirs. 1st Am. Bank, Jackson. Lobbyist for edn. and children's issues State of Miss., 1980—; charter mem. Jackson Assn. for Children with Learning Disabilities, bd. dirs., historian, mem. adv. bd. Miss. chpt.; active many civic groups. Recipient Book of Golden Deeds award Exch. Club North Jackson, 1989, Disting. Tchr. award White House Commn. Presdl. Scholars, 1996. Mem. Jackson Profl. Educators (pres. 1988-90), Jackson Area Reading Coun. (pres. 1975-76, Outstanding Svc. award 1987), Miss. Hist. Soc. (bd. dirs. 1998-2000), Jackson-Hinds Ret. Tchrs. Assn., Miss. Ret. Tchrs. Assn., Sigma Lambda, Kappa Delta Pi, Phi Kappa Phi, Delta Kappa Gamma (workshop presenter 1985, pres. Tau chpt. 1986-88, Woman of Distinction 1990, Disting. Svc. to Edn. award 1984). Methodist. Avocations: volunteer activities, church activities, reading. Home: 4164 Crestview Pl Jackson MS 39211

ANGLIN, MICHAEL WILLIAMS, lawyer; b. Chelsea, Mass., Dec. 3, 1946; s. John M. and Lillian Rogene (Williams) A. BS, Tex. A&M Commerce, 1969; JD, U. Tex., 1976. Bar: Tex. 1976, U.S. Dist. Ct. (no. dist.) Tex. 1979, U.S. Dist. Ct. (we. and ea. dists.) Tex. 1987, U.S. Dist. Ct. Ariz. 1992, U.S. Ct. Appeals (5th and 11th cirs.) 1981, U.S. Supreme Ct. 1986. With Passman & Jones, Dallas, 1976-87; sr. ptnr. Fulbright & Jaworski, LLP, Dallas, 1987—. Trustee Ofcl. Panel Bankruptcy Trustees for No. Dist. Tex., 1980—. Corp. mem. Dallas Mus. Fine Arts, 1984; ct. apptd. spl. advocate, 1990-95; bd. dirs. Dallas Opera, 1992-95; active Greater Dallas Planning Coun., 1994—, Greater Dallas Crime Commn., 1994—, Youth Crime Coun., 1994—; chair bd. dirs. Kessler Sch., 2001—; chair Dallas Tax Increment Fin. Bd., 2003—. Mem. ABA, Tex. Bar Assn., Dallas Bar Assn., Am. Bankruptcy Inst. Office: Fulbright & Jaworski LLP 2200 Ross Ave Ste 2800 Dallas TX 75201-2784 Office Phone: 214-855-8000. Business E-Mail: anglin@fulbright.com.

ANGOFF, GERALD HARVEY, cardiologist; b. Cambridge, Mass., Feb. 6, 1944; s. Nathan Robert and Evelyn (Kanter) A.; m. Rosalind Norma Tarko, Nov. 23, 1975; children: Elizabeth, Rebekah. AB, Harvard Coll., 1966; MD, Harvard U., 1970; MBA, U. Mass., 2006. Diplomate Am. Bd. Internal Medicine, Am. Bd. Cardiovascular Disease, Nat. Bd. Echocardiography; cert. physician exec. Resident internal medicine Cleve. Met. Gen. Hosp., 1970-72; fellow in cardiology Harvard Med. Sch., Peter Bent Brigham Hosp., Boston, 1975-77, Harvard Sch. Pub. Health, Boston, 1977-78; cardiologist The Heart Ctr., Manchester, NH, 1978-99, New Eng. Heart Inst., 1999—2005; dir. noninvasive cardiology New England Heart Inst., 1999—2002; physician exec. Cerner Corp., 2005—. Chief cardiology Elliot Hosp., Manchester, 1979-82, 86-93; instr. Harvard Med. Sch., Boston, 1978-96; pres. The Heart Ctr., 1995-99. Bd. dirs. Jewish Fedn. Greater Manchester, 1984-94; v.p. Temple Adath Yeshurun, Manchester, 1994-96, pres., 1996-98. Maj. U.S. Army, 1972-75. Recipient award of acad. achievement in med. mgmt., Am. Coll. Physician Execs. Fellow Am. Coll. Cardiology, Am. Heart Assn. (Coun. on clin. cardiology). Avocations: computers, skiing. Office: Cerner Corp 2800 Rockcreek Pkwy Kansas City MO 64117-2551 Home Phone: 603-494-7334. Business E-Mail: gerry.angoff@cerner.com.

ANGONES, FRANK R. (FRANCISCO ANGONES), lawyer; b. Havana, Cuba, July 21, 1950; BA, U. Miami, 1972, JD, 1976. Bar: Fla. 1976, US Ct. Appeals (5th Cir.) 1976, US Ct. Appeals (11th Cir.) 1976, US Supreme Ct. 1981. Ptnr. Angones McClure & Garcia PA, Miami. Dir. Victoria Hosp., 1985—87, chmn., 1988; mem. judicial nom. com. US Dist. Ct. (So. Dist. Fla.). Fellow: Am. Bar Found.; mem.: Eugene Spellman Am. Inns of Ct., ABA (house of delegates 1992—95), Dade County Bar Assn. (dir. 1985—88, treas. 1990, sec. 1991, v.p. 1992, pres.-elect 1993, pres. 1994), Cuban-Am. Bar Assn. (dir. 1979—81, pres. 1982), Internat. Assn. Def. Counsel, Def. Rsch. Inst., Fla. Bar (pres.-elect 2006—07), Am. Bd. Trial Advocates. Office: Angones McClure & Garcia PA Courthouse Tower 8th Floor 44 W Flagler St Miami FL 33130 Office Phone: 305-371-5000. Office Fax: 305-371-3948.

ANGRESANO, JAMES, economics professor; BS, Lehigh U., 1968; MBA, NYU, 1971; PhD in Econs., U. Tenn., 1981. Mktg. rsch. analyst, NYC, 1968—71; asst. prof. Am. Coll. Switzerland, 1972—74; asst. to assoc. prof. econs. Hampden-Sydney Coll., Va., 1980—91; adj. assoc. prof. econs. Sweet Briar Coll., 1984—91; tutor adult degree prog. Mary Baldwin Coll., 1985—; Fulbright scholar Varna U. Econs., Bulgaria, 1991—92; acad. coord. Civic Edn. Project, Czech Republic, 1992—93; vis. prof. econs. Prague U. Econs., Czech Republic, 1992—93; rsch. assoc. Ctr. Post-Soviet and East European Studies U. Tex., Austin, 1993—95; prof. polit. economy Albertson Coll. Idaho, Caldwell, 1995—. Vis. acad. Mansfield Coll., Oxford U., 1987; vis. scholar Inst. Econs., Budapest,

Hungary, 1990; vis. fellow Stanford U. Hoover Instn., 1997; vis. prof. China Agrl. U., 2001, 02; vis. prof. internat. economy U. Trento, Italy, 2002, 03, 04, 05; sr. Fulbright specialist U. Cairo, 2004, 03. Contbr. articles to profl. publs., chapters to books; author: The Political Economy of Gunnar Myrdal: An Institutional Basis for Transformation Policy, 1997, French Welfare State Reform: Idealism Versus Swedish, Kiwi and Dutch Pragmatism, 2007. Recipient US Prof. of Yr. award, Carnegie Found. for Advancement of Tchg. and Coun. for Advancement and Support of Edn., 2006. Mem.: European Cmty. Studies Assn., European Assn. Comparative Econ. Studies, Assn. Comparative Econs., Phi Kappa Phi. Office: Dept Polit Economy Albertson Coll Idaho 2112 Cleveland Blvd Caldwell ID 83605 Office Phone: 208-459-5480. E-mail: jangresa@hotmail.com.*

ANGRIST, JOSHUA D., economics educator; b. Columbus, Ohio, Sept. 18, 1960; 2 children. BA in Economics with highest honors, Oberlin Coll., 1982; MA in Economics, Princeton U., 1987, PhD in Economics, 1989. Faculty rsch. fellow Nat. Bur. Econ. Rsch., Cambridge, Mass., 1989—94, rsch. assoc., 1994—; asst. prof. economics dept. Harvard U., Cambridge, 1989—91; sr. lectr. in economics, dept. economics Hebrew U., 1991—95, assoc. prof., economics dept., 1995—96, affiliated prof. economics, 2003—; vis. assoc. prof., economics dept. MIT, 1994—95, assoc. prof., economics dept., 1996—98, prof., economics dept., 1998—. Dir., rsch. program in human resources Falk Inst., 1991—94; rsch. fellow Centre for Econ. Policy Rsch., 1992—95; vis. scholar Fed. Reserve Bd., 1995, Ctrl. Bank of Columbia, 1999, U. Coll. London, 1999, Mathematical Economics Forum, Wake Forest U., 2002; co-organizer Jerusalem Conf. on Edn. Reform, 1999; vis. scholar and instructor European; invited spkr., panelist Cornell Employment and Disability Policy Inst., 2001; Hooker Disting. vis. prof. McMaster U., 2002; cons. US Social Security Adminstrn., Manpower Demonstration Rsch. Corp., for the Israeli govt. after the Oslo peace negotiations, 1994; instructor IZA Summer Sch. in Labor Economics, 2002, Beijing U./CCER Workshop for PhD Students, 2005; Smith chair Brigham Young U., 2003; Lady Davis Fellow Hebrew U. Jerusalem, 2004. Reviewer of articles, assoc. editor Jour. Bus. and Econ. Statistics, 1992—2001, advisory editor Economics Letters, 1993—2000, mem. editl. bd. Econmetrica, 1994—97, Am. Economic Review, 2001—03, co-editor Jour. Labor Economics, 2002. Recipient Griliches prize, honorable mention, Quarterly Jour. Economics, 1999, Sargan Lecture, Royal Economic Soc., 2003; Rsch. Fellow, IZA-Bonn, 2000. Fellow: Econometric Soc., Soc. Labor Economics, Am. Acad. Arts & Sciences; mem.: Population Assn. Am., Am. Statistical Assn., Am. Econ. Assn. Avocations: hiking, skiing, skating, sailing. Office: MIT Dept Economics E52-353 50 Memorial Dr Cambridge MA 02142-1347 Office Phone: 617-253-8909. Office Fax: 617-253-1330. Business E-Mail: angrist@mit.edu.

ANGST, GERALD L., lawyer; b. Chgo., Dec. 29, 1950; s. Gerald L. Sr. and Audrey M. (Hides) A.; m. Candace Simning, Jan. 29, 1983. BA magna cum laude, Loyola U., Chgo., 1972, JD cum laude, 1975. Assoc. Sidley Austin, Chgo., 1975-82, ptnr., 1982—. Mem.: ABA (constrn. litigation com. litigation sect.), Chgo. Bar Assn. (civil practice com.). Office: Sidley Austin One S Dearborn St Fl 34 Chicago IL 60603 Office Phone: 312-853-7757. Business E-Mail: gangst@sidley.com.

ANGSTROM, WAYNE RAYMOND, communications executive; b. Chgo., Mar. 26, 1939; s. Raymond Harry and Dorothy Louise (Dixon) A.; m. Sandra Sue Weber, Oct. 5, 1963; children: Mark, Carl, David, Kristina. AA in Bus. Adminstrn., Chgo. City Coll., 1962; student, Northwestern U., 1963-68. Mfg. mgr. R.R. Donnelley & Sons Co., Chgo., 1962, div. dir., v.p., 1981-87; exec. v.p. Maxwell Communications Corp., St. Paul, 1987-90, Quebecor Printing Inc., Boston, 1990-91; pres., CEO St. Ives Inc. USA, 1992—; also bd. dirs. Home: 7082 Valencia Dr Boca Raton FL 33433-7404 Office: Saint Ives Inc 2025 Mckinley St Hollywood FL 33020-3139

ANGUIANO, LUPE, advocate; b. La Junta, Colo., June 12, 1929; d. Jose and Rosario (Gonzalez) A. Student, Ventural Jr. Coll., Calif., 1948, Victory Noll Jr. Coll., Huntington, Ind., 1949-52, Marymount Coll., Palos Verdes, Calif., 1958-59, Calif. State U., LA, 1965-67; MA, Antioch-Putney, Yellow Springs, Ohio, 1978. S.W. regional dir. NAACP Legal Def. and Ednl. Fund, LA, 1965-69; civil rights specialist HEW, Washington, 1969-73; S.W. regional dir. Nat. Coun. Cath. Bishops, Region X, San Antonio, 1973-77; pres. Nat. Women's Employment and Edn. Inc., LA, 1979-91; cons. Cisco Sys. Inc., 1998-99; pres., cons. Lupe Anguiano & Assocs., 1981—; dir. devel. La Jolla Inst., Van Nuys, Calif., West Valley Alliance; fund devel. dir. Girl Scouts of the San Fernando Valley, Chatsworth, Calif.; rep. Primerica, Valencia, Calif.; mktg. and fund devel. cons. self employed. Cons. Tex. Dept. Human Resources, Dept. Labor, Women's Bur., U.S. Office Pers. Mgmt., USCG, Washington, 1990-92; tech. cons. Cisco Sys. Inc.; developer regional networking acad., Oxnard Coll.; part-time faculty mem. Ventura (Calif.) Coll.; proposal reader U.S. Office Edn., Women's Equity Act; mem. Tex. Adv. Coun. on Tec.-Vocat. Edn., Calif. del. White House Conf. on Status of Mex.-Ams. in U.S., 1967; founding mem. policy coun. Nat. Women's Polit. Caucus, 1971—; Tex. and nat. del. Intrnat. Women's Yr., 1976-77; chmn. Nat. Women's Polit. Caucus Welfare Reform Task Force, 1977—; co-developer Cisco Networking Acad. in Ventura County high schs. Author (with others): U.S. Bilingual Edn. Act, 1967, Tex. AFDC Employment and Edn. Act, 1977; manuals for Women's Employment and Edn. Model program. Co-chmn. Nat. Peace Acad. Campaign, 1977-81; founder, bd. dirs. Nat. Chicana Found. Inc., 1971-78; bd. dirs. Calif. Coun. Children and Youth, 1967, Rio Grande Fedn. Chicano Health Ctrs., S.W. rural states, 1974-76, Women's Lobby, Washington, 1974-77, Rural Am. Women, Washington, 1978—, Small Bus. Coun. Greater San Antonio; mem. Pres.'s Coun. on Pvt. Sector Initiatives, 1983. Recipient Cmty. award Coalition Mex.-Am. Orgns., 1967, Outstanding Svc. award Washington, 1968, Thanksgiving award Boys' Club, 1976, Outstanding Svc. award Tex. Women's Polit. Caucus, 1977, Liberty Bell award San Antonio Young Lawyers, 1981, Vista award for Exceptional Svc. to end poverty, 1980, Headliner award San Antonio Women in Comm., 1978, Woman of Yr. award Tex. Women's Polit. Caucus, 1978, Pres.'s Vol. Action award 1983, Leadership award Nat. Network Hispanic women, 1989; named Outstanding Woman of Yr., L.A. County, 1972, Woman of the 80's, Ms. Mag., 1980, Nat. Pres.'s award Nat. Image Inc., 1981, Wonder Woman Found. award, 1982, Pres.'s Vol. Action award, 1983, Adv. of Yr., San Antonio SBA, 1984; selected one of Am.'s 100 Most Important Women, Ladies Home Jour., 1988, 89; featured in CBS TV series An American Portrait, 1985, Leadership award Nat. Network Hispanic Women, 1989. Mem. Nat. Assn. Female Execs., Pres.'s Assn., Am. Mgmt. Assn. Roman Catholic. Office: Primerica 25060 Stanford Ave Valencia CA 91355-3411 Home: 1031 Kumquat Pl Oxnard CA 93036-1533 Home Phone: 805-983-2733; Office Phone: 805-983-8517. Personal E-mail: languiano@verizon.net.

ANGULA, HELMUT KANGULOHI, Prime Minister of Namibia; b. Ontananga, Oshikoto, Namibia, Nov. 11, 1945; s. Onesmus and Adda (Thomas) A.; div. Nov. 1992; children: Adda Kaone, Vita, Priscilla, Magdalena, Monica, Justus K., Mutaleni H. Cert., Nikumbi Internat. Coll., 1969; MSc in Biology, Voronezh State U., USSR, 1975. Cert. Tchr. Biology and Chemistry. Tchr. SWAPO Edn. Ctr., Nyango, Zambia, 1975-76, adminstr., 1976-77; head of diplomatic mission SWAPO Mission, Havana, Cuba, 1977-86; head of mission SWAPO Observer Mission, UN, NYC, 1986-89; deputy min. Mines and Energy Republic of Namibia, 1990-91, min. Fisheries and Marine Resources, 1991-95, min. of fin., 1995-96; min. Agr., Water and Rural Devel., 1997—2004. Author: Haimbodi Ya Haufiku 1000 Days, 1991. Activist South West Africa People's, Windhoek, 1964; youth activist Organization SWAPO, Zambia, 1966. Mem. Revival Volley Ball Club (patron), Parliamentary Football Team (capt. 1993—).

ANGULO, CHARLES BONIN, foreign service officer, lawyer; b. NYC, Aug. 6, 1943; s. Manuel R. and Carolyn C. (Bonin) A.; m. Kathleen Fisher, Oct. 1, 2005. BA, U. Va., 1966; cert., U. Madrid, 1966; JD, Tulane U., 1969. Bar: Va. 1969. Assoc. Michael & Dent, Charlottesville, Va., 1969-73; assoc. editor The Michie Pub. Co., Charlottesville, 1973; fgn. svc. officer U.S. Dept. State, Washington, 1973-75, Am. Embassy U.S. Dept. State, Brussels, 1976-78, Santo Domingo, 1981-85, Office of the Legal Advisor, U.S. Dept. State, Washington, 1978-81; exec. dir. office of insp. gen. U.S. Dept. State, Washington, 1985-86; asst. chief protocol U.S. State Dept., Washington, 1986-88, Am. Consulate Gen. U.S. Dept. State, Jeddah, Saudi Arabia, 1988-93; fgn. svc. officer Am. Embassy U.S. Dept. State, Quito, Ecuador, 1993—. Home and Office: 117 Chestnut Dr River Green Canton GA 30114

ANGUS, JOHN COTTON, chemical engineering educator; b. Grand Haven, Mich., Feb. 22, 1934; s. Francis Clark and Margaret (Cotton) A.; m. Caroline Helen Gezon, June 25, 1960; children: Lorraine Margaret, Charles Thomas. BSChemE, U. Mich., 1956, MS, 1958, PhD in Engring, 1960; DSc (hon.), Ohio U., 1998. Registered profl. engr., Ohio. Research engr. Minn. Mining & Mfg. Co., St. Paul, 1960-63; prof. Case Inst. Tech. (now Case Western Res. U.), Cleve., 1963-67, prof. chem. engring., 1967—2004, prof. emeritus, 2004—, chmn. dept., 1974-80, interim dean engring., 1986-87. Vis. lectr. U. Edinburgh, Scotland, 1972-73; vis. prof. Northwestern U., 1980-81. Trustee Ohio Scottish Games. NSF fellow, 1956-57; NATO sr. fellow, 1972-73 Fellow AIChE, Electrochem. Soc. (Pioneer award); mem. NAE, Am. Chem. Soc., Sigma Xi, Tau Beta Pi, Phi Lambda Upsilon. Achievements include research in fields of crystal growth, diamond synthesis, conducting diamond, electrochemical devices, thermodynamics. Office: Case Western Res U Dept Chem Engring Cleveland OH 44106-7217

ANGUS, PATRICIA MARIE, lawyer; b. Rockville Centre, NY, May 13, 1964; d. John Wakefield and Patricia Gerard Angus. BA cum laude, Amherst Coll., 1986; M in Internat. Affairs, Columbia U., 1990; JD, George Washington U., 1992. Bar: N.Y. 1993. Atty. Coudert Bros., NYC, 1992—96; v.p. wealth advisor JP Morgan Pvt. Bank, NYC, 1996—99; atty. Hughes and Whitaker, 1999—2003; ind. contractor Hughes & Whitaker/Day Berry & Howard, 2003; pres. Angus Adv. Group LLC, NYC, 2003—04; v.p. Asset Mgmt. Advisors, Greenwich, Conn., 2004—06; mng. dir., head wealth adv. svcs. Svcs., Shelterwood Fin. Svcs., LLC, 2006—. Presenter in field. Contbr. articles to profl. jours. Mem. advocacy coun. Citizens Com. Children N.Y., NYC, 2001—; devel. com. N.Y. Women's Found., NYC, 2001—. Mem.: ABA, Assn. Bar City N.Y. Office: Asset Mgmt Advisors 60 E 42nd St #3410 New York NY 10165 Office Phone: 212-937-1030.

ANIOL, SCOTT MICHAEL, pastor; b. Dearborn, Mich., Mar. 30, 1980; s. Robbie and Deborah Aniol; m. Rebecca Apelian, June 19, 2004. MusB, Bob Jones U., Greenville, SC, 2003; MusM, Northern Ill. U., DeKalb, 2006. Assoc. pastor First Bapt. Ch., Rockford, Ill., 2003—. Office: First Bapt Ch 5304 Charles St Rockford IL 61108 Home: 118 S Van Buren St Cherry Valley IL 61016 Office Phone: 815-395-0550.

ANISE, NADER, lawyer; Pres., CEO Nader Anise Lawyer Mktg., Boca Raton, Fla.; ptnr. Anise & Anise Attys. at Law, Boca Raton, Fla. Adj. prof. managerial mktg. and entrepreneur law Nova SE Univ., Fort Lauderdale, Fla. Mem.: Am. Mktg. Assn., Legal Mktg. Assn., Nat. Speakers Assn., Am. Lawyers Public Image Assn. (founder, pres. 2000—), Fla. Bar. Office: Anise & Anise Attys Ste 358 1900 Glades Rd Boca Raton FL 33431 also: Lawyer Mktg Inc PO Box 11138 Fort Lauderdale FL 33339 Office Phone: 561-417-2324, 888-510-1520. Business E-Mail: nader@naderanise.com.

ANISSIMOVA, SVETLANA VLADIMIROVNA, physicist, researcher; b. Pavlovo, Nizhegorodskaya region, Russia, Dec. 25, 1975; arrived in US, 2000; d. Vladimir Mikhailovich Anissimov and Nina Prokhorovna Anissimova. BS, Nizhniy Novgorod State U., Russia, 1997; MS, Northeastern U., Boston, 2002, PhD, 2005. Tchg. asst. Northeastern U., Boston, 2000—02, grad. rsch. scholar, 2002—05, post-doctoral fellow, 2005—. Referee Phys. Rev. Letters, Phys. Rev. B Jours., 2005—; spkr. in field. Contbr. articles to profl. jours. Grantee, NSF, 2004—05. Mem.: Assn. Computing Machinery, Am. Phys. Soc. Achievements include development of new method for studying magnetic properties of nano-scale devices involving measurements of electric currents at a femto-ampere level; design of experiments on magnetocapacitance, magneto-transport, and magnetization studies of semiconductor devices; first to construct a current preamplifier with an ultra low noise in the areas of metal-insulator transition, strongly correlated electrons; observe temperature dependence of the strength of electron-electron interaction; research in electron transport phenomena in & thermodynamic properties of 2 dimension; electron gas in ultra-clean silicon metal-oxide-semiconductor field-effect transistors at low temperatures & high magnetic fields. Office: Northeastern Univ Physics Dept 110 Forsyth St 111 Boston MA 02115 Personal E-mail: svan25@hotmail.com.

ANISTON, JENNIFER, actress; b. Sherman Oaks, Calif., Feb. 11, 1969; d. John and Nancy (Dow) Aniston; m. Brad Pitt, July 29, 2000 (div. Oct. 2, 2005). Attended, Fiorello La Guardia School of Music, Art & Performing Arts, NYC. Actor: (TV series) Ferris Bueller, 1990, Molloy, 1990, The Edge, 1992, Muddling Through, 1994, Friends, 1994—2004 (Screen Actors Guild outstanding ensemble performance in comedy series, 1995, Emmy award best actress, 2002, Golden Globe award best actress, 2003, People's Choice award favorite female television performer, 2001, 2002, 2003, 2004), (guest appearances) Herman's Head, 1992—93, Quantum Leap, 1992, Burke's Law, 1994; host (TV Documentary) Growing Up Grizzly 2, 2004; actor: (TV films) Camp Cucamonga, 1990, Sunday Funnies, 1993; (films) Leprechaun, 1993, She's the One, 1996, Dream for an Insomniac, 1996, Til There Was You, 1997, Picture Perfect, 1997, The Thin Pink Line, 1998, The Object of My Affection, 1998, The Iron Giant (voice), 1999, Office Space, 1999, Rock Star, 2001, The Good Girl, 2002, Bruce Almighty, 2003, Along Came Polly, 2004, Derailed, 2005, Rumor Has It., 2005, Friends With Money, 2006, The Break-Up, 2006 (with Vince Vaughn Movies-Choice Chemistry, Teen Choice Awards, 2006), (off-broadway play) For Dear Life, Dancing on Checkers' Grave, (music videos) I'll Be There For You, 1995, Walls, 1996, I Want To Be In Love, 2001. Named Most Intriguing People, People Weekly, 1995, Favorite Female Star, People's Choice Awards, 2007; named one of Most Beautiful People in the World, People, 1999, 50 Most Beautiful People, 2002, 2003, 2004, 2005, 100 Most Powerful Celebrities, Forbes.com, 2007. Office: c/o Kevin Huvane Creative Artists Agy 9830 Wilshire Blvd Beverly Hills CA 90212*

ANITESCU, MIHAI, computer scientist, mathematician; b. Bals, Romania, Aug. 10, 1968; arrived in U.S., 1993; s. Ilie and Marioara Anitescu; m. Magdalena Anitescu, Nov. 14, 1992; 1 child, Julia Christine. MS, Poly. U., Bucharest, Romania, 1992; PhD, U. Iowa, 1997. Asst. prof. math. U. Pitts., 1999—2004, adj. assoc. prof., 2004—; computer scientist Argonne (Ill.) Nat. Lab., 2002—. Vice chair optimization sect. Inst. Ops. Rsch. & Mgmt. Sci., 2005—. Contbr. articles to profl. jours.; assoc. editor Math. Programming, software editor Optimization Methods and Software. Sgt. Inf. Romanian Mil., 1986—87. Wilkinson fellow, Argonne Nat. Lab., 1997. Office: Argonne Nat Lab MCS Bldg 221 9700 S Cass Avenue Lemont IL 60439 E-mail: anitescu@mcs.anl.gov.

ANJULIS, STANLEY JOSEPH, retired church administrator; b. Jersey City, Feb. 4, 1948; s. Stanley and Lorraine Anjulis; m. Alane Hope Berney, Oct. 30, 1982. B in Bible Theology, Internat. Bible Inst., M in Bible Theology, 1987, DD (hon.), 1988; M in Christian Counseling, Internat. Sem., 1990; PhD, Carolina Christian U., 1990. Clin. Pastoral Counselor Acad. Prof. Clin. Therapists, 1991, Marriage & Family Therapist Acad. Prof. Clin. Therapists, 1992. Asst. regional dir. Servants of The Good Shepherd, NYC, 1984—85; vicar-gen. Ecumenical Orthodox Ch., Balt., 1985—87, oeconomus, 1985—87; provost Am. Orthodox Ch., Balt., 1987—87, diocesan ordinary LA, 1991—2000; superior gen. (ex-officio) Comm. Order of St. Benedict, LA, 1991—2000; ret. with full faculties Am. Orthodox Ch./O. St. Benedict, Hudson, Wis., 2001—. CEO Ecumenical Orthodox Ch., Balt., 1985—87, dean of presbyterium, 1985—87, dean of sem., 1985—87. Orthodox Catholic. Office Phone: 651-261-0674. Personal E-mail: anjulisstan@yahoo.com.

ANKA, PAUL, singer, composer; b. Ottawa, Ont., Can., July 30, 1941; came to US, 1959; s. Andrew Emile and Camilia (Tannis) A.; m. Anne Alison de Zogheb, Feb. 16, 1963 (div. Oct. 2000); children: Alexandra, Amanda, Alicia, Anthea, Amelia. Grad. high sch., Ottawa; Doctorate Music (hon.), St. Johns U., NYC, 1981. Owner, prin. Spanka Music Corp., 1958—, Flanka Music Corp., 1958—, Camy Prodns., Inc., 1961-66; owner Panka Musci, 2001—. Internat. performer, 1956—; films include The Longest Day, 1961 (also wrote title song), Girl's Town, Look in Any Window, Captain Ron, 1992, Ordinary Magic, 1993, Shake, Rattle and Rock!, 1994, Mr. Playback: An Interactive Movie, 1995, Mad Dog Time, 1996, 3000 miles to Graceland, 1999, TV film Perry Mason: The Case of the Maligned Mobster, 1991; TV appearances include Larry King Live, Barbara Walters, The View, Ed Sullivan Show, Danny Thomas, Perry Como, Johnny Carson, Dean Martin, Hollywood Palace, Open Mind, Atlantic City USA, Happy Birthday, America, 1976, Sinatra: The First Forty Years; appeared syndicated variety show, 1973; replacement in Broadway mus. What Makes Sammy Run?, 1954; appeared at Copacabana, NYC, Sands Hotel, Caesars Palace, Hilton Hotel, all Las Vegas, Caribe Hilton Hotel, San Juan, PR, Paladium, London, Olympia, Paris, Uris, NYC, Waldorf Astoria, NYC, Golden Nugget Hotels, Las Vegas and Atlantic City; participated San Remo Music Festival, 1964; recs. include My Way, 1968, (You're) Having My Baby, 1974, One Man Woman/One Woman Man, 1974, I Don't Like To Sleep Alone, 1975, (I Believe) There's Nothing Stronger Than Our Love, 1975, Times of Your Life, 1975, Anytime (I'll Be There), 1976, Happier, 1976, My Best Friend's Wife, 1977, Everybody Ought To Be in Love, 1977, Headlines, 1979, Both Sides of Love 1981, Walk a Fine Line, 1983, Songs, 1983, Italiano, 1987, In Vegas, 1995, Amigos, 1996, A Body of Work, 1998, Christmas, 2000, Live, 2001, Live in Las Vegas, 2002, Live & In Concert, 2003, Rock Swings, 2005, Classic Songs, 2007; wrote: (with Burt Bacharach) score for film Together?, 1979; composer Diana, 1957, Crazy Love, Lonely Boy, 1959, Put Your Head on My Shoulder, 1959, Time to Cry, 1959, The Longest Day, 1962, Ogni Volta, 1964, Do I Love You, 1971, Tonight Show theme music; others; also compositions for other artists including My Way for Frank Sinatra and She's A Lady for Tom Jones. Named a Chevalier, Order of Arts & Letters, France, 1991; named 21st most successful artist in Billboards history., Entertainer of Yr., Internat. Gaming Assn., 1991, Songwriters Hall of Fame, Nat. Acad. Popular Music, 1991; named an Officer, Order of Can., 2005; named to, Can. Music Hall of Fame, 1980, Hollywood Walk of Fame, Can. Walk of Fame, 2005. Mem. Broadcast Music, Inc. (22 songwriting awards: 18 for most performed songs, 4 for songs performed more than one million times). Clubs: Friars NYC. Eastern Orthodox. Achievements include being a holder of 15 gold records for million dollar world-wide sellers, and having to his credit more than 42 million single sales and over 900 songs. Office: Paul Anka Prodns Penthouse 32 9200 Sunset Blvd Los Angeles CA 90069 also: William Morris Aby 1 William Morris Pl Beverly Hills CA 90212 E-mail: fan@paulanka.com.*

ANKROM, CHARLES FRANKLIN, golf course architect, consultant; b. Parkersburg, W.Va., Nov. 7, 1936; s. Donsel and Elva Dale (Cale) A.; m. Alice Lynell Glass, Aug. 24, 1968; children: Steven Charles, Cheryl Lyn, Jan Ellen Lambert, Beverly Lyn Webster. Student, W.Va. U., 1955, Eli Frank Sch. Design Arts, Tampa, Fla., 1956, Indian River C.C., Stuart, Fla., 1993—94, student, 2007—. Exec. dir. golf, corp. golf course arch. Gen. Devel. Corp., Miami, Fla., 1964-70; exec. dir. golf, golf course arch. Boise Cascade Recreation Communities Group, Palo Alto, Calif., 1970-73; pres. Charles F. Ankrom, Inc., Internat. Golf Course Archs., Cons. & Planners, Stuart, Fla., 1973—. Prin. works include Panther Woods Country Club, Ft. Pierce, Fla., Sabal Trace C.C., Port Charlotte, Fla., Sun 'N Lake Country Club, Turtle Run Golf Course, Sebring, Fla., Cocoa Beach Mcpl. Golf Course, Cocoa Beach City, Fla., Ft. Lauderdale (Fla.) Country Club, Boca Raton (Fla.) Mcpl. Golf Course, The Cypress Golf Course at Woodmont Country Club, Tamarac, Fla., The Club at Emerald Hills, Hollywood, Fla., The Habitat Golf Course, Brevard County, Fla., Aquarina Beach & Country Club, Melbourne, Fla., Crane Creek C.C., Palm City, Fla., Indian River Plantation Resort, Hutchinson Island Marriott Beach Resort and Marina, Jensen Beach, Fla., Metro Country Club Resort, Dominican Republic, Osprey Creek Golf Course, Palm City, Fla., San Miguel Country Club, Venezuela, numerous others; over 60 planned cmtys. including Indian River Plantation Marriott Resort, Hutchinson Island, Fla., Joe's Point, Hutchinson Island, Stuart West, Martin County, Fla., Pinecrest Lakes, Jensen Beach, Crystal Lakes, Okeechobee, Fla., Panther Woods, Ft. Pierce, Crane Creek, Palm City, Fla., River Ridge, Tequesta, Fla., River Landing, Palm City. Donated design & adminstrv. svcs. for Bulldog Sportsturf Complex, Martin County (Fla.) Schs. Recipient Outstanding Achievement by Ind. in Bus. or Industry award State of Fla. Coun. on Vocat. Edn., 1992, Bus. Ptnr. award Martin County Sch. Dist., 1991. Achievements include profl. svc. multi-disciplinary cons. assignments provided to clients in 28 states and 9 countries or territories, including approxmamtely 300 assignments to both the govt. and pvt. sectors, profl. orgns., coll. and univ. and the edn. industry, natl. and internat. conf. as the lectr. for seminars, including svcs. to resort ops., pvt. amenities and public ops., 2001; formed AMI (Ankrom and Miartus Internat.) for the internat. design of golf course projects, with offices in Fla. and Venezuela. Office: Charles F Ankrom Inc PO Box 898 Stuart FL 34995-0898 Office Phone: 772-283-1440. Personal E-mail: cfankrom@adelphia.net, cfankrom@comcast.net.

ANLYAN, WILLIAM GEORGE, surgeon, educator, academic administrator; b. Alexandria, Egypt, Oct. 14, 1925; s. Armand and Emmy (Nazar) A.; children: William George, John Peter, Louise. BS magna cum laude, Yale U., 1945, MD, 1949; DSc (hon.), Rush Med. Coll., 1973. Diplomate Am. Bd. Surgery, Am. Bd. Thoracic Surgery. Intern, resident, instr., assoc. in surgery Duke Hosp., Durham, NC, 1949-53, asst. prof. surgery, 1953-58, prof. surgery, 1961-89; assoc. dean Duke U. Sch. Medicine, 1963, dean, 1964-69, v.p. health affairs, 1969-83, chancellor health affairs, 1983—89, exec. v.p., 1987—89; chancellor Duke U., 1989—90, chancellor emeritus, 1990—. Chmn. Durham VA Chancellor's Com., 1963—89; chmn. Pearle Health Svcs., Inc., 1983—85; surg. cons. Durham VA Hosp.; Markle scholar med. sci., 1953—58; bd. regents Nat. Libr. Medicine, 1971—72; trustee N.C. Sch. Sci. and Math., 1978—85, chmn. phys. facilities com., 1979, vice-chmn. bd. trustees, 1981—84; mem. bd. visitors The U. Tex. Health Sci. Ctr. at Houston, 1980—88, Stanford U., 1985—87; chmn. Yale U. Coun. Com. on Med. Affairs, 1985—93. Mem. editl. bd. Pharos, 1968-93. Trustee The Duke Endowment, 1990—, vice chmn., 2004-, Commn. Future Structure Vet. Health Care, 1990-92; chmn. Gov.'s Task Force Better Health NC in 2000, 1991-97; mem. White House Sci. Coun., 1988-89. Recipient Disting. Achievement award Modern Medicine, 1974; Gov.'s Disting. Meritorious Svc. award, 1978; Abraham Flexner award, 1980, Disting. Surgeon Alumnus award Yale U. Sch. Medicine, 1979, Award of Merit Duke U. Hosp. and Health Adminstrn. Alumni Assn., 1987,

Lifetime Achievement award Duke U. Med. Alumni, 1995, Lifetime Achievement award Rsch. Am., 1997, Disting. Meritorius Svc. medal, Duke Univ., 2002, N.C. award in sci., presented by the gov., 2002, Lifetime Achievement award City of Medicine, 2003. Fellow ACS; mem. AMA (adv. com. med. sci. 1972—), Soc. Univ. Surgeons, Soc. Vascular Surgery, Internat. Cardiovasc. Soc., Soc. Clin. Surgery, Am. Heart Assn., Soc. Med. Adminstrs. (pres. 1983-85), Inst. Medicine of NAS, Coun. Deans (chmn. 1968-69), AAMC (exec. com. 1965-71, chmn. 1970-71), AAMC Coun. Deans (chmn. 1968-69), So. Med. Assn., Coord. Coun. Med. Edn. (chmn. 1973-74), Surg. Biology Club II, Am. Surg. Assn., So. Surg. Assn., Halsted Soc., Allen O. Whipple Surg. Soc., Assn. Am. Med. Colls. (chmn. 1970-71), Ind. Rsch. Roundtable NAS, Assn. Acad. Health Ctrs. (pres. 1975), Rsch. Am. (bd. dirs. 1989-2005, chmn. 1992-96), Rotary, Phi Beta Kappa, Sigma Xi, Alpha Omega Alpha. Home: 1516 Pinecrest Rd Durham NC 27705-5817 Office: Duke Med Ctr PO Box 3626 Durham NC 27710-0001 Home Phone: 919-489-3196; Office Phone: 919-684-3438. Business E-Mail: anlya001@mc.duke.edu.

ANMA, SO, engineer, consultant; b. Hamamatsu, Shizuoka, Japan, Nov. 7, 1936; s. Yu and Chie (Matsumoto) A.; m. Fumie Kishikawa, Mar. 15, 1964; children: Ryo, Akitsu, Mizuho, Yashima. BS, Hokkaido U., Sapporo, Japan, 1959; DEng, Tokai U., Tokyo, 1987. Registered engring. geologist; profl. civil engr. Rschr. Hukada Chisitsu Inst., Tokyo, 1959-67; pres. Kisokogaku Co., Tokyo, 1967-70; exec. Kensetsu Kiso Chosa Sekkei Co., Shizuoka, Japan, 1970-91, pres., 1991—2002; rep. Artemis Inst. Forensic Geology and Geoenvironment, 2006—. Lectr. Tokai U., Shizuoka, 1988-2006; bd. dirs. Shizuoka Environ. and Resources. Co-author: The First Ascent of Mt. Chamlang, 1965, Geology of Nepal Himalaya, 1967 (Chichibunomiya prize 1968), Patagonian Mountain Climb, 1968, Mt. Dhaulagiri-I Midwinter, 1985. Recipient Chichibunomiya prize Chichibunomiya Meml. Found., Tokyo, 1968, Hokkaido prize Hokkaido Regional Govt., 1983, Asahi Sports prize Asahi Newspaper Inc., Tokyo, 1984. Fellow Japan Soc. Civil Engrs.; mem. Internat. Geosynthetic Soc., Geol. Soc. Japan, Japanese Soc. Snow and Ice, Japanese Alpine Club (chpt. chmn. 1986-95). Avocations: mountain climbing, forest watching. Home and Office: Artemis Inst FGG 574-6 Miyajima Fuji Shizuoka Japan Office Phone: 81-545-62-0611. Business E-Mail: anma.sf@tx.thn.ne.jp.

ANNAKIN, KENNETH COOPER, film director, writer; b. Beverly, Yorkshire, Eng. came to U.S., 1979; s. Edward C. and Hannah J. (Gains) A.; m. Pauline Mary Carter, 1960; children: Jane, Deborah. DLitt (hon.), Hull U., 1935. Writer, dir. 14 documentaries, 1941-46; movie dir. Holiday Camp, 1946, Miranda, 1948, Quartette, 1948, Trio, 1950, Hotel Sahara, 1951, Planter's Wife, 1952, Robin Hood and Her Merry Men, 1952, Sword and the Rose, 1953, Loser Takes All, 1956, Three Men in a Boat, 1956, Across the Bridge, 1957, Third Man on the Mountain, 1959, The Swiss Family Robinson, 1960, A Very Important Person, 1961, The Hellions, 1961, Crooks Anonymous, 1962, The Fast Lady, 1962, The Longest Day, 1962, Those Magnificent Men in Their Flying Machines, 1965, The Battle of the Bulge, 1965, The Biggest Bundle of Them All, 1967, Those Daring Young Men in Their Jaunty Jalopies, 1969, Call of the Wild, 1972, Paper Tiger, 1974, The Fifth Musketeer, 1977, The Pirate Movie, 1982, Pippi Longstocking, 1986, 99; screenwriter Coco Chanel, 1999, Chiffon, 2001, Fair Play, 2001, Lady With the Redwing, 2005; author (autobiography): So You Wanna Be A Director?, 2001. Decorated Order Brit. Empire. Office: 9233 Swallow Dr West Hollywood CA 90069-1145 Personal E-mail: flyingmachines@earthlink.com.

ANNAS, GEORGE J., health law educator; b. St. Cloud, Minn., July 13, 1945; s. George J. and Margaret L. (Pallansch) A.; m. Mary Frances Roche, Aug. 17, 1969; children: Katie, David. BA, Harvard U., 1967, JD, 1970, MPH, 1972; LHD, Salem State Coll., 1994. Bar: Mass., Minn. Law Clk. to Justice John V. Spalding Supreme Judicial Ct., Boston, 1970—71; research fellow (med. ethics) Harvard U, 1971—72; vis. asst. prof. of law Boston Coll. Law Sch., 1972—73; dir. Boston U. Ctr. for Law and Health Scis., 1973—78; assoc. prof. health law Boston U. Sch. Medicine, 1978—83; prof. health law, chair dept. health law Boston U. Schs. Medicine and Pub. Health, 1983—; founder & dir. (law, medicine and ethics prog.) Boston U., 1989—; Edward R. Utley prof. of health Law, chair Boston U, Boston. Editor in chief Emeritus, Law, Medicine and Health Care (now jour. law, medicine & ethics) 1980chair Mass. Health Facilities Appeals Bd., Boston, 1973-77; vice chair Mass. Bd. Registration in Medicine, Boston, 1976-82; chair Mass. Task Force on Organ Transplantation, 1983-84; co-founder Global Lawyers and Physicians: Working Together for Human Rights, 1996. Author: The Rights of Patients, 1975, 2d edit., 1989, 3rd, 2004, Juding Medicine, 1988, Standard of Care: The Law of American Bioethics, 1993, Some Choice: Law, Medicine and the Market, 1998, American Bioethics: Crossing Human Rights and Health Law, 2005; co-author: (with Glantz, L.H. & Katz, B.F) Informed Consent to Human, 1975, Experimentation: The Subject's Dilemma, Rights of Doctors, 1981, (with Eliass. S) Reproductive Genetics and the Law, 1987, American Health Law, 1990,; co-editor: Genetics and Law I, II and III, 1976, 81, 86, The Nazi Doctors and the Nuremburg Code, 1992, Gene Mapping: Using Law & Ethics as Guides, 1992, Health and Human Rights: A Reader, 1998; columnist on health law Hastings Ctr. Report, Am. Jour. Pub. Health, New Eng. Jour. Medicine; editor-in-chief emeritus Law Medicine and Health Care; contbr. jours. Recipient Life time award Am. Soc. Law, Medicine and Ethics, 1990, Health Law Tchr.'s award, 1993, Joseph P. Kennedy, Jr. Found. Fellowship, Harvard University, 1971-72, Humanitarian award, APHA, 1982, Cmty. Svc. award, Health Planning Coun. for Greater Boston, 1984, Nat. Health Law Teachers award, Am. Soc. of Law, 1993, Doctor of Humane Letter, Salem State Coll., 1994, Milton Greenblatt Award, Mass. Psychiatry Soc., 1995, Jennifer Robbins award, APHA (Health Law Forum), 2001, Humanist of Year award, Ethical Soc., Boston, 2003. Mem. ABA (chmn. com. on legal problems in medicine sci. and tech. sect.), Minn. Bar Assn., APHA , Mass. Psychiatric Soc., Inst. Medicine 1997, Am. Soc. of Law, (medicine & ethics) 1981, Phi Beta Kappa, Fellow Am. Assn. for Advancement of Sci., 1996, Am. Coll. of Legal Medicine, 2000. Office: Boston U Sch Pub Health 715 Albany St Talbot Bldg Boston MA 02118-2526 Office Phone: 617-638-4640. Office Fax: 617-638-5299.

ANNAUD, JEAN-JACQUES, film director, producer, scriptwriter; b. Juvisy, France, Oct. 1, 1943; s. Pierre and Madeleine (Tripoz) A.; m. Monique Rossignol, 1970 (div. 1980); 1 child, Mathilde; m. Laurence Duval; 1 child, Louise. Student, Ecole Louis Lumière, Institut Des Hautes Etudes Cinematographiques, Paris, 1966; Lic. Lettres, The Sorbonne, Paris, 1967. Freelance film dir., screenwriter, Paris, 1967—. Sreenwriter, dir.: Black and White in Color, 1976 (Oscar award Best Fgn. Film 1977), Hot head, 1978, Quest for Fire, 1981, (César award 1982), Name of the Rose, 1986 (César award 1987, Donatello award), The Bear, 1988 (César award best dir. 1988), The Lover, 1991 (Best Dir. award Japan Critics Assn., 1992); screenwriter, dir., prodr.: Wings of Courage, 1994 (in IMAX 3D), Seven Years in Tibet, 1997 (Best Fgn. Film Gilde Filmpreis, Germany, 1998), Enemy at the Gates, 2000, Two Brothers, 2004. Decorated commandeur Ordre des Arts et Lettres; recipient Grand Prix Nat. du Cinema, prix du Cinéma de L'Académie Française. Home: 9 rue Guénégaud 75006 Paris France also: Repérage SAS 10 rue Lincoln 75008 Paris France Office: ICM c/o Jeff Berg 10250 Constellation Blvd Los Angeles CA 90067 Office Phone: 33 140769411. Business E-Mail: jj@reperage-films.fr.

ANNCHILD, CYNTHIA, educational consultant; b. Kilgore, Tex., Sept. 9, 1946; d. Walter Charles Hewitt and Blanche Ann Fraser; children: Lincoln McNulty, Anson McNulty. BA in Sociology, Wagner Coll., SI, NY, 1968; postgrad., NYU, NYC, 1968—69; Cert. Practitioner, Acad. Orton-Gillingham Educators, Amenia, NY, 1997. Tchr. U.S. Peace Corps, Abadeh, Iran, 1968—71, cross-cultural dir. Hamehdon, Iran, 1971—72; epidemiologist N.Y.C. Health Dept., 1972—73; owner The Bathhouse, Natural Toiletries, NYC; instr. ESL, King Abdul Azziz U. Women's Coll., Jeddah, Saudi Arabia, 1993—94; learning specialist Kildonian Sch., Amenia, NY, 1994—98, Ann Arbor Acad., Mich., 1998—2001, Emerson Sch., Mich., 2001—. Bd. dirs. Ann Arbor Acad., Mich.; program cons. Sch. Without Walls; spkr. in field. Founding mem. Artist Way Ann Arbor, Mich., 2000—06. Recipient Notable New Tchr. award, Kildonian Sch., 1994, Svc. Recognition award, Ann Arbor Acad., 2001. Mem.: Child and Adults with Attention Deficit Disorder and Hyperactivity Disorder, Internat. Dyslexia Assn., Learning Disabilities Assn. (bd. dirs. 1998). Avocations: creating multi-sensory learning games, travel, camping, hiking, sketching. Office: Emerson Sch 5425 Scio Church Rd Ann Arbor MI 48103 Office Phone: 734-665-9005 ext. 122. Office Fax: 734-665-8126. E-mail: cannchild@emerson-school.org.

ANNENBERG, LEONORE A., foundation administrator; m. Walter H. Annenberg; 2 children. BA, Stanford U.; PhD (hon.), Pine Manor Coll., LaSalle U., U. Pa., Brown U.; DHL (hon.), U. So. Calif., 1998. Former chief of protocol for U.S.A. Pres., chair, sole dir. Annenberg Found.; founding mem. governing bd. Annenberg sch. comm. U. Pa., Annenberg sch. comm. U. So. Calif.; founder Am. Friends Covent Garden; past chmn., hon. chmn. Friends Art and Preservation Embassies; mem. trustee's coun. Nat. Gallery Art; mem. Com. Preservation White House; mng. dir. Met. Opera; mem. Acad. Music Com.; past pres., hon. trustee Palm Springs Desert Mus.; hon. trustee performing arts coun. LA Music Ctr.; trustee emeritus U. Pa.; former bd. dirs. Pa. Acad. Fine Arts, Phila. Orch. Assn.; bd. dirs. Met. Mus. Art, Phila. Mus. Art. Decorated Cavaliere Dell'Ordine Al Merito Della Republica Italiana, Grand Officio Order of Orange-Nassau (Netherlands); recipient Wagner medal Robert F. Wagner grad. sch. pub. svc. NYU, Colonial Williamsburg Churchill Bell award, Nat. Medal of Arts, NEA, 1993; named one of 400 Richest Ams. Forbes mag., 2006. Fellow Am. Acad. Arts and Scis.; mem. Disting. Daus. Pa. Office: The Annenberg Found St Davids Ctr 150 Radnor Chester Rd Ste A-200 Wayne PA 19087-5293

ANNESI, ADELE MARY, editor; b. Bayshore, NY, July 21, 1957; d. John Carmine and Adele (Frattini) Annesi. BA with honors, Bentley Coll., Waltham, Mass., 1981; Cert. Computer Graphics, Fairfield U., 1993; Cert., Wesleyan Writers Conf., 1999; Cert. Writing, Fairfield U., 2000. Adminstr. Mass. Fin. Svcs., Boston, 1981—82; asst. mgr. C-Systems, Ridgefield, Conn., 1982—83; advt. prodn. mgr. Christian Herald Mag., Chappaqua, NY, 1983—86; pub. rels. mgr. Housatonic Area Regional Transit, Danbury, Conn., 1986—87; mktg. mgr. Digitech, Danbury, 1987—2000; editor Scholastic Pub., Danbury, Conn., 2001—06, Gartner, Stamford, Conn., 2006—; writer Hersam Acorn Newspapers, Conn., 2000—06. Writers residency Wisdom House, Harwinten, Conn., 2001, Harwinten, 06. Meals provider Dorothy Day Hospitality House, Danbury, Conn., 1994—98; contbr. Cir. Lit. Jour., 2002—05. Recipient Editor's Choice award, Nat. Libr. of Poetry, Md., 1998. Mem.: Ridgefeld Writer's Guild, Conn. Authors and Pub. Assn., Shepaug River Writer's Group, Conn. Authors and Publishers Assn., Wellspring Writers' Group (coord. 2002—03). Democrat. Avocations: hiking, reading, singing, travel.

ANNEXSTAD, ALBERT T., insurance company executive; b. Sept. 17, 1940; s. Alice Annexstad. BA, Mankato State Univ., 1967; DHL (hon.), Gustavus Adolphus Coll., 2005. Mktg. & mgmt. positions Federated Mutual Ins., Owatonna, Minn., 1965—86, dir. mktg, 1986—99, pres., CEO, 1999—, chmn., 2000—. Bd. gov. Property Casualty Insurers Assn. Am. Trustee Gustavus Adolphus Coll.; mem. exec. com. Minn. Bus. Partnership. Recipient Connecting with Youth Lifetime Achievement award, Minn. Bus. Partnership. Office: Federated Mutual Insurance PO Box 328 121 E Park Sq Owatonna MN 55060-0328

ANNING, ROBERT DOAN HOPKINS, brokerage company executive; b. Cin., Apr. 16, 1940; s. Robert H. and Marjorie Thuma Anning; m. Sydney Ann Fish, July 6, 1963; children: Sydney A. Raidy, Robert H. II, John H. II, Elizabeth A. Mullin. BA, Trinity Coll., 1963. 1st v.p. investments Merrill Lynch Global Pvt. Client Group, 1967—. Commr. Cin. Bd. Pk. Commrs., 2006—; bd. trustees Convalescent Hosp. for Children, 1985—2005, emeritus trustee, 2005—, chmn., 1988—94; bd. trustees The Children's Hosp., Cin., 1989—, pres., 2004—, chmn., 2003—; bd. trustees Cin. Children's Hosp. Med. Ctr., 1990—, Cerebral Palsy Svcs. Ctr., United Cerebral Palsy Cin., 1994—2003, Cin. Parks Found., 1995—2007, pres., 1999—2000; bd. trustees Found. Family Svc., 1997—, Family Svc. Cin. Area, 1998—99. Lt. USNR, 1963—67. Named one of All-Pro Stockbrokers Money mag., 1990, All-Star Brokers, 1994-96, Blue-Chip Brokers Town and Country mag., 1992. Mem.: Commonwealth Club, Queen City Club, Univ. Club, Camargo Club, Cin. Country Club. Home: 25 Weebetook Ln Cincinnati OH 45208-3330 Office Phone: 513-579-3673.

ANN-MARGRET, (ANN-MARGRET OLSSON), actress, performer; b. Stockholm, Apr. 28, 1941; came to U.S., naturalized, 1949; d. Gustav and Anna Olsson; m. Roger Smith, May 8, 1967. Student, Northwestern U. Performer radio shows, band tours; appeared with: George Burns, Las Vegas, 1961; headliner numerous appearances, Las Vegas, 1961—; made NYC debut Radio City Music Hall, 1991; actress numerous films including Pocketful of Miracles, 1961, State Fair, 1961, Bye Bye Birdie, 1962, Viva Las Vegas, 1963, The Pleasure Seekers, 1964, Kitten With a Whip, 1964, Bus Riley's Back in Town, 1964, Once A Thief, 1965, Cincinnati Kid, 1965, Stagecoach, 1966, Made in Paris, 1966, The Swinger, 1966, Murderers' Row, 1967, The Tiger and the Pussycat, 1967, R.P.M., 1970, C.C. & Company, 1971, Carnal Knowledge, 1971, Train Robbers, 1972, Outside Man, 1972, Tommy, 1975, Joseph Andrews, 1976, The Last Remake of Beau Geste, 1977, Magic, 1978, The Cheap Detective, 1978, Lookin' To Get Out, 1978, The Villain, 1979, Middle-Age Crazy, 1980, The Return of the Soldier, 1982, I Ought To Be in Pictures, 1982, Twice in a Lifetime, 1985, 52-Pick-up, 1987, A Tiger's Tale, 1988, A New Life, 1988, Something More, Newsies, 1992, Grumpy Old Men, 1993, Grumpier Old Men, 1995, Seduced by Madness, 1996, The Limey, 1999, Any Given Sunday, 1999, The Last Producer, 2000, Interstate 60, 2002, Taxi, 2004, Mem-o-re, 2005, Tales of the Rate Fink, 2006, The Break-Up, 2006, The Santa Clause 3: The Escape Clause, 2006; several TV spls., 1975-76; TV films Who Will Love My Children, 1983, A Streetcar Named Desire, 1984, Our Sons, 1991, Nobody's Children, 1994, Seduced by Madness: The Diane Borchardt Story, 1996, Blue Rodeo, 1996, Life of the Party: The Pamela Harriman Story, 1998, Happy Face, 1999, The 10th Kingdom, 2000, Perfect Murder, Perfect Town, 2000, A Woman's a Helluva Thing, 2001, A Place Called Home, 2004; mini-series The Two Mrs. Grenvilles, 1987, Alex Haley's Queen, 1993, Scarlett, 1994, Blonde, 2001; TV series Four Corners, 1998; author: (with Todd Gold) Ann-Margret: My Story, 1994. Recipient 2 Acad. award nominations, 4 Emmy nominations, 5 Golden Globes. Office: William Morris Agy 151 S El Camino Dr Beverly Hills CA 90212-2775*

ANNS, ARLENE EISERMAN, publishing company executive; b. Pearl River, NY; d. Frederick Joel and Anna (Behnke) Eiserman. Student, Fairleigh Dickinson U., 1946—48; BS, Utah State U., 1950; postgrad., Traphagen Sch. Design, 1957, NYU, 1958, Hunter Coll., 1959—60. Rsch. and promotion asst. Archtl. Record, NYC, 1952-56; asst. rsch. dir. Esquire Mag., NYC, 1956-62; rsch. mgr. Am. Machinist publ. McGraw-Hill, Inc., NYC, 1962-67, mktg. svc. mgr., 1967-69, 69-71, sales mgr., 1976-77, dir. mktg., 1977-78; v.p. mktg. svcs. Morgan Gramplan, Inc., NYC, 1971-72; mktg. dir. Family Health and Diversion mag., 1972-74; dist. sales mgr. Postgrad. Medicine, 1974-76; advt. sales mgr. Contempory Ob/Gyn, 1976-78, dir. profl. devel., 1978-80; pub. graduating engr., dir. mktg. Aviation Week Group, 1980-90; pub. World Aviation Directory; dir. comms. Aviation Week Group, 1990-92; v.p. Phase, Ltd., 1993—; owner, mgr. Barnahill Loblolly Tree Farm, 1993—. Mem.: Va. Forestry Assn., Am. Soc. Pers. Adminstrs., Employment Mgmt. Assn., Sales Exec. Club, Advt. Club NY, Advt. Women NY, Pharm. Advt. Club, Am. Mktg. Assn., Dir. Assn., Svc. Corps Ret. Execs. (chair), U. Va. Libr. Assn. Bd., Coll. Placement Coun., Nat. Orgn. Disability (bd. dirs.), Internat. Platform Assn., Wings Club, Pi Sigma Alpha. Home: Barnahill Farm 6653 Celt Rd Stanardsville VA 22973-3638 Personal E-mail: theanns@earthink.net.

ANNS, PHILIP HAROLD, brokerage house and pharmaceutical executive; b. London, Eng., June 24, 1925; came to U.S., 1950; s. Harold Falkner and Dorothy Louise (Torckler) A.; m. Jacqueline Estelle Wyrtzen, Dec. 27, 1952 (div. 1975); 1 child, Jean Anns; m. Arlene Claire Eiserman, Apr. 1, 1978. BA in Econs., Christ Coll., Cambridge, Eng., 1948, MA in Econs., 1950. Asst. to pres. BASF Inc., NYC, 1954-58; gen. mgr. Squibb Australia E.R. Squibb and Sons, Princeton, NJ, 1958-68, dir. animal health New Brunswick, NJ; gen. mgr. animal health Am. Hoechst, Kansas City, Mo., 1968-72; exec. v.p. Lakeside Labs., Milw., 1972-75; sr. v.p., gen. mgr. internat. div. A.H. Robins Co., Inc., Richmond, Va., 1975-85, sr. v.p. corp. govt. relations Washington, 1986-90; pres. Phase Ltd., Arlington, Va., 1990—; prin., owner Barnahill Tree Farm. With Va. Dist. Export Coun.; mem. Congl. staff U.S. Ho. of Reps., 1990—. Mem. Indsl. Devel. Authority, Greene County, Va. Served to lt. Brit. Royal Navy, 1943-46, ETO. Mem.: Va. Forestry Assn., Rotary. Home and Office: 6653 Celt Rd Stanardsville VA 22973-3638 Personal E-mail: theanns@earthlink.net.

ANNUS, JOHN AUGUSTUS, artist; b. Riga, Latvia, Oct. 25, 1935; U.S., 1949; s. Augustus and Irma (Gustavs) Annus; m. Edite Zeile, Oct. 18, 1981; children from previous marriage: Aurelia, Fabiola. BFA, Pratt Inst., 1959; postgrad., Art Students League, 1958—59, Nat. Acad. Design, 1958—59, Academia de Belli Arti, 1962—64. One-man shows include Am. Acad. in Rome, 1960, Arte al Berge, Palermo, 1963, Archtl. League, N.Y., 1965, Vendo Nubes, Phila., 1965, 70, 76, Galleria del Vantaggio, Rome, 1962, 71, 73, 74, Galerie Clasing, Germany, 1982, T.L.C. Gallery, Toronto, 1985, Jacobi Gallery, Hamburg, 1987, 92, Raitern Gallery, Riga, Latvia, 1989, Gallery K. Munster, Germany, 1992, Internat. Mus., Riga, 1993, Jannus Image, Munster, 1993, 95, Design Technik GmbH Gallery-Verlag, Hamburg, 1995, Kunsthaus Schone, Anderhach, Germany, 2002-03; group shows include Spectrum 5, N.Y.C., 1972, 73, Skidmore Coll., N.Y.C., 1975, U. Pa., 1976, NAD, 1958, 59, 64, 67, 68, 75, 80, 91, Nat. Acad. Design Mems., 1993, Nat. Acad. Design Academician, 1995, Images Photokina, Cologne, Germany, 1996, 2nd internat. HRS Exhibition-Riga Latvia, 1998, Nat. Acad. Design, 2003, I Werkschaz, 2005, II Werkshave, Spinnerei-Leipzig, Germany, 2006, Galerie Daugava, 2006; represented in permanent collections NAD, Balt. Mus., Collection of the Italian Govt., Henry Ranger Fund, Am. Acad. in Rome. Recipient Gold medal for oil painting Labyrinth, 1962; recipient Wallace Truman prize for oil painting Agrigento, 1967, Ranger Purchase prize for By the Sea, 1965, Reflection, 1965, award of Excellence for By the Sea, 1982; Nat. Acad. Design grantee, 1958-59, Albert Hallgarten traveling grantee, 1958-59; Prix de Rome Am. Acad. in Rome, 1959-60; Italian Govt. grantee, 1962— Mem. Nat. Acad. Design (academician), Soc. Fellows, Am. Acad. Rome (Centennial Directory listee), Nat. Soc. Mural Painters, others Lutheran. Office Phone: +49 341 498 0371. Personal E-mail: johnaugustusannus@hotmail.com.

ANOATUBBY, BILL, governor of Chickasaw Nation; b. Nov. 8, 1945; m. Janice Marie Loman, Dec. 23, 1967; children: Chris, Brian. AS, Murray State Coll., 1970; BS, East Ctrl. State Coll., 1972. Acct., office mgr. Am. Plating Co., 1972-74; acct., systems & budgetary contr. Little Giant Corp., 1974-75; dir. health svcs. The Chickasaw Nation, Ada, Okla., 1975-76, dir. acctg., 1976-78, spl. asst. to gov., 1978-79, lt. gov., 1979-87, gov., 1987—. Trustee Morris K. Udall Scholarship and Excellence in Nat. Environ. Policy Found., 1994-2000. Mem. adv. com. Okla. Dept. Commerce, 1990; mem. Trail of Tears Nat. Historic Adv. Com., 1990-92; trustee Oklahoma City U., 1991-98; trustee Native Am. Cultural Edn. Authority, 1998—. Recipient Gov.'s ARTS award, 1997; named Okla. Minority Bus. Advocate of Yr., U.S. SBA, 1995; named to Okla. Hall of Fame, 2004, Honored One and Friend of the Ct., Supreme Ct. Okla., 2005. Mem. Inter-Tribal Coun. of Five Civilized Tribes (past v.p., pres.), Ada Area C. of C. (bd. dirs.), Okla. Indian Affairs Commn. Democrat. Office: Chickasaw Nation PO Box 1548 Ada OK 74821-1548 Office Phone: 405-436-2603. Business E-Mail: bill.anoatubby@chickasaw.net.

ANOOSHIAN, ROBERT VAHAN, plastic surgeon; b. Garden City, NY, Aug. 20, 1956; s. Arsen George Anooshian and Mary Ann Burgujian. BA, U. Pa., 1978, MSc, 1979; MD, Boston U., 1984. Intern, resident gen. surgery Buffalo Gen. Hosp., 1984—86; resident, chief resident Wash. Hosp. Ctr., Washington, 1986—90; chief resident plastic surgery Lahey Clin., Burlington, Mass., 1990—92; fellow U. Southern Calif. Med. Ctr., 1992—93; physician, emergency svcs. Kaiser Hosp., Los Angeles, 1993—96; pvt. practice Los Angeles, 1996; staff physician Kaiser Hosp., San Francisco, 1996—2001, chief plastic surgery, 2001—. Mem.: San Francisco Med. Assn, Calif. Med. Assn., Calif. Soc. Plastic Surgeons, Am. Soc. Plastic Surgeons. Office: 2238 Geary Blvd San Francisco CA 94115

ANQUETIL, PATRICK ARMAND, investment company executive, researcher; b. Boulogne Billancourt, France, Oct. 11, 1973; arrived in U.S., 1998; m. Nitasha Manchanda, May 31, 2005. Diploma in Engring., Swiss Fed. Inst. Tech., Zurich, Switzerland, 1998; degree, The U. Tokyo, Japan, 1999; PhD, MIT, Cambridge, Mass., 2004. Lic. Nat. Assn. Securities Dealers, 2005. Rsch. scientist MIT, 1999—; sr. equities analyst Susquehanna Internat. Group, Boston, 2004—06; CEO, Aretais, Inc., 2006—. Contbr. articles to profl. jours. Achievements include patent for molecular actuators. Office: MIT 77 Massachusetts Avenue Room 3-147 Cambridge MA 02139 Office Phone: 617-258-8628.

ANSARI, AMIR, digital home and multimedia management technology company executive; BSEE and Computer Sci., George Mason U. Co-founder, chief tech. officer Telecom Technologies, Inc. (TTI) (acquired by Sonus Networks, Inc.), 1993—2000; served in the IP divsn. Sonus Networks, Inc.; co-founder, chief tech. officer Prodea Systems, Inc., Plano, Tex., 2006—. Contbr. to numerous technical papers. Mem., trustee X-Prize Found. Vision Circle. Along with Anousheh Ansari (sister-in-law) made a multi-milion dollar contribution for the first non-governmental organization to launch a reusable manned spacecraft into space twice within two weeks to the X-Prise Foundation on May 5, 2004, To honor this donation the X-prize was renamed the Ansari X Prize; several US patents filed in areas of voice over IP and multimedia services. Office: Prodea Systems Inc 6101 W Plano Pkwy Ste 210 Plano TX 75093

ANSARI, ANOUSHEH, digital home and multimedia management technology company executive, first female civilian space traveler; b. Tehran, Iran, 1966; emigrated to the US in 1984; m. Hamid Ansari, 1991. BSEE and Computer Sci., George Mason U., 1988; MSEE, George Washington U. Held engring. positions MCI Telecommunications Corp., Comm. Satellite Corp. (COMSAT); co-founder, pres., CEO Telecom Technologies, Inc. (TTI) (acquired by Sonus Networks, Inc.), 1993—2000; co-founder, chmn. Prodea Systems, Inc., Plano, Tex., 2006—. US Delegate at ITU SG VII, SG XI and SG XVII; rep. Am. Nat. Standard Inst. T1S1 and T1X1. Contbr. to numerous technical papers. Mem., bd, trustee X-Prize Found. Vision Circle; past bd. dir. Make-a-Wish Found. (North Tex.), Collin County Children's Advocacy Ctr.; Ashoka Found. Named one of 40 Under 40, Fortune, 2001; recipient Ernst and Young Entrepreneur of Yr., Southwest Region, Tech. and Comm. category, 1999, Nat. Entrepreneurial Excellence award, Working Women, 2000, George Mason U. Entrepreneurial Excellence award, George Mason Univ. Alumni Assn., 2001, George Washington U. Disting. Alumni Achievement award. Mem.: Nat. Soc. Profl. Engineers, IEEE, Eta Kappa Nu. Along with Amir Ansari (brother-in-law) made a multi-milion dollar contribution for the first non-governmental organization to launch a reusable manned spacecraft into space twice within two weeks to the X-Prise Foundation on May 5, 2004. To honor this donation the X-prize was renamed the Ansari X Prize; becoming the first Iranian in space and the first female civilian space tourist; will be the fourth space tourist part of the primary crew on the Soyuz TMA-9 mission in September, 2006, launching from Baikonur Cosmodrome in Kazakhstan; patents on Automated Operator Services and Wireless Service Node. Office: Prodea Systems Inc 6101 W Plano Pkwy Ste 210 Plano TX 75093

ANSARI, HAMID, digital home and multimedia management technology company executive; m. Anousheh Ansari. Master's Degree in Computer Sci., George Washington U.; completed advanced credits towards doctorate of comm. Various positions MCI Comm.; co-founder Telecom Technologies, Inc. (TTI) (acquired by Sonus Networks, Inc.), 1993—2000; CEO, pres. Prodea Systems, Inc., Plano, Tex., 2006—. Office: Prodea Systems Inc 6101 W Plano Pkwy Ste 210 Plano TX 75093

ANSARY, CYRUS A., investment company executive, lawyer; b. Shoraz, Oram, Nov. 20, 1933; s. A. R. and Jamali (Mostmand) Ansary; m. Janet C. Hodges, Aug. 1, 1970; children: Douglas C., Pary Ann, Jeffrey C., Bradley C. BS, Am. U., 1955; JD, Columbia U., 1958. Bar: Md. 1959, D.C. 1960, Va. 1961. Pvt. practice, Washington, 1959-72; sr. ptnr. firm Ansary, Kirkpatrick and Rosse, 1964-72; chmn. bd. Industry Reports, Inc., Washington, 1960-72; organizer, 1st chmn. bd., pres. Woodland Nat. Bank, Alexandria, Va., 1963-67; lectr. Sch. Bus. Adminstrn., Am. U., 1967-71; chmn. bd. Fin. Dynamics Corp., Washington, 1967-72, Campbell Music Co., Washington, 1968-72, John L. Lindstrom and Assocs., Inc., Washington, 1962-86, IK Investment A.G., Zurich, Switzerland, 1974-79; pres. Investment Svcs. Internat. Co. LLC, Washington, 1973—; chmn. MACO Bancorp, Washington, 1988—95. Chmn. Washington Mut. Investors Fund; bd. dirs. J. P. Morgan Value Opportunities Fund, Am. Funds Tax-Exempt Series I; chmn. Fort Knox Nat. Co. Trustee Am. U., 1968—96, chmn. bd., 1982—91; trustee Internat. Law Inst., 1976—88, Wolf Trap Found., Vienna, Va., 1977—82, Fried Krupp Found., Essen, Germany, 1977—79, Washington Opera Soc., 1982—89; pres. Ansary Found., Washington, 1983—; mem. Woodrow Wilson Coun., Washington, 2000—. With USMCR, 1959—64. Mem.: CFA Soc. Washington, Nat. Economists Club, Washington Assn. Money Mgrs., Nat. Press Club, Econ. Club Washington, Washington Soc. Investment Analysts, Life Guard Hist. Mt. Vernon, Congressional Country Club, City Club, Chevy Chase Country Club (Bethesda), Met. Club (Washington), Rotary. Office: 1725 K St NW Ste 410 Washington DC 20006-1401 Business E-Mail: cansary@isicollc.com.

ANSBACHER, BARRY BARNETT, lawyer; b. Jacksonville, Fla., Jan. 7, 1963; s. Lewis and Sybil Ansbacher; m. Elaine Kenny, Aug. 30, 1992. BA, U. Fla., 1985, JD, 1988. Bar: Fla. 1989, D.C. 1989; bd. cert. real estate atty. Fla. Atty. Ansbacher & Schneider PA, Jacksonville, 1989—97, Ansbacher & McKeel PA, Jacksonville, 1997—. Pres. Attys. Real Property Coun. NE Fla., Inc., Jacksonville; pub. rep. on Pvt. Provider Task Force Fla. Bldg. Commn., 2004. Author: Complex Real Estate Transactions-Subdivisions, 1997, 98, Issues of Transboundary Pollution in North America, 1988. Named Outstanding Young Men of Am., 1986. Mem. Fla. Bar Assn. (exec. coun. cir. rep. real property, probate and trust law sect. 1998—, chmn. problem studies 2005—), Jacksonville Bar Assn. Jewish. Avocation: equestrian sports. Office: 8818 Goodbys Executive Dr Jacksonville FL 32217 Office Phone: 904-396-8050. Business E-Mail: Info@ansbacher.net.

ANSBACHER, RUDI, physician; b. Sidney, NY, Oct. 11, 1934; s. Stefan and Beatrice (Michel) A.; m. Elisabeth Cornelia Vellenga, Nov. 19, 1965; children— R. Todd, Jeffrey N. Grad., Harvard Coll., 1951; BA, Va. Mil. Inst., 1955; MD, U. Va., 1959; MS, U. Mich., 1970. Diplomate Am. Bd. Ob-Gyn. Staff ob-gyn, chief clin. investigation Brooke Med. Ctr., San Antonio, 1971-75, asst. chief ob-gyn, 1975-77; chief dept. ob-gyn Letterman Army Med. Ctr., San Francisco, 1977-80; from prof. ob-gyn to prof. emeritus U. Mich., Ann Arbor, 1980—2001, prof. emeritus, 2002—. Cons. Biomed. Adv. Com. Population Resource Ctr., 1978-81; bd. dirs. Health Policy Internat. Contbr. articles to profl. jours., chpts to books; mem. editorial bds., reviewer jours. Served to col. U.S. Army, 1960-80. Named Disting. Mil. Grad. Va. Mil. Inst., Lexington, Va., 1955; NIH grantee, 1973-78 Fellow ACOG (Chmn.'s award 1970), AAAS; mem. Am. Fertility Soc. (dir. 1979-82), Am. Soc. Andrology (sec. 1978-80, pres. 1984-85), Central Assn. Ob-Gyn, Assn. Mil. Surgeons U.S., Soc. for Study Reprodn., Mich. State Med. Soc. (bd. dirs. 1995-2005, sec. 2005-06), Mich. State Med. Soc. Found. (bd. dirs. 2003—), Physicians Rev. Orgn. Mich. (bd. dirs. 2000-), U. Mich. Med. Ctr. Alumni Soc. (bd. dirs. 2004—). Republican. Presbyterian. Avocations: tennis, softball, gardening, skiing. Home: 3755 Tremont Ln Ann Arbor MI 48105-3022 Home Phone: 734-665-2396; Office Phone: 734-763-4344. Business E-Mail: ansbache@med.umich.edu.

ANSBRO, JOHN JOSEPH, philosopher, educator; b. NYC, Nov. 16, 1932; s. Thomas and Katherine (Reilly) Ansbro. BA, St. Joseph's Sem., Yonkers, NY, 1954, postgrad., 1955; MA, Fordham U., Bronx, NY, 1957, PhD, 1964. Lectr. philosophy Manhattan Coll., Riverdale, NY, 1958-59, instr., 1959-63, asst. prof., 1963-68, assoc. prof., 1968-79, prof., 1979-96; ret., 1996; writer, 1996—. Curriculum guidance supr. faculty counselors Sch. Arts & Scis. Manhattan Coll., 1962—73, chmn. co-curricular interdisciplinary arts program, 1962—70, chmn. com. faculty rsch. projects and grants, 1976—78, 1989—92, chmn. dept. philosophy, 1977—81, chmn. sabbatical leave com., 1989—91, dir. rsch. peace studies program, 1990—91, com. faculty rsch. projects, mem. instnl. rev. bd. human subjects, task force acad. programs, liaison officer Danforth Found., others; adj. asst. prof. philos. resources contemporary problems program Grad. Sch. Arts & Scis., Fordham U., 1975; chmn. Met. Round Table Philosophy, 1972—75; project field coord. NY State Dept. Edn., 1965—67; founder, pres. Manhattan Coll. Coun. World Hunger, 1977—85. Author Martin Luther King, Jr.: The Making of a Mind, 1982, Martin Luther King, Jr.: The Making of a Mind, Mex. trans., 1985, Martin Luther King, Jr.: Nonviolent Strategies and Tactics for Social Change, 2d edit., 2000, The Credos of Eight Black Leaders: Converting Obstacles into Opportunities, 2004; contbr. 40 articles in philos., ednl. and civil rights jours. US, Europe, Asia, numerous philos. reviews. Grantee Travel and Study, Ford Found., 1973, Summer, Am. Can. Co. Found., 1985, Samuel Rubin Found., 1985; scholar, Fordham U. Grad. Sch., 1956—57. Mem.: AAUP, Gandhi-King Soc., Soren Kierkegaard Soc., Soc. Ancient Greek Philosophy, Hegel Soc. Am., Am. Philos. Assn., Soc. Advancement Am. Philosophy.

ANSCHUTZ, PHILIP F., communications and professional sports team executive; m. Nancy Anschutz; 3 children. BS, Univ. Kans., 1961. Dir. chair. QCC, 1993—; founder Anschutz Corp., Denver, 1965; dir. chair. Anschutz Co., Denver, 1991—; CEO, dir. Anschutz Corp., Denver, 1992—; dir. So. Pacific Rail Corp., San Francisco, 1988-96; chair. So Pacific Rail Corp., 1988-96; vice chmn. (merger with So Pacific Rail Corp) Union Pacific, San Francisco, 1996—; dir. Forest Oil Corp., 1995—, Qwest Comm., 1997—, chmn., 1997—2002; co-owner L.A. Kings, 1995—; owner L.A. Galaxy, 1996—; investor-operator Major League Soccer, 1995—; owner San Francisco Examiner, The Ind., Grant Printing Co., San Francisco, 2004—. Dir. Regal Entertainment Group. Named one of 200 Top Collectors, ARTnews Mag., 2004, 2006, Forbes Richest Americans, 1999—, World's Richest People, Forbes Mag., 1999—2007; recipient Disting. Svc. Citation, Kans. U., 1992, Horatio Alger Award. Republican. Avocations: Collecting 19th and 20th century Am. art, especially Western, tennis, squash, running marathons.*

ANSELL, EDWARD ORIN, lawyer; b. Superior, Wis., Mar. 29, 1926; s. H. S. and Mollie (Rudnitzky) A.; m. Hanne B. Baer, Dec. 23, 1956; children: Deborah, William. BSEE, U. Wis., 1948; JD, George Washington U., 1955. Bar: D.C. 1955, Calif. 1960. Electronic engr. FCC, Buffalo and Washington, 1948-55; patent atty. RCA, Princeton, NJ, 1955-57; gen. mgr. AeroChem. Rsch. Labs., Princeton, 1957-58; patent atty. Aerojet-Gen. Corp., La Jolla, Calif., 1958-63, corp. patent counsel, 1963-82, asst. sec., 1970-79, sec., 1979-82, assoc. gen. counsel, 1981-82; dir. patents and licensing Calif. Inst. Tech., Pasadena, Calif., 1982-92; pvt. practice Claremont, Calif., 1992—; co-founder Gryphon Pharms., South San Francisco, 1993, Ciphergen BioSystems, Fremont, Calif., 1993. Adj. prof. U. La Verne (Calif.) Coll. Law, 1972-78; spl. advisor, task force chmn. U.S. Commn. Govt. Procurement, 1971 Editor: Intellectual Property in Academe: A Legal Compendium, 1991; contbr. articles to profl. publs. Recipient Alumni Svc. award George Washington U., 1975. Mem.: Am. Intellectual Property Law Assn., Ea. Bar Assn. LA County, LA Intellectual Property Law Assn., Assn. Univ. Tech. Mgrs., State Bar Calif. (exec. com. intellectual property sect. 1983—86), Athenaeum Club Pasadena, Univ. Club Claremont. Office: 427 N Yale Ave # 204 Claremont CA 91711 Home Phone: 909-625-1244; Office Phone: 909-621-1985. Personal E-mail: anselaw@verizon.net.

ANSELL, JULIAN S., urologist, educator; b. Portland, Maine, June 30, 1922; s. Jacob M. and Anna Gertrude (Fieldman) A.; m. Eva Ruth Ballin, June 17, 1951; children: Steven, Jody, Carol, Ellen, Peter. BA, Bowdoin Coll., 1946; MD, Tufts U., 1951; PhD, U. Minn., 1959. Intern in surgery U. Minn. Hosps., Mpls., 1951-52, resident in urology, 1952-54; NIH fellow U. Minn., Mpls., 1954, instr., 1956-59; asst. prof., head urology U. Wash., Seattle, 1959-62, assoc. prof., head urology, 1962-64, prof., chair urology, 1965-87, prof. urology, 1987-92, prof. emeritus, 1992—. Contbr. scientific papers pub. to profl. jour. Chair Post Grad. Seminar Am. Urological Assn., 1978; pres. Soc. Univ. Urologists; med. quality assurance commn. Wash. State, 1992—2005, chair., 2001. With US Army, 1943—46. Mem. Am. Alpine Club. Achievements include development of neonatal closure of exstrophy of bladder; urology residency objectives; research in renal sparing surgery in bilateral renal cancer; total body potassium in patients with urinary diversion; smoking as a cause of bladder cancer; discordant urinary defects in monozygotic twins; healing in infected and irradiated tissues; reflux and renal failure. Office: 3827 49th Ave NE Seattle WA 98105-5233

ANSELME, JEAN-PIERRE LOUIS MARIE, chemist; b. Port-au-Prince, Haiti, Sept. 22, 1936; came to U.S., 1955, naturalized, 1960; s. Pierre F. and Jeanne (Kieffer) A.; m. Marie-Celine Carrie, Dec. 31, 1960; children: Fabienne, Veronika, Vanessa. BA, St. Martial Coll., Haiti, 1955; BS, Fordham U., 1959; PhD, Poly. Inst., Bklyn., 1963. Research asso. Poly. Inst. Bklyn., 1963, 65, sr. instr., 1965. NSF fellow Institut fur Organische Chemie, Munich, 1964; asst. prof. chemistry U. Mass. at Boston, 1965-68, asso. prof., 1968-70, prof., 1970—; pres. Organic Preparations and Procedures, Inc., Newton, Mass.; vis. prof. Research Inst. Indsl. Sci., Kyushu U., Fukuoka, Japan, 1972, U. Miami, Coral Gables, Fla., 1979 Author: (with others) Organic Compounds with Nitrogen-Nitrogen Bonds, 1966, N-Nitrosamines, 1979; founder, editor: Organic Preparations and Procedures, 1969-70, Organic Preparations and Procedures Internat, 1971—; contbr. (with others) articles to profl. jours. Recipient Seymour Shapiro award as outstanding grad. student organic chemistry Poly. Inst. Bklyn., 1963; Sloan fellow, 1969-71 Fellow Japan Soc. for Promotion Sci.; mem. Am. Chem. Soc., Chem. Soc. London, Sigma Xi, Phi Lambda Upsilon. Office: U Mass Dept Chemistry Harbor Campus Boston MA 02125-3393 Office Phone: 617-287-6141. Business E-Mail: jp.anselme@umb.edu.

ANSELMO, ROBERT LOUIS, writer; b. Yonkers, NY, Sept. 22, 1953; s. Albert Peter and Anna Marie (Zegarelli) Anselmo; 1 child, Jason. Florist, designer, East Meadow, NY, 1971—93; fed. govt. Manhaset (N.Y.) P.O., 1993—95; author Levittown, NY. Author: I Will Always Love My Grandma and Grandpa Too, 2004, We're All Different, and Yet Still the Same, 2006; composer: (country rock song) Halfway to Hel. Avocation: collect sports memorabilia. Personal E-mail: anselmobooks@aol.com.

ANSETH, KRISTI S., tissue engineer, educator; b. ND; BS in Chem. Engring., Purdue U., 1992; PhD in Chem. Engring., U. Colo., 1994. Rsch. assoc. Purdue U., West Lafayette, Ind., 1995; rsch. fellow Mass. Inst. Tech., Cambridge, Mass., 1995—96; asst. prof. chem. engring. U. Colo., Boulder, Colo., 1996—98, Patten asst. prof. chem. engring., 1998—99, Patten assoc. prof. chem. engring., 1999—2002, asst. investigator Howard Hughes Med. Inst., 2000—; assoc. prof. surgery U. Colo. Health Sci. Ctr., Denver, 2000—; prof. chem. engring. U. Colo., Boulder, 2002—03, Tisone prof. chem. and biol. engring., 2003—, assoc. faculty dir. initiative in molecular biotech., 2003—, prof. (by courtesy), 2004—. Vis. rschr. Ecole Nationale Superieure de Chimie, Mulhouse, France, 1994. Recipient Career award, NSF, 1998—2002, First award, NIH, 1998—2003, Dow Outstanding New Faculty award, Am. Soc. Engring. Edn., 1999, Outstanding Young Investigator award, Materials Rsch. Soc., 2001, Curtis W. McGraw award, Am. Soc. Engring. Edn., 2003, Allan P. Colburn award, AIChE, 2003, Alan T. Waterman award, NSF, 2004, others; fellow, Am. Inst. Med. and Biol. Engring., 2001. Office: Dept Chem and Biol Engring ECCH 128 Univ Colo Boulder CO 80309-0424 Office Phone: 303-492-3147. Office Fax: 303-492-4341. E-mail: kristi.anseth@colorado.edu.

ANSLEY, JULIA E., retired elementary school educator, poet, writer; b. Malvern, Ark., Nov. 10, 1940; d. William Harold and Dorothy Mae (Hamm) Smith; m. Miles Ansley, Nov. 8, 1964 (div. June 1976); children: Felicia Dianne, Mark Damon. BA in Edn., Calif. State U., Long Beach, 1962; postgrad., UCLA Ext. Early childhood edn., life, gen. elem., kindergarten/primary, Miller-Unruh reading specialist credentials, Calif. Elem. tchr. L.A. Unified Sch. Dist., 1962—2003; ret., 2003. Coord. Proficiency in English Program, L.A., 1991-93, 98-2001; mem., advisor P.E.P. Instrnl. Tchrs. Network, 1993-2001, workshop presenter, staff devel. leader, and classroom demonstration tchr. in field; also poetry presentations, L.A., 1989—; owner Poetry Expressions, L.A.; self-markets own poetry posters; creator, presenter KIDCHESS integrated lang. arts program, 1987—. Author: (poetry vols.) Out of Heat Comes Light, From Dreams to Reality. Bd. dirs. New Frontier Dem. Club, L.A., 1990-93; mem. exec. bd. L.A. Panhellenic Coun., rec. sec., 1993-95; vol., cmty. orgns. Greater South L.A. Affirmative Action Project, 1995-96; elected tchr. rep. Ten Schs. Leadership Team, 1992-93; active local sch. leadership 6 schs. L.A. Unified Sch. Dist., elected mem. sch. site coun., local sch. leadership coun., shared-decision-making coun.; mem. Dem. Senatorial Campaign Com., Dem. Congl. Campaign Com., Cmty. Coalition, United Tchrs., LA, Action Grassroots Empowerment and Neighborhood Devel. Alternatives. Honored by Teacher mag., 1990; recipient Spirit of Edn. award Sta. KNBC-TV, L.A., 1990, Shiny Apple award L.A. Tchr. Ctr., 1992, Dedicated Tchr. award Proficiency in English Program, 1994; grantee L.A. Ednl. Partnership, 1985, 87, 89, 93. Mem. L.A. Alliance African-Am. Educators (exec. bd. 1991-94, parliamentarian 1992-94), Black Women's Forum, Black Am. Polit. Assn. (edn. co-chair 1993-95), Calif. Tchrs. Assn., So. Pverty Law Ctr., Sigma Gamma Rho. Mem. FAME Ch. Avocations: reading, listening to music, writing, playing chess (cert. chess instr. for grades K-3), political activist. Home: 3828 Sutro Ave Los Angeles CA 90008-1925 Home Phone: 323-293-8013; Office Phone: 323-964-2322.

ANSLEY, SHEPARD BRYAN, lawyer; b. July 31, 1939; s. William Bonneau and Florence Jackson (Bryan) A.; m. Boyce Lineberger, May 9, 1970; children: Anna Ansley Davis, Florence Bryan. BA, U. Ga., 1961; LLB, U. Va., 1964. Bar: Ga. 1967. Assoc. Carter & Ansley and predecessor firm Carter, Ansley, Smith & McLendon, Atlanta, 1967-73, ptnr., 1973-84, of counsel, 1984-91; with Attkisson Carter & Akers Inc., Atlanta, 1997—2000, Attkisson Carter & Co., Atlanta, 2001—04, Carter, Terry and Co., Inc., Atlanta, 2004—. Bd. dirs. Prime Bancshares, Inc., Prime Bank, FSB; chmn. bd. dirs., pres. Sodamaster Co. Am.; exec. v.p. Woodridge Realty, Inc.; sr. v.p., Inc.; fin. cons. Carter, Terry and Co. Inc.; bd. dirs., sec. CRM Co., LLC, LA County, Calif., bd. dirs., sec. CRM of Am., LLC, Queen Creek, Ariz. Vestry mem. St. Luke's Episc. Ch., Atlanta, 1971-74; treas., exec. com., bd. dirs. Alliance Theatre Co., Atlanta, 1974-85; trustee Atlanta Music Festival Assn., Inc., 1975—; v.p., bd. dirs. Atlanta Preservation Ctr. Inc., pres., 1988-90, hon. bd. mem. 1999-; bd. vis. Lineberger Cancer Rsch. Ctr. U. NC, Chapel Hill, 1987-92; pres., Study Hall at Emmaus Ho., Inc., 1988-1992, bd. 1992—; bd. dirs. Margaret Mitchell Ho., Inc.; bd. govs. Ga. Pub. Policy Found., Inc., 1999-2001. Capt. US Army, 1965-67. Mem. ABA, Ga. Bar Assn., Atlanta Bar Assn., Piedmont Driving Club. Office Phone: 404-364-2040. Personal E-mail: sbansley@bellsouth.net.

ANSOHN, JOHN HUGO, emergency physician, educator; b. Houston, Nov. 3, 1949; s. John Ludwig and Ruth Ida Ansohn; m. Lori Woods Ansohn; children: Gena Joan Ansohn Ohert, Travis Jason, James Tyler, Katelyn Mae. AA, San Jacinto Coll., Pasadena, Tex., 1975; BS, Baylor U., Houston, 1975; MA, U. Houston, Clear Lake, 1980; DO, U. North Tex., Ft. Worth, 1985. Bd. cert. family practice Am. Coll. Osteo. Family Practice Bd. Physician asst., instr. U. Tex., Galveston, 1976—78, resident, 1981—86; family practice physician Southlake Med. Clinic, Tex., 1986—98; EMS med. dir. Baylor Regional Med. Ctr., Grapevine, Tex., 1987—, emergency physician, 1998—. EMS med. dir. rep., exec. bd. mem. North Tex. Tng. Regional Adv. Coun., 1999—; apptd. mem. med. dirs. com. Govs. EMS and Trauma Adv. Counsel, 2002—; assoc. prof. medicine U. Tex. Southwestern, Dallas, 2003—, U. Tex. Med. Br., Galveston, 2003—. With USN, 1969—73, with USPHS, 1978—81, col. USAR, 1981—2004. Named EMS Med. Dir. of Yr., Tex. Dept. Health, 2003, Med. Health Hero of Yr., Ft. Worth Bus. Press, 2004. Fellow: Am. Acad. Family Practitioners; mem.: Am. Coll. Emergency Medicine, Am. Osteo. Assn., Masons (master mason Grapevine Lodge 288). Avocations: hunting, ranching, fishing, camping. Office: Baylor Regional Med Ctr 1650 W College St Grapevine TX 76051

ANSOLABEHERE, STEPHEN DANIEL, political science professor; BA, Univ. Minn., 1984, BS in Econ., 1984; PhD in Polit. Sci., Harvard Univ., 1989. Asst. prof., polit. sci. UCLA, 1989—93; nat. fellow Hoover Inst., 1993—94; assoc. prof., polit. sci. MIT, 1995—98, Elting R. Morison prof. polit. sci., 1998—, assoc. head, 2002—05. Author: (book) The Media Game, 1993, Going Negative, 1996 (Goldsmith Book Prize, 1996), The End of Inequality, 2007. Named Carnegie Scholar, 2000—02; recipient Harry S Truman Fellowship, 1982—86. Fellow: Am. Acad. Arts & Scis. Office: Dept Polit Sci E53-449 MIT 77 Massachusetts Ave Cambridge MA 02139-4307 Office Phone: 617-253-5236. Business E-Mail: sda@mit.edu.*

ANSORGE, IONA MARIE, musician, educator, real estate agent; b. Nov. 3, 1927; d. Edgar B. and Marie Louise (Bleeke) Bohn; m. Edwin James Ansorge, Sept. 13, 1949; children: Richard, Michelle. BA, Valparaiso U., Ind., 1949; cert. in tchg., Drake U., Des Moines, Iowa, 1964; MA, U. Iowa, Iowa City, 1976. Min. of music Our Savior Luth. Ch., Des Moines, 1949-63; dir. chorus, concert choir Johnston (Iowa) HS, 1964—75; instr. Iowa Meth. Sch. Nursing, Des Moines, 1978-87; owner, pres. Bed and Breakfast in Iowa, Ltd., 1982-86; realtor Better Homes and Gardens First Realty, Des Moines, 1986-92. Dir.: Valparaiso U. Glee Club, 1948—49, Luth. Hour Mass Children's Choir, Johnston Concert Choir European concert tour, 1972; piano soloist: Grieg Piano Concerto, 1947; composer: If Winter Comes, 1949, The Moldau, 1948, Piano Salon Recitals, 1995, Organ Salon Recital, 2006. Pres. Des Moines Jaycee-ettes; spearheaded drive Des Moines Zoo; founder Messiah Luth. Ch., Des Moines, 1978; started Iowa Bed and Breakfast Industry, 1982; owner, pres. Bed and Breakfast in Iowa, Ltd.; mem. First Luth. Ch.; permanent sec. Class of 1949, Valparaiso U. Mem. LWV, AAUW, Am. Choral Dirs. Assn., Des Moines Bd. Realtors, Women's Coun. Realtors, Realtor's Million Dollar Club, Jaycee-ettes (pres. Des Moines chpt. 1957-58), Valparaiso U. Guild (charter mem. Des Moines chpt.), Mortar Bd. Lutheran. Avocations: playing piano and organ, tennis, bridge, reading, painting. Home: 8345 Twinberry Pt Colorado Springs CO 80920-5394

ANSPACH, ROBERT MICHAEL, lawyer; b. Tiffin, Ohio, Feb. 29, 1948; s. William Charles and Evelyn Helen (Smith) A.; m. Jane Evelyn Friedman, Oct. 29, 1983; children: Michael Robert, Robert Joseph, John William. BA, Cornell U., 1970, JD, 1973. Bar: Ohio 1973, U.S. Dist. Ct. (no. dist.) Ohio 1974, U.S. Ct. Appeals (6th cir.) 1976, U.S. Supreme Ct. 1976, U.S. Tax Ct. 1985. Assoc. Shumaker, Loop & Kendrick, Toledo, 1973-79, ptnr., 1979-83, mng. ptnr., 1984, adminstr. trial dept., 1985; founder, mng. ptnr. Anspach, Meeks & Nunn, L.L.P. and predecessor firm, Toledo, 1986—. Co-author: Winning in Court—The Accountant's Role in Litigation, Arbitration and Dispute Resolution, 1986. Trustee Toledo Repertoire Theatre, 1993—96, Boys and Girls Clubs Toledo, 1993—, Historic Perrysburg, Inc., 1998—99, pres., 1998—2000; trustee Toledo Cultural Arts Commn. at the Valentine Theatre, bd. chmn., 2001—. Recipient award of merit Ohio Legal Ctr., 1986. Fellow: Am. Bar Found., Ohio State Bar Found.; mem.: ABA, Def. Rsch. Inst., Nat. Assn. R.R. Trial Counsel, Toledo Bar Assn., Ohio Bar Assn. (vice chmn. jud. adminstrn. and legal reform com. 1982, lawyer's assistance com. 1986—). Avocations: singing, piano, art collecting, musical composition, tennis. Home: 535 E Front St Perrysburg OH 43551-2135 Office: Anspach Meeks & Nunn LLP Ste 1600 300 Madison Ave Toledo OH 43604-2633

ANSPAUGH, LYNN RICHARD, research biophysicist; b. Rawlins, Wyo., May 25, 1937; s. Solon Earl and Alice Henrietta (Day) A.; m. Barbara Anne Corrigan, Nov. 2, 1965 (div.); children: Gregory, Heidi; m. Larisa Fedorovna Kornushina, Sept. 27, 1993. BA, Nebr. Wesleyan U., 1959; M in Bioradiology, U. Calif., Berkeley, 1961, PhD, 1963. Biophysicist Lawrence Livermore (Calif.) Nat. Lab., 1963-74, group leader, 1974-75, sect. leader, 1976-82, div. leader, 1982-92, dir. Risk Scis. Ctr., 1992-95, dir. Dose Reconstruction program, 1995-96; rsch. prof. radiobiology divsn. Univ. Utah, Salt Lake City, 1997—. Tchr. extension U. Calif., Berkeley, 1966-69; lectr. San Jose (Calif.) State U., 1975; guest lectr. UCLA, Stanford U., U. Calif., Davis, 1992-96; faculty affiliate Colo. State U., Ft. Collins, 1979-83; cons. EPA, Washington, 1984-85, U. Utah, Salt Lake City, 1983-88, NAS/NRC, 1998, 2005; mem. U.S. del. UN Sci. Com. on Effects of Radiation, Vienna, 1987—; mem. Nat. Coun. on Radiation Protection and Measurements, 1989-2001, hon. mem., 2002—; mem. radiation adv. com. EPA, 1999-2005. Contbr. articles to profl. jours. AEC fellow, 1959-61; fellow NSF, 1961-63. Fellow Health Physics Soc. (pres. environ. radiation sect. 1984-85, pres. No. Calif. chpt. 1986-87); mem. AAAS, Soc. for Risk Analysis, Internat. Union Radioecology, Radiation Rsch. Soc., Sigma Xi. Office: PO Box 77777 Henderson NV 89077 Office Phone: 702-616-0914. E-mail: LAnspaugh@aol.com.

ANSTAETT, JENNIFER GRIFFIN, lawyer; b. Sikeston, Mo., Dec. 14, 1975; m. Patrick Anstaett. BA in Eng., Ctr. Coll. Ky., 1998, BA in Hist., 1998; JD, Washington & Lee U. Sch. of Law, 2001. Bar: Ohio 2001, US Dist. Ct., Southern Dist. Ohio, US Supreme Ct. Assoc. Beckman Weil Shepardson LLC, Cin., 2004—. Planned giving com. Alzheimer's Assn., Ky., exec. com., Young Professionals, Ky.; bd. dir. Franciscan Haircuts from the Heart. Named one of Ohio's Rising Stars, Super Lawyers, 2005, 2006. Mem.: Assn. Professionals in Aging, Am. Health Lawyers Assn., Ohio Bar Assn., Cin. Bar Assn. (Basic Estate Planning Seminar Com.). Office: Beckman Weil Shepardson LLC American Book Bldg 300 Pike St Ste 400 Cincinnati OH 45202 Office Phone: 513-621-2100. Office Fax: 513-621-0106.

ANSTEAD, HARRY LEE, state supreme court justice; b. Jacksonville, Fla., Nov. 4, 1937; m. Sue Anstead; children: Chris, Jim, Laura, Amy, Michael. BA, JD, U. Florida; grad., Nat. Coll. of State Judiciary. With Nat. Security Agency, Wash., DC; trial and appellate lawyer Fla., 1963—76; judge, then chief judge Fla. Ct. Appeals. (4th dist.), Fla., 1976—94; justice Fla. Supreme Ct., Tallahassee, 1994—, chief justice, 2002—04. Mem. Supreme Ct. Commn. on Structure of Florida's Courts; mem., vice-chair Supreme Ct. Com. on Civil Jury Instructions; mem. bd. governors Shepard Broad Law Ctr. Nova Southeastern U., St. Thomas U. Law Sch.; former chair Fla. Supreme Ct. Commn. on Professionalism. Published numerous articles relating to legal education, constitutional law, appellate practice. Founder, mem. Urban League of Palm Beach County, Beautiful Palm Beaches, Inc. Named to Hall of Fame, Boys and Girls Clubs of Am. Mem.: Fla. Bar Assn. (mem. steering com. for continuing legal edcuation), ABA, Sons of the Am. Revolution. Office: Fla Supreme Ct 500 S Duval St Tallahassee FL 32399-6556*

ANSTICE, DAVID W., pharmaceutical executive; B in Econs., U. Sydney, 1970. Economist Australian Pharm. Mfrs. Assn., 1969—74; various positions Merck Sharp & Dohme Australia, 1974—81; with corp., domestic divsn. Merck Rsch. Labs., 1981—82; dir. mktg. and sales Merck Sharp & Dohme South Africa, 1982—84; dir. sales Merck Sharp & Dohme Australia, 1984—85, dir. mktg. and sales, 1985—86, mng. dir., 1986—88; v.p. internat. human health mktg. Merck Sharp & Dohme Internat., 1988—89; v.p. mktg. Merck Sharp & Dohme USA, 1989—91; sr. v.p. human health divsn., pres. human health Merck & Co., Inc., 1991—92, sr. v.p. Europe human health divsn., 1993, pres. human health U.S./Can., 1994—97, pres. human health for the Americas Whitehouse Station, NJ, 1997—2002, pres. human health, 2003—05, pres. human health Asia-Pacific, 2005—06, exec. v.p., 2006—. Bd. dirs. Am. Found. Pharm. Edn.; bd. dirs., exec. com. Biotech. Industry Orgn., Washington; bd. dirs. Nat. Pharm. Coun., Reston, Va., chmn., 1997; bd. trustees U. Scis., Phila., Found. for Managed Care Pharmacy, Alexandria, Va., U.S. Found. of U. of Valley of Guatemala; mem. pres.'s coun. Gwynedd-Mercy Coll., Ambler, Pa.; mem. corp. adv. coun. COSSMHO, Nat. Coalition Hispanic Health and Human Svcs. Orgn., Washington; mem. corp. exec. bd. Phila. Mus. Art; mem. corp. coun. Children's Health Fund., Pitts. Chmn. steering com. Merck United Way , 1995—97. Office: Merck and Co Inc One Merck Dr Whitehouse Station NJ 08889-0100*

ANTALEK, EILEEN ELIZABETH, educational psychologist, consultant; b. Burtonwood, Eng., Jan. 16, 1957; d. Henry and Sarah Louise O'Connor; m. Michael Antalek, Feb. 16, 1980; children: Peter, Sarah. BA, Framingham State Coll., 1991; M in English, Clark U., 1994, EdD, 2004. House maintenance, Grafton, Mass., 1989-90; tutor Framingham (Mass.) State Coll., 1990-91, Clark U., Worcester, 1991-93, asst. dir. spl. needs, 1993-94, tchg. asst., 1994-95; asst. dir. Educational Directions, Westborugh, Mass., 1995—. Cable access prodr. Grafton Cable Network, 1986—88. Publicity dir. North Grafton United Meth. Ch., 1986—88, Sunday sch. tchr., 1989—95, Sunday sch. supt., 1992—95, chair bd. edn., 1988—92, chair pastor parish rels., 1999—2003, chair space needs com., 2000—03, mem. stewardship com., 2007. Scholar Resident, Clark U., 1991—96, Nat. Merit, 1975, 1976, David O. Wilson, Anderson Coll., 1976. Mem.: APA, Internat. Dyslexia Assn. (bd. dirs., Mass. br.), Coun. Exceptional Children, Ind. Edn. Cons. Assn., Internat. Dyslexia Assn., Consortium Learning Disabilities, Sigma Tau Delta, Phi Eta Sigma. Avocations: textile art, motorcycling, painting, music, hiking. Office: Educational Directions 57 E Main St Ste 220 Westborough MA 01581 Office Phone: 508-870-1515. Office Fax: 508-870-1505. Business E-Mail: eileen@educationaldirections.com.

ANTELL, DARRICK EUGENE, plastic surgeon, educator; b. Cleve., Feb. 22, 1951; s. E. James and Wanda H. (Kociecki) A.; m. Elizabeth Ann Sobottka, July 14, 1984; children: Gillian Elizabeth, Darrick Eugene Jr., Leslie Jane, Helen Greer, Meredith James. BS in Biology, Hobart Coll., 1973; DDS, Case Western Res. U. Dental, 1978; MD, Med. Coll. of Ohio, 1982. Diplomate Am. Bd. Plastic Surgery. Surgery intern Stanford (Calif.) U. Med. Ctr., 1982-83, surgery resident, 1983-85; plastic surgery resident N.Y. Hosp. Cornell, NYC, 1985-87; plastic and reconstructive surgeon St. Luke's/Roosevelt, NYC, 1987—; asst. clin. prof. plastic surgery Columbia U., NYC, 1989—; med. dir., founder Lenox Hill Ambulatory Surgery, PC, NYC. Author: Plastic Surgery, 1991; contbr. articles to profl. jours. Trustee East Side House Settlement, N.Y.C., 1991, Hist. Soc. of the Town of Greenwich, 1999, Univ. Sch. Cleve., 2000; trustee adv. Girl Scouts U.S.A., N.Y.C., 1991. Facial Proportions grantee Am. Soc. for Aesthetic Plastic Surgery, 1987; Maliniac fellow Plastic Surgery Edn. Found.; recipient Pres. Citizenship award N.Y. State Med. Soc., 1992. Fellow: ACS, Plastic Surgery Ednl. Found.; mem.: AMA, Lipoplasty Soc., Interplast, Am. Acad. Cosmetic Dentistry, Internat. Acad. Dental Facial Aesthetics (founding), Internat. Soc. for Aestheic Plastic Surgery, N.Y. Regional Soc. Plastic and Reconstructive Surgeons, Am. Soc. Maxillofacial Surgeons Parliamentarian, Am. Soc. Aesthetic Plastic Surgery, Am. Soc. Plastic and Reconstructive Surgeons, Univ. Sch. Alumni Adv. Coun., Herbert Conway Soc., Greenwich Skating Club, Mill Reef Club (Antigua, W.I.), Cleve. Skating Club, Fishers Island Yacht Club, Stanwich Country Club, Union Club. Avocations: squash, fly fishing, golf, skiing. Office: 850 Park Ave New York NY 10021-1845 Office Phone: 212-988-4040. E-mail: dea@antell-md.com.

ANTEZANO, ANTONIO, investment company executive; s. Tulio and Alicia (Chavarri) Antezano; m. Maria Scelza. BSc in Indsl. Engring., Pontificia Cath. U., Lima, Peru, 1990; MBA, J.L. Kellogg Grad. Sch. Mgmt., Evanston, Ill., 1997. Assoc. sales & mktg. Eli Lilly & Co., Lima, Peru, 1990—91; asst. brand mgr. Procter & Gamble, Lima, 1991—94; assoc. corp. staff GE, Cleve., 1996; sr. analyst, overseas and domestic fin. GM, NYC, 1997—98, mgr. capital planning, 2000, sr. analyst, corp. fin. Brussels, 1999—2000; sr. mgr., bus. devel. Entopia, San Francisco, 2000—01; assoc. equity analyst AllianceBernstein, NYC, 2001—03; sr. equity analyst Bear Stearns & Co, NYC, 2004—05, sr. equity analyst and mng. dir., 2006—. Mem.: Chartered Fin. Analyst Inst. (cert.), NY Soc. Security Analysts. Achievements include research in international transfer of technology. Avocations: tennis, soccer, chess. Home Phone: 646-862-3976; Office Phone: 212-272-2357. Personal E-mail: aantezano@gmail.com.

ANTEZZO, MATTHEW J., artist; b. Hartford, Conn., 1962; Attended, U. Utah, 1982—84; degree, Parsons Sch. Design, NYC, 1985—88. One-man shows include Randy Alexander, NYC, 1991, Galerie George-Philippe Vallois, Paris, 1991, 1993, Basilico Fine Arts, NYC, 1993, 1994, Interim Art, London, 1994, Gian Enzo Sperone, Rom I, Galerie Georges Philippe Vallois, Paris, 1995, Blum & Poe, Santa Monica, Calif., 2000, Eleni Koroneou Gallery, Athens, 2001, Spüth Magers Projekte, Münich Arena, Mexico, 2003, Michele Maccarone Inc., NYC, 2005, exhibited in group shows at Am. Fine Arts, 1989, Galerie Georges-Philippe Vallois, Paris, 1990, Home For Contemporary Theatre and Art, NYC, 1991, John Post Lee Gallery, 1991, Andrea Rosen Gallery, 1993, Backstage, Kunstverein, Hamburg, Germany, 1993, ghost-limb, Basilico Fine Arts, NYC, 1993, Desire and Loss, Carl Solway Gallery, Cin., 1994, Crash, Thread Waxing Space, 1994, When Attitudes Become Form, Monclair Art Mus., NJ, 1994, I Love New York, Edinburgh Internat. Arts Festival, 1997, Influence, Anxiety and Gratitude, MIT List Visual Arts Ctr., Cambridge, 2002, Living with Duchamp, The Tang Teaching Mus. and Art Gallery, Skidmore Coll., 2003, Reanimation, Kunstmuseum Thun, 2004.

ANTHAMATTEN, MITCHELL LEWIS, chemical engineer, educator; b. Independence, Mo., Mar. 23, 1974; s. Paul Dean and Sharon Jeanette Anthamatten; m. Sandra Doreen Kuechler, June 26, 1998. BSChemE, U. Mo., 1996; MSChemE, MIT, 2001, PhD in Chem. Engring., 2001. Staff scientist Lawrence Livermore (Calif.) Nat. Lab., 2002—04; asst. prof. U. Rochester, NY, 2004—. Office: U Rochester Dept Chem Engring 250 Gavett Hall Rochester NY 14627 Office Phone: 585-273-5526. Office Fax: 585-273-1348. Business E-Mail: anthamatten@che.rochester.edu.

ANTHOINE, ROBERT, lawyer, educator; b. Portland, Maine, June 5, 1921; s. Edward S and Sara B (Pinkham) Anthoine; m. Margarita M. Hamilton, Dec. 12, 2006; children from previous marriage: Alison, Robert Neal, Nelson, Nina. AB, Duke U., 1942; JD, Columbia U., 1949. Bar: NY 1949, US Ct Appeals (2d cir) 1956, US Supreme Ct 1970. Rsch. assoc. Am. Law Inst. fed. income tax project Columbia U., NYC, 1949—50; assoc. Cleary, Gottlieb, Friendly and Cox, 1950—52; assoc. prof. law Columbia U., 1952—56, prof. law, 1956—64, adj. prof., 1964—93; ptnr. Winthrop, Stimson, Putnam and Roberts, 1963—86, sr. counsel, 1987—2000, in charge London office, 1972—76; sr. counsel Pillsbury Winthrop Shaw Pittman LLP, NYC, 2001—. Vis. prof. Law Sch. Ind. U., Bloomington, Ind., 1986; vis. prof. Law Sch. U. Tex., Austin, 1988; vis. prof. Law Sch. U. NC, Chapel Hill, 1991, U. Pa., Philadelphia, 1996, Seattle U., 1997. Author, editor: survey Tax Incentives for Investment in Developing Countries, 1979; contbr. articles to profl jours. Trustee Royal Shakespeare Theatre Trust, 1977—; hon. gov. Royal Shakespeare Theatre, Stratford-upon-Avon, England, 1977—; chmn. emeritus, bd. dirs. Aperture Found., 1978—; active Coun Fgn. Rels., 1982—; trustee, dir. Grosvenor Gallery (Fine Arts) Ltd., London, 1994—; pres. S K Yee Found., 1995—; vice chair, trustee Internat. Photog. Coun., 1996—; vice-chmn, bd dirs Am. Friends Theater, 1998—; hon. dir. Hazen Polsky Found., 2000—; bd. dirs., v.p. Morris Graves Found., 2000—; chmn. Lucid Art Found., 2005—; trustee Sevenarts, Ltd., London; bd. dirs. emeritus Eric and Salome Estorick Found, Vol. Lawyers Art. Lt. USN, 1942—46. Mem.: ABA, Asn Litèraire et Artistique Int (US), Int. Fiscal Assn., Assn. Bar City NY, Am. Law Inst. (life), Queen's, Hurlingham Club (London), River Club (New York, NY), Century Assn. Club. Democrat. Office: Pillsbury Winthrop Shaw Pittman LLP 1540 Broadway New York NY 10036-4039 Office Phone: 212-858-1127. Business E-Mail: robert.anthoine@pillsburylaw.com.

ANTHONISEN, GEORGE RIOCH, sculptor, artist; b. Boston, July 31, 1936; s. Niels Landmark and Margaret (Rioch) A.; m. Ellen Friedman, Feb. 16, 1966; children: Rachel, Daniel. BA, U. Vt., Burlington, 1961; postgrad., Nat. Acad. Design, NYC, 1961—62, Art Students League, 1962—64, Dartmouth Coll. Med. Sch., Hanover, NH, 1967. One-man shows include Hopkins Ctr. Dartmouth Coll., 1966, Ctr. Art Gallery, NYC, 1969, Moody Gallery, Pasadena, Calif., 1979, Bjorn Lindgren Gallery, NYC, 1981, 82, U. Scranton Art Gallery, Pa., 1986, Rotunda Cannon House Office Bldg., US Capitol, Washington, 1989, The Woodmere Art Mus., Phila., 1992, Bianco Gallery, Buckingham, Pa., 1994, 98, Phila. Flower Show-Gale Nurseries, 1995, Berman Mus. Art, Collegeville, Pa., 1996, Festival of Faiths, The Gardens of Louisville, 1999, Jonathan Edwards Coll., Yale U., 2006, Cooley Gallery, Old Lyme, Conn., 2007; exhibited in group shows NAD, N.Y., 1971, Port of History Mus., Phila., 1987, James A. Michener Art Mus., Doylestown, 1988, 00, Millersville U., Pa., 1991, Nat. Sculpture Soc., 1993, Morani Gallery, Med. Coll. Pa., 1994, Monuments Conservancy, Samuel Dorsky Symposium on Pub. Monuments/Time and Life Bldg., NYC, 1997, Bianco Gallery, Buckingham, Pa., 1995-2002, Salmagundi Club, NYC, 2000, Phila. Sketch Club, Travis Gallery, 2002, 03, 04, 05, Sculpture Along Bear Creek, Keller, Tex., 2005, Bee & Thistle Inn, Old Lyme, Conn., 2007; represented in permanent collections at WHO, Geneva, US Capitol Bldg. Hall of Columns, Washington, Carnegie Hall, NYC, Ctr. for Interfaith Rels., Louisville, Please Touch Mus., Phila., Dartmouth-Hitchcock Med. Ctr., Lebanon, NH, Washington Sch. Psychiatry, Keneseth Israel, Elkins Park, Pa., Doylestown Hosp., Pa., Pa. Acad. Music, Lancaster, Atlanta U. Trevor Arnett Libr., U. Alaska, Fairbanks, James Michener Art Mus., Doylestown, Pa., Phila. Coll. Osteo. Medicine, Berman Mus. Art, Collegeville, Pa., Martin Art Gallery, Muhlenberg Coll., Allentown, Pa. With US Army, 1955-57. Sculptor-in-residence Augustus St. Gaudens Nat. Hist. Site, US Dept. Interior, 1971; recipient James Augustus Suydam bronze medal, 1968, Sen. Ernest Gruening award Alaska State Coun. on Arts, 1976, Exemplary Achievement in Arts award Bucks County C. of C., Pa., 1985. Fellow Nat. Sculpture Soc. (bd. dirs. 1993-94), hon. mem. Phila. Sketch Club, 2002. Avocations: fishing, baseball. Home and Office: PO Box 147 Solebury PA 18963-0147 Home Phone: 215-297-5318. Personal E-mail: ellena@voicenet.com.

ANTHONY, ANDREW JOHN, lawyer; b. Newark, Jan. 26, 1950; s. Andrew and Mary (Norton) A.; children: Nicholas, Natalie. BA, Kean Coll., 1973; JD cum laude, U. Miami, Coral Gables, 1976. Bar: Fla. 1977, US Dist. Ct. (so. dist.) Fla. 1977, US Dist. Ct. (mid. dist.) Fla., US Supreme Ct. Assoc. Knight, Peters, Hoeveler, Pickle, Niemoeller & Flynn, Miami, Fla., 1977-79, Vernis & Bowling, Miami, 1979, Ligman, Martin, Shiley & McGee, Coral Gables, Fla., 1979-86; sole practice Coral Gables, 1986—. Mem.: ABA, Fla. Bar Assn. Democrat. Roman Catholic. Avocations: coin collecting/numismatics, fishing, reading. Home: 90 Edgewater Dr 202 Coral Gables FL 33133 Office: The Law Offices of Anthony & Associates PA Ste 505 250 Catalonia Ave Coral Gables FL 33134 Home Phone: 305-661-3738; Office Phone: 305-444-8927 ext. 11. Business E-Mail: ajanthony@ajalaw.com.

ANTHONY, BARBARA COX, foundation administrator; b. Dec. 1922; m. Garner Anthony; children: Blair, James Cox Kennedy. Contr. Cox Enterprises, Inc. Chair Daytona Newspapers Cox Enterprises, Atlanta; founder Barbara Cox Anthony Found., Hawaii; rancher, cattle breeder, Australia. Bd. trustees La Pietra: Hawaii Sch. for Girls, 1978—. Named one of World's Richest People, Forbes mag., 1999—, Forbes Richest Ams., 2006. Heiress to James M. Cox, founder of Cox Enterprises, Inc. Office: Cox Enterprises Inc 6205 Peachtree Dunwoody Rd Atlanta GA 30328 Mailing: Barbara Cox Anthony Found 1132 Bishop St Ste 1200 Honolulu HI 96813 Office Phone: 678-645-0000. Office Fax: 678-645-1079.*

ANTHONY, BERTHA M., minister; b. Osceola Mills, Pa., Dec. 28, 1928; d. Samuel Smith and Dovie C. Morgan; m. Ballard James Anthony, 1946 (dec. 1989); children: Eunice J. Thomas, Charles J.(dec.) , Dovie Franquita Mason, Ida Marie Lanansha, Vanessa M. Lynch, Yette S. Cooksey, Vanteria L., Terrence E.(dec.). Ordained min. Ch. of God in Christ, 1987. Caretaker Canoe Creek State Park, Hollidaysburg, Pa.; worker Puritan Sportswear, Altoona, Pa.; custodian Vets. Home, Duncansville, Pa.; glassmaker, shaper PPG Industries, Blair & Perry Co.; sketcher Gween Engr., Altoona; nurses's asst. Valley View Nursing Home, Altoona; bible ministry Loretto State Prison, Pa.; coffee hostess Sheets, Inc., Altoona: pastor Livingwater Ch. of God in Christ, Williamsport, Pa., 1987—. Judge of elections Blair County, Altoona, Pa., 2003—; mem. outreach ministry Ch. of Livingwaters, Williamsport, 1997—. Republican. Pentecostal. Home: PO Box 93 1111 17th Ave Altoona PA 16603

ANTHONY, CARMELO, professional basketball player; b. NYC, May 29, 1984; 1 child, Kiyan. Student, Syracuse U., 2003. Forward NBA Denver Nuggets, 2003—. Mem. US Men's Basketball Team, Athens Olympic Games, 2004. Vol. Family Resource Ctr., Denver. Named NCAA Final Four Most Outstanding player, 2003, NBA Rookie of the Month (6 Times), 2003—04, USA Basketball Male Athlete of Yr., 2006; named one of All-NBA 3rd Team, 2006; named to All-Rookie 1st Team, NBA, 2004, Western Conf. All-Star Team, 2005, 2007. Office: Denver Nuggets 1000 Chopper Cir Denver CO 80204*

ANTHONY, CAROLYN ADDITON, librarian; b. Pitts., Nov. 27, 1949; d. Elwood Prince and Elizabeth Martha (Gruginskis) Additon; m. William W. Anthony, III, July 7, 1973; children: Margaret Susan, Lauren Elizabeth. AB, Colby Coll., 1971; MLS, U. R.I., 1973. Reference libr. Enoch Pratt Free Lib., Balt., 1973-75, head info. and referral svc., 1975-78; head info. svcs. Balt. County Pub. Libr., Towson, Md., 1978-80, head, info. and program svcs., 1980-85; dir. Skokie (Ill.) Pub. Libr., 1985—. Pres. Libr. Adminstr. Conf. No. Ill., 1988—89; chair adv. bd. Pub. Librs., 1986—89; bd. mem. Rush North Shore Med. Ctr., 2004—, pres. women's bd., 2004—06. Recipient Libr. of Yr., North Suburban Libr. Sys., 2004. Mem.: ALA (mem. coun. 1993—97), Ill. Libr. Assn. (pres. 1999—2000, award, Libr. of the Yr. 2003), Am. Libr. Trustee Assn. (bd. dirs.), Pub. Libr. Assn. (new stds. task force com. 1984—87, bd. dirs. 1987—89, 2005—), Met. Libr. Assn. (exec. com. 1990—93), Chgo. Libr. Club (pres. 1991—92), Rotary (pres. Skokie chpt. 1992—93). Democrat. Soc. Of Friends. Office: Skokie Pub Libr 5215 Oakton St Skokie IL 60077-3680 Office Phone: 847-673-7774. Business E-Mail: canthony@skokielibrary.info.

ANTHONY, DONALD BARRETT, engineering executive; b. Kansas City, Kans., Jan. 28, 1948; s. Donald W. and Marjorie (Lifsey) A.; m. Darla S. Donovan, Dec. 16, 1972; children: Jennifer L., Danielle S. BSChemE, U. Toledo, 1970; MS, MIT, 1971, DSc, 1974. Asst. prof., practice sch. dir. dept. chem. engring. MIT, Cambridge, Mass., 1974-75; group supr. coal R&D Std. Oil Co. Ohio, Cleve., 1976-77, mgr. marine planning, 1978-79, mgr. synthetic fuels devel., 1980-83, v.p., gen. mgr. Pfaudler Divsn. Rochester, NY, 1983-85; v.p. R&D Std. Oil Co., Cleve., 1985-87, BP Am., Inc., Cleve., 1987-88, BP Exploration, Inc., Cleve., 1989-90; v.p. tech. Bechtel, Inc., Houston, 1990-94, v.p. ops., 1994-95, v.p. ref., 1995-96; pres. Bailey Controls Co., 1996-98, Process Ind. Group, ABB Automation, 1999—2000; pres., CEO NineSigma, Inc., Cleve., 2001—03; pres. Coun. for Chem. Rsch., Wash., DC, 2004—. Contbr. articles to profl. jours.; patentee in field. Capt. AUS, 1970-78. MIT Esso fellow, 1970-71, Little rsch.-devel. fellow, 1971-72, Procter & Gamble fellow, 1972-73, Bechtel fellow, 1992. Mem. AIChE, Am. Chem. Soc., Sigma Xi, Phi Kappa Phi, Tau Beta Pi, Pi Mu Epsilon, Phi Eta Sigma. Lutheran. Home: 122 Portofino Dr Nokomis FL 34275 Office: Council for Chem Research Ste 302 1730 Rhode Island Ave Washington DC 20036 Office Phone: 202-429-3971, 216-396-8664. Business E-Mail: danthony@ccrhq.org.

ANTHONY, DONALD CHARLES, librarian, educator; b. NYC, Mar. 29, 1926; s. Charles and Margaret Evelyn (Gleason) A.; m. Mary Miserez, Apr. 18, 1957; children— Stephen, Sheila, Irene. BA, U. Wis., 1951, MA, 1954; postgrad., U. Geneva, Switzerland, 1952-53. Library asst. Enoch Pratt Free Library, Balt., 1954-55; librarian Eleutherian Mills-Hagley Found., Wilmington, Del., 1955-59; dir. Fargo (N.D.) Pub. Library, 1959-61; asso. librarian N.Y. State Library, Albany, 1961-66; asst. dir. Columbia Libraries, 1966-69, acting dir., 1969, asso. dir., 1970-74; dir. Syracuse U. Libraries, 1974-85; cons. on preservation of library materials, 1986—; pres. Donmar Assocs., Clinton, NY, 1987—2004. Adj. faculty Mohawk Valley Community Coll., Utica, N.Y., 1989-97; docent Munson-Williams-Proctor Arts Inst., Utica, 1999—; cons. N.Y. State Edn. Dept., 1967-97. Producer; host: TV Museum, KXGO-TV, Fargo, 1960; Contbr. articles to profl. jours. Trustee N.Y. Met. Reference and Research Library Agy., 1969-74, Cen. N.Y. Library Resources Council, 1983-86; chmn. bd. dirs. Five Asso. U. Libraries, Syracuse, 1975-76, 77-79; trustee Bd. Edn., Dobbs Ferry, N.Y., 1971-74, v.p., 1973-74. Served with USNR, 1944-46. Fellow Coun. on Libr. Resources. Home: 120 Paris Rd New Hartford NY 13413-2433

ANTHONY, EDWARD MASON, linguistics educator; b. Cleve., Sept. 1, 1922; s. Edward Mason and Elsie (Haas) A.; m. Ann Louise Terbrueggen, Sept. 18, 1946; children: Lynn Diane Anthony Higgins, Janice Louise, Edward Mason, 4th. AB, U. Mich., 1944, MA, 1946, PhD, 1954. From instr. English to prof. linguistics U. Mich., 1945—64; prof. U. Pitts., 1964—90, prof. emeritus, 1990—, chmn. dept. gen. linguistics, 1964—74; dir. Lang. Acquisition Inst., 1970, dir. lang. orientation programs, 1974—82, dir. Asian Studies program, 1977—82, dir. Lang. and Culture Inst, 1982—90. Vis. lectr., Afghanistan, 1951, Thailand, 1955-57, Mexico, 1964, 65, Poland, 1977, Greece and Yugoslavia, 1981, Singapore and Thailand, 1984, Hong Kong, 1985, 86; dir. S.E. Asian English Project, Thailand, Laos, Vietnam, 1958-61, Rockefeller Found. Thai Project, 1967-72; vis. prof. Regional English Lang. Centre, Singapore, 1974-75, Peking Inst. Fgn. Lang., 1979-80; cons. in field; mem. Nat. Adv. Coun. Tchg. English as Fgn. Lang.; resource person Detroit Bd. Edn., 1964, Pitts. Bd. Edn., 1965; mem. adv. screening com. in linguistics Coun. for Internat. Exch. Scholars, 1976; mem. adv. panel in English tchg. to dir. USIA, 1987-93. Author: Reading Thai Syllables, 1962, (with others) Foundations of Thai, 2 vols, 1968, Towards a Theory of Lexical Meaning, 1975, About Thai, 2001; book rev. editor: Lang. Learning, 1948; editor, 1949. Mellon fellow Nat. Fgn. Lang. Ctr. Washington, 1990; Smith-Mundt grantee, 1951, Lang. Rsch. grantee NDEA, 1965-67, grantee State Dept., 1964, 65, 77, 81, 84, 90; recipient Fulbright award, 1955-57, Plaque of Honor Ramkhamhaeng U., Bangkok, Thailand, 1986, Cert. Appreciation USIA, 1992. Mem. Linguistic Soc., Am. Assn. Applied Linguistics, Assn. Asian Studies, Siam Soc. (life), Assn. Tchrs. English to Speakers of Other Langs. (pres. 1967, Alatis award 1991), Nat. Coun. Tchrs. English. Democrat. Presbyterian. Home: 4118 Northampton Dr Allison Park PA 15101-1532 Office: Dept Linguistics U Pitts Pittsburgh PA 15260 Business E-Mail: emal@pitt.edu.

ANTHONY, HARRY ANTONIADES, retired city planner, architect, educator; b. Skyros, Greece, July 28, 1922; arrived in U.S., 1951, naturalized, 1954; s. Anthony G. and Maria G. (Ftoulis) Antoniades; m. Anne C. Skoufis, Sept. 23, 1950; children: Mary Anne Anthony Smith, Kathryn Harriet. B.Arch., Nat. Tech. U., Athens, Greece, 1945; student, Ecole Nat. Supérieure des Beaux Arts, Paris, 1945-46; M.City Planning, U. Paris, 1947; Docteur de l'Université, Sorbonne, Paris, 1949; PhD in Arch. and Urban Planning, Columbia, 1955. Architect-planner with Constantinos A. Doxiadis, Athens, 1943-45, LeCorbusier, Paris, 1946-47, ECA, Paris, 1949-51; city planner with Maurice E.H. Rotival, NYC, 1951-52; chief planner Brown & Blauvelt, NYC, 1952-54; city planner, urban designer Skidmore, Owings & Merrill, NYC, 1954-56; prin. planning cons. Brown Engrs. Internat., NYC, 1956-60; prin. Brown & Anthony City Planners, Inc., NYC, 1960—69; v.p. Doxiadis Assocs., Inc., Washington, 1971—72; mem. faculty Columbia U., 1953-72, from asst. to assoc. prof., 1956-63, prof. urban planning, 1963-72, dir. grad. div. urban planning Grad. Sch. Architecture and Planning, 1962-65; prof. urban planning Calif. State Poly. U., Pomona, 1972-83, prof. emeritus urban and regional planning, 1983—, chmn. dept., 1972-76. Vis. prof. urban design Tulane U., 1967-68; vis. lectr. U. Calif. at Berkeley, Stanford U., Dartmouth, San Diego State U., CUNY, U. Okla., Ohio U., Auburn U., Salk Inst. Biol. Studies, U.S. Internat. U.; lectr. urban studies and planning U. Calif., San Diego, 1980-82, Chancellor's Assoc., 2001—; scholar-in-residence U. B.C., Vancouver, 1978; planning, zoning, urban renewal and urban design cons. to several cities, U.S. and abroad; also cons. to UN, Am. Med. Bldg. Guild, corps. and pvt. firms, to govts. and univs.; planning commr., Leonia, N.J., 1958-64; master planner, cons. arch. for Ss. Constantine and Helen Greek Orthodox Ch. and Village for the Elderly, Cardiff-by-the-Sea, Calif., 1983-2007 (AIA design awareness program orchid award 1997). Author, co-author, contbr.: Four Great Makers of Modern Architecture: Gropius, Le Corbusier, Mies Van

Der Rohe, Wright, Dictionary of American History, The Challenge of Squatter Settlements-With Special Reference to the Cities of Latin America, La Défense à Paris et le Quartier d'Affaires de Vancouver: Une Comparaison Urbaine, New Orleans Air Rights Study, Woodstock Growth Plan and Land Use Controls, Mt. Vernon Planning Study, Corning Area, N.Y.: Conditions and Prospects, Corning Region: Development Plans, Metairie Shore, La.: Lakefront Recreation and Comty. Devel., U.S. Navy Multiple Activity Master Plan: Norfolk Complex, Aqaba, Jordan: Future Devel., Lands of Kapua, Hawaii: Feasibility Study for Urban, Agricultural and Recreational Devel.; several master plans, city and regional planning reports, urban design plans and programs, environ. impact reports, zoning ordinances, educational videocassettes on urban planning subjects; contbr. articles to profl. jours., mags., newspapers; acad. profl. writings, awards, plans, designs and reports included in Spl. Collections Libr., U. Calif. (San Diego), 1998. Recipient Premier Grand Prix Internat. Exhbn. Housing and City Planning, Paris, 1947, St. Paul's Gold Medal award Greek Orthodox Archdiocese Am., 2003; William Kinne Fellows travelling fellow in planning N.Am., 1956, French Govt. fellow, 1945-47; research award Urban Center of Columbia U., 1969; named Outstanding Prof. Calif. State Poly. U., 1975; founder Met. Opera House, Lincoln Ctr. for the Performing Arts, N.Y.C. Mem. AIA (Arnold W. Brunner scholar 1958), Am. Inst. Cert. Planners (bd. examiners), Am. Planning Assn. (Disting. Svc. award 1984, San Diego Cmty. Design Awareness Program Orchid award 1997), Order of Am. Hellenic Ednl. Progressive Assn., Hellenic Cultural Soc. (Dedication to Perpetuating the Greek Lang. award 2003), Internat. Soc. Greek Writers (Architecture and Poetry award 2004), Internat. Land Econs. Soc. of Lambda Alpha (Richard T. Ely Disting. Educator award 1988), U. Calif. San Diego Faculty Club. Home: 7665 Caminito Avola La Jolla CA 92037-3956 Business E-Mail: hanthony@ucsd.edu.

ANTHONY, JOAN CATON, administrative judge; b. South Bend, Ind., July 28, 1939; d. Joseph Robert and Margaret Catherine (McMeel) Caton; m. Robert Armstrong Anthony, Jan. 3, 1980; 1 child, Peter. BA, Marquette U., Milw., 1961; MA, Northwestern U., Evanston, Ill., 1963; JD, Catholic U. Am., Washington, 1979. Bar: D.C. 1980, Va. 1982. Instr. English Marquette U., Milw., 1963-65, George Washington U., Washington, 1965-69, asst. prof., 1969-70; spl. asst. student affairs HEW, Washington, 1970-72; dir. Office Student and Youth Affairs U.S. Office Edn., Washington, 1972-74, legis. specialist, 1974-78; chief mgmt. ops. br. Fed. Wildlife Permit Office U.S. Fish and Wildlife Svc., Washington, 1978-81; assoc. Cate and Goodbread, Washington, 1981—85; atty., advisor office legis. counsel U.S. Dept. Interior, 1991-95; staff atty. Interior Bd. Land Appeals, 1995—2003; adminstrv. judge Def. Office of Hearings and Appeals, U.S. Dept. Def., 2003—. Mem. U.S. del. to 2d meeting Conf. Parties to Conv. on Internat. Trade in Endangered Species of Wild Fauna and Flora, San Jose, Costa Rica, 1979. Contbr. lit. revs., essays and articles on univ.-cmty. rels., western settlement and internat. negotiations to various publs. Pres. Franklin Forest Frolickers, 1985—86; den leader Cub Scouts, mem. com. Boy Scouts Am., 1990—2000; parent vol. Fairfax County Pub. Schs., 1987—2001; treas. Greater McLean Rep. Women's Club, 1987—88; bd. dirs. McLean Citizens Assn., 1982—83, Fairfax County Humane Soc., 1983. Recipient Spl. Achievement award U.S. Fish and Wildlife Svc., 1981. Mem.: Fed. Bar Assn., DAR (Fauquier Courthouse chpt.), Va. Bar Assn., D.C. Bar Assn. Roman Catholic. Office Phone: 703-696-1802. Business E-Mail: anthonyj@osdgc.osd.mil.

ANTHONY, JULIAN DANFORD, JR., lawyer; b. Boston, Oct. 23, 1935; s. Julian Danford and Eleanor Caroline (Hopkins) Anthony; m. Ellen Nora Brown, Apr. 8, 1961; children: Julian Danford III, Sarah Dodge, David Campbell. AB, Wesleyan U., 1957; LLB, Harvard U., 1960. Bar: Minn. 1961, Conn. 1965. Atty.-advisor U.S. Tax Ct., Washington, 1962-64; assoc. Day, Berry & Howard LLP, Hartford, Conn., 1965-70, ptnr., 1971—2004, of counsel, 2004—. Chmn. Conn. Red Cross Blood Svcs., Farmington, 1981—82; elector Wadsworth Atheneum, Hartford, 1986—95; bd. dirs. J. Walton Bissell Found., Hartford, 1987—2004, pres., CEO, 2004—; corporator Hartford Hosp., 1988—; mem. adv. bd. dirs. Salvation Army, Hartford, 1990—96; bd. dirs. Hartford Symphony Orch., 1993—99; trustee Amistad Ctr. Art & Culture, Hartford, 1997—; bd. dirs. Conn. Children's Med. Ctr., 1994—2005, chmn., 1999—2002; bd. dirs. Coordinating Coun. Founds., Hartford, 1994—99, Conn. Children's Med. Ctr. Found., 1998—2004. Mem.: ABA, Fed. Tax Inst. New Eng. (mem. exec. com. 1987—). Office: Day Berry & Howard LLP Cityplace Hartford CT 06103

ANTHONY, MICHAEL, chef; Chef Daniel, March, L'Astrance, L'Arpege, Jacques Cagna; exec. chef Blue Hill at Stone Barns, Gramercy Tavern, NYC, 2006—. Named one of Americas Best New Chefs, Food and Wine Mag., 2002, NYC's Rising Star, StarChefs.com, 2007; named to Next Generation list, Bon Appetit, 2003. Office: Gramercy Tavern 42 E 20th St New York NY 10003 Office Phone: 212-477-0777.*

ANTHONY, MICHAEL FRANCIS, lawyer; b. Chgo., Dec. 19, 1950; s. Rudolph A. and Margaret M. (Shea) Anthony; m. Megan P. O'Connell; children: Erin Christine, Ian O'Connell, Connor Cullerton, Madeline Shea, McKenzie Galligan. BS cum laude, Xavier U., Cin., 1972, MHA, 1974; JD, U. Balt., 1978. Bar: Md. 1978, Fla. 1979, Ill. 1980, DC 1989. Various adminstrv. positions Johns Hopkins Hosp., Balt., 1973-78; assoc. Ober Kaler Grimes & Shriver, Balt., 1978-80; from assoc. to ptnr. McDermott, Will & Emery, Chgo., 1980-87, 1989—91, nat. head health law dept., 1991—2001, 2006—; sr. v.p. for legal affairs Am. Hosp. Assn., Chgo., 1987-89. Contbr. articles to profl. jours. Mem. adv. bd. De Paul Inst. Health Law. Fellow: Am. Health Lawyers Assn. (past pres.), Am. Coll. Healthcare Execs. (various coms.). Office: McDermott Will & Emery 227 W Monroe St Ste 5300 Chicago IL 60606-5096 Office Phone: 312-984-7635. Business E-Mail: manthony@mwe.com.

ANTHONY, RICHARD E., bank executive; b. May 6, 1946; BS in Fin., U. Ala., 1968; MBA, U. Va., 1971. Various position including exec. v.p. AmSouth Bank, N.A., Birmingham, 1971—85; pres. First Comml. Bancshares, Inc., 1985; chmn. bd., CEO First Comml. Bank, 1985; chmn. First Comml. Bank. (acquired by Synovus), Birmingham, 1985—93; pres. Synovus Finl. Corp., Ala., 1993—95; vice chmn. Synovus, Columbus, Ga., 1995—, COO, 2003—05, pres., 2003—06, pres., CEO, 2005—06, chmn., CEO, 2006—. Dir. Econ. Develop. Partnership Ala.; mem. Fin. Svc. Roundtable, U. Ala. Nat. Adv. Coun., U. Ala. Pres.'s Cabinet; mem. bd. vistors U. Ala. Sch. Commerce and Bus. Adminstrn.; bd. dirs. Bux. Coun. Ala. Mem.: Country Club Birmingham (pres. 1991), Ala. Golf Assn. (pres. 1985), Kiwanis (pres. Birmingham club 1996—97), Morning Quarterback Club (capt. 1993). Office: Synovus Finl Corp PO Box 120 Columbus GA 31902*

ANTHONY, ROBERT ARMSTRONG, lawyer, educator; b. Washington, Dec. 28, 1931; s. Emile Peter and Martha Graham (Armstrong) Anthony; m. Ruth Grace Barrons, Feb. 7, 1959 (div.); 1 child, Graham Barrons; m. Joan Patricia Caton, Jan. 3, 1980; 1 child, Peter Christopher Caton. BA, Yale U., 1953; BA in Jurisprudence, Oxford U., 1955; JD, Stanford U., 1957. Bar: Calif. 1957, N.Y. 1971, DC 1972. Assoc. Pillsbury, Madison & Sutro, San Francisco, 1957-62, Kelso, Cotton & Ernst, San Francisco, 1962-64; assoc. prof. law Cornell U. Law Sch., 1964-68, prof., 1968-75, dir. internat. legal studies, 1964-74; chief counsel, later dir. Office Fgn. Direct Investments, Dept. Commerce, 1972-73; cons. Adminstrv. Conf. U.S., Washington, 1968-71, chmn., 1974-79; ptnr. McKenna, Conner & Cuneo, Washington, 1979-82; pvt. practice Washington, 1982-83; prof. law George Mason U., Arlington, Va., 1983—2002, prof. emeritus, 2002—. Fulbright lectr., Slovenia, 1994; lectr. Acad. Am. and Internat. Law, Southwestern Legal Found., Dallas, 1967—72; instr. Golden Gate U., 1961; cons., chmn. pubs. adv. bd. Internat. Law Inst., 1984—2004; cons. Inst. Pub. Adminstrn., Slovenia, 1994—. Mem. editl. bd. Jour. Law and Tech., 1986—91; contbr. articles to profl. jours. Active Pres.'s Inflation Program Regulatory Coun., 1978—79; chmn. panel U.S. Dept. Edn. Appeal Bd., 1981—83; commr. Sausalito (Calif.) City Planning Commn., 1962—64; active Fairfax County (Va.) Rep. Com., 1984—86; bd. dirs. Nat. Ctr. Adminstrv. Justice, 1974—79, Marin Shakespeare Festival, San Rafael, Calif., 1961—64, Va. Assn. Scholars, 1990—98. Mem.: ABA (coun., sec. sect. adminstrv. law and regulatory practice 1988—94), Washington Inst. Fgn. Affairs, Stanford U. Law Soc. Washington (pres. 1982), Am. Law Inst., Assn. Am. Rhodes Scholars, Cosmos Club. Home: 275 Roebling St Warrenton VA 20186 Office: George Mason U Law Sch 3301 N Fairfax Dr Arlington VA 22201-4426 Personal E-mail: ranthonys@aol.com. Business E-Mail: ranthony@gmu.edu.

ANTHONY, STEPHEN PIERCE, lawyer; b. Concord, Mass., Aug. 30, 1961; s. Reed Pierce and Barbara (Beatley) Anthony; m. Lisa Ann Battalia, June 2, 1990; children: Matthew William, Caroline Grace. AB, Dartmouth Coll., 1983; JD, Columbia U., 1988. Bar: Md. 1989, D.C. 1991, U.S. Dist. Ct. D.C. 1991, U.S. Dist. Ct. Md. 2000, U.S. Ct. Appeals (D.C. Cir.) 1991, U.S. Ct. Appeals (3rd Cir.) 2003. Law clk. to Hon. Patricia M. Wald, US Ct. Appeals (DC cir.), Washington, 1988—89; assoc. Wilmer, Cutler & Pickering, Washington, 1989—91; asst. US atty. US Atty.'s Office, Washington, 1991—96; trial atty. pub. integrity sect. criminal divsn. US Dept. Justice, Washington, 1996—2000; with Covington & Burling LLP, Washington, 2000—, ptnr., 2003—. Barrister Edward Bennett Williams Am. Inn of Ct., Washington, 1997—. Notes and comments editor Columbia Law Rev., 1987-88. Harlan Fiske Stone scholar Columbia U., 1985-86, 87-88, James Kent scholar, 1986-87. Office: Covington & Burling LLP 1201 Pennsylvania Ave NW Washington DC 20004 Office Phone: 202-662-5105. E-mail: santhony@cov.com.

ANTHONY, SYLVIA, social welfare organization executive; b. Boston, Oct. 5, 1929; d. Charles and Josephine (Guastaferro) Caccamesi; children: Lyn Newbury, Edward Charles Souza Jr., Dean Souza. Student, Northeastern U., Boston, 1968-69, Lee Inst., 1966, 86-87. Lic. real estate broker, Mass. Founder, pres. Life for the Little Ones, Inc., Everett, Mass., 1987-94, Sylvia's Haven, Everett, 1994—2006, Devens, Mass., 1997—2006, Revere, 2006—. Recipient Arthur L. Whitaker award Am. Bapt. Ch. of Mass., 1992, Recognition award Commonwealth of Mass. State Senate, Ho. of Reps., Gov. of Mass., 1997, 99, Mass. Gov.'s Hwy Safety Bur., 1998, Mayor Dean J. Mazzarella City of Leominster, 1999, named Hometown Hero WBZ TV, Boston, 2001; Daily Point of Light award Points of Light Found., 2002, Amb. for Peace award The Interreligious and Internat. Fedn. for World Peace, 2002; Commendation from Pres. George Bush, 2002. Achievements include Life for the Little Ones, Inc./Sylvia's Haven celebrating 20 years of service to 996 women and children. Office: Sylvia's Haven 474 Revere Beach Blvd Ste 1004 Revere MA 02151 also: Home for Homeless Women 248 Bellingham Ave Revere MA 02151 Office Phone: 781-284-0560.

ANTHONY, THOMAS DALE, lawyer; b. Cleve., July 23, 1952; m. Susan Shelly; children: Lara, Elizabeth. BS, Miami U., Oxford, Ohio, 1974; JD, Case Western Res. U., 1977. Bar: Ohio 1977. Tax specialist Ernst & Young, Cleve., 1977—79; ptnr. Benesch, Friedlander, Coplan and Aronoff, Cin., 1979—89, Frost and Jacobs, Cin., 1989—98; exec. v.p., chief legal officer, sec. Choice Care, 1996—98; pres., CEO PacifiCare of Ohio, 1998—2002; mem., vice chair corp. dept. Frost Brown Todd LLC, 2001—. Speaker various orgns. Mem. Cin. Coun. on World Affairs, 1980-82; vol. fundraising drive Sta. WVIZ, 1978-79, Sta. WCET, 1980-82; legal counsel Children's Internat. Summer Villages, 1979—; account capt. United Way of Hamilton County, 1986-88, cabinet mem., 1993; pres. State Libr. Bd., Ohio, 1987-89; mem. bus. adv. coun., subcom. ednl. legis. Mariemont City Schs. and Bd. of Edn.; bd. dirs. Greater Cin. Ctr. for Econ. Edn., Am. Heart Assn. (Cin. chpt.), Juvenile Diabetes Found.; bd. mem. Cin. Playhouse in the Park; exec. com., v.p. strategic planning Cin. Nature Ctr. Mem. ABA (taxation sect., tax acctg. problems com., tax shelter subcom., small bus. com., mem. health law forum), Ohio State Bar Assn. (health law com., ins. sect.), Assn. Corp. Growth (bd. dirs. Cin. chpt.), Cin. Bar Assn. (chmn. tax. inst. com. 1990, adminstrn. and fin. com. 1991-93, chmn. tax sect. 1993, health law com.), Cin. C. of C., Miami U. Alumni Assn. (bd. dirs., treas. 1989-91, v.p. 1991-92), Nat. Health Lawyers Assn., Rotary (co-chair youth in city govt. program), Omicron Delta Kappa, Sigma Phi Epsilon. Home: 4337 Ashley Oaks Dr Cincinnati OH 45227-3947 Office: PacifiCare 11260 Chester Rd Ste 800 Cincinnati OH 45246-4096 Office Phone: 513-651-6191. Business E-Mail: tanthony@fbtlaw.com.

ANTHONY, VIRGINIA QUINN BAUSCH, medical association executive; b. Odessa, Tex., June 9, 1945; d. William Francis and Florence Elizabeth (Decker) Quinn; m. E. James Anthony; 1 child, Justin. BA, Mt. Holyoke Coll., 1967. Exec. dir. Am. Acad. Child and Adolescent Psychiatry, Washington, 1973—. Recipient Spl. Presdl. citation Am. Psychiat. Assn., 1995, Exec. Achievement award AMA, 1999. Office: Am Acad Child & Adolescent Psychiatry 3615 Wisconsin Ave NW Washington DC 20016-3007 Business E-Mail: vqanthony@aacap.org.

ANTHONY, WILLIAM GRAHAM, artist; b. Ft. Monmouth, NJ, Sept. 25, 1934; s. Emile Peter and Martha Graham (Armstrong) A.; m. Norma Neuman, Jan. 16, 1983. BA in European History, Yale U., 1958; student, San Francisco Art Inst., 1959. Author: A New Approach to Figure Drawing, 1965, Bible Stories, 1978, Bill Anthony's Greatest Hits, 1988, War is Swell, 2000; exhibited in one-man shows: Legion of Honor, San Francisco, 1962, Stuart Katz Gallery, Laguna Beach, Calif., 1992, Cokkie Snoie Gallery, Rotterdam, 1995, 99, Dorfman Gallery, N.Y.C., 2002, 04, Stalke Gallery, Copenhagen, 2004, others; exhibited in group shows: San Francisco Mus. Modern Art, Art Inst. Chgo., Whitney Mus. Am. Art, N.Y.C., Allan Stone Gallery, N.Y.C., St. Paul Art Center; works represented in collections: Art Inst. Chgo., Bklyn. Mus., Cleve. Mus. Art, Corcoran Gallery Art, Washington, Detroit Inst. Arts, Mus. Fine Arts, Houston, Met. Mus. Art, N.Y.C., Seattle Art Mus., Whitney Mus. Am. Art, N.Y.C., Guggenheim Mus., N.Y.C., others. Served with U.S. Army, 1953-55. Republican. Home: 463 West St Apt 903 New York NY 10014-2010 Office Phone: 212-255-0379. Personal E-mail: normabill@verizon.net.

ANTHONY, WILMA TYLINDA, retired customer service administrator; b. Friars Point, MIss., July 11, 1954; d. John Thomas and Ellen (Ward) Anthony. BS in Edn., Langston U., 1979; postgrad. in interdisciplinary studies, U. Oreg. Sales assoc. Meier & Frank, Eugene, Oreg., 1976—78; vault teller 1st Interstate Bank, Portland, Oreg., 1979—80; mapping analyst Portland GE Co., 1980—97; sales assoc. Nike, Beaverton, Oreg., 1998—99, cashier, 2000—06; ret., 2006. Profl. model, 1987—. Telethon divsn. chief Mt. Hood coun. Campfire, Inc., Gladstone, Oreg., 1982—; loaned exec. Columbia-Willamette United Way, 1982; in-house campaigner Portland GE Co., 1981; mem. planning adv. bd. City of Tualatin, Oreg.; vol. State Games of Oreg., 1987—88; line mem. Marshall for All Joining Hands, 1986; vol. mgr. hospitality U.S. Figure Skating Championship, 2005; active Nat. Fedn. Rep. women, Portland; sec. Multnomah Young Reps., 1986; elected com. person Precinct 7, Washington County, 1986, re-elected, 1988; sec. Washington Young Reps., 1988. Recipient Leadership in Cmty. Svcs. award, Portland GE, 1986, Hon. Mention Vol. of Yr. award, 1986, ACE award, 1998, 2000, Cmty. Involvement award, Nike, 2003. Mem.: Pumpkin Ridge, U.S. Women Open Golf Tournament (chartered mem.), Toastmasters (v.p. 1984, Competence cert. 1984), Kappa Delta Pi. Baptist.

ANTHONY-PEREZ, BOBBIE COTTON MURPHY, retired psychology professor; b. Macon, Ga., Nov. 15, 1923; d. Solomon Richard and Maude Alice (Lockett) Cotton; m. William Anthony, Aug. 22, 1959 (dec.); 1 child, Freida; m. Andrew Silviano Perez, June 20, 1979. BS, DePaul U., 1953, MS, 1954, MA, 1975; MS, U. Ill., 1959; PhD, U. Chgo., 1967. Tchr. Chgo. Pub. Schs., 1954-68; math. coord. U. Chgo., 1965; prof. Chgo. State U., 1968-95, coord. Black Studies Program, 1982-83, 90-94, prof. emeritus, 1995; with psychol. svcs. Chgo. Pub. Schs., 1971-72; rsch. coord. Urban Affairs Inst. Howard U., Washington, 1978; coord. higher edn., careers counseling, campus ministry Ingleside Whitfield Parish, 1978-84, comm. chmn., 1991-92, 95, comms. com., 2006. Contbr. articles to profl. jours., chapters to books. V.p. Cmty. Affairs Chatham Bus. Assn., 1981-85, asst. sec., 1985-86, sec., 1986-87, directory com., 1987, 88; bus. rels. chmn. Chatham Avalon Pk. Cmty. Coun., 1984—, newsletter editor, 1993-01; bd. dirs. United Meth. Found. at U. Chgo., 1980-84, Cmty. Mental Health Coun. Inc., 1979-83; pub. edn. chair Chatham Avalon unit Am. Cancer Soc., 1977-88, 90-97, pub. info. chair, 1988-94; pres. Aux. Chgo. chpt. Tuskegee Airmen, Inc., 1994-95, rec. sec., 1998-99, parliamentarian, 1991-95, newsletter feature writer, reporter Chgo. chpt., 1999—, historian, 2006. NSF fellow, 1957, 58, 59; recipient numerous awards religious, civic and ednl. instns. and assns. Mem. APA, Internat. Assn. Applied Psychology, Internat. Assn. Cross-Cultural Psychology, Internat. Assn. Ednl. and Vocat. Guidance, Assn. Black Psychologists (elder 1995—, pres. Chgo. chpt. 1995-96, past pres.), Chgo. Psychol. Assn., Nat. Coun. Tchrs. Math., Am. Ednl. Rsch. Assn., Midwest Ednl. Rsch. Assn., Am. Soc. Clin. Hypnosis, Midwestern Psychol. Assn., Chgo. Soc. Clin. Hypnosis. Methodist.

ANTIA, KERSEY H., industrial and clinical psychologist, consultant; b. Surat, Gujarat, India, Jan. 7, 1936; arrived in US, 1965; s. Homasji and Dinsi R. (Mistry) Antia; m. Dilshad K. Khambata, Dec. 18, 1966; children: Anahita, Mazda, Jimmy. AB with honors, U. Bombay, 1958; MS, Tata Inst. Social Scis., Bombay, 1960, NC State U., Raleigh, 1969; PhD, Ind. No. U., 1976. Lic. psychologist, Ill.; cert. social worker, Ill. Personnel mgr., welfare officer Tata Steel and Tata Chem., 1960-65; rsch. asst. psychology dept. NC State U., 1966-67, U. NC, 1967—69; project dir. Behavior Systems, Inc., Raleigh, 1969-70; dir. Midwest Inst. Human Resources, Tinley Park, Ill., 1972—. Lang. scholar U. Bombay, 1954-56. Assn. for the Advancement of Psychology, Am. Acad. Pain Mgmt., Am. Bd. Profl. Disability Cons. Zoroastrian. Avocations: photography, yoga, jogging, hiking, travel. Home: 8318 138th Pl Orland Park IL 60462-1746 Office Phone: 708-460-6060. Personal E-mail: kerseyantia@yahoo.com.

ANTICH, PETER, radiologist, educator; m. Miriam Drayer, Feb. 7, 1970; children: Max, Janet, Marjorie, Peter. DSc, U. degli Studi Milan, 1964; PhD, Johns Hopkins U., 1971. Instr. physics U. Milan, 1965—66; rsch. asst. to rsch. assoc. Johns Hopkins U., Balt., 1966—71; rsch. scientist U. Milan Inst. Nat. Nuclear Physics, Inst. Physics, 1971—72; from sr. rsch. scientist to head rsch. scientist, prof. U. Pavia Inst. Nat. Nuclear Physics, Inst. Physics, Italy, 1972—75; rsch. assoc. prof. radiotherapy, med. physicist Mt. Sinai Sch. Medicine, NYC, 1977—83; assoc. prof. radiology U. Tex. Southwestern Med. Ctr., Dallas, 1983—92, prof. radiology, 1992—. Bd. dirs. Bone Quality Rsch. Inst., Dallas; guest scientist Brookhaven Nat. Lab., Upton, NY, 1967—71, collaborating scientist, 1994—95; guest scientist German Krebs Forschungs Zentrum, Heidelberg, 1991, Heidelberg, 95; vis. scientist CERN, Geneva, 1972—75; assoc. attending physicist Parkland Meml. Hosp., Dallas, 1983—92; chmn. grad program biomed. engring. Southwestern Grad. Sch. Biomed. Scis., 1990—; co-organizer meeting on functional imaging Banbury Ctr., LI, NY, 1995; presenter in field. Contbr. articles to profl. jours., chapters to books. 2d lt. Italian Army, 1964—66. Recipient numerous rsch. grants; fellow, ACS-NYCD, 1976; Gilman fellow, Johns Hopkins U., 1966—70. Mem.: IEEE, AAAS, Am. Soc. for Bone and Mineral Rsch., Am. Assn. Physicists in Medicine (program com. 1978—80), Phi Beta Kappa, Sigma Xi. Episcopalian. Achievements include patents for position sensitive radiation detector, position sensitive gamma-ray detector, detection of bone quality using ultrasound critical angle reflectometry megavoltage scanning imager and method for its use; diverging gynecological template, high resolution gamma ray detectors for positron emission tomography, others. Avocations: kayaking, walking, reading, writing, painting. Office: Univ Tex Southwestern Med Ctr 5323 Harry Hines Blvd E6 238 Dallas TX 75390-9058 Business E-Mail: peter.antich@utsouthwestern.edu.

ANTIN, DAVID, poet, critic; b. Bklyn., Feb. 1, 1932; s. Max and Mollie (Kitzes) A.; m. Eleanor Fineman, Dec. 16, 1961; 1 son, Blaise BA, CCNY, 1955; MA, NYU, 1966. Prof. visual arts U. Calif., San Diego, 1968—99, prof. emeritus visual arts, 2000—. Author: Definitions, 1967, Autobiography, 1967, Code of Flag Behavior, 1968, Meditations, 1971, Talking, 1972, Talking at the Boundaries, 1976 , Tuning, 1984, Selected Poems 1963-73, 1991, What It Means to be Avant Garde, 1993, (with Charles Bernstein) A Conversation with David Antin, 2002, I Never Knew What Time it Was, U.C.Press, 2005, John Cage Uncaged is Still Cagey, Singing Horse Press, 2005; contbg. editor: Alcheringa, 1972-80, New Wilderness, 1979-; mem. editl. com. U. Calif. Press, 1972-76. Recipient Creative Arts award U. Calif., 1972; Herbert Lehman fellow NYU, 1966; Guggenheim fellow, 1976-77; NEH fellow, 1983-84, Getty Rsch. fellow, 2002. Home: PO Box 1147 Del Mar CA 92014-1147 Office: U Calif San Diego Visual Arts Dept La Jolla CA 92037 E-mail: dantin@ucsd.edu.

ANTIN, JONATHAN, hairstylist, entrepreneur; b. LA, Aug. 16, 1967; s. Michael and Brenda Antin; 1 child, Asher Jones. Attended, Fairfax Beauty Acad. Owner, hairstylist Jonathan Salon West Hollywood, Jonathan Salon Beverly Hills, 2004—. Released signature hair product line Jonathan Product, 2005. Actor: (TV reality show) Blow Out, 2004—; judge Miss Teen USA Pageant, 2004. Office: Jonathan Salon 901 Westbourne Dr West Hollywood CA 90069 also: Bravo c/o NBC Entertainment 3000 W Alameda Ave Burbank CA 91523 Office Phone: 310-855-0225. E-mail: salon@jonathanproduct.com.

ANTIN, MICHAEL, lawyer; b. Milw., Nov. 30, 1938; s. David Boris and Pauline (Mayer) A.; m. Evelyne Judith Hirsch, June 19, 1960; children: Stephanie, Bryan, Randall BS, Univ. Calif., 1960; JD, U. Calif., 1963. Bar: Calif. 1963; cert. tax specialist. Tax atty. Cruikshank, Antin & Grebow, Beverly Hills, Calif., 1963-81, Antin, Litz & Grebow, Beverly Hills, 1981-91, Antin & Taylor, LA, 1993—99; sole practice LA, 1999—. Bd. dirs. Small Bus. Counsel Am., Washington, The Group, Inc.; speaker in field; instr. Solomon S. Heubner Sch. CLU Studies, 1977-86; vis. prof. law U. Latvia, 2006, Protacky U., Czech Republic, 2007. Author: How to Operate Your Trust or Probate, 1983; contbr. articles to profl. jours. With U.S. Air Force, 1959-67. Fellow Am. Coll. Tax Counsel, Am. Coll. of Trust and Estate Counsel, L.A. County Bowlers Assn. (bd. dirs. 1996-99), Ctr. Internat. Legal Studies. Avocations: jogging, tennis, cross country skiing, bowling. Office: Ste 2000 1925 Century Park East Blvd Fl 20 Los Angeles CA 90067-2721 Office Phone: 310-788-2733.

ANTIOCO, JOHN F., former film rental company executive; b. Bklyn., Nov. 1, 1949; Grad. in Bus. Adminstrn., NY Inst. Tech., 1970. Mgr. tng., v.p. mktg., sr. v.p. ops. Southland Corp., 1970—90; CEO Pearle Vision, Dallas, 1990; COO Circle K Corp., Phoenix, 1991—93, pres., CEO, 1993—96; chmn. Circle K Corp, 1995—96; pres., CEO Taco Bell Corp., 1996-97; pres. Blockbuster Inc., Dallas, 1997—2001, chmn., CEO, 1997—2007. Named to Boys & Girls Clubs of Am. Alumni Hall of Fame, 2006; recipient Phoenix Award, Pub. Rel. Soc. of Am. , Valley of the Sun Chap., DeMateius award, St. Vincent's Services, Herbert Hoover Humanitarian award, Boys & Girls Clubs of Am.*

ANTLE, CHARLES EDWARD, statistics educator; b. East View, Ky., Nov. 11, 1930; s. Bayard Pierpoint and Mary Elizabeth (Blaydes) A.; m. Elna Thomas Hall, Nov. 25, 1953; children— James, Rebecca, Susan Hall, Mark Edward. AA, Lindsey Wilson Coll., 1950; BS, Eastern Ky. State U., 1954, MA, 1955; postgrad., U. Ky., 1954-55; PhD (NDEA fellow), Okla. State U., 1962. Sr. aerophysics engr. Gen. Dynamics Corp., Fort Worth, 1955-57; mem. faculty U. Mo., Rolla, 1957-60, 62-68, prof. math., 1966-68; asso. prof. statistics Pa. State U., University Park, 1968-70, prof., 1970-92, prof. emeritus of stats. University Park, 1992—. Contbr. articles to profl. jours. Served with AUS, 1951-52. Decorated Bronze Star medal. Mem. Am. Statis. Assn. Home: 2303 W Branch Rd State College PA 16801-8043 Office: Pa State U Dept Stats University Park PA 16802 Office Phone: 814-237-4608. Business E-Mail: cea@psu.edu.

ANTMAN, ELLIOT MARSHALL, cardiologist, educator; b. NYC, May 9, 1950; m. Karen Hamm Antman; children: Amy, David. MD, Columbia U. Coll. Physicians and Surgeons, 1974. Cert. Internal Medicine, Cardiovascular Disease. Intern, medicine Columbia-Presbyn. Med. Ctr., NYC, 1974—75, resident, cardiology, 1975—77; fellow Peter Bent Brigham Hosp., Boston, 1977—80; co-dir., coronary care unit Brigham and Women's Hosp., Boston, 1980, dir., coronary care unit (also called Samuel L. Levine Cardiac Unit), 1980—; with Harvard Med. Sch., Boston, 1989—, assoc. prof. medicine, prof. medicine. Prin. investigator TIMI Trials, Boston, 1996—; chair steering com. MAGIC Trial, Boston, 1996—. Contbr. chapters to books Harrison's Principals of Internal Medicine, Heart Disease; editor: Cardiovascular Therapeutics; sr. assoc. editor Circulation. Mem. Am. Coll. Cardiology (Gifted Tchr. of Yr., 2003), Am. Heart Assn. Office: Brigham and Women's Hosp Cardiovascular Divsn 75 Francis St Boston MA 02115-6106 Office Phone: 617-732-7149. Office Fax: 617-975-0990.*

ANTMAN, KAREN HAMM, oncologist, educator, dean; b. NJ, July 26, 1948; m. Elliot Antman; children: Amy, David. Grad. in Chemistry (magna cum laude), Muhlenberg Coll.; MD, Columbia U. Coll. Physicians and Surgeons, 1974. Diplomate Am. Bd. Internal Medicine, Am. Bd. Med. Oncology. Intern Columbia Presbyn. Med. Ctr., NYC, 1974—75, resident, 1975—77; clin. fellow, medicine Harvard Med. Sch., instr. medicine, 1979; clin. fellow, med. oncology Sidney Farber Cancer Inst., Boston, 1977—79; chief med. oncology Columbia U., NYC; clin. dir. Dana-Farber Cancer Inst./Beth Israel Solid Tumor Autologous Marrow Program, 1984; attending physician N.Y. Presbyn. Hosp., 1993; dir. Herbert Irving Cancer Ctr., Nat. Cancer Inst.; Wu prof., medicine & pharmacology, prof. medicine & pharmacology Columbia U. Coll. Physicians and Surgeons, NYC, 1993—2004; dep. dir. translation and clinical services Nat. Cancer Inst., 2004—05; provost, Med. Campus Boston U., 2005—, dean, Med. Sch., 2005—. Assoc. editor New England Journal of Medicine, mem. editl. of several med. jours.; contbr. articles to profl. jours. Bd. observer Muhlenberg Coll., 2007—. Mem.: Am. Soc. for Blood and Marrow Transplantation (past pres.), Am. Assn. for Cancer Rsch. (past pres.), Am. Soc. Clinical Oncology (past pres.). Avocations: backpacking, travel. Office: Boston Univ Medical Sch 715 Albany St L-103 Boston MA 02118 Office Phone: 617-638-5300. Office Fax: 617-638-5258.*

ANTMAN, STUART SHELDON, mathematician, educator; b. Bklyn., June 2, 1939; s. Mitchell and Gertrude (Siegel) A.; m. Wilma Gail Richlin, Mar. 24, 1968; children: Rachel Alexandra, Melissa Dora. BS, Rensselaer Poly. Inst., 1961; MS, U. Minn., 1963, PhD, 1965. Lectr. U. Minn., 1965; vis. mem. Courant Inst. of NYU, 1965-67; asst. prof. math. and aeros. NYU, 1967-69, assoc. prof. math., 1969-72; sr. vis. fellow U. Oxford, 1969-70, Heriot-Watt U., Edinburgh, 1972, 77; prof. math. U. Md., College Park, 1972—2001, disting. prof., 2001—. Prin. investigator NSF grants, 1972—; mem. Applied Math. Summer Inst., Dartmouth Coll., 1973; prof. Ecole d'Eté d'Analyse Numérique, Bréau, France, 1974; vis. prof. U. Paris-Sud, Orsay, 1975, Brown U., Providence, 1978-79, Ecole Polytechnique, Palaiseau, France, 1979, U. Nacional Autónoma de México, 1981, Math. Scis. Rsch. Inst., Berkeley, Calif., 1983, Univ. P. and M. Curie, Paris, 1983, 92, Math. Rsch. Ctr., U. Wis., 1984, Inst. Math. and Applications, U. Minn., 1985, U. Bonn, Germany, 1987, U. Leipzig, Germany, 1995, Tech. U. Darmstadt, Germany, 1999, Max Planck Inst., Leipzig, 1999, City Univ. of Hong Kong, 2000, U. Dortmund, Germany, 2001, U. Rome, 2006; mem. U.S. Nat. Com. on Theoretical and Applied Mechanics, 1980-88. Author: The Theory of Rods, 1972, Nonlinear Problems of Elasticity, 1995, 2d edit., 2005; co-editor: Bifurcation Theory and Nonlinear Eigenvalue Problems, 1969, Metastability and Improperly Posed Problems, 1987, Analysis and Continuum Mechanics, 1989; mem. editl. bd. Archive for Rational Mechanics and Analysis, 1972-89, 99—, editor in chief, 1989-99; editor The Non-Linear Field Theories of Mechanics, 3d edit., 2004; mem. editl. bd. Springer Tracts in Natural Philosophy, 1972-80, Acta Applicandae Mathematicae, 1982—, Jour. Elasticity, 1996—, Electronic Rsch. Announcements of Am. Math. Soc., 1997-2006, Quar. of Applied Math., 1999—, assoc. editor Notices of Am. Math. Soc., 1985-87; mem. editl. com. Proc. of Symposia on Applied Math, 1986-88; mem. editl. bd. (Springer series) Applied Math. Scis., 1998-2001, co-editor-in-chief, 2001—; mem. editl. bd. Interdisciplinary Applied Math., 1998-2001, co-editor-in-chief, 2001—; co-editor-in-chief Texts in Applied Math, 2001, Surveys and Tutorials in the Applied Mathematical Sciences, 2005—. Recipient D. Alcaraz medal, Nat. Autónoma U. Mex., 1997; John S. Guggenheim Meml. Found. fellow, 1978—79. Mem. Am. Math. Soc., Soc. Indsl. and Applied Math. (T. von Kármán prize 1999), Soc. for Natural Philosophy (sec. 1974-76), Soc. for Interaction of Mechanics and Math. (mem. exec. com. 1986-90), Math. Assn. Am. (L.R. Ford award 1987), Pi Mu Epsilon. Office: U Md Dept Math College Park MD 20742-4015 Home Phone: 301-229-8632. Business E-Mail: ssa@math.umd.edu.

ANTOINE, RICHARD L., human resources specialist, consumer products company executive; m. Dorothy O'Brien; 1 child. BS, U. Wis., 1969. Various positions including soap process supr. and plant mgr. Procter & Gamble Co., mgr. N.Am. supply sys., engring., and purchasing divsn., 1992—99, dir. global supply sys., 1999—2001, global human resources officer, 2001—. Bd. dirs. Cinn. Ballet Co. Avocations: travel, golf. Office: Procter & Gamble Co 1 Procter & Gamble Plz Cincinnati OH 45202 Office Phone: 513-983-1100. Office Fax: 513-983-9369.

ANTOKOLETZ, ELLIOTT MAXIM, music educator; b. Jersey City, Aug. 3, 1942; s. Jack and Esther (Leiter) A.; m. Juana Canabal, May 28, 1972; 1 child, Eric. Student, Juilliard Sch. Music, 1960-65; BA in Musicology, Hunter Coll., 1968, MA in Musicology, 1970; PhD in Musicology, CUNY, 1975. Instr. violin Brearley Sch., NYC, 1970-76; theory lectr., instr. chamber music Queens Coll., NYC, 1973-76; prof. musicology U. Tex., Austin, 1976—. Author: The Music of Béla Bartók, 1984, Béla Bartók: A Guide to Research, 1988, 97, Twentieth-Century Music, 1992, Musical Symbolism in the Operas of Debussy and Bartok, 2004; editor: Bartök Perspectives, 2000, Georg Von Albrecht Memoirs, 2004, Internat. Jour. of Musicology; contbr. articles to prof. jours. and mags. Recipient Béla Bartók Memorial award Hungarian Govt., 1981, Tacquard Endowed Centennial Chair, U. Tex., 1983-84, Tchg. Excellence award U. Tex., 1981, Achievement PhD Alumni award CUNY, 1987; E.W. Doty professorship, 1994-95, 2007—. Mem. Am. Musicol. Soc. (Subvention award 1982), Coll. Music Soc., Internat. Musicol. Soc. Avocation: oil and water-color painting. Office: U Tex Music School Austin TX 78712 Business E-Mail: antokoletz@mail.utexas.edu.

ANTOL, JOSEPH J., artist; b. Rexis, Pa., May 2, 1947; s. John J. Antol and Agnes Dorothy Bananto. BFA, Norfolk State U.; MFA, Old Dominion U., 1984. Cert. Artisian Printer Tamarind Inst., N.Mex, 1981. Graphic artist, tech. cons. Harbour Graphics, Virginia Beach, Va., 1998—2001; artist, tchr., technition printer M&G Electronics, Virginia Beach, 2001—. Instr. Govenors Magnet Sch., Norfolk, Va., 1988—90. With US Army, 1967—68, Vietnam. Sculpture fellow, Va. Mus., 1988. Mem.: Blue Spader Assn. (life). Achievements include design of Double Plattened Long Sleeve Pallet For Textile Printing. Avocations: fishing, computers, hiking, travel, swimming. Home: 2565 Shore Dr Virginia Beach VA 23451 Home Phone: 757-481-1949. Personal E-mail: jantol@cox.net.

ANTOLIK, MICHAEL, geophysicist; b. St. Louis, Feb. 29, 1968; s. Edwin J. and June R. Antolik. PhD in Geophysics, U. Calif., Berkeley, 1990—96. Lead geophysicist Quantum Tech. Svcs., Inc., Cocoa Beach, Fla., 2004—; chief sci. US Nat. Data Ctr., Satellite Beach, Fla., 2005—. Contbr. articles to profl. jours. Mem.: Seismol. Soc. Am. Conservative-R. Avocation: golf. Office: Quantum Techology Svcs Inc 1980 N Atlantic Ave Ste 514 Cocoa Beach FL 32955 Business E-Mail: mantolik@qtsi.com.

ANTON, DAVID L., research and development company executive, biotechnologist, researcher; b. Seattle, Mar. 20, 1953; s. Hector R. and Lois M. Anton; m. Johanna Kahalley, Sept. 2, 2000; children: Christopher D, Steven M, Kahalley M. PhD, U. Minn., 1980. From prin. investigator to mgr. rsch. DuPont Ctrl. Rsch., Wilmington, Del., 1983—94, mgr. rsch., 1994—2001; mgr. strategic R&D planning DuPont Crop Protection, Newark, Del., 2001—04; program mgr. biochemical products DuPont ConAgra Visions, LLC, Wilmington, 1991—93; mgr. biofuels devel. DuPont BioBased Materials, Wilmington, Del., 2004—; vp R&D DuPont Tate & Lyle BioProducts LLC, Wilmington, 2004—. Chmn. biocatalysis Gordon Rsch. Conf., 1990; chmn. enzyme engring. conf. Engring. Found., 1999. Editor: Jour. Molecular Catalysis B: Enzymatic, 1994—97. Recipient Bacaner Basic Sci. award, Minn. Med. Found., 1981, Presdl. Green Chemistry Challenge award, U.S. EPA, 2003; fellow, NIH, 1980—82. Mem.: Am. Chem. Soc. (nominating com. 1995—99, biotech rep. 1995—99), Am. Assn. Biochemistry and Molecular Biology, Del. Valley Enzymology Club (founder 1986—89, chmn. 1986—89). Achievements include development of and commercialization of a biological process for 1, 3Propanediol, DuPont's first bioprocess. Avocation: scuba diving. Office: DuPont Bio-Based Materials PO Box 80728 Wilmington DE 19880-0728 Home Phone: 302-793-3939. Business E-Mail: david.l.anton@usa.dupont.com.

ANTON, FRANK A., publishing executive; b. Greensburg, Pa., Dec. 19, 1949; s. Carmen T. and Jeanne Mary (Joseph) A.; m. Grace Praga Spadoro, Nov. 4, 1972; children— Emily Grace, Elizabeth Ann, Margaret Teresa. AB, Dartmouth Coll., 1971; MS in Journalism, Medill Sch. Journalism, 1974. Sr. editor Cahners Pub. Co., Chgo., 1974-79; editor Hanley Wood LLC, Washington, 1979-86, publisher, 1986-93, pres., 1993—. CEO ebuild.com. Mem.: Am. Bus. Media (chair bd. dirs. 2007—). Office: Hanley-Wood Inc One Thomas Cir NW Ste 600 Washington DC 20005-5811 Office Phone: 202-452-0800. Office Fax: 202-785-1974.*

ANTON, JOHN PETER, philosopher, educator; b. Canton, Ohio, Nov. 2, 1920; s. Peter C. and Christine (Giannopoulos) A.; m. Helen Vezos, Nov. 26, 1955; children: James, Christopher, Peter. BS, Columbia U., 1949, MA, 1950, PhD, 1954, U. Athens, 1954, LHD (hon.), 1992; DHL (hon.), U. Patras, 2004, U. Ioannina, 2005. Instr. Pace Coll., 1953-54; vis. lectr. U. N.Mex., 1954-55; asst. prof. U. Nebr., 1955-58; assoc. prof. Ohio Wesleyan U., 1958-62; prof. SUNY, Buffalo, 1962-67, assoc. dean grad. sch., prof., 1967-69; Fuller E. Callaway prof. Emory U., 1969-81, chmn. dept. philosophy, 1969-76; prof., provost New Coll., U. South Fla., Tampa, 1982-83, disting. prof. Greek philosophy and culture, 1983—, dir. Ctr. Greek Studies. Woods vis. prof. Mills. Coll., 1981; vis. prof. Columbia U., 1966. Author: Aristotle's Theory of Contrariety, 1957, Science, Philosophy and Educational Tasks, 1966, Naturalism and Historical Understanding, 1967, Philosophical Essays, 1969, Essays in Ancient Greek Philosophy (5 vols.), 1971-92, Science and the Sciences in Plato, 1980, Critical Humanism as a Philosophy of Culture, 1981, Upward Panic: The Autobiography of Eva Palmer-Sikelianos, 1993, The Poetry and Poetics of C.P. Cavafy, 1995, Categories and Experience, 1996, Archetypal Principles and Hierarchies, 2000, American Naturalism and Greek Philosophy, 2005; co-editor (jour.) Diotima: editl. cons. Jour. History of Philosophy, 1968—, The Humanist, 1967—; mem. editl. bd. So. Jour. Philos., 1974—, Eidos, 1974—, Ancient Philosophy, 1979, Idealistic Studies, 1981, Philos. Inquiry, 1981; founding editor (jours.) Jour. of Neoplatonic Studies, 1991, Revue de Philosophie Ancienne, 1984—, Skepsis, 1997, Phronimos, 2004. Bd. govs. St. Lawrence Coll., 1989. With US Army, 1946—47. Mem. Am. Philos. Assn., Soc. Advancement of Am. Philosophy (founding mem.), Am. Philol. Assn., Am. Soc. Aesthetics (trustee 1973-76, 81-84), Ga. Philos. Soc. (v.p. 1972, pres. 1973), Internat. Soc. Neoplatonic Studies (chmn. exec. com., pres. 1997—2004), Soc. Ancient Greek Philosophy (sec., treas. 1973-81, pres. 1981-83), Internat. Assn. Sports Law (hon.), Modern Greek Studies Assn. (v.p. 1969—72), Soc. Macedonian Studies (hon.), Acad. Athens (corr.), Internat. Assn. Greek Philos. (hon. pres. 1993), Soc. Internat. pour l'Etude de la Philosophie Mediévale, Parnassos Lit. Soc. (hon.), Phi Beta Kappa, Eta Sigma Phi, Phi Sigma Tau. Home: 10012 Oxford Chapel Dr Tampa FL 33647-2870 Office: U South Fla Dept Philosophy Tampa FL 33620 Office Phone: 813-974-3670. E-mail: hanton1@tampabay.rr.com.

ANTONACCI, ANTHONY EUGENE, retired engineer; b. Sept. 21, 1949; s. Salvatore Natali and Odile Estella (Stanton) A.; m. Sherry Lee Kessler, Mar. 6, 1971; children: Don Warren, Lance Anthony. Cadet, USAF Acad., 1968-69; AS, Forest Park Coll., 1971. Lic. power engr. Asst. supr. data processing ops. 1st Nat. Bank, St. Louis, 1969-71; engr. Installation & Svc. Engring. (Mech. & Nuclear) divsn. Gen. Electric Corp., St. Louis, 1971-76; engr. Anheuser-Busch Corp., St. Louis, 1976—2006; ret., 2006. Author software. Trustee, treas. Antonette Hills Trusteeship, Affton, Mo., 1976-80. Mem. Brewers and Maltsters Local 6 (del. 1982-83), Nat. Aerospace Edn. Coun., Apple Programmers and Developers Assn., Am. Legion. Republican. Roman Catholic. Avocations: classic auto restoration, trumpet music. Home: 8971 Antonette Hills Dr Saint Louis MO 63123-6503 Personal E-mail: TonyA2@aol.com.

ANTONACCI, MARK DARRYL, orthopedist, surgeon; b. Teaneck, NJ, Aug. 13, 1966; s. Luke J. and Concetta Antonacci; m. Ana Palomino; children: Caitlin, Luke, Ally. BS in Biology, Georgetown U., Washington, 1988, MD cum laude, 1992. Diplomate Nat. Bd. Med. Examiners, Am. Acad. Orthop. Surgery. Intern dept. gen. surgery Baylor Coll. Medicine, Houston, 1992—93, resident dept. orthop. surgery, 1993—98; fellow in spine surgery U. Miami, Fla., 1998—99; asst. prof. orthop. surgery MCP-Hahnemann U. Sch. Medicine, Phila., 1999—2001; dir. spine diagnostic and treatment ctr. Grad. Hosp., Phila., 1999—2002; dir. acute spine injury program dept. orthop. surgery Hahnemann U. Hosp., Phila., 2000—01; cons. attending spine surgeon Shriners' Hosp. Children, Phila., 2000—; clin. asst. prof. orthop. surgery Mt. Sinai Sch. Medicine, 2001—; pvt. practice dept. orthop. surgery Lenox Hill Hosp., NYC, 2001—; pvt. practice Inst. Spine and Scoliosis, PA, Lawrenceville, NJ, 2001—. Presenter in field. Contbr. articles to profl. jours. Recipient Paul Harrington award for orthop. rsch., Baylor Coll. Medicine, 1998, Golden Stethoscope award, Grad. Hosp., 2002; grantee Paul Harrington award for orthop. rsch., Baylor Coll. Medicine, 1994, Shriners Hosp. Children, 2003. Fellow: Am. Acad. Surgery, Scoliosis Rsch. Soc. (Russell Hibbs Basic Sci. award 2001, 2003), Am. Acad. Orthop. Surgery; mem.: AMA, ACS, NJ Med. Soc., Cervical Spine Rsch. Soc., Am. Acad. Orthop. Surgery, Alpha Omega Alpha. Avocations: tennis, skiing. Office: Inst Spine and Scoliosis PA 3100 Princeton Pike Bldg 1 Lawrenceville NJ 08648 Office Phone: 609-912-1500. Personal E-mail: iss9121500@yahoo.com.

ANTONAKES, STEVEN L., state agency administrator; BA, Pa. State U.; MBA, Salem State Coll.; PhD in Law, Policy and Soc., Northeastern U. Positions including bank examiner, chief dir. CRA exams., sr. dep. commr. adminstrn. and policy and first dep. commr. banks Mass. Divsn. Banks, 1990—, commr. banks, 2004—. Chmn. state liaison com. Fed. Fin. Instns. Exam. Coun.; adj. faculty mem. Emmanuel Coll., Boston. Mem.: Conf. State Bank Suprs. (chmn. dist. I 2005, bd. mgrs. States Regulatory Registry LLC 2006—). Office: Mass Divsn Banks One South Sta Boston MA 02110 Office Phone: 617-956-1500. Office Fax: 617-956-1599.

ANTONAKOS, STEPHEN, sculptor; b. So., Greece, Nov. 1, 1926; came to U.S., 1930; Student, Bklyn. CC. Lectr. Yale, New Haven, 1968; sculptor, working primarily in neon; vis. artist; artist-in-residence (U. Wis.), Madison, 1971, U. Calif.-Fresno, 1972. One-man shows U. Maine, 1958, Avant-Garde Gallery, N.Y., 1958, Miami Mus. Modern Art, 1964, Schramm Gallery, Ft. Lauderdale, 1964, Byron Gallery, N.Y.C., 1964, Fischbach Gallery, N.Y.C., 1967, 68, 69, 70, 72, John Weber Gallery, N.Y.C., 1974, 75, 76, 77, Ft. Worth Art Mus., 1970, 74-75, Contemporary Art Mus., Houston, 1971, SUNY, Albany, 1973, Bernier Gallery, 1977, Young Hoffman Gallery, Chgo., 1978, U. Mass., 1978, Bernier Gallery, 1977, Gillespie/de Laage Gallery, Paris, 1979, Albright-Knox Art Gallery, Buffalo, 1975, Wright State U., Dayton, Ohio, 1975, Galleria Marilena Bonomo, Bari, Italy, 1975, Galerie 26, Paris, 1975, Galleriaforma, Genoa, Italy, 1975, Galerie December, Dusseldorf, Germany, 1976, Art & Project, Amsterdam, 1976, Galerie Bonnier, Geneva, 1976, Nancy Lurie Gallery, Chgo., 1976, Galerie Aronowitsch, Stockholm, 1977, Galerie Tanit, Munich, 1978, 80, Lowe Art Mus., Miami, Fla., 1980, Nassau County Mus. Fine Art, Roslyn, N.Y., 1982, Maison de Culture de Nevers (France), 1983, Le Coin du Miroir, Dijon, France, 1983, Bonnier Gallery, N.Y.C., 1983, Jean Bernier Gallery, Athens, 1983, La Jolla (Calif.) Mus. Contemporary Art, 1984, Davenport (Iowa) Art Gallery, 1985, Ileana Tounta Contemporary Art Ctr., Athens, Greece, 1988, Rose Art Mus., Brandeis U., 1986, Elvehjem Mus. Art U. Wis., Madison, 1986, Burnett Miller Gallery, L.A., G.H. Dalsheimer Gallery, Balt., 1987, Kouros Gallery, N.Y.C., 1989, Galerie d'Art Contemporain, Geneva, 1990, Ileana Tounta Gallery, Athens, Greece, 1992, Carpenter Ctr., Harvard U., 1992-93, Rhodes (Greece) Contemp. Art Space, 1993, Mus. Contemporary Art, Salonika, 1993, Malibu (Calif.) Internat. Sculpt. Exhibition, 1993, Macedonian Mus. Modern Art, Salonika, Greece, 1993, The New Fort, Corfu, Greece, 1995, The Art Inst. Boston, 1996, Smith Coll. Mus. Art, Northampton, Mass., 1997, The Harn Mus., Gainesville, Fla., 1997, Stux Gallery, Athens Greece, 1997, Lucas Gallery Princeton U., 1998, Mitchell Algus Gallery, 1998, Gallery Camino Real, Boca Raton, Fla., 1999, St. Peter's Ch., 1999, Pub. Sch. 1, Long Island City, N.Y., 1999, Found. for Hellenic Culture, N.Y., Rose Art Mus., Brandeis U., Waltham, Mass., 2000, State Mus. Contemp. Art, Thessaloniki, 2000, Salonica, Greece, 2000, Neuberger Mus. Art, SUNY, Purchase, 2000, Corpus Christie Ch., N.Y., 2001, Galerie Denise Rene, Rive Gauche, Paris, 2002, Astrolavos Gallery, Athens, 2003, Macedonian Mus. Contemp. Art, Salonika, 2003, Alexander S. Onassis Pub. Benefit Found., N.Y., 2003, Lafayette Coll., Easton, Pa., 2004, The Kydoniefs Found., Andros, Greece, 2004, The Chapel of St. George, Mystra, Greece, 2004, Gallery of the Graduate Ctr., CUNY, 2005, others; exhibited in group shows Miami Mus. Modern Art, 1958, Martha Jackson Gallery, N.Y., 1960, Allan Stone Gallery, 1961, 62, 64, Byron Gallery, 1963, 64, PVI Gallery, N.Y., 1964, 65, Whitney Mus. Am. Art, 1966, 68, 69, 73, Newark Coll. Engring., 1968, U. N.C., 1968, R.I. Sch. Design, 1969, Worcester Art Mus., 1965, Nelson Gallery of Art, Kansas City, Mo., 1966, 68, Stedelijk von Abbemuseum, Eindhoven, 1966, Walker Art Ctr., Mpls., 1967, L.A. County Mus., 1987, N.J. State Mus. Cultural Ctr., 1967, Carnegie Internat. Mus., Pitts., 1967, Wadsworth Atheneum, Hartford, Conn., 1968, Fort Worth Art Mus., 1969, Smithsonian Instn., 1970, Portland Mus., Maine, 1971, Anne-Marie Verna Gallery, Zurich, 1972, San Francisco Mus. Art, 1973, Indpls. Mus. Art, 1974, Stadtischen Mus., Leverkusen, Federal Republic of Germany, 1975, MIT, Arts on the Line, 1980, Aldrich Mus., Ridgefield, Conn., 1979, 84, Corcoran Gallery of Art, Washington, 1987, Am. Craft Mus., N.Y.C., 1988, UCLA Art Gallery, 1969, U. Nebr., Lincoln, 1969, 70, Documenta 6, Kassel, W.Ger., 1977, Galerie Nancy Gillespie/Elisabeth de Laage, Paris, 1979, Wellesley (Mass.) Coll. Mus., 11th Internat. Sculpture Conf., Washington, 1980, Creative Time Inc., N.Y.C., Mus. Mod. Art, N.Y.C., 1981, Europalia, Brussels, 1982, Mus. Mod. Art of the City of Paris,1983, 24th Annual Print Exbn. Bklyn. Mus., 1986, Sao Paulo Internat. Biennale, Brazil, 1987, Rose Art Mus. Brandeis U., 1987, archtl. show Montreal, 1988, Boston Atheneum, 1988, Ileana Tounta Contemporary Arts Ctr., Athens, Greece, 1988, Artec, Nagoya, Japan, 1989, Fawbush Gallery, N.Y.C., 1990, Nat. Gallery, Athens, 1992, Harn Mus. Art, Gainesville, Fla., 1998, Chrysler Mus. Art., Norfolk, 1999; represented in permanent collections Fed. Bldg., Dayton, Ohio, Hampshire Coll., Amherst, Mass., U. Mass., Amherst, Atlanta Internat. Airport, Whitney Mus. Am. Art, Mus. Modern Art,N.Y.C., Wadsworth Atheneum, Hartford, Conn., Phoenix Art Mus., Weatherspoon Art Gallery, U. N.C., Greensboro, Newark Mus., Milw. Art Center, Guggenheim Mus., La Jolla Mus. Contemporary Art; pub. commns. include Fed. Bldg., Dayton, Ohio, U. Mass., Amherst, Harstfield Internat. Airport, Atlanta, The Atheneum, U. Dijon, France, 14th Dist. Police Sta., Chgo., Hampshire Coll., U. Mass., 42d St, N.Y.C., Bagley Wright Theatre, Seattle, Tacoma (Wash.) Dome, La Jolla Mus. Contemporary Art, Rose Art Mus., Columbus (Ohio) Mus. Arts, Greektown Sta., Detroit, 59th St. Marine Transfer Sta., N.Y., 7475 Wis. Ave., Bethesda, Md., Back Bay/South Sta., Boston, Exch. Pl. Sta., Jersey City, 5th/Hill Sta. L.A., Lawrence St., Denver, Southwestern Bell, Dallas, Davenport (Iowa) Transit Ctr., Charles St. Sta., Balt., South Campus Sta., Buffalo, York Coll., Jamaica, N.Y., Embassy Stes., San Diego, Neon for the 59th St. Marine Transfer Station, N.Y., 1990, Neons for Buttonwood, Phila., 1990, Neons and Drawings Galerie d'Art Contemporain, Geneva, 1990, Neons for Pershong Square, 1991, Neons for Momoci, Fukuoka, Japan, 1992, Neons for Messe Turm Frankfurt, Ger., 1993, Neons for the Stadtsparkasse, Cologne, 1993, Neons for Tachikawa, Tokyo, 1994, San Antonio Pub. Libr., 1995, Neons for Providence Convention Ctr., 1995, Neon for Granpark, Tokyo, 1996, Neon for William Paterson Coll., Wayne, N.J., 1995, Neuberger Gallery SUNY, Purchase, 1997, Neons for the Reading Power Plant, Tel Aviv, 1998—, Hot Glass, Flat Glass & Neon, Chrysler Mus., Norfolk, Va., 1999, Blue Cross: Meditation Chapel, Courthouse Gallery, Portsmouth, Va., 1999, Once Again, Smith Coll. Campus, Northamptron, Mass, 2001, Six Incomplete Circles, Bati, Italy, 2002, Tria, Macedonian Mus. Contemp. Art, Thessaloniki, Greece, 2002, Double Sequence, Gen. Mitchell Internat. Airport, Milw., 2002, Ascension, Nat. Bank of Greece, Athens, 2003, Three Gates, Tsumari, Japan, 2003, Two Entrances, Athena Atrium, Odessa, Ukraine, 2004, Orizzonte, Aeroporto di Bari, Italy, 2005, Presence, European Cult. Ctr., Delphi, Greece, 2005, Jack S. Blanton Mus. Art, Austin, Tex., 2006, Roddard County CC, Suffern, NY, 2006, Collecting Ctr., 2006, The Drawing Rm., 2006, Galleria Bonomo, Bari, Italy, 2006. Recipient award NEA, 1973, N.Y. Creative Artists Pub. Svc. Program, Lifetime Achievement award Neuberger Mus. Art, 2000. Home: 435 W Broadway New York NY 10012-5902 Office Phone: 212-925-5956.

ANTONE, NAHIL PETER, lawyer, civil engineer; b. Baghdad, Iraq, Jan. 17, 1952; came to U.S., 1978; s. Peter and Salima (Kammoo) A. BS in Civil Engring. with highest distinction, U. Baghdad, 1971; MS in Structural Engring., U. Surrey, 1974; JD summa cum laude, Detroit Coll. Law, 1985. Bar: Mich. 1985, U.S. Dist. Ct. (ea. dist.) Mich. 1985; registered profl. engr., Mich. Constrn. engr. Ministry Constrn., Baghdad, 1971-73; project mgr. Ministry Oil, Baghdad, 1974-78; design engr. Harley Ellington Pierce Yee, Southfield, Mich., 1978-79; v.p. Hennessey Engring. Co., Trenton, Mich., 1979-85; assoc. Bodman, Longley & Dahling, Detroit, 1985-88; owner N. Peter Antone Profl. Corp., Southfield, 1988—; ptnr.

Antone, Casagrande & Adwer, P.C., Farmington Hills, Mich., 1989-93; pvt. practice Southfield, 1993—. Lectr. Detroit Coll. Law, 1986—87; adj. prof. immigration law Mich. State U., 2000—. Govt. of Iraq scholar, 1974; scholar Det. Coll. Law, 1982. Mem. ABA, Detroit Bar Assn., ASCE (chmn. legis. com. Southeast Mich. chpt. 1981). Avocations: tennis, swimming, exercise, travel, music. Office: 31555 W 14 Mile Rd Ste 100 Farmington Hills MI 48334 Office Phone: 248-406-4100. Business E-Mail: law@antone.com.

ANTONELLI, JUDITH SARAH, writer; b. Cin., Oct. 25, 1952; d. Robert John and Bernadette Rita Antonelli. BA in Psychology, U. Dayton, Ohio, 1974; MA in Women's Studies, Goddard Coll., Cambridge, Mass., 1978; MS in Journalism, Boston U., 1986. Freelance writer, Dayton, 1975—, Boston, 1976—; editl. asst. Cultural Survival, Inc., Cambridge, 1979—86; assoc. editor The Jewish Advocate newspaper, Boston, 1986—92, contbg. writer, 1994—95; mng. editor Jewish Family & Life! mag., Boston, 1995—96; freelance copy editor, proofreader, indexer Brookline, Mass., 1996—. Lectr. in field, 1995—97. Author: In the Image of God: A Feminist Commentary on the Torah, 1995; contbr. chapters to books. Dir. U. Dayton Women's Ctr., 1973—74. Democrat. Jewish. Achievements include co-founder of one of the first rape crisis centers in the country. Avocations: guitar, mandolin, history, astronomy, puzzles.

ANTONELLI, ROSEMARY, writer; b. Hazleton, Pa. d. Dominic A. and Carmella Antonelli. BA in Journalism, Pa. State U. Newspaper reporter Hazleton (Pa.) Standard-Speaker, Inc.; writer, pub. rels. cons. Orlando, Fla. Contbr. articles to consumer mags., newspapers, and profl. jours. including Design Times, Health Facilities Mgmt., Bldr./Arch., Orbus, Hosp. News of Fla., Fla. Design, Orlando Mag., Orlando Bus. Jour., The Lion, Hazleton (Pa.) Standard-Speaker. Recipient Newswriting award Pa. affiliate Nat. Fedn. Press Women; named Woman of the Yr., Soroptimist Internat. of Greater Hazleton, 1979; featured in Editor and Pub. mag., 1979.

ANTONELLIS, JOSEPH C., investment company executive; married; 3 children. BA, Harvard U., 1976; MBA, Bentley Coll., 1982. Positions including divsn. head mutual fund custody and dep. corp. auditor Bank of Boston; joined mutual fund services group State Street Corp., Boston, 1991, named head global fin. tech. services, 1993, sr. v.p., 1994, exec. v.p., 1999—2006, CIO, 2002—06, vice-chmn., CIO, head No. Am. investor services, 2006—. Bd. dir. Euroclear PLC, Princeton Fin. Systems, Boston Fin. Data Services. Chmn. Boston Partners in Edn.; mem. bus. adv. council Bentley Coll.; mem. United Way Tech. Council. Named one of The Premier 100 IT Leaders, Computerworld, 2005. Office: State Street Corp 1 Lincoln St Boston MA 02111*

ANTONIADIS, DIMITRI ALEXANDER, electrical engineering educator; b. Athens, Greece, Jan. 1, 1947; s. Alexander and Maria (Mastichiadis) A; m. Daphne Carvela, Oct. 29, 1969 (div. 1980); 1 child, Alexander; m. Janet Montgomery, July 8, 1988. BS in Physics, Nat. U. Athens, 1970; MSEE, Stanford U., 1973, PhD, 1976. Fellow Nat. Rsch. Inst., Greece, 1970-71; co-founder, dir. engring. ALDI Rsch. Co., 1972—; instr. Stanford U., Calif., 1976-78, rsch. assoc., 1976-78; prof. MIT, Cambridge, Mass., 1978—, dir. Microsystems Tech. Labs., 1983-90, Ray and Maria Stata chair elec. engring. Vis. faculty IBM T.J. Watson Rsch. Ctr., Yorktown, N.Y., 1979. Co-author: (computer program) SUPREM I and II, 1976; contbr. over 120 articles to profl. jours.; patentee in field. Recipient Solid State Sci. and Tech. Young Author award Electrochem. Soc., 1979. Fellow IEEE; mem. NAE. Avocation: sailing. Office: MIT Rm 39-427 60 Vassar St Cambridge MA 02139 Office Phone: 617-253-4693. Office Fax: 617-324-5341. E-mail: daa@mtl.mit.edu.

ANTONIC, JAMES PAUL, international marketing consultant; b. Milw., Mar. 29, 1943; s. George Paul and Betti Ware (Littler) A.; m. Irene Robson, Dec. 26, 1970; 1 child, Glenn. BS in Psychology, U. Wis., 1964; MBA, Boston U., 1976. Owner JPA Supply and Warehouse Co., Milw., 1966—68; product mgr., market mgr. Delta Oil Products, Milw., 1968—74, v.p. internat. ops. Brussels, 1974—2003; pres. Internat. Market Devel. Group, Barrington, Ill., 1976—2003; CEO Internat. Market Devel. Group, LLC, Ft. Myers, Fla., 1998—2004; pres., COO, Advanced Composite Tech., Inc., Ft. Myers, 2003—04; pres., CEO CBS-Homes Fla. LLC, 2004—, Composite Bldg. Structures Ltd., 2004—. Bd. dirs. ASG LLC, Schaumburg, Ill., Sustainable Bldgs. Industry Coun.; lectr. Cast Metals Inst., Am. Mgmt. Assn., U.S. Dept. Commerce, Ga. World Congress Inst., various colls. Contbr. articles to profl. jours. With U.S. Army Combat Engrs., 1964-66. Fellow Anglo-Am. Acad.; mem. Licensing Execs. Soc., Internat. Trade Club Chgo., MIT Enterprise Forum, World Trade Assn., Japan Mgmt. Cons. Assn., Am. Foundrymen's Assn. (chair legis. task force), Oak Brook Hounds (pres.). Home: 9111 Southmont Cv Apt 406 Fort Myers FL 33908-6298 Office: Ste 102 1500 Colonial Blvd Fort Myers FL 33907-1025 Office Phone: 941-870-4413. Business E-Mail: james.antonic@cbs-homes.com.

ANTONIO, DOUGLAS JOHN, lawyer; b. NYC, Sept. 14, 1955; s. John and Joan (Deitz) A.; m. Sarah Kathrine Nadelhoffer, Aug. 31, 1986; children: Zachary Douglas, Sophia Marie. BS, BA, U. Md., 1977, JD, 1980, MBA, 1981; LLM in Taxation, Georgetown U., 1983. Bar: Md. 1980, D.C. 1981, Mo. 1983, U.S. Ct. Claims 1983, Ill. 1984. Atty.-advisor U.S. Labor Dept., 1980-83; atty. Thompson & Mitchell, St. Louis, 1983-84; assoc. Blumenfeld, Sandweiss, Marx, Tureen, Ponfil & Kaskowitz, St. Louis, 1984-86, Sugar, Friedberg and Felsenthal, Chgo., 1986-87, ptnr., 1988-95; owner Antonio and Assocs., Chgo., 1995-98; ptnr. Holleb & Coff, Chgo., 1998-2000, Duane Morris LLP, Chgo., 2000—. Contbr. articles to profl. jours. Mem. Chgo. Bar Assn. (mem. exec. com. 1996—, chair fed. taxation com. 1999-2000). Home: 1316 N Sutton Pl Chicago IL 60610-2008 Office: Duane Morris LLP 227 W Monroe St Ste 3400 Chicago IL 60606-5098 Office Phone: 312-499-6772. Business E-Mail: djantonio@duanemorris.com.

ANTONIOU, ANDREAS, electrical engineering educator; b. Yerolakkos, Nicosia, Cyprus, 1938; immigrated to Can., 1969. s. Antonios and Eleni Hadjisavva; m. Rosemary C. Kennedy, 1964 (dec.); children: Anthony, David, Constantine, Helen BSc (hon.), U. London, 1963, PhD, 1966; doctorate (hon.), Nat. Tech. U. Athens, Greece, 2002. Mem. sci staff GEC Ltd., London, 1966; sr. sci. officer P.O. Rsch. Dept., London, 1966-69; sci. staff in R & D No. Electric Co., Ottawa, Ont., Canada, 1969-70; from asst. prof. elec. engring. to prof., dept. chmn. Concordia U., Montreal, Que., Canada, 1970-83; founding chmn. elec. and computer engring. dept. U. Victoria, Canada, 1983-90, prof., 1983—2003, prof. emeritus, 2003—. Author: Digital Filters: Analysis, Design, and Applications, 1979, 2d edit., 1993, Digital Signal Processing: Signals, Systems, and Filters, 2005; co-author: Two-Dimensional Digital Filters, 1992, Practical Optimization: Algorithms and Engineering Applications, 2007; contbr. articles to profl. jours. Recipient Chmn.'s award, B.C. Sci. Coun., 2000. Fellow: IEEE, Instn. Engring. Tech. (Ambrose Fleming premium 1969); mem. IEEE Sig. Proc. Soc. (Disting. Lectr. 2003-04), IEEE Cirs. Sys. Soc. (assoc. editor/editor-in-chief Trans. on Cirs. and Sys. 1983-87, bd. govs. 1995-97, gen. chair Internat. Symposium Cirs. and Sys. 2004, Golden Jubilee award 2000, Tech. Achievement award 2005, Disting. Lectr. 2006-07), Assn. Profl. Engrs. and Geoscientists BC (councilor 1988-90). Greek Orthodox. Home: 4058 Jason Pl Victoria BC Canada V8N 4T6 Office: U Victoria Dept Elec & Computer Engring PO Box 3055 STN CSC Victoria BC Canada V8W 3P6 E-mail: aantoniou@ieee.org.

ANTONISHEK, JOSEPH JOHN, chef; b. Detroit, Oct. 20, 1972; s. Joe Antonishek and Margaret Susan Hoffman. AOS, Culinary Inst. Am., Hyde Park, NY, 1992. Exec. chef Mondrian Hotel, West Hollywood, Calif., 1998—97, O-Bar Restaurant, West Hollywood, 2004—06, Minx Restaurant and Lounge, Glendale, Calif., 2006—; exec. chef, food and beverage dir. Raffles L'Ermitage Hotel, Beverly Hills, Calif., 1999—2002. Cons. Cafe Aubette, NYC, 1997—98. Host, prodr. (cooking show in development) Campfire Joe. Home Phone: 323-600-5960; Office Phone: 818.242.9191.

ANTONSEN, ELMER HAROLD, Germanic languages and linguistics educator; b. Glens Falls, NY, Nov. 17, 1929; s. Haakon and Astrid Caroline Emilie (Sommer) A.; m. Hannelore Gertrude Adam, Mar. 24, 1956; children: Ingrid Carol, Christopher Walter. BA, Union Coll., Schenectady, NY, 1951; postgrad., U. Vienna, 1951-52, U. Goettingen, 1956; MA, U. Ill., 1957, PhD, 1961. Instr. German, Northwestern U., Evanston, Ill., 1959-61; asst. prof. U. Iowa, Iowa City, 1961-64, assoc. prof., 1964-67, U. Ill., Urbana, 1967-70, prof. Germanic langs. and linguistics, 1970—, head dept. Germanic langs., 1973-82, head dept. linguistics, 1990-96, assoc. Ctr. for Advanced Studies, 1984. Vis. prof. U. N.C., Chapel Hill, 1972-73, U. Goettingen, 1988. Author: A Concise Grammar of the Older Runic Inscriptions, 1975, Runes and Germanic Linguistics, 2002, Elements of German, 2007; editor: The Grimm Brothers and the Germanic Past, 1989, Studies in the Linguistic Sciences, 1995—2002; co-editor: Staefcraeft: Studies in Germanic Linguistics, 1991; contbr. articles to profl. jours. Served with AUS, 1953-56. Fulbright scholar, 1951—52. Mem. Linguistic Soc. Am., Royal Norwegian Soc. Scis. and Letters, Soc. Advancement of Scandinavian Study, Institut für Deutsche Sprache (corr. mem.), Selskab for nordisk filologi, Soc. for Germanic Linguistics, Phi Beta Kappa. Home: 2210 Plymouth Dr Champaign IL 61821-6542 Office: Univ Ill 4088 Flb Urbana IL 61801 Personal E-mail: elmer.antonsen@insightbb.com.

ANTONUCCIO, JOSEPH ALBERT, management consultant; b. San Pier Niceto, Sicily, Italy, Apr. 25, 1932; came to U.S., 1935, naturalized, 1941; s. Joseph and Nancy (Calogero) A.; m. Patricia B. Damon, June 1, 1957 (div. 1987); children— Joseph Russell, Louise Shaffer, Timothy Damon AB, Rutgers U., 1954. Vice pres. Deluxe Reading Corp., Elizabeth, NJ, 1962-67; ptnr. Peat, Marwick, Mitchell & Co., NYC, 1967-88; exec. v.p. Lex Electronics Inc., Westbury, NY, 1988-90; v.p. Princess Hotels Internat., NYC, 1990-98; mng. ptnr. Veritas Cons., NYC, 1998—. Contbr. aticles on computers to profl. jours. Vice pres., bd. dirs. Sutton-Area Community, Inc., N.Y.C., 1983—; mem. N.Y.C. Bd. Elections task force N.Y.C. Partnership, Inc., 1985. Served to sgt. U.S. Army, 1954-56 Mem. Data Processing Mgmt. Assn. (bd. dirs. 1962-67), Computer Security Inst. (lectr. 1979—), Assn. Systems Mgmt. (project chmn. 1972-79) Clubs: University (N.Y.C.). Avocations: hiking, skiing. Home and Office: 405 E 56th St New York NY 10022-2412 Home Phone: 212-486-0344; Office Phone: 212-754-6202. Personal E-mail: jantonuccio@msn.com.

ANTONY, PAUL T., military officer, physician executive; BS in Biomedical Engring., Johns Hopkins U., Balt., 1978—81; MBA, Harvard U., Boston, 1986—88; MD, MPH, George Wash. U., DC, 1991—96. Diplomate aerospace medicine Am. Bd. Preventive Medicine; lic. pilot FAA. Cons. McKinsey & Co., Paris, 1988—90, NYC, 1988—90; comdr., flight surgeon US Navy & Marine Corps., DC, 1991—; sr. med. officer Marine One Presdl. Helicopter Squadron, 2001—04; chief med. officer PhRMA, DC, 2004—; product mgr. AT&T & Hewlett-Packard. Decorated Medal UN, Parachutist Badge US Mil., Meritorious Svc. medal, Presdl. Svc. Badge White Ho. Mil. Office, Iraq Campaign medal US Mil. Mem.: AMA (rps del. 1997—98), Soc. Naval Flight Surgeons (life; dir. 1998—99, Surgeon General's award 1997), Assn. Mil. Surgeons US (life), Mensa. Home: 12466 Riverside Dr Fort Myers FL 33919 Office: PhRMA 950 F St NW Washington DC 20004

ANTOUN, MIKHAIL, medicinal chemistry and pharmacognosy educator; b. Khartoum, Sudan, Aug. 20, 1946; came to U.S., 1979; s. Daoud and Badia (Boulos) A.; m. Slavomira Kucerova, Sept. 14, 1973; children: Helena, David Emmanuel, Anna Maria. B in Pharm. with distinction, U. Khartoum, 1968; PhD, U. London, 1974. Asst. prof. pharm. U. Khartoum (Sudan), 1974—78, assoc. prof., 1978—81; sr. rsch. scientist Purdue U., West Lafayette, Ind., 1981—86; assoc. prof. medicinal chemistry and pharmacognosy U. P.R. Sch. Pharm., San Juan, 1986—92, prof. medicinal chemistry and pharmacognosy, faculty chair prof., 1993—, dept. head, 1993—2005. Vis. prof., rsch. assoc. Sch. Pharmacy and Pharm. Sci. Purdue U., West Lafayette, 1979-81. Contbr. articles to profl. jours. Sr. scholar U. Khartoum, 1968-69; teaching fellow U. London, 1969-73. Fellow Linnean Soc.; mem. Am. Assn. Colls. Pharmacy, Am. Soc. Pharmacognosy, Am. Assn. Pharm. Scientists, Sigma Xi. Avocations: piano, classical music, reading, chess, swimming. Office Phone: 787-758-2525 ext. 5414. Personal E-mail: anto285@aol.com.

ANTREASIAN, GARO ZAREH, artist, lithographer, educator; b. Indpls., Feb. 16, 1922; s. Zareh Minas and Takouhie (Daniell) A.; m. Jeanne Glascock, May 2, 1947; children: David Garo, Thomas Berj. BFA, John Herron Sch. Art, 1948; DFA (hon.), Ind. U.-Purdue U. at Indpls., 1972. Instr. Herron Sch. Art, Indpls., 1948—59, 1961—64; tech. dir. Tamarind Lithography Workshop, Los Angeles, 1960-61; prof. art U. N.Mex., 1964-87, chmn. dept. art, 1981-84; tech. dir. Tamarind Inst., U. N.Mex., 1970-72; vis. lectr., artist numerous univs. Bd. dir. Albuquerque Mus., 1980-90; printmaker emeritus Southern Graphics Coun., 1994; Fulbright vis. lectr. U. São Paulo and Found. Armando Alvares Penteado, Brazil, 1985. Prin. author: The Tamarind Book of Lithography: Art and Techniques, 1970; one-man shows include Malvina Miller Gallery, San Francisco, 1971, Marjorie Kauffman Gallery, Houston, 1975-79, 84, 86, U. Colo., Boulder, 1972, Calif. Coll. Arts & Crafts, Oakland, 1973, Miami U., Oxford, Ohio, 1973, Kans. State U., 1973, Atlanta Coll. Art, 1974, U. Ga., Athens, 1974, Alice Simsar Gallery, Ann Arbor, 1977-79, Elaine Horwich Gallery, Santa Fe, 1977-79, Mus. of N.Mex., Santa Fe, 1979, Robischon Gallery, Denver, 1984, 86, 90, Moss-Chumley Gallery, Dallas, 1987, Rettig-Martinez Gallery, Santa Fe, 1988, 91, 92, U. N.Mex. Art Mus., 1988, Albuquerque Mus., 1988, Louis Newman Gallery, L.A., 1989, Expositum Gallery, Mexico City, 1989, State U. Coll., Cortland, NY, 1991, Mus. Art, U. Ariz., Tucson, 1991, 2004, Indpls. Mus. Art, 1994, Ruschmon Gallery, Indpls., 1994, Mitchell Mus. Art, Vernon, Ill., 1995, Cline-Lewallen Gallery, Santa Fe, 1997, 2002, Anderson Gallery, Albuquerque, 1997, Fenix Gallery, Taos, NM State U., Las Crucis, 1998, Lewallen Gallery, Santa Fe, 2002, Cline Gallery, Scottsdale, 2002, 03, 04, Cline Fine Art, Scottsdale, Ariz., 2002, Gerald Peters Gallery, Santa Fe, 2005, Fresno Art Mus., 2005, others; exhibited group shows Phila. Print Club, 1960-63, Ind. Artists, 1947-63, White House, 1966, Nat. Lithographic Exhbn. Fla. State U., 1965, Library Congress, 1961-66, Bklyn. Mus., 1958-68, 76, U.S. Pavilion Venice Biennale, 1970, Internat. Biennial, Bradford, Eng., 1972-74, Internat. Biennial, Tokyo, 1972, City Mus. Hong Kong, 1972, Tamarind UCLA, 1985, Roswell Mus., 1989, Pace Gallery, 1990, Worcester (Mass.) Art Mus., 1990, Amon Carter Mus., Ft. Worth, 1990, Albuquerque Mus., 1991, 92, Art Mus. U. N.Mex., 1991, 92, 99, 2001, Norton Simon Mus., Pasadena, Calif., 1999, U. NH, 1999, Cline Fine Art, Scottsdale, Ariz., 2002, 03, Fenix Gallery, Taos, 2003, Fresno Mus. Art, 2005, Gerald Peters Gallery, Santa Fe, 2005; reppresented in permanent collections: Albuquerque Mus., Bklyn. Mus., Guggenheim Mus., NYC, Cin. Mus., Chgo. Art Inst., Ind. State Mus., Mus. Modern Art, NYC, Library of Congress, Met. Mus., NYC, NY Pub. Libr., Mus. Fine Arts, Santa Fe, also, Boston, Indpls., Seattle, Phila., San Diego, Dallas, Worcester Art Museums, Los Angeles County Mus., Roswell Mus. and Art Ctr., Tucson Mus., murals, Ind. U., Butler U., Ind. State Office Bldg., Smithsonian Inst., So. Ill. U., U. Nev., Cinn. Mus. Art, others. Combat artist with USCGR, World War II, PTO. Recipient Distinguished Alumni award Herron Sch. Art, 1972, N.Mex. Annual Gov.'s award, 1987; Grantee Nat. Endowment for Arts, 1983; fellow Nat. Acad. Design, NYC, 1993. Fellow NAD; mem. World Print Coun. (bd. dirs. 1980-87), Nat. Print Coun. Am. (co-pres. 1980-82), Coll. Art Assn. Am. (bd. dirs. 1977-80).

ANTWI, EBENEZER YAW, education educator; b. Bomeng, Ghana, Jan. 12, 1936; s. Kwasi Ofori and Akua Nyame; 7 children , Mavis, Salome, Stella, Beverly, Kwadwd, Kwame. BA, Kans.Wesleyan U., 1978; MA, PhD, Ohio State U., 1981. Pres., CEO MEDCO, Inc., Bronx, NY. Avocation: fishing. Office: 2240 E Tremont Ave 7D Bronx NY 10462 also: MEDCO Inc 2240 E Tremont Ste 7D Bronx NY 10462 E-mail: medco@optonline.net.

ANTZELEVITCH, CHARLES, research and development company executive; b. Israel, Mar. 25, 1951; arrived in US, 1959, naturalized; s. Chaim and Frida (Hassman) A.; m. Brenda Reisner, June 24, 1973; children: Daniel Avi, Lisa Rachel. BA, Queens Coll., 1973; PhD, SUNY, Syracuse, 1977. Postdoctoral fellow Masonic Med. Rsch. Lab., Utica, NY, 1977-80, rsch. scientist, 1980-83, sr. rsch. scientist, 1984, exec. dir., dir. rsch., 1984—; asst. prof. SUNY Health Scis. Ctr. Pharmacology, Syracuse, 1980-83, assoc. prof., 1983-86; prof. pharmacology SUNY Health Scis. Ctr., Syracuse, 1987—. Mem. editl. bd. Jour. Cardiovasc. Electrophysiology, 1990, NASPETAPES, Jour. Cardiovasc. Pharmacology and Therapeutics, Circulation, Current Cardiology Revs., Heart Rhythm, others; contbr. articles to profl. jours. Com. mem. NY State Heart Assn., Syracuse, 1982-87; bd. dirs. Clin. Med. Network, Utica, 1987-94, Jewish Cmty. Ctr., Utica, 1987-92, Royal Arch Masons Med. Rsch. Found., 1989, Ctrl. N.Y. Heart Assn., 1989; v.p. Temple Beth El, Utica, v.p., 1993-95, pres., 1995-97, com. mem., 1991—; instnl. rev. bd. Faxton Hosp., Utica, 1990—2002 Recipient Van Horne award Ctrl. NY Heart Assn., 1981-84, numerous grants; Gordon K. Moe scholar chair in exptl. cardiology Masonic Med. Rsch. Lab., 1987—, Disting. Svc. award RAM Med. Rsch. Found., 1994, Charles Henry Johnson medal Grand Lodge Free and Accepted Masons NY, 1996, Disting. Achievement medal, 2001, Disting. Scientist award Heart Rhythm Soc., 2002. Fellow: Am. Coll. Cardiology (editl. bd. jour. 1989—92, program com. 2001—); mem.: Am. Physiol. Soc. (Carl J. Wiggers award 2006, 2007), N.Am. Soc. Pacing and Electrophysiology (chmn. sci. com. 1995—98, long range planning com. 1995—98, nominations com. 1997—99, bd. dirs. 1997—2003, program com. 1998—2002, sec. 2000—03, exec. com. 2000—03, fin. com. 2000—03, Disting. Scientist award 2002), Internat. Cardiac Electrophysiology Soc. (sec.-treas. 1994—96, pres. 1996—98, sec.-treas. 1998—), Cardiac Electrophysiol. Soc., Internat. Soc. for Heart Rsch., N.Y. Acad. Scis., Am. Heart Assn. (chmn. peer rev. com. 1997—, Excellence in Cardiovasc. Sci. award 2003, Excellence in Cardiovasc. Sci. 2003). Avocation: swimming. Office: Masonic Med Rsch Lab 2150 Bleecker St Utica NY 13501-1738 Home Phone: 315-797-6976; Office Phone: 315-735-2217. Business E-Mail: ca@mmrl.edu.

ANUAKAN, ROBYN ISET, archivist, educator, film producer; b. Cleve., Mar. 20, 1961; d. Charles Tillman Broughton and Audrey Faye Taborn. BA, U. Calif. San Diego, La Jolla, 1985; Masters, U. Calif., Berkeley, 1991, PhD, 2002. Grad. student instr. U. Calif., Berkeley, 1991—2001; grad. student archivist Ctr. for Study of Higher Edn., Berkeley, 2000—01; lectr. San Diego State U., 2002; asst. prof. Calif. State U. Dominguez Hills, Carson, 2002—. Pres. Making History Prodns., Inglewood, Calif., 2004—. Actor: (theatre performance) A Son Come Home; prodr.: (film) The Career of Professor Roy Thomas; prodr., rschr. (DVD) A Vision of CSUDH, author, archivist (biographies) California's Leaders in the Master Plan for Higher Education; author: (internet publishing) The History of History Series; contbr. articles to profl. publs.; host (TV program) Cultural Pluralism, Carson, Calif., 2006. Recipient Romel award, NAACP, 1987, Achievement award, Am. Bus. Women's Assn., 1988, Gold award, World of Poetry, 1992, award, Bullins Meml. Theatre, 1992, Leadership award, Nat. U., 1997, Outstanding Tchg. award, U. Calif., Berkeley, 2000, Wall of Tolerance award, So. Poverty Law Ctr., 2001, Achievement award, Ctr. for Tchg. and Learning, 2005; fellow, U. Calif., Berkeley, 1989—93, Ford Found., 1992, Byrne Rsch. Ctr., 1996—97, West African Rsch. Assn., 1996; grantee, Andrew Mellon Found., 1995, U. Calif., Berkeley Grad. Office, 1995, Heller Found., 1999, Calif. State U., Dominguez Hills Found., 2003, Calif. State U. Dominguez Hills, 2005; scholar, Osher Found., 1990—91; Acad. fellow, Archbishop Riordan, 1997, Fulbright fellow, Calif. State U., Sacramento, 2004. Mem.: Smithsonian, Internat. Soc. Tchg. and Learning, Schomburg Mus., Nat. Black Grad. Students (v.p. 1992—93, Svc. award 1993), Calif. Faculty Assn. (affirmative action rep. 2005—06), San Diego African Am. Alumni Assn. Liberal. Avocations: poetry, painting, gardening, film. Office: California State U Dominguez Hills 1000 East Victoria St Carson CA 90747 Home Phone: 310-427-5868; Office Phone: 310-243-3471. Office Fax: 310-516-4268. E-mail: ianuakan@csudh.edu.

ANUPINDI, RAVI, operations research specialist, educator; PhD, Carnegie Mellon U., Pitts., 1993. Asst. prof. Northwestern U., Evanston, Ill., 1993—2000; assoc. prof. NYU, 2000—02, U. Mich., Ann Arbor, 2002—. Author: (textbook) Managing Business Process Flows, 2d edit., 2006; contbr. articles to profl. jours. Mem.: Coun. Supply Chain Mgmt. Profls. (assoc.), Master Supply Chain Program Soc. (assoc.; v.p. of meetings 2002—03), Inst. Ops. Rsch. and Mgmt. Scis. (assoc. Meritorious Svc. award 1996, 2002). Office: U Mich 701 Tappan Ave W5724 Ann Arbor MI 48109 Home Phone: 734-769-5928; Office Phone: 734-615-8621. Office Fax: 734-936-0279. Business E-Mail: anupindi@umich.edu.

ANUSZKIEWICZ, RICHARD JOSEPH, artist; b. Erie, Pa., May 23, 1930; s. Adam Jacob and Victoria (Jankowski) A.; m. Sarah Feeney, Nov. 26, 1960; children: Adam John, Stephanie, Christine. B.F.A., Cleve. Inst. Art, 1953; M.F.A., Yale U., 1955; BS in Edn., Kent State U., 1956. One-man shows at Butler Art Inst., Youngstown, Ohio, 1955, The Contempories, N.Y.C., 1960, 61, 63, Sidney Janis Gallery, N.Y.C., 1965-67, Dartmouth Coll., 1967, Cleve. Mus. Art, 1967, Kent State U., 1968, Andrew Crispo Gallery, N.Y.C., 1975, 77, La Jolla (Calif.) Mus. Contemporary Art, 1976, Univ. Art Mus., Berkeley, Calif., 1977, Columbus (Ohio) Gallery of Fine Arts, 1977, Charles Foley Gallery, Columbus, 1982, Graham Modern, N.Y.C., 1984, Heckscher Mus., Huntington, N.Y., 1984, Schweyer-Galdo Galleries, Pontiac, Mich., 1985, Tampa (Fla.) Mus., 1986, Richard Green Gallery, N.Y.C., 1987, Galleria Sagittaria, Pordenone, Italy, 1988, Charles Foley Gallery, Columbus, 1988, Galleie Civiche D'Arte Moderna, Ferrara, Italy, 1989, Newark Mus., 1990, Maruzen Co., Ltd., Tokyo, 1990-91, Abante Fine Art, Portland, Oreg., 1992, Ctr. fro Arts, Vero Beach, Fla., 1993, others; exhibited in group shows at Mus. Modern Art, 1960-61, 63, 65, U. Ill., 1961, NYU, 1961, Pa. Acad. Design, 1962, Whitney Mus. Am. Art, 1962, 63-64, 70, 71, Inst. Contemporary Arts, Boston, 1962, Columbus Gallery Fine Arts, 1962, City Art Mus., St. Louis, 1962, Munson-Williams-Proctor Inst., Utica, N.Y., 1962, Tweed Gallery U. Minn., 1962, Silvermine (Conn.) Guild Artists, 1962-63, Atheneum Sch., Helsinki, Finland, 1962, Mus. Modern Art, Sarasota, Fla., 1962, J.B. Speed Art Mus., Louisville, 1962, Meml. Art Gallery, Rochester, N.Y., 1962, Allentown (Pa.) Art Mus., 1963, Krannert (Ill.) Art Mus., 1963, De Cordova Mus., Lincoln, Mass., 1963, Washington Gallery Modern Art, 1963, U. Mich. Mus. Art, 1964, Sidney Janis Gallery, N.Y.C., 1964, 65, Art Inst., Chgo., 1964, 71, Tate Gallery, London, 1964, Far Gallery, 1964, Carnegie Inst., Pitts., 1964, Corcoran Gallery Art, Washington, 1965, Art Fair Cologne, Germany, 1967, Larry Aldrich Mus., Ridgefield, Conn., 1968, 71, Hopkins Center Art Galleries Dartmouth Coll., Hanover, N.H., 1969, Denver Art Mus., 1969, Va. Mus. Fine Arts, Richmond, 1970, Ind. State U., Terre Haute, 1970, Masur Modern Art, Monroe, La., 1970,

Birmingham (Ala.) Mus., 1971, Whitney Mus. Am. Art, N.Y.C., 1972, Hirshhorn Mus. and Sculpture Garden, N.Y.C., 1974, Bklyn. Mus., 1977, Albright-Knox Gallery, Buffalo, 1979, Met. Mus. Art, N.Y.C., 1982, Museo de Arts Moderno, Ciudad Bolivar, Venezuela, 1984, Tel Aviv Mus., 1986, Paris-New York-Kent Gallery, Kent, Conn., 1987, Guggenheim Mus., N.Y.C., 1987-88, Marilyn Pearl Gallery, N.Y.C., 1988, James A. Michener Arts Ctr. Bucks County, Doylestown, Pa., 1988, Centre d'Art Contempora, Geneva, 1989, Provincaal Mus., Hasselt, Belgium, Ctr. d'Art en Sante Monica, Barcelona, Spain, 1989, Galleri Civiche D'Arte Moderna, 1989, Samuel P. Harn Mus. Art, Gainesville, Fla., 1990, 92, DeCordova Mus., Lincoln, Mass., 1991, Nat. Gallery Art, Washington, 1991, Cummer Gallery Art, Jacksonville, Fla., 1992, Harmon Meek Gallery, Naples, Fla., 1993, Nat. Acad. Design, Washington, 1993, Camino Real Gallery, Boca Raton, Fla., 1993, 96, 98, Center for the Arts, Vero Beach, Fla., 1993, Intermission Gallery, John Harms Ctr. Arts, Englewood, N.J., 1993, Williams Center Arts, Lafayette Coll., Easton, P.A., 1994, N.J. State Mus., Trenton, 1994, Harmon Meek Gallery, Naples, Fla., 1995, 2000, OK Harris Gallery, N.Y.C. 2002, ACA Gallery, N.Y.C., 2003others; represented in permanent collections, Mus. Modern Art, Whitney Mus. Am. Art, Cleve. Mus. Art, Corcoran Gallery Art, Allentown Art Mus., Albright-Knox Art Gallery, Butler Art Inst., Akron (Ohio) Art Inst., Yale Art Gallery, Chgo. Art Inst., Larry Aldrich Mus., Ridgefield, Conn., Fogg Art Mus. of Harvard U., Hirshhorn Mus. and Sculpture Garden, artist-in-residence, Dartmouth Coll., 1967, U. Wis., 1968, Cornell U., 1968, Kent State U., 1968; contbr. articles to profl. jours. Home and Office: 76 Chestnut St Englewood NJ 07631-3045 Home Phone: 201-567-9404; Office Phone: 201-567-9404. E-mail: sa22@earthlink.net.

ANVARIPOUR, M. A., lawyer; b. Tehran, Iran, Jan. 23, 1935; arrived in U.S., 1957; s. Ahmed and Monir (Georgi) A.; m. Patricia Matson Lynch (div. 1971); 1 dau., Sandra M.; m. Guilda Eshtehardi, Mar. 31, 1978 (div. 1984); 1 son, Cyrus Ramsey; m. Tess Temel, May 15, 1995 (div. 2002). LLB, U. Tehran, 1956; BS, U. San Francisco, 1959; student, U. Calif. Hastings Coll. Law, San Francisco, JD, 1973. Bar: Ill. 1973, Fed. cts. Asst. field dir. Am. Friends of Middle East, Inc., Iran, 1962-64, field dir., 1964-66; asst. dean students, dean internat. students and faculty affairs Ill. Inst. Tech., Chgo., 1966-81; practiced in Chgo., 1973—, in San Francisco, 1985—; ednl. and legal adviser Consulate Gen. Iran, Chgo., 1973-79; aux. lawyer NAACP, Chgo., 1973-74. Lectr. immigration and law seminar Ill. Inst. Tech.-Chgo.-Kent Coll. Law Sch., 1974 Mem. Am., Iran-Am. (sec.-gen. 1964-66), Chgo. Bar Assn. (chmn. immigration com. 1982-83), Iran Am. Alumni Assn. (sec. 1964-66), Nat. Assn. Fgn. Student Affairs (Ill. chmn. 1968-69), U. Tehran, U. San Francisco, Idaho State U. (hon.), Ill. Inst. Tech., Chgo.-Kent Coll. Law alumni assns., Am. Immigration Lawyers Assn. (sec.-treas. Chgo. chpt. 1976-78, v.p. 1978-80, pres. 1980-81), Armour Faculty Club (pres. 1977-78), Phi Delta Phi. Office: 180 N La Salle St Chicago IL 60601-2501 Office Phone: 312-750-0558. Personal E-mail: anvaripourlaw@yahoo.com. *My biases have made my life extremely rewarding. I have several. I have a strong bias against intolerance. I have a deep-seated bias against hate and bigotry, a bias against war, a bias for peace, and a bias which guides me to have faith in the basic goodness of my fellow human beings.*

ANVERSA, PIERO, medical educator; s. Giuseppe Anversa and Maria Folzani; m. Sandra Zanelli, Sept. 16, 1968; 1 child, Matteo. MD, Med. Sch., Parma, Italy, 1959—65; MD (hon.), Med. Sch., Bologna, Italy, 2002. Prof., medicine N.Y. Med. Coll., Valhalla, 1984—, v.chmn., medicine, 2000—; vis. prof. Albert Einstein Coll. Medicine, NYC, 1992—, Sacred Heart U., Rome, 1989—, U. Vita-Salute, Milan, 2003—, San Diego State U., 2003—. Fellow: Am. Heart Assn. (Rsch. Achievement award 2004, Disting. Scientist 2003). Achievements include research in the identification of cell death in the heart. Avocation: travel. Home Phone: 212-772-7906. Office Fax: 914-594-4406. Business E-Mail: piero_anversa@nymc.edu.

ANWAR, SOHEL, engineering educator; s. Mokhlesur Rahman and Roushan Ara Mostazir; m. Shahriar Shahnaz, Aug. 16, 1992; children: Saffanah children: Jumanah. BSME, Bangladesh U. Engring. and Tech., Dhaka, 1986; PhD, U. Ariz., 1994. Registered profl. engr., Mich. Staff engr. Caterpillar Inc., Peoria, Ill., 1995—99; sr. staff engr. Ford Motor Co. / Visteon Corp., Dearborn, Mich., 1999—2004; asst. prof. Sch. Engring. and Tech. Purdue U., Indpls., 2004—. Contbr. scientific papers to profl. jours. and confs. Organizer Habitat for Humanity, Detroit, 2001—03. Recipient Leading the Way award, Visteon Corp., 2003. Mem.: ASME. Achievements include 12 US patents; first patent on full throttle directional shift. Office: Indiana U/Purdue U Indpls 723 W Michigan St SL 260 Indianapolis IN 46202 Office Phone: 317-274-7640. Business E-Mail: soanwar@iupui.edu.

ANYA, ADAMMA CHUKWUDI, special education educator; b. Nsu, Imo, Nigeria, Aug. 2, 1950; came to U.S., 1982; d. Simeon and Mercillina Osuji Nwaokeafor; m. Conleth Chukwudi Anya, Feb. 28, 1984; 1 child, Uchenna; 2 stepchildren; 1 adopted child BSc, U. Minn., 1983, MS, 1991, MS, 1998; PhD Critical Pedagogy, U. St. Thomas, 2002. Cert. spl. edn. specialist, Minn. Family life educator Fed. Minn. Tech., Lagos, 1979—82; home economist Imo State Schs., Owerri, Nigeria, 1965—78; sous chef Daytons Huston, Mpls., 1988—92; tchr. spl. edn. Mpls. Pub. Schs., 1989—2005. Mem. cmty. youth advocate, Youth Excellence award, vol. Hennepin County, Mpls., 1979—; mem. adv. bd. Nigerian Hotel and Catering; vol., owner Connice Share Internat., Inc., Osseo, Minn., 1973—. Recipient Nat. Youth Svc. award Nigerian Youth Svc., 1997. Mem. AAUW, Am. and Internat. Home Econs. Assn., Am. Fedn. Assn. Tchrs., Stigma Club Avocations: music, dance, sports, sewing, travel. Office: Connice Share Internat Inc PO Box 634 Osseo MN 55369-0634 Office Phone: 763-496-1110. Personal E-mail: cshare5250@yahoo.com.

ANYALEBECHI, PRINCE N., engineering educator, consultant; b. Umuechem-Etche, Rivers State, Nigeria, Mar. 11, 1957; s. Anyalebechi Ebenezer and Cecilia Nwaulo Otamiri; m. Esther O. Anyalebechi, Sept. 30, 1985; children: Jason E., Jamal C., Jerome C., Janel C. MSc, Brunel U., Uxbridge, Eng., 1982, PhD, 1985. Cert. Brit. Engring. Coun., London, 1991. Rsch. engr. Alcoa Tech. Ctr., Alcoa Inc., Pitts., 1985—88, sr. rsch. engr., 1988—89, staff scientist, 1989—92, sci. assoc., 1992—96; assoc. prof. James Madison U., Harrisonburg, Va., 1996—99; tech. specialist Alcoa Tech. Ctr., Alcoa Inc., Pitts., 1999—2001; asst. prof. Grand Valley State U., Grand Rapids, Mich., 2001—05, assoc. prof., 2005—. Recipient Arthur Vining Davis Tech. Excellence award, Alcoa Tech. Ctr., Alcoa Inc., 1990. Mem.: Soc. Mfg. Enrs., Am. Soc. Engring. Edn., Am. Soc. Metals Internat., Minerals, Metals and Materials Soc., Inst. Materials, Minerals, & Mining, Eng., Sigma Xi. Achievements include patent for siloxane coating process for metal or ceramic substrates. Office: Grand Valley State Univ 618 Eberhard Center 301 W Fulton Grand Rapids MI 49504 Home Phone: 616-667-0620; Office Phone: 616-331-6405. Office Fax: 616-331-7215. Personal E-mail: anyalebechi@msn.com. Business E-Mail: anyalebp@gvsu.edu.

ANYANWU, CHUKWUMA UCHENNA, clinical pharmacist, biomedical researcher; b. Owerri, Nigeria, Sept. 22, 1970; s. Max Uchechukwu Anyanwu and Stella Ugochi Nwanguma; m. Akudo Mmaulo Amaechi, Dec. 25, 2004. BSc with honors, U. Nigeria, 1994; PharmD, Temple U., 2003. Rsch. asst. Loyola U. Med. Ctr., Maywood, Ill., 1996—99; rsch. project coord. U. Chgo. Med. Ctr., 1999; post-doctoral pharmacy practice resident Crozer-Keystone Health Sys., Upland, Pa., 2003; clin. and staff pharmacist Lankenau Hosp., Wynnewood, Pa., 2004—. Rsch. intern Temple U. Sch. of Medicine, Phila.; summer intern Bridging The Gaps, Phila., 2000; pharmacy extern Temple U. Hosp., 2000—03. Trustee, mem. of choir Second Bapt. Ch. of Germantown, Phila., 1999; vol., charity and hospice Public Health Edn. to Inner City Dwellers. Academic merit scholarship, Fed. Govt. of Nigeria, 1982—87. Fellow: Royal Inst. of Pub. Health; mem.: Drug Info. Soc., Am. Soc. of Health-Systems Pharmacy, Am. Coll. Clin. Pharmacy, Mbaitoli-Ikeduru Family Meeting. Independent. Achievements include research in the genetics of hypertension, obesity in blacks, cancer genetics and epidemiology studies, anticoagulation monitoring, drug safety. Avocations: music, chess, Scrabble, lawn tennis. Office: Lank Hosp and Lank Inst of Bmd Resc 100 Lancaster Ave Wynnewood PA 19096 Home Phone: 267-934-2171; Office Phone: 610-645-2151. Personal E-mail: chukky70@hotmail.com.

ANZALONE, FILIPPA MARULLO, law librarian, educator; b. Cambridge, Mass., Sept. 27, 1953; d. Gaspar Edward and Patricia Alice (O'Connell) Marullo; m. Antonio Anzalone, Oct. 30, 1983; children: Patricia, Lucia. AB, Smith Coll., 1975; MSLM, Simmons Coll., 1977; JD, Suffolk U., 1985. Bar: Mass. 1985, U.S. Dist. Ct. Mass. 1986. Br. libr. Medford Pub. Libr., Mass., 1975-76, children's libr. Mass., 1976-78; br. dir. Cambridge Pub. Libr., Mass., 1978-80; rsch. libr. Dike, Bronstein, Roberts, Cushman and Pfund, Boston, 1980-81; dir. law libr. Bingham, Dana & Gould, Boston, 1981-91; dir. info. and access svcs. Northeastern U. Sch. Law, Boston, 1991-93, dir. law libr., 1993—2002, dir. info. svcs. and rsch., prof. law; acting dean univ. librs. Northwestern U., Boston, 2000—01; prof. law, assoc. dean libr. and computing svcs. Law Libr. Boston Coll. Sch. Law, Newton, 2002—. Book reviewer Legal Info. Alert; mem. exec. bd. Nellco. Contbr. articles to profl. jours. Mem. Am. Assn. Law Librs. (chair coun. chpt. pres. 1993-94), Assn. Boston Law Librs. (pres. 1989-90), Law Librs. New Eng. (pres. 1992-93), Assn. Am. Law Sch. (mem. Law Librs. Exec. Bd., 2006-). Roman Catholic. Avocations: art, music, reading, swimming. Office: Boston Coll Law Sch Law Libr 885 Centre St Newton Centre MA 02459 Office Fax: 617-552-6809. E-mail: filippa.anzalone.1@bc.edu.*

AO, QI, nuclear engineer, research scientist; s. Chuanfa Ao and Xiaolin Gu; m. Ann Yu, May 15, 1993; children: Bethany R., Zachary X. BE in Applied Geophysics, Chengdu U. Tech., Sichuan, China, 1982, ME in Nuc. Tech., 1988; PhD in Nuc. Engring., NC State U., Raleigh, 1995. Lectr. Chengdu U. Tech., China, 1982—89; rschr. NC State U., Raleigh, 1995—97, Duke U., Durham, NC, 1997—98; prin. scientist Analyser Sys. Inc., Escondido, Calif., 1998—2000, Thermo Electron Corp., San Diego, 2000—01; v.p. Nuc. Solutions, Inc., Washington, 2001—03; prin. engr. GE Energy, Nuc., Wilmington, NC, 2003—. Mem.: Am. Nuc. Soc. (internat. com. 2006—). Achievements include research in computational methods in nuclear science and engineering; nuclear safety; nuclear design and analysis in industry, medicine, and geophysics. Office: General Electric Company 3901 Castle Hayne Rd Wilmington NC 28402

AOKI, MASANAO, economics professor; b. Hiroshima, Japan, May 14, 1931; came to U.S. 1956; BS, U. Tokyo, 1953, MS, 1955; PhD, UCLA, 1960; DSc, Tokyo Inst. Tech., 1966. Prof. elec. engring. and econs. UCLA, 1963-73, 75-81, 85-92; prof. U. Ill., 1973-75, U. Osaka, Japan, 1981-85. Author: Optimization of Stochastic Systems, 1967, 2d edit., 1989, State Space Modeling of Time Series, 1987, 2d edit., 1996, New Approaches to Macroeconomic Modelings: Evolutionary Stochastic Dynamics, Multiple Equilibria, and Externalities as Field Effects, Modeling Aggregate Behavior and Fluctuations in Economics, 2002, Reconstructing Macroeconomics: A Perspective of Statistical Physics and Combinational Stochastic Processes, 2007. Mem.: Soc. Econ. Dynamics and Control (pres. 1982—83), Soc. Instrument and Control Engring. Japan, Japanese Econ. Assn. Office: UCLA Dept Econs 405 Hilgard Ave Los Angeles CA 90095-1477 Home Phone: 310-472-1988; Office Phone: 310-825-2360. Business E-Mail: aoki@econ.ucla.edu.

AOKI, STEVEN, federal agency administrator; children: Genevieve, Lillian, Thalia, Nadege. AB, U. Chgo., 1972, BS, 1973, PhD in Physics, 1979. Scientific staff mem. Lawrence Livermore Nat. Lab., 1978—84; spl. asst. to under sec. for internat. security affairs US Dept. State, with Bur. Politico-Military Affairs and Near East-Asian Affairs, dir. Office Proliferation Threat Reduction; staff mem. Nat. Security Coun., 1993—96; sr. adv. internat. programs and nonproliferation Nat. Nuclear Security Adminstrn., US Dept. Energy, dep. undersecretary for counter-terrorism, 2005—. Office: National Nuclear Security Adminstrn US Dept Energy 1000 Independence Ave SW Washington DC 20585

AON, FRANK JOSEPH GARCIA, lab administrator, materials scientist; b. Portsmouth, Va., May 18, 1953; s. Isaac Aon and Carmen Gomes; m. Joan Marie Lucker, Sept. 22, 1989; children: Orion Dov, Joshua Dylan. Student, Creighton U., 1970—71; BA in Art History, Highlands U., 1973; MA in Geology, Las Companas, N.Mex., 1974; MA in Metulurgy, Delay Guild, 1982. Owner, pres. Orenda Lab., Santa Fe, 1975—. Sr. instr. Sin Lung Kwoon, Denver, 1993—. Author: The Making, 1987. Scholar, Highlands U., 1971—73. Mem.: Beijing Ba Gua Assn., Beijing Chen Assn.

AOUN, JOSEPH, academic administrator, linguistics educator, researcher; b. Beirut, Mar. 26, 1953; came to US, 1978; s. Elie and Josephine (Kikano) A.; m. Zeina El-Imad, June 22, 1979; children: Joseph K., Adrian M. MA, St. Joseph U., Beirut, Lebanon, 1975; Diploma of Advanced Studies, U. Paris VIII, 1977; PhD, MIT, 1981. Asst. prof. linguistics U. So. Calif., LA, 1982-86, assoc. prof., 1986—96, vice dean, dean faculty Coll. Letters, Arts and Scis., 1999—2000, dean, 2000—06; pres. Northeastern U., Boston, 2006—. Author: A Grammar of Anaphora, 1985, Generalized Binding: The Syntax and LF of Interrogatives, 1986; co-author: The Syntax of Scope, 1993. Recipient Phi Kappa Phi Faculty Recognition award, U. So. Calif., 1988, 1993, Assocs. award, 1997. Mem. Linguistic Soc. Am., Phi Kappa Phi. Office: Office of Pres / Northeastern U 110 Churchill Hall 360 Huntington Ave Boston MA 02115 Office Phone: 617-373-2101. Office Fax: 617-373-5015. E-mail: president@neu.edu.*

APANASOV, BORIS N., mathematics professor, researcher; b. Sukhobuzimskoe, Russia, Oct. 24, 1950; s. Nikolay Aleksandrovich and Aleksandra Mikhailovna A.; children: Tatyana, Anton, Nikolay. Magister, Novosibirsk State U., Russia, 1973; PhD in Math., Inst. Math. USSR Acad. Sci., 1976. Spl. researcher Inst. Math. Acad. Sci. USSR, Novosibirsk, 1973, sci. researcher, 1974-80; asst. prof. math. Novosibirsk State U., 1975-80, assoc. prof., 1980-82, Novosibirsk Elektro-Tech. Inst., 1982-88; sr. researcher Inst. Math., Acad. Sci. USSR, Novosibirsk, 1981—; prof. Inst. Math. Kl. Ohridski U., Sofia, Bulgaria, 1986. Mem. Math Sci. Rsch. Inst., Berkeley, Calif., 1989, 96-97; prof. math. Ohio State U., Columbus, 1990, Mittag-Leffler Inst. of Sweden Royal Acad., 1989, U. Autonoma de Barcelona, 1990-91, U. Okla., Norman, 1991—, Tokyo U., 1997, Paris-Sud U. at Orsay, 1998, Centre de Recerca Matematica at Barcelona, 2004. Co-author: Kleinian Groups and Uniformization in Examples and Problems, 1981; author: Discrete Transformation Groups and Manifold Structures, 1983, Discrete Groups in Space and Uniformization Problems, 1991, Geometry of Discrete Groups and Manifolds, 1991, Conformal Geometry of Discrete Groups and Manifolds, 2000; co-editor: Topology 90, 1992, Geometry, Topoloty and Physics, 1997. Mem. Am. Math. Soc., Siberian Math. Soc., Japanese Soc. Promotion of Sci. Office: Univ of Okla Dept Math Norman OK 73019-0001

APAP, ANTONIO, finance educator, portfolio manager; b. NYC, Apr. 15, 1936; s. Emmanuel Charles and Josephine Dolores (Spagna) A.; m. Anna Frances Bradley, July 28, 1990. BS, U. West Fla., 1970; MBA, Tex. A&I U., 1976; MS, Naval Postgrad. Sch., 1977; DBA, U.S. Internat. U., 1982. Real estate license. Commd. ensign USN, 1957, advanced through grades to comdr., 1972, served in Vietnam, ret., 1980; CFO Sand Land Devel. Corp., Pensacola, Fla., 1981-85; pres. Denton Devel. Corp., San Diego, 1985-89; prof. fin. U. West Fla., Pensacola, 1990—. Contbr. articles to acad. and profl. jours. Dir. Pace Water Sys., Fla., 1995-97, 02-04; dir., pres. Solana Shores Owners Assn., Pensacola, 1992-93; dir., CFO Wings of Angels, Inc., 2007—; chair Concerned Citizens for Better Govt., 2007—. Recipient Golden Apple award Found. for Excellence in Edn., Pensacola, 1997, 98, Disting. Tchg. award Student Govt. Assn., Pensacola, 1997. Mem. Am. Acad. Acctg. and Fin., Am. Soc. Bus. and Behavioral Sci., Acad. Econ. and Fin. (dir. 1997-01), Optimists (bd. dirs. West Pensacola 1992-93). Avocations: golf, fishing, travel. Office: Univ West Fla Acctg & Fin 11000 University Pky Pensacola FL 32514-5732 Business E-Mail: aapap@uwf.edu.

APASOV, ALEXANDER MIKHAILOVICH, physicist, educator; b. Gorno-Altaisk, Russia, June 13, 1950; s. Mikhail Petrovich Apasov and Anna Ivanovna Apasova; m. Galina Vasilyevna Yemets, Apr. 26, 1975; 1 child, Andrey. Engr.-Physicist, Polytech. Inst., Tomsk, 1973; Cand.Sci., Polytech. Inst., 1991; ScD, Tech. U., Barnaul, Russia, 2002. Lab. asst. Joint Inst. for Nuclear Rsch., Dubna, Russia, 1971—73; sr. lab. asst. Phys.-Energetic Inst., Obninsk, Russia, 1973—75; engr.-designer Bolshevic Wks., Leningrad, Russia, 1975—77; chief of lab. Machine Wks., Yurga, Russia, 1977—92; chief of office Abrasive Wks., Yurga, 1992—95; v.p. of Branch Campus Tomsk Polytech. U., Yurga, 1995—96, dept. head, dean, 1995—2002, dept. head, 2000—, assoc. prof., 2000—. Author: (monograph) Welding Destruction, 2002, Physical Foundation of Non-Destructive Testing During Welding, 2004, (textbook) Special Electrometallurgy, 2003, Materials Sciences, 2005 (named Best Textbook Kemevovo region, 06), Introduction in the Theory and Technology of Manufacture Special Steels, 2006, Introduction in the Theory and Technology of Production Special Steels, 2006; contbr. articles to profl. jours. Dep. Town Soviet of People's Deps., 1997—99, Yurga, 1990—95. Lt. Russian Mil. Recipient Laureate, Nuclear Physics, Obninsk, 1974, Tech. Physics, Yurga, 1980, Assoc. Prof. of Yr. award, Tomsk Poltechnic Univ., 2003, Best Textbook award, Kemerovo Region, Kuzbass, 2006. Achievements include patents for A.M. Apasov's method to analyse failure of welded joints; method of non-melting revealing. Avocations: stamp collecting/philately, photography, fishing. Home: Moskovskay St 26 Apt 4 Yurga Russia Office: Tomsk PolyTech Univ Leningradskay St 26 Yurga Russia Office Phone: 7-838451-53199. Personal E-mail: mchmyti@rambler.ru. Business E-Mail: mehm@ud.tpu.edu.ru.

APATOFF, DAVID B., lawyer; b. Sept. 28, 1952; BA, Sarah Lawrence Col., 1974; JD, Univ. Chgo., 1977. Bar: Ill. 1977, D.C. 1979, US Ct. Fed. Claims 1983. Ptnr., Intellectual Property & Tech. Practice Group Arnold & Porter, Washington. Contbr. articles to profl. jours. Office: Arnold & Porter 555 Twelfth St NW Washington DC 20004-1206 Office Phone: 202-942-5556. Office Fax: 202-942-5999. Business E-Mail: david.apatoff@aporter.com.

APATOFF, MICHAEL JOHN, entrepreneur; b. Harvey, Ill., June 12, 1955; s. William and Frances (Brown) A; m. Monique Van Blitter, 2005; 1 child, Dante Madison. BA, Reed Coll., 1980. Chief legis. asst. to U.S. Congressman Al Ullman, Chmn. Ways and Means Com., Washington, 1978-80; spl. asst. to U.S. Congressman Tom Foley, Majority Whip, Washington, 1981-85; exec. v.p., COO Chgo. Merc. Exch., 1986-90; pres., COO Dresdner RCM Global Investors, San Francisco, 1991-98, fin. entrepreneur, 1999—. Office: 11 Edwards Ave Sausalito CA 94965 Personal E-mail: mapatoff@mac.com.

APATOW, JUDD, scriptwriter, television and film producer; b. Syosset, NY, Dec. 6, 1967; m. Leslie Mann; 1 child, Maude. Exec. prodr., writer (TV series) The Ben Stiller Show, 1992—93 (Emmy award for best writing, 1993), Freaks and Geeks, 1999—2000, co-exec. prodr., writer, dir. The Larry Sanders Show, 1992—98 (Cable ACE award, 1994, 1995), exec. prodr., writer, dir. Undeclared, 2001—02, prodr., writer (TV films) Life on Parole, 2003, Sick in the Head, 2003, (films) Knocked Up, 2007, assoc. prodr. Crossing the Bridge, 1992, exec. prodr., writer Heavy Weights, 1995, Celtic Pride, 1996; prodr.: (films) The Cable Guy, 1996, Anchorman: The Legend of Ron Burgundy, 2004; prodr.: (films) Talladega Nights: The Ballad of Ricky Bobby, 2006, Superbad, 2007; exec. prodr.: (films) Kicking & Screaming, 2005, American Storage, 2006, The TV Set, 2006; prodr., dir., writer (films) The 40 Year Old Virgin, 2005; author: (screenplays) Fun with Dick and Jane, 2005. Office: United Talent Agy 9560 Wilshire Blvd Ste 500 Beverly Hills CA 90212

APCAR, LEONARD M., online editor; b. 1953; married; 2 children. BA, Claremont McKenna Coll., 1975; MS, Columbia U., 1976. Reporter Wall St. Jour., 1976—89; bus. editor St. Petersburg Times, Fla., 1989—91; asst. bus. editor NY Times, 1991—98, enterprise editor, assignment editor, chief of correspondents, asst. fgn. editor, 1998—2002; editor-in-chief NYTimes.com, 2002—. Adv. bd. Am. Press Inst. Media Ctr., 2003—; bd. dirs. Online News Assoc., 2005—, Nat. Press Found., 2005—. Pres. bd. trustees Scarsdale Pub. Libr., NY, 2004—. Office: NY Times Digital 500 7th Ave 8th fl New York NY 10018 Office Phone: 646-698-8000. E-mail: apcar@nytimes.com.

APEL, ROBERT WILLIAM, actor; b. Elmont, NY, Aug. 5, 1948; s. Harold Robert and Sally Santa (Falcone) Apel; m. Eula Rae Harris, Feb. 14, 1976; children: Shawn, Tina Barley, Dakota. Lic. CNA 1993. Actor, comedian Fosi's Talent Agy., Tucson. Stuntman Old Tucson Movie Location, Tucson, 1970—72, Fosi's Talent Agency, Tucson, 1975—2005; student Pima Coll., Tucson, 1984. Writer, singer, producer: CD Country Girl, 2004; prodr.: (CD) Good bye to Jesse James, 2004, (comedy CD) Hilarity Without Vulgarity, 2004—05; entertainer (comedy CD) Hilarity Without Vulgarity, Armed Forces Radio, 2004—05; writer: standup comedy; performer: Kids Against Drugs, 1988, Adopt Wild Mustang Program, 1985, (TV films) Outlaw Josey Wales, Last Hard Man, A Star is Born, Pursuit, Red Rock West, (Television) The Ascension, Father Murphy, Young Riders, Young Pioneers, Desperado, various TV commercials. Mem.: Nat. Rifle Assn., Screen Actors Guild. Avocations: guitar, music, horseback riding, swimming. Office Phone: 520-795-3534.

APELBAUM, PHYLLIS L., delivery messenger service executive; 1 child, Mark. Instr. Am. United Cab Co., Chgo., 1957-65; gen. mgr. City Bonded Messenger Svc., Chgo., 1960-74; founder, pres. Arrow Messenger Svc., Inc., Chgo., 1974—. 1st chair Affirmative Action Adv. Bd. of Chgo., 1991-92; chair Variety Club Children's Carnival, Chgo., 1990-94; mem. bicycle com. City of Chgo., 1992-95, parking task force, 1993-95; gov. Ill. Coun. on Econ. Edn., Chgo., 1995—; mem. Lakefront SRO Adv. Bd., Chgo., 1989-94; mem. Chgo. Police bd., 1995—. Recipient Small Bus. Innovative Mgmt. award Bank of Am., 1994; named Entrepreneur of the Yr., Ernst & Young, 1992, Nat. Small Bus. Person of the Yr., Small Bus. Assn., 1990; named to Entrepreneurship Hall of Fame, U. Ill., Chgo., 1993. Mem. Messenger Courier Assn. of Am. (bd. dirs. 1989—), Messenger Svc. Assn. Ill. (co-founder, pres.), Nat. Assn. Women Bus. Owners, The Chgo. Network. Office: Arrow Messenger Svc Inc 1322 W Walton St Chicago IL 60622-5340

APFEL, GARY, lawyer; b. NYC, June 2, 1952; s. Willy and Jenny (Last) A.; m. Serena Jakobovits, June 16, 1980; children: Alyssa J., I. Michael, Alanna J., Stephen J., Alexander. BA, NYU magna cum laude, 1973; JD, Columbia U., 1976. Bar: N.Y. 1977, Calif. 1988, U.S. Dist. Ct. (so. and ea. dists.) N.Y. 1977, U.S. Dist. Ct. (cen. dist.) Calif. 1988, U.S. Ct. Appeals (9th cir.) 1988. Assoc. Sullivan & Cromwell, NYC, 1976-80, LeBoeuf,

Lamb, Leiby & MacRae, NYC, 1980-84, ptnr., 1985-88, Kaye, Scholer, Fierman, Hays & Handler LLP, LA, 1988-97, Akin, Gump, Strauss, Hauer & Feld, L.L.P., LA, 1997—2000; chmn. bd. ELSA, Inc., 2000—01; co-mng. ptnr. LA office LeBoeuf, Lamb, Greene & MacRae LLP, 2001—, chmn. corp. dept. Kent scholar Columbia U., 1976. Mem. ABA, Calif. State Bar Assn. (bus. law sect. corps. com.), Phi Beta Kappa. Office: LeBoeuf Lamb Greene & MacRae 725 S Figueroa St Ste 3100 Los Angeles CA 90017 Office Phone: 213-955-7350. Office Fax: 213-955-7399. Business E-Mail: gapfel@llgm.com.

APFELBACH, GEORGE LEONARD, JR., urologist; b. Chgo., Mar. 10, 1931; s. George Leonard and Alice Clothilde (Hotz) Apfelbach; m. Claire Fleischmann Apfelbach, Aug. 8, 1955; children: Martha, Paul, Eric, Edward. AB, Harvard Coll., Cambridge, Mass., 1953; MD, Northwestern U., Chgo., 1957. Diplomate Am. Bd. Urology. Physician Mercy Hosp., Janesville, Wis., 1962—93, chief of staff, chief of surgery, pres. staff. Contbr. articles to profl. jours.; prodr.: (video-hist.) Tour Fish Creek, Wis., 2005. Mem.: Rock County Surg. Soc. (pres.), Rock County Med. Soc. (pres.), Rotary. Independent. Avocations: gardening, boating, theater, opera, symphony. Home: 99 Sunset Dr # 303 Sarasota FL 34236 Home (Summer): PO Box 67 Fish Creek WI 54212

APICELLA, MICHAEL ALLEN, microbiologist, educator; b. Bklyn., Apr. 4, 1938; s. Anthony D. and Fay (Kahn) A.; m. Agnes Dengler, Aug. 19, 1961; children: Michael P., Christopher A., Peter N. AB, Holy Cross Coll., 1959; MD, SUNY, Bklyn., 1963. Diplomate Am. Bd. Internal Medicine, Am. Bd. Infectious Disease. Postdoctoral fellow Johns Hopkins Hosp., Balt., 1966-68; asst. prof. microbiology SUNY, Buffalo, 1970-74, assoc. prof., 1974-78, prof., 1981-92; prof., chmn. dept. microbiology Coll. Medicine U. Iowa, Iowa City, 1993—. Contbr. over 150 articles to profl. jours. Maj. USAF, 1968-70. Office: U Iowa Coll Medicine Dept Microbiology Coll Medicine 3-403 Science Bldg Iowa City IA 52242 E-mail: michael.apicella@uiowa.edu.

APJOHN, NELSON GEORGE, lawyer; b. NYC, June 21, 1956; s. George N. and Catherine A.; m. Mary Joan Greene, June 3, 1978; children: Andrew, Eric, Allan. AB in Polit. Sci., Syracuse U., 1978; JD, Boston Coll., 1981. Bar: Mass. 1981, U.S. Dist. Ct. Mass. 1981, U.S. Ct. Appeals (1st cir.) 1984. Ptnr. Nutter, McClennen & Fish LLP, Boston, 1981—. Mem. Mass. Bar Assn., Boston Bar Assn., Phi Beta Kappa, Order of Coif. Home: 28 Homeward Ln Walpole MA 02081-2210 Office: Nutter McClennen & Fish LLP World Trade Ctr West 155 Seaport Blvd Boston MA 02210-2604 Office Phone: 617-439-2000.

APL.DE.AP, See LINDO, ALLEN

APOLLO, BRIAN, psychologist, poet; b. Chgo., Sept. 30, 1976; s. Carlton and Sarah Apollo. AA, Triton Coll., Melrose Park, Ill., 1997; BS with honors in Psychology, Chgo. State U., 2000; degree in Sch. Psychology, Ill. State U., Normal, 2003. Lic. sch. psychologist Ill. Bd. Edn., 2003. Large rides operator Kiddieland Amusement Pk., Melrose Park, Ill., 1994—98; assoc. Tilt Arcades, Normal, 2001—03; with stock and sales Carson Pirie Scott, North Riverside, Ill., 2002—03; sch. psychologist Chgo. Bd. Edn., 2003—. With crisis intervention Chgo. Bd. Edn., 2004—, mentor new hirees, 2005—, mem. sch. psychology employment panel, 2004—. Author: Spirituality: Uncut, (albums). Usher Crusaders Ch., Chgo., 1992, deacon, 2005, tchr. Sunday sch., 2006. Mem.: Nat. Assn. Sch. Psychologists (licentiate), Ill. Sch. Psychology Assn. (licentiate), Psi Chi (life). Democrat. Avocations: web designing, poetry, music producing, bible reading. Office: Chgo Bd Edn 125 S Clark St Chicago IL 60603 Home Phone: 708-345-6286; Office Phone: 773-553-1000. Personal E-mail: angelofwarr@excite.com.

APONE, CARL ANTHONY, journalist; b. Brownsville, Pa., July 9, 1923; s. Peter P. and Carmela (Puglia) A.; m. Kathleen King, Jan. 23, 1965; 1 child, Elizabeth. BA cum laude, U. Notre Dame, 1949; MA, Boston U., 1950. Dir. pub. rels., lectr. journalism and Am. lit. St. Mary's Coll., Notre Dame, Ind., 1950-53; staff writer UP, Detroit, 1953; city editor Brownsville Telegraph, 1953-57; staff writer Pitts. Sun- Telegraph, 1958-60; music editor Pitts. Press, 1960-89; mem. faculty journalism Duquesne U., 1967-72; free-lance writer, 1950—. Mem. St. Vincent DePaul Soc., 1963—. Served with inf. AUS, 1943-46. Recipient Golden Quill Journalism awards; Pa. Newspaper Pubs. Assn. awards. Home: 2016 Worcester Dr Pittsburgh PA 15243-1542

APONTE, FRANCES, psychologist, educator; MA, Fairfield U., 1995, Cert. Advance Studies, 2004. Cert. sch. psychologist Conn. Spl. edn. ombudsman Bridgeport Pub. Schs., 1997—2004; sch. psychologist Bridgeport Pub. Schools, 2004—. Adj. instr. Sacred Heart U., Fairfield, Conn., 2005—. Mem.: Conn. Assn. Sch. Psycholgist (co-coord. profl. devel. 2005—). Home Phone: 203-374-5024; Office Phone: 203-576-7084. Personal E-mail: faponte01@snet.net.

APONTE MARTINEZ, LUIS CARDINAL, retired archbishop; b. Lajas, P.R., Aug. 4, 1922; s. Santiago E. Aponte and Rosa Martinez. Student, San Ildefonso Sem., San Juan, PR, 1944, St. John's Sem., Boston, 1950; LLD (hon.), Fordham U., 1965. Ordained priest Roman Cath. Ch., 1950. Asst. in Patillas, PR; pastor in Maricao, PR, Sta. Isabel, PR, 1953—55; sec. to bishop of Ponce, PR, 1955—57; pastor in Aibonito, PR, 1957—60; from aux. bishop to bishop of Ponce, 1960—64; archbishop of San Juan, 1964—99; archbishop emeritus, 1999—; created cardinal, 1973. Chancellor Cath. U., Ponce, 1963—64; pres. Puerto Rican Episcopal Conf. Chaplain P.R. N.G., 1957—60. Mem.: Lions. Roman Catholic. Mailing: Archdiocese of San Juan Apartado 901967 Calle San Jorge 201 Santurce San Juan PR 00902-1967

APONTE SAMALOT, MYRELIS, neuroscientist, psychologist, consultant; d. Eric Aponte and Myrna Samalot. BS in Microbiology, Inter Am. U., San Juan, PR, 1995; MS in Counseling, Galladet U., Washington, 2000; DS in Clin. Psychology, Ponce Sch. Medicine, PR, 2006. Cert. Nat. Bd. Cert. Counselors, Wash., 2001, lic. clin. psychologist Bd. Psychology PR, 2006. Dir. program Turabo U., Gurabo, PR, 2003; intern neuropsychology med. ctr. NYU, NY, 2005—. Fellow, Pa. State U., 1994; scholar, Gallaudet U., 2000—01, Hispanic Mental Health Assn., 2006. Mem.: APA (assoc.), Nat. Assn. Deaf (assoc.), Nat. Acad. Neuropsychology (assoc.), Internat. Soc. Neuropsychology (assoc.), Registry Intepreters Deaf (assoc.; pres. affiliate chpt. 1999—2006, Pres.'s Choice award 2004). Achievements include development of sign language intepretation program. Home: PO Box 193891 San Juan PR 00919-3891 Home Phone: 787-529-1584. Home Fax: 1-484-210-5373. Personal E-mail: mapontepsyd@gmail.com.

APOSTOLAKIS, GEORGE E., engineering educator, researcher; Diploma in Elec. Engring., Nat. Tech. U., Athens, Greece, 1969; MS in Engring. Sci., Calif. Inst. Tech., 1970, PhD in Engring. Sci. and Applied Math., 1973. Prof. nuc. sci. and engring. and engring. systems MIT, Cambridge. Founder, sec. Internat. Assn. Probabilistic Safety Assessment and Mgmt.; mem. adv. com. reactor safeguards US Nuc. Regulatory Commn., chmn., 2001—02; chmn. peer rev. panel Internat. Space Sta. Probabilistic Risk Assessment NASA, 2002. Editor-in-chief: Reliability Engineering and System Safety, mem. editl. bd.: Process Safety and Environmental Protection, 1991—, Risk Analysis, 1997—; contbr. articles to profl. jours. Fellow: Soc. Risk Analysis, Am. Nuc. Soc. (Tommy Thompson award Nuc. Installations Safety Divsn. 1999, Mark Mills award 1974); mem.: NAE, Internat. Nuc. Tech. Commn. Office: MIT Dept Nuc Engring 77 Massachusetts Ave Bldg 24-221 Cambridge MA 02139-4307 Office Phone: 617-252-1570. Office Fax: 617-258-8863. E-mail: apostola@mit.edu.*

APOSTOLAKIS, JAMES JOHN, shipping company and pharmaceutical executive; b. NYC, May 31, 1942; s. John George and Ann (Lampros) A. AB, U. Pa., 1962; LLB, Harvard U., 1965. Bar: N.Y. 1965. Atty. Dewey, Ballantine, Bushby, Palmer & Wood, NYC, 1965-67; pres. Transoceanic Tank Ship Mgmt. Group, NYC, 1968-72, Koplik Group Ltd., NYC, 1983-84, A.G. Palmer & Co., Inc., NYC, 1976—, Bradford Shipping, Inc., NYC, 1973—, Bradmar Trading Corp., NYC, 1975—; mng. dir. Poseidon Capital Corp., NYC, 1998—; vice chmn., pres. Columbia Labs, Inc., Miami, Fla., 1999—; pres. Columbia Labs., Inc., Fla., 2000—. Pres. Lexington Shipping and Trading Corp., NYC, 1980—, Bedford Capital Corp., NYC, 1989—93; vice chmn. Koplik Group Ltd., NYC, 1988—93, Columbia Labs. Inc., Livingston, NJ, 1999—; bd. dirs. Macmillan, Inc., Grow Group, Inc., Columbia Labs., Inc. Mem. Union Club, Met. Club, Phi Beta Kappa. Home: 150 E 69th St New York NY 10021-5704 Office Phone: 212-588-1900. Personal E-mail: apostolak@aol.com.

APPEL, ALBERT M., lawyer; b. NYC, May 26, 1945; s. Morris and Belle (Kaplan) A.; m. Irena Uhl, June 10, 1979; 1 child, Elliott. BS in Econs., U. Pa., 1966; JD, NYU, 1969. Bar: N.Y. 1969, U.S. Dist. Ct. (so. and ea. dists.) N.Y. 1971, U.S. Ct. Appeals (2d cir.) 1974, U.S. Ct. Appeals (4th cir.) 1979, U.S. Ct. Appeals (11th Cir.) 2002. Assoc. Spear and Hill, NYC, 1969-75, Webster & Sheffield, NYC, 1976-80, ptnr., 1981-91; spl. counsel Stroock & Stroock & Lavan LLP, NYC, 1991-97, ptnr., 1998—. Mem. ABA, Am. Health Lawyers Assn., N.Y. State Bar Assn., Assn. of Bar of City of N.Y., Beta Alpha Psi. Home: 670 W End Ave New York NY 10025-7313 Office: Stroock & Stroock & Lavan LLP 180 Maiden Ln New York NY 10038-4925 Office Phone: 212-806-6625. Business E-Mail: aappel@stroock.com.

APPEL, BERNARD SIDNEY, marketing professional, consultant, retired electronics executive; b. Boston, Jan. 10, 1932; s. Max and Sophie (Altshuler) A.; m. Ellen Carey, July 1988; children: Ann, Sharon; children by previous marriage: Arlene R., Gerald I. AA Commercial Sci., Boston U., 1959; D Comml. Sci. (hon.), McKenzie Coll., 1991. Store mgr., buyer S & W Distbg. Co., Boston, 1949-59; buyer Radio Shack Co., Boston, 1959-66, mdse. mgr., 1966-70, v.p. merchandising Ft. Worth, 1970-78, sr. v.p. merchandising and advt., 1978-80, exec. v.p. mktg., 1980-84, pres., 1984-92, chmn., 1992-93; sr. v.p. Tandy Corp., 1992-93; bd. dirs. Uniview Corp., 1995—2002; pres. Appel Assocs., Mktg. Cons., 1993—; vice chmn., bd. dirs. Integrated Tech. Inc., 1994-99. V.p. Holbrook (Mass.) Jewish Cmty. Ctr., 1958-59; bd. dirs. Casa Manana Mus., 1978-79, Dan Danciger Jewish Cmty. Ctr., Ft. Worth, 1989-98, Family Svcs., Inc., 1990—, Non-Profit Svc. Ctr., 1999-04, Crime Prevention Resource Ctr., 1997-2005; v.p., founder Temple Aliyah, Needham, Mass., 1969-70; pres. Congregation Ahavath Sholom, Ft. Worth, 1979-81, bd. dirs., 1972—; bd. dirs. Jewish Fedn. Ft. Worth, 1975-97, v.p., 1981-85, pres., 1985-87; mem. adv. bd. Arts Coun. Ft. Worth, 1985—; project renewal cluster chmn. Acco-East, Israel, 1981-94; mem. exec. com. so. regional campaign cabinet United Jewish Appeal, 1980-89; so. regional chmn. United Jewish Appeal's Passage to Freedom Campaign for Soviet Jewry, 1989; co-chmn. fin. rels. United Jewish Appeal Western Region, Jewish Agy. Com., 1992-93, United Jewish Appeal Ctrl. Region, Jewish Agy Com., 1993; mem. exec. com. Network of Ind. UJA Coms., 1994—; mem. internat. bd. visitors M.J. Neeley Sch. Bus., Tex. Christian U., 1990—; hon. life mem. nat. commn. Anti-Defamation League, 1992. With USCG, 1951-54; mem. adv. bd. Crime Stoppers of N. Tex., 2005-; chmn. crime stoppers com. Safe City Commn., 2006-. Recipient Torch of Liberty award Anti-Defamation League of B'nai B'rith, 1988, Defender of Jerusalem award, 1990, Alumni award Boston U. Sch. Mgmt., 1994; named Man of Yr., B'nai B'rith Ft. Worth Jewish, 1984, Anti-Defamation League Ft. Worth, 1990; named to Consumer Electronics Hall of Fame, 2002. Mem. Electronic VIP Club, Ft. Worth C. of C. (bd. dirs. 1981-84), Masons, Shriners, Frog Club (Tex. Christian U.), Colonial Country Club, City Country Club, Ft. Worth, Rotary (bd. dirs. 2005-). Home: 4917 Ranch View Rd Fort Worth TX 76109-3117 Office: Appel Assocs 301 Commerce St Ste 1415 Fort Worth TX 76102-4114 Office Phone: 817-338-9579. E-mail: bappel@flash.net.

APPEL, BRENT ROBERT, state supreme court justice, lawyer; b. Dubuque, Iowa, July 13, 1950; s. Herbert John and Janice Emily (Bardill) A. BA, MA, Stanford U., 1973; JD, U. Calif., Berkeley, 1977. Bar: Calif. 1978, Iowa 1979, U.S. Ct. Appeals (8th cir.), U.S. Dist. Ct. (no. and so. dists.). 1st asst. atty. gen. State of Iowa, Des Moines, 1979-80; campaign mgr. U.S. Sen. John Culver, Des Moines, 1980; dep. atty. gen. State of Iowa, Des Moines, 1981-82, 83-86; shareholder Dickinson, Mackaman, Tyler & Hagen, PC, Des Moines, 1987—2005; prin. Wandro, Baer & Appel PC, 2005—06; justice Iowa Supreme Ct., 2006—. Contbr. articles to profl. jours. Dem. nominee for U.S. Congress, 2d dist. Iowa, 1982. Mem. ABA, ATLA, Iowa Trial Lawyers Assn., Iowa Bar Assn., Polk County Bar Assn. Democrat. Methodist. Office: 1111 E Court Ave Des Moines IA 50319 Home Phone: 515-960-6982. Business E-Mail: bappel@2501grand.com.

APPEL, GERALD, investment advisor; b. NYC, June 2, 1933; s. Samuel and Vivian (Adlerstein) A.; m. Judith Kane, May 26, 1956; children: Marvin Laurence, Marion Fran. BA, Bklyn. Coll., 1954; MSW, NYU, 1956. Adminstr. social agy. Jewish Family Svc., Bklyn., 1958-73; pvt. practice as psychoanalyst Great Neck, N.Y., 1963-95; pres. Signalert Corp., Great Neck, 1973—, Appel Asset Mgmt. Corp., 1995—. Author: Winning Market Systems, 1972, Double Your Money Every Three Years, 1973, 99 Ways to Make Money in a Depression, 1974, Stock Option and No-Load Switch Fund Scalpers Manual, 1979, Winning Stock Selection Systems, 1979, The Big Move, 1981, Time-Trend III, 1988, Portraits of Nature, 1992, American Photographers at the Turn of the Century, Travel and Trekking, 1994, (with others) The Art of the Human Form, 1995, New Directions in Technical Analysis, 1976, Stock Market Trading Systems, 1980, Far Away Faces-A Guide to Better Travel Portraits, 1998; (video) The MACD Trading System, 1990, Day Trading, 1990, Power Tools, 1992, Technical Analysis - Power Tools for the Active Investor, 2005, Opportunity Investing, 2006; contbr. articles to profl. jours. Bd. dirs. Keystone Ctr. of Music and Arts, 1998-2000, Mountain Laurel Ctr. Performing Arts, 2000-2004, The Great Neck Ctr. Performing Arts, 2000—. Mem.: Nat. Psychol. Assn. for Psychoanalysis (bd. dirs., v.p.), Am. Assn. Media Photographers. Avocations: photography, tennis, sailing, music. Home: 97 Myrtle Dr Great Neck NY 11021-1805 Office: Signalert Corp 150 Great Neck Rd Ste 301 Great Neck NY 11021-3339 Office Phone: 516-829-6444. E-mail: gappel6@optonline.net, gappel@signalert.com.

APPEL, JOEL, household cleaner manufacturing executive; With mktg. dept. Quaker Oats; pres. Orange Glo Internat., Greenwood Village, Colo. Office: Orange Glo International 8200 E Maplewood Ave Greenwood Village CO 80111-4822

APPEL, LAURENCE BRUCE, lawyer, retail executive; b. 1961; m. Caren Appel; children: Molly, Rebecca, Michael. BA, U. Va., 1983; JD, U. Pa., 1989. Bar: Ga. 1989. Lawyer King & Spalding, Atlanta, Altman, Kritzer & Levick, Atlanta, 1995—97; sr. corp. counsel for strategic bus. devel. Home Depot Inc., 1997, sr. v.p. legal, 1997—2002; sr. v.p., gen. counsel Winn-Dixie Stores, Inc., Jacksonville, Fla., 2002—, sec., 2003—. Mem.: Atlanta Bar Assn., State Bar Ga., ABA, Order of the Coif. Office: Winn-Dixie Stores Inc 5050 Edgewood Ct Jacksonville FL 32254-3699

APPEL, MARSHA CEIL, advertising executive; b. NYC, Dec. 3, 1953; d. Albert and Stella Joy (Glaser) A.; m. Mark D. Marcellus, Sept. 10, 1978; children: Sam, Jill. BA, SUNY, Albany, 1974; MSLS, Syracuse U., 1975. Info. specialist Am. Assn. Advt. Agys., NYC, 1976-79, mgr. member info. svc., 1979-89, v.p., 1989-97, sr. v.p., 1997—. Author: Illustration Index IV, 1980, Illustration Index V, 1984, Illustration Index VI, 1988, Illustration Index VII, 1993, Illustration Index VIII, 1998; editor What's New in Advertising and Marketing, 1978-80; mem. adv. bd., contbr. Ency. Advt., 2002; contbr. Super Searchers Madison Avenue, 2003. Mem.: Advt. Rsch. Found. (Innovation award, cert. Recognition 2007), Advt. Women of NY, Spl. Librs. Assn. (chmn. advt. mktg. divsn. 1982—83). Office: Am Assn Advt Agys 405 Lexington Ave New York NY 10174-0002

APPEL, NINA SCHICK, law educator, dean, academic administrator; b. Feb. 17, 1936; d. Leo and Nora Schick; m. Alfred Appel Jr.; children: Karen Oshman, Richard. Student, Cornell U.; JD, Columbia U., 1959. Instr. Columbia Law Sch., 1959-60; adminstr. Stanford U., mem. faculty, prof. law, 1973—, assoc. dean, 1976-83; dean Sch. Law Loyola U., 1983—2004, dean emerita, prof. law, 2004—. Mem. Am. Bar Found., Ill. Bar Found., Chgo. Bar Found., Chgo. Legal Club, Chgo. Network. Jewish. Office: Loyola U Sch Law 25 E Pearson St Chicago IL 60611-2055 Home Phone: 847-256-5458; Office Phone: 312-915-7128. E-mail: nappel@luc.edu.

APPEL, STANLEY HERSH, neurologist, educator; b. Boston, May 8, 1933; married; 4 children. AB, Harvard U., 1954; MD, Columbia U., 1960. Diplomate Am. Bd. Psychiatry and Neurology. Intern medicine Mass. Gen. Hosp., 1960-61; resident neurology Mt. Sinai Hosp., 1961-62; rsch. assoc. Lab. Molecular Biology NIH, 1962-64; chief rsch. assoc. Sch. Medicine U. Pa., 1965-66, asst. prof., 1966-67; assoc. of neurology Med. Ctr. Duke U., 1964-65, from assoc. prof. to prof. neurology, 1967-77, assoc. prof. biochemistry, 1968-77, chief divsn. neurology, 1969-77; prof. neurology Baylor Coll. Medicine, 1977—2004, prof., chmn. dept. neurology, 1977—2004, chmn. program neurosci., 1977-89, dir. Jerry Lewis Neuromuscular Disorder Rsch. Ctr., 1977—2004; dir. Vicki Appel MDA/ALS Ctr., 1977—2004; chair dept. neurology Meth. Hosp. Neurol. Inst., Houston, 2005—, dir. MDA/ALS Rsch. and Clin. Ctr., 2005—, Peggy and Gary Edwards disting. endowed chair for the treatment and rsch. of ALS dept. neurology, 2006—; prof. neurology Weill Med. Coll. Cornell U., NYC, 2005—. Recipient Gold Medal award Columbia Coll. Physicians and Surgeons, 1997, Disting. Faculty award Baylor Coll. Medicine Alumni Assn., 2004, Tex. Neurol. Soc. Lifetime Achievement award, 2005, Forbes Norris award Internat. Alliance ALS/MND Assn., 2005. Mem. Am. Acad. Neurology (Sheila Essey award, 2003), Am. Neurol. Assn., Soc. Neuroscience, Am. Soc. Neurochemistry. Achievements include research in etiology of amyotrophic lateral sclerosis, Parkinson's disease, and Alzheimer's disease. Office: Meth Neurological Inst Dept Neurology 6560 Fannin St #802 Houston TX 77030 Office Phone: 713-441-3760.

APPEL, WILLIAM FRANK, pharmacist; b. Mpls., Oct. 8, 1924; s. William Ignatius and Elna Antonia (Mulzahn) A.; m. Louise D. Altman, Sept. 24, 1949; children— Nancy, Peggy, James, Elizabeth. BS in Pharmacy, U. Minn., 1949; D.Sc. (hon.), Phila. Coll. Pharmacy and Sci., 1978. Intern in pharmacy Northwestern Hosp., Mpls.; pres., pharmacist, mgr. Appel Com-Pharm, Inc., Mpls., 1949—; pres. Pharm. Cons. Services, P.A., St. Paul, 1960—. Mem. Minn. Bd. Pharmacy, 1960-65, pres., 1965; preceptor internship requirement program; chmn. Minn. Gov.'s Commn. on Drug Abuse, 1971-73; mem. Mpls. Health Dept. Task Force on Pub. Health Approaches to Chem. Dependency; clin. instr. U. Minn. Coll. Pharmacy, 1970—; cons. HEW; long term care facilities; rep. Nat. Pharmacy/Industry Com. on Nat. Health Ins.; mem. revision com. U.S. Pharmacopeial Conv., 1980— Served with USN, 1942-46. Recipient Good Neighbor award, Sta. WCCO, Mpls., 1973. Mem. Twin City Met. Drug Assn., Minn. Pharm. Assn. (v.p., Harold R. Popp award 1974, mem. continuing edn. faculty 1970—), Am. Pharm. Assn. (pres. N.W. br., nat. pres. 1976-77, Daniel B. Smith award 1970, treas. 1979—) pharm. assns), Minn. Gerontol. Soc., U. Minn. Coll. Pharmacy Alumni Assn. (v.p., Distinguished Pharmacist award 1971) Office: Preferred Choice Pharmacy 900 Long Lake Rd #150 New Brighton MN 55112 Home: 5251 Ashlar Dr Minneapolis MN 55437-3360

APPELBAUM, ANN HARRIET, lawyer; b. Decatur, Ill., 1948; d. Irving and Cecelia (Hecht) A.; m. Neal Borovitz, July 4, 1982; children: Abby, Jeremy. BA, Barnard Coll., 1970; JD, Boston U., 1973. Bar: N.Y. 1974, U.S. Dist. Ct. (so. dist.) N.Y. 1975, U.S. Ct. Appeals (2nd cir.) 1975, U.S. Supreme Ct. 1978. Assoc. Hart & Hume, NYC, 1974-76, Warshaw, Burstein, NYC, 1976-80; counsel Jewish Theol. Sem. & Jewish Mus., NYC, 1980—. Mem. Nat. Assn. Coll. and Univ. Attys. Office: The Jewish Theological Seminary 3080 Broadway New York NY 10027-4650 Office Phone: 212-678-8804.

APPELBAUM, DIANA KARTER, author; b. Ft. Belvoir, Va., Nov. 9, 1953; d. Peter and Elizabeth Carmen (Whitman) Karter; m. Paul Stuart Appelbaum, Mar. 31, 1974; children: Binyamin, Yonatan, Avigail. AB, Columbia U., 1975. Author: Thanksgiving, An American Holiday, 1984, The Glorious Fourth, 1989, Giants in the Land, 1993, Cocoa Ice, 1997, Reflections in Bullough's Pond: Economy and Ecosystem in New England, 2000. Recipient Booklist Mag. Top of the List prize, 1993. Mem. Author's Guild. Home: 39 Claremont Rd Apt 24 New York NY 10027 Office: care Houghton Mifflin Co 222 Berkeley St Boston MA 02116-3748

APPELBAUM, FREDERICK RAY, oncologist; b. Canton, Ohio, Sept. 2, 1946; s. Samuel and Evelyn (Shapiro) A.; m. Janet Wynn Schwarz, Feb. 3, 1980; children: Jacob, David. AB, Dartmouth Coll., 1968; MD, Tufts U., 1972. Intern, resident U. Mich., Ann Arbor, 1972-74; clin. assoc. NIH, Bethesda, Md., 1974-76, investigator, 1976-78; asst. prof. Fred Hutchinson Cancer Rsch. Ctr., Seattle, 1978-83, assoc. prof., 1983-88, clin. rsch. mem., 1988—, dir. clin. rsch., 1993—; prof. med. oncology U. Wash. Sch. Medicine, Seattle, 1988—, dept. head divsn. med. oncology, 1998—. Mem. bd. sci. advisors Nat. Cancer Inst.; exec. dir., Seattle Cancer Alliance, 1998-. Assoc. editor: Blood, 1993-2002; editl. bd., Tumor, Leukemia, Am. Jour. Hematology, Video Jour. Oncology, Bone Marrow Transplantation, Hematological Oncology, Cancer Biotherapy and Radiopharmaceuticals, others; contbr. articles to profl. jours. Grantee NIH, 1980-. Mem. Am. Assn. for Cancer Rsch., Am. Soc. Clin. Oncology (bd. dirs. 1990-93), Am. Soc. Hematology (bd. councillors 1994-98). Am. Soc. Blood and Marrow Transplantation (bd. dir.), Internat. Soc. for Exptl. Hematology, Alpha Omega Alpha. Jewish. Office: Fred Hutchinson Cancer Rsch 1100 Fairview Ave N D5 310 PO Box 19024 Seattle WA 98109-1024 Personal E-mail: fappelba@fhcrc.org.*

APPELBAUM, PAUL STUART, psychiatrist, medical educator, department chairman; b. Bklyn., Nov. 30, 1951; s. Isidore W. and Celia (Bressler) A.; m. Diana Muir Karter, Nov. 9, 1953; children: Binyamin, Yonatan, Avigail. AB, Columbia U., 1972; MD, Harvard U., 1976. Diplomate Am. Bd. Psychiatry and Neurology. Intern Soroka Med. Ctr., Beersheva, Israel, 1976-77; resident Mass. Mental Health Ctr., Boston, 1977-80; clin. fellow psychiatry Harvard Med. Sch., Boston, 1977-80; from asst. prof. to assoc. prof. psychiatry and law U. Pitts., 1980-84; assoc. prof. psychiatry Harvard Med. Sch., Boston, 1984-85; Zeleznik prof. psychiatry, dir. law and psychiatry program U. Mass. Med. Sch., Worcester, 1985—2005, chmn. dept., 1992—2005; vis. interdisciplinary prof. Law Ctr. Georgetown U., Washington, 1988-89; Dollard prof. psychiatry, medicine and law Columbia Coll. Physicians and Surgeons, NYC, 2006—. Mem. commn. on mentally disabled ABA, Washington, 1982-87; task force on involuntary civil commitment Nat. Ctr. for State Cts., Williamsburg, Va., 1984-89, Rsch. Network on Mental Health and Law, John D. and Catherine T.

Macarthur Found., Chgo., 1988-96; fellow Ctr. for Advanced Study in the Behavioral Scis., Stanford, Calif., 1996-97; rsch. network on mandatory outpatient treatment John D. and Catherine T. MacArthur Found., Chgo., 2000-; bd. dirs. neurosci. and behavioral health Inst. Medicine of NAS, 2001-04. Author: Clinical Handbook of Psychiatry and the Law, 1982 (M.F. Guttmacher award 1982), 4th edit., 2006, Informed Consent: Legal Theory and Clinical Practice, 1987, 2d edit., 2001, Paul Appelbaum on Law and Psychiatry, 1989, Almost A Revolution: Mental Health Law and Limits of Change, 1994 (M.F. Guttmacher award 1996), Trauma and Memory: Clinical and Legal Controversies, 1997, Assessing Patients' Capacities to Consent to Treatment, 1998 (M.F. Guttmacher award 2000), Rethinking Risk Assessment, 2001 (M.F. Guttmacher award 2002); contbr. articles to profl. jours. Nat. coord. Med. Mobilization for Soviet Jewry, Waltham, Mass., 1974-80; bd. dirs. Action for Soviet Jewry, Waltham, 1984-85, Torah Ctr., Sharon, Mass., 1987-88, Cmty. Health Link, Worcester, Mass., 1992-2005, Am. Psychiat. Press, 2001-03, Am. Psychiat. Inst. on Rsch. and Edn., 2001-03. Recipient Rsch. Scientist Devel. award NIMH, 1983; Rsch. grantee Pres.'s Commn. on Ethical Problems in Medicine, Washington, 1982, John D. and Catherine T. MacArthur Found., 1988, 2003; fellow Ctr. for Advanced Study in Behavioral Scis., Palo Alto, Calif., 1996-97. Mem.: NAS (elected to Inst. Medicine 2000), Mass. Psychiat. Soc. (pres. 1992—93), Am. Soc. Law and Medicine, Am. Acad. Psychiatry and the Law (councillor 1987—90, pres. 1995—96, Seymour Pollock award 2001), Am. Psychiat. Assn. (chair commn. on jud. action 1984—90, joint reference com. 1984—94, chair coun. on psychiatry and law 1990—94, sec. 1997—99, bd. dirs. 1997—2006, v.p. 1999—2001, pres. 2002—03, chair coun. on psychiatry and law 2004—, Isaac Ray award 1990), Internat. Acad. Law and Mental Health (Philippe Pinel award 2000). Jewish. Avocation: writing for popular mags. Office: NY State Psychiat Inst 1051 Riverside Dr 122 New York NY 10032 Home Phone: 646-734-3684; Office Phone: 212-543-4184. Business E-Mail: psa21@columbia.edu.

APPELBAUM, YONATAN ASHER, administrative assistant, city manager; s. Paul S. and Diana K. Appelbaum; m. Emily Pressman, June 20, 2004. AB, Columbia Coll., 2003. Exec. asst. to pub. adv. City of NY, 2003—04; Crown fellow Brandeis U., Waltham, Mass., 2004—. Recipient Robert Shellow Gerdy prize, Columbia Coll., 2003. Mem.: Phi Beta Kappa.

APPELL, LOUISE SOPHIA, retired consulting company executive; d. Romeo Edward and Phyllis Teresa (Szynal) Fortier; m. Melville Joseph Appell, July 26, 1953 (div. 1975); children: Melissande Foglio, David Maxcim; m. Clifford Harding Querolo, June 1, 1991 (dec. 1992). BA, Smith Coll., 1951; MA, U. Ky., 1966, PhD, 1972. Instr. U. Ky., 1966-68; dir. spl. edn. grad. program Catholic U. Am., Washington, 1969-76; assoc. dir. nat. com. Arts for the Handicapped, Washington, 1976-80; owner, pres. Louise Appell Cons. Svcs., Washington, 1980-82; assoc. Macro Systems, Inc., Silver Spring, Md., 1982-84, dir. edn. product devel., 1984-85, dir. ednl. product devel., 1985—, v.p., 1985—, ret., 1996. Personal E-mail: lsappell@verizon.net.

APPELLA, DANIEL, biochemist, researcher; b. Washington, July 20, 1971; s. Ettore and Charlotte Appella; m. Julia Appella, May 31, 1998; 1 child, Amy Filomena. PhD, U. Wis., Madison, 1998. Prof. Northwestern U., Evanston, Ill., 2001—04; investigator bioorganic chemistry lab Nat. Inst. Diabetes and Digestive and Kidney Diseases, Bethesda, Md., 2005—. Contbr. articles to profl. jours. Recipient Presdl. Early Career award for Scientists and Engrs., Pres. George W. Bush, 2005. Mem.: Am. Chem. Soc. Achievements include patents for small molecule reactivation of mutant p53.

APPELLO, PATRICK PAUL, guitarist, lutenist, educator; b. Jersey City, Feb. 17, 1954; s. Paul James and Frances Theodora Appello; 1 child, Laura Elizabeth. MusB, Manhattan Sch. Music, NYC, 1977; MusM, NJ City U., 2006. Instr. classical guitar Westchester Conservatory, NY, 1975—81, Monmouth Conservatory, Red Bank, 1987—91, instr. guitar and lute, 2002—; dir. Highlander Capital Mgmt./FIA Capital, 1993—2001; instr. Red Bank Regional HS, 2003, Brookdale CC, Lincroft, NJ, 2005; adj. lectr. guitar and theory Georgian Ct. U., Lakewood, NJ, 2006—. Musician: Windows on the World, World Trade Ctr., 1976—93, Augustine Guitar Collection, 2007, (concerts) NY Continuo Collective, Boston Early Music Festival, Ch. of St. Francis of Assisi, Christ and St. Stephen Ch., Our Saviour's Atonement, Advent Luth. Ch., Bargemusic, Ams. for the Arts, Finkelstein Meml. Libr., NJ City U., Monmouth Conservatory of Music, Georgian Ct. U., UN, Princess Grace Found., others. Named co-winner, Oscar Ghilia Master Class Competition, Aspen, Colo., 1976. Mem.: Soc. Classical Guitar, Brit. Lute Soc., USA Lute Soc., Early Music Am., NJ Guitar and Mandolin Soc. Avocation: teaching. Home: 270 Ocean Ave Long Branch NJ 07740 Office: Georgian Ct U 900 Lakewood Ave Lakewood NJ 08701 Office Phone: 732-987-2624. Fax: 732-728-0522. Personal E-mail: patrick.appello@verizon.net.

APPELMAN, EVAN HUGH, retired chemist; b. Chgo., June 6, 1935; s. Harry Louis and Mollie Sarah (Hirsch) A.; m. Mary Frances Goold, Sept. 2, 1960; children: Harold Stewart, Hilary Louise. AB, U. Chgo., 1953, MS, 1955; PhD, U. Calif., Berkeley, 1960. With Argonne (Ill.) Nat. Lab., 1960-95, chemist, 1963-76, sr. chemist, 1976-95, ret., 1995. Contbr. articles to profl. jours. Guggenheim fellow, 1973-74; Recipient award for service at Argonne Nat. Lab., U. Chgo., 1975, E.O. Lawrence award ERDA, 1976, Alexander von Humboldt Research award Fed. Republic Germany, 1988-89; vis. sr. rsch. fellow Brit. Sci. Rsch. Coun.-U. Oxford, 1983-84. Fellow AAAS; mem. Am. Chem. Soc., Phi Beta Kappa, Sigma Xi. Jewish. Home: 224 Lake Dr Kensington CA 94708-1132 Personal E-mail: evhap@anl.gov.

APPENZELLER, OTTO, neurologist, researcher; b. Czernowitz, Romania, Dec. 11, 1927; came to U.S., 1963; s. Emmanuel Adam and Josephine (Metsch) A.; m. Judith Bryce, Dec. 11, 1956; children: Timothy, Martin, Peter. MBBS, Sydney U., Australia, 1957, MD, 1966; PhD, U. London, 1963. Diplomate Am. Bd. Psychiatry and Neurology. Prof. U. N. Mex., Albuquerque, 1970-90; vis. prof. McGill U., Montreal, Canada, 1977; hon. rsch. fellow U. London, 1983; vis. scientist Oxygen Transport Program Lovelace Med. Found., Albuquerque, 1990-92; pres. N.Mex. Health Enhancement and Marathon Clinics Rsch. Found., Albuquerque, 1992—; prof. exptl. neurobiology Bogomoletz Inst. Ukrainian Acad. Sci., Kiev, 1995-2000. U.S.-India exch. scientist NSF, 1992; Fogarty internat. exch. scientist, Kiev, Ukraine, 1993; rsch. com. UNESCO Internat. Coun. Sports and Phys. Edn., 1978-99; ref. Med. Rsch. Coun. New Zealand, 1986-99, reviewer, 1988-99; participant individual health scientist exch. program Fogarty Internat. Ctr., NIH to A.A. Bogomoletz Inst. Physiology, Kiev, 1993. Author: The Autonomic Nervous System, 5th edit., 1997; co-author: Headache, 1984; editor: Pathogenesis and Management of Headache, 1976, Health Aspects of Endurance Training, 1978, Sports Medicine, 3d edit., 1988, Jour. Headache, 1975-77, Annals of Sports Medicine, 1984-88; translator: Neurologic Differential Diagnosis (M. Mumentaler), 2nd edit., 1992; vol. editor: Handbook of Clinical Neurology: The Autonomic Nervous System, Parts I and II, 1998-2000; mem. editl. bd. numerous med. jours. Grantee Diabetes Rsch. and Edn. Found., 1988, Inst. C. Mondino, U. Pavia, Italy, 1992, 95-96, 2000, NMHEMC Rsch. Found., 1992-2007. Fellow ACP (sr.), Am. Acad. Neurology (sr.), Royal Australasian Coll. Physicians (sr.). Achievements include discovery of disease affecting peripheral nerves of Navajo children, of release of opioids and endothelin in human circulatory system after exercise, of chronic neurodegenerative disease in human T-lymphotropic viral II (HTLV II) infection, of peptidergic innervation of blood vessels supplying blood to peripheral nerves in present day and ancient mummified tissues of neurologic dis. in mummy portraits, of neuropathy in chronic pulmonary disease and chronic mountain sickness of fossilized biological rhythm in ancient human teeth, and teeth of extinct archosaurs; of archived biologic rhythms in human and animal hair; of cerebral vasodilatation to nitric oxide as a measure of fitness for life at altitude; leader of Mt. Everest rsch. expedition, 1987, Khachenjunga rsch. expedition, 1989, Stock Kangri rsch. expedition, 1992, Tso Moriri Lake (Ladakh) rsch. expedition, 1994, Cerro de Pasco rsch. expedition, 1997, 99-2000, 03, rsch. expedition Simen Mountains, Ethiopia, 2005, Korzok, Ladakh, 2006, 2007. Business E-Mail: oarun@unm.edu. E-mail: ottoarun12@aol.com, o.appenzeller@comcast.net.

APPERSON, BERNARD JAMES, lawyer; b. Washington, June 28, 1956; s. Bernard James, Jr. and Ann Wentworth (Anderson) Apperson. BA in Polit. Sci., Am. U., 1978; JD, Cumberland Sch. Law, 1981; LLM in Internat. Law, Georgetown U., 1985. Bar: Fla. 1981, Ga. 1981, DC 1983, U.S. Supreme Ct. 1985. Atty., U.S. trustee for so. dist. N.Y. U.S. Dept. Justice, NYC, 1981; atty. EPA, Washington, 1981-83; atty. civil rights div. U.S. Dept. Justice, Washington, 1983-84, atty. office legis. affairs, 1986-87; asst. U.S. atty. Ea. Dist. Va., Alexandria, 1987-97, DC, Washington, 2007—; counsel to dir. Legal Services Corp., Washington, 1985-86; commr. U.S. Dist. Ct., Ea. Dist. Va., Alexandria, 1996-97; sr. counsel com. on govt. reform and oversight, spl. counsel subcom. Nat. Econ. Growth, Natural Resources etc. U.S. Ho. of Reps., Washington, 1997-98; assoc. ind. counsel Office of the Ind. Counsel, Washington, 1998-99, dep. ind. counsel, 1999-2000; chief counsel oversight and investigations Com. on Jud., U.S. Ho. of Reps., Washington, 2001, chief counsel subcom. crime, terrorism & homeland security, 2001—05, chief counsel to U.S. Senator Saxby Chambliss, 2005—07, spl. designation to senate com. on armed svcs., 2006. Instr. FBI Tng. Acad., Quantico, Va., 1990; lectr. law U. London, U. Ga., 1990. Assoc. editor: Am. Jour. Trial Advocacy Cumberland Sch. Law, 1979—81. Nat. staff Citizens for Reagan, Fla., Kansas City, Mo., 1976; cons. Reagan for Pres., Detroit, 1980; northeastern regional dir. Reagan-Bush 1984, Washington, 1984, Lawyers for Bush-Cheney, Washington, 2000; Volusia County chmn. Paula Hawkins for U.S. Senate, 1974. Recipient Lewis F. Powell medal for Excellence in Advocacy, Am. Coll. Trial Lawyers, 1980. Mem.: Federalist Soc. Law and Pub. Policy Studies, St. Andrew's Soc., Order of Barristers. Republican. Anglican. Home: 545 E Braddock Rd Apt 704 Alexandria VA 22314-2171 also: US Atty DC 555 4th St NW Washington DC 20530 E-mail: jay.apperson@usdoj.gov.

APPERSON, JACK ALFONSO, retired army officer, management executive; b. Fredericksburg, Va., Dec. 21, 1934; s. Claude Heywood and Mary Louise (Farmer) A.; m. Alexandra Maynard, Aug. 31, 1957 (dec. Aug. 1992); children: Melissa Heywood, Amy Alexandra, Robert Randall (dec.), Eric Edward; m. Marguerite M. Legin, Nov. 25, 1995. BS, U.S. Mil. Acad., 1957; MS in Nuclear Physics, U. Ala., 1962; AA (hon.), Texarkana C.C., 1979. Commd. 2d lt. U.S. Army, 1957, advanced through grades to brig. gen., platoon leader Ft. Bragg, NC, 1957-58, Ft. Knox, Ky., 1958-59; comdg. officer 546th Ordnance Co. U.S. Army-Europe, 1963-64, materiel officer 66th Maintenance Bn., 1964-65, exec. officer bn., 1965-66; asst. prof., instr. dept. ordnance U.S. Mil. Acad., 1967-69; bn. comdr. and materiel officer 801st Maintenance Bn., Vietnam, 1969-70; assignment officer ordnance br. Office of Personnel Ops., Dept. Army, Washington, 1970-71, chief co. grade assignments, 1971-72; bn. comdr. 1st Inf. Div., Ft. Riley, Kans., 1973-74; office dep. chief of staff for logistics Dept. Army, Washington, 1974-75; chief war res. office Office Dep. Chief of Staff for Logistics, Dept. Army, Washington, 1975-76; exec. to asst. sec. Army Installations and Logistics, Washington, 1976-77; comdr. Red River Army Depot, Texarkana, Tex., 1977-79; dep. comdg. gen. U.S. Army Missile Materiel Readiness Command, Redstone Arsenal, Ala., 1979-81; comdg. gen. U.S. Army Depot System Command, Chambersburg, Pa., 1981-82; sr. v.p. ops. mgmt. div. Day & Zimmermann, Phila., 1982-83, also bd. dirs.; pres. Govt. Systems Group Day and Zimmerman, Phila., 1991-95, Systems Engring. Assocs. Corp., Mt. Laurel, NJ, 1983-91. Bd. dirs. Redstone Fed. Credit Union; vestryman Sharon Chapel Episcopal Ch., Alexandria, Va., 1975-77, St. Paul's Episcopal Ch., Phila., 1984-1988. Decorated DSM, Legion of Merit, Bronze Star (2), Meritorious Svc. medal, others; inducted into U.S. Army Ordnance Hall of Fame, 1994. Mem. Assn. Grads. U.S. Mil. Acad., West Point Soc. Phila. (bd. dirs.), Assn. U.S. Army (pres. chpt. 1983-85), Am. Def. Preparedness Assn., Alumni Assn. U.S. Army War Coll., Phila C. of C., Cherry Hill C. of C., Narragansett C. of C. (pres. 1996—2000), South County Hosp. Found.; trustee R.I. State Investment Commn., Rotary (pres. West Bay Rotary Coun. 2000), Rehoboth-Lewes Rotary, Sigma Pi Sigma. Republican. Home: 4544 Columbus St # 710 Virginia Beach VA 23462-6702 Personal E-mail: japperson@cox.net.

APPLE, DAINA DRAVNIEKS, federal agency administrator; b. Kuldiga, Latvia, July 6, 1944; came to U.S., 1951; d. Albins Dravnieks and Alina A. (Bergs) Zelmenis; divorced; 1 child, Almira Moronne; m. Martin A. Apple, Sept. 2, 1986. BSc, U. Calif., Berkeley, 1977, MA, 1980. Economist Pacific S.W. Rsch. U.S. Forest Svc., Berkeley, 1976-85, mgr. regional land use appeals San Francisco, 1986-88, program analysis officer, engring., 1988-90, asst. regulatory officer, 1990-95, strategic planner nat. forest sys. resources program, 1995-98, policy analyst, 1998—2002; adminstr. workplace rels. Pacific Southwest Region, Vallejo, Calif., 2002—03, staff asst. to dep. chief programs and legislation, 2004—05, staff asst. to the dep. chief for R&D, 2005—. Mem. SAF Bd. Forest Sci. and Tech., 2004—06. Author: Public Involvement in the Forest Service-Methodologies, 1977, Public Involvement, Selected Abstracts for Natural Resource Managers, 1979, The Management of Policy and Direction in the Forest Service, 1982, An Analysis of the Forest Service Human Resource Management Program, 1984, Organization Design-Abstracts for Natural Resources Users, 1986, Social and Legal Forces Changing the Management of National Forests, 1996, Water and the Forest Service, 2000, The Forest Service as a Learning Organization, 2000, Evolution of U.S. Water Policy, 2001; contbg. editor Jour. Women in Natural Resources, 1987—. Fellow Soc. Am. Foresters (chair Nat. Capital Soc. 2000, designated fed. officer), Phi Beta Kappa Fellows; mem. AAAS, Am. Chem. Soc., Am. Inst. Biol. Scis., NY Acad. Sci., Washington Acad. Scis., Am. Water Resources Assn., Forest Rsch. Adv. Coun., Forest History Soc., Am. Latvian Assn. (bd. dirs. 1995-97). Commonwealth Club Calif., Phi Beta Kappa (nat. sec. 1985-88, pres. No. Calif. 1982-84), Sigma Xi. Avocations: politics, ballroom dancing, tennis, films. Office: USDA Forest Svc R&D 1400 Independence Ave SW Washington DC 20250-1120 Office Phone: 202-205-1452. Business E-Mail: dapple@fs.fed.us.

APPLE, GARY WINSTON, writer, educational consultant; b. Kansas City, Mo., Aug. 9, 1948; s. Winston Loyal Apple and Betty Jean Shelton; children: Christine Michelle Apple Blegen, Sarah Beth Apple Rimel, Dylan Winston. BA in Secondary Edn., U. Mo., Kansas City, 1970, MA in Curriculum and Instrn., 1990. Tchr. Kansas City Mo. Sch. Dist., 1984—2005; self-employed writer, cons. Independence, Mo., 2005—. Author: Edutopia: A Manifesto For The Reform of Public Education, 2003. Founder, bd. pres. Jobs for Ams., Independence, 2005—. Mem.: Assn. for Supervision and Curriculum Devel. Avocation: songwriting and recording.

APPLE, JACKI (JACQUELINE B.), artist, educator, writer; b. NYC; Student, Syracuse U.; BFA, Parsons Sch. Design. Curator exhbns. and performance Franklin Furnace, NYC, 1977—80; prodr., host Sta. KPFK-FM, North Hollywood, Calif., 1982—95; prof. Art Ctr. Coll. Design, Pasadena, Calif., 1983—. Mem. faculty adv. com. Art Ctr. Coll. Design, Pasadena, 1993, Faculty Coun. rep., 2000-06, dir. office faculty affairs, 2007—; vis. faculty UCSD, LaJolla, 1995-99. Contbg. writer: L.A. Weekly, 1983-89; contbg. editor: Artweek, 1983-90, High Performance Mag., 1984-95; performance works include The Garden Planet Revisited, 1982, The Amazon, the Mekong, the Missouri and the Nile, 1985, Palisade, 1987, Fluctuations of the Field, 1989, (with J. Adler) A Stone's Throw., 2000, Kokoro No Mai, 2003, After the Fall.A Prophecy, 2004; writer, performer, dir., prodr.: (record) The Mexican Tapes, 1979-80, (performance/installation/audio work) Voices in the Dark, 1989-97, (radio art work) Swan Lake, 1989; artist, prodr.: (installations and audio work) The Culture of Disappearance, # 1-5, 1991-95; author, designer: (book, installation) Trunk Pieces, 1975-78, (cd) Thank You for Flying American, 1995, Ghost Dances/On the Event Horizon 1996; six part radio art series Redefining Democracy in America Parts, 1991-92; (site specific installation) Zeitghosts: Angels in the Architecture, 1996, Sanctuary, 1996, Hidden Desires, 1998, A Stone's Throw.The Last Witnesses, 2001; (photowork) ghost.dance series 1995—, (installation) Aviary of the Lost. 1994/2004, (photo/audio performance) You Don't Need a Weatherman, 1999; pub. art projects Aliso-Pico Cmty. Ctr., 1997-2000, Venice Oakwood Cmty. Ctr., 2000-03, Martin Luther King Rehab Ctr., 2000-03, Little Tokyo br. L.A. Pub. Libr., 2002-05; author: Doing It Right in L.A., 1990; prodr. EarJam Music Festival, 2000, 01, 02, 04. Recipient Vesta award Media Arts Women's Bldg., 1990, Faculty Enrichment grant Art Ctr. Coll. Design, 2001, 07; NEA visual artists fellow, 1979, 81; InterArts program grantee NEA, 1984-85, 91-92; Calif. Arts Coun. Visual Arts/New Genres fellowship, 1996; grantee Durfee Foundation, 2003, 07. Mem.: Internat. Art Critics Assn., Nat. Writers Union, Coll. Art Assn. (edn. com. 2005—). Home: 3532 Jasmine Ave Los Angeles CA 90034-4947 E-mail: jaworks@sprintmail.com.

APPLE, JAMES GLENN, lawyer, educator; b. Huntington, W.Va., Sept. 20, 1937; s. David French and Bernice (Stewart) A.; m. Emory O'Shee, June 9, 1959 (div. May 15, 1990); children: Meredith Ellen, Miles Stewart; m. Elizabeth Fitzpatrick Jones, Nov. 10, 1990. BA (with honors), U. Va., 1959, JD, 1962; LLM, U. Edinburgh, Scotland, 1990. Bar: Va. 1962, Ky. 1962, U.S. Dist. Ct. (ea. and we. dists.) Ky., U.S. Ct. Appeals (6th cir.), U.S. Supreme Ct. Pvt. practice law Wheeler & Marshall, Paducah, Ky., 1964-67; adminstrv. asst. Gov. of Ky., Frankfort, 1967-69; exec. asst. Ky. Commr. of Hwys., Frankfort, 1969-70; assoc. Stites & Harbison Law Firm, Louisville, 1970-72, ptnr., 1972-90; spl. asst., counsel to dir. Fed. Jud. Ctr., Washington, 1990-92; chief Interjudicial Affairs Office, Fed. Jud. Ctr., 1992-99; chmn., pres. Internat. Jud. Acad., Washington, 1999—. Adj. prof. Bellarmine Coll., Louisville, 1988-90; adj. prof. internat. law dept. polit. sci. George Washington U., 1995, Am. U., 1996; adminstr. justice program George Mason U., 2004. Comments and projects editor Va. Law Rev., 1961-62; editor State-Fed. Jud. Observer, 1993-99, Internat. Jud. Observer, 1994-98; co-author: A Primer on the Civil Law System (Fed. Jud. Ctr.), Manual for Cooperation Between State and Federal Courts (Fed. Jud. Ctr.); co-editor Internat. Jud. Monitor, 2006—; contbr. articles to profl. jours. Bd. dirs. Ky. Authority for Ednl. TV, Lexington, 1971-75; chmn. bd. Transit Authority of River City, Louisville, 1981-85; pres. Louisville Bar Found., 1986-87; mem. Leadership Louisville, 1983-84; bd. dirs, treas. Jud. Leadership Devel. Coun., Washington, 2001—. Lt. USAR, 1963-68. Recipient Award of Merit, Louisville Bar Assn., 1980, Pres.'s award Washington Combined Fed. Campaign, 1990, 91, Spl. Svc. award, 1990; first prize Brit. Red Cross Essay Contest, 1990; resident fellow Henri Dunaut Inst., GEneva, 1990. Fellow Am. Coll. Trial Lawyers; mem. Am. Law Inst., Am. Soc. Internat. Law (chair, tillar house com.), Am. Bd. Trial Advocates, Nat. Press Club, Univ. Club of Washington. Avocations: reading, writing, gardening, travel, walking. Office: Internat Jud Acad 1616 H St NW Ste 204 Washington DC 20006 Home Phone: 703-379-4814; Office Phone: 202-628-7801. Fax: 202-628-7803. E-mail: jgapple@verizon.net.

APPLE, MARTIN ALLEN, science executive and educator; b. Duluth, Minn., Sept. 17, 1938; m. M. Daina; children: Deborah Dawn, Pamela Ruth, Nathan, Rebeccah Lynn AB, ALA, U. Minn., 1959, MSc, 1962; PhD, U. Calif., 1968. Chmn. Multidisciplinary Drug Rsch. Group U. Calif., San Francisco, 1974-78; pres. IPRI, San Carlos, Calif., 1978-81; with EAN-Tech., Inc., Daly City, Calif., 1982-84, chmn. bd., 1983-84; with Adytum Internat., Mountain View, Calif., 1982-90, CEO, 1983-90, LEADERS, Washington, 1989—; pres., Coun. Sci. Soc. Presidents, Washington, 1993—; CEO Sci. Watch, Inc., 1996-98. With Hon. Doug Walgren co-chair Leadership Network, 1995-97; adj. prof. U. Calif., San Francisco, 1982-84; cons. SRI Internat. Dept. Edn., EPA, NIH, NSF, The Network, Hughes-GM, Nat. Cancer Inst., AAAS, Nat. Sci. Tchrs. Assn., others; adj. rsch. prof. George Mason U., Fairfax, Va., 1991-92; vis. scholar Nat. Humanities Ctr., 1990-91; nat. project mgr. NSTA Scope Sequence and Coordination Project, 1991-92; bd. dirs. Am. Med. Progress Ednl. Found.; bd. dirs. ACCTION, Inc., chmn. trustees, 1995-96; expert advisor Dept. of Edn., 1996-2001; mem. blue ribbon panel USDA, 2000-01; chmn. bd. trustees Ctr. Advanced Rsch. Behavioral Neurobiology U. Ill., Chgo., 2002-03; chmn. bd. visitors U. Md./U. Md. Biotech. Inst., 1999-2004; bd. govs. Nat. Economists Club, 2005—; mem. USDA Nat. Agrl. Rsch., Edn., Econs. and Ext. Bd., 2006—. Author: (with F. Myers) Review Medical Pharmacology, 1976; (with M. Fink) Immune RNA in Neoplasia, 1976; (with F. Becker et al) Cancer: A Comprehensive Treatise, 1977; (with M. Keenberg et al) Investing in Biotechnology, 1981; (with F. Ahmad et al) From Genes to Proteins: Horizons in Biotechnology, 1983; (with J. Kureczka) Status of Biotechnology, 1987; (with M. Baum) Business Advantage, 1987 (winner Excellence award Software Pubs. Assn. 1987), (with R. Yager) Translating and Using Research for Improving Teacher Education in Science and Mathematics, 1998; mem. editl. bd. Computers in Medicine Mem. Calif. Coun. Indsl. Innovation, 1982. Recipient citation, East West Ctr. Bd. of Govs., 1988, Leadership citation, Coun. Sci. Soc. Pres., 1995, Support of Sci. award, 2002. Fellow Am. Coll. Clin. Pharmacology, Am. Inst. Chemists (chmn. bd. dirs. 2005—), Phi Beta Kappa (Disting. Svc. award 1984, 85); mem. Assn. Venture Founders (bd. govs. 1982-83), East-West Ctr. Assn. (trustee 1982-88, vice chmn. 1983-85), Profl. Software Programmers Assn., Leaders of Tomorrow (chmn. 1987-88), Commonwealth Club Calif., Phi Beta Kappa, Sigma Xi (bd. dirs., chmn. long-range strategic planning com. 1988-92). Office: Coun Sci Soc Presidents PO Box 33999 Washington DC 20033-0999 also: PO Box 905 Benicia CA 94510-0905 E-mail: cssp@acs.org.

APPLEBAUM, ANNE, journalist, writer; b. Washington, 1964; m. Radek Sikorski; children: Alexander, Tadeusz. Grad, Yale U., 1986. Correspondent The Independent, London, 1988—90; journalist Economist, London, 1988—92; fgn. editor Spectator Mag., London, 1993—94, deputy editor, 1994—; columnist The Daily Telegraph, London, 1994—; columnist, mem. editl. bd. Wash. Post, 2002—. Author: (book) Between East and West: Across the Borderlands of Europe, 1995, Gulag, A History, 2004 (Nat. Book award nominee, 2003, Pulitzer Prize for general nonfiction, 2004), several writings have appeared in The Wall St. Jour., the Fin. Times, The Internat. Herald Tribune, Fgn. Affairs, Boston Globe, The Ind., The Guardian, Commentaire, Suddeutsche Zeitung, Newsweek, The New Criterion, others. Recipient Charles Douglas Home Meml. Trust award, 1992; Marshall Scholar, London Sch. Economics, St. Antony's Coll., Oxford. Office: Washington Post 1150 15th St NW Washington DC 20071

APPLEBAUM, CHARLES, lawyer; b. Newark, May 19, 1947; s. Harry I. and Francis (Gastwirth) A.; m. Patricia (Gyurko) Applebaum; children: Matthew, David, Michael, Amanda. BA, U. Pa., 1969; JD, Rutgers U., 1973; LLM, NYU, 1978. Bar: U.S. Dist. Ct. N.J. 1973. Law clk. to Hon. Samuel A. Larner, Jersey City, 1973-74; assoc., then ptnr. Greenbaum, Rowe, Smith, Ravin, Davis & Himmel LLP, Woodbridge, NJ, 1974-89; gen. counsel Alfieri Orgn., Edison, NJ, 1989—2002, Kara Homes Inc., East Brunswick, NJ, 2002—. Adj. prof. Rutgers Law Sch., Newark, 1985-88. Co-author: New Jersey Real Estate Forms, 1988; contbr. articles to profl.

jours. Mem. ABA (real property probate and trust, chmn. significant lit. and publs. 1985-97, co-editor The Acrel Papers 1992-94), Am. Coll. Real Estate Lawyers (editor publs. 1991—). Office: Kara Homes Inc 197 Rte 18 Ste 101N East Brunswick NJ 08816 Office Phone: 732-565-0720. Business E-Mail: capplebaum@karahomes.com.

APPLEBAUM, EDWARD LEON, otolaryngologist, educator; b. Detroit, Jan. 14, 1940; s. M. Lawrence and Frieda Applebaum; m. Eva Redei; children: Daniel Ira, Rachel Anne. AB, Wayne State U., 1961, MD, 1964. Diplomate: Am. Bd. Otolaryngology. Intern Univ. Hosp., Ann Arbor, Mich., 1964-65; resident Mass. Eye and Ear Infirmary Harvard Med. Sch., Boston, 1966-69; practice medicine specializing in otolaryngology Chgo., 1972—2007; assoc. prof. Northwestern U. Med. Sch., 1972-79, prof., acting chmn. dept. otolaryngology Chgo., 2000—06, acting chmn. dept. otolaryngology, 2002—04, chmn. dept. otolaryngology, 2002—06; prof., head dept. otolaryngology, head and neck surgery Coll. Medicine, U. Ill., 1979-2000. Mem. staff Northwestern Meml. Hosp. Author: Tracheal Intubation, 1976; editor: Am. Jour. Otolaryngology, 1982-87; mem. editl. bd. Am. Jour. Otolaryngology, Laryngoscope. Served as maj. U.S. Army, 1969-71. Recipient Anna Albert Keller Rsch. award Wayne State U. Coll. Medicine, 1964, Disting. Alumni award, 1989, William Beaumont Soc. Original Rsch. award, 1964, Disting. Faculty award, U. Ill. Coll. Medicine, 1996. Fellow ACS, Am. Soc. for Head and Neck Surgery, Surgery, Am. Acad. Otolaryngology, Head and Neck Surgery, Am. Laryngol., Rhinol. and Otol. Soc. (v.p. 1993, pres. 2000), Am. Laryngol. Assn., Am. Otol. Soc., Soc. Univ. Otolaryngologists, Head and Neck Surgeons (pres. 1988), Assn. Acad. Depts. Otolaryngology-Head and Neck Surgery (pres. 1995-96). E-mail: eapple@northwestern.edu.

APPLEBAUM, STUART S., public relations executive; b. NYC, Sept. 19, 1949; s. Jack and Anne (Miller) A. BA, Queens Coll., 1971. Publicist Alfred A. Knopf Inc., NYC, 1971-73, MGM Pictures, NYC, 1973, Bantam Books Inc., NYC, 1974-77, mgr. publicity, 1977-79, dir. publicity, 1979-87, v.p., dir. pub. rels. and publicity, 1983-90, v.p., dir. pub. rels., 1990-91, v.p., dir. publicity and pub. rels., 1991—; sr. v.p., dir. pub. rels. Bantam Doubleday Dell Pub. Group, NYC, 1987-98, Random House, Inc., NYC, 1998—, exec. v.p. comms., 2002—. Named as one of the People Who Shaped the Book Bus., Pubs. Weekly, 1997. Mem. Publishers Publicity Assn. (bd. dirs. N.Y.C. chpt. 1979-84) Office: Random House Inc 1745 Broadway New York NY 10019 Business E-Mail: sapplebaum@randomhouse.com.

APPLEBY, R(OBERT) SCOTT, history educator; b. Shreveport, La., Dec. 3, 1956; s. John and Joanne (Jackson) A.; m. Margaret Calhoun; children: Benjamin, Paul, Clare, Tony. BA, U. Notre Dame, 1978; MA, U. Chgo., 1979, PhD, 1985. Asst. prof., chair dept. religious studies St. Xavier Coll., Chgo., 1985-87; rsch. assoc. U. Chgo., 1988-94; assoc. dir. The Fundamentalism Project Am. Acad. Arts and Scis., Chgo., 1988—; dir. Cushwa Ctr. for Study of Am. Catholicism U. Notre Dame, Ind., 1994—, assoc. prof. history Ind., 1994—. Cons. Lilly Endowment, 1994—, William Benton Broadcast Project, U. Chgo., 1989-92. Editor: (with Martin E. Marty) Fundamentalisms Observed, 1991. Mem. Am. Acad. Religion, Am. Hist. Assn., Am. Cath. Hist. Assn., Am. Soc. Ch. History, Coll. Theology Soc., Religious Rsch. Assn. (nominations com. 1993—). Office: U Notre Dame 614 Hesburgh Ctr Notre Dame IN 46556-5677

APPLEBY, STUART, professional golfer; b. Cohuna, Australia, May 1, 1971; m. Renay Appleby (dec. 1998); m. Ashley Appleby. Profl. golfer, 1992—; amateur winner Queensland Open, 1991; 2d pl. Bay Hill Invitational; runner-up Sprint Internat.; winner Victorian title, 1991, Victorian PGA Championship, 1994, S. Australia PGA Championship, 1994, Nedlands Masters Classic, 1994, Nedlands Tassie Classic, 1994, Nike Sonoma County Open, 1995, Nike Monterrey Open, 1995, Honda Classic, 1997, Kemper Open, 1998, Coolum Classic, 1998, Shell Houston Open, 1999, CVS Charity Classic, 1999, Las Vegas Invitational, 2003, Mercedes Championship, 2004, 2006, Shell Houston Open, 2006; mem. Dunhill Cup, 1997—99, Pres. Cup, 1998, 2000, 2003, World Cup, 2003. Mem. nat. team Dunhill Cup, 1997, 98, The Pres. Cup, 1998; mem. PGA Tour charity team The Players Championship, 1999; finished in top 25 NEC World Series of Golf, 1998. First qualifying school grad. to earn more than $1 million the following year. Avocations: action sports, motor racing. Office: Ste 1300 One Erie View Plaza Cleveland OH 44114-1715

APPLEGARTH, PAUL VOLLMER, investment and development executive; b. Wilkinsburg, Pa., Apr. 21, 1946; s. William Francis and Alice (Vollmer) A.; m. Linda Davis, Dec. 28, 1971; children: Katharine Davis, Caroline Elizabeth. BA, Yale U., 1968; MBA, JD, Harvard U., 1974. Bar: D.C. 1974, Mass. 1975. Various positions with The World Bank, Washington, 1974-83; sr. v.p. Bank Am., San Francisco, 1983-86, Am. Express/Lehman Bros., NYC, 1987-94; mng. dir. Emerging Markets Corp., Washington, 1994—2003; CEO Millenium Challenge Corp., 2004—05; sr. transatlantic fellow German Marshall Fund of the US, 2005—06; CEO Value Enhancement Internat., 2005—; founder, mng. dir., COO, Emerging Africa Infrastructure Fund, 2001—02. Author: Capital Market and Financial Sector Development in Sub-Saharan Africa. Bd. mem. No. Calif. Resolve, 1985-87, Sales/Svc. Am., 1993-94, various others; CFO United Way Am., Alexandria, Va., 1992-94. Capt. AUS, 1968-70. White House fellow, 1981-82; named Alumnus of Yr., The Marist Sch., 2000. Mem. Mass. Bar Assn., D.C. Bar Assn., Belle Haven Club (bd. dirs. 1991-95, vice commodore 1993-94), Congl. Country Club, White House Fellows Alumni Assn. Office: Value Enhancement Internat 186 Field Point Rd # 4B Greenwich CT 06830 Personal E-mail: valueenhancement@gmail.com.

APPLEGATE, CHRISTINA, actress; b. LA, Calif., Nov. 25, 1971; d. Robert Applegate and Nancy Priddy; m. Johnathon Schaech, Oct. 20, 2001 (div. Aug. 10, 2007). Film appearances include: Jaws of Satan, 1980, Streets, 1990, Don't Tell Mom the Babysitter's Dead, 1991, Across the Moon, 1994, Vibrations, 1995, Wild Bill, 1995, Mars Attacks!, 1996, Nowhere, 1997, Claudine's Return, 1998, The Big Hit, 1998, Mafia!, 1998, The Giving Tree, 2000, Just Visiting, 2001, The Sweetest Thing, 2002, Heroes, 2003, View from the Top, 2003, Wonderland, 2003, Grand Theft Parsons, 2003, Employee of the Month, 2004, Anchorman: The Legend of Ron Burgundy, 2004, Surviving Christmas, 2004, Tilt-A-Whirl, 2005; TV appearances include: (series) Days of Our Lives, 1974, Washingtoon, 1985, Heart of the City, 1986, Married.With Children, 1987-97, All My Life, 1998, Jesse, 1998-2000, Friends, 2002, (TV movies) Grace Kelly, 1983, Dance 'til Dawn, 1988, Prince Charming, 2001, Suzanne's Diary for Nicholas, 2005. Off-broadway appearances include: Sweet Charity, 2005 (Theatre World award, 2005).

APPLEGATE, DEBBY, biographer; b. Feb. 1, 1968; m. Bruce Tulgan. BA summa cum laude, Amherst Coll., Mass., 1989; PhD Sterling Fell. in Am. Studies, Yale U., New Haven, Conn., 1998. Taught Yale U.; prof., Dept. History Wesleyan U., prof., Art History. Contbr. articles Jour. Am. History, NY Times; author: (biography) The Most Famous Man in America, 2006 (chosen as one of the 100 notable books of 2006, NY Times, finalist (biography), Nat. Book Critics Circle Awards, 2006, The Pulitzer Prize for Biography, 2007). Office: 125 Lawrence St New Haven CT 06511 Office Phone: 203-777-5043. Office Fax: 203-772-0886. E-mail: applegate@rainmakerthinking.com.*

APPLEGATE, DONALD EDWARD, history professor; b. Neptune, NJ, May 30, 1973; s. Robert Henry and Carole Erma (Becker) Applegate; m. Marie Victoria Jernoske, Dec. 28, 2003; 1 child, Benjamin Henry. Grad. cum laude, Rutgers U., 1995; MA in Tchg. Hist., U. Wyo., Laramie, 1998. Cert. social studies edn. NJ, 1995. Tchr. Hillsborough Sch. Dist., NJ, 1999—2001; tchr. history Monmouth County Vocat. Sch. Dist., Wall, NJ, 2001—. Attendee Civil War Inst., Gettysburg, Pa., 2005—07. CWI scholard, Lincoln Fellowship PA, 2005. Home: 22 Waltham Dr Tabernacle NJ 08088 Office: Comm High Sch 1740 New Bedford Rd Wall NJ 07719 Home Phone: 609-268-5712; Office Phone: 732-681-1010. Business E-Mail: donald_applegate@chs.mcvsd.org.

APPLEGATE, JEFFREY M., investment company executive; BA, American Univ., 1972; B Litt, Oxford Univ., 1974. Sr. investment advisor Lehman Bros., Credit Suisse, Shearson Lehman, E.F. Hutton, Smith Barney, H.C. Wainwright, 1974—2004; founder Jeffrey Applegate & Co.; exec. v.p., chief investment officer Fiduciary Global Advisors, Franklin Templeton Investments, NYC, 2004—. Mem.: CFA Inst., NY Soc. Securities Analysts. Office: Franklin Templeton Fiduciary Global Advisors 600 5th Ave New York NY 10020-2326*

APPLEGATE, WILLIAM BROWN, dean, researcher, medical educator, department chairman; b. Louisville, Ky., July 28, 1946; s. Henry Lovelace and Margaret (Whitesides) A.; m. Gail Reekers, July 31, 1982; children: Elizabeth Marie, Jennifer Michelle. BA, U. Louisville, 1968, MD, 1972; MPH, Harvard U., 1973. Intern Boston City Hosp., 1973—74, resident in internal medicine, 1974—75; R.W. Johnson clin. scholar U. NC, Chapel Hill, 1975-77; asst. prof. medicine U. N.Mex., Albuquerque, 1977-79; chief divsn. geriatric medicine U. Tenn., Memphis, 1979-93, dir. gen. clin. rsch. ctr., 1993-99, chmn. dept. preventive medicine, 1994-99; chmn., prof. dept. internal medicine Wake Forest U., Winston-Salem, NC, 1999, dean sch. medicine, sr. v.p. health scis., 2002—. Mem. coun. Nat. Inst. Aging, 1989-93, nat. adv. bd. Johnson Found. Clin. Scholars Program; bd. regents, ACP, 2002-. Contbr. articles to med. jours., including Jour. AMA, Archives Internal Medicine, others. Named Alumni fellow U. Louisville, 2003; grantee. Mem. ACP (bd. regents, chair-elect bd. regents, 2007), Am. Geriat. Soc. (editor-in-chief jour. 1993-2000), Rotary. Democrat. Avocation: bicycling. Office: Wake Forest Med Ctr Medical Center Blvd Winston Salem NC 27157-0001 Office Phone: 336-716-5026.

APPLEGET, TERRI LYNN, elementary school educator; d. Richard Louis and Joan Elizabeth (Seatter) Tobias; m. Patrick R. Appleget, Dec. 26, 1971 (div. May 1997); children: Brooke Elizabeth, Patrick Justin-Shaun, Katherine Bethany Anne Aisling, Keir Michael James. BA, U. Wis. Parkside, Kenosha, 1973; MA in Tchg., Coll. of Charleston, SC, 1991. Dir. extended day Ashley Hall, Charleston, 1993; founder, dir. The Children's Ctr., Summerville, S.C., 1993-97; tchr. mid. sch. lit., grammar, history Pinewood Preparatory, Summerville, 1993-97; tchr. kindergarten, early childhood diagnostic, 1st and 3d grade inclusion Charleston County Sch. Dist., 1997—2001; tchr. Charlestowne Acad. Magnet Sch., 2001—02, Ronald McNair Elem., 2002—03, N. Charleston Elem. at McNair, 2003—04; tchr. B-GAP (sci., math., English, social studies) Brentwood Mid. Sch., 2004—, A.C. Corcoran Elem., 2005—. Homesch. tchr. Charleston Prep. Sch., 1998—2001; freelance tutor, 1997—; homebound tchr., 2004—. Tchr. jr. Achievement, Charleston, 2000; sponsor Jr. Beta Club, Summerville, 1993—97; docent Historic Charleston Soc., 1988—98; v.p. Oakleaf Officers Wives Club, Orlando, Fla., 1986—87; pres. Fellowship Wartburg Spouses, Dubuque, Iowa, 1982—83; tchr. adult Sunday ch. sch. St. John's Luth. Ch., Charleston, 1988—, chair social ministry, 1989—2005, mem. vestry, 1989—2005. Mem. NEA, Nat. Assn. for Edn. of Young Children, Nat. Trust, Internat. Reading Assn. (S.C. coun.), Palmetto State Tchrs. Assn., Ladies' Sewing Soc. (life). Republican. Avocations: writing, studying Irish history, reading, gardening. Home: 141 Palmetto Bluff Ct Charleston SC 29418-3017 Office Phone: 843-764-2218.

APPLEMAN, NATE, chef; m. Clarisse Appleman. Grad., Culinary Inst. Am., Hyde Park, NY. Cert. pizzaiolos Verace Pizza Napoletana Assn. Intern Maisonette, Cin.; with Brasa, Seattle, 1999; mgr. meat station Campton Place, San Francisco, 2001; exec. sous chef Tra Vigne, A16, San Francisco, 2003—05, chef de cuisine, co-owner, 2005—06, exec. chef, co-owner, 2006—. Nominee Rising Star Chef, James Beard Found., 2007; named one of San Francisco's Rising Stars, StarChefs.com, 2007. Office: A16 2355 Chestnut St San Francisco CA 94123 Office Phone: 415-771-2216.*

APPLER, THOMAS L., lawyer; b. Washington, Oct. 12, 1943; m. Nancy J. Babb, Dec. 3, 1967; children: Alexandra Whitney. AB in Politics, Princeton U., 1965; JD, George Washington U., 1968. Bar: Va. 1968. Atty. Office of Judge Adv., Surgeon Gen. of Army, 1969-70; ptnr. McGuire, Woods, Battle & Boothe (and predecessor firms), McLean, Va., 1970-99, Crews & Hancock, PLC, Fairfax, Va., 1999—2002, Hancock, Daniel, Johnson & Nagle, P.C., 2002—04, Wilson, Elser, Moskowitz, Edelman & Dicker LLP, McLean, 2005—. Co-author: Damages for Plaintiff and Defense Attorneys, 1987. USAR, 1970-76. Fellow Am. Coll. Trial Lawyers; mem. No. Va. Def. Attys. Assn. (pres. 1975), Va. Assn. Def. Attys. (v.p., bd. dirs. 1977-83), Va. Bar Assn. (bd. dirs. young lawyers sect. 1974-76, appellate judges com. 1989-91, Boyd-Graves Conf. com. chair 2006-), Va. State Bar (coun. 1985-92, malpractice ins. com. 1989-99), Fairfax Bar Assn. (pres. 1984-85, bd. dirs. 1983-86), No. Va. Young Lawyers Assn. (pres. 1974). Home: 9717 Meadowlark Rd Vienna VA 22182-1951 Office: Wilson Elser Moskowitz Edelman & Dicker LLP 8444 Westpark Dr Ste 510 Mc Lean VA 22102 Office Phone: 703-245-9300. Office Fax: 703-245-9301. Business E-Mail: thomas.appler@wilsonelser.com.

APPLETON, KEVIN, academic administrator; s. Bernice and Eugene Appleton; m. Sokhatie Boye, Mar. 16, 1995; children: Khalil, Malik. BS in Acctg., Wilberforce U., 1985. CPA Ohio, 1988. Asst. contr. East Tenn. State U., 1991—94; contr. Wilberforce U., Wilberforce, Ohio, 1994—96; v.p. fin. and adminstrn. Jackson State U., Miss., 1996—2002; v.p. fin. affairs St. Joseph's U., Phila., 2002—03; v.p. fin. and bus. Norfolk State U., Va., 2003—06, Morehouse Coll., 2006—. Participant Civic Leadership Inst. of Hampton Roads, Norfolk, Va., 2004—05, Leadership Jackson, Miss., 2000—01; mem. Jackson Metro Pky. Commn., Miss., 1999—2002. Mem.: Nat. Assn. Coll. and U. Bus. Officers. Avocations: chess, swimming, basketball. Home Phone: 678-489-4631. Business E-Mail: kappleto@morehouse.edu.

APPLETON, MARC, architect; m. Joanna Kerns; 3 children. Grad., Harvard Coll., 1968; MArch, Yale U., New Haven, 1972. With Frank O. Gehry & Assocs., MacAllister, Rinehart & Ring, Benjamin Thompson & Assocs.; prin., pres. Appleton & Assocs., Inc., Santa Monica, Calif., 1976—. Author: George Washington Smith: An Architect's Scrapbook, 2001; co-author (with Melba Levick): California Mediterranean, 2007. Bd. trustees Prescott Coll., Ariz., Cooper Union, NYC; founding mem. Appleton-Whittel Rsch. Ranch Found., Ariz., Mingei Internat. Mus. World Folk Art, San Diego; bd. mem. Inst. Classical Architecture & Classical Am.; mem. Dean's coun. Yale Sch. Architecture. Mem.: AIA. Office: Appleton & Assocs Inc 1556 17th St Santa Monica CA 90404-3402 Office Phone: 310-828-0430. Office Fax: 310-828-0631.*

APPLETON, R. O., JR., lawyer; b. San Francisco, Aug. 17, 1945; s. Robert Oser and Leslie Jeanne (Roth) A.; m. Susan Frelich, June 3, 1971; children: Jesse David, Seth Daniel. AB, Stanford U., 1967; JD, U. Calif., San Francisco, 1970; postgrad., NYU, 1971. Bar: Calif. 1971, U.S. Dist. Calif. (no. dist.) Calif. 1971, Mo. 1973, U.S. Dist. Ct. (ea. dist.) Mo. 1974, U.S. Ct. Appeals (8th cir.) 1975, U.S. Ct. Internat. Trade, 1980. Assoc. Dinkelspiel & Dinkelspiel, San Francisco, 1971-73, Schramm & Morganstern, St. Louis, 1973-75; pvt. practice, 1975-77; ptnr. Braun, Newman, Stewart & Appleton, St. Louis, 1977-82, Appleton, Newman & Kretmar, St. Louis, 1982-84, Appleton, Newman & Gerson, St. Louis, 1984-89, Appleton & Kretmar, St. Louis, 1989—, Appleton, Kretmar & Beatty. Adj. prof. pre-trial litigation Washington U. Sch. Law, St. Louis, 1985-88. Arbitrator, vol. Better Bus. Bur. of St. Louis, 1980—; St. Louis Gymnastic Centre, 1984—; bd. dirs. St. Louis Friends of Tibet, 1991-94. Mem. ABA, Calif. Bar Assn., Met. Bar Assn. of St. Louis, St. Louis County Bar Assn., Am. Arbitration Assn. (arbitrator comml. panel, arbitrator mass claims appeals com. 1999), Stanford Club (pres. 1991—). Democrat. Jewish. Avocations: jogging, swimming, cooking, model trains, reading. Home: 8317 Cornell Ave Saint Louis MO 63132-5025 Office: Appleton Kretmar Beatty & Stolze 8000 Maryland Ave Ste 900 Saint Louis MO 63105-3911 Office Phone: 314-721-8685. Personal E-mail: roajratty1@aol.com.

APPLETON, STEVEN R., electronics executive; b. Mar. 1960; BBA, Boise State U., 1982. Fab supr., prodn. mgr., dir. mfg., v.p. mfg. Micron Tech., Inc., Boise, Idaho, 1983—91, pres., COO, 1991—94, chmn., CEO, pres., 1994—. Chmn. Semiconductor Ind. Assn.; bd. dir. Nat. Semiconductor Inc.; mem. World Semiconductor Council. Trustee Boise State Univ.; mem. Idaho Bus. Council. Office: Micron Tech PO Box 6 8000 South Federal Way Boise ID 83707*

APPLEWHAITE, CARLISLE S., special education educator, consultant; s. John Lancelot and Eulene Gertude Applewhaite; 1 child, Carl William Beshires-Applewhaite. BS, U. of the W.I., Bridgetown, Barbados, 1980; MA in Ednl. Psychology, Andrews U., Berrien Springs, Mich., 1987; PhD in Edn., Andrews U., 1994. Tchr. Ministry of Edn., Bridgetown, Barbados, 1973—76, 1979—87; dir. of student learning/vice prin. Chgo. SDA Acad., 1994—97; spl. edn. cons. Van Buren ISD, Lawrence, Mich., 1997—; mng. dir. P.A.C.E.R.S. Inc., Berrien Springs, Mich., 1996—. Author: (book, diagnostic screening tool) Carlisle-Attention Deficit Diagnostic System. Parent/child adv. P.A.C.E.R.S., Inc., Berrien Springs, Mich., 1998—2006. Recipient Cert. of Recognition, Phi Delta Kappa, 1992. Mem.: NASP (assoc.). Seventh-Day Adventist. Avocations: lawn tennis, soccer, travel, photography, nature walks. Office: Van Buren Intermediate School District 701 South Paw Paw St Lawrence MI 49064 Home Phone: (269) 471-361. Personal E-mail: capplewhaite@yahoo.com.

APPLEY, ALAN J., neurosurgeon; b. Long Beach, Calif., Mar. 2, 1958; s. Stephen N. and Arlene B. Appley; m. Cynthia C. Chicola, May 28, 1983; children: Maya A., Maxwell G. BA in Biology cum laude, Franklin and Marshall Coll., 1979; MD, Tulane U., New Orleans, 1983. Diplomate Am. Bd. Neurol. Surgery. Asst. prof. neurol. surgery Med. Coll., Richmond, Va., 1989—91, Orlando Neurol. Assocs., 1991—92, Fla. Neurosurgery, 1992—2001; neurosurgeon Neurol. Assoc. La., Lafayette, 2001—; clin. asst. prof. dept. neurosurgery Tulane U., New Orleans, 2003—. Chmn. dept. neurosurgery Fla. Hosp. Med. Ctr., Orlando, 1995—96; med. dir. Fla. Hosp. Gamma Knife Ctr., Orlando, 1996—2000, Terrebonne Regional Gamma Knife Ctr., Houma, La., 2002—04; chmn. sect. neurosurgery Winter Pk. Meml. Hosp., Fla., 1996—98; founding med. dir. Fla. Hosp. Neuroscience Inst., Orlando, 1998—2000; surg. dir. Cyberknife Ctr., Lafayette, La., 2007—. Active Am. Cancer Soc., Orlando, Fla., 1994—2001. Named one of Top Drs. in Orlando, Orlando Mag., 2001; recipient Norman Rogers prize, Tulane U. Sch. Medicine, 1982; fellow, Alpha Omega Alpha, 1982. Fellow: ACS; mem.: Leksell Gamma Knife Soc., La. Neurosurgical Soc., North Am. Spine Soc., Am. Soc. for Stereotactic and Functional Neurosurgery, World Soc. for Stereotactic and Functional Neurosurgery, Internat. Stereotactic Radiosurgery Soc., Congress Neurol. Surgeons, Am. Assn. Neurol. Surgeons, Cyberknife Soc. Office: Acad Neurosurgery 913 S College Rd Ste 110 Lafayette LA 70503 Home Phone: 337-261-4048; Office Phone: 337-235-7743. Office Fax: 337-235-7614. Personal E-mail: aappley@gmail.com.

APPLEY, MORTIMER HERBERT, psychologist, retired academic administrator; b. NYC, Nov. 21, 1921; s. Benjamin and Minnie (Albert) A.; m. Dee Gordon, June 5, 1942 (div. Oct. 1969); children: Richard Gordon, John Benton; m. Mariann B. Hundahl, Jan. 10, 1971; stepchildren: Scott, Eric, Heidi Hundahl. BS, CCNY, 1942; MA, U. Denver, 1946; PhD, U. Mich., 1950; DSc (hon.), York U., 1975; DHL (hon.), Northeastern U., 1983; LittD (hon.), Am. Internat. Coll., 1984; LLD (hon.), Clark U., 1984. Instr. U. Denver, 1945-47; instr. U. Mich., 1947-49; asst. prof. Wesleyan U., Middletown, Conn., 1949-52; prof., chmn. psychology Conn. Coll., New London, 1952-60, So. Ill. U., Carbondale, 1960-62, York U., Toronto, Ont., Canada, 1962-67, dean faculty grad. studies, 1965-68; prof., chmn. psychology U. Mass., Amherst, 1967-69; dean Grad. Sch., 1969-74, asso. provost, 1973-74; pres. Clark U., Worcester, Mass., 1974-84; vis. scholar psychology Harvard U., 1984-88, lectr., extension, 1985-95, vis. prof., 1985-86; exec. dir., Commn. on the Future of the Univ. U. Mass., Boston, 1988-89. Cons. NSF, NIMH, NRC of Can., Can. Council, VA., AAAS, MacArthur Found. Author: (with C.N. Cofer) Motivation: Theory and Research, 1964, (with R. Trumbull) Psychological Stress, 1967, (with J. Rickwood) Psychology in Canada, 1967, (with R. Trumbull) Dynamics of Stress, 1986, (with L. Lasagna) Who are the Elderly, 1986, (with W.B. Maher) Social and Behavioral Sciences, 1989, Learning to Lead, 1989; editor: Adaption Level Theory: A Symposium, 1971, Motivation and Emotion, 1976-88; assoc. editor Psychol. Abstracts, 1961-62; editor, contbr. Internat. Ency. Neurology, Psychology, Psychoanalysis and Psychiatry; contbr. articles to profl. jours. Chmn. bd. mgrs. Unitarian Fellowship, Toronto; vestryman King's Chapel, Boston; trustee Nantucket Atheneum. With USAAF, 1942-45. NSF Sci. Faculty fellow, 1959-60, Fulbright fellow, Germany, 1973-74. Fellow AAAS, APA (past chmn. edn. and tng. bd.), Can. Psychol. Assn. (bd. dirs.); mem. Conn. Psychol. Assn. (past pres.), New Eng. Psychol. Assn. (past pres.), St. Botolph Club (Boston, pres. 1997-2000), Worcester Econ. Club (pres. 1980-81), Wharf Rats (Nantucket), Sigma Xi, Psi Chi, Phi Sigma. Democrat. Unitarian Universalist. Home: Two Commonwealth Ave Boston MA 02116 Personal E-mail: mappley@comcast.net.

APPLEYARD, DAVID FRANK, retired mathematics professor; b. South Haven, Mich., July 13, 1939; s. Edwin Ray and Hertense Ruth (Guilford) A.; m. Joey Hierlmeier, Aug. 5, 1967; children: David Wayne, Gregory Jay, Robert James. BA, Carleton Coll., 1961; MS, U. Wis., 1963, PhD, 1970. Teaching asst. in math. U. Wis., Madison, 1961-66; prof. math. and computer science Carleton Coll., Northfield, Minn., 1966—2007, Lloyd P. Johnson Norwest Found. prof. liberal arts, 1993—2007, dean students, 1977—83, faculty pres., 1988-91; ret., 2007. Carleton Coll. faculty athletic rep. to Midwest Collegiate Athletic Conf., 1975-83, pres., 1982-83 Trustee United Ch. Christ, Northfield, 1969—72. Recipient Cowling Cup for career achievement, 2002; NSF fellow, 1964, grantee prin. investigator, 1993—97; NASA traineeship, 1965-66; Sloan Found. grantee, 1969, 73, 84. Mem.: Nat. Coun. Tchrs. Math., Math. Assn. Am. (N. Ctrl. sect., award for disting. coll. or univ. tchg. 2006), Sigma Xi. Avocations: canoeing, vintage baseball. Home: 6450 134th St E Northfield MN 55057-4611 E-mail: dappleya@carleton.edu.

APPLEYARD, DIANE PAIGE, human service administrator; b. Sept. 23, 1947; BA, Birmingham-So. Coll., 1969; MA in English, Vanderbilt U., 1973. Asst. editor Meth. Pub. Co., 1971-73; secondary sch. tchr. Escambia County, Fla., 1973-78; tchr. Dept. Def., Germany, 1973-78; dir. John Appleyard Agy., Inc., 1984—, v.p., 1989—; pres. Healthcare R&D Inst., Inc., Pensacola, Fla. Bd. dirs. U.S. Girls Scout Coun., W. Fla., v.p., 1988-95; bd. dirs. N.W. Fla. Rehab. Found., 1989-95, Pensacola Jr. Coll. Found., 1990—, Pensacola Jr. Coll., 1993—; trustee Nat. Com. Quality Health Care, 1995—, mem. exec. com., 1995—. Office: Healthcare R&D Inst Inc 4400 Bayou Blvd Pensacola FL 32503-2673 Fax: 850-494-0289.

APPS, JEROLD WILLARD, writer; b. Wild Rose, Wis., July 25, 1934; s. Herman E. and Eleaner S. (Witt) A.; m. Ruth Ellen Olson, May 20, 1961; children: Susan, Steven, Jeffrey. BS, U. Wis., 1955, MS, 1957, PhD, 1967. Extension agt. U. Wis., Green Lake, 1957-60, Green Bay, 1960-62, asst. prof. Madison, 1962-67, assoc. prof., 1967-69, prof. adult and continuing edn., 1969-94; prof. emeritus, 1994—. Vis. prof. N.C. State U., Raleigh, 1979, U. Guelph, Ont., Can., 1980, U. Alta., Can., 1982, 89, U. Man., Can., 1986, U. Victoria, Can., 1991, U. Alaska, 1995, 97, No. Ill. U., 1996. Author: The Land Still Lives, 1970, How to Improve Adult Education in Your Church, 1972, Cabin in the Country, 1972, Toward a Working Philosophy of Adult Education, 1973, Ideas for Better Church Meetings, 1975, Barns of Wisconsin, 1977, rev. edit., 1995, Problems in Continuing Education, 1979, Spanish edit., 1983, Mills of Wisconsin and the Midwest, 1980, The Adult Learner on Campus: A Guide for Instructors and Administrators, 1981, Study Skills: For Adults Returning to School, 1981, Improving Your Writing Skills, 1982, Improving Practice in Continuing Education, 1985, Skiing into Wisconsin: A Celebration of Winter, 1985, Higher Education in a Learning Society, 1988, Study Skills for Today's College Student, 1990, Mastering the Teaching of Adults, 1991, Breweries of Wisconsin, 1992, rev. 2004, Leadership for the Emerging Age, 1994, One-Room Country Schools, 1996, Rural Wisdom, 1997, Traveler's Companion, 1997, Cheese: The Making of a Wisconsin Tradition, 1998, When Chores Were Done, 1999, Symbols: Viewing a Rural Past, 2000, Humor from the Country, 2001, The People Came First: A History of Wisconsin Cooperative Extension, 2002, Eat Rutabagas, 2002, Stormy, 2002, The Travels at Increase Joseph, 2003, Ringlingville USA, 2004, Every Farm Tells A Story, 2005, Tents, Tigers and The Ringling Brothers, 2006, Living A Country Year, 2007, In A Pickle: A Family Farm STory, 2007. Capt. U.S. Army, 1956. Recipient Non-Fiction Book award of merit Wis. Hist. Soc., 1978, 81, 93, 99, 2003, Wis. Idea award, 1994, Robert E. Gard Excellence in Lit. award, 1996, Wis. 4-H Alumni award, 1998, Midwest Favorite Book award Upper Midwest Booksellers, 1999, 2000, 02, Pride of Wis. award Barnes and Noble Booksellers, 2001, 02, Major Achievement award Wis. Coun. Writers, 2007; recognized for Outstanding Lit. Achievement, Wis. Libr. Assn. Mem. Am. Assn. Adult and Continuing Edn. (mem. exec. com. 1975-76, Rsch. to Practice award 1982), Commn. Profls. of Adult Edn. (pres. 1972-74), Wis. Acad. Scis., Arts and Letters (pres. 1987), Wis. Assn. Adult and Continuing Edn. (pres. 1969, Outstanding Adult Educator of Yr. award 1986), Wis. Coun. Writers (pres. 1978-80, Best Non-Fiction Book award 1977, Scholarly Book award 1988, 2003, Outstanding Title, 2005, Non-Fiction Book award 2006). Business E-Mail: jwapps@wisc.edu.

APRIKYAN, ANDRANIK ANDREW GOORGEN, molecular biologist, biomedical researcher; b. Yerevan, Armenia, Mar. 27, 1962; arrived in U.S., 1993; s. Goorgen Vardevan and Vera Aprikyan; m. Anoush Oganesian-Aprikyan, Feb. 27, 1988; children: Tatevik, Helen. BS (hon.), Yerevan U., 1983; MS (hon.), Moscow U., 1984; PhD in Molecular Biology, Inst. of Molecular Biology, Moscow, 1988. Scientist, sr. scientist dept. neurochemistry of aging Inst. of Biochemistry, Yerevan, 1989—93; sr. fellow dept. medicine and oncology U. Wash., Seattle, 1994—98, rsch. asst. prof. medicine dept. medicine and hematology, 1999—. Contbr. articles to profl. jours. Mem. supreme adv. bd. Ministry of Economy, Yerevan, 1991—93. Recipient Rsch. Grant award, Amgen, Inc, 1999—2000, Nat. Merit award, Nat. Acad. Sci. Armenia, 1991, Gold Medal of Excellency, Ministry of Sci. and Edn., 1979, Reserach Grant award, Am. Cancer Soc., Inc., 2000—01, Nat. Merit award, Nat. Acad. Sci. Armenia, 1992; grantee U.S. HHS, NIH-NCI, 2001—. Mem.: AAAS, Internat. Soc. of Exptl. Hematology (Merit award 2001), Am. Soc. of Hematology (Merit/Travel award 1996, Merit/Travel Award 1997, 1998). Achievements include patents for substance prolonging the lifespan of experimental animals. Home: Orbeli St 63-32 Yerevan 375028 Armenia Office: U Washington Box 356422 1959 NE Pacific St Seattle WA 98195 Personal E-mail: apri@u.washington.edu.

APRISON, MORRIS HERMAN, retired experimental and theoretical neurobiology educator; b. Milw., Oct. 6, 1923; s. Henry and Ethel Aprison; m. Shirley Reder, Aug. 21, 1949; children— Barry, Robert. BS in Chemistry, U. Wis., 1945, tchrs. cert., 1947, MS in Physics, 1949, PhD in Biochemistry, 1952. Grad. teaching asst. in physics U. Wis., Madison, 1947-49; grad. research asst. in pathology Sch. Medicine, 1950-51, grad. research asst. in biochemistry, 1951-52; tech. asst. in physics Inst. Paper Chemistry, Appleton, Wis., 1949-50; biochemist, prin. investigator, head biophysics sect. Galesburg (Ill.) State Research Hosp., 1952-56; prin. research investigator in biochemistry Inst. Psychiat. Research; asst. prof. depts. biochemistry and psychiatry Ind. U. Med. Sch., Indpls., 1956-60, asso. prof., 1960-64, prof. biochemistry, 1964-78, distinguished prof. neurobiology and biochemistry, 1978-93, disting. prof. emeritus, 1993—, chief neurobiology sect., 1969-74. Mem. exec. com. dept. psychiatry, exec. adminstr. Inst. Psychiat. Rsch., 1973-74, dir. inst., 1974-78, chief sect. applied and theoretical neurobiology, 1978-93; co-chmn. session on neurotransmitters 23d Internat. Physiol. Congress, 1965; chmn. session neurochemistry and neuropharmacology 25th Congress, 1971; ad hoc mem. study sect. psychopharmacology NIMH, 1967-71, mem. neuropsychology study sect., 1970-74; mem. molecular and cellular neurobiology program adv. panel NSF, 1984-86; mem. com. recommendations U.S. Army sci. rsch. Nat. Rsch. Coun. Bd. Physics and Astronomy, 1987-89; mem. gov. bd. Inst. for Advanced Study Ind. U., Bloomington, 1989-92; vis. prof. 4th ASPET Workshop, Vanderbilt U., 1972; guest scholar Grad. Sch., Kans. State U., 1973. Adv. editor Neurosci. Rsch., 1968-73, Jour. Biol. Psychiatry, 1968-83, Neuropharmacology, 1969-93, Jour. Neurochemistry, 1972-75, Pharmacology, Biochemistry and Behavior, 1973-89, Jour. Comparative and General Pharmacology, 1974-75, Jour. Gen. Pharmacology, 1975-93, Jour. Developmental Psychobiology, 1974-77; regional editor Life Scis., 1970-73; co-editor Advances in Neurochemistry, 1973-92; mem. editorial bd. Jour. Neurochemistry, 1975-79, dep. chief editor, 1980-83; mem. editorial bd. Neurochem. Rsch., 1975-82, Jour. Neurosci. Rsch., 1984-92; co-editor 10 books; contbr. more than 355 rsch. articles and abstracts to profl. jours., chpts. to books, including one in History of Neuroscience in Autobiography, vol. 3, 2001. Mem. Ind. regional adv. bd. Anti-Defamation League, 1973-76; bd. overseers St. Meinrad Sem., 1974-77. Served with USNR, 1944-46. Recipient First 50th Univ. award, Inst. Psychiat. Rsch., 2007. Mem. Am. Physiol. Soc., Biophys. Soc., Soc. Biol. Psychiatry (program com. 1974-75, co-chmn. 1975-76, gold medal 1975), Internat. Brain Rsch. Orgn., Internat. Soc. Neurochemistry (co-chmn. session 1st internat. meeting Strasbourg, France 1967, 4th meeting Tokyo 1973, 7th meeting Jerusalem 1979, coun. 1973-75, sec. 1975-79, chmn. 1979-81, publicity com. 1975-83, nominating com. 1983-87, policy adv. com. 1985-98, ad hoc and founding rules com. 1998-2000, standing rules com., 2000—), Am. Soc. Neurochemistry (co-chmn. sci. program com. 1972, mem. 1973), Soc. for Neurosci. (pres. Indpls. chpt. 1970-71), Sigma Xi. Achievements include development of the Morris Aprison lecture in biological psychiatry 2006-; having the department of psychiatry at Indiana Universities School of Medicine create awards in his honor from 1999-2005 for the best research towards a PhD in medical neurobiology. Home: 9268 Spring Forest Dr Indianapolis IN 46260-1266

APRUZZESE, PHILIP JOHN, educational association administrator, educator; s. Philip John and Margaret Rose Apruzzese; m. Margaret R. Tarascio, June 14, 1969; children: Jason Miles, Aaron Matthew, Ian Douglas, Jennifer Elizabeth. BS, Ctrl. Conn. State Coll., 1971; MS, Ctrl. Conn. State U., 1978. Cert. tchr. State Dept. Edn., Conn., 1971. Educator Wethersfield (Conn.) Bd. Edn., 1971—97; treas. Conn. Edn. Assn., Hartford, Conn., 1997—2000, v.p., 2000—06, pres., 2006—. Pres. Conn. Edn. Found., Hartford, 2000—06; presenter Conn. Sch. Indoor Environ. Resource Team, Hartford, 2003—04. Lobbyist Conn. Edn. Assn., 1996—2006. Recipient Nat. Environ. award, U.S. EPA, 2003, Environ. Merit award, 2004, Sch. Drug Testing Panel award, Gov.'s Prevention Partnership, 2005. Fellow: Conn. Acad. Math, Sci. and Tech.; mem.: Phi Delta Kappa. Independent. Achievements include development of training model of school teams to detect indoor quality issues in Connecticut schools. Avocations: swimming, golf, fishing, woodworking, fly tying. Office: Connecticut Education Association 21 Oak Street Hartford CT 06106 Office Phone: 860-525-5641. Office Fax: 860-725-6388. Personal E-mail: phila@cca.org. Business E-Mail: phila@cea.org.

APRUZZESE, VINCENT JOHN, lawyer; b. Newark, Nov. 1, 1928; s. John and Mildred (Cerefice) A.; m. Marie A. Yeager, July 10, 1955; children: Barbara, John, Donald, Lynn, Kathy. BA, Rutgers U., 1950; LLB, U. Pa., 1953. Bar: N.J. 1954, U.S. Dist. Ct. N.J. 1954, U.S. Ct. Appeals (3d cir.) 1962, U.S. Supreme Ct. 1970, U.S. Ct. Appeals (D.C. cir. 1973), U.S. Ct. Appeals (4th cir.) 1973, D.C. 1976, N.Y. 1983. Assoc. Lum, Fairlie & Foster, Newark, 1953-54; sole practice Newark, 1954-55, 58-65; sr. ptnr. Apruzzese & McDermott, Newark, 1965-70, pres. Springfield, N.J., 1970-90, Liberty Corner and Newark. Mem. legal adv. bd. Martindale-Hubbell, 1991-98. Bd. dirs. St. Barnabas Hosp., Papermill Playhouse. With JAGC, USAF, 1956-57. Mem. ABA (mem. coun. labor and employment law sect. 1984-94, chair labor & employment law sect. 1992-93, bd. govs. 1988-91), Coll. of Labor and Employment Lawyers, Fed. Bar Assn., Internat. Labor Law Soc. (treas.), Am. Coll. Trial Lawyers, Am. Bar Found., Fed. Bar State N.J., N.J. State Bar Assn. (pres. 1982-84), Essex County Bar Assn., Somerset County Bar Assn., Baltusrol Country Club (Springfield), Chatham (Mass.) Beach and Tennis Club, Eastward Ho Country Club (Chatham). Office: Apruzzese McDermott Mastro & Murphy PO Box 112 25 Independence Blvd Liberty Corner NJ 07938 E-mail: vapruzzese@excite.com.

APSEL, ALYSSA, electrical and computer engineer; BS in Elec. Engring., Swarthmore Coll., 1995; MS in Elec. Engring., Calif. Inst. Tech., 1996; PhD in Elec. Engring., Johns Hopkins U., 2002. Undergraduate research fellow U. of Pa, SUNFEST, 1994; grad. research asst., electrical engineering Calf. Institute of Technology, 1995—97; grad. research asst., electrical and computer engineering Johns Hopkins U., 1998—; grad. research asst., army research lab Adelphi, 2000—. Teaching asst., engineering methodology Swarthmore College, 1993; teaching asst., integrated electronics Johns Hopkins U., 1998, teaching asst., lab asst., Advanced Integrated Circuits, 99. Fellow Caltech Institute Fellowship, California Institute of Technology, 1995—96, Abel Wolman Fellowship, Johns Hopkins University, 1997—98. Achievements include patents for Integrated electronic-optoelectronic devices and method of making the same, 2000; Low Power, Differential Optical Receiver in Silicon on Sapphire, 2001. Office: Johns Hopkins U Dept Computer & Electrical Engineering 3400 N Charles St Baltimore MD 21218

APT, CHARLES, artist; b. NYC, Dec. 10, 1933; s. Gustav Lee and Tami (Vera Salzman) A.; m. Ursula Edith Betz, July 24, 1959; children— Gregory, Sam. B.F.A., Pratt Inst., 1956. Exhibited in group shows at Mus. Fine Art, Springfield, Mass., 1966, Expn. Intercontinentale, Monaco, France, 1966, 68, NAD, 1965, 68, 77-81, 83, 85, 87, 99, 2001, 03, 05, 07, Am. Watercolor Soc., 1965-66, 68-69, Allied Artists Am., 1964-65, 67, 69-70, 72, Nat. Mus. Racing, Saratoga, N.Y., 1967, Atlantic City Race Track, 1967, Nat. Arts Club, 1967; one-man shows Ground Floor Art Gallery, N.Y.C., 1967-69, Aqueduct Race Track Art Gallery, N.Y.C., 1967, Grand Central Art Galleries, 1969, Far Gallery, N.Y.C., 1972, 78, Palm Beach (Fla.) Galleries, 1973, Talisman Gallery, Bartlesville, Okla., 1976, Gallery 52, South Orange, N.J., 1976-77, Lorings Gallery, Cedarhurst, N.Y., 1985, 87, Dassin Gallery, L.A., Loring Gallery, Sheffield, Mass., 2007. Served with AUS, 1956-58. Recipient Gold medal Am. Vets. Soc. Artists, 1965; Best in Show award Saratoga Mus. Racing Ann., 1967; 2d Benjamin Altman award for figure painting NAD, 1968; Le Prix Prince Souverain Monaco, 1968; Bronze medal Nat. Arts Club, 1971; Sutherland prize Annual Open Oil Exhbn., 1972; Ject-key prize Salmagundi Club, 1972, prize, 1966, 68-69, 71, Williams award Salmagundi Club, 1966, 68, 1st prize Product Design award for Aquarelle fabric collection Resource Coun., 1984, 1st prize Am. Artists Profl. League, 1965, Talens award, 1966 Mem. NAD (academician, Briggs Meml. award 1989), Artists Equity Assn. N.Y. Studio: 152 South Almont Dr Los Angeles CA 90048 Personal E-mail: chazapt@yahoo.com.

APT, LEONARD, physician; AB with highest honors, U. Pa., 1942; MD with highest honors, Jefferson Med. Coll., 1945. Diplomate Am. Bd. Pediat., Am. Bd. Ophthalmology. Intern Jefferson Med. Coll. Hosp., Phila., 1945-46; rsch. fellow in pathology-hematology, resident in pediat. Children's Hosp., Detroit, 1946-49, resident in pediat. Cin., 1949—50, Children's Med. Ctr., Boston, 1950-52, chief med. resident, 1952-53, asst. physician, 1953-55; resident in ophthalmology Wills Eye Hosp., Phila., 1955-57; first spl. fellow in pediat. ophthalmology NIH, Bethesda, and Children's Hosp., Washington, 1957—59; first fellow in Pediat. Ophthalmology Wills Eye Hosp., Phila., 1959—61; from asst. prof. to prof. ophthalmology Sch. Medicine, UCLA, 1961—72, prof., 1972—; disting. prof. UCLA, 1993—; attending surgeon Jules Stein Eye Inst., UCLA, founding dir. divsn. pediat. ophthalmology, 1961—81, founder, 1966, dir. emeritus, 1981—, co-dir. ctr. to prevent childhood blindness, 2005—. Tchg. fellow in pediat. Harvard U. Med. Sch., Boston, 1950—52, instr. pediat., 1953—55; sr. physician radioisotope unit Boston VA Hosp., 1953—55; cons. pediat. ophthalmology Cedars-Sinai Med. Ctr., LA, St. John's Hosp., Santa Monica, Calif., Bur. Maternal and Child Health, Dept. Pub. Health Calif., Dept. Health, LA. Author: Diagnostic Procedures in Pediatric Ophthalmology, 1963; mem. editl. bd.: numerous med. jours.; contbr. articles to profl. jours., chapters to books. Founder L.A. Philharmonic Assn.; presdl. circle mem. L.A. County Mus. of Art; v.p. fin. UCLA Grunwald Ctr. for Graphic Arts, Hammer Mus.; bd. dirs. Royce Ctr. Cir., UCLA Performing Arts Dept.; bd. dirs. Cmty. Outreach Program UCLA Design for Sharing; founder John Wooden UCLA Athletic Ctr.; exec. coun. mem. UCLA Divsn. of Humanities; founder UCLA Acosta Athletic Tng. Complex; judge Wines of Am. Ann. Competition. 1st lt. M.C. US Army, 1943—46. Recipient F.T. Stewart Surgery prize, Jefferson Med. Coll., 1945, Arthur J. Bedell Resident Rsch. prize, Wills Eye Hosp., Phila., 1957, Disting. Alumnus Achievement award, Jefferson Med. Coll., 1992, 1st Escalon Sci. award, 1992, Hall of Fame Distinction award, Cin. Pediat. Hist. Soc., 1994, 1st Disting. Alumni award, Sch. Arts and Scis. U. Pa., 1995, Alumni Univ. Svc. award, UCLA, 1996, William Feinbloom 1st Disting. Achievement award, 1999, Profl. Achievement award, UCLA Med. Alumni Assn., 1999, 1st Disting. Achievement award, Ethicon Inc.-Johnson & Johnson Co., 1999, S. Rodman Irvine prize, Jules Stein Eye Inst., UCLA, 2005. Mem.: AMA, Am. Med. Writers Assn., Pacific Coast Oto-Ophthal. Soc., Internat. Strabismol. Assn., Am. Assn. Pediat. Ophthalmology and Strabismus (1st Disting. Achievement award 1996, Honor award 1995), Soc. Pediat. Rsch., Assn. for Rsch. Ophthalmology, Am. Ophthal. Soc., Am. Acad. Pediats. (Lifetime Achievement award 2000, Ann. Leonard Apt Lectureship named in his honor 2000), Am. Acad. Ophthalmology (Honor award 1968), L'Ordre Mondial des Gourmets Deguistaeurs, Confrerie de la Chaine des Rotisseurs, Internat. Wine and Food Soc., Shriner, Masons (32d deg.), Alpha Omega Alpha. Avocations: sports, art, theater, gourmet food, oenology. Office: UCLA Sch Medicine Jules Stein Eye Inst 100 Stein Plz Los Angeles CA 90095-7000 Office Phone: 310-825-3986. Office Fax: 310-206-3652.

APTED, MICHAEL DAVID, film director; b. London, Feb. 10, 1941; BA, Downing Coll., Cambridge, Eng., 1963. Pres. Directors Guild Am., 2003—; mem. bd. govs. Acad. Motion Picture Arts and Scis. (documentary br.), 2002—. Dir.: (films) Triple Echo, 1972, Stardust, 1974, The Squeeze, 1976, Agatha, 1977, Coalminer's Daughter, 1980 (DGA nominee), Continental Divide, 1981, Gorky Park, 1983, Kipperbang, 1983 (Brit. Acad. TV and Film award nominee), Firstborn, 1984, Critical Condition, 1986, Gorillas in the Mist, 1988, Class Action, 1990, Thunderheart, 1991, Blink, 1993, Nell, 1994, Extreme Measures, 1996, Always Outnumbered, 1998, The World Is Not Enough, 1999, Enigma, 2000, Enough, 2002, Lipstick, 2002, Amazing Grace, 2006; (play) Strawberry Fields, 1978 (BAFTA, Emmy award); (documentaries) 14 UP, 21 UP (Internat. Emmy), 28 UP (Brit. Acad. award, Internat. Emmy), 1985, Bring On the Night, 1984 (Emmy, Grammy awards), The Long Way Home, 1989, Incident at Oglala, 1991, 35 UP, 1992 (BAFTA award), Moving the Mountain, 1993 (IDA award), Inspirations, 1997, 42 Up, 1998, Me & Isaac Newton, 1999, Married in America, 2002, 49 Up, 2005; (Brit. TV) Slattery's Mounted Foot, 1970 (Brit. Critics Best Play), The Mosedale Horshoe, 1971 (Brit. Critics Best Play), Another Sunday and Sweet F.A., 1972 (Brit. Critics Best Play), Follyfoot, 1972 (Best Children's Svcs.), Kisses at Fifty (Brit. Critics Best Play, SFTA Best Dir.), The Collection (Internat. Emmy), (Am. TV) Big Breadwinner Hog, 1969, The Lovers, 1970, Follyfoot, 1971, My Life and Times, 1991, Crossroads, 1992, New York News, 1995, Rome, 2005 (Outstanding Directorial Achievement in Dramatic Series Night Directors Guild Am., 2005).*

APTEKAR, DORIS MAE WEINBERG, psychotherapist, school psychologist, hypnotherapist; b. Bronx, NY; d. Jack Weinberg and Mildred Rosofsky; m. Seymour Aptekar, May 31, 1987; children: Liandra Heather, Jordanne Arielle Weinstein. BA, Boston U., 1965; MS, Queens Coll., 1975; PhD, Fordham U., 1987. Cert. sch. psychologist NY, bilingual sch. psychologist, educator NY, 1987, elem. tchr. NY, advanced hypnotherapist NY, lic. mental health counselor NY. Elem. tchr., spl. edn. tchr., NYC, 1961—74; sch. psychologist Amityville Union Free Sch. Dist., NY, 1975—2003, Nassau County Bd. Coop. Edn. Sys., 1977—78; pvt. practice Roslyn Estates, NY, 1975—. Pre-sch. cons. Manchester Recreation Ctr., Vt., 2003—; cons. South Shore Health Ctr., Freeport, NY, 2004—, Willow Rd. Sch., Franklin Sq., NY, 2006, Vincent Smith Sch., Pt. Washington, NY, 2006—; evaluator, counselor Quality Evaluations, Rego Pk., NY, 2005—. Active Planned Parenthood. Recipient Svc. award, NYC Works Cmty. Workshop, 1989. Mem.: NOW, NE Psychol. Assn., NC Psychol. Assn., US Charter Students Against Drunk Driving, Mothers Against Drunk Driving, Naral, Nature Conservancy, Sierra Club, Nat. Honor Soc. Psychology. Avocations: tennis, travel, reading, ecology. Home: Roslyn Estates 30 The Hemlocks Roslyn NY 11576 also: 633 McNamara Rd Dorset VT 05251 Office Phone: 516-484-6351. Personal E-mail: doctordma@msn.com.

APTEKAR, KEN, painter; b. Detroit, May 13, 1950; BFA, U. Mich., 1973; MFA, Pratt Inst., 1975. Studio artist, NYC. Solo shows include Jack Shainman Gallery, NYC, 1994, 96, Palmer Mus. Art Pa. State U., 1995, Corcoran Gallery Art, 1997, Cummer Mus. Art, Jacksonville, Fla., 1998, Steinbaum-Krauss Gallery, NYC, 1999, Victoria and Albert Mus., London, 2001, Meml. Art Gallery, Rochester, NY, 2002, Kemper Mus., Kansas City, 2001, Coll. Wooster, Ohio, 2002, Pamela Auchincloss Projects, NYC, 2001, Contemporary Art Ctr. Va., 2001-02, Bernice Steinbaum Gallery, 2001, 03;, Douglas Cooley Gallery, Reed Coll., Portland, Oreg., 2004, Espace Camille Lambert, Juvisy, France, 2005, James Graham and Sons Gallery, NYC, 2006, Musee Robert Dubois-Corneau, Brunoy, France, 2006; exhibited in group shows at Carnegie-Mellon U. Mus., Pitts., 1991, Corcoran Gallery, Washington, 1993-94, 97-98, Flint (Mich.) Inst. Art, 1993, Wight Gallery UCLA, 1994, Yerba Buena Ctr. Contemporary Art, San Francisco, 1994, Walters Art Gallery, Balt., 1995, Calif. Ctr. Contemporary Art, Escondido, 1996, Kohler Arts Ctr., Wis., 1996, Jewish Mus., N.Y.C., San Francisco, 1996, Armand Hammer Mus., L.A., 1996, Islip Art Mus., N.Y., 1998, Ashville Mus. Art, 2003; represented in permanent collections Kemper Mus., Kansas City, Mo., Corcoran Gallery Art, Washington D.C., Victoria & Albert Mus., London, Meml. Art Gallery, Rochester, Niagara U., Denver Mus. Art, Progressive Corp., Jewish Mus., Bell Atlantic Corp., Nat. Mus. Am. Art, Washington, Harvard U. Recipient Pollock-Krasner Found. award, 1989; NEA fellow, 1987, 95, Bellagio residency Rockefeller Found., 1992, artist residency Ucross Found., Wyo., 1992, painting residency Resident Artists Program Djerassi, 1991, 94, Mid Atlantic Arts Found. award, 1998. Home: 201 W 85th St Apt 7E New York NY 10024-3909 Home Phone: 646-736-7513. E-mail: kenaptekar@verizon.net.

APUD, JOSE ANTONIO, psychiatrist, educator; b. San Miguel de Tucuman, Argentina, May 25, 1948; came to U.S., 1987; s. Jose and Emelin (Chagra) A.; m. Graciela Varela, Jan. 25, 1979; children: Maria Macarena, Jose Sebastian. MD, U. Tucuman, 1975; degree in pharmacology, U. Milan, 1980, degree in exptl. endocrinology, 1983; PhD, U. Buenos Aires, 1985. Diplomate Am. Bd. Psychiatry and Neurology. Investigator CONICET, Buenos Aires, 1985—98; prof. pharmacology U. Buenos Aires, 1985-93; psychiatrist in residence St. Elizabeth's Hosp. NIMH, Washington, 1991—95; clin. assoc. neuropsychiatry br. NIMH, Washington, 1995-98; faculty psychiatry residency tng. program Commn. on Mental Health Svcs., 1998—2000; dir. psychopharmacology divsn. St. Elizabeths Hosp. Commn. on Mental Health Svcs., 1998—2000; med. dir. schizophrenia inpatient rsch. program NIMH, 2002—05; clin. dir. genes, cognition and psychosis program, clin. brain disorder br. NIMH/NIH, 2005—. Cons. Farmitalia Carlo Erba Labs, Milan, 1979-83; vis. prof. pharmacology Georgetown U., Washington, 1987-91, instr. dept. psychiatry, 1995-98, prof. psychiatry, 1998—; mem. editl. bd. Endocrinologia Clinica y Metabolism, 1982—, Neuroendocrinologia Latinoamericana, 1982—. Contbr. numerous articles to profl. jours. Fellow Nat. Atomic Energy Commn., 1976, Dept. Endocrinology French Hosp., 1978, Inst. Pharmacology U. Milan, 1978-84, sr. staff fellow St. Elizabeth's Hosp. NIMH, 1994-98; recipient Cediquifa award in pharmacology, 1992, Upjohn award NIMH, 1993. Mem. AMA, Am. Psychiat. Assn. (sci. com. 1993-95, Burroughs Wellcome award 1993), Am. Soc. Clin. Psychopharmacology, Washington Psychiat. Soc., Italian Soc. Neurosci., Italian Soc. Pharmacology, Soc. for Neurosci., Sociedad Argentina de Farmacologia Exptl., Internat. Soc. Psychoneuroendocrinology, Internat. Soc. Neuroendocrinology, Argentina Soc. Biology and Nuclear Medicine, Serotonin Club. Roman Catholic. Achievements include identification of Gabaergic system in rats; study of the mechanism of action of psychotropic drugs; studies on schizophrenia and tardive dyskinesia, pharmacogenomics in schizophrenia; identification of an endogenous ligand for the serotonin-2 receptor in the rat brain. Office: NIMH Clin Brain Disorders Br Bldg 10 Rm CRC 7-3342 10 Center Dr Bethesda MD 20892 E-mail: apudj@intra.nimh.nih.gov.

APUZZO, MICHAEL LAWRENCE JOHN, neurological surgeon; b. New Haven, 1940; BA, Yale U., 1961; MD, Boston U., 1965. Intern in neurosurgery Yale U.; resident in surgery McGill U., 1966; resident in neurosurgery Yale U., New Haven, 1967-73; prof. neurol. surgery, radiation oncology, biology and physics U. So. Calif. Sch. Medicine, LA. Editor Neurosurgery on-line; contbr. over 600 articles to profl. jours. Office: U So Calif Sch Medicine Ste 5046 1200 N State St Los Angeles CA 90033-1029 Office Phone: 323-442-3001. Business E-Mail: apuzzo@usc.edu.

AQUILA, FRANCIS JOSEPH, lawyer; b. NYC, Feb. 3, 1957; s. Frank Joseph and Evelyn Jane (Farrell) A.; m. Catherine Spinella, June 10, 1984; children: Jessica Lynn, Jillian Rose, Elaina Kathryn. AB, Columbia U., 1979; JD summa cum laude, Bklyn. Law Sch., 1983. Bar: NY 1984. Ptnr. mergers and acquisitions Sullivan & Cromwell, NYC, 1991—. Exec. dir. Young Dems. of Am., Washington, 1981-83; v.p. US Youth Coun., Washington, 1982-84; mem. Dem. Nat. Com., 1979-81; Trustee exec. com. St. Peter's Univ. Hosp. and Health System, New Brunswick, NJ, 1998—; mem. Nat. Adv. Bd., NALP Found. for Edn. and Training, Washington,

1997—, Adv. Bd. Salavation Army of Greater NY, 2001—. Recipient Burton award, 2005. Mem. ABA, NY State Bar Assn., Assoc. of the Bar of the City of NY Democrat. Roman Catholic. Office: Sullivan & Cromwell 125 Broad St Fl 28 New York NY 10004-2489 Office Phone: 212-558-4048. Office Fax: 212-558-3588. Business E-Mail: aquilaf@sullcrom.com.

AQUILINO, DANIEL, banker; b. Needham, Mass., Feb. 4, 1924; s. Michael Aquilino and Anna (Bruno) A.; m. Theresa H. Barberio, Nov. 9, 1946; children: Donna Lee, Daniel C., Michael D. BS magna cum laude, Northeastern U., 1949; grad., Rutgers U., 1962. With Fed. Res. Bank Boston, 1949-85, exec. v.p., 1970-85, Bank of New Eng., Boston, 1985-89; cons. Boston, 1990—. Served with AUS, 1943-45. Recipient Sears B. Condit award Northeastern U., 1947, 49; recognition award Italian-Am. Soc., Inc., 1972. Home: 3 N Bennet Ct Apt 1 Boston MA 02113-1904

AQUILINO, THOMAS JOSEPH, JR., federal judge, educator; b. Mt. Kisco, NY, Dec. 7, 1939; s. Thomas Joseph and Virginia Burr (Doughty) A.; m. Edith Luise Berndt, Oct. 27, 1965; children: Christopher T., Philip A., Alexander B. Student, Cornell U., 1957-59, U. Munich, 1960-61; BA, Drew U., 1962; postgrad., Free U., Berlin, 1965-66; JD, Rutgers U., 1969. Bar: N.Y. 1972, U.S. Dist. Ct. (so., ea. and no. dists.) N.Y. 1973, U.S. Ct. Appeals (2nd cir.) 1973, U.S. Supreme Ct. 1976, U.S. Ct. Appeals (3rd cir.) 1977, Interstate Commerce Commn. 1978, U.S. Ct. Claims 1979, U.S. Ct. Internat. Trade 1984. Law clk. to Hon. John M. Cannella U.S. Dist. Ct. (so. dist.) N.Y., NYC, 1969-71; atty. Davis Polk & Wardwell, NYC, 1971-85; judge U.S. Ct. Internat. Trade, NYC, 1985—2005, sr. judge, 2005—. Adj. prof. law Benjamin N. Cardozo Sch. of Law, 1984-95; mem. bd. visitors Drew U., 1997—. With U.S. Army, 1962-65. Mem. N.Y. State Bar Assn., Fed. Bar Coun. Roman Catholic. Avocations: sports, travel, linguistics, cinema. Office: US Ct Internat Trade 1 Federal Plz New York NY 10278-0001 Office Phone: 212-264-2854.

AQUINO, JOSEPH MARIO, clinical psychologist; b. NYC, Nov. 21, 1947; s. Joseph and Rose (Nasi) A.; m. Kathleen Ann Ryan, Oct. 6, 1990; children: Joseph Patrick, Ryan Thomas, Erin Rose. BA in English, So. Ill. U., 1969, MS in Secondary Edn., 1976; PhD in Clin. Psychology, St. John's U., Jamaica, NY, 1987. Lic. psychologist, N.Y. Tchr. English Wappingers Cen. Schs., Wappingers Falls, NY, 1969-79; intern psychology Maimonides Med. Ctr., Bklyn., 1983-84; specialist in applied behavior sci. Builders for Family and Youth, Bklyn., 1984-85; trainee psychology and psychologist St. Vincent's Svcs., Bklyn., 1984-89; psychologist St. Christopher-Ottilie Svcs., Sea Cliff, NY, 1989-96; pvt. practice psychology NYC area, 1989—. Guest lectr. St. John's U., 1990. Co-author: Situational Leadership for Principals, 1983; mem. editl. bd. Jour. Urban Psychiatry, 1982-84; guest The Women's Line, WVOX 1460 AM, 1994; cited in newspaper articles; contbr. articles to profl. jours. Recipient citation VFW, Wappingers Falls, N.Y., 1977; Bethany House Achievement award Bethany House II, 1991; psychology teaching fellow St. John's U., 1981; cited in article Emergency mag., 1991. Mem. APA, N.Y. State Psychol. Assn., Westchester County Psychol. Assn., Nat. Register of Health Svc. Providers in Psychology, Am. Coll. of Advanced Practice Psychologists (founding fellow). Office: 10 Rye Ridge Plz Ste 214 Rye Brook NY 10573-2857 Office Phone: 914-253-9429. Personal E-mail: werpsyched@aol.com.

ARABATZIS, CONSTANCE ELAINE, lawyer; b. Dania, Fla., Jan. 23, 1961; BS in Health Services Adminstrn., summa cum laude, CUNY, 1986; JD, NYU, 1989. Bar: Conn. 1990, NY 1991, DC 1991, US Dist. Ct. (so. dist.) NY 1992, Fla. 1993. Asst. dist. atty. King's County Dist. Atty. Office, Bklyn., 1989—92; assoc., comm. real estate litig. Finkelstein Borah Schwartz Altschuler & Golstein, 1992—94; in-house counsel Investments Ltd., Fla., 1994—95; sr. assoc. Stephens Lynn Klein & McNicholas, Fla., 1995—98; assoc. Baer Marks & Upham, 1998—2001; sr. assoc., Litig. & Dispute Resolution Group Dickstein Shapiro Morin & Oshinsky LLP, NYC, 2001—, diversity/pro bono coun. Mem.: Fla. Bar, DC Bar, Soc. Human Resource Mgrs., Phi Alpha Delta. Office: Dickstein Shapiro Morin & Oshinsky LLP 1177 Avenue of the Americas New York NY 10036-2714 Office Phone: 212-896-5430, 212-997-9880. Business E-Mail: arabatzise@dsmo.com.

ARABI, MAZDAK, hydrologist, researcher; b. Tehran, Iran, Sept. 11, 1975; s. Habib Arabi and Mahmoudi Mehrbanoo; m. Sybil Elizabeth Sharvelle, Aug. 15, 2003; 1 child, Sybil Elizabeth. BSc in Civil Engring., U. Tehran, 1998, MSCE, 2000; PhD, Purdue U., West Lafayette, Ind., 2005. Grad. rsch. asst. Purdue U., 2001—05, postdoctoral rsch. assoc., 2005—. Cons. Water Resources Rsch. Ctr., Tehran, 1998—2000. Recipient Estus H. and Vashti L. Magoon Outstanding Tchg. award, Purdue U., 2004, Jacques W. Delleur award, 2004, Estus H. and Vashti L. Magoon Outstanding Tchg. award, 2005; Blooser Environ. grantee, 2005. Mem.: ASCE (assoc.). Avocations: playing the tar, soccer. Home: 516 Parkridge Dr West Lafayette IN 47906 Office: ABE Purdue U 225 S University St West Lafayette IN 47907 Home Phone: 765-430-4119; Office Phone: 765-494-1134. Office Fax: 765-496-1115. Business E-Mail: marabi@purdue.edu.

ARABIAN, ARMAND, arbitrator, mediator, lawyer; b. NYC, Dec. 12, 1934; s. John and Aghavnie (Yalian) A.; m. Nancy Arabian, Aug. 26, 1962; children: Allison Ann, Robert Armand. BSBA, Boston U., 1956, JD, 1961; LLM, U. So. Calif., LA, 1970; LLD (hon.), Southwestern Sch. Law, 1990, Pepperdine U., 1990, U. West LA, 1994, We. State U., 1997, Thomas Jefferson Sch. of Law, 1997, Am. Coll. Law, 2001. Bar: Calif. 1962, US Supreme Ct. 1966. Dep. dist. atty. LA County, 1962-63; pvt. practice law Van Nuys, Calif., 1963-72; judge Mcpl. Ct., LA, 1972-73, Superior Ct., LA, 1973-83; assoc. justice Calif. Ct. Appeal, LA, 1983-90, Supreme Ct. Calif., San Francisco, 1990-96. Adj. prof. sch. law Pepperdine U., 1996-98. Contbr. articles to profl. jours. 1st lt. US Army, 1956-58. Recipient Stanley Lintz Meml. award San Fernando Valley Bar Assn., 1986, Lifetime Achievement award San Fernando Valley Bar Assn., 1993, Outstanding Jurist of the Yr., Malibu Bar Assn., 1996, Mesrob Mashdots medal Aram I Catholicos, Beirut, Lebanon, 1999, Mekhitar medal Brotherhood in Venice, Italy, 1999, Gold medal of honor of Peter the Great, Russian Acad. Sci., 1999, Mekhitar Gosh medal Pres. of Armenia Robert Kocharian, 2001, St. James the Apostle medal Beatitude Torkom Manoogian, Jerusalem, 2001, Albert Einstein Gold medal of honor, Russian Acad. Natural Scis., 2003, Ellis Island Medal Honor award, 2004, St. Gregory the Illuminator medal Karekin II Catholicos Yerevan, Armenia, 2004, Women of LA Highlight award, 2005, Fernando Cmty. award vol. efforts, 2006, FErnando award, 2006; Pappas Disting. scholar Boston U. Sch. Law, 1987; Justice Armand Arabian Resource and Comm. Ctrs. named in honor of Van Nuys and San Fernando Calif. Courthouses, 1999; reception area of Chatsworth Superior Courthouse named in honor, Los Angeles County, 2005. Republican. Office: 6259 Van Nuys Blvd Van Nuys CA 91401-2711 Home Phone: 818-708-0010; Office Phone: 818-997-8900. Fax: 818-781-6002. Business E-Mail: honarabian@aol.com.

ARABIE, PHIPPS, marketing educator, researcher; b. Mar. 13, 1948; s. Wade Joseph and Betty Jo (Thomason) A.; m. Terry Feldstein, Feb. 24, 2000. Diploma, Phillips Acad., Andover, 1966; AB, Harvard U., 1970; PhD, Stanford U., 1974. Asst. prof. psychology U. Minn., Mpls., 1974-77, assoc. prof., 1977-80; prof. psychology and sociology U. Ill., Champaign-Urbana, 1980-90; prof. Rutgers U. Sch. Mgmt., Newark, 1990—; chair mktg. Rutgers U. Bus. Sch., Newark, 1990-96, 2000—02. Cons. AT&T Bell Labs, Murray Hill, N.J., 1975-82; Fulbright vis. prof. computer sci. U. Coll., Dublin, Ireland, 1986-87; vis. prof. psychology U. Santiago de Compostela, Spain, 1993; mem. adv. panel on methods, measures and stats. NSF, 1996-97. Co-author: Three-way Scaling and Clustering, 1987, Combinatorial Data Analysis: Optimization by Dynamic Programming, 2001, The Structural Reprentation of Proximity Matrices with MATLAB; co-editor: Clustering and Classification, 1996, Classification, Clustering, and Data Mining Applications, 2004; editor Jour. Classification, 1983-02; contbr. articles to profl. jours.; author computer programs for multidimensional analysis of data. Grantee, NSF, Office Naval Rsch., Nat. Inst. Justice, AT&T; Beckman assoc., U. Ill., 1983—84. Fellow: AAAS, APA, Am. Statis. Assn., Am. Psychol. Soc.; mem.: INFORMS, Thomas Wolfe Soc., Am. Mktg. Assn., Soc. Math. Psychology, Psychonometric Soc. (trustee 1987—89, pres. 1990—91), Classification Soc. N.Am. (bd. dirs. 1983—, pres. 2004—). Office: Rutgers U Business Sch 180 University Ave Newark NJ 07102-1893 Office Phone: 973-353-1020.

ARAC, JONATHAN, literature and language professor; b. NYC, Apr. 4, 1945; s. Benjamin and Evelyn (Charm) A. AB, Harvard U., 1967, MA, 1968, PhD, 1974. Jr. fellow Soc. Fellows Harvard U., Cambridge, Mass., 1970-73; asst. prof. English Princeton U., 1973-79; assoc. prof. U. Ill., Chgo., 1979-85, prof., 1985-86; prof. grad. program lit. Duke U., 1986-87; prof. English and comparative lit. Columbia U., 1987-90; prof. English U. Pitts., 1989-2000, Mellon prof. English, 2000-01, 2006—; Harriman prof. English and comparative lit. Columbia U., 2001—06. Assoc. dir. Inst. Humanities, U. Ill., Chgo., 1983-84, dept. chair, 2001-05; Drue Heinz disting. vis. prof. Oxford U., 2000, 05; Avalon disting. vis. prof. humanities Northwestern U., 2000. Author: Commissioned Spirits, 1979, Critical Genealogies, 1987, Huckleberry Finn as Idol and Target, 1997, The Emergence of American Literary Narrative, 2005; editor: The Yale Critics: Deconstruction in America, 1983, Postmodernism and Politics, 1986, After Foucault, 1988, Consequences of Theory, 1990, Macropolitics of 19th Century Literature, 1991; mem. editl. bd. Comparative Lit., 1989—, Am. Lit., 2000-02, Boundary 2: Jour. Postmodern Lit. and Culture, 1979—. Am. Coun. Learned Socs. fellow, 1978-79, NEH fellow, 1986-87, 94-95. Mem. MLA (mem. publs. com. 1997-2000), Soc. Critical Exch. (bd. dirs. 1983-90), English Inst. (mem. supervisory com. 1985-88, chmn. 1987-88), PMLA (mem. adv. com. 1990-94). Office: U Pitts Dept English 526 Cathedral Learning 4200 Fifth Ave Pittsburgh PA 15260 Office Phone: 412-624-6506. Business E-Mail: jarac@pitt.edu.

ARAD, MICHAEL SAHAR, architect; b. Israel, 1969; arrived in US, 1991; s. Moshe and Rivka Arad; m. Melanie Ann Fitzpatrick, 2001; 1 child, Nathaniel. BA, Dartmouth Coll., 1994; MA, Ga. Inst. Tech., 1999. Arch. Kohn Pedersen Fox, 1999—2002; arch. design dept. N.Y.C. Housing Authority, 2002—04; ptnr. Handel Architects, NYC, 2004—. Spkr. in field. Reconnaissance unit of an infantry brigade Israeli Def. Force, 1988—91. Named co-winner, World Trade Ctr. Site Meml. Competition, 2003; recipient Young Architects award, Am. Inst. Architects, 2006. Office: Handel Architects 150 Varick St 8th Fl New York NY 10013*

ARAFAT-JOHNSON, DANYAH, secondary school educator, director; b. Ft. Worth, Jan. 10, 1969; d. Husam Rashed and Margaret Miller Arafat; m. Clinton Heath Johnson, May 18, 1955; children: Clay Elias, Brooks Husam. BA in English, Tex. A&M U., College Station, 1991, BA in Theatre Arts, 1991; MEd, U. North Tex., Denton, 2003. Cert. profl. educator Tex. Bd. Edn., 1993. Speech tchr. Cypress-Fairbanks Ind. Sch. Dist., Katy, Tex., 1993; speech/theatre arts dept. chair Humble (Tex.) Ind. Sch. Dist., 1996—97; theater arts dir., tchr. Keller (Tex.) Ind. Sch. Dist., 1997—2000; asst. dir. Huntington Learning Ctr., Watauga, Tex., 2001—02; theatre arts dir., tchr. Carroll Ind. Sch. Dist., Southlake, Tex., 2002—. Recipient Disting. Scholar award, Coll. Liberal Arts - Tex. A&M U., 1990; grantee Mid. Sch. Broadcast Journalism Unit, Keller Ind. Sch. Dist., 1999; Aggie Players Undergraduate Scholarship/Assistantship Award, Tex. A&M U., 1987—91. Mem.: United Educators Assn., Tex. Assn. for the Gifted and Talented (assoc.), Tex. Ednl. Theatre Assn. (assoc.; curriculum cons. 2005—06). Democrat. Office: George Dawson Middle School/Carroll ISD 400 South Kimball Ave Southlake TX 76092 Home Phone: 817-337-1316; Office Phone: 817-949-5556. Office Fax: 817-949-5555. Business E-Mail: arafatd@cisdmail.com.

ARAGONES, TESA, advertising executive; b. 1970; BS in Mktg., Entrepreneurial Studies, Babson Coll., Wellesley, Mass., 1991. Pub. rels. intern Arnold Fortuna Ln., Boston, 1991—92; asst. media planner, profl. devel. program D'arcy Masius, Benton & Bowles Inc., Troy, Mich., 1992—93, asst. account exec., Pontiac GMC divsn., 1993—94, account exec., Pontiac GMC divsn., 1994—97; mktg., advt. mgr. Volkwagon of Am. Inc., Auburn Hills, Mich., 1997—2000, dir, e-bus. & brand innovation, 2000—04, dir media & interactive mktg., 2004—06; mng. dir. digital branding, brand innovation David and Goliath, LA, 2006—07, mng. ptnr., digital branding, brand innovation, 2007—. Named one of 40 under 40, Advt. Age, 2007. Office: David and Goliath Inc 1230 S Myrtle Ave #401 Clearwater FL 33756 E-mail: tesa_aragones@yahoo.com.*

ARAI, TOSHIHIKO, retired microbiology and immunology educator; b. Niigata, Japan, Sept. 12, 1937; s. Hachiro Sisido and Kazue Arai; m. Hatsue Aoki, Dec. 1, 1963; children: Masako, Tomoko, Kazuhiko. MD, Keio U., Tokyo, 1962; PhD, Keio U., 1968. Instr. dept. microbiology Keio U. Sch. Medicine, 1967-73, asst. prof., 1973-85, assoc. prof., 1985; prof. microbiology and immunology Meiji Coll. Pharmacy, Tokyo, 1985-97; ret., 1997. Rsch. assoc. U. Tex., Dallas, 1970—72; lectr. Ochanomizu U. Sch. Sci., Tokyo, 1978—79, Chiba U. Sch. Medicine, Japan, 1978—82, Josai Dental U., Sakado, Japan, 1978—87, Aoyama Gakuin U., Tokyo, 1988—2003; cons. Kitasato Inst., Tokyo, 1981—84. Author (15 books); contbr. Mem.: NY Acad. Scis., Am. Soc. Microbiology, Japan Soc. Ningen Dock, Japan Soc. Chemotherapy, Japan Soc. Bacteriology. Zen Buddhist. Home: 5-1-23 Yatsu Narashimo-shi Chiba 275-0026 Japan Office: St Maguerite Hosp 450 Kami-kouya Yachiyo-shi Chiba 276-0022 Japan Home Phone: 81 47 473 5768, 81 090 3689 4086; Office Phone: 81-47-485-5111. Business E-Mail: ya5-1-23@mxm.mesh.ne.jp.

ARAIZA, FRANCISCO (JOSÉ FRANCISCO ARAIZA ANDRADE), opera singer; b. Mexico City, Oct. 4, 1950; s. José and Guadalupe (Andrade) A.; m. Vivian Jaffray, Sept. 30, 1977 (div. 1995); children: José Riccardo, Maria del Carmen Cecilia; m. Ethery Inasaridse, children: Abessalom Rodrigo, Laura Imeda. Grad. in Bus. Adminstrn., U. Mexico City, 1972; grad., Nat. Sch. Music, Mexico City, 1974, Nat. Conservatory, 1974, Musikhochschule, Munich, 1975. Tchr. vocal technique and style Internat. Opera Studio, Zurich, 2005—; mem. mng. bd. Liz Mohn Kúltúr-únd Músikstiftúng, Bertelsmann, Konzertgesellschaft München; jury mem. numerous internat. singing contests. Tenor roles (lyric repertory as well as dramatic parts till Wagner's Lohengrin in 1990) include performances in opera hos. Zurich, Munich, Vienna, Rome, Hamburg, Berlin, Milan, London, Parma, Florence, Venice, Barcelona, Madrid, Tokyo, Mexico City, Chgo., San Francisco, N.Y.C.; performed at Salzburg Festival, Bayreuth Festival; numerous recordings include works by Mozart, Rossini, Beethoven, Donizetti, Offenbach, Schubert, Verdi, Puccini, Gounod, Massenet, Weber and others; also six solo albums including opera arias, lieder, popular songs. Bd. dirs. Opernstudio, Zurich, Switzerland, 2006; mem. mng. bd. Bertelsmann Stiftung, Germany. Recipient Orphée d'Or, 1984, Deutscher Schallplattenpreis, 1984, Otello d'Oro performer prize, 1995, Golden Merkur best performance award, 1996, Mozart medal of Mex., 1991; named Kammersänger of Vienna State Opera, 1988, prof. of the Music and Art Hochschule Stuttgart, Germany, 2003. Address: c/o Elene Tschaidse Opern-und Konzertagentur Tal 28 80331 Munich Germany Personal E-mail: faraiza@aol.com.

ARAKAWA, KASUMI, physician, educator; b. Toyohashi, Japan, Feb. 19, 1926; came to U.S., 1954, naturalized, 1963; s. Masumi and Fayuko (Hattori) A.; m. Juen Hope Takahara, Aug. 27, 1956; children: Jane Riet, Kenneth Luke, Amy Kathryn. MD, Tokyo Med. Coll., 1953; PhD, Showa U., 1984. Diplomate Am. Bd. Anesthesiology. Intern Iowa Meth. Hosp., Des Moines, 1954—56; resident in internal medicine U. Kans. Med. Ctr., Kansas City, 1956—58, instr. anesthesiology, 1961—64, from asst. prof. to prof., 1964—94; prof. emeritus, 1994—; Arakawa Disting. prof. anesthesiology U. Kans. Med. Ctr., Kansas City, 1990, Kasumi Arakawa professorship, 1994. Clin. assoc. prof. U. Mo.-Kans. City Sch. Dentistry, 1973—; dir. Kansas City Health Care, Inc. Fulbright scholar, 1954; nat. cons. to surgeon gen., USAF, 1990—. Recipient Outstanding Faculty award Student AMA, 1970 Fellow Am. Coll. Anesthesiology; mem. Assn. Univ. Anesthetists, Acad. Anesthesiology (pres. 1986-87), Japan-Am. Soc. Midwest (v.p. 1965, 71). Office: Univ Med Ctr 3901 Rainbow Blvd Kansas City KS 66160-0001 Home: 2190 Rosa Vista Terr Camarillo CA 93012 Personal E-mail: kcarakawamdphdca@verizon.net.

ARAMBURÚZABÁLA, MARIA ASUNCIÓN, food products executive; b. Mexico, May 2, 1963; d. Pablo Aramburuzabala Ocaranza; m. Tony Garza, Feb. 26, 2005; 2 children. BA in Accounting, Technological Inst. of Mexico. Chairwoman Grupo Modelo (brewer of Corona), 1996—. Bd. dir Grupo Televisa. Named one of most powerful women, Forbes mag., 2005, 50 Women to Watch, Wall Street Journal, 2005, 50 Most Powerful Women in Global Bus., Fortune mag., 2005; recipient Golden Plate award, Acad. Achievement, 2004. Achievements include being Mexico's richest woman. Mailing: Grupo Modelo Campos Elíseos #400 8th Fl Colonia Lomas de Chapultepec 11000 Mexico City Mexico*

ARAMS, FRANK ROBERT, electronics executive; b. Danzig; came to U.S., 1939, naturalized, 1945; s. Richard and Alice (Frank) A.; m. Edith Knoll, July 24, 1952; children: Mark, Ronald. BEE, U. Mich., 1947; MS in Applied Physics, Harvard U., 1948; MS in Bus. Mgmt, Stevens Inst. Tech., 1953; PhD in Electrophysics, Poly. U. N.Y., 1961. Group leader RCA Microwave div., Harrison, NJ, 1948-56; cons. AIL div. Eaton Corp., Melville, NY, 1956-65, head electrooptics and infrared dept., 1965-71; v.p. LNR Communications, Inc., Hauppauge, NY, 1971-99, also bd. dirs.; mgmt. cons., patent tech. expert, 2000—. Author: Infrared-to-Millimeter Wave Detectors, 1972; contbr. articles to profl. jours. Served with AUS, 1942-44. Fellow IEEE. Home: 37 School House Ln Great Neck NY 11020-1322 Office Phone: 516-466-8597.

ARANAS, PAULINE, law librarian, educator; BA, UCLA; JD, U. So. Calif.; MLIS, U. Calif., Berkeley. Reference libr. law libr. U. So. Calif. Gould Sch. Law, LA, 1984, assoc. dir., adj. assoc. prof. law, 1992, assoc. dean, COO, 2004—06, assoc. dean, dep. dir. law libr., 2006—; dir. Alyne Queener Massey Law Libr., Vanderbilt U. Law Sch., 1994—2002, asst. dean libr. and info. tech., assoc. prof. law; assoc. law libr. UCLA Sch. Law, 2002—04. Mem.: State Bar of Calif., Am. Assn. Law Libraries. Office: USC Gould Sch Law 699 Exposition Blvd, 210 Los Angeles CA 90017 Office Phone: 213-740-6482. Office Fax: 213-740-7179. E-mail: paranas@law.usc.edu.

ARAND, FREDERICK FRANCIS, accountant, finance company executive; b. Chgo., Mar. 14, 1954; s. Bernard Anthony and Millicent Catherine (Schweizer) A.; m. Judith Mary Utz, May 22, 1982; children: Joseph, Diana, Thomas, Amanda, Laura. AB, Dartmouth Coll., 1976; MBA, U. Mich., 1978. CPA Mich. Staff acct. Ernst & Young, Chgo., 1978-79, advanced staff acct., 1979-80, sr. staff acct., 1980-82, supr., 1982-85, sr. mgr., 1985—94; contr. Ancilla Sys., Inc., Hobart, Ind., 1994—97, v.p. fin. svcs., 1997—. Bd. dirs. Simmons Ambulance Co., treas., 2004—, Ancilla Domini Sisters; bd. dirs. L. Gilbraith SPC Ltd. Leader Jr. Achievement, Wheaton, Ill., 1981—83; mgr., coach Niles Baseball and Soccer Leagues, 1989—94, Park Ridge Softball and Soccer Leagues, 1993—94, Schererville Soccer League, 1994—2004, St. John Softball League, 1996, CYO Soccer League, 1997—2004; adv. bd. St. John Evangelist Sch.; bd. dirs. Schererville Soccer Club, treas., 1998—99; bd. dirs. Gary Citywide Devel. Corp., treas., 2004—07; bd. dirs. PHJC Cmty. Support Trust, St. Joseph Med. Ctr. of Ft. Wayne, St. Mary's Hosp. Health Found., Sisters of Providence Cmty. Support Trust, Gary Cmty. Health Found., Ancilla Ins. Trust, Catherine Kasper Life Ctr., treas., 2004—07; bd. dirs. Linden Ho. of Mishawaka, treas., 2004—; bd. dirs. Simmons Ambulance Co., treas., 2004—; bd. dirs. Advantage Health Solutions. Mem. AICPA (grassroots panel, 2003-), Math. Assn. Am., Ill. CPA Soc., Ind. CPA Soc. (leadership cabinet, 2003-), Fin. Mgr. Soc. (mem. fin. mgmt. com. 1986-91, vice chmn. 1987-88, chmn. 1988-90, mem. accounting issues com. 1991-92), Healthcare Fin. Mgmt. Assn., Fin. Execs. Internat., Dartmouth Alumni Club, Met. Club, Toastmasters (area gov. 1985-86). Avocations: soccer, golf, tennis, softball. Home: 9123 Olcott Ave Saint John IN 46373-9729 Office: Ancilla Systems Inc 1419 S Lake Park Ave Hobart IN 46342

ARANDA, BENJAMIN, architect; BArch, U. Calif., Berkeley; MArch, Columbia U., NYC. Co-founder Aranda/Lasch, NYC, 2003—. Non-Linear Systems Orgn. fellow U. Pa. Sch. Design, 2005—06. Prin. works include Grotto, Baskets; co-author (with Chris Lasch): Tooling, 2006. Named Co-winner of Young Archs. Forum, Archtl. League NY, 2007. Office: Aranda/Lasch 212 Forsyth St New York NY 10002 Office Phone: 917-534-9767. Office Fax: 707-281-1543.*

ARANGO, JORGE SANIN, architect; b. Bogota, Colombia, Nov. 29, 1916; s. Fernando Arango and Maria Sanin A.; m. Elizabeth Leighton, 1944; 1 child, Peter; m. Judith Brooks Wolpert, Dec. 14, 1951; children: Richard, Virginia; m. Penelope Corey, Aug. 18, 1976. Student, Universidad Catolica de Chile Sch. Architecture, 1935-42, Harvard Grad. Sch. Design, 1942-43. Head archtl. firm Arango & Murtra, Bogota, 1946-59; prof. architecture and urban design Nat. U., Bogota, 1945-47; vis. prof. Sch. Architecture U. Calif., Berkeley, 1956, 58; Pub. bldgs. dir. Colombia, 1948-49; pres. Colombian Soc. Architects, 1946-51, Colegio Engrs. and Architects of Colombia, 1955. Co-creator (with Le Corbusier) basic plan for devel. Bogota, 1948. Author: (with C. Martinez) Architecture in Colombia, 1951, The Urbanization of the Earth, 1970, Segunda Edad Media, 1994, Ecophila: The Future is Waiting, 2000, Villa Sofia, 2003, Jorge Arango-Architect, 2003; mem. bd. contbrs. Miami Herald, 1984-91; contbr. articles to mags. Recipient Excellence in Design awards Miami and Fla. chpts. AIA, 1967; named Living Legend, Ocean Drive Mag., 2006. Mem. AIA (mem. emeritus). Achievements include being invited to U.S. by State Dept. and Mus. Modern Art, N.Y.C. Home: 5153 SW 71st Pl Miami FL 33155-5640

ARANGO, PENELOPE COREY, psychologist, consultant; b. San Francisco, Oct. 10, 1943; d. George Raymond Corey Jr. and Katherine Barnard; m. Jorge Arango, Aug. 18, 1976. Diploma de cultura Española, U. Madrid, 1962; cert. de langue et litterature Francais, Universite de Grenoble, 1964; BA in art, U. Miami, Fla., 1965; MA in psychology, U. No. Colo., 1977. Psychol. asst. dept. clin. psychology U. Fla., 1966—68; asst. psychologist - Spanish Dade County Pub. Schs., Miami, 1968—76; dir., healthcare divsn. Helmsley-Spear of Fla., Miami, 1986—91; dir., CQI, tng. & devel. CAC-United HealthCare of Fla., Miami, 1991—98; LAO continuing improvement facilitator Carrier Corp., Latin Am. Hdqs., 1998—2000; faculty mem. Bayer Inst. Healthcare Comms., West Haven, Conn., 1995—2005; v.p. Arango Group, Quality Mgmt. Cons., Miami, 2000—. Quality adv. bd. mem. Coral Gables C. of C., Coral Gables, Fla., 1992—93. Office: Arango Group 5153 SW 71st Pl Miami FL 33155 Office Phone: 305-665-3133.

ARANGO-LASPRILLA, JUAN CARLOS, medical educator; b. Medellin, Colombia, Nov. 1, 1973; s. Dario Arango-Correa and Blanca Isabel Lasprilla-Rojas; m. Heather Lynn Rogers, July 12, 2002. PhD, Autonomous U. Madrid, 2002. Adj. prof. psychology U. San Buenaventura,

Medellin, 1997—98; postdoctoral fellow Kessler Rehab. Rsch. and Ednl. Corp., West Orange, NJ, 2004—06; asst. prof. U. Medicine and Dentistry, Newark, 2006—07, Va. Commonwealth U., Richmond, 2007—. Editor: (textbook) Dementia: Clinical, Neuropsychological, and Treatment Characteristics, 2003 (CANIEM award Nat. Publ. Bd. Mex., 2003), Neuropsychological Rehabilitation, 2006; guest editor: Jour. Head Trauma and Rehab., 2007. Recipient Best Nat. Investigation in the Scis., Alejandro Escobar Found., 1997, Excellence in Sci. award, Colombian Inst. for the Devel. Sci. and Tech., 1999, Bd. Trustees award, Kessler Rehab. Rsch. and Edn. Corp., 2005, Founders' award, Brain Injury Assn. NJ, 2006, Excellence in Rsch. award, Colombian Psychol. Soc., 2006. Mem.: APA (Presdl. Latino/Am. Leadership Citations for Students and Early Career Psychologist award 2005), Hispanic Neuropsychological Soc., Am. Congress Rehab. Medicine, Nat. Acad. Neuropsychology, Internat. Neuropsychological Soc. Liberal. Avocation: travel. Office: MCV Campus West Hosp PO Box 980542 1200 E Broad St 3rd Fl Rm 3-102 Richmond VA 23298-0542 Home Phone: 804-918-7671; Office Phone: 804-828-8797. Personal E-mail: jcarango@psi.ucm.es.

ARANHA, GERARD V., surgeon; b. Bangalore, India, 1943; MB BS, Bangalore Med. Coll., 1969. Diplomate Am. Bd. Surgery. Intern Christ Hosp., Oak Lawn, Ill., 1970-71; resident in surgery Loyola Affiliated Hosp., Maywood, Ill., 1971-75; fellow in surg. oncology U. Minn. Hosps., Mpls., 1975-77; chief surg. oncology Loyola U.-Stritch Sch. Medicine, Maywood, 1990—, dir. breast care ctr., 1992—, prof. Fellow ACS, Royal Coll. Surgery; mem. Internat. Surg. Soc., Am. Surg. Assn., Assn. Acad. Surgery, Ctrl. Surg. Assn., Midwest Surg. Soc., Soc. Surgery Alimentary Tract, Soc. Surg. Oncology, Western Surg. Assn., Soc. Digestive Surgery, Am. Hepto-Pancreato-Biliary Assn., Internat. Hepto-Pancreato-Biliary Assn. Office: Loyola U Med Ctr Dept Surg EMS110-3236 2160 S 1st Ave Maywood IL 60153-3304 Office Phone: 708-327-3430. Business E-Mail: gararha@lumc.edu.

ARANI, ARDY A., marketing professional, sports association administrator; BBA, U. Miami, 1975; JD, Loyola U., New Orleans, 1978. Mktg. dir. Internat. Sports Mktg. Ltd., London, 1978-80; mng. dir., CEO Championship Group Inc., Atlanta, 1980—; exec. prodr. Race Day Fox Sports Radio, 2003—. Mem. editl. bd. Sport Mktg. Quar.; contbr. articles to profl. jours. Bd. dirs. Atlanta Sports Coun., 1986-97, Atlanta Olympic Organizing Com., 1988-96; chmn. TEAM Ga. Recipient Reggie Promotions award, Promotion Mktg. Assn. Am., 1999. Mem. Am. Mktg. Assn., Sports Car Club of Am. (Recognition award 1988), Nat. Assn. Stock Car Auto Racing, Am. Motorcycle Assn., Internat. Motor Sports Assn. Office: Championship Group Inc 1954 Airport Rd Ste 2000 Atlanta GA 30341

ARANOFF, SHARA L., federal official; m. David Korn; 2 children. BA, Princeton U.; JD, Harvard U.; post grad., Institut Universitaire de Hautes Etudes Internationales, U. Geneva, 1984—85. Atty. Steptoe & Johnson LLP; atty. advisor Office Gen. Counsel U.S. Internat. Trade Commn., Washington, 1993—2001, sr. internat. trade counsel, 2001—05, commr., 2005—; mem. senate com. on fin. U.S. Senate, Washington, 2002—05. Office: US Internal Trade Commn 500 E St SW Rm 704 Washington DC 20436 Office Phone: 202-708-2880. Office Fax: 202-205-2798.

ARANSON, ROBERT, physician, director; b. Portland, Maine, Dec. 18, 1953; s. Albert and Golde Leah (Rodman) A. BS in Biology, Trinity Coll., 1976; MD, Tufts U., 1980. Diplomate Am. Bd. Internal Medicine-Pulmonary Diseases, Critical Care Medicine. Resident in internal medicine Maine Med. Ctr., Portland, 1980—83; fellow in pulmonary and critical care medicine Albert Einstein Med. Ctr. & Temple U. Hosp., Phila., 1983—85; clin. instr. of medicine Temple U. Sch. of Medicine, Phila., 1983—85, asst. prof. of medicine, 1985—88, dir. Med. Respiratory ICU, 1985—88; asst. prof. of medicine Tufts U. Sch. of Medicine, Boston, 1988—93; dir. pulmonary fellowship program St. Elizabeth Hosp., Boston, 1988—93, asst. dir. pulmonary critical care divsn., 1988—93, dir. Med. Respiratory ICU, 1988—93; asst. prof. medicine Emory U. Sch. Medicine, Atlanta, 1993—2000; dir. med. ICU and respiratory care dept. Grady Meml. Hosp., Atlanta, 1993—2000; assoc. prof. cardiopulmonary care scis. Ga. State U., Atlanta, 1993—2000, med. dir. Sch. Respiratory Therapy, 1993—2000; pvt. practice Maine, 2000—04; chief pulmonary critical care and sleep medicine Parkview Adventist Med. Ctr., Brunswick, Maine, 2005—, dir. ICU and respiratory care dept., 2005—. Med. physician Phila. Seventy-Sixers Profl. Basketball Team, Phila., 1987-88. Contbr. articles to profl. jours. Fellow ACP, Am. Coll. Chest Physicians (gov. State of Maine chpt. 2007-); mem. Am. Thoracic Soc., Soc. Critical Care Medicine, Nat. Assn. for Med. Direction of Respiratory Care. Jewish. Avocations: basketball, sailing, skiing. Home: 20 Lookout Dr Freeport ME 04032-6272 Office: Parkview Adventist Med Ctr 329 Maine St Brunswick ME 04011 Office Phone: 207-729-5720. Business E-Mail: raranson@parkviewamc.org.

ARANT, EUGENE WESLEY, lawyer; b. North Powder, Oreg., Dec. 21, 1920; s. Ernest Elbert and Wanda (Haller) A.; m. Juanita Clark Flowers, Mar. 15, 1953; children: Thomas W., Kenneth E., Richard W. BS in Elec. Engring, Oreg. State U., 1943; JD, U. So. Calif., 1949. Bar: Calif. 1950. Mem. engring. faculty U. So. Calif., 1947-51; pvt. practice LA, 1950—51; patent atty. Hughes Aircraft Co., Culver City, Calif., 1953-56; pvt. practice LA, 1957—2001, Lincoln City, Oreg., 2001—. Author: The Idea Business: Rules of the Game, 2005; contbr. articles to profl. jours. Mem. La Mirada (Calif.) City Coun., 1958-60; trustee Beverly Hills Presbyn. Ch., 1976-78. Served with AUS, 1943-46, 51-53. Mem. ABA, Am. Intellectual Property Law Assn., State Bar Calif. Democrat. Home: 100 NE Indian Shores Lincoln City OR 97367 Office: PO Box 269 Lincoln City OR 97367 Office Phone: 541-557-1716. E-mail: gwapat@charterinternet.com.

ARANYA, GWENDALIN QI, painter, priest, educator, yoga educator; b. Bklyn., July 25, 1967; d. Carroll Jean Yorgey and Donald Enix; children: Zarathustra Goertzel, Zebulon Goertzel, Scheherazade Goertzel. BA in linguistics, Temple U., 1988; MS in math., U. Nev., Las Vegas, 1992; MFA in painting, Howard U., Washington, DC, 2005. Ordained Zen priest Buddhist Order of the Hsu Yun. Exhibited in group shows at Vox Populi, Phila., 1988—89, Waikato Soc. Arts, New Zealand, 1995, New Century Artists, NYC, 2002—05, Howard U., Washington, 2003—05, Artomatic, 2004—05, Graham Collection Gallery, 2005—, Internat. Visions Gallery, 2006, 2007, Mason Murer Gallery Fine Art, Atlanta, 2006, DC Arts Ctr., Washington, 2006—, Children's Studio Sch. Gallery, 2006, Flashpoint Gallery, Washington, DC, one-woman shows include Local Artist, Las Vegas, Internat. Art Gallery, Australia, 1996, Riverview Arts Ctr., NJ, 1999, Intro Art Gallery, 2001, Howard U., 2005, Cafe Nema, Washington, DC, 2006, Mocha Hut, Washington, 2006, 2006, Artomatic 2007, Mason Murer Gallery, exhibited in group shows at Simon's Rock College of Bard; designer Las Vegas Kardma, 1994, illustrator Linus Pauling: A Life in Science and Politics, 1995, The Evolving Mind, 1993. Mem.: Washington Project for the Arts Corcoran, Coll. Art Assn., Black Artists of DC, DC Arts Ctr., Nat. Conf. Artists, New Century Artists. Home: 4005 Delancy Dr Silver Spring MD 20906 Office Phone: 240-476-4445. Personal E-mail: garanya@yahoo.com.

ARAOZ, DANIEL LEON, psychologist, educator; b. Buenos Aires, Apr. 23, 1930; came to U.S., 1951, naturalized, 1967; s. Jose Daniel and Maria Lia (Suarez) A.; m. Marie Carrese, July 27, 1991; m. Dorita Catherine Smyth, July 17, 1964 (div. 1984); children: Leon Daniel, Nadine Victoria. BA, Gonzaga U., 1953, MA, 1954; MST., U. Santa Clara, 1961; MA, Columbia U., 1964, EdD, 1969; Psychoanalysis Diploma, Am. Inst. for Psychotherapy and Psychoanalysis, 1972. Clin. psychologist, Ill., Pa. Diplomate in counseling psychology and family psychology Am. Bd. Profl. Psychology; diplomate in clin. hypnosis Am. Bd. Psychol. Hypnosis; lic. mental health counselor N.Y., 2006. Asst. chaplain Coll. Mt. St. Vincent, Bronx, N.Y., 1962-64; psychotherapist Cmty. Guidance Svc., NYC, 1965-72, supr., 1972-82; faculty Am. Inst. Psychotherapy and Psychoanalysis, NYC, 1972-82; assoc. prof. counseling L.I. U., 1973-82, prof., 1982—, chmn. dept. counseling and devel., 1995-97. Dir. L.I. Inst. Ericksonian Hypnosis, 1992-97. Editor-in-chief Am. Jour. Family Therapy, 1973-76, jour. adv., 1977—; author: Hypnosis and Sex Therapy, 1982, 98; Hypnosex, 1982; Self-Transformation Through the New Hypnosis, 1984; The New Hypnosis, 1985, 95, The New Hypnosis in Family Therapy, 1987; Selbst Hypnose: Kreative Imagination in Beruf und Alltag, 1992, Reengineering Yourself, 1994, 2d edit., 2003, Chinese edit., 1995, Solution-Oriented Brief Therapy for Adjustment Disorders, 1996, Japanese edit., 1999, Power Over Stress at Work, 1998, Autoreingeniería Para el nuevo Milenio, 2003, The Symptom is not the Whole Story, 2006; co-editor: Hypnosis Questions & Answers, 1986; contbr. articles to profl. jours. Named Hon. Prof. U. peruana Cayetano Heredia, Lima, Peru; recipient LIU Excellence in Tchg., David Newton award, 2003. Fellow APA, Am. Inst. Psychotherapy and Psychoanalysis, Am. Soc. Psychosomatic Dentistry and Medicine, Acad. Counseling Psychology, Acad. Family Psychology, Soc. Clin. and Exptl. Hypnosis; mem. Am. Assn. Sexuality Educators, Counselors and Therapists (diplomate), Am. Assn. Marriage and Family Therapy (supr. 1973—), Nat. Assn. for Advancement of Psychoanalysis, Pa. Psychol. Assn., Ill. Psychol. Assn., Nassau County Psychol. Assn., Am. Mgmt. Assn. (unit trainer 1987-94), N.Y. State Psychol. Assn., N.Y. Soc. Clin. Hypnosis, N.Y. Mental Health Counselors Assn. Home: 66 Gates Ave Malverne NY 11565-1912 Office: LI U CW Post Northern Blvd Greenvale NY 11548-1207 Office Phone: 516-299-2213. Business E-Mail: daniel.araoz@liu.edu.

ARASAKESARI, SUBRAMANIAM, chemical engineer, researcher, consultant; US, 1987; s. S. and Chittal Arasakesari. BE Pulp & Paper, Indian Inst. of Tech., Roorkee, India, 1987; MS Paper Sc, Western Mich. U., Kalamazoo, Mich., 1990; PhD, U. Wash., Seattle, Wash., 1994. Lead developer Andritz Inc., Atlanta, 1995—2000; process tech. cons. Mead-Westvaco Corp, Chillicothe, Ohio, 2000—02; process modeling cons. Procter & Gamble Corp, W. Chester, Ohio, 2002—. Contbr. articles pub. to profl. jour. Recipient Creative Rsch. Scholar, Western Mich. U., 1990, Outstanding Contr., Procter & Gamble Corp, 2004. Mem.: IPPTA, TAPPI (chmn., process engg 2000—). Achievements include first to Advanced pulping model & digester optimizer. Home: 8332 Landmark Ct Apt 101 West Chester OH 45069 Office: Procter & Gamble Corp 8256 Union Ctr Blvd Mail stop IP352 West Chester OH 45069 Home Phone: 513-608-4091. Office Fax: 513-634-9439. Personal E-mail: mani287@gmail.com. Business E-Mail: arasakesari.s@pg.com.

ARAUJO, ILKA VASCONCELOS, musicologist, pianist; arrived in U.S., 1997; d. Jose Mario and Maria Cleomar Vasconcelos Araujo; m. Aleksa Jovanovic, Sept. 18, 2004; 1 child, Isabella Araujo Jovanovic. Tech. Level, Conservatory Music Alberto Nepomuceno, Fortaleza, CE, Brazil, 1989; BMus in Piano Performance, State U. Ceara, Fortaleza, Brazil, 1995; MMus in Piano Performance and Pedagogy, U. Fla., Gainesville, 2001, PhD in Musicology, 2007. Piano and theory tchr. Juvenal de Carvalho H.S., Fortaleza, Brazil, 1993—94; piano tchr. Conservatory Music Alberto Nepomuceno, 1994—95, State U. Ceara, 1994—95; pianist and accompanist Maninha Mota Voice Sch., 1996—97; grad. tchg. asst. U. Fla., Gainesville, 1997—. Choir dir. Friends of Music Soc., Fortaleza, Brazil, 1992—93; co-director and co-founder Brazilian choir Brazilian Student Assn., Gainesville, Fla., 1997—2000; asst. mgr. Prague Internat. Piano Master Classes, Czech Republic, 1998—2001; pvt. instr. piano and accompanist, Gainesville, 1998—; co-organizer events, hostess and translator U. Fla. Sch. Music, 1998—, rep. grad. student coun., 2002—03. Composer: Instants, 2001— (3rd prize Fla. Juried Arts Exhbn., 2002); musician (pianist and lectr.): The Subjective Nationalitic Aspects in Liszt, Villa-Lobos and Ginastera, 2003, 20th Century Compositional Vocabulary featuring works by Villa-Lobos, Ginastera, and Ilka Araujo, 2004, Works of Schubert, Liszt, and Ginastera, 2004; musician: (pianist) Sonata No. 4 by Prokoviev, 2001, Works by Scriabin, Liszt, Villa-Lobos and Ilka Araujo, 2003, Vallee D'Obermann by Liszt, 2004, Works by Schubert, Liszt, Villa-Lobos, and Ginastera, 2004, Works by Villa-Lobos and Ginastera, 2004, Works by Liszt, Villa-Lobos, and Ginastera, 2004; musician: (master class presenter) Conservatory of Music and State Univ. Ceara, 2004—06, Music Acad.; performer: Programa Do Jo, 2004; contbr. scientific papers in musicology; performer: TV Verdes Mares, 2004; interviewed (various mags., TV programs, newspapers), 2005; performer: TV Ceara, 2006. Vol. pianist The Village, Gainesville, Fla., 1999—2000, The Atrium; pianist Lochloosa United Meth. Ch., Hawthorne United Meth. Ch., Hawthorne, Fla., 2000, Dunnellon Presbyn. Ch., 2003; pres. Brazilian Student Assn., Gainesville, Fla., 1998—99, v.p., 1999—2000. Named an Internat. Female Leader, Women's Leadership Conf., Gainesville, 2005; recipient First prize, Piano Competition Young Instrumentalists Festival, Brazil, 1994, Paurillo Barrozo Piano Competition, Brazil, 1995, Alec Courtelis Award, 2004, Presdl. award Outstanding Achievement and Contibn., U. Fla., 1999, 2000, Oustanding Student Recognition, U. Fla. Ctr. Internat. Studies, 1998, 2000, Student Academic award, U. Fla. Coll. Fine Arts, 1998, 2000; Grad. Tchg. assistantship, U. Fla., 1997—. Mem.: Nat. Guild Piano Teachers Assn., Soc. Composers Inc., Coll. Music Soc., Am. Music Soc., Phi Lambda Beta, Pi Kappa Lambda. Avocations: swimming, travel, reading. Business E-Mail: ilkarauj@ufl.edu.

ARB, CARRIE SAMANTHA, adult education educator; d. Carol and adopted d. Stephen Gibbs; m. David Lee Arb, Jr., July 30, 2005. BA, Miami U., Oxford, Ohio, 2002; MS, Xavier U., Cin., 2004. Exec. sec. Hamilton County Pub. Defenders Office, Cin., 1999—2005; program mgr. Inst. for Psychiatry and Law, U. Cin., Cin., 2005—; lead criminal justice instr. Southwestern Coll., Cin., 2006—. Vol. Accountability and Credibility Together, Inc., Cin., 1998—2007, Hilcrest Tng. Sch., Cin., 2003—04. Republican. Avocations: travel, rugby, swimming. Office: Institute for Psychiatry and Law UC 231 Albert Sabin Way Cincinnati OH 45267-0559 Home Phone: 513-871-5168; Office Phone: 513-558-4423. Office Fax: 513-558-3823. Business E-Mail: carrie.arb@uc.edu.

ARBAUGH, JON HALBERT, legal assistant; b. San Francisco, June 13, 1948; s. Peggy Jean Grinstead; m. Julia Carol Arbaugh, Dec. 21, 1995; 1 child, laurel Leigh Johnson. AA, Mt. San Antonio Coll., Walnut, Calif., 1973; BA, Calif. State U., Fullerton, 1976; JD, Western State U. Coll. Law, Fullerton, 1989. Legal rep. Calif. Compensation Ins. Co., Diamond Bar, Calif., 1991—96, Monterey, Calif., 1996—99, Law Office John Amos, Salinas, Calif., 1999, Law Office Bruce Sutherland, Arroyo Grande, Calif., 2000, Law Office Brian Collins, Redlands, Calif., 2001—02, Law Office Larry Kaplan, Tustin, Calif., 2002, Law Office Robert Wheatley, Santa Ana, Calif., 2002—. State dir. legal tng. Calif. Compensation Ins. Co., Calif., 1994—99. Bd. dirs., legal officer US Territorial Marshals, Calif., 1998—2001; dir. Code of West, Calif., 2002—. With US Army, 1967—71. Mem.: NRA (life), ILA, Single Action Shooting Soc., Am. Legion. Avocations: theater, old west performances.

ARBEITER, JOAN, artist, educator; b. NYC, May 8, 1937; d. David and Winifred Arden (Lembke) Berman; m. Jay David Arbeiter, June 15, 1958 (div. May 1990); children: Lisa B., Gail Arbeiter Goldstein. BA, CUNY, 1959; MFA, Pratt Inst., Bklyn., 1982. Lic. art tchr. NY, NJ. Tchr. NYC Sch. Sys. Bd. Edn., 1959-63; dir. Joan Arbeiter Studio Sch., Metuchen, NJ, 1976-90; instr. art, coord. founds. Ducret Sch. Art, Plainfield, NJ, 1978—, instr. color and design, 1978—2006, instr. art history, 1981—2001, instr. art appreciation, 1983—; workshop instr. NJ Teen Arts Festival, 1998—2003; artist in residence NJ Sch. Arts, 1995—2002. Juror various art orgns., NJ, 1981—; cons. Ednl. Testing Svc., Princeton, NJ, 1988; curator travelling art exhibit Age As a Work of Art, Plainfield, Boston, NYC, 1985—86, Lives and Works, NYC, 2000; presenter paper, slides Coll. Art Assn. Conf., San Antonio, 1995, NYC, 2003; presenter, moderator Nat. Mus. Women in Arts, Wash., 1997, Artists Talk on Art, NYC, 1997, 2000, 05; lectr. art appreciation South Brunswick Libr., NJ, 2006, NJ, 07. One-woman shows include Ceres Gallery, NYC, 1987, 1989, 1993, 1997, 2000, 2001, Columbia U., 1986, Stony Brook-Millstone Watershead Assn. Gallery, Pennington, NJ, 1991, Wagner Coll., SI, NY, 1992, Douglas Coll. Ctr., New Brunswick, NJ, 1992, 1996, Union County Coll., Cranford, NJ, 1999, Elizabeth Found., NYC, 2001, Cedar Crest Coll., Allentown, Pa., 2004, Du Cret Sch., Plainfield, NJ, 2006, exhibited in group shows at Ramapo Coll., Mahwah, NJ, 1980, Brookdale Coll., Lincroft, NJ, 1980, Westbeth Gallery, NYC, 1980, Douglas Coll. Libr., New Brunswick, NJ, 1982, Ceres Gallery, 1983—, NY Feminist Art Inst., NYC, 1985—88, Ednl. Testing Svc., Princeton, NJ, 1986, Appalachian State U., Boone, NC, 1989, Soho 20 Gallery, NYC, 1990, 1998, Noyes Mus., Oceanville, NJ, 1995, 1998, 2005, Krasdale Corp. Gallery, Bronx, NY, 1995, 2006, Monmouth Mus., Lincroft, 1996, Kingsbourgh CC, Bklyn., 1999, Kunstler Forum, Bonn, Germany, 1999, EPA, Washington, 2001—02, Solaris Gallery, Califon, NJ, 2004, Pratt Inst., Bklyn., 2006, Woman Made Gallery, Chgo., 2006, U. Wis., Madison, 2007, Represented in permanent collections Noyes Mus., Oceanville, Fairmount Chem., Newark, CSR Group Archs. and Builders-Leon Cohen, Nutley, NJ, JFK Med. Ctr., Edison, NJ, Muhlenberg Regional Med. Ctr., Plainfield, 1st Presbyn. Ch., Metuchen, NJ, MS Found., NYC, pvt. collections; co-author: (book) Lives and Works: Talks with Women Artists, vol. 2, 1999. Recipient 1st pl. mixed media, Westfield Art Assn., 1978, 1st pl. all media award, Metuchen Cultural Arts Commn. Art Exhbn., 1988, Best in Show award, Middlesex County Mus., New Brunswick, NJ, 1989, AIA award, Hunterdon Arts Ctr. NJ, 1996, People's Choice award, Watchung Arts Ctr., NJ, 1998, Excellence award, Manhattan Arts Mag., 2000, 2007, Elan award for Mentoring Women's Studio Ctr., 2004; grantee, Vt. Studio Colony, 1987. Mem.: Varo Registry, Art Table, Women's Caucus Art, Coll. Art Assn., Women's Studio Ctr. (hon.; bd. dirs., NYC), Alpha Beta Kappa. Studio: 41 Victory Ct Metuchen NJ 08840-1430

ARBELBIDE, C(INDY) L(EA), librarian, historian, author; b. Stockton, Calif., Aug. 4, 1949; d. Garrett Walter and Fern Mable (Lea) A. AA in History, Santa Barbara City Coll., Calif., 1969; BS in Health & Phys. Edn., Oreg. State U., 1972; M in Libr. Sci., Emporia State U., 1980. Asst. dir. Child Youth Libr., Rappahannock County Libr., Washington, Va. Vis. author The White House, 1998, 99, 2000, 01; adv. com. Va. Libr. Youth Svc., 2006. Author: White House Easter Egg Roll, 1997; contbr. National Archives mag. prologue. Recipient Yellow Rose of Tex. Govt. award, 1992, Nat. Orgn. Vic. Asst. Achievement award, 1994, NPS Merit Letter, 1999, 2000, George Wash. Hon. medal, Freedoms Found., 2003. Mem. Am. Assn. State & Local History, Assn. Rural and Small librs., Va. Libr. Assn., Woman of Month Ladies Home Jour., US Women's Track & Field Team, Race Walking. Home and Office: 147 Dogwood Blossom Ln Front Royal VA 22630 Office: PO Box 55 Washington VA 22747

ARBER, DANIEL ALAN, hematologist, pathologist; b. Houston, Tex., May 16, 1961; s. Harry D. and Nancy R. Arber; m. Carol A. Park, Apr. 15, 2006. BS, Tex. A&M U., College Station, 1983; MD, U. Tex. Health Sci. Ctr., San Antonio, 1986. Diplomate in anatomic and clin. pathology Am. Bd. Pathology, 1991, in hematology Am. Bd. Pathology, 1993. Intern E.A. Conway Meml. Hosp. La. State U. Shreveport, Monroe, La., 1986—87; resident anatomic and clin. pathology Scott & White Clinic Tex. A&M U., Temple, Tex., 1987—91, asst. prof. pathology Scott and White Clinic, 1993—94; fellow hematopathology City Hope Nat. Med. Ctr., Duarte, Calif., 1991—93, staff pathologist, 1995—2002, dir. hematopathology and molecular pathology, 1997—2002; prof. pathology Stanford U., Stanford, Calif., 2002—, assoc. chmn. pathology, 2005—. Author: Illustrated Pathology of the Bone Marrow, 2006; contbr. chapters to books, over 150 articles to profl. jours. Named to America's Top Doctors for Cancer, 2005, 2006, Best Doctors in Am., 2005—06. Mem.: Arthur Purdy Stout Soc. Office: Stanford Univ Pathology 300 Pasteur Dr H1507 Stanford CA 94306-5627 Office Phone: 650-725-5604.

ARBER, WERNER, microbiologist; b. Gränichen, Switzerland, June 3, 1929; married; 2 children. Student, Aargau Gymnasium, Switzerland, Eidgenössische Technische Hochschule, Zurich, 1949—53. Asst. Lab. Biophysics, U. Geneva, 1953—58, docent, then extraordinary prof. molecular genetics, 1962—70; research assoc. dept. microbiology U. So. Calif., 1958—59; vis. investigator dept. molecular biology U. Calif., Berkeley, 1970—71; prof. microbiology U. Basel, Switzerland, 1971—96, rector, 1986—88. Co-recipient Nobel Prize for physiology or medicine, 1978. Mem.: Internat. Coun. Sci. (pres. 1996—99), Nat. Acad. Scis. (assoc.). Office: Biozentrum der Universität 70 Klingelbergstrasse CH-4056 Basel Switzerland E-mail: Werner.Arber@unibas.ch.

ARBISSER, ATON, lawyer; AB magna cum laude, Princeton U., 1978; MA in Economics, JD, U. Calif., Berkeley, 1982. Bar: NY 1984, Calif. 1990. Assoc., antitrust practice Kaye Scholer, Los Angeles, Calif., 1983—, now ptnr., antitrust & product liability groups. Mem.: ABA (ed. bd. mem., antitrust law devel., antitrust section 1989—92, vice-chmn. Robinson-Patman act com., antitrust section 1993—94), Los Angeles County Bar Assn. (exec. com., trade regulations section 1992—93), Calif. State Bar Assn. Office: Kaye Scholer 1999 Ave of Stars Ste 1700 Los Angeles CA 90067-6048 Office Phone: 310-788-1000. Office Fax: 310-788-1200. Business E-Mail: aarbisser@kayescholer.com.

ARBIT, BERYL ELLEN, legal assistant; b. LA, Aug. 16, 1949; d. Harry A. and Norma K. A. BA, UCLA, 1970. From legal asst. to sr. legal asst. O'Melveny & Myers, LLP, LA, 1977—. Guest lectr. atty. asst. tng. program UCLA, 1991. Mem. UCLA Atty. Asst. Alumni Assn. (bd. dirs. 1980-82), Alpha Omicron Pi (treas. Greater L.A. alumnae chpt. 1993—), Nu Lambda (corp. bd. pres. 1978-80, chpt. adv. 1976-78). Avocations: travel, theater, needlecrafts, bridge. Office: O'Melveny & Myers, LLP 400 S Hope St Los Angeles CA 90071-2899 Business E-Mail: barbit@omm.com.

ARBIT, BRUCE, direct marketing executive, consultant; b. Milw., Nov. 16, 1954; s. Saul B. and Naomi (Chase) A.; m. Tanya Arbit; children: Oren, Carmiel, Eugene. Student, U. Haifa, Israel, U. Wis. Founder, co-mgr., dir. A B Data, Ltd., Milw., 1977—. Chmn., bd. dirs. Integrated Mail Industries Ltd., Asset Devel. Group, Inc.; bd. dirs. Integrated Mail Industries Israel, Ltd.; chmn. Fox Point Capital, LLC, Fox Point Credit Corp Pres., gen. campaign chmn., bd. dirs., pres. Milw. Jewish Fedn. Keshet, Milw. Jewish Day Sch., Habonim Dror Found.; mem. United Jewish Appeal Young Leadership Cabinet; mem. Wexner Heritage Found., Non-profit Mailers Fedn., Campaign Cabinet Devel. Corp. for Israel; trustee United Israel Appeal, sec.; bd. dirs., sec. Jewish Telegraphic Agy.; bd. govs. Jewish Agy. for Israel, co-chmn. ednl. resources devel. com.; mem. nom. com. United Jewish Communities. Recipient Benjamin E. Nickoll Young Leadership award Milw. Jewish Fedn., 1989. Mem. Direct Mktg. Assn., Israel Direct Mktg., Wis. Direct Mktg. Assn. (Direct Marketer of Yr. award 1997), Am. Assn. Polit. Cons. Office: AB Data Ltd 8050 N Port Washington Rd Milwaukee WI 53217-2600 Business E-Mail: barbit@abdata.com.

ARBOGAST, GORDON WADE, systems engineer, educator, consultant , retired military officer; b. Charleston, SC, May 24, 1942; s. Valentine and Teresa Louise Arbogast; m. Dorothy Sheryl Blackwell, Mar. 5, 1966; children: Annette Marie, Christina Theresa, Valentine Scott. BS, U.S. Mil. Acad., 1963; MSEE, MSIM, Ga. Inst. Tech., Atlanta, 1971; PhD, Clemson

U., SC, 1986. Commd. 2d lt. U.S. Army, 1963, advanced through grades to col., 1983, ret., 1990; head, assoc. prof. dept. engring. U.S. Mil. Acad., 1986-89; assoc. dir. engring. and tech. Def. Comm. Agy., 1989-90; v.p. sys. tech. Pacific Bell, San Ramon, Calif., 1991—94; prof. Jacksonville U., Fla., 1994—, assoc. dean, dir. grad. programs Fla., 2005—. Prin. scientist Contel, Chantilly, Va., 1990; instr., cons. Miller Electric, Jacksonville, 1999—2000, Jacksonville Jaguars, 2004—05; instr., cons., ednl. advisor Scott McCrae Group, 2003—06. Contbr. articles to profl. jours. Lector Cursillo Cath. Ch., 1988—, eucharistic min., 1988—. Decorated Legion of Merit, Bronze Stars (2), Air medal, Def. Superior Svc. medal; named Prof. of Yr., Jacksonville U., Adult Degree Program, 2000. Mem.: Armed Forces Comm.-Electronics Assn. (pres. West Point chpt. 1987—89), Inst. Indsl. Engrs. (sr.), West Point Soc. North Fla. (pres. 1998—2001), Phi Kappa Phi. Achievements include initiating systems engineering at The US Military Academy and major work in transforming Defense Communications Agency to Defense Information Systems Agency. Home: 9937 Orchard Hills Rd Jacksonville FL 32256 Office: Jacksonville U Davis Coll Bus 2800 University Blvd N Jacksonville FL 32211-3394 Business E-Mail: garboga@ju.edu.

ARBOGAST, RICHARD TERRENCE, entomologist, researcher; b. Freeport, Ill., Aug. 7, 1937; s. Raymond Dale and Virginia Mabel Arbogast; m. Helen Dee Fortney, Dec. 21, 1958; children: James Raymond, Kimberly Ann, Timothy Scott, Stephanie Ann. BSc, U. Ill., Urbana, Ill., 1959; student, U. Chgo., 1959—60; PhD, U. Fla., Gainesville, Fla., 1965; BS, Armstrong State Coll., Savannah, Ga., 1984. Rsch. entomologist Stored Product Insects R&D Lab. USDA, Savannah, Ga., 1965—94, rsch. leader Stored-Product Insects R&D Lab., 1975—94, lab. dir. Stored-Product Insects R&D Lab., 1990—94, rsch. entomologist , Ctr. for Med. Agrl. and Veterinary Etomology Gainesville, Fla., 1994—. Active Boy Scouts Am., Savannah, 1968—81. Mem.: Fla. Entomol. Soc., Entomol. Soc. Am., Lepidoptorists Soc. Avocations: butterfly collecting, gardening, reading, history. Office: CMAVE Agr Rsch Svc USDA 1700 SW 23rd Dr Gainesville FL 32608

ARBOLEYA, CARLOS JOAQUIN, lawyer, broker; b. Havana, Cuba, Aug. 16, 1958; came to U.S., 1960; s. Carlos Jose and Marta Aurora (Quintana) A. ABA, Miami Dade C.C., 1977; BBA in Fin., U. Miami, 1980, MBA in Fin., 1981, JD, 1987. Bar: Fla. 1989, U.S. Ct. Appeals (D.C. cir.) 1990. From teller to br. mgr. Barnett Bank South Fla. N.A., North Miami Beach, 1975-84; realtor, assoc. Cervera Real Estate, 1980—; pres. Owner's Box Promotions, 1993-95; pvt. practice Coconut Grove, 1988—. Adv. bd. Exec. Nat. Bank, 1994—98, Linda Ray Infant Ctr., 1990—; mem 20th Anniversary Grand Prix of Miami com., 2002; bd. dirs. Pvt. Industry Coun. Jobs for Miami; Hispanic adv. com. U. Miami Sports Mktg., 1992—95. Bd. dirs. Greater Miami Tennis Found., 1995, U. Miami Ear Inst., 1993; vice chma. planning adv. bd. City of Miami, 1993-95, 98-99, chmn. 1995-98, chmn. code enforcement bd., 1990-91, vice chmn. 1989-90; asst. scoutmaster Boy Scouts Am.; participant joint civilian orientation conf. US Dept. Def., 1995; pres. Cocogrove Villas Condominium Assn., 1998—; with U. Miami Golden Canes, 1996, United Way, Miami-Dade, 2000-01; baseball adv. coaches com. 1996-. Named One of 12 Good Men of Miami, Ronald McDonald House, 2000-01. Mem. ABA, Nat. Soc. Hispanic MBAs, Nat. Eagle Scout Assn., Cuban Am. Bar Assn., Builders Assn. South Fla., Am. Title Ins. Co., Attys. Title Ins. Fund, Inc., Fla. Bar Assn., Latin Bus. Assn., Latin Builders Assn., Hispanic Law Students Assn., Coral Gables C. of C., Greater Miami C. of C. (sports coun., chmn., homestead motorsports complex com., 1994-97, co-chmn. existing events com., 1992-94), Leadership Miami (exec. com. 1990-93, task force 1984-88, Coconut Grove Jaycees, Phi Delta Phi, Delta Sigma Pi (Outstanding Alumni award 1982). Republican. Roman Catholic. Office: 2550 S Dixie Hwy Coconut Grove FL 33133-3137 Office Phone: 305-856-0076. Business E-Mail: cja@arboleyalaw.net.

ARBUCKLE, AVERIL DOROTHY (COOKIE ARBUCKLE), healthcare facility administrator; b. Bklyn., May 9, 1934; d. Arnold Drummond and Mildred (Engel) Lloyd; m. Robert V. Arbuckle (dec. Mar. 1990); children: Gregory, Jody, Leann, Kathleen, Mary. Student, Lamson Coll., Phoenix, 1968-71, Colo. State U., 1964-68, U. Ctrl. Okla., 1974, Okla. State U., Oklahoma City, 1976. Flight attendant Pacific Southwest Airlines, San Diego, 1952, Am. Airlines, Chgo., 1953; social worker Dept. Human Svcs., Oklahoma City, 1972-89; mem. task force Gov.'s Task Force on AIDS, Oklahoma City, 1987-88; exec. dir. Other Options, Inc., Oklahoma City, 1989—. Mem. adv. bd. Carter Hospice, Carter Home Health, Red Rock Mental Health Homeless Com., Okla. AIDS Coalition; cons. HIV-AIDS State of Okla., 1985—96; dir. Friends Food Pantry Okla. City. Author: Aids for HIV-AIDS, 4 edit. 1989 (award 1992), Accessing the System Directory, 1995, Physician Compassionate Use Directory, 1995. Bd. dirs. AIDS Support Program, 1986-88, Okla. Epilepsy Found., 1989-93; com. chmn. Cmty. Action Agy., Oklahoma City., 1994-95; bd. mem. Ven Cor Hosp. Ethics Com., 1998; HIV Care Consortium, Okla., 1998, 99, Okla. City Housing Com. HIV/AIDS, 1998, 99; Nat. Fin. Planning Bd. for Disabilities, 1998, 99; dir. fellowship award Okla. Lions Svc. Found., 2002; U.S. coord. Guatemala AIDS Medicine Program. Recipient Jefferson award Presbyn. Health Found., Oklahoma City, 1990, Jacqueline Kennedy award Am. Inst. Pub. Svc., Washington, 1990, Five Who Care award Gannett Found., Arlington, Va., 1992, merit award GLB Polit. Caucus, Oklahoma City, 1993, Book of Yr. award Woman's Front Page News, 1993, Friends of Libr. Book award City of Oklahoma City-Moore Libr., 1989, Cmty. Contbn. award, 1994, Individual award U. Okla. Coll. Pub. Health and Alumni Assn., 4th Annual Pub. Health award for excellence U. Okla. Health Scis. Ctr., 1999, Richard May Humanitarian award Okla. AIDS Care Found., 2006. Mem. Case Mgmt. Soc. Am., Case Mgmt. Soc. Ctrl. Okla. Lions (v.p. Bethany Helping Hands 2002. Lion of the Yr. 2002). Democrat. Avocations: writing, lecturing, consulting, horticulture, geology. Home: PO Box 36 Bethany OK 73008-0036 also: 3005 N May Ave Oklahoma City OK 73107-2120 Home Phone: 405-831-1225; Office Phone: 405-605-8020. E-mail: otheroptions@coxinet.net.

ARBUCKLE, JOHN FINLEY, JR., retired investment advisor; b. Peoria, Ill., Jan. 16, 1938; s. John F. Sr. and Florence (Netter) A. Grad., U. Okla., 1985. V.p. 1st Am. Bank, Peoria, 1975—96; shareholder rels. AT/Investor Svc. & Document Co., Peoria, 1996—2001; ret., 2001. Past bd. dirs. Dist. 150 Sch. Bd., Peoria. Mem. Ill. Valley Yacht Club, Creve Coeur Club, S.W. Kiwanis Club (v.p. 1996—), S.W. Kiwanis Club (pres. 1999-2000).

ARBUCKLE, PEGGY TRAWICK, special education educator, consultant; b. Newville, Ala., Apr. 18, 1939; d. Alex Trawick and Hattie Mae Humphrey; m. George H. Arbuckle (dec.); children: Gary Steven, Sandra. Undergrad., Ala. State U., 1955—57; BA, Kean U., 1976. Tchr. elem. edn. Roselle (N.J.) Bd. Edn., 1976—79; tchr. Ednl. Tng. Cons., East Orange, NJ, 1980—81, Essex County Svc. Commn., West Orange, NJ, 1981—. Dir. summer day camp Park Ave St. John's, East Orange, 1992—99. Lay spkr. United Meth. Ch. Mem.: N.J. Edn. Assn., Nat. Coun. Negro Women, Ala. State U. Alumni (treas. N.J. chpt. 1992—), Order Eastern Stars (grand matron Marth Grand chpt. 1996—). Home: 25 Porter Ave Newark NJ 07112

ARBUTHNOT, ROBERT MURRAY, lawyer; b. Montreal, Quebec, Can., Oct. 23, 1936; s. Leland Claude and Winnifred Laura (Hodges) A.; m. Janet Marie O'Keefe, Oct. 6, 1968; children: Douglas, Michael, Mary Kathleen, Allison Anne. BA, Calif. State U., San Francisco, 1959; JD, U. Calif., San Francisco, 1966. Bar: Calif. 1967, U.S. Dist. Ct. (no. and cen. dists.) Calif. 1967, U.S. Ct. Appeals (9th cir.) 1967, U.S. Supreme Ct. 1975. Assoc. trial lawyer Rankin & Craddick, Oakland, Calif., 1967-69; assoc. atty. Ericksen, Arbuthnot, Brown, Kilduff & Day, Inc., San Francisco, 1970-73, ptnr., 1973-80, chmn. bd., mng. dir., 1980—. Gen. counsel CFS Ins. Svcs., San Francisco, 1990—; pro tem judge, arbitrator San Francisco Superior Ct., 1990—; lectr. in field. Bd. regents St. Mary's Coll. High Sch., Berkeley, Calif., 1988-91. With U.S. Army, 1959-62. Recipient Honors plaque St. Mary's Coll. High Sch., 1989. Mem. Internat. Assn. of Ins. Counsel, No. Calif. Assn. of Def. Counsel, Def. Rsch. Inst., Assn. Trial Lawyers Am., San Francisco Lawyers Club. Avocation: boating. Office: Ericksen Arbuthnot Kicduff Et Al 111 Sutter St #575 San Francisco CA 94104 E-mail: eakdlsf@aol.com.

ARBUZ, JOSEPH ROBERT, lawyer; b. NYC, Nov. 23, 1949; s. Jose Hernan Cortes and Rachel Dweck Arbuz; m. Millicent Luck Fornah July, 1978 (div.); 1 child, Christina. BA, Fla. State U., 1972, MS in Pub. Adminstrn., 1975; JD, Howard U., 1977; MDiv, Southwestern Bapt. Sem., 1981; postgrad. in theology, Westminster Theol. Sem., 1995; D Divinity, Cohen U. & Theol. Sem., 2000. Bar: Fla. 1978, U.S. Ct. Mil. Appeals 1983, U.S. Dist. Ct. (so. dist.) Fla. 1986, U.S. Ct. Appeals (11th cir.) 2000, U.S. Supreme Ct., 2000; lic. min. So. Bapt. Ch., 1982—. EEO investigator Smithsonian Instn., Washington, 1985; asst. atty. gen. Atty. Gen., Miami, Fla., 1986; pvt. practice Miami, Fla., 1987-90, Miami Beach, Fla., 1994—. Evangelism Gambrell St. Bapt. Ch., Ft. Worth, 1980; pastor Biscayne Bapt. Ch., Miami, 1989; choir mem. U. Bapt. Ch., Coral Gables, Fla., 1994-97; performer Miami Christmas Pageant, Miami, 1994, 96; asst. staff judge advocate. 1st lt. Signal Corps., U.S. Army, 1972-74; capt. USAF, 1982-84. J.F.K. Tchg. scholar Miami-Dade C.C., Miami, 1969. Mem. Atty. Title Ins. Fund, South Fla. Hispanic C. of C., Dade County Bar Assn. Democrat. Presbyterian. Avocations: exercise, theater, reading, church activities. Office: PO Box 398843 Miami Beach FL 33239-8843 Office Phone: 305-673-2695. E-mail: joearbuz@aol.com.

ARCANGEL, CORY, artist, computer technician; b. Buffalo, May 25, 1978; BA in Tech. in Music & Related Arts, Oberlin Coll., 2000. Founding mem. BIEGE Programming Ensemble, The 8-bit Construction Set. Curator (web exhibitions) Low Level All Stars, Kingdom of Piracy, (exhibitions), Deitch Projects, 2005, Another Bad Creation, 2003, Psych-Out 2k3, Anthology Film Archives/NYUFF, 2003, The Infinite Fill Grp. Show, Foxy Productions, 2004, (distributed on floppy disk, group shows) 1.44 Megs, with Moving Image Gallery & Rhizome.org; exhibitions include Deadtech Gallery, Chgo., Eye Beam, Lothringer13, Make-World Festival, Munich, Leroy Neiman Gallery, Columbia U., 2004, NY Underground Film Festival, video screenings, Anthology Film Archives, NY Underground Film Festival, 2002, 2003, 2004, 2005, Rodney Graham Film Prog., Whitechapel Gallery, 2002, Art Plus Dance, 2004, Game Engine, NY Video Festival, 2003, Internat. Film Festival Rotterdam, 2004, 2005, Pics 'n Clips, Arthouse, 2004, exhibited in group shows at Interface: Exploring Possibilities, Fassbender Gallery, Chgo., 2001, Unknown Pleasures, Daniel Reich Gallery, 2002, Digital Media, Am. Mus. Moving Image, NY, 2002, Blinky, Foxy Productions, 2003, Throwback, Team Gallery, 2003, Killer Instinct, New Mus. Contemporary Art, 2003, Artbase, 2005, Expander, Royal Acad., London, 2004, Guggenheim, 2004, Pattern Playback, Moore Space, 2004, NY/Liverpool Project, Liverpool Biennial, 2004, Database Imaginary, Banff Centre, 2004, Super Cinema, Guggenheim, 2006, Outside the Box: New Cinematic Experiences, U. of Akron, 2006, Whitney Biennial Am. Art, Whitney Mus. Am. Art, 2004, Premieres, Mus. Modern Art, NY, 2004, one-man shows include welcome to the infinite fill zone, FACT, Liverpool, 2004, The Young Art Fair, LISTE, Swizterland, 2004, Nerdzone Version 1, Migros Mus., Zurich, 2005, Super Mario Movie, Deitch Projects, 2005, disassembling 48k, Brandstorm & Stene, Stockholm, 2005, Team Gallery, NY, 2005, Mix, Temple U. Gallery, 2005, Summer Party Jam, Wood St. Galleries, 2005, Growing up absurd, Herbert Read Gallery, 2005, P.S.1, 2005, Carnegie Mus. Art, 2005, Start Kapital, Standard, Oslo, 2005, Vox, centre de l'image contemporaine, 2005, Collaborations, The Embassy, 2005, The Early Show, White Columns, 2005, Moving Pictures, Dallas Ctr. Contemporary Art, 2005, Space 1026, 2005, Video Cube, Galarie Thaddaeus Ropac, Salzburg, Austria, 2005, Galarie Thaddaeus Ropac, Paris, 2006; performer: The 8bit Constrn. Set, 2003, Summer of HTML, 2003, Paper Rad and Beige, 2004, One Night Only, 2005, New Work, 2005, Nerds Gone Wild, 2005, Media Archeology, 2005, I Heart Garfunkel, 2005. Grantee, turbulence.org, NY State Coun. Arts. Mailing: c/o Team Gallery 527 West 26th St New York NY 10001 E-mail: cory@gmail.com.

ARCARO, THOMAS E., sociologist, educator; m. Ami Arcaro; children: Zac, Bevin, Amelia. Faculty mem. to prof. sociology Elon U., NC, 1985—. Dir. Project Pericles Elon U., 2002—. Author: A Collection of Essays on Being Human. Recipient US Prof. of Yr. award, Carnegie Found. for Advancement of Tchg. and Coun. for Advancement and Support of Edn., 2006. Office: Elon U Holland House 203 2610 Campus Box Elon NC 27244 Office Phone: 336-278-6442. E-mail: arcaro@elon.edu.*

ARCE, A. ANTHONY, psychiatrist, educator; b. San Juan, June 13, 1923; s. Angel and Juana (Baez) A.; m. Malvene Balkind, Oct. 7, 1971; children: Alan I. Scheer, Judith Ann Scheer, Michael Anthony Arce. BS, Washington and Jefferson Coll., 1942; MD, Temple U., 1946. Diplomate: Am. Bd. Psychiatry and Neurology; certified in adminstrv. psychiatry. Intern Mercy Hosp., Bay City, Mich.; Frankford Hosp., Phila., 1946-47; dir. Aguadilla Dist. Hosp., PR, 1947-48; chief health officer Utuado, PR, 1950-51; physician US Mil. Acad., West Point, NY, 1951-52; med. officer Pa. R.R., 1952-53; practice medicine Yonkers, NY, 1953-59; resident psychiatrist Payne Whitney Clinic, NYC, 1959-62; assoc. dir. psychiatry Grasslands Hosp., Valhalla, NY, 1962-67; dir. psychiatry Lincoln Hall Sch., Lincolndale, NY, 1967-68; dir. Bur. Aftercare Svcs. NY State Dept. Mental Hygiene, 1968-71; dir. Manhattan Psychiat. Ctr., Ward's Island, NY, 1971-76, Hahnemann Cmty. Mental Health and Mental Retardation Ctr., Phila., 1976-84; pvt. practice medicine specializing in psychiatry, 1962—; prof. psychiatry, dep. chmn. dept. mental health svcs. Hahnemann U., 1976-85, prof., chmn., 1985-87, prof., dir. amb. svcs., 1987-91; prof., dep. chmn. dept. psychiatry Med. Coll., U. Pa., Phila., 1991-96; chmn. dept. behavioral medicine, med. dir. Girard Med. Ctr., Phila., 1996—. Mem. president's coun. NYU Sch. Social Work, 1963-66; bd. dirs. PR Family Inst., NYC, 1970-72. Served with AUS, 1943-46, 48-50. Mem. Am. Coll. Mental Health Adminstrs., Am. Coll. Psychiatrists, Am. Psychiat. Assn. (chmn. task force continuing care), Phila. Psychiat. Soc., Am. Assn. Psychiat. Adminstrs. (treas., pres.). Home: 1416 Academy Ln Elkins Park PA 19027-2515 Office: Girard Med Ctr 2ADC 8th St & Girard Ave Philadelphia PA 19122-9999

ARCE, PHILLIP WILLIAM, hotel and casino executive; b. NYC, June 25, 1937; s. Joseph F. and Margaret (Degnan) A.; m. Dorothy Fiss, June 25, 1966; children: Joseph, William, Serena. Student, U. Notre Dame, 1955-56; AA, San Diego Jr. Coll., 1958; student, San Diego State U., 1958-60, San Diego U., 1960-62, LaSalle Law Sch., 1963-65. Various positions Del Webb Corp., Las Vegas and Reno, Nev., Oahu, Hawaii, 1963-75; exec. Caesars Palace, Las Vegas, 1975-78; pres. Frontier Hotel, Las Vegas, 1978-84; corp. v.p., v.p. mktg., sr. v.p. Dunes Hotel & Country Club, Las Vegas, 1985-88; hotel and gaming specialist Arce Cons., Las Vegas, 1988—. Tchr. hotel div. U. Nev., Las Vegas, 1966-67, 1976-77 Mem. exec. com. Boulder Dam Area coun. Boy Scouts Am., 1976-88; vice chmn. United Way So. Nev., 1968-70; founder, chmn. Las Vegas Events, Inc., 1980-89; pres. Easter Seals Nev., 1974-76, pres. first nat. telethon, 1975; bd. dirs. Air Force Acad. Found., 1982-89. Served with USMC, 1962. Recipient Appreciation award Easter Seals, 1972, 73, United Way, 1975, Silver Beaver Boy Scouts Am., 1984, others. Mem. Am. Hotel and Motel Assn. (bd. dirs. 1979-82), Nev. Hotel and Motel Assn. (founder, pres. 1980, Hotelier of Yr. award 1981), Las Vegas C. of C. (dir. 1979-85, pres. 1984). Republican. Roman Catholic. Home: 4243 Ridgecrest Dr Las Vegas NV 89121-4949

ARCENEAUX, WILLIAM, historian, educator, association administrator; b. Scott, La., Aug. 19, 1941; s. Teddy and Regina (Begnaud) A.; m. Patricia Boozman; children: Ted, Angelle, Leah, Scott. BA, U. La., Lafayette, 1962; MA, La. State U., 1965, PhD, 1969; LHD, Loyola U., 1982. Instr. La. State U., 1966-67; asst. prof. Northwestern State U., Natchitoches, La., 1967-69; assoc. prof., chmn. dept. history So. U., New Orleans, 1969-72; exec. dir. La. Coordinating Council for Higher Edn., 1972-75; commr. higher edn. La. Baton Rouge, 1975-87; pres. La. Assn. Ind. Colls. and Univs., 1987—. Chmn. CSLA, Inc. Author: Acadian General-Alfred Mouton and the Civil War, 1972, 2d edit., 1981, No Spark of Malice: The Murder of Martin Begnaud, 1999; editor: Postsecondary Education in Transition: Planning for Change in Louisiana, 1975. Bd. dirs., chmn. Student Loan Mktg. Assn., 1979-97; chmn. La. Found. La., 1993—; exec. com. La. Pub. Broadcasting, chair La. Bicentennial Com. of Baton Rouge. Decorated chevalier L'Ordre de la Pleiade, Association Internationale des Parlementaires de Langue Francaise, L'Ordre des Palmes Academique (France); named one of 100 Young Leaders of Academy Change mag., 1978; recipient Jefferson Davis medal UDC, E.T. Dunlap medal Southeastern Okla. State U. Mem.: La. Hist. Assn., World Trade Ctr. New Orleans, Am. Hist. Assn., Nat. Assn. Ind. Coll. and Univ. State Execs., Plimsol Club, City Club of Baton Rouge (bd. govs.), Country Club of La., Phi Alpha Theta, Omicron Delta Kappa. Roman Catholic. Office: La Assn Ind Colls and Univs Ste 104 320 Third St Baton Rouge LA 70801 Business E-Mail: bill@laicu.org.

ARCHABAL, NINA M(ARCHETTI), historic site director; b. Long Branch, NJ, Apr. 11, 1940; d. John William and Santina Matilda (Giuffre) Marchetti; m. John William Archabal, Aug. 8, 1964; 1 child, John Fidel. BA in Music History cum laude, Radcliffe Coll., 1962; MAT in Music History, Harvard U., 1963; PhD in Music History, U. Minn., 1979. Asst. dir. humanities art mus. U. Minn., Mpls., 1975-77; asst. supr. edn. divsn. Minn. Hist. Soc., St. Paul, 1977-78, dep. dir. for program mgmt., 1978-86, acting dir., 1986-87, dir., 1987—, sec. governing bd. Bd. dirs. US nat. com. Internat. Coun. Mus.; mem. Nat. Coun. on Humanities, 2000. V.p. Friends of St. Paul Pub. Libr., 1983-93; Minn. state hist. preservation officer, 1987—; chair State Hist. Records Adv. Bd., 1987—, St. Anthony Falls Heritage Bd., 1988—; trustee, bd. dirs. Am. Folklife Ctr., Libr. of Congress, 1989-98; bd. dirs. N.W. Area Found., 1989-98, St. Paul Acad. and Summit Sch., 1993-2002, St. Paul Riverfront Corp., 2000-03, Rsch. Librs. Group, 2004—; bd. regents St. John's U., Collegeville, Minn., 1997-2004; overseer Harvard Coll., Cambridge, Mass., 1997—; mem. bd. overseers Hill Mus. and Manuscript Libr., 2004—. NDEA fellow U. Minn., 1969-72, U. Minn. grad. fellow, 1974-75; recipient Nat. Humanities medal The White House, 1997. Mem. Am. Assn. State and Local History (sec. 1986-88), Am. Assn. Museums (v.p. 1991-94, chair bd. dirs. 1994-96; named to Centennial Honor Roll, 2006). Office: Minn Hist Soc 345 Kellogg Blvd W Saint Paul MN 55102-1906 Office Phone: 651-296-6126.*

ARCHAMBAULT, LEE JOSEPH, astronaut; b. Oak Park, Ill., Aug. 25, 1960; s. Lee and Mary Ann Archambault; m. Kelly Renee Raup; 3 children. BSc with hon. in Aero. & Astronautical Engring., U. Ill., Urbana, 1982, MSc with hon. in Aero. & Astronautical Engring., 1984. Commd. 2d lt. USAF, 1985, advanced through grades to lt. col., various assignments, 1985—90; assigned to Operation Desert Shield/Desert Storm, Saudi Arabia, 1990—91, Saudi Arabia, 1991—92, Holloman AFB, N.Mex., 1992—94; various assignments USAF, 1995—98; astronaut NASA, Houston, 1998—. Mem. acad. adv. com. U. Ill. Aero. & Astronautical Engring. Dept.; pilot STS-117 Atlantis Mission, 2007. Decorated Disting. Flying Cross USAF, Meritorious Svc. medal with 1 oak leaf cluster, Air medal with 2 oak leaf clusters, Aerial Achievement medal with 4th oak leaf cluster, Commendation medal with 1st oak leaf cluster, Kuwaiti Liberation medal, Achievement medal; recipient Southwest Asia Svc. medal. Mem.: Soc. Exptl. Test Pilots, U. Ill. Alumni Assn., Order of Daedalians. Avocations: weightlifting, golf, running, ice hockey. Office: Astronaut Office CB NASA Johnson Space Center Houston TX 77058*

ARCHAMBAULT, NICOLE MARIE, speech pathology/audiology services professional, consultant; b. Anaheim, Calif., Nov. 24, 1973; d. Guy Rene and Donna Jean Archambault. BA in Speech and Hearing Scis., Wash. State U., 1996; MS in Speech and Hearing Scis., U. N.Mex, 1999. Cert. clin. competence speech-lang. pathology Am. Speech-Language Hearing Assn., 2000, lic. speech-lang. pathologist Calif. Speech-Language Pathology and Audiology Bd., 2000, Nev. Bd. of Examiners for Audiology and Speech Pathology, 1999, cert. Hanen Centre, 2002, interior decorator Decorator Tng. Inst., 2005, speech-lang. pathologist orofacial myofunctional therapist exec., infant massage instr. Internat. Loving Touch Found. Speech-language pathologist The Continuum, Reno, 1999—; pediatric speech-language pathologist Cedars Sinai Med. Ctr., LA; owner, dir. Talk For Tots, Santa Monica. Cons. Step By Step Early Childhood Devel. Ctr., Benjamin Links; sr. cons. Little Lima Bean Prodns.; co-owner Kids Places & Spaces Integrative Develop. Design Co., 2005—07. Recipient ACE award, Am. Speech Lang. Hearing Assn., 2005; Maynard Lee Daggy scholar, Wash. State U., 1995, All-Am. scholar, U.S. Achievement Acad., 1996. Mem.: Internat. Soc. for Devel. Neurosci., Internat. Assn. Orofacial Myology, Internat. Mind, Brain and Edn. Soc., Nat. Coalition Auditory Processing Disorders, Calif. Speech and Hearing Assn., Am. Speech-Lang. Hearing Assn. (Am. Continuing Edn. award 2003, 2005, 2006), Acad. Neurological Comm. Disorders and Sci. (assoc.), Soc. Children's Book Writers and Illustrators (assoc.), Golden Key Nat. Honor Soc. Office: Talk For Tots 1814 14th St Ste 210 Santa Monica CA 90404 Office Phone: 310-936-3020. Business E-Mail: talkfortots@msn.com.

ARCHANGELSKY, DMITRY A., application developer, researcher; b. Kharkov, Ukraine, Nov. 29, 1960; s. Cecilia V and Avenir L Archangelsky; m. Svetlana V Loganova; 1 child, Alexander D. PhD, St.Petersburg State U., 1993. Assoc. prof. Tver State U., Tver, Russia, 1995—99; cons. Global Consulting Group, Haverhill, Mass., 1999—. Contbr. articles to profl. jours. Grant, Internat. Sci. Fund, Russian Fund of Fundamental Researches. Mem.: Am. Math. Soc. (assoc.), NY Acad. Of Sciences (assoc.). Achievements include invention of algorithm of person identification using blood vessel picture; algorithm of understanding of a natural language in a given context; development of a system for computer text book development; research in polinomial algorithm for BR-nets. Home: 3414 138th St E Tacoma WA 98446-1722 Personal E-mail: dm_ar@hotmail.com.

ARCHBOLD, MICHAEL G., consumer products company executive, former retail executive; b. July 7, 1960; m. Laura P. Archbold. BSc in Acctg., Fairfield U., 1982. CPA. Various fin. positions Woolworth Corp., 1988—96; v.p., CFO Booksellers Divsn. Barnes & Noble, Inc., 1996—2002; sr. v.p. Autozone, Memphis, 2002—05, CFO, 2002—05, exec. v.p., 2005; exec. v.p., CFO, chief adminstrv. officer Saks Fifth Ave. Enterprises, 2005—07; exec. v.p., COO, CFO The Vitamin Shoppe, No. Bergen, NJ, 2007—. Office: The Vitamin Shoppe 2101 9th St North Bergen NJ 07047*

ARCHBOLD, WILLIAM CORNELL, JR., lawyer; s. William Cornell Archbold and Barbara Curtis; m. Janice Marie Kendrick, July 27, 1957; children: Cynthia Anne, Cassandra Kendrick. BS, Syracuse U., 1950; JD, George Wash. U., DC, 1955. Bar: Superior Ct. Pa. 1956, US Dist. Ct. (DC) 1955, US Dist. Ct. (ea. dist.) 1965, US Dist. Ct. (middle dist.) Pa. 1965, DC 1955, US Circuit Ct. (DC) 1955, Pa. 1955, Ct. Common Pleas Del. County,

Pa. (judge pro tem) 1971, Pa. Supreme Ct. 1956, US Supreme Ct. 1960, Am. Bd. Trial Advocates. Civil and criminal litigator Hodge, Hodge and Cramp, Media, Pa., 1955—57, Kearns, Archibald Maffei & Kelly, Media, 1957—62, Bloom Archbold Ramsey & Kelly, Chester, 1962—63; pub. defender Delaware County, Pa., 1957—58; founding ptnr. Kassab Archbold O'Brien, Media, Pa., 1963—. Founding mem. Nat. Bd. Trial Advocacy, DC, 1978—; trustee Thomas F. Lambert chair Suffolk U. Sch. Law, Boston, 1987—; founding mem. Pub. Justice Found., DC, 1997—; mem. rules com., ea. dist. Pa. US Dist. Ct., Phila., 2001—. Author: (reference book) Wrongful Death Damages of the Late Good Wife and Mother, 1977, Wrongful Death Damages in Pennsylvania, 1977; co-author: The Pennsylvania No Fault Motor Vehicle Insurance Act, 1979. Chmn. Com. Preserve & Restore 1724 Courthouse, Chester, Pa., 1970—79; founder Roy D. Simmons Sr. Scholarship Fund; dir. Syracuse U. Alumni Assn., 1971—75, Syracuse U. Varsity Club, 1980—2007, Syracuse U. Athletic Dirs. Adv. Bd., 2007; founder Roy D. Simmons, Sr. Scholarship Fund, Syracuse; dir. Hist. Del. County, Inc., Media, Pa., 1970—79, Del. County Legal Assistance Assn., Inc., Media, 1975—77; mem. Syracuse U. Founders Soc., 1990—2007, Orange Pack, Syracuse, 1985—2007, Ernie Davis Fund, Syracuse, 1975—2007. 1st lt. US Army, 1951—52, Korea, asst. batallion surgeon US Army. Decorated Combat Medic's Badge US Army, Bronze Star, UN Medal, Korean Svc. 3 Battle Stars medal, Am. Def. medal; recipient Man of Yr. award, Lawyers' Club, Del. County Bar Assn., 1971, Nat. Bd. Trial Advocacy award, ATLA, 1978, Letterman of Distinction award, Varsity Club, Syracuse U., 1978, Guy G. DeFuria award, Am. Inns Ct., 2000, Elizabeth C. Price award, Del. County Bar Assn., 2003, Melvin A. Eggers Sr. Alumni award, Syracuse U., 2004, Hon. Paul R. Sand award, Del. County Bar Assn., 2006; grantee 1724 Courthouse Restoration Matching grant, HUD, 1972. Mem.: Antique and Classic Boat Soc., Melvin E. Belli Soc. (trustee 1987—), Pa. Bar Assn., Omicron Delta Kappa (life), Tau Theta Upsilon (life), Phi Alpha Delta (life), Phi Delta Theta (life). Avocations: sailing, diving, tennis, water-skiing, skiing. Home: 1012 Robin Dr West Chester PA 19382 Personal E-mail: william@archbolds.com. Business E-Mail: williamarchbold@kassablaw.com.

ARCHER, CHALMERS, JR., retired education educator; b. Tchula, Miss., Apr. 21, 1938; s. Chalmers Sr. and Eva Alcola (Rutherford) A. AS, Saints Jr. Coll., 1969; BS, Tuskegee Inst., 1972, MEd, 1974; post doctorate, U. Ala., 1980; cert., MIT, 1980; PhD, Auburn U., 1979. Asst. to the pres. Saints Coll., Lexington, Miss., 1968-72; asst. v.p. Tuskegee (Ala.) Inst., 1972-83; prof. No. Va. C.C., Manassas, 1983-2001, prof. emeritus, 2001. Author: Growing Up Black in Rural Mississippi (recipient Miss. Inst. of Arts and Letters award for Nonfiction), Green Berets in the Vanguard: Inside Special Forces, 1953-1963; contbg. editor: The Jackson Advocate; contbr. articles to profl. jours. and newspapers. Mem. Dem. Spkr.'s Bur. for Clinton/Gore Re-election Campaign. Recipient Nat. Edn. Articulation Model, Conf. on Blacks in Higher Edn., Washington, 1986. Mem. Rotary (county transportation commnr.). Democrat. Baptist. Avocations: writing, motivational speaking, community service. Home: 7885 Flager Cir Manassas VA 20109-7435 Office Phone: 703-335-5289. Personal E-mail: drarcher97@aol.com.

ARCHER, CRISTINA LOZEJ, meteorologist; b. Como, Italy, Apr. 21, 1970; d. Alessandra Bonfanti; m. Scott Mckinley Archer, Nov. 4, 2000; children: Eva Julia children: Emma Tiffany, Clara Maria. MS, Politecnico di Milano, Italy, 1995, San Jose State U., Calif., 1998; PhD, Stanford U., Calif., 2004. Post doctoral scholar Stanford U., 2004—05; atmospheric modeler Bay Area Air Quality Mgmt. Dist., San Francisco, 2005—07; rsch. assoc. Carnegie Instn. Washington, Stanford, Calif., 2007—. Cons. asst. prof. dept. civil and environ. engring. Stanford U., 2005—. Contbr. articles to profl. jours. Recipient Best thesis in environ. field award, Regione Lombardia, Milano, Italy, 1995. Mem.: Am. Meteorol. Soc. (assoc.). Roman Catholic. Achievements include research in first study on global wind power potential; discovery and study of an atmospheric vortex. Avocations: bicycling, beach, reading, knitting. Office: Carnegie Instn Washington Dept Global Ecology 260 Panama St Stanford CA 94305 Home Phone: 650-321-1376. Personal E-mail: lozej@stanford.edu.

ARCHER, DENNIS WAYNE, lawyer, former mayor; b. Detroit, Jan. 1, 1942; s. Ernest James and Frances (Carroll) A.; m. Trudy Ann DunCombe, June 17, 1967; children: Dennis Wayne, Vincent DunCombe BS, Western Mich. U., 1965; JD, Detroit Coll. Law, 1970; LLD (hon.), Western Mich. U., 1987, Detroit Coll. Law, 1988, U. Detroit, 1988, John Marshall Law Sch., 1991, Gonzaga U., 1991, U. Mich., 1994; D in Pub. Svc. (hon.), Ea. Mich. U., 1994; LLD (hon.), Aquinos Coll., 1996, Marygrove Coll., 1997, Hamline U., 2001, Wayne State U., 2002, U. Balt., 2002, Stetson U., 2003, Temple U., 2004, U. Conn., 2004. Bar: Mich. 1970. Tchr. spl. edn. Detroit Bd. Edn., 1965-70; assoc. Gragg & Gardner, 1970-71; ptnr. Hall, Stone, Allen, Archer & Glenn, P.C., 1971-73, Charfoos, Christensen & Archer, P.C., 1973-85; assoc. justice Mich. Supreme Ct., 1986-90; ptnr. Dickinson, Wright, Moon, Van Dusen & Freeman, Detroit, 1991-93; chmn. Dickinson Wright PLLC, 2001—, Detroit, 2002—; mayor City of Detroit, 1994—2001. Assoc. prof. Detroit Coll. Law, 1972-78; adj. prof. Wayne State U. Law Sch., Detroit, 1984-85; mem. Mich. Bd. Ethics, 1979-83; mem. adv. bd. U.S. Conf. Mayors, 1994—; bd. dirs. Nat. Conf. Black Mayors, 1994—; mem. intergovtl. policy adv. com. U.S. Trade Rep.; bd. dirs. Compuware, Johnson Controls, Inc. Contbr. articles to legal jours. Bd. dirs. Legal Aid and Defenders Assn., Detroit, 1980-82, Nat. Conf. Black Mayors, 1994, CATCH, Henry Ford Health Sys.; co-chmn. Met. Detroit Cmty. Coalition for Dems., 1979-80; bd. trustees Olivet Coll., 1991-93; active numerous local Dem. campaigns, 1970-85; host local pub. svc. radio programs; co-chair platform com. Dem. Conv., 1996; pres. Nat. Conf. Dem. Mayors, 1996; mem. Nat. Com. on Crime Control and Prevention, 1995. Named Most Respected Judge in Mich. Mich. Lawyers Weekly Jour., 1990. Mem. ABA (ho. dels. 1979-93, chmn. drafting com. 1986-88, com. on scope and correlation of work sect. officers liaison 1987-90, chmn. gen. practice sect. 1987-88, chair commn. on opportunities for minorities in the profession 1987-91, sect. legal edn. and admissions to the bar, coun. mem. 1989-95, task force on profl. skills instrn. 1989-91, task force on law schs. and the profession, Narrowing The Gap, 1989-91, chmn. spl. com. prepaid legal svcs. 1981-83, chmn. sect. officers conf. 1988-90, resource devel. coun. 1988-91, bd. editors ABA Jour. 1988-94, bd. editors The Practical Litigator 1989-94, chmn. rules and calendar com. 1990-92, state del. 1990-96, pres. 2003-2004), ATLA, Nat. Bar Assn. (pres. 1983-84), Am. Judicature Soc. (bd. dirs 1977-81), State Bar Mich. (pres. 1984-85), Wolverine Bar Assn. (pres. 1979-80), Detroit Bar Assn. (bd. dirs. 1973-75), Mich. Trial Lawyers Assn. (exec. bd. 1973-74), Econ. Club, Alpha Phi Alpha. Roman Catholic. Office: Dickinson Wright Ste 4000 500 Woodward Ave Detroit MI 48226-3425 Office Phone: 313-223-3500. Office Fax: 313-223-3598. Business E-Mail: darcher@dickinsonwright.com.*

ARCHER, GLENN LEROY, JR., federal judge; b. Densmore, Kans., Mar. 21, 1929; s. Glenn LeRoy and Ruth Agnes (Ford) A.; m. Carole J. Thomas, 1990; children: Susan, Sharon, Glenn, Thomas. BA, Yale U., 1951; JD with honors, George Washington U., 1954. Bar: D.C. 1954. Assoc. Hamel, Park, McCabe & Saunders, Washington, 1956—60, ptnr., 1960—81; asst. atty. gen. US Dept. Justice, Washington, 1981-85; circuit judge US Ct. Appeals (fed. cir.), Washington, 1985-94, chief judge, 1994-97, sr. cir. judge, 1997—. First lt. JAG Corps USAF, 1954—56. Republican. Methodist. Office: US Ct of Appeals Fed Circuit 717 Madison Pl NW Washington DC 20439-0002*

ARCHER, JAMES ELSON, engineering educator; b. Hedley, Tex., Dec. 1, 1922; s. James M. and Mary Minerva (Bolles) A.; m. Reta Faye Turner, Nov. 8, 1942; 1 son, James Elson. BS, Tex. Tech. U., 1947; PhD, Mass. Inst. Tech., 1950. Instr. Mass. Inst. Tech., 1950-52, Sloan fellow in indsl. mgmt., 1963-64; researcher Pitts. Plate Glass Co., Pitts., 1952-53, asst. dir., 1953-54, asso. dir., 1954-56, dir. research, 1956-62; mng. partner Archer Assos., Dallas, 1962-64; corporate dir. mgmt. systems Tex. Instruments, Dallas, 1964-68; prof. Tex. Tech U., Lubbock, 1968-95, prof. emeritus, 1995—. With USAAF, 1943—46. Home: 6208 Lynnhaven Dr Lubbock TX 79413-5332

ARCHER, LILLIAN PATRICIA, academic administrator, dean; b. Lawrenceville, Va., Oct. 31, 1952; d. Wyatt and Marian Archer; m. James Leroy Drewery, July 7, 2000. BS, Morgan State U., 1976; MA, Coll. Notre Dame, 1990; EdD in Higher Edn., Morgan State U., 2002. Counselor CC Balt. County, 1992—99, interim dir. of human rels., 1998—99, dir. counseling, 1999—2001, sr. dir. student support svcs., 2001—02, sr. dir. counseling, acad. advisement and entry svcs., 2002—04, sr. dir. acad. and adminstrv. svcs., 2004—05, campus adminstr., 2005—06, campus dean, 2006—. Sys. appraiser Higher Learning Commn. of North Ctrl. Assn. of Colls. and Schs., Chgo., 2004—. Vol. Wigs for Kids, Cleve., 2004—04, South Balt. Emergency Relief (SOBER), Balt., 1999—2001; bd. dirs. Balt. Med. Sys.; mem. Balt. County Commn. on Women, 2006—. Fellow, Am. Coun. on Edn., 2003—04. Mem.: Am. Coll. Pers. Assn. (ACPA), Am. Assn. of Women in Cmty. Colleges (AAWCC). Avocations: reading, travel, writing. Home Phone: 410-654-9963; Office Phone: 410-455-4300. Personal E-mail: archerfellow@yahoo.com.

ARCHER, RICHARD JOSEPH, lawyer; b. Virginia, Minn., Mar. 24, 1922; s. William John and Margaret Leanore (Duff) A.; m. Kristina Hanson, Jan. 29, 1977 (dec.); children: Alison P., Cynthia J. AB, U. Mich., 1947, JD, 1948. Bar: Calif. 1949, U.S. Supreme Ct. 1962, Hawaii 1982. Partner firm Morrison and Foerster, San Francisco, 1954-71, Sullivan, Jones and Archer, San Francisco, 1971-81, Archer Rosenak & Hanson, San Francisco, 1981-85, Archer & Hanson, San Francisco, 1985—. With USNR, 1942—45. Decorated Bronze Star. Mem. ABA, Am. Bar Found. (life), Am. Law Inst. (life). Home: 3110 Bohemian Hwy Occidental CA 95465-9113 Office Phone: 707-874-3438. Personal E-mail: archerdic@aol.com.

ARCHER, RONALD DEAN, chemist, educator; b. Rochelle, Ill., July 22, 1932; s. Don Adam and Irma Cecil (Olson) Archer; m. Joyce Hilder Carlson, Jan. 31, 1954; children: Paul Dean, Lynn Sue, Sharon Jean, Julie Anne. BS, Ill. State U., 1953, MS, 1954; PhD, U. Ill., 1959. Tchr. Larson Jr. High Sch., Elgin, Ill., 1954; asst. prof. U. Calif., Riverside, 1959-63, Tulane U., New Orleans, 1963-65, assoc. prof., 1965-66, U. Mass., Amherst, 1966-70, prof. chemistry, 1970-99, prof. emeritus, 1999—, head chemistry dept., 1977-83. Cons., 1960—63, 1964—70, 1972—; vis. prof. Tech. U., Denmark, 1972, U. Vienna, 1987; rsch. scientist Naval Rsch. Lab., Washington, 1980; chief chemistry reader advanced placement program Ednl. Testing Svc., 1985—88. Author: (book) Inorg. Organomet Polymass, 2001; contbr. articles to profl. jours. With US Army, 1956—56. Recipient Alumni Achievement award, Ill. State U., 1989; grantee, USAF, Rsch. Corp., NSF, Am. Chem. Soc., NIH, Army Rsch. Office, Office Naval Rsch. Fellow: AAAS; mem.: Masons, Shriners (master mason), New Eng. Assn. Chemistry Tchrs., Am. Chem. Soc. (chmn. Conn. Valley sect. 1979, councilor 1981—, chmn. com. edn. 1987—89, nominating and election com. 1990—94, exec. com. divsn. chem. edn. 1995—98, coun. policy com. 1996—98, chair-elect, chair, past chair divsn. chem. edn. 1996—98, chair adv. bd. gen. chem. curriculum project 1997—2004, com. econ. profl. affairs 1999—2000, chair 2000, sci. com. 2001—03, com. on com. 2001—06, budget and fin. com. 2007—), Rotary Internat. (chpt. bd. dirs. 2005—), Sigma Xi, Phi Lambda Upsilon. Lutheran. Home: 3 Burgundy Ln Amherst MA 01002-3300 Office: U Mass Dept Chemistry Grad Rsch Towers # A Amherst MA 01003-9336 Business E-Mail: archer@chem.umass.edu. *Nothing surpasses the joy in the eyes of a student who has just synthesized a new chemical compound, especially if it has unique properties or may benefit the human endeavor.*

ARCHER, STEPHEN HUNT, economist, educator; b. Fargo, ND, Nov. 30, 1928; s. Clifford Paul and Myrtle Mona (Blair) A.; m. Carol Rosa Mohr, Dec. 29, 1951 (div. Feb. 1971); children: Stephen Paul, Timothy William, David Conrad; m. Lana Jo Urban, Sept. 23, 1972 (dec. Mar. 2003). BA, U. Minn., 1949, MS, 1953, PhD, 1958; postdoctoral student (Ford Found. grantee), U. Calif. at Los Angeles, 1959-60. Mgr. trader J.M. Dain Co., Mpls., 1950, account exec., 1952-53; instr. econs. U. Minn., Mpls., 1954-56; asst. prof. fin. U. Wash., Seattle, 1956-60, assoc. prof., 1960-65, prof., 1965-73, chmn. dept. fin., bus. econs. and quantitative methods, 1966-70; dean Grad. Sch. Adminstrn. Willamette U., Salem, Oreg., 1973-76, 83-85, prof., 1976-79, Guy F. Atkinson prof., 1979-96. Fulbright sr. lectr. Bocconi U., Milan, Italy, 1982; v.p. Hinton, Jones & Co., Inc., Seattle, 1969-70; cons. Wash. Bankers Assn., 1971-72, Weyerhaeuser Co., 1971, Bus.-Econs. Adv. & Research Inc., 1969-77, State of Oreg., 1984, 86, 88, 91; vis. prof. Manchester Bus. Sch., Manchester, Eng., 1990-91, Aomori (Japan) Pub. coll., 2000-01. Author: Introduction to Mathematics for Business Analysis, 1960, Business Finance: Theory and Mgmt, 1966, rev. edit., 1972, The Theory of Business Finance, 1967, 2d rev. edit., 1983, Portfolio Analysis, 1971, rev. edit., 1979, Introduction to Financial Management, 1979, rev. edit., 1983, Cases and Readings in Corporate Finance, 1988; editor Jour. Fin. and Quantitative Analysis, 1966-70, Economic Perspectives, Economica Aziendale, Jour. Bus. and Entrepreneurship. Served with USNR, 1950-52. Mem.: Phi Beta Kappa, Beta Gamma Sigma. Home: 520 SE Columbia River Dr Apt 425 Vancouver WA 98661-8035 Personal E-mail: sarcher75@comcast.net.

ARCHERD, ARMY (ARMAND A. ARCHERD), columnist, retired commentator; b. Bronx, NY, Jan. 13, 1922; m. Selma Archerd. Grad., UCLA, 1941, U.S. Naval Acad. Postgrad. Sch., 1943. With Hollywood bur. AP, 1945—2005; columnist Herald-Express, Daily Variety, 1953—2005; ret. Master of ceremonies numerous Hollywood premieres, Acad. Awards shows; co-host People's Choice Awards shows. Served to lt. USN. Recipient awards Masquers, L.A. Press Club, Hollywood Fgn. Press Club, Newsman of Yr. award Publicists Guild, 1970. Mem. Hollywood Press Club (founder). Office: care Daily Variety 5700 Wilshire Blvd Ste 120 Los Angeles CA 90036-5804 Office Phone: 323-965-4431. Business E-Mail: aarcherd@reedbusiness.com.

ARCHIBALD, CHESTINA MITCHELL, minister; d. Thomas Mitchell and Rosa Lee Horne; m. Albert John Archibald II (dec. 1969); 1 child, Albert John III. BA, U. Dubuque, 1967; MDiv, Interdenominational Theol. Ctr., 1985; JD, Howard U., 1971. Dir. Wesley Found. Fisk U., Nashville, 1985—, univ. chaplain, 1987—97; pastor Key United Meth. Ch., Murfreesboro, Tenn., 2000—06. Freelance writer and motivational speaker. Editor: Say Amen, A.A. Book of Prayer, 1997; Secret of the Psalms; contbr. articles to profl. publs. Avocation: piano. Office: Wesley Found Fisk U 1034 17th Ave N Ste C Nashville TN 37208 Office Phone: 615-321-1134.

ARCHIBALD, JAMES KENWAY, lawyer; b. Greenfield, Mass., Mar. 29, 1949; s. John Lawrence and Jean (Kenway) A.; m. Joanne Mary Ricciuti, Aug. 16, 1975; children: Kathryn, John. BA, Johns Hopkins U., 1971; JD, U. Md., 1975. Bar: Md. 1975, DC 1985, U.S. Dist. Ct. Md. 1976, US Ct. Appeals (4th cir.) 1978, US Supreme Ct. 1979, U.S. Ct. Appeals (9th cir.) 1984, Maine 1998. Assoc. Venable LLP, Balt., 1975-83, ptnr., 1983—. Co-author: Pleading Causes of Action in Maryland, 1990, Model Witness Examinations, 1997. Chmn. bd. trustees Md. State Colls. and Us., 1984-86; trustee Johns Hopkins U., 1997-2000; bd. dirs. Roland Park Country Sch., Inc., Balt., 1989-94; pres. Homeland Assn., Inc., Balt., 1990. Recipient Disting. Svc. award Litigation Sect. Md. State Bar, Md., 1981, Disting. Svc. Award, Md. Inst. for Continuing Edn. of Lawyers. Mem. ABA (litigation sect., co-chair com. 1987-2002), Internat. Assn. Def. Counsel, Def. Rsch. Inst. (Exceptional Performance award 1989, Md. state chair 1989-93), Md. Assn. Def. Trial Counsel (pres. 1988-89), Bar Assn. of Balt. City, Product Liability Adv. Coun., DC Bar, Md. State Bar., U. Md. Law Sch. Alumni Assn. (bd. mem.), Johns Hopkins Alumni Coun. (v.p. 1996-98, pres. 1998-2000), Johns Hopkins Second Decade Soc. (nat. chair 1989-91), Am. Law Inst. Avocation: running. Home: 13037 Jerome Jay Dr Cockeysville MD 21030-1523 Office: 1800 Mercantile Bank Bldg 2 Hopkins Plz Ste 2100 Baltimore MD 21201-2982 also: Venable LLP 575 7th St NW Washington DC 20004 Office Phone: 410-244-7525, 202-344-4901. Office Fax: 202-344-8300, 410-244-7742. E-mail: jkarchibald@venable.com.

ARCHIBALD, NOLAN D., household and industrial products company executive; b. Ogden, Utah, June 22, 1943; m. Margaret Hafen, June 8, 1967. AA, Dixie Coll., 1966; BS, Weber State Univ., 1968; MBA, Harvard U., 1970. Exec. v.p., gen. mgr. Sno Jet, Inc. div. Conroy, Inc., Burlington, Vt., 1970-77; sr. v.p., and pres. non-foods cos. Beatrice Foods, Chgo., 1977-85; pres., COO The Black & Decker Corp., Towson, Md., 1985—86, pres., CEO, 1986—87, chmn., pres., chief exec. officer, 1987—. Former All Am. basketball player.; bd. dir Huntsman Corp.; bd. dir Lockheed Martin Corp., Brunswick Corp. Named one of 10 Most Wanted Execs in U.S., Fortune Mag., Six Best Mgrs. in U.S., Bus. Week Mag.; recipient Edison Achievement award, Am. Mktg. Assn. Avocation: theater.*

ARCHIBEQUE, CHARLENE PAULLIN, retired music educator; b. Mt. Sterling, Ohio, July 15, 1935; d. Howard Samuel and Roberta Mae (Miller) Paullin; 1 child, Melissa. BME, U. Mich., Ann Arbor, 1957; MA, San Diego State Coll., 1965; DMA, U. Colo., Boulder, 1969. Tchr. San Diego Unified Sch. Dist., 1957—69; dir. San Jose State U. Choraliers, Calif., 1970—2005, ret., 2005. Cons., guest lectr. many univs.; condr. choirs in 43 states and Can. Contbr. articles to profl. jours. Dir. chorus San Jose Symphony, 1970-2000, bd. dirs. 1993-2001; v.p. emeritus Faculty Assn.; v.p. Silicon Valley League of San Francisco Symphony; mem. exec. com. San Francisco vol.; bd. mem., chair devel. com., Am. Beethoven Soc. Named Woman of Vision Career Ctr., Disting. Alumni U. Colo., 1986, Woman of Achievement in Arts San Jose Mercury News and Women's Fund, 1998, Outstanding Prof. San Jose State U., 1984-85; recipient Pen award, 1996; Pres.'s scholar San Jose State U., 1992-93 Mem. Am. Choral Dirs. Assn. (state pres. 1971-73, nat. chair 1973-75), Music Educators Nat. Conf., Internat. Choral Fedn. Avocations: travel, reading, cooking, entertaining. Home: 11511 Summit Wood Rd Los Altos Hills CA 94022-4512 Personal E-mail: chara@pacbell.net.

ARCHULETA, KEITH ANTHONY, entrepreneur, business and management consultant; b. Denver, Mar. 13, 1955; s. Willie M. and Judith Ruth (Archuleta) Suggs; m. Iris Curtis, May 27, 1995; 1 child, Dorian. BA in Comm., Stanford U., 1978, BA in African and African Am. Studies, 1978; MA, U. San Francisco, 1992. Founder, bus. mgr. Stanford Black Media Inst., 1976; dir. So. Africa Media Ctr., San Francisco, 1979-80; program coord. Student Arts at Stanford (Calif.), 1982-84; asst. dir. Stanford Residential Edn., 1984-88; founder/dir. Black Cmty. Svcs. Ctr., Stanford, 1987-92; exec. dir., asst. dean students Oakland (Calif.) Youth Chorus, 1993; project adminstr. Arts Edn. Funders Collaborative, San Francisco, 1994-99; site adminstr. Young African Am. Achievers Program, San Francisco, 1995-97; interim exec. dir. LEAP.Imagination in Learning, San Francisco, 1996, Oakland Asian Cultural Ctr., Oakland, 1998; founder, CEO Ur At Work, Inc., 1999—2001; cons. East County Bus.-Edn. Alliance, 2000—; exec. dir. CASA Contra Costa County, 2001—. Founder/pres. Emerald Consulting, Antioch, Calif., 1992—; mem. adv. bd. CIIS MBA Program, San Francisco, 1994-97; mem. bd. devel./mktg. chair LEAP.Imagination in Learning, San Francisco, 1995-97; mem. bd. emeritus Theatre Works, 1992—; rev. panelist Arts Coun. Santa Clara County, San Jose, Calif., 1996-97, NEA, Washington, 2001-02, 07; bd. dirs. Micro Credit Loan Fund, Inc., Regional Tng. Inst., 2002-05, CBO Ctr., 2004—, Opportunity Junction, 2006—. Author: (play) Their Spirits are Free, 1982; prodr., editor (ednl. video) Song for Melvin Truss, 1986. Fellow Calif. State Legislature, Sacramento, 1978-79; vol. Crossroads Africa, Liberia, West Africa, 1979, San Francisco Sch. Vols., 1995-99; founder Kuumba Arts Ensemble, 1979, East Palo Alto Youth Theatre Project, 1985; congrl. dist. coord./del. Jesse Jackson for Pres., Santa Clara County, Calif., 1984, 88; bd. regents John F. Kennedy U., 2005—. Mem. ASCD, Calif. Alliance Arts Edn., Calif. Assn. Non-Profits, PowerPac, Co-Op Am. Bus. Network, Fellowship Cos. Christ Internat., Bus. Social Responsibility (founding mem.), Antioch Christian Ctr., Am. Assn. Christian Counselors, Youth for Christ (mem. nat. adv. bd. 1997-99), Nat. Alliance of Bus., Calif. CASA Assn. (bd. dirs. 2003—). Avocations: poetry writing, theater, music, cinema, travel. Office: 1883 Mt Conness Way Antioch CA 94531-7492 Office Phone: 925-755-9291. E-mail: keith@emeraldconsulting.com.

ARCILLA, JUANITA R., physical therapist; b. Manila City, Phillippines, June 24, 1942; d. Eliseo Rivera and Dominga Dimla; m. Denny B. Arcilla Jr., Mar. 25, 1973; 1 child, Jeandell R. BA in English, U. St. Tomas, Manila City, Phillipinnes, 1966; MD, Far Eastern U., Manila City, Phillipinnes, 1970; cert., Harvard U., 2006. Lic. physician Pa., Tex., R.I. Rsch. assoc. Northwestern U., Chgo., 1975—77, U. Tex., Houston, 1977—80; resident in phys. medicine and rehab. La. State U., New Orleans, 1980—81, Baylor Coll. Medicine, Houston, 1981—83; fellow in pediat. rehab. Tex. Children's Hosp., Houston, 1983—84; staff physiatrist Profl. Rehab. Outpatient Svcs., Pitts., 1985—86; clin. dir. Phys. Handicap Offender Program, Jester III, Tex. Dept. Correction, Hunsville, Tex., 1986—87; cons. Tex. Dept. of Mental Health and Mental Retardation (MHMR), Richmond, 1987; med. cons. Phys. Handicap Offender Program, Jester III, Tex. Dept. Corrections, 1987—89; med. dir. Richmond State Sch., Richmond, 1987—97; med. staff Tex. Dept. of Mental Health & Mental Retardation (TDMHMR), Richmond, 1997—. Clin. instr. Baylor Coll. Medicine, Houston, 1981—83; asst. prof. U. Tex., Galveston, 1987—; faculty position appt. Tex. A&M U., 1988—94; med. dir. Adult & Children Rehab. Ctr., Houston, 1987—; med. cons. Total Care Med. Clinic, Houston, 1994—; designated Phys. with Tex. Dept. Worker Compensation Comm., Austin, 1994—; WC patient's phys. of Richmond State Sch., Richmond. Contbr. articles to profl. jour., med. mission vol. Catanduanes Internat. Assoc., Inc. (Academic Scholarship Award, 2002). Med. mission vol. Catanduanes Internat. Assn. Inc., 1993, Catanduanes Internat. Assoc. Inc., 2002; mem. fund raising Tex. Asian Rep. Caucus, Houston, 1989—. Named Outstanding Career Woman Yr., IC Metro Houston, Inc., 1996, Mrs. Valentine, Fil-Am Women's Club, 2005; recipient Svc. award, Gov. Leandro Verceles, Jr. and Ea. Bico Med. Ctr., 2002, Exemplary Svc. award, CIA, Inc., 2003, Merit cert., Pres. George W. Bush, 2005, Disting. Svc. award, 2005; fellow, United Cerebral Palsy Rsch. Edn. Found., 1983—84. Mem.: Am. Acad. Phys. Medicine and Rehab., Internat. Rehab. Medicine Assn., Am. Cong. Rehab. Medicine, Harris County Med. Soc., Tex. Med. Assn., Tex. Assn. Phillipinnes Physicians Inc. (pres. 1997—98, past v.p., coord. Feed the Hungry Opn. 1998, plaques for charity work 1997, 1998). Roman Catholic. Avocations: gardening, cooking, home decorating, travel, crocheting, winner of Trophy 1st. of Tango Compet. Office: Adult & Children Rehab Ctr PO Box 270301 Houston TX 77277-0301

ARCINIEGA, ARMANDO, mathematics professor; b. La Flor, Durango, Mexico, Apr. 9, 1975; s. Ignacio and Apolonia Arciniega; m. Rosa M Arciniega, Sept. 13, 2001; children: Adrián A, Emanuel. BA in Math. (hon.), Ea. N.Mex U., 1998, MA in Math., 2000; PhD in Math., Tex. Tech U., 2003. Asst. prof. math. St. Mary's U., San Antonio, 2003—04, U. Tex., San Antonio, 2004—. Home Phone: 210-767-0951; Office Phone: 210-458-5551. Office Fax: 210-458-4439. E-mail: armando.arciniega@utsa.edu.

ARCINIEGA, TOMAS ABEL, university president; b. El Paso, Tex., Aug. 5, 1937; s. Tomas Hilario and Judith G. (Zozaya) Arciniega; m. M. Concha Ochotorena, Aug. 10, 1957; children: Wendy H. Heredia, Lisa Gannon, Judy Shackleton, Laura. BS in Tchr. Edn., N. Mex. State U., 1960; MA, U. N. Mex., 1966, PhD, 1970; postdoc., Inst. for Ednl. Mgmt., Harvard U., 1989. Asst. dean Grad. Sch. U. Tex.-El Paso, 1972-73; co-dir. Southwestern Schs. Study, U. Tex.-El Paso, 1970-73; dean Coll. Edn. San Diego State U., 1973-80; v.p. acad. affairs. Calif. State U., Fresno, 1980-83, pres. Bakersfield, 1983—. Prof. ednl. adminstrn. and supervision U. N.Mex., U. Tex.-El Paso, San Diego State U., Calif. State U., Fresno, Calif. State U., Bakersfield; cons. in edn. to state and fed. agys., instns.; USAID advisor to Dominican Republic U.S. Dept. State., 1967-68; dir. applied rsch. project U. N.Mex., 1968-69, dep. chief party AID Project, Colombia, 1969-70; cons. in field. Author: Public Education's Response to the Mexican-American, 1971, Preparing Teachers of Mexican Americans: A Sociocultural and Political Issue, 1977; co-author: Chicanos and Native Americans: The Territorial Minorities, 1973; guest editor: Calif. Jour. Tchr. Edn., 1981; editor Commn. on Hispanic Underrepresentation Reports, Hispanic Underrepresentation: A Call for Reinvestment and Innovation, 1985, 88. Trustee emeritus Carnegie Corp. N.Y.; trustee Ednl. Testing Svc., Princeton, N.J., The Aspen Inst.; bd. dirs. Math., Engring., Sci. Achievement, Berkeley, Calif.; mem. bd. dirs. Air U., Hispanic Scholarship Fund; mem. Am. Coun. on Edn.; founding mem., trustee Tomas Rivera Policy Inst.; dir. Civic Kern Citizens Effective Local Govt.; mem. adv. bd. Beautiful Bakersfield; advisor Jr. League Bakersfield. Vis. scholar Leadership Enrichment Program, 1982; recipient Legis. commendation for higher edn. Calif. Legislature, 1975-78, Meritorious Svc. award Am. Assn. Colls. Tchr. Edn., 1977-78, Meritorious Svc. award League United L.Am. Citizens, 1983, Svc. award Hispanic and Bus. Alliance for Edn., 1991, Pioneer award Nat. Assn. Bilingual Edn., 1994; named to Top 100 Acad. Leaders in Higher Edn. Change Mag., 1978, Top 100 Hispanic Influentials Hispanic Bus. Mag., 1987, 97. Mem. Am. Ednl. Rsch. Assn. (editl. com. 1979-82), Am. Assn. State Colls. and Univs. (bd. dirs.), Hispanic Assn. Colls. and Univs. (bd. dirs.), Assn. Mexican Am. Educators (various commendations), Am. Assn. Higher Edn. (instl. rep.), Western Coll. Assn. (past pres.), Rotary, Stockdale Country Club, Bakersfield Petroleum Club. Democrat. Roman Catholic. Home: 30450 Palomar Vista Dr Valley Center CA 92082-4537 *Ensuring the right of every American youngster to a first-rate public education has been a driving interest in my life. I consider myself extremely fortunate in having had numerous opportunities to become involved in meaningful efforts to ensure that basic right in our country.*

ARCONES, MIGUEL A., mathematics professor; arrived in US, 1987; s. Valentin Arcones and Juana Vicente. PhD, CUNY, NY, 1991. Assoc. prof. SUNY, Binghamton, 2001—06, prof., 2006—. Contbr. articles to profl. jours. Grantee, NSF, 1993—95. Mem.: Internat. Statis. Inst. (assoc.). Democrat. Home: 18 Lennox Dr Binghamton NY 13903 Office: Binghamton Univ Dept Math Scis Binghamton NY 13902 Home Phone: 607-723-5120; Office Phone: 607-777-2593. Office Fax: 607-777-2450. Business E-Mail: arcones@math.binghamton.edu.

ARCOS, CRESENCIO S., ambassador; b. San Antonio, Nov. 10, 1943; m. Patricia Cordova; 2 children. BA, U. Tex., 1966; MA, Johns Hopkins U., 1973. Various pub. and cultural affairs positions, Leningrad, USSR, Sao Paulo, Brazil; consulate gen. Leningrad, Russia; various pub. and cultural affairs positions Am. Embassy, Lisbon, Portugal, from 1973, counselor pub. affairs Tegucigalpa, Honduras, 1980-85; dep. dir. Nicaraguan Humanitarian Assistance Office, Dept. State, Washington, 1985-86, dep. coord. Latin Am. and Caribbean pub. diplomacy, 1986-87, dep. asst. sec. state for Cen. Am., 1988-89; coord. pub. diplomacy White House Office Communications and Planning, Washington, 1987-88; amb. to Honduras, Am. Embassy, Tegulcigalpa, 1990-93; sr. dep. asst. sec. state for internat. narcotics and crime Dept. State, 1993-95; v.p. for L.Am. and Can. AT&T Corp, IPA, Coral Gables, Fla., 1995—2002; dir. internat. affairs Dept. Homeland Security, Washington, 2003—05, asst. sec. internat. affairs, 2005—06; counselor, govt. affairs Kirkpatrick Lockhart & Gates, 2006—. Mem. White House Pres.'s Fgn. Intelligence Adv. Bd., 1999-2003; mem. res. forces policy bd. Dept. Def. Mem. Hispanic Coun. on Internat. Rels., Washington; bd. dirs. Caribbean-Latin Am. Action, Coun. of the Americas, N.Y.C., Pan Am. Devel. Found., Visit Fairfax; adv. com. Fla. Internat. Univ. Latin Am. Carribean Ctr.; bd. visitors Zamorano Agr. Sch., Honduras; dir. United Negro Coll. Fund Inst. Internat. Pub. Policy; bd. dirs. Fla. Foster Care Rev., 1999-02; mem. corp. adv. bd. Pacific Coun. on Internat. Policy; mem. corp. bd. Cuban-Am. Nat. Coun. Decorated Orden de Morazan (Honduras); recipient awards USIA, Superior Honor awards State Dept.; Regents' fellow U. Calif., 1998-99. Mem. Coun. Fgn. Rels., Am. Fgn. Svc. Assn., Coun. of Ams. (bd. dirs.), Interam. Dialogue, Pacific Coun. Internat. Policy. (mem. corp. adv. bd.), Pan Am. Devel. Found. Home Phone: 203-821-0602. Personal E-mail: arcoscs@yahoo.com.

ARCURI, MICHAEL A., congressman; b. Utica, NY, June 11, 1959; s. Carmen and Elizabeth (Timpano) Arcuri; children: Carmen Joseph, Dominique. BA in Hist., SUNY Albany, 1981; JD, NY Law Sch., NYC, 1984. Bar: NY 1985. Pvt. law practice, Utica, NY, 1989; atty., Bd. Edn. New Hartford Ctrl. Sch. Dist.; dist. atty. Oneida County, NY, 1994—2006; adj. prof. Utica Coll.; asst. varsity football coach Notre Dame High Sch.; mem. US Congress from 24th NY dist., 2007—, mem. transp. & infrastructure com., 2007—, mem. rules com., 2007—. Involved with Utica Rescue Mission, Big Brothers-Big Sisters, Utica Safe Schools, March of Dimes, The Charity One, Children's Mus. of Utica. Recipient Person of Yr. award, YWCA Mohawk Valley, 1997. Mem.: NY State Dist. Attorneys' Assn. (former pres.), Blue Dog Coaltion. Democrat. Roman Catholic. Office: 17 E Genesee St Auburn NY 13021 Office Phone: 315-223-9280, 315-252-2777. Office Fax: 315-223-9283, 315-252-2779.*

ARCUS, SAM GEORGE, social worker, educator, writer; b. Bklyn., Oct. 19, 1921; s. Nathan Louis and Mollie (Srulowitz) Arcus; m. Adele Rosenthal, Jan. 27, 1946; children: Norman Louis, Rochelle Linda Arcus/Ting. B in Social Sci., cum laude, CCNY, 1947; MSW, Columbia U., 1949. Supr. Pride of Judea Children's Home, Bklyn., 1942—44; casework counselor Jewish Family Svc., NYC, 1949—50; program dir. Jewish Cmty. Ctr., Albany, NY, 1950—52, YM-YWHA, Elizabeth, NJ, 1952—53; asst. dir. Jewish Cmty. Ctr., Houston, 1953—56; exec. dir. Jewish Cmty. Alliance, Jacksonville, Fla., 1956—57; area dir. Niles Twp. Jewish Cmty. Ctr., Skokie, Ill., 1957—61, exec. dir. Dallas, 1961—66, exec. dir. North Shore Marblehead, Mass., 1966—79, exec. dir. Tucson, 1979—86; coord. Ct. Visitor's Program, Superior Ct., Tucson, 1986—89; coord. long-term care advocacy program, Ariz. Ombudsman program Pima Coun. on Aging, Tucson, 1989—. Faculty Albany Tchrs. Coll., NY, 1950—52; field work supr. Columbia U., Elizabeth, NJ, 1952—53; faculty sociology U. Houston, 1953—55; field work supr. Lady of Lake Coll., San Antonio, 1962—65; instr. Bishop Coll., Dallas, 1963—65; field work supr. Brandeis U./Heller Sch. Communal Svc., Waltham, Mass., 1967—69; part-time faculty North Shore C.C., Beverly, Mass., 1970—73; overall supr. field work students Salem State Coll., 1973—74, asst. prof., 1974—79; field work supr. Ariz. State U. Sch. Social Work, Tucson, 1981—86, field work supervisor, 1987—93. Author: Deja Views of An Aging Orphan, 2000, Journeys-Sequel to Deja Views of an Aging Orphan, 2003, Kola: Episodes in the Life of A Siberian Husky, 2005, The Affluent American Dog and Other Tails, 2007; co-editor: HNOH: Memories of Orphanage Life, 2001; author: Handbook for Volunteers in LTC Ombudsman Program, 1998; contbr. An Orphan Has Many Parents, 1999; contbr. numerous articles to profl. jours.; editor: alumni newsletter. Life mem. Jewish Cmty. Ctr.; mem. Jewish Hist. Soc. of So. Ariz. Recipient Ward medal in sociology, CCNY, 1947, Ariz. Ombudsman Achievement award, 1998, Aging and Adult Adminstrn. award, Ariz. Dept. Econ. Svc., 2001, Making a Difference award, Ariz. Gov. Adv. Coun., 2003, Ret. Sr. Vol. Program Achievement award, 2004, 20 Yr. Svc. award, LTC Ombuds, 2007. Mem.: HHH Alumni Assn., Columbia U. Alumni Assn., CCNY/Hunter Coll. Alumni Assn. Progressive. Jewish. Avocations: reading, walking, classical music, crafts, art. Business E-Mail: sarcus@pcoa.org.

ARD, HAROLD JACOB, library administrator; b. Herrick, Ill., Aug. 26, 1940; s. Jacob S. and Hazel E. (Taylor) A.; m. Erma Chapman, Jan. 30, 1960 (div. June 1974); children— Teri Ann, Mark Alan. BS in Edn, Ill. State U., 1962, MS in Psychology, 1964; M.L.S., Rosary Coll., River Forest, Ill., 1968. Tchr., materials cons. Decatur (Ill.) Pub. Schs., 1962-64; head librarian Barrington (Ill.) Pub. Library, 1964-68; exec. librarian Arlington Heights (Ill.) Meml. Library, 1968-72; library system dir. Jackson (Miss.) Met. Library System, 1972-77; assoc. dir. Rowland Med. Library, U. Miss. Med. Ctr., Jackson, 1978-84; mgr. bus., sci. and tech. units Fort Worth Pub. Libr., 1985-91; mgr. Wedgwood Libr., Ft. Worth, 1991-94; dir. S.W. Regional Libr., Ft. Worth, 1994-97; ret., 1997; part-time instr. U. Tex., Arlington, 2001—05. Reference libr. Burleson Pub. Libr., 2004—; owner Antiques, Etc., Arlington; cons., lectr. in field. Mem. ALA, Tex. Library Assn., Med. Library Assn., Beta Phi Mu. Clubs: Rotary. Methodist. Home: 4952 Stadium Dr Fort Worth TX 76133-1742 Personal E-mail: hard730939@aol.com.

ARDALAN, PEZHMAN CHRISTOPHER, lawyer; b. Tehran, Iran, Aug. 26, 1973; arrived in U.S., 1977; s. Ali and Jessica Ardalan; m. Anavelle Ardalan, July 3, 1996; children: Ethan, Devin. BA cum laude, Calif. State U. Northridge, 1996; JD cum laude, Order of Coif, Loyola Law Sch., LA, 2000. Bar: Calif. 2000, U.S. Dist. Ct. (cen., ea., so. and no. dists) Calif. 2000, U.S. Ct. Appeals 2000. Paralegal, counsel Law Offices of Robert J. Vars, Encino, Calif., 1996—2000; counsel, pres. Vars & Ardalan PLC, Encino, 2001—02, Ardalan & Assocs. PLC, Sherman Oaks, Calif., 2002—. Commr. San Fernando Valley Pub. Safety Commn., Van Nuys, Calif., 2001—. Mem.: ATLA, ABA, Consumer Attys. Assn. L.A. Avocations: basketball, dance, tutoring. Office: Ardalan & Assocs PLC 15060 Ventura Blvd Ste 201 Sherman Oaks CA 91403 Office Phone: 818-926-4222. Business E-Mail: pca@ardalanlaw.com.

ARDANS, ALEXANDER ANDREW, veterinarian, educator, lab administrator; b. Ely, Nev., June 6, 1941; s. Jean Baptiste and Eleanora (Campbell) A.; m. Janice Gae Sanford, Dec. 23, 1961; children: Tamara Marie, Stephanie Marie, Melanie Alexandra, Angela Rosanne, Jeanette Alison. Student, U. Nev., 1959-61; BS, U. Calif., Davis, 1963, DVM, 1965; MS, U. Minn., St. Paul, 1969. Instr. Colo. State U., Ft. Collins, 1965-66, U. Minn., St. Paul, 1966-69; asst. prof., Sch. Vet. Medicine U. Calif., Davis, 1969-74, assoc. prof., 1974-80, prof., 1980—, chmn. dept. medicine, 1983-87; dir. Calif. Animal Health and Food Safety Lab Sys., Davis, 1987—. Recipient Outstanding Tchr. award U. Calif.-Davis Sch. Vet. Medicine, 1970, 73, Alumni award Sch. Vet. Med. U. Calif. Davis, 2000. Mem. Nat. Acad. Practitioners, AVMA, Am. Assn. Vet. Lab. Diagnosticians (Pope award 2000), Calif. Vet. Med. Assn., Conf. Rsch. Workers in Animal Disease. Republican. Roman Catholic. Avocations: swimming, fishing, hunting. Office: Univ Calif Sch Vet Medicine CAHFS Davis CA 95617 Home Phone: 530-758-9191; Office Phone: 530-752-8709. Business E-Mail: aaardans@ucdavis.edu.

ARDASH, GARIN, mechanical engineer; b. Detroit, July 14, 1963; s. Berge and Lucy Alice (Souldourian) Ardash. BSME, U. Mich., 1986, MME, 1988. Grad. rsch. asst. U. Mich. Coll. Engring., Ann Arbor, 1986-87, Los Alamos (N.Mex.) Nat. Lab., 1987; analysis engr. Naval Reactors Facility, Idaho Falls, Idaho, 1989-92, rsch. analysis engr. materials tech. dept., 1992—94, sr. rsch. analysis engr. materials tech. dept., 1994—2001; sr. analysis engr. refueling engring. Bechtel Bettis Inc., Bettis Atomic Power Lab., West Mifflin, Pa., 2001—. Fellow U. Mich. Coll. Engring. 1986-87; scholar State Mich. Coop. 1982-83; recipient Best Landscape Photograph, Pitts. Salon 2002, Best Water Photgraph, Pitts. Salon 2007. Mem. AAAS, ASME, Internat. Legion Intelligence, Photog. Soc. Am., Acad. Sci. and Art Pitts. (photog. sect.), Mensa. Avocations: photography, soccer, skiing, chess. Office: Bettis Atomic Power Lab Ctrl Office Bldg 2 MDP PO Box 79 West Mifflin PA 15122-0079 Home: 111 Maple Ave Apt 9 Pittsburgh PA 15218 Office Phone: 412-476-6534. Personal E-mail: garinard7@netscape.net.

ARDELEAN, EMIL VALENTIN, mechanical engineer, researcher; b. Ceanu Mare, Romania, Oct. 7, 1966; s. Valentin and Ana Ardelean. BS, U. Tech., Cluj-Napoca, Romania, 1992, MS, 1994; PhD, Duke U., Durham, NC, 2003. Design engr. S.C. Sinterom S.A., Cluj-Napoca, 1993—97; engr., co-owner Gimati SRL, Turda, Romania, 1995—97; pc mfg. assembling, configuration, testing IBM Corp., Research Triangle Park, NC, 1997—98; mapper, drafter ASI Landmark, Cary, NC, 1998—99; grad. rsch. asst. Duke U., Durham, 1999—2003; sr. mech. engr. SAIC, Albuquerque, 2003—. Mem.: ASME, AIAA, Romanian Engring. Soc. Achievements include development of V-stack piezoelectric actuator and application for active flutter control; research in lightweight, low frequency acoustic barrier. Home: 12529 Apache Ct NE Albuquerque NM 87112 Office: SAIC 2109 Air Park Rd SE Albuquerque NM 87106 Home Phone: 505-715-3235; Office Phone: 505-846-9383. Personal E-mail: ardelean@duke.edu. Business E-Mail: emil.ardelean@saic.com.

ARDEN, BRUCE WESLEY, retired computer scientist, retired engineering educator; b. Mpls., May 29, 1927; s. Wesley and Clare Montgomery (Newton) A.; m. Patricia Ann Joy, Aug. 25, 1951 (dec. 2003); children: Wayne Wesley, Michelle Joy; m. Margaret Greif, Dec. 2004. Student, U. Del., 1944; BS in Elec. Engring., Purdue U., 1949; postgrad., U. Chgo., 1949; MA, U. Mich., 1955, PhD, 1965. Detail engr. Allison div. Gen. Motors Corp., Indpls., 1950-51; asst. prof. dept. computing and communication scis. U. Mich., Ann Arbor, 1965-67, assoc. prof., 1967-70, prof., 1970-73, chmn. dept., 1971-73, from research asst. to assoc. dir. Computing Facilities, 1951-73; prof., chmn. dept. elec. engring. and computer sci. Princeton U., 1973-85, Arthur Le Grand Doty prof. engring., 1981-86; prof. elec. engring., computer sci., dean engring. and applied sci. U. Rochester, 1986-94, vice provost computing, 1992-94, William F. May Prof. Engring., 1993-95, dean emeritus, 1994—; William F. May Prof. Engring. Emeritus, 1995—. Vis. prof. U. Grenoble, France, 1971-72; guest prof. Siemens Research, Munich, Germany, 1983, also cons.; cons. to Gen. Motors Corp., Ford Corp., Westinghouse Co., RCA, Xerox Data Systems, IBM.; mem. sci. council USRA Inst. for Computer Applications in Sci. and Engring., 1973-79, 82-88; mem. sci coun. USRA Inst. Advanced Computer Sci., 1982-88; chmn. com. on anti-ballistic missile data processing Nat. Acad. Sci., 1966-71; mem. panel Inst. Computer Sci. and Tech., 1980-86; mem. acad. adv. council Wang Inst., 1978-87; mem. study sect. NIH, 1985-88; reviewer Guggenheim Found., 1985-91. Author: An Introduction to Digital Computing, 1963; (with K. Astil) Numerical Algorithms: Their Origins and Applications, 1970; editor: What Can Be Automated?, 1980. Served with USNR, 1944-46, 49-50. Fellow AAAS; mem. IEEE (sr.), Assn. for Computing Machinery, Univs. Space Research Assn. (bd. dirs. 1982-88), Sigma Xi, Tau Beta Pi, Eta Kappa Nu.

ARDEN, EUGENE, retired university provost; b. NYC, June 25, 1923; s. Harry and Gussie (Shevach) A.; m. Sandra E. Rose, July 11, 1948; children: Stacey, Jonathan. BA, NYU, 1943; MA, Columbia U., 1947; PhD, Ohio State U., 1953. Mem. faculty Ohio State U., Columbus, Queen's Coll., Hofstra U., 1947-56; from asst. prof. to prof., chmn. dept. English and humanities div. C.W. Post Coll., Greenvale, N.Y., 1956-62, dean, 1962-64; dean grad. faculties L.I. U., 1964-70, dean Conolly Coll., 1970-71, exec. dean Bklyn. Ctr., 1971; vice chancellor, dean acad. affairs U. Mich., Dearborn, 1972-89, provost, 1989-91, ret., 1991. Editor: Boca Chase Newsletter, 1995—; contbr. articles to profl. jours., mags. Bd. dirs. Mid-Island YM and YWHA, 1962-64, Temple Beth Hillel, Margate, Fla; mem. nat. exec. com. Hillel Founds.; asso. chmn. civil liberties com. Jewish Cmty. Coun. Met. Detroit. Served with AUS, 1943-46, ETO. Mem. AAUP (editor Academe jour. 1991-93), B'nai Brith (pres. Ctrl. Nassau lodge 1966-68). Home: 18102 Clear Brook Cir Boca Raton FL 33498-1943

ARDERY, PHILIP PENDLETON, lawyer; b. Lexington, Ky., Mar. 6, 1914; s. William Breckenridge and Julia (Spencer) A.; m. Anne Stuyvesant Tweedy, Dec. 6, 1941; children: Peter Brooks (dec.), Philip Pendleton, Jr., Joseph Lord Tweedy, Julia Spencer. AB, U. Ky., 1935; JD, Harvard U., 1938; MBA, U. Louisville, 1957. Bar: Ky. 1938. Practice law, Frankfort, 1938-40, 45-50, Louisville, 1952—; ptnr. Frost Brown Todd, 1972—. Sec. Ky. Aero. Commn., 1946-48; commr. Jefferson County, 1958-61 Author: Bomber Pilot: A Memoir of World War II, 1978, Heroes and Horses, Tales of the Bluegrass, 1996; also articles. Bd. dirs. Frazier Rehab. Ctr., 1953-93, Schizophrenia Found., Ky., 1981—, Thomas D. Clark Found., 1994—, Nat. Alliance Rsch. in Schizophrenia and Depression, 1985-92, Norton Hosp. Found., 1985-94, Ky. Mental Health Assn., 1985—, Jewish Hosp. Healthcare Svcs., 1986—, Ky. Shakespeare Festival, 1989-90, Ky. Humanities Coun., 1989-94; pres. Ky. Heart Assn., 1955, chmn. bd., 1956; incorporator, dir. Ballet Español, 1984—; chmn. bd. Am. Heart Assn., 1966-69; dep. Episcopal Gen. Convs., 1970, 73, 76, 79; mem. exec. com. Ky. Hist. Soc., 1983-95; trustee U. of South, 1977-80, Episcopal Theol. Sem. in Ky., 1985-90; sec. Ky. Horse Park Found., 1985—. Col. USAAF, 1940-45, col. USAF, 1950-52, maj. gen. USAFR, ret., 1974—. Decorated Silver Star, D.F.C. (2), Air medal (4); Croix de Guerre with palm (France) Mem. ABA, Ky. Bar Assn., Louisville Bar Assn., Soc. Cin., Order First Families of Va. (Burgess), Pendennis Club, Filson Club (bd. dirs. 1986-96), Phi Beta Kappa. Democrat. Episcopalian. Home: 448 Swing Ln Louisville KY 40207-1444 Office: 3200 Providian Ctr Louisville KY 40202-2873 Office Phone: 502-895-5400. Personal E-mail: pardery1@aol.com.

ARDITI, RALPH, lawyer; b. NYC, 1948; BA, Yale Coll., 1970; JD, Yale Law Sch., 1973. Bar: NY 1974. Law clerk Hon. Morris E. Lasker, US Dist. Ct. for Southern Dist., NY, 1973—75; ptnr., mergers and acquisitions, securities and general corporate matters Skadden, Arps, Slate, Meagher & Flom LLP, NYC. Editor: Yale Law Jour., 1972—73. Mem.: Phi Beta Kappa. Office: Skadden Arps Slate Meagher & Flom LLP Four Times Sq New York NY 10036 Office Phone: 212-735-3860. Office Fax: 917-777-3860. Business E-Mail: rarditi@skadden.com.

ARE, AYOKUNNU OLANREWAJU, financial advisor, investment banker; arrived in Canada, 1985; s. Lalekan Ayokunnu and Olabisi Abike Are; m. Emiko Yoshida, July 10, 1989; children: Ayo Jr., Francois. BA in Polit. Sci. with an emphasis on Internat. Rels., U. Mich., Flint, 1986; MPA with an emphasis on Econs. and Fin., U. Mich., Ann Arbor, 1989. Mgr. and fin. advisor Prudential Fin. Svcs., Livonia, Mich., 1988—95; pres., CEO Money Mgrs. Internat. Ltd., Toronto, Canada, 1988—. Author: (poetry book) A Voice From Apatanganga, 1981; author: (and editor) (bill proposal) Canadian Ho. of Commons, 1985. Christian. Avocations: writing, poetry, reading, running, international relations and politics. Office: Money Mgrs Internat Ltd 675 Cochrane Dr E Twr 6th Fl L3R 0B8 Markham ON Canada Home: 12-16715 Yonge St Ste 1084 l3X 1X4 Newmarket ON Canada Office Fax: 800-294-0087. Business E-Mail: moneymanagersinternational@msn.com.

AREEN, JUDITH CAROL, law educator; b. Chgo., Aug. 2, 1944; d. Gordon Eric and Pauline Jeanette (Payberg) A.; m. Richard M. Cooper, Feb. 17, 1979; children: Benjamin Eric Cooper (dec.), Jonathan Gordon Cooper. AB, Cornell U., 1966; JD, Yale U., 1969. Bar: Mass. 1970, D.C. 1972. Program planner for higher edn. Mayor's Office City of N.Y., 1969-70; dir. edn. voucher study Ctr. for Study Pub. Policy, Cambridge, Mass., 1970-72; mem. faculty Georgetown U., Washington, 1972—, assoc. prof. law, 1972-76, prof., 1976—, prof. cmty. and family medicine, 1980-89, assoc. dean Law Ctr., 1984-87, dean, exec. v.p. for law affairs, 1989—2004, emeritus, 2004—, Paul Regis Dean prof. law, 2004—. Gen. counsel, project coord. Office Mgmt. and Budget, Washington, 1977—80; spl. counsel White House Task Force on Regulatory Reform, Washington, 1978—80; cons. NIH, 1984, NRC, 1985. Author: Youth Service Agencies, 1977, Cases and Materials on Family Law, 5th edit., 2006, Law, Science and Medicine, 1984, 3d edit., 2005. Mem. Def. Adv. Com. Women In Svcs., Washington, 1979-82; trustee Cornell Univ., 1997-01; bd. dir. Eqaul Justice Works, 2004-, Pro Bono Inst., 2004-, Women's Law and Public Policy Fellowship Program, 2004-. Woodrow Wilson Internat. Ctr. Scholars fellow, 1988-89, Kennedy Inst. Ethics Sr. Rsch. fellow, Washington, 1982-98, Janet Reno Torchbearer award, Women's Bar Assn., 2007. Mem. ABA (coun. legal edn. sect. 2000-04), DC Bar Assn., Am. Law Inst., Assn. Am. Law Schs. (exec. com. mem. 2005-, pres. 2006). Business E-Mail: areen@law.georgetown.edu.

AREF, HASSAN, fluid mechanics engineer, educator; b. Alexandria, Egypt, Sept. 28, 1950; s. Moustapha and Jytte (Adolphsen) A.; m. Susanne Eriksen, Aug. 3, 1974; children: Michael, Thomas. Cand.Sci., U. Copenhagen, Denmark, 1975; PhD, Cornell U., 1980. Asst. prof. Brown U., Providence, 1980-85, assoc. prof., 1985; assoc. prof. fluid mechanics U. Calif., San Diego, 1985-88, prof. fluid mechanics, 1988-92; chief scientist San Diego Supercomputer Ctr., 1989-92; prof., head dept. theoretical and applied mechanics U. Ill., Urbana-Champaign, 1992—2003; dean engring. Va. Tech., 2003—05, Reynolds Metals prof., 2003—. Niels Bohr vis. prof. Danish Tech. U., 2006—; lectr. in field. Editor Cambridge Texts in Applied Math., 1987-94, Advances in Applied Mechanics, 2001—; assoc. editor Jour. Fluid Mechanics, 1984-93; contbr. articles to profl. jours. Recipient Presdl. Young Investigator award, NSF 1985, Otto Laporte award, Am. Physical Soc., 2000. Fellow: World Innovation Found., Am. Acad. Mechanics, Am. Phys. Soc.; mem.: Danish Ctr. Applied Maths. Mechanics, Soc. Indsl. and Applied Math. Office: Va Polytech Inst 320 Norris Hall Blacksburg VA 24061 Home Phone: 217-664-3623; Office Phone: 540-231-5626. Business E-Mail: haref@vt.edu.

AREGOOD, RICHARD LLOYD, editor; b. Camden, NJ, Dec. 31, 1942; s. Lloyd Samuel and Ruby Odell (Trousdale) A.; m. Barbara Sue Wittenberger, Oct. 6, 1962 (div. June 1978); children: Laurie, Christopher; m. Doris Joan Sampieri, Apr. 21, 1979 (div. July 1992); children: Deborah, David, Jennifer, William Sampieri; m. Kathleen Shea, Feb. 20, 1993; 1 child, James. BA in English, Rutgers U., 1965. Reporter, editor Burlington County Herald, Mount Holly, NJ, 1964-65; reporter Burlington County Times, Willingboro, NJ, 1965-66, Phila. Daily News, 1966-71, features editor, 1971-73, news editor, 1973-74, editor editorial page, 1975-95, dep. sports editor, 1976; editor the editl. page The Star Ledger of Newark (N.J.), 1995—2005; Clendinin prof. journalism U. South Fla., 2006; sr. v.p. The Marcus Group, 2006—. Co-author: Beyond Argument: A Handbook for Editorial Writers, 2001, The Journalist's Craft: A Guide to Writing Better Stories, 2002. Pres. local 10 Newspaper Guild, Phila., 1978-79, v.p., 1973-77. Recipient Pulitzer prize for editorial writing, 1985, Walker Stone award Scripps-Howard Newspapers, 1993; inducted into Rutgers Hall of Disting. Alumni, 1993. Mem. Am. Soc. Newspaper Editors (dir. 1996-2002, disting. writing award 1984, 90, 94), Nat. Conf. Editl. Writers. Episcopalian. Office: The Star Ledger Star Ledger Pla Newark NJ 07102-1200 Home Phone: 908-647-5640; Office Phone: 201-902-9000. Personal E-mail: raregood@yahoo.com. Business E-Mail: raregood@verizon.net.

AREHART-TREICHEL, JOAN, writer; b. Louisville, May 19, 1942; d. Oscar Martin Arehart and Isabelle Rebecca Turner; m. Horst Klaus

Treichel, May 13, 1972; children: Tamara Treichel, Heidi Treichel. BA, Ind. U., Bloomington, 1964; postgrad., NYU, Georgetown U., Washington. Med. writer Sci. News Mag., Washington, 1971—83; freelance sci. writer various mags., 1983—98; sr. staff writer Psychiat. News, Arlington, Va., 1999—. Author: Biotypes - The Critical Line Between Your Personality and Your Health, 1980. Mem.: Nat. Assn. Sci. Writers. Avocations: hiking, gardening, birdwatching, reading. Home: 1800 R St NW #606 Washington DC 20009 Office: Psychiat News Am Psychiat Assn 1000 Wilson Blvd Ste 1825 Arlington VA 22209

AREHOLE, SHALINI, audiologist, educator; d. Narasimhayya Arehole and Shakuntala Narasimhayya; m. Shankar Aithal, Aug. 26, 1988; children: Mitra Aithal, Vikas Aithal, Ritvik Aithal. PhD, U. Tex., Dallas, 1986. Cert. in audiology Am. Speech Language Hearing Assn., 1987. Audiologist Univ. La., Lafayette, 1986—2007, prof., 1987—. Contbr. articles to profl. jours. Mem.: Am. Auditory Soc. (licentiate), Am. Acad. Audiology (licentiate). Home Phone: 337-984-5685; Office Phone: 337-482-6723.

ARELL, BOBBY RAY, JR., pharmaceutical executive, management consultant; b. San Jose, Calif., Mar. 15, 1970; s. Bobby Ray and Marie Celeste (Cecil) Arell; m. Kimberly Dawn Harding, May 21, 2001; m. Barbara Lynn Castillo, July 3, 1998 (div. Jan. 12, 1999); children: Derek William Lawrance, Alexander Morgan. A in Bus. Mgmt., Pillips Jr. Coll., Campbell, Calif., 1992; B in Info. Tech., Am. Intercontinental U., Ga., 2007. Mgr. Bally's Alladins Castle, San Jose, 1988—92; retail pharmacutical mgr. Walgreens, Las Vegas, Nev., 1998—. Cons. in field. Coord. mgr. Rep. Party, Fallbrook, Calif., 1995—96. Sgt. USMC, 1992—98. Decorated Cert. of Commendation USMC, Meritorous Mast, Good Conduct medal. Independent. Roman Catholic. Avocations: reading, writing. Office: Walgreens Las Vegas Blvd Las Vegas NV 89125 Home Phone: 702-438-5852; Office Phone: 702-836-0818. Personal E-mail: brarellj@netzero.com.

AREM, LAWRENCE JAY, lawyer; b. Bklyn., Feb. 2, 1950; s. Gilbert and Renee (Rothman) A.; m. Marcia Susan Clark, May 4, 1980; children: Nathaniel, Hannah, Jacob. BS, NYU, 1972, LLM in Taxation, 1978; JD, U. Pa., 1975. Bar: Pa. 1975, U.S. Dist. Ct. (ea. dist.) Pa. 1975, U.S. Tax Ct. 1976. Assoc. Eilberg, Carson, Getson & Abramson, Phila., 1975-76, Krekstein, Wolfson & Krekstein, Phila., 1977-79, Klehr, Harrison, Harvey, Branzberg & Ellers, Phila., 1979—83, ptnr., 1983—, chmn. tax dept. Mem. ABA, Pa. Bar Assn., Phila. Bar Assn. Democrat. Jewish. Home: 645 Hazelhurst Ave Merion Station PA 19066-1406 Office: Klehr Harrison Harvey Branzberg & Ellers 260 S Broad St 3d Fl Philadelphia PA 19102 Office Phone: 215-569-4142. Business E-Mail: larem@klher.com.

ARENA, ALBERT A., museum director; b. Waltham, Mass., Nov. 12, 1929; s. John Giovanni and Jennie (Inferrera) A.; m. Jean Marie MacDonald; children: Albert A. Jr., Andrew A., Arthur A. BS, Mass. Maritime Acad., 1952. Licensed Chief Marine Engr. Marine engr. Gulf Oil Co., NYC, 1952, Farrell Lines, Inc., Bklyn., 1952-54; naval engr. officer USS New Jersey, Norfolk, Va., 1954-56; engr. Commonwealth of Mass., various locations, 1957-59, Harvard U., Roxbury, Mass., 1960; marine engr. SS America, NYC, 1960-62; boiler and machine inspector Factory Mutual Ins., Norwood, Mass., 1963-70; assoc. prof. Mass. Maritime Acad., Buzzards Bay, Mass., 1970-72; engr. instr. Raytheon Co., Lexington, Mass., 1973-74; chief stationary engr. Allied Maintenance Corp., Boston, 1974-80; museum dir. Waltham (Mass.) Museum, 1971—. Producer, narrator This Was Waltham for Waltham Cable Access TV, 1989—. Recipient Ship Safety Achievement award Am. Merchant Marine Inst., 1962, Citation of Svc. for efforts associated with Waltham Mus. Mass. Ho. of Reps., 1994. Roman Catholic. Home: 17 Noonan St Waltham MA 02453-4212 Office: Waltham Museum 25 Lexington St Waltham MA 02452 Office Phone: 781-893-9020. Personal E-mail: aaarena@hotmail.com.

ARENA, BRUCE, professional soccer coach; b. Bklyn., Sept. 21, 1951; m. Phyllis Arena; 1 child. Student, Nassau CC, NY, 1969-71; BS in Bus., Cornell U., 1973. Asst. lacrosse coach, asst. soccer coach Cornell U., Ithaca, NY, 1973-76; head soccer coach U. Puget Sound, Tacoma, 1976-78; head soccer coach, asst. men's lacrosse coach U. Va., Charlottesville, 1978-95; head coach DC United, Washington, 1995-98, US Nat. Soccer Team, Chgo., 1998—2006; dir., head coach NY Red Bulls, 2006—. Mem. U.S. nat. teams in both soccer and lacrosse and competed professionally in both sports; past chmn. ACC soccer coaches, ISAA Divsn. I nat. poll; "A" coaching lic. from U.S. Soccer Fedn.; mem. NCAA Divsn. I soccer com., 1989-95; head coach U.S. Olympic team 1996, U.S. World Cup Team 2002, 2006. Named ACC Coach of Yr., 1979, 84, 86, 88, 89, 91, South Atlantic Region Coach of Yr., 1982, 83, 87, nat. Coach of Yr. by Lanzera, 1993. Inducted into Cornell Athletic Field Hall of Fame, 1986, Long Island Lacrosse Hall of Fame, 1990. Named MLS Coach of Year, 1997. Achievements include career record of 295-58-32 (.808) in 18 yrs. at U. Va., leading U. Va. to NCAA titles in 1989, 91, 92, 93, 94, taking U. Va. to 6 of the last 7 NCAA semi-finals and 8 straight quarter finals, directing U. Va. to 15 straight NCAA tournament appearances (longest active streak in U.S.), Major League Soccer Cup Championships, 1996, 97, U.S. Open Cup Championship, 1996, World Cup quarterfinals 2002. Mailing: NY Red Bulls One Harmon Plz Third Fl Secaucus NJ 07094

ARENAL, JULIE (MRS. BARRY PRIMUS), choreographer; Tchr. Herbert Berghof Studio; asst. on tng. program Lincoln Center Repertory Theatre. Dancer with cos. of Anna Sokolow, Sophie Maslow, John Butler, Jack Cole, Jose Limon; choreographer: Marat/Sade for, Theatre Co. of Boston, Harvard U. Loeb Theatre, Municipal Theatre, Atlanta, Hair, on Broadway (Most Original Choreographer of Year award Sat. Rev. 1968), also London; dir., choreographer Hair, Stockholm (Best Dir.-Choreographer of Yr. award 1969); choreographer, dir. Isabel's a Jezebel; choreographer: Indians on Broadway, Fiesta for Ballet Hispanico, 1972, 20008 1/2, Boccaccio, 1975, A Private Circus, 1975, Free to Be You and Me, 1976, The Referee, 1976, El Arbito, 1978; choreographer for San Francisco Ballet, Nat. Ballet de Cuba, (film) King of the Gypsies, Great Expectations, Fur. Friends, 1980, Mistress, 1991, Once Upon a Time in America, Houston Grand Opera Co., Porgy and Bess, 1995, Great Expectations, 1997, (movie) The Good Shepherd, 2006; dir., choreographer (stage) Funny Girl, Tokyo, 1979-80; dir. N.Y. Express Hip Hop Dance Co., commd. by Spoleto Festival of the Two Worlds, N.C. and Italy; toured 7 cities in People's Republic of China. Grantee NEA, 1973, Oreg. Shakespeare Festival, 1997, Porgy and Bess City Opera, N.Y.C. Opera, 2000, Am. Family PBS TV Series, 2002, Hair Downtown Cabaret, Bridgeport, Conn., 2005; nominated Outstanding Dir. Choreographer Prodn. Ensemble award Conn. Critic Cir.; recipient Outstanding Dir. award 2005. E-mail: borbos@aol.com.

ARENAS, GILBERT, professional basketball player; b. Jan. 6, 1982; s. Gilbert; 1 child, Amay Semaya. Student, U. Ariz. Basketball player Golden State Warriors, Calif., 2001—03, Washington Wizards, 2003—. Mem. US Men's Sr. Nat. Team. Host Gilbert's Christmas Dream. Named Most Improved Player, NBA, 2002—03, MVP, NBA Got Milk? Rookie Challenge, 2003; named to All-NBA 3rd Team, 2005, 2006, Ea. Conf. All-Star Team, NBA, 2005—07. Office: Washington Wizards Verizon Ctr 601 F St NW Washington DC 20004*

ARENBERG, IRVING KAUFMAN KARCHMER, otolaryngologist; b. East Chicago, Ind., Jan. 10, 1941; s. Harry and Gertrude (Field) Kaufman; divorced; children: Daniel Kaufman, Michael Harrison, Julie Gayle. BA in Zoology, U. Mich., 1963, MD, 1967. Diplomate Am. Bd. Otolaryngology. Intern Chgo. Wesley Meml. Hosp., 1967-68; resident Barnes and Allied Hosps., St. Louis, 1969-74; asst. prof. surgery U. Wis., Madison, 1976-80; chief otolaryngology VA Hosp., Madison, 1976-80; CEO Ear Ctr. PC, Englewood, Colo., 1989—96; chmn. bd., CEO IntraEar, Neurobiometrix Inc., Inc., 1994—99; pres., CEO, chmn. Arenberg and Assocs. Ltd., LLC, 2000—04. Dir., founder Internat. Meniere's Disease Rsch. Inst., Denver, 1971—; guest of honor 39th Chinese Nat. ENT Congress, Taipei, 1985, U. Antwerp, 1995, West German ENT Soc., 1996; vis. scientist Swedish Med. Rsch. Coun., 1975-76; vis. prof. U. Mich., Ann Arbor, 1988, 94, St. Mary's Hosp. and Med. Sch., London, 1988, U. Verona (Italy) Med. Sch., 1989, U. N.C., Chapel Hill, 1989, U. Wurzburg (Germany) Med. Sch., 1989, 90, 92, U. Ark., Little Rock, 1990, 95, U. Innsbruck, Austria, 1991, U. Sydney, Australia, 1992, U. Tex., Dallas, 1993. Editor: Meniere's Disease, 1983, Inner Ear Surgery, 1991, Dizziness and Balance Disorders, 1993; assoc. editor AMA Archives of Otolaryngology, 1968-81; mem. editorial bd. Am. Jour. Otology, 1978-91, Head and Neck Surgery Jour., 1992—; guest editor Otolaryngologic Clinics N.Am., 1980, 83, Neurologic Clinics N.Am., 1990; editor Inner Ear Surgery, 1991; mem. rev. bd. Rev. de Laryngologie et Otology (France), 1984—; contbr. over 400 articles to profl. peer-reviewed jours. Recipient Pietro Caliceti prize and Gold Medal Honor award U. Bologna, Italy, 1983, Spl. Tchr. Investigation Tng. award NIH, 1970-1975; fellow Barnes and Allied Hosps., 1968-69, 75, NIH, 1971-76, U. Uppsala-Royal Acad. Hosp., Sweden, 1975-76; grantee NIH, 1971-77, Deafness Rsch. Found., 1971-73. Fellow ACS, Am. Acad. Otolaryngology; mem. AMA, Am. Neurotology Soc., N.Y. Acad. Scis., Colo. Otologic Rsch. Ctr. (founder, pres., bd. dirs. 1980-88), Internat. Meniere's Disease Rsch. Inst. (dir. 1971—), Assn. Rsch. in Otolaryngology, Barany Soc., Triological Soc., Politzer Soc., Prosper Meniere Soc. (founder, exec. dir. 1981-99), Acoustical Soc. Am., Ogura Soc., Sigma Xi. Achievements include 10 U.S. and fgn. patents in field. Avocations: skiing, golf, biking, tennis.

ARENBERG, JULIUS THEODORE, JR., retired accounting company executive; b. Chgo., May 29, 1923; s. Julius Theodore and Ellen A. (Foran) A.; m. Jean E. Young, June 19, 1948; children— Robert, Thomas, Mary, James, Michael, Douglas. BS in Acctg, U. Ill., 1947. C.P.A., Ill. With Arthur Andersen & Co., Chgo., 1947—, ptnr., 1962—, head fin. services div., 1975—; chmn. C.P.A. adv. com. Nat. Assn. Ins. Commrs., 1974-75. Mem. faculty Bank Adminstrn. Inst. Sch., U. Wis., 1966-69, Nat. Installment Credit Sch., U. Chgo., 1965-70 Mem. Lombard (Ill.) Elementary Bd. Edn., 1960-66, pres., 1962-66. Served with USNR, 1943-46. Mem. Am. Inst. C.P.A.'s (chmn. com. ins. acctg. and auditing 1966-73), Ill. Soc. C.P.A.'s. Clubs: St. Charles Country, Bay Hill. Roman Catholic. Personal E-mail: payde369@aol.com.

AREND, ANTHONY CLARK, social studies educator, academic administrator; b. Balt., Oct. 24, 1958; s. Paul Joseph and Cora Allen (Clark) A. BSFS magna cum laude, Georgetown U., 1980; MA, U. Va., 1982, PhD, 1985. Rsch. asst. U. Va. Sch. Law, Charlottesville, Va., 1981-84, sr. fellow, 1985-86; professorial lectr. dept. govt. Georgetown U., Washington, 1986, asst. prof., 1988-93, assoc. prof., 1993-2000, chair main campus exec. faculty, 1997-2001, prof., 2000—, co-dir. Inst. for Internat. Law and Politics, 2003—, v.p. univ. faculty senate main campus, 2001—06. Vis. asst. prof. Pa. State U., Harrisburg, 1987, Georgetown U., 1987—88; co-dir. Inst. for Internat. Law and Politics. Author: Pursuing a Just and Durable Peace: John Foster Dulles and International Organization, 1988, Legal Rules and International Society, 1999; co-author: International Law and the Use of Force: Beyond the United Nations Charter Paridigm, 1993; editor: The United States and the Compulsory Jurisdiction of the International Court of Justice, 1986; co-editor: The Falklands War: Lessons for Strategy, Diplomacy and International Law, 1985, International Rules: Approaches from International Law and International Relations, 1996; mem. bd. advisors Va. Jour. Internat. Law, 1992—; contbr. chpts. to books, articles to profl. jours. Chmn. adminstrv. coun. Severn United Meth. Ch., 1984-89, lay leader, 1990—2006; gov. bd. govs. Georgetown U. Alumni Assn., 2001-07, senator, 2007-. Margaret Nils Butler Meml. DACOR fellow, 1980-81, Richard M. Weaver fellow, 1982-83, Lassen fellow, 1983-84, Philip Francis du Pont fellow, 1983-84. Mem. Am. Soc. Internat. Law, Georgetown U. Alumni Assn. (bd. govs. 2001-07, senator 2007-), Coun. on Fgn. Rels., Phi Beta Kappa Democrat. Avocations: golf, squash. Home: 1301 33rd St NW Apt 1 Washington DC 20007-2850 Office: Georgetown U Dept Govt Washington DC 20057-0001 Office Phone: 202-687-6237. Business E-Mail: arenda@georgetown.edu.

ARENDS, ANN M., elementary school educator, pianist; b. Fairbury, Ill., July 28, 1962; d. Leland George Wycoff and Barbara Jean Bauerle-Wycoff; m. Michael Alan Arends, June 20, 1987; children: Stephanie, Erica, Alyssa. BA, Carthage Coll., Kenosha, Wis., 1984. Cert. tchr. Ill. Elem. music tchr. St. Mary's of Kickapoo, Edwards, Ill., 1984—86; music tchr. Metamora Grade Sch., Ill., 1986—87, Franklin Elem. Sch., Boona, Iowa, 1987—88; elem. libr. Illini Ctrl., Mason City, Ill., 1989—90; accompanist Lincoln Coll., Lincoln, Ill., 1990—91; pvt. piano tchr., 1984—99; music tchr. AFC Sch. Dist., Franklin Grove, Ill., 1996—2006, P.H. Miller Sch., Plano, Ill., 2006—. Pres. and corres. sec. Indian Creek Edn. Found., Ill., 1999—; pres., v.p. Waterman Elem. Parent Club; organist Waterman United Meth. Ch., Ill., 1995—, chair worship com., 2002—. Mem.: Music Educators Nat. Conf. Lutheran. Avocations: reading, piano. Home: 130 W Eisenhower St Waterman IL 60556

ARENDS, HERMAN JOSEPH, former insurance company executive; b. 1945; M of Math., Mich. State U., 1967. Tchr. Laningsburg (Mich.) H.S., 1967-72; chmn., CEO Auto-Owners Ins. Co., Lansing, Mich., 1972—2004. Office: Auto-Owners Insurance Co 6101 Anacapri Dr Lansing MI 48917-3994

ARENELLA, PETER LEE, law educator; b. Boston, Nov. 28, 1947; s. Nicholas Peter and Joanne (Issacson) Arenella; children: David Mack, Katherine Mack; m. Mia Arenella, July 1, 2002; children: Mara, Paloma. BA magna cum laude, Wesleyan U., 1969; JD cum laude, Harvard U., 1972. Bar: Mass. 1972. Law clk. to presiding chief justice Mass. Supreme Jud. Ct., Boston, 1972-73; atty. Mass. Pub. Defender's Office, Boston, 1973; sole practice Boston, 1974-75; asst. prof. law U. Mass., Boston, 1974-75, Rutgers U., Camden, N.J., 1975-78, assoc. prof., 1978-80, prof., 1980-82, Boston U., 1982-87, UCLA, LA, 1987—. Cons., expert witness Congl. Hearings on Grand Jury Reform Insanity Def., Washington, 1982, 85; legal cons. ABC News (O.J. Simpson Case), 1994-97, Nat. Pub. radio and KNX radio and KTLA Channel 5 LA. Contbr. articles to profl. jours. Recipient Metcalf Tchg. Excellence prize Boston U., 1984, Rutter Tchg. Excellence award UCLA, 1999; Woodrow Wilson fellow, 1969. Mem. ABA (grand jury com. 1979-85, reporter model grand jury act 1980), Soc. Am. Law Tchrs. Unitarian Universalist. Avocations: swimming, tennis, softball, jogging. Office: UCLA Law Box 951476 Los Angeles CA 90095-1476 Office Phone: 310-825-4841. E-mail: arenella@law.ucla.edu.

ARENOWITZ, ALBERT HAROLD, psychiatrist; b. NYC, Jan. 12, 1925; s. Louis Isaac and Lena Helen (Skovron) A.; m. Betty Jane Wiener, Oct. 11, 1953; children: Frederick Stuart, Diane Helen. BA with honors, U. Wis., 1948; MD, U. Va., 1951. Diplomate Am. Bd. Psychiatry, Am. Bd. Child Psychiatry. Intern Kings County Gen. Hosp., Bklyn., 1951-52; resident in psychiatry Bronx (N.Y.) VA Hosp., 1952-55; postdoctoral fellow Youth Guidance Ctr., Worcester, Mass., 1955-57; dir. Ctr. for Child Guidance, Phila., 1962-65, Hahnemann Med. Service Eastern State Sch. and Hosp., Trevose, Pa., 1965-68; dir., tng. dir. Child and Adolescent Psychiat. Clinic, Phila. Gen. Hosp., 1965-67; asst. clin. prof. psychiatry Jefferson Med. Coll., Phila., 1974-76; exec. dir. Child Guidance and Mental Health Clinics, Media, Pa., 1967-74; med. dir. Intercommunity Child Guidance Ctr., Whittier, Calif., 1976—. Cons. Madison Pub. Schs., 1957-60, Dane County Child Guidance Ctr., Madison, 1957-62, Juvenile Ct., Madison, 1957-62; clin. asst. prof. child psychiatry Hahnemann Med. Coll., Phila., 1966-74; asst. clin. prof. psychiatry U. Wis., Madison, 1960-62, clin. asst. prof. psychiatry, behavioral scis. and family medicine U. So. Calif., L.A., 1976—; mem. med. staff Presbyn. Intercommunity Hosp., Whittier, 1976—. Pres. Whittier Area Coordinating Coun., 1978-80; chmn. ethics com. Presbyn. Intercommunity Hosp. Flight officer, navigator USAF, 1943-45. Decorated Air medal, POW medal. Fellow Am. Psychiat. Assn. (disting. life), Am. Acad. Child Psychiatry; mem. AAAS, Los Angeles County Med. Assn., So. Calif. Psychiat. Soc., So. Calif. Soc. Child Psychiatry, Phila. Soc. Adolescent Psychiatry (pres. 1967-68), Peace Sci. Soc. Avocations: study of violence and aggression, ethnic travels, ethnic folk music, photography. Office: Intercommunity Child Guidance Ctr 10155 Colima Rd Whittier CA 90603 Home Phone: 562-693-9805; Office Phone: 562-692-0383.

ARENSON, GREGORY K., lawyer; b. Chgo., Feb. 11, 1949; s. Donald L. and Marcia (Terman) A.; m. Karen H. Wattel, Sept. 4, 1970; 1 child, Morgan Elizabeth. BS in Econs., MIT, 1971; JD, U. Chgo., 1975. Bar: Ill. 1975, US Dist. Ct. (no. dist.) Ill. 1975, NY 1978, US Dist. Ct. (so. and ea. dists.) NY 1978, US Supreme Ct. 1985, US Ct. Appeals (2d cir.) 1987, US Dist. Ct. (ctrl. dist.) Ill. 1995, US Ct. Appeals (7th cir.) 1997, US Ct. Appeals (3rd cir.) 2007. Assoc. Rudnick & Wolfe, Chgo., 1975-77, Schwartz, Klink & Schreiber P.C., NYC, 1977-81, ptnr., 1982-87, Proskauer, Rose, Goetz & Mendelsohn, NYC, 1987-93, Kaplan Fox & Kilsheimer LLP, NYC, 1993—. Mediator U.S. Dist. Ct. (so. dist.) N.Y., 1993—; mem. MIT Corp., 1997—2002; mem. corp. devel. com. MIT, 1994—, mem. alumni/alumnae fund bd., 1989—2006, chair, 1994—96; mem. adv. bd. Fed. Discovery News, 1999—. Co-editor: Federal Rules of Civil Procedure, 1993 Amendments, A Practical Guide, 1994; contbr. articles to profl. jours. Mem. ABA, NY State Bar Assn. (comml. and fed. litigation sect., chair com. on discovery 1989-97, chair com. fed. procedure 1997—), NY Bar Found., Assn. Bar City NY. Home: 125 W 76th St Apt 2A New York NY 10023-8334 Office: Kaplan Fox & Kilsheimer LLP 850 3d Ave New York NY 10022-7237 Office Phone: 212-687-1980. Business E-Mail: garenson@kaplanfox.com.

ARENSON, KAREN WATTEL, reporter; b. Long Beach, NY, Jan. 3, 1949; d. Harold Louis and Sara (Gordon) Wattel; m. Gregory Keith Arenson, Sept. 4, 1970; 1 child, Morgan Elizabeth. S.B., MIT, 1970; M.Pub. Policy, Harvard U., 1972. Assoc. dir. Nat. Affiliation of Concerned Bus. Students, Chgo., 1972-73; corr. Bus. Week Mag., 1973-77, editor, 1977-78; reporter NY Times, NYC, 1978-84, asst. fin. editor, 1985-86, editor Sunday Bus. Sect., 1987-89, asst. bus. editor, 1989-90, dep. bus. editor, 1991-94, higher edn. reporter, 1995—. Mem. vis. com. dept. econs. MIT, 1980-88, dept. nuclear engring., dept. linguistics and philosophy, 1989-96, dept. polit. sci., 1991-96, also ednl. counselor. Author: The New York Times Guide to Making the New Tax Law Work for You, 1981. Recipient Matrix award Women in Communications, 1982; recipient Journalism award Washington Monthly, 1981 Mem. MIT Alumni Assn. (bd. dirs. 1986-88, v.p. 1991-93, pres. 1995-96), MIT Corp. (bd. dirs. 1989-94, 95-96, exec. com. 1992-94). Home: 125 W 76th St New York NY 10023-8318 Office: NY Times 229 W 43rd St New York NY 10036-3959 E-mail: arenson@nytimes.com.

ARENZ, DALE WESLEY, lawyer, law educator; b. Eagle, Wis., June 14, 1935; s. Wesley E. and Dorothea Augusta Arenz; m. Susan Jane Arenz, July 26, 1938; children: Deborah, Peter. JD, Marquette Law Sch., Milw., 1963. Pres. Arenz, Molter, Macy and Riffle, Waukesha, Wis., 1980—2002. Lectr. law Marquette Law Sch., Milw., 1968, U. Wis. Law Sch., Madison, 1968—90, League Wis. Municipalities, Madison, 1968—90. Contbr. articles to profl. jours. Mem.: Ruffed Grouse Soc. (chpt. chmn. 1975—2005), Nat. Rifle Assn., Wis. Water Fowl Assn. (life; pres., dir. 2003—). Republican. Avocations: hunting, fishing, reading, fly tying. Office: Arenz Molter Macy and Riffle 720 N East Ave Waukesha WI 53186

ARESTY, JEFFREY M., lawyer; b. Framingham, Mass., Dec. 31, 1951; s. Victor Joseph and Pola (Granek) A.; m. Ellen Louise Gould, Aug. 15, 1976; children: Joshua, Abigail, Joanne. BA, Johns Hopkins U., 1973; JD, Boston U., 1976, LLM in Taxation, 1978, LLM in Internat. Banking, 1993. Bar: Mass. 1977, DC 1982. Tax specialist Coopers & Lybrand, Boston, 1976-78; assoc. Meyers, Goldstein & Crossland, Brookline, Mass., 1978-79; ptnr. Crossland, Aresty & Levin, Boston, 1979-87, Aresty & Levin, Boston, 1987-91, Aresty Internat. Law Offices, Boston, 1992—. Cons. editor Tax Shelter Investment Rev., 1981-85. Recipient Disting. Achievement award Boston Safe Deposit and Trust, 1976, Grad. Banking Alumni Achievement award Boston U. Law Sch., 1993. Mem. ABA (membership chmn. 1981-84, coun. 1985-91, vice chmn. computer divsn. 1985-90, reporter e lawyering 1999-2004, chmn. internat. interest group 1992-96, chmn. internat. negotiations task force 1992-96, chmn. Mass. membership com. 1985-91, internat. law sect., chair law practice com. 1995-98, co-editor ABA Guide Internat. Bus. Negotiations 1994-00, prodr. ABA/AT&T CD-Rom on Cross-Cultural Comm. 1997, chmn. task force on e-commerce, 2002-07), Am. Bar Found. (standing com. tech. and info. systems 1998-99, 05-06, pub. bd. gen. practice 1998-99), Mass. Bar Assn. (bd. dels., exec. com. 1981-83, chmn. law practice sect. 1983-85), Mass. Bar Found. (chmn. 2005). Home: 35 Three Ponds Rd Wayland MA 01778-1732 Office: Aresty Internat Law Offices Bay 17 Union Wharf Boston MA 02109 Personal E-mail: jaresty@cyberspaceattorney.com, jaresty@msn.com.

ARFFA, ALLAN J., lawyer; b. New Haven, Aug. 26, 1955; s. Stanley H. and Shirley (Levinson) A.; m. Kay Marschullart, Dec. 10, 1983; children: Kathryn, Leslie, Travis. BA magna cum laude, Harvard U., 1977, JD cum laude, 1980. Bar: NY 1982, US Dist. Ct. (so. dist.) NY, 1982, US Dist. Ct. (ea. dist.) NY 1991, US Ct. of Appeals (2nd cir.), DC Ct. Appeals. Law clk. to hon. J. Edward Lumbard US Ct. Appeals (2nd cir.) NY, 1980-81; assoc. Paul, Weiss, Rifkind, Wharton & Garrison, NYC, 1981-88, ptnr., 1989—. Mem. Assn. Bar City of N.Y. (mem. various coms.). Office: Paul Weiss Rifkind Wharton & Garrison 1285 Ave of Americas New York NY 10019-6028 Office Phone: 212-373-3203. Office Fax: 212-373-2116. Business E-Mail: aarffa@paulweiss.com.

ARGERS, HELEN, writer, playwright; b. Valisburg, NJ; BA; graduate studies, Europe. Writer advt. copy. Lectr. in field. Author: A Lady of Independence, 1982, Noblesse Oblige, 1994, (play) The Home Visit, 1986 (Winner Nat. One-Act-Play Competition 1986, Weisbrod award 1987), A Scandalous Lady, 1991, A Captain's Lady, 1991, An Unlikely Lady, 1992, The Gilded Lily, 1998, (short story) The Ozymandias Bush, Repossession (Writer's Digest Short Story Competition award); author (under pseudonym Helen Archery) The Age of Elegance, 1992, The Season of Loving, 1992, Lady Adventuress, 1994, Duel of Heats, 1994; humor columnist Worrall Newspapers, 2003—; contbr. articles to profl. jours.; reviewer in field. Recipient Resolution of Honor, State of N.J., 1994, 97. Mem.: Poetry Soc. Am.

ARGIRION, MICHAEL, editor; b. Chgo., May 2, 1940; s. Gus and Angela A.; m. Sherrie Berlant, Feb. 10; children: Carrie, Glen. Student, DePaul U., 1958-59, Northwestern U., 1959-60, U. Chgo., 1961-62. Copy editor Chgo.'s Am., 1959-68, wire editor, 1969; news editor Chgo. Today, 1970-71, Sunday and features editor, 1971-74; asst. Sunday editor Chgo. Tribune, 1974-75, features editor, 1975-79, asst. mng. editor features, 1979-81, asst. mng. editor news editing, 1981-82, exec. news editor, 1982-83, assoc. editor, 1983; editor Tribune Media Services, 1984, v.p., editor, 1985-93. Co-creator internationally syndicated newspaper word puzzle Jumble, That Scrambled Word Game, 1994—. Editor: History of Your World, 1969. Served with U.S. Army, 1962. Mem. Legacy Club Alaqua Lakes. Office: Argirion 1212 St Albans Loop Heathrow FL 32746

ARGIRIS, ATHANASSIOS, oncologist, researcher; b. Athens, Oct. 7, 1966; s. Stavros and Anna Argiris; m. Nektaria Koulaki. MD, Athens Med. Sch., 1990. Diplomate Am. Bd. Internal Medicine, Am. Bd. Med. Oncology. Resident in radiation oncology Areteion U. Hosp., Athens, 1992—94; resident in internal medicine Beth Israel Med. Ctr., NYC, 1994—97; fellow in hematology-oncology Yale U., New Haven, 1997—2000; attending physician Northwestern Meml. Hosp., Chgo., 2000—05; asst. prof. medicine Northwestern U., Chgo., 2000—05; assoc. prof. medicine U. Pitts., 2005—. Attending physician Shadyside Hosp., 2005—, Presbyn. Hosp., 2005—, U. Pitts. Med. Ctr., 2005—; co-dir. head and neck program U. Pitts. Cancer Inst./Hillman Comprehensive Cancer Ctr., 2005—. Recipient Young Investigator award, Am. Assn. Cancer Rsch., 2000. Fellow: ACP; mem.: AMA, Am. Soc. Clin. Oncology. Business E-Mail: argirisae@upmc.edu.

ARGON, ALI SUPHI, mechanical engineering educator; b. Istanbul, Turkey, Dec. 19, 1930; came to U.S., 1948, naturalized, 1980; s. Mehmet Ali Suphi and Seniha Margaret (Grosche) A.; m. Xenia Mary Lacher, Sept. 6, 1953; children: Alice Leyla, Arif Kermit. BS, Purdue U., 1952, DEng (hon.), 2005; SM, MIT, 1953, ScD, 1956. Project engr. High Voltage Engring. Corp., Burlington, Mass., 1956-58; lectr. Middle East Tech. U., Ankara, Turkey, 1959; mem. faculty MIT, 1960—, prof. mech. engring., 1968—, Quentin Berg prof. mech. engring., 1982—2001, Quentin Berg prof. emeritus, 2001—. Vis. prof. polymer physics U. Leeds, 1972; vis. scientist U. Göttingen, Germany, 1992; cons. indsl. and govt. labs. Author: (with F.A. McClintock) Mechanical Behavior of Materials, 1966, (with U.F. Kocks and M.F. Ashby) Thermodynamics and Kinetics of Slip, 1975, Strengthening Mechanisms in Crystal Plasticity, 2007; editor: Physics of Strength and Plasticity, 1969, Constitutive Equations in Plasticity, 1975, Topics in Fracture and Fatigue, 1992; contbr. articles to profl. jours. Recipient Charles Russ Richards Meml. award ASME, 1976, Nadai medal, 1998, Humboldt award, 1992, ETH Switzerland Staudinger-Durrer medal, 1999, Heyn medal German Soc. Materials, 2004, Outstanding Mech. Engr. award Purdue U., 2004; hon. fellow Internat. Congress Fracture. Fellow Am. Phys. Soc.; mem. NAE, Soc. Engring. Sci. (bd. dirs.), Inst. Mech. Materials (bd. govs.). Home: 16 Plymouth Ave Belmont MA 02478-4220 Office: MIT Room 1-306 Dept of Mech Engring Cambridge MA 02139 Office Phone: 617-253-2217. Business E-Mail: argon@mit.edu. *Always strive for perfection, but never take yourself seriously.*

ARGOTI, ANDRES, chemical engineer, researcher; b. Pasto, Nariño, Colombia, Mar. 31, 1975; s. Alvaro Argoti and Betty Caicedo. BS, U. Nat. de Colombia, Bogotá, 1998; MS, Kans. State U., Manhattan, 2003, PhD, 2007. Grad. rsch. asst. Kans. State U., Manhattan, 2000—. Contbr. articles to profl. jours. William H. and Virginia Honstead scholar, Kans. State U. Coll. Engring., 2006—. Mem.: AIChE, Sigma Xi. Office: Kans State Univ 1005 Durland Hall Manhattan KS 66506 Office Phone: 785-532-5584. Office Fax: 785-532-7372.

ARGUE, DON HARVEY, college president, minister; b. Winnipeg, Man., Can., July 12, 1939; came to U.S., 1948; s. Andrew Watson and Hazel Bell (May) A.; m. Patricia Jean Opheim, Sept. 23, 1961; children: Laurie, Lee, Jonathan. BA, Cen. Bible Coll., Springfield, Mo., 1961; MA, Santa Clara U., 1967; EdD, U. of the Pacific, 1969; postdoctoral study, Gordon-Conwell Theol. Sem., 1990, Regent Coll., Vancouver, Can., 1990. Ordained to ministry Assemblies of God, 1964. Pastor 1st Assembly of God, Morganville, Calif., 1965-67; dean of students/men Bethany Coll., Santa Cruz, Calif., 1967-69; asst. prof., dean of student life, dean of students Evangel Coll., Springfield, 1969-74; dean, v.p. North Cen. Bible Coll., Mpls., 1974-79; pres. North Ctrl. Bible Coll., Mpls., 1979—2002, Northwest Univ., 1998—. Gen. presbyter Assemblies of God, Springfield. Recipient Decade of Growth award Christianity Today, 1990. Mem. Nat. Assn. Evangs. (1st v.p.), Soc. for Pentecostal Studies (pres.), Rotary. Home: PO Box 579 Kirkland WA 98083-0579 Office: Northwest University 5520 108th Ave NE Kirkland WA 98033*

ARGUEDAS, CRISTINA CLAYPOOLE, lawyer; b. 1953; BA, U. NH; JD summa cum laude, Rutgers U., 1979. Bar: Calif. Supreme Ct. 1979, US Dist. Ct., No. Dist. Calif. 1979, So. Dist. Calif. 1983, Ctrl. Dist. Calif. 1982, Ea. Dist. Calif. 1982, Dist. Ariz. 1991, US Ct. Appeals: Ninth Cir. 1980, Tenth Cir. 1985, US Supreme Ct. 1983, US Tax Ct. 1994. Dep. fed. defender US Dist. Ct. (no. dist.) Calif.; ptnr. Arguedas, Cassman & Headley (formerly Cooper, Arguedas & Cassman), Emeryville, Calif., 1982—. Lawyer rep. US Ct. Appeals (9th cir.) Jud. Conf.; adj. prof. Benjamin N. Cardozo Sch. Law, Yeshiva U., Boalt Hall Sch. Law. Named one of 50 Top Lawyers, Nat. Law Jour., 1998, 100 Most Influential Lawyers, 2006, The 50 Most Influential Women Lawyers in Am., 2007, Top Ten Lawyers in Bay Area, San Francisco Chronicle, 2003, America's Leading Lawyers for Bus., Chambers USA, 2005. Fellow: Am. Coll. Trial Lawyers; mem.: ABA Sect. of Litigation Trial Advisory Bd., Bd. Western Ctr. on Law and Poverty, Am. Bd. Criminal Lawyers, Am. Inns of Ct. (master 1999—), Internat. Acad. Trial Lawyers, Calif. Attys. for Criminal Justice (past pres.). Office: Arguedas Cassman & Headley 803 Hearst Ave Berkeley CA 94710 Office Phone: 510-654-2000.*

ARGYROS, GEORGE L., real estate company executive, former ambassador; b. Detroit, 1937; m. Judie Argyros. Student, Mich. State U.; BS in Bus. and Econs., Chapman Coll., 1959. Pres. Arnel Devel. Co., 1968; chmn. bd. Arnel Mgmt.; chmn., CEO Arnel & Affiliates; chmn., dir. Air Cal, 1981—87; dir. comml. financing services Newport bancorp and Coast Thrift and Loan Co.; prin. owner Seattle Mariners Baseball Team, 1981-89; U.S. amb. to Spain & Andorra U.S. Dept. State, 2001—04. Mem. Baseball's Revenue sharing Com., Restructuring Com., Commr. Selection Com.; bd. dirs. Am. League Chmn. Western Wash.'s United Cerebral Palsy Telethon; chmn. fundraising Nat. Multiple Sclerosis Soc., Puget Sound chpt.; active NCCJ, Boy Scouts Am., World Affairs Council, Young Pres.'s Orgn.; chmn. bd. dir. Chapman Coll, 1976-2001, bd. dir; internat. coun., trustee, Ctr. for Strategic and Internat. Studies, Washington, DC.; bd. dir. U.S. C.of C.; mem. bd. visitors, M.D. Anderson Cancer Ctr.; former chmn. Richard Nixon Libr. & Birthplace Found.; founding chmn. Nixon Ctr., Washington, DC; former chmn. and bd. dir. Orange County Coun. Boy Scouts of Am. Named one of Forbes' Richest Americans, 2006. Mem.: Horatio Alger Assn. (pres., CEO 1995—98, chmn. 1998—2000, treas., chmn. emeritus, Norman Vincent Peale award 2003).

ARIAS, ILEANA, psychiatrist, educator; AB, Bernard Coll., Columbia U.; MA, SUNY Stony Brook, PhD in Psychology. Rsch. assoc. SUNY, Stony Broko; asst. prof. U. Ga., 1985—2000, dir. clin. tng., clin. psychology prof.; chief etiology and surveillance br., divsn. violence prevention Centers for Disease Control, 2000—04, acting dir. Nat. Ctr. Injury Prevention and Control, 2004—. Contbr. articles to profl. jours.; mem. editl. bd. Jour. of Aggression, Maltreatment and Trauma, Rev. of Aggression and Violent Behavior, Violence and Victims. Office: Nat Ctr Injury Prevention and Control Vanderbilt Bdlg Koger Ctr 2858 Woodcock Blvd Rm 1017B Atlanta GA 30333 Office Phone: 770-488-4696.

ARIAS, RICARDO ALBERTO, ambassador, lawyer; b. Panama City, Panama, Sept. 11, 1939; s. Ricardo Alberto Arias Espinosa and Olga Arias de Arias; children: Makelin de Perez, Alexandria Arias, Ricarco Arias, Lolitin Arias. BS in Fgn. Svc., Georgetown U., Washington, 1961; LLB, U. PR, 1964; LLM, Yale U., New Haven, 1965. Fgn. trainee Sherman & Sterling, 1966; assoc. Fabrega, Lopez & Pedreschi, 1967-68; founding mem., ptnr. Galindo, Arias & Lopez, Panama City, 1968—2004; prof. fiscal law and adminstrn. law Santa Maria La Antigua U., Panama, 1973—78; amb. to US Govt. Panama, 1994—96, fgn. min., 1996—98, amb., permanent rep. to UN NYC, 2004—. V.p., dir. Corporacion La Prensa, Panama; dir. Banco Gen., S.A., Panama, Assa Compania de Seguros, Panama, Copa Airlines. Mem. Internat. Bar Assn., Interamerican Bar Assn., Colegio de Abogados de Panama. Office: Permanent Mission of Panama to UN 866 United Nations Plz Ste 4030 New York NY 10017 Office Phone: 212-421-5420. Office Fax: 212-421-2694.*

ARIEFF, ALLEN IVES, physician; b. Chgo., Sept. 30, 1938; BS in Math. and Chemistry, U. Ill., 1960; MS in Physiology, Northwestern U., 1964, MD, 1964. Intern Phila. Gen. Hosp., 1964-65; resident SUNY, Bklyn., 1967-68; renal fellow U. Colo., Denver, 1968-69; rsch. and edn. assoc., clin. investigator Wadsworth VA Med. Ctr., LA, 1970-74; asst. prof. medicine, rsch. scientist UCLA Med. Ctr., 1971-74; asst. prof. medicine, dir. hemodialysis U. Calif. VA Med. Ctr., San Francisco, 1975-76, assoc. prof. medicine, dir. nephrology sect., 1976-83, prof. medicine, chief clin. nephrology, 1983-86, prof. medicine, dir. rsch. & edn. geriatrics, 1986—. Cons. and spkr. in field. Author: 10 books; contbr. articles 98 chpts. med. textbooks, over 400 articles to profl. jours. Fellow: ACP; mem.: Soc. Neurosci., Internat. Soc. Nephrology, We. Soc. Clin. Rsch., We. Assn. Physicians, Assn. Am. Physicians, Am. Soc. Bone and Mineral Rsch., Am. Soc. Clin. Investigation, Am. Soc. Neurochemistry, Am. Physiol. Soc., Am. Diabetes Assn., Am. Fedn. Med. Rsch., Am. Soc. Nephrology. Office: Penthouse 9400 Brighton Way Ph Beverly Hills CA 90210-4712 Office Phone: 310-276-2033. Business E-Mail: allen.arieff@ucsf.edu.

ARIETI, JAMES ALEXANDER, classics educator, writer; b. NYC, May 12, 1948; s. Silvano and Jane (Jaffe) A.; m. Barbara Ann Mapes, May 23, 1976; children: Samuel Abraham, Ruth Sophia. BA, Grinnell Coll., 1969; MA, PhD, Stanford U., 1972. Asst. prof. Stanford (Calif.) U., 1972-74, Pa. State U., University Park, 1974-75, Cornell Coll., Mt. Vernon, Iowa, 1975-77; prof. dept. classics Hampden-Sydney (Va.) Coll., 1978—. Author: Love Can Be Found, 1975, Longinus on the Sublime, 1985, Interpreting Plato: The Dialogues as Drama, 1991, Discourses on the First Book of Herodotus, 1995, The Scientific and the Divine: Conflict and Reconciliation from Ancient Greece to Today, 2003, Philosophy in the Ancient World: An Introduction, 2005, Plato's Gorgias (translation), 2007; editor: Hamartia, 1983; translator Plato's Gorjias, 2007; contbr. articles to profl. jours. Woodrow Wilson fellow, 1969; NEH fellow, 1977-78. Mem. Am. Philol. Assn., Classical Assn. Middle West and South, Classical Assn. Va., Phi Beta Kappa, Phi Alpha Theta, Eta Sigma Chi. Jewish. Home and Office: Hampden Sydney Coll PO Box 746 Hampden Sydney VA 23943-0746 Office Phone: 434-223-6252.

ARIETTI, MICHAEL RAY, ambassador; b. LA, Oct. 25, 1947; s. Michael John and Margaret Mary (Schiller) A.; m. Lesley Gwenllian Latter, May 24, 1980; 1 child, Rachael. BA, Johns Hopkins U., 1970. Fgn. svc. officer US Dept. State, Washington, 1973—, dep. staff mem. Am. Embassy Lusaka, Zambia, dep. perm. rep. of US Mission to UN Washington, dir. Office West African Affairs, US amb. to Rwanda Kigali, 2005—. Avocation: tennis. Office: Am Embassy 2210 Kigali Pl Washington DC 20521

ARIFI, FATANA BAKTASH, artist, educator; arrived in US, 2000, naturalized, 2006; d. Mohammed Arif and Bibishreen Arifi. Diploma in Art (hon.), Women Orgn. Afghanistan, Kabul, 1983; diploma in Painting, Maimanagi Art Inst., Kabul, Afghanistan, 1983; MFA, Kabul U., Afghanistan, 1987; AA in Art, Thompson Coll. Edn. Direct, 2004. Cert. picturer Framing Gallery, US. Art instr. Kabul (Afghanistan) U., 1989—92; freelance artist, designer Afghan Internat. Orgn., 1994—99; dir. Maimanagi Fine Arts Ctr., Peshawar, Pakistan, 1995—99; art instr. Inst. of Fine Arts, Peshawar, 1996; founder, editor Art and Culture Jour., Peshawar, 1997—99; art instr. Hunarkada Acad. Visual and Performance Arts, Peshawar, 1998; sr. cert. framer Michael's Art and Crafts, Alexandria, Va., 2001—, instr. drawing and watercolor, 2005—; freelance artist, 2001—. Mem. selection com. Afghan Artistic Competitions, Peshawar, Pakistan; art dir. Afghan Musaic, 1999; artist mem. Gallery West, Alexandria, Va. Author: Drawing and Painting, 1988, Painting and it's Status in Afghanistan, 1998, Drawing Technical Metodes, 1999. Finalist Exptl. Category, Artists Mag. Competition, 2007; recipient award, Artist Festival, Japan, 1981, Nat. Painting award, Ministry of Culture, Afghanistan, 1983, 1985, 1987, award, Women Orgn., Afghanistan, 1983, Army Mus., Afghanistan, 1986, Nat. Assn. Artists of Afghanistan, 1986, Youth Orgn. Afghanistan, 1985. Mem.: Empowered Women Internat., Nat. Assn. Women Artists. Muslim. Achievements include development of Handasism. Avocations: writing, poetry, cooking. Personal E-mail: fatana_ba@hotmail.com.

ARIMILLI, RAVI K., computer engineer; b. 1963; arrived in US, 1969; BEE, La. State U. Joined IBM, 1985, fellow & chief tech. officer Austin, Tex. Named Asian Am. Engr. of Yr., Chinese Inst. Engring. in US, 2004. Achievements include holding more patents than any other IBM employee.

ARIMURA, AKIRA, biomedical researcher, educator; b. Kagoshima, Japan, Dec. 26, 1923; arrived in U.S., 1965; s. Jyojiro and Kiyoko (Kajiwara) A.; m. Katsuko Yamashita, July 31, 1957; children: Jerome J., Mark M., Margaret M. BS, 7th Nat. Coll., Kagoshima, 1943; MD, Nagoya U., Japan, 1951, PhD, 1957; diploma (hon.), Pécs Med. Sch., Hungary, 1995. James Hudson Brown postdoctoral fellow Yale U., New Haven, 1956-58; instr., rsch. assoc. Hokkaido U., Sapporo, Japan, 1961-65; instr. Tulane U., New Orleans, 1958-61, asst. prof., 1965-68, assoc. prof., 1968-73, prof. medicine, 1973—, dir. U.S.-Japan Biomedical Rsch. Lab. Belle Chasse, La., 1985—. Rsch. physician VA Hosp., New Orleans, 1965-80; mem. Endocrine Study Sect., NIH, 1978-82; adj. prof. anatomy Tulane U., New Orleans, 1979—, Physiology, 1989—, founder, dir. clin. RIA Lab., Tulane U. Med. Ctr., 1980-87, molecular neuroendo and diabetes lab. Belle Chasse, 1980-85, dir., 1985; vis. prof. Keio U., Tokyo, 1990—; founder U.S.-Japan Biomed. Rsch. Labs., Belle Chasse, 1985—; reviewer Jour. Clin. Endocrinology and Metabolism, Am. Jour. Physiology, Jour. Clin. Investigation, Sci., Life Sci., Procs. Soc. Exptl. Biology and Medicine, others. Mem. editorial bd. Peptides, Turkish Jour. Med. and Endocrine Jour.; contbr. articles to scholarly and profl. jours. Planner, initiator student exch. program Tulane U. and Keio U., New Orleans and Tokyo, 1986, Tulane U. and Nagoya (Japan) U., Showa U. Decorated with Order of Rising Sun, Gold Rays with Neck Ribbon, Govt. of Japan, 1995; named Fulbright scholar 1956. Mem. AAAS, Internat. Soc. Neuroendocrine, Endocrine Soc. U.S., Japan Endocrinology Soc. (hon.), Hungarian Soc. for Endocrinology and Metabolism (hon.), Am. Physiology Soc., Am. Soc. Neurosci., Soc. Exptl. Biology and Medicine, N.Y. Acad. Scis., Japan Physiol. Soc. (hon.), Japan Neuroenscience Soc. (hon.). Achievements include co-development of LHRH, somatostatin, Interleukin-1, pituitary adenylate cyslau activating polypeptide; discovery of PACAP. Office: Tulane U Herbert Rsch Ctr US-Japan Biomed Rsch Labs 3705 Main St Belle Chasse LA 70037-3001 Home Phone: 504-393-7887. Business E-Mail: arimura@tulane.edu.

ARIOLA, DANTE, television commercial and video director; Television comml. director Method Studios. Dir.: (TV Commercials) Infiniti Hand, 2002, Infiniti Heart, 2002, Lee Dungarees Cheese and Emu, 2002, Nintendo Moth, 2003, Nintendo Flower, 2003, Diet Coke Movie House, 2003, Anti-Smoking PSA Growth, 2004, Infiniti Blur, 2004, First Taste Coca-Cola, 2006 (Outstanding Directorial Achievement in Commercials, Director's Guild awards, 2007).*

ARISON, MICKY, cruise line company executive, professional sports team owner; b. Tel Aviv, June 29, 1949; married; 2 children. Student, U. Miami; D in Naval Architecture (hon.), U. Genoa. Reservations mgr. Carnival Corp., 1974-76, v.p. passenger traffic, 1976-79, pres., CEO, 1979-90, chmn., CEO, 1990—; mng. gen. ptnr. Miami Heat, Fla.; chmn. NBA Bd. Govs., 2005—. Named Officer of the French Legion of Honor, French Pres. Jacques Chirac; named one of World's Richest People, Forbes mag., 1999—, Forbes' Richest Ams., 1999—; recipient Onorificenza al Merito della Repubblica Italiana, Pres. of Italy, Decoration of Comdr., 1st Class, of the Order of the Lion of Finland, Pres. of Finland. Mem.: Fla. Caribbean Cruise Assn. (chmn.). Office: Carnival Corp 3655 NW 87th Ave Miami FL 33178-2428*

ARISON, SHARI, investment company executive; d. Ted Arison; m. Ofer Glazer; 4 children. Grad., U. Fl. Chmn. Arison Holdings, 1999—, Arison Investments, 1999—; chmn., pres. Ted Arison Family Foundation, 1999—; controller Bank Ha'poalim, Israel. Named one of World's richest people, Forbes mag., 2000—. Achievements include Israel's wealthiest citizen, 1999-2004; shareholder, Carnival Cruise Lines. Office: c/o Carnival Corp 3655 NW 87th Ave Miami FL 33178*

ARIYAN, STEPHAN, plastic surgeon; b. Egypt, July 30, 1941; m. Sandra Ariyan, June 25, 1967; children: Stephen, Christopher, Tiffany. BS, LI U., 1962; MD, N.Y. Med. Coll., 1966; MBA, U. New Haven, 1993; MA (hon.), Yale U., 1981. Diplomate Am. Bd. Surgery, Am. Bd. of Plastic Surgery.; lic. Conn., Calif., NY. Intern, surgery UCLA, 1966-67; asst. resident, gen. surgery U. Calif., San Diego, 1967-68; NIH fellow, Surgery Yale U., 1970—71, asst. resident, gen. surgery, 1971-73, resident, plastic surgery, 1973-74, chief resident, gen. surgery, 1974-75, chief resident, plastic surgery, 1975-76, asst. prof. surgery, 1976-79, assoc. prof. surgery, 1979-81, prof. surgery, 1981-91, chmn. plastic surgery, 1979-91, clin. prof. surgery, plastic surgery, otolaryngology, 1994—; dir. Yale Melanoma Unit, Yale Cancer Ctr., 1976—; fellow, hand surgery Yale U./U. Conn., 1976; Internat. Union Against Cancer (UICC) fellow, melanoma rsch. Sydney U., Australia, 1980. Rsch. on organ preservation and transplantation U. Calif., San Diego, 1969—70, prosector, anatomy, 1969—70; vice-chmn. Am. Bd. Plastic Surgery, 1994—95, chmn., ethics com., 1989—95, dir., 1981—, bd. examiner; mem. joint com. with Am. Bd. Plastic Surgery & Am. Bd. Otolaryngology to consider cert. of otolaryngologists in plastic surgery within the head & neck Am. Bd. Med. Specialties, 1992—95; mem. upper aerodigestive cancer working group organ sys. coordinating ctr. Nat. Cancer Inst., 1986—89; v.p. SpecialtyNet, LLC, 1997—2001; chair, search com., chief gen. surgery Yale U. Sch. Medicine, 1979—91, mem. bd. permanent officers, 1981—, vice-chair, search com., chmn. orthop., 1984—86, search com. for chmn. dept. medicine, 1986—87, mem. med. sch. admissions com., 1995—; mem. exec. com., dept. surgery Yale-New Haven Hosp., 1979—91, mem. trustees' task force for hosp. goverance, 1981, mem. infectious disease com., 1981—86, mem. operating room com., 1981—91, mem. med. staff cabinet, 1983—93, mem. med. staff credentials com., 1984—86, mem. com. residency program dir., 1989—91; mem. search com. for chmn. plastic surgery Hosp. St. Raphael, 1983; bd. dir. Vis. Nurses Assn., 1996—; cons. Am. Medico-Legal Found.; C.I.S. med. dir. Armenian General Benevolent Union-Med. Outreach Program for Ministry of Health, Armenia, 1989—; med. dir. Armenian General Benevolent Union-Yale Program Tng. Soviet Med. Team in Plastic Surgery, 1990—91; evaluation and treatment of injured victims Armenian Earthquake, 1989; mem. med. com. Yale-China Assn., 1990; vol. surgeon Hopital Albert Schweitzer Deschapelles, Haiti, 1973, 82; vis. prof. U. Calif., San Diego, 1976, NYU Med. Ctr., 1977, Brown U. Med. Ctr., RI, 1977, RI, 80, U. Calif., Irvine, 1979, Roswell Park Meml. Inst., Buffalo, 1980, NYU, 1981, 85, Nat. Naval Med. Ctr., Md., 1981, Mass. Gen. Hosp., 1982, McLaren Gen. Hosp., Mich. State U., 1983, U. Conn., St. Francis Hosp., 1984, NY Med. Coll., 1984, U. Singapore, 1985, George Washington U., 1986, U. Mass., 1986, U. Mo., Columbia, 1990, Meml. Sloan-Kettering Cancer Ctr., NYC, 1991, Hopital Gen. Gregorio Maranon, U. Madrid, 1991, Stanford U., 1992, Brown U., RI, 1992, Dartmouth Med. Sch., NH, 1993, Lorna Linda U., Calif., 1994, U. So. Calif., LA, 1994, U. Md., 1994, John Hopkins U., 1994, U. Miami, 1996, Rush U. Med. Coll., Ill., 1996, U. Tenn., 1996, U. Louisville, Ky., 1996; invited spkr. in field; traveling oncology cons. Am. Cancer Soc., 1994. Assoc. editor Plastic and Reconstructive Surgery, 1983-89; editl. bd. Annals of Surg. Oncology, 1993-2001; reviewer Head & Neck Surgery, 1987-93, Annals Plastic Surgery, 1990-, Cancer 1996-2002, Jour. Reconstructive Microsurgery, 1997-2002, Jour. Urology, 1997-2000; author The Hand Book, 1978, 2nd edit. 1983, 3rd edit., 1988, Cancer of the Head and Neck, 1987; co-author Facial Fractures, 1989, Plastic Surgery-Principles and Practice. Vol. surgeon Hopital Albert Schweitzer, 1973, 82; mem. in-svc. examination com., Plastic Surgery Ednl. Found., 1976-81, chmn. head and neck com., 1978-81), mem. evaluation and treatment of injured victims Armenian Earthquake, U.S.S.R., 1989; med. dir. Tng. Soviet Med. Team in Plastic Surgery, 1990-91, Ministry of Health, 1989-91. Named Best Breast Cancer Drs. Good Housekeeping mag., 1989, Outstanding Med. Specialists in U.S. Town and Country mag., 1989, Best Doctors of NY, 2001-05; recipient Kabakjian award Outstanding Contrbn. in a Field of Sci., 1991, Presdl. award, Am. Soc. for Head and Neck Surgery, 1993, Rep. Armenia, CIS, 1994, Presdl. Citation, Am. Head and Neck Soc., 2002. Mem. ACS (mem. commn. on cancer, 1987-95, mem. adv. coun., plastic and maxillofacial surgery, 1992-95, Scholar award. 1973-76, honorable mention, resident papers, Conn. Chpt., 1975), Am. Coll. Physician Execs., Am. Assn. Plastic Surgeons (chmn. scientific program com., 1986-87, chmn. ethics com. 1994-95), Am. Assn. Hand Surgery (honorable mention, resident papers, 1976), Am. Burn Assn., Am. Cleft-Palate-Craniofacial Assn., Soc. for Aesthetic Plastic Surgery, Am. Soc. Maxillofacil Surgeons, Am. Soc. Plastic and Reconstructive Surgeons (first prize in basic rsch., Plastic Surgery Chief Resident's Conf. Ednl. Found., 1974, first prize in head and neck surgery Plastic Surgery Conf. Ednl. Found., 1976, first prize, basic sci. rsch., Ednl. Found., 1976, third prize, clin. rsch., Ednl. Found., 1979, first prize, essay, Ednl. Found., 1996, 1998), Am. Soc. for Reconstructive Microsurgery, Am. Soc. for Surgery of the Hand, Am. Surg. Assn., Assn. for Acad. Surgery, Assn. Acad. Chmn. Plastic Surgery(founding pres., 1985-86), Assn. Am. Med. Colls., Conn. Soc. Am. Bd. Surgeons, Conn. Soc. Plastic and Reconstructive Surgeons (rep. to coun. to regional societies, 1981-86, chmn. ins. liaison com. 1983-88), Internat. Soc. Reconstructive Microsurgery, New England Hand Soc.(mem. exec. coun., 1981-83), New England Soc. Plastic and Reconstructive Surgeons (pres. 1986-87), New England Surg. Soc., N.Y. Acad. Scis., N.Y. Regional Soc. Plastic and Reconstructive Surgeons (first prize, resident papers, 1976), Northeastern Soc. Plastic Surgeons (pres., 1990-91), Pan Pacific Surg. Assn., Plastic Surgery Rsch. Coun., Royal Soc. Medicine (Eng.), Soc. Head and Neck Surgeons (dir. head and neck workshop, 1986-90, pres. 1992-93, Disting. Svc. award, 1989, Nat. Vis. Prof., 1995-96), Soc. Surg. Oncology, Soc. Univ. Surgeons, Conn. Vis. Nurses Assn. (bd. dirs. 1996-2002), Am. Bd. Plastic Surgery (vice chmn., 1989-1995), Nat. Match for Plastic Surgery Residency (founding chmn. 1986-91), Alpha Epsilon Delta, Phi Sigma, Sigma Xi. Office: 60 Temple St Ste 7C New Haven CT 06510 Address: 5 Durham Rd Guilford CT 06437 Office Phone: 203-458-4433.*

ARIYOSHI, GEORGE RYOICHI, lawyer, business consultant, former governor; b. Honolulu, Mar. 12, 1926; s. Ryozo and Mitsue (Yoshikawa) A.; m. Jean Miya Hayashi, Feb. 5, 1955; children: Lynn Miye, Todd Ryozo, Donn Ryoji. Student, U. Hawaii, 1944-45, 47; BA, Mich. State U., 1949, LL.D. (hon.), 1979; JD, U. Mich., 1952; LL.D. (hon.), U. Philippines, 1975, U. Guam, 1975; H.H.D. (hon.), U. Visayas, Philippines, 1977, U. Hawaii, 1986. Bar: Hawaii 1953. Sole practice, Honolulu, 1953-70; mem. Ter. of Hawaii Ho. of Reps., 1954-58, State of Hawaii Senate, 1959-70, chmn. ways and means com., 1963-64, majority leader, 1965-66, majority floor leader, 1969-70; lt. gov. State of Hawaii, 1970-73, acting gov., 1973-74, gov., 1974-86; of counsel Kobayashi, Watanabe, Sugita, Kawashima & Goda, Honolulu, 1986-90, Watanabe, Ing and Kawashima, Honolulu, 1990—; ptnr. Cole, Gilburn, Goldhaber & Ariyoshi Mgmt. Inc.; mnging. ptnr. Ariyoshi, Mills & Assocs. Chmn. Western Govs. Conf., 1977-78; chmn. Western Govs. Assn., 1984-85; dir. Hawaiian Ins. & Guaranty, Ltd., 1966-70, First Hawaiian Bank, 1962-70, Honolulu Gas Co., Ltd. (Pacific Resources Inc.), 1964-70; bus. cons.; pres., CEO Cultured Tech., Inc.; pres. Aina Kamalii Corp. holding co. Mauna Kea Beach Hotel, Maui Prince Hotel, Hapuna Beach Prince Hotel, Hawaii Prince Hotel and golf courses; co-chmn. Asia-Pacific Cons. Group; bd. dirs. Pacific Internat. Ctr. for High Tech. Rsch.; mem. Japan-Hawaii Econ. Coun.; founder pres. Internat. Comml. Dispute Resolution. Mem. adv. bd. Japan Found. Ctr. for Global Partnership; mem. Pres.'s Adv. commn. on Trade Policy and Negotiations; exec. bd. Aloha Coun. Boy Scots Am., 1970-72; pres. Pacific Basin Devel. Coun., 1980-81; bd. mgrs. YMCA, 1955-57; chmn., treas. Earth Cons. Inc.; hon. co-chmn. Japanese-Am. Nat. Mus.; trustee Japanese-Am. Inst. Mgmt. Sci., bd. dirs. Bishop Mus.; bd. govs. Japanese Cultrual Ctr. Hawaii; nat. committeeman Dem. Party Hawaii; adv. mem. Japan-Am. Cooperation in Space Project. Recipient Distinguished Alumni awards U. Hawaii, 1975, Distinguished Alumni awards Mich. State U., 1975, Japan's Order of Sacred Treasure 1st class, 1985, Emperor's Silver Cup award, 1986. Mem. ABA (ho. dels. 1969—), Hawaii Bar Assn. (pres. 1969), Hawaii Bar Found. (charter, pres. 1969—). Clubs: Military Intelligence Service Vets (pres. 1968-69). Democrat.*

ARIYUR, KARTIK BALASUBRAMANIAN, control systems engineer, researcher; US, 1996; s. Balasubramanian M. Ariyur and Usha Baalasubramanian. BTech, Indian Inst. Tech., Chennai, Tamilnadu, India; MS, U. Calif., La Jolla, Calif., 1999, PhD, 2002. Engring. intern United Technologies Rsch. Ctr., East Hartford, Conn., 1998, Qualcomm Inc., La Jolla, 2001—02; scientist Honeywell Labs, Mpls., 2002—. Student mentor Inst. Tech. U. Minn., Mpls., 2002—; program com. Hybrid Sys., Computation and Control Conf., Santa Barbara, Calif., 2005—06; mem. program com. Am. Control Conf., Seattle, 2008. Author: Real-Time Optimization by Extremum Seeking Control, 2003; editor: Internat. Jour. Adaptive Control and Signal Processing, 2005—; contbr. articles to profl. jours. Mem.: IEEE, Soc. Automotive Engrs. (Outstanding paper award 2005). Achievements include discovery of slope seeking, a new technique for adaptive control; patents for pilot estimation using prediction error method-switched filters; patents pending for trending system and method using window filtering; trending system; prediction of dynamic ground effect forces for fixed wing aircraft; collision avoidance involving radar feedback. Avocations: philosophy, law, indian classical music, drawing. Office: Honeywell Labs 3660 Tech Dr Minneapolis MN 55418 Office Phone: 612-951-7129. Business E-Mail: kartik.ariyur@honeywell.com.

ARKANI-HAMED, NIMA, physicist, educator; b. Houston; PhD, U. Calif., Berkeley, 1997. Rsch. assoc. Stanford Linear Accelerator Ctr., Menlo Pk., Calif., 1997—99; prof. physics U. Calif., 1999—2002, Harvard U., 2002—. Contbr. articles to sci. jours. Named one of Brilliant 10, Popular Sci. mag., 2006; recipient Gribov medal, European Phys. Soc., 2003; Packard Found. fellow, David and Lucille Packard Found., 2000—, Sloan fellow, Alfred P. Sloan Found., 2000—02. Achievements include development of the theory of large extra dimensions of space, in collaboration with Savas Dimopoulos and Gia Dvali, to explain the extraordinary weakness of gravity relative to the other forces of nature. Office: Jefferson Lab 570 Harvard U 17 Oxford St Cambridge MA 02138 Office Phone: 617-496-6908. E-mail: arkani@physics.harvard.edu.*

ARKFELD, LOURAINE C., judge; b. Olean, NY, 1948; JD magna cum laude, Ariz. State Univ., 1976. Bar: Ariz. 1977, US Ct. Appeals (9th cir.) 1977, US Dist. Ct. Ariz. 1977. Asst. city prosecutor Phoenix City Prosecutors Off., 1978—83; ptnr. Cohen, Fromm & Crawford, 1983—84; mcpl. ct. judge City of Tempe, Ariz., 1994—. Recipient William H. Rehnquist Award for Judicial Excellence, 2005. Mem.: Ariz. Magistrates Assn. (pres. 1990—92), Nat. Conf. Spl. Court Judges (vice chair 1996—97), ABA (bd. govs. 2005—). Office: Municipal Court Judge 140 E 5th Ste 200 Tempe AZ 85281-3736 Office Phone: 602-350-8454. Office Fax: 602-350-8580.

ARKILIC, GALIP MEHMET, mechanical engineer, educator; b. Sivas, Turkey, Mar. 10, 1920; came to U.S., 1943, naturalized, 1960; s. Sabir Mehmet and Zahra Fatima (Hocazade) A.; m. Ann A. Bryan, Mar. 31, 1956. BME, Cornell U., 1946; MS, Ill. Inst. Tech., 1948; PhD, Northwestern U., 1954. Registered profl. engr., Va. Mech. engr. Miehle Printing Press and Mfg. Co., Chgo., 1948-49, analyst, 1954-56; research and devel. engr. Mech. and Chem. Industries, Turkey, 1949-52; asst. prof. Pa. State U., University Park, 1956-58; assoc. prof. dept. civil engring. George Washington U., Washington, 1958-63, prof. engring. and applied sci., 1963—, prof. emeritus, 1990—, chmn. dept. engring. mechanics, 1966-69, asst. dean, 1969-74. Contbr. articles to sci. jours. Vice pres. Courtland Civic Assn., Arlington, Va., 1965-66; pres. Am. Turkish Assn., Washington, 1967-71. Served to 2d lt. Turkish Army, 1939-41 Recipient Disting. Leadership award Am. Turkish Assn., 1972; Recognition of Service award Sch. Engring. and Applied Sci., George Washington U., 1976, Spl. Appreciation award Engring. Alumni Assn., George Washington U., 1990; Air Force Office of Sci. Research grantee, 1963-69 Mem. ASME, AAUP, Am. Acad. Mechanics, Math. Assn. of Am., Am. Math. Soc., Wash. Soc. Engrs., Sigma Xi. Clubs: George Washington U. (Washington). Home: 8403 Camden St Alexandria VA 22308-2111 Office: George Washington Univ Sch Engring and Applied Sc Washington DC 20052-0001 Office Phone: 202-994-1000. Personal E-mail: gmarkilic@aol.com.

ARKIN, ALAN WOLF, actor; b. NYC, Mar. 26, 1934; s. David I. and Beatrice (Wortis) A.; m. Jeremy Yaffe, 1955 (div. 1960); children: Adam, Matthew.; m. Barbara Dana, June 16, 1964 (div.); 1 child, Anthony; m. Suzanne Arkin. Student, Los Angeles City Coll., 1951-53, Bennington Coll., 1954-55. Broadway appearances include From The Second City, 1961, Enter Laughing (Tony award), 1963, Luv, 1964; motion picture appearances include The Russians are Coming, The Russians Are Coming, 1966 (Golden Globe award as best actor in musical or comedy 1967), Woman Times Seven, 1967, Wait Until Dark, 1967, Inspector Clouseau, 1968, The Heart is a Lonely Hunter (N.Y. Critics award), 1968, Popi, 1969, Catch-22, 1970, Last of the Red Hot Lovers, 1972, Freebie and the Bean, 1974, Rafferty and the Gold Dust Twins, 1975, Seven Per Cent Solution, 1976, The In Laws, 1979 (also exec. prodr.), Chu Chu and the Philly Flash, 1981, Improper Channels, 1981, The Last Unicorn, 1982, Joshua Then and Now, 1985, Big Trouble, 1986, Coupe De Ville, 1990, Havana, 1991, Edward Scissorhands, 1991, The Rocketeer, 1991, Glengarry Glen Ross, 1991, Indian Summer, 1993, So I Married an Axe Murderer, 1993, The Jerky Boys, 1995, Steal Big, Steal Little, 1995, Mother Night, 1996, Grosse Pointe Blank, 1997, Gattaca, 1997, Slums of Beverly Hills, 1998, Jakob the Liar, 1999, Arigo, 2000 (also dir.), Magicians, 2000, America's Sweethearts, 2001, Thirteen Conversations About One Thing, 2001, Raising Flagg, 2003, Noel, 2004, Eros, 2004, The Novice, 2004, Little Miss Sunshine, 2006 (Outstanding Performance by a Cast in a Motion Picture, SAG, 2007, Actor in a Supporting Role, British Acad. Film and TV Arts, 2007, Acad. award best actor in a supporting role, 2007), Firewall, 2006, The Santa Clause 3: The Escape Clause, 2006; TV film appearances include The Other Side of Hell, 1978, The Defection of Simas Kudirka, 1978, Escape From Sobibor, 1987, Cooperstown, 1993, Taking the Heat, 1993, Doomsday Gun, 1994, Heck's Way Home, 1996, Blood Money, 1999, Varian's War, 2001, And Starring Pancho Villa as Himself, 2003; TV series include Sesame Street, 1970-72, Harry, 1987, 100 Centre Street, 2001-02; mem. theatre group, Second City Chicago and Off-Broadway, 1961; rec. of children's music The Babysitters, 1958, Songs and Fun with The Babysitters, 1960, The Family Album, 1965, The Babysitters Menagerie, 1968; short motion pictures include That's Me, 1963, The Last Mohican, 1965; dir. movie short People Soup, motion picture Little Murders, 1971; prodr., dir. films Samuel Beckett is Coming Soon, 1993; dir. Broadway The Sunshine Boys; TV series Fay, 1975; author: (juvenile) Tony's Hard Work Day, 1972, The Lemming Condition, 1979; (adult-jour.) Halfway Through the Door, 1979, The Clearing, 1986, (juvenile) Some Fine Grampa, 1995, (juvenile) One Present From Flekrians, 1998, (juvenile) Cassie Love Beethoven, 2000.*

ARKIN, J. GORDON, lawyer; b. NYC, Jan. 3, 1946; AB summa cum laude, Lehigh U., 1967; JD cum laude, Harvard U., 1970. Bar: N.Y. 1971, Fla. 1976. Gen. counsel Greater Orlando Aviation Authority; ptnr. Foley & Lardner, Orlando, Fla. Co-vice-chmn. legal com. Airport Operators Coun. Internat., 1986-88, chmn. legal com., 1989. Founding chmn. Orlando chapter Nat. Conf. Christians and Jews; trustee Cmty. Found. Ctrl. Fla.; bd. mem. Srs. 1st, Inc., New Hope For Kids. Recipient Cmty. Leadership award, Nat. Points Light Found., Humanitarian award, Orlando chapter Nat. Conf. Christians and Jews, Tree of Life award, Jewish Nat. Fund, Svc. to Mankind award, Leukemia & Lymphoma Soc., George Wolly Cmty. Leadership award, Jewish Family Svc. Greater Orlando, Lynford Lardner Cmty. Svc. award, Foley & Lardner LLP., Best Lawyers in Am., Super Lawyer, Law & Politics Media, Inc, 2006. Mem. Fla. Bar (chmn. corps. com. 1979-80), Orange County Bar Assn., Phi Beta Kappa. Office: Foley & Lardner 111 N Orange Ave Ste 1800 PO Box 2193 Orlando FL 32801-2386 Office Phone: 407-244-3225. Office Fax: 407-648-1743. Business E-Mail: jarkin@foley.com.

ARKIN, MICHAEL BARRY, lawyer, arbitrator, writer; b. Washington, Jan. 11, 1941; s. William Howard and Zenda Lillian (Liebermann) A.; children and stepchildren: Tracy Renee, Jeffrey Harris, Marcy Susan, Chatom Callan, Michael Edwin, Samuel Hopkins, Brandon Maddox, Jessica Remaley, Brandi Remaley Arkin, Casey Remaley Arkin; m. Laura Dorene Haynes, Aug. 16, 1998. AA, George Washington U., 1961; BA in Psychology, U. Okla., 1962, JD, 1965. Bar: Okla. 1965, U.S. Ct. Claims 1968, U.S. Supreme Ct. 1968, Calif. 1970, U.S. Tax Ct. 1970, U.S. Ct. Appeals (3d, 5th, 6th, 9th, 10th cirs.) 1970, U.S. Dist. Ct. (cen. dist.) Calif. 1970, U.S. Dist. Ct. (so. dist.) Calif. 1970, U.S. Dist. Ct. (ea. dist.) Calif. 1987. Trial atty. tax divsn. U.S. Dept. Justice, 1965-68, appellate atty., 1968-69; ptnr. Surr & Hellyer, San Bernardino, Calif., 1969-79; mng. ptnr. Wied, Granby Alford & Arkin, San Diego, 1979-82, Lorenz Alhadeff Fellmeth Arkin & Multer, San Diego, 1982, Finley, Kumble, Heine, Underberg, Manley & Casey, San Diego, 1983; pvt. practice Sacramento and San Andreas (Calif.), 1984-86; ptnr. McDonough Holland & Allen, Sacramento, 1986-87; pvt. practice San Andreas, Calif., 1987—2002; chief trial counsel Calaveras County Child Protective Svcs., 1995—2002; ind. state hearing officer Calif. Spl. Edn. Hearing Office, McGeorge Sch. Law, U. Pacific, 2002—05. Judge pro-tem Calaveras County Consol. Cts., Calif., 1999-02; cons. in field. Author: History of the Bench and Bar of Calaveras County California, 1997—. Bd. dirs. San Bernardino County Legal Aid Soc., 1971-73, sec., 1971-72, pres., 1973; mem. Calaveras County Adv. Com. on Alcohol and Drug Abuse, 1985-94, pres., 1991-92; treas. Calaveras County Legal Assistance Program, 1987—; trustee Calaveras County Law Libr., 1987-98; bd. dirs. Mark Twain Hosp. Dist., 1990-03, treas., 1994—. Named to Hon. Order of Ky. Cols., 1967. Mem. ABA, Calif. Bar Assn. (Wiley F. Manuel pro bono pub. svc. award 1991), San Diego County Bar Assn., San Bernardino County Bar Assn. (bd. dirs., sec.-treas. 1973-75, pilot drug abuse program 1970), Calaveras County Bar Assn. (bd. dirs., v.p. 1988-90, pres. 1990-95), Am. Arbitration Assn. (arbitrator 1987—). Democrat. Jewish. Home: 1041 Angel Rd Corrales NM 87048 Personal E-mail: markin2500@aol.com.

ARKIN, STANLEY S., lawyer; b. LA, Feb. 28, 1938; s. Jerome and Lillian (Rogo) A.; m. Suzanne Arkin, Mar. 3, 1963; children: Adam Arkin, Alexander Arkin, Anthony Arkin. AB magna cum laude, U. So. Calif., 1959; JD cum laude, Harvard U., 1962. Bar: N.Y. 1964, Calif. 1977, D.C. 1982. Sr. ptnr. Stanley S. Arkin, P.C., NYC, 1969-90, Chadbourne & Parke, NYC, 1990-93, Arkin Kaplan Rice, LLP (formerly Arkin Kaplan & Cohen LLP), NYC, 1994—; chmn. Arkin Group LLC (pvt. intelligence agy.), 2000—. Author: (with Matthew Bender) Business Crime, 1982, (with Matthew Bender) Hi Tech Crimes, 1989; columnist, contbr. articles to newspapers and profl. jour. With JAGC US Army, 1962—68. Fellow Am. Coll. Trial Lawyers; mem. Coun. on Fgn. Rels., Phi Beta Kappa. Office: Arkin Kaplan Rice LLP 590 Madison Ave 35th Fl New York NY 10022 Office Phone: 212-333-0200. Business E-Mail: sarkin@arkin-law.com.

ARKING, LUCILLE MUSSER, nurse, epidemiologist, consultant; b. Centre County, Pa., Jan. 26, 1936; d. Boyd Albert and Marion Anna (Merryman) Musser; m. Robert Arking, May 8, 1958; children: Henry David, Jonathan Jacob. RN, Episcopal Sch. Nursing, 1958; BSN, U. Pa., 1968; MSN, Wayne State U., 1986; Doctoral Studies in Evaluation Stats., Wayne State U., Detroit, 1991—96. Psychiat. rsch. nurse Boston City Hosp., 1958; hosp. supr. Phila. Psychiat. Ctr., 1959-61; pub. health nurse Cmty. Nursing Svc., Phila., 1961-64; DON Green Acres Nursing Ctr., Phila., 1966-67; head nurse U. Va., Charlottesville, 1967-68; asst. DON U. Ky., Lexington, 1968-70; asst. dir. nursing edn. Rio Hondo Hosp., Downey, Calif., 1973-75; DON Bellwood Hosp., Bellflower, Calif., 1974-75; nurse epidemiologist Henry Ford Hosp., Detroit, 1975-84, dir. hosp. epidemiology, 1984-89, sr. clin. epidemiologist, 1990-94; v.p. clin. svcs. Great Lakes Rehab. Hosp., Southfield, Mich., 1994-96; adminstr. Cadillac Nursing Ctr., Detroit, 1997-99; exec. dir. St. Anthony Nursing Care Ctr., Warren, Mich., 1999—2001; with office of internat. affairs Pusan (South Korea) Nat. U., 2001; with St. James Nursing Ctr., Detroit, 2002—03, Arking Cons. Assocs., 2003—. Lectr. drug abuse Fountain Valley, Calif., 1970-75; instr. Santa Ana Coll., 1971-73. Contbr. articles to profl. jours. Co-founder Parents and Friends Learning Disabilities Orgn., 1968-70; den leader Cub Scouts, Fountain Valley and Troy, Mich., 1968-75; founding mem., bd. dirs. Wellness Networks, Detroit, 1982-86; mem. Mich. Gov. AIDS Task Force, 1985-86, Mich. Med. Soc. AIDS Task Force, 1986, chair religious affiliation social action com., 1984-90; sr. coun. mem. Oakland County, Mich., 2007; precinct delegate, Democratic Part, 2006-; chair of nom. com., Troy Democratic Club, 2006. Women's Club of Centre County scholar, 1954-58; recipient edn. grant Phila. Cmty. Nursing Svc. Ednl., 1963-64; USPHS nursing trainee, 1965. Mem. APHA (mem. epidemiology sect. 1975-99), ANA, Mich. Nurses's Assn. (AIDS task force 1987-89, HIV adv. com. 1989-90), Assn. Practitioners Infection Control, Sci. Rsch. Soc., Assn. Women in Sci., Sigma Xi. Democrat. Jewish. Avocations: gardening, cooking, genealogy. Home Phone: 248-689-5286; Office Phone: 248-689-5286. Personal E-mail: arkinglm@aol.com. Business E-Mail: brkac@aol.com.

ARKING, ROBERT, geneticist, gerontologist, educator; b. Bklyn., July 1, 1936; s. Henry and Mollie (Levinson) A.; B.S., Dickinson Coll., 1958; Ph.D., Temple U., 1967; m. Lucille Mae Musser, May 8, 1958; children—Henry David, Jonathan Jacob. Sci. tchr. Phila. Public Schs., 1959-61; asst. prof. zoology U. Ky., Lexington, 1968-70; research biologist Devel. Biology Ctr., U. Calif., Irvine, 1970-75; asst. prof. biology Wayne State U., Detroit, 1975-81, assoc. prof. 1981—93, prof., 1993—, undergraduate officer, 1997-. Grant reviewer Fulbright Found., 2000-; faculty assoc. Inst. Gerontology Wayne State U.; founder, coord. molecular biotech. program; expert vis. prof. Pusan Nat. U., 2001; Fulbright disting. chair natural sci. U. Salzburg, Austria, 2006; speaker in field. NSF fellow, 1964-66, NIH fellow, 1967-68; NIH and NSF grantee, 1970-85, NIH grantee, 1995—99. Fellow Gerontology Soc. Am.; mem. AAAS, Genetics Soc. Am., Sigma Xi. Author: Biology of Aging: Observations and Principles, 1991, 2006; contbr. articles to profl. jours. Personal E-mail: arkingr@aol.com. Business E-Mail: aa2210@wayne.edu.

ARKLESS, DAVID, employment services executive; With Hewlett-Packard; founder Caden Corp.; v.p. Manpower, Inc., Milw., 1992, with global mktg. and strategic svcs. divsns., founder The Empower Group subs., 1999, sr. v.p. corp. affairs, 2004—, mem. exec. mgmt. team. Bd. mem. Internat. Orgn. Migration, UN High Commn. Refugees; spl. envoy End Human Trafficking Now!. Office: Manpower Inc 5301 N Ironwood Rd Milwaukee WI 53217 Office Phone: 414-961-1000.*

ARLEDGE, DAVID A., energy executive; b. 1944; BBA, U. Tex., 1965, JD, 1968. With Touch Ross & Co., CPA's, 1968-72, ptnr., 1975-80, Penfold & Arledge, 1972-75; pres., CEO, COO Coastal Corp., West Memphis, Ark., 1980—2001; vice chmn. bd. dirs. El Paso Energy Corp. (formerly Coastal Corp.), 2001; dir. Enbridge Inc., Calgary, Alta., Canada, 2002—, chmn., 2005—. Bd. dir. AmerUS Group, Realty Group of Naples LLC, Fla. Office: Enbridge Inc 3000 Fifth Ave Pl 425 W 1st St SW Calgary AB T2P 3L8 Canada Office Phone: 713-420-2600. Office Fax: 713-420-4417.*

ARLEN, JENNIFER HALL, law educator; b. Berkeley, Calif., Jan. 7, 1959; d. Michael John and Ann (Warner) A.; m. Robert Lee Hotz, May 21, 1988; children: Michael Arlen Hotz, Robert Arlen Hotz. BA, Harvard U., 1982; JD, NYU, 1986, PhD in Econ., 1992. Bar: NY 1987, US Ct. Appeals (11th cir.) 1987. Summer clk. US Dist. Ct. (ea. dist.), Bklyn., 1984; summer assoc. Davis Polk & Wardwell, NYC, 1985; law clk. US Cir. Judge, 11th cir., Savannah, Ga., 1986-87; asst. prof. law Emory U., Atlanta, 1987-91, assoc. prof. law, 1991-93; prof. law U. So. Calif., LA, 1994—2002, Ivadelle and Theodore Johnson prof. law and bus., 1997—2002; prof. law NYU, 2002—03, Norma Z. Paige prof. Law, 2003—. Vis. prof. law U. Southern Calif., 1993, dir. Ctr. Law, Econs. & Orgn., 2000—02; vis. prof. law Calif. Inst. Tech., 2001, Yale U., 2001—02; mem. acad. bd. Ctr. Law and Bus. NYU, 2003—, dir. Ctr. Law Econ. & Orgn., 2005—; Eli Goldston prof. Harvard Law Sch., 2006. Olin fellow, U. Calif. Sch. Law, Berkeley, 1991. Mem. ABA, Am. Assn. Law Schs. (chair remedies sect. 1994, chair elect 1993, exec. com. 1990-91, 95, chair torts sect. 1995, chair-elect 1994, treas. 1991, sec. 1992-93, exec. com. bus. assns. sect. 1995-96, 2000—, chair law and econ., sect. 1996, chair-elect law and econs. sect. 1995, chair 1996), Am. Law and Econ. Assn. (bd. dirs. 1991-93, 2006-07, program com. 1999), Am. Econ. Assn., Order of Coif, Am. Law Inst., Soc. Empirical Legal Studies (pres. 2006-07, organizing com. conf. 2005—). Democrat. Office: NYU Law Sch 40 Washington Square S New York NY 10012

ARLEN, MICHAEL J., writer; b. London, Dec. 9, 1930; s. Michael and Atlanta (Mercati) A.; m. Ann Warner, 1957 (div. 1971); children—Jennifer, Caroline, Elizabeth, Sally; m. Alice Albright Hoge, 1972; stepchildren— Alicia, James Patrick, Robert Hoge. Grad., St. Paul's Sch., Concord, NH, 1948, Harvard U., 1952; LLD (hon.), Colby Coll., 1984. Reporter Life mag., 1952-56; contbr., TV critic The New Yorker mag., 1957-82; juror Columbia U.-Dupont awards for broadcast journalism, 1969-72, 78-80; faculty Bread Loaf Writers Conf., 1980. Bd. dirs. Nat. Arts Journalism Program. Author: Living-Room War, 1969, Exiles, 1970, An American Verdict, 1973, Passage to Ararat, 1975, The View from Highway 1, 1976, Thirty Seconds, 1980, The Camera Age, 1981, Say Goodbye to Sam, 1984. Recipient award for television criticism Screen Dirs. Guild, 1968; Nat. Book award for contemporary affairs, 1976; Le Prix Brémond, 1976 Mem. Authors Guild (exec. coun.), PEN Am. Ctr., Knickerbocker Club, Century Assn., Harvard Club of N.Y.

ARLIDGE, JOHN WALTER, retired utilities executive; b. Rochester, NY, Feb. 4, 1933; s. Harold Wesley and Grace Edith (Kempshall) A.; m. Sandra Marie Koswar, Feb. 4, 1955; children: James William, Edward John. BS, L.A. State Coll., 1962. Registered profl. engr., Calif., Nev., Utah. Comm. sys. engring. design and purchase City of L.A., 1961—62, power sys. resource planning R & D, 1962—74; asst. to v.p. Nev. Power Co., Las Vegas, 1974—82, v.p. resource planning and power dispatch, 1982—89, sr. v.p. govt. affairs, 1989—93; v.p., dir. Nev. Electric Investment Co., Las Vegas, 1982—89; cons. on energy resources and regulation Las Vegas, 1995—. Advisor electric-lignite sector Ministry Indusry and Trade, Warsaw, Poland, 1992-95; mem. Nev. Engr.'s Adv. Com. on Geothermal Devel., 1974-76, Nev. Solar Energy Devel. Adv. Group, 1976-86; mem. energy task force WEST, 1972-84, mem. energy engring. planning com., 1978; mem. advanced energy sys. divsnl. com. Electric Power Rsch. Inst., 1973-92; mem. We. Utility Group on Fed. Land, 1977; mem. endangered species subcom., rail issues group Edison Elec. Inst., 1977; cons. on air, land and water We. Regional Coun., 1977; mem. Nev. adv. bd. U.S. Bur. Land Mgmt., 1975-77, mem. adv. coun. Las Vegas dist., 1980-92; mem. rsch. adv. bd. U. Nev.; trustee Corp. Devel. Sci. Tech. Nev. Contbr. articles on energy resources to various publs. Mem. Nev. adv. bd. Nature Conservancy; mem. Sec. Energy's Nat. Coal Coun., 1988-93. With USMC, 1950-54. Mem. IEEE, Geothermal Resources Coun. (dir.), Utility Coal Gasification Assn. (chmn.), Internat. Solar Energy Assn., Nat. Coal Coun. (advisor to sec. energy), Pacific Coast Elec. Assn., So. Nev. Off-Road Vehicle Assn., Slurry Transp. Assn. (dir. 1979), Masons.

ARLING, BRYAN JEREMY, internist; b. Mpls., Dec. 10, 1944; s. Leonard Swenson and Marion (Schroeder) A.; m. Donna Dickson; children: Elissa, Jeremy, Timothy. BA summa cum laude, U. Minn., 1965; MD, Harvard U., 1969. Diplomate Am. Bd. Internal Medicine. Intern Stanford Affiliated Hosp., Calif., 1969-70, resident in internal medicine Calif., 1970-71; spl. asst. to adminstr. health sci. mental health adminstrn. USPHS, Rockville, Md., 1971-73; instr., chief resident medicine George Washington U. Hosp., Washington, 1973-74, asst. prof. medicine, 1974-77; pvt. practice Washington, 1977—; clin. prof. medicine George Washington U., 1988—, Georgetown U., Washington, 1997—. Adminstrv. bd. Chevy Chase United Meth. Ch.; devel. com. Maret Sch., 1985-98, trustee, 1991-98, v.p., 1994-98; question relevance reviewer Am. Bd. Internal Medicine, 1991-92, com. on certifying and recertifying exam., 1992-93. Fellow ACP; adv. coun. on med. ed., Harvard Med. Sch., 2003-; mem. AMA, Am. Soc. Internal Medicine, DC Med. Soc., Acad. Medicine (mem. exec. com. 1995—), Acad. of Sci. of Washington DC (v.p. 2001—), Smithsonian Assocs., Friends of Kennedy Ctr., Harvard Club Washington (chmn. med. sch. alumni meetings 2007), Nat. Trust for Hist. Preservation, Friends of Nat. Zoo, Common Cause, ACLU, Physicians for Social Responsibility, Columbia Country Club, Bahamas Air-Sea Rescue Assn. Home: 3803 Taylor St Bethesda MD 20815-4117 Office: 2440 M St NW Ste 817 Washington DC 20037-1404 Office Phone: 202-833-5707. Personal E-mail: rhonda@arlingpat.com. *1. Good medicine is more thoroughness than brilliance.2. The sickest body is smarter than the brightest doctor.3. Learn as though you'll never die - live as though you'll die tomorrow.*

ARLING, DONNA DICKSON, social worker; b. Jersey Shore, Pa., July 8, 1945; d. Eugene Robert and Helen (Bardo) Dickson; m. Bryan Jeremy Arling, Aug. 28, 1969; children: Elissa, Jeremy, Timothy. BS, Pa. State U., 1967; MSW, Smith Coll., 1969; PhD, Clinical Social Work Inst., Wash., DC, 2003. Bd. cert. diplomate in clin. social work; cert. social worker, Md.; cert. ind. clin. social worker, D.C. Clin. social worker N. County Mental Health Ctr., Palo Alto, Calif., 1969-71, VA Hosp., Washington, 1971-77; pvt. practice clin. social work Washington, 1978—. Mem. Nat. Assn. Social Workers, Greater Washington Soc. Clin. Social Work, Smith Coll.

Sch. Social Work Alumni Assn. (nat. exec. com. 1979-82, Washington exec. com. 1976-86). Home: 3803 Taylor St Chevy Chase MD 20815-4117 Office: 1015 33rd St NW Washington DC 20007-3523 Office Phone: 202-337-7115.

ARLINGHAUS, SANDRA JUDITH LACH, mathematical geographer, educator; b. Elmira, NY, Apr. 18, 1943; d. Donald Frederick and Alma Elizabeth (Satorius) Lach; m. William Charles Arlinghaus, Sept. 3, 1966; 1 child, William Edward. AB in Math., Vassar Coll., 1964; postgrad., U. Chgo., 1964—66, U. Toronto, 1966—67, Wayne State U., 1968—70, MA in Geography, 1976; PhD in Geography, U. Mich., 1977. Vis. instr. math. U. Ill., Chgo., 1966; vis. asst. prof. geography Ohio State U., Columbus, 1977—78, lectr. math., 1978—79, Loyola U., Chgo., 1979—81, asst. prof. math., 1981—82; lectr. math. and geography U. Mich., Dearborn and Ann Arbor, 1982—83; founding dir. Inst. Math. Geography, Ann Arbor, 1985—; pres. Arlinghaus Enterprises LLP, Ann Arbor, 1998—. Guest lectr. U. Chgo., 1979, 87, 2000-01, U. Calif., 1979, Syracuse U., 1991, U. No. Iowa, 1991; guest lectr. U. Mich., Ann Arbor, 1983, 90-93, adj. prof. math. geography, population-environ. dynamics Sch. Natural Resources and Environ., 1994—, adj. prof. Coll. Architecture and Urban Planning, 1997, 2001-2004; cons. Transp. Rsch. Inst., Coll. Architecture, 1985-86, Coll. Edn., 1992, Cmty. Sys. Found., 1993—; prodr. Ann Arbor Cmty. Access TV, 1988-90; dir. spatial analysis divsn. Cmty. Sys. Found., 1996—, dir. fellowship tng. divsn., 1996; program chair AAG/TFI Learning Workshop, 2006; program chair Unleashing the Power of GIS/GPS, Taylor & Francis/Assn. Am. Geographers Workshop, Chgo. Author: Down the Mail Tubes: The Pressured Postal Era, 1853-1984, Essays on Mathematical Geography, 1986, Essays on Mathematical Geography-II, 1987, An Atlas of Steiner Networks, 1989, Essays on Mathematical Georgraphy-III, 1991, (eBook) Spatial Synthesis, 2005; co-author: Population-Environment Dynamics, Sectors in Transition, 1992 and later editions through 1998, Mathematical Geography and Global Art, 1986, Environmental Effects on Bus Durability, 1990, Fractals in Geography, 1993, (eBook) Graph Theory and Geography: An Interactive View, 2002, Spatial Synthesis Vol. I, Book I, 2005; editor, co-author: 3D Atlas of Ann Arbor, 2006; founder, editor, co-author Solstice, 1990—, Image Interactive Atlases, Image Game Series, Image Discussion Papers, Internat. Soc. Spatial Scis., 1995—; author, editor-in-chief Practical Handbook of Curve Fitting, 1994; co-author: (book chpt.) Handbook of Engineering, 2004; co-author, editor-in-chief Practical Handbook of Digital Mapping: Terms and Concepts, 1994; editor-in-chief Practical Handbook of Spatial Stats., 1995; editor internat. monograph series; reviewer Mathematical Reviews, 1992—; contbr. articles, book reviews to profl. jours. in field of geography, psychology, math., biology, history, philately. Mem. City of Ann Arbor Planning Commn., 1995-2003, sec., 1997-2002, chair, 2002-2003, vice-chmn., 2003; mem. City of Ann Arbor Environ. Commn., 2000-03; bd. dirs., chmn. Bromley Homeowners Assn., Ann Arbor, 1989-93, pres., 1990-93, 95-96; mem. ordinance revisions com. City of Ann Arbor, 1996-2003, mem. master planning com., 2002-03; donation GIS analysis City of Ann Arbor, 2003—, 3D virtual reality models downtown devel. task force, 2004, 3D Atlas of Ann Arbor, 2001—; bd. dirs. World Jr. Bridge Championships, Ann Arbor, 1990-91, Dolfins Inc., 1993-96; co-chair ACBL Compuware Spring North Am. Bridge Championships, Detroit, 2004; artist Math. Awareness Week, Lawrence Tech. U., 1988; trustee Cmty. Sys. Found., 1995-2001; co-vice chair citizens adv. com. NE Ann Arbor master plan revision, 1999-2000; adv. bd. City of Ann Arbor Police Dept. Neighborhood Watch, 2001—; mem. exec. com. Cmty. Sys. Found., 2003—, sec. bd. trustees, 2003—; donation GIS analysis Am. Contract Bridge League, 2005—. Finalist Pirelli Internat. award, 2002; recipient Cmty. Svc. award, City of Ann Arbor, 1999, Pres.'s Vol. Svc. award, Pres. Bush's Coun. Svc. and Civic Participation, 2003—, Pirelli Internat. award semifinalist, 2001, 2003. Fellow Am. Geog. Soc. (rep. search com. for curator of collection in Golda Meir Libr. U. Wis.-Milw. Libr. 1993-94); mem. AAAS, Am. Math. Soc., Math. Assn. Am., Assn. Am. Geographers, Internat. Soc. Spatial Scis. (founder), Regional Sci. Assn. Achievements include discovery of exact fractal characterization of the geometry of central place theory and its electronic interpretation; creator Spatial Synthesis; alignment of earth marking sculptures to solstices and equinoxes in Minnesota, Washington, Alaska, New Brunswick, Canada, and USSR; creator of one of world's first refereed electronic journals; creator of applications of chaos theory in geography and population environment dynamics, maps for major international projects for Syria and Pakistan; creator Google Earth models of 3D Ann Arbor, 2006. Office: U Mich Sch Natural Resources and Envrion Ann Arbor MI 48109 Business E-Mail: sarhaus@umich.edu.

ARLOOK, IRA ARTHUR, advocate, communications executive; b. NYC, Apr. 7, 1943; s. George G. and Shirley (Meyers) A.; m. Karen Beth Nussbaum, July 9, 1978; children: Gene, Jack, Eleanor. BA, Tufts U., 1964; MA in History, Stanford U., 1966; PhD in Pub. Policy, Union Inst., 1978. Asst. prof. Cleve. State U., 1975—80; exec. dir. Ohio Pub. Interest Campaign, Cleve., 1976—83, Citizen Action, Cleve., Chgo. and Washington, 1980—97; mng. dir. Fenton Comms., Washington, 2004—. Exec. dir. New Economy Comms., 1998—. Woodrow Wilson Nat. fellow, 1965, NSF fellow, 1980. Mem. Citizens for Tax Justice (pres. 1980-97), Nat. Conf. Alternative State and Local Pub. Policies (bd. dirs. 1976-80), Citizen Labor Energy Coalition (bd. dirs. Washington 1978-90), Nat. Campaign Against Toxic Hazards (bd. dirs. 1983-87). Avocations: sports, music. Office: New Economy Comm 1320 18th St NW 5th fl Washington DC 20036-1811 Personal E-mail: ira@fenton.com. Business E-Mail: ira@neweconomy.org.

ARLOTTA, JOHN J., pharmaceutical executive; BS in Mktg., U. Notre Dame. With Baxter Internat.; pres., COO Caremark Pharmaceutical Services; vice-chmn. Genesis Health Ventures; pres., chmn., CEO NeighborCare Inc. Office Phone: 410-528-7300. Office Fax: 410-528-7447.

ARMACOST, MARY-LINDA SORBER MERRIAM, educational consultant; b. Jeannette, Pa., May 31, 1943; d. Everett Sylvester Calvin and Madeleine (Case) Sorber; m. E. William Merriam, Dec. 13, 1969 (div. 1975); m. Peter H. Armacost, July 10, 1993. Student, Grove City Coll., 1961-63; BA, Pa. State U., 1963-65, MA, 1965-67, PhD, 1967-70; HHD (hon.), Carroll Coll., 1991; LLD (hon.), Wilson Coll., 1994. Rsch. assoc. Pa. State U., University Park, 1970-72; asst. prof. speech Emerson Coll., Boston, 1972-79, dir. continuing edn., 1974-77, spl. asst. to pres., 1977-78, v.p. adminstrn., 1978-79; asst. to pres. Boston U., 1979-81; pres. Wilson Coll., Chambersburg, Pa., 1981-91, Moore Coll. Art and Design, Phila., 1991-93; sr. fellow Office of Women in Higher Edn. Am. Coun. on Edn., 1994—; interim pres. Moore Coll. Art and Design, Phila., 1998-99; pres. emerita, 2000; prof. assoc. faculty U. Pa. Grad Sch. Edn., 2003—. Cons. Govt. Edn. and Secondary Edn. Act Title III, Alameda County, Calif., 1968. Bd. govs. New Eng. chpt. NATAS, 1980-81; bd. dir. Sta. WITF, Inc., Harrisburg, Pa., 1982-91, chmn. bd., 1988-91; bd. dir. Chambersburg Hosp., 1984-89, vice chmn. bd., 1987-89; bd. dir. Elderhostel, 1997-2002; vice-chmn., 2000-2002; trustee Monmouth U., N.J., 1994-99, Sta. WHYY-FM-TV, Phila., 1992-93, Boston Zool. Soc., 1980-81, Arts Boston, 1979-81, Scotland Sch. Vets. Children, Pa., 1984-90, Randolph-Macon Woman's Coll., Lynchburg, Va., 2001-02; bd. dir. Fla. Orch., 1993-97, co-chair edn. com., 1995-97, exec. com., 1995-97; exec. com. Found. Ind. Colls., 1989-91, WEDU-TV, 1998-2002, chair planning com., exec. com., bd. dir., 1998-2002; pres. Chambersburg Area Coun. Arts, 1988-90; chmn. higher edn. com. Gen. Assembly Presbyn. Ch., 1987-90; elder Falling Spring Presbyn. Ch., 1988-90; fellow Am. Coun. Edn., 1977-78, commn. on govtl. rels., 1985-89, commn. on women, 1992-93; exec. com. Pa. Assn. Colls. and Univs., 1984-90, Assn. Presbyn. Colls. and Univs., 1983-88, pres., 1986-87; edn. adv. com. John S. and James L. Knight Found., 1998-2000; bd. dir., exec. com. Presbyn. Edn. Bd., Lahore, Pakistan 2003—; bd. dirs. Queen Mary Coll., Lahore, 2006-. Recipient Disting. Alumna award Pa. State U., 1984, Disting. Dau. of Pa., 1986, Athena award Chambersburg C. of C., 1988, Outstanding Alumnae award Sch. Dist. Jeannette, 1991. Mem.: Phi Kappa Phi. Personal E-mail: mlsma@cs.com.

ARMACOST, PETER HAYDEN, academic administrator; b. NYC, July 12, 1935; s. George Henry and Verda Gay (Hayden) A.; m. Suzanne Lee Sadosky, June 22, 1957 (dec. Feb. 1991); children: Martha Hayden, David Keys, Sarah Jane, Rebecca Ann; m. Mary-Linda Merriam, July 10, 1993. BA, Denison U., 1957; PhD, U. Minn., 1963. Dean students, chmn. dept. psychology Augsburg Coll., Mpls., 1959-65; program dir. Assn. Am. Colls., Washington, 1965-67; pres., prof. psychology Ottawa U., Kans., 1967-77; pres. Eckerd Coll., St. Petersburg, Fla., 1977—2000, pres. emeritus, 2000—; sr. adviser Coun. Ind. Colls., 2001—; pres., prin. Forman Christian Coll., 2002—. Author materials in field. Chmn. Kansas City (Mo.) Regional Coun. Higher Edn., 1972-74; pres. Am. Bapt. Chs. U.S., 1974-75, So. Univ. Conf., 1997; bd. dirs. United Way of Pinellas County, 1995—. Recipient Disting. Alumnus citation Denison U.; Woodrow Wilson fellow; Danforth fellow; named to Tampa Bay Bus. Hall of Fame, 1999. Mem. Assn. Am. Colls. (bd. dirs.), Am. Coun. Edn., Nat. Assn. Student Pers. Adminstrs. (bd. dirs. divsn. rsch., publs. and conf. chmn. Disting. Svc. award), Assn. Ind. Colls. Kans. (pres. 1970-72), Young Pres. Orgn. (chmn. Fla. chpt. 1983-84), So. Assn. of Colls. and Schs. (appeals com.), Am. Assn. Higher Edn., Soc. Values in Higher Edn., Nat. Assn. Ind. Coll. and U. Pres., Fla. Assn. Colls. and Univs. (pres. 1989-90), Ind. Colls. and Univs. Fla. (sec. 1984-86, treas. 1986-88, vice chmn. 1990-91, chmn. 1991-93), Coun. Ind. Colls. (bd. dirs. 1993—, sec. exec. com.), Nat. Assn. Ind. Colls. and Univs. (bd. dirs. 1995-98), Suncoast C. of C. (chmn. 1984-85), Pinellas Econ. Devel. Coun. (bd. dirs. 1989—), Fla. Coun. of 100, St. Petersburg C. of C. (bd. dirs. 1995—), St. Petersburg Yacht Club, Suncoasters Club, Rotary, SunTrust Bank of Tampa Bay (bd. dirs. 1983—), Blue Key, Phi Beta Kappa, Omicron Delta Kappa, Pi Gamma Mu, Psi Chi. Republican. Home: 555 5th Ave NE #914 Saint Petersburg FL 33701 Office: Eckerd Coll 4200 54th Ave S Saint Petersburg FL 33711-4744 Office Phone: 92-42-587-4312. E-mail: peterarma@brain.net.pk.

ARMAINGAUD, FRANCK, engineer; b. Marseille, France, July 3, 1939; s. Maurice Armaingaud and isabelle Marguerite Lourde-Rocheblave; m. Claude Alice Heer, May 25, 1963; children: Patrick, Yves, Agnes. BA, Lycee Toulon, France, 1959. Field engr. and European support, Switzerland, France, Tunisia, Belgium, 1962-73; tng. mgr. Burroughs, France, Europe, 1973-75, internat. product mgr. Detroit, 1975-77, internat. tng. mgr., 1977-79; country svc. mgr. Burroughs, Columbia and Equador, Bogota, 1979-80, Data Gen., France, 1980-81; gen. mgr. SFR/Ins., Monaco, 1981-83; country svc. mgr. Prime Computer, France, 1983-85, country sales mgr., 1985-87; v.p. svc. South Europe ICL, Paris, France, 1987-89; pres. ICL-Sorbus, Europe, London, 1994-97; v.p. Jane Pannier, Marseille, 1998—2001. Mem. AFSMI (chmn., pres. 1992), Lions Club (pres. 2000-01). Avocations: gardening, painting. Personal E-mail: franck_clande@noos.fr.

ARMAN GELENBE, DENIZ, concert pianist; b. Ankara, Turkey, Oct. 8, 1944; came to U.S., 1962; d. Abdul Kerim and Ayse Mediha (Raif) A.; m. Erol Gelenbe, June 8, 1968; 1 child, Pamir Emre. Student, Eastman Sch. Music, 1962-64; MusB, Juilliard, 1967, MusM, 1968; postgrad., U. Mich., Ann Arbor, 1970-71. Founder, artistic dir., prof. piano Semaines Musicales de Rouen Paris U., 1985—93; founder, artistic dir. Arman Ensemble, NC, 1994—, Arman Ensemble, Arman Trio, Paris, 1994—. Dir. summer music program, Normandy, France, 1999—; vis. assoc. prof. piano U. Ctrl. Fla., Orlando, 1998—2003, artist in residence, assoc. prof. piano, 2001—03; sr. lectr., keyboard coord. for collaborative performance Trinity Coll. Music, London, 2003—; founder Schubertiad, Winter Park, Fla., 2000. Musician (recitals): Carnegie Weill Hall, Salle Gaveau, Nat. Gallery Art, Tonhalle, Wigmore Hall, 2003—05, Concerts de Midi, Blackheath Hall, 2007; musician: (soloist) Ensemble Orchestral Paris, Dartington Internat. Summer Sch., 2006, New Japan Philharm., Ankara Presdl. Symphony Orch., Presdl. Symphony Orch., N.C. Symphony, Ripon Festival; musician: (CD) with Haydn Quartet, 1994, 2000, Arman Ensemble, 1996, Arman Trio, 2000, 2004;: Arman Trio, 2005, 2003;: Arman Trio, 2005, Wigmore Hall, 2006. Emerging Artist grantee, Durham, N.C., 1984. Mem. European Piano Tchrs. Assn., Chamber Music Am., Coll. Music Soc. Avocations: painting, reading, walking. Office: Trinity Coll Music King Charles Ct Old Royal Naval Coll, Greenwich London SE10 9JF England Home: Flat 813 St Johns 79 Marsham St Westminster London SW1 England Personal E-mail: dgelenbe@aol.com.

ARMANI, FRANK HENRY, retired lawyer; s. Ezzelin M. and Edvige A.; m. Natalie Mary Mozo, July 1, 1950; children: Deborah M., Dorina A. AB, Syracuse U., 1950, JD, 1956. Bar: N.Y. 1956, U.S. Dist. Ct. (no. dist.) N.Y. 1958, U.S. Ct. Appeals (2d cir.), 1962, U.S. Supreme Ct. 1964. Counsel Legal Aid, Onondaga County, N.Y., 1956-57; pvt. practice, Syracuse, 1957-62m 68-88; ptnr. Armani, Welch & Welch, Syracuse, 1962-68; asst. dist. atty. Onondaga County, 1961-70; ptnr. Armani, Fitzpatrick, Snyder & Armani, P.C., Camillus, N.Y., 1988-89; ret., 1989. Lectr. legal ethics, Syracuse U., Detroit Law Sch., U. Va., U. La.; participant profl. confs. and symposia.; prodn. and tech. advisor to movie Sworn to Silence, 1987; lectr. Syracuse U. Law, St. John's Law Sch. Author (with Tom Alibrandi): Privileged Information, 1984. Membership chmn. Onondaga County Young Reps., 1948-50, chmn. Law Day com., 1970; bd. dirs. Onondaga Coun. on Alcoholism, 1979—; del. Rep. Nat. Conv., 1980; com. mem. VA Med. Ctr.; del. U.S.-China Joint Session on Trade, Investment and Econ. Law, Beijing, 1987. Supply sgt. US Army, 1946—47, 2nd lt., air intelligence officer USAF Intelligence Sch., 1950, Lowery Air Force Base, Denver, capt. USAFR, 1950—54. Recipient Law Day award, Catharagus County Bar Assn., 1985, commendation, La. Senate, Onondaga County Disting. Lawyer award, 2006. Mem. ABA (nominee Michael Frank Profl. Responsibility award 2007), ATLA, NY State Bar Assn., Onondaga County Bar Assn. (bd. dirs. 1979-81, chmn. alcohol and drug abuse com. 1977—), Upstate Trial Lawyers Assn. Republican. Roman Catholic. Featured on Sta. WETA-TV documentary Ethics on Trial. Home and Office: 121 Munro Dr Camillus NY 13031-1934 Personal E-mail: farmani926@aol.com.

ARMANI, GIORGIO, fashion designer; b. Piacenza, Emilia Romagna, Italy, July 11, 1934; Student, U. Bologna, Italy; D (hon.), Royal Coll. Art, London, 1991. Fashion coord., buyer La Rinascente, Milan, 1957-64; designer, product developer Cerutti Co., Milan, 1964-70; freelance designer Milan, 1970—74; co-founder Giorgio Armani SpA, Milan, 1975—; established Giorgio Armani Corp. USA, 1979; pres. and CEO Armani Group. The first Giorgio Armani menswear collection was presented, 1974; launched, in partnership with Galleotti, the first women's line, 75; signs license agreement with L'Oreal (formerly H. Rubinstein), 1980—; creates new accessories divsn., 1999; launched first issue of Emporio Armani Magazine, 89; opens first Emporio Armani Store, Milano, 1981, Giorgio Armani Boutique, Milano, 1982, Armani Junior Store, Milano, 1986, Emporio Armani Express restaurant, London, 1989, A/X Armani Exchange store, Soho, NY, 1991, Giorgio Armani Collezioni stores (Milano, London, Tokyo), 1997, Armani Jeans store, Roma, 1997, Armani Casa Store, Milano, 2000; opens Armani/Chater House, Hong Kong, 2002, Armani/Privè, Milan, 2003, Armani/Three on the Bund, Shanghai, 2004; launched Giorgio Armani Borgonuovo women's and men's ready to wear collections, 1975, Giorgio Armani underwear, swimwear, and accessories collections for men and women, 1975—80, Giorgio Armani Le Collezioni white label diffusion line for men and women (U.S.A. and Can.), 1979, MANI, white label diffusion line for men (U.S.A. and Can.) and women (World Launch), 1979, Armani Junior, Emporio Armani, and Armani Jeans for men and women, 1981, Emporio Armani underwear and swimwear collection for men and women, 1982, Emporio Armani Accessories collections for men and women, 1982, Armani women's perfume, 1982, Armani men's fragrance, 1984, Giorgio Armani Occhiali (eyewear) & Giorgio Armani Calze (hoisery) collections, 1987, Emporio Armani gift collection (items for home and bath), 1989, A/X: Armani Exchange collection for men and women (USA and Asia), 1991, GIO, women's fragrance, 1992, Acqua di Gio women's perfume, 1995, Giorgio Armani Neve (skiwear), 1995, Giorgio Armani Golf, 1995, Acqua di Gio men's fragrance, 1996, Giorgio Armani Classico collection for men and women, 1996, Emporio Armani Orologi collection (watches for men and women), 1997, Emporio Armani fragrance for men and women, 1998, Emporio Armani beauty components, 1999, Easy Pieces (Women's line, identifiable by its unique Royal Blue Label), 1999, Mania Fragrance for women, 2000, Giorgio Armani Cosmetics, 2000, Armani Casa (home furnishings), 2000, Emporio Armani White fragrance for men and women, 2001, Armani Mania fragrance for men, 2002, Emporio Armani Gioielli (small to big items jewelry), 2002, Armani Dolci (Dessert line), 2002, Sensi, Giorgio Armani fragrance for women, 2002, Armani Jeans collection for men and women (U.S.A. dept. stores), 2002, first Emporio Armani Caffe' CD, 2003, Emporio Night fragrance for men and women, 2003, second Emporio Armani Caffe' CD, 2003, Sensi White Notes fragrance for women, 2004; contbr. to several cultural and social events; designer of wardrobe for several films and commercials, wardrobe for several music tours and events, uniforms for several sport events. Served with Italian Army, 1953-54 Recipient Neiman Marcus fashion award, 1979, Cutty award for Sark award the Internat. Top Men's Fashion Designer, 1980, 81, 84, 86, 87, Men's Style award for best fashion designer, GQ mag., 1981, Nanstyle award for best designer in the world, 1982, Ambrogino D'Oro award, Milan, 1982, Leon D'Oro, Lions Club, Paicenza, 1982, Fil D'or award, Festival Internat. du Lin, 1982, 83, 87, Gold medal, Piacenza, 1983, Internat. Designer award, Coun. Fashion Designers Am. for best internat. designer, 1983, Occhio D'Oro award for best designer for Spring/Summer Collections, 1984, 86, 87, 88, 94, Occhiolino D'Oro award for best designer for Autumn/Winter Collections, 1986/87, 88/89, First Designer Laureate , Cutty Sark Men's Fashion award, 1985, Commendatore Dell'ordine al merito della repubblica, 1985, Grand Ufficiale Dell'Ordine al Merito Della Repubblica, Italy, 1986, Gran Cavaliere, Italy, 1987, Lifetime Achievement award, Coun. Fashion Designers Am., 1987, Cristobal Balenciaga award for best internat. designer, Madrid, 1988, Media Key award for Armani perfume commercial directed by Martin Scorsese, 1988, Woolmark award as best indsl. designer NY, 1989, Senken award, Senken Newspaper, Japan, 1989, Publicitá E Successo award for Armani jeans commercial, 1989, People for the Ethical Treatment of Animals award, 1990, Fiorino d'Oro, Florence, for promoting "Made in Italy", 1992, Woolmark award best internat. menswear collection, 1992, Occhio de oro award for best Italian designer of year, 92-94, Aguja de Oro award for best designer of yr., Madrid, 1993, Telva Triunfador award for best designer of yr., Madrid, 1993, Lifetime Achievement award for arts & fashion, Nat. Italian Am. Found., Washington, DC 1994, Together for Peace Found. award, Rome, 1995, Maschera D'oro , Campione d'italia, 1995, Telva Trinunfador de Belleza award, for Acqua di Gio women's fragrance, Madrid, 1995, Designer of Yr., Best Modern Classics, Marie Claire, UK, 1995, 97, Man of Yr., GQ U.S.A. readers, NY, 1996, Award from Il Sole 24 Ore and Bain, Cuneo e Assn. for Best Financial Results in Italy, 1998, Bambi prize for best internat. designer of yr., Burda Pub. Group, Germany, 1998, Man of Yr. award GQ U.S.A., 2000, David di Donatello award for contbn. to film & cinema, Rome, 2000, FIFI award for Best Women's packaging (MANIA), 2001, CA-FR-FE award for the brand Armani Jeans, 2003, Rodeo Drive Walk of Style award (first-ever), 2003, Giotto for the Arts, Mayor of Padua, 2003; named Most Influential Designer Outside Am., Coun. Fashion Designers Am., 1983, Goodwill Amb. by UN High Commn. for Refugees, 2002; named one of World's Richest People, Forbes mag., 2001—; only fashion designer to have work displayed at Guggenheim Museum, NYC; first fashion designer after Christian Dior to appear on cover of Time Mag., 1982. Office: Giorgio Armani Corp 114 5th Ave Fl 17 New York NY 10011-5607 also: Giorgio Armani SpA Via Borgonuovo 21 20121 Milan Italy also: Giorgio Armani Corp 650 Fifth Ave New York NY 10019-6108 Address: Giorgio Armani SpA Via Borgonuovo 24 20121 Milan Italy Office Phone: 02 80 14 81. Office Fax: 02 29 09 31, 02 65 47 77.*

ARMANIOS, DANIEL ERIAN, mechanical engineer, political science scholar; b. Atlanta, 1984; s. Erian Armanios and Mahera Philobos. BS in Mech. Engring., Univ. Pitts., 2007, BA in Polit. Sci., 2007; MSc student in Drylands Sci., Mgmt., Oxford Univ., 2007—. Contbr. numerous articles to scientific jours. Rhodes Scholar. Mem.: Soc. Advancement of Material and Processing Engring., Am. Helicopter Soc., AIAA, Am. Soc. Mech. Engr. (student). Am. Coptic Christian. Recipient Barry M. Goldwater Scholarship for innovative engring.rsch., 2005 Truman Scholarship for leadership in public svc.; fluent in Arabic, French, and English.*

ARMBRISTER, DOUGLAS KENLEY, surgeon; b. Emory, Va., Feb. 20, 1934; s. Victor Stradley and Naomi Lucile (Byrd) A.; m. Nancy Sheri Douglas, Apr. 30, 1960 (div. Sept. 1995); children: Valere Lynn, Victor Kenley, Christopher Douglas, Karen Leigh; m. Barbara Ann Atwell, Sept. 9, 2000. BA in English/German, BS in Chemistry/Biology, Emory and Henry Coll., 1955; MD, U. Va., Charlottesville, 1959, MS in Surg. Rsch., 1962. Diplomate Am. Bd. Surgery. Intern surgery U. Va., 1959—60, resident surgery, 1960—62, 1964—67; pvt. practice Marion, Va., 1967—. Regional adv. group Va. Regional Med. Program, 1971; subarea coun. chmn. Health Systems Agy.; bd. dirs. Va. Health Quality Ctr.; pres. Smyth County Cmty. Hosp. Med Staff, 1973, chair surg. svcs., 1978-2006. Bd. visitors Emory and Henry Coll., 1982—2006, trustee, 2006-. Capt. USAF, 1962-64. Fellow Am. Col. Surgeons: mem. Va. Surg. Soc. (malpractice review panel mem. 1972—), Med. Soc. Va. (review bd. dirs. 1985-95), Southwest Va. Med. Soc., Muller Surg. Soc., Nat. Eagle Scout Assn., Blue Key Nat. Honor Soc. (chpt. pres. 1953). Methodist. Avocations: tennis, classical music, singing, piano. Office: 592 Radio Hill Rd Marion VA 24354-4224 Home Phone: 276-783-2554; Office Phone: 276-783-7226.

ARMBRUST, JOSEPH W., JR., lawyer; b. 1943; BS, Boston Coll., 1965; LLB, Univ. Va., 1968. Bar: NY, Va. Ptnr. Sidley Austin LLP, NYC, 1976—, now ptnr. corp. securities group and co-head NYC office. Mem. mgmt. and exec. committees Sidley Austin Brown & Wood LLP; lectr. on securities laws and corp. governance Univ. Va., Univ. Texas, Univ. Md. Mem.: ABA, Assoc. of the Bar of the City of NY, Am. Bar Found. Office: Sidley Austin LLP 787 Seventh Ave New York NY 10019 Office Phone: 212-839-5390. Office Fax: 212-839-5599. E-mail: jarmbrust@sidley.com.

ARMBRUSTER, PAULA, social worker, director, child mental health educator; b. NYC, June 30, 1935; d. William and Anna Bertha Armbruster; children: K. Levni, Elif-Lale A., Murat A. Student, Smith Coll., Geneva, 1954—55; BA, U. Conn., 1956, MSW, 1974; MA, Yale U., 1964. Intelligence analyst Nat. Security Agy., Washington, 1956—62; Nat. Def. Act fellow Yale U., New Haven, 1962—66; clin. instr. social work Yale Child Study Ctr., Sch. Medicine, Yale U., New Haven, 1974—80, assoc. clin. prof., 1980—, dir. social work tng., 1984—2006, dir. outpatient svcs., 1985—2006. Fellow Pierson Coll., Yale U., 1976—; assoc. project dir. HEW tng. grant, asst. prof. residence U. Conn. Sch. Social Work, West Hartford, 1979-80; mem. adv. coun. U. Conn. Sch. Social Work, So. Conn. State U. Sch. Social Work; Johnson Wax fellow, vis. prof. U. Surrey, Eng., 1984. Author, editor works in field. Founder The Neighborhood Place, New Haven; founder, bd. dirs Leadership, Edn. Athletics in Partnership for Youth of Conn.; dir. children's programs Yale Behavioral Health, 1997; 1st. v.p. New Haven Mus. and Hist. Soc.; past pres. Edgerton Park Conservancy; nat. steering coun. Habitat for Humanity Mental Health Partnership;

rep. of the Nat. Assn. Social Worker to the Nat. Consortium on Children's Mental Health Svcs., Washington, sec., 1994—96, pres., 1996—98; bd. dirs. New Haven Ballet, YWCA, New Haven, Sylvan House, New Haven Dept. Edn. Sch. Based Clinics Bd., Arts Coun., New Haven; pres. bd. dirs. New Haven Land Trust; bd. dirs. Inst. for Victims of Trauma, Summerbridge, New Haven; chmn. regional adv. coun. Conn. Dept. Children and Youth Svcs., chmn. regional adv. couns.; mem. Yale Sch. Medicine Adv. Com. on Sch. Based Clinics, adv. faculty, Yale Child Study Ctr.; mem. manage care/med. oversight coun. Conn. Legislature, chair quality assurance, 1995—, mem. behavioral health partnership oversight com.; vice chair Quality Mgmt. and Access Sub Com.; nat. task force managed care implementation U. Pa.; nat. task force Sch. Bd. Mental Health Svcs. U. Pa.; expert adv. panel Office Adolescent Medicine; bd. dirs. New Haven Chorale; cons. Robert Wood Johnson Found., Bur. Maternal & Child Health, Substance Abuse and Mental Health Svcs. Adminstrn. Mem.: NASW (sec. Conn. chpt.), Southern Conn. State U. Found., Conn. Soc. Clin. Social Work, Nat. Acad. Cert. Social Workers, Mory's Assn., New Haven Lawn Club, Yale Club N.Y.C., Yale Club New Haven. Office: Yale Child Study Ctr 230 S Frontage Rd New Haven CT 06519-1124 Office Phone: 203-641-3572. Personal E-mail: parmbruster@snet.net. Business E-Mail: Paula.Armbruster@yale.edu.

ARMELLINO, MICHAEL RALPH, retired portfolio manager; b. Jersey City, Jan. 30, 1940; s. Ralph Michael and Florence (Arturo) A.; m. Patricia Ann Beckett, Mar. 3, 1963; children: Tracy, John, Joseph, Peter. BS in Econs., U. Pa., 1961; MBA, NYU, 1963. Chartered Fin. Analyst. Jr. analyst F.I. DuPont, NYC, 1963-64; transp. analyst Standard & Poors, NYC, 1964-67, Goodbody & Co., NYC, 1967, Lord, Abbett & Co., NYC, 1967-69; sr. transportation analyst Goldman, Sachs & Co., NYC, 1970-90, dir. rsch., 1984-88, ptnr. in charge rsch., 1989-90; chmn., chief exec. officer Goldman, Sachs Asset Mgmt., 1991-94; ret. ptnr. GS & Co., 1995—. Mem. N.Y. Stock Exch. (allied); bd. dirs. , chmn. strategic planning com. Canadian Nat. Ry. Bd. Trustee Peddie Sch., 1996—, also mem. investment com., fin. com., exec. com. Mem. Benjamin Franklin Soc., U. Pa. Alumni Assn., Soc. Airline Analysts (pres. 1983-84). Roman Catholic. Home: Apt 2301 900 Palisade Ave Fort Lee NJ 07024 E-mail: mrarmellino@aol.com.

ARMEN, GARO H., research and development company executive; BA in Chemistry, Queens Coll.; PhD in Physical Chemistry, CUNY. Rsch. fellow Brookhaven Nat. Lab., Long Island, NY; sr. v.p. rsch. Dean Witter Reynolds, 1986—89; mng. gen. ptnr. Armen Ptnrs. LP, 1990—; assoc. prof. Merchant Marine Acad.; first v.p. rsch. E.F. Hutton & Co.; co-founder, chmn., CEO Antigenics Inc. (formerly Antigenics LLC), NYC, 1994—, pres., 1994—2002. Dir. Color Kinetics Inc.; bd. dir. Elan Corp. plc (non-exec. chmn. 2002-), Dublin, 1994—; founder and pres. Children of Armenia Fund. Office: Antigenics Inc Ste 2100 630 Fifth Ave New York NY 10111

ARMEN, MARGARET MEIS, lawyer; d. Joseph John and Florence Catherine Meis. BA, Carlow Coll., 1969; JD, Cleveland State U., 1978. Bar: Ohio 1978, Washington, DC 1980. Tchr. Pitts. City Sch., 1969—70, Archdiocese of Washington, DC, 1970—73; pers. adminstr. Stouffer Foods Corp., Cleve., 1973—75, Hospitality Motor Inns, Inc., Cleve., 1976—78; atty. adv. US Govt. Accountability Office, Washington, 1978—, sr. atty., 1986—2006. Dir. Am. Assn. for Budget and Program Analysis, Washington, 1986—93, pres., 1993—94; dir. Pub. Fin. Pub., Inc., Washington, 1990—2002, pres., 2003—. Exec. editor: Cleve. State U. Law Rev., 1977—78; contbr. articles to profl. jours. Mem.: Exec. Women in Govt. (v.p. 2002—03), Internat. Alliance for Women (sec. 2004—05, counsel 2006—).

ARMEN, ROBERT K. (KELLY), III, federal judge; b. Pa., 1949; BA, Duquesne, U., 1973; JD, Georgetown U., 1973, M in Taxation (MLT), 1984; LLM, Cleve. State U., 1979. Bar: Ohio 1973, US Tax Ct. 1973, DC 1999. With Office of Chief Counsel, Cleve. Dist. Counsel, IRS, 1973—78, Criminal Tax Divsn., 1978—79, Wash. Dist. Counsel, 1979—81; law clk. to Hon. Howard A. Dawson, Jr. US Tax Ct., 1981—83, asst. clk., 1983—85, dep. counsel to the chief judge, 1986—93, spl. trial judge, 1993—. Adj. prof. No. Va. Cmty. Coll., 1981—89, U. Balt. Law Sch., 1988—90. Office: US Tax Ct 400 Second St NW Washington DC 20217

ARMENAKAS, ANTHONY EMMANUEL, aerospace engineering educator; b. Mytilene, Greece, Aug. 23, 1924; came to U.S., 1946; s. Emmanuel Anthony and Efterpe (Sakis) A.; m. Stella Dimitri Petroutsa, Jan. 3, 1950 (dec. Jan. 1988); children: Alexandra Daphne, Noel Anthony, Melina Cybel. BSCE, Ga. Inst. Tech., 1950; MSCE, Ill. Inst. Tech., 1952; PhD in Applied Mechanics, Columbia U., 1959; DCE (hon.), Democretion U. Greece, 2006. Registered profl. engr., N.Y., N.J., Greece. Instr. Ill. Inst. Tech., Chgo., 1950—52; sr. structural engr. Edwards Kelcey and Beck Cons. Engrs., Newark, 1952—54; ptnr. Rynar Armenakas and McCann Cons. Engrs., Newark, 1954—59; lectr. civil engring. CUNY, NYC, 1954—57; assoc. prof. civil engring. Cooper Union for the Advancement Sci. and Art, NYC, 1958—65; prof. engring. sci. U. Fla., Gainesville, 1965—67; prof. aerospace Poly. U., Bklyn., 1967—; Fulbright lectr. to Greece, 1972—73, 1973—74; prof., dir. Inst. Structural Analysis Nat. Tech. U., Athens, Greece, 1977—84. Vis. prof. divsn. engring. Brown U., Providence, 1964-65; cons. Vector Engring., Springfield, N.J., 1954-59; rsch. cons. Poly. Inst., Bklyn., 1962-67, Northwestern U., Evanston, Ill., 1962-65; pres. Stress-Optics, Inc., Queens, N.Y., 1970-72; bd. dirs. Greek r.r.s, 1978-80; vice-chmn. bd. dirs. Greek agy. for design and rsch. earthquake protection, 1989-92. Author: Free Vibrations of Circular Cylindrical Shells, 1969, Tensor Analysis for Engineers, 1974, Classical Structure Analysis-A Modern Approach, 1988, Modern Structural Analysis-The Matrix Method Approach, 1991, Advanced Mechanics of Materials and Applied Elasticity, 2005; patentee in field; contbr. articles to profl. jours. Chmn. bd. dirs. Poulos Philanthropic Found., Athens, Greece. Fellow ASCE, ASME. Avocation: photography. Address: Kifissou 3A Xalandri Attica 15234 Athens Greece Office: Polytechnic Univ 333 Jay St Brooklyn NY 11201-2990 Home: 500 E 77th St Apt 1832 New York NY 10162

ARMENAKAS, NOEL ANTHONY, medical educator; b. Orange, NJ, Sept. 29, 1958; s. Anthony E. and Stella P. (Petroutsa) A.; m. Macrene R. Alexiades, Oct. 26, 1996; children: Sophie Stella, Anthony Emmanuel. MD, U. Athens, Greece, 1985. Diplomate Am. Bd. Urology. Intern surgery Lenox Hill Hosp., NYC, 1985-86; resident surgery Monmouth Med. Ctr., Long Branch, N.J., 1986-87; resident urology Lenox Hill Hosp., NYC, 1987-91; fellow trauma and reconstructive surgery U. Calif., San Francisco, 1991-92, clin. instr. dept. urology, 1991-92; clin. instr. dept. surgery Cornell U. Med. Coll., NYC, 1992-94; clin. asst. prof. dept. urology Cornell U. Med. Sch., NYC, 1994—2002, clin. assoc. prof. dept. urology, 2002—. Mem. oper. rm. com. Lenox Hill Hosp., 1990, outpatient clinic com., 1993—; mem. ChubbHealth Physician Adv. Panel, 1994-00; mem. scholarship com. Hellenic Med. Assn.; attending staff San Francisco Gen. Hosp., 1991-92; dir., physician-in-charge Outpatient Urologic Clinics Lenox Hill Hosp., 1992-05, assoc. program dir. sect. urology, 1992-; attending staff NY Presbyn. Hosp., NYC, 1992—, Lenox Hill Hosp., NYC, 1992—; lectr. in field. Contbr. chpts. to books and articles to profl. jours. Fellow ACS; mem. Internat. Soc. Urology, Am. Assn. Clin. Urologists, Am. Urol. Assn., Hellenic Med. Assn., Soc. for Urology and Engring., Soc. Genitourinary and Reconstructive Surgeons, N.Y. Acad. Medicine. Avocations: skiing, tennis, travel. Office: New York Urological Assocs 880 5th Ave New York NY 10021-4951 E-mail: drarmenakas@nyurological.com.

ARMENTEROS, EDUARDO CARLOS, psychologist, educator; b. Havana, Cuba, Nov. 4, 1955; s. Pedro L. and Maria E. Armenteros; m. Maria A. Perez, June 26, 1982; children: Erika M., Javier E. AA, Miami-Dade Coll., 1976; BS, Fla. Internat. U., 1978, MS, 1986, EdS in Sch. Psychology, 1995. Lic. sch. psychologist Fla., cert. profl. tchg. Fla., lic. mental health counselor Fla. H.S. math. tchr. Miami-Dade County Pub. Sch., Miami, Fla., 1979—82, sch. psychologist, 1986—; h.s. tchr., counselor Christopher Columbus H.S., Miami, 1982—86; psychotherapist pvt. practice S.Miami, Fla., 1995—. Adj. prof. spl. edn. Barry U., Miami-Shores, Fla., 1997—98; adj. instr. Miami-Dade Coll., 1998—2000; adj. prof. Nova Southeastern U., Ft. Lauderdale, Fla., 2004—. Contbr. articles to profl. jours. Recipient Outstanding Tchr. award, Miami-Dade Pub. Sch., 1980, Outstanding Sch. Psychologist award, 2004. Mem.: ACA, Dade Assn. Sch. Psychologists (pres. 2002—03, Outstanding Svc. award 2003), Phi Kappa Phi, Psi Chi. Democrat. Roman Catholic. Avocations: hiking, swimming, reading, travel, coin collecting/numismatics. Office: Miami-Dade County Pub Sch Region Ctr VI 698 N Homestead Blvd Homestead FL 33033 Office Phone: 305-246-5934. Business E-Mail: ecarmenteros@dadeschools.net.

ARMENTROUT, CHARLES EDWARD, secondary school educator; b. Harrisonburg, Va., July 24, 1944; s. Ernest Biedler and Mary Lee Armentrout; m. Carol Lynne Armentrout, May 2, 1969; children: Heather A., Christopher C. Student, Shepherd Coll., Shepherdstown, W.Va., 1962—63; BS, US Naval Acad., Annapolis, Md., 1967. Naval sci. tchr. South Florence HS, SC, 1987—91, Adm. Faragut Acad., Pine Beach, NJ, 1991—93, Colleton County HS, Walterboro, SC, 1993—. Lt. comdr. USN, 1967—87. Named Tchr. of the Yr., Colleton County Sch. Dist., 1997. Mem.: VFW, Mil. Purple Heart, Am. Legion. Home: 340 Chamblee Rd Walterboro SC 29488

ARMERDING, HUDSON TAYLOR, retired college president, consultant; b. Albuquerque, June 21, 1918; s. Carl Armerding and Eva May Taylor; m. Miriam Lucile Bailey, Dec. 26, 1944 (dec. July 2006); children: Carreen, Taylor, Paul, Miriam, Jonathan. AB, Wheaton Coll., 1941; AM, Clark U., 1942; PhD, U. Chgo., 1948; DD (hon.), Gordon-Conwell Sem., 1972, Reformed Episcopal Sem., 1990; LLD (hon.), Houghton Coll., 1973; HumD (hon.), John Brown U., 1983; STD (hon.), Greenville Coll., 1976; LittD (hon.), Asbury Coll., 1977, Colo. Christian U., 2000. Prof. Wheaton Coll., Ill., 1946—48, 1961—82; provost Wheaton U., 1963—65, pres., 1965—82; prof. Gordon Coll., Wenham, Mass., 1948—49, 1950—61, dean, acting pres., 1950—61. V.p. Quarryville (Pa.) Presbyn. Retirement Cmty., 1982-99; min-at-large Officers Christian Fellowship, Englewood, Colo., 1979-2005; chmn. Site Acquisition Com., Batavia, Ill., 1975; pres. Nat. Assn. Evang., Wheaton, 1970-72; chmn. World Evang. Fellowship, Wheaton, 1974-80. Comdr. USN, 1942-46, USNR, 1946-66 Recipient Excellence in Leadership award Officers Christian Fellowship, 2001 Mem. Am. Legion, Mil. Officer Assn., Naval Inst Republican. Presbyterian. Avocations: travel, walking, camping, reading. Home: Apt C219 130 Windsor Park Dr Carol Stream IL 60188 Personal E-mail: harmerding@juno.com.

ARMES, ROY V., manufacturing executive; married; 2 children. BSME, U. Toledo. Mgmt. positions Whirlpool Corp., 1975—2006; corp. v.p., gen. dir. Whirlpool Mexico; pres., mng. dir. Whirlpool Greater China; corp. v.p., global procurement ops. Whirlpool Corp., sr. v.p., project mgmt.; pres., CEO Cooper Tire & Rubber Co., Findlay, Ohio, 2007—. Office: Cooper Tire & Rubber Co 701 Lima Ave Findlay OH 45840 Office Phone: 419-423-1321. Office Fax: 419-424-4108. E-mail: cooperinfo@coopertire.com.*

ARMEY, DICK (RICHARD KEITH ARMEY), state representative; b. Cando, ND, July 7, 1940; s. Glen Forest and Marion (Gutschlog) A.; m. Susan Byrd; children: Kathryn, David, Scott A., Chip, Scott Oxendine. BA, Jamestown Coll., ND, 1963; MA, U. N.D., 1964; PhD, U. Okla., Norman, 1969. Mem. econs. faculty U. Mont., 1964-65; asst. prof. West Tex. State U., 1967-68, Austin Coll., 1968-72; assoc. prof. North Tex. State U., 1972-77, chmn. dept. econs., 1977-84; mem. US Congress from 26th Tex. dist., Washington, 1985—2003; majority leader, 1995—2003; chmn. ho. rep. conf. com., 1992-94; sr. policy adv., co-chmn Homeland Security Task Force DLA Piper LLP, Washington, 2003—. Chmn. FreedomWorks (formerly Citizens for a Sound Economy), 2003—. Author: Price Theory, 1977, The Freedom Revolution: The New Republican House Majority Leader Tells Why Freedom Works, and How We Will Rebuild America 1995, The Flat Tax-A Citizen's Guide to the Facts on What It Will Do For You, Your Country, and Your Pocketbook, 1996, Armey's Axioms: 40 Hard-Earned Truths from Politics, Faith and Life, 2003; co-author: (with James Tobin, Edward J. Harpham & Wilson Gray) Moral Values in Liberalism and Conservatism, 1995 Republican. Office: DLA Piper 1200 Nineteenth St NW Washington DC 20036 Office Phone: 202-861-6007.

ARMFIELD, DIANA MAXWELL, artist, educator; b. Ringwood, Eng., June 11, 1920; d. Joseph Harold Armfield and Gertrude Mary Uttley; m. Bernard Dunstan, 1949; 3 children. Student, Slade Sch. Art, Ctrl. Sch. Arts and Crafts. Tchr. Byam Shaw Sch. Art, 1959-89. Artist-in-residence, Perth, Australia, 1985, Jackson, Wyo., 89. One-woman shows include Browse & Darby, London, 1979-2003, 06, Royal Acad. Friends Rm. Gallery, 1995, 2004-05, Royal Cambrian Acad., 2001, Albany Gall, Cardiff, 2001, Albany Gallery, Cardiff, 2002, 05, 06, New Acad. Gallery, 2005; author: Mitchell Beazley Pocket Guide to Painting in Oils, Mitchell Beazley Pocket Guide to Drawing, The Art of Diana Armfield (Julian Halsby); represented in pub. collections at Yale Ctr. for Brit. Art, Govt. Eng., Faringdon, Mercury Asset Mgmt., Lancaster City, Victoria and Albert Mus. Textiles. Commr. HRH Prince of Wales, Reuters, Contemporary Art Soc. Wales, Natural Trust. Mem. Royal Acad. Art, New English Art Club (hon.), Royal Cambrian Acad. (hon. ret.), Pastel Soc. (hon.), Royal Watercolor Soc., Royal West of Eng. Acad. (hon. ret.). Avocations: music, gardening. Address: 10 High Park Rd Kew Richmond TW9 4BH England also: Llwynhir Parc Bala Gwynedd LL23 7YU Wales Office Phone: 0208-876-6633.

ARMFIELD, TERRI ELAINE, music educator, musician; b. Lincoln, Nebr., Sept. 29, 1955; d. Jesse Lee and Charlotte Irene Smith; m. Ted Duane Armfield, Dec. 18, 1976 (dec. May 12, 1995); children: Lisa Renee, Ben Jared. MusD in Oboe Performance, U. Ky., 2003; MusM, U. Northern Iowa, 2000; BFA in music edn., 1976. Adj. prof. oboe Asbury Coll., Wilmore, Ky., 2000—03; vis. instr., oboe and music theory Western Carolina U., Cullowhee, 2004—; 2d prin. oboist Asheville (NC) Symphony Orch. 2nd prin. oboist Asheville (N.C.) Symphony Orch., 2004—; freelance oboist. Mem.: Internat. Double Reed Soc. Avocations: travel, sewing, reading, exercise. Office: Western Carolina Univ 265 Coulter Cullowhee NC 28723 Home: PO Box 141 Cullowhee NC 28723-0141 Home Phone: 828-506-0937; Office Phone: 828-227-2471. E-mail: tarmfield@email.wcu.edu.

ARMINANA, RUBEN, academic administrator, educator; b. Santa Clara, Cuba, May 15, 1947; came to U.S., 1961; s. Aurelio Ruben and Olga Petrona (Nart) A.; m. Marne Olson, June 6, 1954; children: Cesar A. Martino, Tuly Arminana. AA, Hill Jr. Coll., 1966; BA, U. Tex., 1968, MA, 1970; PhD, U. New Orleans, 1983; postgrad. Inst. of Applied Behavioral Scis., Nat. Tng. Labs., 1971. Nat. assoc. dir. Phi Theta Kappa, Canton, Miss., 1968-69; dir. ops. and tng. Inter-Am. Ctr. Loyola U., New Orleans, 1969-71; adminstrv. analyst City of New Orleans, 1972, adminstrv. analyst and orgnl. devel. and tng. cons., 1972-78; anchor and reporter part time STA. WWL-TV, New Orleans, 1973-81; v.p. Commerce Internat. Corp., New Orleans, 1978-83; exec. asst. to sr. v.p. Tulane U., New Orleans, 1983-85, assoc. exec. v.p., 1985-87, v.p., asst. to pres., 1987-88; v.p. fin. and devel. Calif. State Poly U., Pomona, 1988-92; pres. Sonoma State U., 1992—. TV news cons., New Orleans, 1981-88; lectr. Internat. Trade Mart, New Orleans, 1983-89, U.S. Dept. Commerce, New Orleans. Co-author: Hemisphere West-El Futuro, 1968; co-editor: Colloquium on Central America-A Time for Understanding, Background Readings, 1985. Bd. dirs. Com. on Alcoholism and Substance Abuse, 1978-79, SER, Jobs for Progress, Inc., 1974-82, Citizens United for Responsive Broadcasting, Latin Am. Festival Com.; dir. bd. advisors Sta. WDSU-TV, 1974-77; mem. Bus. Govt. Rsch., 1987-88, Coun. Advancement of Support to Edn.; mem. League of United Latin Am. Citizens, Mayor's Latin Am. Adv. Com., Citizens to Preserve the Charter, Met. Area Com., Mayor's Com. on Crime. Kiwanis scholar, 1966, Books scholar, 1966. Mem. Assn. U. Related Rsch. Prks., L.A. Higher Edn. Roundtable, Soc. Coll. and U. Planning, Nat. Assn. Coll. and U. Bus. Officers Coun., Am. Econ. Assn., Assn. of Evolutionary Econs., Am. Polit. Sci. Assn., AAUP, Western Coll. Assn. (pres. 1994-95), Latin Am. C. of C. (founding dir. New Orleans and River Region 1976-83), Cuban Profl. Club, Phi Theta Kappa, Omicron Delta Epsilon, Sigma Delta Pi, Delta Sigma Pi. Democrat. Roman Catholic. Avocation: mask collecting. Office: Sonoma State U 1801 E Cotati Ave Rohnert Park CA 94928-3609 Office Phone: 707-664-2156. Business E-Mail: ruben.arminana@sonoma.edu.

ARMINAS, SCOTT ARNOLD, chemist, poet, writer; b. S.I., NY, Feb. 12, 1960; s. Henry Arnold and Josephine Antoinette Arminas; m. Mariá Basora-Ruiz, Sept. 12, 1987. Student, Rutgers U., 1978—79, student, 1997. Chemist, cosmetic colorist Revlon Rsch. Ctr., Edison, NJ, 1987—2001. Author: Sojourn on Eternity's Edge, 2003, Campfire Tales, 1990; co-author: Tales from the Gallery, 1995. Vol. firefighter Middletown Twp. Fire Dept., Port Monmouth, NJ, 1983—86. Nominee Emily Dickenson award, The Amherst Soc., 1991; recipient Golden Poet award, World of Poetry, Sacramento, 1990, 1991. Mem.: Soc. Cosmetic Chemists, NRA, KC (3d degree, charter mem.). Roman Catholic. Achievements include patents in field. Avocations: scuba diving, music, gymnastics, pen collecting. Home: 67 Citadel Dr Jackson NJ 08527 Personal E-mail: spartaboy@optonline.net.

ARMINE, CINDY A., bank executive; Mgmt. positions with Citigroup Inc., NYC, 1981—, U.S. dir. compliance, corp. & investment banking & Smith Barney, mng. dir., chief compliance officer, global wealth mgmt., mem. mgmt. com., 2004—. Office: Citigroup Inc 399 Park Ave New York NY 10043

ARMINIO, JOSEPHINE MECONI, elementary school educator; b. NYC, Dec. 26, 1922; s. Egidio Meconi and Esther Nardi; m. E. Ralph Arminio, Sept. 11, 1943; children: Robert(dec.) , Richard. BA, Kean U., Union, NJ, 1968. Pole clk. AT&T, Linden, NJ, 1959—61; tchr. elem. sch. St. Joseph's Cath. Sch., Carteret, NJ, 1961—63, Hazlet Bd. Edn., NJ, 1963—81; owner, operator Noah's Ark Day Sch., Waretown, NJ, 1972—81, Manakawkin, NJ, 1976—81. Tchr. ceramics Roselle Sch. Sys., Linden H.S. Adult Classes. Active election bds., 1991—. Mem.: Monmouth County Ret. Tchrs. Assn. Home: 106 Beacon Ln Tinton Falls NJ 07753

ARMISTEAD, (IVOR) CARY, III, lawyer; b. Columbus, Ohio, Jan. 22, 1946; BA, Mich. State Univ., 1967; JD cum laude, Columbia Univ., 1970. Bar: D.C. 1970, Mass. 1979, US Dist. Ct. (D.C., Mass.), US Ct. Appeals (D.C., 1st cir.), US Supreme Ct. Trial atty. Antitrust Div., U.S. Dept. Justice; v.p. & asst. gen. counsel Digital Equipment Corp.; ptnr. corp. dept. Ropes & Gray, Boston, 1996—, vice chmn. corp. dept. & co-head internat. practice group. Mem. London Ct. Internat. Arbitration, England. Harlan Fiske Stone scholar. Mem.: ABA, Boston Bar Assn., New England Antitrust Planning Com. Office: Ropes & Gray 1 International Pl Boston MA 02110-2624 Office Phone: 617-951-7832. Office Fax: 617-951-7050. Business E-Mail: cary.armistead@ropesgray.com.

ARMISTEAD, KATHERINE KELLY (MRS. THOMAS B. ARMISTEAD III), interior designer, travel consultant, civic worker; b. Apr. 14, 1926; d. Joseph Anthony and Katherine Arnold (Manning) Kelly; m. Thomas Boyd Armistead III, Nov. 29, 1952. Grad., Finch Jr. Coll., NYC, 1946. Cert. travel cons. Editor news Sta. WOR, NYC, 1946—51; with Dumont TV, 1951—52; editor Social Svc. Rev., LA, 1956—57; interior designer LA, 1963—; travel cons. Gilner Internat. Travels, Beverly Hills, Calif., 1980—2006, Protravel, Beverly Hills, 2006—. Mem. edit. bd. Previews Mag., 1984—87. Pres. Jrs. Social Svc., LA, 1962—64; nat. chpt. chmn. Assoc. Alumnae of Sacred Heart, 1960—66; pres. Las Floristas, 1967—68; coord. Jr. Mannequin Assisteens, Assistance League So. Calif., 1971—72; pres. docent coun. L.A. County Mus. Art, 1976—77, pres. decorative arts coun., 1977—80, chmn. Am. Antiques Conf., 1979—81, mem. costume coun., mem. past pres.' coun., 1981—, mem. capital gifts campaign com.; pres. L.A. Orphanage Guild, 1969—70, bd. dirs., 1970—. Recipient Eve award, Assistance League So. Calif. Mem.: Inst. Cert. Travel Agts., Am. Soc. Travel Agts., Lady Grand Cross Equestrian Order of the Holy Sepulchre of Jerusalem, Birnam Wood Golf Club. Republican. Roman Catholic. Office Phone: 310-271-9566.

ARMISTEAD, M. KATHRYN, editor; b. Indpls., July 23, 1952; d. John Mason and Thelma LaNelle Garrett; m. Charles Franklin Armistead, June 2, 1973; children: Kristin Lee Helms, Jennifer Elizabeth. BA magna cum laude, Butler U., Indpls., 1974; MA, Vanderbilt U., Nashville, 1988; PhD, Vanderbilt U., Nashville, Tenn., 1992. Ordained deacon United Meth. Ch., 1987. Devel. and br. ops. mgr. Parthenon Fed. Credit Union, Nashville, 1994—2000; devel. editor academic resources Abingdon Press, Nashville, 2000—. Mem. supervisory com. Parthenon Fed. Credit Union, Nashville, 2004—. Author: (non-fiction book) God Images: In the Healing Process, 1995; editor: With God in the Crucible: Preaching Costly Discipleship by Peter Storey, 2003 (Named one of Best Books for Preachers by Preaching Mag.), (academic book) Evolution from Creation to New Creation: Conflict, Conversation, and Convergence, 2005 (Book of Distinction, Templeton Found.). Mem. Bd. Ordained Ministry Tenn. Conf. United Meth. Ch., Nashville, 2002—07. Fellow: Am. Assn. Pastoral Counselors; mem.: Soc. Christian Ethics, Am. Acad. Religion, Soc. Study Psychology and Wesleyan Theology (program chmn. 2007—), Kappa Alpha Theta. Avocations: reading, crafts, travel, gardening. Office: Abingdon Press 201 8th Ave South Nashville TN 37202

ARMITAGE, DAVID RICHARD, historian; b. Stockport, Eng., Jan. 31, 1965; s. Brian Geoffrey Armitage and Margaret Roseanne Hill; m. Joyce Elizabeth Chaplin, July 28, 2000. BA, Cambridge U., Eng., 1986, MA, 1988, PhD, 1992. From asst. to full prof. history Columbia U., NYC, 1993—2004; prof. history Harvard U., Cambridge, Mass., 2004—. Author: (monograph) The Ideological Origins of the British Empire (Longman/History Today Book of Yr., 2001), The Declaration of Independence: A Global History. Recipient Caird medal, Nat. Maritime Mus., London, 2006; fellow, Nat. Humanities Ctr., 1996—97; Harkness fellow, Commonwealth Fund, 1988—90, Jr. Rsch. fellow, Emmanuel Coll., Cambridge U., 1990—93, Warren fellow, Warren Ctr. for Studies in Am. History, Harvard U., 2000—01, Mellon Rsch. fellow, Henry E. Huntington Libr., 2006—07. Fellow: Royal Hist. Soc. Office: Dept History Harvard Univ 35 Quincy St Cambridge MA 02138 Business E-Mail: armitage@fas.harvard.edu.

ARMITAGE, JAMES O., medical educator; b. LA, Dec. 19, 1946; m. Nancy Elaine Roker, Aug. 12, 1967; children: Amy Jolane, Gregory Olen, Anne Marie, Joel Donald. BS, U. Nebr., Lincoln, 1969; MD, U. Nebr., Omaha, 1973. Diplomate in internal medicine, med. oncology and hematology Am. Bd. Internal Medicine. Med. intern U. Nebr. Med. Ctr., Omaha, 1973-74, resident in internal medicine, 1974-75; fellow hematology/oncology U. Iowa Hosps. and Clinics, Iowa City, 1975-77;

clin. asst. prof. medicine U. Nebr. Coll. Medicine, Omaha, 1977-79, assoc. prof., 1982-87, vice chmn. dept. internal medicine, 1982-90; from assoc. prof. to Joe Shapiro prof. internal medicine Epley Inst. for Rsch. in Cancer and Allied Diseases, Omaha, 1985—; chief sect. oncology/hematology U. Nebr. Coll. Medicine, Omaha, 1986-89, prof. internal medicine, 1987—, chmn. dept. internal medicine, 1990-99, dean, 2000—03; pvt. practice hematology/oncology Omaha, 1977-79. Contbr. articles to profl. jours. Recipient Sir William Osler Teaching award, 1988, Arnold Ungerman-Robert Lubin Cancer Rsch. award, 1993, Richard and Hinda Rosenthal Found. award, 1996, numerous others. Fellow ACP, Am. Assn. Cancer Rsch., Am. Soc. Blood and Marrow Transplantation, Am. Soc. Clin. Oncology, Am. Soc. Hematology, Am. Fedn. for Clin. Rsch., Assn. Profs. Medicine, Ctrl. Soc. for Clin. Rsch., European Soc. Med. Oncology, Internat. Soc. Exptl. Hematology, Nebr. Med. Assn., Met. Omaha Med. Soc., Midwest Blood Club, Royal Coll. Physicians Edinburgh, Internat. Soc. for Hematotherapy and Graft Engring., European Hematology Soc., Phi Beta Kappa, Sigma Xi, Alpha Omega Alpha, others. Office: U Nebr Med Ctr Dept Internal Medicine 987680 Nebr Med Ctr Omaha NE 68198-0001

ARMITAGE, KENNETH BARCLAY, retired biology professor; b. Steubenville, Ohio, Apr. 18, 1925; s. Albert Kenneth and Virginia Ethel (Barclay) A.; m. Katie Lou Hart, June 5, 1953; children: Karole, Keith, Kevin BS summa cum laude, Bethany Coll., W.Va., 1949; MS, U. Wis.-Madison, 1951, PhD, 1954. Instr. U. Wis.-Green Bay, 1954-55; instr. U. Wis.-Wausau, 1955-56; asst. prof. biology U. Kans., Lawrence, 1956-62, assoc. prof., 1962-66, prof., 1966-96, William J. Baumgartner disting. prof., 1987-96, chmn. dept. systematics & ecology, 1982-88, dir. environ. studies program, 1976-82, dir. exptl. and applied ecology program, 1974-94, prof. emeritus, 1996—. Vis. prof. U. Modena, Italy, 1989; mem. com. examiners Grad. Record Exam. Biology Test, 1986—92, chmn., 1988—92; sr. investigator Rocky Mountain Biol. Lab, Gothic, Colo., 1962—2004, trustee, 1969—86, pres. bd. trustees, 1985—86; cons. Vancouver Island Marmot Recovery Program; vis. rschr. Queen Mary Coll., London, 1972—73. Author: (lab. manual) Investigations in General Biology, (with others) Principles of Modern Biology; contbr. articles to profl. jours.; co-editor: Holarctic Marmots as a Factor of Biodiversity, 3d Internat. Marmot Conf. proceedings; mem. editl. bd.: Ethology, Ecology and Evolution, 1989—, Ibex Jour. Mountain Ecology, 1994—, Oecologia Montana, 1996—; sci. editor: Die Murmeltiere der Welt. Pres. Douglas County chpt. Zero Population Growth, 1969-71; bd. dirs. Children's Hour, Inc., Lawrence, 1969-70; v.p. Hist. Mt. Oread, Lawrence, 1998-2004, pres., 2004—. Recipient Antarctic medal NSF, 1968, Edn. Service award U. Kans., 1979, Alumni Achievement award Bethany Coll., 1989; Knapp House fellow U. Wis., Madison, 1952-53, NSF fellow, 1952-53, 58. Fellow AAAS, Animal Behavior Soc.; mem. Am. Soc. Naturalists (treas. 1984-86), Am. Inst. Biol. Scis. (mem. task force for 90s), Ecol. Soc. Am., Am. Soc. Zoologists, Am. Soc. Mammalogists (C. Hart Merriam award 1997), Orgn. Biol. Field Stations (v.p. 1986-87, pres. 1988-89), Sigma Xi, Phi Beta Kappa, Beta Beta Beta, Gamma Sigma Kappa. Avocations: stamp collecting/philately, gardening, natural history, western history. Home: 505 Ohio St Lawrence KS 66044-2245 Office: U Kans Dept Ecology & Evolutionary Biology Lawrence KS 66045-7534 Home Phone: 785-841-3303; Office Phone: 785-864-3236. E-mail: marmots@ku.edu.

ARMITAGE, RICHARD LEE, former federal agency administrator; b. Boston, Apr. 26, 1945; s. Leo Holmes and Ruth H. Armitage; m. Laura Alice Samford, Apr. 15, 1968; children: Beth, Lee, Jenny, Paul. BS, U.S. Naval Acad. Naval ops. coordinator Def. Attache Office, Saigon, Vietnam, 1973-75; cons. US Dept. Def., Washington, 1975-76, Iran, 1975-76; ptnr. Agt.-Export, Bangkok, 1976-78, Washington, 1976-78; adminstrv. asst. to U.S. Senator Robert Dole Washington, 1978-79; self-employed cons. Fairfax, Va., 1979-80; fgn. policy advisor Reagan for Pres. campaign, Washington, 1980; trans. advisor U.S. Govt., Washington, 1980-81; asst. sec. def. East Asia US Dept. Def., Washington, 1981-83, asst. sec. def. internat. security affairs, 1983—89; presidential spec. negotiator for Phillippines mil. bases Washington, 1989—92; US amb. to the Newly Independent States of the former Soviet Union US Dept. State, 1992—93; pres. Armitage Assoc., 1993; dep. sec. US Dept. State, Washington, 2001—05; pres. Armitage Internat., Va., 2005—. Mem. strategy group Aspen Inst.; bd. dir. ManTech Internat., 2005—, Conoco Phillips, 2006—. Served to lt. USN, 1967-73, Vietnam. Mem. Assn. Asian Studies Republican. Roman Catholic.

ARMITAGE, ROBERT ALLEN, lawyer, pharmaceutical executive; b. Port Huron, Mich., June 16, 1948; s. George Robert and Deloris Alene (Fitz) A.; m. Deborah Ann Wismer, Dec. 29, 1973; children: Aimee Elizabeth, Emily Ann. BA with highest honors, Albion Coll., Mich., 1970; MS in Physics, U. Mich., 1971, JD with honors, 1973. Bar: Mich. 1974, US Ct. Appeals (fed. cir.) 1983, US Supreme Ct. 1993, DC 1994. Patent atty. The Upjohn Co., Kalamazoo, 1974-78, mgr. patent law dept., 1979-83, patent counsel, exec. dir. patent law, 1983—87, v.p. corp. patents and trademarks, 1987—93, asst. sec., 1988—93; ptnr. Vinson & Elkins, LLP, Washington, 1993—99; v.p., gen. patent counsel Lilly Rsch. Labs., 1999—2003; sr. v.p., gen. counsel Eli Lilly and Co., 2003—. Past bd. dirs. Human Genome Scis. Inc. Pres. Hospice of Kalamazoo, 1985-87. Fellow Woodrow Wilson Nat. Fellowship Found., Princeton, NJ, 1971. Mem. Mich. Bar Assn. (chair intellectual property law sect. 1986), Am. Intellectual Property Law Assn. (pres. 1994), Intellectual Property Owners Inc. (bd. dirs. 1985-93), Assn. Corp. Patent Counsel (pres. 1993), Phi Beta Kappa. Office: Eli Lilly and Co Lilly Corp Ctr Indianapolis IN 46285 Office Phone: 317-276-2000.*

ARMOR, DAVID J., sociologist; b. Long Beach, Calif., Nov. 11, 1938; s. John Edward Armor and Marie (Huffine) White; m. Marilyn Louise Sells, Sept. 7, 1958; children: Adrienne, Daniel. BA with highest honors, U. Calif., Berkeley, 1961; PhD, Harvard U., 1966. Asst. prof. sociology Harvard U., Cambridge, Mass., 1965-70, assoc. prof., 1970-73; sr. social scientist Rand Corp., Santa Monica, Calif., 1973-82; pres. Nat. Policy Analysts Inc., Santa Monica, 1981-86; acting asst. sec. Dept. Def., Washington, 1986-89; rsch. prof. George Mason U., 1992—2000, prof. pub. policy, 2001—. Vis. prof. sociology UCLA, 1972-73, Rutgers U., 1991-92; cons. Nat. Inst. on Alcohol Abuse and Alcoholism, Washington, 1972-73, Dept. Def., Washington, 1982-83, U.S. Commn. on Civil Rights, Washington, 1984-86. Author: American School Counselor, 1968, The Data-Text Primer, 1972, Alcoholism and Treatment, 1976, Forced Justice: School Desegregation and the Law, 1995, Competition in Education, 1997, Maximizing Intelligence, 2003. Mem. L.A. Bd. Edn., 1985-86; assoc. Pepperdine U., Malibu, 1982-86; Rep. nominee for U.S. Congress 23d Calif. dist., 1982. Fellow Woodrow Wilson Found., 1961-62, Ph.D. fellow Russell Sage Found., 1963-65. Mem. Am. Sociol. Assn. Home: 17246 Pepperstock Ln Jeffersonton VA 22724 Office Phone: 703-993-2260.

ARMOR, JOHN N., chemical company scientist, consultant, research manager; b. Phila., Sept. 14, 1944; m. Connie B. Korzuch. BS in Chemistry, Pa. State U., 1966; PhD, Stanford U., 1970. Asst. prof. chemistry Boston U., 1970-74; group leader Allied Signal Corp., Morristown, NJ, 1974-85; prin. rsch. assoc. Air Products and Chems. Inc., Allentown, Pa., 1985—2004; head corp. Catalysis Rsch. Ctr. Air Products, 1999—2004, Global Catalysis.com L.L.C.; global cons. on all aspects of catalysis, 2004—. Chmn. Inorganic Gordon Rsch. Conf., New London, N.H., 1988; gen. chmn. 2d World Congress on Environ. Catalysis. Editor-in-chief CATTECH, 2001—03; editor Applied Catalysis, 1987-96; mem. editl. bd. Jour. Natural Gas Chemistry, Japanese Catalysis Surveys, Jour. Catalysis, others; contbr. more than 120 articles to profl. jours. Recipient Houdry award for excellence in applied catalysis, N. Am. Catalysis Soc., 1997, 2001, E. V. Murpee award, Am. Chem. Soc. Mem. AIChE, Am. Chem. Soc. (organizer 1st symposium on environ. catalysis 1993), The N.Am. Catalysis Soc. (bd. dirs., treas. 1993-01, pres. 2001—), Catalysis Club Phila. (award for Excellence in Catalysis 1995), Catalysis Club N.Y. (bd. dirs.). Achievements include over 50 US patents. Office: 1608 Barkwood Dr Orefield PA 18069-8923 Personal E-mail: jnagcat@verizon.net. Business E-Mail: globalcatalysis@verizon.net.

ARMSTONG, ROBERT G., lawyer; b. 1947; B summa cum laude in Greek, Univ. Calif., San Diego; JD, Univ. San Diego. Bar: Calif. 1976. Ptnr. Armstrong Fishcer & Tutoli PLC, La Jolla, Calif. Co-founder, prin. shareholder Am. Acad. Estate Planning Attys., San Diego, 1992—. With USN, Vietnam. Mem.: ABA, San Diego County Bar, State Bar Calif. Office: Am Acad Estate Planning Attys Ste 850 4365 Executive Dr San Diego CA 92121 Office Phone: 858-453-0626, 858-453-2128. Office Fax: 858-535-8241. Business E-Mail: robert@aaepa.com.

ARMSTRONG, ALDEN ARTHUR, retired elementary school educator, photographer, writer; b. LA, Jan. 8, 1939; s. Ralph Edward and Ida Jeanette Armstrong; m. Linda Jean Keck, July 29, 1966; 1 child, Amy Alice. AA, Glendale Coll., 1966; BA, Calif. State Coll., LA, 1968. Tchr. LA Unified Sch. Dist., 1971—94. Contbr. articles to profl. publs., photographs of railroad locomotives to more than 50 books. With US Army, 1962—63. Mem.: Am. Legion, Kappa Delta Pi, Phi Alpha Theta. Avocation: model railroading. Home: 401 Rana Ct Grand Junction CO 81503

ARMSTRONG, ALEXANDRA, financial planner; b. Washington, Sept. 26, 1939; d. Rhoda Elizabeth (Forbes) Armstrong; m. Jerry J. McCoy, 1994. BA in History, Newton Coll. Sacred Heart, 1960. Cert. fin. planner, 1977. Exec. sec. Ferris & Co., Washington, 1961—66, registered rep., 1966—77; sr. v.p. Julia Walsh & Sons, Washington, 1977—83; pres. Alexandra Armstrong Advisors Inc., Washington, 1983—91; chmn. Armstrong, Welch & MacIntyre Inc., Washington, 1991—2000, Armstrong, MacIntyre & Severns, Inc., Washington, 2001—04, Armstrong, Fleming & Moore Inc., Washington, 2005—. Bd. experts Boardroom Reports, 1987—. Author: On Your Own: A Widow's Passage To Emotional and Financial Wellbeing, 1993, 3d edit., 2000. Vice chmn. Nat. Coun. Friends of Kennedy Ctr., Washington, 1987-91; pres. Nat. Capital coun. Boy Scouts Am., 1999-2000, chmn., 2000-01; mem. bd. visitors Sch. Bus. Georgetown U., 1988-91; v.p. programs Internat. Women's Forum, 1991-93, v.p. membership 1997-99, dir. IWF leadership found., 2001-04; bd. dirs. Reading is Fundamental, treas. 2000-04; chmn. Found. Fin. Planning, 1999-2000, bd. dirs. Named Bus. Woman of Yr. Washington Bus. and Profl. Women's Club, 1978; recipient award of excellence for commerce Boston Coll. Alumni Assn., 1985, Woman Who Makes a Difference award Internat. Women's Forum, 1992, Silver Beaver award Boy Scouts Am., 1991, Loren Dutton award, Internat. Assn. Registered Fin. Cons., 2003, Beta Gamma Sigma chpt. honoree Georgetown U., 1992; named to Washington Bus. Hall of Fame, 2006. Mem. Fin. Planning Assn. (bd. dirs. 1980-87, chmn. emeritus, pres. 1986-87), Nat. Assn. Investment Clubs (columnist monthly mag. 1978—, Disting. Svc. award 1993), Nat. Assn. Securities Dealers (bus. conduct com. dist. 10 1986-89, vice chmn. 1988-89), Nat. Assn. Women Bus. Owners (pres. Capital Area chpt. 1980-81), D.C. Estate Planning Coun., Nat. Capital Area Coun., Econ. Club Washington, Cosmos Club Washington, Econ. Club N.Y.C., Fin. Planning Assn. (Lifetime Achievement award 2001) Republican. Roman Catholic. Home: 3560 Winfield Ln NW Washington DC 20007-2368 Office: 1850 M St NW Ste 250 Washington DC 20036 Office Phone: 202-887-8135.

ARMSTRONG, ANNE LEGENDRE, retired ambassador; b. New Orleans, Dec. 27, 1927; d. Armant and Olive (Martindale) Legendre; m. Tobin Armstrong, Apr. 12, 1950 (dec. Oct. 7, 2005); children: John Barclay, Katharine Love, Sarita A. Hixon, Tobin and James L. (twins). BA in English, Vassar Coll., 1949. Co-chmn. Rep. Nat. Com., 1971-73; counsellor to U.S. Pres., 1973-74; U.S. amb. to Gt. Britain and No. Ireland London, 1976-77; chmn. adv. bd. Ctr. Strategic and Internat. Studies (formerly affiliated with Georgetown U.), 1981—87, chmn. bd. trustees, 1987—99, chmn. exec. com., 1999—2007, vice chair exec. com., 2007—; chmn. Pres.'s Fgn. Intelligence Adv. Bd., 1981-90; dir. Promontory Interfinancial Network, LLC, 2003—. Commn. on Integrated Long Term Strategy, 1987; adv. coun. GM Corp., 1998. Co-chmn. Reagan-Bush Campaign, 1980; mem. U.S. Commn. on Nat. Security/21st Century, 1999—2001, Gov.'s Coun. Sci. and Biotech. Devel., Tex., Gov.'s Task Force on Homeland Security, Tex.; county commr. Kenedy County, Tex., 2005; bd. regents Smithsonian Instn., Washington, 1978—94, emeritus, 1994; bd. overseers Hoover Instn., 1978—97; bd. regents Tex. A&M U., 1997—2003. Recipient Gold medal Nat. Inst. Social Scis., 1977, Rep. Woman of Yr. award, 1979, Texan of Yr. award, 1981, Presdl. Medal of Freedom award, 1987, Golden Plate award Am. Acad. Achievement, 1989; named to Tex. Women's Hall of Fame, 1986. Mem. English-Speaking Union (chmn. 1978-80), Coun. Fgn. Rels., Am. Assocs. of Royal Acad. Trust (trustee 1985-2005, vice-chmn. 1996), Alfalfa Club, Capitol Hill Club, Phi Beta Kappa. Republican.

ARMSTRONG, BILL HOWARD, artist, educator; b. Horton, Kans., Dec. 13, 1926; s. Pearl Marion and Elsie Nettie (Brown) Armstrong; m. Margo Simson, Aug. 16, 1990; children: William Cortney, William Bradford. BFA cum laude, Bradley U., 1949; MFA, U. Ill., 1956. Designer, illustrator Malone Studios, Dallas, 1952—53; art dir. U. Wis. Publ., Madison, 1956—57; asst. prof. art dept. U. Wis., Madison, 1957—63; prof. art Mo. State U., Springfield, 1963—88. Exhibitions include Taipei Fine Arts Mus., Soc. Am. Graphic Arts, 1956, Am. Fedn. Arts, 1956, Watercolor Soc., DC, 1960 (award, 1960), Taipei Arts Mus., Taiwan, Penn Acad. Fine Arts, 1967 (Top award, 1967), Cleve. Art Inst., 1968, The Butler Inst., 1968, Tours, France, 1987, Nat. Watercolor Soc. (Two awards), Watercolor Soc. Ala. (Three Purchase awards), Mo. Art Mus., Springfield (Eight awards), St. Louis Acad., The Boston Mus. (Purchase award), The Bklyn. Mus. (Purchase award), San Francisco Mus. Art (Purchase award). With USAF, 1944—45. Recipient Art Advisor award, Ford Found., 1957—58, Purchase award, West Publ. Co., 1982—83, Lifetime Achievement award, Mo. Arts Coun., 1990, Ozzig award, Springfield Area Arts Coun., 2003, Appreciation award, Mo. State U. Alumni, 2005. Mem.: Watercolor USA Honor Soc. (founder, emeritus pres., Lifetime Achievement award 2006). Home: 3029 Wilshire Springfield MO 65804 Personal E-mail: msba3@mchsi.com.

ARMSTRONG, BILLIE JOE, singer, musician; b. Oakland, Calif., Feb. 17, 1972; m. Adrienne Armstrong, July 2, 1994; children: Joseph Marciano, Jacob Danger. Played with bands such as Blatz, Rancid, The Lookouts, Goodbye Harry and Corrupted Morals; currently with side band Pinhead Gunpowder; co-founder, partial owner Adeline Records; co-founder, singer, musician Sweet Children (changed name to Green Day in 1989), 1988—. Singer: Look for Love; writer (first song) Why Do You Want Him, 1986, singer, musician (first EP) 1,000 Hours, (albums) 1,039/Smoothed Out Slappy Hour, 1991, Kerplunk, 1992, Dookie, 1994 (Grammy award for Best Alternative Music Performance, 1994), Insomniac, 1995, Nimrod, 1997, Warning, 2000, American Idiot, 2004 (Viewers Choice award, MTV Video Music Awards, 2005, Am. Music Awards Favorite Rock Album, 2005), writer (song) Church on Sunday; composer: (films) Angus, 1995, Godzilla, 1998, Varisty Blues, 1999, Austin Powers: The Spy Who Shagged Me, 1999, Freddy Got Fingered, 2001, American Pie 2, 2001; voice (films) Live Freaky Die Freaky, 2003; actor: (films) Dreamland, 2004; guest appearances Saturday Night Live, 1994, 2005, Mad TV, 2001, (voice) King of the Hill, 1997, and several others. Recipient Video of Yr., Best Group Video, Best Rock Video, Best Editing in a Video, Best Direction in a Video for Boulevard of Broken Dreams, MTV Video Music Awards, 2005, Pop Group of Yr., Rock Artist of Yr., Modern Rock Artist of Yr., Hot 100 Group of Yr., Billboard 200 Album Group of Yr., Billboard Music Awards, 2005, Rock Song of Yr. for Boulevard of Broken Dreams, 2005, Alternative Song of Yr. for Boulevard of Broken Dreams, Radio Music Awards, 2005, Favorite Group, People's Choice Awards, 2006, Record of Yr. for Boulevard of Broken Dreams, Grammy Awards, 2006.

ARMSTRONG, BRENDA ESTELLE, pediatrician, cardiologist; b. Rocky Mount, NC, Jan. 19, 1949; d. Wiley Thurber and Marguerite (Carson) A.; 1 child, Bradlee Alexander Carson Armstrong. BA, Duke U., 1970; MD, St. Louis U., 1974. Diplomate Am. Bd. Pediatrics, Am. Bd. Pediatric Cardiology. Intern in pediatrics UCLA Med. Ctr., 1974-75; resident in pediatrics Duke U. Med. Ctr., Durham, N.C., 1975-76, fellow in pediatric cardiology, 1976-79, asst. prof. pediatrics, 1979-89, assoc. prof. pediatrics, 1987—, assoc. prof., 1989—, dir. admissions, 1996—. Chief clin. svcs. div. pediatric cardiology, Duke U., 1986—, chief fellowship tng., 1986—, chief of pediatric cardiac lab., 1984—; cons. to U.S. Army and USAF, 1982—. Mem. N.C. Environ. Mgmt. Commn., Raleigh, 1979-86; bd. dirs. Montessori Children's House of Durham, 1988—, Durham Striders Track and Field Club, 1984—. Recipient Golden Apple Teaching award Duke U. Med. Sch., 1981, Thomas Kinney Teaching award Duke U. Med. Sch., 1985; named YWCA Woman of Achievement, City of Durham YWCA, 1986. Mem. Assn. Black Cardiologists, Old North State Med. Soc. (Dr. of Yr. 1987), Nat. Med. Assn., N.C. Pediatric Soc., Am. Acad. Pediatrics., Links Inc. Democrat. Episcopalian. Avocations: music, reading, sports, knitting. Office: Duke U Div Pediatric Cardiology PO Box 3195 Durham NC 27715-3195

ARMSTRONG, C. MICHAEL, retired communications executive; b. Detroit, Oct. 18, 1938; s. Charles H. and Zora Jean (Brooks) A.; m. Anne Gossett, June 17, 1961; children: Linda, Julie, Kristy. BS in Bus. Econs, Miami U., Oxford, Ohio, 1961; grad., Dartmouth Inst., 1976; LLD (hon.), Pepperdine U., 1997, Loyola Marymount U., 1998; LLD (hon.), Worcester Polytechnic Inst., 2000. With IBM Corp., 1961-92, dir. systems mgmt. mktg. div., White Plains, N.Y., 1975-76, v.p. market ops. East, 1976-78, pres. data processing divsn., 1978-80, v.p., asst. group exec. plans and controls, data processing product group, 1980-83, v.p., group exec., 1983-84, sr. v.p., group exec., 1984-92, also pres. Europe, Paris, until 1988, pres., dir. gen. World Trade Europe/Middle East/Africa, 1987-89, chmn. World Trade Corp., 1989-92; chmn., CEO Hughes Aircraft Co., LA, 1992-93, GM Hughes Electronics (now Hughes Electronics Corp.), 1993—97, AT&T, NYC, 1997—2002; chmn. Comcast Corp., 2003—04. Mem. GM Pres. Coun.; bd. dirs. Travelers Corp., Hartford, Conn., The Times-Mirror-Co., L.A., Citigroup; mem. supervisory bd. Thyssen-Bornemisza Group; chmn. Pres.'s Export Coun., The White House, 1994—. Trustee Johns Hopkins U., chmn. adv. bd. Johns Hopkins Med. Sch.; mem., CEO bd. of adv. U. So. Calif. Bus. Sch.; mem. bus. adv. coun. Miami U.; mem. Coun. on Fgn. Rels., Nat. Security Telecomm. Adv. Com., Def. Policy Adv. Com. on Trade (DPACT); adv. bd. Yale Sch. Mgmt.; vice-chmn. World Affairs Coun., L.A.; chmn. Sabriya's Castle of Fun Found.; bd. trustees Carnegie Hall. Mem. Calif. Bus. Roundtable. Office: Comcast Corp 1500 Market St Philadelphia PA 19102

ARMSTRONG, CATHAL, chef; b. Dublin, 1970; m. Cathal Armstrong; children: Eve, Eamonn. Owner, ptnr. Baytree, Dublin; chef New Heights, Washington, Cities, Washington; sous chef Garbiel Restaurant, Washington, 1994, Vidalia Restaurant, Washington, 1995; head chef Bistro Bis, Washington, 1998; co-owner, chef Restaurant Eve, Alexandria, Va., Eamonn's A Dublin Chipper, Alexandria, Va., 2006—, PX, Alexandria, Va., 2006—. Mem. Share Our Strength Leadership Coun., Am. Farmland Trust. Named one of Washington DC's Rising Stars, StarChefs.com, 2006; recipient Best New Chef award, Food and Wine Mag., 2006. Office: Restaurant Eve 100 S Pitt St Alexandria VA 22309 Office Phone: 703-706-0450.*

ARMSTRONG, CLAY, physiology educator; BA, Rice U., 1956; MD, Washington U., 1960. Postdoctoral fellow NIH, 1961—64, Univ. Coll., London, 1964—66; prof. Duke U., U. Rochester; prof. physiology U. Pa. Sch. Medicine, Phila., 1976—. Mem editorial bd. Journal of General Physiology, Journal of Neurophysiology. Recipient Louisa Gross Horwitz prize Columbia U., 1996, Jacob Javits Neuroscience Rsch. award, NIH, Albert Lasker award for basic med. rsch., Lasker Found., 1999, Gairdner Found., 2001. Mem.: NAS, Soc. General Physiologists, Biophysical Soc., Am. Physiological Soc. Office: U Pa Dept Physiology C701 Richards Bldg/ 6085 Philadelphia PA 19104-6085 Office Phone: 215-898-7816. E-mail: carmstro@mail.med.upenn.edu.

ARMSTRONG, DANIEL WAYNE, chemist, educator; b. Ft. Wayne, Ind., Nov. 2, 1949; s. Robert Eugene and Nila Louise (Koeneman) A.; m. Linda Marilyn Todd, June 11, 1972; children: Lincoln Thomas, Ross Alexander, Colleen Victoria. BS, Washington and Lee U., 1972; MS in Chem. Oceanography, Tex. A&M U., 1974, PhD in Chemistry, 1977. Prof. Bowdoin Coll., Brunswick, Maine, 1978-79, Georgetown U., Washington, 1980-83, Tex. Tech. U., Lubbock, 1983-87; Curators' disting. prof., head ctr. environ. sci. and tech.; head dept. analytical chemistry U. Mo., Rolla, 1987-2000; Caldwell prof. chemistry Iowa State U., 2000—06; Robert A. Welch prof. chemistry and biochemistry U. Tex., Arlington, Tex., 2006—. Bd dirs. Advanced Separations Techs., Whippany, NJ; Moreton lectr. Millsaps Coll., 2001, R.A. Welch lectr., 2002, Dow lectr., 2003; lectr. Columbia U., 2003. Host Univ. Forum Radio Show, Washington, 1981-83; writer, host weekly radio show We're Sci. Nat. Pub. Radio, 1993—; author film, radio shows; contbr. articles to profl. jours. Recipient Tchg. Excellence award U. Mo., 1985, 88-89, 92, 94, Faculty Excellence award U. Mo., 1988-89, Martin medal, 1991, EAS Chromatography award, 1990, Isco award, 1992, Presdl. award, 1993, Perkin Elmer award, 1994, R&D 100 award R&D Mag., 1995, Benedetti-Pichler award Am. Microchem. Soc. 1996, Helen M. Free award, 1998, CLDG Merit award, 2001, Weber medal, 2001, Kenneth A. Spencer award for agr. and food chemistry, 2002, Chirality medal, 2003, Dal Nogre award for separation sci., 2005. Slovak Med. Soc. medal. 2007; named Disting. Scholar Hope Coll., 1999; grantee Rsch. Corp., 1979, Petroleum Rsch. Fund, 1979, 91, NSF, 1981; Rsch. grantee Whatman Corp., 1981, Dept. Energy, 1984, 87, 91, 94, Dow Chem., 1985-90, NIH, 1986, 91, 95, 2000, 03, 05, EPA, 1995, Shell Co., 1989-92. Fellow Am. Assn. Pharm. Scientists; mem. Am. Chem. Soc. (49th Midwest award for chemistry 1993, award in chromatography 1999), Slovak Pharm. Soc. (hon., Vladimir J. Zuffu medal 2004), Sigma Xi, Phi Lambda Upsilon. Achievements include patents in field. Office: Iowa State U Dept Chemistry Gilman Hall Ames IA 50011 Business E-Mail: sec4dwa@iastate.edu.

ARMSTRONG, DAVID LIGON, psychiatrist; b. Ontario, Calif., May 5, 1927; s. John Awdry and Ruth (Harrison) A.; m. Mary Meredith, Mar. 30, 1953 (dec. Feb. 13, 1997); children: Meredith Armstrong Richey, Paul, Adelaide Armstrong Butler. BS in Plant Sci., U. Calif., Berkeley, 1949; PhD in Genetics, U. Calif., Davis, 1956; MD, Creighton U., 1972. Diplomate Am. Bd. Psychiatry and Neurology. Dir. rsch. Armstrong Nurseries, Inc., Ontario, Calif., 1953—68; resident in psychiatry U. Calif., Irvine, 1972—75; staff psychiatrist Met. State Hosp., Norwalk, Calif., 1975—2005; ret., 2005. Pres. med. staff Met. State Hosp., Norwalk, 1985-88, 1997-2005 Pres. West End United Fund, Ontario, 1958-60, Chaffey Young Reps., Ontario, Upland, Chino, Calif., 1958-60, West End Coun. Cmty. Svcs., Ontario, Upland, Chino, 1960-64; chmn. Rep. Ctrl. Com., San Bernardino County, Calif., 1960-62. With USNR, 1945-46. Mem. Calif. State Employed Physicians Assn. (pres. 1984-86), Sigma Xi, Alpha Zeta. Republican. Achievements include patents for roses and peaches. Avocations: politics, travel, gardening. Home: 2809 E Hillside Ave Orange CA 92867-8413 Home Phone: 714-998-2349. Personal E-mail: davidarmstrong22@sbcglobal.net.

ARMSTRONG, DAVID MICHAEL, biology professor; b. Louisville, July 31, 1944; s. John D. and Elizabeth Ann (Horine) A.; children: John D., Laura C. Armstrong-Stone. BS, Colo. State U., 1966; MA in Teaching, Harvard U., 1967; PhD, U. Kans., 1971. From asst. prof. to prof. natural sci. U. Colo., Boulder, 1971-85, prof. ecology and evolutionary biology, 1993—, assoc. chair, 1997-99; sr. scientist Rocky Mountain Biol. Lab., Gothic, Colo., 1977, 79; resident naturalist Sylvan Dale Ranch, Loveland, Colo., 1984—; acting dir. Univ. Mus., 1987-88, dir., 1989-93. Cons. in field. Author: Distribution of Mammals in Colorado, 1972, Rocky Mountain Mammals, 1975, 87, Mammals of the Canyon Country, 1982; co-author: Mammals of the Northern Great Plains, Mammals of the Plains States, Mammals of Colorado. Mem. non-game adv. council Colo. Div. Wildlife, 1972-76, Colo. Natural Areas Council, 1975-80. Mem.: Colo. Wildlife Fedn. (bd. dirs. 2000—02), The Nature Conservancy (trustee Colo. chpt. 1989—99, 2002—, chair 1996—98), Rocky Mountain Biol. Lab. (trustee 1979—83), Southwestern Assn. Naturalists (editor 1976—80), Am. Soc. Mammalogists (editor 1981—87). Avocations: draft horses, conservation activities, writing. Office: U Colo Ecology and Evolutionary Biology PO Box 334 Boulder CO 80309-0334 Personal E-mail: mausmann@aol.com. Business E-Mail: david.armstrong@colorado.edu.

ARMSTRONG, DIANNE OWENS, language educator; d. James Hamilton Jones; m. David Seaton Armstrong, July 6, 1958 (div. June 0, 1967); children: Sydney Pollard, David Seaton Armstrong, Jr., Emily Hines, Malcolm Conger. BA, U. Ill., Champaign Urbana, 1957; MA, St. Johns U., Jamaica, NY, 1976; PhD, U. So. Calif., LA, 1992. Instr. English UCLA, 1984—87; lectr. freshman writing program U. of So. Calif., LA, 1988—93; adj. instr. English Santa Barbara City Coll., Calif., 1993—96; prof. English Ventura Coll., Calif., 1996—. Contbr. articles to profl. jours., ency. Vol. Faulding Hotel Ministry, Santa Barbara, 1999—2001. Named Instr. of the Yr., EOPS, Ventura Coll., 1996—97, Lectr. of the Yr., USC Writing Program, 1992. Democrat-Npl. Episcopalian. Office: Ventura College 4667 Telegraph Rd Ventura CA 93003 Home Phone: 805-568-0575; Office Phone: 805-654-6400 x 2221. E-mail: darmstrong@vcccd.edu.

ARMSTRONG, DOUG, professional sports team executive; b. Sarnia, Ontario, Canada; s. Neil Armstrong; m. Kelly Armstrong; children: Blake, Kayla. Asst. gen. mgr. Dallas Stars, Irving, Tex., 1993—2002, gen. mgr., 2002—. Office: Dallas Stars 2601 Ave Of The Stars Ste 100 Frisco TX 75034-9016

ARMSTRONG, DOUGLAS DEAN, journalist; b. Wichita, Kans., Mar. 12, 1945; s. H. Glenn and Emma F. (Starkey) A.; m. Paige Prillaman, Jan. 3, 1967 (div. Sept. 1982); children: David Douglas, Christine Elizabeth; m. Mary Alyce Dooley, Mar. 8, 1987; children: Patrick Glenn, Gillian Marie. BA, U. Minn., 1967. Entertainment writer Milw. Jour. Sentinel, 1967-72, editl. writer, 1972-74, consumer writer, 1974-81, movie critic, 1981-95, bus. writer, 1995-2000, personal fin. columnist, 1995-2000. Guest lectr. U. Wis., Milw., 1982-89; movie reviewer WISN-TV, Milw., 1984-85; movie critic WKTI-FM, Milw., 1989-97; pres. Lexington Software Corp., 1996—2003; mem. faculty studies com. Whitefish Bay Schs. Contbr. short fiction to Ellery Queen's Mystery Mag., Alfred Hitchcock's Mystery Mag., Boys' Life. Recipient Pub. Interest award Ctr. for Pub. Representation, 1978. Mem. Mystery Writers Am., Allied Authors, Coun. Wis. Writers, Milw. Press Club. Avocations: video, piano, golf. E-mail: doug@douglasarmstrong.com.

ARMSTRONG, EDWARD BRADFORD, JR., oral and maxillofacial surgeon, educator, naval officer; b. Teaneck, N.J., Sept. 24, 1928; s. Edward Bradford and Ruth Elizabeth (Fippinger) A.; AB, U. Pa., 1950; DDS, N.Y.U., 1954; m. Dusanka Vladimirovna Jakovljevic, Nov. 5, 1960; children: Edward Bradford, III, James B., Hugh B. Commd. lt. j.g. U.S. Navy, 1954, advanced through grades to capt. 1971; intern oral surgery Roosevelt Hosp., N.Y.C., 1958, assoc. attending oral surgery, 1959—, attending oral surgeon out-patient dept., 1959—, chmn., moderator Oral Surgery Staff Confs., 1963-70; resident Carle Hosp., Urbana, Ill., 1959; assoc. attending oral surgeon Flower and Fifth Ave. hosps., N.Y.C., 1960-78; asst. attending oral surgeon Hackensack (N.J.) Hosp., 1963-65; adminstrv. officer Naval Res. Dental Co. 3-2, 1965-68, exec. officer, 1968-71, comdg. officer, 1971-73; comdt.'s rep. 3d Naval Dist., Naval Acad., 1972-78, 3d Naval Dist for Dentistry, 1973-75, group staff officer for dentistry and medicine, 1973-75, Ready Res. Unit 502, 1975-77, VTU 0207, 1977-79, ret., 1979; assoc. clin. prof. oral surgery N.Y. Med. Coll., 1963-93; adj. assoc. clin. prof. oral surgery Columbia U. Sch. Dentistry, 1973-89; chmn. bd. E. & R. Armstrong, Inc., Albany, N.Y., 1966-77; pres. Edward B. Armstrong, P.C., N.Y.C., 1979-90; dir. Songtime, Inc., Boston; dir., mem. exec. com. PGP Internat. Corps, Inc. Bd. dirs., trustee Christian Mission Farms of Paraguay, Inc., 1974-84; pres., trustee Central Bible Chapel, Palisades Park, N.J.; area rep., ann. giving U. Pa., 1960-68; Blue and Gold officer Naval Acad. Admissions Com.; sec. bd. dirs., trustee Boys' Club of N.Y. Health Svcs., Inc. Diplomate Am. Bd. Oral Surgery. Fellow N.Y. Acad. Dentistry (sec., dir., pres. 1979-80), Am., Internat. Colls. Dentists (life), Am. Coll. Oral and Maxillofacial Surgeons (founding), Am. Dental Soc. Anesthesiology (hon. life); mem. ADA (life, 1st dist. life), Am. Assn. Oral and Maxillofacial Surgeons (life, N.J. rep. Ho. of Dels. 1963-65), N.Y. Soc. Oral Surgeons (life, chmn. audit and budget com. 1972-79), First Dist. Dental Soc. (life), N.Y. Dental Soc., Bklyn. Dental Soc., Yokosuka Dental Soc. (hon.), Assn. Mil. Surgeons U.S., Mil. Order World Wars, Naval Res. Assn. (life), Union League (chmn. art com. 1973-76, bd. govs. 1974-77, 82-84, v.p. 1977-80, 85-88), Met. Club (bd. gov. 1992-96, 98-2002), N.Y.C., U. Pa. Club, U. Pa. Club of Met. N.J. (dir. 1982—), Acacia, Xi Psi Phi, Psi Omega (hon.), Delta Sigma Delta. Mem. Plymouth Brethren Ch.

ARMSTRONG, F(REDRIC) MICHAEL, retired insurance company executive, consultant; b. Wichita, Kans., Dec. 20, 1942; s. Frederick Dale and Virginia Pauline A.; m. Patricia R. Latif, Dec. 13, 1976 (div. 1996). BSEE, MIT, 1964; MBA, Stanford U., 1966. Mgr. capital appropriations Trans World Airlines, NYC, 1966-69; corp. planner Transam. Corp., San Francisco, 1969-70; v.p. Transam. Film Svc., Salt Lake City, 1970-73, also bd. dirs.; v.p. fin. Europe Transam. Airlines, Madrid, Spain, 1973-75, v.p. planning and info. svcs. Oakland, Calif., 1975-77; exec. v.p. fin. Budget Rent a Car Corp., Chgo., 1977-83, also bd. dirs.; exec. v.p., chief adminstrv. officer Transam. Ins. Group, LA, 1983-93, also bd. dirs.; pres. Century Indemnity Co., Century Reinsurance Co., LA, 1995-96, also bd. dirs. Bd. dirs. Melia Internat. Hotels, Panama, The Canadian Surety Co., Ins. Value Added Network Service, River Thames Ins. Co., London, Fairmont Fin. Inc., Mason-McDuffie Ins. Svc., Inc., The Completion Bond Co. Mem. adv. coun. Pierce Coll.; mem. audit com. City of Sanibel, Fla. E-mail: marmstrong@alum.mit.edu.

ARMSTRONG, GREG L., oil industry executive; BS, Southeastern Okla. State U., 1980. CPA. Formerly with Price Waterhouse; corp. sec. Plains Resources, Inc., 1981—88, treas., 1984—87, v.p., CFO, 1984—91, sr. v.p., CFO, 1991—92, exec. v.p., CFO, 1992, pres., COO, 1992, pres., CEO, dir., 1992—2001; chmn., CEO Plains All Am. Pipeline, LP, Houston, 2001—. Bd. dirs. Petroleum Club of Houston, IPAA Tex. Southeast Regional Bd. of Trustees, Varco Internat., 2004—. Office: Plains All Am Pipeline LP 333 Clay St Ste 1600 Houston TX 77002*

ARMSTRONG, HENRY CONNER, former Canadian government official, consultant; b. Winnipeg, Man., Can., June 16, 1925; s. William Arthur Laird and Archena May (Conner) A.; m. Barbara Fay Jackson, May 20, 1950; children: Barbara E., Nancy M., Scott J. B.Sc. in Metall. Engring., Queen's U., Kingston, Ont., 1949; MBA (Kresge fellow), U. Toronto, 1954; diploma in indsl. adminstrn. (Alcan fellow), Internat. Mgmt. Inst., Geneva, Switzerland, 1958. Various sales and marketing positions Aluminum Co. of Can., Ltd., 1954-64; commodity officer Dept. Trade and Commerce, Ottawa, Ont., 1964-66; comml. counsellor Canadian Embassy, Washington, 1966-74; chief research and planning div., resource industries and constrn. br. Dept. Industry, Trade and Commerce, Ottawa, Ont., Canada, 1974-75; dir. minerals and metals div. Dept. Energy, Mines and Resources, Ottawa, Ont., 1975-81, exec. dir. internat. minerals, 1981-82, mgr. spl. projects, 1982-83; counsellor (metals, minerals and energy) Can. High Commn., Canberra, Australia, 1983-86; counsellor (commercial) Can. Embassy, Washington, 1986-89; pvt. practice cons. Ottawa, 1989—. Served with RCAF and Royal Navy Fleet Air Arm, 1944-45. Mem. Assn. Profl. Engrs. Ont., Canadian Inst. Mining and Metallurgy, Am. Soc. for Materials. Mem. United Ch. of Can. Home and Office: 2159 Delmar Dr Ottawa ON Canada K1H 5P6

ARMSTRONG, HENRY JERE, retired judge; b. Dothan, Ala., Mar. 5, 1941; s. Henry Jordan and Lillian (Taylor) Armstrong; m. Jeanne Bachmann, June 3, 1963; children: April Heather, Ashley Brooke. BA, U. Ala., Tuscaloosa, 1964, JD, 1966; postgrad., JAGs Sch., Charlottesville, Va., 1972-73; grad., Armed Forces Staff Coll., 1978. Bar: Ala. 1966, U.S. Ct. Mil. Appeals 1967, U.S. Supreme Ct. 1972, DC 1974, Va. 1984. Commd. 2d lt. U.S. Army, 1964, advanced through grades to col., 1983; def. counsel, prosecutor Ft. Ord., Calif., 1967-68; chief criminal law, chief civil law, mil. judge Ft. Shafter, Hawaii, 1968-72; chief legis. br. criminal law divsn. Dept. Army, Washington, 1973-75, exec. asst. to JAG, 1975-77; staff judge adv. 2d inf. divsn. Republic of Korea, 1978-79; exec. officer U.S. Army Trial Def. Svc., Falls Church, Va., 1979-82; exec. officer litigation divsn. Dept. Army, Washington, 1982-84; counsel to chief Immigration Judge U.S., 1984-86; judge, asst. chief immigration judge U.S. Dept. Justice, 1986-97, dep. chief immigration judge, 1997—2003; ret., 2003. Profl. responsibility adv. com. Dept. Army; guest lectr. ethics and def. advocacy U.S. Army Europe Continuing Legal Edn. seminars; faculty Nat. Jud. Coll., Reno; adv. bd. Nat. Fgn. Lang. Ctr. Johns Hopkins U. Contbr. articles to profl. jours. Elder Grace Presbyn. Ch., Springfield, Va. Decorated Legion of Merit, Meritorious Svc. medal with 2 oak leaf clusters U.S. Army, Commendation medal; named Hon. Ky. Col., 1982; fellow, Inst. Ct. Mgmt., Nat. Ctr. State Cts., Williamsburg, Va. Mem.: ATLA, Judge Advs. Assn. (bd. dirs.), Fed. Bar Assn., Va. State Bar Assn., DC Bar Assn., Ala. State Bar Assn., Phi Alpha Delta, Kappa Sigma Alumni Assn. Home: 8208 Little River Tpke Annandale VA 22003-2305

ARMSTRONG, J. HORD, III, pharmaceutical company executive; Chmn. bd., CEO D&K Healthcare Resources, Inc., Saint Louis, 1993—. Office: D&K Healthcare Resources Inc PO Box 16989 Saint Louis MO 63105-1389

ARMSTRONG, JACQUE, pre-school educator; b. Camden, NJ, Dec. 28, 1950; d. Willis Franklin and Barbara (Robbins) Beltz; m. Allen W. Armstrong, Mar. 25, 2000; children: Robbin B. Walsh, John H. Walsh. BA in Early Childhood and Elem. Edn., W.Va. Wesleyan Coll., Buckhannon, 1972. Lic. tchr. Ark., N.J., cert. early childhood edn. tchr. Kindergarten tchr. Washington Elem. Schs., Parkersburg, W.Va., 1972—74; 1st grade tchr. Kingwood Twp. Bd. Edn., Kingwood, NJ, 1974—75; day care dir. Creative Playsch., Bloomsbury, NJ, 1975—90; kindergarten tchr. Bloomsbury Elem. Sch., 1990—93, St. Mary's Elem. Sch., North Little Rock, Ark., 1993—. Membership chair, past pres. Ark. Cath. Spl. Interest Reading Coun., North Little Rock, 1996—2006. Leader Girl Scouts U.S., Boy Scouts Am., North Little Rock, 1997—2002. Mem.: Ark. Reading Assn. (com. chair 1998—2006, Educator Literacy award 2003), Internat. Reading Assn., Heritage Seekers. Avocations: sewing, quilting, genealogy.

ARMSTRONG, (ARTHUR) JAMES, minister, educator, consultant, writer; b. Marion, Ind., Sept. 17, 1924; s. Arthur J. and Frances (Green) A.; m. Sharon Owen, Apr. 8, 2000; children from previous marriages: Eve Stoughton, Allison, James, Teresa, John, Rebecca Putens, Leslye Armstrong Hope. AB, Fla. So. Coll., 1948; BD, Candler Sch. Theology, Emory U., 1952; DD, Fla. So. U., 1960, DePauw U., 1965; LHD, Ill. Wesleyan U., 1970, Dakota Wesleyan U., 1970, Westmar Coll., 1971, Ind. Ctrl. U., 1982, Emory U., 1982. Ordained to ministry Meth. Ch., 1948. Minister in Fla., 1945-58; sr. minister Broadway Meth. Ch., Indpls., 1958-68; bishop United Meth. Ch., Dakotas area, 1968-80, Ind. area, Indpls., 1980-83; exec. v.p. conflict resolution firm, Washington, 1984-87; vis. prof. preaching and social ministries Iliff Sch. Theology, Denver, 1985-91; sr. min. 1st Congl. Ch., Winter Park, Fla., 1991-99; exec. dir. Ctr. on Dialogue and Devel., Denver, 1984-96. Adj. prof. Rollins Col., 1992—, Fla. Ctr. Theol. Studies, 1999-2007; instr. Christian Theol. Sem., Indpls., 1961-68; del. 4th Gen. Assembly, World Coun. Chs., 1968, 6th Gen. Assembly, 1983; pres. Nat. Coun. Chs., 1982-83; pres. bd. ch. and soc. United Meth. Ch., 1972-76, chmn. com. for peace and self devel. of peoples, 1972-76, pres. Commn. on Religion and Race, 1976-83; exec. v.p. Pagan Internat., 1982-87. Author: Gentlemen, Start Your Engines, 1967, The Journey That Men Make, 1969, The Urgent Now, 1970, Mission: Middle America, 1971, The Pastor and the Public Servant, 1972, United Methodist Primer, 1973, 77, Wilderness Voices, 1974, The Nation Yet To Be, 1975, Telling Truth: The Foolishness of Preaching in a Real World, 1977, From the Underside, 1981, Feet of Clay, on Solid Ground, 2002; contbg. author: The Pulpit Speaks on Race, 1966, War Crimes and the American Conscience, 1970, Rethinking Evangelism, 1971, What's a Nice Church Like You Doing in a Place Like This?, 1972, The Miracle of Easter, 1980, Preaching on Peace, 1982, Ethics and the Multi-National Enterprise, 1986, The Best of the Circuit Rider, 1987, Prayerfully Pro-Choice, 1999, Connected Spirits, 2007. Vice-chmn. Hoosiers for Peace, 1968; mem. Ind. State Platform Com. Democratic Party, 1968, Nat. Coalition for a Responsible Congress, 1970. With USNR, 1942. Recipient Disting. Svc. award, Indpls. Jr. C. of C., 1959. Mem. Fla. Coun. Chs. (pres. 1996-97), Ctrl. Fla. Interfaith Alliance (co-chair 1994-96). Methodist. Home Phone: 407-678-0840; Office Phone: 407-678-0840. Personal E-mail: jarmstrongjsa@aol.com.

ARMSTRONG, JAMES DAVID, editor, educator, minister; b. Charlotte, NC, Dec. 17, 1932; s. George Eugene and Edna Bleeker Armstrong; m. Gloria Holmes Armstrong, June 15, 1985; children: James David, Deborah Loren, Brenda Carol, Robert Jon. BA, Livingstone Coll., Salisbury, NC, 1955; MDiv, Hood Theol. Sem., Salisbury, NC, 1959; MA, Scarritt Coll., Nashville, 1974. Ordained elder AME Zion Ch. Pastor Henry's Chapel AME Zion Ch., Belmont, NC, 1954—59, Mid. St. AME Zion Ch., Charlotte, 1955—57, Trinity AME Zion Ch., Gastonia, 1957—58, Rudisil Chapel AME Zion Ch., Cherryville, 1958—60, Thomas Chapel AME Zion Ch., Conover, 1960—62, Trinity AME Zion Ch., Birmingham, NY, 1962—67, Hopkins Chapel AME Zion Ch., Asheville, NC, 1967—74, Varick Meml. AME Zion Ch., Hackensack, NJ, 1974—85, Spotswood AME Zion Ch., New Britain, Conn., 1985—89; editor and sec. AME Zion Quar. Rev. and Hist. Soc., Charlotte, NC, 1989—. Mem. Broom County Coun. Churches, NY, 1962—64, Bergen County Coun. Churches, NJ, 1976—82; dir. Com. Orgn. Opportunities for Broome, Binghamton, NY, 1965—67; founder and chmn. Asheville AME Zion Evangelistic Assn., NC, 1969—74; instr. religious studies Allen H.S Girls United Meth. Ch., 1973—74; asst. prof. practical theology Hood Theol. sem., Salisbury, 1973—74; founder and dean AME Zion Dist. Sch. Christian Workers, Hackensack, NJ, 1980—85, New Britain, Conn., 1985—89; mem. Commn. Archives and History United Meth. Ch., Madison, NJ, 2005—. Author: A Brief Historical Survey AME Zion Church, 2004, (monologue) Meet James Varick, 1996; editor: The Zion Pulpit: What Price Freedom and Other Great Sermons from the Zion Pulpit, 1996, (republ. work) A Short Account of the AME Church in America, 2000, History of the AME Church in America, 2004, One Hundred Years of AME Zion Church, 2006. Dir. and co-chair Asheville Human Rels. Coun., NC, 1970—71; adv. bd. Planned Parenthood, Binghamton, NY, 1962—74, Buncombe County Coun. Girl Scouts, 1969—71; pres. Asheville chpt. NAACP, 1969—70. Recipient Outstanding Cmty. Svc. award, Asheville City Coun., 1970, Exemplary Svc. in Evangelism award, AME Zion Bd. Evangelism, 1972, Outstanding Svc. award, AME Zion Minister's and Lay Assn., 2004, Frederick Douglass award, AME Zion Ministerial and Lay Assn., 2006. Mem.: Am. Assn. State and Local Hist. Assns. Democrat. Avocations: carpentry, piano, painting. Office: AME Zion Quarterly Rev and Hist Soc 3225 W Sugar Creek Rd Charlotte NC 28208 Office Phone: 704-599-4630. Business E-Mail: jaarmstrong@2mezhq.org.

ARMSTRONG, JAMES FRANCIS, III, retired language educator, writer; b. Penn Yan, NY, Mar. 17, 1945; s. James Francis Armstrong Jr. and Frances (Grady) Armstrong-Barden. BA in English Edn. cum laude, Hobart-William Smith, 1983; cert., Kellogg Inst., 1989. Cert. English tchr.; cert. devel. educator. English tchr. Penn Yan Jr. High Sch., 1984-85; learning specialist CC Finger Lakes, Geneva, NY, 1986-87, dir. learning ctr. and libr., 1987—2005; ret., 2005. Film maker Kodak, 1970; G.E.D. instr. Bd. Coop. Ednl. Svcs., Stanley, NY, 1986—87. Performer: Feels Like Spyders, 1975; author: The Asexuals, 2001, Subsect, 2002, Rock Hard, 2005; contbr. articles to profl. jours. Avocation: music. Office: PO Box 14 Keuka Park NY 14478 Personal E-mail: armstrjf@bluefrog.com.

ARMSTRONG, JEFFREY LEE, representative, oceanographer; b. Twenty-Nine Palms, Calif., Apr. 18, 1959; s. Alden David and Josephine Frances Armstrong; m. Dawn Lee Embree, July 12, 1979; children: Cassandra Jean, Shannon Elizabeth. BS in Marine Biology, Calif. State U., Long Beach, 1993, MS in Biology, 1997; PhD in Biol. Oceanography, City U. L.A., 2001. Marine biologist, consultant Orange County Sanitation Dist., Fountain Valley, Calif., 1996—97, prin. environ. specialist, 1997—2000, scientist, 2000—04, sr. scientist, 2004—; marine ecol. cons., owner Coastal Environ. Consulting, Dana Point, 1996—98; adj. faculty mem. Calif. State U., Long Beach, Calif., 2005—. Regional rep. Fish and Invertebrate Com. So. Calif. Coastal Water Rsch. Project Regional Monitoring, Westminster, 1997—, regional rep. Toxicity Com., 1997—, regional rep. Benthic Infauna Com., 2003—; mem. nat. monitoring network design com. U.S. Geol. Survey, 2005—06; adv. bd. mem. Chapman U. Bio-Science, 2006—. Contbr. text book. Mem.: Water Environ. Fedn., So. Calif. Acad. Scis., So. Calif. Assn. Marine Invertebrate Taxonomists, Soc. Environ. Toxicology and Chemistry (govt. rep. So. Calif. chpt. 2001—03, historian 2003—05, v.p. 2005—06, pres. 2006—07). Avocations: baseball, sailing, music. Office: Orange County Sanitation Dist 10844 Ellis Ave Fountain Valley CA 92708-7018 Office Phone: 714-593-7455. Business E-Mail: jarmstrong@ocsd.com.

ARMSTRONG, JOHN WALLACE, film producer; b. Mpls., Mar. 24, 1943; s. Wallace David and Mary Garland Armstrong; m. Naomi Fatt, July 10, 1982; m. Marilyn Kay Stageberg, Apr. 11, 1963 (div. Feb. 2, 1966); children: Michael Ian Charles, Stefan Gwilym, Sarah Lilith. BA, Harvard Coll., Cambridge, Mass., 1964; MA, Stony Brook U., NY, 1969. Instr. theater arts Stony Brook U., NY, 1969—70; free lance film editor NYC, 1972—75; assoc. media prodr., dir. Health Scis. Ctr., Stony Brook, 1970—72; media prodr., dir. Health Scis. Ctr., 1975—76; prodr., dir. Don Ln. Pictures, Inc., NYC, 1976—87; pres. John Armstrong & Co., Inc., Bklyn., 1987—. Dir.: (over 150 documentaries about health and medicine); contbr. articles to profl. jours. Mem.: Nat. Assn. Sci. Writers, Am. Sci. Film Assn. (bd. mem. 1979—81). Avocations: skiing, cooking, travel. Home and Office: John Armstrong & Co Inc 519 10th St Brooklyn NY 11215 Home Phone: 718-499-2086; Office Phone: 718-369-1360.

ARMSTRONG, L. C., artist; b. Humbolt, Tenn., Dec. 18, 1954; d. Arlie L. Clenney and Louray Armstrong; m. Philip Arthur Epstein, July 23, 1995; 1 child, Alexandra Armstrong Epstein. BFA, Art Ctr. Coll. of Design, Pasadena, 1982, San Francisco Art Inst., 1987. One-woman shows include Galerie Sophia Ungers Gallery, Cologne, Germany, 1991—92, Marsha Mateyka Gallery, Washington, 1993, 1997, 2000, 2003, John Post Lee Gallery, N.Y., 1993, Bravin Post Lee Gallery, 1994, Angles Gallery, Santa Monica, 1994, 1999, Phillippe Rizzo Gallery, Paris, 1994, USF Contemporary Mus., Tampa, 1995, Bravin Post Lee Gallery, N.Y., 1997, Hofstra Univ., Hempstead, N.Y., 1998, Galerie Huebner, Frankfurt, 1998, 2000, 2005, Postmasters Gallery, N.Y., 1999, 2001, Corcoran Gallery of Art, Washington, 1998, exhibited in group shows at Corcoran Gallery Art Biennial, 1991, Biennial Sydney, Australia, 1993, Van Abbemuseum, Eindhoven, 2000, Laing Art Gallery, Eng., 2002, Bklyn. Mus., 2004, Blaffer Gallery, 2005, Marlborough Chelsea Gallery, NY, 2005, Marlborough Gallery, 2007. Pollack Krasner grantee, 1991. Home: 33 Harrison St New York NY 10013 Office: 55 Washington St #307 Brooklyn NY 11201 Office Phone: 718-852-4670.

ARMSTRONG, LANCE, retired professional cyclist; b. Plano, Tex., Sept. 18, 1971; s. Linda Armstrong Kelly; m. Kristin Richard, May 8, 1998 (div. Dec. 2003); 3 children. Profl. cyclist Motorola Team, 1992—96, Cofidis, 1997, United States Postal Service Cycling Team, 1998—2004, Discovery Channel Pro Cycling Team, 2005. Host ESPY awards, 2006. Author (with Sally Jenkins): (book) It's Not About the Bike: My Journey Back to Life, 2001, Every Second Counts, 2003. Founder Lance Armstrong Foundation for Cancer, 1996—. World Road-Racing Champion, 1993; U.S. Profl. Champion, 1993; Triathlete Rookie of the Year, 1988; winner Tour DuPont, 1995, 1996; Bronze medal Olympics, Sydney, Australia, 2000; Sports Illustrated Man of the Yr., 2002; Male Athlete of the Yr., AP, 2002, 2003, 2004, 2005; overall winner, Tour de France, 1999-2005, Espy Award for Best Comeback Athlete, ESPN, 2000, Espy Award for Best Male Athlete, 2003, 2004, 2006, Centennial Medal for Disting. Pub. Svc., Am. Assn. Cancer Rsch., 2007; named one of The 10 Most Fascinating People of 2005, Barbara Walters Special, Jimmy V Honoree, V Found. for Cancer Rsch., 2007. Achievements include being a former swimmer and triathlete; mem. U.S. Olympic team, 1992, 1996, 2000; recovered from cancer to become only man in history to win 7 Tour de France championships; finished NYC Marathon in 2 hours 59 minutes and 36 seconds, Nov. 2006. Mailing: Lance Armstrong Found PO Box 161150 Austin TX 78716-1150*

ARMSTRONG, LLOYD, JR., academic administrator, physics professor; b. Austin, Tex., May 19, 1940; s. Lloyd and Beatrice (Jackson) A.; m. Judith Glantz, July 9, 1965; 1 son, Wade Matthew. BS in Physics, MIT, 1962; PhD in Physics, U. Calif., Berkeley, 1966. Postdoctoral physicist Lawrence Berkeley Lab., 1965-66, cons., 1976; sr. physicist Westinghouse Rsch. Labs., Pitts., 1967-68, cons., 1968-70; rsch. assoc. Johns Hopkins U., Balt., 1968-69, asst. prof. physics, 1969-73, assoc. prof., 1973-77, prof., 1977-93, chmn. dept. physics and astronomy, 1985-87, dean Sch. Arts and Scis., 1987-93; provost, sr. v.p. for acad. affairs U. So. Calif., LA, 1993—2005, prof. physics, 1993—, prof. edn., 2005—, Univ. prof., 2005—. Assoc. rsch. scientist Nat. Ctr. Sci. Rsch. (CNRS), Orsay, France, 1972—73; vis. fellow Joint Inst. Lab. Astrophysics, Boulder, Colo., 1978—79; program officer NSF, 1981—83, mem. adv. com. for physics, 1985—87, mem. visitors com. physics divsn., 1991; chmn. com. atomic and molecular scis. NAS/NRC, 1985—88, mem. bd. physics and astronomy, 1989—96; mem. adv. bd. Inst. for Theoretical Physics, Santa Barbara, Calif., 1992—96, chmn., 1994—95, Inst. Theoretical Atomic and Molecular Physics, Cambridge, Mass., 1994—97, Rochester Theory Ctr. for Optical Sci. and Engring., 1996—98. Author: Theory of Hyperfine

Structure of Free Atoms, 1971; contbr. articles to profl. jours. Bd. dirs. So. Calif. Econ. Partnership, 1994—2000, Calif. Coun. Sci. and Tech., 1994—2005. NSF grantee, 1972-90; Dept. Energy grantee, 1975-82. Fellow Am. Phys. Soc., Coun. on Fgn. Rels., Pacific Coun. on Internat. Policy (bd. dirs. 1996-05), Inside Track Adv. Bd. Office: U So Calif 3470 Trousdale Pkwy WPH 701 Los Angeles CA 90089-4037 Office Phone: 213-740-7218. Business E-Mail: lloydarm@usc.edu.

ARMSTRONG, NAK, jewelry designer; Co-owner, designer (with Anthony Camargo) Anthony Nak, 1998—. Work featured in Vogue, Harper's Bazaar, Town and Country, WWD, Glamour, InStyle, Elle, W, Marie Claire, People, Nat. Jeweler, Basel Mag., and Jewelry Connoisseur. Recipient Fashion Group Internat. Rising Star award, 2003, Town & Country Editors Choice award, 2004, Swarovski Perry Ellis award for accessory design, Council of Fashion Designers of Am., 2005, Couture Internat. Jeweler Retail Design award, Nat. Jeweler and Couture Internat. Jeweler mag., 2005. Office: Anthony Nak 800 Brazos Austin TX 78701

ARMSTRONG, NEAL EARL, academic administrator; b. Dallas, Jan. 29, 1941; m. Nancy L. Weinerth; 5 children. BA in Zoology, U. Tex., 1962, MA in Zoology, 1965, PhD in Engring., 1968. Lic. Tex. Research engr. Engring. Sci., Inc., 1967—71; asst. office mgr., cons. san. engring., 1968-70; mgr. Washington Research and Devel. Lab., 1970-71; assoc. prof. civil engring. U. Tex., Austin, 1971-79, prof., 1979—, assoc. chmn. dept., 1989-96, assoc. dean acad. affairs Coll. Engring., 1996—2003, vice provost faculty affairs, 2004—. Mem. ASCE, Water Environ. Fedn. (bd. dir., 1999-2003, Svc. award 1976, 84, 96, 2003), Am. Acad. Environ. Engrs. (diplomate, trustee), Internat. Water Assn., Estuarine Rsch. Fedn. (v.p. 1975-77), Am. Soc. Engring. Edn. (bd. trustees 2004-), ABET, Inc., Engring. Accreditation Commn. (commr. 2005-). Office: U Tex Provosts Office MAI 201 Austin TX 78712 Home Phone: 512-346-9558; Office Phone: 512-232-3305. Business E-Mail: neal_armstrong@mail.utexas.edu.

ARMSTRONG, NEIL A., former astronaut; b. Wapakoneta, Ohio, Aug. 5, 1930; s. Stephen A.; children: Eric, Mark. BS In Aero. Engring., Purdue U., 1955; MS in Aero. Engring., U. So. Calif. With Lewis Flight Propulsion Lab., NACA, 1955; then aero. research pilot for NACA (later NASA, High Speed Flight Sta.), Edwards, Calif.; astronaut Manned Spacecraft Center, NASA, Houston, 1962-70; command pilot Gemini 8; comdr. Apollo 11; dep. assoc. adminstr. for aeros. Office Advanced Research and Tech., Hdqrs. NASA, Washington, 1970-71; prof. aerospace engring. U. Cin., 1971-79; chmn. AIL Sys., Inc., 1989-2000, EDO Corp., 2000—02. Mem. Pres.'s Commn. on Space Shuttle, 1986, Nat. Commn. on Space, 1985-86. Served as naval aviator USN, 1949-52, Korea. Recipient numerous awards, including Octave Chanute award Inst. Aero. Scis., 1962, Presdl. Medal for Freedom, 1969, Exceptional Service medal NASA, Hubbard Gold medal Nat. Geog. Soc., 1970, Kitty Hawk Meml. award, 1969, Pere Marquette medal, 1969, Arthur S. Fleming award, 1970, Congl. Space Medal of Honor, Explorers Club medal. Fellow AIAA (hon., Astronautics award 1966), Internat. Astronautical Fedn. (hon.), Soc. Exptl. Test Pilots; mem. Nat. Acad. Engring. Achievements include being the first man to walk on the Moon, July 20, 1969. Office: Edo Corporation 60 E 42nd St New York NY 10165-0006

ARMSTRONG, NELSON WILLIAM, JR., gaming company executive; b. Port Huron, Mich., Mar. 5, 1941; s. Nelson William and Kathryn J. (Clarke) A.; m. Judith A. Roth, Sept. 5, 1964; children: Nelson William III, Tad John. BA, Mich. State U., 1964—64. Acct. Gen. Motors Corp., Warren, Mich., 1964—66; in acctg. and fin. Consumers Power Co., Jackson, Mich., 1966—73; dir acctg. Ramada Inns, Inc., Phoenix, 1973—77, asst. contr., 1977—79, v.p. audit svcs., 1979—82, corp. contr., 1982—85, v.p. adminstrn., 1985—, v.p. audit and adminstrv. svcs., 1985—, v.p. corp. contr., 1987—90; v.p. adminstrn., sec. Aztar Corp., Phoenix, 1990. Office: Aztar Corp 2390 E Camelback Rd Phoenix AZ 85016-3448

ARMSTRONG, PETER F., surgeon, pediatrician, orthopedist; b. Owen Sound, Canada, Dec. 13, 1946; s. Frederick Finlay and Joan Armstrong; m. Mary Catherine McFadden; children: Mark Pierson, Drew Frederick Glenn, Adam John, Mary Elizabeth. MD, U. We. Ont., London, Can., 1972. Cert. orthop. surgeon Royal Coll. Surgeons Can., 1981. Intern St. Joseph's Hosp., London, Ont., 1972—73; med. officer Can. Armed Forces, Lahr, Germany, 1973—76; resident U. Toronto, Ont., Canada, 1976—81; fellow Hosp. Sick Children, Toronto, 1981—82, pediatric orthop. surgeon, 1984—91; rsch. fellow U. Pa., Phila., 1982—84; chief staff Shriners Hosps. Children, Intermountain, Utah, 1991—2000, chief med. officer HQ, 2000—. Prof. orthop. surgery U. Utah, Salt Lake City, 1991—2000; affiliate prof. dept. surgery U. South Fla., Tampa, 2003—; mem. expert workgroup pediatric subspecialty capacity Maternal and Child Health Bur., Washington, 2003—; med. adv. bd. Discovery Health, 2006—; adv. bd. health sector MBA program U. We. Ont., London, 2006—; bd. dirs. US Bone and Joint Decade. V.p. Pregnancy Resource Ctr., Salt Lake City, 1992—99; mem. various coms. Ronald McDonald Ho., Salt Lake City, 1995—99. Fellow, Am. Can. Orthop. Assns., 1981, Hosp. Sick Children, 1981—84; Irving Heward Cameron scholarship, U. Toronto, 1982—83. Fellow: ACS, Royal Coll. Surgeons Can., Am. Acad. Pediat.; mem.: Twentieth Century Orthop. Assn., Can. Orthop. Assn., Assn. Children's Prosthetics and Orthotics Clinics, Am. Telemedicine Assn. (bd. mem. 1999—2003), Am. Orthop. Assn., Am. Coll. Physician Execs., Am. Coll. Healthcare Execs., Am. Burn Assn., Pediatric Orthopaedic Soc. N.Am. (presdl. guest lectr. 2003), Internat. Pediatric Orthop. Think Tank, Christian Med. Dental Assn., Focus on Family Physician's Resource Coun. Office: Shriners Hosps Children 2900 Rocky Point Dr Tampa FL 33607 Office Phone: 813-281-8160. Office Fax: 813-281-8113. Business E-Mail: parmstrong@shrinenet.org.

ARMSTRONG, RANDY LEE, communications educator; b. Sweetwater, Tex., June 19, 1948; s. Alvin Lee and Essie Lee Armstrong; m. Jody Anne Armstrong, June 12, 1987; 1 child, Eric Lee. BA, Tex. Tech. U., Lubbock, Tex., 1971, MA, 1975, EdD, 1997. Prof. Hardin-Simmons U., Abilene, Tex., 1976—, prof. comm., assoc. dean Cynthia Ann Parker Coll. Liberal Arts, 2004—. Co-dir. Four-O Pub., 1988—. Mem.: Am. Journalism Historians Assn., Pub. Rels. Soc. Am., Book Club Tex. Presbyterian. Avocations: history, coin collecting/numismatics, stamp collecting/philately, films, antiques. Home: 1402 Sylvan Dr Abilene TX 79698 Office: Hardin-Simmons Univ 2200 Hickory St Box 16022 HSU Sta Abilene TX 79698 Office Phone: 325-670-1436. Business E-Mail: rarmstrg@hsutx.edu.

ARMSTRONG, RICHARD STOLL, minister, educator, poet; b. Balt., Mar. 29, 1924; s. Herbert Eustace and Elsie Davis (Stoll) A.; m. Margaret Childs, Jan. 31, 1948; children: Ellen, Richard, Andrew, William, Elsie. BA, Princeton U., 1947; MDiv, Princeton Theol. Sem., 1958; DMin, Christian Theol. Sem.-Indpls., 1978; doctoral, Temple U., 1962-68. Ordained to ministry Presbyn. Ch., 1958. Pastor Oak Lane Presbyn. Ch., Phila., 1958-68; dir. devel. Princeton Theol. Sem., NJ, 1968—71, v.p. devel., 1971—74, prof. ministry and evangelism NJ, 1980—90, prof. emeritus NJ, 1990—; pastor 2d Presbyn. Ch., Indpls., 1974-80. Life trustee Fellowship Christian Athletes, Inc., Kansas City, Mo., 1979—; mem. ch. mins. adv. bd. Christian Theol. Sem., 1975-80; bd. dirs. Nat. Conf. Christians and Jews, Ind., 1975-80, Ind. Inter-Religious Commn. on Human Equality, 1975-80. Author: The Oak Lane Story, 1971, Service Evangelism, 1979, The Pastor as Evangelist, 1984, The Pastor-Evangelist in Worship, 1986, Faithful Witnesses, 1987, The Pastor-Evangelist in the Parish, 1990, Enough, Already!, 1993, Now, That's A Miracle!, 1996, Faithful Witnesses MiniCourse, 1997, If I Do Say So Myself, 1997, Are you Really Free?, 2002, Help! I'm a Pastor, 2005, Captured Memories, 2006; contbg. composer Carmina Princetonia, 1968; contbg. author: Westminster Dictionary of Christian Theology, 1983, The New Dictionary of Pastoral Studies, 2002 Bd. dirs. Indpls. Symphony Orch., 1978-80; trustee Am. Boychoir Sch., 1980—; trustee McDonogh Sch., Md., 1980-90; mem. adv. com., ctr. for contextual ministry Pretoria U., South Africa; mem. Nat. Coun. Presbyn. Men, 1995-98; Lt. (j.g.) USN, 1942-46. Recipient Disting. Svc. award Fellowship of Christian Athletes, 1965, Branch Rickey Meml. award, 1974, Alumni Svc. award Princeton Theol. Sem., 1974, Outstanding Svc. award Nat. Conf. Christians and Jews, 1980, Robert L. Peters award Princeton U., 1990; named Man of Week, Princeton Town Topics, 1957, 68. Mem. Presbytery of New Brunswick (v.p.), Acad. for Evangelism Theol. Edn. (pres. 1989-91, Jour. editor 1991-97, Charles Grandison Finney award 1997), Presbyn. Writers' Guild, Gallup Internat. Inst. (fellow 1997-2002), Phila. A's Hist. Soc. Presbyterian. Home: 2118 Windrow Dr Princeton NJ 08540 Office: Princeton Theol Sem PO Box 821 Princeton NJ 08542-0803 Personal E-mail: mail@rsarmstrong.net. Business E-Mail: richard.armstrong@ptsem.edu.

ARMSTRONG, RICHARD WILLIAM, bank executive, management consultant; b. Phila., June 18, 1932; s. Richard Mervyn and Elvina (Burns) A.; m. Barbara Robbins, Sept. 5, 1959; children: Richard W. Jr., James M. AB cum laude, Harvard U., 1954; MA, Johns Hopkins U., 1959. Disarmament specialist AEC, Washington, 1960—62; fin. mgr. NASA and OEO, Washington, 1962—67; Nat. Inst. Pub. Affairs fellow Princeton U., 1967—68; dep. mgr. Head Start, Washington, 1969-70; corp. budget dir. Chase Manhattan Bank, NYC, 1970-78, fin. and adminstrv. officer real estate fin. bus., 1978-84, fin. and adminstrv. officer comml. sector, 1984-89, fin. and adminstrv. officer real estate fin. sector, 1989-91; mgmt. cons. NYC, 1992. Prin. Coun. for Excellence in Govt., 1992—. Audit com. Madison Presbyn. Ch., NJ, 1981; trustee, fin. officer Bethesda Congl. Ch., Md., 1965-67; active NJ Harvard Schs. and Scholarship Com., 1983-88. Lt. USN, 1954-57 Avocations: genealogy, sailing, swimming, travel. Home and Office: 10 Pomeroy Rd Madison NJ 07940-2619

ARMSTRONG, ROBERT BEALL, physiologist, educator; b. Hastings, Nebr., Nov. 13, 1940; s. Edwin Ollis and Elena (Beall) A.; m. Ingrid Elizabeth Vaiciulenas, Apr. 9, 1966; children: Edwin John, Andrew Niel, Sarah Elizabeth. BA, Hastings Coll., 1962; MS, Wash. State U., 1970, PhD, 1973. Asst. prof. biology Boston U., 1973—78; assoc. prof. physiology Oral Roberts U., Tulsa, Okla., 1978—81, prof. physiology, 1981—85; prof. U. Ga., Athens, 1985—90, rsch. prof., 1990—92; Omar Smith prof. health and kinesiology Tex. A&M U., College Station, 1992—, Omar Smith chair, 1995—, disting. prof., 1995—, dept. head, 1992—97, 2000—02. Assoc. zoology Harvard U., Cambridge, Mass., 1977-87; external examiner Nat. U. Singapore, 1984-85; rsch. com. Am. Heart Assn., Athens, 1987-89. Assoc. editor Med. Sci. Sports Exercise, Indpls., 1985-87; contbr. articles to Jour. Applied Physiology, Am. Jour. Physiology. NSF fellow, 1970-73; grantee NIH, 1975-97, Am. Heart Assn., 1981-89, NASA, 1997-2000. Fellow Am. Coll. Sports Medicine (trustee 1986-88); mem. Am. Physiol. Soc. Office: Tex A & M U Dept Health & Kinesiology College Station TX 77843-0001 Home Phone: 979-764-6449; Office Phone: 979-862-2912. Business E-Mail: rb-armstrong@hlkn.tamu.edu.

ARMSTRONG, ROBIN LOUIS, physics professor, physicist; b. Galt, Ont., Can., May 14, 1935; s. Robert Dockstader and Beatrice Jenny (Grill) S.; m. Karen Elisabeth Feilberg Hansen, July 8, 1960; children: Keir Grill, Christopher Drew. BA, U. Toronto, Ont., 1958, MsC, 1959, PhD, 1961; DSc (hon.), U. NB, Can., 2001. Rutherford Meml. fellow Oxford U., England, 1961-62; mem. faculty U. Toronto, 1962, prof. physics, 1971-90, adj. prof. physics, 1990-98, prof. emeritus, 1998—, chmn. dept., 1974-82, dean Faculty of Arts and Sci., 1982-90; pres. U. N.B., Fredericton, St. John, 1990-96, prof. physics, 1990-96, rsch. prof. physics, 1996-2001, Wilfrid Laurier U. spl. advisor to the pres., 1997-2000. Pres. Can. Inst. Neutron Scattering, 1986-89; founding dir. Can. Inst. Advanced Rsch., 1981-82, mem. rsch. coun., 1982-2000; mem. coun. Nat. Sci. and Engring. Rsch. Coun., 1991-97 mem. exec., 1992-97, v.p., 1994-97; mem. Atomic Energy Can. Ltd. R&D Adv. Com., 1999—, vice chair, 2004-05, chair 2006-; chair bd. dirs. Can. Arthritis Network, 2003-; exec. dir. Coll. U. Consortium Coun., 2006-. Co-author: Mechanics, Waves and Thermal Physics, 1970, Electromagnetic Interaction, 1973; contbr. articles to profl. jours. Named to Preston HS Hall of Fame, Ont., Can., 2007; recipient Commemorative medal for 125th Anniversary of Can. Confedn., 1992, Designated Visitante Distinguido, U. Cordoba, Argentina, 1987. Fellow Royal Soc. Can. (Rutherford Meml. fellow 1961); mem. Can. Assn. Physicists (v.p. 1989-90, pres. 1990-91, Herzberg medal 1973, medal for achievement 1990), Can. Assn. Physics, Internat. Soc. Magnetic Resonance Medicine. Home: 383 Ellis Pk Rd Ste 803 Toronto M6S 5B2 Canada Business E-Mail: r.armstrong@utoronto.ca.

ARMSTRONG, RODNEY, librarian; b. Atlanta, Mar. 5, 1923; s. Harold Rodney and Mary Blair (Armstrong) A.; m. Katharine Price Cortesi, June 14, 1969; children: Louise Spencer Barton, Robert Knowlton. BA, Williams Coll., 1948; MS, Columbia U., 1950; HHD (hon.), U. Liberia, 2000. Libr. Phillips Exeter Acad., NH, 1950—73; dir., libr. Boston Athenaeum, 1973—97, dir., libr. emeritus, 1997—. N.E. assoc. Sotheby's. Pres. Trustees Edn. Liberia, 1974—, A Republican Instn. in the Town of Boston, 1819, 2006—07. Decorated Purple Heart; Benjamin Franklin fellow Royal Soc. Arts, 1974 Fellow Am. Acad. Arts Scis., Soc. Antiquaries, Pilgrim Soc. (trustee Pilgrim Hall Mus.); mem. ALA (life), NH Libr. Assn. (past officer, bd. dirs.), Am. Antiquarian Soc., Colonial Soc. Mass., Mass. Hist. Soc., Manuscript Soc. (bd. dirs., past pres.), New Eng. Hist. Geneal. Soc. (pres. 1977-82), Century Assn. (NYC), Grolier Club (NYC), Odd Volumes Club (pres. 1979-83). Home: Penthouse F 65 E India Row Boston MA 02110-3311 Office: Sothebys 67 1/2 Chestnut St Boston MA 02108-1121 Office Phone: 617-367-6323.

ARMSTRONG, ROGER L., lawyer; b. Mason City, Iowa, July 19, 1957; s. Curtis F. and Eva M. Armstrong; m. Mary E. Wilkinson; children: Jessica K., Brett L. BA, U. Calif., La Jolla, 1975—79; JD, Loyola U., LA, 1992—95. Bar: Calif. 1995, Utah 2005. V.p. ICPR Pub. Rels., LA, 1983—85; exec. dir. DeLaurentiis Entertainment Grp., Beverly Hills, Calif., 1986—87; v.p. Universal Pictures, Universal City, Calif., 1987—91, TriStar Pictures, Culver City, Calif., 1991—92; assoc. Baker & Hostetler, LA, 1995—97; ptnr. Manatt, Phelps & Phillips, LLP, LA, 1997—2005; atty. Roger L. Armstrong, Esq., P.C., Park City, Utah, 2006—. Bd. govs. Loyola Law Sch., LA, 1998—2002; co-chair entertainment practice grp. Manatt, Phelps & Phillips, LLP, LA, 2001—04; prof. UCLA Ext., LA, 2004—06. Editor-in-chief Loyola Law Rev., LA, 1994—95. Named So. Calif. Super Lawyer, LA Mag., 2004—06. Mem.: Acad. Motion Picture Arts & Scis. (life), Alpha Sigma Nu (life). Avocations: snow skiing, guitar, fly fishing, flying. Home and Office: Roger L Armstrong Esq PC 2574 Aspen Springs Dr Park City UT 84060 Home Phone: 435-649-9679. Business E-Mail: roger@rogerlarmstrong.com.

ARMSTRONG, RONALD E., corporate financial executive; Ops. controller Paccar Inc., Bellevue, Wash., 1995—2002, v.p., controller, 2002—. Office: Paccar Inc 777 106th Ave NE Bellevue WA 98004

ARMSTRONG, SCOTT ALLEN, oncologist; b. Lawton, Okla., Nov. 13, 1966; s. Howard Armstrong and Armstrong Janet. MD, U. Tex. Southwestern, Dallas, 1996; PhD, U. Tex. Soutwestern, Dallas. Diplomate pediatric oncology Mass. Pedatric oncologist Children's Hosp., Dana Farber Cancer Inst., Boston, 2001—; asst. prof. pediat. Harvard Med. Sch., Boston, 2003—07. Recipient Claire W. and Richard P. Morse Rsch. award, Dana Farber Cancer Inst., 2002, Damon Runyon-Eli Lilly Clin. Investigator award, Damon Runyon Cancer Rsch. Found., 2003, Wilson S. Stone award, MD Anderson Cancer Ctr., 2006. Achievements include research in MLL translocations specify a distinct gene expression profile, distinguishing a unique leukemia. Nature Genetics 2002; inhibition of FLT3 in MLL: validation of a therapeutic target identified by gene expression based classification. Cancer Cell; transformation from committed progenitor to leukaemia stem cell initiated by MLL—AF9. Nature. 2006; gene expression-based chemical genomics identifies rapamycin as a modulator of MCL1 and glucocorticoid resistance. Cancer Cell. Office: Children's Hosp 300 Longwood Ave Boston MA 02115 Office Phone: 617-919-2508.

ARMSTRONG, SONYA M., mathematics professor, researcher; children: Janelle M., Ricardo. BA in Math., CUNY, 1976; MS in Numerical Sci., Johns Hopkins U., 1980; MA in Stats., U. Rochester, 1993, PhD, 1997. Secondary math tchr. Balt. City Pub. Sch., 1976—81; aerospace engr. Westinghouse, Balti., 1981—85; assoc. prof. W.Va. State U., Institute, 1999—. Sr. warden Episcopal Ch., Charleston, W.Va., 2003—05. Named to Hall of Fame, Compeer Program, Rochester, 1995; recipient Excellence in Tchg. award, Clark Atlant U., 2004; fellow, NASA, 2003. Mem.: ACLU (v.p. mem. 2000), Nat. Coun. Tchrs. Math., Gen. Fedn. Women's Club (grants writer), Alpha Kappa Mu (faculty advisor 2002), Zeta Phi Beta (state treas. 2001). D-Conservative. Episcopalian. Avocations: travel, sewing, reading. Home Phone: 304-760-2180; Office Phone: 304-766-3390. Office Fax: 304-766-4272. Personal E-mail: calcgrmn@earthlink.net. E-mail: armstrso@wvstateu.edu.

ARMSTRONG, THEODORE MORELOCK, corporate financial executive; b. St. Louis, July 22, 1939; s. Theodore Roosevelt and Vassar Fambrough (Morelock) A.; m. Carol Mercer Robert, Sept. 7, 1963 (div. 2006); children: Evelyn Anne, Robert Theodore; m. Kathryn Sibbald, Apr. 27, 2007. BA, Yale U., New Haven, Conn., 1961; LLB, Duke U., Durham, NC, 1964. Bar: Mo. 1964. With Miss. River Transmission Corp. and affiliated cos., 1964-85; corp. sec. Mo. Pacific Corp., 1971-75, River Cement Co., 1968-75; asst. v.p. Miss. River Transmission Corp., 1974-75, v.p. gas supply, 1975-79, exec. v.p., 1979-83, pres., chief exec. officer, 1983-85; exec. v.p. Natural Gas Pipeline of Am., 1985; sr. v.p. fin. and adminstrn., CFO Angelica Corp., St. Louis, 1986—2004; pvt. practice fin. cons. St. Louis, 2004—. Bd. dirs. UMB Fin. Corp., Custom Cuts, Inc., Cabela's, Inc., World's Foremost Bank. Bd. dirs., past pres. Boys and Girls Town Mo.; past pres. Tenn. Soc. St. Louis; mem. St. Louis County Boundary Commn.; former alderman, former mem. bd. adjustment City of Frontenac; bd. dirs., pres. Ctrl. Inst. Deaf; mem. fin. com. City of Creve Coeur. Mem. Mo. Bar Assn., Bellerive Country Club (treas., bd. dirs.), Saint Louis Club (past pres. bd. dirs.), Yale Club (St. Louis, NYC), Phi Alpha Delta. Republican. Presbyterian. Office: 7730 Carondelet Ste 103 Saint Louis MO 63105 Home: 424 Twin Creek Rd Saint Louis MO 63141 Office Phone: 314-862-4224. Personal E-mail: tmarmstrong@sbcglobal.net.

ARMSTRONG, THOMAS NEWTON, III, landscape artist; b. Portsmouth, Va., July 30, 1932; s. Thomas Newton, Jr. and Mary Saunders (Tabb) A.; m. Virginia Whitney Brewster, May 18, 1963; children: Thomas Newton IV, Whitney, Eliot, Amory. Attended, Cornell U., 1950-54, Art Students League, summer 1953, Inst. Fine Arts, NYU, 1965-67. Pers. coord., asst. to chmn. bd. Stone & Webster, Inc., NYC, 1957-65; curator, assoc. dir. Colonial Williamsburg, Abby Aldrich Rockefeller Folk Art Collection, Williamsburg, Va., 1967-71; dir. Pa. Acad. Fine Arts, Phila., 1971-73, Whitney Mus. Am. Art, 1974-90, dir. emeritus, 1990—; dir. Andy Warhol Mus., Pitts., 1993-95. Chmn. The Garden Conservancy; mem. scholars selection com. Henry Luce Found., Inc.; cons. Sotheby's. Adv. com. Mt. Vernon; trustee Nat. Bldg. Mus.; garden com. Winterthur; trustee NY Sch. Interior Design.

ARMSTRONG, TIM, information technology executive; Grad., Conn. Coll. With IDG; dir. integrated sales & mktg. Starwave's and Disney's ABC/ESPN Internet Ventures; v.p. sales and strategic partnerships Snowball.com; v.p. advt. sales Google Inc., Mountain View, Calif., 2001, now pres. advt. and commerce N.Am. v.p. Bd. dirs. Interactive Advt. Bur., Associated Content Inc., KnowledgeStorm Inc., 2004—. Bd. trustees Conn. Coll., 2006—. Named one of top 100 People to Know, Media Mag.; recipient Media Maven Award, Advertising Age, 2004. Office: Google Inc 1600 Amphitheatre Pkwy Mountain View CA 94043 Office Phone: 650-253-0000. Office Fax: 650-253-0001.*

ARMSTRONG, WILLIAM TUCKER, III, lawyer; b. Houston, Nov. 13, 1947; s. William Tucker Jr. and Jess (Nettles) A.; m. Nancy Bayliss Armstrong, Feb. 18, 1978; children: Will, Anne, Daniel. BA, Am. U., 1969; JD with honors, U. Tex., 1972. Bar: Tex. 1972, U.S. Ct. Appeals (5th cir.) 1972, U.S. Dist. Ct. (so. & we. dists.) Tex. 1978, U.S. Ct. Appeals (11th cir.) 1982, U.S. Ct. Appeals (D.C. cir.) 1983. Staff counsel for inmates Tex. Dept. Corrections, Huntsville, 1972-73; assoc. Foster, Lewis, Langley, Gardner & Banack, San Antonio, 1973-76, shareholder, 1976-96, Langley & Banack, 1996—. Contbr. articles to profl. pubs. Dir. South Tex. Leukemia Soc., 1989-92; pres. Tex. Coun. Sch. Attys., 2003-04. Mem. Tex. State Bar Assn. (mem. coun. of sch. law sect., past officer), Tex. Coun. Sch. Attys. (dir. 1999-2001, vice chmn. 2002-2003, chmn. 2003-2004), San Antonio Longhorn Club (pres. 1993-94), Tex. Longhorn Club (pres. 1996-97), San Antonio Tex. Exes (pres. 1993-94), Oak Hills Country Club (dir. 1998-2001). Methodist. Avocation: golf. Office: Langley & Banack Inc 745 E Mulberry Ave Ste 900 San Antonio TX 78212-3141 Home Phone: 210-828-3773.

ARMSTRONG-LAW, MARGARET, school administrator; b. Fargo, ND, Jan. 21, 1931; d. Theron L. and Besse Ross Armstrong; m. Robert Harold Law, Sept. 6, 1952 (div. Oct. 1964); children: William Robert, Anne Elizabeth Law Buckingham, Amy Catherine Law Burman. BS in English, N.D. State U., 1952, MS Secondary Sch. Adminstrn., 1974; postgrad., UCLA, Moorhead State U., 1984, Mich. State U., 1985; Cert., Harvard Prin.'s Sch., London, 1986. Cert. tchr., ednl. adminstr. Tchr. Agassiz Jr. High, 1963—66, Ben Franklin Jr. High, 1969—71, North HS, Fargo, ND, 1971—74, asst. prin., 1974—78; secondary head Taipei Am. Sch., Taiwan, 1978-87, Vienna Internat. Sch., Austria, 1987-90; dir. Internat. Sch. Amsterdam, The Netherlands, 1990-97; internat. ednl. cons., 1998—. Prof. devel. com. European Coun. Internat. Schs., London, chmn. bd., 1994-96; mem. No. European Coun. Internat. Schs., head coun., 1990-97; spkr. in field. Author: (booklet, film) Future: The Quality of Life, 1975; contbr. articles to profl. jours. Adv. bd. Coll. Arts, Humanities and Social Scis., N.D. State U., 1998—2004; pres. Fargo-Moorhead Opera Bd., 1999—2001; chmn. bd. Christian edn. Plymouth Congl. Ch., Fargo, 1998—99, coun. mem., 1988—99, vice chair women's fellowship bd., 1999; chair pres. adv. bd. Minn. State U., Moorhead, 2003; bd. dirs. Trollwood Performing Arts Sch., 2002. Recipient Bd. Dirs. award for Extraordinary Svcs. European Coun. Internat. Schs., Promotion of Internat. Edn. award, 1996; named hon. mem. for disting. svcs., European Coun. Internat. Schs., 1997; scholarship named in her honor by bd. govs. Internat. Sch. Amsterdam, 1997—. Fellow: ASCD; mem.: UNICEF, LWV, AAUW, UN Assn. USA, De Amsterdamschekring Club, World Peace Com. (The Hague, Netherlands), World Future Soc., Am. C. of C., Am. Women's Club (Amsterdam), Am. Assn. Sch. Adminstrs., Assn. Advancement Internat. Edn., Rotary (bd. dirs. 1993—94, program chair 1993—94, v.p. 1994—96, pres. 1995—96, Amsterdam), Phi Kappa Phi. Democrat. Congregationalist. Avocations: chinese brush painting, music, reading, tennis, interior decorating.

ARNALL, ROLAND E., ambassador; b. Paris, 1939; m. Dawn Arnall. Founder, chmn. bd. Ameriquest Capital Corp., 1979—2006; US amb. to the Netherlands US Dept. State, The Hague, 2006—. Former mem. Calif. Edn.

Task Force com.; former trustee Calif. State Univ. sys. Founding co-chmn., trustee Simon Wiesenthal Ctr., Mus. Tolerance. Named one of Forbes' Richest Americans, 2006. Office: US Dept State 5770 The Hague Pl Washington DC 20521

ARNAVUT, ZIYA, educator; b. Nicosia, Nicosia, Cyprus, Jan. 31, 1960; s. Ahmet and Huriye Arnavut; m. Meral Abdulazizoglu, Aug. 22, 1994; children: Eliz Huri, Selin. PhD, U. Nebr., Lincoln, 1995. Rsch. analysist, lab. mgr. U. Nebr., Omaha, 1995—97; prof. SUNY, Fredonia, 1997—2007. Liberal. Achievements include development of BWIC coder. Avocation: travel. Office: SUNY 227 Fenton Hall Fredonia NY 14063 Office Phone: 716-673-3864. Office Fax: 716-673-3804. Business E-Mail: arnavut@fredonia.edu.

ARNDT, CHARLES RICHARD, educational consultant; b. Marion, Ohio, Dec. 20, 1942; s. Charles Henry and Ruth Katheryn (Oehler) A.; m. Loretta Ann Keefe, Dec. 21, 1968; children: Cynthia Ruth, Charles Richard II, Camille Rebecca. BA in Edn.; Capital U., Columbus, Ohio, 1964; MS in Edn., St. Francis Coll., Ft. Wayne, Ind., 1972; EdS, Bowling Green State U., Ohio, 1975, PhD, 1981. Tchr. Riverdale Local Sch. Dist., Forest, Ohio, 1964-66, Ridgewood Local Sch. Dist., West Lafayette, Ohio, 1966-67, Marion (Ohio) City Sch. Dist., 1967-72; guidance counselor River Valley Local Sch. Dist., Marion, 1972-75; asst. prin. high sch. Strongsville (Ohio) City Sch. Dist., 1975-76; prin. Marion Cath. High Sch., 1976-78; intern instr. Bowling Green State U. Coll. Edn., 1978-81; adminstrv. asst. River Valley Local Sch. Dist., Marion, 1981--82; supt. schs. Gibsonville (Ohio) Exempted Village Sch. Dist., 1982-85, Pleasant Local Sch. Dist., Marion, 1985—95; dir. tech. prep. Marion Tech. Coll., 1995—98; dir. articulation and transfer Ohio Bd. Regents, 1998—2005; dean undergrad. recruitment and coll. partnership Cleve. State U., 2005—06. Co-author: Ohio Schools: Urban, Suburban, Rural, 1978. Mem. Marion City Coun., 1986-2000; precinct committeeman Marion County Rep. Com., 1987-89; pres. Marion Area United Way, 1993-98. Grantee Bowling Green State U., 1978-80. Mem. Buckeye Assn. Sch. Adminstrs., Rotary, Elks. Roman Catholic. Avocation: golf. Home: 7278 Morning Star Trl Northfield OH 44067-3502

ARNDT, DIANNE JOY, artist, photographer; b. Springfield, Mass., Dec. 20, 1939; d. Samuel Vincent and Carrie Lillian Annino; m. Joseph Vincent Bower, June 16, 1979 (dec.); 1 child by previous marriage, Christabelle Nita Arndt. Student, Art Students League, 1965-71; BFA with honors in Painting, Pratt Inst., 1974; postgrad., Columbia U., 1979-86; MFA, Hunter Coll., 1981. Photojournalist. Photo cons. to mags. and bus., N.Y.C., 1978—; artist, filmmaker, 1962—. One-woman shows include Cinama One, Springfield, Mass., 1966, Panoras Gallery, NY, 1969, 70, Unicorn Gallery, NY, 1975, Women's Interart Ctr., NY, 1976, Bathurst Arms, Cirenchester, Eng., 1987, Modernage, N.Y., 1992, 96, 2000, 01, 02, others; group shows include Islip Art Mus., L.I., N.Y., 1999, White Walls Conceptual Art Jour., Chgo., 2000, St. Francis Coll., Bklyn., 2001, The Gallery, Stamford, NY, 2003, Susquehanna Mus., Harrisburg, Pa., 2004, Pfizer, Inc., NY, 2005, Durst Orgn., NY, 2005, St. Vincent's Hosp., NY, 2006, Gallery Aferro, Newark, 2006, numerous others; exhbns. include Am. Cultural Ctr., U.S., New Delhi and Bombay, 1987, Bathurst Arms Installation, Eng., 1987, Camden Arts, London, 1987, Nat. Inst. Archtl. Edn., 1988, Phillip Morris Traveling Photo Exhibit, 1988, Centennial Libr. Gallery, Isca Graphics, Edmonton, Alta., Can., 1988, Nat. Inst. Archtl. Edn., 1988, N.Y. Sci. & Tech. Gallery, N.Y., USSR, 1989, Mercer Gallery, 1989, Circolo Pickwick, Alessandria, Italy, 1989, Balt. Mus. Industry, 1992, Aaron Davis Hall, 1992, N.Y. City Coll., Alijira Gallery, Newark, 1994, UN, 1994, Phila. Art Alliance, Phila., 1995, Columbia U., 1995, Severoceske Mus., Liberec, Bohemia, 1996, Naproskovo Mus., Prague, 1996, Modern Age, N.Y.C., 1996, Lever House, N.Y.C., 1996, St. Marks/Bowery, N.Y.C., 1997, Eighth Floor Gallery, N.Y.C., 1997, Velan Gallery, Torino, Italy, 1998, Islip Art Mus., 1998, 99, Bound for Glory, N.Y., 1999-2000, In Frame, Chgo., 2000, St. Francis Coll., 2001; represented in permanent collections Archives Can. Postal Mus., Ottawa, Jean Brown Archives, Mass., Franklin Furnace, N.Y., Nat. Inst. Design and Lalit Kala Akademi, Ne WDelhi, Printed Masser, N.Y., Tate Gallery, London; films include Mullenium, N.Y., 1985, A.I.R., N.Y., 1978, Women's Interart Ctr., N.Y., 1976, Artists Space, N.Y., 1975. Mem. Am. Soc. Media Photographers (bd. dirs.), Am. Soc. Picture Profls., Art and Sci. Collaborations, Inc., Artists Talk on Art (bd. dirs.), Profl. Women Photographers. E-mail: arndtpix@rcn.com.

ARNDT, GEORGE ARTHUR, anesthesiologist, consultant; b. Milw., Sept. 4, 1956; s. Harold and Otilla Arndt; children: Lauren Arlene Welton-Arndt, Anna Rae Welton-Arndt. MD, U. Wis., Madison, 1984. Diplomate Am. Bd. Anesthesilogy, 1987. Prof. anesthesiology U. Wis., Madison, 1989—. Inventor in field. Capt. USAR, 1982—92. Office: U Wis 600 Highland Ave Madison WI 53719 Office Phone: 608-263-8100. Office Fax: 608-263-0575.

ARNDT, JANET S., former state legislator, educator; b. Providence, May 23, 1947; m. Kenneth G. Arndt; 4 children. AB, Gordon Coll., 1968; MEd, Boston U., 1970; student, U. Mass., 1998—, CAGS, 2002; EdD, U. Mass. Amherst, 2003; cert., Advanced Grad. Study. Specialist, counselor Early Childhood, 1987—2005; N.H. state rep. Dist. 27, Rockingham, 1992—2002; mem. children, youth and juvenile justice com. N.H. Ho. of Reps., mem. constn. and statutory rev. com., chmn. election law com., 1997—2002; prin. Perley Sch., Georgetown, Mass., 2005—. Asst. prof. Gordon Coll., 1995, N.H. Tech. Coll., 1997—2001, adj. prof., 2001—, chair early childhood, elem. and spl. edn. dept., 2002—. Mem. Friends of the Libr. of Windham, chmn., 1991-92; active Girl Scouts Am., publicity chairperson; scholarship chmn. Nat. Order of Women Legislators; exec. bd. Rockingham County; events chairperson Nesmith Libr.; mem. edn. task force ALEC, mem. ch. early childhood task force; mem. nat. coun. of state legislators Coun. of State Govt.; chair Rockingham County Register of Deeds, 1996-02; mem. early childhood mental health coun., 2003-; mem. bd. N.H. Kids Coll., 2003. Recipient M. Carter award for Outstanding Libr. Svc., 1995; named Leader of Yr. Windham Girl Scouts, 1995. Mem. N.H. Order Women Legislators, Gordon Coll. Alumni Coun. Address: 8 Crestwood Rd Windham NH 03087-1429 Office Phone: 978-867-4814. Business E-Mail: jarndt@gordon.edu.

ARNDT, LAURA DENISE LYONS BODEEN, mathematics educator; b. Memphis, Tenn., Feb. 13, 1952; d. Walter Guy and Laura Deming Lyons; m. Michael Charles Bodeen (div.); children: Matthew Wells Bodeen, Jeffrey Guy Bodeen, William Joseph Bodeen; m. J.T. Arndt, May 31, 2003. BS magna cum laude, Christian Bros. Univ., Memphis, Tenn., 1993. Cert. tchr. 7-12 math., computer sci. Tchr. Fayette County Sch., Somerville, Tenn., 1993—2005. Memphis Symphony advocate Memphis Symphony League, Memphis, 2003—; del. People to People Del. to China, 1999, 2006. Mem.: Nat. Edn. Assn., Tenn. Edn. Assn., Alpha Chi. Avocation: video games.

ARNDT, MATTHEW, scriptwriter; Ed. in Film, NYU. Freelance script reader; staff mem. Pixar Animation Studios. Screenwriter (films) Little Miss Sunshine, 2006 (New Generation award, LA Film Critic Assn., 2006).*

ARNDT, MICHAEL, scriptwriter; Screenwriter (films) Little Miss Sunshine, 2006 (Best Original Screenplay, Kans. City Film Critics Awards, 2006, Best Original Screenplay award, Phoenix Film Critics Cir., 2006, Best Original Screenplay award, Southeastern Film Critics Cir., 2006, Best Screenplay award, NY Film Critics Soc., 2006, Best Original Screenplay award, Washington DC Film Critics Assn., 2006, New Generation award, LA Film Critics Assn., 2006, Best Screenplay award, LA Film Critics Assn., 2006, Original Screenplay award, Brit. Acad. Film and TV Arts, 2007, Original Screenplay, Writers Guild Am., 2007, Best Original Screenplay, Acad. award, 2007).*

ARNDT, RICHARD TALLMADGE, writer, consultant, cultural administrator; b. Phila., Oct. 28, 1928; s. Howard Wilcox Arndt and Eleanor (Shaw) Branigan; m. Edith Robichon (div. 1964); children: Skyler Arndt-Briggs, Matthew Wilcox; m. Dorothy Serlin (div. 1973); children: Daniel Serlin, Sarah L. Piazza; m. Lois W. Roth (dec. 1986). AB, Princeton U., 1949, postgrad., 1971—72; PhD, Columbia U., 1959. Instr., asst. prof. French Columbia U., NYC, 1953-61; cultural attaché U.S. embassies, Beirut, 1961-63, Colombo, 1963-66, Tehran, 1966-71, Rome, 1974-78, Paris, 1978-80; dir. policy and plans Bur. Ednl. and Cultural Affairs, U.S. Info. Agy., 1980-83; cultural coord. Near East/So. Asia, USIA, Washington, 1983-85; with Dept. State, Washington, dep. dir. L.Am., dir. youth and student programs Bur. Ednl. and Cultural Affairs, 1972-74. Adj. prof. George Washington U., 1993—95, 2007—; diplomat-in-residence, dir. mid-career study dept. govt, U. Va., Charlottesville, 1986—89; faculty div. psychopolitics Ctr. Mind and Human Interaction, U. Va., 1997—. Author: The First Resort of Kings: American Cultural Diplomacy in the 20th Century, 2005, Potomac, 2005; prin. editor: The Fulbright Difference, 1948-92, Transaction, 1993; contbr. articles to profl. jours. Pres. Internat. Soc. for Edn. Cultural and Sc. Interchange, 1986—89; mem. Coun. Internat. Programs, 1986—95, v.p., 1991—95, adv. coun., 2002—; adv. bd. Toda inst., Hawaii, 1997—; chmn. US Com. Preservation Ancient Tyre, 1999—; mem. Am. for UNESCO, 1992—, pres., 2002—06, co-chair adv. coun., 2006—; bd. Nat. Peace Found., chmn., 1992—95, chmn. adv. bd., 1995—2002; adv. bd. Am. Iranian Coun.; chmn. bd. Lois W. Roth Endowment, Washington, 1986—; bd. Fulbright Assn., Washington, 1986—92, pres., 1989—91; mem. US Nat. Commn. for UNESCO, 2004—06. Fulbright fellow U. Dijon, France, 1949-50, USIA mid-career fellow, 1971-72; recipient Merit awards USIA, 1963, 66, 71, Peacebuilder award Nat. Peace Found., 2002 Mem.: Cosmos. Avocations: music, cultural diplomacy, political culture, theater, history. Home: 1870 Wyoming Ave NW Washington DC 20009-1802

ARNEL, KEVIN J., lawyer; b. Kansas City, Mo., Apr. 5, 1963; s. James Edward Arnel and Mary Karen Cummins; m. Roxanne R. Kirner, May 17, 1986; children: James Kirner, Weston Byrne. BA with distinction, cum laude, So. Meth. U., 1984; JD magna cum laude, Washburn U., 1987. Bar: Kans. 1987, U.S. Ct. Appeals (10th cir.) 1989. Ptnr. Foulston Siefkin, LLP, Wichita, Kans., 1987—. Guest lectr. Wichita State U., 2003, 04; spkr., moderator in field. Bd. mem., chairperson Bd. Pension and Health Benefits, Kans. West Ann. Conf. United Meth. Ch.; bd. mem., exec. com. mem. Boys and Girls Clubs South Ctrl. Kans., Inc., Sedgwick County Zool. Soc., Inc.; bd. mem. Starkey Found., Inc., Sedgwick County Zool. Found. Named one of 40 Under 40, Wichita Bus. Jour. Mem.: ABA, Am. Health Lawyers Assn., Wichita Bar Assn., Kans. Bar Assn. Office: Foulston Siefkin LLP 1551 N Waterfront Pkwy Ste 100 Wichita KS 67206

ARNELL, RICHARD ANTHONY, radiologist; b. Chgo., Aug. 21, 1938; s. Tony Frank and Mary Martha (Oberman) Yaki; m. Paula Ann Youngberg, June 28, 1964; children: Carla Ann, Paula Marie, Paul Anthony. BA, Grinnell Coll., 1960; MD, U. Iowa, 1964. Diplomate Am. Bd. Radiology, Am. Bd. Nuc. Medicine. With Innc., 1968—93, v.p., 1970-78, sec., 1978-90, pres., 1990—93, trustee pension profit plan, 1979-2000; pres. Moline Radiology Assocs., S.C., 1990-93, Advanced Radiology, S.C., 1993-2001, Radiology Assocs., LLC, 2000—01, Advanced Radiology Diagnostic Ctrs., LLC, 2000—01; with Moline Radiology SC. Mem. staff Luth. Hosp., Moline, 1968-88, dir. continuing mem. edn. prog. for physicians, 1979-83, bd. dirs., 1977-83; mem. staff Moline Pub. Hosp., 1968-88, Hammond Henry Dist. Ill., Geneseo, Ill.; mem. staff United Med. Ctr., 1989-92, chmn. radiology dept., 1992-94, med. dir. radiology dept., 1992-99; pres. Moline Radiology Assocs., Inc., 1990-93; mem. med. staff Mercer County Hosp., 1994-2003, Ill. Hosp., 1995-2003, Trinity Med. Ctr., 1992-2003, ret., 2003; trustee Midstate Found. for Med. Care, 1975-79, mem. exec. com., 1976-79; v.p. Quad City HMO Health Plan, 1979; clin. lectr. U. Iowa. Pres. Moline Mgmt. Assocs., Inc., 1990—; chmn. mng. com. Metro MRI Ctr., Ltd. Partnership, 1990--; supt. Sunday Ch. Sch. St. John's Ch., Rock Island, Ill., 1974-79, mem. ch. cabinet, 1975-76; del. Chs. United of Scott and Rock Island counties, Ill., 1977; mem. nat. exec. com. Augustana Coll., Rock Island, 1977-81; assoc. chmn. profl. div. United Way, 1985; bd. dirs. Luth. Hosp. Found., 1981-84, pres., 1982-84; bd. dirs. Quad Cities Health Care Resources, Inc., 1984-88; chmn. Luth. Health Care Found., 1984-88, United Health Care Found., 1989-91. Recipient David Theophillus trophy for outstanding athlete Grinnell Coll., 1960, Dr. of Distinction award Rock Island Med. Soc. Alliance, 1998. Mem. Am. Coll. Radiology, Ill. Radiol. Soc., Am. Coll. Nuc. Medicine, Soc. Nuc. Medicine, AMA, Ill. Med. Soc. (ho. of dels., 1974-79), Rock Island County Med. Soc. (exec. com. 1974-79, peer rev. com. 1975-79), Iowa-Ill. Ctrl. Med. Soc. (pres. 1978), Ctrl. Ill. Med. Assn. (v.p. 1977, pres. 1978), Ind. Physicians Assn. Western Ill. (dir. 1984-86, v.p. 1985, pres. 1986), World Med. Assn., Am. Coll. Med. Imaging, Short Hills Country Club. Office: 615 Valley View Dr Ste 101 Moline IL 61265 E-mail: rarny@aol.com.

ARNELL, WALTER JAMES WILLIAM, engineering educator, consultant; b. Farnborough, Eng., Jan. 9, 1924; arrived in U.S., 1953, naturalized, 1960; s. James Albert and Daisy (Payne) Arnell; m. Patricia Catherine Cannon, Nov. 12, 1955; children: Sean Paul, Victoria Clare, Sarah Michele. Aero. Engr., Royal Aircraft Establishment, 1946; BSc, U. London, 1953, PhD, 1967; MA, Occidental Coll., LA, 1956; MS, U. So. Calif., 1958. Lectr. Poly. and Northampton Coll. Advance Tech., London, 1948-53; instr. U. So. Calif., LA, 1954-59; asst. prof. mech. engring. Calif. State U., Long Beach, 1959-62, assoc. prof., 1962-66, prof., 1966-71, chmn. dept. mech. engring., 1964-65, acting chmn. divsn. engring., 1964-66, dean engring., 1967-69, rschr.; affiliate faculty dept. ocean engring. U. Hawaii, 1970-74; adj. prof. systems and insdl. engring. U. Ariz., 1981—91; pres. Lenra Assocs. Ltd., 1973—; chmn., project mgr. Hawaii Environ. Simulation Lab., 1971-72. Contbr. articles to profl. jours. Trustee Rehab. Hosp. of the Pacific, 1975—78. Fellow: Ergonomics Soc.; mem.: AAUP, AIAA, IEEE Sys. Man and Cybernetics Soc., Human Factors and Ergonomics Soc., Soc. Engring. Psychology sect., Am. Psychol. Assn. Soc., Royal Aero. Soc., Pi Tau Sigma, Phi Kappa Phi, Tau Beta Pi, Alpha Pi Mu, Psi Chi. Home: 4491 E Fort Lowell Rd Tucson AZ 85712-1106

ARNESEN, MARK R, lawyer; b. Oakland, Calif., Dec. 1, 1952; s. Ralph Otto and Marilyn Vivian (Schmitz) A.; m. Carol Bershad Cole, Jan. 1, 1984; children: Beth Elyse, Brian Kyle, Amy Rose. BA, U. Calif., 1974; JD, Yale U., 1977. Bar: Calif. 1977, U.S. Dist. Ct. (cen. dist.) Calif. 1978, U.S. Supreme Ct. 1991. Assoc. Overton, Lyman & Prince, LA, 1977-78; from asst. corp. counsel to v.p. assoc. corp. counsel First Am. Title Ins. Co., Santa Ana, Calif., 1979-92, v.p., sec., corp. counsel, 1992—; v.p., sec., counsel The First Am. Fin. Corp., Santa Ana, 1992—. Mem. Orange County Bar Assn., Am. Soc. of Corp. Secs., Am. Corp. Counsel Assn. Office: First Am Fin Corp 114 E 5th St Santa Ana CA 92701-4642

ARNESEN, NORMAN HOWARD, pastor, educator; b. San Francisco, Jan. 21, 1941; s. Howard Bernard Arnesen and Clara Esther Rauhut; m. Claire Arlene Arnesen. BA, U. Pacific, Stockton, Calif., 1962, Golden Gate Bapt. Theol. Seminary, 1962; MA, Wheaton Grad. Sch. Theology, Ill., 1970; MDiv, Fuller Theol. Seminary, Pasadena, Calif., 1974. Prof. bibl. lit. Bethany U., Scotts Valley, Calif., 1964—95; pastor Craig Meml. Chapel, Scotts Valley, 1968—78; prof. Johanesburg South Africa Ind. Schs., South Africa, 1994—2000; ret. Contbr. articles to profl. jours. Democrat. Assemblies Of God.

ARNESON, MARGARET SUSAN, lawyer; b. Madison, Wis., Apr. 27, 1960; d. John Louis and Marilyn B. Krismer; m. Rick A. Arneson, Nov. 5, 1988; children: Jessica, Stephanie. BBA, U. Wis., 1982; JD summa cum laude, Nova Southeastern U., 2001. Bar: Fla. V.p. Advanced Temperature Technicians, Inc., Sunrise, Plantation, 1994—; pvt. practice, 2001—. Cons. Advanced Temperature Technicians, Inc., 1994—. Democrat. Roman Catholic. Avocations: skiing, swimming. Office: Margaret Susan Arneson PA 300 S Pine Island Rd #217 Fort Lauderdale FL 33324 Office Phone: 954-472-5077. Office Fax: 954-472-5752. Business E-Mail: margaretarneson@bellsouth.net.

ARNEST, RICHARD T., composer, consultant; b. Richmond, Va., Apr. 27, 1950; s. Richard T. and Susan Oatfield Arnest; m. Nancy Sue Ammerman, Aug. 15, 2004; children: Caitlin Joy, Kristen Kay McClanahan, Anna Zacharias, Darcy Zacharias. MusB in Composition, U. Hawaii, Honolulu, 1972; MusM in Composition, U. Cin., 1986. Composer Music Under Constrn., Milford, Ohio, 1966—; theory instr. Joint Svcs. Sch. Music, Norfolk, 1973—74; flute/piccolo player 371st Army Band, Leavenworth, Kans., 1974—76; artist in residence State Arts Councils (AR, OK, OH), Milford, Ohio, 1976—. Exec. dir. Concordium, Honolulu, 1970—76, Fayetteville, 1976—82; founder Music Under Constrn., Cin., 2003—. Composer: (concertino for flute and strings) Liquescence, (soprano and orchestra) Pisces, (chamber ensemble) Small Music for Dancing, (chamber orchestra) Négociation, Haworth Suite, (trio sonata) Chiese Serenissime, (concert band) Dark Wing, (satb chorus with instruments) Prologue to a Time That Has Forgotten Itself, Carol Fantasia, (satb chorus and orchestra) The Second Coming, (chamber ensemble with narrator) Three Poems by Lily Peter. Referee US Rowing Assn., Princeton, NJ, 2000—06; singer May Festival Chorus, Cin., 2001—06. With US Army, 1973—76. Named Featured Composer, Flute World, 2006; recipient First prize, Ohio Fedn. Music Clubs, 1985, EPIC Music Competition, 2004, ASCAPLUS award, 2005—. Mem.: ASCAP, Am. Fedn. Musicians, Am. Music Ctr., Am. Composers Forum. Office: Music Under Constrn 5380 Overlook Dr Milford OH 45150 Home Phone: 513-576-1544; Office Phone: 513-379-7401. Business E-Mail: info@musicunderconstruction.com.

ARNETT, DAVID LESLIE, former diplomat, speaker, writer; b. Muncie, Ind., Nov. 7, 1943; s. Clyde Earl and Jeanne Arnett; m. Vivi Smiler Ronningsen, May 5, 1990; children: Heather Raine, Nathan Smiler, Wesley Smiler. BA, Wabash Coll., Crawfordsville, Ind., 1965; MA, Tulane U., New Orleans, 1971, PhD, 1973. Cert. fgn. svc. officer USIA, Dept. State, 1974. Counselor pub. affairs Am. Embassy, Ankara, Turkey, 1995—97, min. counselor pub. affairs Bonn and Berlin, Germany, 1997—2000; office dir. bur. European and Eurasian affairs/office press and pub. diplomacy Dept. State, Washington, 2000—02; consul gen., prin. officer Am. Consulate Gen., Istanbul, Turkey, 2002—05; freelance writer, spkr. Sedona, Ariz., 2005—. Chmn. Fulbright Commn. Bd., Ankara, 1995—97, Bonn and Berlin, 1997—2000, Radio Am. Sector Commn., Berlin, 1998—2000. Mem. Am. Friends Turkey, Washington, 2006—. First lt. US Army, 1965—69, Viet Nam. Recipient Presdl. Meritorious Svc. Award, White Ho. (Dept. of State), 2003, Superior Honor Award, Dept. of State, 1999, Nat. Friendship Award, GESIAD (Turkey), 2005. Mem.: Mensa. Avocations: travel, fishing, tennis, hiking. Home Phone: 928-203-0402. Home Fax: 928-203-1063. Personal E-mail: arnettdl3@npgcable.com.

ARNETT, EDWARD MCCOLLIN, chemistry educator, researcher; b. Phila., Sept. 25, 1922; s. John Hancock and Katherine Williams (McCollin) A.; m. Sylvia Gettmann, Dec. 10, 1970; children: Eric, Brian; stepchildren: Elden, Byron, Colin Gatwood. BS, U. Pa., 1943, MS, 1946, PhD, 1949. Rsch. dir. Max Levy & Co., Phila., 1949-53; asst. prof. Western Md. Coll., Westminster, 1953-54, 1954-55; assoc. prof. chemistry U. Pitts., 1957-61, assoc. prof., 1961-64, prof., 1964-80; R.J. Reynolds prof. Duke U., Durham, NC, 1980-92, prof. emeritus, 1992—. Vis. lectr. U. Ill., 1963; vis. prof. U. Kent, Canterbury, Eng., 1970; dir. Pitts. Chem. Info. Ctr., 1967-70; mem. adv. bd. Petroleum Rsch. Fund, 1968-71; mem. com. on chem. info. NRC, 1969-71. Contbr. 200 articles to sci. jours. DuPont fellow, 1948-49; rsch. fellow Harvard U., Cambridge, Mass., 1955-57, Guggenheim fellow, 1968-69, Mellon Inst. adj. sr. fellow, 1964-80, Inst. Hydrocarbon Chemistry sr. fellow, 1980. Fellow AAAS; mem. Am. Chem. Soc. (James Flack Norris award 1977, Pitts. award Pitts. chpt. 1976, Petroleum Chemistry award 1985), NAS, The Chem. Soc., Sigma Xi, Phi Lambda Upsilon. Office Phone: 919-489-4133. Personal E-mail: edward.arnett@duke.edu.

ARNETT, WILL, actor; b. Toronto, May 5, 1970; m. Penelope Ann Miller, 1994 (div. 1995); m. Amy Poehler, Aug. 29, 2003. Actor: (films) Ed's Next Move, 1996, Weekend Getaway, 1998, The Broken Giant, 1998, Southie, 1998, The Waiting Game, 1999, The Acting Class, 2000, (voice) Series 7: The Contenders, 2001, The Great New Wonderful, 2005, Monster-in-Law, 2005, (voice) Ice Age: The Meltdown, 2006, RV, 2006; actor, actor: (films) Wristcutters: A Love Story, 2006, Let's Go to Prison, 2006, Blades of Glory, 2007; (TV series) The Mike O'Malley Show, 1999, Arrested Development, 2003—; (TV films) Undefeated, 2003; appearances include Sex and the City, 1999, Third Watch, 2000, Boston Public, 2001, Yes, Dear, 2002, The Sopranos, 2002, Law & Order: Special Victims Unit, 2002, Will & Grace, 2004. Office: c/o Sutton-Barth & Vennari #310 145 South Fairfax Ave Los Angeles CA 90036 also: c/o Abrams Artists Agency 275 7th Ave, 26th Fl New York NY 10001*

ARNEY, RANDALL, artistic director; b. Effingham, Ill. BA in Theatre Arts, Eastern Ill. U.; MFA in Acting, Ill. State U. Artistic dir. Steppenwolf Theatre Co., Chgo., 1987—95, ensemble mem.; artistic dir. Geffen Playhouse, LA. Instr. master classes and workshops, US & Tokyo; assoc. prof. acting and directing Columbia Coll., Chgo.; assoc. prof. Ill. Stage U. Dir.: (plays) Savages, 1981, Arms and the Man, 1981, Streamers, 1985, Lydie Breeze, 1986, The Caretaker, 1986, Bang, 1986, A Lie of the Mind, 1987, Killers, 1988, A Walk in the Woods, 1989, The Geography of Luck, 1989, The Grapes of Wrath, 1990, Love Letters, 1990, Harvey, 1990, Curse of the Starving Class, 1991, Earthly Possessions, 1991, The Song of Jacob Zulu, 1993, Death and the Maiden, 1993, Picasso at the Lapin Agile, 1994, The Rise and Fall of Little Voice, 1994, A Certain Kind of Denial, 1995, My Thing of Love, 1995, The Beauty Queen of Leenane, 1999, I Just Stopped By to See the Man, 2002, Six Dance Lessons in Six Weeks, 2003, Speed the Plow, 2007; actor: Balm in Gilead, 1981, True West, Fool for Love, 1984, Coyote Ugly, 1985, You Can't Take It With You, 1985, Born Yesterday, 1987, The Homecoming, 1989, Frank's Wild Years, 1986, Ghost in the Machine, 1993; (films) The Color of Money, 1986, Miles from Home, 1988, Chain Reaction, 1996, The Out-of-Towners, 1999, Mystery, Alaska, 1999, Rain, 2001; (TV films) Dream Breakers, 1989, Weapons of Mass Distraction, 1997, Legalese, 1998, Normal, 2003, (appeared in) Judging Amy, 2000, According to Jim, 2001, The Guardian, 2002, Grey's Anatomy, 2005, CSI: Crime Scene Investigation, 2006. Recipient Distng. Alumni award, Eastern Ill. U. Office: c/o Geffen Playhouse 10886 Le Conte Ave Los Angeles CA 90024*

ARNEZ, NANCY LEVI, educational leadership educator; b. Balt., July 6, 1928; d. Milton Emerson Levi and Ida Barbour (Rusk) Levi Washington. AB, Morgan State Coll., 1949; MA, Columbia U., 1954, EdD, 1958. Tchr. English Druid Jr. H.S., Balt., 1949-52, Houston Jr. H.S., Balt., 1952-57; asst. to admissions officer Tchrs. Coll., Columbia U., NYC, 1957-58, grad. asst., 1957; head dept. English Cherry Hill Jr. H.S., Balt., 1958-62; assoc. prof., dir. student teaching Morgan State Coll., Balt., 1962-66; co-founder Cultural Linguistic Early Childhood Follow Through Approach; prof., asst. dir./dir. Ctr. for Inner City Studies, Northeastern Ill. U., Chgo., 1966-74; prof., assoc. dean, acting dean Sch. Edn. Howard U., Washington, 1974-80, chmn. dept. ednl. leadership, 1980-86, prof., 1980-93, prof. emeriti, 1993—. Author: Partners in Urban Education: Teaching the Inner City

Child, 1973, The Struggle for Equality of Educational Opportunity, 1975, Administrative Issues in the Implementation of the Response to Educational Needs Project, 1979, The Besieged School Superintendent, 1981, School Based Administrator Training, 1982; mem. editorial bd.: Phi Delta Kappan, 1975-80, Jour. Negro Edn., 1975-80, Black Child Jour., 1980—; contbr. articles to profl. jours. State treas., mem. exec. com. Md. State council UN Children's Fund, 1965; founder Operation Champ, Balt, 1965; mem. adv. bd. Better Boys Found., Chgo., 1966-74, Mus. African-Am. History, 1969; state chmn. Right to Read, Washington, 1973-80; treas. Com. to Elect Douglass Moore to City Council, 1982. Grantee, African Am. Inst., 1974, Spencer Found., 1976, AAUW, 1977. Mem. Am. Assn. Sch. Adminstrs. (editorial bd. 1982), Assn. for Study of Afro-Am. Life and History, African Am. Heritage Assn., African Am. Writers Guild, Nat. Alliance Black Sch. Educators, D.C. Alliance Black Sch. Educators (pres. 1986-88), Phi Delta Kappa. Presbyterian. Home: 3122 Cherry Rd NE Washington DC 20018-1612

ARNKRA, JOE, legal administrator, writer; b. Newark, Jan. 3, 1960; s. Sam F. and Jill E. Arnkra. BS in Fin., UCLA, 1990. Legal adminstr., Santa Monica, Calif., 1990—; writing cons., trainer, 1990—. Democrat. Roman Catholic. Avocations: freelance writing, skydiving, spelunking, cross-country and super marathon races, competitive sailing. Office: 2272 Colorado Blvd # 1228 Los Angeles CA 90041-1143 Fax: 310-559-2603.

ARNN, NANCY SHANK, secondary school educator; b. Cin., Jan. 20, 1939; d. Ebbert Dexter and Claudine Kaps Shank; children: Roger Edward, Christa Sue. BE, U. Cin., 1961. Secondary tchr. Reading Cmty. Pub. Schs., Ohio, 1961—68; elem. tchr. Milford Pub. Schs., Ohio, 1969—71; v.p., ops. and mgmt. chairperson Sideburn Run Recreation Assn., 1978—84; secondary tchr. Manassas City Pub. Schs., Va., 1983—2004; ret., 2004. Coach girls sports and cheerleading Reading Cmty. Pub. Schs., 1962—69, phys. and health dept. chairperson, 1966—69; coach cheerleading Manassas City Pub. Schs., 1981—90. Treas., v.p. Oakview Elem., Fairfax, 1977—88; edn. chairperson Oakwalk Country Club View Civic Assn., Fairfax, 1980—81; v.p. Falls Run Cmty. Assn., Fredericksburg, Va., 2005—07, v.p. modifications com., 2005—07, capt. Neighborhood Watch; resident adv. Falls Run Bd. Dirs., Fredericksburg, 2005; mem., deacon Hartwood Presbyn. Ch. Mem.: Zeta Tau Alpha Alumnae Assn. Republican. Presbyterian. Avocations: sports, reading, Sudoku, community service. Home: 36 Harborton Ln Fredericksburg VA 22406

ARNOFSKY, ADAM GARETT, cardiothoracic surgeon; b. July 7, 1972; BS summa cum laude in Engring., U. Pa., Phila., 1994, MD, 1998. Cert. Am. Bd. Thoracic Surgery, 2006. Intern Bellevue Hosp. Ctr., 1998—99, resident, 1999—2003, fellow, 2003—05; with Manhattan Vets. Hosp., NYU Hosp.; attending surgeon North Shore Univ. Hosp., Manhasset, NY, 2005—. Vis. surgeon Univ. Med. Ctr., Utrecht, Netherlands. Office: Cardiovasc and Thoracic Surgery North Shore Univ Hosp 300 Community Dr Manhasset NY 11030 Office Phone: 516-562-4970. Office Fax: 516-562-3786. E-mail: aarnofsk@nshs.edu.*

ARNOLD, ALANNA S. WELLING, lawyer; b. Canton, Ohio, Jan. 13, 1951; d. Coen Edward and Clara M. Welling; m. Jack Mitchell Arnold, Aug. 28, 1971; children: Cassandra L., Shanna R. BA in Sociology magna cum laude, Kent State U., 1980, MA in Applied Sociology, 1981; JD, Loyola Law Sch., New Orleans, 1991. Instr. Phillips Jr. Coll., New Orleans, 1988-90; jud. extern U.S. Ct. (ea. dist.) La., New Orleans, 1990-91; ptnr. Milling, Benson, Woodward LLP, New Orleans, 1991—2000, John Brooks Cameron & Assocs., 2000—03; rsch. fellow Case Western Res. U., 2003—04. Pvt. practice, 2000—; legal aid atty. Cmty. Legal Aid, 2004—05; feature legal writer Take Charge! mag., 2005—06. Contbr. articles to profl. jours.; mem. Loyola Law rev., 1989-91. Bd. dirs. Medina County YWCA, 2000-03, v.p., 2003, trustee, 2007—; vol. Medina Rape Crisis Ctr., 2004, Medina Battered Women's Shelter, 2006—, Guardianship Program, 2005-; coord. elect mediator's to pub. office project Cleve. Mediation Ctr., 2005—07. Gordon, Arrata McCullom scholar, 1989-90, Kent State U. Outstanding scholar, 1980. Mem. La. Bar ASsn., Ohio Bar Assn., Medina County Bar Assn., Bar Applicants Admission, Com. Svc Commn. (chmn.), Zonta Club ABC (bd. dirs. 2005—, del. internat. conv. 2006, v.p. 2006—07), Medina Women in Bus. (bd. dirs. 2003-06, program chmn. 2003-06), Cleve. Bar Assn. Democrat. Avocations: painting (watercolor), reading, movies, theater, travel. Home Phone: 330-721-1510; Office Phone: 330-315-3533. Personal E-mail: aswarnold@gmail.com.

ARNOLD, ALBERT JAMES, foreign language educator; b. Ballston Spa, NY, Nov. 8, 1939; s. Albert J. and Florence Emily (Cleveland) A.; m. Josephine Diane Valenza, June 8, 1963; 1 child, Elizabeth. AB, Hamilton Coll., 1961; MA, U Wis. Madison, 1964, PhD, 1968; cert French lang., lit., U. Paris, 1960. Instr. romance langs. Hamilton Coll., Clinton, NY, 1961-62; from asst. to prof. French U. Va., 1966—2007, chair com. comparative lit., 1974-79, 1986-89, co-chair comparative programs in literature and culture, 1989-95; dir. New World Studies, 1991-92, Caribbean Lit. Archive, 2003—07. Vis. exch. prof. U. de Paris III, 1981; external examiner Queensland U., Australia, 1986, U. West Indies, 1991-2007, NYU, 1991, Yale U., 1994, U. West Australia, 2003; external assessor French dept. U. West Indies, 1995, 2002-03; coord. com. on comp. lit. hist. Internat. Comp. Lit. Assoc., 1992-2001; internat. adv. bd. New West Indian Guide, 1992—; adv. bd. Review Lit. and Arts Americas, 2003—; vis. fellow Trinity Coll., Cambridge U., 2007; spkr., cons. in field. Author: Paul Valéry, 1970, Sartre, 1973, Césaire, 1981, 90, Camus, 1983; gen. editor Caraf Books, 1987-93; editor New World Studies, 1992-2005, Plantation Soc. in the Americas, 1999-2007, Critique, 2006; contbr. articles to profl. jours. Fellow ACLS, 1975-76, NEH, 1989-90, Fulbright Found., 1995-96, Queensland U., Australia, 1995, Rock Found. Bellagio Conf. Ctr., 2004, DAAD, 2006; grantee NEH, 1977, 88, 89-90, 2004, U. Va., 1969, 70, 72, 75-76, 78, 80, 81-82, 86, 95-96, 2001-02, Camargo Found., 1981-82, 86, 2001, Va. Found. Humanities, 1992, 94, 2004. Mem. Phi Beta Kappa. Democrat. Avocations: gardening, photography, birding. Home: 310 E Beverley St Staunton VA 24401-4327 Office: U Va Dept French PO Box 400770 Charlottesville VA 22904-4770 Business E-Mail: aja@virginia.edu.

ARNOLD, ANN, artist, illustrator; b. Newcastle-upon-Tyne, 1936; d. Edmund Tefler; m. Graham Arnold, July 29, 1961. Illustrator (books) Fanny at Chez Panisse, 1992, Stop Smelling My Rose, 1997, The Children's Kitchen Garden: A Book of Gardening, Cooking, and Learning, 1997, illustrator, co-author Firehouse Max, 1997; co-author (with John Clare, Brian Patten and Eric Robinson): (books) Clare's Countryside, 1981; author: Gamblers & Gangsters: Fort Worth's Jacksboro Highway in the 1940s and 1950s, 1998, History of the Fort Worth Legal Community, 2000, History of the Fort Worth Medical Community, 2002, The Adventurous Chef: Alexis Soyer, 2002; Represented in permanent collections North Point Gallery, San Francisco, numerous exhibitions in London and the U.S. Mem.: Assn. Art Therapists (founding mem.). Address: c/o Pippin Properties Inc 155 E 38th St Ste 2H New York NY 10016

ARNOLD, BARBARA EILEEN, state legislator; b. North Adams, Mass., Aug. 3, 1924; d. Lester Flemming and Sarah (Van Hagen) Smith; m. William E. Arnold, Dec. 5, 1946; children: Wynn, Jefffrey, Gayle, Christopher. BA in Psychology, U. Mass.; postgrad., Keene State Coll. Spl. edn. tchr. Easter Seal Rehab. Ctr., Manchester, NH, 1967-74; state legislator NH, 1982-95; Rep. floor leader Ho. of Reps., 1989-95; mem. N.H. Coun. Vocat. Tech. Edn., 1986-95, State and Fed. Rels. Commn.; chmn. Manchester Rep. Del.; vice chmn. Ways and Means, 1992—95. Sec. N.E. State Coun. Vocat. Edn.; adv. bd. edn. N.H. Dept. Corrections; mem. adv. coun. adult rehab. Easter Seal Soc., NH, 1990—; state adv. com. Vocat. Child Care Programs, 1993—95; mem. com. for children, families, social svcs. Nat. Conf. of State Legislatures; bd. registration City of Manchester, 1999—, chair, 2003—05; Manchester chmn. Dole for Pres. campaign, 1995, Gov. Judd Gregg for U.S. Senate, 1992, 2004; chair Manchester Rep. Com., 1993—95, George W. Bush for Pres., Manchester, 1999, 2004; chmn. Manchester Rep. Com., 1992—95; chmn. Manchester Senator John E. Sununu Campaign, 2002; past mem. vestry, registered lay leader, mem. diocesan commn., del. gen. conv. Episcopal Ch.; bd. dirs. ARC, 1975—96, chmn. bd. dirs., 1977—80. Mem. Nat. Order Women Legislators, Nat. Fedn. Rep. Women, Greater Manchester Federated Rep. Women's Club, N.H. Kappa Kappa Gamma Alumni Assn. (pres. 1990-91). Address: 374 Pickering St Manchester NH 03104-2744

ARNOLD, BARRY RAYNOR, philosophy educator, medical ethicist; b. Mooresville, NC, Sept. 29, 1951; s. Adrian Leicester and Cleo Agnes (Fisher) A.; m. Margaret Elizabeth Morelock, Aug. 15, 1984. AB cum laude, Davidson Coll., 1973; MDiv magna cum laude, Emory U., 1976, PhD, 1986. Ordained to ministry Presbyn. Ch.; cert. Christian clin. counselor Am. Counseling Assn.; lic. mental health counselor, Ind. Min. various parishes, Ga., Fla., 1976—; instr. religion, assoc. chaplain The Lovett Sch., 1980-82; prof. Andrew Coll., Cuthbert, Ga., 1983-84; from asst. prof. to prof. emeritus U. West Fla., Pensacola, 1986—2007, prof. emeritus, 2007—; pvt. practice clin. counseling, Pace, Fla., 1996—; acting chmn. dept. philosophy/religion U. West Fla., Pensacola, 1997—, chmn. dept. interdisciplinary humanities, philosophy, relig., 2000—, exec. dir. Univ. Office for Applied Ethics, 2000—, joint prof. biology and philosophy divsn. life and health scis., 2003—; prof. Bioethics and Philosophy, dir. Ctr. for Health Care Ethics U. West Fla./Sacred Heart Hosp., Pensacola, 2003—; supr. interns in palliative care and bio-ethics Sacred Heart Hosp., 2004—; dir. Ctr. for Health Care Ethics U. West Fla./Sacred Heart Hosp., 2003—; prof. emeritus biology, allied health U. West Fla., Pensacola, 2007—. Counselor Pace Counseling Ctr., 1996-97; bd. dirs. Unif Ctr. Aging; reviewer med. edn. Coun. Pensacola Fla., 2006—; spkr. in field. Author: The Pursuit of Virtue, 1989; editor: Essays in American Ethics, 1992; gen. editor (11 vols.) The Reshaping of Psychoanalysis, 1992-2002; assoc. editor Explorations: Jour. Adventurous Thought, 1999—; featured as med. ethicist on CBS Radio, 2006; contbr. articles to profl. jours. Bd. dirs. Sacred Heart Hosp., Pensacola, Bapt. Hosp.; mem. instl. rev. bd. U. West Fla., 2006—; pres., bd. dirs. Assn. for Retarded Citizens, Albany, Ga., 1978—79; bioethicist, bd. dirs. West Fla. Regional Med. Ctr., Pensacola, 1990—2003, Bapt. Hosp., 2003—, Sacred Heart Hosp., 2003—, com. on palliative care, com. on blood products, com. on intravenous immunoglobulon, 2006—. Recipient Disting. Tchg. award UWF and Fla. State Legislature, 1988, 90, 95, 6 awards UWF, 1986-2007; fellow Rice U., 1973-75, Emory U., 1975-76, 79-82, U. Glasgow, 1976. Fellow: Am. Coll. Counselors (cert. Christian clin. counselor, chair examiners for cert.), Am. Assn. Integrative Medicine (diplomate, nat. bd. dirs., chair nat. bd. 2002—03), Am. Bd. Child Mental Health Providers; mem.: ACA, Assn. for Cognitive Behavioral Therapists (cert. cognitive forensic therapist, cert. anxiety disorders specialist), So. Soc. Philosophy and Psychology, Am. Acad. Religion, Internat. Thomas Merton Soc., Rotary (sgt.-at-arms 1982—83), Phi Beta Kappa, A£D (hon.), Alpha Epsilon Delta, Phi Kappa Phi (sec. 1988). Democrat. Avocations: antique cards, antique cars, birdwatching. Home: 5820 Kirkland Dr Milton FL 32570-8251 Office: Univ West Fla 11000 University Pkwy Pensacola FL 32514-5750 Home Phone: 850-626-7556. Business E-Mail: barnold@uwf.edu.

ARNOLD, CHARLES BURLE, JR., retired psychiatrist; b. Seattle, Aug. 13, 1934; s. Charles Burle and Ruth Helene (Hadley) A.; m. Sarah J. Slagle, Dec. 16, 1972; children: Geoffrey, Christopher, Jonathan. BS cum laude, U. Puget Sound, 1956; MD, CM, McGill U., 1960; MPH, U. N.C., 1965. Diplomate: Am. Bd. Preventive Medicine. Intern U. Wash. Hosp., Seattle, 1960-61, resident, 1961; physician Peace Corps, Bolivia, Washington, 1961-64; asst. prof. health adminstrn., asso. Carolina Population Center, U. N.C., Chapel Hill, 1965-69; asst. prof. Albert Einstein Coll. Medicine, Bronx, NY, 1969-72; prof. public adminstrn. and clin. assoc. prof. preventive medicine NYU, NYC, 1972-83; med. dir., med. rels. Met. Life Ins. Co., 1983-91, v.p. med. rels., 1991-93; psychiat. resident North Shore Univ. Hosp., Manhasset, NY, 1993-96, chief resident, 1995-96; pvt. practice of psychiatry, 1996-99; attending psychiatrist Augusta (Maine) Mental Health Inst., 1999—2002; ret., 2002. Adj. prof. pub. adminstrn. NYU, 1983—; lectr. cmty. health Mt. Sinai Med. Sch., NYC; lectr. preventive medicine Downstate Med. Sc., SUNY, 1986-92; dir. Mahoney Inst. Health Maintenance, Am. Health Found., 1975-83, v.p. rsch., 1978-83, cons., 1983-86; chair Hitchcock Weekday Sch. Bd., 1986-92; chmn. Worksite Smoking subcom. NY State Commn. on Smoking or Health, 1991-93; psychiatrist Drop-In Ctr., Ctr. Urban Cmty. Svcs., West Harlem, 1996-98; asst. attending psychiatrist NY Presbyn. Hosp. Westchester Divsn.; dir. Open Arms Clinic; asst. clin. prof. psychiatry Cornell Med. Coll., 1998-2000. Editor, mem. exec. coun.: Transactions of Am. Acad. Ins. Medicine, 1988-93; assoc. editor Preventive Medicine Jour., 1975-83, sr. assoc. editor, 1983-85; editor Advances in Disease Prevention, 1981-83; editor-in-chief Statis. Bull., 1983-93; contbr. articles to profl. jours. Milbank Faculty fellow, 1967-74; OEO grantee, 1968-74; Population Council grantee, 1971-75; Health Research Council N.Y.C. grantee, 1972-75; Nat. Cancer Inst. grantee, 1975-83; Nat. Heart, Lung and Blood Inst. grantee, 1977-83; HEW Office Health Promotion grantee, 1978-80 Fellow Am. Coll. Preventive Medicine (pres. 1977-78); mem. N.Y. Acad. Medicine (com. on pub. health 1988—, vice chmn. 1992, chmn. 1993), Health Ins. Assn. Am. (chair com. on prevention and pub. health policy 1989-92). Home: PO Box 479 Topsham ME 04086-0479 Personal E-mail: carnold1@suscom-maine.net.

ARNOLD, CHARLOTTE S., criminal justice agency executive, activist; b. Port Jervis, NY, Sept. 18, 1929; d. Abraham and Jennie Skolnick; m. John Arnold (dec.); children: Seth Ginsburg, Daniel Ginsburg, Deborah Marx. BA, SUNY, Albany, 1951. Vol., pres. Women in the Urban Crisis, Pitts., 1968—73; exec. dir. The Program for Female Offenders, Pitts., 1974—98. Mem. Pa. Gov.s Justice Commn., Harrisburg, 1975—90; mem. justice rev. bd. Pa. Bar Assn., Harrisburg, 1991—95. Author: (book) Get Out of Jail Free, 2005, Over These Prison Walls, 2006. Mem. bd. Urban League, Pitts., Better Bus. Bur.; mem. NAACP, NOW; bd. mem., sec. Palm Beach County Jail Bd., 2006—; mem. B'nai B'rith Women. Named Charlotte Arnold Day, Pitts. City Coun., 1997, Disting. Daughter of Pa., 1997; recipient Martin Luther King award, Hand-in-Hand, Inc., 1974, Person of Yr. award, Thomas Merton Ctr., 1974, Leadership award in Cmty. Svc., YWCA, Pitts., 1984, Human Svcs. award, Kaufmann's Program for Women in Bus., 1986, Liberty Bell award, Allegheny County Bar Assn., 1994. Achievements include first woman board member of the Better Business Bureau; featured in Savvy magazine article, 1985; CBS Morning News, 1985. Avocations: writing, reading, golf.

ARNOLD, CRAIG, manufacturing executive; B in Psychology, Calif. State U., San Bernardino; MBA, Pepperdine U., Malibu, Calif. With GE, 1983, mng. dir. Structured Products Europe for Plastics, 1995—97, corp. v.p., pres. GE Appliances Asia, 1997—98, corp. v.p., pres. GE Plastics Greater China, 1998—99, corp. v.p., pres. GE Lighting Svcs. Ltd. London, 1999—2000; with Eaton Corp., Cleve., 2000—, sr. v.p., pres. Fluid Power bus. Office: Eaton Corp Eaton Ctr 1111 Superior Ave Cleveland OH 44114-2584 Office Phone: 216-523-5000.*

ARNOLD, DAMON THEODORE, physician; b. Bklyn., Mar. 21, 1957; s. Charles William and Dorothy Sinclair Arnold; m. Sharon Elizabeth Johnson-Arnold, Sept. 6. BS, Howard U., Washington, 1980; MD, U. Ill., Chgo., 1987, MPH, 1992; Massage Therapist, Chgo. Sch. Massage Therapy, 2002. Lic. physician and surgeon Ill. Commd. 2d lt. U.S. Army, 1984—, advanced through ranks to col., 2005—; resident in internal medicine Cook County Hosp., Chgo., 1987—90, resident in occupl. medicine, 1990—92; med. dir. occupl. health svcs. and staff physician St. Francis Hosp. and Health Ctrs., Blue Island, Ill., 1992—96; med. dir. for LTV Steel Co. Corporate Health Dimensions, East Chicago, Ind., 1996—97; med. dir. employee health svc., med. and sci. staff Mercy Hosp. and Med. Ctr., Chgo., 1997—. Med. rev. officer Med. Rev. Officers Cert. Coun., 1995—. Contbr. articles toprofl. jours. Col. USAR, 1984—, Res. N.G. Decorated Army Commendation medals. Mem.: AMA, Ill. State Med. Soc., N.G. Assn. Ill., Chgo. Med. Soc., Am. Legion (life), Soc. of U.S. Army Flight Surgeons (life), Assn. Mil. Surgeons U.S. (life), Am. Massage Therapy Assn., Japanese Karate Assn. (Black Belt). Avocations: oil painting, sculpting, photography, martial arts, poetry. Office: Mercy Hospital and Med Ctr 2600 S Michigan Ave Chicago IL 60616 E-mail: d.arnold@us.army.mil.

ARNOLD, DENNIS B., lawyer; b. Apr. 25, 1950; BA magna cum laude, SUNY Buffalo, 1972; JD, Yale U., 1975. Bar: Calif. 1976. Asst.-in-instrn. Yale Law Sch., New Haven, Conn., 1974-75; law clk. to Hon. Murray M. Schwartz U.S. Dist. Ct., Del., 1975-76; ptnr. Irell & Manella, 1980-88, Gibson, Dunn & Crutcher LLP, LA, 1988—. Adj. assoc. prof. law Southwestern U. Sch. Law, 1980-82; advisor Restatement of Law, 2d edit., Suretyship and Guaranty, Am. Law Inst., 1989-95. Contbr. articles to profl. jours. Mem.: ABA, Am. Coll. Real Estate Lawyers, Fin. Lawyers Conf. (bd. govs. 1986—89, 1992—95, 1996—99, pres. 1999—2000), L.A. County Bar Assn. (exec. com. commercial law and bankruptcy sect. 1987—90, exec. com. real property sect. 1987—92, steering com. real estate fin. subsect. 1987—; exec. com. commercial law and bankruptcy sect. 1996—99), State Bar Calif. (real property and bus. law sect. 1978—, standing joint com. anti-deficiency laws 1985—89), Am. Law Inst. Office: Gibson Dunn & Crutcher LLP 333 South Grand Ave Los Angeles CA 90071-3197

ARNOLD, DOUGLAS NORMAN, mathematician; b. NYC, Apr. 30, 1954; s. Justin Bruce and Bernice Shirley (Goertzel) A.; m. Maria Carme Torrescassana Calderer, Aug. 3, 1985; 1 child, Clara Maria. BA in Math., Brown U., 1975; MS in Math., U. Chgo., 1976, PhD in Math., 1979. Asst. prof. math. Dept. Math. U. Md., College Park, 1979-84, assoc. prof., 1984-89, prof., 1989; prof. math. Pa. State U., University Park, 1989-95, assoc. chair for computing, 1991—94, acting dept. chair, 1994—95, disting. prof. math., 1995—2001, assoc. dir., Inst. for High Performance, Computing and Applications, 1996—2001, co-dir., Ctr. for Computing, Math. and Applications, 1997—2001; dir. inst. math. and applications U. Minn., 2001—, prof. math, 2001—. Bd. gov. Inst. for Math. and Its Applications, 1999—2001; lectr. Internat. Congress of Math., Beijing, 2002, mem. program com., Madrid, 2003—06; co-coord. Internat. Math. Sci. Inst. Consortium, 2002—06; mem. external review com. Kavil Inst. Theoretical Physics, 2003; mem. scientific adv. bd. Banff Inst. Rsch. Station, Canada, 2002—05, Centre Math. for Applications, Oslo, 2003—; mem. adv. com. Math. Awareness Month, 2005; mem. adv. bd. Maxwell Inst. for Math. Scis., Edinburgh, 2006—; mem. Ctr. for Gravitational Physics and Geometry; co-dir. Ctr. for Computational Math. and Applications; assoc. dir. Inst. for High Performance Computing Applications; mem. supercomputing inst. task force on initiatives in high performance computing U. Minn., 2006—; lead organizer Math is Coll!/Who Wants to be a Mathematician?, 2006; mem. US Nat. Com. for Math., 2007—; mem. internat. adv. com. for planning Spanish Inst. Math., 2007—; invited lectr. & presenter in field. Editl. adv. bd., Computational Mechanics, 1990-96; editl. bd., Math. Modelling and Numerical Analysis, 1995-99, Electronic Rsch. Announcements, Am. Math. Soc., 1995-2001, SIAM Jour. on Numerical Analysis, 1990-2001, Calcolo, 1997-, Numerische Mathematik, 1998-, Ctrl. European Jour. Math., 2002-, Math. Models and Mathods in Applied Scis. (M3AS), 2002-, Math. Modelling and Numerical Analysis, 2006-, Acta Numerica, 2007-; editor, Advances in Computational Math., 1992-, Studies in Math. and its Applications, 2001-; series editor, Inst. Math. Applications Volumes in Math. and its Applications, 2001-; adv. bd., Found. Computational Math., 2006-;author (article) Computer-Assisted Instruction for Encarta '97 Ency.; wrote and maintain extensive web pages in various areas of math. instruction (My Graphics for the Calculus Classroom & Graphs for Complex Analysis); contbr. numerous articles to profl. jours. NATO fellow, 1982-83; NSF rsch. grantee, 1981—; recipient 1st Internat. Giovanni Sacchi-Landriani prize, Acad. Scis. & Letters, Lombardy Inst., Milan, 1991, Disting. Svc. award, Eberly Coll. Sci., Pa. State Alumni Soc., 2000. Mem. AAAS, Am. Math. Soc., Soc. for Indsl. and Applied Math.(mem. com. sci. policy, 2001-, coun. del. bd. trustees, 2005-2007, mem.-at-large coun., 2004-), Math. Assn. Am. (NSF (mem. math. & phys. adv. com., 2005-2008, mem. math. and phys. scis. directorate, (DIMACS) Ctr. for Discrete Math. and Theoretical Computer Sci.), Phi Beta Kappa, Sigma Xi. Home: 12120 54th Ave N Minneapolis MN 55442-1847 Office: Inst Math and Its Applications Univ Minn 426 Lind Hall 207 Church St SE Minneapolis MN 55455 Office Phone: 612-624-6066. Office Fax: 612-626-7370. Business E-Mail: arnold@ima.umn.edu.*

ARNOLD, EDWARD (EDDY ARNOLD), research scientist, educator; m. Gail Ferstandig Arnold, 1981; children: Elizabeth, Emily. PhD (with Jon Clardy), Cornell U., 1982; Postdoctoral (with Michael G. Rossmann), Purdue U., 1982—87. Prof., chemistry and chemical biology Rutgers U., Piscataway, NJ; resident faculty mem., researcher Rutgers U., Ctr. for Advanced Biotechnology and Medicine (Aaron Shatkin, Dir.), Piscataway, NJ, 1987—. Established laboratory (with wife Gail Ferstandig Arnold) at Rutgers University, Center of Advanced Biotechnology and Medicine in 1987, which has a 20 member research team that has collaborated with scientists at NIH, Nat. Cancer Inst. (Stephen H. Hughes) and Janssen Pharmaceutica (including the late Paul Janssen), among others. The team is working to develop and apply structure-based drug and vaccine designs for the treatment and prevention of serious human diseases (contributed to the discovery of DAPY (diarylpyrimidine) compounds as potential anti-AIDS drugs; is developing chimeric human rhinoviruses as potential vaccines for HIV/AIDS). Dr. Arnold is well known for crystallographic studies of viruses, viral proteins, and polymerases. Office: Rutgers U Chemistry & Chemical Biology Ctr Advanced Biotechnology and Medicine 679 Hoes Ln Room 016 Piscataway NJ 08854 Office Phone: 732-235-5323. Office Fax: 732-235-5788. Business E-Mail: arnold@cabm.rutgers.edu.

ARNOLD, FRANCES HAMILTON, chemistry educator; b. Pitts., July 25, 1956; d. William Howard and Josephine Inman (Routheau) A.; m. Andrew Evan Lange, Mar. 4, 1994; children: James Howard, William Andrew. BS magna cum laude, Princeton U., 1979; PhD in Chem. Engring., U. Calif., Berkeley, 1985. Asst. chem. engring. Calif. Inst. Tech., Pasadena, 1987-92, assoc. prof., 1992—, prof. chem. engring & biochemistry, Dick and Barbara Dickinson prof. chemical engring. and biochemistry. Vis. assoc. chemistry U. Calif., Berkeley, 1986—87; ann. lectr. Advanced Ctr. Biochemical Engring. Univ. Coll., London, 1994; William Rauscher Lectr. in Chemistry Rensselaer Polytechnic Inst., 1996; Purves Lectr. in Chemistry McGill U., 1998; Lindsay Disting. Lectr. Tex. A&M, 2003; Merck-Frosst Invited Lectr. Biochemistry U. Alberta, 2003; Sir Robert Price Lectr. CSIRO, Melbourne, 2003. Contbr. articles to profl. jours. Recipient Office Naval Rsch. Young Investigator award, 1988, NSF Presdl. Young Investigator award, 1989, Van Ness Award, Rensselaer Polytechnic Inst., 1994, Profl. Progress Award, AIChE, 2000; grantee David and Lucile Packard fellow, 1989. Mem.: NAE, AAAS (Sci. Innovation Topical Lectr.), Inst. Medicine, Santa Fe Inst. (Sci. Bd.), Am. Inst. Medical and Biological Engring., Am. Soc. Microbiology, Protein Soc., Am. Inst. Chem. Engrs., Am. Chem. Soc. (David Perlman Lectr. Award, ACS Biochemical Tech. 2003, Francis P. Garvan-John M. Olin medal 2005, Carothers award, ACS Del. divsn. 2003), Tau Beta Pi, Phi

Beta Kappa. Office: Calif Inst Tech Div of Chem & Chem Engring 228B Spalding Pasadena CA 91125-0001 Office Phone: 626-395-4162. Office Fax: 626-568-8743. E-mail: frances@cheme.caltech.edu.

ARNOLD, FRED ENGLISH, lawyer; b. Mexico, Mo., May 10, 1938; s. Charles P. and Mary E. (Blackman) A.; m. Dorothy P. Offutt, Dec. 31, 1966 (div. Aug. 2002); children: Jane E., Charles P. III, Susan J., m. Jo Ann Harmon, Apr. 10, 2004. AB, Harvard U., 1960, LLB, 1963. Bar: Mo. 1963, U.S. Dist. Ct. (ea. dist.) Mo. 1964, U.S. Supreme Ct. 1966. Assoc. Thompson Coburn LLP, St. Louis, 1964-70, ptnr., 1971—2005, sr. counsel, 2006—. Trustee KETC/Channel 9, 2002—. Trustee Mary Inst., St. Louis, 1981—87, v.p., 1985—86; bd. dir. Repertory Theatre of St. Louis, 1982—88, Whitfield Sch., St. Louis, 1990—96, pres., 1991—93; bd. dir. Arts & Edn. Coun. Greater St. Louis, 1991—97, vice chmn., 1996—97; adv. com. Jordan Charitable Found., St. Louis, 1975—; trustee Ctrl. Meth. U., Fayette, Mo., 1997—2006. Mem. ABA, Am. Coll. Real Estate Lawyers, Noonday Club, (bd. govs. 2003-05, pres. 2005), The Racquet Club. Democrat. Methodist. Office: Thompson Coburn LLP One US Bank Plz Saint Louis MO 63101-1693 Home: 921 Cella Rd Saint Louis MO 63124 Business E-Mail: farnold@thompsoncoburn.com.

ARNOLD, GARY HOWARD, film critic; b. Princeton, Ind., Aug. 22, 1942; s. Charles Howard and Ferris (Smith) A.; m. Sue Datz, Dec. 29, 1967; children— Pauline, Jane, Esther. Student, NYU, 1959-60, U. Calif., Berkeley, 1960-63. Film critic Diplomat mag., 1966; film critic, reporter Ind. Film Jour., 1968-69; film critic Washington Post, 1969-84; co-host weekly TV commentary show The Moviegoing Family, 1985-90; arts critic The Connection, Reston, Va., 1987-89; movie critic The Washington Times, Washington, 1989—2005, freelance movie columnist, 2006—. Home: 5133 1st St N Arlington VA 22203-1207 Personal E-mail: garyarnold@verizon.net.

ARNOLD, GEORGE LAWRENCE, retired advertising company executive; b. Kansas City, Mo., Sept. 30, 1942; s. James Robert and Mary Virginia (Ellington) A.; m. Mary Antoinette Turrin, Dec. 31, 1964; children: Margery, Matthew, Molly, Sara. BJ magna cum laude, U. Tex., 1965, MA cum laude, 1966. Advt. and pub. relations trainee Gen. Electric Co., Phila., 1966; advt. asst. Dallas Power & Light Co., 1967-70; dir. comm. Continuum Co. Inc., Austin, Tex., 1970-73; pres. Evans/Dallas Inc., Dallas, 1977-99; ret., 1999. Bd. dirs. Evans Group, Inc., Salt Lake City, operating com. Salt Lake City. Bd. dirs. United Way Met. Dallas, 1978, Lone Star council Camp Fire, Dallas, 1978-84. Recipient Silver Anvil award Pub. Relations Soc. Am., 1980, Gold Effie award Am. Mktg. Assn., 1981. Mem. Tex. Pub. Rels. Assn. (bd. dirs. 1978-80, 92-97, pres. 1998, Silver Spur award 1979, 85, 2003), Dallas Advt. League (pres. 1981). Democrat. Roman Catholic. Achievements include multi-award winning author of five books, both fiction and nonfiction, from Sunbelt Media/Eakin Press. Home: 912 Kneese Rd Fredericksburg TX 78624-7057

ARNOLD, HENRI, cartoonist; b. Bethlehem, Pa. s. Samuel Max and Dora (Schnur) A.; m. Harriet Chefetz, Feb. 14, 1980; children by previous marriage— Nora Sally, Ned Michael. Student, Cooper Union, 1946. Editorial/sports cartoonist Bridgeport (Conn.) Sun. Herald; cartoonist weekly humor page Chgo. Tribune, 1955-65; art dir. Chgo. Tribune-N.Y. News Syndicate, Inc., NYC, 1957-77. Lectr. in field. Creator: This Man's Army, N.Y. Sun. News, 1954-64, Meet Mr. Luckey, N.Y. Daily News, 1991—; writer, cartoonist for Ching Chow, 1977—; producer Jumble, That Scrambled Word Game, 1960—; illustrator: The ABCs of Golf (by Tommy Armour), 63 vols. of Jumble, That Scrambled Word Game, 1962—, Super Jumble Puzzle Book, 1991, Jumble for Kids Book, 1992. Mem. Nat. Cartoonists Soc., Palm-Aire Country Club.

ARNOLD, J(AMES) BARTO, III, marine archaeologist; b. San Antonio, Jan. 9, 1950; s. J. Barto Jr. and Wilnora (Barton) Arnold; children: Kathryn, Julia, Jessica. BA cum laude, U. Tex., 1971, MA, 1973. Rsch. asst. Tex. Archeol. Rsch. Lab. U. Tex., Austin, 1970-72; asst. state marine archaeologist Tex. Antiquities Com., Austin, 1972-75; state marine archaeologist Tex. Hist. Com., Austin, 1975-97; dir. Tex. ops. Inst. of Nautical Archaeology, Tex. A&M U., College Station, 1997—. Cons. NOAA, 1977-91, Nat. Trust Hist. Preservation, Washington, 1979-90, Congl. Office Tech. Assessment, Washington, 1986; mem. Md. Gov.'s Adv. Com. on Marine Archaeology, Annapolis, 1987-90; mem. history area com. nat. park sys. adv. bd. U.S. Dept. Interior, 1994-95; dir. La Salle Shipwreck Project, 1995-96, Confederate Blockade-Runner Denbigh Shipwreck Project, 1997—. Co-author: Nautical Archaeology of Padre Island, 1978, Documentary Sources for the Wreck of the New Spain Fleet of 1554, 1979 (Presidio La Bahaia 1979), others; Plenum series editor Underwater Archaeology, 1995—; contbr. articles to profl. jours. Recipient Achievement award for Hist. Preservation Dept. Interior, 1980. Mem. Soc. Profl. Archaeologists (cert.; sec.-treas. 1987-89, Spl. Achievement award 1990), Soc. Hist. Archaeology (pres. 1993), Tex. Archeol. Soc., Archaeol. Inst. Am., Explorers Club, Phi Beta Kappa. Methodist. Avocations: stamp collecting/philately, science fiction. Office: Tex A&M U Inst Nautical Archaeology PO Drawer HG College Station TX 77841-5137 E-mail: barnold@tamu.edu.

ARNOLD, JAMES RICHARD, chemist, educator; b. New Brunswick, NJ, May 5, 1923; s. Abraham Samuel and Julia (Jacobs) A.; m. Louise Clark, Oct. 11, 1952; children: Robert C., Theodore J., Kenneth C. AB, Princeton U., 1943, MA, 1945, PhD, 1946. Fellow Inst. Nuc. Studies, U. Chgo., 1946—47, faculty, 1948—55; NRC fellow Harvard U., 1947—48; faculty chemistry Princeton U., 1955—59; assoc. prof. chemistry U. Calif., San Diego, 1958—60, prof., 1960—92, Harold C. Urey prof., 1983—92, chmn. dept. chemistry, 1960—63. Assoc. Manhattan Project, 1943-46; dir. Calif. Space Inst., 1980-89, interim dir., 1996-97; prin. investigator Calif. Space Grant Consortium, 1989—; mem. various bds. NASA, 1959—; space sci. bd. NAS, 1970-74, com. on sci. and pub. policy, 1970-77. Mem. editl. bd. Ann. Rev. Nuclear Chemistry, 1972, Revs. Geophysics and Space Physics, 1972-75, Moon, 1972—; contbr. articles to profl. jours. Pres. Torrey Pines Elem. Sch. PTA, 1964-65; pres. La Jolla Dem. Club, 1965-66; nat. coun. World Federalists-U.S.A., 1970-72. Recipient E.O. Lawrence medal AEC, 1968, Leonard medal Meteoritical Soc., 1976, Kuiper award Am. Astron. Soc., 1993; asteroid 2143 named Jimarnold in his honor, 1980; Guggenheim fellow, India, 1972-73. Mem. NAS, AAAS, Am. Acad. Arts and Scis., Internat. Acad. Astronautics, Am. Chem. Soc., Fedn. Am. Scientists, Citizens for Global Solutions. Office: U Calif San Diego Dept Chemistry Code 0524 La Jolla CA 92093 Home Phone: 858-453-0232. Business E-Mail: jarnold@ucsd.edu.

ARNOLD, JANET NINA, health facility administrator, consultant; b. Poughkeepsie, NY, Apr. 23, 1933; d. Paul Dudley and Pauline Katherine (Board) Bartram; m. Robert William Arnold, Dec. 19, 1954; children: Paul Dudley, Janet Elizabeth. AB cum laude, Vassar Coll., 1955; postgrad. Sch. Med. Tech., Albany Med. Coll., 1955—56; MS Microbiology cum laude, Vassar Coll., 1963; MHSM, Webster Coll., 1981. Rsch. asst., med. technologist H. Aird Boswell, M.D., Troy, NY, 1956—59; tchg. supr., adminstrv. cons. Vassar Bros. Hosp., Poughkeepsie, 1959—69; asst. adminstr., lab. mgr. Boulder Meml. Hosp., Colo., 1975—80; cons. hosp. planning Mercy Med. Ctr., Denver, 1981—82; clin. lab. dir., adminstr. Humana, Denver, 1982—85, dir. MRI, 1985—2006. Cons. health care mgmt. Humana, Inc., 1982-96, Columbia/HCA Health Sys., 1992-96; pres. Arnold and Assocs., 1988—; acad./adminstrv. cons. U. Guam, Vassar Coll., Boulder Cmty. Hosp., Humana Int., 1990-97; adj. faculty Vassar Coll., adv. to med. lab., lectr. med. mycology, 1961-63, tchg. fellow 1961-63, chmn. unrestricted fund raising, 1989-96, co-chair major gifts, 2000-05; sec., bd. dirs. Sanitas Fed. Credit Union, 1977-78, pres., 1979-82 Assoc. editor Am. Jour. Med. Tech., 1980-88; contbr. articles to profl. jours Contbr. NMC, 1988-92 NSF rsch. fellow, 1960-62 Mem. Am. Acad. Microbiology, Soc. for Gen. Microbiology, Am. Soc. Med. Technologists, Colo. Pub. Health Assn., Soc. Women Environ. Profls., Med. Mycological Soc. Ams Republican. Episcopalian. Office Phone: 717-464-8536. Personal E-mail: r-j-arnold-assoc@att.net.

ARNOLD, JEROME GILBERT, lawyer; s. Edward F. and Annastacia (Thielen) A.; m. Judith Lindor, Dec. 18, 1971; children: Thomas, Mark, John, Jason, Maria. BS, U. Minn., 1964; LLB, U. N.D., 1967. Bar: Minn. 1967, S.D. 1967, U.S. Dist. Ct. S.D. 1967, U.S. Dist. Ct. Minn. 1973, U.S. Ct. Appeals (8th cir.) 1986. Law clk. U.S. Dist. Ct., Aberdeen, SD, 1967-68; asst. city atty. City of Duluth, Minn., 1968-69; asst. county atty. St. Louis County, Duluth, 1969-70, chief criminal prosecutor, 1970-71; spl. asst. to county atty. County of Carlton, Minn., 1971; ptnr. Hunt & Arnold, Duluth, Minn., 1971—86; U.S. atty. U.S. Dist. Ct. Minn., Mpls., 1986—91; ptnr. Larson, Husby. Brodin & Arnold, Duluth, 1992—93; compensation judge State of Minn., Duluth, 1993—2004, 2005—; mem. Falsani, Balmer, Peterson, Quinn and Beyer, Duluth, Minn., 2004—05; compensation judge State of Minn., 2005—. Mem. adv. com. Supreme Ct. Appointments, St. Paul, 1980; chmn. selection com. 6th Jud. Dist., Duluth, 1978-83. Chmn. St. Louis City (Minn.) Bd. Adjustment, 1978-82; Rep. nominee 8th Congl. Dist. Minn., 1974; mem. state steering com. Reagan for Pres., 1976, 80, 84. Mem. Fed. Bar Assn. (bd. dirs. 1986-91), Minn. Bar Assn., Minn. Trial Lawyers Assn. Roman Catholic. Avocations: fishing, hunting. Office Fax: 218-723-1931.

ARNOLD, JESSE CHARLES, retired statistician; b. Bowie, Tex., Sept. 28, 1937; s. Jesse Connally and Lillie Christine Arnold; m. Peggy Lou Peveto; children: Christa Louise, Jesse Charles Arnold, Jr. BS, Southeastern State U., 1960; MS, Fla. State U., 1963, PhD, 1967. Statistician Communicable Disease Ctr., Atlanta, 1961—63; prof. stats. Va. Tech U., Blacksburg, Va., 1968—2002, head Dept. Stats., 1973—82, ret., 2002. Contbr. articles to profl. jours. Sr. asst. health svc. officer USPHS, 1961—63. Fellow, NSF, 1963—67. Fellow: Internat. Statis. Inst., Am. Statis. Assn. (chmn. stat. edn. sect. 1975—76); mem.: Biometric Soc. (pres. 1976—77). Methodist. Achievements include research in sampling, quality control, nutrition. Avocations: tennis, woodwork, writing, consulting. Home: 2011 Northside Drive Blacksburg VA 24060 Office: Virginia Tech University-Retired Hutcheson Hall Blacksburg VA 24061 Home Phone: 540-552-0132. Business E-Mail: jca@vt.edu.

ARNOLD, JOHN DAVID, management counselor; b. Boston, May 14, 1933; s. I. I. and Edith (Gordon) A.; children by previous marriage: Derek, Keith, Craig; m. Diane Summers, Sept. 1994. BA in Social Rels. cum laude, Harvard U., 1955. Prodn. supr., dealer svc. mgr. Arnold Stretch Mates Corp., Boston, 1957-59; asst. dir. manpower and orgn. devel. Polaroid Corp., Waltham, Mass., 1959-63; dir. internat. ops. Kepner-Tregoe & Assocs., Princeton, NJ, 1963-68; pres. John Arnold ExecuTrak Sys. Inc. and Corp. Breakthroughs! Inc., Boston, 1968—. Merger integration catalyst, conflict resolution/prevention counselor, conf. leader numerous firms; spkr. in field. Author: Make Up Your Mind, 1978, The Art of Decision Making, 1978, Shooting the Executive Rapids, 1981, How To Make the Right Decisions, 1982, Trading Up-A Career Guide: How To Get Ahead without Getting Out, 1984, How To Protect Yourself Against a Takeover, 1986, The Complete Problem Solver! A Total System of Competitive Decision Making, 1992, When the Sparks Fly: Resolving Conflict in Your Organization, 1993; contbr. articles to popular mags. V.p. programming, exec. com., bd. dirs. Orange County Philharm. Soc., 2001-04, bd. dirs. World Music, 1998-00; co-chmn. Laguna Beach Music Festival, 2003-06. 1st lt. U.S. Army, 1955-57. Avocations: skiing, squash, investments, music. Office: John Arnold ExecuTrak Sys and Corp Breakthroughs! Inc 32031 Point Pl Laguna Beach CA 92651-6862 Office Phone: 949-499-5400. Office Fax: 949-499-7608. Personal E-mail: chimo7@cox.net.

ARNOLD, JOHN FOX, lawyer; b. St. Louis, Sept. 17, 1937; s. John Anderson and Mildred Chapin (Fox) Arnold; m. Martha Ann Freeman, June 29, 1963 (div. Oct. 1993); children: Lisa A. Galena, Laura Wray, Lynne A. Binder, Lesli Johnston; m. Ann Ruwitch, Mar. 3, 2003. AB, U. Mo., Columbia, 1959, LLB, 1961. Bar: Mo. 1961, US Dist. Ct. (ea. dist.) Mo. 1961, US Ct. Appeals (8th cir.) 1961, US Supreme Ct. 1971. Ptnr. Green, Hennings, Henry & Arnold, St. Louis, 1963-70; mem. Lashly & Baer, P.C., St. Louis, 1970—, chmn., 1987—. Mem. St. Louis County Charter Revision Com., 1968, Mo. State Governance Rev. Com., 2005; chmn. St. Louis County Bd. Election Commrs., 1981—86; chmn. bd. dirs. Downtown St. Louis Inc., 1996—98, Downtown St. Louis Partnership, Inc., 1997—99; chmn. bd. overseers Lindenwood U., 1992—93, bd. dir., 1993—95. Lt. USAR, 1961—63. Recipient citation of merit U. Mo. Law Sch., Columbia, 1984, Mo. Bar Pres.'s award, 2005, Best Lawyers in Am., 2005, 06, 07, Found. award St. Louis Bar Found., 2006. Fellow Am. Bar Found.; mem. ABA (mem. house of dels. 1986-90), Bar Assn. Met. St. Louis (pres. 1975-76), Mo. Bar (pres. 1984-85), Nat. Conf. Commrs. on Uniform State Laws (life, drafting com. Securities Act, Partnership Act, article 2 sales, 2A leases and 8 investment securities of Uniform Comml. Code), Am. Law Inst. (life). Republican. Office: Lashly & Baer 714 Locust St Saint Louis MO 63101-1699 Office Phone: 314-621-2939. Business E-Mail: jfarnold@lashlybaer.com.

ARNOLD, JOSEPH PATTERSON, artist, small business owner; b. LA, May 17, 1954; s. George Longan and Ellen Pearson; m. Alison Higby Arnold; children: Jason, April. BFA, U. Arts, 1977, cert. in Elem. and Secondary Art Edn., 1978. Prin., owner Jo Arnold Studios, Laramie, Wyo., 1977—. Curator Ann Simpson Artmobile Program U. Wyo. Art Mus., 1996—98. One-man shows include Artwest Gallery, Jackson, Wyo., 2002, Bradford Brinton Mus., Sheridan, Wyo., 2002, Jackson Hole Ctr. for Arts, 2007, exhibited in group shows at Nat. Mus. Wildlife Art, Jackson, Wyo., 2004—, exhibitions include numerous exhibitions including most recently, Buffalo Bill Hist. Ctr., Cody, Wyo., 1990—, Yellowstone Art Mus., 1995, Bighorn Gallery, Cody, Wyo., 2000, Nat. Mus. Wildlife Art, Jackson, Wyo., 2001, Ucross Found. Ctr., Clearmont, Wyo., 2004, U. Wyo. Art Mus., Laramie, Wyo., 2005, Masters of Colo. Landscape Travelling Show, 2007, Represented in permanent collections Wyo. State Mus., U. Wyo. Art Mus., Rock Springs (Wyo.) Fine Art Ctr. Bd. dirs. Solid Rock Outdoor Ministries, Laramie, 1984—. Recipient Best of Show award, Internat. Platform Assn., 1983, Exhbn. award, Nicolaysen Art Mus., Purchase award, Wyo. State Mus., Landscape award, Windriver Valley Art Show, 1997, Best Pastel award, 1997, Fine Arts award, Wyo. State Hist. Soc., 2000. Democrat. Evang. Avocations: mountain climbing, skiing, music. Home and Office: Joe Arnold Studios 701 S 4th St Laramie WY 82070 Office Phone: 307-745-6214. Personal E-mail: artist82070@yahoo.com.

ARNOLD, KEN E., engineering company executive; BS, Cornell U.; MS in Civil Engring., Tulane U. With Shell Oil Co.; cons. Am. Petroleum Inst. (API); founder, former CEO Paragon Engring. Svc., Houston, 1980; now sr. exec. v.p. AMEC Paragon, Houston. Mem. Marine Bd. Transp. Rsch. Bd., 2004—. Contbr. articles to profl. jours. Named Engr. of Yr., Tex. Soc. of Profl. Engrs., 2003; recipient Production Engring. Award, Soc. Petroleum Engrs., 1998. Mem.: NAE. Office: AMEC Paragon 10777 Clay Rd Houston TX 77041 Office Phone: 713-570-1000. Office Fax: 713-570-8920.

ARNOLD, KIRK, information technology executive; BA, Dartmouth Coll. V.p. strategic svcs., cons. group Computer Scis. Corp., pres. cons. group; exec. v.p., COO NerveWire, Inc., pres., CEO; exec. v.p. product mktg. and strategy Human Resources Outsourcing Group FMR Corp.; vice chair, pres., CEO Keane, Inc., Boston, 2007—. Office: Keane Inc 100 City Square Boston MA 02129 Office Phone: 617-241-9200. Office Fax: 617-241-8027.*

ARNOLD, LAUREN, art historian, writer; b. Fox Lake, Ill., Dec. 27, 1949; d. Charles Harvey and Patricia Adelaide (Streeter) Arnold; m. Kenneth Pokorny (div. 1985); 1 child, Rachel Pokorny; m. Reay Stewart Dick, 1989; children: Ian Dick, Connor Dick, Caillie Dick. BA in History, U. Mich., Ann Arbor, 1979, MA in History of Art, 1981; cert. of mus. practice, U. Mich., 1983. Asst. to dir. U. Mich. Mus. Art, Ann Arbor, 1982—86; rsch. assoc. Ricci Inst. for Chinese-Western Cultural History/U. San Francisco, 1997—. Adj. lectr. U. San Francisco, 2002; presener, lectr. in field. Author: Princely Gifts and Papal Treasures: The Franciscan Mission to China and Its Influence on the Art of the West 1230-1350, 1999. Mem.: Coll. Art Assn. Episcopalian. Achievements include discovery of The Heavenly Horse painting, lost for 200 years in Forbidden City Beijing. Office: Ricci Inst for Chinese-Western Cultural History Univ San Francisco 2130 Fulton San Francisco CA 94117 Personal E-mail: laurenarnold@cs.com.

ARNOLD, LEE, library director, archivist; b. Waukegan, Ill., Oct. 18, 1959; s. Louis Douglas and Verona Christina Arnold. BA cum laude, Edgewood Coll., Madison, Wis., 1982; M of Libr. and Info. Sci., U. Wis., Milw., 1987; M of Liberal Arts, Temple U., 2000. Sales support mgr. Marshall Field and Co., Milw., 1982-88; asst. univ. libr. for adminstrv. svcs. Princeton U., 1988-92; tchr. English., Berlitz Schs. Lang., Princeton, 1990-92; dir. of libr. Hist. Soc. of Pa., Phila., 1992—. Contbr. articles to profl. jours.; numerous book reviews and presentations in field. Mem. Delta Epsilon Sigma. Democrat. Roman Catholic. Avocations: reading, travel, outdoors. Office: Hist Soc PA 1300 Locust St Philadelphia PA 19107-5661 Office Phone: 215-732-6200 ext 237.

ARNOLD, MARTIN, editor, journalist; b. NYC, May 14, 1929; s. A.M. and Evelyn (Goodman) A.; m. Irmgard Alexy, May 25, 1952 (div. 1988); children: Mark William, Christopher Curt. BA, Adelphi Coll., 1951. With NY Times, 1951-52, Newsday, 1952-54, NY Herald Tribune, 1954-59; reporter NY Times, 1959-76, asst. met. editor, 1976-77; asst. editor NY Times Mag., 1977-83, dep. editor, 1983-87, law page editor, 1987, spl. asst. to exec. editor, media editor, 1987-95, assoc. styles editor, 1995-97, sr. editor culture and book pub. columnist, 1997—. Friend of Robert F. Kennedy Meml. Found. Served with AUS, 1946-48. Recipient George Polk award, 1968, Page One award NY Newspaper Guild, 1970, Press award Am. Bar Assn., 1974, African-Am. Lit. award Harlem Book Fair, 2001 Mem. Soaring Soc. Am., Soc. Silurians Avocations: drawing, painting. Office: NY Times 620 Eighth Ave New York NY 10018-1405 Office Phone: 212-556-1550. Office Fax: 212-556-1516. Business E-Mail: arnold@nytimes.com.

ARNOLD, MARYGWEN SUELLA, language educator, medical/surgical nurse; d. Clarence Glen and Winifred Opal Arnold. AS in Nursing, Tyler Jr. Coll., Tex., 1974; diploma, Tex. Ea. Sch. Nursing, 1975; BS in Edn., U. Tex., Tyler, 1978, MEd in Reading, 1986, MA in English, 1989. Tchr. biology, life and earth sci. Troup High Sch., Tex., 1979—80; tchr. Spanish Chapel Hill Mid. Sch., 1983—84; tchr. biology, chemistry. Spanish and English Grace Cmty. High Sch., Tyler, 1980—85; instr. devel. writing, reading, English as 2d lang. Tyler Jr. Coll., 1989—2004, instr. English, 2004—. Mem.: Tex. Faculty Assn., Sigma Delta Pi, Alpha Chi. Avocations: piano, classical music.

ARNOLD, MORRIS SHEPPARD, federal judge; b. Texarkana, Tex., Oct. 8, 1941; BSEE, U. Ark., 1965, LLB, 1968; LLM, Harvard U., 1969, SJD, 1971; MA (hon.), U. Pa., 1977, JD (hon.), 1986; LLD (hon.), U. Ark., Little Rock, 1998, U. Conn., 2004. Tchg. fellow law Harvard U., 1969-70; from asst. prof. to prof. Ind. U. Law Sch., 1971-76, prof., 1976-77, dean, 1985; prof. law, history U. Pa., 1977-81; Ben J. Altheimer disting. prof. law U. Ark., Little Rock, 1981-84; judge US Dist. Ct. (we. dist.) Ark., Ft. Smith, 1985-92, US Ct. Appeals (8th cir.), Little Rock, 1992—2006, sr. judge, 2006—. Vis.fellow commoner Trinity Coll., Cambridge U., 1978; v.p., dir. office of the pres. U. Pa., 1980—81; vis. prof. Stanford U. Law Sch., Calif., 1985. Author: Old Tenures and Natura Brevium, 1974, Yearbook 2 Richard II, 1378-79, 1975, On the Laws and Customs of England, 1980, Unequal Laws Unto a Savage Race, 1985, Select Cases of Trespass from the King's Courts, 1307-1399, 2 vols., 1985, 1988, Arkansas Colonials, 1986, Colonial Arkansas 1686-1804: A Social and Cultural History, 1991, The Rumble of a Distant Drum: Quapaws and Old World Newcomers, 1673-1804, 2000, Arkansas: A Narrative History, 2002. Chmn., Rep. party State of Ark., 1983; gen. counsel, Rep. party Ark., 1982; bd. dirs. Nature Conservancy of Ark., 1982—87, Ark. Arts Ctr., 1981—84. Decorated chevalier Ordre Palmes Acad., France; recipient Porter Literary prize, 2001, Worthen Literary prize, 2001, Ragsdale prize, 2002; Frank Knox fellow, Harvard U./U. London, 1970—71, Mus. Sci. Natural History fellow, 1986. Fellow: Am. Soc. Legal History (hon.; pres. 1981—85); mem.: Am. Antiquarian Soc., Grolier Club, Country Club of Little Rock, Union League Club of Phila., Athenaeum Club London. Office: US Ct Appeals PO Box 2060 Little Rock AR 72203*

ARNOLD, PERI ETHAN, political scientist; b. Chgo., Sept. 21, 1942; s. Joseph Evon and Eve (Jacobs) A.; m. Beverly Ann Kessler, Aug. 22, 1965; children: Emma, Rachel. BA, Roosevelt U., Chgo., 1964; MA, U. Chgo., 1967, PhD, 1972. Lectr. Roosevelt U., Chgo., 1966-68; instr. polit. sci. Western Mich. U., Kalamazoo, 1970-71; asst. prof. polit. sci. U. Notre Dame, Ind., 1971-76, assoc. prof. govt. Ind., 1976-86, prof. of govt. and internat. studies Ind., 1986; chair dept. govt., 1986-92. Compton vis. prof. of world politics Miller Ctr., U. Va., 1993-94; dir. Hesburgh Program in Pub. Svc., 1995-2001; dir. Notre Dame Semester in Washington, 1997-2001. Author: Making the Managerial Presidency, 1986 (Louis Brownlow Book award 1987), 2nd rev. ed., 1998; mem. editl. bd. Am. Jour. Polit. Sci., 1991-94, Polity, 1995—2004, Presdl. Studies Quar., 1997—2005; co-editor Jour. of Policy History, 1987-88; mem. editl. adv. bd. Hughes Leadership Series, Tex. A&M U. Press, 1999—; contbr. articles to profl. jours. and edited vols. Bd. dirs. South Bend Hebrew Day Sch., Mishawaka, Ind., 1985—88; chair Cmty. Rels. Coun. of Jewish Fedn. of St. Joseph Valley, South Bend, Ind., 1990—94; mem. acquisitions com. Snite Mus. Art, Notre Dame, Ind., 1994—99; mem. adv. com. Coll. Arts and Scis., Roosevelt U., 2006; trustee congregation Beth El, South Bend, 1994—2000, sec., exec. com., 2000—02; bd. dirs. Jewish Fedn. of St. Joseph Valley, 1999—2002, v.p., 2001—03. Recipient Spl. Presdl. award U. Notre Dame, 1993, Marshall Dimock award Am. Soc. Pub. Adminstrn., 1996; grantee Am. Coun. Learned Socs., 1974; rsch. grantee Herbert Hoover Libr. Assn., 1993-94; Ford Found. fellow, 1978-81. Fellow Nat. Acad. Pub. Adminstrn.; mem. Am. Polit. Sci. Assn. (program chmn., exec. com. presidency sect.), Midwest Polit. Sci. Assn., The Cliff Dwellers Club (Chgo.). Democrat. Jewish. Avocations: literature, music, drama. Home: 1419 E Colfax Ave South Bend IN 46617-3307 Office: U Notre Dame Dept Polit Sci Notre Dame IN 46556 Home Phone: 574-233-9535; Office Phone: 574-631-7430. Business E-Mail: peri.e.arnold.1@nd.edu.

ARNOLD, ROBERT MORRIS, banker; b. Seattle, June 6, 1928; s. Lawrence Moss and Grace Elizabeth (Heffernan) A.; children: Grace Allen Arnold, Lauren McLellan Gorter. BA in Fin. and Bus. Adminstrn., Yale U., 1951; grad., Pacific Coast Sch. Banking, 1963. With Seattle-1st Nat. Bank, 1951, 1955—, v.p., 1965-73, mgr. nat. accounts dept., 1969-73, sr. v.p., mgr. corp. bus. devel., 1973-99, also bd. dirs. Bd. dirs. Seafirst Corp. Bank of Am. Bd. dirs. Centrum Found., Fred C. Hutchinson Cancer Rsch.; trustee Poncho; bd. dirs., exec. com., fin. com. Seattle Art Mus., also mem., joint founder its Contemporary Art Coun. Officer USNR, 1951-55. Mem. Am. Inst. Banking, Mcpl. League Seattle, Yale Assn. Western Wash., Newcomen Soc. (treas. Pacific N.W. com.), Seattle Golf Club, Seattle Tennis Club, Seattle Yacht Club, University Club (Seattle), Bohemian Club (San Francisco), Thunderbird Golf Club (Palm Springs, Calif.), O'Donnell Golf Club (Palm Springs), Mission Hills Country Club (Palm Springs). Home: 1535 Parkside Dr E Seattle WA 98112-3719 Office: 1001 4th Ave Ste 4710 Seattle WA 98154-1198 also: 50 Hilton Head Dr Rancho Mirage CA 92270-1607

ARNOLD, RONALD HENRI, nonprofit organization executive, consultant; b. Houston, Aug. 8, 1937; s. John Andrew and Carrie Virginia (Henri) A.; m. Phoebe Anne Trogdon, Oct. 12, 1963 (dec. Feb. 1974); 1 child, Andrea; m. Janet Ann Parkhurst, Aug. 8, 1974; stepchildren: Andrea Wright, Rosalyn Wright. Tech. publ. Boeing Co., Seattle, 1961-71; cons. Northwoods Studio, Bellevue, Wash., 1971—; exec. v.p. Ctr. for Def. of Free Enterprise, Bellevue, 1984—. Advisor Nat. Fed. Lands Conf., 1988-92. Author: James Watt and the Environment, 1981, Ecology Wars, 1987, The Grand Prairie Years, 1987; author: (with Alan Gottlieb) Trashing the Economy, 1993; author: Politically Correct Environment, 1996, Ecoterror, 1997, Battered Communities, 1998, Undue Influence, Power to Hurt, 2000, Trust Us, 2002, Autocrats and Activists, 2005, Freezing in the Dark, 2006; editor: Stealing theNational Parks, 1987; contbg. editor: Logging Mgmt. mag., 1978—81, We. Conservation Jour., 1974—81. Recipient Editorial Achievement award Am. Bus. Press, 1981. Mem. AFTRA, Forest History Soc. Republican. Avocation: music. Home: 12605 NE 2nd St Bellevue WA 98005-3206 Office Phone: 425-455-5038. Personal E-mail: rarnold@eskimo.com. Business E-Mail: rarnold@cdfe.org.

ARNOLD, SABRINA NICOLE, secondary school educator; b. Bristol, Tenn., Oct. 12, 1973; d. Tommy Ray King and Judy Kaye Holmes-King; m. Daniel Lee Arnold, June 19, 1993; children: Carson Danielle, Cassidy Nicole. BA in English, East Tenn. State U., Johnson City, 1996, BA in Drama, 1996; MEd, Tusculum Coll., Greenville, Tenn., 2000. Drama tchr. Princeton Arts Ctr., Johnson City, Tenn., 1996—97; 7th grade tchr. Holston Mid. Sch., Blountville, Tenn., 1997—2001; English and drama tchr. Sullivan East HS, Bluff City, Tenn., 2001—. Peer leader Ctr. Prevention of Hate Violence, Maine, 2003—. Named Educator of Yr., Dist. 6, Tenn. Hich Schs. Speech and Drama League, 2005; grantee, Found. for Excellence in Edn., 2004. Avocations: reading, travel, scrapbooks, camping. Office: Sullivan East HS 4180 Weaver Pike Bluff City TN 37618-2031 E-mail: nottheteenagewitch@yahoo.com.

ARNOLD, STANLEY NORMAN, management consultant, educator; b. Cleve., May 26, 1915; s. Morris L. and Mildred (Stearn) A.; m. Barbara Anne Laing, Aug. 31, 1946; 1 child, Jennifer Laing BS in Econs., U. Pa., 1937. Co-founder, exec. v.p. Pick-N-Pay Supermarkets, Cleve., 1937-51; exec. v.p., dir. Cottage Creamery Co., Cleve., 1937-51; dir. sales promotion div. Young & Rubicam, NYC, 1952-58; founder, pres. Stanley Arnold & Assocs., Inc., NYC, 1958—. Cons. Ford Motor Co., United Airlines, Gen. Electric, Nat. Cash Register, IBM, Philip Morris, Am. Express, Bank of America, DuPont, Goodyear, Quaker Oats, Readers Digest, Continental Can, Hunt Foods, Moet-Hennessy, Seagram, Pan Am, Chrysler Corp., Pillsbury, Coca Cola, Gen. Mills, Lever Bros., Exxon, Arco, Hallmark, others; mem. adv. bd. Bank of Palm Springs div. Bank of Calif. subs. Mitsubishi Corp., 1989—; vis. exec. prof. Freeman Sch. Bus., Tulane U., 1998—. Author: Tale of the Blue Horse, 1968; Magic Power of Putting Yourself Over with People, 1961; I Ran Against Jimmy Carter, 1977. Syndicated daily columnist, 1943-48. Architect of plan to install new office of v.p. in White House. Contbr. articles to profl. jours. Pres. Ind. Sch. Fund of N.Y.C., 1960-66; mem. fund raising com. U.S. Olympic Team, 1984. Founding mem. Nat. Businessmen for Humphrey, 1968, Nat. Citizens for Humphrey, 1968; candidate for Dem. nomination for v.p. U.S., 1972; chmn. White House Libr. Fund Raising Com., 1961-63; corp. sponsor for The Rose as Nat. Flower, 1983-86; nat. chmn. Golf's Tribute to Ike, 1980; mem. Clinton adv. com., 1991-92; mem. Bush For Pres. Com., 2000, 04; mem. Rep. Nat. Com., 2000—. Recipient Sales Exec. award Sales Exec. Club N.Y., 1965; Wisdom award of Honor Wisdom Soc., 1979 Mem.: Outrigger Canoe Club, La Quinta Fishing Club, Desert Riders Club, Seven Lakes Country Club, Les Amis D'Escoffier, Doubles Dutch Club (N.Y.C.). Home: 162 Desert Lakes Dr Palm Springs CA 92264-5521 also: 2895 Kalakaua Ave Honolulu HI 96815-4003 also: 375 Park Ave New York NY 10152-0002 Office: 162 Desert Lakes Dr Palm Springs CA 92264-5521

ARNOLD, SUSAN E., consumer products company executive; b. Pitts., Mar. 8, 1954; 2 children. BA, U. Pa., 1976; MBA, U. Pitts., 1980. Joined Procter & Gamble Co., Cin., 1980, brand asst., Dawn/Ivory Snow, 1980, sales tng. Phila., 1981, asst. brand mgr., Oxydol Cin., 1981—83, asst. brand mgr., Cascade, 1983—84, brand mgr., Gain/Spl. Assignment, 1984—85, brand mgr., Tide Sheets, 1985—86, brand mgr., Dawn, 1986—87, assoc. advertising mgr., PS& D Advertising, 1987, assoc. advertising mgr., laundry products, PS&D Divsn., 1987—88, assoc. advertising mgr., laundry specialty products, PS&D Divsn., 1988—89, advertising mgr., fabric softeners, BS&HCP Divsn., 1989—90, gen. mgr., Noxell Products, Internat. Divsn. Canada, 1990—92, gen. mgr., deodorants/Old Spice (U.S.A.), 1993—96; v.p., gen. mgr., deodorants/Old Spice and Skin Products-US Procter & Gamble Co. N.Am., 1997—97, v.p., gen. mgr., laundry products-US, 1997—99; v.p., N.Am. Fabric Care Procter & Gamble Co., Cin., 1999, pres., global skin care, 1999—2000, pres., global cosmetics & skin care, 2000, pres., personal beauty care, 2000—02, pres., global personal beauty care & global feminine care, 2002—04, vice chmn. global beauty care, 2004—, vice-chmn., beauty & health (oral care, personal health and pharm. businesses), 2006—07, pres. global bus. units, 2007—. Bd. dir. Reflect.com, Cin. Zoo, Walt Disney Co., 2007—, Goodyear Tire & Rubber Co., 2003—05. Named Top Marketer and One of the 21 to Watch in the 21st Century, Advt. Age, Career Woman of Achievement, YWCA, 2000; named one of 50 Most Powerful Women in Bus., Fortune mag., 2002—, 50 Women to Watch, Wall Street Jour., 2004, 2005, 100 Most Powerful Women, Forbes Mag., 2006, 50 Most Powerful Women in Bus., Fortune mag., 2006; recipient Best Boss award, Cosmetic Exec. Women, 2003. Achievements include first women to reach a president-level position at Procter & Gamble Co; first women to be named to the vice chairman position at Procter & Gamble Co. Avocation: surfing. Office: Procter & Gamble Co 1 Procter & Gamble Plz Cincinnati OH 45202*

ARNOLD, TOM, actor, comedian, television producer; b. Ottumwa, Iowa, Mar. 6, 1959; s. Jack and Ruth (stepmother) A.; m. Roseanne, Jan. 20, 1990 (div. 1994); m. Julie Champnella, July 22, 1995 (div. 1999); m. Shelby Roos, 2002 (separated, August, 2006) AA, Indian Hills Cmty. Coll.; bachelor's degree, U. Iowa. Actor, co-exec. prodr. The Jackie Thomas Show, 1992-93, HBO Tom Arnold the Naked Truth I, II, III; dir. HBO's Roseanne Live from Minn.; exec. prodr. (TV series) Tom, 1994; actor, exec.prodr. (TV series) The Tom Show, 1997-89, Roseanne, 1988-97; actor, prodr: (films) The Kid and I, 2005; actor Backfield in Motion, 1991, Body Bags, 1993, (voice) Hercules, 1998, Jackie's Back!, 1999, Arnold Schwarzenegger: Hollywood Hero, 1999, Bar Hopping, 2000, Romantic Comedy 101, 2001, (voice) Dennis the Menace in Cruise Control, 2002, Hero, 1992, Undercover Blues, 1993, True Lies, 1994, Nine Months, 1995, Big Bully, 1995, The Stupids, 1996, Carpool, 1996, (also co-prodr.) McHale's Navy, 1997, Touch, 1997, Austin Powers: International Man of Mystery, 1997, Hacks, 1997, (voice) Buster and Chauncey's Silent Night, 1998, Golf Punks, 1998, Blue Ridge Fall, 1999, Animal Factory, 2000, We Married Margo, 2000, Civility, 2000, Just Sue Me, 2000, Exit Wounds, 2001, Lloyd, 2001, Fever Pitch, 2001, Ablaze, 2001, Hansel & Gretel, 2002, Children on Their Birthdays, 2002, Cradle 2 the Grave, 2003, After School Special, 2003, (voice) Goose!, 2004, Soul Plane, 2004, Happy Endings, 2005, Chasing Christmas, 2005, Three Wise Guys, 2005, (voice) Lola's Cafe, 2006, Oranges, 2007, Pride, 2007; guest appearances Veronica's Closet, 1999, Baywatch, 2000, Judging Amy, 2003, Hope & Faith, 2004, Life According to Jim, 2004 and others. Office: William Morris Agency care Michael Gruber 151 S El Camino Dr Beverly Hills CA 90212-2775*

ARNOLD, VALERIE DOWNING, lawyer; b. Istanbul, Turkey, Jan. 6, 1967; BA in French, U. Minn., 1988; student, Universite de Savoir, Chambery, France, 1990; MA in French, U. Minn., 1992, JD, 1997. Bar: Minn. 1997, US Dist. Ct. (dist. Minn.) 2004. Shareholder Tuft & Arnold, P.L.L.C., Maplewood, Minn. Named a Rising Star, Minn. Super Lawyers mag., 2006. Mem.: Warren E. Burger Inn of Ct., Minn. Women Lawyers, Ramsey County Bar Assn., Minn. State Bar Assn. Office: Tuft & Arnold PLLC 2109 County Rd D East Ste A Saint Paul MN 55109 Office Phone: 651-771-0050. E-mail: val@tuftarnoldlaw.com.*

ARNOLD, WILLIAM EDWIN, health advocate, consultant; b. Charleston, SC, Aug. 13, 1938; s. Edwin Gustaf and Sara Louise (Hitchcock) A. BA, Yale U., 1960. Pres. Dixon & Rippel, Inc., Saugerties, NY, 1965-70; v.p. Taj Enterprises Ltd., 1965-67, Bellern Rsch. Corp.; pres. Dixon & Rippel divsn., Saugerties, 1970-75; v.p. H & G Industries, Inc.; pres. World Brushworks, Inc., 1982-84; v.p. CFO Optimax III, Inc., NYC, 1983-84; mng. dir. Brush Trading, Ltd., 1983-87; pres. Chestnut Holdings Ltd., 1985-91; part-time mng. dir. Cassi Properties, 1984—; pres. Computerworx, Inc., Washington, 1999—. Pres. Swan Holding Ltd., 1985-88. Bd. dirs. ARCS, 1991-92; chair Dutchess County AIDS Consortium, 1989-95; chmn. Dutchess County HIV Health Svcs. Planning Coun., 1995-96; bd. dirs. ARCS Cmty. Educator, 1989-91; pres. Hudson AIDS Cmty. Progress, Inc., 1992-94; exec. dir. Title II Nat. AIDS Coalition, 1994-95; CEO Title II Cmty. AIDS Nat. Network, Washington, 1995—; chair ADAP Working Group, Washington, 1995—; sec.-treas. AIDS Empowerment and Treatment Internat., Washington, 2002—. 1st lt. U.S. Army, 1961-63. Mem.: Res. Officers Assn., Yale Club (Washington). Home: 1755 Seaton Pl NW Washington DC 20009-2625 Office: 1775 T St NW Washington DC 20009-7124 Home Phone: 202-462-0409; Office Phone: 202-588-1775. E-mail: weaids@aol.com, weaids2@tiicann.org.

ARNOLD, WILLIAM MCCAULEY, lawyer; b. Waco, Tex., May 3, 1947; s. Watson Caulfield and Mary Rebecca Arnold; m. Karen Axtell, May 17, 1980. BA, Duke U., 1969; JD, U. Tex., 1972. Bar: Tex. 1973, Va. 1975, D.C. 1977, Md. 1983, U.S. Dist. Ct. (ea. dist.) Va. 1975, U.S. Ct. Appeals (4th cir.) 1977, U.S. Ct. Claims 1977, U.S. Supreme Ct. 1978. Spl. atty. U.S. Dept. Justice, Newark, 1973-75; asst. county atty. County of Fairfax, Va., 1975-78; ptnr. Cowles, Rinaldi & Arnold, Ltd., Fairfax, 1978-95, McCandlish & Lillard, Fairfax, 1995—. Instr. No. Va. C.C., Alexandria. Pres. Clifton Betterment Assn., Va., 1979-81; chmn. Clifton Planning Commn., 1980-85, mem. Clifton Town Coun., 1985-2006; bd. dirs. Clifton Gentlemen's Social Club, 1981-84. Mem. ABA, Va. State Bar Assn., Fairfax County Bar Assn., Va. Trial Lawyers Assn. Office: McCandlish & Lillard PC 11350 Random Hills Rd Ste 500 Fairfax VA 22030-6044 Office Phone: 703-934-1128. Business E-Mail: marnold@mccandlaw.com.

ARNOLD, WINFRED RAYMON, trade association administrator; b. Palestine, Tex., Feb. 8, 1960; s. Gilbert Andrew Arnold and Eugenia Clare Nettleton. BS in Biology magna cum laude, Stephen F. Austin State U., Nacogdoches, Tex., 1981, MS in Biology, 1982—84; postgrad., Tex. A&M U., College Station, 1985—86; PhD in Biology, U. North Tex., Denton, 1989. Grad. tchg. asst. Stephen F. Austin State U., 1982—84, Tex. A&M U., 1984—85; grad. rsch. and tchg. asst. U. North Tex., 1986—89; environ. scientist Exxon Biomed. Scis., East Millstone, NJ, 1989—91, sr. environ. scientist, 1991—93, staff environ. scientist, 1993—2000; v.p. Copper Devel. Assn., NYC, 2000—. Group head Exxon Biomed. Scis., East Millstone, 1993—97; mem. Green Bldg. Guidelines Group Nat. Assn. Home Builders, 2003—; chmn. tech. adv. com. San Francisco Bay Regional Monitoring Program, 1996—2000, mem., 2000—; mem. toxics subcom. Chesapeake Bay Program, 2000—; mem. Biomonitoring Task Force, Am. Petroleum Inst., 1991—2000, mem. Drilling Mud Task Force, 1997—2000, mem. methyl-tertiary butyl ether water quality criteria task force, 1998—2000; mem. Aquatic Life and Human Health Chem. Specific Objectives Adv. Task Force, Calif., 1995—97, San Francisco Bay Fish Contamination Com., 1996—2000, San Francisco Bay Fish Consumption Com., 1996—2000, San Francisco Bay Risk Assessment Endpoint Subcom., 1996—2000; mem. Environ. and Govt. Affairs Com., US Copper Industry, 2000—; mem. Am. Copper Policy Coun., 2000—. Author numerous abstracts in field; contbr. articles to profl. jours.; mem. editl. bd. Jour. Environ. Toxicology and Chemistry, 1997—2000, invited editor/reviewer Environ. Toxicology and Chemistry Jour., Human and Ecol. Risk Assessment Jour., Bull. of Environ. Contamination and Toxicology, Aquatic Toxicology Jour. Named Disting. Young Alumnus, Stephen F. Austin State U., 1996; recipient Quality Svc. award, Exxon Biomed. Scis., 1991, 1992, Exceptional Achievement award, 1992, 1995; Louis David Scholastic scholar, 1978—81, EPA Trainee scholar, U. North Tex., 1986—87. Mem.: Am. Fisheries Soc., Am. Soc. Limnology and Oceanography, Soc. Environ. Toxicology and Chemistry (expert adv. panel on Whole Effluent Toxicity 1996—2001, student mentor 1997—, expert adv. subcom. on TR/TIE 1998—2000, session chair 2006, 1997, expert participant tech. workshop on Whole-Effluent Toxicity 1995, session chair 1993, sec./treas. Hudson-Del. chpt. 1989—93, counselor South Ctrl. Region 1987—88, Meritorious Platform award 1989, Meritorious Poster award 1988), Beta Beta Beta, Alpha Chi (chpt. v.p.), Sigma Xi. Achievements include development of Private Whys? inquiry-based hands-on science education program; simple surrogate method to replace US EPA saltwater Water-Effects Ratio tests; research in calibrating the Biotic Ligand Model to predict the toxicity of copper to endangered freshwater mussels of the USA and Canada; development of unified approach to derive copper water quality criteria across salinity gradients ranging from fresh to true marine waters; management of project to determine copper recycling rates in the USA; management of projects to determine the fate and effects of copper in the diet of fish; management of project to determine copper toxicity thresholds to benthic organisms using amended sediments in situ; management of studies to develop simple, cost-effective methods for removing copper from stormwater. Avocation: fishing. Home: 108 Lowell Ct # 2 Princeton NJ 08540 Office: Copper Devel Assn 260 Madison Ave New York NY 10016

ARNOLD, WINNIE JO, retired mental health nurse; b. Cromwell, Okla., May 21, 1929; d. Robb Henry and Luella (Odom) Boatman; widowed; children: Linda, Cherie. BSEd, Okla. U., 1962; ADN, Amarillo Coll., 1974; BSN, St. Joseph's Coll., 1977. RN, Tex. Charge nurse Northwest Tex. Hosp., Amarillo; staff nurse, team leader High Plains Bapt. Hosp., Amarillo; adminstr. Healthcare Svcs., Amarillo; dir. nurses Tex. Dept. Corrections, Amarillo, 1989—97; ret., 1997. Vol. ARC. Recipient Vol. award ARC, 1989, Pilot Club, 1989. Mem. Am. Kidney Found., Women's Bus. Assn. (Bus. Woman of Yr. 1989). Home: 216 Ramada Trl Amarillo TX 79108-1128 E-mail: wjatexan@msn.com.

ARNON, STEPHEN SOULÉ, physician, research scientist; b. Oakland, Calif., Oct. 14, 1946; s. Daniel I. and Lucile S. Arnon; m. Joyce M. Meissinger, Aug. 24, 1985; children: Eric, Christina. AB, Harvard U., 1968, MPH, 1972, MD, 1973. Lic. physician Calif. Resident physician U. Colo. Hosps., Denver, 1973—75; med. epidemiologist Ctrs. for Disease Control, Atlanta, 1975—76, Berkeley, Calif., 1976—77; founder, chief infant botulism treatment and prevention program Calif. Dept. Health Svcs., Berkeley and Richmond, 1977—. Contbr. articles and book chpts. to profl. publs. Bd. dirs. Orinda (Calif.) Pks. and Recreation Found., Orinda, 1992—. Lt. comdr. USPHS, 1975—77. Recipient Jens Aubrey Westengard and John Houghton Taylor scholarships, Harvard Med. Sch., 1968—73, Wiley medal, U.S. Pub. Health Svc., 1998, Therapeutic Achievement award, Nat. Orgn. for Rare Disorders, 2004. Fellow: Am. Coll. Epidemiology, Infectious Disease Soc. Am. Achievements include creation and development of pub. svc. orphan drug Botulism Immune Globulin Intravenous (Human) BabyBIG (registered) for treatment of infant botulism; research in orphan drug development; medical and public health management of botulinum toxin if used as bioweapon. Office: Calif Dept Health Svcs 850 Marina Bay Pkwy Richmond CA 94804 Office Phone: 510-231-7600.

ARNOT, WILLIAM G., III, lawyer; b. 1950; BBA, U. Tex., Austin, 1972; JD, Baylor U., Tex., 1975; LLM, U. Va., 1992. Assoc. justice 11th Ct. of Appeals, Abilene, Tex., 1986—93, chief justice, 1994—2005; shareholder Winstead Sechrest & Minick P.C., Houston, 2005—. Bd. dirs. Appellate Judges Inst., So. Meth. U. Dedman Sch. of Law. Bd. trustees Hardin-Simmons U., Abilene. Named Top Lawyer, H Tex. Mag., 2006. Office: Winstead Sechrest & Minick PC 919 Milam St Ste 2400 Houston TX 77002-5895 Office Phone: 713-650-8400. Office Fax: 713-650-2400. Business E-Mail: barnot@winstead.com.

ARNOTT, HOWARD JOSEPH, biology professor, dean; b. LA, Mar. 9, 1928; s. Andrew Hugh and Evelyn Leonore (Donnelly) A.; m. Wanda Jean Cross, Jan. 28, 1950; children: John Joseph, Catherine Jean Arnott-Thornton, Susan Leonore Arnott Garrett, Virginia Anne Arnott Scott. AB, U. So. Calif., 1952, MS, 1953; PhD, U. Calif., Berkeley, 1958. Asst. prof. biology Northwestern U., Evanston, Ill., 1958-64; assoc. prof. dept. botany U. Tex., Austin, 1965-68, prof., 1968-72, acting chmn. dept., 1970-71; prof., chmn. dept. biology U. So. Fla., Tampa, 1972-74; dean Coll. Sci. U. Tex., Arlington, 1974-90, prof. biology, 1974-91, Ashbel Smith prof. biology, 1991-96, dir. Ctr. for Electron Microscopy Coll. Sci., 1984—, Jenkins Garrett prof., 1996—. Vis. mem. dept. biology Tex. A&M U., 1971-75; cons. Ency. Brit. Films, NASA, Alcon Labs., Frito-Lay; bd. dirs. Ft. Worth Nature Ctr., 1985-91; chmn. 2nd Gordon Conf. Calcium Oxalate, 1989, main spkr. 4th Conf., 1993; vis. prof. Purdue U., 1990-91; Bessey lectr. Iowa State U., 1993; visitor Lab. Tree-Ring Rsch., U. Ariz., Tucson, 2006, 07. Advisory editor: Protoplasma; Contbr. articles, abstracts to sci. jours., chpts. to books. With USN, 1946-48. Recipient award for disting. and continued research U. Tex. at Arlington, 1984; postdoctoral fellow U. Tex., NIH, 1964-65; NSF grantee, 1963-65, NIH grantee, 1989. Mem. Am. Soc. Plant Physiology, Bot. Soc. Am., Mycol. Soc. Am., Microscopy Soc. Am., Tex. Soc. Microscopy (hon., pres. 1988-89), Sigma Xi (bd. dirs. S.W. region 1984-91), Phi Sigma (Spl. award 2005). Business E-Mail: arnott@uta.edu.

ARNOTT, JASON, professional hockey player; b. Collingwood, Ont., Can., Oct. 11, 1974; Center Edmonton Oilers, 1993—98, NJ Devils, 1998—2002, Dallas Stars, 2002—06, Nashville Predators, 2006—. Achievements include being a member of Stanley Cup Champion NJ Devils, 2000. Office: Nashville Predators 501 Broadway Nashville TN 37203

ARNOTT, ROBERT DOUGLAS, investment company executive; b. Chgo., June 29, 1954; s. Robert James Arnott and Catherine (Bonnell) Cameron; children: Robert Lindsay, Sydney Allison, Richard James. BA, U. Calif., Santa Barbara, 1977. V.p. Boston Co., 1977—84; pres., chief exec. officer TSA Capital Mgmt., LA, 1984—87; v.p., strategist Salomon Bros. Inc., NYC, 1987—88; mng. ptnr. First Quadrant Corp., Morristown, N.J., Pasadena, Calif., and London, 1988—96, First Quadrant, LP, Pasadena, London, Boston, 1996—2002, chmn., 2002—04; chmn., CEO Rsch. Affiliates, LLC, 2002—. Mem. chmn.'s adv. coun. Chgo. Bd. Options Exch., 1989-94; bd. dirs. Internat. Faculty in Fin.; mem. product adv. bd. Chgo. Mercantile Exch., 1990-96; vis. prof. UCLA, 2001-03. Editor: Asset Allocation, 1988, Active Asset Allocation, 1992, Handbook of Equity Style Management, 1997, Fin. Analysts Jour., 2002-06; mem. editl. bd. Jour. of Investing, 1990—, Jour. Portfolio Mgmt., 1984-2002, Jour. Wealth Mgmt., 1997—; contbr. articles to profl. jours. and chpts. to books. Mem. Inst. Internat. Rsch. (adv. bd. 1990—), Assn. for Investment Mgmt. and Rsch., Inst. Quantitative Rsch. in Fin., Toronto Stock and Futures Exch. (adv. coun. 1992—). Avocations: motorcycling, astrophotography, billiards, sommelier, travel. Office: Rsch Affiliates 155 N Lake Ave Ste 900 Pasadena CA 91101 E-mail: arnott@rallc.com.

ARNOULD, RICHARD JULIUS, economist, educator, consultant, dean; b. Rochelle, Ill., Nov. 18, 1941; s. Elliott and Blanch (Colwell) A.; m. Carol Foster, Aug. 27, 1960; children: Debra, Laura. BS, Iowa State U., 1963, MS, 1965, PhD, 1968. Instr. Iowa State U., Ames, 1963-65; asst. prof. econs. and bus. adminstrn. U. Ill., Champaign, 1967-72, assoc. prof., 1973-82, prof., 1982—2003, prof. emeritus, 2003—, dir. Coll. Rsch. Office, 1995-96, assoc. dean for acad. affairs, Coll. Commerce and Bus. Adminstrn., 1979-87, prof. econs., Coll. Medicine, 1984—, adj. prof. Inst. of Govt. and Pub. Affairs, 1987—, dir. Program in Health Econs., Mgmt. & Policy, 1989—, head dept. econs., 1996—2003; exec. dir. Am. Soc. Health Economists, 2003—. Acting dir. Exec. Devel. Ctr., part-time 1982, 84, mem. Med. Scholars Steering Com., active numerous other univ., coll. and dept. coms.; rsch. economist pricing and competition grp., USDA, 1965-67; vice chmn. Dept. Econs., U. Ill., 1970-73; vis. economist Econ. Policy Office, U.S. Justice Dept., 1973-74; regional economist U.S. Comptroller of Currency, 1976-79; vis. rsch. prof. Duke U., 1977-78; vis. rsch. scholar York (Eng.) U.; cons. Carle Found., chmn. bd., 1989-91; mem. Gov.'s Task Force on Health Care Reform, 1992-95; cons. Auditor Gen. State of Ill., GAO, Health Care Financing Adminstrn., Anti-trust div. U.S. Justice Dept., ABA, AMA, Prepaid Legal Svcs. Inst., others; bd. dirs. First Busey Trust & Investment Co.; expert witness numerous law firms; speaker profl. meetings. Author: Extra Territorial Application and Effects of Certain U.S. and Canadian Laws, 1978, (monograph) Blue Shield Fee Setting in the Physicians' Service Market: A Theoretical and Empirical Analysis, (pamphlets) Diversification and Profitability Among Large Food Processing Firms, USDA, 1970, (with R. Resek) A Comparative Cost Study of Staff Panel and Participating Attorney Panel Prepaid Legal Servcie Plans, ABA, 1982; editor spl. issue Quar. Rev. of Econs. and Bus., 1990, also book chpts. and revs.; co-editor: (with R. Rich and W. White) Competitive Approaches to Health Care Reform, 1993; contbr. numerous articles to profl. jours. Bd. dirs. City Bank Champaign, First Basey Trust and Investment Co.; trustee Carle Found., 1981-93, chmn. fin. com., 1982-86, chmn. bd., 1989-91; elder 1st Presbyn. Ch., Champaign; mem. Gov.'s Task Force on Health Care Reform; mem. U.S. Govt. Study of Econ. Underpinning of Vaccine Markets. Brookings Inst. Econ. Policy fellow, 1973; recipient Outstanding Service award, U.S. Justice Dept., 1974; grantee Internat. Bur. Edn., 1979, Carle Found., 1982-83, Grad. Research Bd., 1983-86; named Outstanding Tchr. U. Ill. various yrs. Mem. Am. Econ. Assn., So. Econ. Assn., Internat. Health Econs. Assn., Midwest Econ. Assn. Avocation: golf. Office: U Ill 1206 S 6th St Champaign IL 61820-6978 Business E-Mail: rarnould@uiuc.edu.

ARNOVE, ROBERT FREDERICK, education educator; b. Chgo. s. Isadore and Julie (Zeplowitz) A.; m. Toby Strout; 1 child, Anthony Keats BA, U. Mich., 1969; MA, Tufts U., 1961; PhD, Stanford U., 1969. Vol. tchr. Peace Corps, Venezuela, 1962-64; Ford Found. edn. advisor Bogota, Colombia, 1969-71; prof. comparative edn. Ind. U., Bloomington, 1969—, Ind. U.-Hangzhou, People's Rep. China, 1983; vis. prof. Stanford U., McGill U. Edn. cons. to Latin Am. ministries and agys.; dir. Overseas Study Program of Ind., Purdue, and Wis. univs. in Madrid, 1989—; USIA Exch. scholar, Ryazan, Russia, 1996, Yaounde, Cameroon, 1997, Salamanca, Spain, 2001; UNESCO-chair vis. scholar U. Palermo, Buenos Aires, 1997-2002; adv. prof. Hong Kong Inst. Edn. Author, editor, co-editor: Student Alienation, Educational Television, Education and American Culture Comparative Education, Philanthropy and Cultural Imperialism, Education and Revolution in Nicaragua, National Literacy Campaign: Historical and Comparative Perspectives, Emergent Issues in Education: Comparative Perspectives, Education as Contested Terrain: Nicaragua 1979-93, 1994, Comparative education: The Dialectic of the Global and the Local, 1999, 07, Civil Society or Shadow State: State NGO Education Relations, 2004; prodr. (documentary) Alternative Public Schools, 1978, Asi Fue: Election Time Nicaragua, 1984; contbr. articles to profl. jours. Citizens Party candidate for U.S. Congress, 8th dist. Ind., 1982 Fulbright grantee, India, 1982; Fulbright lectr. Fed. U. Bahai, Brazil, 1995; Fulbright sr. scholar U. Iberoamericana, Dominican Republic, 2003. Mem. Comparative and Internat. Edn. Soc. (pres. 2001, hon. fellow), Latin Am. Studies Assn., Am. Ednl. Rsch. Assn. Phi Delta Kappa. Office: Ind U Sch Edn Bloomington IN 47405 Office Phone: 812-856-8374. Business E-Mail: arnove@indiana.edu.

ARNOVITZ, BENTON MAYER, editor; b. Butler, Pa., July 21, 1942; s. Paul and Miriam (Shapiro) A. AB, Cornell U., 1964; MA, NYU, 1969; grad., U.S. Army Command and Gen. Staff Coll., 1982; grad. Nat. Security Mgmt. Program, Nat. Def. U., 1986. Editor Macmillan Pub. Co., NYC, 1966-73; sr. trade editor Chilton Book Co., Radnor, Pa., 1973-76; exec. editor Stein and Day Pubs., Briarcliff Manor, NY, 1976-85, v.p., 1984-85; ind. editl. svcs., 1985-89, 91-93; editl. dir. Scarborough House Pubs. divsn. BookCrafters, Peekskill, NY, 1989-91; dir. acad. pubs. U.S. Holocaust Meml. Mus., Washington, 1994—. Contbr. articles to scholarly jour. and newspapers. Trustee Field Libr. Inc., 1985-94, Westchester Libr. Sys., 1992-94; mem. Spirit of Raoul Wallenberg Humanitarian award selection com. Am. Swedish Hist. Mus. Capt. U.S. Army, 1964-66, 70; lt. col. USAR. Mem. Alpha Phi Delta. Home: 13439 Overbrook Ln Bowie MD 20715-1159 Office: 100 Raoul Wallenberg Pl SW Washington DC 20024-2126

ARNOWITT, RICHARD LEWIS, retired physics professor; b. NYC, May 3, 1928; s. Leon and Belle (Feinberg) A.; m. Young In Rhee, Apr. 21, 1961; children: Michael Paul, Myron Philip. BS, MS, Rensselaer Poly. Inst., 1948; PhD, Harvard U., 1953. Rsch. assoc. Radiation Lab. U. Calif., Berkeley, 1952-54; mem. Inst. Advanced Study, Princeton, NJ, 1954-56; asst. prof. Syracuse (N.Y.) U., 1956-59, assoc. prof., 1959-62; prof. Northeastern U., Boston, 1962-86, Tex. A&M U., College Station, 1986-88, disting. prof. physics, 1988—2004, disting. prof. emeritus, 2004—, dir. Ctr. Theoretical Physics, 1986-95, head dept. physics, 1987-93; disting. prof. emeritus, 2004—. Contbr. over 200 articles to profl. jours. Fellow Guggenheim Found., 1975-76. Fellow Am. Phys. Soc. (Dannie N. Heineman prize 1994, Burgess chair high energy physics 1997-04). Office: Texas A & M U Dept Physics College Station TX 77843-4242 Home Phone: 979-696-1101; Office Phone: 979-845-7746. Business E-Mail: arnowitt@physics.tamu.edu.

ARNQUIST, CAROL ANNE, humanities educator; b. Chgo., Oct. 12, 1938; d. William Donald and Mildred E. Baumeister; m. Herbert Arvid Arnquist; 1 child, Eric William. BS, U. Chgo., 1960, MS, 1961. Cert. tchr. Ill., 1961. Tchr. Oak Lawn Cmty. HS, Ill., 1961—73, Triton Coll., River Grove, Ill., 1974—83, 1993—. Pres. PTSA, Oak Lawn, 1969—70; co-chair spl. events PTA, 1991—92, grant writer, 1991—92. Finalist Outstanding Biology Tchr. award, Ill.; Merit fellowship, Shell, 1968. Avocations: camping, singing. Business E-Mail: carnquis@triton.edu.

ARNSTEIN, WALTER LEONARD, retired historian; b. Stuttgart, Germany, May 14, 1930; arrived in U.S., 1939, naturalized, 1944; s. Richard and Charlotte (Heymann) Arnstein; m. Charlotte Culver Sutphen, June 8, 1952; children: Sylvia, Peter. BSS., CCNY, 1951; MA, Columbia U., 1954; PhD, Northwestern U., 1961; postgrad., U. London, Eng., 1956-57. Asst. prof. history Roosevelt U., Chgo., 1957-62, assoc. prof., 1962-66, prof., acting dean grad. divsn., 1966-67; prof. history U. Ill., Urbana, 1968-98, LAS Jubilee prof. history, 1989-98, prof. history and LAS Jubilee prof. history emeritus, 1998—, chmn. dept., 1974-78, assoc. Ctr. for Advanced Study, 1972-73. Vis. assoc. prof. history Northwestern U., 1963—64; vis. fellow Clare Hall, Cambridge U., 1982; hon. fellow U. Edinburgh, 1989. Author: The Bradlaugh Case: A Study in Late Victorian Opinion and Politics, 1965, 2d edit., 1984, Britain Yesterday and Today, 1966, 8th edit., 2001, Protestant Versus Catholic in Mid-Victorian England, 1982, (with William B. Willcox) The Age of Aristocracy, 3d edit., 1976, 8th edit., 2001, Queen Victoria, 2003; editor: The Past Speaks: Sources and Problems in British History Since 1688, 1981, 2d edit. 1993; editor: Recent Historians of Great Britain, 1990; bd. editors The Historian, 1976-2000, Am. Hist. Rev., 1982-85, Albion, 1988-93; mem. bd. advisers: Victorian Studies, 1966-75; contbr. articles profl. jours. Vice chmn. Ill. Humanities Coun., 1983-84. Served with AUS, 1951-53, Korea. Fellow, Am. Coun. Learned Socs., 1967—68; Fulbright scholar, 1956—57. Fellow Royal Hist. Soc.; mem. Am. Hist. Assn., Brit. Hist. Assn., N.Am. Conf. Brit. Studies (exec. com. 1971-76, v.p. 1993-95, pres. 1995-97), Midwest Conf. on Brit. Studies (pres. 1980-82), Midwest Victorian Studies Assn. (pres. 1977-80, annual Walter L. Arnstein Dissertation prize awarded in his name 1992—), Phi Beta Kappa, Phi Alpha Theta. Home: 804 W Green St Champaign IL 61820-5017 Office: U Ill Dept History 309 Gregory Hall 810 S Wright St Urbana IL 61801-3644 Business E-Mail: warnstei@uiuc.edu.

ARNTSON, PETER ANDREW, lawyer; b. Washington, May 23, 1938; s. Paul Lee and Mary Ellen (Garrigan) Arntson; m. Colette Rousseau, July 11, 1962; 1 child, Eric Paul. BA, U. Va., 1960, JD, 1965; LLM in Taxation, Georgetown U., 1971; postgrad., U.S. Army War Coll., 1982. Bar: Va. 1965, US Supreme Ct. 1973. Assoc., then ptnr. Phillips, Kendrick, Gearheart & Aylor, Arlington, Va., 1965-75; ptnr. McCandlish, Lilliard, Church & Best, Fairfax, Va., 1975-84, Miles & Stockbridge, Fairfax, 1984-95, McCandlish & Lillard, Fairfax, 1995—. Chmn. com. taxation Va. State Bar, 1978; dep. commr. accts. Fairfax County, 1994—2006. Chmn. bd. dirs. No. Va. Am. Heart Assn., 1978; bd. dirs. Benedictine Sch. Exceptional Children, Ridgely, Md., 1985—, No. Va. Cmty. Found., 1991—, Arlington Cmty. Found., 1992—96; mem. exec. coun. Nat. Capital area coun. Boy Scouts Am., 1993—; founder, pres. Wakefield Ednl. Found., 1986—; trustee Claude Moore Charitable Found. 1st lt. US Army, 1960—62, col. US Army. Fellow, Va. Law Found., 2007. Mem.: ABA, Fairfax Bar Assn., Va. Bar Assn., Assn. US Army, Rotary. Methodist. Home: 4047 27th Rd N Arlington VA 22207-5237 Office: McCandlish & Lillard 11350 Random Hills Rd Ste 500 Fairfax VA 22030-7429

ARO, EDWIN PACKARD, lawyer; b. Colorado Springs, Colo., July 20, 1964; s. Harold William and Margaret (Packard) A. BA, Denver U., 1986; JD magna cum laude, Boston U., 1989. Bar: Colo. 1989, U.S. Dist. Ct. Colo. 1990, U.S. Ct. Appeals (10th cir.) 1990. Law clk. Hon. Richard P. Matsch, U.S. Dist. Ct. for Colo., Denver, 1989-90; ptnr. Holme, Roberts & Owen LLP, Denver, 1990—, Hogan & Hartson LLP, Denver, dir. labor & employment practice group. Adj. prof. U. Denver Coll. of Law, 1994-2006; mem. Boston U. Law Rev., 1987-89. Mem. Boston U. Law Rev., 1987-89. Mem. ABA, Colo. Bar Assn., Denver Bar Assn., Faculty of Fed. Advocates. Office: Hogan & Hartson LLP One Tabor Ctr 1200 17th St Ste 1500 Denver CO 80202 Office Phone: 303-899-7389. Business E-Mail: eparo@hhlaw.com.

ARON, ADAM M., air transportation executive; b. Phila., Sept. 30, 1954; s. David Henry Lane and Joan (Tobias) A.; m. Abbe Kahn, Aug 25, 1984. AB, Harvard U., 1975, MBA, 1979. System dir. mktg. plans and programs Pan Am. World Airlines, NYC, 1979-85; v.p. mktg. programs Western Airlines, LA, 1985-87; sr. v.p. mktg. Hyatt Hotels Corp., Chgo., 1987-90, United Airlines, Chgo., 1990; pres. & CEO Norwegian Cruise Line, 1993—96; CEO Vail Resorts, Inc., 1996—2006; chmn., CEO World Leisure Partners, Inc; CEO Starwood Hotel and Resorts Worldwide Inc., chmn., 2006—. Bd. dirs. Royal Caribean Cruises, Miami, Bank Northwest, Steamboat Springs, Colo.; chmn. Travel Industry Assn. Am. Dir. Goodman Theater, Chgo. Recipient Mktg. 100 award Advt. Age, 1992, 40 Under 40 award Crain's Chgo. Bus., 1991. Mem. Coun. Fgn. Rels. Democrat. Jewish. Avocations: sports, government affairs, travel, films, theater. Office: Starwood Hotels & Resorts Worldwide Inc 1111 Westchester Ave White Plains NY 10604*

ARON, ALAN MILFORD, pediatric neurology educator; b. White Plains, NY, Oct. 15, 1933; s. Henri Jordan and Rosalind (Weinstein) A.; m. Sarah Deborah Bornstein, Dec. 29, 1963; children: Alexandra, Abigail, Adam. BS, Tufts U., 1954; MD, Columbia U., 1958. Diplomate Am. Bd. Pediatrics, Am. Bd. Psychiatry and Neurology with spl. competence in child neurology. Intern Grace New Haven Hosp. and Yale Med. Ctr., 1958-59; resident in pediatrics Babies Hosp. Columbia Presbyn. Med. Ctr., NYC, 1959-61; Fellow Columbia Presbyn. Med. Ctr. and Neurologic Inst., NYC, 1961—; pediatric neurologist Mt. Sinai Hosp., NYC, 1961-64; dir. child neurology Mt. Sinai Sch. Medicine, NYC, 1975—, prof. pediatrics and neurology, 1982—. Pres. N.Y. Pediatric Soc., N.Y.C., 1980-81. Contbr. articles to profl. jours. Recipient Lucy Moses award Clin. Research Neurologic Inst., N.Y.C., 1964. Mem. AMA, Am. Acad. Pediatrics, Am. Acad. Neurology, Child Neurology Soc., Tri-State Child Neurology Soc. (pres. 1990-91), Profs. Child Neurology, Phi Beta Kappa. Democrat. Jewish. Avocations: music, piano, opera, antiques, art. Office: Mt Sinai Sch Medicine 5 E 98th St New York NY 10029-6501 Home Phone: 914-834-4881; Office Phone: 212-831-4393. E-mail: amaronmd@aol.com.

ARON, LESTER, lawyer; b. Bronx, NY, Aug. 8, 1947; s. Eugene Abraham and Ruth Lea (Levine) A.; m. Hannah Gail Butensky, Dec. 16, 1979; children: Matthew, Sarah, Daniel. BA, Cornell U., 1969; JD, Georgetown U., 1972. Bar: N.J. 1972, D.C. 1972, U.S. Supreme Ct. 1980, NY Third Dist., 2004. Atty. NLRB, Newark, 1972-73; assoc. Law Office of Gerald Dorf, Rahway, N.J., 1973-74; dir. labor relations N.J. Sch. Bd., Trenton, 1974-75; assoc. Grotta, Glassman & Hoffman, Roseland, N.J., 1975-76; ptnr. Aron, Salsberg & Rosen, Nutley, NJ, Sills Cummis Epstein and Gross, Newark; sr. v.p., gen. counsel U. Medicine & Dentistry NJ, Newark, 2007—. Co-adj. prof. Rutgers U., New Brunswick, N.J., 1975-80, St. Peters U., Jersey City, 1981-82, State Wide Adv. Com. Rutgers U. Sch. Mgmt. Labor Rels., chmn. Nat. Inst. Mmgt. Rsch. Annual Conf. Employment Regulations NJ, 1988-1996 Co-author: The Complicated Web of Psychiatric Disabilities Under the American With Disabilities Act, 1997; contbr. Named one of New Jersey Superlawyers, NJ Monthly, 2005. Mem. ABA, N.J. Bar Assn. (mem. exec. bd. 1981-82, chmn. pub. sector bargaining com. 1981-82), N.J. Council of Sch. Attys., NSBA Council of Sch. Attys, Garden State Am. Inst. Banking (mem, employment and labor coun.), Nat. Banking Indus. Labor Law Com., 1988-. Office: U Medicine & Dentistry NJ PO Box 1709 Newark NJ 07101

ARON, NAN, lawyer, association executive; b. NYC, Jan. 4, 1948; d. Jerome I. and Joan B. A.; m. Bernard S. Arons, Dec. 28, 1969; children: Nicholas, Emma, Elena. BA, Oberlin Coll., Ohio, 1970; LLB, Case Western Res. U., 1973. Lawyer EEOC, Washington, 1973-76, Nat. Prison Project, ACLU, Washington, 1976-79; exec. dir. Alliance for Justice, Washington, 1979—. Instr. George Washington U., Washington, 1977; adj. prof. law Georgetown U., 1979—. Author: Liberty and Justice for All-Public Interest Law in the 1980s and Beyond, 1988; contbr. articles to profl. pubs. Bd. dirs. Oyster Sch. Community Coun., Washington, 1980—. Mem. Ams. for Dem. Action (bd. dirs. 1988—), Washington Coun. Lawyers (bd. dirs. 1979—). Jewish. Office: Alliance for Justice 11 Dupont Circle NW 2nd Fl Washington DC 20036

ARON, ROBERTO, lawyer, writer, educator; b. Mendoza, Argentina, Nov. 1, 1915; s. David and Catalina (Trostanetzky) A.; m. Catalina Berstein, May 1, 1940 (dec. Oct. 1965); children: Jaim, Sylvia, Daniel; m. Eva Coriat, Dec. 14, 1968; stepchildren: Sonia, Aileen (twins). BA in Law, U. Chile, 1943; LLM in Internat. Law, NYU, 1977, LLM in Corp. Law, 1979, M in Hebrew and Judaic Studies, 1995. Bar: Israel 1960. Sr. ptnr. Aron and Cia, Santiago, Chile, 1943-57, Arón, Tamir and Arón, Tel Aviv, 1960—. Adj. tchr. NYU, 1983; lectr. Tel Aviv U., 1985—, bd. govs., 1982; vis. prof. faculty of law U. Chile, 1991; bd. dirs. Otzar Itiashvut Hayeudim Bank, Tel Aviv; mem. Israeli del. to UN, 1975; participant Oxford Trial Advocacy Program. Co-author: How To Prepare Witnesses for Trial, 1985, Trial Communications Skills, 1986, Cross-Examination of Witnesses, 1989, Impeachment of Witnesses, 1990. Mem. Nat. Inst. Trial Advocacy (participant workshops on teaching trial advocacy Harvard Law Sch.), Advocates Assn., Assn. Trial Lawyers Am. Avocations: golf, pipe collecting. Home: 985 5th Ave Apt 12A New York NY 10021-0142 Office: Arón and Stern 7 ABA Hillel St Ramat-Gan 52522 Israel E-mail: aronbob@aol.com.

ARONOFF, CRAIG ELLIS, business educator, consultant; b. Atlanta, May 18, 1951; s. Marvin Charles and Patricia (Sabin) Aronoff; m. Jane G. Miller; children: Lara Dorfman, Emily Rose, Alexander Samuel Miller. BS in Journalism, Northwestern U., Evanston, Ill., 1971; MA, U. Pa., Phila., 1974; PhD, U. Tex., Austin, 1975. Asst. prof. mgmt. Ga. State U., Atlanta, 1975-79, assoc. prof., 1979-83; prof. mgmt. Kennesaw State U., Marietta, Ga., 1983—2005, Dinos disting. chair pvt. enterprise, 1983—2005, chmn. dept. mgmt., 1984-86, eminent scholar, 1999—2005, prof. emeritus, 2005—. Founder Cox Family Enterprise Ctr., dir., 1987—2001; chmn. Cobb Transit Adv. Bd., Marietta, 1988—90; exec. dir. Bus. Owner Resources, Marietta, 1989—2000; CEO Family Bus. Comm., Inc., 1989—2002; co-founder, prin. Family Bus. Cons. Group, Inc., 1994—; bd. dirs. Whitacre Oil Co., Nioxin Rsch. Labs. Author, co-author, editor: other books, 1979—; co-editor: The Future of Private Enterprise, 3 vols., 1982—84; co-author: Family Business Leadership Series, 18 vols., 1992—, Public Relations: The Profession and the Practice, 4th edit., 1996; contbg. editor, columnist: Family Bus. Planning, Nation's Bus. mag., 1990—99; mem. editl. bd. Jour. Pvt. Enterprise Edn., 1986—, Family Bus. Rev., 1992—; exec. editor: Family Bus. Advisor, 1991—. Active Leadership Cobb, 1986—87; co-pres. West Side Elem. Sch. PTA, 1992—93; bd. dirs. Southeastern Legal Found., 1990—97; commr. Marietta Bd. Zoning and Planning, 1987—90; bd. advisors Marous Jewish Cmty. Ctr., Atlanta, 2007—; bd. dirs. Temple Kol Emeth, Marietta, 1989—92, co-chmn. capital campaign, 2007—. Named Craig E. Aronoff Professorship in family bus. in his honor, Kennesaw State U., 2004; recipient Leavey award, Freedom Found., 1987, Outstanding Educator award, Nat. Fedn. Ind. Bus. Found., 1989, Disting. Leadership award, Leadership Cobb, 1988. Mem.: Ga. Coun. Econ. Edn. (trustee 1983—2004), Family Firm Inst. (bd. dirs. 1989—94, sec., treas. 1990—92, pres. 1992—94, Richard Beckhard award 1997), Family Bus. Forum (founder, bd. dirs. 1987—), Assn. Pvt. Enterprise Educators (bd. dirs. 1977—91, pres. 1978—79, Kent-Aronoff award 1988), Cobb C. of C. (vice chmn. 1986, 1991—93), Progressive Club (pres. 1976—77), Kiwanis (Outstanding Kiwanian award 1989). Home: 2061 E Side Dr NE Marietta GA 30062-6426 Office: Family Bus Consulting Group Inc 1220-B Kennestone Cir Marietta GA 30066 Office Phone: 678-277-9865. Business E-Mail: aronoff@efamilybusiness.com.

ARONOFF, GEORGE RODGER, medicine and pharmacology educator; b. Peoria, Ill., Mar. 6, 1950; BA in Chemistry with distinction, Ind. U., 1972; MD with honors, Ind. U., Indpls., 1975, MS in Pharmacology, 1984. Diplomate Am. Bd. Internal Medicine; diplomate Am. Bd. Internal Medicine Nephrology. Intern in internal medicine Ind. U., Indpls., 1975-76, resident, 1976-77, clin. fellow div. nephrology, 1977-78, chief resident in internal medicine Wishard Meml. Hosp., 1978-79, rsch. fellow div. nephrology, 1979-80, instr. phys. diagnosis, 1977-78, instr. medicine, 1978-79, from asst. prof. to assoc. prof. medicine, 1980-87, assoc. prof. pharmacology, 1985-87; prof. medicine, prof. pharmacology U. Louisville, 1987—; mem. staff Univ. Louisville (Ky.) Hosp., 1987—. Fellow in clin. pharmacology Eli Lilly & Co., Indpls., 1979-80. Contbr. numerous articles and abstracts to profl. jours. Fellow ACP; mem. Am. Soc. Nephrology, Cen. Soc. Clin. Rsch., Ky. State Med. Assn., Jefferson County Med. Soc. (editorial bd. Louisville Medicine 1989-92, editor 1990), Renal Physicians Assn., Nat. Kidney Found., Phi Eta Sigma, Phi Lambda Upsilon, Phi Beta Kappa, Alpha Omega Alpha, Sigma Xi. Office: U Louisville Kidney Disease Program 615 S Preston St Louisville KY 40202-1715

ARONOFF, VERA, law librarian; b. Kiev, Ukraine, Sept. 17, 1934; arrived in U.S., 1981; d. Joseph and Khasya Davidovich; m. Leonard Aronoff, July 26, 1958; 1 child, Irene Aronoff-Kastanas. BA in Edn. with top honors, Pedagogical Inst., Nezhin, Ukraine, 1956; postgrad., Maywood Coll., 1984—86; MLS Syracuse U., 1989. Tchr. HS # 19, Kiev, 1956—61, Inst. Fgn. Langs., Kiev, 1961—79; asst. libr. Scranton (Pa.) Pub. Libr., 1981—85; rschr. Cornell U., Ithaca, NY, 1985—88; catalog libr. Loyola U. Law Sch., LA, 1989—. Mem.: So. Calif. Assn. Law Librs., Am. Assn. Law Librs. Office: Loyola Law Sch PO Box 15019 919 S Albany St Los Angeles CA 90015-0019 Office Phone: 213-736-1419. Business E-Mail: vera.aronoff@lls.edu.

ARONOW, SAUL, radiological physicist, consultant; b. NYC, Oct. 4, 1917; s. Abraham and Minnie (Mirel) Aronow; m. Alice Pearlman, Feb. 12, 1942; children: Victor A, Frederick D, David B, Nathan J, Louise G, Jessie P Kravette. BEE, Cooper Union, 1939; PhD, Harvard U., 1953. Registered profl engr, Mass, cert. radiological physicist. Engr. Harvey Radio Labs., Cambridge, Mass., 1946-49; med. physicist Mass. Gen. Hosp., Boston, 1953-81; clin. engr. Project Hope, Jamaica, W.I., 1981-83; chmn. bd. Tech. in Medicine, Inc., Holliston, Mass., 1972—. Adj prof Northeastern Univ, Boston, 1975—95; instr MIT, Cambridge, 1969—83. Editor: (book) The Fallen Sky, 1963. Mem. Newton Dem. City Com. Served to 1st lt Signal Corps US Army, 1942—46. Recipient Gano Dunn medal, Cooper Union Inst.Tech., 1981; NSF fellow, Harvard U., 1950, Fulbright fellow, Danmarks Tekniske Hojskole, 1969. Fellow: IEEE; mem.: Harvard Musical Assn., Soc. Nuc. Medicine, Nat. Fire Protection Assn. (mem. stds. coun. 1983—89), Assn. Advancement Med. Instrumentation (bd. dirs. 1979—82), Am. Assn. Physicists in Medicine, Folk Song Soc. Greater Boston. Jewish. Avocations: hiking, folk music. Home and Office: 80C Seminary Ave Auburndale MA 02466 Home Phone: 617-969-9417.

ARONOW, WILBERT SOLOMON, physician, educator; b. NYC, Oct. 30, 1931; s. Simon and Bella (Safrin) A.; m. Ina Gloria Brody, Sept. 20, 1958; children: Michael Steven, Janice Susan. BS, Queens Coll., Flushing, 1953; MD, Harvard U., Cambridge, Mass., 1957. Diplomate Am. Bd. Internal Medicine. Intern Michael Reese Hosp. and Med. Ctr., Chgo., 1957-58, resident, 1958-61; practice medicine specializing in internal medicine and cardiology; cardiologist, chief Noninvasive Cardiovascular Lab., Long Beach VA Hosp., Calif., 1964-72, chief cardiovascular diseases Calif., 1973-82, asst. chief medicine for rsch. Calif., 1975-80; asso. prof. medicine U. Calif., Irvine, 1972-75, prof. medicine, 1975-82, prof. cmty. and environ. medicine, 1975-82, prof. pharmacology and therapeutics, 1976-82, vice chief cardiovascular divsn., chief cardiovascular rsch., 1974-82; prof. medicine, chief cardiovascular rsch. Creighton U., Omaha, 1982-84; chief Cardiology Clinic Westchester Med. Ctr./NY Med. Coll., Valhalla, NY, 2001—. Vis. prof. U. Tex. Southwestern Med. Sch., Dallas, 1976, U. Man., 1979, U. Toronto, 1979, Tex. Tech U. Sch. Medicine, Lubbock, 1983, U. Medicine and Dentistry of NJ-Rutgers Med. Sch., 1983; vis. prof. geriat. U. Rochester Sch. Medicine, 1999; staff cardiology svc. St. Joseph Hosp., Omaha, 1982—84; mem. ad hoc sci. ad. coms. FDA, 1970—72, mem. cardiovascular and renal adv. com., 1973—76; chmn. spl. rev. com. Nat. Cancer Inst., 1980; mem. subcom. on smoking Am. Heart Assn., 1980—83; med. dir. Hebrew Hosp. Home, 1984—2001; adj. prof. geriat. and adult devel. Mt. Sinai Sch. Medicine, 1992—; clin. prof. medicine NY Med. Coll., 2001—; chief cardiology clinic Westchester Med. Ctr./NY Med. Coll., 2001—, sr. assoc. program dir., rsch. mentor fellowship programs dept. medicine, 2003—; cons. in field. Mem. editl. bd. Jour. Pharmacology an Exptl. Therapeutics, guest field editor, 1981, mem. editl. bd. Am. Jour. Cardiology, 1980—82, Jour. Circulation, 1980—83, E R Reports, 1981—84, Physician's Drug Alert, 1982—, Jour. Cardiovascular and Pulmonary Technique, 1983—86, Clin. Pharmacology and Therapeutics, 1977—83, Jour. ACC, 1982—83, Drugs and Aging, 1990—, Am. Jour. Noninvasive Cardiology, 1986—95, Jour. Cardiovascular Diagnosis and Procedures, 1992—, Preventive Cardiology, 1998—, Jour. Am. Med. Dirs. Assn., 1999—2004; mem. editl. bd.: Jour. Am. Med. Dirs. Assn., 2006—; mem. editl. bd. Caring for the Ages, 1999—2001, Jour. Gerontology: Med. Scis., 2000—, Heart Disease, 2000—03, Geriatrics, 2001—, Cardiology in Rev., 2006—, Jour. Cardiac Failure, 2007—, Comprehensive Therapy, 2006—, Jour. Cardiac Failure, 2007—; contbr. articles to profl. jours. Served to capt., M.C. AUS, 1961-63. Fellow: ACP, Soc. Geriatric Cardiology (chmn. program com. 1993—2003, bd. dirs. 1994—2000), Coun. Clin. Cardiology of Am. Heart Assn., Gerontol. Soc. Am., Am. Geriatrics Soc., Am. Coll. Cardiology, Am. Coll. Chest Physicians (gov. So. Calif. 1977—83, vice chmn. coronary disease sect. 1978—79, chmn. coronary disease sect. 1979—81, mem. exec. coun. 1979—81, chmn. forum on cardiovasc. disease 1980—81, sec. coun. on govs. 1981—82, vice chmn. gov.'s coun.); mem.: Orange County Heart Assn. (dir. 1979—81), Long Beach Heart Assn. (dir. 1972—75), Assn. VA Cardiologists (pres. 1975—77), Am. Fedn. Med. Rsch., Am. Soc. Clin. Pharmacology and Therapeutics (chmn. cardiovasc. and pulmonary diseases sect. 1973—74, 1975—77), Phi Beta Kappa. Jewish. Home: 23 Pebbleway Rd New Rochelle NY 10804-3914 Office: Westchester Med Ctr/NY Med Coll Cardiology Divsn Macy Pavilion Rm 138 Valhalla NY 10595 Office Phone: 914-493-5311. Personal E-mail: wsaronow@aol.com. *Concern for the public health as well as for individual patient care has been the motivating force behind my medical research, teaching, and patient care. Performing work in a very careful, scientific fashion, being honest, being helpful and supportive to others, working very hard and efficiently, and being true to my principles of conduct has contributed to my success.*

ARONOWITZ, DAVID M., lawyer, chemicals executive; BA, Haverford Coll.; JD, Yale U. Assoc. Skadden, Arps, Slate, Meagher and Flom; v.p., gen. counsel, sec. Grimes Aerospace Co., Columbus, Ohio; asst. gen. counsel Taylor Pub. Co., Insilco Corp., Dublin; v.p., asst. gen. counsel The Scotts Miracle-Gro Co., Marysville, 1998—2000, sr. v.p., asst. gen. counsel, asst. sec., 2000—01, exec. v.p., gen. counsel, sec., 2001—. Office: Scotts Miracle-Gro Co 14111 Scottslawn Rd Marysville OH 43041 Office Phone: 937-644-0011.*

ARONOWITZ, JOEL ALAN, plastic and reconstructive surgeon; b. Memphis, Dec. 5, 1956; MD, Baylor Coll. Medicine, 1982. Intern in gen. surgery Baylor Coll. Medicine, 1982-83, resident in plastic surgery, 1983-87; attending plastic surgeon Cedars Sinai Med. Ctr., 1987—, vice chmn. plastic surgery divsn., 1997—2005, chmn. plastic surgery divsn., 2005—. Office: 8635 W 3rd St Ste 1090 Los Angeles CA 90048-6104 Office Phone: 310-659-0705.

ARONS, BERNARD S., psychiatrist, educator, health services administrator; Grad., Oberlin Coll.; MD, Case Western Res. U. Psychiatrist, adminstr., instr. psychiat. residents St. Elizabeths Hosp. NIMH, Washington, dir. Dixon implementation office, 1980, chief clin. advisor, dir. med. nursing, psych. social work; assoc. dir. mental health fin. NIMH; legis. asst. to chair Health Subcom. Ways and Means Com., Washington; dir. Ctr.

Mental Health Svcs. U.S. Dept. Health and Human Svcs., Washington, 1993—2003, sr. science advisor to the dir., Ctr. Mental Health Svcs., 2003—. Advisor to Mrs. Tipper Gore Office of V.P. U.S.; instr. Ctr. Mental Health Inc., Washington; clin. prof. psychiatry Georgetown U. Office: NIH/NIMH 6001 Executive Blvd Rm 8218 MSC 9669 Bethesda MD 20892-9669

ARONSON, ARTHUR LAWRENCE, retired veterinarian, toxicologist, educator, pharmacologist; b. Mpls., Aug. 24, 1933; s. Arthur Theodore and Thorene (Elfstrand) A.; m. Marilyn Ann Lundeen, Sept. 15, 1956; children: Brenda Louise, Mark Theodore, Luann Marie. BS, U. Minn., 1955, DVM, 1957, PhD, 1963; MS, Cornell U., 1959. Asst. prof. pharmacology Cornell U., 1964-67, assoc. prof., 1967-71, prof., 1971-80; prof., head dept. anatomy, physiol. sci., and radiology Coll. Vet. Medicine, N.C. State U., Raleigh, 1980-99; prof. emeritus, 1999—. Mem. com. biologic effects atmospheric pollutants NRC; mem. vet. medicine adv. com. FDA.; mem. U.S. Pharmacopeia Adv. Panel Vet. Medicine; chmn. com. recognition of pain and distress in lab. animals, Inst. Lab. Animal Resources, NAS, 1988. Co-editor Jour. Vet. Pharmacology and Therapeutics, 1992-99. Mem. Friends of Scandinavia, Carl Larsson Vasa Lodge; pres. Wake County Literacy Coun., 1997-99; vol. mentor Communities in Sch. of Wake County, 1999—; dir. N.C. State U. Women's Club English conversation classes, 2000—. Mem. AVMA (chmn. coun. on biologic and therapeutic agts. 1986-87), Am. Soc. Pharmacology and Exptl. Therapeutics, Soc. Toxicology (animals in rsch. com.), N.C. Soc. Toxicology (pres. 1985-86), Am. Acad. Vet. Pharmacology and Therapeutics (pres. 1987-89), Am. Coll. Vet. Clin. Pharmacology (pres. 1993-95), Wake County Literacy Coun. (bd. dirs. 1991-2003, pres. 1997-99), Friends Scandinavia (pres.-elect 2006—), Sigma Xi, Phi Zeta. Lutheran. Home: 1213 Glendale Dr Raleigh NC 27612-4772

ARONSON, BENJAMIN, artist; b. Boston, Oct. 4, 1958; s. David and Georgianna (Nyman) A.; m. Margaret Ray Combs, Nov. 5, 1983; children: Jesse Benjamin, Alexander Raymond. BFA in Painting, Boston U., 1980, MFA in Painting, 1982. Tchg. asst. Boston U. Sch. Fine Art, 1980-82; tchr. Beaver Country Day Sch., Chestnut Hill, Mass., 1983-90; mem. U.S. Supreme Ct. Portrait Painting Team, 1989-97; guest lectr. Boston U. Summer Art Inst., 1985, Deerfield Acad., Old Deerfield, Mass., 1986, Salve Regina Coll., Newport, R.I., 1987, Mass. Coll. Art, Boston, 1987, Worcester Craft Ctr., Boston Globe Scholastic Art Awards, 1988, Boston U. Sch. Art Edn., 1988, art dept. Southeastern Middlesex U., 1988, Gordon Coll., Wenham, Mass., 1989, painting dept. Boston U. Sch. Visual Art, 1989, R.I. Sch. Design, 1990, Charrette Corp., 1991, Harvard Grad. Sch. Design, 1995, 96, 97, 98, 99; artist in residence Beaver Country Day Sch., Chestnut Hill, Mass., 1985-88. One-man shows include Nancy Lincoln Gallery, Chestnut Hill, Mass., 1983, 89, Lane Gallery, Gordon Coll., Wenham, Mass., 1986, Julia-Saul Gallery, Sudbury, Mass., 1987, Louis Newman Galleries, Beverly Hills, Calif., 1994, Jerry Solomon Gallery, Hollywood, Calif., 1996, Horwitch Newman Gallery, Scottsdale, Ariz., 1996, M B Modern, N.Y.C., 1997, 99, Sydne Bernard Fine Arts, Hollywood, 1998; exhibited in group shows at Boston U. Art Gallery, 1980, 82, Dana Hall Gallery, Wellesley, Mass., 1984, Quadrum Gallery, Chestnut Hill, 1984, DeCordova Mus., Lincoln, Mass., 1988, Copley Soc., Boston, 1990, Nat. Acad. Design, N.Y.C., 1990, 92, Urban Ctr. Mcpl. Art Soc., N.Y.C., 1991, Mickelson Gallery, Washington, 1992, Security Pacific Gallery, Seattle, 1992, Gwenda Jay Gallery, Chgo., 1992, Louis Newman Galleries, Beverly Hills, 1993, 94, Koplin Gallery, Santa Monica, Calif., 1995, Horwitch Newman Gallery, Scottsdale, 1995, 96, Jerry Solomon Gallery, Hollywood, 1996, 97, Sydne Bernard Fine Arts, Hollywood, 1997, 98, Pepper Gallery, Boston, 1997, M B Modern, N.Y.C., 1997, 98, Mangel Gallery, Phila., 1998, Soma Gallery, la Jolla, Calif., 1998, Alpha Gallery, Boston, 1999; represented in permanent collections at Reading (Pa.) Pub. Fine Art Mus., MIT, Woodshole Oceanographic Inst., Mass.; also corp. and pvt. collections; contbr. articles to profl. jours. Recipient Blanche E. Colman award for painting, 1986, 88, 1st prize in drawing Sudbury Art Assn., 1987, Mass. Lottery grant for painting, 1987, St. Botolph Club Found. grant for painting, 1988, R.I. State Coun. for Arts grant, 1989, William P. and Gertrude Schweitzer painting prize, Nat. Acad. of Design, 1990, Thomas Fisher award Am. Soc. Archtl. Perspectivists, NYC, 1991, Ogden M. Pleissner painting award Nat. Acad. Design, NYC, 1992. Home: 33 Wayside Inn Rd Framingham MA 01701-3021

ARONSON, CARL EDWARD, pharmacology and toxicology educator; b. Providence, Mar. 14, 1936; s. Carl Ivar and Ruth (Workman) A.; m. Marjorie Peck Boutelle, Dec. 17, 1960; children— Linda J., Kristen L. AB, Brown U., Providence, 1958; PhD, U. Vt., Burlington, 1966; MA, U. Pa., Phila., 1973. Asst. prof. pharmacology U. Pa. Sch. Medicine, Phila., 1971-75, assoc. prof. pharmacology, 1975-92; asst. prof. pharmacology and toxicology dept. animal biology U. Pa. Sch. Vet. Medicine, Phila., 1971-73, head labs. of pharmacology and toxicology, 1972-86, assoc. prof. pharmacology and toxicology, 1973-96; retired to emeritus status, 1996; instrument specialist, dept. chemistry Haverford (Pa.) Coll., 1996—. Editor Veterinary Pharmaceuticals and Biologicals, 1978-83, 85-86; contbr. chpts. to books, articles to profl. jours. Active local sch. dist. coms. and other civic assns. 1st lt. USAFR, 1958-65 Recipient Norden award U. Pa. Sch. Vet. Medicine, 1982, Legion of Honor, Chapel of the Four Chaplains, 1984. Fellow: Am. Acad. Vet. and Comparative Toxicology, Am. Acad. Vet. Pharmacology and Therapeutics (newsletter editor 1982—2001, pres. 1983—85, Svc. award 1994, L.E. Davis Career Achievement award 2001); mem.: AAUP, Am. Soc. Pharmacology and Exptl. Therapeutics, Bay Region Mariners Sailing Assn. (treas. 1981—83, vice commodore 1986, commodore 1987), The Haven Yacht Club (charter), Masons, Sigma Xi. Lutheran. Avocations: sailing, photography, woodworking. Office: Haverford Coll Dept Chemistry 370 Lancaster Ave Haverford PA 19041-1392

ARONSON, CLIFFORD HANK, lawyer; b. Phila., Mar. 7, 1955; s. George Leonard and Gloria Harriet (Mort) A.; m. Amy Roberta Benenson, Sept. 21, 1986; children: Chloe Annette, Carter Asher, Fiona Skye BS in Econ., U. Pa., 1977; JD, Georgetown U., 1980. Bar: DC 1980, NY 1985. Assoc. Meagher & Flom, NYC, 1980-88; spl. counsel Skadden, Arps, Slate, Meagler & Flom, NYC, 1988, ptnr. antitrusts, 1989—, ptnr.-in-charge, summer associate program. Instr. Wharton Sch., U. Pa.; regular spkr. on mergers and acquisitions at Wharton's Executive Education Program. Co-editor: Mergers and Acquisitions — Understanding the Antitrust Laws. Mem. ABA (antitrust sect. 7 com.), Century Country Club, American Yacht Club Democrat. Jewish. Avocations: skiing, bicycling, sailing. Home: 560 Polly Park Rd Rye NY 10580-1929 Office: Skadden Arps Slate Meagher & Flom 4 Times Sq New York NY 10036 Office Phone: 212-735-2644. Office Fax: 917-777-2644. Business E-Mail: caronson@skadden.com.

ARONSON, DAVID, artist, retired educator; b. Shilova, Lithuania, Oct. 28, 1923; came to U.S., 1929, naturalized, 1931; s. Peisach Leib and Gertrude (Shapiro) A.; m. Georgianna B. Nyman, June 10, 1956; children: Judith, Benjamin, Abigail. Certificate, Boston Mus. Sch., 1946; LHD (hon.), Hebrew Coll., 1993; DFA (hon.), Boston U., 2005. Instr. painting Boston Mus. Sch., 1943-54; prof. art Boston U., 1962-89, founder art dept., chmn. div., 1954-62, chmn. painting dept., 1962-89, prof. emeritus, 1989—. Author David Aronson: Paintings, Drawings, Sculpture, 2005; contbr. articles to profl. jours.; one man shows include Niveau Gallery, N.Y.C., 1945, 56, Mus. Modern Art, N.Y.C., 1946, Boris Mirski Gallery, Boston, 1951, 59, 64, 69, Downtown Gallery, N.Y.C., 1953, Nordness Gallery, N.Y.C., 1960, 63, 69, Rex Evans Gallery, L.A., 1961, Long Beach (Calif.) Mus., 1961, Westhampton (N.Y.) Gallery, 1961, J. Thomas Gallery, Provincetown, Mass., 1964, Zora Gallery, LA, 1965, Hunter Gallery, Chattanooga, 1965, Kovler Gallery, Chgo., 1966, Bernard Danenberg Galleries, N.Y.C., 1969, 72, Pucker Gallery, Boston, 1976, 78, 86, 90, 94, 99, 2005, Phila. Mus. Judaica, 1990, Louis Newman Gallery, LA, 1977, 81, 84, 86, 89, 92, Sadye Bronfman Art Ctr., Montreal, Que., Can., 1982, Horwitch Newman Gallery, Scottsdale, Ariz., 1995, 96, MB Modern Gallery, N.Y., 1997, Alter & Gil Gallery, L.A., 1999, Sp. Galerie Yoram GIL, L.A., 2002, 04; group shows include N.Y. World's Fair, 1964-65, Bridgestone Gallery, Tokyo, Royal Acad. London, Mus. Modern Art, Paris, Palazzo Venezia, Rome, Congresse Halle, Berlin, Charlottenborg, Copenhagen, Palais Des Beaux Arts, Brussels, Smithsonian Instn., 1965, retrospective exhbns. include Rose Mus., Brandeis U., Waltham, Mass., 1978, Jewish Mus., N.Y.C., 1979, Nat. Mus. Am. Jewish History, Phila., 1979, So. Middlesex U., South Dartmouth, Mass., 1983, Mickelson Gallery, Washington, 1985, Boston U., 2005; represented in permanent collections Art Inst. Chgo., Va. Mus. Fine Arts, Richmond, Bryn Mawr Coll., Brandeis U., Tupperware Mus., Orlando, Fla., Decordova Mus., Lincoln, Mass., Mus. Modern Art, Atlanta U., Atlanta Art Assn., U. Nebr., Krannert Art Mus. U. Ill., Whitney Mus. Am. Art, Colby Coll., U. N.H., Portland Mus. Art, Maine, Corcoran Gallery Art, Washington, Munson Williams Proctor Art Inst., Ithaca, N.Y., Boston Mus. Fine Arts, Smithsonian Instn., Washington, Milw. Art Inst., Pa. Acad. Fine Arts, Johnson Found., Racine, Wis., Worcester (Mass.) Art Mus., Colorado SPrings Fine Arts Ctr., Brockton (Mass.) Mus. Art, Longy Sch. Music, Cambridge, Mass., Boston U., Jewish Community Ctr., Boston, Nat. Acad. Design, N.Y., Joseph Hirschorn Collection, Hebrew Coll., Newton, Mass., David and Alfred Smart Mus., U. Ill., Chgo., Two-Ten Found., Boston, Pa. State U. Mus. Art, Syracuse (N.Y.) U., Beth Israel Hosp., Boston Mass. Guilford Coll. U. N.C., Greensboro Campus, U. Judaism, L.A., Fine Arts Ctr., Cheekville, Tenn., Danforth Mus., Framingham, Mass., Skirball Mus., L.A., Herbert F. Johnson Mus. Art, Cornell U., Museo Sefardi, Toledo, Spain, Flint Inst. Arts, Mich., Colo. Springs Fine Arts Ctr., Colo., Dayton Art Inst., Ohio, Danforth Mus. Art, Framingham, Mass., others; sculpture commns. Container Corp. Am., 1963, 65, Reform Jewish Appeal, 1980, Combined Jewish Philanthropies, 1981, Temple Beth Elohim, Wellesley, Mass., 1982, Brandeis U. Libr., Waltham, Mass., 1983, Brandeis U. Berlin Chapel, 1996. Recipient 1st Judges prize Inst. Modern Art, Boston, 1944, 1st Popular prize, 1944; Choice Friends of Art Art Inst. Chgo., 1946; Purchase prize Va. Mus. Fine Arts, 1946; Travelling fellow Boston Mus. Sch., 1946; Grand prize Boston Arts Festival, 1952, 54; 2d prize, 1953; 1st prize Tupperware Art Fund, 1954, cert. of merit for sculpture NAD, 1990; grantee in art Nat. Inst. Arts and Letters, 1958; Purchase prize, 1961, 62, 63; purchase prize Pa. Acad. Fine Arts, also other purchase prizes; Samuel F.B. Morse Gold medal NAD, 1973; Isaac N. Maynard prize NAD, 1975; Joseph S. Isidor gold medal NAD, 1976; Guggenheim fellow, 1960; Adolph and Clara Obrig prize NAD, 1968, Academician NAD, 1970. Home: 137 Brimstone Ln Sudbury MA 01776-3200

ARONSON, DONALD ERIC, management and tax consultant; b. Boston, Feb. 24, 1934; s. Harry and Nathalie A.; m. Margery Roth, Sept. 27, 1955 (dec. 1981); children: Nancy, Helaine; m. Joan Gelman, Jan. 12, 1986 AB, Dartmouth Coll., 1955; MBA, Columbia U., 1959. CPA, NY, NJ. Mem. audit and tax staff Arthur Young & Co., NYC, 1959-63, tax mgr., 1963-68, tax ptnr., 1968-72, office mng. ptnr. Saddle Brook, NJ, 1972-80; dir. mktg. Arthur Young, NYC, 1980-89; dir. tax mktg. Ernst & Young, NYC, 1989-92; prin., profl. svcs. firms cons. Aronson/Heintz Assocs. LLC, NYC, 1995—; value added tax recovery advisor, cons. and prin. VATAmerica, L.P., NYC and Princeton, NJ, 1993—. Asst. prof. acctg. Upsala Coll., East Orange, NJ, 1963-65; asst. prof. Columbia U. Grad. Sch. Bus., NYC, 1966-67; acctg. adv. bd. Columbia U. Grad. Sch. of Bus., NYC, 1981-89; assoc. prof. bus. NYU, 1992-97; cons. and lectr. in field. Contbr. articles to bus. and profl. jours. Served to 1st lt. USAF, 1955-57 Recipient Montgomery prize Columbia U. Grad. Sch. Bus., 1959; award NY Soc. C.P.A.s, 1959 Mem. AICPA, NY State Soc. CPAs, NJ Soc. CPAs (trustee 1975-78). Democrat. Jewish. Avocations: tennis, skiing, boating. Office: Ste 6D 2 W 67st New York NY 10023 Office Phone: 212-874-4181.

ARONSON, EDGAR DAVID, venture capitalist; b. NYC, June 17, 1934; s. Aaron Solomon and Ida Claire (Minevitch) A.; m. Nancy Carol Pforzheimer, Dec. 23, 1956; children: Edgar David Jr., Alison C., Edith S., Peter Borrah. AB, Harvard U., 1956, MBA, 1962. Successively trainee, asst. cashier, v.p. 1st Nat. Bank of Chgo., 1962-67; v.p. Republic Nat. Bank of N.Y., 1968; trainee Salomon Bros., NYC, 1968-69, ltd. partner, 1970, v.p., 1971-72, gen. partner, 1972-79; mng. dir. Salomon Bros. Internat. Ltd., London, 1971-76; chmn. bd. Dillon, Read Internat., 1979-81; pres. EDACO, Inc., 1981—2002. Bd. dirs. APL N.V., Curacao, Petrogas Ltd., Hong Kong, H.L. Oakes & Co., Inc., Panama, Hertford Internat., N.V., Curacao, Mid-Am. Energy Holdings Co., Inc., 1982-99. Author (with others): New Old World, 1962, Response to Change, 1963. Trustee Lesley Coll., Cambridge, Mass., 1981-84, South St. Seaport Mus., NY, 1996-2002, Marine Mil. Acad., Harlingen, Tex.; bd. dirs. Carl and Lily Pforzheimer Found., NYC; founder Nat. Mus. U.S. Marine Corps. 1st lt. USMCR, 1956-60, maj. FMF ret. res. Mem. Marine Corps Res. Officers Assn., 1st Marine Divsn. Assn., The Cruising Assn. (UK), Mensa, NY Yacht Club, Bass Harbor Yacht Club (Maine), Harvard Club NYC, Royal Cork Yacht Club (Eire), Royal Nova Scotia Yacht Squadron (Halifax), The Brook (NYC), Annabel's (London). Office: 551 Fifth Ave Rm 512 New York NY 10176-0599

ARONSON, JASON, publisher; b. Minn., Jan. 25, 1928; s. Louis and Mollie (Weiner) A.; div.; 1 child, Jane; m. Joyce Kraus. BA, U. Minn., 1949, MD, 1953. Resident in psychiatry U. Minn. Hosps., 1954-57; asst. psychiatrist Harvard Med. Sch. and Mass. Gen. Hosp., 1959-64; editor-in-chief Internat. Jour. Psychiatry, 1962-70; pres. Jason Aronson Pubs. Inc., Northvale, NJ, 1964—. Capt. U.S. Army, 1957-59. Fellow Am. Psychiat. Assn.

ARONSON, JAY RICHARD, economics professor, researcher, academic administrator; b. NYC, Aug. 26, 1937; s. Lester and Rose (Hacken) A.; m. Judith Libby Klein, Sept. 13, 1959; children: Sarah, Miriam, Anne. AB, Clark U., 1959, PhD, 1964; MA, Stanford U., 1961. Asst. prof. econs. Worcester Poly. Inst. (Mass.), 1961-65, Lehigh U., Bethlehem, Pa., 1965-68, assoc. prof., 1968-72, prof., 1972—, dir. Martindale Ctr. for Study Pvt. Enterprise, 1980—, William L. Clayton prof. bus. and econs., 1984—. Vis. scholar U. York (Eng.), 1973, hon. prof., 1996-; cons. Internat. City Mgmt. Assn.; commr. Pa. Pension Fund Study Commn. Author: books including (with J. Hilley) Financing State and Local Governments, Public Finance; editor: books including (with E. Schwartz) Management Policies in Local Government Finance, 1975, 5th edit., 2004; contbr. articles to profl. publs. Recipient Lindback award Lehigh U., 1968; recipient Stabler award Lindback award, 1974; Rockefeller fellow, 1959-61; named hon. fellow Clark U., 1962; grantee Ford Found., 1971-72, 76-77, HEW, 1978-79, Scaife Found., 1982; Fulbright research scholar, 1991, 96. Mem.: Roya Econ. Soc., Am. Fin. Assn., Nat. Tax Assn., Am. Econ. Assn. Democrat. Jewish. Home: 1804 Jennings St Bethlehem PA 18017-5235 Office: Lehigh U Dept Economy Bethlehem PA 18015 Office Phone: 610-758-3411. Business E-Mail: jra1@lehigh.edu.

ARONSON, LOUIS VINCENT, II, manufacturing executive; b. Newark, Jan. 18, 1923; s. Alexander H. and Leona L. (Lazarus) A.; m. Joan Barbara Fisch, Nov. 2, 1945; children: James Richard, Robert A., Kathryn Ann, Diane Barbara. BS, U.S. Naval Acad., 1945. Methods engr. Ronson Corp., Newark, 1947-48, supr. prodn. control, 1948-50, v.p. charge material procurement, 1950-52, v.p. charge ops., 1952-53, pres., 1952—, also bd. dirs. Bd. dirs. NCCJ; trustee emeritus Newark Acad., Livingston, NJ. With USN, 1945-47. Mem. U.S. Naval Acad. Athletic Assn Home: PO Box 9 Oldwick NJ 08858-0009 Office: Ronson Corp PO Box 6707 Somerset NJ 08875-6707

ARONSON, MARK BERNE, retired lawyer, advocate; b. Pitts., Aug. 24, 1941; s. Richard J and Jean (DeRoy) Aronson; life ptnr. Karen K. Shapiro, 1993; children: Robert M., Andrew A., Michael D. BS in Econs., U. Pa., 1962; JD, U. Pitts., 1965. Pvt. practice law, Pitts., 1965-90; sr. ptnr. Behrend & Aronson Law Firm, Pitts., 1967-80, Behrend, Aronson & Morrow Law Firm, Pitts., 1980-83; pres. Current Concepts Corp., Pitts., 1992-2000; ret., 2000. Real estate broker, 1972—94; cons. to attys., 1991—2002; pvt. consumer adv., 1991—2002. Trustee Pitts. Child Guidance Found., 1987—90; mem. Pitts. Coun. Edn., 1986—89; pres. Cmty. Day Sch., Pitts., 1982—84, Rodef Shalom Jr. Congregation, 1970—71, Churchill Mansions Condominium Assn., Pitts., 2006—; trustee Rodef Shalom Congregation, Pitts., 1979—87, Rodef Shalom Jr. Congregation, 1967—71, Brotherhood, 1990—92, 2000—01. Mem.: Am Arbitration Assn. (mem nat panel arbitrators), Tau Epsilon Rho (chancellor Eta chpt 1964—65). Republican. Jewish. Address: Ste 506-507 Churchill Mansions 2525 Greensburg Pike Pittsburgh PA 15221-3691 Personal E-mail: sue4spam@aol.com.

ARONSON, MICHAEL ANDREW, editor; b. Bklyn., Apr. 27, 1939; s. Jesse Besthoff and Marcia (Sacks) A. BA, Johns Hopkins, 1960. Asst. dir. Ind. U. Press, Bloomington, 1966-69; London editor U. Chgo. Press, 1970, sci. editor, 1971-73; editor-in-chief Johns Hopkins U. Press, Balt., 1973-78; sr. editor social scis. Harvard U. Press, Cambridge, Mass., 1978—. Office: Harvard U Press 79 Garden St Cambridge MA 02138-1447 Business E-Mail: michael_aronson@harvard.edu.

ARONSON, NEAL IRWIN, neurosurgeon, medical educator; b. Bklyn., July 22, 1926; s. Gustave Coburn and Lillian Aronson; m. Shirlee Rose Friedman, Nov. 8, 1945; children: Rita Jane Joseph, Andrew Charles. MD, U. Cin., 1949. Chief neurosurgery Sinai Hosp. Balt., Inc., 1966—95; assoc. prof. neurosurgery Johns Hopkins U., Balt., 1980—. Bd. mem. JCC, Balt., 1989—95. Lt. USNR, 1954—56. Recipient Cert. of Merit, AMA, 1971; grantee, NIH, Nat. Inst. Neurol. Diseases and Blindness, 1957—61. Mem.: Assn. Neurol. Surgeons (life). Achievements include design of instrumentation for cervical fusion. Avocations: swimming, golf. Home: 4 Swanhill Dr Baltimore MD 21208-1927 Office: Mid-Atlantic Neurosurgical Associates 2411 W Belvedere Ave Baltimore MD 21215 Home Phone: 410-484-1269; Office Phone: 410-601-8314. Office Fax: 410-601-9974. Personal E-mail: left4golf1@aol.com.

ARONSON, NEIL H., lawyer; b. 1957; BA summa cum laude, with distinction, Boston U., 1979; JD, Cornell U., 1982. Bar: Mass. 1982, US Ct. Appeals (1st Cir.) 1983. Ptnr. Mintz, Levin, Cohn, Ferris, Glovsky & Popeo PC, Boston, chmn., Bus. & Fin. Sect. Contbr. articles to profl. jour.; lectr. in field. Mem.: Boston Estate Planning Coun., Nat. Assn. Corp. Dirs., MIT Enterprise Forum, Boston Chief Exec. Officers Club (former pres.), Boston Bar Assn., Mass. Bar Assn., ABA, Phi Beta Kappa. Office: Mintz Levin Cohn Ferris Glovsky & Popeo PC One Financial Center Boston MA 02111 Office Phone: 617-348-1809. Office Fax: 617-542-2241. Business E-Mail: naronson@mintz.com.

ARONSON, PETER SAMUEL, physiologist, researcher; b. Bklyn., Feb. 3, 1947; s. Harry and Sydelle Aronson; m. Marie Louise Landry, Sept. 25, 1977; children: Paul L., William L. AB, U. Rochester, NY, 1967; MD, NYU, 1970; MA (hon.), Yale U., New Haven, Conn., 1987. Diplomate Nat. Bd. Med. Examiners; diplomate in internal medicine and nephrology Am. Bd. Internal Medicine. Intern and resident in internal medicine U. NC Sch. Medicine, Chapel Hill, 1970-72; clin. assoc. Gerontology Rsch. Ctr., NIH, Balt., 1972-74; fellow in nephrology Yale U. Sch. Medicine, New Haven, 1974-77, asst. prof. medicine and physiology, 1977-81, assoc. prof. medicine and physiology, 1981-87, prof. medicine and cellular and molecular physiology, 1987—, C.N.H. Long prof. internal medicine, 1995—. Chief sect. nephrology Yale U. Sch. Medicine, New Haven, 1987-2002; established investigator Am. Heart Assn., 1981-86. Mem. editl. bd. Am. Jour. Physiology, 1982-86, 87-90, 96-2000, Kidney Internat., 1990-94, Jour. Biol. Chemistry, 1995-2000; cons. editor Jour. Clin. Investigation, 1993-98; contbr. rsch. articles to profl. jours. With USPHS, 1972-74. Recipient Solomon Berson Med. Alumni Achievement award NYU, 1996; co-recipient Charles W. Bohmfalk Tchg. prize in basic sci., Yale U., 2005. Fellow: AAAS; mem.: Soc. Gen. Physiologists, Internat. Soc. Nephrology, Am. Heart Assn. (exec. com. coun. on the kidney 1986—90), Am. Soc. Nephrology (councillor 2002—06, pres.-elect 2006—07, Young Investigator award 1985, Homer Smith award 1994), Am. Soc. Clin. Investigation (councillor 1986—88, editl. com. 1993—98), Am. Physiol. Soc., Am. Fedn. Med. Rsch., Am. Assn. Physicians, Salt and Water Club (sec. 1985—87), Alpha Omega Alpha, Phi Beta Kappa. Office: Yale Sch Medicine Dept Medicine/Nephrology PO Box 208029 New Haven CT 06520-8029

ARONSON, SETH, lawyer; b. NYC, 1955; BBA, Ohio U., 1978; JD, Loyola U., 1981. Bar: Calif. 1981, US Dist. Ct. (Ctrl. Dist. Calif.) 1983, US Dist. Ct. (So. and No. Dist. Calif.) 1985, US Ct. Appeals (9th Cir.) 1985, US Supreme Ct. 1987, US Ct. Appeals (8th Cir.) 1989. Ptnr Practice Group of O'Melveny & Myers, LLP, LA, head office L.A. br., chmn. securities litig. Bd. overseer Loyola Law Sch., 2000—, bd. vistors, 2001—; lectr. and panelist on various litig. topics at programs by the ABA, LA County Bar Assn., Assn. Bus. Trial Lawyers, Practising Law Inst., Directors Roundtable, Nat. Bus. Inst., FBA, and UCLA Law Sch.; chmn. securities litigation practice group O'Melveny & Myers, LLP. Contbr. articles in profl. jours. Bd. advisors UCLA Sch. Pub. Policy and Social Rsch., 2001—; bd. dir. Ninth Cir. Historical Soc., 2000—, Legal Aid Found., LA, 1993—2000, pres., 1998—99; bd. dir. LA C. of C., 2003—. Mem.: Assn. Bus. Trial Lawyers (bd. gov. 1992—2002, pres. 2001—02), LA County Bar Assn. (mem. exec. com., litig. sect. 1999—2003, chair: complex courts com. 2000—05). Office: O'Melveny & Myers LLP 400 S Hope St Los Angeles CA 90071-2899 Office Phone: 213-430-6000. Office Fax: 213-430-6407. Business E-Mail: saronson@omm.com.

ARONSON, STANLEY MAYNARD, physician, educator; b. NYC, May 28, 1922; s. Eliuh and Lena (Hassner) A.; m. Betty Ellis, June 3, 1947; children: Susan, Lisa, Sarah; m. Gale Matheson Holmes, Oct. 12, 2003. BS, CCNY, 1943; MD, NYU, 1947; MA, Brown U., 1971; MPH, Harvard U. Sch. Pub. Health, 1981; DSc (hon.), Tougaloo Coll., 2005; LHD (hon.), RI Coll., 2006; D in Med. Sci. (hon.), Brown. U., 2007. Diplomate Am. Bd. Pathology, Am. Bd. Neuropathology. Resident Bellevue Hosp., Sydenham Hosp., Meml. Sloan-Kettering Ctr. for Cancer, VA Med. Ctr., NYC, 1946-51; fellow Mt. Sinai Hosp., NYC, 1951-54; faculty Armed Forces Inst. Pathology Columbia Coll. Physicians and Surgeons, 1951-54; prof. pathology, asst. dean SUNY, Bklyn., 1954-70; prof. med. sci., dean medicine Brown U., 1970-81, Univ. prof. med. sci., 1981-87, dean medicine emeritus, 1987—. Dir. labs. Kings County Hosp. Ctr., Bklyn., 1965-70; pathologist-in-chief Miriam Hosp., Providence, 1970-75; vis. prof. cmty. medicine Dartmouth Coll. Med. Sch., 1982-; lectr. Yale Sch. Medicine, 1964-65; lectr. pathology Tufts U. Sch. Medicine, 1978-; profl. lectr. Bklyn. Health Ctr., SUNY, 1970—; cons. physician neuropathology Jewish Chronic Disease Hosp., Bklyn., 1951-, NIH, 1962-, RI Hosp., Roger Williams Hosp., Meml. Hosp., Miriam Hosp., Providence VA Hosp., Butler Hosp., Providence, RI Med. Ctr., Luth. Med. Ctr., NYC. Author: (with B.W. Volk) Cerebral Sphingolipidoses, 1962, Inborn Disorders of Sphingolipid Metabolism, 1966, Sphingolipids, Sphingolipidoses and Allied Disorders, 1972, (with A. Sahs and E Hartman) Guidelines for Stroke Care, 1976; (with Adachi and Hirano) The Pathology of the Myelinated Axon, 1985, Tapestry of Medicine, 1999, Worms, Germs and Wayward Physicians, 2000, Smallpox in Colonial America, 2002, (with R. Shield), Aging in Today's World, 2003; also numerous articles; mem. editl. bd. Jour. Submicroscopic Cytology, Jour. Neuropathology and Exptl. Neurology; editl. bd., editor-in-chief RI Med. Jour.; weekly columnist Providence Jour.-Bull. Commr. US Commn. Control of Huntington's Disease, 1976-79; chmn. Legis. Commn. Dementia Related to Aging; vice chmn. RI Bd. of Med. Licensure and Discipline, 1993-2003; pres. Hospice RI, 1989—, Interfaith Health Care Ministries, 1989-91; mem. Nat. Adv. Commn. on Multiple Sclerosis, 1973-74, NIH Perinatal Rsch. Commn., Joint Commn. on Stroke Facilities, med. adv. bd. Nat. Multiple Sclerosis Soc., Dysautonomia Found., Nat. Tay-Sachs Assn., Nat. Fund for Med. Edn.; trustee Finch Univ. Health Sci., Chgo.; cons. for internat. epidemiology programs The Rockefeller Found., 1990—; chmn. bd. trustees Jewish Home for Aged, RI, 1993-94; pres. Shalom Housing for Elderly, 1993-94. With U.S. Army, 1942-46. Named to R.I. Hall of Fame, 1997. Mem. AMA, Am. Neurol. Assn., Am. Assn. Neuropathology (pres. 1971-72), NY Acad. Medicine, Am. Acad. Neurology, Am. Assn. Pathologists and Bacteriologists, Internat. Soc. Neuropathology, Assn. Am. Med. Coll., NY Neurol. Soc., APHA, Am. Osler Soc., Am. Coll. Epidemiology, NAS (com. on nutrition in med. edn. 1983-85, com. on dietary guidelines implementation 1988-90). Achievements include research on genetics, epidemiology, pathology and diagnostic features of cerebral degenerative diseases, population dynamics, pathology and epidemiology of cerebral vascular disease and organic dementia. Home: 530 Blackstone Blvd Providence RI 02906 Office: Brown U Office Med Affairs Providence RI 02912-0001 Home Phone: 401-383-0060. Personal E-mail: smamd@cox.net.

ARONSON, VIRGINIA L., lawyer; b. Bremerton, Wash., June 4, 1947; m. Simon Aronson. BA, U. Chgo., 1969, MA, 1973, JD, 1975. Bar: Ill. 1975. Ptnr. Sidley Austin LLP, Chgo. With U. Chgo. Law Review, 1974—75; mem. exec. and mgmt. com. Sidley Austin LLP. Contbr. articles to profl. jours. Mem. leadership coun. Chgo. Pub. Edn. Fund; mem. bd. dirs. Chgo. Ctrl. Area Com. Mem. Am. Coll. Real Estate Lawyers, Chgo. Mortgage Attys. Assn., The Chgo. Network. Office: Sidley Austin LLP 1 South Dearborn St Chicago IL 60603 Office Phone: 312-853-7741. Office Fax: 312-853-7036. Business E-Mail: varonson@sidley.com.

ARONZON, PAUL S., lawyer; b. LA, 1954; BA cum laude, Calif. State U., Northridge, 1976; JD, Southwestern U., 1979. Bar: Calif. 1979, DC 1995, NY 1996. Mng. dir., exec. v.p., co-head investment banking Imperial Capital, LLC, LA, 2006—. Office: Imperial Capital LLC 2000 Avenue of the Stars 9th Fl Los Angeles CA 90067 Office Phone: 310-246-3631. Business E-Mail: paronzon@imperialcapital.com.

ARORA, SANDEEP, cardiologist; b. Palwal, Haryana, India, July 24, 1974; s. Krishan Lal and Mira Arora; m. Anju Arora, Nov. 24, 2001; children: Ishika, Navya. MBBS, Maulana Azad Med. Coll., India, 1997, MD, 2001, Temple U., 2006. Diplomate Am. Bd. Internal Medicine, 2006. Housestaff Maulana Azad Med. Coll., New Delhi, 1998—2001, Maharaja Agrasen Heart Inst. and Rsch. Ctr., New Delhi, 2001; chief resident Lady Hardinge Med. coll., New Delhi, 2001—02; emergency med. officer Lok Nayak Hosp., New Delhi, 2002—03; housestaff Temple U., Western Pa. Hosp., Pitts., 2003—06, cardiology fellow, 2006—. Contbr. articles to profl. jours., chapters to books. Recipient Best Student Tchr. award, Temple U. Western Pa. Hosp., 2005, Best Housestaff award, 2005, 2006. Mem.: Am. Heart Assn. (Rsch. award 2007), AMA, ACP (Rsch. award 2004), Am. Coll. Cardiology, Am. Bd. Internal Medicine, Cmty. Hangout and Recreation Pl. For All Indo-Ams., Internat. High IQ Soc., Maulana Azad Med. Coll. Alumni Assn. N.Am., Network Indian Profls. N.Am. Achievements include development of evidence based protocol at West Penn Hospital for management of 'Acute Congestive Heart Failure' in emergency department; preparation of guidelines for management and implementation of 'Chronic Congestive Heart Failure' for Clinical Reminder System (CRS) in Western Pennsylvania Hospital; research in accuracy of noninvasive assessment of atherosclerotic plaque composition with multidetector computed tomography: A comparative study using intra-vascular ultrasound virtual histology; incidence of major peripheral vascular complications with micropuncture needle in patients undergoing cardiac catheterization; reducing cardiac enzyme leaks by vasodilatation before percutaneous coronary intervention with intracoronary nicardipine pre-treatment. A double blind randomized placebo-controlled trial; effect of nesiritide on renal functions in patients with acute decompensated heart failure; complications associated with central venous line insertion in hospitalized patients; Safety of cardiac catheterization in very elderly patients. Avocations: photography, travel, music. Personal E-mail: sandeeparora24@hotmail.com.

AROUH, JEFFREY ALAN, lawyer; b. NYC, May 2, 1945; s. Isaac E. and Jean J. (Halfron) Arouh; m. Karen Ann Wieder, Feb. 1, 1969; children: Russell Andrew, Ilonne A. BA, U. Mich., 1966; JD cum laude, NYU, 1969. Bar: NY 1970; sr. cert. relocation profl. Assoc. Gilbert, Segall and Young, NYC, 1969-74, ptnr., 1975-2001, Holland & Knight LLP, NYC, 2001—. Spkr. in field. Editor NYU Law Rev., 1969; contbr. articles to legal publs. Recipient Founders Day award NYU. Mem. ABA (bus. law sect. com. corp. compliance), NY State Bar Assn., Assn. Bar City NY, Employee Relocation Coun. (pub. policy com.), Order Coif, Hampshire Country Club, Ibis Golf Country Club (pP Office: 195 Broadway Fl 24 New York NY 10007 Home: 7997 Crane's Pointe Way West Palm Beach FL 33412 Office Phone: 212-513-3460. Business E-Mail: jeffrey.arouh@hklaw.com.

ARP, ARLENE, elementary school educator; b. Detroit, Sept. 30, 1951; 1 child, Ila Arp-Spratt. BA in Religious Studies (hon.), Ind. U., 1993; cert. in Primary Edn., Montessori Tchr. Coll. Montessori Primary Education Teaching Certificate Montessori Tchr. Coll. NW, 1988, cert. early childhood generalist Nat. Bd. Cert. Profl. Tchg. Stds., 1996. Primary montessori tchr. Nat. Ctr. for Montessori Edn., Seattle, 1987—92; early childhood tchr. Austin Ind. Sch. Dist., Tex., 1992—94, DeKalb County Sch. Dist., Atlanta, 1994—99, Atlanta Pub. Schs., 2007—; pvt. tutor Atlanta, 1999—2007. Recipient recognition for nat. cert., DeKalb County Bd. of Edn., 1996. Mem.: Internat. Honor Soc. and Profl. Assn. in Edn. (hon.). Personal E-mail: arlenearp@bellsouth.net.

ARPEY, GERARD J., air transportation executive; b. July 26, 1958; m. Lisa Arpey; 3 children BA, U. Tex., 1980, MBA, 1982. FAA multi-engine pilots license. Fin. analyst Am. Airlines, 1982, mng. dir. airline profitability analysis, mng. dir. analysis and fleet planning, mng. dir. fin. planning, v.p. fin. planning and analysis, 1989-92, sr. v.p. planning, 1992-95, sr. v.p. fin. and planning, 1995—99; CFO AMR Corp. and Am. Airlines, exec. v.p. ops., 2000—02, pres., COO, 2002—03, pres., CEO, 2003—04, chmn., pres., CEO, 2004—. Bd. dirs. Am. Bracom Advisors, Inc. Avocation: private pilot. Office: AMR Corp Maildrop 5621 PO Box 619616 Dallas TX 75261-9616*

ARPINO, GERALD PETER, performing company executive; b. SI, NY, Jan. 14, 1928; s. Luigi and Anna (Santanastasio) A. Student, Wagner Coll., PhD (hon.), 1980; student ballet under Mary Ann Wells, student modern dance under May O'Donnell and Gertrude Shurr. Dancer Ballet Russe, 1951-52; co-founder Joffrey Ballet, 1956, dancer, to 1962, former assoc. artistic dir., now artistic dir. Chgo., resident choreographer, until 1990, artistic dir.; with faculty Joffrey Ballet Sch., NYC, from 1953, now artistic dir., 1988—, assoc. dir., 1988—, prin. choreographer, 1988—. Bd. dirs. Dance Notation Bur., Dancers in Transition; mem. adv. coun. to dept. dance Calif. State U., Long Beach, also mem. Disting. Artists Forum. Choreographer ballets including Incubus, 1962, Viva Vivaldi!, 1965, Olympics, Nightwings, both 1966, Cello Concerto, Arcs and Angels, Elegy, all 1967, Secret Places, The Clowns, Fanfarita, A Light Fantastic, 1968, Animus, The Poppet, 1969, Confetti, Solarwind, Trinity, all 1970, Reflections, Valentine, Kettentanz, all 1971, Chabriesque, Sacred Grove on Mount Talmalpais, both 1972, Jackpot, 1973, The Relativity of Icarus, 1974, Drums, Dreams on Banjos, 1975, Orpheus Times Light 2, 1976, Touch Me, 1977, Choura, L'Air d 'Esprit, Suite Saint-Saens, all 1978, Epode, 1979, Celebration, 1980, Ropes, Partita for Four, Sea Shadow, Diverdissement, 1980, Light Rain, 1981, Round of Angels, 1982, Italian Suite, Quarter-Tones, 1983, Jamboree (commd. by City of San Antonio) Adv. Sportsmedicine Edn. & Rsch. Found., L.A.; mem. adv. com. N.Y. Internat. Festival of the Arts; mem. nat. adv. coun. ITI/USA Internat. Ballet Competition; mem. hon. com. The Yard Benefit-Vineyard Celebration, 1989; mng. dir., bd. dirs. Found. for Joffrey Balllet, Inc. Served with USCG, 1945-48. Recipient Dancemagazine award, 1974, Bravo award San Antonio Performing Arts Assn., 1984, Disting. Achievement award Nat. Orgn. Italian-Am. Women, 1987, Tiffany award Internat. Soc. Performing Arts Adminstrs., 1989, Outstanding Artistic Achievement award Staten Island Coun. on Arts, 1990, Ammy award Am. Express Corp. Office: Joffrey Ballet Chgo 70 E Lake St Fl 1300 Chicago IL 60601-5917*

ARQUETTE, PATRICIA, actress; b. Chgo., Apr. 8, 1968; d. Lewis and Mardi Arquette; m. Nicholas Cage, Apr. 8, 1995 (div. May 18, 2001) m. Thomas Jane, June 25, 2006, 1 child, Harlow Olivia Calliope; 1 child (with Paul Rossi), Enzo Actress: (films) Pretty Smart, 1986, A Nightmare on Elm Street 3: Dream Warriors, 1987, Time Out, 1988, Far North, 1988, The Indian Runner, 1991, Prayer of the Rollerboys, 1991, Especially on Sunday, 1991, Inside Monkey Zetterland, 1992, Trouble Bound, 1993, Ethan Frome, 1993, True Romance, 1993, Holy Matrimony, 1994, Ed Wood, 1994, Beyond Rangoon, 1995, Flirting with Disaster, 1996, The Secret Agent, 1996, Infinity, 1996, Lost Highway, 1997, Nightwatch, 1997, Goodbye Lover, 1998, The Hi-Lo Country, 1998, Toby's Story, 1998, Stigmata, 1999, Bringing Out the Dead, 1999, Little Nicky, 2000, Human Nature, 2001, The Badge, 2002, Deeper Than Deep, 2003, Holes, 2003, Tiptoes, 2003, Fast Food Nation, 2006; (TV movies) Daddy, 1987, The Girl with the Crazy Brother, 1990, Dillinger, 1991, Wildflower, 1991 (CableACE award, 1991), Betrayed by Love, 1994; (TV series) Medium, 2005- (Emmy award for outstanding lead actress in a drama series, 2005); (TV appearances) thirtysomething, 1990, Tales From the Crypt, 1990. Spokesperson Lee Nat. Denim Day, 1999. Office: UTA 9560 Wilshire Blvd Fl 5 Beverly Hills CA 90212-2401

ARQUIT, KEVIN JAMES, lawyer; b. Ithaca, NY, Sept. 11, 1954; s. Gordon James and Nora (Harris) A. BA cum laude, St. Lawrence U., 1975; JD cum laude, Cornell U., 1978. Bar: Ohio 1978, N.Y. 1980, U.S. Dist. Ct. (so. and ea. dists.) N.Y. 1980, U.S. Dist. Ct. (we. dist.) N.Y. 1983, U.S. Dist. Ct. (no. dist.) Calif. 1983, U.S. Ct. Appeals (3d cir.) 1983, U.S. Dist. Ct. (no. dist.) N.Y. 1985, U.S. Ct. Appeals(2d cir.) 1985, U.S. Supreme Ct. 1989. Assoc. Arter & Hadden, Cleve., 1978, Fish & Neave, NYC, 1978-83, Harris, Beach & Wilcox, Rochester, NY, 1983-86; atty. advisor to chmn. FTC, Washington, 1986-87, chief staff, 1987-88, gen. counsel, 1988-89; dir. Bur. Competition, Washington, 1989-92; ptnr., dep. chmn., head Clifford Chance US LLP Antitrust Practice Group, NYC, 1992—2002; ptnr. STB, 2003—. Republican. Roman Catholic. Office: Simpson Thacher & Bartlett 425 Lexington Ave New York NY 10017-3954 Business E-Mail: karquit@stblaw.com.

ARQUIT, NORA HARRIS, retired music educator, writer; b. Brushton, NY, June 30, 1923; d. Samuel Elton George and Esther Cecelia (Gillen) Harris; m. Gordon James Arquit, Nov. 12, 1948; children: Christine Elaine Arquit, Kevin James Arquit, Candace Susan Arquit-Martel. BS in Music Edn., Ithaca Coll., 1945, MS, 1962; postgrad., St. Lawrence U., 1946-47, 74, Cornell U., 1970-71, N.Y. State Coll., Potsdam, 1973. Cert. aerospace edn. with techicians rating. Music dir., band dir., tchr. N.Y. and N.J. State Schs., 1945—80. Guest conductor U.S. Air Force Band, Washington, Dutch and Am. band students, Schiedam, Holland, opening Am.-Can. Seaway, Massena, N.Y., 1975; U.S. Navy Band, Washington, various massed bands in U.S.A., Canada, Europe; dir. bands Worlds Fair, 1964, 65; 1st woman guest conductor Tri-State Honors Band Phillips U., Enid, Okla.; dir., coord. St. Lawrence County ann. H.S. Band Day, 1973-2002; past supvr. coll. student practice tchrs., N.Y.; mem. Mid-States Commn. Secondary Schs. and Colls. Evaluations. Author: Before My Own Time and Since, 1978, From Hamlet to Cold Harbor, 1989, Our Lyon Line, 1993, The History of the New York State, Society of the National Society of the Daughters of the American Colonists, 1994. Past adjudicator h.s. and coll. band contests; past dir., coord. ann. St. Lawrence County Band Day; past capt. aux. USAF Civil Air Patrol; past John Philip Sousa bd. dirs. rep. to Hall of Fame enshrinement of Sousa NY. Named Dist. Band Master Am., First Chair Am.; recipient Letter of Commendation for People to People Diplomacy for work with student band groups, Embassy at the Hague, Europe, honored for 39 yrs. of svc. on Band Day, St. Lawrence County, 2002. Mem.: AAUW (past divsn. meeting rep.), DAR (life; hon. regent Cayuga chpt., past state com. chmn., genealogical chmn.), Women Band Dirs. Nat. Assn. (past nat. pres., Silver Baton), N.Y. State Ret. Tchrs. Assn., N.Am. Band Dirs. Coordinating Coun. (pres. 1978, past nat. v.p.), Am. School Band Dirs. Assn. (emeritus mem. 1980, N.Y. state chmn. 2003—, past chmn. internat. band com., past nat. and state ofcr., honored nat. covention 2003), Internat. Assn. U. Women, Colonial Daughters of the XVIIC (chpt. councillor 1988-91, past. mem. coms.), De Schilpen Mus. Soc. Netherlands, De Schilpen Soc. (Holland), Kings County Hist. Soc. Nova Scotia, Daughters of Union Vets., Denison Soc., Daughters Am. Colonists (N.Y. state regent 1991—94, hon. state regent, life 1994), Soc. Colonial Dames of Seventeenth Century (past state officer, past state pres, registrar), Colonial Daughters Seventeenth Century (Atlantic Coast chmn. 2000—, nat. com. chmn. 2000—, past pres.), Daus. Colonial Wars, Soc. New England Women, N.Y. Ct. Assts. of Nat. Soc. Women Descendents of Ancient and Honorable Artillery Co. (life; past state officer, corr. sec., com. chmn.), Soc. Magna Charta Dames and Barons, Plantagenet Soc., Colonial Order of The Crown (Charlemagne), Soc. Sons and Daus. of the Pilgrims, Soc. U.S. Daughters 1812 (past pres., past Onondaga chpt. pres., past state ofcr.), Soc. Daughters of Founders & Patriots of Am. (past pres., past state pres., registrar, life mem. Nat. Officers Club), Soc. Sons and Daughters of Colonial Wars, Soc. New England Women, Soverign Colonial Soc., Daughters of Am. Colonists (nat. com chmn. 1994—97, Atlantic sect.chmn genealogy 2003—), Summit N.J. Club (spl. panel), Nat. Fedn. Music Club (past editl.com.), N.Y. State Officers Club DAR, Ithaca Music Club (past pres.), Delta Omicron. Avocations: writing, photography, research. Home: 130 Christopher Cir Ithaca NY 14850-1702

ARRARÁS, MARIA CELESTE, newscaster, journalist; b. Mayagüez, Puerto Rico, Sept. 22, 1961; d. Jose Enrique Arrarás; m. Manny Arvesu Arrarás, 1990 (div. Mar. 27, 2004); children: Julian, Lara Giuliana; 1 adopted child, Vadim. Grad., Loyola U. News anchor Primer Impacto Univision TV, 1994—2002, Al Rojo Vivo Telemundo USA, 2002—; co-host Today Show NBC TV, 2006. Actor: (films) Contact, 1997. Office: Telemundo Comm Group Inc 2290 W 8th St Hialeah FL 33010*

ARRASMITH, WILLIAM W., engineering educator; b. Bad Aibling, Bavaria, Germany, Jan. 7, 1961; s. Billy Gene and Hanna Black (Stepmother); m. Pongrat Lena Intaraphuck, Aug. 1, 1987; children: Christina Lori, Kari Amber. BSEE, Va. Tech U., Blacksburg, 1983; MS in Elec. and Computer Engring., U. N.Mex, Albuquerque, 1991; PhD in Engring. Physics, Air Force Inst. Tech., Dayton, Ohio, 1995. Chief software divsn., teal ruby program USAF Space Divsn., LA, 1983—88; chief sensor calibration lab. Imaging Br., Air Force Weapons Lab., Albuquerque, 1988—91; dir. flood beam expt. Air Force Phillips Lab., Albuquerque, 1991—92; program mgr. Physics Directorate, Air Force Office Sci. Rsch., Wasington, 1995—97; asst. prof. US Naval Acad., Annapolis, Md., 1997—2000; divsn. chief systems and tech. divsn. Applied Tech. Directorate, Air Force Tech. Applications Ctr., Melbourne, Fla., 2000—02, divsn. chief advanced sci. and tech. divsn., 2002—03; assoc. prof., engring. systems dept. Fla. Inst. Tech. Cons. Greywolf Tech. Svcs., Inc, Melbourne, 2003—. Contbr. articles to profl. jours. Mil. cmty. outreach K-12 and Troubled Teens, Melbourne, 2002—03. Lt. USAF, 1983—2003. Scholar, USAF, 1979—83. Mem.: Am. Math. Assn., Internat. Soc. Optical Engring., Am. Soc. Engring. Edn., Nat. Honor Soc., Soc. Am. Mil. Engineers, Tau Beta Pi. Achievements include patents pending for high speed, portable, unconventional imaging system for atmospheric turbulence compensation and adaptive image processing. Avocations: travel, soccer, martial arts. Office: Florida Institute of Technology 150 W University Blvd Melbourne FL 32901 Office Phone: 321-223-4980. Office Fax: 321-674-7270. E-mail: warrasmi@fit.edu.

ARREDONDO, JENNA DOLORES, speech pathology/audiology services professional; b. Oklahoma City, Jan. 16, 1963; d. Ralph Maurice Barnett and Patsy June Lynch; m. Hector Javier Arredondo, Aug. 5, 1995 (dec.); children: Kayleigh Marie, Noelia Elena children: James Ray Velasquez. AA, Tex. Southmost Coll., 1992; BA, U. Tex.-Pan Am., 1997, MA in Comm. Disorders, 1999; student, So. Meth. U. Certificate of Clinical Competence, Am. Speech Hearing Assn., 2000. Staff speech lang. pathologist Aptus Therapy Svcs., McAllen, Tex., 2000, Milestones Therapeutic Assocs., McAllen, Tex., 2000—. Leader U.S. Girl Scouts Tip-O-Texas Coun., Pharr, 1996—97. Mem.: Tex. Speech Hearing Assn. (assoc.), Am. Speech Hearing Lang. Assn. (assoc.). Roman Catholic. Avocations: reading, sewing, cooking, arts and crafts. Office: Milestones Therapeutic Assocs 3300 N McCall St Ste A Mcallen TX 78501 Office Phone: 956-661-0475. Business E-Mail: jenna@milestonestx.com.

ARRINDELL, NICHOLAS J., academic administrator, educator; children: Haile, Craig. BA, Ctrl. State U., 1969; M, CUNY, 1976; PhD, U. Md., 1983; cert. in advanced study, Harvard U., 1995. Cert. guidance and counseling State of N.Y., 1976. Dir. Fairleigh Dickinson U., Teaneck, NJ, 1983—87; asst. dir. City Coll. N.Y., CUNY, NYC, 1987—91; dir. Johns Hopkins U., Balt., 1991—. Mem. Md. Sister State Edn. Com., Balt., 2004—06; advisor Wash. Edn. Coun., Inc, Washington, 2003—06; bd. trustee Holton-Arms Sch., Bethesda, Md., 1994—2003. Named Outstanding Young Man of Am., U.S. Jaycees, 1979; fellow, State of Md., 1977; Fulbright scholar, Dept. of State, 2003. Mem.: European Assn. Internat. Educators, Assn. Internat. Edn. Adminstr. (life), Nat. Assn. Internat. Educators (life). Avocations: swimming, travel, photography. Office: Johns Hopkins Univ 3103 N Charles St Baltimore MD 21218 Home Phone: 301-270-1883; Office Phone: 410-516-1013. Office Fax: 410-516-1018; Home Fax: 410-516-1018.

ARRINGTON, CAROLYN RUTH, school system administrator, consultant; b. May 20, 1942; d. Robert Ray and Grace Dotson; m. Wayne Vernon Arrington; children: Kevin Ray, Kemp Gray, Korey shay, Wayne, Kimberly. AA, Ohio Valley Coll., 1962; BA, Fairmont State Coll., 1964; MA, W.Va. U., 1966, EdD, 1994. Cert. pub. sch. adminstr. Tchr. Greenbrier Bd. Edn., Lewisburg, W.Va., 1964-68; supr. Mason County Bd. Edn., Point Pleasant, W.Va., 1968-70; media specialist Kanawha County Bd. Edn., Charleston, W.Va., 1970-71; asst. dir., dir., asst. divsn. chief W.Va. Dept. Edn., Charleston, 1971-89, asst. state supt. schs., 1989-98; v.p. Arrington Assocs., Inc., 1998—2005; rsch. adv. Chio Valley U., 2005—. Adj. prof. Ohio Valley U., 2005—; cons., spkr. in field. Author: numerous poems, short stories. Bd. dirs. YWCA, Charleston, 1988—91. Recipient Merit medal Edn. Ohio Valley U.; SEA fellow US Dept. Edn., 1984 Mem. Assn. Ednl. Comm. and Tech. (pres. 1979-80, Edgar Dale award 1975, Spl. Svc. award 1982), Wva. Ednl. Media Assn. (pres. 1975-76). Office: Arrington Assocs Inc Charleston WV

ARRINGTON, JOHN LESLIE, JR., lawyer; b. Pawhuska, Okla., Oct. 15, 1931; s. John Leslie and Grace Louise (Moore) A.; m. Elizabeth Anne Waddington, 1956 (div.); children: Elizabeth Anne, John Leslie III, Winifred L., Katherine M.; m. Linda Vance, 1972. Grad., Lawrenceville Sch., 1949; AB, Princeton U., 1953; JD, Harvard U., 1956, LLM, 1957. Bar: Okla. 1956, U.S. Supreme Ct. 1960. Assoc. Arrington, Kihle, Gaberino & Dunn and predecessor firms, Tulsa, 1957-61, ptnr., 1961-93, chmn., CEO, 1994-96; gen. counsel ONEOK, Inc., 1997-98; of counsel Gable & Gotwals, Tulsa, 1998—. Chmn. bd. dirs. Woodland Bank of Tulsa, 1979-94. Prin. draftsman Okla. Supreme Ct. rules governing disciplinary proceedings, 1980-81; bd. dirs. Tulsa County Legal Aid Soc., 1965-70, pres. 1967-70; bd. dirs. Tulsa Family Mental Health Ctr., 1982-89. Named Outstanding Young Man, Tulsa Jaycees, 1963 Mem. ABA, Tulsa County Bar Assn. (Young Lawyer award 1962, pres. 1970, Pres.'s award 1984, Professionalism award 1993), Okla. Bar Assn. (mem. profl. responsiblity commn. 1977-84, vice chmn. 1983-84, Disting. svc. award 1984, Golden Gavel award 1985, Pres.'s award 1991, Masonic award for ethics 1995), So. Hills Country Club (Tulsa), Princeton Club (N.Y.C.). Republican. Episcopalian. Home: 2300 Riverside Dr Unit 3E Tulsa OK 74114-2402 Office: 100 W 5th St Ste 1000 Tulsa OK 74103-4293

ARRINGTON, LAVAR, professional football player; b. Pitts., June 20, 1978; s. Michael; m. Janelle Arrington; 1 child, Keeno Lamoni. Attended, Penn State U. Profl. football player Wash. Redskins, 2000—06, NY Giants, 2006. With Washington Redskins Leadership Coucil's Fields for Tomorrow program. Named to NFL Pro-Bowl, 2001—03; recipient Pigskin Club Oxley award, 2002, Chuck Bednarik award, 1999, Dick Butkus award, 1999.*

ARRINGTON, (JACK) MICHAEL, web publishing company executive, blogger, lawyer; b. Mar. 1970; Attended, U. Calif. Berkeley; BA in Economics, Claremont McKenna Coll.; JD, Stanford Law Sch., 1995. Corp. atty. O'Melveny & Meyers, Wilson Sonsini; with RealNames; co-founder Achex (sold to First Data Corp.); founder Zip.ca, Canada; v.p. ops. Global Name Registry Ltd., London, 2000—01; ind. cons., 2001—02; COO RazorGator, Inc., 2002—03; CEO Pool.com, Inc., 2003—04; founder CrunchNotes.com, 2005—; co-founder, chmn. Edgeio.com, 2006—; founder, editor, author TechCrunch.com, 2006—. Cons. Snap-Names and Verisign; bd. dirs. foldera.com, 2006—. Named one of 50 Who Matter Now, Business 2.0, 2007, Top 25 Web Celebs, Forbes mag., 2007.*

ARRINGTON, MICHAEL BROWNE, foundation administrator; b. Chgo., Mar. 24, 1943; s. W. Russell and Ruth Marian (Browne) Arrington; m. DeEtta Jane Watson, Dec. 15, 1966 (div. 1969); m. Trudi Jeanne Robertson, Dec. 4, 1971 (div. 1992); children: Jennifer Lorraine, Patrick Browne; m. Catherine L. Swainbank, July 14, 2006. AA, Kendall Coll., Evanston, Ill.; BA in Polit. Sci., U. Ill. Adminstrv. asst. to Senate Majority Leader State of Ill., Springfield, 1966-67; dir. pub. affairs Union League Club of Chgo., 1967-68; exec. dir. South Loop Improvement Orgn., Chgo., 1968-69; pres., chief exec. officer The Arrington Found., Chgo., 1979—, Arrington Travel Ctr., Inc., Chgo., 1969-99, Recon Mgmt Svcs., Evanston, Ill., 1999—. Mem. Nat. White House Conf. Travel and Tourism, Disting. Entrepreneurship Bd., U. Ill., Chgo. Bd. dirs. Robert R. McCormick Chgo. Boys & Girls Club, 1982—, Friends of Prentice Hosp., Chgo., 1986—; mem. chancellor's adv. bd. U. Ill., Chgo. Cpl. USMC, 1962-64. Named finalist Entrepreneur of Yr., 1989, 1990, Man of Yr., Ill. Vietnam Vets Leadership Program, 1993; named to Hall of Fame, Nat. Assn. Trade and Tech. Schs., 1988, Entrepreneurship Hall of Fame, 1994; recipient Excellence in Phys. Fitness award, USMC, 1962, Significant Contbn. to Dental Health award, Ill. Dental Health Soc., 1967, Alumni Achievement award, U. Ill., 2001. Mem. World Pres.'s Orgn., Econ. Club of Chgo., Chgo. Club, Westmoreland Country Club, 100 Club Cook County, Chief Execs. Orgn. Republican. Episcopalian. Avocations: golf, boating, skiing, scuba diving. Office: Recon Mgmt Svcs Inc 929 Edgemere Ct Evanston IL 60202-1428 Home Phone: 847-869-1336; Office Phone: 312-726-1800. E-mail: arringtonusa@aol.com.

ARRINGTON, MICHAEL IRVIN, communications educator; s. Jesse Irvin and Charlotte Carolyn Arrington; m. Tamara Bollis, Mar. 19, 2004; 1 child, Mia Elizabeth. BA in Speech Comm., U. So. Miss., Hattiesburg, 1989—93; MA in Comm., U. S.Fla., Tampa, 1995, PhD in Comm., 2001. Prof. Ohio U., Athens, 2001—04; asst. prof. U. Ky., Lexington, 2004—06. Mem.: So. States Comm. Assn., Nat. Comm. Assn. Office: Univ Ky 247 Grehan Bldg Lexington KY 40506 Home Phone: 859-252-7060. Office Fax: 859-257-4103. Business E-Mail: michaelarrington@uky.edu.

ARROTT, ELIZABETH, journalist; b. Detroit, Oct. 1, 1960; d. Anthony Schuyler and Patricia Graham Arrott; m. Rafael Alexeevich Ekimyan, Sept. 16, 1995; children: Alexei Rafaelevich Ekimyan, Elizabeth Rafaelevna Ekimyan, Catherine Rafaelevna Ekimyan. AB, Harvard U., 1983. Moscow corr. Voice of Am., Moscow, 1993-97; anchor NewsNow Voice of Am., Washington, 1998—. Mem. Ch. LDS. Home: 5026 Reno Rd NW Washington DC 20008-2951 Office: Voice of Am 330 Independence Ave SW Washington DC 20547-0003

ARROTT, PATRICIA GRAHAM, artist, educator; b. Pitts., July 27, 1931; d. George Patterson and Helen (Gilleland) Graham; m. Anthony Schuyler Arrott, June 6, 1953; children: Anthony Patterson, Helen Graham, Matthew Ramsey, Elizabeth. BFA in Painting and Design, Carnegie-Mellon Univ., 1954; postgrad., Nat. Acad. Design, NYC, 1985-87, Art Students League, 1980-91. Cert. tchr. art, Pa. Instr. children's ceramics Handcraft House, Vancouver, B.C., Can., 1970-72; courtroom artist Vancouver, B.C., Can., 1972-73; pvt. portrait artist Vancouver, NYC, 1975—; instr. Art Students League, NYC, 1993-99. Group shows include Nat. Acad. Design, 1990, 92, 94, Cork Gallery, Lincoln Ctr., N.Y.C., 1991, Pen & Brush Club, N.Y.C., 1988-98, Silver Point Etc., 1992-93; represented by Eleanor Ettinger Gallery, N.Y.C., 1997—; exbhns include: Carnegie Mellon U. Fine Arts Alumni Regina Gouger Miller Gallery, Pitts., 2006. Recipient Helen M. Loggie Prize, 1990, and cert. of merit, 1994, Nat. Acad. Design; recipient Emily Nicholas Hatch award Pen & Brush Club, 1989-91, Elizabeth Morse Genius award, 1988, 90, 93, 95, others. Mem. Art Student's League (life; mem. bd. 1989-92, women's v.p. 1991-92), Am. Fine Arts Soc. (mem. bd. 1991-92), Mayflower Soc. (life), Kappa Kappa Gamma (life). United Presbyterian.

ARROW, ALLEN H., lawyer; b. NYC, June 1, 1928; s. Herman Arrow and Emma; m. Fran Loffmin Arrow; children: Edward, David, Lynn. BA, Bklyn. Coll., 1950; JD, NYU, 1953. Bar: N.Y. 1954, Calif. 1976, U.S. Dist. Ct. (ea. dist.) 1958, U.S. Dist. Ct. (so. dist.) 1958. Ptnr. Orenstein & Arrow, NYC, 1955—65, Orenstein Arrow Silverman & Parcher, NYC, 1965—76, Arrow Edelstein & Laird, NYC, 1977—93, Shukat Arrow Hafer & Weber, LLP, NYC, 1993—2007, Shukat Arrow Hafer Weber & Herbsman, LLP, NYC, 2007—. Contbr. articles to profl. jours. Dir. Caron Treatment Ctrs. NY, 2003—, exec. com., 2003—, chmn. bd., 2003—. Cpl. US Army, 1953—55. Mem.: ABA, N.Y.C. Bar Assn. Avocations: golf, music. Office: Shukat Arrow Hafer & Weber LLP 111 W 57th St New York NY 10019 Office Phone: 212-245-4580. Business E-Mail: allen@musiclaw.com.

ARROW, KENNETH JOSEPH, economist, educator; b. NYC, Aug. 23, 1921; s. Harry I. and Lillian (Greenberg) Arrow; m. Selma Schweitzer, Aug. 31, 1947; children: David Michael, Andrew. BS in Social Sci., CCNY, 1940; MA, Columbia U., 1941, PhD, 1951, DSc (hon.), 1973; LLD (hon.), U. Chgo., 1967, CUNY, 1972, Hebrew U. Jerusalem, 1975, U. Pa., 1976, Washington U., St. Louis, 1989; D. Social and Econ. Scis. (hon.), U. Vienna, Austria, 1971; LLD (hon.), Ben-Gurion U. of the Negev, 1992; D in Social Scis. (hon.), Yale U., 1974; D (hon.), Université René Descartes, Paris, 1974, U. Aix-Marseille III, 1985, U. Cattolica del Sacro Cuore, Milan, Italy, 1994, U. Uppsala, 1995, U. Buenos Aires, 1999, U. Cyprus, 2000; Dr.Pol., U. Helsinki, 1976; MA (hon.), Harvard U., 1968; DLitt, Cambridge U., Eng., 1985; LLD (hon.), Harvard U., 1999; PhD (hon.), Tel Aviv U., 2001; LLD (hon.), Hitotsubashi U., 2004. Rsch. assoc. Cowles Commn. for Research in Econs., 1947—49; asst. prof. econs. U. Chgo., 1948—49; acting asst. prof. econs. and stats. Stanford, 1949—50, assoc. prof., 1950—53, prof. econs., stats. and ops. rsch., 1953—68; prof. econs. Harvard, 1968—74, James Bryant Conant univ. prof., 1974—79; exec. head dept. econs. Stanford U., 1954—56, acting exec. head dept., 1962—63, Joan Kenney prof. econs. and prof. ops. rsch., 1979—91, prof. emeritus, 1991—. Economist Coun. Econ. Advisers, U.S. Govt., 1962; cons. RAND Corp., 1948—; Fulbright prof. U. Siena, 1995; vis. fellow All Souls Coll., Oxford, 1996; overseas rsch. fellow Churchill Coll., Cambridge, 1963—64, Cambridge, 1970, 73, 86. Author: Social Choice and Individual Values, 1951, Essays in the Theory of Risk Bearing, 1971, The Limits of Organization, 1974, Collected Papers, Vols. I-VI, 1983—85; co-author: Mathematical Studies in Inventory and Production, 1958, Studies in Linear and Nonlinear Programming, 1958, Time Series Analysis of Inter-industry Demands, 1959, Public Investment, The Rate of Return and Optimal Fiscal Policy, 1971, General Competitive Analysis, 1971, Studies in Resource Allocation Processes, 1977, Social Choice and Multicriterion Decision Making, 1985. Capt. US Army, 1942—46. Recipient Alfred Nobel Meml. prize in econ. scis., Swedish Acad. Scis., 1972, Kempé de Feriet medal, Info. Processing for Mgmt. Under Uncertainty, 1998, Medal, U. Paris, 1998, U.S. Nat. Medal of Sci. in Behavioral/Social Sci., 2004; fellow Social Sci. Rsch. fellow, 1952, Ctr. for Advanced Study in the Behavioral Scis., 1956—57, Guggenheim, 1972—73. Fellow: AAAS (chmn. sect. K 1983), NAS Inst. Medicine (mem. coun. 1990—93), Am. Fin. Assn., Am. Econ. Assn. (exec. com. 1967—69, pres. 1973, John Bates Clark medal 1957), Internat. Soc. Inventory Rsch. (pres. 1983—90), Econometric Soc. (v.p. 1955, pres. 1956), Am. Acad. Arts and Scis. (v.p. 1979—81, 1991—93), Am. Statis. Assn., Inst. Math. Stats.; mem.: Royal Soc. (fgn.), Game Theory Soc., Brit. Acad. (corr.), Pontifical Acad. Social Scis., Soc. Social Choice and Welfare (pres. 1991—93), Western Econ. Assn. (pres. 1980—81), Finnish Acad. Scis. (fgn. hon.), Inst. Ops. Rsch. and Mgmt. Sci. (pres. 1963, chmn. coun. 1964, Von Neumann prize 1986, Fellows' award), Am. Philos. Soc., Internat. Econs. Assn. (pres. 1983—86). Office: Stanford U Dept Econs Stanford CA 94305-6072 Home Phone: 650-327-3957; Office Phone: 650-723-9165. Office Fax: 650-725-5702. Business E-Mail: arrow@stanford.edu.

ARROWOOD, CATHARINE BIGGS, lawyer; b. Lumberton, NC, Nov. 27, 1951; d. Isley Murchison and Janis (Bolton) Biggs; 1 child, Catharine Jeannette. BA cum laude, Wake Forest U., 1973, JD cum laude, 1976. Bar: N.C. 1973. Assoc. atty. gen. antitrust sect. Dept. Justice, Raleigh, N.C., 1976-77; ptnr., litig. Parker Poe Adams & Bernstein LLP, Raleigh, NC, 1977—, mem. mgmt. com., 1990—2001. Mem. panel of comml. arbitrators, Am. Arbitration Assn.; chair, Fed. Bar Adv. Council, 1995-96, Civil Justice Reform Act Com., ea. dist NC, 1997; mem. Gov.'s Adminstrv. Rules Review Commn., Raleigh, 1983-90; N.C. rep. Fourth Cir. Rules Com. Editor (assoc.): Wake Forest Law Rev. Chair bd. vis., Wake Forest Univ. Law Sch., 2001-02. Fellow Am. Coll. Trial Lawyers; mem. ABA, N.C. Bar Assn., Wake County Bar Assn. (pres. 2006—), Phi Beta Kappa. Democrat. Baptist. Office Phone: 919-890-4142. Office Fax: 919-834-4564. Business E-Mail: cbarrowood@parkerpoe.com.

ARROWOOD, DEBORAH MESSER, medical transcriptionist; b. Gastonia, NC, Jan. 8, 1961; d. Lloyd Wayne and Jane Godfrey Messer; m. Michael Dean Arrowood; children: Michael Dean Jr., Julia Ellen. Student in Med. Office Adminstrn., Gaston Coll., Dallas, NC, 2005—, cert. in Med. Transcription, 2006. Cert. med. transcriptionist NC, 2006. Buyer, planner CRS, Gastonia, NC, 1985—2004; med. transcriptionist Focus Infomatics, Woburn, Mass., 2006—. Home Phone: 704-866-0160. Personal E-mail: dmarrowood@bellsouth.net.

ARROWSMITH, MARIAN CAMPBELL, secondary education educator; b. St. Louis, Nov. 12, 1943; d. William Rankin and Elizabeth (Mitchell) Arrowsmith; m. William Earl Schroyer, July 23, 1983; stepchildren: Carey Jo, Amy Lynn. BS, La. State U., 1961; MEd, Southeastern La. U., 1978. Lic. tchr., La.; cert. practicum supr. Inst. for Reality Therapy. Tchr. 1st grade McDonough #26, Jefferson Parish Sch. Bd., Gretna, La., 1966; 2nd grade tchr. Woodlawn High Sch., Baton Rouge, 1966-67; kindergarten tchr. Univ. Terrace Elem. Sch., Baton Rouge, summer 1967; 1st grade tchr. Westminster Elem. Sch., Baton Rouge, 1967-72, Elm Grove Elem. Sch., Harvey, La., 1972-73; kindergarten tchr. Westminster Elem. Sch., Baton Rouge, summers 1968, 69, 70, 71, Elm Grove Elem. Sch., summer 1973; 1st grade tchr. St. Andrews Episcopal Sch., New Orleans, 1973-74; kindergarten tchr. St. Tammany Parish Sch. Bd., Folsom, La., 1974-77; early childhood specialist St. Tammany Parish Sch. Bd., Covington, La., 1977-87; prin. Woodlake Elementary Sch., 1987-99; supr. instrn., St. Tammany Parish, 1999-; off-campus coordinating asst. St. Tammany Parish for Dept. Continuing Edn., Southeastern La. U., 1985-87; condr. workshops in field; selected ofcl. pres. Sunbelt Region of Reality Therapists, 1983; regional dir. La. and Miss. Reality Therapists, Sunbelt Bd. of Reality Therapists, 1983. Author: Helping Your Child at Home, 1982-83; Handbook for Early Childhood Tutorial Program, 1983-84. Mem. Ctr. Learning Devel. and Learning, Regina Coedn. Child Devel. Ctr. (HeadStart), Jr. League. Mem. ASCD, La. Assn. Sch. Execs., Nat. Assn. Tchrs. Math., La. Assn. Tchrs. Math., Pontchartrain Yacht Club, Delta Kappa Gamma (v.p. 1986), Alpha Delta Kappa, Kappa Alpha Theta, Phi Delta Kappa. Democrat. Methodist. Avocations: horticulture, reading, fishing, dancing. Home: 1000 Montgomery St Mandeville LA 70448-5517 Home Phone: 985-626-5880; Office Phone: 985-892-2276. E-mail: marianarrowsmith@charter.net.

ARROYO, F. THADDEUS, telecommunications industry executive; b. San Francisco; m. Alyssa Arroyo; 1 child. BS in Math., U. Tex., Arlington, 1986; MBA, So. Methodist U. Info. tech. Southwestern Bell; mgr., dir., v.p. Sabre Corp., sr. v.p., info. tech. svcs., sr. v.p., product mktg. and devel.; chief info. officer Cingular Wireless, Atlanta, 2001—. Named one of 50 Most Important Hispanics in Tech. & Bus., Hispanic Engr. & Info. Tech. mag., 2005; recipient Disting. Alumna award, U. Tex., Arlington, 2001, Ga. Global Chief Info. Officer of Yr., 2002. Mem.: Nat. Soc. of Hispanic MBAs, N. Fulton County C. of C. Office: Cingular Wireless Glenridge Highlands Two 5655 Glenridge Connector Atlanta GA 30342

ARROYO, MARTINA, soprano; b. NYC; d. Demetrio and Lucille (Washington) Arroyo. Studied successively with Marinka Gurevich, Joseph Turnau and Rose Landver; student, Kathryn Long Course Met. Opera.; BA, Hunter Coll. CUNY, 1954, DHL (hon.), 1987. Founder Martina Arroyo Found. Disting. prof. emeritus music Ind. U., Bloomington. Debut, Carnegie Hall, 1958, leading soprano, Met. Opera, NYC; in roles including: Trovatore, Rida, Ballo, Forza, Chenier; performed opening night Met. season, 1970-71, 71-72, 73-74, performed at La Scala, Milan, Munich Staatsoper, Berlin Deutsche Oper, Rome Opera, Vienna State Opera, Covent Garden, Teatro Colon, Buenos Aires, San Francisco, Chgo., and all maj. opera houses; soloist, NY, Vienna, Berlin, Royal (London), Paris philharmonics, San Francisco, Pitts., Phila., Chgo., Cleve. symphonies, Concertgebouw, other maj. orchs.; frequent performer Saratoga, Ravinia, Tanglewood festivals and festivals Vienna, Berlin, Edinburgh, Helsinki; recordings include I Vespri Siciliani, Un Ballo in Maschera; recorded for Columbia, London, Angel, DGG, Philips, EMI, RCA. Former mem. Nat. Endowment of Arts, Washington; trustee Carnegie Hall, NYC; founder Martina Arroyo Found. and Prelude to Performance Program. Named Outstanding Alumna Hunter Coll., NYC; recipient Verdi's medal, Amici di Verdi, London. Fellow: Am. Acad. Arts and Scis. Office: Martina Arroyo Found Inc PO Box 2015 Radio City Sta New York NY 10101-2015

ARRUDA, JOSE, nephrologist; MD, U. Fed. Fluminese, Niteroi, Rio de Janeiro, Brazil, 1967. Diplomate Am. Bd. Internal Medicine and Nephrology. Prof. medicine, physiology U. Ill., Chgo., 1981. Chief of nephrology U. Ill., Chgo., 1985. Contbr. over 230 articles to profl. jours. Office: Univ Ill 820 S Wood St MC 793 Chicago IL 60612 Office Phone: 312-996-6775. Office Fax: 312-996-7378. E-mail: jaarruda@uic.edu.

ARSCOTT, R. LYNDON (RAYMOND LYNDON ARSCOTT), management consultant; b. Sept. 1940; Mgmt. cons., Danville, Calif. Mem.: NAE.

ARSENEAU, JAMES CHARLES, physician; b. Syracuse, NY, Aug. 29, 1942; s. James Howard and Glenna Carolyn (Worth) A.; m. Jane Macy, July 2, 1966; children: Marc, David. AB, Syracuse U., 1964; MD, Albany Med. Coll., 1968. Intern and resident in medicine Strong Meml. Hosp., Rochester, N.Y., 1968-70, fellow in med. oncology, 1973-74; clin. assoc. med. br. Nat. Cancer Inst., Bethesda, Md., 1970-73; asst. prof. medicine U. Rochester, 1974-80, assoc. prof. medicine, 1980-83; head med. oncology unit Rochester Gen. Hosp., 1974-83; clin. assoc. prof. medicine Albany Med. Coll., 1985—; ptnr. Albany Regional Cancer Ctr., 1983—. Pres. med. staff St. Peter's Hosp., Albany, N.Y., 1993-95, bd. dirs., 1997—. Author numerous chpts. in textbooks; contbr. articles to profl. jours. Sr. Asst. Surgeon USPHS, 1970-73. Mem. Am. Soc. Clin. Oncology, Albany County Med. Soc. (exec. com. 1993—), Am Radium Soc., Upstate N.Y. Soc. Med. Oncology/Hematology (pres. 1994—), Gynecologic Oncology Group (chmn. devel. therapeutic com. 1980—), Wolfert's Roost Country Club, Zeta Psi, Alpha Omega Alpha (pres. 1966-67). Avocations: reading, writing, chess, tennis, golf, skiing. Home: 205 Graffunder Dr Albany NY 12204-1301 Office: Albany Regional Cancer Ctr 317 S Manning Blvd Ste 330 Albany NY 12208-1774 Office Phone: 518-489-2607. Business E-Mail: james.arseneau@usoncology.com.

ARSHAM, HOSSEIN, operations research analyst; came to U.S., 1978; s. Gholam Reza and Habebeh (Babai) A.; m. Elaheh-Naaze Khoshghadam, Dec. 20, 1984; 1 child, Aryana. BSc in Physics, Arya-Mehr U. Tech., Tehran, Iran, 1971; MSc, Cranfield Inst., Eng., 1978; DSc, George Washington U., 1982. Cert. info. scientist, specialized in strategic decision making. Postdoctoral rschr. Internat. Water Resources Inst., Washington, 1982-83; prof. U. Balt., 1983—, Harry Wright disting. rsch. prof. mgmt. sci. simulation and stats., chair dept. mgmt. scis. Balt., 1996—; rsch. prof. Info. Systems Rsch. Ctr., Balt., 1996—. Faculty advanced studies Calif. Nat. U., 1991—; faculty adv. bd. Western Govs. U., 1999; faculty cons. Kennedy-Western U., 1995—; mem. exec. adv. coun. Internat. Soc. for Theory and Application of Multi-Objective Decision Analysis; tech. lectr. Bethlehem Steel Co., Balt., 1983-84; host Fulbright vis. scholars European univs. and rsch. insts., 1995—; sci. cons. in field; supv. doctoral dissertations comms. nat. and internat. univs. Editor InterStat: Stats. on the Internet, Ops. Rsch. category for the Netscape Open Directory, Jour. of Interdisciplinary Math.; sr. assoc. editor Computational Stats. and Data Analysis, Internat. Jour. Stats. and Sys., Jour. Environ. Dynamics, Internat. Journ. Stats. and Sys.; mem. editl. bd. IEEE Ednl., Tech. and Soc. Jour., Jour. of End User Computing, Jour. Environ. Dynamics, Internat. Jour. Ops. and Quantitative Mgmt.; mem. editl. bd. Ednl. Tech. and Soc. Jour.; mem. internat. sci. com. Advances in Intelligent Data Analysis, 1997—, Internat. Symposium on Adaptive Systems, 1999—; contbr. articles to profl. jours. Commn. on Office Lab. Accreditation grantee, 1993; NSF grantee, 1995-2002; recipient Black & Decker Corp. Rsch. award, 1987, 88, 98, Excellence in Rsch. award U. Sys. Md., 2000. Fellow Royal Statis. Soc., Operational Rsch. Soc., Inst. Combinatorics and Applications, World Innovation Found.; mem. AAAS, IEEE, Am. Math. Soc., Internat. Assn. Math. and Computer Modeling, Internat. Forecasting Soc., Am. Statis. Assn., Assn. for Computing Machinery, Digital Equipment Computer Users Soc., Info. Resources Mgmt. Assn., Math. Assn. Am., London Math. Soc., Inst. for Ops. Rsch. and Mgmt Scis., Soc. Indsl. and Applied Math., Soc. for Info. Mgmt., N.Y. Acad. Scis., Internat. Soc. for Theory and Application of Multi-Objective Decision Analysis (exec. adv. coun.), Beta Gamma Sigma, Omega Rho. Achievements include research in statistics, applied probability, discrete-event systems simulation, and mathematical programming and modeling. Office: U Balt 1420 N Charles St Baltimore MD 21201-5720 Home Phone: 410-727-6351; Office Phone: 410-837-5268. Business E-Mail: harsham@ubalt.edu.

ARSHT, ADRIENNE, lawyer, broadcast executive, bank executive; b. Wilmington, Del., Feb. 4, 1942; d. Samuel and Roxana (Cannon) Arsht; m. Myer Feldman, Sept. 28, 1980. BA, Mt. Holyoke Coll., 1963; JD, Villanova U., 1966. Bar: Del. 1966. Assoc. Morris, Nichols, Arsht and Tunnell, Wilmington, 1966-69, Bregman, Abel and Kay, Washington, 1979-84; dir. govt. affairs TWA, NYC, 1969-79; pres., chmn. bd. Land Title & Escrow Corp., Washington, 1981-86; v.p. Ardman Broadcasting Corp., Washington, 1984—, also bd. dirs.; chmn. bd. TotalBank Corp. Fla., Miami, 1986—; also bd. dirs. Totalbank Corp. Fla., Miami; chmn. Eve Stillman Corp., NYC, 1989-99, also bd. dirs. Bd. dirs. Ardman, Inc., Washington, Capital Broadcasting, Inc., Kansas City, Mo., Trade Nat. Bank, Miami. Bd. dirs. Washington Opera Co., 1982-84, Am. Ballet Theatre, N.Y.C., 1984-90; founder, chmn. Van Guard Found., Washington, 1987-94, Fit and Fabulous, Washington, 1992-93; mem. exec. com. Lombardi Cancer Ctr., Washington, 1988-92; mem. Com. of 200, Coun. on Fgn. Rels.; chmn. bd. dirs. Kennedy Ctr. Prodns., inc., 1982—; U.S. adv. bd. women's internat. forum Dare to Dream Found.; exec. com., sec. Performing Arts Found., Miami. Named Woman of Yr., Am. Ballet Theatre, 1989. Mem. Del. Bar Assn., Women's Internat. Forum, Miami C. of C., Rana Soc. (founder). Office: Total Bank 2720 Coral Way Miami FL 33145-3271 Home Phone: 305-800-1795; Office Phone: 305-476-6258. *By giving more than you receive, you receive more than you give.*

ARSIC, ANTOINETTE, information specialist; d. Velimir and Elinor (Brannen) A. BSBA, Old Dominion U., 1984; MS in Info. Sci., U. Tenn., Knoxville, 2000. Pub. exec. Double A Pub., Inc., Gordonsville, 1990—96; mag. editor/publisher Va. Country Life, 1990—96; librarian Va. Divsn. Mineral Resources, Gordonsville, 1995—; info. scientist The MITRE Corp., 2001—. Theater prodr. Four County Players, 1993-95, theatre asst. dir., 1997. Avocations: acting, horse training, writing. E-mail: aarsic@adelphia.net.

ARSLAN, HAYDAR, civil engineer, researcher; b. Ankara, Turkey, Feb. 8, 1976; arrived in US, 2003; s. Azimet and Peruze Arslan; m. Gul Arslan. BSc, O. Gazi U., Turkey, 1997; MSc, Bogazici U., Istanbul, Turkey, 2003; PhD, U. Colo., Boulder, 2006. Tchg./rsch. asst. Bogazici U., 2001—03, U. Colo., Boulder, 2003—06, postdoctoral rsch. fellow, 2006—. Contbr. articles to profl. jours. Fellow, U. Colo., 2000. Home: 1350 20th St Apt A-28 Boulder CO 80302 Office: U Colo Boulder Engring Ctr EC-4 441 DCB 428 Boulder CO 80302 Office Phone: 303-215-5466.

ARTEAGA, CARLOS LUIS, medical researcher, director; b. Guayaquil, Ecuador, Dec. 3, 1955; MD with honors, U. Guayaquil, 1980. Cert. internal medicine Am. Bd. Internal Medicine, med. oncology Am. Bd. Internal Medicine. Intern, internal medicine Grady Meml. Hosp., Emory U., Atlanta, 1981—82, resident, 1982—84; fellow U. Tex. Health Sci. Ctr., San Antonio, 1984—87; prof. medicine and cancer biology Vanderbilt U., Nashville, 1988—, Ingram prof. cancer rsch., mem. divsn. hematology, dir. breast cancer rsch. program, dir. breast cancer specialized programs for rsch. excellence, Vanderbilt-Ingram Comprehensive Cancer Ctr., Am. Cancer Soc. Clin. Rsch. Prof., vice-chancellor's chair in breast cancer rsch. Co-chair devel. therapeutics com. Eastern Cooperative Oncology Group; mem. bd. sci. advisors Nat. Cancer Inst., 1999—2004; chmn. spl. conf. com. Am. Assn. Cancer Rsch., 2002—, bd. dirs., 2004—; mem. parent com. for review of cancer ctrs. NIH, 2004—. Assoc. editor, mem. editl. bd. Jour. Mammary Gland Biology & Neoplasia, Clin. Cancer Therapeutics, Jour. Clin. Oncology, Clin. Proteomics, Cancer Biology and Therapy; contbr. articles to profl. jours. Recipient Richard and Hinda Rosenthal Found. award, Am. Assn. Cancer Rsch., 2003. Mem.: Am. Soc. Clin. Investigation. Achievements include research in the role of polypeptide growth factors and receptor tyosine kinases in mammary devel./transformation and breast cancer progression; development of molecular therapeutics in breast cancer. Office: Vanderbilt U Med Ctr 682 Preston Rsch Bldg MRB 11 Nashville TN 37232-6307 also: Vanderbilt-Ingram Cancer Ctr 683 Preston Bldg Nashville TN 37232-6838 Office Phone: 615-936-1919, 615-936-3524. Business E-Mail: carlos.arteaga@vanderbilt.edu.*

ARTEMOV, VLADIMIR NIKOLAEVICH, gymnastics coach; b. Vladimir City, Russia, Dec. 7, 1964; came to U.S., 1990; s. Nikolai Filippovich and Maria vasilievna (Mileshnikova) A.; m. Susan Ann Wallace, July 28, 1991; children: Glenn Vladimirovich, Alexander Vladimirovich. Phys. conditioning instr. USSR Mil., 1987-88; staff mem. South Tex. Gymnastics Acad., 1991-92, Team USA Gymnastics Camp, 1991; head coach Kips Gymnastics, 1993—; coach Pan Am. Tng. Camp, 1994; mem. U.S.A. Nat. Coaching staff, 1990—; cons. Elios Gynmastic Tng. Ctr., Mexico, 1995—. Spkr. in field; head coach, dir. Brown's Gymnastics, San Antonio, 2005—. Contbr. articles to profl. jours. Recipient Master of Sport Internat. Class, 1981, 83, 88. Winner 4 gold medals, 1 silver medal Olympics, Seoul, South Korea, 1988, 1 gold, 1 silver medal World Championships, 1983, 1 gold, 1 silver medal, 1985, 2 gold, 1 silver, 1 bronze medal, 1987, 3 gold, 1 silver, 1 bronze medal, 1989, 1 bronze medal World Cup, 1986, 2 gold, 2 silver medals Univ. Games, 1983. Office: Brown's Gymnastics 21750 Hardy Oak Blvd San Antonio TX 78258 Office Phone: 210-497-5000. E-mail: artemov@mail.ev1.net, artemov@peoplepc.com.

ARTERIAN, HANNAH R., dean, law educator; b. 1949; BS, Elmira Coll., 1970; JD, U. Iowa, 1973. Bar: NY 1974. Assoc. Dewey, Ballantine, Bushby, Palmer & Wood, NYC, 1973—78; vis. assoc. prof. law U. Iowa, 1977, assoc. prof., 1978, Ariz. State U., 1979—82, prof., 1982—2002, assoc. dean, 1992—2001; dean, prof. law Syracuse U. Coll. Law, 2002—. Vis. prof. U. Houston, 1983—84. Mem.: Phi Beta Kappa, Order of the Coif. Office: Syracuse U Coll Law Ste 340 Syracuse NY 13244-1962 Office Phone: 315-443-2524. E-mail: arterian@law.syr.edu.

ARTERO, MARGARET T., academic administrator, military officer; d. Antonio C. and Josepha T. Artero; children: Jesika F., Keana L. PhD, U. Oreg., 1989. Chairwoman, counseling MA program U. Guam, Mangilao, 1989—; maj. Guam Army N.G., Barrigada, 1998—. Bd. mem. Inafa' Maolek, Agana, 2003—, mediator, 2002—; chairwoman Grad. Coun., U. Guam, Mangilao, Student Discipline and Appeals Com., Mangilao, Registration and Admissions Com., Mangilao, Grad. Curriculum Academic Com., Mangilao, U. Guam Commencement Com., Mangilao. Mem. Guam Health Coun., Agana; v.p. Guam Sch. Counseling Assn., Agana. Recipient Whittney Fellowship award, Whittney Fellowship Found. Mem.: Guam Psychol. Assn. (life), ACA (life), APA (life), Phi Delta Kappa (life). Achievements include research in suicide prevention. Avocations: travel, reading, music, multicultural interests, sports. Home: PO Box 2023 Hagatna GU 96932 Home and Office: Sch Education Univ Guam UOG Station Mangilao GU 96923 Home Phone: 671-653-0128; Office Phone: 671-735-2440. Office Fax: 671-734-3651; Home Fax: 671-653-2901. Business E-Mail: martero@uog9.uog.edu.

ARTERTON, JANET BOND, federal judge; b. Phila., Feb. 8, 1944; m. F. Christopher Arterton; two children. BA, Mt. Holyoke Coll., 1966; JD, Northeastern U., 1977. Law clk. to Hon. Herbert J. Stern U.S. Dist. Ct. N.J., 1977-78; ptnr. Garrison & Arterton, 1978-95; judge U.S. Dist. Ct. Conn., New Haven, 1995—. Fellow Am. Bar Found., Conn. Bar Found.; mem. ATLA, Nat. Employment Lawyers Assn., Conn. Employment Lawyers Assn., Conn. State Trial Lawyers Assn. (bd. govs. 1990-95), Conn. Bar Assn. (mem. adv. com. state ct. rules 1992, mem. fed. jud. selection com. 1991-93, mem. exec. com. women and the law sect. 1990-93, chairperson fed. practice sect. 1993-95. Office: US Dist Ct Conn 141 Church St New Haven CT 06510-2030

ARTEST, RON (RONALD WILLIAM ARTEST JR.), professional basketball player; b. LI City, NY, Nov. 13, 1979; s. Ron and Sarah Artest; m. Kimsha Artest; 4 children. Student, St. John's U., 1998—99. Profl. basketball player Chgo. Bulls, 1999—2002, Ind. Pacers, 2002—06, Sacramento Kings, 2006—. Founder, CEO TruWarier Records, Stamford, Conn.; founder clothing line TruWarier Wear. Named NBA's 2003-04 Defensive Player of the Year; named to All Star Team, 2004. Achievements include selection by the Chicago Bulls in the first round (16th overall) of the 1999 NBA Draft; league leader with an average of 3.29 steals for every 48 minutes played in 2002-03. Office: Sacramento Kings Arco Arena One Sports Pkwy Sacramento CA 95834

ARTHINGTON, CAROL ANN, elementary school educator; b. Duluth, Minn., Sept. 17, 1942; d. Harry Matthew Mleziva and Martha Suzannah Busse-Mleziva; m. Gary Lynn Arthington, Sept. 7, 1963; children: Michelle Lynn, Kurt Alan. BA, North Ctrl. Coll., 1964; MA with distinction, Calif. State U., Northridge, 1992; PhD, Union Inst. and U., 2001. Kindergarten tchr. Puffer Elem. Sch., Downers Grove, Ill., 1965—70; kindergarten/1st grade tchr. Bethlehem Christian Sch., Lake Oswego, Oreg., 1980—81; kindergarten tchr. Wilsonville (Oreg.) Elem. Sch., 1981—83; kindergarten art tchr. Hillcrest Christian Sch., Thousand Oaks, Calif., 1983—84; first grade tchr. Cornerstone Christian Sch., Camarillo, Calif., 1984—86; kindergarten tchr. Los Nogales Sch., Camarillo, 1986—87, Dos Caminos Sch., Camarillo, 1987—. Brain based learning presenter Jensen Learning, San Diego, 1997—98; after sch. art club tchr. Dos Caminos Scj., Camarillo, 1995—2006. Missions chair First Christian Ch. Newbury Park, Calif., 1992—2006. Recipient Hon. Svc. award, Dos Caminos PTA, 2006, Tchr. Excellence award, Amgen Corp., 1992. Home: 873 Tamlei Ave Thousand Oaks CA 91362 Office: Dos Caminos Elem Sch 3635 Appian Way Camarillo CA 93010 Office Phone: 805-482-9894. Personal E-mail: carthington@hotmail.com.

ARTHUR, BEATRICE, actress; b. NYC, May 13, 1923; d. Philip and Rebecca Frankel; m. Gene Saks, May 28, 1950 (div. 1978); 2 children, Matthew, Daniel. Student, Blackstone Coll., also Franklin Inst. Sci. and Arts; student acting with, Erwin Piscator, Dramatic Workshop, New Sch. Social Research. Theatrical appearances include: Lysistrata, 1947, Dog Beneath the Skin, 1947, Gas, 1947, Yerma, 1947, No Exit, 1948, The Taming of the Shrew, 1948, Six Characters in Search of An Author, 1948, The Owl and the Pussycat, 1948, Le Bourgeois Gentilhomme, 1949, Yes Is for a Very Young Man, 1949, Creditors, 1949, Heartbreak House, 1949, Three Penny Opera, 1954, 55, Shoestring Revue, 1955, Seventh Heaven, 1955, The Ziegfield Follies, 1956, What's The Rush?, summer 1956, Mistress of the Inn, 1957, Nature's Way, 1957, Ulysses in Nightown, 1958, Chic, 1959, Gay Divorcee, 1960, A Matter of Position, 1962, Mame, 1966 (Tony award best supporting mus. actress), Fiddler on the Roof, 1964, Bermuda Avenue Triangle, 1996, For Better or Worse, 1996; one woman shows, ...And Then There's Bea, San Francisco,2001. An Evening With Bea Arthur, L.A., 2001, Bea Arthur on Broadway: Just Between Friends, 2002; stock appearances with Fiddler on the Roof, Circle Theatre, Atlantic City, summer 1951, State Fair Music Hall, Dallas, 1953, Music Circus, Lambertville, NJ, 1953, resident commedienne, Tamiment (Pa.) Theatre, 1953; numerous TV and nightclub appearances, 1948-; motion picture appearances That Kind of Woman, 1959; Lovers and Other Strangers, 1970, Mame, 1974, History of the World Part I, 1981, Stranger Things, 1995; TV movie: My First Love, 1988; TV appearances include All in the Family, 1971, leading role in TV series Maude, 1972-78 (Emmy award for Best Actress in a Comedy Series 1977), The Golden Girls, 1985-92 (Emmy award for Best Actress in a Comedy Series 1988), The Beatrice Arthur Spl., TV series 30 Years of TV Comedy's Greatest Hits; TV guest appearance: Malcolm in the Middle, 2000, Futurama, 2001, Curb Your Enthusiasm, 2005. Vol. med. tech. USMC, WWII. Mem. Artists Equity Assn., SAG, AFTRA.

ARTHUR, GARY L., JR., energy executive; m. Sheila Arthur; 2 children. BBA, U. Ky.; MBA, Morehead State U. Various positions to v.p. bus. ops. Ashland Petroleum; v.p. supply and distbn. Colonial Grp.; v.p. mktg., supply and transp. Valero Energy Corp., San Antonio, 2000, sr. v.p. retail and speciality products mktg., 2000—. Bd. dirs. St. Peter's/St. Joseph's Children's Home; bd. mem., mem. exec. com. San Antonio Sports Found.; mem. mktg. adv. com. United Way. Office: Valero PO Box 696000 San Antonio TX 78269-6000

ARTHUR, GREER MARTIN, leasing firm executive; b. Champaign, Ill., Feb. 15, 1935; s. Greer Martin and Olive Loretta (Simard) A.; m. Veronica Lattman, Nov. 30, 1968; children: Alexandra, Vincent, Tanya, Greer III. BA, Lafayette Coll., 1956; JD, Columbia U., 1961. Bar: N.Y. 1961. Acct. exec. tng. program Young & Rubicam, 1957-58; assoc. Havens, Wandless, Stitt & Tighe, NYC, 1961—62; mgmt. cons. McKinsey & Co., 1962-67; asst. to v.p. internat. Scovill Mfg. Co., Waterbury, Conn.; internat. market mgr. Scovill France, Paris; market mgr. Hamilton Beach div. Scovill, Waterbury, 1967-69; pres., CEO SSI Container Corp., subs. Itel Corp., San Francisco, 1969-73; founder, chmn., pres., CEO, dir. Trans Ocean Ltd., San Bruno, Calif., 1973-96. Founder, dir., bd. dirs. Inst. Internat. Container Lessors, 1970—73, dir., 1977—96, pres., 1989—90, 1994—95; chmn. bd. dirs. Trans Ocean Distbn., Ltd., Southampton, England. Treas., trustee Phillips Brooks Sch., Menlo Park, Calif., 1980-83; bd. dirs. Nat. Alzheimer's Assn., 1994-2002, San Francisco Opera, 1999—; with Lafayette Coll. Nat. Coun., 1991-93; mem. bd. advisors Columbia Law Sch., 1992-2000; bd mem., Lake Tahoe Lakefront Homeowner's Assn. bd. Mem.: World Pres. Orgn. (No. Calif. chpt. chmn. 1991—92, bd. dirs. 1994—99), Chief Exec. Orgn. (bd. dirs. 1990—91), Sharon Heights Golf Club, Lahontan Golf Club (Lake Tahoe), Lake Tahoe Yacht Club, Bankers Club, Family Club. Office: Trans Ocean Distribution 2105 Woodside Rd Woodside CA 94062

ARTHUR, GWENDOLYNNE LEE, university librarian; d. Paul W. and Emily M. Arthur; m. Thomas L. Whistler. BA, Wesleyan U., Middletown, Conn., 1975; MLS, Columbia U., 1982; MA, U. Pa., 1990. Coord. reference desk services Temple U., Phila., 1985—90, sci. bibliographer, 1990—91; head reference services Bowling Green State U. Librs., Ohio, 1991—95; head pub. and reference services Trinity Coll. Libr., Hartford, Conn., 1995—99; univ. libr. Goddard Libr., Clark U., Worcester, Mass., 1999—. Editor: (assn. publ.) Get Them Talking: Managing Change Through Case Studies; contbr. articles to profl. jours. Mem. ARTSWorcester, Mass. Mem.: ALA, Libr. Adminstrn. and Mgmt. Assn., Assn. of Coll. & Rsch. Libraries, Reference and User Services Assn. (pres. 2004—05), Beta Phi Mu. Office: Clark Univ Goddard Libr 950 Main St Worcester MA 01610 Office Phone: 508-793-7384. Office Fax: 508-793-8871. Business E-Mail: garthur@clarku.edu.*

ARTHUR (II), HUGH THOMAS, lawyer; b. 1945; BA, Wofford Coll., 1967; PhD in economics, U. SC, 1971; JD, Mercer U., Macon, Ga., 1982. Bar: SC 1982. Economics tchr., 1971—79; atty. regulatory affairs SC Electric & Gas Co., 1982—87; v.p., gen. counsel SC Pipeline Corp., 1987—96; v.p., gen. counsel, asst. sec. SCANA Corp., Columbia, SC, 1996—98, sr. v.p., gen. counsel, asst. sec., 1998. Mem. St. David's Episcopal Ch. Mem.: Energy Bar Assn., Ga. Bar Assn., SC Bar Assn., ABA.

ARTHUR, JOHN MORRISON, retired utilities executive; b. Pitts., Aug. 17, 1922; s. Hugh Morrison and Anna Matilda (Crowe) A.; m. Sylvia Ann Martin, June 19, 1948; children: William Robert, John Martin, Andrew Scott. BEE, U. Pitts., 1944, MEE, 1947. With Duquesne Light Co., Pitts., 1944-87, asst. to chmn. bd. and pres., 1966-67, pres., 1967-68, chmn. bd., chief exec. officer, 1968-83, chmn. bd., pres., 1983-85, chmn. bd., 1986-87, ret., 1987. Trustee emeritus U. Pitts. With AUS, 1942-43. Mem. Duquesne Club, Montour Heights Country Club, Rolling Rock Club. Office Phone: 412-264-8224. E-mail: arthur1401@comcast.net.

ARTHUR, LINDA LOUISE, sociologist, educator; d. Tony and Jeanne Gehringer; life ptnr. Michael McIlvenna; children: Joel Boynton, Brendan Boynton. BA, MA, PhD, U. Calif., Davis, 1992. From asst. prof. to prof. U. Hawaii, Honolulu, 1992—2002; prof. Wash. State U., Pullman, Wash., 2002—, curator, 2002—. Author: (book) Idealized Images: Appearance and the construction of feminities, 1986, The Plain People; an Ethnography of the Holdeman Mennonites, 1986, Aloha Attire; Hawaiian Dress in the 20th Century, 2000, The Art of the Aloha Shirt, 2002 (Ka Palapala Po1olela award, 2003), At the Cutting Edge: Contemporary Hawaiian Quilting, 2003 (Ka Palapala Po1olela award, 2003); editor: Traditional Asian Costume (31 countries), 1999, Religion, Dress and the Body, 1999, Undressing Religion, 2000; contbr. articles to profl. jours. Recipient Prof. of the Yr. award, Carnegie Found., 2000, Excellence in U. Tchg. award, USDA, 2000, 2002. Office: Washington State Univ Kruegel Hall Pullman WA 99163 Office Phone: 509-335-7890. Business E-Mail: larthur@wsu.edu.

ARTHUR, LINDSAY GRIER, retired judge, editor, writer; b. Mpls., July 30, 1917; s. Hugh and Alice (Grier) A.; m. Jean Johansen, Sept. 19, 1940; children: Lindsay G., Hugh Emil, Mollie K., Julie A. AB, Princeton U., 1939; postgrad., Harvard U., 1939-40; LLB, JD, U. Minn., 1946. Bar: Minn. 1946, U.S. Dist. Ct. Minn. 1948, U.S. Supreme Ct. 1964. Lawyer Nieman, Bosard & Arthur, Mpls., 1946-54; alderman Mpls. City Coun., 1951-54; judge Mcpl. Ct., Mpls., 1954-61; chief judge juvenile divsn. Dist. Ct., Mpls., 1961-79, 87-93, judge felony, civil divsn., 1979-83, chief judge mental health divsn., 1983-87; mediator, 1987—2003. Arbitrator civil and family cts., 1991—; lectr. Nat. Coun. Juvenile Ct. Judges, 1964—89. Author: Minnesota Practice, 1974, Juvenile Case Law, 1980, Twin Cities Uncovered, 1996, A Manual for Mediators, 1995; editor Digest of Juvenile and Family Law, 1983-93; contbr. over 40 articles to profl. jours. Chmn. Mpls. Pks. Rehab., 1959—60; chmn. boys com. YMCA, 1955—57; chmn. trustees Bethlehem Luth. Ch., 1979—89; bd. dirs. Nat. Ctr. State Cts., Williamsburg, 1974—77, Metro YMCA, Mpls. area, 1981—85. Lt. USNR, 1942—45, PTO. Decorated 7 major battle stars SW Pacific. Mem. Nat. Coun. Juvenile Ct. Judges (pres. 1972-73, Jud. scholar 1985-2005), ABA (disabilities com. 1984-89), Am. Law Inst. (advisor divorce law 1989-93). Avocation: writing. Home: Apt 232 8505 Flying Cloud Dr Eden Prairie MN 55344-3956 Personal E-mail: lgasr@earthlink.net.

ARTHUR, MICHAEL ELBERT, financial advisor, lawyer; b. Seattle, Oct. 9, 1952; s. Theodore E. and Gladys L. (Jones) A.; m. Claire C. Meeker, Dec. 23, 1974; children: Christine, Conor, Austin. BA, U. Calif., Santa Barbara, 1974; JD, Stanford U., 1977. Ptnr. Miller Nash LLP, Portland, Oreg., 1977—2001; fin. advisor UBS Fin. Svcs., Portland, 2001—. Trustee Chiles Found. Home: 13535 NW Lariat Ct Portland OR 97229-7001 Office: UBS Financial Svcs 805 SW Broadway Ste 2600 Portland OR 97205-3365 Office Phone: 503-225-9211. Business E-Mail: mike.arthur@ubs.com.

ARTHUR, PAUL KEITH, retired military officer; b. Kansas City, Mo., Jan. 14, 1931; s. Walter B. and Frieda J. (Burckhardt) A.; m. Joy N. Lim, Apr. 26, 1958; children: Gregory V., Lia F. Student, Ohio No. U., 1947, Taylor U., Upland, Ind., 1948-49; BSEE, Purdue U., 1956; postgrad., N.Mex. State U., 1957-78. Registered profl. engr., N.Mex.; cert. army acquisition profl.; cert. Naval engring. duty officer, Navy material profl. With White Sands Missile Range, N.Mex., 1956—2004; electronic engr. field engring. group, missile flight surveillance office, 1956-60; chief field engring group, 1960-62; project engr. Pershing Weapon Sys. Army Missile Test and Evaluation Directorate, 1962-74; chief high altitude air def. projects br., 1974-82; chief air def. materiel test divsn., 1982-91; dep dir. Materiel Test Directorate, 1991-95; dir., 1995-98; exec. dir. Nat. Range, 1998-99; dep. comdr. White Sands Test Ctr., 1999—2001, comdr., 2001—03; dep. to comdg. gen./tech. dir. White Sands Missile Range, 2003—04; rear adm. ret., 2004; with Phys. Scis. Lab., New Mex. State U., 2006—. Mem. N.Mex. Spaceport Commn., 1994-95, Southwest Regional Space Task Force, Metro Planning Orgn.; past pres. missile range pioneer group; bd. dirs. Dagupan Electric Corp. of the Philippines. Author numerous plans and reports on weapon systems test and evaluation and topics in naval engring. Chmn. adminstrv. bd. Meth. Ch., 1992-95. Served with USN, 1949-53, USNR, 1954-87, rear adm. and sr. engring. duty officer, 1984-87. Decorated Legion of Merit, Meritorious Svc. medal, Navy Achievement medal, Navy Expeditionary medal, Mil. Order St. Barbara, Meritorious Civilian Svc., Army Decoration for Exceptional Civilian Svc.; named to White Sands Missile Range Hall of Fame, 2005; recipient ITEA Lifetime Achievement award, others. Mem. AIAA (past vice chmn.), Internat. Test and Evaluation Assn., Am. Def. Preparedness Assn. (past pres.), Assn. Old Crows, Naval Res. Assn., Res. Officers Assn. (pres. 1983-85), United Vets. Coun. (chmn. 1984-85), Am. Soc. Naval Engrs., Naval Inst., Navy League, Surface Navy Assn., Assn. U.S. Army, Purdue U. Alumni Assn. (past pres.), N.Mex. State U. Alumni Assn., Mesilla Valley Track Club, Bujutsukan Acad. Martial Arts. Home: 2050 San Acacio St Las Cruces NM 88001-1570 Personal E-mail: paul.k.arthur@comcast.net.

ARTHUR, RAY, retail executive; Degree, William Paterson Coll. CPA. With Am. Home Products; with Lederle Labs. Divsn. Am. Cyanamid; with KPMG Peat Marwick; v.p., corp. controller Gen. Signal Corp., Stamford, Conn., corp. controller; from v.p., controller to sr. v.p. pres., toysrus.com Toys R Us, Inc., Wayne, NJ, 2000—02, pres., toysrus.com, 2002—04, CFO, 2004—. Chmn. bd. William Paterson Univ. Found. Office: Toys R Us Inc 1 Geoffrey Way Wayne NJ 07470-2030

ARTHUR, RAYMOND L., retail toy and game company executive; Grad., William Paterson Coll. Plant controller Lederle Labs., Am. Cyanamid Co., 1986—89; mgr. fin. reporting Am. Cyanamid Co., 1989—94; asst. controller, asst. v.p., dir. compliance Am. Home Products Corp., Madison, NJ, 1994—97; v.p., corp. controller Gen. Signal Corp., Stamford, Conn., 1997—99, Toys "R" Us Inc., 1999—2000, Toysrus.com, 2000, v.p. fin. and adminstrn., 2000, sr. v.p., CFO, 2000—02, pres., 2002—04; CFO Toys "R" Us Inc., 2004—. Chmn. bd. William Paterson U. Found. Office: Toys R Us Inc 1 Geoffrey Way Wayne NJ 07470-2030

ARTHUR, ROSE ANN HORMAN, dean; b. Batchtown, Ill., June 13, 1931; d. John Henry and Trena Marie (Snyders) H.; m. Richard Laurence Arthur, May 1, 1971. BS in Religion and Edn. with honors, St. Louis U., 1962; MA in Religion and Edn., St. Mary's Grad. Sch. Theology, 1967; ThD in Theology and Edn., Grad. Theol. Union, 1979. Coord. women's studies Grad. Theol. Union, Berkeley, Calif., 1969-71; tchr. 6th grade Prince George County Schs., Beaver Heights, Md., 1971-72; dir. Ctr. Women Grad. Theol. Union, 1972-73; television tchr. grades 1-3 Govt. of Am. Samoa, 1973-79; rsch./resource assoc. Harvard U. Divinity Sch., Cambridge, Mass., 1979-80; exec. dir. Chgo. Cluster Theol. Schs., 1980-83; dean grad. & undergrad. Heritage Coll., Toppenish, Wash., 1983-88; dean Rivier Coll., Nashua, NH, 1988—96. Dir. distance learning grant Heritage Coll., 1986-88, dir. liberal arts edn. grant, dir. women's studies grant, 1987-88; dir. women's studies grant Rivier Coll./N.H. Humanities Coun., 1991-92; founder, dir. Rivier Inst. for Sr. Edn., 1997—. Author: The Wisdom Goddess: Feminine Motifs in the Nag Hammadi Documents, 1984. Mem. Alderwoman's Campaign, Chgo., 1981-82, Hyde Park Tenants' Assn., Chgo., 1980-82, Merrimack (N.H.) Dem. Orgn., 1993—; v.p. Merrimack Town Com., 1993-2004; mem. NH State Legislature, 1998-2000; candidate N.H. Senate, 2004. Recipient NH Older Worker of Yr. award, Experience Works Prime Time Awards Program, 2006. Mem. Grad. Theol. Union Ctr. Women and Religion. Democrat. Avocations: reading, walking, canoeing, gardening. Home: 25 Island Dr Merrimack NH 03054-4159 Office: Rivier Coll 420 Main St Nashua NH 03060-5043 Office Phone: 603-897-8623. Business E-Mail: rarthur@rivier.edu.

ARTHUR, THOMAS CARLTON, former dean, law educator; b. July 11, 1946; s. Charles Ralph and Mary Ruth (Parker) Arthur; m. Carolyn Scott Fisher, June 15, 1968; children: John, David. BA, Duke U., 1968; JD, Yale U., 1971. Bar: DC 1972, Va. 1972, U.S. Ct. Appeals (D.C. cir.) 1972, U.S. Supreme Ct. 1979. Assoc. Kirkland & Ellis, Washington, DC, 1971—77, ptnr., 1978—82; assoc. prof. Sch. Law Emory U., Atlanta, 1982—, sr. faculty mem. Law and Econs. Ctr., 1983—, interim vice provost internat. affairs, dean, 2002—05; dean of counsel Trotter Smith & Jacobs, Atlanta, 1984—92. Contbr. articles to Law Rev. Pres. Falls Ch. Cmty. Service Coun., 1974—75. Mem.: ABA, Phi Beta Kappa. Methodist. Office: Emory U Sch Law 1301 Clifton Rd Atlanta GA 30322 Office Phone: 404-712-8815. Office Fax: 404-727-0866.

ARTHUR, WILLIAM LYNN, environmental and political program director; b. Spokane, Wash., May 22, 1954; s. Robert Cyril and Mabel Mildred (Collison) A.; m. Debora Lee Donovan, Feb. 2, 1975; children: Kathleen, Jonathan. BA in Econs., Wash. State U., 1976, postgrad., 1982-83. Rsch. asst. Wash. State U., 1976-77; project mgr. Ctr. Environ. Understanding, Cheney, Wash., 1977-78; program dir. Wash. Energy Extension Svc., Spokane, 1978-79; econs. instr. Spokane Falls CC, 1977—81; economist, cons. Biosystems Analysis Inc., Spokane, 1983; assoc. N.W. rep. Sierra Club, Seattle, 1983-87, N.W. rep., 1987-91, N.W./Alaska regional dir., 1992—2003, nat. wildlands campaign com., 2000—04, dep. nat. field dir., 2004—. Chmn. bd. N.W. Conservation Act Coalition, Seattle, 1982-83; adv. com. N.W. Renewable Resources Ctr., Seattle, 1987-91; cons. energy workshops N.W. Regional Found., Spokane, 1982; mem. exec. com. Save Our Wild Salmon Coalition, 1991-95; mem. adv. com. Inland Empire Pub. Lands Coun., 1990-2000; mem. steering com. Campaign for the Northwest, 1998-2000. Chmn., mem. city commn. Environ. Quality Commn., Pullman, Wash., 1976-77; bd. dir. Ryegrass Sch., Spokane, 1978-81; conservation rep. Internat. Mountain Caribou Tech. Com., 1978-81; bd. dirs. Wash. Citizens for Recycling, Seattle, 1980-82; chair Wash. State Environmentalists for Clinton/Gore Com., 1992, 96; environ. rep. N.W. Forest Conf. convened and chaired by Pres. Clinton, Apr. 2, 1993; mem. steering com. on No Initiative 164 Coalition, 1995; mem. Wash. State Steering Com. to Re-elect Clinton/Gore, 1996; mem Wash. State steering com. Gore for Pres., 1999-2000; chair Wash. State Environmentalists for Gore Com., 2000; mem. exec. com. Alaska Def. Initiative, 2001-2003; founding mem. WildPAC, 2000. Recipient Michael McCloskey award, Sierra Club, 2003, Spl. Achievement award, 2005. Avocations: hiking, rafting, fishing, playing guitar. Office: Sierra Club NW Office Ste 202 180 Nickerson St Seattle WA 98109-1631

ARTHURS, HARRY WILLIAM, lawyer, educator, academic administrator; b. Toronto, Ont., Can., May 9, 1935; s. Leon and Ellen (Dworkin) A.; m. Penny Milnes, June 22, 1974. BA, U. Toronto, 1955, LLB, 1958; LLM, Harvard U., 1959; LLD (hon.), Sherbrooke, Brock Law Soc. Upper Can., McGill U., U. Montreal, U. Toronto; D.Litt. (hon.), Lethbridge U.; DCL (hon.), U. Windsor. Prof. Osgoode Hall Law Sch., York U., Toronto, Ont., 1961-95, dean, 1972-77, pres., 1985—92; prof. York U., Toronto, 1995—2005. Chief adjudicator Pub. Svc. of Can., 1967-68; assoc. Can. Inst. Advanced Rsch., 1995-98; arbitrator, mediator. Author various books and articles on labor law, legal history, adminstrv. law and legal edn. to profl. jours. V.p. Can. Civil Liberties Assn., 1964-76, pres., 1976-77; mem. U.A.W. Pub. Rev. Bd., 1967-77; vice chmn. Ont. Ednl. Rels. Commn., 1976-77; chmn. S.S.H.R.C. Study on Legal Resch. and Edn. in Can., 1980-83; bencher Law Soc. Upper Can., 1979-83; mem. Econ. Coun. Can., 1978-81; bd. dirs. Rights and Democracy, 1999-2003; commr. to Rev. Part III of Can. Labour Code, 2004-06, pension legis., Ont., 2006—. Decorated officer Order of Can., Order of Ont. Fellow: Royal Soc. Can. (Killam Prize in the Soc. Scis. 2002), Brit. Acad. (corr.). Home: 11 Hillcrest Pk Toronto ON Canada M4X 1E8 Office: York Univ Osgoode Hall Law Sch 4700 Keele St Toronto ON Canada M3J 1P3 Office Phone: 416-736-5407. Business E-Mail: harthurs@osgoode.yorku.ca.

ARTMAN, CARL JOSEPH, federal agency administrator; b. Mar. 15, 1965; BA, Columbia Coll., 1987; JD, Washington U., 1991; MBA, Wis. U., 1999; LLM, U. Denver, 2003. Legis. counsel to Congressman Michael Oxley US Congress; gen. mgr. devel. and ops. VoiceStream Wireless Corp.; v.p. legal affairs Airadigm Comm.; mem. President's Bd. of Advisors on Tribal Colleges and Universities US Dept. Edn.; chief legal counsel Oneida Tribe of Indians of Wis.; gen. counsel, v.p. bus. devel. CorAccess Sys. LLC, 2002; assoc. solicitor Bur. Indian Affairs, US Dept. Interior, asst. sec. for Indian affairs, 2007—. Office: 1849 C St NW Rm 4160 Washington DC 20240 Office Phone: 202-208-7163. Office Fax: 202-208-5320.

ARTNER, ALAN GUSTAV, art critic, journalist; b. Chgo., May 14, 1947; s. Gustav and Katherine Rose (Lucas) A. BA, Northwestern U., 1968, MA, 1969. Apprentice music critic Chgo. Tribune, 1972-73, art critic, 1973—; contbg. editor The Art Gallery Mag., 1975-76; corr. Artnews Mag., 1977-80. Contbr. to Playbill, 1994—. Decorated Chevalier de l'ordre des Arts et des Lettres; Rockefeller Found. grantee, 1971-72 Office: Chgo Tribune Co 435 N Michigan Ave Chicago IL 60611-4066

ARTUSI, DANIEL A., Internet company executive; b. 1954; BEE, Instituto Tecnologico de Buenos Aires (ITBA), Argentina. Gen. mgr. Motorola RF Semiconductors Divsn., 1996—97; v.p., gen. mgr. Motorola Wireless Infrastructure Systems Divsn., 1997—99; exec. v.p., gen. mgr. Motorola Networking and Computing Systems Grp., 1999—2001; COO Silicon Laboratories Inc., 2001—03, pres., COO, 2003—04, pres., CEO, 2004—05; chmn., CEO ColdWatt, Inc., 2005—07; pres., CEO Conexant Systems, Inc., 2007—. Bd. dirs. Powerwave Technologies, Inc. Office: Conexant Systems Inc 4000 MacArthur Blvd Newport Beach CA 92660-3095 Office Phone: 949-483-4600. Office Fax: 949-483-4078.*

ARTZ, JOHN CURTIS, lawyer; b. Columbus, Ohio, Mar. 4, 1946; s. Curtis Price and Kathryn Lucille (Risley) A.; m. Nancy Eileen Jones, Apr. 5, 1969; children: John Curtis Jr., Alexander Hardie, Kathryn Cullen. BA disting. mil. grad., Allegheny Coll., 1968; JD magna cum laude, U. S.C., 1976. Bar: Pa. 1976, U.S. Dist. Ct. (we. dist.) Pa. 1976, U.S. Ct. Appeals (3d and 6th cirs.) 1996, U.S. Supreme Ct. 1980. From assoc. to ptnr. Eckert Seamans Cherin & Mellott, Pitts., 1976-94; shareholder, dir. Polito & Smock, P.C., Pitts., 1994—2006; shareholder Ogletree, Deakins, Nash, Smoak & Stewart, PC, 2007—. Adj. asst. prof. Grad. Sch. Pub. Health U. Pitts., 1988-92; instr./lectr. Robert Morris U., Pitts., 1998—; presenter Nat. Safety Coun., Western Pa. Safety Coun., Assn. of Iron and Steel Engrs., Pa. Bar Inst., Allegheny County Bar Assn., Pitts. Human Resources Assn., Butler Human Resources Assn., Westmoreland Human Resources Assn.,

SMC Bus. Couns., Constrn. Fin. Mgmt. Assn., Pa. Inst. CPAs, Western Pa. Cmty. Accts., YWCA Mid-Atlantic Regional Coun. Notes editor U. S.C. Law Rev., 1975-76; contbr. articles to profl. jours. Dir. Jr. Achievement S.W. Pa., Pitts., 1994-2005, vice-chair adminstrn., 1998-2005. Capt. USAF, 1968-73. Recipient Bronze Leadership award Jr. Achievement S.W. Pa., 1993, Silver award, 2005, Am. Jursiprudence award in labor law; named Pa. Super Lawyer, Law & Politics and the Pub. of Phila. Mag., 2004, 05, 06. Fellow Allegheny County Bar Found.; mem. ABA (com. on occupl. safety and health law 1981—), Soc. for Human Resource Mgmt., Pa. Bar Assn. (com. on legal ethics and profl. responsibility 1987-94), Pitts. Human Resources Assn. (treas. 1997, sr. profl. human resources 1998—), Order of Wig and Robe, Omicron Delta Kappa. Office: Ogletree Deakins Nash Smoak Stewart PC 444 Liberty Ave Ste 400 Pittsburgh PA 15222-1237 Office Phone: 412-394-3342. Business E-Mail: john.artz@ogletreedeakins.com.

ARTZT, EDWIN LEWIS, consumer products company executive; b. NYC, Apr. 15, 1930; s. William and Ida A.; m. Ruth Nadine Martin, May 12, 1950; children: Wendy Anne, Karen Susan, William M., Laura Grace, Elizabeth Louise. BS, U. Oreg., 1951. Account exec. Glasser Gailey Advt. Agy., LA, 1952-53; with Procter & Gamble Co., Cin., 1953-95, brand mgr. advt. dept., 1955-58, assoc. brand promotion mgr., 1958-60, brand promotion mgr., 1960, 62-65, copy mgr., 1960-62, mgr. advt. dept. paper products div., 1965-68, mgr. food products divsn., 1968-69, v.p. food products divsn., 1969-70, v.p., acting mgr. coffee div., 1970, v.p., group exec., 1970-75, bd. dirs., 1972-75, 80-95, exec. v.p. then vice chmn. internat. ops., 1980-89, group v.p. European ops. Europe, Belgium, 1975-80; pres. Procter & Gamble Internat., 1984-89, chmn., chief exec. officer, 1995-99. Bd. dir. GTE Corp., Delta Air Lines, Am. Express Co., Spalding Holdings Corp., Barilla G.e R.F.lli S.p.A., Italy, Am. Inst. for Contemporary German Studies, Am. Enterprise Inst. for Public Policy Rsch. Bd.; mem. Internat. Adv. Bd. Babson Coll. Internat. councilor Ctr. for Strategic and Internat. Studies, Washington; mem. Coun. on Fgn. Rels., The Jackson Hole Land Trust; bd. trustees Cin. Inst. of Fine Arts; mem. exec. com. The Business Coun.; past chmn. residential div. United Appeal; past chmn. Public Library Capital Funds campaign; past dist. chmn. Capital Fund Raising dr. Boy Scouts Am., past leadership tng. chmn.; past chmn. advt. com. Sch. Tax Levy, County Govt. Issue; past trustee Kansas City Philharmonic, Nutrition Found., Boys' Clubs Greater Cin.; past bd. dirs. Kansas City Lyric Theater; past bd. govs. Kansas City Art Inst. Recipient Martin Luther King, Jr. Salute to Greatness award, 1995, Leadership Conf. on Civil Rights Private Sector Leadership award, 1995; inducted to Nat. Sales Hall of Fame, 1995, Advt. Hall of Fame, 1996. Mem. Am. C. of C. Belgium (v.p.), Conf. Bd. Europe (adv. council), Internat. C. of C. (exec. com. U.S. council), Nat. Fgn. Trade Council, Queen City Club, Commercial Club, Camargo Club, Teton Pines Club. Clubs: Queen City (Cin.), Cin. Country (Cin.), Comml. (Cin.). Office: Procter & Gamble Co 1 Procter And Gamble Plz Cincinnati OH 45202-3393 Home: 3849 Hedgewood Dr Lawrenceburg IN 47025-8047

ARTZT, RUSSELL M., electronics executive; b. 1947; BS, Queens Coll., 1968; MS, NYU, 1975. With Riverside Rsch. Corp., NYC, 1968-72; with Standard Data Corp., 1972-76; co-founder Computer Assocs. Internat. Inc., Islandia, NY, 1976, with, 1976—, v.p., 1978-83, sr. v.p. devel., from 1983, exec. v.p., rsch & devel, 1987—2002, exec. v.p., alliances & eTrust solutions, 2002—05; exec. v.p., products Computer Assocs. Internat. Inc. (now called CA), Islandia, NY, 2005—; bd. dir. Computer Assocs. Internat. Inc., Islandia, NY, 1980—. Mem. Bd. Trustees Queens Coll. Found. Office: Computer Assocs Internat Inc (CA) 1 Computer Associates Plz Islandia NY 11749-7000

ARUM, ROBERT, lawyer, sports events promoter; b. NYC, Dec. 8, 1931; s. Samuel and Celia (Baumgarten) Arum; m. Barbara Mandelbaum, July 2, 1960 (div. 1977); children: John, Richard, Elizabeth; m. Sybil Ann Hamada, Dec. 18, 1977 (div. 1991); m. Lovee Hazan Du Boef, Sept. 14, 1991. BA, NYU, 1953; JD cum laude, Harvard U., 1956. Bar: NY 1956. Atty. firm Root, Barrett, Cohen, Knapp & Smith, NYC, 1956—61; asst. U.S. atty., chief tax sect. U.S. Atty.'s Office, So. Dist. N.Y., 1961—64; ptnr. firm Phillips, Nizer, Benjamin, Krim & Ballon, NYC, 1964—72, Arum & Katz, NYC, 1972—79; chmn. Top Rank, Inc.; Promoter Ali-Frazier Super Fight II, 1974, Evel Knievel Snake River Canyon Jump, 1974, Ali-Norton World Heavyweight Championship, 1976, Monzon-Valdez World Middleweight Championships, 1976, 1977, Ali-Spinks Championships, 1978, Leonard-Duran Championships, 1980, 1989, Top Rank/ESPN Boxing Series, 1980—, Arguello-Pryor Championship, 1983, Moore-Duran Championship, 1983, Hagler-Duran Championship, 1983, Hagler-Hearns Championship, 1985, Hagler-Leonard Superfight Championship, 1987, Leonard-Hearns "The War" Championship, 1989—91, Holyfield-Foreman World Heavyweight Championship, 1991, Holyfield-Holmes World Heavyweight Championship, 1992, Foreman/Morrison Heavyweight Championship, 1993, De la Hoya/Whitaker, 1997, De la Hoya/Chavez, 1996, 1998, De la Hoya/Quartey, 1999, De la Hoya/Trinidad, 1999, De la Hoya/Mosely, 2000, Morales/Barrera, 2002, De la Hoya/Vargas, 2002. Named to Boxing Hall of Fame, 1999. Mem.: Friars Club. Home: 36 Gulf Stream Ct Las Vegas NV 89113-1354 Office: 3980 Howard Hughes Pkwy Las Vegas NV 89109-0992 E-mail: erroa@aol.com.

ARUNDEL, JOHN HOWARD, journalist, publisher; b. Washington, June 4, 1965; s. Arthur W. and Margaret C. (McElroy) A.; married; 1 child. BA in Polit. Sci., Duke U., 1988; MA in Internat. Econs., Johns Hopkins U., 1995. Reporter, trainee The New York Times, NYC, 1988-90; bur. chief States News Svc., Washington, 1991-92; corr. The Washington Post, Kuwait City, Kuwait, 1991; v.p. Citigroup, Washington, 1996—; journalist, editor, publisher The Alexandria Times, Alexandria, Va., 2004—. Bd. mem. Va. Film Found.; bd. dirs. The Kennedy Ctr. Camelot Circle, Washington, 1995—. Author: The Student Guide to Duke, 1988, While America Slept, 2003; contbr. articles to profl. jours. Mem. Nat. Press Club. Democrat. Episcopalian. Home: 6034 Woodmont Rd Alexandria VA 22307-1158 Office: 300 S Washington St Alexandria VA 22314 Home Phone: 703-317-9450; Office Phone: 703-739-0001. Personal E-mail: jonarundel@aol.com. E-mail: johna@alextimes.com.

ARVANITAKIS, ZOE, neurologist, researcher; MD, U. Western Ontario, London, Can., 1994. Diplomate bd. cert. Resident in neurology U. Manitoba, Winnipeg, Canada, 1991; fellow in dementia Mayo Clinic, Jacksonville, Fla., 2001; asst. prof. Rush U. Med. Ctr., Chgo., 2001—. Rsch. mentor Rush U. Med. Ctr., Chgo., 2001—; med. jour. reviewer Neurology Archives of Neurology, 2004—; med. grant reviewer Alzheimer's Assn., Chgo., 2004—; med. course developer Am. Acad. Neurology, Rochester, Minn., 2005—; invited prof. Mayo Clinic, 2005—, Vanderbilt U., Nashville, 2005—; exec. mem. and sec. Women's Adv. Group to Dean Rush Med. Coll., Chgo., 2006—. Contbr. articles to profl. jours. Lobbying neurologist Alzheimer's Assn., Washington, 2006. Grantee, Mayo Clinic, 2000—01, Alzheimer's Assn., 2004—06, Nat. Inst. Aging, 2005—. Mem.: Am. Acad. Neurology (exec. mem. geriatric neurology sect. 2006—, councilor geriatric neurology sect. 2006—). Office: Alzheimers Disease Ctr Rush Univ Med Ctr Ste 8N 710 S Paulina Chicago IL 60612

ARVESON, WILLIAM BARNES, mathematics professor; b. Oakland, Calif., Nov. 22, 1934; s. Ronald Magnus and Audrey Mary (Hichens) A.; m. Lee A. Kaskutas. BS in Math, Calif. Inst. Tech., 1960; MA, UCLA, 1963, PhD, 1964. Benjamin Peirce instr. Harvard U., 1965-68; lectr. dept. math. U. Calif., Berkeley, 1968-69, assoc. prof., 1969-74, prof., 1974—, Miller rsch. prof., 1985—86, 1999—2000. Author: An Invitation to C*-algebras, 1976, A Short Course in Spectral Theory, 2001, Noncommutative Dynamics and E-semigroups, 2003; assoc. editor: Duke Math. Jour, 1975-86, Jour. of Operator Theory, 1977-87, editor, 1987—; contbr. articles to math. jours. Served with U.S. Navy, 1952-55. John Simon Guggenheim fellow, 1976-77 Mem. Am. Math. Soc. (assoc. editor bulletin 1988-91), Edinburgh Math. Soc. (assoc. editor proceedings 1989—). Office: U Calif Dept Math Berkeley CA 94720-0001

ARVIA, ANNE L., bank executive; m. Jack Arvia; 2 children. BS in Acctg., Mich. State Univ. CPA. Acctg. mgr. Crowe, Chizekand Co. LLP; asst. controller ShoreBank Corp., Chgo., 1991—93, v.p., controller, 1993—96, sr. v.p., 1996—98, CFO, 1998—2001, pres., 2001—06, CEO, 2003—06, Nationwide Bank, Columbus, Ohio, 2006—. Bd. dir. Cmty. Investment Corp., Cmty. Initiatives Inc. Mem. Leadership Chgo. Named one of 100 Most Influential Women, Crain's Chgo. Bus., 2004, 25 Most Powerful Women in Banking, US Banker mag., 2005; named to 40 Under 40, Crain's Chgo. Bus., 2002. Mem.: Ill. CPA (Fin. Inst. Com.), Ill. Bankers Assn., Chgo. Fin. Exchange, Leadership Ill. Office: Nationwide Bank One Nationwide Plz Columbus OH 43215 Office Phone: 773-288-1000. Office Fax: 773-493-6609.

ARVIN, ANN MARGARET, microbiology and immunology educator, researcher; BA, Brown U., 1966; MD, U. Pa., 1972. Resident U. Calif. San Francisco Med. Ctr., 1975; fellow Stanford (Calif.) Hosp. and Clinics, 1978; mem. faculty Stanford U. Sch. Medicine, 1978—, Lucille Packard Prof. Pediat., prof. microbiology and immunology, 1989—, assoc. dean rsch., 2001—. Cons. FDA Ctr. Biologics Evaluation & Rsch., 1994—; co-chair rsch. team investigating possible uses of flu virus in bio-terrorism Stanford U., 2003—; life sciences bd. NAS/NRC, 2004—. Trustee Am. Herpes Found.; mem. exec. com. VZV Rsch. Found. Recipient New Investigator award, Nat. Inst. Allergy & Infectious Diseases, 1981—84, Rsch. Career Devel. award, 1984—89, E. Mead Johnson award for rsch. in pediat., 1992, John F. Enders award, Infectious Diseases Soc. Am., 2002. Mem.: Assn. Am. Physicians, Inst. Medicine. Office: Stanford U Sch Medicine 300 Pasteur Dr Stanford CA 94305 Business E-Mail: aarvin@stanford.edu.

ARVIN, LINDA LEE, counselor; b. York, Pa., May 12, 1952; d. Paul Henry and Mary Elizabeth (Stein) Honsermyer; m. Michael Eugene Arvin, Dec. 16, 1978 (div.); children: Melissa Elizabeth, Michael Alexis; m. Daniel A. Hitchcock October 14, 2002. BA, George Washington U., 1981; MS in Clin. Cmty. Counseling, 1999. Lic. Clin. Profl. Counselor Johns Hopkins U. Sr. staff Cmty. Ministry, Rockville, Md., 1989-92; sr. counselor Arlington Cmty. Residences, 1992-93; program dir. Montgomery County Coalition for the Homeless, Rockville, 1993-97; counselor ASG, Silver Spring, Md., 1998—2001; psychotherapist Threshold Svc., Silver Spring, Md., 2003—, Pvt. Practice, Kensington, Md., 2003—. Mem. ACA, AAUW, AMHCA Democrat. Avocations: ballroom dancing, music, travel. Home: 4202 E West Hwy Chevy Chase MD 20815-5911 Office: Threshold Svc 8818 Ga Ave Silver Spring MD also: 3720 Farragot Ave Ste 103 Kensington MD Office Phone: 240-281-5004. Personal E-mail: larvinlcpc@aol.com.

ARVIZU, CHARLENE SUTTER, elementary school educator; b. San Jose, Calif., Mar. 1, 1947; d. Joseph Carl and Marjorie Loreen (Nylin) Sutter; m. Ambrose Emanuel Arvizu, Apr. 7, 1980; children: Joseph Todd Nottingham, Matthew Sutter. BA in Art, San Jose State U., 1964, lifetime tchg. credential grades K-9, 1969, lifetime spl. edn. grades K-14, 1969, specialist/learning handicapped, 1969. Tchr. edn. mentally retarded class grades K-12 Berryessa Union Sch. Dist., 1969-71, resource ctr. dir. grades K-5, 1971-73, kindergarten tchr. Ruskin Sch., 1974—. Instr. Ohlone Coll., Fremont, Calif., 1980—89, chapman Coll., 1985—88, San Jose County Office Edn., 1985—94; cons., lectr. Bur. Edn. and Rsch., 1990—; nat. lectr., cons., presenter in field. Author: Whole Language Strategies in the Classroom, 2001, Strengthening Your Kindergarten Using Thrmatic, Integrate Literature Based Strategies, 2002, Kindergarten 5 Day Institute Book, 1994, Read It Again, 1998, Current Best Strategies to Help All Your Kindergartens to be Successful, 2002, Management for Kindergarten Success, 1999. Recipient Disting. Sch. award Office of Mayor, San Jose, Calif., 1987, award Bur. Edn. and Rsch., 1998, Tchr. of Yr. award Berryessa Dist., 2005-06, Outstanding Tchr. of Yr. award Santa Clara Valley, 2005-06. Mem. Internat. Reading Assn., Calif. Reading Assn., Internat. Book Assn. for Young Readers, Children's Book Coun. Inc., Calif. Sch. Age Consortium, Planetary Citizens-One World-One People, Soc. Children's Book Writers, Delta Kappa Gamma. Avocations: animals, horseback riding. Home: 3010 Daurine Ct Gilroy CA 95020-9552 Office: Ruskin Sch 1401 Turlock Ln San Jose CA 95132-2399 Office Phone: 408-842-1587. Personal E-mail: tradewinz9@aol.com.

ARVIZU, DAN ELIAB, mechanical engineer; b. Douglas, Ariz., Aug. 23, 1950; s. Walter and Ella (Rodriguez) A.; m. Patricia Ann Brady, Feb. 23, 1980; children: Joshua, Angela, Elizabeth, Kayley, Tecia. BSME, New Mexico State U., 1973; MSME, Stanford U., 1974, PhD in Mech. Engring., 1981. Mfg. engring. asst. Texas Instruments, Dallas, 1969-72; mem. tech. staff Bell Telephone Labs., Denver, 1973-77; mem. solar thermal tech. staff Sandia Nat. Labs., Albuquerque, 1977-81, mem. solar photovoltaic tech. staff, 1981-86, supr. photovoltaic cell rsch., 1986-88, mgr. tech. transfer, 1988-91, dir. tech. transfer, 1991-93, dir. adv. energy tech., 1993-97, dir. materials and process scis., 1997-98; v.p. energy, environment and sys. group CH2M Hill, 1998-2000, sr. v.p. tech., 2001—, chief tech. officer energy, environ. and sys. bus., 2002—; chair energy working group CEO Coalition to Advance Sustainable Tech., 2002—; exec. dir. engery and tech. U. Chgo., 2004—. Mem. tech. transfer steering com. Nat. Ctr. for Mfg. Scis., Ann Arbor, Mich., 1992; mem. tech. transfer mgrs. adv. bd. Nat. Tech. Transfer Ctr., Wheeling, W.Va., 1992—96; mem. commercialization adv. bd. Solar II Power Plant, Barstow, Calif., 1996—96; mem. adv. bd. U. Tex.-El Paso model Inst. Excellence Program, 1995—; chmn. indsl. adv. bd. ME Acad. N.Mex. State U., 1995—99, bd. dirs.; mem. com. to rev. DOE's renewable energy tech. program NRC, 1998—2000; mem. corp. adv. bd. Colo. Sch. Mines, 1999—; mem. nat. adv. bd. for Hispanic engr. nat. achievement award conf. HENAAC, 1999—, bd. dirs., 2000—, Nat. Sci. Bd., 2004—; mem. indsl. adv. group U. Tex. El Paso Coll. Engring., 1999—; mem. nat. coal coun. Dept. Energy, 1999—; adv. group G8 Task Force Renewable Energy, 2000—01; mem. Army Sci. Bd. Dept. of Def., 2001—; adv. Divsn. Engring. and Physical Sci. Comm. Nat. Acad. of Engring., 2001—; bd. adv. Greater Metro Denver Salvation Army, 2000—; mem. com. to review Dept. Energy concentrating solar power tech. NRC, 2002—; chair blue ribbon panel on sci. and engring. workforce diversity Coun. on Competition; chmn. Hispanic Nat. Achievement Award conf. Contbr. articles to profl. jours. Recipient Sel. Hispanic Engr. Nat. Achievement award Exec. Excellence, 1996; named Disting. Engring. Alumnus N.Mex. State U., 1988, 96, Ingeniero Eminente, 1990, Outstanding Achievement award Hispanic Alliance for Career Enhancement, 1997, named Rising Star in Sci. Albuquerque Tribune newspaper, 1989, One of top 20 Hispanic Scientists and Engrs. in Am., Hispanic Engr. Mag., 1998, One of 50 Most Important Hispanics in Am. in Tech. and Bus., Hispanic Mag., 2003. Mem. ASME (solar standards com. 1981-83, nat. lab. tech. transfer com. 1990-93), IEEE, IEEE Electronic Device Soc. (adminstrv. com. 1986-91), Am. Soc. Material Internat., Tech. Transfer Soc. Achievements include leadership of national laboratory negotiating teams that resulted in Department of Energy policy changes to improve U.S. Goverment/ Industry partnership agreements, management of research effort that developed 30 percent solar to electric conversion efficiency solar cell, and development of Sandia National Laboratory's technology transfer center including development of policy, maturation of technology, and formal partnerships between industry and laboratories. Office: CH2M Hill Energy Environment and Sys Bus Group 6060 S Willow Dr Greenwood Village CO 80111-5142 E-mail: darvizu@ch2m.com.

ARVYSTAS, MICHAEL GECIAUSKAS, orthodontist, educator; b. Vilnius, Lithuania, Dec. 18, 1942; arrived in U.S., 1949, naturalized, 1961; s. Mykolas and Antanina (Kleiza) Arvystas; m. Jane Grannis, 1969 (div. 1978); m. Mary Ruth Buchness, Nov. 2, 1992. BA, Colgate U., 1965; DMD, Tufts U., 1969. Cert. Columbia U., 1973, diplomate Am. Bd. Orthodontics. Chief orthodontic sect. Morrisania City Hosp., Bronx, NY, 1973—76; dir. orthodontics ctr. for craniofacial disorders and cleft palate ctr. Montefiore Hosp. and Med. Ctr., 1973—; chief orthodontic sect. North Ctrl. Bronx Hosp., 1976—83; clin. prof. N.J. Dental Sch., Newark, 1974—, dir., lectr. undergrad. and postgrad. students, 1974—. Vis. prof. Albert Einstein Coll. Medicine, Bronx; lectr. in field. Author: Orthodontic Management of Agenesis and Other Complexitues: An Interdisciplinary Approach to Functional Aesthetics, 2003; contbr. articles to profl. jours., chpts. to books. Capt. Dental Corps USAF, 1969—71. Mem.: ADA, Am. Acad. Esthetic Dentistry (orgn. com. Greater N.Y. Dental Meeting), N.Y. Acad. Dentistry, Northeastern Soc. Orthodontists, Am. Assn. Orthodontists, Dental Soc. N.Y.C., N.Y. County Dental Soc. (bd. dirs.), Sigma Xi, Colgate U. Alumni Assn., Orthodontic Alumni Soc. Columbia U., Tufts U. Dental Alumni Assn. Office: 24 Washington Sq N New York NY 10011-9168 Office Phone: 212-777-9977. Personal E-mail: marvystas@optonline.net.

ARWADY, GEORGE E., publishing executive; b. Bklyn. 4 children. BA, Hope Coll., Holland, Mich., 1969; MA in Journalism, Columbia U., NYC, 1970. Editorial writer Kalamazoo Gazette, 1970—75, pub., 1988—2004; met. editor Muskegon Chronicle, Mich., 1975—76, editor, pub., 1980—88; editor Saginaw News, Mich., 1976—80; pub. The Star-Ledger, Newark, 2004—. Trustee Ind. Coll. Fund NJ; bd. dirs. Mich. Colls. Found. Recipient Disting. Alumni award, Hope Coll., 1984. Office: The Star-Ledger One Star Ledger Plaza Newark NJ 07102-1200 Office Phone: 973-392-4161. Business E-Mail: garwady@starledger.com.*

ARYANFAR, FARSHID, electrical and electronics engineer; m. Haleh Hazer. BSc in Elec. Engring, U. Tehran, 1994, MSc in Elec. Engring, 1998; PhD, U. Mich., 2004. Rsch. asst. U. Mich., Ann Arbor, Mich., 2000—04; sr. rsch. engr. EMAG Technologies Inc., Ann Arbor, 2003—05; sr. staff engr. Motorola, 2005—. Contbr. articles to profl. jours. Grantee, MDA, 2004, USAF, 2004, DARPA, 2005. Mem.: IEEE (sr.). Achievements include design of miniaturized mm-wave transceivers; development of a novel scaled measurement system for wireless channel characterization; a full 3D physics-based wave propagation simulator; research in through wall imaging technique; design of miniaturized planar filters. Office: Microwave Tech Rsch Lab Motorola Labs Schaumburg IL Personal E-mail: aryanfar@yahoo.com.

ARZOUMANIDIS, GREGORY G., chemist; b. Thessaloniki, Greece, Aug. 16, 1936; arrived in U.S., 1964, naturalized, 1976; s. Gerasimos and Sophia Arzoumanidis; m. Anastasia Anastasopoulos, Jan. 2, 1966; children: Sophia, Alexis. BS in Chemistry, MS in Chemistry, U. Thessaloniki, 1959; PhD in Inorganic Chemistry, U. Stuttgart, Germany, 1964; MBA, U. Conn., 1979. Research assoc. MIT, 1964-66; research chemist Monsanto, Everett, Mass., 1966-69; sr. research chemist Am. Cyanamid Co., Stamford, Conn., 1969-72, Stauffer Chem. Co., Dobbs Ferry, NY, 1972-79; research assoc. Amoco Chem. Co., Naperville, Ill., 1979-94, Argonne (Ill.) Nat. Lab., 1995-96; with Oakwood Cons., 1996—. Contbr. articles to profl. jours. Served to 2d lt. Greek Army, 1959—61. Recipient Acad. award, Govt. of West Germany, 1963, Presdl. award, Amoco Chem. Co., 1990. Mem.: AAAS, Am. Chem. Soc., Sigma Xi. Greek Orthodox. Achievements include invention of commercial catalysts for polypropylene plastics, new processes; patents in field; principal co-inventor Amoco supported polypropylene catalyst. Home: 7 S 610 Carriage Way Naperville IL 60540 Personal E-mail: arzo@sbcglobal.net.

ASAADI, MOKHTAR, plastic surgeon; b. Tehran, Iran, Aug. 28, 1946; came to U.S., 1974; s. Esmael and Talat Asaadi; m. Nejla Nassirzadeh, Jan. 11, 1983; children: Deena, Dara, Neela. Pre-med. coll. arts & scis., Pahlavi U., Shiraz, Iran, 1967—73; MD, Pahlavi Med. Sch., Shiraz, Iran, 1973. Diplomate Am. Bd. Surgery, 1980, Am. Bd. Plastic Surgery, 1983, lic. NJ, 1976, NY, 1977, Fla., 1981, Calif., 1981, Ill., 1981. On rotation St. Thomas Hosp., London U., London, 1971; resident rotating Pahlavi U. Med. Sch., Shiraz, Iran, 1971—72, resident, internal medicine, 1973—74; intern, med. Pahlavi Med. Sch. Hosps., Shiraz, Iran, 1972—73; resident, gen. surgery Meml. Sloan-Kettering Cancer Ctr., NYC, 1976; fellow, microsurgery So. Ill. U. Sch. Medicine, Springfield, Ill., 1981—82; fellow, aesthetic surgery Manhattan Eye, Ear and Throat Hosp., NYC, 1982; intern, surgery St. Barnabas Med. Ctr., Livingston, NJ, 1974—75, resident, gen. surgery, 1975—76, 1977—79, chief resident, gen. surgery, 1978—79, resident, plastic surgery, 1979—81, chief resident, plastic surgery, 1980—81, attending plastic surgeon dept. plastic surgery, 1985—, chmn., operating room com., dept. plastic surgery, 1990—, assoc. chmn., dept. plastic surgery, 1997—98, chmn., dept. plastic surgery, 1998—2001. Instr., physiology Pahlavi Med. Sch., Iran, 1969; instr. med. review course St. Barnabas Med. Ctr., Livingston, NJ, 1982—, tchg. residents, dept. plastic surgery, tchg., microsurgical lab, mem. utilization review com., mem. libr. com., mem. operating and recovery room com., mem. credential com., mem. med. bd.; mem. med. adv. com., Med/Mark Same Day Surgery Ctr., West Orange, NJ; mem. utilization review com. Morristown Meml. Hosp., NJ; lectr. in field. Featured in NY Absolute Mag., NJ Life, New Beauty Mag., , NY Times, Family Health Mag., Plastic Surgery Products Mag., FIRST Mag., NJ Mag., West Orange Chronicle, Star-Ledger, Daily News; featured on NBC, News12, NBC, CN8; contbr. articles to profl. jours. Physician's Recognition award, AMA, 1983-88, 1990-97 Mem.: ACS, Internat. Coll. Surgeons, Med. Soc. NJ, NJ Soc. Plastic Surgery, AMA, NY Regional Soc. Plastic and Reconstructive Surgery, Northeastern Soc. Plastic Surgeons, Lipolysis Soc. N.Am., Am. Soc. for Aesthetic Plastic Surgery, Inc., Am. Soc. Plastic Surgeons, Essex County Med. Soc. (mem. publications com. 1984), Med. Soc. NJ (advisory 1982—83). Avocations: horseback riding, skiing, tennis, western riding and "round-up". Office: 101 Old Short Hills Rd Ste 504 West Orange NJ 07052 Address: 125 E 63rd St New York NY 10021 Office Phone: 201-731-7000, 212-938-0158.*

ASADORIAN, DIANA C., electrical engineer, educator; b. Leninakan, Armenia, June 16, 1950; came to U.S., 1975; d. Eduard and Vartuhi (Seraidarian) Martirosyan; m. William R. Asadorian, July 22, 1978; 1 child, Ronald E. M in Electromech. Engring. Elec. Motors, Polytech. Inst., Odessa, USSR, 1972. Elect. engr. Odessa Cable Plant, 1972-75; draftsman Leviton Co., Bklyn., 1976-77; from engring. asst. to design engr. engring. and devel. CBS, NYC, 1977-86, assoc. dir. engring. lab., 1986-89, dir. engring. lab. and drafting. engring. and devel., 1989-90, dir. tech. tng. and documentation engring., 1990—, assoc. dir. news engring. and document, 1994—99. Mem. Soc. Motion Picture and TV Engring., Am. Soc. News Engring. and Documentation (assoc. dir.). Republican. Baptist. Avocation: concert pianist. Home Phone: 718-461-5130; Office Phone: 212-975-1719. Business E-Mail: dasadorian@cbs.com.

ASAI, RIKA, musicologist, educator; b. Windsor, Ont., Can., Oct. 11, 1974; BMus, U. Sask., Saskatoon, Can., 1997; MA, PhD, Ind. U., Bloomington, 1999. Editl. asst. Jour. Musicology, 2002—04; vis. lectr. Ind. U., Bloomington, 2003—. Contbr. articles to profl. jours. Recipient Kaufmann prize, Ind. U., 2003, Tischler award, 2003; fellow, 2005—06; grantee, 2005; scholar, 1997—2002; Grad. and Profl. Student Orgn. Travel grantee, 2002, A. Peter Brown Travel grantee, 2004. Mem.: Soc. Am. Music, Am. Musicological Soc. Office: Ind U Jacobs Sch Music 1201 E Third St Bloomington IN 47405 Office Phone: 812-855-8252.

ASAI-SATO, CAROL YUKI, retired lawyer; b. Osaka, Japan, Oct. 22, 1951; came to U.S., 1953; d. Michael and Sumiko (Kamei) Asai; 1 child,

Ryan Makoto Sato. BA cum laude, U. Hawaii, 1972; JD, Willamette Coll. Law, 1975. Bar: Hawaii 1975. Assoc. firm Ashford & Wriston, Honolulu, 1975-79; counsel Bank of New Eng., Boston, 1979-81; assoc. counsel Alexander & Baldwin, Honolulu, 1981-83, sr. counsel, 1984-88; of counsel Rush, Moore, Craven, Sutton, Morry, Beh, 1988-89, ptnr., 1989-97, Alston Hunt Floyd & Ing, 1997—2004; ret., 2004. Willamette Coll. Law Bd. Trustees scholar, 1972-73. Mem. ABA, Hawaii Bar Assn., Hawaii Women Lawyers, Phi Beta Kappa, Phi Kappa Phi. Democrat.

ASAKAWA, TAKAKO, dancer, choreographer, educator, director; b. Toyko, Feb. 23, 1939; came to U.S., 1962; d. Kamenosuke and Chiaki Asakawa. Student, Tokyo schs., 1962-91. Prin. dancer Martha Graham Dance Co., NYC, 1962-76, 81—; dancer Alvin Ailey, 1968-69, Pearl Lang, 1967, Lar Lubovitch, 1974-80. Guest tchr. at numerous schs. and univs. throughout world, including Moscow Culture Exch. Program, Martha Graham Sch., Juilliard Sch.; co.-founder Asakawalker Dance Co.; dir. Paris Opera Ballet Co., Am. Ballet Theater, Het Nationale Ballet in Amsterdam and various univs. throughout world. Performed all major roles in GRaham reperatory throughout world, including Paris Opera House, Covent Garden; Broadway and TV performances include Eliza in The King and I, Bell Tel. Hour. Named Legendary Woman of Am., St. Vincent's Hosp. Mem. Am. Guild Musical Artists Home and Office: 20 W 64th St Apt 29-E/F New York NY 10023-7180

ASANI, ALI S., foreign language and religious studies educator; b. Nairobi, Kenya, Oct. 28, 1954; came to U.S., 1973; s. Sultaan Ali and Shirinkhanu (Velji) A. BA summa cum laude, Harvard Coll., Cambridge, Mass., 1977; MA, Harvard U., Cambridge, 1981, PhD, 1984. From instr. to assoc. prof. Indo-Muslim culture Harvard U., Cambridge, Mass., 1983-92, prof. practice of Indo-Muslim lang. and culture, 1992—. Vis. prof. Inst. Ismaili Studies, London, 1992—; dir., co-dir. Al-Ummah Summer Program for Muslim Youth, 1984—. Author: The Bujh Niranjan: An Ismaili Mystical Poem, 1991, The Harvard Collection of Ismaili Literature in Indic Literature, 1992, Celebrating Muhammad, 1995, Ecstasy and Enlightenment: Ismaili Devotional Literature of South Asia, 2002, Let's Study Krdu: An Introductory Course, 2007, Let's Study Krdu: An Introduction to the Scyprt, 2007; editor Jour. Inst. Muslim Minority Affairs. Recipient Harvard Found. medal, 2002; rsch. fellow NEH, 1986; rsch. grantee Inst. Ismaili Studies, London, 1995, Consortium for Lang. Tchg. and Learning, 1993-94, 95-96, 99-2000, 02-03; Aga Khan scholar Harvard U., 1973-84. Mem. Am. Acad. Religion, Assn. for Asian Studies, Phi Beta Kappa. Muslim. Avocation: travel. Home: 203 Pemberton St Apt 3 Cambridge MA 02140-2543 Office: Harvard Univ Study of Religion NELC Barker Ctr 305 12 Quincy St Cambridge MA 02138 Business E-Mail: aliasani@fas.harvard.edu.

ASARI, EIKICHI, information sciences educator, researcher; b. Fonto, Karafuto, Japan, Feb. 10, 1929; s. Shoukichi and Kiku (Kotaki) A.; m. Satsuko Yamada, June 13, 1959; 1 child, Kimie Grad., Military Scis. and Tech. Acad. Imperial Army of Japan, 1945; 1st class radio engr. (hon.), Ministry Telecom. of Japan, 1952; attended sci.: math. and computer sci., Hokkaido U., Sapporo, Japan, 1959-61, Polytech. Nippon Telegraph and Pub. Corp., Tokyo, 1964. Radio engr. Nippon Telegraph and Tel. Pub. Corp., Sapporo, 1951-64, mem. mgmt. staff, 1964-69; assoc. prof. Tokai U., Sapporo, 1969-88, Hokkaido Tokai U., Sapporo, 1988-92; prof. info. scis. Hokkaido Coll. Arts and Scis. , Ebets, 1993-97. Part-time lectr. info. scis. Nat. Otaru U. Commerce, 1970-97, Sapporo Polytech. of Nippon Telegraph and Telephone Pub. Corp., Hokkaido, 1970-85, Rakuno Gakuen U., Ebets, 1997-99. Editor, author: Encyclopedia of Operations Research, 1974-75, Encyclopedia of hokkaido,1979-81; contbr. articles to profl. publs.; inventor complete solution and applications of renewal theory, 1967, microwave propagation in precipitation, 1974, theory of countermeasures for cold damage of rice cultivation in subpolar climate dists., 1973-77, weather forecast method by meteorological noises, 1989, ski resort radiosys., 1989-90 (govt. prize 1992). Commr. com. distbn. in Hokkaido, Ministry Transp., 1975-76; chmn. com. optimazation of rice cultivation in Hokkaido, Hokkaido Govt., 1977-78; chmn. com. establish planning Hokkaido teleport Hokkaido Inst. Future Advancement, 1985-86; chmn. com. ski resort radio systems Ministry Post and Telecom., 1989-90, detection of clear air turbulences, 1999. Technical corp. telecom. Imperial Army Japan, 1945-46. Recipient award of merit of cold dist. devel. Civil Assns. Dist. Devel., Hokkaido, 1991, award of merit for radio sci. devel. Hokkaido br. Ministry Post and Telecom., 1992, fellow Operations Rsch. Soc. of Japan, 1995. Mem. IEEE, UNESCO, N.Y. Acad. Scis., Hokkauido/Mass. Soc., The Planetary Soc., Ops. Rsch. Soc. Japan (councilor 1970-92), Inst. Electronics and Communication Engrs. Japan, Cold Dists. Agrl. Sci. Soc. Ministry Agriculture, Forest and Fishery of Japan. Avocations: travel, photography, mysteries and science fiction, history of wars research. Home and Office: Shinkawa 2-Jo 2-chome Kita-ku Sapporo 001-0922 Japan Office Phone: 81117618856. Office Fax: 81117618865. Personal E-mail: asarie@d2.dion.ne.jp.

ASATO, EVAN MASAMI, artist, architect, designer; b. Honolulu, Feb. 13, 1947; s. Carl Seichi and Helen Hanaye Asato; m. Evelyn Kimiko Tayasu-Asato, Sept. 3, 1977. AA, LA Trade-Tech. Coll., 1967, U. Hawaii, Kahului, 1982; art student, Art Ctr. Coll. Design, Pasadena, 1969—70. Graphic artist ABC TV Ctr., Hollywood, 1967—69, ACE Printing Co., Wailuku, Hawaii, 1978—82; artist Pukalani, Hawaii, 1982—; pvt. practice, 1990—. Exhibitions include Art Maui Juried Exhibit, 1982—95, Artists of Hawaii, 1986, 1988, 1990, 1992, 1993, 1994, Hawaii Craftsman Juried Exhibit, 1990, Art Maui Juried Exhibit, 1997—2004, 2007, SFCA, Hawaii, 1984, 1996, 1999, Contemporary Art Mus., Honolulu, 2000, 2006, Hawaii State Art Mus., 2003, U. Hawaii Art Gallery, 2001, one-man shows include Hui Noeau Visual Arts Ctr., 1991, Territorial Savings, 1992, First Hawaiian Ctr., 2000, 2006. Sgt. US Army, 1968—76. Avocations: surfing, hiking, camping, gardening, music.

ASATRYAN, RUBIK, chemistry professor, researcher; b. Tehran, Iran, May 8, 1955; s. Serob and Khanibek Asatryan; m. Olga Minaeva, Jan. 23, 1982; children: Aram, Mariam. BS/MS, Yerevan State U., Armenia, 1976; PhD, Moscow State Lomonosov U., 1982. Engr.-scientist Moscow State Lomonosov U., 1982—83; rsch. assoc. Inorganic Br. USSR Inst. Chem. Reactives and High Purity Materials, Yerevan, Armenia, 1983; sr. rsch. assoc. Inst. Chem. Physics of Nat. Acad. of Sci., Yerevan, 1990—2001; asst. prof. Yerevan State U., 1989—90; assoc. prof. Yerevan State Med. U., 2001—04; rsch. scholar La. State U., Baton Rouge, 2005, NJ Inst. Tech., Newark, 2005—. Cons. Expertise Ctr. Republic of Armenia, Yerevan, 2003—04; mem. sci. bd. Armenian Br. USSR Inst. Chem. Reactives and High Purity Materials, 1992—94, chmn. coun. of young scientists; vis. scientist La. State U., Baton Rouge, 2004. Author: (book) Fundamentals of Chemistry, 1992, (textbook) Chemistry for Colleges, 1999, sci. articles in various jours. Mem. Green Union of Armenia, Yerevan, 1988—90; chmn. Ctr. for Environ. Studies, NGO, Yerevan, 2003—05; head sci.-ednl. commn. Armenian-Iranian Cultural Club, Yerevan, 2003—05. Sgt. engring. svcs. USSR Army, 1977—78. Fellow, A.N.Nesmeyanov Inst. Organo-Element Compounds, USSR Acad. of Sci., 1975—76, Gorki State U., 1981; grantee, ISF, 1993, Nat. Found. Sci. and Advanced Tech. and Civilian R & D Found., 2004. Mem.: Combustion Inst. (intern), Armenian Chem. Soc. Christian, Armenian Apostolic. Achievements include development of fuel combustion elementary reactions and kinetic models and a new kinetic mechanism has been developed to obtain a fundamental understanding in the formation of dioxins; and other environmental contaminants. Avocations: literature, music, swimming, soccer, travel. Office: NJ Inst Tech University Heights Newark NJ 07102 Office Phone: 973-596-5854. Office Fax: 973-596-3586. Business E-Mail: asatryan@njit.edu.

ASBECK, PETER MICHAEL, engineering educator; BSEE, MIT, Cambridge, 1969; PhD in Elec. Engring., MIT, 1975. With Sarnoff Rsch. Ctr., Princeton, NJ, Philips Lab., Briarcliff Manor, NY, Rockwell Internat. Sci. Ctr., 1978—91, prin. scientist high speed electronics and optoelectronics function, 1991; prof. elec. and computer engring. U. Calif., San Diego, 1991—. Contbr. articles to sci. jours. Fellow: IEEE (David Sarnoff award 2003); mem.: NAE. Achievements include development of heterojunction bipolar transistors, which amplify cell phone signals so they are strong enough to travel from a cell phone antenna to the closest cell phone tower; patents in field. Office: Dept Elec and Computer Engring U Calif San Diego Mail Code 0407 9500 Gilman Dr La Jolla CA 92093-0407 Office Phone: 858-534-6713. Office Fax: 858-534-2486. E-mail: asbeck@ece.ucsd.edu.*

ASBILL, RICHARD M., lawyer; b. Wilmington, Del., Nov. 9, 1943; s. Mac Jr. and Jane (Winchester) A.; m. Jane Cherry (div. 1974); children: R. Brandon, Christopher L.; m. Evelyn M. Judd, May 1, 1976; children: Judd W., Carter M. BA, Princeton U., 1965; JD, U. N.C., 1968. Bar: Ga. 1968. Assoc. Jones, Bird & Howell (name changed to Alston & Bird), Atlanta, 1968-73; ptnr. Harman, Asbill, Roach & Nellis (name changed to Asbill, Porter, Churchill & Nellis), Atlanta, 1973-86, Paul, Hastings, Janofsky & Walker, Atlanta, 1986—, co-chmn. trade regulation & proprietary rights practice group, co-chmn. resort, restaurant & recreation practice group. Co-author: Franchising Law: Practice and Forms, 1992; co-author, co-editor: Fundamentals of International Franchising, 2001. Trustee, mem. exec. com., Schenck Sch., Atlanta, 1990-2000, mem. adv. bd., 2000—. Mem. ABA (governing com. Forum on Franchising 1995-01, chair 1997-99, immediate past chair 1999-01), Internat. Bar Assn. (vice chair internat. franchising com. X 1994-98, chair 1998-02), Capital City Club, Orchard Golf & Country Club. Avocations: golf, skiing, travel. Office: Paul Hastings Janofsky & Walker 600 Peachtree St NE Ste 2400 Atlanta GA 30308-3624 Office Phone: 404-815-2236. Office Fax: 404-685-5236. Business E-Mail: rickasbill@paulhastings.com.

ASBJÖRNSON, KEVIN DONALD, musician, small business owner; b. Brookings, SD, Aug. 9, 1954; s. Donald Carvel and Clarice Elaine Asbjornson; m. Cathrine Anderson Wilson, Sept. 14, 2002. Diploma in European Econ., Legal and Polit. Studies, U. Vienna, Strobl am Wolfgangsee, Austria, 1983; BA cum laude, U. Nebr., Omaha, 1984; MS in Internat. Mgmt., Thunderbird Sch. Global Mgmt., Glendale, Ariz., 1985. Rep. fin. svcs. Am. Express, Frankfurt, Germany, 1976—80; mgr. internat. mktg. Applied Comm. Inc., Amsterdam, 1985—90; internat. mktg. mgr. Am. Tool Companies, Lincoln, Nebr., 1990—93; dir. sales and mktg. Echostar Comm., Englewood, Colo., 1993—94; dir. worldwide mktg. Info. Handling Svcs., Englewood, 1995—96; sr. faculty Ctr. Creative Leadership, Greensboro, NC, 1996—2004; prin., owner PianoOne LLC, Littleton, Colo., 2004—. Performing artist in residence Ctr. Creative Leadership, Greensboro, 1997—, Banff Centre-Leadership Devel., Alta., Canada, 2000—, Thunderbird Sch. Global Mgmt., Glendale, Ariz., 2007—. Prodr.: (films) The Artistry of Leadership-Creating Meaningful Connections (Internat. Telly award for creative excellence, 2005); composer (producer, pianist): (albums) Awakenings-Contemporary Piano Solos by Kevin Asbjornson, 1998, Inner Voices-Contemporary Piano Solos by Kevin Asbjornson, 1999, Collage-Contemporary Piano Solos by Kevin Asbjornson, 2000; composer: (musician, co-prodr.) Acoustitherapy Ambiance, 2001, Acoustitherapy Gentle Passion, 2002, Acoustitherapy Relaxation, 2003. Adv. performing artist in residence Colo. Boys Ranch, La Junta, Colo., Boys & Girls Town Mo., St. James; mem. adv. bd. Am. Bank Commerce, Colo. Springs, 2004—07. With US Army, 1973—76. Finalist Innovation award, Colo. Bus. Com. for Arts; scholar, Goethe Inst., 1983. Mem.: Am. Music Therapy Assn. (life), Am. Soc. Composers, Authors and Pubs. (life), Colo. Bus. Com. Arts (life), Soc. Arts in Healthcare (life), Am. Music Conf. (life), Delta Phi Alpha (life), Phi Gamma Mu (life), Omicron Delta Kappa (life). Office: PianoOne LLC 9693 Las Colinas Dr Littleton CO 80124-4201 Office Phone: 303-768-8712. Business E-Mail: kevin.asbjornson@pianoone.com.

ASBURY, ARTHUR KNIGHT, neurologist, educator; b. Cin., Nov. 22, 1928; s. Eslie and Mary (Knight) Asbury; m. Carolyn Holstein, May 17, 1980; children from previous marriage: Dana, Patricia Knight, William Francis. Grad., Phillips Acad., Andover, Mass., 1946; student, Stanford, 1947—48; BS, U. Ky., 1951; MD, U. Cin., 1958; MA (hon.), U. Pa., 1974. Intern in medicine Mass. Gen. Hosp., Boston, 1958—59, resident, 1959—63, fellow, 1963—65, staff neurologist, 1965—69; chief neurology San Francisco VA Hosp., 1969—74; prof. dept. neurology U. Pa., Phila., 1974—, chmn. dept. neurology, 1974—82, Van Meter prof. neurology, 1983—97; acting dean, exec. v.p. U. Pa. Sch. Medicine, 1988—89, vice dean for rsch., 1990—93, vice dean for faculty affairs, 1993—97, interim dean, 2000—01; tchg. fellow Harvard Med. Sch., 1958—65, instr., 1965—68, assoc., 1968—69; assoc. prof. neurology U. Calif. at San Francisco, 1969—73, vice-chmn., 1969—74, prof., 1973—74. Mem. nat. adv. neurol. disease & stroke coun. NIH, 1990—93; hon. prof. med. scis. Hebei Med. Coll., China, 1995. Sr. editor: Blue Books of Practical Neurology, 1980—2004, assoc. editor: Archives of Neurology, 1975—76, Annals of Neurology, 1976—81, chief editor:, 1985—93, mem. editl. bd.: Muscle and Nerve, 1977—89, Neurology, 1981—85, Jour. Neuropathology and Exptl. Neurology, 1981—83, Jour. Neurol. Scis., 1989—2001; contbr. chpts. to med. textbooks, articles to med. jours. V.p., bd. dirs. Forest Retreat Farms Inc., Carlisle, Ky., 1970—92. With US Army, 1951—53. Recipient Daniel Drake medal, U. Cin., 1988, IS Ravdin Master Clinician award, U. Pa., 1999, Lindback Tchg. award, 2000; grantee, UPHS, 1967—93, Muscular Dystrophy Assn., 1974—82. Fellow: AAAS, Royal Coll. Physicians London, Am. Acad. Neurology (v.p. 1977—79, hon. 2003); mem.: Coll. Physicians Phila. (pres. 2004—06, Meritorious Svc. award 2006), World Fedn. Neurology (v.p. 1989—93, chair rsch. group on neuromuscular diseases 2001—05, Lifetime Achievement award for work in neuromuscular diseases 2002), Assn. Univ. Profs. Neurology (pres. 1980—82, Meritorious Svc. award 2006), Am. Assn. Neuromuscular and Electrodiagnostic Medicine (hon.; hon.), European Neurol. Soc. (hon.), Assn. Brit. Neurologists (hon.), Soc. Neurosci., Am. Assn. Neuropathologists (v.p. 1983—84), Am. Neurol. Assn. (councillor 1976—81, pres. 1982—83, hon. 1995), Inst. Medicine. Achievements include Arthur K. Asbury Ann. award for faculty mentoring established at University Pennsylvania School of Medicine in 2004. Home: 408 S Van Pelt St Philadelphia PA 19146-1233 Office: U Pa Hosp Dept Neurology 3400 Spruce St Philadelphia PA 19104-4283 Home Phone: 215-790-0882; Office Phone: 215-662-2629. Business E-Mail: arthur.asbury@uphs.upenn.edu.

ASCENCAO, ERLETE MALVEIRA, psychologist, educator; b. Manaus, Brazil, Apr. 8, 1954; naturalized, U.S., 03; d. Alvaro de Azevedo and Adelia Malveira Ascencao. AA, Reinhardt Coll., 1978; BA, Berry Coll., 1980; MA, Emory U., 1982, BS in Mental Health Psychology, 1986, PhD, 1986, U. Tenn., 1995. Lic. psychologist. Psychotherapist Luron Mental Health Svcs., Nashville, 1995—97; psychol. examiner Tenn. Prison for Women, Nashville, 1996—97; assoc. prof. psychology Tenn. State U., Nashville, 1998—2004; clrin. psychologist Meharry Cmty. Wellness Ctr., Nashville, 2001—; dir. psychol. treatment svcs. and quality assistance Meharry Med. Coll., Nashville, 2004—, assoc. prof. psychiatry and behavioral sci., 2004—05; assoc. prof. dept. internal medicine Meharry Cmty. Wellness Ctr., 2005—, dir.dept. psychology and treatment svcs. Mem. share mothers project Vanderbilt U., Nashville, 2001; presenter in field. Contbr. articles to profl. publs. HIV outreach educator, pro bono clin. psychologist Meharry Med. Coll., 2001—. Recipient award for outstanding clin. work, Luton Mental Health Svcs., 1997; grantee, Meharry Med. Coll., Ctr. AIDS Rsch., 2004. Mem.: APA (regional trainer HIV/AIDS HOPE 1986—, expert in multicultural psychology, grantee), Tenn. Psychol. Assn. Democrat. Roman Catholic. Avocations: theater, music, literature. Home: 3410 Batavia St Nashville TN 37209 Office: Meharry Med Coll Dept Internal Medicine 1005 DB Todd Jr Blvd Nashville TN 37208

ASCENZO, CARL, information technology executive; BS in Bus. Adminstrn., Western New England Coll. V.p. ops. & chief info. officer Aetna Health Plans; ptner, sys. integration practice Pricewaterhouse Coopers LLP, Hartford, Conn.; sr. v.p. & chief info. officer Blue Cross Blue Shield of Mass. Mem. Soc. for Info. Mgmt. Executives, Healthcare Info. and Mgmt. Systems Soc., Mass. Health Data Consortium (bd. dir.). Office: SVP & CIO Blue Cross Blue Shield of Mass 401 Park Dr Boston MA 02215

ASCH, SUSAN MCCLELLAN, pediatrician; b. Cleve., Dec. 31, 1945; d. William Alton and Alice Lonore (Heide) McClellan; m. Marc Asch, Sept. 10, 1966; children: Marc William, Sarah Susan, Rebecca Janney. AB, Oberlin Coll., Ohio, 1967; MA, Mich. State U., 1968, PhD, 1975; MD, Case Western Res., 1977. Diplomate Nat. Bd. Med. Examiners, Am. Bd. Pediatrics, Am. Bd. Emergency Pediatrics. Instr. sociology Mich. State U., East Lansing, 1971-73; resident in pediatrics Children's Nat. Med. Ctr., Washington, 1977-80, chief resident in ambulatory and emergency pediatrics, 1979-80; asst. to dir. Office for Med. Applications of Rsch. NIH, Bethesda, 1980-81; pvt. practice in pediatrics Millinocket (Maine) Regional Hosp., 1981-84; assoc. dir. emergency Akron (Ohio) Children's Hosp., 1984-87; asst. prof. pediatrics Northeastern Ohio U. Coll. Medicine, 1984-87; dir. emergency St. Paul Children's Hosp., 1987-91; asst. prof. pediatrics U. Minn., 1987-93, clin. asst. prof., 1993—; pvt. practice pediatrics Stillwater, Minn., 1992—; sec. exec. com. med. staff Lakeview Meml. Hosp., 1999—2001, vice chief of staff, 2001—03, chief of staff, 2003—05, past chief of staff, 2005—07, chair pediatrics, 2005—. Nat. faculty PALS Am. Heart Assn., Mpls., Dallas, 1987—94, regional PALS faculty, 1994—, state bd. dirs. Minn. affiliate, 1988—92; mem. task force, sub-bd. emergency pediat. Am. Bd. Pediat., 1987—91, mem. sub-bd. emergency pediat., 1991—93; chmn. SIDS task force Minn. Dept. Maternal and Child Health, St. Paul, 1990—92. Assoc. editor Pediatric Emergency Medicine, 1992, contbr., 1992, 96; author various publs., 1970—. Mem.: Minn. Med. Assn. (emergency svcs. com. 1990, ho. of dels. 1994), Am. Acad. Pediat. (exec. com. sect. on emergency pediat. 1988—90, chair Minn. emergency pediat. com. 1989—91, nat. faculty advanced pediat. life support 1989—, regional faculty neonatal resuscitation program 1994—, nat. svc. commendation 1991), Alpha Omega Alpha. Democrat. Mem. Soc. Of Friends. Avocations: travel, cutting horses. Home: 34 N Oaks Rd North Oaks MN 55127-6325 Office: Stillwater Med Group 921 Greeley St S Stillwater MN 55082-5935 Office Phone: 651-439-1234.

ASCHAUER, CHARLES JOSEPH, JR., retired health products executive; b. Decatur, Ill., July 23, 1928; s. Charles Joseph and Beulah Diehl (Kniple) A.; m. Elizabeth Claire Meagher, Apr. 28, 1962; children: Karen A. Vorwald, Thomas Arthur, Susan A. Baisley, Karl Andrew. BBA, Northwestern U., 1950. Cert. internat. bus. adminstr. Centre d'Etudes Industrielles, 1951. Prin. McKinsey & Co., Chgo., 1955-62; v.p. mktg. Mead Johnson Labs. div. Mead Johnson & Co., Evansville, Ind., 1962-67; v.p., pres. automotive group Maremont Corp., Chgo., 1967-70; v.p., group exec. Whittaker Corp., Los Angeles, 1970-71; v.p., pres. hosp. products div. Abbott Labs., North Chicago, Ill., 1971-76, v.p., group exec., 1976-79, exec. v.p., dir., 1979-89, ret., 1989. Lt. Supply Corps. USNR, 1951—55. Mem.: Shadow Wood Country Club, Sunset Ridge Country Club, Econs. Club Chgo., Univ. Club Chgo.

ASCHER, JAMES JOHN, pharmaceutical executive; b. Kansas City, Mo., Oct. 2, 1928; s. Bordner Fredrick and Helen (Barron) A.; m. Mary Ellen Robitsch, Feb. 27, 1954; children: Jill Denise, James John, Christopher Bordner Student, Bergen Jr. Coll., 1947—48, U. Kans., 1946—47, student, 1949—51. Rep. B.F. Ascher & Co., Inc., Memphis, 1954-55, asst. to pres. Kansas City, Mo., 1956-57, v.p., 1958-64, pres., 1965—2001, chmn. bd., 2001—. Bd. dirs. Childrens Cardiac Ctr., 1964-70, pres., 1968-70; mem. cen. governing bd. Children's Mercy Hosp., 1968-80; bd. dirs. Jr. Achievement of Middle Am., 1970-90, pres., 1973-76, chmn., 1979-81; edn. chmn. Young Pres.'s Orgn. 6th Internat. Univ. for Pres., Athens, 1975. 1st. lt. inf., U.S. Army, 1951-53, Korea Decorated Bronze Star, Combat Infantryman's Badge Mem.: VFW, Consumer Health Care Products Assn., Am. Mgmt. Assn. (pres.'s assn.), Chief Execs. Orgn., World Pres.'s Orgn., Lenexa City C. of C., Indian Hills Country Club, Kansas City Club, Lotos Club, N.Y. Athletic Club, Mercury Club, Delta Chi. Home: 6706 Glenwood St Shawnee Mission KS 66204-1451 Office: 15501 W 109th St Lenexa KS 66219-1307

ASCHER, ROBERT, anthropologist, archaeologist, film producer, educator; b. NYC, Apr. 28, 1931; s. Alfred and Claire (Eliscue) A.; m. Marcia Alper, Mar. 10, 1956 PhD, UCLA, 1960. Prof. dept. anthropology Cornell U., Ithaca, NY, 1960—2002, emeritus prof. anthropology, 2003—, prof. dept. theatre, film and dance Grad. Sch., 1960—. Fieldwork in Turkey, Mex., Eng., Peru, U.S., Israel, 1960—. Co-author: Mathematics of the Incas, 1997; filmmaker: Cycle: An Australian Myth, 1984-86, Bar Yohai: In Celebration of a Visionary, 1987-88, Blue: A Tlingit Odyssey, 1989-91, The Golem, 1992-95; contbr. articles to profl. jours. With US Army, 1954—56. Office: Cornell Univ Dept Anthropology 726 University Ave Ithaca NY 14850-3914 Business E-Mail: ra27@cornell.edu.

ASCHERMAN, JEFFREY ALAN, plastic and reconstructive surgeon; b. Erie, Pa., Mar. 19, 1962; s. Herbert Stanley and Dorothy Rose A.; m. Corinne Fortunee Rouah, June 9, 1988; children: Jeremy, Benjamin, Jonathan, Sarah. Student, Am. U. Paris, 1983; BA, Harvard U., 1984; MD, Columbia U., 1988. Diplomate Am. Bd. Plastic Surgery. Resident in gen. surgery Columbia-Presbyn. Med. Ctr., NYC, 1988-91, rsch. fellow, 1991-92, resident in plastic surgery, 1992-94; fellow in craniofacial and pediat. plastic surgery Hôpital Necker-Enfants Malades, Paris, 1994-95; instr. clin. surgery Columbia U., NYC, 1995-97, asst. prof. surgery, 1998—2006, chief divsn. plastic surgery, 2004—, assoc. prof. clin. surgery, 2006—. Assoc. adj. N.Y. Eye and Ear Infirmary, N.Y.C., 1995-2001, adj. surg., 2001—; asst. attending physician N.Y. Presbyn. Hosp., N.Y.C., 1995—; adj. asst. prof. surgery Cornell Univ., 2002—. Patentee palatal distractor; contbr. articles to profl. jours. Active local synagogues Kehilath Jeshurun, N.Y.C., 1996—. Palatal Distraction Rsch. grantee Columbia U., 1996, Plastic Surgery Edn. Found., 1997; Cranial Ossification Rsch. grantee Columbia U., 1997; Retention Suture Rsch. grantee Columbia U., 1998; Hydroxyapatite Resin Rsch. grantee Columbia U., 1999; Cranial bone rsch. grantee, 2000, Cranial Reossification Rsch. grantee, 2001, Wound Healing Rsch. grantee, 2002, 05, Craniofacial Outcomes Study grantee, 2004, Wound Angiogenesis rsch. grantee, 2004; grantee NIH, 2005. Mem. AMA, ACS, Am. Soc. Plastic Surgeons, Am. Cleft Palate-Craniofacial Assn., Am. Soc. for Aesthetic Plastic Surgery, Am. Soc. Peripheral Nerve, Med. Soc. State N.Y., Assn. Academic Surgery, N.Y. County Med. Soc., N.Y. Regional Soc. Plastic and Reconstructive Surgery, Plastic Surgery Rsch. Coun., No. Soc. Plastic Surgeons, Alpha Omega Alpha. Republican. Avocations: downhill skiing, tennis, travel. Office: Columbia Univ Med Ctr 161 Fort Washington Ave New York NY 10032-3713 Office Phone: 212-305-9612. Business E-Mail: jaa7@columbia.edu.

ASCHHEIM, EVE MICHELE, artist, educator; b. NYC, Aug. 30, 1958; d. Emil and Lydie Aschheim. BA, U. Calif., Berkeley, 1983; MFA, U. Calif., Davis, 1987. Asst. prof. Occidental Coll., LA, 1990, Sarah Lawrence Coll., Bronxville, NY, 1994—97. Vis. critic Md. Inst. Coll. Art, Balt., 1998-2000; lectr. Princeton (N.J.) U., 1991, 93, 98, 2000, sr. lectr., 2001—, dir. visual arts program, 2003—. One-woman shows include Stefan Stux Gallery, 1997, Galerie Rainer Borgemeister, Berlin, 1999, 2001, Galleri Magnus Åklundh, Lund, Sweden, 1999, Galerie Benden and

Klimczak, Cologne, Germany, 1999, U. Mass. Gallery, Amherst, 2003, Larry Becker Contemporary Art, Phila., 2004, Eve Aschheim Guy Coirriero, Patrick Verelst Gallery, Antwerp, 2004, Lori Bookstein Fine Art, 2007; group exhbns. include Sackler Mus., Cambridge, Mass., 1997, Kunstmuseum Winterthur, Switzerland, 1998, Acad. der Künste, Berlin, 1998, Fonds régional d'art contemporain de Picardie and Mus. de Picardie Amiens, 1997, Parrish Mus., L.I., N.Y., 1999, Stark Gallery, N.Y.C., 1999, U. Calif., San Diego, 1999, Landesgalerie Oberosterreich, Linz, Austria, 1999, Pratt Gallery, N.Y.C., 1999, So. Meth. U., 2000, N.Y. Studio Sch., 2000, Hunter Coll. Leubsdorf Gallery, N.Y.C., 2000, Maier Mus., Lynchburg, Va., 2000, Tucson Art Mus., 2000, Mus. Contemporary Art, Miami, 2001, D.A.A.D. Galerie, Berlin, U. Art Mus. Calif. State U., Long Beach, 2001, Colby Coll., 2002, N.Y. Hist. Soc., 2002, O.S.P. Gallery, Boston, 2002, Black and White Gallery, Bklyn., 2003, U. Mass., Amherst, 2003, Bill Maynes Gallery, N.Y.C., 2003, Tang Mus., Saratoga, N.Y., 2004, Larry Becker Contemporary Art, Phila., 2004, Nat. Acad. Design, N.Y.C., 2004, Ins Licht Geruckt-Aus der Grafischen Sammlung, Kunstmuseum, Bonn, Germany, 2004, N.Y.-Hist. Soc., 2004, Lohin-Geduld Gallery, N.Y., 2005, The Am. Acad. Arts and Letters N.Y., Lori Bookstein Gallery, N.Y.C., 2005, Tang Mus., 2006, Pollak Gallery, Dallas; represented in permanent collections at Fogg Mus., Nat. Gallery, Washington, N.Y. Hist. Soc., Hamburger Bahnhof, Berlin, M.O.C.A., Miami, Met. Mus. Art, N.Y.C., Yale U. Art Gallery, Bonn Kunstmus., Mus. Modern Art, N.Y, Ark. Art Ctr., Pollock Gallery Meth. So. U., Dallas, Hood Mus. at Dartmouth Coll., San Diego Mus. Art, Ark. Art Ctr.; artist (catalogs) Eve Aschheim Paintings and Drawings, 1999, Eve Aschheim Drawings, 2003, Eve Aschheim Recent Work, 2005. Recipient Rosenthal award Am. Acad. Arts and Letters, 1997, Purchase prize, 2005; fellow NEA, 1989, Pollock-Krasner Found., 1990, 2001, N.Y. Found. for Arts, 1991; grantee Elizabeth Found., 1997. Mem. Am. Abstract Artists. E-mail: easchh@aol.com.

ASCHHEIM, JOSEPH, retired economist, educator; b. Hanover, Germany, May 28, 1930; s. Max and Sarah (Pfeffer) A.; married; 1 child. AB with highest honors, U. Calif., Berkeley, 1951; A.M. (Charles H. Smith scholar), Harvard U., Cambridge, Mass., 1953, PhD (Thayer scholar, Willard scholar), 1954. Mem. faculty Johns Hopkins U., 1956-63; mem. faculty George Washington U., Washington, 1963-2001, prof. emeritus, 2001. Dir. rsch., econ. advisor to gov. Ctrl. Bank Kenya, 1971-72; faculty advisor D.C. univs. consortium US Naval Res. Officers Tng. Corps Unit, 1984-2001; affiliated scholar Ctr. for Study of Ctrl. Banks, NYU Sch. of Law, 1995-2006. Author books and numerous articles in profl. jours.; editorial bd. So. Econ. Jour, 1960-63, Atlantic Econ. Jour, 1973—2005; Disting. Assoc., Internat. Atlantic Econ. Soc., 2003-. Served with AUS, 1954-56. Ford Found. Faculty Research fellow. Mem. Am. Econ. Assn., Atlantic Econ. Soc. (v.p. 1973-76), Royal Econ. Soc., Phi Beta Kappa. Jewish. Office Phone: 202-337-6777.

ASCHOFF, LAWRENCE MICHAEL (MICK ASCHOFF), computer information scientist; b. NYC, Feb. 14, 1950; s. Edward William and Marie Louise (Marshall) A. BA in Art History, U. Fla., 1971; MBA in Fin., NYU, 1984, advanced profl. cert. in computer applications and info. systems, 1988. Sales rep. VIP Fabrics, NYC, 1979—81; asst. to v.p. mktg. RAM Data, NYC, 1981—82; sales agt. Equitable Life Assurance Soc., NYC, 1982; programmer/analyst Drexel Burnham Lambert, NYC, 1984—86, sr. programmer/analyst, 1986—88, project leader, 1988—89, project mgr., asst. v.p., 1989—90; officer, project mgr. retail banking sys. Mfr.'s Hanover Trust, NYC, 1990—92; asst. v.p. retail banking Chem. Bank (merger with Mfr. Hanover Trust), NYC, 1992—95; v.p. project mgmt. competency ctr. retail banking sys. Nat. Consumer Svcs. Chase Manhattan Bank (merger with Chem.), NYC, 1996—2000; dir. GITSSO Program Mgmt. Office AXA Global I.T. Org., NYC, 2000—01; dir. program mgmt. office AXA Tech. Svcs., NYC, 2002—06, dir. global Sarbanes-Oxley coord., 2006—. Treas. Saunders Owners of Queens, Ltd., 1989-91, 2002—, pres., 1991-2000 Clin. assoc. Suicide and Crisis Prevention Ctr., Gainesville, Fla., 1972; mem. pres.'s coun. U. Fla., 1992— Mem. IEEE, Mensa, Project Mgmt. Inst. (quality program mgr. N.Y.C. chpt. 2005—), Phi Beta Kappa (sec. L.I. Alumni Assn. 1985-87, pres. 1987-93), Alpha Lambda Delta. Democrat. Avocations: travel, exercise, history, amusement parks, arts & sciences. Office: AXA Technology Svcs 1290 AV Americas 13th Fl New York NY 10104

ASEA, ALEXZANDER, research scientist; s. Solomon Bayo and Sandy Asea; m. Jacqueline Asea; children: Edwina, Vanessa, Alexzander Jr. PhD, U. Gothenburg, Sweden, 1990—95. Instr. in radiation oncology Dana-Farber Cancer Inst., Boston, Mass., 1999—2002, Harvard Med. Sch., Boston, Mass., 1999—2002; asst. prof. of medicine Boston U. Sch. of Medicine and Boston U. Med. Ctr., Boston, Mass., 2002—05; assoc. prof. of pathology and lab. medicine Tex. A&M U. Health Sci. Ctr., College Station, Tex., 2005—, Scott & White Meml. Hosp. and Clinic, Temple, Tex., 2005—. Effie and wofford cain centennial endowed chair in clin. pathology Scott & White Meml. Hosp. and Clinic, Temple, Tex., 2005—, chief, divsn. of investigative pathology, 2005—, dir., proteomics core facility, 2005—; dir. of rsch., dept. of pathology Scott & White Meml. Hopsital and Clinic, Temple, Tex., 2005—. Master: Internat. Symposium on Heat Shock Proteins in Biology and Medicine (life; chmn. 2000); mem.: Am. Assn. of Immunologists (AAI) (assoc.), AAAS (AAAS) (assoc.), Am. Assn. for Cancer Rsch. (AACR) (assoc.), North Am. Hyperthermia Soc. (assoc.), Internat. Soc. of Exercise and Immunology (assoc.), Internat. Soc. for Oncodevelopmental Biology and Medicine (assoc.). Office: Scott & White Hospital and Clinic 1901 South First Street Temple TX 76504 Office Phone: 254-743-0201. Office Fax: 254-743-0247. E-mail: asea@medicine.tamhsc.edu.

ASENSI, GUSTAVO, advertising executive, cinematographer; b. Vitoria, Spain; came to the U.S., 1992; s. Gustavo Asensi. Student, Sch. Dramatic Arts, Madrid, 1983, Sch. Cinematography, 1983. Copywriter Delvico Bates, Madrid, 1985-86, J. Walter Thompson, Madrid, 1986-87; creative dir. HDM, Madrid, 1987-89; exec. creative dir., v.p. Publinsa, Madrid, 1989-92; sr. v.p., exec. creative dir. Font & Vaamonde Advt., NYC, 1993-94, mng. ptnr., CCO, 1994—. Recipient Bronze medal Festival San Sebastian, 1990, Silver medal, 1991, Gold medal Houston Internat. Film Festival, 1995, 96, Bronze medal, 1995, Gold medal Charleston Internat. Film Festival, 1995, Grand award, 1995, Gold Clio award, 1995.

ASFAW, ABAY, economist, consultant, research scientist; b. Gonder, Ethiopia, Mar. 20, 1971; s. Fitiftie Alehegn; m. Lishan Akuma; children: Bethany, Nathaniel. BA in Econs., Addis Ababa U., Ethiopia, MSc in Human Resources Econs., 1997; PhD, U. Bonn, Germany, 2002. Lectr. Addis Ababa U., Ethiopian Civil Svc. Coll., 1996—98; jr. rschr. Ctr. Devel. Rsch., Bonn, 1999—2002, sr. rschr., 2002—04; post doctoral fellow Internat. Food Policy Rsch. Inst., Washington, 2004—. Cons. ILO, Bonn, 2004, WHO, Bonn, 2004, German Internat. Coop. Devel., Bonn, Germany, 2004, World Cancer Rsch. Fund, Washington, 2005—06. Author: (book) Costs of Illness the Demand for Medical Care and the Prospect of Community Health Insurance Schemes in Ethiopia, 2003; contbr. articles to profl. jours. Recipient Sci. award, Josef G. Knoll Found., 2002, Theodor Brinkmann prize, U. Bonn., 2003. Mem.: Ethiopian Econ. Assn., Am. Agrl. Econ. Assn. Home: 4921 Seminary Rd Apt 1110 Alexandria VA 22311 Office: 2033 K St NW Washington DC 20006

ASH, BARBARA LEE, education and human services educator; b. Boston, Sept. 2, 1940; d. Charles Edward and Helen Barbara (Elwell) Fox; m. Robert Irvin Ash, July 31, 1971 AS, Norwich U., 1960; BS, Boston U., 1962, MEd, 1966, EdD, 1982. Cert. bus. tchr., Mass. Tchr. Chatham (Mass.) Pub. Schs., 1962-63, Braintree (Mass.) Pub. Schs., 1963-66; asst. prof. Simmons Coll., Boston, 1966-73; prof., dept. chair Bunker Hill Community Coll., Charlestown, Mass., 1973-77; prof. Suffolk U., Boston, 1977—, dir. Human Resources Learning and Performance Grad. Programs, 1977—. Mem. adv. bd. Aquinas Coll., Newton, Mass., 1985—, Bunker Hill C.C., 1985—, LaSell Coll., Newton, 1985—, Mt. Ida Coll., 1985—; disting. lectr. Rider Coll., N.J., 1992. Contbr. articles to profl. jours. Recipient Suffolk U. Evening div. assoc. Outstanding Faculty Mem. award, 1991. Mem. Internat. Soc. Performance Improvement, Assn. Psychol. Type, Am. Soc. Tng. and Devel., Mass. Bus. Educators Assn. (pres. 1992-93, Tchr. of Yr. award 1990), Soc. Human Resource Mgmt., Orgnl. Devel. Network, Nat. Bus. Edn. Assn. (legis. advocacy com. 1993—), New Eng. Bus. Educators Assn. (sec. 1986, v.p. 1987, pres. 1988), Mass. Coalition Adult Edn. (bd. dirs.), N.Y. Assn. Contg. Cmty. Edn., N.E. Human Resources Assn., Phi Delta Kappa, Delta Pi Epsilon (corr. sec. Epsilon chpt. 1964, pres. 1966). Office: Suffolk U Beacon Hill Boston MA 02114 Office Phone: 617-573-8280.

ASH, DOROTHY MATTHEWS, civic worker; b. Dresden, Germany, Nov. 10, 1918; came to U.S., 1924; d. Kurt Horst and Ana Matthesius; m. Harry A. Ash, Apr. 13, 1941 (dec. June 1981); children: Fredrick Curtis, Dorothea Ash Linklater. Dancer, 1933-40; treas. Inheritance Abstractors Inc., Chgo., 1949-70; reporter Miami (Fla.) Sun Post, 1983; reporter, columnist Social Mag., Miami, 1984—. Chmn. Miss Universe Pageant, 1983-85; cruise chmn. Miami U., 1984. Pres. Big Bros. and Big Sisters, 1982-83; founding mem. World Sch. of Arts, 1985—; founding Notable Douglas Gardens 1988: Pres.'s Club U. of Miami, 1989; founding and bd. mem. Cancer Link Rsch., 1990; mem. Bd. Animal Welfare; active Project: Newborn, Am. Cancer Soc., March of Dimes, chmn. quest for the best, 1988-92, winner celebrity gourmet gala, 1988; active Children's Resource, Erase Diabetes, founding and bd. mem. 1990, Cerebral Palsy Found., Theatre Arts League, Linda Ray Infant Ctr., Miami City Ballet, Am. Ballet; bd. dirs. Greater Miami Opera, 1975—; pub. rels. vol. Miami Heart Inst., 1988—; com. mem. Miami Beach (Fla.) Beautification Program, 1984; mem. bd. Miami Mayor's Ad Hoc Com., 1984; mem. com. Challenger Seven Meml., 1988; founding mem., bd. mem. Leading Ladies, Inc., 1998—; active Cousteou Soc.; numerous others. Named Woman of Yr., Big Bros. and Big Sisters, Miami, 1981, Best Dressed, Am. Cancer Soc., 1981, Outstanding Humanitarian and Civic Leader, Mayor City of Miami, 1985, Woman of the Yr., Project: New Born, 1985, Miss Charity, Biscayne Bay Hosp., 1986, Queen of Hearts, Miami Children's Hosp., 1988, Leading Lady, March of Dimes, 1998; recipient Shining Star award Bon Secours Hosp., 1993, Patron Recognition award Mia Heart Rsch. Inst., 1993, Goddess of Love award Villa Maria Hosp., 1995, Shining Angel, 2000, Star of the Century award Miami Heart Rsch. Inst., 2000, Miracle Maker award Big Bros./Big Sisters, 2001, Salute to Dorothy Ash, Mia Heart Inst., 2002, Hero of the Heart award Mia Heart Inst., 2003, Animal Welfare honoree Mia Heart Inst., 2003. Mem. Miami Internat. Press Club. Avocations: reading, writing, painting.

ASH, FREDERICK MELVIN, retired manufacturing executive; b. Columbus, Ohio, June 15, 1941; s. Melvin Edward and Ida Belle (Berry) A.; m. Karen Persichetti, Apr. 7, 1979; children: Jason, Carrie. Student, U. Cin., 1959-61; BS, BA, Ohio State U., 1963; MBA in Mgmt., Rutgers U., 1982. Staff acct. chem. plastics divsn. Gen. Tire & Rubber Co., Akron, Ohio, 1963-65; office mgr., 1965-67; acctg. mgr. Lawrence, Mass., 1968; controller Newcomerstown, Ohio, 1968-70; Lawrence, 1971-73; plant mgr., 1974-76; v.p. film Jeannette, Pa., 1977; pres. Gen Tire & Rubber Plastic Film Co., Jeannette, 1977-78; bus. dir. plastics Tenneco Chems., Inc., Piscataway, 1978-80; gen. mgr. plastics, 1980-82; v.p., gen. mgr. plastics Nuodex, Inc., Edison, NJ, 1982-84; v.p. mkgt. and sales Am. Maize Products, 1985-89; v.p. ops., 1990-92; pres. ingredients divsn., 1993-95; pres., comml. dir. Cerestar USA, Inc., 1995-99; bd. dirs. OceanBoy Farms, Inc., 2002—05. Adv. Jr. Achievement, Akron, 1965; mem. budget com. Merrimack Valley United Fund, Lawrence, 1973-74, budget com. chmn., 1975, campaign chmn., 1976, dir., 1975-76; bd. dirs. Tradewinds Rehab Ctr., Lakeshore Devel. Coun., United Way of Westmoreland County, 1977-78, Lake Area United Way, NW Ind. Fourm, Olympia Fields/Flossmoor United Way, 1985, pres., 1986-87. U.S. Rubber scholar, 1961-63; recipient Pace Setter award Ohio State U., 1963. Mem. Nat. Assn. Accts., Soc. Plastics Industry (vice chmn. film gorup), Ind. Mfrs. Assn. (mem. bd. dirs.), Corn Refiners Assn. (bd. dirs.), Westmoreland County C. of C., Ohio State U. Alumni Assn., Rutgers U. Alumni Assn., Village 2 Homeowners Assn. (v.p.), Sea Chase Condominium Assn. (bd. dirs.), Masons, Scottish Rite, Sigma Chi, Beta Gamma Sigma. Republican. Home: 95136 Captains Way Fernandina Beach FL 32034-4386

ASH, J. MARSHALL, mathematician, educator; b. NYC, Feb. 18, 1940; s. Barney and Rosalyn (Hain) A.; m. Alison Igo, Nov. 24, 1977; children: Michael A., Garrett A., Andrew A. SB, U. Chgo., 1961, SM, 1963, PhD, 1966. Joseph Fels Ritt instr. Columbia U., NYC, 1966-69; asst. prof. math. DePaul U., Chgo., 1970-72, assoc. prof., 1972-74, prof., 1974—. Vis. prof. Stanford U., 1977. Author: Studies in Harmonic Analysis, 1976, Harmonic Analysis: Calderon-Zygmund and Beyond, 2006; co-author: (with R. Jones) Human Analysis: Colderon-Zygmund and Beyond, 2006; contbr. articles to profl. jours. George Westinghouse fellow, 1961, NSF fellow, 1962-66. Mem. AAUP, Am. Math. Soc., Math. Assn. Am., Sigma Xi. Office: De Paul U Math Dept Chicago IL 60614 Home: 2314 N Lincoln Pk W #3S Chicago IL 60614 Office Phone: 773-325-4216. Business E-Mail: mash@math.depaul.edu.

ASH, JOHN, chef; Founder John Ash & Co., Calif., 1980—; culinary dir. Fetzer Vineyards, 1990; dean Brown-Forman Ctr. for Global Wine Edn., 1999; tchr., Profl. Wine Studies Culinary Inst. Am. Greystone; founder, wine dir. Sauvignon Republic Cellars. Home chef Disney Inst., Sur La Table, Crystal Cruises, Fla. Winefest, Taste of the Nation, Telluride; spokesperson Chilean Fresh Fruit Mktg. Assn., Calif. Raisin and Prune Bd., Chinet, Muir Glen Organics, Real Calif. Cheese. Author: American Game Cooking, 1991, From the Earth to the Table: John Ash's Wine Country Cuisine, 1996 (Best Am. Cookbook, Julia Child award, Cookbook of Yr., Internat. Assn. Culinary Professionals, 1996), John Ash Cooking One-on-One: Private Lessons in Simple Contemporary Food from a Master Teacher, 2004 (James Beard award, 2005); contbr. articles Bon Appetit mag., Fine Cooking mag., Winetoday.com, Joy of Cooking, columns in newspapers LA Times Syndicate; host (TV series) John Ash, Food Network, co-host food & wine radio show, Northern Calif. Bd. overseers Chef's Collaborative; bd. adv. Seafood Watch, Monterey Bay Aquarium. Named one of America's Hot New Chef, Food & Wine Mag., 1985. Office: John Ash & Co 4330 Barnes Rd Santa Rosa CA 95403

ASH, KAREN ARTZ, lawyer; b. Bklyn., Dec. 23, 1955; d. Bernard and Helen Artz; m. David Charles Ash, June 11, 1977; 2 children. AB in Econs. with honors, Georgetown U., 1976; JD magna cum laude, N.Y. Law Sch., 1980. Bar: N.Y. 1981, U.S. Dist. Ct. (so. and ea. dists.) N.Y. 1981. Assoc. Kaye, Scholer, Fierman, Hays & Handler, NYC, 1980-83, Amster, Rothstein & Ebenstein, NYC, 1983-88, ptnr., 1988; ptnr., co-chair Intellectual Property Practice Katten Muchin Zavis Rosenman, NYC. Lectr. in field. Author: Grey Goods and What Does It Mean to You, Trademark Licensing Do's and Don'ts, Rule 60(b)(4) F.R.C.P.; research editor N.Y. Law Rev., 1980 (cert. of merit 1980); contbr. articles to profl. jours. Fundraiser Assn. for Help Retarded Children, N.Y.C., 1978—. Mem. ABA (chairperson trademark com. 1982—), Women's Bar Assn., N.Y. State Bar Assn., U.S. Trademark Assn., NOW, N.Y. Humane Soc. Democrat. Office: Katten Muchin Zavis Rosenman 575 Madison Ave New York NY 10022 Office Phone: 212-940-8554. Office Fax: 212-940-8776. E-mail: karen.ash@kmzr.com.

ASH, ROY LAWRENCE, former federal official; b. LA, Oct. 20, 1918; s. Charles K. and Fay E. (Dickinson) A.; m. Lila M. Hornbek., Nov. 13, 1943; children— Loretta Ash Danko, James, Marilyn Ash Hanna, Robert, Charles. MBA, Harvard, 1947. Chief fin. officer Hughes Aircraft Co., 1949-53; co-founder Litton Industries, Inc., Beverly Hills, Calif., 1953-72, dir., 1953-72, pres., 1961-72; chmn. Pres.'s Adv. Coun. on Exec. Orgn., 1969-71; asst. to Pres. U.S.; dir. Office Mgmt. and Budget, Washington, 1973-75; chmn. bd., chief exec. officer AM Internat., 1976-81. Co-chmn. Japan-Calif. Assn., 1965-72, 80-81; mem. vis. com. Harvard U. Kennedy Sch. Govt., 1992—; mem. Bus. Roundtable, 1977-81. Vice chmn. Los Angeles Olympic Organizing Com., 1980-85, chmn. fin. com.; trustee Calif. Inst. Tech., 1967-72, Com. for Econ. Devel., 1970-72, 75—; dir. Los Angeles World Affairs Council, 1968-72, 78— , pres., 1970-72; chmn. adv. council on gen. govt. Rep. Nat. Com., 1977-80; chmn. L.A. Music Ctr. Opera Assn., 1988-93. From pvt. to capt. Army Air Corps, 1942-46. Mem. C. of C. U.S. (bd. dirs. 1979-85, chmn. internat. policy com. 1979-85), Calif. Club, Harvard Club.

ASH, THOMAS PHILLIP, school system administrator; b. East Liverpool, Ohio, June 4, 1949; s. Bobby and Elizabeth Ann (Ludwig) A.; m. Nancy Elizabeth Gauron, June 8, 1951; children: Megan Elizabeth, John Gauron. BS in Edn., Bowling Green State U., Ohio, 1971; MS in Edn., Youngstown State U., Ohio, 1974. Tchr. East Liverpool City Schs., 1971-73, project coord., 1973-78, asst. supt., 1978-84, supt., 1984-99, Mid-Ohio Ednl. Svc. Ctr., 2000—05; dir. Buckeye Assn. Sch. Adminstrs., 2005—. Bd. dirs. CF Bank, Columbiana County Mental Health Assn.; chmn. Lincoln Way Spl. Edn. Resource Ctr., 1988-89, 93-94; treas. Richland County Youth and Family Coun., 2000-05. Exec. coun. Columbiana County coun. Boy Scouts Am., 1989-91, Morrow County Workforce Investment Bd., 2000-2005, state adv. panel for Exceptional Children 2002-2005; pres. East Liverpool Area United Way, 1990-92; mem. State Supt. Adv. Commn. for Spl. Edn., 1993-95, 2002—. Recipient Disting. Alumni award East Liverpool High Sch. Alumni Assn., 1987, Ohio Adminstr. of Yr. award Ohio Ednl. Libr. and Media Assn., 1990. Mem. Am. Assn. Sch. Adminstrs., Buckeye Assn. Sch. Adminstrs. (pres. 1999-2000), East Liverpool Area C. of C. (bd. dirs. 1985-2000, Outstanding Educator award 1982, Disting. Svc. award 1982). Office: Buckeye Assn Sch Adminstrs 8050 North High St Columbus OH 43235

ASHANTI, BARON JAMES, poet, educator; b. NYC, Sept. 5, 1950; s. Gladys Carroll Foxhall, David Lancaster Foxhall; life ptnr. Mary Beithe Chow, May 31, 1999; children: Marcus, Nova. Grad., Evander Childes H.S., Bronx, NY, 1964. Exec. asst. Marie Brown Assoc., NYC, 1987—90; tchr., adminstr. Frederick Douglass Creative Arts Ctr., NYC, 1988—98; founder, pres. The Brilliance Factory, NYC, 1990—. Tchr. Tchrs. & Writers Collaborative, NYC, 1995—99. Author: Nubiana, vol. I, 1977, Nova, 1990, numerous poems (Killeen prize, 1982). Polit. organizer Afrikan Peoples Party, Phila., 1969—80. Sgt. USMC, 1967—71, Viet Nam. Grantee, Pen Writers, 1985. Mem.: New Renaissance Writers Guild (co-founder), Black Writers Union (co-founder), Acad. Am. Poets. Avocations: archery, drawing, shaolin gung-fu, travel, photography. Business E-Mail: briliancefactory@aol.com.

ASHANTI, (ASHANTI SHEQUOIYA DOUGLAS), vocalist; b. Glen Cove, NY, Oct. 13, 1980; Trained as dancer, Bernice Johnson Cultural Arts Ctr. Launched signature fragrance Precious Jewel by Ashanti, 2005. Singer with Ja Rule (songs) Always On Time, singer with Fat Joe What's Luv?, singer with the Notorious B.I.G. Unfoolish; singer: (albums) Ashanti, 2002 (Grammy award, 2002), Foolish/Unfoolish: Reflections on Love, 2002, Ashanti: The 7 Series, 2003 (nominated 2 Grammy awards, 2003), Chapter II, 2003, Ashanti's Christmas, 2003, Concrete Rose, 2004; actor: (films) Bride & Prejudice, 2004, Coach Carter, 2005, John Tucker Must Die, 2006; (TV films) The Muppets' Wonderful Wizard of Oz, 2005; dancer Polly; guest appearances include Sabrina, the Teenage Witch, 2002, American Dreams, 2002, Buffy the Vampire Slayer, 2003, Las Vegas, 2005. Office: Murder Inc 825 8th Ave 20th Floor New York NY 10019

ASHAR, HANSRAJ G., structural engineer, nuclear regulator; s. Girdharlal R. and Diwaliben G. Ashar; m. Kusum H. Sampat, July 16, 1961; 1 child, Bimal H. B in Civil Engring., Lukhdhirji Engring. Coll., Morvi, India, 1955; MSCE, U. Mich., 1958. Registered profl. engr., Ohio, Md. Bridge design engr. Rackoff Assocs., Columbus, Ohio, 1958—61; diploma engr. Julius Berger A.G., Wiesbaden, Germany, 1962—63; sr. engr. various cos., 1963—68; sr. design engr. Burns & Roe, Oradell, NJ, 1969—74; sr. structural engr. U.S. Nuc. Regulatory Commn., Rockville, Md., 1974—. Tech. judge Montgomery Sci. Fair, Gaithersburg, Md., 1996—2001. Fellow: ASCE (award for significant contbn. to profession 1992), Am. Concrete Inst.; mem.: IAEA (spl. cons. 2000—05), Am. Inst. Steel Constrn. (nuc. spec. com. 1996—, chair 2006). Office: US Nuc Regulatory Commn 11555 Rockville Pike Rockville MD 20852 Home Phone: 410-772-0563; Office Phone: 301-415-2851. Business E-Mail: hga@nrc.gov.

ASHBAUGH, DENNIS, artist; One-man shows include Ams. Soc., NYC, 1992, Met. Mus. Art, 1992, Kitchen, 1992, Goode, Crowley Gallery, Houston, 1993, Marisa del Rey Gallery, NYC, 1993, Ralls Collection, Washington, 1993, 2003, Margulies-Taplan Gallery, Miami, Fla., 1994, Galleri Antoinina Zaru, Capri, Italy, 1998, NAS, Smithsonian, Washington, 2006, Kunst-Mus. Ahlen, Germany, 2006, Aspen Inst., Colo., 2006, Mus. Im Kulturspeicher, Wurzburg, Germany, 2006, Mus. Modern Art, NYC, 2007, exhibited in group shows at Butler Mus. Am. Art, Youngstown, Ohio, 1997, Betsy Sr. Gallery, NYC, 1998, one-man shows include Ruth Chandler Williamson Gallery, Scripps Women's Coll., Claremont, Calif., 2000, exhibited in group shows at Regina Gougar Miller Gallery, Carnegie Mellon U., Pitts., 2002, Tulane U. Woldenberg Art Ctr., New Orleans, 2003, Alyce de Roulet Williams Gallery, Art Ctr. Coll. Design, Pasadena, Calif., 2003, Ctr. Art and Visual Culture, U. Md., Balt., 2004, Represented in permanent collections Boca Raton Mus. Art, Fla., Bklyn. Mus., Crocker Nat. Bank, San Francisco, Drew U., Madison, NJ, First City Bank, Houston, First Nat. Bank Minn., Mpls., First Nat. City Bank, NYC, GE, NYC and London, Goldman Sachs, NYC, Hewlett-Packard Corp., Palo Alto, Calif., numerous others. Address: 67 Greene St Ground Fl New York NY 10012

ASHBERY, JOHN LAWRENCE, language educator, poet, playwright, art critic; b. Rochester, NY, July 28, 1927; s. Chester Frederick and Helen Ashbery. Grad., Deerfield Acad., 1945; BA, Harvard U., 1949; MA, Columbia U., 1951; postgrad., NYU, 1957—58; DLitt (hon.), Southampton Coll. of L.I.U., 1979, U. Rochester, Harvard U., Pace Univ. Copywriter Oxford U. Press, NYC, 1951—54, McGraw Hill Book Co., NYC, 1954—55; art critic European edit. N.Y. Herald Tribune, Paris, 1960—65; Paris corr. Art News, 1964—65, exec. editor NYC, 1965—72; prof. English Bklyn. Coll., 1974—90, Disting. prof., 1980—90, Disting. emeritus prof., 1990; Charles P. Stevenson Jr. prof. langs. and lit. Bard Coll., 1990—; editor quar. rev. Art and Lit., Paris, 1964—67; art critic Art Internat., Lugano, Switzerland, 1961—62; editor Locus Solus, Lans-en-Vercors, France, 1960-62; poetry editor Partisan Rev., 1976—80; art critic New York Mag., 1978—80, Newsweek, 1980—85; Charles Eliot Norton prof. poetry Harvard U., 1989—90; conducted spl. rsch. on life and work of Raymond Roussel. Author: Turandot and Other Poems, 1953, Some Trees, 1956, The Poems, 1960, The Tennis Court Oath, 1962, Rivers and Mountains, 1966, Selected Poems, 1967, Three Madrigals, 1968, Sunrise in Suburbia, 1968, Fragment, 1969, The Double Dream of Spring, 1970, The New Spirit, 1970, Three Poems, 1972, The Vermont Notebook, 1975, Self-Portrait in a Convex Mirror, 1975, Houseboat Days, 1977, As We Know, 1979, Shadow Train, 1981, A Wave, 1984, Selected Poems, 1985, April Galleons, 1987, Flow Chart, 1991, Hotel Lautrèamont, 1992, And the

Stars Were Shining, 1994, Can You Hear, Bird, 1995, Wakefulness, 1998, (plays) The Heroes, 1952, The Comprimise, 1955, The Philosopher, 1963, Three Plays, 1978, (poetry) Girls on the Run, 1999, Your Name Here, 2000, As Umbrellas Follow Rain, 2001, Chinese Whispers, 2002; author: (with James Schuyler) (novels) A Nest of Ninnies, 1969, represented in numerous anthologies; contbr. articles to periodicles;, author verse set to music. Named Lit. Lion, N.Y. Pub. Libr., 1984, Poet of Yr., Pasadena City Coll., 1984; recipient Yale Series of Younger Poets prize, 1955, Harriet Monroe Poetry award, Poetry Mag., 1963, Civic and Arts Found. prize, Union League, 1966, award, Nat. Inst. Arts and Letters, 1969, Shelley award, Poetry Soc. Am., 1973, Pulitzer prize, 1976, Nat. Book award, 1976, Nat. Book Critics Circle award, 1976, Jerome J. Shestack Poetry award, Am. Poetry Rev., 1983, Bollingen prize in poetry, Yale U. Libr., 1985, Lenore Marshall poetry prize, The Nation, 1985, Common Wealth award in lit., MLA, 1986, Creative Arts award, Brandeis U., 1989, Ruth Lilly Poetry prize, Poetry Mag. and Modern Poetry Assn. and Am. Coun. for Arts, 1992, Robert Frost medal, Poetry Soc. Am., 1995, Grand prize, Biennales Internat. Poetry, Belgium, 1996, Bingham Poetry prize, Boston Rev. Books, 1998, Walt Whitman Citation of Merit, State of N.Y., N.Y. State Writer's Inst., 2000, Medal for Achievement in the Arts, Signet Soc. Harvard U., 2001, Phi Beta Kappa Poet award, Harvard U., 1979; grantee, Poet's Found., 1960, 1964, Ingram Merrill Found., 1962, 1972; scholar Fulbright scholar, U. Montpellier, France, 1955—56, Rennes, France, 1956—57; Guggenheim fellow, 1967, 1973, Rockefeller Found. fellow, 1979—80, Wallace Stevens fellow, Yale U., 1985, McArthur Found. fellow, 1985—90. Fellow: Acad. Am. Poets (chancellor 1988—99, Wallace Stevens award 2001); mem.: Am. Acad. Arts and Scis., Am. Acad. Arts and Letters (Gold medal 1997). Address: Dept Langs and Lit Bard Coll PO Box 5000 Annandale On Hudson NY 12504-5000

ASHBURN, ROY, state senator; b. Bakersfield, Calif., Mar. 21, 1954; children: Shelley, Shannon, Stacy, Suzy. Student, Coll. of Sequoias; BA in Pub. Adminstrn., Calif. State U., Bakersfield, 1983. Owner Roy Ashburn Signs, 1969—72; field rep. Supr. LeRoy Jackson, 1972—77; dist. rep. Congressman William Thomas, 1979—83; mem. Calif. State Assembly, Sacramento, 1996—2002; mem. dist. 18 Calif. State Senate, Sacramento, 2002—. Mem. rules com. Calif. State Assembly, mem. appropriations com., vice chmn. govt. modernization com., mem. transp. and housing com., vice chmn. pub. employees and ret. com., chmn. senate select com. def. and aerospace industry. Republican. Roman Catholic. Mailing: State Capitol Rm 5094 Sacramento CA 95814 Office: 5001 California Ave Rm 105 Bakersfield CA 93309

ASHBY, DANNY S., lawyer; b. Jacksonville, Fla., Oct. 1, 1964; BA magna cum laude, U. SC, 1986; JD with highest honors, Baylor Law Sch., Waco, Tex., 1990. Bar: Tex. 1990, US Supreme Ct., US Ct. Appeals (5th and fed. dists.). Clk. to Hon. Edith H. Jones US Ct. Appeals (5th cir.); trial atty. criminal divsn. US Dept. Justice; ptnr. Hughes & Luce, LLP, Dallas. Named one of Best Lawyers in Dallas, D Mag., 2005. Mem.: 5th Cir. Bar Assn., Dallas Bar Assn., ABA, Dallas Bar Found., State Bar Tex. Office: Hughes & Luce LLP Ste 2800 1717 Main St Dallas TX 75201 Office Phone: 214-939-5745. Office Fax: 214-939-5849. E-mail: danny.ashby@hughesluce.com.*

ASHBY, EUGENE CHRISTOPHER, chemistry professor; b. New Orleans, Oct. 25, 1930; s. Anthony and Ida (Bruno) A.; m. Carolyn Turner, Sept. 13, 1952; children: Chris, Steven, Terry, Marie, Angela, Julie, Rachel. BS in Chemistry, Loyola U., New Orleans, 1951; MS in Chemistry, Auburn U., 1953; PhD in Chemistry, U. Notre Dame, 1956. Rsch. chemist Ethyl Corp., Baton Rouge, 1956-59, rsch. assoc., 1959-63; asst. prof. Ga. Inst. Tech., Atlanta, 1963-65, assoc. prof., 1965-69, prof., 1969-73, Regents prof., 1973-93, Regents prof. emeritus, 1993—. Cons. Ethyl Corp., 1980-91, Conoco, Ponca City, Okla., 1972-76, U.S. Dept. Energy, 1990-98, Ga. Dept. Edn., 1994-97, Pfizer Pharm., 1996. Contbr. over 270 articles to profl. jours. Recipient Lavoisier medal French Chem. Soc., 1971, Sigma Xi rsch. award, 1968, 75, Herty medal Am. Chem. Soc., 1983, Disting. Prof. award Ga. Inst. Tech., 1988. Avocations: tennis, cattle farming. Home: 2516 Flair Knoll Dr NE Atlanta GA 30345-1316

ASHBY, FRANKLIN CHARLES, JR., corporate financial executive, educator; b. Rockville Centre, NY, Feb. 20, 1954; s. Franklin Charles and Janet Mary (Rauscher) Ashby; m. Rita Sandra Birzkalns, June 26, 1993; 1 child, Daniel Matthew Ashby. BA, Hofstra U., 1976; MBA, N.Y. Inst. Tech., 1984; MA, Columbia U., 1987; Grad. Cert., Columbia Bus. Sch. Exec. Prog., 1987; PhD, American U., UK, 1994. V.p. & chief ed. officer Dale Carnegie & Assocs., Inc., NY, 1984—98, corporate spokesperson NY, 1996—98; pres. Manchester Training, Inc., 1998—2000; exec. v.p. Manchester Ptrns. Internat., Inc., 1998—2000; head Modis U., 1999—2000; incoming pres. The Chubb Inst., 2000; pres. The Leadership Capital Group LLC, 2000—. Dep. U.S. Marshal (WAE), 1975—80; radio talk show host, Career Clinic, 1986—87; doctoral dissertation advisor Columbia U., NYC, 2000—01, U. Southern Miss., 2002—05, U. Mo., 2002—. Author: Contemporary Approaches to Organizational Development and the Improving of Productivity, 1994, World Class, 1995, Revitalize Your Corporate Culture, 1999; author: (foreword) The Complete Idiot's Guide to Team Building, 1999, The Complete Idiot's Guide to Human Resource Management, 2002, The Complete Idiot's Guide to Managing People, 2003; co-author: Embracing Excellence, 2001, The Exponential Effect, 2006; author/editor Effective Leadership Programs, 1999. Chmn. PONSI Bus. Adv. Bd., Am. Coun. on Educ., 1990-93; Commn. on Educ. Credit and Credentials, 1993-98; co-chmn. Comn. on Corporate Development, 1997; designated world's #1 Dale Carnegie instructor, 1984-1998; executive producer, Carnegie Refresher Series, 1986-1997; acting pres., Columbia U. Alumni Asn. (L.I. Region), 1992; chmn. Long Island Colls. & Univs. Comt., 1984-86; Bd. Dirs. Manchester Partners Internat., Inc., 1998-2000, bd. dirs. Chubb Computer Svcs., 2000; Performance Resources Organization, Inc., 1998-99, Coalition for Fair Broadcasting, Inc., 1987-92, Advancement for Commerce & Industry, Inc., 1986-92, North Shore Montessori Sch., 2002-2003; tryout, New York Mets, Shea Stadium, 1976; mem. adv. coun.U. So. Miss. Workplace Learning and Performance Inst., 2004—. Lutheran. E-mail: fashby1@optonline.net.

ASHBY, JEFFREY S., astronaut; BS in Mech. Engring., U. Idaho, 1976; MS in Aviation Systems, U. Tenn., 1993; grad., Naval Test Pilot Sch., Naval Fighter Weapons Sch. Commd. ensign USN, advanced through grades to capt.; ret.; commdg. officer Strike Fighter Squadron 94; astronaut NASA, Houston, 1999; now on spl. assignment Air Force Space Command Hdqrs., Colorado Springs, Colo. Decorated DFC, 4 Navy Air medals, 2 Navy Commendation medals, Navy Achievement medal. Achievements include logged over 7,000 flight hours; 1,000 aircraft carrier landings; logged over 660 hours in space; logged over 11 million miles, flown 436 orbits around the Earth; pilot STS-93 Columbia; pilot STS-100 Endeavour; commander STS-112 Atlantis. Avocations: skiing, soaring, backpacking, fly fishing. Office: Astronaut Office/CB NASA Johnson Space Ctr Houston TX 77058

ASHBY, RICHARD JAMES, JR., bank executive, lawyer; b. Lancaster, Pa., Aug. 18, 1944; s. Richard James and Gloria Marie (Mayer) A.; m. Claire Lundberg, July 1, 1967; children: Douglas R., Elizabeth, Brian J. AB, Wittenberg U., 1966; JD, Ohio State U., 1969. Bar: Pa. 1969, Ohio 1969. Assoc. Arnold Bricker Beyer & Barnes, Lancaster, 1969-71; trust officer First Nat. Bank Strasburg (Pa.), 1971-73, v.p., 1973-78, Fulton Bank, Lancaster, 1978-80, sr. v.p., 1980-86, exec. v.p., 1986-91; chmn., pres., CEO Lafayette Bank, Easton, Pa., 1991-98; chmn, pres., CEO Fulton Bank, Lancaster, Pa., 1999—. Vice chmn. Lehigh Valley Econ. Devel. Corp., 1995-98. Author: Profitability in Community Bank Trust Department, 1977. Mem. adv. bd. Pa. Joint State Govt. Commn., Harrisburg, 1984—; mus. dir. Lancaster Red Rose Chorus, 1976—91; pres. Parish Resource Ctr., Lancaster, 1984—2002, Northampton C.C. Found., 1991—98, 1994—96, State Theatre, Easton, 1991—98, 1993—94, Easton Hosp., 1991—98; dir. Valley Health Found., 1992—99, Northampton County Devel. Corp., 1994—99, LeHigh Valley Partnership, 1993—98; commr. Manheim Twp., Lancaster County, 1988—92; bd. dirs. United Way of Lancaster County, 2002—, Fulton Opera House, 2002—, Lancaster C. of C., 1999—2002; bd. dirs., vice chmn. Two Rivers C. of C., 1993—99. Staff sgt. US Army, 1970—76. Recipient George Beneman Meml. award Ohio State U. Coll. Law, Columbus, 1969, Am. Spirit Honor medal Army & Navy Vets Aux., Ft. Ord, Calif., 1970 Mem.: Pa. Bankers Assn., Am. Bankers Assn., Lancaster Bar Assn., Pa. Bar Assn., Lancaster Country Club, Hamilton Club. Republican. Lutheran. Avocations: barbershop quartet singing, golf, fishing. Office: 1 Penn Sq Lancaster PA 17602-2853

ASHCRAFT, CAROLYN, state librarian; B in English, U. Ark., Monticello; MLS, U. Ala. Head libr. Grant County Libr., Ark.; dir. Saline County Libr., Ark.; prog. adv. ext. services Ark. State Libr., Little Rock, 1993—2004, assoc. dir. libr. devel. and services, 2004—06, state libr., 2006—. Ark. rep. Fed. State Coop. System Steering Com. Mem.: Am. Libr. Assn., Ark. Libr. Assn. (pres.). Office: Arkansas State Library 1 Capital Mall Little Rock AR 72201-1081 Office Phone: 501-682-1526. Office Fax: 501-682-1899. Business E-Mail: cashcraft@asl.lib.ar.us.*

ASHCRAFT, DAVID JOHN, secondary school music educator; s. Clarence and Jane Ashcraft; m. Joan Louise Dively, June 19, 1976; children: Christopher David, Timothy Allen. MusB, U. Ariz., Tucson, 1974, MusM, 1976, D of Music Arts, 1986. Choral dir. Sahuaro HS, Tucson, 1974—2007. Vol. Am. Cancer Soc., Tucson, 1978—; dist. com. Boy Scouts Am., Tucson, 1987—90. Recipient Ariz. Music Educator of Year award, 1988, Fine Arts Disting. Alumnus award, U. Ariz., 1993. Mem.: Music Educators Nat. Conf., Am. Choral Dirs. Assn. Avocations: camping, writing, photography, travel.

ASHCROFT, JOHN DAVID, law educator, former United States attorney general; b. Chgo., May 9, 1942; s. James Robert and Grace Pauline (Larson) Ashcroft; m. Janet Elise Roede, 1967; children: Martha, Jay, Andrew. B cum laude, Yale U., 1964; JD, U. Chgo., 1967. Bar: Mo., U.S. Supreme Ct. Asst. prof. S.W. Mo. State U., Springfield, 1967—71, assoc. prof., 1971—73; pvt. practice Springfield, 1967-73; state auditor State of Mo., 1973-75, asst. atty. gen., 1975-77, atty. gen., 1977-84, gov., 1985-92; atty. Suelthaus and Kaplan P.C., 1993-94; U.S. Senator from Mo., 1995-2001; atty. gen. US Dept. Justice, 2001—05; disting. prof., law & govt. Regent U., Virginia Beach, Va., 2005—; founder The Ashcroft Group LLC, Washington, 2005—. Mem. commerce, sci. and transp. coms., aviation subcom., comm. subcom., chmn. consumer affairs, fgn. commerce & tourism subcom., mfg. and competitiveness subcom., mem. fgn. rels. com., European affairs subcom., Near Ea. & South Asian affairs subcom., Western Hemisphere Peace Corps subcom., mem. jud. com., chmn. constitution, fedn. and property rights subcom.; mem. Presdl. Adv. Coun. Intergovtl. Affairs, The Pres.'s Export Coun.; nat. chmn. Edn. Commn. States, 1987-88, Jud. Com., Subcom., chmn. constn.; chmn. Nat. Govs. Assn. Task Force on Coll. Quality, 1985, Nat. Govs. Assn. Task Force on Adult Literacy; co-chair Renewal Alliance. Author: Lessons From a Father to His Son, 1998, Never Again: Securing America and Restoring Justice, 2006; co-author: (with Janet E. Ashcroft) College Law for Business, 7th, 8th, 9th, 10, 11th edits., It's the Law, 1979-91, (with Gary Lee Thomas) On My Honor: The Beliefs That Shape My Life, 2001; contbr. articles to profl. jours.; gospel singer (records) In the Spirit of Life and Liberty, The Gospel According to John Chmn. Task Force on Adult Literacy, Task Force on College Quality Nat. Gov.'s Assn., 1991; chmn. Rep. Gov.'s Assn., 1990; co-chmn. Rep. Platform Com., 1992. Recipient Nat. Sheriffs Assn. award, 1996; named Christian Statesman of Yr., 1996. Mem. ABA (ho. of dels.), Mo. Bar Assn., Cole County Bar Assn., Nat. Assn. Attys. Gen. (pres. 1980-81, chmn. budget com., exec. com., Wyman award 1983), Nat. Govs. Assn. (vice chmn. 1990, chmn. 1991-92, chmn. Pres.'s Commn. on Urban Families 1992). Republican. Mem. Assembly Of God Ch.*

ASHCROFT, NEIL WILLIAM, physics professor, researcher; b. London, Nov. 27, 1938; m., 1961; 2 children BSc, U. New Zealand, 1958, MSc with honors, 1960; PhD, U. Cambridge, 1964; DSc (hon.), Victoria U., Wellington, New Zealand. Sci. rsch. coun. sr. fellow Cavendish Lab. U. Cambridge, England, 1973-74, vis. fellow Clare Hall, 1973-74; assoc. theoretical physics Cornell U., Ithaca, NY, 1965-66, from asst. prof. to assoc. prof., 1966-75, prof. physics, 1975—, Horace White Chair of Physics, 1990, various adminstrv. and acad. coms., dir. Lab. of Atomic and Solid State Physics, 1979-84; dep. dir. Cornell High Energy Synchrotron Source, Ithaca, NY, 1978-97; dir. Cornell Ctr. for Materials Rsch., Ithaca, 1997-2000. Chaire municipale Joseph Fourier U., Grenoble, France, 1989-93, 2000—; sci. cons. Los Alamos Nat. Lab., 1976-94; adv. com. High Flux Beam Reactor, Brookhaven, 1984-90; sci. cons. Lawrence Livermore Nat. Lab., 1985—; chmn. Gordon Rsch. Conf. on Rsch. at High Pressure, 1986—, trustee 1988-92, chmn. bd. trustees, 1991—; liasion rep. Nat. Rsch. Coun. Rev. Panel on Materials, Am. Phys. Soc. div. of Condensed Matter Physics Physics; vis. com. Brookhaven Nat. Lab., 1986—; Gordon Godfrey vis. prof. U. New South Wales, Australia, 1988; mem. rsch. briefing panel on high temperature superconductivity NAS, adv. panel solid state div. Oak Ridge Nat. Lab.; Erskine fellow Canterbury U., New Zealand, 1990, Ehrenfest lectr. U. Leiden, The Netherlands, 1991; Faraday bicentennial lectr. Electrochem. Soc., 1991; mem. solid state scis. com. NRC, 1993-96; editl. bd. mem. Physics and Chem. of Liquids, 2003-Co-author: Solid State Physics, 1975; mem. editl. bd. Jour. of Physics, 1988-94, The Phys. Rev., 1996—, Australian Jour. of Physics, 1997—, Physics and Chemistry of Liquids, 2003—; contbr. numerous articles to profl. jours. Fellow Royal Soc. guest fellow, 1984—85, overseas fellow, Churchill Coll., Cambridge U., 1984—85, 2001—, Erskine fellow, Canterbury U., 1990; Guggenheim fellow, 1984—85. Fellow AAAS, Am. Phys. Soc., Royal Soc. New Zealand (hon.), Inst. of Physics (London); mem. NAS, Assn. Internat. pour L'Avancement de la Recherche et de la Technologie Aux Hautes Pressions (exec. com. 1995-99, Bridgman prize 2003), fellow The Inst. of Physics (London), 2004- Office: Cornell U Clark Hall Ithaca NY 14853-2501 Home Phone: 607-257-6671. Business E-Mail: nwa@cornell.edu.

ASHDOWN, FRANKLIN DONALD, physician, composer; b. Logan, Utah, May 2, 1942; s. Donald and Theresa Marie (Hill) A. BA, Tex. Tech. U., 1963; MD, U. Tex., 1967. Chief of med. Holloman Air Force Base, New Mexico, 1971-73; chief of staff Gerald Champion Mem. Hosp., Alamogordo, N.Mex., 1976, 91, 92; pvt. practice Alamogordo, 1973—; pres. Otero County Concerts Assn., Alamogordo, 1985-94, Otero County Med. Soc., Alamogordo, 1986. Cons. N.Mex. Sch. for Visually Handicapped, Alamogordo, 1973—76. Composer of more than 100 published and recorded works. Bd. dirs. Otero County Mental Health Assn., Alamogordo, 1973-77, Flickinger Found. for Performing Arts, 1995; bd. trustees Gerald Champion Meml. Hosp., 1992. Mem. Gerald Champion Mem. Hosp., N.M. Med. Soc., Am. Soc. Internal Med., ASCAP (Standard Panel award 2000, 01, 02). Republican. Office: 1301 Cuba Ave Alamogordo NM 88310-5727 Home Phone: 505-437-8807; Office Phone: 505-437-4586. E-mail: fashdown@wayfarer1.com.

ASHDOWN, MARIE MATRANGA, writer, educator, cultural organization administrator; b. Mobile, Ala. d. Dominic and Ave (Mallon) Matranga; m. Cecil Spanton Ashdown Jr., Feb. 8, 1958; children: Cecil Spanton III, Charles Coster; children by previous marriage: John Stephen Gartman, Vivian Marie Gartman. Degree, Maryville Coll. Sacred Heart, Springhill Coll. Feature artist, women's program dir. daily program Sta. WALA, WALA-TV, Mobile; v.p., dir. Met. Opera Guild, NYC, opera instr. in-svc. program, 1970-80, Marymount Coll., NYC, 1979-85; exec. dir. Musicians Emergency Fund, Inc., NYC, 1985—. Internat. adv. coun. Van Cliburn Found., 1998—; cons. No. Ill. U. Coll. Visual and Performing Arts, 1985—; lectr. in field. Author: Opera Collectables, 1979, contbr. articles to profl. jours. Recipient Extraordinary Svc. award March of Dimes, Medal of Appreciation award Harvard Bus. Sch. Club NYC, Cert. Appreciation, Kiwanis Internat., Arts Excellence award NJ State Opera, Cipario award, Albanese-Puccini award Lincoln Ctr., 2002. Mem. AAUW, Nat. Inst. Social Scis., Com. for U.S.-China Rels. Avocations: collecting art, antique porcelain, book binding. Home: 25 Sutton Pl S Apt 16K New York NY 10022-2456 Office: Musicians Emergency Fund Inc PO Box 1256 New York NY 10150-1256 Personal E-mail: dmat807@aol.com, meffndtn@aol.com.

ASHE, ARTHUR JAMES, III, chemistry professor; b. NYC, Aug. 5, 1940; s. Arthur James and Helen Louise (Hawelka) A.; m. Penelope Guerard Vaughan, Aug. 25, 1962; children: Arthur J., Christopher V. BA, Yale U., 1962, MS, 1965, PhD, 1966; postgrad., Cambridge U., 1962-63. Asst. prof. chemistry U. Mich., Ann Arbor, 1966-71, assoc. prof., 1971-76, prof., 1976—, chmn. dept., 1983-86, prof. macromolecular sci. and engring., 2000—. Vis. scientist Phys. Chemistry Inst., U. Basle, Switzerland, 1974 Mem. editorial avd. bds. profl. jours, 1984—. Alfred P. Sloan fellow, 1972-76 Mem. Am. Chem. Soc. Office: U Mich Dept Chemistry Ann Arbor MI 48109 Business E-Mail: ajashe@umich.edu.

ASHE, BERNARD FLEMMING, arbitrator, lawyer, educator; b. Balt., Mar. 8, 1936; s. Victor Joseph Ashe and Frances Cecelia (Johnson) Flemming; m. Grace Nannette Pegram, Mar. 23, 1963; children: Walter Joseph, David Bernard. BA, Howard U., 1956, JD, 1961. Bar: Va. 1961, D.C. 1963, Mich. 1964, N.Y. 1971. Tchr. Balt. Pub. Schs., 1956-58; atty. NLRB, Washington, 1961-63; asst. gen. counsel Internat. Union United Auto Workers, Detroit, 1963-71; gen. counsel N.Y. State United Tchrs., Albany, 1971-96, arbitrator, 1996—. Mem. adj. faculty Cornell Sch. Indsl. and Labor Rels., Albany div., 1981, 87, Fordham U. Law Sch., 1996-00, Roger Williams U. Law Sch., 1996-98. Contbr. articles on labor and constnl. law to profl. jours. Bd. dirs. Urban League Albany, 1979—85, 1st v.p., 1981—85; trustee N.Y. Lawyers Fund for Client Protection, 1981—, Adelphi U., Garden City, NY, 1997—2005. Recipient Nat Weinberg award, Wayne State U., Detroit, Mich., 2001. Fellow Am. Bar Found. (life), Coll. Labor and Employment Lawyers (emeritus); mem. NAACP (Thurgood Marshall Justice award 2000), ABA (chmn. sect. labor and employment law sect. 1982-83, consortium on legal svcs. and the pub. 1979-84, commn. on pub. understanding about the law 1987-91, mem. standing com. on group and prepaid legal svcs. 1996-97, ho. of dels. 1985-96, 97-2003, nominating com. 1988-91, chair drafting com., 1998-2000, bd. govs. 1991-94, exec. com. 1993-94, accreditation com. sect. legal edn. and admission to the bar 1994-98, chmn. standing com. on group and prepaid legal svcs. 1996-97, sr. lawyers divsn. coun. 1994-2000, standing com. on client protection 1998-2001, advisor commn. on judiciary in 21st century 2002-03, jour. editl. bd. 2003—), Am. Law Inst., Nat. Bar Assn., Am. Arbitration Assn. (bd. dirs. 1982-98, Whitney North Seymour Sr. medal 1989), N.Y. State Bar Assn., Albany County Bar Assn. E-mail: bfashe@verizon.net.

ASHE, DIANE DAVIS, psychology professor, sport psychology consultant; d. Trenton Gene and Barbara Kathryn Davis; m. Alan Michael Ashe, Sept. 4, 1988; 1 child, Brandon Colin. BA, East Carolina U., 1983, MA, 1985; PhD, Fla. State U., 1993. Licensed Mental Health Counselor State of Fla., 1993, Sport Psychology Consultant Assn. for the Advancement of Applied Sport Psychology, 1994. Prof. of psychology Valencia Cmty. Coll., Orlando, Fla., 1993—; psychol. specialist Fla. Dept. of Corrections, 1989—91; psychotherapist self-employed, Orlando, Fla., 1993—2005; crisis counselor Apalachee Ctr. for Human Services, Tallahassee, 1988—89; asst. academic advisor for athletics Fla. State U., 1986—88; sport psychology cons. Fla. State Basketball, 1987—89; adj. prof. Stetson U., Celebration, Fla., 2001—03, Troy State U., Orlando, 1997—99. Reviewer N.Am. Jour. Psychology. Co-author (book) Celebrity Worshippers: Inside the Minds of Stargazers, 2004; contbr. articles to profl. jours., to jours. Parent vol. Celebration Sch. PTSA, Celebration, Fla., 2001—05; vol. Celebration Found., Celebration, Fla., 2002—04; mem. Celebration Women's Club, 2002—04, Celebration Booster Club, 2001—03; vol. Fla. Dem. Party, 2004, Cmty. Presbyn. Ch., Celebration, 2002—03; pres. of Fla. chpt. East Carolina U. Alumni Assn., 1995—2000; coach Youth Soccer, Celebration, Fla., 2001—02. Recipient Excellence in Tchg. award, Nat. Inst. for Staff and Orgn. Devel., 1997, Student Choice award, Valencia C.C., 2005. Mem.: APA, Assn. for the Advancement of Applied Sport Psychology, Am. Psychol. Soc. Home: 405 Celebration Ave Celebration FL 34747 Office: Valencia Community College 1800 S Kirkman Rd Orlando FL 32611 Home Phone: 407-566-8255; Office Phone: 407-582-1617. Personal E-mail: diane.ashe@celebration.fl.us. Business E-Mail: dashe@valenciacc.edu.

ASHER, AARON, retired editor, publisher; s. Samuel and Henny (Meyer) A.; m. Linda Wofsey, Oct. 11, 1956; children— Rachel, Abigail. BA with honors, U. Chgo., 1949, MA, 1952. Mem. editorial staff Alfred A. Knopf, Inc., NYC, 1956-58; exec. editor Meridian Books, Inc., NYC, 1958-64; sr. editor Viking Press, Inc., NYC, 1964-69; dir. gen. book dept. Holt, Rinehart and Winston, Inc., NYC, 1969-74; editor in chief Macmillan Pub. Co., Inc., NYC, 1974; editor in chief, v.p. Farrar, Straus and Giroux, Inc., NYC, 1975-81; exec. editor Harper & Row, NYC, 1981-86; pub. Grove Press, NYC, 1986-89, Grove Weidenfeld, NYC, 1989-90, Aaron Asher Books, Harper Collins, NYC, 1990-93; pub. cons., editor, translator, 1993—2005. Served with AUS, 1953-55. Home and Office: 201 W 86th St New York NY 10024-3349 Personal E-mail: asher10024@hotmail.com.

ASHER, SANFORD ABRAHAM, chemist, educator; b. Landesburgh, Federal Republic of Germany, June 18, 1947; came to the US, 1949; s. Leo Dow and Pearl (Lon) A.; m. Trina Asher, 1966 (div. 1974); children: James David, Dianne Louise; m. Nancy Lee Day, June 27, 1976; 1 child, Rachel Marie. BA, U. Mo., 1971; PhD, U. Calif., Berkeley, 1977. Rsch. asst. Petrotile Corp., St. Louis, 1967-71; rsch. fellow Harvard U., Cambridge, Mass., 1977-80; prof. U. Pitts., Pitts., 1980—, dir. Materials Rsch. Ctr.; sci. founder Glucose Sensing Tech. LLC. Cons. EG&G Princeton Applied Rsch., 1986-88, Am. Cyanamid, Stamford, Conn., 1988-90, Bristol-Myers-Squibb, Princeton, NJ, 1990—, Mine Safety Applicances Co., 1992—; McElvain lectr. U. Wis., 1989; established investigator Am. Heart Assn., 1984-89. Contbr. numerous articles to profl. jours. Recipient Spectrochemical Analysis award, Am. Heart Assn., 1996, Bowen Michelson award, 2000, Lippencott award, 2002, Pitts. award, Am. Chem. Soc., 2002, Alumni award, U. Mo. Mem. AAAS, Am. Chem. Soc., Spectroscopy Soc. Pitts. (chmn. aide to edn. 1990), Coblentz Soc. (bd. dir. 1990—). Jewish. Achievements include patents in field. Office: U Pitts Dept Chemistry Pittsburgh PA 15260 Home Phone: 412-661-7557; Office Phone: 412-624-8570. E-mail: asher@pitt.edu.

ASHFAQ, RAHEELA, pathologist, educator; arrived in U.S., 1985; m. M. Hossein Saboorian; children: Nina Saboorian, Amir Saboorian. MB, BChir, Fatima Jinnah Med. Coll., Pakistan, 1976; degree (hon.), Govt. Coll., Rawalpindi, Pakistan. Diplomate Am. Bd. Pathology, 1992. Staff surg. pathologist Zale-Lipshy U. Hosp., Dallas, 1992—; dir. cytopathology Parkland Meml. Hosp., Dallas, 1993—2005; program dir. cytology fellowship U. Tex. Southwestern Med. Ctr., Dallas, 1994—, prof. pathology, 2002—; dir. oncodiagnostic lab. Parkland Health & Hosp. Sys., Dallas,

1996—. Mem. pathology rev. com. Gynecology Oncology Group, 1995—; grant reviewer Susan G. Komen Breast Cancer Found., Dallas, 2003—; jour. reviewer Obs & Gyn, Cancer, Cancer Cytopathology, Diagnostic Cytopathology, JAMA, 1998—. Founding mem. bd. trustees Breast Cancer Risk Stratification Assn., Dallas, 2003—05. Mem.: U.S. and Can. Acad. Pathology, Coll. Am. Pathologists, Am. Soc. for Clin. Pathology, Am. Soc. Cytopathology. Achievements include research in prognostic and predictive tumor markers; evaluation of new technologies in cancer diagnosis and prognosis; makers for targeted therapies. Office: UT Southwestern Medical Center at Dallas 5323 Harry Hines Blvd EE4-206 Dallas TX 75390-9073 Home Phone: 214-358-7210; Office Phone: 214-590-8897.

ASHFORD, JOHN WESSON, JR., psychiatrist, researcher; b. San Francisco, May 29, 1948; s. John Wesson and Jane Ashford; m. Joanne Tackett, Oct. 9, 1976; children: MaryJane Tackett, John Wesson III, Suzanne Smith, Curtis Burkett. BA in Biol. Scis., U. Calif., Berkeley, 1970; MD, UCLA, 1974, PhD, 1984. Diplomate Am. Bd. Psychiatry and Neurology. Tchg. asst. UCLA, 1974—75, rotating intern, 1975—76, resident in psychiatry, 1976—79, chief resident geriatric neuropsychiatry inpatient unit, 1978—79, resident, co-founder Neurobehavior Clinic, 1977—79, fellow in psychiatry, 1979—80, fellow mental health tng. program, 1980—81; assoc. prof. psychiatry, neurology Sanders-Brown Ctr. Aging, 1992—2003; sr. rsch. scientist Stanford / VA Alzheimer Ctr., VA Med. Ctr., Palo Alto, 2003—; staff psychiatrist Palo Alto VA Hosp. Mem. spkrs. bur. Janssen / Ortho-McNeil Pharm. Co.; cons. Bowles-Langley Tech., Cognitive Labs., Neurotez, Inc.; mem. editl. bd. Jour. Mental Health and Aging, 2003—05; staff psychiatryst Atascadero State Hosp., 1979; staff psychiatrist VA Med. Ctr., Martinez, Calif., 1991—92; rsch. dir. geriatric psychiatry ward Brentwood VA Hosp., 1984—85; staff psychiatrist VA Med. Ctr., Lexington, Ky., 1992—2003, dir. Memory Disorders Clinib, 1994—2003, acting chief mental health svc., 2000—01; staff psychiatrist Palo Alto Health Care Sys., 2003—; adj. lectr. dept. psychiatry UCLA, 1983—85; asst. prof. dept. psychiatry So. Ill. U., Springfield, 1985—90; assoc. prof. dept. psychiatry U. Calif., Davis, 1991—92; assoc. prof. dept. psychiatry and neurology, Sanders Brown Ctr. on Aging U. Ky., 1992—93, vice chmn. rsch. dept. psychiatry, 1992—2001. Contbr. articles to profl. jours. Mem. sci. adv. bd. No. Calif. Alzheimer Assn., 2004. Named Tchr. of Yr., So. Ill. U., 1990; recipient Outstanding Article award, Clin. Digest Series, 1993, Nat. Inst. Aging., 1993—97, Eli Lilly Pharm., 1998—2002; grantee, NPI/UCLA, 1984—85, Nat. Inst. Aging., 1987—89, R.J. Reynolds Tobacco Co., Inc., 1987—91, Miles Labs., 1993—96, Dept. Psychiatry and State Dept. Health, 1994—95, Bayer Pharm., 1994—98, DujPont Pharm., 1996—2001, SCIREX Corp., 1998—2002, Gen. Clin. Rsch. Ctr., 2002, U. Ky. Coll. Medicine, 2002—03, Ill. Dept. Pub. Health, 1987—90. Mem.: Soc. Neurosci. (pres. Sangamon chpt. 1991), Internat. Psychogeriatrics Assn. (program com. 2002—03, membership com. 2002—03), Am. Psychiat. Assn., Am. Assn. Geriatric Psychiatry (program com. 2001—03, CME com. 2002—). Office: Stanford / VA Alzheimer's Ctr 3801 Miranda Way Palo Alto CA 94304 Home Phone: 650-365-5010; Office Phone: 650-852-3287.

ASHFORD, KECIA A., voice educator, vocalist; b. Davenport, Iowa, Mar. 16, 1965; d. Charles W. Ashford and Marva K. Livengood; m. David L. Coffield, Mar. 16, 1991. MusB in Vocal Performance, U. Iowa, 1987; MusM in Vocal Performance, Baylor U., 1989; D of Musical Arts in Vocal Performance, Tex. Tech U., 2004. Grad. asst. music Baylor U., Waco, Tex., 1987—89; adj. instr. voice and dir. opera theatre Conn. Coll., New London, 1994—98; voice instr. Thames Valley Music Sch., Stonington, Conn., 1995—98; assoc. prof. voice Hardin-Simmons U., Abilene, Tex., 1998—. Voice area head Hardin-Simmons U., Abilene, 2004—; singer, artist in residence U. Iowa Ctr. for Contemporary Music; apprentice artist Des-Moines Metro Opera. Singer: (Ft. Worth Opera) Hansel and Gretel, (Muddy River Opera) Suor Angelica; singer: (soprano soloist) (Abilene Philharmonic) Mozart Mass in C minor, Bach's Cantata no.140; singer: (soloist) (recording) Vier Lezte Lieder; singer: (Midwest Chorale and Orch.) Mozart's Exultate Jubilate, de Falla's Siete Canciones for soprano and guitar. Mem.: Opera Am., Nat. Assn. Tchrs. Singing, Pi Kappa Lambda. Democrat. Avocations: historic novels, cats, antiques. Office: Hardin-Simmons Univ HSU Box 16230 Abilene TX 79698 Home Phone: 325-690-1770; Office Phone: 325-670-1421. Business E-Mail: kashford@hsutx.edu.

ASHINOFF, REID L., lawyer; b. NYC, June 6, 1949; BA summa cum laude, CUNY, 1970; JD cum laude, Harvard U., 1973. Bar: N.Y. 1974, U.S. Dist. Ct (so., ea., no. dists.) N.Y. 1974, U.S. Ct. Appeals (2d and 3d cirs.) 1974, D.C. 1978. Chief legis. asst. Office U.S. Senator, Washington, 1976-78; ptnr. Sonnenschein Nath & Rosenthal, NYC, 1990—. Nat. coordinating counsel, chief trial counsel Prudential Ins. Co., 1995—2003; chaired Class Action Litig. Summit, 2003; faculty mem. ALI/ABA Inst.'s. Mem. (bd. dir.) Tourette Syndrome Assn., NYC. Recipient leading trial lawyer, Chambers USA, 2005. Mem. ABA, Assn. of Bar NYC, DC Bar Assn., Phi Beta Kappa. Office: Sonnenschein Nath & Rosenthal 1221 Ave Of Americas Fl 24 New York NY 10020-1001 Office Phone: 212-768-6730. Office Fax: 212-768-6800. Business E-Mail: rashinoff@sonnenschein.com.

ASHKENAZY, VLADIMIR DAVIDOVICH, concert pianist, conductor; b. Gorky, Russia, July 6, 1937; arrived in Eng., 1963; s. David and Evstolia (Plotnova) A.; m. Thorunn Johannsdottir, Feb. 25, 1961; children: Vladimir Stefan, Nadia Liza, Dimitri Thor, Sonia Edda, Alexandra Inga. Student, Cen. Music Sch., Moscow, Moscow Conservatory; studies with, Sumbatyan, Lev Oborin. Condr., music dir. Royal Philharm. Orch., London, 1987-95; prin. guest conductor Cleve. Orch., 1987-94; music dir. Deutsches Symphonie Orchester (formerly Radio Symphony Orch.), Berlin, 1989-99, Czech Philharm. Orch., 1998—2003, European Union Youth Orch., 2001—, NHK Symphony Orch., Tokyo, 2004. London debut, 1963, London Symphony Orch. under George Hurst, later solo recital, Festival Hall, 1963, recs., concerts throughout world. Music dir. Czech Philharm. Orch., Prague, 1998-2003, European Union Youth Orch., 2002, NHK Symphony Orch., Tokyo, 2004-. Co-recipient Tchaikovsky Piano Competition award, Moscow, 1962; recipient 2d prize, Internat. Chopin Competition, Warsaw, 1955, Gold medal, Queen Elizabeth Internat. Piano Competition, Brussels, 1956, Grammy awards, 1973, 1978, 1981, 1985, 1987, 1999. Office: care Harrison/Parrott Ltd 12 Penzance Pl London W11 4PA England Office Phone: 44207 229 9166. Business E-Mail: jasper.parrott@harrisonparrott.co.uk.

ASHKIN, RAJASPERI MALIAPEN, marketing executive; b. Penang, Malaysia, Mar. 1, 1956; came to U.S., 1984; d. Maliapen A.M.N. (Annasamy) and Jayaletchemi (Chelliah) M.; m. Ronald Evan Ashkin, Nov. 25, 1984; 1 child, Jacqueline Ariel. BS in Forestry, U. Canterbury, 1978, DBA, 1979. Mktg. asst. Forest Rsch. Inst., Rotorua, Nw Zealand, 1978-79; mktg. officer Consulate Gen. India, Sydney, Australia, 1980-81; nat. mktg. coord. Estee Lauder Ltd., Sydney, 1981-84; assoc. buyer Brown Store Group, Terre Haute, Ind., 1984-85; mktg. mgr. A.T.C. Time Inc., Terre Haute, Ind., 1985-87; v.p. New Concepts Inc., Terre Haute, Ind., 1987-90; chief exec. officer, mng. dir. Excelsior Corp., Terre Haute, Ind., 1990—, also bd. dirs. Mktg. & advt. cons. in field; organizer Christmas Food Drive Salvation Army, Terre Haute, 1985-86; vol. reader Vigo County Pub. Libr. Literacy Program, 1989—. Mktg. com. Leadership Terre Haute, 1986-87; TV moderator Valley Point of View, Terre Haute, 1986—; bd. dirs. YWCA, Terre Haute, 1986—; internat. rels. chairperson Altrusa Club, Terre Haute, 1985-87; cake bake chairperson, on site rep. Century Club, YWCA, 1986; cmty. vol. Am. Embassy, Sarajevo, 1999, cmty. vol. and fundraiser, Internat. Sch. Bucharest, Romania, 2000, Artizanats of Pristina, Kosovo, 2001; fundraiser, Women for Women, Pristina, 2001-02; vol. Internat. Women's Club, Sarajevo, 1999, Almaty Woman's Club, 2002-05, PTA Miras Sch. Kazakhstan, PTA Jakarta Internat. Sch. Indonesia, Toastmasters, Jakarta Indonesia, 2006-07. Recipient Letter of Commendation Ralph Davidson Time Inc., 1986, Nat. System Mktg. award A.T.C. Time Inc., 1986, Grand Prize HBO Summer Sales Campaign, 1986, Letter of Commendation Disney Channel, 1986, Outstanding Creative Contbrn. award, 1987, Tempo TV award, 1987; named to Scholastic Honor Soc. Pamarista Ind. State U., 1989, Literacy Grante Internat. Network for Women. Mem. NAFE, India Assn. Terre Haute, United Hebrew Congregation Terre Haute, Country Club of Terre Haute, M.V.P. Club Larry Bird, Altrusa Club of Terre Haute, YWCA, Leadership Terre Haute. Avocations: travel, gardening, music, fine arts, skiing.

ASHKIN, RONALD EVAN, international executive; b. New Rochelle, NY, Apr. 5, 1957; s. Abraham and Arleen (Wollins) A.; m. Rajasperi Maliapen, Nov. 25, 1984; 1 child, Jacqueline Ariel. AB magna cum laude, Harvard U., 1977; MBA, Wharton Sch., U. Pa., 1982; postgrad., Harvard U., 1993-96. Cert. fin. planner. V.p. Continental Chem. Corp., Terre Haute, Ind., 1978-83, pres., 1983-86, New Concepts Inc., Terre Haute, 1987-90, Excelsior Corp., Terre Haute, 1990-92; dir. internat. sales Gold Eagle Co., Chgo., 1992-95, v.p. internat., 1995-97; dir. cons. The Recovery Group, Boston, 1998—2002, USAID Bus. Cons., Sarajevo, Bosnia, 1998-99, World Bank Pvt. Sector Adjustment Loan Program, Bucharest, Romania, 2000-01; chief of party U.S. AID Kosovo Bus. Support, Pristina, Serbia and Montenegro, 2001—02, U.S. AID Enterprise Devel. Project Ctrl. Asia, Almaty, Kazakhstan, 2003—05, The Pragma Corp., 2003—05, Devel. Alternatives, Inc., 2005—, U.S. AID Senada Indonesia Competitiveness Program, Jakarta, Indonesia, 2005—. Adj. faculty Sch. Bus., Ind. State U., 1991-92. Moderator TV show, Terre Haute, 1985-86; author weekly econs. editl. column Kahoditore newspaper, Pristina, 2001-02. Mem. Terre Haute sch. adv. com., 1984-86; bd. dirs. Glenn Civic Ctr., Terre Haute, 1985-88; mem. mktg. edn. curriculum study com. Ind. Dept. Edn. Group study exch. grantee Rotary Found., Sri Lanka and India, 1985-86; Harvard U. scholar, 1973-76; recipient Ill. Gov.'s Export award, 1995, 96. Mem. Leadership Terre Haute Alumni Assn. (chmn. 1986), Am. Prodn. and Inventory Control Soc. (local v.p. 1982-84, 86, local pres. 1985), Overseas Automotive coun., Automotive Exporters Coun. (v.p. 1994—, pres. 1995-98), Jr. Achievement (vol. cons.), Toastmasters (local v.p. 1981-82), Phi Beta Kappa. Avocations: music, outdoor recreation, travel. Home: 1526 Justin Ln Farmington MO 63640

ASHLER, PHILIP FREDERIC, international trade and development advisor; b. NYC, Oct. 15, 1914; s. Phillip and Charlotte (Barth) Ashler; m. Jane Porter, Mar. 4, 1942 (dec. 1968); children: Phillip Frederic, Robert Porter, Richard Harrison; m. Elise Barrett Duvall, June 21, 1969; stepchildren: Richard Edward Duvall, Jeffries Harding Duvall. BBA cum laude, St. Johns Coll., 1935; MBA, Harvard U., 1937; grad., Indsl. Coll. Armed Forces, 1956; ScD, Fla. Inst. Tech., 1969; LLD (hon.), U. West Fla., 1969; postgrad., U. Oxford, Eng., 1988, 89, 91. Enlisted USMCR, 1932; commd. ensign USN, 1938, advanced through grades to rear adm., 1959; served in D-Day at Normandy Invasion of France, Iwo Jima landings and Korea; dir. Office Small Bus., Dept. Def., Washington, 1948-49; mem. joint staff Joint Chiefs Staff, 1957-59; ret., 1959; dir. devel. Pensacola Jr. Coll., 1960-68; vice chancellor adminstrn. State Univ. System Fla., 1968-70, exec. vice chancellor, 1970-75; treas., ins. commr., fire marshal State of Fla., 1975-76, sec. of commerce, 1977-79; pres. Philip F. Ashler & Assos., Tallahassee, 1979—; chmn. bd. Cambridge Community Care, Inc., Tallahassee, 1981-86, Circle Seven Internat., Tampa, 1988-91. Mem. Fla. Edn. Coun., 1967—68; commr. Fla. Edn. Commn. States, 1967—68; mem. US Dept. Commerce Dist. Export Coun., 1978—92; chmn. bd. dirs. Fla. Internat. Vol. Corps., 1988—90, chmn. emeritus, 2004—; legis. adv. coun. So. Regional Edn. Bd., 1966—68; mem. Fla. Bd. Ind. Colls. and Univs., 1971—75, adv. coun. mil. edn., 1980—85; bd. adv. Ctr. Profl. Devel. Fla. State U., 1988—96; chmn. Fla. Civil Def. Adv. Coun., 1966—69; mem. Fla. Coun. Internat. Devel., 1973—92, vice chmn., 1979—80, chmn., 1980—82, chmn. emeritus, 1990—; mem. Select Coun. Post HS Edn., 1967—68; chmn. Fla. Med. Liability Ins. Commn., 1975—76, Fla. Task Force Auto and Workers Compensation, 1975—76; mem. Yugoslavia Adv. Coun., 1976—87, InterAm. Congress Psychology, Bogota, Colombia, 1974, NATO Advanced Sci. Inst., 1973; guest lectr. U. Belgrade, 1973; adv. econ. devel. to gov. Fla., 1977—78; mission leader Japan/S.E. US Assn., Tokyo, 1977; trustee Fla. Coun. Econ. Edn., 1979—81; svcs. policy adv. com. Office US Trade Rep. Exec. Office of Pres., Washington, 1980—85; mem. Republic of China/USA Econ. Coun., 1979—92. Chmn. bd. dirs. Fla. Heart Assn., 1969—71; bd. dirs., treas. Internat. Cardiology Found.; bd. dirs. Tallahassee Meml. Hosp., Easter Seal Soc., 1963—68; bd. dirs., mem. exec. com. Am. Heart Assn., 1971—77, Internat. Cardiology Fedn., Geneva, 1975—77; founding chmn. Tallahassee Symphony Orch., 1981—82; trustee So. Ctr. Internat. Studies, Atlanta, 1988—91; mem. adv. bd. Fla./China Inst., Miami, Fla., Fla./Japan Inst., Tampa, Fla./Brazil Inst.; mem. Fla. Ho. of Reps., 1963—68; lic. lay eucharistic min. Episc. Ch. Decorated Bronze Star with combat IV; recipient Korean Presdl. citation, French Medill du Jubile, Internat. Disting. Svc. award, Kiwanis Internat., 1965, Legis. award, St. Petersburg Times, 1967, Disting. Svc. award, Am. Heart Assn., 1965, 1971, Disting. Achievement award, 1975, Disting. Floridian award for Life Achievement, 2005. Mem.: S.E. US/Korea Econ. Coop. Coun. (bd. dirs.), Internat. C. of C. (US coun. 1979—87), Nat. Assn. Ins. Commrs. (vice chmn. exec. com. 1976), Fla. Med. Malpractice Joint Underwriting Assn. (chmn. bd. govs. 1975—76), US S.E./Japan Assn. (chmn. 1981—83), Econ. Club Fla. (chmn. 1987—90, chmn. emeritus 1991—), Govs. Club (bd. govs. 1989—93, v.p. fin. 1992—93, bd. govs. 1994—96, treas. 1996), Capital Tiger Bay Club (chmn. bd. dirs.), Rotary, Shriners, Masons (32 degree), Kappa Delta. also: 11 Riad Sultan Kasbah Tangier Morocco Home: 4169 Diplomacy Cir Tallahassee FL 32308

ASHLEY, CHRISTOPHER, performing company executive; BA, Yale U., 1984. Artistic dir. La Jolla Playhouse, Calif., 2007—. Dir.: (Broadway plays) Voices in the Dark, 1999, The Rocky Horror Picture Show, 2000, The Smell of the Kill, 2002, All Shook Up, 2005, The 24 Hours Plays, 2005, Xanadu, 2007; (plays) Das Barbecu, Fires in the Mirror, The White Rose, The Night Hank Williams Died, Buzzsaw Berkeley, Eve's Diary/Story of the Tiger, A Breath of Fresh Air, Miss Ever's Boys, Lips Together, Teeth Apart, Haikin, The Cocktail Hour, Story of the Tiger at Los Angeles Theatre Company, Nine Armenians, I Hate Hamlet, The Naked Truth, Blown Sideways Through Life, Jeffrey (OBIE award outstanding dir., Village Voice, Lucille Lortel award outstanding dir.), Sweeney Todd, Merrily We Roll Along; (films) Jeffrey, 1995, Last Call, 2007. Office: La Jolla Playhouse PO Box 12039 La Jolla CA 92039*

ASHLEY, DAVID B., academic administrator, engineering educator; BS, MIT, 1973, MS in Project Mgmt., 1974; MS in Engring., Stanford U., 1975, PhD in Construction Engring. and Mgmt., 1977. Tchr. Engring. Mgmt. Program U. Santa Clara, 1976—77; spl. studies analyst Guy F. Atkinson Co., San Francisco, 1975—77; asst. prof. civil engring. MIT, 1977—81, assoc. prof., 1981—82, rschr. Grad. Construction Engring. and Project Mgmt. Program; assoc. prof. civil engring. U. Tex., Austin, 1982—88, prof., 1988—89, assoc. chmn. Civil Engring. Dept., 1988—89; prof. civil engring. U. Calif., Berkeley, 1989—97, chair Civil and Environ. Engring. Dept., 1993—97; dean Coll. Engring. Ohio State U., 1997—2001; exec. vice chancellor, provost, Shaffer-George Chair in Engring. U. Calif., Merced, 2001—06; pres. U. Nev., Las Vegas, 2006—. Vis. faculty Danish Tech. U., Lyngby, Denmark, 1982, U. Stellenbosch, South Africa, 1984, South Africa, 85, Chalmers Tech. U., Gothenburg, Sweden, 1984, Royal Swedish Inst. Tech., Stockholm, 1985, Cath. U. of Chile, Santiago, 1988; vis. lectr. Nanyang Tech. U., Singapore, 1990—2002. Contbr. articles to profl. jours. Mem.: Am. Soc. Civil Engrs. (Peurifoy Construction Rsch. Award 2004), Nat. Acad. Engring., Am. Soc. Engring. Edn. (Construction Mgmt. Award 1992). Office: U Nev / Office of Pres 4505 Maryland Parkway Box 451001 Las Vegas NV 89154-1001 Office Phone: 702-895-3201.

ASHLEY, DWAYNE, not-for-profit fundraiser; BA cum laude, Wiley Coll., Marshall, Tex.; MA in Govtl. Adminstrn., U. Pa.; LLD (hon.), U. DC, 2001. Nat. exec. dir., CEO 100 Black Men of Am., Inc.; devel. dir. United Negro Coll. Fund; campaign mgr. United Way; exec. dir. Thurgood Marshall Scholarship Fund, NYC, 1998—99, pres., 1999—, CEO. Co-author (with Juan Williams): I'll Find a Way or Make One, 2004. Named one of 100 Most Influential Black Ams., Ebony mag., 2005, 2006; named to The Ebony Power 150, 2007. Mem.: Phi Beta Sigma (life African-Am. Image award 2003). Office: Thurgood Marshall Scholarship Fund 80 Maiden Ln Ste 2204 New York NY 10038 Office Phone: 212-573-8492. Office Fax: 212-573-8497. Business E-Mail: dashley@tmsf.org.*

ASHLEY, ELIZABETH, assistant dean, educator; b. Waycross, Ga., July 8, 1943; d. James Bryant and Henrietta (Hargreaves) Lewis; m. Rhett Ashley, Sept. 9, 1973 (div. July 1977); m. Stefan Mellin, June 21, 1978 (div. Feb. 1986). AA Stephens Coll., 1963; BA, U. Fla., 1965; MS, Fla. State U., 1969; MA, Ariz. State U., 1975. Cataloging libr. Columbia U., N.Y.C., 1967; circulation libr. Fla. State U., Tallahassee, 1968-69; acquisitions libr. Ariz. State U., Tempe, 1969-76, No. Ariz. U., Flagstaff, 1977-78; approval libr. Baker & Taylor Co., Somerville, N.J., 1979-80; dir. tech. svcs. Golden Gate Sem., Mill Valley, Calif., 1981-87; dir. tech. svcs. Windward C.C., Kaneohe, Hawaii, 1988-2004, prof. humanities, 1995—, acting asst. dean of instrn., 2004—. Author: A Midsummer Madness, 1979, Abraham Steele, 1981, The Skull, 1982, Getting Rich, 2003; actor (theatre) Mardi Gras Follies, 1999—, Dee Dee West in Follies, 2003. Founder, exec. dir. Friends of Trees Soc., 1983—; co-founder, chmn. Menehune Lane Co., 1989-2000. Mem. ALA, Hawaii Libr. Assn., Phi Theta Kappa, Phi Kappa Phi, Beta Phi Mu. Office: Windward Community Coll 45-720 Keaahala Rd Kaneohe HI 96744-3528 Home Phone: 808-237-8028. Business E-Mail: ashleyel@hawaii.edu.

ASHLEY, KATHLEEN LABONIS, elementary school educator; d. Edward Francis and Modesta Bubnis Labonis; m. Richard Raymond Ashley, Nov. 24, 1984; children: Christopher, Lisa. B in music edn., Immaculata Coll., 1979; M in edn., Temple U., 1984. Cert. instrnl. II Pa. Secondary tchr. St. Basil Acad., Jenkintown, Pa., 1979—88; elem. tchr. St. Martin of Tours Dept. of Performing Arts, Phila., 1980—82; pre-sch. tchr. The Curiosity Shoppe, Doylestown, Pa., 1990—96; elem. tchr. Our Lady of Mt. Carmel, Doylestown, 1995—2000, St. Jude Sch., Chalfont, Pa., 1997—. Performing arts camp tchr. Brown Bag Arts Festival, Doylestown, Pa., 1991—96; ch. musician, performer St. Jude, Chalfont, Pa., 1997—. Composer: (songs) St. Jude School Song, 1997; arranger: instrumental music, 1979—; co-author: Pre-sch. and Elem. Sch. shows, 1990—2003. Steering com. for mid. states evaluation St. Basil Acad., Jenkintown, Pa., 1985; tchr. St. Jude Sch., Chalfont, Pa., 1994—. Scholar, Immaculata U., 1975—79. Mem.: Pa. Music Educators Assn., Nat. Cath. Educators Assn., Music Educators Nat. Conf. Avocations: drawing, painting, gardening, writing. Office: St Jude Sch 323 W Butler Ave Chalfont PA 18914 Office Phone: 215-822-9225.

ASHLEY, LYNN, social sciences educator, consultant; b. Rock Island, Ill., Nov. 18, 1920; d. Francis Ford and Cleo Marguerite (Monahan) Haynes; m. Edward Messenger Ashley, Aug. 16, 1946; children: Edward Jr., Ann Rice, Rebecca Pocisk, William. BS in Social Psychology, Union Inst., Cin., 1978; MEd., U. Cin., 1979, EdD, 1985. Clk. Lumberman's Mutual Casualty Co., Chgo., 1940-41; account asst. Quaker Oats Co., Chgo., 1941-43; riveter Douglas Aircraft Co., Chgo., 1943-44; organizer, dir. Forest Park Youth Ctr., Forest Park, Ohio, 1967-73; staffing coord. Presbytery of Cin., 1973-78; grad. tchg. asst. U. Cin., 1978-84; pres. Nat. Corrective Tng. Inst., Cin., 1979—. Cons., trainer Hamilton County Probation Dept., Warren County Juvenile Ct., 1987—, Allen County Juvenile Ct., Worth Ctr., Allen County; adj. faculty Union Inst., 1986—, mem. undergrad. studies bd., mem. doctoral dissertation com. Spkr., adv. women vets. to schs. and orgns.; organizer cmty. rels. coun. City of Forest Park, 1983; mem. Cin.-Harare, Zimbabwe Sister Cities Assn., 1989—, Ohio Gov.'s Adv. Com. on Women Vets., 1993—99; field rep. Women in Mil. Svc. for Am. Found.; mem. ROTC oversight com. U. Cin., 2005—06; councilwoman City of Forest Park, 1981—85. With WAC, 1943—46, maj. ret. USAF. Recipient in Recognition award Forest Park City Coun., 1985, In Appreciation award Union Inst., 1987, Recognition award AMVETS, U. Cin., 1993, award Commonwealth of Ky., 1989, recognition WWII Vet Cin. Warbirds; inducted into Ohio Vets. Hall of Fame, 1999. Mem. Am. Corrections Assn., Nat. Assn. Corrective Tng. Affiliates (pres. 1987), Women's Army Corp Vet. Assn. (selected rep. to dedication of Dole Inst. Politics, Internat. Conf. on WWII D-Day Mus., New Orleans), Assn. Family and Conciliation Cts., Am. Probation and Parole Assn. Avocations: photography, travel, computers, camping, fishing. Office: Nat Corrective Tng Inst 811 Hanson Dr Cincinnati OH 45240-1921 Office Phone: 513-825-9206.

ASHLEY, RICHARD W., pharmaceutical executive; B in Polit. Sci., Northwestern U., MBA; JD, U. Wis. Head global leadership and orgn. practice McKinsey and Co., mng. ptnr. Chgo., sr. dir.; exec. v.p. corp. devel. Abbott Labs., 2004—. Mem. exec. com. of bd. dirs. Jr. Achievement Chgo. Mem.: ABA, Wis. Bar Assn. Office: Abbott Labs 100 Abbott Park Rd Abbott Park IL 60064-6400 Office Phone: 847-937-6100.*

ASHLEY, STEPHEN B., finance company executive; b. Mar. 1940; m. Janice Ashley; 3 children. BS, Cornell U., 1962, MBA, 1964. Chmn., CEO Sibley Mortgage Corp. (formerly Sibley Corp.), Rochester, NY, 1975—95, The Ashley Group, Rochester, NY, 1997—; non-exec. chmn. Fannie Mae, Washington, 2004—. Mem. bd. dirs. The Genesee Corp., 1987—, Fannie Mae, 1995—, Exeter Fund, Inc. Mem.: Mortgage Bankers Assn. Am. (pres. elect 1992—93, pres. 1993—94). Achievements include established with wife Janice, the Stephen B. & Janice Ashley Grad. Fellowship in the Coll of Agrl. & Life Sciences, 1991. Office: The Ashley Group 600 Powers Bldg 16 W Main St Rochester NY 14614 also: Fannie Mae 3900 Wisconsin Ave NW Washington DC 20016

ASHLEY, WILLARD WALDEN C., SR., minister; b. NYC, Nov. 16, 1953; s. Will and Clara (Peterkin) Ashley; m. Veronica Lamb, June 1975 (div. Sept. 1976); 1 child, Willard W.C. Ashley Jr.; m. Diane Theresa Manning, Sept. 29, 1979 (div. June 21, 2001). AAS in Fashion Buying and Mktg., Fashion Inst. Tech., 1974; BA, Montclair State Coll., 1981; MDiv, Andover Newton Sch. Theol., 1984, D of Ministry in Leadership Devel., 1992; cert. in Marriage and Family Therapy, Blanton Peale Grad. Inst., 2000, cert. in Psychotherapy, 2000. Ordained to ministry Am. Bapt. Ch., 1982. Seminarian First Bapt. Ch., Tewksbury, Mass., 1981—82; pastor New Hope Bapt. Ch., Portsmouth, NH, 1982—84; asst. dean students, dir. recruitment Andover Newton Theol. Sch., Newton, Mass., 1984—86; pastor Monumental Bapt. Ch., Jersey City, 1986—96; founder Abundant Joy Bapt. Ch., Jersey City, 1996—; resident pastoral psychotherapy Blanton-Peale Counseling Ctr., NYC, 1996—2000; chmn. Abundant Joy Cmty. Devel. Corp., 1999—; COO Norwood Securities Cons., Columbia, Md., 2001—04; cons., 2005—. Mem. Am. Bapt. Statement of Concerns Com., 1988—90; co-chmn. Interfaith Cmty. Orgn., Jersey City, 2004—, mem. strategy team, 1988—95; strategy team Indsl. Areas Found., Nat. Leaders Team, 1991—92; assoc. prof. NY Theol. Sem., 1992—2001, prof. Blanton Peale pastoral studies program, 1999—2001; assoc. prof. Drew Theol. Sem., 1995—98, Auburn Sem., 1998—99; dir. exec. svcs. Haris & Rothenberg Internat., 1999—2002; coord. pastoral care Barnert Hosp.,

Paterson, NJ, 1994—97; psychotherapist Montclair Counseling Ctr., Upper Montclair, NJ, 1998—2002; staff psychotherapist Riverside Ch., NYC, 2000—; program dir. care for the care giver interfaith project Coun. Churches of City of N.Y., 2002—; lectr. U. Amsterdam, 2003; spritiual support team mem. US Dept. Health and Human Svcs., 2006—; creator We Save Lives Program, 2007; dir. pastoral care dept. Coun. Chs. City NY, 2007—. Preacher: (weekly radio program) Sta. WNJR, Hillside, NJ., 1987-92, Black Entertainment TV, 1992; contbr. Men of Color Study Bible, 2002. Bd. dirs. Vis. Homemakers of Hudson, Jersey City, 1988-93, YMCA of Jersey City, 1989-93, Christ Hosp., Jersey City, 2006-, Disaster Chaplaincy Svcs., NY, 2006—; bd. regents St. Peter's Coll., 1995-99; chmn. NJ Convocation, Christian Disciples of Christ, 2004-07; trustee Canterbury Health Svcs. Corp., 2006—. Recipient Montclair State Coll. award, 1981, H. Otherman Smith Preaching award, 1984, Citation, Phi Delta Kapppa, 1989, Appreciation award, Alpha Kappa Alpha, 1990, Humanitarian award, NCCJ, Matthew Turner award for Environ. Justice, Jersey City Branch NAACP, 2004. Mem. Am. Assn. Pastoral Counselors, Am. Group Psychotherapists Assn., Am. Assn. Marriage and Family Therapists, Clin. Pastoral Edn., Ministers Coun. Am. Bapt. Ch., Blanton Peale Alumni Assn. (pres. 2002-04), North NJ Missionary Bapt. Assn., Black Psychiatrists of Greater NY, Anti-Racism Alliance of Greater NY. Baptist. Avocations: basketball, baseball, weightlifting. Home: 7000 Boulevard E # 48F Guttenberg NJ 07093 Office: 475 Riverside Dr Ste 727 New York NY 10115 also: Abundant Joy Community Church 137 Bowers St Jersey City NJ 07307 Office Phone: 201-795-0200. Business E-Mail: wwca@aol.com.

ASHMUS, KEITH ALLEN, lawyer; b. Cleve., Aug. 19, 1949; s. Richard A. and Rita (Petti) A.; m. Marie Sachiko Matsuoka, Dec. 15, 1973; children: Emmy Marie, Christopher Todd. BA in Policy Sci., Mich. State U., 1971, MA in Econs., 1972; JD, Yale U., 1974. Bar: Ohio 1974, Calif. 1991, US Dist. Ct. (no. dist.) Ohio 1975, US Dist. Ct. (no., so. and ctrl. dists.) Calif. 1991, US Dist. Ct. (so. dist.) Ohio 2000, US Ct. Appeals (6th cir.) 1975, US Ct. Appeals (11th cir.) 2005, US Supreme Ct. 1980. Assoc. Thompson Hine & Flory LLP, Cleve., 1974-82, ptnr., 1982—2000, ptnr.-in-charge Cleve. office, 1996-99, dept. chmn., 1999-2000; founding ptnr. Frantz Ward LLP, Cleve., 2000—. Mediator/arbitrator Am. Arbitration Assn. Comml. Employment Panels, 1995—, Nat. Complex Case Panel, 2007-; mem. employment panel CPR Internat. Inst. Conflict Prevention and Resolution, 2006-. Co-author: Public Sector Collective Bargaining: The Ohio System, 1984. Trustee cmty. arts Baycrafters, Bay Village, Ohio, 1981-84, Hospice Coun. No. Ohio, 1982-84, Inst. for Personal Health Skills, Cleve. 1985-90, Coun. Smaller Enterprises, 1990-96, 98—, 1st vice chmn., 2000-01, chmn., 2001-03, Village Found., 1997—, pres. 2005-07; Vocat. Guidance Svcs. 1999-02, Youth Opportunities Unlimited, 2000-04, Cleve. Saves, 2001—, Greater Cleve. Partnership, 2004—, exec. com., 2006—; sec. George W. Codrington Charitable Found., 1994-2000; chmn. job placement for older persons Skills Available, Cleve., 1980-87; gov.'s appointee to Health Care Quality Adv. Coun., 1996; mem. adv. bd. Greater Cleve. Salvation Army, 1997—, treas., 2000-01, vice chmn., 2001-04, chmn. 2004-06; exec. com. Fund Econ. Future, 2004—07, funders com., 2004-07. Named one of Outstanding Vols. award Nat. Hospice Orgn., 1982, Vol. of Yr. Vocat. Guidance and Rehab. Services, 1985, 86.; recipient Others award, Salvation Army, 2007. Fellow Am. Bar. Found., Ohio State Bar found. (bd. dirs. 2002—); mem. State Bar Calif., Ohio State Bar Assn. (coun. dels. 1995—, bd. govs. 1998-01, pres. 2003-04), Cleve. Bar Assn. (trustee 1985-88, 98-2001, chmn. labor law sect. 1983-84), ABA (ho. delegates 2004—); Def. Rsch. Inst., Pub. Sector Labor Rels. Assn. (exec. com. 1989-93), Am. Arbitration Assn. (chmn. comml. adv. panel 2004-05), Yale Law Alumni Assn. (mem. exec. coun. 2003—), Nat. Small Bus. Assn. (bd. dirs. 2001—, vice chair advocacy 2005-07, treas. 2007—). Avocations: golf, fishing. Office: Frantz Ward LLP 127 Public Sq 2500 Key Ctr Cleveland OH 44114-1230 Home Phone: 440-835-3393; Office Phone: 216-515-1660. Business E-Mail: kashmus@frantzward.com.

ASHTON, BETSY FINLEY, artist, broadcast journalist, author, lecturer; b. Wilkes-Barre, Pa., May 13, 1944; d. Charles Leonard Hancock Jones and Margaretta Betty (Hart) Jones Layton; m. Arthur Benner Ashton, Nov. 5, 1966 (div. 1972); m. Robert Clarke Freed, May 18, 1974 (div. 1981); m. Jacob B. Underhill III, Oct. 17, 1987 (div. 2007). BA, Am. U., 1966; postgrad., Corcoran Sch. Art, 1968; postgrad. in fine arts, Am. U., 1969-71; student in painting, Corcoran Sch. Art, 1968; student, Nat. Acad. Sch. Fine Arts, 2007—. Tchr. art Fairfax County Pub. Schs., Va., 1967—70; reporter, anchor Sta. WWDC, Washington, 1972—73, Sta. WMAL-AM-FM, Washington, 1973—75; corr. Sta. WTTG-TV, Washington, 1975—76, Sta. WJLA-TV, Washington, 1976—82; consumer corr. CBS News and Sta. WCBS-TV, NYC, 1982—86; sr. corr. Today's Bus., 1986—87; contbr. personal fin. CBS Morning Program, 1967, Lifetime Cable TV, 1988—; anchor FNN Money Talk, 1989; exec. editor, producer Great Giving, 2000—06. Bd. dirs. Lowell E. Mellett Fund Free Responsible Press, Washington, 1979-82; courtroom artist, Washington, 1978-81; portrait painter, 2007-. Reporter TV news report Caffeine, 1981 (AAUW award 1982); reporter spot news 6 P.M. News, 1979 (Emmy award); author: Betsy Ashton's Guide to Living on Your Own, 1988; artist, 10th Annual Juried Student Show, Nat. Acad. Mus. and Katzen Gallery, Wash. DC, 2007. Concert master ceremonies Beethoven Soc., Washington, 1979-82. Recipient Laurel award Columbia Journalism Rev., 1984, Outstanding Alumna award Am. U., 1985, Outstanding Media award Am. U., 1986, Best Consumer Journalism citation Nat. Press Club, 1983. Mem. AFTRA, NATAS, Author's Guild, Portrait Soc. Am., Newswomen's Club NY, Soc. Profl. Journalists (pres. NY chpt. 1994, 2000, Washington chpt. 1980-81, bd. dirs. NY chpt., co-chair 2004 nat. conv.), Friends of Thirteen (bd. dirs.), Kenyon Review (trustee, 2004-), Sigma Delta Chi Found. (bd. dirs., v.p. bd. 2004-07), Alpha Chi Omega (v.p. chpt. 1964-66). Episcopalian. Avocations: painting, drawing, golf.

ASHTON, DAWNE BELINDA, retired secondary school educator; b. Chgo., Sept. 15, 1940; d. Arthur Elmer Albach and Ruth Evelyn Christensen Albach; m. Harold Edward Ashton (div.); children: Andrea Gabriela, Alexandra Kristi. BS, Brigham Young U., Provo, Utah, 1962; A of Interior Design, John F. Kennedy U., Orinda, Calif., 1983. Cert. tchr. gen. secondary edn. Calif., in Spanish US Nat. Bd., 2003. Tchr. art, biology Pittsburg Sr. H.S., Calif., 1962—63; vol. US Peace Corps, Santiago, Chile, 1963—65; tchr. art Sequoia Union H.S. Dist., Redwood City, Calif., 1966—68, tchr. art, Spanish, 1970—83, tchr. Spanish, 1985—2005; tchr. art San Dieguito Union H.S. Dist., Cardiff-by-the-Sea, 1969—70; ret., 2006; active vol. US Peace Corps, China, 2007—. Site dir. Calif. Fgn. Lang. Project, Stanford, 1994—98; cons. tchr., peer assistance & rev. Sequoia Union H.S. Dist., 2000—04; Fulbright-Hayes travel study leader, Chile, 2000; instr. English as fgn. lang., China. Author: (booklet) Mentor Teachers & Their Careers, 1993, Fulbrighters Abroad, 2000. Steering com. Stanford U. Edn. Collaborative, Calif., 1992—96; univ. instr. English as fgn. lang. US Peace Corps, China, 2007—. Fellow, Rockefeller Found., Spain, 1986; grantee, Fulbright-Hayes, Argentina, Ecuador, 1988, NEH, Washington, 1994, Fulbright Tchr. Exchange, Chile, 1998—99. Mem.: Nat. Peace Corps Assn., Calif. Tchrs. Assn., Calif. Lang. Tchrs. Assn. Democrat. Mem. Lds Ch. Home: 10343 N Morgan Blvd Cedar Hills UT 84062 Personal E-mail: dashton3@hotmail.com.

ASHTON, DORE, writer, educator; b. Newark; d. Ralph N. and Sylvia (Ashton) Shapiro; m. Adja Yunkers, July 8, 1952 (dec. 1983); children— Alexandra Louise, Marina Svietlana; m. Matti Megged, 1985 (dec. 2003). BA, U. Wis., 1949; MA, Harvard U., 1950; PhD (hon.), Moore Coll., 1975, Hamline U., 1982, Minn. Coll. of Art, 2002. Asso. editor Art Digest, 1951-54; asso. critic N.Y. Times, 1955-60; lectr. Pratt Inst., 1962-63; head humanities dept. (Sch. Visual Arts), 1965-68; prof. Cooper Union, 1968—. Art critic, lectr., dir. exhbns. in arts; mem. Dedalus Found. Author: Abstract Art Before Columbus, 1957, Poets and the Past, 1959, Philip Guston, 1960, The Unknown Shore, 1962, Rauschenberg's Dante, 1964, Modern American Sculpture, 1968, Richard Lindner, 1969, A Reading of Modern Art, 1970, Pol Bury, 1971, Cultural Guide for New York, 1972, Picasso on Art, 1972, The New York School: A Cultural Reckoning, 1973, A Joseph Cornell Album, 1974, Yes, But, A Critical Biography of Philip Guston, 1976, A Fable of Modern Art, 1980, American Art Since 1945, 1982, About Rothko, 1983, Jacobo Borges, 1984, 20th Century Artists on Art, 1985, Out of the Whirlwind, 1987, Fragonard in the Universe of Painting, 1988, Terence La Noue, 1992, Noguchi East and West, 1992, Ursula van Rydingsvard, 1995, Gunther Gerzso, 1995, The Delicate Thread: Teshigahara's Life in Art, 1997, À Rebours: La Rebellión Informalista, 1999, The Black Rainbow: The Work of Fernando de Szyszlo, 2003, The Walls of the Heart: The Work of David Rankin, 2001, William Tucker, 2001, Bonevardi: Chasing Shadows, 2007, also monographs; co-author (with Denise Browne Hare): Rosa Bonheur, A Life and Legend, 1981; editor: The Writings of Robert Motherwell, 2007; co-editor: Redon, Moreau, Bresdin, 1961, The Writings of Robert Matherwell, 2007; assoc. editor Arts, 1974—92, NY contbg. editor Studio Internat., 1961—74, Opus Internat., 1968—74, XXième Siècle, 1955—70, The Brooklyn Rail, 2004—, contbr. to Vision and Value series (Gyorgy Kepes), 1966, The New Art Anthology (Gregory Battcock), 1966. Adv. bd. Guggenheim Found. Recipient Mather award for art criticism Coll. Art Assn., 1963, Art Criticism prize St. Louis Art Mus., 1988; Guggenheim fellow, 1964; Graham fellow, 1963; Ford Found. fellow, 1960; Nat. Endowment for Humanities grantee, 1980 Mem. Internat. Assn. Art Critics, Phi Beta Kappa. Home: 217 E 11th St New York NY 10003-7302 Office: Cooper Union Advancement Sci and Art 41 Cooper Sq New York NY 10003-7136 Office Phone: 212-353-4273.

ASHTON, HARRIS JOHN, lawyer; b. Elizabeth, NJ, June 21, 1932; s. Earle S. and Dorothy (Black) A.; m. Angela Murphy, Oct. 20, 1962; children: Kelly Elizabeth, Victoria Catherine. BA, Yale U., 1954; LLB, Columbia U., 1959. Bar: NY 1960. Assoc. Breed, Abbott & Morgan, 1959-62, Lovejoy, Wasson, Lundgren & Huppuch, 1962-64; partner Lovejoy, Wasson, Lundgren & Ashton, 1964-75, of counsel, 1975-81; pres., chief adminstrv. officer Gen. Host Corp., 1967-69, chmn., pres., chief exec. officer, 1970-97. Bd. dirs. Bar-S Foods Co., of 43 Franklin Templeton Group of Funds. Emeritus mem., former bd. dir. Madison Square Boys and Girls Club; trustee Greenwich Acad., 1977-81, Miss Porter's Sch., 1981-85; emeritus mem., trustee United Cerebral Palsy Rsch. and Ednl. Found., Inc.; emeritus mem., mem. bd. visitors Columbia U. Sch. Law, 1982—2003, Yale New Haven Hosp., 1990-95; bd. overseers Inst. for Civil Justice, 1999, 2002. Mem. Yale Club (NYC), Blind Brook Club, Cypress Point Club, Bohemian Club.

ASHTON, MARK RANDOLPH, lawyer; b. Abington, Pa., Sept. 10, 1955; s. Frank E. and Charlotte (Wagenbaur) A. BA in Internat. Affairs, George Washington U., 1977; JD, John Marshall U., 1980. Bar: Pa. 1980. Law clk. to Hon. Mason Avrigian Ct. of Common Pleas of Montgomery County, Norristown, Pa., 1980-81; assoc. Abrahams & Loewenstein, Norristown, 1982-87; dept. chmn. Riley, Riper, Hollin & Colagreco, 1987-90; ptnr. Fox, Rothschild, O'Brien & Frankel, Exton, Pa., 1990—. Mem. Pa. Bar Assn. (dir. family law sect. 2003), Montgomery Bar Assn. (bd. dirs. 1985-87), Chester County Bar Assn. (chmn. family law sect. 1988-90), Historic Yellow Springs (dir. 2004-05), Wissahickon Valley Hist. Soc. (former pres.), D.J. Freed Am. Inn of Ct. (former pres.). Republican. Episcopalian. Home: 413 Stratford Ave Collegeville PA 19426-2553 Office: Fox Rothschild O'Brien & Frankel 747 Constitution Dr Ste 100 Exton PA 19341-1149 Home Phone: 610-513-5231; Office Phone: 610-458-4942. Business E-Mail: mashton@foxrothschild.com.

ASHTON, RICK JAMES, retired librarian; b. Middletown, Ohio, Sept. 18, 1945; s. Ralph James and Lydia Marie (Thornbery) A.; m. Marcia K. Zuroweste, Dec. 23, 1966; children: Jonathan Paul, David Andrew. AB, Harvard U., 1967; MA, Northwestern U., 1969, PhD, 1973; MA, U. Chgo., 1976. Instr., asst. prof. history Northwestern U., Evanston, Ill., 1972-74; curator local and family history Newberry Libr., Chgo., 1974-77; asst. dir. Allen County Pub. Libr., Ft. Wayne, Ind., 1977-80, dir., 1980-85; city libr. Denver Pub. Libr., 1985—2006; ret., 2006. Mem. Ind. Coop Libr. Svcs. Authority, 1980-85, pres., 1984-85; cons. NEH, Nat. Ctr. Edn. Stats., Northwestern U. Office Estate Planning, Snowbird Leadership Inst., Houston Pub. Libr.; adj. faculty Dominican U., 2006—. Author: The Life of Henry Ruiter, 1742-1819, 1974, The Genealogy Beginner's Manual: A New Edition, 1977, Stuntz, Fuller, Kennard and Cheadle Ancestors, 1987 (with others) Trends in Urban Library Management, 1989, Intelligent Library Buildings, 1999. Bd. dirs. Cmty. Coordinated Child Care, Evanston, 1972-74, Three Rivers Montessori Sch., Ft. Wayne, 1977-80; bd. dirs., sec. Allen County-Ft. Wayne Hist. Soc., 1977-83; trustee Iliff Sch. Theology, 2000-06; conscientious objector. Recipient Old City Hall Hist. Svc. award, 1985, Phil Milstein award Denver AIA, 1998; NDEA fellow, 1967-69, Downtown Denver award, 1996, 97, Bonfils-Stanton Found. award in arts and humanities, 2003; Woodrow Wilson fellow, 1971-72. Mem. ALA, Colo. Libr. Assn. (Libr. of Yr. 2000), Colo. Alliance Rsch. Librs. (pres. 1987-88, sec. 1993-95, chmn. 1995-2000), Urban Librs. Coun., Cactus Club. Home: 217 S Jackson St A Denver CO 80209-3132 Home Phone: 303-322-9261; Office Phone: 303-322-9261. Personal E-mail: rickashton20@msn.com.

ASHTON, THOMAS WALSH, investment banker; b. Rochester, NY, May 11, 1929; s. Charles Edward and Marie Margaret (Walsh) A.; m. Frances E. Hickey, May 16, 1953 (div. 1977); children: Lucy M. Van Atta, Mary B. Ashton Anders, Monica H., William T; m. Mary K Joy, Dec. 20, 1978 (dec. 1997); m. Carolyn B. Richardson, Jan. 26, 2002. BS, U.S. Mil. Acad., 1952; MBA, Harvard U., 1957. Assoc. corp. fin. Eastman Dillon Union Securities, NYC, 1957-61, gen. ptnr., 1967-69; asst. v.p. Harris Upham & Co., NYC, 1961-67; v.p. duPont Glore Forgan, Inc., NYC, 1971-73; sr. v.p. ABD Securities Corp., NYC, 1973-75; fin. cons. Am. Cancer Soc. of N.Y.C., East West Group Inc. Chmn. Peninsular Investments, Treasure Island, Fla., 1977-87; cons. Dept. Commerce, 1971; chmn. Ashton Investments, Inc., 1987—. Chmn. parents's coun. Smith Coll., 1974-76. With AUS, 1946-48, 52-55. Mem. Soc. Harvard Engrs. and Scientists (gov. 1974-75), West Point Soc. N.Y. (dir. 1971-75), Army and Navy Club (Washington), Ponte Vedra Inn and Club. Republican. E-mail: tashton749@aol.com.

ASHWORTH, BESSIE, benefits compensation analyst, writer; d. John Henry and Vivian Kennedy; m. Joe T. Ashworth, May 5, 1973; 1 child, Robert F. Kennedy. A in Bus. Adminstrn., Strayer U., 1992. Sr. adminstrv. asst. ANA, Washington, 1983—99; benefits asst. George Wash. U., Washington, 2005—. Founder, pres. Woman Thou Are Called Ministry, Washington, 2001—. Author: (book) Stagnated Christian, Special Special Woman Thou Art Called. Supporter So. Poverty Law Ctr., Montgomery, Ala., 2005—06; elder Jericho City of Praise, 2004. Democrat. Avocations: swimming, travel, writing, sports. Home Phone: 202-561-0415. E-mail: bashworth1@verizon.net.

ASHWORTH, BRENT FERRIN, lawyer; b. Albany, Calif., Jan. 8, 1949; s. Dell Shepherd and Bette Jean (Brailsford) Ashworth; m. Charlene Mills, Dec. 16, 1970; children: Amy, John, Matthew, Samuel(dec.) , Adam, David, Emily, Luke, Benjamin. BA, Brigham Young U., 1972; JD, U. Utah, 1975. Bar: Utah 1977. Asst. county atty. Carbon County, Price, Utah, 1975-76; assoc. atty. Frandsen & Keller, Price, Utah, 1976-77; v.p. legal affairs, sec., gen. counsel Nature's Sunshine Products, Provo, Utah, 1977—2003; v.p., gen. counsel Neways Internat., Springivlle, Utah, 2003—04; pvt. practice, 2004—05; ptnr. Ashworth & Sandberg, Provo, 2005—. Bd. dirs., gen. counsel Carbon County Nursing Home, Price, 1976—77; active Provo Landmarks Commn., 1997—, co-chair sesquicentennial com., 1998—99, chmn., 2002—05; active Provo Libr. Bd., 2000—06, chmn., 2003—04, Utah County Cancer Crusade Com., 1981—83, Provo LCOC Arts subcom., 1998—99; pres. Desert Village Spani Fork, Utah, 1988—90; gen. counsel Brigham Young Acad. Found., 1995—2001; founder, chmn. George E. Freestone Boy Scout Mus., Provo, 2000—; exec. bd. Utah Nat. Pk. coun. Boy Scouts Am., 2000—; city councilman, planning commn. Payson City, Utah, 1980—82, mayor pro tem, 1982; bd. dirs. ARC, Utah County chpt., 1988—94, Springville Mus. Art, 1998—2001, Celebration Health Found., 1999—, Provo Sch. Dist. Found., 2001—03; bd. mem. Am. Heritage Sch., Am. Fork, Utah, 2002—05. Recipient Silver Beaver award, Boy Scouts Am., 2006. Mem.: ATLA, SAR (pres. Utah County chpt. 1989—90, state chpts. 1st v.p. 1990—91, state soc. pres. 1991—92, chancellor 1992—94), ABA, Am. Corp. Counsel Assn. (sec. intermountain chpt. 1990—91), Utah State Bar Assn., Southeastern Utah Bar Assn. (sec. 1977), Sons Utah Pioneers, Emily Dickinson Soc. Utah (pres. 1995—97), Kiwanis Club (v.p. 1995—96, pres. 1997—98, lt. gov. Utah Idaho dist. 2001—02), Phi Eta Sigma, Phi Kappa Phi. Home: 1377 Cambridge Ct Provo UT 84604-4178 Office: Ashworth & Sandberg c/o B Ashworth's Inc 127 W Center St Provo UT 84601 Personal E-mail: bashworths@hotmail.com.

ASHWORTH, JULIE, elementary school educator; Tchr. Hawthorne Elem. Sch., Sioux Falls, SD, 1990—. Participant Internat. Space Camp, Huntsville, Ala., 1993; S.D. tchr. participant Goals 2000 Forum, U.S. Dept. Edn., Washington, 1993; mem. S.D. Gov.'s Adv. Coun. on Cert. for Tchrs., 1994—; mem. exceptional needs standards com. Nat. Bd. for Profl. Tchg. Stds., Washington, 1994—; initiator, organizer S.D. Tchrs. Forum, 1994. Named S.D. Tchr. of Yr., Sioux Falls Sch. Dist., 1992, S.D. Elem. Tchr. of Yr., 1993. Home: 2015 Pendar Ln Sioux Falls SD 57105-3022 Office: Hawthorne Elem Sch 601 N Spring Ave Sioux Falls SD 57104-2721

ASHWORTH, KENNETH HAYDEN, public information administrator; b. Abilene, Tex., Feb. 24, 1932; s. Harold Laverne and Mae Beatrice (Grote) A.; m. Emily Yaung; children: Rodney Brian, Karen Grace. BA, U. Tex., 1958, PhD, 1969; M. Pub. Adminstrn., Syracuse U., 1959. Asst. commr. Tex. Higher Edn. Coordinating Bd., Austin, 1965-69, commr. higher edn., 1976-97; vice chancellor for acad. affairs U. Tex. System, Austin, 1969-73; exec. v.p. U. Tex. at San Antonio, 1973-76. Vis. prof. govt. and pub. affairs U. Tex., Austin, 1997—, Tex. A &M U., College Sta., 1997—. Author: Scholars and Statesmen, 1972, American Higher Education in Decline, 1979, (with Norman Hackerman) Conversations on the Uses of Science and Technology, 1996, Caught Between the Dog and the Fireplug or How to Survive Public Service, 2001. Served with USN, 1951-55. Mem. Philos. Soc. Tex., Phi Beta Kappa, Phi Delta Kappa, Phi Kappa Phi, Pi Sigma Alpha. Clubs: Town and Gown. Democrat. Unitarian Universalist. Home: 7616 Rustling Rd Austin TX 78731-1365 Office: U Tex LBJ Sch Pub Affairs PO Box Y Austin TX 78713-8925 also: Tex A&M U Bush Sch Govt And Pub Svc College Station TX 77843-0001 Home Phone: 512-345-9521; Office Phone: 512-232-4019.

ASHWORTH, RONALD BROUGHTON, health facility executive, accountant; b. San Francisco, Apr. 19, 1945; s. Robert William and Tracy Marie (Parks) A.; m. Carol Lynn Heaps, Oct. 2, 1970; 1 dau., Christina Ann. B.B.A., U. Mo.-Columbia, 1967, M.A., 1968. C.P.A., Mo., N.C., Ill., La. With Peat Marwick Mitchell & Co., 1968-91 , ptnr., 1975-91 , in charge St. Louis Office health care practice, 1975-77, nat. dir. health care practice, 1978-91 , Chgo., 1979-91, exec. v.p., COO, Sisters of Mercy Health System, 1991-99, pres., CEO, 1999-. Bd. dirs. Chgo. Lung Assn., Mid-Am. chpt. ARC. Recipient Haskins and Sells award, 1967; Fin. Execs. Inst. award, 1967; Alpha Kappa Psi scholar, 1967. Mem. Healthcare Fin. Mgmt. Assn., Am. Inst. C.P.A.s, Fedn. Am. Hosps., Am. Hosp. Assn., Ill. Soc. C.P.A.s. Clubs: Tavern, Medinah Country, Country Club of Mo. Office: Sisters of Mercy Health System 14528 S Outer Forty Chesterfield MO 63017

ASIABANPOUR, BAHRAM, engineering educator; arrived in U.S., 1999; PhD in Indsl. Engring., U. So. Calif., LA, 2003. Computer-aided design and mfg. engr. Automotive Industry Rsch. and Innovation Ctr., Tehran, 1997—99; rsch. asst. U. of So. Calif., LA, 1999—2003; asst. prof. of mfg. engring. Tex. State U., San Marcos, 2003—. Author: (book chpt.) Rapid Prototyping: Theory and Practice; contbr. scientific papers to profl. jours. Recipient Highly Commended award, Emrald Publ. Literati Club, 2004, Best Paper award, Iran's 6th Indsl. Engring. Conf., 1999, Rsch. and Tchg. assistantship, U. of So. Calif., 1999—2003. Mem.: Inst. of Indsl. Engrs., Soc. of Mfg. Engrs. Home Phone: 512-665-4617. Office Fax: 512-245-3052; Home Fax: 512-245-3052. Personal E-mail: asiabanpour@yahoo.com.

ASIKA-ENAHORO, CHIDI MAUREEN, rehabilitation services professional, consultant, writer; d. Anthony Ukpabi and Gloria Nwamaka Asika; m. Victor Maurice Enahoro, May 20, 1991; children: Tara Peaches Enahoro, Ritchie Anthony Enahoro. BA, Quinnipiac U., Hamden, Conn., 1983; MA, U. New Haven, West Haven, Conn., 1985; PhD in Progress, Fla. Bible Christian and Theol. Sem., Deerfeild Beach, Fla., 2004. Cert. rehab. counselor Nat. Rehab. Assn., 1996; sr. disability analyst Am. Bd. Disability Analysts, 1998. Mental health counselor State Fla., Miami, 1987—89, rehab. cons., trainer, 1989—95; owner, CEO New Alternatives, Inc, Miami, Fla., 1996—2004; owner, dir. Neighborhood Anchor, Miami, 1998—2002; owner, exec. dir. Taritch, Inc, Miami, 2000—02; co-owner, exec. dir. Taritch Internat. Corp, Miramar, Fla., 2004—. Contract mgr., trainer State Fla., Miami, 1995—99; spkr. in field. Author: (self help book) A Slice of Africa, Innocence Interrupted, Till Cheating Do Us Part; internet radio talk show host Love and Balance with Chidi Asika-Enahoro. Mem.: Fla. Rehab. Assn. (pres., recruiting dir. 1996, Leadership award 1996), Ameriacn Bd. Disability Assocs. Conservative. Roman Catholic. Avocations: reading, dance, theater, travel, horseback riding. Office: Taritch Internat Corp 18455 Miramar Pwy #149 Miramar FL 33029 Home Phone: 954-394-6633; Office Phone: 954-394-6633. Office Fax: 954-443-9259; Home Fax: 954-443-9259. Personal E-mail: misschidi@aol.com. Business E-Mail: taritch@aol.com.

ASIMAKAKIS, PANAGIOTA, mathematics educator; b. Carlisle, Pa., July 12, 1976; d. Andreas and Georgia Asimakakis. BS (hon.), Shippensburg U., 2004. Cert. math. and secondary edn. Pa. Math. tchr. Carlisle H.S., 2004—. Tchr. Greek lang., Chambersburg, Pa., 2004. Mem.: Kappa Mu Epsilon. Office: Carlisle H S W Penn St Carlisle PA 17013 Office Phone: 717-240-6800. E-mail: carlisleschools.org.

ASIMOV, ERIC, wine critic; b. 1959; BA, Wesleyan U., 1980; graduate work, U. Texas, Austin, 1982—83. Editor Chgo. Sun-Times, 1983—84; copy editor NY Times, 1984—89, dep. editor, The Living Section, 1989—91, editor, The Living Section, 1991—94, editor, Styles of the Times, 1994—95, Style columnist, 1995—2004, chief wine critic, 2004—. Columnist $25 and Under restaurant reviews, 1992—; To Go columnist; Tastings columnist, 1999—; The Wine Panel host, 1999—. Host A.M. Restaurant Report, WQXR-FM; author: $25 and Under: A Guide to the Best Inexpensive Restaurants in New York, 1995—98; co-author: NY Times Guide to Restaurants, 2004. Office: NY Times Dining Sect 229 W 43rd St New York NY 10036 Office Phone: 212-556-4220. Office Fax: 212-556-1481. E-mail: asimov@nytimes.com.

ASIMOW, PAUL D., geophysicist, educator; AB summa cum laude in Geol. Scis., Harvard U., 1991; MS in Geology, Calif. Inst. Tech., Pasadena, 1993, PhD in Geology, 1997. Postdoctoral rsch. fellow Columbia U. Lamont-Doherty Earth Obs., Palisades, NY, 1997—99; asst. prof. geology and geochemistry Calif. Inst. Tech., Pasadena, 1999—2005, assoc. prof. geology and geochemistry, 2005—. Contbr. articles to sci. jours. Recipient CAREER award, NSF, 2003—; grantee Alfred P. Sloan Found. fellowship, 2003—05. Mem.: AAAS, Mineral. Soc. Am., Geochemical Soc. (F. W. Clarke medal 2003), Am. Geophys. Union (James B. Macelwane medal 2005). Office: Divsn Geol and Planetary Scis Calif Inst Tech Mail Code 170-25 Pasadena CA 91125 Office Phone: 626-395-4133. Office Fax: 626-568-0935. E-mail: asimow@gps.caltech.edu.*

ASIRVATHAM, ANGELA LILY, science educator; d. Arthur Samuel and Jothi Suthanthra Asirvatham; m. Jay Richard Stine, Mar. 10, 2005. DVM, Madras Vet. Coll., Chennai, India, 1992; MS, U. Wyo., Laramie, 1994; PhD, Kent State U., Ohio, 1999. Postdoctoral fellow Oreg. Health & Scis. U., Portland, 2000—07; asst. prof. Coll. Misericordia, Dallas, Pa., 2003—. Mem.: AAAS. Office Phone: 570-674-6378.

ASKANAS, MARK S., lawyer; b. 1960; m. Aynah V. Askanas. BA, U. Calif., Berkeley, 1982; JD, U. Calif., Davis, 1985. Bar: Calif. 1986. Assoc. Jackson, Lewis, Schnitzler & Krupman, San Francisco, 1988—93, ptnr., 1993—2001; sr. v.p. human resources, gen. counsel Ross Stores Inc., Pleasanton, Calif., 2001—. Office: Ross Stores Inc 4440 Rosewood Dr Bldg 4 Pleasanton CA 94588-3050*

ASKENASE, PHILIP WILLIAM, medicine and pathology educator; b. Bklyn., June 7, 1939; s. Irving and Hilda Askenase; m. Marjorie Dopkin, June 21, 1967; children: Hilary, Isabel. BA in Physics magna cum laude, Brown U., 1961; MD cum laude, Yale U., 1965. Diplomate Am. Bd. Internal Medicine, Am. Bd. Allergy and Immunology. Intern, asst. resident in medicine Boston City Hosp., 1965-67; clin. assoc. arthritis and rheumatism sect. Nat. Inst. Arthritis and Metabolic Disease, NIH, 1957-59; Brit. Am. Heart fellow of Am. Heart Assn., London Hosp. Med. Coll., 1969-70; postdoctoral trainee in inflammatory diseases Yale U. Sch. Medicine, New Haven, 1970-71, asst. prof. medicine, 1971-75, assoc. prof., 1975-82, assoc. prof. pathology, 1981-82, prof. medicine and pathology, 1982—, chief sect. clin. immunology dept. medicine, 1985—. Attending physician Yale-New Haven Hosp., 1971—, West Haven (Conn.) VA Hosp., 1971—; vis. scientist immunoparasitology div. Nat. Inst. Med. Rsch., London, 1977-78; lectr. biology Yale U., 1981—, vis. prof. molecular immunology unit, 1991; hon. rsch. fellow tumor immunology unit dept. zoology Univ. Coll., London, 1984-85; mem. Yale Comprehensive Cancer Ctr., 1987—; ad hoc reviewer numerous med. jours; vis. prof., Woods Hole, Mass., 1980-84; mem. U.S.-Israel Binat. Sci. Found., 1982—, Med. Rsch. Coun. Can., NSF, Netherlands Cancer Found., Wellcome Truste, London, Med. Rsch. Coun., London, Can. Med. Rsch. Coun.; mem. adv. bd. spl. program in tropical diseases WHO; mem. pathology-A/study sect. NIH, 1976, mem. immunol. scis. study sect., 1983-87, ad hoc mem. allergy and immunology study sect. NIH, 1987-89 Mem. editl. bd. Jour. Clin. Immunology, 1983-88, Jour. Allergy and Clin. Immunology, 1980-85, Clin. and Diagnostic Lab. Immunology, 1983—; assoc. editor Jour. Immunology, 1976082; mem. editl. adv. bd. Jour. Molecular and Cellular Immunology, 1983—; contbr. over 200 articles, abstracts and revs. to med. jours., chpts. to books. Laurens Hammond grantee for cancer rsch., 1975-77, grantee NIH, 1987—. Fellow Am. Acad. Allergy; mem. AAAS, Am. Assn. Immunologists (membership com. 1978-82), Am. Assn. Physicians, Am. Fedn. Clin. Rsch., Am. Rheumatism Assn., Am. Soc. Clin. Investigation, Am. Soc. Tropical Medicine and Hygiene, Am. Thoracic Soc., Brit. Soc. Immunology, Clin. Immunology Soc., Collegium Internat. Allergogium, Conn. Allergy Soc., Histamine Rsch. Soc. N.Am., Reticuloendothelial Soc., Serotonin Soc., Skin. Pharmacology Soc., Soc. Investigative Dermatology, Interurban Clin. Club, Polish Acad. Arts and Scis. (fgn. corr.), Phi Beta Kappa, Alpha Omega Alpha. Office: Yale Univ Sch Medicine PO Box 208013 333 Cedar St New Haven CT 06520-8013 Office Phone: 203-785-4143.

ASKER, JAMES ROBERT, magazine editor; b. Louisville, 1952; BA, Rice U., 1974. Reporter, columnist Houston Post, 1974—88; freelance reporter, 1988—89; mng. editor Electronic Bus., 1989—; space tech. editor Aviation Week & Space Tech., Washington, 1989—95, Washington bur. chief, 1995—, mng. editor, 2003—. Recipient Knight Sci. Journalism fellow, MIT, Cambridge, 1987—88. Office: Aviation Week & Space Tech 1200 G St NW Ste 900 Washington DC 20005-3814 Home Phone: 703-560-3238; Office Phone: 202-383-2300. Business E-Mail: asker@aviationweek.com. E-mail: jim_asker@yahoo.com.

ASKEW, GLORIA YARBROUGH, dietician; d. Charlie Yarbrough and Maggie Yarbrough Dotson; m. Divorced; 1 child, None. BS, U. Memphis, 1970; MS, Rush U., 1980. Registered dietitian Commn. Dietetic Registration, 1975, cert. arobics instr. Am. Coun. Exercise, 1995, exercise leader Am. Coll. Sports Medicine, 1995. Therapeutic dietitian St. Mary Hosp., Gary, Ind., 1974—75; coord. clin. dietetics U. Chgo. Hosps., 1975—80; clin. nutrition mgr. Meth. Hosps., Memphis, 1981—86; nutrition svcs. cons. Hillhaven Corp., Memphis, 1986—90; clin. nutrition mgr. King Fahad Hosp., Al Baha, Saudi Arabia, 1991—92; dep. chief dietitian Riyadh Armed Forces Hosp., Saudi Arabia, 1992—95; nutrition cons. Martha Gregory & Assoc., Louisville, 1996—2000; dir. dietary svcs. Diversified Health Svcs., Memphis, 2000—02; dir. nutrition svcs. Graceland Nursing Ctr., Memphis, 2002—04; regional dir. of nutritional services Tara Cares, Orchard Park, NY, 2004—. Preceptor Dietary Managers Certification Course, Memphis, 1985—98. Mem.: Internat. Assn. Fitness Profls., Am. Dietetic Assn., River City Investors Investment Club (fin. ptnr. 2003—06). Home: 1835 Parkway Terr Memphis TN 38114 Office: Tara Cares 3690 Southwestern Blvd Orchard Park NY 14127 Home Phone: 901-278-8300. Office Fax: 901-278-0084. Business E-Mail: gaskew@tarahc.com.

ASKEW, JENNIFER P., pharmacist; PharmD, U. NC, Chapel Hill, 2003. Clin. pharmacist practitioner Tileston Outreach Health Clinic, Wilmington, NC, 2003—; coord. outpatient pharmacy svcs. New Hanover Regional Med. Ctr., Wilmington, 2004—. Bd. dirs. Tileston Outreach Health Clinic, Wilmington, 2006—. Mem.: NC Assn. Pharmacists (bd. dirs. 2004—). Office: New Hanover Regional Medical Center 2239 South 17th St PO Box 9000 Wilmington NC 28402 Office Phone: 910-343-7000.

ASKEW, KIM JUANITA, lawyer; b. Savannah, Ga., Nov. 14, 1957; BS summa cum laude, Knoxville Coll., 1979; JD, Georgetown U., 1983. Bar: US Supreme Ct., DC 1983, Tex. 1984, US Ct. Appeals (4th, 5th, and 8th cirs.), US Dist. Ct. (no. and ea. dists. Tex.). Law clk. US Dist Ct. (no. dist. Tex.); ptnr. Hughes & Luce, LLP, Dallas. Contbr. articles to profl. publs. Mem. bd. regents Georgetown U.; bd. dirs. Victims Outreach; dir., treas. Dallas Mus. Art; former dir. Greater Dallas C. of C.; former trustee Paul Quinn Coll.; former dir. Jr. League Dallas. Named Tex. Super Lawyer, Law & Politics Mag., 2003; named one of Best Lawyers in Am., Corp. Counsel, 2003, Best Lawyers in Dallas, D Mag., 2005; recipient Louise Raggio award, Dallas Women Lawyers Assn., 2003, Trailblazer award, J.L. Turner Legal Assn., 2003. Mem.: ABA (mem. com. commn. on women in profession 1993—97, mem. com. on meetings and travel 1997—2000, mem. continuing legal edn. com. 2000—03, sec. litig. sect. 2002—04, chair litig. sect. 2006—, mem. ho. of dels., mem. coun. fund for justice and edn., mem. membership com.), Tex. Women Lawyers, Dallas Bar Assn. (former co-chair judiciary com.), State Bar Tex. (chair continuing legal edn. com. 1997—2000, chair litig. sect. 2001—02, chair bd. dirs. 2003—04, former chair evidentiary panel dist. 6A grievance com., bd. dirs., Presdl. Citation 2000, Gene Cavin award 1999), Am. Law Inst. (chair com. on size, fed. judiciary com.). Office: Hughes & Luce LLP 1717 Main St Ste 2800 Dallas TX 75201 Office Phone: 214-939-5579. Office Fax: 214-939-5849. E-mail: kim.askew@hughesluce.com.*

ASKEW, LAURIN BARKER, JR., architect; b. Richmond, Va., May 29, 1942; s. Laurin Barker and Ellen (White) A.; m. Theda Bundy; children: Laurin Barker, Portia Elizabeth. Student, N.C. State U., Sch. Design, 1965. Registered architect, Md. Designer Architecture Coop., Stockholm, 1964; designer, job capt. RTKL Assocs., Inc., Balt., 1965-68; designer Gehry, Walsh, O'Mally, Balt., 1968-69; designer, job capt. Ballard McKim & Sawyer, Wilmington, N.C., 1969; dir. design, v.p. The Rouse Co., Columbia, Md., 1969-99; pres. Monk LLC, Balt., 1999—. Adv. bd. Md. Inst. Coll. of Art; selection com. The Vernon F. Shogren Endowment N.C. State U. Fellow AIA. Office: Monk LLC 176 Village Sq # I 5100 Falls Rd Baltimore MD 21210 Office Phone: 410-323-7950. Business E-Mail: monk@monkllc.com.

ASKEW, RILLA, author; b. Poteau, Okla., Jan. 26, 1951; d. Paul and Carmelita Askew; m. Paul Austin, Aug. 6, 1983. BFA, U. Tulsa, 1980; MFA, Bklyn. Coll., 1989. Author: Strange Business, 1992, The Mercy Seat, 1997, Fire in Beulah, 2001. Recipient Okla. Book award, Okla. Ctr. for the book, 1993, 1998, Western Heritage award, Cowboy Hall of Fame, 1998, O'Henry award, Soc. Arts and Scis., 1993, Am. Book award, Before Columbus Found., 2002, Myers Book award, Gustavas Myers Ctr., 2002. Mem.: PEN, Authors Guild, Assoc. Writing Programs.

ASKEY, RICHARD ALLEN, mathematician, educator; b. St. Louis, June 4, 1933; s. Philip Edwin and Bessie May (Yates) Askey; m. Elizabeth Ann Hill, June 14, 1958; children: James, Suzanne. BA, Washington U., St. Louis, 1955; MA, Harvard U., Cambridge, Mass., 1956; PhD, Princeton U., NJ, 1961. Instr. in math. Washington U., St. Louis, 1958-61; instr. U. Chgo., Chgo., 1961-63; asst. prof. U. Wis., Madison, 1963-65, asso. prof., 1965-68, prof., 1968-86, Gabor Szego prof., 1986-95, John Bascom prof., 1995—2003, prof. emeritus, 2003—. Author: (book) Orthogonal Polynomials and Special Functions, 1975; author: (with G. E. Andrews and R. Roy) Special Functions, 1999; editor: Theory and Application of Special Functions, 1975, Collected Papers of Gabor Szego, 1982. Recipient Edyth May Stiffe award; fellow Guggenheim, 1969—70. Fellow: AAAS, Am. Acad. Arts and Scis., Indian Acad. Sci. (hon.); mem.: Soc. Indsl. and Applied Math., Math. Assn. Am., Nat. Acad. Sci., Am. Math. Soc. Home: 2105 Regent St Madison WI 53726-3941 Office: U Wis Van Vleck Hall Madison WI 53706

ASKEY, THELMA J., federal agency administrator; b. Lakehurst, NJ; BA, Tenn. Tech. U., 1970; postgrad., George Washington U., Am. U. Press asst. Rep. John Duncan, 1972-74; editor Nat. Rsch. Coun. Marine Bd., 1974-76; asst. minority trade counsel Ho. Com. Ways and Means, 1976-79, minority trade counsel, 1979-94; staff dir. subcommitttee trade Ho. Com. on Ways and Means, 1995-98; commr. U.S. Internat. Trade Commn., Washington, 1998—2000; dir. U.S. Trade and Devel. Agy., Arlington, Va., 2001—. Office: US Trade and Devel Agy Office Dir 1000 Wilson Blvd Ste 1600 Arlington VA 22209-3901 Office Phone: 703-875-4357.

ASKEY, WILLIAM HARTMAN, United States magistrate judge; b. Williamsport, Pa., June 21, 1919; s. Charles Fisher and Marguerite Kirlin (Hartman) A.; m. Betty Arlene Moore, July 3, 1942; 1 dau., Elizabeth Powell. BA, Bucknell U., Lewisburg, Pa., 1941; JD, U. Pitts., 1951. Bar: Lycoming County Cts., 1951, Pa. 1952, U.S. Dist. Ct. (mid. dist.) Pa. 1952, U.S. Supreme Ct. 1960. U.S. commr. U.S. Dist. Ct. (mid. dist.) Pa., 1964-71; part-time U.S. magistrate judge, 1971—. With AAA, North Penn. Bd. dirs. Appalachia Ednl. Lab., Charleston, W.Va., 1967-85. Served to maj. USAAF, 1941-46. Mem. Lycoming Law Assn. (pres. 1968-69), Pa. Bar Assn., ABA, Fed. Bar Assn. (hon.), Fed. Magistrate Judges Assn., Masons, Ross Club (Williamsport). Office Phone: 570-323-9881.

ASKIN, FRANK, law educator; b. Balt., Jan. 8, 1932; s. Abraham and Rose (Mervis) A.; m. Marilyn Klein, Aug. 6, 1960; children: Andrea Marcy, Jonathan Michael, Daniel Simon; 1 son from previous marriage, Steven. BA, CCNY, 1966; JD, Rutgers U., 1966. Bar: N.J. 1966, N.Y. 1983, U.S. Dist. Ct. (ea. dist.) N.Y., U.S. Ct. Appeals (2d, 3d cirs.), U.S. Supreme Ct. 1971. Journalist N.Y. Post, Bergen Record, Newark Star-Ledger; disting. prof. law Rutgers Law Sch., Newark, 1975—. Vis. prof. U. Hawaii Law Sch., 1975; spl. counsel edn. and labor com. U.S. Ho. of Reps., 1976-77, cons. govt. ops. com., 1989-92; gen. counsel ACLU, 1976—. Author: Defending Rights: A Life in Law and Politics, 1997; co-editor: Enforcing Fair Housing Laws, 1970; contbr. articles to profl. jours. Nat. bd. dirs. ACLU, 1968—, sec., 1971-75, gen. counsel, 1976—; del. Dem. Nat. Conv., 1980, 88; Dem. candidate 11th dist. U.S. Ho. of Reps., N.J., 1986—. Named one of Best Lawyers in America, Woodward & White. Mem. Soc. Am. Law Tchrs. (treas. 1974-75). Office: Rutgers Law Sch 123 Washington St Newark NJ 07102-3192 Office Phone: 973-353-5687. Business E-Mail: faskin@kinoy.rutgers.edu.

ASKIN, WALTER MILLER, artist, educator; b. Pasadena, Calif., Sept. 12, 1929; s. Paul Henry and Dorothy Margaret (Miller) A.; child from previous marriage, Nancy Carol Oudegeest; m. Elise Anne Doyle, Apr. 17, 1993. BA, U. Calif., Berkeley, 1951, MA, 1952; postgrad., Ruskin Sch. Drawing and Fine Art, Oxford. Asst. curator edn. Legion of Honor Mus., San Francisco, 1953-54; prof. art Calif. State U., LA, 1956-92; pub. Nose Press, Pasadena, 1984—; vis. artist Pasadena Art Mus., 1962-63, U. N.Mex., 1972, Calif. State U., Long Beach, 1974-75, Cranbrook Acad. Art, Mich., 1978, Ariz. State U., Tempe, 1979, Art Ctr. Athens Sch. Fine Arts, Mykonos, Greece, 1973, Kelpra Studio, London, 1969, 73. Chief reader Advanced Placement Program, Ednl. Testing Svc., 1982—85; chmn. visual arts panel Art Recognition and Talent Search Nat. Found. Advancement in Arts-Commn. on Presdl. Scholars; advanced placement studio art exam. com. Coll. Bd., 1985—96, chmn., 1992—96, mem. Commn. of Future of Advanced Placement Program, 1999—2001, mem. acad. coun., 1989—94, chair arts adv. com., 1987—93; bd. dirs. Internat. Assn. for Humor Studies, 1989; adj. prof. Ariz. State U., 1988—90; artist-in-residence Ragdale Found., Lake Forest, Ill., 1986, John Michael Kohler Art Ctr., Sheboygan, Wis., 1987, Hambidge Ctr. for Arts & Sci., Ga., 1991, Vt. Studio Colony, 1988, U. Dallas, 2001; co-dir. 1st Internat. Conf. on Humor in Art, Chateau de la Bretsche, Brittany, France, 1989, 92; vis. prof. Ariz. State U., Tempe, 2001; invited artist 12 lithos Hullaballoo in Winter in collaboration with Wayne Kimball, Brigham Young U., 2001; historian art alumni group U. Calif., Berkeley, 2001—; curator Jest for Fun Channel Islands Art Ctr., 2004; juror various exhibitions. One-man shows include Contemporary Art in Pasadena, 1960-74, Santa Barbara Mus. Art, 1966, Hellenic-Am. Union, Athens, Greece, 1973, Hank Baum Gallery, San Francisco, 1970, 74, 76, Ericson Gallery, NYC, 1978, Abraxas Gallery, Calif., 1979-81, Kunstlerhaus, Vienna, Austria, 1981, USIA, Yugoslavia, 1985-86, Fla. State U., Tallahassee, 1988, Lizardi/Harp Gallery, Pasadena, 1988, 91, 95, LA Valley Coll., 1989, Armory Ctr. for Arts, 1991, Taipei Mus. Art, 1998, Norton Simon Mus., 1999, Taipei Fine Arts Mus., 1999, Gertrude Herbert Art Inst., Ga., 1999, Schafler Gallery, Pratt Inst., Bklyn., 1999, Kittredge Gallery, U. Puget Sound, Tacoma, 1999, Cmty. Visual Art Assn., Jackson Hole, Wyo., 1999, Wayland Bapt. U., Plainview, Tex., 1999, Norton Simon Mus., 2000, Bradley U., Peoria, Ill., 2000, Brand Libr., Glendale, Calif., 2001, U. Dallas, 2001, Brigham Young U., 2002, Calif. State U., Channel Islands, 2002, Pasadena Playhouse Gallery, 2003, Floating Rock Gallery, Pasadena, 2004, Village Sq. Gallery, Montrose, 2005, LA City Coll., 2005, Painting Ctr., NY, 2006, Brattleboro Mus. and Art Ctr., Vt., 2006, Internat. Print Ctr. NYC, 2007; exhibitions include LA Met. Transit Authority, 2003, Gallery LeLong, NYC, 2003, N.W. Watercolor Soc., Art Inst. Seattle, 2004, Art of Humor Studio Channel Islands Art Ctr., 2004, Artful Jesters Painting Ctr., NYC, 2006, Brattleboro Mus. Art Ctr., Vt., 2006, Palm Desert El Paseo, 2006—, So. Graphics Coun., 2006—, Rocky Mt. Nat. Watermedia Exhbn., 2006, El Paso Invitational, Tex., 2006, Foothills Art Ctr., Golden, Colo., 2006, LA City Coll., 2006, others; author: A Briefer History of the Greeks, 1983, Another Art Book to Cross Off Your List, 1984, Modern Manifesto Match Game, 1998, Hideous Headlines, 1998, Womsters and Foozlers, 1998, On Becoming an Artist, 1999, (calendar) Man, Dog, Bone Artists' Calendar; represented in permanent collections Norton Simon Mus., Pasadena, Getty Ctr. for the Arts, LA, Mus. Modern Art, NYC, Whitney Mus. Art, NYC, San Francisco Mus. Contemporary Art, Albright Knox Mus., Buffalo, LA County Mus. Art, others; contbr. articles to profl. jours. and mags. Trustee Pasadena Art Mus., 1963-68; bd. dirs. LA Inst. Contemporary Art., 1978-81, Pasadena Gallery Contemporary Arts; bd. govs. Baxter Art Gallery, Calif. Inst. Tech., 1980-86; bd. dirs. The Calif. Artist, Book Program, 1985-2000; dir. The Visual Humor Project, 1989—. Recipient Outstanding Prof. award Calif. State U., 1973, Artists award Pasadena Arts Coun., 1970, award 61st ann. exhbn. N.W. Watercolor Soc., 2001, Past Pres.' award 80th ann. exhbn. Nat. Watercolor Soc., 2000, Purchase prize 3d nat. print biennial Frederick R. Weisman Mus., Mpls., 2001; named Disting. Alumnus, Pasadena City Coll.; grantee Ruth G. Jansen Edn. Meml., Pasadena Arts Commn., 1990, Calif. State U., 2006; also over 50 awards in competitive exhbns. art. Mem.: Kauai Soc. Artists, So. Graphics Coun., LA Printmaking Soc. (pres. 2002—04, founding mem.), Nat. Watercolor Soc. (1st v.p. 1960), Coll. Art Assn. Am. Home and Office: PO Box D South Pasadena CA 91031-0120 *What can we do today that has any kind of meaning and value? We can search for a means to escape from conventions, from ordinariness, and from the limitations of everyday existence. We can help create the emergent fiction that is the world we live in. We can regenerate the key myths and archetypes so that life doesn't seem worth living unless one is on the side of the liberating and transformative. We can learn to play again - to not know what we are looking for, to break through the ice of habit, to know what it means to be truly alive and to experience the specialness of even the most ordinary things. We can find the god within, inspiration, magic, once again be visionaries, bring peace. The real joy is in making a better, more calm, more serene, more alive, more playful, more energized, more focused, more directed, more life filled existence for the time we're here.*

ASKINS, ARTHUR JAMES, accountant, auditor; b. Dec. 2, 1944; s. William J. and Rita M. (O'Brien) A.; m. Nancy E. Paulsen, Apr. 28, 1979. BS, LaSalle U., 1967; MA, Rider Coll., 1971. Cert. of specialization hospitality acctg. and mgmt. Am. Hotel and Motel Assn.; CPA, Pa., NJ; cert. fraud examiner, hotel adminstr. Tchr. Cardinal Dougherty HS, Phila., 1967-70; pvt. practice acctg., 1967—. Recipient cert. of Commendation Twp. of Abington, Pa., 1967, Disting. Svc. award Cmty. Accts., Phila., 1982, Superstar award Resorts Internat. Casino-Hotel, 1982, Brotherhood award NCCJ, Atlantic City, 1983, Mgmt. award Resorts Internat. Casino Hotel, 1986, 1st Mgrs. award Resort Internat. Casino-Hotel, 1986, Outstanding Vol. Svc. award Big Bros./Big Sisters, 1987. Mem. AICPA, Inst. Mgmt. Accts. (nat. bd. dirs. 1983-85, pres. South Jersey Shore chpt. 1979-81, Cmty. Affairs award Suburban NE Phila. 1978), Inst. Internal Auditors (bd. dirs. 1984-89, audit com. 1979-83), NJ Soc. CPAs, Pa. Inst. CPAs, Greater Mainland C. of C., Forensic CPA Soc. Republican. Roman Catholic. Office: Seneca Nation of Indians Seneca Gaming Authority PO Box 425 Niagara Falls NY 14302 Home: PO Box 428 Youngstown NY 14174-0428 Office Phone: 716-299-1246. Personal E-mail: ajacpa@roadrunner.com.

ASKINS, JARI, lieutenant governor, former state representative; b. Duncan, Okla., Apr. 27, 1953; d. Ollie M. and Jarita Askins. BA in Journalism, U. Okla., 1975, JD, 1980. Bar: Okla. V.p. closing office Stephens County Abstract Co., Duncan, Okla.; spl. dist. judge Stephens County, Okla., 1982—90; chmn. Okla. Pardon and Parole Bd., Okla. City, 1991—92; dep. gen. counsel Gov.'s Office, 1992—94; rep. Ho. of Reps., State of Okla., Okla. City, 1995—2006; lt. gov. State of Okla., 2007—. Dep. majority fl. leader Okla. Ho. Reps., Okla. City, 2001; mem. Okla. Judicial Conf., Okla. City; dir. Arvest Bank, Duncan, Okla. Mem Leadership Okla.; mem., bd. dirs. Goodwill Industries; bd. trustees Cottey Jr. Coll., Nevada, Mo. Named Outstanding Legislator, Am. Acad. Pediatrics, Am. Acad. Family Physicians, AHA, Okla. Assn. County Commissioners, Okla. County Clerks Assn., Okla. Pub. Employees Assn., Okla. Cattlemen's Assn.; named to Okla. Woman's Hall of Fame, 2001; recipient Disting. Svc. award, Duncan Jaycees, Pres. award, Okla. Wildlife Fedn., Friend of Medicine award, Okla. State Med. Assn. Mem.: ABA, Okla. Acad. of State Goals, Duncan C. of C. (Woman of Yr. 1995), Stephen's County Bar Assn., Okla. Bar Assn., Lions Club. Democrat. Office: Lieutenant Governor State Capitol Rm 211 Oklahoma City OK 73105 Office Phone: 405-521-2161. Office Fax: 405-525-2702. E-mail: askinsja@lsb.state.ok.us.*

ASKINS, NANCY ELLEN PAULSEN, training services executive; b. St. Paul, Nov. 2, 1948; d. Charles A. and Stasia (Sawicki) Paulsen; m. Arthur J. Askins, Apr. 28, 1979. BS in Home Econ., U. Cin., 1970, BS in Edn., 1971, MEd, 1972; postgrad., SUNY-Buffalo, 1974—76, Temple U., 1976, Walden U., 1988—92, Inst. Fin. Edn., 1982—85; student, Capella U., 2002—. Cert. gaming supr. Edn. Inst. Am. Hotel and Motel Assn., strategic planning facilitator, mgr. of quality and organizational effectiveness Am. Soc. for Quality, 2006-. Asst. aquatic supr. Cin. Recreation Commn., 1969—72; adminstr. student affairs U. Cin., 1970—72; mem. faculty student affairs adminstrn. Tex. Luth. Coll., 1972—73; mem. faculty, student affairs adminstr. SUNY-Geneseo, 1974—76; student affairs adminstr. Temple U., Phila., 1976—78; tchr. drug awareness coord. Adams Sch. Harlandale Sch. Dist., San Antonio, 1973—74; career life ins. agt., fin. planning cons. Phoenix Mut. Life Ins. Co., Phila., 1978—81; registered rep., securities agt. Phoenix Equity Planning Corp., Phila., 1980—81; mem. women's task force Phoenix Cos., 1980—81; owner, exec. corp. cons. Askins Tng. and Cons., 1981—; coord. tng. svcs. Collective Fed. Savs. & Loan Assn., Egg Harbor City, NJ, 1981—82, asst. v.p., tng. dir., 1982—84; mgr. tng. Shore Meml. Hosp., Somers Point, 1984—85, instr. wellness, 1984—88, dir. edn.l. devel., 1986—89; dir edn. svcs. Holy Cross Hosp., Ft. Lauderdale, Fla., 1990—91, dir. cmty. and vol. svcs., 1991—94, part-time instr. wellness program, 1991—94; v.p. tng. and assoc. devel. Grand Casino, Biloxi, 1994—96; coord. tng. svcs. Gulf Coast Bus. Svcs., Gulfport, Miss., 1996—98; dir. quality Hollywood Casino Resort/Tunica, Robinsonville, Miss., 1998—2001; adj. prof. Webster U., Memphis, 2003; dir. Ctr. Renewal Retreat & Conf. Ctr. at Stella Niagara, 2005—. Adj. prof. bus. and social scis. Atlantic C.C. Coll., Mays Landing, N.J., 1986-89; facilitator Assertiveness Tng. Group, Interpersonal Comms. Group, orgnl. and leadership devel. seminars and cons.; mem. bd. examiners Malcolm Baldrige Nat. Quality Award, 2001,02, 03, Pres.'s Quality Award, 2000, Tenn. Quality Award, 2000, Miss. Quality Award, 1999, 2000 (judge 2002); instr. Inst. Fin. Edn., 1982-85, Ednl. Inst.; nat. seminar leader, Fred Pryor / Career Track, 2000-05; workshop presenter and spkr. in field; writer in field. Agy. chmn. United Way Campaign, Phila., 1979, 80; bd. dir. South Jersey Regional Theater, 1983-86, chmn., 1983-84; active ann. Muscular Dystrophy Telethon, Phila.; active Girl Scouts U.S., 1956-74, 84—; mem. Parish coun., parish enrichment com., 1984-88, cantor St. Joseph Roman Cath. Ch., Somers Point, 1979-89; mem., lector Christ the King Cath. Ch., Southaven, Miss., 1998-2003; chmn. com. Women's Club St. Luke's Cath. Ch., Coconut Creek, Fla., 1992-94, parish coun., 1993-94; bd. dir. Holly Shores Coun. Girl Scouts U.S., 1984-85; host fgn. exch. students Am. Scandinavian Student Exch. Program, 1985-87; mem. Somers Point Bd. Edn., 1986; mem. Libr. Adv. Bd. City of Margate, Fla., 1991-94, fundraising chmn., vice chmn., chmn.; originator Niagara Frontier Faith Heritage Trail. Recipient Brotherhood-Sisterhood Achievers award NCCJ, 1985, Rising Star award, 1997, Gold Dir. award, 1998 Carlson Learning Co.,

Inscape Publishing, Minn.; named Biloxi Career Woman Bus. Profl. Women/Lighthouse of Biloxi, 1995, Women of Achievement Woman of Yr. Bus. Profl. Women Clarksdale, Coahoma County, Miss., 1999. Mem. ASTD (treas. South Jersey chpt., nat. dir. savs. and lending industry group 1983-84, hosps. and healthcare industry group 1984-86, nat. conf. spkr. 1984-86, sec. Greater Broward/Ft. Lauderdale chpt. 1991, pres.-elect 1992, pres.1993, nat. dir.-elect 1990-91. dir. 1991-92, Interfaith Trainers Cons. Network), Internat. Cons. Assn., Am. Hotel & Motel Assn. (No. Miss. chpt. charter pres. 1999, instr. 1999-2001), Bus. and Profl. Women Buffalo (individual devel. prgram co-chair 2004-05), Women Robinsonville, Miss. (charter pres. 1999-2000), Bus. and Profl. Women Clarksdale (legis. com. chair, 1998-2000), Bus. and Profl. Women Lighthouse of Biloxi (v.p. membership, newsletter editor, chair 1997 Nat. Bus. Women's Week), Bus. and Profl. Women Miss. (state 2d v.p., state membership chair, 1996-97, state legis. chair, 1999-2000, nat. leadership chair, state pres.-elect 2002-03, state pres. 2003-04, nat. leadership chair 2004-05), Greater Camden Assn. Life Underwriters (state pres. 2003-04, chmn. Life Ins. Week for South Jersey 1978-79, bd. dir. 1979-81, pub. rels. chmn. 1979-81, chmn. state edn. 1981), Am. Soc. for Quality (features editor Competitive Advantage quality divsn. 2000-03), Am. Hosp. Assn., Am. Soc. Health Edn. and Tng., Am. Mgmt. Assn., Fla. Soc. Healthcare Edn. and Tng., Greater Mainland C. of C. (v.p., treas., membership coord. 1979-89, Pres. award 1983), Internat. Assn. Facilitators, U. Cin. Alumni of Greater Phila. Area (pres. 1980-89), Greater Ft. Lauderdale C. of C. (diplomat 1992-93, edn. com. 1993-94), Alliance/The Women's Network (bd. dir. 1983-84), Rotary Internat., Rotary of Gulfport, Rotary of Robinsonville, (sect. 1999, newsletter editor 1998-99, pres.-elect 1999-2000, pres. 2000-2001), Rotary (chairperson, long range planning com. 1999-2001, group study exch. com. 1999-2000, youth study exch. com. 1999-2000, chmn. matching grants com. 2001-2002). Democrat.

ASKINS, WALLACE BOYD, manufacturing executive; b. Chgo., June 2, 1930; s. Wallace Fay and Evelyn Mae (Baker) A.; m. Trieste M. Olivieri, May 20, 1954 (div. Sept. 23, 1994); 1 child, Justin Wallace. BA, Lake Forest Coll., Ill., 1952; JD with honors, John Marshall Law Sch., Chgo., 1961. Bar: Ill. 1961; CPA, Ill. Sr. accountant Ernst & Young (CPAs), Chgo., 1952-55; controller, house counsel Nat. Lock Co., Rockford, Ill., 1955-65; asst. corp. controller Xerox Corp., Stamford, Conn., 1965-77; exec. v.p., chief fin. officer White Motor Corp., Cleve., 1977-81, chmn. bd., chief exec. officer, 1981-84; exec. v.p., chief fin. officer Armco Inc., Parsippany, NJ, 1984-92, also bd. dirs. Bd. dirs. Trump Entertainment Resorts, Inc. Mem. ABA, AICPA, Ill. Soc. CPA's, N.Y. Soc. CPA's, Ill. Bar Assn. Home: 4324 Butterfly Orchid Ln Naples FL 34119 Office Phone: 239-254-7836. Personal E-mail: walgator@aol.com.

ASKLAND, ANDREW, law educator, director; b. NY, Aug. 16, 1951; JD, U. Md., 1978; MA, U. Colo., 1992, PhD, 1995. Instr. law Ariz. State U. Coll. of Law, dir. Ctr. for Study of Law, Sci., and Tech., 1999—. Contbr. articles to law jours. Office: Ariz State U Coll of Law PO Box 877906 Tempe AZ 85287-7906 Office Phone: 480-965-2465. E-mail: sandy.askland@asu.edu.

ASK-NANKO, LORRAINE CHARLOTTE, music educator; b. Bronx, NY, Sept. 13, 1939; d. Charles Bernt Ask and Loretta Hilda Merkel; m. Joseph Nanko, Aug. 18, 1968 (dec.). MusB, Manhattan Sch.Music, 1962, MusM, 1964. Music faculty Notre Dame H.S., NYC, 1969—72, Cardinal Hayes H.S., Bronx, NY, 1969—, fine arts chmn., 1994—. Adv. bd. City Is. Players, Bronx, 1996—. Dir. music First Presbyn. Ch. of Throggs Neck, 1979—. Recipient Outstanding H.S. Choral Conductor, 1980, Distinguished Faculty award, Cardinal Hayes H.S., 2004. Mem.: Presbyn. Assn. Musicians, Am. Guild Organists, Am. Choral Dir. Assn. Republican. Presbyn. Avocations: reading, crafts. Office: Cardinal Hayes HS 650 Grand Concourse Bronx NY 10451 Office Phone: 718-292-6100. Business E-Mail: lnanko@cardinalhayes.org.

ASKOV, EUNICE MAY, adult education educator; b. St. Louis, Nov. 20, 1940; d. David Hull and Marjorie Jane (Gutgsell) Nicholson; m. Warren Hopkins Askov, Jan. 22, 1967; children: David, Karen. BA in English, Denison U., 1962; MA in English, U. Wis., 1966, PhD in Curriculum and Instrn., 1969. English and reading tchr. Rich Twp. High Sch., Park Forest, Ill., 1962-64; reading svc. reading specialist U. Wis., Madison, 1965-66, project asst. Wis. R & D Ctr. for Cognitive Learning, 1966-67, rsch. assoc., 1969-72, lectr. dept. curriculum and instrn., 1968-69; coord. adult basic edn. programs U. Wis. Extension, 1966-67; remedial reading specialist Lincoln Jr. High Sch., Madison, 1966; adult basic edn. tchr. Madison Vocat., Tech. and Adult Schs., 1967-68; asst. prof. elem. edn. Minn. State U., Bemidji, 1972-74; assoc. prof. Pa. State U., University Park, 1974-79, prof. edn., 1980—2001, disting. prof., 2001—. Presenter seminars on adult edn., Germany, 1986, 93; cons., speaker in field; mem. editorial bd. Jour. Ednl. Rsch., Adult Edn. Quarterly, Adult Basic Edn., Am. Reading Forum Yearbook; mem. steering com. Adult Literacy and Tech.; mem. panel nat. work group on cancer and literacy Nat. Cancer Inst.; organizer, coord. Pa. State Coalition for Adult Literacy; mem. adv. coun. Nat. Coalition for Literacy. Contbr. articles to profl. publs. Fulbright sr. scholar, 1983; Literacy Leader fellow Nat. Inst. for Literacy, 1994-95; recipient Alumni Achievement award U. Wis.-Madison Sch. Edn., 1994, Career Achievement award Pa. State Coll. Edn.; Disting. fellow Flinders U. Inst. Internat. Edn., Australia, 1998; named to Reading Hall of Fame, 2005, Internat. Adult and Continuing Edn. Hall of Fame, 2007. Mem. Am. Assn. Adult and Continuing Edn. (chair, mem. various coms., bd. dir.),Commn. Profs. of Adult Edn., Am. Edn. Rsch. Assn., Am. Reading Forum, Internat. Reading Assn. (chair, mem. various coms.), Keystone State Reading Assn., Mid-State Literacy Coun. (bd. dir., pers. com., long range planning com.), Mid-State Reading Coun. (pres.), Pa. Assn. Adult and Continuing Edn., Phi Beta Kappa, Phi Delta Kappa. Democrat. Methodist. Avocations: travel, aerobics, hiking, reading. Office: Pa State U Inst for Study Adult Lit 200 Rackley Bldg University Park PA 16802-3202 Business E-Mail: ena1@psu.edu.

ASKREN, STAN A., manufacturing executive; BA Business Administration, U. of Northern Iowa; MBA, Washington U. Group v.p. The HON Co., 1998—99; Pres. Allsteel Inc., 1999—2003; exec. v.p. HNI Corp., Muscatine, Iowa, 2001—03, pres., 2003—04, chmn., pres., CEO, 2004—. Office: HNI Corp PO Box 1109 408 E 2d St Muscatine IA 52761-0071*

ASLAN, MADALYN, writer, educator; d. George Vincent Shea and Donna Marie Todd. BA with honors, U. London, 1984; BA, Cornell U., 1987; MFA, Sarah Lawrence Coll., 1991. Lectr. Coll. Psychic Studies, London, 2001—. Monthly astrologer AOL, 2006—. Author: What's Your Sign? A Cosmic Guide for Young Astrologers, 2002, Madalyn Aslan's Jupiter Signs, 2003; actor: (TV series) The Martian Chronicles, 1980; (films) D.H. Lawrence. Mem.: Nat. Coun. Geo-Cosmic Rsch., Nat. Campaign for Tolerance (life; founder), Am. Fedn. Astrologers (life).

ASLIN, RICHARD N., psychology professor, researcher; b. Aug. 9, 1949; married; 2 children. BA in Psychology with High Honors, Mich. State U., 1971; PhD in Child Psychology, Inst. Child Develop., U. Minn., 1975. Asst. prof., dept. psychology Ind. U., 1975—79, assoc. prof., dept. psychology, 1979—82, prof., dept. psychology, 1982—84, U. Rochester, 1984—95, prof., Ctr. for Visual Sci., 1984—, chair, dept. psychology, 1988—91, dean, Coll. Arts & Sciences, 1991—94, vice provost, dean of the coll., 1994—96, prof., dept. brain and cognitive sciences, 1995—, dir., Ctr. for Language Sciences, 2000—03; dir. Rochester Ctr. for Brain Imaging, 2003—. Vis. scientist, Regional Primate Rsch. Ctr. U. Wash., 1981; vis. prof., Ctr. for Rsch. in Human Learning U. Minn., 1982; vis. prof., dept. psychological and brain sciences Dartmouth Coll., 1999; mem. NIH Study Sect. on Human Development and Aging- I, 1985—89, NSF Review Panel on Human Cognition and Perception, 1997—2000. Contbr. articles to profl. jours., chapters to books; series editor Neural and Behavioral Development-Advances, Monographs and Books, 1982—87, mem. editl. bd. Infant Behavior and Development, 1982—85, 1989—98, Child Development, 1983—85, 1989—96, Developmental Psychology, 1984—85, 1998—2003, Journal of Experimental Child Psychology, 1997—2003, Cognition, 2001—, Infancy, 1998—2003; editor: Infancy, 2003—; assoc. editor Developmental Psychology, 1986—88. Recipient Rsch. Career Development award, Nat. Inst. Child Health and Human Develop., 1979—84, Robert and Pamela Goergen award for Disting. Contributions to Undergraduate Learning in the Coll., U. Rochester, 2001; NSF Undergraduate Rsch. Fellowship, 1970, NIH Mental Health Predoctoral Traineeship in Child Psychology, 1971—75, Summer Faculty Fellowship, Ind. U., 1976, James McKeen Cattell award (sabbatical), 1984—85, John Simon Guggenheim Meml. Found. Fellowship, 1988—89, Fellow, Ctr. for Advanced Study in Behavioral Sciences, Stanford, 1988—89, Bridging Fellowship, Departments Biology and Human Genetics, U. Rochester, 1997. Fellow: Am. Acad. Arts & Sciences, AAAS; mem.: Soc. for Rsch. in Child Develop., Soc. for Language Develop., Psychonomic Soc., Internat. Soc. for Infancy Studies, Cognitive Sci. Soc., Cognitive Develop. Soc., APA (Boyd R. McCandless Young Scientist award (Divsn. 7) 1981, Early Career award, Develop. Psychology 1982), Acoustical Soc. Am. Office: Dept Brain and Cognitive Sciences U Rochester Meliora Hall Room 406 Rochester NY 14627-0268 Office Phone: 716-275-8687, 716-275-4621 (lab). Office Fax: 716-444-9216. Business E-Mail: aslin@cvs.rochester.edu.

ÅSLUND, ANDERS, economist; b. Karlskoga, Sweden, Feb. 17, 1952; s. Ivan and Ingrid (Åblad) Å. BA, U. Stockholm, Sweden, 1976; MSc, Stockholm Sch. Econs., 1976; PhD, U. Oxford, England, 1982. Second sec. Swedish Embassy, Kuwait, 1977-78; first sec. Swedish Permanent Delegation, Geneva, 1982-84, Swedish Embassy, Moscow, 1984-87; rsch. scholar Kennan Inst. Advanced Russian Studies, Washington, 1987-88; prof., dir. Stockholm Inst. E. European Econs., Stockholm Sch. Econs., 1989-94; sr. assoc. Carnegie Endowment for Internat. Peace, Washington, 1994—2005, dir. Russian and Eurasian program, 2003—05; sr. fellow Peterson Inst. Internat. Econs., Washington, 2006—. Fellow World Econ. Forum, Geneva, 1991—; adj. prof. Georgetown U., Washington, 2002—. Author: Private Enterprise in Eastern Europe, 1985, Gorbachev's Struggle for Economic Reform, 1989, 1991, Post-Communist Economic Revolutions: How Big a Bang?, 1992, How Russia Became a Market Economy, 1995, Building Capitalism: The Transformation of the Former Soviet Bloc, 2002, How Capitalism was Built: The Transformation of Central and Eastern Europe, Russia, and Central Asia, 2007, Russia's Capitalist Revolution, 2007; co-author: Getting It Wrong; editor 12 books on Soviet, post-Soviet and Russian econ. affairs. Sr. econ. advisor to Russian Govt., 1991—94, Ukrainian Govt., 1994—97; pres. Akaev Kyrgyz Republic, 1998—2004. Mem. Cosmos Club (Washington). Office: Peterson Inst Internat Econs 1750 Massachussetts Ave Washington DC 20036 Business E-Mail: aaslund@iie.com.

ASMA, EVREN, medical researcher; b. Ankara, Turkey, Aug. 5, 1978; s. Tahir and Muzeyyen Asma. BSc, Bilkent U., 1999; MSc, U. Southern Calif., 2000, PhD, 2004. Rsch. asst. U. Southern Calif., 1999—2004, postdoctoral rsch. assoc., 2004—; mem. staff GE Global Rsch. Ctr., 2005—. Recipient Outstanding Acad. achievement, U. Southern Calif., 2001, 2003, Student Travel award, IEEE, 2001, Rsch. assistantship, U. Southern Calif., 1999—2004. Mem.: IEEE. Avocation: swimming.

ASMA, LAWRENCE FRANCIS, priest; b. Waukegan, Ill., Oct. 21, 1947; s. Francis Victor and Isabelle Amelia (Recktenwald) A. BA in English, U. Wis., Whitewater, 1969; MA in English, Ill. State U., 1974; MA in Scripture magna cum laude, De Andreis Sem., 1982, MDiv, 1983. Ordained priest Roman Cath. Chr., 1983. Dir. spritual formation Cardinal Glennon Coll., St. Louis, 1983-85, instr. theology dept., 1983-85; chaplain St. Vincent's Div. DePaul Health Ctr., St. Louis, 1985—. Bd. dirs. Rosati Stabilization Ctr., St. Louis, 1988-94; vice chmn. Rosati Stabilization Ctr., 1990-94; advisor Explorers, 1991-92. Local religious superior Congregation of the Mission, 1994-99; chaplain Knights Columbus, 1996—. With USNR, 1970-72, Vietnam. Mem. Assn. Profl. Chaplains (bd. cert.), Cath. Biblical Assn., Soc. Biblical Lit., Congregation of Mission, Sigma Tau Delta. Avocations: ornithology, photography, drawing. Office: DePaul Health Center 12303 De Paul Dr Bridgeton MO 63044-2588 Home Phone: 314-843-0108; Office Phone: 314-344-7080. E-mail: revlasma@yahoo.com.

ASMAN, BUB (HENRY B. ASMAN), sound editor; b. Louisville, Ky., Aug. 17, 1949; Editor: (films) Abby, 1974, Sheba, Baby, 1975, Grizzly, 1976, Day of the Animals, 1977, The Manitou, 1978; sound effects editor (films) The Bad News Bears Go to Japan, 1978, Escape from Alcatraz, 1979, North Dallas Forty, 1979, Bronco Billy, 1980, Any Which Way You Can, 1980, The Postman Always Rings Twice, 1981, Nighthawks, 1981, Zorro, the Gay Blade, 1981, Conan the Barbarian, 1982, Firefox, 1982, Honkytonk Man, 1982, Sudden Impact, 1983, Uncommon Valor, 1983, The Last Starfighter, 1984, Red Dawn, 1984, Windy City, 1984, City Heat, 1984, Hard to Kill, 1990, The Last Boy Scout, 1991, Radio Flyer, 1992, True Romance, 1993, Demolition Man, 1993, The Stars Fell on Henrietta, 1995, Quest for Camelot, 1998, The Replacements, 2000, Heartbreakers, 2001, sound editor (films) First Blood, 1982, Vacation, 1983, The Last Starfighter, 1984, Lethal Weapon 2, 1989, White Hunter Black Heart, 1990, Die Hard 2, 1990, New Jack City, 1991, Lethal Weapon 3, 1992, Maverick, 1994, Speed 2: Cruise Control, 1997, supervising sound editor (films) The Bridges of Madison County, 1995, Eraser, 1996, Absolute Power, 1997, Midnight in the Garden of Good and Evil, 1997, True Crime, 1999, co-supervising sound editor (films) Lara Croft: Tomb Raider, 2001, Blood Work, 2003, Star Trek: Nemesis, 2002, Mystic River, 2003, Million Dollar Baby, 2004, The Legend of Zorro, 2005, Flags of Our Fathers, 2006, Letters from Iwo Jima, 2006 (Acad. award for achievement in sound editing, 2007), dialogue editor Up Close & Personal, 1996.*

ASMUS, DAVID F., lawyer; b. Hinsdale, Ill., Aug. 6, 1959; BS in geology and geophysics, magna cum laude, Yale U., 1981; JD, Harvard U., 1985. Ptnr. Baker Botts LLP, Houston, 1993—, ptnr. in charge global oil and gas practice. Mem.: Internat. Bar Assn. (past chmn. oil and gas com.), Houston Bar Assn., State Bar Tex. (oil, gas, and mineral law sects., internat. law sect.), Assn. Internat. Petroleum Negotiators (past pres.). Office: Baker Botts LLP One Shell Plz 910 Louisiana St Houston TX 77002-4995 Office Phone: 713-229-1539. Office Fax: 713-229-2839. E-mail: david.asmus@bakerbotts.com.

ASMUS, JOHN FREDRICH, physicist; b. Pasadena, Calif., Jan. 20, 1937; s. William F. and Eleanor E. (Kocher) Asmus; m. Barbara Ann Flaherty, Feb. 23, 1963; children: Joanne M., Rosemary H. BSEE, Calif. Inst. Tech., 1958, MSEE, 1959, PhDEE and Physics, 1965. Head optical systems dept. Aero Geo Astro Corp., Alexandria, Va., 1960-64; head laser dept. Gulf Gen. Atomic, San Diego, 1964-69; research staff Inst. Def. Analyses, Arlington, Va., 1969-71; v.p., bd. mem. Sci. Applications, Inc., Albuquerque, 1971-73; lectr. U. Calif., Davis, 1974, research physicist, co-founder art and sci. center San Diego, 1973—. Co-dir. JASON nat. laser program study Office of Pres. of US; keynote spkr. Laser World Trade Fair, Munich, 2003, Munich, 05, Munich, 07; mem. editl. bd. Springer Verlag, Elsevier Pub.; cons. in field. Mem. editl. bd.: Jour. Cultural Heritage, 2004—; contbr. scientific papers to profl. jours. Decorated knight Holy Sepulchre of Jerusalem; named George Eastman lectr., Optical Soc. Am., 1994, Rank Prize mentor, 2004, winner, IBM Supercomputing Competition for Image Enhancement fo Mona Lisa, 1989; recipient Rolex Laureate for Enterprise award for restoration Xian terra cotta warriors, Montes Rolex SA, 1990, Best Scholarly Article award, Soc. Tech. Com., 1988; fellow, Oberlin Coll., 1990; Schlumberger fellow, 1959—60, Tektronix fellow, 1960—61, Getty fellow, 1989, Explorers Club fellow, 1997. Mem.: IEEE, Soc. Photo-Optical Instrumentation Engrs. (editl. bd. mem. 2002—), Venice Soc., Nat. Trust Hist. Preservation, Am. Inst. Conservation, Internat. Inst. Conservation Hist. and Artistic Works, Lasers Conservation Artworks (sci. bd. mem., hon. pres.), Bay Area Art Conservation Guild, Sigma Xi, Tau Beta Pi. Achievements include patents for metallic vapor laser; embedded pinch laser; plasma pinch annealing system; chemical decontamination with ultraviolet; research in laser, ultrasonic and computer image enhancement techniques to art conservation; laser cleaning to the field of paleontology, and revealed new features of da Vinci's Mona Lisa; restored Cremona Cathedral; restored California State Capital; restored White House mural; restored Venice Ducal Palace Sculpture; development of laser-robotic technique for the decontamination of the Hanford nuclear weapons facility of US Department of Energy; laser, flashlamp and pinchlamp systems for depainting stealth aircraft and decontaminating the JET TOKAMAK thermonuclear fusion reactor; laser system for branding bowhead whales at a distance. Home: 8239 Sugarman Dr La Jolla CA 92037-2222 Office: IPAPS 0360 U Calif San Diego 9500 Gilman Dr La Jolla CA 92093-5004 Business E-Mail: jfasmus@ucsd.edu. *The lessons and adventures that pervade our stories are manifestations of God's grace.*

ASNER, EDWARD, actor; b. Kansas City, Kans., Nov. 15, 1929; s. Morris David and Lizzie (Seliger) A.; m. Nancy Lou Sykes, Mar. 23, 1957 (div., 1988), m. Cindy Gilmore, Aug. 2, 1998; children: Matthew and Liza (twins), Kathryn, Charles. Student, U. Chgo., 1947-49. Debut at Playwrights Theatre, Chgo., 1953; appeared on TV, in Off-Broadway and Broadway shows, N.Y.C., 1955-61; appeared in numerous motion pictures and TV shows, Los Angeles, 1961—; appeared in TV miniseries Rich Man, Poor Man, 1976, Roots, 1977; appeared on Slattery's People, CBS-TV, 1964-65, Mary Tyler Moore Show, CBS-TV, 1970-77, Lou Grant Show, CBS-TV, 1977-82, Off The Rack, ABC-TV, 1985, This Side of Eden, The Bronx Zoo, 1987-88, The Trials of Rosie O'Neil, 1991, Fish Police (voice) 1991, Hearts Afire, 1992-93, Thunder Alley 1994-95, Center of the Universe, 2004-; narrator TV film Narco; appeared in cable and TV films The Doomsday Flight, 1966, Doug Selby, D.A., 1969, House on Greenapple Road, 1969, Daughter of the Mind, 1970, The Old Man Who Cried Wolf, 1970, The Last Child, 1971, The Haunts of The Very Rich, 1971, Hey, I'm Alive, 1975, Life and Assassination of the Kingfish, 1977, The Gathering, 1977, The Family Man, 1979, A Small Killing, 1981, A Case of Libel, 1983, Anatomy of an Illness, 1984, Tender Is The Night, 1985, Vital Signs, 1986, The Christmas Star, 1986, Cracked up, 1987, Friendship in Vienna, 1988, Not a Penny More, Not a Penny Less, 1990, Switched at Birth, 1991, Yes, Virginia, There Is a Santa Claus, 1991, Silent Motive, 1991, Cruel Doubt, 1992, Gypsy, 1993, Christmas Vacation 2: Cousin Eddie's Island Adventure, 2003; appeared in motion pictures The Murder Men, 1961, Kid Gallahad, 1962, The Slender Thread, 1965, The Satan Bug, 1965, The Venetian Affair, 1967, Peter Gunn, 1967, Change of Habit, 1969, Halls of Anger, 1970, They Call Me Mister Tibbs, 1970, Skin Game, 1971, Gus, 1976, Fort Apache, The Bronx, 1980, O'Hara's Wife, 1982, Daniel, 1983, Moon Over Parador, 1988, JFK, 1991, (voice) Happily Ever After, 1993, Down on the Watefront, 1993, The Animal, 2001, The Kid (voice), 2001, Elf, 2003; Higher Education (TV); Gargoyles: The Heroes Awaken (voice), 1994; Gargoyles (TV series, voice), 1994; Spider-Man (TV series, voice), 1995 & 2003; Freakazoid (TV series, voice), 1995; The Story of Santa Claus (TV), 1996; Gargoyles: The Goliath Chronicles (TV series, voice), 1996; Bruno the Kid (TV series, voice), 1996; Prep, 1997; Dog's Best Friend (TV), 1997; 187 Documented, 1997; Batman: Gotham Knights (TV series, voice), 1997, Superman (TV, voice), 1998; Payback (TV)(also prodr.), 1997; The Long Way Home (voice), 1997; Ask Harriet (tv series), 1998; Hard Rain (aka The Flood), 1998; The Closer (TV series), 1998; More Tales of the City (aka Armistead Maupin's More Tales of the City, TV series), 1998; X-Men Legends (video, voice), 2004; guest appearances on: The Untouchables, 1962 & 1963, Dr. Kildare, 1963, Gunsmoke 1964 & 1966, F.B.I., 1966, 1968, 1969, Mission Impossible, 1969, Police Story, 1974 & 1976, Rhoda, 1974, Hawaii Five-O, 1975, Highway to Heaven, 1986, Mad About You, 1996, 1997, 1998, Roseanne, 1996, The Practice, 1997 & 2004, The X-Files, 1998, The Simpsons (voice), 1999 & 2002, Buzz Lightyear of Star Command (voice), 2000, King of Hill (voice), 2001, The Wild Thornberrys (voice), 2000, Dharma & Greg, 2001, The Family Guy (voice), 2001, The Ellen Show, 2001, ER, 2003, Justice League, 2004 and numerous others. Served with Signal Corps U.S. Army, 1951-53. Recipient 5 Golden Globe Awards, 7 Emmy Awards, Flame of Truth Award, Fund for Higher Education, 1981; inducted into TV Acad. Hall of Fame, 1996. Mem. Screen Actors Guild (pres. 1981-85) Office: William Morris Agency care Brian Dubin 1325 Avenue Of The Americas New York NY 10019-6026

ASNESS, CLIFFORD S., investment company executive; BS in Economics, summa cum laude, U. Pa., BS in Engring., summa cum laude; MBA with high honors, U. Chgo., 1991, PhD in Fin. Economics, 1994. Mng. dir., dir. Quantitative Rsch., Asset Mgmt. Divsn. Goldman, Sachs and Co.; founder, mng. prin. AQR Capital Mgmt. Mem. leadership coun. Robin Hood Found.; mem. investment com. U. Chgo.; gov. bd. Courant Inst. Math. Fin. NYU, Coun. on Grad. Sch. Bus.; editl. bd. Jour. Portfolio Mgmt., Fin. Analysts Jour. Office: AQR Capital Mgmt Two Greenwich Plz Greenwich CT 06830 Office Phone: 203-742-3600. Office Fax: 203-742-3100.

ASNIEN, PHYLLIS ARLINE, humanities educator, writer; b. Cleve., June 23, 1937; d. Morris and Rebecca Berman Asnien; m. Michael Jay Tabor, Apr. 24, 1973 (div. Nov. 30, 1983); 1 child, Xanthe Rebecca Tabor. BS in Vocal Music Edn., Ohio State U., 1959; MA in Am. and English Lit., John Carroll U., 1967. Tchr. English lit., composition, dramatics Westlake (Ohio) Sr. H.S., 1964—68; adj. faculty remedial speech Cuyahoga C.C., Cleve., 1984; prof. humanities Lakeland C.C., Kirtland, Ohio, 1969—. Textbook revisionist Harper Collins Pubs., NYC, 1990—97; spkr. in field. Author: (textbook) Humanities Considered, 1966; dramatist (plays) To the Sound of the Heartbeat, 1965, A Sudden Conviction, 1966. Bd. dirs. Carl Jung Soc., Cleve., 1993—95. Recipient scholarship, Citizens Exch. Corps., 1971, grant, NEH, 1984—85. Mem.: Ams. for the ARts Action Fund, Nat. Mus. Women in Arts (charter mem.), Delta Omicron. Achievements include development of year-long humanities inter-disciplinary program. Avocations: singing, swimming, Ikebana, yoga. Office: Lakeland CC 7700 Clocktower Dr Kirtland OH 44094 Office Phone: 440-525-7193. E-mail: phyllisa1973@earthlink.net.

ASOH, DEREK AJESAM, information scientist, educator; arrived in US, 2000; s. Jacob Angwa and Miriam Adoh Asoh; life ptnr. Viviane Solange Asoh, May 17, 1990; children: McWashington Ekeh Ajesam, Miriam Farahanitra Ajesam, Andriantsoa Nchayekwah Ajesam, Marie-Tina Aboh Ajesam. MSc, Water Transport Inst., St. Petersburg, Russia, 1984—90; PhD in Info. Sci., SUNY, Albany, 2000—04. Lectr. U. Yaounde I, Cameroon, 1991—2000; tchg. asst. sch. bus. adminstrn. SUNY, 2002—04; asst. prof. info. sys. and applied tech. So. Ill. U. Carbondale, 2004—07. Network mgr. HealthNet Cameroon, Yaounde, 1993—95; network cons. SatelLife, Boston, 1993—95, UN Office Project Svcs., NYC, 1995—95, UN Econ. Commn. Africa, Addis Ababa, Ethiopia, 1996; network/info. specialist UN Devel. Program, Yaounde, 1996—97; co-chair World Info. Tech. Forum Empowerment and Participation Commn., 2006—07. Co-guest editor: Internat. Jour. Health Care Tech. and Mgmt., 2005—. Recipient Nat. Outstanding Candidate, Ministry Edn. Cameroon, 1981; Fulbright Scholar, US Dept. State, 2000. Mem.: Info. Resource Mgmt.

Assn., Assn. Computing & Machinery, Am. Health Info. Mgmt. Assn., Am. Assn. Med. Informatics, Acad. Mgmt. Office: So Ill Univ Carbondale 1365 Douglas Dr ASA Bldg 106 Carbondale IL 62901 Office Fax: 618-453-7254. Personal E-mail: derekasoh@yahoo.com. Business E-Mail: dasoh@siu.edu.

ASONEVICH, WALTER JOZEF, English educator; b. Springfield, Vt., July 29, 1950; s. Joseph Stanley and Evelyn Audrey (Bowers) A.; m. Kimberly Ann Lee, Feb. 14, 1993; step-children Micah McDowell, Heather Richman. BA in English, Keene State Coll., NH, 1977; MA in English, U. Vt., 1982; PhD in English, U. Del., 1986. Asst. prof. Cumberland County Coll., Vineland, NJ, 1986; assoc. prof. Potomac State Coll., Keyser, W.Va., 1986—98, coord. English, 1991—2000, interim dean acad. affairs, 1998—2000, cood. cmty. edn., 2000—02, prof. English, 1999—2002; v.p., dean academic affairs Corning CC, NY, 2002—. Evaluator Middle States Commn. 2005-. Author: (short stories) A Very Dark Tea, 1986, Victims of the Heat, 1992.; contbr. articles to profl. jours. Bd. dir. Steuben Sr. Svcs. Fund, 2004—; pres., bd. dir. Schuyler County Childcare Coord. Coun., 2005—. U. Vt. fellow, 1980-82, U. Del. fellow, 1985. Mem. MLA, SUNY Connect Advisory Council, League for Innovation in CCs, Am. Assn. CC, Chief Academic Officers of SUNY, NY State Transfer & Articulation Assn., Nat. Coun. Instructional Adminstrs., Am. Conf. Academic Deans, Chair Acad., Corning Rotary. Democrat. Roman Catholic. Avocations: swimming, culinary arts, snorkeling. Office: Corning CC Corning NY 14830 Office Phone: 607-962-9231. Business E-Mail: asonevich@corning-cc.edu.

ASONGU, JANUARIUS JINGWA, business executive; arrived in US, 1997; s. Nicholas Jingwa Asongu and Monique Nkeng; m. Christine Nkwayep Ngangsic, Dec. 1, 2000; children: Maria Yorkzah Ngangsic-Asongu children: Jude Jingwa Ngangsic-Asongu. PhB, Pontifical Urban U., Rome, 1993; cert. in mass. comm., U. Lagos, Nigeria, 1995; diploma in Latin, St. Thomas Aquinas Maj. Sem., Bambui, The Southern Cameroons, 1992, diploma in Greek, 1992; PhD, Pacific Western U., Hawaii, 1998; MS in Info. Tech., U. Md., Adelphi, 2002, cert. CIO officer, 2002; cert., Fed. CIO U., Washington, 2002. CEO Global Thrust Comm., Inc., Hyattsville, Md., 1999—2005, Sevire Group, LLC, 2005—; exec. dir. US-So. Cameroons Found., Inc., Hyattsville, 1999—; journalist various publs., Houston, 1997—99. Author: The Problem of National Unity in Cameroon, 1993, The Media & Nationalism: The Case of the Southern Cameroons (Nuffield Press Fellowship, 1998); editor: Houston Chronicle (AFPF, 1997), (mag.) Telecom Bus. (Telecom Profl. of the Yr., 1999), (online mag.) Global Tech. Trends; contbr. articles to profl. publs. Named Best African Journalist in the US, Assn. of African Publishers, 1998; fellow, Alfred Friendly Press, 1997, Nuffield Press fellowship, Wolfson Coll., Cambridge U., 1998. Achievements include building a company from scratch to a multi-million dollar firm within 9 months. Home: 1666 Wilson Manor Cir Lawrenceville GA 30045 Office: Sevire Group LLC 6975 New Hampshire Ave Ste 504F Hyattsville MD 20783 Personal E-mail: asongu@yahoo.com.

ASP, WILLIAM GEORGE, librarian; b. Hutchinson, Minn., July 4, 1943; s. George William and Blanche Irene (Mattson) A. BA, U. Minn., 1966, MA, 1970; postgrad., U. Iowa, 1972-75. Dir. East Cen. Regional Libr., Cambridge, Minn., 1967-70; asst. prof. Sch. Libr. Sci. U. Iowa, 1970-75; dir. Minn. Office Libr. Devel. and Svcs., St. Paul, 1975-96, Dakota County Libr., Eagan, Minn., 1996—2003. Mem. Nat. Coun. Quality Continuing Edn. for Info., Libr. and Media Pers., 1979-85; bd. dirs. Bakken Libr. Electricity and Life, Mpls.; vice chmn. White House Conf. on Libr. and Info. Svcs. Task Force, 1980-81, chmn., 1982, mem. adv. com., 1989-91; pres. Continuing Libr. Edn. Network and Exch., 1986-87. Mem. Minn. Regional Network Bd., 1992-96. Mem. ALA (mem. coun. 1985-88, 00-02), Minn. Libr. Assn., Chief Officers State Libr. Agys. (chmn. 1979-80), Minn. Ednl. Media Orgn., Minn. Assn. Continuing and Adult Edn., Assn. Specialized and Coop. Libr. Agys. (pres. 1989-90), Am. Field Svc. Home: 2095 Batello Dr Venice FL 34292

ASPAAS, JENNIFER, lawyer; b. Spokane, Wash., Nov. 9, 1968; BA, Univ. Wash., 1991; JD, Gonzaga Univ., 1996; LLM in Taxation, Univ. Wash., 1997. Bar: Wash. 1996, Ore. 2003. Former clerk US Bankruptcy Judge, Ea. Dist., Wash., 1997—98; assoc. atty., creditor bankruptcy; real estate foreclosure; real estate title Insurance; mortgage insurance; litig. Bishop, White & Marshall, P.S., Seattle, 1998—. Spkr. in field. Contbr. articles to numerous profl. jours. Named Seattle Rising Star, SuperLawyer Mag., 2006. Mem.: Seattle Bar Assn., ABA. Office: Bishop White and Marshall PS 1301 720 Olive Way Seattle WA 98101

ASPEL, PAULENE VIOLETTE, retired language educator; b. Condé-sur-Noireau, Normandy, France, Mar. 19, 1920; arrived in U.S., 1946; d. Oscar Emile Flon and Martha Chaille de Néré; m. Alexander Aspel, Dec. 20, 1945 (dec. Mar. 1975); 1 child, Amandine. MA in philosophy, U. Paris, The Sorbonne, 1945; BS in anthropology, U. Paris, 1953; MA in romance lang., U. Iowa, 1958, PhD in French & comparative lit., 1969. Iowa Secondary Sch. Tchg. Cert., 1957. Prof. philosophy Lycée Molière, Paris, 1945—46; prof. French lang. & lit. Mt Holyoke Coll., Mass., 1948—49; prof. French lang. Middlebury Coll., Vt., 1952—53; prof. French civilization & phonetics U. Paris, summers, 1954—58; prof. French civilization NDEA Inst., Cedar Rapids, Iowa, 1961—62; prof. French lang. U. Iowa, 1953—54; prof. Iowa Wesleyan Coll., 1962—75, head foreign lang. dept., 1969—74. Author (book of poems) Gout D'Une Autre Terre, 1954, Les Comptines de Colette, 1960, Traverses/Crossings, 1966, 2 chapbooks, 1999, 2004. Recipient Chevalier dans L'Ordredas Palmes Academiques, Fernch Govt., 1965; grantee U. Iowa Alumni Assn. for French textbook for children, 1970; name on Wall of Tolerance, 2005. Mem.: Heartland Leadership Coun. Democrat. Presbyterian. Avocations: writing, poetry, gardening. Home: 101 Lusk Ave Iowa City IA 52246-2419

ASPERGER, JAMES, lawyer; b. Fresno, Calif., 1953; BA with highest honors, U. Calif., Davis, 1975; JD, U. Calif., LA, 1978. Bar: Calif. 1978, DC 1980. Law clerk to Hon. Stanley Mosk Supreme Ct. Calif., 1978—79; law clerk to Hon. William H. Rehnquist US Supreme Ct., 1979—80; asst. US atty. Central Dist. Calif., 1983—93; dep. chief, major frauds sect. LA US Attorney's Office, 1987—90, chief, major frauds sect., 1990—93; ptnr. O'Melveny & Myers LLP, LA, mem. policy com., chair global enforcement and criminal defense group. Lectr. continuing legal education courses on criminal law, civil enforcement actions, and the RICO statute; bd. dir. Western Ctr. on Law and Poverty, 1997—, Office of Pub. Counsel, 1998—. Assoc. editor UCLA Law Review, 1976—77, editor-in-chief, 1977—78; contbr. articles to profl. jours. Named one of Top Trial Lawyers in So. Calif., LA Bus. Jour., 1999; recipient Alumni award for Academic Distinction, U. Calif., LA. Fellow: Am. Coll. of Trial Lawyers; mem.: Fed. Bar Assn. (bd. dir., LA Chpt. 1997—), ABA (former chair, West Coast White Collar Crime Com. 1998—2000, vice-chair, Nat. White Collar Crime Com. 2000—02), Assn. Trail Lawyers of Am., Order of Coif, Phi Beta Kappa. Office: O'Melveny & Myers LLP 400 S Hope St Los Angeles CA 90071-2899 Office Phone: 213-430-6491. Office Fax: 213-430-6407. Business E-Mail: jasperger@omm.com.

ASPERO, BENEDICT VINCENT, lawyer; b. Newton, NJ, Sept. 3, 1940; s. Umberto S. and Rose (Cerreta) A.; m. Sally Hennen, June 26, 1971; children: Benedict Vincent, Alexander Morgan. AB, U. Notre Dame, 1962, JD, 1966. Bar: NJ 1970, NY 1982, D.C. 1983, US Dist. Ct. NJ 1970, US Supreme Ct. 1981. Assoc., then ptnr. Meyers, Lesser & Aspero, Sparta, NJ, 1971-76; atty. Benedict V. Aspero, Sparta and Morristown, NJ, 1976-82; ptnr. Broderick, Newmark, Grather & Aspero, Morristown, 1982-89, Courter, Kobert, Laufer, Purcell & Cohen, 1989-91; prin. Benedict V. Aspero, Esq., P.C., 1992—. Mem. adv. bd. First Morris Bank. Trustee Harding Twp. Civic Assn., Loyola Retreat House, 1992—99, Craig Sch., 1985—, pres. bd., 1992—2002. Mem. ABA, NJ Bar Assn., Morris County Bar Assn., Sussex County Bar Assn., St. Thomas More Soc., Sorin Soc. (bd. govs., sec.), Morristown Club, Essex Hunt Club. Republican. Roman Catholic. Office: 222 Ridgedale Ave PO Box 1573 Morristown NJ 07962-1573 E-mail: bvatty@GTI.net.

ASPINWALL, DAVID CHARLES, lawyer, insurance company executive; b. Denver, Apr. 15, 1955; s. Darrell David and Gwendolyn Beth (Skeels) Aspinwall; m. Inez Bussey Merritt, Dec. 5, 1981; children: Courney Merritt, Johnathan Westbrook. BA, Denver U., 1977, JD, 1980. Bar: Colo. 1980, U.S. Ct. Appeals (10th cir.), U.S. Supreme Ct. Assoc. Dunn, Crane & Burg, Denver, 1980—81, Michael S. Burg, P.C., Denver, 1981—83, Burg & Aspinwall, P.C., Denver, 1983—88; chief legal officer, litig. and corp. compliance Gt. West Life & Annuity Ins. Co., Greenwood Village, Colo., 1988—; mem. Legal Adv. Group AHIP, 2003—. Mem. class action working group ACLI, 1995—2000; faculty, life ins. litig. ALIABA; legal adv. com. Employment Retirement Income Security Act, 1998, 2001, 06; adv. work group AAHP, 2001—03; instr. in field; legal adv. group Am. Health Ins. Plans, 2003—, adv. group, 2003—. Mem. auction underwriting com. St. Anne's Episc. Sch., 1988—89; pre-marital facilitator Christ Episc. Ch., 1988—94; pres. Sundance Pride, 1987—90. Mem.: Gen. Counsel Roundtable, Am. Corp. Counsel Assn., Internat. Assn. Def. Counsel, Internat. Claims Assn. (law com. 1990—93, panel law com. presentation ann. conv. 1992), Colo. Bar Assn., Def. Rsch. Inst., Arapahoe County Bar Assn., Phi Beta Kappa. Republican. Office: Great West Life & Annuity Ins Co 8525 E Orchard Rd Ste 200 Greenwood Village CO 80111-5097 Business E-Mail: david.aspinwall@gwl.com.

ASPLUNDH, CHRISTOPHER B., tree service company executive; b. Aug. 26, 1939; BBA, U. Pa. Joined Asplundh Tree Expert Co., Willow Grove, Pa., 1963, v.p., 1966, pres., 1992-2001, CEO, chmn. bd. dir., 2001—. With USMC. Office: Asplundh Tree Expert Co 708 Blair Mill Rd Willow Grove PA 19090-1784

ASPNES, DAVID ERIK, physicist, researcher; b. Madison, Wis., May 1, 1939; s. Erik A. and Anita L. (Knabe) A.; m. Edna Joyce Hall, Jan. 27, 1964 (dec. 1996); children: James D., Gary E., Ann K.; m. Cynthia Jean Ball, July 26, 1997. BSEE, U. Wis., 1960, MSEE, 1961; PhD, U. Ill., 1965. Postdoctoral rsch. assoc. U. Ill., Urbana, 1965-66, Brown U., Providence, 1966-67; mem. tech. staff Bell Labs., Murray Hill, NJ, 1967-83; sr. scientist Max-Planck-Inst., Stuttgart, Fed. Republic Germany, 1976-77; dist. mgr. Bellcore, Red Bank, NJ, 1983-92; prof. physics dept. NC State U., Raleigh, 1992—99, disting. univ. prof. physics, 1999—. Contbr. more than 450 articles to Phys. Rev., Applied Optics, Thin Solid Films and other jours.; U.S. editor Applied Surface Sci., 1996-2001. Recipient Sr. Scientist award Alexander von Humboldt Found., 1976-77, John Yarwood medal Brit. Vacuum Coun., 1993, Max Planck Rsch. Award for Internat. Coop., 1997, Outstanding Rsch. award N.C. State U. Alumni Assn., 1997; named Alumni Disting. Grad. Prof. NC State U. Alumni Assn., 2005. Fellow AAAS, Am. Phys. Soc. (councillor divsn. condensed matter physics 1996-99, exec. coun. 1998-99, Frank Isakson prize 1996), Optical Soc. Am. (Wood prize 1987), Am. Vacuum Soc. (chmn. electronic materials and processing divsn. 1982-83, chmn. electronics materials and processing divsn. Internat. Union Vacuum Sci., Techniques and Applications 1986-89, bd. dirs. 1991-92, trustee 2001-03, pres. 2005, Medard W. Welch award 1998), Soc. Photo-Optical Instrumentation Engrs., World Innovation Found.; mem. IEEE, Nat. Acad. Scis., Materials Rsch. Soc., Alexander von Humboldt Assn. Am., Sigma Xi. Mem. Lds Ch. Achievements include discovery and development of reflectance-difference spectroscopy and low-field electroreflectance; development of spectroscopic ellipsometry with applications to process control; contributions to solid-state physics including 3rd derivative interpretation of low-field electroreflectance, ordering of the lower conduction bands of GaAs, elucidation of the kinetics of crystal growth by organometallic chemical vapor deposition, virtual-interface theory, arisotropic bond model of nonlinear optics. Office: NC State U Physics Dept Raleigh NC 27695-8202 Business E-Mail: aspnes@unity.ncsu.edu.

ASRYAN, LEVON V., physicist, electronics engineer, materials scientist; m. Anna V. Sharonova. MSc in Radiophysics and Electronics, Yerevan State U., 1985; PhD in Physics and Math., Ioffe Inst., St. Petersburg, 1988; DSc in Physics and Math., Ioffe Physico-Technical Inst., St. Petersburg, 2002. Sr. rschr. Ioffe Physico-Tech. Inst., St. Petersburg, Russia, 1992—2005; rsch. assoc. prof. dept. elec. and computer engring. SUNY, Stony Brook, 2000—04; assoc. prof. dept. materials sci. and engring. Va. Tech., Blacksburg, 2004—. Reviewer Applied Physics Letters and IEEE jours., 1998—; mem. program com. summer topical workshop on nanostructures and quantum dots IEEE LEOS, San Diego, 1999; presenter in field. Contbr. articles, series of papers to profl. publs. Recipient Best Paper award, IEEE Jour. Quantum Electronics, 2001, State Prize in Sci. and Tech., Russia, 2001. Achievements include patent for semiconductor laser with reduced temperature sensitivity; first to theory of threshold characteristics of quantum dot lasers. Office: Va Tech Dept MSE 207 Holden Hall MC 0237 Blacksburg VA 24061

ASSAEL, HENRY, marketing educator; b. Sofia, Bulgaria, Sept. 12, 1935; s. Stanley Isaac and Anna (Behar) A.; m. Alyce Friedman, Aug. 19, 1961; children: Shaun Eric, Brenda Erica. BA cum laude, Harvard U., 1957; MBA, U. Pa., 1959; PhD, Columbia U., 1965. Asst. prof. mktg. Sch. Bus. St. John's U., Jamaica, NY, 1962—65; asst. prof. mktg. Hofstra U., Hempstead, NY, 1965—66; prof. mktg. Stern Sch. Bus. NYU, 1966—, chmn. dept., 1979—91. Cons. AT&T, N.Y. Stock Exch., Nestle Co., Inc., CBS. Author: Educational Preparations for Positions in Advertising Management, 1966, The Politics of Distributive Trade Associations: A Study in Conflict Resolution, 1967, Consumer Behavior and Marketing Action, 1981, 6th edit. 1998, Marketing Management: Strategy and Action, 1985, Marketing: Principles and Strategy, 1990, 2d edit., 1993, Marketing: Core Concepts, 1998, Consumer Behavior: A Strategic Approach, 2004; editor: A Century of Marketing, 33 vols., 1978, Early Development and Conceptualization of the Field of Marketing, 1978, History of Advertising, 40 vols., 1985; contbr. numerous articles to profl. jours. Mem. Am. Mktg. Assn., Assn. Consumer Rsch. Office: 44 W 4th St New York NY 10012-1106 Office Phone: 212-998-0514. Business E-Mail: hassael@stern.nyu.edu.

AS-SALAAM, JAMAAL (WILLIAM LOUIS WILLIAMS JR.), poet, film producer, writer; b. Albany, NY, Apr. 20, 1955; s. William Louis Williams Sr. and Helen Virginia Williams-Smith; m. Veronica Foster, June 20, 1980 (div. June 1985); children: Qwinde, Shani O.; m. Arlene Hooks (div. Sept. 1992); 1 child, Jamar Williams; m. Terisita Ann Lopez; 1 child, Mieko O. Lopez. Student, SUNY, Purchase, 1972—76, U. No. Colo., 1984—86, Nat. U., Encino, Calif., 1990—92, Calif. Arts Partnership, 1995—98. Cert. Microsoft cert. sys. engr. Ednet Career Inst., Microsoft software trainer, Microsoft cert. profl., A+ cert. computer svc. technician. Track laborer Burlington No. RR, 1978-85; computer specialist Denver Pub. Schs., 1980—86; Saks cons. Tom Hopkins Sales Tng., Denver, 1984-86; tech. support Telepoetics, LA, 1988-94; computer technician LA County Schs., Bellflower, Calif., 1987-94; video editor Calif. Arts Cmty. Ptnrs., LA, 1994-99; rschr. Sales, Inc., Beverly Hills, Calif., 1996-97; ind. prodr. Lightland Prodns., LA, 1999—. Freelance prodr. Mile High Cable Co., Denver, 1983-86; radio announcer Sta. KUVO, Denver, 1984-85. Author: One-Eyed Dogs, 2006, (anthology) Portraits of Life, 1997 (Editors Choice award), (chapbook) Facing East, 1995; actor: (TV) Naked Truth, General Hospital, also commls. and theatrical prodns.; dir., writer, prodr.: (film) Leimert Park, 1996; (theatre) New Age Perspective, The Muse; (video) Poetry 101, Leimert Park: Unlocking the Pyramid, Coming Full Circle, 2002; dir., writer: (theatre) Persona Suite, Kwanzaa Adatation; dir., prodr.: (video) History Revisited. Vol. Inner City Cultural Ctr., 1989-95; founding mem. Denver Black Arts Theater Co., 1980-85; mem. Win/Win Bus. Forum, Denver, 1984; vol., mem. Telepoetics, LA, 1994; vol. LA In Support of Gang Truce, 1996; mem. Black Radical Congress, 1999. Recipient Calif. Arts Cmty. Project award Calif. Inst. of Arts, 1996, 98, 1st prize Upstate Photography, Albany, NY, 1973. Mem. Black Radical Congress. Buddhist. Avocations: reading, sports, swimming, conga, martial arts, art restoration. Home and Office: PO Box 815 Englewood CO 80110 Personal E-mail: jamaal21@hotmail.com.

ASSELIN, HEATHER E., lawyer; BA, Calif. State U., Fresno, 1993; JD, Creighton U. Sch. Law, 1996. Bar: Tex., US Dist. Ct. (so. dist.) Tex., US Dist. Ct. (no. dist.) Tex., US Dist. Ct. (ea. dist.) Tex. Dir. litigation and constrn./surety sects. Coats Rose. Named a Rising Star, Tex. Super Lawyers mag., 2006, 2007. Mem.: Assn. Gen. Contractors (Houston chpt.), Assn. Women Attys. (former mem. jud. reception com., bd. dirs.), Houston Bar Assn. (litigation and constrn. sects.) (mem. CLE com.). Office: Coats Rose Yale Ryman Lee 3 E Greenway Plz Ste 2000 Houston TX 77046 Office Phone: 713-653-7386. E-mail: hasselin@coatsrose.com.

ASSELIN-CONNOLLY, JOHN THOMAS, lawyer; b. Manchester, Conn., May 13, 1951; s. Oliver Joseph and MaryRose Mildred (Dondero) A.; children: Jessica Lynn, Kristina Anne. BA, U. Conn., 1973, JD, 1976. Bar: Conn. 1976, U.S. Dist. Ct. Conn. 1976. Pvt. practice, New London, Conn., 1976—. Lectr. Practicing Law Inst. N.Y., Profl. Edn. Systems Inc. Author: Connecticut Workers' Compensation Practice Manual, The Trial Handbook for Connecticut Lawyers; contbr. articles to profl. jours. Served Conn. gov. Thomas J. Meskill, U.S. Rep. Robert Steele. Grantee Deerfield Found. Mem. ABA (lectr.), Conn. Bar Assn. (exec. com. civil justice sect.), Assn. Trial Lawyers Am., Conn. Trial Lawyers Assn. (bd. govs. 1981—), Phi Beta Kappa, Phi Kappa Phi, Pi Sigma Alpha. Roman Catholic. Avocations: horses, team penning. Office: 38 Granite St New London CT 06320-5931 Office Phone: 860-447-0708. Business E-Mail: jta@lawmatters.com.

ASSINI, VINCENT PAUL, financial executive; b. Newark, Dec. 1, 1950; s. Vincent A. and Jean L. (Di Pietro) A.; m. Elisabeth Schmidt, May 2, 1979. BSBA, U. Fla., 1972. CPA, N.Y. Contr. Ingersoll-Rand, Vienna, 1976-81; mgr. planning OTIS, Paris, 1982-86, dir. fin. Munich, 1987-90; divsn. contr. J.I. Case, Paris, 1990-92; divsn. gen. mgr. Alusuisse-Lonza, Singen, Germany, 1993-96; CFO, Leica AG, St. Gallen, Switzerland, 1996-98. Bd. dirs. Leica Microsys., Wetzlar, Germany, Leica Geosys., Heerbrugg, Switzerland. Mem. AICPA, Swiss Fin. Execs. Home and Office: 4321 Dewey Dr New Port Richey FL 34652-3114

ASSINK, NELLIE GRACE, agricultural executive; b. Yakima, Wash., July 5, 1920; d. Martin Gilde and Grace Byl; m. George H. Assink, July 9, 1943 (dec. Nov. 1982); children: Macile Assink Zais, Jon Martin. BA, Whitman Coll./Conserv. Music, 1942, tchr.'s diploma in music and piano, 1942; postgrad., U. Wash. and Cen. Coll., 1944-59. Gen. cert., Wash.; cert. supr. music. English tchr., libr. Mabton (Wash.) H.S., 1943-45; libr. Wide Hollow Sch., Yakima, 1948-49; English tchr., libr. Lower Naches (Wash.) Sch., 1960-80; pres. Assink Acres, Inc., Naches, 1982—. Ch. organist Meml. Bible Ch., Yakima, 1946-82; chmn. Christian Edn. Bd., 1981-82; bd. dirs., sec. Yakima County Farm Bur., 1985-99; libr. Meml. Bible Ch., Yakima, 1960—. Mem. Naches Union Irrigation Dist. (sec. 1993—), Yakima County Farm Bur. (past sec. 1997), Lower Naches Women's Club (pres. 1984-86, 2000-02), Yakima Music Club, Ch. Librs.-N.W. (past pres.). Republican. Avocations: genealogy, photography, classical piano. Home: 681 N Gleed Rd Naches WA 98937 Office: Assink Acres Inc 681 N Gleed Rd Naches WA 98937

ASSOUSA, GEORGE ELIAS, information technology executive, physicist, corporate executive; b. Jerusalem, Mar. 15, 1936; emigrated to U.S., 1953, naturalized, 1965; divorced; children: Mark Andrew, Virginia Noel. BA, Earlham Coll., 1957; postgrad. (Rockefeller Bros. fellow), Union Theol. Sem., 1957-58; MA, Columbia U., 1960; PhD (Nuclear Sci. fellow, Grad. fellow), Fla. State U., 1968. Mem. faculty Earlham Coll., Richmond, Ind., 1960-63; rsch. asst., instr. nuclear physics Fla. State U., Tallahassee, 1963-68; fellow Carnegie Instn. of Washington, 1968-70, rsch. prof., mem. sci. staff, 1970-80, sr. fellow, 1980-81; chief sci. and tech. advisor Coats Viyella, PLC, London, 1987—91; chmn. Coats Viyella Techs., Ltd., London, 1987—91; chmn. London sect. Mgmt. Cons. Ctrl. and Ea. Europe, 1991—. Sci. and ednl. affairs v.p. Ideas, Inc., Washington, 1974-75; cons. Princeton U. Obs., 1971-72; cons. on Mid-East sci. Nat. Acad. Scis., 1975; advisor sci. and tech. policy to Crown Prince Hassan of Jordan, 1976-78; cons. N.J. Marine Scis. Consortium, 1980-87; Presdl. fellow, fellow program in sci., tech. and humanism Aspen Inst. for Humanistic Studies, 1978-80 Contbr.: articles in field to Phys. Rev.; co-discoverer supernova induced star formation, 1977. Co-founder, pres. Found. for Arab-Israeli Reconciliation, Washington, 1974-77, co-chmn. bd., 1977-78; founder, dir. Salzburg Internat. Affairs Seminar, 1979-81; dir.-gen. Trust for Internat. Devel. and Edn., London, 1979-86; pres. Partnership for Internat. Devel., Inc., Washington, 1981-86; vice chmn. Internat. Scholars for Environ. Studies Inc., 1987—; pres. Gryphon Tech. Investors, 1987-88. Mem. Internat. Astron. Union, Am. Astron. Soc., AAUP, Am. Phys. Soc., Council Fgn. Relations, Royal Inst. Internat. Affairs, Sigma Xi. Clubs: Cosmos, Athenaeum. Office: Multi Techs Group 15 Stratton St Mayfair London W1J 8LQ England

AST, THESESA LYNN, history professor; b. Harlingen, Tex., Aug. 11, 1954; d. Jacek Z. Ast and Betty Jo Baker; m. Russell O-Neal Clay, Dec. 20, 1972 (div.); children: Jeremy J. Clay, Benjamin O. Clay, Christopher N. Clay. BA, Marietta, Ga., 1988; MA in History, PhD in History, Emory U., Atlanta. Instr. State U. West Ga., Carrollton; instr. to asst. prof. Reinhardt Coll., Waleska, Ga., assoc. prof. Lectr. Sr. Enriched Living, Roswell, Ga., 1999—2007. Recipient Exemplory Tchg. award, United Meth., Reinhardt Coll., 2004; fellow, Gov. of Ga. Fellow: Holocaust Project Emory U.; mem.: So. Hist. Assn., Am. Hist. Assn. Avocations: reading, films, sewing. Office: Reinhardt Coll 7300 Reinhardt Col Cir Waleska GA 30183

ASTER, RUTH MARIE RHYDDERCH, business owner; b. Cleve., Aug. 15, 1939; d. Roy William and Ruth Marie (Teckmeyer) Rhydderch; m. Ferdinand Aster, Nov. 23, 1963; children: Anneliese Ruth Aster Wilt, Christian Josef Roy Student, Cooper Sch. Art, Cleve., 1957; BS, Kent State U., Ohio, 1962. Tchr. art North Olmsted Jr. and Sr. H.S., Ohio, 1962—64; chmn. art dept. Andrews Sch. for Girls, Willoughby, Ohio, 1963—64; co-owner, treas. Aster Cabinet Shop, Chesterland, Ohio, 1963—; co-owner, v.p., treas. Ferdl Aster Ski Sch., Chesterland, 1964—; owner, v.p., sec., treas. Ferdl Aster Ski Shop, Chesterland, 1972—; owner, v.p., advt. designer, fashion buyer, tour advisor Ferdl Aster Sport Ctr., Chesterland, 1985—. Chmn. region IV U.S. Ski Assn., Colorado Springs, 1980—84, Alpine ofcl., 1983—88; ski racing coach U.S. Ski Coaches Assn., Park City, Utah, 1980—89; ski racing coach, Alpine ofcl. Fedn. Internat. Ski, Bern, Switzerland, Alpine ofcl.; adv. bd. First County Bank, Chesterland, 1992—2000; adv. coun. U.S. Postal Svc., Chesterland, 1993—2000; v.p., bd. mem. in charge zoning space Lake Cardinal Timbering Corp., 2002—. Exhibitions include Akron Mus. Art, 1959, Cleve. Gallery, 1962—64, Willoughby Fine Arts, 1963—65, Wagrain, Austria, 1979—, Fairmont Fine Arts, 1980—. Creator blind ski program Cleve. Sight Ctr., 1969; trustee Chesterland Hist. Found., 1985—, past pres., past v.p., past treas.; past chair, vice chair Chester Twp. Zoning Commr., 1987—; life friend Geauga West Libr., 1989—, bd. dirs., historian; dir. history ARC, Cleve., amb.,

1999—; grad. Leadership Geauga, 1997; bd. dirs. Geauga County Libr. Found.; v.p. bd. dirs., mem. mktg. com. Geauga County Coun. for Arts and Culture, 2002—. Mem.: North Ea. Ohio Ski Retailers Assn. (bd. dirs.), Orchesis, Cmty. Improvement Corp. Geauga County (re-orgn. com., nominating com., trustee 1990—), Chesterland C. of C. (past pres., v.p., treas., trustee 1985—, sec. to exec. bd. 2001—, Bus. Person of Yr. 1993), Kent State U. Alumni Pvt. Sector Bus. Alliance, Internat. Platform Assn., Kent State U. Alumni Assn. (life), Chester Study Club (past v.p., pres. 1997—2003), Gamma Delta, Alpha Psi Omega, Chi Omega. Lutheran. Avocations: reading, hiking, hunting, collecting classic autos and historic homes. Office: Ferdl Aster Ski Shop 8330 Mayfield Rd Chesterland OH 44026-2520 Home Phone: 440-729-4227; Office Phone: 440-729-9472. E-mail: fasterskier@prodigy.net.

ASTHANA, RAJIV, engineering educator, researcher; b. Lucknow, India, June 18, 1957; s. Hari S. and Kamala Asthana; m. Neerja Prakash, Apr. 22, 1987; children: Ankur, Akansha. BS, Indian Inst. Tech., Kharagpur, 1980, MS, 1983; PhD, U. Wis., Milw., 1991. Staff scientist Coun. Sci. and Indsl. Rsch., Bhopal, India, 1983-87; tchg. and rsch. asst. U. Wis., Milw., 1987-91; resident rsch. assoc. NASA Lewis Rsch. Ctr., Cleve., 1991-95, project scientist, 1993; asst. prof. mfg. engring. U. Wis. Stout, Menomonie, 1995-99, assoc. prof., 1999—2004, prof. engring. and tech., 2005—. Vis. assoc. prof. U. Wis., 2000-04; NSF vis. scientist Foundry Rsch. Inst., Poland, 2002 Author: Solidification Processing of Reinforced Metals, 1998, Materials Processing and Manufacturing Science, 2006; assoc. editor Jour. Materials Engring. and Performance; mem. editl. bd. Bull. Polish Acad. Scis.; referee in field; contbr. articles to profl. jours. NRC postdoctoral rsch. assoc., 1994-95; Barker Meml. fellow, 1988-89, Faculty fellow NASA, 2004-05; recipient Cert. Recognition award NASA, 1996, Rschr. award U. Wis.; named Stout Outstanding scholar U. Wis. Mem. Am. Soc. Materials (Howe medal, Grossman award selection com.), The Minerals, Metals and Materials Soc., Am. Foundrymen's Soc., Am. Soc. Engring. Edn., Am. Ceramic Soc. Office: U Wis Stout 326 Fryklund Hall Menomonie WI 54751-3841 Home: 2615 Schabacker Ct Menomonie WI 54751-3760 Office Phone: 715-232-2152. Business E-Mail: asthanar@uwstout.edu.

ASTI, ALISON LOUISE, lawyer; b. Phila., July 25, 1954; d. Andrew Paul and Elsie Aileen (Sincavage) Asti. BA, Duke U., 1975, MA in Pub. Fin., 1976; JD, U. Md., 1979. Bar: Md. 1979. Assoc. Gordon, Feinblatt et al, Balt., 1979-86, ptnr., 1986-90; gen. counsel Md. Stadium Authority, 1990—2004, exec. dir., 2004—. Presenter Nat. Confs. on Sports Facility Fin. Chair editl. bd. The Daily Record, 1998—. Mem. Gov. Glendening's Task Force on Jud. Nominating Com., 1995; mem. U. Md. Law Sch. Bd. Vis., 1997—; pres. Gibson Island County Sch. Parents Assn., 1996-98; pres. Met. Bar Caucus, 1999-2000; mem. sect. coun. Nat. Conf. Bar Presidents, 2000-03; dir. U. Sys. Md. Found. Recipient Leadership in Law award The Daily Record, 2005; named one of Md.'s Top 100 Women Warfield's Bus. Record, 1996, Md. Superlawyers, 2007. Fellow Am. Bar Found.; mem. ABA (ho. of dels. 1995-98, 2006—), Md. Bar Assn. (bd. govs. 1986-88, 95-97, 2003-04, pres.-elect 2006-07), Bar Assn. Balt. City (pres. 1994-95), Md. State Bar Found. (pres. 1999-2001), Balt. Women's Bar Assn. Md. (pres. 1986-87), Balt. City Bar Found. (pres. 1994-95), U. Md. Sys. Found (dir. 2005-). Avocations: water sports, running, skiing, horseback riding, photography. Home: 527 Sylview Dr # A Pasadena MD 21122-5523

ASTILL, KENNETH NORMAN, mechanical engineering educator; b. Westerly, RI, July 16, 1923; s. John Henry and Mabel Nellie (Robotham) A.; m. Hazel Patricia Lamb, Apr. 10, 1948; 1 child: Kenneth John. BS, U. R.I., 1944; MA in Engring., Chrysler Inst. Engring., 1946; MS, Harvard U., 1953; PhD, MIT, 1961. Lab engr. Chrysler Corp., Detroit, 1944-47; prof. mech. engring. Tufts U., Medford, Mass., 1947-91, assoc. dean engring., 1980-88, prof. emeritus, 1991—. Mem. energy facilities siting coun. Commn. of Mass., 1989-92; mng. dir. U. Rsch. Engring. Assn., 1989—1997; cons. Sylvania Electric Co., Natick Labs., Kaye Instruments, C.S. Draper Labs.; vis. fellow U. Leeds, 1976, U. Sussex, 1983. Author: (with B. Arden) Numerical Algorithms, 1970, Elementary Experiments in Mechanical Engineering, 1971, (with others) Laboratory Demonstrations in Heat Transfer and Fluid Mechanics, 1968. Trustee Charles River Mus., 1992-2003. Recipient Ralph R. Teeter award Soc. Automotive Engrs., 1981; NSF fellow, 1968 Fellow ASME (life, chmn. Boston sect. 1981-82); mem. AAUP, Am. Soc. Engring. Edn., Engring. Soc. New Eng. (bd. dirs. 1982-87), Sigma Xi, Tau Beta Pi. Home: 72 Yale St Winchester MA 01890-2331 Office: Tufts U Anderson Hall Medford MA 02155

ASTIN, SEAN PATRICK, actor, film director, film producer, writer; b. Santa Monica, Calif, Feb. 25, 1971; s. Michael Tell and Patty Duke, adopted s. John Astin; m. Christine Louise Astin, July 11, 1992; children: Alexandra Louise, Elizabeth Louise, Isabella Louise. BA in History and English with honors, UCLA. Actor: (films) The Goonies, 1985 (Young Artist award, 1986), White Water Summer, 1987, Like Father, Like Son, 1987, Staying Together, 1989 (Young Artist award, 1990), The War of the Roses, 1989, Memphis Belle, 1990, Toy Soldiers, 1991, The Willies, 1991, Encino Man, 1992, Where the Day Takes You, 1992, Rudy, 1993, Safe Passage, 1994, The Low Life, 1995 (Pres. award Ft. Lauderdale Internat. Film Festival, 1995), Courage Under Fire, 1996, Bulworth, 1998, Boy Meets Girl, 1998, Kimberly, 1999, Deterrance, 1999, Icebreaker, 1999, The Last Producer, 2000, Dish Dogs, 2000, The Sky is Falling, 2000, The Lord of the Rings: The Fellowship of the Ring, 2001, The Lord of the Rings: The Two Towers, 2002 (Visual Effects Soc. award, 2003), The Lord of the Rings: Return of the Kings, 2003 (Best Supporting Actor award, Seattle Film Critics Soc., Best Supporting Actor award, Las Vegas Film Critics Soc.), 50 First Dates, 2004, Elvis Has Left the Building, 2004, (voice only) Balto III: Wings of Change, 2004, Smile, 2005, Bigger Than the Sky, 2005, Marilyn Hotchkiss' Ballroom Dancing and Charm School, 2005, Click, 2006; (TV films) Please Don't Hit Me Mom, 1981, The Rules of Marriage, 1982, The B.R.A.T. Patrol, 1986, Harrison Bergeron, 1995; (TV series) Jeremiah, 2003—04, (voice) Party Wagon, 2004,: (TV miniseries) Hercules, 2005, Into the West, 2005; guest appearances: (TV series) Perversions of Science, 1997; Las Vegas, 2004; The Shield, 2006; actor, co-prodr.: (films) Slipstream, 2005; dir.(producer): On My Honor, 1988; co-dir.(producer): Kangaroo Court, 1994 (nominated Acad. award Best Live Action Short, 1995); dir.(producer, writer): The Long and Short of It, 2003,: (TV films) Perversions of Science, 1997, Nickelodeon's 100 Good Deeds for Eddie McDowd; (TV series) Angel, Jeremiah; author (with Joe Layden): There and Back Again: An Actor's Tale, 2004. Active Pres.'s Coun. Svc. and Civic Participation. Mem.: Am. Fedn. Television and Radio Artists, Screen Actors Guild, Dirs. Guild Am.

ASTLEY, AMY, editor-in-chief; married; 2 children. BA in English Lit., Mich. State U., East Lansing, 1989. Editl. asst. House and Garden mag., asst. editor, assoc. editor; beauty assoc. Vogue mag., 1993—94, beauty dir., 1994—2005; editor-in-chief Teen Vogue, 2005—. Named one of Most Powerful Fashion Editors, Forbes.com, 2006. Office: Teen Vogue 4 Times Sq New York NY 10036*

ASTMAN, BARBARA ANN, artist, educator; b. Rochester, NY, July 12, 1950; d. George William and Bertha Dinah (Meisel) A.; m. Noel Robert Harding, Feb. 23, 1977 (div. 1983); m. Joseph Anthony Baker, Aug. 29, 1984; children: Amy Astman Baker, Laura Astman Baker. A degree, RIT, 1970; grad., Ont. Coll. Art, Toronto, 1973. Prof photography dept. Ont. Coll. Art and Design (formerly Ont. Coll. Art), Toronto, 1975—; faculty York U., Toronto, 1978-80, 86. Lectr. in field. One-woman shows include: Baldwin St. Gallery Photography, Toronto, 1973, Ryerson Photo Gallery, Toronto, 1974, Nat. Film Bd. Can., Ottawa, 1975, S.A.W. Gallery Inc., 1976, Sable-Castelli Gallery Ltd., Toronto, 1977, 79-84, 86, 88, 90, Jean Marie Antone Gallery, Annapolis, Md., 1979, Whitewater Gallery, North Bay, Ont., Bruce Art Gallery, Canton, NY, 1980, Mendel Art Gallery, Saskatoon, Sask., 1981, So. Alta. Art Gallery, Edmonton, 1981, Art Gallery Peterborough, Ont., 1982, Galerie du Musee, Musee du Quebec, 1986, Ctr. d'Animation et de Diffusion de la Photographie, Quebec, 1986, Thunder Bay Art Gallery, Ont., 1992, Robert McLaughlin Gallery, Oshawa, Ont., 1993, McIntosh Gallery, London, Ont., 1994, Gallery Stratford, Ont., 1994, Art Gallery Hamilton, 1995, Edmonton Art Gallery, Kamloops Art Gallery, BC, 1996-2005, Jane Corkin Gallery (now Corkin Gallery), 1997, 99, 2001, 03, 05, 07, Art Gallery Windsor, 2004, Yukon Art Ctr., Whitehorse, Yukon, 2005, Koffler Art Gallery, Toronto, 2006, Corkin Gallery, 2007; group exhbns. include: Lamkin Camerawork Gallery, San Francisco, 1975, Art Gallery Ont., Toronto, 1975, 80, 84, 93, Rochester Meml. Art Gallery, Montreal Mus. Fine Arts, 1975, Harbourfront Art Gallery, Toronto, 1977, 80, Sable-Castelli Gallery Ltd., 77, 81, Anna Leonowens Gallery, Halifax, N.S., 1977, London Regional Art Gallery, Ont., 1978, 83, Edmonton Art Gallery, Ont., 1978, Winnipeg Art Gallery, 1979, Everson Mus., Syracuse, NY, 1979, Galerie Luca Polazzoli, Milan, 1979, H.F. Johnson Mus. Art, Ithaca, NY, 1979, George Eastman House, Rochester, 1979, Hamilton Art Gallery, La Galerie Powerhouse, Montreal, 1981, YYZ Gallery Toronto, 1982, Forum des Halles, Paris, 1985, Graves Art Gallery, Sheffield, U.K., 1985, San Diego Art Ctr., 1986, Hallwalls Gallery, Buffalo, 1986, La Galerie des Arts Lavalin, Montreal, 1988, Pro Mus. Contemporary Art, Finland, 1988, Kamloops Art Gallery, 1989, Koffler Gallery, Toronto, 1990, Art Gallery Peterborough, Ont., 1992, Art Gallery Hamilton, 1993, So. Alta. Art Gallery, Lethbridge, 1994, Art Gallery Hamilton, Gallerie Arts Tech., Montreal, Basel Art Fair, Switzerland, 1998-2006, Basel Art, Miami, 2002-06, Chgo. Art Fair, 1999, Nat. Gallery Can., Ottawa, 2000, Can. Mus. Contemporary Art, North York, Ont., 2000, Can. Mus. Contemporary Photography, Ottawa, 2000-01, Nat. Gallery Can., Ottawa, Art Gallery Hamilton, 2001, Kitchener-Waterloo Art Gallery, Ont., 2001, Art Basel, 2002-06, Basel Art Fair, 2002-06, Toronto Photgraphers Workshop, 2002, Confedn. Art Ctr. Art Gallery, Prince Edward Island, 2003, Art Gallery Bishop's U., Que., 2003, McMichael Gallery, Kleinburg, Ont, 2004, Les Revenants Le Mois de la Photo Mai, Montreal Quebec, 2005, Art Gallery Peterborough, Ont., Can., 2006 White Box, NY, 2007; public collections include: Agnes Etherington Art Ctr., Kingston, Ont., Art Gallery Hamilton, Art Gallery Ont., Toronto, Bibliotheque Nationale, Paris, Gallery/Stratford, Nickle Arts Mus., Calgary, Alta., Robert McLaughlin Gallery, Oshawa, Winnipeg Art Gallery, Victoria and Albert Mus., London. Coord. Colour Xerox Artists' Program, Visual Arts Ont., Toronto, 1977-83; bd. dirs. Art Gallery at Harbourfront, Toronto, 1983-85; apptd. mem. City of Toronto Pub. Art Commn., 1986-89; mem. curatorial team WaterWorks Exhbn., Toronto, 1988; chmn. Toronto Arts Awards, Visual Arts Jury, 1988; bd. dirs. Arts Found. of Greater Toronto, 1989-92; mem. ednl. adv. com. Art Gallery Ontario, 1999-2000; mem. Toronto Cmty. Found., Arts on Track Com., Toronto Bay Crest Hosp Art Com., 2006—. Recipient Silver award, Photographic Still Life, Can., Nat. Mag. award. Mem.: Royal Can. Acad. Arts. Office: 23 Alcina Ave Toronto ON Canada M6G 2E7 Address: Corkin Gallery 55 Mill St Bldg 61 Toronto ON Canada M5A 3C4 Home Phone: 416-537-0808. Personal E-mail: astmanba@aol.com.

ASTON, SHERRELL JERONE, plastic surgeon, educator; b. Nansemond County, Va., July 14, 1942; s. Walter Mathew, Jr. and Mary Louise (Bracy) A.; B.A., U. Va., 1964, M.D., 1968; m. Michelle Sykes, Nov. 24, 1967 (dec. July 1995); children: Walter Mathew III, Sherrell Jerone, Bradford Sykes; m. Miriam (Muffie) Isabelle Potter, Dec. 27, 1996; children: Ashleigh Tatiana and Bracie Potter (twins). Intern, UCLA, 1968-69, resident, chief resident in surgery, 1969-73; Halsted fellow Johns Hopkins Hosp., 1971; resident, chief resident in plastic surgery NYU, 1973-75; chief plastic surgery service Manhattan VA Hosp., 1975-79; assoc. prof. plastic surgery NYU Med. Center, 1977-93, prof. surgery, 1993—; attending surgeon Inst. Reconstructive Plastic Surgery, NYU Med. Center; surgeon dir., chmn. dept. plastic surgery, Manhattan Eye, Ear and Throat Hosp., Bellevue Hosp. Named one of NY's Top Doctors, NY Mag. Guest appearances on Oprah, Today Show. Diplomate Am. Bd. Surgery, Am. Bd. Plastic Surgery. Fellow ACS, N.Y. Acad. Medicine, Am. Soc. Plastic and Reconstructive Surgery; mem. N.Y. State, N.Y. County med. socs., Soc. Academic Surgeons, Pan Am. Med. Assn., Brazilian Plastic Surgery Soc., Am. Soc. for Aesthetic Plastic Surgery (pres. 1993-94, Walter Scott Brown award, Simon Fredricks award, Best Sci. Exhibit award), Am. Assn. for Accreditation Ambulatory Plastic Surgery Facilities (founding mem., dir. 1980), Am. Assn. Plastic Surgeons. Author numerous surg. publs. Known for developing the FAME (finger-assisted malar elevation) facelift technique, which repositions not only the skin, but also the soft tissue of the face. Office: 728 Park Ave New York NY 10021-4945 Home Phone: 212-737-3223; Office Phone: 212-249-6000. Business E-Mail: sjaston@sjaston.com.*

ASTOR, DAVID WARREN, journalist; b. Bronx, Mar. 29, 1954; s. Harold Milton and Thelma (Oppenberg) A.; m. Laurel Cummins, May 15, 2004; 1 child from previous marriage, Maggie Elizabeth. BA in English, Rutgers U., 1976; MS in Journalism, Northwestern U., 1978. Rutgers corres. New York Times, NYC, 1974-76; reporter Red Bank Register, Shrewsbury, N.J., 1976-77, Passaic (N.J.) Herald-News, 1978; assoc. editor, sr. editor Mktg. Communications Mag., NYC, 1978-83; sr. editor Editor & Pub. Mag., NYC, 1983—; freelance humor columnist Montclair (N.J.) Times, 2003—. Avocations: reading, guitar-playing, bicycling, cartooning. Office: Editor and Publisher 770 Broadway New York NY 10003-9595 Home Phone: 973-783-9009. E-mail: dastor@editorandpublisher.com.

ASTRIAB, STEVEN MICHAEL, military officer; b. Pitts., Mar. 10, 1952; s. Steven Leonard and Anna (Popivchak) Astriab; m. BettyLou Elaine Gimmi, Dec. 27, 1975. BA in Psychology, Washington and Jefferson Coll., 1974; MSW in Manpower Planning, W.Va. U., 1976; grad., Commd. & Gen. Staff Coll., 1985. Commd. 2d lt. U.S. Army, 1974, advanced through grades to lt. col., 1992; div. social work officer 1st Cav. Div., Ft. Hood, Tex., 1976-77, med. platoon leader, then med. co. comdr. 15th med. bn., 1977-79; med. ops. officer 1st Cav. Div. Hdqs., Ft. Hood, Tex., 1979-81; chief M.C. procurement Office Army Surgeon Gen., Washington, 1982-85; chief combat medicine Office Project Mgr. Saudi Arabian Nat. Guard, Riyadh, 1985-88; pers. officer 62 Med. Group, Ft. Lewis, Wash., 1988-90; asst. chief staff for med. civil and mil. ops. 3d U.S. Army (Army Cen. Command), Riyadh, 1990-91; med. ops. officer Hdqrs. I Corps, Ft. Lewis, 1991-93; chief med. plans for S.W. Asia Hdqs. 3d U.S. Army, Atlanta, 1993-95, chief coalition integration for S.W. Asia, 1995-96; chief med. plans and intelligence S.W. Asia Hdqrs. 3d U.S. Army, 1996; sr. med. and fgn. mil. sales advisor U.S. Mil. Tng. Mission for Saudi Arabia, Riyadh, 1996-98; chief of ops. Divsn., exec. officer Pacific Regional Med. Command, 1998-2000; dep. surgeon U.S. Army Pacific, 2000—01, ret., 2001; project mgr. Eagle Group Internat. Ltd., Kosovo, 2001—03; proposal coord., mgr. Eagle Group Internat., Inc., Atlanta, 2003, tech. writer 9/11 project, 2003—05, sr. tech. writer, 2005—06, dir. proposal devel., 2006—; project mgr. emergency exercise program Ga. DPH, 2003. Assoc. faculty Ctr. Excellence Disaster Mgmt. and Humanitarian Assistance, 1999—2003. Author: (book) Vendetta: Military Med. Peace Operations in Kosovo, 2003, Knights of the New Millennium, 2005. Decorated Legion of Merit, Bronze Star, Def. Meritorious Svc. medal, Meritorious Svc. medal (7), Army Commendation medal (2), Joint Meritorious Unit award, Nat. Def. Svc. medal (2), S.W. Asia Campaign medal (3), Armed Forces Expeditionary medal, Liberation of Kuwait medal Army Ranger, Parachutist, Saudi Arabia, Kuwait. Mem.: Order Mil. Med. Merit. Republican. Baptist. Avocations: running, weight training, computer applications. Home Phone: 770-603-3142; Office Phone: 404-464-6760. Personal E-mail: sastriab@comcast.net.

ASTROTH, MARGO FOLTZ, mental health nurse, nurse psychotherapist; b. Washington, Feb. 17, 1945; d. Charles Tage Foltz and Margaret Edna Bell; m. Dennis J. Astroth, Sept. 16, 2000; m. W. David Wilson, June 24, 1967 (div. Sept. 9, 1987); children: Kimberly Margo Martin, Brett David Wilson, Colleen Jennifer Warthan. BSN, Wagner Coll., SI, NY, 1967; MS in Nursing, U. Calif., San Francisco, 1970. RN U. of State of N.Y. Edn. Dept., lic. clin. nurse specialist, adult psychiat. and mental health nursing, ANA, 1983, psychiat. mental health nurse, Calif. Bd. Mental Health Nursing, cert. clin. nurse specialist, Calif. Bd. Registered Nursing; group psychotherapist Nat. Registry Group Psychotherapists. Clin. nurse specialist inpatient mental health U.S. VA Hosp., Palo Alto, Calif., 1970—76; asst. prof. nursing baccalaureate program Point Loma Coll., San Diego, 1976—82; instr. nursing office of continuing edn. U. Calif. Sch. of Medicine, San Diego, 1976—78; clin. nurse specialist outpatient mental health U.S. VA Hosp., San Diego, 1983—84; pvt. practice nurse psychotherapist, cons. Garmisch-Partenkirchen, Bavaria, Germany, 1984—86; program dir. outpatient mental health svcs. Douglas Young Clinic, San Diego, 1986—89; instr. RN to BSN program U. Phoenix, San Diego, 1988—96; quality mgmt., program rev. and devel. San Diego County Mental Health Svcs., San Diego, 1989—95; pvt. practice nurse psychotherapist Encinitas, Calif., 1989—2005; psychosocial specialist emergency and ambulatory svcs. Sharp Grossmont Hosp., La Mesa, Calif., 1989—95; instr. RN to BSN/MSN/nurse practitioner program U. San Diego, 1994—2003; clinician psychiat. liaison team Scripps Health, Scripps Mercy Hosp., San Diego, 1996—2004, charge psychiat. liaison team, 2004—. Author: (book) Group Theory/Process for Nursing Practice, 1985, (vignettes) Touched by a Nurse; contbr. articles to profl. jours. Psychotherapist, critical incident stress debriefing Scripps Health, Response to Santana H.S. Shooting, Santee, Calif., 2001; bd. dirs. Western Inst. Found. for Mental Health, San Diego, 1989—90. Recipient Psychiat. Mental Health Nurse of the Yr., Advanced Practice/Expanded Role, Psychiat. Mental Health Clin. Nurse Specialists of San Diego, 2000. Mem.: Am. Psychiat. Nurses Assn., San Diego Group Psychotherapy Assn., Am. Group Psychotherapy Assn., Internat. Soc. of Psychiat. Mental Health Nurses, San Diego Soc. of Psychiat. Mental Health Nurses (chair 1996—97), Sigma Theta Tau (life). Lutheran. Avocations: travel, scrapbooking, hiking, jogging. Office: Scripps Health Scripps Mercy Hosp 4077 5th Ave San Diego CA 92103 Home Phone: 760-943-8681; Office Phone: 619-686-3763. E-mail: astroth.margo@scrippshealth.org.

ASTROTH, MICHAEL PATRICK, military officer; b. Springfield, Ill., July 28, 1961; s. Robert John and Mary Jean Astroth; m. Laverne Astroth, Aug. 10, 1990. AA in Transp. Movement, City Coll. Chgo., 1995; BS in Liberal Arts, Excelsior Coll., Albany, 2001; MBA in Mgmt., Columbus U., Picayune, Miss., 2006. Sgt. first class US Army, 1983—2007. Decorated 3 Meritorious Svc. medals US Army, 7 Good Conduct medals, 3 Army Commendation medals, Army Achievement medal, 2 Nat. Def. Svc. medals. Avocation: reading.

ASTRUE, MICHAEL JAMES, lawyer; b. Ft. Dix, NJ, Oct. 1, 1956; s. James Walter and Mary Patricia (Connelly) A.; m. Laura Whitney Mali, June 16, 1979; children: James Connelly, Caitlin Whitney. BA magna cum laude, Yale U., 1978; JD cum laude, Harvard U., 1983. Bar: Mass. 1983. Law clk. to fed. dist. judge, Boston, 1983-84; assoc. Ropes & Gray, Boston, 1984-85; acting dep. asst. sec. for legis. HHS, Washington, 1985-86, legal counsel to dep. commr. for programs and policy, Social Security Adminstrn., Balt., 1986-87, counselor to commr., 1987-88, gen. counsel, Washington, 1989-92; assoc. counsel to Pres. White House Office, Washington, 1988-89; ptnr. Mintz, Levin, Cohn, Ferris, Glovsky and Popeo, Boston, 1992—; commr. Social Security Adminstrn. Office Pub. Inquiries, Baltimore, Md., 2007—. Mem. Adminstrv. Conf. of U.S., Washington, 1989-92. Trustee French-Am. AIDS Found., Del., 1989-92; bd. govs. World AIDS Found., Geneva, 1989-92; mem. U.S. Archtl. and Transp. Barriers Compliance Bd., Washington, 1989-92. Republican. Roman Catholic. Office: Social Security Adminstrn Office Pub Inquiries 6401 Security Blvd Windsor Park Bldg Baltimore MD 21235

ASTRUP, JENS LEO, retired civil engineer; b. Plentywood, Mont., Sept. 21, 1934; s. Jens Legend and Dagmar (Jensen) Astrup; m. Susanne Elizabeth Laime, Nov. 25, 1967 (div. Nov. 1985); children: Moriah Ann, Jens Aaron. BS, ND State U., 1956; MBA, Keller Grad. Sch. Mgmt., 1983. Registered profl. engr., Ill.; patent agt. Civil engr. City of Chgo. Dept. Urban Renewal, 1964—65, Harza Engring. Co., 1965—69; city engr. City of Williston, ND, 1969—70; civil and resident engr. Bauer Engring., Inc., Chgo., 1970—71; civil and structural sr. engr. Brown and Root, Inc., 1971—82; project engr. Lester B. Knight & Assocs., 1983—85, Comstock Engring., Inc., Oak Brook, 1985—86; sr. civil engr. Allen Engring. Co., Villa Park, 1986—88; project engr. Globetrotters Engring. Corp., Chgo., 1988—92; sr. civil engr. Clark Dietz, Inc., 1993—94. Mem.: ASCE, Am. Pub. Works Assn. N.D. (past state sec. 1969—70), Ill. Soc. Profl. Engrs. (state v.p. 1979—80, chmn. state activities com. 1976—77; chpt. pres. 1977—78). Home: 5801 Fairglen Ave 216 Fort Worth TX 76137 Home Phone: 817-306-8760. Personal E-mail: leoa2@juno.com.

ASTUCCIO, SHEILA MARGARET, educational administrator; b. Biddeford, Maine, Apr. 24, 1943; d. James T. III and Margaret H. (Cameron) Rollinson; m. Joseph Kevin Astuccio, Aug. 22, 1976 (dec. Apr. 1992); children: James M., Sheila E. BS in Edn., Salem Coll., Mass., 1968, MEd, 1975; cert. advanced grad. studies, Lesley Coll., Cambridge, Mass., 1983; Cert. Distributive Edn. Leader, Nova Southeastern U., Fla. Cert. elem. tchr. and prin., supr., dir., Mass.; cert. instrnl. tech. grades K-12. Elem. educator Hood Elem. Sch., Lynn, Mass., 1968-79; tchr. grades 3 and 4 Lynn (Mass.) Pub. Schs., comp. coord., facilitator, 1981-84, tchr. academically talented, 1979-81, 84-85, computer program specialist, 1986-87, computer implementation team leader, MIS dir., 1987-98; adminstr. IS/MIS, 1998—; owner operator Pilot Imaging Computer Imaging, Lynn, Mass., 1991-92. Tchr. adult edn. North Shore C.C., 1982-87; part-time real estate broker, 1979—; part-time mktg. cons. IDN, 1993-95; presenter Beijing Dist. Edn. Bur., 2001; presenter in field. Mem. Chpt. II adv. coun., 1979-83; nat. grad. alumni rep. Lesley Coll., 1984-85; chair Mayor's Computer Adv. Com., 1985-86; participant Educators in Industry GE/Salem State Coll., 1983; People to People Amb. to China, 2000, 2001; sec.-gen. United Cultural Convention, 2001—. Recipient Educators in Industry cert., 1983, Novell Netware Adminstr. and Sys. Installation/Configuration certs., 1994-95, Letters of Commendation Mass. Dept. Edn., 2000, 2001, Distributive Edn. Leader Cert., 2005. Mem. ASCD, AAUW, NAFE, NSBA, DECUS, PEI Nat. Users Group, New Eng. Pentamation Users Group, Boston Computer Soc. Office: Data Ctr LVTI 80 Neptune Blvd Lynn MA 01902-4570 Home Phone: 781-842-1931; Office Phone: 781-595-5794. Personal E-mail: astuccio@comcast.net. Business E-Mail: astuccios@lynnschools.org.

ASTUTO, PHILIP LOUIS, retired language educator; b. NYC, Jan. 5, 1923; s. Salvatore and Anna (Insalaco) A.; m. Natella M. Digia, July 4, 1953; children: Philip, Anne Marie. BA, St. John's U., 1943; MA, Columbia, 1947; PhD, Columbia U., 1956. Mem. faculty St. John's U., 1947-89, prof. Spanish, 1958-89, prof. emeritus, 1991—, dir. Latin Am. studies, 1957-60, chmn. dept. modern fgn. langs., 1961-65. Participant Prof.-Student Summer Seminar, sponsored State Dept., 1950; OAS research fellow, Quito, Bogota, 1973-74 Contbr. articles to profl. jours. Mem. coll. coun. SUNY, Farmingdale, 1988-98. 1st lt., inf. AUS, 1943-46, ETO. Recipient Pietas medal St. John's U., 1977, Faculty Outstanding Achievement medal, 1986 Mem. Am. Assn. Tchrs. Spanish and Portuguese, Am. Hist. Assn., Assn. Latin Am. Studies, MLA, Nat. Acad. History of Ecuador (fgn. corr.) Home: 11 Steuben Dr Jericho NY 11753-1414 Personal E-mail: pnastuto@aol.com.

ASWADY, ADIYATWIDI ADIWOSO, diplomat; Exec. dir. Non-Aligned Movement Ctr. for South-South Tech. Cooperation; charge d'affaires a.i., dep. permanent rep. to UN Govt. Indonesia, NYC. V.p. bur. UN Devel. Programme, 2006. Office: Permanent Mission of Indonesia to UN 325 E 38th St New York NY 10016 Office Phone: 212-972-8333. Office Fax: 212-972-9780. E-mail: ptri@indonesiamission-ny.org.

ASWANI, SHANKAR (SHANKAR ASWANI-CANELA), anthropologist, educator; b. Spain; BA in Marine Affiars/Anthropology, U. Miami, 1988; MA in Anthropology, U. Hawaii, 1992, PhD in Anthropology, 1997. PADI Divemaster 1988, Patron Motor Segunda (Boat Lic.-up to 360 hp) 1989, Research Diver Cert. U. Calif. Santa Barbara, 2003. Mil. adminstrv. asst. Spanish Infantry Divsn. Jaen 25, Barcelona, 1989—90; rsch. assoc. Internat. Ctr. for Living Aquatic Resources Mgmt., 1994—95; field mgr. for research on the socio-cultural aspects of the Hawaiian troll and handline fishery U. Wash., 1997—99; postdoctoral rsch. fellow U. Auckland, 1998—2000, hon. sr. rsch. fellow, 2000—; asst. prof. U. Calif., Santa Barbara, 2000—04, assoc. prof., 2004—, assoc. prof., interdepartmental grad. program in marine sci. With Solomon Islands Rsch. Ctr., U. Auckland; field work experience at Hawaii Islands and Solomon Islands, 1992—2005; spkr. in field at nat. and internat. conferences. Contbr. articles to profl. and peer-reviewed jours.; mem. editl. adv. bd. Collegiate Press, San Diego, 2003—. Established a network of marine protected areas in the Western Solomons, 1999—2005; established various develop. projects in the Roviana and Vonavona areas, 2002—05. Nominee U. Calif. Santa Barbara Plous award, 2004; named one of the Five Most Innovative Scholars in Ocean Sci., Pews Fellow Program, 2005; recipient Faculty Early Career Develop. award, NSF, 2003, Edward T. Foote II Alumnus of Distinction award, U. Miami, 2005; fellow Pews Fellow Program in Marine Conservation, 2005; recipient of several profl. grants. Mem.: Soc. Applied Anthropology, Melanesia Interest Group, European Soc. for Oceanists, Soc. for Scientific Anthropology, Anthropology and Environment, Am. Anthropology Assn., Assn. for Social Anthropology in Oceania. Office: Dept Anthropology U Calif Santa Barbara Santa Barbara CA 93106-3210 Address: Dept Antropology U Auckland Private Bag 92019 Auckland New Zealand Office Phone: 805-893-5285. Fax: 64-9-373-7441; Office Fax: 805-893-8707. Business E-Mail: aswani@anth.ucsb.edu, s.aswani@auckland.ac.nz.

ATAEVA, AKSOLTAN, diplomat; b. Ashgabat, Nov. 6, 1944; m. Tchary Pirmoukhamedov, Apr. 25, 1969; children: Avnabat, Azat. Dipl. medicine, Turkmen State Med. Inst., 1968; DMS (hon.), Soviet Union Sci. Rsch. Inst., 1989; A (hon.), Internat. Acad. Computer Scis., Kiev, Ukraine, 1993; PhD in Pub. Health. Staff, asst. to chief doctor Hosp. No. 1, Ashgabat, Turkmenistan, 1968-80; vice dir. Regional Health Dept., Ashgabat, 1980-85; vice min., min. Health of Turkmenistan, Ashgabat, 1985-94; min. Social Security Turkmenistan, Ashgabat, 1991—94; now permanent rep. Mission Turkmenistan UN, NYC, 1995—; chmn. Trade Unions Turkmenistan, 1994—95. Contbr. numerous articles to profl. jours. Mem. Supreme People's Coun. Turkmenistan, 1993—. Mem. Dem. Party of Turkmenistan. Avocations: art, reading, sports. Office: Permanent Mission Turkmenistan UN 866 United Nations Plz Rm 424 New York NY 10017-1822

ATAI, MANUCHER, retired surgeon; b. Tabriz, Azerba, Iran, Sept. 26, 1935; arrived in U.S., 1960; s. Rasoul and Ismat Atai. MD, Tabriz Med. Sch., 1960. Cert. Bd. Gen. Surgery, Bd. Thoracic Surgery. Surgeon Heart Hosp., Tehran, Iran, 1973—84; staff surgeon Mercy Hosp., San Diego, 1985—2001; ret., 2001. Assoc. prof. clin. surgery U. Calif. San Diego, 1985—2001. Contbr. articles to profl. jours. Mem.: ACS. Avocations: reading, tennis, skiing. Home: 6656 Muirlands Dr La Jolla CA 92037

ATAL, BISHNU SAROOP, retired speech research executive, educator; b. Kanpur, Uttar Pradesh, India, May 10, 1933; came to U.S., 1961; s. Jagannath Prasad and Lakshmi Devi (Lakshmi) A.; m. Kamla Atal, July 3, 1959; children: Alka, Namita. BS with honors, U. Lucknow, India, 1952; elec. engring. degree, Indian Inst. Sci., Bangalore, 1955; PhD in Elec. Engring., Poly. Inst. Bklyn., 1968. Sr. rsch. asst. Indian Inst. Sci., Bangalore, 1955-56, lectr., 1957-60; sr. rsch. fellow Cen. Elec. Engring. Rsch. Inst., Pilani, Rajasthan, India, 1960-61; mem. tech. staff AT&T Bell Labs., Murray Hill, N.J., 1961-85, head acoustics rsch., 1985-90, head speech rsch., 1990-97; tech. dir. AT&T Labs., Florham Park, NJ, 1997—2002; affiliate prof. U. Washington, Seattle, 2002—. Contbr. articles to various publs. Fellow Acoustical Soc. Am., IEEE (Acoustics, Speech and Signal Processing Sr. Tech. Achievement award 1975, ASSP Sr. award 1980, Centennial medal 1984, Morris N. Liebman Meml. Field award 1986); mem. NAE, NAS (Franklin medal 2003). Home: 6226 95th Pl SW Mukilteo WA 98275-3533 E-mail: catchall@bishnu.net.

ATALA, ANTHONY JOHN, surgeon; b. July 14, 1958; m. Katherine Atala, May 13, 1985. BA, U. Miami, 1984; MD, U. Louisville, 1985. Cert. Am. Bd. Urology. Intern in surgery U. Louisville Sch. Medicine, 1985-86, resident in surgery, 1985—87, resident in urology, 1987-89, chief resident in urology, 1989-90; rsch. fellow dept. surgery Children's Hosp., Harvard Med. Sch., Boston, 1990-91, clin. fellow dept. surgery, 1991-92, instr., 1992-93, asst. prof., 1993—2003, mem. investigations rev. bd., 1994—; dir. lab. tissue engring. and cellular therapeutics Children's Hosp. and Harvard Med. Sch., 1993—; W.h. Boyce prof., chair dept. urology, dir. Inst. Regenerative Medicine and Tissue Engring. Inst. Wake Forest Univ. Baptist Med. Ctr., 2004—. Mem. study sect. NIH, 1996; mem. scientific adv. bd., Regenerate Internat. Conf. Editor Tissue Engring., 1995—; cons. Jour. Urology, 1993-, editor investigative urology sect., editor, Lancet, 1994, (book) Current Concepts in Tissue Engineering, 1995, Jour. Rejuvenation Rsch., The Scientific World: Tissue Engring., Stem Cell Therapy, Regenerative Medicine, and Stem Cells and Development; editor investigative urology sect., Urology, Current Opinion in Urology, Current Reviews in Urology, Jour. Laparoendoscopic, Advanced Surgical Techniques: Endosurgery and Innovative Techniques, The Scientific World: Cell Biology; mem. editl. bd. Expert Opinion on Biol. Therapy; contbr. articles to profl. jours. Bd. dirs. Nat. Kidney Found., Boston, 1996-; chmn. bd. dirs. Nat. Bladder Found.; mem. investigations rev. bd. Harvard Med. Sch., Boston, 1994. Rsch. award ACS, 1990, Am. Acad. Pediat., 1993, 94, 96, Am. Soc. Plastic Surgery, 1994, Christopher Columbus Found. award, Gold Cystoscope award; named Med. Treatments Leader of the Yr., Scientific American. Mem. AMA, AAAS, Am. Urol. Assn. (program com. 1995), Soc. for Basic Urol. Rsch. (program com. 1995), Soc. of Regenerative Medicine (bd, dir., v.p.), Tissue Engring. Soc. (bd. gov.), Achievements include patents in field, inventions in area of tissue engineering and medicine. Office: Wake Forest Univ Baptist Med Ctr Reynolds Tower Main Fl Medical Ctr Blvd Winston Salem NC 27157 Office Phone: 336-716-4131. Office Fax: 336-716-9042, 336-716-5711. Business E-Mail: cmontgom@wfubmc.edu, aatala@wfubmc.edu.

ATASHILI, JULIUS, epidemiologist; s. Nicholas Tita Sangbong and Mary Siri. MD, U. Yaounde I, Cameroon, 2002; MPH, U. NC, Chapel Hill, 2005. Interim chief med. officer Fondation Ros, Yaounde, 2002, Quality Health Clinic Shemka Found., Yaounde, 2002—03; gen. practice U. Tchg. Hosp., Yaounda, 2002—03; fellow U. NC, 2003—. Summer intern WHO, Geneva, 2005—05; presenter in field. Recipient Internat. Internship award, U. Ctr. Internat. Studies, U. NC, 2005, Young Investigator award, 2007. Mem.: Cameroon Nat. Med. Coun. Office: U NC Chapel Hill McGavran-Greenberg Chapel Hill NC 27599-7435 Home Phone: 919-602-4268. Business E-Mail: atashili@email.unc.edu.

ATCHER, JOSEPH RAY, director; b. Louisville, Ky., Sept. 19, 1949; s. Francis Aloysius Atcher and Mary Louise Neuling. BA, Marquette U., Milw., 1972; MA, U. Notre Dame, South Bend, Ind., 1975. Cert. tchr. Wis., 1972. Asst. prin., campus min. Carmel H.S. for Boys, Mundelein, Ill., 1978—84; prin. Crespi Carmelite H.S., Encino, Calif., 1985—89; pres., prin. Mt. Carmel H.S., Chgo., 1989—96; assoc. pastor, dir. cemetery Our Lady Mt. Carmel, Tenafly, NJ, 1996—98; pastor, dir. cemetery St Therese Parish, Cresskill, NJ, 1998—2002; pastor Our Lady Mt. Carmel, Louisville, 2002—04; dir. total edn. Archdiocese Louisville, 2004—, vicar, 2004—. Bd. dirs. Louisville Sci. Ctr.; adv. bd. Holy Cross H.S., Louisville, 2002—04; consultor Archdiocese Louisville, 2004—. Mem.: Chief Administrators Cath. Edn. Roman Catholic. Office: Archdiocese of Louisville 1935 Lewiston Dr Louisville KY 40216 Home Phone: 502-366-5651; Office Phone: 502-448-8581. Office Fax: 502-448-5518; Home Fax: 502-448-5518. Business E-Mail: jatcher@archlou.org.

ATCHER, ROBERT WHITEHILL, chemist, educator; b. Chgo., June 12, 1951; s. Robert O. and Marguerite (Whitehill) Atcher; m. Lisa Laidlaw, 1990 (div. 1995); 1 child, Robert Andrew Laidlaw; m. Sharon Ciessau, 1998. BA, Washington U., St. Louis, 1972; MS, U. Rochester, NYC, 1974, PhD, 1980; MA, U. Mo., Columbia, 1976; MBA, U. N.Mex., Albuquerque, 2004. Rsch. fellow Harvard Med. Sch., 1979-82, Peter Bent Brigham Hosp., 1979-82; rsch. affiliate nuc. engring. MIT, Cambridge, 1979-82; rsch. assoc. radiology Harvard Med. Sch., 1982-83, Brigham & Women's Hosp., 1982-83; rsch. affiliate Nuc. Reactor Lab. MIT, 1982-83; cancer expert, radiation oncology br. div. cancer treatment Nat. Cancer Inst., NIH, Bethesda, Md., 1983-86; adj. prof. dept. chemistry U. Md., College Park, 1984-86; group leader nuclear medicine rsch. chemistry div. Argonne Nat. Lab., Ill., 1986-93; radiochemist Michael Reese/U. Chgo. Ctr. Radiation Therapy, 1986-94; asst. prof. radiation oncology dept. U. Chgo., 1986-94; assoc. prof. medicine, assoc. prof. radiation oncology U. Ala., Birmingham, 1994-97; tech. staff mem. Los Alamos Nat. Lab., N.Mex., 1997-99; group leader Los Alamos Nat. Lab Bioscience Divsn., N.Mex., 1999—2003; program mgr. US Dept. Health and Human Svcs., 2003—. Tchg. asst. dept. chemistry U. Rochester, 1972-74; tchg. asst. Sch. Journalism, U. Mo., 1974-75; advisor lab. grad. participant program Argonne Nat. Lab., 1986-93, advisor undergrad. student rsch. program, 1986-93; cons. Cytogen Corp., Princeton, NJ, 1986-90, NeoRx Corp., Seattle, 1987-2005, Sterling Drug, 1989-93; mem. task force Isotope Prodn./Distbn., US Dept. Energy, Washington, 1990-2005; U. N.Mex./Los Alamos Nat. Lab. prof. pharmacy U. N.Mex., Albuquerque, 1997—; mem. adv. bd. N.Mex. Ctr. for Isotope in Medicine, 2004— Bd. reviewers Jour. Nuclear Medicine, 1989—; editorial bd. Bioconjugate Chemistry, 1989-93. Fellow Am. Inst. Chemists; mem. AAAS, Radiation Rsch. Soc., Soc. Nuc. Medicine (pres. radiopharm. sci. coun., assoc. chair sci. porgram com., 1999—, v.p. elect, 2006-07, pres.-elect 2007—), Am. Chem. Soc., Fedn. Am. Scientists, NY Acad. Scis., Sigma Xi, Beta Gamma Sigma. Roman Catholic. Office: Biosci Divsn MS M888 Los Alamos NM 87545-0001 Office Phone: 505-667-0585. Business E-Mail: ratcher@lanl.gov.

ATCHESON, SUE HART, business educator; b. Dubuque, Iowa, Apr. 12; d. Oscar Raymond and Anna (Cook) Hart; m. Walter Clark Atcheson (div.); children: Christine A. Hischar, Moffet Zoe, Claye Williams. BBA, Mich. State U.; MBA, Calif. State Poly. U., Pomona, 1973. Cert. tchr. and adminstr. Instr. Mt. San Antonio Coll., Walnut, Calif., 1968-90. Bd. dirs. faculty assn. Mt. San Antonio Coll., mem. acad. senate, originator vol. income tax assistance; spkr. in field; lectr. in bus. mgmt. Calif. State Poly. U., Pomona, 1973—75; cons., trainer Joint Venture between Mt. San Antonio Coll. and County of Los Angeles Dept. Pub. Social Svcs., summer, 2001. Author: Fractions and Equations on Your Own, 1975. Charter mem. Internat. Commn. on Monetary and Econ. Reform; panelist infrastructure funding reform, Freeport, Ill., 1989. Mem. Cmty. Concert Assn. Inland Empire (bd. dirs.), Scripps Coll. Fine Arts Found.(bd. dirs. 2006—, co-pres. 2006—), Recyclers Club (pres. 1996).

ATCHISON, DOUG, film director, writer; Dir.: (films) Ellen's Father, 1990, Akeelah and the Bee, 2006; dir., prodr.: (films) The Pornographer, 1999; author: (films) Ellen's Father, 1990, The Pornographer, 1999, Akeelah and the Bee, 2006 (NAACP Image award, 2007).*

ATCHISON, JOSEPH EDWARD, pulp and paper industry consultant; b. Barnum, W.Va., Dec. 25, 1914; s. Edward Washington and Frederica Catherine (Kerns) A.; m. Frances Julia Winebrinier, July 3, 1951 (dec. Apr. 1965); m. Betty Jeanne Pugh, May 30, 1968; children: Leah, Robert, Scott (dec.), Kevin (dec.). BSCE, La. State U., 1938; MS in Pulp & Paper Tech., Inst. Paper Chem., 1940, PhD in Pulp & Paper Tech., 1942. Tech. dir. John Strange Paper Co., Menasha, Wis., 1946-48; chief pulp & paper br. Marshall Plan, Washington, Paris, 1948-52; mill mgr., project dir. Portarican Paper Products, Inc., San Juan, P.R., 1952-53; v.p., sr. v.p. Parsons & Whittemore, Inc., NYC, 1953-67; pres., owner Joseph E. Atchison Cons., Inc., NYC, 1968-97, Atchison Cons., Inc., Sarasota, Fla., 1997—. Spkr. internat. confs. *Dr. Atchison has specialized in the utilization of all types of non-wood plant fibers for the manufacture of pulp and paper and of all types, including newsprint. These fibers include sugar cane bagasse, wheat straw, rice straw, reeds, grasses, bamboo, cotton linters, He has developed appropriate processes for utilizing these raw materials and assisted many companies, in the developing countries, who do not have adequate wood, to design and build pulp and paper mills, based on whatever raw materials they had available. He has provided technical services in some 50 different countries. Enabling many countries to establish pulp and paper industries, based on using these raw materials, especially in wood-poor countries.* Author: Waste Paper Recycling, 1972, Kenaf for Paper Pulp, 1976; contbr. articles to profl. jouors. Lt. col. US Army, 1942—46. Decorated DSM Bronze Star with oak leaf cluster; named to Paper Industry Internat. Hall of Fame, 1997; named Man of Quarter, In Paper Internat., 1999. Mem. TAPPI (Gunnar Nicholson Gold medal 1996), Internat. Soc. Sugar Cane Technologists. Presbyterian. Avocations: tennis, exercise, dance, travel, theater. Office Phone: 941-377-3922. Personal E-mail: atchconsul@comcast.net.

ATCHISON, RICHARD CALVIN, trade association director; b. Altadena, Calif., Aug. 4, 1932; s. Floyd and Clara (Warwick) A.; m. Mildred Platt, Jan. 24, 1957; children: Tracey, Hayley. BS, UCLA, 1958. Salesman, product mgr. Lever Bros., NYC, 1958-61; group product mgr., then regional sales mgr. Purex Corp.; pres. Van Camp Seafood Co. div. Ralston Purina Co., 1965-81; pres. Mitsubishi Foods (USA) Inc., 1981-91; exec. dir. Am. Tuna Boat Assn., San Diego, 1991-93; pres. Internat. Bus. Cons., 1993—. With USAF, 1952-56. Office Phone: 858-481-0036.

ATCHISON, RODNEY RAYMOND, retired lawyer, arbitrator; b. Hanford, Calif., Nov. 14, 1926; s. Clyde Raymond and Velma May (Watts) A.; m. Evaleen Mary McFadden, June 27, 1948; children: Cathlin Atchison, Susan Barisone, Kerry Atchison, Brian. Student, San Jose State Coll., Calif., 1946-49; JD, U. Santa Clara, Calif., 1952. Bar: Calif. 1953, U.S. Dist. Ct. (all dists.) Calif. 1953, U.S. Ct. Appeals (9th cir.) 1953, U.S. Supreme Ct. 1971. Assoc. Mullen & Filippi, Attys., San Francisco, 1953-55; dep. county counsel Santa Clara Calif. County Counsel, San Jose, 1955-57; city atty. City of Mountain View, Calif., 1957-62, City of Santa Cruz, Calif., 1962-90; pres. Atchison, Anderson, Hurley & Barisone, Profl. Law Corp., Santa Cruz, 1980-96; of counsel Atchison Barisone & Condotti, Profl. Law Corp., Santa Cruz, 1996, Law Offices of Rodney R. Atchison, 1996-2001. Arbitrator Am. Arbitration Assn., San Francisco, 1970—2004. Pres. Rotary Club Mountain View, Calif., 1961-62, Santa Cruz (Calif.) County Bar Assn., 1973. With USNR, 1944-46. Mem. ABA, Santa Cruz Rotary Club, Elks Lodge (life). Roman Catholic. Avocations: travel, golf.

ATCHISON, STEVEN, real estate company executive; b. 1969; Internal auditor Pulte Homes Inc., 1995, v.p., fin., Las Vegas divsn., pres. Tucson, Houston, Mich., 2005—. Named one of 40 Under 40, Crain's Detroit Bus., 2006. Office: Pulte Homes Incorporated 450 W Fourth St Royal Oak MI 48067-0956 Office Phone: 248-546-2300. Office Fax: 248-541-5533.

ATCHISON, TIMOTHY B., education educator, neuropsychologist; b. Clifton, Tex., Dec. 12, 1959; s. Thomas Carl and Kathleen Atchison; m. Iris B. Blessen, Nov. 19, 1983; children: John Isaac, Joseph Isaiah. BA, U. Tex., Austin, 1991; MS, Abilene Christian U., 1996; PhD in Clin. Psychology, U. Houston, 2002. Lic. Psychologist Tex. State Bd. Examiners Psychologists, 2004. Asst. prof. West Tex. A&M U., Canyon, 2002—. Mem.: Tex. Brain Injury Assn. (bd. mem. 2005—), Internat. Neuropsychological Soc. (assoc.). Mem. Ch. Of Christ. Avocations: fly fishing, camping. Office: West Tex A&M U PO Box 60876 Canyon TX 79016 Home Phone: 806-655-7146; Office Phone: 806-651-2729. Office Fax: 806-651-2728. Business E-Mail: tatchison@mail.wtamu.edu.

ATCHLEY, RAYMOND DEVAL, technology company executive; b. Blackfoot, Idaho, Apr. 15, 1915; s. Claude Deval and Marie Himmelgarn Atchley; m. Virginia Gifford, Jan. 26, 1946; 1 child, Susan Virginia. BSME, MIT, 1951; bus. cert., UCLA, 1966. Chief tool designer, co-founder Rohr Aircraft, San Diego, 1939-41; design engr. USN Underwater Sound Lab., San Diego, 1942-46; assoc. rsch. engr. MIT Dynamic Analysis and Control Lab., Cambridge, Mass., 1946-51; v.p. engring. Midwestern Instruments Inc., Tulsa, 1951-54; owner, pres. Raymond Atchley, Inc., West Los Angeles, Calif., 1954-59; gen. mgr. Raymond Atchley divsn. Am. Brake Shoe, West Los Angeles, 1959-63; cons. aerospace divsn. Abex Corp., Oxnard, Calif., 1964-65; pvt. practice cons., 1966-68; pres. Deval Industries, Inc., West Los Angeles, 1969-84, Atchley Controls, Inc., Canoga Park, Calif., 1985-90; sr. tech. advisor fluid controls divsn. BW/IP Internat., Inc., Van Nuys, Calif., 1991-94; sr. tech. advisor E-Sys. Raytheon, West Los Angeles, 1996-97, Salt Lake City, 1995-96; cons., 1998—. Patentee pressure control valve for hydraulic actuator, end effector, component locating apparatus, electrical component testing apparatus, coating apparatus, writing surface and temporary eraseable ink composition for marking thereon, electro-hydraulic servovalve, others. Cpl. USMC, 1933-37. Mem. MIT Alumni Assn., UCLA Alumni Assn. Republican. Avocations: photography, fishing, sports cars, computers. Home: 3470 Mandeville Canyon Rd Los Angeles CA 90049-1020

ATER, AL, former state official; b. Ferriday, La., Dec. 15, 1953; m. Susie Beard; children: Whitney, Thomas, Elliott. Attended, Northwestern State U. Farmer; mem La. Ho. of Reps., 1984—92; mem. House and Governmental Affairs com., Legis. Svcs. com., House Ways and Means com., Agrl. com.; vice chmn. Transp., Highways and Pub. Works com., 1987; chief dep. commr. Dept. Ins., 2005; first asst. to sec. state Fox McKeithen State of La., 2001—04, first asst. sec. state, 2005, sec. state Baton Rouge, 2006—07. Bd. dirs. Concordia Parish Farm Bur., Catalyst Energy; bd. trustees La. Sch. Employees' Retirement Sys., La. Tourist Devel. Commn., La. Workmen's Compensation, Second Injury Bd., Gov. Advisory Coun. on Disability Affairs, Internat. Assn. Copr. Administrs., Nat. Assn. Secretaries of State; others.*

ATES, J. ROBERT, lawyer; b. New Orleans, Sept. 12, 1945; s. Loten Arthur Jr. and Eugenia Lea (Carpenter) A. BA, Tulane U., 1967; JD, Loyola U., New Orleans, 1972. Bar: La. 1973, U.S. Dist. Ct. (ea., mid. and we. dists.) La., U.S. Ct. Appeals (5th cir.), U.S. Supreme Ct., Colo. 1990. Prof., chmn. sci. dept. East Jefferson High Sch., Metairie, La., 1967-72; law clk. to judge La. Ct. Appeals (4th cir.), New Orleans, 1972-73; assoc. Kierr, Gainsburgh, Benjamin, Fallon & Lewis, New Orleans, 1974-78, ptnr., 1979-87, Gainsburgh, Benjamin, Fallon, David & Ates, New Orleans, 1987-94; prin. J. Robert Ates, A Profl. Law Corp., New Orleans, 1994-95, Ates & Assocs., A Profl. Law Corp., New Orleans, 1996—2003, Ates Law Firm, New Orleans, 2003—. Lectr. in field; mem. adj. law faculty and skills faculty, Continuing Legal Edn. Programs, Tulane U., Loyola Law Schs. Mem. ATLA, FBA, La. Bar Assn. (vice chmn. civil law sect. 1986-87, chmn. 1987—, sec., treas. 1985—, chmn. pub. rels. and edn. com. 1987—, mem. ho. of dels. 1987-94, bd. govs. 1993—, gen. sec. and editor La. Bar Jour. 1993-95), Orleans Bar Assn., Jefferson Bar Assn., La. Trial Lawyers Assn. (pres.'s adv. com.), Soc. Am. Law Tchrs., Am. Soc. Law and Medicine. Democrat. Baptist. Avocations: photography, skiing, water-skiing, hunting, fishing. Home: 29 Turnberry Dr La Place LA 70068-1617 Office: Ates Law Firm 13726 River Rd # A Destrehan LA 70047-5012 E-mail: jra@ateslawfirm.com.

ATHANASIOU, KYRIACOS A., biomedical engineer; BS summa cum laude, NY Inst. Tech., 1984; MS, Columbia U., 1985, PhD, 1988. Lic. profl. engr., Tex. Adj. prof. orthopaedics U. Tex. Houston Med. Sch.; adj. prof. oral & maxillofacial surgery U. Tex. Houston Dental Sch.; dir. Musculoskeletal Bioengineering Ctr. U. Tex. San Antonio, 1998—2002; dir. Musculoskeletal Bioengineering Lab. Rice U., Houston, 1999—2002, Karl F. Hasselman prof. bioengineering. Co-founder OsteoBiologics, Salix Med., VidaCare, Cytex; assoc. editor Annals of Biomedical Engring., 2003; editorial bd. Tissue Engring., 2002—, Jour. Foot & Ankle Surgery, 2003—, Evidence-Based Preventive Medicine, 2005—; scientific adv. com. Whitaker Found., 2001—06; scientific adv. bd. TMJ Assoc., 2003—. Reviewer med. journals; contbr. scientific papers, articles, chapters to books. Recipient Van C. Mow medal, Am Soc. Mech. Engrs., Bioengineering Div., 2005. Fellow: Am. Inst. Med. & Biol. Engring.; mem.: Soc. Biomaterials, Am. Acad. Orthopaedic Surgeons, Cyprus Soc. Biomedical Engring. & Med. Physics, Cyprus Assn. Profl. Engrs., Am. Soc. Biomechanics, Am. Soc. Mech. Engrs., Orthopaedic Rsch. Soc., Biomedical Engring. Soc. (chair finance com. 2000—01, bd. dirs. 2000—03, exec. com. 2000—05, chair membership com. 2000—, pres. 2002—04, Fellow 2005). Office: Rice U Dept Bioengineering MS-142 PO Box 1892 Houston TX 77251-1892 Office Phone: 713-348-6385. Office Fax: 713-348-5877. E-mail: athanasiou@rice.edu.

ATHAS, GUS JAMES, lawyer; b. Chgo., Aug. 6, 1936; s. James G. and Pauline (Parhas) A.; m. Marilyn Carres, July 12, 1964; children: Paula C. Vlahakos, James G., Christopher G. BS, U. Ill., 1958; JD cum laude, Loyola U., Chgo., 1965. Bar: Ill. 1965, U.S. Dist. Ct. (no. dist.) Ill. 1965, U.S. Ct. Appeals (7th cir.) 1970. With Isham, Lincoln & Beale, Chgo., 1965-69; group gen. counsel, asst. sec. ITT, Skokie, Ill., 1969-87; assoc. gen. counsel Itel Corp., Chgo., 1987; sr. v.p., gen. counsel, sec. Eagle Industries, Inc., Chgo., 1987-97; exec. v.p. adminstrn., gen. counsel, sec. Falcon Bldg. Products, Inc., Chgo., 1994-99; sr. v.p., gen. counsel Great Am. Mgmt. and Investment, Inc., Chgo., 1995-97; ptnr. Stamos & Trucco, Chgo., 2000—. Contbr. articles to profl. jours. 1st lt. U.S. Army, 1958-62. Mem. ABA, Ill. Bar Assn., Chgo. Bar Assn. Greek Orthodox. Home: 1240 Hawthorne Ln Downers Grove IL 60515-4503 Office: Stamos & Trucco 30 W Monroe Ste 1600 Chicago IL 60603 Office Phone: 312-630-7979. Business E-Mail: gathas@stamostrucco.com.

ATHERTON, BARBARA KLEIN, elementary school educator; b. LA, Sept. 1, 1944; d. Harry and Pearl Zwick; m. Michael Evans Atherton, Dec. 17, 1995; children: Lillian Shavon Klein, Zeva Julia Pettigrew. MS, Nova U., Fla., 1981. Cert. tchr. Calif. Adminstr. Vocat. and Tech. Coll., LA, 1989—90; facilitator, instr. Dade County Pub. Schs., Miami, Fla., 1966—89; curriculum writer, grant coord. Long Beach Unified Sch. Dist.,

Calif., 1990—95; curriculum coord. Long Beach (Calif.) Unified Sch. Dist.; math /sci. camp planner, facilitator Washington Mid. Sch., Long Beach. Dir. interns Dade County Schs., Miami, 1970—88; guest instr. Fla. Internat. U., Miami, 1986—88; new tchr. coach Long Beach Unified Sch. Dist., 1995—; presenter in field. Mem. Mid. Sch. Adv. Com. Recipient award, Mid. Sch. Adv. Com. Mem.: AAUW (assoc.), Phi Delta Kappa (life Outstanding mem. 2002). Avocations: exercise, travel, sewing. Home Phone: 562-926-4821.

ATHERTON, CHARLES HENRY, federal commission administrator; b. Kingston, Pa., June 24, 1932; s. Thomas Henry and Mary A.; m. Mary Bringhurst Davis, Dec. 15, 1967; children: Sarah Scott, Thomas Henry, Charles Henry. BA summa cum laude, Princeton U., 1954, MFA, 1957. Registered architect, D.C. Asst. sec. Fine Arts Commn., Washington, 1960-64, sec., adminstrv. officer, 1964—2004; ret., 2004. Trustee Nat. Child Rsch. Ctr., 1975-79; v.p. Washington Hist. Soc.; bd. dir. Hist. Am. Bldg. Survey Found. (elected fellow 2003), Navy Art Found.; mem. Citizens Commemorative Coin Adv. Com., 1994-2003; bd. dirs. Heurich House Found., 2003—. Lt. (j.g.) USNR, 1957—60. Recipient Martin Luther King Leadership award D.C. Pub. Libr. Sys., 1992, Centennial medal Washington chpt. AIA, 1993, Lifetime Achievement award Comm. of 100 on the Federal City, Mayor's award lifetime achievement in hist. preervation, 2004, Thomas Jefferson award for pub. architecture AIA, 2005; inductee Washington D.C. Hall of Fame, 2004. Mem.: Cosmos Club, Potomac Boat Club. Home: 3127 Newark St NW Washington DC 20008-3344 E-mail: charleshatherton@yahoo.com.

ATHERTON, MICHAEL WARD, music educator; b. Silver Spring, Md., Dec. 5, 1950; s. James Kenneth Ward and Patricia Hall Atherton; m. Kathy Alice Lewis, Jan. 23, 1973; children: Corey Lewis, Kier James; 1 child, Luke Stiles. BA, U. Mont., 1987, B in Music Edn., 1989, M in Music Edn., 1998; Master Recording II diploma, Conservatory Rec. Arts and Scis., 2003. Cert. music tech. Tech. Inst. Music Edn. Music tchr. Eureka (Mont.) Pub. Schs., 1987—. Leader, guitarist, vocalist Street Legal, Trego, Mont., 1990—; musician, bassist Don Lawrence Orch., Kalispell, Mont., 2000—01; musician, octave mandolin Cup O' Tea, Whitefish, Mont., 2004—. Prodr.: (CD) Eureka Kitchen Serenade, 2004, Ellithorpe Sisters, 2006; rec./mixing engr.: CD Girl From Montana, 2005, 90 Years of Oldtime Country Music, 2005. Profl. Devel. grantee, Mont. Arts Coun., 1999, Swan Sch. Alliance Tech. grantee, 2000—01, 2003. Mem.: NEA, Am. Choral Dirs. Assn., Music Educators Nat. Conf. Avocations: fly fishing, hiking, kayaking, sailing. Office: Lincoln County HS PO Box 2000 Eureka MT 59917 Office Phone: 406-297-2525. E-mail: mwatheaton@montanasky.net.

ATHERTON, WILLIAM, actor; b. New Haven, July 30, 1947; s. Robert Atherton Knight and Myrtle (Robison) Raymond; m. Bobbi Goldin, Dec. 8, 1980. BFA, Carnegie-Mellon U., 1969. Film appearances include The Sugarland Express, The Day of the Locust, The Hindenburg, Looking for Mr. Goodbar, Real Genius, Ghostbusters, No Mercy, Die Hard, Die Hard 2: Die Harder, Grim Prairie Tales, Oscar, The Pelican Brief, Frank and Jesse, Biodome; stage appearances include title roles in The Basic Training of Pavlo Hummel and Suggs (Drama Desk award, Outer Circle Critics award, two Obie nominations, Theatre World award), role of Ronnie in original prodn. of House of Blue Leaves, Kennedy Ctr. prodn. The Scarecrow, Misalliance. Broadway prodn. The American Clock, The Caine Mutiny Court Martial; TV appearances include mini-series Centennial, The House of Mirth, Tomorrow's Child; series The Equalizer; numerous other made-for-TV movies; also actor, singer in musical comedies; sang theme song What'll I Do? in movie The Great Gatsby.

ATHEY, SUSAN CARLETON, economics professor; b. Boston, Nov. 1970; d. Whit and Elizabeth (Johansen) Athey; m. Guido Imbens; children: Carleton, Annalise. BA in Economics, Math. and Computer Sci., Duke U., 1991; PhD in Economics, Stanford U. Bus. Sch., 1995. Asst. prof. economics MIT, 1995—97, Castle Krob Career Develop. asst. prof. economics, dept. economics Cambridge, 1997—99, Castle Krob Develop. assoc. prof. economics, dept. economics, 1999—2001; assoc. prof. economics, dept. economics Stanford U., 2001—04, Holbrook Working Prof. Economics and Prof. (by courtesy) Grad. Sch. Bus., dept. economics, 2004—06; prof. economics Harvard U., 2006—. Vis. asst. prof. economics Cowles Found. for Econ. Rsch., Yale U., 1997—98; faculty rsch. fellow Nat. Bur. Econ. Rsch., 1997—2001; vis. prof. Institut d'Economie Industrielle, Toulouse, 1998; prin. Market Design, Inc., 2001—; cons. Govt. BC; cons. rsch. dept Mpls. Fed. Reserve Bank, 1999—2001; mem. NSF Economics Panel, 2004—06; co-dir., Market Design Program Stanford Inst. for Econ. Policy Rsch., 2004—06; sr. cons. Criterion Auctions, 2006—; chair, program com. N.Am. Winter Meetings, 2006. Co-editor: American Economic Journals: Microeconomics; co-editor Journal of Economics and Management Strategy, 1997—2001, assoc. editor B.E. Journals in Theoretical Economics, 2000—, Quarterly Journal Economics, 2001—, fgn. editor Review of Economic Studies, 2001—04, assoc. editor RAND Journal Economics, 2002—04, American Economic Review, 2002—05, Theoretical Economics, 2005—, Econometrica, 2006—; contbr. articles to profl. jours.; referee for several profl. jours. Named to Toulouse Lectures in Economics, 2007; recipient Elaine Bennett Rsch. award, 2001; fellow, Ctr. for Advanced Studies in Behavioral Sci., Stanford U., 2004—05; Sloan Found. Rsch. Fellowship, 2000—02, Nat. Fellow, Hoover Institution, Stanford U., 2000—01, Stanford U. Fellow, 2002—04, Guggenhime Faculty Scholar, Stanford U., 2004—06. Fellow: Econometric Soc. (fellos nominating com. 2006, program com. summer mtgs. 1997, 1998, mem. 8th World Congress 2000, mem. winter mtgs. 2001, 2005); mem.: Am. Econ. Assn. (chair Elaine Bennett Rsch. Prize Com. 2002, nominating com. 2003, chair Elaine Bennett Rsch. Prize Com. 2004, 2006, mentor, CeMent Monitoring Workshop 2006, John Bates Clark medal (First Female to win) 2007), Status of Women in the Economics Profession, Phi Beta Kappa. Avocations: running, bicycling, rollerblading. Office: Dept Economics Harvard U Littauer M-25 Cambridge MA 02138-3001 Office Phone: 617-496-1939. Office Fax: 617-495-8570. Business E-Mail: athey@fas.harvard.edu.*

ATIBA, JOSHUA OLAJIDE OLUWABUNMI, internist, philanthropist, oncologist, educator, pharmacologist; b. Enugu, Nigeria, July 6, 1956; arrived in US, 1983, naturalized, 1995; s. Joseph Ojo and Abigail Olayo A.; m. Stella N. Mordi, June 26, 1981; children: April, Annamarie, Joseph. MD, U. Lagos, Nigeria, 1979; MHA, St. Mary's Coll., Moraga, Calif., 1999. Diplomate Am. Bd. Internal Medicine, Am. Bd. Oncology. Rotating intern Ahmadu Bello U. Tchg. Hosp., Kaduna, Nigeria, 1979-80; resident in internal medicine Lagos U. Tchg. Hosp., 1981-85; fellow in med. oncology Cancer Control Agy., Vancouver, B.C., Can., 1988-90; fellow in clin. pharmacology Stanford U. Med. Ctr., Palo Alto, Calif., 1983-86; pvt. practice Irvine, Calif.; med. oncologist Drs. Pomeroy, Choate and Atiba, Soquel and Watsonville, Calif., 2004—05, Cancer and Blood Inst. Lucy Curci Cancer Ctr., Rancho Mirage, Calif., 2005—06. Dir. clin. investigation U. Calif., Irvine, 1991-95; mem. U. Calif. Irvine Med. Ctr., Orange, North Bay Med. Ctr., Fairfield, Calif., Vaca Valley Hosp., Vacaville, Calif.; asst. prof. medicine, pharmacology U. Calif., Irvine; med. dir. N. Bay Hosp., 1997-99; pres. NOAH Med. Svc. Corp.; med. dir. NOAH, Inc.; rancher. Med. dir. North Bay Hospice, Fairfield, Calif.; pres. Newport Oncology and Healthcare Found. Fellowship in clin. pharm., Merck Internat., 1984—86, PHARMA Jr. Faculty fellowship award, 1991—95, Dean's Fellowship award, Stanford U., 1983. Fellow Royal Coll. Physicians Can.; mem. ACP, AMA, Am. Fedn. for Clin. Rsch., Am. Soc. of Clin. Pharmacology and Therapeutics, Am. Soc. Clin. Oncology, Calif. Med. Assn., Solano County Med. Soc. (sec./treas., pres.-elect, pres.), Physician Peer Rev. Orgn. (dir.), KC (knight 1997). Republican. Roman Catholic. Home (Winter): 15 Spyglass Cir Rancho Mirage CA 92270 Home Phone: 831-761-1100; Office Phone: 703-631-0921. Personal E-mail: jatiba@yahoo.com.

ATILGAN, TIMUR FAIK, retired structural engineer; b. Adana, Turkey, July 15, 1943; arrived in U.S., 1972; s. Faik Ahmet and Sacide (Togman) Atilgan; m. Gulsum Z. Kuzuoglu, Dec. 7, 1977 (div. 1980); m. Mirat Gurol, July 20, 1992 (div. 2002). BS in Civil Engring., Aegean U., Izmir, Turkey, 1967; MS in Structural Engring., U. Md., 1979. Registered profl. engr., Va. Civil engr. NATO/Infrastructure Dept., Ankara, Turkey, 1970-72; structural engr. Bendix Field Engring., Columbia, Md., 1977-79; sr. design engr. Northrop Svcs. Inc., NASA, GSFC, Greenbelt, Md., 1979-82; sr. antenna engr. COMSAT Gen. Corp., Washington, 1982-83; sr. structural engr. OAO Corp., Greenbelt, 1983-84; engring. specialist PRC-Kentron, Inc., Hampton, Va., 1984-86; prin. engr. Fairchild Space Co., Greenbelt, 1986-91; sr. engr. Def. Systems, Inc., McLean, Va., 1991-94; sr. staff engr. Astro Space divsn. Lockheed Martin, Valley Forge, Pa., 1995-98; sr. prin. engr. Canada-France-Hawaii Telescope Corp., Kamuela, Hawaii, 1999-2000; sr. staff engr. Lockheed Martin Corp., Moorestown, NJ, 2001—05; ret., 2005. Mem.: AIAA (sr.). Avocations: music, reading, swimming, cinema. Home Phone: 609-518-6990. Personal E-mail: tatilgan@netzero.net.

ATIYAH, SIR MICHAEL FRANCIS, mathematician; b. London, Eng., Apr. 22, 1929; s. Edward Selim and Jean (Levens) A.; m. Lily J. Brown, July 30, 1955; children: John (dec.), David, Robin. BA, Trinity Coll., Cambridge, 1952, PhD, 1955; DSc (hon.), Bonn, 1968, U. Durham, 1977, Trinity Coll., Dublin, 1983, U. Chgo., 1983, Cambridge U., Eng., 1984; DSc (hon.), Harvard U., 2006. Fellow Trinity Coll., Cambridge, 1954-58, 97—, hon. fellow, 1976-97, master, 1990-97; hon. prof. sch. math. U. Edinburgh, Scotland, 1997—; lectr., fellow Pembroke Coll., Cambridge, 1958-61, hon. fellow, 1983. Commonwealth Fund fellow Princeton, 1955-56, prof. Inst. Advanced Study, 1969-72; reader Oxford U., 1961-63, Savilian prof. geometry, fellow New Coll., 1963-69, hon. fellow, 2000; Royal Soc. rsch. prof., fellow St. Catherine's Coll., 1973-90, hon. fellow, 1991; dir. Isaac Newton Inst. for Math. Scis., Cambridge, Eng., 1990-96; chancellor Leicester U., 1995-05; pres. Pugwash Confs. Sci. and World Affairs, 1997-02; mem. bd. adjudicators, The Shaw Prize (Hong Kong), 2005-, chmn. selection com. math. sciences, 2005- Author: K-Theory, 1966, Commutative Algebra, 1969; contbr. articles to math. jours., also collected works, 1987, 2004. Decorated knight; recipient Fields medal Internat. Congress Mathematicians, Moscow, 1966, DeMorgan medal London Math. Soc., 1980, Feltrinelli prize Accademia Nazionale dei Lincei, 1982, King Faisal Found. Internat. prize for sci., Saudi Arabia, 1987, Order of Merit, 1993, Abel prize Norwegian Acad. Sci. and Letters, 2004. Fellow Royal Soc. (pres. 1990-95, Royal medal 1969, Copley medal 1988), Royal Soc. Edinburgh (hon., pres. 2005-, Royal medal 2003), Royal Instn. (hon.), Royal Acad. Engring. (hon.), Acad. Med. Scis. (hon.), Faculty Actuaries (hon.), Internat. Math. Union (exec. co 1966-74), Math. Assn. (pres. 1981), London Math. Soc. (pres. 1975-77); mem. Nat. Acad. Scis. U.S.A. (fgn.), Leopoldina Acad. (fgn.), Am. Acad. Arts and Scis. (fgn.), Swedish Royal Acad. (fgn.), Academie des Scis. (fgn.), Royal Irish Acad. (fgn.), Am. Philos. Soc. (fgn., Benjamin Franklin medal 1993), Third World Acad. Scis., Indian Nat. Sci. Acad. (fgn.), Chinese Acad. Sci. (hon. prof.), Ukrainian Acad. Scis. (fgn.), Venezuelan Acad. Sci., Australian Acad. Sci., Russian Acad. Sci., Georgian Acad. Sci., Accademia Nazionale dei Lincei, Royal Norwegian Soc. Sci. and Letters, Spanish Royal Acad. of Sci., Order Andres Bello Venezuela, Order Cedars of Lebanon, Order of Merit Lebanon (first class). Office: U Edinburgh Sch Math James Clerk Maxwell Bldg Mayfield Rd Edinburgh EH9 3JZ Scotland Home Phone: +44-131-667-0898; Office Phone: +44-131-650-4883.

ATKIN, J. MYRON, science educator; b. Bklyn., Apr. 6, 1927; s. Charles Z. and Esther (Jaffe) A.; m. Ann Spiegel, Dec. 25, 1947; children— David, Ruth, Jonathan. BS, CCNY, 1947; MA, NYU, 1948, PhD, 1956. Tchr. sci. Ramaz H.S., NYC, 1948—50; tchr. elem. sch. sci. Great Neck Pub. Schs., NY, 1950—55; prof. sci. edn. Coll. Edn., U. Ill., Urbana, 1955—79, assoc. dean, 1966—70, dean, 1970—79; prof. Sch. Edn., Stanford U., Calif., 1979—2004, prof. emeritus, 2004—, dean, 1979—86. Cons. OECD, Paris, Nat. Inst. Edn.; mem. edn. adv. bd. NSF, 1973-76, 84-86, vice-chmn., 1984-85, sr. advisor, 1986-87; mem. Ill. Tchr. Certification Bd., 1973-76; Sir John Adams lectr. U. London Inst. Edn., 1980, vis. scholar com. scholarly commn. Nat. Acad. Scis., People's Republic China, 1987; math. sci. edn. bd. NRC, 1985-89, nat. com. sci. edn. standards and assessment, 1992-96, com. on sci. edn. K-12, 1996-2002, vice chair, 1998, chair, 1999-2002; invited lectr. Nat. Sci. Coun., Taiwan, 1989—; resident Rockefeller Found., Bellagio Ctr., 1999; nat. assoc., Nat. Acads. of Sci., 2001-. Author children's sci. textbooks. Served with USNR, 1945-46. Fellow: AAAS (v.p. sect. Q 73 1974); mem.: NAS (assoc.), Am. Edni. Rsch. Assn. (exec. bd. 1972—75, chmn. govt. and profl. liaison com.), Coun. Elem. Sci. Internat. (pres. 1969—70), Sigma Xi (chmn. com. on sci., math. and engring. edn.). Office Phone: 650-450-3514. Business E-Mail: atkin@stanford.edu.

ATKIN, JERRY C., air transportation executive; b. 1948; m. Carolyn Jones; 4 children. Degree, Dixie Coll., 1969; BS, MBA, U. Utah; HHD (hon.), Dixie Coll., 1995. CPA, 1972—74; dir. fin. SkyWest Airlines, St. George, Utah, 1974—75, pres., CEO, 1975—, chmn., 1991—. Bd. dir. Regence Blue Cross & Blue Shield of Utah, The Regence Group, Portland, Oreg., Zions Bancorporation, Regional Airlines Assn.; state bd. regents Utah Sys. Higher Edn., 1999—. Named to Hall of Fame in Bus., Dixie State Coll., 1999; recipient Outstanding Young Businessman of Yr. award, St. George C. of C., 1981. Office: SkyWest Inc 444 South River Rd Saint George UT 84790*

ATKINS, HOWARD IAN, bank executive; b. NYC, Feb. 12, 1951; s. Maurice and Gertrude Atkins; m. Vivian Leslie Katz; children: Jacqueline, Naomi. BS in Math., CCNY, 1972; MS in Econs., Ohio State U., 1974. Fin. analyst Chase Manhattan Bank, NYC, 1974-78, global funding coord., 1978-80, global funding exec., 1980-82, area treasury exec., Europe, 1982-86, portfolio and funding exec., 1986-88, corp. treas., 1988—91, sr. v.p., 1991—96; v.p., CFO New York Life, 1996—2001; exec. v.p., CFO Wells Fargo & Co., San Francisco, 2001—05, sr. exec. v.p., CFO, 2005—. Treas. Blackstone Coop. Assn., N.Y.C. Mem. Bankers Assn. for Fgn. Trade (Washington), N.Am. Corp. Treasurers. Jewish. Avocations: tennis, skiing, chess. Office: Wells Fargo & Co 420 Montgomery St San Francisco CA 94163*

ATKINS, JOHN L., III, architect; b. Durham, NC, Dec. 16, 1943; s. J. Leeslie Jr. and Delores (Camp) A.; m. Sandra Kelly; children: Margaret Kelly, Ashley Jane. BArch, N.C. State U., 1966; M of Regional Planning, U. N.C., 1970. Registered architect, N.C., N.J., Va., N.Y.; cert. NCARB. Architect John D. Latimer & Assocs., Durham, NC, 1970-75; pres., CEO O'Brien/Atkins Assocs., Research Triangle Park, NC, 1975—. Founding mem., chmn. bd. visitors N.C. State U., Raleigh, 1992—; mem. exec. U. N.C. State U. Design Found., Raleigh, 1991—, also past pres.; mem., past pres. N.C. Bd. Architecture, Raleigh, 1977-87; bd. dirs., chmn. Wachovia Bank and Trust Co., 1987—. Founding mem., bd. dirs., former chmn. Research Triangle Regional Partnership, Research Triangle Park, 1989—; founding mem., chmn. exec. com. Greater Triangle Regional Coun., Research Triangle Park, 1993—; bd. dirs. Durham Ambulatory Surg. Ctr., 1996—. With U.S. Army, 1966-68. Named to NC Bd. Architecture, 1978, emeritus mem., 1988; recipient Civic Honor award, Durham C. of C., 1994. Mem.: AIA (Coll. Fellows 1991—, F. Carter Williams Gold Medal 2005). Office: O'Brien Atkins Assocs PA PO Box 12037 Research Triangle Park NC 27709-2037

ATKINS, NOLAN THOMAS, meteorologist, educator; b. Brookings, SD, Dec. 29, 1964; s. Thomas and Leona Atkins; m. Bridget Mary-Teresa Colasanti, Aug. 6, 1999; children: Nathaniel Nolan, Benjamin Thomas, Gabrielle Mary Teresa. BS in Physics, U. Minn., Mpls., 1988; MS in Atmospheric Scis., UCLA, 1991, PhD in Atmospheric Scis., 1995. Post-doctoral rsch. scientist Nat. Ctr. Atmospheric Rsch., Boulder, Colo., 1995—97; asst. prof. meteorology Lyndon State Coll., Lyndonville, Vt., 1997—2003, assoc. prof. meteorology, 2003—07, co-chmn. meteorology dept., 1998—2001. Contbr. articles to profl. jours. Pres. KC, Littleton, NH, 2005—07. Grantee Rsch. grant, NSF, 2001—07. Mem.: Am. Meteorol. Soc. Avocations: skiing, hiking, kayaking, swimming, bicycling. Home: 64 Heather Ln Littleton NH 03561 Office: Lyndon State Coll 1001 College Rd Lyndonville VT 05851 Office Fax: 802-626-9770. Business E-Mail: nolan.atkins@lyndonstate.edu.

ATKINS, PAUL S., commissioner; married; 3 children. AB, Wofford Coll., 1980; JD, Vanderbilt U. Sch. of Law, 1983. Bar: NY, Fla. Assoc. Davis, Polk & Wardwell, NYC & Paris, 1990—94; exec. asst. to chmn. Richard C. Breeden SEC, Washington, 1990—94, counsellor to chmn. Arthur Levitt, 1990—94, commr., 2002—; ptnr. Coopers & Lybrand, 1994—98, PricewaterhouseCoopers, 1998—2001. Mem.: Phi Beta Kappa. Office: SEC 100 F St NE Washington DC 20549

ATKINS, PETER ALLAN, lawyer; b. NYC, June 29, 1943; m. Lorraine Marilyn Feuerstadt, Apr. 3, 1966; children: Aileen Debra, Karen Jennifer. BA magna cum laude, CUNY, 1965; LLB cum laude, Harvard U., 1968. Bar: N.Y. 1969. Assoc. Skadden, Arps, Slate, Meagher & Flom LLP, NYC, 1968—74, ptnr., 1975—. Mem. dean's adv. bd. Harvard Law Sch.; bd. dirs. A Better Chance, Inc.; N.Y. regional bd. mem. Anti-Defamation League. Contbr. articles to profl. jours. Mem.: ABA, Assn. of Bar of City of N.Y., N.Y. State Bar Assn. Office: Skadden Arps Slate Meagher & Flom LLP 4 Times Sq Fl 46 New York NY 10036-6595 Office Phone: 212-735-3700. Business E-Mail: patkins@skadden.com.

ATKINS, RICHARD BART, film and television producer; b. Paterson, NJ, May 11, 1951; s. S. Stephen and Alice B. (Stein) A.; m. Joanna Pang; 1 child, David. AB in Polit. Sci., Princeton U., 1973. With Cadence Industries, NYC, 1973-74; mgr. TV program devel. Benton & Bowles, NYC, 1977-79, mgr. daytime programming, 1980; v.p. prodn. Telecom Entertainment, NYC, 1981-83; pres. Atkins Pictures Inc./A-Films, West Orange, NJ, 1984—. Programming and prodn. cons. Hearst Entertainment, Whittle Communications, D'Arcy Masius Benton & Bowles, King World Prodns., 1989-91, Quartier Latin, Paris, 1992, TeleVest, 1997-98, Sta. Court TV, 2004, CBS-TV, 60 Mins., 2005. Prodr. (TV films) Shocktrauma, 1982, Murder in Coweta County, 1983, The Gift of Love: A Christmas Story, 1983, Trapped in Silence, 1986; exec. in charge prodn. About Sarah, 1998, Christmas in America, 1990; prodr., writer (videocassette) Knowing Childbirth, 1985; prodr., writer (feature film) Forced March, 1989; producer: (feature film) Asunder, 2000; dir. (documentary) Mongolia, 1995; author: Method to the Madness: Hollywood Explained, 1975, (musical plays) Getting to Know You, 1994, 97, In the Mirror, 1995, 98, Independence, 1996. Mem. Friar's Club, Princeton Club. Jewish. Avocations: golf, computers. Home and Office: A-Films 105 Barringer Ct West Orange NJ 07052 E-mail: datk@aol.com, afilms@aol.com.

ATKINS, RODNEY, musician; b. Knoxville, Tenn., Mar. 28, 1969; married; 1 child, Elijah. Singer: (albums) Rodney Atkins, 1997, Honesty, 2003, If You're Going Through Hell, 2006. Recipient Top New Male Vocalist award, Acad. Country Music, 2007. Office: c/o CAA Inc Ste 500 3310 W End Ave Nashville TN 37203-1087 Office Phone: 615-383-8787. E-mail: info@rodneyatkins.com.

ATKINS, RONALD RAYMOND, lawyer; b. Kingston, NY, Mar. 8, 1933; s. A. Raymond and Charlotte S. A.; m. Mary-Elizabeth Empringham, June 23, 1956; children: Peter Herrick, Timothy Barnard, Suzanne Elizabeth. BS in Econs., U. Pa., Phila., 1954; JD, Columbia U., NYC, 1959. Bar: NY 1959. Assoc. Pell, Butler, Curtis & LeViness, NYC, 1959-61, ptnr., 1962-67; ptnr. Bisset & Atkins, NYC, 1967—, also Greenwich, Conn., 1982—; also of counsel Davidson, Dawson & Clark, LLP, NYC; vis. com. Dept. Medieval Art and Cloisters, Met. Mus. Art.; mem. Coun. of Friends, NYU Inst. Fine Arts; trustee Mianus Gorge Preserve, Inc., chmn., 1984-94, trustee Yale Libr. Assoc. 2004-. 1st lt. U.S. Army, 1954-56. Fellow Frick Collection, Pierpont Morgan Libr.; mem. ABA, NY State Bar Assn., Assn. Bar City NY, Medieval Acad. Am., Coll. Art Assn., Internat. Ctr. Medieval Art chmn. fin. com. 2005-. Republican. Episcopalian. Club: Univ. Club (NYC), Grolier Club (NYC), Field Club (Greenwich, Conn.), Penn Club (NYC), Greenwich (Conn.) Croquet Club, St. Nicholas Soc. City of NY, Soc. Colonial Wars, Pilgrims of US. also: 777 North St Greenwich CT 06831-3105 Office Phone: 203-661-8100.

ATKINS, VERONICA, philanthropist; b. Russia; m. Robert C. Atkins (dec.). Profl. opera singer, 1963—76; mem. bd. dir. Atkins Nutrition, 2003, Robert Atkins Found., 1999—, chmn., 2005—. Co-author (with Robert Atkins): (cookbooks) Dr. Atkins' Quick and Easy New Cookbook, 1997. Named an 50 Most Generous Philanthropists, Fortune Mag., 2005.

ATKINS, VICTOR KENNICOTT, JR., private investor; b. Seattle, Feb. 8, 1945; s. Victor Kennicott and Elizabeth (Tanner) A. AB, Harvard U., 1967, MBA, 1972. Assoc. Blyth Eastman Dillon & Co., NYC, 1972-75, v.p., 1976-78, 1st v.p., 1978-79, E.F. Hutton & Co., NYC, 1979-81, sr. v.p., 1981-84; pres. Covington Ptnrs., 1984-85, Equity Income Ptnrs. Capital Corp., Southampton, 1987-94, also bd. dirs.; chmn. Polaris Industries Capital Corp., Southampton, 1987-94, also dir.; pres., dir. Am. Nat. Security Inc., Omaha, 1992-95. Internat. adv. bd. Laidlaw Holdings, Inc., N.Y.C., 1995-96. Lt. USNR, 1967-70, Vietnam. Decorated Bronze Star, Cross of Gallantry Republic of Vietnam. Mem. Brook Club NYC, Southampton Club, Nat. Golf Links, Pacific Union Club San Francisco, Bohemian Club San Francisco, Meadow Club Southampton, Valley Club Montecito, Birnam Wood Golf Club Montecito, Santa Barbara Yacht Club, U. Club Santa Barbara.

ATKINS, WILLIAM AUSTIN, SR., (BILL ATKINS), former state legislator; b. Tate, Ga., Aug. 16, 1933; s. Austin and Gladys Atkins; m. Jennifer Lee Atkins; children: Chip, Paige; stepchildren: Stacy, Justin. BS in Pharmacy, Mercer U., 1954. Former owner Atkins Pharmacy, Smyrna, Ga.; mem. Ga. Ho. of Reps., 1982-94, mem. appropriations, regulated beverages and industry coms.; dir. Drugs and Narcotics Agy. State of Ga., 1994—. Past chair Cobb County Joint House and Senate Legis. Delegation; past chmn. Ga. State Bd. Pharmacy. Leader, vocalist Bill Atkins Band. Adminstrv. bd. 1st United Meth. Ch., 1998-2003; bd. dirs. Mercer U. Sch. Pharmacy; governing bd. Brawner Hosp., 1993-96; long-range planning bd. Smyrna Hosp., 1993-96 With US Army, 1955—57. Recipient Appreciation plaque Ga. div. Am. Cancer Soc., 1991, Legislator of Yr. Friendship award Personal Care Homes of Ga., 1991, Liberty Bell award Cobb County Bar Assn., 1991, Pharmacist of Yr. in Ga. award, Phi Delta Chi, 1978, One of a Kind award Cobb Clean Commn., 1992, Meritorious Svc. award Mercer U., So. Sch. Pharmacy, 1992, Carlton Henderson award, Mercer U., 2007, others. Mem. Ga. Pharm. Assn. (award for dedication and svc. to profession of pharmacy 1986, Cmty. Svc. award 1997, Bowl of Hygiea award 1997), Ga. Pharmacists Assn. (past bd. dirs.), Ga. Assn. Chiefs of

Police, 7th Dist. Pharmacists Assn. (past pres.), Atlanta Metropol, Cobb C. of C., Moose (named Mr. Cobb County 1993), Nat. Sheriff's Assn. Home: 4719 Windsor Dr SW Smyrna GA 30082-4465 Office Phone: 404-656-5100. Business E-Mail: batkins@gdna.ga.gov.

ATKINS, WILLIAM PAUL, lawyer; b. Balt., Mar. 17, 1962; s. Raymond Melvin and Julia Anne (Lacey) A.; m. Lesley Moira Brand, Jan. 22, 1994. BS in Phys. Scis., U. Md., 1986; MBA, JD, U. Balt., 1992; LLM in Intellectual Property, George Washington U., 1996. Bar: Md. 1992, D.C. 1993, Va. 2001; U.S. Patent and Trademark Office, 1995; US Dist. Ct. (Md., DC, ea., we. Va.), US Ct. Appeals (4th, DC, Fed. cir.), US Supreme Ct. Assoc. Cushman Darby & Cushman I.P. group Pillsbury Madison Sutro, Washington, 1992—99; ptnr. Pillsbury Winthrop LLP, Washington and McLean, Va., 2000—05; ptnr. & co-chair, intellectual property section, mem. mng. bd. Pillsbury Winthrop Shaw Pittman LLP, McLean, Va., 2005—. Editor in chief U. Balt. Law Forum, 1991-92. Mem. ABA, Md. Bar Assn., D.C. Bar Assn., Bar Assn. of DC (pres. 2005) Office Phone: 703-770-7777. Office Fax: 703-770-7901. Business E-Mail: william.atkins@pillsburylaw.com.

ATKINS, YVETTE, special education educator; d. Jacob Mintz and Frieda Levy; m. David Harris Atkins, Jan. 6, 1963; 1 child, Faith Lisa. BA summa cum laude with honors, Fairleigh Dickinson U., Teaneck/Hackensack, NJ, 1982; MA, Columbia U., NYC, 1985, MEd, 1987. Reading specialist State of NJ, 1983, special edn. tchr., 1983, sch. libr., 1988, media supr., 1990—. Advisor Virtual Classroom for Chronically Ill, Paramus, NJ, 2004—06, Buddy Club, Paramus, 1992—2006; learning therapist Westwood Learning Ctr., Ridgewood, NJ, 1988—2002. Developer: ednl. materials in field. Adviser, developer Cultural Connection youth exch., 1992—93; co-chmn. mid. sch. diversity Kean U., Union, NJ, 1994—; chmn. Blue Ribbon Sch. Walk program Am. Diabetes Assn., 2003—. Recipient Spl. Educator of Yr., Gov. of NJ, 1998, Tchr. of Yr. commendation, Bergen County, 1999, Best Practice award, NJ Intercultural Youth Exch., Citizenship award, Assn. Help Retarded Children, 1968. Mem.: Coun. Exceptional Children, Phi Omega Epsilon. Jewish. Avocations: gardening, music, boating, writing. Home: 253 Allen Rd Bayville NJ 08721 Office: Paramus Bd Edn West Brook Mid Sch 550 Roosevelt Blvd Paramus NJ 07652

ATKINSON, ARTHUR JOHN, JR., pharmacologist, educator, consultant; b. Chgo., Mar. 22, 1938; s. Arthur John and Inez (Hill) Atkinson; m. Mary Jo Yunker, May 12, 1984. AB in Chemistry, Harvard U., 1959; MD, Cornell U., 1963. Intern, asst. resident medicine Mass. Gen. Hosp., Boston, 1963-65; chief resident, Howard Carroll fellow medicine Passavant Meml. Hosp., Chgo., 1967-68; fellow clin. pharmacology U. Cin., 1968-69, asst. prof. pharmacology, 1969; vis. scientist dept. toxicology Karolinska Inst., Stockholm, 1970; from asst. prof. to assoc. prof. medicine and pharmacology Northwestern U., Chgo., 1970—76, prof., 1976-94; corp. v.p. clin. devel. and med. affairs Upjohn Co., 1994-95; v.p. clin. R & D and worldwide clin. pharmacology Pharmacia & Upjohn, Inc., 1995-96; adj. prof. pharmacology Ctr. for Drug Devel. Sci., Georgetown U., 1996—2003. With NIH, USPHS, 1965—67; sr. advisor clin. pharmacology to dir. clin. ctr. NIH, 1998—2005; vice chair safe medication use expert com. U.S. Pharmacopeia, 2000—05; cons. in field. Recipient Faculty Devel. award in clin. pharmacology, Pharm. Mfrs. Assn., 1970—72, award of excellence in clin. pharmacology, 2002; scholar Burroughs Wellcome, 1972—77. Master: ACP; mem.: Assn. Am. Physicians, Am. Soc. Clin. Pharmacology and Therapeutics (pres. 1995—96, Rawls Palmer award 1983, Henry W. Elliott award 2004, Oscar B. Hunter award 2005), Am. Soc. Pharmacology and Exptl. Therapeutics (Harry Gold award 1989), Gibson Island Club, Chgo. Yacht Club, Alpha Omega Alpha. Home: 6176 Hidden Lake Cir Richland MI 49083 Office Phone: 269-349-8830. Personal E-mail: art_atkinson@msn.com.

ATKINSON, BARBARA F., dean, medical educator, executive vice chancellor; b. Mpls., Oct. 19, 1942; MD, Jefferson Med. Coll., Thomas Jefferson Univ., 1974. Diplomate Am. Bd. Anatomic and Clin. Pathology, Am. Bd. Cytopathology. Intern Hosp. U. Pa., Phila., 1974—75, resident in pathology, 1975—78; mem. faculty U. Kans., Kansas City; dir. resident program U. Kans. Med. Ctr., Kansas City, exec. vice chancellor, dean Sch. Medicine. Assoc. scientist Wistar Inst. Anatomy and Biology, 1983—87; mem. staff dept. pathology Hosp. of U. Pa., 1978—87, dir. cytopathology, 1978—87, med. program dir. Sch. Cytotech., 1978—86; chmn. dept. pathology and lab. medicine Med. Coll. Pa., 1987—94; dir. Delaware Valley Regional Lab. Svcs., Med. Coll. Hosps. and St. Christopher's Hosp. for Children, 1991—96; chmn. dept. pathology and lab. medicine Med. Coll. Pa. and Hahnemann U., 1994—96; trustee Am. Bd. Pathology, 1992—95, pres., 1998—. Mem. editl. bd. Lab. Investigation, 1988—94, Modern Pathology, 1990—94, Human Pathology, 1992—94, manuscript reviewer Cancer, Diagnostic Cytopathology, Modern Pathology, 1988—94, abstract rev. bd. U.S. and Can. Acad. Pathology, 1989—92, rev. panel Am. Soc. Clin. Pathology Abstract, 1991—96; contbr. articles to profl. jours., chapters to books. Bd. dirs., treas. Laennec Soc. Phila., 1979—81; bd. dirs. Thyroid Soc. Phila., 1982—84; exec. com., bd. dirs. Med. Coll. Pa., 1994—96; bd. trustees Hahnemann U., 1994—96. Recipient Golden Apple Tchg. award for excellent sci. tchg., 1994; grantee, NIH, 1985—88, Takeda-Abbott R&D, 1989—94, NIA, 1991—94. Fellow: ASIM, Coll. Am. Pathologists; mem.: NAS (mem. Inst. Medicine), U.S. and Can. Acad. Pathology, Am. Soc. Clin. Pathology (Janet M. Glasgow Meml. scholarship 1974), Am. Soc. Cytopathology. Office: U Kans Med Ctr Mail Stop 2015 3901 Rainbow Blvd Kansas City KS 66160 Office Phone: 913-588-1440. Business E-Mail: batkinson@kumc.edu.

ATKINSON, CHRISTOPHER LEE, county official; s. Debra Lynn Atkinson; m. Allison Meredith Close, Sept. 10, 2005. BA in English cum laude, George Wash. U., Washington, 1998, MPA, 2000; AS in Bus. Adminstrn., Sinclair C.C., Dayton, OH, 2000; ABD in Public Administration, Fla. Atlantic U., Ft. Lauderdale, 2000—. Contract specialist FTC, Washington, 1999—2000; grad. intern Broward County Office Equal Opportunity, Ft. Lauderdale, Fla., 2001—03, compliance officer, 2003—05, small bus. devel. mgr., 2005—06, asst. to dir., 2006—. Adj. instr. Fla. Atlantic U., Ft. Lauderdale, 2003—. Mem.: Bugle Corps Booster Club, Phantom Rgt. Drum, Golden Key Nat. Honor Soc., Phi Theta Kappa, Pi Alpha Alpha. Roman Catholic. Home: No 1 3013 N Oakland Forest Dr Oakland Park FL 33309 Office Phone: 954-357-7800.

ATKINSON, DAVID NEAL, law educator; b. Leon, Iowa, Feb. 12, 1940; s. Cecil L. and Lena M. (Enarson) A. BA, U. Iowa, 1962, JD, 1965, MA, 1966, PhD, 1969. Bar: Iowa 1965, U.S. Supreme Ct. 1971. Asst. prof. polit. sci. U. Mo., Kansas City, 1967-71, assoc. prof. polit. sci., 1971-75, prof. polit. sci. and law, 1986—, chmn. dept. polit. sci., 1979-81, 89-91, Curators' Distinguished Tchg. Prof., 1999—. Author: Leaving the Bench: Supreme Court Justices at the End, 1999; mem. editl. bd. The Am. Rev. of Politics, 1990-93; contbr. articles to profl. jours. Recipient Shelby Storck award for outstanding undergrad. teaching U. Mo.-Kansas City, 1976, Alumni Reunion Tchg. award, 1995. Mem. Am. Polit. Sci. Assn. (Outstanding Tchg. award 1999), Supreme Ct. Hist. Assn. Home: 6502 W 49th St Mission KS 66202-1715 Office: Univ of Mo Dept Polit Sci 213 Haag Hall 5100 Rockhill Rd Kansas City MO 64110-3143 Office Phone: 816-235-2793. Business E-Mail: atkinsond@umkc.edu.

ATKINSON, DOROTHY SCOTT, retired accountant; b. July 23, 1926; BA in Math., Western Md. Coll., Westminster, 1948; postgrad., Anne Arundel CC, Arnold, Md., 1982. Cryptologist Navy Security Sta., Washington, 1948—51; acct. ABCJ Inc., Atkinson's Acctg. and Tax Svc., West River, Md., 1980—2001, pres., 1994—2001. Mem.: Md. Fedn. Women's Clubs (Outstanding Club Woman 2003). Home: 4909 E Chalk Point Rd West River MD 20778-2209

ATKINSON, GEOFF, marketing executive; b. 1982; Grad., Dartmouth U. Brand mktg. Smith Sport Optics; dir. email and website mktg. Overstock.com Inc., 2005—07, mktg. chief of staff, 2007—. Named one of 40 under 40, Advt. Age, 2007. Office: Overstock.com Inc 6350 S 3000 E Salt Lake City UT 84121 Office Phone: 801-947-3100. Office Fax: 801-944-4629.*

ATKINSON, GORDON C., lawyer; b. Kansas City, Mo., May 16, 1955; BA cum laude, Harvard Univ., 1977; JD, Univ. Chgo., 1981. Bar: NY 1982, Calif. 1986, US Dist. Ct. (so., ea. dist. NY, so., ea., no., ctrl. dist. Calif.). Assoc. Rogers & Wells, NYC, 1981—85; ptnr., litigation Cooley Godward, San Francisco, 1985—, vice chmn. litigation dept. Founder & past pres. Chgo. Law Found.; adj. prof. Univ. Calif., Hastings. Trustee San Francisco Day Sch.; past pres. & mem. exec. com. Sunny Hills Children's Garden. Mem.: ABA, Bar Assn. San Francisco, Calif. State Bar, NY State Bar Assn., Santa Clara County Bar Assn. Office: Cooley Godward Llp 101 California St Fl 5 San Francisco CA 94111-5800 Office Phone: 415-693-2088. Office Fax: 415-951-3699. Business E-Mail: atkinsongc@cooley.com.

ATKINSON, HOLLY GAIL, physician, journalist, educator, human rights activist, writer; b. Detroit, Oct. 20, 1952; d. John S. and Patricia Atkinson; m. Galen Jay Guengerich, Nov. 18, 2000. BA in Biology magna cum laude, Colgate U., 1974; MD, U. Rochester, NYC, 1978; MS in Journalism, Columbia U., NYC, 1981. Diplomate Nat. Med. Bds. Intern in internal medicine Strong Meml. Hosp., Rochester, NY, 1978-79; rschr. Walter Cronkite's Universe show CBS News, NYC, 1981-82; med. reporter CBS Morning News, NYC, 1982-83; on-air co-host Bodywatch health show PBS, 1983-88; contbg. editor and health columnist New Woman mag., 1983-88; on-air corr., med. editor, sr. v.p. programming/med. affairs Lifetime Med. TV, 1985-93; assoc. editor Journal Watch, 1986-90; med. corr. Today Show NBC News, NYC, 1991-94; editor HealthNews, 1994—2006; exec. v.p. Reuters Health, NYC, 1994-98, pres., CEO, 1998-2000; CEO New Media Health Answers Inc., 2000; pres. allHealth.com (iVillage health), 2000—01; med. editor-in-chief, columnist Everydayhealth.com, 2006—. Lectr. dept. pub. health Cornell U. Med. Coll., 1997-2003, asst. prof., 2003—; asst. prof. medicine Mt. Sinai Med. Sch., 2006—. Author: Women and Fatigue, 1986. Vol. nat. and local level Am. Heart Assn., 1984-91, bd. dirs., chmn. nat. comms. com. Am. Heart Assn., 1987-91; bd. dirs. Phys. Human Rights, 1994—, pres. 2002-07, NOW Legal Def. and Edn. Fund, 1996-2006, Soc. Advancement Women's Health Rsch., 1997-99, Am. Lyme Disease Found, 1997-98. Recipient Young Achievers award Nat. Coun. Women, 1986, Achievement award Soc. Advancement Women's Health Rsch., 1995, Health and Human Rights award Physicians for Human Rights, 2006. Mem. Phi Beta Kappa.

ATKINSON, JAMES BLAKELY, writer, editor; b. Honolulu, Nov. 24, 1934; s. Edward Clay and Gertrude (Blakely) A.; m. Starr Koester, Sept. 10, 1960 (dec. Oct. 1978); 1 child, Andrew Edward; m. Gretchen A. Holm, June 28, 1980; stepchildren: Nils, Katrina. AB in History, Swarthmore Coll., 1956; MA in Am. Lit. with honors, Columbia U., 1961, PhD in Comparative Lit. with distinction, 1968. Tchr. English Coll. Benjamin Franklin, Orléans, France, 1958-59; tchr. French, English and Am. history St. David's Sch., NYC, 1960-62; asst. prof. English Dartmouth Coll., Hanover, N.H., 1966-73, Earlham Coll., Richmond, Ind., 1973-78; mem. core faculty Capital U., Dayton, Ohio, 1978-79; asst. prof. English Rutgers U., Camden, N.J., 1979-87; vis. scholar dept. Romance langs. U. Pa., 1987-89; ind. scholar, 1989—. Author: Machiavelli: The Prince, 1976; co-author: Machiavelli, The Complete Comedies, 1985, Machiavelli and His Friends: Their Personal Correspondence, 1996, Footprints of the Past, 1996, The Sweetness of Power: Machiavelli, Discourses on Livy and Guicciardini, Considerations of Discourses, 2002, Massacre at Oradour, 2004, New Hampshire's Cornish Colony, 2005; contbr. articles to profl. jours.; translator Pres. Cornish (N.H.) Hist. Soc., 1992—. With inf. U.S. Army, 1956-58. Mem. AAUP, MLA, Renaissance Soc. Am. Democrat. Mem. Soc. Of Friends. Avocations: hiking, gardening, art and antiques. Home: 117 Town House Rd Cornish NH 03745-4639 Personal E-mail: atholm@valley.net.

ATKINSON, JOSEPH MATTHEW, lawyer; b. Mt. Vernon, Ill., Jan. 4, 1958; s. Obbie O. and Doris V. Atkinson; m. Frances Ann Rightnowar, June 6, 1982; children: Matthew, Luke, Blake, Grant. BA, U. Ill., Urbana, 1980; JD, U. Chgo., 1983. Bar: Ariz. 1983, US Dist. Ct. Ariz. 1983, US Ct. Appeals (9th cir.) 1983, cert.: Ariz. Bd. Legal Specialization (specialist real estate law) 1991. Shareholder Fennemore Craig, Phoenix, 1983—91, Kalish & Forrester, Phoenix, 1991—96; pres., shareholder Atkinson, Hamill & Barrowclough, Phoenix, 1996—, also bd. dirs. Governing coun. real property sect. State Bar Ariz., Phoenix, 1990—93. Author: Advanced Real Estate Law in Arizona, 1994; editor-in-chief: Real Property Jour., 1990—93. Pres. Rosson House Heritage Sq. Found., Phoenix, 1987—92, bd. dirs., 1987—92. Avocation: flying (licensed pilot). Office: Atkinson Hamill & Barrowclough PC 3550 N Central Ave Ste 1150 Phoenix AZ 85012 Office Phone: 602-222-4828. Office Fax: 602-222-4820. Business E-Mail: joseph.atkinson@azbar.org.

ATKINSON, JUNE ST CLAIR, school system administrator; m. William Gurley. BS in Bus. Edn., Radford U., 1969; MS in Vocational and Tech. Edn., Va. Tech. U., 1974; EdD in Ednl. Leadership and Policy, NC State U., 1996. Chief cons., dir. bus. edn., career and tech. edn., and instructional svcs. NC Dept. Pub. Instrn., 1976—2004, supt. pub. instrn., 2005—. HS tchr., bus. edn., Roanoke, Va., Charlotte, NC; pres. So. Regional Edn. Bd.'s HS that Work, 1995—96, 1996—97, Nat. Assn. of State Dirs. of Career and Tech. Edn. Consortium, 2001—03; spkr. in field. Author: Help with Computers, Exploring Business and Computer Careers; contbr. articles to profl. jours. Mem.: Nat. Bus. Edn. Assn. (past pres.). Office: State Supt Office 6301 Mail Service Center Raleigh NC 27699-6301 Office Phone: 919-807-3430. E-mail: jatkinson@dpi.state.nc.us.*

ATKINSON, RICHARD CHATHAM, academic administrator, cognitive scientist; b. Oak Park, Ill., Mar. 19, 1929; s. Herbert and Margaret Atkinson; m. Rita Loyd, Aug. 20, 1952; 1 dau., Lynn Loyd. Ph.B., U. Chgo., 1948; PhD, Ind. U., 1955. Lectr. applied math. and stats. Stanford (Calif.) U., 1956—57, assoc. prof. psychology, 1961—64, prof. psychology, 1964—80; asst. prof. psychology UCLA, 1957—61; dep. dir. NSF, 1975—76, acting dir., 1976, dir., 1976—80; chancellor, prof. cognitive sci. and psychology U. Calif., San Diego, 1980—95; pres. U. Calif. Sys., 1995—2003, pres. emeritus, 2003—. Author: (with others) Introduction to Psychology, 14th edit., 2003, Computer Assisted Instruction, 1969, An Introduction to Mathematical Learning Theory, 1965, Contemporary Developments in Mathematical Psychology, 1974, Mind and Behavior, 1980, Stevens' Handbook of Experimental Psychology, 1988. With AUS, 1954—56. Guggenheim fellow, 1967; fellow Ctr. for Advanced Study in Behavioral Scis., 1963; recipient Disting. Rsch. award Social Sci. Rsch. Coun., 1962, Vannevar Bush award, 2003. Fellow APA (Disting. Sci. Contbn. award 1977, Thorndike award 1980), AAAS (pres. 1989-90), Am. Psychol. Soc. (William James fellow 1985), Am. Acad. Arts and Scis.; mem. NAS, Soc. Exptl. Psychologists, Am. Philos. Soc., Nat. Acad. Edn., Inst. of Medicine, Cosmos Club (Washington), Explorers Club (N.Y.C.). Home: 6845 La Jolla Scenic Dr S La Jolla CA 92037-5738 Office: U Calif San Diego Rm 5320 Atkinson Hall La Jolla CA 92093-0436 Business E-Mail: RCA@ucsd.edu.

ATKINSON, RICHARD LEE, JR., internal medicine educator; b. Petersburg, Va., May 15, 1942; s. Richard Lee and Ruth (Scarborough) A.; m. Susan Stayner Hume, Aug. 13, 1966; children: Catherine Crane, Barbara Hill, Deborah Gildea. BA, VA Mil. Inst., 1964; MD, Med. Coll. Va., 1968. Divsn. surgeon 101st Airborne Divsn., 1973; chief, dept. medicine Ft. Campbell Army Hosp., Ft. Campbell, 1973—74; liaison endocrinologist Vanderbilt U., Nashville, 1973-74; adj. asst. prof. UCLA, 1975-77; asst. prof. internal medicine U. Va. Sch. Medicine, Charlottesville, 1977-83; assoc. prof. internal medicine U. Calif., Davis, 1983-87; prof. internal medicine Ea. Va. Med. Sch., Norfolk, 1987-93; assoc. chief staff for rsch. and devel. VA Med. Ctr., Hampton, Va., 1987-93; prof. medicine and nutritional scis., dir. Beers-Murphy Clin. Nutrition Ctr. U. Wis., Madison, 1993—2002; emeritus prof. medicine and nutritional scis. U. Wis., Madison, 2002—; dir. Obesity Inst. Medstar Rsch. Inst., Washington, 2002—04; pres. Obetech, LLC, Richmond, Va., 2004—, dir. Obesity Rsch. Ctr., 2004—. Clin. prof. pathology Va. Commonwealth U., Richmond, 2005—; nutrition study sect. NIH, 1991-95, chair, 1993-95; chair subcom. on obesity in the mil. NAS, 1999-2003; chair USDA Intramural Peer Rev. Com., 2003-04, USDA Retrospective Rev. Panel on Human Nutrition Rsch., 2006-07. Contbr. articles to profl. jours. Maj. US Army, 1970—74. Decorated Army Commendation medal. Mem. N.Am. Assn. Study Obesity (pres. 1990-91; Richard L. Atkinson-Judith S.Stern award for Disting. Public Svc. 2006), Am. Soc. Clin. Nutrition (pres. 1994-95), Am. Obesity Assn. (pres. 1995-2006). Home: 6077 Barkers Mill Rd Mechanicsville VA 23111 Office: Obetech LLC Va Biotech Rsch Pk 800 E Leigh St Ste 50 Richmond VA 23219 Office Phone: 804-344-5360. Business E-Mail: ratkinson2@vcu.edu.

ATKINSON, TRACEY BLAKE, artist, educator; b. Raleigh, NC, Jan. 16, 1976; d. Robert Claytor and Jane Barry Bishop Atkinson. MA in Art Edn., Teachers Coll., Columbia U., 2002—04; BFA in Illustration, Pratt Inst., 1995—99. Cert. tchr.in visual arts NY State, 2004. Catalogue prodn. artist Christie's, NYC, 1999—2001; visual arts tchr. N.Y.C. Pub. Schools, Bklyn., 2004—. Freelance illustrator, Bklyn., 1999—. Illustration, Body Of Illustration Work (Cert. of Excellence award for Outstanding Merit in Illustration, 1999). Mem. LWV, Washington, 2003—05. Presdl. grant, Pratt Inst., 1997. Mem.: Nat. Art Edn. Assn., United Fedn. Tchrs. Avocations: painting, travel, reading. Home Phone: 917-658-7385.

ATLAS, DAVID, meteorologist, research scientist; b. Bklyn., May 25, 1924; s. Isadore and Rose (Jaffee) A.; m. Lucille Rosen, Sept. 26, 1948; children: Joan Linda, Robert Fred. BSc, NYU, 1946; MSc, MIT, Cambridge, Mass., 1951, DSc in Meteorology, 1955. Chief weather radar br. Air Force Cambridge Rsch. Labs., Bedford, Mass., 1948-66; prof. meteorology U. Chgo., 1966-72; dir. atmospheric tech. divsn. Nat. Ctr. for Atmospheric Rsch., 1972—74, dir. nat. hail rsch. experiment, 1974-75; dir. lab. for atmospheric sci. NASA Goddard Space Flight Ctr., Greenbelt, Md., 1977-84, disting. vis. scientist, 1988—; sr. research assoc. dept. meteorology U. Md., 1985-87; disting. vis. scientist Jet Propulsion Lab. Calif. Inst. Tech., 1984-92. Chmn. panel on remote atmospheric probing, also mem. com. on atmospheric scis., NAS, 1975-82, mem. on modernization of the Nat. Weather Svc., 1996-99—; mem. weather radar beyond NEXRAD, 2001-02; vis. scientist Coop. Inst. for Marine and Atmospheric Scis., U. Miami, 1988-99. 1st lt. USAAF, 1943—46. Recipient Loeser award Air Force Cambridge Rsch. Labs., 1957, O'Day award, 1964; Robert M. Losey award AIAA, 1966; NASA Outstanding Leadership medal, 1982; Presdl. Meritorious Sr. Exec. award, 1983; NSF sr. postdoctoral fellow Imperial Coll., London, 1959-60 Fellow Am. Meteorol. Soc. (councilor 1961-64, 72-74, Meisinger award 1957, assoc. editor publs. 1957-74, pres. 1975, Cleveland Abbe award 1983, Remote Sensing award 1991, Carl Gustav Rossby medal 1996, hon. 2001), Am. Geophys. Union, Am. Astron. Soc., Royal Meteorol. Soc. (Symons Meml. medal 1989), AAAS (chmn. atmospheric and hydrospheric scis. sect. 1986); mem. NAE, IEEE (Dennis J. Picard medal for radar techs. and applications 2004), Internat. Radio Sci. Union (pres. inter-union commn. on radio meteorology 1969-72). Achievements include invention of weather radar devices. Personal E-mail: davnlu@comcast.net. Business E-Mail: datlas@alum.mit.edu.

ATLAS, JAMES ROBERT, editor, writer; b. Chgo., Mar. 22, 1949; s. Donald and Nora (Glassenberg) Atlas; m. Anna O'Conor Sloane Fels, Aug. 2, 1975; children: Amelia Eyre, William Easton. BA, Harvard U., 1971; postgrad. (Rhodes scholar), Oxford U., Eng., 1971-73. Staff writer Time, NYC, 1977-78; asst. editor book rev. NY Times, 1978-81; assoc. editor Atlantic Monthly, 1981-85; contbg. editor Vanity Fair, NYC, 1985-87; asst. editor NY Times Mag., 1987-97; staff writer The New Yorker, 1997-99. Founding editor Penguin Lives. Author: Delmore Schwartz: The Life of an American Poet, 1977, The Great Pretender, 1986, Battle of the Books, 1992, Bellow: A Biography, 2000, My Life in the Middle Ages: A Survivor's Tale, 2005; contbr. articles to nat. mags. Office: Atlas Books 15 W 26th St New York NY 10010 Business E-Mail: atlas@atlasbooks.net.

ATLAS, JAY DAVID, philosopher, consultant, linguist, educator; b. Houston, Feb. 1, 1945; s. Jacob Henry and Babette Fancile (Friedman) A. AB summa cum laude, Amherst Coll., Mass., 1966; PhD, Princeton U., NJ, 1976. Mem. common rm. Wolfson Coll., Oxford, England, 1978, 1980; vis. fellow Princeton U., 1979; rsch. assoc. Inst. for Advanced Study, Princeton, 1982-84; vis. lectr. U. Hong Kong, 1986; prof. Pomona Coll., Claremont, Calif., 1989—, chair dept. linguistics and cognitive sci., 2001—03, 2006—, Peter W. Stanley Prof. linguistics philosophy, 2003—. Sr. assoc. Jurecon, Inc., LA; lectr. 2d European Summer Sch. in Logic, Lang. and Info., 1990; examiner U. Edinburgh, Scotland, 1993, U. Groningen, Netherlands, 1991, 93-97, vis. rsch. prof., 1995, 2005; vis. prof. UCLA, 1988-95, Max Planck Inst. for Psycholinguistics, Nijmegen, Netherlands, 1997, 2005; vis. fellow Amherst Coll., 2004; disting. scholar faculty linguistics U. Cambridge, 2006. Author: Philosophy Without Ambiguity, 1989, Logic, Meaning, and Conversation, 2005; contbr. articles to profl. jours., popular mags. Mem. Am. Philos. Assn., Linguistic Soc. Am., Phi Beta Kappa, Sigma Xi. Office: Pomona Coll 333 N College Way Claremont CA 91711-4410 Office Phone: 909-621-8947. E-mail: jatlas@alumni.princeton.edu.

ATLAS, LIANE WIENER, writer; b. NYC; d. Louis and Frances (Ferne) Wiener; m. Martin Atlas, Mar. 5, 1944 (dec. Mar. 1997); children: Stephen Terry, Jeffrey L. AB, Vassar Coll., 1943; postgrad., Johns Hopkins U., 1953-55. Cert. fin. planner 1986. Fgn. affairs officer Dept. State, Washington, 1962-68; sr. economist U.S. Commerce Dept., Washington, 1968-75, U.S. Treasury Dept., Washington, 1975-79, Riggs Nat. Bank, Washington, 1980-82; v.p. Fintapes Inc., Washington, 1984-87, pres., 1987-95; freelance writer Washington, 1995—. Mem. U.S. delegation UN Econ. Orgns., N.Y.C., Geneva, 1963, 64, 68, 79. Author: Middle East Financial Institutions, 1977, (audio cassettes) What Every Wife Should Know, 1986, rev., 1992, Financial Planning for Divorce, rev. edit. 1992; freelance writer Changing Times and other mags., 1982-87. Treas. Entertaining People/Washington Home, 1986—90, Smithsonian Craft Show, 1993—95, Smithsonian Women's Com., 1996—97; mem. Kennedy Ctr. Cirs. Bd., 1999—; info. specialist Nat. Gallery Art, 2004—; treas. NCC-OWL, 2005—06. Fellow in econs. Johns Hopkins U., Balt., 1954-55; recipient Cert. of Appreciation U.S. Treasury Dept., Washington, 1977. Mem.: OWL (treas. Nat. Capitol chpt. 2005—06), Washington Ind. Writers, Inst. CFPs, Smithsonian Women's Com., Washington Print Club, Vassar Club of Washington. Avocations: print collecting, travel. Home: 2254 48th St NW Washington DC 20007-1035

ATLAS, SCOTT J., lawyer; b. Austin, Tex., Jan. 15, 1950; s. Morris and Rita Jean (Willner) A.; m. Nancy Ellen Friedman, Mar. 26, 1983; 2 children. BA magna cum laude, Yale U., 1971; JD with honors, U. Tex.,

1975. Bar: Tex. 1975, U.S. Dist. Ct. (so. dist.) Tex. 1976, U.S. Ct. Appeals (5th cir.) 1976, U.S. Supreme Ct. 1979, U.S. Ct. Appeals (11th cir.) 1981, U.S. Dist. Ct. (we, no. and ea. dists). Law clk. to judge Thomas Gibbs Gee U.S. Ct. Appeals (5th cir.), Austin, 1975—76; assoc. Vinson & Elkins, Houston, 1976—82, ptnr., 1982—2006, Weil, Gotshal & Manges, Houston, 2006—. Mem. bd. visitors U. Tex. Law Sch., 1982-90; mem. Chancellors Coun. U. Tex., exec. com., 2001-; mem. Com. of 125, U. Tex., Austin, 2003--; lectr. numerous law schs. and legal orgns. Chancellor, Coif, editor-in-chief Tex. Law Rev.; contbr. numerous articles to profl. jours. Founding pres. Houston Shakespeare Festival, 1980-82; vice chair, co-founder Tex. Lyceum Assn. Inc., 1983-85; exec. com. Alley Theatre, Houston, 1983—, ex-officio, 1989—; bd. dirs. ADL S.W. Region, 1998—, exec. com., 1999-, vice chair, 2001—; past bd. dirs. Tex. Opera Theatre, Cultural Arts Coun. of Houston, Young Audiences Houston, others; county coord. U.S. Sen. Lloyd M. Bentsen, 1987-92; mem. adv. com. Law Firm Project of the Pro Bono Inst., 1991-, chmn., 1997-2001. Named one of Outstanding Young Houstonians, Jaycees, 1984-85, Outstanding Young Lawyer in Houston, Houston Young Lawyers Assn., 1984, Outstanding Young Tex. Exes, Tex. Ex-Students Assn., 1989, Tex. Monthly's Tex. Super Lawyers in Bus. Litigation, 2003, 04, 05, EEOC's 40th Ann. Civil Rights All Stars, 2005, 100 Best Lawyers in Houston, 2005; named Lawyer of the Yr., Mex.- Am. Bar Assn. Tex., 1996, Disting. Alumnus for Cmty. Svc., U. Tex. Law Alumni Assn., 2000; recipient Azteca Civil Rights award, LULAC Dist. XVIII, 1993, spl. recognition for contbns. to cross-border relationships Tex.-Mex. Bar Assn., 1997, Pub. Interest award Tex. Law Fellowship, 1998, ADL Karen Susman Jurisprudence award, 2002. Fellow Houston Bar Found. (founder, life), Tex. Bar Found. (life), Am. Bar Found. (life); mem. ABA (chmn. litig. sect. 2002-03, chmn. appellate practice com. litigation sect. 1985-89, coun. mem. litigation sect. 1989-92, 2000-06, exec. com. 1992-96, 2000-06, standing com. on pro bono and pub. svc. 1995-98, co-chair strategic planning implementation task force litigation sect. 1996-97, dir. divns. litigation sect. 1997-98, co-chair fed. practice task force litigation sect. 1998-2000, liaison to civil adv. com. jud. conf. on rules of practice and procedure 1998-2000, planning com. mem. London 2000 meeting 1996-2000, working group on UCITA 2001-2002, task force on advocacy for the assn. and profession 2002-2003, Pro Bono Publico award 1986), Am. Law Inst., State Bar Tex. (jud. selection funding com. 1985-87, liaison with law schs. 1988-90, legal aid to indigent com. 1986, numerous coms. 1986-87), Alliance for Jud. Funding (bd. dirs. 1992-95, 2003—), Tex. Law Rev. Assn. (past pres., bd. dirs. 1977-95, ex officio, bd. dirs. 1995— Leon Green award 1997), U. Tex. Ex-Students Assn. (exec. coun. 1992-98), Houston Bar Assn. (vol. lawyers program bd. 1998-2000), Houston U. Tex. Ex-Students Assn. (bd. dirs. 1991-92), Yale U. Alumni Club (class sec. 1991-96, coun. 1986-87, local dir. 1982-89, 90-91), Govs. Criminal Justice Adv. Coun. (ex officio). Avocations: golf, books. Office: Weil Gotshal & Manges LLP Ste 1600 700 Louisiana Houston TX 77002 Office Phone: 713-546-5115. Business E-Mail: scott.atlas@weil.com.

ATLAS, TERRY, journalist; b. Washington, 1952; BA in Econs. and Polit. Sci., U. Rochester, 1974. Energy reporter Chgo. Tribune, Washington, 1978—83, Washington corr., 1983—86, chief diplomatic corr., Washington bur., 1986—97, Washington news editor, 1997—99; asst. mng. editor (nation and world) U.S. News & World Report, Washington, 1999—. Named Bagehot fellow, Columbia U., 1976—77. Office: US News and World Report 1050 Thomas Jefferson St NW Washington DC 20007-3837 Home Phone: 703-325-3382; Office Phone: 202-955-2297. Business E-Mail: tatlas@usnews.com.

ATLEE, JOHN LIGHT, retired physician, consultant; b. Lancaster, Pa., Feb. 22, 1941; s. John Light Jr. and Ann (Stevens) A.; m. Barbara Sheaffer, June 20, 1964 (dec. Apr. 14, 1967); m. Barbara Sanford, Feb. 3, 1968; children: Sarah Sanford, John Light. BA, Franklin and Marshall Coll., 1963; MD, Temple U., 1967, MS in Pharmacology, 1971. Diplomate Am. Bd. Anesthesiology. Intern Germantown Hosp., Phila., 1967-68; resident in anesthesiology Temple U. Hosp., Phila., 1968-70; postdoctoral rsch. fellow pharmacology Temple U. Grad. Sch. Medicine, 1970-71; staff anesthesiologist U.S. Naval Hosp, Bethesda, Md., 1971-73; asst. prof. anesthesiology U. Wis., Madison, 1973-78, assoc. prof. anesthesiology, 1978-85, prof. anesthesiology, 1985-88, Med. Coll. Wis., Milw., 1988—2005; ret., 2005. Cons. in field; co-founder, v.p. sci. and tech. Esotech Innovations, Inc., Concord, Mass., 2006—. Author: Perioperative Cardiac Arrhythmias, 1985, 2d edit., 1990, Arrhythmias and Pacemakers, 1996; editor: Perioperative Management of Pacemaker Patients, 1992, Complications in Anesthesia, 1999, 2d edit., 2007, Critical Care Cardiology in the Perioperative Period, 2001, 2d edit., 2007, Complicanze in Anestesia (Italian), 2001; mem. editl. bd. Anesthesia & Analgesia, Am. Heart Jour., Am. Jour. Physiology, Anesthesiology, Med. and Biol. Enging. and Computing, Jour. Cardiothoracic and Vascular Anesthesia; contbr. articles to profl. jours. Lt. comdr. USN, 1971—73. Grantee, NIH, 1978—96. Fellow: Am. Heart Assn., Am. Coll. Cardiology and Anesthesiology; mem.: Am. Soc. Exptl. Pharmacology and Therapeutics, Soc. Register Assn., Heart Rhythm Soc., Assn. Univ. Anesthesiologists, Am. Soc. Anesthesiologists, Sigma Xi. Republican. Episcopalian. Achievements include 11 patents in field; patents pending in field. Home: W 309 N 6698 Caddy Ct Hartland WI 53029-9249 Home Fax: 262-966-1866. Personal E-mail: jatlee@wi.rr.com.

ATRAK, TAISSER M., pediatrician, director; b. Lebanon, Beirut, Jan. 10, 1959; m. Amani Noor Hashisho, Jan. 5, 1971. Cert. neonatal-perinatal medicine Am. Bd. Pediat., 1997. Attending neonatologist St Mary's Hosp., Grand Rapids, Mich., 1990—91, St Mary's Hosp./Columbia Hosp., West Palm Beach, Fla., 1991—96; cons. neonatologist Aramco Oil Co., Dharhan, Saudi Arabia, 1996—2002; attending neonatologist West Boca Med. Ctr., Boca Raton, Fla., 2002—04; dir. neonatology Lake Norman Med. Ctr., Moorsville, NC, 2004—. Dir. neonatal ICU Lake Norman Med. Ctr. Fellow, U. Mo. Columbia Sch. Medicine, 1990. Office: Lake Norman Regional Med Ctr 171 Fairview Rd Huntersville NC 28078 Home: 18617 Peninsula Cove Ln Cornelius NC 28031-7752 Home Phone: 704-896-6710; Office Phone: 704-660-4390.

ATREYA, SUSHIL KUMAR, planetary-space science educator, astrophysicist; b. Apr. 15, 1946; came to U.S., 1966, naturalized, 1975; s. Harvansh Lal and Kailash Vati (Sharma) A.; 1 child, Chloè E. ScB, U. Rajasthan, India, 1963, MSc, 1965; MS, Yale U., 1968; PhD, U. Mich., 1973. Rsch. assoc. physics U. Pitts., 1973-74; asst., then assoc. rsch. scientist U. Mich., Ann Arbor, 1974-78, asst. prof., 1978-81, assoc. prof. atmospheric sci., 1981-87, prof. atmospheric and space sci., 1987—, dir. planetary sci. lab. Assoc. prof. U. Paris, 1984-85, vis. prof., 2000-01; vis. sr. rsch. scientist Imperial Coll., London, 1984; vis. astronomer Paris Observatory, 2006-; disting. vis. scientist Jet Propulsion Lab, Calif. Inst. Tech., 2006-; mem. sci. expt. and investigation team Mars Sci. Lab., Sample Analysis Mars Ste., Juno-Jupiter Polar Orbiter, Cassini-Huygens Probe to Saturn-Titan, Galileo Jupiter Probe, Nozomi, Mars Express and Venus Express Missions, Russian Mars '96 and Soviet Phobos projects, Voyager spacecraft missions to the giant planets, Comet Rendezvous/Asteroid Flyby, 1986-92, Japanese Mars Mission, 1999-2004, and SpaceLab I; guest observer/investigator on Spitzer Telescope, Hubble Space Telescope, Internat. Ultraviolet Spectrometer and Copernicus Orbiting Astron. Obs.; sci. working groups, adv. coms. NASA, Jet Propulsion Lab., European Space Agy. Author: Atmospheres and Ionospheres of the Outer Planets and their Satellites, 1986; editor: Planetary Aeronomy and Astronomy, 1981, Outer Planets, 1989, Cometary Environments, 1989, Origin and Evolution of Planetary and Satellite Atmospheres, 1989; contbr. numerous articles to books and profl. jours. Recipient NASA award for exceptional sci. contbns. Voyager Project, 1981, NASA Group Achievement award for Voyager Ultraviolet Spectrometer Investigations, 1981, 86, 90, NASA Group Achievement awards for Galileo Probe Mass Spectrometer experiment, and for Significant Outstanding Contbns. to the Galileo Probe and Orbiter to Jupiter, Excellence in Rsch. award U. Mich. Coll. Engring., 1995, Disting. Faculty award U. Mich., 2007. Fellow AAAS; mem. Internat. Assn. Meteorology and Atmospheric Scis. (pres. commn. planetary atmospheres and their evolution 1987-95, sec. 1983-87, pres. emeritus, 1995—), Am. Geophys. Union (assoc. editor Geophys. Rsch. Letters jour. 1986-89), Internat. Astron. Union, Am. Astron. Soc., Internat. Acad. Astronautics (academician 1993—). Office: Space Rsch Bldg Univ Mich Ann Arbor MI 48109-2143

ATTAL, LAURENT, cosmetics executive; b. Tunisia; married; 2 children. MD in Dermatology, Paris, 1984; MBA, INSEAD. Sales rep. L'Oreal, France, 1986, with Active Cosmetics, CEO Vichy Internat. brand, 1994—98, pres. Active Cosmetic Divsn., 1998, mem. exec. com., 2002—; pres., CEO L'Oreal USA, NYC, 2005—. Office: L'Oreal USA 575 5th Ave New York NY 10017 Office Phone: 212-818-1500.*

ATTANASIO, JOHN BAPTIST, dean, law educator; b. Jersey City, Oct. 19, 1954; s. Gaetano and Madeline (Germinario) A.; m. Kathleen Mary Spartana, Aug. 20, 1977; children: Thomas, Michael. BA, U. Va., 1976; JD, NYU, 1979; diploma in law, Oxford U., 1982; LLM, Yale U., 1985. Bar: Md. 1979, U.S. Dist. Ct. Md. 1980, U.S. Ct. Appeals (4th cir.) 1980, U.S. Supreme Ct. 1983. Pvt. practice, Balt., 1979-81; vis. asst. prof. law U. Pitts., 1982-84; assoc. prof. law U. Notre Dame, Ind., 1985-88, prof. law Ind., 1988-92; Regan dir. Kroc Inst. for Internat. Peace Studies, 1991-92; dean Sch. of Law St. Louis U., 1992-98; dean, William Hawley Atwell chair constnl. law So. Meth. U. Sch. Law, Dallas, 1998—. Prin. investigator Rule of Law Forum. Co-author: Constitutional Law, 1989, Understanding Constitutional Law, 1993. Chair adv. bd. Ctr. for Civil and Human Rights, 1990-92; mem. Fulbright awards area com., 1994-96; bd. dirs. Legal Svcs. Ea. Mo., 1996-98; bd. dirs. Ctr. for Internat.; mem. Law Sch. Adv. Com., Access to Justice Comm. Recipient Fulbright Award, 1990, Legal Teaching award Sch. of Law, NYU, 1994. Mem. ABA (chair out-of-the-box com., legal edn. sect., mem. fellows adv. rsch. com.), Dallas Bar assn. (coun. mem.), Ctrl. States Law Sch. Assn. (v.p. 1992-94), Soc. Internat. Bus. Fellows, Phi Beta Kappa, Alpha Sigma Nu. Roman Catholic. Office: So Meth U Dedman Sch Law PO Box 750116 3315 Daniel Ave Dallas TX 75205-0116 Business E-Mail: jba@smu.edu.

ATTANASIO, MARK L., investment banker, professional sports team executive; AB, Brown U., Providence; JD, Columbia U., NYC. Atty. Debevoise & Plimpton; various positions in High Yield Bond and Investment Banking Depts. up to mng. dir. Drexel Burnham Lambert Inc., 1985—91; co-CEO, co-founder Crescent Capital Corp.; with Trust Co. of West, LA, 1995, group mng. dir. Leveraged Fin. Group; chmn., prin. owner Milw. Brewers, 2005—. Dir. TCW Group, Inc. and TCW Asset Mgmt. Co. Bd. trustees Heal the Bay; mem. Pres.'s Leadership Coun. Brown U. Office: Milw Brewers One Brewers Way Milwaukee WI 53214-3652 also: TCW 865 S Figueroa St Los Angeles CA 90017 Office Phone: 414-902-4400, 213-244-0000.*

ATTAWAY, JOHN A., JR., lawyer; b. Charleston, W.Va., July 17, 1958; BA in Mgmt. Scis., Duke U., 1980; JD, Stetson U., 1982; LLM in Taxation, U. Fla., 1984. Bar: Fla. 1983. Assoc. atty. Raymond, Rupp & Wienberg, Boca Raton, Fla., 1984—86; ptnr. Lane, Trohn, Bertrand & Vreeland, Lakeland, Fla.; corp. counsel Publix Super Markets Inc., Lakeland, Fla., 1997—2000, gen. counsel, sec., 2000—04, sr. v.p., gen. counsel, 2005—. Chmn. United Way of Ctrl. Fla., 1997—98. Office: Publix Super Markets PO Box 407 Lakeland FL 33802-0407*

ATTEBERRY, LINDA ROSE, surgeon, retired military officer; b. Indpls., Oct. 8, 1951; d. Carlysle L. and Marjorie Elizabeth Atteberry. MD, Wake Forest U., 1991. Diplomate Am. Bd. Surgery. Commd. pvt. 1st class U.S. Army, 1972, advanced through grades to col.; resident Health Sci. Ctr. U. Fla., Jacksonville, 1991—97; chief of surgery Irwin Army Hosp., Ft. Riley, Kans., 1998—99, fellow critical care, 2006—07; chief of surgery 10th Combat Support Hosp., Tuzla, Bosnia-Herzegovina, 1999, Winn Army Hosp., Ft. Stewart, Ga., 1999—2001; divsn. surgeon 24th Infantry Divsn., Ft. Riley, Kans., 2001—03; surgeon 250th Forward Surg. Team, Kirkuk, Iraq, 2003—04, comdr. Ft. Lewis, Wash., 2003—05; ret., 2005. Contbr. articles to profl. jours. Decorated Legion of Merit, Legion of Merit with one oak leaf cluster. Fellow: Am. Coll. Surgeons; mem.: Duval County Med. Soc., Assn. Mil. Surgeons of U.S., Alpha Omega Alpha. Office: 1120 15th St Augusta GA Personal E-mail: linda.atteberry@us.army.mil.

ATTEBERY, LOUIE WAYNE, language educator; b. Weiser, Idaho, Aug. 14, 1927; s. John Thomas Attebery and Tressie Mae (Blevins) Attebery Miller; m. Barbara Phyllis Olson, Dec. 31, 1947; children: Bobby Lou, Brian Leonard. BA, Albertson Coll. of Idaho, 1950; MA, U. Mont., 1951; PhD, U. Denver, 1961. Tchr. Middleton H.S., Idaho, 1949-50, Payette H.S., Idaho, 1951-52, Nyssa H.S., Oreg., 1952-55, East H.S., Denver, 1955-61; prof. English Albertson Coll. Idaho, Caldwell, 1961-99, holder Eyck-Berringer chair English, 1987-98, acting acad. v.p., 1983-84; pres. West Shore Press, 1998—. Vis. fellow Harvard U., Cambridge, Mass., 1993-94. Author: The College of Idaho, 1981-91, A Centennial History, 1991, Sheep May Safely Graze: A Personal Essay on Tradition and A Contemporary Sheep Ranch, 1993, The Most of What We Spend, 1998, Albertson College of Idaho: The Second Hundred Years, 1999, J.R. Simplot: A Billion the Hard Way, 2000; editor: Idaho Folklife: Homesteads to Headstones, 1985; editor Northwest Folklore, 1985-91; gen. editor U. Idaho Northwest Folklife series, 1991-2004. Trustee Idaho Hist. Soc., 1984-91, Albertson Coll. Idaho, 2003—. With USN, 1945-46. Bruern fellow, U. Leeds, Eng., 1971—72. Mem. Western Lit. Assn. (exec coun. 1964-65), Assn. Lit. Scholars and Critics, 1995-. Methodist. E-mail: lattebery@albertson.edu.

ATTEBURY, WILLIAM HUGH, construction company executive; b. Amarillo, Tex., Jan. 8, 1929; s. Arnold Gentry and Lula Vivian (Dunn) A.; m. Joyce B. Kallin, June 7, 1951; children: Julie Anne, William Arnold, Nancy Ellen, Elizabeth Grace, Edward Anton. BA, Okla. U., 1951. V.p. Attebury Elevators, Inc., Amarillo, 1954—; pres. Bison Devel. Co., 1960—, A & S Steel Bldgs. Inc., Houston, 1962-69; CEO, U.S. I. A&S, 1969-72, El Poso Oil Co., Amarillo, 1969—, Bison Chem. Co., Port Neches, Tex., 1969-74; ptnr. Tex. Beef Prodrs. Group, 1978—. Bd. dirs. Western Data, Inc., 1st Nat. Bank Am. Mem. adv. bd. Salvation Army, 1973-77; mem. bd. mgrs. Amarillo Hosp. Dist., 1978-79; bd. dirs. Amarillo Children's Home, 1978-82, Village of Hope, 1972-74; chmn. bd. dirs. Harrington Cancer Ctr.; elder Westminster Presbyn. Ch., 1970—. Served with USNR, 1951-54, Korea. Mem. Panhandle Prodrs. and Royalty Owners, Tex. Cattle Feeders Assn. (bd. dirs. 1981-83, 90-94), Nat. Cattleman's Assn. (bd. dirs. 1990-94), Amarillo Club, Amarillo Country Club. Home: 3202 S Lipscomb St Amarillo TX 79109-3536 Office: PO Box 7446 Amarillo TX 79114-7446

ATTENBOROUGH, BARON RICHARD SAMUEL, actor, film director, producer, ambassador; b. Cambridge, England, Aug. 29, 1923; s. Frederick Attenborough; m. Sheila Beryl Grant Sim, 1945; 3 children. Leverhulme scholar to Royal Acad. Dramatic Art, 1941 (Bancroft Medal); DLitt (hon.), U. Leicester, 1970, U. Kent, 1981, U. Sussex, 1987; DCL (hon.), U. Newcastle, 1974; LLD (hon.), Dickinson Coll., 1983; DLit (hon.), Am. Internat. U., 1994; DLitt (hon.), Cape Town, 2000. Fleming Meml. lectr. R.T.S., 1989; Cameron Mackintosh vis. prof. of theatre Oxford U., 1996; pro-chancellor U. Sussex, 1970-98, chancellor 1998—. First stage appearance as Richard Miller in Ah, Wilderness, Intimate Theatre, Palmers Green, 1941; Ralph Berger in Awake and Sing, Arts (West End debut), 1942; The Little Foxes, Piccadilly, 1942; Brighton Rock, Garrick, 1943. Joined RAF 1943; seconded to RAF Film Unit for Journey Together, 1944; demobilized, 1946. Returned to stage in The Way Back (Home of the Brave), Westminster, 1949; To Dorothy a Son, Savoy, 1950, Garrick, 1951; Sweet Madness, Vaudeville, 1952; The Mousetrap, Ambassadors, 1952-54; Double Image, Savoy, 1956-57, St. James's, 1957; The Rape of the Belt, Piccadilly, 1957-58; film appearances: In Which We Serve (screen debut), 1942, Schweik's New Adventure, 1943, The Hundred Pound Window, 1944, A Matter of Life and Death, 1946, School for Secrets, 1946, The Man Within, 1947, Dancing With Crime, 1947, Brighton Rock, 1947, London Belongs to Me, 1948, The Guinea Pig, 1948, The Lost People, 1949, Boys in Brown, 1949, Morning Departure, 1950, Hell is Sold Out, 1951, The Magic Box, 1951, Gift Horse, 1952, Father's Doing Fine, 1952, Eight O'Clock Walk, 1952, The Ship That Died of Shame, 1955, Private's Progress, 1956, The Baby and the Battleship, 1956, Brothers in Law, 1957, The Scamp, 1957, Dunkirk, 1958, The Man Upstairs, 1958, Sea of Sand, 1958, Danger Within, 1959, I'm All Right Jack, 1959, Jet Storm, 1959, SOS Pacific, 1959, The League of Gentlemen, 1959, The Angry Silence (also co-prod.), 1960, All Night Long, 1961, Only Two Can Play, 1962, The Dock Brief, 1962, The Great Escape, 1963, Seance On a Wet Afternoon (also prod., Best Actor, San Sebastian Film Festival and Brit. Film Acad.), 1964, The Third Secret, 1964, Guns at Batasi (Best Actor, Brit. Film Acad.), 1964, The Flight of the Phoenix, 1965, The Sand Pebbles (Hollywood Golden Globe), 1966, Dr. Dolittle (Hollywood Golden Globe), 1967, The Bliss of Mrs. Blossom, 1968; Only When I Larf, 1968, The Magic Christian, 1969, Loot, 1970, The Last Grenade, 1970, A Severed Head, 1970, 10 Rillington Place, 1971, (voice) Cup Glory, 1972, And Then There Were None, 1974, Rosebud, 1975, Brannigan, 1975, Conduct Unbecoming, 1975, The Chess Players, 1977, The Human Factor, 1979, Jurassic Park, 1993, Miracle on 34th St., 1994, E=mc2, 1996, Hamlet, 1996, The Lost World: Jurassic Park, 1997, Elizabeth, 1998, Puckoon, 2002 (also writer, dir.); (video-voice) The Trespasser, 1998; (video) Joseph and the Amazing Technicolor Dreamcoat, 1999; (TV series-voice) Tom and Vicky, 1999; (TV) David Copperfield, 1969, The Railway Children, 2000, Jack and the Beanstalk: The Real Story, 2001; producer: Whistle Down the Wind, 1961; The L-Shaped Room, 1962; producer, dir. Oh! What a Lovely War (16 Internat. Awards including Hollywood Golden Globe and BAFTA UN Award), 1968, Young Winston (Hollywood Golden Globe), 1972, Gandhi (8 Oscars, 5 Brit. Acad. TV and Film Artists Awards, 5 Hollywood Golden Globes, Dirs.' Guild of Am. Award for Outstanding Directorial Achievement), 1980-81, Cry Freedom (Berlinale Kamera, BFI award tech. achievement), 1987, Chaplin, 1992, Shadowlands, 1992 (Alexander Korda award for outstanding Brit. film of yr., BAFTA), In Love and War, 1997, Grey Owl, 1998; dir. A Bridge Too Far (Evening News Best Drama Award), 1976, Magic, 1978, A Chorus Line, 1985; publications: In Search of Gandhi, 1982, Richard Attenborough's A Chorus Line (with Diana Carter), 1986, Cry Freedom, A Pictorial Record, 1987; actor: Light Keeps Me Company (Europe), 2000, The Railway Children, 2000 (TV), Joseph and the Amazing Technicolor Dreamcoat, 2000. Goodwill amb. UNICEF, 1987—; mem. Brit. Actors' Equity Assoc. Council, 1949-73, Cinematograph Films Council, 1967-73, Arts Council of Great Britain, 1970-73; formed Beaver Films with Bryan Forbes, 1959, Allied Film Makers, 1960; dir. Chelsea Football Club, 1969-82, life v.p., 1993—; dir. Young Vic, 1974-84; chmn. The Actor's Charitable Trust, 1956-88, pres., 1988—; chmn. European Script Fund, 1988-96, hon. pres., 1996—, Combined Theatrical Charities Appeals Council, 1964-88, pres., 1988—; chmn. Brit. Acad. Film and TV Artists (v.p. from 1971-94, chmn. trustees, 1970-, pres. 2002-), 1969-70, Royal Acad. Dramatic Art, mem. council 1963—, chmn., 1972—, Capital Radio, 1972-92, life pres., 1992—, Help a London Child, 1975—; trustee King George V Fund for Actors and Actresses, 1973—; chmn. U.K. Trustees Waterford-Kamhlaba Sch., Swaziland (gov. 1987—), 1976—, Duke of York's Theatre, 1979-92, Brit. Film Inst., 1981-92, Goldcrest Films & TV, 1982-87, Com. of Inquiry into the Arts and Disabled People, 1983-85, Channel Four TV (dep. chmn. 1980-86), 1987-92, Brit. Screen Adv. Council, 1987—; Gov. Nat. Film Sch., 1970-81, 96, hon. pres. 96; pres. Muscular Dystrophy Group of Great Britain (v.p. 1962-71), 1971-96, hon. pres. 1996—; pres. The Gandhi Found., 1983—, Brighton Festival, 1984-95, Brit. Film Yr., 1984-86; trustee Tate Gallery, 1976-82, 94-96, Tate Found., 1986—, Found. Sport and Arts, 1991—; pres. Arts for Health, 1989—, Gardner Centre Arts, Sussex U., 1990—; gov. Motability, 1977—; patron Kingsley Hall Community Ctr., 1982—; R.A. Centre Disability & Arts, Leicester, 1990-; life v.p. Chelsea Football Club. Decorated Commander Brit. Empire, 1967, Knighted 1976; recipient Evening Std. Film award, 40 yrs. svc. to Brit. Cinema, 1983, Praemium Imperiale award, 1998, Martin Luther King Jr. Peace Prize, 1983, Padma Bhushan, India, 1983, award of merit for humanitarianism in film making, European Film awards, 1988, Shakespeare prize Outstanding Contbn. European culture, 1992, Patricia Rothermere award for lifelong service to theatre, London Evening Standard Theatre award, 2003; named Commandeur, Ordre des Arts et des Lettres, France, 1985; Chevalier, Order de la Legion d'Honneur, France, 1988; named Freeman of City of Leicester, 1990; named fellow Kings Coll. London, 1993; named Baron, Life Peer of Long Borough of Richmond upon Thames, 1993; recipient hon. fellowship U. Wales, Bangor, 1997, Manchester Poly., 1994, Kings Coll., 1993. Fellow BAFTA, Brit. Film Inst.; mem. Garrick Club, Beefsteak Club. Avocations: collecting paintings and sculpture, listening to music, watching football. Home: Old Friars Richmond Green Surrey England Office: Richard Attenborough Prodns Twickenham Studio Saint Margaret's Middlesex TW1 2AW England

ATTIG, RICK, editor; b. Oreg., 1962; married; 2 children. BA cum laude, U. Oreg., 1983. Police reporter Springfield (Oreg.) News, 1983—86; sr. writer, editl. page editor, exec. editor Bend (Oreg.) Bulletin, 1986—98; assoc. editor, lead editl. writer The Oregonian, Portland, 1998—. Mem. editl. bd. The Oregonian, 1998—. Recipient 2 best writing awards, Oreg. Newspaper Pubs. Assoc., 7 best editl. awards, Pulitzer Prize for pub. svc., 2001, Pulitzer Prize for editl. writing, 2006; fellow, Nat. Press Assoc. Agendas, 1999; journalism fellow, Casey Found. Children & Families, 1996. Office: The Oregonian 1320 SW Broadway Portland OR 97201 Office Phone: 503-294-5091. E-mail: rickattig@news.oregonian.com.

ATTINGER, CHRISTOPHER ERNST, medical educator; b. Lausanne, Switzerland, July 20, 1947; came to the U.S., 1952; s. Ernst Otto and Françoise (Daubige) A.; m. Lydia Henri, June 20, 1975; 1 child, Thalia. BS cum laude, Washington & Lee U., 1977; MD, Yale U., 1981. Bd. cert. plastic surgery. Resident in gen. surgery Brigham & Women's Hosp., Boston, 1981-86, vascular fellow, 1986-87; plastic surgery resident NYU, NYC, 1987-89, hand surgery fellow, 1989-90; asst. prof. plastic, orthopedic surgery, otolaryngology Georgetown U., Washington, 1990-94, assoc. prof. plastic, orthopedic surgery, otolaryngology, 1994—. Recipient Edward James Olmos award for Advocacy in Amputation Prevention, DF Con, Global Conf. on the Diabetic Foot, 2007; named one of Top Doctors in Washington area, N. Va. mag., 2007. Fellow ACS, Am. Foot and Ankle Surgery (hon.); mem. Am. Soc. Plastic and Reconstructive Surgery, Am. Soc. for Reconstructive Microsurgery, Phi Beta Kappa. Avocations: tennis, skiing, birding. Office: Georgetown Univ Hosp Pasquerilla Healthcare Ctr 3800 Reservoir Rd NW Washington DC 20007-2196 Office Phone: 202-444-3059.*

ATTOH-OKINE, NII OTOKUNOR NII, civil and environmental engineering educator; b. Accra, Ghana, Oct. 10, 1958; came to U.S., 1990; s. Richard Attoh-Okine and Georgina Quaynor; children: Nii Attoh, Naa Djama. MS in Civil Engring., Rostov U., Russia, 1986; PhD, U. Kans., 1992. Profl engr., Kans. Lectr. engring. U. Sci. and Tech., Kumasi, Ghana, 1987-89; instr. soil mechanics U. Kans., Lawrence, 1990-91, rsch. assoc., 1992, rsch. engr., 1993; project engr. Mng. Tech. Inc., Overland Park, Kans., 1993; rsch. assoc., adj. prof. civil engring. Fla. Internat. U., Miami,

1993-94, sr. rsch. assoc., 1994, adj. prof., sr. rsch. assoc., 1995, assoc. prof. civil and environ. engring., 1995-99; asst. prof. civil and environ. engring. U. Del., Newark, 1999—. Organizer, chmn. 2d Internat. Workshop on Artificial Intelligence and Math. Mehods in Pavement and Geomch. Systems, Newark, 2000, 1st Internat. Workshop, Miami, 1998; external examiner U. Miami, 1994; mem. Dade County Brownfield Task Force, 1996—; mem. Transp. Rsch. Bd.; reviewer, spkr. in field. Contbr. articles to profl. jours., chapters to books. Eisenhower fellow, Fed. Hwy. Adminstrn., 1999. Mem. ASCE, IEEE (sr.), Ghana Instn. Engrs. (asst. hon. sec. no. sector 1987-90), Phi Beta Delta. Office: U Del Dept Civil & Environ Engrg 137 Dupont Hall Newark DE 19716 Office Phone: 302-831-4532. Business E-Mail: okine@ce.udel.edu.

ATTOLE, MARY BERTHA, writer; b. Lafayette, La., Dec. 12, 1958; d. Antoine and Elia Guillory Attole. Student, So. U., Baton Rouge, La., 1976—80. Tchr.'s aide Glendale Elem., Eunice, La., 1980—82; mem. staff Fred's Dept. Store, Eunice, 1983—85, John's IGA Grocery Store, Eunice, 1985—88. Author: My Brother's Keeper, 2001. Vol. So. Poverty Law Ctr.'s Civil Rights Meml. Visitors Ctr. Wall of Tolerance; active Creole Heritage Found., Northwestern State U., 2005—; vol. St. Matilda Cth. Ch., Eunice, 1991—. Mem.: Alpha Mu Gamma. Democrat. Roman Catholic. Avocations: reading, genealogy, comedy, classic television, pets. Home: 310 N Martin Luther King Dr Eunice LA 70535

ATTRIDGE, DANIEL F., lawyer; b. Washington, Oct. 4, 1954; s. Patrick and Teresa A.; m. Anne Asbill, Aug. 23, 1980; children: James, William, and Thomas. BA magna cum laude, U. Pa., 1976; JD cum laude, Georgetown U., 1979. Bar: D.C. 1980, U.S. Dist. Ct. D.C. 1980, U.S. Ct. Appeals (D.C. cir.) 1980, U.S. Supreme Ct. 1983, U.S. Dist. Ct. Md. 1985, U.S. Ct. Appeals (fed. cir.) 1985, U.S. Ct. Appeals (2d.cir.) 1987, U.S. Ct. Claims 1988, U.S. Ct. Appeals (4th and 6th cirs.) 1990, U.S. Ct. Appeals (8th cir.) 1997, U.S. Ct. Appeals (1st cir.) 2000, U.S. Ct. Appeals (11th cir.) 2003, U.S. Ct. Appeals (9th cir.) 2004, U.S. Ct. Appeals (5th cir.) 2005. Law clk. to judge Oliver Gasch U.S. Dist. Ct. D.C., Washington, 1979-80; assoc. Kirkland & Ellis LLP, Washington, 1980-85, ptnr., 1985—. Faculty Nat. Inst. Trial Advocacy, 1991—. Exec. editor Georgetown U. Law Jour., 1978-79. Trustee Fed. City Coun., 2003—. Fellow Am. Bar Found.; mem. ABA (vice chmn. antitrust sect. Sherman Act sect. 2 com. 1999-2002), D.C. Bar Assn. (bd. govs. 1996-99, co-chair litigation sect. 1993-96). Roman Catholic. Home: 1249 Cherry Tree Ln Annapolis MD 21403-5023 Office: Kirkland & Ellis LLP 655 15th St NW Fl 12 Washington DC 20005-5793 Office Phone: 202-879-5012. Business E-Mail: dattridge@kirkland.com.

ATTRIDGE, RICHARD BYRON, lawyer; b. Atlanta, Oct. 14, 1933; s. Archibald Angus and Katherine Elizabeth (Babb) A.; m. Florence Law, Dec. 14, 1963; children: Anne Habersham, Elizabeth Barnes, R. Byron Jr. BA, Princeton U., 1955; LLB, Emory U., 1961. Bar: Ga. 1960. Ptnr. King & Spalding, Atlanta, 1960—. Chmn. State Bd. of Bar Examiners, Ga., 1978-83. Vice chmn. Cmty. Rels. Com., Atlanta, 1968-73; various local charities; vestry Episc. Ch. 1st It. U.S. Army, 1956-57. Fellow Am. Coll. Trial Lawyers; mem. ABA, State Bar Ga. (bd. govs. 1974-83), Atlanta Bar Assn. (pres. 1971-72), Lawyers Club Atlanta, Capital City Club (bd. dirs. 1989—), Piedmont Driving Club. Avocations: hunting, fishing, tennis. Home: 2820 Habersham Rd NW Atlanta GA 30305-2959 Office: King & Spalding LLP 1180 Peachtree St NE Ste 1700 Atlanta GA 30309-7525 Office Phone: 404-572-4787. E-mail: battridge@kslaw.com.

ATTWOOD, DAVID THOMAS, physicist, researcher; b. NYC, Aug. 15, 1941; s. David Thomas and Josephine (Banks) A.; divorced; children: Timothy David, Courtney Catherine, Kevin Richard; m. Linda Jean Geniesse, Aug. 3, 1991. BS, Hofstra U., 1963; MS, Northwestern U., 1964; D Engring. Sci., NYU, 1972. Physicist Lawrence Livermore Nat. Lab., Livermore, Calif., 1972-83, Lawrence Berkeley Nat. Lab., Berkeley, Calif., 1983—; sci. dir. Advanced Light Source, 1985—88; prof. in residence U. Calif., Berkeley, 1989—, founding chair applied sci. and tech. PhD program. Founder Ctr. for X-Ray Optics, Lawrence Berkeley Lab., 1983; assoc. dir. NSF EUV Sci. Tech. Ctr., 2003—. Author: Soft X-Rays and Extreme Ultraviolet Radiation: Principles and Applications, 2000; editor: (with B.L. Henke) X-Ray Diagnostics, (with J. Bokor) Short Wavelength Coherent Radiation, (with F. Zernike) Extreme Ultraviolet Lithography, (with W. Meyer-Ilse and T. Warwick) X-Ray Microscopy; reviewer numerous sci. jours.; contbr. numerous articles to profl. publs. Fellow: Optical Soc. Am.; mem.: AAAS, Am. Phys. Soc. Achievements include research on x-ray optics and microscopy, extreme ultraviolet lithography, synchrotron radiation, partially coherent x-rays, and laser-plasma interactions. Office: Lawrence Berkeley Nat Lab Ctr X-ray Optics Berkeley CA 94720

ATTWOOD, JAMES ALBERT, JR., investment company executive; b. Lake Forest, Ill., Apr. 20, 1958; s. James Albert and Pauline Veryl (Ellwood) A.; m. Leslie Kim Williams. BA in Applied Math., summa cum laude, Yale U., 1980, MA in Stats., 1980; MBA, JD, Harvard U., 1985. Bar: Mass., N.Y., D.C. Assoc. Hewitt Assocs., Rowayton, Conn., 1980-81; v.p. Goldman, Sachs & Co., NYC, 1985-96; exec. v.p. strategic devel. and planning GTE Corp., Irving, Tex., 1996-2000; exec. v.p. strategy, devel. and planning Verizon Comm., NYC, 2000; mng. dir. The Carlyle Group, NYC, 2000—. Democrat. Presbyterian. Office: The Carlyle Group 520 Madison Ave New York NY 10022

ATWATER, BRIAN F., geologist, educator; BS in Geology, Stanford U., Calif., 1973, MS in Geology, 1974; PhD, U. Del., 1980. Geologist US Geol. Survey, mem. Pacific NW Earthquake Hazards Team; affiliate prof. dept. earth & space scis. and quaternary rsch. ctr. U. Wash., Seattle. Guest rschr. U. Tokyo, Geol. Survey Japan. Contbr. articles to sci. jours.; assoc. editor: Quaternary Rsch., 1994—2001; author: The Orphan Tsunami of 1700, 2005. Named one of 100 Most Influential People, Time mag., 2005. Mem.: NAS. Office: Dept Earth & Space Scis U Wash Johnson Hall 070 Box 351310 Seattle WA 98195-1310 Office Phone: 206-553-2927. Office Fax: 206-553-8350. E-mail: atwater@u.washington.edu.*

ATWATER, PHYLLIS Y., municipal official; b. Memphis, Nov. 4, 1947; d. Jeff D. and Thelda E. A.; m. John R. Ernst, Dec. 28, 1972. BA, Vassar Coll., 1968; MA, Boston U., 1970; postgrad., New Sch. Soc. Rsch., NYC, 1974-82. Lectr. math. Tufts U., Medford, Mass., 1970-72; instr. math. higher edn. program Boston Model Cities Adminstrn., 1970-74, coord. program, 1971; instr. econs. SUNY, Old Westbury, 1977-82; dep. dir. adminstrn. and fin. Divsn. Solid Waste Mgmt., Commonwealth of Mass., 1984-88; pres. and chief operating officer Recoverable Resources/R2B2, Inc., Bronx, NY, 1989-91; dir. divsn. solid waste N.Y. State Dept. Environ. Conservation, 1992-93, regional dir. NYC, 1993-95; pvt. practice computer svcs. cons., 1995-99; computer specialist N.Y.C. Dept. Employment, 1999—2002, assoc. commr. for info. tech. and adminstrn., 2002—03; admin. staff analyst N.Y.C. Dept. Small Bus. Svcs., 2003—. Assoc. Recycling Adv. Coun., EPA, Washington, 1990-93; vice chair Manhattan Solid Waste Adv. Bd., NYC, 1991-92. Mem. founding bd. advisors N.Y. Feminist Art Inst., NYC, 1979—81; bd. advisors The Labor Inst., NYC, 1985—97, West Harlem Environ. Action Inc., NYC, 1996—99; founder, pres., bd. dirs. Inst. for Labor and the Cmty., NYC, 1997—; sec. bd. dirs. O.R.E., Inc., NYC, 1998—; bd. dirs. Scenic Hudson, Inc., Poughkeepsie, NY, 2001—. Ford Found. fellow Nat. Fellowship Fund, 1975-78, Danforth Found., 1980-82.

ATWATER, VERNE STAFFORD, finance educator; b. Pitts., Aug. 22, 1920; s. Verne L. and Priscilla (Brodeur) Atwater; m. Evelyn Lowe, May 29, 1943 (dec. Dec. 16, 2005); children: Lynda Mary Atwater Pyfrin, Louise Christine Atwater Cross. BA, Heidelberg Coll., 1942; MBA, Harvard U., 1943; PhD, NYU, 1961; LHD, Heidelberg Coll., 1989. Asst. prof. bus. adminstrn. Syracuse U., 1946-50; asst. to chmn. bd. N.J. Bank, Paterson, 1950-56; dir. adminstrn. Ford Found., 1956-61; rep. Argentina/Chile, 1961-63; dir. Latin Am. and Caribbean Program, 1963-64, v.p., 1964-68; pres. Westinghouse Learning Corp., NYC, 1968-71; chmn., chief exec. officer Central Savs. Bank, NY, 1971-81; prof. fin. Lubin Grad. Sch. Bus., Pace U., NYC, 1981-90, vice dean, 1984-86, prof. emeritus in residence, 1990-2001; lead ind. dir. Hudson City Bancorp, 2003—04. Mem. Nat. Commn. Electric Fund Transfers, 1975—77, Pres.'s Task Career Devel., 1967—68, N.J. Housing Fin. Agy., 1966—70. Chmn. Woodlawn Cemetery, 1994—98, James T. Lee Found.; chmn. bd. trustees Heidelberg Coll., 1982—89. Lt. USNR, 1943—46. Mem.: Univ. Club (N.Y.C.), Arcola Country Club (dir. Paramus, N.J.). Home: PO Box 1176 232 Boston Post Rd Amherst NH 03031-1176 Personal E-mail: singndo@aol.com.

ATWELL, GEORGE MICHAEL, composer, conductor, musician; b. Roanoke, Va., July 8, 1946; s. William Lee and Ann Atwell; m. Teresa Ann Nichols, Jan. 19, 1967; children: Michael Wayne, Jennifer Lauren. BA in Piano Performance, U. Ctrl. Fla., Orlando, 1987. Staff prodr. Bee Jay Rec. Studios, Orlando, 1977—83; assoc. dir. music, organist First Presbyn. Ch. Orlando, 1994—. Composer: (choral, soloists, and orchestra) Mass for a New Millennium (Carnegie Hall premier, 2007), Bread for a Hungry World (ASCAP Spl. award, 1988), Tears, (choral) Fly!, (children and piano) A Nut for a Jar of Tuna (established MIJEN PRESS Publishing). Democrat. Presbyterian. Avocations: chess, travel. Office: First Presbyterian Church of Orlando 106 E Church St Orlando FL 32801 Office Phone: 407-423-3441. Office Fax: 407-423-2094. Personal E-mail: gatwell@cfl.rr.com. Business E-Mail: gatwell@fpco.org.

ATWELL, NEDRA WHEELER, education educator, consultant; b. Louisville, Ky., Sept. 24, 1950; d. James Riley and Elsie Parsley Skaggs; m. Charles William Atwell, Aug. 10, 2000; children: Donald Wheeler, Jonathan Wheeler. BA in hist. and psychology, Western Ky. U., 1972, MA in exceptional child edn., 1988; EdD in ednl. leadership, Vanderbilt U., 1995. Cert. dir.special edn. U. Ky., Lexington, 1989, Ky. Standard Cert. for Tchrs. of Exceptional Children. LBD tchr. New Providence Sch., Clarksville, Tenn., 1972—75; prin. and ednl. therapist Rivendell America, Bowling Green, 1986—88; area program cons. Ky. Dept. Edn., Frankfort, 1988—90; dir. profl. devel. consortia Ky. Valley Ednl. Consortia, Hazard, 1990—97; special edn. faculty Alice Lloyd Coll., Pippa Passes, Ky., 1994—97; adj. grad. faculty Morehead State U., Ky., 1996—97; dir. tchr. edn., assoc. prof. Va. Intermont Coll., Bristol, 1997—2000; assoc. prof., personnel preparation grant coord. Radford U., Va., 2000—02; assoc. prof. special instrnl. programs, exceptional edn. Western Ky. U., Bowling Green, 2002—. Co-editor Tchr. Educators Jour. ATE-VA; copy editor Southeast Regional Assn. Tchr. Educators Jour., editl. bd. Author: (book) KVEC Principal Institute 1, 1992, KVEC Principal Institute 2, 1993, Affective Data Interpretation, 1993, Beans, Buses, and Basketball, 1993, Building School Communities for All, 1994, Change Process, 1995, The Instructional Leader's Primer in Systems Thinking, 1995, SMART: Science and Math Appalachian Regional Teachers Instructional Manual, 1996, Implementing School Centered Decision-Making, 1996, HEART: Humanities Education Appalachian Regional Teachers Integrated Curriculum Guide, 1996, Kentucky and Missouri School Improvement Models, 1997, Lighting Strikes Twice, 1997, Troubled Students and School, 1999, Appalachian Women, 2005, Voius, 2006. Mem.: Ky. Inst. Women Sch. Adminstrn. (mentor), Southeast Regional Assn. Tchr. Educators, Am. Assn. Tchr. Educators, Va. Assn. Tchr. Educators (exec. bd., editl. bd.), Nat. Staff Devel. Coun., Am. Coun. Rural Special Edn., Coun. Exceptional Children, VA Declaration (editor), Coun. Children Behavioral Disorders, VA Fedn. (past pres.), Coun. Exceptional Children, VA Fedn. (past pres.), Ky. Reading Assn., Internat. Reading Assn., Am. Ednl. Rsch. Assn., Am. Assn. U. Women, Appalachian Studies Assn., Phi Delta Kappa (v.p. membership, Radford U. chpt.). Office: Western Ky U 1 Big Red Way Bowling Green KY 42101 Home Phone: 270-846-1929; Office Phone: 270-745-4647. E-mail: nedra.atwell@wku.edu.

ATWELL, ROBERT HERRON, academic administrator; b. Washington, Pa., Jan. 26, 1931; s. R. Boice and Elsie (Herron) A.; m. Suzanne Fogg, Apr. 22, 1989; children by previous marriages: Mary, Robert, John, Nancy, Carl, Catherine, Cynthia. BA, Coll. Wooster, 1953; MA in Pub. Adminstrn, U. Minn., 1957. Budget examiner U.S. Bur. Budget, Washington, 1957-60; fiscal economist, loan officer U.S. Devel. Loan Fund, Dept. State, 1960; budget examiner, program analyst for higher edn. and med. research programs U.S. Bur. Budget, 1961-62; program planning officer, asst. chief Cmty. Mental Health Ctrs. br. NIMH, HEW, 1962-65; vice chancellor for adminstrn. U. Wis., Madison, 1965-70; pres. Pitzer Coll., Claremont, Calif., 1970-78; v.p. Am. Coun. Edn., 1978-84, pres., 1984-96, pres. emeritus, 1996—. Chmn. coun. Claremont Coll., 1971—72; pres. Ind. Colls. So. Calif., 1974—75; trustee Eckerd Coll., Argosy U., Western State U. Coll. Law; mem. adv. bd. Inside Track Learning; bd. dirs. Nat. Ctr. for Pub. Policy and Higher Edn. With AUS, 1953-55. Home: 447 Bird Key Dr Sarasota FL 34236-1805

ATWOOD, CHARLES L., recreational facility executive; b. Pascagoula, Miss., Dec. 29, 1948; s. George L. and Mary Frances (Lewis) A. BS, Univ. So. Miss., 1970; MBA in Fin., Tulane U., 1973. CPA, Tenn. Asst. to CFO NEI Properties, New Orleans, 1973—78; controller Canal Pl. Ventures, New Orleans, 1978—79; from sr. fin. analyst to v.p. Harrah's Entertainment Inc., Las Vegas, 1979—96, v.p., 1996—2001, treas., 1996—2003, sr. v.p., CFO, 2001—06, bd. dir., 2005—, vice-chmn., 2006—. Bd. dir. Equity Residential Trust. Pres. Annesdale Snowden Hist. Dist., Memphis, 1984; bd. dirs. Memphis Heritage, 1986—. Mem.: AICPA. Republican. Office: Harrahs Entertainment Inc One Harrahs Ct Las Vegas NV 89119*

ATWOOD, DONNA ELAINE, retired financial manager; b. Sewickley, Pa., Apr. 17, 1933; d. Donovan E. and Hazel Marie (Rush) Oelschlager; m. G. Richard Atwood, Oct. 22, 1955; children: Stephen Parker Atwood, Elaine Alden Atwood Henderson. BS in Commerce and Fin., Grove City Coll., 1955. Acctg. clk. 1st Nat. Bank, Coraopolis, Pa., 1949; asst. libr. Coraopolis Pub. Libr., 1949—51; acctg. asst. Aluminum Co. of Am., Pitts., 1951—55; sec. to dean Grad. Sch. Indsl. Adminstrn. Carnegie Mellon U., Pitts., 1955—56; fin. sec., acct. Third Presbyn. Ch., Pitts., 1956—65; fin. mgr., acct. Dominican Sisters of the Sick Poor, Ossining, NY, 1972—92; ret. Mother advisor Internat. Order Rainbow for Girls NY, 1980—83; state chmn., 1986—, mem. state adv. bd., 1987—, sec., 1997—, gen. chmn. Grand Assembly, 1987—94; pubs. chmn. Ossining Woman's Club, 1965—69, pres., 1969—71, house mgr., 1971—72; yearbook chmn. AAUW, Chappaqua, NY, 1964; treas. trustees Pleasantville United Meth. Ch., 1980—83, pastor parish rels. com., 1989—91, sec. United Meth. Women, 1993—96, auditor, 1988—2003, choir, 1980—2003; mem. Grand Assembly Com., 1994—. Mem.: PEO (guard 2006—), DAR (chpt. libr. 1957, state page 1957—68), Women Descs. of Ancient and Honorable Arty. Co., Huguenot Soc., Colonial Dames XVII Century, Daus. Am. Colonists (state page 1957—76, chpt. sec. 1961—64, nat. page 1972—79, state chmn. Golden Acorns and Pages 1970—73, nat. chmn. Golden Acorns and Pages 1973—79, state rec. sec. 1976—79, state chmn. pages 2000—03, state marshal 2003—06, state chair 2006—), Hudson Fortnightly Club, St. Officer's Club (pres. 2006—), Order Ea. Star (past matron 1962—63, grand Esther 1991, past matron 1996, chmn. com. 1997—2003, trustee 1997—2004). Home Phone: 518-325-1222. Personal E-mail: gratwood@aol.com.

ATWOOD, EDWARD CHARLES, economist, educator; b. NYC, Dec. 2, 1922; s. Edward Charles and Bertha Margaret (Moloney) A.; m. June Matilda Ruschmeyer, Mar. 30, 1946; children— Edward Terrell, Jeffrey Terrell. AB, Princeton U., NJ, 1946, MA, 1950, PhD in Econs, 1959. Tchg. fellow U. Buffalo, 1946-47; part-time instr. Princeton U., 1948-50; instr. Denison U., 1950-52; from asst. to assoc. prof. Washington and Lee U., 1952-60, dean students, 1961-69, dean Sch. Commerce, 1969-86, Lewis W. Adams Prof. of Econs., 1986-93, prof. econs. emeritus, 1993—. Econ. cons. Bankers Trust Co., NYC, 1956; economist Gen. Electric Co., 1960-61; tchr. courses Am. Inst. Banking, Va. Sch. Banking, 1957-59; co-chmn. Va. Council Higher Edn. Bus. Adminstrn. Task Force, 1985-86; dir. United Va. Bankshares/Rockbridge, Lexington; vis. prof. Tamkang U., Taiwan, Fall, 1986; vis. fellow U. Coll., Oxford U., Spring, 1987. Pres. Rockbridge Area Housing Corp., 1974-75; trustee Lawrenceville Fathers Assn; mem. Southbury-Middlebury Scholarship Fund, 2000-2001; mem. Waterbury Found., 2001—; deacon United Ch. Christ, Southbury, 2001—. Served with USNR, 1942-46. Mem. Am. Assembly Collegiate Schs. Bus. (initial accreditation com., continuing accreditation com. 1969-86), Am., So. econ. assns., Am. Bankers Assn (selection com. 1973-74), Beta Gamma Sigma, Omicron Delta Kappa, Omicron Delta Epsilon. Congregationalist. Home: 389B Heritage Vlg Southbury CT 06488-1717

ATWOOD, HOLLYE STOLZ, lawyer; b. St. Louis, Dec. 25, 1945; d. Robert George and Elise (Sauselle) Stolz; m. Frederick Howard Atwood III, Aug. 12, 1978 (div.); children: Katherine Stolz, Jonathan Robert. BA, Washington U., St. Louis, 1968; JD, Washington U., 1973. Bar: Mo. 1973. Jr. ptnr. Bryan Cave, St. Louis, 1973-82, ptnr., 1983—2001, mem. exec. com., 1995-2000, of counsel, 2002—. Bd. dirs. St. Louis coun. Girl Scouts U.S., 1976-86; trustee John Burroughs Sch., St. Louis, 1983-86. Mem. ABA, Met. St. Louis Bar Assn., Washington U. Law Sch. Alumni Assn. (pres. 1983-84), Noonday (St. Louis) (bd. govs. 1983-86). Office: Bryan Cave One Metropolitan Sq 211 N Broadway Saint Louis MO 63102-2733 E-mail: hsatwood@bryancave.com

ATWOOD, JOHN BRIAN, dean; b. Wareham, Mass., July 25, 1942; s. Ellsworth Savary and Bernice Anita (Perkins) A.; m. Susan Johnson, Aug. 3, 1991; children: John, Deborah, Michelle. BA, Boston U., 1964; postgrad., Am. U., 1970, LLD (hon.), 1995. Mgmt. intern Nat. Security Agy., Washington, 1964-66; fgn. svc. officer U.S. Dept. State, Washington, 1966-71; legis. asst. to Senator Thomas F. Eagleton, 1971-77; dep. asst. sec. for congl. rels. U.S. Dept. State, Washington, 1977-79, asst. sec., 1979-81; dean, profl. studies and acad. affairs Fgn. Svc. Inst., Washington, 1981-82; v.p. Internat. Reporting and Info. Systems, Washington, 1982—; exec. dir. Dem. Senatorial Campaign Com., Washington, 1982-84; pres. Nat. Dem. Inst. for Internat. Affairs, Washington, 1985-93; adminstr. U.S. AID, Washington, 1993-99; pres. Citizens Internat., Boston, 1999—2002; prof. Harvard U., Cambridge, Mass., 1999—; dean Hubert H. Humphrey Inst. Pub. Affairs U. Minn., Mpls., 2002—. Mem. Coun. Fgn. Rels., UN Assn. Bd. dirs. Nat. Dem. Inst., Freedom House, World Peace Found., Acad. Ednl. Devel. Recipient Harvard Prize Book award, 1959. Mem. Boston U. Alumni Assn. Office: Hubert H Humphrey Inst for Public Affairs 300 Humphrey Ctr 301 19th Ave Minneapolis MN 55455 Home Phone: 952-935-5443; Office Phone: 612-625-0669. E-mail: jbatwood@hhh.umn.edu.

ATWOOD, MARGARET ELEANOR, writer; b. Ottawa, Ont., Can., Nov. 18, 1939; d. Carl Edmund and Margaret Dorothy (Killam) A. BA, U. Toronto, 1961; AM, Radcliffe Coll., 1962; postgrad., Harvard U., 1962-63, 65-67; LittD (hon.), Trent U., 1973, Concordia U., 1980, Smith Coll., Northampton, Mass., 1982, U. Toronto, 1983, U. Waterloo, 1985, U. Guelph, 1985, Mt. Holyoke Coll., 1985, Victoria Coll., 1987, Univ. de Montréal, 1991, McMaster U., 1996; LLD (hon.), Queen's U., 1974. Lectr. in English U. B.C., 1964-65, Sir George Williams U., 1967-68, U. Alta., 1969-70; asst. prof. English York U., Toronto, 1971-72; writer-in-residence U. Toronto, 1972-73, U. Ala., Tuscaloosa, 1985. Berg Chair NYU, 1986; writer-in-residence Macquarie U., Australia, 1987, Trinity U., San Antonio, 1989. Author: (poetry) Double Persephone, 1961, The Circle Game, 1967, The Animals in That Country, 1968, The Journals of Susanna Moodie, 1970, Procedures for Underground, 1970, Power Politics, 1973, Poems for Voices, 1970, You Are Happy, 1975, Selected Poems, 1976 (Am. edit. 1978), Selected Poems, 1966-84, 1990, Margaret Atwood Poems, 1965-75, 1991, Two-Headed Poems, 1978, True Stories, 1981, Interlunar, 1984, Selected Poems II: Poems Selected and New, 1976-1986, 1986, Morning in the Burned House, 1995; (novels) The Edible Woman, 1969 (Am. edit. 1970), Surfacing, 1972, (Am. edit. 1973), Lady Oracle, 1976, Life Before Man, 1979, Bodily Harm, 1981, The Handmaid's Tale, 1985, Cat's Eye, 1988 (City Toronto Book award 1989, Coles Book of the Yr. 1989, Can. Booksellers Assn. Author of the Yr., 1989, Book of the Yr. award Found. for Advancement of Can. Letters, Periodical Marketers Can., 1989, Torgi Talking Book award 1989), The Robber Bride, 1993 (award for Fiction Can. Authors Assn., 1993, Trillium award for Excellence in Ont. Writing 1993, Regional Commonwealth Lit. award), Alias Grace, 1996 (Giller Prize 1996, Medal of Honor for Literature, Nat. Arts Club 1997), The Blind Assassin, 2000 (The Booker Prize 2000, nominee for Internat. IMPAC Dublin Literary award, Dashiell Hammett Prize, Internat. Assn. of Crime Writers, 2001), Oryx and Crake, 2003 (Booker prize shortlist, 2003), The Tent, 2006; (short stories) Dancing Girls, 1977, Bluebeard's Egg, 1983, Murder in the Dark, 1983, Wilderness Tips, 1991 (Trillium award 1992, Book of the Yr. award Periodical Marketers of Can., 1992), Good Bones, 1992; (juvenile) Up in the Tree, 1978, Anna's Pet, 1980, For the Birds, 1990, Princess Prunella & the Purple Peanut, 1995; (non-fiction) Survival: A Thematic Guide to Canadian Literature, 1972, Second Words: Selected Critical Prose, 1982, Strange Things: The Malevolent North in Canadian Literature, 1995, Negotiating with the Dead, 2002, Writing With Intent: Essays, Reviews, Personal Prose: 1983-2005, 2005; Curious Pursuits, 2005. Recipient E.J. Pratt medal, 1961, Pres.'s medal U. Western Ont., 1965, YWCA Women of Distinction award, Gov. Gen.'s award, 1966, 1st pl. Centennial Commn. Poetry Competition, 1967, Union Poetry prize Chicago, 1969, Bess Hoskins prize of Poetry Chicago, 1974, City of Toronto Book award, 1977, Can. Booksellers Assn. award, 1977, award for short fiction Periodical Distbr. Can., 1977, St. Lawrence award for Fiction, 1978, Radcliffe Grad. medal, 1980, Molson award, 1981, Internat. Writer's prize Welsh Arts Council, 1982, Book of Yr. award Periodical Distbrs. of Can. and Found. for Advancement Can. Letters, 1983, Los Angeles Times Fiction award, 1986, Gov. Gen.'s Lit. award, 1986, Ida Nudel Humanitarian award, 1986, Toronto Arts award, 1986, Arthur C. Clarke award for Best Sci. Fiction, 1987, shortlisted for Ritz Hemingway prize, Paris, 1987, Commonwealth Lit. Prize regional award, 1987, 94, Silver medal for Best Article of Yr. Council for Advancement and Support of Edn., 1987, Nat. Mag. award 1st prize, 1988, Sunday Times award for literary excellence, YWCA Women of Distinction award 1988, Centennial medal Harvard U., 1990, John Hughes prize Welsh Devel. Bd., 1992, Commemorative medal 125th Anniversary of Can. Confedn., 1992, Trillium award for excellence in Ont. writing, 1995; Guggenheim fellow, 1981; decorated companion Order of Can., 1981, Order of Ont., 1990; named Woman of Yr. Ms. Mag., 1986, Humanist of Yr., 1987, Chevalier de l'Ordre des Arts et des Lettres, 1994. Fellow Royal Soc. of Can., Am. Acad. Arts and Scis. (fgn. hon. lit. mem. 1988). Achievements include invention of a remote-controlled pen, LongPen, that allows writers to sign books for fans from thousands of miles away. Office: c/o Carrol & Graf Avalon Publishing NY Divsn 245 W 17th St New York NY 10011-5300

ATZORI, MARCO, neuroscientist, educator; b. Oristano, Sardinia, Italy, May 6, 1963; permanent resident, USA, 2004; s. Gianni Atzori and Marisa Murru. BS in Physics, U. Trieste, Italy, 1989; PhD in Biophysics, Internat. Sch. for Advanced Studies, Trieste, 1995. Rsch. asst. prof. Blanchette Rockefeller Neurosci. Inst., Johns Hopkins U., Rockville, Md., 2001—04; asst. prof. U. Tex., Richardson, 2004—. Recipient Young Investigator award, Nat. Alliance for Rsch. on Schizophrenia and Depression, 2003—04, NIH/Nat. Inst. Deafness and other Comm. Disorders, 2004—; fellow, U. Tenn., 1997, NIH, 1999; Fulbright fellow, US Internat Agy./Commn. for Internat. Exch. of Scholars, 1996. Mem.: Assn. Rsch. in Otolaryngology (assoc.), Soc. Neurosci. (assoc.). Liberal. Achievements include animal research suggesting that psychoses are caused by monoaminergic disruption of the physiological function of acetylcholine; development of patch clamp dual recording. Office: Univ Texs at Dallas 2601 N Floyd Rd Richardson TX 75080 Home Phone: 972-231-3656; Office Phone: 972-883-4311. Office Fax: 972-883-2491. Personal E-mail: marco_atzori@hotmail.com. Business E-Mail: marco.atzori@utdallas.edu.

AUBERGER, MARCIA A., lawyer; b. Rochester, NY, Nov. 8, 1963; BA, SUNY, Buffalo, 1985; JD, South Tex. Coll. of Law, 1989. Bar: Tex. 1989, DC 1998. Ptnr. Trademark Venable LLP, Washington, DC. Lectr. in field. Contbr. articles top profl. jours. Mem.: ABA (mem. Intellectual Property Sect.), Intellectual Property Owners Assn. (mem. US Trademark Law Com.), Women's Bar Assn. of DC, DC Bar (mem. Intellectual Property Sect.), Assn. for Protection of Intellectual Property, Am. Intellectual Property Law Assn., Internat. Trademark Assn., State Bar Tex. Office: Venable LLP 575 7th St NW Washington DC 20004 Office Phone: 202-344-4969. Office Fax: 202-344-8300. E-mail: maauberger@venable.com.

AUBERTIN, MADELINE KATHERINE, retired nursing educator, medical/surgical nurse, mental health services professional; b. Detroit, May 16, 1930; Grad., Providence Hosp. Sch. Nursing, 1951; BS in Nursing Edn., Mercy Coll., Dobbs Ferry, NY, 1959; MEd, Wayne State Coll., Nebr., 1995. RN, Mich. Staff nurse Vets. Hosp., Dearborn, Mich., 1951-58; staff nurse, nursing educator St. John's Hosp., St. Louis, 1960-64; staff nurse U. Mich., Ann Arbor, 1965-66; instr., staff nurse Harper Hosp., Detroit; insvc. dir., nursing instr. Holy Cross Hosp., Detroit, 1966-68; insvc. instr., dir. Grace Hosp., Detroit, 1968-72; nursing instr. Wayne County Community Coll., Detroit, 1972-96; ret., 1996. Mem. ARC, Detroit, 1962-92, Am. Heart Assn., Southfield, Mich., 1962-92, Assn. for Learning Disabilities, Farmington, Mich., 1972-92, Nat. League of Nursing, Detroit, 1962-92. Democrat. Roman Catholic. Avocations: singing, church choir, sewing, reading. Home: 36550 Grand River Apt 904 Farmington MI 48335

AUBERY, STEPHEN ROYSTON EDMUND, film producer; b. Kingston Upon Hull, Yorkshire, Eng., July 4, 1951; came to U.S., 1964; s. Gerald Royston and Doreen (Stevens) A.; m. Rose Marie Marks, Feb. 23, 1973 (div. Dec. 1991); children: Suzanne Marie, Julia Dawn, Wendy Lynn, Katrina Rose; m. Tamara Phizacklea, Oct. 4, 1994 (div. May 2000). Student, U. Utah, Salt Lake City, 1968—70, Brigham Young U., Provo, Utah, 1974—75; BA in Mktg., Stafford U., London, 2004. Sound dept. mgr. Brigham Young U. Motion Picture Studio, Provo, Utah, 1972—76; film prodr., ptnr. Linton Prodns., Salt Lake City, 1976—79; prodr., gen. ptnr. Seven Star Pictures, Salt Lake City, 1979—82; news editor KUTV Inc., Salt Lake City, 1982—84; film prodr., mgr. LDS Audiovisual, Salt Lake City, 1984—94; film prodr. Challenger Schs., Salt Lake City, 1994—95; film prodr., owner Encore Prodns., Salt Lake City, 1995—96; film prodr. Mountain Prodns., Inc., Draper, Utah, 1997—99, Mark Phillips Philms & Telephision, LA, 1999—2000; film prodr., owner flixnpix.com, LA, 2000—01; sr. dir. mktg., video prodr. Arbor E&T, LLC, Austin, Tex., 2001—. Film dept. instr. U. Utah, Salt Lake City, Brigham Young U., Provo; mgr., lead singer, guitarist Tapestry top 40 soft rock dance band, 1980-98 Co-author, prodr., cinematographer (screenplay, book, film) Knocking at Heaven's Door, 1980; prodr. (film) Temple Open House, 1992 (Telly award 1993); prodr., dir. (film) Phonics Fun, 1993 (two Telly awards 1994), From Thoughts to Things, 1997 (Telly & Communicator award 1997); prodr., dir., dir. photography, editor, Undercover Stings, Learning Channel, 1999, The Jer-Z Games, Disney Channel, 2000, K-9 Cops-The Learning Channel, 2000, Bridges to Freedom, 2000, First Impressions, 2000 (Videographer Excellence award and Communicator award and Cindy Award 2001), A Unique Alternative Education Experience, 2003 (Communicator award 2003, Videographer award 2004, MCA-I award 2004); author, contbg. editor Super 8 Filmaker Mag., 1975-80. Bd. dirs. World Firefighters Assistance League, Salt Lake City. Mem. Internat. TV Assn., Soc. Motion Picture and TV Engrs. (presenter tech. paper L.A. conv. 1974-80, cert. presentation 1995), Media Comm. Internat. Avocations: vocal performing, playing guitar, computers. Mailing: 2011 Campfield Pwy Austin TX 78745-6347 Office Phone: 512-344-4014. Business E-Mail: saubery@arboret.com.

AUBIN, BARBARA JEAN, artist; b. Chgo., Jan. 12, 1928; d. Philip Theodore and Dorothy May (Chapman) A. BA, Carleton Coll., 1949; B Art Edn., Sch. Art Inst. Chgo., 1954, M Art Edn., 1955. Lectr. Centre D'Art & Haitian Am. Inst., Port-Au-Prince, Haiti, 1958-60; asst. prof. Sch. Art Inst. Chgo., 1960-67, Loyola U., 1968-71; lectr. Calumet Coll., Hammond, Ind., 1971-75; prof. art Chgo. State U., 1971-91; ret., 1991. Vis. prof., artist Wayne State U., Detroit, 1965; vis. artist St. Louis CC, Forest Park, Mo., 1980, 81, U. Wis., Green Bay, 1981; co-curator Art for the Next Millennium Kimo Theatre Gallery, Albuquerque, 1997; spkr. and exhibiting artist, Womens's Caucus For Art Regional Conf./Exhbn., 1999. One-woman shows include Countryside Arts Ctr., Arlington Heights, Ill., 1954, 87, Avant Arts Gallery, Chgo., 1954, Riccardo's Restaurant and Gallery, Chgo., 1956, Evanston Twp. HS, Ill., 1958, Centre d'Art, Port-au-Prince, Haiti, 1960, Chgo. Pub. Libr., 1960, Chgo. Acad. Fine Arts, 1965, Oxbow Summer Sch. Fine Arts, 1965, Lewis Towers Gallery, Loyola U., Chgo., 1970, Chgo. State U., 1971, 74, 85, North River Cmty. Gallery, Northeastern Ill. U., Chgo., 1974, Ill. Arts Coun., Chgo., Crossroads-Jr. Mus., Art Inst. Chgo., 1976, Fairweather Hardin Gallery, Chgo., 1978, 80, 85, 90, U. Wis., 1981, Illini Union Gallery, U. Ill., Urbana, 1986, Artemisia Gallery, Chgo., Katerina's, Chgo., 2002, Woman Made Gallery, Chgo., 2006; exhibited in group shows at Art Inst. Chgo., 1960, 78, 80, 85, 89, Vanderpoel Art Assn., Beverly Art Ctr., Chgo., 1992, Ancient Echoes, Chgo., 1992, Renaissance Ct., Chgo. Cultural Ctr., 1993, 2001, 02, Artemisia Gallery, Chgo., 1994, Art Place Gallery, Chgo, 1994, Chgo. State U., 1994, Chgo. Women's Caucus for Art, 1994, 95, 98, 2000, 02-06, Eastern Ill. U., Charleston, 1991, 1993-2001, ARC Gallery, Chgo., 1995, 97, 2004, 05, N.Mex. Art League, Albuquerque, 1996, Mirage Gallery, Albuquerque, Barrington Arts Coun., 1997, Meridian Ctr., Washington, 1997, Chgo. Women's Caucus for Art, No. Ill. U., 1998, Peter Jones Gallery, 2000, Springfield Art Mus., Mo., 1999, (Patron Purchase award), Beacon St. Gallery, Chgo., 1999, DeKalb Area Women's Ctr., Ill., 1999, Mini-Millennium Women's Caucus For Art Nat. Gallery, 2000, Eastern Ill. U., Charleston, 2000, 01, Chgo. Cultural Ctr., 2001-05, 07, Arts Club Chgo., 2003, 05, Oakton CC, 2004, 2005, Peter Jones Gallery, 2005, 06, Women's Day Art Exhibits Oakton CC, 2005, 06, A.R.C. Gallery, Chgo., 2005, Art of the Book Plate Printworks Gallery, 2005, 2006; represented in permanent collections at Art Inst. Chgo., Ill. State Mus., Ball State Mus., Calumet Coll., Hammond, Ind., Shimer Coll., Waukegan, Ill., Ill. Inst. Tech., Chgo., Kemper Group Collection, Long Grove, Ill., State of Ill. Bldg., Chgo., Seyfarth, Shaw, Fairweather & Geraldson, Washington, Ernst & Ernst, Chgo., Foote, Cone & Belding, Chgo., US League of Savs. and Loans, Chgo., Northside Industries, Chgo., Keck, Cushman, Mahin & Cate, Chgo., Gould, Inc., Rolling Meadows, Ill., First Nat. Bank Chgo., Internat. Mineral and Chem., Skokie, Ill., Wellesley Coll. Davis Mus., Mass.; reporter Women Artists News, 1977, 80, 83-86. V.p. Midwest region Womens Caucus Art, Chgo., 1982-88; founding mem. local chpt. Chgo. Women's Caucus Art, 1974, bd. dirs., 2002-07; bd. dirs. Chgo. Artists' Coalition, 1992-94. Recipient honorable mention Sr. Artist's Network South Shore Cutural Ctr., Chgo., 2006, George D. Brown Fgn. Travel fellow Sch. Art Inst. Chgo., 1955-56; Art grant Fulbright fellow, 1958-60, Huntington Hartford Fedn. grant, 1963, Project Completion grant Ill. Arts Coun., 1978-79, Chgo. Cultural Ctr., 2002, CAAPS grant, 2002. Mem. Arts Club Chgo., Chgo. Artists' Coalition, Chgo. Womens Caucus for Art. Home: The Hallmark 2960 N Lake Shore Dr #405 Chicago IL 60657-5645 Office Phone: 773-348-0589. E-mail: dittofeline@aol.com.

AUBREY, DOUGLAS P., ecologist, researcher; b. Kirkwood, Mo., Dec. 21, 1975; s. James S. Aubrey and Aubrey Lou Mary; m. LeAnn M. Pressey, Feb. 23, 2002; 1 child, Olivia M. BS in Ecology, Evolution and Systematics, Mo. State U., 2002, MS in Biology, 2004. Lead biol. sci. technician USDA Forest Svc., New Ellenton, SC, 2004—. Milt Topping Rsch. fellow, Mo. State U., 2002, Rsch. grantee, Mo. State U. Grad. Coll., 2002, Mo. State U., 2002. Mem.: Ozarks Biol. Grad. Soc. (vice-president 2002—03, pres. 2003—04), Internat. Assn. Ecology, Ecologiocal Soc. Am., Mo. Stream Team, Sierra Club. Achievements include research in the effects of fire on oak and hickory seedling physiology; degree of niche overlap in dendriculous bat species; the effects of fire on bat roosting preferences; the effects of fertilization and irrigation on loblolly pine's response to ice damage; the effect of seasonal changes on the Q10 of soil respiration; separating autotrophic and heterotrophic components of soil respiration; variation of soil chemistry as a function of allocthanous inputs. Home Phone: 803-641-8275; Office Phone: 803-652-3754. E-mail: daubrey@fs.fed.us.

AUBUCHON, RICHARD E., engineering executive; b. Crystal City, Mo., Feb. 7, 1945; s. Earl L. and Estelle L. Aubuchon; m. Nancy C. Sweat, Sept. 8, 1969 (div. Aug. 27, 1973); 1 child, Denise Michelle Stellhorn. BS, Washington U., St. Louis, 1974; MBA, U. Wis., Milw., 1999. Cert. quality auditor; quality engr., mgr. of quality and organizational excellence; six sigma Black Belt. Lab. technician United Nuc. Corp., Hematite, Mo., 1968—72, Indsl. Testing Labs., St. Louis, 1972—73; quality engr./gage lab supr. Carter Carburetor, St. Louis, 1973—74; quality control engr. J. I. Case, Rock Island, Ill., 1974—78, sr. quality engr. Wausau, Wis., 1978—82; quality control mgr. Brandt, Inc., Watertown, Wis., 1982—92, quality assurance mgr., 1992—97; quality sys. supr. Waukesha (Wis.) Engine, 1997—98; quality engring. mgr. Broan-NuTone LLC, Hartford, Wis., 1998—. Forward award examiner State of Wis., Madison, 1998—2000; mem. trade and industry adv. bd. Madison Area Tech. Coll., Watertown, 1992—97. Sgt. US Army, 1966—67. Fellow: Am. Soc. Quality (sect. chmn. 2000—01, chmn. soc. examining com. 2007—); mem.: Mensa. Home: 1522 Bridge St Watertown WI 53094 Office: Broan-NuTone LLC 926 W State St Hartford WI 53027 Home Phone: 920-261-8278; Office Phone: 262-673-8764.

AUCH, WALTER EDWARD, security firm executive; b. Detroit, Apr. 12, 1921; s. Fred J. and Beatrice H. (Higgins) A.; m. Patricia H.; children: Walter Edward, Timothy R., Terrance H. Student, Albion Coll., also U. Detroit, 1939-42, Cornell U., 1959. Stockbroker William C. Roney & Co., Detroit, 1946-55; sr. partner Bache & Co., NYC, 1955-64, Paine, Webber, Jackson & Curtis, NYC, 1964-70; pres. Nat. Securities & Research Corp., NYC, 1970-72; exec. v.p. duPont, Glore, Forgan, Inc., NYC, 1972-73; pres. duPont Walston, Inc., 1973-74; COO Paine, Webber, NYC, 1974-79; chmn., chief exec. officer Chgo. Bd. Options Exchange, 1979-86, cons., 1987—. Bd. dirs. Smith Barney Trak Fund, Legg Mason Allocation Series Funds, Multiple Discipline Trust, Nicholas/Applegate Funds, UBS Funds, US Bancorp Advisors Funds, Sound Surgical Tech. Trustee Albion Coll., 1981-1990, Hillsdale Coll., 1991-. With USAAF, 1942-45. Mem. Bond Club N.Y., Bond Club Chgo., Chgo. Club, Greenwich Country Club, Paradise Valley Country Club (Scottsdale), Crystal Downs Country Club (Crystal Lake, Mich.), Sigma Chi. Home (Summer): 2700 Crystal Dr Crystal Lake Beulah MI 49617 Address: 6001 N 62nd Pl Paradise Valley AZ 85253 *When I was a boy, my grandfather advised me to "live every day in such a way that the line behind the hearse gets longer." I've tried hard to follow that advice.*

AUCHLY, CHRISTOPHER M., music educator; s. William J. and M. Dione Auchly. B in Music Edn., Ctrl. Meth. Coll., Fayette, Mo., 1991. Pcii DESE, 1991. Dir. of bands Tipton H.S., Tipton, Mo., 1991—94; asst. dir. of bands Lee's Summit H.S., Mo., 1994—95; dir. of bands Lee's Summit North H.S., Mo., 1995—98, Festus H.S., Mo., 1999—. Dist. band v.p. Kansas City (Mo.) Metro Dist., 1996—98, East Ctrl. Dist., Festus, Mo., 2004—. Mem.: Nat. Band Assn., Mo. Music Educators, Mo. Bandmasters, Phi Beta Mu, Phi Mu Alpha. Independent. Roman Catholic. Avocations: biking, walking, photography, travelilng. Office: Festus High School 501 Westwind Drive Festus MO 63028 Home Phone: 636-933-0323; Office Phone: 636-937-5410.

AUCHUS, RICHARD J., internist, endocrinologist; MD, Washington U., 1988, PhD in Pharmacology, 1988. Resident, internal medicine U. Iowa Hosp. & Clinics, 1988—91; endocrinology fellow Univ. Tex. Health Sci. Ctr., Houston, 1991—93; assoc. prof., internal med. and endocrinology Grad. Sch. Biomedical Sciences, Southwestern Med. Sch. Contbr. articles to several publications. Recipient Atlantic Richfield prize, MIT, 1981, Alpha Chi Sigma prize, 1982, Air Force Commendation medal, USAF, 1995; Merck Scholar, U. Tex. Southwestern Med. Ctr. Dallas, 1999. Mem.: Tex. Med. Assn., Dallas County Med. Soc., Am. Soc. Internal Medicine, Am. Coll. Physicians, Endocrinology Soc., Phi Beta Kappa, Xi Chpt. Office: U Tex Southwestern Med Ctr at Dallas 5323 Harry Hines Blvd Dallas TX 75390-8857

AUCUTT, RONALD DAVID, lawyer; b. St. Paul, Dec. 28, 1945; s. Howard Lewis and Eleanor May (Malcolm) A.; m. Grace Diane Kok, Apr. 3, 1976; children: David Gerard, James Andrew. BA, U. Minn., 1967, JD, 1975. Bar: Minn. 1975, D.C. 1976, Va. 1978, Tex. 1999, U.S. Supreme Ct. 1978, U.S. Tax Ct. 1980, U.S. Dist. Ct. D.C. 1980, U.S. Ct. Appeals (D.C. cir.) 1980, U.S. Ct. of Claims 1980, U.S. Claims Ct. 1982, U.S. Ct. Appeals (fed. cir.) 1982, U.S. Dist. Ct. (ea. dist.) Va. 1986, U.S. Ct. Appeals (4th cir.) 1986. Assoc. Miller & Chevalier, Chartered, Washington, 1975-81, ptnr., 1982-98, McGuireWoods LLP, McLean, Va., 1998—. Mem. bd. advisors IRS Practice Alert, NYC, 1987—93; adj. prof. Sch. Law U. Va., 1998—2003; mem. adv. com. Philip E. Heckerling Inst. on Estate Planning U. Miami, 1999—. Bd. adv. Jour. Taxation Exempt Orgns., 1989—, Bus. Entities, 1999—; mem. editl. bd. Estate Planning, 1993—, adv. bd. Tax Mgmt. Estates, Gifts, and Trusts Jour., 1999—, Bus. Valuation Update, Portland, Oreg., 1999—; contbr. articles to profl. jours. Orgn. Security and Coop. in Europe internat. observer Bulgarian Parliamentary Election, 1997; sec.-treas. Miller and Chevalier Charitable Found., Washington, 1980—82, pres., 1993—97; bd. dirs. Coun. for Ct. Excellence, Washington, 1993—99, Advocates Internat., Fairfax, Va., 1997—2000, vice chmn., 1999—2000; mem. adv. bd. Trinity Law Sch., Santa Ana, Calif., 1998—2001; bd. visitors U. Minn. Law Sch., 1998—2004; bd. regents Trinity Internat. U., Deerfield, Ill., 2000—06; bd. dirs. Evang. Free Ch. Am., Mpls., 1986—92, vice moderator, chmn. bd. dirs., 1993—95, moderator, 1995—97, 2007—. Lt. USN, 1970—73. Fellow: Am. Coll. Trust and Estate Counsel (bd. regents 1996—2005, chmn. bus. planning com. 1997—2000, sec. 1999—2000, treas. 2000—01, v.p. 2001—02, pres.-elect 2002—03, pres. 2003—04), Am. Coll. Tax Counsel, Am. Bar Found.; mem.: ABA (chair taxation sect., com. on estate and gift taxes 1986—88, vice chmn. com. on govt. submissions 1989—91, liaison to sect. real property, probate and trust law 1990—, chmn. com. on govt. submissions 1991—93, coun. 1993—97, vice chair com. ops. 1998—2000), Christian Legal Soc., Internat. Acad. Estate and Trust Law (exec. coun. 2000—04, academician), U. Minn. Law Alumni Assn. (bd. dirs. 1998—2004), Met. Club Washington. Home: 3417 Silver Maple Pl Falls Church VA 22042-3545 Office: McGuireWoods LLP 1750 Tysons Blvd Ste 1800 Mc Lean VA 22102-4215 Office Phone: 703-712-5497. Business E-Mail: raucutt@mcguirewoods.com.

AUDEN, BRUCE JAMES, chef, restaurateur, consultant; b. London, Mar. 7, 1955; came to U.S., 1973; s. Peter Derrick Auden and June Elliot (Povey) Ives; m. Debra Dawn Irwin, Jan. 29, 1989; 1 child, Berean. Cook Northmoor Country Club, Highland Park, Ill., 1973-75, Le Bistro, Denver, 1975-76; from cook to exec. sous chef Crickets, Chgo., 1976-82; chef Exposure, Dallas, 1982-84, Charley's 517, Houston, 1984-86, Polo's, Fairmount Hotel, San Antonio, 1986-89; chef, owner LocuStreet Bakery, San Antonio, 1991, Restaurant Biga, San Antonio, 1991—. Opening cons. EZ's, San Antonio, 1990. Named Best New Chef in 1988 Food & Wine Mag; nominee Best Chef: Southwest, James Beard Found., 2001-05. Avocations: biking, hiking, photography.*

AUDET, PAUL L., diversified financial services company executive; BA in Acct. and Econs. with honors, Rutgers U. Sr. acct. Price Waterhouse & Co.; mgr. fin. reportingand analysis Paine Webber Inc.; sr. v.p. corp. fin. First Fidelity BankCorp; CFO, sr. v.p. PNC, 1991—98; mng. dir. Black-Rock Inc., NYC, 1998—, CFO, 1998—2005, head cash mgmt. bus., 2005—, interim CFO, 2007. Office: BlackRock Inc 40 East 52nd St New York NY 10022*

AUERBACH, ALAN JEFFREY, economist, educator; b. NYC, Sept. 27, 1951; s. William and Tess (Kasper) A.; m. Gay Cameron Quimby, June 25, 1978; children: Ethan, Andrew. BA, Yale U., 1974; PhD, Harvard U., 1978. Asst. prof. dept. econs. Harvard U., Cambridge, Mass., 1978-82, assoc. prof., 1982-83; assoc. prof. dept. econs. U. Pa., Phila., 1983-85, prof., 1985-94, chmn. dept., 1988-90, prof. Sch. Law, 1990-94; Robert D. Burch prof. of tax policy and pub. fin. U. Calif., Berkeley, 1994—, chmn. dept., 2001—02. Author: The Taxation of Capital Income, 1983 (David A. Wells prize); co-author: Dynamic Fiscal Policy, 1987, Macroeconomics: An Integrated Approach, 1995, Generational Accounting Around the World, 1999; editor: Corporate Takeovers, 1988, Mergers and Acquisitions, 1988, Fiscal Policy: Lessons from Economic Research, 1997; co-editor: Handbook of Public Economics, Vol. I, 1985, Vol. II, 1987, Vol. III, 2002, Vol. IV, 2002, Demographic Change and Fiscal Policy, 2001, Ageing, Financial Markets, and Monetary Policy, 2002, Toward Fundamental Tax Reform, 2005, Public Policy and the Income Distribution, 2006; editor Jour. Econ. Perspectives, 1995-96; editor Am. Econ. Jour.: Econ. Policy, 2007—. Fellow Am. Acad. Arts and Scis., Econometric Soc.; mem. Am. Econ. Assn. (exec. com. 1992-94, v.p. 1999), Phi Beta Kappa. Home: 110 El Camino Real Berkeley CA 94705-2823 Office: U Calif Berkeley Dept Econs 549 Evans Hall Berkeley CA 94720-3880 Business E-Mail: auerbach@econ.berkeley.edu.

AUERBACH, ANDREW DANIEL TRETTER, consulting executive; s. Jeffrey I. Auerbach and Terry H. Tretter. GG, AJP, Gemological Inst. Am., Carlsbad, Calif., 2006. Cert. jewelry design with rhino and tech gems level I Robert McNeel & Assocs., 2005. Sr. advisor Redline Motorsports Racing, LLC, Takoma Park, Md., 2003—06; mgr., designer, gemologist Creative Goldsmiths, Bethesda, Md., 2004—06; CEO, founder Mille Dynamics, LLC, Rockville, Md., 2006—. Internat. del. leader USAID - Pakistan, Las Vegas, Nev., 2005. Aide to pres. county coun. Montgomery County Coun., Rockville, Md., 2001—02. Home Phone: 202-957-4202; Office Phone: 202-957-4202.

AUERBACH, ANITA L., clinical psychologist; b. Flushing, NY, Dec. 23, 1946; d. Ben and Gussie (Zuckerman) Weiss; m. Steven Miles Auerbach, May 25, 1969. BA cum laude, SUNY, Buffalo, 1968, MA, 1970; PhD, George Washington U., 1977. Diplomate Am. Bd. Med. Psychotherapists, Internat. Acad. Behavioral Medicine. Chief rsch. Youth Crime Control Project D.C. Dept. Corrections, 1970-74; intern clin. psychology No. Va. Tng. Ctr., Fairfax, 1974-75, staff psychologist, then chief psychol. svcs., 1975-79; pvt. practice clin. psychology Commonwealth Psychol. Assocs. PLC, McLean, Va., 1979—; founder,dir. Commonwealth Psychol. Assocs., 1979—, pres., 1979—. Lectr. Washington Tech. Inst., 1972-74, George Mason U., 1978—82; asst. clin. prof. psychology George Washington U., 2004—; chair RXP Task Force Va. Acad. Clin. Psychologists, 2006-; cons. in field. Contbr. articles to profl. jours. Mem. adv. bd. World Children's Choir, 2000—02; mem. family edn. project Joseph P. Kennedy Jr. Found., 1977—79; mem. regional appeals bd. No. Va. Pub. Sch. Sys., 1977—79; mem. adv. bd. Value Options Behavioral Health, 2001—03. Fellow N.Y. State Regents 1968-70; recipient N.Y. State Scholar Incentive award, 1969. Mem. APA, Am. Soc. Clin. Hypnosis (approved cons.), Va. Acad. Clin. Psychologists, Va. Psychol. Assn., No. Va. Soc. Clin. Psychologists, Washington Soc. Study Clin. Hypnosis, Assn. Advancement Applied Sports Psychology, Psi Chi, Alpha Lambda Delta. Office: 1479 Chain Bridge Rd Mc Lean VA 22101-5730 Office Phone: 703-734-0787.

AUERBACH, ERNEST SIGMUND, lawyer, insurance company executive, writer; b. Berlin, Dec. 22, 1936; arrived in U.S., 1938; s. Frank L. and Gertrude Auerbach; m. Jeanette Taylor, 1990; 1 child, Hans Kevin. AB, George Washington U., 1958, JD, 1961; postgrad., U.S. Army Gen. Staff Coll., 1975. Bar: D.C. 1962, Pa. 1978. Atty. So. Ry. Co., Washington, 1961-62; commd 1st lt. U.S. Army, 1962, advanced through grades to col.; served in Germany, Vietnam, Pentagon; div. counsel Xerox Corp., Stamford, Conn., 1970-75; mng. atty. NL Industries, Inc., NYC, 1975-77; from asst. to assoc. gen. counsel, staff v.p. INA Corp., Phila., 1977-79; sr. v.p. INA Svc. Co., 1979-82; sr. v.p., chief of staff INA Internat., 1982-83; pres. internat. life and group ops. CIGNA Worldwide Corp. div. CIGNA Corp., 1984-89; mng. dir. Crusader Life Ins. PLC, Reigate, England, 1984-86, chmn., 1986-89; pres., COO N.Y. Life Worldwide Holding, Inc., NYC, 1989-90; pres., CEO Paperless Claims, Inc., NYC, 1991-92; dir. gen. Seguros Azteca Ins. Co., Mexico City, 1992—93; sr. cons. Anderson Consulting, Mexico City, 1993-95; sr. v.p. United Ins. Cos., Inc., Irving, Tex., 1995-97, also pres., CEO student ins. divsn., 1996-97, pres., CEO ins. group, 1997; pres., COO Software Testing Assurance Corp., NYC, 1998; pres., CEO Tesia Corp., NYC, 1998—2001, chmn., bd. dirs., 2002; sr. v.p. Strickland Group, NYC, 2001—03; v.p. ALICO divsn. AIG Corp., 2003—04; cons. AIG Life, Tokyo, 2004; regional v.p. AIA divsn. AIG Corp., Hong Kong, 2004—05, v.p. exec. devel. life divsn. NYC, 2005—06, v.p. global real estate divsn., 2006—. Mem. adv. bd. revbox.com, 1998—2001. Author: Joining the Inner Circle: How To Make It As A Senior Executive, 1990; contbg. author: The Wall St. Jour. on Mng., 1990; contbr. articles to legal, fin., news, and def. jours. Mem. Am. Coun. on Germany, 1980-2000; computer sys. tech. adv. com. Dept. Commerce, 1974-76; mem. bd. adv. dirs. Salvation Army, Mexico City, 1993-94; commr. bd. adjustment City of Coppell, Tex., 1996-97. Ret. col. U.S. Army, 1985. Decorated Legion of Merit with oak leaf cluster, Bronze Star. Mem.: Westchester-Fairfield Corp. Counsel Assn. (founding officer 1973—78), Ret. Army Judge Advocate Assn., Audubon Soc. (pres., bd. dirs. Greenwich chpt. 1999—2002, bd. dirs. Conn. chpt. 2002—04), Spl. Forces Assn., Army and Navy Club (Washington chpt.), Nat. Arts Club (N.Y.C.), Univ. Club (N.Y.C.). Office Phone: 212-770-2204. Personal E-mail: colauerbach@earthlink.net.

AUERBACH, FRANK, artist; b. Berlin, Apr. 29, 1931; s. Max and Charlotte Auerbach; m. Julia Wolstenholme, 1958; 1 child. Student, St. Martin's Sch. Art, London, Royal Coll. Art. One man shows: Beaux-Arts Gallery, London, 1956, 59, 61, 62, 63, Marlborough Fine Art, London, 1965, 67, 71, 74, 83, 87, 90, 97, Marlborough Gallery Inc., N.Y.C., 1969,

82, 94, 98, Villiers Art Gallery, Sydney, 1972, U. Essex, Colchester, 1973, Galleria Bergamini, Milan, 1973, Municipal Art Gallery, Dublin, 1975, Marlborough, Zurich, 1976, Anthony d'Offay, London, 1978, Retrospective Exhbn., Arts Coun., Hayward Gallery, London, Fruit Market Gallery, Edinburgh, 1978, Bernard Jacobson, N.Y.C., 1979, Brit. Pavilion Venice Biennale, 1986, Kunstverein, Hamburg, 1986, Folkwang Mus., Essen, 1987, Centro De Arte Reina Sofia, Madrid, 1987, Rijksmus. Vincent Van Gogh, Amsterdam, 1989, Marlborough Graphics, 1990, Yale Ctr. Brit. Art, New Haven, 1991, Nat. Gallery, London, 1995, Campbell-Thiebaud Gallery, San Francisco, 1995, Rex Irwin, Sydney, 1996, 2000, Charlottenborg, Copenhagen, 2000, R.A., London, 2001, Marlborough Gallery, NYC, 2006; group shows include: Tooths Gallery, London, 1958, 71, Carnegie Internat. Exhbn., Pitts., 1958, 61, Dunn Internat. Exhbn., London, 1963, Gulbenkian Exhbn., London, 1964, Peter Stuyvesant Found. Collection, London, 1967, L.A. County Mus., 1975, European Painting in the Seventies, 1976, TheHuman Clay, Hayward Gallery, London, New Spirit in Painting, R.A., London, 1981, Westkunst, Cologne, 1981, Eight Figurative Painters, Yale Ctr. Brit. Art, 1981, The Hard-Won Image, The British Show, Tate Gallery, London, 1984, Gallery Western Australia, Perth, 1985, R.A., London, 1987, British Art in the Twentieth Century, Kunstnernes Hus, Olso, 1987, The Pursuit of the Real, Manchester City Art Gallery, 1991, Israel Mus., Jerusalem, 1992-93, A Sch. London, Astrup Fearnley Mus. Moderne Kunst, Oslo, 1994, Scottish Nat. Gallery Modern Art, Edinburgh, 1995-96, L'Ecole de Londres, Found. Dina Vierny-Musée Maillol, Paris, La Mirada Fuerte, Pintura Figurativa de Londres, Museo de Arte Moderno, Mexico, 2000; works in pub. collections in U.K., Australia, Brazil, U.S.A., Mex., Israel. Recipient Sivler medal for painting Royal Coll. Art; joint winner Golden Lion prize Venice Biennale, 1986. Office: c/o Marlborough Fine Art 6 Albemarle St London W1S 4BY England

AUERBACH, JEROLD S., academic administrator, educator; b. Phila., May 7, 1936; s. Morry M. and Sophie (Soloff) A.; m. Susan H. Levin, May 16, 1982; children: Shira, Rebecca; children from previous marriage Jeffrey, Pamela. BA, Oberlin Coll., 1957; MA, Columbia U., 1959, PhD, 1965. Lectr. Queens Coll. CUNY, 1964-65; asst. prof. Brandeis U., Waltham, Mass., 1965-71, Wellesley (Mass.) Coll., 1971-72, assoc. prof., 1972-77, prof., 1977—. Vis. scholar Harvard Law Sch.; Fulbright lectr. Tel Aviv U., 1974-75. Author: Labor and Liberty, 1966, Unequal Justice, 1976, Justice Without Law?, 1983, Rabbis and Lawyers, 1990, Jacob's Voices, 1996, Are We One?, 2001, Explorers in Eden, 2006. Guggenheim Meml. Found. fellow, 1974-75; fellow NSF, 1979-80, NEH, 1986-87, 91-92. Office: Wellesley Coll 106 Central St Wellesley MA 02481-8268 Personal E-mail: jsauerbach@comcast.net.

AUERBACH, JOHN M., city health department administrator; MBA. With Uhpham's Corner Health Ctr., Dorchester, Mass.; linked city's health centers with Boston City Hosp. City of Boston, 1986—88; chief of staff state commr. public health Mass Dept. Pub. Health, 1988—90; dir., AIDS bur. and asst. commr. Mass. Dept. Pub. Health, 1990—97; exec. dir. Boston Pub. Health Commn., 1998—. Office: Boston Pub Health Commn 1010 Massachusetts Ave Boston MA 02118 Office Phone: 617-534-5395. Business E-Mail: john_auerbach@bphc.org.

AUERBACH, JOSEPH, former lawyer, educator; b. Franklin, NH, Dec. 3, 1916; s. Jacob and Besse Mae (Reamer) A.; m. Judith Evans, Nov. 10, 1941; children: Jonathan L., Hope B. Pym. AB, Harvard U., 1938, LLB, 1941. Bar: N.H. 1941, Mass. 1952, U.S. Ct. Appeals (1st, 2d, 3d, 5th, 7th and D.C. cirs.), U.S. Supreme Ct. 1948. Atty. SEC, Washington and Phila., 1941—43, prin. atty., 1946—49; fgn. svc. staff officer U.S. Dept. State, Dusseldorf, Germany, 1950—52; ptnr. Sullivan & Worcester, Boston, 1952—82, counsel, 1982—; lectr. Boston U. Law Sch., 1975—76, Harvard Bus. Sch., Boston, 1980—82, prof., 1982—83, Class of 1957 prof., 1983—87, prof. emeritus, 1987—; prof. Harvard Ext. Sch., 1988, Harvard Ext,. Sch., 1991—95. Bd. dirs. Nat. Benefit Life Ins. Co., N.Y.C. Author: (with S.L. Hayes, III), Investment Banking and Diligence, 1986, Underwriting Regulation and Shelf Registration Phenomenon in Wall Street and Regulation, 1987, also chpt. to book, papers and articles in field. Trustee Mass. Eye and Ear Infirmary, Boston, 1981—, chmn. devel. com., 1985-88, chmn. nominating com., 1993-94; mem. adv. bd., former chmn. devel. com. Am. Repertory Theatre, Cambridge, Mass., 1985—; bd. dirs., past pres. Friends of Boston U. Librs., 1972—; past v.p., bd. dirs. Shakespeare Globe Ctr., N.A., 1983-90; overseer New Eng. Conservatory of Music, 1992-98, mem. fin. com.; bd. dirs. English Speaking Union, Boston, 1995-98; chair 1938 Harvard Pres. Assn.; active Harvard Coll. Fund, Harvard Law Sch. Fund. Decorated Army Commendation medal; recipient Disting. Svc. award Harvard Bus. Sch., 1996, Disting. Teaching award 1993, Exemplary Svc. award Harvard Extension Sch., 1995. Mem. ABA, Mass. Bar Assn., Boston Bar Assn., Harvard Mus. Assn., St. Botolph Club, Harvard Club N.Y.C., Shop Club, Downtown Club. Home: 300 Boylston St Apt 512 Boston MA 02116-3923 Office: Sullivan & Worcester 1 Post Office Sq Ste 2300 Boston MA 02109-2129 also: Harvard Bus Sch Cumnock Hall Rm 300 Boston MA 02163

AUERBACH, MARSHALL JAY, lawyer; s. Samuel M. and Sadie (Miller) A.; m. Carole Landsberg, July 3, 1960; children: Keith Alan, Michael Ward Student, U. Ill.; JD, John Marshall Law Sch., 1955. Bar: Ill. 1955. Sole practice, Evanston, Ill., 1955-72; ptnr. in charge matrimonial law sect. Jenner & Block, Chgo., 1972-80; mem. firm Marshall J. Auerbach & Assocs., Ltd., Chgo., 1980—. Mem. faculty Ill. Inst. Continuing Legal Edn. Author: Illinois Marriage and Dissolution of Marriage Act, enacted into law, 1977; Historical and Practice Notes to Illinois Marriage and Dissolution of Marriage Act, 1980-88; contbr. chpts. to Family Law, Vol. 2 Fellow Am. Acad. Matrimonial Lawyers; mem. Ill. State Bar Assn. (chmn. family law sect. 1971-72), ABA (vice-chmn. family law sect. com. for liaison with tax sect. 1974-76) Home and Office: Marshall J Auerbach & Assoc Ltd 30 N La Salle St Ste 3440 Chicago IL 60602 Office Phone: 312-853-3300.

AUERBACH, PAUL IRA, lawyer; b. NYC, Dec. 30, 1932; s. Joseph and Fannie (Steingard) Auerbach; children: Stuart Andrew, Beth Royce. LLB, Bklyn. Law Sch., 1954; CLU, Am. Coll., 1980, ChFC, 1982. Bar: N.Y. 1955, Fla. 1991, U.S. Dist. Ct. (so. and ea. dists.) N.Y., U.S. Dist Ct. (so. dist.) Fla. 1991. Trial counsel Cosmopolitan Mutual Ins. Corp., NYC, 1955-57, Hertz Corp., NYC, 1957-59; ptnr. Brent, Phillips, Auerbach & Dranoff, Rockland, NY, 1959-63; prin. Paul I. Auerbach, Atty. at Law, NYC and Bronx, 1963-97, Palm Beach Gardens, Fla., 1990—. Founder Young Dem. Com., Bronx, 1955-60; committeman Rep. Com., South Orangeton, N.Y., 1970-76. Mem.: KP, Rotary (chmn. drug prevention com. 1970—74, pres. W. Palm Beach Sunrise 2005—06), ABA, South Palm Beach County Bar Assn. (co-chmn. elder law commn.), Nat. Acad. Elder Law Attys., Planned Giving Coun. of Palm Beach County (v.p.), Tax Inst. of Palm Beach County, Fla. Bar Assn., Palm Beach County Bar Assn., North Palm Beach County Bar Assn. (pres. 1999—2000), Bronx Bar Assn. (chmn. criminal law com. 1990—91), N.Y. State Bar Assn., West Palm Beach Rotary Club, Masons. Avocations: tennis, gourmet food. Home: 11215 Curry Dr Palm Beach Gardens FL 33418 Office Phone: 561-775-2734. Personal E-mail: piaesq@yahoo.com.

AUERBACH, SEYMOUR, architect; b. NYC, May 28, 1929; s. Nathan and Jennie (Norman) A.; m. Alyce Kelly, Oct. 21, 1963 (div. 1977); children: Kalin Marie Hyman, Alison Kelly; m. Patricia Sullivan, July 31, 1985 (div. 1991). B.Arch., Yale U., 1951. Assoc. firm Satterlee & Smith (Archs.), Washington, 1955-59; ptnr. Cooper & Auerbach (Archs.), Washington, 1960-69, Walton, Madden, Cooper & Auerbach (Archs.), Washington, 1970-71; pvt. practice Washington, 1971—. Pres. Kamak Enterprises, Inc., sole propr. for patent commercialization; developer, architect Battery Subdiv., Washington, Buck's Knoll Farm, Yellow Spring, W.Va.; prof. architecture Cath. U. Am., 1960-99; cons. constn. failures, 1982—. Prin. works include Nat. Visitor Ctr., Washington, campus plan and dormitories, Georgetown U., Olam Tikvah Synagogue, Fairfax, Va., Brith Sholom Synagogue, Bethlehem, Pa., resort cmtys., Rehoboth Beach, Del., campus for Bowling Brook prep; cons. in field; patentee in unrelated fields. Bd. mgrs. Chevy Chase Village, Md., 1973-77, vice chmn. bd., 1976-77; mem. archtl. adv. panel Union of Am. Hebrew Congregations. With C.E. U.S. Army, 1951-54. Decorated knight honor and merit Imperial Russian Order St. John of Jerusalem; recipient award excellence in architecture Met. Washington Bd. Trade, 1964, Papal Benemerenti medal, 1994, Rsch. Ctr. award Georgetown U., 1964; winner award competition for design of Copley Plaza, Boston, 1967, award for excellence in arch. Washington Bd. Trade, 1964, Potomac Valley award, 1964; William Wirt Winchester fellow, 1951. Fellow AIA; mem. AAUP, Soc. Archtl. Historians, Guild Religious Architecture, Cosmos Club Washington, Yale Club Washington. Republican. Jewish. Home and Office: 115 Hesketh St Chevy Chase MD 20815-4222 Personal E-mail: syauer@comcast.net. *I consider it to be of the highest calling to be involved in the improvement of man's physical environment: not only his shelter, but also his public environment and the implements he uses. In this context I have held architecture to be an Applied, rather than a Fine, Art. I consider it to be a higher calling to be a designer than to be an architect and I find the greatest of personal pleasure in solving individual problems of design for man, by myself, without regard to "style", and without regard to political or other irrelevant considerations.*

AUFDERHEIDE, ARTHUR CARL, pathologist; b. New Ulm, Minn., Sept. 9, 1922; s. Herman John and Esther (Sannwald) A.; m. Mary Lillian Buryk, Jan. 26, 1946; children: Patricia Ann, Tom Paul, Walter Herman. MD, U. Minn., 1946; DSc (hon.), Coll. of St. Scholastica, 1983. Chief dept. pathology Mpls. VA Hosp., 1952-53, St. Mary's Hosp., Duluth, Minn., 1953-57; chief dept. pathology Sch. Medicine U. Minn., Duluth, 1970-87, dean Sch. Medicine, 1974-75, dir. paleobiology lab. Sch. Medicine, 1977—. Mem. Plaisted Polar Expdn., 1968; rsch. cons. anthropology lab. U. Colombia, Bogota, 1989—, Pigorini Mus., Rome, 1988, Archeol. Mus. of Tenerife, Canary Islands, 1989-90; chmn. sci. com. Cronos Rsch Project, Santa Cruz, Tenerife, 1991—. Author: Cambridge Ency. Author: Scientific Study of Mummies 2002 Human Paleopathology, 1998; co-editor: Paleopathology, 1991; author: (documentary film) Copper Eskimo, 1970; contbr. numerous articles to profl. publs. Chmn. civil com. to devel. a degree-granting med. sch., Duluth, 1988. Capt. U.S. Army, 1947-49. Fellow AAAS; mem. Paleopathology Assn., N.Y. Acad. Scis. Democrat. Lutheran. Achievements include research in soft tissue paleopathology. Home: 4711 Colorado St Duluth MN 55804-1512 Office: U Minn 10 University Dr Duluth MN 55812-2403 Home Phone: 218-525-2572; Office Phone: 218-726-7911. Business E-Mail: aaufderh@d.umn.edu.

AUFHAUSER, DAVID D., lawyer, former federal agency administrator; b. NYC, Nov. 19, 1950; married; 3 children. A.B., Wesleyan U., 1972; MBA, Harvard U., 1974; JD, U. Pa., 1977. Bar: Pa. 1977, D.C. 1978. Lawyer Williams & Connolly LLP, Washington, 1977—2001, counsel, 2003—04; gen. counsel US Dept. Treasury, Washington, 2001—03; global gen. counsel, gen. counsel for the Americas UBS Investment Bank, 2004—; sr. adv. Ctr. for Strategic & Internat. Studies. Mem. steering com. Civil Justice Reform Task Force, 1992; gen. counsel credentials com. Rep. Convention, 1992; mem. legal adv. group Rep. House Leadership Conf., 1993—94; counsel President's Group on Financial Markets, 2001—03; chmn. Nat. Security Coun. Policy Coordinating Com. on Terrorist Financing, 2001—03; Treasury Rep. U.S. Dept. Justice, Corp. Fraud Task Force, 2002—03; sr. fellow Ctr. for Strategic & Internat. Studies, 2004—. Recipient The U.S. Treasury Dept. Alexander Hamilton award for Disting. Service, 2003, CIA Disting. Svc. award and seal, 2003, FBI Disting. Svc. and Leadership Citation, 2003, U.S. Secret Svc. Dir.'s Honor award, 2003. Mem.: bd., Fed. Financing Bank, 2001-03, Civil Justice Reform Task Force, 1992, Edward Bennett Williams Inns of Ct., 2002-03, Bush-Cheney Election Contest Legal Representation Team, 2000-01, Phi Beta Kappa. Republican. Office: UBS Investment Bank 1 Finsbury Ave EC2M 2PP England E-mail: daufhauser@wc.com.*

AUFSES, ARTHUR HAROLD, JR., surgeon, educator; b. NYC, Feb. 8, 1926; s. Arthur Harold and Beatrice (Hauser) A.; m. Harriet Whitman, Dec. 28, 1947; children: Arthur Harold III, Carolyn Aufses Blashek. Student, Columbia U., 1942-43; BS, Union Coll., 1944; MD, Columbia U. Coll. Physicians and Surgeons, 1948. Diplomate Am. Bd. Surgery. Intern Presbyn. Hosp., NYC, 1948-49, resident in surgery, 1950-51, 53-54, Mt. Sinai Hosp., NYC, 1954-56; practice medicine specializing in surgery NYC, 1956-97; prof. Mt. Sinai Med. Ctr., NYC, 1974—; chmn. dept. surgery Mt. Sinai Sch. Medicine, NYC, 1974-96, L.I. Jewish Med. Ctr., 1971-74; prof. surgery SUNY-Stony Brook, 1971-74; surgeon-in-chief Mt. Sinai Hosp., NYC, 1974-96. Contbr. articles to med. jours. Bd. dirs. 92d St. YMHA, 1974—. 1st lt. U.S. Army, 1951-53. Recipient Jacobi medallion Mt. Sinai Med. Ctr., 1979; recipient Gold Headed Cane award Mt. Sinai Med. Ctr., 1982 Fellow ACS (2nd v.p. 1996-97), Am. Surg. Assn. (2nd v.p. 1995-96), Am. Coll. Gastroenterology (pres. 1986-87), Assn. of Program Dirs. Surgery (pres. 1989-91), N.Y. Acad. Medicine; mem. Soc. Surg. Oncology, Am. Gastroent. Assn., N.Y. Surg. Soc. (pres. 1979-80), Soc. Surgery Alimentary Tract, Brazilian Coll. Surgeons, Chilean Congress Surgeons, Portuguese Soc. Gastroenterology. Jewish. Home: 1185 Park Ave New York NY 10128-1308 Office: Mt Sinai Sch Medicine Box 1077 1 Gustave L Levy Pl New York NY 10029-6500 Home Phone: 212-410-6056; Office Phone: 212-659-9560. Business E-Mail: arthur.aufses@mssm.edu.

AUGELLI, JOHN PAT, geographer, educator, writer, consultant, rancher; b. Celenza, Italy, Jan. 30, 1921; s. Pat John and M. Antoinette (Iacaruso) A.; divorced; children: John, Robert. BA, Clark U., 1943; MA, Harvard U., 1949, PhD, 1951. Teaching fellow Harvard U., Cambridge, Mass., 1948—49; from asst. to assoc. prof. geography U. P.R., Rio Piedras, 1949—51; assoc. prof. U. Md., College Park, 1952—61; prof. U. Kans., Lawrence, 1961—70, 1971—91; prof. geography, dir. Ctr. Latin Am. Studies U. Ill., Champaign-Urbana, 1970—71. Lectr., travel cons. Mediterranean and Latin Am. cruises, 1991-95; mem. Bd. Fgn. Scholarships, Washington, 1967-70; cons. Nat. Geographic Soc., Washington, 1984-87; del. U.S. Acad. Scis., New Delhi, 1968; sec. Coun. of Inter-Am. Affairs, Washington, 1959-60. Author: Carribean Lands, 1965, Puerto Rico, 1973, Middle America, 3d edit., 1989; cons.: (atlas) World & North America, 1984; contbr. 76 articles to profl. jours. Served to 1st lt. U.S. Army, 1943-46, PTO, Res., 1949-51. Recipient Fulbright research grant, 1982. Fellow Am. Geog. Soc.; mem. Assn. Am. Geographers (sec. 1966-69), Latin Am. Studies Assn. (pres. 1969), Nat. Council Geographic Edn. (master tchr. 1979), Conf. of Latin Americanist Geographers (outstanding contbn. to research and teaching award 1982). Democrat. Roman Catholic. Avocations: travel, fishing. Address: 35 Mediterranean Blvd E Port Saint Lucie FL 34952-8557

AUGER, JESSIE L., elementary school educator; BA, Colby Coll., Maine, 1989. Elem. tchr. Watertown, Mass., 1990; tchr. Cambridge-El Salvador Sister City Project, San José Las Flores, El Salvador, Puerto Rico, Boston Pub. Sch. Sys., 2001—; elem. generalist/Spanish bilingual tchr. Rafael Hernandez Two-Way Bilingual Sch., Roxbury, Mass., 2004—. Named Mass. Tchr. of Yr., 2007; named to All-USA Teacher Team for outstanding teaching, USA Today, 2005. Avocation: guitar. Office: Rafael Hernandez Two-Way Bilingual Sch 61 School St Boston MA 02119 Business E-Mail: jauger@boston.k12.ma.us.*

AUGSPURGER, MARK CHRISTIAN, elementary school educator; b. Bloomfield, Iowa, July 6, 1972; s. David L. and Karen M. Augspurger. BA, Simpson Coll., Indianola, Iowa, 1995. 7th grade history tchr. Norwalk Mid. Sch., Iowa, 1997—. Mem.: Nat. Coun. Social Studies. Office: Norwalk Mid Sch 200 Cherry St Norwalk IA 50211 Home Phone: 515-279-8328; Office Phone: 515-981-0435.

AUGUR, MARILYN HUSSMAN, distribution executive; b. Texarkana, Ark., Aug. 23, 1938; d. Walter E. and Betty (Palmer) H.; m. James M. Augur, Dec. 29, 1962; children: Margaret M. Hancock, Elizabeth H. Taylor, Ann Louise Hardaway. BA, U. N.C., 1960; MBA, So. Meth. U., 1989. Pres. North Tex. Mountain Valley Water, Dallas, 1989—. Bd. dirs. Camden News Pub. Co., Little Rock, Living Waters, Dallas, 2005—. Trustee Hussman Found., Little Rock, 1991—2005, Marilyn Augur Family Found., Dallas, 1991—, U. Tex. Southwestern Med. Found., 1993—, Nat. Jewish Hosp., 1993—2000; bd. dirs. Baylor Health Sys. Found., 1992—2001, chmn., 1995; mem. Tex. Bus. Hall Fame, 1992—98, exec. com., 1994—95; mem. Dallas Citizens Coun., 1994—2004; bd. dirs. Tate Lectr. Series, 1994—2000, Dallas County CC Dist. Found., 1995—, mem. exec. com., 2006—; bd. dirs. Dallas Helps, 1995—99; mem. adv. bd Salvation Army, 1996—, chmn., William Booth Soc., 1999—2000; mem. adv. bd. Charter 100, 1998—; bd. dirs. Baylor Oral Health Found. Bd., 1998—2001, So. Meth. U. Dedman Law Sch., 1998—; mem. exec. bd. Cox Bus. Sch., 1998—; mem. vestry St. Michael and His Angels Ch., 2003—06; bd. dirs. Children's Health Care Sys. Found., 1998—. Mem. Dallas Country Club, Crescent Club, Dallas Women's Club, Beta Gamma Sigma. Episcopalian. Avocations: travel, skiing, trekking. Office: North Tex Mountain Valley Water 4209 McKinney Ave Ste 202B Dallas TX 75205-5439 Personal E-mail: ntmvw1@aol.com.

AUGUST, DAVID ALLEN, surgeon; b. NYC, Apr. 16, 1955; s. Robert Irwin and Rhoda (Greene) A.; m. Barbara Ann Peck; children: Sandy, Harry, Eitan. BS in Life Scis., MIT, 1976; MD, Yale U. Sch. Medicine, 1980. Diplomate Am. Bd. Surgery. Resident in surgery Yale - New Haven Hosp., 1980-86; fellow in surg. oncology Nat. Cancer Inst., Bethesda, Md., 1982-84; surgeon RW Johnson Med. Sch. - U. Hosp., New Brunswick, N.J.; educator UMDNJ. Bd. dirs. N.J. Am. Cancer Soc., 1996—. Mem. Soc. Univ. Surgeons, Assn. Acad. Surgery, Am. Coll. Surgeons, Am. Soc. Parenteral and Enteral Nutrition. Office: Cancer Inst NJ 195 Little Albany St New Brunswick NJ 08901-1914 Office Phone: 732-235-7701.

AUGUST, ROBERT OLIN, retired journalist; b. Ashtabula, Ohio, Oct. 6, 1921; s. Frank and Lillian (Olin) A.; m. Marilynn Eccles, Sept. 23, 1943; 1 dau., Alison. BA, Coll. Wooster, 1943. With Cleve. Press, 1946-82, staff sports dept., 1950—, covered profl. football, 1953-58, exec. sports editor, 1957-58, sports editor, 1958-64, sports columnist, 1964-67, sports columnist, sports editor, 1967-79, gen. columnist, sports editor, 1979-81, assoc. editor, 1981-82; sports editor Lake County News-Herald, 1982-89. Sports columnist 4 Ingersoll newspapers, 1982—2003; nationally syndicated columnist Wiser Side of 60 Universal Press Syndicate, 1982-86. Author: Fun and Games, 2001, And The Wiser Side of 60, 2002. Served from ensign to lt. (j.g.) USNR, 1943-46. Recipient Cleve. Newspaper Guild awards, 1958, 61, 81, 82, 83; inducted into Cleve. Journalism Hall of Fame, 1988. Mem. Sigma Delta Chi (Disting. Svc. award 1981). Home: 1140 Hedgecliff Dr Wooster OH 44691-3088 Personal E-mail: raugust106@aol.com.

AUGUST-DEWILDE, KATHERINE, banker; b. Bridgeport, Conn., Feb. 13, 1948; d. Edward G. and Benita Ruth (Miller) Burstein; m. David deWilde, Dec. 30, 1984; children: Nicholas Alexander, Lucas Barrymore. AB, Goucher Coll., 1969; MBA, Stanford U., 1975. Cons. McKinsey & Co., San Francisco, 1975-78; dir. fin. Itel Corp., San Francisco, 1978-79; sr. v.p., CFO PMI Group, San Francisco, 1979-85, pres., CFO, 1988-91; CEO, pres. First Republic Thrift & Loan of San Diego, 1988-96; exec. v.p. First Republic Bank, San Francisco, 1987—96, sr. v.p. , chief fin. officer, 1985-87, COO, 1996—. Mem. policy adv. bd. Ctr. for Real Estate and Urban Econs., U. Calif., Berkeley, 1987—2000; bd. dirs. First Republic Bank, Trainer, Wortham & Co., Inc. Bd. dirs. San Francisco Zool. Soc., 1993-2001, vice-chair, 1995-2000; trustee Carnegie Found., 1999-2004, Town Sch. for Boys, San Francisco, 1999-2004, vice chmn., 2004-06; mem. adv. coun. Stanford U. Grad. Sch. Bus., 2003-; trustee Mills Coll., 2004-07. Mem. Women's Forum (bd. dirs.), Bankers Club, Belvedere Tennis Club, Villa Taverna. Home: 2650 Green St San Francisco CA 94123-4607 Office: First Republic Bank 111 Pine St San Francisco CA 94111-5602 Office Phone: 415-296-3707. Business E-Mail: kaugust@firstrepublic.com.

AUGUSTINE, CYNTHIA H., educational services company executive, lawyer; b. Oct. 30, 1957; married; 2 children. BA, Sarah Lawerence Coll., 1979; JD, Rutgers U., 1982. Bar: N.J., N.Y. Lawyer Pitney, Hardin, Kipp & Szuch, 1982; sr. atty. legal dept. The NY Times Co., 1986-93; ptnr., employment law Sabin, Bermant & Gould LLP, 1993—98; sr. v.p., human resources The NY Times Co., NYC, 1998—2004; sr. v.p., talent mgmt. Time Warner, NYC, 2004—07; sr. v.p., human resources & employee svcs. Scholastic Corp., NYC, 2007—. Bd. dirs. Urban Pathways. Mem. ABA. Office: Scholastic Corp 557 Broadway New York NY 10012

AUGUSTINE, HENRY JOSEPH, secondary school educator; s. Joseph Henry and Barbara Jean Augustine; m. Laura Ann Nalipi, June 27, 1987; children: Joseph, Rebecca. BS, Northern Mich. U., Marquette, 1985, MA, 1992. Tchr. L'Anse Area Schs., Mich., 1985—, coach, 1985—. Guitarist with Augustine Family Band: CD First Time Around, 2003, Family Time, 2005. Avocations: football, hunting, fishing, camping, backpacking. Office: L'Anse High Sch 201 N 4th St Lanse MI 49946

AUGUSTINE, HILTON H., JR., computer company executive; Degree in Elec. Engring., U. Wis. Salesman IBM; founder Global Mgmt. Sys. Inc., 1988—, chmn., CEO Bethesda, Md., 1996—. Office: Global Mgmt Sys Inc GMSI 2201 Wisconsin Ave NW Ste 300 Washington DC 20007-4105 Office Phone: 202-471-4674. Office Fax: 202-625-9016. E-mail: Hilton.Augustine@gmsi.com.

AUGUSTINE, JEROME SAMUEL, merchant banker; b. Racine, Wis., May 7, 1928; s. Lester Samuel and Pearl (Hilker) A.; m. Camilla Sewell, Feb. 7, 1953; children: Theodore Samuel Purnell, Julia Sewell Augustine Marshall, Elizabeth Stroebel Augustine Burgoyne. AB cum laude, Harvard U., MBA, 1952. Cons. Scudder, Stevens & Clark, Boston, 1952-56; founder, treas., dir. Vencap, Inc., Boston, 1956-58; treas., dir. Consumer Products, Inc., Boston, 1956-58; founder, treas., dir. Microsonics, Inc., Hingham, Mass., 1956-58; treas., dir. Capitol Mgmt. Corp., Boston, 1956-58; cons. Kidder, Peabody & Co., Boston, 1958-64; pres. Cosmos Am. Corp., NYC, 1964-66; founder, pres., dir. Cosmos Securities Corp., 1965-70, Cosmos (Bahamian) Ltd., Nassau, 1964-70; mng. dir. J. Samuel Augustine & Co., Ltd., Toronto, Ont., Can., 1966—. 1st v.p. Van Alstyne, Noel & Co., N.Y.C., 1973-74; v.p. Wright Investors' Svc., Bridgeport, 1974-87, sr. v.p., 1987-92; pres. Kredietbank (Belgium) Global Asset Mgmt., Stamford, 1992-94. Trustee Low-Heywood Sch.; trustee The Augustine Family Charitable Trust; chmn. bd. The Hannaford St. Silver Band. Named to Washington Hall of Fame, 1986. Mem. Boston Fin. Rsch. Assocs. (gov. 1960-64, v.p. 1963-64), New Eng. Amateur Rowing Assn. (past pres.), Union Boat Club, Harvard Club, Noroton Yacht Club, Royal Canadian Yacht Club, Ox Ridge Hunt Club, Centaur Polo Club, Royal Ascot Polo Club, East India Club (London). Anglican. Office: 3219 Yonge St Ste 119 Toronto ON Canada M4N 3S1 Home Phone: 416-802-1611; Office Phone: 416-250-7762. Personal E-mail: augustco@hotmail.com.

AUGUSTINE, NORMAN RALPH, not-for-profit executive, business executive, educator, government agency administrator; b. Denver, July 27, 1935; s. Ralph Harvey and Freda Irene (Immenga) A.; m. Margareta Engman, Jan. 20, 1962; children: Gregory Eugen (dec.), René Irene. BSE magna cum laude, Princeton U., 1957, MSE, 1959; DEng (hon.), Rensselaer Poly. Inst., 1988; DSc (hon.), U. Colo., 1989; DEng (hon.), McDaniel Coll., 1990, U. Md., 1992; D in Mgmt. (hon.), Embry Riddle U., 1992; DEng (hon.), Stevens Inst., 1993; HHD (hon.), Wheeling Jesuit U., 1994; DSc (hon.), SUNY, 1994; DEng (hon.), U. Ctrl. Fla., 1995; LHD (hon.), U. Denver, 1996; DEng (hon.), Worcester Polytech., 1996; LHD (hon.), Georgetown U., 1997, Trinity Coll., 1997; DEng (hon.), U. Ariz., 1997; LLD (hon.), Duke U., 1997; DEng (hon.), Milw. Sch. Engring., 1998, Colo. Sch. Mines; DSc (hon.), Arcadia U., 1998; D in Nat. Security Affairs (hon.), Nat. Def. U., 2005; D in Bus. Adminstrn. (hon.), Drexel U., 2006; DEng (hon.), Princeton U., 2007. Rsch. asst. Princeton U., 1957-58; program mgr., chief engr. Douglas Aircraft Co., Inc., Santa Monica, Calif., 1958-65; asst. dir. def. rsch. and engring. US Govt., Office of Sec. Def., Washington, 1965-70; v.p. advanced systems Missiles and Space Co., LTV Aerospace Corp., Dallas, 1970-73; asst. sec. army The Pentagon, Washington, 1973-75, undersec. army, 1975-77; v.p. ops. Martin Marietta Aerospace Corp., Bethesda, Md., 1977-82; pres. Martin Marietta Denver Aerospace Co., 1982-85, sr. v.p. info. systems, 1985, from pres., COO to chmn., CEO, 1986-95, also bd. dirs.; pres. to chmn. & CEO Lockheed Martin Corp., Bethesda, 1995—97. Chmn. exec. com. Lockheed Martin Corp., Bethesda, Md., 1998-2004; bd. dirs. ConocoPhillips Co., Procter & Gamble Co., Black & Decker, New Am. Schs. Devel. Corp.; US adv. bd. Deutches Bank, 2006-; cons. office Sec. of Def., 1971—, Nat. Security Coun., Exec. Office Pres., 1971-73, Dept. Army, Dept. Air Force, Dept. Navy, FAA, Dept. Energy, Dept. Transp., Dept. Homeland Security, Dept. Commerce; mem. USAF Sci. Adv. Bd.; chmn. Def. Sci. Bd., 1997—; mem. NATO Group Experts on Air Def., 1966-70, NASA Rsch. and Tech. Adv. Coun., 1973-75, chmn. Space Sys. and Tech. Adv. Bd., 1985-89; mem. Chief of Naval Ops. Exec. Bd., 1989-92; chmn. def. policy adv. com. on trade, 1988-91, 93—; lectr. with rank of prof. Princeton U., 1997-99; chaired NRC study panels such as the Com. on the Orgn. and Mgmt. of Rsch in Astronomy and Astrophysics; served on Com. on the Orgnl. Structure, NIH, co-chair NIH Panel on Conflicts of Interest; chmn. Nat. Acads. Competitiveness Com., Aerospace Industry Assn.; mem. Pres.'s Com. Advisors on Sci. and Tech.; mem. adv. bd. Dept. Homeland Security.; mem. Hart/Rudman Commn. on Nat. Security. Author: Augustine's Laws, Augustine's Travels, 1997; co-author: The Defense Revolution, 1990, Shakespeare in Charge, 2001; mem. adv. bd. Jour. Def. Rsch., 1970—; assoc. editor Def. Systems Mgmt. Rev., 1977-82; mem. editl. bd. Astronautics and Aerospace. Trustee Johns Hopkins U., Princeton U., MIT; mem. bd. govs. Colonial Williamsburg, 1996-2006; mem. bd. trustees Callaway Gardens Found.; chmn. White House/NASA Adv. Com. on Future of US Space Program, 1991, Nat. Security Telecomm. Adv. Com., US Antarctic Program Rev. Com., 1996-97; nat. program evaluation com., coun. v.p. Boy Scouts Am., pres., 1993-95; chmn. , prin. officer ARC, 1993-2002. Recipient Meritorious Svc. medal Dept. Def., 1979, 5 Disting. Civilian Svc. medals Dept. Def., Nat. Engring. award Am. Assn. Engring. Socs., 1991, Am. Acad. Achievement Golden Plate award, 1995, James Madison medal Princeton U., 1995, Blumenthal award Johns Hopkins U. Sch. Engring., 1996, Gold Eagle award Soc. Am. Mil. Engrs. Acad. of Fellows, 1996, Ralph Coates Roe medal ASME, 1996, M. Eugene Merchant Mfg. medal, 1997, Nat. Medal of Technology, 1997; named Personality of Yr., Flight Internat. Aerospace, 1996, 05 AAAS Philip Hauge Abelson prize, 2006, Pub. Welfare medal, NAS, 2006, Bower award for Bus. Leadership, Franklin Inst., 2007. Fellow IEEE (Founders' award 1996), AIAA (hon., bd. dirs. 1978-85, pres. 1983-84, Goddard medal 1988), Am. Astron. Soc., Am. Helicopter Soc. (dir. 1974-75), Royal Aero. Soc., Explorers Club; mem. NAE (chmn. 1994-96, Arthur M. Bueche award 1991), Am. Acad. Arts and Scis., Am. Philos. Soc., Internat. Acad. Astronautics, Assn. US Army (pres. 1980-84, chmn. 1990—, George C. Marshall medal), Nat. Security Indsl. Assn. (Forrestal medal 1988), Indsl. Coll. Armed Forces (Eisenhower award 1990), Armed Forces Comm. and Electronics Assn. (Sarnoff medal 1990), Hart Rudman Commn., US Mil. Acad. (Thayer medal, A.F. Acad. Thomas White award), Nat. Space Club (Goddard Trophy 1991), Rotary (Nat. Space Trophy 1992), Planetary Soc. (bd. dirs.), Phi Beta Kappa, Sigma Xi, Tau Beta Pi. Presbyterian. travelled extensively around the world, including dogsledding in the Arctic, exploring volcanoes in Antarctica, canoeing the Boundary Waters of Canada, snorkeling on the Great Barrier Reef, Trans-Siberian Railroad and Silk Route, and stood on both poles of the Earth. Personal E-mail: norm.augustine@lmco.com.

AUGUSTUS, SEIMONE, professional basketball player; b. Baton Rouge, La., Apr. 30, 1984; d. Seymore Augustus, Kim. BA, La. St. Univ., 2005. Guard Minn. Lynx, 2006—. Vol. Gus Young Ctr. Named Nat. Player Yr., Women's NCAA Basketball, 2005—06, WNBA Rookie of Yr., 2006; named to Western Conf. All-Star Team, WNBA, 2007; recipient Cmty. Svc. award, NAACP, 2001. Achievements include being selected by Minn. Lynx with first overall pick in WNBA draft, 2006; three-time All-Am., 2004-2006, three-time All-SEC, three-time regional honors; four-time All-SEC Tournament, 2003-2006; mem. Kodak All-Am. Team, 2004-2006. Office: Minn Lynx 600 First Ave N Minneapolis MN 55403*

AUH, YANG JOHN, librarian, educational administrator; b. Chulla Namdo, Korea, Mar. 18, 1934; came to U.S., 1962, naturalized, 1971; s. Sam Hyuck and So Yae (Suh) A.; m. Karen Kyung-ja Kim, Mar. 11, 1969; 1 child, Alice Kim. BA, Chung-ang U., 1957; MA in LS, Western Mich. U., 1964; Cert. in Libr. Adminstrn. Devel., U. Md., 1973; Cert. in Advanced Librarianship, Columbia U., 1975; Cert. in Mgmt., Clarkson U., 1978; MBA, St. John's U., 1979; postgrad., NYU, 1996, Oxford U., Eng., 1997. Asst. libr. Korean Nat. Libr., Seoul, 1957; tech. svcs. libr. Korean Mil. Acad. Libr., Seoul, 1958-61; asst. libr. Branch County Libr., Coldwater, Mich., 1964; head union catalog L.I. U. Librs., Greenvale, NY, 1965-68; head catalog dept., tech. svcs. coord. Wagner Coll. Libr., SI, NY, 1968-71, libr. dir., 1972-84, dir. Libr. and Learning Resources Ctr., 1984-2000; dir. Internat. Exch. program Wagner Coll., SI, NY, 2000—; vis. prof. Chung-Ang U., Seoul, 2000—; pres. Highland Realty Mgmt., 1984—; dean internat. study & program Daebul U., Mokpo, Republic of Korea, 2001—. Evaluator, Commn. Higher Edn., Middle States Assn. Colls. and Schs., 1984; trustee Am. Friends of Chung-ang U., 1979—, vis. prof., 2000—; dean internat. study and program Daebul U., Mokpo, Korea, 2001—; life dep. gov., bd. govs. Am. Biographical Inst., Inc., Raleigh, N.C., 1998—; adv. coun. Internat. Biographical Ctr., Cambridge, Eng., 1999—. Fellow, HEW, 1973, 1978. Mem. ALA, N.Y. State Libr. Assn., Korean Libr. Assn., N.Y. Librs. Club, Omicron Delta Kappa (chpt. admintrv. mem. 1995). Office: Wagner Coll Horrmann Libr One Campus Rd Staten Island NY 10301-4428

AUKLAND, DUNCAN DAYTON, lawyer; b. Delaware, Ohio, July 6, 1954; s. Merrill Forrest and Elva Sampson (Dayton) A.; m. Diane Sue Clevenger, Aug. 7, 1982. BA, Va. Polytech. Inst., 1978; JD, Capital U., 1982. Bar: Ohio 1982, U.S. Dist. Ct. (so. dist.) Ohio 1982. Legal intern Ohio EPA, Columbus, 1982, staff atty., 1982-83, legal cons., 1983; sole practice Columbus, 1983-90; judge adv. USNG, Columbus, 1990—. Atty. Clean Up and Recycling Backers of Clintonville, Columbus, 1983-89; deacon Overbrook Presbyn. Ch., Columbus, 1986-89. With JAGC, USAR, 1984-90. Mem. Ohio Bar Assn., Va. Poly. Alumni Assn. Cen. Ohio (pres. 1984-85), Ohio Gamma Alumni Corp. (trustee 1983-88, 91-95). Republican. Avocations: golf, home repairs. Home: 5789 Crescent Ct Worthington OH 43085-3804 Office: Ohio Adj Gen's Dept Attn: AGOH-JA 2825 W Dublin Granville Rd Columbus OH 43235-2789 Home Phone: 614-431-9538; Office Phone: 614-336-7022. Business E-Mail: duncan.aukland@us.army.mil.

AUKOFER, FRANK ALEXANDER, journalist; b. Milw., Apr. 6, 1935; s. Herbert Anselm and Wanda Mary (Kaminski) A.; m. D. Sharlene Talatzko, Aug. 6, 1960; children: Juliann Navarrete, Matthew P., Becky Hawryluk, Joseph J. BA in Journalism, Marquette U., 1960; Fellowship Cert., Northwestern U., 1967. With The Milw. Jour. Sentinel (merger The Milw. Jour., Sentinel), 1960-2000; with Washington Bur. The Milw. Jour. Sentinel, 1970-2000, bur. chief; ret., 2000. Writer syndicated column on automobiles DriveWays, 1985—; automobile columnist Artists & Writers Syndicate, Scripps Howard News Svc. Bd. dirs. Haven of No. Va., 2005—. With USAF Res., 1952-60. Recipient Byline award for lifetime achievement in journalism Marquette U., 1992, Profl. Merit award Marquette U., awards from Wis. Press. Assn., Milw. Press Club, Soc. Profl. Journalists; Vis. Profl. Freedom Forum First Amendment scholar Vanderbilt U., 1994-95. Mem. Nat. Press Club (pres. 1978, bd. dirs. bldg. corp., Corr. award), Nat. Press Found. (pres., chmn. bd. 1980-85, bd. dirs., 1978-2005), Soc. Profl. Journalists, Standing Com. Corr. U.S. Congress (sec. 1976), Washington Automotive Press Assn. (pres. 1987-88), Gridiron Club Washington. Roman Catholic. Home: 6325 Beachway Dr Falls Church VA 22044 E-mail: faukofer@gmail.com.

AULBACH, GEORGE LOUIS, retired real estate company executive; b. York, Pa., July 9, 1925; s. George A. and Mary N. (Goulden) Aulbach; m. Gertrude Frisby, June 24, 1949 (dec. Apr. 2004); children: Jeanne, Cynthia, Patricia, Kathleen, Barbara; m. Florence Hipschman, July 9, 2005. BSCE, Villanova U., 1945. Registered profl. engr., Pa., Ga. Field engr., estimator, chief engr., project mgr., exec. v.p R.S. Noonan, Inc., York, Pa., 1946-63; pres., CEO R.S. Noonan, Inc. & Noonan Engring. Corp., York, Pa., 1963-72; pres. systems bldg. divsn. McCrory-Sumwalt, Columbia, SC, 1972-76; pres., CEO Laing Properties, Inc., Atlanta, 1976-90; ret., 1990. Adv. bd. dirs. Bank South, Atlanta; vice-chmn., dir. Cath. Continuing Care Retirement Cmtys., Inc.; adv. bd. Ga. Tech. Rsch. Inst.; dir., treas. York, Pa. Meml. Osteo. Hosp., 1966—72; pres. York ABC Corp., 1966—72. Bd. dirs. Northside Hosp. Found., Cath. Housing Initiative; trustee So. Tech. Found.; cons. non-profit corp. developing affordable housing; chmn. sch. implementation com. Cath. Archdiocese of Atlanta, chmn. fin. com.; vice chmn. Cath. Continuum Care Com. Lt. (j.g.) USN, 1943—46. Decorated Knight Comdr. St. Gregory Vatican. Roman Catholic. Business E-Mail: imdutchman@citcom.net.

AULD, FRANK, psychologist, educator; b. Denver, Aug. 9, 1923; s. Benjamin Franklin and Marion Leland (Evans) A.; m. Elinor James, June 29, 1946 (dec. June 1990); children: Mary, Robert, Margaret; m. Elinor Leah Levine, Dec. 8, 1996 (dec. Dec. 2004). AB, Drew U., 1946; MA, Yale U., 1948, PhD, 1950. Cert. psychologist, Mich., Ont. Instr. psychology Yale U., New Haven, 1950-52, asst. prof., 1952-59; assoc. prof. Wayne State U., Detroit, 1959-61, prof., 1961-67, dir. clin. psychology tng. program, 1960-66; prof. U. Detroit, 1967-70, dir. psychol. clinic, 1967-69; prof. U. Windsor, Ont., Canada, 1970—91, prof. emeritus, 1992—. Cons. in field. Author: Steps in Psychotherapy, 1953, Scoring Human Motives, 1959, Resolution of Inner Conflict, 1991, 2d edit., 2005; contbr. articles to profl. jours. Chmn. Dearborn CC, Mich., 1962; mem. adv. com. on coll. work Episcopal Diocese Mich., 1962-71. Recipient Alumni Achievement award Drew U., 1965 Fellow APA (evaluation com. 1961-66); mem. Mich. Psychol. Assn., Ont. Psychol. Assn. (edn. and tng. bd. 1976-91, Lifetime Achievement award 1998), Conn. State Psychol. Soc. (pres. 1958), Soc. Psychotherapy Research, Phi Beta Kappa, Sigma Xi. Home: 200 Chester St Apt 220 Birmingham MI 48009-1427 Home Phone: 248-433-1886. Business E-Mail: frankauld@aya.yale.edu.

AULD, JAMES S., educational psychologist; Grad., U. Nebr. Cert. sch. counselor, profl. counselor. Dir. testing, asst. prof.; K-12 dir. guidance; kindergarten-12 dir. psychol. svcs. Author: Real Personality. Mem. APA, AACD, ASCD, Can. Psychol. Assn., Nebr. Profl. Counselors, Gold Key, nat. Disting. Svc. Registry for Counselors, Phi Delta Kappa. Office: PO Box 6228 Lincoln NE 68506-0228

AULD, ROBERT HENRY, JR., biomedical engineer, educator, consultant, writer; b. Akron, Ohio, Sept. 19, 1942; s. Robert Henry Sr. and Elsie Mae (Rollans) A.; children: Sheila Kay, Jason Craig; stepson: Christopher William Weiss. BSBA, Biomed. Engr., U. San Francisco, 1978. Registered profl. engr., Calif.; cert. clin. engr. Reg. svc. mgr. scientific products div. AHSC, Sunnyvale, Calif., 1963-68; founder, gen. mgr. Lab. Instrument Svc., Campbell, Calif., 1968-77; nat. mgr. Biomed. Svcs. Group Pilot Project Honeywell, Inc., Denver, 1977-79; internship Stanford U. Med. Ctr., 1976, UCSF, 1978; profl. engr. Robert Auld Enterprises, San Jose, Calif., 1979-86; dir. clin. engring. St. Louis Reg. Med. Ctr., 1987-89; engring. mgr. Robert Auld Engring.-West, Imperial, Mo., 1989—, biomedical engr. cons. Santee, Calif., 1989—; nat. svc. mgr. R.C. Network, Cleveland, OH, 1990-99; expert examiner State of Calif. Bd. Registration for Profl. Engrs., Sacramento, 1995-99. Seminar dir. ASMT, Phoenix AZ., 1968-79; instrument workshop seminar coordinator, Stanford U. Med. Ctr., 1980-84; engring. advisor St. Louis Reg. Career Access Ctr., 1987-89, U. Mo., Rolla and St. Louis. Author: The Clone Factory (A True Story About Police), 1992; contbr. articles to profl. jours. Apptd. hazardous waste com. State of Mo., 1988—90; del. at large Rep. Legion of Merit, Imperial, Mo., 1990—93; registrar of voters, precinct inspector San Diego County, 2004, 2005, 2006; precinct rep. San Diego, 2006—. Recipient Govs. Golden Spike award, Calif., 1986. Mem. IEEE, N.Y. Acad. Scis., Am. Soc. Hosp. Engrs., NSPE, Mo. Soc. Profl. Engrs. (chmn. 1988-89, chmn. minority Math Counts pilot project 1987-89), Order Demolay (life). Republican. Achievements include development of device for equilibrating gases in a liquid or blood for measurement of gases in blood; patent pending for dual halogen colormetric light source; Innovator "Single Source Service", "Parts Banks" for Clinical Equipment for Health Care Facilities. Office: Robert Auld Engring West 943 Tenth Ave Ste 226 San Diego CA 92101 Mailing: PO Box 40541 San Diego CA 92164 Business E-Mail: bauld@cox.net.

AULD, SKIP (HAMPTON AULD), library director; m. Noreen Cullen; children: Patrick, Stephanie. Grad. in Psychology, Davidson Coll., NC; MLS, U. NC, Chapel Hill, 1980; grad. cert. in Pub. Mgmt., Va. Commonwealth U., 2005. With Pub. Libr. Charlotte and Mecklenburg County, Duke U. Librs.; cons. Montgomery County Md. Pub. Libr. sys.; br. mgr. Carroll County Pub. Libr. sys., Westminster, Md.; asst. libr. dir. Chesterfield County Pub. Libr., Va.; dir. Durham County Libr., NC, 2006—. Contbr. articles to profl. jours. Mem.: ALA, Pub. Libr. Assn. Office: Durham County Pub Libr 300 N Roxboro St Durham NC 27701 Office Phone: 919-560-0100. Office Fax: 919-560-0137.

AULETTA, JOAN MIGLORISI, construction company executive, mortgage and insurance broker; b. July 23, 1940; d. Angelo George and Ann (Passa) Miglorisi; m. E.V. Auletta, Oct. 5, 1958; children: Ann, Vincent, George, Jeanne. ABS, Bklyn. C.C., 1957. Owner, mgr. Auletta Realty, 1947-76, E&J Pancake House, LI, N.Y., 1947-76; office and fin. mgr. Larchwood Constrn. Co., Farmingville, N.Y., 1976-77; prodn. mgr. Lawlor Industries, Holtsville, N.Y., 1977-79; real estate and fin. adv. Family Home Improvement Corp., Queens Village, N.Y., 1979-81; co-owner Total Home Constrn. Co., N.Y.C., 1981-86; owner, mgr. Century 21, Echo Hills Realtors Inc., Miller Place, N.Y., 1987-92, Auletta Realty, 1989—, Tone-O-Matic, 1988-89; owner, mgr. comml. property, 1970—. Bd. dirs. Multiple Listing Svc. of L.I., 1986-91, L.I. d. Realtors, 1986-92, Fin. Dept. Waste Industry, 1992-99. Mem. Miller Pl.-Mt. Sinai C. of C. (pres. 1988-90). Roman Catholic. Home: 7901 NW 83d St Tamarac FL 33321 E-mail: jma6715@hotmail.com.

AULETTA, KEN, columnist; b. Bklyn., 1942; married; 1 child. BA in History, SUNY, Oswego, 1963; MA in Polit. Sci., Syracuse U., 1965; LittD (hon.), SUNY, 1990. Exec. editor Manhattan Tribune; first exec. dir. NYC Off Track Betting Corp.; staff writer and weekly columnist Village Voice; contbg. editor NY Mag.; chief polit. corr. NY Post, 1974; polit. columnist Daily News, NYC, 1977—93; media critic, columnist New Yorker mag., NYC, 1993—. Nat. judge Livingston Awards; trustee, mem. exec. com., chmn. of nominating com. Pub. Theatre/NY Shakespeare Festival; mem. Columbia Journalism Sch. Task Force; juror Pulitzer Prize; trustee Nightingale-Bamford Sch. Author: Three Blind Mice: How the TV Networks Lost Their Way, Greed and Glory on Wall Street, The Highwaymen: Warriers of the Information Superhighway, others, The Streets Were Paved With Gold, Hard Feelings, The Underclass, The Art of Corporate Success, World War 3.0; Microsoft and Its Enemies, Random House, Backstory: Inside the Business of News, Penguin Press, 2003; guest editor: The Best Business Stories of the Year 2002, Random House. Named a Literary Lion, NY Pub. Libr.; recipient Nat. Mag. award, 2001, America's Premier Media Critic, Columbia Journalism Review. Office: The New Yorker 4 Times Sq New York NY 10036-6561

AULL, ELIZABETH BERRYMAN, real estate development executive; b. Independence, Mo., 1951; d. Homer Hayter and Mary Elizabeth (Wulfert) A. AA, Christian Coll., 1971; BS, U. Mo., 1973; master gardener, U. Mo. ext., Columbia, 1996; grad., Econ. Devel. Inst., 1992. With Mo. Senate Staff and Dept. Revenue, Jefferson City, 1973-74; administrv. asst. B. State Devel. Agy., St. Louis, 1974-76, Bingham Sketches, Inc., St. Louis, 1976; rate/routing analyst Mo. Pacific R.R., St. Louis, 1976-78; sr. property mgmt. specialist Burlington No. Inc., St. Louis, Springfield, Mo., 1978-87; dir., prop. mgmt. Glacier Park Co. subs. Burlington No., Inc., 1987-88; indsl. devel. mgr. Burlington No. R.R., Omaha, 1989-91, with Ft. Worth, 1991-95; indsl. and market devel. exec. Bd. dirs. Indpendence Ctr., St. Louis, 1982-83, Mental Health Assn. Greater St. Louis, 1982-83, Mental Health Assn. of Ozarks, Springfield, 1983-87; mem. Jr. League St. Louis, 1980-83, Jr. League Springfield, 1984-88, Jr. League, Omaha, 1989-92, Jr. League Ft. Worth, 1992—; chmn. bldg. subcom. Ozark Food Harvest Springfield Coun. of Chs., 1987-88; pres. Greater St. Louis Area Christian (Columbia) Coll. Alumni Assn., 1981-83; greeting card chmn. UNICEF Com. S.W. Mo., 1997. Named one of Outstanding Young Women Am., 1978, 80, 81. Mem. DAR, Dau. Am. Colonists, Colonial Dames 17th Century, Celtic Soc., German, Austrian and Swiss Soc., Friends of the Springfield Art Mus. Republican. Avocations: travel, art, herb gardening, genealogy. Home: 2391 E Wayland St Springfield MO 65804-3332

AULL, JAMES STROUD, retired bishop; b. Winnsboro, SC, Mar. 3, 1931; s. Luther Bachman and Ruth (Bull) A.; m. Virginia Kloeppel, Aug. 9, 1958; children: Diane, James Jr. (dec.), Virginia Ruth. AB magna cum laude, Newberry Coll., 1953; MDiv cum laude, Luth. Theol. So. Sem., Columbia, SC, 1960; M in Systematic Theology, Luth. Sch. Theology, Chgo., 1970; PhD, Duke U., 1971; DD (hon.), Newberry Coll., 1988. Ordained to ministry United Luth. Ch. in Am., 1961. Pastor St. Timothy Luth. Ch., Camden, SC, 1961-62; instr., staff mem. Luth. Theol. So. Sem., Columbia, SC, 1962-79; sec. S.C. Synod, Luth. Ch. in Am., Columbia, 1979-87, bishop, 1988-96; ret., 1996. Author: Obey My Voice: a Form Critical Study of Selected Prose in the Book of Jeremiah", 1971. Trustee Newberry Coll., 1972-96, sec., 1977-82; trustee Luth. Homes SC Found., White Rock, 1988-96, 2004-, chair, 2005-; trustee Lutheridge/Lutherock Ministries, Inc., 1988-96; bd. dirs. divsn. edn. Evang. Luth. Ch. Am., Chgo., 1988-91, mem. ch. coun., 1991-96, trustee, mem. bd. pensions, 1997-2003; mem. adv. bd. Lowman Home, 2003-2004. Mem. Soc. Bibl. Lit., Rotary (bd. dirs. 1987-90, pres. 1996-97). Lutheran. Home: PO Box 608 White Rock SC 29177-0608 E-mail: jimaull3@aol.com.

AULL, SUSAN, physician; b. NYC; d. Eugene and Ines Aull. BA, Vassar Coll., 1981; MD, N.Y. Med. Coll., 1986. Diplomate Am. Acad. Phys. Medicine and Rehab., Am. Acad. Pain Mgmt. Intern L.I. Coll. Hosp., Bklyn., 1986-87; phys. medicine and rehab. PGY II, III Westchester County Med. Ctr., Valhalla, NY, 1987-89; phys. medicine and rehab. PGY IV Lincoln Hosp., Bronx, NY, 1989-90, Ctrl. Fla. Physicians Rehab., Orlando, 1990-91; med. dir. dept. phys. medicine and rehab. Halifax Med. Ctr., Daytona Beach, Fla., 1992-99; med. dir. 21st Century Rehab. and Wound Mgmt. Ctr., Maitland, Fla., 1992; staff dept. internal medicine Winter Park (Fla.) Meml. Hosp., 1991-96; pvt. practice WWPM&R, Winter Park and Sarasota, 1991—2002; multi-specialty group practice, dir. phys. medicine and rehab. Ctrl. Fla. Physicians Rehab., Orlando, 1990-91; physician Advanced Sports Medicine Ctr., 2002—04, S. Aull MD PA, 2002—, IOM Svcs. Inc., 2004—07. Electrodiagnostic cons. SEA Med. Svcs., PA, Goldenrod, Fla., 1990-96; adj. clin. prof. U. Ctrl. Fla., Orlando, 1991-96. Author: (with others) Strength Conditioning for Preventive Medicine, 1992, ISC Control Points - New Generation of Pressure Points, 1993. Recipient Leadership award Defensive Tactics Newsletter, 1993; grantee PPCT Mgmt. Systems, Inc., 1992. Fellow Am. Acad. Phys. Medicine and Rehab.; mem. AMA, Am. Acad. Pain Mgmt., Am. Coll. Sports Medicine. Office: 1921 Waldemere St Ste 609 Sarasota FL 34239 Office Phone: 941-917-6500.

AULT, ANDREW JARED, music educator, disc jockey; b. Wheeling, W.Va., Dec. 29, 1978; s. Ronald Kenneth Ault and Virginia Elaine Biliter. BA in Music Edn./Applied Performance, Alderson-Broaddus Coll., 2002. Music educator Brooke County Schs., Wellsburg, W.Va., 2002—04, Robertson County Schs., Greenbrier, Tenn., 2004—. Mem. Bluecoats Drum and Bugle Corps, Canton, Ohio, 1999—2000. Recipient W. Lee and Alberta Williams Music award, Alderson-Broaddus Coll., 2003, Charles Ervin Music award, 2004. Home: 124 Green Meadow Ct Greenbrier TN 37073 Office: Greenbrier HS 126 Cuniff Dr Greenbrier TN 37073 Office Phone: 615-643-4526. Office Fax: 615-643-8873. E-mail: ault2002@hotmail.com.

AUMANN, R. KARL, commissioner, former state official; b. Balt., May 17, 1960; s. Frederick Carl and Marjorie Patterson (Rue) A.; m. Susan Langley Mueller, Sept. 20, 1986, children: Lang, Katherine BA, Loyola Coll., Balt., 1982; JD, U. Balt., 1985. Bar: Md. 1986, U.S. Dist. Ct. Md. 1986. Assoc. Power and Mosner PA, Towson, Md., 1986-88, Miles & Stockbridge, Balt., 1988—91; counsel, sr. policy advisor Appalachian Regional Commn., 1991—94; chief adminstr., dist. dir. for Congressman Robert L. Ehrlich US Congress, 1995—2003; sec. state State of Md., Annapolis, 2003—05; commr. Md. Workers Compensation Commn., Balt., 2005—, chmn., 2005—. Mem. SAR. Roman Catholic. Office: Md Workers Compensation Com 10 E Baltimore St Baltimore MD 21202

AUMANN, ROBERT JOHN, economics professor; b. Frankfurt on the Main, Fed. Republic Germany, June 8, 1930; arrived in Israel, 1956; s. Siegmund and Miriam (Landau) A.; m. Esther Schlesinger (dec.), Apr. 21, 1955; children: Shlomo (dec.), Tamar, Yehonatan, Miriam, Noga Judith. BS in Math., CCNY, 1950; SM in Math., MIT, 1952, PhD in Math., 1955; PhD (hon.), U. Bonn., Fed. Republic Germany, 1988, Cath. U. Louvain, Louvain-la-Neuve, Belgium, 1989, U. Chgo., 1992, CUNY, 2006, Bar Ilan U., 2006. Rsch. assoc., Econometric Rsch. Program Princeton U., 1960—61; instr. Hebrew U. Jerusalem, 1956—58, lectr., 1958—61, sr. lectr., 1961—64, assoc. prof., 1964—68, prof., 1968—2001, prof. emeritus, 2001—; vis. prof., Dept. Statistics and Cowles Found. Rsch. in Economics Yale U., 1964—65, vis. scholar, Cowles Found. Rsch. in

Economics, 1989; outside tchr., Statistics Dept. Tel Aviv U., 1969—93; Ford vis. rsch. prof. economics U. Calif., Berkeley, 1971, 1985—86; vis. prof., Ctr. for Ops. Rsch. and Econometrics Universite Catholique de Louvain, 1972, 1978, 1984; vis. prof. economics Stanford U., 1975—76, 1980—81; prof., Inst. for Decision Sci. and Econbmics Dept. SUNY, Stony Brook, 1986—89, 1991—2003; Oskar Morgenstern vis. prof. economics NYU, 1997; Nemmers prof. economics Northwestern U., 1999—2000; cons. E.I. du Pont de Nemours & Co., Wilmington, Mathematica, Inc., Princeton, US Arms Control and Disarmament Agy., Washington, Rand Corp., Santa Monica, Everyman's U., Tel Aviv. Chmn., Inst. Mathematics The Hebrew U., 1966—68, fellow, Inst. for Advanced Studies, 1979—80, mem., Ctr. for Rationality, 1991—; mem., Inst. for Mathematics and its Applications U. Minn., 1984; mem. Mathematical Sci. Rsch. Inst., Berkeley, 1985—86; lectr. in field. Author: Lectures on Game Theory, 1989, (with L.S. Shapley) Values of Non-atomic Games, 1974, (with M. MAschler) Repeated Games with Incomplete Information, 1995, (with S. Hart) Handbook of Game Theory, 2002; mem. editl. bd. Internat. Jour. of Game Theory, 1971-, SIAM Jour. on Applied Mathematics, 1976-80, Games and Economic Behavior, 1989-; adv. bd. mem. Jour. of Methematical Economics, 1974-, Mathematics of Operations Rsch., 1979-; assoc. editor Jour. Economic Theory, 1974-79, Econometrica, 1975-78, Jour. of the European Mathematical Soc., 2000-; contbr. numerous articles to profl. jours. and orgns. Served in Israeli Army, 1969—84. Recipient Harvey prize for sci. and tech. Haifa (Israel) Inst. Tech., 1983, Israel prize Econ., 1994, Lanchester prize in ops. rsch., 1995, Erwin Plein Nemmers prize in Econ., Northwestern U., 1998, EMET prize in Econ., 2002, Nobel Meml. Prize in Econ. Sci., 2005, John von Neumann Theory prize, Inst. for Operations Rsch. and the Mgmt. Sciences, 2005. Fellow: Econometric Soc. (coun. 1977—82, exec. com. 1982—85), British Acad. (corr.); mem.: Israel Acad. Sciences and Humanities (mem. 1989—), NAS (mem. 1985—), Am. Econ. Assn. (hon.), AAAS (hon.; fgn. mem. 1974—), Game Theory Soc. (founding pres. 1998—2003), Israel Mathematics Union (pres. 1990—92). Jewish. Avocations: hiking, climbing, skiing, cooking.

AUNE, DEBRA BJURQUIST, lawyer; b. Rochester, Minn., June 13, 1956; d. Alton Herbert and Violet Lucille (Dutcher) Bjurquist; m. Gary ReMine, June 6, 1981 (div. June 1993); children: Jessica Bjurquist ReMine, Melissa Bjurquist ReMine; m. David Aune, Jan. 1, 1995. BA, Augsburg Coll., 1978; JD, Hamline U., 1981. Bar: Minn. 1981. Assoc. Hvistendahl & Moersch, Northfield, Minn., 1981-82; adjuster Federated Ins. Cos., Owatonna, 1982-84; advanced life markets advisor Federated Life Ins. Co., Owatonna, 1984-87; mktg. svcs. advisor Federated Ins. Cos., Owatonna, 1987-89, 2d v.p., corp. legal counsel, 1989-92, v.p. gen. counsel, 1992-95, 1st v.p., gen. counsel, 1996-99; ind. cons., 1999—. Mem. Hamline Law Rev., 1979-80. Pres. Owatonna Ins. Women, 1983-84; charter commr. City of Owatonna, 1992—. Mem. ABA, Minn. State Bar Assn., 5th Dist. Bar Assn., Steele County Bar Assn. (sec. 1986-87, v.p. 1987-88, pres. 1988-89), Assn. Life Ins. Counsel, Alliance Am. Insurers (legal com. 1989—). Lutheran. Office Phone: 952-250-9587. E-mail: db.aune@gmail.com.

AUPING, MICHAEL G., curator; b. Portland, Oreg., Oct. 17, 1949; s. Jack Louis and Jane (Hammel) A.; m. Patricia Contreras, Aug. 22, 1974; children: Alicia Contreras, Jonathan Contreras. AA, Santa Ana Coll., 1969; BA, Calif. State U., Fullerton, 1971; MA, Calif. State U., Long Beach, 1975. Editor #1 Powell Libr. UCLA, 1975-77; assoc. curator Univ. Art Mus., Berkeley, Calif., 1977-80; head of curatorial, curator 20th century art Ringling Mus. Art, Sarasota, Fla., 1980-84; chief curator Albright-Knox Art Gallery, Buffalo, 1984-93, Modern Art Mus. of Ft. Worth, 1993—. Instr. art history Citrus Coll., Azusa, Calif., summer, 1977, San Francisco Art Inst., spring, 1978; adj. lectr. U. Calif., Santa Barbara, fall, 1977, U. Buffalo, 1988—89; guest curator Artist's Space , NY, 1988; panelist mus. aid program N.Y. State Coun. on Arts, 1988—89, Fed. Adv. Com. for Internat. Exhbns., NEA and Rockefeller Found., 1992—; curator Whitney Biennial, 2000; cons. commr. Am. Pavilion 1990 Venice Biennale, Italy; mem. adv. com. Intermus. Conservation Lab., CARE Pub., Art in Pub. Places, Met.-Dade area, 1984—, The Bush Found., St. Paul, 1985; cons. L.A. County Dept. Parks Cultural Arts sect., 1973; grant panelist mus. programs spl. exhbns. NEA, Washington, 1985; panelist, on-site evaluator Artists Orgn., NYC, 1983; visual arts panelist Divsn. Cultural Affairs State of Fla., Tallahassee, 1980, Tallahassee, 81. Author: Francesco Clemente, 1985, Jenny Holzer, 1992, Drawing Rooms: Jonathan Borofsky, Sol LeWitt, Richard Serra, 1994, Arshile Gorky: The Breakthrough Years, 1995, Tatsuo Miyajima: Big Time, 1996, Susan Rothenberg Paintings, 1996, Georg Baselitz: Portraits of Elke, 1997, Agnes Martin/Richard Tuttle, 1998, House of Sculpture, 1999, Natural Deceits, 2000, Philip Guston Retrospective, 2003, Anselm Kiefer: Heaven and Earth, 2005; TV appearances including CBS Sunday Morning, 1988; mng. editor L.A. Inst. Contemporary Art Jour., 1976-77; contbr. articles to profl. jours.; organizer exhbns. Office: Modern Art Mus 3200 Darnell St Fort Worth TX 76107

AURAND, CHARLES HENRY, JR., music educator; b. Battle Creek, Mich., Sept. 6, 1932; s. Charles Henry and Elisabeth Dirk (Hoekstra) A.; m. Donna Mae Erb, June 19, 1954; children: Janice, Cheryl, Sandra, Charles III, William. MusB, Mich. State U., 1954, MusM, 1958; PhD, U. Mich., 1971. Cert. tchr., Mich., Ohio. Asst. prof. music Hiram Coll., Ohio, 1958-60; dean, prof. music Youngstown State U., 1960-73; dean No. Ariz. U., Flagstaff, 1973-88, prof. music, 1988-94, prof. emeritus, 1994—. Chmn. Ariz. Alliance for Arts Edn., 1974-77; solo clarinetist Flagstaff Symphony; solo, chamber music and orch. musician, 1973-86; fine arts cons. Miami U. of Ohio, 1982 Author: Selected Solos, Methods, 1963; solo clarinetist Sonora Winds, 2002—; musician: Foothills Chamber Choir, Soranan Winds. Elder Presbyn. Ch., 1965; chmn. Boy Scouts Am., Coconino dist., 1974-78; bd. dir. Ariz. Com. Arts for the Handicapped, 1982-88, Flagstaff Symphony Orch., 1973-85, Flagstaff Festival of Arts, 1973-89, Sedona Chamber Mus. Soc., 1989-99, Sedona Med. Ctr., 1998-2002, Civic Orch. Tucson, 2003-04; conf. dir. Internat. Clarinet Soc., 1991; pres. Citizens for an Alt. Route, 1995-98; mem. Ariz. Town Hall, 1996-98; bd. dir. Sedona Med. Ctr. Found., 1998-2002; mem. Foothills Chamber Music Ensemble, Catalina Chamber Ensemble, 2004-; mem. Ariz. Town Hall, 1996-2002; solo clarinet Sonora Winds, 2002-05. 1st lt. USAF,1955-57 Recipient award of merit Boy Scouts Am., 1977; cert. appreciation John F. Kennedy Ctr. Performing Arts, 1985. Mem. SAR (pres. No. Ariz. chpt. 2000-02, pres. Ariz. Soc. 2003—, state pres. 2003-04, sec.-treas. Tucson chpt. 2007-), Am. Assn. Higher Edn., Ariz. Humanities Assn., Music Educators Nat. Conf., State Adminstrs. Music Schs. (chmn. 1971-73), Internat. Clarinet Soc./ClariNetwork Internat. (conf. dir. 1991), No. Ariz. U. Retirees Assn. (pres. 1997-98), Kiwanis (pres. 1984-85). Republican. Presbyterian. Avocations: golf, tennis, bridge. Home: 37738 S Hill Side Dr Tucson AZ 85739-2221 Personal E-mail: cdaurand2@msn.com.

AURELIAN, LAURE, medical sciences educator; b. Bucharest, Romania, June 17, 1939; came to U.S., 1963, naturalized, 1971; d. George I. and Stella (Ben-Joseph) A.; M.S., Tel-Aviv U., 1962; Ph.D., Johns Hopkins U., 1966; m. I.I. Kessler, Nov. 24, 1970; 1 dau., Amalia D. Asst. prof. dept. lab. animal medicine and microbiology Johns Hopkins U. Sch. Medicine, Balt., 1969-74, assoc. prof. dept. biophysics and biochemistry, 1975-82, assoc. prof. dept. comparative medicine and biophysics, 1974-82, prof. div. biophysics, 1982—; prof. dept. pharmacology U. Md., 1982— , dir. virology/immunology labs., 1984—; mem. NIH study sects. internat. teaching, 1973; mem. sci. adv. com. Internat. Biomed. Inst. UNESCO, 1987—. Recipient Hon. medal Disting. Contribution to Gynecol. Oncology U. Bologna, Italy, award Premio XXIV Casalli 90 ASS, Pro Loco Bronte Edizione Speciale Medicina, Catania, K. Vephvadze Meml. award Georgian Soc. Oncologists; ACS grantee, 1970-74; NIH grantee, 1969—; WHO grantee, 1980—; others; named Disting. Young Scientist, Md. Acad. Sci., 1970. Mem. David Boyes Soc. Gynecol. Oncology, Brit. Coll. Can. (hon.) Am. Soc. Microbiology, AAAS, Am. Assn. Immunologists, Soc. Exptl. Biology and Medicine, Md. Acad. Sci., N.Y. Acad. Sci., Am. Assn. Cancer Research, Reticuloendothelial Soc. Editor Jour. Soviet Oncology, 1980-86, European Jour. Gynecol. Oncology, 1982—, Internat. Jour. Oncology, 1993—, In Vivo, 1994-2004, Clin. and Diagnostic Lab. Immunology, 2000—, Frontiers in Biosci, 1997—, Genetics Vaccine and Therapy, 2003—, Cancer Therapy, 2003—; contbr. articles to profl. jours. Home: 3404 Bancroft Rd Baltimore MD 21215-3105 Home Phone: 410-358-3706; Office Phone: 410-706-3895. Business E-Mail: laurelia@umaryland.edu.

AURELL, JOHN KARL, lawyer; b. Tulsa, Sept. 26, 1935; s. George E. and Maxine (Reagor) A.; m. Jane Brevard Collins, Oct. 1, 1960; 1 child, Jane B. BA, Washington and Lee U., 1956; LLB, Yale U., New Haven, Conn., 1964. Bar: Fla. 1964, D.C 1971, U.S. Dist. Ct. (no., mid. and so. dists.) Fla., U.S. Ct. Appeals (5th and 11th cirs.), U.S. Supreme Ct. Gen. counsel to Gov. State of Fla., Tallahassee, 1979-80; pvt. practice, 1964—79, 1980—. Mem. Fed. Jud. Nominating Commn. Fla.; chmn. No. Dist. Fla., 1993—97. Mem. exec. com., v.p. Yale Law Sch. Assn., 1975-80; mem. Orange Bowl Com. 1st lt. U.S. Army, 1956-57. Fellow Am. Bar Found., Internat. Soc. Barristers, Am. Coll. Trial Lawyers; mem. ABA, Fla. Bar Assn. (bd. govs. young lawyers sect. 1966-71), Am. Law Inst., Exch. Club, Yale Club (N.Y.C.), Chattooga Club, Econ. Club Fla. (chmn. 1997-98), Havana Country Club, Capital City Country Club. Democrat. Home: 1225 Live Oak Plantation Rd Tallahassee FL 32312-2509 Office: PO Box 13505 Tallahassee FL 32317 Home Phone: 850-385-8844; Office Phone: 850-556-8001. Personal E-mail: aurellj@comcast.net.

AURIEMMA, GENO, women's college basketball coach; m. Kathy; children: Jenna, Alysa, Michael. BA in Polit. Sci., West Chester U., 1981. Coach boys' basketball Bishop Kenrick HS, 1979-81; asst. coach U. Va., 1981-85, St. Joseph's U., Phila., 1984; head coach U. Conn., 1985—. Mem. Kodak All-Am. Selection Com., chair, 1992; voting mem. USA Today/Women's Basketball Coaches Assn. Top 25 Poll-In; co-head coach Nat. Sr. All-Stars; coach USA Basketball Select Team, Colorado Springs; asst. coach USA World U. Games Women's Basketball Team, 1995; head coach West Team US Olympic Festival, San Antonio, 1993; spkr. Nat. HS Coaches Assn. Conv., Conn. Co-author: (autobiography) Geno: In Pursuit of Perfection, 2006. Chair Why-Me of New Eng.; chair (hon.) Am. Heart Assn. Named Women's Basketball Nat. Coach of Yr., 1997, 2000, 02, Naismith Nat. Coach of Yr., 1995, 97, 2000, 02, Coach of Yr., AP, 1995, 97, 2000, 03; recipient Victor award, Women's Basketball Coaches Assn., 1995, 96, 2000; named to Women's Basketball Hall of Fame, 2006, Naismith Memorial Basketball Hall of Fame, 2006. Achievements include leading the Huskies to five national championships, 1995, 2000, 02, 03, 04. Office: U Conn Divsn Athletics Womens Basketball 2095 Hillside Rd Unit 1173 Storrs Mansfield CT 06269-1173 Office Phone: 860-486-4756. E-mail: GENO.AURIEMMA@uconn.edu.*

AURIN, ROBERT JAMES, entrepreneur; b. St. Louis; m. Kathryn L. Engel, 1998. B in Journalism, U. Mo., 1965. Copywriter Leo Burnett Co., Chgo., 1971-72, Young & Rubicam, Inc., Chgo., 1972-73; from copywriter to v.p., creative dir. Foote, Cone & Belding, Inc., Chgo., 1973-79; exec. v.p., dir. creative services Grey-North Inc., Chgo., 1979-82; pres. Robert Aurin Assocs., Chgo., 1982—; owner ROMAR Investments Co., Chgo., 1984-99. Exec. creative dir. DraftWorldwide, Inc., 1996-99. Lt. USN, 1965—70, Vietnam.

AURNER, ROBERT RAY, II, retail development executive; b. Madison, Wis., Mar. 24, 1927; s. Robert Ray and Kathryn (Dayton) A.; m. Phyllis Barrett, 1951 (div. 1966); children: Sheryl, Roxanne, Kathryn, Suzanne, Robert III; m. Deborah Marion Lucas, Jan. 31, 1976 (div. 1999); children: William Lucas, Christopher Ray. AA, Monterey Peninsula Coll., 1949; BA, Calif. State U. Fresno and Occidental Coll. Eagle Rock, 1950; postgrad., U. Calif., Berkeley, Duquesne U., Pitts. Lic. in real estate, Calif., Pa., NY; registered investment advisor. Announcer Radio Sta. WSUI, Iowa City, 1946-48; featured celebrity Cowboy Bob, William Randolph Hearst Radio Sta. WISN-CBS, Milw., 1950-51; sr. sales supr. Shell Oil Co., San Francisco, 1952-60; dir. devel. ctrl. Calif. coast svc. sta. Gulf Oil Corp., 1960-67; ea. divsn. mgr. ops. Sunray DX Oil Co. (merger Sunoco), Tulsa, 1967-72; mgr. site devel. Milex Auto Diagnostic Tune-Up and Brakes, Inc., Plymouth Meeting, Pa., 1972-74; mgr. real estate store devel. Pitts. divsn. Atlantic & Pacific Tea Co. Supermarkets, 1974-77; real estate adminstr. store devel. N.E. U.S. region Steak and Ale - Bennigan's Restaurant divsn.; real estate mgr. N.Y. and Phila. regions Burger King Corp. restaurant divsn. Pillsbury Cos., Md., Va., NY, NJ, Pa., Del. and Conn., 1977-87; real estate mgr. Ky. Fried Chicken and Pizza Hut divsns. Pepsico, Inc., Metro SMSA, NYC and No. N.J., 1987-89; nat. dir. real estate, cons. store devel. Nathan's Famous Coney Island Hot Dog Restaurants, Inc., NYC, 1989-90; ret., 1990. Founder, chmn. bd. dirs., pres., CEO Bristlecone Trading and Devel., Inc., Carmel, Calif.; pres., CEO Aurner and Assocs., Consultants, Carmel, 1987—, chmn. bd. dirs., 1990—; tower devel. cons. So. NJ Nextel Wireless Telecom. Corp., NJ, 1994-95; founder Trader Bob Fashions Inc., Carson City, Nev., 1997; career counselor US Coast Guard Acad. and Pub. Affairs. Officer and flotilla comdr. Flotilla 64 C.G. Aux., Coast Guard Sta., Monterey, Calif., 2000—07; divsn. chmn. Nat. Safe Boating Week, USCG Aux., 2001—07; membership chmn. Monterey Bay Sail and Power Squadron, Unit U.S. Power Squadrons Hdqrs., Raleigh, NC, 2003—, squadron comdr., 2005—07; dist. safety officer San Francisco Bay region Unit U.S. Power Squadrons Hdqrs., 2004—. With USN, 1944—46, PTO. Named to Hon. Order Ky. Col., Gov. of Ky., Commodore in Okla. Navy Gov. Johnston Murray of Okla. Mem.: Moss Landing Harbor Safe Boating Com., Moss Landing C. of C., Navy League Monterey Peninsula, Carmel Valley (Calif.) C. of C. (bd. dirs., sec. 1999—2003), USS Yellowstone Assn. (USNR), Compari Club of Monterey Peninsula, Monterey Peninsula Yacht Club, Buccaneer Club of NY (past pres. NY and Conn.), Rotary Club of Monterey, Pacheco Club of Monterey, Elkhorn Yacht Club, Monterey Elks Club, Sigma Alpha Epsilon. Republican. Episcopalian. Avocation: Civil War history. Office: Aurner & Assocs Inc PO Box 222135 Carmel CA 93922-2135 also: Bristlecone Trading & Devel Carmel CA 93923 Personal E-mail: traderbob2@aol.com.

AURORA, SHEENA KAUR, neurologist; b. India, Sept. 3, 1966; B Medicine B Surgery, Christian Med. Coll., Ludhiana, India, 1989. Intern Christian Med. Coll., 1989; intern in internal medicine Wayne State U., Detroit, 1991; resident in neurology Henry Ford Hosp., Detroit, 1992-94, chief resident in neurology, 1994-95, fellow in headache and neurophysiology, 1995-96, staff neurologist, 1997—. Mem. Am. Acad. Neurology, Am. Acad. Study, Am. Assn. Electrodiagnostic Acad. (Jr. Mem. Recognition award 1996), Internat. Headache Soc. (Fellowship award 1995, Harold G. Wolff award for headache rsch. 1999), Am. Assn. for Study of Headache.

AUSBROOK, J. KEITH, lawyer; b. 1958; AB, Princeton Univ.; JD, Univ. Va., 1985. Bar: DC 1986. Atty. Collier Shannon Rill & Scott, Washington, 1985—97; chief counsel subcommittee Nat. Econ. Growth, Natural Resources & Regulatory Affairs, U.S. Ho. Rep., Washington, 1997—99; dep. ind. counsel in re: Madison Guaranty Savings & Loan Assn., Washington, 1999—2001; chief counsel, oversight & investigations Com. Judiciary, U.S. Ho. Rep., Washington, 2001—03; chief counsel Com. Govt. Reform, U.S. Ho. Rep., Washington, 2003—. Republican. Office: Committee on Government Reform 2157 Rayburn HOB Washington DC 20515-6143

AUSIELLO, DENNIS ARTHUR, nephrologist; b. Chelsea, Mass., Sept. 12, 1945; s. Hugo Italo and Gilda (Santosuosso) A.; m. Susan Johnson, May 10, 1969; children: Jeffrey, John. BA, Harvard Coll., 1967; MD, Univ. Pa., 1971. Diplomate Am. Bd. Internal Medicine, Am. Bd. Nephrology. Intern, resident in medicine Mass. Gen. Hosp., Boston, 1971-73; rsch. fellow NIH, Bethesda, Md., 1973-75, Mass. Gen. Hosp., Harvard Medical Sch., Boston, 1976-77; clinical staff medical svcs. Mass. Gen. Hosp., Boston, 1976—; instr., asst., assoc. prof. Harvard Medical Sch., Cambridge, 1976-93, prof. medicine, 1993—96; physician in chief medical svcs. Mass. Gen. Hosp., Boston, 1996—; Jackson prof. clin. medicine Harvard Medical Sch., 1996—. Recipient Dr. O.H. Perry prize Univ. Pa., 1971, NIH Merit award NIH, 1988, 1996. Fellow Molecular Medicine Soc.; mem. Am. Soc. Nephrology, Internat. Soc. Nephrology, Am. Fedn. for Clinical Rsch., Am. Soc. for Clinical Investigation, Assn. Am. Physicians, Assn. Profs. Medicine, Am. Acad. Arts and Sci. (elected mem.), Inst. Medicine. Office: Massachusetts Gen Hosp 55 Fruit St # St740 Boston MA 02114-2696

AUSLANDER, MITCHELL J., lawyer; b. NYC, July 1, 1956; BA, NYU, 1977; JD, Rutgers U., 1980. Bar: NY 1981, US Dist. Ct., (so. dist.) NY 1981, US Dist. Ct. (ea. dist.) NY 1981, US Ct. Appeals, (2nd cir.) 1988, US Supreme Ct. Ptnr. litig. dept. Willkie Farr & Gallagher LLP, NYC. Panelist Gen. Counsel Leadership Series, 2007. Mem.: ABA, Assn. Bar of City NY, NY County Lawyers Assn. Office: Willkie Farr & Gallagher LLP 787 Seventh Ave New York NY 10019 Office Phone: 212-728-8201. Office Fax: 212-728-9201. E-mail: mauslander@willkie.com.*

AUSMAN, ROBERT K., surgeon, research and development company executive; b. Milw., Jan. 31, 1933; s. Donald Charles and Mildred (Shafrin) A.; m. Christine McCann, 1992. Student, Kenyon Coll., 1953; MD, Marquette U., 1957. Damon Runyon cancer fellow U. Minn., 1958-61; dir. Health Research Inc. Roswell Park Meml. Inst., 1961-69; dep. dir. Fla. Regional Med. Assn., 1969-70; v.p. clin. research Baxter Travenol Labs., 1970-82, pres. advanced devel. group, 1982-90; pres. Mildon Corp., 1985—, Citation Pub. Co., 1991—. Clin. prof. surgery Med. Coll. Wis., 1972—. Named Outstanding Young Man in N.Y. Buffalo Evening News, 1966, Citizen of Year, 1967 Mem.: Am. Assn. Cancer Rsch., Am. Soc. Clin. Oncology, Masons. Home: PO Box 3538 Long Grove IL 60047 Office: Willow Valley Rd Long Grove IL 60047

AUSNEHMER, JOHN EDWARD, lawyer; b. Youngstown, Ohio, June 26, 1954; s. John Louis and Patricia Jean (Liguore) A.; m. Carole Marie Ausnehmer; children: Jill Ellen, Amber Layne. BS, Ohio State U., 1976; JD, U. Dayton, 1980. Bar: Ohio 1980, U.S. Dist. Ct. (no. dist.) Ohio 1981, U.S. Ct. Appeals (6th cir.) 1984, U.S. Supreme Ct. 1984. Law clk. Ohio Atty. Gen., Columbus, 1978, Green Schiavoni, Murphy, Haines & Sgambati Co., L.P.A., 1978; assoc. Dickson Law Office, Petersburg, Ohio, 1979-85; sole practice Youngstown, 1984—. Asst. pros. atty. Mahoning County, Ohio, 1986—89, 1992—; pres., co-owner Drunken Jacks' Saloon, Boardman, Ohio. Mem.: Columbiana County Bar Assn., Mahoning County Bar Assn., Cleve. Acad. Trial Attys. Ohio, Ohio State Bar Assn., Ohio Acad. Trial Lawyers, Ohio State U. Alumni Club (Mahoning County chpt. bd. dirs. 2003—06), Mahoning Valley Soccer Club (rep. 1982—84), Phi Alpha Delta. Democrat. Roman Catholic. Home: 51 S Shore Dr Boardman OH 44512-5926 Office: PO Box 3965 120 Marwood Cir Youngstown OH 44513-3965 Office Phone: 330-726-1654 Ext. 12. Personal E-mail: jealaw1302@aol.com.

AUST, JOE BRADLEY, surgeon, educator; b. Buffalo, Sept. 8, 1926; s. Joe Bradley and Edith (Derby) A.; m. Constance Ann MacMullin, June 18, 1949; children— Jay Bradley, Bonnie Jean, Barbara Ann, Linda Lee, Mary Louise, Tracey Roberta. MD, U. Buffalo, 1949; MS in Physiology, U. Minn., 1957, PhD in Surgery, 1958. Diplomate: Am. Bd. Surgery, Am. Bd. Thoracic Surgery. Intern U. Minn. Hosps., 1949-50, resident, 1950-58; scholar Am. Cancer Soc. U. Minn., 1957-62, mem. faculty, 1957-66, prof. surgery, 1964-66; prof. surgery, chmn. dept. U. Tex. Med. Sch., San Antonio, 1966-96, prof. dept. surgery, 1996—. Cons. Minn. State Prison, 1958-62, Anoka State Hosp., 1962-65, Brooke Army Med. Hosp., 1967— , Wilford Hall USAF Hosp., 1967— , Audie Murphy Meml. VA Hosp., 1973—; nat. cons. to surgeon gen. USAF, Washington, 1975-78 Served with M.C. USNR, 1950-52. Fellow ACS; mem. Am. Surg. Assn., Western Surg. Assn., So. Surg. Assn., Cen. Surg. Assn., Soc. U. Surgeons, Soc. Head and Neck Surgeons, Am. Assn. Cancer Rsch., Soc. Surg. Oncology, San Antonio Surgical Soc., Am. Assn. Cancer Edn., Halsted Soc., Soc. Clin. Oncology, Transplantation Soc., Sigma Xi, Alpha Omega Alpha, Phi Ch. Achievements include spl. research cancer immunity, regional cancer chemotherapy, shock, homotransplantation. Office: U Tex Med Sch 7703 Floyd Curl Dr San Antonio TX 78284-6200

AUST, STEVEN DOUGLAS, biochemistry, biotechnology and toxicology educator; b. South Bend, Wash., Mar. 11, 1938; s. Emil and Helen Mae (Crawford) A.; m. Nancy Lee Haworth, June 5, 1960 (dec.); children: Teresa, Brian; m. Karen Hurley, July 16, 2004. BS in Agr., Wash. State U., 1960, MS in Nutrition, 1962; PhD in Dairy Sci., U. Ill., 1965. Postdoctoral fellow dept. toxicology Karolinska Inst., Stockholm, 1966; New Zealand facial exzema sr. postdoctoral fellow Ruakura Agrl. Rsch. Ctr., Hamilton, 1975-76; mem. faculty dept. biochemistry Mich. State U., East Lansing, 1967-87, prof., 1977-87, assoc. dir. Ctr. for Environ. Toxicology, 1980-85, dir. Ctr. for the Study of Active Oxygen, 1985-87; dir. biotech. ctr. Utah State U., Logan, 1987-91, prof. chem. biochemistry, 1987—. Dir. basic rsch. and tng. program Super Fund Nat. Inst. Environ. Health Scis., 1988-96; mem. toxicology study sect. NIH, 1979-83; mem. environ. measurements com., mem. sci. adv. bd. EPA, 1980-83; mem. toxicology data bank, mem. peer rev. com. Nat. Libr. Medicine, 1983-85; mem. Mich. Toxic Substance Control Commn., 1979-82, chmn., 1981-82; pres., founder Intech One-Eighty Corp., North Logan Utah, 1993-99, pres. 1999—; mem. adv. panel for metabolic biochemistry program NSF, 1998; mem. EPA/DOE/NSF/ONR Joint Program on Bioremediation, 1998. Contbr. articles to profl. jours. Recipient Nat. Rsch. Svc. award NIH, USPHS, Dupont Sci. and Engring. award, 1988, Alumni Achievement award Wash. State U., 1998, Gov.'s Sci. and Tech. medal, 2002, Univ. Outstanding Grad. Mentor award, 2003, Disting. Alumnus in Sci., Edn., Rsch. award Washington State U., 2007; named D. Wynne Thorne Rschr. of Yr., 2003; NRC Facial Eczema fellow Ruakura Agrl. Rsch. Ctr., Hamilton, 1975. Fellow Acad. Toxicology Scis., Oxygen Soc.; mem. Am. Soc. Biol. Chemists, Am. Soc. Pharmacology and Exptl. Therapeutics, Soc. Toxicology, Am. Chem. Soc. (Kenneth A. Spencer award 2004), Am. Soc. Microbiology Avocations: raising, training quarter horses, fly fishing. Office: Utah State U Ctr Integrated BioSys Logan UT 84322-4705 Home Phone: 208-852-3611; Office Phone: 435-797-2730. E-mail: sdaust@cc.usu.edu.

AUSTAD, ERIC DAVID, plastic and reconstructive surgeon; b. Biloxi, Miss., Oct. 4, 1944; s. Myron Theodore and Marjorie (Larsen) A.; m. Carol Campbell, June 7, 1969; 1 child, Nissa Kristine. MD, U. Mich., 1969. Diplomate Am. Bd. Plastic Surgery. Intern Charity Hosp., New Orleans, 1969-70; resident in gen. surgery St. Joseph Hosp., Ann Arbor, Mich., 1970-71, 73-74; resident in neurosurgery U. Mich., Annr Arbor, 1974-76, resident in plastic surgery, 1976-78; staff surgeon Henry Ford Hosp., Detroit, 1978-80; prin. Eric D. Austad, M.D., P.C., Ann Arbor, 1980—2003; pvt. practice San Diego, 2003—. Clin. asst. prof. surgery U. Mich., 1978—; staff surgeon Catherine McAuley Health System, Ann Arbor, 1981—, Chelsea (Mich.) Cmty. Hosp., 1980—. Contbg. author 6 books on plastic surgery; contbr. articles to profl. jours.; patentte in med. devices. Trustee Emerson Sch., Ann Arbor, 1989-97. Lt. comdr. USN, 1971-73. Am. Cancer Soc. grantee, 1977-78. Fellow ACS; mem. AMA,

Am. Soc. Plastic Reconstructive Surgeons (implant com. 1988—, 1st pl. in clin. rsch. 1980's), Mich. Med. Soc., Mich. Acad. Plastic Surgeons (pres. 1988-90), Assn. Acad. Surgeons. Avocations: tennis, photography. Office: 4510 Executive Dr Ste 105 San Diego CA 92121 also: 351 SANTA FE Dr Ste 1 Encinitas CA 92024 Office Phone: 760-635-2448.*

AUSTAN, FRANK ACOSTA, clinician, educator; b. Medellin, Colombia, Apr. 29, 1951; arrived in U.S., 1959; s. Guillermo Austan and Lillian Acosta; m. Joan Robin Pliner, July 14, 1974; children: Lara Nicole, Jason Michael. AB, U. Miami, 1980; MSc, Nova Southeastern U., Ft. Lauderdale, Fla., 1983. Lic. Bd. Medicine, Fla., Pa., Nat. Bd. for Respiratory Care, 1978. Dir. respiratory care Berlin West Jersey Hosp., Berlin, NJ, 1986—99, Temple U. Hosp. and Med. Sch., Phila., 1999—. Asst. prof. Miami-Dade C.C., Miami, Fla., 1980—82; clin. instr. Respiratory Therapy Inst., Miami, 1982—83; sr. instr. dept. medicine Hahnemann Med. Coll. and Hosp., Phila., 1983—86; clin. instr. Univ. Medicine and Dentistry, Newark, 1992—. Contbr. articles to profl. jour. Mem.: Am. Coll. Chest. Physicians, Am. Thoracic Soc., Am. Assoc. Respiratory Care (Respironics Fellowships Prize 2000). Democrat. Achievements include Contrb. to med. lit. via Heart & Lung Jour., Am. J clin. hypnosis in the clin. area of ventilator weaning, treatment of asthma and chronic obstructive pulmonary disease, artery puncture pain reduction. E-mail: austanf@te.temple.edu.

AUSTEN, K(ARL) FRANK, internist, educator; b. Akron, Ohio, Mar. 14, 1928; s. Karl and Bertle (Jehle) Austen; m. Joycelyn Chapman, Apr. 11, 1959; children: Leslie Marie, Karla Ann, Timothy Frank, Jonathan Arthur. AB, Amherst Coll., 1950; MD, Harvard U., 1954. Intern in medicine Mass. Gen. Hosp., 1954—55, asst. resident, 1955—56, sr. resident, 1958—59, chief resident, 1961, asst. in medicine, 1962—63, asst. physician, 1963—66, chief pulmonary unit, 1964—66, also cons. in medicine; practice medicine, specializing in internal medicine, allergy and immunology Boston, 1962—66; USPHS postdoctoral research fellow Nat. Inst. Med. Research, Mill Hill, London, 1959—61; asst. in medicine Harvard Med. Sch., 1961, instr., 1961—62, assoc. in medicine, 1962—64, asst. prof., 1965—66, assoc. prof., 1966—68, prof., 1969—72, Theodore Bevier Bayles prof. medicine, 1972—; physician-in-chief Robert B. Brigham Hosp., Boston, 1966—80; chmn. dept. rheumatology and immunology Brigham and Women's Hosp., Boston, 1980—95, dir. lab. inflammation and allergic disease rsch. sect., 1995—. Mem. fellowship subcom. Arthritis Found., 1968—71, chmn., 1971; mem. coun. Infectious Disease Soc. Am., 1969—71; mem. arthritis tng. grants com. Nat. Inst. Arthritis and Metabolic Diseases, NIH, 1970—73; NHLB adv. coun., 1994—; mem. directing group, task force on immunology and disease Nat. Inst. Allergy and Infectious Diseases, 1972—73; bd. dirs. Arthritis Found., 1972—75, chmn. manpower study com., 1972—73, chmn. rsch. com. Multipurpose Arth. Ctr., 1972—76; chmn. rsch. com. Med. Found., Inc., 1972—76; mem. Am. Bd. Allergy and Immunology, 1973—78, Nat. Commn. on Arthritis and Related Musculoskeletal Diseases, 1975—76, Allergy and Immunology Rsch. com., NIAID, 1975—79, chmn., 1976—79; chmn. nomenclature com. Internat. Union Immunol. Socs., 1983—; mem. adv. com. to the dir. NIH, 1986—90, mem. nat. heart, lung and blood adv. com., 1966—80. Mem. editl. bd.: Arthritis and Rheumatism, 1968—81, Proc. of Transplantation Soc., 1968—82, Jour. Infectious Diseases, 1969—79, Jour. Exptl. Medicine, 1971—, Immunol. Comm., 1972—85, Clin. Immunology and Immunopathology, 1972—89, Proc. of NAS, 1978—83, Clin. and Exptl. Immunology, 1978—88, Internat. Jour. Immunopharmacology, 1984, Advances in Immunology, 1985—, Advances in Pharmacology, 1989—; contbr. articles to profl. jours. Trustee Amherst Coll., 1981—. Capt. M.C. US Army, 1956—58, Walter Reed Army Inst. Rsch. Recipient Warren Alpert Found. prize, 1999. Mem.: ACP, NAS (chmn. sect. on med. microbiology and immunology 1983—86), Internat. Soc. Immunopharmacology (pres. 1994), Internat. Assn. Allergology and Clin. Immunology, Fedn. Am. Soc. Exptl. Biology, Am. Acad. Allergy and Immunology (exec. com. 1970—72, sec. 1977—80, pres. 1981), Assn. Am. Physicians (recorder 1978—84, pres. 1989—90), Am. Acad. Arts and Scis., Transplantation Soc., Am. Rheumatism Assn., Am. Soc. Clin. Investigation, Brit. Soc. Immunology, Am. Assn. Immunologists (pres. 1977—78), Am. Soc. Exptl. Pathology, Am. Soc. Pharm. and Exptl. Therapeutics, Inst. Medicine, Interurban Clin. Club. Office: BWH Dept Rhem & Allergy Smith Bldg Room 638 75 Francis St Boston MA 02115 Office Phone: 617-525-1300. Office Fax: 617-525-1310.

AUSTEN, KARL RAMSDELL, lawyer; b. Boston, Aug. 29, 1964; s. W. G. and Patricia (Ramsdell) A. BA, Amherst Coll., Mass., 1986; JD, Harvard U., 1989. Bar: Calif. 1989. Assoc. Gipson, Hoffman & Pancione, LA, 1989—94, Armstrong, Hirsch, Jackoway, Tyerman & Wertheimer, LA, 1994—2004; ptnr. Jackoway Tyerman Wertheimer Austen Mandelbaum & Morris, LA, 2004—. Office: Jackoway Tyerman Wertheimer Austen Mandelbaum & Morris 1888 Century Park E 18th Fl Los Angeles CA 90067

AUSTEN, W(ILLIAM) GERALD, surgeon, educator; b. Akron, Ohio, Jan. 20, 1930; s. Karl and Bertl (Jehle) Austen; m. Patricia Ramsdell, Jan. 28, 1961; children: Karl Ramsdell, William Gerald Jr., Christopher Marshall, Elizabeth Patricia. BS, MIT, 1951; MD, Harvard U., 1955; HHD (hon.), U. Akron, 1980; DSc (hon.), U. Athens, 1981, U. Mass., 1985, Northeastern Ohio U. Coll. Medicine, 1996. Diplomate Am. Bd. Surgery, Am. Bd. Thoracic Surgery. Intern, then resident in surgery Mass. Gen. Hosp., Boston, 1955—61, chief surg. cardiovasc. rsch. unit, 1963—69, chief surgery, 1969—97, surgeon-in-chief, 1989—97, surgeon-in-chief emeritus, 1997—; surgeon clinic surgery Nat. Heart Inst., 1961—62; CEO, pres. Mass. Gen. Physicians Orgn., Boston, 1994—98, CEO, chmn., 1998—99, chmn., 1999—2000, hon. trustee, chmn. emeritus, 2000—. Assoc. in surgery Harvard Med. Sch., 1963—65, assoc. prof. surgery, 1965—66, prof. surgery, 1966—74, Edward D. Churchill prof. surgery, 1974—; mem. residency review com. surgery Accreditation Coun. Grad. Med. Edn., 1988—93; bd. dirs. Abiomed, Inc., The Smithers Group, Inc. Author, editor: med. textbooks; contbr. articles to profl. jours. Mem. corp. MIT 1972-2005, life mem. corp., 1982-2005, life mem. corp. emeritus, 2005—, mem. exec. com. corp., 1986-98; trustee John S. and James L. Knight Found., 1986-, vice chmn., 1991-96, chmn., 1996-; bd. dirs. Found. Biomed Rsch., 1988-2000; trustee Mass. Eye and Ear Infirmary, 1991-, Ptnrs. HealthCare System Inc., 1994-97, Mass. Gen. Hosp., 1997-99, Dana Farber/Ptnrs. Cancer Care Inc., 1999-, Mass. Taxpayers Found., 2000—, North Shore Med. Ctr., 2001—; hon. trustee Mass. Gen. Hosp., 1999—; hon. trustee Akron Art Mus., 2004— Markle scholar, 1963-68. Fellow AAAS, Royal Coll. Surgeons Eng. (hon.), Am. Acad. Arts and Scis.; mem. NAS Inst. Medicine, Am. Heart Assn. (pres. 1977-78, Gold Heart award 1980), Am. Surg. Assn. (sec. 1979-84, pres. 1985-86), Am. Assn. Thoracic Surgery (v.p. 1987-88, pres. 1988-89), Am. Bd. Surgery (mem. bd. 1969-74, sr. mem. 1974-), Am. Bd. Thoracic Surgery (bd. dirs. 1984-90), ACS (regent 1982-91, chmn. bd. regents 1989-91, pres. 1992-93), Assn. Acad. Surgery (pres. 1970), Soc. Univ. Surgeons (sec. 1967-70, pres. 1972-73), New Eng. Surg. Soc. (Distinguished Svc. award 2002), New Eng. Cardiovasc. Soc. (pres. 1972-73), Mass. Heart Assn. (pres. 1972-74, Paul Dudley White Cardiac award 1981). Home: 330 Beacon St Apt C66 Boston MA 02116-1190 Office: Mass Gen Hosp BUL 3 Boston MA 02114-2696 Office Phone: 617-726-2050. E-mail: wgausten@partners.org.

AUSTER, NANCY EILEEN ROSS, economics professor; b. NYC, Aug. 19, 1926; d. Norman L. and Edith Cornelia (Jacobson) Ross; m. Donald Auster, Aug. 18, 1946; children: Carol J., Ellen R. AB, Barnard Coll., 1948; MBA, Ind. U., 1954. Rsch. assoc. The Conf. Bd., NYC, 1948-51; editor publs. Bur. Bus. Rsch. Ind. U., Bloomington, 1954-56; lectr. St. Lawrence U., Canton, NY, 1962-66; from asst. prof. to prof. SUNY, Canton, 1966-82, disting. svc. prof. econs., 1982-91, disting. svc. prof. econs. emeritus, 1991—. Pres. univ. faculty senate SUNY, 1973-75; mem. chancellor's adv. com. disting. tchg. prof. SUNY, 1983-86, chair, 1986-87. Author: (with Donald Auster) Men Who Enter Nursing: A Sociological Analysis, 1970; contbr. articles to profl. jours. Chair adv. coun. St. Lawrence County CETA, Canton, 1977-82. Recipient Professions Excellence award N.Y. State/United Univ. Professions, 1991; USPHS grantee, 1966-70. Unitarian-Universalist. Avocations: running, skiing, birding, quilting. Home: 21 Craig Dr Canton NY 13617-1211

AUSTER, PAUL, writer; b. Newark, Feb. 3, 1947; s. Samuel and Queenie (Bogat) A.; m. Lydia Davis, Oct. 6, 1974 (div. 1979); 1 child, Daniel; m. Siri Hustvedt, June 16, 1981; 1 child, Sophie. BA, Columbia U., 1969, MA, 1970. Lectr. Princeton (N.J.) U., 1986-90. Author: (poetry) Unearth, 1974, Wall Writing, 1976, Fragments From Cold, 1977, Facing the Music, 1980, Disappearances: Selected Poems, 1988, Collected Poems, 2004, (non-fiction) White Spaces, 1980, The Invention of Solitude, 1982, The Art of Hunger, 1982, expanded edit., 1992, Why Write?, 1996, Translations, 1997, Hand to Mouth, 1997, The Red Notebook, 2002; author: (with Sam Messer) The Story of My Typewriter, 2002; author: Collected Prose, 2005, (fiction) City of Glass, 1985, Ghosts, 1986, The Locked Room, 1986, In the Country of Last Things, 1987, Moon Palace, 1989, The Music of Chance, 1990, Leviathan, 1992, Mr. Vertigo, 1994, Timbuktu, 1999, The Book of Illusions, 2002, Oracle Night, 2003, Auggie Wren's Christmas Story, 2004, The Brooklyn Follies, 2006, Travels in the Scriptorium, 2007, (films) Smoke, 1995 (Ind. Spirit award, 1996), Blue in the Face, 1995, Lulu on the Bridge, 1998, The Inner Life of Martin Frost, 2007; editor: The Random House Book of Twentieth-Century French Poetry, 1982, I Thought My Father was God and Other True Tales from NPR's National Story Project, 2001, Samuel Beckett: The Grove Centenary Edition, 2006. Decorated commandeur de l'Ordre des Arts et des lettres (France), Prix Médicis Etranger; recipient Morton Davwon Zabel award, Am. Acad. Arts & Letters, Asturias prize for lit., 2006; fellow, NEA, 1979, 1985. Mem. PEN, Am. Acad. Arts and Letters. Office: care Carol Mann Agy 55 5th Ave New York NY 10003-4301

AUSTERMANN, CHRISTOPHER BRENT, language educator; b. Rolla, Mo., Nov. 5, 1971; s. Charles Ross and Dorothy Karen (Matlock) Austermann. BS summa cum laude in Mgmt. Info. Sys., Maryville U., 1994. Tchr. English and Internat. Studies Shiunji Bd. Edn., Japan, 1994—2003; liaison Sister City Relationship, 1998—, St. James, Mo., 1998—; translator Cultural Liaison Nagano Olympics, 1998—; translator, cultural liaison World Cup Soccer, Nigata, Japan, 2002, Tokyo, 2002. Counselor AM. Field Svc., U.S., 1989-94, Japan, 1994—. Mem. Japan Assn. Lang. Tchrs. (publicity chair 1997-98). Home: 285-122 Choomchonprachavives 3 surn3 Soi Watbua Khwan Northaburi 11000 Thailand also: 1626 N Humboldt Blvd Apt 3w Chicago IL 60647-5020 E-mail: newdeai2003@yahoo.com.

AUSTILL, ALLEN, dean emeritus; b. Newton, Mass., June 22, 1927; s. William E. and Anna (Pifer) A.; m. Joan Mildred Sellery, June 4, 1950; children: Randolph Allen, Christopher Scott, Lara Anne. BA, U. Chgo., 1948, MA, 1951; LHD (hon.), New Sch. U., 1987. Research asso. Council State Govts., Chgo., 1951-52; mem. faculty, dir. admissions and placement St. Johns Coll., 1953-55; dir. student housing U. Chgo., 1955-57; tchr., dean students SUNY-Stony Brook, 1957-61; cons. Ford Found., Middle East, Amman, Jordan, 1962; mem. faculty, asso. dean New Sch. Social Research, 1962-64, dean, 1964-79, v.p. acad. affairs and exec. dean, 1979-82, dean, 1982-87, chancellor, 1987-89. Cons. Chatham Coll., 2000, Corcoran Gallery Coll., 2003, Coll. for Creative Studies, 2006; cons. title I Higher Edn. Act, State N.Y.; mem. council academic fellows Shimer Coll., 1971-80; mem. N.Y. Regents Adv. Task Force for Adult Edn., 1972-77, chmn., 1976-77; chmn. bd. dirs. Harpers Mag. Found., 1988—; bd. dirs. Ednl. Mgmt. Network, 1985-95; chmn. vis. com. Am. Mus. Natural History, 1990. Author: (with others) Higher Education in the Forty-Eight States, 1952; Summary of State Legislation and Elections (with others), 1953. Pres. Friends of Cresskill Libr., 1969-71; mem. vis. com. continuing edn. Harvard U., 1977-83; mem. Boston Ctr. for Adult Edn., 1990—, chair bd. trustees, 1991-95; trustee New Eng. Coll. Fin., 2006, chair, bd. trustees, 2007-. With AUS, 1945—46. Home: 103 Belmont St Somerville MA 02143 Personal E-mail: aaustill@comcast.net.

AUSTIN, ANN SHEREE, lawyer; b. Tyler, Tex., Aug. 25, 1960; d. George Patrick and Mary Jean (Brookshire) A. BA cum laude, U. Houston, 1983; JD, South Tex. Coll., 1987. Bar: Tex. 1987, U.S. Dist. Ct. (no. dist.) Tex. 1988, U.S. Ct. Appeals (5th cir.) 1989, U.S. Dist. Ct. (we. dist.) Tex. 1990, U.S. Ct. Appeals (D.C. cir.) 1992, U.S. Supreme Ct. 1992, U.S. Dist. Ct. (ea. dist.) Tex. 1993. With First City Ops. Ctr., Houston, 1980-85; law clk. Lipstet, Singer, Hirsch & Wagner, Houston, 1985-86, Pizzitola, Hinton & Sussman, Houston, 1986-87; briefing atty. Hon. Hal M. Lattimore Ct. Appeals, 2d Jud. Dist., Ft. Worth, 1987-88; assoc. Cantey & Hanger, Ft. Worth and Dallas, 1988-93, Smith, Ralston & Russell, Dallas, 1993-94, Russell, Austin & Henschel, Dallas, 1994-95; pvt. practice Arlington, 1995-96; prin. Landau, Omahana & Kopka, Ltd., Dallas, 1996-97; asst. city atty. City of Dallas, 1997—2002; atty. Law Offices of W. Blake Hyde, 2002—. Tchr. Project Outreach State Bar of Tex., 1992. Author: Personnel Rules, Park & Recreation Department, City Dallas, 2000; co-author Annual Meeting of Invited Attorneys, Construction Law, 1992; chpt. editor: Cases and Materials on Civil Procedure, 1987. Mem. Ft. Worth Hist. Preservation Soc., com. mem., 1992; fundraiser Prevention of Child Abuse in Am., 1988—, Women's Haven. Mem. Tex. Young Lawyers Assn. (jud. rev. com. 1990, women in the profession com., profl. ethics and grievance awareness com. 1992-94), Dallas Bar Assn. (jud. com. 1992-94, ethics com. 1999-2001, cmty. involvement com., employment law sect. CLE com. 1999-2000), Dallas Assn. Young Lawyers, Dallas Women's Bar Assn., Ft. Worth Tarrant County Young Lawyers Assn. (treas. 1989-90, dir. 1989, co-chair Teen Ctr., co-chair Adopt-A-Sch. program, tchr. Constl. Rights, 5th grade class, chair CLE program), Tarrant County Women's Bar Assn., Am. Inns. of Ct., Garland Walker Inn; vol. Texas Mock Trial Competition. Methodist. Avocations: walking, reading, sky diving. Office: Law Offices of W Blake Hyde Ste 490/LB11 1301 E Collins Blvd Richardson TX 75081 Office Phone: 214-570-6296. E-mail: aaustin@stpaultravelers.com.

AUSTIN, ARTHUR DONALD, II, lawyer, educator; b. Staunton, Va., Dec. 2, 1932; s. George Milnes and Mae (Eichner) A.; m. Irene Clara Wittenberg, June 12, 1960; 1 son, Brian Carl. BS in Commerce, U. Va., 1958; JD, Tulane U., 1963. Bar: Va. 1964, D.C. 1970. Asst. prof. Coll. of William and Mary, Williamsburg, Va., 1963-64, Bowling Green State U., Ohio, 1964-66; asst. prof. law Cleve. State U., 1966-68; prof. law Case Western Res. U., Cleve., 1968-70, 72-78, Edgar A. Hahn prof. jurisprudence, 1978—. Atty. Dept. Justice, Washington, 1970-71 Author: Antitrust: Law, Economics, Policy, 1976, Complex Litigation Confronts the Jury System, 1984, The Empire Strikes Back: Outsiders and the Struggle Over Legal Education, 1998; contbr. articles to law revs. Served with U.S. Army, 1952-54. Decorated Bronze Star medal with V, Purple Heart. Home: 1174 Stony Hill Rd Hinckley OH 44233-9538 Office: 11075 East Blvd Cleveland OH 44106-5409 Office Phone: 216-368-3289.

AUSTIN, CATHERINE DEADY, retired school librarian, musician; b. San Antonio, Tex., Dec. 22, 1944; d. William Robert and Beatrice Butland Deady; m. David Willard Austin, Sept. 1, 1967; children: Michelle Lea, Kimberly Austin Wanke(dec.) , Candace Austin Schoenert(dec.). BA, SW Tex. State U., San Marcos, 1982; MEd, Our Lady of Lake U., San Antonio, 1989; MusB in Organ Performance, U. Tex., San Antonio. Cert. secondary edn. English and biology tchr. Tex., 1982, learning resource specialist Tex., 1989, elem. edn. tchr. Tex., 1998. English and sci. tchr. East Ctrl. Ind. Sch. Dist., San Antonio, 1982—89, sch. libr., 1989—99, San Antonio Ind. Sch. Dist., 1999—2003; music min. St. Stephen's Episc. Ch., San Antonio, 2001—07, Holy Cross, St. Stephen's Episc, Ch., San Antonio, 2006—. Mem.: Am. Guild Organists. Episcopalian. Avocations: music, reading, tennis, volleyball. Office: Holy Cross St Stephen's Episc Ch 3726 S New Braunfels San Antonio TX 78223 Office Phone: 210-534-5400. Office Fax: 210-534-9161. Personal E-mail: austincat@aol.com. Business E-Mail: ccpim@sbcglobal.net.

AUSTIN, CHRISTOPHER, neurologist, researcher; b. Balt., Md., Sept. 23, 1960; s. Perry and Sally Austin; m. Judy Roy, May 10, 1986; children: Ashley, Genevieve, Shelley. AB, Princeton U., NJ, 1982; MD, Harvard Med. Sch., Boston, 1986. Bd. cert. neurologist Am. Bd. Psychiatry and Neurology, 1992. Intern medicine Mass. Gen. Hosp., Boston, 1986—87, resident and clin. fellow in neurology, 1987—90, chief resident in neurology, 1990—91; rsch. fellow in genetics Harvard Med. Sch., 1991—96, 1991—96; sr. rsch. fellow Merck Rsch. Labs., West Point, Pa., 1996—2002, dir., genomic neuroscience, 1999—2002; sr. advisor to the dir. for translational rsch. NIH, Nat. Human Genome Rsch. Inst., Bethesda, Md., 2002—; dir., chem. genomics ctr. NIH, 2004—. Assoc. editor Ann. Rev. of Medicine, Palo Alto, Calif., 2001—. Recipient Molecular Librs. Roadmap Initiative Dirs. award, NIH, 2005, Trans-NIH Mouse Transcriptome Project Dirs. award, 2005, Merit award, Nat. Human Genome Rsch. Inst., 2004. Mem.: Sigma Xi. Achievements include research in design and implementation of research programs to translate the Human Genome Project into benefits for human health; initiation of Mouse Knockout Project to produce knockout mice for all genes; discovery of multiple new genes involved in human disease; Discovery of the role of the Notch gene in vertebrate neurogenesis. Avocation: opera performance. Office: Nat Human Genome Rsch Inst National Institutes of Health 31/4B09 Bethesda MD 20892 Home Phone: 301-424-2062; Office Phone: 301-496-0844. Office Fax: 301-402-0837. Business E-Mail: austinc@mail.nih.gov.

AUSTIN, CLAUDE LIDELL, retired surgeon; b. Winona, Miss., Jan. 4, 1919; s. Luther Barksdale Austin and Cora Claudine Carter; m. Elizabeth Hightower, Sept. 2, 1944 (dec. Mar. 1990); children: Larry, Richard; m. Merry Cobb Lowry, Feb. 1, 1991. BA, U. Miss., 1940, BS, 1944; MD, Jefferson Med. Sch., 1946. Pvt. practice, Hattiesburg, Miss., 1947—91; ret., 1992. Pres. med. staff Hattiesburg Hosp., 1969—80; established vol. med. office and ongoing med. care Home of Grace, 1997—. Pres. Belle Fontaine Beach Assn., Ocean Springs, Miss., 1995; bd. dirs. Rotary Club, Hattiesburg, 1947. Fellow: Internat. Coll. Surgeons; mem.: AMA, Miss. State Med. Assn. Republican. Methodist. Avocation: deep sea fishing. Office: Home of Grace 14200 Jericho Rd Ocean Springs MS 39565 Home: 2311 Sunset Dr Hattiesburg MS 39402-2732

AUSTIN, DANFORTH WHITLEY, media executive; s. Whitley and Mary Frances (Danforth) Austin; m. Gail Ellen Davenport, Sept. 2, 1967; children: Stephen D., Richard D. BS, U. Kans., 1968. Staff reporter The Wall St. Jour., Dallas, Detroit, 1970—76, spl. writer NYC, 1976—78, news editor, 1978, bur. chief Pitts., 1978—83, from asst. to deputy nat. editor NYC, 1984—86, spl. reports editor, 1986—87, v.p. circulation, 1992—95, v.p., gen. mgr., 1995—2002; dir. corp. rels. Dow Jones and Co. Inc., NYC, 1987—89; dir. circulation Wall St. Jour., Barron's, Princeton, NJ, 1989-95; v.p. Dow Jones & Co. Inc., 2002—06. Vice chmn. Ottaway Newpapers Inc. (subsidiary Dow Jones & Co.), Campbell Hall, NY, 2002—03; chmn., CEO Ottaway Newpapers Inc., Campbell Hall, NY, 2003—06; dir. Voice of Am., Washington, 2006—. Trustee William Allen White Found., U. Kans., Lawrence, 1996—; sr. warden St. Peter's Episcopal Ch., Brentwood, Pa., 1981; lay reader Episcopal Diocese of Pitts., 1981—83, Diocese of Newark, 2001—; vestryman St. George's Episcopal Ch., Maplewood, NJ, 1985—88; bd. dirs. Episcopal Ch. Found., NYC, 2002—; bd. dir. NY Newspaper Assn., 2000—02, Am. Press Inst., Reston, Va., 2005—06. Sgt. US Army, 1968—70, Vietnam. Decorated Bronze Star, Air medal. Mem.: Soc. Profl. Journalists, Kappa Sigma. Episcopalian. Home: 51 Joanna Way Short Hills NJ 07078-3206 Office Phone: 202-203-4500. Personal E-mail: dwaustin@att.net.

AUSTIN, DANIEL WILLIAM, lawyer; b. Springfield, Ill., Feb. 24, 1949; s. Daniel D. and Ruth A. (Ahrenkiel) A.; m. Lois Ann Austin, June 12, 1971; 1 child, Elizabeth Ann. BA, Millikin U., Decatur, Ill., 1971; JD, Washington U., St. Louis, 1974. Bar: Ill. 1974, US Dist. Ct. (cen. dist.) Ill. 1979, US Ct. Appeals (7th cir.) 1980, US Supreme Ct. 1980, US Tax Ct. 1986. Assoc. Miley & Meyer, Taylorville, Ill., 1974-78; ptnr. Miley, Meyer & Austin, Taylorville, 1978-81; prin. Meyer, Austin & Romano P.C., Taylorville, 1981—. Pres. United Fund, Taylorville, 1980, Christian County YMCA, Taylorville, 1983-85, St. Vincent Meml. Hosp. Found., 1998-05, Christian County Crimestoppers, 2004-05; trustee St. Vincent Meml. Hosp., 2007-, Lincoln Land C.C., 2007—. Named one of Outstanding Young Men Am., 1985, Outstanding Citizen of City of Taylorville, 1993. Mem. ABA, Ill. Bar Assn., Christian County Bar Assn., Order of Barristers, Sangamo Club, Millikin U. Alumni Assn. (pres. 2006-07). Democrat. Presbyterian. Avocations: golf, photography. Home: 14 Westhaven Ct Taylorville IL 62568-9064 Office: Meyer Austin & Romano PC 210 S Washington St Taylorville IL 62568-2245 Home Phone: 217-824-4110; Office Phone: 217-824-4931.

AUSTIN, GRANT WILLIAM, real estate appraiser; b. Toronto, July 15, 1954; m. Joanne Austin; 1 child, Kelly Rae. BA summa cum laude, York U., 1983; MS, U. St. Thomas, 2003. Cert. gen. appraiser Fla. Pres. Am. Valuation, Inc., Ft. Lauderdale, Fla., 1998—. Author: Calculator Skills for the HP 19B, 1995, Property Owner's Guide to Condemnation, 1998. Mem.: Royal Instn. Chartered Surveyors, Assn. Eminent Domain Profls. (v.p., dir. 1994—95), Mkt. Rsch. Soc., Appraisal Inst. (chair pub. rels. com. 1995—97), Lambda Alpha Internat. (pres. 1997—99). Avocations: golf, tennis. Office Phone: 954-349-9725. Personal E-mail: amervalu@bellsouth.net.

AUSTIN, H(ARRY) GREGORY, lawyer; b. NYC, Mar. 18, 1936; s. Harry Gregory and Pauline (Moore) Austin; m. Deanna Ruth Anderson, Nov. 28, 1970; children: Sabrina Elizabeth, Harry Gregory III, Anne Catherine. BE, Yale U., 1957, postgrad., 1958; JD, U. Mich., 1961; LLD (hon.), Lincoln U., 1976. Bar: Colo. 1961, U.S. Supreme Ct. 1974. Assoc. Holland & Hart, Denver, 1962—73, ptnr., 1977—2001, of counsel, 2002—; gen. counsel SBA, Washington, 1973—75; solicitor, gen. counsel U.S. Dept. Interior, Washington, 1975—77; dir. Rocky Mountain Pub. Broadcasting Network, 2004—. Trustee Colo. Legal Aid Found., Denver, 1984—91, chmn., 1988—91; mem. adv. com. Colo. Sec. of State, 1996—; bd. dirs. Children's Hosp., Denver, 1985—97, Denver Police Found., 2004—. 1st lt. USAR, 1957—64. Fellow: Am. Bar Found.; mem.: Denver Bar Assn., Colo. Bar Assn. (chmn. bus. entities subsect. bus. law sect. 1987—89, vice chmn. bus. law sect. 1989—91, chmn. 1991—93, chmn. partnership laws com. 1993—), Am. Law Inst., Metro Denver C. of C. (bd. dirs., sec. 1995—97). Republican. Office: Holland & Hart LLP 555 17th St Ste 3200 Denver CO 80202-3979 Business E-Mail: gaustin@hollandhart.com.

AUSTIN, JACOB (JACK AUSTIN), Canadian government official; b. Calgary, Alta., Can., Mar. 2, 1932; s. Morris and Clara Edith (Chetner) A.; m. Natalie Veiner Freeman, Apr. 2, 1978; children: Edith Clare, Sharon Jill, Barbara Joan. BA, LLB, U. B.C.; LLM, Harvard U.; postgrad., U. Calif., Berkeley; ScD in Social Sci., U. East Asia. Bar: B.C. 1958, Yukon 1966. Chief of staff to prime min., 1974-75; dep. min. energy, mines and resources, 1970-74; mem. Senate, 1975—2007; leader of the govt. in the Senate, 2003—06; min. of state, 1981-82; min. of state for social devel., 1982-84. Mem. Vancouver Club. Liberal. Jewish. Office: The Senate 267 EB Ottawa ON Canada K1A 0A4

AUSTIN, JESSE HINNANT, III, lawyer; b. Jacksonville, NC, Feb. 12, 1954; s. Jesse Hinnant and Helen (Canady) A.; m. Deborah Pitman, Oct. 16, 1982; children: Emily Katherine, Anne Elizabeth. BS, U. N.C., 1976; JD with distinction, Emory U., 1980, MBA, 1980. Bar: Ga. 1980, U.S. Dist. Ct. (no. dist.) Ga. 1980, U.S. Dist. Ct. (mid. dist.) Ga. 1983, U.S. Ct. Appeals (4th, 5th and 11th cirs.) 1983, U.S. Dist. Ct. (no. dist.) Tex. 1989. Ptnr. Powell, Goldstein, Frazer & Murphy, Atlanta, 1980—94, Paul, Hastings, Janofsky & Walker LLP, Atlanta, 1994—, head bankruptcy practice group. Mem. ABA (litigation and business law sect., bankruptcy com., subcom. second creditors and chpt. 11), Am. Bankruptcy Inst., Ga. State Bar Assn. (litigation and bankruptcy sect.), Order of Coif, Order of Barristers, Phi Beta Kappa, Phi Eta Sigma, Beta Gamma Sigma, Beta Alpha Psi. Office: Paul Hastings Janofsky & Walker LLP 600 Peachtree St NE Ste 2400 Atlanta GA 30308-2222 Office Phone: 404-815-2208. Office Fax: 404-815-2424. Business E-Mail: jessaustin@paulhastings.com.

AUSTIN, JOHN D., corporate financial executive; CPA. Acct. Deloitte & Touche LLP; asst. controller Gen. Med. Corp., 1991—95; corp. controller Performance Food Group, 1995—98, corp. treas., 1998—2001, sec., 2000—01, v.p., 2001—03, sr. v.p., CFO, 2003—. Office: Performance Food Group PO Box 29269 Richmond VA 23242-0269*

AUSTIN, JOHN DAVID, retired financial executive; b. Memphis, Jan. 16, 1936; s. Thomas L. and Vela M. (Davis) Austin; m. Dorothy Clemans, Dec. 31, 1959 (div.); children: Laura Jan, David John; m. Marilyn C. Brewster, Nov. 2, 1985; 1 child, Christopher Brewster. BBA, Ga. State U., 1961. Acct. Price Waterhouse & Co., Atlanta, 1961—64, sr. tax acct. Miami, 1964—67; audit mgr. N.C. Nat. Bank Corp., Greensboro, 1968, v.p., gen. auditor Charlotte, 1969—73; sr. v.p., dir. corp. planning 1st Nat. Bank Mobile, Ala., 1973—74; sr. v.p. Southeast Nat. Bank. Pa., Malvern, 1974—75, exec. v.p., 1975—83, acting pres., CEO, 1978—80; sr. v.p. Va. Fed. Savs. and Loan, Richmond, 1984, exec. v.p., 1985, pres., also bd. dirs., 1986—88; exec. v.p. and CEO, also bd. dirs. Citizens Fed. Savs. & Loan, Salisbury, NC, 1988—90; self employed Marietta, Ga., 1990—91; v.p., CFO Atlanta Cutlery Corp, Conyers, Ga., 1991—96, COO, 1993—96, ret. Former pres. United Arts Coun. of Rowan; former bd. dirs. Chester County Mental Health/Mental Retardation Bd., The Chester Group, Del. County Econ. Devel. Com., Del. County Cmty. Coll. Found., St. John's Hosp. With US Army, 1957—59. Home: 1303 Spring Gate Cir Woodstock GA 30189-5489

AUSTIN, JOHN DELONG, retired judge; b. Cambridge, NY, May 31, 1935; s. John DeLong and Mabel Cowles (Bascom) A.; m. Marcia Kay Behan, Aug. 15, 1969 (dec.); children: John DeLong, Susan Behan. AB, Dartmouth Coll., Hanover, NH, 1957; postgrad., U. Minn., Mpls., 1959; JD, Albany Law Sch., NY, 1969. Bar: N.Y. 1970. Editl. dir. Glens Falls (N.Y.) Times, 1960-66; sole practice Glens Falls, 1970-79; law asst. Warren County Judge and Surrogate, 1975-79, N.Y. State Supreme Ct., 1980-84; judge Warren County Family Ct., NY, 1984-99, Warren County Ct. and Surrogate's Ct., 1999—2003; ret. Instr. Adirondack Comm. Coll., Glens Falls. Editor New Eng. Hist. and Geneal. Register, 1970-73; contbr. hist. and geneal. articles to various periodicals. Councilman Town of Queensbury, N.Y., 1969-71, supr., 1972-74; budget officer Warren County, N.Y., 1974; mem. N.Y. State Local Govt. Records Adv. Coun.; historian Warren County NY, 2007—. With U.S. Army, 1958-60. Recipient Adminstrv. Law prize Albany Law Sch., 1969. Fellow Am. Soc. Genealogists; mem. N.Y. State Bar Assn., Warren County Bar Assn., Mohican Grange, Elks. Republican. Personal E-mail: jaqby@adelphia.net.

AUSTIN, JOHN H., health care administrator; MD, Univ. Calif., San Francisco, 1970; MPH, Harvard Univ., 1972. Cert. internal medicine. COO HealthAmerica, Nashville, 1982—87; exec. v.p. Health Plan Am., 1987—92; dir. Coventry Health Care, 1988—, chmn. bd., 1995—2004; chmn., CEO Arcadian Mgmt. Svcs., 1997—; pres. profl. svcs. divsn. Unihealth, 1997—; health care cons., 1992-94; dir. QuadraMed Corp., 1995-98. Fax: 801-493-0752.

AUSTIN, JOHN H.M., radiologist; b. Boston, 1939; MD, Yale U., 1965. Cert. Diagnostic Radiology. Prof., radiology Columbia U. Coll. Physicians and Surgeons, 1973—; resident, radiology UCSF Med. Ctr., San Francisco, 1966—68, fellowship, radiology, 1968—70; radiologist N.Y.-Presbyn. Hosp., Columbia U. Med. Ctr., NYC, 1973—. Former pres. Fleischner Soc. Office: NY Presbyn Hosp Dept Radiology 622 W 168th St MHB 3-202C New York NY 10032-3784

AUSTIN, JOHN NORMAN, classics educator; b. Anshun, China, May 20, 1937; s. John Alfred and Lillian Maud (Reeks) A. BA, U. Toronto, 1958; MA, U. Calif.-Berkeley, 1959, PhD, 1965. Vis. lectr. Yale U., New Haven, 1971; asst. prof., then assoc. prof. UCLA, 1966-76; Aurelio prof. Greek Boston U., 1976-78; prof., chmn. dept. classics U. Mass., Amherst, 1978-80; prof. classics U. Ariz., Tucson, 1980—, acting dean humanities, 1987-88, head dept. classics, 1995—2000, prof. emeritus, 2000—. Vis. prof. Leeds U., 1999. Author: Archery at the Dark of the Moon, 1975, Meaning and Being in Myth, 1990, Helen of Troy and Her Shameless Phantom, 1994; editor: (with others) The Works of John Dryden, vol. III; sr. editor Calif. Studies Classical Antiquity, vols. VI and VII. Jr. fellow Ctr. for Hellenic Studies, 1968-69, J.S. Guggenheim Found. fellow, 1974-75 Episcopalian. Home: 3200 NE 36th St #1216 Fort Lauderdale FL 33308 Office Phone: 954-566-4883. Personal E-mail: normana764@aol.com.

AUSTIN, JOHNTA, musician; Signed to RCA, 1994—95, So So Def Recordings, Atlanta, 2005—, singer, songwriter, 2003—. Co-author: (songs) Sweet Lady, 1998, Get Gone, 1999, Miss You, 2002, Be Without You, 2005 (Grammy award for Best R&B Song, 2007), It's Like That, 2005, Shake It Off, 2005, We Belong Together, 2005 (Grammy award, Best R&B Song, 2006); performer Lil More Love, 2005, (albums) Ocean Drive, 2006.

AUSTIN, LINDA S., psychiatrist; b. 1951; m. Marshall Austin (div.); children: Stephanie, Matt; m. John W. Hallett. At, Stanford U.; BA, Duke U., 1973; MD, Duke U. Sch. of Medicine, 1976. Resident in psychiatry Duke U.; clin. instr. psychiatry Georgetown U., Washington; pvt. practice Chevy Chase, Md.; staff Med. U. S.C., 1986—89, asst. prof. psychiatry, 1989—99, assoc. dean pub. edn., 1996, prof. psychiatry, 1999—2000; staff Ea. Maine Med. Ctr. Heritage Psychiat. Assn., Bangor, Maine, 2000—. Dir. Obsessive-Compulsive Disorder program Med. U. S.C., 1989, mem. Hurricane Hugo response team, 89; featured in Depression: The Storm Within Am. Psychiat. Soc., 1990; host What's on Your Mind Nat. Pub. Radio, 1990—; TV appearances. Author: (books) What's Holding You Back? Eight Critical Choices for Women's Success, 1999, Heart of the Matter: How to Find Love. How to Make it Work., 2003; editor: Responding to Disaster: A Mental Health Clinician's Guide, 1989. Fellow child psychiatry, Georgetown U. Address: Heritage Psychiat Assn Ea Maine Med Ctr 2016 Wappoo Dr Charleston SC 29412 Office Phone: 843-795-5858. Personal E-mail: lindaaustinmd@aol.com.

AUSTIN, LOLA HOUSTON, psychologist; b. San Antonio, Dec. 27, 1939; d. Albert and Sarah Leola Houston; m. Craig L. Austin, July 4, 1972; children: Madie Grabda, Polly Toro, Julia Austin Bingamon, Carrie Austin Young. BA in Edn., North Tex. State U., 1966; MA in Edn., U. Incarnate Word, 1973; PhD in Clin. Psychology, Fielding Inst., 1987; postgrad. study in neuropsychol. evaluation, Santa Barbara, Calif., 2000. Elem. sch. tchr. Edgewood Ind. Sch. Dist., San Antonio Ind. Sch. Dist., Northside Ind. Sch. Dist., San Antonio, 1960—75; reading specialist Northside Ind. Sch. Dist., San Antonio, 1971—76; owner, dir. D & R Reading Clinic, San Antonio, 1976—2005; psychologist San Antonio, 1997; neuropsychol. evaluator Child Protective Svcs., San Antonio, 2000—. Co-chmn. fair King William Hist. Orgn., San Antonio, co-chair food booths. Mem.: APA, Nat. Acad. Neuropsychology, Delta Kappa Gamma (charter mem. Iota Beta chpt.). Office: McCullough Ctr for Mental Health Ste 101 2515 McCullough San Antonio TX 78212 Office Phone: 210-736-1762.

AUSTIN, PAMELA KAY, voice educator; b. Kirbyville, Tex., Aug. 23, 1956; d. John Thomas and Florene Deloris Morris; children: Jonathan Steele, Ledah LeeAnne. MusB in Edn., Lamar U., 1991, MusM in Vocal Performance, 1993. Cert. Provisional Music All Levels Tex. Asst. choral dir. Nederland (Tex.) HS, 1993—94; choral dir. Port Neches-Groves HS, Tex., 1994—98; music tchr. Oak Forest Elem., Vidor, Tex., 1998—2000, Tyrrell Elem., Port Arthur, Tex., 2000—02; choral dir. Meml. HS 9th Gr. Campus, Port Arthur, 2002—04; asst. choral dir. Sam Rayburn HS, Pasadena, Tex., 2004—. Organist First United Meth. Ch., Port Neches, 2004—06. Recipient NATS Intern, Nat. Assn. Tchrs. of Singing, 1995; Grad. scholarship, Tex. Music Educators Assn., 2006. Office: Sam Rayburn HS 2121 Cherrybrook Ln Pasadena TX 77502 Office Phone: 713-477-3601 1538. Personal E-mail: pam_austin@sbcglobal.net. Business E-Mail: pgoza@pasadenaisd.org.

AUSTIN, PHILIP, research scientist; b. Pitts., Jan. 5, 1957; s. Martin and Jacqueline Austin; children: Jade, Rachel. BA in History, Widener U., 1977, BS in Math., 1977; MS in Astronomy, U. Tex., 2002, MS in Physics, 2002, phD in Theoretical Astrophysics, 2005; degree (hon.), Oxford U., Eng., 1973, Seria Coll., Italy, 1976. With Zayre Corp., 1977—89, Sams Stores/Walmart Corp., 1989—94; scientist Fla., 2002—; prof. astronomy U. Fla. Pres., CEO Austin Finl. Group. Writer: Am. Scientist, 1993—2001; co-author: Astron. Jour., 2000. Named to Empire Who's Who in Profl. Honors, 2005; recipient Rice medal honors, N.Y.C., Manchester medal in Sci. honors, 2005. Mem.: ACLU, Am. Scientists, Union League, Widener Alumni Club, Space Telescope Team, Univ. Club, Mensa Soc., Sigma Xi. Democrat. Jewish. Avocations: collecting rare old books, collecting and restoring old cars. Mailing: 3829 Nimblewill Ct Port Saint Lucie FL 34952-3151

AUSTIN, PHILIP EDWARD, economics professor, former academic administrator; b. Fargo, ND, 1942; s. William and Angelyn A. Austin; children: Patrick William, Phillip James. BS, N.D. State U., 1964, MS, 1966; MA, Mich. State U., 1968, PhD, 1969; D (hon.), Autonomous U. Guadalajara, Mex., N.D. State U., U. Ala. Economist U.S. Office of Mgmt. and Budget, Washington, 1971-74; dep. asst. sec. HEW, Washington, 1974-77, acting asst. sec., 1977; dir. doctoral program in edn. policy George Washington U., Washington, 1977-78; v.p. acad. affairs, prof. econs. and fin. Bernard Baruch Coll., NYC, 1978-84; pres., prof. econs. Colo. State U., Fort Collins, 1984-89; chancellor U. Ala. Sys., Tuscaloosa, 1989-96; pres. U. Conn., Storrs, 1996—2007, prof. econs., 2007—. With US Army, 1969—71. Decorated Bronze Star. Office Phone: 860-486-2337. Business E-Mail: philip.austin@uconn.edu.

AUSTIN, ROBERT CLARKE, naval officer; b. Cleve., Sept. 5, 1931; s. Clarke Albert and Margaret Jane (Richardson) A.; m. Joyce Ann Bisese, Apr. 22, 1957; children— Susan Lynn, James Holden, Robert Clarke, Cecelia Ann. BS, U.S. Naval Acad., 1954; MS in Physics, Naval Postgrad. Sch., 1963. Enlisted U.S. Navy, 1948, commd. ensign, 1954, advanced through grades to rear adm., 1980; commdg. officer USS Finback, 1968-72; comdr. Submarine Devel. Group Two, 1974-76; commdg. officer Naval Submarine Sch., 1976-78; chief of staff submarine force U.S. Atlantic Fleet, 1979-80; dep. dir. for internat. negotiations for Plans and Policy Directorate, Joint Chiefs of Staff, Pentagon, Washington, 1981-82; chief naval tech. tng., 1982-86; supt. Naval Postgrad. Sch., 1986-89; ret. USN, 1989; pres. Austin Assocs., Inc., Alexandria, Va., 1989-97. Decorated Def. Superior Service Medal, Legion of Merit with 4 gold stars, Meritorious Service medal, others. Mem. Sigma Xi. Episcopalian. E-mail: rcaustinva@aol.com.

AUSTIN, ROBERT EUGENE, JR., lawyer; b. Jacksonville, Fla., Oct. 10, 1937; s. Robert Eugene and Leta Fitch A.; children: Robert Eugene, George Harry Talley; m. Carolyn Rhea Songer BA, Davidson Coll., 1959; JD, U. Fla., 1964. Bar: Fla. 1965, D.C. 1983, U.S. Supreme Ct. 1970; cert. in civil trial law Nat. Bd. Trial Advocacy. Pvt. practice law, 1965—. Asst. state atty., 1972; mem. Jud. Nominating Commn. and Grievance Com. 5th Dist. Fla.; gov. Fla. Bar, 1983; trustee U. Fla. Law Ctr.; mem. com. on std. jury instns. Fla. Supreme Ct Chmn. Lake Dist. Boy Scouts Am.; asst. dean Leesburg Deanery Diocese Cen. Fla.; trustee Fla. House, Washington, U. Fla. Law Ctr., 1983—, chmn., 1988-90 Named one of The Best Lawyers in Am., Leading Fla. Lawyers. Mem. Am. Law Inst., Lake County Bar Assn., Roscoe Pound Am. Trial Found., Kappa Alpha, Phi Delta Phi Democrat. Episcopalian. Home: PO Box 490200 Leesburg FL 34749-0200 Office: 1330 Citizens Blvd Ste 401 Leesburg FL 34748-3942 Office Phone: 352-782-1020. E-mail: reajr@robertaustinlaw.com.

AUSTIN, ROBERTA JONES, elementary school educator; b. Clearwater, Fla., July 28, 1930; d. Wallace Theodore and Eloise (Knight) Jones; m. Ned Payne Austin, Oct. 18, 1952; children: David, Robin, Samuel, Frances, Genevieve, Laura. BS in Pub. Sch. Music, Queens Coll., Charlotte, NC, 1952; postgrad. Sch. Edn., U. Colo., 1962-64; MA in Adminstrn. and Supervision, Appalachian State U., 1981. Cert. elem. and music tchr., sch. adminstr., N.C. Tchr. music grades 7 and 8 Denver Pub. Schs., 1961-62, tchr. grade 6, 1970-71; tchr. music grades 1 through 6 Adams County Sch. Dist. 12, Northglenn, Colo., 1962-63, elem. tchr., 1963-70; tchr. Playhouse Presch., LA, 1972; elem. tchr. Watauga County Schs., Boone, N.C., 1973-97; retired, 1997; home sch. dir., tchr., 1998-99. Chairperson curriculum com. Adams County Sch. Dist. 12, 1965-70; chairperson/liaison calendar com. Watauga County Schs., 1975-80, instr. writing workshop for tchrs., 1982, 86, 90, 92; dir. after-sch. program and cmty. sch. Hardin Pk. Sch., Boone, 1980-85. Editor: (compilation of children's writings) Out of Our Children's Minds, 1967, (compilation of tchr.'s writings) In the Shadow of Howard's Knob, 1990. Com. woman Dem. Precinct, Denver, 1968-71, pres., Boone, N.C., 1999—2003; vol. coord. Summer Youth Employment Program, Denver, 1969; active Boone chpt. N.C. Ctr. for Internat. Understanding, 1993—, Blue Ridge Cmty. Theatre, 1979—; tutor, coord. ESL program High Country Amigos, Boone, 2000-2004; treas. Boone Unitarian Universalist Fellowship, 2000-2002, v.p., 2002-2003, pres., 2003-2004, choir dir., 2000—; pres. Parents, Family, and Friends of Lesbians and Gays of Boone, 2001-2005. Recipient trip to Russia, named N.C. Tchr. of the World, Children's Mus. About the World, Raleigh, N.C., 1993. Mem. NEA, N.C. Edn. Assn. (faculty rep. 1973—81), Internat. Friendship Link. Avocations: music, drama, reading, writing. Home: 1561 Winklers Creek Rd Boone NC 28607-8904

AUSTIN, SAM M., physicist, educator; b. Columbus, Wis., June 6, 1933; s. A. Wright and Mildred G. (Reinhard) A.; m. Mary E. Herb, Aug. 15, 1959; children: Laura Gail, Sara Kay. BS in Physics, U. Wis., 1955, MS, 1957, PhD, 1960. Rsch. assoc. U. Wis., Madison, 1960; NSF postdoctoral fellow Oxford U., Eng., 1960-61; asst. prof. Stanford U., Calif., 1961-65; assoc. prof. physics Mich. State U., East Lansing, 1965-69, prof., 1969-90, univ. disting. prof., 1990-2000, univ. disting. prof. emeritus, 2000—, chmn. dept., 1980-83, acting dean Coll. Natural Sci., 1994, assoc. dir. Cyclotron Lab., 1976-79, rsch. dir., 1983-85, co-dir., 1985-89, dir., 1989-92. Guest Niels Bohr Inst., 1970; guest prof. U. Munich, 1972-73; sci. collaborator Saclay and Lab. Rene Bernas, 1979-80; vis. scientist Triumf-U. B.C., 1993-94; invited prof. U. Paris, Orsay, 1996; mem. grant selection com. sub-atomic physics, NSERC (Can.), 1996-99; mem. com. nuc. physics NRC, 1996-99; mem. steering com. Nuc. Physics Summer Sch.; mem. internat. adv. com. and exec. com. NSF Joint Inst. Nuc. Astrophysics, 2003- Author, editor: The Two Body Force in Nuclei, 1972, The (p,n) Reaction and Nucleon-Nucleon Force, 1980; editor: Phys. Rev. C., 1988—2002, Virtual Jour. Nuc. Astrophysics, 2003—; editor: (assoc.) Atomic Data and Nuc. Data Tables, 1990—; contbr. over 125 pubs. to profl. jours. Fellow NSF, 1960-61, Alfred P. Sloan Found., 1963-66; recipient Mich. Assn. of Governing Bds. Disting. Prof., 1992 Fellow AAAS (chair nominating com.), Am. Phys. Soc. (vice chmn. nuc. physics divsn. 1981-82, chmn. 1982-83, exec. com. 1983-84, 86-89, coun. 1986-89, coun. exec. com. 1987-88, panel on pub. affairs 1996-98); mem. APS, Sigma Xi (Sr. rsch. award 1977). Achievements include research in nuclear physics, nuclear astrophysics and nitrogen fixation. Home: 1201 Woodwind Trl Haslett MI 48840-8994 Office: Mich State U Nat Supercondr Cyclotron Lab East Lansing MI 48824 Business E-Mail: austin@nscl.msu.edu.

AUSTIN, SANDRA IKENBERRY, nursing educator, consultant; b. Lexington, Va., Dec. 22, 1941; d. William Peters and June Virginia (Blackwell) Ikenberry; m. Joseph M. Austin, Apr. 10, 1965; children: Joseph M. Jr., Susan C., Christopher M. BSN, U. Va., 1963; MSN, U. Calif., LA, 1967; EdD, U. Mass., 1997. RN, Mass. Pub. health nurse Dept. Health, Waynesboro, Va., 1963-64; instr. U. Va., Charlottesville, 1964-65; staff nurse Santa Monica (Calif.) Hosp., 1965-66; faculty nursing Boston U., 1968-69, Quinsigamond C.C., Worcester, Mass., 1969-70, Fitchburg (Mass.) State Coll., 1973-96; assoc. prof. nursing Framingham (Mass.) State Coll., 1997—; project dir., sr. health edn. cons. HealthCo Consulting Inc., Shrewsbury, Mass., 1996—. Mem. Shrewsbury Town Meeting, 1992—95; chair steering com. Framingham State Coll. Nursing Honor Soc., 1998, faculty counselor/advisor, 1999—, pres., 1999—; people to people ambassador program delegate China Healthcare Info., 2004. HBO and Co. Nurse scholar, 1995. Mem.: Assn. Critical Care Nurses, Nat. League Nursing (awards com. 1999—2001), Assn. Women's Health, Obstet. and Neonatal Nurses, Am. Ednl. Rsch. ASsn., Sigma Theta Tau (Epsilon Beta edn. chair 1993—95, Rho Phi chpt. pres. 2002—04, chpt. pres. 2005, faculty counselor 2000—, rsch. grant 1996), Pi Lambda Theta. Republican. Congregationalist. Avocations: computer multimedia production, reading, walking. Home: 100 Harrington Farms Way Shrewsbury MA 01545-4081 Office: Framingham State Coll Nursing Dept Framingham MA 01701 Office Phone: 508-626-4715.

AUSTIN, SKI, sports association executive; m. Teresa Austin; 1 child, Hayley. BFA in Directing and Theatrical Design, Baylor U. Mgr. Safaris, Inc.; mgr. spl. events NBA Entertainment, Secaucus, NJ, 1989—91, dir. spl. events, 1991—95, event dir. NBA Dream Team, 1992, v.p. spl. events., 1995—97, sr. v.p. events & attractions, 1997, exec. v.p. events & attractions. Achievements include creation of NBA Jam Session. Office: NBA Entertainment 450 Harmon Meadow Blvd Secaucus NJ 07094 Home: 29 Sherwood Rd Tenafly NJ 07670-2734*

AUSTIN, STUART, lawyer; BS, Cornell U., Ithaca, NY, 1988; JD, SUNY, Buffalo, 1993. Bar: NY 1993, NJ 1993. Dep. bur. chief, atty. Legal Aid Soc. Nassau County, Hempstead, NY, 1994—2007; atty. Law Offices of Stuart Austin, Garden City, NY, 2007—. Adj. prof. SUNY Law Sch., Buffalo, 2007. Mem.: Nat. Assn. Criminal Def. Lawyers. Office: Law Offices of Stuart Austin 595 Stewart Ave Ste 700 Garden City NY 11530 Home Phone: 516-897-3696; Office Phone: 516-317-2767. Office Fax: 516-706-3190. Personal E-mail: repugnantverdict@aol.com.

AUSTIN, TERRY LEE, director, conductor; b. Evansville, Ind., Apr. 1, 1952; s. Nettie Brown Austin; m. Tracia Everton, June 27, 1992; children: Joshua Adams, Seth Thomas. MusB, Ind. U., Bloomington, 1974; MA, U. Hawaii, Honolulu, 1978; PhD, U. Wis., Madison, 1984. Band dir. Southmont Jr.-Sr. H.S., Crawfordsville, Ind., 1974—76, Orange H.S., 1978—81, U. Mo., St. Louis, 1984—86, Va. Commonwealth U., Richmond, 1986—. Bd. dirs. John Philip Sousa Found., 1996. Recipient Award of Excellence, Va. Commonwealth U. Sch. of Arts, 2005. Mem.: Nat. Assn. for Music Edn. (bd. dirs. so. divsn. 2000—02), Va. Music Educators Assn. (pres. 2000—02), Nat. Band Assn. (Citation of Excellence 1997, 1998, 2005), Coll. Band Dirs. Nat. Assn., Am. Bandmasters Assn. (bd. dirs. 2007—). Baptist. Avocations: travel, bicycling, theater. Office: Virginia Commonwealth Univ 922 Park Ave Richmond VA 23284-2004 Office Phone: 804-828-1660.

AUSTIN, WANDA MURRY, systems engineer; b. NYC, Sept. 08; d. Murry Pompey and Helen Lewis; m. Wade Austin Jr.; children: Wade, Wendell. MS in Sys. Engring., U. Pitts., 1977; PhD in Sys. Engring., U. So. Calif., 1988. Engr. Rockwell Internat., Anaheim, Calif., 1977-79, Aerospace Corp., El Segundo, Calif., 1979—. Contbr. chpt. to book: Quantitative Simulation, 1991. Recipient Outstanding Achievement award Women in Aerospace, 1996, King Spirit of the Dream award Space and Missile Sys. Ctr., 1999. Fellow AIAA; mem. Soc. Women Engrs. (sr., award 1996). Office: Aerospace Corp 15049 Conference Ctr Dr Chantilly VA 20151

AUSTON, DAVID HENRY, former academic administrator, electrical engineer, educator; b. Toronto, Ont., Can., Nov. 14, 1940; arrived in U.S., 1963; BS, U. Toronto, 1962, MS, 1963; PhD, U. Calif., Berkeley, 1969. Rsch. physicist GM, Santa Barbara, Calif., 1963—66; tech. staff AT&T Bell Labs., Murray Hill, NJ, 1969—82, head dept., 1982—87; former prof. Columbia U., NYC, chmn. elec. engring. dept., 1990, dean sch. engring. and applied sci., 1991—94; provost Rice U., Houston, 1994—99; pres. Case Western Res. U., Cleve., 1999—2002, Kavli Found. and The Kavli Inst., Oxnard, Calif. Author 1 book; contbr. scientific papers. Fellow: IEEE (Quantum Elecs. award 1990, Morris E. Leeds award 1991), Am. Phys. Soc., Am. Acad. Arts and Scis., Optical Soc. Am. (R.W. Wood prize 1985); mem.: NAE, Nat. Acad. Scis. Achievements include patents in field.

AUSUBEL, JESSE HUNTLEY, environmental researcher; b. NYC, Sept. 27, 1951; s. Herman and Anne (Weisinger) A. BA, Harvard U., 1974; M in Internat. Affairs and MBA, Columbia U., 1977. Fellow NAS, Washington, 1977-79; rsch. scholar Internat. Inst. for Applied Systems Analysis, Laxenburg, Austria, 1979-81; staff officer, Bd. on Atmospheric Sciences and Climate NRC, Washington, 1981-83; dir. programs NAE, Washington, 1983-88; dir. studies Carnegie Commn. on Sci., Tech., Govt., NYC, 1989—93; fellow in sci. and pub. policy Rockefeller U., NYC, 1989—93, dir., Program for the Human Environ., sr. rsch. assoc., 1994—; prog. dir. Alfred P. Sloan Found., 1994—. Main organizer for the first UN World Climate Conf., Geneva, 1979, led the Climate Task of the Resources and Environ. Program, Internat. Inst. for Apllied Systems Analysis, 1979-81; mem. panel on global warming NAS, 1989; directorate Sci., Tech. and Internat. Affairs adv. bd. NSF, Washington, 1989; mem. U.S. Com. for Internat. Inst. for Applied Systems Analysis, Am. Acad. Arts and Scis., Cambridge, 1990; univ. fellow of resources for the future; guest investigator Woods Hole Oceanographic Instn., 1991-, adj. faculty mem. Editor: Climate Impact Assessment, 1985, Cities and Their Vital Systems, 1988, Technology and Environment, 1989; mem. editorial bd. Climatic Change, Tech. Forecasting and Social Change, Jour. Indsl. Ecology; co-author (paper) Dematerialization, 1989; published first paper on the concept of "decarbonization" of the energy system, 1991; published in the Proceedings of the NAS, Nature, American Scientist and The Sciences; contbr. articles to profl. publs. Columbia U. Internat. fellow, 1976. Mem. AAAS, Am. Meteol. Soc., N.Y. Acad. Scis., Coun. Fgn. Relations (com. on studies), Sigma Xi, Beta Gamma Sigma. Office: Program for the Human Environment Rockefeller U 1230 York Ave Box 234 New York NY 10021-6399 Address: Alfred P Sloan Found 630 Fifth Ave Ste 2550 New York NY 10111 Office Phone: 212-327-7917, 212-649-1649. Office Fax: 212-327-7519, 212-757-5117.*

AUTELITANO, PHILIP M., marketing professional, consultant, writer; b. Schenectady, NY, Jan. 23, 1973; s. Philip Sr. M and Patricia M Autelitano; m. Tamara Leigh Robinson, Feb. 9, 1999; children: Ezekiel, Bruno. Cert. Guerrilla Mktg. Coach Guerrilla Mktg. Internat., 2004. Pres. P. M. Autelitano & Associates, Inc., Delray Beach, Fla., 1992—; ceo Mojo Beverage Co., Boca Raton, Fla., 1999—2001; pub./editor-in-chief Beachcomber Mag., Delray Beach, Fla., 2001—. Author: (book) 250 Ways to Save Money, Increase Sales and Maximize Your Profits!, Simplified Marketing Management, (e-book) 36 Ways to Promote Your Book Online-.for Free!. Philanthropic and fundraising activities Mr. Holland's Opus Found., Caring Ho. Project, et al, Delray Beach, Fla., 2001—; pro bono mktg. and mgmt. consulting to minority entrepreneurs and start-ups Delray Beach, Fla., 2001—; philanthropic and fundraising activities Make-A-Wish Found., Albany, NY, 1995—96, Ronald McDonald Ho., 1995—96. Democrat-Npl. Roman Catholic. Achievements include Health & Fitness, 1998-1999, Credited with developing and introducing the first branded electrolyte-enhanced bottled water to the world. Avocations: writing, reading, classical guitar, travel. Office: P M Autelitano & Assoc Inc PO Box 7203 Delray Beach FL 33482-7203 Office Phone: 561-276-0931. E-mail: phil@urguru.com.

AUTEN, DAVID CHARLES, lawyer; b. Phila., Apr. 4, 1938; s. Charles Raymond and Emily Lillian (Dickel) A.; m. Suzanne Crozier Plowman, Feb. 1, 1969; children: Anne Crozier, Meredith Smedley. BA, U. Pa., 1960, JD, 1963. Bar: Pa. 1963. Ptnr. Reed Smith LLP (and predecessors), Phila., 1963—2004. Author articles in field. V.p. N.E. Cmty. Mental Health Ctr., 1971-72; vice chmn. alumni ann. giving U. Pa., 1975-77, 81-82, chmn., 1982-84, trustee, 1977-80, 83-88; pres. Gen. Alumni Soc., 1977-80; chmn. Benjamin Franklin Assocs., 1975-77, 81-82, bd. overseers Sch. Arts and Scis., 1983-96; trustee U. Pa. Health Sys., 1995—, Pa. Medicine, 2002-, Springside Sch., 1985-88, v.p., 1987-88; pres. Soc. of Coll., 1975-77; v.p. Assn. Reps. for Educated Action, 1971-79; bd. mgrs. Presbyn.-U. Pa. Med. Ctr., 1980—, vice chmn., 1983-85, 88-95, chmn., 2002—; trustee Presbyn. Found. for Phila., 1986—, vice chm., 1996-98, chmn., 1998-2005; bd. mgrs. Phila. City Inst., 1981—, treas., 1990-99; bd. dirs. Kearsley Home, 1974-2002, treas., 1990-96, chmn., 1996-2002, 2005—; bd. mgrs. St. Peter's Sch., 1975-88, pres., 1978-79; bd. dirs. Greater Phila. Internat. Network, 1989-94, Com. of Seventy, 1990-2003, Courtland Found., Del Pres Health Care Inc., New Courtland Elder Svs., chmn., 1998-2005; mem. econ. devel. com. Greater Phila. First Corp.; rector's warden Christ Ch., Phila., 1996-2001. Mem. ABA, Pa. Bar Assn. (vice chmn. real property sect. 1985-87, chmn. 1987-88), Am. Land Title Assn., Phila. Bar Assn. (vice chmn. young lawyers sect. 1971-72), Juristic Soc. (pres.), Am. Coll. Real Estate Lawyers, Interfrat. Alumni Coun. U. Pa. (pres. 1970-74), French Am. C. of C. (bd. dirs. 1989—), Phi Beta Kappa, Theta Xi (pres. 1974-76, chmn. found. 1977-86), Rittenhouse Club (pres. 1979-82), Union League (bd. dirs., v.p., pres. 1993-94, chmn. Lincoln Found. 1996-2002), Fourth St. Club (bd. dirs. 1998-2000, 2005—), Phila. Club. Episcopalian (vestryman). Home: 120 Delancey St Philadelphia PA 19106-4303 Office: Reed Smith LLP 2500 One Liberty Pl Philadelphia PA 19103

AUTEN, DONALD R., lawyer; b. Phila., July 27, 1946; BA cum laude, U. Pa., 1968, JD cum laude, 1971. Bar: Pa. 1972, Mass. 1998, US Tax Ct., US Dist. Ct. Ea. Dist. Pa., Supreme Ct. Pa., Supreme Ct. Mass. Judicial clk. to Hon. Thomas A. Masterson US Dist. Ct. Ea. Dist. Pa., 1971—72; assoc. Duane Morris LLP, Phila., 1972—77, ptnr., 1978—, chair firm tax dept., 1994—99, co-chair firm health law dept., 1999—, mem. partners bd. Fellow Am. Coll. Tax Counsel; mem. ABA (chair affiliated and related corporations com. 1983-85, mem. taxation sect.), Pa. Bar Assn. (mem. tax law sect.), Phila. Bar Assn. (bd. governors 1995-96, mem. tax sect., vice chair 1993-94, chair 1995-96, mem. bus. law sect. healthcare subcom.), Am. Health Lawyers Assn., Pa. Soc. Healthcare Attorneys. Office: Duane Morris LLP 30 South 17th St Philadelphia PA 19103-4196 Office Phone: 215-979-1969. Office Fax: 215-979-1020. Business E-Mail: auten@duanemorris.com.

AUTH, ROBERT RALPH, art educator; b. Bloomington, Ill., Oct. 27, 1926; s. Phillip C. and Frances E. A. BFA, Ill. Wesleyan U., 1953; MFA, Wash. State U., 1963. Art tchr., Burley, Idaho, 1959, Boise (Idaho) Ind. Sch. Dist., 1960-81; art supr. Boise Ind. Sch. Dist., Boise, ID, 1981-87. Author: ID State Humanities Curriculum Guide, 1985; creator historic prints, paintings, sculptures; exhibited works in more than 25 one-man shows and more than 50 group shows including Smithsonian, 1983-84, 98, 99, internat. tour, 2000. Cmty. svc. adv. Boise's Jr. League; mem. Allied Arts Coun.; bd. dirs., Boise Gallery of Art, Boise Edn. Assn., Alliance for Arts in Edn.; calligrapher Am. Air Mail Soc., 1985—. Recipient Allied Arts Coun. Artist of the Year award, 1972, Nat. Art Edn. award, 1979, Idaho Hist. Soc. Hon. Curator of Military Hist. award, 1983, Gov. of Idaho medal for Excellence in the Arts, 1988, The Idaho Statesman's Distinguished Citizen award, 1988, Phi Delta Kappa Friend of Edn. award, 1989. Roman Catholic. Avocations: hunting, fishing. Home: PO Box 91 Yellow Pine ID 83677-0091 Office Phone: 208-323-0535.

AUTHELET, KEITH A., information technology executive; Sr. dir., bus. process and tech. mgmt. Lotus Services Group; v.p. & chief info. officer Gilbane Bldg. Co., Providence. Bd. dir. WhyData. Named one of top 10 CIOs, Info. Week mag., 2001. Office: VP & CIO Gilbane Bldg Co Seven Jackson Walkway Providence RI 02903 Business E-Mail: kauthelet@gilbaneco.com.

AUTHEMENT, RAY PAUL, college president; b. Chauvin, La., Nov. 19, 1928; s. Elias Lawrence and Elphia (Duplantis) A.; m. Barbara B. Braud, June 1, 1950; children: Kathleen Elizabeth, Julie Ann. BS, U. Southwestern La., 1950; MS, La. State U., 1952; PhD, 1956. Instr. La. State U., Baton Rouge, 1952-56; asso. prof. McNeese State Coll., Lake Charles, La., 1956-57, U. Southwestern La., 1957-59, prof. math., from, 1959, acad. v.p., 1966-73, pres., 1973—. Vis. prof. U. N.C., Chapel Hill, 1962-63 Mem. Downtown Devel. Com. Lafayette, 1972—; commr., mem. exec. com. Lafayette Econ. Devel. Authority, 1988—94; mem. La. Bicentennial Commn., 1973, Lafayette Bicentennial Commn., 1973, Econ. Devel. Com., Lafayette, 1973, Sch. Bd. Fatima Parish, Lafayette, 1963-65; bd. dirs. United Way, 1973, U. Southwestern La. Found., 1967, Gulf South Rsch. Inst., 1985-91; trustee Lafayette Gen. Hosp., 1981—; mem. bd. advisers John Gray Inst., 1982-91, St. Joseph Sem., 1967; mem. Commn. Colleges So. Assn. Colls., 1981-83; active Cajundome Commn., 1988—; bd. dirs. Lafayette Health Ventures, Inc., 1989—2000, 2007, Enterprise Ctr. of La., Inc., 1990—, Affiliated Blind of La., Inc., 1991—98, La. Partnership for Tech. and Innovation, 1989—, chmn., 1993; chmn. Acadiana Navigation Channel Task Force, 1990—; bd. dirs. Coun. for a Better La., 1992—, La. chpt. Leukemia and Lymphoma Soc., 2005. Named Outstanding Citizen of Acadiana Internat. Rels. Assn. Acadiana, 1991; recipient Lafayette Civic Cup award, 1991. Mem. AAAS, Lafayette C. of C. (dir. 1983—), Blue Key, Phi Kappa Phi, Kappa Mu Epsilon, Sigma Pi Sigma, Phi Kappa Theta. Roman Catholic. Home: PO Drawer 41008 Lafayette LA 70504 Office: U La at Lafayette PO Drawer 41008 Lafayette LA 70504 Office Phone: 337-482-6203. Business E-Mail: president@louisiana.edu.

AUTOR, ROBERT S., finance company executive; BS in Bus. & Computer Sci., SUNY. Past mgr. info. tech. and fin. svc. industry Price Waterhouse; mng. cons., gen. mgmt. consulting divsn. Towers Perrin, NY; sr. v.p., chief info. officer Nellie Mae, 1993—2000, COO Edn. Loan Svcs. Inc. (ELSI), 1994—96, COO loan origination ops., 1999—2000; v.p. SLM Corp. (Sallie Mae), 1999—2000, v.p. application devel., info. tech. divsn., 2000—02, exec. v.p. consumer ops., chief info. officer, 2002—. Past mem. bd. Reston's Children's Ctr., Va. Named one of Premier 100 IT Leaders, Computerworld, 2006. Office: Sallie Mae 12061 Bluemont Way Reston VA 20190*

AUTREY, WESLEY, Construction Worker; b. Pensacola, FL, 1956; s. Robert and Mary; children: Wesley Jr., Shuqui, Syshe. Mailman Postal Service; construction worker NYC. Veteran soldier USN. Named one of The World's Most Influential People, TIME Mag., 2007; recipient Bronze Medallion, NY Mayor Michael Bloomberg, 2007; grantee received 10,000$, Donald Trump, multiple prizes including 5,000$ GAP Gift Card, season tickets to the New Jersey Nets, a signed jersey from Jason Kidd, a brand new Jeep Patriot, The Ellen DeGeneres Show. Mem.: Laborers' Internat. Union of North Am. Achievements include achieving internat. recognition after he saved Cameron Hollopeter, a 19-year-old film student who had suffered a seizure and fallen onto the tracks from being struck by a New York City subway train on Jan 2nd, 2007; being interviewed for several nat. morning news programs, invited to be a guest by David Letterman, Charlie Rose and Ellen DeGeneres, among others; being the personal guest and salutation by President Bush during his 2007 State of the Union adrdess.*

AUTRY, ALAN, film company executive, mayor, actor, former professional football player; b. Shreveport, La., July 31, 1952; m. Kimberlee Autry; children: Lauren, Heather, Austin. BA, U. Pacific, 1975. Quarterback Green Bay Packers; founder & pres. Dirt Road Prodns.; CEO Autry Entertainment Group; mayor City of Fresno, Calif., 2001—. Mem. Advisory Council on Historic Preservation; mem. strengthening communities secretarial adv. com. U.S. Dept. Commerce; mem. adv. bd., ed. standing comm. U.S. Conf. Mayors; bd. dirs. League Calif. Cities; mem. authority bd. Fresno County Transp.; founding bd. mem. Operation Clean Air, Regional Jobs Initiative. Actor: (films) Remember My Name, 1978, North Dallas Forty, 1979, Popeye, 1980, Southern Comfort, 1981, Roadhouse 66, 1984, O.C. and Stiggs, 1985, Brewster's Millions, 1985, House, 1986, At Close Range, 1986, Amazing Grace and Chuck, 1987, World Gone Wild, 1988; writer, prodr., dir., actor (TV films) The Legend of Jake Kincaid, 2002; actor: (TV series) Best of the West, 1982, Cheers, 1983, The Dukes of Hazzard, 1984, Newhart, 1986, St. Elsewhere, 1986, In the Heat of the Night, 1988—93, Grace Under Fire, 1995—96. Office: 2600 Fresno St 2nd Fl Fresno CA 93721-3600 E-mail: mayor@fresno.gov.*

AUTRY, CAROLYN, artist, educator; b. Dubuque, Iowa, Dec. 12, 1940; d. William Tilden and Vela (Laseman) A.; m. Peter Elloian, May 27, 1966; 1 dau., Cybele Justine. BA, U. Iowa, 1963, MFA, 1965. Instr. art, art history Baldwin-Wallace Coll., Berea, Ohio, 1965-66; adj. assoc. prof. art history dept. Ctr. for Visual Arts U. Toledo, 1966-2001. Artist-in-residence Sch. Arts in France, Lacoste, 1984, Lacoste, 87, adj. instr. in printmaking, 87. Numerous exhbns. from 1966 to present including most recently 25th Ann. Nat. Print Exhbn., 2005, Artlink Contemporary Art Gallery, Ft. Wayne, Ind., Calif. Soc. Printmakers 91st Ann. Exhbn., San Francisco Bay Model Visitor Ctr., Sausalito, 2004, Soc. Am. Graphic Artists, Art Students League of NY, 2005, Print Club Albany Artist Mem. Show, Cooperstown (NY) Art Assn. Gallery, 2005, Sidney Larsen Gallery, Columbia Coll., Mo., 2006, Artlink 26th Ann. Nat. Print Exhbn., Fort Wayne, Ind., 2006, The Soc. Am. Graphic Artists, 2006, Hollar Soc. Gallery, Praha, Ceska Republicka, 2006, others; represented in permanent collections Libr. of Congress, Phila. Mus. Art, Worcester Art Mus., Mount Holyoke Coll., U. Colo., Bradley U., Calif. State U., San Diego, Ga. State U., U. S.D., U.N.D., U. Louisville, St. Lawrence U., U.Dallas, Hunterdon Art Ctr., Clinton, N.J., Fitchburg (Mass.) Mus., Duxbury (Mass.) Art Complex, Elvehjem Mus. Art U. Wis.-Madison, Inst. per la Cultura E L'Arte, Catania, Italy, Lakeview Mus. Arts and Scis., Peoria, Ill., Nat. Mus. Fine Arts, Hanoi. Recipient Boston Printmakers N.Am. Print Exhbn. award 1971, 79, 80, 81, 87, Pennell award Libr. Congress, 1971, 75, Phila. Print Club awards, 1972, 73, 77, 79, Wesleyan Coll. Internat. award of merit, 1980, Anne Steele Marsh award Hunterdon Art Ctr., Clinton, N.J., 1975, 1991, Bradley U. Nat. award, 1991, Friends of the Janet Turner Gallery Nat. Exhbn. award Chico State U., Calif., 1995, Exhbn. award 16th Nat. Print Exhbn., Artlink, 1996, Exhbn. award 17th Nat. Print Exhbn., 1997, Counterpoint, 2000, Nat. Exhbn. award The Hill Country Arts Found., 2000, Exhbn. award 5th Nat. Print Exhbn., Calif. State U., Chico, 2004, Exhbn. award, Hunterdon Art Ctr., 1991; Ford Found. grantee, 1961-63, Ohio Arts Coun. grantee, 1979, 90, Yale-Norfolk Summer Sch. Art and Music scholar, 1962. Mem.: The Print Club of Albany (Ledyard Cogswell Jr. Meml. prize 1995), Coll. Art Assn. Am., Calif. Soc. Printmakers, Soc. Am. Graphic Artists (Jo Miller award 1985, Phillip Monteith award 1986, George Sherman Purchase prize 2005), LA Printmakers Soc., Boston Printmakers (Louis Black award 1971, Ture Bewgtz award 1981), Phi Beta Kappa. Address: 26114 W River Rd Perrysburg OH 43551-9128 Personal E-mail: autello@aol.com.

AUTRY, HERMAN ALLEN, SR., lobbyist, writer, music executive; b. Wilmington, NC, Apr. 29, 1941; s. George Herman and Bessie Mae Autry; m. Deanna Wilson Autry, Nov. 30, 1963; 1 child, Herman Allen Jr. AA, Chowan U., Murfreesboro, NC, 1961; BA, Wake Forest U., Winston-Salem, NC, 1963, JD, 1966. Pension cons., Fla., 1966—80, NC, 1966—80; chmn. bd. Ameriserv, Inc., Ft. Lauderdale, Fla., 1980—94; prin., owner Horizon Energy, Inc., Ft. Lauderdale, 1988—2005; chmn. bd. TRIAM Cons., Inc., Margate, Fla., 1990—2006; co-founder Autry Music Inst., Inc., Margate, Fla., 1999—. Advisor Fla. Dept. Ins., Tallahassee, 1994—96; trustee Ft. Lauderdale C. of C., 1994—96; music pub. Bayview Prodns., Inc., Nashville, 1992—95. Author: Miracle in a Small Mountain Town; contbr. to various pubs. Leader Boy Scouts Am., Carteret County, NC, 1966—68; chmn. regional fin. George H. Bush Rep. Party, 1984—86; founder, CEO Broward 2000, Ft. Lauderdale, 1985—2003; chmn. county campaign U.S. Sen. Paula Hawkins Rep. Party, Ft. Lauderdale, 1986—88; chmn.visitors com., tchr. evangilism explosion First Bapt. Ch., Ft. Lauderdale, 1975—2006; chmn. bd. South Fla. Mus. Natural History, Dania, Fla., 2000—03; bd. dirs. Hope Pregnancy Ctr., Ft. Lauderdale, 1990—98, Mission of St. Francis Rehab. Ctr., Ft. Lauderdale, 1988—2000. Named Leading Rep. Fundraiser Broward County, Broward 2000 PAC, 2005. Mem.: Nat. Assn. Music Mdse. (assoc.), Tower Club Ft. Lauderdale (assoc.). Republican. So. Bapt. Avocations: writing, guitar, boating, scuba diving, snorkeling. Home: 6146 NW 53 Cir Coral Springs FL 33067 Office Phone: 954-568-1402. Personal E-mail: aautrysr@triamgroup.com.

AUTRY, LOLA MAE, music educator; d. William Marion Lineberry and Alice May Anderson-Lineberry; m. Ewart Arthur Autry, Feb. 21, 1941 (dec. Sept. 1981); children: Jerry Duane, Lanny Lemuel, Martha Lynn Autry Crawford stepchildren: Ewart Ronald, James Arthur. BS, U. Memphis, 1939. Profl. photographer Self-employed, Hickory Flat, Miss., 1963—, tchr. piano, organ, voice, stringed instruments, art, 1939—, author, journalist, 1947—, lectr., 1982—, artist, 1987—, musician, 1932—. Vol. missionary related to ch. and writing careers, 1982—; dir. choirs Pine Grove Bapt. Ch., Hickory Flat, 1982—2000; spkr. in field. Author (with E.A. Autry): (novel) The Turtle and the Oak (1st Pl. Fiction award Miss. Media Profls., 1992); author: (non-fiction) 52 Devotions with Original Songs for Primary Children; author: (with E.A. Autry) (non-fiction.) Bible Puppet Plays, (non-fiction) Don't Look Back Mama; author: Please God, I'm a City Girl. What Am I Doing In the Country?, 2004; oil painting, Little Girl with Yellow Daisy (First Pl. award Tupelo Women's Club and N.E. Miss. Art Assn., 2001); contbr. articles to mags. and jours. Nat. and internat. missions vol. So. Bapt. Conv., Richmond, Va., 1982—; vol.-tchg. and entertaining with music and slide programs, Bible study Nursing Homes, Ashland, Miss., 1981—. Named one of 4 Top Photographers in the State, Miss. Inst. Arts and Letters, 1992; recipient Statewide Ageless Hero award in field of creativity, Miss. Blue Cross and Blue Shield, 2003, several writing awards. Office Phone: 662-224-8518.

AUTRY, PHILIP EARL, music educator, musician; b. Humboldt, Tenn., Apr. 9, 1965; s. Max E. and Evelyn Mayo Autry. BS, David Lipscomb U., 1987; MA, Middle Tenn. State U., 1989; D. Musical Arts, U. Okla., 1996; Program Cert., Russian Piano Inst. of Internat. Fine Arts Inst., Moscow, 1998, Russian Piano Inst. of St. Petersburg Conservatory, 1999. Independent studio tchr. Pvt. Piano Studio, 1987—2002; asst. prof. music Angelo State U., San Angelo, Tex., 1996—2001; assoc. prof. music, chair dept. music Fisk U., Nashville; solo performer, orch. pianist Tenn. Discussion leader Nat. Conf. on Keyboard Pedagogy, Oak Brook, Ill., 2001, Group Piano Forum, Cin., 2004; panelist World Piano Pedagogy Conf., 2006; presenter in field. Contbr. articles to profl. jours., Hymnal Praise for the Lord, 1992. Mem.: Tenn. Music Tchrs. Assn. (pres. 2005—07), Music Tchrs. Nat. Assn. (South-Ctrl. Divsn. Competition chair 1995—2001), Phi Kappa Phi, Pi Kappa Lambda, Phi Mu Alpha Sinfonia. Office: 1000 17th Ave N Nashville TN 37208-3045 Office Phone: 615-329-8702. Business E-Mail: PAutry@fisk.edu.

AUTTONBERRY, SHERI E., lawyer; BA, La. Tech U., 1996; JD, Vanderbilt U. Law Sch., 1999. Bar: Ohio 1999. Assoc. Katz, Teller, Brant & Hild, Cin., dir., Fine Arts Fund. Mem. Vol. Lawyers for the Poor. Named one of Ohio's Rising Stars, Super Lawyers, 2006. Mem.: Cin. Bar Assn. (legal adv.), Class X, Cin. Acad. Leadership for Lawyers. Avocations: reading, gardening, sports. Office: Katz Teller Brant & Hild 255 E 5th St Ste 2400 Cincinnati OH 45202-4724 Office Phone: 513-721-4532. Office Fax: 513-762-0012.

AUWAERTER, PAUL GISBERT, physician, educator; b. East Patchogue, NY, Mar. 3, 1962; s. Gisbert Paul and JoAnn Elizabeth Auwaerter; m. Karen M. Manzo, May 23, 1992; children: Alec, Bennett. AB, Columbia U., 1984, MD, 1988; MBA, John Hopkins U. Sch. Profl. Studies in Bus. and Edn., Balt., 2003. Diplomate Am. Bd. Internal Medicine, Am. Bd. Infectious Diseases. Intern, infectious disease Johns Hopkins Hosp., Balt., 1988-89, resident, internal medicine, 1989-91, chief resident, medicine, 1991-92; fellow, infectious diseases Johns Hopkins U. Sch. Medicine, Balt., 1992-96, asst. prof., assoc. prof., medicine (gen. internal medicine and infectious diseases), chief med. officer, Point of Care-Info. Tech. Ctr., Lighthouse Point, dir., gen. internal medicine, Green Spring Station. Mng. editor John Hopkins Antibiotic Guide. Office: John Hopkins Greenspring Station 10753 Falls Rd Ste 325 Lutherville Timonium MD 21093 Office Phone: 410-583-2774. Office Fax: 410-583-2883. Business E-Mail: pauwaert@jhmi.edu.*

AUWERS, LINDA S., lawyer; Grad., Stanford U.; PhD, Brandeis U.; JD, U. Houston Law Ctr. Prof. history Temple U.; atty. Schlanger, Cook, Cohn, Mills & Grossberg; v.p., asst. gen. counsel Compaq Computer Corp., Houston, 1995—99, v.p., assoc. gen. counsel, sec., 1999—2001, v.p., dep. gen. counsel, sec., 2001—02; sr. v.p., gen. counsel, sec. ABM Indus., San Francisco, 2003—. Mem.: Am. Corp. Counsel Assn. (mem. corp. & securities law com.), Am. Soc. of Corp. Secretaries (mem. public co. affairs com.). Office: ABM Industries 160 Pacific Ave Ste 222 San Francisco CA 94111

AUWERS, STANLEY JOHN, motor carrier executive; b. Grand Rapids, Mich., Mar. 22, 1923; s. Joseph T. and Cornelia (Moelhoek) A.; m. Elizabeth Kruis, Apr. 6, 1946; children— Ellen (Mrs. William Northway), Stanley John, Thomas. Student, Calvin Coll., 1940-41; BBA, U. Mich., 1943. C.P.A., Mich. With Ernst & Ernst, Detroit, 1943-51; controller Interstate Motor Freight System, Grand Rapids, Mich., 1951-61, v.p., controller, 1961-65, v.p. finance, 1965-69, exec. v.p., 1969-72; also dir.; pres. Transam. Freight Lines, Detroit, 1973—. Chmn. cost com. Mich. Trucking Adv. Bd. to Mich. Pub. Service Commn., 1958-63; mem. citizens com. to study Mich. tax structure advisory Mich. Ho. Reps., 1958 Mem. Am. Motor Carriers Central Freight Assn. (gov. regular common carrier conf.), Mich. Motor Carriers Central Freight Assn. (v.p., gov.), Tax Execs. Inst., Am. Inst. C.P.A.s, Trucking Employers. Presbyterian. Home: 3099 Lakeshore Dr Douglas MI 49406 Office: 3684 28th St SE Grand Rapids MI 49512-1606 E-mail: sauwers@umich.edu.

AUYANG, GRACE CHAO, education educator, consultant; d. C.P. Chao and T.C. Chang; m. King Auyang, Aug. 4, 1974; children: Edward, Elizabeth. PhD, Temple U., Phila., 1978. Dept. chair U. Cin., 1994—2000, prof., 1999—. Cons. mgmt. and academic assessment U. Cin., 1994—. Editor: (textbook) Sociological Outlook (Diversity award, 1995); author: Writing, Editing, and Reviewing (Tchg. awards, 2005), articles to profl. jours. Mem. governing coun. Am. Women Studies Assn., Washington, 1995—97; bd. mem. Cin. Chinese Learning Assn., Cin., 1990—2000. Grantee, U. Cin., 1990, 1994, 1995, 1997, 2000, 2005, 2006. Mem.: AAUP, Am. Sociol. Assn. (sect. chair 1994—95), AAUW (assoc.). Protestant. Achievements include research in Global Culture and World Issues, Teaching Pedagogy, Science, Technology and Society, etc; Study Gender and Education Issues. Avocations: reading, writing, travel, painting, music. Office: Univ Cincinnati 9555 Plainfield Rd Cincinnati OH 45236 Office Phone: 513-745-5656. Business E-Mail: grace.auyang@uc.edu.

AVAKOFF, JOSEPH CARNEGIE, medical and law consultant; b. Fairbanks, Alaska, July 15, 1936; s. Harry B. and Margaret (Adams) Avakoff; m. Teddy I. Law, May 7, 1966; children: Caroline, Joe E., John. AA, U. Calif., Berkeley, 1956, AB, 1957; MD, U. Calif., San Francisco, 1961; JD, Santa Clara U., 1985. Bar: Calif. 1987; diplomate Am. Bd. Surgery, Am. Bd. Plastic Surgery. Physicist U.S. Naval Radiol. Def. Lab., San Francisco, 1957, 59; intern So. Pacific Gen. Hosp., San Francisco, 1961-62; resident in surgery Kaiser Found. Hosp., San Francisco, 1962-66; resident in plastic surgery U. Tex. Sch. Medicine, San Antonio, 1970-72; pvt. practice specializing in surgery Sacramento, 1966-70; pvt. practice specializing in plastic surgery Los Gatos and San Jose, Calif., 1972-94; cons. to med. and legal professions, 1994—. Clin. instr. Sch. Medicine U. Calif., Davis, 1967—70; chief dept. surgery Mission Oaks Hosp., Los Gatos, 1988—90; chief divsn. plastic surgery Good Samaritan Hosp., San Jose, 1988—91; expert med. reviewer Med. Bd. Calif., 1995—2001; spl. cons. Calif. Dept. Corps., 1997—2002; presenter numerous med. orgns. Contbr. articles to profl. jours. Mem. San Jose Adv. Commn. Health, 1975—82; bd. govs. San Jose YMCA, 1977—80. Mem.: AMA, Union Am. Physicians and Dentists, Santa Clara County Med. Assn., Calif. Med. Assn., Phi Beta Kappa, Phi Eta Sigma. Republican. Presbyterian. Avocations: music, photography, computer programming. Home: 6832 Rockview Ct San Jose CA 95120-5607

AVALOS, HECTOR IGNACIO, language educator; b. Nogales, Sonora, Mexico, Oct. 8, 1958; s. Magdalena Avalos Bernal and Ignacio Arizmendi; m. Cynthia Dee Schultz, May 8, 2000. PhD, Harvard U., 1991. Carolina minority postdoctoral fellow U. N.C., Chapel Hill, 1991—93; assoc. prof. Iowa State U., Ames, 1993—. Dir. U.S. Latino studies program Iowa State U., Ames. Author: (book) Illness and Health Care in the Ancient Near East: The Role of the Temple in Greece, Mesopotamia, and Israel. Exec. dir. sci. exam. of religion com. Coun. for Secular Humanism, Amherst, NY, 1997. Independent. Avocations: travel, music, debate. Home: 3604 Grand Ave Ames IA 50010 Office: Iowa State Univ 402 Catt Hall Ames IA Office Phone: 515-294-0051. Office Fax: 515-294-0780. E-mail: havalos@iastate.edu.

AVANT, GAYLE, political scientist, educator; b. Mercedes, Tex., Aug. 23, 1940; s. George Clarence and Winnie Lela (Bagley) Avant; m. Patricia Kay Coalson, Sept. 1, 1970; children: Samantha, Celia. BA, U. Tex., 1962; MA, U. N.C., 1965, PhD, 1969. Devel. officer AID/State Dept., Washington, 1966—68; asst. prof. Miami U., Oxford, Ohio, 1968—70; assoc. prof. polit. sci. Baylor U., Waco, Tex., 1970—. Vis. prof. polit. sci., sr. lectr. U. Ballarat, Australia, 1996—97. Editor: Foundations of Citizenship, 1990. State dir. Fellowship of Baptist Educators, 2005; dir. Baylor Washington Program, 1985—92; treas. Am.-Thai Found. Bd., 1993—; sec. treas. Coins for Tchrs., 2001—. Mem.: Internat. Assn. Christian Higher Edn., Am. Polit. Sci. Assn. Baptist, Tex. Coun. Social Studies, Nat. Coun. Social Studies, S.W. Social Sci. Assn.

AVANT, PATRICIA KAY, nursing educator; b. Dallas, Aug. 15, 1941; d. Lem Barrett and Georgia Evelyn Coalson; m. Gayle R. Avant, Sept. 6, 1963; children: Samantha Gay Foss, Celia Kay Drews. RN, Meth. Hosp., Dallas, 1962; BSN, Tex. Christian U., Ft. Worth, 1963; MSN, U. N.C., Chapel Hill, 1965; PhD, Tex. Woman's U., Denton, 1978. Chair family nursing U. Tex. Health Sci. Ctr., San Antonio, 2005—. Fellow Am. Acad. Nursing; mem. Royal Coll. Nursing (Australia), ANA (pres. Dist. 10 1983-84), Nat. League Nursing, (1st v.p. Tex. 1985-89), N.Am. Nursing Diagnosis Assn. (taxonomy chair 1994-98, pres. 2000-02). Democrat. Baptist. Home: 7601 Tallahassee Rd Waco TX 76712-3814 Office: U Tex Health Sci Ctr 7703 Floyd Curl Dr San Antonio TX 78229-3900 Office Phone: 210-567-5881. Business E-Mail: avantk@uthscsa.edu.

AVANT, ROBERT FRANK, retired physician; b. Chisholm, Minn., 1937; m. Betty Jensen, Dec. 28, 1962; children: Paul, Gregory, Todd. MD, U. Minn., 1963. Intern San Bernardino County Hosp., Calif., 1963-64; chief of family practice Glenwood Hills Hosp., Golden Valley, Minn., 1970—71, chief of staff, 1972; dir. family practice residency North Meml. Hosp., Mpls., 1973-77; asst. prof. dept. family practice and cmty. health U. Minn., 1973—77; chmn. dept. family medicine Mayo Clinic, Rochester, 1977—91, assoc. prof. family medicine, 1977—84; prof. family medicine Mayo Med. Sch., 1984—93; Sanders prof. primary care Mayo Clinic, 1986—93; chmn. dept. family medicine Mayo Clinic Jacksonville, Fla., 1991—93; dep. exec. dir. Am. Bd. Family Medicine, Lexington, Ky., 1991—97, exec. dir., 1998—2002, sr. exec., 2003—05, exec. dir. emeritus, 2005—. Capt. MC, USAF, 1964-66. E-mail: ravant@theabfm.org.

AVARY, ROGER ROBERTS (FRANK BRAUNER), film director, producer, writer; b. Flin Flon, Manitoba, Canada, Aug. 23, 1965; s. Edwin Roberts and Brigitte (Bruninghaus) A. Student, Art Ctr.Coll. Design, Pasadena, Calif., 1985—88. Writer D'Arcy, Masius, Benton & Bowles, LA, 1989-90, J. Walter Thompson, LA, 1990—. Writer: (film) 99 Days, 1991, (with Mario Puzo) The Lorch Team, 1992, Silent Hill, 2006; writer, dir. (film): Killing Zoe, 1994 (Yubari Internat. Film Festival Best Film award, 1994, Mystfest Best Film award, 1994, Mystfest Critics prize, 1994, Cannes Prix Tres Spl. Best Film award, 1994), True Romance, 1993; exec. prodr. (film): The Last Man, 1999; writer, prodr., dir. (film): The Worm Turns, 1993, The Rules of Attraction (screenplay), 2002, Glitterati, 2004; co-exec. prodr. (film): Boogie Boy, 1997; co-writer (film): Pulp Fiction, 1994 (L.A. Film Critics Assn. Best Screenplay award, 1995, N.Y. Film Critics Cir. Best Screenplay award, 1995, Boston Soc. Film Critics Best Screenplay award, 1995, Nat. Soc. Film Critics Best Screenplay award, 1995, Chgo. Soc. Film Critics Best Screenplay award, 1995, BAFTA Best Screenplay award, 1995, Acad. award best screenplay 1995), Hatchetman, 1995, (children's book) Marshall's Dreams, 1991, (music video) for the group The Go Go's song The Whole World Lost Its Head, 1994; writer, dir., prodr. (TV movie) Mr. Stitch, 1995, Odd Jobs, 1997; actor: Phantasm IV: Oblivion, 1998 Office: Creative Artists Agy Care Rob Paris 9830 Wilshire Blvd Beverly Hills CA 90212-1804

AVEDON, MARCIA J., diversified industrial products company and former pharmaceutical executive; b. 1961; BA summa cum laude in Psychology, U. N.C., 1983; MS in Indsl. and Orgnl. Psychology, George Washington U., 1987, PhD with hons. in Indsl. and Orgnl. Psychology, 1989; MS in Exec. Program, Rutgers U. Intern U.S. Army Civilian Ctr., 1984; assoc. cons., sr. cons., cons. Booz-Allen & Hamilton, Inc., 1985—90; program mgr. Anheuser-Busch Cos., Inc., 1990—92, sr. cons., 1992—93, mgr. corp. succession planning, 1993—94, dir. mgmt. and orgn. devel. Campbell Taggart Inc., 1994—95; dir. orgn. and leadership devel. Honeywell Internat., 1995—97, v.p. human resources and comms. Performance Polymers, 1997—2000, v.p. human resources and comms. Performance Polymers and Chems., 2000—01, v.p. corp. human resources, 2001—02; v.p. talent mgmt. and orgn. effectiveness Merck & Co., Inc., Whitehouse Station, NJ, 2002, sr. v.p. human resources, 2003—07; sr. v.p. human resources & comm. Ingersoll-Rand Co. Ltd., Montvale, NJ, 2007—. Adv. bd. Human ResourcesOfficer's Acad., mem. corp. leadership coun. Bd. dirs. Jersey Battered Women's Svcs., 2000—; mem. adv. bd. Masters in Human Resources U. S.C., 1998—; corp. sponsor Cornell Ctr. for Advanced Human Resource Studies, 2001—. Mem.: Pharm. Human Resources Assn., Healthcare Businesswomen's Assn., Am. Psychol. Assn., Human Resources Policy Assn. (mem. personnel roundtable), Soc. for Human Resources Mgmt., Soc. for Indsl. and Orgnl. Psychology. Office: Ingersoll-Rand Co Ltd PO Box 0445 155 Chestnut Ridge Rd Montvale NJ 07645*

AVELLA, JOSEPH RALPH, university professor; b. NYC, Nov. 13, 1942; s. Salvatore Ralph and Bianca (Artoni) A.; m. Elizabeth Theresa Eberhardt, Aug. 12, 1967 (dec. Aug. 2000); children: Edward Jay, James Joseph. BS in Chemistry, Rensselaer Poly. Inst., Troy, NY, 1964; MA, Cath. U. Am., Washington, 1992, PhD, 1995; MBA, Capella U., Washington, 2001. Mgr. Md. ops. Great Atlantic and Pacific Tea Co., Inc., 1978-83; program mgr. Honeywell Fed. Sys., Inc., McLean, Va., 1984-86, mgr. integration svcs., 1987-89; dep. dir. mobilization Office Sec. Def., Washington, 1990-92, dir. internat. programs, 1992-93; sr. fellow global strategy program Potomac Found., McLean, 1995-98; prof. and acad. dean Am. Mil. U., Manassas, Va., 1995-98; exec. v.p. Capella U., 1998—2001, prof. bus., 2001—. Seminar moderator US Naval War Coll., Newport, RI, 1989-91; sec. NATO Forces Com., Brussels, Belgium, 1992-94; cons. Masi Rsch. Cons., Inc., Boston, 1995-; pres. Delphic Consulting Inc., 1998; mem. faculty Touro U., 2004-. Contbr. articles to profl. jours. With USNR, 1964—95. Recipient Achievement award No. Va. Navy League, 1989, Cert. of Appreciation Sec. of Navy, 1986, 88, Award of Appreciation U.S. Naval Sea Cadet Corps, 1986. Mem. Assn. Naval Aviation (past chpt. sec.), Navy League US (former mem. bd. dirs.), Pi Sigma Alpha. Roman Catholic. Office: Capella Univ 225 S 6th St Fl 9 Minneapolis MN 55402 Home: 313 Pine Glen Way Englewood FL 34223 Office Phone: 941-460-0247. Personal E-mail: javella@aol.com.

AVENT, SHARON L. HOFFMAN, manufacturing company executive; b. St. Paul, Feb. 7, 1946; d. Ebba and Harold Hoffman; m. Terry Avent; 2 children. Student, Hamline U., St. Paul. With Smead Mfg. Co., Hastings, Minn., 1965—, pres., CEO, 1998—; acquired The Atlanta Group (now Smead-Europe), Hoogezand, Netherlands, 1998—. Bd. dirs. Hastings Public Sch. Found. Named Minn. World Trader of the Year, World Trade Week, Inc., 2002; recipient Spirit of Life honoree, City of Hope, 2003. Office: Smead Mfg Co 600 Smead Blvd Hastings MN 55033-2219

AVERA, STEPHEN R., food products company executive, lawyer; b. Tallahassee, Fla., Oct. 19, 1956; m. Anne Avera; children: Harrison, Leigh, Hunter. BA magna cum laude, U. Ala., 1978, JD, 1981. Bar: Ala. 1981, Army Ct. Mil. Rev. 1981, U.S. Ct. Mil. Appeals 1982, Fla. 1987, Ga. 1988. Assoc. gen. counsel labor rels. Flowers Foods, Inc. (formerly Flower Industries), Thomasville, Ga., 1986—92, gen. counsel, 1992—2002, sec., gen. counsel, 2002—04, sr. v.p., sec. gen. counsel, 2004—; v.p., gen. counsel Flowers Bakeries, 1998—2002. Capt. U.S. Army JAGC, 1981-86. Mem. ABA, Fla. Bar Assn., Ala. State Bar, State Bar Ga. Office: Flowers Foods Inc 1925 Flowers Cir Thomasville GA 31757-1137

AVERILL, BRUCE ALAN, chemistry professor; b. Bucyrus, Ohio, May 19, 1948; s. Kenneth L. Averill and Mildred (Reid) Krug; m. Patricia Ann Eldredge, Aug. 23, 1986; children: Lindsay Patricia, Alan Eldredge, Ryan Eldredge. BS, Mich. State U., 1969; PhD, MIT, 1973. Asst. prof. chemistry Mich. State U., East Lansing, 1976-81, assoc. prof. chemistry, 1981-82, U. Va., Charlottesville, 1982-88, prof. chemistry, 1988-94; prof. biochemistry U. of Amsterdam, 1994-2001; disting. univ. prof. chemistry U. Toledo, 2001—; Jefferson Sci. fellow U.S. Dept. State, 2004—05, William C. Foster fellow, 2006—. Mem. biophysics adv. panel NSF, Washington, 1985-88; mem. faculty forum for sci. rsch. U. Va., Charlottesville, 1984-88; group leader protein rsch. and coord. chemistry working parties Dutch Found. Chem. Rsch., 1995-2001, mem. exec. com. protein rsch. working party, 1996-99. Acquisitions editor ChemTracts-Inorganic Chemistry, 2002—; contbr. more than 140 articles to sci. jours. A.P. Sloan fellow, 1981-83; recipient creativity award NSF, 1991. Mem. AAAS, Am. Soc. Biochemistry and Molecular Biology, Am. Chem. Soc., Royal Soc. Chemistry, Soc. Biol. Inorganic Chemistry, Sigma Xi. Office: U Toledo Dept Chemistry 2801 W Bancroft Rd Toledo OH 43606-3390 Business E-Mail: baa@utoledo.edu.

AVERILL, ELLEN CORBETT, retired secondary education science educator, administrator; b. Milledgeville, Ga. d. Felton Conrad and Vivian Iris (Brookins) Corbett; m. George Edmund Averill, July 31, 1971; 1 child, John Conrad BS, U. Ga., 1966, MS, 1971; tchg. cert., Columbus Coll., 1979, EdS, 1994. Cert. master gardener Ala., 2006, Ga., 2006. Grad. tchg. asst. U. Ga., Athens, 1966—68; tchr. sci. Decatur City Schs., Ga., 1971—72; tchr. sci., chair dept. Kendrick H.S., Columbus, Ga., 1980—2004; ret., 2004. Rsch. asst. Caretta Rsch. Project, Savannah (Ga.) Sci. Mus., 1985, NEWMAST, Kennedy Space Ctr., 1986; rsch. assoc. Inhalation Toxicology Rsch. Inst., Albuquerque, summer, 1990; instr. sci. Gov.'s Honor Program Valdosta State Coll., summer, 1991, Woodrow Wilson Biotech. Inst., Princeton, N.J., 1993 Contbr. articles to newspapers, jours.; inventor The Wrap-All, 1992 Vol. Hope Harbour, 2004—; v.p. Green Glove Master Gardeners, 2007—. Mem. NSTA (program com., regional conf. 1993), Nat. Assn. Biology Tchrs. (Outstanding Biology Tchr. 1990-91), Ga. Sci. Tchrs. Assn. (dist. VI rep. 1988-90, secondary rep. 1990-91, pres.-elect 1991-92, pres. 1992-93, conf. coord. ann. conf. 1992, Dist. VI Sci. Tchr. of Yr. 1995), Coalition for Excellence in Sci. Edn. (orgnl. com. 1992-93), Ga. Sci. Tchrs. Edn. Found. (chair 1994-98), Valley Area Sch. Tchrs. (charter, pres.-elect 1996-97, pres. 1997-98), Muscogee Area Literacy Assn. (treas. 1992-93), Phi Delta Kappa (Tchr. of Yr. 1992, v.p. 2002-), Delta Kappa Gamma (treas. 2006—). Unitarian-Universalist. Avocations: art, gardening, radio. Home: 126 Waterway Dr Cataula GA 31804-4407 Personal E-mail: eaverill@mchsi.com.

AVERILL, JAMES REED, psychology professor; b. San Francisco, Nov. 29, 1935; s. Dupree Reed and Rosalie Averill. BA, San Jose U., 1959; PhD, UCLA, 1966. Psychologist U. Calif.-Berkeley, 1966-71; mem. faculty U. Mass., Amherst, 1971—, prof. psychology, 1976—. Served with U.S. Army, 1954-57. Fulbright fellow W. Germany, 1959-60 Mem. APA, Am. Psychol. Soc., Internat. Soc. for Rsch. on Emotion. Office: U Mass Dept Psychology Amherst MA 01003 Business E-Mail: averill@psych.umass.edu.

AVERSA, DOLORES SEJDA, educational administrator; b. Phila., Mar. 26, 1932; d. Martin Benjamin and Mary Elizabeth (Esposito) Sejda; m. Zefferino A. Aversa Jr., May 3, 1958; children: Dolores Elizabeth, Jeffrey Martin, Linda Maria. BA, Chestnut Hill Coll., 1953. Owner Personal Rep. & Pub. Rels., Phila., 1965-68; ednl. cons. Franklin Sch. Sci. and Arts, Phila., 1968-72; pres., owner, dir. Martin Sch. Bus., Inc., Phila., 1972—. File reader, cons. for ct. reporting and travel tng. Southwestern Pub. Co., 1990; mem. ednl. planning com. Ravenhill Acad., Phila., 1975-76. Active Phila. Mus. ARt, Phila. Drama Guild; mem. Met. Opera Guild, 2002; sec. Rep. Exec. Com., Phila.; mem. 8th Ward Rep. Exec. Com. Mem.: Lower Bucks County C. of C., Am. Soc. Travel Agts. (PAC chmn. 1997—, sch. divsn., nat. educators com., sec. Del. chpt., edn. chmn.), Hist. Soc. Pa., World Affairs Coun. Phila., Phila. Hist. Soc., Pa. Sch. Counselors Assn., Am. Bus. Law Assn., Pa. Bus. Edn. Assn., Nat. Bus. Edn. Assn., Andrea Doria Survivor Assn., Chestnut Hill Coll. Alumnae Assn. (sec. class '53), Phila. Orch., Am.-Italy Soc., Met. Opera Guild, Stone Harbor Golf Club (Rep. exec. com. 8th ward Phila.). Roman Catholic. Home: 2111 Locust St Philadelphia PA 19103-4802 Office: 2417 Welsh Rd Philadelphia PA 19114-2213 Personal E-mail: msb-aversa@erols.com.

AVERY, BRUCE EDWARD, lawyer; b. Boonville, NY, Aug. 16, 1949; s. Edward Cecil and Marian Alma (Pierce) A.; m. Margaret Calvert, June 21, 1969; children: Sarah, Prudence. BA in Sociology, Polit. Sci., Hobart Coll., 1971; JD, U. Louisville, 1976. Bar: Ky. 1976, U.S. Ct. Mil. Appeals 1977, U.S. Army Ct. Mil. Rev. 1984, U.S. Supreme Ct. 1984, Md. 1992, D.C., 1993, U.S. Ct. Vet. Appeals 1992, U.S. Dist. Ct. Md. 1993. Commd. capt. U.S. Army, 1976, advanced through grades to maj., 1983; rschr. U.S. Army Rsch. Inst., Ft. Knox, Ky., 1972-76, atty., 1976-77, U.S. Army, Camp Zama, Japan, 1977-80, U.S. Army Recruiting, Ft. Meade, Md., 1980-83, U.S. Army Claims Svc., Ft. Meade, 1984-87, U.S. Armed Forces Claims Svc., Seoul, Korea, 1987-89; chief claims V Corps, Frankfort, Germany, 1989-91; pvt. practice Rockville, Md., 1991—. Mem. Ft. Knox Bd. Edn., Ky., 1975-76. Mem. ABA, ATLA, FBA, D.C. Bar, Md. State Bar, Ky. Bar Assn. Office: 51 Monroe St Ste 701 Rockville MD 20850-2421 Office Phone: 301-762-7644. Business E-Mail: bea@averyuptonlaw.com.

AVERY, DONALD HILLS, metallurgist, educator; b. Hartford, Conn., May 7, 1937; s. Charles Raymond and Loma Ellinor (Mulholland) A.; m. Marianna Pinchot, Dec. 3, 1994; children: Jon Weymouth, Nathaniel Caleb, Jessica van Voast. Student, Loomis Inst., 1951-55; BS, MIT, 1959, ScD, 1962; MA, Brown U., 1969. Lic. profl. engr.; lic. pvt. dectective. Pres. Strathmore Research Co., Cambridge, Mass., 1961-69; dir. research Armor Flite Group, Rangely, Maine, 1973-83; pres. A.T.S. Cons. Engrs., 1980—; dir. A.P.C. Engrs., East Providence, RI, 1977-82; asst. prof. M.I.T., 1962-66, Brown U., 1966-69, asso. prof., 1969-74, prof. engring., 1974-97, prof. emeritus, 1997—. Vis. scholar, prof. U. Capetown, 1974, 76, 79, 82, 83; vis. fellow Yale U. Sch. Forestry, New Haven, 1995; vis. prof. Wharton Sch. U. Pa., 1999-01. Contbr. articles to profl. jours.; patentee in field. NSF fellow, 1959-62; Ford fellow, 1965; rsch. scholar Tanzania, 1976, 79; rsch. scholar Malawi, 1982, 83 Mem. AIME (Metall. Soc.), AAAS, AAU, AAW, WCS (MW chpt. chair), Am. Soc. Metals (past chmn. R.I., Howe medal 1965), Soc. Plastics Engrs., Soc. Automotive Engrs., Hist. Metall. Soc., History Sci. Soc., Soc. History Tech., Hope Club, Explorers Club, Athenaeum, Barrington Yacht Club, Kasungu Farmers. Home: 142 Toandos Rd Quilcene WA 98376-9687 Office: Brown U Div Engring Providence RI 02912-0001

AVERY, GORDON BENNETT, medical educator, neonatologist; b. Beirut, Dec. 10, 1931; s. Bennett Franklin and Margaret Anne (Scales) A.; m. Ruth Elizabeth Butler, June 12, 1954 (div.); children: Melody Anne, Wendy Jean, Heidi Elizabeth; m. Penny Glass, Nov. 4, 1989; children: Alexander, Andrew, Anthony. AB, Harvard U., 1953; MD, U. Pa., 1958, PhD, 1959. Dir. div. neonatology Children's Hosp. Nat. Med. Ctr., Washington, 1963-90, physician-in-chief, chief acad. officer, 1990-98; prof. dept. pediats. George Washington U., Washington, 1971-98, prof., chmn. dept. pediatrics, Sch. Med. and Health Scis., 1990-98; prof. pediats. emeritus, 1998—; chief oper. officer Children's Rsch. Inst., Washington, 1990-98. Adv. com. FDA, Washington, 1979-83, 88-91; cons. Nat. Inst. Child Health and Human Devel., 1978—, Bethesda Naval Hosp., 1980—, Walter Reed Army Hosp., 1981—; mem. Mayor's adv. bd. on maternal and infant health, 1986-90. Editor: Neonatology, Pathophysiology and Management of the Newborn, 1975, 3d edit., 1987, 4th edit., 1994, 6th edit., 2005; co-editor: Atlas of Neonatal Procedures, 1983; edtl. bd. Pediat. Jour., 1980-86. Bd. dirs. Pathfinder, Boston, 1975-86, Children's Rsch. Inst., Washington, Children's Hosp., Children's Nat. Med. Ctr. Lt. Med. Svc. Corps., USN, 1958-63. Mem. Soc. for Pediatric Research, Am. Pediatric Soc., Am. Acad. Pediatrics (chmn. fetus and newborn com. 1977-90), National Capital Med. Found. (chmn. perinatal mortality com. 1979-82), Peruvian Pediatric and Surg. Socs. (hon.), Nat. Perinatal Assn. (legis. com.). Avocations: cello, tennis. Home: 4655 36th St S # 2B Arlington VA 22206-1748 Office: Children's Nat Med Ctr 111 Michigan Ave NW Washington DC 20010-2916

AVERY, KARIN F., lawyer; JD, U. Detroit, 1991. Atty. Hertzberg & Golden, Birmingham, Mich., 1992—93, Silverman & Morris, PLLC, West Bloomfield, Mich., 1993—. Mem.: FBA, Am. Bankruptcy Inst., Mich. Bar Assn. Office: Silverman Morris PLLC 7115 Orchard Lake Rd Ste 500 West Bloomfield MI 48322 Office Phone: 248-539-1330. Office Fax: 248-539-1355. Business E-Mail: avery@silvermanmorris.com.

AVERY, MARY ELLEN, pediatrician, educator; b. Camden, NJ, May 6, 1927; d. William Clarence and Mary (Miller) Avery. AB, Wheaton Coll., Norton, Mass., 1948, DSc (hon.), 1974, Trinity Coll., 1976, U. Mich., 1975, Med. Coll. Pa., 1976, Albany Med. Coll., 1977, Med. Coll. Wis., 1978, Radcliffe Coll., 1978; DSc, U. So. Calif., 2003; DSc (hon.), Harvard U., 2005, MA (hon.), 1974; MD, Johns Hopkins U., 1952; LHD (hon.), Emmanuel Coll., 1979, Northeastern U., 1981, Russell Sage Coll., 1983, Meml. U., Newfoundland, 1993; DHL, Johns Hopkins U., 1999; LLD, Queen's U., Kingston, Ont., 2000, U. So. Calif., 2003; DSc (hon.), Harvard U., 2005. Intern Johns Hopkins Hosp., 1953—54, resident, 1954—57; rsch. fellow in pediat. Boston, 1957—59, Balt., 1959—69; assoc. prof. pediat. Johns Hopkins U., 1964—69; prof., chmn. dept. pediat. McGill U. Med. Sch., 1969—74; physician-in-chief Montreal Children's Hosp., 1969—74; Thomas Morgan Rotch prof. pediat. Harvard U. Med. Sch., Boston, 1974—97; physician-in-chief Children's Hosp. Med. Ctr., Boston, 1974—85; prof. emerita Harvard U. Med. Sch., Boston, 1997—. Mem. Med. Rsch. Coun. Can.; mem. study sect. NIH, 1968—71, 1984—88. Author: The Lung and Its Disorders in the Newborn Infant, 4th edit., 1981; author: (with A. Schaffer) Avery's Diseases of the Newborn, 8th edit., 2004; author: (with G. Litwack) Born Early, 1984, editor (with H.W. Taeusch and R. Ballard); author: (with L. First) Pediatric Medicine, 1988, 2d edit., 1994, also articles:, mem. editl. bd.: Pediatrics, 1965—71, Am. Rev. Respitory Diseases, 1969—73, Am. Jour. Physiology, 1967—73, Jour. Pediatrics, 1974—84, Medicine, 1985, Johns Hopkins Med. Jour., 1978—82, Clin. and Investigative Critical Care Medicine, 1990—96, New Eng. Jour. Medicine, 1990—95. Trustee Wheaton (Mass.) Coll., 1965—85, Radcliffe Coll., Johns Hopkins U., 1982—88. Recipient Mead Johnson award in pediatric rsch., 1968, Trudeau medal, Am. Thoracic Soc., 1984, Nat. Medal of Sci., NSF, 1991, Marta Philipson award, Karolinska Inst., Stockholm, 1998; Markle scholar in med. scis., 1961—66. Fellow: NAS (mem. coun. 1997—), AAAS (dir. 1989, pres. 2004—05), Royal Coll. Physicians of Edinburgh, Am. Acad. Arts and Scis., Am. Acad. Pediat., Internat. Pediatric Assn. (standing com. 1986—89); mem.: Am. Pediatric Soc. (pres. 1990, John Howland award 2005), Royal Coll. Pediat. and Child Health (hon.), Inst. Medicine (coun. 1987, Walsh McDermott award 2000), Soc. Pediatric Rsch. (pres. 1972—73), Am. Physiol. Soc., Can. Pediatric Soc., Alpha Omega Alpha, Phi Beta Kappa. Home Phone: 781-235-7168; Office Phone: 617-355-8330. Business E-Mail: mary.avery@tch.harvard.edu.

AVERY, MELISSA J., lawyer; b. Columbus, Ohio, May 29, 1969; d. Joe Morris Toeller and Sharon Lee Parker; m. Bryan Keith Avery, Nov. 8, 1997; children: Preston James, Paige Evelyn. BS, Ohio U., 1991; JD, Capital U., 1994. Bar: Ohio 1995, U.S. Dist. Ct. (so. dist.) Ohio 1995, Ind. 1997, U.S. Dist. Ct. (no. and so. dists.) Ind. 1997. Assoc. Terry L. Thomas Co., LPA, Columbus, 1994—98, Phelps & Fara, Indpls., 1998—2003; ptnr. Avery & Cheerva LLP, Indpls., 2003—. Mem. Marion County Family Ct. Task Force, Indpls., 2000—, Marion County Family Law Rules Com., Indpls., 2002—; lectr. in field. Fellow: Ind. State Bar Assn. (cert. family law specialist 2002, com. co-chair 2002—04); mem.: ABA (com. vice chair 2003—04, family law sect., mem. coun., com. vice chair 2006), Indpls. Bar Assn. (chair family law sect. 2002). Office: Avery & Cheerva LLP 230 E Ohio St 6th Fl Indianapolis IN 46204 Office Phone: 317-637-7575. Business E-Mail: mavery@averycheerva.com.

AVERY, ROBERT DEAN, lawyer; b. Youngstown, Ohio, Apr. 23, 1944; s. Donald and Alta Belle (Simon) Avery; m. Ann Mitchell Lashen, May 16, 1993; 1 child from previous marriage, Benjamin Robert. BA, Northwestern U., 1966; JD, Columbia U., 1969. Bar: Ohio 1971, Calif. 1973, Ill. 2001. Law clk. to Hon. Robert P. Anderson U.S. Ct. Appeals 2d Cir., NYC, 1969-70; assoc. lawyer Jones Day, Cleve., 1970-74, LA, 1974-76, ptnr., 1977-98, adminstrv. ptnr., 1990-92, ptnr. Chgo., 1999—. Editor: Columbia Law Rev., 1968—69. Dir. Wilshire YMCA, LA, 1981—88; mem. bd. govs. Northwestern U. Libr., 2004—. Harlan Fiske Stone scholar. Home: 45 E Division St Chicago IL 60610-2316 Office: Jones Day 77 W Wacker Dr Chicago IL 60601-1662 Office Phone: 312-269-4103. Business E-Mail: rdavery@jonesday.com.

AVERY, ROBERT LOGAN, ophthalmologist; s. Thomas and Frances Avery; m. Kelly Elhatton, July 1, 1994; children: Olivia Nicole, Logan Patrick, Georgia Michelle, Kincade Jackson. BA, Rice U., Houston, 1982; MD, Johns Hopkins U., Balt., 1987. Cert. ophthalmologist Am. Bd. Ophthalmology, 1992. Intern Santa Barbara Coll. Hosp., 1987—88; ophthalmology resident Johns Hopkins U., Balt., 1988—91, asst. chief svc., ophthalmology dept., 1992—93; retina fellow Duke U., Durham, NC, 1991—92; rsch. biologist U. Calif., Santa Barbara, 1993—; CEO Calif. Retina Cons., Santa Barbara, Calif., 1995—. Dir. Calif. Retina Rsch. Found., Santa Barbara, 2000—. Fellow, Ronald G. Michels Found., 1993. Fellow: Am. Acad. Ophthalmology (Achievement award 2006); mem.: Calif. Med. Assn., Calif. Assn. Ophthalmology, Assn. Rsch. in Vision and Ophthalmology, Am. Soc. Retina Specialists, Phi Beta Kappa. Achievements include patents for retinal drug delivery devices. Office: Calif Retina Cons 515 E Micheltorena St Ste C Santa Barbara CA 93103 Office Phone: 805-963-1648. Office Fax: 805-965-5214. Personal E-mail: avery1@jhu.edu.

AVERY, ROBERT NEWELL, sculptor; b. May 22, 1940; s. Robert Newell and Margaret (Andrews) A.; m. Karen Lissol, Aug. 27, 1963 (div. 1978); 1 child, Robert Walter; m. Amanda Fair Jones, May 5, 1979; 1 child, Melinda Hopkins. BFA, Calif. Coll. Arts and Crafts, Oakland, 1962; postgrad., Coll. of San Mateo, Calif., 1969-70, Coll. of Redwoods, 1975-76. Freelance comml. artist, Mendocino, Calif., 1971-75; exec. dir. Mendocino Art Ctr., Inc., 1975-79; proprietor Missing Link Prodns., Mendocino, 1979-93; mng. dir. Mezzanine Gallery at Daly's, Ft. Bragg, Calif., 1986-87, 91-93; exec. dir. Staunton/Augusta Art Ctr., Staunton, Va., 1995-96; proprietor Avery Studio Gallery, Staunton, 1996—. Art dir. The Mendocino Rev., 1983-91; judge Sonoma County Fair, Santa Rosa, Calif., 1977; auctioneer many arts/ednl./polit. events; art dir. The Mendocino Rev. #3, 1975; disc jockey Radio Sta. KMFB-FM, Mendocino, 1971-73, KJAZ-FM, Berkeley, Calif., 1960-61; lead player (play) The Great American Desert, 1975, Candida, 1977, Mousetrap, 1978, Rain, 1979, The Real Inspector Hound, 1984; prodr.: Twin Peaks (stage play), 1985; host interviewer: Art View, 1987-89, The Now and Then Show, 1985-91; prodr., programmer radio show: Odd Bob Comedy Show, KZYX-FM, 1989-90. Contbr. articles, photographs, illustrations to profl. jours.; columnist The Mendocino Daily Planet, 1972-73, The Mendocino Beacon, 1975-79, The New Settler Interview, 1986, Mendocino Grapevine, 1977-82; illustrator: The House that Jack Built; one man shows include Winona Gallery, Mendocino, 1990, Stock Exch. Deli, Waynesboro, Va., 1995, Augusta County Libr., Fishersville, Va., 1996; group shows include Mendocino Art Ctr., 1986, 1990, 91-93, Mayhew Wildlife Gallery, Mendocino, 1986-93, Mezzanine Gallery, Ft. Bragg, 1986-88, Caspar Studios Gallery, 1990, Shenandoah Valley Art Ctr., Waynesboro, Va., 1994-95, Beverley St. Studio Sch., Staunton, Va., 1995, Jordan Gallery, Charlottesville, Va., 1995, Lynchburg Fine Arts Ctr., 1995, Augusta Art Ctr., 1997, others Master of ceremonies 4th of July Parade, Mendocino, 1976-93; judge Bodega Bay Fisherman's Festival Ann. Arts Show, 1976; chmn. art acquisition com. Augusta Hosp. Corp., 1997; mem. founding bd. Mendocino Performing Arts Co., Inc.; past pres. Mendocino Cmty. Land Trust, Inc.; trustee Mendocino Unified Sch. Dist., 1973-77, pres., 1977; past dir. Mendocino Bus. and Profl. Coun.; mem. citizen's adv. coun. Coll. of the Redwoods, 1979-80; mem. exec. com. Calif. Arts Coun., Rural Arts Svcs., 1978-79; trustee Mendocino Art Ctr., Inc., 1980-85, chmn. citizen's adv. com., 1991, hon. life mem. Recipient numerous sculpture awards various art assns. Mem. Assn. of Sci. Fiction Artists, Internat. Sculpture Commn. Home and Office: 4855 Morris Mill Rd Swoope VA 24479-2323 Personal E-mail: goodartmaker@yahoo.com.

AVERY, STEPHEN NEAL, playwright, writer; b. Hot Springs, Ark., Mar. 20, 1955; s. Leo A. Avery and Dedette Carol (Miles) Andree; m. Kathleen Annette Twin, Sept. 7, 1979. Free-lance reporter Hot Springs Sentinel-Record and New Era, 1970-73. Author: (plays) Hungry: 3 Plays, 1991, Because, 1991, Insidious, 1992, Burning Bridges, 1999; prodn. ptnr. (Moriah Films documentary) Ever Again, 2005. Active US Holocaust Meml. Mus., 2001—; leadership coun. So. Poverty Law Ctr., 2002—; founding mem. The Nat. Campaign for Tolerance, 2002—; founders cir. Ark. State U./Mountain Home Cultural Arts Ctr., 2002—; active Simon Wiesenthal Ctr., 2002—, Beil Hashoah Mus. of Tolerance, 2003—; mem. scholarship com. Am. Indian Edn. Found., 2005—; mem. Internat. Rescue Com., 2004—, AmeriCares, 2004—, Friends of Sesame Workshop, 2005—; founding sponsor Martin Luther King, Jr. Nat. Meml., 2005—, Flight 93 Nat. Meml., 2006—; active Nat. Rep. Congl. Com., 2004—; hon. co-chair President's Dinner for George W. Bush, 2004, 2005; active Am. Jewish Com., 2003—, World Jewish Congress, pres. coun., 2005—. With USN, 1973—77. Named to inclusion in Rep. Presdl. Honor Roll, chmn., exec. comm. Nat. Rep. Congl. Com., 2005; recipient Congl. Order of Merit, 2006. Mem.: Drama League, Theatre Comms. Group, Authors League Am., Dramatists Guild Inc., World Trade Ctr. Meml. Found. (charter), US Naval Inst., Americans for the Arts Action Fund (charter), Save Ellis Island (charter), Nat. Mus. Am. Indian (charter), Nat. D-Day Mus. (charter), Carter Ctr., Nat. Mus. Women in Arts, Nat. Trust Hist. Preservation, Habitat for Humanity Internat., Nat. Campaign Tolerance. Avocation: museum and gallery exhbns.

AVERYT, GAYLE OWEN, retired insurance executive; b. Montgomery, Ala., Oct. 13, 1933; s. Edwin Franklin and Asenath Pratt (Murfee) A.; m. Margaret Rosborough Finlay, June 15, 1963; children: Caroline Averyt Lord, Margaret McQueen, Elinor Finlay. BS cum laude, Davidson Coll., 1955; MBA, Harvard U., 1958; D Pub. Svc. (hon.), U. S.C., 1989. Chmn. bd. Colonial Cos., Inc., Columbia, SC, 1970-93. Bd. dirs. UNUM Cor., 1993-99; bd. dirs., treas. Palmetto Bus. Forum, 1977-94;. mem. S.C. Ins. Commn., 1976-84, S.C. State Ports Authority, 1994-99. Trustee Davidson Coll., N.C., 1980-84; pres. S.C. Orch. Assn., 1986-88. Recipient Order of Palmetto State of S.C., 1994, Disting. Alumnus award Davidson Coll., 1997—, Disting. Svc. award U. S.C., 2006; named Business Man of Yr. S.C. C. of C., 1989, Man of the Decade Columbia Met. Mag., Humanitarian of Yr. Palmetto Soc. of United Way of Midlands, 2004; inducted into S.C. Bus. Hall of Fame, 1998. Mem. Phi Beta Kappa. Home: 1717 Greene St Columbia SC 29201-4014 Office: Colonial Supplemental Ins 1200 W Colonial Life Blvd Columbia SC 29210-7646

AVI, (AVI WORTIS), author; b. NYC, Dec. 23, 1937; s. Joseph and Helen (Zunser) Wortis; children: Shaun Wortis, Kevin Wortis; m. Linda Wright; stepchildren: Katie Spina, Robert Spina, Jack Spina. BA, U. Wis., 1959, MA, 1962; MS in Libr. Sci., Columbia U., 1964. Staff mem. Lincoln Ctr. Libr. of Performing Arts, NYC, 1962-70, Lambeth Pub. Lib., London, 1968; asst. prof., humanities libr. Trenton (N.J.) State Coll., 1970-86; writer, 1968—. Dir. workshop Young People's Fiction, Ill. Wesleyan U. Writers Conf., 1983, course in children's lit., 1986; tchr. course in writing for Children, UCLA Extension, 1987, course in aesthetics and ideology of children's lit., Simmons Coll., Boston, 1987, course in history of children's lit. Simmons Coll., 1988, course The Writers's Achievement, Simmons Coll., spring 1990; condr. more than 2000 workshops and seminars with children, parents and educators in U.S. and abroad. Author: Things That Sometimes Happen, 1970, Snail Tale, 1972 (One of Best Books of Yr. Brit. Book Coun. 1973), No More Magic, 1975 (Spl. award Mystery Writers Am. 1975), Captain Grey, 1977, Emily Upham's Revenge, 1978 (Spl. award Mystery Writers Am. 1979, Book of Month PCRRT, 1978), Encounter at Easton, 1980 (Christopher award 1980), The History of Helpless Harry, 1980 (Book of the Month PCRRT 1980), Man from the Sky, 1980 (IRA Children's Choice 1980), A Place Called Ugly, 1981, Who Stole the Wizard of Oz, 1981, Sometimes I Think I Hear My Name, 1982, Shadrach's Crossing, 1983 (Spl. award Mystery Writers Am. 1983), Devil's Race, 1984 (ALA Best Books Hi-Lo 1984), The Fighting Ground, 1984 (O'Dell award 1984, ALA Notable Book, One of Best Books for Young Adults 1984, Notable Children's Trade Books in Social Studies 1984, Jefferson Cup award Honor Book Va. Libr. Assn. 1985, Book of the Month PCRRT 1984), Wolf Rider, 1986 (named One of Best Books for Young Adults, ALA 1986, N.Y. Pub. Libr. 1986, One of Best Books of the 80s, Booklist 1989, , Recommended Book for Reluctant Readers 1986, Va. Young Readers award 1990), Romeo and Juliet—Together (and Alive!)—at Last, 1987 (LA/YASD Recommended Book for Reluctant Readers, 1988, IRA Children's Choice 1988, named One of Best Books of Yr. , Bank St. Coll. Children's Book Com., Wis. Children's Book Ctr. 1988), Something Upstairs, 1988 (Rhode Island award 1991, named One of Best Books of Yr. Libr. Congress 1989), The Man Who Was Poe, 1989, (named One of Best Books of Yr., N.Y. Pub. Libr. 1989, Notable Children's Book, NCTE 1990, One of Best Books of Yr., Libr. Congress 1990), The True Confessions of Charlotte Doyle (IRA Children's Choice award 1990, Lopez Meml. Found. award 1990, Golden Kite award Soc. Children's Book Authors 1991, named One of Best Books of Yr., Child Study Assn. 1990, Notable Childrn's Trade Book in the Lang. Arts 1990, N.Y. Pub. Lib. Best Books for Teens 1990, Editors' Choice, Booklist 1990, ALA Notable Book, 1990, YASD Best Books for Young Adults 1991, Newbery Honor Book 1991), Nothing But the Truth, 1991, (Newbery Honor Book, 1992, Horn Book-Boston Globe award Honor Book, 1992, ALA Notable Book, 1992, named One of Best Books of Yr.-Hornbook, SLJ, 1991, YASD Best Books for Young Adults, 1992, Pub. Weekly Best Books of 1991, Am. Booksellers Children's Choice List, 1992, Best Books for Teens, N.Y. Pub. Libr., 1992, Notable Nat. Coun. Social Studies/Children's Book Council, 1991, Blue Ribbon Book Bulletin of Ctr. Children's Books), Windcatcher, 1991, Who Was that Masked Man, Anyway?, 1992, Blue Heron, 1992, City of Light, City of Dark, 1993, The Bird, The Frog and the Light, 1994, The Barn, 1994, Tom, Babette & Simon, 1995, Poppy, 1995, Beyond the Western Sea, 1996, Crispin: The Cross of Lead, (Newbery Medal Winner 2003); contbr. articles to jours. in field. Mem.: Authors Guild. Avocation: photography. Home: 859 S York St Denver CO 80209-4646

AVIDAN, ALON Y., physician; b. Jerusalem, May 13, 1966; s. Kami and Tova Avidan. BS, UCLA, 1988; MD, MPH, George Washington U., 1994. Diplomate in neurology Am. Bd. Psychiatry and Neurology, cert. Am. Bd. Sleep Medicine. Dir. sleep disorders clinic U. Mich., Ann Arbor, Mich., 2002—06; assoc. dir. sleep medicine program UCLA, 2005—, dir. outpatient neurology clinic Reed neurol. rsch. ctr., 2005—, assoc. prof. neurology David Geffen sch. medicine, 2007—. Office: UCLA Dept Neurology Rm 1-169 Reed Bldg 710 Westwood Plz Los Angeles CA 90095-1769 Office Phone: 310-825-0703. Office Fax: 310-825-6956. Business E-Mail: avidan@mednet.ucla.edu. E-mail: alonavidan@gmail.com.

AVIL, RICHARD DANIEL, JR., lawyer; b. Phila., Nov. 28, 1948; s. Richard Daniel and Elizabeth (McGinley) Avil; m. Karen Mudry, May 27, 1972; children: Sierra Soo, Brier Sung, Winston Richard. BEE, Villanova U., 1970; JD, Cornell U., 1974. Law clk. US Dist. Ct. Northern Dist. NY, 1974-75, 75-76, US Ct. Appeals Second Cir., NYC, 1976-77; assoc. Jones Day, Cleve., 1977-83, ptnr., 1984-91, Washington, 1991—. Spkr. in field. Mem.: Energy Bar Assn. Office: Jones Day 51 Louisiana Ave NW Washington DC 20001-2113 Office Phone: 202-879-5401. Business E-Mail: rdavil@jonesday.com.

AVILA, CHARLIE A., physics researcher, inventor; b. Arecibo, P.R., May 7, 1950; s. Manuel Antonio Avila and Natalia Rivera; children: Carlos Jr., Rolando, Elias, David; m. Shelia Diana Avila. BEd in Chemistry, NYU, 1976, BA, 1978, MEd in Sci. Edn., 1986; BAW in Chemistry and Gen. Sci., Inter Am. U., PR, 1988; MA in Sci. Edn., NYU, 1992; DSc Astrophysics of Particles, U. Oxford, Eng., Postdoctoral degree in Quantum Physics and Artificial Intelligence. Tchr. of sci. Dept. Edn., P.R., 1976-86, tchr. chemistry lab. P.R., 1992-93; rschr. physics dept. U. P.R., 1993—; pres., owner EBINC-CINCE, Inc.; rschr. sci. and tech. divsn. U. S. Fla. Spanish cmty. svcs. staff Dept. Edn., Penns Grove, N.J., 1982-83; substitute tchr. Dept. Edn., Meml. H.S., 1983-84; owner, pres. CINCE; with Mission to Planet Earth and Earth Observing System programs, NASA. Songwriter: Men Should Understand, others; author: Space is Not Empty - It is the 5th State of the Matter, Beyond Einstein Equation & Modifying Einstein Equation: E=Mc2 singularity was modified to Up=ME.C, Universe Not Expanding; contbr. scientific papers. Special elite US Army, 1971—75, with US Army, 1991—92. Nominee Nobel Prize in Physics, Internat. Peace prize; named Internat. Outstanding Scientist of Yr., 2005—06. Mem. Nat. Sci. Assn., IP&R Inventors and Pub./Rsch. Corp. (recipient Internat. Personality of Yr., Cambridge, Eng., others), Am. Fedn. Tchrs., Puerto Rico Fedn. Tchrs., Am. Legion. Achievements include invention of Thermoelectric battery and power plant using the same; development of Avila's Singunification Theory; antigravity technology; theory of antigravitational equilibrium; technology to restore ozone holes in the stratosphere; a seismograph to detect earthquakes up to 5 minutes before destructive waves reach populated cities; Thermoelectric Generator in orbit to capture sun radiation and transform it into electricity to light up the international space station; technology to debilitate or desintegrate hurricanes and tornados to disperse them using bombs of freeze zero absolute (-273 C) dissoclution; biochemical substances biodegradable at -273 C or absolute; postulated and warned that there are already formed micro ozone holes; research in centrifucal, kinetic and inertial forces. Avocations: reading, music. Personal E-mail: charliefisico21@yahoo.com.

AVILA, NILO ALONSO, radiologist; b. Havana, Cuba, Oct. 31, 1957; arrived in US, 1970; s. Nilo Avila and Hilda Sanchez. BS, Fordham U., Bronx, NY, 1979; MD, SUNY, Syracuse, 1983. Diplomate Am. Coll. Radiology. Resident Bridgeport Hosp., Conn., 1983—87; fellow in ultrasound and MRI U. Mich., Ann Arbor, 1987—88; staff radiologist NIH, Bethesda, Md., 1992—2007. Contbr. scientific papers to profl. jours. Fellow: Am. Coll. Radiology (counselor phys. health serv.); mem.: Radiol. Soc. N.Am., Am. Roenteen Ray Soc. Office: Warren G Magnuson Clin Ctr NIH 10 Medical Ctr Dr Bethesda MD 20892

AVILES, ALICE ALERS, psychologist; b. NYC; d. Jose Oscar and Pauline (Irizarry) Alers; m. Jose A. Aviles, Aug. 13, 1954 (div. Oct. 1981); children: Jeffrey (dec.), Brian, Gregory; m. Clifford M. Goldman, June 29, 1997. BS magna cum laude, SUNY, Oswego, 1955; MA, Queens Coll., 1978; PhD, Yeshiva U., 1984; postdoctoral diploma in psychoanalysis and psychotherapy, Adelphi U., 1991. Lic. psychologist, N.Y. Tchr. elem. schs., Spring Valley, NY, 1955, Erlangen Am. Sch., Germany, 1955—56, Uniondale, NY, 1956, Freeport, NY, 1957—58, Island Park, NY, 1973—75; psychology clk. Fifth Ave. Ctr. for Counseling and Psychotherapy, NYC, 1978—80; psychology intern St. Vincent's Hosp. and Med. Ctr., NYC, 1980—81; psychologist Kingsboro Psychiat. Ctr., Bklyn., 1981—84; psychologist to assoc. psychologist South Beach Psychiat. Ctr., Bklyn., 1984—86; pvt. practice Valley Stream, NY, 1985—. From staff psychologist to sr. psychologist Luth. Med. Ctr., Bklyn., 1986-95; cons. Beach Terrace Care Ctr., Long Beach, N.Y., 1995-97; mem. adv. com. Hispanic Counseling Ctr. of Family Svc. Assn. of Nassau County, Hempstead, N.Y., 1978-80; cons. Nassau County Extended Care Ctr., Hempstead, 1997-99, Resort Nursing Home, Far Rockaway, N.Y., 1998-2000, Woodmere (N.Y.) Rehab. and Health Care Ctr., 1999-2000. Ford found. grad. fellow, 1978-81. Mem. APA, N.Y. State Psychol. Assn., Nassau County Psychol. Assn. (mem. pvt. practice com. 1992-93), Adelphi Soc. Psychoanalysis and Psychotherapy. Office Phone: 516-791-8326.

AVILES, DIONEL MICHAEL, civilian military employee, former federal agency administrator; b. Bryan, Tex. BS in Mech. Engring., U.S. Naval Acad., 1983; MBA, George Washington U., 1993. Program engr. Naval Air Systems Command; asst. to dir. nat. security divsn. Office Mgmt. & Budget, Exec. Office of the Pres., Washington, 1991—95; profl. staff mem. US Ho. Rels. Com. on Armed Services, Washington, 1995—2001; asst. sec. (fin. mgmt. & comptr.) Dept. of Navy, US Dept. Def., Washington, 2001—04, under sec., 2004—. Served in USN, 1983—88. Office: USN 1000 Pentagon Washington DC 20350

AVILES MIRANDA, MAXIMO, insurance company executive; b. Humacao, PR, Sept. 23, 1946; s. Maximo Aviles and Rosa Miranda; m. Blanca Rodriguez, 1970; children: Blanca, Frances. MBA magna cum laude, World U., PR, 1982. Sales and mktg. exec. Blue Shield of P.R., 1972—94; prof. Puerto Rico Jr. Coll., 1985—93; investment exec. Oriental Bank & Trust, 1994—96; pres. Max Group Ins. & Employee Benefits, Caguas, PR, 1996—. Mem.: P.R. Assn. Merchants and Profls., Am. Mktg. Assn., Mental Retardation Assn., Am. Cancer Assn., Lions (pres. Caguas chpt. 1983—86). Roman Catholic. Avocations: travel, art, history, die-cast car replicas. Office: PO Box 4956 PMB 121 Caguas PR 00726-4956

AVIV, DIANA L., public policy analyst, psychotherapist; b. Johannesburg, Nov. 17, 1951; came to U.S., 1975; d. Ervin Biderman and Miriam Weissman; m. Abraham Aviv (div.). BSW, Haifa U., 1972, U. Witwatersand, Johannesburg, 1974; M in Social Work, Columbia U., 1977. Psychotherapist S.E. Nassau Guidance Ctr., NYC, 1977-79; exec. dir. Alternatives to Domestic Violence, N.J., 1979-81; dir. programs Nat. Coun. of Jewish Women, NYC, 1981-86; assoc. v.p. Jewish Coun. for Pub. Affairs, 1986-94; v.p. pub. policy United Jewish Communities, Washington, 1994—2003; pvt. practice in psychotherapy NJ, NY, Washington, 1979—; pres., CEO Ind. Sector, Washington, 2003—. Cons. Pub. Defenders Office, N.J., N.Y., 1980—. Steering com. Amos, 1999; bd. dirs. Coalition on Human Needs, 1999; v.p. Nat. Immigration Forum, 1999—. Recipient Profl. Excellence award N.Y. Assn. of New Am., 1999. Mem. NASW. Jewish. Avocations: hiking, exercising, reading, gardening, beadwork. Office: Ind Sector 1200 Eighteenth St NW Ste 200 Washington DC 20036

AVIV, OREN R., film company executive; b. 1961; s. David and Rena Aviv; m. Katie Locke, Nov. 24, 1990; children: Alexandra Madeline, Avery, Andie. BA in English and History, Columbia U. Dir. special projects CapCities/ABC; v.p. creative services. Buena Vistas Pictures Mktg., 1991—97, sr. v.p. mktg., creative dir., 1997—2000, pres., 2000; pres. mktg., chief creative officer Walt Disney Co., 2005, pres. production Walt Disney Pictures, 2006—. Office: Walt Disney Studios 500 South Buena Vista St Burbank CA 91521

AVOSEH, MEJAI BOLA MIKE, adult education educator, researcher; PhD, U. Ibadan, 1991. Tchr. NYC Pub. Sch., Bklyn., 2002—04; asst. prof. U. S.D., Vermillion, 2004—. Sr. lectr. U. Namibia, Windhoek, 1989—2001. Contbr. articles to profl. jours. Recipient Internat. award Literacy Rsch.-Spl. Mention, UNESCO, 1992; fellow, Commonwealth Learning, 1999, German Adult Edn. Assn., 2000; grantee, U. S.D., 2004, Can. Internat. Devel. Assn., 1999. Mem.: AAUP, Mo. Valley Adult Edn. Assn., Assn. World Edn. Denmark (Danish Min. Fgn. Affairs Travel fellow 2001), Am. Assn. Adult and Continuing Edn. Democrat. Avocation: travel. Office: U SD Sch Edn Vermillion SD 57069 Home Phone: 605-624-4895. Office Fax: 605-677-5438. E-mail: mavoseh@usd.edu.

AVOURIS, PHAEDON, chemical physicist; b. Athens, Greece, June 16, 1945; came to U.S., 1970. s. Dionisios and Ourania (Nomikos) A.; m. Alice Laura Dearden, Oct. 7, 1976; 1 child, Ann. BS, Aristotle U., Thessaloniki, greece, 1968; PhD, Mich. State U., 1974. Postdoctoral fellow U. Calif., LA, 1975-77; rsch. assoc. AT&T Bell Labs., Murray Hill, NJ, 1978; rsch. staff IBM Watson Rsch. Ctr., Yorktown Heights, NY, 1978-84, mgr. chem. physics, 1984—, now mgr. nanoscale sci. & tech. group. Panel for chem. sci. Nat. Rsch. Coun., Washington, 1990—. Editor: (book) Atomic and Nanoscale Modifications of Materials; contbr. articles to profl. jours. including Phys. Rev., Sci., Jour. Chem. Physics. Recipient Medard W. Welch award in vacuum sci. Am. Vacuum Soc., 1997. Fellow Am. Phys. Soc.; mem. Am. Chem. Soc. (adv. editl. bd. 1990—). Achievements include pioneering the study of surface chemistry on atomic scale with scanning tunneling microscopy, the manipulation of individual atoms; contbutions to understanding of electronically excited states at surfaces. Office: IBM Watson Rsch Ctr PO Box 218 Yorktown Heights NY 10598

AVRIT, RICHARD CALVIN, defense consultant, career officer; b. Tilamook, Oreg., Feb. 18, 1932; s. Roy Calvin and Mary Louise (Morgan) A.; m. Alice Jane Tamminga, July 10, 1959; 1 dau., Tamra Jane. BS in Engring, U.S. Naval Acad., 1953; MS in Engring. Electronics, U.S. Naval Postgrad. Sch., 1960; postgrad., U.S. Naval War Coll., 1971-72. Commd. ensign U.S. Navy, 1953, advanced through grades to rear adm., 1979; served weapons dept. U.S.S. George K. Mackenzie, 1953-54; ops. dept. U.S.S. Willis A. Lee, 1954-57; comdg. officer U.S.S. Sumner County, 1960-63; project officer, staff of comdr. Operational Test and Evaluation Force, Key West, Fla., 1963-66; exec. officer U.S.S. Berkeley, 1966-68; ops. officer, AAW project officer Comdr. Cruiser Destroyer Florilla Nine, 1968-70; comdg. officer U.S.S. Sellers, 1970-71; mil. asst. for surface guns and missiles to asst. dir. Ocean Control Directorate, Def. Research and Engring., Office Sec. of Def., 1972-76; comdg. officer U.S.S. Harry E. Yarnell, 1976-78; chief of staff, comdr. Naval Surface Force U.S. Atlantic Fleet, 1978-79; project mgr. for Saudi Naval Expansion Program, Naval Material Command, Washington, 1979-82; dir. navy logistics plans Office Chief of Naval Ops., Washington, 1982-84; cons. Info. Spectrum, Inc., 1984-88; pres. Mil. Data Corp., Arlington, Va., 1989-91; small bus. cons., 1992—. Decorated D.S.M., Legion of Merit (3), Bronze Star with Combat V, Meritorious Service Medal (2). Mem. Naval Inst., IEEE. Methodist. Home: 4839 Keswick Ct Dumfries VA 22025-1084 Personal E-mail: dick.avrit@verizon.net.

AVZARADEL, BOB, music educator; s. Avzaradel. MusB in Edn., Calif. State U., Long Beach, 1984. CA Clear Tchg. Credential Dept. of Ed, 1985. Dir. of instrumental music San Clemente H.S., 1985—92; dir. of jazz studies Saddleback Coll., Mission Viejo, Calif., 1993—2001; dir. of instrumental music, dept. chair Irvine H.S., Calif., 1993—. Asst. dir. Sydney Olympic Marching Band, 2000. Recipient Tchr. of Yr., Capistrano Unified Sch. Dist., 1992, Most Outstanding Arts Educator, Orange County, 2003. Mem.: So. Calif. Sch. Bank and Orch. Assn. Office: Irvine HS 4321 Walnut Ave Irvine CA 92604 Office Phone: 949-936-7138. E-mail: ravzarad@iusd.org.

AWAIS, GEORGE MUSA, obstetrician, gynecologist; b. Ajloun, Jordan, Dec. 15, 1929; arrived in U.S., 1951; s. Musa and Meha (Koury) A.; m. Nabila Rizk, June 24, 1970 AB, Hope Coll., 1955; MD, U. Toronto, 1960. Diplomate Am. Bd. Obstetrics and Gynecology. Intern U. Toronto Hosps., Ont., Canada, 1960—61, resident in ob-gyn, 1961—64, chief resident, 1965, Harlem Hosp., Columbia U., NYC, 1966; asst. ob-gyn Cleve. Met. Gen. Hosp., 1967, assoc. ob-gyn, 1969; instr. ob-gyn Case We. Res. U., Cleve., 1967—70, asst. ob-gyn MacDonald House, 1970, asst. prof., 1970, asst. clin. prof. dept. reproductive biology, 1971, asst. ob-gyn Univ. Hosps., 1971; mem. staff, dept. gynecology Cleve. Clinic Found., 1971—91. Chmn. dept. ob-gyn. King Faisal Specialist Hosp. and Rsch. Ctr., Riyadh, 1975-76; cons. panel mem. Internat. Corr. Soc. Obstetricians and Gynecologists, 1971; emeritus staff Cleve. Clinic Found., 1991; pres. Task Force on Humanitarian Aid and Relief Inc., 1997. Contbr. articles to publs. in field, papers, reports to confs., TV appearances, Saudi Arabia Named Grand Officer of Order of Independence His Majesty King Hussein of Jordan, 1992. Fellow ACS, Am. Coll. Obstetricians and Gynecologists, Royal Coll. Surgeons Can.; mem. AMA, AAAS, Am. Infertility Soc., Arab Am. Med. Assn. (pres. 1991—, chmn. humanities relief 1996), Acad. Medicine of Cleve. Office: Cleve Clinic Found Emeritus Office EE/40 9500 Euclid Ave Cleveland OH 44195-0001 Office Phone: 216-444-6814. Business E-Mail: awaisg@ccf.org.

AWAKUNI, GENE I., academic administrator, psychologist; BA, MA, Univ. Hawaii, Manoa; PhD in psychol., Harvard Univ. Dir. counseling & psychol. svc. Univ. Calif., Irvine, asst. vice chancellor Santa Barbara; v.p. student affairs Calif. Poly., Pomona; vice provost, student affairs Stanford Univ.; chancellor Univ. Hawaii, West Oahu, 2005—. Co-author: Resistance to Multiculturalism: Issues and Interventions. Named one of 25 People for the Next 25 Years, Hawaii Bus. Mag., 2007. Mem.: Asian Pacific Americans in Higher Edn. (past pres.). Office: Univ of Hawaii West Oahu 96-129 Ala'Ike Pearl City HI 96782 Office Phone: 808-454-4750. Office Fax: 808-453-6076.*

AWAZU, YUKIKA, corporate executive, researcher, consultant, writer; MBA, MA in Econs., U. Ill., Chgo., 2002; BA in Polit. Studies, Gakushuin U., Tokyo, 1993. Founder YA Rsch. & Solutions, 2004—05; rsch. fellow Inst. for Engaged Bus. Rsch., Chgo., 2004; co-founder, v.p. Engaged Enterprise, Chgo., 2004—. Author: Engaged Knowledge Management, 2005; contbr. articles to profl. jours. Recipient H.B. Earhart student fellow Hoover Instn., Stanford U., 1997—99; Henry. E. Rauch doctoral fellow, McCallum Grad. Sch. Bus., Bentley Coll., 2006—. Home Phone: 312-804-7327.

AWOMOYI, AGNES ABIOLA, microbiologist, researcher; b. Ibadan Nigeria, Nigeria, May 13, 1967; d. William Ojo-Dada and Florence Ayeyemi (Olofin) Awomoyi; 1 child, Anthonia Ore-Oluwa Olatunde. PhD, Open U., Milton Keynes, England, 2000. Rsch. scholar U. Md., Coll. Pk., 2001—03, Balt., 2003—. Reviewer profl. jours. in field. Recipient First Travel award, Brit. Soc. Histocompatibly and Immunogenetics, 1999; Chevening fellowship, Brit. Coun., 1992. Mem.: Internat. Endotoxin and Innate Immunity, Am. Soc. Human Genetics. Achievements include research in link between infections, autoimmunity and cancers. Avocations: travel, walking. Home Phone: 410-340-5533; Office Phone: 410-706-4716. Office Fax: 410-706-8607. Business E-Mail: aawomoyi@som.umaryland.edu.

AWSCHALOM, DAVID DANIEL, physics professor; b. Baton Rouge, Oct. 11, 1956; s. Miguel and Evelyn A.; m. Nancy L. Kawalek, Aug. 6, 1988. BSc in Physics, U. Ill., Urbana-Champaign, 1978; PhD in Exptl. Physics, Cornell U., 1982. Exxon rsch. fellow Cornell U., Ithaca, NY, 1981—82; postdoctoral fellow IBM Watson Rsch. Ctr., Yorktown Heights, NY, 1982—83, rsch. staff mem., 1984—89, mgr. nonequilibrium physics dept., 1989—92; prof. physics U. Calif., Santa Barbara, 1991—, prof. elec. and computer engring., 2001—. Mem. NRC Panel on Magnetic Semiconductors, 1990, NRC Panel on Naval Rsch., 1991, NSF Ctr. Quantized Electronics Structures, 1992; dir. Ctr. Spintronics and Quantum Computation; assoc. dir. Calif. Nanosystems Inst.; seminar spkr. in field. Contbr. articles to profl. jours. Named James scholar U. Ill., 1976-78; recipient Lyman Physics prize U. Ill., 1978, IBM Outstanding Innovation award, 1987, Internat. Magnetism prize, Internat. Union of Pure and Applied Physics, 2003, Néel medal, 2003, Agilent Europhysics prize, European Phys. Soc., 2005. Fellow Am. Phys. Soc. (Oliver E. Buckley prize, 2005), Am. Acad. Arts & Scis., AAAS (Newcomb Cleveland prize, 2006); mem. Materials Rsch. Soc. (Outstanding Investigator prize 1992), NAS. Achievements include development and application of an ultrafast optical technique for exploring electronic and magnetic interactions in quantum systems; invented new time- and spatially-resolved magnetic spectroscopies using superconducting and optical devices. Office: U Calif Dept Physics Broida Hall 4125 Mail Code 9530 Santa Barbara CA 93106-9530 Office Phone: 805-893-2121. Office Fax: 805-893-4170. E-mail: awsch@physics.ucsb.edu.*

AWTAR, SHORYA, engineering educator, consultant; ScD, Mass. Inst. Tech., Cambridge, 2000—04; MS, Rensselaer Poly. Inst., Troy, NY, 1998—2000; BTech, Indian Inst. Tech., Kanpur, UP, India, 1994—98. Asst. prof. U. Mich., Ann Arbor, Mich., 2007—; mech. engr. Gen. Electric Global Rsch. Ctr., Niskayuna, NY, 2004—06. Conf. symposium organizer 30th Mechanisms and Robotics Conf., ASME, Philadelphia, 2006; conf. session chair, compliant mechanisms 29th Mechanisms and Robotics Conf., Long Beach, Calif.; jour. referee ASME Jour. of Mech. Design, IEEE Transactions on Robotics, IFAC Mechatronics. Author articles to profl. jours. Recipient Notional award for academic excellence, Indian Inst. Tech., Kanpur, 1996, Founder's award for academic excellence and leadership, Rensselaer Poly. Inst., 1999, Mark Darlow Meml. award for outstanding achievement in Mechatronics, 1999, Michael A. Sadowsky award for best MS thesis in Mech. Engring., 2000, Inventor's Bronze Medal, Gen. Electric Global Rsch. Ctr., 2005; fellow Rosenblith Fellowship for grad. studies, Mass. Inst. Tech., 2000—01, Standford Grad. Fellowship, Stanford U.; scholar Nat. Talent Search Scholarship, Govt. of India, 1992—98. Mem.: Am. Soc. Precision Engrs. (assoc.), ASME (assoc.), Sigma Xi (assoc.). Achievements include numerous patents pending in field. Office: University of Michigan 2268 GG Brown 2350 Hayward Street Ann Arbor MI 48109 Office Phone: 734-615-0285. Office Fax: 734-647-3170. Business E-Mail: awtar@umich.edu.

AX, EMANUEL, pianist; b. Lvov, Poland, June 8, 1949; s. Joachim and Hellen (Kurtz) A.; m. Yoko Nozaki, Nov. 23, 1974; 2 children. Student of Mieczyslaw Munz, Juilliard Sch. Music; BA, Columbia U. Appeared as soloist Chgo., Los Angeles, Phila., Rochester, Seattle, St. Louis and London, Philharm. orchs., NY Philharm., Israel Philharm., Pitts. Symphony; recitalist (with Yo-Yo Ma) Avery Fisher Hall, Carnegie Hall, NYC, festival at Tanglewood, Hollywood Bowl and Ravinia; toured extensively in C.Am. and S.Am., performed in joint recital (with violinist Nathan Milstein), extensive tours, Europe, Japan; with major orchs.; also recs. Winner Arthur Rubinstein Internat. Competition 1974, Avery Fisher prize 1979; recipient Young Concert Artist's Michaels award 1975; 4 Grammy awards. Fellow, Am. Acad. Arts & Scis. Office: care ICM Artists 40 W 57th St New York NY 10019-4001 or: care Harold Holt Ltd 31 Sinclair Rd London W14 ONS England*

AXEL, BERNARD, finance executive; b. Bklyn., May 23, 1946; s. Joseph and Irene (Rosen) A.; m. Tobie Reznik, Sept. 3, 1995. BS, U. Ala., 1967; grad., Am. Inst. Banking, 1970. Asst. cashier, comptroller Nat. Bank of Commerce (formerly Am. Nat. Bank), Birmingham, Ala., 1967-72; supr. internat. travel Travel Anywhere, Birmingham, 1972; acctg. and purchasing agt. U.S. Dept. Justice, Texarkana, Tex., 1972-74; mgr. Styslinger Realty, Birmingham, 1974-75; pres. Christian's Inc., Birmingham, 1975-92, Christian's Tutwiler, Inc., Birmingham, 1992-98; mgr. Tucker Cos., Tuscaloosa, Ala., 1998—; v.p. Tucker Fin. Co., Tucker Title Co., Tuscaloosa, 1998—; v.p., COO Tucker Fin. Co., 2001—03, pres., 2003—07, Tucker Title Co., 2004—, gen. mgr., 2007—. Gourmet chef Top of Morning show Sta. WVTM-T-V, Birmingham, 1991—, Good Day Ala. WBRC-TV, Birmingham, 1996—. Contbr. recipes to mags. Judge March of Dimes Gourmet Gala, Birmingham, 1986, Miss Ala.-U.S.A. Pageant, 1990, 91, Miss Teen Ala., 1992; mem. gov.'s staff State of Ala., Montgomery, 1968-70, mem. lt. gov.'s staff, 1980-84; bd. dirs. Temple Beth El, 1969-72; mem. adv. bd. U. Ala. Sch. Restaurant Hospitality Mgmt., 1989—, chmn. adv. bd., 1992—. Awarded Key to City of Birmingham, Ala., 1991. Mem. Nat. Restaurant Assn. (cert. foodsvc. mgmt. profl., mem. adv. bd. polit. action com. 1987-98, state chmn. 1993-98, bd. dirs. 1996-98), Am. Culinary Fedn. (bd. dirs. Birmingham chpt., medal 1986, Appreciation award 1991), Ala. Restaurant and Food Svc. Assn. (bd. dirs. 1983-98, pres. 1990-92, trustee self-ins. fund 1994-96, Restaurateur of Yr. 1992, Polit. Eagle award 1994), Birmingham-Jefferson County Restaurant Assn. (bd. dirs. 1981-83, 89-98, Restaurant Operator of Yr. 1995), Birmingham-Jefferson Restaurant Assn. (pres. 1995), Chaine des Rotisseurs (L'Order Mondial des Gourmets Degustateurs 1989, coord. culinaire south ctrl. 1996-97), Les Disciples d'Auguste Escoffier Assn. Gastronomique, Commanderie des Cordon Bleus France. Republican. Avocations: travel, cooking. Home: 1716 Dauphine Dr Tuscaloosa AL 35406-3070 Office: Tucker Cos 3302 Mcfarland Blvd E Tuscaloosa AL 35405-2424 Home Phone: 205-366-3660; Office Phone: 205-556-3636. E-mail: baxel@comcast.net.

AXEL, RICHARD, pathology and biochemistry educator; b. NYC, July 2, 1946; AB magna cum laude, Columbia U., 1967; MD, Johns Hopkins U., 1970. Intern dept. pathology Columbia U. Coll. Physicians and Surgeons, NYC, 1970-71; fellow Inst. Cancer Research, 1971-72; vis. fellow dept. pathology Columbia U., 1971-72; research assoc. USPHS, NIH, 1972-74; asst. prof. dept. pathology Inst. Cancer Research, Columbia U., 1974-78, prof., dept. pathology and biochemistry, 1978—. Mem. molecular biology study sect. NIH, 1981-, Ctr. for Neurobiology and Behavior; Univ. lectr. Columbia U., 1983; investigator, Howard Hughes Med. Inst. Assoc. editor: Cell, 1976-; contbr. articles to profl. jours. Recipient Irma T. Hirschl Career Scientist award, 1976, Young Scientist award Passano Found., 1979, Alan T. Waterman award, 1982, Eli Lilly award, 1983, Scientific Award, Moet Hennessy, Louis Vuitton, 1992, Disting. Scholar award, Kappa Chpt., Columbia, Sigma Xi Scientific Rsch. Soc., 1998, Mayor's award (NY)for Excellence in Science and Tech., 1998, Bristol Myers Squibb award for disting. achievement in neuroscience rsch., 1998, Perl/Univ. of NC Neuroscience prize, 2003, Gairdner award, Gairdner Found., 2003, Golden Plate award, Acad. Achievement, 2005; co-recipient Nobel Prize in Medicine, 2004. Mem. NAS (Richard Lounsbery award 1989), Am. Acad. Arts and Scis., Phi Beta Kappa, GM Adv. Council, Cancer Rsch. Found., Am. Philosophical Soc. Achievements include discovery of odorant receptors and the organization of the olfactory system. Office: Howard Hughes Med Inst Columbia U Hammer Health Scis Ctr 701 W 168th St Room 1014 New York NY 10032-2704 Office Phone: 212-305-6915. Office Fax: 212-923-7249. E-mail: ra27@columbia.edu.*

AXELROD, CHARLES PAUL, lawyer; b. NYC, Oct. 23, 1941; s. Abraham and Lillian Rose (Neidetch) A.; m. Susan J. Schneider; children: Seth Jordan, Tracy Brooke. BS, NYU, 1963; JD, Bklyn. Law Sch., 1966. Bar: N.Y. 1966, U.S. Ct. Appeals (2d cir.) 1967, U.S. Dist. Ct. (so. dist.) N.Y. 1970, U.S. Supreme Ct. 1974, U.S. Dist. Ct. (ea. dist.) N.Y. 1975, U.S. Ct. Appeals D.C. 1979. Ptnr. Goldstein & Axelrod, NYC, 1980-94, Camhy, Karlinsky & Stein LLP, NYC, 1994-99, Greenberg Traurig LLP, 1999—. Chmn. legis. sub-com. study of securities laws N.Y. State Assembly, 1972; adj. prof. law Pace U., Pleasantville, N.Y., 1976-77. Vol. atty. City of N.Y. Com. on Human Rights, 1972. Mem. ABA (com on corp governance, com. on fed. regulation of securities, sub-com. on civil lit. and SEC enforcement matters, sub-com. on NASD corp. financing rules), N.Y. State Trial Lawyers Assn., N.Y. County Lawyers Assn., N.Y. State Bar Assn., Nat. Assn. Securities Dealers (bd. arbitrators), Com. on Securities and Exchs. (N.Y.C.). Democrat. Jewish. Office: Greenberg Traurig LLP 200 Park Ave New York NY 10016 Office Phone: 212-801-9200. Business E-Mail: axelrodc@gtlaw.com.

AXELROD, DEBORAH MONA, surgeon; b. NYC, Aug. 31, 1957; m. Noel Raskin; children: Ben, Max. MD, Tel Aviv U. Sackler Sch. Medicine, 1982. Diplomate Am. Bd. Surgery. Intern, gen. surgery Beth Israel Med. Ctr., NYC, 1982-83, resident, surgical oncology, 1983-88, attending surgeon; physician-in-charge, Louis Venet MD CompBrest Svc. Beth Israel Hosp. and Med. Ctr., NYC, 1988—99; fellow in surg. oncology Meml. Sloan Kettering, NYC, 1985-86; asst. prof. surgery Albert Einstein Med. Sch., NYC; chief, Comprehensive Breast Ctr. St. Vincent's Hosp. and Med. Ctr., NYC, 1999—2004; dir., clin. breast svcs. and breast surgery NYU, 2004—, med. dir., cmty. cancer edn. and outreach, 2004—; assoc. prof. surgery NYU Sch. Medicine, 2004—; oncologist NY, 1988—; mem. NYU Breast Surgery Associates. Invited spkr. in field; mem. adv. bd. Cancerand-Careers.org. Founder, host (ednl. website) breastdoc.com; contbr. several articles to peer-reviewed jours.; co-author (with Rosie O' Donnell and Tracy Chuterian-Semler): Bosom Buddies: Lessons and Laughter About Breast Health and Cancer, 1999; guest appearance Rosie O'Donnell Show, 2000. Initiated Cmty. Lecture Series Program, NYC; initiated Artist-In-Residence Program St. Vincent's Med. Ctr.; bd. dir. SHARE (Self-Help Group for Women with Breast or Ovarian Cancer), NYC, Susan G. Komen Found., Northern NJ Affiliate, Cancer 101; mem. med. resource coun. Gilda's Club, NYC; mem. health adv. bd. Hadassah; mem. med. adv. bd. Young Survival Coalition, Judges and Lawyers Breast Cancer Alert; founder Say Ahh (say art helps heal); active with Nat. Alliance Breast Cancer Organizations; chairperson Cultural Arts Program, Summit Schs., NJ; bd. dir. Summit Jr. Baseball. Named honoree, SHARE-A-WALK in Ctrl. Park, 2000, 5th Ann. Pink Tie Ball, Susan G. Komen Found., North NJ Affiliate, 2001; recipient Spl. Recognition award, Judges and Lawyers Breast Cancer Alert, 2000, Humanitarian Tower of Hope award, Israel Cancer Rsch. Fund, 2000, Creative Spirit award, Creative Ctr. for Women with Cancer, 2001, Ann. Gilda's Club, It's Always Something award, 2003; Craft grant, Susan G. Komen Found., 2001. Fellow ACS; mem. AMA, I.A.B.C.R., Israel Med. Assn., N.Y. Assn. Medicine, N.Y. Surg. Soc. Avocations: weightlifting, hiking. Address: 160 E 34th St New York NY 10016 Office Phone: 212-731-5366.*

AXELROD, EVAN M., psychologist, educator; s. David and Carrie Axelrod; m. Michelle Axelrod; children: Sam children: J. T. BA in Psychology, U. Puget Sound; D of Psychology, U. Denver. Bd. cert. traumatic stress expert Am. Acad. Experts Traumatic Stress, 2004. Clin. police psychologist Nicoletti-Flater Assocs., Lakewood, Colo., 2000—. Adj. prof. U. Denver Grad. Sch. Profl. Psychology. Contbr. text book. Grantee, U. Puget Sound, 1996—97. Mem.: APA, Colo. Psychol. Assn., Soc. Police and Criminal Psychology, Am. Acad. Experts Traumatic Stress, Internat. Assn. Chiefs of Police, Colo. Assn. Peer Support (hon.), Psi Chi. Achievements include research in Interpersonal Violence on the Internet and Cyber-Terrorism; Impact of Divorce on the Adjustment of College Students. Office: Nicolettii-Flater Assocs 3900 S Wadsworth Blvd Denver CO 80235 Home Phone: 303-359-9706; Office Phone: 303-989-1617. Personal E-mail: e2axe@aol.com.

AXELROD, GLEN SCOTT, publishing and pet product company executive; b. Newark, Nov. 4, 1953; s. Alan Robert and Janet Lee Axelrod; m. Jennifer Anderson, June 24, 1979; children: Jason Aaron, Daniel Jay. BA in Biology, Rutgers U., 1975; MSc in Zoology/Ichthyology, Rhodes U., Grahamstown, South Africa, 1978. Rschr. in phylogenetics Rhodes U. and Mus. Comparative Zoology, Harvard U., 1978-79; asst. to pres., sr. editor TFH Pubs., Inc., Neptune City, NJ, 1979-81; asst. to prin. Six Star Cablevision Group, Englewood, NJ, 1981-82; exec. v.p. Breckenridge Devel. Corp., Wayne, NJ, 1985-92; pres., CEO Design Svcs., Riverdale, NJ, 1992-95; pres. GJA Prodn. Corp., Colts Neck, NJ, 1982—; exec. v.p. TFH Pubs., Inc., Neptune City, 1996-97, pres., CEO, 1997—. Bd. dir. TFH Pubs., Inc. Exec. editor Tropical Fish Hobbyist mag., 1998—; contbr. articles to profl. jours. Trustee, treas. Deerhaven Assn., Mahwah, 1990—97. Recipient Best New Dog and Cat Product award, Pet Industry Distbrs. Assn., 1999, 2000, Best New Product award, PETCO, 2001, Spirit Recognition award, 2003, Best New Gift-Gen. Merchandise Product award, Am. Pet Products Mfrs. Assn., 2002, Best New Product-Dog and Cat, 2003. Fellow The Zool. Soc. London (sci.), Masons. Achievements include patents in field; over 200 patents pending in field; research in taxonomic description of new Pisces species. Avocations: skiing, diving, hiking, aquarium hobbyist, writing. Office: TFH Publications Inc One TFH Plz 3d & Union Neptune City NJ 07753

AXELROD, JONATHAN GANS, lawyer; b. NYC, Oct. 23, 1946; s. Arthur and Rosalind (Gans) Axelrod; m. Carol Jean Zachary, Jan. 16, 1983; children: Zachary Arthur, Tristan Gans. AB, Dartmouth Coll., 1968; JD, Columbia U., 1971; LLM in Labor Law, George Washington U., 1975. Bar: NY 1971, DC 1975. Trial atty. App. Ct. Br. NLRB, 1971-74; asst. gen. csl Fed. Conf. Teamsters, 1974-80; ptnr. Beins, Axelrod, Osborne, Mooney & Green, Washington, 1980-96, Beins, Axelrod, P.C., Washington, 1996—. Contbr. articles to profl. jours. Mem. ABA, DC Bar Assn. (co-chmn. sect. on labor law 1985-89, steering com. 1990-91). Office: Beins Axelrod PC 1625 Mass Ave NW Washington DC 20036 Home Phone: 202-686-0363; Office Phone: 202-328-7222. Business E-Mail: jaxelrod@beinsaxelrod.com.

AXELROD, LEONARD, management consultant; b. Oct. 27; s. Morris and Doris S. A. BA, Ind. U., 1972; MPA, U. So. Calif., 1974; JD, Hamline U., 1982. Asst. dir. Ind. Jud. Ctr. Ind. U. Sch. Law, Indpls., 1974-76; cons. Booz, Allen & Hamilton, Washington, 1976-77; staff assoc. Nat. Ctr. State Cts., St. Paul, 1977-82; ptnr. Ct. Mgmt. Cons., Mpls., Va., 1982-87, Friedman, Farrar & Axelrod, Mpls., 1984-86; prin. Ct. Mgmt. Cons., Mpls., 1987-94; v.p. CMC Justice Svcs., Inc., Mpls., 1994—; project mgr. Legal Rsch. Ctr., Mpls., 1996-97; ct. adminstr. U.S. Bankruptcy Ct., Mpls., 1997—2005; govt. acct. mgr. Thomson-West, Mpls., 2005—. Cons. Ctr. Jury Studies, Vienna, Va., 1979-82, Calif. Atty. Gen., 1972-73, Control Data Bus. Advisers, Mpls., 1982-88; arbitrator BBB, 2002—; adj. prof. Coll. Mgmt. Met. State U., 1998— Author: North Dakota Bench Book, 1982; contbr. articles to profl. jours.; assoc. editor Law Rev. Digest, 1982. Mem. presdl. search com. Hamline U., 1980-81; reporter Minn. Citizen Conf. on Cts., 1980; appointed to The Petrofund Bd., 1994. Samuel Miller scholar, 1981. Mem. ABA, ASPA, So. Calif. Soc. Pub. Adminstrn., Booz, Allen & Hamilton Alumni (pres. Minn. 1980), The Brandeis Soc. (exec. dir. Mpls. 1980), U. so. Calif. Midwest Alumni (exec. bd. Chgo. 1974), Phi Alpha Alpha, Phi Alpha Delta. Office: PO Box 11967 Saint Paul MN 55111-0967 Office Phone: 651-398-7345. E-mail: cmc@justice.com.

AXELROD, NORMAN N(ATHAN), technology and product development consultant; b. NYC, Aug. 26, 1934; s. Louis E. and Sadie (Katz) A.; m. Victoria Ann Grant, Mar. 21, 1975; children: Lauren Grant, Brian George. AB, Cornell U., 1954; postgrad., U. Paris, France, 1958; PhD in Optics and Physics, U. Rochester, 1959. Aerospace scientist NASA, Goddard Space Flight Ctr., Washington, 1959-60; rsch. fellow U. London, 1960-61; asst. prof. U. Del., 1961-65; mem. tech. staff Bell Labs., Murray Hill, NJ, 1965-72; prin. Axelrod Assocs., NYC, 1972—. Bd. dirs. World Resources Devel. Corp., Input-Output Tech., Inc.; mem. adv. bd. Del. Dept. Edn., 1963-64; participant vis. scientist program Am. Inst. Physics, 1963-64; advisor to White House, 1969-70, French Ministry Nat. Def. and War, 1971, Am. Consumer Products, Inc., Baker-Botts, Calor plc, Compuscan, Corning, CPC, Delco, Finnegan, Henderson et al, GE, Gen-Probe, Honeywell, IBM, ITT, Internat. FiberCom, Konishiroku, Jones Day, Johnson & Johnson, Labatt, Lear Siegler, Lockheed Martin, Medtronic, Recognition Equipment Inc., Perkin-Elmer, Sharp, Procter & Gamble, Samsung, Sensar, Symbol Techs., Teledyne Sci. and Imaging, Teradyne, Timken Co., Unilever Rsch., Wall St. Jour., Wheatland Tube, Woodgrain Millwork; advisor, cons. Bausch & Lomb, expert witness before Internat. Trace Commn.; guest cons. Marine Biol. Lab., Woods Hole, Mass., 1993—; pro bono Met. Mus. Art, 1969-72, CUNY Grad. Vision Rsch. Biology, 2001—, Georgetown U. Med. Sch., 2005—. Editor: Optical Properties of Dielectric Films, 1968; book reviewer, cons. John Wiley & Sons, 1965-68, Rheinhold-Van Nostrand, 1968-70, Pergamon Press, 1969-70; contbr. articles to profl. jours. Patentee in field. Boldt scholar; recipient Fortune 500 Corp. award for tech. contbn., 1990; grantee NATO, NSF, Office of Naval Rsch. Fellow AAAS; mem. IEEE, Am. Phys. Soc., Am. Optical Soc., Soc. Mfg. Engrs. (cert. by stature as CMfgE in machine vision), Del. Acad. Sci., N.Y. Acad. Sci., Electrochem. Soc., Sigma Xi, Sigma Pi Sigma, Pi Mu Epsilon. Home: 445 E 86th St New York NY 10028-6433 Office: Norman Axelrod Assocs 121 W 27th St Ste 601 New York NY 10001-6207 Office Phone: 212-741-6302. E-mail: naxelrod@axelrodassociates.com.

AXELSON, CHARLES FREDERIC, retired accounting educator, food products executive; b. Chgo., Apr. 24, 1917; m. Dorothy L. Jepson, July 23, 1940 (dec. Oct. 1994); children: Linda Axelson Masters, Fred, Lorraine Axelson Gresty; m. Marion I. Murray, Mar. 11, 1995. AB, MBA, U. Chgo., 1937. Staff acct. Lybrand, Ross Bros. & Montgomery, Chgo., 1938-41; with U.S. Gypsum Co., Chgo., 1941-70, asst. controller, 1946-52, controller, 1952-60, controller, asst. treas., 1960-70; v.p. controller Libby, McNeill & Libby, Chgo., 1970-78; v.p., chief fin. officer Lawry's Foods, Inc., LA, 1978-82; prof. acctg. U. So. Calif., LA, 1982-85; vis. lectr. Darling Downs Inst. Advanced Edn., Toowoomba, Queensland, Australia, 1985; lectr. acctg. Calif. State Poly. U., Pomona, 1985-92; lectr. emeritus, 1992—95. Lectr. acctg. Northwestern U., 1946-53; bd. dirs. Air Conditioning Co., 1982-96; bd. dirs. Goodwill Industries So. Calif., 1982—. Trustee emeritus Nat. Louis U.; bd. dirs. Ability First (formerly Crippled Children's Soc. So. Calif.), chmn., 1986-89, vice-chmn., 1990-99. Named to Calif. Poly. Acctg. Hall of Fame, 1996; named Lipton Vol. of Yr., 1997. Mem. AICPA, Fin. Execs. Internat. (past dir. L.A. chpt., past pres. Chgo. chpt., past nat. dir., past v.p. Midwestern area), Phi Delta Theta. Clubs: Town Hall (Los Angeles). Presbyterian. Home: 888 S Orange Grove Blvd # 2-w Pasadena CA 91105-1790 *Whatever successes I've had - business and personal - can be traced to self-discipline, a good education, a reputation for integrity, much reading, good health, outside interests to offset business pressures and lots of advance planning.*

AXELSON, JOSEPH ALLEN, professional sports team and publishing executive; b. Peoria, Dec. 25, 1927; s. Joseph Victor Axelson and Florence (Ealen) Massey; m. Malcolm Rae Smith, Oct. 7, 1950 (dec.); children: David Allen, Mark Stephen, Linda Rae. BS, Northwestern U., Evanston, Ill., 1949. Cert. judge Kansas City Barbeque Soc. With sports dept. Augusta Herald, Ga., 1955; sports info. dir. Furman U., Greenville, SC, 1956, Ga. So. U., Statesboro, 1957-60, Nat. Assn. Intercollegiate Athletics, Kansas City, Mo., 1961-62; tournament dir. Bowling Proprs. Assn. Am., Park Ridge, Ill., 1963-64; asst. exec. sec. Nat. Assn. Intercollegiate Athletics, Kansas City, Mo., 1964-68; exec. v.p., gen. mgr. Cin. Royals Profl. Basketball Team, Cin., 1969-72; mgr. Cin. Gardens, 1970-72; pres., gen. mgr. Kansas City Kings Profl. Basketball Team, Kansas City, Mo., 1972-79, 82-85; lectr. Fred Pryor Seminars, Overland Park, Kans., 1978—83; pres., gen. mgr. Sacramento Kings Profl. Basketball Team, 1985-88, exec. v.p., 1988-90; pres. Arco Arena, Sacramento, 1985-88; exec. v.p. Sacramento Sports Assn., Arco Sports Complex, 1988-90, Profl. Team Publs., Inc., Stamford, Conn., 1991-92; pub. Between The Vines Newsletter, 1993—2005. Exec. v.p. ops. NBA, NYC, 1979-82, chmn. competition and rules com., 1975-79; trustee Naismith Basketball Hall of Fame; co-host The Sports Page, Sta. KFMB-AM, San Diego, 1994-97. Author: Basketball Basics, 1987. Mem. Emil Verban Meml. Soc., Washington. Capt. Signal Corps. AUS, 1949-54. Named Nat. Basketball Exec. of Yr. The Sporting News, St. Louis, 1973, Sportsman of Yr., Rockne Club, Kansas City, 1975; recipient Annual Dirs. award Downtown, Inc., Kansas City, Mo., 1979, Nat. Assn. Intercollegiate Athletics Frank Cramer Nat. Svc. award, 1983, Man of Yr. award Sacramento C. of C., Calif., 1986, Sacramento Bus. Cmty. award, 1986; named to Ga. So. U. Sports Hall of Fame, 1990, Ill. Alpha Phi Kappa Psi Hall of Fame, 2006. Mem. Am. Philatelic Soc., Soc. for Am. Baseball Rsch., Morse Telegraph Club, Inc., Phi Kappa Psi (Hall of Fame Ill. 2006). Republican. Presbyterian. Home and Office: 230 B Ave Coronado CA 92118-1970

AXELSON, LINDA RAE, business director, event planning specialist; b. Statesboro, Ga., May 22, 1959; d. Joseph Allen and Malcolm Rae (Smith) Axelson; m. Aug. 29, 1981 (dec.). BA in Spanish, Baker U., 1981. Acct. Lois A. Brozey, CPA, San Diego, 1981-82; bus. mgr. San Diego Chicken, Inc., 1983; discount brokerage mgr. Union Bank and Trust, Bartlesville, Okla., 1984; bus. mgr. ARCO Arena, Sacramento, 1985-86, box office mgr., 1987-91, San Diego Sports Arena, 1991—93, Arrowhead Pond of Anaheim, Calif., 1993—96; asst. contr. Stamford Ctr. for the Arts, 1997-98, box office mgr., 1999—2001; corp. events mgr. Allied Domecq Spirits and Wine N.Am., 2000—05; acct. supr. Relay Event Mktg., NYC, 2005; bus. mgr. Greenville Drive Profl. Baseball Club, SC, 2005—07; mgr. nat. events BMW Car Club Am., Greenville, 2007—. Cons. Don Chargin Boxing Prodns., L.A., 1987—. Recipient scholarship Baker Univ., 1981. Mem. Alpha Chi Omega (sch. com. chmn. 1981), Sigma Delta Pi, Alpha Mu Gamma. Republican. Presbyterian. Avocation: collector of mystery novels and miniatures. Home: 32 Oak Grove Lake Rd Greenville SC 29615

AXENTE, LIVIU MIRCEA, management consultant; b. Bucharest, Romania, June 6, 1966; s. Aurelian and Maria (Vatra) A. Cert. internat. financier, U. of the Ams., 1995; degree in freelance press photography, Freelance Photogs. Orgn., Lewisville, NC, 1996; grad., Alexander Hamilton Inst., 1998. Cert. Profl. Cons., Cons. Inst. Freelance journalist, Bucharest, 1982-89; country rep. Sipa Press Paris, Bucharest, 1990-95; dir. Global Network Corp., Wilmington, Del., 1997—; pres. Atlantis Internet Svcs. Corp., Wilmington, Del., 1999—. Contbr. photos to numerous mags. Sgt. Romanian Army, 1985-86. Recipient Spl. Excelence prize Nat. Daily Last Word, 1994. Mem. Internat. Sport Press Assn., Internat. Freelance Photographers Orgn., Assoc. mem., Assn. of Cert. Fraud Examiners Region, Natl. Geographic Soc., The Highlander Club, The Oxford Club. Avocations: fishing, travel, reading, writing. Office: 3422 Old Capitol Trl Wilmington DE 19808-6124

AXFORD, ROY ARTHUR, nuclear engineering educator; b. Detroit, Aug. 26, 1928; s. Morgan and Charlotte (Donaldson) A.; m. Anne-Sofie Langfeldt Rasmussen, Apr. 1, 1954; children: Roy Arthur, Elizabeth Carole, Trevor Craig Charles. BA, Williams Coll., 1952; BS, MIT, 1952, MS, 1955, DSc, 1958. Supr. theoretical physics group Atomics Internat., Canoga Park, Calif., 1958-60; assoc. prof. nuc. engring. Tex. A&M U., 1960-62, prof., 1962-63; assoc. prof. nuc. engring. Northwestern U., 1963-66; assoc. prof. U. Ill., Urbana, 1966-68, prof., 1968—. Cons. Los Alamos Nat. Lab., N.Mex., 1963— Vice-chmn. MIT Alumni Fund Drive, 1970-72, chmn., 1973-75; sustaining fellow MIT, 1984. Mem. ASME, Am. Nuc. Soc. (Excellence in Undergrad. Tchg. award 1990, 95, 97, 99, 2002, 04, disting. faculty Alpha Nu Sigma 1991), SAR (sec.-treas. Piankeshaw chpt. 1975-81, v.p. chpt. 1982-83, pres. chpt. 1984-86), Kiwanis (charter life patron fellow 1992), Sigma Xi, Tau Beta Pi, Phi Kappa Phi.

AXILROD, STEPHEN HARVEY, global economic consultant, economist; b. NYC, June 21, 1926; s. Jacob James and Pearl (Feltenstein) A.; m. Katherine Podolsky, July 1, 1950; children: Peter, Emily Axilrod Hildner, Richard. Student, So. Meth. U., 1943-44; AB magna cum laude, Harvard U., 1948; MA, U. Chgo., 1950, postgrad., 1951-52. Assoc. dir. div. research and statistics Fed. Res. Bd., Washington, 1970-73, advisor to bd. govs., 1973-76, staff dir. for monetary and fin. policy, 1976-86; economist domestic fin. Fed. Open Market Com., Washington, 1974-78, economist, 1978-81; staff dir., sec. Fed. Open Market Commn., Washington, 1981-86; vice chmn. Nikko Securities Internat., NYC, 1986-94; cons. internat. orgns. and ctrl. banks on policy ops., 1994—; cons. global econs. and markets pvt. practice, 1994—. Advisor Brookings Panel on Econ. Activity, Washington, 1986-89; mem. investment com. Japan Soc., 1987-03; mem. adv. coun. Ctrl. Bank of Oman, 1993-99; mem. bd. Fin. Svcs. Vol. Corps, 2005-, chmn. audit com. Contbr. articles on monetary policy, credit and securities markets, transformation of policy ops. and markets in emerging countries and related matters to books, newspapers, mags. and profl. jours. With USN, 1944—46. Mem.: Phi Beta Kappa. Avocations: tennis, writing poetry and prose, reading, hiking, squash. Office Phone: 212-439-6048. E-mail: staxil@aol.com.

AXINN, GEORGE HAROLD, rural sociology educator; b. Jamaica, NY, Feb. 1, 1926; s. Hyman and Celia (Schneider) A.; m. Nancy Kathryn Wigsten, Feb. 17, 1945; children: Catherine, Paul, Martha, William. BS, Cornell U., 1947; MS, U. Wis., 1952, PhD, 1958. Editorial asst. Cornell U. Geneva, N.Y., 1947; bull. editor U. Md., College Park, 1949; chmn. dept. rural communication U. Del., Newark, 1950; mem. faculty Mich. State U., East Lansing, 1953—, assoc. dir. coop. extension service, 1955-60; coordinator U. Nigeria program, 1961-65, prof. agrl. econs., 1970-85, prof. resource devel., 1985-95, prof. emeritus, 1996—, asst. dean internat. studies and programs, 1964-85; pres., exec. dir. Midwest Univs. Consortium for Internat. Activities, Inc., 1969-76, 1969-76. FAO rep. to Nepal, 1983-85, India and Bhutan, 1989-91; cons. World Bank, 1973-74, Ford Found., 1968, UNICEF, 1978, FAO, 1974, 87, 89, Govt. of India, 1988; vis. prof. Cornell U., Ithaca, N.Y., 1958-60, U. Ill., Urbana, 1969-70 Author: Modernizing World Agriculture: A Comparative Study of Agricultural Extension Education Systems, 1972, New Strategies for Rural Development, Rural Life Associates, 1978, FAO Guide Alternative Approaches to Agricultural Extension, 1988, Collaboration in International Rural Development - A Practitioner's Handbook (with Nancy W. Axinn), 1997; contbr. articles to various publs. Served with USNR, 1944-46. Recipient Outstanding Alumni award Cornell U. Coll. Agrl. and Life Sci., 1993; W.K. Kellogg Found. fellow, 1956-57. Home: The Fountains at La Cholla 2001 W Rudasill Rd #5211 Tucson AZ 85704 Personal E-mail: axinn@msu.edu.

AXINN, STEPHEN MARK, lawyer; b. NYC, Oct. 21, 1938; s. Mack N. and Lili H. (Tannenbaum) A.; m. Stephanie Chertok, May 12, 1963; children: Audrey, David, Jill. BS, Syracuse U., NY, 1959; LLB, Columbia U., NYC, 1962. Bar: NY 1962, US Supreme Ct. 1962. Assoc. Cahill & Gordon, NYC, 1963-64, Malcolm A. Hoffman, NYC, 1964-66, Skadden, Arps, Slate, Meagher & Flom, NYC, 1966-69, ptnr., 1970-97, Axinn, Veltrop & Harkrider LLP, NYC, 1997—. Adj. prof. Law Sch. NYU, 1981-83, Law Sch. Columbia U., 1983-85; counsel Bellsouth in acquisition by AT&T; lead counsel WorldCom-Sprint merger investigation and litigation Antitrust Divsn. US Dept. Justice, 1999-2000; special counsel US Dept. Justice Antitrust Dir., 1999—2000. Author: Acquisitions Under H-S-R, 1980; contbr. articles to profl. jours. Chmn. lawyers div. United Jewish Appeal, NYC, 1985-87; mem. exec. com., treas. Jewish Theol. Sem. Am., 1984-96; mem. bd. visitors Columbia Law Sch., 1993-98; mem. adv. panel on environ. crimes by orngs. US Sentencing Commn., 1992-94. Capt. US Army, 1965-68. Mem. ABA (council antitrust sect. 1983-85), NY State Bar Assn. (chmn. antitrust sect. 1982-83). Office: Axinn Veltrop & Harkrider LLP 1370 Ave of the Americas New York NY 10019-6708 Office Phone: 212-728-2200. Business E-Mail: sma@avhlaw.com.

AXLEY, FREDERICK WILLIAM, lawyer; b. Chgo., June 23, 1941; s. Frederick R. and Elena (Hoffman-Pinther) A.; m. Cinda Jane Russell, Mar. 29, 1969; children: Sarah Elizabeth, Elizabeth Jane. BA, Holy Cross Coll., 1963; MA, U. Wis., 1966; JD, U. Chgo., 1969. Bar: Ill. 1969, U.S. Dist. Ct. (no. dist.) Ill. 1969, U.S. Ct. Appeals (7th cir.) 1970. Assoc. McDermott, Will & Emery, Chgo., 1969-74, jr. ptnr., 1974-80, sr. ptnr., 1980—. Trustee Wilmette Elem. Sch. Dist. #39, Ill., 1976-81, Ill. chpt. Nature Conservancy, 1983-91; bd. dirs. Bus. and Profl. People for the Pub. Interest, Chgo., 1984—; bd. dirs. Friends of the Chgo. River, 1994—, pres., 1998—; bd. dirs. Shore Line Place, 1994—, pres. 2001—, Interfaith Housing Devel. Corp., 1997—; 1st. v.p., 2000—. Served to lt. USN, 1963-65. Mem. Mich. Shores Club (Wilmette). Democrat. Roman Catholic. Office: McDermott Will & Emery 227 W Monroe St Ste 3100 Chicago IL 60606-5096 E-mail: faxley@msn.com.

AXLEY, HARTMAN, retired estate planner, underwriter; b. Madison, Wis., Apr. 17, 1931; s. Ralph Emerson and Katharine Nella (Hartman) A.; m. Marguerite Ann Thessin, Sept. 4, 1954; children: Colleen Lynn Axley Patrick, Timothy Hartman Axley. BA, U. Wis., 1952, JD, 1956; MSFS, Am. Coll., Bryn Mawr, Pa., 1983. CLU, cert. fin. planner, accedited estate planner; chartered fin. cons.; registered health underwriter. Assoc. atty. Holland & Hart, Denver, 1956—58; life underwriter Colo. Assocs. of Allmerica Fin. (formerly State Mut. Cos.), Denver, 1958—2003. Mem. bd. editl. advisors Fin. Svc. Advisors (formerly Life and Health Insurance Sales), Lexington, Ky.; mem. Colo. Ethics in Bus. Alliance Bd., 1995—, v.p., 2001—; mem. Denver Estate Planning Coun., pres., 1968-69; founding mem. Boulder County Estate Planning Coun., 1976—. Author: National Ski Patrol Ski Lift Evacuation Manual, 1975, National Ski Patrol Awards Manual, 1980. Bd. dir. Met. Denver YMCA, 1978-81, S.W. Denver Family YMCA, chmn., 1978-81; mem. First Aider Mile High chpt. ARC, Denver, 1956-86; bd. dir., officer Cmty. Concert Assn. Denver, 1962-65; bd. dir. Colo. Ski Mus., vice chair, 2003-; chair Colo. Ski Hall of Fame, 1996-99; mem. Nat. Ski Patrol Sys., 1948—, asst. nat. dir., 1969-76, Rocky Mountain divsn. dir., 1963-69 (Minnie Dole award 1988, Schobinger Outstanding Adminstr. award 1973); mem. Olympic Ski Patrol, Squaw Valley, Calif., 1960; mem., patroller Arapahoe Basin Ski Patrol, 1956-85, front range dir., 1961-63; coord. badminton Rocky Mountain Sr. Games, 1987—. Capt. USAF (JAG), 1952-60. Named to Roll of Honor, Mile High ARC, 1974, Met.Denver YMCA Hall of Fame, 1987, Colo. Ski Hall of Fame, 1993; recipient Award of Merit (Lifesaving) ARC, 1959, J. Stanley Edwards award Colo. and Denver Assn. Life Underwriters, 1980, Badminton medal Rocky Mountain Sr. Games, 1987—, U.S. Badminton Assn. Sr. Championship, 1988, 92, U.S. Nat. Sr. Games, 1991, 93, 95, 97, 99, 2001, 03, 2005. Mem. ABA (real property, probate and trust sect.), Nat. Assn. Estate Planners and Couns. (bd. dir. 1970-76, pres. 1974-75, dir. emeritus 1989—, patron chair 1975—, accreditation com. 1991—, Hartman Axley award outstanding svc. and achievement 2004), Nat. Assn. Estate Planners (founder, bd. dir. 1987), Soc. Fin. Svcs. Profls. (bd. dir. 1992-95, we. region v.p. 1994-95, nat. pub. rels. com. 1990-94, vice chair 1992, chair baby boomer rsch. project 1990, Colo.-Wyo. liaison 1992-97), Estate Planning Law Specialists, Inc. (founder, bd. dir.), Am. Soc. CLU and ChFC (Rocky Mountain chpt. bd. dirs. 1985-91, pres. 1989-90), Assn. Advanced Life Underwriters (Colo. liaison, 1996-2000), Nat. Assoc. of Ins. and Fin. Advisors (Wesley Whitney award 1995, qualifying and life, Million Dollar Round Table 1970-85), Colo. Ins. Commr.'s Adv. Coun. (chmn. 1990—), Colo. Assn. Commerce and Industry (Health Care Task Force 1990-94), Nat. and Colo. Assoc. of Ins. and Fin. Advisors (Nat. Quality award, Nat. Sales Achievement award), Life Underwriter Charities, Inc. (founder, bd. dir. 1989-92), Metro Denver Assn. Health Underwriters (founder, bd. dir. 1990-92, legis. chair 1990-92), Colo. State Assn. Health Underwriters (charter 1986—, founder, bd. dirs. 1986-92, legis. chair 1986-92), Nat. Assn. Health Underwriters (leading prodrs. roundtable 1981-89), U.S. Badminton Assn. (staff vol. Olympic Games Atlanta 1996), U. Wis. Alumni Assn. (bd. dir. 1970-89, Spark Plug award 1977), Wis. Bar Assn., Scabbard and Blade, Provost Corps, Denver Athletic Club (bd. dir. 1984-87, Sr. Athlete of Yr. 1997, Legend 2003), Phi Delta Phi, Phi Mu Alpha Congregationalist. Avocations: skiing, badminton, deltiophile, singing, travel. Home and Office: 1845 S Jay Way Lakewood CO 80232-7095 Office Phone: 720-941-9703.

AXON, DONALD CARLTON, architect; b. Haddonfield, NJ, Feb. 27, 1931; s. William Russell Sr. and Gertrude L. (Ellis) A.; m. Rosemary Smith, Sept. 1952 (div. Oct. 1967); children: Donald R., James K., Marianne Axon Flannery, Darren H., William R. II; m. Janice Jacobs, Mar. 16, 1968; stepchildren: Jonathan Lee, Elise Marie. BArch, Pratt Inst., 1954; MS in Arch., Columbia U., 1966. Registered architect, NY, Pa., Calif. Designer, drafter Keith Hibner, Assoc., Hicksville, NY, 1954-56; designer Charles Wood, Riverhead, NY, 1956-59; architect, prin Donald C. Axon, Assoc., Wantaugh, NY, 1959; ptnr. Bailey-Axon & Assoc., Long Beach, NY, 1960-66; project mgr. Caudill Rowlett Scott, Houston, 1966-69; in-house arch. Kaiser Permanente Hosp., LA, 1969-75; dir. med. facilities Daniel Mann Johnson Mendenhall, LA, 1975-78, Lyon Assoc., LA, 1979-80; pres. Donald C. Axon, FAIA, Inc., LA, 1980—. Tchr. bldg. sci. program U. So. Calif., 1978-82; lectr. in field; profl. advisor dept. architecture U. Tex., 1968-69; advisor to chmn. Sch. Architecture Rice U., Houston, 1968-69; profl. dir. Future Architect Am., 1965-66. Mem. Crestwood Hills Assn., bd. dir. 1971-75, pres., 1973-75, archtl. rev. com., 1987—; bd. dir. Brentwood Community Fedn., 1973-75, v.p., 1974-75. Recipient LA Beautiful award KPH Norwalk Hosp. Fellow AIA, Royal Soc. Health, Health Facilities Inst., Am. Coll. Healthcare Arch. (founding fellow),(Calif. regional bd. dir. 1987-89, mem. various subcoms., chair steering com. 1980, liaison 1991—, bd. dir. L.A. chpt. 1983-84, pres. 1986, chair com. on architecture for health 1974, chair health facilities com. Calif. coun. 1975, Disting. Svc. citation 1992), mem. Am. Soc. Healthcare Engr., Archtl. Found. LA (founding, v.p. 1985-89, pres. 1989-90), Internat. Conf. Bldg. Ofcl., Am. Hosp. Assn., Forum for Health Care Planning (bd. dir. 1982—, pres. 1993-94). Office: 24302 Carlton Ct Laguna Niguel CA 92677-3718 Office Phone: 949-360-8112. Fax: 949-360-8114. E-mail: donaxon@aol.com.

AXTELL, JAMES LEWIS, history professor; b. Endicott, NY, Dec. 20, 1941; s. Arthur James Axtell and Laura (England) Levinsky; m. Susan Carol Hallas, Aug. 31, 1963; children: Nathaniel Harsen, Jeremy England. BA, Yale U., 1963; PhD, U. Cambridge, Eng., 1967. Asst. prof. Yale U., New Haven, 1966-72; assoc. prof. Sarah Lawrence Coll., Bronxville, NY, 1972-75; vis. prof. Northwestern U., Evanston, Ill., 1977-78; prof. Coll. of William and Mary, Williamsburg, Va., 1978—; William R. Kenan Jr. prof. of humanities Coll. William and Mary, Williamsburg, Va., 1986—. Author: The Educational Writings of John Locke, 1968, The School Upon a Hill, 1974, The European and the Indian, 1981, The Invasion Within, 1985 (prize, 1985, 2 prizes, 1986), After Columbus, 1988, Beyond 1492, 1992, The Indians' New South, 1997, The Pleasures of Academe, 1998, Natives and Newcomers, 2001, The Making of Princeton University, 2006; editor: The Indian Peoples of Eastern America, 1981; contbr. articles to profl. jours. in field. Recipient Outstanding Faculty award Va. State Coun. Higher Edn., 1988; NEH fellow, 1975-77, 86, 92, J.S. Guggenheim Meml. Found. fellow, 1981-82, Am. Coun. Learned Socs. fellow, 1987. Fellow Am. Acad. Arts and Scis.; mem. Soc. Am. Historians, Am. Soc. for Ethnohistory (pres. 1988-89), The Champlain Soc., Am. Hist. Assn., Orgn. Am. Historians, Colonial Soc. Mass., Pilgrim Soc., Mass. Hist. Soc., Am. Antiquarian Soc. Democrat. Avocation: book collecting. Home: 109 Walnut Hills Dr Williamsburg VA 23185-3426 Office: Coll of William & Mary Dept History Williamsburg VA 23187-8795 Office Phone: 757-221-3730. E-mail: jlaxte@wm.edu.

AXTHELM, NANCY, advertising executive; V.p., head prodn. group Grey Worldwide (formerly Grey Advt. Inc.), sr. v.p., dep. dir. broadcast prodn., 1990—92, sr. v.p., dir. broadcast prodn., 1992—93, exec. v.p., dir. broadcast prodn., 1993—. Office: Grey Worldwide 777 3rd Ave Fl 10 New York NY 10017-1302

AYAD, JOSEPH MAGDY, retired psychologist; b. Cairo, May 21, 1926; arrived in U.S., 1949, naturalized, 1961; s. Fahim Gayed and Victoria Gabour (El-Masri) Ayad; m. Widad Fareed Bishai, May 29, 1954; children: Fareed Merritt, Victor Maher, Michael Joseph, Mona Elaine. BA in Social Scis., Am. U., Cairo, 1946; MA in Clin. Psychology, Stanford U., 1952; PhD in Clin. Psychology, U. Denver, 1956. Trans. Hoover Inst. War and Peace Stanford U., 1950—51; asst. to chief psychologist Colo. Psychopathic Hosp., 1952—54; cons. Child Guidance Clinic State Dept. Pub. Welfare, Denver, 1953—56; cons. psychologist Dept. Pub. Welfare State of Tex., 1957—72; cons. psychologist Dept. Insts. Social and Rehab. Svc. State of Okla., 1960—72; cons. psychologist N.Mex. Dept. Pub. Welfare, 1960—72; lectr. Fitzsimmons Army Hosp., Denver, 1953—54; vis. psychologist Child Guidance Clinic State Dept. Pub. Welfare, Pueblo, Colo., 1953—54; staff psychologist Cons. Psychol. Svc., Denver, 1956—57, High Plains Neurol. Ctr., Amarillo, Tex., 1973—2002; pres. JMA Cattle Co., Amarillo, 1973—2002; v.p., treas. Filigon Inc., Amarillo, 1962—75, pres., 1976—2002, ret., 2002. Mem. profl. adv. bd. Amarillo Mental Health Assn., 1968—69. Contbr. articles to profl. jours. Mem. Amarillo Child Welfare Bd., 1961—63; area chmn. U. Denver Fund Raising Campaign, 1963; mem. profl. adv. bd. St. Paul's Meth. Ch. Sch. for Children with Learning Disabilities, Amarillo, 1969—70. Recipient Grad. Sr. award in philosophy, Am. U. at Cairo, 1946. Mem.: APA, Calif. Psychol. Assn., Tex. Psychol. Assn., Potter-Randall County (Tex.) Psychol. Soc. (pres. 1974), Am. Assn. Marriage and Family Therapists, Internat. Assn. Applied Psychology, Am. Psychol. Soc., Amarillo Country Club. Presbyterian. Office Phone: 806-352-8840.

AYADI, MARY OLUFEMI, health economist, educator; arrived in U.S., 1992; d. David Adebayo and Rachel Foluke Alao; m. Olusegun Felix Ayadi, May 29, 2004. BSc. in Agr.- Fisheries Mgmt., U. of Ibadan, 1989; MA in Econs., Ga. State U., Atlanta, 1996, PhD in Econs., 2001. Devel. intern Womens' Internat. League for Peace and Freedom, NYC and Geneva, Switzerland, 1992; instr., grad. rsch. asst. dept econs. Ga. State U., Atlanta, 1993—99; rsch. fellow Ctrs. for Disease Control and Prevention, Atlanta, 1999—2001, prevention effectiveness fellow, 2001—03, health economist, 2003—05; asst. prof. U. of Houston Clear Lake, 2005—. Cons. Ctrs. for Disease Control and Prevention, Atlanta, 2005—. Contbr. articles to profl. jours. Patron St Barnabas Anglican Primary Sch., Ode-Erinje, Ondo State, Nigeria; bd. mem. Students Image Career Consulting Inc, Atlanta, 2002—05. Recipient Nat. Ctr. for Chronic Disease Prevention and Health Promotion Group Award for Operational Rsch., Ctrs. for Disease Control and Prevention, 2003, Cert. of Achievement, 2001, Cert. of Appreciation for Providing Outstanding Contbns. and Leadership, Prevention Effectiveness Br., Ctrs. for Disease Control and Prevention, 2001. Mem.: APHA, Am. Congress of Healthcare Execs., Internat. Acad. of African Bus. and Devel. (track chair 2006), Internat. Health Econs. Assn., Phi Beta Delta. Avocation: travel. Office: U Houston Clear Lake 2700 Bay Area Blvd Box 73 Houston TX 77058-1098 Business E-Mail: ayadim@uhcl.edu.

AYAFOR, MARTIN CHUNGONG, ambassador; b. Awing, Bamenda, Cameroon, Mar. 15, 1947; arrived in US, 1980; s. Joseph Chungong and Regina Ngwing; m. Justina Melo Chinda, Dec. 26, 1973; children: Akwesey Ngwenyi, Ayafor Temengye, Ngwingmba Aziseh, Apiseh Ayakeh, Aziwoh Afeseh, Nchinda Sehlakwe. BA wih honors in hist., U. Cameroon, Cameroon, 1972; MPhil in polit. sci., Internat. Rel.; doctorate in internat. rels., Inst. of Cameroon, Cameroon, 1974; MBA in pub. mgmt., Higher Inst. of Pub. Mgmt. of Cameroon, 1985. Cert. Pub. Svc. Diplomat Pub. Svc. Bd. Exams., Cameroon, 1980. Head UN divsn. Min. of Fgn. Affairs, Yaounde, Cameroon, 1977—80; second counselor Cameroon Mission to UN, NYC, 1981—83; head diplomatic affairs' divsn. Presidency of the Republic, Yaounde, 1983—89; permanent sec. Min. of Livestock, Fisheries and Animal Ind., Yaounde, 1989—90, Min. of External Rels., Yaounde, 1990—92; min., dir. Cabinet of the Prime Min., Head of Govt., Yaounde, 1992—96; ambassador, dep. permanent rep. Cameroon to the UN, NYC, 2002—. Mem. UN Sec.-Gens. Adv. Bd. on Security and Disarmament Matters, NYC, 1992—96; chmn. Panel of Experts on Sierra Leone, UN, NYC, 2000—01, Panel of Experts on Liberia, UN, 2001—02; dir. publication Peace and Security Studies, Yaounde Internat. Inst., 1992. Contbr. articles various profl. jours. Mem. Cameroon Nat. Scholarships Commn., 1977—79; examiner, mem. Cameroon Gen. Cert. of Edn. Jury, 1977—79; mem. bd. dirs. Trans-Cameroon Railway Corp., 1984—89, Cameroon Nat. Water Corp., 1985—90; chmn. bd. dirs. Nat. Fin. Credit Corp., 2000—03. Recipient Knight Order of Valor, Govt. of Cameroon, 1986, Officer Order of Valor, 1989, Comdr. Order of Valor, 2002. Mem.: Cameroon Assn. of Diplomats (permanent sec. 1980—), Club '58 Social Club, Pub. Works Social Club (v.p. 1978—80). Avocations: reading, soccer, basketball, music, hunting. Home: 184-15 Avon Rd Jamaica NY 11432 Office: Cameroon Mission To The UN 22 E 73rd St New York NY 10021 Office Phone: 212-794-2295. Office Fax: 212-249-0533. Business E-Mail: vivifad@aol.com.

AYALA, FRANCISCO JOSÉ, geneticist, educator; b. Madrid, Mar. 12, 1934; came to U.S., 1961, naturalized, 1971; s. Francisco and Soledad (Pereda) A.; m. Hana Lostakova, Mar. 8, 1985; children by previous marriage: Francisco José, Carlos Alberto. BS, Universidad de Madrid, 1954; MA, Columbia U., 1963, PhD, 1964; D honoris causa, Universidad de León, Spain, 1982, Universidad de Barcelona, 1986, Universidad de Madrid, 1986, U. Athens, Greece, 1991, U. Vigo, Spain, 1996, U. Islas, Baleares, Spain, 1998, U. Valencia, Spain, 1999, U. Bologna, Italy, 2001, U. Vladivostok, Russia, 2002, Masaryk U., Czech. Rep., 2003, U. Padua, Italy, 2006, Nat. U. de la Plata, Argentina, 2007. Research assoc. Rockefeller U., 1964-65; asst. prof. Providence Coll., 1965-67, Rockefeller U., 1967-71; assoc. prof. to prof. genetics U. Calif., Davis, 1971-87, disting. prof. biology Irvine, 1987-89, Donald Bren prof. of Biol. scis., 1989—, univ. prof., 2003—. Bd. dirs. basic biology NRC, 1982-91, chmn., 1984-91, mem. commn. on life scis., 1982-91; mem. nat. adv. coun. Nat. Inst. Gen. Med. Scis.; mem. exec. com. EPA, 1979-80; mem. adv. com. directorate sci. and engring. edn. NSF, 1989-91; mem. nat. adv. coun. for human genome rsch. NIH, 1990-93; mem. Pres. com. advisors sci. and tech., 1994-2001. Author: Human Evolution. Trails from the Past, 2007, Darwin's Gift to Science and Religion, 2007, Systematics and the Origin of Species. On Ernst Mayr's 100th Anniversary, 2006, Variation and Evolution in Plants and Microorganisms. Toward a New Synthesis 50 Years after Stebbins, 2000, Evolutionary and Molecular Biology: Scientific Perspectives on Divine Action, 1998, Population and Evolutionary Genetics, 1982, Modern Genetics, 1980, 2d edit., 1984, Evolving: the Theory and Processes of Organic Evolution, 1979, Evolution, 1977, Molecular Evolution, 1976, Studies in the Philosophy of Biology, 1974. Recipient medal Coll. de France, 1979, Mendel medal Czech Republic Acad. Scis., 1994, Hon. Gold medal Acad. Nat. dei Lincei, Rome, 2000, U.S. Nat. Medal of Sci. award 2001, gold medal Stazione Zoological Naples, 2003; Guggenheim fellow, Fulbright fellow. Fellow AAAS (Sci. Freedom and Responsibility award 1987, bd. dirs. 1989-93, pres.-elect 1993-94, pres. 1994-95, chmn. of bd. 1995-96, chmn. com. on health of sci. enterprise 1991—, mem. nat. coun. for sci. and edn. for phase II, project 2061 1990—), Am. Acad. Microbiology; mem. NAS (sect. population biology evolution and ecology chmn. 1983-86, councillor 1986-89, bd. dirs. Nat. Acad. Corp. 1990—), Am. Acad. Arts and Scis., Am. Soc. Naturalists (sec. 1973-76), Genetics Soc. Am., Am. Genetic Assn. (hon. life, Wilhelmine E. Key award), Ecology Soc. Am., Am. Philos. Soc., Soc. Study Evolution (pres. 1979-80), Royal Acad. Scis. Spain (fgn. mem.), Russian Acad. Natural Scis. (fgn. mem.), Mex. Acad. Scis. (fgn. mem.), Acad. Nat. dei Lincei (Rome) (fgn.), Serbian Acad. Scis. & Arts (fgn. mem.), Sigma Xi (William Proctor prize 2000, pres. 2003—). Home: 2 Locke Ct Irvine CA 92617-4034 Office: U Calif Dept Ecology & Evolution Irvine CA 92697-0001 Office Phone: 949-824-8293. Business E-Mail: fjayala@uci.edu.

AYALA, JOE SERRANO, marketing professional, personal trainer; b. Tabucca, PR, May 10, 1953; s. Jose and Aracelas Serang Ayala; m. Janice Estelle Molina, Oct. 24, 1984. BA, Pa. StateU., State College, 1975; MA, Nat. U., San Deigo, 2001. Family therapist Hispanic Ctr. Daniel Torres, Reading, Pa., 2001—03, dir. mktg. & devel., 2003—. Chair anti-gang initiative City of Reading, 2006—; mem. Berks County Conflict Resolution Task Force, 2005—, City of Reading Trash Graffiti Task Force, 2005—; bd. dirs. Berks County Conservancy, Reading, 2002—05, PR Latin Assn., Reading, 2002—04, ARC, Reading, 2006—, Berks County Pks. and Recreation, Pa., 2006—. Sgt. USMC, 1981—2001. Fellow: Am. Fundraising Profls. (bd. dirs. 2006—). Republican. Roman Catholic. Home: 510 Snyder Rd Reading PA 19609 Office: Hispanic Ctr Daniel Torres 501 Washington St Reading PA 19601

AYALA, JOHN L., retired librarian, dean; b. Long Beach, Calif., Aug. 28, 1943; s. Francisco and Angelina (Rodriguez) Ayala; m. Patricia Marie Dozier, July 11, 1987 (dec. Jan. 19, 2001); children: Juan, Sara; m. Gloria Ann Aulwes, Dec. 28, 2002. BA in History, Calif. State U., Long Beach, 1970, MPA, 1981; MLS, Immaculate Heart Coll., LA, 1971. Libr. paraprofl. Long Beach Pub. Lib., 1963-70; libr. L.A. County Pub. Libr., 1971-72, Long Beach City Coll., 1972-90, assoc. prof., 1972-90, pres. acad. senate, 1985-87; dean, Learning Resources Fullerton Coll., 1990—2006, evening/weekend supr., 1997—99, adminstr. study abroad program, 2000—06, ret., 2006; interim dir. libr. & learning resources Compton Coll., 2006—07. Chmn. Los Angeles County Com. to Recruit Mexican-Am. Librs., 1971-74; mem. acad. senate Calif. Cmty. Colls., 1985-90; pres. Latino Faculty/Staff Assn., NOCCD, 1993-2000. Editor: Calif. Librarian, 1971. Served with USAF, 1966-68, Vietnam. U.S. Office Edn. fellow for libr. sci., 1970-71. Mem. ALA (com. mem. 1971—, Melvil Dewey award com. 1998—), Calif. Libr. Assn., REFORMA Nat. Assn. to Promote Spanish Speaking Libr. Svc. (founding mem., v.p., pres. 1973-76), Arnulfo Trejo Libr. of the Yr. Award 2001, from Reforma), Calif. State U.-Long Beach Alumni Assn. (treas. 2003—). Democrat. Roman Catholic. Home: 607 E Las Palmas Dr Fullerton CA 92835-1617 Office Phone: 310-900-1648 2170. Personal E-mail: ayala_j@fcompton.edu.

AYALA, KARA J., speech educator, researcher; d. Lester William and Shirley Jean Zempel; m. Jose Mario Ayala, Nov. 11, 2004. MA, Northwestern U., Evanston, Ill., 1999, PhD, 2004. Speech pathology lic. Ill. State

Speech-Language-Hearing Assn., 2002, Tex. State Speech-Lang.-Hearing Assn., 2006. Speech-lang. pathologist Northwestern Meml. Hosp., Chgo., 2000—01; adj. prof. Govs. State U., University Park, Ill., 2001—02; sr. speech-lang. pathologist Gottlieb Meml. Hosp., Melrose Park, Ill., 2002—06; asst. prof. St. Xavier U., Chgo., 2002—06, U. Tex. Pan Am., Edinburg, Ill., 2006—. Communication sciences speech lab coord. U. Tex. Pan Am., Edinburg, 2006—, cmty. health fair supr., 2006—07. Contbr. articles to profl. jours. Vol. Food Bank So. Tex., McAllen, Tex., 2007. Scholar, Northwestern U., Evanston, 1997—2002. Mem.: Am. Speech-Lang.-Hearing Assn. (licentiate cert. clin. competence), Mortar Bd., Golden Key. Avocations: running, travel, bicycling, reading, rollerblading. Office: U Tex Pan American HSHW 1308 1201 W University Dr Edinburg TX 78541 Office Phone: 956-318-5275.

AYALA, ORLANDO, information technology executive; b. Bogota, Colombia; married; 4 children. BA in Mgmt. Info. Sys. With NCR Corp., Dayton, Ohio, 1981—91, product & sales mgr., 1985—88; sr. dir. Latin Am. region Microsoft Corp., Miami, 1991—95, sr. v.p., intercontinental region Redmond, Wash., 1995—98, sr. v.p., South Pacific & Amer. region, 1998—2000, group v.p., worldwide sales, mktg. & svc. group, 2000—03, sr. v.p., small & midmarket solutions & ptnr. group, 2003—. Office: Microsoft Corp One Microsoft Way Redmond WA 98052-6399

AYALA, RAYMOND See DADDY YANKEE

AYANSO, ANTENEH WONDIMU, information systems educator; arrived in Can., 2004; BA, Addis Ababa U., Ethiopia, 1993; MBA, Syracuse U., 2000; PhD, U. Conn., Storrs, 2004. Cert. in prodn. and inventory mgmt. Assn. For Ops. Mgmt. (formerly Am. Prodn. and Inventory Mgmt.), 2000. Asst. lectr. Addis Ababa U., 1994—98; rsch. and tchg. asst. U. Conn., Storrs, 2000—04; asst. prof. Brock U., St. Catharines, Ontario, Canada, 2004—. Recipient Excellence in Fin. award, Sch. Mgmt., Syracuse U., 2000; Fulbright fellow, Inst. Internat. Edn., 1998—2000. Mem.: Phi Beta Delta (life), Beta Gamma Sigma (life). Office: Brock Univ 500 Glenridge Ave Saint Catharines ON Canada L2S3A1 Home Phone: 905-684-8883; Office Phone: 905-688-5550 ext. 3498. Business E-Mail: aayanso@brocku.ca.

AYAR, DIVYANG, radiologist; arrived in US, 1989; s. Chhaganbhai and Samjuben Ayar; m. Pooja Ayar, Nov. 28, 2004; 1 child, Krishna. MD, U. Ala., Birmingham, 1995; BS summa cum laude, Creighton U., 1991. Diplomate Am. Bd. Radiology, 2000. Resident diagnostic radiology U. Ala., Birmingham, 1995—99; fellow interventional radiology Vanderbilt U. Med. Ctr., Nashville, 1999—2000; interventional radiologist Radiology and Imaging South Tex., Corpus Christi, 2000—. Mem.: Soc. Interventional Radiology, Am. Coll. Radiology, Radiol. Soc. N.Am., Phi Sigma. Office: Radiology and Imaging South Tex 3226 Reid Dr Corpus Christi TX 78404 Office Phone: 361-853-4503. Personal E-mail: dayar@mail.com.

AYARS, PATTI, human resources specialist, health products executive; B in Bus. Adminstrn. with highest distinction, U. Neb. Various internat. and domestic human resources positions Monsanto Corp./Pharmacia, 1981—2001; sr. v.p. human resources Roche Diagnostic Corp., Indpls., 2001—. Co-author: (book) Mastering Momentum: A Practical and Powerful Approach for Successful Change. Office: Roche Diagnostics Corp 9115 Hague Rd Indianapolis IN 46256-1025 Office Phone: 317-521-2000. Office Fax: 317-845-2221. Personal E-mail: payars01@aol.com.

AYASO, MANUEL, artist; b. Coruna, Galicia, Spain, Jan. 1, 1934; came to U.S., 1947, naturalized, 1955; s. Jose and Dolores (Dios) A.; m. Lucia Rivas, May 2, 1959; children: Monica, Jose Luciano. Student, Newark Sch. Fine and Indsl. Art, NJ, 1953-56. One-man shows include Cober Gallery, N.Y.C., 1961—68, Forum Gallery, 1970—74, Ft. Worth Art Ctr., 1964, SUNY-Oswego, 1965, Witt meml. Mus., San Antonio, 1967, Casa de Galicia, Madrid, Spain, 1994, N.Y. Armory, 1995, Casa da Parra, Santiago de Compostela, Spain, 1997 (Silver Patelle), Santiago de Composte, Spain, exhibited in group shows at 22d Biennial Internat. Watercolor Exhbn., Bklyn. Mus., 1963, U. Mex., Mexico City, 1963, Exhibit Contemporary Am. Artists, Nat. inst. Arts and letters, 1962—71, Whitney Mus. Am., 1963, Vatican Exhibit Contemporary Am. Spiritual Art, Rome, 1976, The Fine Line: Drawing with Silver in Am., 1985—86, Objects and Drawings from the Sanford M. and Diane Besser Collection, 1992—93, Casa da Cultura, Riveira La Coruna, Museo Valleinclan Puebla del Caraminal, La Coruna, 2001, retrospective exhbn., Fundacion Museo del Grabado, Artes, Riviera, Spain, 2002—03. Served with U.S. Army, 1956-58. Recipient St. Paul Gallery and Sch. Art Purchase award, 1961; Tiffany Found. Award, 1962; Ford Found. grantee, 1964; recipient Nat. Inst. Arts and Letters Childe Hassam Purchase award, 1971, hon. mention 2d Ann. Int. Exhibit of Miniature Art, Del Bello Gal, Toronto, Can., 1987; named Artists of Yr., Asociacion Artistas Plasticos Gallegos, 2007. Mem. Nat. Geog. Soc., Smithsonian Instn., Whitney Mus. Am. Art, N.J. State Mus. Roman Catholic. Address: 12 Vincent Pl Verona NJ 07044-3022

AYASOUFI, ANAHITA, engineer, researcher; b. Tehran, Iran, May 28, 1973; d. Kazem Aiassofi and Farideh Shahla; m. Ramin Rahmani, May 5, 1997; children: Cyrus Rahmani, Darius Rahmani. PhD, U. Toledo, 2004. Rschr. Niroo Rsch. Inst., Tehran, 1999—2000; rschr., tchg. asst. U. Toledo, 2000—04; postdoctoral rschr. U. Ala., Birmingham, 2005—. Contbr. articles to profl. jours. Mem.: ASME, Am. Inst. Aeronautics and Astronautics. Office: UAB Dept Mech Engring 1530 3rd Ave S HOEN 259C Birmingham AL 35294

AYAZ, SANDRA M., educational association administrator; m. Mehmet Ayaz. Attended, Santa Fe Cmty. Coll.; BA, Fla. Atlantic U., MA in English, EdS; EdD in Adult Edn. Asst. dir., minority students svcs. Fla. Atlantic U.; adj. instr. Edison Cmty. Coll.; exec. dir., pub. schools enrichment partnerships Fla. Gulf Coast U.; mgr. Coll. Survival, Houghton Mifflin. Co-dir. College Reach Out Prog. Author: Contemporary Sanguines: The Metamorphosis of the Vampire Myth in Literature; co-author: Hitching A Ride to Success: A Roadmap For Collegiate Travelers. Recipient Disting. Faculty award, Omega Psi Phi, Karl F. Ijams Humanitarian award, Student Affairs Disting. Svc. award, Fla. Atlantic U., Davis Productivity award, State of Fla. Mem.: Am. Assn. Higher Edn., Coll. Reading and Learning Assn., Nat. Assn. Devel. Edn., Internat. Mentoring Assn., Nat. Tutoring Assn. (pres.), Phi Theta Kappa, Phi Kappa Phi, Sigma Tau Delta. Office: National Tutoring Association PO Box 6840 Lakeland FL 33807-6840 Office Phone: 863-529-5206.*

AYCOCK, JAMES J., lawyer; b. McCamey, Tex., May 1, 1944; BA, U. Tex., Austin, 1966, JD, 1969. Cert.: Tex. Bd. Legal Specialization (estate planning and probate law). Ptnr. Bayern & Aycock, P.C., San Antonio. Named one of Top 100 Attys., Worth mag., 2005. Mem.: Am. Coll. Trust & Estate Counsel, San Antonio Bar Assn., San Antonio Estate Planning and Probate Law Assn., Probate Law Assn., San Antonio Estate Planners Coun. (past pres.), State Bar Tex. (estate and gift tax editor and editor-in-chief of the Reporter, past chair real estate, probate and trust law sect.). Office: Bayern & Aycock PC 745 E Mulberry Ste 300 San Antonio TX 78212 Office Phone: 210-731-8300. E-mail: jjaycock@estplanning.com.*

AYCOCK, JOSEPH WILLIAM, music educator, auto racing official; b. Charlotte, NC, Sept. 6, 1979; s. Joseph William and Patricia Dale Aycock. MusB in Music Edn., Appalachian State U., Boone, NC, 2002. Orch. dir. Charlotte-Mecklenburg Schools, 2002—; race ofcl. Lowe's Motor Speedway, Concord, NC, 2003—; dir. of music Meml. United Meth. Ch., Charlotte, 2004—05. Adjudicator Fla. Fedn. of Judge's Assn., Frostproof, 2005—; vol. Bands of Am., Indpls., 2001—; prin. percussionist Winthrop U. Olde English Wind Ensemble, Rock Hill, SC, 2004—. Contest dir. Carolina Winter Ensemble Assn., Charlotte, 2004—05. Mem.: Am. Guild of English Handbell Ringers, Fla. Fedn. of Judge's Assn., Music Educators Nat. Conf., Phi Mu Alpha Sinfonia (sec. 2001—02). Reform. Methodist. Avocations: golf, travel, cooking. Home: 2061 University Heights Ln Charlotte NC 28213 Home Phone: 704-594-6831; Office Phone: 980-343-5750. Personal E-mail: joey@joeyaycock.com.

AYDELOTTE, MYRTLE KITCHELL, retired nursing administrator; b. Van Meter, Iowa, May 31, 1917; d. John J. and Larava Josephine (Gutshall) Kitchell; m. William O. Aydelotte, June 22, 1956; children: Marie Elizabeth, Jeannette Farley. BS, U. Minn., 1939, MA, 1947, PhD, 1955; postgrad., Columbia U. Tchrs. Coll., 1948. Head nurse Charles T. Miller Hosp., St. Paul, 1939—41; surg. tchg. St. Mary's Hosp. Sch. Nursing, Mpls., 1941—42; instr. U. Minn., 1945—49; dir., dean State U. Iowa Coll. Nursing, 1949—57, prof., 1957—62; assoc. chief nurse VA Hosp. Rsch. for Nursing, Iowa City, 1963—64, chief nursing rsch., 1964—65; prof. U. Iowa Coll. Nursing, 1964—76, 1982—88; exec. dir. ANA, 1977—81; ret., 1988. Dir. nursing U. Iowa Hosps. and Clinics, 1968—76; mem. sci. adv. bd. Ctr. Health Rsch. Wayne State U., 1972—76, Inst. Medicine, 1973—; cons. U. Minn., 1970, 82, 90, U. Rochester, 1971, U. Mich., 1970, 73, U. Colo., 1970—71, U. Hawaii, 1972—73, Ariz. State U., 1972, U. Nebr., 1972—73. Mem. editl. bd.: Nursing Forum, 1969—72, Jour. Nursing Adminstrn., 1971; contbr. articles to profl. jours. Mem., v.p. Iowa City Libr. Bd., 1961—67; mem. Johnson County Bd. Health, 1967—70; mem. adv. com. family living courses Iowa City Bd. Edn., 1970—72. With Nurse Corps. US Army, 1942—46. Mem.: ANA, Am. Acad. Nursing, Inst. Medicine, Sigma Theta Tau (rsch. com. 1968—72). Home: 158 Johnsarbor Dr W Rochester NY 14620

AYDIN, LEVENT, electrical engineer; BSEE, Mid. East Tech. U., Ankara, Turkey, 1989; MSEE, U. So. Calif., LA, 1991, PhD, 1996. Sys. engr. Qualcomm Inc, San Diego, 1996—. Achievements include patents for efficient finite impulse response filter implementation For CDMA waveform generation; simplified quality indicator bit test procedures; system, method and computer program for controlling a transmit signal using and expected power level. Office Phone: 858-658-5505.

AYEDUN, KEHINDE PETER, information systems executive; b. Lagos, Nigeria, Sept. 20, 1965; came to U.S., 1987; s. Joseph Olukayode and Ayoka Olapeju (Ogun) A.; m. Faosatu Olubunmi Ogunnowo, July 27, 1990; children: Folashade Olivia, Lolade Alexis., U. Lagos, Nigeria, 1984-87, ITT Tech. Inst., Schaumburg, Ill., 1990-91. Programmer, cons. Sage Internat., Schaumburg, Ill., 1987-92; MIS mgr. Andrew Corp., Itasca, Ill., 1992—. Info. tech. cons. Algol Techs., Cary, Ill., 1994—. Co-author Windows NT, Server, Installation, Configuration and Customization. Mem. IEEE Computer Soc. Avocations: music, chess, reading, magic.

AYER, DONALD BELTON, lawyer; b. San Mateo, Calif., Apr. 30, 1949; m. Anne Norton; children: Christopher, Alison BA in History with great distinction and honors, Stanford U., 1971; MA in History, Harvard U., 1973, JD cum laude, 1975. Bar: Calif. 1975, D.C. 1978. Law clk. to Judge Malcolm R. Wilkey US Ct. Appeals DC Cir., 1975-76; law clk. to Justice William H. Rehnquist, U.S. Supreme Ct., Washington, 1976-77; asst. U.S. atty. criminal div. No. Dist. Calif., San Francisco, 1977-79, in charge San Jose office, 1978-79; assoc. Gibson Dunn & Crutcher, San Jose, Calif., 1979-81; US atty. Eastern Dist. Calif., Sacramento, 1982-86; prin. dep. solicitor gen. Dept. Justice, 1986-88; ptnr. JonesDay, Washington, 1988—; dep. atty. gen. US Dept. Justice, Washington, 1989-90; adminstrv. ptnr. Jones, Day, Reavis & Pogue, Washington, 1991-93, chair gov. disputes sect., 1993-96, office chair pro bono com., 2003—06, firm-wide chair pro bono com., 2004—, chmn., gov. regulatory practice, 2005—. Mem. Calif. State Bar Fed. Cts. Commn., 1983-86; mem. exec. com. 9th Cir. Jud. Conf., 1983-85; mem. Atty. Gen.'s Adv. Com. of U.S. Attys., 1986; publs. com. U.S. Supreme Ct. Hist. Soc., 1991—; adj. prof. Georgetown U. Law Sch., 2006—, NYU Law Sch., 2007—. Articles editor Harvard U. Law Rev., 1974-75; contbr. articles to legal jours. Pres. Stanford Young Reps., 1970-71; mem. vestry St. Mary's Episc. Ch., 1987-90; bd. dirs. Langley Non-Profit Housing Corp., 1990-98; mem. Fed. City Coun., 1991-93; mem. adv. com. State and Local Legal Ctr., 1992—; trustee Potomac Sch., McLean, Va., 1994-2000; bd. dirs. Am. Rivers, Inc., 1997—2006, treas., 1998-2004; bd. advisors Supreme Ct. Inst. of Georgetown U., 1999—. Fellow: Am. Bar Found. (life); mem.: ABA (task force on internat. criminal ct. 1991—94, litigation sect.), Legal Aid Soc. DC (bd. dirs. 2006—), Edward Coke Am. Inn of Ct. (pres. 2006—07, master), NYU Inst. Jud. Adminstrn. (bd. dirs. 2000—07), DC Bar Assn. (ct. funding com. 2000—01), Calif. State Bar, DC Bar Found. (adv. bd. 1992—), Am. Law Inst., Am. Acad. Appellate Lawyers (mem. com. 1997—2002, sec. 2006—07, treas. 2007—). Office: Jones Day 51 Louisiana Ave NW Washington DC 20001 Office Phone: 202-879-3939. Personal E-mail: dbatrout@aol.com. Business E-Mail: dbayer@jonesday.com.

AYER, RAMANI, insurance company executive; BS, Indian Inst. Tech., Bombay; MS in Chem. Engring., D in Chem. Engring., Drexel U. With The Hartford, Hartford, Conn., 1973—, asst. sec., staff asst. to chmn. and chief exec., 1979-83; v.p. HartRe, 1983-86; pres. Hartford Specialty Co., 1986-89; sr. v.p. The Hartford, 1989-90, exec. v.p., 1990-91; pres., COO property-casualty ops. Hartford Fire Ins. Co., 1991-97; chmn., CEO, pres. The Hartford Fin. Svcs. Group, Inc., 1997—2007, chmn., CEO, 2007—. Past chmn. Ins. Svcs. Office; bd. dirs. Ins. Info. Inst. Trustee Mark Twain House, Hartford, Conn.; chmn. Metro Hartford Regional Econ. Alliance; bd. dirs. Hartford Hosp.; trustee Drexel U.; mem. Bus. Roundtable. Mem. Am. Ins. Assn. (bd. dirs., past chmn. task force catastrophic issues, past vice chmn. spl. bd. com. workers compensation), Am. Inst. Property and Liability Underwriters (trustee), Ins. Inst. Am. (trustee). Office: Hartford Plz 60 Asylum Ave Hartford CT 06115*

AYER, WILLIAM S., air transportation executive; m. Pam Ayer; 1 child. Degree, Stanford U.; MBA, U. Wash. From v.p. strategy and route planning to sr. v.p. ops. Horizen Air Industries, 1985—95, sr. v.p. ops., 1995; from v.p. mktg. and planning to pres. Alaska Air Group, Inc., Seattle, 1995—2003, chmn., pres., CEO, 2003—. Office: Alaska Air Group Inc 19300 Pacific Hwy South Seattle WA 98188*

AYERS, ANNE LOUISE, small business owner, consultant, counselor; b. Albuquerque, Oct. 22, 1948; d. F. Ernest and Gladys Marguerite (Miles) A. BA, Kans. U., 1970; MEd, Seattle Pacific U., 1971. Staff cons. in student devel. Cen. Wash. State U., Ellensburg, 1971-72; dir. Aerospace Def. Command Resident Edn. Ctrs. for N.D. and Mont. Chapman U., Orange, Calif., 1972-74; instr. psychology Hampton U., Va., 1973-75; edn. svc. specialist Gen. Edn1. Devel. Ctr., Fort Monroe, Va., 1975-77; edn. specialist US Army Transp. Sch., Ft. Eustis, Va., 1977-79, Nat. Mine Health and Safety Acad., Beckley, W.Va., 1979-89; edn. svcs. specialist NASA Hdqrs., Washington, 1989-96; ret., 1996. Pres. Appalachian Love Arts, Martinsburg, W.Va., 1983—; tchr. undergrad. and grad. evening classes in psychology, 1972-74; program mgr. NASA Tchr. Resource Ctr. Network Program; sub. counselor Berkley County, W.Va. Mem. Nat. Soc. Inventors, Nat. Assn. Women Deans Adminstrn. and Counselors, Internat. Soc. Photographers, Alumnus of Growing Vision Century in Edn. (award), Mayflower Soc. Methodist. Achievements include invention of decorative pen, thermometer holder, corsage, psychedelic jewelry process. Avocations: travel, collecting gems and shells, coin collecting/numismatics, rock and fossil collecting, oboe and clarinet. Home and Office: 480 Tanbridge Dr Martinsburg WV 25401-4695

AYERS, CHRISTOPHER JAMES, special education educator; b. Pequannock Township, NJ, Apr. 17, 1979; s. James Loring and Judith Eileen Ayers; m. Jessica Kathleen McLelland, Dec. 28, 2003; 1 child, Samantha Marion. BS in Telecom. Mgmt., DeVry U., 2001; BA in tchr. of handicapped summa cum laude, Kean U., 2004. Cert. handicapped tchr. Kean U., NJ, 2004. Spl. edn. tchr. Perth Amboy Bd. Edn., 2002—. Asst. varsity football coach Perth Amboy H.S., 2002; supplemental instr. Perth Amboy Bd. Edn., 2002—; club leader 21st Century, Perth Amboy, NJ, 2004—. Vol. Edison Youth Svc. Corps, 2001—05. Mem.: Coun. Exceptional Children. Home: 22 Paul St Fords NJ 08863 Home Phone: 732-738-8737. Personal E-mail: yellowstonenp44@aol.com.

AYERS, EDWARD L., academic administrator, history professor; m. Abby Ayers; children: Hannah, Nate. BA, U. Tenn., 1974; PhD, Yale U., 1980. Asst. prof. U. Va., 1980—86, assoc. prof., 1986—92, prof., 1992—93, Hugh P. Kelly prof. history, 1993—2007, Buckner W. Clay dean Coll. and Grad. Sch. Arts and Scis., 2001—07; pres. U. Richmond, Va., 2007—. John Adams prof. Am. studies U. Groningen, Netherlands, 1995; fellow Ctr. for Advanced Study in the Behavorial Scis., Palo Alto, Calif., 1999—2000. Author: Vengeance and Justice: Crime and Punishment in the Nineteenth-Century American South, 1984, The Edge of the South: Life in Nineteenth Century Virginia, 1991, The Promise of the New South: Life after Reconstruction, 1992 (James Rawley prize Orgn. Am. Historians, 1992), The Strange Career of Thomas Jefferson: Race, Slavery, and American Memory, 1943-1993, 1993 (Frank L. and Harriet C. Owsley award So. Hist. Assn., 1993), All Over the Map: Rethinking American Regions, 1996, The Oxford Book fo the American South: Testimony, Memory, and Fiction, 1997, American Passages: A History of the United States, 2000, The Valley of the Shadow: Two Communities in the American Civil War--The Eve of War, 2000, In the Presence of Mine Enemies: War in the Heart of America, 1859-1863, 2003 (Bancroft prize, 2004), What Caused the Civil War: Reflections on the South and Southern History, 2005. Named Univ. Prof. of Yr., Carnegie Found., 2003; recipient James Willard Hurst prize, Law and Soc. Assn., 1986. Mem.: Am. Assn. Arts and Scis. Office: Office of Pres Maryland Hall, Rm 203 U Richmond Richmond VA 23173 Office Phone: 804-289-8100.*

AYERS, HARRY BRANDT, editor, publisher, columnist; b. Anniston, Ala., Apr. 8, 1935; s. Harry Mell and Edel Olga (Ytterboe) A.; m. Josephine Ehringhaus, Dec. 9; 1 child, Margaret. BA in History, U. Ala., Tuscaloosa, 1959; LHD (hon.), U. Ala., Birmingham, 1994, U. Ala., 1994. Polit. writer The Raleigh (N.C.) Times, 1959-61; corr. Bascom Timmons Bur., Washington, 1961-63; mng. editor The Anniston Star, 1963-69, editor, pub., 1969—. Chair Consolidated Publ. Co., 1998—; commentator Pub. Radio, NPR "Morning Edition." Mem. adv. bd. Inside Story, Pub. Broadcasting System, N.Y.C., 1981-85; co-editor: You Can't Eat Magnolias, 1972; co-author: A Bicentennial Portrait of the American People, U.S. News Books, 1976, Inaugural Book President Carter, 1977, Dixie Dateline, 1983; frequent contbr. to internat. and nat. newspapers. Trustee Talladega (Ala.) Coll., 1972-89, Wooster Sch., Danbury, Conn., 1989-90, Century Found., 1985—, Ctr. for Excellence in Govt., 1985-88, Am. Com., Internat. Press Inst., Vienna, 1985—; bd. dirs. So. Ctr. for Internat. Studies, Atlanta, 1979—, Bd. Fgn. Scholarships, Washington, 1981-84; mem. adv. bd. Am. Ditchley Found., London; mem. Coun. Fgn. Rels., N.Y.C., 1983—; bd. dirs. Inter-Am. Press Assn., Miami, 1992-93, 2003—; chmn. UN Day Ala., 2000. Named Disting. Journalism Grad., U. Ala., 1967; recipient Human Rels. award Am. Jewish Com., 1977, Green Eyeshade award Soc. Profl. Journalists, 1985, Editl. Leadership award, Soc. Newpaper Editors, 2003; named to Ala. Acad. Honor, 1991; fellow Nieman Found., Harvard U., 1968, sr. fellow Gannett Ctr., Columbia U., 1989; inductee Hall of Fame, U. Ala. Sch. Comm., 2000, Tutwiler dist. svc. award, 2002, Lifetime achievement award, Ala. Press Assn., 2003 Mem. Ala. Press Journalism Found. (founding pres. 1969), Am. Soc. Newspaper Editors (Editl. Leadership award 2003), So. Newspaper Pubs. Assn. (dir. 1981-84), Century Assn. N.Y.C., Met. Club Washington, The Summit Club Birmingham. Democrat. Episcopalian. Home: 1 Booger Holw Anniston AL 36207-6805 Office: Anniston Star PO Box 189 Anniston AL 36202-0189

AYERS, HOWARD T., lawyer; b. St. Louis, 1944; BA in Econ. & Bus. Adminstrn., Rice U., 1966; JD with honors, U. Houston, 1969. Bar: Tex. 1969. Ptnr., Real Estate Andrews Kurth LLP, Houston, mng. ptnr. of firm, 1997—, chmn. mgmt. com., 2001—. Bd. dir. U. Houston Law Found.; adv. bd. Tex. State Bank. Mem.: Tex. Coll. Real Estate Attys., ABA, State Bar Tex., Houston Real Estate Lawyers Coun., Houston Bar Assn., Order of Barons, Phi Kappa Phi, Phi Alpha Delta. Office: Andrews Kurth LLP 600 Travis St Ste 4200 Houston TX 77002-3090 Office Phone: 713-220-4044. Office Fax: 713-238-7151. Business E-Mail: hayers@andrewskurth.com.

AYERS, JAMES CORDON, lawyer; b. Raleigh, NC, Aug. 2, 1934; s. Edwin White and Laura Cordon (Stedman) A.; m. Leona Bell Weston, Aug. 1, 1965; children: James Cordon Jr., Alan Andrew. BSBA, U. N.C., 1958; JD, Ohio State U., 1977. Bar: Ohio 1977, U.S. Dist. Ct. (so. dist.) 1978, U.S. Ct. Appeals (6th cir.) 1983, U.S. Supreme Ct. 1992. Dist. sales mgr. Gen. Tel. Dir. Co., 1965-71; pres. Cols. Advt. co., 1971-74; sr. v.p. Assoc. Ind. Dir., 1972-74, exec. v.p. univ. dir., 1972-74; asst. atty. gen. workers' compensation sect. State of Ohio, Columbus, 1977-79; pvt. practice James C. Ayers Law Office, Columbus, 1979—; ind. hearing examiner Ohio Dept. Pub. Safety, 1993-99. Mem. Armed Forces Disciplinary Bd., N.C. 1960; bd. dirs. Post Exch., Camp Lejeune, 1960; summary ct. martial jurisdiction USMC Camp Lejeune, 1960. Chmn. Columbus County March of Dimes, 1961; pres. SBA; jud. panelist Ohio Mock Trial, 1995—2001; trustee The Reserve, 2002—. 1st lt. USMC, 1957—60. Mem. Ohio Bar Assn., Men's Golf Assn. (dir. 1990-92, treas. 1990-91, v.p 1992), Scarlet and Gray (dir. 1988, v.p 1989), Phi Delta Phi (Grad. of Yr.). Avocation: golf. Office: 165 N High St Columbus OH 43215-2402 Home: 8559 Stonechat Loop Dublin OH 43017-8625 Home Phone: 614-932-9515; Office Phone: 614-221-0770. Personal E-mail: ayersj@sbcglobal.net.

AYERS, JEFFREY DAVID, lawyer; b. Grant, Nebr., Nov. 30, 1960; s. William D. and Lela R. (Gilmore) A.; m. Shelly Jo Dodds, June 11, 1988; children: Sydney Elizabeth, Bailey Anne. BS, Graceland U., 1982; MBA, JD, U. Iowa, 1985. Bar: Mo. 1985. Assoc. Stinson, Mag & Fizzell, Kansas City, Mo., 1985—88, Bryan, Cave, McPheeters & McRoberts, Kansas City, 1989—92; ptnr. Blackwell Sanders Peper Martin LLP, Kansas City, Mo., 1992—95, mng. ptnr. London, 1996—99; sr. v.p., gen. counsel and corp. sec. Aquila Mcht. Svcs., Inc., Kansas City, 1999—2002; v.p., assoc. gen. counsel GE Ins. Solutions, Kansas City, 2003—05; sr. v.p., gen. counsel, corp. sec. NovaStar Fin., Inc., 2005—. Mayor City of Lake Tapawingo, Mo., 1993-96. Trustee Little Blue Valley Sewer Dist., 1994-95. Democrat. Office: NovaStar Fin Inc Ste 380 8140 Ward Pkwy Kansas City MO 64114 Personal E-mail: jayers@kc.rr.com. Business E-Mail: jeff.ayers@novastar1.com.

AYERS, RICHARD WAYNE, electric power industry executive, writer, journalist; b. Atlanta, Aug. 23, 1945; s. Harold Richard and Martha Elizabeth Ayers; m. Nancy Katherine Martin, Aug. 9, 1969. BBA, Ga. State Coll., 1967; MBA, Ind. U., 1969. Specialist mktg. comm. rsch. GE, Schenectady, NY, 1969—70, copywriter lamp divsn. Cleve., 1970—73, supr. distbr. advt. & sales promotion, 1973—75, supr. comml. & indsl. promotional programs Lighting Bus. Group, 1975—79, mgr. comml. & indsl. market distbr. and promotional programs, 1979—87, mgr. comml. & indsl. comm., 1987—91, mgr. mktg. comms., 1992—2000; reporter, feature writer Tampa Bay newspapers, 2000—. Lectr. in field. Author: Winning Through Promotion, 1987, 1996, Cleveland and the Western Reserve, 2000, 2004, Ohio's Lake Erie Vacationland, 2000, St. Petersburg: The Sunshine City, 2001, Tampa Bay's Gulf Beaches: The Fabulous 1950's and 1960's, 2004, Tampa Bay Gulf Beaches, 3d edit., 2005, Florida's Grand Hotels From the Gilded Age, 2005, Indian Rocks As It Was: A Pictorial History, 2006. Bd. dirs. Indian Rocks Beach Hist. Mus.; chmn. Belleair Beach Parks Bd., 2003—; dir.-at-large Ga. Young Reps., 1966—67. Recipient Best Indsl. Promotion award, Advt. Age, 1974, Incentive Showcase award, Nat. Premium Sales Exec. Assn., 1975, 1976, 1987, 1991, Golden Communicators award, Factory mag., 1976, Leader award, Direct Mktg. Assn., 1983, Top prize, Am. Lighting Assn., 1990—92, 1995—98, Addy award, Am. Advt. Assn., 1992, Gold Tower award, Bus. Mktg. Assn., 1998, ProComm award, 1998, Best Original Writing award, Cmty. Papers Fla., 2003. Mem.: Eflun Soc., Blue Key, Beta Gamma Sigma, Delta Sigma Pi. Home and Office: 2900 Gulf Blvd Apt 304 Belleair Beach FL 33786 Office Phone: 727-593-2686. Personal E-mail: ayersrw@msn.com.

AYI, BERTHA SERWA, infectious disease specialist, internist; b. Akim Oda, Eastern Region, Ghana, Feb. 1, 1971; d. Samuel Kwaku and Hannah Akua Gyamerah; m. Richard Sowah Ayi, May 22, 1999; children: Michael Okpoti, Henry- Josiah Ako, Richmond- Joshua Anyiteye. MB. ChB, U. Ghana Med. Sch., 1997. Diplomate Am. Bd. Internal Med., Am. Bd. Internal Med. subspecialty Bd. Infectious Disease, 2004. House staff pediat., gen. surgery, urology, orthops., trauma Korlebu Tchg. Hosp., Accra, Ghana, 1997—98; intern, jr. and sr. resident Good Samaritan Hosp., Balt., 1999—2002; infectious disease fellow tng. Creighton U. Med. Ctr., U. Nebr. Med. Ctr., Omaha, 2002—04; jr. faculty fellow Creighton U. Med. Ctr., Omaha, 2002—04; assoc. med. dir. Mercy Infectious Disease and Epidemiology Ctr., 2004; adj. asst. prof. internal medicine Nebr. Med. Ctr., Omaha, 2004—. Reviewer Clin. Infectious Diseases Jour., Chgo., 2003—, Chest jour. Co-author: Blastomycosis. In Conn's Current Therapy, 2005, Infections of Leisure; contbr. articles to profl. jours. Motivational spkr. and spkr. on reproductive health issues Planned Parenthood Assn. Ghana, Accra, 1995—97; spkr. marriage, counselling Internat. Ctrl. Gospel Ch., Accra, 1997—98. Recipient Opthalmology Award for Graduating Med. Students, Alcon-Paracelsus Pharmacy, 1997, Deans Award for Acad. Excellence, U. Ghana Med. Sch., 1995, Honors in Surgery, Pathology, Microbiology, Biochemistry, 1997—97. Fellow: ACP; mem.: Infectious Disease Soc. Am. Avocations: sewing, baking. Office: Mercy Infectious Disease and Epidemiology Ctr 801 5th St Sioux City IA 51101

AYKROYD, DANIEL EDWARD, actor, writer; b. Ottawa, Ont., Can., July 1, 1952; came to U.S., 1975; s. Peter Hugh and Lorraine G. (Gougeon) A.; m. Maureen Lewis May 10, 1974 (div.); m. Donna Dixon, April 29, 1983; children: Danielle, Belle, Stella. Attended, Carleton U., 1969, Doctorate (hon.), 1994. Mem. Toronto Co. of Second City Theater; star in CBS TV series Coming Up Rosie; writer, actor: NBC's Saturday Night Live, 1975-79; motion picture appearances include (actor) Love at First Sight, 1974, 1941, 1979, Mr. Mike's Mondo Video, 1979, Neighbors, 1981, Doctor Detroit, 1983, Trading Places, 1983, Twilight Zone, 1983, Nothing Lasts Forever, 1984, Into the Night, 1985, Caddyshack II, 1988, The Great Outdoors, 1988, My Stepmother is an Alien, 1988, Driving Miss Daisy, 1989, My Girl, 1991, Sneakers, 1992, Chaplin, 1992, My Girl 2, 1994, Exit to Eden, 1994, (voice) Antz, 1998, 50 First Dates, 2004, Christmas with the Kranks, 2004, I Now Pronounce You Chuck and Larry, 2007; (actor, co-screenwriter) The Blues Brothers, 1980, Ghostbusters, 1984, Spies Like Us, 1985, Dragnet, 1987, Ghostbusters II, 1989, Coneheads, 1993, Canadian Bacon, 1994, Tommy Boy, 1995, Rainbow, 1995, Casper, 1995, Sgt. Bilko, 1996, My Fellow Americans, 1996, getting Away With Murder, 1996, Feeling Minnesota, 1996, Celtic Pride, 1996, Grosse Pointe Blank, 1997, Blues Brothers 2000, 1997, The Arrow, 1997, Susan's Plan, 1998, Diamonds, 1999 (actor, dir., screenwriter) Nothing But Trouble, 1991, (exec. prodr.) One More Saturday Night, 1986; performed (with John Belushi) as the Blues Brothers; albums include: Briefcase Full of Blues, Made in America, The Blues Brothers (motion-picture soundtrack), Best of the Blues Brothers, The Essential Blues Brothers; guest-columnist for Premiere magazine, 1992; TV guest appearances include All You Need is Cash, Steve Martin's Best Show Ever, Tales From the Crypt, HBO, 1992, Soul Man, 1997, The Nanny, 1993, 94, Home Improvement, 1997, According to Jim, 2002, 03. Recipient Emmy award 1976-77. Mem. Writers Guild Am. West, AFTRA. Office: Creative Artists Agy care Fred Specktor 9830 Wilshire Blvd Beverly Hills CA 90212-1804

AYLESWORTH, OWEN ROY, retired firefighter, genealogist, philanthropist; b. Appleton, Wisc., Jan. 21, 1926; s. Frederick Donovan and Adeline Louise Minnie (Hauert) A.; m. Mary Hildred Horton, Aug. 23, 1946 (div. Sept. 1949); children: Sheldon Roy, Earl Lynn; m. Mary Corrine Patti Gray, Dec. 26, 55 (div. Nov. 1964); 1 child, Nancy Denise. AA, Santa Barbara City Coll., 1973. Fireman City of Santa Barbara, Calif., 1950-56, alarm operator Calif., 1956, fire engr. Calif., 1956-62, fire capt. Calif., 1962-69, 76-79, fire tng. officer Calif., 1969-76, acting fire batallion chief Calif., 1976. Webmaster, Aylesworth.net; dir. v.p., pres. City Employee's Assn., 1961-69; coord. fire sci. Santa Barbara City Coll., 1969-74, instr. 1972-74. Author, editor: Caleb Sheldon Aylesworth His Descendents, 1963, 82, Hauert Family Genealogy, 1965, 73, Baron/Bertino Family, 2003. Instr. advanced first aid and emergency care ARC; cardiopulmonary resustation instr. Am. Heart Assn.; life mem., bd. dirs. Santa Barbara Fireman's Relief Assn., 1952-64, v.p. 1964-66. With U.S. Navy, 1944-47. Mem. Calif. State Fire Tng. Officers Assn. (life), Calif. Firefighters Assn. (life, state conf. del. 1955-61), Santa Barbara High Sch. Alumni Assn. (life, bd. dirs. 1974-76, treas. 1976-94, exec. sec. 1994-96, sec. 1996—, dir. membership 2002—, Disting. Alumnus award 1993). Avocations: genealogy, research, woodworking, aestheometry, metal sculpture. Home: 621 W Arrellaga St Santa Barbara CA 93101 Personal E-mail: olenug@aol.com.

AYLING, HENRY FAITHFUL, editor, consultant, journalist, poet; b. Bklyn., Dec. 30, 1931; s. Albert Edward John and Mina Campbell McCurdy (Lindsay) A.; m. Julia Corinne Gornto, 1954; children: Campbell, Eben, Corey, Harry, Faith. BA, Grinnell Coll., 1953; MA, Columbia U., Calif. State U., Carson, 1984; 2 grad. teaching certs., Calif. State U., Carson, 1985. Asst to registrar Columbia U., NYC, 1958-59; supr. crew scheduling Pan Am World Airways, Jamaica, NY, 1959-62, supr. payload control, 1963-65; mgr. crew scheduling Seabd. World Airlines, Jamaica, 1962-63, 65-68, mgr. system control, 1968-80; mgr. ops. control Flying Tiger Line, 1980-84; instr. English, ESL Long Beach (Calif.) City Coll., 1984-85; mng. editor IEEE Expert, IEEE Computing Futures IEEE Computer Soc., Los Alamitos, Calif., 1985-90, editorial dir. Computer Soc. Press, 1990-93; writer, editor, cons., 1993—. Mem. editorial bd. Expert Mag., 1986-90, CamAm Programming Inc., 1987-88; columnist Mag. Design and Prodn. mag., 1988-89; contbr. articles to profl. mags. and tech. books; contbr. poetry to various mags. and anthologies. Bd. dirs. Playa Serena Home Owners Assn., Playa Del Rey, Calif., 1983-85. Recipient Maggie awards Western Publs. Assn., 1988-89, IEEE Computer Soc. Golden Core award, 1997. Avocations: music, fine arts. Home and Office: 78291 Allegro Dr Palm Desert CA 92211-1894 Personal E-mail: jcayling@msn.com.

AYLOR, JAMES HIRAM, engineering educator; b. Charlottesville, Va., May 30, 1946; s. Melvin Winfrey and Mary Yager (Payne) A.; m. Sherry Lynn Kendall, Oct. 20, 1973; children: Jennifer K., David A. BSEE, U. Va., 1968, MSEE, 1971, PhD in elec. engring., 1977. Mem. faculty elec. engring. U. Va., Charlottesville, 1978—, chair dept. elec. engring., 1996—2003, assoc. dean. academic programs Sch. Engring. and Applied Sciences, 2003—, interim dean. Sch. Engring. and Applied Sciences, 2004—, Louis T. Rader Prof. Author: Performance and Fault Modeling with VHDL, 1991, Codesign of Embedded Systems: A Unified Hardware/Software Representation, 1996; contbr. articles to numerous profl. jours. Recipient Outstanding Svc. award Va. Engring. Found., Charlottesville, 1991. Fellow: IEEE (pres. computer soc. 1993, editor-in-chief IEEE Computer). Methodist. Office: U Va Sch Engring and Applied Sciences Box 400246 Charlottesville VA 22904-4246

AYLWARD, RONALD LEE, lawyer; b. St. Louis, May 30, 1930; s. John Thomas and Edna (Ketcherside) A.; m. Margaret Cecilia Hellweg, Aug. 10, 1963; children: Susan Marie Jotte, Stephen Ronald, Carolyn Ann Dolan. AB, Washington U., St. Louis, 1952, JD, 1954; student, U. Va., Charlottesville, 1955. Bar: Mo. 1954, Ill. 1961, US Supreme Ct. 1968. Assoc. Heneghan, Roberts & Cole, St. Louis, 1958-59; asst. counsel Olin Corp., East Alton, Ill., 1960-64; asst. gen. counsel INTERCO, Inc., St. Louis, 1964-66, assoc. gen. counsel, mgr. law dept., 1966-69, asst. sec., 1966-74, gen. counsel, 1969-81, mem. oper. bd., 1970-92, v.p., 1971-81, mem. exec. com., dir., 1975-92, exec. v.p., 1981-85, vice chmn. bd. dirs., 1985-92; chmn., pres. Aylward & Assocs., Inc., St. Louis, 1992—. Mem. dist. export coun. US Dept. Commerce, 1974-77; dir., mem. exec. com. Boatmen's Nat. Bank St. Louis, 1982-91, trust estates com., 1982-85, chmn. audit com., 1986-91; bd. dirs. Boatmen's Bancshares, Inc., mem. audit com., 1984-91, mem. compensation com., 1986-91; trustee Maryville U., 1989-92, chmn. bd., 1991-92. Trustee St. Louis Coun. World Affairs, sec., 1977—84; chmn. lay bd. DePaul Health Ctr., 1979—81; mem. exec. com. lay bd., 1981—89; mem. lay adv. bd. Chaminade Coll. Prep. Sch., 1980—84, chmn. bd. trustees, 1981—84; mem. lay bd. Acad. of the Visitation, 1981—85; bd. dirs. Cath. Charities of St. Louis, 1994—2001, vice chmn., 1995—97, chmn., 1997—99; mem. coun. Archdiocesan Devel. Appeal, 1994—97, chmn., 1996—97, vice chmn., 1995—97, mem. exec. com., 1995—97, chmn. rev./planning com., 1995—96, chmn., 1996—, hon. life mem.; mem. fin. coun. Archdiocese of St. Louis, 1995—98, mem. investment com., 1995—97; bd. dirs. St. Louis chpt. Nat. Found. March of Dimes, 1974—84, sec., 1976—78, chmn., 1979—82; bd. dirs. Cardinal Ritter Inst., 1975—90, chmn. pers. com., 1986—90; bd. dirs. St. Louis chpt. ARC, 1977—82, Linda Vista Montessori Sch., 1975—77, BBB Greater St. Louis, 1978—81, YMCA Greater St. Louis, 1981—2001, adv. dir., 2001—, NCCJ, 1992—93; bd. dirs. Carindal Glennon Children's Hosp., 1991—96, mem. exec. com., 1992—96, bd. dirs. Found., 1996—2001, dir.emeritus, 2001—; bd. dirs., fin. United Way Greater St. Louis, 1986—2001; mem. investment com. St. Louis Cmty. Found., 1993—95. With US Army, 1955—58. Recipient of Order of St. Louis's King, Archdiocese of St. Louis. Mem.: NAM (taxation com. 1970—76, pub. affairs com. 1973—76, govt. ops./expenditures com. 1973—78), St. Louis Bar Assn., Mo. Bar Assn. (sr. counselor), Innsbrook Resort, Am. Soc. Corp. Secs. (pres. St. Louis regional group 1972—73), Am. Apparel Mfrs. Assn. (bd. dirs. 1983—85), Am. Footwear Industries Assn. (nat. affairs vice chmn. 1970, chmn. 1971—75), Assoc. Industries Mo. (bd. dirs. 1973—80, 2d v.p. 1974—76, exec. com. 1974—80, pres. 1976—78), Serra Internat., St. Louis C. of C. (legis. and tax com. 1966—74, vice-chmn. 1970—71), Old Kinderhood Golf Club, Bellerive Country Club, Mo. Athletic Club, Rotary (bd. dirs. St. Louis Club 1976—79), Bellerive Country Club (bd. dirs. 1981—84), Serra Club (trustee 2004—05), Order of St. Louis King, Knights of Malta (hospitaller), Knights of Holy Sepulcher, Delta Theta Phi (pres. St. Louis Alumni 1963, dist. chancellor Mo. 1970—79). Home: 55 Muirfield Saint Louis MO 63141-7372 Office: Aylward and Assoc Inc 55 Muirfield Ct Saint Louis MO 63141 *Having something to achieve is the essence of my career. Continuing to set higher goals throughout life has made it both interesting and rewarding.*

AYOTTE, KELLY A., state attorney general; b. Nashua, NH, 1968; BA with honors in Polit. Sci., Pa. State U., 1990; JD, Villanova U., 1993. Bar: N.H., Maine. Law clerk for Hon. Sherman Horton NH Supreme Ct., 1993—94; litigator McLane, Graf, Raulerson and Middleton, Nashua, NH, 1994—98; asst. atty. gen., homicide unit State of NH, 1998—2000, sr. asst. atty. gen., chief, homicide unit, 2000—02, legal counsel to gov., 2003, dep. atty. gen., 2003—04, atty. gen., 2004—. Named among 11 Remarkable Women in NH, NH Mag.; recipient Kirby award, Bar Found., 2004. Republican. Office: Office of Atty Gen State House Annex 33 Capitol St Concord NH 03301-6397 Office Phone: 603-271-3658.*

AYOUB, ELSA, lawyer; b. Beirut, Sept. 24, 1978; arrived in U.S., 2001; d. Gharamy Habib and Marcelle Farid Ayoub. Baccalaureate in French, Acad. Paris, 1996; licence en droit, Universite Pantheon Assas, 2000; M, Universite Pantheon-Assas, 2001; M in law, Washington Coll., 2002. Bar: N.Y. 2003. Atty. at law Gleason & Koatz, LLP, NYC, 2000—, Shamy & Shamy Law Offices, New Brunswick, NJ, 2003—04, Schulte Roth & Zabel, LLP, NYC, 2004. Cons. Embassy & Consulate Gen. of Lebanon, NYC, 2003—. Dean's fellow for grant devel., 2002. Mem.: N.Y. State Bar Assn., ABA, Am. Immigration Lawyers Assn. Maronite. Avocations: travel, politics. Office: Gleason & Koatz LLP 230 Park Ave New York NY 10166 Office Phone: 212-986-1544. Office Fax: 212-986-1379. Business E-Mail: eayoub@gleasonkoatz.com.

AYOUB, JUDITH LORENE, retired nursing educator; b. Lima, Ohio, Nov. 14, 1941; d. Clarence William and Marjorie Avenell Croft; m. Waheeb Fahmy Ayoub (dec.). Nursing diploma, Miami Valley Hosp., Dayton, Ohio, 1963; BSN, Wright State U., Dayton, 1977; MSN, U. Cin., 1982; PhD, U. Ariz., Tucson, 1997. Staff nurse Miami Valley Hosp., Dayton, 1963—64, 1973—77, USAF, Maxwell AFB, Ala., 1964—66; nurse educator Lima Meml. Hosp. Sch. Nursing, Ohio, 1967—68; head nurse Ohio State U. Hosps., Columbus, 1969—72; nurse educator Lima Tech. Coll., 1977—81, Huron Rd. Hosp., Cleve., 1982—85, U. Ariz., Tucson, 1985—99, Mercy Coll. NW Ohio, Toledo, 1999—2006; ret., 2006. Bd. mem., treas. Ohio League for Nursing, Ohio, 2002—06. Co-editor: (on-line jour.) Jour. Undergrad. Scholarship, 1999—2006. Bd. mem. Am. Inst. Archeology, Toledo, 2002—06. Capt. USAF. Mem.: Nat. League Nursing (articulation task force 2003—04), Sigma Theta Tau. Republican. Presbyterian. Avocations: travel, singing. Home: 2323 Oaks Edge Dr Toledo OH 43617

AYRAULT, EVELYN WEST, psychologist, writer; b. Mar. 3, 1922; d. John and Evelyn (West) A. BS, Fla. State Coll. for Women, 1945; MA, U. Chgo., 1947. Chief psychologist, asst. prin. Crippled Children's Sch., Jamestown, ND, 1947-48; psychologist, tchr. spl. edn. dept. Sharon (Pa.) Pub. Schs., 1948-50; chief psychologist, instr. Med. Coll. Va., Richmond, 1950-52; pvt. practice psychology NYC, 1952-68; clin. psychologist Erie, Pa., 1968—. Dir. psychol. svcs. United Cerebral Palsy Assn., Miami, Fla., 1952-54, Erie County (Pa.) Crippled Children's Soc., 1968-78; mem. med. staff HealthSouth Great Lakes Rehab. Hosp., Erie, Pa., 1986—; psychol. cons. Shriners Hosp. for Crippled Children, Erie. Author: Take Step, 1963, You Can Raise Your Handicapped Child, 1964, Helping the Handicapped Teenager Mature, 1971, Growing Up Handicapped, 1978, Sex, Love, and the Physically Handicapped, 1981, Beyond a Physical Disability: The Person Within, 2001. Mem. APA, CEC, Pa. Psychol. Assn., Psi Chi. Home: 227 W 22nd St # 4B Erie PA 16502-2614 Home Phone: 814-897-0341. Home Fax: 814-897-0341. Personal E-mail: evfscw@att.net.

AYRES, JANICE RUTH, social services administrator; b. Idaho Falls, Jan. 23, 1930; d. Low Ray and Frances Mae (Salem) Mason; m. Thomas Woodrow Ayres, Nov. 27, 1953 (dec. 1966); 1 child, Thomas Woodrow Jr. (dec.). MBA, U. So. Calif., 1952, M in Mass Comms., 1953. Asst. mktg. dir. Disneyland, Inc., Anaheim, Calif., 1954-59; gen. mgr. Tamasha Town & Country Club, Anaheim, Calif., 1959-65; dir. mktg. Am. Heart Assn., Santa Ana, Calif., 1966-69; state exec. dir. Nev. Assn. Mental Health, Las Vegas, 1969-71; exec. dir. Clark Co. Easter Seal Treatment Ctr., Las Vegas, 1971-73; mktg. dir., fin devel. officer So. Nev. Drug Abuse Coun., Las Vegas, 1973-74; exec. dir. Nev. Assn. Retarded Citizens, Las Vegas, 1974-75; assoc., cons. Don Luke & Assocs., Phoenix, 1976-77; program dir. Inter-Tribal Coun. Nev., Reno, 1977-79; exec. dir. Ret. Sr. Vol. Program, Carson City, Nev., 1979—. Chair sr. citizen summit State of Nev., 1996; apptd. by Gov. Guinn, Nev. Commn. Aging, 2001; presenter in field; apptd. del. by Gov. of Nev. White House Conf. on Aging, 2005. Del. White Ho. Conf. on Aging, 2005; bd. suprs. Carson City, Nev., 1992—; obligation bond com., legis. chair; commr. Carson City Parks and Recreation, 1993—; bd. dirs. Nev. Dept. Transp., 1993; active No. Corp. for Nat. and Cmty. Svc. by Gov., 1994, V&TRR Commn., 1993, re-appointed by Gov., 2005—, chair, 1995, vice-chair, chair pub. rels. com., bd. dirs. Hist. V&TRR Bd.; chair PR Cmty./V&RR Commn. Nev. Home Health Assn.; appointed liaison Carson City Sr. Citizens Bd., 1995; chair summit Rural Nev. Sr. Citizens, Carson City; pres. No. Nev. RR Found., 1996—; chair Tri-Co-RR Commn., 1995, Gov.'s Nev. Commn. for Corp. in Nat. and Cmty. Svc., 1997—, pres., 1998, Carson City Pub. Transp. Commn., 1998—; Carson City Commn. for Clean Groundwater Act, 1998—; chairperson Celebrate Svc. Conf. Americore, 2000; apptd. by Gov. of Nev. Commn. on Aging, 2001—; apptd. by Nev. Gov. New Nev. Commn. to Restructure the Historic V&T RR, 2002—; mem. Nev. Commn. on Aging, 2001—; apptd. rep. of gov. to Nev. Commn. Recruitment V&T RR, 2002; apptd. by Nev. Treas. Brian Krolicki Women's Commn. Fin., 2003—; re-appointed to commn. by Gov. Nev. Commn. for Nat. and Cmty. Svc., 2005—; apptd. del. to White House Conf. on Aging Nev. Gov., 2005; apptd. to bd. dirs. Chinese Workers Mus. Am. Constrn. Project, 2007. Named Woman of Distinction, Soroptimist Club, 1988, Oustanding Dir. of Excellence, Gov. State of Nev., 1989, Outstanding Nev. Women's Role Model, Nev. A.G., 1996, Woman of Distinction, Carson Valley Optimist, 2002, Nev.'s Outstanding Older Worker for Experience-Works, 2002, Oldest CEO in Nev., 2002, Outstanding Nev. Pvt. Citizen, Nev. Gov. Kenny Guinn, 2003, Outstanding Dir., Vol. Action Ctr., J.C. Penney Co., invitee to White Ho. for outstanding contbns. to Am.; named to White House Conf. on Aging as Gov. del., 2005; recipient Gold award, Western Fairs Assn., 2000, Woman of Distinction award, Soroptimist, 2003, Carson City Optimist, 2003, Nat. Optimist Conv., Reno, Nev., 2003, Outstanding Svc. to Seniors Blue Star award, Sanford Ctr. on Aging, 2004, Outstanding Contbn. to Success of Women in Bus., Carson Valley Sorpotomists. Mem.: AAUW, Nat. Assn. Ret. and Sr. Vol. Dirs., Inc. (pres. 2003, nat. pres. 2003—), Internat. Assn. Bus. Commentators, No. Nev. Railroad Found. (pres. 1996—, 2005—08), Am. Soc. Assn. Execs., Nev. Assn. Transit Svcs. (bd. dirs., legis. chmn.), Nev. Fair and Rodeo Assn. (pres.), Nat. Soc. Fund Raising Execs., Women in Radio and TV, Pub. Rels. Soc. Am. (chpt. pres., Outstanding 25 Yr. Svc. award 2004), Internat. Platform Assn., Am. Mktg. Assn. (bd. dirs. 1999—), Am. Mgmt. Assn. (bd. dirs.), Nat. Women's Polit. Caucus, Nev. Women's Polit. Caucus. Office: 3303 Butto Wau Bldg 1 Carson City NV 89701 Office Phone: 775-687-4680 ext. 2. Business E-Mail: branded@rsvp.carson-city.nv.us.

AYRES, JEFFREY PEABODY, lawyer; b. Waltham, Mass., Sept. 23, 1952; s. John Cecil and Dora Hoxie A.; m. Janet Diehl, May 31, 1980; children: Brendan Peabody, Caroline Bradfield, Gordon Pettit. BA cum laude, Harvard U., 1974; JD magna cum laude, George Washington U., 1977. Bar: D.C. 1977, Md. 1978, U.S. Ct. Appeals (3d, 4th and D.C. cirs.), U.S. Dist. Ct. Md., U.S. Dist. Ct. D.C., U.S. Supreme Ct. 1985. Assoc. Arent, Fox, Kintner, Plotkin & Kahn, Washington, 1977-78, Venable, Baetjer & Howard, Balt., 1978-85, ptnr., 1986; ptnr., chair Ethics Com. Venable LLP, Towson, Md. Contbr. articles to profl. jours. Alt., del., parliamentarian Episcopal Diocesan Conv.; sr. warden Ch. of the Redeemer, 2002-05 Mem. ABA, Md. Bar Assn., Balt. Bar Assn. (chair labor and employment sect. 1998-2000), Md. Atty. Grievance Commn. Peer Review Com., Harvard Club Md. (pres. 1989-94, v.p. 1994-2002), Harvard Alumni Assn. (regional dir. 1995-98). Democrat. Episcopalian. Avocations: swimming, bicycling. Home: 7120 Sheffield Rd Baltimore MD 21212-1629 Office: Venable LLP 210 Allegheny Ave PO Box 5517 Towson MD 21204 Office Phone: 410-494-6282. Office Fax: 410-821-0147. E-mail: jpayres@venable.com.

AYRES, MARY ELLEN, federal official; b. Spokane, Wash., June 23, 1924; d. Frank H. and Marion (Kellogg) A. Student, U. Wash., 1942-43; BA, Stanford U., 1946; postgrad., Am. U., 1960. With Henry von Morpurgo, Advt., 1946-47; reporter Wenatchee Daily World, Wash., 1947-50, Washington Post, 1951-52; with U.S. Fgn. Service, Dept. State, 1950-51; mem. editorial staff Changing Times, 1952-61; editor Family Guide, Kiplinger Washington Editors, 1958-61, Bur. Labor Stats., Manpower Adminstrn., U.S. Dept. Labor, 1962-67; pub. info. specialist Bur. Indian Affairs, U.S. Dept. Interior, 1967-75; writer-editor Bur. Labor Stats., 1975—. Tchr. newsletter class Dept. Agriculture Grad. Sch., 1975-89, editing style and technique class, 1987-89; past treas. Govt. Info. Orgn. Mem. publicity com. Nat. Capitol YWCA, 1982-83; dir. Wenatchee High Sch. Scholarship Found., 1988-95. Mem. Nat. Assn. Govt. Communicators (founding treas., dir. 1975-80, 89-91, chmn. Blue Pencil Contest 1987, nat. capital chpt. treas. 1989), Nat. Press Club (Washington), Washington Athletic Club (Seattle), Am. News Women's Club, Stanford U. Alumnae Assn., Kappa Kappa Gamma. Episcopalian. Home: 2400 Virginia Ave NW Apt C802 Washington DC 20037-2657 Office: Bur Labor Stats 2 Massachusetts Ave NE Washington DC 20212-0022 Office Phone: 202-691-5856. Office Fax: 202-691-7890. Business E-Mail: ayres_m@bls.gov.

AYRES, ROBERT MOSS, JR., retired university president; b. San Antonio, Sept. 1, 1926; s. Robert Moss and Florence (Collett) A.; m. Patricia Ann Shield, Sept. 10, 1955; children: Robert Atlee, Vera Patricia. Student, Tex. Mil. Inst., 1944; BA, U. South, 1949, DCL, 1974; postgrad., Oxford U., Eng., 1949; MBA, U. Pa., 1952. With Kidder, Peabody & Co., Phila., NYC, 1950-52; with Dittmar & Co., San Antonio, 1952-53; pres., dir. Russ & Co., Inc., San Antonio, 1953-73; sr. v.p., dir. Rotan Mosle Inc., San Antonio, 1973-77; pres. U. South, Sewanee, Tenn., 1977-88, pres. emeritus, 1988—; past pres. So. Univ. Conf.; chmn. So. Coll. and Univ. Union. Former allied mem. N.Y. Stock Exch., Am. Stock Exch.; bd. dirs. Rail Tex. Corp., Howell Corp., James Avery Craftsman. Past pres. Assn. Alumni U. of South; past pres. bd. dirs. Bexar County chpt. ARC; past pres. bd. trustees Tex. Mil. Inst.; trustee, past chmn. bd. regents U. of South; trustee Brother's Bro. Found.; mem. exec. coun. Episcopal Ch., 1976-82, also mem. nat. and world mission com., dir., past pres. St. Mary's Episcopal Ctr.; mem. Commn. on Ministry Com. Diocese of Tex.; past bd. dirs. Inst. European Studies, Presiding Bishop's Fund World Relief, Alfalit, Internat.; vol. exec. dir. Vol. in Mission, 1976; bd. dirs. Inst. of Servant Leadership, Soc. Promotion of Christian Knowledge/U.S.A., Salvation Army, Episcopal Hist. Soc. With USN, 1944-46; lt. Res. 1949-60. Mem. San Antonio Soc. Fin. Analysts (past pres.), Securities Industries Assn. (past mem. governing coun.), Investment Bankers Assn. Am. (past chmn. Tex. group), Nat. Assn. Securities Dealers (past mem. dist. com.) Young Pres. Orgn., Order of Alamo, Tex. Cavaliers, Argyle, Am. Soc. Order of St. John, Sigma Alpha Epsilon. Episcopalian (mem. exec. bd. diocese W. Tex.; vestryman). Clubs: San Antonio German, San Antonio Country. Home: 5705 Scout Island Cv Austin TX 78731-3386

AYRES, TED D., lawyer; b. Hamilton, Mo., July 14, 1947; m. Marcia Sue Busselle; children: John Corbett, Jackson Frazer, Joseph Dean. BSBA, Ctrl. Mo. State Coll., 1969; JD, U. Mo., 1972. Bar: Mo. 1972, US Dist. Ct. (we. dist.) Mo. 1972, US Ct. Appeals (8th cir.) 1977, US Supreme Ct. 1977, Colo. 1984, US Dist. Ct. Colo. 1984, US Ct. Appeals (10th cir.) 1984, Kans. 1987. Law clk. to presiding justice Mo. Supreme Ct., Jefferson City, 1972-73; ptnr. Stubbs & Ayres, Chillicothe, Mo., 1973-74; atty. Southwestern Bell Tel. Co., St. Louis, 1974-76; counsel U. Mo., Columbia, 1976-84; gen. counsel U. Colo., Boulder, 1984-86, Kans. Bd. Regents, Topeka, 1986-92, gen. counsel, dir. govtl. rels., 1992-96; acting pres. Pitts. State U., 1995; gen. counsel, assoc. to pres. Wichita State U., Kans., 1996—2002, interim dir. Edwin A. Ulrich Mus. Art, 1999-2000, 2006—07, v.p., gen. counsel, 2002—, dir. equal employment opportunity, 2003—. Adj. asst. prof. coll. bus. adminstrn. U. Colo., Denver, 1984-85, adj. assoc. prof.,

1985-86; spl. asst. atty. gen. State of Colo., 1984-86, State of Kans., 1986—; presenter region II conf. Assn. Coll. Unions Internat., U. Mo., Rolla, 1983; spkr. Soc. Colo. Archivists, U. Colo., Boulder, 1985; adj. prof. Washburn U., Topeka, 1989; adj. prof. kinesiology and sport studies Wichita State U., 1999—; spl. cons. to pres. Southwestern Coll., Winfield, Kans., 2003-05. Contbr. articles to profl. jours., reviews to profl. pubs. Mem. adv. com. Boone County (Mo.) Cmty. Svcs.; com. social concerns Mo. United Meth. Ch., 1979-81, supervisory com. Mothers' Morning Out program, 1980-84; adminstv. bd., com. on fin. and stewardship 1st United Meth. Ch., Topeka, 1989-91, family life coun., 1994-95; trustee Mid-Mo. chpt. Nat. Multiple Sclerosis Soc., 1981-84; bd. mgrs. Topeka YMCA-Downtown Br., 1991-96, fedn. coun. Indian Guides program, 1988-91; pack treas. Boy Scouts Am., 1990-95; bd. dirs. Innovative Tech. Enterprise Corp., 1991-94, S.W. Youth Athletic Assn., Inc., 1994-96, Friends of Topeka Zoo, 1995-2000, Wichita Tech. Corp., 1997-, Wichita State U. Hist. Preservation Commn., 1998-; chair collections com. Ulrich Mus. Art, 2003—; parents coun. Truman State U., 1997-99. Curator scholar, 1969-70, Omar E. Robinson scholar, 1970-71, John M. Dalton Ednl. Trust scholar 1971-72. Mem. Mo. Bar Assn., Nat. Assn. Coll. and Univ. Attys. (chairperson Southwestern region 1979-81, bd. dirs. 1985-88, com. mem. 1979-84, del. and presenter numerous CLE workshops), U. Mo. Alumni Assn. (life; bd. dirs. Wichita chpt. 2004—, pres. 2005-07), Wichita State U. Alumni Assn. (life). Avocations: reading, running, photography, travel, gardening. Home: 2820 Tallgrass St Wichita KS 67226-1815 Office: Wichita State Univ 203 Morrison Hall Wichita KS 67260-0001 Office Phone: 316-978-3001. Business E-Mail: ted.ayres@wichita.edu.

AYSCUE, EDWIN OSBORNE, JR., lawyer; b. May 21, 1933; s. Edwin Osborne and Grace Elizabeth A.; m. Emily Mizell Urquhart, Aug. 17, 1957; children: Grace, E. Osborne, Emily Hassel, Margaret Certain. Grad. cum laude, Phillips Acad., Andover, Mass., 1951; AB in Polit. Sci., U. NC, Chapel Hill, 1954, LLB with honors, 1960. Bar: NC 1960, US Supreme Ct. 1979. Of counsel Helms Mulliss & Wicker, PLLC (and predecessor firms), 1960—. Mem. Civil Justice Reform Act Com., Western Dist. N.C., 1991—95. Editor-in-chief: NC Law Rev., 1959-60; contbr. articles to profl. jours. Bd. dirs. Legal Svcs. of So. Piedmont, 1983-85, Am. Judicature Soc. , 1985-89, Legal Svcs. of NC, 1984-85, 88-94, US Supreme Ct. Hist. Soc., 1999-2003; bd. visitors U. NC Chapel Hill, 2000-04; trustee St. Mary's Sch., Raleigh, NC, 2000-04; sr. warden Christ Episcopal Ch., 1990-91. Lt. USNR, 1955-57. Fellow: Am. Coll. Trial Lawyers (pres. 1998—99), Am. Bar Found. (life); mem.: ABA (ho. of dels. 1991—95, standing com. fed. judiciary 2001—04), People's Republic of Cuba Legal Exch. (chair 2001), People's Republic of China Legal Exch. (chair 1987), Anglo-Am. Legal Exch. (co-chair 1999—2000), Mecklenburg County Bar (pres. 1980—81), NC State Bar, NC Bar Assn. (pres. 1984—85, Gen. Practice Hall of Fame), 4th Cir. Jud. Conf., Nat. Conf. Bar Pres., U. NC Chapel Hill Law Alumni Assn. (pres. 1999—2000), Order of Coif, Order Golden Fleece, Charlotte Country Club, Phi Beta Kappa. Democrat. Episcopalian. Office: Helms Mulliss & Wicker PLLC PO Box 31247 Charlotte NC 28231-1247 Office Phone: 704-343-2058. Business E-Mail: ozzie.ayscue@hmw.com.

AYUS, JUAN CARLOS, nephrologist; b. Buenos Aires, Feb. 25, 1941; arrived in U.S., 1973; s. Jose and Matilde A.; m. Linda Maria Giudici; children: Sebastian, Mariana. BS, Nat. Coll., 1959; MD, U. Buenos Aires, 1967. Diplomate Am. Bd. Internal Medicine, Am. Bd. Nephrology. Resident in internal medicine U. Buenos Aires, 1968-71, fellow in nephrology, 1971-72; resident in internal medicine U. Mass., Worcester, 1973-74, U. Minn., Mpls., 1974-75; fellow in nephrology U. Calif., San Francisco, 1975-77; chief renal svc. Ben-Taub Regional hosp., Houston, 1977-84; from assoc. prof. to prof. medicine Baylor Coll. Medicine, Houston, 1984—2001; prof. medicine U. Tex. Health Sci. Ctr., San Antonio, 2001—. Recipient Gold Insignia, Spanish Soc. Nephrology, 1999. Fellow ACP; mem. L.Am. Soc. Nephrology (sec.-treas. 1993-96, v.p. 1996-99), Argentine Soc. Critical Care (founder). Home: 2412 Westgate Houston TX 77019 Office Phone: 713-502-0543. Personal E-mail: carlosayus@yahoo.com.

AYYUB, BILAL M., engineer, company executive, educator, researcher; b. Shweikeh, Tulkaram, Palestine, Jan. 5, 1958; came to U.S., 1980; s. Mohammed S. and Thuraya Ayyub; m. Deena L. Ziadeh, June 27, 1987; children: Omar, Rami, Samar, Ziad. BSCE, U. Kuwait, 1980; MSCE, Ga. Inst. Tech., 1981, PhD, 1983. Registered profl. engr., Md. Asst. prof. dept. civil engring. U. Md., College Park, 1983-88, assoc. prof., 1988-93, prof., 1993—, gen. dir. Ctr. for Tech. and Sys. Mgmt.; pres. BMA Engring. Inc., Md., 1988—; CEO Decide-Now.com, Inc., 2000—03. Cons. prof. Carderock divsn. of Naval Surface Warfare Ctr., USN; cons. USCG, Groton, Conn., 1987-90, USN, Crystal City, Va., 1990—, ASME, Washington, 1990—, Internat. Monetary Fund, Washington, 1993, Chevron Rsch. and Tech. Corp., Richmond, Calif., 1992-94, U.S. Army Corps. of Engrs., Washington, 1994—; mem. adv. bd. to internat. jours. and Naval Engrs. Jour., 1989-2005; gen. chmn. Internat. Symposium on Uncertainty Modeling and Analysis, 1990, 93, 95, 2003; dir. Ctr. for Tech. and Sys. Mgmt. Editor: Analysis and Management of Uncertainty, 1992, Uncertainty Modeling and Analysis, 1995, Uncertainty Modeling in Finite Element, Fatigue and Stability of Systems, 1997, Uncertainty Modeling in Vibration, Control and Fuzzy Analysis in Structural Systems, 1997, Uncertainty Modeling and Analysis in Civil Engrineering, 1998, Uncertainty Modeling and Analysis in Engineering and the Sciences, 1997; editor: (textbooks) Numerical Methods for Engineers1995, Elicitation of Expert Opinions for Uncertainty and Risks, 2001, Probability, Statistics and Reliability for Engineers, 2d edit., 2003, Risk Analysis in Engineering and Economics, 2003; contbr. articles to profl. jours. Recipient Cert. of Appreciation, U.S. Army C.E., 1995; grantee, NSF, 1985—92, Md. State Hwy. Adminstrn., 1986—90, USN, 1990—95, U.S. Army C.E., 1994—95. Fellow ASCE (Outstanding Rsch. Oriented Paper award 1988, Edmund Friedman award 1989, Walter L. Huber Civil Engring. Rsch. award 1997, chmn. reliability of offshore structures com. 1993-96, assoc. editor Jour. Structural Engring., mem. com. on fatugue and fracture reliability, mem. tech. adminstrv. com. on structural safety and reliability 1993-96), Soc. Naval Archs. and Marine Engrs. (chmn. panel on design procedure and philosophy of the hull structures com., Jour. Ship Rsch. com.), ASME (polit. action com. 1990—, risk-based tech. rsch. com.); mem. IEEE (sr.), NRC (working groups of marine bd.), Am. Soc. Naval Engrs. (life, Jimmie Hamilton award 1986, 93, 2000, 02, chmn. naval engrs. jour. com.), Am. Concrete Inst., Am. Acad. Mechanics, N.Am. Fuzzy Info. Processing Soc. (K.S. Fu award 1995, gen. chmn. ann. conf. 1995), Computer Soc. Achievements include risk and uncertainty analysis in engineering, homeland security and protection of critical infrastructure and key assets, design guidelines for posttensioned composite bridges, general guidelines for risk-based inspection, structural reliability assessment using variance reduction techniques, uncertainty modeling and analysis in engineering, fuzzy logic in civil engineering, reliability-based design of marine structures, reliability assessment and reliability-based design of navigation structures. Office: U Md Dept Civil & Environ Engr College Park MD 20742-0001 Office Phone: 301-405-1956. Business E-Mail: ba@umd.edu.

AZAD, NILOFER SABA, oncologist; d. Mushtaq Husain Azad and Manik Husain. MD, Baylor Coll., Houston, 2001. Oncologist Nat. Cancer Inst., Bethesda, Md., 2004—. Clin. rschr. Nat. Cancer Inst., 2005. Office Phone: 301-496-4916. E-mail: azadn@mail.nih.gov.

AZAD, SUSAN STOTT, lawyer; BS, Oreg. State U., 1984; JD, UCLA, 1989. Bar: Calif. 1989. With Latham & Watkins, LA, 1989—, ptnr., 1997—. Mem. assocs. com. Latham & Watkins, LA, 1992—94, fin. com., 1995—97, ethics com., 2001—. Mem.: ABA, LA County Bar Assn. (litigation sect., former mem. jud. election evaluations com., former mem. Calif. and state bar ct. rules com.). Office: Latham and Watkins LLP 633 W Fifth St Ste 4000 Los Angeles CA 90071 Home Phone: 818-790-7454; Office Phone: 213-485-1234. Business E-Mail: susan.azad@lw.com.

AZADPUR, MOHAMMAD, philosopher, educator; s. H. Azadpur and S. Eslami; m. Avissa H. Tehrani, Feb. 9, 2005. BA, Bucknell U., Lewisburg, Pa., 1986; MA, U. Pitts., 1993; PhD, U. Va., Charlottesville, 1999. Mellon postdoctoral fellow Johns Hopkins U., Balt., 1999—2001, CRCL postdoctoral fellow, 2001—02, instr., 2002—03; prof. San Francisco State U., 2003—. Contbr. articles to profl. jours. Recipient CSU Summer Rsch. award, San Francisco State U., 2004, 2007, Presdl. award, 2007; Pres. fellow, U. Va., 1994—97, Dupont Dissertation fellow, 1997—98. Mem.: Am. Philos. Assn. (programming com. 2006). Muslim. Office Phone: 415-338-1598.

AZADZOI, KAZEM M., urologist, educator; b. Feb. 10, 1957; s. Nasim and Amena Azadzoi; m. Jamila Azadzoi; children: Naweed Azad, Roya Azad, Michelle Azad. MD, Kabul U., Afghanistan, 1983; MA, Boston U., 1990. Prof., pathology and urology Boston U. Med. Sch., 2002—; dir., urology rsch. VA Boston Healthcare Sys., 2002—. Mem. adv. bd. European Urol. Soc. Ann. Meeting, Istanbul, Turkey, 2000; ad hoc cons. NIH, Veterans Affairs Ctrl. Office. Contbr. articles to profl. jours., chpts. to books; mem. editl. bd. Brit. Jour. Urology Internat. Recipient prize in med. rsch., Jean-Francois Ginestie, 1990, 1996, Endourology Soc., 1993, Jack Lapides, 1998, AVA/Circon, 2000; grantee, NIH, 1987—88, 1992—97, 2000—05, Veterans Affairs Ctrl. Office, 1991—94, 1998—2001, 2001—05, Gentronics Inc., 1998—99, Pfizer Pharmaceuticals, 2000, 2001, 2002, 2003, POM Wonderful Inc., 2003—05, Ely-Lilly Pharmaceuticals, 2004, Yamanouchi Pharmaceuticals, 2005. Mem.: N.E. Smooth Muscle Soc., Nat. Bladder Found., Internat. Soc. for Impotence Rsch., Internat. Continence Soc., Am. Urol. Assn. Achievements include development of the first experimental model of pelvic ischemia. Office: VA Boston Healthcare Sys 150 S Huntington Ave Boston MA 02130 Home Phone: 617-964-4673; Office Phone: 617-232-9500 5602. E-mail: kazadzoi@bu.edu.

AZANK, ROBERTO, artist; b. Buenos Aires, Nov. 3, 1955; came to U.S., 1979; s. Neazi and Dora Margarita (Estevez) A.; m. Monika Schifler, Oct. 20, 1990; 1 child, Rudi Vinicius. Student, U. Arch., Buenos Aires, 1975-78. One-man shows include Marcos J. Alegria Sch. Fine Arts, P.R., 1991, Consulate Gen. of Argentina, N.Y.C., 1997, Lizan Tops Gallery, East Hampton, N.Y., 1998, Albers Fine Arts, Memphis, 1998, Albert White Gallery, Toronto, 1998, Hooks-Epstein Galleries, Houston, 1998, Brewster Arts Ltd., N.Y.C., 1999, Addison-Ripley Fine Art, Washington, 1999, 2003, Byron Cohen Gallery, Kansas City, Mo., 2000, Albert Einstein U., N.Y.C., 1999, Eleonore Austerer Gallery, San Francisco, 2001, 02, 03, 04, Palm Springs, Calif., 2003, Gomez Gallery, Balt., 2001, Bachelier-Cardonsky Gallery, Kent, Conn., 2001, 2003, 2006, Austerer-Crider Gallery, Palm Springs, 2002, Ctr. of Earth Gallery, Charlotte, N.C., 2003, Eleonore Austerer Gallery, Palm Desert, Calif., 2003, 05, 06, 07, Simmons Gallery, San Francisco, 2004, 05, Patricia Rovzar Gallery, Kirkland, Wash., 2004; group exhbns. include Olympia and York Gallery, N.Y., 1991, Galaxy Gallery, Miami Beach, Fla., 1990, SUNY, Albany, 1993, Ramis Barquet Gallery, Miami, 1997, N.Y. Arts Mag. 2d City-wide Biennial, 1997, Mulligan Shanoski Gallery, San Francisco, 1998, Elite Fine Art, Miami, 1998, Art Miami, '98, 1998, Lyons Wier Gallery, Chgo., 1998, Artspace/Va. Miller Gallery, Miami, 1998, Meredith Kelly Fine Arts, Santa Fe, 1998, 2000, 02, 03, Kougeas Gallery, Boston, 1999, William Havu Gallery, Denver, 1999, Art Miami, 2000, 01, Palm Springs Art Fair, 2000, 01, Eleonore Austerer Gallery, 2000, Ctr. of Earth Gallery, Charlotte, N.C., 2002-06; represented by Robert Miller Gallery, N.Y., Artspace/Virginia Miller Gallery, Miami, Eleonore Austerer Gallery, Palm Desert, Calif.; works featured in publs. including N.Y. Arts Mag., New Am. Painting, Waterfront Week, Kansas City Star, The Washington Post, Miami Herald, Palm Springs Life; included in pub. collections at Washington Conv. Ctr., Am. Express Fin. Advisors, Spring Telecomms., also pvt. collections. Avocations: classical music, astronomy, chess, bridge. Office: Roberto Azank Studio 8 Watch Hill Rd New Paltz NY 12561-2705 Office Phone: 845-255-3525. E-mail: RobertoAzank@mac.com.

AZAR, ALEX MICHAEL, II, former federal agency administrator, lawyer; b. 1967; m. Jennifer Azar; 2 children. AB, Dartmouth U., 1988; JD, Yale U., 1991. Bar: Md. 1993, DC 1995. Law clk. to Hon. J. Michael Luttig US Ct. Appeals 4th Cir., 1991—92; law clk. to Assoc. Justice Antonin Scalia US Supreme Ct., 1992—93; assoc. Kirkland & Ellis, Washington, 1993—94; assoc. ind. counsel Whitewater Investigation, 1994—96; ptnr. Wiley, Rein & Fielding, Washington, 1996—2001; gen. counsel US Dept. Health & Human Services., Washington, 2001—05; dep. sec. US Dept. Health & Human Svcs., Washington, 2005—07; sr. v.p. corp. affairs and comm. Eli Lilly & Co., 2007—.

AZAR, HENRY AMIN, retired medical historian, educator; b. Egypt, Dec. 21, 1927; s. Amin Antonios and Agnes Garabed (Nazaretian) A.; m. Rose Theresa Connell, Apr. 19, 1960; children: Henry Amin Jr., Philip John. BA, Am. U., Beirut, 1948, MD, 1952; PhD in History, U. NC, Chapel Hill, 1998. Diplomate Am. Bd. Pathology. Intern NYC Hosp., 1952-53; resident Columbia-Presbyn. Hosp. Med. Ctr., NYC, 1955-56, NY-Cornell, Med. Ctr., NYC, 1956-57, Mass. Meml. Hosp., Boston, 1957-58; asst. prof. pathology Am. U., Beirut, 1958-60; asst. prof. and assoc. prof. pathology Coll. Physicians and Surgeons, Columbia U., 1960-70; dir. surg. pathology, prof. U. Kans., 1970-72; chief lab. service James A. Haley Vets. Hosp., Tampa, Fla., 1972-83, chief anatomic pathology, 1983-92; prof. U. South Fla., 1973-92, prof. emeritus, 1992. Rsch. prof. pathology U. NC, 1998—. Author: Multiple Myeloma and Related Disorders, 1973, Diagnostic Electron Microscopy: The Hemopoietic System, 1979, Pathology of Human Neoplasms, 1988, Ibn Zuhr (Avenzoar): The Translation of His Work into Latin and His Image in Medieval Europe, 1998; contbr. articles to profl. jours. Fellow Coll. Am. Pathologists; mem. Assn. Vet. Chiefs Lab. Svc. (pres. 1981-83), Arthur Purdy Stout Soc. (sec. 1983-87, pres. 1990-91), Pathology Alumni Found. (emeritus trustee) Harvey Soc., Internat. Acad. Pathology (emeritus), Hematopathology Soc., Am. Assn. for History of Medicine, Soc. Internat. History of Sci. and Philosopy Arab Islam, Am. U. Beirut Alumni Assn. (pres. Tampa Bay chpt. 1985-87), History of Pathology Soc. (pres. 1996-97). Syrian Orthodox. Home: 1700 Old Oxford Rd Chapel Hill NC 27514-2132

AZAR, J. J., engineering educator; b. Tripoli, Lebanon, Sept. 19, 1937; arrived in U.S., 1957; s. Joseph and Sarah Azar; m. Zaetta Jean Bradshaw, Dec. 23, 1961; children: Scott J., Steven Zay. BS, U. Okla., Norman, 1960; MS, U. Okla., 1961, PhD, 1965. Lic. profl. engr., Okla. Asst. prof. U. Tulsa, 1965—69, assoc. prof., 1969—75, prof., 1975—96, McMen Chair prof., 1996—2002, prof. emeritus, 2002—. Dir. U. Tulsa Drilling Rsch. Projects, 1975—96; chmn. award com. AIME, NYC, 1997. Author: Matrix Structural Analysis, 1972, Aircraft Structures, 1982, Drilling Fluids, 1986, Drilling Engineering, 2006; contbr. articles to profl. jours. Mem.: Nat. Acad. Engring., Soc. Petroleum Engrs. (chmn. award com. 1994—, Disting. Achievement Prof. in Petroleum Engring. 1997, Drilling Engring. award 1998, Disting. Mem. award 2004). Republican. Presbyterian. Avocations: tennis, golf, skiing. Office: U Tulsa 600 S College Tulsa OK 74104 Home: 20603 Fairway Meadow Ln Spring TX 77379 Office Phone: 918-631-5170. Personal E-mail: adc.training@sbcglobal.net.

AZARIA, HANK, actor; b. NYC, Apr. 25, 1964; m. Helen Hunt, July 17, 1999 (div. Dec. 18, 2000). BA, Tufts U., 1987. Actor: (films) Cool Blue, 1988, Pretty Woman, 1990, Quiz Show, 1994, Now and Then, 1995, Heat, 1995, The Birdcage, 1996, Grosse Pointe Blank, 1997, Godzilla, 1998, Great Expectations, 1998, Homegrown, 1998, Celebrity, 1998, The Cradle Will Rock, 1999, Alligatropolis, 1999, Mystery Men, 1999, Mystery Alaska, 1999, Tuesdays With Morrie (Emmy award, 2000), 1999, C-Scam, 2000, America's Sweethearts, 2001, Bark, 2002, Along Came Polly, 2004, Dodgeball: A True Underdog Story, 2004, The Simpsons Movie (voice), 2007; (TV movies) Frank Nitti: The Enforcer, 1988, Tuesdays with Morrie, 1999, Fail Safe, 2000, Uprising, 2001; (TV appearances) Family Ties, 1988, Growing Pains, 1985, The Fresh Prince of Bel-Air, 1990, Babes, 1990, Herman's Head, 1991, Friends, 1994, 2001, 2002, 2003, Tales From the Crypt, 1995, If Not for You, 1995, Mad About You, 1996-97; voice characterizations The Simpsons (voice of Apu, Chief Wiggum, Moe Syzlak, and others), 1989— (Emmy award for animation voice-over, 1998, 2001, 2003), Beethoven, 1994, Spider-Man, 1995, Anastasia, 1997, Stressed Eric (also prodr.), 1998, Futurama, 1999, Bartok the Magnificent (also co-prod.), 1999, CyberWorld, 2000; actor, prodr., dir., writer: (film) Nobody's Perfect, 2004; exec. prodr.: (TV series) Imagine That, 2002; actor, prodr.: Huff, 2004-; broadway: Monty Python's Spamalot, 2005 (Theatre World award, 2005). Recipient: Light on the Hill award, Tufts U., 1999. Office: The Simpsons c/o Twentieth Television PO Box 900 Beverly Hills CA 90213*

AZARNOFF, DANIEL LESTER, pharmaceutical executive, consultant; s. Samuel J. and Kate (Asarnow) A.; m. Joanne Stokes, Dec. 26, 1951; children: Rachel, Richard, Martin. BS, Rutgers U., 1947, MS, 1948; MD, U. Kans., 1955. Asst. instr. anatomy U. Kans. Med. Sch., 1949—50, rsch. fellow, 1950—52, intern, 1955—56, resident, Nat. Heart Inst. research fellow, 1956—58, asst. prof. medicine, 1962—64, assoc. prof., 1964—68, dir. clin. pharmacology study unit, 1964—68, assoc. prof. pharmacology, 1965—68, prof. medicine and pharmacology, 1968, dir. Clin. Pharmacology-Toxicology Ctr., 1967—78, Disting. prof., 1973—78, also prof. medicine, 1965—67, pres. Sigma Xi Club, 1968—69, clin. prof. medicine, 1982—96, prof. medicine, 1997—; Nat. Inst. Neurol. Diseases and Blindness spl. trainee Washington U. Sch. Medicine, St. Louis, 1958—60; asst. prof. medicine St. Louis U. Sch. Medicine, 1960—62; sr. v.p. worldwide R&D, G.D. Searle & Co., Skokie, 1978; pres. Searle R&D, Skokie, 1979—85, Azarnoff Assocs., Inc., Evanston, Ill., 1986—87, D.L. Azarnoff Assocs., So. San Francisco, Calif., 1987—; prof. pathology, clin. prof. pharmacology Northwestern U. Med. Sch., 1978—85; sr. v.p. clin. regulatory affairs Cellegy Pharms., San Francisco, 1998—2003; sr. v.p. clin. devel., pharmacology Congentus Pharms., 2006—; commr. Nat. Commn. on Orphan Diseases, 1985—87; chmn. bd. dirs. Alpha RX Corp., South San Francisco, Calif., 1992—94; clin. prof. med. Stanford U. Sch. Med., 1998—2002. Professorial lectr. U. Chgo., 1978-86; dir. Second Workshop on Prins. Drug Evaluation in Man, 1970; chmn. com. on problems of drug safety NRC-NAS, 1972-76; chmn. bd. dirs. Oread, Inc., Lawrence, Kans., 1998-99; CEO Cibus Pharms., Burlingame, Calif., 1996-97; cons. numerous govt. agys.; chmn. bd. dirs. Cibus Pharm., Inc., 1996-97; CEO, chmn. bd. dirs. Vitalsensor, Inc., 2004-05. Editor: Devel. of Drug Interactions, 1974-77, Yearbook of Drug Therapy, 1977-79; series editor: Monographs in Clin. Pharmacology, 1977-84; mem. editl. bd. Drug Investigation, Brit. Jour. Clin. Pharmacology, Clin. Pharmacol. Therapy, Clin. Pharmacokinetics, Clin. Drug Investigation, 1989—, others. Served with U.S. Army, 1945-46. Recipient Ginsburg award in phys. diagnosis U. Kanas. Med. Ctr., 1953, Outstanding Intern award, 1956, Ciba award for gerontol. rsch., 1958, Rectors medal U. Helsinki, 1968, Nathanial T. Kwit Meml. Disting. Svc. award Am. Coll. Clin. Pharmacology, 2002; named Disting. Med. Alumnus, U. Kans. Coll. Health Sci., 1995; John and Mary R. Markle scholar, 1964, William N. Creasy vis. prof. clin. pharmacology Med. Coll. Va., 1975; Bruce Hall Meml. lectr. St. Vincents Hosp., Sydney, 1976, 7th Sir Henry Hallett Dale lectr. Johns Hopkins U. Med. Sch., 1978; Fulbright scholar Karolinska Inst., Stockholm, 1968. Fellow ACP, N.Y. Acad. Scis., Am. Assn. Pharm. Scientists (Rsch. Achievement award in clin. scis. 1995), AAAS (chmn. elect pharm. sect. 2001, chmn. pharm. divsn. 2002-03); mem. AMA (vice chmn. coun. on drugs 1971-72, editl. bd. jours.), Am. Soc. Clin. Nutrition, Am. Nutrition Instn., Am. Soc. Pharmacology and Exptl. Therapeutics (chmn. clin. pharmacology divsn. 1969-71, mem. exec. com. 1966-73, 78-81, del. 1975-78, bd. publ. trustees), Am. Soc. Clin. Pharmacology and Therapeutics (Oscar B. Hunter Meml. award 1995), Am. Fedn. Clin. Rsch., Brit. Pharmacol. Soc., Ctrl. Soc. Clin. Rsch., Royal Soc. for Promotion Health, Inst. Medicine of Nat. Acad. Scis., Soc. Exptl. Biology and Medicine (councillor 1976-80), Internat. Union Pharmacologists (sec. clin. pharmacology sect. 1975-81, internat. adv. com. Paris Congress 1978), GPIA (blue ribbon com. on generic medicine 1990), Sigma Xi. Office: DL Azarnoff Assoc LLC 433 Airport Blvd Ste 225 Burlingame CA 94010-2011 Office Phone: 650-343-9222. Business E-Mail: dan@azarnoffassociates.com.

AZCUENAGA, MARY LAURIE, government official; b. Council, Idaho, July 25, 1945; AB, Stanford U., 1967; JD, U. Chgo., 1973. Bar: Dist. of Columbia, Calif., U.S. Supreme Ct. Atty. FTC, Washington, 1973-75, asst. to gen. counsel, 1975-76; staff atty. San Francisco regional office, 1977-80, asst. regional dir., 1980-81, asst. to exec. dir., 1981-82; litigation atty. Office of Gen. Counsel, 1982, asst. gen. counsel for legal counsel, 1983-84, commr. Washington, 1984-98; atty., shareholder Heller & Ehrman LLP, 1998—. Mem. Adminstrv. Conf. of the U.S., 1990-95. Trustee Food and Drug Law Inst., 1990-97, Advisory Bd. FDLI, 1997-98, Natl. Advertising Review Bd., 1998-2000, ERA Review Bd., 1998-2000. Office: 1717 Rhode Island Ave NW Washington DC 20036-3001

AZER, SAMY AZIZ, gastroenterologist, educator; b. Cairo, Mar. 28, 1953; s. Aziz Azer and Sania Sedrak; m. Mary Azer; children: Sarah, Diana. B in Medicine and Surgery, Ain Shams U., Cairo, 1977, M in Medicine, 1983; MEd, U. New South Wales, 1993, MPH, 2005; PhD, U. Sydney, 1995. Resident in internal medicine Govt. of Health, Egypt, 1979-80, cons. in medicine, 1983-84, Saudi Arabia, 1984-89; vis. med. officer Ain Shams U. Hosps., 1980-83; postdoctoral fellow U. Kans. Med. Ctr., 1994; sr. lectr. in med. edn. U. Melbourne, Australia, 1999—2006, dir. problem-based learning tng. program faculty medicine, dentistry and health scis., 2001—, chair semesters 1 - 5, faculty medicine, dentistry and health scis., 2002—, chair faculty excellence in tchg. awards comm., faculty of medicine, dentistry, and health scis., 2003—04, anti-discrimination advisor, 2004—; prof. med. edn., head of The Unit Sch. Medicine, U. Teknologi, Mara, Malaysia, 2007—. Cons. NIHS, Australia, 1995; lectr. spkrs. bur. ACG, Australia, 1996; instr. pathology and grad. med. program, faculty medicine U. Sydney, 1997, sr. lectr. in med. edn., 1998—99; vis. prof. med. edn. Sch. Medicine, U. Toyama, Japan, 2006; chair, prof. med. edn., faculty of medicine U. Teknologi Mara, Malaysia. Author: Core Clinical Cases in Basic Biomedical Science, 2006, Navigating Problem-based Learning; co-author: Our Children, 1987; writer med. column El-Telegraph, Australia, 1996-97; contbr. chpts. to books, articles to profl. jours. Mem. ch. coun. Fairfield Anglican Chs., Australia, 1994, 95; elder Presbyn. Ch. of Australia, South Yarra, Victoria, 2002. Scholar Ministry of Edn., Egypt, 1968-71, undergrad. scholar, 1972-77, postgrad. scholar U. Sydney, 1993-94. Fellow Am. Coll. Gastroenterology, Royal Soc. of Health; mem. U. New South Wales Union (life), Gastroenterol. Soc. Australia, Am. Assn. for Study Liver Disease, Am. Coll. Gastroenterology. Presbyterian. Avocations: painting, soccer, history of medicine. Office: Univ Tecknologi Mara Faculty Medicine Level 7 Tower 1 Shah Alam Selangor 40450 Malaysia Business E-Mail: azer2000@optusnet.com.au.

AZINGER, PAUL, professional golfer; b. Holyoke, Mass., Jan. 6, 1960; m. Toni Azinger; 2 children. Student, Broward Jr. Coll., Fla., Fla. State U. Profl. golfer, 1981—. Mem. US Team World Cup, 1989, Ryder Cup, 1989, 91, 93, 2002, capt. US Team, 06; co-capt. US Team Pres.'s Cup, 1994, mem. US Team, 2000. Author: Zinger, 1995. Named PGA Tour Player of Yr., 1987, Golf World Player of Yr., 1987; receipient Ben Hogan award

Golf Writers Assn. of Am., 1995. Achievements include winning PGA Tour events including the Phoenix Open, 1987, Panasonic Las Vegas Invitational, 1987, Canon Sammy Davis Jr.-Greater Hartford Open, 1987, 89, Hertz Bay Hill Classic, 1988, MONY Tournament of Champions, 1990; winner, AT&T Pebble Beach Nat. Pro-Am, 1991, THE TOUR Championship, 1992, Meml. Tournament, 1993, New England Classic, 1993, PGA Championship, 1993, Sony Open in Hawaii, 2000; winner, internat. events including the BMW Internat. Open, 1990, 92. Office: PGA Tour 112 Tpc Blvd Ponte Vedra Beach FL 32082-3077*

AZIZ, ADNAN, manufacturing engineer, marketing products engineer; b. 1982; BS in Bioengring., U. Pa., BA in. Polit. Sci. Founder First Flavor, Inc., Bala Cynwyd, Pa., 2005—. Named one of Best Entrepreneurs Under 25, Bus. Week, 2006; recipient Snider Seed Capital award, Wharton Venture Initiation Program; grantee Weiss Tech. House, U. Pa. Achievements include patents for Peel 'n Taste, 2005. Office: First Flavor Inc 143 Bala Ave Bala Cynwyd PA 19004 Office Phone: 610-785-1325. Office Fax: 610-785-1334. E-mail: info@firstflavor.com.

AZIZ, FAISAL, surgeon; b. Attock, Punjab, Pakistan, Aug. 29, 1977; s. Aziz Ur Rehman and Gul Yasmine Aziz; m. Amina Mahmood, July 11, 2005; 1 child, Faizaan F. MD, King Edward Med. Coll., Pakistan, 2001. Rsch. fellow Yale U., Sch. Medicine, New Haven, 2002—03, resident surgery, 2004—05, Nort Oakland Med. Ctrs., Pontiac, Mich., 2005—06, NY Med. Coll., Valhalla, NY, 2006—, chief resident surgery, 2007—. Contbr. articles to profl. jours. Fellow, Yale U., Sch. Medicine, 2003; scholar Quaid-e-Azzm scholar Medal, Pakistan Govt., 1993. Mem.: AMA (licentiate), ACS (assoc.). Achievements include research in shear stress-stimulated endothelial cells induce smooth muscle cell chemotaxis via platelet-derived growth factor-BB and interleukin-1alpha; development of differential effects of orbital and laminar shear stress on endothelial cells; research in abstract Differential responsiveness of early and late-passage endothelial cells to shear stress; support groups play a role in weight loss after laparoscopic adjustable gastric banding; free full text retroperitoneal fibrosis, a rare cause of both ureteral and small bowel obstruction; hemorrhage, intestinal angina and ectopic pregnancy; natural history of an aspirated foreign body; Buschke-Lowenstein tumors. Personal E-mail: faisalaziz116@yahoo.com.

AZIZ, KHALID, petroleum engineering educator; b. Bahawalpur, Pakistan, Sept. 29, 1936; arrived in US, 1952, naturalized; s. Aziz Ul and Rshida; m. Mussarrat Rizwani, Nov. 12, 1962; children: Natasha, Imraan. BS in Mech. Engring., U. Mich., 1955; BSc in Petroleum Engring., U. Alta., 1958, MSc in Petroleum Engring., 1961; PhD in Chem. Engring., Rice U., 1966. Jr. design engr. Massey-Ferguson, 1955-56; various position to asst. prof. petroleum engring. U. Alta., 1960-62; various positions, chmn. bd. Neotech. Cons. Ltd., 1972-85; mgr., dir. Computer Modelling Group, Calgary, Alta., 1977-82; various positions to chief engr. Karachi (Pakistan) Gas Co., 1958-59, 62-63; various positions to prof. chem. and petroleum engring. U. Calgary, 1965-82; hon. prof., 1994—2001; prof. petroleum engring. dept. Stanford U., Calif., 1982—2006, assoc. dean rsch. Sch. Earth Scis., 1983-86, chmn. petroleum engring. dept., 1986-91, 94-95, Otto N. Miller prof. in earth scis., 1989—, prof. energy resources engring. dept., 2006—. Co-author: Flow of Complex Mixtures in Pipes, 1972, Petroleum Reservoir Simulation, 1979; contbr. articles to profl. jours. Recipient Diploma of Honor, Pi Epsilon Tau, 1991, Killam Resident fellow U. Calgary, 1977, Blaise Pascal Earth Scis. medal 2005, Lifetime Achievement award Petroleum Soc. Can.; Chem. Inst. Can. fellow, 1974. Mem. AIME (hon.), European Assn. Geoscientists and Engrs., Soc. Petroleum Engrs. (disting. mem., Ferguson award 1979, Reservoir Engring. award 1987, Lester C. Uren award 1988, Disting. Achievement award for Petroleum Engring. Faculty 1990, hon. mem. 1996), Nat. Acad. Engring., Russian Acad. Natural Scis. (fgn.), European Acad. of Sci. (Blaise Pascal medal in Earth Scis., 2005). Muslim. Achievements include rsch. in multiphase flow of oil/gas mixtures & steam in pipes & wells, multiphase flow in porous media, reservoir modeling and optimization, natural gas engring., hydrocarbon fluid phase behavior. Office: Stanford U Dept Energy Resources Engring Stanford CA 94305-2220

AZIZ, SHAHNAZ, psychology professor; PhD, Bowling Green State U., Ohio, 2002; BS in Psychology, U. Calgary, 1997. Adj. prof. Bowling Green State U., 2002—03; asst. prof. E. Carolina U., Greenville, NC, 2003—. Contbr. articles to profl. jours. Recipient Indsl./Orgnl. Acad. Challenge Non-Svc. Assistantship, Bowling Green State U., 2000—01; fellow, 2001—02; grantee, NSF, 2005. Mem.: N.C. Indsl./Orgnl. Psychologists, APA, Soc. Indsl./Orgnl. Psychology. Office: E Carolina Univ Dept Psychology 104 Rawl Greenville NC 27858-4353 Office Phone: 252-328-1379. Office Fax: 252-328-6283. E-mail: azizs@ecu.edu.

AZMY, YOUSRY YOUSSEF, computational scientist; b. Cairo, Jan. 1, 1956; came to U.S., 1980; s. Youssef H. and Jannette F. (Gerges) A.; m. Inas T. Messiha, Nov. 4, 1984; children: Christina N., Joseph G. BSc with honors, U. Alexandria, Egypt, 1978; MS, U. Ill., 1982, PhD, 1985. Asst. prof. U. Va., Charlottesville, 1986; sr. rsch. scientist Oak Ridge Nat. Lab., Tenn., 1986—2002; prof. nuc. engring. Pa. State U., U. Park, Pa., 2002—. Vis. scientist U. Bologna, Italy, 1990; adj. asst. prof. NC State U., Raleigh, 1995-99. Mem. editl. bd. Progress in Nuclear Energy; reviewer Nuclear Sci. & Engring., NAS, Jour. Computational Physics; contbr. articles to profl. jours. Fellow Am. Nuc. Soc. (vice-chmn. tech. jours. com., treas. math. and computation divsn. 1990, exec. com. 1991-94, Mark Mills award 1986, Young Mem. Engring. Achievement award 1995); mem. Soc. Indsl. and Applied Math., Am. Math. Soc., Am. Soc. Engring. Edn., Alpha Nu Sigma, Phi Kappa Phi. Achievements include devel. of arbitrarily high order transport methods for neutral particle transport problems; innovator of adjacent-cell preconditioners for transport methods convergence acceleration; development of angular domain decomposition schemes for transport methods on several multi-processor architectures. Home: 339 Norle St State College PA 16801-6970 Office: Pa State Univ 229 Reber University Park PA 16802 Home Phone: 814-867-1082; Office Phone: 814-865-0039. Business E-Mail: yya3@psu.edu.

AZUA, MARIA, computer company executive, computer engineer; b. Cuba; m. Ben Himmel. B magna cum laude, U. PR, 1982; MS in Computer Sci., U. Miami; MBA, Fla. Atlantic U. Cert. IT Architect IBM, Project Mgr. IBM. With Gould Electronics, Fla., Data Gen., NC; joined IBM, 1989, SWG fin. sector and industry standards architect mgr., disting. engr., 2004. Mem. La Red Familiar. Named to IBM Acad. Tech., 2002, WITI Hall of Fame, Women in Tech. Internat., 2006; recipient Technical Innovation award, Women of Color Tech. Conf., 2003. Achievements include over 30 patents. Office: IBM 294 Rte 100 Somers NY 10589

AZUONYE, FELIX O., pharmacist; arrived in US, 1997; s. Nathaniel Onu and Margaret Enti Azuonye; m. Chinonye Ogelhi Onuchnicwu, Nov. 21, 2003; 1 child, Chinedu Daniel. PharmD, Tex. So. U., Houston, 2004. Cert. ACLS, 2005, BLS, 2005, HAMAT tng., 2006, ACPE for pharmacy-based immunization. Rsch. asst. Mental Health Mental Retardation Authority, Houston, 1997—99, Drug Info. and Outcomes Ctr., Houston, 1999—2001; pharmacy technician Meml. Hermann Hosp., Houston, 2000—03; pharmacy intern Wal-Mart Pharmacy, Houston, 2002—04, part-time pharmacist, 2004—; pharmacy practice resident U. Tex. Med. Br., Galveston, 2004—05; adminstr. GraceFaith Healthcare Svcs., Inc., Houston, 2006—; clin. pharmacy specialist Bayshore Med. Ctr., Pasadena, Tex., 2006—. Adj. prof. Tex. So. U., Houston, 2006—; presenter in field. Vol. Am. Sickle Cell Assn., Breast Cancer Survival Walk, Diabetes Walk, Minority and Effective Healthcare Delivery; music dir. Master's Vessel Ministries Praise Band; mem. Impact Campus Fellowship, 1998—2001, UN Student Coun., 2000—03; mem. Internat. Students Assn. Tex. So. U., 1998—2003. Recipient Douglas Honor award, 1998, Most Outstanding Male Participant award Student Support Svc. Program, Tex. So. U., 1999, Pres. Acad. Excellence award, 2002. Mem.: Am. Pharmacists Assn., Am. Soc. Health-Sys. Pharmacists, Soc. Critical Care Medicine, Am. Coll. Clin. Pharmacy (assoc.), Golden Key (life award 1998). Pentecostal. Avocations: reading, singing, soccer. Office: Bayshore Med Ctr 4000 Spencer Hwy Pasadena TX 77504

AZZOLI, VAL, music company executive; b. Toronto, Can., 1955; Grad. in bus. admin., Seneca Coll., Ontario, Canada, 1977. Sr. vp., gen. mgr. Atlantic Recording Corp., NYC, 1991—93, exec. v.p., gen. mgr., 1993—95, co-chmn., co-CEO, 1995—. Office: Atlantic Group 1290 Avenue Of The Americas New York NY 10104-0101

AZZOLINA, DAVID SEAN, librarian; b. East Orange, NJ, May 22, 1957; s. Alexander and Helen (Fitzpatrick) A. BA, U. Pa., 1978, MA, 1991, PhD, 1996; MS, Columbia U., 1979. Social sci. libr. Rice U., Houston, 1980-82; ref. libr. Johns Hopkins U., Balt., 1982-86, U. Pa., Phila., 1986—, adj. prof. English, 1997—. Mem. adv. bd. Lesbian Gay Bisexual Ctr. U. Pa. Author: Tale Type and Motif Indexes, 1987, The Circle Always Grew: Folklore and Gay Identity 1945-1960, 1996; contbr. (book) Guide to Reference Books, 11th edit., 1997; reviewer various jours. Democrat. Episcopalian. Home: 256 S 44th St Philadelphia PA 19104-2944 Office: University of Pennsylvania Library 3420 Walnut St Philadelphia PA 19104-3411 Business E-Mail: azzolina@pobox.upenn.edu.

BAAB-HOHMAN, ROBERTA (ROBIN), artist, scriptwriter, state manager; b. Greeley, Colo., June 26, 1935; d. Robert Sinclair Baab and Dorothy Bass; m. Glenn William Hohman, Mar. 20, 1958; children: Jonathan David Hohman, Taaron Glennanne Hohman Meikle, Glenn Erin-Ahren Hohman. BFA, U. Colo., Boulder, 1957; attended, Columbia U., NYC, 1957—60, New Sch., 1957—60; MFA, San Diego State U., 1960. With idea dept., NYC, 1957—59; social worker Dept. Welfare, Norfolk, Va., 1959—60, Newport, RI, 1959—60; math. tchr. Key West HS, Fla., 1960; prof. painting San Diego Adult Edn., 1960, Port Washington Adult Edn., NY, 1962, So. Coll., Orlando, Calif., 1963—69; freelance art guide NYC, 1963—80; stage mgr. Orlando Opera Co., NYC, 1972—2006; CEO, pres. Baab-Hohman Studios, Winter Park, Fla., 1963—95, owner, CEO, 1973—. Spkr. in field. Designer furniture; one-man shows include Chgo. Biennial, 1963 (1st place watercolor), San Diego Triannual, 1963 (1st place watercolor), Newport, RI, 1964, Bedell Gallery, NYC, 1965. Bd. trustees Orlando Opera Co., 1970—, exec. com., 1972—, trustee emeritus, 2006; exec. com. Fla. Symphony Adv. Bd., Orlando, 1970—78; assoc. bd. Fla. Symphony, Orlando, 1972—82; chmn. steering com. Designer's Show-house, Orlando, 1980—; patron United Arts Ctrl. Fla., Orlando, 1985—; family counselor WPFB Ch., Winter Park, 1980—. Recipient Woman of Yr., Orlando Opera Co., 1984. Mem.: Orlando Opera Guild (exec. com. 1972—), Metro. Opera Guild, Orlando Opera, Opera Am., Delta Phi Delta. Republican. Avocations: piano, travel, pugs.

BAACK, LAWRENCE JAMES, energy executive, history professor; b. Berkeley, Calif., May 13, 1943; s. Ernest Charles and Frieda Baack; m. Jane Ellyn Williams, Sept. 12, 1964; children: James Hamilton, Sally Ann. BA with honors in History, U. Calif., Berkeley, 1964; MA in History, Stanford U., 1970, PhD in History, 1973. Officer USN, 1964—69; history prof. U. Nebr., 1973—80; various positions Pacific Gas & Electric, San Francisco, 1980—95; bus. prof. U. Calif., Berkeley, San Francisco, 1981—2003; sr. v.p. Solem & Assoc., San Francisco, 1995—96; pres. Bay Area Econ. Forum, San Francisco, 1996—98; vis. scholar, dept. history U. Calif., Berkeley, 2003—. Chmn., univ. libr. commn. U. Nebr., 1975—79, head, area studies program in bus. & internat. affairs, 1975—79; guest prof., dept. strategy US Naval War Coll., Newport, RI, 1979; chmn. Bay Area Def. Conversion Task Force, 1996—98; chair Bay Area Regional Trade Development Alliance, San Francisco, 1996—98, Bay Area Regional Technology Alliance, San Francisco, 1996—98; co-chair Bay Area Task Force Water-based Transportation, San Francisco, 1998. Author: (book) Agrarian Reform in 18th Century Denmark, 1977, Christian Bernstoff and Prussia, 1980; editor: The Worlds of Brutus Hamilton, 1975. Chair pub. edn. com. San Francisco C. of C., 1981—85; mem. exec. com. Bay Area Ethics Consortium, Grad Theological Union, Berkeley, 1982—87; mem., bd. dirs. Berkeley Pub. Edn. Found., 1982—88; mem. Calif. Commn. Pub. Schs., Sacramento, 1986—87; mem., vice-chair Bay Area Urban League, 1986—91; bd. trustees Hispanic Cmty. Fund Bay Area, 1986—94; mem. pres. strategic planning task force Calif. Maritime Acad., 1987—89; mem. dirs. blue ribbon commn. Calif. State Pk. Sys., Sacramento, 1989; mem., bd. dirs. United Way Bay Area, 1991—96, No. Calif. Coun. Cmty., 1996—98; mem. regional planning com. Assn. Bay Area Govts., 1996—98. Lt. USN, 1964—69, Vietnam and Coronado, Calif. Decorated Achievement medal USN, Presdl. Unit citation; recipient Chairman's Excellence award, Pacific Gas & Electric Co., 1993, Northern Calif. Social Responsibility award, Mex. Am. Legal Def.and Edn. Fund, 1990; fellow, Hist. Commn. Berlin, 1971, 1976, NSF, 1979—80. Fellow: Order Golden Bear, U. Calif. (pres. 1964—); mem.: Am. Hist. Assn., Sierra Club, Inverness Yacht Club, Phi Beta Kappa. Democrat. Presbyn. Avocations: cello, hiking, gardening, travel, cooking. Home: 160 Brookside Dr Berkeley CA 94705

BAACK, PAULA D., music educator, director; b. Omaha, June 13, 1949; d. Paul and Wilma I. Teigeler; m. Robert A. Morris, May 10, 1969 (div. Oct. 1979); m. L. Thomas Baack, July 26, 1980; 1 child, Paul R. BS, U. Nebr., 1971, MusM, 1973. Cert. tchr. Nebr., Cmty. Coll. Tchr. Ariz. Dir. choral Lincoln Pub. Schs., Nebr., 1971—97; dir. choral, voice coach Scottsdale C.C., Ariz., 1998—2007; dir. scarlet and cream singers, 1995—97; dir. vocal jazz, peak performance voice studio founder U. Colo., Colorado Springs, 2007—. Asst. prof. U. Nebr., Lincoln, 1995—97; dir., vocal coach Peak Performance Voice Studio; music and pvt. voice instr. Named Nat. Anthem Singer for Phoenix Coyotes Hockey Game. Mem.: Nat. Assn. Tchrs. Singing, Ariz. Music Educators Assn., Music Educators Nat. Conf., Nebr. Choral Dirs. Assn. (exec. bd. 1995—97), Nebr. Music Educators Assn. (exec. bd. 1993—95). Republican. Avocations: bicycling, singing, dance. Home: 15963 Bridle Ridge Dr Monument CO 80132 Office: U Colo at Colorado Springs 1420 Austin Bluffs Pkwy Colorado Springs CO 80918 Personal E-mail: bachsingr@comcast.net. Business E-Mail: pbaack@uccs.edu.

BAADH, VALERIE, choreographer, movement educator, theater producer, production designer; b. Burbank, Calif., Sept. 16, 1952; d. Uffe and Shirley (Goldberg) Baadh; m. Michael Earl Garrett, May 20, 1979; 1 child, John David Garrett; 1 child, Rose Kaiulani Garrett. BFA, Calif. Inst. Arts, 1973; MM, Spatial Dynamics Inst., 1996. Choreographer Pacific Ballet, 1975—77, Dancers' Group, San Francisco, 1981—83; ind. choreographer, 1984—. Dir. Kadeka Dances for Kids, San Francisco, 1982—84, Dancers Group/Footwork, 1983; faculty mem. San Francisco Waldorf Sch., 1990—2006; dir. San Francisco Movement Studio, 2005—; trustee Spatial Studies Inst., NYC, 1994; internat. trainer Hands in Peace Festivals, 2001—. Choreographer Places, 1976, Half Past Eight, 1981, White Dance, 1982, Spy in the House of Love, 1983, Mother Goose Suite, 1984, Threefold Suite, 1993, Madeleine's Duet, 1995, Lambarena, 1996, with clarinetist Dov Goldberg Istanbul Late Night, San Francisco, 2003; prodr.: Bay Area Theatre Week, 1986, Event of the Year, 1986, Nina Watt Solos, 1986, Rosa Montoya Bailes Flamencos, 1987; prodn. designer: An Evening of Comedy and Dance with Robin Williams and Friends, 1985; author: The Autumn Adventure of Uffe the Gnome, 1998, The Valentines Adventure of Uffe the Gnome, 2000, Dance As Movement History, 2001; author: (with Joan Carr Shiner) Games We Play and Sing, 2001; author: Uffe the Gnome and the Tree of Light, 2005, The Hill of the Hawk Adventures of Uffe the Gnome, 2006. Home: 120 Solano St Brisbane CA 94005-1333 Office Phone: 415-218-7088. Personal E-mail: vbaadh@earthlink.net, valerie@stmovement.com.

BAAS, JACQUELYNN, museum director, art historian; b. Grand Rapids, Mich., Feb. 14, 1948; BA in History of Art, Mich. State U.; PhD in History of Art, U. Mich. Registrar U. Mich. Mus. Art, Ann Arbor, 1974-78, asst. dir., 1978-82; editor Bull. Museums of Art and Archaeology, U. Mich., 1976-82; chief curator Hood Mus. Art, Dartmouth Coll., Hanover, NH, 1982-84, dir., 1985-89, U. Calif. Berkeley Art Mus. and Pacific Film Archive, 1989—99, emeritus dir., 1999—; program dir. Awake: Art and Buddhism, 1999—2004. Collaborating curator 6th Gwangju Biennale, 2006; cons. in field; organizer exhbns.; ind. art historian; lectr. in field. Author: Smile of the Buddha: Eastern Philosophy and Western Art, 2005; co-editor: Buddha Mind in Contemporary Art, 2004; contbr. articles and essays to jours. and books. Mem. Internat. Assn. Art Critics, Coll. Art Assn. Am., Am. Assn. Mus. Address: PO Box 5 The Sea Ranch CA 95497-005 Home Phone: 510-406-4455; Office Phone: 510-406-4455. Business E-Mail: jbaas@mcn.org.

BABA, MARIETTA LYNN, anthropologist, academic administrator; b. Flint, Mich., Nov. 9, 1949; d. David and Lillian (Joseph) Baba; m. David Smokler, Feb. 14, 1977 (div. 1982); 1 child, Alexia Nicole Baba Smokler. BA with highest distinction, Wayne State U., 1971, MA in Anthropology, 1973, PhD in Phys. Anthropology, 1975; MBA, Mich. State U., 1994. Asst. prof. sci. and tech. Wayne State U., Detroit, 1975-80, assoc. prof. anthropology, 1980-88, prof., 1988—, spl. asst. to pres., 1980-82, econ. devel. officer, 1982-83, asst. provost, 1983-85, assoc. provost, 1985-89, dir. internat. programs, interim assoc. dean Grad. Sch., 1988-89, assoc. dean Grad. Sch., 1989-90, acting chair dept. anthropology, 1990-92, chair dept. anthropology, 1996-2001; dean, prof. anthropology Mich. State U. Coll. Social Sci., East Lansing, 2001—. Program dir. transformations to quality orgns., dir. social, behav., and econ. scis. NSF, 1994—96; evolution rschr. Wayne State U., 1975—82; cons. GM Rsch. Labs., 1988—92, Electronic Data Sys., 1990—93, McKinsey Global Inst., 1991; rsch. contractor GM/EDS, 1990—94; vis. scholar IBM Almaden Svcs. Rsch. Inst., 2005; lectr. in field. Adv. for editor orgnl. anthropology: American Anthropologist, 1990-93; issued letters patent for method to map joint ventures and maps produced thereby; contbr. articles to profl. jours.; patentee in field. Mem. State Rsch. Fund Feasibility Rev. Panel, 1982—84; mem. adv. panel on tech. innovation and U.S. trade U.S. Congl. Office Tech. Assessment, 1990—91, mem. panel on electronic enterprise, 1993—94; active Leadership Detroit Class IV, 1982—83; dir. Mich. Tech. Coun. (S.E. divsn.), 1984—85. With USAF, 1992—94. Job Partnership Tng. Act grantee, 1981-90, NSF grantee, 1982, 84-85, 99-01. Fellow Am. Anthrop. Assn. (bd. dirs. 1986-88, exec. com. 1986-88, del. to Internat. Union Anthrop. and Ethnol. Sci. 1990-94, chair global commn. anthropology 1993-98), Nat. Assn. Practice Anthropology (pres. 1986-88), Soc. Applied Anthropology, Phi Beta Kappa, Sigma Xi (Morton Fried award 1991), Beta Gamma Sigma. Office Phone: 517-355-6675.

BABAO, DONNA MARIE, retired community health and psychiatric nurse, educator; b. St. Louis, May 6, 1945; d. Wilbert C. and Cecelia (Hogan) Bremer; widowed; 1 child, Tonya J. Diploma, Henry Ford Hosp. Sch. Nursing, Detroit, 1966; BSN, Calif. State U., Sacramento, 1978, MS in Nursing, 1990; MA in Edn., Calif. State U., Chico, 1985. Cert. pub. health nurse; master tchr. cert.; cert. clin. use of interactive guided imagery. Staff nurse U. Calif. Med. Ctr., San Franicsco, 1968-72; staff and charge CCU nurse Children's Hosp. of San Francisco, 1972-78; pub. health nurse II Sutter-Yuba Health Dept., Yuba City, Calif., 1979-81; prof. nursing Yuba Coll., Marysville, Calif., 1981-2000; psychiat. charge nurse Sunridge Hosp., Yuba City, 1994-96; RN case mgr. Home Health Care Mgmt. Inc., Chico, Calif., 2004—05; office nurse, case mgr. First Care Med. Clinic, Oregon House, 2005—. Mem. exam. item writing panel NCLEX-RN, 1998. Writer health column, 1986-90; chpt. to textbooks; reviewer nursing textbooks and jour. articles; contbr. articles to profl. jours. 1st lt. Nurse Corps, U.S. Army, 1966-68. Mem. Vietnam Vets. Am., Imagery Internat., Henry Ford Hosp. Alumni Assn. Nursing. Personal E-mail: dbabao@hotmail.com.

BABAR, SARDAR IJLAL, pulmonologist; b. Karachi, Sindh, Pakistan, Aug. 12, 1966; s. Babar Hamid Chauhan and Seemeen Babar; m. Nosheen Zaki Nosheen Zaki, Dec. 27, 1996; children: Naahin, Maham, Parisay. MBBS, Aga Khan U., Karachi, Pakistan, 1990. Cert. pulmonary medicine Am. Bd. of Internal Medicine, 1998, critical care medicine Am. Bd. Internal medicine, 1999, sleep medicine Am. Assn. Sleep Medicine, 2005. Internship, residency internal medicine Tucson Hosps. Med. Edn. Program, Ariz., 1992—95; pulmonary/critical care fellowship U. Ariz., Tucson, 1995—98, asst. prof. medicine, 2002—03; asst. prof. medicine and anesthesiology Aga Khan U., Karachi, 1998—2002; pulmonologist, intensivist, sleep specialist in pvt. practice Gulf Shore Med. Cons., Ocean Springs, Miss., 2003—. Chmn. intensive care com. Aga Khan U., Karachi, Sindh, Pakistan, 1999—2002; co dir. intensive care unit Ocean Springs Hosp., Miss., 2003—. Fellow: Am. Coll. Chest Physicians (Fellowship 2006); mem.: Am. Thoracic Soc., Pulmonary Hypertension Assn., Am. Assn. Sleep Medicine (mem. clin. practice rev. com. 2006—). Home Phone: 228-872-5579; Office Phone: 228-872-1951.

BABAUTA, JUAN NEKAI, former governor, congressional representative; b. Saipan, No. Mariana Islands, Sept. 7, 1953; s. Santiago Miyasaki and Carmen (Nekai) B. BS, MA, Ea. N.Mex. U., 1976; MS, U. Cin., 1979. Health planner TTPI Dept. Health Services, Saipan, 1977; dep. exec. dir. No. Mariana Islands State Health Planning & Devel. Agy., Saipan, 1979; exec. dir. Saipan, 1980-86; senator No. Mariana Islands Legis., Saipan, 1986—90; resident rep. to U.S. Commonwealth of No. Mariana Islands, Saipan, 1990—2002, gov., 2002—06. Co-chmn. 902 Covenant Negotiation team; instr. No. Marianas Coll., Saipan, 1986. Chmn. bd. regents No. Marianas Coll., 1982-83, 84-86; chmn. Bd. Edn., Saipan, 1982-83, 84-86; mem. Med. Profession Licensing Bd., Saipan, 1983-86, Nat. State Bd. Edn., Saipan, 1982-86. Mem. Phi Kappa Phi. Republican. Roman Catholic. Avocation: reading. Office Phone: 670-664-2280.

BABAYANS, EMIL, financial planner; b. Nov. 9, 1951; arrived in U.S., 1969; s. Hacob and Jenik (Khatchatourian) B.; m. Annie Ashjian. BS, U. So. Calif., 1974, MS, 1976. CLU; cert. fin. planner. Pres. Babtech Internat., Inc., Sherman Oaks, Calif., 1975—85; sr. ptnr. Emil Babayans & Assocs., Woodland Hills, Calif., 1985—. Mem.: Million Dollar Round Table, Am. Soc. CLU and Chartered Fin. Cons., Internat. Assn. Fin. Planners, Inst. Cert. Fin. Planners, Nat. Assn. Life Underwriters, Am. Mgmt. Assn. Armenian Orthodox. Office: 21700 Oxnard St Ste 1100 Woodland Hills CA 91367-7574 Home Phone: 818-888-8680. Personal E-mail: embco@aol.com.

BABAYEV, DJANGIR ALI IKRAM, physicist, researcher; b. Baku, Azerbaijan, July 10, 1930; arrived in U.S., 1992; s. Ali Ikram Melik Bakhish Babayev and Rugiya Jahangir Babayeva; m. Sevil Yusuf Huseinova; 1 child, Rauf Djangir. B.Engring., Moscow Inst. Physics and Engring., 1953; PhD in Physics and Math., Inst. Problems of Mechanics, USSR Acad. Scis., Moscow, 1962; Dr.Engring. Scis., Inst. Cybernetics, Acad. Scis. of Ukraine, Kiev, 1974. Engr. aerodynamics diploma, Moscow Inst. Physics and Engring., 1954; cert. sr. fellow scientist, computational math. diploma USSR High Attestation Bd., 1963, prof. computerized mgmt. and control sys. diploma USSR High Attestation Bd., 1984. Engr., sr. engr., lead engr. Ctrl. Inst. Aero-Hydrodynamics, Moscow, 1954—62; dep. dir. of inst., dir. dept. ops. rsch. Inst. Cybernetics, Acad. Scis. of

Azerbaijan, Baku, 1962—92; mem. tech. staff U.S. West Advanced Technologies, Boulder, Colo., 1992—2000; sr. rsch. scientist Cox Assocs., Inc., Denver, 2000—. Prof. computational math. Baku State U., 1970—77; prof. computational math., optimization theory and methods Azerbaijan State Oil Acad., 1977—85; prof. math. methods of econs. Azerbaijan State U. Econs., 1985—92; supr. PhD dissertations on ops. rsch. Inst. Cybernetics of Azerbaijan Acad. Scis., 1972—92; on info. and comm. tech. UN Devel. Programs, NYC, 2002—. Mem. editl. bd. Internat. Jour. Applied and Computational Math., 2001—; contbr. more than 120 sci. articles to profl. jours.;, translator books. Recipient State Prize of Azerbaijan on Sci. and Tech., Azerbaijan, 1984, prize for outstanding applications of ops. rsch. in mng. bus., Ops. Rsch. Soc. Am., 1994. Mem.: Lofti Zade Internat. Acad. Modern Scis. Achievements include development of nonlinear theory of the delta wing on supersonic flow; patents for on methods and systems of solving different classes of management problems in communication industry. Home: 4834 Macintosh Pl Boulder CO 80301 Office: Cox Associates Inc 503 Franklin St Denver CO 80218-3623

BABAYI, ROBERT S., lawyer; b. Tehran, Iran, Jan. 18, 1959; BSEE, Fla. Internat. U., 1981; JD, U. Miami, 1992. Bar: Fla. 1992, DC 2000, US Patent and Trademark Office. Of counsel Patent Prosecution and Intellectual Property Litig. Depts. Venable LLP, Washington, DC. Contbr. articles to profl. jours. Mem. Washington DC Cmty. for Family Life Svcs., Coalition for Homeless. Mem.: ABA, Am. Intellectual Property Law Assn. Office: Venable LLP 575 7th St. NW Washington DC 20004 Office Phone: 202-344-4045. Office Fax: 202-344-8300. E-mail: rsbabayi@venable.com.

BABB, BARBARA A., lawyer, educator; BS with highest distinction, Pa. State Univ., 1973; MS, Cornell Univ., 1978, JD, 1981. Bar: N.Y., Md. Mng. atty. Legal Aid Bureau, Balt., 1986—89; assoc. prof. Univ. Balt., 1989—; dir. Ctr. for Families Children & the Courts, Univ. Balt. Vis. prof. George Washington Univ., 1999. Contbr. articles to prof. jour. Mem. Soros Grant Oversight Com.; mem. Chief Judge's ad hoc com. Family Divisions Md.; co-founder Domestic Law Pro Se Assistance Project, Md.; mem. bd. dir. People's Pro Bono Action Ctr., 1990—94; mem. editl. adv. bd. Family Ct. Rev., Md. Family Law Monthly. Recipient Regent's award, Univ. Sys. Md., Benjamin L. Cardin Disting. Svc. award, Md. Legal Svc. Corp. Mem.: Md. State Bar Assn., Assn. Am. Law Sch. (chair, Family & Juvenile Law sect.), ABA (mem. Adv. Council, standing com. substance abuse). Office: University of Baltimore School of Law 1420 N Charles St Baltimore MD 21201-5779 Office Phone: 410-837-5661. Business E-Mail: bbabb@ubalt.edu.

BABB, HAROLD, psychologist, educator; b. Mosheim, Tenn., Sept. 4, 1926; s. Ray Edward and Mary Louise (Brown) B.; m. Marjorie Craig Leask (Sept. 27, 1947); children: Patricia Craig, Barbara Lou, David Edward. BA, Wayne State U., 1950; MA, Ohio State U., 1951, PhD, 1953. Asst. prof., assoc. prof., chmn. dept. psychology Coe Coll., 1953-58; prof., chmn. dept. psychology Hobart and William Smith Colls., 1958-63; NIH, NIMH exec. sec., grants specialist, 1963-64; prof., chmn. dept. psychology U. Mont., Missoula, 1964-71; prof. psychology SUNY-Binghamton, 1971-95, prof. emeritus, 1995—, chmn. dept., 1971-74. Contbr. articles on psychology to profl. jours. Served with USNR, 1944-46. NIMH research grantee, 1960-62; NSF research grantee, 1968-69 Fellow Am. Psychol. Assn., Am. Psychol. Soc.; mem. AAAS, AAUP, Ea. Psychol. Assn., Midwestern Psychol. Assn., Psychonomic Soc., Sigma Xi Home: RR 1 Box 1957 Stanley Lake Rd Friendsville PA 18818 E-mail: hbabb@epix.net.

BABB, JOSEPH DOLBY, physician; b. Columbus, Ohio, Apr. 16, 1939; s. Joe A. and Dorothe (Dolby) B.; m. Anne Tanner Hammerlund, Sept. 2, 1969 (div. Apr. 1985); children: Elizabeth Anne, Peter Dolby; m. Margo Tregenza, Oct. 6, 1990. BA magna cum laude, Kenyon Coll., Gambier, Ohio, 1961; MD, Johns Hopkins U., Balt., 1966. Diplomate in internal medicine and cardiovascular diseases Am. Bd. Internal Medicine; cert. physician, Pa., Conn., NC. Intern Mass. Gen. Hosp., Boston, 1966-67, resident in internal medicine, 1967-68, clin. and rsch. fellow, 1970-72; teaching fellow Harvard Med. Sch., Boston, 1970-72; asst. prof. med. cardiology Pa. State U. Sch. Medicine, Hershey, 1972-76, assoc. prof., 1976-80; chief of cardiology Bridgeport Hosp., Conn., 1980-95; clin. assoc. prof. medicine (cardiology) Yale U., New Haven, 1980-95; prof. medicine (cardiology) East Carolina U. Sch. Medicine, Greenville, 1995—. Bd. dir., pres. Alcohol and Drug Dependency Coun., Westport, Conn., 1987-95. Maj. US Army, 1968—70, Vietnam. Fulbright fellow, Utrecht, Netherlands, 1961-62. Fellow Am. Coll. Cardiology (gov. 1987-90, 02-05), Am. Heart Assn. (coun. clin. cardiology), Soc. Cardiac Angiography and Intervention (trustee 1993-99, pres. 2001-02), Coalition Cardiovasc. Orgns. (pres. 2004-05). Avocations: fishing, hiking. Office: East Carolina U Sch Med PCMH Teaching Annex Rm 352 Greenville NC 27858-4354 Business E-Mail: babbj@ecu.edu.

BABB, LISA MARIE, physical education educator; b. Abington, Pa., June 8, 1970; d. Janet Marie and Bruce James Lewis (Stepfather); 1 child, William Samuel. BS in Bible, Phila. Bible U., Langhorne, Pa., 1993; BS in Ednl., Phila. Bible U., 1999; MS in Edn., Wilkes U., Wilkes-Barre, Pa., 2005. Cert. Level II in edn. Pa., 2005. Tchr. Heartland Christian Sch., Sebring, Fla., 1993—94, Plumstead Christian Sch., Plumsteadville, Pa., 1994—98; head cross country coach CB East, Doylestown, Pa., 1995—99; health and phys. edn. tchr. Quakertown Cmty. Sch. Dist., Pa., 2003—. Youth leader First Bapt. Ch., Newtown, Pa., 1989—99. Recipient Randall C. Ostein award, PBU, 1993; scholar Leadership scholar, 1988—2003. Mem.: APHERD (assoc.), PSEA (assoc.). Democrat-Npl. Christian. Avocations: running, reading, photography, cooking. Office: Rishland Elementary School 500 Fariview Ave Quakertown PA 18951 Home Phone: 215-828-6872; Office Phone: 215-529-2492. Office Fax: 215-529-2451; Home Fax: 215-529-2451. Personal E-mail: lbabb@qcsd.org.

BABB, RALPH W., JR., bank executive; b. Sherman, Tex., Feb. 4, 1949; s. Ralph Wheeler and Billie Margaret (Odneal) B.; m. Barbara Louise Alexander, Aug. 30, 1970; children: Dana P., Derek R. BS in Acctg., U. Mo., Columbia, 1971. CPA, Mo. Audit mgr. Peat, Marwick, Mitchell & Co., CPA's, St. Louis, 1971-78; contr., sr. v.p. Mercantile Bancorp. Inc., St. Louis, 1978-83, treas., sr. v.p., 1979-83, CFO, exec. v.p., 1983-94, vice chmn., 1987-95; EVP, CFO Comerica Bank, Comercia Inc., Detroit, 1995—99, vice chmn., CFO, 1999—2001, CFO, 2002, chmn., pres., CEO, dir., 2002—. Mem. Fin. Execs. Inst. (pres. St. Louis chpt. 1986-87). Methodist. Office: Comerica Inc PO Box 75000 Detroit MI 48275-0001*

BABB, ROBERTA JOAN, educational administrator; b. East Chicago, Ill., Jan. 5, 1944; d. Joseph A. and Katherine Phillips; m. Donald L. Babb, July 30, 1966; children: Sasha M., Holly S. BS in Edn., Ind. U., 1966; postgrad., De Paul U., 1972—73. Tchr. East Chicago Pub. Schs., 1969—70, Hammond Pub. Schs., Ind., 1966—68, 1970—71; head tchr. The Lab Sch., Washington, 1968—69, The Lab. Sch., Washington, 1974—79; co-founder, dir. Creme de le Creme, Houston, 1982—. Scholar Ind. U., PTA. Mem. Nat. Child Care Assn., Tex. Lic. Child Care Assn.

BABBEL, DAVID FREDERICK, finance and insurance educator; b. Salt Lake City, Apr. 12, 1949; s. Frederick William and June (Andrew) Babbel; m. Mary Jane Benson, Aug. 27, 1975; children: Tara Nicole, Elise Kiera, Karisa Rose, Tyson Frederick. BA, Brigham Young U., 1973; MBA, U. Fla., 1975, PhD, 1978; MA (hon.), U. Pa., 1986. Prof. fin. U. Calif., Berkeley, 1978—85; prof. fin. and ins. Wharton Sch., U. Pa., Phila., 1985—. V.p. Goldman, Sachs & Co, NYC, 1987, cons.; pres. A/L Tech., Bryn Mawr, Pa. Author: over 100 books and sci. articles. Sr. advisor CRA Internat. (formerly Charles Rivers Assocs.), 2006—; pres. Brasilia, Brazil Mission LDS Ch., 2002—05. Fellow Fulbright, 1976—77. Independent. Office: U Pa Wharton Sch 3620 Locust Walk 3000 Philadelphia PA 19104 Office Phone: 617-425-3775. Business E-Mail: babbel@wharton.upenn.edu. *Any idea, without at least some element of absurdity, is probably not worth further consideration.*

BABBIN, JED LLOYD, lawyer, former deputy undersecretary of defense; b. NYC, Mar. 16, 1950; s. Harold H. and Pearl (Bander) B.; m. Frances Kloker, June 22, 1975 (div. 1990); children: Jacob Harold, Norman Tyler; m. Sharon Cohen. BE, Stevens Inst. Tech., Hoboken, NJ, 1970; JD, Samford U., 1973; LLM, Georgetown U., 1978. Bar: Ala. 1973, D.C. 1978. Assoc. McKenna, Connor & Cuneo, Washington, 1977-81; v.p., gen. counsel Shipbuilders Coun., Washington, 1977-81; dir. contract policy Lockheed Corp., Washington, 1985-90; dep. under sec. for acquisition planning US Dept. Def., Washington, 1990-91; ptnr. McGuire, Woods, Battle & Boothe, Washington, 1991-94, Tighe, Patton, Tabackman & Babbin, Washington, 1994-2000, O'Connor & Hannan, LLP, Washington, 2000—06. Columnist Am. Spectator Online, RealClearPolitics.com. Author: Legacy of Valor, 2000, Inside the Asylum: Why the United Nations and Old Europe are Worse Than You Think, 2004; co-author (with Edward Timperlake): Showdown: Why China Wants War with the United States, 2006; editor: Human Events and Human Events.com, 2007—; co-editor: In the Words of Our Enemies, 2007—; contbg. editor: The American Spectator Mag., 2001—07. Bd. dirs. Columbia Lighthouse for the Blind, 2002—05, Royal Air Force Mus. Am. Found., 2006—. Capt. USAF, 1973—77. Conservative. Jewish. Avocations: fishing, bird hunting. Office Phone: 202-216-0601. E-mail: jbabbin@humanevents.com.

BABBITT, MARGARET SARGENT, museum administrator; b. New Haven, Conn., Jan. 16, 1957; d. Theodore Fisher and Betsy Hurd Babbitt; m. Jerry Lynn Fields; 1 child, Alexandra Margaret Fields. BA, Kirkland Coll., Clinton, NY, 1978. Dir. of devel. Figge Art Mus., Davenport, Iowa, 2003—. Mem. arts and cultural com. Downtown Partnership, Davenport, Iowa, 2005—. Mem.: Assn. Fundraising Profls. Democrat. Avocation: visual arts. Home: 3912 8th Ave Rock Island IL 61201 Office: Figge Art Mus 225 W 2d St Davenport IA 52801 Home Phone: 309-788-7087; Office Phone: 563-326-7804. Business E-Mail: mbabbitt@figgeartmuseum.org.

BABBITT, MARTHA E., science educator; d. Nelson Benjamin and Pearl Leone Betts; m. Donald W. Babbitt, July 8, 1995; children: Mary Ellen Crowley, William Christopher children: Kenneth Scott, Katharine Doreen Hubbard. MS in Edn., Western Conn. State U., Danbury, 1973; BS, N.Y. State U. Coll., Cortland, 1966. Tchr. Scotia-Glenville Ctrl. Schs., Scotia, NY, 1966—69, Newtown Mid. Sch., Conn., 1969—. Tchr. Amateur Radio Relay League Edn. and Tech. program, Newtown, Conn., 2003—. Sec. Northville Amateur Radio Assn., Candlewood Amateur Radio Assn.; mem. choir Salem Covenant Ch., Washington, Conn., 2001—, bldg. upkeep. Mem.: Candlewood Amateur Radio Assn. (sec.), Bridgewater Grange #153 (overseer 2001—). Home: P O Box 477 Bridgewater CT 06752 Office: Newtown Mid Sch 11 Queen St Newtown CT 06470 Home Phone: 860-350-8804; Office Phone: 203-426-7638. E-mail: babbittm@newtown.k12.ct.us.

BABBITT, SAMUEL FISHER, retired university official; b. New Haven, Feb. 22, 1929; s. Theodore and Margaret (Fisher) B.; m. Natalie Zane Moore, June 28, 1954; children: Christopher Converse, Thomas Collier, Lucy Cullyford. BA, Yale U., 1953, MA, 1957, PhD, 1965; LLD (hon.), Hamilton Coll., Clinton, NY, 1968. Asst. dean Yale Coll. Grad. Sch., New Haven, 1953-57, 63-66; dean of men Vanderbilt U., Nashville, 1957-62; chief coll. and univ. liaison Office Pub. Affairs, U.S. Peace Corps, Washington, 1962-63; pres. Kirkland Coll., Clinton, NY, 1966-78; v.p. program planning and resources Meml. Sloan-Kettering Cancer Ctr., NYC, 1979-83; v.p. devel. Brown U., Providence, 1982-90, sr. v.p. The Campaign, 1990-93, sr. advisor to pres. for Far Eastern Affairs, 1993-96. Mem. N.Y. State Commn. on Civil Rights, 1968-76. Author: The 49th Magician, 1966, Limited Engagement: Kirkland College 1965-1978, 2006; producer: (film) The Eyes of the Amaryllis, 1981. Bd. dirs. Sandra Feinstein-Gamm Theatre. With inf. U.S. Army, 1948-51, Korea. Decorated Silver Star. Mem. Century Assn. (N.Y.C.). Democrat. E-mail: sambabb1@cox.net.

BABBY, ELLEN REISMAN, educational association executive; b. Montreal, Que., Can., Oct. 21, 1950; came to U.S., 1973; d. Mark Reisman and Rose Gutwillig (Reisman); m. Lon Scott Babby, June 17, 1973; children—Kenneth Robert, Heather Lynn. Student, McGill U., 1968-70; BA, Beaver Coll., 1972; MA, Lehigh U., 1973, Yale U., 1976, M.Phil., 1977, PhD, 1980. Tchr. elem. schs. to coll. levels; instr. resident assoc. program Smithsonian Instn., Washington, 1980-82; exec. dir. Assn. for Can. Studies in U.S., Washington, 1982—91; with Nat. Fgn. Lang. Ctr. Johns Hopkins U., Washington, 1992-94; sr. dir. planning and devel. Assn. Internat. Educators, Washington, 1995—98; v.p. Am. Coun. on Edn., Washington, 1999—. Author: Play of Language and Spectacle: A Structural Reading of Selected Texts by Gabrielle Roy, 1986. Contbr. articles on Quebec lit. to profl. jours. Mem. Am. Soc. Assn. Execs., Assn. Fund Raising Profls., Yale Alumni (del. 1989-92). Office: Am Coun On Edn One Dupont Cir #800 Washington DC 20036 Business E-Mail: ellen_babby@ace.nche.edu. E-mail: ellen@babby.com.

BABBY, LON S., lawyer; b. Bklyn., Feb. 21, 1951; BA, Lehigh U., 1973; JD, Yale U., 1976. Bar: Conn. 1976, DC 1977, U.S. Supreme Ct. 1981, U.S. Claims Ct., 1986; cert. agt. Nat. Basketball Players Assn., Maj. League Baseball Players Assn. Law clk. to Hon. M. Joseph Blumenfeld Dist. Conn., 1976-77; mem. Williams & Connolly, Washington, 1977—. Adj. faculty George Washington U. Law Sch., 1991-92. Editor Yale Law Jour., 1974-76; contbr. articles to profl. jours. Trustee Naismith Meml. Basketball Hall of Fame, 2002—. Mem. ABA, D.C. Bar, Conn. Bar Assn., Phi Beta Kappa, Omicron Delta Kappa. Office: Williams & Connolly 725 12th St NW Washington DC 20005-5901 Office Phone: 202-434-5561. Business E-Mail: lbabby@wc.com.

BABCOCK, CHARLES LUTHER, classics educator; b. Whittier, Calif., May 26, 1924; s. Robert Louis and Margarette Estelle (Fuller) B.; m. Mary Ayer Taylor, Aug. 6, 1955; children: Robert Sherburne, Jennie Rownd Chapman, Jonathan Taylor. AB in Latin, U. Calif., Berkeley, 1948, MA in Latin, 1949, PhD in Classics, 1953. Asst. in classics U. Utah, Salt Lake City, 1949-50; instr. classics Cornell U., Ithaca, N.Y., 1955-57; acting. instr. Stanford U., Calif., summer 1956; asst. prof. classical studies U. Pa., Phila., 1957-62, assoc. prof., 1962-66, asst. dean, vice dean of coll., 1960-62, 62-64, acting dean, spring 1964; prof. classics Ohio State U., Columbus, 1966-92, prof. emeritus, 1992—, chmn. dept., 1966-68, 80-88, dean Coll. of Humanities, 1968-70. Prof.-in-charge summer sch. Am. Acad. in Rome, 1966, resident in classical studies, 1986, acting Mellon prof.-in-charge sch. classical studies, 1988-89, chmn. adv. coun. sch. classical studies, 1992-94; Latin exam. com. Advanced Placement Program, 1967-74, chmn., 1972-74; prof.-in-charge Intercollegiate Ctr. Classical Studies, Rome, 1974, chair mng. com., 1975-82; scholar in residence Hope Coll., 1993. Co-author: Aspects of Roman Civilization, humanities, 1980; contbr. articles on Latin lit. (especially Horace), Latin epigraphy, Roman civilization. Served to capt. inf. US Army, 1943—47, ETO. Univ. fellow in classics U. Calif., Berkeley, 1951-53; Fulbright scholar in classics, Rome, 1953-55. Fellow Am. Acad. in Rome (trustee 1981-83, trustee emeritus 1994—); mem. Am. Philol. Assn. (bd. dirs. 1968-72), Classical Assn. of Mid. West and South (Ovatio award 1982, pres. 1977-78), Vergilian Soc. Am. (pres. 1975-76), Assn. Depts. Fgn. Langs. (pres. 1986), Archeol. Inst. Am., Ohio Classical Conf., Phi Beta Kappa (pres. Epsilon of Ohio 1969-70), Phi Kappa Phi, Phi Sigma Kappa (chpt. pres. U. Calif., regional dep. 1949-51), Scabbard and Blade Club (Pa., hon.), Philomathean Soc. (Pa. hon.), Greater Columbus Latin Club. Home: 969 Village Brook Way Columbus OH 43235-5039 Office: Ohio State U Dept Greek & Latin 230 N Oval Mall Columbus OH 43210-1319 Office Phone: 614-292-3280. E-mail: babcock.2@osu.edu.

BABCOCK, CHARLES LYNDE, IV, lawyer; b. Bklyn., June 23, 1949; s. Charles Lynde III and Dorothy (Yates) B.; children: Katherine Kester, Barbara Yates. AB, Brown U., 1971; JD, Boston U., 1976. Bar: Tex. 1977, U.S. Dist. Ct. (no. dist.) Tex. 1977, U.S. Dist. Ct. (so. dist.) Tex. 1979, U.S. Ct. Appeals (5th and 11th cirs.) 1979, U.S. Supreme Ct. 1980, U.S. Dist. Ct. (we. dist.) Tex. 1981, U.S. Ct. Appeals (9th and 10th cirs.) 1982, U.S. Dist. Ct. (ea. dist.) Tex. 1982. Sportswriter Phila. Inquirer, 1971-73; law clk. to presiding justice U.S. Dist. Ct. (no. dist.) Tex., Dallas, 1976-78; assoc. Jackson, Walker, Winstead, Cantwell & Miller, Dallas, 1978-83, ptnr., 1983—, now Jackson Walker LLP, Dallas. Chmn. Tex. Supreme Court Rules Adv. Com., 2006—. Author: Business Law for Executives, 1977, Texas Media Law handbook, 1984; contbr. articles to legal jours. Bd. dirs. Freedom of Info. Found. Tex., 1995—. Recipient Disting. Pro Bono Svc. award North Tex. Legal Svcs. Found., 1986. Fellow Tex. Bar Found., Am. Coll. Trial Lawyers; mem. ABA, Tex. Bar Assn. Mem. Soc. Of Friends. Avocation: sports. Office: Jackson & Walker LLP Ste 6000 901 Main St Dallas TX 75202-3797

BABCOCK, CHARLES WITTEN, JR., lawyer; b. Kansas City, Mo., Dec. 6, 1941; s. Charles W. and Esther L. (Marcy) B.; m. Sharon K. Chamberlain, June 26, 1976; children: David, William, Susan, Stephen. BA with honors, U. Mo., 1963; JD, Harvard U., 1966. Bar: Mo. 1966, Mich. 1971, Pa. 2003. Judge advocate USMC, various locations, 1966-69; assoc. Blackwell, Sanders, Kansas City, 1969-71; staff atty. Gen. Motors Corp., Detroit, 1971—2003; of counsel Lavin, O'Neil, Phila., 2004—. Contbr. articles to profl. jours. Bd. dirs. Mothers Against Drunk Driving, 1992-99, nat. chmn., 1996-98. Avocation: amateur radio. Home: 630 Woodbine Rd West Chester PA 19382-8539

BABCOCK, JO, artist, educator; b. St. Louis, Feb. 24, 1954; s. Boyd Leon and Shirley Lynn (Hamm) B.; m. Kitty Costello, May 25, 2003. Student, UCLA, 1975; BFA, San Francisco Art Inst., 1976, MFA, 1979. Color printer Rolling Stone mag., San Francisco, 1976, Outside mag., San Francisco, 1977; cameraman 1st Calif. Press, San Francisco, 1977-80; electrician Bros. Electric, San Francisco, 1984-89; exhibit designer Levi Strauss & Co., 1989—2004; assoc. prof. San Francisco Art Inst., 1989-93, Visual Studies Workshop, Rochester, NY, 1991; assoc. prof. photography faculty Acad. Art U., San Francisco, 2007—. Author: The Invented Camera, 2005; one-man shows include Chgo. Art Inst., 1982, Zwinger Gallery, Berlin, 1987, Marcuse Pfeiffer Gallery, N.Y.C., 1988, CEPA, Buffalo, 1988, Artspace, San Francisco, 1989, Visual Studies Workshop, Rochester, N.Y., 1990, Kyle Roberts Gallery, San Francisco, 1992, Ctr. for the Arts, San Francisco, 1995, Oakland (Calif.) Mus., 1997, Addison Gallery Am. Art, Andover, Mass., 1997, Joyce Gordon Gallery, Oakland, Calif., 2005, Butte Coll., Chico, Calif., 2007, others; exhibited in group shows at Friends of Photography Gallery, Carmel, 1976, Cal Arts, Valencia, Calif., 1979, The Alternative Mus., N.Y., 1981, Wooster St. Gallery, N.Y., 1981, Living Mus., Rejkjavik, Iceland, 1983, 10 on 8, N.Y., 1983, Windows on White, N.Y., 1984, Public Image, N.Y., 1984, Otis Parsons Gallery, L.A., 1985, Hotel Project, Oakland, Calif., 1986, Roanoke (Va.) Mus. Fine Art, 1988, Ctr. for contemporary Arts, Santa Fe, 1988, Artists at the Rock, Alcatraz, Calif., 1988, Sao Paulo (Brazil) Bienal, San Francisco Mus. of Modern Art, 1989, Rena Bransten Gallery, San Francisco, 1991, Oliver Art Ctr., CCAC, 1991, Lieberman & Saul, N.Y., 1991, Tampa Mus. Art, 1992, San Jose Mus. Art, 1992, Palm Springs Desert Mus., 1993, 100 Years of Landscape Art in the Bay Area, M.H. de Young Mus., San Francisco, 1995, Bay Area Landscapes, 1995, Tex. Tech. U., Lubbock, 2006, Ohio Wesleyan U., Delaware, 2007, The Mattress Factory, Pitts., 2007, others; represented in permanent collections at San Francisco Mus. Modern Art, Bklyn. Mus., Newport Harbor Art Mus., Lightwork, Syracuse, N.Y., La Biblioteque, Avignon, France, San Francisco Pub. Libr., San Francisco Arts Commn., George Eastman House, Rochester, N.Y., Nat. Collection, Smithsonian Instn., Lit. Getty Inst., L.A., others. Recipient Govs. award NY State Coun. on Arts, 1989; grantee City of Oakland, 1985, NY State Coun. on Arts, 1988, Nat. Endowment for Arts, 1990. Mem. Primitive Hunting Soc. Avocation: building pinhole cameras. Studio: 378 San Jose Ave Apt B San Francisco CA 94110-3700 Personal E-mail: jobabcock@jobabcock.com.

BABCOCK, KEITH MOSS, lawyer; b. Camden, NJ, Aug. 5, 1951; s. William Strong Jr. and Dinah Leslie (Moss) B.; m. Jacquelyn Sue Dickman, Aug. 16, 1975; children: Michael Arthur, Max William. AB, Princeton U., NJ, 1973; JD, George Wash. U., Washington, DC, 1976. Bar: SC 1977, U.S. Dist. Ct. SC 1977, US Ct. Appeals (4th cir.) 1977, US Supreme Ct. 1980. Staff atty. S.C. Atty. Gen.'s Office, Columbia, 1977-78, state atty., 1978-79, asst. atty. gen., 1979-81; ptnr. Barnes & Austin, Columbia, 1981-82, Austin & Lewis, Columbia, 1982-84, Lewis & Babcock, LLP, Columbia, 1984—. Mem. civil justice adv. com. for dist. SC, 1991-94; mem. SC Bd. Bar Examiners, 2001-06. Bd. dirs. Columbia Jewish Cmty. Pre-Sch., 1984, chmn., 1985-86; bd. dirs. Columbia Jewish Cmty., 1986-88, 2006—, Jewish Fedn. Columbia, 2007—, Greater Columbia Ednl. Advancement Found., 2007—. Mem. ABA, SC Bar Assn. (chmn. prof. resp. com. 1985-86), Richland County Bar Assn., Princeton Alumni Assn. of SC (v.p. 1980-86, 88-89, pres. 1990-93, 96-98), George Washington U. Law Sch. Alumni Assn. (bd. dirs. 1983-87), Summit Club, Spring Valley Country Club (Columbia). Democrat. Episcopalian. Home: 233 W Springs Rd Columbia SC 29223-6912 Office: Lewis & Babock LLP 1513 Hampton St Columbia SC 29201-2928 Business E-Mail: kmb@lewisbabcock.com.

BABCOCK, LYNDON ROSS, JR., environmental engineer, educator; b. Detroit, Apr. 8, 1934; s. Lyndon Ross and Lucille Kathryn (Miller) B.; m. Betty Irene Immonen, June 21, 1957; children: Lyndon Ross III, Sheron Lucille Babcock Fruehauf, Susan Elizabeth Babcock Williams, Andrew Dag BSChemE, Mich. Tech. U., 1956; MSChemE, U. Washington, 1958, PhD in Environ. Engring., 1970. Chem. engr. polymers Shell Chem. Co., Calif., N.J., N.Y., 1958-67; assoc. prof. environ. engring., geography, pub. health U. Ill., Chgo., 1970-75, prof. environ. engring., geography, pub. health, 1975-90, prof. emeritus, 1990—, dir. environ. health scis. program Sch. Pub. Health, 1978-79, dir. environ. and occupational health scis. program Sch. Pub. Health, 1979-84, assoc. dean Sch. Pub. Health, 1984-85. Cons. WHO, 1985, Interam. Devel. Bank, 1990-91, Environ. Secretariat Fed. Dist., Mexico City, 1995-97; USA coord. air quality project for Gestión de la Calidad del Aire, Mexico City, 1986-92; environ. cons./lectr. Tech. Instns., Mexican Secretariat of Pub. Edn., 1993-95; vis. prof. El Colegio de Mexico, Mexico City, 1996-2000. Mem. editorial bd. The Environ. Profl., 1979-90; contbr. environ. articles to profl jours.; patentee plastics composition and processing. Bd. dirs. Chgo. Lung Assn., 1981-92. Fulbright lectr., Turkey and India, 1975-76, Mexico, 1986-87, 1992-93; fed. and state environ. research and ednl. grantee Mem. Air and Waste Mgmt. Assn. (chmn. Lake Michigan sect. 1977-78), UN Assn.-USA, League Am. Bicyclists, League Mich. Bicyclists, Chicagoland Bicycle Fedn. (v.p. 1985-86). Office: U Ill Sch Pub Health EOHS MC922 2121 W Taylor St Chicago IL 60612-7260 Office Phone: 517-455-7532. E-mail: lyndonrb@comcast.net.

BABCOCK, MARGUERITE LOCKWOOD, addictions treatment therapist, educator, writer; b. Jacksonville, Fla., Jan. 1, 1944; d. Allen Seaman and Emilie (Lockwood) B. BA in Art History, Am. U., Washington, DC, 1965; M in Counselor Edn., U. Pitts., 1982. Lic. profl. counselor, Pa.; cert. nat. cert. counselor, nat. cert. master's addiction counselor. Addictions therapist South Hills Health Sys., Pitts., 1979—81; addiction therapist, clin. supr., clin. dir. Alternatives Turtle Creek Mental Health/Mental Retardation/D&A Ctr., Pitts., 1981—86; addictions therapist, coord. Ligonier Valley Treatment Ctr., Stahlstown, Pa., 1986—88; addictions clin. supr., unit dir. Ctr. for Substance Abuse Mon-Yough, McKeesport, Pa., 1988—96; quality assurance Mon-Yough, McKeesport, 1996—97; clin. supr. Sojourner House, Pitts., 1997—2000; co-founder, addictions cons. consortium Outcomes Builders, 2000—. Adj. instr. in addictions courses Seton Hill Coll., Greensburg, Pa., 1989-91, C.C. Allegheny County, West Mifflin, Pa., 1989-91, Pa. State U., McKeesport, 1993-97; pvt. trainer, writer, Acme, Pa., 1985—; ind. info. profl. in addictions, 2003—. Co-author, co-editor: Challenging Codependency: Feminist Critiques, 1995; mem. editl. bd. Jour. Tchg. in Addictions, 2000—; contbr. articles to profl. jours. Fellow Andrew Mellon Found., 1966-68, NSF, 1967. Mem.: Alpha Lambda Delta, Phi Kappa Phi. Home and Office: 3533 Rt 130 Acme PA 15610-9712 Office Phone: 724-593-7139. E-mail: margueritebabcock@yahoo.com.

BABCOCK, MICHAEL WARD, economics professor; b. Bloomington, Ill., Dec. 10, 1944; s. Bruce W. and Virginia (Neeson) B.; m. Virginia Lee Brooks, Aug. 4, 1973; children: John, Karen. BSBA, Drake U., 1967; MA in Econs., U. Ill., 1971, PhD in Econs., 1973. Tchg. asst. U. Ill., Urbana, 1968, rsch. asst., 1971—72; prof. econs. Kans. State U., Manhattan, 1972—. Cons. Santa Fe, Burlington No., and Union Pacific RR, Brotherhood of Maintenence Way, United Transp. Union, Kans. Dept. Transp., Kans. Dept. Agr., US Dept. Agr., Kans. Dept. Commerce. Gen. editor Jour. Transp. Rsch. Forum; contbr. articles to profl. jours., newspapers, mags. Apptd. to Kans. Govs. RR Working Group to Evaluate Class I RR Mergers, 1995, 96, 2000. With US Army, 1969-71. Recipient A.T. Kearney award Transp. Rsch. Forum, 1987, 89, Edgar S. Bagley award Kans. State U., 1989, 1993, 1997, 2004, UPS Found. award, 1990, Outstanding Rsch. in Agrl. Transp. award Burlington No. R.R., 1994, Rail-Tex. Corp. award Transp. Rsch. Forum, 1997, Herbert O. Whitten Svc. award Transp. Rsch. Forum, 2005, Edgar S. Bagley award Kans. State U., 1989, 93, 97, 2004, Professorial Performance award, 2007; grantee U.S. Army CE, 1978-79, USDA, 1978-80-82, 84-85, 96-97, 2000, Kans. Dept. Agr., 1987, Kans. Wheat Commn., 1989, 92, 93, Midwest Transp. Ctr., 1989, 92-93, Kans. Dept. Transp., 1991—, Mid-Am. Transp. Ctr., 1995-96. Mem. Am. Assn. Agrl. Economists, Missouri Valley Econ. Assn., Mid-Continent Regional Sci. Assn., So. Regional Sci. Assn., Transp. Rsch. Forum (gen. editor Jour., Herbert O. Whitten Svc. award 2005), Transp. Rsch. Bd., Coun. Logistics Mgmt., So. Econs. Assn., We. Econs. Assn., Beta Gamma Sigma, Omicron Delta Epsilon. Home: 720 Harris Ave Manhattan KS 66502-3614 Office: Kans State U Dept Econs Manhattan KS 66506 Office Phone: 785-532-4571. Business E-Mail: mwb@ksu.edu.

BABCOCK, MIKE, professional hockey coach; b. Saskatoon, Sask., Can., Apr. 29, 1963; m. Maureen Babcock; children: Allie, Michael, Taylor. Grad., McGill U. Head coach Cin. Mighty Ducks, 2000—02, Mighty Ducks of Anaheim, 2002—04, Detroit Red Wings, 2005—. Coach Can. World Junior Team, 1997, Team Ca., World Championships, Prague, 2004. Office: Detroit Red Wings Joe Louis Arena 600 Civic Center Dr Detroit MI 48226

BABCOCK, SANDRA L., lawyer, educator; BA in Internat. Rels., Johns Hopkins U., Balt., 1986; JD, Harvard U., 1991. Pub. defender Hennepin County, Minn.; dir. Mex. Capital Legal Assistance Prog., 2000; clin. assoc. prof. law, clin. dir. Ctr. Internat. Human Rights Northwestern U. Sch. Law, Chgo., 2006—. Adj. law prof. South Tex. Coll. Law; of counsel Govt. of Mex.; cons. Human Rights Com., Inter-Am. Commn. Human Rights, Inter-Am. Ct. Human Rights. Recipient Aguila Azteca, Govt. of Mex., 2003. Office: Bluhm Legal Clinic Northwestern U Sch Law 357 E Chgo Ave Chicago IL 60611-3069 Office Phone: 312-503-0114. E-mail: s-babcock@law.northwestern.edu, sandrababcock@earthlink.net.*

BABER, BOB, dean; b. Utica; BA in Pub. Rels. and Journalism, Utica Coll.; M in News/Editl. Journalism, Ball State U. Instr. journalism Utica Coll., Syracuse U., Syracuse, NY; dir. pub. relations SUNY Inst. Tech., Utica/Rome; dir. comm. & devel. Pratt at Munson-Williams-Proctor Arts Inst., Utica, NY, 1999—2002, dir. comm. & interim Dean Sch. Art, 2002—03, Dean Sch. Art, 2003—. Co-author (with Joe Chilberg): N.Y. Wine Country, 1980. Former pres. Downtown Utica Devel. Assn., Utica, NY; sec, bd. Oneida County Conv. & Visitors Bur.; bd. dirs. GroWest Inc.; former pres. Utica Kiwanis Club, SUNY Coun. U. Advancement & Devel. Office: Office of the Dean Pratt MWP Arts Inst 310 Genesee St Utica NY 13502

BABER, BRETT D., lawyer; b. Iowa City, Iowa; BA, U. Southern Maine, 1982; JD magna cum laude, U. Maine, 1985. Bar: US Supreme Ct., US Ct. Appeals (1st Cir.), US Dist. Ct. (Dist. Maine), Maine. Pvt. law practice, Bangor, Maine. Contbr. articles to scholarly journals. Mem.: Maine State Bar Assn. (pres.-elect 2006—07). Office: Atty at Law Ste 2E 304 Hancock St Bangor ME 04401 Office Phone: 207-945-6111. Office Fax: 207-945-6118. E-mail: brett@bangorattorney.com.

BABER, WALTER FRANKLIN, political science professor; b. Oklahoma City, Aug. 18, 1953; s. Eldon Clay and Evalena Baber; m. Carolyn Diane Pearson, Aug. 8, 1975; children: Katherine Ann, John Jay. PhD, U. NC, Chapel Hill, 1980; JD, U. San Diego, 1991. Bar: Calif. 1990. Assoc. prof. Calif. State U., Long Beach, 2001—. Author: Deliberative Environmental Politics, Organizing the Future, (articles) Social Sci. Jour., Public Integrity, Natural Resources Jour., Kansas Jour. Law and Pub. Policy, Pub. Adminstrn. Quarterly, Jour. Mgmt. History, The Bureuacrat, Internat. Jour. Pub. Adminstrn. Mem.: Western Polit. Sci. Assn., Am. Polit. Sci. Assn. (life). Democrat. Unitarian-Universalist. Home: 17047 Abra Way San Diego CA 92128 Office: Calif State Univ 1250 Bellflower Blvd Long Beach CA 90840 Home Phone: 858-451-9428; Office Phone: 562-985-5747. Business E-Mail: wbaber@csulb.edu.

BABIN, CLAUDE HUNTER, history professor; b. Baton Rouge, Feb. 6, 1924; s. Ventress Victor and Essie (Bond) B.; m. Barbara Ann Murphy, Dec. 29, 1947; 1 son, Claude Hunter. BA, La. State U., 1945; MA, U. Wis., 1946; PhD, Tulane U., 1954; LLD, Hendrix Coll., 1965. Instr. history U. Miami, Fla., 1946-49; grad. fellow Tulane U., 1949-54; asst. prof., asso. prof., then prof. history Ark. A. and M. Coll., Monticello, 1954-60, acad. dean, 1960-62, pres., 1962-71; chancellor U. Ark. at Monticello, 1971-77, prof. history, 1977-92, chancellor, prof. emeritus, 1992—. Ford fellow, 1951-52 Mem. Am. Hist. Assn., Ark. Hist. Assn., Ark. Farm Bur. Fedn., Drew County Hist. Soc., Kappa Sigma, Phi Alpha Theta, Pi Sigma Alpha. Democrat. Methodist. Home: 135 Ross Ave Monticello AR 71655-4249

BABIN, STEVEN MICHAEL, atmospheric scientist, researcher; b. Lawton, Okla., Sept. 6, 1954; s. Cleveland Victor Jr. and Delys Lilian (Lowry) B.; m. Pamela Gail Nee, June 23, 1990; 1 child, Heather Rebecca. BS in Engring. Physics spl. distinction, U. Okla., 1976; MD, U. Okla., Oklahoma City, 1980; MSEE, U. Pa., 1983; MS in Meteorology, U. Md., 1994, PhD in Meteorology, 1996. Diplomate Am. Bd. Med. Examiners. Assoc. instr. pathology and lab. medicine U. Pa. Hosp., Phila., 1980-82; sr. engr. Applied Physics Lab. Johns Hopkins U., Laurel, Md., 1983—. Presenter in field. Contbr. articles to profl. jours. Engring. scholar Frontiers Sci. Found., 1972, Spl. scholar Nat. Merit Found., 1972. Mem. IEEE (sr.), Am. Meteorol. Soc., Am. Geophysics Union (life), Am. Mensa (life), Union Radio-Sci. Internat., Sigma Xi, Tau Beta Pi, Alpha Epsilon Delta, Phi Eta Sigma. Achievements include discovery of hurricane effects on open ocean phytoplankton blooms; investigation of meteorological effects on microwave propagation in the marine boundary layer; design and development of data acquisition and analysis software in use on helicopters, rocketsondes, buoys, etc.; development of optical waveguide pH sensor; design and creation of working proportional counter for exo-electron research. Office: Johns Hopkins U Applied Physics Lab Johns Hopkins Rd Laurel MD 20723-6099

BABITZKE, THERESA ANGELINE, health facility administrator; b. Madison, Ill., Dec. 19, 1925; d. Victor Joseph and Angela (Ziolkowski) Sobolewski; m. Douglas Christ Babitzke, May 2, 1953; children: Charlotte, Mary Ann, Rose Marie, Helen. Student, Quincy Coll., 1943; diploma, St. John's Sch. Nursing Edn., Springfield, Ill., 1949; student, U. Ill., Chgo., 1970; BA, St. Francis Coll., 1973; MA in Gerontology summa cum laude, Sangamon State U., 1982. Co-founder, admin. dir. Mayslake Village, Oakbrook, Ill., 1962, St. Paschal's Infirmary, Oakbrook, 1962; night supr. Godair Home, Hinsdale, Ill., 1958-72; DON King Bruwaert House, Hinsdale, 1973-76; head nurse Mt. Sinai Hosp., Chgo., 1976-82; DON Rosary Hill Home, Justice, Ill., 1989—. Election judge Rep. Com. DuPage County, 1953-98, 2003; adv. bd. Gower Grade Sch., 1973-76; adv. com. Burr Ridge Marriot Brighton Gardens Assisted Living, 1996— Named Ill. Nurse of Yr. of the Midwest, 1981, Catholic Woman of Yr. 1962, St. Mary's Ch., Joliet, Ill. Mem. Downers Grove and Suburban Nurses Club (pres. Downers Grove chpt.), U. of Ill. Gerontology, Forty and Eight, Premier Nurse Ill., Am. Legion Aux., Sigma Phi Omega (Eta chpt. U. Ill.). Roman Catholic. Avocations: travel, bicycling, doll collecting, reading.

BABIUK, LORNE ALAN, virologist, immunologist, researcher; b. Canora, Sask., Can., Jan. 25, 1946; s. Paul and Mary (Mayden) Babiuk; m. Betty Lou Carol Wagar, Sept. 29, 1973; children: Shawn, Kimberley. BSA, U. SK, Saskatoon, 1967, MSc, 1969, DSc, 1987; PhD, U. BC, Vancouver, 1972; DSc in Infectious Diseases, Colo. State U., Ft. Collins, 2007. Postdoctoral fellow U. Toronto, Ont., Canada, 1972-73; asst. prof. Western Coll. Vet. Medicine, Saskatoon, SK, 1973-75, assoc. prof., 1975-79, prof., 1979—. Cons. Molecular Genetics, Mpls., 1980—84, Genentech, San Francisco, 1981—84, Ciba Geigy, Basel, Switzerland, 1984—91; assoc. dir. rsch. Vet. Infectious Disease Orgn., Saskatoon, 1984—93, dir., 1993—2007; v.p. rsch. U. Alberta, 2007—. Contbr. chapters to books, articles to profl. jours. Recipient award, Can. Soc. Microbiology, 1990, Am. Vet. Immunology, 1992, Xerox-Can. Forum, 1993, Emerging Sci. and Tech. award for innovation, 1995, Pfizer award in animal health, 1998, Nat. Merit award, 1998, Bill Snowden Meml. award, 2000, Saskatchewan Order of Merit, 2004, Saskatchewan Centennial medal, 2005, Officer of Order of Can., 2005, Centennial medal, Province of Saskatchewan, 2005, Prix Galien Can. Rsch. award, 2005. Fellow: Can. Acad. Health Scis., Royal Soc. Can., Infectious Disease Soc. Am. (chair Can. rsch. in vaccinology and biotech. 2001—07), Royal Coll. Physicians and Surgeons Can. (hon.); mem.: Internat. Soc. Antiviral Rsch., Soc. Gen. Microbiology, Can. Soc. Microbiology, Am. Soc. Virology, Am. Soc. Microbiology, Internat. Soc. Interferon Rsch. Achievements include 25 patents in field. Office: Vaccine and Infectious Disease Orgn U SK 120 Veterinary Rd Saskatoon SK Canada S7N 5E3 Home: 2130 Haddow Dr. Edmonton AB T6R 3C9 Canada Office Phone: 306-966-7465, 780-492-5353. Business E-Mail: lorne.babiuk@ualberta.ca.

BABLER, WAYNE E., JR., lawyer; b. Detroit, Apr. 29, 1942; s. Wayne E. and Mary E. (Blome) Babler; m. Patricia A. Ward, Feb. 5, 1972; children: Dean W., Anne E. BA, Wittenberg U., 1964; JD, U. Wis., 1967. Bar: Wis. 1967, US Dist. Ct. (ea. and we. dists.) Wis. 1967, US Ct. Appeals (7th cir.) 1971, US Supreme Ct. 1980, US Ct. Appeals (9th and 10th cirs.) 1981, US Ct. Appeals (DC cir.) 1983, US Dist. Ct. (ctrl. and no. dists.) Ill. 1987, US Dist. Ct. (ea. and we. dists.) Mich. 1990. Assoc. Quarles, Herriott, Clemons, Teschner & Noelke, Milw., 1971-74, Quarles & Brady, Milw., 1974-76, ptnr., 1976—. Rep. of chief justice Wis. Supreme Ct. to Wis. Jud. Compensation Com., 1983—84. Author (with others): Business and Commercial Litigation in Federal Court, 1998; rsch. editor: Wis. Law Rev., 1966—67, Antitrust, Federal Civil Litigation, State Civil Litigation. Campaign cabinet United Performing Arts Fund, Inc., Milw., 1977—78; bd. dirs. Milw. Bar Found., 1976—79, Wis. Bar Found., 1983—2000, pres., 1985—87; bd. dirs. Legal Aid Soc., Milw., 1997—2006; mem. U. Wis. Benchers Soc. With JAGC USN, 1967—71. Fellow: Wis. Law Found., Am. Coll. Trial Lawyers (state chair 2002—04), Am. Bar Found.; mem.: ABA (ho. of dels. 1984—96), Bar Assn. 7th Fed. Cir., State Bar Wis. (bd. govs. 1983—87), Milw. Bar Assn. (bd. dirs. 1976—83, pres. 1981—82), Delray Dunes Country Club, Order of Coif. Office: Quarles & Brady 411 E Wisconsin Ave Milwaukee WI 53202-4497 Home: 2 Acacia Dr Boynton Beach FL 33436 Office Phone: 414-277-5529. Business E-Mail: web@quarles.com.

BABLIN, MARK EDWARD, security administrator, mortgage consultant; b. Amsterdam, NY, Oct. 30, 1949; s. Edward and Diane B.; m. Mediatrix Ferrer, Aug. 8, 1983 (div. May 1989); children: Francis, Michael, Alex. BS, Siena Coll., 1971; student, Albany State U., 1972. Real estate mgr. Kasow Estates, Phila., 1972-76; credit mgr. Pub. Fin. and Assoc. Fin., Montclair, N.J., 1976-84; security cons. Arboc Security, Reading, Pa., 1984-87; with chem. sales dept. HyTest Industry, Springfield, NJ, 1988—90; dir. corp. security Benjamin Moore/Ingersoll Rand, Woodcliff Lake, NJ, 1990—2005; mortgage sales cons. Mercury Mortgage, Fairfield, NJ, 1998—2006; corp. security dir. Reckson Assocs., Short Hills, NJ, 2005—. Mem. N.J. Rep. State Com., Trenton, 1988—. Mem. N.J. Rep. Heritage Coun. (nat. vice chair 2000--, Ethnic Leader of Yr. 1989). Roman Catholic. Avocations: photography, travel, history, sports, literature. Home: 53 Linden St Millburn NJ 07041-2132

BABLITCH, WILLIAM A., lawyer, retired state supreme court justice; b. Stevens Point, Wis., Mar. 1, 1941; BS, U. Wis., Madison, 1963, JD, 1968; MA, U. of Virginia, 1987. Bar: Wis. 1968. Pvt. practice law, Stevens Point, Wis.; dist. atty. Portage County, Wis., 1969-72; mem. Wis. Senate, 1972-85, senate majority leader, 1976-82; justice Wis. Supreme Ct., Madison, 1983—2003; atty. Michael Best & Friedrich, Madison, 2003—. Volunteer US Peace Corp., Liberia, 1963—65. Mem.: Nat. Conf. State Legislators (exec. com. 1979). Office: Michael Best & Friedrich One S Pinckney St Ste 700 Madison WI 53703 Office Phone: 608-283-0100. Office Fax: 608-283-2275. E-mail: wabablitch@michaelbest.com.

BABROWSKI, CLAIRE HARBECK, retail executive; b. Ottawa, Ill., July 25, 1957; d. John Clayton Harbeck and Corrine Ann (Lavender) French; m. David Lee Babrowski, July 3, 1982; 2 stepdaughters. Student, U. Ill., 1975-77; MBA, U. NC, 1995. Dental asst., Ottawa, 1975-76; crew person McDonald's Corp., Ottawa, 1974-76, mem. restaurant mgmt. Champaign, Ill., 1976-80, ops. and tng. cons. St. Louis, 1980-84, ops. mgr., 1984-86, dir. nat. ops. Oak Brook, Ill., 1986-88, dir. ops. Phila., 1988-89, sr. regional mgr. Raleigh, NC, 1989—92, regional v.p., 1992—95, corp. v.p. ops., 1995—97, sr. v.p. ops., 1997—98, exec. v.p. U.S. Restaurant Sys., 1998—99, exec. v.p. Worldwide Restaurant Sys., 1999—2001, pres. McDonald's Asia/Pacific/the Middle East and Africa, 2001—03, chief restaurant ops. officer, 2003—04; exec. v.p., COO RadioShack Corp., Fort Worth, Tex., 2005—06, acting CEO, 2006; exec. v.p., COO Toys "R" Us, Inc., Wayne, NJ, 2007—. Chmn. NC Ronald McDonald's Children's Charities, Raleigh, 1989-95; relationship ptnr. Donatos Pizza, Pret A Manger, Chipotle Mexican Grill, chmn. bd. dirs.; mem. Com. of 200.; bd. dir. Delhaize Group, 2006-. Author: (manual) Training Consultants Development Program, 1987. Named one of Named one of Next 20 Female CEOs, Pink Mag. & Forté Found., 2006; recipient Emerging Leader award, US Women's Svc. Forum. Mem. NC Restaurant Assn. (bd. dirs. 1992-95). Republican. Roman Catholic. Avocations: tennis, gardening. Office: Toys R Us Inc 1 Geoffrey Way Wayne NJ 07470*

BABSKI-REEVES, KARI, industrial and systems engineering educator; b. Silver Spring, Md., Oct. 21, 1972; d. Wayne and Linda Havard; m. Tory Reeves, June 10, 2000; children: Kyler Reeves, Tanner Reeves. AA, SW Miss. C.C., Summit, 1992; BS, Miss. State U., 1995, MS, 1998, PhD, 2000. Co.-dir. Indsl. Ergonomics and Biomech. Lab. Va. Inst. Tech. and State U., Blacksburg, 2000—06, asst. prof., 2000—06, affiliate faculty mem. Ctr. Gerontoloty, 2000—06, affiliate faculty mem. Sch. Biomed. Engring., 2003—06, mem. Ctr. Applied Biomech., 2005—06, mem. Ctr. for Innovation in Constrn. Safety and Health, 2005—06, co-dir. Safety Lab., 2005—06; asst. prof. Miss. State U., 2006—, co-dir. human sys. performance lab., 2006—, faculty Ctr. Advanced Vehicular Sys., 2006—. Author: (conf. procs.) Annual Human Factors and Ergonomics Conference; contbr. articles to profl. pubs. Grantee, NIOSH, 2000—, Honda of Am., Inc., 2003, Hyundai Motor Corp., 2005—06; Athletic scholar, SW Miss. C.C., 1990—92, Dean's scholar, Miss. State U., 1993—2000, Pres.' scholar, 1993—2000, Honda fellow, 1995, Barrier fellow, 1996. Mem.: Soc. Women Engrs., Am. Soc. Engring. Edn., Soc. Automotive Engrs., Inst. Indsl. Engrs., Human Factors and Ergonomics Soc., Golden Key, Alpha Pi Mu, Phi Kappa Phi. Achievements include research in modeling total body fatigue of construction workers; investigating muscle activation patterns using thermography to prevent WMSDs of the upper extremity; performance evaluations of the ABNOSTRAIN; performance evaluations of micro-climate cooling products. Office: Miss State U PO Box 9542 Mississippi State MS 39762 Office Phone: 662-325-1677. Office Fax: 662-325-7618. Business E-Mail: kari@isc.msstate.edu.

BABSKY, ANDRIY M., biologist, researcher; b. Sokal, Ukraine, Mar. 18, 1957; arrived in U.S., 1995; s. Myroslav M. Babsky and Hanna A. Babska; m. Uliana Babska; children: Yaromyr, Ostap. BS, Lviv State U., Lviv, Ukraine, 1979, PhD, 1985. Rschr. Inst. of Biol. Physics, Pushcino, Russia, 1983—86; rschr., head of the lab. Lviv State U., Lviv, Ukraine, 1986—95; vice-dean Lviv State U., Sch. of Biology, Lviv, Ukraine, 1994—95; post-doctoral rschr. U. Pa., Biochemistry/Biophysics, Phila., 1995—2001; rsch. assoc. Ind. U., Radiology, Indpls., 2002—. Lectr. Lviv State U., Lviv, Ukraine, 1990—95. Editor: (editing) The Galician Herald; contbr. scientific papers over 130 pub. worldwide to profl. jour. Recipient Diploma for Winner of the All-Ukrainian Competition for Bachelor's Projects, 1979. Mem.: Ukrainian Physiol. Soc., Internat. Soc. for Magnetic Resonance in Medicine. Achievements include patents for #MBL 00769036 Succinic Acid as an Adrenomimetic Compound (Ukraine). Avocations: bicycling, soccer, sports, painting, photography. Office: Ind Univ 950 W Walnut St R2 E124 Indianapolis IN 04602 Business E-Mail: ababsky@iupui.edu.

BABSON, JANE FRANCES, artist, writer; b. Leitchfield, Ky., Aug. 17, 1925; d. William Winstead McCall and Matilda Caroline Hahn; m. David Frederick Babson, Aug. 7, 1954; children: David Winstead, Leila Jane. BA, Mt. Holyoke Coll., 1947; MFA in Art and Art History, U. Ill., 1949. Registrar The Corcoran Gallery of Art, Washington, 1952—54, curator of prints, 1953—54. Author: The Epsteins: A Family Album, 1984, The Search for the Indian, 2001, (childrens books) The Nest on the Porch, 1988, Babson's Bestiary, 1990, A Story of Us, 2003, (DVD) Toward Freedom, (CDs) The Christmas Songs, Babson Singers; contbr. woodcut prints to collection of Nat. Air and Space Mus. Founder Stamford (Conn.) Art Assn., 1970. Named hon. citizen, City of Wakayama, Japan, 1984. Mem.: Nat. Trust for Historic Preservation, Am. Crafts Coun., Soc. Archtl. Historians, Greater N.Y. Ind. Pubs. Assn. (bd. dirs. 2002—07). Avocations: swimming, travel, clothing design. Home and Office: The Winstead Press Ltd Diva Leila Prodns 202 Slice Dr Stamford CT 06907 Home Phone: 203-322-4941; Office Phone: 203-322-4941. Office Fax: 203-629-2545. Personal E-mail: winstead.press@verizon.net.

BABULA, WILLIAM, dean, writer; b. Stamford, Conn., May 19, 1943; s. Benny F. and Lottie (Zajkowski) B.; m. Karen L. Gemi, June 19, 1965; children: Jared, Joelle. BA, Rutgers U., 1965; MA, U. Calif., Berkeley, 1967, PhD, 1969. Asst. prof. English U. Miami, Coral Gables, Fla., 1969-75, assoc. prof., 1975-77, prof., 1977-81, chmn. dept. Eng., 1976-81; dean of arts and humanities Sonoma State U., Rohnert Park, Calif., 1981—. Author: Shakespeare and the Tragicomic Archetype, 1975, Shakespeare in Production, 1935-79, 1981; (short stories) Motorcycle, 1982, Quarterback Sneak, 1983, The First Edsel, 1983, Ransom, 1983, The Last Jogger in Virginia, 1983, The Orthodontist and the Rock Star, 1984, Greenearth, 1984, Football and Other Seasons, The Great American Basketball Shoot, 1984, Ms. Skywriter, Inc., 1987; (plays) The Fragging of Lt. Jones (1st prize Gualala Arts Competition, 1983), Creatures (1st prize Jacksonville U. competition 1987), The Winter of Mrs. Levy (Odyssey Stage Co., New Play Series 1988), Nat. Playwright's Showcase, 1988, Theatre Americana, 1990 (James Ellis award), Basketball Jones, Black Rep of Berkeley, 1988, West Coast Ensemble, Festival of One Acts, 1992, Mark Twain Masquers, 9th Ann. Festival One Act Plays, 1994 (2d Place award), The Last Roundup, 1991 (Odyssey Stage Co.); (novels) The Bombing of Berkeley and Other Pranks (1st prize 24th Ann. Deep South Writers' Conf. 1984), St. John's Baptism, 1988, According to St. John, 1989, St. John and the Seven Veils, 1991, St. John's Bestiary, 1994, St. John's Bread, 1999; contbr. articles to profl. pubs. and short stories to lit. mags. Mem. Shakespeare Assn. of Am., Dramatists Guild, Assoc. Writing Programs, Mystery Writers Am., Phi Beta Kappa. Democrat. Episcopalian. Office: Sonoma State U Sch Arts and Humanities Rohnert Park CA 94928 Business E-Mail: william.babula@sonoma.edu.

BABULAK, EDUARD, computer scientist, educator, researcher, consultant; arrived in Can., 1993, naturalized, 1998; BSc in Engring., MSc in Engring., Kosice Tech. U., 1982; MSc in Computer Sci., U. East London, 1991; PhD in Computer Sci., Staffordshire U., UK, 2003. Cert. in computing Brighton Coll. Tech., 1990; chartered engr., 2002, European engr., 2002, cert. profl. engr., Can., 2004. Export engr. Travel Agy., Prague, Czech Republic, 1982—85; lectr. Coll. Transp., Prague, Czech Republic, 1985—86, Electrotech. Coll., Kosice, Slovakia, 1986—87, Coll. Bratislava, Slovakia, 1987—88; head dept. House of Tech., Kosice, Slovakia, 1988—89; European director Joint Venture Services, Brighton, Sussex, England, 1992—93; rschr. Polytechnic of Montreal, Quebec, Canada, 1993—95; rsch. asst. U. Ottawa, Ottawa, Ontario, Canada, 1996—99; lectr. computer engring. Pa. State, Erie, Pa., 1999—2000; assoc. prof. computer sci. Azusa Pacific U., Calif., 2000—01; sr. lectr. computing Staffordshire U., Stafford, England, 2001—06; prof. Am. U. Cyprus, 2006—07; expert European Commn., 2007. Expert cons. European Commn., Brussels, 1992—2002; advisor Bd. Trade, Erie, 1999—2000; lectr. calculus and linear algebra U. Ottawa, Canada, 1998—99; cons. Whitebird Cons., Montreal, Canada, 1993—95; vis. prof. computing sci. and engring. U. Que., 2004—05; vis. prof. electrical engring U. Pardubice, Czech Republic, 2005—06; vis. prof. telecom. engring., Spain, 2006—; keynote lectr. MIT, Boston. Contbr. articles to profl. jours.; guest editor, mem. editl. bd. Jour. Physician and Tech., 2002, hon. mem. editl. bd. Internat. Jour. Mfg. Engring., 2002; editor: Jour. Wireless Comm. Mem.: IEEE (sr.), Am. Math Soc., U.K. Engring. Coun. (chartered mem.), Instn. Electrical Engrs. (corp. mem.), Brit. Computer Soc. (profl. mem.), Inst. Dirs. (advisor 1992), Inst. Corp. Dirs. (advisor 1993), Math. Assn. Am. (mem. math. jour. 2000), Assn. Computer Machinery (profl. mem. 2000). Avocations: travel, swimming, walking. Address: PO Box 133 Ontario Canada K0B 1C0 Office Phone: (418) 7241806. Personal E-mail: babulak@yahoo.com.

BABUSKA, IVO MILAN, mathematics professor; b. Prague, Czechoslovakia, Mar. 22, 1926; PhD in Civil Engring., Tech. U. Prague, 1951; PhD in Math., Czech Acad. Sci., 1955, DSc in Math., 1960. Rsch. fellow Math. Inst., Czech Acad. Sci., 1951—55, dept. head, 1956—68; disting. prof. math. U. Md., College Park, 1968—95; Robert Trull chair engring., TICAM sr. rsch. scientist, prof. aerospace engring. and engring. mechanics, and math. U. Tex., Austin, 1995—. Contbr. articles to profl. jours. Recipient Czechoslovak State award for Math., 1968, Alexander von Humboldt Sr. Scientist award, 1977, 1994, Bolzano Medal, Czech Acad. Scis., 1996. Fellow US Assn. Computational Mechanics; mem. NAE, Am. Math. Soc. (George David Birkhoff Applied Math. prize, 1994), Soc. Indsl. Appl. Math., Czech Learned Society (hon. fgn.). Achievements include research on numerical analysis of partial differential equations, applied mathematics related to continuum theory. Office: U Tex Austin Dep Aerospace Engring 105 W Dean Keeton St, SHC 328 Austin TX 78712 Office Phone: 512-471-2156. Office Fax: 512-471-8694. E-mail: babuska@ticam.utexas.edu.

BACA, JIM, mayor; BSBA, U. N.Mex. Mayor City of Albuquerque, 1997—. Former dir. alcohol and beverage control State of N.Mex., press sec. to gov., commr. pub. lands; past asst. to mayor, gen. mgr. Rio Grande Conservancy Dist.; former dir. Fed. Bur. Land Mgmt.; nat. cons. pub. land and conservation issues. Served with USAF.

BACA, JOE, congressman; b. NM, Jan. 23, 1947; m. Barbara Baca; children: Joe Jr., Jeremy, Natalie, Jennifer. BS in Sociology, Calif. State U., LA, 1971. Ptnr. Interstate World Travel, San Bernardino, Calif.; formerly with cmty. rels. divsn. GTE; spkr. pro tempore Calif. State Assembly, Sacramento, 1992-97, asst. spkr. pro tempore, spkr.'s fed. govt. liaison, mem. rules com., 1997-98; mem. rules com., vet. affairs com., pub. employment and ret. com., energy, utilities and comm. com., local govt. com., govtl. orgn. com. Calif. State Senate, 1998-99; mem. US Congress from 43rd (formerly 42nd) Calif. dist., Washington, 1999—; mem. agriculture and sci. coms. US Ho. Reps. Trustee San Bernardino Valley Coll. Dist., 1979—. With U.S. Army, 1966-68, Vietnam. Named Citizen of Distinction San Bernardino Area LWV, Kiwanian of Yr. Greater San Bernardino Kiwanis Club, Disting. Citizen Inland Empire Dist. Boy Scouts Am., Outstanding Legislator Calif. Rifle and Pistol Assn., VFW, 1994-95, Legislator of Yr. Am. Legion, Dept. Calif.; recipient Minority Male of Yr. award Greater Riverside Area Urban League. Democrat. Office: US Ho Reps 328 Cannon Ho Office Bldg Washington DC 20515-0543 also: Ste 102 201 N E St San Bernardino CA 92401-1520*

BACA, JOSEPH FRANCIS, retired judge; b. Albuquerque, Oct. 1, 1936; s. Amado and Inez (Pino) Baca; m. Dorothy Lee Burrow, June 28, 1969; children: Jolynn, Andrea, Anna Marie. BA in Edn., U. N.Mex., 1960; JD, George Washington U., 1964; LLM, U. Va., 1992. Asst. dist. atty. 1st Jud. Dist., Santa Fe, 1965-66; pvt. practice Albuquerque, 1966-72; dist. judge 2d Jud. Dist., Albuquerque, 1972-88; justice N.Mex Supreme Ct., Santa Fe, 1989—2002, chief justice, 1995-97; ret., 2002. Spl. asst. to atty. gen. Office of N.Mex Atty. Gen., Albuquerque, 1966—71. Bd. dirs. State Justice Inst., 1994—, vice chmn., 1999—; Dem. precinct chmn. Albuquerque, 1968; del. N.Mex Constl. Conv., Santa Fe, 1969. Named one of 100 Most Influential Hispanics, Hispanic Bus. Mag., 1997, 1998; recipient Judge of the Yr. award, People's Commn. Criminal Justice, 1989, Quincentennial Commemoration Achievement award, La Hispanidad Com., 1992, Luchando pro la Justicia award, Mex. Am. Law Students Assn. U. N.Mex Law Sch., 1993, J. William Fulbright Disting. Pub. Svc. award, George Washington U. Alumni Assn., 1994, Recognition and Achievement award, Commn. Opportunities for Minorities in the Profession, 1992, others. Mem.: ABA, N.Mex Hispanic Bar Assn. (Outstanding Hispanic Atty. award 2000), Santa Fe Bar Assn., Albuquerque Bar Assn., Am. Jud. Soc. (bd. dirs. 1999—), Scribes (bd. dirs. 1998—2006), Am. Law Inst., N.Mex Bar Assn. (Outstanding Jud. Svc. award 1998, Disting. Jud. Svc. award 2002), Hispanic Nat. Bar Assn. (Lincoln-Juarez award 2000), Alumni Assn. (pres. 1980—81), KC, Kiwanis (pres. Albuquerque chpt. 1984—85, dep. grand knight 1968). Roman Catholic. Avocation: reading. Office Phone: 505-821-6881. E-mail: jbaca01@msn.com.

BACA, VERA JENNIE SCHULTE, art educator; b. Albuquerque, Mar. 2, 1950; d. Hugo Ross Schulte and Vera Loisa Pacheco-Schulte; m. Samuel Valdez Baca, Sept. 28, 1968; children: Jennifer Carisa, Paul Brian. Degree in interior decorating, Stratford Career Inst., Washington, 2002; cert. reiki pratcitioner, Miami Valley Reiki Ctr., Kettering, Ohio, 2002. Substitute tchr. Los Lunas Pub. Sch., N.Mex., 1979—88, St. Charles and St. Mary's, Belen and Albuquerque, N.Mex., 1983—88; teller, new accts. First Nat. Bank, Bosque Farms, N.Mex., 1988—90; art tchr. Resurection Cath. Sch., Lakeland, Fla., 1997—2000. Mem.: N.Mex. Art League. Republican. Roman Catholic. Avocations: stained glass, reading, tennis. Home: 5000 Cumbre Del Sur Ct NE Albuquerque NM 87111 Office Phone: 505-550-3442. Personal E-mail: finelinebyjennie@msn.com.

BACAL, KIRA, emergency physician, educator; d. Kenneth Lee Kauffman and Jessica Bonnie Bacal. Student in Divinity, Harvard U., Cambridge, Mass., 1993—94; MD, PhD, Baylor Coll. Medicine, Houston, Tex., 1996; MPH, U. Tex., Galveston, 2001. Diplomate Am. Coll. Preventive Medicine, 2002. Resident emergency medicine Albany Med.Ctr. Hosp., NY, 1996—99; resident aerospace medicine U. Tex., Galveston, 1999—2001; emergency medicine physician S.E. Physicians Assn., Houston, 2000—04; robert wood johnson fellow health policy US Senate, Washington, 2004—06; asst. prof. coll. osteo. medicine Ohio U., Athens, 2006—. Dir. Bacal Enterprises, Houston; cons. in field. Author: (short story) First Impressions; contbr. chapters to books, articles to profl. jours. Maj. Res. USAF, 1998—2006. Recipient Spl. Profl. Achievement award, NASA Johnson Space Ctr. Space and Life Scis. Directorate, 2002, 2003; fellow, NIH, 1988—96, Robert Wood Johnson Found., 2004—05, White Ho. Fellows, 2004. Fellow: Am. Coll. Emergency Physicians. Jewish. Avocations: hiking, martial arts, target shooting, writing, horseback riding. Office: Ohio Univ Coll Medicine 245 Grosvenor Athens OH 45701 Home Phone: 740-447-1282; Office Phone: 740-593-2259. Business E-Mail: bacal@ohio.edu.

BACALL, LAUREN (BETTY JOAN PERSKE), actress; b. NYC, Sept. 16, 1924; m. Humphrey Bogart, May 21, 1945 (dec. Jan. 14, 1957); children: Stephen, Leslie; m. Jason Robards, July 4, 1961 (div. Sept. 10, 1969); 1 child, Sam. Student pub. schs., Am. Acad. Dramatic Art. Actress in Broadway plays Franklin Street, 1942, Goodbye Charlie, 1959, Cactus Flower, 1966-68, Applause, 1969-71 (Sarah Siddons award 1975); also road co., 1971-72, London co., 1972-73 (Tony award for best actress in a musical 1970), Woman of the Year, 1981 (Tony award for best actress in a musical 1981, Sarah Siddons award 1983), Sweet Bird of Youth, 1983 (London, 1985, Australia, 1986, L.A., 1987; (Films) To Have and Have Not, 1944, Confidential Agent, 1945, The Big Sleep, 1946, Dark Passage, 1947, Key Largo, 1948, Young Man With a Horn, 1949, Bright Leaf, 1950, How To Marry a Millionaire, 1953, Woman's World, 1954, The Cobweb, 1955, Blood Alley, 1955, Written on the Wind, 1956, Designing Woman, 1957, The Gift of Love, 1958, Flame Over India, 1959, Shock Treatment, 1964, Sex and the Single Girl, 1965, Harper, 1966, Murder on the Orient Express, 1974, The Shootist, 1976, Health, 1980, The Fan, 1981, Tree of Hands, 1987, Appointment With Death, 1987, Mr. North, 1988, Misery, 1990, A Star for Two, 1991, All I Want for Christmas, 1991, Ready to Wear (Prêt-à-Porter), 1994, My Fellow Americans, 1996, The Mirror Has Two Faces, 1996 (Golden Globe award, 1997, SAG award, 1997), The Line King: Al Hirschfield, 1996, Le Jour et la Nuit, 1997, Diamonds, 1999, Dogville, 2003, The Limit, 2003, Birth, 2004, (voice only) Howl's Moving Castle, 2004, Firedog, 2005, Manderlay, 2005, These Foolish Things, 2006; TV movies: The Paris Collections, 1968, Applause, 1973, A Commercial Break (Happy Endings), 1975, Perfect Gentlemen, 1978, Dinner at Eight, 1989, The Portrait, 1992, A Foreign Field, 1993, From the Mixed Up Files of Mrs. Basil E. Frankweiler, 1995, The Man Who Had Everything, 1998, Madeline: Lost in Paris, 1999 Too Rich: The Secret Life of Doris Duke, 1999; TV appearances include: "What's My Line?", 1953, 1965, The Rockford Files, 1979, Chicago Hope, 1998, So Graham Norton, 2000, The Sopranos, 2006; Author: Lauren Bacall: By Myself, 1978, Now, 1994, By Myself and Then Some, 2005 Recipient Am. Acad. Dramatic Arts award for achievement, 1963, Standard award London Evening, 1973, Nat. Book award, 1980; decorated comdr. Order of Arts and Letters (France), 1995; named 50 Most Beautiful People in the World, People, 1997. Office: care Johnnie Planco William Morris Agy 1325 Avenue of the Americas New York NY 10019-6026

BACANI, NICANOR-GUGLIELMO VILA, civil and structural engineer, consultant; b. Dagupan City, Pangasinan, Philippines, Jan. 10, 1947; s. Jose Montero and Felisa (Vila) B.; m. Julie Bacani, June 24, 1972; children: Julinor, Jazmin, Joymita, Normina, Nicky, Noel. BSCE, U. Philippines, 1968, M in Engring. Stuctures, 1973. Registered profl. engr., Philippines. Structural engr. FR Estuar, PhD. Assocs., Quezon City, Philippines, 1970-72; civil structural engr. BestPhil Cons., Dagupan City, 1972-73; engring. mgr. Supreme Structural Products, Inc., Manila, 1974; chief engr. Tecphil Cons., Quezon City, 1974-76; v.p. Erectors, Inc., Makati, Philippines, 1977-81; pres. NGV Bacani & Assocs., various locations, 1981—. Advisor, cons. Met. Manila Office of Commr. Planning, 1980-85; profl. lectr. U. Manila Grad. Sch., 1982-83; resource person Nat. Engring. Ctr. U.P., Quezon City, 1983—; cons. Geo. J. Fosdyke Assocs., L.A., 1985-86, Victor Constrn. & Devel., 1986-87, Stanley Assocs. Internat., 1988, H.A. Simons Internat., 1988-90, Azlon Devel. Corp., 1990—; pres. Mgmt. Design & Investment Co., 1987—; sr. structural cons. Seismic Engring. Ltd., 1990—; sr. cons. Davey Gibson Cons., 1991-92; pres. Bestphil Can., 1992—, Seismic Cons., 1993—; cons. Chemetics Internat., 1994—; sr. cons. Sturdy Engring. Corp., Wash., 1997—; pres. Bestphil Enterprises Internat., 2000—. Author: A Reference for Engineers and Builders, 1983. Mem. Internat. Assn. Bridge and Structural Engrs. Switzerland, Assn. Structural Engrs. Philippines (life, bd. dirs. 4 terms), U. Philippines Alumni Engrs. Assn. (life), Nat. Geog. Soc., Nature Conservancy. Avocations: guitar playing, choir, dance. Home: 1119 Chase Park Dr Bacliff TX 77518-2486

BACARELLA, FLAVIA, artist, educator; b. Bklyn. d. Salvatore John and Angeline Mary B. MA, New Sch. for Social Rsch., NYC, 1975; MFA, Bklyn. Coll./CUNY, 1983; student, N.Y. Studio Sch., 1980. Assoc. prof. Herbert H. Lehman Coll., Bronx, 1995—. Grantee N.Y. Found. Arts, 1986. Mem. Coll. Art Assn. Office: Herbert H Lehman Coll Bedford Park Blvd W Bronx NY 10468 Office Phone: 718-960-8259. Business E-Mail: flavia.bacarella@lehman.cuny.edu.

BACAS, ANDREW R., data processing executive; BA, Yale U.; MS, NYU; MBA, Wharton Sch. V.p. Simmons & Co. Internat.; vice chmn., CEO ImageMAX Inc., Fort Washington, Pa.; with Key Prin. Ptnrs., San Francsico. Vis. faculty Assn. Corp. Growth. Former flight officer USN.

BACCHUS, HAROLD MUSTAPHA, physician; b. New Amsterdam, Guyana, June 19, 1946; arrived in US, 1964; s. H. M. Bacchus Sr. and Saira Bacchus; m. Kathleen Mary Brouillet, 1968 (div.); children: Timothy, Lisa, Jamy; m. Fazia Deen, 1985 (div.); children: Jannah, Jibril, Maryam. BA, Minn. State U., Mankato, 1967, MA, 1970; BS, U. Iowa, 1974; MD, Am. U. Caribbean, 1981. Emergency rm. physician St. Vincent's Hosp., Winchester, Ind., Lee Meml. Borgess, Dowagiac, Mich.; med. dir. MED-I-Qwik, Inc., Ft. Wayne, Ind. Med. dir. Spiece Lifestyle Med. Ctr., Ft. Wayne, 2005. Lt. col. USAF Res., 1985—. Fellow: Am. Acad. Family Physicians; mem.: Am. Assn. Physician Specialists (diplomate, gov.), Lions, Jaycees. Democrat. Islam. Avocations: music, dance, travel. Home: 12002 Woodbourne Ct Fort Wayne IN 46845 Office: MED-I-Qwik Inc 1719 Cremer Ave Fort Wayne IN 46818 Office Phone: 260-490-9150. Business E-Mail: mediqwikine@aol.com.

BACCIGALUPPI, ROGER JOHN, agricultural products executive; b. NYC, Mar. 17, 1934; s. Harry and Ethel (Hutcheon) B.; m. Patricia Marie Wier, Feb. 6, 1960 (div. 1978); children: John, Elisabeth, Andrea; m. Iris Christine Walfridson, Feb. 3, 1979; 1 child, Jason. BS, U. Calif., Berkeley, 1956; MS, Columbia U., 1957. Asst. sales promotion mgr. Maco Mag. Corp., NYC, 1956-57; merchandising asst. Honig, Cooper & Harrington, San Francisco and L.A., 1957-58, 1958-60, asst. dir. merchandising, 1960-61; sales rep. Blue Diamond Growers (formerly Calif. Almond Growers Exch.), Sacramento, 1961-64, mgr. advt. and sales promotion, 1964-70, v.p. mktg., 1970-73, sr. v.p. mktg., 1973-74, exec. v.p., 1974-75, pres., 1975-91; founder RB Internat., Sacramento, 1992—. Vice chmn., bd. dirs. Agrl. Coun. Calif., 1975-91; mem. consumer-prodr. com., adminstrn. com.; bd. dirs. AgriNova Corp.; mem. U.S. adv. com. Trade Policy and Negotiations, 1983-2002; mem. Agrl. Policy Adv. Com., 2005—; mem. U.S. adv. bd. Rabobank Nederlands, 1988-91; mem. Calif. World Trade Commn., 1993-2001; mem. adv. coun. Nat. Ctr. for Food and Agr. Policy Resources for Future, 1990-99. Vice chmn. Calif. State R.R. Mus. Found.; bd. dirs. Cmty. Colls. Found.; vice chmn. Grad. Inst. Cooperative Leadership, 1986-87, chair, 1987-89; bd. dirs. Valley Vision, Inc., 1995-03, AgriNova Corp., 2004-. With AUS, 1957. Mem. Calif. C. of C. (chmn. internat. trade com. 1988-94, bd. dirs. 1988—, vice chmn. bd. 1992-94, chmn. bd. 1995, Sacramento Host Com. (chmn. 1997, 98), Calif. for Higher Edn., Grad. Inst. Coop. Leadership (chmn., trustee), Grocery Mfrs. Am., Inc. (bd. dirs. 1988-91), Sutter Club. Office: RB Internat 777 Campus Commons Rd Ste 200 Sacramento CA 95825-8343

BACCUS, R. EILEEN TURNER, academic administrator; b. Oxford, N.C., Aug. 8, 1944; d. Nathaniel Benjamin and Gloria Constance (Davis) Turner; B.A., Fisk U., 1964; M.B.A., U. Conn., 1975, Ph.D., 1978; 1 son, Christopher Lloyd. Programmer, systems analyst IBM, N.Y., Mo., 1964-66; substitute tchr., Lakenheath AFB, Eng., 1967-69; asst. dir. fin. aid U. Conn., Storrs, 1970-74, asst. to dean Sch. Edn., 1974-77, dir. personnel services div., 1977-81; adminstr. treasury ops. Aetna Life & Casualty Co., Hartford, Conn., 1981-82, ops. mgr. discretionary asset mgmt., 1982-86; pres. Thames Valley State Tech. Coll., Norwich, Conn., 1986-92; pres. Northwestern Conn. Community Tech. Coll., Winsted, 1992-2004, pres. emeritus, ret.; cons. Ford Found., 1976, Tchr. Corps, 1977, Meriden (Conn.) Schs., 1979—, R&B Consulting; dir. Conn. Savs. & Loan Assn. Mem. planning com. Conn. Legis. Black Caucus, 1980; mem. mgmt. team Ujima, Inc., Hartford, 1978-80; co-chmn. bd. Hartford Scholarship Found., 1971-75; treas. bd. Cmty. Coun. Capitol Region, 1982-86; mem. community adv. bd. Jr. League Hartford, Inc., 1982—84. Mem. Am. Ednl. Rsch. Assn., Internat. Platform Assn., Links, Inc., Rotary Internat., Phi Delta Kappa, Pi Lambda Theta, Delta Sigma Theta. Democrat. Episcopalian. Home: 87 Woodland Ave Bloomfield CT 06002-1806 Office Phone: 860-478-2926. E-mail: rebaccus@mindspring.com.

BACELO, DANIEL ENRIQUE, chemist, educator; b. Buenos Aires, Sept. 22, 1966; s. Enrique Alberto Bacelo and Maria Elena Gomez; m. Silvina Ethel Fioressi, Mar. 10, 1968; children: Nicolas Oscar, Mercedes Elena, Lucia Daniela. PhD with hons. in Phys. Chemistry, U. PR, 1998; degree en Ciencias Quimicas, U. Buenos Aires, 1994. Mgr. prodn. Beril S. A., Buenos Aires, 1988—91; rsch. scientist Nat. Inst. Drugs, Buenos Aires, 1991—93; asst. prof. U. Metropolitana, San Juan, 1998—2004, assoc. prof., 2004—. Contbr. articles to profl. jours. Recipient Carrera de investigador cientifico award, Consejo Nacional de Investigaciones Científicas y Técnicas, 2004; grantee, NIH, 2002—04, PR Space Grant consortium- NASA, 2002, 2004, NSF, 2007—. Mem.: Nat. Assn. Equal Opportunity in Higher Edn. (presdl. adv. com. of biotechnology and astrobiology). Achievements include development of combination of statistical and quantum mechanics methodologies. Office: Universidad Metropolitana Av Ana G Mendez Km 03 San Juan PR 00927 Home Phone: 787-758-1477; Office Phone: 787-766-1717 6117. Office Fax: 787-759-7663. Personal E-mail: dbacelo@yahoo.com.

BACEVICIUS, JOHN ANTHONY, V, (JOHN BACE), research and development company executive; b. Chgo., Mar. 8, 1953; s. John Anthony IV and Mary Ann (Slazas) B.; m. Irene Joyce Rooney, Oct. 16, 1976; 1 child, John Anthony VI. BS in Psychology, Polit. Sci., Rockford Coll., 1975; MS in Journalism, Northwestern U., 1982; postgrad., Union Inst., John Marshall Law Sch. Accredited pub. rels. profl.; cert. compliance and ethics profl. Reporter, editor United Press Internat., Chgo., 1974-79; managing editor WCFL-AM, Mutual Broadcasting, Chgo., 1979-80; writer, editor WIND. Group W Westinghouse, Chgo., 1980-81; reporter, writer WBBM-AM, CBS News, Chgo., 1981-82; comms. advisor IBM Corp., Chgo., 1982—91; pres. J.A. Bace Comms., Inc., 1991—; dir. mktg., rsch. and industry rels. Technology Solutions Co., Chgo., 1995-97; v.p., dir. rsch. and knowledge assets Gartner, Inc., Chgo., 1997—. Asst. prof. Northwestern U., Evanston, Ill., 1988-92; mgr. media rels. Zenith Data Systems, 1992-93. Nat. Sea Explorer Boy Scouts Am. Com., Irving, Tex., 1986-95, recipient Quartermaster award, 1972, Silver Beaver award, 1990; Vigil honor, 1971. Gannett fellow, Northwestern U., 1981. Mem. NATAS, Pub. Rels. Soc. Am., Internat. Assn. Bus. Comms., US Naval Inst., Publicity Club Chgo., Soc. Profl. Journalists, Soc. Corp. Compliance and Ethics, Radio-TV News Dirs. Assn., US Navy League (life). Roman Catholic. Avocations: backpacking, hiking, sailing, photography. Home: 252 W Washington Ave Lake Bluff IL 60044-2036 Office: Gartner Inc Sears Tower 233 S Wacker Dr Ste 1810 Chicago IL 60606 Office Phone: 312-612-6548. E-mail: john.bace@gartner.com.

BACH, JAN MORRIS, composer, educator; b. Forrest, Ill., Dec. 11, 1937; s. John Nicholas and Anne (Morris) B.; m. Dalia Zakaras; children: Dawn, Eva. MusB, U. Ill., 1959, MusM, 1961, MusD, 1971; postgrad., U. Va., Arlington, 1963—65, Yale U., 1960, Berkshire Music Ctr., 1961. Instr. music U. Tampa, Fla., 1965—66; prof. music No. Ill. U., DeKalb, 1966—2002, Presdl. Rsch. prof. Dekalb, 1982—86, Disting. Rsch. prof., 1986—; composer-in-residence Institut de Hautes Etudes Musicales, Montreux, Switzerland, 1976; editor for brass compositions M.M. Cole, Chgo., 1968—72. Mem. Ill. Arts Coun., 1986-89, Ind. Arts Coun., 1992. Composer: Skizzen, 1967, Woodwork, 1970, Eisteddfod, 1972, Turkish Music, 1968, Four Two-Bit Contraptions, 1971, The System, 1973, Dirge for a Minstrel, 1974, Three Choral Dances, 1975, Laudes, 1975, Piano Concerto, 1975, Three Bagatelles, 1978, Hair Today, 1978, The Happy Prince, 1978, My Wilderness, 1979, Student from Salamanca, 1979, Rounds and Dances, 1980, Horn Concerto, 1982, Helix, 1984, Escapade, 1984, Dompes & Jompes, 1986, Harp Concerto, 1986, Trumpet Concerto, 1987, A Solemn Music, 1987, Triptych, 1989, Euphonium Concerto, 1990, With Trumpet and Drum, 1991, Anachronisms String Quartet, 1991, People of Note, 1993, Concerto for Steelpan and Orchestra, 1994, The Last Flower, 1995, Foliations, 1995, Bassoon Concertino, 1996, Pilgrimage, 1997, Variations on a Theme of Brahms, 1997, Kimberly's Song, 1998, Dear God, 1998, NIU MIUSIC, 1999, In the Hands of the Tongue, 1999, The Duel, 1999, Songs of the Streetwise, 2000, Music for a Low Budget Epic, 2001, If Music be the Food of Love, 2001, Tuba Concerto, 2003, Choral Fanfare, 2003, The Haunted Palace, 2004, Penny Poems, 2004, A Prayer of Intercession, 2004, A Little Knight Music, 2005, The Song of Simeon, 2005, Triple Play, 2005, Oompah Suite, 2006, Baptism of Christ, 2006, Duologue Concertante, 2007, Berceuse, 2007, Blowout, 2007 (CDs) The Happy Prince, 1980, Laudes: The NY Brass Quintet, 1980, Rounds and Dances: Premieres, 1984, Four Two-Bit Contraptions: Is This the Way to Carnegie Hall?, 1986, Introducing the Bowie Brass Quintet, 1989, Skizzen: American Wind Music, 1990, Eisteddfod: Chamber Music for Flute, Harp, and Strings, 1990, Meridian Arts Ensemble, 1991, Heavy Metal, 1993, 20th Century Wind Chamber Music, 1994, Clockworks, 1995, Concert Variations: Eu-Fish, 1995, Fanfare and Fugue: Contrasts for Trumpets, 1995, Eisteddfod: In the Shadow of a Miracle, 1996, Triptych: Premier, 1996, Praetorius Suite: Jubilee, 1997, Eisteddfod: Garten von Freuden und Traurigkeit, 2000, The Duel: Spring Flowers, 2000, Concert Variations: Obsessions, 2002, Steelpan Concerto: Paul Freeman Introduces Exotic Concertos, 2002, My Very First Solo: My Very First Solo, 2003, Concert Variations: Everyone But Me, 2003, Gala fanfare, Concerto for Horn and Orch., French Suite, Helix, Four Two-Bit Contraptions: The Music of Jan Bach, 2006, Concert Variations: The Real Euphonium, II, 2007; commns. include Tuba Brotherhood, 1977, Internat. Trumpet Guild, 1978, 86, Internat. Brass Congress, 1980, Greenwich Philharmonia, 1981, Orch. of Ill., 1982, NACWPI, 1982, Minot Symphony, 1984, Am. Brass Quintet-Chamber Music Am., 1988, Sacramento Symphony-N.C. Symphony, 1989, Camarata Singers, 1991, WFMT-Vermeer Quartet, 1991, Woodstock Chimes Fund, 1994, Ronen Chamber Ensemble, 1994, Stockholm Chamber Brass, 1994, Eileen Gress-N.C. Symphony, 1995, Elmhurst Symphony, 1996, Ramon Parcells, 1996, Palos Park Cmty. Chorale, 1997, Cantori of Hobart and William Smith Colls., 1998, No. Ill. Children's Chorus, 1999, South Bend Chamber Singers, 1999, Robert Sims, 1999, Regina H. Helcher, 2000, Jeff Nesseth, 2001, Jay Hunsberger-Fla. West Coast Symphony, 2002, Gloria Musicae, 2003, Diane Ragains, 2004, Kaneland Cmty. Schs., 2005, Zephyr Brass Trio, 2005, Walker Bowman, 2005, Internat. Double Reed Soc., Nebr. Brass, others. With US Army, 1962—65. Recipient BMI student composers 1st prize, 1957, Koussevitsky composition award, 1961, Harvey Gaul composition award, 1973, Mannes Opera award, 1973, Pulitzer prize nomination, 1973, 81, 82, 84, 92, SAI composition award, 1974, Excellence in Tchg. award No. Ill. U., 1978, choral composition award Brown U., 1978, Nebr. Sinfonia Chamber Orch. contest, 1979, N.Y.C. Opera contest, 1980; named to Fox Valley Arts Hall of Fame, 2004. Mem. Broadcast Music, Phi Eta Sigma, Phi Mu Alpha, Phi Kappa Phi, Pi Kappa Lambda, Omicron Delta Kappa. Office Phone: 630-513-7166. E-mail: janbach@janbach.com.

BACH, MARY IRENE, music educator; b. Dallas, Nov. 25, 1944; d. Forrest Bedford McCord, Sr. and Mary Estelle McCord; children: Kari Lynn Glasco, Kent McCord Glasco;. MusB in Edn., Sam Houston State U., Huntsville, Tex., 1967. Cert. tchr. Tex. Edn. Agy., 1967. Dallas Cowboys cheerleader, 1960—62; music tchr., choir dir. Conroe ISD - Elem. Pub. Schs., Tex., 1967—81; asst. dir. choir, accompanist Conroe ISD - McCullough H.S., The Woodlands, 1981—84; tchr. music, choir dir. Conroe ISD - Intermediate Sch., 1984—. Ch. organist, accompanist various schs., 1967—2007; accompanist civic choir Montgomery County Choral Soc., 1984—2000; ch. organist, accompanist First Presbyn. Ch., 2002—; Kodaly clinician Tex. schs., 1977—84; performer Studio One Singers, Conroe and The Woodlands, 1982—; music dir. little theatre Crighton Playhouse, Conroe, 1987—2006; singer Conroe Chorale - Civic Choir, 1998—2004. Recipient Tchr. Yr., Wilkerson Intermediate Sch. - ConroeISD, 1985, Reaves Intermediate Sch. - ConroeISD, 2000; scholar, Sam Houston State U., 1963—67, Dallas Rotary Club, 1963; Powell scholar, Sam Houston State U., Music Dept., 1966. Mem.: Orgn. Am. Kodaly Educators (assoc.), Gulf Coast Orff Assn. (assoc.), Tex. Choral Dirs. Assn. (assoc.; ways and means com. 2005—06), Orgn. Am. Kodaly Educators (assoc.), Kodaly Educators Tex. (assoc.), Assn. Tex. Profl. Educators (assoc.), Tex. Music Educators Assn. (assoc.), Delta Kappa Gamma (hon.; music dir. 1983—99). Methodist. Avocations: travel, scrapbooks, gardening, snorkeling.

BACH, RICHARD GORDON, internist, cardiologist, educator; b. 1956; BS in Biology, Georgetown U., 1977; MD, NYU, 1984. Resident internal medicine NYU Med. Ctr., NYC, 1984-87, fellow cardiology, 1987-91; dir. CCU St. Louis U. Hosp., 1997—99, Barnes-Jewish Hosp., St. Louis, 1999—. Assoc. prof. medicine St. Louis U. Hosp., 1996-99, Washington U. Sch. Medicine, St. Louis, 1999—. Fellow Am. Coll. Cardiology, Soc. for

Cardiac Angiography and Interventions; mem. ACP, Am. Fedn. Clin. Rsch. Office: Box 8086 660 S Euclid Ave Saint Louis MO 63110 Office Phone: 314-362-1963. E-mail: rbach@wustl.edu.

BACH, ROBERT J. (ROBBIE BACH), information technology executive; b. Peoria, Ill., Dec. 31, 1961; m. Pauline Bach; 3 children. BA in Econ., U. NC, Chapel Hill, 1984; MBA, Stanford U., 1988. Fin. analyst Morgan Stanley & Co.; with Microsoft Corp., Redmond, Wash., 1988—, bus. ops. mgr., Microsoft Europe, 1990—92, v.p. mktg., desktop applications divsn., v.p., learning, entertainment, & productivity divsn., 1996—99, v.p., home and retail, 1999—2000, sr. v.p. games divsn., chief Xbox officer, 2000—05, pres., entertainment & devices divsn., 2005—. Co-leader Microsoft Consumer Leadership Team. Chmn. Microsoft Giving Campaign, Bellevue Boys and Girls Club. Mem.: Entertainment Software Assn. (chmn.). Office: Microsoft Corp One Microsoft Way Redmond WA 98052-6399*

BACH, THOMAS HANDFORD, lawyer, investor; b. Vineland, NJ, Dec. 25, 1928; s. Albert Ludwig and Edith May (Handford) B. AB, Rutgers U., 1950; LLB, Harvard U., 1956. Bar: N.Y. State bar 1957. Assoc. firm Hawkins, Delafield & Wood, NYC, 1956—61, Reed, Hoyt, Washburn & McCarthy, NYC, 1961—62; ptnr. Bach & Condren, NYC, 1963—71, Bach & McAuliffe, NYC, 1971—79, Stroock & Stroock & Lavan, NYC, 1979—88, Sullivan & Donovan, NYC, 1989—2000, of counsel, 2000—02, Sullivan, Donovan & Gentile, NYC, 2002—03, Gentile & Turpen, NYC, 2003—05; arbitrator Nat. Assn. of Securities Dealers Reg., NYC, 2000—. Co-counsel N.Y. State Senate Housing and Urban Devel. Com., 1971; fiscal cons. N.Y.C. Fin. Adminstrn., 1967-70; asst. counsel State Fin. Com., N.Y. State Constl. Conv. of, 1967; del. U.S./Japan Bilateral Session, 1988, Moscow Conf. on Law and Bilateral Econ. Rels., 1990; spkr. Practicing Law Inst., Mcpl. Bond Workshop, N.Y., 1995-97. Contbr. articles to profl. jours.; co-author: A Guide to Certificates of Participation, 1991, the Handbook of Municipal Bonds, 1994. Mem. N.Y. State Commn. to Study Constl. Tax Limitations, 1974-75; chmn. subcom. Pub. Securities Assn., 1990-91. Served with U.S. Army, 1951-53, 1st lt. U.S. Army, 1952-53, Japan. Mem. ABA (state and local govt., dispute resolution and internat. law. sects.), N.Y. State Bar Assn., Assn. of Bar of City of N.Y., Market Technicians Assn. (affiliate), Internat. Fin. Svcs. Vol. Corps. Episcopalian. Office: Thomas H Bach Esq 4 East 89th St 5fl New York NY 10128

BACHAND, GEORGE D., research scientist; b. Providence, July 4, 1970; s. George Leo and Jeanie Kramer Bachand; m. Marlene Dennis, Sept. 6, 1997; children: Nicholas, MayLiana. BS, Elizabethown Coll., Pa., 1992; PhD, SUNY, Syracuse, 1997. Rsch. assoc. Cornell U., Ithaca, NY, 1998—2001; prin. mem. tech. staff Sandia Nat. Labs., Albuquerque, 2001—. Adj. asst. prof. U. N.Mex., Albuquerque, 2006—. Named to Frontiers in Engring. Symposium, NAE. Mem.: AAAS, Fedn. Am. Socs. for Exptl. Biology, Am. Chem. Soc., Materials Rsch. Soc., Am. Acad. Nanomedicine. Achievements include research in active assembly of dissipative nanocomposites materials; biomolecular motor-driven capture and transport of viruses and bacteria. Office: Sandia National Laboratories PO Box 5800 MS 1413 Albuquerque NM 87185-1413 Home Phone: 505-796-0624; Office Phone: 505-844-5164. Business E-Mail: gdbacha@sandia.gov.

BACHARACH, BURT, composer, conductor; b. Kansas City, Mo., May 29, 1929; s. Bert and Irma (Freeman) Bacharach; m. Paula Stewart, 1953 (div. 1958); m. Angie Dickinson, 1965 (div. 1980); 1 child, Lea Nikki (dec.); m. Carole Bayer Sager, Mar. 30, 1982 (div. 1991); 1 child, Cristopher Elton; m. Jane Hanson, 1993; children: Oliver, Raleigh. Student, McGill U.; pupil Darius Milhaud at, New Sch. for Social Rsch.; pupil Henry Cowell at, Music Acad. West, Santa Barbara, Calif. Accompanist Vic Damone, 1952, Polly Bergen, Georgia Gibbs, Joel Gray, Ames Bros., Marlene Dietrich; composer songs, film scores, stage musicals Carole Bayer Sager. Composer: Raindrops Keep Fallin' on My Head (Best Original Song Acad. award, 1970, ASCAP award for Most Performed Feature Film Standards, 1988, Academy award, 1969), Magic Moments, The Story of My Life, Don't Make Me Over, Walk on By, Trains and Boats and Planes, Close to You, Anyone Who Had a Heart, What the World Needs Now, I'll Never Fall in Love Again, Do You Know the Way to San Jose?, The Look of Love, One Less Bell to Answer, Alfie (Grammy award for Best Instrumental Arrangement, 1967), Heartlight, On My Own, Arthur's Theme (Best Music, Original Song Acad. award, 1982, ASCAP award for Most Performed Feature Film Standards, 1991), That's What Friends Are For (Grammy award, 1986, Grammy award for Song of Yr., Academy award, 1981), (film scores) The Man Who Shot Liberty Valence, 1962, Wives and Lovers, 1963, Send Me No Flowers, 1964, A House is Not a Home, 1964, Who's Been Sleeping in My Bed, 1964, What's New Pussycat?, 1965, Alfie, 1966, Promise Her Anything, 1966, After the Fox, 1966, Casino Royale, 1967, The April Fools, 1969, Butch Cassidy and the Sundance Kid, 1969 (Best Music for Motion Picture Acad. award & Grammy award, 1969), Lost Horizon, 1972, Together?, 1979, Arthur, 1981, Night Shift, 1982, Best Defense, 1984, Baby Boom, 1987, Arthur 2: On the Rocks, 1988, Love Hurts, 1991, (TV series) Any Day Now, 1998, (albums) At This Time, 2005 (Grammy award for Best Pop Instrumental Album, 2006); contbr. songs Grace of My Heart, 1996, composer music for play Promises, Promises, 1969 (Drama Desk award, 1968, Grammy award for Best Musical Show Album, 1969); actor: The Bacharach-David Song Book, 1970; (films) cameo roles in Austin Powers film series. With AUS, 1950—52. Co-recipient (with Hal David) Trustees award, Nat. Acad. Recording Arts & Scis., 1997; named (with David) Entertainers of Yr., Cue Mag., 1969; recipient 3 Acad. awards, 7 Grammy awards, 2 Emmy awards, Tony award. Mailing: c/o Linda Dozoretz Communications # 996 8033 Sunset Blvd Los Angeles CA 90046

BACHARACH, MELVIN LEWIS, venture capitalist; b. Oakland, Calif., May 14, 1924; s. Max and Ellen Mildred (LeValley) B.; m. Vera Patricia Mortimer, Aug. 20, 1950; children: Kimberly Bacharach Arnone, Craig Ronald. BSBA, U. Calif., Berkeley, 1948. With Levi Strauss & Co., 1948—79, v.p., then exec. v.p., 1973—79, pres. U.S. group, 1975—79, also bd. dirs., mem. exec. com.; pres., CEO Internat. Bus. Sponsors, Inc., 1979—86, also bd. dirs.; pres., CEO VMB, Inc., San Francisco, 1986—; mng. ptnr. Diamond View LP, San Francisco, 1973—. Bd. dirs. Internat. Bus. Sponsors, Inc., Above the Belt, Inc. Patentee in field. Served as pilot USNR, 1942-46, 51-53. Decorated Air medal. Mem. U. Calif. Bus. Adminstrn. Alumni Assn., Beta Gamma Sigma, Pi Lambda Phi. Clubs: Marine Meml., Palm Valley Country Club.

BACHE, ROBERT JAMES, physician, educator; MD, Harvard U. Diplomate Am. Bd. Internal Medicine, Am. Bd. Cardiovasc. Disease. Resident in internal medicine Duke U., Durham, NC, assoc. prof. medicine; prof. medicine U. Minn., Mpls. Contbr. articles to profl. jours. Fellow Am. Coll. Cardiology; mem. Am. Soc. for Clin. Investigation, Assn. of Am. Physicians, Assn. Univ. Cardiologists, Am. Heart Assn. Office: U Minn Med Sch Med Box 508 Mayo 420 Delaware St SE Minneapolis MN 55455-0374 Office Phone: 612-624-8970. Business E-Mail: bache001@umn.edu.

BACHELDER, BEVERLY BRANDT, secondary school educator, assistant principal, director; b. Fort Dodge, Iowa, June 24, 1954; d. Olaf Ottesen and Eleanor Berg Brandt; m. Robert Stephen Bachelder, Sept. 17, 1977; children: Stephen Edward, Elizabeth Margrethe. BA, Luther Coll., Decorah, Iowa, 1976; MusM, Yale U., New Haven, Conn., 1978; MA in Modern English Lit., U. Kent, Eng., 1979. Lic. asst. prin., secondary tchr., tchr. K-12 vocal music, 7-12 English Mass. Vocal music tchr. Douglas Sch. Sys., Mass., 1980—81; dir. music Zion Luth. Ch., Worcester, Mass., 1980—97; English lang. arts tchr. Douglas Jr., Sr. HS, 1982—2004; dir. music First Congl. Ch., Auburn, Mass., 1997—2000; English dept. chair Douglas HS, 2003—04, acting asst. prin., 2004—05, asst. prin., 2005—06, dir. curriculum and instrn., 2006—, title I dir., 2006—. Co-founder, advisor Nat. Jr. Honor Soc., Roberta Wagner Chpt., 1990—2003; organist, choir dir. Christ Episcopal Ch., Rochdale, Mass., 2000—; co-chair accreditation steering com. New Eng. Assn. Schs. and Colls., 2002—06. Mem. First Congl. Ch., Oxford, Mass., 1984. Finalist Mass. Tchr. of Yr. award, Mass. Dept. Edn., 1986; recipient Internat. Understanding award, Rotary Found., 1978-79, Douglas Tchr. of Yr. award, Douglas Jr./Sr. HS, 1986, Horace Mann Tchr. award, 1986-87. Mem.: ASCD, Nat. Assn. Secondary Sch. Prins., Am. Guild of Organists, Mass. Secondary Schs. Adminstrs.' Assn. Home: PO Box 67 North Oxford MA 01537 Office: Douglas Pub Schs 21 Davis St Douglas MA 01516 Home Phone: 508-987-5131; Office Phone: 508-476-4065. Personal E-mail: bjbach@charter.net.

BACHELDER, CHERYL ANNE, former food service company executive; b. Columbus, Ohio, May 4, 1956; d. Max Edwin and Margaret Anne Stanton; m. Christopher Frank Bachelder, June 13, 1981; 2 children. BS, Ind. U., 1977, MBA, 1978. Asst. product mgr. Procter & Gamble Co., Cin., 1978-81; product mgr. The Gillette Co., Boston, 1981-84; sr. product mgr. R.J.R. Nabisco, Planters Life Savers Co., Parsippany, N.J., 1984, group product mgr., 1985-87, dir. mktg. Winston-Salem, NC, 1987, v.p. mktg., 1988-91; v.p., gen. mgr. Life Savers Div., Nabisco Foods Group, 1991-92; pres. Bachelder & Assoc., 1992-95; v.p. mktg. & product devel. Domino's Pizza, Inc., Ann Arbor, Mich., 1995—2001; pres., chief concept officer KFC Corp., divsn. Yum! Brands, 2001—03. Bd. dirs. True Value Co., 2006—, AFC Enterprises, Inc., 2006—. Named one of 100 Best and Brightest Women in Advt. Advt. Age mag., Chgo., 1988; featured in Fortune Mag. People to Watch column, 1990.*

BACHELDER, JOSEPH ELMER, III, lawyer; b. Fulton, Mo., Nov. 13, 1932; s. Joseph Elmer and Frances Evelyn (Gray) B.; m. Louise Este Mason, June 12, 1955; children: Louise Stewart Bachelder Alcock, Christina Cathryn Bachelder Dufresne, Hilary Houston. BA magna cum laude, Yale U., 1955; LLB, Harvard U., 1958. Bar: NY 1959. Assoc. Mudge, Rose, Guthrie & Alexander, NYC, 1958-67, McKinsey and Co., Inc., NYC, 1967-69; ptnr. Satterlee and Stephens, NYC, 1969-72, Leboeuf, Lamb, Lieby & MacRae, NYC, 1972-80; founder, sr. ptnr. Law Offices of Joseph E. Bachelder, NYC, 1980—; chmn. The Bachelder Group, Inc., 1989—. Lectr. NYU Ann. Inst. on Fed. Taxation, 1972—74, Practicing Law Inst., 1977—80, 2000, Am. Law Inst., 1980, 97, 99, The Conf. Bd., 1986, 2004—06; spkr. Academia Symposia, 1999—2006; mem. adv. bd. Program on Corp. Governance Harvard Law Sch. Co-author, editor: Employee Stock Ownership Plans, 1979, 99-06; columnist NY Law Jour. 1977—. Mem. Princeton Twp. Zoning Bd., NJ, 1981-82; trustee Concord Acad., Mass., 1986-92. Fellow Am. Coll. Tax Counsel; mem. ABA, N.Y. State Bar Assn., Assn. of Bar of N.Y.C. Clubs: The Down Town Assn. (N.Y.), Yale Club N.Y.; Bedens Brook (Princeton), Nassau (Princeton); Siasconset Casino (Nantucket, Mass.). Republican. Congregationalist. Home: 226 Constitution Dr Princeton NJ 08540-6712 Office: 780 3rd Ave New York NY 10017-2024

BACHELDER, ROBERT STEPHEN, minister; b. Middletown, NY, Nov. 2, 1951; s. Stephen and Dorothy Esther (Gunderson) B.; m. Beverly June Brandt, Sept. 17, 1977; children: Stephen, Elizabeth. AB, Dartmouth Coll., 1973; MDiv, Yale U., 1978. Ordained to ministry United Ch. of Christ, 1978. Money markets trader RI Hosp. Trust Nat. Bank, Providence, 1973-75; pastor United Ref. Ch., Pangbourne, England, 1978-79; min. 1st Congl. Ch., Shrewsbury, Mass., 1980-84; min. for mission and svc. Worcester (Mass.) Area Mission Soc., 1984—. Advisor to religious congregations for charitable giving. Author: Mystery and Miracle, 1983, Between Dying and Birth, 1983; contbr. chpts. to books, articles to profl. jours. Vice chmn. Housing for All, 2003—; v.p. Colony Retirement Homes, 2005—; bd. dirs. Mass. Coun. of Chs., 1991—93, Worcester Interfaith, 1992—94, Worcester County Ecumenical Coun., 1992—96, Mass. Conv. Congl. Mins., 1983—85, Ctrl. Assn. Mass. Conf., United Ch. of Christ, 1983—, Worcester Coop. Coun., 1985—89, Accord: The Ctr. for Human Rels., 1991—93, Corx, Inc., 1993—95, WCHR Securities, Inc., 1993—, Mass. Congl. Fund, 1999—, New Am. Cmty. Forum, 1995—97, Pakachoag Cmty. Music Sch., 1996—98, Congl. Christian Hist. Soc., 1997—, Worcester Pastoral Counseling Ctr., 1998—2000, Greater Worcester Cmty. Found. Exec. Com., 1998—, Colony Retirement Homes, 1998—, Worcester Area Campus Ministry, 1998—2005, Jeremiah's Hospice, 2000—, Accion Worcester, 2002—, United Way of Ctrl. Mass., 2000—; chair Bus. Advisory Coun Martin Luther King Jr. Bus. Empowerment Ctr., 1999—, bd. dirs., 1993—99; chair Capital Devel., 1996—2001; mem. City Mgr.'s Housing Task Force, 1990—92; distbn. com. mem. Fed. Emergency Mgmt. Agy., Ctrl. Mass., 1984—86, Housing Ind. Fund, 1989—92, Greater Worcester Cmty. Found., 1994—2000, chair, 1998—2000; bd. dirs. Higgins Armory Mus., 1993—2002, pres., 1997—99; v.p. Worcester Housing Partnership, 1991—93; pres. Habitat Worcester, 1984—86, Worcester Cmty. Loan Fund, 1986—90, Worcester Com. on Homelessness and Housing, 1988—91, Worcester Cmty. Housing Resources, 1993—95. Recipient award Pernet Family Svc., 1993, Outstanding Charitable Svc. award United Ch. of Christ, 1995, Nipmuc Women's Health Coalition award, 1999, Spirit in Art award, 2002, Exemplary Leadership award Nat. Conf. on Cmty. and Justice, 2002. Mem.: Worcester Com. on Fgn. Rels., United Ch. of Christ Ministers' Fellowship (pres. 1982—83), St. Wulstan Soc., Dartmouth Club of Ctrl. Mass. (pres. 1991—93). Home: PO Box 67 North Oxford MA 01537-0067 Office: Worcester Area Mission Soc 128 Central St Auburn MA 01501-2820 Personal E-mail: wamsucc@bigplanet.com.

BACHICHA, JOSEPH ALFRED, physician, educator; b. Rock Springs, Wyo. s. Alfred and Helen B BA, Stanford U., Calif., 1977; MD, Boston U., 1982. Diplomate Am. Bd. of Ob-Gyn. Intern St. Luke's-Roosevelt Hosp., NYC, 1982—83; resident ob-gyn Stanford U. Hosp., Palo Alto, Calif., 1983—86; pvt. practice Chgo., 1986—95; asst. prof. ob-gyn U. Calif., San Francisco, 1996—97, assoc. prof., 1997—99; med. dir. Pacific Occupl. Health Med. Assocs., South San Francisco, 1999—2003; sr. physician Kaiser Permanente, 2000—, chief, patient edn. and health promotion Hayward, Calif., 2004—. Cons. WHO, UN Family Planning Assn.; asst. prof. Northwestern U., Chgo., 1986-95; Gen. Hosp., 1996-99, dir. student edn. dept. ob-gyn., San Francisco, 1995-99, dir. obstetrics, 1998-99; dir. Excelsior Group Health Care for Women and Children, San Francisco, 1995-99; dir. low-risk obstetrics, coord. undergrad. med. edn. Prentice Women's Hosp., Chgo., 1990-95; mem. Liaison Com. on Med. Edn.; physician, educator Carnegie Found., Ghana, 1989, Project Hope, Nicaragua, 1992 Contbr. articles to profl. jours. Mem. Chgo. Coun. Fgn. Rels Grad. fellow Rotary Found., 1980; mem. Harvard Macy Scholars Inst., 1995 Fellow ACOG, Assn. Profs. Gynecology and Obstetrics, Internat. Coll. Surgeons, Royal Soc. Medicine; mem. AMA, APHA, Nat. Bd. Med. Examiners (bd. dirs.), Am. Assn. Maternal and Neonatal Health, Am. Fertility Soc., Chgo. Gynecol. Soc., San Mateo County Med. Soc., Stanford U. Alumni Assn., Boston U. Sch. Medicine Alumni Assn., Commonwealth Club Calif Roman Catholic. Avocations: mystery books, cross country skiing, weight training, running, aerobics. Office: 27400 Hesperian Blvd Hayward CA 94545 Business E-Mail: joseph.bachicha@kp.org.

BACHMAN, ARTHUR, lawyer; b. Phila., Nov. 18, 1947; s. Stanley Bachman and Ann (Rosen) Flashner; div.; children: Helene, Allison. BBA, Temple U., 1969, JD, 1972, postgrad., 1980. Bar: Pa. 1972. Atty., advisor legis./regulations divsn. Office Chief Coun. IRS, Washington, 1972—76; assoc. Fox, Rothschild, O'Brien & Frankel, 1976—79; ptnr. Blank Rome L.L.P., Phila., 1979—. Instr. Am. Coll., 1986, 88, Temple U., 1988; lectr. Estate Planning Coun. Lehigh Valley, 1983, C. of C. of Cherry Hill, N.J., 1985, Nat. Conf. CPA Practitioners, 1988, Am. Soc. Pension Actuaries, 1988, Internat. Soc. Employee Benefit Specialists, 1991; guest spkr. Harry S. Gross radio program Sta. WCAU, 1987, 88, 89. Co-author: (booklets) The REA's Joint and Survivor Annuity Rules--Coping with the Regulations, 1986, How to Defer Income with IRA's and Sec. 401(k) Plans, 1987, Evaluation of Probable Impact of Proposed Nondiscrimination Regs: An Interview with 8 Pension Experts, 1990, An Evaluation of the Proposed Regulations on Separate Lines of Business, 1991, ERISA: A Comprehensive Guide, 1991-97, A Second Look at Final Regulations on FICA and FUTA Tax on Non-Qualified Deferred Compensation; contbr. articles to jours., chpts. to books. Mem. Pa. Bar Assn. (lectr. 2001), Phila. Bar Assn., Am. Soc. Pension Profls. and Actuaries Benefits Coun. Del. Valley (bd. dirs. 1997—, lectr. 2001, 04, v.p. of bd. dirs.), Phi Alpha Delta, Alpha Epsilon Pi, Beta Gamma Sigma. Office: Blank Rome LLP Fls 2-13 One Logan Square Philadelphia PA 19103-2521 Home Phone: 215-988-9922; Office Phone: 215-569-5715. E-mail: Bachman@BlankRome.com.

BACHMAN, DAVID CHRISTIAN, orthopedic surgeon; b. Peoria, Ill., Apr. 11, 1934; s. Leland Alvin and Elsie May (Springer) B.; m. Betty June Foster, Sept. 9, 1956; children: Lynne Allison, Laura; m. Karen Jean McDaniel, Oct. 21, 2006. BA, Goshen Coll., 1958; MD, Northwestern U., 1962. Intern Cook County Hosp., Chgo., 1962-63; resident in orthopaedic surgery Northwestern U. Med. Sch., 1963-67; practice medicine specializing in orthopaedic surgery Chgo., 1967-80; practice specializing in ski injuries, 1980-93; with Mountain Med. Services, Telluride, Colo., 1982-87, Ouray Mountain Rescue Team, Inc., Ouray Med. Ctr., Ouray, Colo.; coroner Ouray County, Colo., 1982-93; mem. staffs Northwestern Meml. Hosp., Children's Meml. Hosp., Grant hosp., Chgo., 1967-80, Montrose Meml. Hosp., Colo., 1984-93; med. cons. Western Area U.S. Postal Svc. Dir. Ctr. for Sports Medicine, Northwestern U. Med. Sch., 1978-80; team physician Chgo. Bulls, Nat. Basketball Assn., 1967-80; asst. prof. dept. orthop. surgery Northwestern U. Med. Sch., 1967-80; syndicated columnist on sports medicine Dr. Jock, 1976-90; cons. Western area U.S. Postal Svc., 1996-97; sr. area med. dir. Western Area U.S. Postal Svc., 1997-2002, Pacific Arae U.S. Postal Svc., 2002-06, nat. med. adminstr. U.S. Postal Svc., 2006—. Author: (with Marilyn Preston) Dear Doctor Jock.The Peoples Guide to Sports and Fitness, 1980, (with others) The Diet That Lets You Cheat, 1983, (with Tod Bacigalupi) The Way it Was, 1990, (with Robert Pickering) The Use of Forensic Anthropology, 1996. Elder Presbyn. Ch., 1965—; rsch. assoc. anthropology dept. Denver Mus. Natural History, 1994-99. Mem. ACS, Am. Acad. Orthop. Surgery, Am. Orthop. Soc. for Sports Medicine, Phi Rho Sigma. Presbyterian. Home and Office: 849 W Golf Course Pl Green Valley AZ 85614 Office Phone: 520-388-5202. Business E-Mail: david.c.bachman@usps.gov.

BACHMAN, GREGG PAUL, communications educator; s. Norman and Elaine Bachman; m. Sherrie Teddy, May 29, 1983; children: Shayna, Elayna. PhD, Union Inst., Cin. Prof., chmn. dept. comm. U. Tampa, Fla., 1991—. Editor: American Silent Film: Discovering Marginalized Voices. Named Tchr. of Yr., Coll. Liberal Arts and Sciences U. Tampa, 2004. Office: Univ Tampa 401 W Kennedy Blvd Tampa FL 33606 Home Phone: 727-785-6045; Office Phone: 813-253-3333. Business E-Mail: gbachman@ut.edu.

BACHMAN, HENRY LEE, electrical engineer, company executive; b. Bklyn., Apr. 29, 1930; s. Solomon and Frances (Cortese) B.; m. Doris Engelhardt, Dec. 8, 1951; children: Steven, Diane, Lorraine. BEE, Poly. U., NYC, 1951, MSEE, 1954; postgrad. Advanced Mgmt. Program, Harvard U., Cambridge, Mass., 1972. Engr., mgr. Wheeler Labs., Great Neck, NY, 1951-55, exec. v.p., dir., 1967-68, pres., dir., 1968-70; product line dir. BAE sys. Sensor Sys., Green Lawn, NY, 1970—72; v.p. quality assurance and logistics Marconi Aerospace Systems, Green Lawn, 1973-75, v.p. quality assurance and customer svc., 1975-78, v.p. ops., 1978-84, v.p. engring., 1985-90, v.p. market planning, 1991, v.p. spl. projects, 1992-95, ret. v.p., 1996, dir. tech. mktg., 1996—; bd. dirs. wireless telecom. group, 1999—. Chmn. LI Forum Tech., 1985—86, dir., 1987—; cons. Rsch. Found. SUNY, 2001—. Contbr. articles to profl. jours. Pres., bd. dirs. Friends of LI Mus. Sci. and Tech., 1994-96, 2006—; bd dirs. Huntington Arts Coun., 1994-96; mem. Pres.'s Adv. Com. on Indsl. Innovation, 1979. Named Fellow and Disting. Alumnus Poly. Inst., NY, 1986; recipient Engring. Mgr. of Yr. award IEEE/Engring. Mgmt. Soc., 1985. Fellow AAAS, IEEE (life, Centennial medal 1984, Haradem Pratt award 1995, exec. v.p. 1984, treas. 1985, pres. 1987, pres. IEEE Found. 1994-99, v.p. projects 2000-02, dir. 1986-2002, pres. emeritus 2003, fellow com. 2004—, 3d Millennium medal 2000), Sigma Xi, Tau Beta Pi, Eta Kappa Nu (eminent mem.). Avocations: sailing, opera, piano. Home: 5 Brandy Rd Cold Spring Harbor NY 11724-2401 Office: BAE Systems Mail Sta 1-30 Greenlawn NY 11740 E-mail: h.bachman@ieee.org.

BACHMAN, KATHARINE ELIZABETH, lawyer; b. Harrisburg, Pa., Oct. 28, 1953; d. Neal D. and Helen (Alexander) B. BA summa cum laude, Dickinson Coll., 1975; JD, NYU, 1978. Bar: Mass. 1978. Sr. ptnr., hiring ptnr. Hale & Dorr, Boston, 1978—2004; ptnr., vice chmn. Real Estate dept. Wilmer Cutler Pickering Hale & Dorr, Boston, 2004—. Bd. dirs. Greater Boston Legal Services. Editor (articles): Annual Survey of Am. Law. Mem. single family adv. com. Mass. Housing Fin. Agy., Boston, 1985-90; trustee Dickinson Coll., Carlisle, Pa., 1987-2005; mem. New Eng. Adv. Com. Trust for Pub. Land; past chmn. Develop. & Fin. Task Force Boston 2000; past mem. exec. com. Mass. chpt. Nat Assn. Indsl. & Office Properties. Named a Mass. Super Lawyer, Boston Mag., 2004; named one of Top 50 Female Mass. Lawyers, 2004; Root Tilden scholar. Mem. Am. Coll. Real Estate Lawyers, Mass. Bar Assn., Boston Bar Assn., New Eng. Women in Real Estate (past pres.), Phi Beta Kappa. Office: Wilmer Cutler Pickering Hale & Dorr 60 State St Boston MA 02109-1816 Office Phone: 617-526-6216. Office Fax: 617-526-5000. Business E-Mail: katharine.bachman@wilmerhale.com.

BACHMAN, KENNETH LEROY, JR., lawyer; b. Washington, Aug. 24, 1943; s. Kenneth Leroy and Audrey Teresa (Torrence) B.; m. Sharon Abel, June 18, 1966; children— Laura Ann, Eric Kenneth. A.B. summa cum laude, Ohio U., 1965; J.D. cum laude, Harvard U., 1968. Bar: D.C. 1968, U.S. Ct. Appeals (D.C. cir.) 1971, U.S. Supreme Ct. 1981. Law clk. to judge U.S. Dist. Ct. So. Dist. N.Y., 1968-70; assoc. Cleary, Gottlieb, Steen & Hamilton, Washington, 1970-76, ptnr., 1976—. Mem. ABA. Contbg. editor Oil and Gas Price Regulation Analyst, 1978-83, Natural Gas Journal, 1983-85; contbr. articles to profl. jours. Home: 5332 Falmouth Rd Bethesda MD 20816-2915 Office: 1752 N St NW Washington DC 20036-2904

BACHMAN, MARIA K., English professor; BA in Internat. Affairs, George Washington U., Washington, DC, 1987; MA in English, George Mason U., Fairfax, Va., 1991; PhD in English, U. Tenn., Knoxville, 1998. Asst. editor Telocator Network Am., Washington, 1984—87; mng. editor NOW, Washington, 1987—89; sr. tech. writer GTE Spacenet Corp., McLean, Va., 1989—91, No. Telecom, Raleigh, NC, 1992—93; task mgr./sr. tech. writer EDS/Sherikon, Inc., Frederick, Md., 1991—92; instr. U. Tenn., 1998—99; asst. prof. English Coastal Carolina U., Conway, SC, 1999—2004, assoc. prof., 2004—, dir. Women's and Gender Studies Prog., 2006—. Contbr. articles to profl. publs., chapters to books; co-editor: Reality's Dark Light: The Sensational Wilkie Collins, 2003. Recipient US Prof. of Yr. award, Carnegie Found. for Advancement of Tchg. and Coun. for Advancement and Support of Edn., 2006. Mem.: Babel Working Group, Wilkie Collins Soc., Victorians Inst., Nineteenth-Century Studies Assn. (bd. dirs. 2005—), South Atlantic Modern Lang. Assn. (chair, sec.

mystery/detective fiction sect. 1999—2001), Modern Lang. Assn. Office: Dept English Communication & Journalism Coastal Carolina U PO Box 261954 Conway SC 29528-6054 Office Phone: 843-349-2747. E-mail: mbachman@coastal.edu.*

BACHMANN, BILL, photographer; b. Pa., Mar. 4, 1946; s. Ernest Edward and Helen May (Himler) B. BS, Roberts Wesleyan Coll., Rochester, NY, 1967; MBA, NYU, 1971; postgrad., U. London, U. Calif., Berkeley, Rochester Inst. Tech., U. Pitts., Ft. Lauderdale Art Inst. Freelance comml. and advt. photographer, Miami, NYC, Orlando, 1972—. Worked in over 170 countries worldwide; instr. photography Triangle Inst., 1992, S.E. Ctr. for Creative Arts, Daytona, 1990—; vis. instr. photography at many colls. and univs.; guest numerous TV programs, 1978—; lectr. in field. Prin. works include Miami Herald, 1978-80, Fla. Tourism, 1982—, Sheraton Hotels, 1982—, Gen. Mills Restaurants, 1983—, Olive Garden, 1986—, Marriott Hotels, 1992—, Bahamas Tourism, 1984-, Radisson Hotels, 1986—, Grosvenor Hotels, 1988—, Revlon, 1991—, Harris Corp., 1993—, Sea Escape Cruises, 1988—, Century Club, 2000—, Regent China Tours, 1999—, Burger King, 1988—, Caribbean Travel & Life, 1990—, Fuji Films, 1990—, Far & Wide, 2000—, Nickelodeon, 1989—, Merv Griffin's Paradise Island, Bahamas, 1990—, Kodak Films, 1976—, McDonalds, 1987—, Stern Mag., 1987—, AAA, 1985—, Regal Boats, 1990—, Renaissance Cruises, 1996-2001, Universal Studios, 1990—, Citibank VISA, 1990—, Delta Airlines, 1991—, Am. Showcase, 1991—, Creative Black Book, 1994—, PepsiCo, 1994—, Hilton Hotels Internat., 1992—, NuSkin, 1995—, Pizza Hut, 1996—, Grey Poupon, 1995—, Atlantis Resort, 1996—, Arnold Palmer, 1996—, Home Depot, 1996—, Whale Cay, 1997—, Sandals Resorts, 1997—, People Mag., 1998—, La Quinta Hotels, 1998—, Grand Circle Tours, 1999—, Pitcom, 1999, Saga Holidays, 1999-2001, Regent China Tours, 1999—, Bachmann Tour Overdrive, 1999—, Backstreet Boys, 2000, Cooper Tires, 2000—, Brendan Tours, 2001—, General Tours, 2002—, SIKA, 2002—, Condor Adventures, 2004—, Sony, 2003—, Venus Williams, 2003—, Reebok, 2003—, Sony, 2003—, Smithsonian, 2003—, Vantage Tours, 2004, Kodak World Calendar, 2004, United Way, 2004, Continental Airlines, 2004, Bank of Am., 2004—, Ed McMahon, 2004—, Condor Adventures, 2005, Tauck World Tours, 2006—, Lear Jets, 2006—, SONY, 2006—, Caribbean Travel and Life, 2006, Bank of America, 2006—; dir. TV commls. and videos, 1987—; author: Clicking the Shutter is the Easy Part, 1988, Introspective World, 1996, Welcome Back Berlin, 1990, Bali-Paradise in Indonesia, 1994, Shooting Figure Studies, 1990, Kathmandu, A Jewel Discovered, 1996, One Dream Too Many, 1989, Treasures of the Caribbean, 1992, China's Greatest Resource, It's Diverse People, 1997, Orlando-The City Beautiful, 1998, Traveling After Terrorism, 2002, Travel Hints for Photographers, 2003, Images of Woman, 2004, Send Me Anywhere, 2005, Remember the Joy, 2006, Hilton Vacation Club, 2006—, Bachmann Tour Overdrive: Exlporing Our Planet, 2007; photographer 295-Day Kodak World Photo Tour, 1992-95, Photo Pro Mag., 1991—; photgraphed over 1000 mag. covers; contbr. articles to profl. jours. Bd. dirs. Big Bros.; active Vols. in Action, 1989—. Named Photographer of Yr. Fla. Peoples Choice Awards, 1987, Photographer of Yr. Asia, 1993; recipient Addy awards, 1976—. Mem. One Club (bd. dirs. 1988—), Sales and Mktg. Execs. (bd. dirs., officer), Am. Soc. Media Photographers N.Y., Orlando C. of C. (pres.' club 1983—), Cen. Fla. Photographers Assn. (v.p., bd. dirs. 1983—), Fla. Motion Pictures and TV Guild, Heathrow Club (social dir. 1986—), Orlando Camera Club, Rotary. Republican. Methodist. Avocations: skiing, tennis, golf, writing. Home and Office: PO Box 950833 Lake Mary FL 32795-0833 Home Phone: 407-322-4444; Office Phone: 407-333-9988. Personal E-mail: bill@billbachmann.com.

BACHMANN, JOHN WILLIAM, security firm executive; b. Centralia, Ill., Nov. 16, 1938; s. George Adam and Helen (Johnston) B.; m. Katharine I. Butler; children: John C., Kristene Ellen Bachmann. AB, Wabash Coll., 1960; MBA, Northwestern U., 1962; LLD (hon.), Wabash Coll., 1990. Rschr. Edward Jones, St. Louis, 1962-63, investment rep., 1963-70, gen. ptnr., 1970-80, mng. ptnr., 1980—2003, sr. ptnr., 2004—. Bd. dirs. Am. Airlines, Inc., The Monsanto Co., Nat. Assn. Securities Dealers. Trustee Wabash Coll., Crawfordsville, Ind., 1980—; chmn. bd. visitors Drucker Ctr. Claremont (Calif.) Grad. Sch., 1987—; past chmn., bd. dirs. Arts and Edn. Coun. Greater St. Louis; commr. St. Louis Art Mus.; chmn. St. Louis Symphony Soc.; past chmn. St. Louis Regional Chamber and Growth Assn.; past chmn. US C. of C., 2004-05, chmn. exec. com. 2005-06. Mem. Nat. Assn. Securities Dealers (past dist. chmn., bd. dirs.), Securities Industry Assn. (bd. dirs., chmn. 1976-79), Securities Industry Found. for Econ. Edn. (chmn. trustees 1988-92), St. Louis Club, Bogey Club. Office: Edward Jones 12555 Manchester Rd Saint Louis MO 63131

BACHMANN, MICHELE, congresswoman, former state legislator; b. Waterloo, Iowa, Apr. 6, 1956; m. Marcus Bachmann; 5 children. BA, Winona State U., 1978; JD, Coburn Sch. Law, 1986; LLM, Coll. William & Mary, 1988. Tax litigation atty. US Fed. Tax Ct., St. Paul, 1988—93; mem. Minn. State Senate from Dist. 52, 2000—07, asst. minority leader, 2004—05, mem. capital investment com., edn. com., taxes com., jobs, housing and cmty. devel. com., E-12 edn. budget divsn. com.,property tax budget divsn. com; mem. US Congress from 6th Minn. dist., 2007—, mem. fin. svcs. com. Named a Friend of the Taxpayer, Taxpayers League Minn., 2001—02; named Best Friend of the Taxpayer, 2003—04. Republican. Wis. Evangelical Lutheran Synod. Office: 412 Cannon House Office Bldg Washington DC 20515*

BACHMANN, RICHARD H., lawyer, energy executive; b. Ft. McClellan, Ala., 1953; BA, Southwestern U., 1974; JD, U. Houston, 1977. Bar: Tex. 1977. Ptnr. Butler & Binion, Houston, 1988—93, Snell & Smith, P.C., 1993—98; exec. v.p., chief legal officer, sec. Enterprise Products Ptnrs., LP, Houston, 1999—, Enterprise GP Holdings LP, 2005—. Fellow Tex. Bar Found., Houston Bar Found.; mem. ABA, State Bar Tex., Houston Bar Assn., Order Barons, Phi Delta Phi. Office: Enterprise Products Ptnrs LP PO Box 4324 Houston TX 77210-4324 E-mail: rbachmann@eprod.com.*

BACHNER, BARBARA LAVERDIERE, artist; b. Waterville, Maine, Sept. 14, 1934; d. Thaddeus Eugene and Bernadette Arthemise (Vashon) LaVerdiere; m. Robert Lawrence Bachner, Mar. 22, 1959; 1 child, Suzanne Jouvé. BA in Fine Arts magna cum laude, NYU, 1968; student, Nat. Acad. Sch. Design, 1975-78, Art Students League, 1977-80, 82-84; MFA in Studio Art, Johnson State Coll., 1999. Lectr. Ulster County Art Assn., 1992, Woodstock Sch. Art, 1994, tchr., 1999—2000; co-curator Belmont Towbin Mus., Woodstock Artists Assn., 2002—; panelist Women on Men, Denise Bibro, 2000; juror in field. One-woman shows include Kleinert/James Arts Ctr., Woodstock, N.Y., 2004, Kleinert Arts Ctr., Woodstock, NY, 1992, TAI Gallery, NYC, 1994, 1998, 2003, Fletcher Gallery, Woodstock, 1995, Pen and Brush, NYC, 1995, 1999, Woodstock Artist Assn., 1997, Julian Scott Meml. Gallery, Johnson State Coll., Johnson, Vt., 1999, Studio Dars, Milan, Italy, 2001, Gallery @49, NYC, 2002, Lab. Inst. Merchandising, 2003, A.I.R. Gallery, 2004, one-man shows include Roessler Gallery, Ravensburg, Germany, 2002, exhibited in group shows at Pastel Soc. Am., NYC, 1978, 1980, Five Towns Juried Show, Woodmere, N.Y., 1983, Nat. Arts Club, NYC, 1984, 1995, Woodstock Artists Assn., 1989—, Artists of Ulster County, Kingston, NY, 1989, Pen & Brush, NYC, 1990—, Springfield (Mo.) Art Mus., 1990, U. Tex., Tyler, 1991, A.I.R. Gallery, NYC, 1992, 2002, SUNY, New Paltz, 1992, 1996, Gallery Korea, NYC, 1993, CUNY, Bayside, 1994, Barrett House, Poughkeepsie, N.Y., 1994, Woodstock Sch. Art, 1994—, Krasdale Corp. Galleries, White Plains, N.Y., 1995—96, Nat. Assn. Women Artists, 1996, 1999—2001, Harper Collins, NYC, 1996, The Art Studio, Bearsville, NY, 1997, Woodstock Artists Assn., 1997, Cork Gallery, Lincoln Ctr., NYC, 1998, NY State Mus., Albany, 1998, Dist. Coun. 37, NYC, 1999, Orensanz Found., 1999, Schoharie County Art Assn., Cobbleskill, N.Y., 1999, Interfaith Ctr., NYC, 1999, Biennale Internat. Dell'Arte Contemporanea, Florence, Italy, 1999, LA Printmaking Soc., No. Hollywood, Calif., 1999—2001, Elements 2000 Ernest Rubenstein Gallery, NYC, 2000, Florence New York Orensanz Found., 2000, It's About Time Barrett Art Ctr., Poughkeepsie, N.Y., 2000, Utopia/Dystopia Kleinert Art Ctr./Byrdciffe, Woodstock, NY, 2000, Nat. Assn. of Women Artists, Balt., 2000, Attleboro Mus., Mass., 2000, Denise Bibro Fine Art, NYC, 2000, About Shoes Studio, D'Ars, Milan, 2001, Grounds for Sculpture, Hamilton NJ, 2001, Lankershim Arts Ctr., N. Hollywood, Calif., 2001, Purdue U. Galleries, West Lafayette, Ind., 2001, Roessler Gallery, Ravensburg, Germany, 2002, Poughkeepsie (N.Y.) Art Mus., 2004, Max Planck Inst. Human Devel., Berlin, Germany, 2004, Marshall Area Fine Arts Coun., 2005, Samuel Dorshy Mus. Art, SUNY, New Paltz, 2005, NY Arts Beijing Gallery, Chao Yang Qu, 2006, Karpeles Libr. Mus., Newburgh, NY, 2006, The Tang Gallery, Bisbee, Ariz., 2006, Gaggle Works, Reading, Pa., 2006, William Whipple Art Gallery, U. So. Minn., Marshall, CVB space, N.Y.C., others, Represented in permanent collections Texaco Corp., Houston, Printmaking Workshop, NYC, Kaatsbaan Internat. Dance Ctr., Tivoli, NY, Four Seasons Hotel Corp., Las Vegas, Nev., Nat. Assn. Women Artists, numerous pvt. collections, Monique Goldstrom, NYC, 2003; author: Behind Closed Eyes, 1999; subject of articles:. Travel grant, US Embassy, Berlin, Germany, 2004. Mem.: Ulster Arts Alliance, Woodstock Artists Assn. (exhbn. com. 1991—94, svc. in the arts dir., dir. 1992—95, trustee 1995—2002, exhbn. com. 1998—2002, Dan Gottschalk award 1991, Breth-Borkmann award 1995), Pen & Brush (co-chair graphics divsn. 1994—98, Solo Show award 1993, 1996), NY Artists Equity Assn., Coll. Art Assn., Women's Caucus Art, Nat. Assn. Women Artists (rec. sec. 1999—2000, Medal of Honor 1998, Elizabeth Stanton Blake meml. award 1998), Art Students League (life Concours award 1978, 1981, 1984, Merit scholar 1979, 1983). Avocations: music, theater, travel. Home: 25 Sutton Pl S Apt 19N New York NY 10022-2455 Office Phone: 212-675-4323. E-mail: blbachner@earthlink.net.

BACHNER, JOHN PHILIP, business consultant; s. Barnard and Bertha (Bellar) B.; m. Patricia B. Gartenhaus, June 14, 1997. AB, Harvard U., 1966. Screenplay writer Screen Presentations Inc., Washington, 1967-68; account exec. Hoffman Assocs. Inc., Silver Spring, Md., 1968-71; pres. Bachner Communications Inc., Silver Spring, 1971—. Pres. Bachner Mgmt. Systems, 1973—; exec. v.p. Cons. Engrs. Coun. of Met. Washington, Silver Spring, 1971-96, Property Mgmt. Assn., Silver Spring, 1973-96, Washington Area Coun. Engring. Labs., Silver Spring, 1975-93; exec. v.p. ASFE/The Best People on Earth, 1973—; pres., chmn. bd. Constrn. Industry Tech. Inc., Silver Spring, 1973—; dir. commn. Nat. Lighting Bureau, 1977-; pres. Most for the Lease, 1982—; v.p. Bachner R.E., 1985-97; exec. v.p. Mid-Atlantic Coun. of Shopping Ctr. Mgrs., 1986-93; exec. v.p. Inst. Profl. Practice, Silver Spring, 1988-94, Coll. Property Mgmt. Found., Silver Spring, 1988-96; pres. Cons. Engrs., Ednl. Found. Inc., 1990-99; exec. dir. Profl. Liability Agts. Network Inc., 1991-98, Mid-Atlantic Cancer Rsch. Found., Silver Spring, 1992-95, Internat. Found. Advancement of Thrombosis and Hematosis Rsch. Inc., Silver Spring, 1992-98, Design and Constrn. Quality Inst., 1992-95, Calif. R.E. Inspection Assn., 1993-98, Metro Washington Heat Pump Assn., 1994-99, Intelligent Bldgs. Inst., 1994; pres. Bus. Art and Graphics, 1993-97; exec. dir. Inst. Brownfield Profls., 2005-, Engrs. Leadership Found., 2004-. Author: Marketing and Promotion for Design Professionals, 1977, Guide to Practical Property Management, 1991, Practice Management for Design Professionals, 1991, ASFE Contract Reference Guide, 3d edit., 1996, 3.1 edit., 1998, ECS Contract Reference Guide, 1997, 2nd edit., 1999, RA&MCO Contract Reference Guide, 1997, 2d edit., 2002, Derailed by Dispute, 2003; writer 25 motion picture screenplays; contbr. over 1500 articles to profl. publs., popular mags.; columnist, author contract reference guides, 1996-2000. Pres. Engrs.' Leadership Found., 1999—2003; bd. govs. Found. for Profl. Practice, 2001—04. Home: 9206 Sterling Montague Dr Great Falls VA 22066-4002 Office Phone: 301-589-9121. Business E-Mail: john@bachner.com.

BACHOP, WILLIAM EARL, JR., retired anatomist, zoologist; b. Youngstown, Ohio, Aug. 31, 1926; s. William Earl Sr. and Mary Agnes (Murray) B.; m. Annabelle Adams, Dec. 27, 1958 (dec. 2001); children: Alice Mary, Margaret Anne. BA, Western Res. U., 1950; MS, Ohio State U., 1958, PhD, 1963. Asst. prof. biology U. Omaha, 1963-65; postdoctoral fellow U. Wash., Seattle, 1965-69; asst. prof. zoology Clemson (S.C.) U., 1969-73; gross anatomy studentship Bowman Gray Med. Sch., Winston-Salem, N.C., 1973-74; asst. prof. anatomy Nat. Coll. Chiropractic, Lombard, Ill., 1974-77, assoc. prof. anatomy, 1977-81, prof. anatomy, 1981-96, prof. emeritus, 1996—, also acting chmn. dept. anatomy, 1974-76, chmn. dept. anatomy, 1976-86; ret., 1996. Vis. scientist NSF, Omaha, 1963-65, Inst. Marine Scis., Morehead City, N.C., summer 1972; gen. anatomy examiner Bd. Chiropractic Examiners, Boulder, Colo., 1975-76; summer fellowship NSF, Columbia U., N.Y.C., 1960. Author: (chpt.) Early Embryology of Fish, 1974, Development of the Spine and Spinal Cord, 1995; contbr. articles to profl. jours. Served to cpl. U.S. Army, 1951-53. Recipient Nebr. Coop. grant NSF, 1964, Rsch. associateship U. Mich., 1964, Tuition scholarship NIH, 1973. Mem. Am. Assn. Anatomists, Am. Assn. Clin. Anatomists, Ill. State Acad. Scis. Achievements include research establishing that giant nuclei in yolk sac syncytium of oviparous teleostean embryos contains polyploid amounts of DNA; establishing that respiratory deficient strains of bakers yeast lacked elementary particles in their mitochondria. Home: 1133 S Finley Rd Apt 410 Lombard IL 60148-3872

BACHRACH, CHARLES LEWIS, advertising agency executive; b. NYC, Feb. 22, 1946; s. Herbert and Lilla Clare (Blumberg) B.; m. Lois Susan Davis, Sept. 12, 1968; 1 dau., Jennifer Leigh. BS, Ithaca Coll., NY, 1968. Assoc. producer MPO Sports Co., NYC, 1968-69; unit mgr. NBC, NYC, 1969; with Ogilvy & Mather, Inc., NYC, 1969—, sr. v.p. broadcast, 1978-83, dir. Network and Programming Dept; sr. v.p. network and programming Western Internat. Media, 1983-89, exec. v.p., 1989—; pres. Western Internat. Syndication, 1983—; sr. v.p., dir. network and program purchasing Rubin Postaer & Assocs., LA, 1990-92, exec. v.p., dir. media and resources and programming, 1992—. Vis. prof. Ithaca Coll. Sch. Communications; vis. lectr. New Sch.; guest lectr. UCLA, Calif. State, L.A., Marymount Coll.; guest commentator NPR, CNN, NBC. Contbr. articles to profl. publs. Judge Internat. Emmy Awards.; Lobbyist N.Y. State pvt. colls.; bd. dirs. Caption Ctr., 1992. Recipient Disting. Alumni award Ithaca Coll., 1980, Aid to Advt. Edn. award Am. Advt. Fedn., 1986, Media Maven award Advt. Age, 1996; named One of Top 100 Young People in Advt., 1985. Mem. AAAA (com. broadcast network and programming), TV Acad. Arts and Scis., L.A. Advt. Club (bd. dirs. 1989). Office: Rubin Postaer and Assocs 1333 2d St Santa Monica CA 90401-1100 Home: 2200 Colorado Ave Apt 514 Santa Monica CA 90404-5541

BACHRACH, HOWARD L., biochemist; b. Faribault, Minn., May 21, 1920; s. Harry and Elizabeth (Panovitz) Bachrach; m. Shirley F. Lichterman, June 13, 1943; children: Eve E., Harrison J. BA in Chemistry, U. Minn., 1942, PhD in Biochemistry, 1949. Research chemist synthetic rubber Jos. E. Seagram & Co., 1942; Research asst. explosives research lab. Nat. Def. Research Com. project Carnegie Inst. Tech., Pitts., 1942—45; research asst. U. Minn., Mpls., 1945—49; biochemist, foot-and-mouth disease mission USDA, Denmark, 1949—50; research biochemist virus lab. U. Calif-Berkeley, 1950—53; chief scientist, head biochem. and phys. investigation Plum Island Animal Disease Ctr., Greenport, NY, 1953—80, research chemist, advisor to dir., 1981—89, sci. collaborator, 1989—95. Charter mem. Sr. Exec. Svc. U.S. Govt., 1979; mem. viral and rickettsial grants subcom. Walter Reed Army Inst. Tech., 1982—85; cons. Pan Am. Health Orgn., Brazil, 1981, Coop. State Res. Svcs. USDA, 1982—83; cons. Office Sec. Assessment U.S. Congress, 1984—85, cons. 1988—89, Nat. Cancer Inst., 1984—87, Tex. A&M U. Inst. Bioscis. and Techs., 1987—89; Theobald Smith lectr. Am. Soc. Microbiology, 1981. Contbr. 20 chpts. to books, more than 150 original articles to sci. publs. Named Internat. Sci. of Yr., Internat. Biog. Ctr., Cambridge, England, 2006; named to USDA Agr. Sci. Hall of Fame, 1987; recipient Naval Ordnance Devel. award, 1945, Cert. of Merit, USDA, 1960, Disting. Svc. award, 1982, U.S. Presdl. citation, 1965, U.S. Sr. Exec. Svc. award, 1980, Newcomb Cleveland prize, AAAS, 1982, Nat. Award for Agrl. Excellence, 1983, Alexander von Humboldt award, 1983, Nat. Medal Sci., Pres. Ronald Reagan, 1983, ISI Citation Classics Publ., 1986. Fellow: N.Y. Acad. Sci.; mem.: AAAS, Am. Soc. Virology, Am. Chem. Soc. (Kenneth A. Spencer medal 1983, 50 yr. mem. 1997), Am. Coll. Vet. Microbiologists (hon.), Nat. Acad. Scis. U.S. (Nominated to Wisdom Hall of Fame 2000), Sigma Xi, Phi Lambda Upsilon, Gamma Alpha. Achievements include development of first purification and electron microscopic visualization of polio and foot-and-mouth disease viruses; subunit vaccines--protection of swine with a protein isolated from foot-and-mouth disease virus; reported first effective recombinant DNA cloned viral protein vaccine for use in animals or humans; described comparative molecular pathways of replication for all classes of animal and human viruses. Home: 10220 Andover Coach Cir Apt G2 Lake Worth FL 33467-8137 Personal E-mail: howshy@aol.com.

BACHRACH, NANCY, retired advertising executive; b. Providence, Jan. 29, 1948; d. David and Maida Horovitz. BA magna cum laude, Conn. Coll. for Women, 1969; MA with honors, Brandeis U., 1973, PhD, 1975. Assoc. dir. Grey France, Paris, 1980—84; sr. v.p., account mgmt. Grey Advt., NYC, 1985—91, exec. v.p., 1992—2001, chief mktg. officer, 2001. Author: The Irrefutability of Skepticism, 1975. Named one of 100 Best and Brightest Women, Advt. Age, 1988; named to Acad. Women Achievers, 1992. Office: Grey Advt Inc 777 3rd Ave New York NY 10017-1401

BACHULA, GARY R., federal official; b. Saginaw, Mich., Jan. 1, 1947; s. Joseph F. and Frieda P. Rexius; m. Jane D. Woodfin, Mar. 29, 1984; 1 child. AB cum laude, Harvard Coll., 1968; JD cum laude, Harvard U., 1973. Chief of staff Rep. Bob Traxler, 1975-86; chaired Mich. Gov.'s Cabinet Coun., 1986—90; chmn. Gov.'s Cabinet Coun. Human Investment State of Mich., 1987-90; v.p. Consortium Internat. Earth Sci. Info. Network, 1991-93; dep. under sec. tech. Tech. Adminstrn., Dept. Commerce, Washington, 1993-97, acting under sec. tech. Tech. Adminstrn. Wash., 1997—; v.p. for external rels. Internet 2, Wash., DC. With US Army, 1968—70. Lutheran. Office: Internet 2 1150 18th St NW Ste 1020 Washington DC 20036 Office Phone: 202-331-5373. Office Fax: 202-872-6648. Business E-Mail: gbachula@internet2.edu.

BACHUS, SPENCER T., III, congressman, lawyer; b. Birmingham, Ala., Dec. 28, 1947; m. Linda; children: Warren, Stuart, Elliott, Candace, Lisa. BA, Auburn U., 1969; JD, U. Ala., 1972. Atty., 1972—; mem. Ala. State Senate, 1982-83, Ala. Ho. of Reps., 46th dist., 1984—86; repr. 6th dist. Ala. State Bd. of Ed., 1987—91; sr. ptnr. Bachus, Dempsey, Carson, & Steed; mem. US Congress from 6th Ala. dist., 1993—, mem. banking com., transp. and infrastructure com., jud. com., ranking minority mem. fin. services com., 2007—. Vice chmn. Jefferson County Legis. Del. Mgr. Guy Hunt's Gubernatorial campaign, 1986; del. Rep. Nat. Conv., 1988; mem. Ala. Bd. Edn.; chmn. Ala. State Rep. Exec. Com., 1991. Served in USAR, 1969—71. Recipient Commr's. merit award as Outstanding Rep. Ala. Dept. Human Resources, 1986, Henry M. Somerville award U. Ala. Republican. Office: US Ho of Reps 442 Cannon Bldg Washington DC 20515-0106 also: Dist Off 1900 Internat Park Dr Birmingham AL 35243 Office Phone: 202-225-4921. Office Fax: 202-225-2082.*

BACHYNSKI, MORREL PAUL, physicist; b. Bienfait, Sask., Can., July 19, 1930; s. Nick and Karolina (Bachynski) B.; m. Slava Krkovic, May 1959; children: Caroline Dawn, Jane Diane. B.Eng., U. Sask., 1952, M.Sc., 1953; PhD, McGill U., 1955; LLD (hon.), U. Waterloo, 1993; DSc (hon.), McGill U., 1994; LLD (hon.), Concordia U., 1997. Mem. sci. staff RCA Ltd., Montreal, Que., 1955-58, dir. microwave physics lab., 1958-65, dir. research, 1965-72, dir. research and devel. labs., 1972-75, v.p. research and devel., 1975-76; pres. MPB Technologies Inc., Pointe Claire, Que., 1976—; Scitec, 1974-75. Author: (with Johnston and Shkarofsky) The Particle Kinetics of Plasmas, 1968; contbr. Recipient David Sarnoff Gold medal, 1963, Prix Scientifique du Quebec, 1973, Can. Enterprise Devel. award, 1977, Prix PME Que., 1984, Medal of Achievement Can. Rsch. Mgmt. Assn., 1988, Can. awards for Business Excellence-Entrepreneurship, 1989, 90, Prix award Assn. Que. Dirs. Indsl. Rsch., 1991, Prix Lionel Boulet, 2001. Fellow: IEEE, Can. Acad. Engring. (pres. 2003—04), Can. Aero. and Space Inst., Royal Soc. Can. (Thomas W. Eadie medal 2003), Am. Phys. Soc.; mem.: Sci. Coun. Can., Can. Assn. Physicists (pres. 1968, medal of achievement 1984, Applied Physics medal 1995), Engring. Inst. Can. (hon.). Home: 78 Thurlow Rd Montreal PQ Canada H3X 3G9 Office: MPB Techs Inc 151 Hymus Blvd Pointe-Claire PQ Canada H9R 1E9 Office Phone: 514-694-8751. Personal E-mail: m.p.bachynski@mpbc.ca.

BACIGALUPI, DON, museum director; BA summa cum laude, U. Houston; MA, PhD, U. Tex., Austin. Dir., chief curator Art Mus. at U. Houston; curator contemporary art San Antonio Mus. Art; exec. dir. San Diego Mus. Art, 1999—2003; dir. Toledo Mus. Art, 2004—. Named one of 50 People to Watch, San Diego Mag., 2000. Office: Toledo Museum Art PO Box 1013 Toledo OH 43697

BACK, MICHAEL WAYNE, lawyer; b. Gary, Ind., Oct. 27, 1949; s. Virlan and Eunice Inez (Dooley) B.; m. Deborah Lynn Martinez, Oct. 1, 1988; children: Michael Christiaan, Amelia Michelle, Mark W., Hillary E. BS, Purdue U., 1976; postgrad., John Marshall Law Sch., 1979, 1979. Bar: Ind. 1979, U.S. Dist. Ct. (no. and so. dists.) Ind. 1979. Pvt. practice (atty.), Crown Point, Ind., 1979-87; hearing officer Lake County Circuit Ct., Crown Pl., 1980-87, pvt. practice, 1987--. Sargeant USAF, 1969-71. Ind. State Bar Assn., Lake County Bar Assn. (bd. dirs. 1996—), Ind. Trial Lawyers Assn. (bd. govs. 1996—), Innsbrook Country Club, Merrillville Club (sec. 1986-87, bd. dirs. 1985-93, pres. 1991-93). Democrat. Roman Catholic. Avocations: golf, tennis. Office: Lake County Circuit Ct 1 Professional Ctr Ste 204 Crown Point IN 46307-1882

BACK, ROBERT WYATT, investment company and pharmaceutical executive, consultant; b. Omaha, Dec. 22, 1936; s. Albert Edward, Jr. and Edith (Elliott) Back; m. Linaya Gail Hahn, Aug. 30, 1964; children: Christopher Frederick, Gregory Franklin. BA, Trinity Coll., 1958; postgrad., London Sch. Econs. and Polit., 1959-60, Harvard U., 1960-61; MA, Yale U., 1960. CLU; CFA, ChFC. Head equity trader, reinsurance rep., security analyst Lincoln Nat. Life Ins. Co., Fort Wayne, Ind., 1964—69; sr. investment analyst Allstate Ins. Co., Northbrook, Ill., 1969-72; investment adv. acct. mgr. Brown Bros. Harriman & Co., Chgo., 1972-74; asst. v.p., investment analyst Harris Trust & Savs. Bank, 1974-82; v.p. instnl. rsch. Prescott Ball & Turben, 1982-83, Blunt, Ellis & Loewi, Inc., 1983-84; v.p. instnl. equity sales Rodman & Renshaw, Inc., 1984-87; v.p. instnl. rsch. ins. Legg, Mason, Wood & Walker, Inc., 1987-89; mng. dir. instnl. dept. J.E. Liss & Co., 1989-92; sr. v.p., sales mgr. SNC Capital Mgmt., 1991—; CEO Iposite.com, Inc. Mng. dir. investor pub. rels. CCR Assocs.; sr. advisor Ivy Coll. Privileges; mng. dir. Ivy Coll. Privileges Ltd. Liability Cos., Revenyouniverse; arbitrator NY Stock Exchange, 2002—04; expert witness Nat. Assn. Security Dealers, 2004; exec. chmn. Skull and Bones Coll. Presenters; mng. dir. Sarbanes-Oxley Nat. Pub. Awareness Forum; cons. exec. Pension Protection Act, 2006; sec. 12 Walker Garden Condominium Assn., 2006—; lectr. in field; advisor families and employee groups 401K Adv. Svcs. Co-author: Yale in the Modern World: The Yale Presidential

Succession, Yale in the Modern World: Bush/Clinton/Bush, Big Money and the Presidential Elections, Adult Authors: Big Money Hurting Yale's Future; contbr. articles to profl. jours. Active founding coun. Nat. Edn. Access Fund, 1992; pres. Buffalo Grove Police Pension Fund, 1973—90; mem. long-range planning com. Adlai Stevenson HS, Prairie View, Ill., 1980—82; chmn. investments Ill. Police Pension Fund Assn., Chgo., 1985—87; fund mgr. AIDS/HIV Select Fund, 1992—; mem. corp. Scholarships for Ill. Residents; vice chmn. Wheaton Cmty. Media Commn., 1996—2007; deacon Presbyn. Ch. Capt. USAFR, 1958—67. Woodrow Wilson fellow, Yale U., 1958, English-Speaking Union fellow, London Sch. Econs., 1959, Russian Rsch. fellow, Harvard U., 1960—61. Fellow: Fin. Analysts Fedn. (internat. del. 1974—); mem.: Am. Coll. CLUs and ChFCs (bd. dirs. 1986—87), Inst. CFAs (sec., bd. dirs. Chgo. chpt. 1980—84, lectr.), Am. Assn. Individual Investors (life), Soc. First Divsn. (life), Yale Club Ft. Wayne (pres., alumni bd. mem.), Trinity Club (mem. scholarship Ill. residents inc. 1973—, mem. exec. com. Chgo. chpt. 1987—90, fin. com.), Yale Club Chgo. (bd. dirs. alumni assn. del. 1972—, founding coord. grad. and profl. alumni, Assn. Yale Alumni founding coord. grad. and profl. programs), Harvard Club Chgo. (schs. com.), Am. Legion, Phi Beta Kappa, Pi Gamma Mu. Republican. Avocations: skiing, travel, homeland security. Home and Office: Ivy College Privileges Ltd Liability Cos 225 N Dorchester Ave Wheaton IL 60187-4707 Office Phone: 630-668-3277. Personal E-mail: backfocus_bob2002@yahoo.com.

BACKEN, HOWARD J., architect; m. Lori O'Kane Backen; 1 child, Annie. BArch, U. Oreg., Eugene, 1962. Founder, prin. Backen, Arrigoni and Ross, Inc., San Francisco, 1966—96, Backen Gilliam Archs., Sausalito and St. Helena, Calif. Prin. works include Delancey St. Found. hdqs., San Francisco (Award of Excellence, Urban Land Inst., 1992). Recipient Ellis F. Lawrence award, U. Oreg. Sch. Architecture and Allied Arts, 2006. Fellow: AIA (juror AIA Calif. awards 2001). Office: Backen Gilliam Archs 1028 Main St Saint Helena CA 94574 Office Phone: 707-967-1920. Office Fax: 707-967-1924.*

BACKER, WILLIAM EARNEST, food products executive; b. Fulton, Mo., Dec. 3, 1922; s. William Earnest and Ida Lorraine (Smith) B.; m. Marjorie Jean Keller, Dec. 25, 1943; children: W. Dale, Vicki Lynn McDaniel, Carolyn Sue Cave. BA in Chemistry, Westminster Coll., 1943; postgrad., Wayne U., 1954. Chemistry lab. technician Delco Remy, Muncie, Ind., 1943—44; gen. mgr. Backer Potato Chip Co., Fulton, Mo., 1946—50, pres., CEO, 1957—88, chmn. of bd., 1988—; regional sales exec. A.P. Green Refractories, Mexico, Mo., 1950—51, salesman Detroit, 1951—53; test engr. Ford Motor Co., Dearborn, Mich., 1953—57. Patentee M39-20mm Cannon components, package machine components, socket holder, socket wrench sorter having Braille for the blind. Pres. Fulton C. of C., 1977, also bd. dirs., chmn. planning and zoning; v.p. adminstrn./product sales Great Rivers coun. Boy Scouts Am., Columbia, Mo., 1980-92, also current trustee; chmn. bldg. and grounds Westminster Coll., Fulton, 1990-91; chmn. nominating com. Children's Hosp., Columbia; established Fulton Visitor Ctr./Collector Vehicle Mus., 1996; founding bd. dirs. The Carpenter's Kids, 1999. Recipient Resolution, donation for bldg., Callaway County Commrs., Fulton, 1989, Disting. Eagle Scout award Nat. Eagle Scout Assn., 1995, Disting. Eagle Scout award Mo. Ho. of Reps., 1996, Excellence in Cmty. Svc. award Daughters of the Am. Revolution, 2000; named Disting. Indsl. Developer, Fulton Rotary, 1994. Mem. Kiwanis Internat. (lt. gov. Mo./Ark. divsns 1987-88), Fulton Kiwanis (pres. 1968, Kiwanian of Yr. 1984, 94), Kingdom of Callaway (pres.-elect 2003). Republican. Presbyterian. Avocation: collector of vintage automobiles. Home: PO Box 128 Fulton MO 65251-0128 Office: Backer Potato Chip Co One Industrial Rd Fulton MO 65251 Office Phone: 573-642-5344. E-mail: w.e.backer@sbcglobal.net.

BACKLIN, JIM, legislative staff member; b. Mpls., July 4, 1942; Grad., West Point Mil. Acad., 1966. With mfg. dept. Procter & Gamble; plant mgr. Potlatch Corp., Scranton, Pa.; with Nat. Life Vt.; v.p. Anderson Products Inc.; chmn. Minn. 5th Congl. dist. Ronald Reagan Presdl. Campaign; with office intergovtl. affairs Sec. VA; chief of staff U.S. Rep. Roscoe G. Bartlett. Founder, organizer Cheboygan Mich. Hockey Assn.; active Harvest Christian Fellowship, Frederick, Md. Office: US Rep Roscoe G Bartlett 2412 Rayburn Ho Office Bldg Washington DC 20515-0001

BACKLIN, WILLIAM WAYNE, music educator, composer; b. Mason City, Iowa, Apr. 24, 1957; s. Rodney Joseph and Shirley Ruth Backlin; m. Jolene Kay Thompson, Mar. 20, 1958; children: Aaron Scott, Jeffrey Thomas. A, North Iowa Area C.C., 1977; MusB in Edn., Drake U., 1979; MusM, U. No. Iowa, 2003. Cert. ministrerial Iowa, 1995; tchg. Iowa, 2001. Vocal music instr. Nora Springs-Rock Falls Cmty. Schools, Iowa, 1977—86; choral music instr. Mason City H.S., 1986—92; piano, music theory and history educator North Iowa Area C.C., Mason City, 1995—. Bd. dirs. Ter. Hill Piano Scholarship, Des Moines, 1986—90; project scholar team leader North Iowa Area Edn. Agy., Iowa, 1986; headline spkr. Iowa Choral Dir.'s Assn., Mason City, 1989; edn. evaluator North Ctrl. Accreditation Team, Sioux City, Iowa, 1991, Ames, Iowa, 91; presenter at numerous confs. Composer: (songs) We Who Live in America, Civil War Chronicles, Psalm 145, Nicea, Agnus Dei, Little Bird (Holocaust Memoires), Spirit of the Lord, When We Build, Psalm 99, Daughters of Jerusalem, Kyrie, others, (commissioned choral work) U. Northern Iowa, Waldorf Coll., Iowa Choral Dirs. Assn. (Choral Composition Commissioning Competition, 2005), North Iowa Area C.C.; contbr. articles to profl. jours. Named Outstanding Educator, Mason City Cmty. Sch. Dist., 1991, winner composition competition, Iowa Choral Dirs. Assn./Iowa Composers Forum, 2005. Mem.: Nat. Fedn. H.S. (assoc.). Home: 6 Hampshire CT Mason City IA 50401 Office: North Iowa Area Community College 500 College Dr Mason City IA 50401

BACKMAN, GERALD STEPHEN, retired lawyer; b. NYC, Apr. 16, 1938; s. Morris and Marion (London) B.; m. Susan Pergament, Sept. 3, 1961 (dec. May 1978); children: Jonathan A., Kenneth S.; m. Barbara Fried Kaynes, Nov. 3, 1979 (dec. Jan. 2003); children: Jonathan J. Kaynes, Adam R. Kaynes. BA, U. Pa., 1959; LLBcum laude, Harvard U., 1962. Assoc. Weil, Gotshal & Manges LLP, NYC, 1962-70, ptnr., 1970—2004; ret., 2004. House counsel The Associated Merchandising Corp., N.Y.C., 1965-68; lectr. N.Y.U., 1973, Irving Trust Co., N.Y.C., 1981-88; adj. prof. law Fordham U. Sch. Law, N.Y.C., 2000-05, Miami U. Sch. Law, 2004—; mem. Tri-Bar Opinion Com., 2000—. Bd. dirs. Hewlett-East Rockaway (N.Y.) Jewish Ctr., 1976-97, chmn. legal com., 1974-85, sec., 1980-82; bd. dirs. 25 E. 86th St. Corp., N.Y.C., 1996-99. Mem.: ABA (chmn. securities law opinions subcom. 2002—05), NY State Bar Assn. (trustee bus. law sect. 2000—03, chmn. securities regulation com. 2000—03), Am. Arbitration Assn. (arbitrator), Nat. Assn. Corporate Dirs. (former chmn., pres. N.Y. chpt., mem. blue ribbon commn. on audit coms.), Masons, Phi Beta Kappa. Republican. Jewish. Avocations: golf, skiing, fishing, boating, sailing. Home: 10 Pink Creek Ave 301W Fairfield CT 06824 Personal E-mail: gback16@aol.com. Business E-Mail: Gerald.Backman@Weil.com.

BACKMAN, VADIM, biomedical engineer, educator; b. St. Petersburg, Russia, May 7, 1973; arrived in U.S., 1996, naturalized, 2002; s. Yuri and Galina Backman. MS, St. Petersburg Technical U., 1996, MIT, 1998; PhD, Harvard U., 2001. Rsch. asst. Ioffe Phys. Tech. Inst. Russian Acad. Sci., St. Petersburg, 1993—96; rsch. asst. MIT, Cambridge, Mass., 1996—2000, rsch. assoc., 2000—01; asst. prof., dir. biomed. optical imaging & spectroscopy lab. Northwestern U., Evanston, Ill., 2001—. Cons. MIT, Cambridge, 2001—. Author: Handbook of Optical Biomedical Diagnostics, 2002, Biomedical Optical Engineering, 2002; contbr. articles to profl. jours. Named one of 100 Most Innovative People Under 35, Tech. Rev. Mag., 2005; recipient Best Paper award in New Techs. in Biomedical Optics and Med. Imaging, Nat. Sci. Found., 2002, Nat. Sci. Found. Career award, 2003, Translational Rsch. award, Coulter Found., 2006; fellow, George Soros Internat. Sci. Found., 1995, Lester Wolfe fellow, 1999, Poitras fellow, 2000; scholar, GM Cancer Rsch. Found., 2002. Mem.: Am. Physical Soc., Optical Soc. Am. Achievements include invention of light scattering spectroscopy; tri-modal spectroscopy of tissue. Office: BME Dept Northwestern Univ 2145 Sheridan Rd Evanston IL 60208 Home Phone: 773 404-8219; Office Phone: 847-491-3536. Office Fax: 847-491-4928. Business E-Mail: v-backman@northwestern.edu.

BACKSTEDT, ROSEANNE JOAN, artist; b. San Francisco, Dec. 15, 1941; d. Anthony and Tillie LaRocca; m. Lawrence Henry Backstedt, Aug. 9, 1964 (dec. May 2004); 1 child, Simone Rose. Student, San Francisco Art Inst., 1960-64, U. Oreg., Eugene, 1966-68, Aesthetic Realism Found., 1976—. Mem. Ceres Gallery, NYC, 1991—. One-woman shows include Sullivan County Mus., Hurleyville, NY, 1972, Hansen Gallery, NYC, 1973-77, The Viewing Rm., NYC, 1978, Noho Gallery, NYC, 1987, Ceres Gallery, NYC, 1991—; group shows include Elysian Art Gallery, San Francisco, 1962-64, Portland Art Mus., 1969, Terrain Gallery, NYC, 1979-85, 00, 05, 06, Ligoa Duncan Gallery, NYC, 1980, Krasdale Food Corp., Bronx, 1989, 91, 94, Z Gallery, NYC, 1991-92, World Trade Ctr., NYC, 1991, Triplex Gallery, NYC, 1992, Snug Harbor Cultural Ctr., SI, NY, 1992, Lincoln Ctr., NYC, 1994, Cedco Calendars, 1994-97, JCB Internat. Co., NYC, 1996, Univ. Luth Ch., Harvard Square, Mass., 1996, Mills Pond House, St. James, NYC, 1997, Artemisia Gallery, Chgo., 1997, Künstlerforum, Bonn, 1998, Orange County CC, Middletown, NY, 1998, Soho 20 Gallery, NYC, 1999, Kingsbourgh CC, Bklyn., 1999, Caelum Gallery, NYC, 2000-03, SUNY, Buffalo, 2000, Commerce Bank, NYC, 2004, Walter Wickiser Gallery, NYC, 2005, Noho Bid Blick Windows, 2005; presenter ART TALK, Aesthetic Realism Found., NYC, 1998-01; author: Pathways; art reproduced in Marshall Cavendish, vol. 8, 2005, Krasdale Gallery, 2006, Mass. Gen. Hosp. Cancer Ctr., Boston, 2007. Office: Ceres Gallery 547 W 27th St 2d Floor New York NY 10001

BACKSTROM, C. STEPHEN, communications executive; Degree, Drexel U. CPA. Accountant Touche Ross & Co. (now Deloitte & Touche LLP), Phila.; from founder Tax Dept. to v.p. Comcast Corp., Phila., 1981—86, v.p., taxation, 1986—. Bd. dir. Comcast Found, Comcast Capital Corp. Bd. trustees Medford (N.J.) United Meth. Ch., chmn. fin. com. With US Army. Mem.: Media Industry Tax Group, Coun. of State Taxation, Inst. for Professionals in Taxation, Tax Exec. Inst., Broadband Tax Inst. (bd. dir., past pres.), Little Mill Country Club, Men's Golf Assn. (mem. greens com., officer). Office: Comcast Corp 1500 Market St Philadelphia PA 19102

BACKSTROM, NIKLAS, professional hockey player; b. Helsinki, Finland, Feb. 13, 1978; Goalie Karpat Oulu (Finnish Elite League), 2002—06, Minn. Wild, 2006—. Co-recipient William M. Jennings Trophy, 2007. Office: c/o Minn Wild 317 Washington St Saint Paul MN 55102*

BACKUS, ELAINE ATHENE, entomologist, educator; b. LA, Sept. 22, 1956; d. Henry Floyd and Penelope (Mihalakis) B.; m. Ned M. Gruenhagen, July 30, 1988. BS, Brigham Young U., 1978; PhD, U. Calif., Davis, 1983. Postdoctoral assoc. U. Calif., Davis, 1983—84; asst. prof. U. Mo., Columbia, 1984—90, assoc. prof. entomology, 1990—2002, prof., 2002; rsch. entomologist US Dept. Agriculture, Agrl. Res. Svc., Parlier, Calif., 2003—. Contbr. articles to profl. publs., chpt. to book. Mem. AAAS, Entomol. Soc. Am. (Comstock award 1983, Pres.'s prize for Student Paper, 192, Provost's award for Outstanding Jr. Faculty Teaching 1990, William T. Kemper fellow excellence in teaching, 1994), Sigma Xi. Achievements include discovery and study of the sensory organs that mediate feeding in leafhoppers, understanding how the feeding of Empoasca leafhoppers cause damage to crop plants to develop resistant crops via genetic engineering, research in and development of advanced electrical penetration graph monitors for study of hemipteran feeding behavior, including screening crop plants for resistance and mechanisms of transmission of plant pathogens, especially Xylella fastidiosa. Office Phone: 559-596-2925.

BACKUS, GEORGE EDWARD, theoretical geophysicist; b. Chgo., May 24, 1930; s. Milo Morlan and Dora Etta (Dare) B.; m. Elizabeth Evelyn Allen, Nov. 15, 1961 (div. 1971); children: Benjamin, Brian, Emily; m. Varda Esther Peller, Jan. 8, 1977 PhB, U. Chgo., 1947, BS in Math., 1948, MS in Math. and Physics, 1950-53, PhD in Physics, 1956; D honoris causa, Inst. de Physique de Globe, Paris, 1995. Jr. mathematician Inst. for Air Weapons, Chgo., 1951-53; physicist Project Matterhorn, Princeton, NJ, 1957-58; asst. prof. math. MIT, Cambridge, 1958-60; assoc. prof. geophysics U. Calif. San Diego, La Jolla, 1960-62, prof. geophysics, 1962-94, rsch. prof. geophysics, 1994-99, prof. geophys. emeritus, 1999—. Mem. vist. com. Institut de Physique du Globe de Paris, 1987; co-chmn. Internat. Working Group on Magnetic Field Satellites, 1983-90; chair acad. senate U. Calif., San Diego, 1992-93. Contbr. articles to profl. jours. Guggenheim Found. fellow, 1963, 71; Royal Soc. Arts fellow, London, 1970— Fellow Royal Astron. Soc. (Gold medal 1986), Am. Geophys. Union (John Adam Fleming medal 1986); mem. NAS (com. on grants and fellowships Day Fund 1974-79, com. on sci. and pub. policy 1971-74), Académie des Sciences (France), Am. Math. Soc., Math. Assn. Am., Soc. for Indsl. and Applied Math., Am. Geophys. Union. Avocations: skiing, swimming, bicycling, hiking, history. Office: IGPP U Calif San Diego La Jolla CA 92093-0225 Home Phone: 858-452-8972. E-mail: gbackus@ucsd.edu.

BACKUS, JOHN KING, former chemical company research administrator; b. Buffalo, May 22, 1925; s. Arthur Osgood and Lois V. (King) B.; m. Marjorie North, June 18, 1950; children: David King, Lois Victoria, Laura North Scott, Ruth Ellen Grillo. BA in Chemistry and Math., Hamilton Coll., 1947; MS in Phys. Chemistry, Cornell U., 1950, PhD, 1952. Rsch. chemist Procter & Gamble Co., Cin., 1952-53; rsch. chemist, supr. Gen. Mills, Inc., Tonawanda, NY, 1953-61; rsch. specialist Mobay Corp. (now Bayer Corp.), Pitts., 1962-64, group leader, 1964-67, mgr. applications rsch., 1967-68, mgr. rsch. svcs., 1968-90; ret., 1990. Participant profl. confs. Patentee in field (3); contbr. articles to tech. jours. Chmn. bd. dirs. Bach Choir Pitts., 1969-70; bd. dirs. Western Pa. Safety Coun., 1975-90, mem. exec. com., 1983-90, chair safety and health conf., 1980; mem. Pitts. Concert Chorale, 1989-2000; mem. coun. First Luth. Ch., Pitts., 1978-80, 84-87, 92-93, pres., 1979; mem. coun. southwestern Pa. synod Evang. Luth. Ch. in Am., 1992-97, 2002-05; co-pres. chpt. AFS Internat. Scholarships, 1972-75, host parent, 1969-70, 79; pres. H.S. Parent-Faculty Assn., 1970-71; advisor Explorer Post, 1967-68; chair corp. sect. United Way Western Pa., 1981-82; organizer, dir. Bayer Choir, 1978-90. With U.S. Army, 1944-46. Mem. Am. Chem. Soc. (environ. improvement com. 1990-95, chmn. elect Pitts. sect. 1992, chmn. 1993, dir. 1995-2003, chmn. elect chemists club group 2000, chmn. 2001-03), NY Acad. Scis., Soc. Plastics Industry (chair tech. conf. of urethane divsn. 1977), Sigma Xi. Republican. Avocations: music, gardening, swimming. Home: 9441 Katherine Dr Allison Park PA 15101-2020 E-mail: backusmj@comcast.net.

BACKUS, KERIANN M., chemistry scholar, Latin American studies scholar; d. Ned Backus and Carol Sorbie. Student, Universidad San Francisco de Quito, Ecuador, 2006; BS in Chemistry, Latin Am. Studies, Brown Univ., 2007; DPhil in Chemical Biology, Oxford Univ., 2007—. Vol. sci. tchr. Providence pub. sch. sys. Rhodes Scholar. Achievements include raising guide dog puppies for the blind, vaccinating dogs against rabies in Bolivia; sailing, with family, around world on small boat. Avocations: bassoon, running, bicycling.*

BACKUS, MARCIA ELLEN, lawyer; b. Melrose, Mass., Sept. 8, 1954; d. Milo Morlan and Barbara (Cairns) B. BA, U. Tex., 1976, JD, 1983. Bar: Tex. 1983. Assoc. Vinson & Elkins, Houston, 1983-90, ptnr., 1991—. Mem. ABA, State Bar Tex., Houston Bar Assn. Office: Vinson & Elkins 1101 Fannin St Ste 2300 Houston TX 77002-6910 E-mail: mbackus@velaw.com.

BACON, A. SMOKI, television host; b. Brookline, Mass., Jan. 29, 1928; d. Alfred Leon and Ruth Dorothy (Burns) Ginepra; m. Edwin Conant Bacon, May 11, 1957 (dec. July 1974); children: Brooks Conant, Hilary Conant Bacon Gabrieli; m. Richard Francis Concannon, Oct. 13, 1979. Student, Art Inst. Boston, 1947; grad., Jackson Von Ladau Sch. Design, 1951. Pub. rels. cons., Boston, 1968—; pres. Bacon-Concannon Assocs., Boston, 1979—95, ptnr.; dir. craftsmobiles Summerthing Program, Boston, 1966—73; dir. exhibits Citifair, Boston, 1974; dir. Victorian exhibits Bicentennial Boston 200, 1975, dir. spl. events, 1976; cons. spl. events. Inst. Contemporary Art, 1977—78; cons. spl. events Boston Tea Party Ship, 1976—79; fundraiser Mass. Assn. Mental Health, 1979; dir. promotions Met. Ctr., 1979; coord. grand finale celebration Boston Jubilee 350, 1979—80; coord. Elliot Norton Awards, 1983; pub. rels. Dyansen Gallery, Boston, 1987—88, French Speaking League, 1987; cons. spl. events Jordan Marsh, 1987; fundraiser, pub. rels. Boston Philharm., 1988; coord. 30th anniversary celebration Charles Playhouse, 1988; fundraiser Elliot Norton Awards, 1989; coord. benefit New Eng. Premiere of film Glory Afro-Am. Mus., 1990; pub. rels. cons. Boston Chamber Music Soc., 1990; pub. rels. Paul Sorota Gallery Fine Arts, 1990—91; fundraising cons. Internat. Inst., 1991; pub. rels., fundraiser Brookline H.S. Sesquicentennial Celebration, 1992—93; co-host radio show Celebrity Time, 1980—; co-host TV show On the Town, The Literati Scene. Guest lectr. Boston U. Sch. Pub. Rels., 1979, Mass Polit. Women's Conf., 1983, YMCA, 1986, ARC, 1987, Radcliffe Coll. 4 O'Clock Forums, 1989, Publicity Club Boston, 1990, Women's Italian Club, 1993, Brookline Rotary, 1995, Harvard Coll. Rotary Club, 1995, Ward 5 Dem. Com., 2004; contbg. editor Design Times Mag. Social calendar editor Boston Tab Newspaper, 1987-90; contbg. editor Design Times Mag.; columnist BeaconHill News, Beacon Hill Chronicle, The Tab, Commuter Mag. Candidate Dem. State Rep., Mass., 1980; Bastille Day chmn. French Libr. Boston, 1994—; local adv. com. Nat. Trust for Historic Preservation; bd. dirs. Boston Lit. Hour, Artvision; host parents com. Harvard Coll.; bd. dirs. Mugar Libr., Spl. Collections, 1994—; vis. com. Mus. Fine Arts, Egyptian Dept., 1994—; bd. trustees Boston Arts Festival, 1960-63; bd. dirs., treas. Samaritans, Boston, 1974-84; art auction chairperson WGBH-Pub. Radio-TV, Boston, 1969-70; bd. dirs. Urban League Ea. Mass., Boston, 1975-85, Elders Living at Home Program, Boston City Hosp. Kids Fund; hon. chairperson City on a Hill benefit, 2007; former mem. numerous civic coms. Recipient Woman of Great Achievement award Cambridge Young Women's Assn., 1991, appreciation award The Samaritans, 1991, Leadership award Friends of Pub. Garden, 1975, Pub. Action for the Arts award, MUSE award Pub. Action for Arts, 2006; named one of Boston's 100 Female Leaders, Boston Mag., 1980, Boston Area Schs. Notable Grad. List Boston Globe, 1994; Honors on 70th birthday Gov. Argeo Paul Cellucci, Pres. of Senate Thomas Birmingham, Spkr. Ho. of Reps. Thomas Finnerman and Mayor of Boston Thomas Menino, 1998; Guest of Honor Womens' City Club Ann. Dinner Dance, 1979; honored Those Who Help Keep Boston's Non-Profit Agencies Alive Horizons for Youth, 1972, Charitable and Civic Endeavors Boston Italian Women's Club, 1995; donated personal ofcl. documents Women's Time Capsule Schlesinger Libr. Radcliffe Coll., 1981; honoree Gibon House Mus., 2003. Mem. AAUW, Harvard Club Boston, Women's City Club. Democrat. Avocation: artistics graphics. Home: 94 Beacon St Ste 1 Boston MA 02108-3329 Office: Bacon Concannon Assocs 94 Beacon St Boston MA 02108-3329 Home Phone: 617-523-1998; Office Phone: 617-523-1188. Office Fax: 617-523-1998. Personal E-mail: SmokiBacon@aol.com.

BACON, BRETT KERMIT, lawyer; b. Perry, Iowa, Aug. 8, 1947; s. Royden S. and Aldeen A. (Zuker) B.; m. Bonnie Jeanne Hall; children: Jeffrey Brett, Scott Michael. BA, U. Dubuque, 1969; JD, Northwestern U., 1972. Bar: Ohio 1972, U.S. Ct. Appeals (6th cir.) 1972, U.S. Supreme Ct. 1980. Assoc. Thompson, Hine & Flory, Cleve., 1972-80, ptnr., 1980-2000; founding ptnr. Frantz Ward, Cleve., 2000—. Spkr. in field. Author: Computer Law, 1982, 84. V.p. profl. sect. United Way, Cleve., 1982-86; pres. Shaker Heights Youth Ctr., Inc., Ohio, 1984-86; elder Ch. of Western Res., 1996—. Mem. Fedn. Ins. and Corp. Counsel, Bar Assn. Greater Cleve., Cleve. Play House Club (officer 1986-94, pres. 1991-93, pres. men's com. 1993-96), Pepper Pike Civic League (trustee and treas. 1994-97). Home: 8190 Devon Ct Chagrin Falls OH 44023 Office: Frantz Ward LLP Key Ctr Ste 2500 127 Public Sq Cleveland OH 44114 Office Phone: 216-515-1613. Business E-Mail: bbacon@frantzward.com.

BACON, BRIAN JAMES, JR., music and liturgy director; b. Phoenixville, Pa., Feb. 4, 1981; s. Brian James Bacon, Sr. and Barbara Ann Salley; m. Amanda Marie Threet, June 16, 2001; 1 child, Autumn Catherine. BA, Maryville Coll., Tenn., 2004. Interim dir. choir 1st Christian Ch., Rockwood, Tenn., 2001; dir. music United Ch., Oak Ridge, Tenn., 2001—05; dir. music ministries Sand Branch United Meth. Ch., Knoxville, Tenn., 2005; dir. music, liturgy Our Lady Guadalupe, St. Joseph, Mo., 2006—. Adjudicator RSCC Acad. Festival, Harriman, Tenn., 2003—05. Recipient Barraclough award, Maryville Coll., 2004. Mem.: Am. Guild English Handbell Ringers, Am. Choral Dirs. Assn., Knights of Columbus (mem. Coun. 571). Office: Our Lady Guadalupe 4503 Frederick Ave Saint Joseph MO 64506

BACON, BRUCE RAYMOND, physician; b. Amherst, Ohio, Nov. 7, 1949; s. Raymond Clifford and Cathryn E. (Fowell) B.; children: Jeffrey Dale, Laurie Katherine. BA in Chemistry, Coll. Wooster, 1971; MD, Case We. Res. U., 1975. Diplomate Am. Bd. Internal Medicine and Gastroenterology. Asst. prof. medicine Case We. Res. U., Cleve., 1982—87, assoc. prof. medicine, 1987—88; assoc. prof. medicine, chief gastroenterology sect. La. State U., Shreveport, 1988—90; prof. internal medicine, dir. gastroenterology divsn. St. Louis U. Sch. Medicine, 1990—. Chair subsplty. bd. gasteroenterology Am. Bd. Internal Medicine, 1999-2003, chair subsplty. bd. transplant hepatology, 2004-. Co-author: Essentials of Clinical Hepatology, 1993; co-editor: Liver Disease: Diagnosis and Management, 2000, Comprehensive Clinical Hepatology, 2006; contbr. numerous articles to profl. jours. Fellow ACP, Am. Coll. Gastroenterology, Am. Soc. Clin. Investigation; mem. Am. Assn. Study Liver Disease (pres. 2004). Presbyterian. Avocation: photography. Office: St Louis U Health Sci Ctr 3635 Vista Ave PO Box 15250 Saint Louis MO 63110-0250 Office Phone: 314-577-8764. Business E-Mail: baconbr@slu.edu.

BACON, CAROLINE SHARFMAN, investor, consultant; b. Ann Arbor, Mich., Aug. 27, 1942; d. Mahlon Samuel and Mary Patricia (Potter) Sharp; m. William Lee Sharfman, Sept. 5, 1964 (div. 1985); m. James Edmund Bacon, Nov. 4, 1989. BA with distinction, U. Mich., 1964; MBA, Columbia U., 1975; MAR, Yale U., 2004. Assoc. Goldman, Sachs & Co., NYC, 1975-80, v.p., 1980-83, Goldman Sachs Money Markets Inc., NYC, 1983-90; sr. cons. investor rels. Burson-Marsteller, 1991; mng. dir. Johnnie D. Johnson & Co. Investor Rels., NYC, 1992-95. Mem. Phi Beta Kappa, Phi Sigma Iota, Beta Gamma Sigma. Episcopalian.

BACON, DONALD CONRAD, writer, editor; b. Jacksonville, Fla., Jan. 15, 1935; s. Francis Herbert and Myrtis Ann (Gunter) B.; m. Barbara Lee Barnwell, June 22, 1957; children— Elizabeth, Jennifer (dec.). BS in Journalism, U. Fla., 1957. Staff writer Wall St. Jour., 1957-61; Congl. fellow, 1961-62; staff writer Washington Star, 1962-63; successively Congl. corr., White House corr., sr. corr. and columnist Newhouse News Service, 1963-75; asso. editor U.S. News & World Report mag., Washington, 1975-79, sr. editor, 1979-81, asst. mng. editor, 1981-88; sr. editor Nation's Business, 1988-89; project dir. Ency. of U.S. Congress, Washington, 1989-95; pres. Fund for the Study of Congress, 1989—. Author: Congress and You, 1969; co-author: The New Millionaires, 1961, Rayburn-A Biography, 1987 (Best Biography award Tex. Hist. Commn. 1987, Best Book award Washingtonian mag. 1987); co-editor: Encyclopedia of the United States Congress, 1995 (Best Reference Source Libr. Jour., 1995). Recipient (with others) Loeb award U. Conn., 1961; award for excellence in journalism Lincoln U., Jefferson City, Mo., 1977, Disting. Alumnus award, U. Fla. Coll. Journalism, 2001. Home: 3809 E West Hwy Chevy Chase MD 20815-5918 Personal E-mail: donbacon@erols.com.

BACON, GEORGE EDGAR, pediatrician; b. NYC, Apr. 13, 1932; s. Edgar and Margaret Priscilla (Anderson) B.; m. Grace Elizabeth Graham, June 30, 1956; children: Nancy, George, John BA, Wesleyan U., 1953; MD, Duke U., 1957; MS in Pharmacology, U. Mich., 1967. Diplomate Am. Bd. Pediatrics, subsplty. Bd. Pediatric Endocrinology. Intern in pediatrics Duke Hosp., Durham, NC, 1957-58; resident in pediatrics Columbia-Presbyn. Med. Ctr., NYC, 1961-63; from instr. to prof. emeritus U. Mich., Ann Arbor, 1963—86, prof. emeritus, 1986—, chief pediatric endocrinology svc., dept. pediatrics, 1970-83, dir. house officer programs, dept. pediatrics, 1981-86, assoc. chmn. dept. pediatrics, 1983-86, mem. senate assembly, 1978-80; vice chmn. dir.'s adv. coun. Univ. Hosp., Ann Arbor, 1981-82; prof. pediatrics Tex. Tech U., Lubbock, 1986—90, chmn. dept., 1986—90, chmn. med. practice income plan, 1989; chief staff pediatrics Lubbock Gen. Hosp., 1986—90; dir. med. edn. and rsch. Butterworth Hosp., Grand Rapids, Mich., 1990-91, med. dir. dept. pediatrics, 1991—95; prof. pediatrics Mich. State U., East Lansing, 1990—95; pediatric endocrinologist Univ. Mich. Hosp., Ann Arbor, 1995—2007, Detroit Med. Ctr., Southfield, Mich., 1996—2001. Coord. profl. svc. C.S. Mott Children's Hosp., 1973-83, mem. exec. com. for clin. affairs, 1975-76, 77-79, assoc. vice chmn. med. staff, 1978-79; chmn. exec. com. Women's Hosp., Holden Hosp., Ann Arbor, 1973-82. Author: A Practical Approach to Pediatric Endocrinology, 1975, 3d edit., 1990; contbr. articles to profl. jours. Capt. U.S. Army, 1958-61. Fellow Am. Acad. Pediatrics (treas. Mich. chpt. 1983-86, alt.-at-large 1995-2001, coun. Tex. chpt. 1986-89, Pediatrician of Yr. Mich. chpt. 2002); mem. Am. Pediatric Soc., Pediatric Endocrine Soc. Home: 3911 Waldenwood Dr Ann Arbor MI 48105-3008 Office: U MIch Med Ctr Dept Pediatrics PO Box 718 Ann Arbor MI 48109-0718 Office Phone: 734-764-5175. E-mail: gbacon4999@aol.com.

BACON, KEVIN, actor; b. Phila., July 8, 1958; s. Edmund and Ruth Bacon; m. Kyra Sedgwick, Sept. 3, 1988; 2 children: Travis and Sosie Ruth. Actor: (off-Broadway debut) Getting Out, Marymount Manhattan Theatre, 1978, (Broadway debut) Slab Boys, Playhouse Theatre, 1983, other stage prodns. include Glad Tidyings, 1979-80, Mary Barnes, 1980, Album, 1980, Forty-Deuce, 1981, Flux, 1982, Poor Little Lambs, 1982, Men Without Dates, 1985, Loot, 1986, (feature films) National Lampoon's Animal House, 1978, Starting Over, 1979, Hero at Large, 1980, Friday the 13th, 1980, Only When I Laugh, 1981, Diner, 1982, Footloose, 1984, Quicksilver, 1985, White Water Summer, 1987, Planes, Trains and Automobiles, End of the Line, 1988, She's Having a Baby, 1988, Criminal Law, 1989, The Big Picture, 1989, Tremors, 1990, Flatliners, 1990, Queens Logic, 1991, He Said/She Said, 1991, Pyrates, 1991, JFK, 1992, A Few Good Men, 1992, The Air Up There, 1994, The River Wild, 1994, Murder in the First, 1995, Apollo 13, 1995, Balto (voice only), 1995, Sleepers, 1996, Destination Anywhere, 1997, Telling Lies in America, 1997, Picture Perfect, 1997, Digging to China, 1997, My Dog Skip, 1999, Stir of Echoes, 1999, Hollow Man, 2000, Novocaine, 2001, Trapped, 2002, Mystic River, 2003, In the Cut, 2003, Cavedweller, 2004, Beauty Shop, 2005, Where the Truth Lies, 2005, The Air That I Breath, 2007, Death Sentence, 2007, Rails & Ties, 2007; actor, exec. prodr. Wild Things, 1998, The Woodsman, 2004; actor, dir., prodr. Loverboy, 2005; (TV movies) The Gift, 1979, Enormous Changes at the Last Minute, 1982, The Demon Murder Case, 1983, Mister Roberts, 1984, The Little Sister, 1984, Lemon Sky, 1988; actor, dir; Losing Chase, 1996; (TV series) Search for Tomorrow, 1979; (TV appearances) Frasier (voice only), 1994, Mad About You, 1996, Will & Grace, 2002; dir. (TV Series) (2 episodes) The Closer, 2006-2007; musician (albums with The Bacon Brothers) Forosoco, 1997, Getting There, 1997, Can't Complain, 2001 Office: William Morris Agy 151 S El Camino Dr Beverly Hills CA 90212-2775*

BACON, LEONARD ANTHONY, accounting educator; b. Santa Fe, June 10, 1931; s. Manuel R. and Maria (Chavez) Baca; m. Patricia Balzaretti; children: Bernadine M., Jerry A., Tiffany A. BE, U. Nebr.-Omaha, 1965; MBA, U. of the Americas, Mex. City, 1969; PhD, U. Miss., 1971. CPA, cert. mgmt. acct., internal auditor. Commd. 2d lt. U.S. Army, 1951, advanced through grades to maj., 1964, served fin. and acctg. officer mainly Korea, Vietnam, ret., 1966; asst. prof. Delta State U., Cleveland, Miss., 1971—76; assoc. prof. West Tex. State U., Canyon, 1976—79; prof. acctg. Calif. State U., Bakersfield, 1979—. Cons. Kershen Co. (now Atlantic Richfield Oil Co.), Canyon, 1979—80. Contbr. articles pub. to profl. jours., scientific papers U.S., Mex., Can., confs. Leader Delta area Boy Scouts Am., Cleveland, 1971—76; min. Christians in Commerce, 1990—; min Kern Youth Facility, Bakersfield, 1983—; dir. United Campus Ministry, Canyon, 1976—79. Paratrooper Brazilian Army, 1955. Mem.: Inst. Cost Estimators and Analysts, Inst. Internal Auditors, Acad. Internat. Bus., Calif. Faculty Assn., Inst. Mgmt. Acctg., Am. Mgmt. Assn., Inst. Mgmt. Accts. (pres. Bakersfield chpt. 1981—82, Most Valuable Mem. award 1981), Am. Assn. Spanish Speaking CPA's, Am. Inst. CPA's, Am. Acctg. Assn., Jockey (Rio de Janeiro), Kiwanis (v.p. 1974—79, A Whale of a Guy award, Cleveland 1975, Plaque of Appreciation 1992—93), Lions (v.p. Cleveland 1971—73), Beta Gamma Sigma, Omicron Delta Epsilon, Alpha Kappa Psi (Dedicated Svc. award 1979). Office: Calif State U 9001 Stockdale Hwy Bakersfield CA 93311-1022 Business E-Mail: lbacon@csub.edu.

BACON, LESLIE EDWARD, operations analysis manager; b. Oklahoma City, Aug. 13, 1972; s. Robert Drew (Stepfather); m. Courtney Luedtke; m. Holly Easttom, Mar. 28, 1991 (div. May 2, 1996); 1 child, James Schuyler. BS, U. Md., Lajes Field, Portugal, 1999. Mechanic Texaco, Midwest City, Okla., 1996—97; security Capone's Night Club, Midwest City, 1996—97; records adminstr. US Govt., Lajes Field, Azores, Portugal, 1997—99; computer technician Dell Inc., Austin, Tex., 1999—2001, tng. mgr., 2001—02, prodn. mgr., 2003—05; gen. mgr. Maxfire Apparatus, Castle Rock, Colo., 2005—06; ops. analysis mgr. Echosphere LLC, Englewood, Colo., 2006—. Chmn. del. Dem. Party, Round Rock, Tex., 2002—04; del. Rep. Party, Austin, Tex., 2004—05; mem. ch. growth com. Christ's Episcopal Ch., Castle Rock, Colo., 2005, co-chmn., 2006—. Sgt. US Army, 1990—96. Decorated Army Commendation medal US Army; recipient Student of Today award, Masonic Lodge, 1984—85, Bronze award World Wide Quality Day, Dell Inc., 1999—2000. Mem.: Mensa. Achievements include member of chasis design team for Dell production. Home Phone: 303-663-2857; Office Phone: 720-514-5053.

BACON, LOUIS ALBERT, retired consulting civil engineer; b. Champaign, Ill., Apr. 10, 1921; s. Harrison Waxler and Mabel Mae (Watson) B.; m. Clara Elizabeth Manny, Aug. 28, 1943; children: Robert Louis, David Kenneth, William Harrison. BSCE, U. Ill., 1943. Registered profl. engr., Ga., Ill.; registered structural engr., Ill. Wing designer Douglas Aircraft Co., El Segundo, Calif., 1943-44; structural designer C.A. Metz Engring. Co., Chgo., 1946-47; chief structural engr. Shaw, Metz & Dolio, architects-engrs., Chgo., 1947-53; chief structural engr., assoc. ptnr. Shaw, Metz & Assocs., Chgo., 1953-66; pres. P&W Engrs., Inc., cons., Chgo., 1966-74; v.p., head Atlanta div. Stanley Cons., Inc., 1974-76; v.p., dir. engring. div. Heery Internat., Inc., Atlanta, 1976-84, dir. mktg. to fed. govt., 1984-89; ret. Mem. planning com. City of Brookfield, Ill., 1951-54, mem. bd. local improvements, village trustee, 1954-59; mem. Glen Ellyn (Ill.) Environ. Protection Commn., 1971-74; pres. Ridgeview Neighborhood Civic Assn., Atlanta, 1980-82, sec.-treas. 1991—2003; chmn. Fulton County Developers Adv. Com., 1981; bd. dirs. Literacy Vols. Am.-Met. Atlanta, 1992-95, 1996-2002, pres., 1993-94; commr. Housing Authority Fulton County, 1995—2003, vice chmn., 1998-99, chmn., 1999-2003; vol. Habitat for Humanity, Atlanta, 1994-96, Atlanta Olympics, 1995-96; vol. bd. dirs. Cancer Network St. Joseph's Hosp. Atlanta, 1995-99, 2003-04; founder, chmn., Ga. Prostate Cancer Coalition, 1998-2004. With USNR, 1944-46. Recipient Outstanding Achievement award Engrs. of Met. Atlanta, 1980, medal of honor Ga. Engring. Found., 2003; named Engr. of Yr., Engrs. of Met. Atlanta, 1984 Fellow ASCE, Soc. Am. Mil. Engrs. (v.p. 1988-89), NSPE (life, dir. 1966-69, v.p. 1969-71, pres.-elect 1982-83, pres. 1983-84, divsn. chmn. profl. engrs. in pvt. practice 1971-72, Chmn.'s award profl. engrs. in pvt. practice 1972, PEPP award 1976, Disting. Svc. award 1993); mem. Ill. Soc. Profl. Engrs. (hon. mem., pres. 1964-65, Ill. award 1968), Ga. Soc. Profl. Engrs. (Pres.'s award Sandy Springs chpt. 1980, Engr. of Yr. award 1982), Engrs. Greater Atlanta (Engr. of Yr. 1984), U. Ill. Civil Engring. Alumni Assn. (pres. 1980-82, Disting. Alumnus award 1985), U. Ill. Alumni Assn. (Loyalty award 1985, Constituent award 1988), Chi Epsilon. Methodist. Home: 1431 Parkview Blvd Stone Mountain GA 30087-6722

BACON, MARLENE PARKINSON, dean, nursing educator; b. St. Anthony, Idaho, May 8, 1949; d. Reid and Leora Virgin Parkinson; m. Jeffrey Douglas Bacon, Apr. 23, 1947; children: Brandon, Natalie, Kevin. BS, Westminster Coll., Salt Lake City, 1975; MS, U. Utah, Salt Lake City, 1984, PhD, 2000. Lic. Utah, 1975. Prof. nursing Salt Lake C.C., Westminster Coll., 2000—05; dean sch. health scis. Salt Lake C.C., 2005—. Nursing dir., program mgr. Primary Children's Med. Ctr., Salt Lake City, 1991—96. Advocacy Utah Compact Higher Edn., Salt Lake City, 2003—04. Grantee, NIH, 1996. Mem.: NW Accreditation Commn. Colls. (assoc.; accreditor 2005). Democrat. Avocations: travel, writing, reading, hiking, boating. Home: 7883 Danish Downes Court Salt Lake City UT 84121 Office: Salt Lake Community College 4600 South Redwood Road Salt Lake City UT 84130 Home Phone: 801-944-0400; Office Phone: 801-957-4569. Office Fax: 801-957-2762; Home Fax: 801-957-2762. Business E-Mail: marlene.bacon@slcc.edu.

BACON, PHILLIP, geographer, author, consultant; b. Cleve., July 10, 1922; s. Hollis Phillip and Emma (Schneider) B.; m. Dorothy Willey, 1951 (div. 1980); children: Laura Bacon Fraser, Phillip Everett; m. Jane Lowrie, 1980 (dec. 1991); m. Sandra Sullivan, 1995. Cadet, The Citadel, 1940-42; AB, U. Miami, 1946; MA, George Peabody Coll. for Tchrs. (now Vanderbilt U.), 1951, EdD, 1955. Tchr. social studies, tactical officer Castle Heights Mil. Acad., Lebanon, Tenn., 1946-47; tchr. social studies, tactical officer Army and Navy Acad., Carlsbad, Calif., 1948-53; grad. asst. geography George Peabody Coll. for Tchrs. (now Vanderbilt U.), 1953-55; dean Grad. Sch., 1963-64; acting dir. Library Sch., 1964; asst. prof. geography U. Pitts., 1955-57; vis. asst. prof. geography Columbia U. Tchrs. Coll., 1956-57, assoc. prof., 1957-60, prof., 1960-63, 64-66; prof. geography and social studies edn. U. Wash., Seattle, 1966-71, co-dir. tri-univ. project in elementary edn., 1967-71; prof. geography U. Houston, 1971-85, chmn. dept., 1973-78, prof. geography and anthropology emeritus, 1985—. Instr. history George Peabody Coll. for Tchrs., 1951; vis. prof. geography U. Colo., 1961, U. Wash., 1965, 79; Jennings lectr., 1963; vis. scholar N.C. Central U., 1966; vis. lectr. geography U. Tex., 1966, NSF vis. scientist, 1970-72; Disting. vis. prof. social studies edn. and geography Seattle Pacific U., 1977-79, vis. prof., geographer-in-residence, Coll. Edn., U. N.Mex., 1993-95; co-coord. N.Mex. Geog. Alliance, 1993-97; mem. editl. adv. bd. World Book Ency., 1965-84; bd. cons. World Book Atlas, 1965-70; cons. editor Golden Press, 1958-61; ednl. dir. Golden Book Inst. Knowledge, 1960-61; cons. book divsn. Time, Inc., 1960-69; cons. social sci. project Ednl. Rsch. Coun. Am., 1962-70; steering com. HS Geography Project, 1965-70; cons. U.S. Office Edn., 1964-71; mem. Wash. State Social Studies Adv. Commn., 1968-71; dir. Follett Social Studies Program, 1980-83, Allyn and Bacon elem. social studies program, 1983-85, dir. Summer Geography Inst., N.Mex. Geographic Alliance, 1993-97; social scis. cons. Harcourt Brace, 1985-2002, Holt, Rinehart and Winston, 1989-97; prof. geography grad. faculty U. Colo., Boulder, 1999-2000; geography cons. Harcourt Brace Elem. Social Studies Program Stories in Time, 1997, 2000, SWAP Project, Colo. Dept. Edn., 1998, Social Studies Texan, 2003-; cons. in field. Author: Australia, Oceania, and the Polar Lands, 1961, North America, 1961, Children's Picture Atlas of the World, 1966, (with Norman Carls and Frank E. Sorenson) Knowing Our Neighbors in the United States and Canada, 1966, Regions Around the World, 1970, (with R.R. Boyce) Towns and Cities, 1970, (with others) The United States and Canada, 1970, (with P.V. Greco) The Story of Latin America, 1970, (with others) America: In Space and Time, 1976, Exploring Our World, 1982, (with Donald C. Fairweather) World Regions, 1983, (with James B. Kracht) Our World Today, 1983, (with M. Evelyn Swartz) Our State: California, 1983, World Geography, The Earth and Its People, 1989; editor: Focus on Geography, Key Concepts and Teaching Strategies, 1970; co-editor (with Lorrin G. Kennamer) Foundations of World Regional Geography Series, 1970; cons. editor: (with others) Life Pictorial Atlas of the World, 1961; mem. adv. bd.: (with others) Jour. of Geography, 1967-70, Social Edn., 1975-78; editl. dir.: (with others) Field Social Studies Program, 1972-73; co-dir.: (with others) Addison-Wesley Elementary Social Studies Program, 1973-80; ednl. cons. The American Nation, Reconstruction to the Present, 1986, The American Nation, Beginnings Through Reconstruction, 1986, Triumph of the American Nation, 1986, World History: People and Nations, 1990, The Story of America, 1994; sr. editl. advisor HBJ Social Studies, K-7, Landmark edits., 1988; contbr. articles to profl. jours., chpts. to books. Mem. adv. bd. Grad. Sch., U. Colo., 1987-93. With USNR, 1942-45. Recipient Teaching Excellence award U. Houston, 1975, 79, 80 Mem. NEA (life), Assn. Am. Geographers (coun. 1976-79, chmn. publs. com. 1976-78), Nat. Coun. for Geog. Edn. (life, pres. 1966, disting. svc. award 1974), Alaska Geog. Soc., Nat., Tex., N.Mex. (exec. bd. 1992-95), Social Studies Couns. (exec. bd. 1992-95), Vanderbilt U. Alumni Assn. (dir. 1979-83), Peabody Coll. Alumni Assn. (pres. 1981-83, Disting. Alumnus award 1986, alumni bd. 1994-95), Peabody Coll. Roundtable, Sigma Xi, Sigma Alpha Epsilon, Phi Delta Kappa, Kappa Delta Pi, Kappa Phi Kappa (life), Omicron Delta Kappa, Gamma Theta Upsilon, Pi Gamma Mu. Presbyterian. Personal E-mail: sanphil@aol.com.

BACON, SYLVIA, judge, educator; b. Watertown, SD, July 9, 1931; d. Julius Franklin and Anne Rae (Hyde) B. AB, Vassar Coll., Poughkeepsie, NY, 1952; cert., London Sch. Econs., 1953; LLB, Harvard U. Law Sch., 1956; LLM, Georgetown Law Ctr., Washington, 1959. Bar: DC 1956, US Supreme Ct. 1963. Law clk. to fed. judge, 1956-57; asst. US Atty. Washington, 1957-65; assoc. dir. Pres. Commn. on Crime in DC, 1965-67; trial atty. spl. projects US Dept. Justice, 1967-69; exec. asst. US atty. Washington, 1969-70; judge DC Superior Ct., Washington, 1970-92; judge-in-residence Columbus Sch. Law Cath. U. Am., Washington, 1993-95, adj. prof., 1995—2002, disting. lectr., 2002—; adjudicator Office of Compliance, US Legis. Br., Washington, 1996—. Adj. prof. Georgetown Law Ctr., 1960-70, 72-74; faculty Nat. Inst. Trial Advocacy, 1973-75, 91-2002, Nat. Jud. Coll., 1974-79, participant, presenter fed. and local jud. confs., 1970-90; bd. dirs. Nat. Ctr. State Cts., 1975-79, Nat. Jud. Coll., 1980-87, DC Law Students in Ct., 2002-; lectr. Am. Acad. Jud. Edn., 1972-82, Nat. Coll. Criminal Def., 1975-82. Recipient Lever award, DC Law Students In Ct., 2005. Mem. ABA (gov. 1988-91), AAUW, DC Bar Assn. (bd. dirs. 1965-67), DC Women's Bar Assn., Am. Inns of Ct., Exec. Women in Govt., Bus. and Profl. Women's Assn., Nat. Assn. Women Judges, Supreme Ct. Hist. Soc., Phi Beta Kappa. Home: 2500 Q St NW Washington DC 20007-4373 Office: Cath U Am Columbus Sch Law 3600 McCormack Dr NE Washington DC 20064-0001 Office Phone: 202-319-6618. Business E-Mail: bacon@law.edu.

BACON, VICKY LEE, lighting services executive; b. Oregon City, Oreg., Mar. 25, 1950; d. Herbert Kenneth and Lorean Betty (Boltz) Rushford; m. Dennis M. Bacon, Aug. 7, 1971; 1 child, Randene Tess. Student, Portland C.C., 1974—75, Mt. Hood C.C., 1976, Portland State Coll., 1979. With All Electric Constrn., Milwaukie, Oreg., 1968—70, Lighting Maintenance Co., Portland, Oreg., 1970—78; mgr. svc. GTE Sylvania Lighting Svcs., Portland, 1976—80, br. mgr., 1980—83; divsn. mgr. Christenson Electric Co. Inc., Portland, 1983—90, v.p. mktg. and lighting svcs., 1990—91, v.p. svc. ops. and mktg., 1991—2000; CEO, owner Dryer Electric, Inc., 2002—. Chmn. Oreg. Ltd. Energy Com., 1993—; vice chmn. to labor commr. Oreg. State Apprenticeship Coun., 1996—. Mem. Energy Contractors Assn., Illuminating Engring. Soc., Nat. Elec. Contractors Assn. (bd. dirs. Oreg. Columbia chpt.), Nat. Assn. Lighting Maintenance Contractors, Elec. Contractors Assn., Office: Dryer Electric Inc PO Box 3514 Portland OR 97208-3514

BACOT, MARIE, management consultant, researcher; b. Jackson, Miss., Oct. 2, 1942; d. James Peter and Marie (Moore) B. BA, Millsaps Coll., 1964; MEd, U. New Orleans, 1974, PhD, 1992. Tchr. Houston Ind. Sch. Dist., 1964-68, Jefferson Parish Sch. Bd., Gretna, La., 1968-86; dir. Ednl. Testing Assocs., New Orleans, 1982-86, Marie Bacot Innovation & Creativity Cons., New Orleans, 1987—. Presenter Acad. Mgmt., 1989, So. Mgmt. Assn., 1989, Decision Scis. Inst., 1990. Co-author chpt.: Understanding Students with High Incidence Exceptionalities: Categorical and Non-categorical Perspectives, 1991; contbr. articles to profl. jours. Recording sec. The New Orleans City Ballet, 1986-87; publicity chmn. book fair New Orleans Symphony Orch., 1986-87; spl. donor chmn. opera ball New Orleans Opera Assn. 1986-87; soloist, quartet/trio choir mem. Trinity Episcopal Ch., 1981-88. Mem. Ctr. for Rsch. in Applied Creativity, Creative Edn. Found., Acad. Mgmt., Am. Soc. for Quality Control. Republican. Episcopalian. Achievements include developer Bacot Orgnl. Learning and Innovation Scale (BOLIS), instrument used to assess orgns. Office: PO Box 15695 New Orleans LA 70175-5695

BACOW, LAWRENCE SELDON, academic administrator, environmental scientist, educator; b. Detroit, Aug. 24, 1951; s. Mitchell Leon and Ruth Wertheim Bacow; m. Adele Fleet, June 1, 1975; children: Jay, Kenneth. SB, MIT, 1972; JD, M in Pub. Policy, Harvard U., 1976, PhD, 1978. Bar: Mass. 1978. Asst. prof. law and environ. policy MIT, Cambridge, 1977-84, assoc. prof. law and environ. policy, 1984-90, dir. Ctr. for Real Estate, 1990-92, prof. law and environ. policy, 1992-97, Lee and Geraldine Martin prof. environ. studies, 1997—2001, chmn. faculty, 1995-97, chancellor, 1998—2001; pres. Tufts U., 2002—. Vis. assoc. prof. law Hebrew U., Jerusalem, 1981-82; rsch. assoc. Harvard Law Sch., Cambridge, 1982-88; vis. prof. Politecnico di Torino, Italy, 1990, U. Bari, Italy, 1991, Gabriela Mistral U., Santiago, Chile, 1992, 93, 94, 95, 97, Faculty Econs.-U. Amsterdam, The Netherlands, 1993-94; rsch. fellow The Tinbergen Inst., Amsterdam, 1993-94. Author: Bargaining for Job Safety and Health, 1980; co-author: (with M. O'Hare and D. Sanderson) Facility Siting and Public Opposition, 1982, (with L. Susskind and M. Wheeler) Resolving Environmental Regulatory Disputes, 1983, (with M. Wheeler) Environmental Dispute Resolution, 1984. Mem. presdl. transition team Occupl. Safety and Health Adminstrn., 1977; mem. socio-econ. subcom. NAS Com. on Surface Mining and Reclamation, 1978-79; advisor Mass. Spl. Legis. Commn. on Hazardous Water, 1980; gubernatorial appointee Mass. Hazardous Waste Facility Site Safety Coun., 1980-83; Town Meeting mem., Arlington, Mass., 1981-83; advisor Israel Environ. Protection Svc., 1981-83; chair citizens adv. com. Mass. Water Resources Authority, 1989; exec. com. One Thousand Friends Mass., 1989-95; advisor Cross Israel Hwy. Commn., 1994-95; dir. MIT Hillel, Cambridge, 1995-98, Jewish Cmty. Housing for the Elderly, Brighton, Mass., 1995—; trustee Hebrew Coll., Brookline, Mass., 1999—, Wheaton Coll., Norton, Mass., 1999—, dir. Am. Coun. on Edn., 2003—. Recipient William S. Ballard award Am. Soc. Real Estate, 1991; adminstrn. fellow Harvard U., 1972-76, post-doctoral fellow Ford Found., 1977; Legal scholar Ctr. for Pub. Resources, 1985. Mem. Am. Acad. Arts and Scis., Mass. Bar Assn., Phi Beta Kappa. Jewish. Avocations: sailing, skiing, running. Office: Tufts University President's Office Ballou Hall Medford MA 02155 E-mail: bacow@tufts.edu.*

BADALAMENT, ROBERT ANTHONY, urologist, oncologist; b. Detroit, Mar. 20, 1954; s. Louis F. and Grace D. (Costello) B.; m. Providence F. Vitale, Nov. 9, 1980; children: Louis F., Peter P., Grace F. BS in Biology, So. Meth. U., 1976; MD, Emory U., 1980. Diplomate Am. Bd. Urology. Surg. intern Henry Ford Hosp., Detroit, 1980-81, surg. resident, 1981-82, urologic resident, 1982-85; fellow in urologic oncology Meml. Sloan Kettering Cancer Ctr., NYC, 1985-87; asst. prof. Ohio State U., Columbus, 1987-92, assoc. prof., 1992-95, prof. Sch. Pub. Health, 1995—; mem. attending staff Arthur James Cancer Ctr., Columbus, 1990-95, Crittenton Hosp., Rochester Hills, Mich., 1995—, chief dept. surgery, 2007—. Contbr. chpt. to book, articles to profl. jours. Fellow ACS; mem. AMA, Soc. Urologic Oncology. Office: Rochester Urology PC 1135 W University Dr Ste 420 Rochester Hills MI 48307-1893

BADALAMENTI, FRED LEOPOLDO, artist, educator; b. Long Island City, NY, June 25, 1935; s. Leopoldo and Concetta (Vitale) B.; m. Barbara J. Frankenfield, June 14, 1959; children: Katherine, Alexander, Frederick. Student, Pratt Inst., 1953-55, U. Alaska, 1957-58; BS, SUNY, New Paltz, 1961; MFA, Bklyn. Coll., 1967. Art tchr. Newburgh (NY) Pub. Schs., 1960-63, Deer Park (NY) High Sch., 1963-65; prof. emeritus Bklyn. Coll., 1967-92. Vis. prof. art, lectr. SUNY, Stony Brook, 1977-78, 80, 81, 83; dep. chmn. studio art Bklyn. Coll., 1990-92, dep. chmn. grad. art, 1972-89; dir. First St. Gallery, NYC, 1978; adj. faculty art dept. Bklyn. Coll., 1992-93, Stony Brook U., 1993-99; art exhbn. jurist One man shows include Suffolk Community Coll., 1971, First Street Gallery, 1973, 76, 80, 89, Nassau County Mus. Fine Arts, 1987, St. Joseph's Coll., 1987, Alfred Van Loen Gallery, South Huntington, NY, 1998; exhibited paintings, drawings representational art in NYC, LI, 1967—. With USAF, 1955-59. Bklyn. Coll. grad. fellow, 1965-67. Mem. Coll. Art Assn., AAUP. Avocations: travel, tennis, gardening. Home: 182 Lower Sheep Pasture Rd East Setauket NY 11733-1826 E-mail: pasture@optonline.net.

BADAR, M. AFFAN, engineering educator; b. Madhubani, Bihar, India; arrived in US, 1995, permanent resident, 2005; s. M. Badar Alam and Noor-un Nisa; m. Sadia Saba, 1997; children: Isra children: Sidrah. BME, Aligrah Muslim U., India, 1988, MS in Indsl. Engring., 1990; MME, King Fahd U. Petroleum & Minerals, Dhahran, Saudi Arabia, 1993; PhD, U. Okla., Norman, 2002. Cert. indsl. technologist, Nat. Assn. Indsl. Tech. Lectr. petroleum and minerals King Fahd U., Dhahran, Saudi Arabia, 1993—95; asst. prof. Ind. State U., Terre Haute, 2002—. Asst. dir. Ctr. for Sys. Modeling and Simulation, Terre Haute, 2004—; Lilly Found. undergraduate fellow faculty mentor Ind. State U., 2005. Contbr. articles to profl. jours. Named Lilly Found. Promising Scholar, Ind. State U., 2006; Collaborative Linkage Travel grant, NATO Security through Sci. Program, 2005. Mem.: ASME, Nat. Assn. Indsl. Tech., Inst. Indsl. Engrs. (dir. engring. economy divsn. 2005—07), Soc. Mfg. Engrs. (assoc.), Muslim Alliance Indiana (bd. dirs. 2007—), Alpha Pi Mu, Epsilon Pi Tau. Muslim. Office: Ind State U Coll Tech Dept IMT Terre Haute IN 47809 Office Phone: 812-237-3982. Office Fax: 812-237-4527. Business E-Mail: mbadar@indstate.edu.

BADASH, LAWRENCE, science history educator; b. Bklyn., May 8, 1934; s. Joseph and Dorothy (Langa) B.; children: Lisa, Bruce. BS in

Physics, Rensselaer Poly. Inst., 1956; PhD in History of Sci., Yale U., 1964. Instr. Yale. U., New Haven, 1964—65, research assoc., 1965-66; from asst. to assoc. prof. U. Calif., Santa Barbara, 1966-79, prof. history of sci., 1979—2002, prof. emeritus, 2002—. Dir. summer seminar on global security and arms control U. Calif., 1983, 86, energy rsch. group, 1992, pacific rim program mem., 1993-95; cons. Nuclear Age Peace Found., Santa Barbara, 1984-90. Author: Radioactivity in Am., 1979, Kapitza, Rutherford, and the Kremlin, 1985, Scientists and the Development of Nuclear Weapons, 1995; editor: Rutherford and Boltwood, Letters on Radioactivity, 1969; Reminiscences of Los Alamos, 1943-45, 1980. Bd. dirs. Santa Barbara chpt. ACLU, 1971-86, 96—, pres., 1982-84, 96-98; nat. bd. dirs. Com. for a Sane Nuclear Policy, Washington, 1972-81; mem. Los Padres Search and Rescue Team, Santa Barbara, 1981-94. Lt. (j.g.) USN, 1956-59. Grantee, NSF, Cambridge, Eng., 1965-66, 69-72, 90-92, Am. Philos. Soc., New Zealand, 1979-80, Inst. on Global Conflict and Cooperation, Univ. Calif., 1983-87; J.S. Guggenheim fellow, 1984-85. Fellow AAAS (sect. mem. at large 1988-92), Am. Phys. Soc. (chmn. divsn. of history of physics 1988-89, exec. com. forum on physics and society 1991-93); mem. History of Sci. Soc. (founder West Coast chpt., chpt. bd. dirs. 1971-73, nat. coun. 1975-78). Democrat. Jewish. Avocation: backpacking. Office: Univ Calif Dept History Santa Barbara CA 93106-9410

BADASH, SANDI B., artist, art educator; b. Hartford, Conn., Mar. 2, 1936; d. Samuel Harry and Ann Evelyn (Olanoff) Borr; m. Lawrence Badash (div.); children: Bruce Alan, Lisa Dale Jones; life ptnr. Frank Montemurro. BS in Edn., Lesley U., Cambridge, Mass., 1958; postgrad., Paer Sch. Art, New Haven, 1963; MS in Art Edn., So. Conn. State U., New Haven, 1964. Art dir. Art Guild Santa Barbara, Forms Gallery, Delray Beach, Fla.; art instr. Bauder Coll., Ft. Lauderdale, Fla., 1984—86; art tchr. Marathon HS, Keys, Fla., 1992; art sales rep. Lela Bruce Gallery, Big Pine Key, Fla., 1995, Four Winds Gallery, Naples, 2002—; instr. Art Inst. Naples, Fla., 1996—98. Guest lectr. Most Maj. Cruise Lines, 1998—; lectr. in art, Naples, 1998—. Exhibitions include Ft. Lauderdale Mus. Art, 1990, Naples Von Leibig Art Ctr., 2006, Amsterdam Whitney Gallery, Forins Gallery, Medici Gallery, Ruth Schafner Gallery, Kotler Gallery, Gallery d'Silva; author: (musical, books and lyrics) The Gallery, 2000. Recipient 3d pl., Key West Body Bldg., 1992. Mem.: Naples Art Assn. Avocations: ballroom dancing, tennis, travel, reading, American Indian jewelry. Home and Studio: 75 Glades Blvd # 1 Naples FL 34112

BADDING, JOHN VICTOR, chemistry professor; b. Buffalo, May 6, 1962; s. Victor George and Nancy (Clark) B.; m. Mizue Abe, Dec. 28, 1993. BS, Manhattan Coll., NYC, 1984; PhD, U. Calif., Berkeley, 1989. Asst. prof. chemistry Pa. State U., University Park, 1991-97, assoc. prof. chemistry, 1997—. Contbr. articles to profl. jours. Packard fellow, 1993; NSF Young Investigator awardee, 1993. Office: Pa State U Dept Chemistry University Park PA 16802 E-mail: jbadding@chem.psu.edu.

BADDOUR, ANNE BRIDGE, pilot; b. Royal Oak, Mich. d. William George and Esther Rose (Pfiester) Bridge; m. Raymond F. Baddour, Sept. 25, 1954; children: Cynthia Anne, Frederick Raymond, Jean Bridge. Student, Detroit Bus. Sch., 1948—50; BA, Pine Manor Coll., Chestnut Hill, Mass. Stewardess Ea. Airlines, Boston, 1952—54; instr. aero. Powers Sch., Boston, 1958; co-pilot, flight attendant Raytheon Co., Bedford, Mass., 1958—63; flight dispatcher, ferry Pilot Comerford Flight Sch., Bedford, 1974—76; adminstrv. asst., ferry pilot Jenney Beachcraft, Bedford, 1976; mgr., pilot Balt. Airways, Inc., Bedford, 1976—77; rsch. test pilot Lincoln Lab. Flight Test Facility MIT, Lexington, 1977—97. Aviation cons., corp. pilot Energy Resources, Inc., Cambridge, Mass., 1974-84; holder World Class speed records for single-engine aircraft; Boston to Goose Bay, Labrador, 1985, Boston to Reykjavik, Iceland, 1985, Portland, Maine to Goose Bay, 1985, Portland to Reykjavik, 1985, Goose Bay to Reykjavik, 1985; records for twin-engine aircraft: Sept Isles to Goose Bay, 1988, Mont Joll to Goose Bay, 1988, Presque Isle to Goose Bay, 1988, Millinocket to Goose Bay, 1988, Bedford to Goose Bay, 1988, Goose Bay to Narssassrag, Greenland, 1988, Narssassrag to Klevelevic, Iceland, 1988, Narssassrag to Reykjavik, 1988, Bedford to Narssassrag, 1988, Millinochet to Narssassrag, 1988, Presque Isle to Narssassrag, 1988, Bedford to St. John, 1991, Bedford to Charlottetown, 1991, Charlottetown to Kennebunk, 1991, Charlottetown to Portsmouth, 1991, Muncton to Bedford, 1991, St. John, to Kennebunk, 1991, St. John to Bedford, 1991, World Class Speed Records Single-Engine Aircraft, 1991, Bedford, Mass. to Sydney, Nova Scotia, Bedford, Mass. to Sydney, Nova Scotia to Bedford, Mass., Portsmouth, New Hampshire to Sydney Nova Scotia to Portsmouth, Brunswick to Sydney Nova Scotia to Brunswick. Mem. campaign coun. Mus. Transp., Boston; mem. coun. assocs. French Libr. in Boston; commr. Commonwealth of Mass., Mass. Aero. Commn., 1979—83; trustee bd. adminstrn. Amelia Earhart Birthplace Mus., 1992—93; trustee Daniel Webster Coll., Nashua, NH, 1995—; v.p., trustee Friends of the Libr. Spl. Collections Boston U., 1997—; trustee Viscaya Mus., 2002—; bd. dirs. Smithsonian Nat. Air and Space Mus., 1998—2005, Cambridge Opera, 1977—79, Key West, Fla. Maritime Mus., 2004—. Named Pilot of Yr., New Eng. sect. Internat. Women Pilots Orgn./The Ninety-Nines Inc., 1992; named to Internat. Aviation Forest of Friendship, Atchison, Kans., 1991, Women in Aviation Internat. Pioneer Hall of Fame, 2005; recipient trophy, Phila. Transcontinental Air Race, 1954, New Eng. Air Race, 1957, Clifford B. Harmon trophy, Internat. Aviatrix, 1988, recipient Spl. Recognition award, FAA, 1990. Mem.: DAR, OX5 Aviation Pioneers, Tailhook Assn., Women in Aviation Internat. (Pioneer Hall of Fame award 2005), Friends of Switzerland, Soc. Exptl. Test Pilots, Assn. Women Transcontinental Air Race, Bostonian Soc., U.S. Sea Plane Pilots Assn., Fedn. Aeronautique Internat., Nat. Aero. Assn., Ninety-Nines (New Eng. Safety trophy 1986), Aircraft Owners Pilots Assn., Nat. Pilots Assn., Beach Colony Club, Fairchild Tropical Garden Club, Harvard Travellers Club, Boston Women's Travel Club, Chilton Club, Belmont Hill Club, Aero Club New Eng. (v.p. 1978—80, dir. 1978—2002).

BADDOURA, RASHID JOSEPH, emergency physician; b. Beirut, Aug. 4, 1947; came to U.S., 1974; s. Joseph and Renée Baddoura; m. Rola Tohme, July 15, 1989; children: Joseph, Philip, Karen. BS, Am. U. Beirut, 1970, MD, 1974. Diplomate Am. Bd. Emergency Medicine (examiner 1984-89), Am. Bd. Internal Medicine, Am. Bd. Pulmonary Diseases. Intern Am. U. Med. Ctr., Beirut; resident in internal medicine St. Joseph's Hosp. & Med. Ctr., Paterson, NJ, 1974-76; fellow in pulmonary and critical care Duke U., 1976-79; dir. emergency dept. Meml. Hosp., Danville, Va., 1981-84; corp. med. officer, mem. med. adv. bd. Coastal Healthcare Group, Durham, NC, 1981-86; assoc. dir. emergency dept. Valley Hosp., Ridgewood, NJ, 1986-90, dir. emergency dept., 1990—2000; ptnr., bd. dirs. Valley Emergency Assocs., 1986—, Valley Regional Emergency Group, 1999—; pres. Valley Emergency Assocs., 2002—; ptnr., bd. dirs. Bergen Regional Emergency Group, 1998—2003; trustee Valley Hosp. Found., 2006—. Mem. bd. Coastal Found. for Med. Edn., Durham, 1984-89; clin. asst. prof. emergency medicine Georgetown U., Washington, 1986-89; bd. trustees Valley Hosp. Found., 2006—. Reviewer: Journal of Critical Care Medicine, 2004—. Fellow: Am. Coll. Chest Physicians, Am. Coll. Emergency Physicians; mem.: Soc. Critical Care Medicine. Avocations: hunting, fishing, philosophy, classical music, architecture. Office: Valley Hosp Dept Emergency Medicine Ridgewood NJ 07451 Office Phone: 201-447-8318.

BADEER, HENRY SARKIS, physiology educator; b. Mersine, Turkey, Jan. 31, 1915; arrived in US, 1965, naturalized, 1971; s. Sarkis and Persape Hagop (Koundakjian) B.; m. Mariam Mihran Kassarjian, July 12, 1948; children: Gilbert H., Daniel H. MD, Am. U., Beirut, Lebanon, 1938. Gen. practice medicine, Beirut, 1940—51; asst. instr. Am. U. Sch. Medicine, Beirut, 1938—45, adj. prof., 1945—51, assoc. prof., 1951—62, prof. physiology, 1962—65, acting chmn. dept., 1951—56, chmn., 1956—65; rsch. fellow Harvard U. Med. Sch., Boston, 1948—49; prof. physiology Creighton U. Med. Sch., Omaha, 1967—91, emeritus prof., 1991—, acting chmn. dept., 1971—72. Vis. prof. U. Iowa, Iowa City, 1957-58, Downstate Med. Center, Bklyn., 1965-67; mem. med. com. Azounieh Sanatorium, Beirut, 1961-65; mem. research com. Nebr. Heart Assn., 1967-70, 85-88. Author textbook Spanish translation; contbr. chpts. to books, articles to profl. jours. Recipient Golden Apple award Students of AMA, 1975, Disting. Prof. award, 1992; Rockefeller fellow., 1948-49; grantee med. research com. Am. U. Beirut, 1956-65 Mem. Internat. Soc. Heart Rsch., Am. Physiol. Soc., Internat. Soc. for Adaptive Medicine (founding mem.). Home: 2808 S 99th Ave Omaha NE 68124-2603 Office: Creighton U Med Sch 2500 California Plz Omaha NE 68178-0001 *My success seems to be related to having set a goal and persevering in achieving it; satisfaction in or enjoyment of the performance of my daily task no matter how mundane; and eagerness to learn from personal experience or the experience of others.*

BADEL, JULIE, lawyer; b. Chgo., Sept. 14, 1946; d. Charles and Saima (Hrykas) Badel. Student, Knox Coll., 1963—65; BA, Columbia Coll., Chgo., 1967; JD, DePaul U., 1977. Bar: Ill. 1977, U.S. Dist. Ct. (no. dist.) Ill. 1977, U.S. Ct. Appeals (7th and D.C. cirs.) 1981, U.S. Supreme Ct. 1985, U.S. Dist. Ct. (ea. dist.) Mich. 1989, U.S. Dist. Ct. (no. dist.) Ind. 2002, U.S. Dist. Ct. (we. dist.) Mich. 2005. Hearings referee State of Ill., Chgo., 1974-78; assoc. Cohn, Lambert, Ryan & Schneider, Chgo., 1978-80, McDermott, Will & Emery, Chgo., 1980-84, ptnr., 1985-2001, Epstein, Becker & Green, PC , Chgo., 2001—. Legal counsel, mem. adv. bd. Health Evaluation Referral Svc. Chgo., 1980-89; mem. Finnish Coun. Finlandia U., 2006—. Author: Hospital Restructuring: Employment Law Pitfalls, 1985; editor DePaul U. Law Rev., 1976-77. Bd. dirs. Alternatives, Inc., 1990—2002, Chgo. chpt. Asthma and Allergy Found., 1993—94, Glenwood Sch.; mem. bus. adv. coun. Lake Forest Grad. Sch. Mgmt. Mem.: ABA, Finnish Am. Lawyers Assn., Chgo. Bar Assn., Labor and Employment and Animal Law (vice chair 2005—06, chair 2006—07), Columbia Coll. Alumni Assn. (1st v.p., bd. dirs. 1981—86), Pi Gamma Mu. Office: Epstein Becker & Green 150 N Michigan Ave 35th Fl Chicago IL 60601-7553 Business E-Mail: jbadel@ebglaw.com.

BADEN, MICHAEL M., pathologist, educator; b. Bronx, NY, July 27, 1934; s. Harry and Fannie (Linn) B.; m. Judianne Densen-Gerber June 14, 1958 (div. 1997), 3 children; m. Linda Kenney, 2000 BS, CCNY, 1955; MD, NYU, 1959. Diplomate Am. Bd. Pathology. Intern, first med. div. Bellevue Hosp., NYC, 1959-60, resident, 1960-61, resident in pathology, 1961-63, chief resident in pathology, 1963-64, fellow in pathology, 1964-65; pvt. practice in pathology NYC, 1965—; asst. med. examiner City of NY, 1961-65, jr. med. examiner, 1965-66, assoc. med. examiner, 1966-70, dep. chief med. examiner, 1970-78, 79-81, 83-86, chief med. examiner, 1978-79; dep. chief med. examiner, dir. labs. Suffolk County, NY, 1981-83; dep. chief med. examiner NYC, 1983-86; dir. forensic scis. unit NY State Police, 1986—; instr. in pathology NYU, NYC, 1964-65, asst. prof. pathology, 1966-70, assoc. prof. forensic medicine, 1970-89. Adj. prof. law NY Law Sch., NYC, 1975-88, John Jay Coll. Criminal Justice, NYC, 1989-90, 93; vis. prof. pathology Albert Einstein Sch. Medicine, NYC, 1975—; lectr. pathology Coll. Physicians and Surgeons, Columbia U., NYC, 1975—, adj. prof. pathology and lab. medicine, 1993—; asst. vis. pathologist Bellevue Hosp., NYC, 1965-75; adj. prof. pathology and lab. medicine Albany (NY) Med. Sch.; lectr. Drug Enforcement Adminstrn., Dept. Justice, 1973—; vis. lectr. Fairleigh Dickinson Dentistry, Hackensack, NJ, 1968-70; spl. forensic pathology cons. NY State Organized Crime Task Force, 1971-75; chmn. forensic pathology panel US Ho. of Reps. select coms. on assassinations of Pres. John F. Kennedy and Dr. Martin Luther King, Jr., 1977-79; mem. med. adv. bd. Andrew Menchell Infant Survival Found., 1969-74; mem. cert. bd. Addiction Svcs. Agy., NYC, 1966-69; preceptor health research tng. program NYC Dept. Health, 1968-79; v.p. Coun. for Interdisciplinary Communication in Medicine, 1967-69; forensic pathology cons. NY State Police, 1985—. Author: Alcohol, Other Drugs and Violent Death, 1978, Unnatural Death, 1989 (with Marion Roach) Dead Reckoning: New Science of Catching Killers, 2001, (novels with Linda Kenney) Remains Silent, 2005; contbr. articles on forensic medicine to profl. jours.; mem. editorial bd. Am. Jour. Drug and Alcohol Abuse, 1973—, Internat. Microfilm Jour. Legal Medicine, 1969-73, Contemporary Drug Problems, 1971; host, HBO series, Autopsy, 1995-2000. Active NY adv. bd. Odyssey House, Inc., 1966-76; bd. dirs. NY Coun. on Alcoholism, sec., 1969-79; bd. dirs. Belco Scholarship Found., Inc., 1971-87. Recipient Great Tchr. award NYU, 1980 Fellow Coll. Am. Pathologists (chmn. toxicology subcom. 1972-74), Am. Soc. Clin. Pathologists (mem. drug abuse task force 1973—), Am. Acad. Forensic Scis. (program chmn. 1971-72, sec. sect. pathology and biology 1970-71, exec. com. 1971-74, v.p. 1982-83); mem. Med. Soc. County NY (mem. pub. health com. 1966-76), Soc. Med. Jurisprudence (corr. sec. 1971-78, v.p. 1979-81, pres. 1981-85, chmn. bd. 1985—), Nat. Assn. Med. Examiners, NY Path. Soc., NY State Med. Soc., AMA, Internat. Royal Coll. Health Office: 142 E End Ave New York NY 10028-7503

BADEN, SHERI LOUISE, primary school educator; b. Beaumont, Tex., July 29, 1944; d. Charles Thomas and Elsie Louise (Stapleton) Barrett; m. Joseph R. Baden (dec.); children: Brandan Kyle, Derek Paul. BS in Elem. Edn., Lamar U., Beaumont, Tex., 1970. 3d grade tchr. French Elem. Sch., Beaumont, 1968—69; 2d grade tchr. Longfellow Elem. Sch., Beaumont, 1969—71; kindergarten tchr. All Sts. Sch., Beaumont, 1973—. Named Nat. K Tchr. of Yr., Staff Devel. Educators, Tchr. of Yr., All Sts. Sch.; named to Hall of Fame for Educators, Lamar U., 2004. Mem.: SE Tex. Hike and Bike Coalition (bd. dirs.), Citizen's Police Acad. Alumni Assn., Golden Triangle Sq. and Round Dance Assn. (sec. 2007—), Order Ea. Star (Worthy Matron Beaumont chpt. 1984—85), Delta Kappa Gamma (program chmn. 2004—06, pres. 2006—). Episcopalian. Avocations: cycling, square dance, country and western dance. Office: All Sts Episcopal Sch 4108 Delaware Beaumont TX 77706

BADEN, THOMAS JAMES, dermatologist; b. Coral Gables, Fla., Dec. 29, 1951; s. Thomas Benjamin and Helen (Threadgill) B.; m. Sandra Louise Bradley, June 22, 1974; children: Craig, Scott, Michael. AB in Chemistry, Duke U., 1973; MD cum laude, Emory U., 1977. Diplomate Am. Bd. Internal Medicine, Am. Bd. Dermatology. Internal medicine resident N.C. Meml. Hosp., Chapel Hill, 1977-80, dermatology resident, 1983-86; internist Toe Valley Med. Assn., Spruce Pine, NC, 1980-83; dermatologist West Piedmont Dermatology Assn., Morganton, NC, 1986—. Consulting dermatologist Western Carolina Ctr., Broughton Hosp., Morganton, 1986—; staff dermatologist Grace Hosp., Morganton, 1986—. Contbr. articles to profl. jours. Troop leader Boy Scouts Am.; deacon First Bapt. Ch., Morganton. Fellow ACP, Am. Acad. Dermatology, Am. Soc. Dermatology Surgeons; mem. AMA, Christian Med. Soc. Avocations: music, hiking, photography. Office: West Piedmont Dermatology 111 Foothills Dr Morganton NC 28655-5152

BADER, ALFRED ROBERT, chemist; b. Vienna, Apr. 28, 1924; came to U.S., 1947, naturalized, 1964; s. Alfred and Elizabeth Maria (Serenyi) B.; m. Isabel Overton, Jan. 26, 1982; children from previous marriage: David, Daniel. BS in Engring. Chemistry, Queens U., Can., 1945, BA in History, 1946, MS in Organic Chemistry, 1947, LLD (hon.), 1986; MA, Harvard U., 1949, PhD, 1950; DS (hon.), U. Wis.-Milw., 1980, Purdue U., 1984, U. Wis.-Madison, 1984, Northwestern U., 1990; D.Univ. (hon.), U. Sussex, Eng., 1989; DSc (hon.), U. Edinburgh, 1998, Glasgow U., 1999, Masaryk U., 2000, Simon Fraser U., 2005, U. Ottawa, 2006. Rsch. chemist PPG Co., Milw., 1950-53, group leader, 1953-54; chief chemist Aldrich Chem. Co., Milw., 1954-55, pres., 1955-81, chmn., 1981-91; pres. Sigma-Aldrich Corp., 1975-80, chmn., 1980-91, chmn. emeritus, 1991-92; pres. Alfred Bader Fine Arts, Milw., 1991—. Author: Adventures of a Chemist Collector, 1995; patentee in field. Guest curator Milw. Art Mus., 1976, 89. Recipient Winthrop-Sears medal Chem. Industry Assn., 1980, J.E. Purkyne medal Acad. Scis., Czech Republic, 1994, Gold medal Am. Inst. Chemists, 1997, Boron USA award, 1997; named Entrepreneur of Yr. Rsch. Dirs. Assn., 1980, Hon. Citizen, U. Vienna, 1995, Comdr. of the Brit. Empire, 1998. Fellow: Royal Soc. Arts, Royal Soc. Chemistry (hon.); mem.: Appraisers Assn. Am., Am. Chem. Soc. (award Milw. sect. 1971, Parsons' award 1995, named one of the top 75 disting. contbrs. to the chem. enterprise in the last 75 years 1998). Jewish. Office: Alfred Bader Fine Arts 924 E Juneau Ave Ste 622 Milwaukee WI 53202-2748 Office Phone: 414-277-0730. Fax: 414-277-0709. E-mail: alfred@alfredbader.com, baderfa@execpc.com.

BADER, DIEDRICH, actor; b. Alexandria, Va., Dec. 24, 1966; s. William and Gretta Bader; m. Duley Rodgers, 1998. Actor in feature film debut in dual role as twins Jethro and Jethrine in remake of TV series: The Beverly Hillbillies; actor (film): Teresa's Tattoo, 1994, Office Space, 1999, The Assassination File, Certain Guy, 1999, Couple Days.A Period Place, 2000, Jay & Silent Bob Strike Back, 2001, Kim Possible, 2002, Evil Alien Conquerors, 2002, (voices in films) Baby Blues, 2000, The Zeta Project, 2001, Lloyd in Space, 2001, Recess: School's Out, 2001, Ice Age, 2002, The Country Bears, 2002, Dead and Breakfast, 2004, (voice) Dinotopia: Curse of the Ruby Sunstone, 2004, Napoleon Dynamite, 2004, Eurotrip, 2004, Miss Congeniality: Armed and Fabulous, 2005, Balls of Fury, 2007; (TV movies) Preppie Murder, 1989; (tv series): Danger Theatre, 1993, The Drew Carey Show, 1995—2004, (voice) Hercules, 1998-99, Center of the Universe, 2004-05; tv guest appearances include: 21 Jump Street, 1987, Fresh Prince of Bel-Air, 1990, Star Trek: The Next Generation, 1987, Cheers, 1982, Quantum Leap, 1989, Broken Badges, 1990, Flying Blind, 1992, Diagnosis Murder, 1993, Frasier, 1993, Gargoyles, 1994, Murphy Brown, 1988, Happy Hour, 1999, (voice) King of the Hill, 1999, (voice) The Simpsons, 2000, The Norm Show, 2001; exec. prodr. Jimmy Scott: If You Only Knew, 2002. Office: c/o Joel Rudnick Paradigm Agy 360 N Crescent Dr N Bldg Beverly Hills CA 90210*

BADER, GERALD L., JR., lawyer; b. St. Louis, Mar. 15, 1934; s. Gerald L. and Mabel A. (Stephens) B.; (div.); children: Gerald L. III, Stephanie, Cynthia, Carlie, Deborah; m. Barbara Anne Lien, June 2, 1979; children: Matthew Stephen, Mary Rachel. BA, Washington U., 1956; LLB, U. Mich., 1959. Bar: Colo. 1960, Mo. 1960, N.Y. 1961, U.S. Supreme Ct. 1972. Assoc. White & Case, NYC, 1960-62, 64-65, Hodges, Silverstein & Harrington, Denver, 1965-68; pres. Bader and Assocs. P.C., Denver, 1969—. Sec. Denver Rep. Ctrl. Com., 1969-73; pres. Rocky Mountain Child Devel. Fedn., Denver, 1982-90; dir. Ctrl. City Opera House Assocs., Denver, 1984-2002, emeritus dir., 2002—; dir. Legal Ctr., Denver, 1992-98. 1st lt. US Army, 1962-64. Mem.: Phi Beta Kappa. Republican. Roman Catholic. Avocations: golf, skiing. Office: Bader & Assocs LLC 14426 E Evans Denver CO 80014 Office Phone: 303-534-1700. Business E-Mail: gbader@bader-associates.com.

BADER, JOHN MERWIN, retired lawyer; b. Wilmington, Del., June 29, 1919; s. Merwin Oldrin and Escelyn (Connell) Bader; m. Constance Wulffaert, Dec. 27, 1944 (div. Oct. 1965); children: Andrew M., Mary Donley, Eileen Williams, Matthew J.; m. Anne S. Shane, Jan. 15, 1973 (dec. Jan. 5, 2003). BA, Villanova U., 1941; LLB, U. Pa., 1948. Bar: Del. 1948, U.S. Supreme Ct. 1956. Pvt. practice, Wilmington, 1948—56, 1966—70; ptnr. Balick and Bader, Wilmington, 1956—59, Bader and Biggs, Wilmington, 1959—66, Bader, Dorsey & Kreshtool, Wilmington, 1970—81; pvt. practice Wilmington, 1981—88; of counsel Tomar, O'Brien, Kaplan, Jacoby & Graziano, Wilmington, 1988—2001, Thomas S. Neuberger, PA, Wilmington, 2001—03; ret., 2003. Counsel Rep. State Com., Wilmington, 1975-85; mem. Ethics Commn., City of Wilmington, 1998-2001. 1st lt. U.S. Army, 1941-45. Mem. Del. Bar Assn. (v.p. 1969-71), ATLA (bd. govs. 1969-73, 75-80), Del. Trial Lawyers Assn. (pres. 1977-80), Elks, Kiwanis. Home: Apt 4316 4830 Kennett Pike Wilmington DE 19807 Personal E-mail: baderj@aol.com.

BADER, KATHLEEN M., chemicals executive; B in Liberal Arts, Notre Dame; MBA, U. Calif., Berkeley. Joined Dow Chem. Co., Chgo., 1973—2005, corp. v.p. Quality and Business Excellence, 1999, pres. bus. group styrenics and engineered products, corp. v.p., quality and bus. excellence Zurich, Switzerland, 2000—04; chmn., pres., CEO Dow Cargill, Minnetonka, Minn., 2004—05; pres., CEO NatureWorks LLC (formerly known as Cargill Dow LLC), Mpls., 2005—. Chair dept. pvt. sector sr. advisory com. Homeland Security; adv. coun. US Homeland Security, 2002—; bd. dirs. Textron Inc., Providence, 2004—. Internat. bd. dir. Habitat for Humanity; dean's coun. Harvard Sch. Govt. Named One of 50 Most Powerful Women in Internat. Bus., Fortune Mag., 2001—03; recipient Henry Laurence Gantt medal, ASME, 2005. Office: NatureWorks LLC PO Box 5830 Minneapolis MN 55440-5830 Office Phone: 877-423-7659.

BADER, ROBERT SMITH, biology and zoology educator, researcher; b. Falls City, Nebr., June 18, 1925; s. Ray Jay and Grace (Smith) B.; m. Joan Larson; children: Douglas, Jonathan, Eric, Joel. BS, Kans. State U., 1949; PhD, U. Chgo., 1954. From instr. to asst. prof. biology U. Fla., 1952-56; from asst. prof. to prof. zoology U. Ill., Urbana, 1956-68; prof. biology, dean Coll. Arts and Scis., U. Mo., St. Louis, 1968-83, rsch. prof., 1983-85; rsch. assoc. dept. history U. Kans., 1985-91. Adj. prof. history Kans. State U., 1986-91. With USNR, 1943-45. Achievements include research on Kansas history, prohibition history, Biblical theology. Home: 2165 Squirrel Rd Neosho Falls KS 66758-7122 E-mail: jlbader@terraworld.net.

BADER, SAMUEL DAVID, physicist; b. NYC, Feb. 4, 1947; s. Fred and Norma (Blake) Bader; m. Karen Deborah Natal, Dec. 23, 1971 (dec. Aug. 1994); children: Ari, Danya. BS, U. Calif., Berkeley, 1967, PhD, 1974. Postdoctoral fellow Argonne Nat. Lab., Ill., 1974-76, asst. physicist materials sci. divsn., 1976-79, physicist, 1979-90, group leader, 1987—, sr. physicist, 1990—. Chair editl. bd. Jour. Vacuum Sci. and Tech., Argonne, 1988-91. Assoc. editor Applied Physics Letters, 1986—; adv. editor Jour. of Magnetism and Magnetic Materials, 1990-97, editor, 1998—; contbr. numerous articles to profl. jours. Recipient Material Sci. Rsch. Competition award for outstanding sci. achievement in solid state physics US Dept. Energy, 1992, U. Chgo. Award for Disting. Performance at Argonne Nat. Lab., 1994. Fellow Am. Phys. Soc. (mem. exec. com. divsn. materials physics 1992-95, sec.-treas. 1996—, David Adler Lectureship award in Field of Materials Physics); mem. Am. Vacuum Soc. (chmn. publ. com. 1988-91). Achievements include 1 patent in magneto-optical storage materials. Office: Argonne Nat Lab MSD-223 9700 Cass Ave Argonne IL 60439-4803 E-mail: Bader@ANL.gov.*

BADER, WILLIAM BANKS, historian, former corporate executive, foundation executive; b. Atlantic City, Sept. 8, 1931; s. Edward L. and Celeste Bader (Burkhardt) B.; m. Gretta Lange, Dec. 19, 1953; children: Christopher, Katharine, John, Diedrich. BA, Pomona Coll., 1953; MA, Princeton U., 1960, PhD, 1964. With Libr. of Congress, 1954—55, Office Nat. Estimates, 1962—64; lectr. history Princeton U., 1964—65; with Dept. State, 1965—66, U.S. Senate Fgn. Rels. Com., 1966—69; program officer, then European rep. Ford Found., Paris, 1969—73; program officer Office European and Internat. Affairs, 1973—74; fellow Woodrow Wilson Internat. Ctr. Scholars, 1974—75; dir. fgn. intelligence task force U.S. Senate, 1975—76; asst. dep. under sec. for policy Dept. Def., 1976—78; dir. staff U.S. Senate Fgn. Rels. Com., 1978—81; v.p. SRI Internat.-Washington, Arlington, 1981—87; sr. v.p. SRI Internat., Menlo Park,

Calif., 1988—92; pres. Eurasia Found., Washington, 1992—96; with World Bank Group, Washington, 1996—97, Ctr. Strategic and Internat. Studies, 1997—98; asst. sec. of state ednl. and cultural affairs Dept. State, 1998—2001; with World Bank Group, Washington, 2001—02; v.p. Nat. Def. U., 2000—04, Internat. Fin. Corp., 2005—06; prof. history and politics Grad. Inst. Internat. Studies, Geneva, 2006—. Adj. prof. Georgetown U. Author: Austria Between East and West: 1945-1955, 1966, The U.S. and the Spread of Nuclear Weapons, 1968, The Taiwan Relations Act: A Decade of Implementation, 1989, Österreich im Spannungsfeld Zwischen Ost und West 1945 bis 1955, 2002; contbr. articles to profl. jours. Bd. dirs. Samuel H. Kress Found. Served as officer USNR, 1955-58, capt. Res. ret. Recipient Meritorious Svc. medal Dept. State, 1966, Sec. Def. medal for outstanding pub. svc., 1979, Österreichische Ehrenkreuz für Wissenschaft und Kunst 1. Klasse Republic of Austria (officer's cross), 1991. Mem. Coun. Fgn. Rels., Internat. Inst. Strategic Studies, Cosmos Club Washington Roman Catholic. Office: Grad Inst Internat Studies Geneva Rue de Lausanne 132 PO Box 36 CH 1211 Geneva Switzerland

BADER, W(ILLIAM) REECE, lawyer; b. Portland, Oreg., Oct. 31, 1941; s. William Lange and Phyllis Harriet (Cole) B.; m. Jean McCarty, Aug. 3, 1963 (div. 1993); children: Lawson R., Cole R.; m. Alicia Spatafore, June 14, 1998. BA, Williams Coll., 1963; JD, Duke U., 1966. Bar: D.C. 1967, Calif. 1969, U.S. Dist. Ct. D.C., U.S. Dist. Ct. (no., ctrl., ea. and so. dists.) Calif., U.S. Ct. Appeals (D.C., 2d, 3d, 7th, 9th and fed. cirs.), U.S. Tax Ct., U.S. Claims Ct., U.S. Supreme Ct. Law clk. to judge U.S. Ct. Appeals (D.C. cir.), Washington, 1966-68; assoc. Orrick, Herrington & Sutcliffe LLP, San Francisco, 1968-74, ptnr., 1974—. Mem. legal adv. bd. Hastings Law Ctr. Found., 1981-87; mem. securities disputes resolution com. Ctr. for Pub. Resources, 1990—; mem. nat. arbitration and med. com. NASDR, 1994-98; mem. ad hoc com. on ct. facilities and design U.S. Jud. Conf., 1969-72, mem. adv. com. on civil rules, 1982-87, mem. standing com. on rules of practice and procedure, 1987-90; lectr., panelist Practicing Law Inst., ABA Am. Law Inst., Internat. Franchise Assn., Calif. Electronic Assn., many others; arbitrator, mediator Nat. Assn. Securities Dealers Regulation Inc., 1979—, Am. Arbitration Assn., 1979-2006, N.Y. Stock Exch., 1984—, Nat. Futures Assn., 1985—, Pvt. Adjudication Found., 1987-96. Mem. editl. bd. Alternatives, 1991—; editor: Securities News, 1993-94, Securities Arbitration, 1999--, Private Securities Litigation Reform Act Reporter, 1996—; contbr. article to profl. jours. Trustee North Park Coll. and Theol. Sem., Chgo., 1984-89, sec., 1985-86, chmn., 1986-89. Fellow Am. Bar Found., Environ. Law Inst.; mem. ABA (litig., bus., natural resources, dispute resolution sects.), State Bar Calif. (litig., bus., environ. sects.), Securities Industry Assn. (compliance and legal divsn.), Futures Industry Assn. (compliance and legal divsn.), Bar Assn. San Francisco, D.C. Bar Assn. Avocations: collecting toy trains, squash, reading, travel. Office: Orrick Herrington Sutcliffe LLP 3050 K St NW Washington DC 20007 Home: 1858 Venetian Point Dr Clearwater FL 33755 Office Phone: 202-334-8564. Office Fax: 202-339-8500. Business E-Mail: wrbader@orrick.com.

BADERTSCHER, DAVID GLEN, law librarian, consultant; b. Morrow, Ohio, Jan. 31, 1935; s. Glen C. and Blanche (Cluff) Badertscher; m. Betty Jo Shafer, June 25, 1965. BS, Ind. State U., 1957, MS, 1962, Rosary Coll., 1967. Tchr. Rockville HS, Ind., 1957-59, Medinah Elem. Sch., Ill., 1961-63; libr. Elgin Acad., Ill., 1963-64; tchr. Beachwood HS, Ohio, 1964-65; libr. Chgo. Pub. Libr., 1965-66; circulation, asst. reference libr. U. Chgo. Law Sch., 1966-70; libr. Schiff Hardin Waite Dorschel & Britton, Chgo., 1970-73; exec. libr. Georgetown U. Law Ctr., Washington, 1973-78; dir. libr. Milbank, Tweed, Hadley & McCloy, NYC, 1978-80; prin. law libr. N.Y. Supreme Ct., NYC, 1980—. Cons. Urban Rsch. Corp., Chgo., 1970—73, Herner & Co., 1977—87, R. R. Bowker & Co., 1981—91, Nat. Ctr. State Cts., 1992—96; advisor Computer Law Svc., 1972—82, EIS, 1978—; adj. prof. Baruch Coll., 1982—2002; bd. dirs. N.Y. Met. Reference and Rsch. Libr. Agy., chmn. bd. pers. com., 1989—93; mem. judges com. automation and tech. State of N.Y. Unified Ct. Sys., 1994—96. Contbr. articles to profl. jours. Mem. corp. adv. bd. Tech. Forum Internat., 1997—, mem. internat. soc., 2003—. With US Army, 1959—61. Mem.: ABA (assoc.; mem. com. sci. and tech. criminal justice sect. 2000—), Assn. Info. Mgrs., Am. Soc. Info. Sci. (editor SIG/Law Newsletter 1975—79), Chgo. Assn. Law Librs. (pres., conf. chmn. 1970—72, mem. com. automation and tech. judges N.Y. 1994—96), Am. Assn. Law Librs. (chmn. com. automation, sci. devel. 1970—72, chmn. state, city, and county law librs. sect. 1989—90, mem. adv. com. law libr. jour. 1989—91, conv. grantee 1970), Medinah Tchrs. Assn. (pres. 1962—63). Home: 257 Orchard St Apt 8 Westfield NJ 07090-3130 Office: NY Supreme Ct 100 Centre St New York NY 10013-4308

BADGER, DAVID HARRY, lawyer; b. Indpls., June 16, 1931; s. David Henry and Mayme Pearl (Wright) B.; m. Donna Lee Bailey, June 24, 1954; children: David Mark, Lee Ann, Steven Michael. BEE, Rose Poly. Inst., 1953; JD, Ind. U., 1964. Bar: Ind. 1964, U.S. Dist. Ct. (so and no. dists.) Ind. 1964, U.S. Patent Office 1964, U.S. Ct. Customs and Patent Appeals 1971, U.S. Ct. Appeals (fed. cir.) 1982. Engr. GE, 1953-56, Ransburg Corp., Indpls., 1956-62; chief elec. engr. Rex Metal Craft, Inc., Indpls., 1963-64; patent counsel, corp. sec. Ransburg Corp., Indpls., 1964—76; legal counsel Ball Corp., Muncie, Ind., 1976-77; ptnr. Jenkins, Coffey, Hyland, Badger & Conard, Indpls., 1977-82; mng. ptnr. Brinks, Hofer, Gilson & Lione, Indpls., 1982-98. Contbr. articles to profl. jours.; patentee in U.S. and fgn. countries. With USN, 1953-55, lt. comdr. USNR. Named Hon. Alumnus Rose Hulman Inst. Tech., 1987. Mem. ABA (various coms.), IEEE, Ind. Bar Assn. (various coms.), Am. Intellectual Property Law Assn. (various coms.), Licensing Execs. Soc. (various coms.), Indpls. Bar Assn., Internat. Assn. Intellectual Property Law, Indpls. Jazz Club (bd. dirs. 1983-85, 95-97), Junto of Indpls. (bd. dirs. 1997-99). Office: Brinks Hofer Gilson & Lione 1 Indiana Sq Ste 1600 Indianapolis IN 46204-2045 Home Phone: 317-876-7556; Office Phone: 317-636-0886. Personal E-mail: badger938@aol.com.

BADGER, PHILLIP CHARLES, agricultural engineer; b. Lodi, Ohio, Jan. 7, 1948; s. Clifford Russell and Helen Pauline (Fair) B.; m. Cheryl Lynn Baker, Aug. 14, 1971 (div. Feb. 1999); children: Brian, Scott, Mark; m. Bonnie Watkins, Aug. 14, 1999. BS in Agrl. Engring., Ohio State U., 1971, MS in Agrl. Engring., 1973; MBA, Vanderbilt U., 1993. Registered profl. engr., Ohio, Ala. Design engr. Ideanamics, Columbus, Ohio, 1972—74; rsch. assoc., project engr. Ohio State U. and Ohio Agrl. R & D Ctr., Wooster, 1975—78, ext. specialist, rsch. assoc., 1978—79; mgr. waste heat utilization project TVA, Muscle Shoals, Ala., 1979—80, mgr. small scale fuel ethanol project, 1980—82, mgr. fuel ethanol from non-woody cellulose program, 1982—84; mgr. Regional Biomass Energy program Dept. Energy, Muscle Shoals, 1984—, leader TVA biomass applications group, 1994—, leader mgr. regional biomass energy program, 1994—99; pres. Gen. Bioenergy, Inc., Florence, Ala., 1999—; pres., chief mgr. Renewable Oil Internat., Florence, 2000—, ROI Ala. Ops. LLC, Florence, ROI Mass. Ops. LLC, Springfield. Mem. biomass and waste energy com. Electric Power Rsch. Inst., Palo Alto, Calif., 1990—; mem. Renewable Energy and Efficiency Inst. Quality Control Bd., 1996—. Author: Conserving Energy in Ohio Greenhouses, 1979 (Am. Soc. Agr. Engrs. blue ribbon award 1979); mem. editl. bd. CIGR Electronic Jour.; contbr. articles to profl. jours. Bd. dirs. New Uses Coun., 1997—. Recipient Tech. Achievement award Dept. Energy, 1985, 96, 98, Outstanding Tech. Presentation award WATTec '89, 1989, Cert. of Environ. Achievement, Nat. Awards Coun. for Environ. Sustainability, 1994-99, Industry Leader award Fiber Fuels Inst., 1993. Mem. Am. Soc. Agrl. and Biol. Engrs. (v.p. energy com. 1990-91, pres. energy com. 1991-92, trustee 2006—), Am. Solar Energy Soc., Am. Assn. Indsl. Crops, Internat. Solar Energy Soc., Nat. Mgmt. Assn., Am. Assn. Indsl. Crops, Biomass Energy Rsch. Assn. (bd. dirs. 1987—), New Uses Coun. (bd. dirs. 1997—), Coun. of Forest Engring., Coun. Agrl. Sci. and Tech., Florence Exch. Club (bd. dirs. 1985-86). Office: Gen Bioenergy Inc Renewable Oil Internat LLC and ROI Ala Ops PO Box 26 Florence AL 35631-0026

BADGER, RONALD KAY, lawyer; b. Horton, Kans., Aug. 24, 1933; s. Clarence E. and Josephine L. (Rick) Badger; m. Janet L. Horner, Feb. 16, 1963; children: Hellen L. Badger Haag, Ronald K. Jr., Laura J. Badger Davis. BS in Bus., U. Kans., 1958, BS in Law, 1961, JD, 1968. Bar: Kans. 1961, U.S. Dist. Ct. Kans. 1961, U.S. Ct. Appeals (10th cir.) 1973, U.S. Supreme Ct. 1982, U.S. Ct. Claims 1990. Law clk. to Hon. Arthur J. Stanley Jr., U.S. Dist. Ct. Kans., Kansas City, 1961—62; spl. asst. to U.S. atty. for dist. of Kans., Dept. Justice, Topeka, 1962—64; assoc. Foulston & Siefkin, Wichita, Kans., 1964—66; atty. in contract adminstrn. Boeing Co., Wichita, 1966—68; pvt. practice Wichita, 1968—. Bd. dirs. Envision, 2002—, Comp Hyde Inc., 1997—, pres., 2006—. Mem. bd. edtiors Kans. Bar Jour., 1966—82; contbr. articles to profl. jours. Bd. dirs. Wichita Symphony Soc., 1970—2003. Mem.: FBA (pres. Kans. chpt. 1978—80), Christian Legal Soc. (pres. Wichita chpt. 2001—03), Wichita Estate Planning Coun. (sec. 1996—97, pres. 1997—98), Wichita Bar Assn., Kans. Bar Assn., Internat. Assn. Lions Clubs (pres. Wichita Downtown Club 1984—85, dist. gov. 1990—91). Republican. Office: 330 N Main St Wichita KS 67202 Office Phone: 316-263-8762.

BADGER, WILLIAM JOHN, urologist, surgeon; b. Canton, Ohio, May 7, 1975; s. William Budd and Beverly Jane Badger; m. Sarah Duval, Aug. 14, 1999; 1 child, Ellen Duval. BS in Chemistry, Hobart Coll., Geneva, NY, 1997; MD, Ohio State U., Columbus, 2002. Resident neurol. surgery Albany Med. Ctr., NY, 2002—. Contbr. articles to profl. jours. Recipient Best Rsch. award, 2006. Mem.: Am. Urol. Assn., Phi Beta Kappa. Home Phone: 518-262-3296. Personal E-mail: billbadger1@gmail.com.

BADGEROW, JOHN NICHOLAS, lawyer; b. Macon, Mo., Apr. 7, 1951; s. Harry Leroy Badgerow and Barbara Raines (Buell) Novaria; m. Teresa Ann Zvolanek, Aug. 7, 1976; children: Anthony Thornton, Andrew Cameron, James Terrill. BA in Bus. and English with honors, Principia Coll., 1972; JD, U. Mo., Kansas City, 1975. Bar: Kans. 1976, US Dist. Ct. Kans. 1976, US Ct. Appeals (10th cir.) 1977, US Ct. Appeals (4th cir.) 1979, US Supreme Ct. 1982, US Ct. Appeals (fed. cir.) 1985, US Ct. Appeals (8th cir.) 1986, Mo. 1986, US Dist. Ct. (we. dist.) Mo. 1986, Civil Lit., Nat. Bd. Trial Advocates, 1994. Ptnr. McAnany, VanCleave & Phillips, P.A., Kansas City, Kans., 1975-85; ptnr.-in-charge Spencer, Fane, Britt & Browne, Kansas City, Mo. and Overland Park, Kans., 1986—. Chmn. ethics grievance com. Johnson County, 1988—; mem. Kans. Jud. Coun., 1995—, Kans. Bd. Discipline for Attys., 2000—, chmn. Ethics 2000 Commn., 2002—, chmn. Kans. ethics adv. opinion com., 2005—. Co-author: Kansas Employment Law, 1992, 2d edit., 2001; co-author, co-editor Kansas Lawyer Ethics, 1996; contbr. articles to jour. Co-chmn. Civil Justice Reform Act Commn., Dist. of Kans., 1995-96; chmn. Kans. Ethics Adv. Opinion Com., 2005-. Mem.: ABA, Earl O'Connor Am. Inn of Ct. (pres. 1996), Kans. Assn. Def. Counsel, Kans. Bar Assn. (ethics adv. opinion com. 1997—, Outstanding Svc. award 1995), Kans. Jud. Coun., Mission Valley Hunt Club (Stilwell, Kans.). Republican. Christian Scientist. Avocations: horseback riding, carpentry, reading. Office: Spencer Fane Britt & Browne 9401 Indian Creek Pkwy Ste 700 Shawnee Mission KS 66210-2038 Office Phone: 913-345-8100. Business E-Mail: nbadgerow@spencerfane.com.

BADGLEY, CLIFFORD W., music educator; b. Garden City, Mich., Sept. 5, 1964; s. Carl and Martha Badgley; m. Marcia Klinder-Badgley, Oct. 23, 1993. MusB with honors, U. Wyo., Laramie, 1986; MusM in Performance, Ariz. State U., Tempe, 1991. Dir. of music, organist Mountain View Luth. Ch., Phoenix, 1993—2000; choral tchr. Reyburn Intermediate Sch., Clovis, Calif., 2002—. Music dir. Second Take Singers, Madera, Calif., 2001—. Finalist Tchr. of Yr., Calif. League Mid. Schs., 2006. Mem.: Fresno/Madera Calif. Music Educators Assn., Calif. Music Educators Assn., Am. Choral Dir.'s Assn. Avocations: dogs, boating, hiking, house restoration. Home: 644 E Terrace Ave Fresno CA 93704 Office: Reyburn Intermediate Sch 2901 N DeWolf Clovis CA 93611 Home Phone: 559-304-7139; Office Phone: 559-327-4730. Personal E-mail: cliffordbrd93@earthlink.net. Business E-Mail: cliffordbadgley@cusd.com.

BADGLEY, JOHN ROY, architect; b. Huntington, W.Va., July 10, 1922; s. Roy Joseph and Fannie Myrtle (Limbaugh) B.; m. Janice Atwell, July 10, 1975; 1 child, Adam; children by previous marriage: Dan, Lisa, Holly, Marcus, Michael AB, Occidental Coll., LA, 1943; MArch, Harvard U., Cambridge, Mass., 1949; postgrad., Internat. Ctr., Vincenza, Italy, 1959. Lic. Calif. Pvt. practice, San Luis Obispo, Calif., 1952—65; chief arch., planner Crocker Land Co., San Francisco, 1965—80; v.p. Cushman & Wakefield Inc., San Francisco, 1980—84; pvt. practice San Rafael, Calif., 1984—2001. Prof. Calif. State U., San Luis Obispo, 1952—65. Bd. dirs. Ft. Mason Ctr., Angel Island Assn. With USCGR, 1942-54 Mem. AIA (emeritus), Am. Arbitration Assn., Golden Gate Wine Soc Home and Office: Unit C 403 Avenida Castilla Laguna Woods CA 92637 Home Phone: 949-458-9444; Office Phone: 949-855-6637. Personal E-mail: jrbadgley@comline.com.

BADGLEY, MARK, fashion designer; b. East St. Louis, Ill., Jan. 12, 1961; Student, Univ. So. Calif., 1982; BFS in Fashion Design, Parsons Sch. Design, NYC, 1985. Apprentice, Jackie Rodgers, Donna Karan, NYC, 1985—88; co-founder, ptnr. Badgley Mischka, NYC, 1985—; ptnr. Badgley Mischka Dress. Recipient Mouton Cadet Young Designer award, 1989, Dallas Internat. Apparel Rising Star award, 1992; named one of Top 10 American Designers, Vogue. Office: 525 7th Ave Fl 18 New York NY 10018-4901*

BADGLEY, THEODORE MCBRIDE, retired psychiatrist, neurologist; b. Salem, Ala., June 27, 1925; s. Roy Joseph and Fannie (Limbaugh) B.; m. Mary Bennett Wells, Dec. 30, 1945; children: Justice O'Neil, Jan Badgley, Mona Jean Covey, Jason Wells, James John, Mary Rose Bleier. Student, Occidental Coll., 1942-44; MD, U. So. Calif., 1949. Diplomate: Am. Bd. Psychiatry and Neurology. Intern Letterman Gen. Hosp., San Francisco, 1949-50, resident in psychiatry, 1950-53; commd. capt. M.C. U.S. Army, 1950, advanced through grades to lt. col., 1967; chief mental hygiene cons. service Ft. Gordon, Ga.; and asso. clin. prof. psychiatry and neurology Med. Coll. Ga., 1954-55; resident in neurology Walter Reed Gen. Hosp., Washington, 1955-57, asst. chief psychiatry service, 1957-59, chief psychiatry service, 1959-62, asst. chief dept. psychiatry and neurology, 1962-63, dir. edn. and tng. psychiatry, 1957-63; chief dept. psychiatry and neurology U.S. Army Gen. Hosp., Landstuhl, Germany, 1963-66; chief psychiatry outpatient dept. Letterman Gen. Hosp., 1966-67; ret., 1967; dir. Kern View Mental Health Center, Bakersfield, Calif., 1967-69; pvt. practice medicine specializing in med. and forensic neuropsychiatry Bakersfield, 1967-93; pres. Sans Doloroso Inst., Bakersfield, 1969-93. Lectr. community health service orgns., profl. confs., seminars. Contbr. articles to profl. jours. Fellow Am. Psychiat. Assn. (disting. life); mem. Kern County Psychiat. Soc. (pres. 1972-93), Kern County Med. Soc. (pres. 1981). Personal E-mail: mcbadge@juno.com.

BADHAM, JOHN MACDONALD, motion picture director; b. Luton, Eng., Aug. 25, 1939; came to U.S., 1945; s. Henry Lee and Mary Iola (Hewitt) B.; 1 child, Kelly MacDonald; m. Julia Laughlin, 1992. BA, Yale U., 1961, MFA, 1963. Assoc. producer Universal Studios, 1969-70; pres. Gt. Am. Picture Show; CEO Badham Co. Guest lectr. UCLA, Yale U., U. So. Calif., Amherst Coll; prof. film media Chapman U. Assoc. producer TV movies Night Gallery, 1969, Neon Ceiling, 1970; assoc. producer, dir. TV movies The Senator, 1970 (Emmy award nomination 1971); dir. numerous episodes of The Bold Ones, others; motion pictures for TV include The Law (Emmy nomination 1974), 1974 (ARD reihe 'das film festival award 1975), Isn't It Shocking, 1973, Reflections of Murder, 1973, The Impatient Heart (Christopher award 1971), The Gun, (So. Calif. Motion Picture Council award 1974), The Godchild, 1974, Sorrow Floats, 1998; theatrical motion pictures include The Bingo Long Travelling All Stars and Motor Kings (NAACP image award nomination 1976), Saturday Night Fever, 1977, Dracula, 1979 (Grand prize 9th Internat. Sci. Fiction Festival of Paris, Best Horror Film award and, 1st George Pal Meml. award, both Acad. of Sci. Fiction Fantasy and Horror Films), Whose Life Is It Anyway, 1981, Blue Thunder, 1983, War Games (Best Dir., Acad. of Sci. Fiction Fantasy and Horror Films), 1983, American Flyers, 1985, Short Circuit, 1986, Stakeout, 1987, Bird on a Wire, 1989, The Hard Way, 1990, Point of No Return, 1993, Another Stakeout, 1993, Drop Zone, 1994, Nick of Time, 1995, Incognito, 1998, Floating Away, 1998, (TV) The Jack Bull, 1999, The Last Debate, 2000, My Brother's Keeper, 2002, Obsessed, 2002, Footsteps, 2003, Evel, 2004; exec. prodr. motion picture Rebound, 1996, Blind Justice; author: The Creative War Between Directors and Actors, 2006. Bd. dirs. Indian Spring Sch. Served with U.S. Army, 1963-64. Mem. Dirs. Guild Am., Am. Film Inst., Acad. Motion Picture Arts and Scis., Yale Drama Alumni Fund (chmn.).

BADIC, MIHAI, research scientist; b. Bucharest, June 15, 1951; s. Theodor Badic and Maria Popescu; m. Cristiana Pasoi, Nov. 17, 1973; children: Alina-Adriana, Alexandru-Theodor. MSc in Elec. Engring., U. Polytech. Bucharest, 1975, PhD in Elec. Engring., 2001. Dipl engr. Siderma Factory, Bucharest, 1975-79; rsch. scientist Rsch. Inst. Electrical Engring., Bucharest, 1979-90, dep. dir., 1990-92, chief lab., 1992-99, project mgr., 1999—. Contbr. articles to profl. jours. Mem. IEEE EMC Soc., Romanian EMC Soc. ACER. Avocations: philosophy, astronomy, astrology, swimming. Home: Str Campia Libertatii no 5 Bucharest 030361 Romania Office: Rsch Inst EE-ICPE Splaiul Unirii 313 Bucharest 030138 Romania Home Phone: 4021 324 55 28; Office Phone: 4021 346 49 40. Office Fax: 4021 346 72 68. Business E-Mail: mbadic@icpe.ro.

BADILLO, ALEJANDRO, lawyer; BA in Polit. Sci., Haverford Coll., 1996; M in Pub. Policy, U. Mich., 1998; JD, Columbia U., 2001. Bar: NJ 2001, NY 2002, DC 2006. Assoc. Kelley Drye & Warren, LLP, NYC, 2001—05, Dickstein Shapiro LLP, Washington, 2005—. Fellow Woodrow Wilson Pub. Policy and Internat. Affairs, Woodrow Wilson Nat. Found., Princeton, 1995, Rackham Grad. Sch., 1996; scholar Lawrence A. Wien, Columbia U. Sch. Law, 2000. Avocation: discussing pub. policy issues, investments, baseball. Office: Dickstein Shapiro LLP 1825 Eye St NW Washington DC 20006 Office Phone: 202-420-3036. Business E-Mail: badilloa@dicksteinshapiro.com.

BADKE, FREDERICK ROBERT, cardiologist; b. Colo. Springs, Colo., Sept. 8, 1948; MD, U. Colo. Sch. Medicine, 1973. Cert. Internal Medicine, Cardiovascular Disease. Intern, internal medicine U. Calif. , San Diego, La Jolla, 1973—74, resident, cardiology, 1974—75, fellow, 1975—77; hosp. appointment St. Alphonsus Regional Med. Ctr., Boise, Idaho, 1983—, bd. trustee, sec. treas., also corp. compliance and organizational integrity com., 2001—; hosp. appointment St. Luke's Regional Med. Ctr., Boise, Idaho, St. Luke's Wood River, West Valley Med. Ctr., McCall Meml. Hosp.; asst. clin. prof. medicine U. Wash. Sch. Medicine; co-founder, cardiologist Idaho Cardiology Associates, PA, 1994—. Fellow: Am. Coll. Cardiology. Avocations: boating, fishing, golf, skiing, tennis, financial investing. Office: Idaho Cardiology Associates PA 6140 Curtisian Ave Ste 200 Boise ID 83704-0107

BADLER, NORMAN IRA, computer and information science educator; b. LA, May 3, 1948; s. Bernard and Lillian Lorraine Badler; m. Virginia Renke, June 14, 1968; children: Jeremy, David. BA in Creative Studies, U. Calif., Santa Barbara, 1970; MS in Computer Sci., U. Toronto, Toronto, 1971, PhD in Computer Sci., 1975. Lectr. U. Toronto, 1973-74; asst. prof. computer and info. sci. U. Pa., Phila., 1974-79, assoc. prof., 1979-86, prof., 1986—, Cecilia Fitler Moore prof., 1990-94, dir. Ctr. for Human Modeling and Simulation, 1994—, assoc. dean Sch. Engring. and Applied Sci., 2001—05. Mem., chmn. program coms. numerous confs. and workshops. Co-author: Simulating Humans, 1993; co-editor: Making Them Move, 1990; contbr. numerous articles to profl. jours. Grantee Advanced Rsch. Projects Agy., NASA, NSF, U.S. Army, USAF. Mem. IEEE Computer Soc., Assn. for Computing Machinery (vice chmn. spl. interest group on graphics 1979-81, mem. spl. interest group on artificial intelligence), Am. Assn. for Artificial Intelligence, Phi Beta Kappa. Democrat. Jewish. Avocations: home renovation, cooking. Office: U Pa Computer & Info Sci Dept Philadelphia PA 19104-6389 Office Phone: 215-898-5862. Business E-Mail: badler@seas.upenn.edu.

BADR, GAMAL MOURSI, legal consultant; b. Helwan, Egypt, Feb. 8, 1924; came to U.S., 1970; s. Ahmad Moursi and Aisha Morshida (Al-Alaily) B.; m. Fatima al-Zahraa Barakat, June 18, 1950; children: Hefni, Hussein. LLB, U. Alexandria, Arab Republic of Egypt, 1944, LLD summa cum laude, 1954; diploma in econs., U. Cairo, 1945, diploma in pvt. law, 1946. Asst. dist. atty. Mixed Cts. Egypt, Alexandria, 1945-49; from assoc. to ptnr. Vatimbella, Catzeflis, Garrana & Badr, Alexandria, 1949-63; legal advisor UN Congo Operation, Kinshasa, Congo, 1963-64; justice Supreme Ct. Algeria, Algiers, 1965-69; from mem. to dep. dir. legal dept. UN Secretariat, NYC, 1970-84; legal advisor Mission of Qatar to UN, NYC, 1984-94; advisor Mission of Saudi Arabia to UN, NYC, 1998—. Permanent bur. mem. Pan-Arab Lawyers' Fedn., Cairo, 1959-61; adj. prof. law NYU, 1982-98; lectr. The Hague Acad. Internat. Law, 1984. Author: Agency, 1980, State Immunity, 1984; gen. editor Commercial Law of the Middle East; contbr. articles to profl. jours. Mem. Internat. Law Assn. (London), Am. Soc. Internat. Law, Am. Arbitration Assn. (panel of arbitrators), Am. Fgn. Law Assn. (v.p. 1985-87, 89-92), Egyptian-Am. Assn. (pres. 1987-90), Rotary (pres. Alexandria Club 1962-63). Muslim. Home: 211 Harris Farm Rd Mooresville NC 28115-5790

BADRA, ROBERT GEORGE, theology studies and humanities educator; b. Lansing, Mich., Dec. 8, 1933; s. Razouk Anthony and Anna (Paul) Badra; m. Maria Theresa Beer, Oct. 25, 1968 (div. 1973); m. Kristen Lillie Stuckey, Dec. 30, 1977 (div. 2001); children: Rachal Jennifer, Danielle Elizabeth Jane. BA, Sacred Heart Sem., 1957; MA, Western Mich. U., 1968; MDiv, St. John's Provincial Sem., 1985. Ordained priest Roman Cath. Ch., 1961. Mem. faculty Kalamazoo Valley CC, 1968—, prof. philosophy, religion and humanities, 1968—. Adj. prof. Nazareth Coll., 1985—91, Siena Heights U., 1993—; mem. faculty ministry formation Cath. Diocese Kalamazoo, 1999—2003. Bd. dirs. Kalamazoo Coun. Humanities, 1983—86, Van Buren Youth Camp, 1993—2007, v.p. bd. dirs., 2002—07. Recipient Edn. award, Exxon, 1996; grantee NEH, 1991—. Mem.: Assn. Religion and Intellectual Life. Office: Kalamazoo Valley CC PO Box 4070 Kalamazoo MI 49003-4070 Personal E-mail: bbadra1579@aol.com.

BAE, FRANK S.H., law librarian, educator; b. Chung King, Szechuan, China, Dec. 19, 1941; came to U.S., 1967; s. Tse H. and Yu F. (Wang) B.; m. Anne Rita Donavan, March 15, 1975; children: Stephen, David, Marie, Elizabeth. LLB, Nat. Taipei U., 1965; MCL, U. Miami, Fla., 1968; MS, U. Wis., 1970; JurD (hon.), New England Sch. Law, Boston, 1977. Dir. law libr. New England Sch. Law, 1970—, asst. prof. law, 1970-73, assoc. prof. law, 1973-74, prof. law, 1974—. Co-author: Searching the Law, 3d edit., 2005, Surety's (Secondary Obligor's) Rights under the Restatement of the Law. Mem. New England Law Libr. Consortium (bd. dirs.). Office: New

Eng Sch Law Libr 154 Stuart St Boston MA 02116-5616 Home Phone: 781-431-7075. Business E-Mail: fbae@faculty.nesl.edu.

BAE, HANHONG, molecular biologist, researcher; b. Hwacheon, Gangwon-Do, Republic of Korea, Jan. 7, 1965; arrived in US, 1987; s. Kwang-Suk Bae and Ok-Nam Song. BS, Seoul Nat. U., 1987; MS, Oreg. State U., Corvallis, 1992; PhD, Iowa State U., Ames, 2001. Rsch. asst. Oreg. State U., Corvallis, 1988—92; rsch. scientist Korea Forest Rsch. Inst., Seoul, 1993—95; rsch. asst. Iowa State U., Ames, 1995—2001; plant molecular biologist USDA-ARS-Plant Scis. Inst., Beltsville, Md., 2001—. Mem.: Am. Soc. Plant Biologists. Roman Catholic. Achievements include research in effect of trehalose on plant growth; necrosis- and ethylene-inducing protein in fungi; responses of cacao plants to biotic and abiotic stresses. Office: USDA-ARS-Plant Scis Inst 10300 Baltimore Ave Beltsville MD 20705 Office Phone: 301-504-5262. Office Fax: 301-504-1998. Business E-Mail: rino.bae@ars.usda.gov.

BAE, SUNGKOO, aeronautical engineer, aerospace engineer, researcher; s. Won Bae and Keum-Hee Lee; m. Kyungsun Na, Dec. 23, 1990; children: Minwoo, Hyejee. BS in Astronomy, MS in Astronomy, Yonsei U., Seoul; PhD in Aerospace Engring. and Engring. Mechanics, U. Tex., Austin, 1998. Rsch. scientist Ctr. Space Rsch., Austin, 1999—. Office: Ctr Space Research 3925 W Braker Ln Ste 200 Austin TX 78759 Home Phone: 512-249-8034. Business E-Mail: bae@csr.utexas.edu.

BAECHER, GREGORY B., civil and environmental engineer, educator; BSCE, U. Calif., 1968; MSc, MIT, 1970, PhD in Civil Engring., 1972. Rockefeller found. post doctoral fellow Internat. Inst. Applied Sys. Analysis, Vienna, Va., 1974—75; prof. Dept. Civil Engring. MIT, Cambridge, Mass., 1975—88; pres., CEO ConSolve Inc., Lexington, Mass., 1988—95; prof., past chmn. Dept. Civil and Environ. Engring. U. Md., College Park, 1995—. Vis. prof. Technical U., Munich, 1980—81. Co-author: Reliability and Statistics in Geotechnical Engineering, 2003, Risk and Uncertainty in Dam Safety, 2004; contbr. articles to profl. jours. Captain USAR, 1972—80. Mem.: NAE. Office: U Md Dept Civil and Environ Engring College Park MD 20742 Office Phone: 301-405-1972. Office Fax: 301-405-2585. E-mail: gbaecher@eng.umd.edu.

BAECHLER, DONALD, painter; b. Hartford, Conn., 1956; Student, Md. Inst. Art, 1974-76, Cooper Union, NYC, 1977-78, Staatliche Hochschule Kunste, Frankfurt, Germany, 1978-79. Exhibited in group shows at Wadsworth Atheneum, Hartford, Conn., 1975, Whitney Mus. Am. Art, N.Y.C., 1989, Parallel Visions, Modern Artists and Outsider Art, L.A. County Mus. Art, 1992, Extravagant: The Economy of Elegance, Tony Shafrazi, NY, 1993, Works on Paper, Baron/Boisante, NY, 1994, Eblems and Contours, Sperone Westwater, NY, 1995, The Baseball Show, Curt Marcus, NY, 1996, Chanel, Any Warhol Mus, Pitts., 97, Knowing Children, David Beitzel Gallery, NY, Road Show, DFN Gallery, NY, 1999, Painting, Paul Kasmin Gallery, NY, 2000, Mythic Proportions: Painting in the 1980s, MoCA, Miami, 2001, New York Expression, Bergen Kommune, Norway, 2002, Funny Papers: Cartoons and Contemporary Drawings, Daniel Weinberg Gallery, LA, 2003, Pop Art and Minimalismus, Albertina, Vienna, 2004, I Am the Walrus, Cheim & Read, NY, 2004; one-man shows include Sperone Westwater, N.Y.C., 1993, 95, Paul Kasmin Gallery, NYC, 1993, Erika and Otto Friedrich, Bern, Switzerland, 1994, Pace Prints, NYC, 1994, Stephen Wirtz Gallery, San Francisco, 1994, Laura Carpenter Fine Art, Santa Fe, 1994, Galerie Thaddaeus Ropac, Paris, 1994-95, Tony Shafrazi Gallery, NYC, 1995, Galeria Leyendecker, Tenerife, Spain, 1996, New Flowers, Harley Baldwin, Aspen, 1997, Works on Paper, Locks Gallery, Phila., 1998, Globes and More, Thaddeaus Ropac, Paris, 1999, Baldwin Gallery, Aspen, Colo., 2000, Five Easy Pieces, Tony Shafrazi, NY, 2001, Alain Noirhomme, Brussels, 2002, Recent Paintings, Galerie Bernd Klueser, Munich, 2003, The Enemies of the Rose, Kunst Meran, Merano, Italy, 2004; represented in permanent collections of MoMA, NY, Whitney Mus. Am. Art, NY, Guggenheim Mus., NY, NY Pub. Libr., Mus. Fine Arts, Boston, Mus. Contemporary Art, LA, Eli Broad Found., LA, Chase Manhattan Bank, NY, Deutsche Bank, NY, Sony Corp., NY. Office: Paul Kasmin Galleryl 293 10th Ave New York NY 10001-7003

BAECKLER, VIRGINIA VAN WYNEN, librarian, writer; b. Englewood, NJ, June 18, 1942; d. Kenneth Gregg and Esther Grace (Thompson) Van Wynen; m. William W. Baeckler, Apr. 9, 1971; children: Gregg William, Sarah Angela. BA, Cornell U., 1964, MA, 1967; postgrad., Moscow State U., 1967—69; MLS, Rutgers U., 1972. Head Slavic acquisitions Princeton U. Library, 1969—71; head Mercer County Library, Ewing, NJ, 1972—75; dir. Sources, Hopewell, NJ, 1975—, Plainsboro Pub. Libr., NJ, 1991—. Vol., tchr. YWCA of Princeton, NJ, 1979. Author: Go, Pep and Pop!, 1976, PR for Pennies, 1978, Sparkle!, 1980, Storytime Science, 1986. Recipient Librarian award, NY Times, 2006. Mem. Nat. Sci. Tchrs. Assn., Alliance for Arts and Edn., ALA, Ednl. Media Assn. (lobbyist). Democrat. Office: Plainsboro Public Library 641 Plainsboro Rd Plainsboro NJ 08536*

BAEHR, THEODORE, religious organization administrator, writer, communications executive; b. NYC, May 31, 1946; m. Liliana Milani, 1975; children: Theodore Peirce, James Stuart Castiglioni, Robert Gallatin, Evelyn Noelle. Student in French lit., U. Bordeaux and Toulouse, France, 1967; student in English lit., Cambridge U., Eng., 1967; student in German lit., U. Munich, 1968; BA in Comparative Lit., Dartmouth Coll., Hanover, NH, 1969; JD, NYU, 1972; postgrad. Inst. Theology, Cathedral St. John the Divine, 1978—80; HHD, Belhaven Coll., Jackson, Miss., 2006. Ordained Internet Ministerial Fellowship. Rsch. engr. Precision Sci. Co., Chgo., 1964-65; legal cons. firm Dandeub, Fleissig & Assocs., NYC, 1970-71; law student asst. US Atty.'s Office, so. Dist. NY, 1971-72; pres. Agape Prodns., NYC, 1972-79, chmn. bd., 1979-82; exec. dir. Good News Comm., Inc., NYC, 1978-80, chmn. bd., 1980—; pres. Episc. Radio-TV Found., Inc., Atlanta, 1981-82, Trinity Concepts, 1982; cons. media; dir. TV Ctr. CUNY at Bklyn. Coll., 1979-80, 82—; pub. Movieguide Mag., 1985—. Episc. Communicators, 1981-84; exec. prodr. Ch.'s Presence at World's Fair, Knoxville, Tenn., 1982; dir. Am. Theater Actors, Episc. Comm. Hollywood's Reel of Fortune, 1993, The Media-Wise Family, 1998, Faith in God and Generals, 2003, What Can We Watch Tonight, 2003, Frodo and Harry, 2003, So You Want To Be In Pictures, 2005; author: Getting the Word Out, 1986, Narnia Beckons: C.S. Lewis' The Lion, The Witch and The Wardrobe and Beyond, 2005, Amazing Grace/Freedom, 2007, Culture-Wise Family, 2007; editor (commentator): NYU Law Sch. newspaper, 1969—72, Contemporary Drug Problems, 1971—72, Atlanta Area Christian News; creator, coord. Communicate Workshops, 1979, creator, writer, editor Episc. Ch. Video Resource Guide and Episcopal Video/TV Newsletter, 1979; prodr.(dir., writer): (various TV and radio programs including) Movieguide®, Joy of Music, Perspectives, PBS, 1981—82, Religionwise on WGST, CBS, 1981— (Religion in Media award); dir.: Runaways (Chgo. Intercom Gold plaque and Religion in Media award, 1989); prodr.: In Their Own Words, Was It Love (Religion in Media award). V.p. Ctr. for TV in Humanities, 1982; chmn. bd. Christian Film & TV Commn., 1978—; bd. dirs. Nat. Religious Broadcasters, Celebrate Life, Religious Heritage of Am., Dorsey Theatre, Nat. Think Tank, Mission Am., Nehemiah Inst., Coalition on Revival; mem. steering com. Theol. Summit Conf.; bd. dirs. Am. Theatre of Actors, Nat. Coun. on Bible Curriculum in Pub. Schs., United Srs. Assn., Campus Renewal Ministries Nat. Broadcast Day of Prayer; bd. dirs., nat. adv. bd. United Srs. Assn. Recipient Pres.'s award, LifeNET, 1998, Eagle award, Nat. Religious Broadcasters, 2001. Mem. Mission Am., Bishop in Ind. Christian Chs. Internat., Nat. Press Club. Office: Movieguide(r) 1151 Avenida Acaso Camarillo CA 93012 Office Phone: 805-383-2000. Office Fax: 805-383-4089. Personal E-mail: Ted@TedBaehr.com.

BAEHREN, JAMES W., lawyer; b. Toledo, June 11, 1950; BS, Ohio State U., 1972, MBA, 1974; JD, U. Toledo, 1978. Assoc. Fuller & Henry, 1978—85, ptnr., 1985—92; asst. gen. counsel Owens-Illinois Inc., Toledo, 1992, sec., 1998, dir. fin., sr. v.p., gen. counsel, corp. sec. Mem.: ABA, Ohio State Bar Assn., Toledo Bar Assn. Office: Owens-Illinois 1 Michael Owens Way Perrysburg OH 43551-2999 Office Phone: 419-247-5000. Office Fax: 419-247-7107. E-mail: jim.baehren@owens-ill.com.*

BAEK, EUN-OK, instructional technology educator; d. Jae-Heum Baek and Gyong-Ja Kim. BEd, Chinju Nat. U. Edn., South Korea, 1987; MEd, Korea Nat. U. Edn., South Korea, 1993; MA, Ind. U., Bloomington, 2001, PhD, 2002. Tchr. NamJung Elem. Sch., ChangWon, GyongNam, Republic of Korea, 1987—94, TaeBang Elem. Sch., ChangWon, GyongNam, Republic of Korea, 1994—96; instrnl. designer St. Meinrad Sch. Theology, St. Meinrad, Ind., 1998—2000; grad. tchg. asst. DePauw U., Greencastle, Ind., 2000—02; grad. rsch. asst. Ind. U., Bloomington, 2001—02; asst. prof. Calif. State U. San Bernardino, 2002—. Online cmty. coord. Preparing Tomorrow's Tchrs. to Use Tech. grant U.S. Dept. Edn., Calif. State U., San Bernardino, Calif., 2002—05; adv. bd. com. mem. Fund for the Improvement of Post Secondary Edn., U.S. Dept. Edn., U. Calif., Riverside, 2002—04; rev. bd. mem. for techtrends Assn. for Ednl. Comm. and Tech., Bloomington, Ind., 2005—. Contbr. articles to profl. jours., chapters to books. Recipient Scholarship of Tchg. and Learning, Tchg. Resource Ctr., Calif. State U. San Bernardino, 2004—05, Tchg. Skills Study award, 2003—04; fellow Summer Rsch. fellow, Faculty Profl. Devel. Coordinating Com., Calif. State U. San Bernardino, 2003; grantee Rsch. grantee, Ind. U., 2001; Mini grantee, Faculty Profl. Devel. Coordinating Com., Calif. State U. San Bernardino, 2003—05. Mem.: Assn. for the Advancement of Computing in Edn., Assn. for Ednl. Comm. and Tech., Am. Ednl. Rsch. Assn., Phi Beta Delta. Office: California State University 5500 University Pkwy San Bernardino CA 92407 Home Phone: 909-241-0124; Office Phone: 909-537-5454. Office Fax: 909-537-7522. Business E-Mail: ebaek@csusb.edu.

BAEK, KWANG-HYUN, research scientist; b. Seoul, Republic of Korea, Nov. 23, 1967; arrived in US, 1998; s. Seung-Khee Paik and Chung-Ja Yi; m. Jin-Kyung Kang, July 29, 1998; 1 child, Daniel S. B in Electronics and Computer Engring., Korea U., 1990, M in Electronics Engring., 1998; PhD, U. Ill. at Urbana-Champaign, 2002. Assoc. rschr. Samsung Electronics, Kiheung, Republic of Korea, 1990—96; rsch. asst. U. Ill., Urbana, 1998—2001; sr. scientist Rockwell Sci. Co., Thousand Oaks, Calif., 2000—. Contbr. scientific papers pub. to profl. jpur. Recipient Team of the Yr., Rockwell Sci. Co., 2002; fellow, Korean Airline, 1998, SRC, 1998-2001. Mem.: IEEE. Achievements include patents pending for Hardware efficient phase-to-amplitude mapping design for direct digital frequency synthesizers; patents for Dual port static RAM; Multi-purpose I/O for analog and digital signals; Access method of display SRAM built in micro-controllers; Dual port SRAM for display in micro-controllers; On screen display cir. Office: Rockwell Scientific Company 1049 Camino Dos Rios Thousand Oaks CA 91360 Home Phone: 805-517-1323; Office Phone: 805-373-4222. Personal E-mail: kbaek@ieee.org. Business E-Mail: kbaek@rwsc.com.

BAER, AMY BOSLEY, film company executive; Grad. in English Lit., Georgetown U. Dir. devel. Guber-Peters Entertainment Co.; exec. v.p. prodn. Columbia Pictures. Mem. LA adv. bd. Georgetown Entertainment & Media Alliance. Named one of 100 Most Powerful Women in Entertainment, Hollywood Reporter, 2006. Office: Columbia Pictures 10202 W Washington Blvd Culver City CA 90232 Office Phone: 310-244-4000. Office Fax: 310-244-2626.*

BAER, HAROLD, JR., senior federal judge; b. NYC, Feb. 16, 1933; s. Harold and Edna (Jacobus) B.; m. Suzanne Harris, Aug. 18, 1957; children: Elizabeth Jane, Linda Gail. Grad. magna cum laude, Hobart Coll., 1954; LLB, Yale U., 1957. Bar: N.Y. 1959, U.S. Dist. Ct. (so. dist.) N.Y. 1961, U.S. Ct. Appeals (2d cir.) 1961, U.S. Supreme Ct. 1964. Asst. U.S. atty., chief organized crime unit, U.S. Atty.'s Office for So. Dist. N.Y., NYC, 1961-66, 1st asst. U.S. atty., chief criminal divsn., 1970-71; exec. dir. civilian complaint rev. bd. N.Y.C. Police Dept., 1966-67; ptnr. Guggenheimer & Untermyer, NYC, 1968-70, 72-82; justice N.Y. State Supreme Ct., 1982-92; exec. jud. officer Jud. Arbitration and Mediation Svcs./Endispute, 1992-94; judge U.S. Dist. Ct. (so. dist.) N.Y., NYC, 1994—. Mem. N.Y.C. mayoral com. alleged police corruption, 1993, 94. Contbr. articles to law jours. Mem. N.Y. State Bar Assn. (ho. of dels. 1977-89, 93-96), N.Y. County Lawyers Assn. (pres. 1979-81, bd. dirs., mem. exec. com.), Assn. Bar City N.Y. (criminal justice coun. 1980-82, judiciary com. 1993-94), Network Bar Leaders (founder, chmn. 1981-83), Assn. Justices N.Y.C. and N.Y. State (officer). Home Phone: 212-974-0140; Office Phone: 212-805-0184.

BAER, JOHN RICHARD FREDERICK, lawyer; b. Melrose Park, Ill., Jan. 9, 1941; s. John Richard and Zena Edith (Ostreyko) B.; m. Linda Gail Chapman, Aug. 31, 1963; children: Brett Scott, Deborah Jill. BA, U. Ill., Champaign, 1963, JD, 1966. Bar: Ill. 1966, US Dist. Ct. (no. dist.) Ill. 1967, US Ct. Appeals (7th cir.) 1969, US Ct. Appeals (DC cir.) 1975, US Ct. Appeals (9th cir.) 1979, US Supreme Ct. 1975. Assoc. Keck, Mahin & Cate, Chgo., 1966-73, ptnr., 1974-97; of counsel Sonnenschein Nath & Rosenthal LLP, Chgo., 1997-99, ptnr., 2000—. Mem. Ill. Atty. Gen.'s Franchise adv. bd., 1992-94, 96—, chair 1996—. Editor Commerce Clearing House Sales Representative Law Guide, 1998—; mem edit1. bd. U. Ill. Law Forum, 1964-65, asst. editor, 1965-66; contbg. editor: Commercial Liability Risk Management and Insurance, 1978. Mem. Plan Commn., Village of Deerfield, Ill., 1976-79, chmn., 1978-79, mem. Home Rule Study Commn., 1974-75, mem. home rule implementation com., 1975-76. Mem.: ABA (topics and articles editor Franchise Law jour. 1995—96, assoc. editor 1996—99, editor-in-chief The Franchise Lawyer 1999—2002, governing com. Forum on Franchising 2003—06), N.Am. Securities Adminstrs. Assn. Franchise Project Group (mem. industry adv. com.), Internat. Bar Assn. (officer franchising com. 2006, sec. franchising com. 2007—), Ill. State Bar Assn. (competition dir. Region 8 nat. moot ct. 1974, profl. ethics com. 1977—84, spl. com. on individual lawyers advt. 1981—83, chmn. 1982—83, profl. responsibility com. 1983—84, standing com. on liaison with atty. registration and discplinary commn 1989—93, ISBA/CBA com. on ethics 2000 1999—2006), Inter-Pacific Bar Assn., Internat. Franchise Assn. (legal/legis. com. 1990—). Office: Sonnenschein Nath & Rosenthal LLP 7800 Sears Tower 233 S Wacker Dr Chicago IL 60606-6404 Home Phone: 312-255-0282; Office Phone: 312-876-2604. Business E-Mail: jbaer@sonnenschein.com.

BAER, MAX, state supreme court justice; b. Pitts., Dec. 24, 1947; s. Henry and Helen Baer; m. Beth Love Hartman; 2 children. BA, U. Pittsburgh, 1971; JD, Duquesne U., 1975; Ms of Tax Program, Robert Morris Coll., 1985—86. Dep. atty. gen. State of Pa., 1975—79; atty. priv. practice, 1980—89; judge Allegheny County Ct. of Common Pleas, 1989—2003; justice Pa. Supreme Ct., 2003—. Former chair Domestic Relations Procedural Rules Com.; ex officio rep. Juvenile Ct. Judges Commn.; former mem. Joint State Govt. Commn. on Adoption Law & Services to Children; former chair Pa. Conference Trial Judges Family Law Section. Named Adoption Advocate of Yr., Pa. Dept. Public Welfare, 1997, Most Valuable Peacemaker, Pa. Council of Mediators, 2004; recipient Adoption Excellence award for Jud. Innovation, 1998, Robert S. Steward award for disting. service to Pa. families, 1998, Champion of Children award, Homeless Children's Edn. Fund, 2003. Mem.: Pa. Bar Assn. (Named Child Advocate of Yr. 2000). Office: Pa Supreme Ct 2325 One Oxford Ctr Pittsburgh PA 15219 Office Phone: 412-467-2220. Business E-Mail: justice.baer@pacourts.us.*

BAER, MICHAEL ALAN, political scientist, educator; b. Atlanta, Feb. 4, 1943; s. Kurt Arthur and Beulah (Mendelson) Baer; m. CHarlotte Glazer, Aug. 16, 1964; children: Daniel Noach, Naomi Aviva. BA, Emory U., 1964; MA, U. Oreg., 1966, PhD, 1968. Rsch. asst. Ctr. Advanced Study Ednl. Adminstrn., U. Oreg., 1964-68; faculty U. Ky., Lexington, 1968-90, prof. polit. sci. and pub. adminstrn., 1980-90, chmn. dept. polit. sci., 1977-81, dean Coll. Arts and Scis., 1981-90; polit. analyst WAVE-TV, Louisville; prof. polit. sci. Northeastern U., Boston, 1990-2000, provost, sr. v.p. acad. affairs, 1990-98; sr. v.p. programs and analysis Am. Coun. Edn., Washington, 1998—2005; dir. Ctr. Policy Analysis, Washington, 1998-2000; v.p. Isaacson, Miller Inc., Washington, 2005—, also bd. dirs. Bd. dirs. Strategic Partnerships, LLC, 2007—. Co-author: (book) Lobbying: Influence and Interaction in American State Legislatures, 1969; co-editor: Political Science in America, 1991; mem. editl. bd.: State and Local Govt. Rev., 1977—81; contbr. articles to profl. jours. Bd. dirs. Coun. Colls. Arts and Scis., 1983—89, pres., 1988; rec. sec. Bluegrass chpt. Ky. Assn. Gifted Edn., 1983—85; mem. Mayor's com. to establish Lexington Children's Mus., 1988—90, bd. dirs., 1990; mem. coun. Inter Univ. Consortium for Polit. and Social Rsch., U. Mich., 1988—94, chmn., 1990—92; bd. dirs. Congregation Ohavay Zion, Lexington, 1976—78, Ctrl. Ky. Jewish Assn., 1970—74, pres., 1973—74; bd. dirs. Ctrl. Ky. Civil LIberties Union, 1973—77, Bluegrass chpt. NCCJ, 1980—81, Jamaica Pond Assn., 1992—97. Fellow Leverhulme, 1974—75. Mem.: Nat. Capitol Area Polit. Sci. Assn. (bd. mem. 2001—06, pres. 2004—05), Nat. Assn. Univ. and Land Grant Colls. (commn. on arts and scis. 1986—90, chmn. 1990), Ky. Conf. Polit. Sci., So. Polit. Sci. Assn. (chmn. nominating com. 1993—94, 1996), Brit. Politics Group (exec. coun. 1978—80), Midwest Polit. Sci. Assn. (exec. coun. 1980—83), Am. Polit. Sci. Assn. (endowed programs com. 1993—94, 1995—98, centennial celebration com. 2002—03, com. on tchg. and learning 2004—06). Home: 4103 38th St NW Washington DC 20016-2217 Office: Isaacson Miller Inc 1875 Connecticut Ave NW Ste 710 Washington DC 20009 Home Phone: 202-244-8203; Office Phone: 202-682-1504. E-mail: mbaer@imsearch.com.

BAER, RICHARD N., lawyer, telecommunications industry executive; b. Glen Cove, NY, Mar. 30, 1957; married; 2 children. BA, Columbia U., NYC, 1979; JD, Duke U., Durham, NC, 1983. Bar: NY 1984, Colo. Asst. dist. atty., Bklyn., 1983—88; staff atty. SEC, Washington, 1988; assoc. Rosenman & Colin, NYC, 1988—92; chmn. litig. dept. Sherman & Howard, Denver, 1992—2000; spl. legal counsel to chmn. and CEO Richard C. Notebaert Qwest Comm. Internat. Inc., Denver, 2001—02, exec. v.p., gen. counsel, 2002—. Office: Qwest Comm Internat Inc Legal Dept 1801 California St Denver CO 80202 Office Phone: 303-992-2811. Office Fax: 303-383-8444. E-mail: rich.baer@qwest.com.*

BAER, SUSAN M., airport executive; married; 1 child. BA in Urban Studies and Anthropology, Barnard Coll.; MBA, NYU. Mgmt. analyst Port Authority of NY and NJ, mgr. pub. svcs. divsn. Tunnels, Bridges and Terminals Dept., mgr. Lincoln Tunnel, 1985—86, mgr. Port Authority Bus Terminal Manhattan NYC, 1986—88, gen. mgr. Aviation Customer and Mktg. Svcs., 1988—94, gen. mgr. LaGuardia Airport Flushing, NY, 1994-98, gen. mgr. Newark Internat. Airport NJ, 1998—. Office: Newark Int & Teterboro Airports Conrad Rd, Bldg 1 Newark NJ 07114

BAER, TIMOTHY R., lawyer, retail executive; b. 1960; BA, Princeton Univ.; JD, Univ. Minn. Bar: Minn. 1985. Asst. gen. counsel Target Corp., Mpls., 1994—2002, v.p., 2002—04, sr. v.p., gen. counsel, corp. sec., 2004—. Bd. dir. Catholic Charities of Mpls. & St. Paul. Office: Target Corp 1000 Nicollet Mall Minneapolis MN 55403*

BAER, WALTER S., think-tank executive; b. Chgo., July 27, 1937; s. Walter S., Jr. and Margaret S. (Mayer) B.; m. Miriam R. Schenker, June 18, 1959 (div. 1987); children: David W., Alan B.; m. Jeri Weiss, Oct. 23, 1988. BS, Calif. Inst. Tech., 1959; PhD (NSF fellow), U. Wis., 1964. Rsch. physicist Bell Telephone Labs., Murray Hill, NJ, 1964-66; White House fellow Washington, 1966-67; White House sci. adv. staff, 1967-69; cons. and sr. scientist RAND Corp., Santa Monica, Calif., 1970-81, dir. energy policy program, 1978-81; dir. advanced tech. Times Mirror Co., Los Angeles, 1981-89; deputy v.p. domestic rsch. RAND Corp., Santa Monica, Calif., 1990—2006; sr. fellow U. So. Calif., Annenberg Sch. Comm., LA, 2006—. Cons. UN, maj. U.S. corps, 1970—; dir. Aspen (Colo.) Cable TV Workshop, 1972-73, L.A. Ednl. Partnership; pres. KCRW Found., Santa Monica, Calif.; adv. bd. Columbia U. Inst. Tele-Info., U.S. Com. for Internat. Inst. Applied Systems Analysis; dir. Am. Tng. Internat.; mem. gov. coun. on info. tech. State of Calif. Author: Interactive Television, 1971, Cable Television: A Handbook for Decisionmaking, 1973, also articles; editor: The Electronic Box Office, 1974, w/ RAND Cable Television Series, 1974; editorial bd.: Telecommunications Policy, 1976— , Internat. Ency. Communications. Mem. European Community Visitor, 1978. Recipient U. Wis. award for excellence in teaching, 1960; Preceptor award Broadcast Industry Conf., 1974— Fellow AAAS (chmn. Indsl. Sci. Sec. 1992-93); mem. IEEE (mem. com. on comm. and info. policy 1994—), Am. Phys. Soc., Internat. Inst. Communications, Sigma Xi. Office: U So Calif Annenberg Ctr Comm Los Angeles CA 90089-7725 Office Phone: 310-488-3444. Business E-Mail: wbaer@usc.edu.

BAER, WERNER, economist, educator; b. Offenbach, Germany, Dec. 14, 1931; came to U.S., 1945, naturalized, 1952; s. Richard and Grete (Herz) B. 58776, CUNY, NYC, 1953; MA, Harvard U., 1955, PhD, 1958; D honoris causa, Fed. U. Pernambuco, Brazil, 1988, New U. Lisbon, Portugal, 2000; D honoris causa (hon.), Fed. U. Ceara, Brazil, 1993. Instr. Harvard U., 1958-61; asst. prof. Yale U., New Haven, 1961-65; asso. prof. Vanderbilt U., Nashville, 1965-69, prof., 1969-74; prof. econs. U. Ill., Urbana, 1974—. Vis. prof. U. São Paulo, Brazil, 1966-68, Vargas Found., Brazil, 1966-68; Rhodes fellow St. Antony's Coll., Oxford (Eng.) U., 1975. Author: The Brazilian Economy: Growth and Development, 6th edit., 2007, Privatization in Latin America, vol. 17, 1994, The Changing Role of International Capital in Latin America, 1998; co-author: (with P. Elosegui and A. Gallo) The Achievements and Failures of Argentina's Neo-Liberal Policies, 2002, (with J. Bang) Privatization and Equity in Brazil and Russia, 2002, (with E. Amann) Anchors Away: The Costs and Benefits of Brazil's Devaluation, 2003; co-editor: Latin America-Privatization, Property Rights and Deregulation, 1993, (with W. Maloney) Neo-Liberalism and Income Distribution in Latin America, 1997, (with W. Miles, A. Moran) The End of the Asian Myth, 1999, The State and Industry in the Development Process, 1999 (with E. Amann) Neoliberalism and it's Consequences in Brazil, 2002; contbr. articles to profl. jours. Decorated Order So. Cross (Brazil). Mem. Am. Econ. Assn., Latin Am. Studies Assn. Home: 1703 Devonshire Dr Champaign IL 61821-5901 Office: U Ill 1407 W Gregory Dr Urbana IL 61801-3606 Office Phone: 217-333-8388. Business E-Mail: wbaer@uiuc.edu.

BAER, WILLIAM J., lawyer; b. May 31, 1950; s. Joseph and Roses B.; m. Nancy Hendry; children: Michael Hendry, Andrew Hendry. BA, Lawrence U., 1972; JD, Stanford U., 1975. Bar: Wis., 1975, D.C., 1981, U.S. Ct. Appeals D.C., 1989, U.S. Supreme Ct. 1999. Trial atty. divsn. nat. advertising FTC, Washington, 1975-76, asst. to dir. bureau consumer protection, 1976-77, atty. advisor to chmn., 1977-78, asst. gen. counsel for legis., 1978-80; assoc. Arnold & Porter, Washington, 1980-83, ptnr., 1984-95; dir. Bur. of Competition FTC, Washington, 1995-99; ptnr., head antitrust practice group Arnold & Porter, Washington, 2000—. Contbr. articles to profl. jours. Trustee Lawrence U. Mem.: ABA. Democrat. Avocations: tennis, golf. Office: Arnold & Porter LLP 555 12th St NW Ste 810 Washington DC 20004-1200 Office Phone: 202-942-5936. Office Fax: 202-942-5999. Business E-Mail: william.baer@aporter.com.

BAERG, RICHARD HENRY, podiatrist, surgeon; b. LA, Jan. 19, 1937; s. Henry Francis and Ruth Elizabeth (Loven) B.; children from previous marriage: Carol Elizabeth, William Richard, Michael David, Niccolo, Monica, Arianna, Mia, Reagan. AA, Reedley Coll., 1956; BS, Samuel Merritt U., Sch. Podiatric Medicine, 1965, DPM, 1968, MSc in Foot Surgery, 1970; MPH in Med. Adminstrn., U. Calif., Berkeley, 1971; ScD (hon.), N.Y. Coll. Podiatric Medicine, 1980; LittD (hon.), Ohio Coll. Podiatric Medicine, 1984; postgrad. Sch. Edn. and Pub. Health, U. Mich., 1973—74; postgrad. Sch. of Bus. and Sch. of Edn., Harvard U., 1975. Diplomate Am. Bd. Podiatric Surgery (foot and ankle surgery), Am. Bd. Podiatric Orthopedics and Primary Podiatric Medicine (exec. dir. 1980-90), Am. Bd. podiatric Pub. Health (bd. dirs. 1980-89). Intern Highland Alameda County Gen. Hosp., Oakland, Calif., 1969; resident in surgery Pacific Coast Hosp., San Francisco, 1970; acad. dean N.Y. Coll. Podiatric Medicine, NYC, 1971-74; v.p., dean Samuel Merritt U., Sch. Podiatric Medicine, Oakland, Calif., 1974-76; chief podiatric medicine Los Angeles County-U. So. Calif. Med. Ctr., 1976-78; dir. So. Calif. Podiatric Med. Ctr., 1976-78; pvt. practice Beverly Hills, Calif., 1976-78; dean Roseland Franklin U. Coll. Podiatric Medicine, Chgo., 1978-79; mem. spl. med. adv. group to sec. Dept. Vets. Affairs, Washington, 1976-79, dir. podiatric service, dept. medicine and surgery, 1979-84, acting dir., 1984-86; health resources adminstrn. cons. Dept. Health and Human Svcs., Washington, 1974-88; chief podiatry VA Med. Ctr., Loma Linda, Calif., 1984-89; dir. residency tng. Loma Linda Foot Clinic, 1990; exec. v.p., med. dir. Dr. Footcare Corp., Montclair, Calif., 1988-90; faculty podiatry U. N.C. Hosps., Chapel Hill, 1992—; clin. prof. Sch. of Podiatric Medicine Barry U., Miami, Fla., 1993—; clin. prof. Med. Sch., U. N.C., 1992—; staff podiatrist Morehead Hosp., Eden, NC, 1997-2000. Mem. podiatric staff Chapel Hill Surg. Ctr., 1993—; chief of podiatry Umstead Hosp., Butner, N.C., 1997-2000, VA Med. Ctr., Huntington, W.Va., dir. residency tng. chief podiatry sect., 2000-02; assoc. clin. prof. Stanford U. Med. Sch., 1974-76; clin. prof. Temple U. Coll. Podiatric Medicine, 1979-86, Des Moines U. Medicine and Health Sci., 1984-, U. NC Sch. Medicine, 1980-90; prof. dept. surgery Marshall U. Sch. Medicine, Huntington, W.Va., clin. prof. podiatric medicine and surgery Pikeville Coll. Sch. Osteopathic Medicine; pres. Baerg & Assocs.; cons. foot surgery, Las Vegas, 2002—; mem. podiatry adv. panel NAS Inst. Medicine, 1974; mem. bd. podiatric medicine Calif. Dept. Consumer Affairs, 1989-90, chmn. residency, edn. and hosp. inspection com. Contbg. author: (text) Podiatric Medicine and Public Health, 1987; mem. editl. bd. Jour. Podiatric Edn., Yearbook of Podiatric Medicine and Surgery, Mil. Medicine Jour.; contbr. over 30 articles to profl. jours., 3 chpts. to textbooks. With M.C. U.S. Army and USN, 1958-64. Mead-Johnson fellow, 1968-69. Fellow USPHS, Am. Podiatric Med. Assn. (com. on pub. health 1971-84, coun. podiatric edn. 1975-84, chmn. profl. edn. com. 1977-78, com. on hosp. 1980-85, Kenison award 1984, cert. appreciation 1990, com. on pub. health and preventive medicine), Am. Coll. Foot and Ankle Surgeons, Am. Coll. Foot & Ankle Orthopedics and Medicine (exec. dir. 1980-90), Acad. Ambulatory Foot Surgery; mem. APHA (governing coun. 1977-80, chmn. podiatric health sect. 1991-94, chmn. nominating com. 1994-96), Am. Acad. Podiatric Adminstrs. (exec. dir. 1990-91), Nat. Bd. Podiatric Med. Examiners (bd. dirs.), Assn. Podiatrists in Fed. Svc., Am. Assn. Colls. Podiatric Medicine (exec. com. 1973, pres. 1980-81), Assn. Mil. Surgeons U.S., Nat. Acads. of Practice (podiatric medicine 1985), N.C. Foot and Ankle Soc. (bd. dirs. ins. com. 1994-97, cons. 1997-2000, chmn. zone III 1994-97, rep. N.C. Health Care Reform Com. 1994-97), Coun. Med. Sch. Affiliated Podiatrists (bd. dirs., dir. region 10), N.C. Symphony Assn., Palm Mortuaries (Las Vegas), Mason (Scottish Rite, 32 degree), Sigma Pi Epsilon, Pi Delta. Republican. Home and Office: Po Box 660538 Arcadia CA 91066-0538 Home Phone: 702-364-9943; Office Phone: 702-241-9006. Personal E-mail: rhbaerg@aol.com.

BAERMANN, DONNA LEE ROTH, real estate property executive, retired insurance analyst; b. Carroll, Iowa, Apr. 28, 1939; d. Omer H. and Mae Lavina (Larson) Real; m. Edwin Ralph Baermann, Jr., July 8, 1961 (dec. Aug. 1997); children: Beth, Bryan, Cynthia. BS, Mt. Mercy Coll., Ames, 1973; student, Iowa State U.-Ames, 1957-61. Cert. profl. ins. woman; fellow Life Mgmt. Inst. ins. agt. Luthern Mut. Ins. Co., Cedar Rapids, Iowa, 1973; home economist Iowa-Ill. Gas & Electric Co., Cedar Rapids, Iowa, 1973-77; supr. premium collection Life Investors Ins. Co. (now Aegon USA), Cedar Rapids, Iowa, 1978-83, methods and procedures analyst, 1987-94; pres., CEO Baermann Apts. Inc., 1992-94, owner, pres., 1992—. Mem. telecom. study group com. 1982-83, mem. productivity task force, 1984-94, TAB cert. facilitator, 2001—. Vol. Mercy Med. Ctr., Cedar Rapids, Iowa, 2002—; apptd. by Mayor and City Coun. Housing Bd. Appeals, Cedar Rapids, 2003. Mem. Internat. Platform Assn., Citizens Com. for Person with Disabilities, Nat. Assn. Ins. Women, Nat. Mgmt. Assn. (bd. dirs. Cedar Rapids chpt.), DAR, Knights of Malta (named Damsel of Ancient Order of St. John, N.Y.C.), Chi Omega. Republican. Presbyterian. Home: 361 Willshire Ct NE Cedar Rapids IA 52402-6922 Personal E-mail: dlrbaer@peoplepc.com.

BAERNSTEIN, ALBERT, II, mathematician, educator; b. Birmingham, Ala., Apr. 25, 1941; s. Albert and Kathryn (Wiesel) B.; m. Judith Haynes, June 14, 1962; children— P. Renée, Amy. Student, U. Ala., 1958-59; AB, Cornell U., 1962; MA, U. Wis., 1964, PhD, 1968. Instr. math. U. Wis., Whitewater, 1966-68; asst. prof. math. Syracuse U., NY, 1968-72; assoc. prof. math. Washington U., St. Louis, 1972-74, prof. math., 1974—. Fulbright sr. research scholar Imperial Coll., London, 1976-77 Mem. Am. Math. Soc., Math. Assn. Am. Office: Washington U Dept Math Saint Louis MO 63130

BAERWALD, SUSAN GRAD, television broadcasting company executive producer; b. Long Branch, N.J., June 18, 1944; d. Bernard John and Marian Grad; m. Paul Baerwald, July 1, 1969; children: Joshua, Samuel. Degre des Arts and Lettres, Sorbonne, Paris, 1965; BA, Sarah Lawrence Coll., 1966. Script analyst United Artists, L.A., 1978-80; v.p. devel. Gordon/Eisner Prodns., L.A., 1980-81; mgr. mini-series and novels for TV, NBC, Burbank, Calif., 1981-82, dir. mini-series and novels for TV, 1982, v.p. mini-series and novels for TV, 1982-89; exec. producer NBC Prodns., 1989-95, Savoy Pictures TV, 1995-96, Citadel Entertainment, 1996-97; sr. lectr. Am. Film Inst., 1999. Producer (TV movies) Blind Faith, 1990, One Spl. Victory, 1991, Cruel Doubt, 1992, A Time to Heal, 1994, Inflammable, 1995 (TV miniseries) Lucky/Chances, 1990. Bd. dirs. The Paper Bag Players, N.Y.C., 1974—, Women in Film Found., 2000, Non-Profit Alliance W.O.M.E.N., Inc., 1998; vol. L.A. Children's Mus., 1978-80; mem. awards com. Scott Newman Found., 1982-84; bd. dirs. L.A. Goal, 1996—. Recipient Vol. Incentive award NBC, 1983. Mem. ATAS (bd. govs. 1993-97, nat. awards chmn. 1997-98), Am. Film Inst., Hollywood Radio and TV Soc.

BAESEMAN, JENNY L., environmental scientist, educator; BS, U. Wis., Stevens Point, 1998; MS, U. Minn., Mpls., 2000; PhD, U. Colo., Boulder, 2004. NSF microbial biology postdoctoral rschr. Princeton U., NJ, 2004—06; asst. prof. of microbial ecology Kent State U., Ohio, 2006—. U.S. rep. Internat. Polar Yr. Youth Steering Coordinatory, Cambridge, 2005—; presenter for Al Gore's Climate Project. Contbr. articles to profl. jours. Mem. bd. dirs. Alumni Assn. for U. Wis. - Stevens Point, Wis., 2006—. Recipient Montgumery Watston/ Harza Masters Thesis award, Assn. Engring. and Environ. Sci. Profs., 2001. Mem.: Assn. Polar Early Career Scientists (bd. dirs.), Am. Geophys. Union, Internat. Soc. Microbial Ecology, Am. Soc. Microbiology. Achievements include discovery of over 100 new speices of bacteria from streams in the McMurdo Dry Valleys, Antarctica; selected as presenter of Al Gore's Climate Project; creation of International Network for early career polar scientists. Office: Kent State University Department of Biological Sciences Kent OH 44244 Office Phone: 330-672-2957. Business E-Mail: jbaesema@kent.edu.

BAETZHOLD, HOWARD GEORGE, retired language educator; b. Buffalo, Jan. 1, 1923; s. Howard Kuster and Harriet Laura (Hofheins) B.; m. Nancy Millard Cheesman, Aug. 5, 1950; children: Howard King, Barbara Millard. Student, Brown U., 1940-43, MIT, 1943-44; AB magna cum laude, Brown U., 1944, A.M., 1948; PhD, U. Wis., 1953. Asst. dir. Vets. Coll., Brown U., Providence, 1947-48, dir., 1948-49, admissions officer, 1948-50; teaching asst. U. Wis.-Madison, 1950-51; asst. to assoc. dean Coll. Letters and Sci., 1951-53; asst. prof. English Butler U., Indpls., 1953-57, assoc. prof., 1957-67, prof. English, 1967-88, Rebecca Clifton Reade prof., 1981-88, Rebecca Clifton Reade prof. emeritus, 1988—, head dept., 1981-85. Vis. prof. U. Del., summer 1963. Author: Mark Twain and John Bull: The British Connection, 1970; co-editor: The Bible According to Mark Twain: Writings on Heaven, Eden and the Flood, 1995, paperback edit., 1996, Three Decades of Odes, 1997; contbr. articles to profl. jours., Dictionary Lit. Biography, Mark Twain Ency. Mem. OASIS (Older Adult Svcs. and Info. Sys.) adv. coun., 1996-2002, Indpls. Art Ctr., Indpls. Mus. Art. Served to lt. A.C., AUS, 1943—46. Recipient Butler Svc. medal, 2004; named Sagamore of the Wabash, 1988; faculty fellow Butler U., 1957-58, 69-70, Butler U. fellow, 1986, 87, John S. Tuckey meml. rsch. fellow Elmira Coll. Ctr. for Mark Twain Studies at Quarry Farm, 1990—, Henry Nash Smith fellow, 2001—; grantee Am. Philos. Soc., 1967, Am. Coun. Learned Socs., 1958. Mem. AAUP (v.p. state conf. 1955), MLA, Ind. Coll. English Assn. (exec. bd. 1983-85), Am. Lit. Assn., Mark Twain Cir. Am. (exec. com. 1987-88, hon. life mem. 1995), Am. Philatelic Soc., Greater Ind. Masters Swimming Assn., Indpls. Lit. Club (2d v.p. 1985-86, 1st v.p. 1987-88, 92-93, pres. 1993-94), Butler U. Odd Topics Soc., Ovid Butler Soc. (exec. com. 1998—), Delta Upsilon. Home: 6723 Riverview Dr Indianapolis IN 46220-1628

BAEZ, JOAN CHANDOS, vocalist; b. SI, NY, Jan. 9, 1941; d. Albert V. and Joan (Bridge) B.; m. David Victor Harris, Mar. 1968 (div. 1973); 1 son, Gabriel Earl. Appeared in coffeehouses, Gate of Horn, Chgo., 1958, Ballad Room, Club 47, 1958-68, Newport (R.I.) Folk Festival, 1959-69, 85, 87, 90, 92, 93, 95, extended tours to colls. and concert halls, 1960s, appeared Town Hall and Carnegie Hall, 1962, 67, 68, U.S. tours, 1970—, concert tours in Japan, 1966, 82, Europe, 1970-73, 80, 83-84, 87-90, 93—, Australia, 1985; rec. artist for Vanguard Records, 1960-72, A&M, 1973-76, Portrait Records, 1977-80, Gold Castle Records, 1986-89, Virgin Records, 1990-93, Grapevine Label Records (UK), 1995-97, Guardian Records, 1995-97, European record albums, 1981, 83, award 8 gold albums, 1 gold single; albums include Gone From Danger, 1997, Rare, Live & Classic (box set), 1993, Dark Chords on a Big Guitar, 2003, Bowery Songs, 2005; author: Joan Baez Songbook, 1964, (biography) Daybreak, 1968, (with David Harris) Coming Out, 1971, And a Voice to Sing With, 1987, (songbook) An Then I Wrote, 1979. Extensive TV appearances and speaking tours U.S. and Can. for anti-militarism, 1967-68; visit to Dem. Republic of Vietnam, 1972, visit to war torn Bosnia-Herzegovina, 1993; founder, v.p. Inst. for Study Nonviolence (now Resource Ctr. for Nonviolence, Santa Cruz, Calif.), Palo Alto, Calif., 1965; mem. nat. adv. coun. Amnesty Internat., 1974-92; founder, pres. Humanitas/Internat. Human Rights Com., 1979-92; condr. fact-finding mission to refugee camps, S.E. Asia, Oct. 1979; began refusing payment of war taxes, 1964; arrested for civil disobedience opposing draft, Oct., Dec., 1967. Office: Diamonds & Rust Prodns PO Box 1026 Menlo Park CA 94026-1026 Office Phone: 650-328-0266.

BAEZ, JOANNE MARIE, school psychologist; b. Chgo., June 4, 1962; d. Rafael Marino and Maria Ana (Lopez) B. BA, Bradley U., Peoria, Ill., 1984; MS, Northwestern State U., Natchitoches, La., 1991; PsyD, Ctrl. Mich. U., 1997. Sch. psychologist Milw. Pub. Schs., 1992—. Mem. Hispanic women's adv. coun. Alverno Coll., Milw., 1992—. Mem. Hispanic Women's Adv. Coun., Alverno Coll., Milw., 1992—. Mem. Nat. Assn. Sch. Psychologists, 1986—, Psychologists Assn. of Milw. Pub. Schs. (sec. 1996—). Roman Catholic. Office: Milw Pub Schs Div Spl Svcs Ctr Psychol Svcs 6620 W Capitol Dr Milwaukee WI 53216-2040

BAEZ-FELICIANO, DORIS V., demographer, educator; d. Pedro A. Baez-Santiago and Doris Feliciano-Torres; m. Alvin Seda, Nov. 17, 2001. BA with honors in Social Scis., U. PR, Mayaguez, 1998; MS with honors in Demography, U. PR, San Juan, 2006. Rsch. asst. demography program med. scis. campus U. PR, San Juan, 1998—, demographer family planning program med. scis. campus, 1999—; biostatistician U. Ctrl. Del Caribe, Bayamon, PR, 2001—. Coord. symposium U. PR, Mayaguez, 1997—; prof. U. Sagrado Corazon, San Juan, 2003—; adj. actuary Cooperativa De Seguros De Vida-cosvi, San Juan, 2000—01; reviewer profl. jours. Contbr. articles to profl. jours. Recipient Blue Ribbon award, Population Assn. Am., 2000. Mem.: Am. Assn. Pub. Health. Home Phone: 787-383-5550; Office Phone: 787-787-8710. Office Fax: 787-787-8733; Home Fax: 787-787-8733. Personal E-mail: dorita30pr@gmail.com. Business E-Mail: dbaez@uccaribe.edu.

BAGALAY, JOHN EARL, information technology executive, venture capitalist, consultant; b. San Antonio, Sept. 22, 1933; s. John Earl and Katherine Louise Bagalay; m. Julia Cunningham, Dec. 27, 1989; children: George Trowbridge Elliman, Julia Smither Elliman, Christopher Dow, Peter Bogert Elliman. PhD, Yale U., New Haven, 1957; JD, U. Tex., Austin, 1964. Instr. polit. philosophy U. Tex., 1957—64, dir. undergrad. studies, dir. Am. studies program; atty. Baker & Botts, Houston, 1964—73; gen. counsel Tex. Commerce Bancshares, Inc., Houston, 1973—81, Houston First Fin. Group, 1981—84, Lower Colo. River Authority, Austin, 1984—88; mng. dir. venture fund and other positions Boston U., 1989—2005; exec. in residence EuroUS Ventures LLC, 2006—; chmn. Wave Systems Corp., Lee, Mass., 2003—. Bd. dirs., chmn. audit & fin. com. Cytogen Corp., Princeton, NJ. Trustee Houston Ballet Found., 1975—84, Houston Grand Opera, 1979—81; pres., trustee Houston Chamber Orch. Soc., 1970—84; dir. Austin Ballet Theatre, 1984—88. Fellow, Woodrow Wilson Found., 1957. Mem.: ABA (licentiate), Tex. Bar Assn. (licentiate). Republican. Episcopalian. Avocations: squash, tennis, rowing, horseback riding. Home: 15 Raymond St Cambridge MA 02140 Office: EuroUS Ventures 2000 Commonwealth Ave Newton MA 02466 Home Phone: 617-354-3231; Office Phone: 617-244-2304. Business E-Mail: jbagalay@eurousventures.com.

BAGAN, MARK G., grain exchange executive; m. Anne Bagan; children: Lindsay, Alyssa, Shaley, Drayton. BA, Mankato State U. Trading fl. clerk Mpls. Grain Exch. (MGEX), 1987, various pos. in operations, compliance, membership and regulation, v.p. of market adminstrn., 1997—2005, corp. sec., 2002—05, pres., CEO, 2005—. Mem. bd. Nat. Futures Exch. Office: Mpls Grain Exch 130 Grain Exch Bldg 400 South 4th St Minneapolis MN 55415-1413 Office Phone: 612-321-7166. E-mail: mbagan@mgex.com.*

BAGAN, MERWYN, neurological surgeon; b. Phila., Jan. 25, 1936; s. Frank and Shirley (Lindenbaum) B.; m. Carol Augusta Joseph, Nov. 14, 1964; children: Eric, Seth, Karin. AB, Dartmouth Coll., 1957; MD, Boston U., 1962, MPH, 1995. Diplomate Am. Bd. Neurol. Surgery. Neurol. surgeon Surg. Neurology Profl. Assn., Concord, NH, 1970-93; chmn. Healthsource, Inc., Hooksett, 1985-97. Chmn., pres. Healthsource N.H., Concord, 1985-93; adj. asst. prof. clin. surgery (neurosurgery) Dartmouth Med. Sch., 1981-88; vis. prof. dept. surgery Tribhuvan U. Inst. Medicine, Kathmandu, Nepal, 1997-2000. Chmn. bd. visitors Boston U. Sch. Medicine; mem. bd. overseers Boston U. Lt. comdr. USPHS, 1963—65. Recipient Disting. Alumnus award Boston U. Sch. Medicine, 1993, alumni award Boston U., 1999, Suprabal Gorkha Dakshina Bahu award, 2000. Fellow ACS; mem. AMA, Am. Assn. Neurol. Surgeons (pres. 1992-93, humanitarian award 2000), N.H. Med. Soc. (pres. 1983), Congress of Neurol. Surgeons (Disting. Svc. award 1990), Found. Internat. Edn. Neurol. Surgery (chmn.), Alpha Omega Alpha. Home: 173 School St Concord NH 03301-2568

BAGBY, JOSEPH RIGSBY, financial investor; b. Banner Elk, NC, Aug. 23, 1935; s. Wesley Marion and Ila Paunee (Rigsby) B.; m. Martha Green, Jan. 1, 1965; 1 child, Meredith Elaine. Student, Fla. State U., 1955; BBA, U. Miami, 1959; MCR, Inst. Corp. Real Estate, West Palm Beach, Fla., 1977. Employee and supr. Miami Herald Pub. Co., 1953-63; rsch. and sales asst. Oscar Dolly Assocs., Miami, 1961-63; sales, appraising and property mgr. Jack Thomas Realty, Miami, 1963-65; dir. corp. real estate Burger King Corp., Miami, 1965-70; founder, pres. Internat. Assn. Corp. Real Estate Execs., Coral Gables, Fla., 1969-88; chmn. bd. trustees Nat. Assn. Corp. Real Estate Execs., Coral Gables, Fla., 1973-88, bd. dirs., 1971—; pres., founder Property Resources Corp. and 20 other investment cos., Miami and Palm Beach, 1970—. Founder merger and acquisition investment co., 1997; mem. businessman's adv. com. U.S. Postal Svc., Washington, 1984-88. Author: Real Estate Financing Desk Book, 1975, rev. edits. 1977, 81, Real Estate Directory, 1975. Pres. interfraternity coun. U. Miami (co-editor campus newspaper); mem., chmn. fin. com. St. Edward's Cath. Ch., Palm Beach, Fla., 1985-93. With U.S. Army, 1959-61. Named to Hall of Fame, Nat. Assn. Corp. Real Estate Execs., 1991. Mem. Nat. Assn. Location Analysts and Negotiators (founder), Internat. Corp. Real Estate Execs. Assn. (life hon. mem., bd. dirs. Corenet Global), Progress Club of Miami (co-founder), Optimist (founding mem. Miami Downtown club), Rotary (Harris fellow), Interfaith Cotillian (co-founder), Sigma Chi (pres. 1958), Alpha Kappa Psi. Democrat. Avocations: swimming, tennis. Home: 125 Brazilian Ave Palm Beach FL 33480-4221 Office: Property Resources Corp PO Box 3149 Palm Beach FL 33480-1349 Office Phone: 561-655-9510.

BAGBY, MARTHA L. GREEN, real estate holding company executive, writer, publishing executive; b. West Palm Beach, Fla., June 17, 1937; d. Hampton and Louise (Lambert) Green; m. Joseph R. Bagby, 1966; 1 child, Meredith E. AA, Palm Beach Jr. Coll., 1957; AB, U. Miami, 1959; MA, Pa. State U., 1964. Tchr. journalism, english Palm Beach County, 1959—62; instr. journalism Pa. State U., 1962—63; city editor, writer Palm Beach News and Life, 1963—64; editor Alfred Hitchcock Mag., Riviera Beach, Fla., 1964; editor, supr. editl. svc., pub. rels. employee newspaper Nat. Airlines, Inc., Miami, Fla., 1965—73; corp. sec., chmn. bd. Property Resources Co., Palm Beach, Fla., 1971—. Life dir. CareNet Global, 2002—; Ill. franchisee Burger King Corp.; founder Internat. Health Awareness Assn.; lectr. journalism Dade, Palm Beach counties; instr. Barry Coll., Miami; pub. The Bagbys Health Digest, 1985—. Author: Stranglehold, 1977, The Complete Real Estate Dictionary, 1992, The Real Estate Financing Deskbook, 1979-90; author: (with others) The Complete Real Estate Book. Mem. exec. bd. Childbirth and Parent Edn. Assn., Miami. Mem.: Internat. Assn. Corp. Real Estate Execs. (founder, trustee, exec. editor, dir. life), Women in Comm. (pres.), Air Transport Assn. Am., Airline Editors Conf. (chmn.), S. Fla. Indsl. Chmn. Internat. Council Indsl. Editors, Fla. Pub. Relations Assn. Office: 125 Brazilian Ave Palm Beach FL 33480-4221 Office Phone: 561-655-9510.

BAGBY, ROBERT L., investment company executive; Former br. adminstr. S.W. region, regional officer, asst. dir. br. div. A.G. Edwards, Inc., 1979—95, dir. br. div. St. Louis, 1995—2001, chmn., CEO, 2001—. Office: AG Edwards Inc 1 N Jefferson Ave Saint Louis MO 63103*

BAGDIKIAN, BEN HAIG, journalist, educator; b. Marash, Turkey, Jan. 30, 1920; came to U.S., 1920, naturalized, 1926; s. Aram Theodore and Daisy (Uvezian) B.; m. Elizabeth Ogasapian, Oct. 2, 1942 (div. 1972); children: Christopher Ben, Frederick Haig; m. Betty L. Medsger, 1973 (div.); m. Marlene Griffith, 1983 AB, Clark U., 1941, LittD, 1963; LHD, Brown U., 1961, U. R.I., 1992. Reporter Springfield (Mass.) Morning Union, 1941-42; assoc. editor Periodical House, Inc., NYC, 1946; successively reporter, fgn. corr., chief Washington corr. Providence Jour., 1947-62; contbg. editor Saturday Evening Post, 1963-67; project dir. study of future U.S. news media Rand Corp., 1967-69; asst. mng. editor for nat. news Washington Post, 1970-71, asst. mng. editor, ombudsman, 1971-72; nat. corr. Columbia Journalism Review, 1972-74; prof. Grad. Sch. Journalism U. Calif., Berkeley, 1976-90, dean, Grad. Sch. Journalism, 1985-88, prof. emeritus, Grad. Sch. Journalism, 1990—. Keynote spkr. Coun. Europe Ministerial Conf. on Mass Media Policy, Kiev, Ukraine, 2005. Author: In the Midst of Plenty: The poor in America, 1964, The Information Machines: Their Impact on Men and the Media, 1971, The Shame of the Prisons, 1972, The Effete Conspiracy, 1972, Caged: Eight Prisoners and Their Keepers, 1976, The Media Monopoly, 1983, 6th edit., 2000, Double Vision: Reflections on My Heritage, Life and Profession, 1995, The New Media Monopoly, 2004; also pamphlets; contbr.: The Kennedy Circle, 1961; editor: Man's Contracting World in an Expanding Universe, 1959; mem. editl. bd. Investigative Reporters and Editors, 1980-88. Mem. steering com. Nat. Prison Project, 1974-82; trustee Clark U., 1964-76; bd. dirs. Nat. Capital Area Civil Liberties Union, 1964-66, Com. to Protect Journalists, 1981-88, Data Ctr., Oakland, Calif., 1990-97; pres. Lowell Mellett Fund for Free an Responsible Press, 1965-76; acad. adv. bd. Nat. Citizens Com. for Broadcasting, 1978—; judge Ten Most Censored Stories, 1976-98. Recipient George Foster Peabody award, 1951, Sidney Hillman Found. award, 1956, Most Perceptive Critic citation Am. Soc. Journalism Adminstrs., 1978, Career Achievement award Soc. Profl. Journalists, John and Catherine Zenger award, 1996, James Madison award ALA, 1998, Wayne Danielson award, U. Tex., 2005, Lifetime Achievement award Nat. Soc. Profl. Journalists, 2007, Nat. Conf., Free Press, Memphis, 2007; named to RI Journalism Hall of Fame, 1992; fellow Ogden Reid Found., 1956, Guggenheim fellow, 1961-62. Mem. ACLU. Home: 25 Stonewall Rd Berkeley CA 94705-1414 Personal E-mail: benmar@berkeley.edu. *Personal philosophy: The most compelling principles in my life have been, in private life the pervasive need of love and trust in human relations, in public life dignity of the individual combined with devotion to the common good, in intellectual life a distrust of detachment from the human condition, and in journalism honesty and clarity.*

BAGERT, DONALD JOSEPH, computer scientist, educator; b. Okinawa, Japan, Mar. 4, 1956; s. Donald and Betty Bagert. BS, Tulane U., 1977; MS, U. La., Lafayette, 1979; PhD, Tex. A&M U., 1986. Cert. Software Devel. Profl. IEEE Computer Soc., Wash. DC; Profl. Engr., Tex. Bd. Profl. Engr., Tex. Instr. computer sci. U. La., Lafayette, 1979—80, Tex. A&M U., College Sta., 1980—86; asst. prof. computer sci. U. La., Monroe, 1986—88; faculty mem. Tex. Tech U., Lubbock, 1988—2002, assoc. chair computer sci., 1999—2001; dir. software engring. Rose-Hulman Inst. Tech., Terre Haute, Ind., 2002—07, prof. computer sci., software engring., 2002—07; prof., chair dept. computer sci. S.E. Mo. State U., Cape Girardeau, 2007—. Dir. regional contests, internat. collegiate programming contest Assn. Computing Machinery, NYC, 1998—99; steering com. chair, conf. software engring. edn. and tng. IEEE Computer Soc., Washington, 2000—05, chair, cert. software devel. profl. cert. com., 2003—04. Interim dir. campus ministry St. Elizabeth's U. Parish, Lubbock, Tex., 2001—02. Recipient First Profl. Engr. award in Software Engring., Tex. Bd. Profl. Engrs., 1998. Mem.: AAUP, NSPE, IEEE (chair, computer soc. CSDP cert. com. 2003—04, Computer Soc. Outstanding Contbn. award 2002, 2003), Am. Soc. Engring. Edn. (chair, software engring. 2005—06), Assn. Computing Machinery (dir. regional contests, internat. programming contest 1998—99, Outstanding Svc. award, Internat. Collegiate Programming

Contest 2000), Order of Engr., Upsilon Pi Epsilon. Roman Cath. Office: Rose Hulman Inst Tech 5500 Wabash Ave CM 97 Terre Haute IN 47803 Office Phone: 812-877-8327, 573-651-2244. Office Fax: 812-872-6060. E-mail: don.bagert@rose-hulman.edu, bagert@computer.org.

BAGGECH, MELODY A., music educator; b. Melrose Pk., Ill., Oct. 3, 1964; d. Robert Harold and Mary Joan Baggech; m. Alan Lee Marshall, Aug. 29, 1992; 1 child, Adie. MusB, Millikin U., 1986; MusM, West Tex. A&M U., 1990; MusD, U. Okla., 1998. Adj. voice instr. Okla. Panhandle State U., 1990—92; asst. voice prof. East Ctrl. U., Ada, Okla., 2001—. Performer: Washington Savoyards, Ltd., 2005; translator: Treatise on Rhythm, Color and Omithology, 1998; performer: Amarillo Opera, Cimarron Circuit Opera Co., Cross Timbers Theatre Co. Recipient Gail B. deStwolinsky award, U. Okla., 1997; Janet Mertz scholarship, Millikin U., 1984—86, grant, Okla. Arts Coun., 2004. Mem.: Nat. Opera Assn., Okla. Music Educators Assn., Nat. Assn. of Tchrs. of Singing. Avocations: sewing, reading. Home: 2100 Fullview Ada OK 74820

BAGGER, RICHARD HARTVIG, pharmaceutical executive; b. Plainfield, NJ, Mar. 27, 1960; s. Donald Hartvig and Elizabeth Claire (Broback) Bagger; m. Barbara Jane Laird, May 14, 1988; Katherine Bianca, Jennifer Anne, Meredith Skye. AB, Princeton U., 1982; JD, Rutgers U., 1986. Bar: NJ 1986, US Dist. Ct. NJ 1986. Legis. aide NJ Gen. Assembly, Trenton, 1979-82; mem. profl. staff Select Com. on Aging US Congress, Washington, 1982-83; assoc. McCarter & English, Newark, 1986-91; asst. gen. counsel Blue Cross and Blue Shield of NJ, Inc., Newark, 1991-93; mgr. civic affairs Pfizer, Inc., NYC, 1993-96, dir. state corp. affairs, 1996-99, nat. dir. state govt. rels., 1999—2002, v.p. govt. rels., 2002—03, sr. v.p. govt. rels., pub. affairs and policy, 2003—06, sr. v.p. worldwide pub. affairs and policy, 2006—. Trustee NJ Hist. Trust, Trenton, 1986-89, Westfield Found., 1995-2001, Westfield United Way, 2003-, Overlook Found., 2001-04, Citizens Budget Commn. NY, 2003-06, Healthcare Inst., NJ, 2004-, NJN Found., 2005-07, NJ Performing Arts Ctr. 2005—, US C. of C., 2006—, United Hosp. Fund, 2007—; bd. govs. NJ Hist. Soc., 1989-98. Editor, author Rutgers Law Rev., 1985-86. Active Westfield Planning Bd., 1987—92; councilman Town of Westfield, NJ, 1984—90, mayor, 1991—92; mem. N. J. Gen. Assembly, 1992—2002, N.J. Senate, 2002—03; dist committeeman Union County Reps., Westfield, NJ, 1980—83, 1987. Episcopalian. Office: Pfizer Inc 235 E 42nd St New York NY 10017-5755 Office Phone: 212-573-7646. E-mail: rich.bagger@pfizer.com.

BAGGETT, DONNIS GENE, newspaper publisher; b. Livingston, Tex., July 16, 1952; s. Sam Jr. and Mavis Baggett; m. Beverly Brown; children: Valerie Shaddix, David Shaddix. BA, Stephen F. Austin State U., 1973. Reporter, photographer East Tex. Eye, Livingston, Tex., 1973-74, co-editor, 1974; reporter Longview (Tex.) Morning Jour., 1974-75, East Tex. editor, 1975-76; reporter The Dallas Morning News, 1976, asst. night city editor, 1977, asst. state editor, 1977-82, state editor, 1982-94, asst. mng. editor, 1994-95; pub., editor The Eagle, Bryan-College Station, Tex., 1996—. Chmn. Tex. Agrl. Summit Exec. Com., 1997—98; bd. dirs. Brazos Valley Mus. Natural History, Am. Heart Assn.; bd. dirs., campaign chair Brazos Valley United Way, 2000; mem. adv. bd. Washington-on-theBrazos State Park Assn. Recipient Mayborn award for Cmty. Leadership, Tex. Daily Newspaper Assn., 2005. Mem.: Soc. Profl. Journalists, Tex. Press Assn. (bd. dirs.), Tex. Daily Newspaper Assn. (pres. 2004), Press Club of Dallas (pres. 1992—94). Methodist. Avocation: ranching.

BAGGETT, FRED W., lawyer; b. Stuttgart, Ark., May 15, 1945; BA, Univ. Fla., 1967; JD, Fla. State Univ., 1970. Bar: Fla. 1970. Exec. asst. to Chief Justice Supreme Ct. Fla., 1970—72; shareholder, chair, nat. govt. affairs practice Greenberg Traurig, Tallahassee. Adj. prof. law Fla. State Univ. Chmn. Tallahassee/Leon County Planning Agy., Capital Cultural Center, Tallahassee; sec. Florida Judicial Coun., Ounce of Prevention Fund of Fla. Fellow: Am. Bar Found.; mem.: Internat. Bar Assn., Tallahassee Bar Assn. Office: Greenberg Traurig 101 E College Ave PO Drawer 1838 Tallahassee FL 32302 Office Phone: 850-222-6891. Office Fax: 850-681-0207. Business E-Mail: baggettf@gtlaw.com.

BAGGETT, STEVEN RAY, lawyer; b. Fayetteville, Ark., July 3, 1963; s. Harold Ray and Norma June (King) B.; m. Amy Lynn Griggs, Jan. 2, 1999; c. Lauren Michelle, Brooke Lindsey. BA, U. Ark., 1985; JD, So. Meth. U., 1988. Bar: Tex. 1988, U.S. Dist. Ct. (no. dist.) Tex. 1988, U.S. Ct. Appeals (5th cir.) 1992, U.S. Dist. Ct (so. and ea. dists.) Tex., 2005. Assoc. Thompson & Knight, Dallas, 1988-95, shareholder, ptnr., 1996—. Recipient Am. Jurisprudence awards Bancroft-Whitney Co., 1985-86. Fellow Dallas Bar Found.; mem. Tex. Bar Assn., Dallas Bar Assn. (spkrs. com. 1997-2004, media rels. com. 2004—, state fair trial by jury com. 1998-2001, jud. com. 1999-2001, 04, cmty. involvement com. 1999-2001, law in schs. and cmtys. com. 1999), Ark. U. Alumni Assn., So. Meth. U. Law Sch. Alumni Assn., Phi Beta Kappa. Avocations: weight training, running, ice skating, music. Office: Thompson & Knight 1700 Pacific Ave Ste 3300 Dallas TX 75201-4693 Home Phone: 972-671-0059; Office Phone: 214-969-1700. E-mail: steve.baggett@tklaw.com.

BAGGETT, W. MIKE, lawyer; b. Waco, Tex., Nov. 8, 1946; s. Bill R. and Jenna (Robertson) B.; m. Jo Kilpatrick, May 28, 1968; children: Carl, Cary. BBA, Tex. A&M U., 1968; JD cum laude, Baylor U., 1973. Bar: Tex. 1973. Law clk. Tex. Supreme Ct., Austin, 1973—74; assoc. Winstead, Sechrest & Minick, Dallas, 1974-79, shareholder, 1979—, chmn. and chief exec. officer, 1992—2006. Chair reverse mortgage rules com., chair home equity loan rules com. Tex. Supreme Ct. Author: Texas Foreclosure: Law & Practice, 1983, Texas Practice Series West, 2nd edit., 2001, Real Estate Litigation, Texas Practice Guide West, 2002; co-author: Lender Liability Law and Litigation, 1989. Trustee Tex. A&M Found., 1989-98, chmn., 1992-93; mem. Joint Select Com. on Judiciary, 1988; bd. dirs. Tex. Higher Edn. Coordinating Bd., 1989-95, North Tex. Commn., Dallas Citizens Coun., State Bar of Tex., Baylor Oral Health Found., Southwestern Bell-SMU Athletic Forum; chmn. Dallas Ft. Worth Regional Sports Commn.; chmn., CEO, Cotton Bowl Athletic Assn. 1st lt. US Army, 1968—71, Vietnam. Decorated Bronze Star; named Tex. Aggie Lawyer of Yr., 2004; named one of Top 10 Bus. Litigators in Dallas/Ft. Worth, Dallas Bus. Jour., Best Lawyer in Am., D Mag., Super Laywer, Top 100 in Dallas/Ft. Worth, Tex. Monthly; recipient Neiman Marcus award, 2002, Judge Sam Williams Leadership award State Bar Tex., 2005; Torch of Conscience award Am. Jewish Congress, 2006. Master: Patrick E. Higginbotham Am. Inn Ct.; fellow: Am. Bd. Trial Advocates, Ctr. for Am. and Internat. Law (chair of fellows, trustee), Dallas Bar Found. (chmn. and trustee), Tex. Bar Found. (sec./treas. of fellows), Am. Bar Found.; mem.: Dallas Bar Assn. (pres., chmn., bd. dirs.), Tex. State Bar Assn. (bd. cert. civil trial com. 1983, bd. dirs., exec. com., adminstrn. justice com.), Greater Dallas C. of C. (bd. dirs.), Baylor Law Sch. Alumni Assn. (pres., bd. dirs.), Assn. Former Students Tex. A&M U. (pres. 1988, Outstanding Alumni Coll. Bus. 1996, Disting. Alumni 1998), Ctrl. Dallas Assn. (Downtown Dallas) (chmn.), City Club, Royal Oaks Club. Methodist. Office: Winstead PC 5400 Renaissance Tower 1201 Elm St Ste 5400 Dallas TX 75270-2199 Home Phone: 214-348-4132; Office Phone: 214-745-5303. Business E-Mail: mbaggett@winstead.com.

BAGHI, HEIBATOLLAH, medical educator; b. Shahreza, Isfahan, Iran; s. Abdol-Khalegh and Dineh Baghi. BA in Sci. Edn., U. Isfahan, 1974; MS in Adult and Continuing Edn., Iowa State U., 1975, PhD in Adult and Continuing Edn., 1979; PhD in Rsch. Design and Stats., Fla. State U., 1988. Sr. psychometrician Am. Nurses Credentialing Ctr., Washington, 1995—2001; assoc. prof. stats. Coll. Nursing and Health Sci., George Mason U., Fairfax, Va., 2001—; rsch. assoc., stats. Del. Dept. Pub. Instrn., Dover, 1993—95; specialist Md. Dept. Edn., Balt., 1987—93; rsch. assoc., data analyst Fla. Dept. Edn., Tallahassee, 1981—87. Vol. psychometric, stats. cons. Am. Bd. Nursing Specialities, 2000—. Contbr. articles to profl. jours. Mem.: Nat. Coun. on Measurement inEdn., Am. Ednl. Rsch. Assn., Am. Stats. Assn. Achievements include research in statistical and psychometric modeling techniques in healthcare research; computer adaptive testing; application of techniques for detecting differential item functioning across subpopulations. Office: George Mason Univ Coll Health and Human Svcs 4400 Univerisity Dr MSN3C4 Fairfax VA 22030

BAGIAN, JAMES PHILIP, former astronaut, public health service officer, medical educator; b. Phila., Feb. 22, 1952; s. Philip and Rose Barbara (Mollick) G.; m. Tandi Marie Benson, June 1, 1984; children: Krista, Kimberly, Brian. BSME, Drexel U., 1973, LLD (hon.), 1988; MD, Jefferson Med. Coll., 1977. Diplomate Nat. Bd. Med. Examiners, Am. Coll. Preventive Medicine; cert. aerospace medicine; registered, cert. profl. engr., Pa. Process engr. 3M Co., Bristol, Pa., 1973; gen. surgery resident Geisinger Med. Ctr., Danville, Pa., 1977—78; flight surgeon NASA, Houston, 1978—79, astronaut, 1980—95; anesthesia resident U. Pa., Phila., 1979—80; dir. Nat. Ctr. for Patient Safety, Vets. Health Adminstrn., Ann Arbor, Mich., 1998—. Adj. asst. prof. mil. and emergency medicine Uniformed Svcs. U. Health Scis.; clin. asst. prof. preventive medicine and cmty. health U. Tex. Med. Br. Patentee in field. Bd. dirs. City of Seabrook (Tex.) Parks Bd., 1986-89. Col. USAF, 1989—. Recipient Sikorsky Helicopter Rescue award Sikorsky Helicopters, 1990, Spaceflight award Internat. Aeronautical Fedn., 1990. Mem. NAE, Aerospace Med. Assn., Am. Human Factor Soc., Inst. Medicine, 2004. Office: National Center for Patient Safety PO Box 486 Ann Arbor MI 48106-0486

BAGINSKI, MAUREEN A., former federal agency administrator; b. Feb. 3, 1955; m. Michael Baginski. BA in Russian and Spanish, SUNY, Albany, MA in Slavic lang.; at, Moriz Torez Fgn. Lang. Inst., Moscow; LHD (hon.), U. Albany, 2005. Russian lang. instr. Nat. Security Agy./Ctrl. Security Svc., 1979, sr. ops. officer, nat. ops. ctr., signals intelligence nat. intelligence officer Russia, exec. asst. to the dir., dep. chief global access program, chief, directorate of ops., consumer products and svcs., asst. dep. dir. tech. and sys., chief, officer of the dir., dir. signals intelligence, 2001—03; exec. asst. dir. Office of Intelligence FBI, Washington, 2003—05; dir. intelligence sector BearingPoint, Inc., McLean, Va., 2005—06; pres., Nat. Security Systems Sector SPARTA, Inc., Arlington, Va., 2006—. Bd. dirs. SI Internat. Inc., 2006—, Argon ST, 2006—. Recipient Sustained Exec. Leadership award, Dir. Ctrl. Intelligence, Exceptional Civilian Svc award, Nat. Security Agy., Outstanding Leadership award, Dir. of Mil. Intelligence's Leadership award, Presdl. Rank award (2). Avocations: gardening, kayaking. Office: SPARTA Inc 1911 N Ft Myer Dr Ste 1100 Arlington VA 22209*

BAGLEY, EDYTHE SCOTT, theater educator; b. Marion, Ala. d. Obie and Bernice (McMurry) Scott; m. Arthur Moten Bagley, June 5, 1954; 1 child, Arturo Scott. BEd, Ohio State U., 1949; MA in English, Columbia U., 1954; MFA in Theater Arts, Boston U., 1965. Instr. Elizabeth City State U., NC, 1953—56; asst. prof. Albany (Ga.) State Coll., 1956-57, A&T U., Greensboro, N.C., 1957-58, Norfolk State U., Va., 1963—65; assoc. prof. theater Cheyney (Pa.) U., 1971—96, chair dept. theater arts; ret. Cons. in black theater Mich. State U., East Lansing, 1969-71. Dir. coll. prodns., 1968-71. Spl. asst. to Coretta Scott King; charter mem. Kimmel Ctr. for Performing Arts, Phila., Nat Constn. Ctr, Phila. Mem. NAACP, Nat. Coun. Negro Women, The Links Inc. (platinum mem.), The Phila. Martin Luther King Jr. Assn. Nonviolence (bd. dirs.), The Martin Luther King Jr. Ctr. Nonviolent Social Change (bd. dirs.). Baptist. Achievements include being featured in the book Sisters. Home: 2 Derry Dr Cheyney PA 19319

BAGLEY, JAMES W., semiconductor equipment company executive; b. Jan. 19, 1939; BS, MS, Miss. State U. With Tex. Instruments, 1966-79; sr. v.p. Applied Materials, Inc., 1979-87, pres., CEO, 1987-96; CEO Lam Rsch. Corp., Fremont, Calif., 1997—98, chmn., CEO, 1998—2005, exec. chmn., 2005—. Bd. dirs. KLA-Tencor, Kulicke & Soffa Industries, Teradyne, Micron Tech., Inc., Semi/SEMATECH. Office: 4650 Cushing Pkwy Fremont CA 94538-6401*

BAGLEY, PHILIP JOSEPH, III, lawyer; b. Richmond, Va., Nov. 24, 1941; s. Philip Joseph Jr. and Louise (Bourne) B.; m. Sally Ann Twedell, Aug. 18, 1967; children: Elizabeth Bourne Faulkner Sgro, Anne Tunstall Twedell. BA, U. Richmond, 1963; LLB, U. Va., 1966. Bar: Va. 1966, U.S. Supreme Ct. 1972. Assoc. Troutman Sanders LLP, Richmond, 1970—74, ptnr., 1974—, practice group leader, comml. develop. and real estate investments group; v.p. Richmond Real Estate Group, 2002—03, pres., 2003—04. Chmn. state adv. coun. Nat. Legal Svcs. Corp., Richmond, 1977-79; bd. dirs. Legal Svc. Corp. Va., 1978-86. Legal advisor Jr. League Richmond, 1977—; bd. dirs. Richmond Symphony, 1986-96, pres. 1992-94; bd. dirs. Richmond Eye and Ear Hosp., 1988—, pres. 1991-96; trustee Benedictine H.S., 1994-2002, pres., 1996-2002; bd. dirs. Carpenter Ctr. Performing Arts, 1995-96, mem. exec. com., 1998—; bd. dirs., mem. exec. com. Va. Performing Arts Found., 2001—; bd. dirs. Richmond Renaissance, 2002—. Fellow Am. Law Found., Va. Bar Found.; mem. ABA (lectr. real estate financing com. 1984, title ins. com. 1987, leasing 1992, coun. real property, probate and trust law sect. 1993-98, sec. 1998-2000, vice-chair real property divsn. 2000-02, chair-elect 2002-03, chair 2003-04), Am. Coll. Real Estate Lawyers (bd. govs. 1988-97, treas. 1991-93, v.p. 1993-94, pres. 1995-96), Anglo-Am. Real Property Inst. (bd. govs. 1995—, sec. 1998-99), Coun. for Am.'s 1st Freedom (bd. govs. 1994-2000, pres. 1996-2000), Internat. Coun. Shopping Ctrs. (co-chair law conf. com. 1996-98), Va. Bar Assn., Richmond Bar Assn., Country Club Va., Commonwealth Club, Order of Coif, Phi Beta Kappa, Omnicron Delta Kappa, Raven Soc., Phi Alpha Delta. Roman Catholic. Office: Troutman Sanders Llp PO Box 1122 Richmond VA 23218-1122 Home Phone: 804-355-3177; Office Phone: 804-697-1444. Office Fax: 804-698-5199. Business E-Mail: phil.bagley@troutmansanders.com.

BAGLEY, PRISCILLA ANNETTE, music educator, performing arts association administrator; b. Laurel, Md., June 3, 1969; d. Christopher Timothy and Sharon Ann Bagley. MusB, Loyola U., New Orleans, 1990; BFA, LI U., Greenville, NY, 1992, MusM, 1994. Founder Priscilla Bagley Voice Studio, Orlando, Fla., 1996—2006; mem. voice faculty U. Ctrl. Fla., Orlando, 2003—. Artistic coord. Intermezzo Inc. HS, NYC, 2005—06, artistic dir., 2006—; pres. Dramatic Inst. Vocal Arts, Winter Park, Fla., 2006—; mem. voice faculty U. Ctrl. Fla. Vocal Arts Summer, Orlando, 2006—. Singer: (Operas) Madame Butterfly, 1998, La Traviata, 1999, Il Pagliacci, 2000. Master class clinician HS Performing Arts, St. Petersburg, Fla., 2002, Palotti HS, Laurel, Md., 2006, Robin Woods Acad., Lakelake, Fla., 2006. Recipient Young Artist award, Pinellas Opera League, 1998. Mem.: Nat. Assn. Tchrs. Singing. (master class clinician), Fla. Fedn. Music Clubs (opera chmn. 2002—06). Home: 1213 Burning Tree Ln Winter Park FL 32792

BAGLEY, TERRENCE M., lawyer; b. Richmond, Va., 1955; BA, Va. Commonwealth U., Richmond, 1977; JD, Campbell U., Buies Creek, NC, 1982. Bar: Va. 1982, Pa. 1991, US Ct. Appeals 4th Cir. 1982, US Cir. Ct. We. & Ea. Districts Va. Ptnr. McGuireWoods LLP, Richmond, Va., 1993—, chair firm complex products liability & mass tort litig. dept., 2004—. Mem.: Def. Rsch. Inst., Pa. Bar Assn. Office: McGuireWoods LLP One James Ctr 901 E Cary St Richmond VA 23219 Office Phone: 804-775-4371. Office Fax: 804-698-2008. Business E-Mail: tbagley@mcguirewoods.com.

BAGLEY, WILLIAM THOMPSON, lawyer; b. San Francisco, June 29, 1928; s. Nino J. and Rita V. (Thompson) Baglietto; m. Diane Lenore Oldham, June 20, 1965; children: Lynn Lorene, William Thompson, Walter William, Shana Angela, Tracy Elizabeth. AB, U. Calif., Berkeley, 1949, JD, 1952. Bar: Calif. 1953, U.S. Supreme Ct. 1967. Atty. Pacific Gas & Electric Co., 1952-56; assoc. Gardiner, Riede & Elliott, San Rafael, Calif., 1956-60; ptnr. Bagley Bernt & Bianchi, San Rafael, 1961-74; mem. Calif. Legis., 1961-74; chmn. Commodity Futures Trading Commn., Washington, 1975-79; ptnr. Nossaman, Guthner, Knox and Elliott, San Francisco, 1980—. Mem. Calif. Pub. Utilities Commn., 1983-86; mem. Calif. Transp. Commn., 1983-89, chmn., 1987-88. Bd. editors Calif. Law Rev., 1951-52. Bd. regents U. Calif., 1989-2002; trustee Marin Cmty. Found., 2004—; bd. dirs. Nat. Futures Assn., Calif. Coun. Environ. and Econ. Balance, Edmund G. Brown Inst. Govtl. Affairs, L.A.; chmn. bd. Calif. Rep. League, 1980-82. Recipient Freedom of Info. award Sigma Delta Chi, 1970, Golden Bear award Calif. Pk. Commn., 1973; named Most Effective Assemblyman, Capitol Press Corps, 1969, Legislator of Yr., Calif. Trial Lawyers Assn., 1970, Alumnus of Yr., U. Calif. Alumni Assn., 2002. Mem. ABA, Calif. State Bar Assn., Three Stooges Fan Club, Elks Club (life), Phi Beta Kappa, Alpha Tau Omega. Presbyterian. Office Phone: 415-398-3600. Personal E-mail: diane_bagley@comcast.net. Business E-Mail: wbagley@nossaman.com.

BAGLIO, VINCENT PAUL, aerospace transportation executive; b. Patchogue, NY, Feb. 18, 1960; s. Lorenzo and Nancy (Morello) B.; m. Katerina Barnova, Apr. 3, 2002. BS, Princeton U., 1982; MS, Poly. U., Bklyn., 1986; MBA, Hofstra U., 1993. Product mgr. integrated sys. and aerostructures sector Northrop Grumman Corp., Bethpage, N.Y., 1982-99; mgmt. cons. Beacon Cons. Svcs. Inc., 1999-2000; sr. mgr. bus. devel. Cubic Transp. Sys., Inc., NYC, 2000—02; dir. engring. and program mgmt. Smiths Aerospace-Electronic Sys., LI, NY, 2002—04; v.p., gen. mgr. Farmingdale ops. Herley Industries, NY, 2004; program mgr. advanced concepts and integrated solutions Northrop Grumman Corp., Bethpage, NY, 2004—. Contbr. articles to profl. jours. Alumni schs. com. Princeton (N.J.) U.; chmn. Princeton Alumni Assn. of L.I. Mem. AIAA (tech. com. 1995-97), Soc. Automotive Engrs. (indsl. lectr. 1990-91), Internat. Coun. Aero. Scis. (program com. 1989-93), Friends Princeton Football. Avocations: golf, running. Office: Northrop Grumman Corp Mail Stop X04 14 925 S Oyster Bay Rd Bethpage NY 11714 Office Phone: 516-704-3870. Business E-Mail: vincent.baglio@ngc.com.

BAGLIVO, MARY L., advertising executive; m. James Meguerian; children: John, Martha. Bachelors, Rutgers U.; M in Advt., Northwestern U. Account exec. Euro RSCG Tatham, Chgo., 1981-91, sr. ptnr., 1991-94, mng. ptnr., 1994-96, CEO, 1996-99; chief mktg. officer, exec. v.p., N.Am. J. Walker Thompson (unit of WPP Group), 1999-2000, COO, global bus. dir., N.Am., 2000—04; CEO, worldwide mktg. dir. Saatchi & Saatchi, NYC, 2004—. Bd. dir. Evanston Northwestern Healthcare, Advertising Week, 2005—. Mem.: The Advertising Club (bd. dirs. sr. v.p.), Phi Beta Kappa. Avocation: fashion. Office: Saatchi & Saatchi 375 Hudson St New York NY 10014-3620 Office Phone: 212-463-2000. Office Fax: 212-463-9855.

BAGLOW, DAVID RICHARD, marine facility administrator; b. Manchester, Eng., May 14, 1939; s. Wilfrid Charles and Edith (May) B. Cert. heat engines/gas industry supply; cert. comms. engr. Engr. indsl. gas supply N.W. Gas Bd., Manchester, 1958-62; comms. engr. Cable & Wireless Ltd. various locations worldwide, 1962-74, Saigon, Vietnam, 1970-72; asst. mgr. The Moorings Ltd., Tortola, British Virgin Islands, 1974-75; mgr., v.p. W.I. Yacht Charter, Tortola, 1975-78; gen. mgr., v.p. Nanny Cay Marine Ctr., Tortola, 1978-80; ops. mgr. South Pacific Yacht Charter, Tonga, Tahiti, Logan, Utah, 1980-85; base mgr., rschr. The Moorings Ltd., Tortola, Tonga, Grenada, Bahamas, 1985-94; ops. mgr., co-dir. The Moorings Australasia Pty./Ltd., Sydney/Whitsunday Islands, Australia, 1994-2000; property mgmt. divsn. Land Office Inc., Hawaii, 2003—04. Author: Cruising Guide to Isles Sous le Vent Tahiti and Vava'u Islands of Tonga, Tonga Guide, 1980, Tahiti Guide, 1982. Avocations: yachting, music, yacht engineering research, reading nonfiction, travel. Home and Office: PO Box 6454 Ocean View HI 96737-6454 Home Phone: 808-939-7105; Office Phone: 808-939-7368. E-mail: baglowdavidr@aol.com.

BAGNALL, LINDSAY LOMAX, not-for-profit executive; d. Victor William and Jacqueline (Bryant) Lomax; m. Kent Alan Bagnall, May 4, 1985; 2 children. BA, U. Mo., Rolla, 1976. Co-owner, v.p. human resources Kent Jewelry and Fine Gifts, Rolla, 1985—; exec. v.p. Mo. Sch. Mines U. Mo. - Rolla, 2002—. Adv. Panhellenic, 2003—05. Vol. Ozark Actors Theater, Rolla, 1985—, Pub. Radio Sta. KUMR, Rolla, Mo., 1985—; mem. Arts Rolla!, 1990—, Friends of Rolla Pub. Libr., 1990—, Champions Rolla Edn., 1995—; vol. Mark Twain Elem. PTO, Rolla, Mo., 1995—2002; vol. parent adv. com. Mark Twain Elem. Sch., Rolla, 2003—05. Mem.: Coun. Advancement and Support Edn., Rolla Area C. of C., U. Mo. Rolla, Mo. Sch. Mines Alumni Assn. (exec. dir.), P.E.O. Internat. (rec. sec. 1997—99, chair publicity 1999—2003, chair auditing 2000—, initiation corr. sec. 2001—04), Duston-Dustin Family Assn. (life), Coterie U. Mo.-Rolla, Phelps County Alumnae Panhellenic (treas. 1990—91, tel. chair 1990—91, chair scholarship com. 2000—01, co-chair cotillion 2000—02, 2006—). Avocations: theater, art collecting, travel, reading. Home: 16541 State Route F Rolla MO 65401 Office: MSM-UMR Alumni Association Castleman Hall 1870 Miner Circle Rolla MO 65409-0650 Office Phone: 573-341-6327. Personal E-mail: bagnall@socket.net. Business E-Mail: lindsayb@umr.edu.

BAGNALL, ROGER SHALER, history professor, director; b. Seattle, Aug. 19, 1947; m. 1969; 2 children BA, Yale U., 1968; MA, U. Toronto, Ont., Can., 1969; PhD in Classical Studies, U. Toronto, 1972. Asst. prof. classics Fla. State U., 1972-74; asst. prof. Greek and Latin Columbia U., NYC, 1974-79, assoc. prof. classics and history, 1979-83, prof., 1983—2007, dean Grad. Sch. Arts and Scis., 1989-93; dir. Inst. for Study of Ancient World NYU, 2007—. Pres. Egyptological Sem. of N.Y., 1981-83; vis. prof. U. Florence, Italy, 1981, 89, Bar-Ilan U., Israel, 1986, U. Warsaw, Poland, 1989, U. Helsinki, Finland, 1994, Am. U. Cairo, 2004; Hamilton vis. rsch. fellow Christ Ch., Oxford, 1995-96; Sather prof. U. Calif.-Berkeley, 2005. Author: The Administration of the Ptolemaic Possessions, 1976, Ostraka in Amsterdam Collections, 1976, The Florida Ostraka: Documents from the Roman Army in Upper Egypt, 1976, Bullion Purchases and Landholding in the 4th Century, 1977, Egypt in Late Antiquity, 1993, Reading Papyri, Writing Ancient History, 1995, Kellis Agricultural Account Book, 1997; co-author: Ostraka in the Royal Ontario Museum, 2 vols., 1971-76, The Chronological Systems of Byzantine Egypt, 1978, 2d edit., 2004, Columbia Papyri VII, VIII, 1978, 90, Consuls of the Later Roman Empire, 1987, Demography of Roman Egypt, 1994. Recipient Disting. Achievement award Andrew W. Mellon Found., 2004; Am. Coun. Learned Soc. grantee, 1975, fellow, 1976-77; Am. Philos Soc. grantee, 1984, 84; NEH fellow, 1984-85, Guggenheim fellow, 1990-91, Fowler Hamilton Vis. Rsch. fellow Christ Church, Oxford, England, 1995-96. Fellow Am. Numismatic Soc., Am. Acad. Arts and Scis.; mem. Am. Philol. Assn. (sec.-treas. 1979-85, bd. dirs. 1988-91), Am. Philos. Soc., Am. Soc. Papyrologists (pres. 1993-96), Acad. Royale de Belgique, Am. Acad. Arts Scis.; corr. fellow British Acad. Office: NYU Inst for the Study of Ancient World 70 Washington Sq S New York NY 10012

BAGNOLI, DANNELLE M., school psychologist; BS in Psychology, The Ohio State U., Columbus, 1998, MA in Sch. Psychology, 2001. Nat. Cert. Sch. Psychologist Nat. Assn. Sch. Psychologist, 2002. Intern sch. psychologist Columbus Pub. Schs., 2001—02, sch. psychologist, 2002—.

Sch. psychology practicum supr. The Ohio State U., 2004—06; mem. Ethics & Stds. Com., Columbus Pub. Schs., 2005—. Mem.: Nat. Assn. Sch. Psychologists. Office: Columbus Pub Schs 2571 Neil Ave Columbus OH 43202 Business E-Mail: bagnoli.1@osu.edu.

BAGNOLI, DAVID CHRISTOPHER, architect; b. Zanesville, Ohio, Mar. 1, 1969; s. Joseph Paul and Lillian Abood Bagnoli; m. Margareth Lp Paz, Oct. 10, 1998; children: Elena Nicole Paz, Gabrielle Irene Paz. BA in Art History, U. Notre Dame, 1992, BArch, 1992; MArch, U. Pa., 1998, Cert. in Urban Design, 1998. Cert. Nat. Coun. Archtl. Registration Bd., Ohio. Assoc. William Rawn Assoc., Arch. Inc., Boston, 1998—2004, Cunningham and Quill Arch., Washington, 2004—. Prin. works include Carneros Inn, Calif. (Boston Soc. Arch. Honor award, 2004), North Pk. Grad. Housing, Dartmouth Coll. (Pillar of Industry, Builder Choice award, 2004), Sugarloaf Mountain Vineyard, Md. Capt. USAF, 1992—97. Recipient Neighborhood Dist. Corridor Charter award, Congress New Urbanism, 2007, Takoma Walk, Md. Block, Bldg., Scale Charter award, 2007. Mem.: AIA (Nat. Urban and Regional Design Honor award 2006). Roman Catholic. Office: Cunningham and Quill Arch 1054 31st St NW Washington DC 20007 Home Phone: 202-363-1220; Office Phone: 202-337-0090. Personal E-mail: dpbagnoli@verizon.net. Business E-Mail: dbagnoli@cunninghamquill.com.

BAGSHAW, BRADLEY HOLMES, lawyer; b. Salem, Mass., Mar. 26, 1953; s. James Holmes and Hope (Bradley) Bagshaw. AB summa cum laude, Bowdoin Coll., 1975; JD cum laude, Harvard U., 1981. Bar: Wash. 1981, US Dist. Ct. (we. dist.) Wash. 1981, US Dist. Ct. (ea. dist.) Wash. 1989, US Ct. Appeals (9th cir.) 1989. Assoc. Helsell Fetterman, Seattle, 1981-88, ptnr., 1988—, mng. ptnr., 1991-97, ptnr., 1997—. Office: Helsell Fetterman LLP 1001 4th Ave Ste 4200 Seattle WA 98154-1154 E-mail: bbagshaw@helsell.com.

BAGSHAW, JOSEPH CHARLES, molecular biologist, educator; b. Niagara Falls, NY, Sept. 2, 1943; s. Joseph Stanley and Nancy Jo (Pannabaker) Pash; children: Joseph Scott, Alan David. BA, Johns Hopkins U., 1965; PhD, U. Tenn., Oak Ridge, 1969. Research fellow Mass. Gen. Hosp., Boston, 1970-71; asst. prof. molecular biology Wayne State U., Detroit, 1971-77, assoc. prof., 1977-84; prof. biology and biotech. Worcester (Mass.) Poly. Inst., 1984—. Dir Worcester Consortium PhD Program Biomedical Sci, 1985—. Editor (with others): Cell and Molecular Biology of Artemia Development, 1989. Predoctoral fellow, NSF, rsch. grantee, NIH, USDA. Mem.: AAAS, Am. Soc. Cell Biology, Am. Soc. Biochemistry and Molecular Biology. Office: Worcester Poly Inst Dept Biology/Biotech Worcester MA 01609-2280 Office Phone: 508-831-5930. Business E-Mail: jbagshaw@wpi.edu.

BAGWILL, JOHN WILLIAMS, retired pension fund administrator; b. Seattle, Aug. 9, 1930; s. John Williams and Amy (Munday) B.; m. Emily Bend Sedgwick, Dec. 28, 1953; children: John Williams III, David Sedgwick, Elizabeth Bagwill Komjathy. BA, Hamilton Coll., 1952; MBA, Harvard U., 1958. CFP. Asst. to pres. George O. Muir, Inc., NYC, 1961-64; v.p. Fin. Instns. Retirement Fund, White Plains, N.Y., 1964-85, exec. v.p., 1985-87, pres., 1987-94; ret., 1994. Gov. Newport (R.I.) Health Care Corp., 1997; cons. long-term care issues, 1999—. Bd. dirs. Town Club New Castle, Chappaqua, N.Y., 1975-79, pres., 1978-79; alumni coun. Hamilton Coll., 1977-82, pres., 1980-82; trustee, treas. Newport Art Mus., 1997-2006; mem. pension fund investment com, Middletown, RI. Mem.: Newport Reading Rm., Quindecim Club. Episcopalian.

BAHA, CHRISTIAN J., investment company executive; b. Vienna, Oct. 30, 1968; s. Helmut and Christine Baha; 1 child, Dorian. Grad., Vienna Police Acad.; attended, U. Vienna. Co-founder, CEO Superfund Asset Mgmt. (formerly Quadriga Investment Group), 1995—; founder, CEO TeleTrader, 1995, now chmn. supervisory bd. Former policeman, Vienna. Avocations: skiing, tennis, jogging. Office: Superfund Asset Mgmt, Inc 489 Fifth Ave New York NY 10017 Office Phone: 212-750-6300. Office Fax: 212-750-2206. E-mail: nyc@superfund.com.

BAHADUR, BIRENDRA, displays research specialist; b. Gorakhpur, India, July 1, 1949; came to Can., 1981; s. Bijai Bahadur and Shakuntala Srivastva; m. Urmila Bahadur, May 29, 1970; children: Shivendra, Shachindra. BS in Physics, Chemistry and Math., Gorakhpur U., 1967, MS in Physics, 1969, PhD, 1976. Rsch. scholar physics dept. Gorakhpur U., 1969-76, asst. prof. physics dept., 1976-77; sr. sci. officer Nat. Phys. Lab. India, New Delhi, 1977-81; v.p. R&D Data Images, Ottawa, Ont., Canada, 1981-85; mgr. R&D Litton Data Images, Ottawa, 1985-91; engr. mgr. liquid crystal display material and process Litton Systems, Can., Toronto, 1988-97; prin. engr. Display Ctr. Rockwell Collins Inc., 1997—. Adj. prof. dept. computers and elec. engring. Waterloo (Can.) U., 1995; active various Internat. Confs. on Liquid Crystals; participant numerous profl. meetings; mem. liquid crystal tech. com. SID, 1993—. Author: Liquid Crystal Displays, 1984; editor: Liquid Crystals--Applications and Uses, vol. I, 1990, vol. II, 1991, vol. III, 1992; mem. editl. bd. Displays, 1993-2006, Liquid Crystal Today, 1995—; abstracting panel Liquid Crystal Abstracts, 1978-80; contbr. articles to profl. jours. V.p. nat. capitol region India Can. Assn., 1989-90, pres., 1990-91. Grantee Indsl. Rsch. Assistance Program, NRC Can., 1982-85, 84-87, 88-91, Wright Patterson AFB, 1991-94. Mem. Internat. Liquid Crystal Soc., Soc. Info. Displays (dir. Upper Midwest chpt. 2003--, Spl. Recognition award 1993, LC tech. com. 1993—, chmn. 1997), Inst. Physics, Soc. de Chimie Physique. Achievements include patent for Process for Production of Printed Electrode Pattern for Use in Electro-Optical Display Devices (India); co-development of technology of various liquid crystal displays; patent for wide viewing angle dye doped TN LCDs with retardation sheets. Home: 935 71st St NE Cedar Rapids IA 52402-7295 Office: Rockwell Collins Inc Mail Sta 106-191 400 Collins Rd Cedar Rapids IA 52498-0001 Home Phone: 319-294-8891; Office Phone: 319-295-9251. E-mail: bbahadur@rockwellcollins.com.

BAHAR, EZEKIEL, electrical engineering educator; US citizen; s. Silas and Hannah Bahar; m. Ophira Rodoff; children: Zillah, Ruth Iris, Ron Jonathan. BS, Technion IIT, Haifa, Israel, 1958, MS, 1960; PhD, U. Colo., Boulder, 1964. Instr. Technion, Haifa, Israel, 1960—62; rsch. assoc. U. Colo., Boulder, 1962—64, asst. prof., 1964—67; assoc. prof. U. Nebr., Lincoln, 1967—71, prof., 1971—80, Durham prof., 1981—89, George Holmes disting. prof., 1989—, u. disting. prof., 1999—, dir. program revs., 1981—83. Vis. prof. NOAA, Boulder, 1979; prin. investigator radio wave propagation in complex media, metamaterials with chiral properties, remote sensing, nanotechnology rsch., 1964—. Pres. faculty senate U. Nebr., Lincoln, 1980. Recipient Outstanding Rsch. and Creative Activities award U. Nebr., Lincoln, 1980, Scholarship citation U. Colo., Boulder, 1964 Fellow IEEE (life); mem. Internat. Union Radio Sci. (rep. 1978, 81, 84, 87, 90, 93, 96, 99, 2002). Avocation: swimming. Home: 2431 Bretigne Dr Lincoln NE 68512-1913 Office: U Nebr WSEC 218 N Lincoln NE 68588-0511 Office Phone: 402-472-1966. Business E-Mail: ebahar@unl.edu.

BAHASH, ROBERT J., information technology executive; b. New Brunswick, NJ, 1945; BS in Acctg., Mt. St. Mary's Coll., 1966; MBA in Fin., NYU, 1972. CPA. Joined as mgr. fin. auditing McGraw-Hill, Inc., NYC, 1974, various finance-related positions, 1974—83, exec. v.p., fin., McGraw-Hill Book Co., 1983; sr. v.p. corp. fin. operation The McGraw-Hill Companies, NYC, 1985, exec. v.p. & CFO, 1988—. Bd. dir. AnswerThink Inc. Mem. Am. Inst. of CPAs, Fin. Executives Inst., NJ Soc. CPAs. Office: McGraw-Hill Inc Ste 383 1221 Avenue Of The Americas New York NY 10020-1095*

BAHBAH, BISHARA ASSAD, investment company executive, consultant; b. Jerusalem, Apr. 10, 1958; came to U.S., 1976; s. Assad R. and Filomene H. Bahbah; children: Leila Jean, As'ad Victor, Jubran Ronald, Remzi Robert. BA, Brigham Young U., 1979; MA, Harvard U., 1981, PhD, 1983; cert., George Washington U., 1988. Cert. mktg. and fund raising profl. Wharton Sch. Bus., 2003, Chartered Inst. Mgmt. Accts., investment cons., sr. investment cons. 2004, estate planning cons. Am. Coll., 2004, wealth strategist Cannon Fin., 2006. Editor-in-chief Al-Fajr Newspaper, Jerusalem, 1983-84; dir. United Palestinian Appeal, Washington, 1985-87; pres., chmn., CEO Internat. Mktg. and Fund Raising Assocs., Inc., Scottsdale, Ariz., 1987—2002; editor-in-chief The Return Mag., Washington, 1988-90; exec. com. mem. Ctr. Policy Analysis on Palestine, Washington, 1990-96; assoc. dir. Middle East Inst., Kennedy Sch., Harvard U., 1992-96; pres., CEO TV Devel. Ptnrs., Inc., NYC, 1997; regional rep. Middle East and Africa RSL COM and RSL Studios, NYC, 1997-98; pres., CEO BHB Enterprises, Woodbridge, Va., 1998—2002, Holy Land Enterprises, Woodbridge, 1999-2000; pres. Eden Advisors, Mass., 1994—96. Vis. prof. Brigham Young U., Provo, Utah, 1985, adj. prof. polit. sci., 1985-90; sr. fellow Kennedy Sch. Govt. Harvard U., 1996-98; guest columnist The Arizona Republic, 2000—. Author: Israel and Latin America-The Military Connection, 1986; mem. adv. bd. Internat. Ency. Comm., 1984—. Chmn., bd. trustees Palestine Children's Relief Fund, USA, 1999-2002; bd. dirs. Givat Haviva, USA, Palestine Consultancy Group, Jerusalem: mem. Nat. Policy Coun., Arab Am. Inst., Washington; mem. Palestinian Del. to the Multi-Lateral Peace Talks on Arms Control and Regional Security, 1991-2000; bd. dirs. Ariz. Acad. Decathlon. Mem. Am. Polit. Sci. Assn., Assn. Fundraising Profls., Direct Mktg. Assn. Washington, Arab Am. Med. Assn. Ariz. (chmn., relief com. 2004—), Acad. Polit. Sci. Personal E-mail: bisharabahbah@yahoo.com.

BAHL, GAUTAM, radiologist; BS in Elec. and Biomed. Engring., Yale U., New Haven, 2001; MD, U. Calif., San Diego, 2005. Intern in internal medicine U. Calif., San Diego, 2005—06; resident in diagnostic radiology Detroit Med. Ctr., Wayne State U., 2006—. Radiology rschr. U. Calif., San Diego, 2001—07; presenter in field. Contbr. articles to profl. jours. Vol. Free Clinic, San Diego, 2001—03. Mem.: Radiological Soc. N. Am. Office: Wayne State U Dept Radiology DRH-3L 4201 St Antoine St Detroit MI 48201-2153 Home Phone: 530-893-2437.

BAHL, ROY WINFORD, economist, educator, consultant; b. Miami, Fla., June 28, 1939; s. Roy Winford and Vista Lee (Becks) B.; m. Marilyn Seifried, Dec. 22, 1963; children: Renee, Alexandra, Martin, Ashley. BA, Greenville Coll., Ill., 1961; MA, U. Ky., 1963, PhD in Econs., 1965. Asst. prof. econs. W.Va. U., Morgantown, 1965-67; economist IMF, Washington, 1967-71; prof. econs. Syracuse (N.Y.) U., 1971-88, Maxwell prof. polit. economy, 1985-88; prof. econs. Ga. State U., Atlanta, 1988—2006, dir. Policy Rsch. Ctr., 1988-96, dean Andrew Young sch. policy studies, 1996—2007, regents prof., 2006—. Bd. dirs. N.Y. State Energy Authority, Albany, 1979-87, Lincoln Found., Phoenix, 1986-93; mem. So. Growth Policies Bd., 1997—; cons. World Bank, Washington, 1971—. Author: Urban Public Finance in LDCs, 1992, Economic Growth and Fiscal Plan, 1992, Fiscal Policy in China, 1999; editor: The Jamaican Tax Reform, 1991, Restructuring Local Government Finance, 2003. Recipient Fiscal medal Govt. of Philippines, 1986, Disting. Economist award State of Ky., 1989. Mem. Nat. Tax Assn. (pres. 1986), Am. Econs. Assn., So. Econs. Assn. (v.p. 1993). Democrat. Office: Ga State U Andrew Young Sch Policy Studies 14 Marietta St 14W Ste 635 Atlanta GA 30303

BAHL, SAROJ MEHTA, nutritionist, educator; b. New Delhi, Apr. 4, 1946; came to U.S., 1972; d. L.D. and G.D. Mehta; m. Vishwa Mittar Bahl; children: Rahul, Ragini. BS in Home Sci., Delhi U., 1965, MS in Nutrition, 1967, PhD in Nutrition, 1973. Lectr. Lady Irwin Coll., New Delhi, 1970-71; instr. U. N.D., Grand Forks, 1972-74; from rsch. assoc. med. sch. to assoc. prof. dental sch. U. Tex. , Houston, 1976—2002, assoc. prof. dental sch., 2002—. Program dir. Peace Corps, Houston, 1984. Author: Nutritional Management of the AIDS Patient; contbr. articles to profl. jours. Den leader Boy Scouts Am., Houston, 1983; mem. ednl. com. March of Dimes, Houston, 1986—; mem. exec. bd. Indo-Am. Charity Found. of Houston, 1995-98. Recipient several awards for tchg. excellence including John P. McGovern award, 1992, 95; named Outstanding Dietetic Educator Tex. Tex. Dietetic Assn., 1995; nominated for U.S. Prof. of Yr., 1993, 94. Mem. Am. Inst. Life Threatening Illness (assoc.), Soc. Nutrition Edn. (editor newsletter), Minority Faculty Assn. (pres. 1996-97), Vivekananda Vedanta Soc. (pres. 1993-1998). Avocations: painting, music, reading. Office: U Tex Dental Sch Rm B-30 6516 MD Anderson Blvd Houston TX 77030 Home Phone: 281-265-3459; Office Phone: 713-500-4586. Business E-Mail: saroj.m.bahl@uth.tmc.edu.

BAHL, TRACY L., healthcare executive; Student, Whittier Coll. Sch. Law; grad. in Bus. and Health, Gustavus Adolphus Coll.; diplomat, Am. Coll. Healthcare Exec. With UniHealth Am., Calif., Maxicare Healthplans, Calif.; dir. provider rels. CIGNA HealthCare Calif., Calif.; v.p., exec. dir. CIGNA HealthCare NY; pres., gen. mgr. CIGNA HealthCare Mid-Atlantic; pres. strategic bus. svcs. United HealthCare Corp., Hartford, Conn., 1998; pres. Uniprise Strategic Solutions, 1998—2002; sr. v.p. comml. health plan CIGNA HealthCare; sr. v.p., chief mktg. officer UnitedHealth Grp., Minnetonka, Minn., 2002—; CEO Uniprise, 2004—. Office: UnitedHealth Grp 9900 Bren Rd East Minnetonka MN 55343

BAHLER, GARY M., lawyer; BA, Houghton Coll., 1973; JD, Cornell U., 1976. Bar: NY 1977. V.p., sec., gen. counsel Woolworth Corp., NYC; sec., dep. gen. counsel Foot Locker, Inc., NYC, 1991—93, v.p., gen. counsel, sec., 1993—98, sr. v.p., gen. counsel, sec., 1998—. Office: Foot Locker Inc 112 W 34th St New York NY 10120 Office Phone: 212-720-3700.

BAHLKE, CONRAD GEORGE, lawyer; b. Phila., Sept. 17, 1958; m. Roxane Orgill; children: Charlotte, Nolan. BA, Oberlin Coll., 1980; MBA, JD, U. Chgo., 1984. Bar: Mass. 1985, N.Y. 1988. Atty. Fed. Res. Bd., Washington, 1984-87; assoc. White & Case, NYC, 1987-94; assoc., spl. counsel Schulte Roth & Zabel LLP, NYC, 1994-2000; ptnr. Weil, Gotshal & Manges LLP, NYC, 2000—. Contbr. articles to profl. publs. Trustee Oberlin (Ohio) Coll., 1980—83. Mem.: ABA (mem. com. futures and derivative investments, chmn. subcom. 2000—), Assn. Bar City of NY (mem. com. futures regulation 1992—95, 1996—99, 2000—), Phi Beta Kappa. Episcopalian. Avocations: art, music, travel, sports. Office: Weil Gotshal & Manges LLP 767 5th Ave New York NY 10153 Office Phone: 212-310-8630. Business E-Mail: conrad.bahlke@weil.com.

BAHLMAN, WILLIAM THORNE, JR., retired lawyer; b. Cin., Jan. 9, 1920; s. William Thorne and Janet (Rhodes) B.; m. Nancy W. DeCamp, Mar. 21, 1953; children: Charles R., William Ward, Baker D. BA, Yale U., 1941, LL.B., 1947. Bar: Ohio 1947. Prin. Paxton & Seasongood, L.P.A., Cin., 1947-67, 73-88; ptnr. Paxton & Seasongood, Cin., 1954-67, Thompson Hine, LLP, Cin., 1989-94; prof. law U. Cin. Coll. Law, 1967-73, lectr., 1965-67, 73-77; ret., 1994. Served with USAAF, 1942-46. Mem. Am. Law Inst., ABA, Ohio State Bar Assn., Cin. Bar Assn. Office: Thompson Hine LLP 312 Walnut St Fl 14 Cincinnati OH 45202-4024 Office Phone: 513-352-6716. E-mail: WilliamBahlman@ThompsonHine.com.

BAHL-MOORE, ELIZABETH ANN, artist, educator; b. Sayre, Pa., Dec. 29, 1978; d. John Anthony Bahl and Margaret Marie Hildebrandt; m. William Andrew Moore, June 13, 1998. BFA magna cum laude, Longwood U., Farmville, Va., 2002. Cert. tchr. Va. Instr. art Longwood Ctr. Visual Arts, Farmville, Va., 2003; tchr. art Culpeper (Va.) County Pub. Schs., 2003—. Instr. art summer enrichment Culpeper (Va.) County Pub. Schs., 2004; founder After Sch. Art Club Program Culpeper, 2004—05. One-woman shows include Artistic License, Culpeper, Va., 2005, Windmore Artist Mems. Show, Culpeper, 2005, Windmore Patron Art Show, 2006, exhibitions include Heart Va. Art and Craft Outdoor Festival, 2003—05, Windmere Artist Group Show, Colpeper, Va., 2005. Vol. Prince Edward Elem., Farmville, 2003; bd. dirs. Voices of Blue Ridge, Culpeper, 2004—. Mem.: NEA, Va. Edn. Assn., Nat. Art Edn. Assn., Va. Art Edn. Assn., Phi Kappa Phi. Office: Culpeper Middle Sch 14300 Achievement Dr Culpeper VA 22701

BAHLS, STEVEN CARL, academic administrator, educator; b. Des Moines, Sept. 4, 1954; s. Carl Robert and Dorothy Rose (Jensen) B.; m. Jane Emily Easter, June 18, 1977; children: Daniel David, Timothy Carl, Angela Emily. BBA, U. Iowa, 1976; JD, Northwestern U., Chgo., 1979. Bar: Wis. 1979, Mont. 1989; CPA, Iowa. Assoc. Frisch, Dudek & Slattery, Milw., 1979-84, dir., 1985; assoc. dean and prof. U. Mont. Sch. of Law, Missoula, 1985-94; dean., prof. law sch. Capital U. Law Sch., Columbus, Ohio, 1994—2003; pres. Augustana Coll., Rock Island, Ill., 2003—. Coordinating exec. editor Northwestern U. Law Rev., 1979. Pres. Illowa coun. Boy Scouts Am.; bd. dirs. Quad Cities United Way, 2004—; treas. Ill. Quad Cities C. of C., 2007, Quad Cities Symphony Orch.; vice chmn., bd. dirs. Putnam Mus., 2007; bd. visitors U. Mont. Sch. Law, 2006—. Mem. ABA, Nat. Assn. Ind. Colls. (bd. dirs.), Am. Agrl. Law Assn. (pres. 2000), Wis. Bar Assn., Mont. Bar Assn., Order of Coif. Avocations: photography, travel, hiking. Office: Augustana College 639 38th Street Rock Island IL 61201-2296

BAHNER, THOMAS MAXFIELD, lawyer; b. Little Rock, 1933; m. Sara M. Bahner; 3 children. BS, Carson-Newman Coll., 1954; JD, U. Va., 1960. Bar: Tenn. 1960, Va. 1960, U.S. Dist. Ct. (ea. dist.) Tenn. 1961, U.S. Supreme Ct. 1970, U.S. Ct. Appeals (6th cir.) 1971, U.S. Ct. Appeals (8th cir.) 1971, U.S. Ct. Appeals (4th cir.) 1975, U.S. Ct. Appeals (3d cir.) 1988, U.S. Ct. Appeals (fed. cir.) 1991, U.S. Ct. Appeals (9th cir.) 1999, U.S. Ct. Appeals (11th cir.) 1999, U.S. Dist. Ct. (we. dist.) Tenn. 2002. Assoc. Kefauver, Duggan and McDonald, Chattanooga, 1960—62; ptnr. Duggan, McDonald & Bahner, Chattanooga, 1962—64, Chambliss, Bahner, Crutchfield, Gaston and Irvine (name changed to Chambliss, Bahner & Stophel), Chattanooga, 1964—. Chmn. adv. commn. civil rules Tenn. Supreme Ct., 1982—89, chair adv. com. drafting Tenn. rules of evidence, 1983—89, mem. bd. profl. responsibility, 1982—85, chmn fin. com., 1984—85, mem. continuing legal edn. blue ribbon com.; bd. commrs. Hamilton County Law Libr.; chair standing com. on atty. admissions to Chattanooga divsn. US Dist. Ct. Ea. Dist. Tenn., 2007—. Sr. contbg. editor Evidence in America, the Federal Rules in the United States, 1987; contbr. chapters to books. Bd. dirs. Orange Grove Ctr., Chattanooga, 1962—99, pres., 1974—75, chmn., 1976—77; mem. bd. trustees, sec. BOTA Found., 1985—; mem. bd. trustees Carson-Newman Coll., Jefferson City, Tenn., 1975—2002, chmn. bd. trustees, 1983—87, 1990—92, mem. pres. search com., 1977, 1999—2000; mem., dir., organizer Ea. Dist. Tenn. U.S. Dist. Ct. Hist. Soc., v.p. Ea. Dist. Tenn., 1993—; mem., organizer, bd. dirs. Tenn. Supreme Ct. Hist. Soc., pres., 1997; active Hamilton County Sch. Bd., 1970—75; bd. dirs. Chattanooga Symphony, 1980—83, Chattanooga United Way, 1990—96, chmn. fund drive profl. divsn., 1992; mem. merit selection panel for Bankruptcy Judges U.S. Dist. Ct., 1993—94; mem. award com. Liberty Bell; bd. dirs. Chattanooga Cmty. Found., 2005—, U. Chattanooga Found., 2006—. Recipient Disting. Alumni award, Carson-Newman Coll., 1984. Fellow: Va. State Bar, Chattanooga Bar Found. (life; founder), Tenn. Bar Found. (life; founder); mem.: ABA (Tenn. Bar del. 1984—90, nominating com. 1990—99, bd. govs. 1999—2002, exec. com. 2001—02, exec. dir. search com. 2005—06, standing com. ethics and profl. responsibility 2005—, state del.), Tenn. Continuing Legal Edn. (Blue Ribbon Com.), Tenn. Supreme Ct., Chattanooga Bar Assn. (pres. 1969—70, med.-legal com. 2004—, pres.'s award 1995, Ralph H. Kelley Humanitarian award), Tenn. Def. Lawyers Assn., Tenn. Bar Assn. (bd. govs. 1975—82, pres. 1980—81), Conf. So. Bar Pres. (chmn. 1980—81), 6th Cir. Jud. Conf. (life), Am. Bd. Trial Advs., Estate Planning Coun. (bd. dirs. 1971—72), Am. Coll. Trial Lawyers (state com. 1995—99, profl. com. 1998—), Am. Judicature Soc., Internat. Assn. Def. Counsel, Chattanooga Rotary Club (sec. 1989—91, 1st v.p. 1997—98, pres. 2001—02), Signal Mountain Golf and Country Club, Mountain City Club, Am. Inns Ct. (master), Delta Theta Phi. Baptist. Home: 718 Parsons Ln Signal Mountain TN 37377-2704 Office: Chambliss Bahner & Stophel PC 1000 Tallan Bldg 2 Union Sq Ste 1000 Chattanooga TN 37402-2500 Office Phone: 423-756-3000. Business E-Mail: mbahner@cbslawfirm.com.

BAHR, DONALD WALTER, retired chemical engineer; b. Chgo., Dec. 13, 1927; s. Walter James and Justine Antonia (Schwegler) Bahr; m. Mary Estelle Zieverink, Oct. 15, 1960; children: Donald Walter Jr., Susan Mary. BS ChemE, U. Ill., 1949; MSChemE, Ill. Inst. Tech., 1951, MS in Gas Tech., 1951. Registered Profl. Engr., Ohio. Aero rsch. scientist Lewis Flight Propulsion Lab. NASA, Cleve., 1951—54; chem. engr. GE Co., Cin., 1956—62, engring. mgr. Phila., 1962—68, GE Aircraft Engines, Phila., 1968—94. Vice chmn. jet engine fuels panel NASA Lewis Rsch. Ctr., Cleve., 1973—76. Contbr. articles to profl. jours. 1st lt. USAF, 1954—56. Named to Propulsion Hall of Fame, GE Co., 1995; recipient Outstanding Engring. Achievement award, 1982. Fellow: ASME (combustion and fuels com. 1975—, vice chmn. combustion and fuels com. 1985—87, chmn. combustion and fuels com. 1987—89, Tom Sawyer award 1998, Aircraft Engine Tech. award 2003), AIAA (Air Breathing Propulsion award 1983); mem.: NAE, Coordinating Rsch. Coun. (aviation fuel, lubricant and other equpment com.), Gen. Aviation Mfrs. Assn. (environ. com.), Aerospace Industries Assn. (chmn. aircraft engine emissions com. 1971—95), Combustion Inst. (bd. advisors ctrl. states sect. 1986—, chmn. bd. advisors 1993—95, chmn. ctrl. states sect. 1995—97). Republican. Roman Catholic. Home: 12195 Pickwick Pl Cincinnati OH 45241-1791 Office Phone: 513-793-3685. Personal E-mail: donbahr@msn.com.

BAHR, EHRHARD, Germanic languages and literature educator; b. Kiel, Germany, Aug. 21, 1932; came to U.S., 1956; s. Klaus and Gisela (Badenhausen) B.; m. Diana Meyers, Nov. 21, 1973; stepchildren: Gary, Timothy, Christopher. Student, U. Heidelberg, Germany, 1952-53, U. Freiburg, 1953-56; MS Ed. (Fulbright scholar), U. Kans., 1956-58; postgrad., U. Cologne, 1959-61; PhD, U. Calif., Berkeley, 1968. Asst. prof. German UCLA, 1968-70, assoc. prof., 1970-72, prof., 1972—2003, prof. emeritus, 2003—, chmn. dept. Germanic langs., 1981-84, 93-98, chair grad. council, 1988-89. Author: Irony in the Late Works of Goethe, 1972, Georg Lukacs, 1970, Ernst Bloch, 1974, Nelly Sachs, 1980, Weimar on the Pacific: German Exile Culture in Los Angeles and the Crisis of Modernism, 2007; editor: Kant, What is Enlightenment?, 1974, Goethe, Wilhelm, Meister's Apprenticeship, 1982, Goethe, Wilhelm, Meister's Journeyman Years, 1982, History of German Literature, 3 vols., 1987—88, 2nd edit., 1998—99, The Novel as Archive: The Genesis, Reception and Criticism of Goethe's Wilhelm Meisters Wanderjahre, 1988; co-editor: The Internalized Revolution: German Reactions to the French Revolution, 1789-1989, 1992; commentary Thomas Mann: Death in Venice, 1991, reprint, 2005, Goethe: Wilhelm Meister's Apprenticeship, 1982; contbr. articles to profl. jour. Recipient Disting. Teaching award UCLA, 1970, Humanities Inst. award, 1972, summer stipend NEH, 1978 Mem. MLA, Am. Soc. 18th Century Studies, Am. Assn. Tchrs. German, Western Soc. 18th Century Studies, German Studies Assn. (pres. 1987-88), Pacific Ancient & Modern Lang. Assn., Lessing Soc., Goethe Soc. N.Am. (exec. sec. 1979-89, pres. 1995-97). Office: UCLA Dept Germanic Langs Los Angeles CA 90095-1539 Office Phone: 310-825-3955. Business E-Mail: bahr@humnet.ucla.edu.

BAHR, JANE MARIE, writer, retired language educator; BS in English, U. Wis., River Falls, 1971; MST in English, U. Wis., Whitewater, 1978. English tchr. Whitewater (Wis.) H.S., 1973—82, Eau Claire (Wis.) Meml. H.S., 1985, Glenwood City H.S., summers 1990-91; freelance writer Wis. Fellowship of Poets, 1981—, Wis. Regional Writers' Assn., 1985—, Wis. Arts Bd. Grant, 1998. Author poems in numerous publs. including Wis. Poets' Calendars, Poetry Out of Wis. V, The WFOP Museletter, Free Verse, Poetry Motel, Wallpaper Broadside Series, Poesy, Hummingbird and others. Scholar WRWA Soar scholar, Sch. of Arts, U. Wis., Madison, 1999.

BAHR, LAUREN S., publishing executive; b. New Brunswick, NJ, July 3, 1944; d. Simon A. and Rosalind J. Bahr. Student, U. Grenoble, France, 1964; BA (Branstrom scholar); MA, U. Mich., 1966. Asst. editor New Horizons Pubs., Inc., Chgo., 1967, Scholastic Mags., Inc., NYC, 1968-71; supervising editor Houghton Mifflin Co., Boston, 1971; product devel. editor Appleton-Century-Crofts, NYC, 1972-74; sponsoring editor McGraw-Hill, Inc., NYC, 1974-75; editor Today's Sec. mag., 1975-77; sr. editor Media Systems Corp., NYC, 1978; sr. editor coll. dept. CBS Coll. Pub., NYC, 1978-82, mktg. mgr. fgn. langs., dir. mktg. adminstrn., 1982-83; dir. devel. coll. divsn. Harper & Row, NYC, 1983—88, pub. cons., 1988—91; v.p., editl. dir. Atlas Edits., Inc., NYC, 1991-98; dir. publs. Bank St. Coll. Edn., NYC, 1999—2000; mng. editor Inkwell Pub., NYC, 2000—02; editl. dir. 4 Lakes Colorgraphics, NYC, 2002—07, exec. dir., 2007—. Democrat. Jewish. Home: 444 E 82nd St #8A New York NY 10028-5903

BAHRAMI, HOSSEIN, epidemiologist, physician; s. Abdolazim and Mahboobeh Bahrami. MD, Tehran U., 2001; MPH, Johns Hopkins U., 2004. Lic. physician 2001. Intern Tehran U., 1999—2001; methodolgist, epidemiologist Digestive Disease Rsch. Ctr., Trauma Rsch. Ctr. Cardio-vasc. Rsch. Ctr., Daryani GI Clinic, 1999—; rsch. fellow cardiology divsn. and Wilmer Eye Inst. Johns Hopkins U., Balt., 2003—. Mem. Sci. Adv. Bd., Arlington, Md.; physician, rschr. Iranian Charity Hepatic Patients Support. Author: (book) Nutrition in Digestive Diseases, Hepatitis; contbr. articles to profl. jours. Vol. physician Iranian Charity Hepatic Patients Support; mem. Hurricane Katrina Relief Com., JHSPH-SA; councilor APHA Governing Coun., 2005—; bd. mem. Sci. Bd., Washington, 2005—. Recipient Ruth Rice Puffer award, Johns Hopkins U., 2005, Eskridge award, 2005, Silverman award, 2005, Dyar Mem. award, 2006, Jay S. Drotman Mem. award, APHA, 2006. Mem.: APHA (mem. governing coun. 2005—, Jay Drotman Meml. award 2006), Soc. Epidemiologic Rsch., Assn. Rsch. Vision and Ophthalmology, Am. Heart Assn., Amercian Coll. Epidemiology (assoc.), Delta Omega. Achievements include invention of New Methods for Improving Scientific Papers; research in New Treatment of Hepatitis B; New PC-Based Eye Tests; Finding different patterns of Fatty Liver in developing countries. Avocations: travel, music, swimming, dancing, camping, hiking. Office: Johns Hopkins Hosp 110 D Nelson 600 N Broadway Baltimore MD 21205 Personal E-mail: nbahrami@gmail.com.

BAHRICK, HARRY PHILLIP, science educator, researcher; b. Vienna, Dec. 22, 1924; arrived in US, 1939; s. Kurt and Margaret Bahrick; m. Phyllis Olwyn Edwards, Aug. 7, 1948; children: Lorraine Ellen, Audrey Susan, Thomas L. BA, U. West Va., 1946, MA, 1948; PhD, Ohio State U., Columbus, 1950. From instr. to prof. dept. psychology Ohio Wesleyan U., Del., 1949—90, rsch. prof., 2006—. Sr. fellow NSF, 1968; vis. prof. U. Hamburg, Germany, 1969—70, U. South Fla., Tampa, 1983—2006, rsch. prof., 1991—; endowed univ. chair Ohio Wesleyan U., 1991; lectr. in field. Contbr. articles to sci. jours. (Am. Psychol. Found. Career Tchg. award, 1996). Sgt. US Army, 1944—46. Recipient Outstanding Tchg. award, Ohio Wesleyan U., 1970, rsch. grants, NIH and NSF, 1961—. Fellow: APA (pres. divsn. exptl. psychologists 1999—2000, Sr. Fulbright Prof. 1959). Achievements include research in Developed Methods for investigating long term maintenance of knowledge throughout the human life span. Avocations: skiing, tennis, sailing, reading, travel. Home: 127 Elmwood Dr Delaware OH 43015 Office: Ohio Wesleyan Univ Dept Psychology Sandusky St Delaware OH 43015 Office Phone: 740-368-3805. Office Fax: 740-368-3812. Business E-Mail: hpbahric@owu.edu.

BAHRIM, CRISTIAN, physicist, educator, researcher; b. Bucharest, Romania, June 8, 1967; arrived in US, 1998; s. Corneliu and Elena Bahrim; m. Bogdana Mioara, June 28, 1967. BS, H.S. Math & Physics, Bucharest, 1985; MS, U. Bucharest, 1991; PhD, U. Paris XI, 1997. Rsch. asst. Nat. Inst. Lasers, Plasma and Radiation, Bucharest, 1991-97, prin. sci. rschr., 1998-99; rsch. assoc. J. R. MacDonald Lab. Kans. State U., Manhattan, 1998—2001; asst. prof. dept. chemistry and physics Lamar U., Beaumont, Tex., 2001—, asst. prof. dept. elec. engring., 2005—. Contbr. articles to profl. jours. Scholar French Govt., 1992-96. Mem. Romanian Phys. Soc., French Optical Soc., Am. Phys. Soc., Am. Assn. Advancement Sci. Romanian Orthodox. Avocations: history, astronomy, biology, sports. Office: Lamar U Dept of Chem and Physics Beaumont TX 77710 Office Phone: 409-880-8290. Business E-Mail: cbahrim@my.lamar.edu.

BAI, CHUNLI, professional society administrator, educator; b. Dandong, Liaoning, P.R. China, Sept. 26, 1953; s. Fuxin Bai and Feng Yun Li; m. Chunfang Li; 1 child, Bing Bai. BS, Peking U., China, 1978; MS, Chinese Acad. Scis. Inst. Chemistry, Beijing, 1981, PhD, 1985. Postdoctoral rsch. assoc. Calif. Inst. Tech., Pasadena, 1985-87; head rsch. grp. Chinese Acad. Scis. Inst. Chemistry, Beijing, 1987-91, dep. dir., 1992-96, v.p., 1996—; vis. prof. Tohoku U. Inst. Materials Rsch., Sendai, Japan, 1991-92. Prof. U. Scis. Tech. China, Hefei, 1994—, China Univ. Geosciences, Beijing, 1994—, Tsingua U., Beijing, 1995—; chief scientist Nat. Steering Com. Nanoscience and Related Tech.; dir. China Nat. Ctr. Nanoscience and Tech.; pres. Chinese Acad. Scis. Grad. Sch. Author: Scanning Tunneling Microscopy and its Application, 1995. Mem. Chinese People's Polit. Consultative Conf., 1993-98. Recipient second prize state sci. tech. advancements, 1990, first prize of sci. and tech. advancement award, Chinese Acad. Scis., 1991, second prize of natural scis. award, 1994, Young Scientist award, 1994, Outstanding Young Scholars award Hong Kong Qiushi Found., 1995; named Nat. level Expert with Outstanding Contributions, 1990, one of top 10 Outstanding young Persons in China, 1992. Fellow Third World Acad. Scis.; mem. Chinese Acad. Scis. (academician 1997—, dir. divsn. chemistry, mem. exec. com. presidium), Chinese Chem. Soc. (sec. gen., exec. coun. 1994-98, pres. 1998—), China Assn. Sci. and Tech (v.p.), China Material Rsch. Soc. (exec. coun. 1992-99, v.p. 1999—), Chinese Crystallographic Soc. (coun. mem. 1994—), All China Youth Fedn. (v.p. 1995—), Western Returned Scholars Assn. (v.p. 1995—), China Youth Scientists Assn. (v.p. 1993-96, pres. 1996), Chinese Vacuum Soc. (coun. mem. 1994—), Internat. Union Pure and Applied Chemistry (bur. mem. exec. com.); fgn. assoc. NAS; fgn. mem. Mongolian Nat. Acad. Scis. Office: Chinese Acad Scis Beijing 100864 China

BAI, HAOWEI, aerospace engineer, aerospace scientist; b. China; arrived in US, 1999, permanent resident; m. Haiying Deng. BS in Info. and Comm. Sys., Xi'an Jiaotong U., China, 1994; MSc in Elec. and Computer Engring., U. Dayton; PhD in Elec. and Computer Engring., U. Minn. Rsch. scientist Honeywell Labs, Mpls., 2001—04; sr. scientist Honeywell Aerospace Advanced Tech., Mpls., 2004—06; sr. sys. engr. Honeywell Space Applications, Glendale, 2006—, lead sys. arch. NASA human and robotics tech. proposal team, 2006—, lead sys. engring. Orion Crew Exploration Vehicle C3I, 2006—, lead comm. product devel. human space enterprise team, 2006—. Presenter in field. Contbr. articles to profl. jours., chapters to books, scientific papers to mags. and confs. Bd. dirs. Honeywell Asian Network, Mpls., 2003—05. Recipient Achievement awards, Shaanxi Province Sci. and Tech. Devel. Commn., 1998, Tech. Achievement awards, Honeywell Aerospace, 2004, Outstanding Engr. award, Honeywell, 2006. Mem.: IEEE, Soc. Automotive Engrs. (mem. com., handbook editor). Achievements include patents pending for devices and methods to monitor aircraft engine health by high-temperature wireless sensors; devices and methods for a dependable avionics data bus architecture based on IEEE-1394b high-performance serial bus; invention of devices and methods to provide reliable onboard wireless communication for entertainment and critical control functions; devices and system to help in-space assembly of multiple spacecrafts. Office: Honeywell Space Applications 19019 N 59th Ave Glendale AZ 85308 Business E-Mail: haowei.bai@honeywell.com.

BAI, YONG, engineering executive, educator; b. Jiang Xi, China, May 30, 1963; came to U.S., 1999; s. J. Bai and M. Liu; m. Hua Peng, Aug. 26, 1986; children: Lihua, Carl Junhua. PhD in Engring., Hiroshima U., Japan, 1989. Rschr. CRC Rsch. Ctr., Osaka, Japan, 1989-90; postdoctoral fellow Danish Tech. U., Copenhagen, 1990-91, Norwegian Tech. U., Trondheim, 1991-92; sr. engr. Det Norske Veritas, Oslo, 1992-96; postdoctoral fellow U. Calif., Berkeley, 1994; mgr. advanced engring. JP Kenny, Stavanger, Norway, 1996-99; mgr. offshore tech. Am. Bur. Shipping, 1999—2001, Shell Oil Co., Houston, 2002—03; v.p. engring. MCS, Houston, 2003—. Prof. U. Stavanger, 1997-2001. Contbr. articles to profl. jours. Norwegian Rsch. Coun. fellow, Oslo, 1991. Mem. Internat. Soc. Offshore and Polar Engrs. (com., chair), Internat. Conf. Offshore Mechanics and Arctic Engring. (com., chair, Best Paper award), Soc. Naval Architects and Marine Engrs., Internat. Congress Ship and Offshore Structures. Avocations: jogging, swimming, ping pong/table tennis. Home: 3415 Hackberry Ct Spring TX 77388-2712 Office: OPR 11999 Katy Fwy Ste 504 Houston TX 77079 Personal E-mail: yongbai1@yahoo.com. Business E-Mail: bai@opr-inc.com.

BAI, ZONGWU, polymer engineer; s. Xiufeng and Shurong Bai; m. Qiuhong Zhang, July 13, 1985; children: Betty, James Yang. PhD, Beijing U., China, 1992—95. Assoc. prof. Hebei U. Tech., Tianjin, China, 1989—92; rsch. assoc. U. Akron, Ohio, 1996—98; sr. engr. Wright Material Rsch., Beavercreek, Ohio, 1999—2002; polymer scientist U. Dayton Rsch. Inst., Ohio, 2002—. Contbr. articles to profl. jours. Mem.: Am. Chemistry Soc., Dayton Am. Chinese Assn. (program dir. 2004—06). Achievements include patents for sulfonated polymer for proton exchange membranes; patents pending for fluorinated polymers for proton exchange membranes. Home Phone: 937-429-1676.

BAICA, MALVINA FLORICA, mathematician, educator, researcher; b. Oravita, Banat, Romania, Nov. 3, 1942; came to U.S., 1968, naturalized, 1973; d. Adam and Cornelia (Stefan) Bunghiu; m. Adrian Baica, Sept. 14, 1963. BS in Math. and Physics, U. Timisoara, Romania, 1964, MS in Math., 1965, Ill. Inst. Tech., 1974; PhD in Math., U. Houston, 1980. Asst. prof. Western Ill. U., Macomb, 1978-80, Marquette U., Milw., 1980-81, Marshall U., Huntington, W.Va., 1981-83, Valparaiso U., Ind., 1983-84, U. Wis., Whitewater, 1984—89, assoc. prof., 1989—92, prof., 1992—. Contbr. more than 60 articles to profl. jours. on algebraic number theory, number theory and engring.; author The Euler System for the Algebraic Number Theory and Mathematical Models in Pollution, 2000, The Algorithmic Solution of the Original Euclidean Fermat's Last Theorem, 2001, Several Star Problems in Analitic Number Theory, 2005. Recipient U. Wis. Excellence in Rsch. award, 1988, hon. diploma, Romanian ASTRA Assn., 2003. Mem. NY Acad. Scis., Pi Mu Epsilon. Achievements include development of an algorithm in a complex field which turned out to be the Generalized Euclidean Algorithm and The Euler System of the Algebraic Number Theory used to approach unsolved problems in algebraic number theory and number theory including Fermat's Last Theorem in Euclidean; discovery of Baica's trigonometric identities; for the first time in collaboration with Mircea Cardu introduced and developed the non-classical trigonometries such as: the infratrigonometry, ultratrigonometry, transtrigonometry, extratrigonometry and paratrigonometry; also discovered Baica Cardu trigonometry; Using these Trigonometries developed mathematical models for their applications in engineering; research in algebraic number theory and number theory; contributor for the solution of Goldbach's problem and mathematical models for mechanical engineering applications. Office: U Wis Dept Math and Computer Sci Whitewater WI 53190 Home: 122 N Esterly Ave Whitewater WI 53190-1313 Office Phone: 262-472-1716. Business E-Mail: baicam@uww.edu.

BAICKER, KATHERINE (KATE), federal official, economics professor; b. May 23, 1971; BA magna cum laude in Econ., Yale U., New Haven, Conn., 1993; PhD in Econ., Harvard U., Cambridge, Mass., 1998. Asst. prof. econs. then assoc. prof. Dartmouth Coll., NH, 1998—2005; rsch. faculty. Nat. Bur. Econ., 2001—; assoc. prof. pub. policy UCLA, 2005—; sr. economist Coun. Econ. Advisers, Exec. Office of the Pres., Washington, 2001—02, mem., 2005—. Vis. prof. U. Chgo., 2003; spkr. in field. Contbr. articles to numerous profl. jours. Recipient William Masse award for outstanding record, Yale Univ., Tiffin Prize for outstanding academic record, Outstanding Tchr., Harvard Univ., 1998, Dissertation Prize Hon. Mention, Nat. Tax Assn., 1999, Dissertation Prize Winner, Nat. Academy of Soc. Ins., 1999; grantee John Heinz Meml. Fell., Yale Univ., Grad. Fell., Nat. Sci. Found., 1993—96, Health and Aging Fell., NBE/NIA, 1996—98. Office: Coun Econ Advisers 1800 G St NW 8th Fl Washington DC 20502*

BAIER, BRET, news correspondent; B in Polit. Sci. and English, DePauw U., Greencastle, Ind. Production asst. CNN; anchor, reporter WJWJ-TV, Beaufort, SC; polit. reporter, substitute anchor WRAL-TV (CBS), Raleigh, NC; weekend anchor WREX-TV (NBC), Rockford, Ill.; reporter FOX News Channel, Atlanta, 1998, nat. security corr. Recipient SC Associated Press award for Superior TV Journalism. Office: FOX News Channel 1211 Avenue of the Americas New York NY 10036

BAIER, EDWARD JOHN, retired public health service officer, industrial hygiene engineer, consultant; b. Pitts., Apr. 1, 1925; s. Edward O. and Lucy M. Baier; m. Grace Cecelia McDonald, Jan. 15, 1947; children: Edward Michael, Grace Cecelia. BS, U. Pitts., 1946, MPH (fellow), 1955. Lic. indsl. hygienist Ill., cert. internat. hazard control mgmt. Hazard Control Mgr. Cert. Bd., hazardous materials mgmt. Inst. Hazardous Materials Mgmt., safety profl. Bd. Cert. Safety Profls. Chief indsl. hygiene sect. Dept. Health State of Pa., 1956-68, dir. divsn. occupl. health, 1968-71, Dept. Environ. Resources, 1971; dir. Bur. Mines and Occupl. Health and Safety, 1971-72; dep. dir. Nat. Inst. for Occupl. Safety and Health, HEW, Rockville, Md., 1972-78; corp. dir. indsl. hygiene and toxicology Diamond Shamrock Corp., Cleve., Dallas, 1978-82; dir. tech. support OSHA, Dept. Labor, 1982-89; cons. in occupl. and environ. health and safety, 1989—. Lectr. in field. Contbr. articles to profl. jours. Chmn. West Shore coun. Boy Scouts Am., 1970-71; sec. Upper Allen Twp. (Pa.) Sewer Authority, 1970-72. Fellow Am. Indsl. Hygiene Assn. (pres. 1975-76, Cummings Meml. award 1982, Edward J. Baier Tech. Achievement award 1984); mem. Am. Conf. Govt. Indsl. Hygienists (chmn. 1968-69), Am. Acad. Indsl. Hygiene (founder, pres. 1987-88), Indsl. Hygiene Roundtable (steward 1975-76), Inst. Hazardous Materials Mgmt. (cert. hazardous materials mgrs. bd. examiners 1991—, bd. dirs., vice chmn. 1993-2001, Disting. Diplomate award 2001, 05), Nat. Am. Indian Safety Coun., N.Y. Acad. Scis., Pa. Soc. Profl. Engrs., Am. Bd. Indsl. Hygiene (bd. dirs. 1970-76). Roman Catholic. Home Phone: 703-743-5186; Office Phone: 703-743-5186.

BAIER, ROBERT EDWARD, chemist, educator; b. Buffalo, Oct. 31, 1939; s. Harry Edward Baier and Florence Elizabeth (Manno) Militello; m. Corinne May Bongiovanni, Sept. 9, 1961; children: Valerie Ann, Anne Marie. BS in Engring. and Physics, Cleve. State U., 1962; PhD in Biophysics, SUNY, Buffalo, 1966. Registered profl. engr., Ohio, N.Y. Postdoctoral fellow NAS-NRC, Washington, 1966-68; rsch. physicist Cornell Aero. Lab., Buffalo, 1968-72; staff scientist Calspan Advanced Tech. Ctr., Buffalo, 1972-84; rsch. prof. biophys. scis. SUNY, Buffalo, 1983—, exec. dir. NSF Industry/U. Coop. Rsch. Ctr., 1988—; exec. dir. Ctr. for Advanced Tech. in Healthcare, Buffalo, 1985-89; prof., dir. biomaterials grad. program SUNY, 1998—. Mem. Soc. Biomaterials (mem. coun., sec.-treas., pres. 1974—). Home: 37 Rosedale Blvd Buffalo NY 14226-3347 Office: SUNY 110 Parker Hall Buffalo NY 14214-3007 Home Phone: 716-832-9864; Office Phone: 716-829-3560. Business E-Mail: baier@buffalo.edu.

BAIGIS, JUDITH ANN, nursing educator, academic administrator; b. Washington, Pa., July 26, 1941; d. Andrew J. and Mary Margaret (Mitchell) Baigis; m. Robert Wachbroit, June 26, 1989. Diploma, Geisinger Hosp. Sch. Nursing, Danville, Pa., 1962; BS, NYU, 1968, PhD, 1979. RN, Md., D.C. Instr. nursing NYU, NYC, 1970-73, CUNY Lehman Coll., Bronx, N.Y., 1973-79; dir. community health nursing program U. Pa. Sch. Nursing, Phila., 1979-87; dir. long-term care Johns Hopkins U. Sch. Nursing, Balt., 1987-92; assoc. dean for rsch. Georgetown U. Sch. Nursing, Washington, 1992—, interim dean, 1998-99, prof., 1992—. Contbr. articles to nursing jours. Nat. Inst. Nursing Rsch. grantee, 1988-96. Mem. ANA, APHA, Am. Acad. Nursing, Assn. Community Health Nursing Educators. Office: Georgetown U Sch Nursing Box 571107 3700 Reservoir Rd NW Washington DC 20007-2111 Office Phone: 202-687-5127. Business E-Mail: baigisj@georgetown.edu.

BAILAR, BARBARA ANN, retired statistician; b. Monroe, Mich., Nov. 24, 1935; d. Malcolm Laurie and Clara Florence (Parent) Dezendorf; m. John Francis Powell (div. 1966); 1 child, Pamela; m. John Christian Bailar; 1 child, Melissa. BA, SUNY, 1956; MS, Va. Poly. Inst., 1965; PhD, Am. U., 1972. With Bur. of Census, Washington, 1958-88, chief Ctr. Rsch. Measurement Methods, 1973-79, assoc. dir. for statis. standards and methodology, 1979-88; exec. dir. Am. Statis. Assn., Alexandria, Va., 1988-95; sr. v.p. for survey rsch. Nat. Opinion Rsch. Ctr., Chgo., 1995—2001. Instr. George Washington U., 1984-85; head dept. math. and stats. USDA Grad. Sch., Washington, 1972-87. Contbr. articles, book chpts. to profl. publs. Pres. bd. dirs. Harbour Sq. Coop., Washington, 1988-89. Recipient Silver medal U.S. Dept. Commerce, 1980. Fellow Am. Statis. Assn. (pres. 1987); mem. AAAS (chair sect. stats. 1984-85), Internat. Assn. Survey Statisticians (pres. 1989-91), Internat. Statis. Inst. (Pres.'s invited speaker 1983, v.p. 1993-95), Cosmos Club. Personal E-mail: babailar@aol.com.

BAILAR, GREGOR S., finance company executive; BSEE, Dartmouth Coll. Various positions Perot Sys. Corp., Next Computer, Inc., and Hewlett Packard Co.; mng. dir. and v.p. for advanced devel. for global corp. banking Citicorp, 1994—98; chief info. officer & exec. v.p. ops. and tech. NASD, 1997—2001; exec. v.p. & chief info. officer Capital One Fin., Va., 2001—. Bd. dir. Digitas, Inc. Office: EVP & CIO Capital One Fin 1680 Capital One Dr Mc Lean VA 22102

BAILAR, JOHN CHRISTIAN, III, retired public health educator, physician, statistician; b. Urbana, Ill., Oct. 9, 1932; married; 4 children. BA, U. Colo., 1953; MD, Yale U., 1955; PhD in Stats., Am. U., 1973. Intern U. Colo. Med. Ctr., Denver, 1955-56; field investigator, biometry br. Nat Cancer Inst., NIH, Bethesda, Md., 1956-62, head demography sect., 1962-70, dir. 3d nat. cancer survey, 1967-70, dep. assoc. dir. for cancer control, 1972-74; editor-in-chief JNCI, 1974-80; dir. research service VA, Washington, 1970-72; lectr. in biostats. Harvard U., Cambridge, Mass., 1980-87; prof. McGill U., Montreal, 1987-95, chair dept. epidemiology and biostats., 1993—95; sr. scientist Office Disease Prevention and Health Promotion, Dept. HHS, Washington, 1983-92; chair dept. health studies U. Chgo., 1995—99, prof. dept. health studies, 1995—2001, assoc. faculty Harris Sch. Pub. Policy, 1999-2000, prof. emeritus, 2001—. Sr. scientist health and environ. rev. divsn. EPA, 1980-83; lectr. epidemiology and pub. health Yale U., New Haven, Conn., 1958-83; mem. faculty math. and stats. USDA Grad. Sch., Washington, 1966-76; vis. prof. stats. SUNY, Buffalo, 1974-80; professorial lectr. George Washington U., Washington, 1975-80; cons. in biostats. and epidemiology Dana-Farber Cancer Inst., Boston, 1977-83; vis. prof. Harvard U., 1977-79; spl. appointment grad. faculty U. Colo. Med. Ctr., Denver, 1979-81; scholar in residence NAS, 1992-96, 2002—. Mem. editl. adv. bd. Cancer Rsch., 1968-72; statis. cons. New Eng. Jour. Medicine, 1980-91; mem. bd. editors New Eng. Jour. Medicine, 1992-96; contbr. numerous articles to profl. jours.; editor JNCI, 1974-80. John D. and Catherine T. MacArthur Found. fellow, 1990-95. Fellow AAAS (chair sect. U 2000-01), Am. Coll. Epidemiology, Am. Statis. Assn. (chair-elect and chair biometric sect. 1979-81, founding chair sect. stats. and environment 1990); mem. Am. Med. Writer's Assn. (hon.), Inst. of Medicine, Internat. Statis. Inst., Coun. Biology Editors (chair publishing policy com. 1983-89, pres.-elect, pres., past pres. 1986-89), Soc. Risk Analysis (founding chair Boston chpt. 1985-86). Office: Apt 8 2101 Connecticut Ave NW Washington DC 20008 Office Phone: 202-334-3784. Business E-Mail: jcbailar@midway.uchicago.edu.

BAILE, CLIFTON A., biologist, researcher; b. Warrensburg, Mo., Feb. 8, 1940; s. Harold F. and Salome (Mohler) B.; m. Beth Lucile Hoover, Aug. 21, 1960; children: Christopher A., Marisa B. BS in Agr., Bus., Cen. Mo. State U., 1962; PhD in Nutrition, U. Mo., 1965; MA (hon.), U. Pa., 1979. NIH rsch. fellow Sch. Pub. Health Harvard U., Boston, 1964-66, from instr. to asst. prof. Sch. Pub. Health, 1966-71; mgr. neurobiol. rsch. SmithKline Animal Health, Phila., 1971-75; from assoc. prof. to prof. Sch. Vet. Medicine U. Pa., Phila., 1975-82; disting. fellow, dir. R & D Monsanto Agrl. Co., St. Louis, 1982-95; adj. prof. nutrition Sch. Medicine Washington U., St. Louis, 1982-95; adj. prof. dept. animal sci. U. Mo., 1982-95; dist. prof. animal sci. and food and nutrition U. Ga., Athens, 1995—; Ga. Rsch. Alliance Eminent scholar Agrl. Biotech., Athens, 1996—; CEO, ProLinia, Inc., 1999—. Presenter in field. Contbr. over 300 articles to sci. publs. Rsch. fellow Ralston Purina, 1962-64, spl. postdoctoral fellow NIH, 1969; recipient Georgia Lamar Dodd award, 2002. Mem. Am. Soc. Animal Sci. (bd. dirs. 1990-93, animal growth and devel. award 1989), Am. Physiol. Soc., Am. Inst. Nutrition, Am. Dairy Sci. Assn. (Am. Feed Mgmt. award 1979), Soc. Neurosci., Endocrine Soc. Achievements include 17 patents in field; research in control and feed intake and regulation of energy balance. Office: U Ga 444 ADS Complex Athens GA 30602-2771 Office Phone: 706-542-4094. Business E-Mail: cbaile@uga.edu.

BAILES, SHAWN MICHAEL, criminalist; b. June 1, 1978; BS in Biology, Ark. Tech. U., Russellville, 2000; MS in Cell, Molecular Biology, U. Ark., Fayetteville, 2006. Lab. tech. U. Mo., Columbia, 2000—03; rsch. asst. U. Ark., Fayetteville, 2003—05; criminalist Mo. State Hwy. Patrol, Jefferson City, 2005—. Contbr. articles to profl. jours. Mem.: Midwestern Assn. Forensic Sci. (assoc.). Office: GHQ CLD 1510 E Elm St Jefferson City MO 65101

BAILESS, ROBERT R., lawyer; b. Birmingham, Ala., Nov. 2, 1951; BBA, U. Miss., 1973, JD, 1976. Bar: Miss. 1976, US Dist. Ct. (No. Dist. Miss.) 1976, US Dist. Ct. (So. Dist. Miss.) 1976, US Supreme Ct. 1980, US Ct. Appeals (5th Cir.) 1990. Ptnr. Wheeless Shappley Bailess & Rector LLP, Miss. Mem.: ABA, Warren County Bar Assn., Miss. Bar (pres.-elect 2006—07). Office: Wheeless Shappley Bailess & Rector LLP PO Box 991 Vicksburg MS 39181-0991 Office Phone: 601-636-8451. Office Fax: 601-636-8481.

BAILEY, ANNETTE F., librarian; m. Godmar Back. BA in English Lit., NC State U., 1996; MS in Libr. and Info. Sci., U. Ill., Urbana-Champaign, 2001. Tech. and pub. svcs. staff U. Utah Marriott Libr.; life scis. libr. SRI

Internat., Menlo Park, Calif., 2002—04; digital assets libr. Va. Poly. Inst. and State U., Blacksburg, 2005—. Presenter Faculty Devel. Inst. Va. Poly. Inst. and State U. Co-developer (with Godmar Back) Firefox LibX ext., 2005. Co-recipient Brett Butler Entrepreneurship award, Libr. and Info. Tech. Assn., 2007. Office: Univ Librs Va Tech U Blacksburg VA 24060 Office Phone: 540-231-9266. E-mail: afbailey@vt.edu.

BAILEY, BARBARA, library director; Libr. dir. Wells-Turner Meml. Libr., Glastonbury, Conn. Recipient Outstanding Libr. award, Ct. Libr. Assn., 2006, ProQuest-SIRS State and Regional Achievement award, ALA Intellectual Freedom Round Table, 2007, Paul Howard award for Courage, ALA, 2007. Achievements include challenging the constitutionality of FBI National Security Letters and gag orders imposed under the USA PATRIOT Act, as one of four Connecticut "John Does". Office: Wells-Turner Memorial Library 2407 Main St Glastonbury CT 06033 Office Phone: 860-652-7719.

BAILEY, BEATRICE NAFF, language educator, researcher; b. Roanoke, Va., July 7, 1957; d. Wesley W. Jr. and Angelia (Hunt) Naff; m. William Glenn Bailey, Nov. 5, 1994. BA in English, Longwood Coll., 1979; MA in Theology, Bethany Theol. Sem., 1981; EdD, Va Tech., 1987. Prof. Clemson (S.C.) U., 1991—, dir. Clemson Writing Project, 1993—. Author: Our Upcountry: Teachers and Students Write About Place, 2000, Literacy Clubs for At Risk Girls, 1988, (with others) Religious Schools and America, 1988, Planning Models Matter in English Education, 1989. Recipient A.L. Burruss Rsch. and Svc. award, 1991, Good Apple award SCCTE, 1998, Career Woman of Yr. award Easley Bus. and Profl. Women, 1998. Mem. Nat. Coun. Tchrs. English (Promising Researcher award 1988, Richard Meade rsch. award 1990), Nat. Conf. Rsch. English, Phi Delta Kappa (Rsch. award 1988). Avocations: golf, tennis, collecting nativity scenes. Office: Clemson U 401 Tillman Hl # B Clemson SC 29634-0001

BAILEY, CHAMP, professional football player; b. June 22, 1978; m. Hanady Bailey; 1 child. Student, U. GA. Defensive back Washington Redskins, 1999—2003, Denver Broncos, 2004—. Named NCAA All-American, 1998; named to NFC Pro-Bowl Team, 2000, 2002—05, NFL All-Pro Team, 2005—06; recipient Bronko Nagurski Award, 1998. Office: c/o Denver Broncos 13655 Broncos Pkwy Englewood CO 80112*

BAILEY, CHARLES-JAMES NICE, linguistics educator; b. Middlesborough, Ky., May 2, 1926; s. Charles Wise and Mary Elizabeth (Nice) B. AB magna cum laude with highest honors in Classical Philology, Harvard U., 1950, MTh, 1955; DMin, Vanderbilt U., 1963; AM, U. Chgo., 1966, PhD, 1969. Faculty dept. linguistics U. Hawaii, Manoa, 1968-71, Georgetown U., 1971-73; u. prof. Technische U. Berlin, 1974-91, u. prof. emeritus, 1991—; mem. Electronics Lab. MIT, 1966—67. Vis. prof. U. Mich., Ann Arbor, 1973, U. Witwatersrand, Johannesburg, 1976, U. Brunei, Darussalam, 1990; Forcheimer prof. U. Jerusalem, 1986; propr. Orchid Land Publs.; hon. col. Staff Gov. of Ky. Author: Essays on Time-Based Linguistic Analysis, 1996. Recipient medal, Edn. Ministry Finland, 1976. Fellow: Internat. Soc. Phonetic Scis. (life), Netherlands Inst. Advanced Study (life); mem.: AAAS (life), NY Acad. Scis., European Acad. Scis., Arts and Letters (corr.), Am. Dialect Soc. (life), Linguistic Soc. Am. (life), Phi Beta Kappa. Personal E-mail: orlapubs@orlapubs.com.

BAILEY, CHRISTOPHER, apparel designer; b. Yorkshire, Eng., 1971; MA, Royal Coll. of Art, 1994. Womenswear designer Donna Karen, 1994—96; sr. designer womenswear, reporting to Tom Ford Gucci, Milan, 1996—2001; creative dir. Burberry, 2001—. Recipient Designer of Yr. award, Brit. Fashion Awards, 2005. Fellow: Royal Coll. Art (hon.). Office: Burberry 18-22 Haymarket London SW1Y 4DQ England

BAILEY, CLAUDIA JEAN, artist, retired librarian; b. Akron, Ohio, July 2, 1936; d. Lloyd Carl Lowe and Vergie P. Hively; m. Richard E. Bailey; children: Laurel Lynn Bailey-Wallace, Robert E. BA, Asbury Coll., 1960; MAL.S., U. Mich., 1966; MA, Ohio State U., 1970; BFA, U. R.I., 1992. Ref. libr. Columbus Pub. Libr., Columbus, Ohio, 1966—68; head journalism, acting head social work libr. Ohio State U., Columbus, Ohio, 1969—70; head fine arts libr. Bridgeport Pub. Libr., Bridgeport, Conn., 1970—72; head providence campus libr. CC of R.I., Providence, 1972—76, head Lincoln campus libr. Lincoln, RI, 1976—82, coord. ref./collection devel., 1982—87, ref. libr. Warwick, RI, 1987—97. Co-sponsored libr. concerts and art exhibits Bridgeport Pub. Libr., Bridgeport, Conn., 1971—72; chairperson, faculty sabbatical com. CC of R.I., Warwick, RI, 1979—80. Author: A Guide To Reference And Bibliography For Theatre Research, 1971, A Guide To Reference And Bibliography For Theatre Research., 2d edit., 1983. Scholar Grad. Libr. Sci., State Of Ohio, 1965-66, Scholar Grad., London Theatre Libraries, 1968, Ohio State U., 1968. Mem.: NEA, Ariz. Edn. Assn., Westbrook Village Fine Arts Assn., Ariz. Art Alliance. Liberal. Avocations: art collages, mixed media, painting, singing, opera. Home: 19483 N 90th Ln Peoria AZ 85382-8560 Personal E-mail: cjbailey20@cox.net.

BAILEY, COLIN BARRY, curator; b. London, Oct. 20, 1955; arrived in U.S., 1985, arrived in Can., 1995, arrived in U.S., 2000; s. Max and Hilda (Feldman) B.; life ptnr. Alan P. Wintermute. BA, Brasenose Coll., Oxford, Eng., 1978; diploma in history of art, U. Paris IV, Sorbonne, 1982-83; MA, Oxford U., 1982, PhD, 1985. Asst. curator European painting and sculpture The Phila. Mus. Art, 1985-89; curator European painting and sculpture Kimbell Art Mus., Ft. Worth, 1989-90, sr. curator, 1990-94; chief curator Nat. Gallery Can., Ottawa, Ont., 1995-98, dep. dir., chief curator, 1999-2000; chief curator The Frick Collection, NYC, 2000—07, Peter Jay Sharp, NYC, 2007—. Vis. prof. U. Pa., 1988; vis. prof. dept. art Bryn Mawr Coll., 1989; vis. prof. dept. art history Columbia U, 2005. Author: The First Painters of the King, 1985, The Loves of the Gods: Mythological Painting from Watteau to David, 1992, Renoir's Portraits, 1997, Jean-Baptiste Greuze, The Laundress, 2000, Patriotic Taste: Collecting Modern Art in Prerevolutionary Paris, 2002; co-author: Masterpieces of Impressionism & Post-Impressionism, 1989, Renoir's Landscapes, 1865-1883, 2007; gen. editor: Gustav Klimt, Modernism in the Making, 2001;co-author, gen. editor: The Age of Watteau, Chardin and Fragonard: Masterpieces of French Genre Painting, 2003; mem. editl. bd. The Oxford Art Jour., 1982-84. Decorated Chevalier de l'ordre des Arts et des Lettres (France); recipient Mitchell prize, 2002—03; Clark fellow, Sterling and Francine Clark Art Inst., Williamstown, 1999, Paul Mellon sr. vis. fellow, Ctr. Advanced Studies Visual Arts, Nat. Gallery Art, Washington, 1994. Mem.: Assn. Art Mus. Curators (trustee 2003—). Avocations: running, tennis, piano, opera. Home: 419 E 57th St New York NY 10022-3060 E-mail: Bailey@frick.org.

BAILEY, DANIEL ALLEN, lawyer; b. Pitts., Aug. 31, 1953; s. Richard A. and Virginia (Henry) B.; m. Janice Abraham, Oct. 10, 1981; children: Jeffrey, Megan. BBA, Bowling Green State U., 1975; JD, Ohio State U., 1978. Bar: Ohio 1978, U.S. Dist. Ct. (so. dist.) Ohio 1978, U.S. Tax Ct. 1979. Ptnr. Arter & Hadden, Columbus, Ohio, 1978—2003, chair exec. com., 2000—03; mem. Baily Cavalieri LLC, Columbus, 2003—, chair bd. mgrs., 2003—. Co-author: Handbook for Corporate Directors, 1985, Liability of Corporate Officers and Directors, 7th edit., 2002. Bd. dirs. Columbus Met. Community Action Orgn., 1979-80, Franklin County Head Start, Columbus, 1979-80, Faith Luth. Ch., Whitehall, Ohio, 1985-90, Luth. Social Svcs. Ctrl Ohio, 1991-2000, 2006—, Concorde Counseling Svcs., 2000—. Mem. ABA, Ohio Bar Assn., Columbus Bar Assn., Phi Kappa Phi, Beta Gamma Sigma, Omicron Delta Kappa. Office: Bailey Cavalieri LLC 10 W Broad St Ste 2100 Columbus OH 43215-3422 Office Phone: 614-229-3213.

BAILEY, DANIEL B., lawyer, entrepreneur; b. Topeka, Sept. 13, 1959; s. Daniel J. Bailey and Paula R. Upton; m. Kimberly A. Peacock, Apr. 1, 2007; children: Catherine Clare, Colin Daniel. BBA, Washburn U., Topeka, 1981; JD, Washburn U., 1987. Bar: Kans. 1987, U.S. Dist. Ct. Kans. 1987, Wyo. 1993, U.S. Dist. Ct. Wyo. 1993, U.S. Ct. Appeals (10th cir.) 1993, U.S. Supreme Ct. 2004. Pres. Lubnau & Bailey PC, Gillette, Wyo., 1992—. Mem. The Jealous Mistress, LLC, Gillette, Wyo., 1991—, Parallel Properties, LLC, 2005—; pres. Simplify, Inc. d/b/a Sir Speedy, 2004—, Destination X, 2005—; v.p. Zone Inc. d/b/a Letko Cycles, 2005—. Mem.: Gillette Energy Rotary Club (pres. 1998—99, asst. dist. gove. dist. 5440 1999—2000). Republican. Roman Catholic. Office: Lubnau & Bailey PC PO Box 1028 300 S Gillette Ave #2000 Gillette WY 82716 Home: 300 S Gillette Ave # 2000 Gillette WY 82716-3706 Office Phone: 307-682-1313. Personal E-mail: sirspeedy@vcn.com. Business E-Mail: dan@etseq.com.

BAILEY, DANIEL CARL, higher education administrator; b. Manchester, Conn., June 10, 1967; s. Donald James and Mary Ann (Reilly) Bailey. BA, Antioch Coll., 1989; MSW, Wash. U., St. Louis, 1993. Rsch. asst. St. Louis Regional Med. Ctr., 1992—93; rsch. assoc. Bklyn. Acad. Music, 1993—94; devel. rschr. U. Mass., Amherst, 1994—95, asst. mgr. devel. rsch., 1995—97; asst. dir. corp./found. prospect mgmt. sys. Wash. U., St. Louis, 1997—99; dir. corp. and found. rels. Kennedy Krieger Inst., Balt., 1999—2001, U. Del., Newark, 2001—. Active Pa./NJ/Del. Regional Corp. and Found. Rels. Roundtable, Phila., 2001—; founder, chmn. Balt. region Assn. Fundraising Profls. Corp. and Found. Rels. Roundtable, 2000—01; bd. dirs. Mo.-Kans. chpt. Am. Prospect Rsch. Assn., St. Louis, 1992—93; cmty. adv. coun. partnership initiative Rohm and Haas Electronic Materials CMP, Inc., Newark, 2002—; mem. Stine-Haskell Rsch. Ctr. Newark cmty. adv. panel E.I. du Pont de Nemours and Co., Newark, 2003—. Alumni bd. devel. and admissions coms. Antioch Coll., Yellow Springs, Ohio, 2000—01; devel. com. Abe and Pearl Kristol Ctr. for Jewish Life, U. Del., 2005—; active Yellow Springs Havurah, 1989—90, Gay and Lesbian Havurah, Balt., 1999—2003; co-pres., mem. St. Louis Lesbian and Gay Havurah, 1991—93; educator Jewish Cmty. Amherst, Mass., 1994—96, Brith Sholom Kneseth Israel Congregation, Richmond Heights, Mo., 1998—99, Ctrl. Agy. Jewish Edn. Jewish Cmty. HS, St. Louis, 1998—99; prin. Congregation Ahavas Achim, Keene, NH, 1996—97; cons., educator Ctrl. Reform Congregation, St. Louis, 1997—98; chmn. cemetery com., bd. dirs. Chestertown Havurah, Md., 2002—04; bd. dirs. Hotline for Help Inc., Brattleboro, Vt., 1995—97, Skinker-DeBaliviere Cmty. Coun., St. Louis, 1998—99. Julia Lathrop fellow, Wash. U., 1991—93. Mem.: Am. Assn. Grant Profls. Democrat. Jewish. Office: U Del George Evans House 5 W Main St Newark DE 19716 Business E-Mail: dbailey@udel.edu.

BAILEY, DARLYNE, social worker, educator; b. NYC, July 21, 1952; d. Arthur and Iris B. AB in Psychology and Secondary Edn., Lafayette Coll., 1974; MSc in Pychiatric Social Work, Columbia U., NYC, 1976; PhD Orgn. Behavior, Case Western Reserve U., 1988. Lic. ind. social worker, Ohio. Coord. specialized treatment Essex County Guidance Ctr., East Orange, N.J., 1976-82; dir. emergency access svcs. Cmty. Mental Health Orgn., Englewood, N.J., 1980-83; field instr. NYU Sch. Social Work, 1981-82; instr. Weatherhead Sch. Mgmt., Case Western Reserve U., Cleve., 1986-87; asst. prof. Mandel Sch. Applied Social Sci., Case Western Reserve U., Cleve., 1988-94, dean and assoc. prof., 1994-99, dean and prof., 1998—2001; dean and v.p. acad. affairs Tchrs. Coll., Columbia U., NYC, 2002—, acting pres., 2003. Cons. to numerous profl. groups; orgnl. devel. specialist Mid-Atlantic Regional Med. Edn. Ctr. VA, Brecksville, Ohio, 1985-88, Shaker Heights (Ohio) Sch. Dist., 1988-90, Cuyahoga Plan, Cleve., 1989-90; trainer 9-to-5 Nat. Assn. Working Women, Cleve., Family Children and Adult Svcs., Columbus, 1988, Exec. Tng. Inst., 1988-90, The Free Med. Clinic of Greater Cleve., Cuyhoga County Dept. Human Svcs., Sr. and Adult Svcs., Luth. Chaplaincy Svc., Cleve., 1993, KPMG Peat Marwick project, Chgo., 1990-91, Ghana Assn. Pvt. Vol. Orgns. in Devel., Accra, 1992-94, Old Stone Ch. Project, Cleve., 1994, Cleve. Rape Crisis Ctr. Project, 1995 Co-author: (book) Strategic Alliances Among Health and Human Services Organizations: From Affiliations to Consolidations, 2000, Managing Human Resources in the Human Services, 2001; contbr. articles to profl. jours., chapters to books and book reviews. Mem. exec. com. bd. trustees Heights Youth Ctr., Inc., Cleveland Heights, Ohio, 1983-95; mem. Human Resources Devel. Com., Neighborhood Ctrs. Assn., Cleve., chair mgmt. and governance task force, 1988-90; bd. trustees Neighborhood Ctrs., Cleve., 1991-94, Tiffin U., 1992-95, Fedn. for Cmty. Planning, Cleve., 1995, Nat. Coun., Cleve., 1995; mem. book rev. com. NASW Press, Washington, 1992-95; cons. editor Social Work, 1996; mem. philantropy and volunteerism adv. com. Kellogg Found., Battle Creek, Mich., 1992; chairwoman Mandel Ctr. Nonprofit Orgn. Named Nat. Group XIII fellow, W.K. Kellogg Nat. Leadership Program; recipient George Washington Kidd award, Lafayette Coll., Easton, Pa., 1994, Crain's Cleveland Bus. Women Influence award, 1997; fellow, Salzburg Seminar, Austria, 1997. Fellow: Nat. Assn. Social Workers, Am. Othopysciatric Assn.; mem.: Coun. Social Work Edn. (bd. dirs.), Nat. Bd. Organizational Behavior Tchg. Soc. (past co-chair), Leadership Cleveland Class. Office: Tchrs Coll Columbia U 525 W 120th St New York NY 10027

BAILEY, DAVID NELSON, pathology educator, dean, academic administrator; b. Anderson, Ind., June 21, 1945; s. Omer Nelson and Louise Genevieve (Hurst) B. BS with high distinction, Ind. U., 1967; MD, Yale U., 1973. Diplomate Nat. Bd. Med. Examiners, Am. Bd. Pathology (Clin. and Chem. Pathology). Clin. fellow dept. lab. medicine Yale U., 1973-75; asst. resident specializing in clin. pathology Yale-New Haven Hosp., 1975-76, chief resident specializing in clin. pathology, 1976-77; asst. prof. pathology U. Calif., San Diego, 1977-81, assoc. prof. pathology, 1981-86, prof. pathology, 1986—, head div. lab. medicine, 1983-89, 94-98, acting chmn., 1986-88, chmn. dept. pathology, 1988—99, 2000—01; dir. toxicology lab. U. Calif. Med. Ctr., San Diego, 1977—, dir. clin. labs., 1982-99, interim vice chancellor for health scis., dean, 1999-2000, 2006—, dep. vice chancellor for health scis., 2001—, dean for faculty/student matters, 2003—. Mem. editorial bd. Jour. Analytical Toxicology, 1979—, Clin. Chemistry Jour., 1983-93, Am. Jour. Clin. Pathology, 1991—; contbr. articles to profl. jours. Recipient Gerald T. Evans award Acad. Clin. Lab. Physicians and Scientists, 1993; Merit scholar Ind. U., 1963-65, Arthur R. Metz scholar, 1965-67. Mem. Calif. Assn. Toxicologists (pres. 1981-82), Acad. Clin. Lab. Physicians and Scientists (pres. 1988-89), Am. Assn. Clin. Chemistry, Am. Chem. Soc., Assn. Pathology Chmn. (sec.-treas. 1996-99), Phi Lambda Upsilon, Alpha Omega Alpha. Office: U Calif San Diego Sch Medicine 9500 Gilman Dr La Jolla CA 92093-0602 Office Phone: 858-822-5577. Business E-Mail: dnbailey@ucsd.edu.

BAILEY, DIANDREA MICHELLE, rehabilitation services professional; b. Petersburg, Va., Nov. 28, 1979; d. William Oscar and Gloria Turner Bailey. BA in english and speech pathology, Norfolk State U., 1997—99; MA, Norfolk State U., Norfolk, VA, 2000—02; MS degree in rehab counseling, Virginia Commonwealth U., 2001—03; Post-Master's Cert. in Sch. Counseling, George Mason U., 2002—04; Post-Master's Cert. in Profl. Counseling, Va. Commonwealth U., 2003. Licensed Professional Counselor Va. Bd. of Counseling/Va., 2004, Certified Rehabilitation Counselor CRCC/ Nat., 2003, Certified Rehabilitation Provider Va. Bd. of Counseling, 2003. Vocat. rehab. counselor Va. Dept for the Blind and Vision Impaired, Richmond, Va., 2002—04, U.S. Dept. of Veterans Affairs, Harrisburg, Pa., 2004—. Mem.: Va. Rehab. Counselor Assn., Va. Counselor Assn., Nat. Rehab. Counselor Assn., Nat. Rehab. Assn., Chi Sigma Iota (life). Office: US Dept of Veterans Affairs 228 Walnut St Ste1150 Harrisburg PA 17108 Home: PO Box 266 Hopewell VA 23860-0266 Home Phone: 804-283-3997; Office Phone: 717-221-3750. Office Fax: 717-224-4570. Personal E-mail: diandrea151@cs.com. E-mail: vrcdbail@vba.va.gov.

BAILEY, DONALD KEITH, music educator, composer, musician; b. Paterson, NJ, Nov. 22, 1954; s. John Alexander and Gertrude Bailey; m. Terri Lee Christensen, June 3, 1983; children: Brooke Renee Cowart, Shane Matthew, Alexis Jordan. MusB in Edn., Iowa Wesleyan Coll., Mt. Pleasant, 1976; MA in Music, U. No. Iowa, Cedar Falls, 1985. Dir. bands Norwalk Mid. Sch., Iowa, 1976—83; grad. asst. jazz studies U. No. Iowa, Cedar Falls, 1983—85; prof., dir. jazz studies U. Ark., Ft. Smith, 1985—. Music min. Faith Assembly God Ch., Ft. Smith, 1985—88; choir dir. Harvest Time Tabernacle Ch., Ft. Smith, 1988—91; worship leader Life Christian Ctr. Ch., Ft. Smith, 1991—2004; tchr, workshop leader Internat. Worship Inst., Dallas, 1997—; studio musician Omega Sound Rec. Studio, Ft. Smith, 1985—; pres., co-founder New Song Pub. Co., Ft. Smith. Composer (producer): (iowa telethon theme song) Reach Out With Love; composer: (arranger) (adventureland theme park musical) Dance to the Music, (sacred work for mass choir & orchestra) Adoration and Exultation, (orchestral ste.) Jazz Suite for Orchestra; composer: (oklahoma city bombing dedication song) Carry On. Clinician performer Ft. Smith Area Pub. Schs., 1985—2007; musician, event coord. City-wide Cross Denom. Religious Events, 1985—2007; bd. mem. Ft. Smith Symphony Assn., 2005—07. Recipient Addy awards, Greater Ft. Smith Ad Club, 1991—94, Nat. Tchg. Excellece award, U. Tex., Austin, 1987, Lucille Speakman Excellence in Tchg. award, Westark C.C., 1986, Mayor's Civic Honor award Contbns. Arts, Ft. Smith Mayor, Ray Baker, 2007. Mem.: Coll. Music Soc. (corr.), Ark. Sch. Band and Orch. Assn. (corr.), Internat. Assn. Jazz Edn. (corr.; pres. Ark. chpt. 1995—97), Internat. Assn. Jazz Edn. (corr.; v.p. Ark. chpt. 1994—95), Ft. Smith Symphony Assn. (assoc.; bd. mem. 2005—07), Kappa Kappa Psi (hon.), Phi Mu Alpha (corr.). Achievements include development of the first comprehensive summer high school jazz band camp in Arkansas; the only jazz improvisation for orchestral strings camp in Arkansas; a series of jazz improvisation clinics for junior high and high school students; a How to Teach Jazz Improvisation workshop for band directors; a series of music workshops for elementary school students; a concert series bringing world-renowned jazz artists to Eastern Arkansas. Avocations: composing/arranging, travel. Home: 8200 Williamsburg Rd Fort Smith AR 72903 Office: U Ark 5210 Grand Ave Fort Smith AR 72913 Home Phone: 479-452-9488; Office Phone: 479-788-7554. Office Fax: 479-788-7559; Home Fax: 479-788-7559. E-mail: dbailey@uafortsmith.edu.

BAILEY, EXINE MARGARET ANDERSON, soprano, educator; b. Cottonwood, Minn., Jan. 4, 1922; d. Joseph Leonard and Exine Pearl (Robertson) Anderson; m. Arthur Albert Bailey, May 5, 1956. BS, U. Minn., 1944; MA, Columbia U., 1945; profl. diploma, 1951. Instr. Columbia U., 1947-51; faculty U. Oreg., Eugene, 1951—, prof. voice, 1966-87, coordinator voice instrn., 1969-87, prof. emeritus, 1987—; faculty dir. Salzburg, Austria, summer 1968, Europe, summer 1976. Vis. prof., head vocal instrn. Columbia U., summers 1952, 59; condr. master classes for singers, developer summer program study for h.s. solo singers, U. Oreg. Sch. Music, 1988—, mem. planning com. 1998-99 MTNA Nat. Convention. Profl. singer, N.Y.C.; appearances with NBC, ABC symphonies; solo artist appearing with Portland and Eugene (Oreg.) Symphonies, other groups in Wash., Calif., Mont., Idaho, also in concert; contbr. articles, book revs. to various mags. Del. fine arts program to Ea. Europe, People to People Internat. Mission to Russia for 1990. Recipient Young Artist award N.Y.C. Singing Tchrs., 1945, Music Fedn. Club (N.Y.C.) hon. award, 1951; Kathryn Long scholar Met. Opera, 1945 Mem. Nat. Assn. Tchrs. Singing (lt. gov. 1968-72), Oreg. Music Tchrs. Assn (pres. 1974-76), Music Tchrs. Nat. Assn. (nat. voice chmn. high sch. activities 1970-74, nat. chmn. voice 1973-75, 81-85, NW chmn. collegiate activities and artists competition 1978-80, editorial com. Am. Music Tchr. jour. 1987-89), AAUP, Internat. Platform Assn., Kappa Delta Pi, Sigma Alpha Iota, Pi Kappa Lambda. Home: 17 Westbrook Way Eugene OR 97405-2074 Office: U Oreg Sch Music Eugene OR 97403 *My chief goal in life is to realize my potentials through perfecting my innate talents and capabilities.*

BAILEY, F. LEE (FRANCIS LEE BAILEY), lawyer; b. Waltham, Mass., June 10, 1933; m. Florence Gott (div. 1961); m. Froma Portney (div. 1972); m. Lynda Hart, Aug. 26, 1972 (div. 1980); m. Patricia Shiers, June 10, 1985. Student, Harvard U., 1950—52, student, 1957; LLB, Boston U., 1960. Bar: U.S. Dist. Ct. Mass. 1961, U.S. Ct. Appeals (1st cir.) 1963, U.S. Tax Ct. 1964, U.S. Ct. Appeals (6th cir.) 1964, U.S. Supreme Ct. 1964, U.S. Ct. Appeals (2d cir.) 1967, U.S. Ct. Appeals (10th cir.) 1968, U.S. Ct. Appeals (3d cir.) 1969, U.S. Ct. Appeals (9th cir.) 1970, U.S. Ct. Appeals (4th and 7th cirs.) 1971, U.S. Dist. Ct. (we. and no. dists.) Tex. 1980, U.S. Ct. Mil. Appeals 1981, U.S. Ct. Appeals (8th and 11th cirs.) 1984, U.S. Ct. Appeals (5th cir.) 1985, U.S. Dist. Ct. (ea. dist.) Wis. 1991. Prin. Law Offices of F. Lee Bailey, West Palm Beach, Fla.; chmn. and CEO IMPAC Control Systems, Inc. Author (with Harvey Aronson): The Defense Never Rests, 1971; author: Cleared for the Approach, 1977; author: (with John Greenya) For the Defense, 1976; author: Novel Secrets, 1979, How to Protect Yourself Against Cops In California and Other Strange Places, 1982, To Be a Trial Lawyer, 1983; author: (with Henry Rothblatt) numerous works in field of criminal law. Lt. USMC, 1952—56. Mem.: ATLA, ABA. Office: Impac Control Systems Inc 955 W Retta Esplanada Punta Gorda FL 33950 Office Phone: 941-639-6677.*

BAILEY, FRED COOLIDGE, retired engineering consulting company executive; b. Claremont, NH, Oct. 5, 1925; s. Howard Perry and Helen Gare (Coolidge) B.; m. Mary Beecroft Cunningham, June 26, 1948; children: Susan Bailey Hunter (dec.), Stephen Coolidge, Elizabeth Bailey George. BS, MIT, 1948, MS, 1949. Registered profl. engr., Mass. Research engr. Caterpillar Tractor Co., Peoria, Ill., 1949-51; asst. tech. dir. com. ship structural design Nat. Acad. Scis., Washington, 1952-55; engr. Lessells & Assocs., Inc., Boston, 1955—65; pres. Teledyne Engring. Services, Waltham, Mass., 1965—86, chmn., 1986-87; group exec. Teledyne Inc., Waltham, Mass., 1983-87, cons., 1987-90, ret., 1990. Chmn. exec. com. Lexington Savs. Bank, 1989-94, chmn. bd. dirs., 1994-97; dir. Affiliated Cmty. Bancorp, 1995-98. Mem. Bd. Selectmen, 1969—78; trustee Cary Meml. Libr., Lexington, 1971—78, pres., 1972—77; trustee Symmes Hosp., Arlington, Mass., 1969—2001, mem. exec. com., 1977—89, v.p., 1978—80, pres., 1980—81; trustee Brookhaven at Lexington, 1986—2007, chmn. pres., 1994—96; chmn. Choates-Symmes Health Svcs., 1981—83; v.p. Charles River Mus. Industry, 1983—86, trustee, 1984—2007, pres., 1986—89; mem. bd. Fire Commrs., Lexington, Mass., 1964—69, chmn., 1968—69. With USNR, 1944—46. Fellow Soc. for Exptl. Mechanics (pres. 1968-69, recipient Tatnall award 1974, hon. mem. 1992); mem. Soc. Naval Architects and Marine Engrs. (recipient Linnard prize 1972), ASME, Am. Welding Soc. Home: 1010 Waltham St H-499 Lexington MA 02421

BAILEY, GLENDA, editor-in-chief; b. Derbyshire, Eng. BA in Fashion Design, Kingston U. Editor Honey, 1986; launch editor Folio mag., British Marie Claire, 1988; internat. editl. cons. Marie Claire, 1995, editor-in-chief, 1996—2001, Harper's Bazaar, NYC, 2001—. Organizer What Women Want event, 1999. Named Editor of Yr., Adweek, 2001; recipient Mag. Editor of Yr. awards. Office: Harpers Bazaar 1700 Broadway 37th Fl New York NY 10019 Office Phone: 212-903-5086. Office Fax: 212-262-7101.*

BAILEY, GREGORY EMMETT, systems engineer; b. Scottsdale, Ariz., Feb. 6, 1969; s. Walter Osbra and Judith Marian Bailey; m. Brenda Lynne Martinez, Aug. 6, 1994; children: Nicholas Emmett, Stephen Gregory, Sophia Elise. BS, N.Mex State U., Las Cruces, 1992. Cert. engr. Red Hat, Inc., 2007. Software developer IBM, Boulder, Colo., 1992—94; sr. software developer Am. Stores Co., Salt Lake City, 1994—98; network mgmt. software engr. I-Link, Inc., Draper, Utah, 1998—2003; sr. info. tech.

adminstr. AlphaGraphics, Inc., Salt Lake City, 2003—04; software sys. engr. Inter-Tel, Inc., Chandler, Ariz., 2004—. Cons. LXPRO.COM, Phoenix, 2000—. Adminstr. Salt Lake Christian Ch., 1997—2004. Mem.: Mensa. Home: 4434 E Cathedral Rock Dr Phoenix AZ 85044-6808 Office: Inter-Tel Inc 7300 W Boston Chandler AZ 85226 Home Phone: 480-275-5275; Office Phone: 480-961-8040. Personal E-mail: gbailey@lxpro.com. Business E-Mail: gebailey@inter-tel.com.

BAILEY, HAROLD RANDOLPH, surgeon, educator; b. Palestine, Tex., Jan. 20, 1943; m. Kelly Curry Bailey. BA in Biology summa cum laude, Rice U., 1964; MD, U. Tex., Dallas, 1968. Diplomate Am. Bd. Surgery, Am. Bd. Colon and Rectal Surgery. Intern straight surg. Parkland Hosp., Dallas, 1968-69; resident gen. surgery U. Tex. Med. Sch./Hermann Hosp., Houston, 1969-73; fellow colon and rectal surgery Ferguson-Droste-Ferguson Hosp., Grand Rapids, Mich., 1973-74; clin. faculty U. Tex. Med. Sch., Houston, 1974—, dir. residency tng. program colon and rectal surgery, 1984—2005, clin. prof. surgery, 1986—; clin. faculty Baylor Coll. Medicine, 1986—, clin. prof. surgery, 1999—; chief div. colon rectal surgery Methodist Hosp., Houston, 2006—. Assoc. examiner Am. Bd. Colon and Rectal Surgery, 1985—89, chmn. exam. com., 1995—97, pres., 1996—97, sr. examiner, 1997—; chief staff Park Plaza Hosp., Houston, 1988—90. Bd. dir. Am. Cancer Soc., Greater Houston unit, 1989-93, v.p., 1991-93, pres., 1993-95; mem. vestry Palmer Meml. Episcopal Ch., Houston, 1979-83, 84-86, chmn. fin. com., 1984-86; mem. fund coun. Rice U., Houston, 1993-95, class fund drive chmn. 1993-95). Recipient George Waldron award Hermann Hosp., 1970, Violet Keller award, 1973; named to Good Housekeeping mag. 400 Best Doctors in U.S., 1991, Good Housekeeping mag. Best Cancer Doctors in U.S., 1993; named Disting. Alumnus, Rice U., 2000. Fellow ACS (chmn. adv. coun. colon and rectal surgery 1996-2001, chmn. membership svcs. com. 2005—, bd. govs. 2002-04, bd. regents 2003—), Internat. Soc. Univ. Colon and Rectal Surgeons (program com. 1986), Am. Soc. Colon and Rectal Surgeons (treas., exec. coun. 1993-99, pres. 1999-2000), Tex. Surg. Soc.; mem. AMA, Tex. Soc. Colon and Rectal Surgeons (pres. 1981, exec. sec. 1982-88), Tex. Med. Assn., Tex. Soc. Gastrointestinal Endoscopy, Harris County Med. Soc., Houston Surg. Soc., Phi Beta Kappa, Alpha Omega Alpha. Office: Colon & Rectal Clinic 6550 Fannin St Ste 2307 Houston TX 77030-2723 Office Phone: 713-790-9250. Personal E-mail: hrbailey@swbell.net. Business E-Mail: h.randolph.bailey@uth.tmc.edu.

BAILEY, HELEN MCSHANE, historian, consultant; b. Gardner, Kans., Oct. 17, 1916; d. Harry Cramer and Maude Ethel (Kramer) McShane; m. James Edwin Bailey, Feb. 23, 1946; children: James Edwin, Barbara Ann Bailey Crawford. BA, Bethany Nazarene Coll., 1938. Adminstrv. asst. Office Chief of Staff, U.S. Army, Washington, 1941—48; historian U.S. Army ofcl. history of World War II, U.S. Army, Washington, 1948—58; rsch. asst. George C. Marshall Rsch. Found., Washington, 1958—59; historian Orgn. Joint Chiefs of Staff, Dept. Def., Pentagon, Washington, 1968—87; cons., 1987—. Mem.: Am. Hist. Assn., Soc. Historians Am. Fgn. Rels., World War Two Studies Assn., Soc. History in Fed. Govt. Republican. Lutheran. Home and Office: 180 N Henderson Rd Travelers Rest SC 29690

BAILEY, HERBERT SMITH, JR., retired publisher; b. NYC, July 12, 1921; s. Herbert Smith and Viola (Howe) B.; m. Elizabeth M. Brown, June 26, 1943; children: John R., James C., Robin E., George W. AB, Princeton U., 1942, LLD (hon.), 1986; LHD (hon.), Yale U., 1976. Sci. editor Princeton U. Press, 1946-52, editor, 1952-54, dir., 1954-86; ret., 1986. Past bd. dirs. Nat. Enquiry into Scholarly Publ., Franklin Book Programs, Princeton Bank; past mem. adv. com. on tech. publs. AEC; bd. govs. Wesleyan U. Press; past mem. bd. visitors Duke U. Press; past chmn. sci. info. coun. NSF; vis. fellow Nat. Humanities Ctr., 1984; R.R. Bowker lectr., 1977; mem. publs. com. Am. Scientist. Author: The Art and Science of Book Publishing, 1970; contbr. articles to profl. jours. Past mem. Princeton Regional Bd. Edn.; past mem. and chmn. long range planning Princetown Twp. Bd. of Edn.; past commr. Commn. on Preservation and Access; bd. dirs. Triangle Opera. Lt. USNR, 1942-45. Mem. Am. Book Pubs. Coun. (past bd. dirs.), Assn. Am. Pubs. (past bd. dirs., Curtis Benajmin award for creative pub. 1987), Assn. Am. Univ. Presses (past bd. dirs. and pres.), Am. Philos. Soc. (mem. publs. and program coms.), Sigma Xi. Home: 6 Carolina Meadows Apt 302 Chapel Hill NC 27517-8525

BAILEY, HIGGINS D., health products executive; BA in Biology, Eastern Wash. U.; MS in Program Planning and Pers., U. Calif., Berkeley, EdD in Adminstrn. and Mgmt. Bud. mgr. Thomas T. Anderson Law Firm, Indio, Calif., 1991—; pres., CEO Pharm. Ednl. and Devel. Found. at Med. U. S.C., Charleston, SC, 1995—96; officer, dir. Entropin, Inc., Indio, Calif., 1992—, now chmn. bd. dirs. Office: Entropin Inc 13314 Lost Key Pl Bradenton FL 34202-5002

BAILEY, HUGH COLEMAN, academic administrator; b. Berry, Ala., July 2, 1929; s. Coleman Costello and Susie (Jenkins) B.; m. Ahleida Joan Seever, Nov. 17, 1962; children: Debra Jane, Laura Joan. AB with honors, Samford U., 1950; MA, U. Ala., 1951, PhD, 1954. Instr. history and polit. sci. Samford U., 1953-54, asst. prof., 1954-56, assoc. prof., 1956-59, prof., 1959-75, chmn. dept., head div. social scis., 1967-70; dean Howard Coll. Arts and Scis., 1970-75; v.p. for acad. affairs Francis Marion U., Florence, SC, 1975-78; pres. Valdosta (Ga.) State Univ., 1978—2002, pres. emeritus, 2002—. Mem. commn. colls. So. Assn. Colls. and Schs., 1974-75; v.p. Ala. Acad. Sci., 1968-69; pres. Ala. Writers Conclave, 1971-73 Author: John Williams Walker, 1964, 2003, Hinton Rowan Helper: Abolitionist-Racist, 1965, 2003, Edgar Gardner Murphy: Gentle Progressive, 1968, 2003, Liberalism in the New South, Southern Social Reformers and the Progressive Movement, 1969, America: The Framing of a Nation, 2 vols, 1975. Vice pres. Homewood City Bd. Edn., 1972-75; pres. Valdosta chpt. ARC, 2001-03; bd. dirs. Salvation Army; chmn. Valdosta Habitat's Jimmy Carter Work Project, 2002-03, Partnership for Health. Guggenheim fellow, 1963-64; Am. Council Learned Socs. fellow, 1965-66; recipient award merit Am. Assn. State and Local History, 1967 Fellow Royal Soc. Arts; mem. Valdosta C. of C., Pi Gamma Mu (trustee, nat. trustee-at-large 1969-71, nat. 1st v.p. 1978-84, pres. 1984-90), Kiwanis. Episcopalian. Home: 3224 Wildwood Plantation Circle Valdosta GA 31605-1031 Office: Valdosta State Univ 1500 N Patterson St Valdosta GA 31698-0001

BAILEY, JAMI LEA, pharmacist; d. James A. and Glenda J. Bailey. BA in Biology, Transylvania U., Lexington, Ky., 2000; PharmD, U. Md., Balt., 2005. Pharmacy practice resident VA Med. Ctr., Lexington, Ky., 2005—06, clin. pharmacy specialist ambulatory care Lebanon, Pa., 2006—07; clin. pharmacist Lexington, Ky., 2007—. Recipient Pharmacy Practice Residency Rsch. award, 2006. Mem.: Am. Coll. Clin. Pharmacy, Am. Soc. Health-System Pharmacists. Democrat. Baptist. Achievements include research in Valproic acid-use and parkinsonian symptoms in a Veterans Affairs population. Avocation: running.

BAILEY, JANET DEE, publishing executive; b. Newark, Aug. 23, 1946; d. Richard and Mary Louise (Dee) Shapiro; m. John Frederick Bailey, May 9, 1971; children: Jason David, Juliana Dee. BA, U. Del., 1968; MBA, Pace U., 1981. Prodn. editor Prentice-Hall, Inc., Englewood Cliffs, NJ, 1968-70; dir. publs. Spl. Libraries Assn., NYC, 1970-76; dir. mktg. services Knowledge Industry Publs., White Plains, NY, 1978-81, v.p., 1984-85; dir. inventory and contracts Macmillan Book Clubs, NYC, 1981-84; group pub. Elsevier Sci. Pub. Co., NYC, 1985-95, v.p. global mktg., 1996-99; v.p. STM books and ref. John Wiley & Sons, 1999—. Mem. Assn. Am. Publishers (chmn. jours. com., PSP exec. coun., book award judge), Soc. for Scholarly Publishing.

BAILEY, JEROME H. (JERRY BAILEY), mercantile exchange executive; m. Irene Bailey; 2 children. BS in Acctg., U. Nebr., 1974. With Price Waterhouse, NYC, 1974, The Hague, The Netherlands, 1978-81, ptnr., 1985; with Morgan Stanley, 1986, controller, 1987-90, mng. dir., 1990-93; with Salomon Brothers, 1993-97; CFO Salomon Inc. and Salomon Brothers, 1993-97; mng. dir. Salomon Brothers; exec. v.p., CFO Dow Jones & Co., 1998—2001, cons., 2001—02; CFO Marsh & Co., 2002—06; COO, CFO NY Mercantile Exch., NYC, 2006—. Named to Accountancy Hall of Fame, U. Nebr., 1995. Office: NYMEX World Fin Ctr One North End Ave New York NY 10282-1101

BAILEY, JOHN PRESTON, federal judge, lawyer; b. Wheeling, W.Va., May 2, 1951; BA, Dartmouth Coll., 1973; JD, W.Va. U., 1976. Bar: W.Va. 1976, Ohio 1981, U.S. Dist. Ct. (no. and so. dists.) W.Va. 1976, U.S. Dist. Ct. (so. dist.) Ohio 2000, U.S. Ct. Appeals (4th cir.) 1977, U.S. Supreme Ct. 1981. Law clk. to Hon. Charles H. Haden, II, US Dist. Ct. (no. and so. dists.) W.Va., 1976—78; spl. asst. prosecuting atty. Marshall County, W.Va., 1985—90; asst. prosecuting atty. Ohio County, W.Va., 1985—86; atty. Bailey, Riley, Buch & Harman, LC, Wheeling, W.Va., 1978—2007; judge US Dist. Ct. (no. dist.) W.Va., 2007—. Chmn. Workers' Compensation Appeal Bd., 1985—91. Mem.: ABA, Nat. Assn. Criminal Def. Lawyers, W.Va. Trial Lawyers, W.Va. State Bar (bd. govs. 1992—95, 1998—2001, pres. 2003—04, 2003), Ohio County Bar Assn., W.Va. Bar Assn. (exec. coun. 1988—94, pres. 1992—93), Order of Coif, Phi Delta Phi. Office: US Dist Ct PO Box 1518 300 Third St Elkins WV 26241*

BAILEY, JUDITH IRENE, academic administrator, educator, consultant; b. Winston-Salem, NC, Aug. 24, 1946; d. William Edward Hege Jr. and Julia (Hedrick) Hege; m. Brendon Stinson Bailey, Jr, June 8, 1968. BA, Coker Coll., 1968; MEd, Va. Tech., 1973, EdD, 1976; postgrad., Harvard U., 1994, 1994—95. Tchr. Chariho Regional H.S., Wood River Junction, RI, 1969—70, Prince William County Pub. Schs., Woodbridge, Va., 1968—72; asst. prin. Osbourn H.S., Manassas, Va., 1973; secondary sch. coord. Stafford (Va.) County Schs., 1973—74; middle sch. coord. Stafford County Schs., 1975—76; human rels. coord. Coop. Extension Svc. U. Md., College Park, 1976—79; dep. dir. Coop. Extension Svc. U. D.C., Washington, 1980-88; asst. v.p., dir. Coop. Extension U. Maine, Orono, 1988—92, interim v.p. for rsch. and pub. svc., 1992—93, v.p. rsch. and pub. svc., 1993—95, v.p. acad. affairs, provost, 1995—97; pres. No. Mich. U., Marquette, 1997—2003, Western Mich. U., Kalamazoo, 2003—06, prof. ednl. leadership, 2006—. Adj. prof. George Mason U., Fairfax, Va., 1978; grad. student adv. U. Md., 1979—80; spkr. and cons. in field; trustee Bronson Healthcare Group, Kalamazoo, 2003—; mem. steering com. Mich. Tri-Tech. Corridor, 2003—05; mem. governing bd. Bioscis. Rsch. and Commercialization Ctr., 2003—06; pres. Western Mich. U. Rsch. Found., 2006—06; mem. Mich. Strategic Econ. Investment and Commercialization Bd., 2006. Co-author: Contingency Planning for a Unitary School System; contbr. articles to profl. jours. Co-vice chmn. Lake Superior Cmty. Partnership, 1997—2003; bd. trustees Marquette (Mich.) Gen. Health Sys., 1998—2003; mem. Mich. Humanities Coun., 1999—2002, sec., treas., 2002; mem. adv. bd. Huntington Bank, 2003—; apptd. by gov. to Mich. Quarter Commn., 2004; mem. Am. Coun. Edn. Commn. on Women, 2004; trustee Southwest Mich. First; vice chmn. Greater Kalamazoo United Way, 2006; bd. dirs. Pine Tree State 4-H Found., 1988—97, Maine Toxicology Inst., 1992—95, Bangor (Maine) Symphony Orch, 1991—97, Shorebank, 1997—2003, Gilmore Keyboard Festival, 2003—. Recipient Disting. Alumni Achievement award, Coker Coll., 1998, Northwoods Woman Educator of Yr. award, 1999, Case V Chief Exec. Leadership award, 2002, Disting. Grad. Alumni Achievement award, Va. Tech., 2005; fellow Susan Coker Watson fellow, 1967. Mem.: AAUW, Grand Rapids Econ. Club, Econ. Club Marquette County (bd. dirs. 1997—2003), Rotary (Paul Harris fellow 2004), Epsilon Sigma Phi (sec. Mu chpt. 1987, v.p. 1988, State Disting. Svc. award), Phi Kappa Phi, Phi Delta Kappa. Republican. Avocations: cooking, hiking. Home: 1201 Short Rd Kalamazoo MI 49008 Office: Western Mich U Coll Edn 1903 W MIchigan Kalamazoo MI 49008-5202 Business E-Mail: judi.bailey@wmich.edu.

BAILEY, K. RONALD, lawyer; b. Sandusky, Ohio, July 30, 1947; s. Kenneth White and Virginia McClung (Sheddan) B.; m. Sara Ann Geary Bressler, Mar. 14, 1969 (div. June 1973); 1 child, Matthew Scott; m. Lynn Darlene Kammer, Aug. 31, 1973; children: Thomas Keith, Kenneth Richard. B in Liberal Studies summa cum laude, Bowling Green State U., 1979; JD, Cleveland-Marshall Law Sch., 1982; grad., Gerry Spence's Trial Lawyers Coll., 1994. Bar: Ohio 1983, U.S. Dist. Ct. (no. dist.) Ohio 1983, U.S. Dist. Ct. (D.C. cir.) 2000, U.S. Ct. Appeals (6th cir.) 1985, U.S. Supreme Ct. 1992. Tool, diemaker Gen. Motors, Sandusky, 1968-84; sole practice Huron, Ohio, 1983-87; sr. trial atty. K. Ronald Bailey & Assocs. Co., Legal Profl. Assn., Sandusky, 1987—. Chmn. Charter Rev. Com. of Huron, 1984. Mem. adv. bd. Salvation Army, 2004—06. Mem. ABA (criminal justice sect., white collar crimes com.), Nat. Assn. Criminal Def. Lawyers, Ohio Bar Assn. (coun. dels. 1998—, criminal justice sect., white collar crimes com., criminal law com.), Erie County Bar Assn., Ohio Assn. Criminal Def. Lawyers (bd. dirs., v.p. publs. 1991-93, 97-98, treas. 1994, pres. 1995-96, chmn. capital litigation 1997—, Pres.'s award 1989-95, 97-98, v.p. CLE, 1997-98). Democrat. Pentecostal. Avocations: reading, photography, painting, swimming, drag racing. Home: 121 Sycamore Dr Norwalk OH 44857-1914 Office: K Ronald Bailey & Assocs Co Legal Profl Assn 220 W Market St Sandusky OH 44870-2515 Office Phone: 416-625-6740. Business E-Mail: krbailey@baileyandassoc.com.

BAILEY, KAY WOOD, management consultant; b. Wilmington, Del. m. Richard H. Bailey. Adminstr. prison arts program Del. Dept. Correction, Dover, 1986—2002; pres., founder A.B.C. Consulting, Smyrna, Del., 2002—. Founder, pub., editor Wyoming (Del.) Gazette, Internat. Correctional Arts Network Jour.; career adv. bd. Wesley Coll., Dover, Del., 2004—. Friend of the libr. bd. Del. State U., Dover, 2004—; corres. sec. Underground Railroad Coalition Del., Wilmington, 2004—; past bd. dirs. Del. Symphony, Grand Opera House. Named Del. Trailblazer of the Yr., Agenda of Del. Women, 1991, hon. African Am., Star Hill A.M.E. Ch., 1995, Del. Mother of the Yr., Del. Chpt. Am. Mothers, 1997, Del. Art Educator of the Yr., Art Educators Del., 2000, Del. Communicator of Achievement, Del. Press Assn., 2002; recipient She Knows Where She's Going award, Girls Inc., 1993, Nat. Communicator of Achievement, Nat. Fedn. Press Women, 2002—03. Mem.: Sons of Civil War Union Vets. (v.p. Mary Torbert aux.). Home: 105 Front St Camden Wyoming DE 19934-1123

BAILEY, KELLEY, foundation administrator; b. Houston, Mar. 17, 1962; d. Myron Edgar Bailey and Georgia Numsen (Reynolds) White BA in Art History and Comm. cum laude, U. St. Thomas, 1993. Lic. FCC. Coord. sch. svcs., asst dir. vis. svcs. Houston Mus. Natural Sci., Edn. Sch. Svcs., Houston, 1991—94; coord. vol. svcs. and cmty. partnerships Hermann Hosp., Houston, 1996—98; adminstr. Vols. in Pub. Schs. Cmty. Partnerships Houston Ind. Sch. Dist., 1998—2001; prin. Cmty. Devel. Resources, Houston, 2001—04; dir. vol. svcs. and cmty. outreach Bering Omega Cmty. Svcs., Houston, 2002—04; dir. vol. svcs. Houston Symphony, 2005; pres., CEO Gulf Coast chpt. Lupus Found. Am., 2006—. Presenter Internat. Conf. on Vol. Adminstrn., Chgo., 1999—; instr. Vol. Mgmt. Acad. Houston CC and Rice U., 2001—04; cons. Susan G. Komen Breast Cancer Found., 2004; dir. Greater Houston Area Breast Health Summit, 2004—05; instr. Rice U., 2005—06. Mem. Jr. League of Houston, Inc., 1990-94; floor presenter Mus. Natural Sci., 1991-94; vol. Houston SPCA; mem. adv. bd. Houston Internat. Festival, 1992-93, chmn. curriculum guide com., 1992-93; bd. dirs. country selection com. Chrysalis Repertory Dance Co., 1995-97; bd. dirs., membership chair Houston Assn. Vol. Adminstrs., 1998-2000, bd. dirs. 2002-2004; mem. adv. coun. Ret. Srs. Vol. Program, Interfaith Ministries Greater Houston, 1999-2000; vol. team capt. Houston Mayor's Summit on Women, 1999; mem. com. Internat. Yr. of Vols., 2000-2003; mem. bd. advocates Planned Parenthood Houston and Southeast Tex., 2000-01; dir. vol. svcs. Houston Symphony Soc., 2005— Named Vol. of Yr. Jr. League Houston, 1991 Home: 4216 Purdue Houston TX 77005 Office: Lupus Founds Am 3720 Kirby Dr Ste 720 Houston TX 77098 Office Phone: 713-529-0126. Home Fax: 713-668-9576. Business E-Mail: kbailey@lupustexas.org.

BAILEY, LEONARD LEE, surgeon; b. Takoma Park, Md., Aug. 28, 1942; s. Nelson Hulburt and Catherine Effie (Long) B.; m. Nancy Ann Schroeder, Aug. 21, 1966; children: Jonathan Brooks, Charles Connor. BS, Columbia Union Coll., 1964; postgrad., NIH, 1965; MD, Loma Linda U., Calif., 1969. Diplomate Am. Bd. Surgery, Am. Bd. Thoracic Surgery. Intern Loma Linda U. Med. Ctr., 1969-70, resident in surgery, 1970-73, resident in thoracic and cardiovasc. surgery, 1973-74; resident in pediatric cardiovasc. surgery Hosp. for Sick Children, Toronto, Ont., Canada, 1974-75; resident in thoracic and cardiovasc. surgery Loma Linda U. Med. Sch., 1975-76, asst. prof. surgery, 1976-86, prof. surgery, 1986—, dir. pediatric cardiac surgery, 1976—, chief divsn. cardiothoracic surgery, 1988-92, chair dept. surgery, 1992—. Mem. ACS, Am. Assn. Thoracic Surgery, Am. Surg. Assn., Am. Coll. Cardiology, Western Thoracic Surg. Assn., Soc. Thoracic Surgery, Western Soc. Pediatric Rsch., Internat. Soc. for Heart Transplantation, Am. Heart Assn., Internat. Assn. for Cardiac Biol. Implants, Am. Soc. for Artificial Internal Organs, Pacific Coast Surg. Assn., Western Assn. Transplant Surgeons, Internat. Soc. for Cardiovasc. Surgery, United Network for Organ Sharing, The Transplant Soc. Democrat. Adventist. Office: Loma Linda U Med Ctr and Children's Hosp 11175 Campus St Ste 21120 Loma Linda CA 92350-1700 Office Phone: 909-558-8744. Business E-Mail: lbailey@som.llu.edu.

BAILEY, LOUISE HOWE, columnist, educator; b. Hendersonville, NC, July 6, 1915; d. William Bell White Howe and Elizabeth Anderson Glasgow; m. Joseph Peden Bailey, Sept. 16, 1945 (dec.); children: Joseph P. Jr., William Howe(dec.) , Robert Woodward. AB, Winthrop Coll., Rock Hill, SC, 1936; postgrad., U. So. Calif., LA, 1938; BLS, Columbia U., NYC, 1940. Tchr. Edgefield Pub. Sch., SC, 1937—39; supr. libr. sci. Winthrop Coll., Rock Hill, 1940—44. Spkr. in field. Author: (newspaper) Along the Ridges, The Times-News, 1967—, From Rock Hill to Connemara - The Story Before Carl Sandburg, 2006, Along the Ridges, Go Home wi' Me, Draw up a Chair, St. John in the Wilderness - 1836, Fifty Years with the Vagabonds, Generations of Excellence: History of Margaret R. Pardee Memorial Hospial, Remembering Henderson County; co-author: Hendersonville and Henderson County: A Pictorial History (Religious Bood award NC Soc. Historians, 1995). Bd. dirs. Henderson County Pub. Libr.; trustee Blue Ridge CC Found., Hist. Flat Rock; mem. com. Hendersonville's sesquicentennail celebration; bd. visitors Kanuga Episcopal Conf. Ctr.; lay reader St. John in Wilderness Episcopal Ch., Flat Rock. Named Western NC Historian of the Yr., 1997. Mem.: Nat. League Am. Penwomen, Delta Kappa Gama (hon.). Episcopalian. Avocations: reading, writing. Home: PO Box 338 Flat Rock NC 28731

BAILEY, MICHAEL KEITH, lawyer; b. Washington, Feb. 19, 1956; s. Alda Merrill and Joan (Moyers) B.; m. Linda Ann Braswell, Dec. 18, 1982; children: Julia Anne, David Allen. AB in Econs. and Polit. Sci., Coll. William and Mary, 1978; JD, Stetson U., 1981. Bar: Fla. 1981, U.S. Dist. Ct. (mid. dist.) Fla. 1982, U.S. Ct. Appeals (11th cir.) 1982, U.S. Supreme Ct. 1986. Assoc. Pitts, Eubanks, et al, Orlando, Fla., 1981-86; ptnr. Parrish, Bailey & Myers, P.A., Orlando, 1986-98, Bailey & Myers, P.A., Maitland, Fla., 1998—. Mem.: ATLA (charter, pres.'s club), ABA, Fla. Bar Bd. Ctr. (civil trial atty.), Nat. Bd. Trial Adv. (cert. civil trial advocate), Acad. Fla. Trial Lawyers (eagle patron), Orange County Bar Assn., So. Trial Lawyers Assn. Republican. Presbyterian. Home: 701 Lake Sue Ave Winter Park FL 32789-5807 Office: Bailey And Myers Pa 875 Concourse Pkwy S Ste 195 Maitland FL 32751-6147 Home Phone: 407-740-5955; Office Phone: 407-628-2929. Business E-Mail: mbailey@baileymyers.com.

BAILEY, NAN HUTCHINS, mathematician, educator; b. Tyler, Tex., July 2, 1952; d. Lemuel Conner and Martha (Hawes) Hutchins; m. Blake Henry Bailey, Nov. 1, 1984 (div. May 1998); children: Laura Elizabeth, Katherine Conner. Premier deg., Sorbonne U., 1972; BA in Math and French, Hollins U., 1974; MS in Math., George Mason U., 1977. Tchr. Math. London County Ind. Sch. Dist., Sterling Park, Va., 1974—75; tchr. h.s. Dept. Def., Okinawa, Japan, 1977—78; tchr. Math., French Carlsbad Ind. Sch. Dist., Carlsbad, Calif., 1979—81; tchr. Math. Crooked Oak Ind. Sch. Dist., Oklahoma City, 1981—83; instr. Math. U. Tex. Tyler, 1984—85, Tyler Jr. Coll., Tyler, 1987—94; tchr. Math. Tyler Ind. Sch. Dist., Tyler, 1997—. Bd. regents Tex. Women's U., Denton, 1992—98. Named Educator of Distinction, Coca Cola Found., 2002, Secondary Tchr. of Yr., Tyler Ind. Sch. Dist., 2002. Democrat. Presbyterian. Avocations: hiking, reading, pen and ink drawing, philosophy. Home: 800 Fox Cove Tyler TX 75703 Office: John Tyler High Sch 1120 NNW Loop 323 Tyler TX 75704

BAILEY, PRESTON EDWARD, music educator; b. Hollywood, Calif., Mar. 27, 1950; s. Lemuel Conner and Myradelle Peck Bailey; children: Celeste Michelle, Crystal Danielle. BA in Music Edn., Sonoma State U., 1992. Customer svc. Betnun Music & Stein on Vine, Hollywood, Calif., 1977—81; various prodn. positions Las Palmas Prodns., 1979—83; musician Music Americana, LA, 1976—83; ind. tchr. music various schs., Sonoma, 1988—92, Marin, 1988—92; dir. elem. music Petaluma City Schs., Calif., 1992—2000; music and activities dir. Petaluma Jr. HS, 2000—. Recipient Hon. Svc. award, McKinley Sch. PTA, Petaluma, 1994, Cir. Excellence award, Sonoma State U., Sch. Edn., 2001. Mem.: Calif. Band Dirs. Assn. Home: 114 Post St Petaluma CA 94952 Office: Petaluma Jr HS 700 Bantam Way Petaluma CA 94952 Office Phone: 707-762-2944. E-mail: bsharp@sonic.net.

BAILEY, REEVE MACLAREN, museum curator; b. Fairmont, W.Va., May 2, 1911; s. Joseph Randall and Elizabeth Weston (Maclaren) B.; m. Marian Alvinette Kregel, Aug. 13, 1939; children— Douglas M., David R., Thomas G., Susan Helen. Student, Toledo U., 1929-30; AB, U. Mich., 1933, PhD, 1938. Instr. zoology Iowa State Coll. (now univ.), 1938-42, asst. prof., 1942-44; asst. prof. zoology U. Mich., 1944-50, asso. prof., 1950-59, prof., 1959-81, prof. emeritus, 1981—. Assoc. curator Mus. Zoology, 1944-48, curator, 1948—; rsch. assoc. Am. Mus. Nat. History, 1964—. Contbr. over 160 articles, bulls., revs. to profl. jours. on ichthyology and herpetology. Fellow Iowa Acad. Sci.; mem. Am. Soc. Ichthyologists and Herpetologists (editl. bd., v.p. 1954, pres. 1959, Robert H. Gibbs Jr. Meml. award 1995), Am. Fisheries Soc. (pres. 1974, hon. mem. 1979—, recipient Award of Excellence 1980, Meritorious Svc. award 1989, Justin W. Leonard award of excellence Mich. chpt. 1985), Am. Inst. Fisheries Rsch. Biologists (Outstanding Achievement award 1996), AAAS (coun. 1968-72), Ecol. Soc. Am., Soc. Study Evolution, Soc. Systematic Biologists, Soc. Limnology and Oceanography, Mich. Acad. Sci., Arts and Letters. Avocation: ichthyology expeditions in US, Bermuda, Bolivia, Guatemala, Paraguay, and Zambia. Home: 4001 Glacier Hills Dr Apt 325 Ann Arbor MI 48105-3652 Office: Univ Mich Museum Zoology Ann Arbor MI 48109 Home Phone: 313-769-0493. E-mail: reevemarian@yahoo.com.

BAILEY, RITA MARIA, investment advisor, psychologist; m. William W. Bailey; children: Anne Christine, Cynthia Patricia. BS in Psychology, Austin Peay U., 1975, MA in Psychology, 1977, postgrad., 1977—79. Cert. counselor Tenn. Editor U.S. Army Spl. Warfare Inst., Ft. Bragg, NC,

1970—74, edn. officer, 1979-82, Augsburg (Germany) Cmty. Ctr., 1982-85; pvt. practice counseling Leavenworth, Kans., 1985-90; pvt. practice investments, 1990—. Author: Extroversion and Introversion, 1978, Special Warfare Training Plan, 1981; author, editor: tng. manual Foreign Small Arms, 1982. Dir. Energy Conservation Campaign, Clarksville, 1976; founder, dir. Women's Support Ctr., Leavenworth, 1986. Mem.: Nat. Assn. Investors, Alpha Mu Gamma. Roman Catholic. Avocations: long distance swimming, gardening, German poetry.

BAILEY, ROBERT, JR., advertising executive; b. Kansas City, Kans., Apr. 27, 1945; s. Robert and Sarah (Morgan) B.; m. Rita Carol Burdinie, June 26, 1971; children: Rebecca, Sarah. AB, U. Kans., 1967; MA, Northwestern U., 1968, PhD, 1972, MBA, 1979. Rsch. supr. Energy BBDO, Chgo., 1973-78, v.p. rsch. dir., 1978-82, sr. v.p., mktg. svcs. dir., 1982-85, exec. v.p., rsch. dir., 1985—. Author: Radicals In Urban Politics, 1974; contbr. articles to profl. jours. Mem. Am. Mktg. Assn. Office: Energy BBDO 410 N Michigan Ave Ste 8 Chicago IL 60611-4273

BAILEY, ROBERT C., opera company executive; b. Metropolis, Ill., Dec. 28, 1936; m. Sally McDermott, July 13, 1958. BA in Speech, U. Ill., 1958, MA in English, 1960; BM in Applied Voice, Eastman Sch. Music, 1965; MM in Applied Voice, New Eng. Conservatory Music, 1969. Music prodr. Nat. Pub. Radio, Washington, 1971-73, dir. cultural programming, 1973-75; mgr. Western Opera Theatre, San Francisco, 1975-79; instr. arts mgmt. Golden Gate U., San Francisco, 1977-82; cons. arts mgmt. San Francisco, 1980-82; gen. dir. Portland Opera Assn., Oreg., 1982—; dir. Opera Am., 1995—2001. Cons. On-Site Program Nat. Endowment Arts, Washington, 1982—; judge Met. Opera Auditions, 1977—. Recipient Chevalier in the Order of Arts and Letters French Govt., 1999. Mem. Bohemian Club (San Francisco), City Club (Portland), Arlington Club, Rotary Club.

BAILEY, ROBERT CONVERSE, epidemiologist, anthropologist, educator; b. NYC, Sept. 27, 1946; s. Charles Wesley and Katharine (Palmer) B.; m. Nadine Ruth Peacock, Sept. 6, 1985; children: Nathan T., Alexander Morgan Peacock. AB, Harvard U., 1969, PhD, 1985; MPH, Emory U., 1997. Resident biologist Tarpon Zoo, Inc., Amazonas, Colombia, 1972-74; field dir. Ituri Project, Zaire Harvard U., Cambridge, Mass., 1980-84; acting asst. prof. anthropology UCLA, 1984-85, asst. prof. anthropology, 1985-91, assoc. prof. anthropology, 1991-96, prof. anthropology, 1996-97. Prof., divsn. epidemiology, U. Ill. Sch. Pub. Health, Chgo, adj. prof. anthropology, U. Ill. at Chgo., 1996—; NIMH Nat. Rsch. fellow HIV/AIDS Rsch. Tng. Program, Emory U. Rollins Sch. Pub. Health and Nat. Ctrs. Disease Control, Atlanta, 1994-96; invited spkr. and presenter in field.; co-organizer, co-chair symposia on tropical forest ecology, Washington, 1989, 90; cons. to World Bank Environ. Sect., 1990; rsch. assoc. Nat. Ctr. Human Nutrition, Kinshasa, Zaire, 1980-90; mem. scientific com. UNESCO Symposium on Food and Nutrition in the Tropical Forest, 1991; mem. Population Rsch. Ctr., Harbor-UCLA Med. Ctr., 1988-92; cons. Global Environ. Fund World Bank, 1992, 93; co-chair exec. com. and adv. bd. Ituri Forest Peoples Fund/Cultural Survival, 1989—; co-dir. Ituri Project, 1980—; dir. Project MenSH, Uganda, 1997—; reviewer manuscripts and proposals NSF, Nat. Ctrs. Disease Control, Wenner Gren Found. Rsch. and Exploration, Swan Fund, numerous other instns. and orgns; dir. Ituri Forest Peoples Fund, Dem. Republic of Congo, 1989—. Author: The Behavioral Ecology of Efe Pygmy Men in the Ituri Forest, Zaire, 1991; co-author: The Time Allocation of Efe Pygmies in the Ituri Forest, Zaire, 1989, Efe: Investigating Food and Fertility in the Ituri Rain Forest, 1994; co-editor: Tropical Deforestation: The Human Dimension, 1996; co-editor spl. issue (jour.) Human Ecology, Human Foragers in Tropical Rain Forests, 1991; contbr. over 60 articles and papers to profl. jours. and conf. procs.; book rev. editor (jour.) Ethology and Sociobiology, 1985-89. Rsch. grantee USPHS/Ctr. Disease Control Coop. Agreement, 1996-98, other agys. and instns., 1973-96. Fellow Am. Anthropol. Assn.; mem. APHA, Am. Assn. Phys. Anthropologists (rev. bd. 59th-67th Ann. Meetings 1988-96), Human Biology Assn., Human Behavior and Evolution Soc., Internat. Soc. Human Ethology, Internat. Epidemiol. Soc. Avocation: birding. Home: 907 N Euclid Ave Oak Park IL 60302-1319 Office: Sch Public Health 2121 W Taylor St Chicago IL 60612-7260 Office Phone: 312-355-0440.*

BAILEY, ROBERT ELLIOTT, financial executive; b. Logansport, Ind., Mar. 29, 1932; s. Edwin William and Elizabeth Carolyn (Elliott) B.; m. Geraldine E. Hershberger, Jan. 31, 1954; children: Susan Elaine, Kathryn Jane. BS in Acctg., Ind. U., 1954; LLB, South Tex. Coll. Law, 1962. CPA, N.Y. Ptnr. Arthur Andersen & Co., Chgo., 1958-72; exec. v.p., dir., CFO Damson Oil Corp., NYC, 1972-82, Gearhart Industries, Inc., Ft. Worth, 1985-88; exec. v.p., CFO ENI Cos., Seattle and Houston, 1982-85; corp. fin. cons., 1988-91; chmn. fin. The Turner Corp., NYC, 1991-93; sr. v.p., CFO Rotondo Cos., Avon, Conn., 1993-94; dir. fin. UCAR, Danbury, Conn., 1995-96; acting CFO Tauck Tours, Inc., Westport, Conn., 1996-98, 2005. Bd. dirs. Berlin Steel Constrn. Co., Kensington, Conn. Capt. USAFR, 1958. Mem. AICPA, Tex. Bar Assn., N.Y. CPA Soc., Fla. CPA Soc. Home: #209 988 Boulevard of the Arts Sarasota FL 34236-4833

BAILEY, ROBIN KEITH, medical educator; b. St. Petersburg, Fla., Jan. 8, 1951; s. Albert Hugh and Kathleen Elizabeth (Badgley) B.; m. Patricia Celeste Bailey. AA, St. Petersburg Jr. Coll., 1973; BS in Pub. Rels. in Criminal Justice, U. Fla., 1976, B Health Sci., 1984; cert., Newark Beth Israel Med. Ctr., 1990; Masters in Physician Assts. Studies, U. Nebr., 1998. Cert. physician Nat. Cert. Commn. of Physician Assts. Paramedic Alachua County Emergency Med. Svc., Gainesville, Fla., 1972-78; perfusionist U. Fla./VA Med. Ctr., Gainesville, 1980-96; physician asst. U. Fla., 1984-96; chief perfusionist, physician asst. U. South Fla.-VA Med. Ctr., Tampa, 1996—2002; prof. otolaryngology-head and neck surgery U. South Fla. Coll. Medicine, 2005—. Air ambulance medic/perfusionist Shands Hosp., Gainesville, 1995-97; cons. in field. Contbr. articles to profl. publs. Lt. col. U.S. Army, 1978-81, USAFR, 1981-2002. Mem. Am. Acad. Physician Assts., Fla. Acad. Physician Assts. (v.p. 2007-), Assn. Mil. Surgeons, Am. Heart Assn. (exec. com., ACLS instr., BCLS instr./trainer). Avocations: golf, fishing. Home: 2944 Sunset Point Rd Clearwater FL 33759-1614 Office Phone: 813-972-2240. Personal E-mail: RKBaileypa@yahoo.com, rkbaileypa@gmail.com.

BAILEY, SANDRA, secondary school educator, department chairman; d. Robert Jordan and Florence Husby; m. Tom Bailey, June 22, 1974. Student, U. Uppsala, Sweden, 1965—66; BA in Social Sci., San Diego State U., 1967; MA in Internat. Rels., U. Wash., Seattle, 1970. Cert. K-12 tchr. Wash., secondary tchr. Calif. English tchr. Skiffgarden Hosp., Uppsala, 1965—66; tutor Urban League, San Diego, 1967—68; spl. edn. tchr. reading, math, English, biology Shasta Union H.S. Dist., Redding, Calif., 1968—69; tchr., advisor, chmn. dept. Edmonds Sch. Dist., Wash., 1970—2000; tchr., chmn. dept. Shoreline Sch. Dist., Wash., 2000—. Leader/tchr. Internat. Baccalaureate, Edmonds, 1993—2000; adj. prof. learning styles Seattle Pacific U., 1994. Contbr. articles to profl. publs. Commr., supporter, rep. to Japan Edmonds Sister City Commn., 1988—95; v.p. guild, chmn. various jobs Olympic Ballet, Edmonds, 1984—2003; coun. leader, tchr., youth leader, mem. Russian com. First Luth. Ch., Shoreline, 1978—2006. Recipient Fulbright-Hays scholar to China, US Govt., 1999, Excellent tchg. award, Shorewood HS, 2001, award, Edmonds Sch. Dist., 1985—88, 1991, 1995—98, Civic Svc. award, Edmonds City Coun., 1995, Angel award, Olympic Ballet, 1999; grantee, NSF, 1963; Howard I Neff scholar, Parent Orgn., 1963—64, U. Uppsala scholar, King of Sweden, 1965—66. Mem.: NEA (assoc.), Alpha Lambda Delta. Democrat. Avocations: writing, painting, travel. Home: 18355 Ridgefield Rd NW Shoreline WA 98177 Office: Shoreline School Dist 18560 1st Ave NE Shoreline WA 98155 Home Phone: 206-542-9037.

BAILEY, STEPHANIE B.C., city health department administrator; married; 3 children. BS, Clark U., Worchester, Mass.; MS in health svcs. adminstrn., Coll. of St. Francis; MD, Meharry Med. Coll., Nashville. Dir., health Metro Pub. Health Dept. of Nashville/Davidson Co., 1995—. Bd. dirs. Centerstone Cmty. Health Ctrs. Inc., 2002—. Mem. Nat. Adv. Com. on Rural Health, Nat. Adv. Com. for Elimination of Tuberculosis, Nat. Adv. Com. to CDC Dir. Recipient Excellence in Pub. Health award, ASTHO, 1999, Milton and Ruth Roemer Prize for Creative Local Public Health Work, Am. Public Health Assn., 2004, Dr. Nathan Davis award for Outstanding Govt. Service, AMA, 2005. Mem.: Nat. Assn. of County and City Health Officials (bd. mem.). Office: Metro Pub Health Dept 311 23rd Ave N Nashville TN 37203

BAILEY, STEPHEN FAIRCHILD, retired museum director, ornithologist, birding tour guide; b. Stamford, Conn., Feb. 7, 1948; s. Edwin Montgomery and Frances (Sherman) B.; m. Karen Lynn Burtness, Aug. 18, 1971 (div. July 1987). BA in Biology magna cum laude, Beloit Coll., 1971; PhD in Zoology, U. Calif., Berkeley, 1978. Mus. dir. Pacific Grove (Calif.) Mus. of Natural Hist., 1992—2004; ret., 2004; birding tour guide Rockjumper Birding Tours, South Africa, 2005—. Collections mgr. for ornithology and mammalogy Calif. Acad. Scis., San Francisco, 1984-92; biol. cons., 1979-92; adj. prof. biology San Francisco State U., 1986—; tchr. Albany Adult Sch., Calif., 1979-85. Co-author Atlas of the Breeding Birds of Monterey County, 1993; co-author, photographer Audubon Society Master Guide to Birding 3 vols., 1983; regional editor Am. Birds, 1985-98; contbr. articles to profl. jours. Rsch. fellowship Christensen Rsch. Inst., Papua New Guinea, 1989. Mem. Am. Birding Assn. (elected), Ecol. Soc. Am. (life), Am. Ornithologists Union, Cooper Ornithol. Soc. (life), Pacific Seabird Group, Phi Eta Sigma, Phi Beta Kappa. Avocations: birding, travel, nature study, military history. Home: 4564 Valley West Blvd Apt C Arcata CA 95521 E-mail: sfbailey@reninet.com.

BAILEY, SUSAN RUDD, physician; BS, Tex. A&M U., 1979, MD, 1981; postgrad., Mayo Grad. Sch. Medicine, 1981-84, 84-86. Diplomate Am. Bd. Pediatrics, Am. Bd. Allergy and Immunology; lic. Tex. Assoc, cons. dept. pediatrics Mayo Clinic, Rochester, Minn., 1987; pvt. practice, allergy and clin. immunology Fort Worth (Tex.) Allergy and Asthma Assocs., 1988—. Instr. in pediatrics Mayo Med. Sch., 1986-87; bd. dirs. Accreditation Coun. on Continuing Med. Edn., 2004—; presenter in field. Mem. editl. bd. Annals Allergy, Asthma and Immunology, 1997—2003; contbr. articles to profl. jours. Bd. visitors Scott and White Clinic, 1994—; adv. bd. M.D. Anderson Physicians, 1992-94; bd. regents Tex. A&M U. Sys., 1999-2005; mem. AMA Coun. Med. Edn. Exec. Com., 2005- Recipient Residents' award Northwest Pediatric Soc., 1984, Leon Unger award Am. Coll. Allergists, 1985, Geigy fellow, 1987, travel grantsee, dist. fellow Am. Coll. Allergy, Asthma & Immunology, 1998. Mem. AMA (chmn. med. student sect. 1980-81, chmn. com. on women in medicine 1987-89, coun. med. edn. 2004—, chair Tex. del. 2006), Mayo Assn. Fellows (treas. 1984-85), Mayo Alumni Assn. (exec. com. 1983-87, 95-02), Conjoint Com. Continuing Med. Edn., The Mayo Alumnus (adv. bd. 1983-87), Tarrant County Med. Soc. (bd. dirs. 1990—, v.p. 1994-95, pres.-elect 1995-96, pres. 1996-97, trustee 1998-01), Minn. Med. Assn. (trustee 1984-85), Tex. Med. Assn. (vice spkr. 1997-01, spkr. 2001-05, various coms.), Am. Acad. Pediats., Am. Coll. Allergy and Immunology (bd. regents 1994-97, chair publs. com. 2003-), Am. Assn. Cert. Allergists, Alpha Omega Alpha, Alpha Zeta, others. Office: 5929 Lovell Ave Fort Worth TX 76107-5029 Office Phone: 817-315-2550. E-mail: susanruddbailey@yahoo.com.

BAILEY, T. WAYNE, political science professor; BA in polit. sci. with honors, U. Fla.; MA in polit. sci. and history, Peabody Coll., Vanderbilt U.; PhD in polit. sci., U. Fla. Prof. polit. sci. Stetson U., DeLand, Fla., 1983—. Cons. in field; advisor on charter changes numerous Am. Cities; chmn. Volusia Co. Charter Revisions Com. Vol. Am. Lung Assn., Fla., pres., 1994—95; mentor to students in govt. careers; vol. Dem. Party; past del. Dem. Nat. Convention. Named J. Ollie Edmunds chair, 1984—85; recipient Will Ross medal, Am. Lung Assn., Hubert H. Humphrey Outstanding Statesman award, Fla. Dem. Party, 1983, Ed Dunn Leadership award, Tiger Bay Club, Volusia County, Discovery Health Channel Med. Honors, 2004, Will Ross Medal, Am. Lung Assn., 2005. Achievements include urged the Am. Lung Assn. of Fla. to shift its focus from small ednl. programs to lobbying for stronger legis. The 2002 Fla. Clean Indoor Air Act has improved the health of Fla. residents lungs. Office: Stetson Univ 421 N Woodland Blvd Deland FL 32720 Office Phone: 386-822-7574. E-mail: wbailey@stetson.edu.

BAILEY, THOMAS ANTHONY, lawyer; b. Milw., Nov. 20, 1942; s. Lawrence C. and Phyllis E. (Croasdaile) B.; m. Barbara Mary Dobbin, June 10, 1967; children: Mary Elizabeth, Kathleen, Erin, Brian, Sean, Bridget, Kevin, Michael. BS in Fin., Marquette U., 1964, JD, 1967; postgrad., U. Va. Law Sch., 1968-70. Bar: Wis. 1967, U.S. Supreme Ct. 1977. Asst. dist. atty. Milw. County, Milw., 1967-68; ptnr. Fricker & Bailey, Milw., 1972-92, Bailey Law Offices, Whitefish Bay, Wis., 1992—. Supr. Milw. County Bd., 1979—. Capt., U.S. Army, 1968-72. Fellow Am. Acad. Matrimonial Lawyers; mem. Milw. Bar Assn. (pres. 1984-85, chmn. family law sect.), Wis. Bar Assn., Wis. Acad. Trial Lawyers, St. Thomas More Lawyers Soc. (pres. 1980-81). Home and Office: Bailey Law Offices 130 W Silver Spring Dr Milwaukee WI 53217-4707

BAILEY, THOMAS CHARLES, lawyer; b. Rochester, NY, Nov. 26, 1948; s. Charles George and Teckla Barbara (Driscoll) B.; m. Rosalie Stoll, Sept. 24, 1974; children: Leah Isabelle, Molly Driscoll, Elizabeth Rose. BA, Princeton U., 1970; JD, SUNY, Buffalo, 1974. Bar: N.Y. 1975, Fla. 1977. Assoc. Little & Burt, Buffalo, 1974-78, ptnr., 1978-80, Saperston & Day, PC, Buffalo, 1980-92; pvt. practice Buffalo, 1992-97; mem. Albrecht Maguire Heffern and Gregg PC, Buffalo, 1997-2000, Phillips Lytle LLP, Buffalo, 2000—. Bd. dirs., sec. Buffalo Therapeutic Riding Ctr. Inc., 1999-2001. Pres. St. Thomas Moore Guild, 1981; trustee Shea's O'Connell Preservation Guild, 1986-96, chmn., 1994; bd. dirs. Opera Niagara, Ltd., 1999—, pres., 2001-. Mem. ABA, N.Y. State Bar Assn. (exec. com. of real property law sect. 1994-2000), Fla. Bar Assn., Saturn Club (dean 2000), Princeton U. Alumni Assn. Western N.Y. (pres. 1990-91), Brookhaven Trout Club. Avocations: fly fishing, sailing. Office: Phillips Lytle LLP 3400 HSBC Tower Buffalo NY 14203 Office Phone: 716-847-5410.

BAILEY, TRACEY L., educational association administrator; married; 8 children. BS in Sci. Edn., Fla. Inst. Tech., MS in Instructional Tech. Tchr. Satellite High Sch., Satellite Beach, Fla.; dir. office of charter schs. Fla. Dept. of Edn.; dir. nat. projects Assn. Am. Educators Found. Recipient State Teacher of the Yr. awd., Florida, Coun. of Chief State School Offices, 1993, Nat. Teacher of the Yr. awd., Coun. of Chief School Offices, 1993. Office: Nat Projects Dir Assn American Educators 1645 Prince St Alexandria VA 22314 Office Phone: 703-739-2100.*

BAILEY, WILLIAM HARRISON, artist, educator; b. Council Bluffs, Iowa, Nov. 17, 1930; s. Willard Kendall and Marjorie Esther (Cheyney) Bailey; m. Sandra Stone, May 28, 1958; children: Ford Hamilton, Alix Brook. Student, U. Kans., 1948-51; BFA, Yale U., 1955, MFA, 1957; HHD (hon.), U. Utah, 1987; DFA (hon.), Adelphi U., Pa. Acad. Fine Arts, 2004. Instr. art Yale U., New Haven, 1957-61, asst. prof., 1961-62, adj. prof., 1969-73, prof., 1973-79, Kingman Brewster prof., 1979-95, Kingman Brewster prof. emeritus, 1995—, dean Sch. Art, 1974-75; asst. prof., assoc. prof. Ind. U., 1962—68, prof., 1968-69. Mem. Nat. Coun. Arts, 1992—97. Exhibitions include Kanegis Gallery, Boston, 1958, 1959, 1961, Robert Schoelkopf Gallery, NYC, 1968, 1971, 1974, 1979, 1982, 1986, 1990, 1991, Galerie Claude Bernard, Paris, 1978, 2001, Galleria Il Gabbiano, Rome, 1985, 1989, 1993, 1997, John Berggruen Gallery, San Francisco, 1988, Andre Emmerich Gallery, NYC, 1992, 1994, 1995, Alpha Gallery, Boston, 1998, Robert Miller Gallery, NYC, 1999, 2003, Palace of the Legion of Honor, San Francisco, 2003, Betty Cuningham Gallery, NYC, 2005, Represented in permanent collections Mus. Modern Art, Whitney Mus., Hirshorn Mus., St. Louis Art Mus., Neu Galerie Der Stadt Aachen, Germany, Pa. Acad., Yale Art Gallery, Ark. Art Ctr., Art Inst. Chgo., Phillips Collection, Washington, Boston Mus. Fine Arts, Nat. Acad. Design, J.B. Speed Mus., Louisville, Des Moines Art Ctr. With US Army, 1951—53. Alice Kimball English Travelling fellow, 1955, Guggenheim fellow, 1965, Ingram Merrill fellow, 1975. Mem.: Conn. Acad. Arts and Scis., Academia di Belli Arti, Perugia, Acad. San Luca, Rome, Am. Acad. Arts and Letters, Nat. Acad. Design, Smithsonian Archives Am. Art (trustee), Tiffany Found. (bd. dirs.), Yaddo (mem. corp.). Office: Yale U Sch Art Dept Painting Printmaking New Haven CT 06520

BAILEY, WILLIAM WADDELL, writer, communications executive; s. George W. and Phyllis K. Bailey; m. Rita Maria Fleischmann. BA in Psychology, U. Miss., 1973; MA in Internat. Rels., U. So. Calif., 1985; disting. grad., Command and Gen. Staff Coll., 1987. Cert. software engr. Commd. 2d lt. U.S. Army, 1973, advanced through grades to lt. col., officer Ft. Bragg, N.C., 1973-82; software mgr. U.S. Govt., Augsburg, Germany, 1982-85, modernization mgr. Leavenworth, Kans., 1985-90, divsn. chief Arlington, Va., 1990-92, spl. exec., 1992-93; sr. advisor to pvt. orgns. Washington, 1993-97; pres. Writer's Ink, Fayetteville, N.C., 1997—; resident artist Urban Arts Prgm., 1998, Arts and Tech., 1999. Cons. Sierra Cybernetics, Yorba Linda, Calif., 1993—. Author, editor: 2004 Future Architecture, 1987, Modernization Plan, 1989; author: Desert Storm Lessons Learned, 1991; contbr. articles, stories and poems to mags. and jours. Mem. fundraising com. Hist. Mus., Fayetteville, 1981; mem. Arts Coun., 1996—. Decorated Legion of Merit. Avocations: astronomy, fencing.

BAILEY-WELLS, DEBORAH, lawyer; BA with honors, Mills Coll., 1980; JD, Univ. San Francisco, 1984. Bar: Calif. 1984, US Dist. Ct. (no., ctrl., so. & ea. Calif.), US Ct. Appeals (9th & Fed. cir.), US Supreme Ct. Adminstrv. ptnr. & mem. mgmt. com. Kirkpatrick & Lockhart Nicholson Graham LLP, San Francisco. Contbr. articles to profl. jours. Mem.: ABA, Am. Intellectual Property Bar Assn., Internat. Trademark Assn., San Francisco Intellectual Property Law Assn., Silicon Valley Intellectual Property Assn. Office: Kirkpatrick & Lockhart Nicholson Graham LLP 10th Fl 4 Embarcadero Ctr San Francisco CA 94111-4121 Office Phone: 415-249-1065. Office Fax: 415-249-1001. Business E-Mail: dbaileywells@klng.com.

BAILIN, MICHAEL TRAHERNE, physician; BS in biology, Mass. Inst. Tech., 1980; MD, Harvard Med. Sch., Boston, 1984. Bd. cert. anesthesiologist Am. Bd. Anesthesiology, 1988. Resident and chief resident in anesthesiology Mass. Gen. Hosp., Boston, 1985—88, anesthesiologist, 1988—2003, anesthetist dept. anesthesia and critical care, 2007—; chief, anesthesiologist St. Vincent Hosp., Worcester, Mass., 2003—04; pres. Narragansett Bay Anesthesia, Providence, 2004—07; chief dept. anesthesiology The Miriam Hosp., Providence, 2004—07. Pres. Boston Anesthesia Edn. Found., 1996—2003; mem. pre health adv. coun. MIT, 1994—; bd. adv. Health Scis. and Tech. Divsn. Harvard Med. Sch., 2007—. Editor-in-chief (CD Rom textbook) Harvard Electronic Anesthesia Libr., 2001. Named one of Best Drs. in Am., 2007—. Office: Mass Gen Hosp Fruit St Boston MA 02114 Personal E-mail: bailin@mit.edu.

BAILLARGEON, RENEE, psychology professor; b. Quebec; BS with first class honors, McGill Univ., Montreal; PhD, Univ. Pa., 1981; postdoctoral fellow, MIT Ctr. for Cognitive Sci., 1981—82. Asst. prof., psychology Univ. Tex., Austin, 1983—84; asst. prof. Univ. Ill. Urbana-Champaign, 1984—89, assoc. prof., 1989—94, prof., 1994—, and dir., Infant Cognition Lab. Fellow: Am. Acad. Arts & Scis. Office: 613 Psychology Bldg Univ Ill 603 East Daniel St Champaign IL 61820 Office Phone: 217-333-5557. Business E-Mail: rbaillar@uiuc.edu.*

BAILLIE, JAMES LEONARD, lawyer; b. Mpls., Aug. 27, 1942; s. Leonard Thompson and Sylvia Alfreda (Fundberg) B.; m. Jacqueline McGlamery; children: Jennifer, Craig, John. AB in History, 1964; JD, U. Chgo., 1967. Bar: Minn. 1967, U.S. Dist. Ct. Minn. 1968, U.S. Ct. Appeals (8th cir.) 1969, U.S. Ct. Appeals (5th cir.) 1980. Law clk. to presiding justice U.S. Dist. Ct., Mpls., 1967-68; assoc. Fredrikson & Byron, P.A., Mpls., 1968-73, shareholder, 1973—. Mem. ABA (litigation sect. co-editor Bankruptcy Litigation 1998, bus. law sect. editl. bd. Bus. Law Today 1993-98, bus. sect. chair pro bono com. 1999-2003, section coun 2003—, standing com. on lawyer pub. svc. responsibility 1991-96, chmn. 1993-96, nat. pro bono award 1984, John Minor Wisdom award 1999), Minn. State Bar Assn. (chmn. bankruptcy sect. 1985-88, sec. 2000-01, treas. 2001-02, pres. elect., 2003-03, pres. 2003-04), Hennepin County Bar Assn. (sec. 1992-93, treas. 1993-95, pres. elect., 1995-96, pres. 1996-97). Office: Fredrikson & Byron PA 200 S 6th St # 4000 Minneapolis MN 55402 Office Phone: 612-492-7013. Business E-Mail: jbaillie@fredlaw.com.

BAILLIE, RICHARD THOMAS, economist, educator; b. London, Feb. 14, 1948; arrived in US, 1979; s. Thomas Edward and Muriel Hervét (Podmore) Baillie; m. Anne Rosalind Waller, Nov. 2, 1974. BS, Middlesex U., London, 1970; MS, U. Kent, Canterbury, Eng., 1972; PhD, London Sch. Econs., 1978. Prof. Mich. State U., East Lansing, 1988-92, 93-98, A. J. Pasant prof., 1998—; prof. Georgetown U., Washington, 1992-93. Cons. Fed. Res. Bank, Cleve., 1994—98, vis. scholar, St. Louis, 1994; part-time prof. Queen Mary U., London, 1999—. Fellow, Jour. Econometrics, 1997; grantee, NSF, 1992, 1993, 1999. Fellow: Am. Statis. Assn.; mem.: Am. Econ. Assn., Am. Fin. Assn., Econometric Soc. Avocations: travel, tennis, wine, films, cricket. Home: 1090 Whittier Dr East Lansing MI 48823 Office: Mich State U Dept Econ East Lansing MI 48824 Office Phone: 517-355-1864. Business E-Mail: baillie@msu.edu.

BAILLIEUL, JOHN BROUARD, aerospace engineering and applied mathematics educator; b. Boise, Idaho, May 13, 1945; s. Paul Brouard and Geneva (Gillam) B.; m. Patricia Pfeiffer; children: Emily, Charlotte, John Paul. BA, U. Mass., Amherst, 1967; M in Math., U. Waterloo, Waterloo, Can., 1969; MS, Harvard U., 1973, PhD in Applied Math., 1975. Asst. prof. math. Georgetown U., Washington, 1975-79; sr. mathematician Sci. Systems, Inc., Cambridge, Mass., 1979-83; Vinton Hayes vis. scientist Harvard U., Cambridge, 1983-85; prof. aerospace and mech. engring. Boston U., 1985—, prof. mfg. engring., 1988—, prof. elec. and computer engring., 2001—, dir. div. engring. and applied sci., 1990-93, assoc. dean Coll. Engring., 1993—96, chmn. dept. mfg. engring., 1994-99, chmn. dept. aerospace/mech. engring., 1999—. Cons. Sci. Systems, Inc., Cambridge, 1985-87, AMD Corp., Stratford, Conn., 1986, Computational Engring., Inc., Laurel, Md., 1988-89; vis. sr. scientist Lab. for Info. and Decision Systems, MIT, 1991; chmn. dept aerospace/mech. engring., 1992-93. Author: Mathematical Control Theory, 1998; assoc. editor IEEE Transactions on Automatic Control, 1984—85, 1989—92, editor-in-chief, 1992—98, SIAMJ on Control and Opt.; assoc. editor: IEEE Robotics and Automation Soc. newsletter, Bifurcation and Chaos in Applied Scis. and Engring.; mem. editl. bd. Procs. IEEE, Comm. in Info. and Systems, Robotics and Computer Integrated Mfg.; contbr. articles to profl. jours. US Dept. Energy grantee, USAF Office Sci. Rsch. grantee Boston U., 1985—, NSF grantee, Army Rsch. Office grantee; frequent grantee for study nonlinear control theory and mechanics Fellow IEEE (bd. dirs. 2007—, v.p. pubs., products and svcs. 2007, mem. publs. bd., 40th pres. Control Sys. Soc. 2006, 3D Millennium medal 2000). Office: Boston U Aero Mech Engring 110 Cummington St Boston MA 02215-2407 Home: 3 Ludwig Rd Needham Heights MA 02494-1042

BAILON, GILBERT, newspaper executive; From mem. staff to v.p., exec. editor Dallas (Tex.) Morning News, 1986—97, exec. editor, 1997—2004, v.p., 1997—2004; pres., editor Al Dia (Spanish language newspaper of Dallas Morning News), 2002—04, pub., editor, 2004—. Mem.: Am. Soc. Newspaper Editors (treas. designate 2003—04, treas. 2004—05, sec. 2005—06, v.p. 2006—07, bd. dir., pres. 2007—08), Nat. Assn. Hispanic Journalists (past pres.). Office: The Dallas Morning News PO Box 655237 508 Young St Dallas TX 75202-4828

BAILYN, BERNARD, historian, educator; s. Charles Manuel and Esther (Schloss) Bailyn; m. Lotte Lazarsfeld, June 18, 1952; children: Charles David, John Frederick. AB, Williams Coll., 1945, LittD (hon.); MA, Harvard U., 1947, PhD, 1953, LLD (hon.), 1999; LHD (hon.), Lawrence U., Bard Coll., Clark U., Yale U., Grinnell Coll., Trinity Coll., Manhattanvill Coll., Dartmouth Coll., U. Chgo., Coll. of William and Mary, Georgetown U., Pa. State U.; LittD (hon.), Rutgers U., Fordham U., La Trobe U., Australia, Washington U., St. Louis. Mem. faculty Harvard U., Cambridge, Mass., 1953—, editor in chief John Harvard Libr., 1962—70, Winthrop prof. history, 1966—81, Adams U. prof., 1981—93, emeritus, 1993—, dir. Charles Warren Ctr. for Studies in Am. History, 1983—94. Sr. fellow Soc. Fellows Harvard U., 1982—2005; Trevelyan lectr. Cambridge U., 1971; mem. inst. advanced study Princeton (N.J.) U., 1980—81, trustee, 1989—94; Pitt prof. Cambridge U., 1986—87; dir. Internat. Seminar on Atlantic History Harvard U., 1995—. Co-author (with Lotte Bailyn): Mass. Shipping 1697-1714, A Statis. Study, 1959; author: New Eng. Merchants in the 17th Century, 1955, Edn. in the Forming of Am. Society, 1960, The Ideological Origins of the Am. Revolution, 1967 (Pulitzer prize, 1968, Bancroft prize, 1968), The Origins of Am. Politics, 1968, The Ordeal of Thomas Hutchinson, 1974 (Nat. Book award, 1975), The Peopling of Br. North Am.: An Intro., 1986, Voyagers to the West, 1986 (Pulitzer prize, Saloutos award Immigration History soc., Triennial Book award Soc. of the Cin.), Faces of Revolution, 1990, On The Tchg. and Writing of History, 1994, To Begin the World Anew, 2003, Atlantic History: Concept and Contours, 2005; co-author: The Gt. Republic, 1977; editor: Pamphlets of the Am. Revolution 1750-1776, 1965, The Apologia of Robert Keayne, 1965, The Debate on the Constitution, 2 vols., 1993; co-editor: The Intellectual Migration, Europe and Am., 1930-1960, 1969, Law in Am. History, 1972, Perspectives in Am. History, 1967—77, 1984—86, The Press and The Am. Revolution, 1980, Strangers Within the Realm, 1990. With AUS, 1943—46. Recipient Robert H. Lord award, Emmanuel Coll., 1967, medal, Fgn. Policy Assn., 1998, Catton prize for lifetime achievement in writing of history, Soc. Am. Historians, 2000, Centennial medal, Harvard Grad. Sch. Arts and Scis., 2001; hon. fellow, Christ Coll., Cambridge U., Jefferson lectr., NEH, 1998, Millenium lectr., White House, 1998. Fellow: Royal Hist. Soc. (corr.); mem.: Academia Europaea, Russian Acad. Scis., Mex. Acad. History and Geography, Brit. Acad., Mass. Hist. Soc. (Kennedy medal 2004), Royal Soc. Edinburgh (hon.), Am. Philos. Soc. (Thomas Jefferson medal 1993, Henry Allen Moe prize 1994), Nat. Acad. Edn., Am. Acad. Arts and Scis., Am. Hist. Assn. (pres. 1981). Home: 170 Clifton St Belmont MA 02478-2604 Office: Harvard U History Dept Cambridge MA 02138

BAILYN, LOTTE, psychologist, educator; b. Vienna, July 17, 1930; came to U.S., 1937; d. Paul Felix Lazarsfeld and Marie (Jahoda) Albu; m. Bernard Bailyn, June 18, 1952; children: Charles, John. BA in Math. with high honors, Swarthmore Coll., 1951; MA in Social Psychology, Harvard U., 1953, PhD in Social Psychology, 1956; PhD (hon.), U. Piraeus, Greece, 2000. Rsch. assoc. Grad. Sch. Edn., Harvard U., Cambridge, Mass., 1956-57, rsch. assoc. dept. social rels., 1958-64, lectr., 1963-67; instr. dept. econs. and social sci. MIT, Cambridge, 1957-58, rsch. assoc. Sloan Sch. Mgmt., 1969-70, lectr., 1970-71, from sr. lectr. to prof., 1971-91, T Wilson prof. mgmt., 1991—2005, prof. mgmt., 2005—, chair MIT faculty, 1997-99; acad. visitor Imperial Coll. Sci., Tech. and Medicine, London, 1991, 1995, 2000; disting. vis. prof. Radcliffe Coll., 1995-97. Trustee Cambridge Savs. Bank, 1975-98; mem. adv. coun. Suffolk U. Mgmt. Sch., Boston, 1983-86; mem. sr. coun. Leadership Devel. Inst., Rutgers U., 1986-89; panel mem. NAS, NRC, Washington, 1988-90; mem. task force in career devel. and maintenance IEEE, Washington, 1982-90; vis. scholar Imperial Coll. Sci. and Tech., London, 1982, New Hall, Cambridge (Eng.) U., 1986-87; scholar-in-residence Rockefeller Found. Study and Conf. Ctr., Bellagio, Italy, 1983; vis. fellow U. Auckland, N.Z., 1984. Author: Mass Media and Children, 1959, Living with Technology, 1980, Breaking the Mold: Women, Men, and Time in the New Corporate World, 1993, Breaking the Mold: Redesigning Work for Satisfying Lives, 2006; co-author: Working with Careers, 1984, Relinking Life and Work: Toward a Better Future, 1996, Beyond Work-Family Balance: Advancing Gender Equity and Workplace Performance, 2002; mem. editl. bd. Jour. Engring. and Tech. Mgmt., Cmty., Work and Family, Human Rels.; contbr. chpts. to books and articles to profl. jours. Trustee Radcliffe Coll., 1974-79, Cambridge Fin. Group, Inc., 1998-2005; bd. dirs. Families and Work Inst., 1995—, Cambridge Savings Bank, 1998-2005; adv. group, Creating Options: Models for Flexible Faculty Career Pathways, Office of Women in Higher Edn., Am. Coun. Edn., 2003-; com. Women in Sci. and Engring., Nat. Acad. Sci., 2004—, Women in Acad. Sci. and Engring., Nat. Acads., 2005-2006. Recipient Grad. Soc. medal Radcliffe Coll., 1998, Everett Cherrington Hughes award for careers scholarship Acad. of Mgmt., 2003, Work Life Legacy award, Families and Work Inst., 2005. Fellow APA; mem. Acad. Mgmt., Am. Sociol. Assn. Home: 170 Clifton St Belmont MA 02478-2604 Office: MIT Sloan Sch Mgmt 50 Memorial Dr Cambridge MA 02142-1347 Business E-Mail: lbailyn@mit.edu.

BAIM, ERIC M., lawyer; b. Pitts., Jan. 23, 1972; BA in Psychology with highest honors, U. NC, Chapel Hill, 1994; MA in Clin. Psychology, U. Cin., 1998; MA in Pub. Policy, Duke U., 2001, JD, 2001. Bar: Va. 2001, DC 2002, US Ct. Appeals 4th Cir. Assoc. Shaw Pittman LLP, Sonnenschein Nath & Rosenthal LLP, Washington, 2003—. Mem.: ABA (mem. health law sect.), Va. Bar Assn., DC Bar Assn. (mem. health law sect.), Am. Health Lawyers Assn. Office: Sonnenschein Nath & Rosenthal LLP Ste 600, E Tower 1301 K St NW Washington DC 20005 Office Phone: 202-408-9160. Office Fax: 202-408-6399. Business E-Mail: ebaim@sonnenschein.com.

BAIN, C. RANDALL, lawyer; b. Greeley, Colo., Feb. 1, 1934; s. Walter Lockwood and Harriet Lucille (Stewart) B.; m. Joanne Berg, Aug. 4, 1956 (div.); children: Jennifer Harriet, Charles Alvin; m. Lois Jean Frazier, Feb. 1, 1973 (dec.); 1 child, Frazier; m. Anna Scalise, Dec. 16, 2000. BA, Yale U., 1955, LLB, 1960. Bar: Ariz. 1961, U.S. Dist. Ct. Ariz. 1961, U.S. Ct. Appeals (9th cir.) 1963, U.S. Supreme Ct. 1968, U.S. Ct. Appeals (fed. cir.) 1992. Ptnr. Brown & Bain, Phoenix, 1961—2003, pres., 1972—87, exec. v.p., 1987—96, of counsel, 2003—04, Perkins, Coie, Brown & Bain, 2004—. Adj. prof. law Ariz. State U. Sch. Law, 2000-01. Trustee Phoenix Country Day Sch., 1983-94; chmn. bd. dirs. Ariz. Audubon, 2003—. Fellow Am. Bar Found.; mem. ABA, Ariz. Bar Assn. (chmn. fee arbitration com. 1982-86), Am. Law Inst., Yale U. Law Sch. Alumni Assn. (exec. com. 1982-85, 93-97), Audubon Ariz. (chmn. bd. dirs. 2003-). Office: Perkins Coie Brown & Bain PA 2901 N Central Ave Ste 2000 Phoenix AZ 85012-2788

BAIN, CONRAD STAFFORD, actor; b. Lethbridge, Alta., Can., Feb. 4, 1923; came to U.S., 1946, naturalized, 1946; m. Monica Marjorie Sloan, Sept. 4, 1945; children: Kent Stafford, Mark Alexander, Jennifer Jean. Grad., Am. Acad. Dramatic Art, 1948. Founder Actors Fed. Credit Union, 1962. Broadway appearances include Candide, 1957, Lost in the Stars, 1958, Hot Spot, 1963, Advise and Consent, 1961, Twigs, 1971, Uncle Vanya, 1973, On Borrowed Time, 1991; off-Broadway appearances include The Iceman Cometh, 1957, Hogan's Goat, 1966, Scuba Duba, 1967, The Kitchen, 1968, Steambath, 1969, The Dining Room, Pasadena Playhouse, 1991, On Borrowed Time, 1992, Ancestral Voices, 1999; film appearances A Lovely Way to Die, 1967, Who Killed Mary Whats er Name, 1968, Up the Sand Box, 1970, C.H.O.M.P.S, 1979, Child Bride of Short Creek, 1982, Postcards from the Edge, 1990; Pasadena Playhouse The Dining Room, 1991; co-star: (TV) Maude, 1971-78; star: (TV) Diff'rent Strokes, 1978-86, Mr. President, 1987—. Served with Canadian Army, World War II. Mem. Actors Equity Assn. (councilor 1962-76), ANTA West (dir. since 1977) Clubs: Players (N.Y.C.). Office: 1230 Chicory Ln Los Angeles CA 90049-1403 *I have come to realize that each job no matter how small must be an end in itself, and that each day of whatever character must be lived for that day, in all its fullness. Yesterday is gone, regret is a waste, and tomorrow is unknown.*

BAIN, DONALD KNIGHT, lawyer; b. Denver, Jan. 28, 1935; s. Francis Marion and Jean (Knight) B.; divorced; children: Stephen A., Andrew K., William B. AB, Yale U., 1957; LLB, Harvard U., 1961. Bar: Colo. 1961. Assoc. Holme Roberts & Owen, Denver, 1961—67, ptnr., 1967—2004, chmn. exec. com., 1988-90, counsel, 2005—; chmn. Colo. Rep. Com., 1993-97. Bd. dirs. Fairmount Cemetery Co.; mem. grievance com. Colo. Supreme Ct., 1975-80, chmn., 1980. Trustee Denver Pub. Libr. Friends Found., 1978—96, Denver Found., 1989—95, chmn., 1993—95; trustee Berger Found., 1994—96; trustee, chmn. Colo. Coun. on Arts, 1999—2005; trustee Human Svcs., Inc., 1970—81, chmn., 1979—80; trustee Colo. Humanities Program, 1975—78; mem. Denver Pub. Libr. Commn., 1983—91; active Rep. Nat. Com., Washington, 1993—97; candidate for mayor City of Denver, 1987, 1991; bd. dirs. Rocky Mountain Corp. Pub. Broadcasting, 1975—83, Downtown Denver, Inc., 1977—2004, Denver Metro C. of C., 1998—, BigHornAction.org, 1999—2003, Auraria Found., 1986—, Legal Aid Found., Colo., 1999—2005, Auraria Higher Edn. Ctr., 1978—89, Denver Archtl. Found., 2002—; chmn. Auraria Higher Edn. Ctr., 1986—89. Fellow Royal Geog. Soc., Am. Coll. Trial Lawyers, Explorers Club; mem. ABA, Colo. Bar Assn., Denver Bar Assn., Colo. Yale Assn. (pres. 1974-76), Assn. Yale Alumni (bd. govs. 1982-85), Selden Soc., Am. Antiquarian Soc., Internat. Wine and Food Soc., Confrerie des Chevaliers du Tastevin, Western Stock Show Assn., Cactus Club, Denver Country Club, Mile High Club, Denver Law Club, Grolier Club, Yale Club, Colo. Mountain Club, Capitol Hill CLub, Univ. Club (Denver), Garden of Gods Club. Republican. Avocation: antiquarian book collecting. Home: 1201 Williams # 13C Denver CO 80218 Office: Holme Roberts & Owen LLP 1700 Lincoln St Ste 4100 Denver CO 80203-4541 Office Phone: 303-861-7000. Business E-Mail: don.bain@hro.com.

BAIN, DOUGLAS G., retired aerospace transportation executive, lawyer; b. Charlottesville, Va., Mar. 12, 1949; m. Cindy Bain; children: Tyler, Emily, Allison. BA, U. Va., 1971, JD, 1974. Bar: Calif. 1974, Wash. 1982, Ill. 2005. Atty. Office Gen. Counsel USAF, Washington, 1975—77; atty. Pillsbury, Madison & Sutro; various positions in legal dept. including sr. counsel & asst. gen. counsel The Boeing Co., Chgo., 1982—96, v.p. legal, contracts, ethics and govt. rels. comml. airplanes group, 1996—99, v.p., gen. counsel, 1999—2000, sr. v.p., gen. counsel, 2000—06.

BAIN, JAMES WILLIAM, lawyer; b. Suffern, NY, Dec. 19, 1949; s. William James and Agnes (Hoey) B.; m. Colleen K., Mar. 23, 1974; children: Rebecca, Meghan. BA, U. Conn., 1972; JD, U. Fla., 1976. Bar: Fla. 1977, U.S. Dist. Ct. (ea. dist.) Tenn. 1980, Tenn. 1984, U.S. Ct. Appeals (11th cir.) 1984, U.S. Ct. Appeals (D.C. cir.) 1984, Colo. 1986, U.S. Dist. Ct. Colo 1986, U.S. Ct. Appeals (10th cir.) 1988, U.S. Supreme Ct. 1998. Counsel TVA, Knoxville, 1977—85; dir. Roath & Brega, P.C., Denver, 1985—89, Brega & Winters, P.C., Denver, 1989—2003; ptnr. Benjamin, Bain & Howard LLC, Greenwood Village, Colo., 2003—. Instr. U. Fla., Gainesville, 1976, U. Colo., Boulder, 1987-90; seminar chmn. Inst. for Advanced Legal Study, Denver, 1987. Contbr. articles to profl. jours.; editor constrn. law column Colo. Lawyer. Recipient Civil Litigation Writing award for 1986-87, Denver Colo. Bar Assn., 1987. Mem. ATLA, Colo. Bar Assn., Fla. Bar Assn., Am. Judicature Soc., Am. Arbitration Assn. (arbitrator 1986). Avocations: soccer, skiing, biking, basketball. Office: Benjamin Bain & Howard LLC 7315 E Orchard Rd Ste E400 Greenwood Village CO 80111 Office Phone: 303-290-6600. Business E-Mail: jamesbain@bbhlegal.com.

BAIN, SCOTT E., lawyer; b. Windom, Minnesota, Apr. 12, 1971; BSEE summa cum laude, Univ. of Minn., 1994; JD, Boalt Hall School of Law, Univ. of CA. Berkeley, 1997. Bar: D.C., Minnesota, U.S. Supreme Ct., U.S. Ct. of Appeals Fourth, Ninth Fed. Circuits, U.S. Dist. Ct., Minn., U.S. Patent and Trademark Office. Mng. editor Berkeley Tech. Law Jour.; law clk. to the Hon. Randall R. Rader U.S. Ct. Appeals (Fed. cir.), 1998—99; partner Wiley Rein & Fielding LLP, 2005—. Mem.: Am. Intellectual Property Law Assoc., Am. Bar Assoc. Office: Wiley Rein & Fielding 1776 K Street NW Washington DC 20006 E-mail: sbain@wrf.com.

BAIN, TRAVIS WHITSETT, II, manufacturing and retail executive; b. San Antonio, Mar. 4, 1934; s. Travis Whitsett and Zelma Gladys (Middleton) B.; m. Karlen Jo Bruner, May 30, 1957; children: Travis W. III, James Henry III. B in Chem. Engring., U. Tex., 1956; MBA, Harvard U., 1958. Mfg. supt. Tex. Instruments, Dallas, 1958-61; sr. assoc. McKinsey and Co., L.A. and Chgo., 1961-65; exec. v.p., COO Trend Line Corp., Jackson, Miss., 1965-81; pres., CEO W.E. Walker Stores, Inc., Jackson, 1981-86; CEO Sunbelt Nursery Group, Inc., Ft. Worth, 1986-87; investor, cons. Bain Assocs., Ft. Worth, 1987-88; pres. Jarman Shoe Co. div. Genesco Inc., Nashville, 1988-92, Bain Enterprises, Inc. dba Sandler Pools, Plano, Tex., 1993-99; chmn. Tex. Custom Pools, Inc., Plano, 1999—. Bd. dirs. Atmos Energy Corp., Dallas, 1988—, Tex. Commerce Bank, Ft. Worth, 1986-88, Delta Industries, Inc., Jackson, 1984—; chmn. bd. dirs. Master Pools Guild, 1997-99. Bd. dirs. New Stage Theatre, Jackson, 1980-86, Boy Scouts Am., Ft. Worth, 1986-88, Miss. Ballet Internat., Jackson, 1984-86; bd. dirs., exec. com. Nashville Ballet, 1989-92; mem. placement coun. Owen Sch. Mgmt. Vanderbilt U., Nashville, 1984-92; mem. adv. bd. CBA Found. U. Tex., Austin, 1987—. Mem. Dallas Exec. Assn. (pres. 1998-99). Republican. Presbyterian. Avocations: gardening, tennis, jogging, travel, scuba diving. Office: Tex Custom Pools Inc 4016 W Plano Pkwy Plano TX 75093-5696 Office Phone: 972-596-7393. Fax: 972-596-9460. E-mail: tbain@texascustompools.com.

BAIN, WILLIAM DAVID, electronics engineer, writer; b. Flint, Mich., Sept. 3, 1958; s. William David and Frances Geraldine B. Student, Jordan Coll., 1984-85. Theater mgr. asst. Northwest Theater, Flint, 1975-81, Commonwealth Theater, Denver, 1981-82; theater mgr., promotions asst. Towne Cinemas, Flushing, Mich., 1987-91; pvt. practice Flint, 1991—. Author: Oasis, 1995, Inspirational Collection, 1997, Tear Drops Fall Like Rain, 1997, Romantic Collection, 1997, Verses From The Heart, 1999, Rite of Passage, 2005. Mem. Comms. com. Democratic Party, 1994-98, Greater Flint Arts Coun.; delegate Democratic Party, 1996-98, 2006-; elected exec. bd. trustees UAW, 1999—2002. Grantee, Flint Arts Coun., 2004—. Mem.: United Automobile, Aerospace, Agrl. Implement Workers, Jerry B. Jenkins Christian Writers Guild, Poetry Soc. Am. Avocations: writing, nature photography, gardening, cookouts. Home and Office: PO Box 70 Flushing MI 48433 E-mail: Author58@yahoo.com.

BAIN, WILLIAM DONALD, JR., lawyer, chemicals executive; b. Rochelle, Ill., July 1, 1925; s. William Donald and Gretchen (Kittler) B.; m. Pauline Thomas, Jan. 14, 1950 (dec. Nov. 1991); children: Elizabeth Kittler Zibart, Anne Alexander, Nancy Hemenway Cotè; m. Barrie Feighner, Mar. 30, 1996. BS in Econs, U. Pa., 1947; JD, Washington and Lee U., 1949. Bar: SC 1952. Mortgage loan field rep. Travelers Ins. Co., Hartford, Conn., Cleve.; Orlando, Fla., 1949-51; with Moreland-McKesson Chem. Co., Spartanburg, SC, 1951-83, pres., 1965-83, also dir.; v.p., gen. mgr. McKesson Chem. Corp., San Francisco, 1982-84. Bd. dirs. Cote Color & Chem. Co., Inc., Spartan Comms. Corp., Tietex Corp.; co-founder, bd. dirs. Affiliated Chem. Group, Bermuda; ptnr. Triple B Ptnrs. Mem. Spartanburg Sch. Bd., 1958—72, chmn., 1963—72; trustee Converse Coll., 1968—92, chmn. bd., 1985—92; chmn. alumni bd. Washington and Lee U., 1979—82; trustee Hollins (Va.) Coll., 1992—98; bd. dirs. Mary Black Meml. Hosp., 1975—96, chmn., 1980—82; trustee Mary Black Found., 1996—2002; trustee, former chmn. Spartanburg County Found.; bd. dirs. Spartanburg Animal Shelter, 2002—; mng. dir. Bain Found. With USAAC, 1943—45. Mem. S.C. Bar, Rotary. Presbyterian.

BAIN, WILLIAM JAMES, JR., architect; b. Seattle, June 26, 1930; s. William James and Mildred Worline (Clark) B.; m. Nancy Sanford Hill, Sept. 21, 1957; children: David Hunter, Stephen Fraser (dec.), Mark Sanford, John Worthington. BArch, Cornell U., 1953. Lic. 1st class architect, Japan, lic. architect in U.K., Wash. Consulting design ptnr. NBBJ (formerly Naramore, Bain, Brady & Johanson), Seattle. Mem. affiliate program steering com. Coll. Architecture and Urban Planning, 1969-71; organizer founding bd. dirs. Pacific N.W. Bank; lectr. U. Wash., Wash. State U., NYU, Harvard U., Cornell, Tech. Transfer Inst. Japan. Prin. works include U. Wash. South Campus, U.S. Pavilion at Expo '74 Worlds Fair, Honolulu Mcpl. Bldg., Two Union Square High-Rise Office Bldg., Four Seasons Olympic Hotel and Sun Mountain Lodge, , U.S. District Courthouse, Seattle, Bagley Wright Theater, Paramount Theater renovation, Saitama Prefecture Demonstration Housing, Japan, Pacific Place Retail Complex, others. Bd. dirs. Arts Fund, 1989—, Arboretum Found., 1971-; bd. dirs. Downtown Seattle Assn., 1980—, 1st vice-chmn., 1990-91, chmn., 1991-92; bd. dirs. Seattle Symphony Orch., 1974-87, pres., 1977-79, lifetime dir.; mem. adv. coun. Coll. Architecture, Art & Planning, Cornell U., 1987-91, 94—, vis. com. U. Washington, 1999—; archl. adv. to bd. dirs. Seattle Pub. Libr.; adv. bd. Mus. History and Industry, Arcade Mag.; Citizen's Adv. Bd., 1997. With C.E., U.S. Army, 1953-55. Recipient Cert. of Achievement Port of Whittier, Alaska, 1955, Disting. Alumnus award Lakeside Sch., 1985, Jim Richards Founders award, Outstanding Alumnus, 2004; named to Hall Fame, Nat. Assn. Indsl. and Office Pks., 2004. Fellow AIA (pres. Seattle chpt. 1969, chmn. N.W. regional student profl. fund 1971, pres. Wash. coun. 1974, co-commn. Seattle centennial yr., Seattle medal 1997, Hall of Fame, 2004), N.W. Regional Archtl. Found. (pres. 1975); mem. Royal Inst. Brit. Architects, Japan Inst. Architects, Seattle C. of C. (bd. dirs. 1980-83), Urban Land Inst., Pacific Real Estate Inst., N.W. Forum, Am. Arbitration Assn. (comml. panel 1975—), L'Ogive Soc., Seattle Athletic Club, Seattle Tennis Club, Town Hall (bd. dirs. 2002—), Rotary (bd. dirs. 1970-72, svc. found. bd. 1976-80), Lambda Alpha Internat. (Robert Filly award 2003), Phi Delta Theta. Clubs: Rainier, Wash. Athletic, Tennis (Seattle); University. Episcopalian. Home: 2033 1st Ave Seattle WA 98121-2132 Office Phone: 206-223-5120. Office Fax: 206-621-2333. Business E-Mail: bbain@nbbj.com.

BAINBRIDGE, FREDERICK FREEMAN, III, architect; b. Charlottesville, Va., Sept. 15, 1927; s. Frederick Freeman and Cornelia Winston (Burnley) B.; m. Binki Baker, Jan. 6, 1948 (div. Nov. 1972); children—Burnley, Susan Winifred, Meriwether, Robin; m. Anna Bacon, Jan. 1976; 1 son, Nicholas Gordon. B.Arch., U. Va., 1950; M. Indsl. Design, Kansas City Art Inst., 1952. Asst. prof. Sch. Architecture Clemson (S.C.) U., 1952-55; asso. firm Toombs, Amisano & Wells (Architects), Atlanta, 1955-62; prin. firm Martin & Bainbridge, Atlanta, 1962-70, Bainbridge & Assos., 1970—. Southeastern project architect U. Ky. civil defense research project, 1964; vis. critic Ga. Inst. Tech., 1964-67 Chmn. archtl. rev. com. Atlanta Civic Design Commn., 1967—. Served with USNR, 1944-46. Recipient honor awards S. Atlantic Region AIA, 1964, 66, 68, 70; honor award prestressed Concrete Inst., 1967 Mem. AIA. Clubs: Fairington Golf and Tennis, Amelia Island Plantation; Farmington Country (Charlottesville, Va.). Home: Oldham Farm PO Box 317 Ivy VA 22945-0317 Office: 6795 Brandon Mill Rd NW Atlanta GA 30328-2028

BAINES, HAROLD DOUGLASS, retired professional baseball player, baseball bench coach; b. St. Michaels, Md., Mar. 15, 1959; m. Marla Henry, Oct. 29, 1983; 4 children: Antoinette, Britni, Harold, Jr., and Courtney. With Chgo. White Sox, 1980-89, 96-97, Texas Rangers, 1989-90, Oakland Athletics, 1990-92, Balt. Orioles, 1997—2000, Cleve. Indians, 2000, Chgo. White Sox, 2001; baseball analyst ESPN, 2002; bench coach Chgo. White Sox, 2004—. Named to Am. League All-Star Teams, 1985, 86, 87, 89, 91; named Outfielder Am. League Sporting News All-Star Team, 1985, designated hitter, 1988-89, Sporting News Am. League Silver Slugger Team, 1989. Office: Chgo White Sox 333 W 35th St Chicago IL 60616

BAINES, HENRY T., SR., supermarkets executive; CEO Baines Mgmt., Balt., Stop Shop Save, Balt., 2006—; operates 8 inner-city supermarkets Balt. Home and Office: Stop Shop Save Sixth Fl Ste 601-A 1100 Wicomico St Baltimore MD 21230 Home Phone: 410-783-8185; Office Phone: 410-608-7090. Personal E-mail: hbaines@comcast.net.

BAINES, KEVIN HAYS, astronomer, planetary scientist; b. Norwalk, Conn., Feb. 11, 1954; s. Elliot A. and Martha Ellen (Ashcroft) B.; m. Jenine Bsharah, June 4, 1982; children: Emily Ansara, Christopher Lewis. BA, Amherst Coll., 1976; MA, Washington U., St. Louis, 1978, PhD, 1982. Resident rsch. assoc. NRC-JPL, Pasadena, Calif., 1982-84; rsch. scientist Jet Propulsion Lab. Calif. Tech. Inst., Pasadena, 1984—2003, prin. scientist, Jet Propulsion Lab., 2003—. Contbr. articles to profl. jours. Flight dir. Aero Assn. Calif. Tech. Inst., 1986, 99--, treas., 1987-99. Virgil I. Grissom Astronaut fellow Washington U., 1976-79. Mem. AAAS (planetary scis. divsn.). Republican. Achievements include research in determination of vertical cloud/haze structures of Uranus and Neptune; role of asteroid-impact generated sulfuric gases on dinosaur extinctions; first to detect the spectrally-identifiable discrete ammonia ice clouds in Jupiter; determination of methane and ortho/para hydrogen above solar averages in Uranus and Neptune; near-infrared spectral imagery and analysis of the atmospheric cloud and compositional structures of Jupiter, Saturn and Titan from the Galileo, Cassini and New Horizons spacecraft; near-infrared imagery and spectroscopy of Venus surface from Galileo, Cassini and Venus Express spacecraft; near-infrared photometry of rings and satellites of Uranus and Saturn. Avocations: flight instructing, scuba diving. Home: 778 Forest Green Dr La Canada Flintridge CA 91011 Office Phone: 818-354-0481. Business E-Mail: kbaines@aloha.jpl.nasa.gov.

BAINS, HARRISON MACKELLAR, JR., retired corporate financial executive; b. Pasadena, Calif., July 8, 1943; s. Harrison MacKellar and Celeste Adele (Callahan) B.; m. Leslie E. Tawney, Mar. 7, 1970; children: Harrison MacKellar, III, Tawney Elizabeth. BA, U. Redlands, Calif., 1964; MBA, U. Calif., Berkeley, 1966. Asst. v.p. Citibank N.A., 1968-72; asst. treas. Richardson-Merrell Inc., 1972-76; v.p. treas. Nabisco Inc., East Hanover, NJ, 1976-81; sr. v.p., treas. Nabisco Brands, Inc., East Hanover, NJ, 1981-85; v.p., treas. RJR Nabisco, Inc., Winston-Salem, NC, 1985-87; sr. v.p. Chase Manhattan Bank, NYC, 1987-88; v.p., treas. Bristol-Myers Squibb Co., NYC, 1988—2002, acting CFO, 2002, v.p., treas., 2002—04; ret. Mem.: Fin. Execs. Inst.

BAINS, LESLIE ELIZABETH, banker; b. Glen Ridge, NJ, July 28, 1943; d. Pliny Otto and Dorothy Ethel (Keeley) Tawney; m. Harrison Mackellar Bains Jr.; Harrison III, Tawney Elizabeth. BA, Am. U., 1965. Asst. treas. Citicorp, NYC, 1965-73; v.p. Mfrs. Hanover, NYC, 1973-80; v.p., divsn. exec. Chase Manhattan Bank, NYC, 1980-86, v.p., group exec., 1986-87, sr. v.p. group exec., 1987-91; mng. dir. Global Pvt. Banking Group Citibank, NYC, 1991-93; exec. v.p. Republic Nat. Bank, NYC,

1993-2000; sr. exec. v.p. HSBC Bank USA, NYC, 2000—03, mem. sr. mgmt. com., 2000—03; ptnr. Raycliff Capital, 2005; vice-chmn., head private banking Modern Bank, NYC, 2006—. Bd. dirs., chair fin. com. Interplast, 1991. Chmn. Ednl. Cable Consortium, Summit, NJ, 1987—91; bd. dirs., chair fin. com. Interplast Found.; bd. dirs. Junior Achievement of N.Y.; mem. exec. com., bd. dirs., chair devel. com. Roundabout Theater; bd. trustees Am. Univ., 1994—2005, vice-chmn., chmn., 2001—05; bd. dirs. Jr. Achievement, NYC, 1996—, chair investment com.; bd. visitors Terry Sanford Inst. Pub. Policy Duke U., Duke U. Med. Sch. Named Achiever of Yr. YWCA, 1985, One of Top 100 Women in Corp. Am., Bus. Month., 1989. Fellow Fgn. Policy Assn; mem. Am. Bankers Assn. (bd. dirs. pvt. banking coun.), Fin. Women Internat. (vice chmn. Edn. Found. 1980-81, treas. 1981-83, v.p. 1983-84, pres. 1984-85), Fin. Women's Assn., Women and Founds., Coun. Fgn. Rels., The Econ. Club of N.Y. Office: Modern Bank 667 Madison Ave New York NY 10021*

BAINTON, DONALD J., diversified manufacturing company executive; b. NYC, May 3, 1931; s. William Lewis and Mildred J. (Dunne) B.; m. Aileen M. Demoulins, July 10, 1954; children: Kathryn C., Stephen L., Elizabeth A., William D. BA, Columbia U., 1952, postgrad., 1960. With Continental Group, Inc., 1954—67, gen. mgr. prodn. planning, 1967—68, gen. mgr. mfg. Ea. divsn., 1968—73, gen. mgr. Pacific divsn., 1973—74, gen. mgr. Ea. divsn., 1974—75; v.p., gen. mgr. ops. U.S. Metal, 1975—76; exec. v.p., gen. mgr. CCC-USA, 1976—78, corp. exec. v.p., pres. diversified ops., 1978—79; pres. Continental Can Co., 1979—81, Continental Packaging, 1981—83, exec. v.p., operating officer parent co., bd. dirs., 1979—83; chmn., CEO, dir. Viatech Inc., Syosset, NY, 1983—92; chmn., CEO Continental Can Co., Inc., Boca Raton, Fla., 1992—99; chmn., CEO, dir. Continental Can Co., Sunrise, Fla., 1999—. Bd. dirs. Viatech Inds., LLC. Bd. dirs. Columbia Coll. With USN, 1952-54, Korea. Mem. Inst. Applied Econs. (dir.), Milbrook Country Club (Greenwich, Conn.), Winged Foot Club (Mamaroneck, N.Y.), Union League Club (N.Y.C.), Royal Palm Yacht and Country Club (Boca Raton, Fla.). Republican. Roman Catholic.

BAINTON, DOROTHY FORD, pathologist, educator; b. Magnolia, Miss., June 18, 1933; d. Aubrey Ratcliff and Leta (Brumfield) Ford; m. Cedric R. Bainton, Nov. 28, 1959; children: Roland J., Bruce G., James H. BS, Millsaps Coll., 1955; MD, Tulane U. Sch. of Medicine, 1958; MS, U. Calif., San Francisco, 1966. Postdoctoral rsch. fellow U. Calif., San Francisco, 1963-66, postdoctoral rsch. pathologist, 1966-69, asst. prof. pathology, 1969-75, assoc. prof., 1975-81, prof. pathology, 1981—, chair pathology, 1987-94, vice chancellor acad. affairs, 1994—2004; ret. Mem. Inst. of Medicine, NAS, 1990—. Grantee, NIH, 1968—98. Fellow AAAS, Am. Acad. Arts & Scis.; mem. FASEB (bd. dirs.), Am. Soc. for Cell Biology, Am. Soc. Hematology, Am. Soc. Histochemists and Cytochemists, Am. Assn. of Pathologists. Democrat. Address: 50 Ventura Ave San Francisco CA 94116 E-mail: dbainton@mac.com.

BAINTON, J(OHN) JOSEPH, lawyer; b. Long Branch, NJ, May 21, 1947; s. Robert L. and Elizabeth (Dowling) B.; 1 child, John Joseph Jr. BA, Kenyon Coll., 1969; JD, Rutgers U., Newark, 1973. Bar: N.Y. 1973. Assoc. Burke & Burke, NYC, 1972-76; ptnr. Reboul, MacMurray, Hewitt, Maynard & Kristol, NYC, 1976-89, Shea & Gould, NYC, 1989-90, Whitman & Ransom, NYC, 1991-92, Ross & Hardies, NYC, 1993-98, Bainton McCarthy LLC, NYC, 1998—. Contbr. articles to legal jours. Mediator Mandatory Mediation Program So. Dist. N.Y. Mem.: Nat. Inst. Trial Advocacy (faculty), Products Liability Adv. Coun., Internat. Anti-counterfeiting Coalition (bd. dirs. 1986—92), Internat. Trademark Assn. (editor The Trademark Reporter 1976). Avocation: yacht racing. Office: Bainton McCarthy LLC 3 Stamford Landing 46 Southfield Ave Stamford CT 06902 also: Bainton McCarthy LLC 320 Carleton Ave Central Islip NY 11722-4502 also: Bainton McCarthy LLC 774 Broad St Newark NJ Office Phone: 212-480-3500. E-mail: bainton@baintonlaw.com.

BAINUM, PETER MONTGOMERY, aerospace engineer, consultant; b. St. Petersburg, Fla., Feb. 4, 1938; s. Charles J. Bainum and Mildred (Trincher) Salyer; m. Carmen Cecilia Perez, Sept. 7, 1968; 1 child, David P. BS, Tex. A&M U., 1959; SM, MIT, 1960; PhD, Cath. U., 1967. Asst. engr. Naval Supersonic Lab. MIT, Cambridge, 1959—60; sr. engr. Martin Co., Orlando, Fla., 1960—62; staff engr. Fed. Sys. divsn. IBM, Bethesda, Md., 1962—65; sr. staff, aerospace engr., cons. Applied Physics Lab. Johns Hopkins U., Laurel, Md., 1965—69, 1969—72; assoc. prof. Howard U., Washington, 1969—73, prof., 1973—90, disting. prof., 1990—2002, disting. prof. emeritus, 2003—. V.p. rsch., cons. WHF & Assocs., Bethesda, 1977-86; mem. NASA/PSN Tether Applications Simulation Working Group, 1987; lectr. various internat. univs., rsch. ctrs. and confs.; hon. vis. prof. Universidad Francisco Marroquin, Guatemala, 1991. Editor, co-editor 20 books, 1981-2004; contbr. articles to profl. jours. Judge, D.C. Sci. Fair, Washington, 1973; vol. docent Nat. Air and Space Mus., Smithsonian Instn., 2004—. Recipient Ralph R. Teetor award Soc. Automotive Engrs., 1971. Fellow: AAAS, AIAA (capital sect. cmty. action com. 1975—76, space transp. com. 1989—93, astrodynamics com. 3 terms, Sustained Svc. award 2005), Brit. Interplanetary Soc., Am. Astronautical Soc. (v.p. internat. 1986—96, bd. dirs., Brouwer award 1990, Spark M. Matsunaga Meml. award 2001); mem.: Internat. Astronautical Fedn. (materials and structures com. 1992—, chair 2006—), Japanese Rocket Soc. (hon.), Internat. Acad. Astronautics, Sigma Xi. Office: Howard Univ Dept Of Mechanical Engr Washington DC 20059-0001 Home Phone: 301-530-9690; Office Phone: 202-806-6612. Business E-Mail: pbainum@howard.edu. *With a doctoral degree comes significant responsibilities: to search out truth scientifically, to safeguard it, and to apply it to the shaping of both private and public life.*

BAIO, JOSEPH T., lawyer; b. NYC, July 24, 1953; BA, Columbia U., 1975; JD cum laude, NYU, 1978. Bar: NY 1979. Ptnr., litig. dept. Willkie Farr & Gallagher LLP, NYC, chair Mktg. Com. Lectr. Columbia U.; dir. inMotion, 1998—. Mem.: Assn. Bar of City NY. Office: Willkie Farr & Gallagher LLP 787 Seventh Ave New York NY 10019 Office Phone: 212-728-8203. E-mail: jbaio@willkie.com.

BAIR, BRUCE BLYTHE, lawyer; b. St. Paul, May 26, 1928; s. Bruce B. and Emma N. (Stone) B.; m. Jane Lawler, July 19, 1952; children: Mary Jane, Thomas, Susan, Barbara, Patricia, James, Joan, Bruce, Jeffrey. BS, U. N.D., 1950, JD, 1952. Bar: ND 1952, US Dist. Ct. ND 1955, U.S. Ct. Appeals (8th cir.) 1971, US Supreme Ct. 1974. Assoc. Lord and Ulmer, Mandan, ND, 1955-57; ptnr. Bair, Bair, and Garrity, Mandan, 1957—2001, of counsel, 2002—. Spl. asst. atty. gen. ND Milk Mktg. Bd., 1967—; chmn. bd. Bank of Tioga, 1984-2003, also bd. dirs.; Rep. precinct committeeman, 1956-70, chmn. Morton County Rep. Com., 1958-62, mem. ND Rep. State Ctrl. Com., 1962-67; pres. sch. bd. St. Joseph's Cath. Ch., 1967-68; bd. dirs. Mandan Pub. Sch. Dist. #1, 1971-77; exec. com. Internat. Assn. Milk Control Agys., 1970-2000; bd. regents U. Mary, Bismarck, ND, 1984—. 1st lt. JAG Corps USAF, 1952-55. Mem.: ABA, ND Bar Assn., Am. Coll. Barristers (sr. counsel), Am. Legion, Elks, Rotary. Roman Catholic. Home: 901 3rd St NW Mandan ND 58554-2537 Office: 210 1st St NW Mandan ND 58554-3115

BAIR, ROYDEN STANLEY, retired architect; b. New Rochelle, NY, Jan. 21, 1924; s. Roy S. and Ruth Irene (Farmer) B.; m. Margaret Davis Powell, Sept. 7, 1946 (dec. July 1972); children: Katherine, David, Laurence (dec. 1990), Andrew, Matthew; m. Martha Ann Cooper, July 7, 1973. BS in Civil Engring., Purdue U., 1947; BArch, MIT, 1950. Registered architect, Tex, Fla.; registered profl. engr., Tex. Construction adminstrn. Skidmore, Owings & Merrill, Chgo., 1950—51; draftsman J.N. MacCammon, Dallas, 1953-56; sr. assoc. Harrell & Hamilton, Dallas, 1956-67; sr. architect Lloyd Morgan Jones, Houston, 1967-68; owner R.S. Bair, Architects, Houston, 1969-95; ptnr. Turner & Bair Architects, Houston, 1996—2002. Capt. U.S. Army, 1942-46, 51-53. Mem. AIA (fellowship 1988, pres. Houston chpt. 1982), Construction Specifications Inst. (nat. pres. 1979, fellowship 1972), Construction Scis. Rsch. Found. (v.p. 1980-87), Tex. Soc. Architects. Home: 9573 Doliver Dr Houston TX 77063-1010 E-mail: stanandmartha@houston.rr.com.

BAIR, SHEILA COLLEEN, federal agency administrator; b. Wichita, Kans., Apr. 3, 1954; d. Albert E. and Clara F. (Brenneman) B.; m. Scott P. Cooper; children, Preston, Colleen. BA in Philosophy, U. Kans., 1975, JD, 1978. Bar: Kans. 1979. Teaching fellow U. Ark. Sch. Law, Fayetteville, 1978-79; atty.-advisor HEW, Kansas City, Mo., 1979-81; legal and policy advisor to Senator Bob Dole US Senate, Washington, 1981-86; of counsel Kutak, Rock & Campbell, Washington, 1986-87; dir. rsch. Bob Dole for Pres., Kans., 1987-88; legis. counsel NY Stock Exch., Washington, 1988-91, sr. v.p. govt. rels., 1995—2000; commr. Commodity Futures Trading Commn., Washington, 1991—95, acting chmn., 1993; asst. sec. for fin. institutions US Dept Treasury, Washington, 2001—02; Dean's prof. fin. regulatory policy U. Mass., Amherst, 2002—06; mem. FDIC, Washington, 2006—, chmn., 2006—. Author: Rock, Brock, and the Savings Shock, 2006. Recipient Treasury medal, 2002, Disting. Achievement award, Assn. Edn. Publishers, 2005. Mem.: Soc. Children's Book Writers & Illustrators, Exchequer Club, ABA, Women's Campaign Fund, Mass. Savings Makes Cents, NASD Ahead-of-the-Curve Adv. Com., Women in Housing & Fin. Ctr. for Responsible Lending, Ins. Marketplace Standards Assn. Office: FDIC 550 17th St NW Washington DC 20429*

BAIR, THOMAS J., publishing executive; married; 1 child. BA, Pa. State U. Ad dir. Fairchild Sports Group, 1992—93; territory mgr., New England Men's Health, NY, 1993—95, advertising mgr. NY, 1995—97, advertising dir. NY, 1997—2000, assoc. pub. NY, 2000—01, Golf Digest Cos., 2001—04, v.p., publisher, 2004—. Office: Golf Digest Co 20 Westport Rd PO Box 850 Wilton CT 06897 Office Phone: 212-286-2888.*

BAIR, WILLIAM ALOIS, engineer; b. Bklyn., Aug. 13, 1931; s. Henry Auchu and Anna Margaret (Zidar) B.; m. Patricia Anne Doyle, July 23, 1955; children: William A. Jr., Joseph M. Student, Pa. State U., 1949-51; BS in Engring., U.S. Naval Acad., 1955; BS in Civil Engring., Rensselaer Poly. Inst., 1958; MS in Nuclear Engring., U. Calif., 1966; grad. advanced mgmt. program, Wharton Sch., 1987. Registered profl. engr., N.Y., N.J., Pa., Conn., Md., Del., Va., S.C., Ga., D.C. Commd. ensign USN, 1955, advanced through grades to comdr., 1969; with USN Civil Engr. Corps, 1957—77; ret. USN, 1977; project mgr. Ebasco Svc. Inc., Princeton, NY, 1977—85, Raytheon Engrs. & Constrn., NYC, 1988—96; dir. program planning and devel. Ebasco Svcs. Inc., NYC, 1985—88; pres. Bair Engring. Cons., 1996—. Appointed mem. spl. 3 man NATO tech. com. to evaluate effectiveness of European Airfield Phys. Protection Program to counter damage from attack by Warsaw Pact Nations, 1972-75. Author: Helium 3 Neutron Spectrometer, 1966; contbr. articles to profl. jours. Scoutmaster Boy Scouts Am., Rockville, Md., 1969-70; coun. mem. European br., Casteau, Belgium, 1971-75. Decorated Legion of Merit, Bronze Star with V, Joint Svc. Commendation medal, Vietnamese Cross of Gallantry, Vietnamese Medal of Honor 1st class. Fellow ASCE; mem. Am. Nuclear Soc., Soc. Am. Mil. Engrs., Am. Legion, VFW. Republican. Roman Catholic. Achievements include research and development of innovative processes/procedures for decontamination and demolition of radioactive contaminated structures. Home and Office: Bair Engring Cons 21 Lorrie Ln Princeton Junction NJ 08550-5112 Home Phone: 609-799-0624; Office Phone: 609-799-0624.

BAIR, WILLIAM J., retired radiobiologist; b. Jackson, Mich., July 14, 1924; s. William J. and Mona J. (Gamble) B.; m. Barbara Joan Sites, Feb. 16, 1952; children: William J., Michael Braden, Andrew Emil. BA in Chemistry, Ohio Wesleyan U., 1949; PhD in Radiation Biology, U. Rochester, 1954. NRC-AEC fellow U. Rochester, 1949-50, rsch. assoc. radiation biology, 1950-54; biol. scientist Hanford Labs. of GE, Richland, Wash., 1954-56, mgr. inhalation toxicology sect., biology dept., 1956-65, Battelle Meml. Inst., 1965-68; mgr. biology dept. Pacific Northwest Nat. Labs., Richland, 1968-74, dir. life scis. program, 1973-75, mgr. biomed. and environ. rsch. program, 1975-76, mgr. environ. health and safety rsch. program, 1976-86, mgr. life scis. ctr., 1986-93, sr. advisor health protection rsch., 1993—2002; ret., 2002. Demonstrated toxicology of plutonium and carcinogenisis of radioactive particles in lung; lectr. radiation biology Joint Ctr. Grad. Study, Richland, 1955-75; cons. to adv. com. on reactor safeguards Nuc. Regulatory Commn., 1971-87; mem. com. on plutonium toxicology; subcom. inhalation hazards, com. pathologic effects atomic radiation NAS, 1957-64, ad hoc com. on hot particles of subcom. biol. effects ionizing radiation NAS-NRC, 1974-76, vice-chmn. com. on biol. effects of ionizing radiation, BEIR IV Alpha radiation, 1985-88, battlefield radiation exposure com., 1997-99; chmn. task force on biol. effects of inhaled particles Internat. Commn. on Radiol. Protection, 1970-79, com. 2 on permissible dose for internal radiation, 1973-93, chmn. task group on respiratory tract models, 1984-93; mem. Nat. Coun. on Radiation Protection and Measurements, 1974-92, hon. mem., 1992-, com. on maximum permissible concentration of radionuclides for occupl. and nonoccupl. exposure, 1970-74, com. basic radiation protection criteria, 1975-93, chmn. ad hoc com. on hot particles, 1974, chmn. ad hoc com. internal emitter activities, 1976-77, com. on internal emitter stds., 1977-92, chmn. com. mgmt. of persons contaminated with radionuclides, 2004—, Lauriston S. Taylor lectr., 1997; radiation adv. com. and sci. adv. bd. EPA, 1993-99; founder, pres. Herbert M. Parker Found., 1987-94, bd. trustees, 1994-; cons. in field, 2002-. Author 200 books, articles, reports, chpts. in books. With US Army, 1943—46. Decorated Bronze Star; recipient Combat Infantry Badge US Army, E.O. Lawrence Meml. award AEC, 1970, cert. of appreciation AEC, 1975, Alumni Disting. Achievement citation Ohio Wesleyan U. Fellow AAAS (life), Health Physics Soc. (life, bd. dirs. 1970-73, 83-86, pres. elect 1983-84, pres. 1984-85, Disting. Sci. Achievement award 1991, Herbert H. Parker award Columbia chpt. 1998, J.N. Stannard lectr. No. Calif. chpt. and Sierra Nev. chpt. 2004); mem. Internat. Commn. Radiological Protection, Radiation Rsch. Soc., Soc. Exptl. Biology and Medicine (vice chmn. N.W. chpt. 1967-70, 74-75), Sigma Xi. Avocations: wildlife photography, woodcarving, fly fishing, orchids, wood turning. Home: 578 Clermont Dr Richland WA 99352-1966

BAIRD, ALICE KNAR, retired education educator; b. Sivas, Turkey, Nov. 11, 1918; arrived in U.S., 1920; d. Harry and Marguerite Seradarian Shamlian; m. James Abington Baird, Dec. 2, 2000; m. Lloyd William Barter, 1940 (div. 1958); 1 child, Andrea Marguerite Barter. BA, Eastern Mich. U., 1939; MA, U. Mich., 1944, PhD, 1957. Tchr. Mich. Pub. Sch., 1939—55; asst. prof. edn. U. Detroit, 1957—60; asst. to assoc. prof. English and edn. Miami U., Oxford, Ohio, 1960—67; prof. English Chgo. State U., 1967—89, chmn. dept. English and speech, 1980—83, acting dean coll. arts and scis., 1984. Vis. prof. Nanjing U., Nanjing, China, 1986. Author: Spelling by Sound and Sequence: A Phonemic Speller, 1975, Tools: A Guide to Basic Grammar and Writing, 1987, Saroyan's Armenians: An Anthology, 1992, Theaters of the Heart and Mind, 1998; contbr. articles to profl. jours. Avocation: sculpting. Home: 85Nottingham Cross Bowling Green OH 43402-9384

BAIRD, BRIAN N., congressman; b. Chama, N.Mex., Mar. 7, 1956; m. Rachel Nugent; 2 children. BS in Psych., U. Utah, 1977; MS, U. Wyo., 1980, PhD in Clin. Psych., 1984. Mem. faculty dept. psych. Pacific Luth. U., 1986—97; mem. US Congress from 3rd Wash. dist., 1999—, mem. transp. and infrastructure com., mem. budget com., mem. sci. com., mem. select com. on continuity in govt. Cons. clin. psychologist St. Charles Med. Ctr., 1994-96. Author: The Internship Practicum Handbook, Are We Having Fun Yet?. Mem.: Wash. State Psychol. Assn., APA. Democrat. Office: US Ho Reps 1421 Longworth Ho Office Bldg Washington DC 20515-0001 Office Phone: 202-225-3536.*

BAIRD, BRUCE ALLEN, lawyer; b. Cin., Mar. 26, 1948; s. William Wendell and Audrey (Geignetter) B.; m. Erica Borden, July 27, 1975 (div. 1993); 1 child, Jessica; m. Nicolette Adair Heidepriem, Sept. 17, 1993; 1 child, William. BA, Cornell U., 1970; JD, NYU, 1975. Spl. asst. to dep. atty. gen. U.S. Dept. Justice, Washington, 1975-76; law clk. to presiding judge U.S. Ct. Appeals (2d cir.), Brattleboro, Vt. and NYC, 1976-77; assoc. Davis, Polk & Wardwell, NYC, 1977-80; asst. U.S. atty. U.S. Attys. Office (so. dist.) N.Y., NYC, 1980-86, dep. chief criminal div., 1986-87, chief narcotics unit, 1987, chief securities and commodities frauds unit, 1987-89; of counsel Covington & Burling, Washington, 1989-91, ptnr., 1991—. Editor in chief NYU Law Rev., 1974-75. Mem. ABA (co-chair securities and commodities fraud subcom. of white collar crime com. of criminal justice sect. 1994-2004), N.Y. State Bar Assn. (profl. jud. ethics com. 1982-89), Assn. of Bar of City of N.Y. (profl. jud. ethics com. 1979-82, 86-89), Fed. Bar Coun., D.C. Bar Assn. Republican. Presbyterian. Home: 5404 Edgemoor Ln Bethesda MD 20814-1326 Office Phone: 202-662-5122. E-mail: bbaird@cov.com.

BAIRD, C. RONALD, lawyer; b. Wichita, Kans., Sept. 3, 1945; s. Charles Lester and Olive Claire Baird; m. Paula A. Paird, June 7, 1969; children: Kristen Roubal, Teresa, Patrick. Assoc., Joplin Jr. Coll., Mo., 1965; BA, Washington U., St. Louis, 1967; JD, U. Mo., Columbia, 1974. Cert.: Am. Acad. Matrimonial Lawyers. Shareholder Baird, Lightner, Millsap & Marpool PC, Springfield, Mo., 1974—. Lt. (j.g.) USN, 1967—71. Mem.: Mo. Bar (pres. 2006—07). Avocations: reading, golf, travel. Home: 2916 S Versailes Springfield MO 65804 Office: Baird LIghtner Millsap & Marpool PC 1949 E Sunshine Ste 2-102 Springfield MO 65804

BAIRD, CHARLES BRUCE, lawyer, consultant; b. DeLand, Fla., Apr. 18, 1935; s. James Turner and Ethelyn Isabelle (Williams) B.; m. Barbara Ann Fabian, June 6, 1959 (div. Dec. 1979); children: C. Bruce Jr., Robert Arthur, Bryan James; m. Byung-Ran Cho, May 23, 1982; children: Merah-Iris, Haerah Violet. BSME, U. Miami, 1958; postgrad., UCLA, 1962-64; MBA, Calif. State U., 1966; JD, Am. U., 1971. Bar: Va. 1971, U.S. Dist. Ct. (ea. dist.) Va. 1971, D.C. 1973, U.S. Dist. Ct. D.C. 1973, U.S. Ct. Appeals (4th cir.) 1974, U.S. Supreme Ct. 1975. Rsch. engr. Naval Ordnance Lab., Corona, Calif., 1961-67; aerospace engr. Naval Air Systems Command, Washington, 1967-69; cons. engr. Bird Engring. Rsch. Assts., Vienna, Va., 1969-71; prof. Def. Systems Mgmt. Coll., Ft. Belvoir, Va., 1982; spl. asst. for policy compliance USIA Voice of Am., Washington, 1983-84. Cons. Booz, Allen & Hamilton, Inc., Bethesda, 1975-82, IBM, Bethesda, Md., 1984, Logistics Mgmt. Inst., McLean, Va., 1986-98, 2002—, TelcoExchange.com, 1998-2000, 2001; adj. prof. Fla. Inst. Tech., 1988. Contbr. articles to profl. jours.; inventor computer-based comm. systems for the gravely handicapped. Bd. govs. Sch. Engring. U. Miami, 1957; trustee Galilee United Meth. Ch., Arlington, Va., 1983-87. Officer USN, 1958-61. Mem. ACLU, NRA, Va. Trial Lawyers Assn., Am. Assn. Justice, Internet. Soc., Fed. Comm. Bar Assn., Sigma Alpha Epsilon. Home and Office: 5396 Gainsborough Dr Fairfax VA 22032-2744

BAIRD, DEBRA, dean, education educator; b. Birmingham, Ala., Aug. 3, 1954; d. Clyde Leon Baird and Mardie Beatrice Mullinax; m. Alton Leonard Wilson, Jr. BS, Auburn U., Ala., 1976; MA, U. Ala., Tuscaloosa, 1987, PhD, 1990. Instr. U. Ala., Tuscaloosa, 1987—90; asst. prof. Austin Coll., Sherman, Tex., 1990—94; assoc. prof. U. W. Ala., Livingston, 1994—99; prof., chair Stillman Coll., Tuscaloosa, 1999—2004; prof., dean Athens State U., Ala., 2004—. Home: 3491 County Rd 3459 Haleyville AL 35565 Office: Athens State U 300 N Beaty St Athens AL 35611

BAIRD, DONNA SELMA, counselor, educator; d. David Hilton and Flora Baird; life ptnr. Richie Benaud Habib; 1 child, Kennedi Kyla White. BS, U. Md.; PhD, Capella U., Mpls., 2002. Cert. counselor Nat. Bd. Cert. Counselors, lic. clin. profl. counselor Md., profl. counselor Washington. Postdoctoral rsch. fellow Georgetown U., Washington, 2005—; adj. asst. prof. U. Md. Univ. Coll., College Park, 2005—; clinician Potomac Ridge Behavioral Health, Rockville, Md., 2006—. Clinician Pro Bono Counseling Project, Balt., 2005; amb. Capella U., 2005. Grantee, Georgetown U., Dept. Internat. Health-Sch. Nursing and Health Studies, 2006; Minority Rsch. Supplement fellow, Nat. Insts. Drug Abuse, 2005—. Mem.: APA (assoc. Dissertation Rsch. award 2002), Internat. AIDS Soc. (assoc.), Chi Sigma Iota. Seventh Day Adventist. Avocations: travel, bicycling, reading. Office: Georgetown U 3700 Reservoir Rd NW Washington DC 20057-1107 Home Phone: 301-871-3744; Office Phone: 202-687-9454. Office Fax: 202-687-9466. Business E-Mail: dsb39@georgetown.edu.

BAIRD, DOUGLAS GORDON, law educator, dean; b. Phila., July 10, 1953; s. Henry Welles and Eleanora (Gordon) B. BA in English summa cum laude, Yale U., 1975; JD, Stanford U., 1979; LLD (hon.), U. Rochester, 1994. Law clk. to Hon. Shirley M. Hufstedler US Ct. Appeals 9th Cir., 1979, law clk. to Hon. Dorothy W. Nelson, 1980; asst. prof. law U. Chgo. Law Sch., 1980-83, prof., 1984—87, Harry A. Bigelow prof. law, 1988—96, Harry A. Bigelow disting. svc. prof. law, 1996—, assoc. dean, 1984-87, dean, 1994-99. Vis. prof. law Stanford U., 1987—88, Yale U., 2000; Robert Braucher vis. prof. law Harvard U., 1993. Author: The Elements of Bankruptcy, 1992, 4th edit., 2006; co-author:(with Gertner & and Picker) Game Theory and the Law, 1994. Fellow: Am. Coll. Bankruptcy, Am. Acad. Arts and Scis. Office: U Chgo Sch Law 1111 E 60th St Chicago IL 60637-2776 Office Phone: 773-702-9571.

BAIRD, DOUGLAS JAMES, investment banker; b. Rochester, NY, Feb. 3, 1962; s. James David and Carol Agatha (Pascale) B.; m. Sarah Lee Stevenson, Dec. 12, 1987; children: David Harrington, Henry Stevenson, Roxanna Margaret. Diploma, Deerfield (Mass.) Acad., 1980; AB Dartmouth Coll., 1984; MBA, Amos Tuck Sch., Hanover, NH, 1989. Fin. analyst pub. fin. group Merrill Lynch Capital Markets, NYC, 1984-85, jr. assoc. internat. fin. group, 1985-86; assoc. equity transactions group Merrill Lynch Europe Ltd., London, 1986-87; assoc. mergers and acquisitions Merrill Lynch Capital Markets, NYC, 1988, Alex. Brown & Sons, Balt., 1989-91, v.p. corp. fin. environ. svcs., 1991-93, mng. dir. equity capital markets, 1993-99; co-head U.S. equity capital mkts. Deutsche Bank Securities, NYC, 2000—07; head equity capital markets The Bank Am. Corp., 2007—. Mem. adv. bd. applied corp. fin. program U. Wis., Madison; mem. bd. advisors Ind. Securities Rsch., LLC; trustee Boys' Latin Sch. of Md.; bd. dirs. PACT: Helping Children with Spl. Needs; intern, White House Office of Media Relations and Planning, 1983. Mem. Yale Club of N.Y.C., Maryland Club, Webhannet Country Club, Balt. Country Club, Univ. Club, Downtown Assn. Republican. Episcopalian. Office: The Bank Am Corp 100 N Tryon St Charlotte NC 28255*

BAIRD, DUGALD EUAN, automotive executive; b. Aberdeen, Scotland, Sept. 16, 1937; came to U.S., 1979; s. Dugald and Matilda Deans (Tennant) B.; m. Angelica Hartz, May 24, 1961; children: Camilla N., Maiken E. MA in Geophysics, Cambridge U., 1960; LLD, Aberdeen U., 1995, Dundee U., 1998; DSc, Heriot-Watt U., 1999. Joined Schlumberger, 1960, various field assignments worldwide, 1979—86, chmn., CEO, 1986—2003; ret., 2003; chmn. Rolls-Royce Plc, 2003—. Mem. Prime Min. Com. Nat. de la Sci., France, 1998—2002, Prime Mins. Coun. Sci. and Tech, England, 2000—, adv. com. Banque de France, 2001—; mem. bd. ScottishPower. Trustee Carnegie Instn., Washington, 1998—. Office: Rolls-Royce plc 65 Buckingham Gate London SW1E 6AT England

BAIRD, EDWARD ROUZIE, JR., retired lawyer; b. Norfolk, Va., Aug. 29, 1936; s. Edward Rouzie and Eleanor Gray (Perry) B.; m. Nell McGlaughon, Oct. 8, 1967 (dec. Oct. 1973); 1 child, Eleanor Gray; m. Abby St. John Starke, Feb. 5, 1977; children: Abby St. John, Edward Rouzie V. BA, U. Va., 1960, LLB, 1967. Assoc. Baird, Creshaw & Ware, Norfolk, 1967—68; asst. dist. counsel U.S. Army C.E., Norfolk, 1968—73; asst. U.S. Atty. U.S. Atty.'s Office, Norfolk, 1973—77; sole practice Norfolk, 1977—82, 1999—2004; ptnr. Willcox & Baird, Norfolk, 1982—99. Served to lt. (j.g.) USN, 1960-63. Mem. Soc. Cin., Va. Club (Norfolk). Home: 1711 Cloncurry Rd Norfolk VA 23505-1717 E-mail: edwardbaird@mac.com.

BAIRD, JAMES, lawyer; b. Ann Arbor, Mich., Oct. 23, 1943; BA, Mich. State Univ., 1965; JD, Univ. Wis., 1968; LLM highest honors, George Washington Univ., 1970. Bar: Wis. 1968, Ill. 1972. Articles editor Wis. Bar Jour., 1967-68; atty. to bd. mem. NLRB, 1968-70; asst. dir. Labor Mgt. Rels. Svc., Washington, 1970—72; ptnr. Seyfarth & Shaw, Chgo., 1978—. Chmn. Ill. State C. of C. Labor Rels. Comm., 1978—80. Mem. ABA (mgmt. chmn. com. state labor law devels. 1975-76, com. state and local govt. bargaining 1976-79, sect. labor rels. law, chmn. com. pub. employee bargaining, sect. urban, state and local govt. law 1981-84, mem. gov. coun. sect. urban, state and local govt. law 1991-92, sect. chair, urban, state and local govt. law 1994-95, ho. del. 1994-, bd. gov. 2004-), Fed. Bar Assn. (mem. state and local govt. reaction panel 1972—). Office: Seyfarth Shaw LLP 131 S Dearborn St Ste 2400 Chicago IL 60603*

BAIRD, JAMES ABINGTON, retired judge; b. Kirksville, Mo., Jan. 28, 1926; s. James Abington and Dorothy (LaGest) Baird; m. Georgia Jane Suliburk, Mar. 29, 1948 (dec. Dec. 1999); children: James Abington III, Mary J.; m. Alice K. Barter, Dec. 2, 2000. BS, U. Mich., 1949; JD, U. Toledo, 1957. Bar: Ohio 1957. Sales rep. Fruehauf Trailer Co., Chgo., 1949-50, Warren-Teed Products Co., Toledo, 1951-52, Dictaphone Corp., Toledo, 1952-53; pres. Kaiser-Frazer dealership, Caro, Mich., 1950-51; claims adjuster Nationwide Ins. Co., Toledo, 1953-57; pvt. practice Toledo; judge Sylvania Ohio Mcpl. Ct., 1970-82; ret., 1982. Chmn. Sch. Levy campaigns Sylvania Pub. Sch. Sys., 1968—69, candidate sch. bd., 1969. With USNR, 1944—46. Mem.: Toledo Bar Assn., U. Toledo Alumni Assn., U. Mich. Alumni Assn., Bowling Green Country Club, Phi Delta Theta. Home: 85 Nottingham Cross Bowling Green OH 43402-9384 E-mail: baird@wcnet.org.

BAIRD, JAMES KERN, educator, consultant, academic administrator; b. Pitts., Aug. 24, 1941; s. Paul Erwin and Helen Elizabeth (Kern) B.; m. Peggy Lorane Flanagan, 1967; 1 child, David Kern. BS, Yale U., 1963; AM, Harvard U., 1965, PhD, 1969. Physicist Oak Ridge (Tenn.) Nat. Lab., 1970-81; unit mgr. Knolls Atomic Power Lab., Schenectady, N.Y., 1981-82; prof., chmn. chemistry dept. U. Ala., Huntsville, 1982—90, 2001—05. Cons. Chrysler Acutron Div., Huntsville, 1988-89, Morton Thiokol, 1988-89, SCI, Huntsville, 1989, Urisphere, Arlington, Va., 1999-2000, Wilmer and Lee, Huntsville, 2002—; vis. prof. chemistry Yale U., 1998-99, 2007. Contbr. numerous articles to profl. jours. Disting. summer faculty rsch. fellow Naval Rsch. Lab., Washington, 1993, NASA/MSFC, 2001. MEM. Am. Chem. Soc. (Charles H. Stone award Carolina Piedmont sect. 1991), Am. Phys. Soc. Home: 4023 Lucerne Dr SE Huntsville AL 35802-1244 Office: U Ala Dept Chemistry Huntsville AL 35899-0001 Office Phone: 256-824-6441. E-mail: jkbaird@matsci.uah.edu.

BAIRD, JOHN ABSALOM, JR., retired academic administrator; b. Honolulu, Sept. 13, 1918; s. John Absalom and Helen (Bates) Baird; m. Virginia Walton, Mar. 8, 1941 (dec. 1983); m. Clare A. Emmons, May 12, 1984 (dec. 1998). AB, Princeton U., 1940; postgrad., Johns Hopkins U., 1941. Asst. supt. Charles S. Walton Co., 1942-47, asst. sec. and dir., 1947-52, v.p., 1952-72; asst. pres. Ea. Bapt. Theol. Sem., Phila., Ea. Coll., St. Davids, Pa., 1952-61, v.p., 1961-88, advisor to pres., 1988—2002; ret., 2002. Author: A Leap of Faith, 1972, The Whole Gospel for the Whole World, 1975, All Things are Thine, 1976, Profile of a Hero, 1977, The Shining Fire, 1979, Horn of Plenty, 1982, Great House, 1984, Promises to Keep, 1989, More Than Knowledge, 1992, Power of One, 1997, Inheritance of Value, 1999; contbr. articles to profl. jours. Trustee, v.p. Pa. Lupus Found.; trustee Ludington Libr., Bryn Mawr, Ralston House, Phila., Vol. Svcs. for the Blind, Phila., 1971—85; vice chmn. Main Line br. YMCA Greater Phila., 1947—63; Phila. Main Line dist. chmn. Valley Forge coun. Boy Scouts Am., 1952—54, dist. commr., 1954—56; mem. adv. bd. Phila. Inglis House, 1963—2003; bd. dirs. Am. Ednl. Film and Video Ctr., 1964—2002; chmn. bd. trustees Shipley Sch., Bryn Mawr, Pa., 1972—78; v.p. Pa. chpt. Lupus Found. Am., 1973—95; trustee 4th Bapt. Mission Found., 1976—80, Seaman's Ch. Inst., Phila., 1998—2003; bd. dirs. Pa. United Theol. Sem. Found., Pitts.; v.p., bd. dirs. Am. Sunday Sch. Union, Phila., 1957—69; mem. adv. bd. Phila. Inglis House, 1963—2003; bd. dirs. Watchman Examiner Corp., NYC, 1958—70, Athenaeum, Phila., Beaumont Retirement Cmty.; bd. corporators, bd. dirs. Covenant Life Ins. Co., 1968—92; mem. Union League. Recipient Honor medal, Freedom Founds., 1973. Mem.: Geneal. Soc. Pa. (dir. 1988—2003), Am. Coll. Pub. Rels. Assn., Hist. Soc. Pa. (dir. 1992—2001), Pa. Acad. Fine Arts, U.S. Naval Found., Am. Alumni Coun., Am. Bapt. Pub. Rels. Assn., U.S. Naval Inst., Am. Assn. Sem. Staff Officers (pres. 1966—68), Am. Philatelic Soc., Am. Rose Soc., Merion Cricket Club (Haverford, Pa.), Right Angle Club, Penn Club, Soc. Colonial Wars (gov. 1991—94), English-Speaking Union, S.R., Order Fgn. Wars, Colonial Soc. Pa. (gov. 1994—97), Soc. of Cin. (pres. Del. 1972—75, sec. gen. 1977—83), Loyal Legion. Republican. Presbyterian. Home: 74 Pasture Ln # 116 Bryn Mawr PA 19010-1766

BAIRD, JULIAN THOMPSON, JR., entrepreneur; b. Harlingen, Tex., Jan. 28, 1938; s. Julian Thompson and Faye Devilbiss Baird; m. Carol Friedell Baird (div. 1985); m. Elaine Fraser Baird, Jan. 9, 1986. AB magna cum laude, Harvard U., 1960, PhD, 1968; BA, Oxford U., Eng., 1962, MA, 1967. Assoc. prof. Boston U., 1967-80; pres. Baird Enterprises, Orleans, Mass., 1981—. Lectr. Cape Mus. Fine Art, Old Lyme Acad. Art, St. Botolph Club, Boston, others; keynote spkr., organizer Nat. Conf. on Representational Painting, 2004. Contbr. articles to profl. jours. Mem. Orleans Charter Commn., 1989-90; pres. Orleans Bd. of Trade, 1983-84, Orleans Taxpayers Assn., 1985-87; fine wine charity auctioneer Cape Mus. Fine Arts, 1994-96. Recipient Spl. Distinction award Boston U. Alumni Assn., 1990; named one of 400 People Who Brighten Our LIves, Cape Cod Life mag., 2005. Mem. St. Botolph Club, Oxford and Cambridge Soc. Avocations: collecting art, wine and books, boating, gardening, computers, investing. Home: 4 Mayflower Cir PO Box 1145 Orleans MA 02653-0666 Personal E-mail: jbaird@pobox.com.

BAIRD, LEONARD LYNN, social scientist, educator, researcher, editor; s. Russel Thomas and Edith Isabel Baird; m. Rosanne Clark Baird, Oct. 19, 1962; children: William Russell, Diana Ragan. BA, U. Calif., LA, 1962, MA, 1965, EdD, 1966. Rsch. psychologist Am. Coll. Testing Program, Iowa City, 1966—69; sr. rsch. psychologist Ednl. Testing Svc., Princeton, NJ, 1969—83; prof. U. Ky., Lexington, 1983—94, Ohio State U., Columbus, 1994—; editor Jour. of Higher Edn., Columbus, 1994—. Editl. bd. Rsch. in Higher Edn., 1987—96. Author: (books) The Elite Schools, 1977; author: (and editor) Understanding Student and Faculty Life, 1980, Increasing Grad. Student Retention, 1993; contbr. chapters to books, articles to profl. jours. Recipient Sydney Suslow award for outstanding rsch., Assn. for Instl. Rsch., 1991, Sr. Scholar award, Am. Coll. Pers. Assn., 2003. Office: Ohio State U 301 Ramseyer Columbus OH 43210 Business E-Mail: baird.62@osu.edu.

BAIRD, LISA P., marketing executive; m. Robert Baird; 2 children. Grad., Pa. State U. Brand mgr. General Motors; with Proctor & Gamble, Bristol-Myers Squibb, Warner Lambert; v.p., worldwide advertising IBM, 2000—03, v.p., worldwide integrated marketing communications, 2003—05; sr. v.p., marketing NFL, 2005—. Office: c/o NFL 280 Park Ave New York NY 10017

BAIRD, MARIANNE SAUNORUS, critical care clinical nurse specialist, administrator; b. Chgo., Dec. 15, 1953; d. John and Irene Saunorus; m. Thomas W. Baird, Sept. 10, 1983; 1 child, Rachel BSN, Loyola U., Chgo., 1975; MSN, Emory U., 1982. Critical care RN; cert. instr. ACLS, Ga. Supr. surg. nursing Rush U. Med. Ctr., Chgo., 1978—80; from dir. med. surg. unit to staff nurse Intensive Care to clin. nurse specialist Critical Care St. Joseph's Hosp., Atlanta, 1982—96, case mgr. depts. pulmonary and nephrology, 1996—2001; clin. assoc. faculty Emory U., Atlanta, 1990—; clin. nurse specialist Critical Care and Med.-surg. Nursing St. Joseph's Hosp., Atlanta, 2001—. RN preceptor, ednl. staff Genentech, Inc., 1995-2002; vice-chairperson Ga. Hosp. Assn. Diabetes Spl. Interest Group, 2003— Author several nursing textbooks; contbr. articles to profl. jours Mem. med. supply com. Atlanta Com. for Olympic Games, 1994-96 Recipient Fed. traineeship Emory U., 1980-81; named one of Outstanding Young Women Am., 1991 Mem. AACN (bd. dirs. Atlanta chpt. 1984-86), Soc. Critical Care Medicine, Am. Holistic Nurses Assn., Am. Assn. Diabetes Educators, Am. Nephrology Nurses Assn., Blue Key, Kappa Gamma Pi, Sigma Theta Tau Office: 5665 Peachtree Dunwoody Rd NE Atlanta GA 30342-1701 Business E-Mail: mbaird@sjha.org.

BAIRD, PATRICIA ANN, physician, educator; b. Rochdale, Eng. arrived in Can., 1955; d. Harold and Winifred (Cainen) Holt; m. Robert Merrifield Baird, Feb. 22, 1964; children: Jennifer Ellen, Brian Merrifield, Bruce Andrew BSc in Biol. Sci. with honors, McGill U., 1959, MD, CM, 1963; DSc (hon.), McMaster U., 1991; D (hon.), U. Ottawa, 1991; LLD (hon.), Wilfrid Laurier U., 2000. Intern Royal Victoria Hosp., Montreal, Que., Canada, 1963-64; resident, fellow in pediat. Vancouver Gen. Hosp., B.C., Canada, 1964-67; instr. pediat. U. B.C., Vancouver, 1968-72, from asst. prof. to prof., 1972-94, Univ. Killam Disting. prof., 1994—; head dept. med. genetics Grace Hosp., Vancouver, 1981-89, Children's Hosp., Vancouver, 1981-89, Health Scis. Centre Hosp., 1986-89. Med. cons. B.C. Health Surveillance Registry, 1977-90; chmn. genetics grants com. Med. Rsch. Coun., Ottawa, Ont., Can., 1982-87, mem. coun., 1987-90; mem. Nat. Adv. Bd. on Sci. and Tech. to Fed. Govt., 1987-91; genetic predisposition study steering com. Sci. Coun. Can., 1987-90; chair Royal Commn. on New Reproductive Technologies, 1989-93, Premier's Coun. on Aging Sr. Issues, 2005-06; co-chair Nat. Forum Sci. and Tech. Couns., 1991; v.p. Can. Inst. for Advanced Rsch., 1991-2002, vice chmn. bd., 2002—; bd. dirs. Biomed. Rsch. Centre, 1986-89; bd. govs. U. B.C., 1984-90; temporary cons. WHO, 1999-2001, human genetics ELSI planning group, 2000-02, expert adv. panel on human genetics, 2002—03. Contbr. articles to med. jours. Decorated officer Order of Can., 2000, Order of B.C., 1992; recipient Commemorative medal for Confedn. of Can., 1992, Queen's Golden Jubilee medal, 2002. Fellow RCP Can., Royal Soc. Can., Can. Coll. Med. Geneticists (v.p. 1984-86); mem. Am. Soc. Human Genetics (chair nominating com. 1987-89), B.C. Med. Assn., Can. Med. Assn., Genetics Soc. Can., Genetic Epidemiology (adv. bd. 1991-94), Internat. Fedn. of Gyn. and Obs. (mem. ethics com. 1997-99). Avocations: skiing, bicycling, music. Address: 3267 Point Grey Rd Vancouver BC V6K 1B3 Canada Business E-Mail: pbaird@interchange.ubc.ca.

BAIRD, PENNY DRUE, interior designer; b. NYC, July 19, 1951; d. Philip Robert and Terri Baird; m. Fred Deutsch, Dec. 31, 1991; children: Alexander Baird Deutsch, Benjamin Baird Deutsch, Philip Baird Deutsch; 1 child, Adam Baird Alpert. BA, U. Rochester, 1973; PsychD, Yeshiva U., 1991; attended, NY School of Interior Design. Pres. Dessins LLC, NYC, 1982—. Archtl. Digest, 1997, 1998, 2000. Pres. City Meals on Wheels, NYC, 1985—90; mem. women's com. N.Y. Hosp., NYC, 1994—; mem. women's bd. Albert Einstein Coll. Medicine, NYC, 1990—. Mem.: Phi Beta Kappa. Office: Dessins LLC 787 Madison Ave New York NY 10021

BAIRD, RICHARD, human resources specialist; m. Linda Baird; children: Ben, Jessica, Blythe. Grad., Albion Coll., 1978. Dir. fin. and human resources Coopers & Lybrand, Detroit, various positions including ops. ptnr. U.S. bus. assurance practice; pres., CEO LAI Compass; global ops. leader assurance and bus. adv. svcs. Pricewaterhouse Coopers, LLP, 1999—. Head INSEAD-Pricewaterhouse Coopers rsch. initiative for high performance orgns.; bd. dirs. Albion Coll., chmn. bd. trustees, chmn. Liberal Arts at Work. Office: PricewaterhouseCoopers LLP 300 Madison Ave 24th Fl New York NY 10017

BAIRD, ROBERT DAHLEN, retired theology studies educator; b. Phila., June 29, 1933; s. Jesse Dahlen and Clara (Sonntag) Baird; m. Patty Jo Lutz, Dec. 18, 1954; children: Linda Sue, Stephen Robert, David Bryan, Janna Ann. BA, Houghton Coll., 1954; BD, Fuller Theol. Sem., 1957; STM, So. Meth. U., 1959; PhD, U. Iowa, 1964. Instr. philosophy and religion U. Omaha, 1962-65; fellow Asian religions Soc. Religion in Higher Edn., 1965-66; asst. prof. religion U. Iowa, Iowa City, 1966-69, assoc. prof., 1969-74, prof., 1974-2001, prof. emeritus, 2001—, acting dir. Sch. Religion, 1985, dir., Sch. Religion, 1995—2000; Leonard S. Florsheim Sr. Eminent Scholar's chair New Coll., U. South Fla., Sarasota, 1988-89. Vis. prof. Grinnell Coll., 1983; Goodwin-Philpot Eminent chair in religion Auburn U., 2001—03; adj. prof. Ripon (Wis.) Coll., 2005—. Author: Category Formation and the History of Religions, 1971, 2d paperback edit., 1991; author: (with W. R. Comstock et al) Religion and Man: An Introduction, 1971, Indian and Far Eastern Religious Traditions, 1972; editor: Methodological Issues in Religious Studies, 1975, Religion in Modern India, 1981, 4th edit., 2001, Essays in History of Religions, 1991, Religion and Law in Independent India, 1993, 2d edit., 2005; book rev. editor: Jour. Am. Acad. Religion, 1979—84; contbr. articles to profl. jours. Ford Found. fellow, 1965—66, Sr. fellow, Am. Inst. Indian Studies, 1972, 1992, Faculty Devel. grantee, U. Iowa, 1979, 1986, 1992. Mem.: N.Am. Assn. Study Religion, Assn. Asian Studies, Am. Acad. Religion. Democrat. Presbyterian. Office: 113 Glenn Dr Cottage Grove WI 53527 Home Phone: 608-839-1509. E-mail: robert-baird@uiowa.edu.

BAIRD, WILLIAM MCKENZIE, chemical carcinogenesis researcher, biochemistry professor; b. Phila., Mar. 23, 1944; s. William Henry Jr. and Edna (McKenzie) Baird; m. Elizabeth A. Myers, June 21, 1969; children: Heather Jean, Elizabeth Joanne, Scott William. BS in Chem., Lehigh U., 1966; PhD in Oncology, U. Wis., 1971. Postdoctoral fellow Inst. Cancer Rsch., London, 1971—73; from asst. to assoc. prof. biochemistry Wistar Inst., Phila., 1973—80; assoc. prof. medicinal chem. Purdue U., West Lafayette, Ind., 1980—82, prof., 1982—97, Glenn L. Jenkins prof. medicinal chem., 1989—97, dir. Cancer Ctr., 1986—97, faculty participant, biochemistry program Cancer Ctr., 1980—97; dir. environ. Health Sci. Ctr. Oreg. State U., Corvallis, 1997—2000, prof., dept. environ. and molecular toxicology, 1997—, prof. dept. biochemistry and biophysics, 1997—. Adv. com. on biochemistry and chem. carcinogenesis Am. Cancer Soc., 1983—86; mem. chem. pathology study sect. NIH, 1986—90. Assoc. editor: Cancer Rsch., 1986—98; contbr. articles to profl. jours. Grantee NCI. Mem.: AAAS, Soc. Toxicology, Environ. Mutagen Soc., Am. Soc. Biochemistry and Molecular Biology, Am. Chem. Soc., Am. Assn. Cancer Rsch., Internat. Soc. for Study of Xenobiotics. Office: Oreg State U Environ and Molecular Toxicology 1007 ALS Bldg Corvallis OR 97331-7301 Home Phone: 541-758-6491; Office Phone: 541-737-1886. Business E-Mail: william.baird@orst.edu.

BAIRD, ZOË, lawyer; b. Bklyn., June 20, 1952; d. Ralph Louis and Naomi (Allen) B.; 2 children. AB, U. Calif., Berkeley, 1974, JD, 1977. Bar: Washington, 1979, Calif. 1977, Conn. 1989. Law clk. Hon. Albert Wollenberg, San Francisco, 1977-78; atty., advisor Office Legal Counsel U.S. Dept. Justice, Washington, 1979-80; assoc. counsel to Pres., The White House, Washington, 1980-81; assoc., then ptnr. O'Melveny & Myers, Washington, 1981-86; counsellor, staff exec. GE, Fairfield, Conn., 1986-90; v.p., gen. counsel Aetna Life & Casualty, Hartford, 1990-93, sr. v.p., gen. counsel, 1993-96; pres. Markle Found., NYC, 1998—. Bd. dirs. Chubb Corp., Boston Properties. Bd. dirs. Lawyers for Children Am., Brookings Inst. Mem. Am. Law Inst., Coun. on Fgn. Rels., Convergys Corp. Office: Markle Found 10 Rockefeller Plaza 16th Fl New York NY 10020-1903 Business E-Mail: info@markle.org.

BAIRSTOW, FRANCES KANEVSKY, arbitrator, mediator, educator; b. Racine, Wis., Feb. 19, 1920; d. William and Minnie (DuBow) Kanevsky; m. Irving P. Kaufman, Nov. 14, 1942 (div. 1949); m. David Steele Bairstow, Dec. 17, 1954; children: Dale Owen, David Anthony. Student, U. Wis., 1937-42; BS, U. Louisville, 1949; student, Oxford U., England, 1953-54; postgrad., McGill U., Montreal, Que., Can., 1958-59. Rsch. economist U.S. Senate Labor-Mgmt. Subcom., Washington, 1950-51; labor edn. specialist U. P.R., San Juan, 1951-52; chief wage data unit WSB, Washington, 1952-53; labor rsch. economist Can. Pacific Ry. Co., Montreal, Que., Canada, 1956-58; asst. dir. indsl. rels. ctr. McGill U., 1960-66, assoc. dir., 1966-71, dir., 1971-85, lectr., indsl. rels. dept. econs., 1960-72, from asst. prof. to assoc. prof. faculty mgmt., 1972—83, prof., 1983-85; lectr. Stetson Law Sch., Fla.; spl. master Fla. Pub. Employees Rels. Commn., 1985-97. Cons. Nat. Film Bd. Can., 1965—69; arbitrator Que. Consultative Coun. Panel Arbitrators, 1968—83, Ministry Labour and Manpower, 1971—83, United Air Lines and Assn. Flight Attendants, 1990—95, Am. Airlines and Transport Workers Union, 1997—98, State U. Sys. Fla., 1990—2003, FDA, 1996—98, Social Security Adminstrn., 1996—2003, Am. Airlines, 1997—, Tampa Gen. Hosp., 1996—, Cargo Internat. Airlines, 2001, Govt. of Fla. and Fla. State Police, 2002—, Bell South and Comm. Workers Am., 2003—, USAF at Warner Robins and AFGE, 2003—; mediator Can. Pub. Svc. Staff Rels. Bd., 1973—85, So. Bell Tel., 1985—, AT&T and Comm. Workers Am., 1986—; cons. on collective bargaining arbitration OECD, Paris, 1979. Contbg. columnist: Montreal Star, 1971—85. Chmn. Nat. Inquiry Commn. Wider-Based Collective Bargaining, 1978; dep. commr. essential svcs. Province of Que., 1976—81. Recipient Sefton award, U. Toronto, 2005, Fireside Chat. award, Nat. Acad. Arbirtrators, 2007; Fulbright fellow, 1953—54. Mem.: Ctrl. Fla. Indsl. Rels. Rsch. Assn. (pres. 1999), Nat. Acad. Arbitrators (bd. govs. 1977—80, program chmn. 1982—83, v.p. 1986—88, nat. coord. 1987—90, Fireside Chat Spkr. award 2007), Indsl. Rels. Rsch. Assn. Am. (mem. exec. bd. 1965—68, chmn. nominating com. 1977), Can. Indsl. Rels. Rsch. Inst. (mem. exec. bd. 1965—68). Home and Office: 4650 54th Ave S # 511 Saint Petersburg FL 33711

BAIRSTOW, RICHARD RAYMOND, retired lawyer; b. Waukegan, Ill., Sept. 26, 1917; s. Fred Raymond and Mildred (Wright) B.; m. Mary Kelley, Aug. 8, 1942 (dec. June 19, 1979); children: Kathleen Bairstow Young, Suzanne Bairstow Hicks, Mary Bairstow Neely; m. Agnes Macaitis Caldwell, July 22, 1980 (dec. July 22, 1995). AB, U. Ill., 1939, JD, 1947; postgrad., George Washington U., 1939-41. Bar: Ill. 1947, U.S. Dist. Ct. (no. dist.) Ill. 1964, U.S. Ct. Mil. Appeals 1963, U.S. Supreme Ct. 1963. Assoc. Hall, Meyer & Carey, Waukegan, 1947-49; asst. state's atty. Lake County, Waukegan, 1949-53; ptnr. McClory & Bairstow, Waukegan, 1953-60, McClory, Bairstow, Lonchar & Nordigan, Waukegan, 1960-66; prin. Richard R. Bairstow & Assocs., Waukegan, 1966-98; ret., 1998. Dist. atty. Fox Lake Fire Protection Dist., Ingleside, Ill., 1953-89; adminstrv. law judge Ill. Dept. Revenue, Chgo., 1953-87. Bd. dirs. ARC, Lake County, 1947-73; mem., pres. Salvation Army, Waukegan, 1954-66; bd. dirs. Lake County Family YMCA, 1990-91. Col. U.S. Army, 1941-46, ETO, USAR, 1946-71, ret. U.S. Army Command and Gen. Staff Coll., 1965. Mem. ABA, Ill. Lake County Bar Assn., Assn. U.S. Army, Mil. Officers Assn. Am., Am. Legion, Glen Flora Country Club, Elks, Waukegan City Club, Delta Tau Delta, Phi Alpha Delta. Republican. Episcopalian. Home: 2050 Walnut St Waukegan IL 60087-4984

BAISDEN, ELEANOR MARGUERITE, retired airline compensation executive, consultant; b. Bklyn., Nov. 7, 1935; d. Vernon McKee and Ethel Mildred (Cockle) Baisden. BA, Hofstra U., 1970. Clk. Trans World Airlines, NYC, 1953-55, sec., 1955-64, compensation analyst, 1964-75, compensation mgr., 1975-85, dir. compensation and orgn. planning, 1985-88, dir. compensation and adminstrn., 1988-97; ret., 1997; owner, mgr. Embassy Estates Rental Properties, 1997—. Bd. dirs., treas. Weatherby Lake Improvement Co., 1997-2001. Mem. Airline Pers. Dirs. Conf. (pers. com. 1984-86), Airline Tariff Pub. Co. (pers. com. 1978-86), Nat. Fgn. Trade Coun. (cmpensation com. 1980-84), Internat. Pers. Assn. (co. rep. 1980-84), Mensa, Weatherby Lake Yacht Club (Mo.), BIG Investment Club (treas. 1998-2001), DAR, Kansas City Lyric Opera Guild, Kansas City Symphony Guild, (treas. 2006—), Red Hat Soc. (chpt. pres. 2003-05), Alpha Sigma Lambda (scholar 1965-66). Republican. Methodist. Avocations: boating, swimming, piano, travel. Home: 7818 NW Scenic Dr Kansas City MO 64152-1643

BAISLEY, JAMES MAHONEY, retired lawyer; b. Dec. 21, 1932; s. Charles Thomas and Katherine (Mahoney) B.; m. Barbara Brosnan, Sept. 7, 1960; children— Mary Elizabeth, Katherine, Barbara, Paul, Genevieve, Charles, James BS, Fordham U., 1954, LLB, 1961. Bar: N.Y. 1961, Ill. 1969. Assoc. Naylon, Aronson, Huber & Magill, NYC, 1961-66; asst. counsel GTE Corp, 1966-69; v.p., gen. counsel GTE Automatic Electric Inc., Northlake, Ill., 1969-81; gen. counsel, v.p. W. W. Grainger Inc., Skokie, Ill., 1981-92, corp. sec., 1991-2000, ret., 2000. Bd. dirs. EAC, Inc. Served with USMC, 1954-57 Mem. ABA, Chgo. Bar Assn., Union League Club Chgo., North Shore Country Club. Republican. Roman Catholic. Home: 2936 Iroquois Rd Wilmette IL 60091-1105

BAITY, JOHN COOLEY, lawyer; b. South Bend, Ind., June 22, 1933; s. Roscoe Flake and Gladys Paula (Kline) B.; m. Patricia Ann Bowen, Nov. 9, 1985; children: Keith F., John C. Jr., Cheryl R., Michael P., Philip J., Mark A. AB with highest honors and highest distinction, U. Mich., 1955, JD summa cum laude, 1958. Bar: Ill. 1958, N.Y. 1961, Calif. 1977, D.C. 1979. Assoc. Cravath, Swaine & Moore, NYC, 1960-62, Donovan Leisure Newton & Irvine, NYC, 1962-65, ptnr., 1966-83, Hunton & Williams, NYC, 1983-84, Baity & Joseph, LA, 1984-86, Milbank, Tweed, Hadley & McCloy LLP, NYC, 1986—. Gen. counsel U.S. Golf Assn., Far Hills, NJ, 1980—85. Chmn. fin. com., coun. and exec. com. Union Internat. Contre le Cancer, 1995—2006; trustee Am. Cancer Soc. Found., 2003—, treas., 2004—; trustee Nat. Hypertension Assn., NYC, 1981—91; bd. dirs. Am. Cancer Soc., Atlanta, 1983—87, 1990—2002, treas., 1994—98, vice chmn., 1998—99, chmn.-elect, 1999—2000, chmn., 2000—01. Mem. N.Y. State Bar. Assn., Calif. Bar Assn., Order of Coif, Phi Beta Kappa, Phi Kappa Phi. Office: Milbank Tweed Hadley & McCloy LLP 1 Chase Manhattan Plz Fl 56 New York NY 10005-1413 Office Phone: 212-530-5168. Office Fax: 212-822-5219. Business E-Mail: jbaity@milbank.com.

BAITZ, JON ROBIN, playwright; b. LA, 1961; Playwright-in-residence N.Y. Stage and Film Co., NYC. Author: The Film Society, 1987, Dutch Landscape, 1989, The Substance of Fire, 1991, The End of the Day, 1992, Three Hotels, 1993, People I Know, 2002, The Paris Letter, 2005 (Ted Schmitt award for world premiere of outstanding new play LA Drama Critics Cir., 2005); writer, exec. prodr.: (TV series) Brothers & Sisters, 2006; actor: (films) Last Summer in the Hampton, 1995, One Fine Day, 1996, Sam the Man, 2000 Playwrights Horizon Revson fellow; recipient Playwright USA award Theatre Comm. Group, 1987, Academy award in Lit. Am. Acad. of Arts and Letters, 1994. Mailing: Roundabout Theatre 231 W 39th St Ste 1200 New York NY 10018

BAJA, LAURO LIBOON, JR., diplomat; b. Alangilan, The Phillippines; m. Norma Baja; children: Maria Elizabeth Baja Facundo, Lauro III. B of Laws, U. of Philippines, BS in Jurisprudence; Fgn. Svc. course, Oxford U. Legal officer Office of Legal Affairs, Dept. of Fgn. Affairs, 1962—63, Office of Adminstrn., Dept. of Fgn. Affairs, 1964; chief Treaties Divsn., Dept of Fgn. Affairs, 1965—66; third sec., then second sec. Philippine Embassy, London, 1967—72; first sec., then career min. Philippine Mission to UN, NYC, 1973—76; exec. dir. Office of UN and other Internat. Orgns., NYC, 1977—79; chief coord. and spl. asst. to sec. of fgn. affairs Dept. of Fgn. Affairs, 1980—95; asst. sec. for Asian and Pacific Affairs, 1993—97; Philippine amb. to Brazil, 1986—93, to Italy, 1997—98; sr. undersecretary of fgn. affairs, 1998—2003; permanent rep. of Philippines to UN, NYC, 2003—; mem. Security Coun. Summit, 2005. Recipient Outstanding Amb. of Yr., Brazil, 1991, Carlos Gomes Gold medal, Sao Paolo, Brazil, 1992, Ordem de Gran Cruz de Rio Branco, Brazil, 1993, Ufficiale nell Ordine, Italy, 1998. Office: Philippine Ctr Bldg 556 5th Ave New York NY 10036

BAJAJ, MANDEEP, medical researcher, educator; s. Jasbir and Avninder Bajaj; m. Kavita Bajaj, Feb. 11, 1997; 1 child, Kabir. MD, All India Inst. of Med. Scis., 1989. Diplomate Am. Bd. of Internal Medicine, 1994, Am. Bd. of Endocrinology, Diabetes and Metabolism, 1997. Fellow dept. of medicine Harvard Med. Sch., Boston, 1994—97; asst. prof. of medicine U. Tex. Health Sci. Ctr., San Antonio, 2000—04; assoc. prof. of medicine U. Tex. Med. Br., Galveston, 2004—. Dir. diabetes rsch. unit U. Tex. Health Sci. Ctr., San Antonio, 2000—04; dir. diabetes edn. U. Tex. Med. Br., Galveston, 2004—. Nat. task force on intensive insulin treatment Am. Coll. Of Endocrinology, Fla., 2004. Recipient Leo Davidoff award, Albert Einstein Coll. Medicine, 1994. Fellow: ACP, Am. Coll. Endocrinology. Achievements include Original Contributions To The Understanding Of The Pathophysiology Of Type 2 Diabetes And The Role Of Free Fatty Acids In The Causation Of Insulin Resistance And Type 2 Diabetes; Original Contributions To The Understanding Of The Role Of Adipocytokines In The Pathogenesis Of Insulin Resistance And Type 2 Diabetes.

BAJICH, MILENA TATIC, psychologist; b. Bosanski Novi, Bosnia-Herzegovina, Mar. 3, 1964; arrived in U.S., 1971; d. Stevo and Ljubica Tatic; m. Stojan Bajich, Oct. 23, 1994; 1 child, Stevan. BS, Loyola U., Chgo., 1986; PsyD, Chgo. Sch. Profl. Psychology, 1994. Lic. clin. psychologist Ill. Asst. tng. dir., program coord. Miwest Mental Health Care Providers, Chgo., 1992—97; clin. psychologist Albany Care/Greenwood Care Rehab. Homes for Severe Psychopathology, Evanston, Ill., 1996—2001, Milena Tatic Bajich, PsyD, Chgo., 1996—, Paladin, LLC, Chgo., 1997—2004, Fabian Carbonell, M.D., S.C., Chgo., 2000—; allied profl. staff St. Joseph Hosp./Resurrection Healthcare, Chgo., 2003—. Mem. ethics com. Adm. at The Lake, Chgo., 2005—; adj. faculty Ill. Sch. Profl. Psychology, Chgo., 1996—2000. Exhibitions include paintings and drawings, invited, Commemmorative 911 Exhibit, Samuel Akainyah, 2002. Choir pres. Stevan St. Mokranjac Choir, Chgo., 2003; mem. Serbian Nat. Fedn., Pitts., 1994. Named Ea. Europe-Poland, Chekoslovakia invitee, Global Initiatives, 2004; recipient Recognition in Behavioral Scis. award, 1998; scholar, Chgo. Sch. of Profl. Psychology, 1987, 1990. Mem.: APA (assoc.), Psi Chi. Serbian Orthodox. Avocation: travel. Office: # 408 2800 N Sheridan Chicago IL 60657 Home Phone: 773-561-5403; Office Phone: 773-561-5524. Office Fax: 773-561-5524. E-mail: mbajich@aol.com.

BAJOR, RENEE ALLYSON, special education educator; b. LA, Calif., Feb. 26, 1964; d. Andrew Donald Bajor and Sandra Lee Ladd. AA, L.A. Pierce Coll., Woodland Hills, California, 1985; BA in Deaf Studies cum laude, Calif. State U., Northridge, 1991; MBA, Internat. U. Japan, Niigata, 2001. Interpreter for deaf L.A. Pierce Coll., 1985, profl. clear multiple subject tchg. credential State of Calif. Commn. Tchr. Credentialling, 1993, clear crosscultural, lang. and academic devel. State of Calif. Commn. Tchr. Credentialling, 2002, cert. gifted and talented edn. U. Calif., Riverside, 2006. Sign lang. interpreter Calif. State U., Northridge, 1984—93, San Bernardino Valley Coll., 1993—2005; math. tchr. Landmark Mid. Sch., Moreno Valley, 1996—2004; fourth grade tchr. Creekside Elem. Sch., Moreno Valley, 2004—. Home and hosp. tchr. Moreno Valley Unified Sch. Dist., Calif., 1996—; tech. advisor Creekside Elem. Sch., 2004—, English lang. devel. specialist, 2006. Troop leader Girl Scouts USA, Van Nuys, Calif., 1985—93, San Bernardino, 1996—97; vol. L.A. Marathon, 2005; altar server Christ the Redeemer Cath. Ch., Grand Terrace, 1993—99. Recipient Gold award, Girl Scouts USA, 1982, Gold and Silver Leadership awards, 1982, Tchr. of Yr., Landmark Mid. Sch., 1998. Mem.: Moreno Valley Educators' Assn., Calif. PTA (auditor 2006), Girl Scouts USA (life). Roman Catholic. Avocations: travel, quilting, reading, cooking, languages. Office: Moreno Valley Unified Sch Dist 13563 Heacock St Moreno Valley CA 92553 Home Phone: 951-778-9950; Office Phone: 951-571-4560. Office Fax: 951-571-4565. E-mail: rbajor@mvusd.k12.ca.us.

BAJURA, RICHARD ALBERT, academic administrator, mechanical engineer, educator; b. Duquesne, Pa., Feb. 2, 1941; BSME, Notre Dame, 1962, MSME, 1964, PhD, 1967. Energy rsch. dir. W.Va. U., Morgantown, 1984-90; rsch. engr. Babcok & Wolcox R&D Ctr., Alliance, Ohio, 1967-68; postdoctoral rschr. Johns Hopkins U., Balt., 1968-69; prof. mech. engring. W.Va. U., Morgantown, 1969—, assoc. provost, 1990-94; dir. Nat. Rsch. Ctr. for Coal and Energy, 1994—. Editor: Polyphase Flow Transport Technology, 1980. Mem. ASME (v.p. basic engring. 1998-2001), Am. Soc. Am. Engring., Washington Coal Club (pres. 1999). Office: WVa U Nat Rsch Ctr for Coal & Energy PO Box 6064 Morgantown WV 26506-6064 Office Phone: 304-293-2867. Business E-Mail: richard.bajira@mail.wvu.edu.

BAJWA, HASHEM, advertising executive; b. Aug. 2, 1980; BA Internat. Rels., New Sch. U., 2002. Spl. asst. UN, 2000—02; account exec. McCann Worldgroup, 2003—05; comm. planner Goodby, Silverstein & Partners, 2005—06, digital planning dir., 2006—. Named one of 40 under 40, Advt. Age, 2007. Mem.: SFMOMA, D&AD, One Club, Cooper-Hewitt Nat. Design Mus. Office: Goodby Silverstein & Partners 720 Calif St San Francisco CA 94108 Office Phone: 415-392-0669. Office Fax: 415-788-4303. E-mail: hb@hashembajwa.com.*

BAJWA, SREEKALA G., agricultural engineer, educator; arrived in US, 1996; d. Gopala Pillai and Savithri Amma; m. Dilpreet S. Bajwa, Sept. 5, 1999; children: Tejas, Ritu. B of Tech. in Agrl. Engring., Kerala Agrl. U., Tavanur, India, 1991; M of Tech., Indian Inst. Tech., Kharagpur, 1994; PhD, U. Ill., Urbana-Champaign, 2000. Asst. prof. Kerala Agrl. U., Tavanur, 1994—96; rsch. assoc. U. Ill., Urbana, 2000—01; asst. prof. U. Ark., Fayetteville, 2001—. Chair, editor AR Precision Agrl. Working Group, Fayetteville, Ark., 2003—05. Contbr. articles to profl. jours. Adult literacy campaign State Govt. Kerala, Tavanur, 1990—91. Recipient Best Conf. Paper award, Soc. Automotive Engrs., 1999. Mem.: Am. Soc. for Photogrammetry and Rem. Sens. (bd. dirs. Ctrl. region 2003—05), Am. Soc. Engring. Edn., Am. Soc. Agrl. and Biol. Engrs. (assoc. editor 1997—2005, com. chair 2003—05, Best Poster award Ark. region 2003—04), Rotary, Gamma Sigma Delta, Phi Kappa Phi. Achievements include patents pending for low density composite made from recycled plastic. Avocations: badminton, hiking, dance, poetry, reading. Office: Univ Ark 203 Engineering Hall Fayetteville AR 72701 Business E-Mail: sgbajwa@uark.edu.

BAKAKOS, DIANA, middle school educator; b. NYC, Apr. 2, 1952; d. Michael and Catherine (Itsines) Constant; m. Constantine Bakakos, Nov. 24, 1974; children: Chris Fotis, Vikki. BA with honors, Coll. of S.I., 1973, MS in Edn., 1976; PhD in Psychology, Neotarian Coll. of Philosophy, 1979; MS in Computer Edn., L.I. U., 1987. Tchr. I.S. 391 Bd. of Edn., Bklyn., 1978—. Instr. adult edn. Bklyn. Coll., 1988; adj. prof. Fordham U., Bronx, 1990; tchr. asst. Peer Intervention Program, N.Y.C., 1995; instr. grad. credits QUIPP N.Y.C. Pub. Schs., Bklyn., 1990. Civilian vol. N.Y.C. Police Dept., Bklyn., 1978; mem. Petrina Brotherhood Assn., Bklyn., 1978—, Laconian Assn. Can. and N.Am., Bklyn., 1978—, Hellenic Am. Edn. Assn., N.Y.C., 1982. Recipient Tchr. of Yr. Arista, 1988, N.Y. Alliance award, 1990, Wall of Tolerance hon., 2002. Mem. Doctorate Assn. N.Y. Educators, United Fedn. Tchrs. (chpt. mem.-at-large, del. 2003, dean 2004), Ctrl. Bklyn. Ind. Dem. Club, Epsilon Delta Chi. Democrat. Greek Orthodox. Avocations: travel, swimming, dance, art, word games. Home: 8620 21st Ave Brooklyn NY 11214-4004

BAKAL, RON SHARONE, urologist; b. Tel Aviv, Apr. 29, 1967; s. Eli and Tikva Bakal. MD, U. Med. Dentistry NJ, Newark, 1995. Cert. Am. Bd. Urology, 2003. Assoc. Midtown Urol. Assocs., NYC, 2001—05; pres. Ron Bakal Md Pc, NYC, 2005—. Contbr. articles to profl. jours. Mem.: Am. Urol. Assn. Achievements include research in scrotal island flap urethroplasy in the management of anterior urethral strictures. Office: Ron Bakal Md Pc 461 Park Ave S Ste 5 New York NY 10016 Home Phone: 212-673-2742; Office Phone: 212-679-6464. Office Fax: 212-679-6472; Home Fax: 212-679-6472.

BAKALAR, JOHN STEPHEN, printing company and publishing executive; b. Lynn, Mass., Feb. 10, 1948; s. Leo and Ann Beatrice (Lepie) B.; m. Christine Lake Heilman, Sept. 24, 1972; children: Brooke Heilman, Jessica Heilman, Luke Heilman. BA, U. Pa., 1970; MBA, Stanford U., 1973. Investment mgr. First Chgo. Corp., Chgo., 1973-76; treas. Rand McNally & Co., Skokie, Ill., 1976-78, v.p. fin., treas., 1978-86, exec. v.p., 1986-93, pres., chief oper. officer, 1993-98. Dir. RC2, Hygenics, Corp. Adv. bd., dir. Broader Urban Involvement and Leadership Devel., Chgo., 1976—; dir. Friends for Health; fellow Leadership Greater Chgo., 1987-88; trustee North Shore Country Day Sch. Found., Winnetka, Ill., 1997—. Mem. Econ. Club Chgo., Northmoor Country Club (Highland Park, Ill.), Country Club of the Rockies (Edwards, Colo.), Eagle Springs Country Club (Wolcott, Colo.). Home: 1760 Dale Ave Highland Park IL 60035-3303

BAKALY, CHARLES GEORGE, JR., lawyer, mediator; b. Long Beach, Calif., Nov. 15, 1927; s. Charles G. Sr. and Doris (Carpenter) B.; m. Patricia Murphey, Oct. 25, 1952; children: Charles G. III, John W., Thomas B. AB, Stanford U., 1949; JD, U. S.C., 1952. Assoc. O'Melveny & Myers, LA, 1956-63, ptnr., 1963-94; mem. JAMS, LA, 2000—. Mem. Commn. on Calif. State Govt. Orgn. and Economy, 1991-94, President's Nat. Commn. on Employment Policy, 1992-94; mem. 9th Cir. Jud. Conf. Lawyer Del. Ch., 1984-87, mem. indigent def. panel, 1992-94; chmn. Calif. Dispute Resolution Adv. Coun., 1987-88; pres. Dispute Resolution Svcs. Bd. Dirs., Calif. Dispute Resolution Coun. Author: (with Joel M. Grossman) Modern Law of Employment Relationships, 1983, 2d edit. 1989; contbr. chpts. to books. Capt. JAG USMC, 1952—56. Named one of Top 50 Mediators in Calif., LA Daily Jour., 2004. Fellow Am. Coll. Trial Lawyers, Coll. Labor and Employment Lawyers, Internat. Acad. Mediators; mem. ABA (chmn. sect. labor and employment law 1981-82, sect. dispute resolution), L.A. County Bar Assn. (trustee, chmn. labor law sect. 1976-77, dispute resolution sect.), Lincoln Club (pres. 1989-91), Chancery Club, Valley Hunt Club (Pasadena, Calif.), Calif. Club (L.A.), Bohemian Club (San Francisco). Office: JAMS 707 Wilshire Blvd Ste 4600 Los Angeles CA 90017 Office Phone: 213-253-9758. Business E-Mail: cbakaly@jamsadr.com.

BAKANOWSKY, LOUIS JOSEPH, artist, architect, educator; b. Conn., Oct. 8, 1930; s. Louis Joseph Bakanowsky and Alice (Sullivan) Derda; m. Marie A. Golas, Jan. 27, 1951; 1 child, Louis J., III. BFA, Syracuse U., 1957; MArch, Harvard U., 1961. Registered arch. Asst. prof. architecture Cornell U., Ithaca, NY, 1961; assoc. prof. Harvard U., Cambridge, Mass., 1963-71, prof. architecture, 1972—, prof. visual arts., 1975-97, Osgood Hooker prof. visual studies emeritus, 1997—, chmn. dept. visual and environ. studies, 1976-86. Prin. Cambridge Seven. Assocs., 1962—99; vis. scholar, artist Am. Acad., Rome, 1983, 91; dir. Carpenter Ctr. Visual Arts, 1984—90; prin. Rosebud Environ. Design Group, 2000—. Prin. works include U.S. Pavillion for Expo '67, Montreal, Can., Henry DuPont Libr., Pomfret Sch., Conn., Columbia Sch., Rochester, N.Y., Rostropovich residence; (sculpture) Carl Siembab Gallery, Boston, 1958; sculpture exhbn. Dietrich Gallery, Cambridge, Mass., 2006; represented in various pub. an pvt. collection. With USAF, 1951—53. Grantee Nat. Endowment Arts, 1979, 83, Graham Found. for Advanced Studies in Fine Arts, 1983. Fellow AIA (design awards 1967, 70). Office: Harvard U Carpenter Ctr for Visual Arts 24 Quincy St Cambridge MA 02138-3804

BAKARI, ROSENNA, educational psychology professor, consultant; d. Robbie and George Jackson; m. Ronald Sentwali Bakari, Aug. 2, 1991; children: Sentwali Jelani, Nailah Myisha. BS, Cornell U., Ithaca, NY, 1984; MS, SUNY, Brockport, 1985; PhD, U. No. Colo., Greeley, 2000. Ednl. opportunity program counselor SUNY, Brockport, 1984—85; alcoholism counselor Anthony Jordan Health Ctr., Rochester, NY, 1985—86; chem. dependency counselor Park Ridge Chem. Dependency, Rochester, 1986—88; psychiat. technician Inst. Pa. Hosp., Phila., 1988—99; asst. prof. SUNY, Oneonta, 2000—03; adj. prof. Drake U., Des Moines, 2004—. Cons. Nazareth Coll. Urban Tchg. Ctr., Rochester, NY, 2002—, Rochester Sch. Dist. Tchr. Ctr., NY, 2003—; counselor SUNY, Oswego, 1989—91, U. Wis., LaCrosse, 1991—92; acad. advisor Aims C.C., Greeley, Colo., 1996—97, adj. faculty, 1997—2000; tchg. intern U. No. Colo., Greeley, 1997—99, tchg. asst., 1997—99. Author: Self-Love, Developing and Maintaining Self-Esteem for the Black Woman, 1994; contbr. articles to jour. Mayor apptd. voting mem. Human Rights Commn, Oneonta, 2002—03. Mem.: Am. Edn. Rsch. Assn., Sisters on Target (treas. 2004—05). Avocation: Tae Kwon Do. Home: 413 39th St West Des Moines IA 50265 Office Phone: 515-271-4647. Personal E-mail: rosennab@msn.com.

BAKAY, ROY ARPAD EARLE, neurosurgeon, educator; b. Chgo., Mar. 5, 1949; s. Archie Joseph and Marjory (Jordahl) B.; m. Joann P. Feiertag; children: Mark, Scott, Candace, Jacqueline. BS, Beloit Coll., 1971; MD, Northwestern U., 1975. Diplomate Am. Bd. Med. Examiners, Am. Bd. Neurol. Surgeons. Intern U. Mich., Ann Arbor, 1975-76; resident in neurosurgery U. Wash., Seattle, 1976-82; acting instr., asst. in neurosurgery U. Wash. Med. Sch., Seattle, 1980-82, NIH fellow, 1981-82; asst. prof. sect. neurol. surgery Emory U. Med. Sch., Atlanta, 1982-88, dir. neurol. surgery resident rsch., 1984-2000, assoc. prof., 1988-93, prof., 1993-2000; mem. R & D Com. VA Med. Ctr., Decatur, Ga., 1982-86, sect. chief neurol. surgery, 1982-95; affiliate scientist neurobiology Yerkes Regional Primate Rsch. Ctr., Atlanta, 1982—, vice chmn. dept. neurol. surgery, 1995-2000; prof., vice chmn. Rush-Presbyn.-St. Luke's Med. Ctr., Chgo., 2000—, dir. Movement Disorder Surg. Ctr., 2000—; with Chgo. Inst. Neurosurgery and Neurorsch., 2000—. Author: (with others) Yearbook of Science and Technology, 1989; abstractor Jour. Surg. Gynecology and Obstetrics, 1978-86; mem. editorial bd. Jour. Contemporary Neurosurgery, 1987-93; mem. editorial rev. bd. Neurosurgery, 1994—; contbr. articles to profl. jours., chpts. to books. Chmn. profl. adv. bd. Ga. chpt. Epilepsy Found. Am., 1987-88; mem. adv. panel U.S. Congl. Office Tech. Assessment, Washington, 1988-90; profl. rep. Am. Cancer Soc., Atlanta, 1987-90. Recipient Resident Rsch. award Western Neurosurgery Soc., 1979, No. Pacific Soc.Neurology and Psychiatry, 1979, Soc. Neurology Anesthesists and Neurology Supportive Care, 1981; named one of Outstanding Athletes of Am., 1971, Am. Best Doctor, 1994—. Mem. AAAS, Soc. Neurosci., Am. Stereotactic and Functional Neurosurgeons (v.p. 1988-91, pres. 1991-93), Am. Assn. Neurol. Surgeons (chmn. GRAFT Registry Com. 1987-95), Congress Neurol. Surgeons (v.p. joint com. 1988-91, pres. 1991-93), Am. Soc. Neural Tranplantation and Repair (founding 1992, counsilor, 1992-99, pres.-elect 1999, pres. 2000). Presbyterian. Avocations: hiking, camping, skiing, fishing, team sports. Office: Rush Presbyn St Lukes Med Ctr 1725 W Harrison St Chicago IL 60612

BAKEMAN, CAROL ANN, travel writer, singer; b. San Francisco; d. Lars Hartvig and Gwendolyne Beatrice (Zimmer) Bergh; m. Delbert Clifton Bakeman; children: Laurie Ann, Deborah Ann. Student, UCLA, 1954-62. Singer Roger Wagner Chorale, L.A. Master Chorale, 1964-86, The Wagner Ensemble, 1991—; libr. Hughes Aircraft Co., Culver City, Calif.; head econs. libr. Planning Rsch. Corp., LA, 1961-63; corp. libr. Econ. Cons., Inc., LA, 1963-68; head econs. libr. Daniel, Mann, Johnson & Mendenhall, archs. and engrs., LA, 1969-71, corp. libr., 1971-77, mgr. info. svcs., 1978-81, mgr. info. and office svcs., 1981-83, mgr. adminstrv. svcs., 1983-96, sr. assoc., 1996-98, assoc. v.p., 1998—; travel mgr. AECOM Tech. Corp., 1996—2004. Assoc. v.p. Corp. Consol. Svcs., Inc., (divsn. AECOM), 1997-2004; pres., Creative Libr. Sys., L.A., 1974-83; libr. cons. ArchiSystems (divsn. SUMMA Corp.), L.A., 1972-81; contbr. Business Travel Executive, 2005— Contbr. articles to profl. jours. Mem. Assistance League, So. Calif., 1956-86, nat. auxilaries com., 1968-72, 75-78, nat. by-laws com., 1970-75, assoc. bd. dirs., 1966-76. Mem. AFTRA, SAG, Am. Guild Musical Artists, Adminstrv. Mgmt. Soc. (v.p. L.A. chpt. 1984-86, pres. 1986-88, internat. conf. chmn. 1988-89, internat. bd. dirs. 1988-90, internat. v.p. mgmt. edn. 1990-92), L.A. Master Chorale Assn. (bd. dirs. 1978-83), Wagner Ensemble (bd. dirs.), L.A. Bus. Travel Assn. (hon., bd. dirs. 1995, sec. 1997, v.p. 1998, pres. 1999, past pres. 2000, bd advisor 2001-2002), Nat. Bus. Travel Assn. (nat. conv. seminar com. 1994-95, conv. vol. chmn. 1994, 2000, nat. conv. panelist 2001, 03, profl. svc. award 2001).

BAKER, AL, journalist; Reporter New York Times. Finalist Press Media Award on Eco-Terrorism, 2002, 2004. Office: The New York Times 229 W 43rd St New York NY 10036

BAKER, ALTON FLETCHER, III, editor, publishing executive; b. Eugene, Oreg., May 2, 1950; s. Alton Fletcher Jr. and Genevieve B.; m. Wendy, Jan. 27, 1979; children: Benjamin A., Lindsay A. BA in Comms., Washington State U., 1972. Reporter Associated Press, 1972-79; asst. city editor The Register-Guard, Eugene, 1979-80, city editor, 1980-82, mng. editor, 1982-86, editor, 1986-87, editor, publisher, 1987—; pres. Guard Publishing Co., Eugene, 1987—. Pres. Cmty. Newspapers, Inc., Portland. Pres. YMCA, Eugene, 1989, United Way of Lane County, Eugene, 1985-01, Eugene Festival Musical Theatre, 1990-94. Mem.: Oreg. Newspaper Pubs. Assn. (pres. 1999), Eugene Country Club (pres. 1999). Avocation: golf. Office: Guard Publishing Co 3500 Chad Dr Eugene OR 97408-7348 Office Phone: 541-338-2318.

BAKER, ANITA, singer; b. Toledo, Jan. 26, 1958; m. Walter Bridgeforth, Jr., Dec. 24, 1988; 1 child, Walter Baker Bridgeforth. Mem. funk band Chapter 8, Detroit, 1978-80; receptionist Quin & Budajh, Detroit, 1980-82; ind. singer, songwriter, 1982—. Rec. artist: (with Chapter 8) I Just Wanna Be Your Girl, 1980, (solo albums) The Songstress, 1983, Rapture, 1986 (Grammy award for best rhythm and blues vocal performance 1987), Giving You the Best That I Got, 1988 (Grammy awards for best rhythm and blues song, 1988, best rhythm and blues performance, female, single, 1988, best album, 1989), Compositions, 1990 (Grammy award for best rhythm and blues performance, 1990), Rhythm of Love, 1994 (Grammy award nominee for best album 1995, best female vocal 1995, best song 1995); songs include No More Tears, Angel, Caught Up in the Rapture, Sweet Love (Grammy award best rhythm and blues song 1987), Same Ol' Love, You Bring Me Joy, Been So Long, No One in the World. Recipient Grammy award gospel, soul, best performance, duo, group, choir or chorus, 1987, NAACP Image award, best female vocalist and best album of yr. also: 8216 Tivoli Cove Dr Las Vegas NV 89128-7446

BAKER, ANITA DIANE, lawyer; b. Atlanta, Sept. 4, 1955; d. Byron Garnett and Anita (Swanson) B.; m. Thomas Johnstone Robison III, Sept. 26, 1995. BA summa cum laude, Oglethorpe U., 1977; JD with distinction, Emory U., 1980. Bar: Ga. 1980. Assoc. Hansell & Post, Atlanta, 1980—88, Kitchens, Kelley, Gaynes, Huprich & Shmerling, 1989—90; asst. gen. counsel NationsBank Corp., 1991—97; v.p., gen. counsel Adaris Corp., 1997—99; pvt. practice Atlanta, 1999—2004; ptnr. Baker Law Group, LLC, Roswell, Ga., 2005—, Baker & Stalzer, LLC, Roswell, 2006—. Trustee Oglethorpe Univ. Mem.: ABA, North Fulton Bar Assn., Stormy Petrel Bar Assn. (past pres.), Ga. Bar Assn., Ga. Elder Care Network, Oglethorpe U. Nat. Alumni Assn. (past pres.), Pace Acad. Alumni Assn., Atlanta Soc., Ravinia Club, Omicron Delta Kappa, Alpha Chi, Phi Alpha Theta, Phi Alpha Delta, Order of Coif. Office: 555 Sun Valley Dr Ste N4 Roswell GA 30076

BAKER, ANNETTE L., pediatric nurse practitioner; BSN, Boston U., Boston, 1981; M in Nursing, Yale U., New Haven, 1989. Cert. pediat. nurse practitioner, ANCC, 1998. Cardiovasc. nurse practitioner Children's Hosp., Boston, 1989—. Office: Dept Cardiology-Childrens Hospital 300 Longwood Ave Boston MA 02115 Office Phone: 617-355-7579. Office Fax: 617-730-0600. Business E-Mail: annette.baker@cardio.chboston.org.

BAKER, BLANCHE, actress; b. NYC, Dec. 20, 1956; d. Jack Garfein and Carroll Baker; m. R. Bruce Vandusen; children: Zane Vandusen, Dara Vandusen, Wynnie Vandusen; m. Mark Magill, Jan. 1, 2003; 1 child, James Magill. BA, SUNY, 2006. Actor: (films) The Hamdmaid's Tale, Shakedown, Raw Deal, Sixgteen Candles, The Seduction of Joe Tynan, Living Large, Bum Rap; The Girl Next Door; actor: (films) Science Fair, Jersey Justice, Underdogs, Jackrabbit Sky, 2007; (TV series) Law and Order; (TV films) Nobody's Child, The Day the Bubble Burst, Holocaust; (Broadway plays) Lolita, (off Broadway shows) Steel Magnolias, Young Playwrights Festival, Hannay, Poor Little Lambs, The Wild Duck, White Marriage. Address: 2501 Palisade Ave Bronx NY 10463-6104

BAKER, BRENT HAROLD, foundation executive, blogger; b. Pitts., Mar. 15, 1963; s. Burnham H. and Florence E. (French) B. BA with Spl. Honors in Polit. Sci., George Washington U., 1985. With Conservative Digest; editor, Newswatch Nat. Conservative Found., Alexandria, Va., 1985-87; co-creator, exec. dir. Media Rsch. Ctr., Alexandria, 1987—, now Steven P.J. Wood Sr. fellow and v.p., rsch. publications, and editor, CyberAlert email report, 1996—, editor, newsbusters.org, 2005—. Author: How to Identify, Expose and Correct Liberal Media Bias, 1994; co-editor: And That's The Way It Isn't: A Reference Guide to Media Bias, 1990; editor Notable Quotables newsletters, 1988-, Media Watch, 1988-99, CyberAlert 1996-; editor-at-large (blog) NewsBusters.org 2005-; oversaw (newsletter) MediaWatch ConventionWatch, 1992, 1996; edited Campaign 2000 Media Reality Check, 2000; contbr. works to NY Post, Wall Street Journal, Investor's Business Daily, Washington Times, Colorado Springs Gazette-Telegraph, Union Leader (Manchester, NH), Orange County Register and Human Events; contbr. articles to National Review and Journalism Quarterly. Republican. Home: 4090 Championship Ct Annandale VA 22003-2425 Office: Media Rsch Ctr 325 S Patrick St Alexandria VA 22314*

BAKER, BRIDGET, publishing executive; b. Eugene, Oreg., Sept. 14, 1955; d. Edwin Moody and Patricia Baker; m. Guy Dominique Wood, June 30, 1977 (div. Oct. 1981); m. Rayburn Keith Kincaid, June 27, 1987; stepchildren: Benjamin Kincaid, Jacob Kincaid. BA in English, French and Theatre, Lewis and Clark Coll., 1977; MA in Journalism, U. Oreg., Eugene, 1985. Circulation dist. supr. Register-Guard, Eugene, 1978—80, pub. rels. coord., 1980—83, promotion dir., 1983—86, mktg. dir., 1986—88, corp. pub. rels. dir., 1989—. Sec. Guard Pub. Co., 1987—, bd. dirs., 1987—. Bd. dirs. Art Found. Western Oreg., chmn., 1997—99; pres. Baker Family Found., 1998—; bd. dirs. Wilani Coun. Camp Fire, 1982—88, pres. bd. dirs., 1986—88; bd. dirs. Lane County United Way, 1982—88, cmty. info. com. chairperson, 1982—84, chair planning com., 1987—88; bd. dirs. Eugene Opera, 1988—91, pres. bd. dirs., 1990—91; bd. dirs. Lane C.C. Found., 1995—97, Lane Metro Partnership, 2003—, treas., 2005, v.p., 2006, pres., 2007—. Named Woman of the Yr., Lane County Coun. Orgns., 1994; recipient 1st pl. advt. award, Editor and Pub. Mag., 1984, 1st pl. TV promotion, 1st pl. newspaper rsch. award, 1988, Best Mktg. Idea/Campaign award, Oreg. Newspaper Pub. Assn., 1984, 1985. Mem.: Pub. Rels. Soc. Am. (pres. greater Oreg. chpt. 1995—96, Spotlight award 1986), Internat. Mktg. Assn. (bd. dirs. western region 1986—88, internat. bd. dirs. 1995—2001, 1st pl. Best in the West awards 1983—91), Round Table of Eugene (treas. 2005, sec. 2005—06, v.p. 2006—07, pres. 2007—), Eugene C. of C. (bd. dirs. 1989—92), U. Oreg. Alumni Assn. (bd. dirs. 1990—93), Eugene Yacht Club, Downtown Athletic Club, Town Club (bd. dirs. 1995—97), Zonta Internat. (pres. Eugene Club 1994—96, area dir. 1997—98, lt. gov. Dist. 8 1998—2000, gov. 2000—02, internat. pub. rels. chair 2002—04, Woman of the Yr. 2002). Republican. Avocations: sailing, hunting, performing arts. Office: Guard Pub Co PO Box 10188 Eugene OR 97440-2188

BAKER, BRUCE EDWARD, orthopedic surgeon, consultant; b. Oswego, NY, Mar. 22, 1937; s. Elbert J. and Reatha (Hartranft) B.; m. Patricia Therese Gormel, Aug. 19, 1961; children: Brett, Clayton, Sean, Reatha BSME, Syracuse U., 1959; MD, SUNY Syracuse, 1965. Intern State U. Iowa, Iowa City, 1965—66, asst. resident, 1966—67; resident orthop. SUNY Upstate Med. Ctr., Syracuse, 1969—72, NIH orthop. rsch. fellow, 1972—73, asst. prof. orthop. surgery, 1973—79, assoc. prof., 1979—86, prof., 1986—89. Dir. univ. sports medicine svc. divsn. dept. orthop. surgery 1980-89; team physician, dir. sports medicine athletic dept., Syracuse U., 1973-93, orthop. cons. Student Health Ctr., 1973-93, staff SUNY Hosp., Syracuse, 1973-89, Syracuse VA Hosp., 1973-89, A.C. Silverman Pub. Health Hosp., 1973-77, Crouse-Irving Meml. Hosp., 1973—; cons. in field Contbr. numerous articles to profl. jours Capt. M.C. USAF, 1967—69. Recipient Bronze medal Am. Roentgen Ray Soc., 1980, Gold medal Sound Slide Prodn. Conditioning, 1977; Syracuse U. scholar, 1955; N.Y. State Regents scholar, 1955-59; grantee USPHS, 1973-74, Hendricks Rsch. Fund, 1973-75, NIH, 1974-77 Fellow ACS, Am. Acad. Orthop. Surgeons; mem. AMA (Physicians Recognition award 1978), Med. Soc. State N.Y., Onondaga County Med. Soc., Orthop. Rsch. Soc., Am. Coll. Sports Medicine, N.Y. Soc. Orthop. Surgeons, Royal Soc. Medicine, Internat. Soc. Arthroscopy, Knee Surgery and Orthop. Sports Medicine, Am. Orthop. Soc. Sports Medicine, European Soc. Sports Trauma, Knee Surgery and Arthroscopy, Arthroscopy Assn. N.Am Office: 600 E Genesee St Ste 117 Syracuse NY 13202-3108 Home Phone: 315-655-2220; Office Phone: 315-476-2670.

BAKER, BRUCE JAY, lawyer; b. Chgo., June 18, 1954; s. Kenneth and Beverly (Gould) B. Student, U. Leeds, Eng., 1974-75; BS, U. Ill., 1976; JD, Washington U., 1979. Bar: Ill. 1979, U.S. Dist. Ct. (no. dist.) Ill. 1984. Asst. atty. gen. antitrust divsn. State of Ill., Chgo., 1979-83; assoc. Mass, Miller & Josephson Ltd., Chgo., 1983-86; sr. counsel Discover Card Services Inc., Riverwoods, Ill., 1986-89; sr. legis. counsel Dean Witter Fin. Svcs. Group, Riverwoods, 1989-91; gen. counsel Ill. Commr. Banks and Trust Cos., Chgo., 1991-94; ptnr. Schiff Hardin & Waite, Chgo., 1994-99, of counsel, 1999-2001, Barack, Ferrazzano, Kirschbaum, Perlman & Nagelberg, Chgo., 2001—; exec. v.p., gen. counsel Ill. Bankers Assn., 1999—. Gen. editor Advising Illinois Financial Institutions, 2002, 2006; contbr. articles to profl. jours. Registered lobbyist Ill. Legislature, Springfield, 1985-91, 94—. Named Ill. State scholar, 1972. Mem. ABA (antitrust com., banking com., chmn. state banking law devels. task force 1998—2000), Ill. State Bar Assn. (comml. banking and bankruptcy sect.), Chgo. Bar Assn. (fin. insts. com.), Ill. Bankers Assn. (legis. counsel 1985-86, gen. counsel 1994—, Disting. Bank Counsel award 1991, 97). also: Barack Ferrazzano Et Al 333 W Wacker Dr Ste 2700 Chicago IL 60606 Office: Illinois Bankers Assn 181 W Madison St Ste 790 Chicago IL 60602-4510 E-mail: bbaker@ilbanker.com.

BAKER, BRUCE ROY, artist, illustrator; b. Syracuse, NY, July 18, 1937; s. Morse Roy and Gladys Irene (Hilton) B.; m. Helen Louise Butler, Apr. 16, 1965; children: Paul, Suzanne, Diana, Amy BS Art Edn., New Paltz Coll., 1959; MS Art Edn., Syracuse U., 1966. Cert. tchr. N.Y. Tchr. art Catskill Pub. Schs., NY, 1959—62, Cortland City Schs., NY, 1964—66, Marcellus Ctrl. Schs., NY, 1966—92; pvt. practice artist, illustrator Marcellus, 1992—. Tchr. art Mex. (N.Y.) Acad., 1975-76 Exhibited in group shows at Artists Ctrl. NY-Munson-Williams-Procter Inst., Utica, 1969, N.Y. State Fair, Syracuse, 1973-75, 2005, Cooperstown (N.Y.) Ann., 1974, Everson Biennial, Syracuse, 2006; contbg. painter Leopold F. Landsberger, N.Y.C., 1979-86; contbg. illustrator Firestone Pub. Corp., Miami Lakes, Fla., 1982-2001, Spartacus/Centurian, Reno, 1983—, Quadriga Art, Inc., N.Y.C., 1993—; illustrator (book) Erotic Art of Bruce Baker, 1995; contbr. articles to profl. jours With U.S. Army, 1962-64 Recipient Hon. Mention for sculpture NY State Fair, 1975, 2004, 1st prize for graphics, 2004, 1st prize for wood, 2006, 1st prize for pastel, 2006. Avocations: reading, golf. Home: 11 1st St Marcellus NY 13108-1114

BAKER, C. MARK, lawyer; BA summa cum laude, Yale Univ., 1981; JD with highest honors, Duke Univ., 1984. Bar: Tex. 1984. Law clk. Hon. John R. Brown US Ct. of Appeals (5th cir.), 1984—85; ptnr., co-head firmwide internat. dept. and arbitration dept. Fulbright & Jaworski, Houston. Arbitrator and mediator World Intellectual Property Assn.; bd. dirs., arbitrator London Ct. Internat. Arbitration. Contbr. articles to profl. journals; lectr. in field. Named one of 100 Most Influential Lawyers, Nat. Law Jour., 2006, 20 Worldwide Experts in Internat. Arbitration, PLC, 2006. Fellow: Tex. Bar Found., Houston Bar Found., Chartered Inst. of Arbitrators, London, England; mem.: ICC Commn., Am. Arbitration Assn. (bd. dir, internat. panel, nat. sports resolution panel), Ct. of Arbitration for Sport, Lausanne, Switzerland, Internat. Bar Assn., Coll. of the Bar of Tex., State Bar Tex. Avocations: fishing, hunting, tennis, opera. Office: Fulbright & Jaworski Ste 5100 1301 McKinney Houston TX 77010-3095 Office Phone: 713-651-5151. Office Fax: 713-651-5246. Business E-Mail: mbaker@fulbright.com.

BAKER, CAMERON, lawyer; b. Chgo., Dec. 24, 1937; s. David Cameron and Marion (Fitzpatrick) B.; m. Katharine Julia Solari, Sept. 2, 1961; children: Cameron III, Ann, John. Student, U. Notre Dame, 1954—57; AB, Stanford U., 1958; LLB, U. Calif., Berkeley, 1961. Bar: Calif. 1962, U.S. Dist. Ct. (so. dist.) Calif. 1962, U.S. Dist. Ct. (no. dist.) Calif. 1963, U.S. Ct. Appeals (9th cir.) 1963. With Adams, Duque & Hazeltine, LA, 1961-62, Pettit & Martin, San Francisco, 1962-95, mng. ptnr., 1972-81, 84-87, exec. com., 1971-82, 84-88; with Farella, Braun & Martel, San Francisco, 1995—. Mayor City of Belvedere, Calif., 1978-79; mgr. Larkmead Vineyards, Napa Valley, Calif. Mem. ABA (sects. on bus. law and internat. law and practice), Calif. Bar Assn. (sect. bus., real property and internat. law), Bar Assn. San Francisco (bd. dirs. 1966, 72-73), Boalt Hall Alumni Assn. (dir. 1982-84), Bohemian Club, Tiburon Peninsula Club. Home: 38 Alcatraz Ave Belvedere CA 94920-2504 Office: Farella Braun & Martel LLP 235 Montgomery St San Francisco CA 94104-2902 Office Phone: 415-954-4460. E-mail: cbaker@fbm.com.

BAKER, CARL GWIN, retired science administrator, educator; b. Louisville, Nov. 27, 1920; s. Edward Forrest and Naomi (Taylor) B.; m. Lois Eleane Oxsen, Mar. 24, 1949 (div. May 1975); children: Cathryn, Jeannette; m. Catherine Valerie Smith, May 23, 1975. AB in Zoology, U. Louisville, 1942, MD, 1944, DSc (hon.), 1980; MA in Biochemistry, U. Calif., Berkeley, 1949. Lic. med. practice, Ky., Calif. Rsch. investigator Biochemistry Lab. Nat. Cancer Inst., NIH, Bethesda, Md., 1949-52, 53-55, staff grants and fellowships br., 1952-53, asst. to NIH assoc. dir., 1956-57, asst. dir., acting sci. dir., 1958-61, assoc. dir. program, 1961-67, sci. dir. etiology, 1967-69; dir. Nat. Cancer Inst., Bethesda, 1969-72; dir. program policy staff Health & Human Svcs. Adminstr., Rockville, Md., 1975-76; med. dir. Ludwig Inst. Cancer Rsch., Zurich, Switzerland, 1977-85, ret., 1985; adj. instr. U. Md., College Park, 1989—. Mem. gov. coun. Internat. Agy. for Cancer Rsch., Lyon, France, 1969-72. Assoc. editor Jour. of the Nat. Cancer Inst., 1954-55; mem. editl. adv. bd. Cancer Jour., 1965-73; contbr. articles to jours. Biochemistry, Oncology, Mgmt. Sci. Del. State Bd. Edn., Annapolis, Md., 1957; mem. exec. com. adv. panel on health Am. Revolution Bicentenial Commn., Washington, 1970-72; v.p. 10th Internat. Cancer Congress, Houston, 1970. Asst. surgeon gen. USPHS, 1970—. Decorated PHS Meritorious Svc. medal; Jane Coffin Childs Fund fellow, 1946-48, Spl. fellow Nat. Cancer Inst., NIH, 1949. Mem. Am. Assn. Cancer Rsch. (bd. dirs. 1972-76), Am. Chem. Soc. (divsn. biol. chemistry, sec. 1955-57, councillor 1958-61), Am. Soc. Biochemistry and Molecular Biology, Soc. Exptl. Biology and Medicine, Cosmos Club, Sigma Xi, Alpha Omega Alpha, Phi Kappa Phi. Achievements include research in application of systems analysis and planning to strategic planning in medical research and laying the foundations for development of national cancer plan. Home: 19408 Charline Manor Rd Olney MD 20832-1044 Personal E-mail: baker1934@comcast.net.

BAKER, CARLETON HAROLD, physiology educator; b. Utica, NY, Aug. 2, 1930; s. Harold George and Loretta (Darling) B.; m. Sara Frances Johnson, July 20, 1963; children: Elizabeth Ann, Janet Lee. BA, Utica Coll. Syracuse U., 1952; MA, Princeton U., 1954, PhD, 1955. Asst. instr. Princeton U., NJ, 1952—54, asst. rsch., 1954—55; asst. prof. Med. Coll. Ga., Augusta, 1955—61, assoc prof., 1961—67, prof., 1967; prof. physiology and biophysics U. Louisville Health Scis. Ctr., 1967—71; prof., founding chmn. dept. physiology and biophysics U. South Fla. Coll. Medicine, Tampa, 1971—92, dep. dean rsch. and grad. studies, 1980—82, prof surgery, physiology and biophysics, dir. surg. rsch., 1992—95; prof. emeritus U. South Fla., 1995—. Rsch. com. mem. Am. Heart Assn., Louisville, 1969-71; rsch. com., bd. dirs. Am. Heart Assn. Fla., Tampa, 1971-85; NIH program project site visit team, 1982-84, mem. LCME Accreditation Survey Team, 1980-81; cons. U. Louisville Grad. Sch., East Carolina U. Grad. Program; rsch. prof. physiology U. S.C. Coll. Medicine, Columbia, 1994-2001 Editor: Microcirculatory Technology, 1986; mem. numerous editl. bds.; contbr. numerous articles in field Pres. Augusta Choral Soc., 1963; v.p. Blount Rd. Homeowners Assn., Lutz, Fla., 1986-93; bd. dirs. Friends of Augusta Grantee NIH, 1960-92, Am. Heart Assn., 1968-97; recipient Svc. awards Am. Heart Assn. Fla., 1974, 77, Disting. Scientist award U. South Fla. Coll. Medicine, 1981, Dean's Citation, 1991, Founder award, 1992, Outstanding Artist/Scholar award Phi Kappa Phi, 1991 Fellow: Am. Heart Assn., Am. Physiol. Soc. (fellow cardiovasc. sect.); mem.: Shock Soc. (program coms.), European Microcirculatory Soc., Microcirculatory Soc., Torch Club Internat. Republican. Avocations: golf, fishing. Home: 4039 Old Waynesboro Rd Augusta GA 30906-9254 Personal E-mail: microves@bellsouth.net.

BAKER, CAROLYN SIMMONS, library director, consultant, researcher; AAS in Libr. Sci., LCC, Kinston, NC, 1979; MLS, NC Ctrl. U., 1998; BSBA, NC Wesleyan Coll., 1985. Instr. Wake Tech. CC, Raleigh, NC, 1988—98; libr. III NC A&T, Greensboro, 1997—98; Greensboro libr. dir., 1998—99; dir. archives Shaw U., Raleigh, 1999—. Mem.: Order Ea. Star. Home Phone: 919-749-0261.

BAKER, CHARLES D., health insurance company executive; Former founder, co-dir. The Pioneer Inst.; former sec. health and human svcs., sec. adminstrn. and finance to former Gov. Mass. William Weld, 1991—98; pres., CEO Harvard Vanguard Med. Assocs., 1998, Harvard Pilgrim Health Care, Quincy, Mass., 1999—. Office: Harvard Pilgrim Healthcare 90 Worcester St Wellesley MA 02481

BAKER, CHARLES DUANE, business administration educator; b. Newburyport, Mass., June 21, 1928; s. Charles Duane and Eleanor (Little) B.; m. Alice Elizabeth Ghormley, 1955; children: Charles D., Jonathan G., Alexander K. AB, Harvard, 1951, MBA, 1955. With Westinghouse Electric Corp., Elmira, NY, 1955-57, Jersey City, 1957-61; v.p., treas. United Research, Inc., Cambridge, Mass., 1961-65; various positions through chmn., chief exec. Harbridge House, Inc., Boston, 1965-69, 72-83; prof. bus. adminstrn. Northeastern U., Boston, 1985—. Dep. under sec. U.S. Dept. Transp., Washington, 1969-70, asst. sec. policy and internat. affairs, 1970-71; under sec. U.S. Dept. HHS, Washington, 1984-85; presiding dir. Millipore Corp., 1986-87; adv. bd. dept. health policy Harvard Med. Sch.; chmn. McLean Health Svcs. Inc. Author various studies dealing with mgmt. transp., health care, pub. policy. Mem. vis. com. Harvard U.; bd. dirs. Pioneer Inst. for Pub. Policy, Millipore Corp., Am. Med. Response, Inc.; trustee, chmn. McLean Hosp.; pres. Hall-Mercer Hosps.; trustee Harvard Med. Ctr., 1996-99; mem. Group Ins. Commn. Lt. (j.g.) USNR, 1946-48, 51-53. Recipient Award for Outstanding Achievement U.S. Govt., 1971 Mem. Pi Eta, Beta Gamma Sigma (Hon.). Clubs: Essex County; Harvard, Comml., Clover (Boston); E. India (London); Metropolitan (Washington). Republican. Congregationalist. Office: Northeastern U 319 Hayden Hall 360 Huntington Ave Boston MA 02115-5000 Home: 64 Caldwell Farm Rd Byfield MA 01922-2823

BAKER, CHARLES E., lawyer; b. Dallas, June 1, 1957; BA in Econs., U. Cambridge, UK, 1978; JD, U. Toronto, 1981; MBA, U. Denver, 2001. Assoc. Fraser & Beatty, 1983—88, ptnr., 1988—93; dir. bus. devel. Ball Corp., Broomfield, Colo., 1993—95, dir. corp. compliance, 1994—97, sr. dir. bus. devel., 1995—99, assoc. gen. counsel, 1999—2004, gen. counsel, asst. corp. sec., 2004—05, v.p., gen. counsel, asst. corp. sec., 2005—. Mem.: Can. Bar Assn., Am. Corp. Counsel Assn., Law Soc. Upper Can., ABA, Colo. Bar Assn. Office: Ball Corp 10 Longs Peak Dr Broomfield CO 80021-2510 Office Phone: 303-460-2586. Office Fax: 303-460-2691. E-mail: cbaker@ball.com.*

BAKER, CHARLES STEPHEN, music educator; b. Cleve., July 25, 1942; s. LeRoy Williams and Nellie Angela (Burskey) B. BMus, Oberlin Coll. Conservatory, 1964; MA, Case Western Reserve U., 1967. Cert. music educator, Ohio. Tchr. music Madison Local Schs., Mansfield, Ohio, 1964-65, Wickliffe (Ohio) City Schs., 1967-96; pvt. clarinet instr., freelance clarinet performer Sch. of Fine Arts, Willoughby, Ohio, 1969—. Prin. clarinet, assoc. condr. Lakeland Civic Orch., Mentor, Ohio, 1972—. Named to Hall of Fame, City of Wickliffe, OhiO, 2005; recipient Disting. Svc. award, Sch. of Fine Arts, 1992. Mem. NEA, Ohio Music Edn. Assn. (gen. music com. mem. 1972-99, 25 Yr. Svc. award 1991), Music Educators Nat. Conf. (N.E. region chair 1986-92, 94-98, all-state orch. chair 1990-92), Lake County Music Educators (sec. v.p., pres.), Ohio Edn. Assn., Am. Fedn. Musicians, U.S. Figure Skating Assn. Roman Catholic. Avocations: figure skating, photography, gardening, travel. Home: 5476 A Wildwood Ct Willoughby OH 44094-3261 Personal E-mail: cbakermus@aol.com.

BAKER, CLORA MAE, business educator; b. Bedford, Ind., Jan. 21, 1948; d. Howard Perry and Bethel (Newlin) B.; BS, Ball State U., 1970, MAE, 1971. Cert. office automation profl. Sec. to dir. human performance lab. Ball State U., Muncie, Ind., 1967-70; bus. tchr. Carmel (Ind.) High Sch., 1970-85; teaching assoc. Ohio State U., Columbus, 1985-89; asst. prof. So. Ill. U., Carbondale, 1989-1995, assoc. prof., 1996; instr. evening div. Ind. U./Purdue U., Indpls., 1979-85. Active Reach to Recovery Am. Cancer Soc. Mem. DAR (Last River chpt.), Internat. Word Processing Assn. (educator's adv. council 1979-81), Ill. Bus. Edn. Assn.(Disting. Svc. award, 2003), Ill. Assn. of Career and Tech. Edn. (Adminstr. of Yr. award, 2004), Ind. Vocat. Assn., Am. Vocat. Assn., NEA, Ind. Tchrs. Assn., Nat. Bus. Edn. Assn., Delta Pi Epsilon (nat. council rep. 1978-90, nat. v.p. 2004-05, nat. pres. 2006-07), Am. Bus. Women's Assn. (named Woman of Yr., Hamilton chpt. 1980), Omicron Tau Theta, Phi Delta Kappa, Epsilon Pi Tau. Mem. Christian Ch. Home: 1214 W Hill St Carbondale IL 62901-2464 Office: So Ill U Dept Workforce Edn and Devel 212 Pulliam Hall Carbondale IL 62901 Home Phone: 618-549-1701; Office Phone: 618-453-3321. E-mail: cmbaker@siu.edu.

BAKER, CONSTANCE H., lawyer; b. Washington, Sept. 2, 1948; AB summa cum laude, Vassar Coll., 1969; JD, Cath. U. Am., 1975. Bar: Md. 1975, DC 1998. Asst. atty gen., prosecutor Md. Bd. Physicians State Md., 1979-81; ptnr. Health Care Group Venable LLP, Balt. Editl. bd. mem. Physician Orgns. and Med. Staff, 1997; contbr. articles to profl. jours. Bd. dirs. HopeWell Cancer Support. Named one of Best Lawyers in Am., 1995—, Top 100 Women in Md., Daily Record, 2000, Leading Health Care Lawyers in US, Chambers USA: Am.'s Leading Lawyers for Bus., 2006—, Leading Health Care Attys., Guide to Leading US Healthcare Lawyers, 2006. Mem. ABA (sect. on healthcare law), AMA (mem. Doctors Adv. Svc. 1993-2005), Md. State Bar Assn. (sect. on health care law), Am. Health Lawyers Assn. (bd. dirs. 1977-88), Wranglers Law Club. Office: Venable LLP 1800 Mercantile Bank & Trust Bldg 2 Hopkins Plz Ste 1800 Baltimore MD 21201-2982 Office Phone: 410-244-7535. Office Fax: 410-244-7742. Business E-Mail: chbaker@venable.com.

BAKER, CORNELIA DRAVES, artist; b. Woodbury, NJ, Mar. 2, 1929; d. Carl Zeno and Cornelia (Powell) Draves.; m. Philip Douglas Baker, July 16, 1955; children: Brinton, Todd, Claudia, Samuel. Student, Ohio Wesleyan U., 1947-50, Goethe U., Frankfurt, Germany, 1950-52. Travel dir. Am. Youth Hostels, Inc., NYC, 1953-57. Artist Cornelia Gallery, Kumamoto, Japan, 1990—; gallery dir. Presbyn. Ch., Franklin Lakes, N.J., 1988-97, Marcella Geltman Gallery, New Milford, N.J., 1993-96; bd. dirs. Bergen Mus. Art and Sci., N.J., 1996-2000, corr. sec., mem. exec. com., 1999-2000. One-woman shows include Ramapo Coll., 1986, Shimada Mus., Kumamoto, 1990, Sekaikan Gallery, Tokyo, 1990, Am. Ctr., Fukuoka, 1990, Bergen Mus. Art and Sci., 1993, L'Atelier Inc. Gallery, 1994, N.Y. Theol. Sem., N.Y.C., 1996, The Gallery, Franklin Lakes, 1997, 2003, Office Congressman S.R. Rothman, Hackensack, N.J., 1997, Lee Hecht Harrison, Paramus, N.J., 1998, Willows Cafe, Ramsey, N.J., 2000, The Gallery, Franklin Lakes, 2003; represented in permanent collections Bergen Mus. Art and Sci., Paramus, Beekley Internat. Skiing Fine Art and Graphics. Chair social problems com. Borough of Franklin Lakes Coun., 1973-76. Recipient Best of Show award Ringwood Manor Assn. of the Arts, 1987, Bergen Mus. Art and Sci., 1989, Emeriti award for excellence N.J. Ctr. for Visual Arts, 1989, Excellence cert. Internat. Art Competition, 1988, Women Making History in Arts award Bergen County, N.J., 1993, Crabbie award Art Calendar, 1994, Gold prize RISO Edn. Found., Japan, 1997, Artist Showcase award Manhattan Art Internat., 2000, merit award Salute to Women in Arts. 2000. Mem. Nat. Assn. Women Artists (printmaking jury chmn. 1992-94), Salute to Women in the Arts (pres. 1988-90), Mastodon Artists Soc. (life), Altrusa Club of Bergen County, N.J. Republican. Presbyterian. Avocation: travel. Home: 293 Green Ridge Rd Franklin Lakes NJ 07417-2011 Personal E-mail: cdbaker@optonline.net.

BAKER, D. JAMES, oceanographer, administrator, science and management consultant; b. Long Beach, Calif., Mar. 23, 1937; s. Donald James and Lillian Mae (Pund); m. Emily Lind Delman, Sept. 7, 1968. BS in Physics, Stanford U., 1958; PhD in Exptl. Physics, Cornell U., 1962; LHD (hon.), Nova U., 1993; DSc (hon.), Morgan state U., 2006. Rsch. assoc. in phys. oceanography U. R.I., Kingston, 1962-63; NIH postdoctoral fellow in chem. biodynamics U. Calif., Berkeley, 1963-64, Harvard U., Cambridge, Mass., 1964-66, asst. prof. oceanography, 1966-70, assoc. prof., 1970-73; group leader deep-sea physics Pacific Marine Environ. Lab. Nat. Oceanog. and Atmospheric Adminstrn., Seattle, 1977-79; rsch. assoc. prof. dept. oceanography U. Wash., Seattle, 1973-75, rsch. prof. dept. oceanography, 1975-79, sr. oceanographer Applied Physics Lab., 1973-86, adj. prof. dept. atmospheric scis., prof. Sch. Oceanography, 1979-86, chmn. dept. oceanography, 1979-81, dean Coll. Ocean and Fishery Scis., 1981-83; disting. vis. scientist Jet Propulsion Lab., Calif. Inst. Tech., Pasadena, 1982-93; pres. Joint Oceanog. Instns. Inc., Washington, 1983-93; under sec. commerce oceans and atmosphere, adminstr. NOAA, Washington, 1993—2001; pres., CEO Acad. Natural Scis., Phila., 2002—06; vis. fellow London Sch. Econs. and Polit. Sci., 2006—; cons. H. John Heinz Ctr. for Sci., Econs. and Environment, Washington, 2006—, UNESCO Intergovtl. Oceanographic Commn., 2006—. Guest investigator Woods Hole Oceanographic Instn., 1968-69, vis. scholar, 1970; mem. adv. com. NAS, NOAA and other internat. bodies; co-chair environ. and natural resources com. Nat. Sci. and Tech. Coun., 1993-2001; chair White House Coun. on Environ. Quality, 1993-94; ex-officio mem. Pres.'s Coun. on Sustainable Devel., 1993-2001; chair Fed. Com. for Meteorol. Svcs. and Supporting Rsch., 1993-2001; mem. Govt.-Univ.-Industry Rsch. Roundtable Coun., NAS/NRC, 1993-2001. Author: Planet Earth-The View from Space, 1990; co-editor-in-chief Geophys. Fluid Dynamics 1975-79; mem. editl. bd. Dynamics of Atmospheres and Oceans, 1979-88, Marine Tech. Soc. Journ., 1986-89, Oceanus Mag., 1992-93, Jour. Environ. Sci. Policy, 2001-; contbr. articles to profl. jours. Recipient COSPAR Vikram Sarabhai award, 1998; spkr., Whitehouse/Smithsonian Inst. Millennium celebration, 2000. Fellow: AAAS, Am. Meteorol. Soc. (coun. 1982—88, pub. awareness com. 1991—93); mem.: Am. Soc. Limnology and Oceanography, Meteorol. and Oceanog. Soc., Challenger Soc. Marine Sci. Can., Marine Tech. Soc., Oceanography Soc. (interim pres. 1988—89, pres. 1989—92, past pres. 1992—93), Am. Geophys. Union, Am. Philos. Soc., Sigma Xi. Achievements include patent for deep-sea pressure gauge with two colleagues. Avocations: piano, banjo, woodworking. E-mail: djamesbaker@comcast.net.

BAKER, DANIAL EDWIN, pharmacist, educator; b. Whitefish, Mont., May 25, 1955; s. Arby and Cathaline Baker, Arby E. and Cathy Lee (Yarroll) Baker; 1 child, Kristin Nicole; m. Susan Reinsel, June 24, 2007. B in Pharmacy, Wash. State U., 1978; PharmD, U. Minn., 1980. Lic. pharmacist, Wash. Instr. in pharmacology for respiratory therapist St. Paul Tech. Vocat. Inst., 1980; asst. prof. U. Okla., 1980-83, Wash. State U., Spokane, 1983-88, dir. Drug Info. Ctr., 1983—, assoc. prof., 1988-95, prof., 1995—, dir. clin. pharmacy programs, interim chmn. pharmacy dept., 1994—97, dir. continuing edn., 1997—, assoc. dean clin. programs, 2002—. Drug formulary adv. com. divsn. med. assistance Wash. Dept. Social and Health Svcs., Olympia, 1990, chmn., 1990-92, cons. 1999-03; cons. panel The Upjohn Co., Kalamazoo, 1990-93; adv. panel on drug info. sci. U.S. Pharmacopeial Conv., Inc., Rockville, Md., 1990-95; mem. Inst. for Safe Medication Practices, Inc., Huntington Valley, Pa., 1990—, Inst. Rev. Bd., Spokane, 1992-2002, Wash. State U., 1993-97; mem. adv. bd. Syntex Area Adv. Bd., Denver, 1994-96; cons., pharmacy and therapeutics com. Medco Health Solutions, Franklin Lakes, N.J., 1995—; pharmacy and therapeutics com. Whatcom Med. Bur., Bellingham, Wash., 1996-98; pharmacy adv. bd. Accredo Health, Memphis, 2007—. Sect. editor Rev. Gastroenterology Disorders, 2001—; asst. editor Hosp. Pharmacy, 2000—. Outdoor emergency care adminstr. Inland Empire region Nat. Ski Patrol, 1999—, sr. patrol, 1998—, instr., trainer, 1999—, asst. OEC supr. pacific N.W. divsn., 2001-04; 49 degree North Chewelah, Wash., 1994— Recipient Pharmacist Achievement award Merck Sharp and Dohme, 1993; named Outstanding Outdoor Emergency Care Instr. Inland Empire Region, Nat. Ski Patrol, 1999-2000, Pacific N.W. Divsn., 1999-2000, Outstanding Instr.

Pacific N.W. Divsn., Nat. Ski Patrol, 1999-2000. Fellow Am. Soc. Cons. Pharmacists, Am. Soc. Hosp. Pharmacists; mem. Am. Assn. Colls. Pharmacy, Am. Coll. Clin. Pharmacy, Am. Pharm. Assn., Wash. Pharmacists Assn. (senator 1991-95, continuing edn. com. 1988—, award com. 1989-95, co-chmn. undergrad. affairs com. 1990-92, del. quinquinnel conv. 1987—, Pharmacist of Yr. award 1992), Wash. Soc. Hosp. Pharmacists (coun. edn. and manpower 1989-92, chmn. 1990-92, bd. dirs. 1989-93, pres. Spokane chpt. 1992-93), Wash. Pharmacy Coun. Avocations: skiing, snow shoeing, photography, bicycling, kayaking. Office: Wash State U PO Box 1495 Spokane WA 99210-1495 Office Phone: 509-358-7660. Business E-Mail: bakerdan@wsu.edu.

BAKER, DANIEL CLIFTON, III, plastic surgeon, educator; b. NYC, Dec. 11, 1942; s. Daniel Clifton B. Jr. and Geraldine B.; m. Nina Griscom, Dec. 8, 1990. MD, Columbia Coll., 1968. Bd. cert. Med. Examiners, bd. cert. plastic surgery. Resident surgery UCLA, 1969—70, NYU Med.; clin. fellow Columbia Presbyn. Med. Ctr., 1977—78; assoc. prof. plastic surgery NYU Med. Ctr. Sch. Medicine, NYC; pvt. practice; surgeon dir. Manhattan Eye, Ear and Throat Hosp. Recipient Disting. Achievement award, Farleigh Dickinson U., Am. Acad. of Achievement award. Mem.: Am. Soc. Aesthetic Plastic Surgeons, Am. Soc. Plastic and Reconstructive Surgeons. Office: NYU Sch Medicine 65 E 66th St New York NY 10021 Office Phone: 212-734-9695. Office Fax: 212-744-5410. E-mail: daniel.baker@med.nyu.edu.*

BAKER, DANIEL PAUL, advertising executive, entrepreneur; b. Kenitra, Morocco, Aug. 3, 1967; s. David A. and Donna C. Baker; life ptnr. Timothy J. Keaveny. V.p. product devel. IFILM Inc., L.A., 1999—2001; pres. Absinthe Pictures, LLC, West Hollywood, Calif., 2001—04, Viricom, L.A., 2004—. Educator Literacy Project, L.A., 2007. D-Conservative. Home Phone: 323-654-1000; Office Phone: 323-654-1000.

BAKER, DANIEL RICHARD, computer company executive; b. Copenhagen, Mar. 19, 1932; came to U.S., 1936; s. Arthur and Molly (Needman) B.; m. June Ellin Nebenzahl, Oct. 2, 1960; children: David Charles, Jill Alison. Student, Tufts Coll., 1949—51; BA, Bklyn. Coll., 1957; postgrad., Fairleigh Dickinson U., 1961—64, Am. U., 1968—69; grad. Realtors Inst., U. Va., 1972. Math tchr. N.Y.C. Pub. Schs., 1958—59; computer programmer Sys. Devel. Corp., Paramus, NJ, 1959—61; programmer analyst ITT, Paramus, 1961—64; sr. mathematician Melpar Corp., Falls Church, Va., 1964—65; sys. analyst Wolf R & D Corp., Bladensburg, Md., 1965—66, Aries Corp., McLean, Va., 1966—68; sr. sys. analyst N. Am. Rockwell Corp., Roslyn, Va., 1968—70; pres. Data Assocs., Fairfax Station, Va., 1970—. Real estate broker. Group leader Dale Carnegie Sales Courses; vol. Ann. Fund Campaign Tufts Coll., 1976—. With AUS, 1954-55, vet. Korean War. Recipient Eagle Scout, Boy Scouts Am., 1945. Mem.: No. Va. Assn. Realtors Pioneer Club, Va. Assn. Realtors (dir. 1977—80, 1983—97, Lifetime award 1992, 1994—2005), Nat. Assn. Realtors (No. Va. chpt. multilist com., edn. com., pub. rels. com., 5-yr. Million Dollar Sales Club award), Charles Tufts Soc., Silvanus Packard Soc., Washington Tufts Club (v.p. 1975). Avocations: art, music, antique automobiles. Office: Data Assocs 5622-G Ox Rd Fairfax VA 22039-1018 Office Phone: 703-824-1848. Personal E-mail: would_i_kid_you@yahoo.com, ryde_em_cowboy@yahoo.com.

BAKER, DAVID, biochemist; BA, Harvard U.; PhD in Biochemistry, U. Calif., Berkeley. Prof. biochemistry U. Wash., Seattle. Sci. adv. bd. Codon Devices, Cambridge, Mass.; investigator Howard Hughes Med. Inst., 2000—. Contbr. articles to sci. jours. Recipient Overton prize, Internat. Soc. Computational Biology, 2002, Feynman prize, Foresight Inst., 2004. Mem.: NAS. Office: U Wash Dept Biochemistry J Wing Health Scis Bldg Box 357350 Seattle WA 98195

BAKER, DAVID A., obstetrician, gynecologist, educator; s. Milton and Sonia Baker; m. Judy Marshel, May 26, 2001; children: Dara A., Dawn G., Erica J. BS, Bklyn Coll., 1967; MS, U. Rochester, 1969; MD, SUNY, Bklyn., 1973. Diplomate Am. Bd. Ob-Gyn. Instr. ob-gyn U. Vt. Med. Ctr., Burlington, 1977—79; asst. prof. ob-gyn SUNY, Stony Brook, 1979—85; assoc. prof. dept. ob-gyn. SUNY Health Sci. Ctr., Stony Brook, 1985—98, prof. dept. ob-gyn., 1998—; assoc. prof. SUNY Dental Sch., Stony Brook, 1985—. Contbr. articles to profl. jours. Cons. LI HELP group, Beth Page, NY. Grantee Westat, NIAID, 1992—2003. Fellow: ACOG. Achievements include research in management and treament of Herpes virus infections. Avocation: gardening. Office: Dept Ob-gyn Health Scis Ctr SUNY Stony Brook NY 11794-8091 Office Phone: 631-444-3944. E-mail: dbaker@notes.cc.sunysb.edu.

BAKER, DAVID ARTHUR, retired small business owner, manufacturing executive; b. Cranston, RI, Jan. 5, 1941; s. Andrew Harris and Phyllis Evelyn (Partridge) B.; m. Anne Marie Perron, July 14, 1959; children: Susan Marie, Pamela Phyllis. Diploma, Brit. Inst. Homeopathy, Middlesex, Eng., 1995, DHM, 1996. With Supreme Coat Co., Worcester, Mass., 1960-74; owner D.A. Baker Mfg. Co., Auburn, Mass., 1975—2000, Eagle's Nest Video Prodns., Auburn, 1985—90; operator NORFED Currency Redemption Ctr., Leicester, Mass.; ret. Treas. Tax Law Rsch. Group, 2005. *Although retired in principal, spends much time studying law and researching the tax code, monetary policy and Social Security system of the United States. Active in the tax honesty movement, and also in the reform of our monetary, legal, and Social Security systems, and has goals to present some of the evidence before a Congressional or Senate committee. Wrote and published a book titled Beliefs, about income tax.* Prodr. (video) Popular Amazons, 1986, Macaws, 1987, Cockatoos, 1988, Parrot Keeping, 1989, others; author: Beliefs. Pres. bd. dirs. Royal Arts Found. Belcourt Castle, Newport, RI; res. dep. sheriff Worcester County; active Madison Found., U.S. Navy War Coll. Found., We the People Congress. Recipient Cert. of Merit, Les Comités des Vins de France, 1982; Decorated knight Order of St. John. Fellow Brit. Inst. Homeopathy; mem. NRA (Nat. Patriots medal), Patron Am. Coll. Heraldry, Homeopathic Acad. Naturopathic Physicians, Internat. Platform Soc., Internat. Soc. Food and Wine, Nat. Trust Hist. Preservation, Fully Informed Jury Assn., Tax Law Rsch. Group, Am. Jury Assn., Tax Law Rsc. Group, Save-A-Patriot Fellowship, Tax Truth Alliance, Free Enterprise Soc., Boston Soc. Aviculture (treas. 1983-85, Outstanding Svc. award 1984), Preservation Soc. Newport County, Exotic Cage Bird Soc. (co-founder, bd. dirs. 1986-88, Outstanding Svc. award 1985), Friends of Ballroom Dancing, Friends of the Royal Arts Found. (v.p.), Freedom Found., Rolls Royce Owners Club (life), Daimler and Lanchester Club, Club Maxine's, Health Scis. Inst., Leicester Bus. Assn. (v.p.), Tax Truth Alliance, Knight Cottage Assn. (past pres.), St. Andrew Soc. RI, Higgins Armory, Frohsinn Club, Salamander Club. Avocations: art, antiques, shooting, boating, aviculture. Office: Eagles Nest Villa 196 Leicester St Auburn MA 01501-1406

BAKER, DAVID HARRIS, lawyer; b. Rome, NY, Aug. 27, 1955; s. Abraham Harris and Ruth Elizabeth (Flanagan) B. BA in History and French, Hamilton Coll., 1976; JD, George Washington U., 1979. Bar: DC, 1979. Assoc. Pope Ballard & Loos, Washington, 1978-81; ptnr. Holland & Knight, Washington, 1982-97, Thompson Hine & Flory, LLP, Washington, 1997—2006. Instr. U.S. Dept. Def., Falls Church, Va., 1983-85. Mem. ABA (vice chmn. rate-making com. 1985-86, vice chmn. Consumer Product Safety Commn. com. 1991-92, chmn. 1992—), Bar Assn. D.C. (chmn. adminstrn. law sect. 1986-87, editor jour. 1986, bd. dirs. 1986-91), Assn. Transp. Practitioners (chmn. D.C. chpt. 1984-85, nat. treas. 1988-95, pres. 1997-8), Met. Club (Washington), Barristers, Columbia Country Club. Republican. Roman Catholic. Home: 3226 Farmington Dr Chevy Chase MD 20815-4827 Office: Law Offices David H Baker LLC 1700 Penn Ave NW Ste 400 Washington DC 20006 Office Phone: 202-349-4190. Business E-Mail: dhbakerlaw@aol.com.

BAKER, DAVID HIRAM, nutritionist, educator; b. DeKalb, Ill., Feb. 26, 1939; s. Vernon T. and Lucille M. (Severson) B.; m. Norraine A. Baker; children: Barbara G., Michael D., Susan G., Debora A., Luann C., Beth A. BS, U. Ill., 1961, MS, 1963, PhD, 1965. Sr. scientist Eli Lilly & Co., Greenfield, Ind., 1965-67; mem. faculty U. Ill., Champaign-Urbana, 1967—, prof. nutrition, dept. animal sci., nutritional biochemist, 1974—, dept. head, 1988-90. Author: Sulfur in Nonruminant Nutrition, 1977, Bioavailability of Nutrients for Animals, 1995; mem. editorial bd. Jour. Animal Sci., 1969-73, Jour. Nutrition, 1975-79, 89-99, Poultry Sci., 1978-84, Nutrition Revs., 1983-92; contbr. numerous articles to sci. jours. Chmn. bd. Champaign-Urbana Teen Challenge Drug Rehab. Program, 1977-80. Recipient Disting. Svc. award USDA, 1987; Univ. Scholar award, 1986; Nutrition Rsch. award, 1986; Am. Feed Mfrs., 1973; Merck award, 1977; Paul A. Funk award, 1977; H. H. Mitchell Tchg. award, 1979, 85; Broiler Rsch. award, 1983. Mem. NAS, Am. Soc. Animal Sci. (Young Scientist award 1971, Gustaf Bohstedt award 1985, Hoffman LaRoche award 1985, Morrison award 1994, Frontiers in Animal Nutrition award 2006, Charles A. Black award 2007), Poultry Sci. Assn., Am. Soc. Nutritional Sci. (Borden award 1986, Dannon award 2003), Fedn. Am. Socs. Exptl. Biology, Sigma Xi, Phi Kappa Phi, Alpha Zeta, Gamma Sigma Delta. Home: 2609 Wadsworth Ln Urbana IL 61802-9403 Office: U Ill Nutrition Dept Urbana IL 61801 Office Phone: 217-333-0243. Business E-Mail: dhbaker@uiuc.edu.

BAKER, DAVID REMEMBER, lawyer; b. Durham, NC, Jan. 17, 1932; s. Roger Denio and Eleanor Elizabeth (Ussher) B.; m. Myra Augusta Mullins, Nov. 2, 1955 PhB, U. Chgo., 1949; BA, Birmingham-So. Coll., 1951; JD, Harvard U., 1954. Bar: Ala. 1954, NY 1963, U.S. Supreme Ct. 1972. Assoc. Cabaniss & Johnston, Birmingham, Ala., 1957-62, Chadbourne, Parke, Whiteside & Wolff, NYC, 1962-66, ptnr., 1967-86, Jones, Day, Reavis & Pogue, NYC, 1986-93, Afridi, Angell & Baker, NYC, 1993-96, Gersen, Baker & Wood LLP, NYC, 1997-98, Baker, Johnston & Wilson LLP, Birmingham and NYC, 1998—2003; of counsel Haskell Slaughter Young & Rediker, LLC, Birmingham and NYC, 2003—. Gen. counsel Econ. Club N.Y., 1977—. Co-editor Due Diligence, Disclosures and Warranties in the Corporate Acquisition Practice, 1988, 2d edit., 1992; author articles and book chpts. Pres. NY Legis. Svc., NYC, 1975-98, chmn., 1998—; mem. adv. com. Ctr. for NYC Law, 2000—; sec., dir. Jr. Achievement of NY, 1973-99; dir. Jr. Achievement of Greater Birmingham, 1999-2007; life trustee Birmingham-So. Coll., 1985—. With US Army, 1954—57. Mem.: ABA (liaison com. fin. acctg. stds. bd.), Ala. Law Inst., Musica Viva N.Y. (pres. 1994—96), NY State Bar Assn. (exec. com. bus. law sect. 1987—89, exec. com. internat. law and practice sect. 1991—92, chmn. internat. investment and devel. com. 1991—92), Assn. Lloyd's Mems. (N.Am. adv. bd.), Internat. Bar Assn. (vice chmn. bus. orgn. com. 1986—90, rep. to U.S. mems. N.Y. area 1988—2000, chmn. com. on trusts for bus. 1990—94, prin. rep. to UN in N.Y. 1993—), Birmingham Bar Assn. (chmn. history and archives com. 2002), Ala. Bar Assn., NYC Bar Assn. (chmn. com. on state legis. 1968—70), Am. Law Inst., Am. Arbitration Assn. (nat. panel), Met. Club NYC, Harvard Club NYC, Summit Club Birmingham. Democrat. Unitarian Universalist. Avocation: bridge. Home: 1200 Beacon Pkwy E Apt 500 Birmingham AL 35209-1041 Office: Haskell Slaughter Young & Rediker LLC 1400 Park Pl Tower 2001 Park Pl N Birmingham AL 35203-2700 also: Haskell Slaughter Young & Rediker LLC 515 Madison Ave Fl 30 New York NY 10022 Office Phone: 205-251-1000, 212-752-5507. Business E-Mail: drb@hsy.com.

BAKER, DAVID WARREN, earth scientist; b. Great Falls, Mont., Nov. 9, 1939; s. Roy Earnest Baker and Thora Leona Martin; m. Evelyn Elizabeth Herbstrith, 1962 (div. 1978); children: Erik Conrad, Andrew Craig, Paula Alicia. PhD, UCLA, 1969; MS in Natural sci., Swiss Fed. Inst. Tech., 1964; BS, MIT, 1961. Cons. earth scientist, owner Little Belt Cons. Svcs., Monarch, Mont., 1984—; rsch. geologist Gulf R & D Corp., Pitts., 1976—83; asst. prof. U. Ill., Chgo., 1970—76. Cons. Export Bd. Zambia, Lusaka, 1995, World Bank, Lusaka, 1995. Scoutmaster Boy Scouts Am., Oak Park, Ill., 1970—76, New Alexandria, Pa., 1976—82. Mem.: Tobacco Root Geol. Soc., Mont. Geol. Soc., Nat. Ctr. Sci. Edn., Geol. Soc. Am., Am. Geophys. Union. Unitarian. Achievements include first to reconstruct plate tectonic history of central Montana; research in plate tectonic origin of Yogo Sapphire Deposit in Montana; first to develop technique to analyze extremely deformed rock (mylonite) using X-rays and spherical harmonic analysis; Conducted field courses for Montana teachers on plate tectonic history of Montana. Home and Office: Little Belt Consulting Svcs PO Box 906 1 Paine Gulch Monarch MT 59463

BAKER, DEBORAH, editor, writer; b. Charlottesville, Va., Mar. 28, 1959; d. Jeffrey John Wheeler and Barbara Ann Baker; m. Amitav Ghosh, Feb. 15, 1990; children: Lila, Nayan. Affiliated degree, Cambridge U., Eng., 1980; BA, U. Va., 1981. Editl. dir. Overlook, NYC, 1986-88; assoc. pub. Sheep Meadow, The Bronx, 1993-95; exec. editor Kodansha, NYC, 1995-99; sr. editor Little Brown, NYC, 2000—. Author: In Extremis: The Life of Laura Riding, 1993 (finalist for Pulitzer prize), Making a Farm: The Life of Robert Bly, 1982. Office: 40 McCormick Williams 6th Fl 27 W 20th St New York NY 10011

BAKER, DEBORAH, medical educator; BA in Spanish and Geology, U. Tex., Austin, 1982; postgrad. in Astronomy, Ocean Geology, Biology, U. Tex., San Antonio, 1989; postgrad. in Rocket Sci., U. Ala., Huntsville, 1991; postgrad. in Marine Biology, Tex. A&M U., Galveston, 1992; postgrad. in Neurology and Environ. Sci., MD Anderson Cancer Ctr., Austin, 2003—06. Cert. Assn. Christian Schs. Internat., Aircraft Owners and Pilots Assn., Tex. Assn. Health, Phys. Edn., Recreation and Dance. Tchr. health, anatomy and physiology SACS, San Antonio; tchr. biology, life sci., dept. head Cornerstone, San Antonio; tchr. pre-chemistry, life sci., computer St. Mary's Hall, San Antonio; tchr. ESL U. Novgorod, Russia; head dept. geology Anson Jones Mid. Sch., San Antonio; tchr. Spanish I and II, life sci., biology Castle Hills HS, San Antonio. Docent Friedrich Wilderness Park, San Antonio; CPR instr. Am. Red Cross; leader and mentor Nat. Youth Leadership Conf., Washington. Author: (poetry collections) New Wings, YHWH, Thirsting, 1985—92; various media, 1999—. Sponsor knitting club Warm Up Am., Texas, Mont., 2005—06; team mem. Konnarock, CREW, Appalachian Tr., Va., Gospel of John, Chisinau, Moldova, 1995—98. Named to Outstanding Coll. Student of Am., 1989; recipient Thanks to Tchrs. Excellence, KENS-TV 5, 1992, Yuri Gagarin Cosmonaut award, Star City Cosmonaut Training, Russia, 1994. Mem.: Assn. Christian Schs. Internat., Assn. Pilots, Alpha Sigma Alpha. Avocations: hiking, swimming, crafts, music.

BAKER, DEXTER FARRINGTON, manufacturing executive, director; b. Worcester, Mass., Apr. 16, 1927; s. Leland Dyer and Edith (Quimby) B.; m. Dorothy Ellen Hess, June 23, 1951; children: Ellen L., Susan A., Leslie A., Carolyn J. BS, Lehigh U., 1950, MBA, 1957. Sales engr. Air Products & Chem., Inc., Allentown, Pa., 1952-56, gen. sales mgr., 1956-57, mng. dir., 1957-64, chief exec. ops. in Europe, bd. dir., 1964-67, exec. v.p., 1967-78, pres., 1978-86, 90-91, chmn., pres., 1990-91, chmn., chief exec. officer, 1986-92, chmn. exec. com. bd. dir., 1992-98. Former chmn. investment policy US Trade Rep. Bd. assocs. Muhlenberg Coll.; trustee Harry C. and Mary M. Trexler Found. Served with USNR, 1945-46; with U.S. Army, 1950-52. Mem. AIChE, Am. Mgmt. Assn., Nat. Assn. Mfrs. (former chmn.), Theta Chi. Presbyterian (elder). Office: Air Products and Chems Inc 7201 Hamilton Blvd Allentown PA 18195-1501

BAKER, DIANE R.H., dermatologist; b. Toledo, Nov. 17, 1945; BS, Ohio State U., 1967, MD cum laude, 1971. Diplomate Am. Bd. Dermatology. Intern U. Wis. Hosp., Madison, 1971-72, resident in dermatology, 1972-74, Oreg. Health Sci. Ctr., Portland, 1974-76; pvt. practce, Portland, 1976—. Clin. prof. dermatology Oreg. Health Sci. U., 1986—; mem. med. staff Meridian Park Hosp., Tualatin, Oreg., 1981—; dir. Am. Bd. Dermatology, 1995—, v.p., 2001. Mem.: AMA (del. 1995—), Oreg. Dermatol. Soc., Am. Dermatol. Assn. (v.p. 2001), Am. Acad. Dermatology (v.p. 1990), Alpha Omega Alpha. Office: 1706 NW Glisan St Ste 2 Portland OR 97209-2225

BAKER, DON L., band director; b. Dover, NJ, Jan. 18, 1967; s. Donald B. and Elaine Baker. MusB, Rutgers U., 1993. Cert. music tchr. Dept. of Edn., N.J. Dir. of bands Lincoln H.S., Jersey City, 1993—95, Rutherford H.S., NJ, 1995—. Drill instr. Columbia H.S., Maplewood, NJ, 1985—96. Mem.: Internat. Assn. of Jazz Educators, Music Educators Nat. Conf., Porsche Club of Am. (Enthusiast of the Yr. 1993). Home: 30-L Garden Terr North Arlington NJ 07031 Office: Rutherford H S 56 Elliott Pl Rutherford NJ 07070 E-mail: leadtrupet@aol.com.

BAKER, DONALD, lawyer, director; b. Chgo., May 28, 1929; s. Russell and Elizabeth B.; m. Gisela S. Carli, Oct. 6, 1960; children: Caryna, Andrew, Russell. Student, Deep Springs Coll., Calif., 1947-49; JDS., U. Chgo., 1954. Bar: Ill. 1955, N.Y. 1964. Ptnr. Baker & McKenzie, Chgo., 1955-94, ret., 1994; sec., gen. counsel, bd. dirs. Air South, Inc., Columbia, SC, 1994-95. Bd. dirs. Trimedyne, Inc., Cardiomedics, Inc. Bd. dirs. exec. com. Mid-Am. Com., Chgo., 1980-94. Mem. ABA. Clubs: Michigan Shores (Wilmette, Ill.). E-mail: dbaker5727@aol.com.

BAKER, DONALD, literature educator; b. Kansas City, Oct. 7, 1944; s. Elmer and Arneda Veronica Baker; m. Anjail Sullivan, Apr. 4, 1993; 1 child, Anjail Ahneda; m. Sharon Elizabeth Allison (dec.); children: Akilah, Aminah, Musa, Donald; 1 child, Kenyatta. BA, Cal State, LA, 1973, MA, 1975. English tchr. LA Unified Sch. Dist., 1979—2004; English tchr., dean Muhammad U., 1973—76; publisher Precocious Publishing Co., 1970—. Author: CRIPS, 1986, Inhale Gasoline & Gun Smoke, 1995, N*GG**S - The Black Curse, 2006; co-author: (screenplays) South Central, 1992. Pres. Internat. Black Writers & Artists, LA, 1983. With US Army, 1966—67, Vietnam. Independent. Muslim. Avocations: tennis, acting, bowling, poetry. Home: 8817 Dartford Pl Inglewood CA 90305 Office: Precocious Publishing Co 149 E 74th St Los Angeles CA 90003 Business E-Mail: dbakeer107@sbcglobal.net.

BAKER, DONNA M., research and development company executive, lawyer; m. Bill Baker; 1 child, Patrick. BA, Loyola Marymount U.; MBA, JD, UCLA. Assoc. Morrison & Foerster LLP; ptnr. Burke, Williams & Sorensen, LLP; v.p., gen. counsel Gemological Inst. Am., 2001, sr. v.p., gen. counsel, 2001—06, acting pres., 2006, pres., 2006—. Mem.: North San Diego County Bar Assn., San Diego Bar Assn., Calif. State Bar Assn., ABA, Am. Corp. Counsel Assn. Office: Gemological Institute of America Robert Mouawad Campus 5345 Armada Dr Carlsbad CA 92008 Office Phone: 760-603-4000. Office Fax: 760-603-4080.*

BAKER, DOUGLAS B., federal official; BA, Tex. U.; JD, South Tex. U. Assoc. staff counsel energy and commerce com. U.S. Ho. of Reps., 1990; policy analyst Agy. Internat. Devel.; law clerk to Hon. John D. Rainey U.S. Dist. Ct., Houston, 1991—92; atty. Looper, Reed, Mark & McGraw, 1993—98; exec. dir., dep. gen. counsel Harris County Houston Sports Authority, 1999—2001; dep. asst. sec. svc. industries, tourism and fin., internat. trade adminstrn. U.S. Dept. Commerce; spl. asst. to Pres., dir. border and transp. security, homeland security coun. Exec. Office of Pres., 2005—. Office: Eisenhower Exec Office Bldg 1650 Pennsylvania Ave NW Rm 492 Washington DC 20502-0001 Office Phone: 202-456-5785.

BAKER, DOUGLAS M., JR., service industry executive; Various mktg. and mgmt. positions Proctor & Gamble Co.; with Ecolab Inc., St. Paul, 1989, sr. v.p. inst. sector, 2001—02, pres., COO, 2002—04, pres., CEO, bd. dir., 2004—, chmn., 2006—. Office: Ecolab 370 Wabasha St N Saint Paul MN 55102*

BAKER, DUSTY (JOHNNIE B. BAKER JR.), former professional baseball team manager, retired professional baseball player; b. Riverside, Calif., June 15, 1949; s. Johnnie B. Baker Sr. and Christine Baker; m. Melissa Baker; children: Natosha, Darren. Student, Am. River Coll. Outfielder Atlanta Braves, 1968-75, L.A. Dodgers, 1976-83, San Francisco Giants, 1984, Oakland A's, 1985-86, San Francisco Giants, 1988-92, 1993—2002, Chgo. Cubs, 2002—06. Mem. Nat. League All-Star Team, 1981-82; baseball analyst ESPN, 2006. Recipient Silver Slugger award, 1980-81, Gold Glove, 1981; named to Sporting News All-Star Team, 1980.*

BAKER, EDWARD KEVIN, retail executive; b. Chester, Ill., Nov. 25, 1948; s. Edward Louis and Betty Lou (Huch) B.; m. Janet Lynn Verbal, Oct. 26, 1967 (div. 1973); 1 child, Shawn Allen; m. Doris Mary Kubala, June 12, 1975; stepchildren: Jimmy Lee, Jennifer Lou Godard. Mgr. F.W. Woolworth Co., St. Louis, then Dallas, 1968-74; pres. Baker Mktg. Co., Dallas, 1974-76; mgr. E.B. Mott Co., Dallas, 1976-83; mkt. mgr. Michaels Stores Inc., San Antonio, 1983-86, dir. merchandising Irving, Tex., 1986-88, dir. mgmt. devel., 1988-89, v.p. ops., 1989-91; sr. v.p. ops., distbn. mktg. Silk Greenhouse Inc., Tampa, 1990-91; dir. ops. mdse. Crafts & More div. Ames Dept. Stores, Rocky Hill, Conn., 1991-92; pres. E.K. Baker Group, Inc., Treasure House Stores, Inc., Seattle, 1993—, chief oper. officer, bd. dirs. Author The Edge 1988; producer (video) Framing Technique 1989; editor (video) Art Materials 1989. Mem. Southwest Craft & Hobby Assn. (bd. dirs. 1987-93), Am. Soc. Tng. Dirs., Art Materials Trade Assn., Am. Soc. Decorative Painters, Profl. Picture Framers Assn. Lutheran. Avocation: restoring antique furniture. Personal E-mail: ekdbaker@sbcglobal.net.

BAKER, EDWARD L., JR., public health physician; b. Chattanooga, Nov. 18, 1946; s. Edward Lamar and Sue B. Baker; m. Pamela Taylor, June 21, 1969; children: Justin, Ryan, Lindsay. BA, Vanderbilt U., 1968; MD, Baylor U., 1972; MPH, Harvard U., 1979, MS, 1980. Diplomate Am. Bd. Internal Medicine, Am. Bd. Occupational Medicine. Commd. USPHS, 1974—2003, asst. surgeon gen.; dep. dir. Nat. Inst. for Occupational Safety; asst. prof. Harvard U. Sch. Pub. Health, Boston, 1980-82, assoc. prof., 1982-85; asst. dir. Nat. Inst Occupl. Safety and Health Ctr. Disease Control, Atlanta, 1985-88, dep. dir. Nat. Inst. Occupl. Safety and Health, 1988-90, dir. Pub. Health Practice Program Office, 1990—2003; dir. NC Inst. for Pub. Health U. NC Sch. Pub. Health, Chapel Hill, 2003—; prof. Dept. Health Policy and Adminstrn. U. NC, Chapel Hill. Bd. dirs. Internat. Commn. on Occupl. Health, 1986-92. Author, editor 100 sci. articles and book chpts. Fellow Am. Coll. Epidemiology; mem. APHA, Am. Coll. Occupl. and Environ. Medicine (authorship award 1988), Soc. Occupl. and Environ. Health, Royal Soc. Medicine (London, vis. fellow). Office: NC Inst Public Health Univ North Carolina Campus Box 8165 Chapel Hill NC 27599-8165 Office Phone: 919-966-1069. Office Fax: 919-966-0478. Business E-Mail: ed_baker@unc.edu.

BAKER, EDWARD MARTIN, engineering and industrial psychologist; s. Harold H. and Paula B.; m. Shige Jajiki; 1 son, Evan Keith. BA, CCNY, 1962, MBA, 1964; PhD (Research fellow), Bowling Green State U., 1972. Human factors research engr. environ. and safety engring. staff Ford Motor Co., Dearborn, Mich., 1972-77, tech. tng. assoc. mgmt. and tech. tng. dept. Detroit, 1977-79, orgn. devel. cons., personnel and orgn. staff, 1979-81, statis. assoc., ops. support product quality office, 1981-83, statis methods mgr. Asia-Pacific and Latin-Am. automotive ops., 1983-87, dir. total quality planning, cons. and statis. methods corp. quality office, 1987—, dir. quality strategy and ops. support, 1990-92; sr. fellow Aspen Inst., Wye, Md., 1992-95. Deming scholars MBA program adv. bd. Fordham U., 1992—, adj. faculty MBA program, 1994—; cons. in field. Author: Scoring a Whole in One, 1999; contbr. articles to profl. jours.; editorial referee: Jour. Quality Tech, 1974-75, 77-81. Trustee W. Edwards Deming Inst., Washington, 1993-2003. Capt. US Army, 1964—67. Fellow Am. Soc. Quality (Brumbaugh award 1975, Craig award 1976, 79, 86, 88, Ishikawa medal 1995, Deming medal 1997). Home and Office: PO Box 5797 Scottsdale AZ 85261-5797 Personal E-mail: lifemap@ix.netcom.com.

BAKER, ELENORA FRANCES, retired elementary school educator; b. Hollidaysburg, Pa., Feb. 28, 1919; d. James Lester Dannals and Alverna Ellen Gordon; m. James Thompson Baker (dec.); children: Sandra Anita Askew, Debra Jeanine Chang. Student, Livingstone Coll., Salisbury, NC, 1938—40; BA, Fla. A&M U., 1958; EdM, Loyola Marymount U., 1977. Instr. English and Math. soldier GED program, Gelnhausen, Germany, 1960—62; instr. 6th grade Holy Spirit Cath. Sch., LA, 1963—66; instr. 2d-3d grade 107th St. Sch., LA, 1966—78; instr. 3d-4th grade Tweedy Sch., South Gate, Calif., 1978—84, St. Teresa of Avila Cath. Sch., LA, 1987—89; instr. jr. HS pvt. sch., LA, 1989—91; program asst. Crystal Stairs Inc., LA, 1991—2001; ret., 2001. Guild pres., membership chmn. Mus. African Am. Art, LA; chmn. hospitality Dorothy Chandler Music Ctr, LA; CCD tchr. Mil. Coun. Cath. Women, Gelnhausen, Germany, 1960—61. Mem.: Officers Wives Club (pres.), Alpha Kappa Alpha (fin. sec. 1957), Kappa Delta Pi (corr. sec. 1957). Democrat. Roman Catholic. Home: 688 N Rimsdale Ave # 59 Covina CA 91722

BAKER, ELIZABETH CALHOUN, magazine editor; b. Boston; d. John Calhoun and Elizabeth Marshall Evans B. BA cum laude, Bryn Mawr Coll.; MA, Radcliffe Coll. Fulbright scholar Inst. d'Art et d'Archeologie and Ecole du Louvre, Paris; Instr. art history Boston U., Wheaton Coll., Norton, Mass.; assoc. editor Art News, NYC, 1963-65, mng. editor, 1965-73; editor Art in Am. mag., NYC, 1973—. Instr. art history Sch. Visual Arts, N.Y.C., 1968-74; freelance art criticism. Recipient Lifetime Achievement award Coll. Art Assn., 1992; Nat. Endowment for Arts grantee, 1972 Office: Art in America Brant Publications 575 Broadway Fl 5 New York NY 10012-3230

BAKER, ELLEN SHULMAN, astronaut, physician; b. Fayetteville, NC, Apr. 27, 1953; d. Melvin Shulman; m. Kenneth J. Baker; 2 daughters. BA in Geology, SUNY, Buffalo, 1974; MD, Cornell U., 1978; grad. Air Force Aerospace Medicine Course, Brooks AFB, San Antonio, Tex., 1981; MS in Public Health, U. Tex., 1994. Diplomate Am. Bd. Internal Medicine. Resident U. Tex. Health Sci. Ctr., San Antonio; med. officer NASA Lyndon B. Johnson Space Ctr., Houston, 1981-84, astronaut candidate, 1984-85, astronaut, 1985—, mission specialist Shuttle Orbiter Atlantis flight STS-34, 1989, mission specialist Shuttle Columbia flight STS-50, 1992, mission specialist Shuttle Atlantis flight STS-71, 1995, lead astronaut for med. issues; astronaut rep. Edn. Working Group at Johnson Space Ctr. Achievements include having logged more than 686 hours in space. Avocations: skiing, swimming, running, movies, music, reading. Address: NASA Johnson Space Ctr Astronaut Ofc 2101 NASA Parkway Houston TX 77058

BAKER, EVA LEE, education educator, researcher; b. LA, May 31, 1940; d. David Brainin and Janice Frances Funk; m. Peter S. Baker, July 27, 1960 (div. Oct. 2, 1978); children: Tristan Bickman, Christopher; m. Harold F. O'Neil, Sept. 15, 1984. BA in English, UCLA, 1963, MA in Edn., 1965, EdD, 1967. Peace Corps instr UCLA, 1965—67; mem. profl. staff S.W. Regional Lab., 1967—68; asst. prof. UCLA, 1968—72, assoc. prof., 1973—78, prof. edn., 1978—2004, dir. Ctr. for the Study of Evaluation, 1975—, dir. Nat. Ctr. for Rsch. on Evaluation, Stds. and Student Testing, 1985—, acting dean Grad. Sch. Edn. and Info. Studies, 1995—97, disting. prof. edn., 2004—. Chair Stds. for Ednl. and Psychol. Testing, 1993—99, Bd. on Testing and Assessment, Washington, 2000—04; mem. Adv. Coun. on Ednl. Stats., Washington, 2002; presenter in field; cons. in field; cert. performance technologist, 2003—. Editor (with M.C. Wittrock): Testing and Cognition, 1991; co-editor (with H.F. O'Neil Jr.): Technology Assessment in Software Applications, 1994, Technology Assessment in Education and Training, 1994; contbr. chapters to books, articles to profl. jours.; mem. editl. bd., spl. issue editor: Am. Jour. Edn., internat. adv. bd. mem.: Assessment in Education: Principles, Policy & Practice, mem. editl. bd.: Educational Assessment; editor: Educational Evaluation and Policy Analysis; mem. editl. bd.: The Education Researcher, Jossey-Bass, guest editor: Jour. Ednl. Rsch., mem. editl. bd.: Jour. Ednl. Psychology; co-editor: Jour. Learning & Evaluation. Mem. Nat. Acad. Edn., 2007—. Grantee, L.A. Annenberg Met. Project, 1996—2000, Stuart Found., 1997—2000, 1998—2001, L.A. Unified Sch. Dist., 1995—2000, State of Wyo. Dept. Edn., 1999—2000, The Joyce Found., 1999—2000, others. Mem.: APA, Nat. Acad. Edn., Am. Ednl. Rsch. Assn. (pres. 2006—07), Nat. Coun. on Measurement in Edn., Am. Psychol. Soc. Office Phone: 310-206-1530. Business E-Mail: eva@ucla.edu.

BAKER, FLOYD WILMER, surgeon, retired military officer; b. Leavenworth, Kans., May 25, 1927; s. Floyd Winfield and Lolita Clare (Somers) B.; m. Darlene Marie Fulk, Apr. 10, 1949; children: Linda Marie, Diane Louise, Barbara Jayne. BA, U. Kans., 1950, MD, 1953; grad., Army Command and Gen. Staff Coll., 1964, Indsl. Coll. Armed Forces, 1967. Diplomate: Am. Bd. Surgery. Commd. 1st lt. U.S. Army, 1953, advanced through grades to maj. gen., 1980; intern Madigan Gen. Hosp., Tacoma, 1953-54; resident in gen. surgery Fitzsimons Army Hosp., Denver, 1955-59; dir. personnel and tng. Office of Surgeon Gen., 1970-71; comdg. gen. Brooke Army Med. Center, Ft. Sam Houston, Tex., 1974-78; Letterman Army Med Center, Presidio of San Francisco, 1978-81; chief surgeon U.S. Army, Europe; comdg. gen. U.S. Army 7th Med. Command, 1981-83, U.S. Army Health Services Command, Ft. Sam Houston, 1983-86; retired U.S. Army, 1986. Served with USNR, 1945-46. Decorated Legion of Merit (2), Meritorious Service medal, Army Commendation medal (3), Air medal (2), Disting. Service medal. Fellow Am. Coll. Physician Execs.; mem. AMA, Soc. U.S. Army Flight Surgeons. Republican. Baptist. Home and Office: 1413 Wiltshire Ave San Antonio TX 78209-6050 E-mail: fbaker1@satx.rr.com.

BAKER, FREDERICK MILTON, JR., lawyer; b. Flint, Mich., Nov. 2, 1949; s. Frederick Milton Baker and Mary Jean (Hallitt) Rarig; m. Irene Taylor; children: Jessica, Jordan. BA, U. Mich., 1971; JD, Washington U., St. Louis, 1975. Bar: Mich. 1975, U.S. Dist. Ct. (we. dist.) Mich. 1980, U.S. Dist. Ct. (ea. dist.) Mich. 1981, U.S. Ct. Appeals (6th cir.) 1983, U.S. Supreme Ct. 1986. Instr. law Wayne State U., Detroit, 1975-76; rsch. atty. Mich. Ct. Appeals, Lansing, 1976-77, law clk. to chief judge, 1977; asst. prof. T.M. Cooley Law Sch., Lansing, 1978-80; ptnr. Willingham & Cote, Lansing, 1980-86, Honigman, Miller, Schwartz & Cohn, Lansing, 1986—2004; commr. Mich. Supreme Ct., 2005—. Adj. prof. T.M. Cooley Law Sch., 1980—86, 1995—96, Detroit Coll. Law Mich. State U., East Lansing, 2001—. Author: Michigan Bar Appeal Manual, 1982; editor Mich. Bar Jour., 1984—; contbr. articles to profl. jours. Founder, pres. Sixty Plus Law Ctr., Lansing, 1978-87, bd. dirs., 1987—; mem. cmty. adv. bd. Lansing Jr. League, 1983-90; co-founder, dir., sec.-treas. John D. Voelker Found., 1989—; bd. dirs. Greater Lansing chpt., ACLU 1997-2004; treas. Kehillat Israel, 1996-98; trustee Thoman Found., 2000-, Lansing Area Cmty. Trust, 2003—; pres. Gerald Beckwith Fund, 2002-04. Recipient Disting. Brief award T.M. Cooley Law Rev., 1988, 99. Fellow Mich. State Bar Found.; mem. ABA (Outstanding Single Project award 1980), Mich. Bar Assn. (vice chmn. jour. adv. bd. 1984-87, chmn. jour. adv. bd. 1987—, young lawyers sect. coun. 1980-84, grievance com. 1982-84, John W. Cummiskey award 1984), Ingham County Bar Assn. (Disting. Vol. award 2000), Big Oak Club (Baldwin, Mich.). Unitarian Universalist. Avocations: photography, fishing, running, frisbee, writing. Home: 5127 Barton Rd Williamston MI 48895-9304 Office: Mich Supreme Ct PO Box 30104 Lansing MI 48909 Home Phone: 517-655-5501; Office Phone: 517-373-0260. E-mail: bakerf@courts.mi.gov.

BAKER, GAIL, director, ESL educator; b. Brynmawr, Breconshire, Wales, Apr. 19, 1954; d. William John Price and Glenys June Edwards; m. Kenneth Baker, Apr. 12, 1980. EdB, Normal Coll., Bangor, Wales, 1977; BA, Open U., Milton Keynes, Eng., 1985; MA in Linguistics and TESOL, U. Surrey, Eng., 2002. Cert. TEFLA Cambridge U., 1997. Substitute tchr. Gwent Edn. Authority, Brynmawr, 1977—78, tchr., 1978—85, prin., 1985—88; ESL instr. Omaha Pub. Schs., 1989—92; prin. KCIS Internat. Sch., Hong Kong, 1993—94; corp. trainer Tender Heart Treasures, Omaha, 1996; tech. writer Brumko Magnetics, Elkhorn, Nebr., 1997—98; ESL instr. Bellevue Univ. and Met. C.C., Omaha, 1998—2002; ESL program coord. Met. C.C., Omaha, 2002—. Mem.: NAFSA (assoc.), Mid-TESOL Orgn. (assoc.), Nat. Literacy Coun. Am. (assoc.), Nat. TESOL Orgn. (assoc.). Home: 13616 Polk St Omaha NE 68137-4123 Office: Metropolitan Community College PO Box 3777 Omaha NE 68103-0777 Home Phone: 402-894-1824; Office Phone: 402-738-4090. Office Fax: 402-738-4553; Home Fax: 402-894-1824. Personal E-mail: kgbaker@aol.com. Business E-Mail: gabaker@mccneb.edu.

BAKER, GEORGE HAROLD, III, physicist, educator; b. Cheverly, Md., Mar. 23, 1949; s. George Harold, Jr. and Betty (Frost) Baker; m. Donna Prillaman, June 21, 1975; children: Matthew C., Jeffrey P., Virginia E. BA, Western Md. Coll., 1971; MS, U. Va., 1974; PhD, USAF Inst. Tech., Dayton, Ohio, 1987. Tchg. asst. U. Va., Charlottesville, 1971-73; physicist Harry Diamond Labs., Adelphi, Md., 1973-77, Def. Nuc. Agy., Alexandria, Va., 1977-87, group leader, 1987-89, asst. for program devel., 1989-94; chief innovative concepts divsn., 1994-96; Def. Threat Reduction Agy. dir. Springfield (Va.) Rsch. Facility, 1996-99; sr. scientist Northrop-Grumman, Alexandria, 1999—2000; assoc. prof. Coll. Integrated Sci. and Tech. James Madison U., Harrisonburg, Va., 1999—, dir. Inst. Infrastructure and Info. Assurance, 2002—03; mem. Congl. Electromagnetic Pulse Commn. Staff, 2002—07. Exec. adv. bd. Inst. Infrastructure and Info. Assurance, 2003—, mem. IIIA exec. adv. bd., 2006—; exec. bd. Nat. Def. Indsl. Assn. Homeland Security, 2005—; infrastructure roundtable NRC, 2005—, com. on burec security; cons. in field. Contbr. articles to profl. jours. Canvasser Citizens Sensible County Planning, Fairfax County, Va., 1989—2000; tchr. Agape Christian Fellowship, Chantilly, Va., 1974—94, elder, 1994—2000; music and youth leader New Life Fellowship, Annandale, Va., 1979—83. Fellow: Nuc. Electromagnetic Soc. (chmn. program com. 1984, co-chair non-proliferation and arms control underground focus group 1996—99, session chair 1998, chmn. nat. HPM conf. steering group 1999, mem. Amerem nat. com. 2001—, session chair 2002); mem.: NAS (mem. infrastructure roundtable 2006—07), IEEE (sr.; session chmn. 1987, 1992), Forum Mil. Application Directed Energy, Directed Energy Profl. Soc. (charter), Assn. Old Crows, Phi Delta Theta. Achievements include patents for optically coupled differential voltage sensor; co-developer sea-going nuclear EMP simulator concept; development of Defense Nuclear Agency EMP underground test program; High Power Microwave program; space nuclear power. Office: Coll Integrated Sci and Tech James Madison U MSC 4102 Harrisonburg VA 22807 Business E-Mail: bakergh@jmu.edu.

BAKER, GERALD DAVID, marketing executive, consultant; b. Boston, Mar. 14, 1929; s. Arthur Haskell Baker and Esther Etta Miller; m. Peggy Joyce Zager, Sept. 6, 1954; children: Suzanne, Wayne, Jill. BA, Colby Coll., Waterville, Maine, 1950; MA, Boston U., 1951; MBA, Harvard Bus. Sch., Boston, 1956. Ad agency account exec., Boston, 1956—64; gen. sales mgr. Regina Corp., Rahway, NJ, 1964—69; exec. v.p. and gen. mgr. Sanyo Electric Corp., Linden, 1969—74, Electric Char-B-Que, Tinton Falls, 1974—79; pres. Lumiscope Co., Inc., Edison, 1979—90, Mega Mktg., 1990—92, Mark of Fitness, Inc. divsn. NISSEI, Shrewsbury, 1992—2003, sr. advisor, 2004—. Cons. Maverick Industries, Inc., Edison, NJ, 1981—2005; radio spokesperson, 2002—04. Vol. fundraiser, Colts Neck, NJ, 1965—2005; leadership mem. Dem. Party, Monmouth City, Colts Neck, 1979—2002, candidate twp. com., 1988, 1990; mem. Brotherhood Ch. Group, pres., 1965—2000. 2d lt. US Army, 1951—53. Achievements include helping launch home blood pressure devices in 1979. Avocations: painting, stamp collecting/philately, tennis, exercise. Office: Mark of Fitness Inc 621 Shrewsbury Ave Shrewsbury NJ 07702

BAKER, GERALD L., bank executive; BS, Univ. So. Calif.; MBA, Calif. State Univ., Long Beach. Sr. mgmt. positions Bank of Am., Countrywide Credit Industries, Fleet Mortgage Group, 1983—98; pres. mortgage banking group First Horizon Nat. Corp., Memphis, 1998—2001; pres. First Horizon Home Loan Corp., Memphis, 2001—06; COO First Tenn. Bank N.A., Memphis, 2005—07, First Horizon Nat. Corp., Memphis, 2005—07, pres., CEO, bd. dir., 2007—. Office: First Horizon Nat Corp 165 Madison Ave Memphis TN 38103*

BAKER, GLORIA MARIE, artist; b. Petersburg, Ind. m. James Daniel Baker; children: David, Christopher. Pvt. practice, Evansville, Ind., 1976—. Painting tchr. Ivy Tech. C.C., Evansville, Ind. Chgo. Art Rev., 4th edit., The Complete Best of Watercolor, Vol.s 1 & 2, Landscape Inspirations, The Ascent (Houston B. Adams award, Evansville Mus. Arts & Sci.), The Dedicated, 1991 (Brown and Williamson Tobacco Corp. award, 1991, Dr. Martin Hydrus award Ga. Watercolor Soc., 03), 1993, Aztec Village, 1994 (Grumbacher Gold Medallion and The Excellence Gold award, 1994), The Domes, 1997 (2d pl.), Past, Present & Future, 1997, Ascent to the Cathedral, 1998 (St. Cuthbert's Mill award, 1998, Grumbacner Bronze award), Double Ascent, 1999 (Winsor & Newton award, Document Framing Svc. award, 1999, 1st pl. Evansville Art Guild, Peabody Coal Co. award), Cathedral of Light, 2000 (2d pl., Dir.'s Choice award, 2000), one-woman shows include Mus. Arts and Sci., Evansville, 2003. Chmn. Celia Sprue Assn., Evansville, 1995—. Nominee Internat. Visual Artist of the Yr., Internat. Biog. Ctr./Cambridge, England, 2004. Mem.: Niagara Frontier Watercolor Soc., Watercolor Soc. Ala. (bronze signature mem., Recognition award 2006), Ga. Watercolor Soc. (winner Nat. Exhibit 2003, Dr. Martin Hydrus award 2003), Pa. Watercolor Soc., Ky. Watercolor Soc., Petroleum Wives Club (v.p. 2003). Avocations: golf, gardening, reading, ballroom dancing. Home: 2711 Knob Hill Dr Evansville IN 47711 Personal E-mail: james_18510@msn.com.

BAKER, HARRIET KUGLEY, elementary school educator; b. Charleston, SC, June 10, 1943; d. Henry Asbury and Helen Halsall Kugley; m. Douglas Neil Baker, Mar. 30, 1968 (dec.); 1 child, David Nelson. BA, Furman U., 1965. 3d grade tchr. Aragona Elem. Sch., Virginia Beach, Va., 1965—67, Monaview Elem. Sch., Greenville, SC, 1967—70; 4th grade tchr. Armstrong Elem. Sch., Greenville, 1989—94, 5th grade tchr., 1994—. Mem. supt.'s cabinet, mem. dist. steering com. Greenville County Schs., 1991—93. Numerous leadership roles Berea First Bapt. Ch., Greenville, 1968—2006; mission trip Tanzania, 2007. Named Tchr. of Yr., Alliance for Quality Edn., 1992—93, Educator of Yr., Berea Lions Club, 2006; recipient Bus. Edn. Partnership Pro award, 1991, Exemplary Sci. Tchr. award, Alliance for Quality Edn., 1992; grantee, 1991- -95, 2004, 2006. Avocations: travel, piano, writing poetry. Home: 320 Westcliffe Way Greenville SC 29611 Office: Armstrong Elem Sch 8601 White Horse Rd Greenville SC 29611

BAKER, HARRISON SCOTT, application developer, consultant; b. Marion, Ohio, Mar. 12, 1950; s. Stanley Wallace and Starling (Dixon) Baker. BA, BS, Fla. State U., 1972-80; MBA, Embry-Riddle Aeronaut. U., 1986. MCSE, cert. computing tech. Computing Tech. Industry Assn., network assoc. Cisco Sys., Inc., 2003, A+, Network+, Security +, Server +, iNet + Comptia, Microsoft cert. database adminstr., Microsoft cert. sys. adminstr.; lic. radiotelephone with radar endorsement FCC. Mgr. Vincent Auto Parts, Inc., Marathon, Fla., 1972-78; maintenance supr. Eastern Air Lines, Inc., Miami, 1980-92; computer cons. Upper Sandusky, Ohio, 1992—. Author: Index to the Muster Rolls of PA in War of 1812, 1995, Early Settlers of Wyandot County, 1995, 1890 Veterans Census For Wyandot County, Ohio, 2004; indexer Obituaries in Upper Sandusky newspapers 1868-1911, 1994, Obituaries in Upper Sandusky newspapers 1912-1937, 1996, Obituaries in Upper Sandusky newspapers 1938-1958, 1997, Obituaries in Upper Sandusky newspapers 1959-1979, 1997, Journal of William Kennedy Beall, 1999, Civil War Soldiers Buried in Wyandot County, Ohio, 2000, Civil War Veterans Buried at the Ohio Veterans Home, 2001, American Prisoners of War Held at Halifax During the War of 1812, 2004, Marriage License and Records 1845-1868 Wyandot County, Ohio, 2006, others. Trustee Wyandot County Geneal. Soc., 1995—2001. Mem.: SAR (pres. Hancock chpt. 1995—96), Assn. Computing Machinery, IEEE Computer Soc., Sons of Vets. Res. (capt., pub. info. officer 2000—03), Sons of Union Vets. (camp sec. 1994—98, Dept. of Ohio signals officer 1999—2000, nat. chief of staff 2002—03), Soc. War of 1812 (Ohio pres. 1996—99). Avocations: electronics, genealogy. Home: 353 Hilltop Dr Upper Sandusky OH 43351-9241 Business E-Mail: hsbaker@udata.com.

BAKER, HENRY S., JR., retired bank executive; b. Balt., June 10, 1926; s. Henry S. and Frances (Robinson) B.; m. Marian Stockton Towsend, June 12, 1948; children— Frances, Sandra, Stockton. BA, Johns Hopkins U., 1950; grad. with honors, Rutgers U., 1957. With Md. Nat. Bank, Balt., 1950-86, sr. exec. v.p., 1973-86. Chmn. Redwood Capital Mgmt. Co., AAA Md., Ins. Agy. Inc., 1983-90, Ind. Coll. Fund Md., 1984-89; v.p., bd. dirs. Manab Properties. Chmn. Md. chpt. Nature Conservancy, 1984-90; chmn. investment com. Kennedy Inst. for Handicapped Children, 1985-88, Episcopal Diocese Md., 1974-80; trustee, treas. Garrison Forest Sch., 1962-88, St. Paul's Sch. for Girls, 1968-77; pres. Jr. Achievement Met. Balt., 1971, Florence Crittenden Home, 1964-66; bd. dirs. Keswick, Home for Incurables, 1965, 1991, 1979; gen. campaign chmn. United Way Cen. Md., 1979. With USNR, 1944-46. Mem. Assn. Res. City Bankers, Md. Bankers Assn. (pres.), Md. State C. of C. (treas., dir.) Republican.

BAKER, HERMAN, medical educator, writer; b. NYC, Jan. 22, 1926; s. Harry and Fannie Baker; m. Shirley Levitz, Nov. 15, 1952; children: Elliott Robert, Joel Martin. BS, CCNY, 1946; MS, Emory U., 1948; PhD, NYU, 1956. Cert. specialist human nutrition Am. Bd. Nutrition. Research asst. Columbia U., NYC, 1949-50; research assoc. Mt. Sinai Hosp., NYC, 1950-60; assoc. prof. medicine N.J. Med. Sch., Jersey City, 1960-70, prof. medicine and preventive medicine Newark, 1970—. Author: Clinical Vitaminology: Methods and Interpretation, 1968; contbr. articles to profl. jours. Fellow: Am. Coll. Nutrition. Avocation: music. Home: 27 Wilk Rd Edison NJ 08837-2726 Office: NJ Med Sch ADMC 1618A 30 Bergen St Newark NJ 07107-3001 Office Phone: 973-972-4664. Business E-Mail: bakerhe@umdnj.edu.

BAKER, HOLLIE L., lawyer; b. 1953; BA, Baylor Univ., 1975; JD, Univ. Denver, 1982. Bar: Colo. 1982, DC 1987, Mass. 1997, US Ct. Appeals (Fed cir.), US Patent & Trademark Office. Ptnr., vice chmn. Intellectual Property dept. Wilmer Cutler Pickering Hale & Dorr, Boston. Contbr. articles to profl. jours. Mem.: ABA (council mem., Intellectual Property Law sect.), Am. Intellectual Property Law Assn., Boston Patent Law Assoc., Licensing Exec. Soc., Patent & Trademark Office Soc. Office: Wilmer Cutler Pickering Hale & Dorr 60 State St Boston MA 02109 Office Phone: 617-526-6110. Office Fax: 617-526-5000. Business E-Mail: hollie.baker@wilmerhale.com.

BAKER, HOLLIS MACLURE, furniture manufacturing company executive; b. Allegan, Mich., Apr. 27, 1916; s. Hollis Siebe and Ruth (MacClure) B.; m. Betty Jane Brown, Aug. 2, 1947; children: Tomelyn Ann, Susan MacClure; m. Elsie Margarite Leigh, Aug. 27, 2003. Student, U. Va., 1935-37. With Baker Furniture, Inc., Holland, Mich., 1938-40, 45-73, v.p., treas., 1959-61, pres., 1961-70, chmn. bd., 1970-73; v.p., gen. mgr. Grand Rapids Chair Co., Mich., 1959-61, pres., 1961-70. V.p., dir. Manor House, Inc., N.Y.C., 1958-70; pres. Boyne City R.R. Co., Mich., 400 Bldg. Corp., Palm Beach, Fla.; dir. Mich. Nat. Bank, Lansing, 1968-83, Am. Seating Co., Grand Rapids, 1973-83, Mich. Nat. Bank, Grand Rapids, 1959-84, Norton Gallery, Palm Beach, 1984-91. Author: A Brief History of Schloss Branzoll, 1975, A History of the Chateau de Caussade, 1980, A History of the Chateau de la Roque, 1985, Five Castles Are Enough, 1989. Bd. dirs. USCG Found., 1981-91. Lt. (s.g.) USNR, 1941-45. Mem. Nat. Assn. Furniture Mfrs. (dir.), Furniture Mfrs. Assn. Grand Rapids (dir., past pres 1970-84), Zeta Psi. Clubs: Brook (N.Y.C.), River (N.Y.C.), New York Yacht (N.Y.C.), Leash (N.Y.C.); Kent Country (Grand Rapids), University (Grand Rapids), Indian (Grand Rapids), Peninsular (Grand Rapids); Everglades (Palm Beach), Bath and Tennis (Palm Beach); Buck's (London). Episcopalian. Home: 301 Chapel Hill Rd Palm Beach FL 33480-4124 Office: 2220 Wealthy St Grand Rapids MI 49506

BAKER, HOWARD HENRY, JR., lawyer, former ambassador, senator; b. Huntsville, Tenn., Nov. 15, 1925; s. Howard Henry and Dora (Ladd) B.; m. Joy Dirksen, Dec. 22, 1951 (dec. 1993); children: Darek Dirksen, Cynthia; m. Nancy Landon Kassebaum, Dec. 7, 1996. Student, U. of South, Tulane U.; LLB, U. Tenn., 1949; diploma (hon.), Yale U., Dartmouth Coll., Georgetown U., Bradley U., Pepperdine U., Centre Coll. U.S. senator from, Tenn., 1967-85; minority leader, 1977-81; majority leader, 1981-85; ptnr. Vinson & Elkins, Washington, 1985-87; chief of staff to Pres. The White House, Washington, 1987-88; ptnr. Baker, Worthington, Crossley, Stansberry & Woolf, Knoxville, Tenn., 1985-87, 88-95, Baker, Donelson, Bearman & Caldwell, Washington, 1995—2000; U.S. amb. to Japan U.S. Dept. State, Tokyo, 2001—05; sr. counsel Baker, Donelson, Bearman, Caldwell & Berkowitz, Washington, 2005—. Bd. dirs. Pennzoil Co., Forum Internat. Policy; chmn. bd. dirs. Cherokee Aviations; mem. internat. adv. bd. Barrick Gold Corp; vice chmn. Senate Watergate Com.; mem. President's Fgn. Intelligence Bd., 1985-90; mem. Coun. Fgn. Rels., Wash. Inst. Fgn. Affairs; internat. councilllor Ctr. Strategic and Internat. Studies. Author: (books) No Margin for Error, 1980, Howard Baker's Washington, 1982, Big South Fork Country, 1983, Scott's Gulf, 2000. Bd. regents Smithsonian Instn. With USN. Named to Hall of Fame, Photo Mktg. Assn., 1994; recipient Jefferson award for Greatest Pub. Svc. performed by elected or apptd. ofcl., 1982, Presdl. Medal of Freedom, 1984, Internat. award, Am. Soc. Photographers, 1993. Office: Baker Donelson Bearman Caldwell & Berkowitz Lincoln Sq 555 Eleventh St NW 6th Fl Washington DC 20004

BAKER, IAN ARCHBALD, explorer, educator, writer, photographer; b. NYC, Dec. 10, 1957; s. John Milnes and Virginia Lea Busser Baker. BA in Art History cum laude, Middlebury Coll., 1980; MA in English Lit., Oxford U., 1985; postgrad., Columbia U. Field work Explorer's Club N.Y., India, Sikkim, and Nepal, 1981-82; acad. dir. semester abroad programs Sch. Internat. Tng., Brattleboro, Vt., 1983-90; freelance writer, photographer, 1993—. Tour leader Smithsonian Instn., Boston Mus. Fine Arts, Distant Horizons; rsch. assoc. Found. Shamanic Studies; acad. advisor U. Wis., 1985-93; cons. Tibetan and Himalayan art Togendo Collection, Kyoto, Japan, 1990-92; founder Red Panda Expdns., Ltd., 1993—; leader rsch. expdns. in Namche Barwa-Tsangpo gorge region of Tibet, 1993-98. Author: The Tibetan Art of Healing with foreword by Dalai Lama, 1997, The Dalai Lamas' Secret Temple: Wall Paintings from the Lukhang with forword by the Dalai Lama, 2000, Celestial Gallery, 2000; co-author: Tibet: Reflections from the Wheel of Life with foreword by Dalai Lama, 1993;

co-prodr. (documentary film) Buddhist Hunters of Tsangpo Gorge, 1998; contbr. writings and photography to mags., books in Holland, France, Germany, U.S., Britain. Nat. Merit fellow Columbia U., 1990; Presdl. scholar Bread Loaf Sch. English, Lincoln Coll., Oxford U., 1985; selected by Rolex Awards for Enterprise for explorator rsch. in field of Himalayan sacred geography, 1990, named one of seven explorers for the millennium, Natl. Geographic Soc., 1999. Mem. The St. Nicholas Soc. N.Y., Colonial Lords of Manors in Am., The Explorers Club (Internat. fellow 1997, Rsch. grantee 1980). Achievements include leading Natl. Geographic Soc. expedition into Tsangpo Gorge's previously unexplored section and documented and measured 110' high falls that had previously been only subject of speculation. Named it Hidden Falls of Dorje Phagmo, 1998. Home: GPO Box 1373 Kathmandu Nepal Office Phone: 977-1-442-7790. Fax: 914-232-7306; 9771-423391. E-mail: ianbaker@mos.com.np.

BÁKÉR, J. A., II, executive management advisor and consultant, monetary architect, financial engineer emeritus; b. NYC, Dec. 12, 1944; s. Leonard Ernest and Miriam Violet (Roché) B. MS in Mgmt., Am. Coll., Bryn Mawr, Pa., 2005; postgrad., U. Phoenix, 2007—. ChFC 1987, CLU 1981, FPA 1985. Cons. mgr. Life Ins., NYC, 1964—79; supr. Physician's Planning Group, Atty.'s Planning Svc., Bus. Planning Svcs., Profl. Svc. Corp., NYC, 1979—81; chief satisfaction officer J A L B Enterprises, East Garden City, NY, 1980—91, emeritus, 1991—2005. Monitor NY State continuing edn. program, 1996—2006, instr. continuing profl. edn. program, 1996—99; instr. licensing courses, 1996—99. Bd. dirs. Medic Alert, Nassau County, N.Y., 1985-87; rep. The Living Bank, Houston; nominated mem.: Citizen Ambassador Program Internat. Recipient Cert. of Appreciation, VFW D.C., 2002. Fellow: Life Underwriters Coun.; mem.: Gen. Agts. Mgrs. Assn. Internat. (charter), NYC Life Underwriters Assn., Soc. Fin. Svc. Profls., Am. Automobile Assn. (Wash. State), Nat. Assn. Life Underwriters (emeritus, pres. Cortland NY chpt. 1974—75, legis. chair 1972—74, v.p. pub. info. Nassau County 1980—87, instr. Bklyn. 1987—90, Queens 1991—92), Am. Mgmt. Assn., The Srs. Coalition, Fraternal Order of Police, Smithsonian Instn. Assn. (Washington nat. assoc.), Am. Assn. NYC, Sovereign Mil. Order of Malta NYC (pilgrim 1999), NYC Civil Svc. Ret. Employee Assn., Nat. Orgn. for Men, Ithaca (NY) Jaycees (past dir.).

BAKER, J. CRAIG, electric power industry executive; BA, Walsh Coll., Troy, Mich., 1970; MBA, U. Akron, Ohio, 1980. With Am. Electric Power Svc. Corp., Columbus, Ohio, 1968—, various positions in info. systems, sys. ops., corp. planning and budgeting and sys. power markets, sr. v.p. AEP Energy Svcs. subs., v.p. transmission policy, 1998, sr. v.p. regulatory svcs. Office: Am Electric Power Svc Corp 1 Riverside Plz Columbus OH 43215-2373 Office Phone: 614-716-1000.*

BAKER, JACK SHERMAN, architect, educator; b. Champaign, Ill., Aug. 8, 1920; s. Clyde Lee and Jane Cecilia (Walker) B. BA with honors, U Ill., 1943, MS, 1949; cert., N.Y. Beaux Art Inst. Design, 1943. Aero engr., designer Boeing Aircraft, Seattle, 1943-44; assoc. Atkins, Barrow & Lasswith, Urbana, 1947-50; pvt. practice architecture Champaign, 1947—; mem. faculty U. Ill. Sch. Architecture, Urbana, 1947—, prof. architecture, 1950-90, acting prof. emeritus, 1990—97, Disting. prof. emeritus, 1997—, former mem. exec. com. Hon. bd. dirs. Gerhart Music Festival, Guntersville, Ala., Stravinsky awards, Champaign, Conservatory of Cen. Ill.; hon. bd. dirs. Ruth Hindman Found., Huntsville, Ala.; dir., performer personal performance loft space for Interaction of the Arts and Architecture, 1960—; participant U. Ill. Exploring the Arts course (Act-NCEA award), 1970—, campus honors program, 1995—; former mem. Chancellor's com. on graphic design and art acquisition and installation, former mem. adv. bd., designer of exhbn., Krannert Mus., U. Ill., engr. basic, Ft. Leonard Wood, Mo., topog. engr., Ft. Blevoir, Va. Exhibitions include watercolors, archtl. drawings and photography, Monograph and Retrospective Arch. Exhibit: "I" Space Gallery, Chgo., 1997, U. Ill. Temple Buell Arch. Gallery, 1998, Temple Buell Hall Gallery, 2000, Japanese House Drawings Exhibit, Krannert Art Mus., U. Ill., 1998; contbr. articles to numerous jours. and confs. Mem. U. Ill. Pres.'s Coun., U. Ill. Bronze Cir., 1986; mem. mus. bd. and affiliate World Heritage Mus.; former mem. adv. bd. Krannert Ctr. for Performing Arts, Assembly Hall U. Ill.; exhbn. designer World Heritage Mus., U. Ill. Served with U.S. Army, AFH, 1945-46, Caserta, Italy, ETO. Recipient "prix d'Emulation Societe des Architectes Diplomes par le Gouvernment" Beaux-Arts medal, 1942, cert. for dedicated and disting. svc., Nat. AIA Com. on Environ. and Design, 1955, Decade of Achievement award, World Heritage Mus., 1992, Art and Humanities award, 1981, 1982, Honor award for advancing profession architecture, CIC/AIA, 1983, Excellence in Edn. award and medal, IC/AIA, 1989, Heritage award, PACA, 1997, numerous other honors and design excellence awards in field, Recognition award, U. Ill. Found., 2001, U. Ill. Sch. Arch., 2006. Fellow: AIA (medal 1977), Nat. Coun. Archtl. Registration Bds. (cert.); mem.: Soc. Archtl. Historians, Ill. Coun./AIA, The Nature Conservancy, Nat. Resources Def. Coun., Gargoyle, Scarab, Cliff Dwellers Club (Chgo.), Alpha Rho Chi. Home: 71 1/2 E Chester St Champaign IL 61820-4149 Office: U Ill 117 Temple Hoyne Buell Hall 611 Taft Dr MC-621 Champaign IL 61820-6922 Office Phone: 217-333-1330.

BAKER, JAMES ADDISON, III, (JIM BAKER), lawyer, former secretary of state; b. Houston, Apr. 28, 1930; s. James A. and Ethel Bonner (Means) B.; m. Susan Garrett, Aug. 6, 1973; 8 children. BA, Princeton U., 1952; LLB, U. Tex., 1957; LLD (hon.), U. Pa., 2007. Bar: Tex. 1957. Assoc. Andrews Kurth Campbell & Jones, Houston, 1957-81; under sec. US Dept. Commerce, Washington, 1975-76; deputy chmn. del. ops. Pres. Ford Com., Washington, 1976; chmn. George Bush campaign for republican presdl. nomination, 1979-80; sr. adv. Reagan-Bush Com., 1980-81; mem. Reagan Transition Team, Washington, 1980-81; chief of staff to Pres. The White House, Washington, 1981-85; sec. US Dept. Treasury, Washington, 1985-88; chmn. George Bush's Presdl. campaign, 1988; sec. US Dept. State, Washington, 1989-92; chief of staff, sr. counselor to Pres. The White House, Washington, 1992-93; sr. ptnr. Baker & Botts, LLP, Washington and Houston, 1993—; personal envoy of UN Sec. Gen. for Western Sahara UN, 1997—2004; spl. envoy to Iraq for debt reduction The White House, 2003—. Hon. chmn. James A. Baker III Inst. for Public Policy Rice U., 1993—; sr. counselor, The Carlyle Group, 1993-2005, co-chair Iraq Study Group, 2006 Author: The Politics of Diplomacy: Revolution, War and Peace, 1989-1992, 1995, "Work Hard, Study.and Keep Out of Politics!": Adventures and Lessons from an Unexpected Political Life, 2006. Trustee Woodrow Wilson Internat. Ctr. for Scholars, Smithsonian Inst., 1977—; bd. dirs. Rice U., hon. chmn. James A. Baker III Inst. for Pub. Policy, 1993—. Recipient Presdl. Medal Freedom, 1991, Woodrow Wilson award Princeton U., Jefferson award The Am. Inst. for Pub. Svcs., John F. Kennedy Sch. Govt. award Harvard U., The Hans J. Morganthau award, The George F. Kennan award, Alexander Hamilton award US Dept. Treasury, Disting. Svc. award US Dept. State. Mem. ABA, Tex. Bar Assn., Houston Bar Assn., Am. Judicature Soc., Phi Delta Phi, bd. dirs, Electronic Data Corp., 1996-2003. Avocations: hunting, fishing, tennis, golf. Office: Baker & Botts LLP 1 Shell Plz 910 Louisiana Houston TX 77002 also: The Carlyle Group 1001 Pennsylvania Ave NW Ste 220 S Washington DC 20004-2505

BAKER, JAMES BARNES, architect; b. NYC, Feb. 18, 1933; s. William Edgar and Violet (Twachtman) B.; children: Mary Morgan, James Edgar, Catriona Griswold, Frederick Alden; m. Rosemary Burgis, June 14, 1997 (dec. 2001). AB, Princeton U., 1954; M.Arch., Yale U., 1960. With firms Blake & Neski, NYC, 1960-62, George Lewis, NYC, 1962-63, Kahn & Jacobs, NYC, 1963-64; ptnr. firm Baker & Blake, NYC, 1964-72, Baker/Grinnell, NYC, 1972-74; cons., 1974-77; dir. Llewelyn Davies Assocs., NYC, 1976-78; pres. Tower Devel. Group Inc., Ohio, 1978-83, Park-Tower Devel. Co., Ltd., Bermuda, 1978-83, Springland Assocs. Inc., 1983-90; prin. Baker & Baker, Architects, NYC, 1990—; pres. Tech. Panel Systems, 1992-93; mng. dir. William McDonough Archs., 1993-94, Forge Co., NYC, 2002; chief exec. Forge Llewellyn, London, 1994—2004, The Forge Co. LTD, 2004—. Vis. prof. Sch. Architecture, CUNY, 1964-89. Trustee Darrow Sch., Mt. Lebanon Shaker Village. Recipient design awards HUD, others. Fellow AIA (bd. dirs., design awards, pres., 2005—); mem. Am. Arbitration Assn., Holland Soc., St. Nicholas Soc., Squadron A. also: Crossways House Mayfield East Sussex TN20 6AB England

BAKER, JAMES CLIFFORD, school system administrator; b. Bangor, Maine; s. John Donald Baker and Helen Mae Fallon; m. Camille Diana Baker, Apr. 21, 1968; children: James, Jay, Kristan. BS, Rutgers U., New Brunswick, NJ, 1969, MEd, 1975, EdD, 1986. Asst. supr. NJ Dept. Edn., Trenton; asst. dir. Govs. Coun. Fitness, Trenton; dir. edn. NJ Dept. Health, Trenton, chief intoxication driver program; dir. edn. Saddle Brook Bd. Edn.; supt. Califon Borough Bd. Edn., Middlesex Borough Bd. Edn. Capt. US Army, 1969—72. Mem.: APA, Rutgers Alumni Fedn. Avocations: sailing, tennis, golf, reading. Home: 10 Norton Rd Monmouth Junction NJ 08852 Office: Middlesex Borough Bd Edn 300 Kennedy Dr Middlesex NJ 08846

BAKER, JAMES EDGAR, federal judge, educator; BA, Yale Coll., 1982; JD, Yale Law Sch., 1990. Attorney adv., Law Enforcement and Intelligence US Dept. State, 1990—93, atty. adv., Bur. Oceans & Internat. Environ. & Scientific Affairs, 1993; dep. legal adv. NSC, Washington, 1994—97; spl. asst., legal adv. to Pres. The White House, Washington, 1997—2000; judge US Ct. Appeals for the Armed Forces, Washington, 2000—. Vis. lecturer Yale Law Sch. Co-author (with W.M. Reisman): (non-fiction) Regulating Covert Action, 1992. Office: US Ct Appeals Armed Forces 450 E St NW Washington DC 20442 also: Yale Law Sch PO Box 208215 New Haven CT 06520 E-mail: james.baker@yale.edu.*

BAKER, JAMES EDWARD, city planner; b. San Antonio, Tex., Aug. 4, 1961; s. Jim and Dora Pitts B. BA, BBA, BFA, So. Meth. U., Dallas, 1983; MS, Trinity U., San Antonio, Tex., 1995, U. Tex., 1997; student, U. Phoenix Online, 2001—; MS, Tex. A&M U., 2006. Tech. writer II JANA, Inc., San Antonio, 1985-86; adminstrv. asst. United Svcs. Automobile Assn., San Antonio, 1987-89; Brackenridge fellow Trinity U., San Antonio, 1993-95; HUD fellow U. Tex., Austin, 1995-97; city planner City of New Braunfels, Tex., 1997-2000; devel. planner City of Georgetown, Tex., 2000; sr. planner City of Dallas, Tex., 2001—05; online course facilitator Western Internat. U., 2005—06, U. Houston., Univ. Pk., 2006—; diversity fellow Tex. A&M U., Coll. Sta., Tex., 2005—06. Presenter in polit. sci., 2005. Mem. emerging leaders program Nat. Congress Cmty. Econ. Devel., 2001. With US Army, 1989—93, with USAR, 1993—2004, with USAFR, 2004—. Decorated 3 Army Commendation medals, 3 Army Achievement medals, Kuwait Liberation medal, Joint Svc. Achievement medal, Joint Meritorious Unit award, Good Conduct medal, Army Reserve Component Achievement medal, Nat. Def. Svc. medal, Armed Forces Expeditionary medal, S.W. Asia Svc. medal, Global War on Terrorism Expeditionary medal, Global War on Terrorism Svc. medal, Armed Forces Svc. medal, Army Res. Components Overseas Tng. Ribbon, Army Forces Res. medal with 2 M Devices, Army Non-comm. Officer Profl. Devel. ribbon, Small Arms Expert Marksmanship Rifle ribbon, Army Svc. ribbon, NATO medal, Kuwait Liberation medal Kingdom Saudi Arabia, Govt. Kuwait, 3 AF outstanding Unit awards; named to The Chancellor's List, Austin, Tex. Mem. Am. Planning Assn., Internat. Econ. Develop. Coun., Urban Land Inst., Air Force Sgts. Assn., VFW, Am. Inst. Cert. Planners, Nat. Assn. Indsl. and Office Properties, Kiwanis, Prince Hall Freemasons, Delta Sigma Phi (pres. Lambda chpt. 1981-82). Avocations: outdoor photography, wing chun, weight tng.

BAKER, JANET, insurance company executive; BS magna cum laude in Mgmt., Troy U., Ala., M in Human Resources Mgmt. With AFLAC Inc., 1982—, various positions including second v.p. human resources and second v.p. client svcs., v.p. mktg. svcs., 1999—2002, v.p. account implementation, 2002—04, sr. v.p. client svcs., 2004—. Mem.: Kiwanis Club. Office: AFLAC Inc 1932 Wynnton Rd Columbus GA 31999 Office Phone: 706-323-3431.*

BAKER, JEAN HARVEY, history professor; b. Balt., Feb. 9, 1933; d. F. Barton and Rose (Lindsay) Hopkins Harvey; m. R. Robinson Baker, Sept. 12, 1953; children— Susan Dixon, Robinson Scott, Robert W., Jean Harvey. AB, Goucher Coll., Towson, Md., 1961; MA, Johns Hopkins U., Balt., 1965, PhD, 1971. Lectr., instr. history Notre Dame Coll., Balt., 1967-69; instr. history Goucher Coll., Balt., 1969, asst. prof. history, 1969-75, assoc. prof. history, 1975-78, prof. history, 1979-82, Elizabeth Todd prof. history, 1981—. Author: The Politics of Continuity, 1973, Ambivalent Americans, 1976, Affairs of Party, 1983, Maryland: A History, Mary Todd Lincoln: A Biography, 1986, The Stevensons: A Family Biography, 1995, Sisters: The Lives of American Suffragists, 2005; co-author: Civil War and Reconstruction, 2002; editor: Md. Hist. Mag., 1979, Votes for Women: The Suffrage Battle Revisited, 2001, James Buchanan, 2004, Sisters: The Lives of the Suffragists, 2005. Am. Coun. Learned Socs. fellow, 1976, NEH fellow, 1982, Newberry Libr. fellow, 1991, Rockefeller Found. fellow, 1998; recipient Faculty Teaching prize Goucher Coll., 1979, Willie Lee Rose prize in Southern history, 1989. Mem.: Am. Hist. Assn., Orgn. Am. Historians, Berkshire Conf. Women Historians, Phi Beta Kappa. Democrat. Office: Goucher Coll History Dept 1021 Dulaney Valley Towson MD 21204 Home Phone: 410-363-3731; Office Phone: 410-337-6267. Business E-Mail: jbaker@goucher.edu.

BAKER, JIMMY H., former state finance administrator; BA, Troy State U.; Master degree, Auburn U. Asst. state supt. Dept. Edn., Montgomery, Ala., dep. supt. edn. adminstrv. and fin. svcs.; dir. fin. State of Ala., Montgomery. Office: 105 N State Capitol 600 Dexter Ave Montgomery AL 36104-3734

BAKER, JOANNE EVELYN, retired government agency administrator; b. Crucible, Pa., Dec. 1, 1933; d. George Joseph and Anna Leona (Kagle) Cormack; m. James Clair Baker, July 7, 1956 (dec. May 1968); m. James Lewis Wilson, June 2, 1970 (div. Sept. 1984); stepchildren: John Thomas Wilson, Charles Edward Wilson, Debra Ruth Wilson, Jeff Lee Wilson, James Lloyd Wilson. Cert. in applied music, Waynesburg Coll., 1951. Various clerical positions including Exec. Offices Pres., Washington, 1951-66; supr. USN, Washington, 1966-71; pres., treas. Little Round Top Farm, Inc., Gettysburg, Pa., 1971-86; logistician USN-U.S. Army, Gettysburg, Pa., 1974—90; ret., 1990. Program mgr. electronic comm. end items and Ship Alterations (SHIPALT), 1974—77; program mgr. Ship Parts Control Ctr. (SPCC), Mechanicsburg, Pa.; Army stock fund program mgr., 1977—80, 1984—90; chief consol. property account US Army Garrison (USAG), Ft. Ritchie, Md., 1980—81, logistics directorate, Ft. Detrick, Md.; insp. Office of Insp. Gen. 7th Signal Command, US Army, Ft. Ritchie, 1981—84, chief supply and svcs. divsn., 1984—89, chief plans and resources mgmt. divsn., 1989—90; mgmt. cons., 1991—. Author: Reflections, 1974. Bd. dirs. Adams County Mental Health Assn., Gettysburg, 1982—87. Named Outstanding Woman of Yr., Ft. Detrick, 1986; recipient Sustained Superior Achievement award, Dept. Navy, 1975, Dept. Army, 1986, Comdr.'s award, 1990. Mem.: World Inst. Achievement (life). Roman Catholic. Avocations: handwriting analysis, writing, ceramics, piano. Home: 5605 Shookstown Rd Frederick MD 21702-2704

BAKER, JOHN DAVID, health facility administrator, not-for-profit fundraiser, real estate agent; b. Orleans, France, Mar. 4, 1964; arrived in US, 1968, arrived in Germany, 1974, arrived in US, 1979; s. Raymond Alfred and Anna (vonPalts) Baker. BS in Commerce, Rider U., Lawrenceville, NJ, 1987; MPA, Rutgers U., Camden, NJ, 1997. Officer Commerce Bank Holding Co., Cherry Hill, NJ, 1988—97; CEO, exec. dir. AIDS Del., Wilmington, 1997—. Pres., tenant coun., bd. dirs. Cmty. Svcs. Bldg. and Corp., Wilmington, 2005—. Pres. Lambda Cycling Found., Ft. Lauderdale, Fla., 2006—; treas. Del. Liberty Fund, Just for Youth, Mayors Health Planning Coun., Wilmington, Del. Named Extraordinary Fundraiser, Del. HIV Consortium, Wilmington, 2005; recipient Svc. Achievement award, Christ Found., Wilmington, 2007. Mem.: Assn. Fundraising Profls. (bd. dirs. 2005—), Tocqueville Soc., Williams Club, Nat. Pub. Admin. Honor Soc. Democrat. Episcopalian. Avocations: running, swimming, bicycling, gardening. Office: AIDS Del 100 W 10th St Ste 315 Wilmington DE 19801

BAKER, JOHN MILNES, architect; b. Port Jefferson, NY, Oct. 15, 1932; s. Alan Griffin and Lucy Hayden (Milnes) B.; m. Virginia Lea Busser (div. 1969); children: Ian Archbald, Jennifer Lea (Mrs. Christopher Warren); m. Elizabeth Jennings Morrison, Jan. 17, 1970; children: James Morrison, Hayden Sheffield. BA, Middlebury Coll., 1955; March, Columbia U., 1960. Designer, draftsman Sir Basil Spence, London, 1960-61; project mgr., later project architect Rogers & Butler, NYC, 1962-64; project architect John A. Pruyn, AIA, NYC, 1965-66; pvt. practice architecture NYC, 1967—68, 1975—79; ptnr. Manice & Baker, 1968—74; pvt. practice architecture specializing in residential design Katonah, NY, 1979—2005. Pres. J.M. Baker Houses Inc.; lectr. New Sch. for Social Rsch., N.Y.C. Author: How to Build a House with an Architect, 1977, rev. edit., 1988, The Baker Family and the Edgar Family of Rahway, N.J. and New York City, 1972, American House Styles: A Concise Guide, 1994. Past trustee N.Y. Revels Inc.; past trustee Bedford Free Libr.; past mem. Katonah Hist. Dist. Adv. Commn.; cons. Town of Bedford; mem. Historic Buildings Preservation Commn. Home designs included among Better Homes and Garden Top Ten Homes Plans, 1982; 3 designs selected by USIA for Design U.S.A., a traveling exhibit in USSR, 1989-90. Mem. AIA, Nat. Coun. Archtl. Registration Bds., Am. Arbitration Assn. (panel mem.), Soc. Archtl. Hists., St. Nicholas Soc. (past pres.), Holland Soc. N.Y. (past trustee), Colonial Lords of Manors in Am. (v.p.), Order Founders and Patriots, Soc. Colonial Wars, Pilgrims, Corinthians, Coffee House, Squadron A, Century Assn. (N.Y.C.), Bedford Golf and Tennis Club, Norwalk Yacht Club. Home: 76 Spooner Hill Rd South Kent CT 06785

BAKER, JOHN RUSSELL, utilities executive; b. Lexington, Mo., July 21, 1926; s. William Frederick and Flora Anne (Dunford) B.; m. Elizabeth Jane Torrence, June 16, 1948; children— John Russell, Burton T. BS, U. Mo., 1948, MBA, 1962. With Mo. Public Service Co., Kansas City, 1948—, treas., 1966-68, v.p. fin., 1968-71, sr. v.p., 1971-73, exec. v.p., 1973—, also dir. Lectr. fin. U. Mo.; vice-chmn. Aquila Inc., 1991—. Vice-pres. Mid-Continent coun. Girl Scouts U.S., 1981; mem. adv. coun. Sch. Acctg., U. Mo., Columbia. Recipient Outstanding alumnus award Sch. Adminstrn. U. Mo., Kansas City, 1965; citation of merit U. Mo., 1995. Mem. Tax Execs. Inst. (pres. Kansas City 1968), U. Mo. Sch. Adminstrn. Alumni Assn. (pres. 1965). Clubs: Kansas City. Republican. Methodist. Home: 205 NW Oxford Ln Lees Summit MO 64063-2118 Office: Aquila Inc 20 W 9th St Kansas City MO 64105-1704

BAKER, JOHN STEVENSON (MICHAEL DYREGROV), writer; b. Mpls., June 18, 1931; s. Everette Barrette and Ione May (Kadletz) B. BA cum laude, Pomona Coll., Claremont Colls., 1953; MD, U. Calif. Berkeley and San Francisco, 1957. Writer, 1958—; book cataloger Walker Art Ctr., Mpls., 1958—59; editor, writer neurol. rsch. articles Lewis E. Phillips Psycho-biol. Rsch. Fund, Mpls., 1960—61. Contbr. articles and poetry to various publs. in Eng. and U.S.; author 65 pub. poems, 21 short essays and 10 sets of aphorisms. Donor numerous species of native plants and seeds to Minn. Landscape Arboretum, U.S. Nat. Arboretum and Arnold Arboretum, Harvard U., papers of LeRoi Jones and Hart Crane to Yale U., Brahms recs. to Bennington Coll., cartoons and comics about psychoanalysis and clinical psychology to Ohio State U., several others; pres. Mission Lakes Assn., Merrifield, Minn., 1989-90. Recipient Disting. Service award Minn. State Hort. Soc., 1976; Cert. of Appreciation U.S. Nat. Arboretum, 1978; property registered as a Minn. Natural Area Minn. chpt. Nature Conservancy, 1990. Mem. AAAS, NAACP, Nat. Resources Def. Coun., So. Poverty Law Ctr., Ctr. for Plant Conservation, Nat. Audubon Soc., Nature Conservancy, Nat. Mus. Am. Indian, Nat. Trust for Hist. Preservation, Soc. for Ecol. Restoration Internat., Met. Opera Guild, Sierra Club, Phi Chi, Nu Sigma Nu. Office: PO Box 16007 Minneapolis MN 55416-9998

BAKER, JOY DOREEN, art educator, artist; d. Herman D. and Sylvia Newfield Bragin; children: Amy Beth Baker-Bridge, Lawrence Adam. Assoc., Fashion Inst. Tech., 1957; Cert. in Graphic Design and Textile Design, Sch. Visual Arts, NYC, 1980; student, Trotta Sch. Fine Arts, Queens. Asst. buyer active sportswear Lord & Taylor, NYC, 1956; showroom sales rep. Brooks & Co., 1956—57; owner, designer, ptnr. Studio J, Inc., Washington, 1968—78; pub. rels., direct mail campaign Abbeville Press, Inc., NYC, 1978—85; mktg. rschr. EJ Rhodes Assocs., NYC, 1985—90; owner, designer, adminstr. Joy Designs, Inc.; mem. faculty Fine Arts Sch., Ednl. Alliance, NYC, 1992—96; instr. dept. fashion Acad. Art Univ., San Francisco, 2002—. Mem. exec. com. Washington Fashion Group. Exhibitions include Fla., Washington, N.Y.C., San Francisco. Mem. Internat. Women's Mus., San Francisco, Nat. Mus. Women in Arts, Washington; active Sunday youth and family program Congregation Emanu-El. Avocations: museums, theater, travel, reading, learning Italian. Office: Acad Art Univ Fashion Dept Fl 7 180 New Montgomery St San Francisco CA 94105 Office Phone: 415-752-7596.

BAKER, JUDITH ANN, retired computer technician; b. Junction City, Kans., Mar. 2, 1947; d. David Daniel and Mildred Elaine Bates; m. Jimmy Ray Baker, Oct. 8, 1972; 1 child, Jimmy Ray Jr. Student, East Ctrl. U., 1993—98. Cert. travel and tourism Draughon Coll., 1988. ADA support group leader, newsletter editor Multiple Sclerosis Assn. Am., Okla., 1995—2006, ednl. amb., 2006—. Leader support group Multiple Sclerosis Soc. Am., Ada, Okla., 2003—06, vol. ednl. amb., 2006—. Recipient Best Support Group Leader award S.E. region and 10 state area, Multiple Sclerosis Soc. Am., 2005. Mem.: Ada Writing Club. Avocations: writing, painting, crafts, decorating, jewelry making. Home: 3816 US Hwy 377 Ada OK 74820 Home Phone: 580-310-0181; Office Phone: 580-310-0181. E-mail: paradise@adacomp.net.

BAKER, KATHERINE JUNE, elementary school educator, minister, artist; b. Dallas, Feb. 3, 1932; d. Kirk Moses and Katherine Faye (Turner) Sherrill; m. George William Baker, Jan. 30, 1955; children: Kirk Garner, Kathleen Kay. BS, BA, Tex. Women's U., 1953, MEd, 1979; cert. in religious edn., Meadville Theol. U., 1970; postgrad., North Tex. State U., 1987—; DD (hon.), Am. Fellowship Ch., 1981. Cert. elem. and secondary tchr., adminstr., Tex.; lic. and ordained min. Kingsway Internat. Ministries, 1991. Mgr. prodn. Woolf Bros., Dallas, 1953-55; display mgr. J.M. Dyer and Co., Corsicana, Tex., 1954; advt. artist Fair Dept. Store, Ft. Worth, 1954-56; artist, instr. Dutch Art Gallery, Dallas, 1960-65; dir. religious edn. 1st Unitarian Ch., Dallas, 1967-69; edn. dir. day care, tchr. Richardson (Tex.) Unitarian Ch., 1971-73; dir. camp Tres Rios YWCA, Glen Rose, Tex., 1975-76; dir. program of extended sch. instrn. Hamilton Park Elem. Sch. Richardson Ind. Sch. Dist., 1975-78, tchr. Dover Elem. Sch., 1979—80, tchr. Jess Harben Elem. Sch., 1980—92; founder ednl., editorial and arts/evang. assn. Submitted Ministries, Richardson, 1992—. Dir. Flame Fellowship Internat., 1987—94, state rep., 1994—99, asst. state overseer (Tex.), 1999—2001, chaplain, 2002—; mem. Extended Sch. Day Program Employee Manual, Extended Sch. Day Courses, Day+ Extended Day Newsletter, RISD Magnet Sch., 1975—79. Contbr. articles to ch. newspaper, 1967-69, newsletters; editor Metro Dallas Chpt. Newsletter, 1992—; one-woman show Dutch Art Gallery - Northlake Ctr., Dallas, 1965; exhibited in group show at Tex. Art Assn., 1966. Advocate day care Unitarian Universalist Women's Fedn., Boston, 1975—76, mem. nominating com., 1976—77; cert. instr. aquatics program Arthritis Found. YMCA AFYAP, Plano Rehab. Hosp., 1997—99, Aquatics Inst. Oak Point Ctr., Plano, 1999—, Aquatics Inst. Fun Fit Crew, 2001—04; overseer Mosaics singles group First Family Ch., 2004—. Mem. NEA, ASCD, Nat. Coun. Social Studies, Tex. State Tchrs. Assn. (treas. Richardson chpt. 1984-85), Tex. Ret. Tchrs. Assn., Richardson Ret. Tchrs. Assn., Women's Ctr. Dallas, Sokol Athletic Ctr., Smithsonian Assn., Dallas Mus. Assn., Alpha Chi, Delta Phi Delta (pres. 1952-53), Phi Delta Kappa. Avocations: gospel and folk singing, guitar, volleyball, camping, travel. Office Phone: 972-235-1178. Personal E-mail: junebaker3693@sbcglobal.net, junedraws@yahoo.com.

BAKER, KEITH LEON, lawyer; b. Columbus, Ind., Jan. 22, 1950; s. Richard Leon and Sarah Elizabeth (Wisehart) B. A.B., Princeton U., 1972; J.D., Syracuse U., 1975; LL.M. with highest honors, George Washington U., 1978. Bar: N.Y. 1976, D.C. 1976, Va. 2000, U.S. Ct. Appeals (D.C. cir.) 1983, U.S. Ct. Internat. Trade 1983. Asst. bank examiner U.S. Treasury Dept., N.Y.C., 1974; law clk. U.S. Dept. of Justice, Syracuse, N.Y., 1974-75; atty.-adviser GAO, Washington, 1975-78; atty.-adviser U.S. EPA, Washington, 1978-80; pvt. practice, Washington, 1980-99; ptnr. Barton, Baker, McMahon & Tolle, 1999—. Author: Small Business Financing, 1983; contbr. articles to profl. jours. Mem. ABA, Fed. Bar Assn., Nat. Contract Mgmt. Assn. Methodist. Home: 6645 Hawthorne St Mc Lean VA 22101-4423 Office: Barton Baker McMahon & Tolle The Madison Bldg Ste 440 1320 Old Chain Bridge Rd Mc Lean VA 22101 Business E-Mail: kbaker@bbmtlaw.com.

BAKER, KEITH MICHAEL, history professor; b. Swindon, Eng., Aug. 7, 1938; arrived in US, 1964; s. Raymond Eric and Winifred Evelyn (Shepherd) B.; m. Therese Louise Elzas, Oct. 25, 1961 (div. 1999); children— Julian, Felix. BA, Cambridge U., 1960, MA, 1963; postgrad., Cornell U., 1960-61; PhD, U. London, 1964. Instr. history and humanities Reed Coll., 1964-65; asst. prof. European history U. Chgo., 1965-71, assoc. prof., 1971-76, prof., 1977-89, master collegiate div. social scis., 1975-78, assoc. dean coll., 1975-78, assoc. dean div. social scis., 1975-78, chmn. commn. grad. edn., 1980-82; chmn. Coun. Advanced Studies in Humanities and Social Scis., 1982-86; prof. European history Stanford U., 1989—, J.E. Wallace Sterling prof. in humanities, 1992—, chair dept. history, 1994-95; Anthony P. Meier family prof. humanities, dir. Stanford Humanities Ctr., 1995-2000, cognizant dean humanities, 2000—03; Jean-Paul Gimon dir. France-Stanford Ctr. for Interdisciplinary Studies, 2002—. Vis. assoc. prof. history Yale U., 1974; mem. Inst. Advanced Study, Princeton, NJ, 1979-80; vis. prof., dir. studies Ecole des Hautes Etudes en Scis. Sociales, Paris, 1982, 84, 91; fellow Ctr. for Advanced Study in Behavioral Scis., Stanford U., Calif., 1986-87, Santora Humanities Ctr., 2005-06; vis. prof. UCLA, 1989; vis. fellow Clare Hall, Cambridge U., Eng., 1994; chair scholars com. Am. Com. on the French Revolution, 1989. Author: Condorcet: From Natural Philosophy to Social Mathematics, 1975, Inventing the French Revolution, 1990; prin. author: Report Commission on Graduate Education, U. Chgo., 1982; editor: Condorcet: Selected Writings, 1977, The Political Culture of the Old Regime: The Old Regime and the French Revolution, 1987, The Terror, 1994; co-editor Jour. Modern History, 1980-89, What's Left of Enlightenment?, 2001; contbr. chpts. to books. Decorated chevalier Ordre des Palmes Académiques; fellow, NEH, 1967—68; ACLS study fellow, 1972—73, Guggenheim fellow, 1979. Fellow AAAS, Am. Philos. Soc.; mem. Am. Hist. Assn. (com. on coms. 1991-94), Soc. French History Studies (co-pres. 2005), Am. Soc. for 18th Century Studies (v.p. 1999, pres. 2000-01), Internat. Soc. Eighteenth Century Studies (pres. 2007-). Office: Stanford Univ Dept History Stanford CA 94305-2024 Home Phone: 650-493-4970; Office Phone: 650-723-2791. Business E-Mail: kbaker@stanford.edu.

BAKER, KENDALL L., academic administrator; b. Clearwater, Fla., Nov. 1, 1942; s. Robert B. and Anne E. Baker; m. Tobin Ratliff McGough, Apr. 12, 1981; children: Kraig, Kris, John, Shannon, Brian. BA with honors, U. Md., 1963; MA, Georgetown U., 1967, PhD, 1979. Instr., Dept. Polit. Sci. U. Wyo., Laramie, 1967-69, asst. prof., 1969-73, assoc. prof., 1973-77, prof., 1977-82, chmn., 1979-82, asst. v.p. for Acad. Affairs, 1976-77; dean, Coll. Arts & Scis., Bowling Green State U., Ohio, 1982-87; v.p., provost No. Ill. U., DeKalb, 1987-92; pres. U. N. D., 1992-99, Ohio Northern U, 1999—. Cons. survey rsch. to various agys. and polit. candidates, 1967—; panel chmn. Rocky Mt. Social Sci. Conv., 1973, We. Social Sci. Conv., 1975, Coun. Colls. Arts and Scis., 1983, 86; guest participant study trip to Germany, 77. Author: The Wyoming Legislature: Lawmakers, the Public, and the Press, 1973; author: (with R. Dalton and K. Hildebrandt) Germany Tranformed: Political Culture and the New Politics, 1981; contbr. articles to profl. jours. Coach Laramie Soccer Assn., 1978—81; election observer Germany, 1980. Mem.: Conf. Group German Politics (mem. exec. com. 1984—87, co-editor newsletter 1985—91), Midwest Polit. Sci. Assn, (chmn. panel ann. conv. 1985, 1986), Am. Polit. Sci. Assn. (chmn. panel ann. conv. 1983), Pi Sigma Alpha, Omicron Delta Kappa, Phi Kappa Phi. Home: 920 West Lima Ada OH 45810 Office: President's Office 525 S Main St Ada OH 45810-1599 Office Phone: 419-772-2030. Business E-Mail: k-baker@onu.edu.

BAKER, KENT ALFRED, broadcasting and publishing company executive; b. Sioux City, Iowa, Mar. 22, 1948; s. Carl Edmund Baker and Miriam M. (Hawthorn) Baker Nye. Student, Iowa State U., 1966-70. Editor Iowa State Daily, 1969-70; mem. U.S. Peace Corps., 1971-72; editor The Glidden (Iowa) Graphic, 1973-75; bur. chief The Waterloo (Iowa) Courier, Iowa, 1975; state editor The Des Moines Register, 1976-77; news dir. Sta. WQAD-TV, Moline, Ill., 1978; Sunday editor The Des Moines Sunday Register, 1979; news dir. Sta. KHON-TV, Honolulu, 1980-95; v.p., gen. mgr. KHON-TV, Honolulu, 1996-2000; pres. Baker Newspapers, 2000—. Pub. The Moville Record, 2000—. Mem. Hoover Libr. Assn., Iowa State U. Alumni Assn., Iowa Newspaper Assn., Iowa Hist. Soc. Home: PO Box 419 Moville IA 51039 Office: Moville Record 238 Main St Moville IA 51039 Office Phone: 712-873-3141. Personal E-mail: record@netins.net.

BAKER, KERRY ALLEN, management consultant; b. Selmer, Tenn., Sept. 21, 1949; s. Austin Clark and Betty Ann (Brooks) B.; m. Ellen Fleming. BIE, Ga. Inst. Tech., 1971; MBA, Ga. State U., 1973; JD, Memphis State U., 1987. With dept. law State of Ga., 1971—73; engr. N.W. Ga. divsn. Gold Kist Inc., Ellijay, 1977—80; sr. mfg. engr. Plough, Inc., Memphis, 1980—82, mgr. indsl. engring., 1983—86, supr. mfg. engr., 1986—90; mgr. plant bus. Clorox Co., Dyersburg, Tenn., 1990—95; mgr. ops. Huish Detergents, Inc., Dyersburg, 1995; exec. dir. Mgmt. Recruiters of Dyersburg, 1996—97; mgr. adminstrn. Gabriel Ride Products, Pulaski, Tenn., 1998—99; pres. Rock Ridge Ventures, Inc., Dyersburg, 1997—2000, Rock Ridge Ventures, Arden, NC, 2000—; contr. MAHLE Motorsports, Inc., Fletcher, NC, 2000—07. Decorated Order of St. Barbara. Mem. Inst. Indsl. Engrs., Am. Prodn. and Inventory Control Soc., Scabbard and Blade, Masons, Phi Delta Phi. Methodist. Home: PO Box 87 Arden NC 28704-0087 Business E-Mail: kerry.baker@us.mahle.com. E-mail: kbaker151@earthlink.net.

BAKER, KIM PEARSON, education educator; b. Hartford, Conn., Jan. 31, 1950; d. Herbert and Charlotte Speare Pearson; children: Jamie, Kristen. BA, Washington U., St. Louis, 1972; MS, SUNY, Albany, 1991, PhD in Reading, 1997. Cert. tchr. elem., reading NY State Edn. Dept., 1991. Tchr. elem. sch. St. Louis Pub. Schs., 1972—74; term substitute East Greenbush Pub. Schs., NY, 1990—91; rsch. asst. SUNY, Albany, 1991—97; prof. The Sage Colls., Troy, NY, 1997—. Mem. higher task force quality inclusive schooling, NY, 1998—. Contbr. chapters to books. V.p. The Ark, Troy, 1998—. Mem.: Nat. Reading Conf. (reviewer area 3, asst. program chmn.), The Jr. League Troy (chmn. ways and means, pub. affairs 1981—). Democrat. Avocations: children's literature, travel, dogs. Office: The Sage Colls The Sch Edn 45 Ferry St Troy NY 12180 Home Phone: 518-785-4898; Office Phone: 518-244-3132. Home Fax: 518-244-2334. Personal E-mail: bakerk2@sage.edu.

BAKER, LAURA KAY, art gallery owner, writer; b. Urbana, Ill., July 25, 1951; d. Warren Henry and Christie Ann Schuetz; m. Thomas Hall Baker, Mar. 19, 1972; children: Nicholas Warren, Allison Whitney. Student, St. Andrews U., Scotland, 1969, Ill. State U., Normal, 1969—71, Ga. State U., 1980—82; Assoc., Parkland Coll., Champaign, Ill., 1972. Owner Silver Shaman, Albuquerque, 1974—80, Tanner Chaney Gallery, Albuquerque, 1987—; novelist Albuquerque, 1993—. Nat. workshop coord. Romance Writers Am., Dallas, 1996—96; sec., treas. Land of Enchantment Romance Authors, Albuquerque, 1993—96. Author: (novels) Stargazer, 1998 (Daphne du Maurier, 1999, Nat. Readers Choice Nominee, 1998, Golden Quill nominee, 1999, Aspen Gold best single title, 1998), Legend, 1998 (Daphne du Maurier, 1999, RITA nominee, 1999), Broken In Two, 1999 (Daphne du Maurier, 2000), Raven, 2001 (Daphne du Maurier, 2002); contbr. articles to profl. jours. Seminar tchr. numerous orgns.; writing judge numerous writers orgns.; pres. PTA Manzano H.S., Albuquerque, 2001—04. Recipient Svc. award, YMCA, 1996, Romance Writers Am., 1998. Mem.: Novelists, Inc. (conf. coord. 2002, 2004). Independent. Avocations: embroidery, piano. Office: Tanner Chaney Gallery 323 Romero NW #4 Albuquerque NM 87104 Personal E-mail: lbaker10@aol.com.

BAKER, LEE EDWARD, biomedical engineering educator; b. Springfield, Mo., Aug. 31, 1924; s. Edward Fielding and Oneita Geneva (Patton) B.; m. Jeanne Carolyn Ferbrache, June 20, 1948; children: Carson Phillips, Carolyn Patton. BEE, U. Kans., 1945; MEE, Rice U., 1960; PhD in Physiology, Baylor U., 1965. Registered profl. engr., Tex. Asst. prof. electrical engring. Rice U., Houston, 1960-64; asst. prof. physiology Baylor U. Coll. Medicine, Houston, 1965-69, assoc. prof., 1969-75; prof. biomed. engring. U. Tex., 1975-82, Robert L. Parker Sr. Centennial Prof. Engring. Austin, 1982-2000, prof. emeritus, 2000—. Co-author: Principles of Applied Biomedical Engineering, 1968, 3d edit., 1989; author, co-author scientific papers. Served to lt. USN, 1943-46, PTO, 1951-53. Spl. research fellow NIH, 1964-65. Fellow Am. Inst. Med. and Biol. Engring., Royal Soc. Medicine; mem. IEEE (sr.), Biomed. Engring. Soc. (sr.), Am. Physiol. Soc. Avocation: gardening. Office: Univ Tex ENS 610 Biomed Engring Program Austin TX 78712

BAKER, LEONARD MORTON, manufacturing executive; b. Medford, Mass., Oct. 2, 1934; s. Abraham and Sarah B.; m. Ruth Lee Edelstein, June 15, 1958; children: Charles Harold, Andrew Mark, Douglas Jon. BS in Chemistry, Harvard U., 1956; PhD in Phys.-Organic Chemistry, MIT, 1960. With Union Carbide Corp., 1959-92, assoc. dir., then dir. rsch. and devel., 1969-77, v.p. rsch. and devel. NYC, 1977-80, v.p., gen. mgr. coatings materials div., 1980-82, v.p. splty. chems. div., 1982-84, corporate dir. tech., 1984-86, v.p. spltys. and services Bus. Group., 1986, corp. v.p. tech., 1986; sr. v.p. tech., chief tech. officer Praxair, Inc., Danbury, Conn., 1992—2002; cons. Tech. Planning and Assesment, 2003—. Bd. dirs. Rogers (Conn.) Corp. Exec. bd. Cornell Inst. Biotech.; mem. sci. adv. com. MIT; mem. materials sci. adv. bd., vis. com. U. Conn.; industry rep. Nat. Acad.-Industry Program, NRC; industry adv. panel NSF; mem. industry adv. bd. Presdl. Sci. Adv. Commn.; mem. sci. adv. bd. Conn. Coll.; active Nat. Industry Coun. for Sci. Edn., adv. bd. Coun. for Competitiveness Rsch. Devel. MIT fellow, 1956-57; NSF fellow, 1957-58; Sun Oil Corp. fellow, 1958-59 Mem. AICE, N.Y. Acad. Scis. (sci. policy com.), Am. Chem. Soc., Indsl. Rsch. Inst. (fed. sci. and tech. com. pre-coll. edn. com., rsch. com.), Council Chem. Rsch. (gov. bd., univ./industry liaison com.), Soc. Chem. Industry, Dirs. Indsl. Rsch., Am. Mgmt. Assn. (rsch. and devel. council), Conn. Acad. Sci. and Engring. Home: 60 Lyons Plains Rd Westport CT 06880-1305 Personal E-mail: lenmbaker@aol.com.

BAKER, LESLIE DAVID, actor; b. Chicago, Feb. 19, 1958; BS in Psychology, Loyola U.; MS in Human Services Adminstrn., Spertus Coll. Judaica, Chgo. Staff AIDS program and policy Chgo. Dept Health; staff Chgo. Office Cable and Comm., Chgo. Bd. Edn. Actor: (TV series) The Office, 2005— (SAG award outstanding performance by an ensemble in a comedy series, 2007), Malcolm in the Middle, 2000, The Guardian, (guest appearance) That '70s Show, 2001, Scrubs, 2003, Just Shoot Me, Road to Redemption, Judging Amy.*

BAKER, LYNNE RUDDER, philosophy educator; b. Atlanta, Feb. 14, 1944; d. James Maclin and Virginia (Bennett) Rudder; m. Thomas B. Baker III, Feb. 1, 1969. BA, Vanderbilt U., 1966, MA, 1971, PhD, 1972; student, Johns Hopkins U., 1967-68. Asst. prof. philosophy Mary Baldwin Coll., Staunton, Va., 1972-76, Middlebury (Vt.) Coll., 1976-79, assoc. prof., 1979-84, prof., 1984-94, acting dean arts and humanities, 1982, chairperson humanities divsn., 1982-85, acting chairperson philosophy, 1986-87; prof. U. Mass., Amherst, 1989—, dir. philosophy grad. program, 1994—. Mem. panel to select summer seminars NEH, Washington, 1982, mem. panel to select fellows, 1989—90; Gifford lectr. U. Glasgow, Scotland, 2001. Author: Saving Belief: A Critique of Physicalism, 1988, Explaining Attitudes: A Practical Approach to the Mind, 1995, Persons and Bodies: A Constitution View, 2000; contbr. scholarly articles to profl. jours. Trustee Vanderbilt U., Nashville, 1969-70, mem. alumni bd. dirs., 1985-89. Mellon fellow, 1974, NEH fellow, 1983-84, Nat. Humanities Ctr. fellow, 1982-83, Woodrow Wilson Internat. Ctr. for Scholars fellow, 1988-89. Mem. Am. Philos. Assn. (program com. 1983, exec. com. 1992-95), Soc. for Philosophy and Psychology, Soc. Christian Philosophers (exec. com. 1992-95), Soc. Women in Philosophy, Phi Beta Kappa. Democrat. Episcopalian. Office: U Mass Dept Philosophy Amherst MA 01003

BAKER, MARGARET MOORE-FRITZ, retired school librarian, humanities educator; b. Washington, May 26, 1934; d. James Fritz; m. Claud Henry Baker, Jr., Sept. 8, 1956; children: Peter Fritz, Elizabeth Blair Baker Naime. BA, BEd, U. Colo., 1956. Cert. tchr. 1956. Libr. U. Colo., Boulder, 1956—57; tchr. grades 3,4,5 Superior Sch., Boulder County, Colo., 1957—59; tchr. Longmont H.S., Longmont, Colo., 1959—60; sub. tchr. Salt Lake City County Sch., 1969—72; libr. Salt. Lake County Libr., Peterson Br., 1969—72; sub. sch. libr. Stonewall Jackson Mid. Sch., Manassas, Va., 1972—77; office mgr. U. Kans., 1980—93; book rev. Glencoe Wordsmithing, Baldwin City, 1993—. Book rev.: review books for radio, press, internet Baldwin Bookworm, Kansas Bookworm, 1994. Mem. Bladwin C. of C.; voter edn., newsletter, v.p. League of Women Voters, Grand Forks, ND, 1963—66, active environ. portfolio Salt Lake County, Utah, 1966—72, organizer, v.p. Manassas, Va., 1972—78, mem. pub. rels. newsletter edn. Lawrence-Douglas County, Kans., 1978—, newsletter editor, 1986—90; libr. Oread Friends Meeting, Lawrence, Kans., 1995—. Mem.: Sister in Crime, Collie Club of Am. Mem. Soc. Of Friends. Avocations: reading, needlecrafts, bagpipe, dogs. Home and Office: Glencoe Wordsmithing 1009 N 600 Rd Baldwin City KS 66006-7205 Personal E-mail: glencoe@knetconnect.net.

BAKER, MARJANE L., social studies educator; b. Bryan, Ohio, May 28; d. Clyde B. Evan and Marjorie M. Eakins Evans Sickmiller; m. Leland O. Baker; 1 child, Troy Judson. BS in Edn., Defiance Coll., Ohio, 1965; MS in Edn., U. Toledo, 1969. Elem. tchr. Defiance Pub. Schs., Ohio, Paulding Village Pub. Schs., Ohio, Sylvania Pub. Schs., Ohio, 1966—71; coop. tchr. Ea. Mich. U., UM, UT, 1970—2002; student tchr., supr. U. Toledo, 1972; tchr., cons. Mich. Geographic Allicance, 1990—; adj. prof., elem. and mid. sch. Ea. Mich. U., 2002—03; tchr. online course Wayne County, 2003; lectr. Ea. Mich. U., 2006; elem. tchr. Plymouth Canton Cmty. Schs., Plymouth, Mich., 1975—2005; curriculum designer Detroit 300, 2002; lesson designer Detroit Hist. Mus., 2004—05; curriculum designer Grosse Pointe Hist. Soc., 2005—; lectr. Ea. Mich. U., Ypsilanti, 2006—. Cons. Mich. Geog. Assn., Mt. Clemons, 1991—, M. D. Environ. Quality, Lansing, Mich., 2005—; presenter in field; taught numerous profl. workshops in environ. and geog. issues. Dir.: Run to Read TV Program, 1989; contbr. articles to profl. jours. Grant writer Plymouth Hist. Mus., Mich., 2005—; com. mem. Plymouth Symphony Orch., 2000—, Detroit Hist. Mus.; singer U. Mich. Choral Union. Recipient Friends of Rouge award, 2005, Outstanding Achievement award, Defiance Coll., 2000, Golden Apple Outstanding Achievement award, 1991; grantee, Edn. Excellence Found., 2005, Showcasing Pub. Schs., Mich. Hist. Lighthouse Project, 2005, Nat. Wildlife Assn., 1998, Nat. Geog. Soc. Mem.: ASCD, Detroit Hist. Soc., Mich. Coun. Hist. Edn., Mich Coun. Social Studies, Nat. Coun. Social Studies, Mich Geog. Alliance, Mich. Sci. Tchrs. Assn., Phi Delta Kappa. Presbyterian. Avocations: singing, reading, bicycling, tennis.

BAKER, MARK BRUCE, lawyer, educator; b. Bridgeport, Conn., Dec. 27, 1946; s. Phillip and Lillian (Islovitz) Bader; m. Sandra Fay Wolf, June 9, 1968 (div. 1982); 1 dau. Rachel Barrett Bader; m. Nora Kay Mandell, Dec. 30, 1984; 1 dau. Lisa Anne Baker. BBA, U. Miami, Coral Gables, Fla., 1968; JD, So. Meth. U., Dallas, 1974. Bar: Tex. 1974. Assoc. firm Herndon, Girand and Dooley, Dallas, 1974-76; ptnr. firm Pailet and Bader, Dallas, 1976-80; prof. internat. law U. Tex., Austin, 1980—; of counsel Bard and Groves, Houston, 1981—83, Goodall and Davison, Austin, 1991—; gen. counsel Embree Constrn. Group, Inc., Austin, Tex., 1987—2000; corp. counsel Kinnect, Inc., A Lloyds of London Co., 2005—. Chmn. bd. Embree Health Care Group, Inc. Contbr. articles to legal publs. Bd. dirs. Jewish Cmty. Coun. Austin, 1983-86, Big Bros./Big Sisters Program, 1999—, Vol. Svcs. of Children's Hosp. of Austin, 2003—. Recipient Outstanding Asst. Prof. award U. Tex., 1982, Outstanding Class Lectr. award, 1984, Tex. Excellence Tchg. award U. Tex. Alumni Assn., 1983. Mem. ABA, Union Internat. des Avocats, Am. Friends Wilton Park (sec.-treas. 1982-84), Tex. Bar Assn. (internat. law sect.), Austin Fgn. Trade Coun., Am. Bus. Law Assn. (internat. law sect., pres. 1990-91). Office: Bldg 3 Ste 601 1250 Capital of Tx Hwy S Austin TX 78746 Home: 1500 W Lynn #107 Austin TX 78703 Office Phone: 512-422-3003. Business E-Mail: m.baker@mail.utexas.edu.

BAKER, MARK M., lawyer, law educator; b. Long Beach, NY, Nov. 20, 1947; s. Barbara and Matt Baker; m. Lorna Hayim-Baker; children: Cory M., Lindsay N. BS, Syracuse U., 1969; JD, Bklyn Law Sch., 1972. Bar: N.Y. 1973, U.S. Ct. Appeals (11th cir.) 1989, U.S. Supreme Ct. 1976, U.S. Ct. Appeals (2d cir.) 1975, U.S. Dist. Ct. (so. dist.) N.Y. 1975, U.S. Dist. Ct. (ea. dist.) N.Y. 1975, U.S. Ct. Appeals (3d cir.) 1989, U.S. Ct. Appeals (4th cir.) 1989, U.S. Ct. Appeals (5th cir.) 1989, U.S. Ct. Appeals (9th cir.) 1989. Asst. dist. atty. Kings County Dist. Atty., Bklyn., 1972—76; ptnr. Rhodes, Baker and Fisher, 1976—77; spl. asst. atty. gen. Office of Spl. State Prosecutor, NYC, 1977—83; ptnr. Slotnick and Baker, 1983—94; of counsel Brafman & Assocs., P.C. (formerly Brafman & Ross, P.C.), 1994—. Adj. prof. of law Touro Coll. Law Ctr., Huntington, 1999—2000. Author: (N.Y. criminal practice handbook supp) Defenses; contbr. articles to profl. jours. Mem., bd. of trustees Hebrew Inst. of Riverdale, 1975—2002, SAR Acad., 1987—90, Westchester Hebrew H.S., Mamaroneck, 1992—96; pres. River Ter. Apartments Assn., Riverdale, NY, 1980—82. Mem.: N.Y. County Lawyers Assn. (assoc.), N.Y. Coun. Def. Lawyers (assoc.), N.Y. Criminal Bar Assn. (assoc.), N.Y. State Assn. Criminal Def. Attorneys (assoc.), Nat. Assn. Criminal Def. Attorneys (assoc.), Assn of Bar City of N.Y. (assoc.). Achievements include research in federal and NY criminal appeals, post conviction and habeas corpus litigation. Avocations: skiing, running, reading political novels and non-fiction. Office: Brafman & Assoc PC 767 Third Ave 26th Fl New York NY 10017 Office Phone: 212-750-7800. Business E-Mail: mbaker@braflaw.com.

BAKER, MARSHINA, physical education educator; b. Shelby, NC, May 6, 1957; d. James Winifred and Selma Patricia Baker; 1 child, Antwon Mendes. BS, St. Augustine's Coll., Raleigh, NC, 1980; MS, N.C. Ctrl. U., Durham, 1984. Phys. fitness specialist Washington Srs. Wellness Ctr., 1985—90; program assoc. Am. Heart Assn., Washington, 1990—91; tchr. D.C. Pub. Sch., Washington, 1994—97; lectr. Bowie State U., Md., 1994—; tchr. Prince George's Pub. Sch., Upper Marlboro, Md., 1997—2000; lectr. No. Va. C.C., Alexandria, 1999—, Prince George's C.C., Largo, Md., 1999—. Author: Foundations of a Health Lifestyle, 2003. Mem.: ASCD, AAHPERD, Nat. Assn. for Sport and Phys. Edn., Am. Assn. for Health Edn. Democrat. Baptist. Avocations: travel, reading, exercise, gardening, music. Office: Bowie State Univ 14000 Jericho Park Rd Bowie MD 20715 Office Phone: 301-860-3780. Office Fax: 301-736-1236. Personal E-mail: marshina5503@aol.com.

BAKER, MARY EVELYN, retired librarian; b. Columbus, Ohio, May 8, 1912; d. Abram Jackson and Martha Maria (Dailey) Shoemaker; m. Richard Heinley Baker, Sept. 18, 1937 (dec.); children: Richard Shoemaker, David Guy. BA, Ohio State U., 1934; BS in Libr. Sci., Western Res. U., Cleve., 1935. Mem. staff libr. Ohio State U., Columbus, 1935-37, 38-44, 1955-74, part-time libr., 1955-66, adminstrv. asst. to the dir., 1958, serial cataloger, 1958-67, asst. reviser, sr. cataloger, 1967-68, head serial div. catalog dept., 1968-71, head catalog dept., 1971-74. Libr. com. First Congl. Ch., Columbus, 1941-97, libr. co-chmn., 1962-65, 74-75, libr. chmn., 1976-97; sec. serials sect., resources and tech. divsn. ALA, 1970-73. Den mother Boy Scouts Am., Columbus, 1953-58; libr. co-chmn. Friendship Village, Dublin, Ohio, 1981-97, chmn., 1997—, pres. Mem. Ohioana Libr. Assn. (past chmn. various coms., life), PEO (telephone chmn. chpt. V 1987—), DAR (Indians com.), Ohio State Univ. Women's Club (past pres.), Agrl. Circle (past pres.), Franklin Co-Ret. Tchrs. Assn. (life), Ohio Ret. Tchrs. Assn. (life), Ohio State Alumni Assn. (life), Polar Bear Alumni Assn. Columbus North H.S. (life), Alumni Assn. Univ. Sch. (life), Ohio State U. Retirees Assn. (life, bridge chmn. 1984-2002), Women's Assn. (pres. 2003-2004), Ohio State U. Friends of the Librs., Ohio Hist. Soc., Worthington Hist. Soc. (life), Columbus Hist. Soc. (life), Ch. Women United of Columbus and Franklin County, Columbus Mus. Art, Columbus Zoo, Gypsies Travel Club, Motts Mil. Mus. (charter), Phi Mu (various offices including pres. active and alumni chpts.). Republican. Home: 6000 Riverside Dr Apt C302 Dublin OH 43017-5072

BAKER, MERL, engineering educator; b. Cadiz, Ky., July 11, 1924; s. Jesse F. and Argie (Coyle) B.; m. Emily Wilson, Sept. 14, 1946; children: Merl Wilson, Marilyn Ruth. BS in Mech. Engring., U. Ky., Lexington, 1945; MS, Purdue U., 1948, PhD, 1952. Grad. asst. Purdue U., 1946-48; mem. faculty U. Ky., 1948-63, prof. mech. engring., 1955-63; exec. dir. Ky. Rsch. Found., 1953-63; coordinator, dir. U. Ky. coop. programs with AID, 1956-63, exec. dir. research and relations with industry, 1957-63; dean U. Mo. Sch. Mines and Metallurgy, 1963; chancellor U. Mo., Rolla, 1964-73, spl. asst. to pres. statewide system, 1973-77; coordinator energy conservation program Oak Ridge Nat. Lab., 1977-79, energy mgmt. specialist, 1979-82; provost U. Tenn.-Chattanooga, 1982-85, prof. engring., 1985-97, dir. Ctr. for Career Enhancement, 1985-97; engring. cons. Lexington, Ky., 1997—. Recipient Disting. Alumnus award U. Ky., 1965, Disting. Engring. Alumnus award Purdue U., 1968; named Outstanding Mech. Engr., 1991; named to U. Ky. Engring. Hall of Distinction, 2003. Fellow Am. Soc. Engring. Mgmt. (bd. dirs.), Am. Soc. Engring. Edn.; mem. NSPE (pres.

Tenn. Soc. 1995-96), U. Mis.-Rolla Acad. Engring. Mgmt. (hon.), Am. Soc. Heating, Refrigerating and Air-Conditioning Engrs. (award of merit tchg. 1959, chmn. edn. com. 1960-61, Disting. Svc. award 1971), Ky. Acad. Sci., Newcomen Soc. N.Am., Cosmos Club (Washington), Blue Key, Scabbard and Blade, Sigma Xi, Phi Kappa Phi, Phi Eta Sigma, Tau Beta Pi, Pi Tau Sigma, Sigma Pi Sigma, Omicron Delta Kappa, Chi Epsilon, Rotary. Home and Office: 1973 Blairmore Rd Lexington KY 40502-2432 Office Phone: 859-268-6190. Business E-Mail: m.baker40@insightbb.com.

BAKER, MITCHELL, computer software developer, foundation administrator; AB in Asian Studies, U. Calif., Berkeley, JD. Former assoc. gen. counsel Netscape Comm. Corp.; joined mozilla.org, 1998, gen. mgr., 1999—; pres. Mozilla Found., 2003—. Bd. dirs. Open Source Applications Found.; adv. bd. SpikeSource. Named one of 100 Most Influential People of 2005, Time mag. Office: Mozilla Corp 1981K Landings Dr Mountain View CA 94043-0801

BAKER, NANCY L., university librarian, educator; BA with honors, U. Conn., Storrs, 1972; MLS, U. Mich., Ann Arbor, 1973; MA in English Lit., SUNY, Binghamton, 1978. Asst. reference libr. SUNY, Binghamton, 1973—76; sr. reference libr. Middlebury Coll., Vt., 1976—78; head reference dept. U. Ky., Lexington, 1978—81; head gen. reference dept. U. Utah, Salt Lake City, 1981—84; asst. dir. librs. for undergrad. svcs. U. Wash., Seattle, 1984, assoc. dir. librs. pub. svcs., 1984—91; dir. librs. Wash. State U., Pullman, 1991—2000; univ. libr. U. Iowa, Iowa City, 2000—. Instr. libr. sci. Coll. Libr. Sci., U. Ky., 1978—81, Grad. Sch. Libr. and Info. Sci., U. Wash., 1990, Sch. Libr. and Info. Sci., U. Iowa, 2002—04, adv. com., 2000—. Contbr. articles to profl. jours. Recipient Scholarship Award, Conn. Libr. Assn., 1972. Mem.: ALA, Iowa Libr. Assn., Assn. Rsch. Librs. (bd. dirs. 2000—03). Office: U Iowa Librs 100 Main Library Iowa City IA 52242-1420 Home: 30 Alder Court Iowa City IA 52246 Office Phone: 319-335-5897. Office Fax: 319-335-5900. E-mail: nancy-l-baker@uiowa.edu.*

BAKER, NATHAN ADAM, music theorist; b. Plains, Mont., Dec. 9, 1976; s. Gary Stephen and Emma Katherine Baker; m. Cari Lyn Silvester, July 14, 1999. MusB magna cum laude, Utah State U., Logan, 2002; MA in Music Theory, U. Oreg., Eugene, 2006. Undergrad. tchg. fellow, dept. music Utah State U., 1999—2002; grad. tchg. fellow U. Oreg. Sch. Music, 2003—. Missionary Ch. Jesus Christ LDS, Puebla, Mexico, 1997—98. Recipient Excellence in Tchg. award, U. Oreg. Sch. Music, 2004. Mem.: Soc. Music Theory. Independent. Mem. Lds Ch. Avocations: cooking, literature. Business E-Mail: nbaker@uoregon.edu.

BAKER, OTIS MCDOWELL, small business owner; b. Baton Rouge, Sept. 21, 1973; s. Otis Mcdowell Baker, Sr. and Yvonne Bell Baker; 1 child, Taylor Marie. BA, La. State U., Bator Rouge, 1999. Owner Baker Tile and Cabinets, Inc., La., 1994—. Community action project, 2 on your Side (Cmty. Action Appreciation award, 1998). Mem.: Omega Psi Phi (assoc.; mentor 2001—07). Home: 13804 Longvue Dr Baker LA 70714 Office: Baker Tile and Cabinets Inc 13804 Longvue Dr Baker LA 70714 Home Phone: 225-774-0583; Office Phone: 225-774-0583. Personal E-mail: ombj@yahoo.com.

BAKER, P. JEAN, lawyer, mediator; b. June 28, 1948; BS summa cum laude, Wright State U., Dayton, Ohio, 1973; MBA, Northeastern U., Boston, 1989; JD, Calif. Western U., San Diego, 1993. Bar: Calif. 1993; cert. mediator. With GenRad Inc., Boston, 1974-82; mktg./sales staff GE Co., Boston, 1982-84; major accounts mgr. Fluke Mfg. Co., Boston, 1984-89; pub. rels. mgr. Racal Dana, Irvine, Calif., 1989-90; legal intern Pub. Defenders Dependancy, San Diego, 1992; law clk. Civil divsn. U.S. Atty., San Diego, 1992; personal injury atty. L.H. Parker, Long Beach, Calif., 1993; mediator/atty. Baker & Assocs., San Diego, 1993-94; dir. Orange County region Am. Arbitration Assn., Irvine, 1994-97, v.p. Washington, 1997—. Mediator San Diego Mediation Ctr., 1993-97; trainer mediation skills Am. Arbitration Assn., 1994-97, staff mediator, 2006—; adj. prof. Western State U., Irvine, 1995-96; MCLE presenter San Diego County Bar, 1994, State Bar of Calif., 1996, ABA, 1997; mediator Superior Ct., San Diego, 1994-97, U.S. Bankruptcy Ct. (cen. dist.) Calif., 1995-97; adj. prof. Columbus Sch. of Law, Washington, 1997-2001, Georgetown Law Sch., 2005-; coach Georgetown Law Sch., 2003—. Bd. dirs. Legal Aid Soc., San Diego, 1994, T. Homann Law Assn., San Diego, 1994, Counsel for Ct. Excellence, 2003-04. Recipient Am. Jurisprudence awards, 1992. Mem. ABA (co-editor sect. litit. newsletter, 2006—), D.C. Bar Assn., State Bar of Calif., Energy Bar Assn., Va. Bar Assn., Md. Bar Assn., Women's Bar Assn. Avocations: tennis, golf. Office: American Arbitration Assn 1776 Eye St NW Ste 850 Washington DC 20006 Home Phone: 703-641-9227; Office Phone: 202-223-7093. Business E-Mail: BakerJ@adr.org.

BAKER, PAMELA, lawyer; b. Detroit, Apr. 6, 1951; d. William D. and Lois (Tukey) Baker; m. Jay R. Franke, June 10, 1972; children: Baker Eugene, Alexandra Britell. AB, Smith Coll., 1972; JD, U. Wis. Madison, 1976. Bar: Ill. 1976, Wis. 1976. Ptnr. Sonnenschein, Nath & Rosenthal, Chgo.; chair nat. employee benefits and exec. compensation practice group. Contbr. articles to profl. jour. Fellow Am. Coll. Employee Benefits Counsel (charter), Am. Bar Found.; mem. ABA (mem. employee benefits com. 1984—, chair-elect 1998-99, chair 1999-2000, mem. plan mergers and acquisitions com. 1985— mem. fed. regulation of securities com. 1989—, chair 1989-95), Ill. State Bar Assn. (sec. employee benefits sect. coun. 1989-90, vice chair 1990-91, chair 1991-92), Chgo. Bar Assn. (employee benefits com. 1978—, sec. 1984-85, vice chair 1985-86, chair 1986-87, fed. taxation com. 1980—, exec. coun. 1982-85). Office: Sonnenschein Nath & Rosenthal Sears Tower 233 S Wacker Dr Ste 7800 Chicago IL 60606-6491

BAKER, PATRICIA, health foundation administrator; BS, Wayne State U.; MS, U. Wis. Dir. Conn. govt. program Oxford Health Plans; exec. dir. The Women's Ctr., Waukesha, Wis., 1978-85; assoc. editor, dir. Planned Parenthood, Wis., 1985—87; exec. dir. Planned Parenthood Conn.; nat. program dir. March of Dimes Birth Defects Found., until 1999; exec. dir. Conn. Health Found., Farmington, 1999—.

BAKER, PAUL RAYMOND, historian, educator; b. Everett, Wash., Sept. 28, 1927; s. Loren Robbins and Alma Irene (Ball) B.; m. Elizabeth O. Kemp, Feb. 11, 1972; 1 dau., Alice Elizabeth. AB, Stanford U., 1949; MA, Columbia U., 1951; PhD, Harvard U., 1960. Staff editor Ency. Americana, NYC, 1952-55; instr., asst. prof. Calif. Inst. Tech., Pasadena, 1960-63; lectr. U. Calif.-Riverside, 1963-64, U. Oreg., Eugene, 1964-65; assoc. prof., then prof. history NYU, NYC, 1965-99, emeritus prof., 1999—, dir. Am. civilization program, 1972-92. Mem. media panel NEH, 1978; vis. schlar Am. Acad. in Rome, 1959. Editor: Views of Society and Manners in America, 1963; gen. editor: American Problem Studies series, 40 vols., 1968—; author: The Fortunate Pilgrims, 1964, Richard Morris Hunt, 1980, Stanny: the Gilded Life of Stanford White, 1989; compiler: The Atomic Bomb, 1968, The Atomic Bomb, rev. edit., 1976; co-author: The American Experience, 5 vols., 1976, 79, (Spanish translation) Nueva Historia de los Estados Unidos, 1986; (with others) Master Builders, 1985, The Architecture of Richard Morris Hunt, 1986, (French translation) Richard Morris Hunt Architecte, The Italian Presence in American Art, 1860-1920, 1992, Henry Adams and His World, 1993, Greenwich Village, Culture and Counterculture, 1993, La Virtù e la Libertà, 1995, Exploration, Vision and Influence--The Art World of Brattleboro's Hunt Family, 2005. Mem. Glen Ridge Hist. Preservation Commn., 1994-96. Recipient Author's award NJ Lit. Hall of Fame, 1993; Kennedy travel fellow Harvard U., 1958-59, NEH fellow, 1982. Mem. Am. Studies Assn. (pres. met. N.Y. chpt. 1968-69, Mary C. Turpie prize for outstanding contbns. to tchg. advisement and program devel. 1994), Orgn. Am. Historians, Victorian Soc. in Am., Phi Beta Kappa (v.p., pres. Beta of N.Y. 1966-70). Home: 90 Hillside Ave Glen Ridge NJ 07028-2212 Office: NYU Dept History 53 Washington Square South New York NY 10012-1098

BAKER, PAUL THORNELL, anthropology educator; b. Burlington, Iowa, Feb. 28, 1927; s. Palmer Ward Baker and Viola Isabelle (Thornell) Loughlin; m. Thelma Marion Shoher, Feb. 21, 1949; children: Deborah C., Amy L., Joshua S., Felicia B. Student, U. Miami, 1947—49; BA, U. N.Mex., 1951; PhD, Harvard U., 1956. Rschr. U.S. Army Q.M., Natick, Mass., 1952—57; asst. prof. anthropology Pa. State U., University Park, 1957—61, assoc. prof., 1961—65, prof., 1965—81, Evan Pugh prof. anthropology, 1981—87, Evan Pugh prof. emeritus, 1987—, head dept., 1980—85. Sci. advisor Wenner-Gren Found., NYC, 1980—83; mem. U.S. Commn. for UNESCO, 1982—84, exec. commn., 1983—84. Editor: Biology of Human Adaptability, 1966, Man in the Andes, 1976, Biology of High Altitude Peoples, 1978, The Changing Samoans, 1986; co-author (with G.A. Harrison, J.M. Tanner, D.R. Pilbeam): Human Biology, 1988. With US Army, 1945—47. Decorated Yugoslavian Order of the Golden Star with Necklace; recipient Huxley medal, Royal Anthrop. Inst. Gt. Brit., 1982; fellow, Guggenheim Found., 1974—75; scholar Fulbright rsch. scholar, 1962. Fellow: Am. Anthrop. Assn. (assoc. editor jour. 1973—76); mem.: NAS, Internat. Union Anthropol. and Ethnol. Scis. (hon. life, v.p. 1988—93, sr. v.p. 1993—98), Internat. Assn. Human Biologists (pres. 1980—89, Franz Boas Disting. Achievement award), Human Biology Coun. (pres. 1974—77), Am. Assn. Phys. Anthropologists (pres. 1969—71, Charles R. Darwin Lifetime Achievement award 1993).

BAKER, PETER MITCHELL, science association director, laser scientist; b. London, July 18, 1939; arrived in U.S., 1966; s. George Edward and Clarice Baker; m. Sunny Baker, Oct. 15, 1988; 1 child, Scott George. BSc in Physics with honors, London U., 1963. Sr. physicist Itek Corp., Lexington, Mass., 1966-69; sr. v.p. Micronetic Sys., Burlington, Mass., 1969-74; tchr. physics Hillcrest Sch., Nairobi, Kenya, 1975-77; pres. Quantrad Corp., Torrance, Calif., 1977-84, Ebtec Calif., Huntington Beach, 1985-88; exec. dir. Laser Inst. Am., Orlando, Fla., 1988—. Lectr. lasers UCLA Ext., 1986—88; chmn. Bd. Laser Safety Inc., 2003. Contbr. articles to profl. jours. Recipient CEO award for Outstanding Small Bus., 1982. Fellow: Laser Inst. Am. (pres. 1987); mem.: Coun. of Engring. and Sci. Soc. Execs. (pres. 2004—05). Avocations: walking, tennis. Office: Laser Inst Am 13501 Ingenuity Dr Ste 128 Orlando FL 32826-3009 *My guiding principle is "Do What You Say."*.

BAKER, PHILIP STEVEN, dentist, educator; m. Jacqulyn Bennett, June 25, 1995. BS in Biology, Regis Coll., 1974; DDS, Loyola U., 1978. Diplomate Am. Bd. Prosthodontics, 2005. From clin. instr. to asst. prof. Sch. Dentistry Loyola U., Chgo., 1978—85; from asst. prof. to assoc. prof. Coll. Dentistry U. Fla., Gainesville, Fla., 1987—98; assoc. prof. Sch. Dentistry Med. Coll. Ga., Augusta, Ga., 1998—. Named Outstanding Tchr. of Yr., U. Fla. Coll. Dentistry, 1989. Fellow: Am. Coll. Prosthodontists (pres. Ga. sect. 2003—04). Office: MCG Sch of Dentistry 1459 Laney Walker Blvd Augusta GA 30912 Home Phone: 706-869-0711; Office Phone: 706-721-2554.

BAKER, R. ROBINSON, surgeon; b. Balt., Dec. 30, 1928; s. Henry Scott and Frances (Robinson) B.; m. Jean Harvey, Sept. 12, 1953; children: Susan, Scott, Robert, Jean. AB, Johns Hopkins U., 1950, MD, 1954. Diplomate Am. Bd. Surgery, Bd. Thoracic Surgery. Intern Johns Hopkins U., 1954-55; sr. asst. surgeon Nat. Heart Inst., 1955-57; asst. resident Johns Hopkins Hosp., 1957-58, resident, 1958-61, chief surg. resident, 1961-62; surgeon-in-charge Johns Hopkins Hosp. (Breast Clinic), 1970—, Johns Hopkins Hosp. (Oncology Center), 1976; prof. surgery Johns Hopkins U., 1967—, prof. oncology, 1975—, Warfield M. Firor porf. surgery, 1991—; mem. (Coop. Lung Cancer Detection Group), 1971—. Recipient grants Am. Cancer Soc., 1966-71, grants John A. Hartford Found., 1968-73, grants Upjohn Co., 1973, grants Sterling-Winthrop Rsch. Inst., 1975—; named hon. fellow Royal Coll. Surgeons of Ireland. Fellow ACS, Royal Coll. Surgeons (hon.); mem. Soc. Univ. Surgeons, Am. Assn. Thoracic Surgery, So. Thoracic Surg. Assn., Soc. Head and Neck Surgeons, AMA, Am., So. Surg. Assns., Elkridge (Balt.) Club, Fishers Island (N.Y.) Club, Hay Harbor Club (Fishers Island). Home: 8717 Mcdonogh Rd Baltimore MD 21208-1021 Office: 600 N Wolfe St Baltimore MD 21287-0005 E-mail: rrbaker@jhmi.edu.

BAKER, R. SCOTT, education educator; b. Balt., Aug. 3, 1956; s. R. Robinson and Jeal H. Baker; m. Beth Thompson, May 16, 1997; 1 child, Luke. BA, Evergreen State Coll., Olympia, Wash., 1979; MA, Tufts U., Medford, Mass., 1985; PhD, Columbia U., NYC, 1993. Tchr. Brookline H.S., Mass., 1981—87; instr. Smith Coll., Northhampton, Mass., 1992—94; from asst. to assoc. prof. Wake Forest U., Winston-Salem, NC, 1994—. Author: Paradoxes of Desaregation, 2006; mem. editl. bd.: History of Edn., 1997—2000. Bd. mem. Cmty. Alliance for Edn., Winston-Salem, 2006—. Grantee, Mellon Found., 2006. Mem.: NAACP, Am. Ednl. Rsch. Assn., So. Hist. Assn. Democrat. Avocations: gardening, hiking. Office: Wake Forest Univ Dept Edn PO Box 7266 Winston Salem NC 27109

BAKER, RICHARD, physician, consultant; b. Frankfort, 1958; MB, BChir, Monash U., Australia, 1992; BA, Oxford U., Eng., 1997; LLB, Deakin U., Australia, 2004; MA in Psych. Med., Monash U., Victoria, Australia, 2005. Registered Gen. Med. Coun., 1993. Registrar Monash Med. Ctr., Melbourne, Australia, 2001—; dir. Specialist Consultants, NYC, London, Melbourne, 2001—. Recipient prize, Supreme Ct. Victoria/Deakin U., 2004. Mem.: RCP of Glasgow, Royal Coll. Physicians (London), Am. Coll. Emergency Medicine, Law Inst. of Victoria (assoc.), Brit. Psychol. Assn. (assoc.), Australian Assn. Neurologists (assoc.), Oxford and Cambridge U. Club. Home Phone: 212-727-9857.

BAKER, RICHARD GRAVES, geologist, palynologist, educator; b. Merrill, Wis., June 12, 1938; s. Dillon James and Miriam Baker; m. Debby J.Z. Baker; children: Kristina Kae, James Dillon, Charity Ann. BA, U. Wis., 1960; MS, U. Minn., 1964; PhD, U. Colo., 1969. Asst. prof. geology U. Iowa, Iowa City, 1970-75, assoc. prof., 1975-81, prof., 1981—, chmn. dept., 1992-95, prof. botany, 1988-92, prof. biol. scis., 1992-2000, prof. emeritus, 2000—. Contbr. articles to profl. jours., chapters to books. Chmn. Iowa chpt. Nature Conservancy, Des Moines, 1981-82. Grantee NSF, 1984-86, 88-90, 94-97, NOAA, 1992-93; recipient Disting. Scientist award Iowa Acad. Sci., 2001. Fellow Geol. Soc. Am., Iowa Acad. Sci.; mem. Am. Quaternary Assn. (disting. career award 2005), Ecol. Soc. Am. Office: Univ Iowa 121 Trowbridge Hall Dept Geosci Iowa City IA 52242-1319 Home Phone: 563-946-3958; Office Phone: 319-335-1805. Business E-Mail: dick-baker@uiowa.edu.

BAKER, RICHARD HUGH, congressman; b. New Orleans, May 22, 1948; m. Kay Carpenter; children: Brandon, Julie. BA, La. State U., 1971. State rep. La. Dist. 64, former chmn. com. on transp., hwys. and pub. works, 1981-82, state rep.; mem. La. Ho. of Reps., 1972—86, US Congress from 6th La. Dist., 1987—, mem. transp. & infrastructure com., vets. affairs com., chmn. Banking & Fin. Svcs. subcom. on Capital Mkts., Securities & Govt. Sponsored Enterprises; also real estate broker. Recipient Congl. Leadership award, Nat. Urban League, 2006. Republican. Methodist. Office: US Ho Reps 341 Cannon Ho Office Bldg Washington DC 20515-1806*

BAKER, RICK, make-up artist; b. Binghamton, NY, Dec. 8, 1950; s. Ralph B. and Doris (Hamlin) Baker; m. Elaine Parkyn (div. 1984); m. Silvia Abascal, Nov. 10, 1987. Spl. effects makeup artist on the following films Octaman, 1971, The Thing With Two Heads, 1972, Pirahna, 1972, Bone, 1972, The Exorcist, 1973, Schlock, 1973, Live and Let Die, 1973, Hell Up in Harlem, 1973, It's Alive, 1974, Death Race 2000, 1975, Black Caesar, 1975, Squirm, 1976, Food of the Gods, 1976, King Kong, 1976, Track of the Moonbest, 1976, Zebra Force, 1976, Kentucky Fried Movie, 1977, Star Wars, 1977, The Incredible Melting Man, 1978, It's Alive 2, 1978, The Fury, 1978, Tanya's Island, 1980, The Funhouse, 1980, The Incredible Shrinking Woman, 1981, An American Werewolf in London, 1981 (Acad. award Best Makeup), Videodrome, 1983, Greystoke: The Legend of Tarzan, Lord of the Apes, 1984, Starman, 1984, My Science Project, 1985, Cocoon, 1985, Ratboy, 1986, Captain Eo, 1986, Harry and the Hendersons, 1987 (Acad. award Best Makeup), Summer School, 1987, Missing Link, 1988, Coming to America, 1988, Gorillas in the Mist, 1988; co-prodr.: Gorillas in the Mist, 1988; Spl. effects makeup artist on the following films Gremlins 2; The New Batch, 1990; co-prodr.: Gremlins 2; The New Batch, 1990; Spl. effects makeup artist on the following films The Rocketeer, 1991, Ed Wood, 1994 (Acad. award Best Makeup), Wolf, 1994, Batman Forever, 1995, The Amazing Panda Adventure, 1995, Just Cause, 1995, The Nutty Professor, 1996 (Acad. awd. Best Makeup), The Frighteners, 1996, Escape from L.A., 1996, Men in Black, 1997 (Acad. awd. Best Makeup, 1997), Mighty Joe Young, 1998, Life, 1999, TV work includes (movies) The Autobiography of Miss Jane Pittman, 1974 (Emmy award Best Makeup), An American Christmas Carol, 1979, Something Is Out There, 1988, Body Bags, 1993, TV work includes (series) Davey and Goliath, 1960—65, Werewolf, 1987—88, Beauty and the Beas, 1987—90, designed spl. makeup effects for Michael Jackson's Thriller, 1983, The Klumps, How the Grinch Stole Christmas (Acad. awd. Best Makeup), Planet of the Apes., Men in Black II, 2002, The Ring, 2002, Haunted Mansion, 2003, Hell Boy, 2003, Cursed, 2005, The Ring II, 2005. Office: IATSE Local 706 828 N Hollywood Way Burbank CA 91505-2831

BAKER, ROBERT ERNEST, JR., retired foundation executive; b. Tuscaloosa, Ala., Oct. 17, 1916; s. Robert Ernest and Faye (Whitson) B.; m. Billye Louise Driskell, June 25, 1947; 1 son, Brent Driskell. BS in Indsl. Engring, U. Ala., 1939. Registered profl. engr., Tex. Indsl. engring., mgmt. and fin. cons., 1939-62; exec. adminstr., sec. Moody Found., Galveston, Tex., 1962-97; ret., 1997. Mem.: Arty. (Galveston). Presbyterian. Home: 6 Adler Cir Galveston TX 77551-5828

BAKER, ROBERT FRANK, molecular biologist, educator; b. Weiser, Idaho, Apr. 9, 1936; s. Robert Clarence and Beulah (Hulet) B.; m. Mary Margaret Murphy, May 29, 1965; children: Allison Leslie, Steven Mark. BS, Stanford U., 1959; PhD, Brown U., 1966. Postdoctoral rsch. assoc. Stanford (Calif.) U., 1966-68; asst. prof. dept. biol. scis. U. So. Calif., LA, 1968-72, assoc. prof., 1972-83, prof., 1983—, dir. molecular biology div., 1978-80, mem. Comprehensive Cancer Ctr., 1984—. Vis. assoc. prof. Harvard U. Med. Sch., Boston 1975-76; mem. genetic study sect. NIH, Bethesda, Md., 1977-79, 82 Contbr. articles to profl. jours. Grantee NIH, NSF, 1968—. Mem. Am. Soc. Zoologists, Am. Soc. Microbiology, Sigma Xi. Avocations: amateur radio, electronics. Home: 607 Almar Ave Pacific Palisades CA 90272-4208 Office: U So Calif Dept Molecular Biology Mc 1340 Los Angeles CA 90089-1340 Home Phone: 310-459-2454; Office Phone: 213-740-5565. Business E-Mail: baker@molbio.usc.edu.

BAKER, ROBERT I., manufacturing executive; b. Bridgeport, Conn., Sept. 28, 1940; s. Irwin Henry and Anna (Keane) B.; m. Patricia Turoczi, Nov. 28, 1968; children: Scott Allen, Christopher Keane. BA, U. Conn., 1962; postgrad., Syracuse U., 1975, U. Pa., 1978. With U.S. Electric Motors div. Emerson, Milford, Conn., 1963-66; with Henry G. Thompson div. Vt. Am., Branford, Conn., 1966-75, pres., gen. mgr. Magna div. Elizabethtown, Ky., 1977-84, corp. v.p., 1982-84, pres., CEO, Louisville, 1984-91; pres., owner Distbrs. Source, Portsmouth, N.H., 1991-92; CEO The Chamberlain Group, Inc., Elmhurst, Ill., 1992-96, The Chamberlain Group, Elmhurst, 1996—2000; ret., 2000. Cons. in field; bd. dirs. Chamberlain, Durasol, Brinkmann. Mem. Medinah Country Club, Abenaqui Country Club. Avocations: skiing, golf, woodworking. Home: 56 Old Bay Rd PO Box 2164 New Castle NH 03854

BAKER, ROBERT LEON, military officer; b. Oak, Nebr., Feb. 7, 1925; s. Oscar E. and Ada Veru (Davis) B.; m. Rebecca Chandler, Dec. 12, 1956; children: Rebecca Ann, Jay Milton, Betsy Jean, Robert Leon, Bruce Chandler, Brenda Carole. BS in Liberal Arts, La. Poly. Inst., 1945; BS in Medicine, U. Ark., 1949, MD with highest honors, 1949; grad. program health systems mgmt., Harvard U. Grad. Sch. Bus., 1972. Diplomate: Am. Bd. Obstetrics and Gynecology. Apprentice seaman U.S. Navy, 1943, commd. lt. (j.g.), M.C., 1949, advanced through grades to rear adm., 1973; rotating intern Tripler Gen. Hosp., Honolulu, 1949-50; resident in obstetrics and gynecology U.S. Naval Hosp., Oakland, Calif., 1954; assigned U.S. and overseas as obstetrician-gynecologist; chmn. dept. obstetrics and gynecology Naval Hosp., Portsmouth, Va., 1969-72; med. aide Office Comdr. in chief, NATO, 1970-72; dir. grad. tng. and chmn. dept. ob-gyn. Naval Regional Med. Center, Oakland, 1973-75, comdg. officer Phila., 1975-77, Naval Aerospace and Regional Med. Center, Pensacola, Fla., 1977-79; chief ob-gyn. service Baxter Gen. Hosp., Mountain Home, Ark., 1980-82. Clin. prof. Va. Commonwealth U. Med. Sch., 1971—72; med. dir. Hospice of Ozarks, 1984—96. Contbr. articles to med. jours. Bd. dirs. Phila. YWCA, 1975-77, USO, Phila., 1976-77, Pensacola, Fla., 1978-80, Baxter County Regional Hosp., 1985-87, also various bds. tng. insts., 1980—; bd. dirs. Ctrl. Ark. Radiation Therapy Inst., 1990-96, 2000-05, chmn. adv. bd. Mountain Home, 1990—; pres. Baxter County chpt. Am. Cancer Soc., 1995-96; founding mem. Internat. Coll. Hospice/Palliative Care, 1995; mem. Make A Wish Found.; bd. dirs. Internat. Hospice Inst. and Coll., 1996-99. Decorated Legion of Merit, Meritorious Service medal, Navy Commendation medal; recipient Letters of Commendation Comdr. in Chief NATO, Sec. Navy; recipient Wish Team award for Ark., Make A Wish Found., 1996. Fellow: ACOG (chmn. armed forces dist. Navy sect. 1967—69, vice chmn. armed forces dist. 1971—74, asst. sec. 1977—79); mem.: AMA (del. 1976—77), Acad. Hospice Physicians (founding mem.), Ark. Med. Soc. (del. 1982—2002), Baxter County Med. Soc. (v.p. 1982—84), Assn. Mil. Surgeons U.S. (chpt. pres. 1973—74), Union League (Phila.), Phi Chi, Alpha Omega Alpha. Mem. Christian Ch. (Disciples Of Christ). Home: PO Box 44 Mountain Home AR 72654-0044 Office: 3763 Highway 5 S Mountain Home AR 72653-5944 E-mail: admbak@mtnhome.com. *Time is critical for top management. It is divided into People time and Paper time. People time, almost invariably, must take precedence at any moment, but paper time still demands and must be accomplished. People time demonstrates concern. This perception by people of concern by management is the essential element of true leadership, and the essence of morale. One who can follow this precept while, at the same time completing paper work, is a top manager. This takes time.*

BAKER, ROBERT (ROBBIE) MICHAEL, protective services official; b. Winnfield, La., June 26, 1957; s. Robert E. and Gay Worsham Baker; life ptnr. Donna Kaye Stewart; children: Robert Christopher, Jason Michael. Completion, La. State U., Baton Rouge, LA, 1997—2006, Tex. A&M, Coll. Sta., Tex., 1998, Nat. Fire Acad., Emmitsburg, Md., 2000—06; Studied, Northwestern State U., Natchitoches, La., 2000—04. Cert. fire inspector 1 IFSAC, 2002, fire inspector II IFSAC, 2004, fire fighter 1 IFSAC, 2005. Dep. sheriff Winn Parish Sheriff's Office, 1976—78; police sgt. Winnfield Police Dept., 1978—94; owner, investigator So. Cross Investigations, Winnfield, 1994—97; insp. La. State Fire Marshal's Office, Baton Rouge, 1997—. Asst. supr. La. State Fire Marshal's Office, Shreveport, La., 2003—. Pres. Winn Jaycees, Winnfield, 1980—97. Flotilla staff officer USCG, 2006—07, Alexandria, La. Named Outstanding Law Enforcement Officer, Winn Jaycees, 1982; recipient Outstanding Local Pres. award, La. Jaycees, 1984. Mem.: Nat. Mus. US Army (Commendation), La. Fire Fighter Assn., Scottish Rite Freemasonary, S.J., U.S.A., Ea. Star Lodge, Masonic Lodge. R-Conservative. Baptist. Avocations: boating, scuba diving, hunting, fishing, golf. Home Phone: 318-780-0299; Office Phone: 318-676-7145.

BAKER, ROBERT M.L., JR., academic administrator, research scientist; b. LA, Sept. 1, 1930; s. Robert M.L. and Martha (Harlan) Baker; m. Bonnie Sue Vold, Nov. 14, 1964; children: Robert Randall, Robert M.L. III, Robin Michelle Leslie Fell. BA summa cum laude, UCLA, 1954, MA, 1956, PhD, 1958. Cons. Douglas Aircraft Co., Santa Monica, Calif., 1954—57; sr. scientist Aeronutronic, Newport Beach, 1957—60; head Lockheed Aircraft Rsch. Ctr., West L.A., 1961—64; assoc. mgr. math. analysis Computer Scis. Corp., El Segundo, 1964—80; pres. West Coast U., LA, 1980—97. Faculty UCLA, 1958—72; dir. Internat. Info. Systems Corp., Pasadena, Transp. Scis. Corp., LA; appointee Nat. Accreditation Adv. Com. U.S. Dept. Edn., 1987—90. Author: An Introduction to Astrodynamics, 1960, 2d edit., 1967, Astrodynamics-Advanced and Applied Topics, 1967, 1987; editor: Jour. Astron. Scis., 1961—76, SCL. To maj. USAF, 1960—61. Named Outstanding Young Man of Yr., 1965; recipient Dirk Brouwer award, 1976. Fellow: AAAS, AAIA (assoc.), Brit. Astro. Soc., Meteoritical Soc., Am. Astro. Soc.; mem.: Am. Phys. Soc., Sigma Pi Sigma, Sigma Xi, Phi Beta Kappa. Achievements include seven patents in field. Office: Gravwave LLC 8123 Tuscany Ave Playa Del Rey CA 90293-7856 Home Phone: 310-823-4143; Office Phone: 310-823-4143, 310-666-0517. Business E-Mail: drrobertbaker@gravwavellc.com.

BAKER, ROBERT W., lawyer; b. Wilmington, Del., Sept. 7, 1956; B in bus., economics, and acctg., U. Del.; JD, U. Tex., Austin. Bar: Tex. 1981, La. 1986. Joined Tenneco Energy, 1983, named v.p., assoc gen. counsel, 1995, sr. v.p., assoc. gen. counsel; named sr. v.p., assoc. gen. counsel El Paso Corp., Houston, 1996, sr. v.p., dep. gen. counsel, 2002—03, exec. v.p., 2003—, pres. El Paso Merchant Energy, 2003, gen. counsel, 2004—. Office: El Paso Corp 1001 Louisiana St PO Box 2511 Houston TX 77002-2511*

BAKER, ROLAND JERALD, finance educator; b. Pendleton, Oreg., Feb. 27, 1938; s. Roland E. and Theresa Helen (Forest) B.; m. Judy Lynn Murphy, Nov. 24, 1973; children: Kristen L., Kurt F., Brian H. BA, Western Wash. U., 1961; MBA, U. Mich., 1968. Cert. purchasing mgr., profl. contract mgr. Asst. dir. purchasing and stores U. Wash., Seattle, 1970-75; mgr. purchasing and material control Foss Launch & Tug Co., Seattle, 1975-79; faculty Shoreline C.C., 1972-79, 98—, Pacific Luth. U., 1977-79, Edmonds C.C., 1974-79; chmn. educators group Nat. Assn. Purchasing Mgmt., Tempe, Ariz., 1976-79, exec. v.p., 1979-98; pres. Nat. Assn. Purchasing Mgmt. Svcs., Tempe, Ariz., 1989-95. Faculty Ariz. State U., Tempe, 1988-91; world bus. adv. Coun. Am. Grad. Sch. of Internat. Mgmt., Glendale, Ariz., 1994-98; adv. bd. blockbuy.com, Inc., 1999-01, Perfect-.com, Inc., 2000—; exec. v.p. MyGroupbuy Inc., 2000-03, also bd. dirs.; mem. faculty Shoreline C.C., Seattle, 1998—. Author: Purchasing Factomatic, 1977, Inventory System Factomatic, 1978, Policies and Procedures for Purchasing and Material Control, 1980, rev. edit., 1992. With USN, 1961-70, comdr. Res., 1969-91. Recipient Disting. Achievement award Ariz. State U. Coll. Bus., 1997; U.S. Navy postgrad. fellow, 1967. Mem. Purchasing Mgmt. Assn. Wash. (pres. 1978-79), Nat. Minority Supplier Devel. Coun. (bd. dirs.), Am. Prodn. and Inventory Control Soc., Nat. Assn. Purchasing Mgmt. (exec. v.p 1979-97), Nat. Contract Mgmt. Assn., Internat. Fedn. Purchasing and Materials Mgmt. (exec. com. 1984-87, exec. adv. com. 1991-98). Office: Shoreline CC 16101 Greenwood Ave N Seattle WA 98133-5667 Personal E-mail: gbaker206@comcast.net. Business E-Mail: jbaker@shoreline.edu.

BAKER, RONALD JAMES, language educator, academic administrator; b. London, Aug. 24, 1924; s. James Herbert Walter and Ethel Frances (Miller) B.; m. Helen Gillespie Elder, Sept. 3, 1949; children: Ann, Lynn, Ian, Sarah, Katherine; m. Frances Marilyn Frazer; 1 son, Ralph Edward. BA, U. B.C., Can., 1951, MA, 1953; LLD (hon.), U. N.B., Can., 1970, Mt. Allison U., 1977, U. P.E.I., 1989, Simon Fraser U., 1990. Lectr. U. B.C., 1951-53, instr., 1953-54, 56-57, asst. prof., 1957-62, sec. Senate Com. Acad. Orgn., 1961-62, assoc. prof., 1962-63; prof. English Simon Fraser U., 1964-69, dir. acad. planning, 1964-65, head dept. English, 1964-68; first pres. U. P.E.I., Charlottetown, Can., 1969-78, univ. prof., 1979-91. Dir. Inst. Dept. Leadership, U. P.E.I., David MacDonald Stewart prof. Can. studies, 1988-91; disting. vis. prof. U. New Eng., Australia, 1984; mem. Acad. Bd. B.C., 1963-69, Joint Bd. Tchr. Edn. B.C., 1964-66; mem., chmn. various selection coms. including Can. Coun., 1971-77, Nat. Def. Dept., 1981-98, Can. Radio-TV and Telecomm. Commn., 1982-87; bd. govs. N.S. Tech. Coll., Holland Coll., 1968-78, Killam Prize Com., 1984-87, Molson Prize Com., 1987-88; chair mil. and strategic studies com. Nat. Def. Can., 1989-98. Editor: The Faculty Handbook, 1960; author (with W. G. Hardwick): North Shore Regional College Study, 1965, Regional College Study: Delta, Langley, Richmond, Surrey, 1966; contbr. articles to profl. jours. Mem. interim coun. U. No. BC, 1989-90; presiding officer Can. Citizen Ct., 1990-2005; vol. advisor First Nations Bands, Can. Exec. Svc. Orgn., 1984-2004. Served with RAF, 1943-47. Decorated Officer Order of Can., 1978; recipient Can. Centennial medal, 1967, Jubilee medal, 1977, Disting. Mem. award Can. Soc. Study of H.E., 1988, Can. 125 medal, 1992, Golden Jubilee medal, 2002, President's 40th Anniversary award, 2006; Humanities Rsch. Coun. Can. fellow, 1954, 55, grantee, 1968; Royal Soc. Can. fellow, 1954-56; Can. Coun. rsch. grantee, 1969. Mem. Assn. Univs. and Colls. Can. (dir. 1972-78), Assn. Atlantic Univs. (pres. 1976-78), Can. Soc. for Study Higher Edn. (v.p. 1974, pres. 1975-76, named Disting. Mem. 1988), Assn. Can. Univ. Tchrs. English (pres. 1967-68), Can. Linguistic Assn. (exec. 1966-67). Home Phone: 604-591-2562. Personal E-mail: rjfbaker@hotmail.com.

BAKER, RONALD LEE, folklore educator; b. Indpls., June 30, 1937; m. Catherine Anne Neal, Oct. 21, 1960; children: Susannah Jill, Jonathan Kemp. BS, Ind. State U., Terre Haute, 1960; MA, Ind. State U., 1961; postgrad., U. Ill., 1963-65; PhD, Ind U., 1969. Instr. English U. Ill., Urbana, 1963-65; teaching assoc. Ind. U., Ft. Wayne, 1965-66; prof. English Ind State U., Terre Haute, 1966—2006, chmn. dept., 1980—2006, chair and prof. emeritus, 2006—; vis. lectr. U. Ill., 1972-73; vis. assoc. prof. Ind. U., Bloomington, 1975, vis. prof., 1978, 84. Author: Folklore in the Writings of Rowland E. Robinson, 1973, Hoosier Folk Legends, 1982, Jokelore, 1986, French Folklife in Old Vincennes, 1989, The Study of Place Names, 1991, From Needmore to Prosperity: Hoosier Place Names in Folklore and History, 1995, Homeless, Friendless, and Penniless: The WPA Interviews with Former Slaves Living in Indiana, 2000; (with others) Indiana Place Names, 1975. Fellow Am. Folklore Soc.; mem. MLA, Am. Name Soc. (v.p. 1981-82), Hoosier Folklore Soc. (pres. 1970-79, exec. sec.-treas. 1988-2000). Home: 3688 N Randall St Terre Haute IN 47805-9736 Office: Indiana State University Terre Haute IN 47809-9989 Home Phone: 812-877-9627; Office Phone: 812-237-3163. E-mail: ronbaker@indstate.edu.

BAKER, RONALD PHILLIP, service company executive; b. Kansas City, Mo., Feb. 15, 1942; s. Harry and Ruth Sarah (Bornstein) B.; m. Marilyn Gitterman, Dec. 27, 1964 (div. Dec. 1993); children: Kevin, Corey; m. Kendra F.; m. Dierdre Christensen, May 8, 1994. Student, U. Okla., 1960—63; BA in Sociology and Govt., U. Mo. Kansas City, 1965, postgrad., 1965. Acct. rep. Am. House and Window Cleaning Co., Kansas City, 1965—69; dist. mgr. ops. Am. Bldg. Svcs., Kansas City, 1969—72; pres. BG Maintenance Mgmt., Kansas City, 1972—86; chmn. bd. dirs. BGM Industries, Kansas City, 1987—. Bd. dirs. Flo Harris Supporting Found. V.p. Jewish Cmty. Ctr., Kansas City, 1985—88, pres., 1989—90, Jewish Vocat. Svcs., Kansas City, 1985—88; v.p. Jewish Fedn. Greater Kansas City, 1992—93; bd. dirs. Village Shalom, 1998—, chmn.,. CEO search com., 2002, chmn. bd. dirs., 2003—; bd. dirs. Jewish Cmty. Campus of Greater Kansas City, 2004, Beth Shalom Synagogue, Kans. City, 1985—89, Jewish Cmty. Rels. Bur.; exec. com. Jewish Cmty. Campus, 2005; bd. dirs. Flo Harris Supporting Found., Jewish Cmty. Ctrs. Assn., 1989—93, mem. exec. com., 1990—91; bd. dirs. Jewish Fedn. Greater Kansas City, 1986—92, Jewish Cmty. Found. Greater Kansas City, 1991—94, mem. strategic planning com., 1997. Mem. Bldg. Svc. Contractors Assn. Internat. (bd. dirs., chmn. seminars, conv. spkr., pres. club 1981-93, edn. com. 1981-90, chmn. edn. com. 1989—, info. ctrl. com. 1985-93, chmn. ann. conv. 1988, exec. com. 1988—, treas. 1989, v.p. 1990-92, pres. 1994, chmn. fin. com. 1990, exec. com., chmn. strategic planning task force 1989-90, chmn., CEO seminar com. 1997-99, strategic planning com. 1996—, govt. affairs com. 1996—), Bldg. Owners and Mgrs. Assn. Kansas City, Jewish Fedn. Kansas City (v.p. 1986-87, 91-93, co-chmn. fin. resources planning com., Young Leadership award 1981), Menninger Found. (pres. Topeka chpt. 1986—), Hallbrook Country Club, Sonnanalys Country Club, Sigma Alpha Mu, Delta Sigma Pi. Republican. Avocations: water sports, boating, skiing, running, reading. Office: BGM Industries 1225 E 18th St Kansas City MO 64108-1605 Office Phone: 816-421-8088. Personal E-mail: rbaker@bgserve.com.

BAKER, ROSALYN HESTER, state senator; b. El Campo, Tex., Sept. 20, 1946; BA, Southwest Tex. State U., 1968; grad., U. Southwestern La., 1969. Lobbyist, asst. dir. Govt. Rels. Nat. Edn. Assn., Washington, 1969-80; owner, retail sporting goods store Maui, Hawaii, 1980-87; legis. aide to Hon. Karen Horita Hawaii Ho. of Reps., Honolulu, 1987, mem., 1989-93, house majority leader, 1993, state senator Hawaii, 1993-98, majority leader, 1995-96; dir. office econ. devel. County of Maui, Hawaii, 1999—2002, chair senate health com. Hawaii, 2003—, asst. majority floor leader. Co-chair ways and means com., 1998, rules com. Hawaii State Dem. Conv., 1990, resolutions com. 1994; mem. energy environ. com., trans., mil. affairs, govt. ops. com.; vice chmn. consumer protection and housing com; former unit pres. Am. Cancer Soc. Del.-at-large Dem. Nat. Conv., 1984, 92, 96; mem. exec. com. Maui County Dem. Com., 1986-88; mem. Maui Workforce Investment Bd., Lahaina Town Action Com.; former vice chmn. Maui Svc. Area Bd. om Mental Health and Substance Abuse; former unit pres. Am. Cancer Soc., bd. dir., Hawaii-Pacific, Inc., Maui Econ. Devel. Bd.; mem. sub-com. pediat. emergency svcs. Inst. Medicine, 2004-06. Mem.: Maalaea Cmty. Assn., Kihei Cmty. Assn., West Maui Taxpayers Assn., Rotary Club Lahaina Sunrise. Democrat. Home: PO Box 10394 Lahaina HI 96761-0394 Office: State Capitol Rm 220 Honolulu HI 96813 Office Phone: 808-586-6070. Business E-Mail: senbaker@capitol.hawaii.gov.

BAKER, RUSSELL WAYNE, columnist, writer; b. Loudoun County, Va., Aug. 14, 1925; s. Benjamin Rex and Lucy Elizabeth (Robinson) B.; m. Miriam Emily Nash, Mar. 11, 1950; children: Kathleen Leland, Allen Nash, Michael Lee. BA, Johns Hopkins U., 1947, L.H.D., Hamilton Coll., Franklin Pierce Coll., Princeton U., Yale U., Long Island U., Conn. Coll.; LL.D., Union Coll.; D.Litt., Wake Forest U., U. Miami, Rutgers U., Columbia U.; H.H.D., Hood Coll. With Balt. Sun, 1947-54; mem. Washington bur. NY Times, 1954-62; columnist editorial page NY Times, 1962—98; column Observer nationally syndicated NY Times News Svc. Author: City on the Potomac, 1958, American in Washington, 1961, No Cause for Panic, 1964, All Things Considered, 1965, Our Next President, 1968, Poor Russell's Almanac, 1972, The Upside Down Man, 1977, So This Is Depravity, 1980, (with others) Home Again, Home Again, 1979, Growing Up, 1982, The Rescue of Miss Yaskell and Other Pipe Dreams, 1983, The Good Times, 1989, There's a Country in My Cellar, 1990; editor The Norton Book of Light Verse, 1986, Russell Baker's Book of American Humor, 1993; host: Masterpiece Theatre, 1992-. Served with USNR, 1943-45. Recipient Frank Sullivan Meml. award, 1976, George Polk award for commentary, 1979, Pulitzer prize for disting. commentary, 1979, Pulitzer prize for biography, 1983, Elmer Holmes Bobst prize for nonfiction, 1983, Howland Meml. prize Yale U., 1989, Fourth Estate award Nat. Press Club, 1989. Mem. Am. Acad. and Inst. Arts and Letters (elected 1984), Am. Acad. Arts and Scis. (fellow 1993). Office: Masterpiece Theater Pub Broadcasting Svc 2100 Crystal Dr Arlington VA 22202*

BAKER, SAUL PHILLIP, geriatrician, cardiologist, internist; b. Cleve., Dec. 7, 1924; s. Barnet and Florence (Kleinman) B. BS in Physics, Case Inst. Tech., 1945; postgrad., Western Res. U., 1946-47; M.Sc. in Physiology, Ohio State U., 1949, MD, 1953, PhD in Physiology, 1957; JD, Case Western Res. U., 1981. Intern Cleve. Met. Gen. Hosp., 1953-54; sr. asst. surgeon Gerontology Br. Nat. Heart Inst, NIH, now Gerontology Research Ctr., Nat. Inst. Aging, 1954-56; asst. vis. staff physician dept. medicine Balt. City Hosps. (now Francis Scott Key Hosp.) and Johns Hopkins Hosp., 1954-56; sr. asst. resident in internal medicine U. Chgo. Hosps., 1956-57; asst. prof. internal medicine Chgo. Med. Sch., 1957-62; assoc. prof. internal medicine Cook County Hosp. Grad. Sch. Medicine, Chgo., 1958-62; assoc. attending physician Cook County Hosp., 1957-62; practice medicine specializing in geriatrics, cardiology, internal medicine Cleve., 1962-70, 72-93; cons., 1993—. Head dept. geriatrics St. Vincent Charity Hosp., Cleve., 1964-67; cons. internal medicine and cardiology Bur. Disability Determination, Old-Age and Survivors Ins., Social Security Adminstrn., 1963—; cons. internal medicine City of Cleve., 1964—; medicare med. cons. Gen. Am. Life Ins. Co., St. Louis, 1970-71; cons. internal medicine and cardiology Ohio Bur. Worker's Compensation, 1964—; cons. cardiovascular disease FAA, 1973—; cons. internal medicine and cardiology State of Ohio, 1974—. Contbr. articles to profl. and sci. jours. Mem. sci. coun. Northeastern Ohio affiliate Am. Heart Assn.; former mem. adv. com. Sr. Adult div. Jewish Community Ctr. Cleve.; mem. vis. com. colls. Case Western Res. U.; former mem. com. older people Fedn. Community Planning Cleve. Fellow AAAS (life), Am. Coll. Cardiology, Gerontol. Soc. Am. (former Ohio regent), Am. Geriatrics Soc., Cleve. Med. Libr. Assn. (life); mem. Am. Physiol. Soc., AMA, Ohio Med. Assn., N.Y. Acad. Scis. (life), Chgo. Soc. Internal Medicine, Am. Fedn. Clin. Rsch., Soc. Exptl. Biology and Medicine, Am. Diabetes Assn., Diabetes Assn. Greater Cleve. (profl. sect.), Am. Heart Assn. (fellow council arteriosclerosis), Nat. Assn. Disability Examiners, Nat. Rehab. Assn., Am. Pub. Health Assn., Acad. Medicine Cleve., Internat. Soc. Cardiology (coun. epidemiology and prevention), Am. Soc. Law and Medicine, Cleve. Clinic Club(past sec.), Lake County Med. Soc. (hon.) Masons (32 degree), Shriners, Sigma Xi, Phi Delta Epsilon, Sigma Alpha Mu (past pres. Cleve. alumni club). Home and Office: PO Box 24246 Cleveland OH 44124-0246

BAKER, SHIRLEY KISTLER, academic administrator, university librarian; b. Lehighton, Pa., Mar. 16, 1943; d. Harvey Daniel and Miriam Grace (Osenbach) Kistler; m. Richard Christopher Baker, Oct. 22, 1966; children: Nicholas Christopher, India Jane. BA in Economics, Muhlenberg Coll., 1965; MA in Libr. Sci., U. Chgo., 1974, MA in South Asian Languages and Civilizations, 1974. Undergrad. libr. Northwestern U., Evanston, Ill., 1974-76; access libr. Johns Hopkins U., Balt., 1976-82; assoc. dir. librs. MIT, Cambridge, 1982-89; dean univ. librs. Washington U., St. Louis, 1989—, vice chancellor for info. tech., 1995—. Contbr. articles to profl. jours. Mem. ALA, Nat. Info. Standards Orgn. (bd. dirs. 1990-94), Assn. Rsch. Librs. (bd. dirs. 1996-2002, pres. 2000-01), Coalition for Networked Info. (steering com. 1999—), Mo. Libr. Network Corp. (bd. dirs. 1990-00). Democrat. Avocations: reading, travel. Home: 6310 Alexander Dr Saint Louis MO 63105-2223 Office: Washington Univ Campus Box 1061 1 Brookings Dr Saint Louis MO 63130-4899 E-mail: baker@wustl.edu.*

BAKER, STANLEY BECKWITH, education educator; b. Mpls., Sept. 3, 1935; s. Stanley Forrest and Dorothy Ruth (Beckwith) Baker; m. Barbara Ann Laufenburger, Aug. 17, 1957 (dec.); children: Susan Elizabeth, David Alan; m. Mary Esther Clark Martin, June 10, 2000. BA, Augsburg Coll., 1957; MA, U. Minn., 1963; PhD, SUNY, Buffalo, 1971. Lic. profl. counselor N.C., nat. cert. counselor. Tchr. social studies Spring Valley (Wis.) HS, 1957-63; tchr. history Janesville (Wis.) HS, 1963-66, sch. counselor, 1964-67, Parker HS, Janesville, 1967-69; from asst. prof. to assoc. prof. edn. Pa. State U., University Park, 1971—84, prof., 1984—94, N.C. State U., Raleigh, 1994—, head dept., 1994—2001. Office: NC State U PO Box 7801 Raleigh NC 27695-7801 Office Phone: 919-515-6360. Business E-Mail: stanley_baker@ncsu.edu.

BAKER, STEPHEN C., lawyer; b. Harvey, Ill., 1953; AB, Duke Univ., 1975; JD, Villanova Univ., 1980. Bar: Pa. 1980. Ptnr. Stradley Ronon Stevens & Young, Phila., 1981—2001; ptnr., chair insurance practice group Drinker Biddle & Reath LLP, Phila., 2001—. Dir. Royer-Greaves Sch. for the Blind. Mem.: ABA, Pa. Bar Assn. Office: Drinker Biddle & Reath LLP One Logan Sq' 18th & Cherry Sts Philadelphia PA 19103-6996 Office Phone: 215-988-2769. Office Fax: 215-988-2757. Business E-Mail: stephen.baker@dbr.com.

BAKER, STEPHEN DENIO, physics professor; b. Durham, NC, Nov. 30, 1936; s. Roger Denio and Eleanor Elizabeth (Ussher) B.; m. Paula Eisenstein, June 24, 1962; children: Hannah Hitzhusen, Sarah Topper. BS, Duke U., 1957; MS, Yale U., 1959, PhD, 1963. Lectr. physics Rice U., Houston, 1963-66, asst. prof., 1966-69, assoc. prof., 1969-73, prof., 1973—2004, prof. emeritus, 2004—. Office: Rice Univ Dept Physics-MS 61 6100 Main St Houston TX 77005-1892

BAKER, STEWART ABERCROMBIE, federal agency administrator, lawyer; b. Poughkeepsie, NY, July 17, 1947; s. Henry Irving and Ruth (Abercrombie) B.; m. Anne Kornhauser, Dec. 31, 1974; children: Margaret, Catherine, Gordon. AB, Brown U., 1970; JD, UCLA, 1976. Chief articles editor UCLA Law Review, 1975—76; law clk. to Hon. Shirley M. Hufstedler US Ct. Appeals (9th cir.), LA, 1975; law clk. to Hon. Frank M. Coffin US Ct. Appeals (1st cir.), Portland, Maine, 1976-77; law clk. to Justice John Paul Stevens US Supreme Ct., Washington, 1977-78; assoc. Steptoe & Johnson LLP, Washington, 1978—79, ptnr., 1981—92, 1994—2005; dep. gen. counsel, spl. asst. to sec. U.S. Dept. Edn., Washington, 1979-81; gen. counsel Nat. Security Agy., Ft. Meade, Md., 1992—94; asst. sec. for policy US Dept. Homeland Security, Washington, 2005—. Chmn. legal adv. bd. State and Local Legal Ctr., Washington, 1983-92; mem. Markle Found. Task Force on Nat. Security in the Info. Age, Def. Sci. Bd. Task Force on Info. Warfare, 1995-96, 1999-2001; gen. counsel, Commn. on the Intelligence Capabilities of the US Regarding Weapons of Mass Destruction, 2004 Co-author: The UNCITRAL Arbitration Rules in Practice, 1992, The Limits of Trust: Cryptography, Governments, and Electronic Commerce, 1998; contbr. articles to law revs., popular press. Recipient Alumni award for Acad. Distinction, UCLA. Office: US Dept Homeland Security 3801 Nebraska Ave Washington DC 20528

BAKER, STUART DAVID, lawyer; b. NYC, July 2, 1935; s. Stuart and Edith (Kennelly) B.; m. Alixandra Fitzwilliam-Tate Collins, June 16, 1980; children from previous marriage— Stuart Richard, David Michael, Elisabeth Kendall BA, Hamilton Coll., 1957; LLB, Columbia U. Bar: N.Y. 1960. Assoc. Chadbourne, Parke, Whiteside & Wolff, NYC, 1960-69, ptnr., 1969-85, Chadbourne & Parke, NYC, 1985—, mem. mgmt. com., 1985-95, 96—. Exec. v.p., counsel to bd. Purdue Pharma L.P.; dir. Napp Pharm. Group Ltd. UK, Mundipharma Labs. GmbH, Mundipharma AG Switzerland; mem. supervisory bd. Mundipharma GmbH, Germany, 1994—. Vestryman St. Mary's Ch., Scarborough-on-Hudson, N.Y., 1967-76, sr. warden, 1974-76; chmn. zoning bd. appeals Town of Ossining, N.Y., 1968-78; mem. Coun. of Diocese of N.Y., 1974-79; bd. dirs. Legal Aid Soc., 1993-99; bd. trustees St. Peters Sch., 1975-99. Mem. N.Y. State Bar Assn., Conn. Bar Assn., Westchester County Bar Assn., Assn. Bar City of N.Y., Suffolk County Bar Assn., Internat. Bar Assn. (rapporteur), Inter-Am. Bar Assn., Union Internat. des Avocats, Swiss Am. C. of C., SAR, Sleepy Hollow Country Club, River Club (N.Y.C.), Netherlands Club (N.Y.C.), Water Mill Beach (N.Y.) Club (pres. 1991-96). Episcopalian. Avocations: fly fishing, tennis, golf, windsurfing. Home: 16 Sutton Pl New York NY 10022-3057 Office: Chadbourne & Parke LLP 30 Rockefeller Plz Fl 31 New York NY 10112-0129

BAKER, SUSAN L., performing company executive, retired investment banker; b. 1950; BA, Wellesley Coll.; MBA, Harvard Bus. Sch. Investment banker Goldman Sachs & Co., Kidder, Peabody & Co., Lehman Bros. Chmn. Collegiate Chorale, NYC, 2000—, New York City Opera, 2003—; v.p. Shakespeare Soc., NYC; bd. dirs. New York City Opera, 1999—, Collegiate Chorale, Sch. Am. Ballet, Lincoln Ctr. Performing Arts, Inc., Women's Venture Fund, Inc. Office: New York City Opera NY State Theater at Lincoln Ctr New York NY 10023

BAKER, TANIA ANN, biology professor, researcher; b. Dane County, Wis., Nov. 27, 1961; BS with distinction in Biochemistry, U. Wis., Madison, 1983; PhD in Biochemistry, Stanford U. Med. Sch., 1988. Postdoctoral fellow dept. biochemistry Stanford U. Med. Sch., 1988—89; postdoctoral fellow NIH Nat. Inst. Diabetes and Digestive and Kidney Disease, 1989—92; asst. prof. dept. biology MIT, 1992—97, assoc. prof., 1997—2002, prof., 1999—, E.C. Whitehead prof. biology, 2002—; asst. investigator Howard Hughes Med. Inst., 1994—97, assoc. investigator, 1997—2002; investigator Howard Hughes Medical Inst., 2002—. Asst. molecular biologist Mass. Gen. Hosp., Boston. Contbr. articles to profl. jours.; co-author: DNA Replication, 2nd ed., 1992, Molecular Biology of the Gene, 5th ed., 2003. Recipient Surdna Found. Rsch. award for support of rsch. of jr. faculty in life scis., 1992—93, Robert A. Swanson Career Devel. Professorship in the Life Scis., 1992—94, Young Investigator award, NSF, 1993, Harold E. Edgerton award, 1999; Undergraduate Rsch. Fellowship to Cold Springs Harbor Lab., 1982, Mary Shine Peterson Fellowship for Undergraduate Rsch., 1982—83, Helen Hay Whitney Found. Fellowship for Postdoctoral Rsch., 1989—92. Fellow: AAAS, Am. Soc. Microbiology (Eli Lilly and Co. Rsch. award 2001), Am. Acad. Arts & Scis.; mem.: NAS, Am. Soc. Biochemistry & Molecular Biology (Schering-Plough Rsch. Inst. award 1998). Office: Dept Biology MIT 77 Massachusetts Ave Room 68-523 Cambridge MA 02139-4307 Office Phone: 617-253-3594. Office Fax: 617-252-1852. E-mail: tabaker@mit.edu.*

BAKER, THOMAS EUGENE, law educator; b. Youngstown, Ohio, Feb. 25, 1953; s. John M. and Helen Marie (Kish) B.; m. Jane Marie Schussler, June 15, 1974; 1 child, Thomas Athanasius. BS cum laude, Fla. State U., Tallahassee, 1974; JD with high honors, U. Fla., Gainesville, 1977. Bars: Fla. 1979, U.S. Dist. Ct. (no. dist.) Tex. 1979, U.S. Supreme Ct. 1982, U.S. Ct. Appeals (5th cir.) 1979, U.S. Ct. Appeals (11th cir.) 1981. Law clk. to presiding judge U.S. Ct. Appeals (5th cir.) Ga., Atlanta, 1977—79; prof. law Tex. Tech. U., Lubbock, 1979—98, Alvin R. Allison prof., 1992—98; jud. fellow U.S. Supreme Ct., Washington, 1985—86, acting adminstrv. asst. to chief justice, 1986—87; James Madison chair constnl. law, dir. constnl. law ctr. Drake U. Law Sch., Des Moines, 1998—2002; mem.

founding faculty Coll. of Law, Fla. Internat. U., Miami, 2002—. Mem. adv. bd. Am. Criminal Law Rev., Washington, 1981-85; standing com. rules and procedures US Jud. Conf., 1990-95; vis. prof. U. Fla., 1994, Coll. William and Mary, 2007; Fulbright prof. U. Athens, Greece, 1993; bd. editors Preview US Supreme Ct. Cases, 1991—. Author: Rationing Justice on Appeal: The Problems of the U.S. Court of Appeals, 1994, The Most Wonderful Work: Our Constitution Interpreted, 1996, Federal Court Practice and Procedure: A Third Branch Bibliography, 2001; co-author (with T. Floyd): Can a Good Christian Be a Good Lawyer?, 1998; co-author: (with J. Williams) Constitutional Analysis in a Nutshell, 2d edit., 2003; co-author: (with R. Jarvis and A. McClurg) Amicus Humoriae: An Anthology of Legal Humor, 2004; co-author: (with J. Stack) At War with Civil Rights and Civil Liberties, 2005; co-author: (with A. Hellman & W. Araiza) First Amendment Law: Freedom of Expression and Freedom of Religion, 2006; co-author: (with D. Meador & J. Steinman) Appellate Courts: Structures,Functions, Processes and Personnel, 2d edit., 2006; mem. editl. bd. Jour. Supreme Ct. History, 1991—93; contbr. articles to profl. jours. Recipient Faculty Rsch. award Tex. Tech U., 1996, 94, 83, Outstanding Law Prof. award, 1988, 89, Spencer A. Wells U. Tchg. award, SBA Pres.'s award Drake Law Sch., 2002, Pioneer award Fla. Internat. U. Coll. Law, 2004; Justice Tom C. Clark fellow Jud. Fellows, 1986. Mem. ABA (various sects. and coms.), Am. Law Inst. (elected), Am. Judicature Soc. (bd. dirs. 2000-02), Order of Coif. Byzantine Catholic. Avocations: pottery, racquetball. Office: Fla Internat U Coll Law University Park RDB Miami FL 33199 Business E-Mail: thomas.baker@fiu.edu.

BAKER, THOMAS WILLIAM, lawyer; b. Buffalo, Mar. 29, 1950; s. David Clayton Jr. and Marjorie Lois (Hagen) B. AB, Syracuse U., 1972; MBA, Ga. State U., 1978; JD, Vanderbilt U., 1981. Assoc. Smith, Cohen, Ringel, Kohler & Martin, Atlanta, 1981-84, Harkleroad Hardy, Atlanta, 1984-85, Fortson & White, Atlanta, 1985-86; spl. asst. to gen. mgr. Pitts. Pirates Baseball Club, 1986; ptnr., corp. securities practice group Troutman Sanders LLP, Atlanta, 1998—. Mem. ABA, Atlanta Bar Assn. Clubs: Atlanta Renegades Rugby (pres. 1984—). Lutheran. Office: Troutman Sanders LLP 600 Peachtree St NE Atlanta GA 30308-2216 Office Phone: 404-885-3198. Office Fax: 404-962-6505. Business E-Mail: tom.baker@troutmansanders.com.

BAKER, THURBERT E., state attorney general; b. Rocky Mount, NC, Dec. 16, 1952; m. Catherine Baker; children: Jocelyn, Chelsea. BA in Polit. Sci., U. NC, Chapel Hill, 1975; JD, Emory U., 1979. With US Environ. Protection Agy.; private pratice; mem. Ga. Ho. of Reps., 1988—90, asst. adminstrn. fl. leader, 1990—93, adminstrn. fl. leader, 1993—97; atty. gen. State of Ga., 1997—. Mem. Coun. on Fgn. Rels. Trustee Statewide Ga. Diabetes Bd., Ebenezer Bapt. Ch., Atlanta; bd. dir. DeKalb Coll. Found.; mem. DeKalb County Libr. Bd.; bd. dir. Nat. Med. Soc., Emory U. Named one of America's Top Black Lawyers, Black Enterprise Mag., 2003. Mem.: State Bar Ga. (bd. governor, mem., jud. nominating commn.), Nat. Assn. of Atty. Gen. (v.p., vice-chair, Homeland Security Com., rep., ABA House of Delegates, pres.), Nat. Med. Soc.-Emory U., DeKalb County C. of C. (bd. dirs.). Democrat. Office: Atty Gen Dept Law 40 Capitol Sq SW Atlanta GA 30334-1300*

BAKER, TIMOTHY DANFORTH, physician, educator; b. Balt., July 4, 1925; s. Frank A. and Alice Elizabeth (Chandler) Baker; m. Susan Lowell Pardee, June 23, 1951; children: Timothy, David, Susan. BA, Johns Hopkins U., 1948, MPH, 1954; MD, U. Md., 1952. Intern U. Md. Hosp., Balt., 1952-53; resident pub. health N.Y. State Dept. Pub. Health, Albany, 1953-56; health officer Syracuse, NY, 1958-59; asst. and acting chief health USAID, India, 1956-58; assoc. prof. Johns Hopkins U. Sch. Pub. Health, Balt., 1959-67, asst. dean, 1959-77, prof. internat. health, health svcs. adminstrn., and environ. health, 1967—, pres. faculty gen. assembly, 1987—, dir. Hubert H. Humphrey scholars program, 1987—. V.p., dir. Univ. Assocs., 1973-77; vis. prof. epidemiology U. Minn., 1976; dir. Intermed., 1982—; external examiner U. Singapore; vis. prof. Am. U., Armenia, 1999; mem. Surgeon Gen.'s Com. on Global Health, 2004; mem. Md. Gov.'s Commn. on Minority Health, Md. Gov.'s Task Force on Violence; cons. in field. Author: Health Manpower in a Developing Economy, Assessment of Health Status and Needs, International Health Perspectives; contbr. articles to profl. publs. First vice chmn. Balt. com. Rep. Party; del., nominating com. Rep. party; bd. dirs., treas. Pan Am. Health Edn. Found. With USAF, 1943-45; USPHS, 1956-58. Recipient Disting. Grad. award, Balt. Poly Inst., Heritage award, Johns Hopkins U. Fellow: AAAS; mem.: APHA (chmn. epidemiology sect., internat. health sect., Lifetime Achievement award 1994), Balt. Med. Soc. (chmn. med. care com.), Md. Pub. Health Assn. (pres.), Md. Med. Soc. (chmn. health manpower com., ho. of dels., editl. bd., guest editor Md. Medicine), Delta Omega, Omicron Delta Kappa. Republican. Office: Johns Hopkins U Sch Hygiene 615 N Wolfe St Baltimore MD 21205-2103 Home: Broadmead E6 13801 York Rd Cockeysville MD 21030 Office Phone: 410-614-3819. Business E-Mail: tbaker@jhsph.edu.

BAKER, TIMOTHY LOUIS, retired naval officer; b. Bklyn., Dec. 21, 1948; s. Halmer Loren and Sheila Ann (Gallaher) B.; m. Noreen Elaine Nugent, June 16, 1973; children: Grant Loren, Reid Francis, Keith Michael. BS in Edn., Villanova U., Pa., 1971; MS in Oceanography with distinction, U.S. Naval Postgrad. Sch., 1978; MA in Nat. Security and Strategy Studies with distinction, U.S. Naval War Coll., 1985. Commd. ensign USN, 1971, advanced through grades to capt., 1971—91; exec. officer USS Eisenhower, 1991-92; commdg. officer USS Sylvania, 1992-94; ret., 1994; chief plans and ops. divsn. Cubic Applications, Inc., Hampton, Va., 1994-2001; dep. chief tng. and exercises divsn. U.S. Joint Forces Command, Suffolk, Va., 2001—05; fed. sr. exec., tech. dir., bus. mgr. U.S. Joint Forces Command, Joint Warfighting Ctr., 2005—. Capt. USNR, 1987-94. Decorated Legion of Merit, Pres. of the U.S., Norfolk, 1994. Mem. Sigma Xi. Roman Catholic. Avocations: skiing, coaching sports. Home: 1041 Downshire Chase Virginia Beach VA 23452-6154 Office: US Joint Forces Command Joint Warfighting Ctr 116 Lakeview Pkwy Suffolk VA 23435-2697 Office Phone: 757-203-7002. Office Fax: 757-686-6058. Business E-Mail: timothy.bakert@jfcom.mil.

BAKER, TOM, utilities executive; married; 2 children. BSME, Univ. Tex., Austin. Engring. & mgmt. positions TXU Corp., Dallas, 1968—; sr. v.p. TU Elec. & TU Services, Dallas; prin. fin. officer Tex. Utilities Co., Dallas; chmn., CEO TXU Elec. Delivery, Dallas; vice-chmn. TXU Corp., Dallas, 2007—. Bd. mem., past. chmn. Greater Dallas C. of C.; exec. bd. mem. Boy Scouts Am. Circle Ten Council; bd. dir. Children's Med. Ctr. Dallas; past chmn. Ctrl. Dallas Assn., Downtown Improvement Dist., Dallas, Dallas Together Forum; past trustee Paul Quinn Coll. Nuclear missile launch officer USAF. Office: TXU Corp Energy Plz 1601 Bryan St Dallas TX 75201*

BAKER, VALERIE L., federal judge; b. Mpls., June 25, 1949; d. Glen R. and Lorraine (Guselc) Baker. BA in English, U. Calif Santa Barbara, 1971, MA, 1972; JD, UCLA, 1975. Bar: Calif. 1975. Assoc. Overtich, Lyman & Prince, LA, 1975—77; asst. US atty. US Atty.'s Office Ctrl. Calif. dist., LA, 1977—80; assoc. Lillick, McHose & Charles, LA, 1980—82, ptnr., 1982—86; judge LA Mcpl. Ct., 1986—87, Superior Ct. (LA County) Calif., 1987—2007, US Dist. Ct. (Ctrl. dist.) Calif., 2007—. Del. 9th Cir. Jud. Conf., 1985. Mem.: Santa Monica Bar. Assn. (antitrust sect.), LA County Bar Assn., Bus. Trial Attys. Assn., Fed. Bar Assn., Pacific Palisades Tennis, Santa Monica Tennis. Office: US Dist Ct Ctrl Calif 312 N Spring St Los Angeles CA 90012 Office Phone: 213-984-1565. Office Fax: 213-894-2215.*

BAKER, VERNON G., II, lawyer, automotive executive; BA, Dartmouth Coll.; JD, Am. U. Assoc. Schnader, Harrison, Segal & Lewis, 1978—80; counsel Scott Paper Co.; assoc. gen. counsel Advanced Material Group; v.p., gen. counsel, Corp. Rsch. Tech. Hoechst Celanese Corp; sr. v.p., gen. counsel, sect. Meritor (now ArvinMeritor), 1999—. Recipient Trailblazer award, Minority Corp. Counsel Assn. Office: Arvin Meritor Inc 2135 W Maple Inc Troy MI 48084

BAKER, VINCENT LAMONT, professional basketball player; b. Lake Wales, Fla., Nov. 23, 1971; 3 children. BA in Comm., Hartford U., 1993. Player Milw. Bucks NBA, 1993—97; forward Seattle Supersonics NBA, 1997—2002, Boston Celtics NBA, 2002—04, NY Knicks NBA, 2003—05, Houston Rockets NBA, 2005, LA Clippers NBA, 2005—06, Minn. Timberwolves NBA, 2006. Cameo appearence (films) He Got Game. Founder The Stand Tall Found.; volunteer, In The Bag Milw. MACC Fund. Named NBA All Star, 1995—97; named one of 99 Good Guys in Sports, The Sporting News, 1999; named to NBA All-Rookie First Team, 1994, All-NBA Third Team, 1996—97, All-NBA Second Team, 1997—98. Avocations: singing, cooking, pool. Mailing: Houston Rockets 1510 Polk St Houston TX 77002

BAKER, W. RANDOLPH, brewery company executive; With Anheuser-Busch Cos. Inc., St. Louis, 1970—, various positions to chief exec. and chmn. Busch Entertainment Corp., 1983—96, v.p., CFO, 1996—. Bd. dirs. St. Louis Chpt. of the Asthma and Allergy Found. Am. Office: Anheuser-Busch Cos Inc One Busch Pl Saint Louis MO 63118 Office Phone: 314-577-2000.*

BAKER, WALTER ARNOLD, lawyer; b. Columbia, Ky., Feb. 20, 1937; s. Herschel T. and Mattie B. (Barger) B.; m. Jane Stark Helm, Apr. 24, 1965; children: Thomas Herschel, Ann Tate. AB magna cum laude, Harvard U., 1958, LLB, 1961; LHD (hon.), Pikeville Coll., 2006. Assoc. Brown, Ardery, Todd & Dudley, Louisville, 1961-63; ptnr. Wilson, Baker, Herbert and Garmon, Glasgow, Ky., 1963-67; pvt. practice Glasgow, 1967-81, 83—; asst. gen. counsel Office Sec. Def., Washington, 1981-83; justice Supreme Ct. of Ky., Frankfort, 1996. Rep. Ky. Ho. of Reps., 1968-71, senator State of Ky., 1972-81, 89-96; active Ky. Coun. on Postsecondary Edn., 1997—; pres. Ky. Hist. Soc., 2001-03; mem. Ky. Judicial Campaign Conduct Com., 2005—. Lt. col. USAFR. Mem. Ky. Bar Assn., Barren County Bar Assn., Glasgow Rotary, Glasgow Golf and Country Club, Phi Beta Kappa. Republican. Episcopalian. Address: 917 S Green St Glasgow KY 42141-2086 Office: 213 S Green St Glasgow KY 42141-2694 Home Phone: 270-651-8116; Office Phone: 270-651-3715. Business E-Mail: wbaker@glasgow.com.

BAKER, WARREN J(OSEPH), university president; b. Fitchburg, Mass., Sept. 5, 1938; s. Preston A. and Grace F. (Jarvis) B.; m. Carol Ann Fitzsimons, Apr. 28, 1962; children: Carrie Ann, Kristin Robin, Christopher, Brian. BS, U. Notre Dame, 1960, MS, 1962; PhD, U. N.Mex., 1966. Rsch. assoc., lectr. E. H. Wang Civil Engring. Rsch. Facility, U. N.Mex., 1962-66; assoc. prof. civil engring. U. Detroit, 1966-71, prof., 1972-79, Chrysler prof., dean engring., 1973-78, acad. v.p., 1976-79; NSF faculty fellow MIT, Cambridge, 1971-72; pres. Calif. Poly. State U., San Luis Obispo, 1979—. Mem. Bd. Internat. Food and Agrl. Devel., USAID, 1983-85; mem. Nat. Sci. Bd., 1985-94, Calif. Bus. Higher Edn. Forum, 1993-98; founding mem. Calif. Coun. on Sci. and Tech., 1989—; trustee Amigos of E.A.R.T.H. Coll., 1991-96; bd. dirs. John Wiley & Sons, Inc., 1993—; bd. regents The Am. Archtl. Found., 1995-97; co-chair Joint Policy Coun. on Agr. and Higher Edn., 1995—; mem. Bus.-Higher Edn. Forum, 2001—; bd. dirs. Westport Innovations, Inc., 2002-. Contbr. articles to profl. jours. Mem. Detroit Mayor's Mgmt. Adv. Com., 1975-76; mem. engring. adv. bd. U. Calif., Berkeley, 1984-96; bd. dirs. Calif. Coun. for Environ. and Econ. Balance, 1980-85, Soc. Mfg. Engrs. Edn. Found., 2001-, bd. dirs., 2002-04; trustee Nat. Coop. Edn. Assn.; chmn. bd. dirs. Civil Engring. Rsch. Found., 1989-91, bd. dirs., 1991-94. Fellow Engring. Soc. Detroit, ASCE (chmn. geotech. divsn. com. on reliability 1976-78, civil engring. edn. and rsch. policy com. 1985-89); mem. NSPE (pres. Detroit chpt. 1976-77), Am. Soc. Engring. Edn., Am. Assn. State Colls. and Univs. (bd. dirs. 1982-84), Nat. Assn. State Univ. and Land-Grant Coll. (commn. on info. tech. 1995-, chair 2003-, bd. dirs. 2003-). Office: Calif Poly State U Office of Pres 1 Grand Ave San Luis Obispo CA 93407-1000 Office Phone: 805-756-6000. Business E-Mail: presidentsoffice@calpoly.edu.

BAKER, WILLIAM DUNLAP, lawyer; b. St. Louis, June 17, 1932; s. Harold Griffith and Bernice (Kraft) B.; m. Kay Stokes, May 23, 1955; children: Mark William, Kathryn X., Beth Kristie, Frederick Martin. AB, Colgate U., 1954; JD, U. Calif., Berkeley, 1960. Bar: Calif. 1961, Ariz. 1961, U.S. Supreme Ct. 1969. Practice in, Coolidge, 1961, Florence, 1961-63, Phoenix, 1963—; law clk. Stokes & Moring, 1960; spl. investigator Office Pinal County Atty., 1960-61, dep. county atty., 1961-63; partner McBryde, Vincent, Brumage & Baker, 1961-63; assoc. atty. Rawlins, Ellis, Burrus & Kiewit, 1963-65, partner, 1965-81; pres., atty. Ellis & Baker, P.C., 1981-84, Ellis, Baker, Lynch, Clark & Porter P.C., 1984-86, Ellis, Baker, Clark & Porter, P.C., 1986-89, Ellis, Baker & Porter, P.C., 1989-92, Ellis Baker & Porter Ltd., Phoenix, 1992-95, Ellis, Baker & Porter, P.C., Phoenix, 1995-99, Ellis & Baker, P.C., 1999—. Referee Juvenile Ct. Maricopa County Superior Ct., 1966-85 Contbr. articles to profl. jours. Mem. Gov.'s Adv. Coun., Phoenix, 1969-71, Ariz. Environ. Planning Commn., 1974-75; bd. dirs. Agri-Bus. Coun., 1978—, sec., 1978-82; pub. mem. State Bd. Accountancy, 1995-03, sec., 1998-99, treas., 1999-00, pres., 2000-02, law com., 2004-; mem. Nat. Assn. Bds. Accountancy, litig. com., 2001-03, nominating com., 2002-04; legal counsel Ariz. Com. Rep. Party, 1965-69, mem. exec. com., 1972-78; vice-chmn. Maricopa County Rep. Com., 1968-69, chmn., 1969-71; bd. dirs. San Pablo Home for Youth, 1964-72, pres., 1971; bd. dirs. Maricopa County chpt. Nat. Found. March of Dimes, 1966-71, campaign chmn., 1970; trustee St. Luke's Hosp., 1976-85, sec., 1978-82, chmn., 1982-85; bd. dirs. Luke's Men, 1971-80, pres., 1976-77; bd. dirs. Combined Health Resources, 1982-85, St. Luke's Health Sys., 1977-95, chmn., 1985-89; bd. dirs. St. Luke's Health Initiatives, 1995—, vice chair, 2000-02; bd. dirs., v.p. Ariz. Anglican Cursillo Movement, 1982-86, treas. 2005-06; Western dist. layman rep. Nat. Episcopal Cursillo Com., 1996-98; regional v.p. Colgate Alumni Corp., 1977-82; vice chancellor Episcopal Diocese Ariz., 1970-96, ch. atty, 1996-03; sr. warden Christ Ch. of Ascension, 1983-86, 2001-03, chancellor, 2004—; bd. dirs. Ariz. Anglican Coun., Ltd., 2003-06. Served to 1st lt. USAF, 1954-57. Mem. ABA, Nat. Water Resources Assn. (life, co-chmn. task force on reclamation law 1990-97, resolutions com. 1990-93, chmn. state caucus 1993—, mem. fed affairs com 2000-, chair water supply task force 2000—, Pres.'s award 1991), Ariz. Soc. CPAs (hon.), Ariz. Bar Assn., Calif. Bar Assn., State C. of C. (bd. dirs. 1988-92), Maricopa County Bar Assn., Flagstaff Golf Assn. (bd. dirs. 1992-93, 94-96, pres. 1994-95), Phoenix Country Club, Ariz. Srs. Golf Assn. (bd. dirs. 1990-, mem. chmn. 2005, sec., treas. 2006, v.p. 2007, pres. 2007-), Sigma Chi, Phi Delta Phi. Episcopalian. Home: 1627 E Cactus Wren Dr Phoenix AZ 85020 Office: Ste 102 7301 N 16th St Phoenix AZ 85020 Business E-Mail: wdb@ellisbaker.com.

BAKER, WILLIAM FRANKLIN, retired broadcast executive; b. Cleve., Sept. 20, 1942; s. William Franklin and Rita Marie (Huebner) Baker; m. Jeannemarie Gelin, June 22, 1968; children: Christiane, Angela. BA in Comms. and Organizational Behavior, Case Western Res. U., 1965, MA, 1968, PhD, 1972; DSc St. John's U. (hon.), NYC, 1981; LLD (hon.), St. Elizabeth Coll., 1995; DHL (hon.), L.I. U., 2000; PhD (hon.), New Sch. Univ., 2002, Seton Hall U., 2003, Fordham U., 2007. Exec. prodr. Sta. WEWS-TV, Cleve., 1971—75, asst gen. mgr., 1975—77; v.p., gen. mgr. Sta. WJZ-TV, Balt., 1977—78; pres. Group W. Prodns., Hollywood, Calif., 1978—79, Group W-TV, NYC, 1979—87; chmn. Group W-TV Satellite Comm., NYC, 1981—87; pres., CEO Sta. WNET Channel 13, NYC, 1987—2007. Bd. dirs. Playhouse Pictures Internat., PBS, Leitch Video Ltd., The Consumers Union, Rodale Press; owner Rudder Mag., Schneider Vineyards, Grey Island Sys., Freedom Comm., Summit Media Co., Pub. Broadcasting Sys. (PBS). Author: Down the Tube: An Insider's View of American Television, 1998, Lighthouse Island, Our Family Retreat, 2004; exec. prodr.: (films) The Face: Jesus in Art, 2001, Picturing Mary, 2006. Trustee Intrepid Air-Space Mus.; vice chmn. N.Y. Arts, 1997; bd. dir. Lamont-Doherty Earth Obs., Mus. Bibl. Art. Named to Broadcasting and Cable Hall of Fame, 2004, N.Y. State Broadcasting Hall of Fame, 2005; recipient 8 Emmy awards, 2 Twyla M. Conway awards, Dupont Columbia Journalism award (2), Triscort award (2), 1991, Modern Lang. award, Iona Coll., 1991, Silver Cir. award, N.Y. TV Acad., Humanitarian award, So. Manhattan Arts Coun., 1999, Frank Knox Media medal, U.S. Navy League, 1999, Comm. honor, U. San Diego, Sarnoff citation, Radio Club Am., 2002, medal, St. Nicholas Soc., 2004. Fellow: Am. Acad. Arts and Scis., Explorers Club (South Pole expdn. 1974, North Pole expedn. 1983, South Pole expdn. 1984, 1988, 1996); mem.: NATAS (past pres. N.Y. chpt., Gabriel award for outstanding broadcaster 1998, trustees' award), N.Y. Yacht Club. Roman Catholic.

BAKER, WILLIAM HARRIS, lawyer; b. Richmond, Va., Oct. 16, 1945; s. Edgar DeWitt and Helen Byrd (Harris) B.; m. Susan Leslie Morgan, Aug. 15, 1970; children: Marisa Whitney, Morgan DeWitt. BA, Yale U., 1968; JD, Harvard U., 1972. Bar: Calif. 1972, Mass. 1974, NY, Ill., US Dist. Ct. Mass. 1974, US Ct. Appeals (1st cir.) 1974, US Ct. Appeals (9th cir.) 1972, US Ct. Appeals (fed. cir.), US Dist. Ct. (so. & ea. dists.) NY, US Dist. Ct. (no. dist.) Ill., US Supreme Ct. 1979. Assoc. Gibson, Dunn & Crutcher, LA, 1972-74, Hale and Dorr, Boston, 1974-77, Nutter, McClennan & Fish, Boston, 1977-80, jr. ptnr., 1980-83, ptnr., 1983--; assoc. gen. counsel Sears, Roebuck and Co., Boston; atty. Marshall, Gerstein & Borun, Chgo.; Counsel Ropes & Gray, NYC. Contbr. articles to profl. journs., spkr. in fields. Former mem., bd. dir. Assn. Patent Law Firms, Greater Boston C. of C., Internat. Litig. Com., International Arbitration Coms., Arbitration and Mediation Com., Litig. Mgmt and Economics Com. (litig. sect. ABA), Harvard Law Sch. Trial Advocacy Program, Assn. Yale Alumni. Mem. ABA, Boston Bar Assn. Democrat. Office: Ropes & Gray 1251 Ave Americas New York NY 10020 Office Phone: 212-596-9057. Office Fax: 646-728-2968. Business E-Mail: william.baker@ropesgray.com.

BAKER, WILLIAM I., application developer; s. Edwin and Dorothy Baker; m. Michiko Ochiai; children: Tsuyoshi Edwin, Chiemi Keelyn. BS in Environ. Scis., Mich. State U., E.Lansing, 1968—72, MS in Botany, 1974—78; MS in Elec. Engring., Wash. State U., Pullman, 1982—86, PhD in Elec. Engring., 1986—94. Software engr. CFI ProServices, Portland, Oreg., 1994—98; software devel. mgr. Harland Fin. Solutions, Portland, 1998—2005, creditquest devel. mgr., 2005—. Com. mem. Citizens Adv. Com. for 20 yr. Vancouver Transp. Plan, Wash., 1999—2000; judge Intel Internat. Sci. & Engring. Fair, Portland, 2004; tech. judge Oreg. Robotcs Tournament & Outreach Program, Portland, 2002—04. Mem.: AAAS (assoc.), IEEE (assoc.). Office: Harland Fin Solutions 400 SW 6th Ave Portland OR 97204 Business E-Mail: bill.baker@harlandfs.com.

BAKER, WILLIAM PARR, lawyer; b. Balt., Sept. 5, 1946; s. George William and Jane (Parr) B.; m. Christine Corbett, Oct. 23, 1982; children: William Corbett, Brendan Parr, Laura Elizabeth. BA, St. Francis Univ., Loretto, Pa., 1968; JD, U. Md., 1971. Bar: Md. 1971, US Dist. Ct. Md. 1972, US Tax Ct. 1978, US Supreme Ct. 1980, US Ct. Appeals (4th cir.) 1982. Law clk. Md. Ct. Appeals, 1971-72; ptnr. Baker and Baker, PA and predecessors, Balt., 1972—. Civil case mediator Cir. Ct. for Balt. County; adj. prof. U. Md. Sch. Law. Contbr. articles to profl. jours. V.p. bd. dirs. Santa Claus Anonymous, 1973-76; bd. dirs. Balt. Assn. Retarded Citizens, 1981-96. Mem. ABA, Md. Bar Assn., Bar Assn. Balt. City, Golfers Charitable Assn. (bd. dirs. 1989—), Am. Mensa (nat. nominating com. 2004-), Md. Mensa (pres. 2006-), Balt. Country Club. Roman Catholic. Office: Baker and Baker PA 1000 Mercantile Trust Bldg 409 Washington Ave Baltimore MD 21204-4920 Office Phone: 410-823-8500. Business E-Mail: wpbaker@baker-baker.net.

BAKER, WILLIAM THOMPSON, JR., lawyer; b. NYC, Jan. 19, 1944; s. William Thompson and Elizabeth (Baird) B.; children: Alice Whetherly, Richard Cass, Heather Thompson. BA cum laude, Yale U., 1965; JD, U. Va., 1968. Bar: NY 1968, US Dist. Ct. (so. and ea. dists.) NY 1969, US Supreme Ct. 1990, US Ct. Appeals (DC cir.), 1992. Assoc. Thelen, Reid, Brown, Raysman & Steiner (formerly known as Thelen, Reid & Priest), NYC, 1968—74, ptnr., 1975—, mng. ptnr., 1986—87, mem. exec. com., 1980—82, mem. exec. com, 1986—91, chmn. exec. com., 1990—91. Chmn. or co-chmn. Utility/Energy Svcs. Group Dept., 1991—2002; chmn. legal com. Edison Electric Inst., 1997-99; chmn. Electric Policy and Regulatory Group, 2003-. Trustee Episcopal Sch. in City of NY, 1969-71, Chase Wildlife Found., 2003—. Mem. ABA (chmn. subcom. pub. utility holding company act 1990-2005, vice chmn. subcom. pub. utility sect. 2004—), NY County Lawyers Assn., Assn. Bar City NY, Hotchkiss Sch. Alumni Assn. (bd. govs. 2003—, sec., treas. 2005—), Union Club NYC, Yale Club NYC, NY Anglers Club. Republican. Episcopalian. Avocations: fishing, fly tying, rod building, wood working. Office Phone: 212-603-2106. Business E-Mail: wbaker@thelen.com.

BAKER, YVONNE BELL, elementary school educator; d. Sylvia Collins and Victor Bell; 1 child, Otis McDowell Baker, Jr. BS, So. U., Baton Rouge, La., 1970, MEd, 1977. Reading Specialist La. Dept. of Edn., 1981, Supr. Student Tchg. La. Dept. of Edn., 1981, Elem. Grades La. Dept. of Edn., 1977, Art La. Dept. of Edn., 1970, English La. Dept. of Edn., 1970. Tchr. Assumption Parish Sch. Bd., Napolenville, La., 1970—72, St. Francis Xavier Cath. Sch., Baton Rouge, 1973—74, Ascension Parish Sch. Bd., Donaldsonville, 1974—. Mem.: NEA (assoc.). Home: 13313 ALBA Dr Baker LA 70714 Home Phone: 225-774-6855. Business E-Mail: bakerbrown@apsb.org.

BAKER, ZACHARY MOSHE, librarian; b. Mpls., June 8, 1950; s. Michael Harry and Margaret Esther (Zanger) B. BA, U. Chgo., 1972; MA, Brandeis U., 1974; MA in LS, U. Minn., 1975. Head tech. svcs. Jewish Pub. Libr., Montreal, Que., Canada, 1981-87; asst. libr. Yivo Inst. for Jewish Rsch., NYC, 1976-80, assoc. libr., 1980-81, head libr., 1987-99; Reinhard family curator Judaica & Hebraica collections Stanford U. Librs., 1999—, head humanities resource group, 2006—. Hist. cons. Que. Inst. Rsch. on Culture, Montreal, 1983; libr. cons. U.S. Holocaust Meml. Coun., Washington, 1984-85, Fla. Atlantic U., Boca Raton, 1994, Ariz. State U., Tempe, 1998. Contbg. author: From a Ruined Garden, 1983, 98; author, contbg. editor Toledot, 1978-82, Judaica Librarianship, 1983--; editor: Yiddish Catalog and Authority File of the Yivo Library, 1990, Judaica in the Slavic Realm, 2003, Ira Nowinski, Photographer as Witness, 2004. Crown fellow Brandeis U., 1973-74; travel and rsch. grantee Andrew W. Mellon Found., 1997, Lucius N. Littauer Found., 1990, 94, 96, 98/ Mem. ALA, Assn. Jewish Librs. (pres. 1994-96), Assn. for Jewish Studies, Coun. Archives and Rsch. Libr. in Jewish Studies (pres. 1998-02), Phi Beta Kappa, Beta Phi Mu. Avocations: map and atlas collecting, current events, travel. Office Phone: 650-725-1054. Business E-Mail: zbaker@stanford.edu.

BAKER, III, REX GAVIN, lawyer, educator; b. Houston, Tex., Apr. 22, 1952; s. Rex Gavin Baker, Jr and Jeannette Russell Baker; m. Cynthia Distene Grenrood, Mar. 28, 1981; children: Narlen Douglas Baker, Rex Gavin Baker IV, Catherine Neil Baker. BA in Econs., U. Tex., Austin, 1974,

JD, 1977. Ptnr. Baker, Brown, Sharman & Parker (now Thompson & Knight), Houston, 1983—90; mng. ptnr. Baker & Assocs., Dripping Springs, Tex., 1991—; pres. Southwestern Title Co., Dripping Springs, Tex., 1994—. Justice of peace precinct 4 Hays County, Tex., 1995—2006; commr. Tex. Commn. Jud. Conduct, Austin; faculty Tex. Justice Ct. Tng. Ctr., Austin; organizer Pioneer Bank, Dripping Springs. Author: (book) Enforcement of Restrictive Covenants in Texas. Mem. exec. com. chancellor's coun. U. Tex. Sys., Austin; mem. bd. visitors McDonald Obs., Ft Davis, Tex.; mem. liberal arts adv. coun. U. Tex., Austin, mem. dean's roundtable sch. law; bd. dirs. Dripping Springs Ednl. Found., 1992—98. Recipient Counsel award, U. Tex. Sch. Law, 1977, Faculty award, Tex. Justice Ct. Tng. Ctr. Mem.: Justice of Peace and Constables Assn. (chmn. edn. com. 2004—06), Hays County Bar Assn., State Bar Tex. (mem. jud. ethics com. 1998—2000), Tex. Lyceum (life), Ex-Students Assn. U. Tex. (pres.), Delta Theta Phi (dean), Alpha Tau Omega. Avocations: hunting, sports. Office: Baker & Assocs 800 Hwy 290 W Bldg A Ste 100 Dripping Springs TX 78620 Home Phone: 512-894-0890; Office Phone: 512-894-0890. Office Fax: 512-894-0346. Business E-Mail: rexbaker@bakerattorneys.com.

BAKER-GARDNER, JEWELLE, interior designer, business consultant; b. Ayden, NC, May 23, 1925; d. Roland Ray and Helen Wingate (Jackson) Cannon; m. Paul Thomas Baker, July 25, 1956 (dec. 1963); children: Paula Jewelle Baker Bryan, Paul Thomas Jr.; 1 stepchild, Blanche Baker Miller; m. Fred Calvin Gardner, Apr. 19, 1969 (dec. May 1983); 1 stepchild, Angela Gardner Jones Hollowell. Student, Woods Bus. Sch., New Bern, NC, 1942—45; BA, Am. Sch. Design, NYC, 1948; BFA, U. NC, Greensboro, 1950. Dept. head Navy Supply, Cherry Point, N.C., 1941-45; ptnr. Cannons Paint & Wallpaper Co., Ayden, 1945-70; exec. v.p. Baker Furniture Co., Kinston, N.C., 1950-63, pres., treas., 1963-69; operator Cannon Farms, Ayden, 1956—; with consumer program Drexel Co., 1965-66; owner Jewelle Baker Cons., Kinston, 1969—; v.p. Gardner Homes, Elizabeth City, N.C., 1972-81, CEO, 1982—; bus. cons. Gardner Constrn. Co., Kinston, 1975-81, chmn. bd. dirs., CEO, 1982—; bus. cons. Lenoir Plumbing & Heating Co., Kinston, 1975-81, chmn. bd. dirs., CEO, 1982—; owner, moderator GenealogyPITT Co. N.C. Friends in Rsch., 1998—. Cons. Carolina Power & Light, 1963-65, N.C. Solar Energy Assn., 1977-79, Nutritional Therapy, Durham, N.C., 1979-81; lectr., 1950-63; del. U.S.-China Joint Session on Industry, Trade and Econ. Devel., Beijing, 1988. Columnist Ayden Dispatch and Greenville News Leader, 1940-56; prodr. Performer Baker's Commls., 1960-69. Mem. Devel. Auth. of Neuse River Coun. of Govts., 1984-85. Mem. C. of C. Kinston (bd. dirs., v.p., chmn. retail mchts. divsn.), So. Retail Furniture Assn., Nat. Retail Furniture Assn., N.C. Mchts. Assn., N.C. Farm Assn., Assn. Gen. Contractors Am., Cmty. Coun. for the Arts, Internat. Platform Assn., N.C. Zool. Assn., N.C. Art Soc., Kinston Country Club, Coral Bay Club, Pineknoll Golf and Country Club, Sea Water Marina Club. Democrat. Mem. Ch. Disciples Of Christ. Home: 1708 Elizabeth Dr Kinston NC 28504-3416 Office: Gardner Constrn Co PO Box 856 Kinston NC 28502-0856 E-mail: jewelle@coastalnet.com, jewellebaker@suddenlink.net.

BAKER-JOHNSON, MARCIA J., dental hygienist; b. Cleve., Dec. 16, 1949; d. Bernard Exsall and Aletha Odessa (Mason) Baker; m. Gregory Carl Johnson, Apr. 24, 1987; children: Bernard Johnson, Cecelia Johnson. Grad. dental hygienist, U. Minn., Mpls., 1972. Cert. Registered Dental Hygienist Wash., Nat. Bd. Cert. Minn. Dental hygienist Children's Hosp., Mpls., 1972—74, Dr. McDonald and Dr. Kinneberg, St. Paul, 1974—77, Dr. Lorenzo Patelli, Seattle, 1978—82, Dr. Terry Thomas, Seattle, 1983—90, Dr. Charles Wallace and Dr. Al. Solhaug, Seattle, 1991—98, Dr. Kathy Curtis and Dr. John Larsen, Seattle, 1999—2003, Dr. Linda FuKuda, Seattle, 2000—. Author: (poetry) Expressions from My Heart, 2004. Vol. Planned Parenthood, Seattle, 1984—87; pres. PTA, Seattle, 1996—97; Sunday sch. tchr. Grace United Meth. Ch., Seattle, 1997—99, chair women, 2001—03. Recipient Vol. Cert., John Muir Elem. Sch., 1996—2002. Mem.: Seattle Dental Hygiene Soc. Democrat. Methodist. Avocations: flower arranging, poetry, reading, writing, walking. Home: 9212 39th Ave S Seattle WA 98118-4827

BAKER KNOLL, CATHERINE, lieutenant governor; b. Pitts. d. Nicholas James and Theresa Mary (May) Baker; m. Charles A. Knoll Sr. (dec.); children: Charles A. Jr., Mina B., Albert B., Kim Eric. BS in Edn., Duquesne U., 1952, MS in Edn., 1973. Dir. western Pa. region Safety Adminstrn. Dept. Transp., Pitts., 1971-79; exec. dir. community svc. Dept. of Adminstrn., Allegheny County, Pa., 1980-88; treas. Pa. Treasury Dept., Harrisburg, 1988—2003; lt. gov State of Pa., 2003—. Owner, operator pvt. bus. firm, Pitts., 1952-70. Mem. Pa. Dem. State Com., Pa. Fedn. Dem. Women, YMCA Bd., Pitts., Harrisburg, Duquesne U. Alumni Bd., Mom's House, Zontas Inc. Bd. Mem. Nat. Assn. State Treas., Women Execs. in State Gov., Coun. State Gov. (exec. com. ea. region). Democrat. Roman Catholic. Office: Office Lt Governor 200 Main Capitol Bldg Harrisburg PA 17120 Office Phone: 717-787-3300. Office Fax: 717-783-0150.

BAKER-MORRIS, KAY, special education educator; b. Tulsa, Nov. 25, 1952; d. Charles Fred and Virginia L. Robinson; m. Don Baker (div.); children: Chandler Baker, Kyle Baker; m. Ron Morris. BEd, Northeastern State U., 1975, MEd, 1978. Cert. spl. edn. tchr. Okla. Spl. edn. tchr. Nowata (Okla.) Pub. Sch., 1975—78, Copan (Okla.) Pub. Sch., 1978—86, Bartlesville (Okla.) Pub. Schs., 1986—, dist. contact for individual edn. program for computers, 2004—, tchr. summer testing program, 1995—. Assessor Nat. Bd. Tchr. Cert., Tulsa, 2002; cons. Coun. Exceptional Children, 2000; presenter in field. Author: Case Study of Exceptional Child, Exceptional Children in Group Home Setting, 1975; contbr. Past pres., v.p., sec. Bartlesville Fraternal Order of Police; active State Bd. Fraternal Order of Police, Ladies Aux. Named Tchr. of Yr., Copen Pub. Schs., 1985, Outstanding Educator, Coun. for Exceptional Children, 1995. Mem.: NEA (rep.), Okla. Edn. Assn., Bartlesville Edn. Assn. (v.p. 1995—2004). Democrat. Baptist. Office: Bartlesville Pub Schs 1100 SE Jennings Bartlesville OK 74003 Home: 801 SE 13th Bartlesville OK 74006

BAKHOS, CHARLES TANOS, surgeon; b. Tahwitat Nahr, Beirut, Lebanon, July 25, 1976; s. Tanos Bakhos. MD, St. Joseph U., Beirut, 2001; MS, U. Claude Bernard, Lyon, France, 2002. Mem. internal medicine housestaff Cleve. Clinic Found., 2002—03; mem. gen. surgery housestaff Hosp. St. Raphael, New Haven, 2003—. Contbr. articles to profl. publs. Recipient Intern of Yr. award, Hosp. St. Raphael, 2004, Devon Philip Sinha award, 2005, Med. Staff Pres.' award, 2006; grantee, Lebanese Nat. Rafik Hariri Found., 1994, French Govt. and St. Joseph U., 2001. Mem.: ACS (resident mem. 2003—06, Surgeons Resident Competition award Conn. chpt. 2006), Soc. Am. Gastrointestinal and Endoscopic Surgeons, Cleve. Clinic Alumni Assn. Achievements include research in vital capacity as a predictor of outcome in elderly patients with rib fractures; early postoperative hemorrhage after roux-en-y gastric bypass; role of purinergic cotransmission in the sympathetic control of arterial pressure variability in conscious rats; clinical pulmonary embolus in gastric bypass patients; clinical predictors of pulmonary embolism in post-operative patients; staged arterial embolization and surgical resection of a giant splenic artery aneurysm; endovascular repair of transplant nephrectomy external iliac artery pseudoaneurysm. Office: Hosp San Raphael MOB 315 1450 Chapel St New Haven CT 06511 Home Phone: 203-287-1172; Office Phone: 203-789-3000. Business E-Mail: bakhos1@srhs.org.

BAKHT, BAIDAR, civil engineer, researcher, educator; b. Delhi, India, Sept. 4, 1940; arrived in Can., 1973; s. Mukhtar and Anwar Jehan Chishti; m. Anita Das, Sept. 11, 1968; children: Natasha, Sacha. BSc in Engring., Aligarh (India) U., 1962; MSc, Imperial Coll., London, 1972; DSc, London U., 1990. Registered profl. engr., Ont., Can. Asst. engr. Heavy Engring. Corp., Ranchi, India, 1962-66; engr. Dept. Environ., London, 1967-73; prin. rsch. engr. Ministry Transp. Ont., 1974-97; pres. JMBT Stuctures Rsch., Inc., Toronto, Ont., 1997—. Adj. prof. civil engring. U. Toronto, U. Man., 2000—; vis. prof. engring. and Urdu lit. Jamia Millia, New Delhi, 2005-06. Co-author: Bridge Analysis Simplified, 1985, Bridge Analysis by Microcomputer, 1988, Soil-steel Bridges: Design and Construction, 1993, Bridge Engineering, Recent Innovations, 1994; Bridge Superstructures, New Developments, 1996; translator 17 books of Urdu poetry to English, 1985—; contbr. over 190 articles to profl. jours.; co-inventor unique deck slab of bridges, inventor of stressed-log bridge. Recipient Moisseif award ASCE, 1982, President's medal Road and Transp. Assn. Can., 1985, Profl. Engrs. Ont. Engring. medal, 1997. Fellow: Profl. Engrs. Ont. (Engring. medal 1996), Engring. Inst. Can. (Gzowski medal 1983), Can. Soc. for Civil Engring. (Pratley award 1988, 1994, Vance award 1996, award for outstanding contbn. to bridge engring. 2002, A.B. Sanderson award 2004), Instn. Engrs. (India) (cert. of merit 1990). Avocation: translating urdu poetry into english. E-mail: bbakht@rogers.com.

BAKKE, DENNIS W., energy company executive; m. Eileen Bakke. MBA, Harvard U. With Fed. Energy Agy.; with Energy Productivity Ctr., Carnegie Mellon U.; co-founder The AES Corp., Arlington, Va., 1981, pres. & CEO, 1994—2002; now pres., CEO Imagine Schools. Co-author: Creating Abundance-America's Least Cost Energy Strategy, 1984, author: Joy at Work: A Revolutionary Approach to Fun on the Job, 2005. Pres. Mustard Seed Found. Mem. Am. Gas Assn. (past dir.). Address: PVG Press PO Box 70525 Seattle WA 98127 Office: Imagine Schools Ste 610 1005 N Glebe Rd Arlington VA 22201 Fax: 703-528-4510.

BAKKE, MERLIN RUSSELL, application developer; b. LaCross, Wis., Apr. 1, 1945; s. Victor S. Bakke and H. Ester Flugstad; m. Leslie Ronica Garrison, Oct. 5, 1985; 1 child, Kimberly Evanna. Student, St. Olaf Coll., Northfield, Minn., 1963—67; BSEE, Airforce Inst. Tech., Dayton, Ohio, 1973; postgrad., U. Utah, 1973—76; MSEE, U. Bridgeport, Conn., 1981. Commd. 2d lt. USAF, 1968, advanced through grades to capt.; ret., 1978; software engr. Trans-lux, Norwalk, Conn., 1978—85, Comtel, Santa Maria, Calif., 1985—86, Digital Families, Ltd., Huntington Beach, Calif., 1986—89, Transdigital, Brea, Calif., 1996—2001, Ziehm Imaging, Riverside, Calif., 2003—05; ret. Mem.: Menas (nat. chmn. 2005—).

BAKKEN, ERIC ALLEN, lawyer; b. June 22, 1967; BS, St. Mary's U.; JD, William Mitchell Coll. Law. Bar: 1994. With Regis Corp., Edina, Minn., 1994—, v.p. law, 1998—2004, v.p., gen. counsel, sec., 2004—, sr. v.p. and gen. counsel, 2006—. Mem.: ABA, Beauty Industry Fund, Minn. Bar Assn., Hennepin County Bar Assn. Office: Regis Corp 7201 Metro Blvd Edina MN 55439 Office Phone: 952-947-7777.*

BAKKEN, GORDON MORRIS, law educator; b. Madison, Wis., Jan. 10, 1943; s. Elwood S. and Evelyn A. H. (Anderson) B.; m. Erika Reinhardt, Mar. 24, 1943; children: Angela E., Jeffrey E. BS, U. Wis., 1966, MS, 1967, PhD, 1970, JD, 1973. From asst. to assoc. prof. history Calif. State U., Fullerton, 1969-74, prof. history, 1974—, dir. faculty affairs, 1974-86. Cons. Calif. Sch. Employees Assn., 1976-78, Calif. Bar Commn. Hist. Law., 1985—; mgmt. task force on acad. grievance procedures Calif. State Univ. and Colls. Systems, 1975; mem. Calif. Jud. Coun. Com. Trial Ct. Records Mgmt., 1992-97. Author 7 books on Am. legal history; contbr. articles to profl. jours. Placentia Jusa referee coord., 1983. Russell Sag resident fellow law, 1971-72, Am. Bar Found. fellow in legal history, 1979-80, 84-85; Am. Coun. Learned Socs. grantee-in-ai d, 1979-80. Mem. Orgn. Am. Historians, Am. Soc. Legal History, Law and Soc. Assn., Western History Assn., Calif. Supreme Ct. Hist. Soc. (v.p.), Phi Alpha Theta (v.p. 1994-95, pres. 1996-97). Democrat. Lutheran. Office Phone: 714-278-3048. Business E-Mail: gbakken@fullerton.edu.

BAKKENSEN, JOHN RESER, lawyer; b. Pendleton, Oreg., Oct. 4, 1943; s. Manley John and Helen (Reser) B.; m. Ann Marie Dahlen, Sept. 30, 1978; children: Michael, Dana, Laura. AB magna cum laude, Harvard U., 1965; JD, Stanford U., 1968. Bar: Oreg. 1969, Calif. 1969, U.S. Dist. Ct. Oreg. 1969. Ptnr. Miller, Nash, Wiener, Hager & Carlsen, Portland, Oreg., 1968-99; pvt. practice lawyer, arbitrator, mediator, spl. master and trustee. Lawyer del. 9th Cir. Jud. Conf., San Francisco, 1980-82. Author: (with others) Advising Oregon Businesses, 1979, Arbitration and Mediation, supplement, 2000, 2d edit., 2007. Past bd. dirs. Assn. for Retarded Citizens, Portland; advisor Portland Youth Shelter House; mem. and counsel to bd. dirs. Friends of Pine Mountain Observatory, Portland. Mem. ABA (forum on constrn. industry), Am. Arbitration Assn., Oreg. State Bar, Oreg. Assoc. Gen. Contractors (legal com. 1991, counsel to bd. dirs. 1992), Arbitration Svc. Portland, Inc. (arbitrator), Multnomah Athletic Club. Avocation: astronomy. Office Phone: 503-245-0385.

BAKKER, THOMAS GORDON, lawyer; b. San Gabriel, Calif., Aug. 18, 1947; s. Gordon and Eva Marie (Hoekstra) B.; m. Charlotte Anne Kamstra, Aug. 1, 1969; children: Sarah, Jonathan. AB in History, Calvin Coll., Grand Rapids, Mich., 1969; JD, U. Mich., 1973. Bar: Ariz. 1973, U.S. Dist. Ct. Ariz. 1973, U.S. Ct. Appeals (9th cir.) 1973. Staff reporter Ariz. Criminal Code Revision Com., Phoenix, 1973-75; asst. atty. gen. State of Ariz., Phoenix, 1975-77; staff atty. div. 1 Ariz. Ct. Appeals, Phoenix, 1977-79; assoc. Burch, Cracchiolo et al, Phoenix, 1979-80; from assoc. to ptnr. Olson, Jantsch, Bakker , Phoenix, 1980—. Vice chmn. tort and ins. practice sect. Appellate Advocacy Commn., 1982-83; judge pro tem div. 1 Ariz. Ct. Appeals, 1985, 92. Served with U.S. Army, 1969-71. Fellow Ariz. Bar Found. (founding fellow); mem. Ariz. Bar Assn., Maricopa County Bar Assn., Am. Health Lawyers Assn., Def. Rsch. Inst., Ariz. Assn. Def. Counsel 163. Mem. Christian Reformed Ch. Avocations: reading, golf, aerobics, fishing. Office: Olson Jantsch Bakker 7243 N 16th St Phoenix AZ 85020-5203 Office Phone: 602-861-2705. E-mail: tgb@ojbb.com.

BAKKUM-GAMEZ, JAMIE NADINE, obstetrician, gynecologist; b. Viroqua, Wis., Dec. 9, 1975; d. Orlan Dean and Denise Eileen Bakkum; m. Jeffrey Daniel Gamez, Aug. 27, 2005. BA, Wartburg Coll., Waverly, Iowa, 1998; MD, U. Wis., Madison, 2002. Diplomate Am. Bd. Ob/gyn. Resident in ob-gyn. Mayo Clinic, Rochester, Minn., 2002—06, fellow in gynecologic oncology, 2006—. Mem.: Soc. Gynecologic Oncologists. Avocations: running, scuba diving, travel. Office: Mayo Clinic 201 1st St SW Rochester MN 55905 Office Phone: 507-266-7712. Office Fax: 507-266-9300. Personal E-mail: jamie_bakkum@hotmail.com.

BAKLANOFF, ERIC NICHOLAS, economist, educator; b. Graz, Austria, Dec. 9, 1925; came to U.S., 1937, naturalized, 1943; s. Nicolas W. and Lucille (King) B.; m. H. Christina Janes, June 17, 1956 (div. June 1973); children: Nicholas, Tanya, Ana-Maria; m. Joy Driskell, June 6, 1982. Student, Antioch Coll., 1943-44; AB, Ohio State U., 1949, MA, 1950, PhD, 1958; postgrad. (Fulbright scholar), U. Chile, 1957, Harvard Grad. Sch. Bus. Adminstrn., 1959; postgrad. (NDEA postdoctoral fellow), U. Tex., summer 1963. Instr. econs. Ohio State U., 1957-58; asst. prof. La. State U., 1958-61, assoc. prof., 1961-62; prof. econs., dir. Latin Am. Studies Inst., 1965-68; assoc. prof. econs., dir. Grad. Center for Latin Am. Studies, Vanderbilt U., 1962-65; prof. econs., dean for internat. studies and programs U. Ala., 1969-73, bd. visitors rsch. prof. econs., 1974-92, rsch. prof. econs. emeritus, 1992—. Disting. vis. prof. Luther Coll. summer 1965; cons. Am. Council on Edn., USAF Inst., Pres.'s Southeastern Council on Latin Am. Studies, 1963-64, U.S. Dept. Edn., Centro de Estudios y Communicacion Economica, Am. Enterprise Inst. Pub. Policy Rsch., Fed. Rsch. divsn., Hispanic divsn. Libr. of Congress. Author: Expropriation of U.S. Investments in Cuba, Mexico and Chile, 1975, The Economic Transformation of Spain and Portugal, 1978, La Transformation Economica de Espana y Portugal: La economia del Fanquismo y del Salazarismo, 1980; author: (with Jeffrey Brannon) Agrarian Reform and Public Enterprise in Mexico: The Political Economy of Yucatan's Henequen Industry, 1987; author: (with Edward H. Moseley) Competing for Latin American Markets: A Business Perspective on the Spanish-American War Centennial, 1999; author: (with others) Revolutionary Change in Cuba, 1971, Modern Brazil: New Patterns and Development, 1971, Background to Revolution: The Development of Modern Cuba, 1979, Yucatan: A World Apart, 1980, The Iberian-Latin America Connection: Implications for U.S. Foreign Policy, 1986, State Shrinking: A Comparative Analysis of Privatization, 1987, The Alabama Economy: Issues for the 1990s, 1990, Portugal: Ancient Country, Young Democracy, 1990, Portugal: A Country Study, 1994, Cuba in Transition, 2001; contbg. author: others, editor, contbg. author: The Shaping of Modern Brazil, 1969, New Perspectives of Brazil, 1966, Mediterranean Europe and the Common Market, 1976, Competing for Latin American Markets: A Business Perspective on the Spanish American War Centennial, 1999, The Handbook of Portuguese Studies, 1999, El Triángulo Económico: España-USA-America Latina, 2002; contbr. articles to profl. jours. Active Boy Scouts Am. Served with USNR, 1944-46, PTO. Decorated Knight of Grace, Hospitaler and Mil. Order St. Lazarus of Jerusalem, Malta obedience; named Outstanding Scholar U. Ala., 1980-81; fellow Ctr. Advanced Study Behavioral Scis., 1964-65; grantee U.S. Dept. State, Spain, 1974; rsch. fellow Andrew W. Mellon Found., 1987. Mem. Delta Chi, Beta Gamma Sigma, Sigma Delta Pi, Omicron Delta Epsilon, Phi Beta Delta. Eastern Orthodox. Office: U Ala PO Box 870224 Tuscaloosa AL 35487-0154 Office Phone: 205-348-7842. Business E-Mail: Ebaklano@cba.ua.edu.

BAKRIS, GEORGE L., nephrologist, educator, clinical researcher; b. Athens, June 15, 1952; arrived in U.S., 1952; s. Louis George Bakris and Athena Petros Marolias; m. Demetria Mary Arges, Nov. 26, 1983; children: Athena, Louis. BA in Biology/Psychology, Ind. U., 1974; MA in Human Devel., U. Chgo., 1975, MD in Medicine, 1981. Diplomate Am. Bd. Internal Medicine, Am. Bd. Nephrology, bd. cert. specialist in clin. hypertension Am. Soc. Hypertension. Staff nephrologist Ochsner Clinic, New Orleans, 1988-91, dir. renal rsch., 1988—91; asst. prof. medicine U. Tex. Health Sci. Ctr., San Antonio, 1991-93, dir. nephrology fellowship program, 1991—93; assoc. prof. preventive medicine and internal medicine Rush U. Med. Ctr., Chgo., 1993-98, prof. preventive medicine and internal medicine, 1998—2006, vice chmn. dept. preventive medicine and internal medicine, 1998—2006, dir. Hypertension Clinic Rsch. Ctr., 1998—2006; prof. medicine, Hypertension Ctr. Diabetes Inst. U. Chgo. Sch. Medicine, 2006—, dir. Hypertension Ctr. Diabetes Inst., 2006—. Adj. asst. prof. medicine Tulane U. Sch. Medicine, New Orleans, 1988—91; cons. cardiorenal divsn. FDA, Rockville, Md., 1993—2003; chmn. hypertension exec. coun. Nat. Kidney Found., NYC, 1998—2000. Editor: (book) Hypertension: A Clinician's Guide to Diagnosis and Treatment, 2d edit., 2000, The Kidney in Hypertension, 2004; co-editor: Hypertension: Practice and Principles, 2004; jour. guest editor: Jour. Mineral and Electrolyte Metabolism, 1998; contbr. articles to profl. jours.; editor: Am. Jour. Nephrology, 2002. Grantee, Nat. Inst. Diabetes and Digestive Diseases, 1994—2001, 2002—, heart, lung and blood divsn. NIH, 1996—2001, Clin. Rsch. Tng., prin. investigator, 1999—. Fellow: ACP, Am. Heat Assn. Coun., Am. Heart Assn. (coun. high blood pressure rsch. 1992—), Am. Coll. Clin. Pharmacology (pres. 2000—02). Greek Orthodox. Avocations: writing music, guitar, golf, bowling. Office: Univ Chgo Sch Medicine 5841 S Maryland Ave MC1027 Rm P328A Chicago IL 60637 Office Phone: 773-702-7936. Office Fax: 773-834-0486. Personal E-mail: gbakris@earthlink.net.

BAKSHI, NANDINI, neurologist; arrived in US, 1988; d. Prem Sagar and Usha Bakshi. B Medicine B Surgery, U. Pune, India, 1985. Diplomate Am. Bd. Psychiatry and Neurology. Intern St. Francis Hosp., NJ, 1989—90; resident in neurology Kaiser Permanente, LA, 1990—93, UCLA, 1993; postdoctoral fellow U. Calif., Davis, 1995—96; neurologist Tex. Permanente, Dallas, 1993—94, Permanente Med. Group, Oakland, Calif., 1996—. Assoc. clin. prof. U. Calif., Davis, 1996—. Capt. Indian Army Med. Corps, 1983—88. Recipient Leo Munoz award for excellence in neurology, Kaiser Permanente, LA, 1992, Neurology award for best resident, 1993; Fulbright scholar, Coun. Internat. Exch. Scholars, Washington, 2004. Mem.: Alameda Contra Costa Med. Assn., Am. Assn. Neuromuscular Electro Diagnostic Medicine, Am. Acad. Neurology. Office: 1425 S Main St Walnut Creek CA 94596

BAKTIR, SELCUK, electrical and computer engineer, researcher; b. Kayseri, Turkey, Feb. 14, 1978; s. Ayse and Mehmet Baktir. BSc, Bilkent U., 2001; MSc, Worcester Poly. Inst., 2003. Tchg. asst. Elec. and Computer Engring. Dept. Worcester Poly. Inst., Mass., 2001—02, rsch. asst. Cryptography and Info. Security Lab. Elec. and Computer Engring. Dept., 2001—. Contbr. articles to profl. jours. Bd. of Trustees Scholarship, Bilkent U., Ankara, Turkey, 1997—2001. Mem.: Internat. Assn. Cryptologic Rsch., IEEE Info. Theory Soc., IEEE Computer Soc., IEEE. Achievements include invention of new finite field representation called Optimal Tower Fields, DFT modular multiplication algorithm; implemented first ever elliptic curve cryptographic processor operating in the frequency domain; discovery of new methods for fingerprinting integrated circuits and detecting Trojan circuitry. Home Phone: 508-615-1614; Office Phone: 508-615-1614. Personal E-mail: selcukbaktir@gmail.com.

BAKULA, SCOTT, actor; b. St. Louis, Mo., Oct. 9, 1954; Student, Kans. U. Appearances include roles in regional prodns. of Godspell, Fiddler on the Roof, Joseph and the Amazing Technicolor Dreamcoat, Shenandoah, 2006, No Strings, 2007; Off-Broadway prodns. of Accentuate the Positive, Three Guys Naked from the Waist Down, Broadway prodns. of Marilyn: An American Fable, 1983, Romance/Romance, 1988 (Tony award nominee 1988); starred in TV series Eisenhower and Lutz, 1988, Gung Ho, 1986, Quantum Leap, 1989-93 (Emmy award nominee, Golden Globe award), Mr. & Mrs. Smith, 1996; guest appearances include (TV series) Matlock, Designing Women, My Sister Sam, Murphy Brown, Dream On; (TV movies) The Last Fling, The Infiltrator, I-Man, An Eye for an Eye, In the Shadow of a Killer, The Bachelor's Baby, 1996,; (TV mini series) The Invaders, 1995, Mr. and Mrs. Smith, 1996, Netforce, 1999; appeared in films Sibling Rivalry, 1990, L.A. Story, 1991, Necessary Roughness, 1991, The Color of Night, 1994, Lord of Illusions, 1995, My Family, 1995, Cats Don't Dance, 1997, Major League: Back to the Minors, 1998, Luminarias, 1999, American Beauty, 1999, Life as a House, 2001; dir. Quantum Leap.*

BAKULIN, ANDREY, geophysicist; b. Timashevsk, Russia, Mar. 24, 1971; arrived in U.S., 2001; s. Viktor Nikolaevich Bakulin and Anna Ivanovna Ruban; m. Svetlana Shaporova, Sept. 3, 1998; children: Dmitry Shaporov, Alexandra Bakulina. BSc in Geology (Geophysics), St. Petersburg State U., Russia, 1993, MSc in Geology and Geophysics with honors, 1995, PhD in Phys. and Math. Sci. (Geophysics), 1996. Asst. prof. St. Petersburg State U., 1996—99; sr. rsch. scientist Schlumberger Cambridge (Eng.) Rsch., 1999—2001; rsch. geophysicist Shell Internat. E & P Inc., Houston, 2001—. Vis. scientist Colo. Sch. Mines, Golden, 1998. Contbr. articles to profl. jours. Recipient Best Student Paper award, Euro-Asian Geophys. Soc., 1994, Best Young Scientist award, St. Petersburg State U., 1995, E&P Spl. Meritorious award for engring. innovation, Hart E&P for Virtual Source Tech., 2007. Mem.: European Assn. Geoscientists and Engrs. (corr.), Acoustical Soc. Am. (corr.), Am. Geophys. Union (corr.), Soc. Petroleum Engrs. (corr.), Soc. Exploration Geophysics (corr.; assoc. editor Geophysics 2004, J. Clarence Karcher award 2005). Achievements include first to use of time-reversed acoustics for geophysical imaging and monitoring; use of seismic data for estimation of subsurface stresses; research in areas of imaging scattering series, time-lapse seismic monitoring, inversion and processing on anisotropic media, rock physics and fracture characterization; patents in field. Office: Shell International E & P Inc 3737 Bellaire Blvd Houston TX 77025 Home Phone: 713-668-1984. Office Fax: 713-245-7532. Business E-Mail: andrey.bakulin@shell.com.

BAKWIN, EDWARD MORRIS, banker; b. NYC, May 13, 1928; s. Harry and Ruth (Morris) B BA, Hamilton Coll., 1950; MBA, U. Chgo., 1961. With Nat. Stock Yards Nat. Bank, National City, Ill., 1953—55; with Mid-City Nat. Bank Chgo., 1955—2001, pres., 1962—72, chmn. bd., CEO, 1967—2001, Darling-Del. Corp., Chgo., 1972—86, Mid-City Fin. Corp., 1982—2001, Nat. Stock Yards Co., 1985—93; chmn. bd. MBFI, Chgo., 2001—06. Bd. dirs. Duncan-Med. YMCA, 1963-72, Northwestern Meml. Hosp., 1980-88, West Ctrl. Assn., 1962-67, pres., 1962-65; mem. global bd. U. Chgo.; trustee Am. Mus. Fly Fishing, 1990—, Art Inst. Chgo. With AUS, 1951-52 Mem. Am. Bankers Assn., Ill. Bankers Assn. (bd. govs. 1966-69), Explorers Club, Adventurers Club (Chgo.), Chgo. Yacht Club, Mid-Am. Club, N.Y. Yacht Club Home: 0433 W US Hwy 20 La Porte IN 46350

BALA, GARY GANESH, lawyer; b. Feb. 10, 1958; s. T.N. and Susila Bala. BA summa cum laude, Temple U., 1979; JD, Villanova U., 1982. Bar: Pa. 1982, NJ 1986, US Dist. Ct. (ea. dist.) Pa. 1982, US Dist. Ct. NJ 1986, US Ct. Appeals (3d cir.) 1986, US Supreme Ct. 1986, DC 1989. Law clk. to judge Phila. Ct. Common Pleas, 1982-84; assoc. Harvey, Pennington, Herting & Renneisen Ltd., Phila., 1985-86, Thompson & Pennell, Phila., 1986-91; mng. trial atty. Law Offices of Gary G. Bala, Staff Counsel for CNA, Mt. Laurel, N.J., 1991-98; pvt. practice in immigration and estate planning Pa., 1998—. Mem. Am. Immigration Lawyers Assn. Democrat. Avocations: sports, reading, travel, tennis. Office: Law Offices of Gary G Bala 201 Ellis Rd Ste 1 Havertown PA 19083-1011 E-mail: garybala@visa-attorney.com.

BALABAN, ALEXANDRU T., chemistry professor, researcher; b. Timisoara, Romania, Apr. 2, 1931; s. Teodor and Florica Balaban; m. Cornelia Florea Balaban, Dec. 3, 1955; children: Teodor-Silviu, Irina-Alexandra Buhimschi. Chem. Engr., Poly. U., Bucharest, 1953, PhD in Organic Chemistry, 1959, DrHabil, 1974; Dr. honoris causa, U. Timisoara, 1997. Radiochemist Inst. Atomic Physics, Bucharest, Romania, 1957, head lab., 1957-75; sr. rsch. officer Internat. Atomic Energy Agy., Vienna, 1967-69; asst. prof. chemistry Poly. U., Bucharest, 1957-65, assoc. prof., 1965-70, prof., 1970—99; prof. chemistry Tex. A & M U., Galveston, 1993—95, 2000—. Author: Steric Fit in Quantitative Structure-Activity Relations, 1980, Pyrylium Salts, 1982, Olefin Metathesis and Ring-Opening Polymerization of Cyclo-Olefins, 1985, Annulenes, Benzo-, Hetero-, Homo-Derivatives and Their Valence Isomers, 1986, Labelled Compounds and Radipharmaceuticals Applied in Nuclear Medicine, 1986, Modeling of Cancer Genesis and Prevention, 1990; editor: Chemical Applications of Graph Theory, 1976, From Chemical Topology to the Three-Dimensional Geometry, 1997, Topological Indices and Related Molecular Descriptors in QSAR/QSPR, 1999; mem. editl. bd. Revue Roumaine de Chimie, Match, Polycyclic Aromatic Compounds and others. Fellow World Acad. Theoretical Organic Chemists, European Acad. Arts and Sci.; mem. Acad. of Romania (v.p. 1995-98, N. Teclu prize 1962), Hung Acad. Sci. (hon. 2001), Internat. Acad. Math. Chem. (pres. 2005-07), Am. Chem. Soc. (H. Skolnik award 1994), Royal Soc. Chemistry. Home: Apt C4 3220 69th St Galveston TX 77551 Office: Tex A & M U Galveston 5007 Ave Galveston TX 77551 Office Phone: 409-741-4313. Business E-Mail: balabana@tamug.edu.

BALABAN, BOB, actor, film director; b. Chgo., Aug. 16, 1945; s. Elmer and Elenore (Pottasch) B.; m. Lynn Grossman, Apr. 1, 1977; children: Mariah, Hazel. BA, NYU; studied with Uta Hagen, Viola Spolin. Studied with Second City comedy troupe, Chgo.; theatrical appearences include (off-Broadway) You're a Good Man Charlie Brown, 1967, Up Eden, 1968, The Basic Training of Pavlo Hummel, 1971, The Children, 1972, Marie and Bruce, 1980, The Three Sisters, 1982, Some Americans Abroad, 1991, (Broadway) Plaza Suite, 1968, The White House Murder Case, 1970, Some of My Best Friends, 1977, The Inspector General, 1978 (Best Featured Actor in Play Tony award nominee 1979), Speed the Plow, 1991, (regional theatre) The Boys Next Door, 1986, Who Wants to be The Lone Ranger?, 1971; dir. play: Girls, Girls, Girls, 1980; film debut in Midnight Cowboy, 1969; film appearences include Me Natalie, 1969, The Strawberry Statement, 1970, Catch-22, 1970, Making It, 1971, Bank Shot, 1974, Report to the Commissioner, 1975, Close Encounters of the Third Kind, 1977, Girlfriends 1978, Altered States, 1980, Absense of Malice, 1981, Prince of the City, 1981, Whose Life Is It Anyway?, 1981, 2010, 1984, In Our Hands, 1984, End of the Line, 1987, Dead Bang, 1989, Alice, 1990, Little Man Tate, 1991, Bob Roberts, 1992, Greedy, 1994, City Slickers Two, 1994, Waiting for Guffman, 1996, Deconstructing Harry, 1996, Clockwatchers, 1997, Jakob the Liar, 1999, Three to Tango, 1999, Tex, the Passive Aggressive Gunslinger, 2000, Natural Selection, 2000, Ghost World, 2000, The Mexican, 2001, The Majestic, 2001, A Mighty Wind, 2003, Marie and Bruce, 2004, Scene Stealers, 2004, Trust the Man, 2005, Capote, 2005, Not a Genuine Black Man, 2006, Lady in the Water, 2006; dir. films: Parents, 1989, My Boyfriend's Back, 1993, The Last Good Time, 1996, Subway Stories, 1997; TV debut in The Mod Squad; TV appearences include (film) Marriage: Year One, 1971, The Face of Fear, 1990, Giving up the Ghost, 1998, Swing Vote, 1999 (series episodes) Seinfeld, 1993; dir. TV series: Legend, 1995, Strangers with Candy, 1999, Now and Again, 1999-2000, Deadline, 2000-01, Dead Last, 2001, Twilight Zone, 2002-03; dir. TV films: The Brass Ring, 1983, No Joking, 2004, The Exonerated, 2005; actor, dir. TV series: Hopless Pictures, 2005; writer, prodr films: The Last Good Time, 1994; exec. prodr. films: The Definite Maybe, 1997; actor, prodr. films: Godsford Park, 2001. Mem. AEA, SAG, AFTRA, Astoria Found. (bd. dirs.).

BALABAN, MURAT OMER, food science educator; b. Ankara, Turkey, Feb. 5, 1952; came to U.S., 1977; s. Faruk Mehmet and Selma (Fetgeri) B.; m. Canan Bayezit, Aug. 10, 1977; 1 child, Denis Tan. BChemE, Mid. East Tech. U., 1976; PhD in Food Sci. & Tech., U. Wash., 1984. Ind. software cons., 1984-85; postdoctoral rsch. assoc. food sci. dept. Rutgers U., New Brunswick, NJ, 1985-86; asst. prof. food processing & engring. U. Fla., Gainesville, 1986-91, assoc. prof. food processing & engring., 1991-97, prof., 1997—. Mem. scientific adv. bd. FMC Corp., 1991—; ops. analysis group Singleton Seafood, Tampa, Fla. Assoc. editor Jour. Aquatic Food Product Tech., 1997-99; editl. bd. Food Tech. in Turkey. Recipient Food Engring. award and medal Food Process Engring. Inst., 1998, U. Fla. Productivity award, 1999; Fulbright scholar, 1995. Mem. Nat. Assn. Colls. & Tchrs. Agr., Inst. Food Technologists (exec. com. food engring. group 1989-92, ann. program com., exec. com. seafood divsn. 1995-99), Am. Soc. Agrl. Engrs., Inst. Thermal Processing Specialists, Tropical and Subtropical Fisheries Soc. (exec. com. 1994-99), Gamma Sigma Delta. Home: 4008 NW 122nd St Gainesville FL 32606-3631 Office: U Fla FSHN 359 Gainesville FL 32611

BALABANIAN, NORMAN, electrical engineering educator; b. New London, Conn., Aug. 13, 1922; s. Adam B. and Elizabeth (Seklemian) B.; m. Jean Tajerian, Aug. 16, 1947 (div. 1977); children: Karen J., Doris R., Gary N., Linda C.; m. 2d, Rosemary Lynch, Jan. 19, 1979. BSEE, Syracuse U., 1949, MSEE, 1951, PhD, 1954. From instr. to prof. Syracuse U., 1949-91, prof. emeritus, 1991—; mem. tech. staff Bell Labs., Murray Hill, N.J., 1956, IBM Devel. Lab, Poughkeepsie, N.Y., 1962; vis. prof. U. Calif., Berkeley, 1965-66; mem. UNESCO field staff Inst. Politecnico Nacional, Mexico City, 1969-70; Fulbright fellow U. Zagreb, Zagreb, Jugoslavia, 1974-75; acad. advisor Inst. Nat. d'Elec. et d'Elec., Boumerdes, Algeria, 1977-78; chmn. Dept. of Elec. & Computer Engring. Syracuse U., 1983-90. Vis. scholar MIT, 1990-95, Tufts U., 1990-95; courtesy prof. U. Fla., 1995—. Author: Network Synthesis, 1958, Fundamentals of Circuit Theory, 1961, Fourier Series, 1976, Ensenanza Programada en la Educacion Activa (in Spanish), 1974, Activne RC Mreze (in Serbo-Croatian), 1977, Electric Circuits, 1994; co-author: Linear Network Analysis, 1959, Electrical Network Theory, 1969, Electrical Science: Resistive Networks, 1970, Electrical Science: Dynamic Networks, 1973, Linear Network Theory, 1981, Digital Logic Design Principles, 2001; editor: Undergraduate Physics and Mathematics in Electrical Engineering, 1960, Electrical Engineering Education, 1961; editor (jour.) IEEE Transactions on Circuit Theory, 1963-65, (mag.) IEEE Technology and Society, 1979-86, 1993-95. Dist. commr. Dem. Party, Syracuse, N.Y., 1959-61; pres. Cen. N.Y. Civil Liberties Union, Syracuse, 1963-64, 79-80 (Civil Liberties award 1966); congl. candidate Liberal Party, People's Peace Party, Syracuse, N.Y., 1966. S/Sgt. Army AC, 1943-46. Recipient peace award Syracuse Peace Coun., 1966. Fellow AAAS, IEEE (life fellow, Centennial award 1984, Third Millenium medal 2000), IEEE Soc. Implications Tech. (v.p., pres. 1988-91); DK. mem. Am. Soc. for Engring. Edn. (life mem., pres. EE div. 1966-67), AAUP (pres. Syracuse U. chpt. 1964-65). Office: U Fla Dept ECE Gainesville FL 32611-6200 Personal E-mail: balabanian@cox.net.

BALACHANDRAN, PRIYA, environmental scientist; d. Uma Balachandran; m. Sailesh Munagala, Dec. 13, 1998; 1 child, Aditya Munagala. PhD, U. Ala., Birmingham, 1996—2001. Postdoctoral fellow U. Calif., San Francisco, 2001—. Grantee U.Calif. Microbial Pathogenesis Tng. grant, NIH, 2004. Mem.: Am. Soc. Microbiology. Achievements include research in host factors involved in resistance to bacterial disease. Home Phone: 415-476-3433.

BALAGURU, PERUMALSAMY, civil engineering educator; b. Tamil Nadu, India, Mar. 26, 1947; s. Perumal and Kengammal (Perumal) Ramasamy; m. Suryaprabha Venkatesalu, June 6, 1974; children: Balasoundhari, Balamuralee. BS with honors, U. Madras, Coimbatore, India, 1968; MS with distinction, Indian Inst. Sci., Bangalore, 1970; PhD, U. Ill., 1977. Assoc. lectr. U. Madras, 1970-73; asst. prof. Rutgers State U., Piscataway, NJ, 1977-82, assoc. prof., 1982-88, prof., 1988—2002, dist. prof., 2002—; program dir. Nat. Sci. Found., 2002—07. Presenter in field. Author: Fiber Reinforced Cement Composites, 1992; editor books; contbr. more than 250 articles to profl. jours. Named Outstanding Alumni, U. Ill.-Chgo., Tchr. of Yr., Rutgers U., 1985, 1992, Outstanding Alumni, Coimbatore Inst. Tech., India; recipient Long Standing Contbrn. award, Internat. Ferrocement Soc., Best Paper award, SAMPE, 2005. Fellow Am. Concrete Inst.; mem. ASCE. Office: Rutgers U 623 Bowser Rd Piscataway NJ 08854 Business E-Mail: balaguru@rci.rutgers.edu.

BALAJI, KETHANDAPATTI C., urologist, oncologist, researcher; b. India; m. Shoba Balaji. MBBS, Madras U., India, 1986. Dir., asst. prof. urol. oncology Southern Ill. U., Springfield, 1999—2000; assoc. prof. urologic surgery U. Nebr. Med. Ctr., Omaha, 2000—05, dir. urological oncology rsch., 2000—06, prof. urol. surgery, 2005—06; chief urology svcs. Vets. Affair Med. Ctr., 2000—06; dir. robotic surgery and urol. rsch. U. Mass. Meml. Healthcare, Worcester, 2006—; leader genitourinary cancer ctr. U. Mass. Med. Sch. Cancer Ctr., 2006—; residency program dir. U. Mass., 2006—, prof. surgery, cell biology and cancer biology, 2006—, prof., chief urology, 2006—. Co-dir. gu oncology program U. Mass., 2006—; primary site investigator Vets. Adminstrn., co-investigator. Named one of America's Top Physicians, Consumer Rsch. Coun. Am., 2004—05; grantee Merit Rev. Grant, Dept. Vet. Affairs, New Investigator Grant, Dept. Def. Mem.: Am. Urol. Assn. (New Eng. Sect.), AAAS, Am. Assn. Cancer Rsch., Am. Soc. Clin. Oncologists, Soc. U. Urologists, Soc. Basic Urol. Rsch., Endourological Soc., Am. Urol. Assn., Mass. Assn. Practicing Urologists. Office: U Mass Meml Health Care 55 Lake Ave N Worcester MA 01655 Office Phone: 508-856-5821. Office Fax: 508-856-3137. Business E-Mail: balajik@ummhc.org.

BALAJI, RENGARAJAN V., grant specialist; b. Tiruchirapalli, Tamil Nadu, India, Apr. 11, 1975; s. Rengarajan Tirumalai and Suguna Rengarajan; m. Deepa Narayanan, Dec. 8, 2002; 1 child, Anushil. BSc, Acharya NG Ranga Agrl. U., Hyderabad, India, 1998; MBA, Ohio U., Athens, 2001. Cert. rsch. adminstr. Racc, Va., 2006. Project mgr., tech. officer NeuroBioTex, Inc., Galveston, Tex., 2001—04; grants specialist U. Tex. Med. Br., Galveston, Tex., 2004—05; rsch. grants devel. coord. Ohio U., 2005—. Contbr. articles to profl. jours. Recipient Excellence award, OU-COM, 2007. Mem.: NCURA (assoc.).

BALAKRISHNAN, P. V. (SUNDAR), marketing educator; s. P.B. and Lakshmi Venkatasubramanian; m. Shobana Srinivasan, Apr. 18, 1989; children: Tara, Maya, Lila. B in Tech., I.I.T., Delhi, 1976—81; MS, U. Tex., Arlington, 1981—83; MA, PhD, Wharton Sch., U. Pa., Phila., 1988. Asst. prof. Ohio State U., Columbus, 1988—94, Univ. Wash., Bothell, 1994—96, assoc. prof., 1996—2004, acting dir., bus. program, 1998—2000, prof. mktg., 2004—. Vis. assoc. prof. U of Chgo, Grad. Sch. of Bus., 2001—02. Contbr. scholarly research. Fellow AMA Doctoral Consortium, Wharton Sch., Univ. Pa, 1986. Mem.: Beta Gamma Sigma. Achievements include first to introduce aritificial intelligence methodologies to marketing; research in business negotiations and new product marketing; development of software for negotiations and product line designs. Office Phone: 425-352-5384. Business E-Mail: sundar@u.washington.edu.

BALAKRISHNAN, RADHESH, marketing professional; s. Em and Padmaja Balakrishnan; m. Meena Sivakumar, May 2, 1997; children: Mira Menon, Vikram Menon. B in Engring., Coimbatore Inst. Tech., India, 1992; MBA, Pondicherry U., India, 1994, William E. Simon Grad. Sch. Bus. Adminstrn., Rochester, NY, 1999. Product mgr. Sonata Software Ltd., Bangalore, India, Karnataka, India, 1994—97, Microsoft Corp., Redmond, Wash., 1999—2002, lead product mgr., 2002—04, group product mgr., 2004—06; chief competitive officer Microsoft India Pvt Ltd, Gurgaon, Haryana, 2006—. Mem.: Mensa, Beta Gamma Sigma. Office: Microsoft Corp One Microsoft Way Redmond WA 98052 Home Phone: 425-996-0678. Business E-Mail: radheshb@microsoft.com.

BALAMACEDA, CASILDA, neurologist, oncologist; b. Buenos Aires, Apr. 1, 1960; (parents Am. citizens); d. Eudoro Geronimo Balmaceda and Margarita Mercedes Sastre de Balmaceda; children: Cristan, Adrian. BS, Tufts U., Medford, Mass., 1981; diploma in French Lang., U. Sorbonne, Paris, 1982; MD, Columbia Coll. Physicians and Sugeons, NYC, 1987. Intern in internal medicine Montefiore Hosp., Bronx, NY, 1987—88; resident in neurology Columbia Presbyn. Hosp., NYC, 1988—91; fellow in neurology Meml. Sloan Kettering Cancer Ctr., 1991—93; asst. prof. neurology Columbia U., 1991—2006; assoc. prof. clin. neurology and neurosurgery N.Y. Presbyn. Hosp., 2006—. Vol. physician, Dominican Republic, 2005, 2006; bd. dir. Richard Brodkey Found. Brain Tumor and HIV Rsch., 2004, Salawskins Found Brain Tumor Rsch., 2004—. Avocations: art, classical music, piano. Home: 24 Hamilton Ter New York NY 10031 Office: Neurol Inst 710 W 168 St New York NY 10031 Office Phone: 212-305-6990, 212-305-4572. Business E-Mail: cb116@columbia.edu.

BALANDIN, ALEXANDER A., electrical engineer, educator; b. Nizhny Novgorod, Russia, Apr. 30, 1968; came to US, 1993; s. Alexei A. and Tania A. (Ovechkin) Balandin; m. Maria P. Spitsin, Jan. 12, 1996. BS in Applied Math., Moscow Inst. Physics & Tech., 1989, MS in Applied Physics, 1991; MSEE, U. Notre Dame, Ind., 1995, PhD in Elec. Engring., 1996. Rsch. asst. dept. elec. engring. U. Notre Dame, Ind., 1993-96; rsch. assoc. dept. elec. engring. Quantum Device Lab. U. Nebr., Lincoln, 1996-97; rsch. engr. dept. elec. engring. Device Rsch. Lab. UCLA, 1997-99; asst. prof. dept. elec. engring. U. Calif., Riverside, 1999-2001, assoc. prof. dept. elec. engring., 2001—05, prof. dept. elec. engring., 2005—, dir. Nano-Device Lab., 2000—, chair materials sci. and engring. program, 2007—. Recipient Career award, NSF, Young Investigator award, ONR, Regents Faculty award, U. Calif. Mem. AAAS, IEEE, Am. Phys. Soc., Electrochem. Soc., Eta Kappa Nu. Achievements include development of nano-phononics; research in theory of quantum dots; flicker noise reduction in high-power transistors; thermal transport in nanostructures; investigation of optical properties of nanostructures. Office: Univ Calif Dept Elec Engring Riverside CA 92521-0425 Business E-Mail: balandin@ee.ucr.edu.

BALANIS, CONSTANTINE APOSTLE, electrical engineering educator; b. Trikala, Thessaly, Greece, Oct. 29, 1938; arrived in US, 1955; s. Apostolos G. and Erini (Vlahocostas) B.; m. Helen Jovaras, May 21, 1972; children: Erini, Stephanie. BSEE, Va. Tech. U., 1964; MEE, U. Va., 1966; PhDEE, Ohio State U., 1969; Doctorate (hon.), Aristotle U. Thessaloniki, Greece, 2004. Electronics engr. NASA, Hampton, Va., 1964-70; asst. professorial lectr. George Washington U. Extension, Hampton, 1968-70; vis. assoc. prof. dept. elec. engring. W.Va. U., Morgantown, 1970-72, assoc. prof., 1972-76, prof., 1976-83; prof. dept. elec. engring. Ariz. State U., Tempe, 1983-91, Regents' prof., 1991—, dir. Telecommunications Rsch. Ctr., 1988-99. Cons. Motorola Inc., Scottsdale, Ariz., 1984-94, Loral Def. Systems, Litchfield Park, Ariz., 1986-88, Gen. Dynamics, Pomona, Calif., 1986-87, Naval Air Warfare Ctr., Patuxent River, Md., 1977-90, Naval Surface Warfare Ctr., Dahlgren, Va., 1985-86, Nat. Radio Astronomy Observatory, Green Bank, W.Va., 1972-74; Boeing, Seattle, 1996, Rockwell Internat., Cedar Rapids, Iowa, 1997. Author: Antenna Theory: Analysis and Design, 1982, 3d edit., 2005, Advanced Engineering Electromagnetics, 1989; editor: Antennas and Propogation, Computational Electromagnetic Series; patentee in field. Recipient Halliburton Best Rschr. award W.Va. U., 1983, Russ award for Rsch., Ohio U., 1984, Tchg. Excellence award Ariz. State U., 1988, Outstanding Grad. Mentor award, 1996-97; grantee NASA, Army Rsch. Office, NSF, Office Naval Rsch., Dept. of Energy, Dept. of Transp., Naval Air Warfare Ctr., Naval Surface Warfare Ctr., Motorola Inc., Gen. Dynamics, Boeing Helicopter Sys., Sikorsky Aircraft, Rockwell Internat., Boeing Helicopters, IBM, 1972—. Fellow (life) IEEE (Individual Achievement award region 6, 1989, Spl. Engring. Professionalism award Phoenix sect. 1992, Third Millennium award 2000, AP Soc. Chen-To Tai Disting. Educator award 2005); mem. Sigma Xi, Phi Kappa Phi, Eta Kappa Nu, Tau Beta Pi. Avocations: golf, jogging, tennis, bowling. Home: 3154 E Encanto St Mesa AZ 85213-6110 Office: Ariz State U Dept Elec Engring Tempe AZ 85287-5706 Office Phone: 480-965-3909. Business E-Mail: balanis@asu.edu.

BALANOFF, CLEM, county election director; b. Chgo., Apr. 14, 1953; m. Virginia Balanoff; 2 children. Student, Ripon Coll., 1971-73. Mem. Ill. House, 1989-95; Dem. candidate U.S. House, 1994, 96. Home: 5606 S Blackstone #3 Chicago IL 60637 Office: Cook County Clerk 69 W Washington 5th flr Chicago IL 60602 Office Phone: 312-603-0925. Business E-Mail: cbalan@cookcountygov.com.

BALAS, EDITH, art historian, educator; b. Cluj, Romania, June 20, 1929; came to U.S., 1967; d. Alexander and Klara (Rooz) Lövy; m. Egon Balas, Dec. 21, 1948; children: Anna Balas, Vera Balas Koutsoyannis. Lic. in philosophy, C.I. Parhon U., Bucharest, 1952; diploma in philosophy, C.I. Parhon U., 1952; MA, U. Pitts., 1970, PhD, 1973. Editor Pub. House of the Acad., Bucharest, 1952-55; instr., lectr. C.I. Parhon U., Bucharest, 1955-58; tchr. Matei Basarab High Sch., Bucharest, 1958-66; instr. U. Pitts., 1975-77, rsch. assoc., 1978—; assoc. prof. art history Carnegie Mellon U., Pitts., 1978-91, prof., 1991—. Author: Brancusi and Rumanian Folk Tradition, 1987, Michelangelo's Medici Chapel: A New Interpretation, 1995, Joseph Csàky: A Pioneer of Modern Sculpture, 1998, The Mother Goddess in the Italian Renaissance, 2002, The Holocaust in the Paintings of Valentin Lustig, 2002, The Early Work of Henry Koerner, 2003, Michelangelo's Double Self-Portraits, 2004, Brancusi and Romanian Folk Tradition, 2d edit., 2006; co-author (with K. Passuth): Brâncuşi és Brancusi, 2005; contbr. articles to profl. jours. Fellow Andrew Mellon Found., 1972-73, 73-74, AAUW, 1971-73. Mem. Coll. Art Assn. Avocations: classical music, swimming, tennis, volunteer work. Home: 136 Beechwood Ln Pittsburgh PA 15206-4526 Office Phone: 412-268-2411. Business E-Mail: ebalas@andrew.cmu.edu.

BALAS, EGON, mathematician, educator; b. Cluj, Romania, June 7, 1922; came to U.S., 1967, naturalized, 1973; s. Ignat and Boriska B.; m. Edith Lovi, 1948; children: Anna, Vera. Diploma licenciae, Bolyai U., Cluj, 1949; D.Sc.Ec. summa cum laude, U. Brussels; D.U. in Math., U. Paris; PhD (hon.), U. Miguel Hernandez, Spain, 2002; Doctorate in Math. (hon.), U. Waterloo, 2005. Asso. prof. econs. Inst. Econ. Sci., Bucharest, 1949-58; analyst Designing Inst. Forestry and Timber Industry, Bucharest, 1959-64; head math. programming sector Center Math. Stats. of Romanian Acad., 1964-66; research mathematician Internat. Computation Centre, Rome, 1966; vis. prof. ops. research U. Toronto, 1967, Stanford U., 1967; Ford disting. research prof. Carnegie Mellon U., 1967-68; prof. indsl. adminstrn. and applied math. Carnegie-Mellon U., 1968—, univ. prof., 1990—, holder GSIA alumni chair, 1980—, Thomas Lord prof. ops. rsch., 1997—. Vis. ops. rsch. analyst Fed. Energy Adminstrn., 1976; cons. NSF grantee, 1972—; vis. prof. Maths. Inst. Köln, 1980-81. Author: Will to Freedom: A Perilous Journey Through Fascism and Communism, 2000 (transl. into Hungarian, Italian, Romanian and French); assoc. editor: Ops. Rsch., 1967-96, Zeitschrift für Ops. Rsch.; adv. editor: Discrete Applied Math., Jour. Combinatorial Optimization, Naval Rsch. Logistics; mem. editl. bd. Computational Optimization and Applications, Discrete Optimization, Annals of Operations Rsch., European Jour. Operational Rsch.; contbr. articles to profl. jours. Recipient Alexander von Humboldt Sr. U.S. Scientist award, 1980-81, John von Neumann Theory award, 1995, Euro Gold medal, 2001, Citation Classic, Current Contents, 1982; named to Hall of Fame Internat. Fedn. Operational Rsch. Socs., 2006; INFORMS fellow, 2002. Mem. NAE, SIAM, Math. Programming Soc. (coun. 1989-92), Inst. Mgmt. Scis. (coun. 1972-75), Oper. Rsch. Soc., Inst. Ops. Rsch. and Mgmt. Scis., Hungarian Acad. Sci. Achievements include research in math. programming, integer and disjunctive programming, combinatorial optimization, graphs, networks, crew scheduling, machine sequencing, energy models; devel. of scheduling system for steel rolling. Home: 136 Beechwood Ln Pittsburgh PA 15206-4526 Office: Tepper School Business Carnegie Mellon Univ Pittsburgh PA 15213 Office Phone: 412-268-2285. Business E-Mail: eb17@andrew.cmu.edu.

BALASA, MARK EDWARD, investment consultant; b. Petoskey, Mich., July 2, 1958; s. Edward S. and Mary N. (Wiklanski) B.; m. Laurel Marie Monaco, July 6, 1985; children: Bryant, Brett. AS, North Ctrl. Mich. Coll., Petoskey, 1978; BSBA, Ctrl. Mich. U., Mt. Pleasant, 1980; MA, Coll. Fin. Planning, Denver, 1992. CPA, Ill.; cert. fin. planner. Contr. Perfection Machinery Sales, Wheeling, Ill., 1981-87; investment cons. Elite Adv. Svcs., Schaumburg, Ill., 1987-89; investment cons., ptnr. Burton Investment Mgmt., Schaumburg, Ill., 1989-97, Balasa & Hoffman, Inc., Schaumburg, Ill., 1998-2001; ptnr. Balasa, Dinverno & Foltz LLC, Schaumburg, Ill., 2001—. Tchr. Mundelein Coll., Chgo., 1988; mem. adv. fin. bd. TIAA-CREF Inst., N.Y. Mem. adv. bd. Jour. Retirement Planning; regular columnist CCH's Rtirement Planning Jour. Named One of Best 120 Planners for Physicians, Med. Econs. mag., 1998, 1999, 2000, 2002, 2006; named one of 200 Best Fin. Advisors in the Country, Worth mag., 1996, 1997, 1998, 1999, 2001, 2002, 2004, 2006, 2007, the Best 100 Fin. Advisors in the Country, Mutual Funds Mag., 2001. Mem. AICPA, Fin. Planning Assn. (v.p. 1990-91, pres. 1991-92, exec. com. 1992-93), Internat. Assn. Fin. Planning (pres. Chgo. chpt. 1992-93). Roman Catholic. Avocations: running, racquetball, chess. Home: 1219 N Lakeview Ct Palatine IL 60067-2086 Office: Balasa Dinverno & Foltzs LLC 500 Park Blvd Itasca IL 60143-3121 Home Phone: 847-358-1772; Office Phone: 630-875-4900.

BALASH, JEFFREY LINKE, investment banker; b. NYC, Nov. 2, 1948; s. George Everett and Jeanne Marie (Linke) B. BA in Econs. summa cum laude, Princeton, 1970; MBA, Harvard U., 1974, JD cum laude, 1974. Bar: N.Y. 1974. Asst. to CEO, Louis-Dreyfus Corp., NYC, 1974-76; dir. Avon Products, NYC, 1976-79; mng. dir. Lehman Bros., NYC, 1979-85, Drexel Burnham Lambert, Beverly Hills, Calif., 1985-90; founding ptnr. Anthem Ptnrs., L.A. and NYC, 1991-92; chmn. Comstock Ptnrs., L.L.C., Beverly Hills, Calif., 1992—; chmn., co-founder JL Furnishings, L.L.C., Gardena, 1991—2002; CFO, chief strategic officer Telephony at Work, 1999—2002; co-founder Comstock Captial Ptnrs. LLC, 2002—. Bd. dirs. Joffrey Ballet, NYC, and LA, 1986-89; alumni coun. Harvard U. Bus. Sch., Boston, 1989-92; mem. major gifts com. Princeton U. Class 1970; founder Sons of Bacchus. Baker scholar Harvard U. Sch. Bus. Adminstrn., 1974. Mem. Harvard Bus. Sch. Assn. So. Calif. (bd. dirs. 1999-2003), Phi Beta Kappa. Republican. Roman Catholic. Avocations: travel, wine, jazz, art, films. Home: 9430 Readcrest Dr Beverly Hills CA 90210-2552 Office Phone: 310-278-6444. Personal E-mail: jbalash@alumni.princeton.edu. Business E-Mail: jbalash@comstockpartners.com.

BALASI, MARK GEOFFREY, architect; b. Chgo., Feb. 29, 1952; s. Alfred Victor and Betty Lou (Biggs) B.; m. Barbara Jane Ritt, May 25, 1985; children: Geoffrey Adam, Maria Elizabeth. Student, Ecole-des-Beaux-Arts, Versailles, France, 1974—75; BS in Archtl. Studies, U. Ill., 1975; postgrad., U. Wis., 1986, postgrad., 1989, postgrad., 1992. Lic. arch., Ill., Mich., Ohio. Arch. Davy McKee, Chgo., 1976-80, Perkins & Will, Chgo., 1980-82; prin. Hansen Lind Meyer Inc., Chgo., 1982-95; v.p. Phillips Swager Assocs., Naperville, Ill., 1995—2003, HDR Architecture, Inc., Chgo., 2003—. Lectr. Italian Nat. Ctr. Hosp. Bldg. and Technique. Editor: Balasi Archives, U. Iowa Librs. Spl. Collections; author: Sgt. Balasic WWI Album-Austro-Hungarian Army, 1996, Balasic Family Vaudeville Album, 1994; contbr.: (with Paul F. Stevens) Low Level Liberators in World War II, 1998; contbr. articles to profl. jours.; prin. works include Villa Schaefer, Mattoon, Ill., Nunamaker House, Mattoon, Mary Brown Stephenson Radiation Oncology Ctr., Zion, Ill. Active Hist. Preservation Commn., McHenry County, Ill. Mem. AIA (Nat. Coun. Archtl. Registration Bds. cert.), Am. Soc. Hosp. Engring., Acad. Architecture for Health, Health Facility Inst., PB4Y Assn., U. Ill. Alumni Assn. Avocations: genealogy, entomology, travel. Office: HDR Architecture Inc 8550 W Bryn Mawr Ave Ste 900 Chicago IL 60631-3223 Office Phone: 773-380-7900. Business E-Mail: mark.balasi@hdrinc.com.

BALASUBRAMONIAN, RAJEEV, computer science educator; b. Pune, Maharashtra, India, May 26, 1977; s. Balasubramonian Srikrishnan and Brinda Balasubramonian; m. Deepthi Eswaran, Jan. 20, 2003. PhD, U. Rochester, NY, 2003. Asst. prof. U. Utah Sch. Computing, Salt Lake City, 2003—. Contbr. articles to profl. jours. Recipient Outstanding Jr. Faculty Career award, Nat. Sci. Found., 2006. Mem.: IEEE. Achievements include three US patents in field. Office: Univ Utah Sch Computin 50 S Central Campus Dr Rm 3190 Salt Lake City UT 84112 Office Phone: 801-581-4553.

BALAS-WHITFIELD, SUSAN, artist; b. NJ; m. Marshall Whitfield. BA, Douglass Coll., New Brunswick, 1961, Rutgers U., Newark, 1964, NYU, NYC, 1964. Tchr. WM. R. Satz. Sch., Holmdel, NJ, 1976—89; artist, 1976—. Author: (novels) Into The Triangle, A Teacher's Trot, 1989. Pres. Ranch Property Owners Assoc., Durango, Colo., 2000—03. Named Artist of Yr., Durango County C. of C., 2003; recipient award for Excellence, Am. Artist's Profl. League, 2004. Mem.: Pastel Soc. Am. (signature mem.), NY Salmagundi Club. Avocations: motorcycling, skiing, running, hiking. Home: 308 CottonWood Creek Rd Durango CO 81301 Studio: 22521 E Rowland Dr Aurora CO 80016 Office Phone: 970-259-0774. Business E-Mail: susan@balasart.com.

BALAY, ROBERT ELMORE, editor, librarian; b. Wichita, Kans., Oct. 6, 1930; s. Loren Elmore and Gladys Lois (Crites) B.; m. Harriette Shirley Anderson, Dec. 23, 1961; children— Christopher Loren, Anne Gladys, Jean Mary BA, Macalester Coll., St. Paul, Minn., 1952; MA, U. Minn., 1954; MS in Libr. Sci., Columbia U., NYC, 1959. Tech. writer Beech Aircraft Corp., Wichita, 1956-58; asst. librarian Grumman Aircraft Corp., Bethpage, NY, 1959-62, Gen. Precision, Little Falls, NJ, 1962-64; asst. sci. librarian Wayne State U., Detroit, 1964-68, adj. instr. library sci., 1966-67; head reference dept. Yale U. Library, New Haven, 1968-86; reference editor Choice mag., Middletown, Conn., 1986—2005. Author: Early Periodical Indexes, 2000; editor: Guide to Reference Books, 11th edit., 1996; contbr. articles to profl. jours. Served with US Army, 1954-56 Recipient Isadore Gilbert Mudge-R.R. Bowker award for reference svc., ALA, 2004. Democrat. Home: 97 Livingston St New Haven CT 06511-2411

BALAZS, ANDRÉ T., hotel executive; b. Boston, Jan. 31, 1957; s. Endre and Eva Balazs; m. Katherine Ford, 1985 (div.); 2 children. Studied at, Cornell U.; MA in Journalism and Bus., Columbia U. Co-founder Biomatrix, 1980; owner André Balazs Properties, NYC. Adv. bd. Niche Media LLC; spkr. in field. Trustee The Public Theater. Office: André Balazs Properties The Puck Bldg 295 Lafayette St, 7th Fl New York NY 10012 Office Phone: 212-226-5656.*

BALBACH, HAROLD EDWARD, environmental scientist; b. Chgo., Sept. 26, 1936; s. Harold Edward and Lillian Mildred (Best) B.; m. Margaret Ann Kain, Sept. 2, 1961. BE, Chgo. State U., 1959; MS, U. Ill., 1961, PhD, 1965. Cert. profl. agronomist, 1982; cert. sr. ecologist, 2002. Prof. Ea. Ill. U., Charleston, 1966—72; environ. scientist rsch. lab. U.S. Army C.E., Champaign, Ill., 1972—90; sr. rsch. fellow Army Environ. Policy Inst., Champaign, 1990—92; mgr. rsch. program U.S. Army C.E., Champaign, 1992—95, sr. rsch. scientist, 1995—96, 1999—, divsn. chief land mgmt. lab., 1996—99. Co-author: Environmental Assessment, 1993, 2001. Bd. trustees Champaign County Hist. Mus., 1995—, pres., 1996—. Fellow Soc. Am. Mil. Engrs. (life, pres. Illini Post 1990-92, 96-97, nat. bd. dirs. 1999-2002); mem. Am. Soc. Agronomy (bd. dirs. 1985-89, 99-2002, chair biosecurity com. 2003—), Am. Soc. Hort. Sci., Ecol. Soc. Am., Internat. Soc. Hort. Sci., Soc. for Am. Archeology, Nat. Trust for Hist. Preservation, Ill. Hist. Soc., Assn. for Southeastern Biology, Gopher Tortoise Coun., Ptnrs. in Amphibian and Reptile Conservation. Avocations: historic preservation, prairie restoration. Office: US Army Engr Rsch and Devel Lab PO Box 9005 Champaign IL 61826-9005

BALBACH, STANLEY BYRON, lawyer; b. Normal, Ill., Dec. 26, 1919; s. Nyle Jacob and Gertrude (Cory) B.; m. Sarah Troutt Witherspoon, May 22, 1944; children: Stanley Byron Jr., Nancy Ann Fehr, Barbara Haines, Edith. BS, U. Ill., 1940, LLD, 1942. Bar: Ill. 1942, Fla. 1980, U.S. Ct. Appeals (7th cir.) 1961, U.S. Supreme Ct. 1950. Ptnr. Couchman & Balbach, Hoopeston, Ill., 1945-48, Webber & Balbach, Urbana, 1948—78, Balbach & Fehr, Urbana, 1978—. Nat. chmn. Jr. Bar Conf., 1955. Author: Reverse Mortgages, 1997, The Lawyers Guide to Retirement: Serving a New Clientele in a Second Career in Real Estate, 1998. Capt. USAAF, 1942-45 (pilot). Mem. ABA (ho. of dels. 1956, lawyer title guaranty fund com., past mem. coun. law office practice and real property, probate and trust law sects.), LWV, Ill. State Bar Assn. (elder law com., Laureate of the Acad. Ill. Lawyers 2002), Am. Judicature Soc., Masons, Rotary, Phi Delta Phi, Alpha Kappa Lambda. Home: 1009 S Douglas Ave PO Box 217 Urbana IL 61803 Office: Balbach & Fehr Box 301 102 E Broadway Ave Urbana IL 61801-2705 Office Phone: 217-367-1011.

BALBI, KENNETH EMILIO, environmental specialist, researcher; s. George Emilio and Blanca Amelia B.; m. Julie Ann Balbi, Feb. 19, 1989; children: Danielle Elizabeth, Joshua Emilio. MD, U. Ctrl. del Este, Dominican Republic, 1985; BS, SUNY, Albany, 1989. Rsch. assoc. Montefiore Med. Ctr., 1988-94; govtl. and instnl. cons. SCITEC Corp., Kennewick, Wash., 1994-95; dir. tng. and profl. svcs. US Lead, Oyster Bay, NY, 1995-97; v.p., co-founder ANDO Internat., Bklyn., 1995—2002; dir. franchise ops. PRO-TECT Franchising Inc., Oyster Bay, NY, 1996-97; v.p. rsch. & design AIA Environ. Corp., Astoria, NY, 1997-99; pres., founder "E" The Solution, Douglaston, NY, 2002—; instr. Nat. Asbestos Environ. Training Inst., Ocean, NJ, 2002, Am. Indoor Air Quality Control, Glendale, Ariz., 2004—. Adj. asst. prof. St. John's U., Jamaica, NY, 2003—. Contbr. articles to profl. jours. Mem. St. Michael's Hispanic Assn., Flushing, NY, 1991—, Cuban-Am. Assocs., Flushing, 1988—, Alliance to End Childhood Lead Poisoning, Washington, 1992—; bd. mem. Am. Indoor Air Quality Coun., Glendale, Ariz., 2006-. Mem.: ASTM, AAAS, Am. Indoor Air Quality Coun., Nat. Environ. Health Assn., Am. Indsl. Hygiene Assn., United Internat. Med. Grads., NY Acad. Scis., InterAm. Coll. Physicians and Surgeons, Nat. Assn. for Search and Rescue. Roman Catholic. Home: 24015B Oak Park Dr Douglaston NY 11362 Office: "E" The Solution PO Box 620790 Douglaston NY 11362 Office Phone: 718-229-8859. Personal E-mail: kbalbi@aol.com.

BALBOA, MARCELO, professional soccer player; b. Cerritos, Calif., Aug. 8, 1967; s. Luis Balboa; m. Cindy Balboa. Grad., San Diego State U., 1988. Player U.S. Nat. Team, 1988—, San Diego Nomads, APSL, 1989, San Francisco Blackhawks, APSL, 1990—91, Colo. Foxes, APSL, 1992, Leon, Mex. 1st Divsn., 1995—96, Colo. Rapids, 1996—. Mem. U.S. World Cup Team, 1994—. Named MVP, World Cup, 1994, Colo. Rapids, 1997. also: US Soccer Fedn 1801 S Prairie Ave # 1811 Chicago IL 60616-1319 Office: 1000 Chopper CIR Denver CO 80204-5805

BALCER, CHARLES LOUIS, college president emeritus, educator; b. McGregor, Iowa, May 23, 1921; s. Ludwig Frank and Iva (Vaughan) B.; m. Martha Elizabeth Belgum, Jan. 6, 1944; children— Mary Elizabeth, Mark Lewis, Beth Louise, Brian Charles. BS, Winona State Tchrs. Coll., Minn., 1942; MA, State U. Iowa, 1949, PhD, 1954; DHL (hon.), Augustana Coll., 2003. Tchr. Minn. and Iowa high schs., 1942-43, 46-47; instr. State U. Iowa, 1947-50; high sch. prin. Detroit Lakes, Minn., 1950-54; assoc. prof. speech St. Cloud (Minn.) State Coll., 1954-56, prof., acad. dean, 1958-64; prof. speech SUNY-Oswego, 1956-57; pres. Augustana Coll., Sioux Falls, SD, 1965-80, pres. emeritus, 1980—. Disting. Service prof., 1980-95, interim chair edn. dept., 1999-00. Interim pres., CEO Good Samaritan Soc., 1997-98. Author: (with H. F. Seabury) Teaching Speech. Bd. dirs. Evang. Luth. Good Samaritan Soc.; active Marquette Bank SD, Sioux Falls Symphony Assn. Served with AUS, 1943-46 Decorated knight 1st class Royal Order St. Olav (Norway); named to S.D. Hall of Fame, 2003. Mem. Speech Communication Assn. Am., Central States Speech Assn. (pres. 1954), NEA, Assn. Higher Edn., Delta Sigma Rho, Kappa Delta Pi, Phi Delta Kappa. Democrat. Home: 111 W 17th St 234 Sioux Falls SD 57104-4901 Home Phone: 605-731-5234. Personal E-mail: clbalcer@aol.com. *I have learned that the purpose of this earthly life is not happiness. It is to be useful, to be honorable, to be compassionate. It is to matter— to have it made some difference that you lived at all.*

BALCERZAK, STANLEY PAUL, retired hematologist, oncologist, director, medical educator; b. Pitts., Apr. 27, 1930; BS, U. Pitts., 1953; MD, U. Md., 1955. Diplomate Am. Bd. Internal Medicine, Am. Bd. Hematology, Am. Bd. Oncology. Instr. medicine U Chgo., 1959-60, U. Pitts., 1962-64, asst. prof., 1964-67; assoc. prof. medicine Ohio State U., Columbus, 1967-71, prof., 1971-99, prof. emeritus, 1999—, dir. div. hematology and oncology, 1969-94, dep. dir. Ohio State U. Comprehensive Cancer Ctr., 1984-97, assoc. chmn. dept. medicine, 1984-98, dir. Hemophilia Ctr., 1975-79, 1981-99. Mem. clin. rev. com. Am. Cancer Soc., N.Y.C., 1976-82 Contbr. chpts. to books, numerous articles to profl. jours. Served to capt. U.S. Army, 1960-62 Recipient numerous grants Fellow ACP; mem. Central Soc. for Clin. Research (chmn. subsplty. council in hematology 1980-81, councillor 1980-83), Am. Soc. for Clin. Oncology, Am. Assn. for Cancer Research, Am. Soc. Hematology, Phi Beta Kappa, Alpha Omega Alpha Home: 3113 N 3 Bs And K Rd Sunbury OH 43074-9582 Office: Ohio State U Divsn Hematology Oncology 320 W 10th Ave Columbus OH 43210-1240 Home Phone: 740-524-7191; Office Phone: 614-293-8729. Business E-Mail: balcerzak.1@osu.edu.

BALCH, CHARLES M., surgeon, educator; b. Milford, Del., Aug. 24, 1942; m. Carol Mitchell; 4 children. BS cum laude, U. Toledo, 1963; MD, Columbia U., 1967. Diplomate Am. Bd. Surgery (bd. dirs. 1986-1992). Intern in surgery Duke U. Med. Ctr., Durham, N.C., 1967-68; resident in gen. surgery U. Ala., Birmingham, 1970-71, 73-75, asst. prof. to assoc. prof. dept. surgery, 1975-81, prof. 1981-85, chief sect. surg. oncology, 1979-85, asst. to assoc. prof. dept. microbiology, 1975-82, prof., 1982-85; assoc. scientist to sr. scientist, sr. investigator cellular immunobiology unit Comprehensive Cancer Ctr., U. Ala., 1975-85, assoc. dir for clin. studies, 1979-85, acting dir., 1982-83; head div. surgery and anesthesiology U. Tex.-M.D. Anderson Cancer Ctr., Houston, 1985-94, v.p. hosp. and clinics, 1993-94, chmn. dept. surgical oncology, 1985-94, prof. surgery, 1993-96, exec. v.p. health affairs, 1994-96; pres., CEO City of Hope, 1996—98; exec. v.p. Am. Soc. Clinical Oncology, Alexandria, Va. Assoc. chmn. dept surgery U. Tex., 1985-94; staff surgeon, chief oncology rsch. VA Hosp., Birmingham, 1975-85; vis. prof., Eleanor Roosevelt internat. fellow U. Sydney, Australia, 1983; chmn. nat. intergroup melanoma com. , Nat. Cancer Inst., NIH, 1981—, mem. subcom. bd. sci. counselors, 1980-86, mem. bd. sci. counselors, 1987-1991, other coms., 1978—; mem. Kettering selection com. GM Cancer Rsch. Found., Inc., 1986, vice chmn., 1987-88, mem. awards assembly, 1988—; prof. surgery & oncology, Johns Hopkins Med. Institutions, 2000-. Author: (with G.W. Milton) Cutaneous Melanoma: Clinical Management and Treatment Results Worldwide, 1985; author, editor: Surgical Approaches to Cutaneous Melanoma, 1985; author over 100 book chpts. including Hardy's Textbook of Surgery, 1988, The Physiologic Basis of Modern Surgical Care, 1988, Textbook on Clinical Oncology, 1991, Advances in Surgery, 1991, Cancer: Principles and Practice of Oncology, 1989, Current Surgical Therapy, 3d edit., 1989; author over 280 jour. articles, abstracts; mem. editorial bds. Practical Rev. in Cancer Mgmt., 1979-85, Ala. Jour. Med. Scis., 1979-81, Jour. Biol. Response Modifiers, 1981—, Am. Jour. Clin. Oncology, 1981-84, Jour. Surg. Rsch., 1982-88, Jour. Immunology, 1982-85, Cancer Treatment Reports, 1984— (also adv. bd.), Jour. Clin. Oncology, 1986—, Archives Surgery, 1986—, Surgery, 1986—, European Jour. Cancer, 1989—, Melanoma Rsch., 1990—, Postgrad. Gen. Surgery, 1991—, many others; editor The Melanoma Letter, 1986-93, Breast Diseases: A Year Book Quarterly, 1990—, Annals of Surgical Oncology, 1993—; assoc. editor Advances in Surgery, 1986—, Cancer Rsch., 1989—. Program specialist USPHS, 1968-70. Immunology fellow Lab. Dr. J. Feldman, La Jolla, Calif., 1971-73; NIH grantee, 1980-84, 83-85, 84-87, 84-86,87-1993, VA, 1981-84, 84-89. CEP grantee, 1990-92, NCI grantee, 1987-94. Fellow ACS (various coms. on commn. on cancer, 1980—, chmn. edn. com. 1981-84, chmn. cancer mgmt. course con. 1981-83, assoc. Internat. Fedn. Surg. Colls. 1988—, mem. surg. forum 1985-91, grantee 1984-88, 85-91); mem. AMA, Am. Cancer Soc. (bd. dirs. Ala. divsn. 1983-85, exec. bd. Bay Area chpt. Houston 1986—, clin. fellowship nat. divsn. 1985-87, mem. profl. edn. subcom. clin. fellowship 1988), Am. Radium Soc. (chmn. publs. com. 1982-84), Am. Soc. Clin. Oncology (sci. and publs. coml 1987-90, bd. dirs.), Assn. Acad. Surgery (sec.-treas. 1981-83, pres.-elect 1983-84, pres. 1984-85, exec. coun. 1982-86), Assn. Surg. Edn., Conjoint Coun. Surg. Edn. (cancer com. 1985—), Soc. Biol. Therapy, Soc. Surg. Oncology (sec. 1986-88, v.p. 1989-90, chmn. membership com. 1986-89, clin. rsch. and govt. rels. com. 1983-85, pres. elect 1990-91, pres. 1991-92), Soc. Univ. Surgeons (councilman 1982-85), Southeastern Cancer Study Group (chmn. surg. com. 1978-85, exec. com. 1979-85, chmn. melanoma/sarcoma com. 1983-85), Am. Soc. Clin. Investigation, Am. Assn. Cancer Edn., Am. Assn. Cancer Rsch., Am. Assn. Immunologists, Am. Assn. Transplant Surgeons, Am. Surg. Assn., European Soc. Surg. Oncology, Harris county Med. Soc., Houston Surg. Soc., Jefferson County Med. Soc., John Kirklin Soc., Pan-Pacific Surg. Assn., Reticuloendothelial Soc., Soc. Internat. de Chirurgie, Soc. Surg. Chmn., Tex. Surg. Soc., WHO Melanoma Group, others. Office: Am Soc Clinical Oncology 1900 Duke St #200 Alexandria VA 22314

BALCH, GLENN MCCLAIN, JR., academic administrator, minister, writer; b. Shattuck, Okla., Nov. 1, 1937; s. Glenn McClain and Marjorie (Daily) Balch; m. Diana Gale Seeley, Oct. 15, 1970; children: Bryan, Gayle, Wesley, John. Student, Panhandle State U., 1958-60, So. Meth. U., summers 1962-64; BS, S.W. State U., Okla., 1962; BD, Phillips U., 1965; postgrad., U. Okla., 1965-66; JD, L.A. Coll. Law, 1969; MA, Chapman U., 1973, MA in Edn., 1975, MA in Sch. Counseling, 1975, MA in Psychology, 1975; PhD, Alliant Internat. U., 1978; LLM, L.A. Coll. Law, 1970; postgrad., Claremont Grad. Sch., 1978—80. Ordained to ministry Meth. Ch., 1962. Sr. min. First Meth. Ch., Eakly, Okla., 1960-63, Calumet, Okla., 1963-65, Goodrich Meml. Ch., Norman, Okla., 1965-66, First Meth. Ch., Barstow, Calif., 1966-70, Brea United Meth. Ch., Calif., 1978-89; asst. dean Chapman U., Orange, Calif., 1970-76; assoc. to v.p. Pepperdine U., 1976—77; v.p. Hope Internat. U., Fullerton, Calif., 1977—79; pres., CEO So. Calif. Inst., Fullerton, 1988-95; pres. Westmar U., Le Mars, Iowa, 1995-96; exec. v.p. Advance Cons. Network (name now Synergistics, Inc.), Rochester, NY, 1996—; pres. Synergistics Tng., LLC, Churchville, NY, 2003—. Mental health cons. U.S. Army, 1969; edn. cons. USAF, 1974—75. Bd. dirs. Found. Internat. Cmty. Assistance, 1988—96. With USMC, 1956—57. Named Man of the Yr., Jr. C. of C., Bartow, 1969; recipient Eastern Star Religious Tng. award, 1963, 1964; Broadhurst fellow, 1963—65. Mem.: Am. Assn. Clin. Hypnosis, Nat. Assn. Sports Psychologists (diplomate), Calif. Assn. Family Therapists, Elks, Shriners, Masons, Rotary (pres. chpt. 1969—70, 1983—84, dist. gov. 1987—88, 1988—89, pres. chpt. 1999—2000, 2007—). Home and Office: Synergistics Tng LLC 39 Bowen Rd Churchville NY 14428-9737 Business E-Mail: glenn@synergistictraining.com.

BALCH, SAMUEL EASON, lawyer; b. Madison, Ala., Sept. 5, 1919; s. Joseph Austin and Clara Irene (Vaughn) B.; m. Elizabeth Gordon Brock, Apr. 17, 1943 (dec.); children: Samuel Eason Jr., Elizabeth Gordon Balch Lanier, Gene Austin Balch Limbaugh, Ann Warwick Balch Miano. BS in Commerce and Bus. Adminstrn, U. Ala., 1940; LLB, U. Va., 1948, JD, 1970. Bar: Va. 1947, Ala. 1948, U.S. Supreme Ct. 1960, U.S. Ct. Appeals (11th cir.) 1981, U.S. Ct. Appeals (5th cir.) 1965. Assoc. Martin, Turner & McWhorter, 1948; sr. ptnr. Balch & Bingham (and predecessor firms), 1962-89, of counsel, 1990—. Bd. dirs. Ala. Power Co., 1970-90; chmn. legal com. Edison Electric Inst., 1979-81, chmn. econs., pub. policy and strategic planning, exec. adv. com., 1986-88. Served to major AUS, 1941-46, ETO, PTO. Life fellow Am. Bar Found.; mem. ABA (mem. coun. pub. utility law, telecomms. and transp. sect.), Fed. Energy Bar Assn., Ala. Bar Assn., Birmingham Bar Assn., Newcomen Soc., Am. Judicature Soc., Farrah Law Soc., Mountain Brook Club, The Summit Club, The Club (Birmingham, Ala.), Kappa Sigma. Episcopalian. Home: 4227 Old Leeds Rd Birmingham AL 35213-3211 Office: PO Box 306 1710 6th Ave N Birmingham AL 35203-2015 Office Phone: 205-226-3400. Business E-Mail: ebalch@balch.com.

BALCH, STEPHEN HOWARD, professional society administrator; b. Bklyn., Jan. 31, 1944; s. Harry and Florence (Frey) B.; m. Maria Weston Schelz, Aug. 31, 1979; children: Leah, Daniel. BA magna cum laude, Bklyn. Coll., 1964; MA, U. Calif., Berkeley, 1967, PhD, 1972. Lectr. U. San Francisco, 1969-70; acting instr. U. Calif., Berkeley, 1970-71; vis. instr. Rutgers U., New Brunswick, N.J., 1971-72; asst. prof. urban policy Grad. Ctr. CUNY, NYC, 1973-74, asst. prof. govt. John Jay Coll. Criminal Justice, 1974-79, assoc. prof. govt., 1979-92; pres. Nat. Assn. Scholars, Princeton, N.J., 1987—. Bd. dirs. Nat. Alumni Forum, Washington, 1993—. Sr. editor Acad. Questions, 1987-91. Chmn. N.J. State adv. com. U.s. Civil Rights Commn., 1985-91, mem., 1991—; trustee Medille Coll., 1998—; chmn. bd. Theodore Roosevelt Sch. Found., 1999—. Am. Polit. Sci. Assn. congl. fellow, 1972. Mem. Phi Beta Kappa. Office: Nat Assn Scholars 575 Ewing St Princeton NJ 08540-2741 E-mail: vas@nas.org.

BALCI, CEM N, radiologist; b. Istanbul, Levent, Turkey, Apr. 17, 1965; s. Nihat A. and Tulin Balci; m. Yesim Yilanci, Sept. 25, 2001; children: Ege E. Kockesen, Emre N. MD, Istanbul Med. Sch., 1991. Lic. Mo., 2005. Rsch. fellow U. NC, Chapel Hill, 1997—99; assoc. prof. Koceeli U., Turkey, 2003—05, St. Louis U., St. Louis, 2005—. Home: 12559 Postgrove Dr Saint Louis MO 63146 Office: St Louis Univ 3635 Vista Ave Saint Louis MO 63110 Home Phone: 314-680-6046; Office Phone: 314-577-8000. Office Fax: 314-268-5116; Home Fax: 314-268-5116. Business E-Mail: nbalci@slu.edu.

BALCOM, ORVILLE, engineer; b. Inglewood, Calif., Apr. 20, 1937; s. Orville R. and Rose Mae (Argo) B.; children: Cynthia, Steven. BS in Math., Calif. State U., Long Beach, 1958, postgrad., 1958-59, UCLA, 1959-62. Engr. AiResearch Mfg. Co., 1959-62, 64-65; chief engr. Meditron, El Monte, Calif., 1962-64, Astro Metrics, Burbank, Calif., 1965-67; chief engr., gen. mgr. Varadyne Power Systems, Van Nuys, Calif., 1968-71; owner, chief engr. Brown Dog Engring., Lomita, Calif., 1971—. Patentee in field. Mem. IEEE Computer Group, Independent Computer Cons. Assn., Torrance Athletic Club. Home: 24521 Walnut St Lomita CA 90717-1260 Office: PO Box 427 Lomita CA 90717-0427

BALCOMB, MARY NELSON, small business owner; b. Mich., Apr. 29, 1928; d. Andrew and Selma (Martin) Nelson; m. Robert S. Balcomb, July 3, 1948; children: Stuart V., Amis. AA, Am. Acad. Art, 1948; BFA cum laude, U. N.Mex., 1968; MFA, U. Wash., 1971. Advt. mgr. Broome Furniture Co., Albuquerque, 1949-55; designer Custom Interiors, Albuquerque, 1956-66; art tchr. Sandia Girls' Sch., Albuquerque, 1966-68; co-owner Woolcot, Inc., Bellevue, Wash., 1975-80; owner Balcomb Design Studio, Silverdale, Wash., 1981—. Author: Nicolai Fechin, Russian-American Artist, 1975 (Rounce and Coffin award), Les Perhacs, Sculptor, 1975, William F. Reese, American Artist, 1984 (Rounce and Coffin award), Robin-Robin/A Journal, 1995, Sergei Bongart, Russian-American Artist, 2002; contbr. articles to periodic jours. Creator Children's Art Ctr. Found., Seattle, 1972, bd. dirs., 1972-80. Recipient Painting award Frye Art Mus., 1994, Honorarium Prix de West Nat. Cowboy Hall of Fame and We. Heritage Mus., 1995. Mem. Author's Guild, Phi Kappa Phi, Lambda Rho. Home: PO Box 1922 Silverdale WA 98383-1922

BALCOMB, MELANIE S., women's college basketball coach; b. Princeton, NJ, Sept. 24, 1962; d. Alan and Barbara Balcomb. BS, Trenton State Coll., 1984; MEd, 1985. Asst. coach Niagara U., 1985—89, Ohio U., 1989—90, Providence Coll., 1990—93; head coach Ashland U., Ohio, 1993—95, Xavier U., Cin., 1995—2002, Vanderbilt U., Nashville, 2002—. Named Coach of Yr., Atlantic 10 Conf., 2001, NJ Sports Writers Assn., 2001, Greater Cin. Women's Sports Fedn., 2001, Ohio Coll. Coach of Yr., Columbus Dispatch, 2001; named to Greater Cin. Basketball Hall of Fame, 2001. Avocations: golf, travel, reading. Office: Vanderbilt U Womens

Basketball McGugin Ctr 2601 Jess Neely Dr Nashville TN 37212 Office Phone: 615-343-8482. E-mail: melanie.balcomb@Vanderbilt.Edu.*

BALD, RONALD JAMES, military officer; b. Dover, NJ, Mar. 6, 1965; s. Ronald Alan Bald and Jeanette Ann Carlstedt; m. Wanda Hope Yates; children: Matthew children: William. BS Civil Engring., USCG Acad., New London, Conn., 1987; MA Pub. Mgmt., U. Houston, 1995; JD, Tulane U., 2003. Deck watch officer/ops. officer U.S. Coast Guard Cutter Buttonwood, Galveston, Tex., 1987—89; adminstrv. officer/aids to nav. officer U.S. Coast Guard Group Galveston, Galveston, Tex., 1989—93; ops. officer USCG Vessel Traffic Svc. Houston/Galveston, Galena Park, Tex., 1993—96; supply officer U.S. Coast Guard Cutter Boutwell, Alameda, Calif., 1996—98; cmdg. officer U.S. Coast Guard Cutter Cushing, San Juan, 1998—2000; asst. legal officer USCG Acad., New London, Conn., 2003—. Comdr. USCG, 1987—. Recipient Coast Guard Achievement Medal, Eighth Coast Guard Dist., 1990—93, 1990—91, Coast Guard Commendation Medal, 1993—96, Coast Guard Achievement Medal, 1993, Commandant's Letter of Commendation, Coast Guard Group Galveston, 1993, Coast Guard Commendation Medal, Coast Guard Pacific Area, 1996—98, Seventh Coast Guard Dist., 1998—2000, James A. Wysocki Trial Advocacy award, Tulane U. Sch. Law, 2003, Cicero C. Sessions Trial Advocacy award, 2003, Trial Advocacy award, N.Y.C. Bar Assn., 2003, Commandant's Letter of Commendation, Coast Guard Acad., 2005; Stiles scholar for maritime law, Tulane Maritime Ctr., Tulane U. Sch. Law, 2002—03. Mem.: ABA, ASPA, Miss. Bar Assn. Avocation: coaching youth athletics. Office: US Coast Guard Acad 15 Mohegan Ave New London CT 06320-8100 Home: 508 Clayton Ct Slidell LA 70461-5710 Home Phone: 860-464-8869, 985-641-7842; Office Phone: 860-444-8254. Personal E-mail: rhwmbald@charter.net.

BALDACCI, DAVID, writer; b. Va., 1960; married. BA Polit. Sci., Va. Commonwealth Univ.; JD, Univ. Va. Former trial, corp. atty, Washington. Nat. amb. Nat. Multiple Sclerosis Soc.; co-founder Wish You Well Found. Author: (children's books) Freddy and the French Fries: Fries Alive!, 2005, (novels) Absolute Power, 1996 (WH Smith's Thumping Good Read award for fiction, Britain, 1997, Gold Medal for Best Mystery/Thriller, Southern Writers Guild, 1996, made into feature film), Total Control, 1996 (Gold Medal for Best Mystery/Thriller, Southern Writers Guild, 1997), The Winner's, 1997, The Simple Truth, 1998, Saving Faith, 1999 (NY Times bestseller list, Publisher's Weekly bestseller), Wish You Well, 2000 (selected inaugural book for All America Reads nat. reading program), Last Man Standing, 2001 (No. 1 on NY Times bestseller list), The Christmas Train, 2002, Split Second, 2003 (NY Times bestseller list), Hour Game, 2004, The Camel Club, 2005 (Publishers Weekly bestseller list), The Collectors, 2006, Simple Genius, 2007, (children's books) Fries Alive!, 2005; author: (seven) screenplays. Bd. dir. Va. Found. Humanities, Va. Commonwealth Univ. Mailing: c/o Author Mail Warner Books 1271 Ave of Americas New York NY 10020*

BALDACCI, JOHN ELIAS, governor, former congressman; b. Bangor, Maine, Jan. 30, 1955; m. Karen Weston; 1 child, Jack. BA in History, U. Maine, 1986. With Momma Baldacci's Restaurant, Bangor; mem. Bangor City Coun., 1978-81, Maine State Senate, 1982-94, 104th-106th Congress from 2nd dist., 1994—2002; Governor, 2003—. Mem. agr. com. Maine State Senate, transp. com., regional whip North East. Democrat. Office: Office of the Governor #1 State House Station Augusta ME 04333-0001 Office Phone: 207-287-3531. Office Fax: 207-287-6548, 207-287-1034. E-mail: governor@maine.gov.*

BALDAIA, PETER, curator; b. Sept. 12, 1953; BA, R.I. Coll., 1978; postgrad., Brown U., 1979; MA, Boston U., 1982. Curator Fuller Mus. Art, Brockton, Mass., 1986—91; curator exhibits and collections Rockford Art Mus., 1992—94; chief curator Huntsville (Ala.) Mus. Art, 1994—2004, dir. curatorial affairs, 2004—. Office: Huntsville Mus Art 300 Church St South Huntsville AL 35801 Home Phone: 256-534-4566; Office Phone: 256-535-4350 ext. 218. Business E-Mail: pbaldaia@hsvmuseum.org.

BALDASSANO, CORINNE LESLIE, radio executive; b. NYC, May 16, 1950; BA cum laude, Queens Coll., CUNY, 1970; MA in Theatre, Hunter Coll., CUNY, 1975; MBA in Fin., NYU, 1986. Various local and nat. radio programming positions, 1970—89; v.p. programming ABC Radio Networks, 1990-94, Unistar Radio Networks, LA, 1994, SW Networks, NYC, 1994-95, sr. v.p. programming, 1995—97; gen. mgr. radio divsn. AP, 1997-99; v.p. broadcast programming soundsbig.com, 1999—2000; v.p. Content LMiV, 2000; owner Translucent Media, 2001—05; sr. v.p. programming and mktg. Take on the Day LLC, 2005—. Vice chair L.A. Regional Alumni, Stern Sch. Bus., NYU, 2004—. Named one of 20 Most Influential Women in Radio, Radio Ink Mag., 1999. Mem.: NYU Bus. Forum (bd. dirs. 1988—91, v.p., treas. 1990—91). Avocations: travel, theater, dance, music, films.

BALDAUF, KENT EDWARD, lawyer; b. Pitts., Feb. 6, 1943; s. Walter William and Esther Baldauf; m. Kathleen Dian Abels, June 10, 1967; children: Kent Edward Jr., Krista K., Kara K. BS in Metall. Engring., Carnegie Mellon U., 1964; JD, Cleve. State U., 1970. Bar: Pa. 1970, U.S. Patent and Trademark Office 1971, U.S. Ct. Appeals (Fed. cir.) 1990, U.S. Supreme Ct. 1977. Shareholder, v.p., dir. Webb Law Firm, Pitts., 1988—. Mem. ABA, Pa. Bar Assn., Allegheny County Bar Assn., Am. Intellectual Property Law Assn. (pres. 1998-99), Pitts. Intellectual Property Law Assn., Valley Brook Country Club, Duquesne Club. Office: The Webb Law Firm 436 7th Ave Pittsburgh PA 15219-1845

BALDESSARI, JOHN ANTHONY, artist; b. National City, Calif., June 17, 1931; s. Anton and Hedvig B.; divorced; children: Annamarie, Antonio. BA, San Diego State U., 1953, MA, 1957; postgrad., Otis Art Inst., Chouinard Art Inst., LA, 1957-59. Asst. prof. U. Calif., San Diego, 1968-70; mem. faculty Calif. Inst. Arts, Valencia, 1970-85; prof. art U. Calif., LA. One-man shows include La Jolla Mus. Art, Calif., 1960, 66, Southwestern Coll., Chula Vista, Calif., 1962, 64, 75, Molly Barnes Gallery, Los Angeles, 1968, Richard Feigen Gallery, N.Y.C., 1970, Eugenia Butler Gallery, Los Angeles, 1970, Galerie Konrad Fischer, Dusseldorf, Fed. Republic Germany, 1971, 73, Art and Project, Amsterdam, The Netherlands, 1971, 72, Galerie MTL, Brussels, 1972, 75, Antwerp, Belgium, 1974, Galeria Franco Toselli, Milan, Italy, 1972, 74, Jack Wendler Gallery, London, 1972, 74, Sonnabend Gallery, N.Y.C., 1973, 75, 78, 79, 80, 81, 84, 86, 87, 90, 92, Galerie Sonnabend, Paris, 1973, 75, Inst. Modern Art, Brisbane, Australia, 1976, Inst. Contemporary Art, Sydney, Australia, 1976, Ohio State U., Columbus, 1976, Portland Ctr. for Visual Arts, Oreg., 1978, Whitney Mus. Am. Art., N.Y.C., 1978, Inst. Contemporary Art, Boston, 1978, Mcpl. Van Abbemuseum, Eindhoven, The Netherlands, 1980, 81, Mus. Folkwang, Essen, Fed. Republic Germany, 1981, Rudiger Schöttle Gallery, Munich, 1981, Albright-Knox Gallery, Buffalo, 1981, Contemporary Art Ctr., Cin., 1982, Contemporary Arts Mus., Houston, 1982, Samangallery, Genoa, Italy, 1975, 81, Margo Leavin Gallery, L.A., 1984, 86, 88-89, 92, Douglas Drake Gallery, Kansas City, Mo., 1983, Marianne Deson Gallery, Chgo., 1983, Swain Sch. Design, New Bedford, Mass., 1983, Contemporary Arts Mus., Houston, Anderson Gallery, Richmond, Va., 1982, Galerie Peter Pakesch, Vienna, 1984, 86, Galerie-Laage Salomon, Paris, 1984, 88, Univ. Art Mus. U. Calif., Berkeley, 1986, Santa Barbara (Calif.) Mus. Art, 1986, Multiples Inc., N.Y.C., 1986-87, Cen. Nat. D'Art Contemporain de Grenoble, 1987, Dart Gallery, Chgo., 1987, Lisson Gallery, London, 1988, Primo Piano, Rome, 1988, Palais des Beaux-Arts, Brussels,1988, Hanover, Kastner-Gesellschaft, 1989, Cirrus, L.A., 1989, Centro de Arte Regina Sofia, Madrid, 1989, Cape Musée d'Art Contemporain, Bordeaux, Instituto Valenciano de Arte Moderno, Centro Julio Gonzàlez, Valencia, Spain, Lawrence Oliver Gallery, Phila., 1989, Galerie Meert Rihoux, Brussels, 1989, 92, Mus. Contemporary Art, L.A., 1990, Galerie Crousel Robelin, BAMA, Paris, 1991, Galerie Weber, Alexander Y Cobo, Madrid, 1991, traveling to San Francisco Mus. Modern Art, Hirshorn Mus. and Sculpture Garden, Walker Art Ctr., Whitney Mus. Am. Ar, Musée d'art Contemporain de Montréal; various others; group shows include Richard Feigen Gallery, N.Y.C., 1968, U. Calif. San Diego Art Gallery, 1968, Dwan Gallery, N.Y.C., 1969, Eugenia Butler Gallery, Los Angeles, 1969, Hayward Gallery, London, 1969, 80, Jewish Mus., N.Y.C., 1970, Moore Coll. Art, Phila., 1970, Sonnabend Gallery, N.Y.C., 1972, 73, 74, 78, 80-81, 84, 86-87, 90, Contemporary Arts Mus., Houston, 1972, 78, San Francisco Art Inst., 1972, Galerie Sonnabend, Paris, 1973, Kennedy Ctr., Washington, 1974, Paula Cooper Gallery, N.Y.C., 1975, 81, 89, Los Angeles County Mus. Art, 1973, 74, 81, 87, Sch. Visual Arts, N.Y.C., 1977, Mus. Fine Arts, Houston, 1977, Inst. Contemporary Arts, Boston, 1978, High Mus. Art, Atlanta, 1980, Westkunst, Cologne, Fed. Republic Germany, 1981, 5th Internat. Biennale, Vienna, Austria, 1981, Stedelijk Mus., Amsterdam, The Netherlands, 1974, 81, Kestner-Gesellschaft, Hanover, Fed. Republic Germany, 1982, Albright-Knox Gallery, Buffalo, 1982, Multiples Inc., 1982, Donald Young Gallery, Chgo., 1990, Whitney Mus. Am. Art, N.Y., 1969, 72, 76, 77, 78, 79, 83, Marianne Deson Gallery, 1983, 87, Douglas Drake Gallery, N.Y.C., 1987, Mus. Modern Art, N.Y.C., 1970, 71, 72, 75, 77, Art Inst. Chgo., 1979, 85, Mus. Contemporary Art, Chgo., 1969, 77, 79, Mus. Contemporary Art, Los Angeles, 1986-88, Holly Solomon Gallery, N.Y.C., 1986-87, Hoffman Borman Gallery, Santa Monica, Calif., 1987, Mus. Modern Art, Toyama, Japan, 1987, Newport Harbor Art Mus., Newport Beach, 1969, 74, 87, 89, Barbara Krakow Gallery, 1987, Bank of Boston Art Gallery, 1987, Phoenix Art Mus., 1987, Los Angeles Mcpl. Art Gallery, 1987, Castello Di Rivoli, Torino, 1987, Bess Cutler Gallery, N.Y.C., 1987, Marian Goodman Gallery, N.Y.C., 1987, 88, 89, 90, LACE, Los Angeles, 1987, Museums Ludwig in den Rheinhallen der Kolner Messe, Cologne, Fed. Republic of Germany, 1989, Centre Georges Pompidou, Grande Halle-La Villette, Paris, 1989, Met. Mus. Art, N.Y.C., 1989, Mus. Modern Art, N.Y.C., 1989, various others; represented in permanent collections, Mus. Modern Art, N.Y.C., Stedelijk Mus., Amsterdam, Holland, Kunstmuseum, Basel, Switzerland, Australian Nat. Gallery, Mus. Contemporary Art, L.A. and Chgo., Whitney Mus. Am. Art, N.Y.C., Met. Mus. Art, N.Y.C., Houston Mus. Fine Art; contbr. articles to profl. jours., photographic reproductions to books; subject of numerous articles. Nat. Endowment for Arts grantee, 1973, 74, 75. Fellow: Am. Acad. Arts and Scis. Office: Sonnabend Gallery 536 W 22nd St New York NY 10011-1108 also: Margo Leavin Gallery 812 N Robertson Blvd Los Angeles CA 90069-4929 Office: U Calif Dept Art 1100 Kinross Ave Ste 245 PO Box 951615 Los Angeles CA 90095

BALDINO, FRANK, JR., biopharmaceutical executive; PhD, Temple U. Sr. rsch. biologist E.I. duPont de Nemours & Co., 1981—87; founder, pres., CEO Cephalon, Frazer, Pa., 1987—. Chmn. exec. council Harvard Div. Sleep Medicine; adj. prof. pharmacology Temple U. Med. Sch.; adj. prof. physiology and biophysics, adj. prof. neurology Hahnemann U. Hosp.; bd. dirs. ViroPharma, Inc., Pharmacopia Drug Discovery Inc., Biotechnology Industry Assn., Quaker Bioventures LP, Pa. Biotechnology Assn., Ea. Tech. Council, NicOx SA, PhRMA; mem. Healthcap adv. bd., Vantage Point Venture Partners adv. com. Author of over 100 articles in profl. jours. Trustee Temple Univ., Franklin Inst.; bd. dir. Greater Phila. C. of C. Office: Cephalon 41 Moores Rd Frazer PA 19355*

BALDOCK, BOBBY RAY, federal judge; b. Rocky, Okla., Jan. 24, 1936; Grad., N.Mex. Mil. Inst., 1956; JD, U. Ariz., 1960. Bar: Ariz. 1960, N.Mex. 1961, U.S. Dist. Ct. N.Mex. 1965. Ptnr. Sanders, Bruin & Baldock, Roswell, N.Mex., 1960—83; judge US Dist. Ct. N.Mex., Albuquerque, 1983—86, US Ct. Appeals (10th cir.), 1985—2001, sr. judge, 2001—. Adj. prof. Ea. N.Mex. U., 1962—81. Capt. adj. gen. staff, NG, 1960—70, N. Mex. Mem.: Chaves County Bar Assn., Ariz. Bar Assn., N.Mex. Bar Assn., Phi Alpha Delta. Office: US Ct Appeals PO Box 2388 Roswell NM 88202-2388*

BALDRIDGE, J. DOUGLAS, lawyer; b. 1962; BA magna cum laude, Fla. State U., 1984; JD cum laude, George Washington U., 1987. Bar: Fla., Supreme Ct. Fla., Va., Va. Supreme Ct., Md., Md. Ct. Appeals, DC, US Bankruptcy Ct., DC, US Bankruptcy Ct., Md., US Bankruptcy Ct. (ea. dist.) Va., US Ct. Appeals (1st, 3rd, 4th and 11th cirs.), US Ct. Appeals, DC, US Ct. Appeals, Fed. Cir., US Ct. Fed. Claims, US Dist. Ct., DC, US Dist. Ct., Colo., US Dist. Ct., Md., US Dist. Ct. (ea. dist.) Va., US Dist. Ct. (middle dist.) Fla., US Supreme Ct. Ptnr. Comml. Litig. Dept. Venable LLP, Washington, DC. Recipient Justice for All, Voting Rights Project Award, AAPD, 2004. Mem.: Mortar Bd., Phi Delta Phi, Omicron Delta Kappa, Phi Beta Kappa. Office: Vanable LLP 575 7th St NW Washington DC 20004 Office Phone: 202-344-4703. Office Fax: 202-344-8300. E-mail: jbaldridge@venable.com.

BALDRIGE, LETITIA, writer, management consultant; b. Miami Beach, Fla. d. Howard Malcolm and Regina (Connell) B.; m. Robert Hollensteiner; children: Clare, Malcolm. BA, Vassar Coll., 1946; postgrad., U. Geneva, 1946-48; DHL (hon.), Creighton U., 1979, Mt. St. Mary's Coll., 1980, Bryant Coll., 1987, Kenyon Coll., 1990. Personal-social sec. to amb. Am. Embassy, Paris, 1948-51; intelligence officer Washington, 1951-53; asst. to amb. Am. Embassy, Rome, 1953-56; dir. pub. rels. Tiffany & Co., 1956-60; social sec. The White House, 1961-63; pres. Letitia Baldrige Enterprises, Chgo., 1964-69; dir. consumer affairs Burlington Industries, 1969-71; pres. Letitia Baldrige Enterprises, Inc., Washington, 1972—. Author: Roman Candle, 1956, Tiffany Table Settings, 1958, Of Diamonds and Diplomats, 1968, Home, 1972, Juggling, 1976, Amy Vanderbilt's Complete Book of Etiquette, 1978, Amy Vanderbilt's Everyday Etiquette, 1979, The Entertainers, 1981, Letitia Baldrige's Complete Guide to Executive Manners, 1985, Letitia Baldrige's Complete Guide to a Great Social Life, 1987, Complete Guide to the New Manners for the '90s, 1990, New Complete Guide to Executive Manners, 1993, Public Affairs Private Relations, 1990, More Than Manners! Raising Today's Kids to Have Kind Manners and Good Hearts, 1997, In the Kennedy Style, 1998, Legendary Brides, 2000, A Lady, First, 2001, New Manners for New Times, 2003, Taste: Acquiring What Money Can't Buy, 2007. Mem. adv. bd. Woodrow Wilson House, Washington, Malcolm Baldrige Nat. Quality Awards, Woodrow Wilson Nat. Fellowship Found. Republican. Office Phone: 202-328-1626. Personal E-mail: lbaldrige@aol.com.

BALDUCCI, ALESSANDRO, nephrologist, educator; b. Mar. 23, 1951; MD, U. Rome, La Sapienza, 1975. With Des Hopitaux de Paris, 1973—82; chief nephrology San Giovanni Hosp., Rome, 1982—. Prof. U. Rome, 1997—. Mem.: Coun. Italian Nephrology, Italian Soc. Nephrology, Am. Soc. Nephrology, Internat. Soc. Nephrology (past pres. ctrl. Italian sect. 2002—06), European Renal Assn. Office: Uo Nefrologia e Dialisi Azienda Ospedaliera S Giovanni A Via Dell'amba Aradam 9 00184 Rome Italy

BALDVINS, LYNN ANN, medical/surgical nurse, army officer; b. Keene, NH, Sept. 24, 1954; d. Jon Otto and Nancy Edith (Low) B. BSN, U. N.H., 1976; MSN, U. Tex., El Paso, 1985. Commd. officer AUS, 1976, advanced through grades to lt. col., 1992; chief nursing edn. and staff devel. svc. Evans Army Community Hosp., Ft. Carson, Colo., Germany; clin. mgr. neurosurgery staff devel. Evans U.S. Army Community Hosp., Ft. Carson, Colo., 1989—92; retired AUS, 1997; mgr. infection prevention Meml. Hosp., Colorado Springs, Colo., 1997—. Decorated Meritorious Svc. medal. Mem. ANA, Assn. Practitioners in Infection Control and Epidemiology, Sigma Theta Tau. Home: 7550 Colby Ct Colorado Springs CO 80919-3927 Office: Meml Hosp 1400 E Boulder St Colorado Springs CO 80909-5599

BALDWIN, ALEC (ALEXANDER RAE BALDWIN III), actor; b. Massapequa, NY, Apr. 3, 1958; s. Alexander Rae Jr. and Carol (Martineau) B.; m. Kim Basinger, August 19, 1993 (div. Feb. 2002), 1 child, Ireland Eliesse. Attended, George Washington U., 1976—79; BFA in Drama, NYU, 1993; LittD (hon.), Montclair State U., 2004. Actor: (films) Forever Lulu, 1987, She's Having a Baby, 1987, Beetlejuice, 1988, Married to the Mob, 1988, Talk Radio, 1988, Working Girl, 1988, Great Balls of Fire!, 1989 The Hunt for Red October, 1990, Miami Blues, 1990, Alice, 1990, The Marrying Man, 1991, Prelude to a Kiss, 1992, Glengarry Glen Ross, 1992, Malice, 1993, The Getaway, 1994, The Shadow, 1994, Looking For Richard, 1996, (voice only) Two Bits, 1995, The Juror, 1996, Ghosts of Mississippi, 1996, Bookworm, 1997, The Edge, 1997, Thick as Thieves, 1998, Mercury Rising, 1998, Notting Hill, 1999, Scout's Honor, 1999, Outside Providence, 1999, Thomas and the Magic Railroad, 2000, Pearl Harbor, 2001, (voice only) Cats & Dogs, 2001, (voice only) Final Fantasy: The Spirits Within, 2001, (narrator) The Royal Tenenbaums, 2001, The Adventures of Pluto Nash, 2002, The Cooler, 2003 (Acad. Award nomination for Best Supporting Actor, 2004, Golden Globe nomination for Best Supporting Actor, 2004, Screen Actors Guild Award nomination for Best Supportinga Actor, 2004), The Cat in the Hat, 2003, Along Came Polly, 2004, The Last Shot, 2004, (voice only) The Spongebob Squarepants Movie, 2004, The Aviator, 2004, Elizabethtown, 2005, Fun with Dick and Jane, 2005, Mini's First Time, 2006, The Departed, 2006, Running with Scissors, 2006, Brooklyn Rules, 2006, The Good Shepherd, 2006; actor, prodr. (films) Heaven's Prisoners, 1996, The Confession, 1999, State and Main, 2000, The Devil and Daniel Webster, 2001; actor (TV movies) Sweet Revenge, 1984, Love on The Run, 1985, Dress Gray, 1986, The Alamo: 13 Days to Glory, 1986, A Streetcar Named Desire, 1995, Path to War, 2002, Second Nature, 2003, Dreams & Giants, 2003; actor, prodr. (TV movies) Nuremberg, 2000; actor (TV series) The Doctors, 1980-82, Cutter to Houston, 1982, Knot's Landing, 1984-85, (narrator) Thomas the Tank Engine & Friends, 1998-2003, 30 Rock, 2006- (Best Performance by an Actor in a TV Series-Musical or Comedy, Golden Globe award, Hollywood Fgn. Press Assn., 2007, Outstanding Performance by a Male Actor in a Comedy Series, SAG, 2007); (TV appearances) Hotel, 1985, Clerks, 2000-01, Friends, 2002, Nip/Tuck, 2004, Las Vegas, 2004, (voice only) The Simpsons, 2004, Will & Grace, 2005; (Broadway appearances) Loot (Theatre world award 1986), 1986, Serious Money, 1988, Prelude to a Kiss (Obie Award), 1990, A Streetcar Named Desire, 1992, Macbeth, 1998, Twentieth Century, 2004, South Pacific, 2005 Recipient Theater World award Theater World Pubs., 1986, Linda McCartney Meml. Award, People for the Ethical Treatment of Animals, 2005; named Outstanding New Talent on Broadway. Mem. SAG, AFTRA, Actors Equity Assn. Democrat. Roman Catholic. Achievements include hosting Saturday Night Live 13 times. Office: Creative Artists Agy c/o Ron Meyer 9830 Wilshire Blvd Beverly Hills CA 90212-1825*

BALDWIN, ALLEN ADAIL, retired lawyer, writer; b. St. Augustine, Fla., July 15, 1939; s. Larrie Paul and Bertha Mae (Capallia) B. BA, Brigham Young U., 1969; JD, So. U., Baton Rouge, 1975. Bar: Fla. 1975. Tchr. Putnam County Sch. Bd., Palatka, Fla., 1969-71; pvt. practice Palatka, 1975—2006; ret. Author: Tricks to Make the Angels Weep, 1986, Call It Not Heaven, 1991, Redeem Us From Virtue, 1992. Mem. Lds Ch. Avocations: reading, swimming, hiking. Office: 308 St Johns Ave Palatka FL 32177-4723 Office Phone: 386-325-7549.

BALDWIN, BRUCE GREGG, botany educator, researcher; b. San Luis Obispo, Calif., Oct. 24, 1957; s. Robert Lee and Sally Louise (Elrod) B. BA in Biol. Scis. with honors, U. Calif., Santa Barbara, 1981; MS in Botany, U. Calif., Davis, 1985, PhD in Botany, 1989. NSF postdoctoral fellow U. Ariz., Tucson, 1990-92; asst. prof. dept. botany Duke U., 1992-94; curator Jepson Herbarium U. Calif., Berkeley, 1994—, asst. prof. in residence dept. integrative biology, 1994-98, assoc. prof. in residence dept. integrative biology, 1998-2000, assoc. prof. dept. integrative biology, 2000—05, prof. dept. integrative biology, 2005—. Mellon vis. scholar Rancho Santa Ana Bot. Garden, 1994. Contbr. articles to profl. jours. and books, reviewer; chief editor Jepson Flora project, 1994—. Recipient NSF Nat. Young Investigator award, 1994; Calif. Acad. Scis. fellow, 1999—, McBryde fellow, Nat. Tropical Botanical Garden, 2007. Mem. Am. Soc. Plant Taxonomists (publicity com. 1993-96, coun. 2002-05), Calif. Bot. Soc. (pres. 2000-03), Soc. Systematic Biology (coun. 2004-). Achievements include research in plant systematics, phylogenetics, plant cytogenetics and chromosome evolution, plant speciation, California floristics, phytogeography, insular evolution. Home: 2408 Parker St Berkeley CA 94704-2812 Office: U Calif Berkeley Jepson Herbarium Dept Integrative Biology 1001 Valley Life Scis Bldg 2465 Berkeley CA 94720-2465 E-mail: bbaldwin@berkeley.edu.

BALDWIN, CALVIN BENHAM, JR., retired science administrator; b. Radford, Va., Dec. 22, 1925; s. Calvin Benham and Louise (Delp) B.; m. Elizabeth Buell, Mar. 10, 1951; children: Susan B., Sally C., Ann H. AB, U. N.C., 1949, postgrad., 1949—51; MPA, Harvard U., 1961. Rsch. asst. Inst. Rsch. Social Scis., Chapel Hill, NC, 1949-50; methods examiner NIH, Bethesda, Md., 1953-55, budget examiner, 1955-57, adminstrv. officer, 1957-58, adminstrv. officer divsn. gen. med. sci., 1958-61; exec. officer Divsn. Gen. Med. Scis., Bethesda, 1961-62, Nat. Inst. Child Health, Bethesda, 1963-70, Nat. Cancer Inst., Bethesda, 1970-80; assoc. dir. adminstrn. NIH, Bethesda, 1980-86. Mem. Montgomery County Econ. Coun., Rockville, Md., 1982—85, Bethany Beach (Del.) Town Coun., 1991—92, 1994—96; pres. Bethany Beach Landowners Assn., 1998—2002; mem. Bethany Beach Planning Commn., 1998—2004. Recipient W.A. Jump Meritorious award HEW, 1960, Superior Svc. award HEW, 1973 Mem. NIH Alumni Assn. (pres. 1995-97), Phi Beta Kappa. Democrat. Unitarian Universalist. Home: 10705 Weymouth St Garrett Park MD 20896-0017 Personal E-mail: cbbaldwin@aol.com.

BALDWIN, CARLITA ROSE, minister; d. Carl Lamont and Alexinia Young Baldwin. AA, Russell Sage Coll., Troy, NY, 1980; BA, U. Albany, Albany, NY, 1989; MDiv., Howard U., Washington, DC, 2002. Itinerant Elder AME Ch. - Wash. Ann. Conf., 2002. Russian linguist and strategic debriefer USAF, Washington, 1980—2000; educator - mid. sch. (lang. arts) Anne Arundel County Pub. Sch., Millersville, Md., 2001—03; doctoral student U. Conn., Storrs, Conn., 2003—. Assoc. min./youth min. AME Ch., Md., 1997—2005. Tech. sgt. USAF, 1980—2000, various locations. Decorated Joint Svc. Commendation Medals Def. Intelligence Agy. and Nat. Security Agy., Joint Svc. Commendation Medal, Joint Svc. Achievement Medals US Air Force and Nat. Security Agy.; recipient Nat. Dean's Honor List, 2000, Disting. Honor Grad. and Outstanding Speech Award, USAF - NCO Leadership Sch., 1989; scholar Trustee Honor Scholarship, Howard U., 1998 - 2000; Multicultural Honors Fellowship, U. Conn., 2003 - present, Grad. Assistantship, 2003 - present. Mem.: World Coun. for Gifted and Talented (assoc.), Nat. Assn. for Gifted Children (assoc.), Human Resources Mgmt. Assn. (assoc.), Altrusa Internat., Inc. (life), Women in Mil. Svc. (life), DAV (life), Am. Legion (life), Pi Lambda Theta Internat. Honor Soc. and PA in Edn. (life), Delta Sigma Theta Sorority, Inc. (life). Democrat-Npl. African Meth. Episcopal. Avocations: water sports, reading, puzzles. Office: Univ Conn 2131 Hillside Rd Unit 3007 Storrs Mansfield CT 06269-3007 Home Phone: 860-423-4448; Office Phone: 860-486-1790. Office Fax: 860-486-2900. Business E-Mail: carlita.baldwin@uconn.edu.

BALDWIN, CYNTHIA ACKRON, state supreme court justice; b. McKeesport, Pa., Feb. 8, 1945; d. James A. and Iona (Meriweather) Ackron; m. Arthur L. Baldwin, June 17, 1967; children: James Ackron, Crystal A. BA, Pa. State U., 1966, MA, 1974; JD, Duquesne U., 1980; LLD (hon.), Point Park Coll., 1999, Widener U., 2007; HHD (hon.), Carlow U.,

2007. Bar: Pa. 1980, U.S. Dist. Ct. (we. dist.) Pa. 1980, U.S. Ct. Appeals (3d cir.) 1980, U.S. Supreme Ct. 1984. Dep. atty. gen. Office of Atty. Gen. State of Pa., Pitts., 1981-83, atty.-in-charge Western Pa. region, consumer protection div., 1983-86; vis. prof. law Duquesne U., Pitts., 1986-87; assoc. Palkovitz and Palkovitz, McKeesport, Pa., 1988-89; judge family div. Allegheny County Ct. Common Pleas, Pitts., 1989—92, judge civil divsn., 1992—2005; justice Pa. State Supreme Ct., 2005—. Vis. prof. Duquesne U., 1986-87, adj. prof., 1989—; sec., exec. bd. Neighborhood Legal Svc. Assn., Pitts., 1987-89. Bd. dirs. Greater Pitts. YWCA, 1988-89, United Way, Pitts., 1988-95; gubernatorial appointee adv. bd. Mon Valley Ednl. Consortium, 1985—; bd. trustees Pa. State U., 1995-, chair, 2004-07. Recipient Role Model award Chatham Coll., 1982; Reginald Heber Smith fellow Neighborhood Legal Svcs. Assn., 1980-81; recipient leadership award in the professions Greater Pitts. YWCA, 1987, Outstanding Achievement award Duquesne Law Sch., 1996; named Disting. Dau. of Pa., 1996; Fulbright Scholarship lectr., 1994. Mem. ACBA (mem. Pa. commn. on crime and delinquency), Internat. Womens Forum, Allegheny County Bar Assn., Nat. Bar Assn., Homer S. Brown Lawyers Assn. (v.p. 1987-88, bd. govs.), Pa. Bar Assn. (bd. govs. 1997—), Assn. Governing Bds. of Colls. and Univs. (vice chair 2007—), Pa. State U. Alumni Assn. (pres. 1989-91, immediate past pres. 1991-93). Democrat. Avocations: writing, pub. speaking. Office: Pa State Supreme Ct 486 City Hall Philadelphia PA 19107

BALDWIN, CYNTHIA ANN, industrial hygienist; d. Arthur Roy Baldwin and Dolores Mae Hill. BS in Biology, Met. State Coll., Denver, 1973; MS in Environ. Health, Colo. State U., 1981. Cert. in comprehensive practice indsl. hygiene Am. Bd. Indsl. Hygiene, 1988. Clk. typist admissions and records Colo. State U., Ft. Collins, 1974-75, student coordinator, office supr. dept. microbiology, 1975-80, grad. research asst. dept. microbiology, 1980-81; indsl. hygienist Consultation div. Iowa Bur. Labor, Des Moines, 1981-84; dir. occupl. health Amana Refrigeration, Inc., Iowa, 1984—93, mgr. environ. health and safety Iowa, 1993—95; sr. project mgr. Beling Cons., Moline, Ill., 1995-97; sr. indsl. hygienist Pointer Environ. Inc., Cedar Rapids, Iowa, 1997—2002; sr. indsl. hygienist Terracon, Cedar Rapids, 2002—. Mem. adv. coun. U. Iowa Inst. Agrl. Medicine and Occupl. Health, Iowa City, 1986—90. Mem.: Am. Soc. Safety Engrs., Am. Indsl. Hygiene Assn. (diplomate, pres. Iowa-Ill. sect. 1987—88, pres.-elect 2006—). Avocations: beading, needlecrafts. Office: Terracon Cons Inc 5855 Willow Creek Dr SW Cedar Rapids IA 52404-4312

BALDWIN, DAVID SHEPARD, physician; b. Rochester, NY, Sept. 5, 1921; s. Jacob and Anna B.; m. Halee Morris, June 24, 1945; children: Neil, Andrew, Daniel, James. BA, U. Rochester, 1943, MD, 1945. Intern Barnes Hosp., St. Louis, 1945-46; resident in medicine Bellevue Hosp., NYC, 1946-48; renal fellow in medicine and physiology NYU Sch. Medicine, 1948-50, mem. faculty, 1950—, prof. medicine, nephrology, 1972—2004, prof. emeritus, 2004—. Attending physician Bellevue Hosp.; hon. attending physician NYU Hosp.; mem. coun. high blood pressure rsch. AHA. Author papers in med. jours., chpts. in books. Served as officer M.C. AUS, 1953-55. Mem. AHA, Harvey Soc., Am. Soc. Nephrology, Am. Soc. Clin. Investigation, Internat. Soc. Nephrology, N.Y. Soc. Nephrology (pres. 1974-75), N.Y. Heart Assn. Home: 333 E 69th St New York NY 10021-5560 Office: NYU Sch Medicine 550 1st Ave OBV CD679 New York NY 10016-6402 Office Phone: 212-263-5635. Business E-Mail: david.baldwin@med.nyu.edu.

BALDWIN, DEBORAH, editor; b. Washington, Nov. 1, 1949; d. William H. and Eleanor Mead (Griesemer) B.; m. Irwin B. Arieff, July 27, 1974; 1 child, Alexis B. BA, U. Pa., 1970; MA, U. Oreg., 1973. Editor Environ. Action, Washington, 1974-80; mng. editor Nat. Consumer Coop. Bank, Washington, 1980-82; contbg. editor Common Cause mag., Washington, 1982-83, assoc. editor, 1984-85, sr. editor, 1985-87, editor, v.p. for publs., 1987—94; columnist Washington Post, Paris, 1994—2000; House & Home sect. editor, columnist NY Times, 2000—. Editorial cons. Nat. Consumers League, 1982, FTC, 1981-83. Contbr. articles to mags. Trustee Nat. Urban League, 1979-82. Avocations: cooking, gardening, reading, walking. Office: NY Times 229 W 43rd St New York NY 10036 Office Phone: 212-556-7611. Office Fax: 212-556-5999. E-mail: Baldwin@nytimes.com.

BALDWIN, DEWITT CLAIR, JR., pediatrician, educator; b. Bangor, Maine, July 19, 1922; s. DeWitt Clair and Edna Frances (Aikin) B.; m. Michele Albre, Dec. 27, 1957; children: Lisa Anne, Mireille Diane. BA, Swarthmore Coll., 1943; postgrad. Div. Sch., Yale U., 1943-45, MD, 1949; ScD (hon.), Northeastern Ohio U. Coll. Medicine, 2003. Diplomate Am. Bd. Med. Examiners, Am. Bd. Pediatrics, Am. Bd. Family Practice. Intern, then resident in pediatrics U. Minn. Hosps., Mpls., 1949-51; rsch. fellow Yale Child Study Ctr., New Haven, 1951-52; instr., asst. prof. pediatrics U. Washington Sch. Medicine, Seattle, 1952-57; resident in psychiatry Met. State Hosp., Waltham, Mass., 1957-58; chief resident in psychiatry Mass. Meml. Hosps., Boston, 1958-59; fellow in child psychiatry Boston City Hosp., 1959-61; asst. prof. pediatrics Harvard Med. Sch., Boston, 1961-67; prof., chmn. behavioral scis. and community health U. Conn. Health Ctr., Farmington, 1967-71; prof. chmn. behavioral scis. U. Nev. Sch. Medicine, Reno, 1971-73, dir. health scis. program, 1971-81, prof. psychiatry and behavioral scis., 1971-83, asst. dean rural health, 1977-83, prof. emeritus psychiatry and behavioral scis., 1983—; pres. Earlham Coll. and Earlham Sch. Religion, Richmond, Ind., 1983-84, Connor Prairie Pioneer Settlement Mus., Noblesville, Ind., 1983-84; dir. office edn. rsch. AMA, Chgo., 1985-88, dir. divsn. med. edn., rsch., info., 1988-91, scholar-in-residence, 1991—2002, sr. assoc. Inst. Ethics, 1991—2002, scholar-in-residence Accreditation Coun. for Grad. Med. Edn., 2002—; adj. prof. psychiatry and behavioral scis. Northwestern U. Med. Sch., Chgo., 1986—; adj. prof. med. edn. U. Ill. Coll. Medicine, Chgo., 1988-93; pres. Med. Edn. and Rsch. Assocs., Inc., Chgo., 1992—. Trustee Friends World Coll., Huntington, N.Y., 1980-83; bd. dirs. Nat. League Nursing, N.Y.C., 1981-83, Gt. Lakes Colls. Assn., 1983-84, Am. Rural Health Assn., 1985-87; mem. Nat. Bd. Med. Examiners, 1979-88, Nat. Adv. Coun. Nursing Tng., 1978-82; mem. coun. acad. socs. AAMC, Washington, 1987-94. Author: (with others) Behavioral Sciences and Medical Education, 1983, other books; author, editor: (with others) Interdisciplinary Health Care Teams in Teaching and Practice, 1981, Interdisciplinary Health Team Training, 1978; contbr. over 200 articles to scholarly publs. Recipient Rsch. Career Devel. award USPHS, 1961-67, Louis Gorin award in rural health, 1991, John P. McGovern award Health Scis., 1997; Commonwealth Fund fellow, 1951-52, Milbank Fund fellow, 1968, Rural Health fellow WHO, 1976. Mem. Assn. Behavioral Scis. and Med. Edn. (pres. 1978-79, 90-91), Nev. Bd. Oriental Medicine (pres. 1976-83). Democrat. Mem. Soc. Of Friends. Home: 1550 N Lake Shore Dr Chicago IL 60610 Office: Ste 2000 515 State St Chicago IL 60610 Business E-Mail: dbaldwin@acgme.org.

BALDWIN, DONOVAN A., marketing professional, writer; b. Atlanta, Mar. 8, 1945; s. Donovan Appleton and Kate Baldwin; m. Kathleen Mae Doré (div.); children: Jeffrey William Doré, Colleen Gabrielle Doré, Jessica Noel; m. Donna Jean Winters, Feb. 27, 1994; children: Ruth Winters, Sarah Winters. BA in Acctg., U. W. Fla., Pensacola, 1973. Optician Vision Ctrs., Copperas Cove, Tex., 1985—87, optician, lab mgr. Austin, 1992—98; fed. purchasing agt. US Purchasing & Fin. Office, Camp Mabry, Tex., 1987—90; retail mgr. Radio Shack, Temple, Tex., 1990—92; driver Schnider Nat. Carriers, Dallas, 2000—05, instr., 2000—05; pvt. practice Dallas, 2005—. Contbr. articles to profl. jours. Staff sgt. US Army, 1966—95. Mem.: Mensa, Am. Fgn. Legion. Avocations: poetry, travel.

BALDWIN, EDWIN STEEDMAN, lawyer; b. St. Louis, May 5, 1932; s. Richard and Almira (Steedman) B.; m. Margaret Kirkham, July 1, 1958; children: Margaret B. Dozler, Edwin S. Jr., Harold K. AB, Princeton U., 1954; LLM, Harvard U., 1957. Bar: Mo. 1957, U.S. Dist. Ct. (ea. dist.) Mo. 1957. Assoc. Teasdale, Kramer & Vaughan, St. Louis, 1957-64; ptnr. Armstrong Teasdale, LLP, St. Louis, 1965-97, of counsel, 1998—. Fellow Am. Coll. Trust and Estate Counsel, St. Louis Country Club, Noonday Club. Republican. Episcopalian. Avocations: golf, hunting, sailing. Office: Armstrong Teasdale LLP 1 Metropolitan Sq Ste 2600 Saint Louis MO 63102-2740 Office Phone: 314-342-8055. Business E-Mail: tbaldwin@armstrongteasdale.com.

BALDWIN, GEORGE CURRIDEN, physicist, researcher; b. Denver, May 5, 1917; s. Harry Lewis and Elizabeth (Watson) B.; m. Winifred M. Gould, Apr. 27, 1952; children: George T., John E., Celia M. BA, Kalamazoo Coll., 1939; MA, U. Ill., 1941, PhD, 1943. Instr. physics U. Ill., Urbana, 1943-44; rsch. assoc. GE, Schenectady, NY, 1944-55, nuclear engr. Cin., 1955-57; reactor mgr. Argonne Nat. Lab., Ill., 1957-58; physicist Gen. Engring. Lab. GE, Schenectady, 1958-67; adj. prof. nuclear engring. and sci. Rensselaer Poly. Inst., Troy, NY, 1964-67, prof., 1967-77, prof. emeritus, 1977—; staff mem. Los Alamos Nat. Lab., N.Mex., 1975-87; vis. scientist, 1987-99; ret., 1987. Author: An Introduction to Nonlinear Optics, 1969, The Science Was Fun, 2006; contbr. articles on nuclear and radiation physics to sci. publs. Councilman, Niskayuna, NY, 1965-69; mem. Zoning Bd., 1969-77. Recipient Disting. Alumnus award Kalamazoo Coll., 1987. Fellow Am. Phys. Soc.; mem. AAAS, Phi Beta Kappa, Sigma Xi, Phi Kappa Phi, Gamma Alpha. Achievements include discovery of nuclear giant dipole resonance; research on gamma-ray lasers; discovery of 1776 Escalante inscription. E-mail: geoc142857@msn.net.

BALDWIN, GEORGE KOEHLER, retired retail executive; b. Cedar Rapids, Iowa, Nov. 17, 1919; s. Nathan and Ada Lillian (Koehler) B. BBA, State U. Iowa, 1942. From office mgr. to mgr. Wapsie Valley Creamery, Cedar Rapids, Iowa, 1946-60; treas., head payroll, accounts payable, sales audit dept. Armstrong's Inc., Cedar Rapids, 1960-87; also bd. dirs., treas. Armstrong's of Dubuque, Iowa, 1982-87; ret., 1987. Mem. adv. coun. Firstar Club, Firstar Bank, Cedar Rapids; theatre organist, 1961—. Composed and copyrighted for band Kinnick Stadium band march, 1992. Mem. Cedar Rapids Performing Arts Commn.; bd. dirs., pres. Cedar Rapids Cmty. Concert Assn., 1993—; pres. State U. of Iowa Concert Band, 1941-42; sec., treas., asst. conductor El Kahir Shrine Band of Cedar Rapids; bd. dirs. Cedar Rapids Stamp Club, 1997-00; chmn. adminstrv. bd. Trinity United Meth. Ch., 1987-92, head usher and staff parish rels. com. chmn.; apptd. by mayor to Cedar Rapids Mcpl. Band Commn., 1994, vice chmn. 1998—; organist Paramount and Iowa theaters, Cedar Rapids, 1961-. With U.S. Army, 1942-46, ETO. Decorated Bronze Star medal, Knight comdr. Ct. Honor Ancient and Accepted Scottish Rite Bodies Masonry, 2005; named hon. Ky. Col.; George K. Baldwin day proclamation in his honor, Mayor of Cedar Rapids, Apr. 16, 1987. Mem. VFW, Cedar Rapids Consumer Credit Assn. (pres. 1968-69), Am. Theatre Organ Soc. (bd. dirs., treas. Cedar Rapids chpt. 1979-2006), Am. Legion, Rotary, Masons, Shriners (past pres. uniformed units), Rotary Svc. Club (chmn. fellowship com., sgt. of arms), State U. Iowa Pres.'s Club and Alumni Assn. Methodist. Home: 1017 F Ave NW Cedar Rapids IA 52405-2724 Personal E-mail: baldwingeo@aol.com.

BALDWIN, HAROLD SCOTT, pediatrician, educator; b. Honolulu, Dec. 22, 1954; MD, U. Va. Sch. Medicine, 1981. Diplomate Am. Bd. Pediat. Intern U. Rochester/Strong Meml. Hosp., NY, 1982—86, resident in pediat. NY; assoc. prof. Children's Hosp., Phila.; fellow in pediatric cardiology U. Iowa Coll. Med., Iowa City, 1986—90; prof. pediatrics, cell and devel. biology, prof. pediat. Vanderbilt U. Med. Ctr., Nashville; vice chmn. lab. scis. pediat., chief divsn. pediatric cardiology Vanderbilt Children's Hosp., Nashville. Recipient Established Investigator award, Am. Heart Assn., 1995. Office: Vanderbilt U Med Ctr 2204 Childrens Way Ste 5230 Nashville TN 37232 Office Phone: 615-322-7447. Business E-Mail: scott.baldwin@vanderbilt.edu.

BALDWIN, HENRY FURLONG, banker; b. Balt., Jan. 15, 1932; s. Henry du Pont and Margaret (Taylor) B.; div.; children: Mary Stevenson, Severn Eyre. AB, Princeton U., 1954. With Merc.-Safe Deposit & Trust Co., Balt., 1956—2001; pres. Merc. Bankshares Corp. and Merc.-Safe Deposit & Trust Co., Balt., 1970-76, chmn., CEO, 1976-2001; chmn. Merc. Bankshares Corp., Balt., 2001—03. Bd. dirs. W.R. Grace & Co., Wills Group, Inc.; dir. Platinum Underwriters Holdings, Alleghany Energy, NASDAQ Stock Market, Inc., 2000-, chmn. bd., 2003-. Trustee Johns Hopkins Medicine, 1989-94; trustee emeritus Johns Hopkins U., Marine Corps Heritage Found., Va. Hist. Soc. With USMC, 1954-56. Office: 2 Village Sq Ste 258 Baltimore MD 21210 Home Phone: 410-889-7545; Office Phone: 410-237-5251. E-mail: hfbaldwin@merctrust.com.

BALDWIN, JEFFREY KENTON, lawyer, educator; b. Palestine, Ill., Aug. 8, 1954; s. Howard Keith and Annabelle Lee (Kirts) B.; m. Patricia Ann Mathews, Aug. 23, 1975; children: Matthew, Katy, Timothy, Philip R. BS summa cum laude, Ball State U., 1976; JD cum laude, Ind. U., 1979. Bar: Ind. 1979, U.S. Dist. Ct. (so. dist.) Ind. 1979, U.S. Ct. Appeals (7th cir.) 1979, U.S. Dist. Ct. (no. dist.) Ind. 1984. Majority leader's staff Ind. Senate, Indpls., 1976; instr. Beer Sch. Real Estate, Indpls., 1977-78, Am. Inst. Paralegal Studies, Indpls., 1987—; dep. Office Atty. Gen., Indpls., 1979-81; mng. ptnr. Baldwin & Baldwin, Danville, Ind., 1979—. Agt. Nat. Attys. Title Assurance Fund, Vevay, Ind., 1983—; officer, bd. dirs. Baldwin Realty, Inc., Danville; conf. participant White House Conf. on Small Bus. (Ind. meeting 1994), congl. appointee, 1995; bd. dirs. Small Bus. Coun. Bd. dirs. Hendricks Civic Theatre, Inc.; organizer, Hendricks County Young Republicans, 1972; sec. Hendricks County Rep. Com., 1978-84; bd. dirs. Hendricks County Assn. for Retarded Citizens, Danville, 1982-86; cons. Hendricks County Right for Life, Brownsburg, Ind., 1984—; mem. philanthropy adv. com. Ball State U., Muncie, Ind., 1987—; judge Hendricks County unit Am. Cancer Soc., 1987; coordinator region 2 Young Leaders for Mutz, Indpls., 1987-88; cubmaster WaPaPh dist. Boy Scouts Am., 1988, S.M.E. chmn., 1988-89; steering com. Ind. Lawyers Bush/Quayle; founder, chmn. Christians for Positive Reform; candidate for Congress 7th Congl. Dist. of Ind.; del. to Annual Conf. South Ind. Conf. of United Meth. Ch., 1993, 95-98, 2000; host com. Midwest Rep. Leadership Conf., 1997; dist. coord. Hoosier Famiies for John Price for U.S. Senate; advisor John Price for Gov., 1999-2000; v.p. Danville Little League Baseball, 1998—. Recipient Presdl. award of honor Danville Jaycees, 1980; named hon. sec. State Ind., 1980. Mem. ABA, Ind. Bar Assn., Hendricks County Bar Assn., Indpls. Bar Assn., Internat. Platform Assn., Nat. Assn. Realtors, Ind. Assn. Realtors, Met. Indpls. Bd. Realtors (Hendricks County div.), Federalist Soc., Ind. Farm Bur., Nat. Fedn. Ind. Bus., Ind. C. of C., Danville C. of C. (sec. 1986), Moot Ct. Soc., Blue Key, Phi Soc. Methodist. Home: PO Box 63 Danville IN 46122-0063 Personal E-mail: jbbfc@aol.com.

BALDWIN, JOHN, legal association administrator, lawyer; b. Salt Lake City, Feb. 9, 1954; BA, U. Utah., 1977, JD, 1980. Bar: Utah 1980, U.S. Dist. Ct. Utah 1980, U.S. Ct. Appeals (10th cir.) 1984. Assoc. Jardine, Linebaugh, Brown & Dunn, Salt Lake City, 1980-82; asst. atty. gen. Utah Atty. Gen.'s Office, Salt Lake City, 1982-85; dir. Utah Divsn. Securities, Salt Lake City, 1985-90; exec. dir. Utah State Bar, Salt Lake City, 1990—. Adj. assoc. prof. mgmt. Eccles Sch. Bus., U. Utah. Mem. N.Am. Securities Adminstrs. Assn. (bd. dirs. 1987-90, pres. 1988-89), U. Utah Young Alumni Assn. (bd. dirs. 1987-90), U. Utah Beehive Honor Soc. (bd. dirs. 1993-97), U. Utah Alumni Assn. (bd. dirs. 1995-97). Office: Utah State Bar 645 S 200 E # 310 Salt Lake City UT 84111-3837 Office Phone: 801-531-9077. Business E-Mail: jbaldwin@utahbar.org.

BALDWIN, JOHN CHARLES, surgeon, researcher; b. Ft. Worth; BA summa cum laude, Harvard U., 1971; MD, Stanford U., 1975; MA Privatim (hon.), Yale U., 1989. Diplomate Am. Bd. Internal Medicine, Am. Bd. Surgery, Am. Bd. Thoracic Surgery. Fellow in medicine Harvard Med. Sch., Boston, 1975-77; fellow in surgery, resident in surgery Mass. Gen. Hosp., 1977-81; resident in cardiothoracic surgery Stanford (Calif.) U., 1981-82, chief resident cardiothoracic surgery, 1983, asst. prof., 1984-87; dir. heart-lung transplantation transplant rsch. lab. Stanford U., 1986-87; prof. surgery and chief cardiothoracic surgery Yale U., New Haven, 1988-94; cardiothoracic-surgeon-in chief Yale-New Haven Hosp.; DeBakey/Bard prof., chmn. Baylor Coll. Medicine, Houston, 1994-98; sr. attending physician, chief surg. svcs. Meth. Hosp., Houston, 1994-98; sr. attending physician, surgeon in chief Ben Taub Gen. Hosp., Houston, 1994; dean med. sch., v.p. health affairs Dartmouth Coll., 1998—2004; pres., CEO CBR Inst. Biomed. Rsch., Boston, 2005—. Bd. dirs. United Network Organ Sharing, 1984-87; mem. clin. rsch. com. ad hoc rsch. grant rev. Cystic Fibrosis Found.; trustee New Eng. Organ Bank, 1988; mem. solid organ transplant com. Blue Cross & Blue Shield of Conn., 1990-94; mem. sci. adv. bd. Alexion Pharms., Inc., 1991-94; bd. dirs. Baylor Coll. Medicine Healthcare, Inc.; mem. adv. bd. Donate Life Found.; mem. exec. faculty Baylor Coll. of Medicine, pres.'s coun.; bd. dirs. New England chpt. Transplant Recipients Internat. Orgn., 1992-94. Co-editor: Thoracic Surgery, Oxford Textbook of Surgery, 1989—; assoc. editor Jour. Applied Cardiology, 1985-92; editorial bd. Jour. Thoracic and Cardiovascular Surgery, 1990-97, Transplantation, 1990—, Transplantation Sci., 1992-95, Andromeda Interactive Ltd., The Cardiovasc. System Interactive Teaching Program, 1993—; contbr. numerous articles and book chpts. in field. Mem. Harvard Club Schs. Com., Harvard Coll. Fund, Harvard U. Undergrad. Admissions Interview Com.; fellow Timothy Dwight Coll. Yale U., Yale U. Art Gallery Assocs.; mem. appointments and promotions com. Sch. Medicine, Yale U., 1991-94, bd. dirs. Neighborhood Music Sch. New Haven., 1989-92; bd. overseers Harvard U., 1995—; bd. permanent officers Yale U., 1988-94. John Harvard scholar, 1969, 70, Wendell scholar Harvard U., 1969, Rhodes scholar Oxford U., 1971, Alumni scholar Stanford Sch. Medicine, 1974; medalist Gothenburg (Sweden) Thoracic Soc., 1985; recipient Medaille de la Ville de Bordeaux French Thoracic Soc., 1987, travelling lectureship, 1988, Master Tchr. award Cardiovascular Revs. & Reports, 1990; travelling fellow Australia and New Zealand chpt., ACS, 1989; traveling lectureship, 1989. Fellow ACP, ACS, Royal Coll. Surgeons (Eng., traveling lectr. 1989), Am. Coll. Angiology, Am. Coll. Cardiology (mem. transplantation com. 1991-94, chmn. task force cardiac donor procurement Bethesda Conf. 1992), Am. Coll. Surgeons (bd. govs. 1993-97), Am. Coll. Chest Physicians, Mass. Med. Soc.; mem. AMA, AAAS, Am. Assn. Thoracic Surgery (mem. com. grad. edn. thoracic surgery 1992-97, chmn. Evarts A. Graham Meml. Traveling Fellowship com. 1993-99), Am. Soc. Transplant Surgeons (com. on heart transplantation 1986-89, adv. com. in issues 1989—, chmn. subcom. on heart transplantation, physician payment reform commn. 1989-92), Nat. Heart, Lung and Blood Inst. (cons. divsn. extramural affairs rev. br. 1990—), Assn. Acad. Surgery, Am. Physiol. Soc., Am. Heart Assn. (mem. rsch. grant peer rev. subcom 1984-87, coun. circulation, cert. of appreciation for outstanding svc. 1986), Am. Surg. Assn., Am. Thoracic Soc., Am. Soc. Artificial Internal Organs, Am. Soc. Extracorporeal Tech., Am. Assn. Lab. Animal Sci., Am. Organ Transplant Assn., Am. Venous Forum, Internat. Soc. Heart and Lung Transplantation (chmn. program com. 1988), Internat. Assn. Cardiac Biol. Implants, Internat. Fedn. Surg. Colls., Internat. Soc. Cardiovasc. Surgery, Internat. Soc. Cardio-Thoracic Surgeons (pres. 1999), Internat. Soc. for Heart Rsch. (mem. Am. sect.), Internat. Soc. for Artificial Organs, Mediterranean Assn. for Cardiology and Cardiac Surgery, New Century Soc., Thoracic Surgery Found. for Rsch. and Edn., Norman E. Shumway Surg. Soc., New Eng. Surg. Soc., Pan Am. Med. Assn. (coun. on organ transplantation), North Am. Soc. Pacing and Electrophysiology, Societe Internat. de Chirurgie, Royal Soc. Medicine, Soc. Univ. Surgeons, Thoracic Surgery Dirs. Assn. (chmn. curriculum com. transplantation 1993-94), Transplantation Soc., Assn. Alumni of Magdalen Coll. Oxford U., Assn. Rhodes Scholars, Acad. Surg. Rsch., Assn. Surg. Edn., Assn. Program Dirs. in Surgery, Conn. Thoracic Soc., Harris County Med. Soc., Calif. Med. Assn., Calif. Thoracic Soc., Calif. Thoracic Soc. Respiratory Care Assembly, No. Calif. Cystic Fibrosis Found., So. Calif. Transplant Soc., Conn. Med. Soc., Conn. Soc. Am. Bd. Surgeons, Mass. Med. Soc., N.Y. Soc. Thoracic Surgery, Harvard Med. Alumni Assn. (assoc.), Soc. Crit. Care Medicine, Soc. Thoracic Surgeons, Southeastern Surg. Congress, Southern Surg. Assn., Southwestern Surg. Congress, Tex. Surg. Soc., Halsted Soc., Houston Surg. Soc. Soc. for Organ Sharing, San Francisco Surg. Soc., Santa Clara Med. Soc., Stanford Med. Alumni Assn., Stanford Club Conn., Harvard Clubs San Francisco, Peninsula, N.Y.C., So. Conn., Houston, Boston, Mory's Assn., New Haven Lawn Club, Inner Quad Stanford U., The Hasty Pudding Club - Inst. 1770, Quinnipiack Club, Forum World Affairs, Ambs. Roundtable, Oxford Soc., Phi Beta Kappa, others. Office: The CBR Inst Biomeducal Rsch 200 Longwood Ave Boston MA 02115 Office Phone: 617-278-3000. Business E-Mail: baldwin@cbr.med.harvard.edu.

BALDWIN, JOHN EDWIN, chemistry professor; b. Berwyn, Ill., Sept. 10, 1937; s. Francis Miller and Irville (Miller) B.; m. Anne Kruesi Nordlander, Sept. 23, 1961; children: Claire Miller, John Nordlander, Wesley Hale. AB summa cum laude, Dartmouth Coll., 1959; PhD, Calif. Inst. Tech., 1963. Mem. chemistry faculty U. Ill., 1962-68; prof. chemistry U. Oreg., Eugene, 1968-84; dean Coll. Arts and Scis., 1975-80; prof. chemistry Syracuse U., 1984-2000, disting. prof., 2000—, Wm. R. Kenan, Jr. prof. sci., 2005—. Cons. Stauffer Chem. Co., Office Sci. and Tech., NIH; 150th anniversary vis. prof. Chalmers U., 1990; pres. Montessori Soc. and Sch. of Champaign-Urbana, 1966-67. Author: Experimental Organic Chemistry, 1965; contbr. articles.; mem. adv. bd. Organic Reactions, Chem. Revs. Guggenheim fellow, 1967; Sloan fellow, 1966-68; recipient Sr. US Scientist award Alexander von Humboldt Found., 1974-75, Syracuse Sect. award Am. Chem. Soc., 1997. Home: 5 Brattle Rd Syracuse NY 13203-2803

BALDWIN, JOHN WESLEY, history professor; b. Chgo., July 13, 1929; s. Edward N. and H. Gladys (McDaniel) B.; m. Jenny Jochens, Dec. 24, 1954; children: Peter, Ian, Birgit (dec.), Christopher. BA, Wheaton Coll., 1950; MA, Pa. State U., 1951; PhD, Johns Hopkins, 1956; LHD (hon.), Northwestern U., 2007. Instr., then asst. prof. U. Mich., Ann Arbor, 1956-61; mem. faculty Johns Hopkins U., Balt., 1961—, prof. history, 1966—, Charles Homer Haskins prof. history, 1986—, prof. emeritus, 2001—; prof. e'tranger Coll. de France, 1984, 95. Author: The Medieval Theories of the Just Price, 1959, Masters, Princes and Merchants, 2 vols, 1970, The Scholastic Culture of the Middle Ages, 1971, City on the Seine: Paris under Louis IX, 1226-1270, 1975, The Government of Philip Augustus, 1986 (French transl. 1991), Les Registres de Philippe Auguste, 1992, The Language of Sex: Five Voices from Northern France Around 1200, 1994, (French translation) Les Languages de l'amour, 1997, Aristocratic Life in Medieval France: The Romances of Jean Renart and Gerbert de Montreuil, 1190-1230, 2000, Le Livre de Terres et de Revenues de Pierre du Thillay, 2002, Paris 1200, 2006; editor (with Richard Goldthwaite) Universities in Politics: Case Studies from the Late Middle Ages and Early Modern Period, 1972. Decorated Chevalier de la légion d'honneur (France), Chevalier Ordre des Arts et des Lettres (France); Prix Litteraire Etats-Unis-France, 1992; Guggenheim fellow, 1960-61, 83-84, Howard fellow, 1960-61, Fulbright fellow, 1953-55, 65-66, Sr. fellow NEH, 1972-73, 90-91; grantee Am. Coun. Learned Socs., 1965-66. Fellow Medieval Acad. Am. (v.p. 1994, pres. 1996-97, Charles Homer Haskins medal 1990), Am. Acad. Arts and Scis., Am. Philos. Soc., Brit. Acad. (corr.); mem. Soc. for French Hist. Studies, Royal Danish Acad. Scis. and Letters (fgn.), Am. Hist. Assn., Commn. Internat. de Diplomatique (hon.),

Acad. Inscriptions et Belles Lettres (France) (assoc. fgn.), Société Nationale des Antiquaires de France (assoc. corr. fgn.), Institut de France. Office: Johns Hopkins U Dept History Baltimore MD 21218 also: 18 rue de Bièvre 75005 Paris France

BALDWIN, LIONEL VERNON, retired university president; b. Beaumont, Tex., May 30, 1932; s. Eugene B. and Wanda (Wiley) B.; m. Kathleen Flanagan, Sept. 3, 1955; children: Brian, Michael, Diane, Daniel. BS, U. Notre Dame, 1954; SM, MIT, 1955; PhD, Case Inst. Tech., 1959. Rsch. engr. Nat. Adv. Com. Aerosci., Ohio, 1957-59; unit head NASA, 1959-61; assoc. prof. engring. Colo. State U., 1961-64, acting dean Coll. of Engring., 1964-65, dean and prof. Coll. of Engring., 1966-84; pres. Nat. Tech. U., Ft. Collins, Colo., 1984—2000; ret., 2000. Served to capt. USAF, 1955-57. Recipient award for plasma rsch. NASA, 1964, Kenneth Andrew Roe award Am. Assn. Engring. Soc., 1996. Fellow Am. Soc. Engring. Edn. (chmn. engring. deans coun.); mem. ASME, IEEE, NSPE, Sigma Xi, Tau Beta Pi, Sigma Pi Sigma. Achievements include patentee apparatus for increasing ion engine beam density. Home: 1900 Sequoia St Fort Collins CO 80525-1540

BALDWIN, PATRICIA ANN, lawyer; b. Detroit, May 3, 1955; d. Frank Thomas and Margaret Elyne Mathews; m. Jeffrey Kenton Baldwin, Aug. 23, 1975; children: Matthew, Katherine, Timothy, Philip. BA summa cum laude, Ball State U., 1976; JD, Ind. U., 1979. Bar: Ind. 1979, U.S. Dist. Ct. (so. dist.) Ind. 1979. Ptnr. Baldwin & Baldwin, Danville, Ind., 1979-94; dep. pros. atty. Hendricks County, Danville, 1980-90, pros. atty., 1995—; dep. pros. atty. Boone County, Ind., 1990-94. Sec.-treas., dir. T.F.W., Inc., Danville, 1983—90. Active Girl Scouts U.S., 1964—2000; vol. Boy Scouts Am., 1986—; mem. Hendricks County Rep. Women, 1976—, pres., 2001—03; mem. parish coun. Mary Queen of Peace Cath. Ch., 1976—80, 1981—83; bd. dirs. Cath. Social Svcs., Archdiocese of Indpls., sec. bd. dirs., 1986—92; bd. dirs. Cummins Mental Health Ctr., 1982—86, Youth as Resources Hendricks County, 1995—2001. Mem.: Hendricks County Bar Assn., Ind. Pros. Attys. Assn., Nat. Dist. Attys. Assn., Danville Conservation Club. Office: One Courthouse Sq #105 Danville IN 46122 Office Phone: 317-745-9283.

BALDWIN, PETER ARTHUR, psychologist, educator, author, minister; b. Andover, Mass., Apr. 7, 1932; s. Alfred Graham and Katherine (Ashworth) B.; m. Carolyn Whitmore, Sept. 3, 1955; children: Sarah MacDonald Baldwin-Welcome, Judith Helen Baldwin-Gleason, Robert Henry. BA, Middlebury Coll., 1955; S.T.B., Boston U., 1959, PhD, 1964; student, New Coll., U. London, 1957-58. Lic. psychologist, N.H.; approved cons. in clin. hypnosis, Am. Soc. Clin. Hypnosis. Ordained to ministry Unitarian-Universalist Ch., 1959; pastor 2d Ch., Boston, 1955-57, in Dighton, Mass., 1958-62; religious counselor M.I.T., 1959-63; exec. dir. Liberal Religious Youth, Unitarian Universalist Assn., 1963-66; asst. prof. Crane Theol. Sch., Tufts U., 1965-67, Meadville Theol. Sch., U. Chgo., 1967-73; pastor All Souls 1st Universalist Soc., Chgo., 1971-73; assoc. prof. psychology New Eng. Coll., Henniker, NH, 1973-74; vis. assoc. prof. psychology Colby-Sawyer Coll., New London, NH, 1974-76; assoc. prof. dept. clin. psychology Antioch-New Eng. Grad. Sch., Keene, NH, 1976—; pvt. practice, 1976—. Dir. Sr. High and Family Insts., Rowe, Mass., 1967-74; Nat. Edn. Conf. lectr. Williston Acad., 1967; Judy lectr., Omaha, 1970, Hon. Brother St. Benedicitine Ctr., Madison, 1972; invited speaker 5th Internat. Congress on Gestalt Therapy, Valencia, Spain, 1993. Recipient; Disting. Svc. Antioch New Eng. Grad. Sch., 1994, New Hampshire Psychological Assn., Margaret M. Riggs Disting. Contribution award, 1995. Fellow: ISDF, N.H. Psychol. Assn. (pres. 1980—81, 1988—90); mem.: APA, Unitarian- Universalists Mins. Assn., Liberal Religious Youth (life). Democrat. Home: 113 Pancake Hill Rd Gilmanton NH 03237 Office: Univ Assocs in Psychology 222 West St Keene NH 03431-2455

BALDWIN, RALPH BELKNAP, retired manufacturing executive, astronomer; b. Grand Rapids, Mich., June 6, 1912; s. Melvin D. and Julie (Belknap) B.; m. Lois Virginia Johnston, Aug. 3, 1940; children: Melvin Dana II, Pamela, Bruce Belknap. BS, U. Mich., 1934, MS, 1935, PhD, 1937, LLD (hon.), 1975; ScD (hon.), Grand Valley State U., 1989, Aquinas Coll., 1999. Asst. dept. astronomy U. Mich., 1935-36, U. Pa., 1937-38; instr. dept. astronomy Northwestern U., 1938-42; lectr. Adler Planetarium, Chgo., 1940-42; sr. physicist Applied Physics Lab. Johns Hopkins, Silver Spring, Md., 1942-46, cons. East Grand Rapids, Mich., 1946-47; acting supt. schs. East Grand Rapids, 1947; prodn. mgr. Oliver Machinery Co., Grand Rapids, 1947-56, dir., 1948-87, successively personnel dir., prodn. mgr., sec., 1949-56, v.p., 1956-70, pres., 1970-84, chmn. bd., 1984-87. Chmn. bd. Internat. Woodworking Machinery and Furniture Supply Fair-U.S.A., 1969-70, 77-78 Author: The Face of the Moon, 1949, The Measure of the Moon, 1963, The Moon— A Fundamental Survey, 1966, The Deadly Fuze: Secret Weapon of World War II, 1980, They Never Knew What Hit Them, 1999; contbr. articles to profl. jours. Recipient Presdl. Cert. of Merit, 1947, U.S. Naval Bur. Ordnance award, 1945, U.S. Army Chief of Ordnance award, 1945, Disting. Alumnus award U. Mich., 1967, Woodworking and Furniture Digest award Forest Products Rsch. Soc., 1973, J. Lawrence Smith medal Nat. Acad. Scis., 1979, G.K. Gilbert award Geol. Soc. Am., 1986, Disting. Alumni award Ctrl. HS, Grand Rapids, 1997 Fellow AAAS, Am. Geophys. Union, Meteoritical Soc. (Leonard medal 1986, Barringer medal 2000), Am. Acad. Arts and Scis.; mem. Am. Astron. Soc., Royal Astron. Soc. Can. (hon.), Grand Rapids Mus. Assn., NAM (dir. 1963-64), Employers Assn. Grand Rapids (pres. 1960-64), Woodworking Machinery Mfrs. Assn. (pres. 1964-68).

BALDWIN, ROBERT FREDERICK, JR., lawyer; b. Syracuse, NY, Sept. 20, 1939; s. Robert Frederick and Marjorie Elizabeth (Thompson) Baldwin; m. Jeanella M. Mastrobattisto, Apr. 26, 1980; m. Margaret Melissa Richards, Aug. 19, 1962 (div.); children: Robert Frederick, Melissa Brooke. BSBA, Syracuse U., 1962, LLB, 1964. Bar: N.Y. 1964, U.S. Dist. Ct. (no. dist.) N.Y. 1980, Fla. 1982, U.S. Ct. Mil. Appeals 1965, U.S. Tax Ct. 1968, U.S. Ct. of Claims 1980, U.S. Supreme Ct. 1968. Assoc. Hancock, Estabrook Ryan, Shove & Hust, Syracuse, NY, 1968—73; ptnr. Hancock, Estabrook Ryan, Shove & Hust, Syracuse, NY, 1974—84; prin. Green & Seifter, Attys, P.C., Syracuse, NY, 1984—96; ptnr. Baldwin & Sutphen, LLP, Syracuse, 1996—. Atty. Village Fayetteville, Fayetteville, 1974—94; adj. prof. law Syracuse U. Coll. Law, 1977—2004. Contbr. articles to profl. jours. Mem., deferred gifts com. ARC, CNY chpt., Syracuse, 1980—84; vice-chair Onondaga County Indsl. Devel. Agy., Syracuse, 1996—2002, chmn., 2004—, DestiNY USA Benefits Maximization Com., Syracuse, 2002; bd. mem. Planned Parenthod CNY, Syracuse, 1978—84; trustee Fayetteville Cemetary Assn., 1974—80; bd. mem. UN Assn. CNY, Syracuse, 1971—74; trustee Fayetteville Libr. Assn., 1976—79; pres., mem. Onondaga Pastoral Counselling Ctr., Syracuse, 1994—2002; bd. govs. Citizens Found., Syracuse, 1973—76; mem. Assn. Retarded Citizens CNY, Syracuse, 1976—79; mem, steering com. Syracuse U. Tax Inst., 1980—2002. Comdr. USNR, 1965—85. Fellow: Am. Coll. Trust & Estate Counsel (chair, employee benefits com. 1997—2000); mem.: Estate Planning Coun. Ctrl. NY (pres. 1973—74), Nat. Assn. Estate Planning Couns. (pres. 1982—83), Onondaga County Bar Assn. (dir. 1976—79). Home: 5153 Burnside Dr Jamesville NY 13078 Office: Baldwin & Sutphen LLP 100 Clinton Sq Ste 320 Syracuse NY 13202 Office Phone: 315-477-0100. Personal E-mail: rbaldwin@baslaw.com.

BALDWIN, ROBERT LESH, biochemist, educator; b. Madison, Wis., Sept. 30, 1927; s. Ira Lawrence and Mary (Lesh) B.; m. Anne Theodora Norris, Aug. 28, 1965; children: David Norris, Eric Lawrence. BA, U. Wis., 1950; D.Phil. (Rhodes scholar), Oxford U., Eng., 1954. Asst. prof., then asso. prof. biochemistry U. Wis., 1955-59; mem. faculty Stanford, 1959—, prof. biochemistry, 1964-98, prof. emeritus, 1998—, chmn. dept., 1989-94. Vis. prof. Collège de France, Paris, 1972, Tsinghua U., Beijing, 2002; mem. adv. panel biochemistry and biophysics NSF, 1974—76; mem. NIH study sect. molecular and cellular biophysics, 1984—88. Assoc. editor Jour. Molecular Biology, 1964-68, 75-79; mem. editl. bd. Trends Biochem. Sci., 1977-84, Biochemistry, 1984—, Protein Sci., 1992-97. Mem. award panel Searle Scholars, 1993—96, 1997—98; mem. adv. panel in biophysics Burroughs-Wellcome, 1995—2001. Recipient Wheland award U. Chgo., 1995, Merit award NIH, 1988; Guggenheim fellow, 1958-59. Fellow Am. Biophysics Soc. (coun. 1977-81, Founder's award 1999); mem. NAS, Am. Soc. Biol. Chemists (Merck award 1999), Am. Chem. Soc., Am. Acad. Arts and Scis., Protein Soc. (coun. 1993-95, Stein and Moore award 1992). Home: 1243 Los Trancos Rd Portola Valley CA 94028-8125 Office: Stanford Med Sch Dept Biochemistry Beckman Ctr Stanford CA 94305-5307 E-mail: bbaldwin@cmgm.stanford.edu.

BALDWIN, SHAUN MCPARLAND, lawyer; b. Chgo., Oct. 19, 1954; BS, No. Ill. U., 1976; JD with distinction, John Marshall Law Sch., 1980. Bar: Ill. 1980, U.S. Dist. Ct. (no. dist.) Ill. 1980, U.S. Ct. Appeals (7th cir.) 1981. Assoc. McKenna, Storer, Rowe, While & Farrug, Chgo., 1980-86, Tressler, Soderstrom, Maloney & Priess, LLP, Chgo., 1986—87, ptnr., 1987—. Mem. ABA, Ill. Bar Assn., Def. Rsch. Inst. (chair ins. law com. 1996-98)), Ill. Assn. Def. Trial Counsel (bd. dirs. 1996, amicus com. chair 1992—98), Ill. Appellate Lawyers Assn. (bd. dirs. 1987-89), John Marshall Alumni Assn. (bd. dirs. 1982-86), Internat. Assn. Def. Trial Counsel (chair membership com. 1996-97, chair casualty ins. com. 1995-96), Profl. Liability Underwriting Soc. Office: Tressler Soderstrom Maloney & Priess LLP 233 S Wacker Dr Ste 2200 Chicago IL 60606-6399 Office Phone: 312-627-4014. Business E-Mail: sbaldwin@tsmp.com.

BALDWIN, SHAWN D., investment company executive; b. Ohio, 1966; COO Wall St. Strategies, NYC, 1999—2001; pres., CEO CMG Instl. Trading LLC, Chgo., 2001—. Pres. Nat. Assn. Securities Profls. (NASP) (Chgo. chapter). Named to The Hot List: America's Most Powerful Players Under 40, 2005. Office: Capital Mgmt Grp Securities LLC 123 N Wacker Dr Ste 810 Chicago IL 60606-1637 Office Phone: 312-578-0470. Office Fax: 312-578-0474.*

BALDWIN, SHERYL DENISE, chemist, editor, writer; b. Va., Apr. 13, 1948; d. William Jacob and Josephine (Rife) B. BS in Chemistry with high honors, Va. Commonwealth U., 1975, PhD in Phys. Chemistry, 1979. Asst. prof. chemistry U. Richmond, Va., 1980-82; quality control, supr. support Hercules, Inc., Hopewell, Va., 1982-83, rsch. chemist, 1983-86; rsch. sci. R & D Philip Morris, Richmond, 1986-90, sr. rsch. sci., 1991-96, sect. leader, paper devel., 1990-94; mgr. bus. devel. Am. Chem. Soc. Industry Rels., Washington, 1996—. Cons. Bear Island Paper Co., Doswell, Va., 1980-82, Alexandria Pub. Svcs., 1993-95, Environ. Friendly Packaging, Richmond, 1994-96. Editor: Plastics, Rubber and Paper Recycling: A Pragmatic Approach, 1995; contbr. articles to profl. jours. including U.S.-China Rev. Bd. dirs. Sister Cities program Richmond-Zheng Zhou, China, 1994—; del. Environ. Tech. Del. to China, 1994; mem. City of Richmond Com., 1986-94. Recipient Star award Va. Commonwealth U. Alumni, 1997. Mem. Am. Chem. Soc. (mem. cellulose and paper divsn., mem. exec. com. 1991-95, Judge Anselme Payen award 1992-94, indsl. liaison chair 1992-93, mem. exec. coun. Va. sect. 1982—, chmn. 1992. alt. councilor 1994—, councilor 1998—, Disting. Svc. award Va. sect. 1996), U.S.-China People's Friendship Assn. (bd. dirs. 1995-97), Friendship Through Sci. and Tech. (coord. 1997—), Mensa, Sigma Xi (assoc.), Phi Kappa Phi, Kappa Sigma Rho. Achievements include eight patents on novel cigarette papers and cigarettes. Office: Am Chem Soc Industry Rels 1155 16th St NW Washington DC 20036-4800

BALDWIN, STANLEY FORREST, lawyer, insurance company executive; b. 1948; BA, JD, U. Tex. Bar: Tex. 1973, Tenn. 1988, Va. 2004. Various sr. officer and gen. counsel positions CIGNA Healthplans, Inc.; sr. v.p., gen. counsel and sec. EQUICOR-Equitable HCA Corp., Nashville, EPIC Healthcare Group, Dallas, 1990—97; exec. v.p., gen. counsel and sec. Amerigroup Corp., Va. Beach, Va., 1997—. Mem.: Va. State Bar, Va. Bar Assn., State Bar Tex., Tenn. Bar Assn. Office: Amerigroup Corp 4425 Corporation Ln Virginia Beach VA 23462 Office Phone: 757-490-6900. Office Fax: 757-557-6743.

BALDWIN, SUSAN OLIN, commissioner, management consultant; b. Battle Creek, Mich., Sept. 1, 1954; d. Thomas Franklin and Gloria Joan (Skidmore) Olin; m. James Patrick Baldwin, Sept. 15, 1979; children: Christopher Mark, David James. BA, Miami U., Ohio, 1976; JD, U. Cin., 1979. Bar: Ohio 1979, Mich. 1984. Assoc. editor Am. Legal Pub. Co., Cin., 1979—80; corp. atty. Hosp. Care Corp., Cin., 1980—84; legal counsel Peak Health Plan, Cin., 1984; assoc. Cook & Goetz, P.C., Bloomfield Hills, Mich., 1984—91, Pringle & Assocs., P.C., Farmington Hills, Mich., 1991—94; exec. dir. Calhoun County Econ. Devel. Forum, Battle Creek, 1994—2003; owner Am. Computer Svcs., Battle Creek, 2002—07; commr. Battle Creek City, 2003—, mem. Mich. mcpl. league transp. and infrastructure com., 2005—. Mem. steering com. Ctr. Workforce Excellence, 1994—96, Barriers to Employment, 1996—2003; bd. dirs. BC, Cal, Kal Inland Port Devel. Corp., 1996—, Forum Greater Kalamazoo, 1995—2001, Calhoun County Health Improvement Program, 1998—99, Battle Creek Unltd., 2004—; mem. Battle Creek Cmty. Leadership Acad., 1996—97, Battle Creek Area C. of C., 1998—2003, mem. adv. bd., 1998—, S.W. Mich. Healthplan Purchasing Alliance, 1998—2000; adv. bd. Starr Commonwealth Battle Creek Child Guidance Ctr., 1998—2006; mem. Cmty. Devel. Block Grant Coun., 1996—99, Mich. Women in Mcpl. Govt., 2005—, sec., 2006—. Contbr. articles to profl. jours. Pres. Hunter's Green Homeowner's Assn., Independence, Ky., 1982—83; chair Safety Town Cmty. Project, 1993—95; v.p. fin. Jr. League Battle Creek, 1996—98; key communicator Minges Brook PTA, 1993—2001, treas., 1994—96, 1998—99; bd. dirs. Vol. Ctr. Battle Creek, 1999—, sec., 2003—06, pres., 2007—; bd. dirs. Battle Creek Cmty. Found. Philanthropic Devel. Com., 1998—, Lakeview Sch. Dist. Com. Continuous Improvement, 1999—2002; chair S. Ctrl. Mich. Jr. Achievement Campaign, 1999, Calhoun County Crossroads Initiative, 1999—2002; bd. dirs. Habitat for Humanity, 2003—; mem. Mayor's Commr. Compensation Commn., 1997—2003; mem. capital campaign com.-making BC Green Leila Arboretum, 1999—2000; mem. exec. bd. Battle Creek Unltd., 2003—; bd. dirs. Binder Park Zoo, 2004—. Mem.: ABA, Am. Businesswomen's Assn. (v.p. 1980—81, editor 1980), Ohio State Bar, State Bar Mich., Battle Creek Area C. of C. (bd. dirs. 1998—), Birmingham Evening Newcomers Club (treas. 1986—87, pres. 1988), Phi Alpha Delta, Alpha Lambda Delta. Office: 164 W Hamilton Ln Battle Creek MI 49015-4030 Office Phone: 269-963-8124. Personal E-mail: sbaldwin4bc@aol.com.

BALDWIN, TAMMY, congresswoman, lawyer; b. Madison, Wis., Feb. 11, 1962; life ptnr. Lauren Azar. AB in Govt. and Math., Smith Coll., Northampton, Mass., 1984; JD, U. Wis., Madison, 1989. Mem. City Coun., Madison, Wis., 1986; supr. Dane County Bd. Suprs., 1986-1994; atty. pvt. practice, 1989-92; mem. Wis. State Assembly from 78th Dist., 1993-99, US Congress from 2nd Wis. dist., 1999—, mem. energy and commerce com. Mem.: Nat. Women's Polit. Caucus, Wis. State Bar Assn., Internat. Network Lesbian and Gay Officials, ACLU, NOW. Democrat. First woman to serve in the US House of Representatives. from Wis.; first openly gay person to be elected to Congress as a non-incumbent. Office: US Ho Reps 1022 Longworth Ho Office Bldg Washington DC 20515 Office Phone: 202-225-2906.*

BALDWIN, WILLIAM ALLEN, application developer; b. Red Wing, Minn., July 4, 1947; s. Walter Charles Baldwin and Edythe Mae Rose; m. Feng-chuan Hsiao (div.); children: Anna Gloria, Connie Alice. BA in Math. and Chemistry, Graceland Coll., Lamoni, Iowa, 1970; MS in Computer Sci., Iowa State U., Ames, 1978, PhD in Computer Sci., 1983. Asst. prof. U. Mo., Columbia, 1982—83, U. ND, Grand Forks, 1984—90, Pk. Coll., Parkville, Mo., 1990—94; computer analyst, sys. analyst Cubic Applications, Inc., Leavenworth, Kans., 1994—96; pres. Baldwin Computer Sci., Overland Park, Kans., 1995—2006; software developer POINT, Inc. (also Sokkia Tech.), Olathe, Kans., 1996—2003; pres. Computer Freedom, Overland Park, 2004—05, Baldwin Computer Sci., Overland Park, Kans., 2005—. Contbr. articles to profl. jours. Pres. Kans. Strengthening Democracy, Overland Park, 2000—06. Mem.: Mensa. Independent. Mem. Cmty. Christ Ch. Home: 10042 Horton Dr Overland Park KS 66207 Home Phone: 913-381-5467.

BALDWIN, WILLIAM D.G., lawyer; b. Rockford, Ill., Apr. 1, 1967; BA, U. Wis.-Madison, 1989; JD, Northern Ky. U., 1997. Bar: Ohio 1997. Student articles editor Northern Ky. Law Review, 1996—97; worked in instl. trust areas Northern Trust Co., Chgo., Fifth Third Bank, Cin.; ptnr. Vorys, Sater, Seymour and Pease LLP, Cin. Bd. mem., treasurer Hamilton County Alcohol and Drug Addiction. Named one of Ohio's Rising Stars, Super Lawyers, 2006. Mem.: ABA, Cin. Bar Assn. Office: Vorys Sater Seymour and Pease LLP Atrium Two Ste 2000 221 E Fourth St PO Box 0236 Cincinnati OH 45201-0236 Office Phone: 513-723-8595. Office Fax: 513-852-7812.

BALDWIN, WILLIAM RUSSELL, optometrist, foundation administrator; b. Danville, Ind., July 29, 1926; s. Edward Claire and Letha Verona (Russell) B.; m. Honey Esther Fisher, Aug. 16, 1947; children: Linda Marie Smith (dec.), Leslie Ann Baldwin Bloom. BS, Pacific U., 1949, OD, 1951, ScD (hon.), 1991; MS, Ind. U., 1956, PhD, 1964; LHD (hon.), New Eng. Coll., 1982; D.S. (hon.), SUNY, 1998; DS (hon.), Pa. Coll. Optometry, 2003. Pvt. practice, Beech Grove, Ind., 1951-54; dir. optometry clinic Ind. U., Bloomington, 1959-63; dean Coll. Optometry Pacific U., Forest Grove, Oreg., 1963-69; pres. New England Coll. Optometry, Boston, 1969-79; dean Coll. Optometry U. Houston, 1979-90; pres. River Blindness Found., 1990-96, chmn. bd. dirs., 1996—2001. Author: (with C.R. Schick) Corneal Contact Lenses, Fitting Procedures, 1962, (with others) The Refractive State of the Eye, 1969, Pediatric Optometry, 1988; editor Vision Science Symposium, Ind. U., 1988, (with others) Refractive Anomalies, 1991. Mem. exec. com. Rep. Ctrl. Com., Washington County, Oreg., 1963-69; chmn. arts, scis. divsn. Ind. Reps., 1962-63; chmn. Vellore India Hosp. Fund Drive, 1959-61; mem. men's adv. coun. Bloomington Hosp., 1959-63, bd. dirs. Am. Optometric Found., 1998-2003. Recipient Alumni Svc. award Ind. U., 1977, Pacific U., 1995, Gold Medal award Beta Sigma Kappa, 1968, Lifetime Achievement award Prevent Blindness Am., 1995, Disting. Svc. award USPHA Vision Sect., 1998, Social Justice Action award New Eng. United Meth. Conf., 1999, Disting. Svc. award World Coun. Optometry, 2000; named Man of Vision Prevent Blindness Mass., 1994; Disting. scholar Nat. Acad. Practice, 1994, Disting. Svc. award, Vis. Section Am. Pub. Health Assn., 1998. Fellow AAAS, Am. Acad. Optometry (life, chmn. sect. on edn. 1984-87); mem. working group Nat. Rsch. Coun. Com. Vision of NAS, Am. Optometric Assn. (chmn. com. on rsch. 1964-69, chmn. task force on manpower 1968, Disting. Svc. award 1992), Assn. Schs. Colls. Optometry (pres. 1974-76, chmn. internat. optometric edn.), Tex. Soc. to Prevent Blindness (v.p. 1985-90), Nat. Soc. to Prevent Blindness Am. (bd. dirs. 1988-96, chm. 1st World Conf. on Optometric Edn. 1990), Optometric Rsch. Inst. (bd. dirs. 1995-2001), Rotary, Sigma Xi, Sigma Nu Office Phone: 812-323-2013. Personal E-mail: billbald@insightbb.com.

BALDYGA, LEONARD J., retired diplomat, consultant; b. Chgo., Mar. 19, 1932; s. Stanislaw J. and Frances T. (Gorzynski) B.; m. Joyce Brinkley, June 25, 1960; children: Natalya M., Sarah E. AA, J. Sterling Morton Coll., 1954; BS, So. Ill. U., 1959; M Internat. Affairs, Columbia U., 1962. City editor Marion (Ill.) Daily Rep., 1958—59; fin. writer Am. Banker, NYC, 1959—61; overseas, 1963—78; dep. dir. Europe U.S. Info. Agy., Washington, 1979—81, dir., 1981—83; 1992—94; minister, counselor Am. Embassy, Rome, 1983—88, New Delhi, 1988—91; sr. rsch. assoc. Washington, 1994—. Acting dir. Murrow Ctr. Tufts U. Fletcher Sch. Law and Diplomacy, Medford, Mass., 1991-92, adj. prof., 1991-92. Mem. editl. bd. Polish Ency. Britannica. Trustee St. Stephen's Sch., Rome, 1984—88; bd. dirs. Ptnrs. for Dem. Change, Washington, Pub. Diplomacy Coun., Sabre Found., Polish Inst. Arts and Scis., NYC. Decorated Polish Order of Merit Republic of Poland, 1994, Commander's Cross, 2002; recipient Presdl. Disting. Svc. award White House, 1984, Edward R. Murrow award Tufts U., 1988, Presdl. Merit award White House, 1988. Home Phone: 703-524-2479. Personal E-mail: ljbjbb@aol.com.

BALE, CHRISTIAN, actor; b. Haverfordwest Pembrokeshire, Wales, Jan. 30, 1974; s. David Bale and Gloria Steinem (Stepmother); m. Sibi Blazic, Jan. 29, 2000; 1 child. Actor: (TV films) Anastasia: The Mystery of Anna, 1986, Treasure Island, 1990, A Murder of Quality, 1991, Mary, Mother of Jesus, 1999; (TV miniseries) Heart of the Country, 1987; (films) The Land of Faraway, 1987, Empire of the Sun, 1987, Henry V, 1989, Newsies, 1992, Swing Kids, 1993, Royal Deceit, 1994, Little Women, 1994, The Secret Agent, 1996, Portrait of a Lady, 1996, Metroland, 1997, Velvet Goldmine, 1998, All the Little Animals, 1998, A Midsummer Night's Dream, 1999, American Psycho, 2000, Shaft, 2000, Captain Corelli's Mandolin, 2001, Laurel Canyon, 2002, Reign of Fire, 2002, Equilibrium, 2002, The Machinist, 2004, Batman Begins, 2005 (Best Hero, MTV Movie awards, 2006), Harsh Times, 2005, The New World, 2005, The Prestige, 2006, Rescue Dawn, 2006, (voice) Pocahontas, 1995, Howl's Moving Castle, 2004. Actively involved with various civic organizations including Happy Child Mission, Ark Trust, Redwings Sanctuary, Greenpeace, World Wildlife Fund., Dian Fossey Gorilla Fund.*

BALÉE, WILLIAM L., anthropology educator; b. Ft. Lauderdale, Fla., Oct. 12, 1954; s. William Lockert Balée and Lorraine Kathryn Monahan; m. Maria da Conceição Bezerra, Mar. 9, 1987; children: Nicholas, Isabel. BA with high honors, U. Fla., 1975; MA, Columbia U., 1979, MPhil, 1980, PhD, 1984. Assoc. rschr. ecology Museu Paraense Emílio Goeldi, Belém, Brazil, 1988-91, chair ecology, 1990-91; assoc. prof. anthropology Tulane U., New Orleans, 1991-98, prof., chair dept. anthropology, 1998-2001, prof. anthropology, 1998—, dir. environ. studies program, Sch. Liberal Arts, 2007—. Adj. prof. anthropology CUNY, 1983-84, SUNY, Purchase, 1982; adj. prof. social scis. CUNY, 1983; adj. prof. sociology and anthropology Rutgers U., 1984; vis. assoc. prof. Ctr. for L.Am. Studies, U. Fla., 1990; fieldwork with forest peoples in Amazon of Brazil and Bolivia, 1980-2003; acad. cons. Smithsonian Instn., 2000—04. Author: Footprints of the Forest: Ka'apor Ethnobotany, 1994 (award Soc. Econ. Botany, 1996), Annual Review Anthropology, 2006; editor: Advances in Historical Ecology, 1998, Jour. Ethnobiology, 1999—2002; co-editor: Resource Management in Amazonia: Indigenous and Folk Strategies, Advances in Economic Botany, vol. 7, 1989, Hist. Ecology Series, 1998—2006, Time and Complexity in Historical Ecology, 2006; mem. editl. bd.: Jour. Ethnobiology, 2002—04; contbr. articles to profl. jours., chapters to books. Decorated officer Order of the Golden Ark (Netherlands), 1993; NY Bot. Garden fellow, 1984-88, Fulbright-Hays fellow, 1980-81, Newcomb Coll. fellow, 1992-94, Conselho Nacional de Desenvolvimento Tecnológico e Científico fellow, 1988-91; grantee OAS, 1981-82, Ford Found., 1989-90, Jessie Smith Noyes Found., 1990-91, World Wildlife Fund, 1991-92, 2003, Tulane U., 1992, Wenner-Gren Found., 1993-94; apptd. to 60th and 61st Coll. Disting. Lectrs., Sigma Xi, 1997-99; recipient Outstanding Book of Yr. award Soc. Econ. Botany. Fellow Am. Anthrop. Assn.; mem. Soc. Ethnobotanists (India), Soc. Ethnobiology, Soc. Anthropology of Lowland

S.Am. (pres. 2002-05), Soc. Etnobiologia e Etnoecologia, Phi Beta Kappa (pres. Alpha of La. 1997-98), Phi Kappa Phi. Office: Tulane U Dept Anthropology New Orleans LA 70118-5238 Office Phone: 504-865-5336.

BALER, BLANCHE KIMOTO, retired child psychiatrist; b. Ceres, Calif., Nov. 30, 1924; d. Kusutaro Kimoto and Toku Kanazawa; m. Lenin Allen Baler (dec.); children: Laura, Claudia Baler Mellen, Carleton. PhD in Psychology, Boston U., 1951, MD, 1954. Staff psychiatrist Hawthorn Ctr., Northville, Mich., 1976—94; ret. Recipient asst. fellowship in psychology, Boston U., 1946—50; scholar, Dakota Wesleyan U., 1943, 1944, 1945, Boston U. Sch. Medicine, 1953. Mem.: Am. Psychiat. Assn. Avocations: gardening, interior decorating, international travel. Home: 1144 Aberdeen Dr Ann Arbor MI 48104

BALES, JOHN FOSTER, III, retired lawyer; b. Springfield, Mass., July 17, 1940; s. John Foster II and Jean (Torrence) Bales; m. Jane Lee Black, Sept. 11, 1965; children: Patricia, Elizabeth, Susan. BS in Engring., Princeton U., 1962; LLB, U. Va., 1965; LLM, Georgetown U., 1972. Bar: U.S. Supreme Ct. 1972. Staff atty. U.S. SEC, Washington, 1970-72; assoc. Morgan, Lewis & Bockius, Phila., 1972-76, ptnr., 1976—2001. Bd. dirs. Ind. Publs., Inc., 1986—. Trustee U.S. com. refugees, 1998—2001; vice-chmn. bd. trustees Ind. Presbyn. Med. Ctr., Phila., 1988—95, Acad. Natural Scis., Phila., 1995—; trustee Presbyn. Found., Phila., 1995—96, Immigration Refugee Svcs. Am., 1998—2001. Mem.: ABA, Colo. Bar Assn., Phila. Bar Assn., Pa. Bar Assn., Va. Bar Assn. Republican. Home: 407 Newbold Rd Jenkintown PA 19046-2849 Personal E-mail: johnfbales@hotmail.com.

BALES, KENT ROSLYN, language educator; b. Anthony, Kans., June 19, 1936; s. Roslyn Francis and Irene E. (Brinkman) B.; m. Maria Gyorei, Aug. 25, 1958; children— Thomas Imre, Elizabeth Irene BA, Yale U., 1958; MA, San Jose State U., 1963; PhD, U. Calif., Berkeley, 1967. Instr. Menlo Sch., Menlo Park, Calif., 1958-63; acting instr. U. Calif., Berkeley, 1967; asst. prof. English U. Minn., Mpls., 1967-71, assoc. prof. English, 1971-82, prof. English, 1982—, chmn. dept. English, 1983—88, 2000—03. Vis. fellow Lit. Studies Inst., Budapest, Hungary, 1973-74, 80-81, 88-89. Contbr. chpts. to books and articles to profl. jours. Fulbright lectr., Budapest, 1980, Fulbright Rsch. fellow, Budapest, 1988-89. Mem. MLA. Home: 2700 Irving Ave S Minneapolis MN 55408-1049 Office: Univ Minn Dept English 207 Church St SE Minneapolis MN 55455-0134 E-mail: bales@umn.edu.

BALES, ROYAL EUGENE, retired philosophy educator; b. Pratt, Kans., Sept. 23, 1934; s. Harold Thomas and Gladys (German) B.; m. Flossie Kathleen O'Reilly, Apr. 16, 1960; children— David Scott, Elizabeth Laurel B.Music Edn. cum laude, U. Wichita, 1956, MA, 1960; PhD, Stanford U., 1968. Tchr. music Kans. Pub. Schs., 1956-57, 59-60; instr. philosophy Menlo Coll., Atherton, Calif., 1962-69, prof., 1970-2000, prof. emeritus, 2000—, chmn. social scis. and humanities, 1971-74, dean liberal arts, 1974-79, provost, 1979-87, standing mem. president's adv. council, 1971-87. Vis. fellow Harris-Manchester Coll., Oxford U., 1994, 98; Wong vis. prof. Guangdong U. of Law and Bus., Guangzhou, China, 1999. Contbg. author: About Philosophy, 2006; contbr. articles to profl. jours. Pres. El Camino Youth Symphony Assn., 1985-87; hon. gov. Harris-Manchester Coll., Oxford, 1994—. Scholar and fellow U. Wichita, 1952-60, Stanford U., 1966-67; prin. investigator NSF, Menlo Coll./Stanford, 1971-72; Rsch grant Stanford-Warsaw Exchange, Poland, 1969-70. Mem. Am. Philos. Assn., Save The Bay Assn., Phi Mu Alpha Sinfonia. Democrat. Avocations: classical music, designing and constructing furniture. Home: 1255 Sherman Ave Menlo Park CA 94025-6012 Personal E-mail: bales.r@sbcglobal.net.

BALES, VIRGINIA SHANKLE, health science association administrator; BA in Chemistry, Emory U., Atlanta, 1971, MPH, 1977. Dep. dir. Nat. Ctr. Chronic Disease Prevention and Health Promotion Ctrs. for Disease Control and Prevention, 1988—98, dep. dir. program mgmt., 1998—2002, dir. adult and cmty. health divsn. Nat. Ctr. for Chronic Disease Prevention and Health Promotion, 2002—. Office: CDC DHHS Mailstop D14 1600 Clifton Rd NE Atlanta GA 30329-4018

BALES, W. SCOTT, state supreme court justice; BA summa cum laude, Mich. State U., 1978; MA in Econ., Harvard U., 1980; JD magna cum laude, Harvard Law Sch., 1983. Clerk, Office of Solicitor Gen. U.S. Dept. of Justice, 1983; clerk to Judge Joseph T. Sneed U.S. Ct. of Appeals for Ninth Circuit, 1983—84; clerk to Justice Sandra Day O'Connor U.S. Supreme Ct., 1984—85; atty. Meyer, Hendricks, Victor, Osborn & Maledon, 1985—94; special investigative counsel, Office of Inspector Gen. U.S. Dept. of Justice, 1995—97, dep. asst. atty. gen., Office of Policy Develop., 1998—99; asst. U.S. atty. Dist. of Ariz., 1995—99; solicitor gen. Office of Ariz. Atty. Gen., 1999—2001; atty. Lewis and Roca LLP, 2001—05; justice Ariz. Supreme Ct., 2005—. Teaching fellow Harvard U., 1979—83; adjunct prof. of law Ariz. State U., 2001, U. Ariz., 2003—05. Bd. dirs. Ariz. Found. for Legal Services and Ed., 2004—05. Recipient Inspector General's award of merit, 1997, U.S. Atty. General's Disting. Svc. award, 1998, Found. for Justice award, 2005. Office: Ariz Supreme Ct 1501 W Washington Ste 402 Phoenix AZ 85007 Office Phone: 602-452-3528. Office Fax: 602-542-9484.*

BALEY, JOAN MARIE, elementary school educator; d. Alfred J. and Angeline Beitler; m. Frank T. Baley, Mar. 24, 1984. BA in Edn., St. Xavier U., 1976; postgrad., Chapman U., Loyola U. Tchr. 3d grade Archdiocese of Chgo., St. Christina Sch., 1976, Archdiocese of Chgo., St. Thomas More Sch., 1976—98; tchr. 6th grade Archdiocese of Chgo., St. Christina Sch., 1998—2002, tchr. grades 7-8, dir. sci., 2002—. Facilitator Rainbow program St. Thomas More Sch., 1976—98, coord. grade level., 1976—98, St. Christina Sch., 1998—, chair sci., 1998—, mem. liturgy team, 1998—, peer mediator facilitator, 1998—. Nominee Golden Apple award, 1990; recipient, 1991, Disney award, 2000. Mem.: Nat. Sci. Tchrs. Assn. Avocations: golf, interior decorating, crafts. Office: St Christina Sch 3333 W 110th St Chicago IL 60655

BALFE, ROBERT CRAMER, III, prosecutor; b. West Palm Beach, Fla., 1968; m. Jennifer Balfe; children: Ryan, Luke. BS, Ark. State Univ.; JD, Univ. Ark., 1994. Bar: Ark. 1995. Dep. pros. atty. Benton County, Ark., 1995—2001, pros. atty. Ark., 2001—04; US atty. (we. dist.) Ark. US Dept. Justice, 2004—. Office: US Attys Office 414 Parker St Fort Smith AR 72901*

BALICK, KENNETH D., international business development consultant; b. Albany, NY, Nov. 27, 1960; s. Sidney M. and Carole (Kaufmann) B. BS in Indsl. and Labor Rels., Cornell U., 1983; MPA, Harvard U., 1986. Legis. aide to mem. Japan Parliament, Tokyo, 1983-84; dir. Asian programs Carnegie Coun. on Ethics and Internat. Affairs, NYC, 1986-90; pres. Trans-Pacific Consulting Group, NYC, 1990-94; asst. to CEO Nomura Securities Internat., Inc., NYC, 1994-97; dir. internat. bus. devel. Capital Co. of Am., NYC, 1998-99; founder, pres. RockBridge Global Advisors, 1999—. Pub. spkr. in field. Henry Luce scholar. Mem. Coun. on Fgn. Rels.

BALIGA, RADHAKRISHNA, pediatrician, educator, nephrologist, director; b. Bombay; naturalized, U.S. m. Mithra Baliga; children: Priya, Divya. Degree, Loyola Coll, Madras, India, 1962, Kasturba Med. Coll., Manipal, 1968; MB, BS, Mysore U., 1968; diploma in Child Health, Madras U., 1973. Lic. DC, 1976, Calif., 1979, La. La., 1982, Miss., 1993, Am. Bd. Pediat. Nephrology, 1982. Internship Govt. Gen. Hosp. Madras U., 1969—70, sr. house surgency, 1970—71; postgrad. pediat. Inst. Child and Health and Hosp. for Sick Children, Madras U., 1971—73; pediat. level I Jewish Hosp and Med. Ctr. Bklyn., 1974—75; pediat. level 2 St. Vincent's Med. Ctr., Staten Island, 1975—76; fellow pediat. nephrology Children's Hosp Mich. Wayne State U., Detroit, 1976—78; pediatrician New Ctr. Med. Plz. Groups, 1978—80; staff pediatrician South La. Med. Ctr., Houma, 1980—82; clin. asst. prof. pediat. Tulane U., New Orleans, 1980—82, instr. pediat., 1982—83, clin. asst. prof. pediat., 1986—92, asst. prof. pediat., 1985—86, rsch. assoc., 1989—90, clin. asst. prof. pediat., 1985—87, clin. assoc. prof. pediat., 1992—96, clin. prof. pediat., 1996—; clin. asst. prof. pediat. La. State U., 1985—87, asst. prof. pediat., 1986—92, assoc. prof. pediat., 1992—93; prof. pediats. U. Miss., 1993—. Cons. in pediat. nephrology Handicapped Children Svcs. Program, New Orleans, 1985—93; vis. asst. prof. dept. pediat. U. Calif., San Francisco, 1986—87. Contbr. numerous presentations, articles to profl. jour. Grantee Biomedical Rsch. Support Grant, 1991—92, Dept. grant, 1997—98, Dept. Rsch. grant, 2001—03. Fellow: Am. Soc. Nephrology; mem.: Internat. Soc. Pediat. Nephrology, Am. Heart Assn., North Am. Pediat. Renal Transplant Co-operative Study Kidney Coun., Southest Pediat. Nephrology Study Group, Internat. Soc. Nephology, Internat. Soc. Pediat. Nephrology, Am. Soc. Pediat. Nephrology. Office Phone: 601-984-5970. Business E-Mail: rbaliga@ped.umsmed.edu.

BALIGA, RAGAVENDRA RAMAKRISHNA, cardiologist, researcher; b. Mangalore, India, Mar. 17, 1960; s. Ram Krishna and Shanthi Baliga; m. Jayashree Baliga, May 1, 1990; children: Anoop, Neena. MBBS, St. John's Med. Coll., Bangalore, India, 1984; MD, Bangalore Med. Coll., 1988; MBA, U. Mich., Ann Arbor, 2004. Diplomate Nat. Bd. Medicine, New Delhi, 1988; mem. Royal Coll. Physicians, Eng., 1991. Intern, resident St. John's Med. Coll. Hosp., Victoria Hosp., Bangalore, 1983-87; sr. house officer Nat. Spinal Injuries Ctr., Stoke Mandeville, England, 1988-89; clin. rsch. fellow St. Mary's Hosp. Med. Sch., London, 1989-90; clin. tutor U. Aberdeen, Scotland, 1990-92; registrar in cardiology Hammersmith Hosp., London, 1993-95; scientist Harvard Med. Sch./Brigham & Women's Hosp., Boston, 1995-97; heart failure fellow Boston U. Med. Sch., 1997-98; heart transplant fellow U. Tex. Southwestern Med. Sch., Dallas, 1998-99; asst. prof. medicine U. Mich., Ann Arbor, 1999—2005; dir. Cardiology Sect. Ohio State U. Hosp. East, 2005—. Clin. prof. internal medicine Ohio State U., Columbus, Ohio, 2005—. Editor-in-chief St. John's Jour. Medicine, 1988; author: 200 Short Cases in Clinical Medicine, 1993, Multiple Choice Questions in Clinical Medicine, 1994, 250 Short Cases in Clinical Medicine, 3d edit., 2003; editor University of Michigan Cardiology Textbook, 2003; mem. editl. bd. Current Journal Review of American College of Cardiology, 2003. Recipient Nat. Rsch. Svc. award NIH, 1995-97, Astra Found. travel award, Eng., 1995. Fellow: Royal Coll. Physicians Edinburgh, Am. Coll. Cardiology; mem.: Soc. Authors Great Britain, Royal Coll. Surgeons and Physicians Glasgow. Avocations: photography, travel. Office Phone: 619-257-3044.

BALILTY, ODED, photographer; b. Jerusalem, 1979; Photographer Israeli Def. Force Mag., ZOOM 77 agy., Yedioth Ahronot, AP, Jerusalem, 2002—. Photographer (group shows) AP: The Intifada, Visa pour l'Image, Perpignan, France, 2004, Local Testimony: The Best of Israeli Photojournalism, Tel Aviv, 2004. Photographer Israeli Def. Force. Recipient 2nd prize for Photo Stories, Editor & Publisher Awards, 2004, 1st prize for Spot News Photography, Nat. Headliner Awards, 2007, 1st prize for People in the News, World Press Photo, 2007, Sigma Delta Chi award for Photography Spot News, Soc. Profl. Journalists, 2007, Pulitzer Prize for Breaking News Photography, 2007. Office: AP 450 W 33rd St New York NY 10001 Office Phone: 212-621-1500.*

BALINBERG, EDMOND B., physician; b. Braila, Romania, Feb. 1, 1924; s. Maxime and Maria Balinberg; m. Teodora Balinberg, May 15, 2002. MD, Bucharest, Romania, 1949. Clin. asst. Bellevue NYU Med. Ctr., NYC, 1973; med. dir. DHS, NYC, 1974. Fellow: Am. Coll. Physicians; mem.: Am. Diabetes Assn. Office: Diagnostic Health Svc 254 W 31st St New York NY 10001

BALINT, DAVID LEE, communications executive; b. Cleve., June 27, 1946; s. Robert Stephen and Edna Mae (Alward) S. BBA, Cleve. State U., 1969; grad., U.S. Naval War Coll., 1982; MBA, Temple U., 1986. Cert. purchasing mgr., profl. contracts mgr. Commd. ensign USN, 1970, advanced through grades to lt. comdr., retired, 1990; dep. dir. contract adminstrn. Teledyne Brown Engring., Huntsville, Ala., 1990-96, mgr. compliance programs, 1996-2000; mgr. export compliance The Boeing Co., Huntsville, Ala., 2000—04, St. Louis, 2004—07; group mgr. trade compliance ITTAerospace/Comm., Fort Wayne, Ind., 2007—. Adj. faculty Temple U., Phila., 1986-90, Southeastern Inst. Tech., Huntsville, 1991-94, U. Ala., Huntsville, 1994-96. Del. mem. People-to-People Contract Mgmt.; del. People's Republic China, 1986, 1989; pres. Family Svcs. Ctr. Found., 2004, bd. dirs., 1999—2000, North Ala. Internat. Trade Assn., Ala., 1999—2004, Vol. Ctr. Huntsville-Madison County, 1995—97; bd. trustees Employees Cmty. Fun, 2001—04; bd. govs. Sigma Phi Epsilon Ednl. Found., 2001—; bd. dirs. Cleve. State U. Alumni Assn., 2007—. Fellow: Nat. Contract Mgmt. Assn. (nat. v.p. N.E. region 1989—90, nat. v.p. membership 1990—91, nat. functional dir. 1991—98, 2001, Nat. Edn. award 1994, Disting. Svc. award 1995); mem.: Acad. Internat. Bus., Am. Assn. Adult and Continuing Edn., Beta Gamma Sigma (Alumni award 2004). Home: 204 Treeline Cove Fort Wayne IN 46825 Office: ITT Aerospace/Comm 1919 W Cook Rd Fort Wayne IN 46801

BALIS, JANET, Internet company executive; BA, Columbia Coll.; MBA, Harvard Univ. Bus. Sch. Former radio prodr. Newsweek Mag.; mgmt. cons. AT Kearney; with media and entertainment banking investment group Goldman Sachs; co-founder The Mascot Network; former pres. sales, mktg. Time, Inc.; currently sr. v.p., sales mktg. AOL Media Networks. Named one of 40 Under 40, Crain's NY Bus. Mag., 2006. Office: AOL Media Networks 22000 AOL Way Dulles VA 20166

BALIS, MOSES EARL, biochemist, educator; b. Phila., June 19, 1921; s. Harry and Frances (Spector) B.; m. Bernice M. Lamborg, Dec. 30, 1945; children— Frances Andrea, Ellen Joyce. BA, Temple U., 1943; MS, U. Pa., 1947, PhD, 1949. With Sloan-Kettering Inst., 1949-87, head nucleoprotein metabolism sect., 1957—, asso. mem., 1960-65, mem., 1965-87, chief div. cell metabolism, 1970-87; chair inst. senate, 1981-83; cons. Sloan-Kettering Inst., 1987-91; asso. prof. Med. Coll. Cornell U., 1954-66, prof. biochemistry, 1966-87, chmn. biochemistry unit, 1969-74. Vis. lectr. Adelphi U., 1963-64; cons. chemistry dept. Manhattan Coll., 1981-86; mem. study sects. Am. Cancer Soc., NIH.; mem. planning com. Nat. Cancer Plan; mem. rev. com. Nat. Large Bowel Cancer Program, 1977-81; pres. Med. Research Investment Fund, 1984-89. Mem. editl. bd. Cancer Rsch., 1969-73; assoc. editor, 1974-82; contbr. articles to profl. jours. Served to lt. (j.g.) USNR, 1944-46. Recipient Research Career award USPHS, 1963 Mem. Am. Chem. Soc. (past sect. chmn.), AAAS, Am. Cancer Soc., Am. Soc. Biol Chemistry and Molecular Biology, Harvey Soc., Am. Assn. Cancer Rsch., Sigma Xi. Achievements include research on metabolism of purines in normal and malignant tissues; determined biochem. action of anti-cancer drugs, biochemical nature of genetic defects. Home and Office: 2792 Donnelly Dr Apt 2512 Lantana FL 33462 Office Phone: 561-434-4534.

BALK, ALFRED WILLIAM, journalist; b. Oskaloosa, Iowa, July 24, 1930; s. Leslie William and Clara Irene (Buell) B.; m. Phyllis Lorraine Munter, June 7, 1952; children: Laraine M., Diane M. Student, Augustana Coll., Rock Island, Ill., 1948—49; BS, Northwestern U., 1952, MS, 1953. Reporter Rock Island Argus, 1946-50; newswriter, prodr. WBBM (CBS), Chgo., 1952-53; reporter Chgo. Sun-Times, 1956; mag. writer, pub. rels. J. Walter Thompson Co., Chgo., 1957-58; freelance writer nat. mags., including spl. writer Saturday Evening Post, 1958-66; feature editor Saturday Rev., 1966-68, editor at large, 1968-69; vis. scholar Russell Sage Found., 1968-69; lectr. journalism, editor Columbia Journalism Rev., 1969-73; editor World Press Rev., 1974, editor, pub., 1975-84, editl. dir., 1985-86, editl. cons., contbg. editor, 1986-94; mng. editor IEEE Spectrum, NYC, 1989-91; assoc. prof. Syracuse (NY) U., 1991-94; freelance writer, cons., 1994—. Cons., rapporteur 20th Century Fund Task Force on Nat. News Coun., 1971-72, Ford Found., Markle Found.; faculty Bread Loaf Writers Conf., Middlebury, Vt., 1971; exec. sec. NY Gov.'s Com. on Employment Minority Groups in News Media, 1968-69; adv. com. World Press Inst., 1984-96. Author (with Irv Kupcinet): Kup's Chicago, 1962; author: The Free List: Property Without Taxes, 1970, A Free and Responsive Press, 1973, The Myth of American Eclipse: The New Global Age, 1990, Movie Palace Masterpiece: Saving Syracuse's Loew's State/Landmark Theatre, 1998, The Rise of Radio, from Marconi through the Golden Age, 2006; co-editor: Our Troubled Press, 1971. Bd. dir. Am. Jour. Nursing Co., 1990—93, Landmark Theatre Found., 1996—99. Mem. Am. Soc. Mag. Editors (exec. coun. 1977-83), Soc. Mag. Writers (pres. 1967), Soc. Profl. Journalists, Overseas Press Club (gov. 1978-79), Century Assn. Home: 13225 Michigan Ave Huntley IL 60142-7480

BALK, ROBERT A., medical educator; BA, U. Mo., Kansas City, 1976, MD, 1978. Resident internal medicine U. Mo., Kansas City, 1978—81; fellow pulmonary and critical care medicine U. Ark., Little Rock, 1981—83, instr. medicine, 1981—83, asst. prof. medicine, 1983—85; staff physician Little Rock VA Med. Ctr., 1983—85; asst. prof. medicine Rush-Presbyn.-St. Luke's Med. Ctr., Chgo., 1985—88, assoc. prof., 1988—95, prof. medicine, 1995—, asst. dir. sect. pulmonary medicine, 1985—90, med. dir. respiratory care svcs., 1985-93, med. dir. noninvasive respiratory care unit, 1985—87, co-dir. med. intensive care unit, 1986—88, dir. med. intensive care unit, 1988-95, assoc. dir. sect. pulmonary & crit. care medicine, 1993—97, assoc. dir. sect. critical care medicine, 1995—2002, dir. pulmonary & critical care medicine fellowship tng. program, 1994—, dir. pulmonary and critical care medicine, 2002—; J. Bailey Carter prof. med. ctr. Rush Med. Coll., Chgo., 2002. Contbr. articles to profl. jours. Recipient Dedicated Svc. & Superior Individual Effort in Patient Care Alice Sachs Meml. award, 1991, Alfred Soffer Rsch. award, Am. Coll. Chest Physicians, 1995, Take Wing award, U. Mo.-Kansas City Sch. Medicine, 1998. Office: Rush Univ Med Ctr 1653 W Congress Pkwy Chicago IL 60612-3833 E-mail: rbalk@rush.edu.

BALKA, SIGMUND RONELL, lawyer; b. Phila., Aug. 1, 1935; s. I. Edwin and Jane (Chernicoff) B.; m. Elinor Bernstein, May 29, 1966. AB, Williams Coll., 1956; JD, Harvard U., 1959. Bar: Pa. and D.C. 1961, N.Y. 1969, U.S. Supreme Ct. 1966. Sr. atty. Lilco, Mineola, NY, 1969-70; v.p., gen. counsel Brown Boveri Corp., North Brunswick, NJ, 1970-75; asst. gen. counsel Power Authority State N.Y., NYC, 1975-80; gen. counsel Krasdale Foods, Inc., NYC, 1980—, v.p., 2005—. Chmn. Hunts Point Environ. Protection Coun., NYC, 1980—, Soc. for a Better Bronx, 1985—; chair fellows, mem. vis. com. Williams Coll. Mus. of Art, 1996—99; exec. com. bd. trustees Queens Mus. of Art, 2001—; chmn. law com. NYC Cmty. Bd. 6, Queens, 1980—88, chmn. econ. devel. com., 1988—99; chmn. Bronx Borough Pres.'s Adv. Com. on Resource Recovery, 1988—90; bd. dirs. Bronx Arts Coun., 1981—2003, Greater NY Met. Food Coun., 1986—, Jewish Repertory Theatre, 1987—, chmn., 2001—; bd. dirs. Judaica Mus., 2006—; bd. trustees Bronx Mus. Arts, 2007—. Fellow Am. Bar Found., N.Y. Bar Found.; mem. ABA (co-chmn. pro bono project corp. law dept. 1986-88, chmn. 1988-90, com. of corp. gen. counsel 1974—, planning chmn. 1994-96, membership chmn. 1996-98, pro bono chair 2000—), Am. Corp. Counsel Assn. (bd. dirs. Met. N.Y. chpt. 1987—, bd. dirs. Found. 1992-99), Assn. Bar City N.Y., Print Connoisseurs Soc. N.Y. (pres.). Office: Krasdale Foods Inc 400 Food Center Dr Bronx NY 10474-7098 Office Phone: 718-378-1100 x2125.

BALKAN, KENNETH J., lawyer; b. NYC, Oct. 18, 1948; s. Robert and Leona (Brenner) B.; m. Berta Hochman, Aug. 16, 1970; children: Richard, Lauren, Adam. BA, Fairleigh Dickinson U., 1969; JD, St. John's U., 1972. Bar: N.Y. 1973, U.S. Dist. Ct. (so. and ea. dists.) N.Y. 1974, U.S. Ct. Appeals (2d cir.) 1975, U.S. Supreme Ct. 1978. Law intern Dist. Atty.'s Office County of Queens, NYC, 1971; assoc. Kroll, Edelman, Elser & Wilson, NYC, 1972-77; ptnr. Wilson, Elser, Edelman & Dicker, NYC, 1977-81, L'Abbate & Balkan, Garden City, N.Y., 1981-94, L'Abbate, Balkan, Colavita & Contini, L.L.P., Garden City, 1995-98, of counsel, 1999—. Mem. St. John's Law Rev., 1971-72; mediator for U.S. Dist. Ct. (ea. and so. dists.) N.Y.; adminstrv. judge Waterfront Commn. N.Y. Harbor; arbitrator, panel mem. NYSERB; arbitrator 10th Jud. Dist. Nassau County; atty. Client Fee Dispute Resolution Program; lectr. in field. Contbr. articles to profl. jours. Mem. Def. Rsch. Inst. Mem. ABA, N.Y. State Bar Assn. (former mem. com. profl. discipline, mem. ins. negligence and compensation law com., trial lawyers com.), Nassau County Bar Assn. (coms., ins. law, fee conciliation, past profl. ethics chair, mem. exec. subcom.). Office: L'Abbate Balkan Colavita & Contini LLP 1050 Franklin Ave Garden City NY 11530-2929 Home Phone: 516-626-0228; Office Phone: 516-294-8844. E-mail: kbalkan@lbcclaw.com, kbalkan@aol.com.

BALKE, VICTOR H., bishop; b. Meppen, Ill., Sept. 29, 1931; s. Bernard H. and Elizabeth A. (Knese) B. BA in Philosophy, St. Mary of Lake Sem., Mundelein, Ill., 1954, STB in Theology, 1956, MA in Religion, 1057, STL in Theology, 1958; MA in English, St. Louis U., 1964, PhD, 1973. Priest Roman Cath. Ch., 1958. Asst. pastor, Springfield, Ill., 1958—62; chaplain St. Joseph Home Aged, Springfield, 1962—63; procurator, instr. Diocesan Sem., Springfield, 1963—70, rector, instr., 1970—76; ordained, installed 6th bishop Crookston, Minn., 1976—. Mem.: Lions, KC. Office: Chancery Office PO Box 610 Crookston MN 56716-0610

BALKIN, ALFRED, music educator, composer; b. Boston, Aug. 12, 1931; s. Samuel John and Rose Balkin; m. Rita Ann Gross, June 21, 1953; children: Michael Phillip, Linda Ellen. BA, Ind. U., Bloomington, 1952, MA, 1953, Columbia U., NYC, 1963, EdD, 1968. Cert. K-12 tchr. NJ. Profl. pianist, singer, NYC, 1955—59; advt. rep. Music Jour., NYC, 1959—62; K-12 tchr. East Brunswick (NJ) Pub. Schs., 1962—65; 7-8 tchr. Irvington (NJ) Pub. Schs., 1965—66; prof. Ea. Conn. State Coll., Willimantic, 1966—68, Fla. State U., Tallahassee, 1968—71, Western Mich. U., Kalamazoo, 1971—93, prof. emeritus. Composer, lyricist: We Live in the City (21 songs), 1971, City Scene (17 songs), 1977, The Musicians of Bremen, 1982, America The Musical, 1987, Shabbat with Jazz, 2001, Tune Up To Literacy (91 songs), 2004, composer, lyricist: choral works from original songs for mid. schs. and HS. With US Army, 1954—55. Fellow: ASCAP (awards 1985—). Avocation: tennis. Home: 8 Pheasant Run Hilton Head Island SC 29926 E-mail: drbalkin@hargray.com.

BALKO, GEORGE ANTHONY, III, lawyer, educator; b. Bklyn., June 22, 1955; s. George Anthony Jr. and Settimia (Palumbo) B. AB, Yale U., 1977; JD, U. Calif., San Francisco, 1986. Bar: Mass. 1986, U.S. Dist. Ct. Mass. 1987, U.S. Dist. Ct. Conn. 1999, U.S. Ct. Appeals (1st cir.) 1987, D.C 1990. Assoc. Swartz & Swartz, Boston, 1986-87, Bowditch & Dewey, LLP, Worcester, Mass., 1987-95, ptnr., 1996—. Adj. prof. Anna Maria Coll., Paxton, Mass., 1988-2000, mem. paralegal studies adv. bd., 1988-95. Author: Risk Management for Nursing Homes: A Primer In Long-Term Care Adminstration Handbook, 1993, Ambulatory Care and the Law: Lien Claims Where None Exist As of Right, 1995; legal columnist Jour. of Workers Compensation, 1996-99. Mem. Rice Sch. PTA, Holden, Mass., 1989-93; bd. health Town of Holden, 1995-99, chmn. 1996-99; moderator, 1999—; pres., bd. dirs. Elm Park Ctr. for Early Childhood Edn., 1994-96, mem. 1993-97. Recipient Am. Jurisprudence award for Ins. Law Lawyers

Coop. Pub. Co. and Bancroft Whitney Co., 1985. Roman Catholic. Avocations: history, travel, tennis. Home: 4 Chestnut Hill Rd Holden MA 01520-1603 Office: Bowditch and Dewey LLP PO Box 15156 311 Main St Worcester MA 01615-0156 Business E-Mail: gbalko@bowditch.com.

BALKOWIEC, AGNIESZKA ZOFIA, science educator, researcher; b. Sokolow Podlaski, Poland, Sept. 30, 1968; d. Anna and Jerzy Michal Balkowiec. MD, Med. U. Warsaw, Poland, 1993, PhD, 1995. Instr. physiology Med. U. Warsaw, 1993—95, asst. prof., 1995—99; rsch. assoc. Case Western Res. U., Cleve., 1997—2001, instr. neuroscis., 2001—02; asst. prof. Oreg. Health & Sci. U., Portland, 2002—. Reviewer profl. jours. Contbr. articles to profl. jours. Recipient Sci. award, Polish Min. Health and Social Welfare, 1994, 1996, Prime Min. of Poland, 1996; fellow, Found. Polish Sci., 1995; grantee, Am. Heart Assn., 2002—, NIH, 2004—, Nat. Heart, Lung and Blood Inst., 2004—. Mem.: Am. Chem. Soc., Am. Dental Edn. Assn., Am. Heart Assn. (basic cardiovas. scis. coun. 2002, grantee 2002—), Soc. Neurosci. Achievements include discovery of the role of activity of nerve cells in regulation of growth factors; invention of setup for immunodetection of growth factors released from neurons following electrical stimulation. Avocations: travel, gourmet cooking, classical music, photography. Office: Oregon Health & Sci U 611 SW Campus Dr Portland OR 97239 Office Phone: 503-418-0190. Business E-Mail: balkowie@ohsu.edu.

BALKRISHNAN, RAJESH, education educator; s. PV and Shanta Balkrishnan; life ptnr. George W. Simmons. BS, U. Bombay, 1995; PhD, U. N.C., Chapel Hill, NC, 1999. Asst. prof. Wake Forest U., Winston-Salem, NC, 1999—2003; assoc. prof. U. Tex., Houston, 2003—04; Merrell Dow prof. Ohio State U., Columbus, Ohio, 2005—. Contbr. articles pub. to over 200 profl. jour. and books. Recipient Brooks Scholar in Academic Medicine, Wake Forest U., 2001-2003. D-Liberal. Hindu. Avocations: movies, classical music, reading. Home: 1056 Pennsylvania Ave Columbus OH 43201 Office: Ohio State Univ 500 West 12th St Columbus OH 43210 Home Phone: 614-291-8794; Office Phone: 614-292-6415. Office Fax: 614-292-1335. Personal E-mail: rbgws1@sbcglobal.net. Business E-Mail: balkrishnan.1@osu.edu.

BALL, ALAN, screenwriter; b. Atlanta, 1957; Student in theater, Fla. State U. Founding mem., writer, actor, dir. Alarm Dog Rep. Playwright: The M Word, 1991, Five Women Wearing the Same Dress, 1993, Made For a Woman, Bachelor Holiday, Your Mother's Butt, The Amazing Adventures of Tense Guy, All That I Will Ever Be, 2007; Screenwriter, co-prodr. (feature film) American Beauty, 1999 (Oscar for best screenplay 1999, Golden Globe for best screenplay motion picture 2000, Satellite award for best original screenplay 2000; best screenplay BFCA award, DGA award, ALFA award, SEFCA award and WGA Screen award 2000), The M Word, 2004; screenwriter, creator, exec. prodr. (tv series) Grace Under Fire, 1993; co-exec. prodr. (tv series) Cybill, 1995; exec. prodr., creator (tv series) Oh Grow Up, 1999; screenwriter, dir., exec. prod. (tv series) Six Feet Under, 2001-2005 (Emmy for outstanding director for a drama series 2002). Office: c/o Andrew Cannava United Talent Agy 9560 Wilshire Blvd Fl 5 Beverly Hills CA 90212-2401*

BALL, ARMAND BAER, former association executive, consultant; b. Dubach, La., Sept. 30, 1930; s. Armand Baer and Lovera (Sanderson) B.; m. Beverly Jane Hodges, Sept. 15, 1957; children: Kathryn Lynn, Robin Armand. BA, La. Coll., 1951; MRE, Southwestern Bapt. Theol. Sem., 1953; MS, George Williams Coll., 1960. Royal Ambassador dir. Fla. Bapt. Conv., Jacksonville, 1953-57; program dir. Woodlawn Boys' Club, Chgo., 1957-58; camp/youth dir. YMCA, Nashville, 1958-62; exec. dir. YMCA Camps Widjiwagan/duNord, St. Paul YMCA, 1962-74; exec. Am. Camping Assn., Martinsville, Ind., 1974-88; cons., 1988—; assoc. Campaign Assocs., Phila., 1989—. Author: (with Beverly H. Ball) Basic Camp Management, 2004; editor: A Cost Study of Resident Camps, 1985; Internat. Camping Fellowship newsletter, 1987-97; co-editor: Business and Finance, Site and Facilities; Trendlines newsletter. Cons. Ctr. Disease Control, St. Petersburg (Russia) Children's Camps, Malaysian Tourist Bd., Pan-Am. Inst. Phys. Edn. (Venezuela), Heritage Conservation and Recreation Svc., Project Reach, Boy Scouts Am., United Ch. of Christ, YMCA, Episcopal Ch.; mem. Internat. Camping Fellowship; bd. dir., past pres; chair Sanibel Parks and Recreation Com., Cmty. Housing Resources Inc.; mem. adv. bd. Ctr. Environ. and Sustainability Edn., Fla. Gulf Coast U. Recipient Disting. Svc. award Am. Camping Assn., 1989, Druszba award, 2002; named Citizen Yr., Sanibel, Fla., 1999, Disting. Alumni Yr., Aurora U., 2003, Disting. Alumni award, George Williams Coll./Aurora U., 2003. Mem. Am. Soc. Assn. Execs. (cert. assoc. exec. life), World Future Soc., Audubon Soc., Canadian Camping Assn., Kiwanis (Hixon award). Home and Office: 1351 Middle Gulf Dr Apt 2A Sanibel FL 33957-4631 Office Phone: 239-472-0536. Personal E-mail: alphaball@comcast.net.

BALL, BARRY ALLEN, veterinarian, researcher; b. Honaker, Va., Sept. 29, 1956; s. Mack Allen and Virginia Kathleen (Jackson) B.; m. Heidi Allison Hock, May 25, 1985; children: Kaitlin Marie, Laurel Leigh. Student, Va. Tech., 1974-77; DVM, U. Ga., 1981; PhD, Cornell U., 1987. Diplomate Am. Coll. Theriogenologists. Resident in reproduction U. Fla., Gainesville, 1982-84; asst. prof. Cornell U., Ithaca, N.Y., 1987-93, assoc. prof., 1993-96; Hughes Endowed Chair in Equine Reprodn. U. Calif., Davis, 1997—. Cons. Thornbrook Farms, Bedford Hills, N.Y., 1987-94, Burnett Park Zoo, Syracuse, N.Y., 1990-91, Naval Rsch. Lab., Washington, 1991-92; reviewer USDA, Washington, 1990-94. Smithkline Beecham scholar Coll. Vet. Medicine/Cornell U., 1992; Rsch. grant USDA/Cornell U., 1991—; recipient Norden Disting. Tchg. award U. Calif. Davis, 2003, Fulbright Disting. Scholar U. Cambridge, 2004-05. Mem. AAAS, Am. Vet. Med. Assn. (excellence in equine rsch. award 1996), Soc. for Study Reproduction, Internat. Embryo Transfer Soc. (student rsch. award 1987), Am. Assn. Equine Practitioners. Achievements include research in gamete biology embryonic development and embryonic mortality in the horse. Office: 1113 Tupper Hall U Calif Davis CA 95616 E-mail: baball@ucdavis.edu.

BALL, CARROLL RAYBOURNE, anatomist, researcher, medical educator; b. Leakesville, Miss., Oct. 11, 1925; s. Marvin Hugh and Elizabeth (Hillman) B.; m. Jannie Vee Brooks, Sept. 5, 1947 (dec. 1954); children: Hugh Brooks, Peter Stephen; m. Sally Ann Montgomery, Mar. 22, 1963 (div. 1976); 1 child, Lou Ellen. BA, U. Miss., 1947, MS, 1948, PhD, 1963. Grad. asst. in zoology U. Miss., Oxford, 1946-48; instr. Duke U., 1948-51; instr. anatomy Med. Sch. W.Va. U., 1951-57; asst. prof. biology U. So. Miss., 1957-60; asst. prof. U. Miss. Med. Ctr., Jackson, 1963-66, assoc. prof., 1966-71, prof., 1971-99. Contbr. numerous articles to profl. jours. Pres. Jackson Civil War Round Table, 1983-84; chmn. Hist. Coker House Restoration Project, 1984-99; v.p. Magnolia chpt. Nat. Assn. Watch and Clock Collectors, 1980-82; bd. dirs. Miss. Hist. Soc., 1976-79, 85-88, 93-96. Lt. comdr. USNR, 1944-71, PTO. NIH predoctoral trainee, 1960-63; Miss. Heart Assn. grantee, 1963-66 Mem. Am. Assn. Anatomists, Soc. Exptl. Biology and Medicine, Am. Assn. Pathology, So. Assn. Anatomy, Miss. Acad. Sci., Hattiesburg Jr. C. of C. (sec. 1959-60), Order of First Families of Miss. (Gov. Gen. 2001-2003), Sigma Xi, Alpha Epsilon Delta, Theta Nu Sigma, Beta Beta Beta (pres. 1947-48), Omicron Delta Kappa, Pi Kappa Alpha (sec. 1943-44) Methodist.

BALL, CLYDE CURTIS, journalist, public information officer, public relations executive; b. Jeffrey Boone County, W.Va., June 25, 1921; BS in Journalism, Marshall U., Huntington, W.Va., 1943. Reporter Assoc. Press, Huntington, 1945—59; pub. rels. exec. Philco Ford Corp., Washington, 1963—70; pub. rels. officer US Govt. Commerce Dept., Dept., Energy, Dept. Trans., Maritime Adminstrn., Washington, 1970—86; et. Speech writer, science writer Philco Ford, Phila., 1963—70; speech writer US Govt. Spiro Agnew Maritime Adminstrn., Washington, 1970—86. Ghost writer (speeches for Spiro Agnew), 1972—73. 1st lt. USN, 1943—45, South Pacific. Recipient Poetry Works award, Va. Poetry Soc., Charlottesille, 1998. Mem.: Nat. Press Club. Avocations: walking, poetry.

BALL, DAN H., lawyer; BA cum laude, Bradley U., 1974; JD Order of the Coif, U. Mo., 1978. Bar: Mo. 1978, Ill. 1979. Ptnr., group leader Product Liability Bryan Cave LLP, St. Louis. Fellow: Am. Coll. Trial Lawyers. Office: Bryan Cave LLP One Metropolitan Sq 211 N Broadway, Ste 3600 Saint Louis MO 63102 Office Phone: 314-259-2200. Office Fax: 314-552-8200. E-mail: dhball@bryancave.com.

BALL, DEBORAH LOEWENBERG, dean, education educator; BA, Mich. State U., 1976, MA, 1982, postgrad., 1981—83, PhD, 1988. Elementary classroom teacher, 1975—88; mem. faculty Mich. State U., East Lansing, 1988—96; Arthur F. Thurnau prof. U. Mich. Sch. Edn., Ann Arbor, 2000—03, William H. Payne collegiate prof. math., 2003—, interim dean, 2005—. Lead author Stds. for Tchg. sect. Profl. Stds. for Tchg. Math., Nat. Coun. Tchrs. Math., 1989—91; mem. adv. bd. Investigations in Number, Data, Space, 1991—96; mem. Commn. on Behavioral and Social Sci. Edn. Nat. Rsch. Coun., NAS, 1996—99, mem. math. learning study, 1999—2000; chair math. study panel RAND Project: Improving the Quality of Educational Research and Devel., 1999—2000; mem. commn. on undergrad. experience U. Mich., 2000—01; co-chair tchr. edn. study Internat. Commn. on Math. Instrn., 2002—; bd. trustees Math. Scis. Rsch. Inst. U. Calif., Berkeley, 2003—. Contbr. articles to profl. jours.; mem. editl. bd.: Am. Ednl. Rsch. Jour., 1999—, Jour. Ednl. Rsch., 1990—93, Elem. Sch. Jour., 1991—. Recipient Raymond B. Cattell Early Career award for programmatic rsch., Am. Ednl. Rsch. Assn., 1997, Award for outstanding Scholarship on Tchr. Edn., Assn. Colls. and Schs. of Edn. in State Univs. and Land Grant Colls. and Affiliated Pvt. Univs., 1990. Office: U Mich 1110 Sch Edn Bldg 610 E University Ann Arbor MI 48109-1259

BALL, DONALD L., retired language educator; b. Balt., Oct. 25, 1922; s. Ambrose Markley and Daisy Gertrude (Anderson) B.; stepmother Thelma (Bonneville) B.; m. Barbara Jean Stevens, May 3, 1950; children: Helen Ball Williams, Ann S., Allison Ball Miller, Markley Ball Rizzi. BA, U. Richmond, 1948; MA, U. Del., 1951; PhD, U. N.C., 1965. Asst. mgr. resort hotels in Md. and Fla., 1948-53; instr. English Va. Mil. Inst., Lexington, 1953-57; part-time instr. U. N.C., Chapel Hill, 1957-60; faculty Coll. William and Mary, Williamsburg, Va., 1960-89, prof., 1976-89; vis. prof. English U.S. Mil. Acad., West Point, N.Y., 1984-85. Author: Samuel Richardson's Theory of Fiction, 1971, Fighting Amphibs-The LCS(L) in World War II, 1997; contbr. articles to profl. publs. Served to lt. (j.g.) USNR, 1943-46, PTO. Research grantee Coll. William and Mary, 1978. Mem. MLA. Episcopalian. Avocations: genealogy, history, music. Home: 1 Cole Ln Williamsburg VA 23185-3313

BALL, DONALD MAURY, agronomist, consultant; b. Owensboro, Ky., Aug. 5, 1945; s. William Alonzo and Mary Ruth (Waltrip) B.; Vonda Lee Hatcher, June 3, 1967; children: Kelly Wayne, Allison Lee. BS, Western Ky. U., 1968; MS, Auburn U., 1973, PhD, 1976. Cert. profl. agronomist. Ext. agronomist Auburn (Ala.) U., 1976-88, ext. agronomist/prof., 1988-97, alumni prof., 1997—2002. Mem. nat. adv. com. Alfalfa Coun., Davis, Calif., 1983-2003; tech. advisor Oreg. Tall Fescue Commn., Salem, 1990—; tech. liaison Oreg. Clover Commn., Salem, 1994—; del. Internat. Grassland Congress, Nice, France, 1989; spkr. in field. Author: Southern Forages, 1991, Practical Forage Concepts, 1999; contbr. over 550 articles to profl. and applied jours. and trade mags. Elder First Presbyn. Ch., Auburn, 1982-85. With U.S. Army, 1968-71. Recipient Superior Svc. award USDA, Washington, 1986, Extension Excellence award Auburn Univ. Alumni Assn., 1988, Alumnus of Yr. award We. Ky. Univ. Dept. Agrl., Bowling Green, 1990, Disting. Career award Ala. Extension Sys., 2005; named to Hall of Disting. Alumni, 2000. Fellow Am. Soc. Agronomy (Crops and Soils award 1984, ext. Agronomy Edn. award 1993), Crop Sci. Soc. Am.; mem. Am. Forage and Grassland Coun. (pres. 1990-91, Merit award 1984, Medallion award 1993), So. Pasture and Forage Crop Improvement Conf. (chair 1987-88). Democrat. Office: Auburn Univ Dept Agronomy & Soils Auburn AL 36849

BALL, EDWARD DAVID, hematologist, oncologist; b. Syracuse, NY, Mar. 15, 1950; s. Edward and Della Lucille (Koehler) B.; m. Elizabeth Kate Rath, June 20, 1970 (div. 1975); 1 child, David; m. Susan Elaine Blonder, Jan. 15, 1977; children: Brian, Lindsey. BS in Biochemistry, U. Md., 1972; MD, Case Western Res. U., 1976. Resident Hartford Hosp., 1976-79; fellow in hematology and oncology Univ. Hosps. Cleve., 1979-81, Dartmouth-Hitchcock Med. Ctr., 1982-83; asst. prof. Dartmouth Coll., Hanover, NH, 1982-86, assoc. prof., 1986-91; prof. U. Pitts., 1991-98; prof. medicine, chief divsn. bone marrow transplant U. Calif., San Diego, 1998—. Co-founder Medarex, Inc., Princeton, NJ, 1987; dir. bone marrow transplant program Pitts. Cancer Inst., 1993-98, co-dir. leukemia/lymphoma program, 1991-98; mem. staff Montefiore U. Hosp., Pitts., 1991-98, Presbyn. U. Hosp., Pitts., 1991-98; assoc. mem. Hitchcock Clinic, Hanover, NH, 1983-91; mem. clin. staff Mary Hitchcock Meml. Hosp., Hanover, 1983-91; mem. sr. staff Norris Cotton Cancer Ctr., Hanover, 1983-91. Contbr. articles to profl. jours., chpts. to books. Bd. dirs. Leukemia Soc. Am., Pitts., 1991-98. Scholar Leukemia Soc. Am., 1986-91, Stolhman award; Tiffany Blake fellow Hitchcock Found., 1982-83. Mem. AAAS, Am. Soc. Hematology, Am. Soc. Clin. Oncology, Am. Assn. Immunologists, Am. Assn. Cancer Rsch., Am. Soc. for Blood and Marrow Transplantation (bd. dirs. 2001-2004), Am. Soc. for Clin. Investigation, Internat. Soc. for Exptl. Hematology (councilor 2003—), Assn. Subsplty. Profs., Assn. Hematology/Oncology Program Dirs. (pres. 1998-2000), Phi Beta Kappa, Phi Kappa Phi. Avocations: running, skiing, hiking, bicycling, surfing. Office: U Calif San Diego Bone Marrow Transplant Divsn 200 West Arbor Dr San Diego CA 92103 Office Phone: 858-822-6600, 412-624-1115. Business E-Mail: tball@ucsd.edu.*

BALL, F. MACNAUGHTON, JR., architect; b. Charleston, SC; BA, U. NC, 1975; MArch, Yale U., New Haven, 1978. With Cesar Pelli & Assocs., 1979—86; founder, prin. Waggonner & Ball Archs., New Orleans, 1989—. Tchr. archtl. design Yale U., Tulane U., New Orleans. Mem.: AIA. Office: Waggonner & Ball Archs 2200 Prytania St New Orleans LA 70130 Office Phone: 504-524-5308. Office Fax: 504-524-5314. E-mail: m_ball@wbarchitects.com.*

BALL, GEORGE L., investment banker; b. Evanston, Ill., 1938; BA, Brown U., 1960. Pres. E. F. Hutton Group Inc. and E. F. Inc., NYC, 1969-82; pres., CEO Prudential Bache Securities Group, Inc., NYC, 1982-86, chmn., CEO, 1986-91; cons., prod. devel. J&W Seligman & Co., NYC, 1991-92; sr. exec. v.p. Smith Barney Shearson Inc., NYC, 1992—94; non-exec. chmn. Sanders Morris Mundy Inc., Houston, 1992—97; chmn. Sanders Morris Harris Group Inc., Houston, 2002—. Mem. exec. com. Prudential Ins. Co. Am., 1982—91; bd. dirs. Sanders Morris Harris Group, 2000—, Nestor Inc. Trustee Brown U.; mem. Presdl. adv. coun. Pvt. Sector Initiative; mem. bus. com. Met. Mus. Arts.; dir. Paper Mill Playhouse (the State Theatre of N.J.); bd. overseers Duke Comprehensive Cancer Ctr.; trustee Joint Coun. Econ. Edn.; nat. trustee Nat. Symphony Orch.; vice chmn. bd. trustees S. St. Seaport Mus. Mem. Securities Industry Assn., Bond Club N.Y. (v.p.). Office: Sanders Morris Harris Inc 3100 JP Morgan Chase Tower 600 Travis Ste 3100 Houston TX 77002 E-mail: George.Ball@smhgroup.com.

BALL, GREGORY FRANCIS, biological psychology educator; b. Washington, May 6, 1955; s. William Howard and Angela Marie (Hosinski) B. BA, Columbia U., 1977; PhD, Rutgers U., 1983. Postdoctoral fellow Rockefeller U., NYC, 1983-86, asst. prof. biol. psychology, 1986-88, Boston Coll., Chestnut Hill, Mass., 1988-91; from asst. prof. to assoc. prof. biol. psychology Johns Hopkins U., Balt., 1991—98, prof., 1998—. Contbr. numerous articles to profl. jours. Charles Revson Found. biomed. fellow, 1986-88; USPHS fellow, 1983-86. Fellow APA, Am. Ornithologists Union; mem. Soc. for Neurosci., Animal Behavior Soc., Soc. for Integrated and Comparative Biology, Am. Psychol. Soc. Office: Johns Hopkins U 230 Ames Hall 3400 N Charles St Baltimore MD 21218-2680 Home Phone: 410-752-3391; Office Phone: 410-516-7910. E-mail: gball@jhu.edu.

BALL, HOWARD GUY, association administrator, educator; b. Lancaster, Ohio, Aug. 4, 1930; s. Howard Emitt and Edith Mildred (Clark) B.; married; children: Brian, Maryla. BS, Ohio State U., 1952, MS, 1969, PhD, 1972. Edn. specialist Ohio Dept. Edn., Columbus, 1964-71; assoc. prof. NC State U., 1971-74; mem. faculty Ala. A&M U., Normal, 1974—; prof. emeritus Ala. A&M U. (Sch. Library Media); chmn. bd. Communicon, Inc., Huntsville, Ala. Chmn. Media Svcs., Inc.; pres. Higby Inc.; dir. So. Inst. for Black Studies, 1995-96. Mem. editorial bd. Library Scene, 1979-80, Media and Methods: Early Years, 1984-85; contbr. articles to profl. jours.; authored, directed: Training of Librarians in CATV, 1975. Mem. Ala. Coun. Human Relations, 1978— , Ala. Dem. Coun., 1978—; sec. Orgn. Inner City Govts., 1977—. Recipient NAACP Cmty. award, 1976, Raleigh C. of C. educator's award, 1973 Mem. ALA, Assn. Educators Comm. and Tech., Assn. Ednl. Research (regional v.p. 1985-86), Phi Beta Kappa, Phi Delta Kappa, Kappa Alpha Psi. Clubs: Masons. Presbyterian. Office Phone: 256-721-7708. Personal E-mail: ball9888@bellsouth.net.

BALL, JAMES HERINGTON, retired lawyer; b. Kansas City, Mo., Sept. 20, 1942; s. James T. Jr. and Betty Sue (Herington) B.; m. Wendy Anne Wolfe, Dec. 28, 1964; children: James H. Jr., Steven Scott. AB, U. Mo., 1964; JD cum laude, St. Louis U., 1973. Bar: Mo. 1973. Asst. gen. counsel Anheuser-Busch, Inc., St. Louis, 1973-76; v.p., gen. counsel, sec. Stouffer Corp., Solon, Ohio, 1976-83; sr. v.p., gen. counsel Nestle Enterprises, Inc., Solon, 1983-91; gen. counsel, sr. v.p. Nestle USA, Inc., Glendale, Calif., 1991-99. Editor-in-chief St. Louis U. Law Jour., 1972-73. Bd. dirs. Alliance for Children's Rights, L.A., 1992-99, Am. Swiss Found., N.Y.C., 1996-99. Lt. comdr. USN, 1964-70, Vietnam. Mem. Mo. Bar Assn. E-mail: Balljimh@bellsouth.net.

BALL, JOHN FLEMING, advertising and film company executive; b. Evanston, Ill., Apr. 26, 1930; s. Edward Hyde and Kathleen (Fleming) B.; m. Anne Idabelle Firestone, Nov. 9, 1957; children— John Fleming, Jr., David Firestone, Sheila Ball Burkert. BA, Princeton U., NJ, 1952. Assoc. prodr., progam exec. CBS, NYC, 1955-59; with J. Walter Thompson Co., NYC, 1959—, v.p., 1965—, dir. programs, 1965-67, dir. broadcasting, 1967—83, pres., dir. Survival Anglia Ltd. div., 1972—; pres. Trident Anglia Inc., 1976—; chmn. John F. Ball Prodns., John F. Ball Co., 1984—. Trustee Found. Am. Dance; chmn. instructional TV, Archidiocese of NY; bd. dirs. Hist. Soc. Town of Greenwich, Conn. With USN, 1952-54. Mem. Knights of Holy Sepulchre of Jerusalem Knights of Sovereign Mil. Order of Malta, Knights of Order of St. Gregory the Gt., Cap and Gown Club of Princeton U. (NYC), Links Club, Round Hill Club (Greenwich), Nassau Club (Princeton), Am. Club (London), Princeton Triangle Club (chmn. emeritus grad. bd.). Home: Deer Park Greenwich CT 06830 also: Northport Point Northport MI 49670 Office: 4 Woodside Rd Greenwich CT 06830-3819 Office Phone: 203-661-8987. Personal E-mail: jfbp@aol.com.

BALL, JOHN PAUL, publishing company executive; b. NYC, Dec. 15, 1946; s. William Emil and Else (Schmid) B.; m. Jayne Barbara Irwin, Jan. 30, 1970 (div. 1991); m. Eileen M. Mitchell, Oct. 25, 1997. Student, N.Y. Sch. Printing, 1964. Prodn. assoc. Macmillan Co., NYC, 1964-65; asst. to pres. Frederick Fell, Inc., NYC, 1965-69; v.p. William Morrow & Co., Inc., NYC, 1969-86; sr. v.p. mfg. and paper purchasing Macmillan Pub. Co., NYC, 1986-94; pub. and graphic arts cons., chmn. bd. Electronic Pub. Svcs. Inc., NYC, 1994—; exec. v.p., sec. Hungry Minds, Inc., NYC, Calif., 1996—2001; cons. in pub. NYC, 2001—04; sr. v.p. fin. and ops. Dorling Kindersley USA, 2004. Recipient Comet Press award graphic arts, 1964, Columbia Scholastic Press Assn. Best Editorial Writing award, 1965. Office: Electronic Pub Svcs Inc 15 E 32d St 2d Fl New York NY 10016 Business E-Mail: jball@e-p-s.com.

BALL, JOHN ROBERT, healthcare executive; b. Opelika, Ala., July 16, 1944; s. John Cooper Jr. and Ellen Beverly (Williams) B.; m. Cornelia Anne Phillips, Aug. 13, 1966 (div. 1983); children: Kristen Anne, John Robert; m. Pamela Preston Reynolds, Jan. 9, 1988 (div. 2006). AB, Emory U., 1966; JD, Duke U., 1971, MD, 1972. Rsch. assoc. Duke U. Sch. Medicine, Durham, NC, 1971—72, resident in medicine, 1972-74; asst. to dir. office asst. sec. for health USPHS, Rockville, Md., 1974-76; chief med. audit br. bur. quality assurance HEW, Rockville, 1976-77; sr. policy analyst Office Sci. and Tech. Policy Exec. Office of Pres., Washington, 1978-81; assoc. exec. v.p. ACP, Phila., 1981-86, exec. v.p., 1986-94, also master; sr. scholar Assn. Acad. Health Ctrs., Washington, 1994-95; exec. v.p., acting pres., CEO Pa. Hosp., Phila., 1995-96, pres., CEO, 1996-99; sr. v.p. The Lewin Group, Falls Church, Va., 2000; exec. v.p. Am. Soc. Clin. Pathology, Chgo., 2002—. Robert Wood Johnson clin. scholar George Washington U., Washington, 1977-79; bd. mgrs. Pa. Hosp., 1988-97; bd. dirs. Milbank Meml. Fund, Holy Cross Hosp. Assoc. editor Jour. Am. Geriatrics Soc., 1984-86; mem. editorial bd. Internat. Jour. Tech. Assessment in Health Care, 1986-89, European Jour. Internal Medicine, 1988-94, Duke U. Law Jour., 1969-71; contbr. articles to profl. jours. Sr. surgeon USPHS, 1974-77. John Gordon Stipe scholar, Nat. Merit scholar, Emory U., 1962. Mem. Inst. Medicine of NAS, N.C. Bar Assn., Am. Clin. and Climatol. Assn., Soc. Med. Adminstrs. Democrat. Home Phone: 312-245-2814; Office Phone: 312-541-4885. Personal E-mail: johnrball@hotmail.com.

BALL, KAREN ELAINE, elementary school educator; b. Shelby, Ohio, July 17, 1951; d. Walter F. and Learlene D. Ingram; m. Stephen K. Ball, Aug. 4, 1973; children: Jonathan, David. BA, Anderson U., 1973. Cert. K-12 health and phys. edn. Pa. Tchr. Brockway Area Schs., Pa., 1973—. Girls volleyball coach Brockway Area HS, boys tennis coach, cheerleading coach, St. Coun. advisor, 2003—. Advisor food dr. Brockway Area HS, 2005, advisor Quilts for Sr. Citizens, 2006, advisor Project Think Ink, 2007—. Mem.: Delta Kappa Gamma (1st v.p. Psi chpt.). Avocations: painting, sewing, poetry, interior decorating, scrapbooks. Office: Brockway Area Sch Dist Box 225 3621 Game School Rd Brockway PA 15824

BALL, MARION JOKL, academic administrator; b. South Africa; d. Ernst and Erica Jokl. Student, Northwestern U., 1957-58; BA in Math. with distinction, U. Ky., 1961, MA in Math., 1965; EdD, Temple U., 1978. Math tchr. Bryan Station High Sch., Lexington, Ky., 1961-62; programmer, instr. dept. behavioral sci., and computer sci. U. Ky. Med. Ctr., Lexington, 1965-68; asst. dir., med. computer activity, asst. prof. Temple U., Phila., 1968-72; dir. computer systems and mgmt. group, assoc. prof. Temple U. Health Scis. Ctr., Phila., 1972-85; dir. acad. computing U. Md., Baltimore, 1985-87, assoc. v.p. info. resources, prof., 1985-91; v.p. Info. Svcs. U. Maryland, 1991—; adj. prof. sch. nursing Johns Hopkins U., Baltimore; v.p. clin. solutions divsn. Healthlink Inc., Houston, 2001—. Bd. dirs. Intellimed, CliniCom, Inc., 1986-88; panel mem. Nat. Libr. Medicine, 1985-86, 1988—; adv. bd. Systems Dimensions Ltd., 1974-75, Nat. Assn. Hosp. Admitting Mgrs., 1983-85, Sperry Corp., 1984—, MEAD Co., 1985, Office Tech. Assessment, 1987, Educom Consulting Group, 1988-89; chmn. Am. Med. Informatics Assn. Transition Task Force on Membership,

1989; chmn. Am. Med. Informatics Assn. internat. affairs com.; U.S. rep. MEDINFO, 1983—, MEDINFO scientific program com., 1989—; rsch. devel. com. Am. Med. Record Assn., 1978-83; mem. tech. subcom. com. on improving patient records, Inst. Medicine, co chair, 1989-91; cons. in field. Author: Selecting a Computer System for the Clinical Laboratory, 1971, What is AComputer?, 1972, How to Select a Computerized Hospital Information System, 1973; author: (with S Charp) Be a Computer Lieterate!, 1978, author: (with K. Hannah)Using Computers in Nursing (nursing book yr. award 1985), 1984; author: (with others) Healthcare Information Management Systems: A Practical Guide, 1990, New Hospital Information Systems, 1988, Nursing Informatics: Where Caring and Technology Meet, 1988, Cancer Informatics: Essential Technologies for Clinical Trials, 2002. Fellow NSF, Phila. Coll. Physicians. Mem. Am. Med. Informatics Assn. (Morris F. Collen Award, 2002), Am. Assn. for Med. Systems and Informatics, Am. Hosp. Assn., Am. Med. Records Assn., Internat. Med. Informatics Assn. (pres. 1992—), Assn. for Computing Machinery, Healthcare Information and Mgmt. Systems Soc. (bd. dirs. 1989-92), Montessori Soc., Network of Women in Computer Tech., Phila. Coll. Physicians, Inst. Medicine (tech. subcom. and bd. dirs. on improving the patient record 1989—, Mortarboard Sr. Woman's Honor Soc., Delta Phi Alpha, Kappa Delta Pi, Phi Mu Eplison; fellow Am. Coll. Med. Informatics, 1984-. Home: Roland Pk N 5706 Coley Ct Baltimore MD 21210-1344 Office: U of Md Info Svcs 100 N Greene St Baltimore MD 21201-1563

BALL, MARKHAM (ROBERT BALL), lawyer, arbitrator, educator; b. Wilmington, Del., Mar. 24, 1934; s. Robert William and Helen (Slepicka) B.; m. Harriet Laura Janney, July 6, 1957; children: Laurence Markham, Richard Janney, Martha Harriet, Julia Helen. BA magna cum laude, Amherst Coll., 1956; BA with honors, Oxford U., Eng., 1958, MA, 1973; LLB, Harvard U., 1960. Bar: D.C. 1961, U.S. Supreme Ct. 1968. Law clk. U.S. Supreme Ct., Washington, 1960-61; assoc. Covington and Burling, Washington, 1961-64; asst. gen. counsel U.S. Office Econ. Opportunity, Washington, 1964-66; staff dir. U.S. Peace Corps, Washington, 1966-67; from assoc. to ptnr. Leva, Hawes, Symington, Martin and Oppenheimer, Washington, 1967-77; gen. counsel U.S. Agy. for Internat. Devel., Washington, 1977-79, mem. adv. com. on vol. fgn. aid, 1981-88; ptnr. Wald, Harkrader and Ross, Washington, 1980-85, Morgan, Lewis and Bockius, Washington, 1986-98, Holland and Knight, Washington, 1998—2002. Sr. fellow, dir. Alternative Dispute Resolution Ctr. Internat. Law Inst., Washington, 2002—; lectr. Law Sch. U. Va., 1991—2001; adj. prof. Law Sch. Georgetown U., 2002—. Mem. adv. bd. Brasenose Coll. Charitable Found., Oxford, 1988—. Fellow Am. Bar Found.; Rhodes scholar Phi Beta Kappa, 1956-58. Mem. ABA, Internat. Bar Assn., Am. Arbitration Assn. (mem. internat. arbitration adv. panel 2002—), Alexandria Literary Soc. (sec. 1981—). Home: 7223 Stafford Rd Alexandria VA 22307-1806 Office: Internat Law Inst 1055 Thomas Jefferson St NW Washington DC 20007-5259 Home Phone: 703-768-8161; Office Phone: 202-247-6006. Business E-Mail: mball@ili.org.

BALL, MELVYN, medical educator; b. Toronto, Canada, Aug. 30, 1940; s. Louis and Rose Ball; m. Elaine Kagan; children: Lawrence, Tamara, Robert. MD, U. Toronto, Canada, 1963. Prof. neuropathology Oreg. Health and Sci. U., Portland, 1990—2003, prof. emeritus, 2003—. Dir. Oreg. Brain Bank, Portland, 1990—2003. Vol. music therapist oncology ward Oreg. Health Scis. U. Hosp., Portland. Recipient Nicholas Munk award in geriatrics, Baycrest Ctr. U. Toronto, 1978. Fellow: Royal Coll. Physicians Can. Office: Oreg Health and Sci Univ L113 3181 SW Sam Jackson Park Rd Portland OR 97239

BALL, MILLIE (MILDRED PORTEOUS BALL), editor, journalist; b. New Orleans, Nov. 15, 1945; d. Harold Curtis and Mildred (Porteous) B.; m. Keith Cooper Marshall, Oct. 17, 1981. BA, Fla. State U., 1967. Editor young people's page The Times-Picayune, New Orleans, 1967-71, city desk reporter, 1971-79, staff writer Dixie Mag., 1979-82, staff writer living sect., 1982-89, travel editor, 1990—. Author: (with others) Fodor's New Orleans, 1990, Gault Millau New Orleans, 1991. Recipient various writing awards AP, La. Press Assn., Press Club New Orleans, Odyssey House, 1970-90, Lowell Thomas award Soc. Am. Travel Writers Found., 1992, Bronze Travel Journalist of Yr. award, 1994, Silver-Best Self-Illustrated Story award, 1994, Best Fgn. Story in Newspaper award, 1992, Best Newspaper Travel Sect., 1994, 95. Mem. Chi Omega. Presbyterian. Office: The Times-Picayune 3800 Howard Ave New Orleans LA 70125-1429 Home: 1224 Dufossat St New Orleans LA 70115-2924

BALL, PATRICIA ANN, physician; b. Lockport, NY, Mar. 30, 1941; d. John Joseph and Katherine Elizabeth Ball; m. Robert E. Lee, May 18, 1973 (div. 2004); children: Heather Lee, Samantha Lee. BS, U. Mich., 1963; MD, Wayne State U., 1969. Diplomate Am. Bd. Internal Medicine, Am. Bd. Hematology, Am. bd. Med. Oncology. Intern, resident Detroit Gen. Hosp., 1969-71; resident Jackson Meml. Hosp., Miami, Fla., 1971-72; fellow Henry Ford Hosp., Detroit, 1972-74; staff physician VA Hosp., Allen Park, Mich., 1974-77; pvt. practice in hematology and oncology Bloomfield Hills, Mich., 1977—. Faculty dept. medicine Wayne State U. Sch. Medicine, Detroit, 1974—. Mem.: AMA, ACP, Mich. Soc. Hematology and Oncology, Oakland County Med. Soc., Mich. Med. Soc., Detroit Inst. Arts, Founders Soc., Alpha Omega Alpha. Avocations: photography, skiing. Office: 44038 Woodward Ave Ste 101 Bloomfield Hills MI 48302-5036 Office Phone: 248-360-8244. E-mail: pball@dmc.org.

BALL, REX MARTIN, urban planner, architect; b. Oklahoma City, June 14, 1934; s. Ralph Martin and Sarah Mae (Kellner) B. BArch, Okla. State U., 1956; MArch, MIT, 1958. Lic. arch. Nat. Coun. Arch. Registration Bd.; cert. planner Am. Inst. Cert. Planners. With HTB Inc. (archtl., engring., planning firm), Oklahoma City, 1958-94; chmn. emeritus HTB Inc., 1958-94; founder, pres. Planning Assocs. Inc., 1960—; founder, pres., chmn., CEO Mid Continent Design Group, 1968—. Presdl. appt. to U.S. Commn. of Fine Arts, 1994-97. Architect U.S./USSR exhibit "The Socially Responsible Environment, 1980-90; contbr. articles to profl. jours. Chair Tulsa Preservation Com., 1997—; facilitator Internat. Coalition Art Deco Socs., 2003—05; oversite com. Vision 2025, Tulsa, 2003—; bd. dirs. Price Tower Mus., 1998—2002; past treas. Philbrook Mus.'s Pacers. Recipient Bus. in the Arts award, 1988, 5 Who Care Corp. Humanitarian award, Gannett Found., 1988, Curt Schwartz Bus. in the Arts award, 1989, Phoenix award/Downtown Now, 1992, Cityscape award City of Oklahoma City, 1992, Disting. Alumni award Okla. State U., 1995. Fellow: AIA (mem. nat. com. on design, past pres. ea. Okla. chpt.); mem.: Soc. Am. Mil. Engrs. (former sustaining mem.), MIT Alumni Assn. (past Okla. pres.), Nat. Trust Hist. Preservation, Am. Planning Assn., Oklahoma City C. of C. (bd. dirs. 1980—90, former v.p.), Okla. State U. Alumni Assn. (life; past bd. dirs., pres. Tulsa and Okla. counties), Tulsa C. of C. (past bd. dirs.), Tulsa Art Deco Soc. (chair), Tulsa Hist. Soc. (bd. dirs. 2000—, chair 6th World Congress on Art Deco 2001), Air Force Assn. (past pres. Gerrity chpt.), Nat. Bldg. Mus., Okla. Heritage Assn., Blue Key Club, Urban League Greater Oklahoma City (former bd. dirs.), Sigma Nu, Alpha Rho Chi. Home: 2926 E 39th St Tulsa OK 74105-3704 Fax: 918-748-9688. E-mail: ballrexm@aol.com.

BALL, ROBERT M. (ROBERT MYERS BALL), retired social security, welfare and health policy specialist, writer, lecturer; b. NYC, Mar. 28, 1914; s. Archey Decatur and Laura Elizabeth (Crump) Ball; m. Doris Jacqueline McCord, June 30, 1936; children: Robert Jonathan, Jacqueline Ball Smith. AB, Wesleyan U., Middletown, Conn., 1935, MA, 1936, degree (hon.), U Md., Yale U., New Haven, Conn. With Bur. Old Age and Survivors Ins., Social Security Bd., 1939-46, asst. dir., 1949-52, acting dir., 1953, dep. dir., 1953-62, commr. social security, 1962-73; sr. scholar Inst. Medicine, Nat. Acad. Scis., 1973-80; writer, lectr., cons., 1980—. Asst. dir. com. edn. and social security Am. Coun. Edn., 1946—49; staff dir. adv. coun. Social Security, 1948—49, chmn., 1965, mem., 79, 91, 96; staff dir. pension study Nat. Planning Assn., 1950—52; mem. Nat. Commn. Social Security Reform, 1982—83, White Ho. Conf. Social Security, 1998. Author: Pensions in the United States, 1952, Social Security Today and Tomorrow, 1978, Insuring the Essentials, Bob Ball on Social Security, Century Foundation, 2000, The Social Security Protection Plan, 2006; author: (with Thomas N. Bethell) Straight Talk about Social Security, 1998, Because We're All in This Together, Families USA Foundation, 1989; contbr. chapters to books, articles to profl. jours. Named to Health Care Hall of Fame, 1999; recipient Disting. Svc. award, Nat. Civil Svc. League, 1958, Rockefeller Pub. Svc. award, 1961, Arthur J. Atlmeyer award, 1968, Clarence A. Kulp award, Am. Soc. Risk and Ins., 1980, Elizur Wright award, Presdl. award, Am. Soc. Aging, 1988, Arthur S. Fleming award, 1989, Andrus award, AARP, 1990, Cruikshank award, Nat. Coun. Sr. Citizens, 1990, Nat. award, UN Internat. Yr. Older Persons, 1999, Maxwell A. Pollack award for productive living, 2000. Mem.: Nat. Acad. Social Ins. (founding chmn. bd.), Gerontol. Soc. Am. (award 1996), Nat. Coun. Aging (Ollie Randall award 1983), Nat. Acad. Pub. Adminstrn., Inst. Medicine (Lienhard award 1991, Com. to Preserve Social Security and Medicare award 2003, Franklin and Eleanor Roosevelt award for Disting. Svc. 2005), Phi Beta Kappa, Delta Kappa Epsilon. Home and Office: 10450 Lottsford Rd Collington#5112 Mitchellville MD 20721-3302 Office Phone: 301-541-5097. Business E-Mail: robertmball@nasi.org.

BALL, TRAVIS, JR., editor, retired school administrator; b. Newport, Tenn., July 13, 1942; s. Travis and Ruth Annette (Duyck) Ball. BA, Carson Newman Coll., 1964; MA, Purdue U., 1966. Instr., then asst. prof. English Ill. Wesleyan U., Bloomington, 1966—69; vis. prof. English Millikin U., 1969; asst. headmaster, chmn. English Brewster Acad., Wolfeboro, NH, 1969—72; dir. admissions, asst. to headmaster Park Tudor Sch., Indpls., 1972—88; cons. Selwyn Sch., Denton, Tex., 1988—89; pres. Travis Ball & Assocs., 1980—88; dir. comm. Verde Valley Sch., Sedona, Ariz., 1988—91; editor Projects in Enrollment Mgmt., 1992—2000. Commn. on curriculum and grad. requirements Ind. Dept. Pub. Instrn., 1974—76; adv. coun. Ednl. Records Bur.; reviewer Nat. Stds. Project in Sci., Civics and Govt., 1994—95; cons. in field. Editor: Tchrs. Svc. Com. Newsletter for English Tchrs., 1977—82; dept. editor: English Jour., 1976—82, editor/pub.: Contact: Newsletter for Admissions Mgmt., 1980—88, contbg. editor: The Developing Leader, 2003—. Chair bd. deacons First Bapt. Ch., Newport, Tenn., 2005—. Mem.: ASCD, Phi Delta Kappa, Pi Kappa Delta, Nat. Assn. Ind. Schs. (workshop faculty 1986, 1997), Coun. Advancement and Support Edn. (adv. com. on ind. schs.), Nat. Coun. Tchrs. English, Ind. Schs. Assn. Ctrl. States, Ind. Non-Pub. Edn. Assn. (treas., dir., vice chmn.), Sigma Tau Delta. Baptist. Office: 1739 Log Church Rd Newport TN 37821-5535 Personal E-mail: ball1739@bellsouth.net.

BALL, WILLIAM KENNETH, lawyer; b. DeQueen, Ark., Jan. 15, 1927; s. William P. and Lucille (Jeter) B.; m. Ella Hubbard Scaife, Dec. 28, 1950; children— Lucy Jane, William Ramsay, Charles Scaife. JD, U. Ark., 1953. Bar: Ark 1953, U. S. Supreme Ct., 1971. Law clk. to assoc. justice Ark. Supreme Ct., 1953-54; pvt. practice Monticello, 1954—99; ptnr. Ball, Barton & Hoffman, 1958—99; city atty. City of Monticello, 1961—93. Spl. justice Supreme Ct. Ark., 1975. Served with AUS, 1945-47, 50-52. Mem. Fellow Ark. Bar Found.; mem. Ark. Bar Assn., S.E. Ark. Bar Assn. (pres. 1957-58), Rotary (pres. 1962-63), Kappa Sigma, Delta Theta Phi. Presbyterian. Home: 104 Westminster Dr Monticello AR 71655-4814

BALL, WILLIAM LOCKHART, III, lobbyist, former civilian military employee; b. Belton, SC, June 10, 1948; BS, Ga. Inst. Tech., 1969. Commd. officer USN, 1969-75; legis. asst. to Senator John Tower US Senate, Washington, 1975-78, adminstrv. asst. to Senator John Tower, 1981-84, adminstrv. asst. to Senator Herman Talmadge, 1978-80; asst. sec. for legis. affairs US Dept. State, Washington, 1985-86; asst. to the Pres. for legis. affairs The White House, Washington, 1986-88; sec. USN U.S. Dept. Def., Washington, 1988-89; pres. Am. Beverage Assn., 1989—2005; mng. dir. The Loeffler Group, Washington, 2006—. Office: The Loeffler Group 1801 K St NW Ste 340 Washington DC 20006 E-mail: wball@loefflerlip.com.

BALLAL, DILIP RAMCHANDRA, mechanical engineering educator; b. Nagpur, India, Jan. 16, 1946; came to U.S., 1979; s. Ramchandra Govind Ballal and Padma (Balwant) Zadkar; m. Shubhangi Sadashiv Ayachit, Dec. 17, 1975; children: Rahul, Deepti. BSME, Coll. Engring., Bhopal, India, 1967; PhD, Cranfield Inst. Tech., Eng., 1972, DSc in Engring. (hon.), 1983. Registered profl. engr., Ohio. Lectr. mech. engring. Cranfield Inst. Tech., 1972-79; sr. staff engr. GM Rsch. Labs., Warren, Mich., 1979-83; prof. mech. engring. U. Dayton (Ohio), 1983—. Cons. GMR Labs. and GE Aircraft, Warren, Cin., 1987—. Author: (with others) Combustion Measurements and Modern Development in Combustion, 1990, 91; contbr. about 130 articles on combustion, turbulence, heat transfer and pollution to profl. jours. Project leader Engrs. Club Dayton, 1986, 88, 90; judge, organizer "Odyssey of Mind" Sch. Contest, Dayton, 1985, 87, 88; vice chmn. edn. com. Miami Valley Sch., Dayton, 1988, 90. Named Outstanding Engr., Engrs. Club, Dayton, 1988. Fellow ASME (chmn. combustion and fuels com. 1995—, Best Rsch. award 1986, 92), AIAA (Energy Systems award 1993). Achievements include patents on Ignitor Plug for Jet Engine Combustor. Home: 950 Olde Sterling Way Dayton OH 45459-3100 Office: U Dayton KL 465 300 College Park Ave Dayton OH 45469-0001 Office Phone: 937-229-4001. E-mail: dilip.ballal@gmail.com.

BALLANFANT, RICHARD BURTON, lawyer; b. Houston, Aug. 15, 1947; s. Richard Edward and Selma Autrey (Lewis) B.; children: Andrea Lavon, Benjamin Burton, Amy Lamar. BA, U. Tex., 1969, JD, 1972. Bar: Tex. 1972, US Ct. Appeals (5th cir.) 1976, US Ct. Appeals (11th cir.) 1981, US Ct. Appeals (8th cir.) 1988, US Dist. Ct. (so. dist.) Tex. 1974. Atty. FCC, Washington, 1973-74; asst. US atty. Dept. Justice, Houston, 1974-78; sr. asst. city atty. City of Houston, 1978-80; atty. Shell Oil Co., Houston, 1980—. Mem. citizens adv. bd. Met. Transit Auth., Harris County, 1979-83; bd. mem. Harris County Met. Transp. Authority, 2007—; del. Rep. State Conv., 1978, 80, 82, 88, 90, 92, 96; del. to Rep. Nat. Conv., 1992; chmn. Personnel Bd., West Univ. Pl., Tex., 1975-85, city councilman, 1999-2001, mayor, 2003-07; mem. Battleship Tex. Adv. Bd., 1989; pres. Harris County Coun. Mayors and Couns., 2006-07. Capt. USAR, 1972-82. Named Outstanding Asst. US Atty. Dept. Justice, 1976, 77. Mem. Houston Bar Assn., Fed. Bar Assn. (pres. 1979-80), ABA, Houston C. of C. (govt. rels. com.). Episcopalian. Home: 3123 Amherst St Houston TX 77005-3009

BALLANTINE, JOHN TILDEN, lawyer; b. Louisville, Feb. 26, 1931; s. Thomas Austin and Anna Marie (Pfeiffer) B.; m. Mary January Strode, May 15, 1954 (div. 1964); children: John T. Jr., William Clayton, Douglas C.; m. Beverley Jo Hackley, Dec. 8, 1967; 1 child, Susan Marie. BA with high distinction, U. Ky., 1952; JD, Harvard U., 1957. Bar: Ky. 1957, US Dist. Ct. (we. dist. Ky.) 1957, US Ct. Appeals (6th cir.) 1958, US Dist. Ct. (ea. dist. Ky.) 1963, US Supreme Ct. 1982. Law clk. to presiding judge U.S. Dist Ct. (we. dist.) Ky., 1957-58; ptnr., then mem., gen. counsel Stoll Keenon Ogden PLLC, 1958—. Mem. civil rules com. Ky. Supreme Ct., 1988—96; jud. nominating com. Ky. Supreme Ct. and Ct. Appeals, 2004—; adj. prof. Brandeis Sch. Law U. Louisville. Bd. dirs. Family and Children Agy., Louisville, 1965-75, pres., 1971-74; bd. dirs. Our Lady of Peace Hosp., Louisville, 1968-73, 88—, chmn., 1968-69, 91-93; bd. dirs. Met. United Way, Louisville, 1975-81; mem. Hist. Landmarks and Preservation Dists. Commn., Louisville, 1976-88; bd. dirs. Ky. Derby Festival, Louisville, 1975-81, v.p., 1975. 1st lt. USAF, 1952-54. Recipient Outstanding Young Man in Field of Law award Louisville Jaycees, 1966. Fellow Am. Coll. Trial Lawyers; mem. ABA, Ky. Bar Assn. (bd. govs. 1996-2002, ho. of dels. 1985-91, chmn. 1989-90, clients' security fund 1993-96, Ky. evidence rules rev. commn. 1995-2002, ethics com. 1996-2003, Outstanding Lawyer award 2003), Louisville Bar Assn. (bd. dirs. 1969-71, 88, 89, 92, 93, 96-2002, pres. 1970, profl. responsibility com. 1988-93, chmn. physician-atty. com., Judge Benjamin Shobe Civility and Professionalism award 2005), U.S. 6th Cir. Ct. Appeals Jud. Conf. (life), Fed. Def. and Corp. Counsel, Ky. Def. Counsel (pres. 1981-82), Louis D. Brandeis Am. Inn of Ct., Ky. Character and Fitness Com., Pendennis Club, The Law Club, Phi Beta Kappa. Office: Stoll Keenon Ogden PLLC 2000 PNC Plz 500 W Jefferson St Louisville KY 40202-2874 Business E-Mail: john.ballantine@skofirm.com.

BALLANTYNE, RICHARD LEE, lawyer; b. Evanston, Ill., Dec. 10, 1939; s. Frank and Grace (Bowles) B.; children: Richard L. Jr., Brant. BS in Engring., U. Conn., 1965, MBA, 1967; JD with honors, George Washington U., 1969. Bar: Mass., 1970, Fla. 1994, U.S. Dist. Ct. Mass. 1976, U.S. Patent Office 1982. Dir. corp. devel. Itek Corp., Lexington, Mass., 1969-73, assoc. counsel, 1973-75; corp. counsel, sec. Goodhope Industries, Springfield, Mass., 1975-77; gen. counsel, asst. treas., sec. Compugraphic Corp., Wilmington, Mass., 1977-82; v.p., gen. counsel, sec. Prime Computer Inc., Natick, Mass., 1982-89, Harris Corp., Melbourne, Fla., 1989—. Served with U.S. Army, 1958-61. Mem. ABA, N.E. Corp. Counsel Assn. Inc. (pres. 1984-86), Licensing Execs. Soc., Am. Soc. Corp. Secs, Computer Law Forum. Republican. Avocations: jogging, golf. Office: Harris Corp 1025 W Nasa Blvd Melbourne FL 32919-0002

BALLANTYNE, RYAN JOHNS, pipe organ builder, small business owner; b. Riverside, Calif., Mar. 27, 1979; s. Edward Maloof and Beth Wasson Ballantyne; m. Melissa Mary Kjelstrom, Dec. 21, 2000; children: Jacob Allen, Andrew Romney. AA in Computer Sys. Tech., Brigham Young U., Rexburg, Idaho, 2003, BA in Tech. Mgmt., 2003. Cert. A+ Comptia, 2002. Owner R.M. Ballantyne Pipe Organs, Riverside, Calif., 2003—. Missionary LDS Ch., Nicaragua, 1998—2000. Mem.: Friends of Mission Inn Hotel (life; caretaker pipe organ). Republican. Office: RM Ballantyne Pipe Organs 8596 Wild Pony Dr Riverside CA 92509 Home Phone: 951-543-4329; Office Phone: 951-283-1245. Personal E-mail: idiay11@yahoo.com.

BALLARD, CHARLES ALAN, investment banker; b. St. Louis; s. Fred William and Fern Ann (Markham) B. BBA, So. Meth. U., 1963. V.p. fin. Systems Capital Corp., Phila., 1967-69; exec. v.p., dir. Vanderbilt Corp., Phila., 1969-71; assoc. Dillon, Read & Co. Inc., NYC, 1971-72, v.p., 1972-78, sr. v.p., 1979-80, mng. dir., 1980-90, sr. advisor, dir., 1990-99; chmn., dir. Ballard Properties Inc., Phila., 1982—; pres., dir. Ballard Marine, Inc., 1986—; sr. advisor UBS, NYC, 1999—. Mem. council Nat. Municipal League, N.Y.C., 1981-85; mem. adv. bd. Nat. Entrepreneurship Found., Bloomington, Ind., 1983— , The Energy Bur., N.Y.C., 1981—. Recipient Merit award U. Wis.-La Crosse, 1975; recipient Achievement award Lions Club, Houston, 1963 Mem. N.Y. Stock Exchange (assoc.), Securities Industry Assn. (vice chmn. 1980-81, exec. com., bd. dirs. 1984-85), Investment Banking Com. (steering com. 1981—, vice chmn. 1981, 83, 86, 87, chmn. 1985). Clubs: Union League (Phila.); The Links (N.Y.C.); Merion Golf (Ardmore, Pa.); India House; Lighthouse Point (Fla.) Yacht and Racquet. Office: 299 Park Ave New York NY 10171-0002

BALLARD, DAVID EUGENE, anesthesiologist; b. Carlsbad, N.Mex., July 30, 1949; s. Samuel Lafayette and Kathleen (Krebs) B.; m. Patricia Ann Lafferty, June 11, 1972; 1 child, Leslie Christine. BA, U. Kans., 1971; MD, U. N.Mex., 1975. Diplomate Am. Bd. Anesthesiology. Intern and resident N.C. Meml. Hosp., U. N.C., Chapel Hill, 1975-78; pvt. practice Anesthesia Cons. Associated, El Paso, Tex., 1978-86; chief anesthesia sect. VA Med. Ctr., Albuquerque, 1986-88; chmn. dept. anesthesiology Lovelace Med. Ctr., Albuquerque, 1988-98; dir. anesthesiology West Mesa Med. Ctr., Albuquerque, 2003—04; clin. assoc. prof. anesthesiology U. NC, Chapel Hill, 2007—. Clin. asst. prof. anesthesiology, U. N.Mex., 1986-88, mem. resident selection com., 1986-88; asst. prof. anesthesiology U. N.C., Chapel Hill, 1991-96. Mem. Am. Soc. Anesthesiologists (alt. del. 1988-91, mem. com. on physician resources 1993-94), AMA, Internat. Anesthesia Rsch. Soc., Anesthesia Patient Safety Found., Soc. Ambulatory Anesthesia, Tex. Soc. Anesthesiologists (alt. del. dist. 5, 1986), Greater Albuquerque Anesthesia Soc. (pres., v.p. 1987-89), N.Mex. Med. Sch. Alumni Assn. (bd. dirs. 1984-92, exec. com. 1988-90). Avocation: golf. Home: 108 Chesley Ct Chapel Hill NC 27514 Office: N2201 UNC Hosps CB #7010 Chapel Hill NC 27599-7010 Home Phone: 919-929-6456; Office Phone: 919-966-5136. Business E-Mail: davideballard@mac.com.

BALLARD, DAVID M., elementary school educator; b. Quincy, Ill., Oct. 15, 1949; s. Lawrence S. and Frances M. Ballard; m. Pamela J. Mitts, Dec. 21, 1968; 1 child, Kristi M. BS in Edn., Quincy U., Ill., 1971; MEd in Supervision, Stetson U., Deland, Fla., 1980. Tchr., adminstr. Shorecrest Prepratory Sch., St. Petersburg, Fla., 1971—89; tchr. Trinity Prepratory Sch., Winter Pk., Fla., 1989—. Coach men's soccer Shorecrest Preparatory Sch., 1984—89; coach men's golf Trinity Preparatory Sch., 1994—2006. Mem.: NCSS, FACA (hon.). Achievements include David Ballard endowed chair social science department at Trinity Preparatory School created by Warren Stanchina Family in 2007. Avocations: golf, reading. E-mail: dmballard1015@aol.com.

BALLARD, ERNESTA, lumber company executive; BA, U. Pa.; MA, MBA, Harvard U. Regional adminstr. Pacific NW EPA, 1983—86; CEO Cape Fox Corp., 1989-94; founder, prin. Ballard & Assocs., Ketchikan, Alaska, 1994-97; commr., Dept. Environ. Conservation State of AK, Juneau, 2002—04; sr. v.p. corp. affairs Weyerhaeuser Co., Federal Way, Wash., 2004—. Mem. bd. govs. U.S. Postal Svc., Washington, 1997—2005. Bd. dirs. Alaska Forest Assn., S.E. Alaska Regional Aquaculture Assn., Ketchikan Gen. Hosp., LifeCenter NW. Office: Weyerhaeuser Co PO Box 9777 Federal Way WA 98063-9777

BALLARD, FREDERIC LYMAN, JR., lawyer; b. Phila., Sept. 12, 1941; s. Frederic L. Sr. and Ernesta (Drinker) B.; m. Marion Scattergood, Dec. 20 1974; 1 child, Anne A.; stepchildren: William S. Dunning, Robert L. Dunning. BA, Harvard U., 1963, LLB, 1966. Bar: Pa. 1966, D.C. 1978. Assoc. Ballard Spahr Andrews & Ingersoll LLP, 1966, ptnr., 1973—. Author: ABCs of Arbitrage, 2007. Mem.: ABA (vice chair 1994—97, taxation sect.), Am. Coll. Tax Counsel (chair 2006—). Home: 4413 Chalfont Pl Bethesda MD 20816-1812 Office: Ballard Spahr Andrews & Ingersoll LLP 601 13th St NW Washington DC 20005-3807

BALLARD, JOHN STUART, retired mayor, lawyer, educator; b. Akron, Ohio, Sept. 30, 1922; s. Irby S. and Sarah (McCormick) B.; m. Ruth Frances Holden, Oct. 22, 1949; children: Susan, Karen, John H., Mark, Ward; m. 2d, Patricia D. Whittenberger, Oct. 20, 1990. AB, U. Akron, 1943; LL.B., U. Mich., 1948. Bar: Mich. 1948, Ohio 1949. Spl. agt. FBI, 1949-52; atty. pvt. practice, Akron, Ohio, 1952—56, 1964—65; pros. atty. Summit County, 1957-64; mayor City of Akron, 1966-80; ret., 1995. Adj. assoc. prof. dept. pub. adminstrn. and urban studies U. Akron, 1980—95. Candidate for U.S. senator from Ohio, 1962. Served with inf. AUS, 1943-46. Recipient Distinguished Svc. award, Akron Jr. C. of C., 1957. Episcopalian. Home: 171 Granger Rd Unit 144 Medina OH 44256-7312 *It is true that in giving we receive.*

BALLARD, LOUIS WAYNE, composer; b. Miami, Okla., July 8, 1931; s. Charles Guthrie and Leona Mae (Quapaw) B.; m. Ruth Sands, Dec. 6, 1965; children by previous marriage: Louis Anthony, Anne Marie, Charles

Christopher. B.Mus. and Music Edn., U. Tulsa, 1954; M.Mus., 1962; D.Mus. (hon.), Coll. Santa Fe, 1973; D.Mus. (hon.), William Jewell Coll., 2001. Dir. vocal and instrumental music Nelagoney (Okla.) Public Sch., 1954-56; dir. vocal music Webster High Sch., Tulsa, 1956-58; pvt. music tchr., 1959-62; music dir. Inst. Am. Indian Arts, Santa Fe, 1962-65, dir. performing arts, 1965-69; nat. dir. music edn. curriculum and rev. Bur. Indian Affairs, Washington, 1969-79. Lectr., clinician, 1960—; pres. First Am. Indian Films, Inc., 1969—; disting. vis. prof. music Wm Jewell Coll., Liberty, Mo., 2000—. Composer, Santa Fe, 1979—; guest composer West German Music Festival, Saarbrü, 1986, Musik im 20 Jahrhundert, Ariz. State U., 1992, U. Ill. at Champagne, 1992, Ea. Music Festival, Greensboro, N.C., 1994, 95, 96; gala concert Carnegie Hall, 1992; full concert in Beethoven Chamber Music Hall, Bonn (first Am. composer), 1989; (ballet) Koshare, 1964, The Four Moons, 1967, Maid of the Mist and the Thunderbeings, 1991; (orchl. music) Fantasy Aborigine, Nos. I, II, III, IV, V; (chamber music) Rhapsody for Four Bassoons, Incident at Wounded Knee, Desert Trilogy, Ritmo Indio, Katcina Dances for cello-piano suite; (choral cantatas) The Gods Will Hear, Portrait of Will Rogers, Thus Spake Abraham; (oratorio) Dialogue Differentia text in Latin, Lakota-Sioux, English, Live On, Heart of My Nation (choral cantate with native Am. dialect), Manitoo, Gitche Manitoo (Am. Indian Doxology); (band works) Nighthawk Keetowa; (percussion) Cecega Ayuwipi, Music for the Earth and the Sky; (guitar) Quetzalcoatl's Coattails, 1992, The Lonely Sentinel, 1993, The Fire Moon (string quartet), A City of Silver, A City of Fire, A City of Light (piano concert pieces), numerous others.; commd. writer Lila Wallace Reader's Digest Arts Ptnrs./Meet the Composer, 1991; commd. writer (opera) Ministry Lower Saxony (Germany), 1993-94; author: The American Indian Sings, Book 1, 1970, Book 2, 1991, American Indian Chants for the Classroom, Oklahoma Indian Chants for the Classroom, 2004, also articles. Recipient 1st Marion Nevins MacDowell award chamber music, 1969, Nat. Indian Achievement award, 1972, Catlin Peace Pipe award Nat. Indian Lore Assn., 1976, ASCAP award, 1966-88, Lifetime Music Achievement award First Americans in Arts, 1997; F.B. Parriott grad. fellow, 1969; grantee Ford Found., 1970; grantee Nat. Endowment Arts, 1967, 69, 76, 79; commd. by Martha B. Rockefeller Found., 1969, Am. Composers Orch., 1982, commd. by Ministry Lower Saxony for Opera in Norden Gymnasium, West Germany, 1994; named to Okla. Music Hall of Fame, 2004. Mem. ASCAP, Music Educators Nat. Conf. (chmn. minority concerns com. for N.Mex. 1976), Am. Symphony Orch. League, Internat. Soc. for Polyaesthetic Music Edn. and Performance (lectr.), Phi Beta Kappa (alumni mem. Beta chpt. Okla. 1999). Lodges: Masons, Scottish Rite (32d degree). Office: PO Box 4552 Santa Fe NM 87502-4552 Personal E-mail: ogx88@msn.com.

BALLARD, MICHAEL B., archivist; b. Nov. 24, 1946; BA in History, Miss. State U., 1975, MA in History, Archives, 1976, PhD in History, 1983. Archivist Western Carolina Libr., Cullowhee, NC, 1979—80, Miss. State U. Libr., 1983—. Appointed to advisory com. Records of US Congress, 2001—03. Author: A Long Shadow: Jefferson David and the Final Days of the Confederacy, 1986, Landscapes of Battle: The Civil War, 1988, Pemberton: A Biography, 1991 (Best Non-Fiction Work by Miss. Author, Miss. Inst. Arts Letters, 1991), Civil War Mississippi: A Guide, 2000, Vicksburg: The Campaign That Opened the Mississippi, 2004, U.S. Grant: The Making of a General, 1861-1863, 2005; co-author: Sonny Montgomery: The Veteran's Champion, 2003, The Heart of the Mississippi: The People's University, Mississippi State, 1878-2003, 2007; co-editor: Chickasaw: A Mississippi Scout for the Union, The Civil War Memoir of Levi H. Naron, 2005; contbr. chapters to books, articles to profl. jours. Rsch. grant, Am. Philosophical Soc., 1988, Garner fellowship, Miss. State U., 1977—83. Mem.: Historians of Civil War Western Theater (co-founder, co-exec. dir. 1998—), Soc. Civil War Historians, Southern Historical Assn., Soc. Miss. Archivists (pres. 1997), Assn. Ctrs. for Study of Congress, Miss. Historical Soc. (mem. bd. dir., mem. editl. review bd., mem. bd. publications, Dunbar Rowland award 2006), Phi Kappa Phi, Phi Alpha Theta. Office: Miss State U Libr Hardy St PO Box 5403 Mississippi State MS 39762 Office Phone: 662-325-7680. Office Fax: 662-325-3560. Business E-Mail: mballard@library-msstate.edu.

BALLARD, MICHAEL RAY (MICKEY BALLARD), minister, music educator; b. Hammond, La., Apr. 24, 1969; s. Milton Ray Ballard and Carol Ann Carter; m. Sue Ellen Sanders, Jan. 19, 1964; 1 child, Jacob Wayne. BFA, La. Tech U., Ruston, La., 1994; MusM Voice Performance, U. Miss., Oxford, Miss., 1996, MusM Music Edn., 1996; M of Ch. Music, So. Bapt. Theol. Sem., Louisville, Ky., 2003. Vis. instr. voice and vocal jazz Ea. Ky. U., Richmond, Ky., 1997—2000; min. music First Bapt. Ch., Richmond, Ky., 2000—. Adj. Ky. Music Educators Assn., Louisville, 1997—2002, Music in the Pks., Pa., 1999—2002; clinician Stephen Collins Foster Music Camp, Richmond, Ky., 1998—2000. Singer: (musical theater) Anything Goes (Tech Tony Award: Best Supporting Actor, 1993); creator (eku vocal jazz ensemble) Musical Performances; singer: (vocal auditions) Nat. Assn. of Tchrs. of Singing (Divsn. Winner in Regional and State Competitions, 1996), (Operas) Susannah; soloist (choral symphony/requiem) Mozart Requiem; mem.: Ky. Bapt. Men's Chorale, 2005—. Mem./advisor Richmond C. of C., Richmond, Ky., 2000—; min. of music First Bapt. Ch., Richmond, Ky., 2000—; advisor Bapt. Student Union, Richmond, Ky., 1998—99. Recipient Undergraduate Singer of the Yr., La. Tech U., 1994; Grad. Honors Fellowship, U. Miss., 1994-1996. Mem.: Bapt. Ch. Music Conf., Nat. Assn. Tchrs. Singing, Am. Choral Dirs. Assn. (life), Am. Mensa. Bapt. Avocations: travel, golf, sports. Home: 113 Prewitt Dr Richmond KY 40475 Office: First Bapt Ch 425 Eastern Bypass Richmond KY 40475 Home Phone: 859-626-8260; Office Phone: 859-623-4028. Personal E-mail: mickey.ballard@firstbaptistnet.com.

BALLARD, ROBERT DUANE, marine geologist; b. Wichita, Kans., June 30, 1942; s. Chester Patrick and Harriet Nell (May) B.; m. Marjorie C. Jacobsen, July 1, 1966 (div.); children: Todd (dec.), Doug; m. Barbara Earle, Jan. 1991; children: Benjamin, Emily. BS, U. Calif., Santa Barbara, 1965; postgrad., U. Hawaii, 1965—66, U. So. Calif., 1966—67; PhD of Oceanography, U. R.I., 1974. Asst. scientist Woods Hole (Mass.) Oceanog. Instn., 1974-76, assoc. scientist, 1976-83, sr. scientist, 1983-97, scientist emeritus, 1997—; prof. oceanography Grad. Sch. Oceanography, dir. Inst. Archaeol. Oceanography U. R.I., 2001—; explorer-in-residence Nat. Geog. Soc., 1999—. Founder, pres. Inst. for Exploration, Mystic Aquarium, Conn., 1995—; vis. scholar Stanford U., 1979-80, cons. prof., 1980-81, founder and dir. Deep Submergence Lab., 1983—; bd. dirs., founder Jason Found. for Edn.; trustee Sea Rsch. Found. Author: Exploring Our Living Planet, 1983, Discovery of the Titanic, 1989, Discovery of the Bismarck, 1990, The Wreck of the ISIS, 1990, The Lost Ships of Guadalcanal, 1993, Explorations, 1995, Exploring the Lusitania, 1995; author (with Michael Sweeney) Return to Titanic: A New Look at the World's Most Famous Lost Ship, 2004. With U.S. Army, 1965-67; with USN, 1967-70. Recipient Sci. award Underwater Soc. Am., 1976, Newcomb Cleveland prize AAAS, 1981, Cutty Sark Sci. award, 1982, Centennial award Nat. Geog. Soc., 1988, Westinghouse award AAAS, 1990, Golden Plate award Am. Acad. Achievement, 1990, U.S. Navy Robert Dexter Conrad award for Sci. Achievement, 1992, Nat. Humanities medal, 2003. Mem. Geol. Soc. Am., Marine Tech. Soc. (Compass Disting. Achievement award 1977), Am. Geophys. Union, Explorers Club (Lone Sailor award, Hubbard medal). Achievements include being the leader of the first and second expeditions to reach sunken ship Titanic, 1985, 86, discover of Bismarck, 1989, Yorktown, 1998, PT-109, 2002; pioneered the use of manned submersibles for ocean research, participating in or leading more than 110 deep-sea expeditions; discovered chemosynthetic life-forms off the Galápagos Islands, where he was one of the first to see hydrothermal vents. Office: Inst for Exploration 55 Coogan Blvd Mystic CT 06355-1927

BALLARD, SHARI L., retail executive; B, U. Mich., Flint. Asst. store mgr. Best Buy Co., Inc., 1993, gen. mgr. Flint, Mich., dir. human resources - retail, mem. retail change implementation team, 1997, v.p. orgnl. effectiveness, 2000—03, sr. v.p. human resources - retail svc. delivery, 2003—04, exec. v.p. human resources and legal, 2004—06, exec. v.p. entertainment, multichannel and human capital, 2007—. Office: Best Buy Co Inc 7601 Penn Ave S Richfield MN 55423-3645 Office Phone: 612-291-1000.*

BALLARD, STEVEN C., academic administrator; m. Nancy Adams; children: Nathan, Laine. BA in History, U. Arizona, 1970; PhD in Political Science, Ohio State U., 1976. Post-doctoral fellow U. Okla., 1976—78, assoc. dir. sci. & policy, 1978—87, dir. sci. & policy, 1987—89; founding dir. Margaret Chase Smith Ctr. for Pub. Policy U. Maine, Orono, 1989—98; dir. State Govt. Partnership prog. U. Maine System, 1990—92; chair. dept. public admin. U. Maine, 1991—94; vice provost rsch. & dean grad. sch. Bowling Green State U., 1998—2001; provost & vice chancellor academic affairs U. Missouri, Kansas City, 2001—04; chancellor East Carolina U., 2004—. Co-author: (with Mike Devine, and others) Energy From the West: A Technology Assessment of Western Energy Resource Development, 1981, Water and Western Energy: Impacts, Issues, and Choices, 1982, (with Mike Devine, Michael Chartock, D.A. Huettner & Elizabeth Gun) Decentralized Electricity Production, 1987, (with Tom James, Mike Devine, Mark Meo, Time Adams & Lani Malysa) Innovation Through Technical and Scientific Information: Government and Industry Cooperation, 1989; co-editor: (with Thomas E. James) The Future of the Sunbelt: Issues in Managing Growth and Change, 1983. Office: E Carolina U E Fifth St Greenville NC 27858 Office Phone: 252-328-1949.*

BALLAS, DEAN JAMES, graphics designer, educator; b. Allenotwn, Pa., Apr. 10, 1971; MFA in Graphic Design, Miami Internat. U. Art and Design, 2005. Creative dir. CEMENT Mktg., NYC; art dir. The AD Studio, Miami; founder, prin. DJBdesign, Allentown, Pa., 2001—07; asst. prof. comm. design Kutztown U., Kutztown, Pa., 2005—; design cons. Crayola, Easton, Pa., 2006—07. Recipient Gold Addy award, Am. Advt. Fedn., 2006. Mem.: Delta Epsilon Iota (life). Home: 2738 W Greenleaf St Allentown PA 18104 Office: Kutztown U PO Box 730 Kutztown PA 19530 Home Phone: 610-739-6878; Office Phone: 610-683-4528. Personal E-mail: deanballas@yahoo.com. E-mail: ballas@kutztown.edu.

BALLBACH, JOHN M., wholesale distribution executive; BA, Georgetown Coll.; MBA, Harvard Bus. Sch., Cambridge, Mass. With Valspar Corp., 1990—2004, group v.p. packaging, 1998—2000, sr. v.p. EPS, Color Corp. and Ops., 2000—02, pres., COO, 2002—04; pvt. investor Ballbach Consulting LLC, 2004—05, pres., 2004—05; pres., CEO, bd. dirs. VWR Internat., Inc., 2005—. Office: VWR Internat Inc PO Box 2656 West Chester PA 19380-0906 Office Phone: 610-431-1700.*

BALLBACH, PHILIP THORNTON, political consultant, investor; b. Lansing, Mich., May 22, 1939; s. Nathan Anthony and Thelma Frances (Bowes) B. BA, Mich. State U., 1960; student, U. Mich., 1960-61; MA, Mich. State U., 1967. Social worker State of Mich., Corunna, 1961-64; legis. aide State Rep. H. James Starr, Lansing, Mich., 1964-67; exec. asst. State Atty. Gen.'s Dept., Lansing, Mich., 1967-81; county commr. Ingham County, Mason, Mich., 1980-93. Pub., Lansing This Weekend, 1963-64, The Gooseneck Tidings, 1977. Coord. Greater Lansing Assn. for Cmty. Edn., 1961-66; mem. Lansing Bd. Election Canvassers, 1965-69; dir. Cmty. Mental Health Bd., Lansing, 1977-99; treas. Zolton Ferency for Gov. Com., 1977-83; county liaison Eastside Neighborhood Orgn., Lansing, 1980-93; commr. Tri-County Regional Planning Com., Lansing, 1981-84; chairperson Ingham County Emergency Planning Com., Mason, Mich., 1988-93; campaign dir. Citizens for Pub. Recycling, Lansing, 1990; treas. People Achieving Legis. Power, 1992-95; campaign coord. Citizens for a Better Lansing, 1993-2003; bd. dirs. Peace Edn. Ctr., 1999—. Recipient Achievement award Nat. Assn. Counties, 1986, Dem. Party Ferency Activist Achievement award, 1998. Mem. Mich. Assn. Community Mental Health Bds. Democrat. Avocations: writing, history studies, skiing, softball. Home: 2723 E Lake Lansing Rd East Lansing MI 48823-9703

BALLE, JAMES CHRISTIAN, information technology manager; b. Ely, Nev., May 5, 1965; s. Dee J. Balle and Ruby Dell Casto. A of Applied and Computer Sci., Parks Coll., Thornton, Colo., 1999; B of Bus. Adminstrn. and Info. Tech., Colo. Tech. U., Colorado Springs, 2006. Cert. sys. engr. Microsoft Corp., 2003, netware adminstr. Novell, Inc., 2003, CompTIA A+ Computing Tech. Industry Assn., 1999, CompTIA Network+ Computing Tech. Industry Assn., 2003, CompTIA Server+ Computing Tech. Industry Assn., 2003, CompTIA Security+ Computing Tech. Industry Assn., 2004. Info. tech. profl. Highland Mgmt., Longmont, Colo., 2003, Graebel Co., Inc., Aurora, Colo., 2004—. Info. tech. profl. Parks Coll., Thornton, Colo., 1998—99. Recipient W.T. Parks Leadership award, Parks Coll., 1999. Mem.: NRA (life), Internat. High IQ Soc. (life), Mensa (life). Conservative. Latter Day Saints. Avocations: travel, shooting, movies, music. Office: Graebel Co Inc 16346 Airport Cir Aurora CO 80011 Office Phone: 303-214-7414. Office Fax: 303-214-2159. Personal E-mail: james_balle@yahoo.com.

BALLEE, SHAWN ALEXANDER, engineering educator; b. Chicopee, Mass., Oct. 19, 1967; s. William J. and Sally Jo Ballee; m. Debra Louise Vittetow, Mar. 30, 2006; children: Mackenzie John-Anton Mielczarek, Alexander William. BS, No. Ill. U., Dekalb, 1996—2000. Nuc. engring. watch supr. US Navy, Va., 1985—93; elec., electronic team leader Fox River Water Rec Dist., Elgin, Ill., 1994—99; instr., indsl. systems tech. Waubonsee C.C., Sugar Grove, Ill., 1999—2006; owner Bravo Zulu Tech. Consulting, Sycamore, Ill., 2002—06. Indsl. com. chair Vallees, Sugar Grove, 2004—06. Recipient Outstanding Student, Tooling and Mfg. Assn., 2000. Mem.: MENSA. Achievements include development of modular powder coat paint facotry for US Air Force. Home: 330 East State St Apt 2W Sycamore IL 60178 Personal E-mail: sballee@waubonsee.edu.

BALLEN, ROBERT GERALD, lawyer; b. Bridgeport, Conn., Dec. 20, 1956; s. Myron Ronald and Joan Ruth (Miller) B.; m. Debra Ruth Tarnapol, Jan. 5, 1986. AB magna cum laude (hon.), Princeton U, 1978; JD cum laude (hon.), Harvard U, 1981. Bar: DC 1981, US Dist. Ct. DC 1982, US Ct. Appeals (DC cir.) 1982, US Supreme Ct. 1988. Atty. Fed. Res. Bd., Washington, 1981-85; assoc. Morrison & Foerster, Washington, 1985-88, ptnr. Wash., 1989—, Schwartz & Ballen LLP, Wash., DC, 1995—. Author: Banks and Mutual Funds, 1988, Uniform Commercial Code Article 4A and the Automated Clearing House System, 1990; contbr. articles to profl. jours. Mem. ABA (chmn. UCC payments systems subcom. 1989—). Office: Schwartz & Ballen LLP 1990 M St NW Ste 500 Washington DC 20036 Office Phone: 202-776-0707. Business E-Mail: rballen@schwartzandballen.com.

BALLENGER, CASS (THOMAS CASS BALLENGER), former congressman, retired plastics company executive; b. Hickory, NC, Dec. 6, 1926; s. Richard E. and Dorothy (Collins) B.; m. Donna Davis, June 14, 1952; children: Cindy Ballenger Brinkley, Melissa Ballenger Jordan, Dorothy Davis Weaver. Student, U. N.C., 1944-45; BA, Amherst Coll., 1948. Pres. Plastic Packaging, Hickory, 1957-86, chmn. bd., 1986—; pres. Hickory Paper Box Co., 1961-80; mem. 100th-108th Congresses from 10th N.C. dist., 1986—2005; ret.; chmn., founder Plastic Packaging, Inc., Hickory. Mem. edn. and workforce com., internat. rels. com. County commr. Catawba County, N.C., 1966-74, chmn. commn., 1970-74; mem. N.C. Ho. of Reps., Raleigh, 1974-76, N.C. Senate, Raleigh, 1976-86. Mem. Hickory C. of C. Lodges: Rotary (pres. Hickory club). Republican. Episcopalian. Avocations: golf, swimming. Office: Plastic Packaging Inc Box 2029 Hickory NC 28601

BALLENTINE, RON, pharmacist, educator; b. New Carlisle, Ohio, Nov. 27, 1947; s. Rollin E. and Margaret L. Ballentine; m. Lydia P. Prather, June 23, 1984; 1 child, Susan Margaret. BS in Pharmacy, U. Cin., 1971; PharmD, U. Mich., Ann Arbor, 1973. Lic. pharmacist Ohio, 1971, Calif., 1971, Tex., 1974, Va., 1988. Drug info. specialist U. Tex. M.D. Anderson Cancer Inst., Houston, 1974—85; asst. prof. U. Houston, 1974—81, assoc. prof., dept. chair, 1981—85; dir. profl. resources Owen Healthcare, Houston, 1985—87; assoc. prof. pharmacy MCV Sch. Pharmacy, Richmond, Va., 1987—. Mem., past pres. Am. Cancer Soc., Richmond, Va., 1997—2007; mem., past pres., com. mem. Instructive Vis. Nurse Assn., Richmond, 1995—2007. Recipient Lederle Pharmacy Faculty Rsch. award, U. Houston, 1977, George Wash. Honor medal, Freedoms Found. Valley Forge, 1965; scholar, Squibb, Inc., 1974. Mem.: Am. Assn. Colls. Pharmacy (assoc.), Am. Soc. Health Sys. Pharmacists (assoc.). Independent. Avocations: travel, skiing. Office: MCV School Pharmacy Box 980581 Richmond VA 23298-0581 Home Phone: 804-320-8253; Office Phone: 804-828-3004. Office Fax: 804-828-7436. Business E-Mail: rlballen@vcu.edu.

BALLESTEROS, PAULA MITCHELL, nurse; b. Jonesport, Maine, Oct. 18, 1950; d. Paul Frederick and Janice Madeline (Beal) Mitchell; m. Ernesto Gascon Ballesteros, Apr. 4, 1981; children: Christopher, Jonathan. BS in Profl. Arts, St. Joseph's Coll., 1984; BSN, Husson/Ea. Me. Med. Ctr. Baccalaureate Sch. Nursing, 1994; MS in Bus., Husson Coll., 2004. Cert. Nursing Administrn. Patient care mgr. Eastern Maine Med. Ctr., Bangor, 1974—, trustee, 1993-95. Chairperson adv. bd. Ea. Maine Tech. Coll., Bangor, Me., 1993-94; pres. Me. Coun. Nurse Mgrs., 1991-93, Ea. Me. Med. Ctr. auxiliary, Bangor, Me., 1993-95. Contbr. articles to profl. jours. Mem. St. Joseph Hosp. Auxiliary. Mem. Am. Orgn. Nurse Execs., Penobscot Med. Soc. Auxiliary, Me. Assn. Hosp. Auxiliaries (pres. 1994—). Democrat. Protestant. Avocations: skiing, tennis, reading. Home: 78 Packard Dr Bangor ME 04401-2531 Office: Ea Maine Med Ctr 489 State St Bangor ME 04401-6616 Home Phone: 207-947-2119; Office Phone: 207-973-7371. Business E-Mail: pballesteros@emh.org.

BALLEW, LAURIE K., psychiatrist; b. Magnolia, Miss. d. J.E. and Elsie W. Ballew. BS, MS, Murray State U., 1972; EdD, Vanderbilt U., 1983; DO, Univ. Osteopathic Med., Des Moines, 1994. Speech pathologist Pennyroyal MH-MR Ctr., Hopkinsville, Ky., 1972-73, JAMP Spl. Edn., Olmstead, Ill., 1973-80; program devel. assoc. Murray State U., Murray, Ky., 1980-81; pvt. practice speech pathology Paducah, Ky., 1981-90; intern Broadlawns Med. Ctr., Des Moines, 1994-95; resident U. Louisville, 1995-98; psychiatrist Communicare, Inc., Leitchfield, Ky., 1998-2000; asst. prof. U. Louisville, 2000—. Co-dir. GERO psychiatry, dir. adult ADHD svcs. U. Louisville Hosp. Mem. Am. Psych. Assn., AMA, Ky. Med. Psychiat. Assn. (pres. 2003-04), Ky. Psychiat. Assn., Jefferson County Med. Soc. Avocations: reading, music, gardening, old movies. Office: 5 East Psychiatry 530 S Jackson St Louisville KY 40202-1675 also: 5 East Psychiatry 530 S Jackson St Louisville KY 40202-1675

BALLIETT, JOHN WILLIAM, entrepreneur, real estate company executive; b. Rochester, NY, Sept. 10, 1947; s. Charles Garrison and Burnetta Elizabeth (Purtell) B.; m. Betsy Jane Van Patten, Jan. 25, 1969; 1 child, Noelle Elizabeth. BS in Physics, Grove City Coll., 1969; postgrad., U. Rochester, 1969-71. Devel. engr. Eastman Kodak Co., 1969-70; scientist Tropel Inc., 1970, mgr. applied optics, 1971-72, mktg. mgr., 1972-73; exec. v.p., dir. Quality Measurement Sys., Inc., Penfield, NY, 1973-77; pres. QMS Internat., Inc., Penfield, 1974-77, Balliett Assocs., Sarasota, Fla., 1978—, Shore Lane Devel. Corp. subs. (merger Sandbar Devel. Corp.), 1981—, 1990—. Pres., pub. Suncoast TV Facts, Inc., Sarasota, 1979-81; pres. Charter One, Inc., Sarasota, 1981—, Palma Sola Enterprises, Inc., 1990—; chmn., CEO Charter One Hotels & Resorts, Inc., 1989—; pres. Alacho Inc., 1992—; pres. Servus Hotel Group, Inc., N.Y.C., 1997-; mng. ptnr. Bayon Bleu, LLC, 2003; spkr. at nat. and internat. timesharing confs. Contbr. articles on timesharing to profl. publs.; patentee optical sys. Founding dir. Internat. Found. for Timesharing. Mem. Fla. Bar (citizen mem. grievance com.), U.S. C. of C., Sarasota County C. of C., Am. Land Devel. Assn., Nat. Timeshare Coun., Fla. Hotel-Motel Assn. Home: 1404 Westbrook Dr Sarasota FL 34231-3549 Office: 2032 Hillview St Sarasota FL 34239-2334

BALLIN, WILLIAM CHRISTOPHER, international shipping and investment advisor; b. Ft. Wayne, Ind., May 3, 1927; s. Christopher T. and Katherine (Nolles) B.; m. Dolores Mary Witte-Jack, June 18, 1948; children: Stuart, Kirk, Scott, Elizabeth. BA, U. Toledo, 1950; postgrad., Colo. Coll., Am. U.; advanced degree, Imede, Lausanne, Switzerland. Pub. affairs coord. Marathon Oil Co., Findlay, Ohio, 1954-61, Washington rep., 1961-63; European mgr. govt., corp. relations Marathon Internat. Oil Co., Geneva, 1963-69; v.p. Crosby Kelly Investor and Corp. Devel., NYC, 1969-70; sr. v.p. Am. Export Lines, Inc., NYC, 1970-76, exec. v.p., 1976-77; chmn. Overland Trust Fin. Svcs., Geneva and NYC, 1978—. Vice chmn. Contship Holdings, INT, B.M.V.; bd. dirs. Contship Asia, Pacific, Hong Kong, Valley-Kuwait Group, Kuwait, CMA-GGM Am.; advisor Atechma Cie, Paris. Mem. Pres.'s Delegation to Algeria, 1987. Office: Malagnou House-CP 424 1208 Geneva Switzerland

BALLINGER, CHARLES EDWIN, educational association administrator; b. West Mansfield, Ohio, June 3, 1935; s. William E. and Mildred Arlene (Jester) B.; m. Venita Dee Riggs, June 12, 1982. BA, De Pauw U., 1957; MA, Ohio State U., 1958, PhD, 1971. Tchr. pub. schs., Ohio, 1958—62, Ohio State U. Lab. Sch., Columbus, 1962—63; adminstrv. intern Parma Pub. Schs., Ohio, 1963—64; asst. supt. North Canton City Schs., Ohio, 1964—67; cons. Franklin County Schs., Columbus, 1967—70, Ohio Dept. Edn., Columbus, 1970—71; coord. San Diego County Office Edn., 1971—98; exec. dir. Nat. Assn. for Yr.-Round Edn., San Diego, 1980—2000, exec. dir. emeritus, 2000—. Contbr. numerous articles to profl. jours. Home: 4891 Jellett St San Diego CA 92110-2226 Office: Nat Assn for Yr-Round Edn PO Box 711386 San Diego CA 92171-1386 Home Phone: 619-275-2245; Office Phone: 619-276-5296. Business E-Mail: cballinger@nayre.org.

BALLINGER, CHARLES WILLIAM, sanitary engineer, consultant; b. Athens, Ohio, Oct. 24, 1949; s. William Pearl Ballinger and Ruth Virginia Bayless; m. Lynn Dorland Ballinger, July 12, 1996. BSCE, Ohio Univ., Athens, Ohio, 1972, MS in Sanitary and Structural Engr., 1973. Registered civil, Ariz., 1980, sanitary, Ariz., 1993, cert. civil, Calif., 1986, lic. profl., Fla., 2002, cert. Mich., 1979, lic. civil, Nev., 1994, cert. profl., New Mex., 1994, lic. N.C., 2002, Ohio, 1976, Oreg., 1996, Utah, 1994; cert. wastewater treatment 3 Ariz., 1987. Dist. engr. Ohio EPA Southeast Dist., Logan, Ohio, 1973—74; project engr. A.E. Stilson and Assoc., Columbus, Ohio, 1974—76; project mgr./project engr. Gilbert/Commonwealth Assoc., Jackson, Mich., 1976—79; asst. project mgr. Brown and Caldwell, Tucson, 1979—82; cont. supr. (in Saudi Arabia) Bechtel Inc., San Francisco, 1982—83; project mgr./project engr. Moore-Knickerbocker and Assoc., Phoenix, 1984—86; resident engr. and proj. engr. Camp, Dresser, and McKee Inc., Phoenix, 1986—91; project mgr. Coe and Van Loo Cons., Inc., Phoenix, 1991—93; pres. Ballinger Cons. P.C., Scottsdale, Ariz., 1993—. Mem.: NFPA, ASCE, Water Environ. Fedn., Instrumentation, Sys. and Automation Soc., Ariz. Water and Pollution Control Assn., Am. Water

Works Assn., Am. Pub. Works Assn., Am. Coun. Engring. Co. Ariz., Am. Coun. Engring. Co. Avocations: scuba diving, snorkeling, camping, dance. Office: Ballinger Cons P C PO Box 12187 Scottsdale AZ 85267

BALLINGER, WALTER FRANCIS, surgeon, educator; b. Phila., May 16, 1925; s. Robert I. and Frances (Taylor) B.; children: Walter Francis, Christopher Bardin, David Gordon; m. Mary Randolph Gordon Dickson, Oct. 4, 1980. Student, Cornell U., 1942-44; MD, U. Pa., 1948. Intern 1st Surg. Div., Bellevue Hosp., NYC, 1948-49, asst. resident surgery, 1949-50, chief resident surgery, 1955-56; asst. resident surgery Columbia-Presbyn. Med. Center, 1953-55; from instr. to assoc. prof. Jefferson Med. Coll., Phila., 1956-63; assoc. prof. surgery Johns Hopkins Sch. Medicine, 1964-67; Bixby prof., head dept. surgery Washington U. Sch. Medicine, St. Louis, 1967-78, prof. surgery, 1978-92, prof. emeritus surgery, 1992—. Med. dir. health adminstrn. program Wash. U. Sch. Medicine, 1993—99. Editor: Research Methods in Surgery, 1964, The Management of Trauma, 1968, 4th edit., 1985, (with T. Drapanas) Practice of Surgery: Current Review, 1972, 2d edit., 1974; editor-in-chief (with G. Zuidema) Surgery, 1971-97, (with J. Hepner) Best Practices and Benchmarking in Healthcare; mem. editl. bd. Brit. Jour. Surgery, 1989-94. Served to capt. U.S. Army, 1950-52. Markle scholar med. sci., 1961-66 Mem. Am. Surg. Assn., Soc. Clin. Surgery, Soc. Univ. Surgeons, A.C.S., James IV Assn., Halsted Soc. Home: 1203 Log Cabin Ln Saint Louis MO 63124-1528

BALLINTINE, DANIEL JOHN, lawyer; b. 1971; BA in Econs. cum laude, Carleton Coll. (completed at Cambridge U., Eng.), 1993; JD cum laude, U. Minn., 1995. Bar: Minn. 1995, US Dist. Ct. (dist. Minn.) 1997. Shareholder, mem. Employment Law Dept. Larkin, Hoffman, Daly & Lindgren, Ltd., Mpls. Mem. Minn. Bd. Architecture and Engring., 2001—. Named a Rising Star, Minn. Super Lawyers mag., 2006. Mem.: ABA, Minn. State Bar Assn., Hennepin County Bar Assn. Office: Larkin Hoffman Daly & Lindgren Ltd 1500 Wells Fargo Plz 7900 Xerxes Ave S Minneapolis MN 55431 Office Phone: 952-896-3288. E-mail: dballintine@larkinhoffman.com.*

BALLIRO, JOSEPH JAMES, SR., lawyer; b. Boston, May 21, 1928; s. James and Anna (DeLambo) B.; m. Amalia Barreda, Sept. 20, 1986; children by previous marriage: James, Joseph, Jullianne, Patrice, Linda. AA, Northeastern U., 1948; LLB, Boston U., 1951. Bar: Mass. 1951. Asst. counsel Vol. Def. Assn., Boston, 1951-55; sr. counsel Joseph J. Balliro, Atty.-at-Law, Boston, 1955—. Fellow Am. Coll. Trial Lawyer; mem. ABA, Mass. Trial Lawyers Assn. (pres.), Nat. Assn. Trial Defense Lawyers, Mass. Bar Assn. Named one of top Boston lawyers, Boston mag., 2004. Office: 99 Summer St Ste 1650 Boston MA 02110-1200 Office Phone: 617-737-8442.

BALLMAN, CHRIS, public radio reporter; m. Susan McCabe; 1 child, McCabe Emmanuel. Reporter, Living on Earth NPR, Boston, reporter, Here and Now. Co-recipient First Place award for reporting on the environ., Society of Environ. Journalists, 2002, AAAS Sci. Journalism award for radio reporting, 2005, 2006. Office: c/o Living on Earth 20 Holland St Ste 408 Somerville MA 02144-2749 also: WBUR Here and Now 890 Commonwealth Ave Boston MA 02215 Office Phone: 617-353-8158. Business E-Mail: cballman@wbur.bu.edu.

BALLMAN, PATRICIA KLING, lawyer; b. Cin., May 1, 1946; d. John Joseph and Margaret Elizabeth (Stacy) Kling; children: Andrew J., Cara E. BS with honors, St. Louis U., 1967; JD with honors, Marquette U., 1977. Bar: Wis. 1977, U.S. Dist. Ct. (ea. and we. dist Wis.) 1980, U.S. Ct. Appeals (7th Cir.) 1983, U.S. Ct. Appeals (8th Cir.) 1986, U.S. Supreme Ct. 1986. Ptnr. Quarles & Brady, Milw., 1977—. Officer lawyer regulation Dist. II Com. Chair pers. com. United Way, 2000—02; past chair Shorewood Bd. of Rev.; mem. Gov.'s Task Force on Ethics Reform in Govt., 2002; past pres. The Benedict Ctr.; bd. dirs. Wis. Law Found. Master: Fairchild Inns of Ct.; mem.: ABA, Am. Acad. Matrimonial Lawyers (pres. Wis. chpt. 2002—04), Wis. Bar Assn. (pres. 2002—03), Milw. Bar Assn. (pres. 1995—96). Office: Quarles & Brady 411 E Wisconsin Ave #2040 Milwaukee WI 53202-4461 Office Phone: 414-277-5000. Business E-Mail: pkb@quarles.com.

BALLMER, STEVEN ANTHONY, computer software company executive; b. Farmington Hills, Mich., Mar. 24, 1956; s. Frederick and Beatrice (Dworkin) Ballmer; m. Connie Snyder, 1990; 3 children. BA in Applied Math. & Econ., Harvard U., 1977; postgrad., Stanford U., 1979—80. Asst. product mgr. Procter & Gamble Co., 1977—79; with Microsoft Corp., Redmond, Wash., 1980—, v.p. mktg., v.p. corp. staffs, sr. v.p. sys. software, exec. v.p. sales & support, 1992—98, pres., 1998—2001, CEO, 2000—. Bd. dirs. Microsoft Corp., 2000—, Accenture, 2001—06; bd. overseers Harvard U.; adv. coun. Stanford Bus. Sch. Named one of Forbes Richest Americans, 2006—. Avocations: exercise, jogging, basketball. Office: Microsoft Corp 1 Microsoft Way Redmond WA 98052-8300*

BALLO, MATTHEW T., radiation oncologist, educator; MD, Case Western Res. U., Cleve., 1995. Bd. cert. radiation oncologist Am. Bd. of Radiology. Asst. prof. M. D. Anderson Cancer Ctr., Houston, 2000—04, assoc. prof., 2005—, med. dir. radiation oncology outreach, 2006—. Contbr. scientific papers to profl. jours. Achievements include research in Defining the role of radiation for patients with melanoma and soft tissue sarcoma. Office: M D Anderson Cancer Ctr Unit 97 1515 Holcombe Blvd Houston TX 77030 Office Phone: 713-563-2300. E-mail: mballo@mdanderson.org.

BALLOU, JANICE DONELON, research director; b. New Brunswick, NJ, May 13, 1944; s. Peter and Kathryn (Koval) Donelon; m. Donald Thomas Ballou, Nov. 12, 1966 (div. 1984); children: Peter, David. BA, Douglas Coll., 1966; MA, Rutgers U., 1977. Tchr. Sayreville (N.J.) Jr. High Sch., 1966-71; dir. field ops. Eagleton Inst., Rutgers U., New Brunswick, NJ, 1977-80, assoc. dir., 1980-82, dir. Star-Ledger/Eagleton Poll, dir. Ctr. for Pub. Interest Polling, 1989—2001; v.p. divsn. head Louis Harris & Assocs., NYC, 1982-86; v.p. group head Response Analysis, Princeton, NJ, 1986-89; v.p., dep. dir. surveys and info. svc. Mathematica Policy Rsch., Inc., Princeton, NJ, 2001—. Bd. dirs. Inst. Rsch. on Aging and Health Fin., Princeton, N.J., Essex C.C. Found. Contbg. author: Polling America. An Encyclopedia of Public Opinion, 2005. Co-founder Parents Drug and Alcohol Coun., Highland Park, N.J., 1991; bd. dirs. Rutgers Substance Abuse Task Force, New Brunswick, 1990-93, The Citizen's Com. on Biomed. Ethics, Summit, N.J., 1993-98; chair Pathways to Participation Civic Edn. Program com., New Brunswick, 1992; grad. bd. Leadership N.J., 1991-99; pres. Bd. Leadership N.J. Grad. Orgn., 1995; mayor Highland Park Econ. Devel. Com., 1999. Leadership N.J. fellow Partnership for N.J., 1990, Ford Found. fellow, 1990; named Alumnae of Yr. by Highland Park High Sch., 1992. Mem. Am. Assn. Pub. Opinion Rsch. (pubs. chair 1988-90, sec.-treas. 1991-93, standards chair 1999-2001, councillor-at-large 2002—), Nat. Network State Polls (mem. exec. coun. 1989—), Nat. Coun. Pub. Polls (mem. exec. coun. 1993—), N.J. Internat. Forum Women (sec.), N.J. Assn. for Pub. Opinion Rsch. (pres. 2002—), Douglass Soc. (Douglass Coll. assoc. alumnae). Avocations: raising christmas trees, travel, hiking, outdoor activities, reading. Office: Mathematica Policy Rsch PO Box 2393 Princeton NJ 08543-2392 Home Phone: 732-828-9369; Office Phone: 609-750-4049.

BALLOU, KENNETH WALTER, retired business executive, dean; s. Thomas Walter and Anne M. (Blanck) A.; m. Ann Dysart; children—Stephen K., Jeffrey S., Laura A., Ellen S. AB, Ed.M., Tufts U.; postgrad., Rutgers U., Wharton Sch. U. Pa. Dir. admissions Northeastern U., Boston, dean univ. relations, dean Univ. Coll., dean adult edn.; pres. Wellesley Motor Coach Co., Mass., 1978-88; v.p., gen. mgr. Waters Bus. Sys., Inc., Framingham, Mass. Cons. U.S. Office of Edn., various colls.; corporator Framingham Savs. Bank, 1980-85; mem. Spl. Legis. Commn. on Sch. Transp. Safety; sr. lectr. in mngt. Northeastern U., 1979-90. Author monographs in field of adult edn. and sch. transp. Chmn. Framingham Sch. Com.; corporator Framingham Union Hosp.; corporator Northeastern U., mem. nat. coun., bd. overseers, mem. long range planning com., life mem. President's Club; bd. dirs. Mass. Osteo. Hosp.; life mem. Danforth Mus. Art, Framingham Hist. Assn.; mem. Sudbury Valley Trustees, Cahoon Mus.; past mem. bd. assessors 1st Parish, Framingham; endowed Childrens Gallery of Danforth Mus. and established the Dean Kenneth W. Ballou Family Scholarship, Northeastern U.; trustee Cotuit Pub. Libr. Mem. AAUP, Assn. Higher Edn., Am. Mgmt. Assn., Adult Edn. Assn., Am. Assn. Continuing Edn., Coun. Advancement of Edn., Am. Pers. and Guidance Asn., Mass. Audubon Soc., Ariz. Hist. Soc., Zeta Psi, Hyannis Yacht Club, Barnstable Newcomers Club (past pres.). Home: 19 Roosevelt Rd Cotuit MA 02635

BALLOUN, JOSEPH EUGENE, lawyer; b. Hays, Kans., June 16, 1929; m. Patricia Balloun (div.); children: Michael, Kristen; m. Sheila Gail Wombles; children: David, Hannah. BS degree, U. Kans., Lawrence, 1951, JD, 1954. Bar: Kans. 1954, Kans. Supreme Ct., US Dist. Ct. (Kans.), US Ct. Appeals (10th cir.) 1963, US Tax Ct. 1972, US Supreme Ct. Atty. USAF, Enid, Okla., 1955-57, Ostrum & Balloun, Russell, Kans., 1957-62, Turner & Balloun, Great Bend, Kans., 1962-72, Payne & Jones, Olathe, Kans., 1972-80, Balloun & Bodinson, Olathe, Kans., 1980-84; ptnr. Shook, Hardy & Bacon, Overland Park, Kans., 1984—, vice chmn. gen. litig. div. Mem. Kans. 10th judicial dist. nominating commn.; mediator US Dist. Ct. Kans. Bd. mem. Child Abuse Prevention Coalition, Johnson County, Kans., Foster and Adoptive Children. Recipient Justinian award, Johnson County Bar Assn., Whittaker award, Lawyers Assn. Kans. City, William Kahrs Lifetime Achievement award, Kans. Assn. Defense Counsel. Fellow Am. Coll. Trial Lawyers; mem. ABA (Pro Bono award), Kans. Bar Assn. (Disting. Svc. award), Kans. Assn. Def. Counsel (past pres.), Am. Bd. Trial Advocates; master emeritus Kans. Inn of Ct., Order of the Coif. Office: Shook Hardy & Bacon 2555 Grand Blvd Kansas City MO 64108 Office Phone: 816-474-6550. Office Fax: 816-421-5547.

BALLOW, MARK, immunologist, educator; b. Harrisburg, Pa., Sept. 8, 1943; m. Molly Ballow, June 25, 1967; children: Sarah, Mara, Andrew. BA, Rutgers U., 1965; MD, U. Chgo., 1969. Diplomate Nat. Bd. Med. Examiners, Am. Bd. Pediatrics, Am. Bd. Allergy and Immunology, Diagnostic Lab. Immunology. Intern, resident Yale-New Haven Hosp., 1969-71; fellow U. Minn., 1971-73; chief clin./exptl. immunology U. Conn. Health Ctr., Farmington, 1975-79, assoc. prof. pediatrics, 1979-85, prof. pediatrics, 1985—; prof., chief allergy and immunology divsn. Children's Hosp. Buffalo, SUNY at Buffalo, 1988—. Dir. Am. Bd. Allergy and Immunology, 1993-99. Fellow Am. Acad. Allergy and Immunology (Carl Arbesman Meml. lectr. 1994), Am. Coll. Allergy, Asthma and Immunology; mem. Soc. Pediatric Rsch., Clin. Immunology Soc., Am. Pediatric Soc., Phi Beta Kappa. Avocations: skiing, tennis. Office: SUNY-Buffalo/Childrens Hosp Dept Allergy & Immunology 219 Bryant St Buffalo NY 14222-2006 Office Phone: 716-878-7105. Business E-Mail: ballow@buffalo.edu.

BALLOWE, JAMES, writer, educator; b. Carbondale, Ill., Nov. 28, 1933; s. Frank Charles and Wilma Ruth (Maynard) B.; children: Jeffrey, Mary; m. Ruth Ganchiff. BA, Millikin U., 1954; MA, U. Ill., 1956, PhD, 1963. Tchr. pub. schs. Decatur, Ill., 1954-55; grad. asst. U. Ill., 1955-61; asst. prof. English Millikin U., 1961-63; mem. faculty dept. English Bradley U., Peoria, Ill., 1963-99, prof., chmn., 1971-74, dean Grad. Sch., 1974-86, assoc. provost, 1979-86, dean communications and fine arts, 1986-90, disting. prof. emeritus of English, 1999—; chmn. Commn. Instns. Higher Edn., North Central Assn., 1985-86. Narrator Herrin Massacre, Nat. Pub. Radio, 1997. Author: (poetry) The Coal Miners, 1979, (history) The Story of the Morton Arboretum, 2003; editor: George Santayana's America, 1967, Anglo-Welsh Poetry, 1989. Mem. Ill. Arts Coun., 1975-83, Ill. State Mus. Bd., 1976—, Ill. Humanities Coun., 1997-2002. Recipient Poetry award Ill. Arts Coun., 1975, 78, Creative Non-fiction award Ill. Arts Coun., 1993. Mem. Ill. Assn. Grad. Schs. (pres. 1979-80), Midwestern Assn. Grad. Schs. (pres. 1978-79). Home: PO Box 302 Ottawa IL 61350-0302 E-mail: jcballowe@gmail.com.

BALLY, ALBERT W., retired geologist, geology educator; PhD, U. Zurich, Switzerland, 1953. Harry Carothers Weiss prof. geology Rice U., Houston, now prof. emeritus. Contbr. articles to profl. jours. Recipient R.J.W. Douglas Meml. medal Can. Soc. Petroleum Geologists, 1996, Signey Powers Meml. award Am. Assn. Petroleum Geologists. Achievements include research in the structure of foreland folded belts, the formation of allochthonous salt sheets in a continental slope environment, mechanical separation of crust and sediments from the underlying lithosphere, inversion of half-grabens in a major orogenic mechanism. Office: Rice U Dept Geology MS126 6100 S Main St Houston TX 77005-1892

BALMER, THOMAS ANCIL, state supreme court justice; b. Longview, Wash., Jan. 31, 1952; s. Donald Gordon and Elisabeth Clare (Hill) B.; m. Mary Louise McClintock, Aug. 25, 1984; children: Rebecca Louise, Paul McClintock. AB, Oberlin Coll., 1974; JD, U. Chgo., 1977. Bar: Mass. 1977, D.C. 1981, U.S. Dist. Ct. Mass. 1977, Oreg. 1982, U.S. Dist. Ct. Oreg. 1982, U.S. Ct. Appeals (9th cir.) 1982, U.S. Ct. Appeals (D.C. cir.) 1983, U.S. Supreme Ct. 1987. Assoc. Choate, Hall & Stewart, Boston, 1977-79, Wald, Harkrader & Ross, Washington, 1980-82; trial atty. antitrust divsn. U.S. Dept. Justice, Washington, 1979-80; assoc. Lindsay, Hart, Neil & Weigler, Portland, Oreg., 1982-84, ptnr., 1985-90, Ater Wynne LLP, Portland, 1990—93; dep. atty. gen. State of Oreg., Salem, 1993-97; ptnr. Ater Wynne LLP, Portland, 1997—2001; justice Oreg. Supreme Ct., Salem, 2001—. Adj. prof. of law Northwestern Sch. Law Lewis and Clark Coll., 1983-84, 90-92. Contbr. articles to law jours. Active mission and outreach com. United Ch. of Christ, Portland, 1984-87, Met. Svc. Dist. Budget Com., Portland, 1988-90; bd. dirs. Multnomah County Legal Aid Svc., Inc., 1989-93, chair 1992-93; bd. dirs. Chamber Music Northwest, 1997-2003, Classroom Law Project, 2000—, chair, 2007-, U.S. Dist. Ct. Hist. Soc., 2003-, Oreg. Law Inst., 2005—. Mem. Oreg. Bar Assn. (chmn. antitrust sect. 1986-87, mem. fed. practice and procedure com. 1999-2001). Home: 2521 NE 24th Ave Portland OR 97212-4831 Office: Oreg Supreme Ct Supreme Ct Bldg 1163 State St Salem OR 97310 Office Phone: 503-986-5717. Business E-Mail: thomas.balmer@ojd.state.or.us.

BALMORI, DIANA, landscape designer; b. Gijon, Spain, June 4, 1936; d. Clemente and Dorothy (Ling) Hernando-Balmori. Diploma in architecture, U. Tucuman, Argentina, 1960; BA in Urban History, UCLA, 1968, PhD, 1973; student in Landscaping, Radcliffe U., 1989. Asst. prof. SUNY, Oswego, 1974-78, assoc. prof., 1978-79; assoc. Cesar Pelli & Assocs., New Haven, 1977-81, prin. for landscape and urban design, 1981-90; prin. Balmori Assocs., New Haven, 1990—; critic Yale U. Sch. Architecture, 1990—; lectr. Yale U. Sch. Forestry and Environ. Studies, 1990—; Davenport Chair of Archtl. Design Yale Sch. of Architecture, 2004. Apptd. mem. Commn. Fine Arts, 2003. Author: Beatrix Farrand, Beatrix Jones Ferrand (1872-1959) Fifty Years Of American Landscape Architecture, 1982, Beatrix Farrand's American Landscapes, 1985, Transitory Gardens, Uprooted Lives, 1993, Redesigning the American Lawn, 1993, Saarinen House and Garden: A Total Work of Art, 1995; contbr. Beatrix Farrand At Dumbarton Oaks: The Design Process of a Garden; co-author: The Land and Natural Development (LAND) Code: Guidelines for Environmentally Sustainable Land Development. Chmn. civic alliance World Trade Ctr. Meml. Com., NYC; mem. program com. N.Y. New Visions; bd. dirs. Minetta Brook Com. for Comprehensive Design Landscape Plan for White Ho. Recipient Pub. Space award Conn. chpts. AIA/Am. Soc. Landscape Architects, 1990, Judges award Harry Chapin Media Aawards, 1995; grantee Ossabaw Found., 1980, N.Y. State Coun Arts, 1987, Carolyn Found., 1990, Nat. Endowment for the Arts, 1990, 92; rsch. fellow NYU, 1982. Mem. Am. Soc. Landscape Architects, Catalog of Landscape Records (bd. dirs.), Van Alen Inst. (mem. exec. com.), Am. Hist. Assn. Office: Balmori Assocs 820 Greenwich St Fl 3 New York NY 10014-5137 E-mail: diana.balmori@yale.edu.

BALMUTH, MICHAEL A., retail executive; With Bamberger's; exec. v.p., gen. mdse. mgr. Karen Austin Petites, 1986—88; sr. v.p., gen. mdse. mgr. Bon Marche, Seattle, 1988—89; joined Ross Stores, 1989, various positions including sr. v.p., gen. merchandise mgr., exec. v.p. merchandising, 1993-96, CEO, vice chmn., 1996—2005, CEO, vice chmn., pres., 2005—. Office: Ross Stores Inc 4440 Rosewood Dr Pleasanton CA 94588*

BALOGH, ARISTOTLE N., information technology executive; BSEE and Computer Sci., Johns Hopkins Univ., MS in Elec. Engring, Computer Engring. Sr. engr., mgmt. positions SRA Corp., UPS's Roadnet Technologies, Westinghouse Electric Corp., Network Solutions; v.p. engring. VeriSign Inc., Mountain View, Calif., 1999—2002, sr. v.p., ops., infrastructure, 2002—06, exec. v.p., ops., infrastructure, 2006—07, exec. v.p., chief tech. officer, 2007—. Named one of Top 25 Chief Tech. Officers, InfoWorld mag., 2007. Office: VeriSign Inc 487 East Middlefield Rd Mountain View CA 94043 Office Phone: 650-961-7500.*

BALOGLU, SEYHMUS, hospitality and tourism educator; b. Diyarbakir, Turkey, July 1, 1966; s. Cahide and Zulfikar Baloglu; m. Zerrin Kezban Keklik; children: Deniz Dogukan, Derin Burak. BS, Mersin Turizm Isletmecilik ve Otelcilik Y.O., 1989; MBA, Hawaii Pacific U., 1993; PhD, Va. Poly. & State U., 1996. Cert. Hospitality Educator Am. Hotel and Motel Assn., 1999. Rsch. assoc. Mersin Turizm Isletmecilik ve Otelcilik Y.O., Mersin, Turkey, 1989—91; gen. mgr. IKM Turizm Ltd., Alanya, Turkey, 1987—89; assoc. prof. U. of Nev., Las Vegas, 1996—. Cons. Asis, 1999—2002, The Edn. Found. of PCMA, 2000, Sta. Casinos, Inc., Las Vegas, 1999—2000, McCarran Internat. Airport, Las Vegas, 1999—2000, The Ednl. Inst. of Am. Hotel and Lodgry Assn., 1997—98; presenter in field various confs., including World Gaming Congress Casino Ops. CHRIE Conv. Svcs. Mktg. Conf. Symposium on Consumer Psychology. Contbr. articles and revs. to profl. jours., 2001 (Emerald Mgmt. Revs. Citation of Excellence, 2001), chapters to books. Bd. mem. Coral Edn. Corp., Reno, 1998—2002. Fellow Turkish Higher Edn. Coun., 1991—96. Mem.: Internat. Soc. Travel and Tourism Educators, Hospitality Sales and Mktg. Assn., Travel and Tourism Rsch. Assn. (awards), Internat. Coun. on Hotel, Restaurant and Instn. Edn., Am. Mktg. Assn. Office: U Nev Las Vegas 4505 Maryland Pkwy Box 456023 Las Vegas NV 89154-6023 Office Phone: 702-895-3932. Business E-Mail: baloglu@ccmail.nevada.edu.

BALOGUN, RASHEED ABIODUN, medical educator; s. Ishaq Ayinde and Morinat Bisi Balogun; m. Seki A. Balogun; children: Aisha Ayodele, Zainab Ayoade, Ishaq Opeyemi. MBBS, U. Ibadan, Nigeria, 1991. Diplomate Am. Bd. Internal Medicine, Am. Bd. Nephrology. Asst. prof. medicine U. Va., Charlottesville, 2001—. Chmn. med. adv. bd. Nat. Kidney Found. of the Virginias, Richmond. Named to Acad. Disting. Educators, U. Va. Sch. Medicine, 2005; recipient Willem J. Kolff Young Investigator award, ASAIO, 2002. Fellow: ACP, Am. Soc. Nephrology; mem.: Am. Soc. for Artificial Internat. Organs. Avocations: bicycling, tennis. Office: U VA Nephrology Divsn 1215 Lee St Box 800133 Charlottesville VA 22911 Office Phone: 434-924-5125. Office Fax: 434-948-2458.

BALON, RICHARD, psychiatrist, educator; b. Olomouc, Czechoslovakia, Oct. 11, 1951; s. Ota and Marie (Sindylek) B.; m. Helena Rachel Zador, July 24, 1976. MD, U. Karlova, 1976. Diplomate Am. Bd. Psychiatry and Neurology; bd. cert. in psychiatry in Czechoslovakia, cert. clin. psychopharmacology Am. Soc. Clin. Psychopharmacology, 1998. Resident in psychiatry and clin. rsch. Psychiat. Rsch. Inst., Prague, 1978—81; resident in psychiatry Lafayette Clinic, Detroit, 1983—87; asst. prof. Wayne State U., Detroit, 1987—90, assoc. prof., 1990—96, prof., 1996—, assoc. dir. residency tng. in psychiatry, 2002—. Dir. jr. med. students program in psychiatry Wayne State U., Detroit, 1989-92, dir. med. student edn. psychiatry, 1993-97; staff psychiatrist Lafayette Clinic, Detroit, 1987-92, pres. med. staff, 1990-92; co-chair Mich. Tech. Adv. Rsch. com., 1991-99. Contbr. chpts to books and articles to profl. jours.; author, editor 4 books; co-author 2 books. Travel fellow Am. Coll. Neuropsychopharmacology, 1987. Fellow: Am. Coll. Psychiatrists, Am. Psychiat. Assn. (1st Nancy C.A. Roeske award 1991, George Tarjan award 1998); mem.: AMA, Mich. Psychiat. Soc. (pres. 2000—01), Assn. Dirs. Med. Student Edn. in Psychiatry, Collegium Internat. Neuro-Psychopharmacologicum, Soc. Biol. Psychiatry, Am. Assn. Suicidology, Internat. Soc. Psychoneuroendocrinology. Avocations: movies, books, politics, geography. Office: Univ Psychiat Ctr 2751 E Jefferson Ave Ste 200 Detroit MI 48207-4100 Business E-Mail: rbalon@wayne.edu.

BALOUN, JOHN CHARLES, retired wholesale distribution executive; b. Chgo., May 1, 1934; s. John Nicholas and Anne (Giera) B.; m. Lynette Anne Jehs, July 27, 1963 (dec. Apr. 1998); children: John Christopher, Michael Warren. BSc, DePaul U., 1956. CPA, Ill. Audit staff Arthur Andersen & Co., Chgo., 1956-63; contr., asst. sec. Super Food Svcs., Inc., Chgo., 1963-67, treas., 1967-68, Dog'N Suds, Inc., Champaign, Ill., 1968-69; dir. planning and control distbn. divsn. Champion Internat., Inc., Chgo., 1969-74; treas. IGA, Inc., Chgo., 1974-77, v.p., 1977-80; v.p. fin. IGA Inc., Chgo., 1986-93, contr., 1993-96; ret. IGA, Inc., 1996; v.p. fin. Allied Van Lines, Inc., Broadview, Ill., 1980-83; contr., dir. corp. devel. Altair Corp., Northbrook, Ill., 1984-86. Pres. bd. dirs. No. Ill. Food Bank, St. Charles, Ill., 1990-91, bd. dirs., 1988-93, 96-2002. 2d lt. AUS, 1957. Republican. Home: 610 Western Ave Glen Ellyn IL 60137-4058 E-mail: jbaloun@netscape.com.

BALOW, IRVING HENRY, retired education educator; b. Wabasha, Minn., Jan. 19, 1927; s. Laurence Christian and Katherine (Yost) Balow; m. Joyce Elizabeth Binner, June 8, 1950 (dec. 1980); children: Mary, Thomas, Michael, Robert, Ann; m. Alta Sitton, June 27, 1981. BS, U. Minn., 1951, MA, 1957, PhD, 1959. Elem. sch. tchr., Theilman, Minn., 1951-53; tchr. elem. sch. Wabasha, 1953-54, 56-57; instr. U. Minn., 1957-59; mem. faculty U. Calif., Riverside, 1959—, prof. edn., 1968—, chmn. dept., 1963-70, assoc. dean, 1970-71, acting dean, 1971-72, dean, 1972-87, acting dean Grad. Sch. Mgmt., 1990-92; ret., 1992. Reading cons., 1959—. Contbr. articles to profl. jours. With USAAF, 1945—47. Home: 29410 Winding Brook Dr Menifee CA 92584 Personal E-mail: iabalow@verizon.net.

BALSER, ROBERT EDWARD, animation film producer, director; b. Rochester, NY, Mar. 25, 1927; s. Syrel Jesse and Goldie (Weisenberg) B.; m. Cima Diane Feinberg, June 25, 1950; 1 child, Trevel Morley. BA, UCLA, 1950. Dir. animation TVC, London, 1967-68, WorldWide Prodn., Barcelona, 1969-70, Halas and Batcheler, London, 1971-72; owner, dir. Pegbar Prodns., Barcelona, 1972-93; dir. TV series Cromosoma, Barcelona, 1994-95; retired cons. Barcelona, 1995. Pres. "CARTOON" (media program), 1988-2004; v.p. ASIFA Internat., 1979-94, pres. Spain, 1980-93; animation cons. Egypt, 1996, Turkey, 1996-99, Eng., 2000-05, France, 2000-05, Spain, 2000-05, USA, 2005-07; lectr. in field. Co-dir. The Yellow Submarine, 1967-68; supv. dir. The Jackson 5, 1971; producer numerous ednl. and TV series. V.p. Benjamin Franklin Found., Barcelona, 1986-

2005, Am. Soc. Barcelona, 1986-90; pres. Benjamin Franklin Sch. Bd., Barcelona, 1986-95. With USN, 1945-46. Recipient EMMY award NATAS, 1980; 1st prize publicity Venice and Annecy Festivals, Italy and France, 1964, Acad. Motion Picture Arts Scis. Democrat. Jewish. Avocations: film, collecting stamps and coins.

BALSIGER, DAVID WAYNE, television director, writer, television producer, television director, researcher; b. Monroe, Wis., Dec. 14, 1945; s. Leon C. and Dorothy May (Meythaler) B.; children from previous marriages: Jennifer Anne, Lisa Atalie, Lori Faith. Student, Pepperdine U., Malibu, Calif., 1964-66, Cypress Jr. Coll., 1966, Chapman Coll. World Campus Afloat, Orange, Calif., 1967-68, Internat. Coll., Copenhagen, 1968; BA, Nat. U., San Diego, 1977; LHD (hon.), Lincoln Meml. U., Harrogate, Tenn., 1978. Chief photographer, feature writer Anaheim (Calif.) Bull., 1968-69; pub., editor Money Doctor, consumer mag., Anaheim, 1969-70; media dir. World Evangelism, San Diego, 1970-72; dir. mktg. Logos Internat. Christian Book Pubs., Plainfield, NJ, 1972-73; pres., dir. Master Media, advt. agy., Costa Mesa, Calif., 1973-75; pres. Balsiger Lit. Svc., Costa Mesa, 1973-78; v.p. communications Donald S. Smith Assocs., Anaheim, Calif., 1975-78; dir. creative devel. Sunn Classic Pictures, L.A., Salt Lake City, 1976-78; owner Writeway Lit. Assocs., Costa Mesa, 1978-92, Balsiger Enterprises, Loveland, Colo., 1978—, Bibl. News Svc., 1980-90; v.p. Donald S. Smith Assocs., Anaheim, 1982-86; owner BNS Publs., 1986-92; v.p. Am. Portrait Films Internat., Anaheim, 1990-91; chief rschr., field prodr., dir. Sun Internat. Pictures, Salt Lake City, 1992-94; exec. producer, dir. audio-video-media divsn. Group Pub., Loveland, Colo., 1994-98; sr. v.p., prodr., rights supr. Grizzly Adams Prodns., Loveland, Colo., 1998—. Vis. prof. Nat. U., San Diego, 1977—80. Author: (amazing stories books) The Satan Seller, 1972, The Back Side of Satan, 1973, Noah's Ark: I Touched It, 1974, One More Time, 1974, It's Good to Know, 1975, In Search of Noah's Ark, 1976, The Lincoln Conspiracy, 1977, Beyond Defeat, 1978, On The Other Side, 1978, 8 Mini Guide Books (travel series), 1975, (amazing coincidence books) Presidential Biblical Scorecard, 1980, 3rd edit., 1988, Protection Scorecard, North Africa, 1987, 3rd edit., 1989, Candidates Biblical Scorecard, 1986, Scoreboard Alert, 1989, Face in the Mirror, 1993, Ancient Secrets of the Bible, 1994, The Incredible Discovery of Noah's Ark, 1995, The Incredible Power of Prayer, 1996, The Evidence for Heaven, 2005; co-author (with Christine Strong): Inspirational Wit and Wisdom from the Internet, 2006; dir.(field producer, writer, researcher): (TV films) Operation Thanks, 1965, The Life and Times of Grizzly Adams, 1976—77, In Search of Noah's Ark, 1976, The Lincoln Conspiracy, 1977, The Bermuda Triangle, 1977, Ancient Secrets of the Bible, 1992, Ancient Secrets of the Bible II, 1993, Mysteries of the Ancient World, 1994, Ancient Secrets of the Bible Collectors Series, 1995 (6 awards including 2 communicator awards of excellence), The Incredible Power of Prayer, 4 vols., 1997; prodr.(6 TV shows and videos): Angels Sent on Assignment, 1996; exec. prodr.: (video) Chadder's Stowaway Adventure, 1996 (Film Adv. Bd, Excellence award, 1996), (videos) Sing and Play Music Video, 1996, Sing and Play Music Jamboree, 1997, Chadder's Wild Frontier Advemture, 1997, Encounter with the Unexplained (series 52 vols.), 2002—03 (21 awards including 3 Telly awards and 1 Omni Intermedia award); prodr.: (TV series, spls.) Secrets of the Bible Code Revealed, 1998, The Bible Code: Future and Beyond, 1999 (5 awards including 1 videographer award of excellence), Millenium Fears: Fact or Fiction?, 1999, Xtreme Mysteries (104 vols.), 2003, Miracle and Wonder of Prayer (series), 2000 (7 awards including 2 communicator awards of distinction); prodr.: (TV series) (spls.) The Search for Heaven, 2004, The Evidence for Heaven, 2004; prodr.: (TV series, spls.) George W. Bush: Faith in the White House, 2004, Breaking the DaVinci Code, 2005, The DaVinci Code Deception, 2005, Twelve Ordinary Men, 2005, Miraculous Mission, 2005, Heroes and Miracles of 9/11, 2006, End Times, How Close Are We, 2006, Miracles In Our Midst, 2006, Apocalypse And The End Times, 2006, Cracking Davinci's Code, 2006, Heroes Among Us, Miracles Around Us, 2006, Fabric of Time, 2007, Miraculous Messages, 2007, The Cure for Christ Resurrection, 2007. Press agt. John G. Schmitz congl. campaign, 1972, Gordon Bishop supr. campaign, Orange County, 1970; press agt. asst. Ronald Reagan for Gov., statewide, 1966; statewide campaign mgr. James E. Johnson for U.S. Senate, 1974; campaign mgr. Dave Gubler Congl. campaign, 1974; candidate Costa Mesa City Coun., 1980; Rep. candidate for Congress from 38th Dist. Calif., 1978; mem. Calif. Rep. Assembly, 1975-78, 81-84, Rep. Assocs. Orange County, 1977-79; mem. World Affairs Coun. Orange County and San Diego, 1969-70; assoc.mem. Calif. Rep. Cen. Com., 1969-70; bd. dirs. Chapman Coll. World Campus Afloat, 1967, Chrisma Ministries, Orange, Calif., 1969-73; founder Ban the Soviets Coalition, 1983-84; exec. com. Anatole Fellowship, 1983-87; founder, pres. Nat. Citizens Action Network, 1984-95; bd. dirs. Internat. Ch. Relief Fund, 1987-92. Recipient Vietnam appreciation citation Am. Soldiers in Vietnam, 1966, George Washington Honor medal Freedoms Found., 1978, 79, Religion in Media Angel trophy, 1981, 85, 87-89, 92-95, 5 Telly awards for Ancient Secrets series, 1996; named Writer of Month Calif. Writer, 1967; grand winner Mercury award for Pub. Affairs, 1987, Gold Mercury award for Pub. Affairs Mag., 1987, Silver Mercury award for affairs video script, 1988, Nat. Faith and Freedom award Religious Heritage of Am., 1994; named to Lit. Hall of Fame, 1977; hon. tourism amb. Rep. of South Africa, 1991. Mem. Nat. Univ. Pres. Assocs., Internat. Christian Visual Media Assn. (bd. mem.), Nat. Religious Broadcasters, Internat. Bible Reading Assn. (adv. bd.), Acad. TV Arts and Scis., Am. Film Mkt. Assn., Christian Booksellers Assn., Internat. Press Assn. (adv. bd.), Fellowship European Broadcasters. Address: PO Box 1987 Loveland CO 80539-1987 Office Phone: 970-663-3820. Personal E-mail: dwbalsiger@ultrasys.net. *I believe successful people have a God given purpose strong enough to make them form the habit of doing things they don't like to do in order to accomplish their purpose. Every single qualification for success is acquired through habit. People form habits and habits form futures.*

BALSILLIE, JIM, information technology executive; b. Seaforth, Feb. 3, 1961; married; 2 children. B of Commerce, U. Toronto, 1984; MBA, Harvard Bus. Sch., 1989; LLD (hon.), Wilfrid Laurier U. Chartered acct., Ont. With Ernst & Young, Toronto; exec. v.p., bd. dirs. Sutherland-Shultz Ltd., Kitchener, Ont.; co-CEO Rsch. in Motion Ltd., Waterloo, Ont., Canada, 1992—, chmn., 1992—2007, also bd. dir. Founder The Centre for Internat. Governance Innovation, 2002. Founding donor Perimeter Inst. for Theoretical Physics; patron Grand River Hosp.; major donor Rsch. In Motion Park in the City of Waterloo; prin. benefactor Balsillie Collection of Roy Studio Images; helped establish Waterloo Regional Children's Mus. Named one of World's 100 Most Influential People, Time Mag., 2005; recipient Golden Plate award, Acad. Achievement, 2006. Fellow: Inst. Chartered Accountants of Ont. Avocations: hockey, golf, coaches soccer and basketball, trains and competes in Men's Long Course Triathlons. Office: Rsch in Motion Ltd 295 Phillip St Waterloo ON N2L 3W8 Canada Office Phone: 519-888-7465. Office Fax: 519-888-7884.*

BALSLEY, PHILIP ELWOOD, entertainer; b. Augusta County, Va., Aug. 8, 1939; s. Henry Elwood and Marjorie Walden (Fielding) B.; m. Wilma Lee Kincaid, July 21, 1962; children— Gregory, Mark, Leah. Grad. high sch. With group Statler Bros., 1961—. Treas. Statler Bros. Prodns., 1973—. Bd. dirs. Happy Birthday U.S.A. Recipient numerous Grammy awards, Country Music Assn. awards. Presbyterian. Office: PO Box 2703 Staunton VA 24402-2703

BALSTAD, ROBERTA, social scientist; b. Mpls., June 25, 1940; d. Gerhard Oliver and Laverne K. (Anderson) Balstad; m. Gary David Lange, Nov. 26, 1959 (div. 1968); m. Floyd John Miller, June 15, 1969 (div. 2004); 1 child, Aaron Gerhard. BA, U. Minn., 1964, MA, 1970, PhD, 1973. Rsch. assoc. AIA, Washington, 1974; staff assoc. Social Sci. Rsch. Coun., Washington, 1975-81; exec. dir. Consortium Social Sci. Assns., Washington, 1981-84; divsn. dir. NSF, Washington, 1984-93; pres., CEO Consortium Internat. Earth Sci. Info. Network (CIESIN), University Center, Mich., 1993-98; adj. prof. natural resources policy behavior U. Mich., 1993-97; sr. rsch. scientist, sr. fellow, dir. CIESIN Columbia U., NYC, 1998—. Guest scholar Woodrow Wilson Internat. Ctr. Scholars, 1994; sr. assoc. mem. St. Anthony's Coll., U. Oxford, England, 1991—92; mem. chmn. NATO adv. panel on Advanced Sci. Insts./Advanced Rsch. Workshops, Brussels, 1988—91; chmn. steering com. space applications and commercialization Nat. Rsch. Coun., 1999—2002, mem. exec. com. Space Studies Bd., 1995—2000, mem. climate rsch. com., 1997—99, mem. com. on global change rsch., 1999—2002; chmn. U.S. Nat. Com. on Sci. and Tech. Data, 2003—; mem. U.S. Nat. Com. IIASA, 1995—; chmn. adv. bd. Luxembourg Income Survey, 1987—91. Author: City and Hinterland, 1979; editor (with Harriet Zuckerman) Science Indicators: Implications for Research and Policy, 1979; contbr. articles to profl. jours.; translator poetry of Jorge Luis Borges, 1989-91, N.P. von Wyk Louw, 1998 Bd. trustees Newport Schs., Kensington, Md., 1986-91, St. Anthony's Coll. Trust, U. Oxford, 1994—, sec., 1997-2000, chair, 2000—, bd. dirs. Open Geospatial Consortium 2003—; adv. trustee Environ. Rsch. Inst. Mich., 1995-98. Recipient NSF Meritorious Svc. award, 1993. Fellow: AAAS (com. mem., chmn. 1987—93), NY Acad. Scis.; mem.: Coun. Fgn. Rels., Am. Lt. Translators Assn., Internat. Social Sci. Coun. (com. 1991—95, v.p. 1992—94), US Man Biosphere Program (com., chmn. 1989—91), Cosmos Club. Lutheran. Business E-Mail: roberta@ciesin.columbia.edu.

BALSTER, ROBERT LOUIS, alcohol/drug abuse services professional, researcher; b. St. Cloud, Minn., Oct. 12, 1944; s. Louis and Marion Balster; m. Sandra Kay Herwig, June 25, 1966; 1 child, Sarah Elizabeth. BS, U. Minn., Mpls., 1966; PhD, U. Houston, 1970. Postdoctoral fellow in psychiatry and pharmacology U. Chgo., 1970-72; rsch. assoc. in psychiatry Duke U., Durham, NC, 1972-73; asst. prof. pharmacology Med. Coll. Va., Richmond, 1973-78, assoc. prof., 1978-84, prof. pharmacology, 1984—2003, Luther A Butler prof. pharmacology, 2003—; dir. Inst. for Drug and Alcohol Studies, 1993—; coord. Humphrey Fellowship Program in Substance Abuse, 2006—. Chmn. Drug Abuse Adv. Com., FDA, Rockville, Md., 1983-84; mem. Robert Wood Johnson Rsch. Network on Etiology of Tobacco Dependence, 1997-2006; mem. adv. bd. Partnership for Drug Free Am. Editor-in-chief Drug Alcohol Dependence, 1998—; contbr. articles to profl. jours. Recipient NIH Merit award, 1993-2004, Va. Commonwealth U. Faculty award of Excellence, 1999, Coll. on Problems of Drug Dependence Mentoring award, 2000, Faculty Tchg. Excellence award Va. Commonwealth U. Sch. Medicine, 2003, Mentoring award NIDA Internat. Program, 2006. Fellow Coll. on Problems of Drug Dependence (charter fellow, pres. 1995-96), Am. Coll. Neuropsychopharmacology, APA (pres. psychopharmacology divsn. 1989-90, chair bd. sci. affairs 1995-96, Disting. Svc. to Psychol. Sci. award, 2006, Brady-Schuster award 2007); mem. European Behavioral Pharmacology Soc. (coun. mem. 1986-94). Achievements include development of laboratory methods for studying the behavioral effects of drugs of abuse and procedures for drug abuse potential evaluation. Office: Va Commonwealth U PO Box 980310 Richmond VA 23298-0310 Business E-Mail: balster@vcu.edu.

BALTAKE, JOE, film critic; b. Camden, NJ, Sept. 16; s. Joseph John and Rose Clara (Bearint) B.; m. Susan Shapiro. BA, Rutgers U., 1967. Film critic Gannett Newspapers (suburban), 1969, Phila. Daily News, 1970-85; movie editor Inside Phila., 1986—; film critic The Sacramento Bee, 1987—; syndicated movie critic Scripps Howard News Svc., 1999—. Leader criticism workshop Phila. Writer's Conf., 1977-79. Contbg. author: Encyclopedia of American Lives, Vol. 6, 2003; contbg. editor: Screen World, 1973-2000; author: The Films of Jack Lemmon, 1977, updated, 1986; contbr. articles to Films in Rev., 1969-00, broadcast criticism for Prism Cable TV, 1985; cons. Jack Lemmon: American Film Institute Life Achievement Award, 1987, Jack Lemmon: A Life in the Movies, 1990. Mem. selection com., program essayist Phila. Internat. Film Festival, 2004—07. Recipient Motion Picture Preview Group award for criticism, 1986, citation Phila. Mag., 1985, First Pl. commentary award Soc. Profl. Journalists, 1995, citation Sacramento News & Rev., 2000. Personal E-mail: joe.baltake@verizon.net. *Life's philosophy: "Living well is the best revenge."*.

BALTAKE, SUSAN, marketing and communications professional; b. Phila., June 10, 1952; d. Irving D. and Sylvianne (Lesnar) Shapiro; m. Joe Baltake, Apr. 10, 1984. BSc in Journalism, Temple U., 1973. V.p. Sommers/Rosen Inc., 1975—86; mktg. dir. Hansen Group, 1986—87, River West Investments, 1987—91, 1993—97; press sec. Calif. Dem. Party, 1991—93; campaign mgr. Phil Angelides for State Treas., 1997—98; asst. state treas. Calif., 1999—2000; pres. Grove St. Solutions, Haddonfield, NJ, 2000—. Bd. mem. Coalition Comml. Real Estate Assns., 2001—06; mktg. and outreach chair Congress for New Urbanism XV, 2005—07. Mem. Haddonfield Zoning Bd., 2003—; founder, chair Haddonfield Farmers Market, 2006—; bd. dirs. Interfaith Caregivers, Haddonfield, 2005—. Mem.: Urban Land Inst., AKA Sr. Counselors Alliance, Rotary. Office: Grove Street Solutions 880 Grove St Haddonfield NJ 08033 Business E-Mail: susan@grovestreetsolutions.com.

BALTARO, RICHARD J., pathologist, medical educator; came to the U.S., 1964; s. Dimitri and Maria Silvana Baltaro; m. Laura E. Neece, 1972; children: Elizabeth B., John C. BA, Earlham Coll., 1972; PhD summa cum laude, U. Rome, Italy, 1977; MD magna cum laude, Cath. U., Rome, 1983. Bd. cert. anatomic and clin. pathology Am. Bd. Pathology, cert. immunopathology Am. Bd. Pathology. Pathology resident Brown U., Providence, 1983-87; clin. pathology fellow George Washington U. Hosp., Washington, 1987-88; asst. in pathology George Washington Med. Sch., Washington, 1987-88; sr. staff fellow NIH Clin. Ctr. Immunology, Bethesda, Md., 1988-90; jr. active staff NIH Clin. Ctr., Bethesda, 1988-90; asst. prof. Marshall U. Sch. Medicine, Huntington, W.Va., 1990-93, dir. pathology residency program, 1991-93; staff pathologist lab. svc. VA Med. Ctr., Huntington, 1990-93; pathologist Med. Arts Lab., Oklahoma City, 1993-98; assoc. clin. prof. Med. Ctr. U. Rochester, 1999—2001; assoc. prof. Creighton U., Omaha, 2001—. Stockholder Med. Arts Lab., 1994-98; ptnr. Med. Arts Pathologists, 1995-98; adj. assoc. prof. U. Okla. Health Sci., Oklahoma City, 1993-99; spkr. in field. Contbr. articles to profl. jours. Recipient NIH grant, 1991. Fellow Coll. Am. Pathologists (lab. insp. 1985—), Am. Soc. Clin. Pathologists, Internat. Acad. Pathology, Acad. Clin. Lab. Physicians and Scientists, Am. Coll. Internat. Physicians, Assn. Clin. Scientists; mem. AMA, AAAS, Am. Soc. Microbiology, Am. Assn. for Clin. Chemistry, Assn. Med. Lab. Immunologists. Avocations: gardening, reading, dance, child raising. Office: Creighton Univ Med Ct Path Dept 601 N 30th St Omaha NE 68131

BALTAY, CHARLES, physicist, educator; b. Budapest, Hungary, Apr. 15, 1937; s. John A. and Ilona T. Baltay; m. Virginia Rohan Baltay, Oct. 7, 1961; children: Peter, Michael, Thomas, Matthew, Annemarie. BS, Union Coll., 1958; MS, Yale U., 1959, PhD, 1963. Lectr. Yale U., New Haven, 1963—64; from instr. to prof. Columbia U., NYC, 1964—88; Higgins prof. physics, prof. astronomy Yale U., New Haven, 1988—. Dir. Nevis Labs. Columbia U., 1978—86; chmn. dept. physics Yale U., 1995—2001. Editor: 3 books; contbr. over 300 articles to profl. jours. Fellow: Am. Phys. Soc.; mem.: Sigma Xi. Home: 86 Lower Rd Guilford CT 06437 Office: Yale Univ Dept Physics New Haven CT 06520 Office Phone: 203-432-3386. Business E-Mail: charles.baltay@yale.edu.

BALTAZZI, EVAN SERGE, retired engineering research consulting company executive; b. Izmir, Turkey, Apr. 11, 1921; came to U.S., 1959, naturalized, 1964; s. Phocion George and Agnes Zoe (Varda) B.; m. Nellie Despina (Biorlaro), July 17, 1945; children— Agnes, James, Maria D.Phys. Scis., Sorbonne U., Paris, 1949; D.Phil. in Chemistry, Oxford U., Eng., 1954. Rsch. dir., prof. rsch. French Nat. Rsch. Ctr., Paris, 1947-59; group leader organic chemistry rsch. Nat. Aluminate Corp., Chgo., 1959-61; mgr. organic chemistry sect. IIT Rsch. Inst., Chgo., 1961-63; dir. rsch. lab. Addressograph-Multigraph Corp., Chgo. and Cleve., 1963-77; pres. Evanel Assocs., Sagamore Hills, Ohio, 1977—. Mem. com. on U.S. currency NRC, 1985-86. Author: Basic American Self-Protection, 1972, Kickboxing, 1976, Stickfighting, 1977, Self-Protection at Close Quarters, 1981, Self-Protection Complete: The A.S.P. System, 1992, Dog Gone West: A Western for Dog Lovers, 1994, Plato and Socrates Trial, 1995, Alternative: Tai Chi Chuan, 2004—05; patentee in field, originator Am. Self-Protection Sys. Mem. judo com. U.S. Olympic Com., 1967-74 Recipient Citizen of Yr. award Citizenship Coun. Met. Chgo., 1964; Outstanding Achievement award in sci. Immigrants Service League, 1965, citation, 1965; Outstanding Program award YMCA, 1967; recognition award Gordon Rsch. Confs., 1976; Ohio Spl. Olympics Gold medal volunteering award, 1999; named Outstanding Scientist of XXth Century Internat. Biog. Ctr., 2000; NRC Can. fellow, 1955, Brit. Coun. fellow, 1952-54 Fellow Am. Inst. Chemists (vice chmn. Chgo. chpt. 1970), Am. Chem. Soc. (sr.), Royal Chem. Soc. U.K., Soc. Photog. Scientists and Engrs. (pres., bd. dirs. Cleve. chpt. 1975-82), Am. Self-Protection Assn. (pres. 1965—), N.Y. Acad. Scis. Avocations: fencing, Judo, Aikido.

BALTER, BERNICE, religious organization administrator; Exec. dir. Women's League for Conservative Judaism, NYC, 1978. Nat. adv. bd. MAZON. Mailing: Women's League for Conservative Judaism 475 Riverside Dr New York NY 10115 Office Phone: 212-870-1260 ext. 7157. Office Fax: 212-870-1261. E-mail: bbalter@wlcj.org.

BALTER, FRANCES SUNSTEIN, civic worker; b. Pitts. d. Elias and Gertrude Susntein; m. James Stone Balter, May 15, 1948; children: Katherine (Mrs. Ross Anthony) (dec.), Julia Frances, Constance Cantor, Daniel Elias. Student, Sarah Lawrence Coll., 1939-41, New Sch. Social Rsch., 1941-43; cert. Inst. Arts Adminstrn., Harvard U., 1973. Adminstrv. asst., assoc. prodr. Ednl. TV Sta. WQED-TV, Pitts., 1963-67; prodr., mng. dir. Freedom Readers, 1964-67; co-founder, incorporator, sec. bd. dirs. Pitts. Coun. Arts, 1967-70; cultural cons. Mayor's Office Dir. Office Cultural Affairs, Pitts., 1968. Initiator Three Rivers Arts Festival 1960; co-dir. Ohio and Miss. River Valley Art Festival, 1961-62; mem. Pa. Coun. Arts, 1972-78; co-founder Pioneer Crafts Coun., Mill Run, Pa., 1972; exec. dir. Poetry on the Buses, 1974—. Author of poems. Bd. dirs. Coun. for Arts MIT, 1985-93, Palm Beach Festival, 1987-89. Named Woman of Yr. Art Post-Gazette, 1969. Mem. Nat. Soc. Arts and Letters (Pitts. chpt.).

BALTER, LESLIE MARVIN, business communications educator; b. NYC, Feb. 27, 1920; s. Harry and Rose Balter; m. Frances Hughes; 1 child by previous marriage, Kenneth Robert (dec. 1979); 1 child by previous marriage, Sheila Beth. BSEE, Columbia U., 1941; postgrad., Rutgers U.; MA, NYU, 1969. Civilian radio engr. Signal Corps Devel. Lab., Ft. Monmouth, N.J., 1941-45, in ETO, 1942; chief engr. Masters Crystal Co., quartz crystal prodn., 1945-46; founder, dir. Jersey City Tech. Inst., 1947—; founder br. operation as Paterson (N.J.) Inst., 1956—; founder Sch. Bus. Machines tchg. IBM machines Plaza Sch., Paramus, N.J., 1958—; cons. test engr. Consumers Rsch., Washington, N.J. Contbr. articles to Electronic Design Mag., Bus. Edn. World, Tech. Edn. News. Mem. N.J. Vocat. Edn. Master Plan Com. Comm.; chmn. Jersey City CD Coun., 1950-53; pres. Ferncroft Park Coop. Mem. IEEE (life, participant Legacies 1994), N.J. Assn. Pvt. Career Schs. (pres. 1971), N.J. Bus. Edn. Assn., Columbia Club N.Y., Delta Pi Epsilon. Home: 41 Ferncroft Park Ramsey NJ 07446-2575 E-mail: lbalter@optonline.net.

BALTIMORE, DAVID, former academic administrator, microbiologist, educator; b. NYC, Mar. 7, 1938; s. Richard I. and Gertrude (Lipschitz) B.; m. Alice S. Huang, Oct. 5, 1968; 1 dau., Teak. BA in Chemistry with high honors, Swarthmore Coll., Pa., 1960; postgrad., MIT, 1960—61; PhD, Rockefeller U., NYC, 1964. Postdoctoral rschr. MIT, Cambridge, Mass., 1964—65; research assoc. Salk Inst. Biol. Studies, La Jolla, Calif., 1965—68; from assoc. prof. microbiology to dir. MIT, Cambridge, Mass., 1968—82, founding dir. Whitehead Inst. Biomed. Rsch., 1982—90; pres. Rockefeller U., NYC, 1990—91, prof., 1990—94; pres. Calif. Inst. Tech., Pasadena, 1997—2006, pres. emeritus, 2006—, Robert Andrews Millikan prof. biology, 2006—. Bd. govs. Weizmann Inst. Sci., Israel; co-chmn. Commn. on a Nat. Strategy of Aids, 1986; ad hoc program adv. com. on complex genome, AIDS rsch. adv. coun. NIH, 1996, chair vaccine adv. com., 1997—2002; bd. dirs. MedImmune, Inc., 2003—. Mem. editorial bd. Jour. Molecular Biology, 1971-73, Jour. Virology, 1969-90, Sci., 1986-98, New Eng. Jour. Medicine, 1989-94; contbr. articles to profl. jours. Bd. govs. Weizmann Inst. Sci., Israel; bd. dirs. Life Sci. Rsch. Found. Recipient Gustav Stern award in Virology, 1970, Warren Triennial prize Mass. Gen. Hosp., 1971, Eli Lilly and Co. award in Microbiology and Immunology, 1971, Nat. Acad. Scis. US Steel award, 1974, Gairdner Found. award, 1974, Nobel prize in physiology & med., 1975, Nat. medal of Sci., 1999, Warren Alpert Found. prize, 2000, Sci. Achievement award, AMA, 2002, 2006. Fellow AAAS (pres.-elect, 2006), Am. Med. Writers Assn. (hon.), Am. Acad. Microbiology; mem. NAS, Am. Acad. Arts and Scis., Inst. Medicine, Am. Philos. Soc., Pontifical Acad. Scis., Royal Soc. (Eng., fgn.), French Acad. Scis. (fgn. assoc.). Office: Calif Inst Tech Mail Code 147-75 1200 E California Blvd Pasadena CA 91125-0001

BALTIMORE, ROBERT SAMUEL, pediatrician, epidemiologist; b. NYC, Nov. 3, 1942; s. Richard Irving and Gertrude (Lipshitz) B.; m. Nancy Virginia Ward, June 16, 1967 (dec. Aug. 1977); 1 child, Gwen; m. Katalin Rachel Radnay, Sept. 24, 1978; 1 child, Richard. AB, U. Chgo., 1964; MD, SUNY, Buffalo, 1968. Diplomate in pediatrics and pediatric infectious diseases Am. Bd. Pediatrics. Intern U. Chgo. Hosps. and Clinics, 1968-69, resident in pediatrics, 1969—71; postdoctoral fellow Walter Reed Army Inst. Rsch., Washington, 1971-74; postdoctoral fellow, instr. Harvard Med. Sch., 1974-76, asst. prof. pediats. and epidemiology, 1976-81; assoc. prof. pediatrics and epidemiology Yale U. Sch. Medicine, New Haven, 1981—95, prof. pediatrics, epidemiology, pub. health, 1995—. Co-editor: Topics in Critical Care Pediatrics, 1984, Pediatric Infectious Diseases: Principles and Practice, 1995, 2d edit., 2002. Asst. dir. health Town of Orange, Conn., 1990—. Maj. U.S. Army, 1971-74. Rsch. grantee NIH, 1981-84, Cystic Fibrosis Found., 1988-90, Ctrs. for Disease Control and Prevention, 1990—. Fellow Infectious Diseases Soc. Am., Pediatric Infectious Diseases Soc., Soc. for Pediatric Rsch., Am. Acad. Pediatrics (mem. com. infectious diseases 2001—), Am. Pediat. Soc., Soc. for Healthcare Epidemiology. Democrat. Jewish. Avocations: gardening, hiking, canoeing. Home: 188 Crocker Ct Orange CT 06477-3025 Office: Yale Univ Sch Medicine 333 Cedar St New Haven CT 06520-8064 E-mail: robert.baltimore@yale.edu.

BALTUCH, GORDON HIRSH, neurosurgeon; b. Montreal, Que., Can., Apr. 24, 1960; arrived in U.S., 1978; s. Siegmar Udo Baltuch and Carol Leila Wevrick; m. Vivian Ariane Barbara Wasmuht-Perroud, Mar. 28, 1997; children: Orphee Sarah, Axel Noah. BA, Harvard U., 1981; MSc, Stanford U., 1982; MD, McGill U., Montreal, 1986, PhD, 1995. Diplomate Am. Bd. Neurol. Surgery. Neurosurgery fellow CHUV, Lausanne, Vaud, Switzerland; neurosurgeon Montreal Gen. Hosp., 1995—96; assoc. prof. neurosurgery U. Pa., Phila., 1996—. Assoc. dir. PADRECC, Vets. Hosp., Phila., 2001—; dir. Ctr. Functional and Restorative Neurosurgery. Named Top Dr., Phila. Mag., 2005; recipient Mastroianni Clinical Innovator award, 2003; grantee, NIH, 1998—, VA, 2001—. Fellow: ACS, Royal Coll. Surgeons Can., Coll. Physicians of Phila.; mem.: Am. Assn. Neurol.

Surgeons. Office: Hosp U Pa 5 Silverstein 3400 Spruce St Philadelphia PA 19104 Home: 268 S 3rd St Philadelphia PA 19106 Office Phone: 215-662-7788. Business E-Mail: baltuch@med.upenn.edu.

BALTZ, ANTHONY JOHN, physicist; b. Indpls., Mar. 10, 1942; m. Marie Lepri Baltz, June 22, 1968; children: Edward Anthony, William Henry. BS, Spring Hill Coll., 1966; MS, Case Western Res. U., 1968, PhD, 1971. Rsch. assoc. Brookhaven Nat. Lab., Upton, NY, 1971—73, assoc. physicist, 1973—76, physicist, 1976—2001, sr. physicist, 2001—; dep. leader theory group RIKEN BNL Rsch. Ctr., 1997—. Vis. scientist Lawrence Berkeley Lab., 1977, U. Sao Paulo, Brazil, 1982, U. of Manchester, England, 1984; nuclear theory monitor U.S. Dept. of Energy, 1984—85, nuclear theory detailee, 1999—2000. Contbr. numerous articles to profl. jours. Fellow: AAAS; mem.: Am. Phys. Soc. Office: Brookhaven Nat Lab Physics Dept 510A Upton NY 11973

BALTZ, PATRICIA ANN (PANN), retired elementary school educator; b. Dallas, June 20, 1949; d. Richard Parks and Ruth Eileen (Hartschuh) Langford; m. William Monroe Baltz, Sept. 6, 1969; 1 child: Kenneth Chandler. Student, U. Redlands, 1967-68; BA in English Lit. cum laude, UCLA, 1971. Cert. tchr. K-8, Calif. Tchr. 4th grade Arcadia (Calif.) Unified Sch. Dist., 1972-74, 92—, substitute tchr., 1983-85, tchr. 3dr grade, 1985-87, tchr. 6th grade, 1987-90, tchr. 4th and 5th grade multiage, 1990—2005, ret., 2005. Sci. mentor tchr. Arcadia Unified Sch. Dist., 1991-94; mentor Tech. Ctr. Silicon Valley, San Jose, Calif., 1991. Tchr. rep. PTA, Arcadia, 1980-93; mem. choir, children's sermon team, elder Arcadia Presbyn. Ch., 1980-93; chaperone, vol. Pasadena (Calif.) Youth Symphony Orch., 1988-90; vol. Am. Heart Assn., 1990-92. Recipient Outstanding Gen. Elem. Tchr. award, Outstanding Tchr. of the Yr. award Disney's Am. Tchr. Awards, 1993, Calif. Tchr. of Yr. award Calif. State Dept. Edn., 1993, Georgie award Girl Scouts of Am., 1993, The Self Esteem Task Force award L.A. County Task Force to Promote Self-Esteem & Personal & Social Responsibility, 1993, Profl. Achievement award UCLA Alumni Assn.; apptd. to Nat. Edn. Rsch. Policies & Priorities Bd., U.S. Sec. Edn. Richard Riley; Pann Baltz Mission Possible Scholar named in her honor. Mem. NEA, Nat. Sci. Tchrs. Assn., Calif. Tchr. Assn., Arcadia Tchrs. Assn. Avocations: reading, singing, calligraphy, book-making, computers. Home: 1215 S 3rd Ave Arcadia CA 91006-4205

BALTZER, CYNTHIA LOUISE, music educator; b. Pitts., Jan. 23, 1955; d. George Edward and Loisan Reisiger Eisenhauer; 1 child, Shannon Evangeline. BS in Edn., Ind. U. Pa., Indiana, 1978. Music educator Derry Area Sch. Dist., Pa., 1978—. Dir. over 20 musicals. Mem-at-large Ligonier Valley Players, 1982—86. Named one of 100 Finalists in Tchr. Excellence, Tchrs. Excellence Ctr., 2004; recipient Ptnrs. in Edn. award, 1992. Mem.: Pa. Music Educators, Westmoreland County Music Educators (pres. 1998—2000). Republican. Meth. Avocations: swimming, water-skiing, singing, playing piano and guitar. Home: 708 James St Latrobe PA 15650 Office: Derry Area Mid Sch 994 N Chestnut St Ext Derry PA 15627 Office Phone: 924-694-8231. Office Fax: 724-694-0288. E-mail: clbaltzer@verizon.net.

BALTZER, REBECCA A., musicologist, researcher, consultant; b. Memphis, June 17, 1940; d. Ralph Neal and Sherard Rawles Baltzer; m. Charles Edward McCarthy, Mar. 17, 1984. AB in English magna cum laude, Randolph-Macon Woman's Coll., 1962; MA in Musicology, Boston U., 1964, PhD in Musicology, 1974. Part-time instr., lectr. in music Boston U., 1964—67; prof. musicology Sch. Music U. Tex., Austin, 1967—, assoc. dean Grad. Sch., 1982—86. Cons. Nat. Endowment for Humanities, Washington, 1979—80, Ednl. Testing Svc., Princeton, NJ, 1986—88; vis. prof. music Princeton U., 1996. Editor, transcriber: Le Magnus liber organi de Notre-Dame de Paris, 1995, co-editor, contbr.: book of essays The Divine Office in the Latin Middle Ages, 2000 (Hon. Mention in Philosophy & Religion, from the Profl. and Scholarly Pub. (PSP) br. of the Assn. of Am. Publishers, 2001); co-editor: The Union of Words and Music in Medieval Poetry, 1991; editor of the music: edition & translation of medieval poetry Guillaume de Machaut: Remede de Fortune, 1988; contbr. articles to profl. jours. Dissertation fellow, AAUW, 1966—67. Mem.: Soc. for Am. Music, Early Music Am., Coll. Music Soc., Medieval Acad. Am. (local arrangements chair ann. meeting 2000), Am. Musicological Soc. (bd. dirs. 1980—82, v.p. 1988—90, treas., mem. exec. com. 1993—2000, Alfred Einstein award 1973), Pi Kappa Lambda, Phi Beta Kappa. Episcopalian. Avocations: reading, photography, travel. Home: 68 Sundown Parkway Austin TX 78746-5258 Home Phone: 512-327-2863. Home Fax: 512-471-7836.

BALU, SANJEEV, pharacoeconomist; b. Mumbai, Maharashtra, India, Apr. 19, 1973; s. Subramani and Raji Balu; m. Sonia Gulrajani. B in Pharmacy, Pune U., India, 1994, MBA, 1995; Ph.D., Purdue U., West Lafayette, Ind., 2005. Pharm. intern Novartis Pvt. Ltd., Mumbai, 1993; pharm. mgmt. intern Wockhardt Pvt. Ltd., Mumbai, 1996; med. sales rep. Raptakos Brett Pvt. Ltd., Satara, India, 1994—95; pharm. sr. rsch. assoc. ORG-MARG Pvt. Ltd., New Delhi, 1999—2000; grad. tchg. asst. U. Cin., 2000—01, Purdue U., 2001—05; grad. intern Aon Consulting Life Scis. Practice, Wellesley, Mass., 2004; sr. pharmacoeconomist/outcomes scientist ABT Assocs. Inc., Lexington, Mass., 2005—. Mem. grades appeal com. Purdue U., 2003—04. Manuscript reviewer P&T Jour., 2005—06, Pharmacotherapy Jour., 2005—06, Value in Health Jour., 2005—. Mem.: Am. Coll. Clinical Pharmacy, Am. Soc. Health-Sys. Pharmacists, Internat. Soc. Pharmacoeconomics and Outcomes Rsch. (sec./treas. Purdue U. student chpt. 2004—05, judge and reviewer 2005—), The Rho Chi Soc. Office: ABT Assocs Inc 181 Spring St 2d Fl Lexington MA 02421 Office Phone: 781-372-6644.

BALZARY, MICHAEL PETER (FLEA), musician, recording artist, actor; b. Melbourne, Australia, Oct. 16, 1962; m. Loesha Zeviar, 1988 (div. 1990); 1 child, Clara; 1 child, Sunny Bebop. Bassist The Red Hot Chili Peppers, 1983—; founder Silverlake Conservatory of Music, LA, 2001—. Musician: (albums) The Red Hot Chili Peppers, 1984, Freaky Styley, 1985, The Uplift Mofo Party Plan, 1987, Mother's Milk, 1989, Blood Sugar Sex Magik, 1991, One Hot Minute, 1995, Californication, 1999, By the Way, 2002, Live in Hyde Park, 2004, Stadium Arcadium, 2006 (Best Album, MTV Europe Music Awards, 2006, Best Rock Album, Best Ltd. Edit. Package, Grammy awards, 2007), (songs) Dani California, 2006 (MTV Video Music award for best Art Direction, 2006, Best Rock Vocal Performance, Best Rock Song, Grammy awards, 2007); actor: (films) Suburbia, 1984, Tough Guys, 1986, Dudes, 1987, Stranded, 1987, Less Than Zero, 1987, The Blue Iguana, 1988, Back to the Future Part II, 1989, Back to the Future Part III, 1990, Motorama, 1991, My Own Private Idaho, 1991, Roadside Prophets, 1992, Son in Law, 1993, The Chase, 1994, The Big Lebowski, 1998, Fear & Loathing in Las Vegas, 1998, Psycho, 1998, Liar's Poker, 1999, Goodbye, Casanova, 2000, (voice actor): (TV series) The Wild Thornberrys, 1998—2001; (TV films) The Wild Thornberrys: The Origin of Donnie, 2001; (films) The Wild Thornberrys Movie, 2002, Rugrats Go Wild!, 2003. Co-recipient Favorite Band, Duo, or Group, Am. Music Awards, 2006, Favorite Alternative Artists, 2006. Office: care Q Prime 131 S 11th St Nashville TN 37206 Office Phone: 615-258-1050. Office Fax: 615-258-1040. E-mail: info@qprime.com.*

BALZEBRE, ANTHONY FRANCIS, SR., real estate developer, investor; b. Newton Center, Mass., Mar. 8, 1928; s. Francis Balzebre and Eva Louise Bragoli; m. Dorothy Pillsbury Wingate, June 26, 1953; children: Anthony Jr., Janet, Richard, Susan, Robert, Thomas. AB, Harvard Coll., 1950; degree in civil engring., MIT, 1951. Pres. Allied Lumber Co., Miami, Fla., 1952—78, Wingate Archt Millworks, Miami, Fla., 1952—76; developer/owner Hilton Hotel, Mobile, Ala., 1973—93, Millers Pond, Miami, 1973—84, Carillon House Internat., Dallas, 1974—, U. Tex. Housing, San Antonio, 1976—, Hilton Hotel South Beach, Fla., 1997—. Mem. adv. bd. Bank Coral Gables, Fla., 1985—95. Sponsor Coral Gables War Meml. Youth Ctr., 1965—75; host Tex. del. Nat. Rep. Conv., Miami, Fla., 1972. Recipient Presdl. award, Pres. Nixon-Rep. Nat. Conv., 1972, Contbn. award, Coral Gables War Meml. Youth Ctr., 1973. Republican. Roman Catholic. Home: 135 Leucadendra Dr Coral Gables FL 33156-2370

BALZEKAS, STANLEY, JR., museum director; b. Chgo., Oct. 8, 1924; s. Stanley and Emily B.; widowed; children— Stanley, III, Robert, Carole Rene. BS, DePaul U., Chgo., 1950, MA, 1951. Pres. Balzekas Motor Sales, Chgo., 1952—, Balzekas Mus. Lithuanian Culture, Chgo., 1966—. Hon. consul for Republic of Lithuania, Palm Beach, Fla. Trustee Lincoln Acad., Cath. Charities, Am.-Lithuanian Coun.; chmn. Sister Cities/Chgo.-Vilnius Friendship Com., Trade & Cultural Ctr.; mem. adv. bd. Chgo. Cultural Affairs. Served with U.S. Army, 1942-45, ETO. Decorated Bronze Star; decorated 3d degree order Grand Duke Gediminas, Pres. Lithuania; recipient Wigilia medal Polish Geneal. Soc. Am., medal DAR, Disting. Alumni award DePaul U., 1991, Zygimantas Augustas medal Vilnius, 2001, Order Lithuanian Numismatics medal, 2003. Mem. Am. Assn. Mus., Ethnic Cultural Preservation Coun. (pres. 1977—), Press Club (Chgo.), Literary Club (Chgo.), City Club (Chgo., ethnic chmn.), Exec. Club (Chgo.), Am. Legion Office: 4030 S Archer Ave Chicago IL 60632-1140 Office Phone: 773-582-6500. E-mail: president@lithuanianmuseum.org.

BALZHISER, RICHARD EARL, research and development company executive; b. Wheaton, Ill., May 27, 1932; s. Frank E. and Esther K. (Merrill Werner) B.; m. Christine Karnuth, 1951; children: Gary, Robert, Patricia, Michele. BS in Chem. Engring., U. Mich., 1955, MS in Nuclear Engring., 1956, PhD in Chem. Engring., 1961. Mem. faculty U. Mich., Ann Arbor, 1961-67; White House fellow, spl. asst. to sec. Dept. Def., Washington, 1967-68; chmn. dept. chem. engring. U. Mich., 1970-71; assoc. dir. energy, environ. and natural resources White House Office of Sci. and Tech., Washington, 1971-73; dir. fossil fuel and advanced systems Electric Power Rsch. Inst., Palo Alto, Calif., 1973-79, sr. v.p. R&D, 1979-87, exec. v.p. R&D, 1987-88, pres., chief exec. officer, 1988-96, pres. emeritus, 1996—. Bd. dirs. Reliant Energy, Electro Source, Aerospace Corp.; mem. adv. bd. Nat. Renewable Energy Lab.; mem. pres. com. on sci. and tech. energy studies I and II, Pres.'s Com. on Sci. and Tech. Energy Studies, 1997-99. Co-author: Chemical Engineering Thermodynamics, 1972, Engineering Thermodynamics, 1977. Mem. Ann Arbor City Coun., 1965-67, mayor pro tem, 1967. Named to Acad. All-Am., U. Mich. Football, 1952, Acad. All-Am. Hall of Fame, 2002. Mem. Nat. Acad. Engring. Lutheran. Office: Electric Power Rsch Inst 3412 Hillview Ave Palo Alto CA 94304-1344 Office Phone: 650-855-2141. Office Fax: 650-855-2090. Business E-Mail: rbalzhis@epri.com.

BAMBERG, LOUIS MARK, wealth planning and business insurance specialist; b. Miami, Fla., Dec. 1, 1948; s. Harold Sidney and Estelle Grace (Nagorski) B.; children: Heather Rae, Elijah Louis; m. Andrea Bamberg. AA, Miami Dade Jr. Coll., Perrine, Fla., 1968; B Bus., Ga. State U., 1970; JD, John Marshall U., Atlanta, 1977. CLU, ChFC; Bar: Ga. 1977. Salesman, buyer, mgr. Levitz, Inc., 1970-78; atty. SBA, Atlanta, 1976-78; salesman Equitable Life Assurance, Miami, 1978-85; estate planning specialist Merrill Lynch Life, Ft. Lauderdale, Fla., 1985-1999; wealth mgmt. specialist, 1999—2003. Bd. dirs. United Hearing & Deaf Svcs., Ft. Lauderdale, 1990. Mem. ABA, Advanced Assn. Life Underwriters, Estate Planning Coun., Top of Table, Internat. Forum (bd. dirs.), Million Dollar Round Table. Avocations: jogging, softball, bike riding, basketball. Home: 310 N Gordon Rd Fort Lauderdale FL 33301-3775 Office: Merrill Lynch 2611 E Oakland Park Blvd Fort Lauderdale FL 33306

BAMBERGER, GERALD FRANCIS, plastics marketing consultant; b. Hannover, Germany, Sept. 20, 1920; came to U.S., 1938, naturalized, 1943; m. Ursula Friede, Mar. 27, 1946; children— Gale, Richard, Annette, Peter. Comml. diploma, Ecole Supérieure de Commerce, Neuchatel, Switzerland, 1938. Pres. A. Bamberger Corp., Bklyn., 1938-54, Interplastics Corp., NYC, 1955-62; prodn. mgr. plastics div. Cities Service Corp., Hicksville, N.Y., 1963-67; pres. Bamberger Polymers, Inc., New Hyde Park, N.Y., 1967-85; plastics mktg. cons., 1985—. Served with M.I. AUS, 1943-46. Decorated Bronze Star. Mem. Soc. Plastics Industry, Soc. Plastics Engrs., Plastics Pioneers Assn. Home Phone: 941-954-5049. Personal E-mail: gfbamberger@att.net.

BAMBERGER, MARY ANN, archivist, consultant; b. Chgo., Feb. 9, 1941; d. Francis Stephen and Julia Mary (Clarett) Bamberger. BS in Humanities, Loyola U., 1963; MA in History, DePaul U., 1966. Tchr. Mother McAuley Liberal Arts H.S., Chgo., 1962—66, history dept. chair, 1965—66; archivist, assoc. prof. U. Libr., U. Ill., Chgo., 1966—2000, assoc. prof. emerita, 2000—; cons., 2000. Grant reviewer Nat. Hist. Pub. and Records Commn., 1985—2000, Nat. Endowment for Humanities, 1985—2000. Contbr. chapters to books, articles to profl. jours. Vol. LaGrange Cmty. Nurses, Ill., 2000—, St. Cletus Missions, LaGrange, 2000—; centennial, exhbn. com. Caxton Club, Chgo., 1990—95; archival adv. bd. Cath. Archdiocese of Chgo., 1984—94, sesquicentennial history, lect. com., 1993—94; steering com., treas. Chgo. Area Women's History Conf., 1976—82. Avocation: hand bookbinding. Home: 11147 Edgebrook Ln Indian Head Park IL 60525-6973

BAMBERGER, MICHAEL ALBERT, lawyer, educator; b. Berlin, Feb. 29, 1936; s. Fritz and Kate (Schwabe) B.; m. Phylis Skloot, Dec. 19, 1965; children: Kenneth A., Richard A. AB magna cum laude, Harvard U., 1957, LLB magna cum laude, 1960. Bar: NY 1960, DC 1982. Assoc. Proskauer Rose Goetz & Mendelsohn, NYC, 1960-69, Finley, Kumble, Wagner, Heine, Underberg, Manley, Myerson & Casey, NYC, 1970, ptnr., 1971-87, Sonnenschein Nath & Rosenthal LLP, NYC, 1987—. Adj. prof. Benjamin Cardozo Sch. Law, Yeshiva U., 2001—; lectr. Boalt Hall, U. Calif., 2006-; mem. faculty various legal seminars and insts.; mem. joint editl. bd. on unincorporated orgn. accts. ABA/Nat. Conf. Commrs. on Uniform State Laws, 1994—, chair, 2003-05; chmn. bd. Transcontinental Music Publs., New Jewish Music Press; lectr. in field. Author: Reckless Legislation: How Lawmakers Ignore the Constitution, 2000; founding editor: State Limited Partnership Laws, 7 vols. and supplements, 1987—; editor Harvard Law Rev., 1958-60; contbr. articles to profl. jours. V.p., bd. dirs. Leo Baeck Inst.; bd. dirs. Ctr. Jewish History, Selfhelp Cmty. Svcs. Fellow Am. Bar Found.; mem. ABA (com. on ltd. partnerships 1980—, chmn. com. on tech. and intellectual property 1992-95, chair, ad hoc com. on security interests in intellectual property 1990-98), First Amendment Lawyers Assn., NY State Bar Assn. (exec. com. comml. and fed. litig. sect. 1989-93), Assn. Bar City NY (com. on fed. legis. 1979-82, com. on civil rights 1982-86, chmn. 1983-86), NY County Lawyers Assn. (securities com. 1980-82). Jewish. Home: 172 E 93d St New York NY 10128-3711 Office: Sonnenschein Nath & Rosenthal LLP 1221 Ave of Americas New York NY 10020-1001 Home Phone: 212-831-8009; Office Phone: 212-768-6756.

BAMBERGER, PHYLIS SKLOOT, lawyer, educator, retired judge; b. NYC, May 2, 1939; d. George Joseph and Martha (Wechselblatt) S.; m. Michael A. Bamberger, Dec. 19, 1965; children: Kenneth, Richard. BA, Bklyn. Coll., 1960; LLB, NYU, 1963. Bar: N.Y. 1963, U.S. Supreme Ct. 1967, U.S. Ct. Appeals (2d cir.) 1965, U.S. Dist. Ct. (so. dist.) N.Y. 1966, U.S. Dist. Ct. (ea. dist.) N.Y. 1979. Assoc. Legal Aid Soc., NYC, 1963-67; assoc.-in-charge criminal appeals Bur. Legal Aid Soc., NYC, 1967-72; atty.-in-charge, fed. def. svcs. unit/appeal Legal Aid Soc., NYC, 1972-88; judge N.Y. State Ct. Claims designated to sit in the N.Y. State Supreme Ct., Bronx County, 1988—2005. Instr. N.Y. State Judicial Inst. and other venues, 1990—; mem. N.Y. State Chief Judge's Jury Project, 1993—94; mem. com. on alternatives to incarceration Office of Ct. Adminstrn., 1994—96, mem. criminal law and procedure adv. com., 1994—98, co-chair, 1998—; mem. N.Y. State Chief Judge's Commn. on the Jury, 2003—06, mem. com. the Future of Indigent Def. Svcs., 2004—06, mem. probation task force, 2006—. Author: Criminal Appeals Handbook, 1984; editor, contbr. Practice Under the Federal Sentencing Guidelines, 1988, 90, 93, 2000 (also supplements); author, compiler Recent Developments in State Constitutional Law, 1985; contbr. numerous articles to publs. Mem. ABA, NY State Bar assn. (co-chair presdl. com. on problems in criminal justice sys. 1986-88, mem. com. on the future of the profession), Assn. of Bar of City NY (mem. coun. on criminal justice 2004—, chair com. on provision of legal svcs. to persons of moderate means 1995-98, 21st century com. 1992-95, chair com. on probation 1993-94, chair task force on town and village cts. 2006-), Phi Beta Kappa.

BAMBURG, JAMES ROBERT, biochemistry professor; b. Chgo., Aug. 20, 1943; s. Leslie H. and Rose A. (Abrahams) B.; m. Alma Y. Vigo, June 7, 1970 (div. Dec. 1984); children: Eric Gregory, Leslie Ann; m. Laurie S. Minamide, June 22, 1985. BS in Chemistry, U. Ill., 1965; PhD, U. Wis., 1969. Project assoc. U. Wis., Madison, 1968-69; postdoctoral fellow Stanford U., Palo Alto, Calif., 1969-71; from asst. to full prof. Colo. State U., Ft. Collins, 1971—, acad. coordinator cell and molecular biol. program, 1975-78, interim chmn. dept. biochemistry, 1982-85, 88-89, assoc. chmn., 1996—99, assoc. dir. neuronal growth and devel., 1986-90, dir. neuronal growth and devel., 1990—96, dir. molecular cell integrative neuroscience, 2002—, assoc. dir. integrated bio med. edn. sci. tech. grad. program, 2005—. Vis. prof. MRC Molecular Biol. Lab., Cambridge, Eng., 1978-79, MRC Cell Biophysics Unit, London, 1985-86, Children's Med. Rsch. Inst., U. Sydney, Australia, 1992-93, U. Calif. San Diego, 1999-2000, Scripps Rsch. Inst., La Jolla, Calif., 2006-07; mem., chmn. NIH Biomed. Scis. Study Sect., Bethesda, Md., 1980-85; ad hoc mem. Physiol. Chem. Study Sec., 1997, Molecular Devel. Cell Neurosci., 1998-99, 2001, Cell Biol. Function, 2001-03; mem. adv. bd. Macromolecular Resources, 1999-2005, Boulder Lab. 3D Fine Structure, 1994-2005, Alaska Basic Neurosci. Program, 2000—; mem. ZNS1 spl. emphasis panel, 2007. Contbr. articles to sci. jours.; mem. editl. bd. Cell Motil Cytoskel. Fellow NSF, 1964-65, Nat. Multiple Sclerosis Soc., 1969-71, J.S. Guggenheim Found., 1978-79, Fogarty Ctr., 1985-86, 92-93, W. Evans Vis. scholar U. Otago, N.Z., 1991; recipient Disting. Svc. award Colo. State U. 1989, 2005, Outstanding Adviser award, 1996, Scholar Impact award, Colo. State U. 2006. Mem. Am. Chem. Soc., Am. Soc. Cell Biology, Am. Soc. Biochem. Mol. Biol., Internat. Neurochem. Soc., Soc. for Neurosci., Sigma Xi (pres. CSU chpt. 1989). Home: 2125 Sandstone Dr Fort Collins CO 80524-1825 Office: Colo State U Dept Biochemistry Mrb Rm 235 Fort Collins CO 80523-1870 Business E-Mail: jbamburg@lamar.colostate.edu.

BAMFORD, JOSEPH CHARLES, JR., gynecologist, obstetrician, educator, medical missionary, author; b. Paterson, NJ, Oct. 23, 1930; s. Joseph Charles and Luise (Whitehead) Bamford; m. Susan Jane Hall, Apr. 13, 1951; children: Joseph Charles III, Elizabeth Ann. BS, Rutgers U., 1952; MD, NY Med. Coll., 1956. Diplomate Am. Bd. Ob-Gyn. Intern U. Vt., 1956—57; resident in ob-gyn NY Med. Coll., NYC, 1957—60, asst. clin. instr. dept. ob-gyn, 1960—64, clin. instr., 1964—65, asst. prof., 1965—70, assoc. prof., 1970—72, asst. dean, 1966—68, assoc. dean, 1968—72, acting v.p. hosp. affairs, 1971—72; sect. chief psychosomatic ob-gyn Met. Hosp. Ctr., NYC, 1963—72, chief svc., 1971—72; practice medicine specializing in ob-gyn Paterson, NJ, 1962—66; practice medicen specializing in ob-gyn St. Johnsbury, Vt., 1972—76; asst. obstetrician and gynecologist Flower and Fifth Ave. hosps., NYC, 1960—66, asst. attending, 1966—70, attending, 1970—72; asst. vis. obstetrician and gynecologist Met. Hosp. Ctr., NYC, 1960—66, assoc., 1968—70, vis., 1970—72; vis. ob-gyn Indian Health Svc. Hosp., Ft. Defiance, Ariz., 1981; clin. asst. ob-gyn Paterson Gen. Hosp., 1962—64, assoc. attending, 1964—66, attending, 1966—67; cons., 1967; attending obstetrician and gynecologist Northeastern Vt. Regional Hosp., St. Johnsburg, 1972—76, cons., 1976—85. Vis. obstetrician and gynecologist St. Jude Missions Hosp., St. Lucia, 1986; med. officer Tumutumu Mission Hosp., Kenya, 1987—88; cons. Beatrice D. Weeks Meml. Hosp., Lancaster, NH, 1972—80; vol. program steering com. for retired physicians Vt. Med. Soc., 1996—2001; chmn. subcom. for fact finding Mayor's Com. for Hosp. Facilities Planning, Paterson, 1964—66. Contbr. articles to profl. jours. Chmn. med. adv. com. Passaic County (NJ) Com. for Planned Parenthood, 1965—67; mem. NJ Com. on Med. Edn., 1965—66; trustee Greater Paterson Gen. Hosp., 1966—2000, So. Vt. Art Ctr., 1997—2002; pres. Lyndon State Coll. Found., 1980—84, Kagando Mission Hosp. Found., 2003—. Lt. comdr. USNR, 1960—62. Fellow: ACOG (mem. com. on course coord. 1977—79); mem.: Caledonia County Med. Soc. (v.p. 1974—75), Vt. Med. Soc. (mem. jud. com. 1975—77), Ob-Gyn. Soc. NY Med. Coll. (mem. exec. com. 1963—66), No. New England Acad. Medicine. Home: Box 724 Myrickview Vlg Dorset VT 05251

BAMGBOLA, OLUWATOYIN FATAI, pediatric renal physician, researcher; MD, U. Ilorin, Nigeria, 1986. Diplomate Am. Bd. Pediat., 2001. Registrar West African Postgraduate Med. Coll., ABU Hosp., Zaria, Nigeria; sr. registrar Nat. Postgraduate Med. Coll., ABU Hosp., Zaria, 1993—96; asst. prof. pediat. U. Okla. Health Sci. Ctr., Oklahoma, 2003—. Contbr. articles to profl. jours. Exec. mem. Full Gospel Bus. Men's Fellowship Internat., NYC, 1997—2003. Fellow, West African Postgraduate Med. Coll., 1989, Nat. Postgraduate Med. Coll., Lagos, Nigeria, 1989, Albert Einstein Coll. Medicine, Bronx, Am. Soc. Transplantation, 2001—03; grantee, Nat. Kidney Found., 2001; scholar, Amgen, 2002. Mem.: Am. Soc. Transplantation, Internat. Pediatric Nephrology Assn. (licentiate), Am. Soc. Pediatric Nephrology (licentiate), Am. Soc. Nephrology (licentiate), Renal Physician Assn. (assoc.). Office: U Okla Health Sci Ctr 940 13th St Oklahoma City OK 73104 Office Phone: 405-271-4409. Office Fax: 405-271-4876. E-mail: oluwatoyin-bamgbola@ouhsc.edu.

BAN, KI-MOON (BAN KI-MOON), Secretary General of the United Nations, former South Korean government official; b. Chunchongbuk-do Umsong, Republic of Korea, June 13, 1944; 3 children. BS in Diplomacy, Seoul Nat. U., 1970; MPA, Harvard U., 1985. With Ministry Fgn. Affairs Govt. of South Korea, Seoul, 1970-72, vice consul, 2d sec., Korean Embassy to India New Delhi, 1972-75, 1st sec., permanent observer, Korean Mission to the UN NYC, 1978-80, dir. UN Divsn., 1980-83, protocol sec. to the prime min. Seoul, 1985-87, consul gen., Korean Embassy to the U.S. Washington, 1987-90, dir. gen. N. Am. Affairs Bur. Seoul, 1990-92, spl. asst. to fgn. min., 1992, min., Korean Embassy to the U.S. Washington, 1992-95, dep. min. for policy planning affairs Seoul, 1995-96, dep. min. for polit. affairs, 1995-96, chief of protocol to the pres., 1996, sr. adv. for fgn. policy and nat. security to the pres., 1996-98, amb. to Austria Vienna, 1998-2000, vice min. fgn. affairs & trade Seoul, 2000—01, amb. to UN NYC, 2001—02, amb. at large min. fgn. affairs and trade Seoul, 2002, adv. to pres. for fgn. policy, 2003—04, min. fgn. affairs & trade, 2004—06; sec.-gen. UN, NYC, 2007—. Office: UN Office Sec Gen Rm S-3800 UN Plz 46th St at First Ave New York NY 10017*

BAN, STEPHEN DENNIS, gas industry executive; b. Hammond, Ind., Dec. 16, 1940; s. Stephen and Mary Veronica (Holecsko) Ban; m. Margie Cahill, Aug. 17, 1963; children: Stephen, Mary Beth, Brian. BSME, Rose Hulman Inst. Tech., 1962; MS in Engring. Sci., Case Inst. Tech., 1964, PhD in Engring., 1967. Chief divsn. fluid and chem. processes Battelle Columbus (Ohio) Labs., 1970-72, chief divsn. emission sys., 1972-76, corp. coord. engring. scis. program, 1972-76; v.p. R & D Bituminous Materials, Inc., Terre Haute, Ind., 1976-81, Gas Rsch. Inst., Chgo., 1981—2000, sr. v.p. R & D ops., 1983-86, exec. v.p., COO, 1986-87, pres.,

CEO, 1987—2000; dir. Office Tech. Transfer Argonne Nat. Lab., 2002—. Mem. indsl. adv. bd. U. Ill., Chgo., 1983—93; mem. Coun. Energy Engring. Rsch., Washington, 1983—87; mem. energy rsch. adv. bd. U.S. Dept. Energy, Washington, 1987—90, mem. adv. com. renewable energy and energy efficiency joint ventures, 1992—95; mem. Natural Gas Coun., 1993—97; bd. dirs. Energen Corp., Birmingham, Ala., UGI Corp., Phila., Amerigas Corp., Phila. Fellow, NDEA, 1962—65, NSF, 1965—67. Mem.: U.S. Energy Assn., Sigma Xi, Tau Beta Pi. Office: 9700 S Cass Ave Argonne IL 60439-4832 Office Phone: 630-252-8111. Business E-Mail: sban@anl.gov.

BANA, ERIC, actor; b. Melbourne, Australia, Aug. 9, 1968; m. Rebecca Gleeson, 1997; children: Klaus, Sophia. Actor: (films) The Castle, 1997, Chopper, 2000, Black Hawk Down, 2001, The Nugget, 2002, Hulk, 2003, Troy, 2004, Munich, 2005, Lucky You, 2007, (voice only) Finding Nemo, 2003; actor, prodr., writer: TV films Eric, 1996—97; actor: (TV series) Full Frontal, 1993—96; actor, writer: TV series The Eric Bana Show Live, 1997; actor: (TV guest appearances) All Saints, 1999, 2000.*

BANAS, C(HRISTINE) LESLIE, lawyer; b. Swindon, Wiltshire, Eng., Oct. 29, 1951; arrived in U.S., 1957; d. Stanley M. and Helena Ann (Boryn) Banas; m. Dale J. Buras, May 1, 1976; children: Eric Buras, Andrea Buras. BA magna cum laude, U. Detroit, 1973; JD cum laude, Wayne State U., Detroit, 1975. Bar: Mich. 1976, US Supreme Ct. 1980. Atty. Hyman & Rice, Southfield, Mich., 1976-77, Hyman, Gurwin, Nachman, Friedman & Winkelman, Southfield, 1977-82, ptnr., 1982-87, Honigman Miller Schwartz and Cohn LLP, Bloomfield Hills, Mich., 1987—. Contbr. articles to profl. jours. Bd. trustees Detroit Pub. TV, 2007—. Mem.: ABA, Urban Land Inst., Fed. Bar Assn., State Bar Mich. (bd. dirs. real property law sect. coun., coun. chair elect), The Parade Co. (bd. trustees), Detroit Athletic Club, Inforum Ctr. Leadership (past pres.). Roman Catholic. Avocations: gardening, photography, skiing. Office: Honigman Miller Schwartz and Cohn LLP Ste 100 38500 Woodward Ave Bloomfield Hills MI 48304-5048 Office Phone: 248-566-8406. Business E-Mail: lbanas@honigman.com.

BANAS, EMIL MIKE, physicist, researcher; b. East Chicago, Ind., Dec. 5, 1921; s. John J. and Rose M. (Valcicak) B; m. Margaret Fagyas Welton, Oct. 9, 1948; children: Mary K., Barbara A. French. BA, Benedictine U., 1943; postgrad. (U.S. Rubber fellow), U. Notre Dame, 1954, PhD, 1955. Author (autobiography): For the Life of Me, 2005. Recipient medal of St. Benedict, Benedictine U., 1999. Mem. Pres. Assocs. of Benedictine U., VFW (life), Sigma Pi Sigma. Home: 425 NW Orion Dr Pullman WA 99163-3526

BANAS, JOHN STANLEY, obstetrician, gynecologist; b. Chgo., May 27, 1955; s. Edward Thomas and Stephanie Victoria (Gatz) B.; m. Kerry Jeanine Keenan, June 7, 1981; children: Melissa, Kevin, Daniel, Amanda. BS in Biology cum laude, Loyola U., Chgo., 1977; MD, Loyola U., Maywood, Ill., 1981. Diplomate Am. Bd. Ob-Gyn. Resident in ob/gyn. SUNY, Buffalo, 1981-85; pvt. practice Ft. Wayne, Ind., 1985-88, Racine, Wis., 1988-90, Rock Island, Ill., 1990—. Fellow ACOG; mem. AMA, Ill. Med. Soc., Rock Island Med. Soc. Roman Catholic. Avocations: swimming, running, bicycling, gardening, reading. Home: 2130 Nathan Ct Bettendorf IA 52722-2100 Office: Trinity Med Ctr 2570 24th St Ste 122 Rock Island IL 61201-5394 Office Phone: 309-779-3868.

BANCEL, MARILYN, fund raising management consultant; b. Glen Ridge, NJ, June 15, 1947; d. Paul and Joan Marie (Spangler) B.; m. Rik Myslewski, Nov. 20, 1983; children: Carey, Roxanne. BA in English with distinction, Ind. U., 1969. Cert. fund raising exec. Ptnr. The Sultan's Shirt Tail, Gemlik, Turkey, 1969-72; prodn. mgr. High Country Co., San Francisco, 1973-74; exec. dir. East Bay Performance, Inc., 1976—79; pub. Bay Arts Rev., Berkeley, Calif., 1976-79; dir. devel. Oakland (Calif.) Symphony Orch., 1979-81; assoc. dir. devel. Exploratorium, San Francisco, 1981-86, dir. devel., 1986-91; prin. Fund Devel. Counsel, San Francisco, 1991-93; v.p. The Oram Group, Inc., San Francisco, 1993—. Co-chmn. capital campaign com. Synergy Sch., San Francisco, 1995-2000; adj. prof. U. San Francisco, 1993-2002. Author: Preparing Your Capital Campaign, 2000. Mentor Assn. Fundraising Profl. Mentor Program, 1994-. Fellow U. Strasbourg, France, 1968. Mem. Assn. Fundraising Profls. (bd. Golden Gate chpt. 1996-98, chmn. National Philanthropy Day, 2000, Outstanding Fundraising Exec. award 2002), Giving Inst., Devel. Execs. Roundtable, Phi Beta Kappa. Democrat. Avocation: gardening. Office: 328 Duncan St San Francisco CA 94131-2022 Office Phone: 415-821-2534. Business E-Mail: mbancel@oramgroup.com.

BANCROFT, ANN E., polar explorer; b. Mendota Heights, Minn., 1955; d. Dick and Debbie Bancroft BS in Phys. Edn., U. Oreg. Former phys. & spl. edn. tchr., coach, St. Paul. Mem. Steger Internat. Polar Expedition, 1986; leader Am. Women's Antarctic Expedition, 1993; mem. The Bancroft Arnesen Expdn., 2000; founder (with Liv Anderson) yourexpedition internat. motivation co. Subject (corp. video) Vision of Teams, 1998, (documentary) Poles Apart, 1999; featured in Remarkable Women of the 20th Century, 1998, Time, People, USA Today, Ms., McCall's, Ladies Home Jour., Vogue, Good Housekeeping, Glamour, National Geographic, Outside, Sports Illustrated, Sports Illustrated for Kids and Sports Illustrated for Women, O, Time for Kids. Founder Ann Bancroft Found; spokesperson Learning Disabilities Assn., Wilderness Inquiry (also co-chair capital campaign, instr.), Girl Scouts U.S.A; bd. dirs. Youth Frontiers; judge Nuclear-Free awards, Nat. Women's Hall of Fame inductions; mem. adv. bd., Melpomene Inst. and Medica. Named Ms. Mag. Woman of Yr., 1987 Glamour Mag. Woman of Yr., 2001; inductee Girls and Women in Sport Hall of Fame, 1992, Nat. Women's Hall of Fame, 1995; recipient Women First award YWCA, 1993 Mem.: Melpomene Inst. and Medica (adv. bd.). Dogsleds 1,000 miles (1,600 km) from the Northwest Territories in Canada to the North Pole as the only female member of the Steger International Polar Expedition, earning the distinction of being the first known woman in history to cross the ice to the North Pole in 1986; leads the first American women's east to west crossing of Greenland in 1992; leads the American Women's Expedition to the South Pole, a 67-day expedition of 660 miles (1,060 km) on skis by four women, earning the distinction of being the first known woman in history to cross the ice to both the North and South Poles in 1993; (with Liv Arnesen) become the first women in history to sail and ski across Antarctica landmass-completing a 94 day, 1,717-mile (2,747 trek) in February, 2001; (with Liv Arnesen) travelled across the North American Great Lakes on May 17 through June 28, 2002; (with Liv Arnesen) (ski, sail & swim) set out to attempt historic first for women: an approximate 1,240 mile (1,996 kilometers) crossing of the mostly frozen Artic Ocean in February 2005 to March 2005, ended because expeditions travelling from Russia toward the North Pole were evacuated due to mounting conflict over economic pwoer of Russian polar travel; (with Liv Arnesen) attempted to ski 530 miles (850 kilometers) across the frozen Arctic Ocean from Canada's Ward Hunt Island to the Geographic North Pole in March 2007, but this expedition ended because Liv Arnesen developed frostbite in three toes. All journeys are followed by millions of children via www.BancroftArnesenExplore.com. Office: Your Expedtion 1920 Oliver Pl S Minneapolis MN 55405-2420 Address: Ann Bancroft Found 808 14th Ave SE Minneapolis MN 55414 Office Phone: 612-676-9410. Fax: 612-333-1325. E-mail: susan@yourexpedition.com.*

BANCROFT, GEORGE MICHAEL, chemical physicist, educator; b. Saskatoon, Sask., Can., Apr. 3, 1942; s. Fred and Florence Jean B.; m. Joan Marion MacFarlane, Sept. 16, 1967; children: David Kenneth, Catherine Jean. B.Sc., U. Man., 1963; M.Sc., 1964; PhD, Cambridge U., Eng., 1967, MA, 1970, Sc.D. (E.W. Staecie fellow), 1979. Univ. demonstrator Cambridge U.; then teaching fellow Christ Coll.; mem. faculty U. Western Ont., London, now prof. emeritus dept. chemistry. Author: Mössbauer Spectroscopy, 1973; also articles in photoelectron spectroscopy, synchrotron radiation studies; revs. Mössbauer Spectroscopy. Recipient Harrison Meml. prize, 1972, Meldola medal, 1972, Rutherford Meml. medal, 1980, Alcan award, 1990, Herzberg award, 1991, Can. Inst. of Chemistry Palladium medal, 1996, Morley medal Am. Chem. Soc., 1998; Guggenheim fellow, 1982-83; named Officer of the Order of Can., 2003. Fellow Royal Soc. Can.; mem. Royal Soc. Chemistry, Can. Chem. Soc., Can. Geol. Soc., Can. Physics Soc. Mem. United Ch. Can. Clubs: Curling, Tennis (London). Office: U Western Ont Chem Dept London ON Canada N6A 5B7 Office Phone: 519-661-4117. E-mail: gmbancro@uwo.ca.

BANCROFT, MARGARET ARMSTRONG, lawyer; b. Mpls., May 9, 1938; d. Wallace David and Mary Elizabeth (Garland) Armstrong; m. Alexander Clerihew Bancroft, Mar. 14, 1964; 1 child, Elizabeth Armstrong. BA magna cum laude, Radcliffe Coll.-Harvard U., 1960; JD cum laude, NYU, 1969. Bar: NY 1971. Reporter Mpls. Star and Tribune, 1960—61, UPI, NY, 1961-66, NJ, 1961—66; ptnr. Law Firm of Dechert LLP, 1998—2004, of counsel, 2004—. Adj. prof. law NYU Sch. Law; vis. prof. Debrecen U. Faculty Law, Hungary, 2006; vis. prof. law Tartu U. Faculty Law, Estonia, 2007. Bd. dirs., exec. com. Vis. Nurse Svc. NY; chair Vis. Nurse Svc. NY Home Care, Inc.; trustee SEC Hist. Soc. Mem. ABA (bus. law sect.), N.Y. State Bar Assn. (securities regulation com.), Assn Bar City N.Y. (com. on investment mgmt. regulation), Am. Law Inst. Office: Law Firm of Dechert LLP 30 Rockefeller Plz 29th Fl New York NY 10112-2200 Office Phone: 212-698-3590. Business E-Mail: margaret.bancroft@dechert.com.

BANDA, SIVA S., research scientist; BS, Regional Engring. Coll., Warangal, India, 1974; MS in Aerospace Engring., Indian Inst.Sci., 1976; MS in Sys. Engring., Wright State U., 1978; PhD in Aerospace Engring., U. Dayton, 1980. Aerospace rsch. engr. Flight Controls Div., Flight Dynamics Lab. Wright-Patterson AFB, Ohio, 1981—86, group leader Flight Dynamics Directorate, Wright Lab., 1986—87, task team leader, 1987—95, branch chief and program mgr., 1995—96, tech. leader Air Vehicles Directorate, Air Force Rsch. Lab., 1996—2000, sr. scientist for control theory, 2000—. Recipient General Benjamin D. Foulois Award, 1987, Royal Aeronautical Society Silver Medal, 2001; fellow Air Force Rsch. Lab., 1990. Fellow: AIAA, IEEE; mem.: NAE. Office: Air Force Rsch Lab Bldg 15, Rm 225 1864 4th St Wright Patterson Afb OH 45433-7131

BANDAR, PRINCE BIN SULTAN BIN ABD AL-AZIZ AL SAUD, former ambassador; b. Taif, Saudi Arabia, Mar. 2, 1949; s. Prince Sultan ibn Abdulaziz al-Saud; m. Princess Haifa bint Faisal ibn Abdulazia al-Saud; children— Lulua, Rema, Khalid, Faisal. B.A., Brit. Royal Air Force Acad., Cranwell, Eng., 1969; Grad., Advanced Fighter and Instr. Pilot Program, USAF, 1979; M.A., Johns Hopkins U., 1980. Fighter pilot Royal Saudi Air Force, Dhahran Air Base, Khamis Mushayt Air Base, Taif Air Base, 1969-82, comdr. 7th Royal Saudi Air Force Squadron, 1976-79, comdr. Peace Hawk Project, Dhahran, 1976-79; in charge spl. AWACS Saudi Arabian Liaison Mission to U.S., 1981; mem. Saudi Arabia Mil. Mission to U.S., def. and mil. attache, 1982-83; mem. Saudi Del. to UN Gen. Assembly, 1983; Saudi Arabian ambassador to U.S., 1983-2005. Served to col. Royal Saudi Air Force. Decorated Flying Hawk medal; King Abdulaziz Sash, for work in attaining Lebanese ceasefire, King Fahd, 1983. Muslim.

BANDEEN, ROBERT ANGUS, management consultant; b. Rodney, Ont., Can., Oct. 29, 1930; s. John Robert and Jessie Marie (Thomson) Bandeen; m. Mona Helen Blair, May 31, 1958; children: Ian Blair, Mark Everett, Robert Derek, Adam Drummond. BA, U. Western Ont., 1952; PhD, Duke U., 1959; LLD (hon.), U. Western Ont., 1975, Dalhousie U., 1978, Queens U., 1982; DCL (hon.), Bishop's U., 1978. Asst. economist Can. Nat. Rys., Montreal, Que., 1955-56, research statistician, 1956-58, staff officer planning, 1958-60, chief costs and stats., 1960, chief devel. planning, 1960-66, dir. corp. planning, 1966-68, v.p. corp. planning and fin., 1968-71, v.p. Great Lakes region, 1971-72, exec. v.p. fin. and adminstrn., 1972-74, pres., CEO, 1974-82; chmn., pres., CEO Crown Life Ins. Co., 1982-84, chmn. CEO, 1984-85; chmn., pres., CEO Cluny Corp., Toronto, Ont., 1986—. Former chancellor Bishop's U.; bd. dirs. Nat. Challenge Sys., Inc. Gov. participation Can. Olympic Trust; senator Shakespearean Festival Found.; mem. Isle Maligne Soc. Duke U. Decorated knight Order St. John, officer Order of Can.; recipient Salzberg medal, Syracuse U., 1982. Mem.: York, Cambridge Club (Toronto), Mount Royal Club (Montreal), Delta Upsilon. Home and Office: Cluny Corp 305-1166 Bay St Toronto ON Canada M5S 2X8 Office Phone: 416-926-0997. Personal E-mail: rbandeen@rogers.com.

BANDER, EDWARD JULIUS, lawyer, librarian emeritus; b. Boston, Aug. 10, 1923; s. Abraham and Ida (Lendman) B. BA, Boston U., 1949, LLB, 1951; MLS, Simmons Coll., 1955. Bar: Mass. 1951. Asst. reference libr. Harvard U., Cambridge, Mass., 1954-55; libr. US Ct. Appeals (1st cir.), Boston, 1955-60; asst. libr., asst. prof. NYU, NYC, 1960-70, assoc. prof., curator, assoc. libr., 1970-78; prof., libr. Suffolk U. Law Sch., Boston, 1978-90, libr., prof. emeritus, 1991—. Author: Mr. Dooley and the Choice of Law, 1963, Mr. Dooley and Mr. Dunne, 1981, Justice Holmes Ex Cathedra, 1966, 91, Searching the Law, 1986, 2d edit., 2005, Shakespeare on Lawyers and the Law, 1998, Bardell V. Pickwick: The Most Famous Fictional Trial in the English Language, 2004, Legal Anecdotes, Wit and Rejoinder, 2007. Served with USN, 1942-46. Recipient Dean Frederick A. McDermott award, Suffolk U. Student Bar Ass, 1980. Mem. Assn. Am. Law Schs., New Eng. Law Librs. (Lifetime Achievement award 2007). Democrat. Jewish. Office: 50 Church St Concord MA 01742-3050 Business E-Mail: ebander@suffolk.edu.

BANDER, MYRON, physics professor, dean; b. Belzyce, Poland, Dec. 11, 1937; came to U.S., 1949, naturalized, 1955; s. Elias and Regina (Zielonka) B.; m. Carol Heimberg, Aug. 20, 1967. BA, Columbia U., 1958, MA, 1959, PhD, 1962. Postdoctoral fellow CERN, 1962-63; research assoc. Stanford Linear Accelerator Center, 1963-66; mem. faculty U. Calif., Irvine, 1966—, prof. physics, 1974—, dean phys. scis., 1980-86; chair dept. physics, 1992-95. Sloan Found. fellow, 1967-69 Fellow Am. Phys. Soc. Office: U Calif Irvine CA 92697-0001 Home Phone: 949-759-0232; Office Phone: 949-824-5945. Business E-Mail: mbander@uci.edu.

BANDERAS, ANTONIO, actor; b. Malaga, Spain, Aug. 10, 1960; m. Ana Leza, July 27, 1987 (div. 1996); m. Melanie Griffith, May 14, 1996; 1 child. Launched signature women's fragrance Diavolo Donna, 1999; launched signature men's fragrance Spirit, 2004. Films include: Labyrinth of Passion, 1982, Pestanas postizas, 1982, Y del sefuro.Ilbranos señor!, 1983,El Senor Galindez, 1983, El Caso Almeria, 1983, The Stilts, 1984, La corte de Faraon, 1985, Requiem por un campesino espanol, 1985, The Puzzle, 1986, 27 Hours, 1986, Matador, 1986, Delirios de amor, 1986, The Way They Were, 1987, Law of Desire, 1987, The Pleasure of Killing, 1988, El Acto, 1987, Baton Rouge, 1988, Women on the Verge of a Nervous Breakdown, 1988, Going South Shopping, 1988, Si que dicen que cai, 1989, The White Dove, 1989, Tie Me Up! Tie Me Down!, 1990, Against the Wind, 1990, New Land, 1991, Woman in the Rain, 1991, Madonna: Truth or Dare, 1991, Borges Tales, Part I, 1991, The Mambo Kings, 1992, Shoot!, 1993, Outrage, 1993, Philadelphia, 1993, The House of the Spirits, 1993, Il Giovane Mussolini, 1993, Of Love and Shadows, 1994, Interview With the Vampire, 1994, Never Talk to Strangers, 1995, Miami Rhapsody, 1995, Four Rooms, 1995, Desperado, 1995, Assassins, 1995, Two Much, 1996, Evita, 1996, The Mask of Zorro, 1997, Crazy in Alabama, 1998, The 13th Warrior, 1999, The White River Kid, 1999, Play It to the Bone, 1999, Dancing in the Dark, 2000, The Body, 2000, Spy Kids, 2001, Original Sin, 2001, Femme Fatale, 2002, Spy Kids: Island of Lost Dreams, 2002, Frida, 2002, Ballistics: Ecks vs. Sever, 2002, Spy Kids 3-D: Game Over, 2003, Imagining Argentina, 2003, And Starring Pancho Villa as Himself, 2003 (TV), Once Upon a Time in Mexico, 2003, Shrek 2 (voice), 2004, The Legend of Zorro, 2005, Take the Lead, 2006; dir. Crazy in Alabama, 1999, Malaga Burning, 2000; prodr. White River Kid, 1999, Forever Lulu, 2000. TV movies: La Otra historia de Rosendo Juarez, 1990 Office: c/o Emanuel Nunez Creative Artists Agy 9830 Wilshire Blvd Beverly Hills CA 90212-1804 also: Agents Assocs/Guy Bonnet 201 Rue du fauborg Saint Honore Paris 75008 France

BANDES, SUSAN JANE, museum director, educator; b. NYC, Oct. 18, 1951; d. Ralph and Bessie (Gordon) Bandes. BA, NYU, 1971; MA, Bryn Mawr Coll., 1973, PhD, 1978; postgrad., Mus. Mgmt. Inst., Berkeley, Calif., 1990. Asst. prof. Sweet Briar Coll., Va., 1978-83; project dir. Am. Assn. Mus., Washington, 1983-84; program officer J. Paul Getty Trust Grant Program, LA, 1984-86; prof., dir. Kresge Art Mus. Mich. State U., East Lansing, 1986—. Author, editor: Caring for Collections, 1984, Affordable Dreams: The Goetsch-Winckler House and Frank Lloyd Wright, 1991; author: Abraham Rattner, The Tampa Museum of Art Collection, 1997, Pursuits and Pleasures: Baroque Paintings from the Detroit Institute of Arts, 2003; editor: The Prints of John S. de Martelly, 1903-1979; author, curator: Pursuits and Pleasures: Baroque Painting from the Detroit Institute of Arts, 2003. Recipient award Am. Philos. Soc., 1981, Publ. award AIA, 1990; Samuel H. Kress fellow, 1972-73, 75-76, Whiting fellow, 1976-77; Fulbright-Hayes grant, 1974-75. Mem. Nat. Inst. for Conservation (treas. 1986-90), Mich. Alliance for Conservation (treas. 1994-95, sec. 1996-97, treas. 1997-98, pres. 1998-2000), Mich. Mus. Assn. (bd. dirs. 1987-92), Mich. Coun. for Humanities (coun. 1988-92), Midwest Art History Soc. (bd. dirs. 1997-2000). Avocation: collecting oriental rugs. Office: Mich State U Kresge Art Mus East Lansing MI 48824 Home Phone: 517-347-3437; Office Phone: 517-353-9834. Business E-Mail: bandes@msu.edu.

BANDIER, MARTIN N., music publisher; b. NYC, July 21, 1941; m. Dorothy Bandier; 3 children. BA in Political Sci., Syracuse U., 1962; JD, Brooklyn Law Sch. Gen. counsel to sr. v.p. LeFrak Org.; atty. Battle, Fowler, Jaffin and Kheel; founding ptnr. Entertainment Music Co., 1975, Entertainment Television Co., 1975; founder SBK Entertainment World Inc. (acquired by EMI), 1986—89; vice chmn. EMI Music Pub., 1989—91, CEO, 1991—2006, chmn., 1992—2007, co-CEO, 2006—07; chmn. & CEO Sony/ATV Music Pub. LLC, 2007—. Bd. dirs. EMI Group plc, 1998—2007. Trustee Syracuse U., T.J. Martell Found.; bd. dirs. United Jewish Appeal, City of Hope, BMI Found. Inc. Named to Songwriters Hall of Fame as Patron of the Arts, 2003; recipient Arents award, Syracuse U., 1994. Mem.: Internat. Music Publishers Assn. (pres.), Nat. Acad. Recording Arts and Sciences, Rock and Rock Hall of Fame (dir.), Songwriters' Hall of Fame (dir.), Nat. Music Publishers' Assn. (dir.). Office: Sony/ATV Music Publishing LLC 5th Fl 550 Madison Ave New York NY 10022 Office Phone: 212-492-1200, 212-833-8000. Fax: 212-492-1863; Office Fax: 212-833-5552.*

BANDLER, DONALD KEITH, international consultant, former ambassador; BA in Polit. Sci., Kenyon Coll., 1969; MA, St. John's Coll., 1974; JD, George Washington U., 1979; LLD (hon.), Kenyon Coll., 2006. Various fgn. svc. assignments, 1976—2002; dir. Israel and Arab-Israeli Affairs US Dept. State, 1994-95; dep. chief of mission, charge d'affaires Am. Embassy, Paris, 1995-97; spl. asst. to pres. and sr. dir. European Affairs NSC, Washington, 1997-99; US amb. to Cyprus US Dept. State, Nicosia, 1999—2002; sr. v.p. Monsanto Co., Washington, 2002—03; sr. dir. Kissinger McLarty Assocs., Washington, 2004—. Participant Sr. Seminar for fgn. affairs profls., 1993-94. Decorated French Legion of Honor, 1998; recipient Superior Honor awards State Dept. Home: 5624 Greentree Rd Bethesda MD 20817 Office: Kissinger McLarty Assocs 900 17th St NW Washington DC 20006

BANDLER, JAMES, reporter; Reporter Wall St. Journal. Author: How to Use Financial Statements: A Guide to Understanding the Numbers, 1994, A Quick Killing, 2000. Co-recipient Polk award for bus. reporting, 2006. Mailing: Wall St Journal 200 Liberty St New York NY 10281 Business E-Mail: james.bandler@wsj.com.*

BANDLER, JOHN WILLIAM, electrical engineering educator, consultant; b. Jerusalem, Nov. 9, 1941; m. Beth; children: Lydia, Zoe. BSc, Imperial Coll. Sci. and Tech., London, 1963, PhD, 1967; DSc, U. London, 1976. With Mullard Rsch. Labs., England, 1966-67; postdoctoral fellow, sessional lectr. U. Man., Canada, 1967-69; asst. prof. McMaster U., Hamilton, Ont., Canada, 1969-71, assoc. prof., 1971-74, prof. elec. engring., 1974-2000, prof. emeritus, 2000—, chmn. dept., 1978-79, dean faculty, 1979-81, coord. group on simulation, optimization and control, 1973-83, dir. rsch. in simulation optimization systems rsch. lab., 1983—. Pres. Optimization Systems Assocs., Inc., 1983-97, Bandler Corp., Inc., 1997—. Contbr. articles to profl. jours. Recipient Automated Measurements Career award Automatic Radio Frequency Techniques Group, 1994, Microwave Application award IEEE Microwave Theory and Techniques Soc., 2004. Fellow IEEE, Inst. Elec. Engrs. U.K., Royal Soc. Can., Engring. Inst. of Can., Can. Acad. of Engring.; mem. Electromagnetics Acad., Assn. Profl. Engrs. Province of Ont. Office: McMaster U Dept Elec & Comp Engring Hamilton ON Canada L8S 4L7 *Proceeding in a direction not sanctioned by my peers has always proved tough, but the results achieved have almost always been worth the effort.*

BANDLER, MARTIN, physician; b. Vienna, Oct. 2, 1930; came to U.S., 1954; s. Sidney and Sara (Feinsinger) B.; m. Frances Feffer; children: Bruce, Gail, Ruth. MD, Dalhousie U., 1954. Diplomate Am. Bd. Internal Medicine. Intern Victoria Genl. Hosp., Halifax, N.S., Canada, 1953-54; resident in medicine Jewish Hosp., Bklyn., 1954-56, fellow in gastroenterology, 1956-57; physician-in-charge divsn. gastroenterology U.S. Naval Hosp., Phila., 1957-59; pvt. practice Bklyn., 1959—; clin. instr. SUNY, 1959-70, clin. asst. prof. medicine, 1970—. With USN, 1957-59. Fellow ACP, Am. Coll. Gastroenterology; mem. AMA, Kings County Med. Soc., N.Y. Med. Soc., Am. Soc. Gastrointestinal Endoscopy, Bklyn. Gastroenterol. Soc. (v.p. 1972-73, pres. 1973-74), N.Y. Soc. for Gastrointestinal Endoscopy. Office: 954 President St Brooklyn NY 11215-1604 Home Phone: 718-859-7377; Office Phone: 718-783-6364. E-mail: fmbandler@aol.com.

BANDON, WILLIAM EDWARD, III, lawyer; b. Bklyn., June 12, 1961; s. William Edward Jr. and Lila Marie (Arida) B.; m. Patricia Linden McKeogh, Sept. 18, 1993; children: John Robert, Isabel Chaobing. AB in History, Princeton U., 1983; JD, NYU, 1987. Bar: NY 1988, US Dist. Ct. (so. and ea. dists.) NY 1988, Conn. 2003. Summer assoc. Cullen and Dykman, Bklyn., 1986, assoc., 1987-96, Brown Raysman Millstein Felder & Steiner LLP, NYC, 1996-99, ptnr., 1999—2003, Wiggin and Dana, Stamford, Conn., 2003—04; sr. counsel, Info. Tech. and Sourcing GE Money, Stamford, 2004—. Trustee Lotte Kaliski Found. for Gifted Children, Inc., NYC, 1996—; active Katonah Hist. Mus., NY, 1996—. Mem. NY County Lawyers Assn. (chmn. com. tech. and automation 1997-2002, bd. dirs. 2003-06), Info. Tech. Law Assn., Somers Hist. Soc. Democrat. Avocation: local history. Home: 101 Lyon Ridge Rd Katonah NY 10536-3731

BANDOW, DOUGLAS LEIGHTON, editor, columnist, consultant; s. Donald E. and Donna J. B. AA, Okaloosa-Walton Jr. Coll., Niceville, Fla., 1974; BS in Econ., Fla. State U., 1976; JD, Stanford U., 1979. Bar: Calif. 1979 D.C. 1984. Sr. policy analyst Reagan for Pres. Com., Los Angeles, 1979-80, Arlington, Va., 1980, Office of Pres. Elect, Washington, 1980-81; spl. asst. to the Pres. for policy devel. White House, Washington, 1981-82; editor Inquiry Mag., Washington, 1982-84; sr. fellow Cato Inst., Washington, 1984—2005; nat. syndicated columnist Copley News Svc., San Diego, 1983—2005; v.p. Citizen Outreach, 2005—; Cobden fellow Inst. for Policy Innovation, 2005—; Bastiat scholar Competitive Enterprise Inst., 2005—. Author: Unquestioned Allegiance, 1986, Beyond Good Intentions: A Biblical View of Politics, 1988, Human Resources and Defense Manpower, 1989, The Politics of Plunder: Misgovernment in Washington, 1990, The Politics of Envy: Statism as Theology, 1994, Tripwire: Korea and U.S. Foreign Policy in a Changed World, 1996, Foreign Follies: America's New Global Empire, 2006; co-author: The Korean Conundrum: America's Troubled Relations with North and South Korea, 2004, Foreign Follies: America's New Global Empire, 2006; editor: U.S. Aid to the Developing World, 1985, Protecting the Environment, 1986; co-editor: The U.S.-South Korean Alliance, 1992, Perpetuating Poverty, 1994; contbr. articles to periodicals. Recipient Nat. Young Am. award Boy Scouts Am., 1977, Freedom Leadership award Freedoms Found., Valley Forge, Pa., 1977, cert. for polit. and journalistic activities Freedoms Found., Valley Forge, Pa., 1979; named Man of Yr. N.Y. State Coll. Reps., 1982. Mem. Calif. Bar Assn., ABA, D.C. Bar Assn., Washington Ind. Writers. Avocations: reading, antiques, travel. Business E-Mail: chessset@aol.com.

BANDROWCZAK, STEVEN J., communications executive; BS in Computer Sci., Long Island U.: C. W. Post Campus, 1989. Systems programmer Unisys Corp., Grumman Corp.; systems programmer, dir. systems and programs, and v.p. bus. tech. devel. Avnet, Inc., 1988—99, v.p. CIO info. services divsn. (ISD), 1999; COO, CTO Seal Consulting Group, 2000; exec. v.p., CIO Americas Info. Services Data Ctr. (AMIS) DHL Worldwide, 2002, exec. v.p., Worldwide CIO; sr. v.p., CIO Lenovo Group Ltd., 2005—07; CIO Nortel Networks Corp., 2007—. Named one of Premier 100 IT Leader, Computerworld mag., 2004. Office: Nortel Network Corp 195 The West Mall Toronto ON M9C 5K1 Canada*

BANDSTRA, EMMALEE S., physician, pediatrician, researcher, educator; b. New Orleans, Oct. 3, 1949; d. James Melvin and Lee (Speir) Shanks; m. Ted E. Bandstra, Feb. 11, 1984; 1 child, Bethany A. BA, U. Ala., Tuscaloosa, 1970; MD, U.Ala., Birmingham, 1974. Diplomate Nat. Bd. of Med. Examiners, 1975, Am. Bd. of Pediat., 1979, Am. Bd. of Pediat. Sub-board of Neonatal-Perinatal Medicine, 1979. Pediat. resident U. Ala., Birmingham, 1974—76, neonatology fellow, 1976—78; asst. prof. pediat. Sch. Medicine, U. Fla., Gainesville, 1978—81, Sch. Medicine, U. Miami, 1982—84, assoc. prof. pediat., 1984—95, prof. pediat. ob-gyn., 1995—, dir. perinatal chem. addiction rsch. and edn. program, 1988—; attending neonatologist Shands Tchg. Hosp., Gainesville, Fla., 1978—81, Jackson Meml. Hosp., Miami, 1982—. Guest editor: Seminars in Perinatology Journal; contbr. articles to profl. jours., chapters to books. Cons., interagency working group on child maltreatment and juvenile delinquency US Dept. Justice, Washington, 1998; mem. State of Fla. Health and Rehab. Svcs. Task Force on Maternal Child Health, Tallahassee, 1982, Miami-Dade County Cocaine Babies Task Force, Miami, Fla., 1989—91, Miami Coalition for a Safe and Drug-free Cmty., Miami, 1989—, State of Fla. Gov.'s Drug Task Force Subcom. on Substance-exposed Infants and Families, Tallahassee, 1989, Healthy Start Coalition for Miami-Dade County, Miami, Fla., 1996—, bd. dirs., 1994—2000, pres., 1996; mem., consensus panel of drug exposed infants Alcohol and Drug Abuse and Mental Health Adminstrn., Bethesda, Md., 1992; mem., tech. expert group on drug exposed infants and young children Substance Abuse and Mental Health Services Adminstrn., Bethesda, 1992—94. Named to Best Drs. in Am., 2005—06; recipient Disting. Alumnus award, pediat. residency program Children's Hosp., U. Ala. Birmingham, 1990, Genevieve Abraham award med. excellence, Project: New Born, U. Miami, 1994; Rsch. grantee, Nat. Inst. Drug Abuse, 1990—, Substance Abuse and Mental Health Svcs. Adminstrn., 1991—96, Svc. grantee, healthy start high risk children's program State of Fla., 1996—99, Health Found. South Fla., State of Fla. Ounce of Prevention Fund, 1998—2001. Mem.: Fla. Soc. Neonatal Perinatologists (pres. 1981—82), So. Soc. Pediat. Rsch. (pres. 1993—94, Founders' award 2007), Soc. Pediat. Rsch., Am. Pediat. Soc. Presbyterian. Avocations: singing, travel, reading, writing, swimming. Office: U Miami Sch Medicine PO Box 016960 R-131 Miami FL 33101 Home Phone: 305-596-0392; Office Phone: 305-243-4078.

BANDURA, ALBERT, psychologist, educator; b. Mundare, Alta., Can., Dec. 4, 1925; arrived in U.S., 1949, naturalized, 1956; m. Virginia Varns; 2 children. BA, U. B.C., 1949, D.Sc. (hon.), 1979; MA in Psychology, U. Iowa, 1951, PhD in Psychology, 1952. Prof. psychology Stanford U., 1953—, David Starr Jordan prof. social sci. in psychology, 1973—. Author: (with R.H. Walters) Adolescent Aggression, 1959, (with R.H. Walters) Social Learning and Personality Development, 1963, Principles of Behavior Modification, 1969, Aggression, 1973, Social Learning Theory, 1977, Social Foundations of Thought and Action: A Social Cognitive Theory, 1986; editor: Psychological Modeling: Conflicting Theories, 1971, Self-Efficacy in Changing Societies, 1995, Self-Efficacy: The Exercise of Control, 1997. Recipient Disting. Lifetime Contbn. award, Soc. for Advancement of Behavior Therapy, 2001, Disting. Achievement Alumni award, U. Iowa, 2005, Lifetime Achievement award, Am. Acad. Health Behavior, 2006;, Guggenheim Found. fellow, 1972. Fellow: Ctr. Advanced Study in Behavioral Sci., Am. Acad. Arts and Scis.; mem.: APA (pres. 1974, Disting. Scientist award divsn. 12 1972, Disting. Sci. Contbn. award 1980, Outstanding Lifetime Contbn. award 2004), Am. Psychol. Found. (Gold medal award 2006), Can. Psychol. Assn. (hon. pres. 1999), Internat. Soc. Rsch. on Aggression (Disting. Contbn. award 1980), Western Psychol. Assn. (pres. 1980, Lifetime Achievement award 2003), Calif. Psychol. Assn. (Disting. Scientist award 1973, Lifetime Disting. Contbr. award 1998, Healthtrac award for disting. contbns. to health promotion 2002, McGovern medal for disting. contbn. to health promotion sci. 2004, Lifetime Achievement award for health promotion rsch. 2006), Inst. Medicine NAS, Am. Psychol. Soc. (William James award 1989, James Cattell award 2003). Office: Stanford U Dept Psychology Stanford CA 94305-2130 Office Phone: 650-724-2409. Business E-Mail: Bandura@psych.Stanford.edu.

BANDURSKI, BRUCE LORD, retired ecologist, environmental scientist; b. Waterbury, Conn., June 28, 1940; s. Stanley Alexander Bandurski and Virginia Ann (VanRensselaer) Bandurski Hinckley; m. Nancy Ann Spaulding, March 17, 2007. BS with honors, Mich. State U., East Lansing, 1962; grad., George Washington U., Washington, DC, 1965, USDA Grad. Sch., 1966. Park ranger Yellowstone Nat. Pk., Nat. Pk. Svc., Wyo., 1962-63; sci. reference analyst USPHS, Washington, 1963-65; intelligence ops. specialist US Army, Washington, 1965-66; analyst planner US Dept. Interior, Washington, 1966-74, coord., br. chief, Nat. Environ. Policy Act officer, 1974-83; on detail as ecologist, ecomgmt. advisor Internat. Joint Commn. US and Can., Washington, 1983-85, sr. ecomgmt. advisor, ecologist, 1985-2000. Dep. game warden Commonwealth Va., 1968-70; mem. faculty USDA Grad. Sch., 1968-96, subcom. Fed. Interagy. Com. on Edn., 1967-74, Internat. Joint Commn. Task Force on Indicators Implementation, 1997-2000; watch dir., dep. and acting mission dir. US Man-in-Sea program, St. John, V.I., 1970; chmn. Conservation Roundtable of Washington, 1970-71; chmn. com. on definitions, spl. com. on environ. protection US nat. com. World Energy Conf., Washington, 1981-85; mem. exec. com. Great Lakes Sci. Adv. Bd., 1986-92; liaison Coun. Great Lakes Rsch. Mgrs.; mem. steering com. Great Lakes-St. Lawrence Ecosys. Model Framework; mem. Steering Group on Marine Environ. Monitoring, Commn. on Engring. and Tech. Studies, NRC, 1986-87; mem. Lake Superior Biodiversity Project Adv. Com. Nat. Wildlife Fedn.; initiator multi year project Ecol. Com. Great Lakes Sci. Adv. Bd., 1990-94; mem. Internat. Joint Commn. Task Force on Indicators for Evaluation, 1994-96; mem. Lake Erie Task Force, 1994-97; co-organizer of first binational conf. on exotic species and the shipping industry; dir. Binat. Workshop on Indicators of Ecosystem Integrity/Diversity, 1998; mgr. Wildcat Mountain Natural Area The Nature Conservancy; guest lectr. in field. Writer planning and recreation impact mgmt. series, 1967-73; author U.S. Bur. Land Mgmt. Environ. Mgmt. Procedures, 1976-84 (Achievement award 1978, 79, 84), Ecology and Economics: Partners for Productivity, 1973; co-author: The Ecosys. Approach: Theory and Ecosys. Integrity, 1993, More Recreation: Implications for the Tropical Ecosystem, 1969, Toward a Transboundary Monitoring Network, 1986, Perspectives on Ecosystems Management for the Great Lakes: A Reader, 1988. Lectr. US Dept Interior Earth Day, 1970. Mem. AAAS, Ecol. Soc. Am. (charter Met. Washington chpt.), Internat. Assn. for Ecology, Am. Soc. Naturalists, The Wildlife Soc., Am. Soc. Mammalogists, Fed. Profl. Assn., Washington Soc. Engrs., Outdoor Ethics Guild, Nature Conservancy, Maine Coast Heritage Trust, Island Inst., Earthwatch, Assn. Ecosystem Rsch. Ctrs., Internat. Soc. for Ecosystem Health (charter), Am. Mus. Women in the Arts (charter), Nat. Campaign Tolerance (founder), Friesian Horse Assn. N.Am., Friesian Horse Soc., Friends of Ky. Ednl. TV, Alpha Zeta, Beta Beta Beta. Achievements include originator of the no action alternative in the US federal government's National Environmental Policy Act process; originator of the concept of tiered/scaled environmental impact statements; catalyzed the first strategic planning endeavor of the International Joint Commission in the US and Canada; development of the first college level course on the National Environmental Policy Act process in 1971-96; standards for recruiting and hiring the first systems ecologist for the federal government. Home: 355 Grover Criswell Rd Cynthiana KY 41031

BANDY, JACK D., lawyer; b. Galesburg, Ill., June 19, 1932; s. Homer O. and Gladys L. (Van Winkle) B.; m. Betty McMillan, Feb. 18, 1956; children: Jean A. Bandy Abramson, D. Michael, Jeffery K. BA, Knox Coll., 1954; LLB, U. La Verne, 1967. Bar: Calif. 1972, U.S. Supreme Ct. 2000. Safety engr. Indsl. Indemnity Co., LA, 1960-65, sr. safety engr., 1965-69, resident safety engr., 1969-72; trial atty. Employers Ins. of Wausau, LA, 1972-79; mng. atty. Wausau Ins. Cos., LA, 1979-92; arbitrator, mediator L.A. Superior Mcpl. Ct., 1992—. Contbr. articles to profl. jours. Youth leader YMCA, Mission Hills, Calif., 1965-72. Served with U.S. Army, 1954-56. Mem. Calif. State Bar, Am. Soc. Safety Engrs. (cert. safety profl.). Personal E-mail: ikwimd@yahoo.com.

BANDYOPADHYAY, AMITABHA, engineering educator; b. Calcutta, West Bengal, India, Dec. 25, 1954; arrived in U.S., 1980; s. Ashoke Kumar and Kalpana Bandyopadhyay; m. Aditi Chattopadhyay, June 19, 1988; 1 child, Anika Banerjee. BE, U. Calcutta, 1976; MS, Pa. State U., 1987, PhD, 1991. Registered profl. engr., N.J., N.Y. Structural engr. M.N. Dastur & Co., Calcutta, 1976—80; lead engr. United Engrs. and Constructors, Phila., 1980—84; instr. Pa. State U., University Park, 1984—90; disting. svc. prof. SUNY, Farmingdale, 1990—. Dept. chair SUNY, Farmingdale, NY; cons. archtl. and constrn. mgmt., 1984—. Contbr. articles to profl. jours. Named Engring. Educator Yr., NSPE, 2001. Mem.: Am. Soc. Engring. Edn. (chmn. Mid Atlantic sect. 2003), ASCE, Chi Epsilon. Office: SUNY Farmingdale Lupton Hall RT 110 Farmingdale NY 11735 Office Phone: 631-420-2378. Business E-Mail: bandyoa@farmingdale.edu.

BANDYOPADHYAY, RAM SHYAMAL, molecular biologist, researcher; b. West Bengal, India, Feb. 6, 1952; arrived in U.S., 1983; s. Ram Sekhar and Geeta Bandyopadhyay; m. Sabita Bandyopadhyay, Feb. 26, 1982. PhD, U. Calcutta, West Bengal, 1982. Fellow U. Fla., Gainesville, 1983—87; rsch. assoc. Tufts U., Boston, 1987—92, Boston U., 1992—2001; pvt. practice, 2001—03; fellow Shriver Ctr. U. Mass. Med., 2003; rsch. asst. Mass. Gen. Hosp., Boston, 2003—04; rsch. assoc. Boston U., 2005—06. Author: Cell Biochemistry and Biophysics, 1999. Avocations: painting, music, sports.

BANE, ALMA LYNN, data research administrator; b. Galveston, Tex., Oct. 3, 1947; d. Clinton LaVon and Betty Jane Lynn; m. Charles William Bane, Feb. 3, 1973; children: Greta Kay Hecker, Deborah Elizabeth Farnsworth, Cynthia Ann Coats. AAS, Alvin C.C., Tex., 1971; BS, Tex. A&M U., Commerce, 1975, MS, 1976. Cert. data processing Inst. for Certification Computer Profls., 1982; vocat. office edn. tchr. Tex. Edn. Agy., 1973. Spl. clk. Tex. Instruments, Dallas, 1966—70; VOE instr. Aldine Ind. Sch. Dist. - McArthur H.S., Tex., 1971—74; computer sci. grad. asst. Tex. A&M U., Commerce, 1975—76; computer sci. tech. instr. Tex. State Tech. Coll., Waco, 1978—80; bus. application programmer analyst So. Farm Bur. Ins. Co., Waco, 1980—89, data security supr., 1989—98, corp. bus. resumption coord., 1999—2000; computer info. systems instr. Tarleton State U. - COBA, Stephenville, Tex., 2000—; data rsch. adminstr. Tarleton State U. - OPEIR, Stephenville, Tex., 2004—. Vice chmn. Tex. Cardinals, Inc., San Antonio, 2003—, Tex. Pot of Gold Found., Dallas, 2004—; worthy grand matron Grand Chpt. Tex., Arlington, 1998—99. Mem.: Assn. Info. Tech. Profls. (student assn. com. 2003—05, pres. Heart of Tex. chpt. 1983—84, Individual Performance Bronze and Silver awards 1982, 1985), Order Ea. Star (worthy matron Waco 7 1982—83, worthy matron Stephenville chpt. #801 2004—06, vision quest coord. for Tex. Gen. Grand chpt. 2006—). Avocations: travel, reading, photography. Office: Tarleton State Univ Box T-0505 Stephenville TX 76402 Home Phone: 254-918-2054; Office Phone: 254-968-9416. Business E-Mail: abane@tarleton.edu.

BANE, MARY JO, dean, political science professor; b. Princeville, Ill., Feb. 24, 1942; d. Fred W. and Helen (Callery) B.; m. Kenneth Winston, May 31, 1975. BS in Internat. Rels., Georgetown U., 1963; MAT, Harvard U., 1966, DEd, 1972. Tchr. English U.S. Peace Corps, Liberia, 1963-65; tchr. social studies Arlington Pub. Schs., Mass., 1966-67; tchr. English and social studies Brookline Pub. Schs., Mass., 1968-71; rsch. assoc. Ctr. Ednl. Policy Rsch. and Huron Inst. Harvard U., Cambridge, Mass., 1971-72, project co-dir. Ctr. Study of Pub. Policy, 1972-75, assoc. prof. edn., lectr. in sociology, 1977-80, assoc. prof. pub. policy, 1981-86, dir. Malcolm Wiener Ctr. for Social Policy, 1987-92, prof. pub. policy, 1986-90; Malcolm Wiener Prof. of Social Policy Kennedy Sch. of Govt., Harvard U., Cambridge, Mass., 1990-92, prof. pub. policy, 1997—98, Thornton Bradshaw prof. pub. policy and mgmt., 1998—, chair mgmt. and leadership, academic dean, 2006—; lectr. in Sociology U. Mass., Boston, 1972-75; assoc. dir. Ctr. Rsch. on Women, asst. prof. edn., lectr. in sociology Wellesley Coll., 1975-77; dep. asst. sec. for program planning and budget analyst Office Planning and Budget U.S. Dept. Edn., Washington, 1980-81; exec. dep. commr. N.Y. State Dept. Social Svcs., 1984-86, commr., 1992-93; asst. sec. Adminstrn. for Children and Families Dept. Health and Human Svcs., Washington, 1993-96. Ida Bean vis. prof. U. Iowa, 1980; chair bd. overseers panel study income dynamics Inst. Rsch. U. Mich., 1982-86; regents lectr. U. Calif., Berkeley, 1987; mem. adv. com. urban poverty NAS, 1986-90, chair com. child devel. rsch. and pub. policy, 1987-90; mem. pres. adv. coun. Columbia U. Tchrs. Coll., N.Y.C., 1988-92; mem. grants adv. coun. Smith Richardson Found., 1989-92; bd. dirs. Manpower Demonstration Rsch. Coun., 1989-92, 97—; active William T. Grant Found. Commn. on Work, Family and Citizenship, 1987-88. Author: (with others) Inequality: A Reassessment of the Effects of Family and Schooling in America, 1972, Here to Stay: American Families in the Twentieth Century, 1974, Japanese translation, 1981, (with George Masnick) The Nation's Families 1960-90, 1980, Welfare Realities: From Rhetoric to Reform, 1994, Lifting Up the Poor: A Dialogue on Religion, Poverty and Wledare Reform, 2003; editor: (with Donald Levine) The Inequality Controversy, 1975, (with Manuel Carballo) The State and the Poor in the 1980s, 1984, (with Kenneth I. Winston) Gender and Public Policy: Cases and Comments, 1993, Who Will Provide? The Changing Role of Religion in American Social Welfare, 2000, Taking Faith Seriously, 2005; contbr. articles to profl. jours. Fellow Nat. Acad. Pub. Adminstrn.; mem. Am. Sociol. Assn., Population Assn. Am., Assn. Pub. Policy Analysis and Mgmt. Avocations: hiking, reading, gardening. Office: Harvard Univ Kennedy Sch Govt 79 John F Kennedy St Cambridge MA 02138-5801 Office Phone: 617-496-9703. Office Fax: 617-496-9053. E-mail: mary_jo_bane@harvard.edu.

BANERJEE, BHASKAR, gastroenterologist, medical educator; s. Santi Priya and Shyamali Banerjee; m. Mousumi Ganguly, Feb. 18, 1992; children: Shoujit, Romit. MBBS, U. London, 1983. Diplomate in internal medicine and gastroenterology Am. Bd. Internal Medicine. House surgeon Ashford Hosp., England, 1983; house physician St. Peters Hosp., England, 1983—84; internal medicine intern U. Conn., 1984—85, resident in internal medicine, 1985—87, fellow in gastroenterology, 1987—89; asst. prof. medicine U. Ark., Little Rock, 1989—94; dir. Biliary-Pancreatic Ctr. Winthrop-U. Hosp., Mineola, NY, 1994—95; assoc. prof. medicine U. Mo., Columbia, 1995—99, Washington U. Sch. Medicine, St. Louis, 1999—2006; prof. medicine Wash. U. Sch. Medicine, St. Louis, 2007—. Presenter in field. Contbr. chapters to books, articles to profl. jours. Fellow: ACP (life), Am. Gastroent. Assn. (life); mem.: Am. Soc. Gastrointestinal Endoscopy (life). Achievements include patents for method of detecting early cancer using a beam of light; development of fiber-optic instrument to detect cancer using a beam of light; research in optical cancer detection using light; high contrast imaging methods in gastroenterology; gastroenterology and endoscopy; high magnification endoscopy and spectral imaging. Office: Washington Univ Sch Medicine Divsn Gastroenterology Dept Medicine 660 S Euclid Ave Campus Box 8124 Saint Louis MO 63110 Business E-Mail: bbanerje@im.wustl.edu.

BANERJEE, GAURAB, research scientist; b. India; BS, Indian Inst. Tech., Kharagpur, 1997; PhD, U. Wash., Seattle, 2006. Analog engr. Intel Corp., Hillsboro, Oreg., 1999—2001; rsch. scientist Circuits Rsch. Lab., Intel, Hillsboro, 2001—06. Scholar Nat. Talent Search Scholar India, Nat. Coun. Ednl. Rsch. and Tng., India, 1990. Mem.: I.E.E.E (Sr. Mem. 2005). Achievements include research in device-circuit co-design for RF/microwave integrated circuits; patents in field of semiconductor devices and circuits. Home Phone: 503-617-0902.

BANERJEE, NEELA, reporter; Energy reporter, religion reporter New York Times. Office: New York Times 229 W 43d St New York NY 10036 Office Phone: 212-556-7377. Office Fax: 212-556-7614.

BANERJEE, PRASHANT, industrial engineer, computer scientist, educator; b. Calcutta, West Bengal, India, Apr. 15, 1962; came to U.S., 1986; s. Prabhat K. and Bani Banerjee; m. Madhumita Banerjee, Dec. 11, 1987; children: Jay, Ann. BSME, Indian Inst. Tech., Kanpur, India, 1984; MS in Indsl. Engring., Purdue U., 1987, PhD, 1990. Indsl. engr. Tata Steel Co., Jamshedpur, India, 1984-85; asst. prof. U. Ill., Chgo., 1990-96, assoc. prof., 1996—. Cons. Caterpillar Inc., Peoria, Ill., 1992, Motorola Inc., 1994—97, Monsanto, Inc., 1996—; tech. adv. bd. mem. Motorola Labs, 2002; chief tech. officer Indsl. Virtual Reality, Inc., 2000—. Author: Automation and Control of Manufacturing Systems, 1991, Object-oriented Technology in Manufacturing, 1992, Virtual Manufacturing, 2001; contbr. articles to profl. jours. Grantee NSF rsch., 1992, 1995, 2000, Nat. Inst. Standards and Tech. rsch., 1995. Fellow: ASME; mem.: Inst. Indsl. Engrs. Avocations: sports, current events, religious discussions. Home: 708 Kirstin Ct Westmont IL 60559 Office: Univ Ill Engring Dept Chicago IL 60607-7022

BANERJEE, PRITH, computer company executive, computer engineering professor; b. India, July 17, 1960; married; 1 child. B Tech, Indian Inst. Tech., 1981; MSEE, Univ. Ill., 1982, PhD, 1984. Asst. prof. elec. & computer engring. Univ. Ill., 1985—89, asst. prof., 1989—93, prof., 1993—96; rsch. assoc. prof. Coordinated Sci. Lab. Univ. Ill., 1989—93, rsch. prof., 1993—96; dir. computational sci. & engring. Univ. Ill., 1994—96; dir. Ctr. for Parallel & Distributed Computing Northwestern Univ., 1996—, dept. chmn. & Walter Murphy prof. elec. & computer engring., 1998—2001, 2002—04; founder, pres., CEO AccelChip Inc., 2000—02, chief scientist, 2002—04; founder, chmn., chief scientist BINACHIP Inc., 2003—; disting. prof., dean Coll. Engring. Univ. Ill., Chgo., 2004—07; exec. v.p. rsch., dir. HP Labs Hewlett Packard Corp., Palo Alto, Calif., 2007—. Contbr. articles to profl. jours., chapters to books; author: Parallel Algorithms for VLSI Computed-Aided Design, 1994. Recipient Pres. of India Gold Medal, Indian Inst. Tech., 1981, Young Faculty Develop. award, IBM, 1986, Presdl. Young Investigators award, NSF, 1987, sr. rsch. award, Xerox, 1992, Frederick Emmons Terman award, Elec. Engring. div. ASEE, 1996. Fellow: IEEE (Taylor L. Booth Edn. award 2001), ACM, AAAS. Achievements include patents in field. Office: HP Labs 1501 Page Mill Rd Palo Alto CA 94304*

BANERJEE, SUBIR KUMAR, science educator; PhD, Cambridge U., 1963, ScD, 1983. Established Inst. Rock Magnetism U. Minn., 1990, disting. prof., dir., Inst. Rock Magnetism, 1990—. Lead spkr. IAGA-IASPEI Conf., Hanoi, Vietnam, 2001; co-convenor Climatic And Human Changes in Latin America (CAHCILA), Buenos Aires, 1999—2000; disting. vis. spkr. series Hawaii Inst. of Geophysics and Planetary Physics, 2000. Contbr. articles to profl. jours. Recipient Louis Néel medal, European Geosciences Union, 2003, 2004. Fellow: Am. Acad. Arts and Scis., Am. Geophys. Union (John A. Fleming medal 2006). Office: U Minn Dept Geology and Geophysics 207 Pillsbury Hall Minneapolis MN 55455-0219 Office Phone: 612-624-5722. Office Fax: 612-625-3819. Business E-Mail: banerjee@umn.edu.

BANERJEE, UTPAL, biology professor, research scientist; b. New Delhi; BS in Chemistry, St. Stephens Coll., New Delhi; M in Phys. Chemistry, Indian Inst. Tech.; PhD in Chemistry, Calif. Inst. Tech., post doctorate in Biology. Asst. prof. univ. Calif., LA, 1988—94, prof., 1994—, chair Molecular Cell & Devel. Biology Dept. Prof. Howard Hughes Med. Inst. Office: 1506D Gonda Neuroscience and Genetics Rsch Ctr 695 Charles Young Dr Los Angeles CA 90095-1761 Office Phone: 310-206-5439, 310-825-2980.

BANERJEE, (BIMAL), artist, educator; b. Calcutta, India, Sept. 4, 1939; naturalized, 1978; s. Dashurathee and Madhabilata B DFA with honors, Indian Coll. Art, Calcutta, 1960; student, Coll. Art, New Delhi, 1965—67, Atelier 17, Paris, 1967—69, Ecole des Beaux-Arts, 1967—70, Pratt Inst., NYC, 1969—72, NYU, 1976; MA, Columbia U, 1980; EdM, Columbia U., 1981, EdD, 1988. Lectr. NAD, NYC, 1969, Bloomfield Coll., NJ, 1980—81, Parsons Sch. Design/New Sch., NYC, 1979, faculty, 1983—88; art therapist St. John's Episc. Hosp., Queens, 1981—83; tchr., art cons. N.Y.C. Pub. Schs., 1984—2001; tchr. art Cath. H.S., NYC, 1987; lectr. Columbia U. Tchrs. Coll., NYC, 1988—2001. Guest lectr. Tchrs. Coll., Columbia U., 1984 Multi-media performance artist shows include Parsons Sch. Design/New Sch., 1986, Columbia U., 1978, 79, 84, Hofstra U., 1979, Just Above Midtown Gallery, N.Y.C., 1977, 78, Bertha Urdang Gallery, N.Y.C., 1976, 91, Fremar Gallery, L.I., N.Y., 1974, Galerie du Haut Pave, Paris, 1968-69, Mcpl. Galeria, Levanto, Italy, 1968, Kumar Gallery, New Delhi, 1970, Arts & Prints Gallery, Calcutta, 1963, 64, Art Heritage Gallery, New Delhi, 1990, Chitrakoot Gallery, Calcutta, 1990, Chemould Gallery, Calcutta, 1993, Cite Internationale des Arts, Paris, 1994, 99; internat. biennials in Paris, Tokyo, Rejika, Miami, Hawaii, Bradford, Eng.,

Biella, Ibiza, Triennale-India, Berlin Triennale, Joan Miro Drawing prize, Barcelona, Ljubljana, others; exhibited in one-man shows, U.S., Europe and India; introduced new media Fumage and Carbontransfer; represented in permanent collections Mus. Modern Art, Paris, Mus. Modern Art, Barcelona, Spain, Mus. Fine Arts, Boston, Mus. Art, Iowa City, Mus. Modern Art de la Ville de Paris, Mus. Internat. Electrography Art, Cuenca, Spain, Ctr. National d'Art Contemporain, Paris, Ministry Cultural Affairs, France, Neil Saek Gallery, Johannesburg, South Africa, Nat. Gallery Modern Art, New Delhi, Nat. Acad. Art, New Delhi, Essex Libr., London, Pallas Gallery, London, Bibliothèque Nat.de France, Paris, Honolulu Acad. Art, Rockefeller Bros. Found., N.Y.C., N.Y. Pub. Libr. Art Collection, Bklyn. Mus., Radford U. Mus., Va.; contbr. articles, poetry, short stories, children's lit. to profl. jours Founding mem. Bill Clinton Presdl. Found., Little Rock, Wall of Tolerance, Nat. Campaign for Tolerance, Montgomery, Ala., Martin Luther King, Jr. Nat. Meml. Found., Washington. Recipient awards Hawaii Biennial, 1971, 73, 79, Arthur Kaplan award, 1978, award Painters and Sculptors Soc., 1972, Culturelle Internat. award, Paris, 1968, award Nat. Art Acad., India, 1967, 70, State Acad. award Bengal State, and Punjab State, 1967, Statue of Victory world cultural prize Nat. Ctr. Study and Rsch., Salsomiggiore, Italy, 1984; grantee Govt. of India, 1965-67, Govt. of France, 1967-70, Adolph and Esther Gottlieb Found., 1989; India Govt. nat. scholar, French Govt. scholar Mem. Mus. Modern Art, Found. for Cmty. Artists of N.Y.C., Coll. Art Assn. Am., Print Club Phila., World Print Coun.ermithsonian Instn., Ancient Art—Paris, Wall of Tolerance (founder, Nat. campaign for tolerance, Montgomery, Ala.). Home: Loft 2C 106 Ridge St New York NY 10002-2554 Office: Bertha Urdang Gallery 23 E 74th St New York NY 10021-2617

BANERJI, RANAN BIHARI, mathematics professor; b. Calcutta, India, May 5, 1928; came to U.S., 1961, naturalized, 1969; s. Bijan Bihari and Setabja (Chatterji) B.; m. Purnima Purkayastha, July 8, 1954; children: Anindita Banerji Spielberg, Sunandita Banerji Ogawa. BS, Patna U., 1947; MS, Calcutta U., 1949, DPhil, 1956. Rsch. scholar Calcutta U., 1950-53, lectr., 1956; vis. asst. prof. Pa. State U., 1953-55; maintenance engr. Indian Statis. Inst., 1956-58; faculty Case Western Res. U., 1958-74, prof. computer sci., 1968-74, Temple U., Phila., 1974-82; prof. math. and computer sci. St. Joseph's U., Phila., 1983-92, prof. emeritus, 1993—. Vis. prof. U. Paris, U. Vienna, U. Calcutta, Czech Tech. U.; asst. prof. engring. U. N.B., Can., 1959-61; cons. in field. Author: Theory of Problem Solving, 1969, Artificial Intelligence, 1980; (with M. Mesarovic) Non-numerical Problem Solving, 1969; (with A. Elithorn) Artificial and Human Intelligence, 1986, Formal Techniques in Artificial Intelligence, 1989, Society, Scientists and the Spirit, 2006; assoc. editor Elsevier Sci. Pubs., Amsterdam; reviewer computing, mathematics reviews; contbr. articles to profl. jours. Gold medalist univs. Patna and Calcutta. Fellow Am. Assn. Artificial Intelligence; mem. ACLU, Common Cause, Sci. within Consciousnes, Computer Profls. for Social Responsibility. Hindu Quaker. Home: 7 Macarthur Blvd Apt N409 Collingswood NJ 08108-3648 Office: St Joseph's U Dept Math and Computer Sci 5600 City Ave Philadelphia PA 19131-1308 Office Phone: 856-869-0021. Personal E-mail: r.banerji@verizon.net. Business E-Mail: rbanerji@sju.edu. *It is my belief that the only successful actions by men and women are those done in selfless service to God. The rest, however laudable, are risky at best.*

BANEY, RICHARD NEIL, retired physician, internist; b. Phila., Apr. 13, 1937; s. Robert Emmet and Mary Elizabeth (Hedges) B.; m. Carolyn Vern Kurey, Feb. 17, 1962; children: Richard N. Jr., Michael D., Marisa V., Brian E. BS, Georgetown U., 1958; MD, U. Pitts., 1963. Diplomate Am. Bd. Internal Medicine, Am. Bd. Rheumatology. Intern VA & Parkland Hosp., Dallas, 1963—64; resident U. Pitts., 1967—70; internist Jess Parrish Hosp., Titusville, Fla., 1971—76, chief med. staff, 1974—76; internist Melbourne (Fla.) Internal Med. Assocs., Holmes Regional Med Ctr., 1976—95; sr. v.p. med. affairs Holmes Regional Med. Ctr., Melbourne, Fla., 1995—96; CEO Health First Physicians, 1995—98; med. officer M.S. Nat. Geog. Endeavor, 1999—2007; ret., 2007. Trustee Holmes Regional Med. Ctr., Melbourne, 1984-95; founding dir., chmn. bd. dirs. Reliance Bank Fla., Melbourne, 1985-95; founding dir., chmn. bd. Bank Brevard, 1996-2004, dir., 2004—. Trustee Fla. Inst. Tech., Melbourne, 1985—, mem. exec. com., 1987—, vice chmn. bd. trustees, 1991—2002; pres. Canaveral chpt. Am. Heart Assn., Rockledge, Fla., 1973—74; chmn. bd. trustees Sea Pines Rehab. Hosp., Melbourne, 1992—94. Lt. comdr. USN, 1964—67. Fellow ACP; mem. Am. Coll. Rheumatology, Am. Coll. Physicians Execs., Brevard County Med. Soc. (pres. 1977-78), Navy League U.S., Eau Gallie Yacht Club (commodore 1985-86), Coast Club (bd. dirs. 1985-91, chmn. bd. 1989-91). Republican. Avocations: bicycling, travel, collecting antique maps, golf. Office Phone: 321-773-4345. Personal E-mail: RNBaney@aol.com.

BANFIELD, JILLIAN, mineralogist, geomicrobiologist, educator; b. Armidale, NSW, Australia, Aug. 18, 1959; BSc, Australian Nat. U., Canberra City, 1981, MSc, 1985; MA, PhD, Johns Hopkins U., 1990. Exploration geologist Western Mining Corp., Australia, 1982—83; rsch. asst. Australian Nat. U., 1985—86; rsch. and tchg. asst. Johns Hopkins U., Balt., 1987—90; asst. prof. geology and geophysics U. Wis., Madison, 1990—95, assoc. prof., 1995-99, prof., 1999—2001; prof. earth and planetary sci. and environ. sci. policy and mgmt. U. Calif., Berkeley, 2001—. Materials sci. adv. com. U. Wis., Madison, 1990-2001, materials sci. ctr. oversight com., 1992-1999, campus com. microscopy and image analysis, 1993-1999, Knapp bequest, 1995, rsch. com., 1995, 1998-1999, affiliate faculty mem. dept. chemistry, 1998-2001, materials sci. prog. grad. sch. com., 1999; assoc. prof. Mineral. Inst. U. Tokyo, 1996-97, prof., 1998; mem. Am. Geophys. Union mineral and rock physics com., 1998-2000; mem. geoscience adv. com., US dept. energy; vis. rsch. fellow ANU, 1998-2000; rschr. Lawrence Berkeley Nat. Lab., 2001- Contbr. scientific papers. Recipient Geol. Soc. of Australia prize 1979; W.B. Clark prize in geology, 1979; Ampol prize, 1980; Australian Nat. U. MSc scholar, 1983-84; Fulbright scholar, 1986; Owen Fellowship award, 1986-89; Eby fellow, 1986-90; Gilman Tuition fellow, 1986-90; JFOL scholar Ariz. State U., 1988; Mineral. Soc. of Am. grantee, 1989; Dept. Energy's award for outstanding rsch., 1995; H.I. Romnes Faculty fellow, 1998; D.A. Brown medal Australian Nat. U., 1999; John D. and Catherine T. MacArthur Found. fellow, 1999-2004; John Simon Guggenheim Found. fellow, 2000; Gast lectr. Geochem. Soc., 2000; NSF Earth Sci. Wk. lectr., 2000; Rosenqvist lectr., 2005 Fellow Mineral. Soc. Am. (Disting. lectr., 1994-95, award, 1997, mem. coun., 1997-1999, chair Roebling award com., 1998, chair mid-career award com., 1998-1999, assoc. editor Am. Mineralogist, 1997-2000); mem. Clay Minerals Soc. (mem. coun, student awards com., Bailey award com., 2000, pioneer lectr., 2005, Marion L. and Christie M. Jackson Mid-Career Clay Scientist award, 2000), Am. Soc. Microbiology, NAS (bd. earth scis. and resources, 2002-2005). Office: U Calif Berkeley Earth and Planetary Sci 369 McCone Berkeley CA 94720-4767

BANG, MICHELE ALENE, protective services official; d. Billy Bang Jr. and Deborah Mae Mangen; m. Darcy Rae Burns, June 1, 1991. BS, U. Nebr., Lincoln, 1991; MBA, U. Nebr., Omaha, 2001. Tchr. Millard Pub. Schs., Omaha, 1992—93; police officer Omaha Police Dept., 1993—2002, police sgt., 2002—07, police lt., 2007—. Small bus. owner Mojo's Coffeehouse, 1997—2002. With USNR, 1987—92. Mem.: Law Enforcement Against Discrimination (v.p. 2004—07), Nebr. Assn. Women Police (v.p., pres. 1999—2007). Democrat. Lutheran. Avocations: reading, gardening, walking, politics, home projects. Office: Omaha Police Dept 505 S 15th St Omaha NE 68102 Office Phone: 402-444-5652.

BANG, SANGCHUL, engineering educator; b. Seoul, Republic of Korea, Mar. 20, 1950; s. Hee K. Bang and Gwi Y. Choi; m. Sookie S. Shin; children: Genie M., Tami J. BS in Civil Engring., Seoul Nat. U., 1972; PhD, U. Calif., Davis, 1979. Profl. engr., SD, 1987. Prof. SD Sch. Mines and Tech., Rapid City, 1985—, dean Coll. Earth Sci., 1994—2003. Lt. j.g. Navy, 1972—75, Korea. Named Outstanding Prof., SD Sch. Mines and Tech., 2004; grantee, Office of Naval Rsch., 1997—2001, NSF, 2001—05, 2002—03; scholar, Nat. Assn. Fgn. Student Advisors, Assn. Internat. Educators, 1998—2000. Mem.: ASCE, Korea NAE, Korean Scientists and Engrs. Assn. (coun. mem. 1999—2002), Internat. Soc. Offshore and Polar Engring., Transp. Rsch. Bd. Achievements include research in offshore piles and anchors. Office: SD Sch Mines & Tech 501 E St Joseph St Rapid City SD 57701 Home Phone: 605-343-5835; Office Phone: 605-394-2439.

BANGA, AJAY, diversified financial services company executive; Mgmt. trainee, various positions in mktg., gen. mgmt. and sales Nestle, 1981—94; with Citigroup, 1996—, divisn. exec. Consumer Bank Ctrl. and Ea. Europe, Middle East, Africa, India, head mkting., sales and bus. devel. Europe, Middle East, Africa region Brussels, head CitiFinancal, U.S. Consumer Assets divisn., exec. v.p. global consumer group, pres. retail banking N.Am. orgn., 2002—05, co-head global consumer group, 2005—. Mem. Fin. Svcs. Roundtable. Bd. dirs. NY Hall of Sci., Nat. Coun. on Econ. Edn.; Enterprise Found. Office: Citigroup Inc 399 Park Ave New York NY 10043

BANGLE, CHRISTOPHER EDWARD (CHRIS BANGLE), automotive company car designer; b. Ravenna, Ohio, Oct. 14, 1956; married; 1 child. Studied liberal arts, U. Wis.; BS with honors, Art Ctr. Coll. Design, Pasadena, 1981. Asst. designer Hartkopf Associates, 1978—81; interior designer Adam Opel AG, 1981—83, dep. head, interior design studio, 1983—85; head exterior studio Fiat Centro Stile, 1985—91, head exterior design, 1991; dir. of the head exterior studio Fiat Centro Stile/Design, 1992; dir. design, chief designer, developmental divsn. BMW AG, Germany, 1992—. Bd. dir. Designworks/U.S.A.; spkr. in field. Achievements include redesigning of the BMW automobile styles, which caused some controversy among BMW enthusiasts; first American chief of design for BMW; also designs and creates multi-media works of art, including large-scale portraits, furniture, carpets and shoes. Office: BMW (Bayerrishe Motoren Werke) AG Petuelring 130 Munich D-80788 Germany

BANGS, CATE (CATHRYN MARGARET BANGS), film production designer, interior designer; b. Tacoma, Mar. 16, 1951; d. Henry Horan and Belva Virginia (Grandstaff) B.; m. Steve Gobin, Nov. 1, 1986 (div. 2002). Student, Hammersmith Coll Art and Bldg., London, 1971; BA cum laude, Pitzer Coll., 1973; MFA, NYU, 1978. Owner Flying Pencil Design, LA, 1981—. Prodn. designer: Lucky Day, 1990; (TV series) My So Called Life, 1994, Fudge-A-Mania, 1994; set designer: (TV series) Picket Fences, 1995-96, (film) Home Alone 3, 1997, Midnight in the Garden of Good and Evil, 1997; art dir.: (film) Volcano, 1997, (TV) Nothing Sacred, 1997-98 (Emmy and SMPTAD-ADG nomination 1998), Charmed, 1998-99, Level 9, 2000, The Huntress, 2000-01, (film) The Fighting Temptations, 2002, (TV) Threat Matrix, 2003, Desperate Housewives, 2004-07 (ADG award 2004, 05, Emmy nomination). 1st v.p. Friends of the Highland-Camrose Bungalow Village, 1985—97; bd. dirs. Ctr. Film and TV Design, 2002—, Hollywood Heights Assn., 1985—87, Cahuenga Pass Property Owners Assn., 1990. Recipient Dramalogue Critics award, 1983. Mem. Art Dirs. Guild (cert.; exec. bd. 1997-99, 2000—, sec. 2005—), Set Designers and Model Makers (cert., exec. bd. 1980—, v.p. 1989-91, pres. 1991-99), United Scenic Artists. Democrat. Buddhist. Home: 9861 Shadow Way St Shadow Hills CA 91040-1543

BANGS, F(RANK) KENDRICK, former business educator; b. Lostant, Ill., May 17, 1914; s. Mark Howard and Mary Hay (Henning) B.; m. Elizabeth Jane Paisley, May 19, 1944; children— John Kendrick, James Paisley. B.E., Ill. State Normal U., 1936; M.P.S., U. Colo., 1946; Ed.D., Ind. U., 1952. Tchr. bus. Rosiclare (Ill.) High Sch., 1936-37, Carmi (Ill.) High Sch., 1937-42; asst. prof. bus. adminstrn. U. Colo., Boulder, 1946-58, assoc. prof., 1958-64, prof., 1964-81, chmn. gen. bus. div., 1964-79; vis. prof. Coll. Bus., Ill. State U., Normal, 1979-80, 84, U. Tex-Austin, 1982, Southwestern La U., Lafayette, 1983, 85, 86, 87, U. Colo., 1987-88. Cons. adminstrv. mgmt., small bus. Chmn. fin. stability bd. Colo. Pvt. Schs. Assn., 1977— Contbr.: articles to Jour. Bus. Edn. Served with inf. U.S. Army, 1942-46. Decorated Bronze Star; recipient Robert L. Stearns award U. Colo. Alumni, 1976; John Robert Gregg award Gregg div. McGraw-Hill Pub. Co., 1978 Mem. Mountain-Plains Bus. Edn. Assn. (pres. 1958-59, Leadership award 1967-68), Nat. Bus. Edn. Assn. (co-editor yearbook 1975, nat. pres. 1967-68), Adminstrv. Mgmt. Soc. (pres. Denver chpt. 1963-64, Diamond Merit award 1967), Colo. Bus. Edn. Assn. (pres. 1956-57), Beta Gamma Sigma, Delta Pi Epsilon (nat. pres. 1968-69, pres. Research Found. 1979—) Clubs: Rotary (Boulder). Presbyterian. Home: 4840 Thunderbird Dr Apt 188 Boulder CO 80303-3829

BANGS, NELSON A. (TONY BANGS), lawyer; BS, Trinity U., 1975; JD, So. Meth. U., 1978. Bar: Tex. 1979. Assoc. atty. Winstead, McGuire, Sechrest & Trimble, 1979-81; staff atty. Dr. Pepper Co., 1981-83, sr. staff atty., asst. sec., 1983-84; gen. counsel and sec. Dr. Pepper Co. & The Seven-Up Co., Dallas, 1986-88, from v.p. to sr. v.p., sec., gen. counsel, 1988—2001; sr. v.p., gen. counsel, sec. Neiman Marcus Group, 2001—. Mem.: ABA, U.S. Trademark Assn., Am. Soc. of Corporate Secretaries, Dallas Bar Assn. Office: Neiman Marcus One Marcus Square 1618 Main St Dallas TX 75201*

BANHAM, SANDRA RODGERS, language educator; b. Washington, June 3, 1947; d. Philip Ray Rodgers and Mildred Elizabeth (Rodgers) Nisonger; m. Richard LeRoy Banham; children: Kassaundra, Richard LeRoy Jr., Philip Rodgers, Jeffrey Edward. BA in English/French magna cum laude, U. Utah, 1969, MA, 1973; MA in English/Sociology, S.W. Tex. State U., 1986; MA in TESOL, U. Miss., 1994, PhD in English Edn., 1995. Tchr. Jordan Sch. Dist., Salt Lake City, 1972-74; instr. Austin (Tex.) C.C., 1974-87, So. Meth. U., Dallas, 1988-89; writing cons./instr. U. Memphis, 1989-91; instr. N.W. Miss. C.C., Senatobia, 1991—. Cons. in field. Author: Resource guide to Teaching Literature, 1980; co-author: Global business Trends Procedures, 1996; editor Acctg. Sys. Jour., 1989-91, British Lit. I & II on-line; contbr. articles to profl. jours. Named Woman of the Yr., Austin C.C., 1986, Tchr. of the Yr., 1981. Mem. MLA, Two Yr. Coll. Assn. (mem. awards selection com.), Nat. Assn. Developmental English, Nat. Coun. Tchrs. English, Am. Coun. on Tchg. Fgn. Lang., Miss. Coun. Tchrs. English (presenter 1993, 99, 2003-), Two Year Coll. English Assn., Phi Kappa Phi, Phi Delta Kappa, Alpha Delta Pi. Avocation: reading. Office: Northwest Miss Cmty Coll 4975 Highway 51 N # 5504 Senatobia MS 38668-1714 Office Phone: 662-562-3202.

BANHOLZER, WILLIAM F., chemical company executive; BS in Chemistry, Marquette U.; MS in Chem. Engring., PhD in Chem. Engring., U. Ill. Staff chemical engr., corp. R&D lab. GE, 1983—89, lab. mgr., Advanced Inorganic Materials, 1989—92, various mgmt. positions, superabrasives bus., 1992—97; v.p., global engring. GE Lighting, 1997—99; v.p., global tech. GE Advanced Materials, 1999—2005; corp. v.p., chief tech. officer Dow Chemical Co., Midland, Mich., 2005—. Mem.: NAE (councillor 2006—). Office: Dow Chemical Co 2030 Dow Ctr Midland MI 48674*

BANIK, SAMBHU NATH, psychologist; b. Joypara, India, Nov. 7, 1935; s. Padma L. and Kadambini B.; m. Promila (Roy), Nov. 16, 1968; children: Sharmila, and Kakali. BS, Calcutta U., 1956, MS, 1958; PhD, Bristol U., 1964. Staff psychologist Des Moines Child Guidance Ctr., 1965; sr. psychologist, dir. internship tng. Univ. Hosp., Saskatoon, Sask., Canada, 1965-69, dir. psychol. svcs., 1969-71; asst. chief mental health svc. Glenn Dale Hosp. and DC Village, 1971-81; chief South Cmty. Mental Health Ctr., Washington, 1981-84, chief child and youth svc., 1984-88; clin. adminstr. NE SE Family Ctr., Washington, 1988—. Pres. Family Diagnostic and Therapeutic Ctr., Washington, 1993—; exec. dir. President's Com. on Mental Retardation HHS, Washington, 1990-93, cons. psychologist, 1993—; pres. Banik and Assoc. Family Diagnostic and Therapeutic Ctr., 1993—; v.p. devel., chmn. Third World Found., 1993—; asst. prof. U. Sask., 1965-71; vis. prof. Bowie State Coll. Md., 1972-81, prof. psychology, 1993; vis. prof. Thakur Hariprasad Inst., India, 1994. Contbr. articles to profj. jours. Mem. nat. adv. coun. on drug abuse, 1987-90; mem. adv. bd. ARC, Washington, 1987-90; founder, pres. Prabashi, Inc., 1974-78, Assn. Indians in Am., 1980-84; pres. E.S.-Asia Found., 1995—; v.p. India Cultural Coordinating Com., 1979-80, Indian Am. Forum for Polit. Edn., 2000; sec. gen. Asian Pacific Am. Cultural Heritage Coun., 1981-82; treas. Asian Pacific Am. Heritage Coun., 1982-84; mem. spl. com. 3d Conv. Asian Indians in N.Am., 1984, chmn. Indian Am. Forum Polit. Edn., Md., 1986-88, 94—; chmn. Third World Found., 1993—; adv. bd. Ednl. India Found., Inc., 1993—, Commonwealth Assn. for the Mentally Handicapped and Developmental Dis., 1992—, Md. com. on diversity, 2000; chmn. Internat. Cooperation and Coordinating Com. 11th World Congress on Mental Retardation, 1993-94; bd. trustees Woodley House, Washington; pub. mem. Svc., Personel, Rev. Bd., Wash., 1996; commr. Commn. People with Disabilities, Montgomery County, Human Rights Commn., 2004—, State Md. Human Rels. Commn., 2005; elected Md. Bush-Cheney del. Rep. Nat. Conv., 2004. Recipient Dept. Humanitarian Svc. Award D.C., 1986; Cmty. Svc. Award U.S. Asia Found., 1995, Disting. Profl. Svc. Award Ariz. Brain Injury Assn., 1999, Mother Teresa Internat. Millennium Award, 2002, Lifetime Achievement award World Bus. Forum, 2004; elected Bush del. to Rep. Nat. Conv. Mem. APA, Am. Group Psychotherapy Assn., DC Psychol. Assn.; Internat. Acad. Forensic Psychology; Nat. Health Svc. Providers in Psychology. Home: 8606 Bradmoor Dr Bethesda MD 20817-3633 Home Phone: 301-530-7589; Office Phone: 202-342-3832. Personal E-mail: sbanik7589@comcast.net.

BANK, BARBARA J., sociology educator; b. Chgo., Dec. 13, 1939; d. Julius Charles and Anna Catherine (Damm) Bank; m. Bruce Jesse Biddle, June 19, 1976. BS in Edn., Ill. State U., Normal, 1961; MA, U. Iowa, 1968, PhD in Sociology, 1974. Tchr. Rich Twp. H.S., Park Forest, Ill., 1961-63; from instr. to prof. emerita U. Mo., Columbia, 1969—, dir. grad. studies dept. sociology, 1978-82, chair dept. sociology, 1981-84. Vis. fellow Australian Nat. U., Canberra, 1984-85, 88, 93. Author: Contradictions in Women's Education, 2003; co-editor: Gender, Equity, and Schooling: Policy and Practice, 1997; assoc. editor Social Psychology of Edn., 1994-2000; contbr. articles to profl. jours.; presenter in field. Recipient Purple Chalk Tchg. award Coll. Arts and Scis., U. Mo., 1998; Fulbright sr. scholar, 1985; William T. Kemper fellow Excellence in Teaching, 2000. Mem. profl. orgns. Avocations: travel, reading. Home: 924 Yale Columbia MO 65203-1874 Office: U Mo Dept Sociology Columbia MO 65211-0001 Home Phone: 573-445-4990; Office Phone: 573-882-9174. Business E-Mail: bankb@missouri.edu.

BANK, MELISSA S., writer; BA in Am. Studies, Hobart & William Smith Colls., 1982; MFA in Fiction, Cornell U., 1988. Editl. asst. Putnam Pub. Group, NYC; copywriter McCann Erickson, NYC. Author: The Girls' Guide to Hunting and Fishing, 1999, The Wonder Spot, 2005; Stories have appeared in Chgo. Tribune, Zoetrope, The North American Rev., Other Voices, Ascent. Office: Penguin Group 375 Hudson St New York NY 10014 Address: c/o Molly Friedrich Aaron Priest Literary Agy 708 Third Ave New York NY 10017

BANK, RITA M., lawyer; b. 1946; BA, Hunter Coll., 1967; JD, Catholic U., 1978. Bar: DC, Md. Ptnr. Ain & Bank , P.C. Instr. Nat. Inst. Trial Advocacy; bd. govs. DC Bar Assn.; spkr. in field. Fellow: Am. Bar Found., Am. Coll. of Trial Lawyers, Am. Acad. of Matrimonial Lawyers; mem.: Bd. of Visitors, Columbus Sch. of Law, Catholic U. Office: Ain & Bank 1900 M St NW Ste 600 Washington DC 20036 Office Phone: 202-530-3300. Office Fax: 202-530-4411. E-mail: rbank@AinBankLaw.com.*

BANK, ROY J., television producer; b. June 13, 1972; Grad. in Bus., U. Pa., Phila. Prodr. Nickelodeon, Reveille; head devel. and ops. Mark Burnett Prodns. Prodr.: (TV series) Wild & Crazy Kids, The Restaurant, 2003, The Casino, 2004; co-exec. prodr. (online game) Flushed Away Underground Adventure, 2006. Avocation: kayaking.*

BANKE, KATHY M., lawyer; b. Glendale, Calif., Mar. 1, 1953; married; 2 children. BA, Calif. State U., Sacramento, 1973; JD, U. Colo., Boulder, 1979. Bar: Calif. 1979, US Dist. Ct. Ea. Dist. Calif. 1979, US Dist. Ct. No. Dist. Calif. 1982, US Dist. Ct. Ctrl. Dist. Calif. 1983, US Ct. Appeals 9th Cir. 1983, US Supreme Ct. 2000, US Ct. Appeals 3rd Cir. 2004. With Crosby Heafey Roach & May (combined with Reed Smith in 2003), 1982—2003; ptnr. Reed Smith LLP, Oakland, Calif., 2003—, also practice group leader appellate group. Adj. asst. prof. law in civil appellate advocacy Hastings Coll. Law, 1990—93; practitioner-advisor in civil appellate advocacy Boalt Hall Sch. Law, 1994—98. Mem.: Calif. Acad. Appellate Lawyers, Am. Acad. Appellate Lawyers. Office: Reed Smith LLP 1999 Harrison St Ste 2400 Oakland CA 94612-3572 Office Phone: 510-466-6765. Office Fax: 510-273-8832. Business E-Mail: kbanke@reedsmith.com.

BANKER, AMY BETH COHEN, artist, writer, educator, curator, actress, poet; b. Bronx, Jan. 9, 1960; d. Morton and Arline Carol (Goldin) Cohen; 1 child, Meredith Elaine. BS in Human Development, Design & Environ. Analysis, Cornell U., Ithaca, NY, 1971—75. Cert. in labor rels. & affirmative action Cornell U., 1992, appraisal studies for fine art, furniture, jewelry, paintings NYU, 2004, decorative arts Isabel O'Neill, 2005. Artist CVB Space, NYC, 2004—; curator, dir. Nat. Assn. Women's Artists, 2006—, 2007—; curator CVB Space, NYC, NY Art World, Artist Ovoworks.com, Artist Kevin Kushel, Gallery Gora, Montreal, Kasia Kay Art Projects, Janos Gat Gallery. Mem. dirs. coun. Whitney Mus., NYC, 1995—; vis. lectr. New Jersey City U. Performed, dir. art and design: The Dead Life, 2005—; prin. works include Warhol Portraits, Opera related expressions, Personal Totem Portraits of Apocalyn, Adelphi U. Faith Ringgold show, Amy Banker Now, Janos Gat Gallery, 2007; contbr. to various publs., The Relicts Project. Agent, Allison Jane Baker fund for Lymphoma and Hodgkins disease cancer Sloan Kettering Hosp., NYC; mem. Feminist Art Project; chair exhibition com. Nat. Assn. Women Artists; mem. dir. coun. Whitney Mus. Named Gershwin superstar, 2007; recipient Top Abstract Artist over 30 Yrs., Art Students League, 1999, 2003, Top Amateur Photographer, ICP, 2005, NOHO Disting. Art award, 2007. Mem.: Greater Barrington Art Assn. and Coop., Coll. Art Assn., NY Acad. Sci., New Marlboro Assn. Democrat. Jewish. Avocations: photography, music, dance, cooking, sewing. Home: 50 E 89 St New York NY 10128 Home Fax: 212-429-2700. Personal E-mail: amycohenbanker@earthlink.net.

BANKER, CAROL ANNE, elementary school educator; b. Denver, June 8, 1954; d. Harry Thomas Stokes and Barbara Jean McCandless; m. Steven Lee Banker, June 4, 1977; children: Kristen, Kimberly. AA, Otero Jr. Coll., LaJunta, Colo., 1974; BS, U. No. Colo., 1976; MA, Lesley Coll., 1996. Classroom tchr. Deerfield (Kans.) Unified Sch. Dist., 1976—79; tchr. Lamar (Colo.) Sch. Dist., 1979—. Named Tchr. of Yr., Lamar Edn. Assn., 1997. Mem.: NEA, Internat. Reading Assn. Avocations: reading, baking, music. Office: Parkview Elem Sch 1105 Parkview Ave Lamar CO 81052

BANKER, MAUREEN JOYCE, artist, educator; d. John and Harriet Kacsur; m. James Roderick Banker, June 24, 1961; children: Pierette, Heather. BA in Art, Meredith Coll., Raleigh, NC, 1979; MA in Printmaking, Villa Shifaroia Grad. Sch. Fine Arts, Florence, Italy, 1985. Assoc. prof. art Meredith Coll., 1988—, dir. galleries, 1990—2000. Vis. artist Am. Acad. in Rome, 2002, 03. One-woman shows include J.J.J. Gallery, Palazzo Guadagni, Florence, 2005. Office: Art Dept Meredith Coll 3800 Hillsborough St Raleigh NC 27607 Business E-Mail: bankerm@meredith.edu.

BANKER, RAJIV D., finance educator, consultant; s. Dushyant D. and Hansa D. Banker; m. Bela R. Banker, Dec. 24, 1982; children: Arjun R., Sachin R., Rishin R., Mohin R. DBA, Harvard U., Cambridge, 1980. Chartered acct., CAII, 1976. Chmn. acctg. and info. tech. Temple U., Phila., 2005—. Contbr. articles to profl. jours. Recipient Best Tchr. Honor award, Carnegie Mellon U., 1984, 1989, 1993. Mem.: Internat. DEA Soc. (life; chmn. 2005—07). Home Phone: 610-645-7774; Office Phone: 215-204-2029.

BANKHEAD, SHERRY L., lawyer; b. Gatesville, Tex., Feb. 12, 1971; BA, U. Tex., Austin, 1994; JD, South Tex. Coll. Law, Houston, 1998. Bar: Tex. 1998. Assoc. atty. Johnson, Spalding, Doyle, West & Trent LLP, Houston. Named a Rising Star, Tex. Super Lawyers mag., 2006. Mem.: ABA, Houston Young Lawyers Assn., Houston Bar Assn. Office: Johnson Spalding Doyle West & Trent LLP 919 Milam St Ste 1700 Houston TX 77002 Office Phone: 713-222-2323. E-mail: sbankhead@js-llp.com.*

BANKO, RUTH CAROLINE, retired library director; b. Phillipsburg, NJ, Mar. 28, 1931; d. Arthur William and Virginia Miller (Wilson) Osborn; m. Marvin Kenneth Banko (dec.); children: David, Sallie, Susan, Joseph, Elisabeth. Cert. libr. tech. asst., Northampton AreaC.C. Salesman Stanley Home Products, 1958-95; dir. Riegelsville (Pa.) Pub. Libr., 1974-97. Social ambudsman County Agy. on Aging, Doylestown, Pa.; asst. dir. Pearl Buck Found., Dublin, Pa.; mem. Riegelsville Fire Aux., 1992—; councilman, Planning Commn., Riegelsville Borough Coun., 1972-89; mem. States Legis. Com., 1972-88; mayor Borough of Riegelsville, 1990-97; disaster chmn., blood chmn., bd. mem. ARC, Doylestown, 1966-86; pres. jr. high and area coun. PTA, Easton, 1966-74; pres. Boro Coun., 1980-81; v.p., trustee Riegelsville Pub. Libr. Recipient Svc. award ARC, Doylestown, Bucks County Libr. Dist., Life Membership award PTA, 1972; named children's rm. in her honor Riegelsville Pub. Libr., 2005 Mem. Pa. Boroughs Assn. (legis. com. 1972-97), Pa. Mayors Assn., Easton Area Coun. PTAs (life). Democrat. Lutheran. Home: 449 Easton Rd Riegelsville PA 18077-0223

BANKOFF, JOSEPH R., art association administrator; b. Newark, Dec. 22, 1945; BS, Purdue U., 1967; JD, U. Ill., 1971. Bar: Ill. 1971, Ga. 1972. Law clk. to Hon. Walter P. Gewin U.S. Ct. Appeals (5th cir.), 1971-72; ptnr. King & Spalding LLP, Atlanta, 1972—2006; pres. Woodruff Arts Ctr., Inc., Atlanta, 2006—, CEO, 2006—. Asst. editor U. Ill. Law Forum, 1969-70. Mem. ABA, Ill. State Bar Assn., State Bar Ga., Atlanta Bar Assn., Nat. Inst. Trial Advocacy (trustee 1995—, chmn. 2005-), Am. Law Inst., Order of Coif, Omicron Delta Kappa. Office: Woodruff Arts Ctr Inc 1280 Peachtree St NE Atlanta GA 30309 Office Phone: 404-572-4600, 404-733-4212.

BANKS, ALICIA, elementary school educator; BA in Speech Comms. and Pre-Law, U. Ill., Urbana-Champaign, 1984; MA in Interpersonal and Orgnl. Comm. summa cum laude, U. Ark., Little Rock, 2001. Lic. non-traditional tchr. Ark. Gen. mgr., announcer, newscaster WUHS Radio, Urbana, Ill., 1979—80; vocal prodn. talent, copywriter WPGU Radio, Urbana, 1980—82; founder, gen. mgr., program dir., host, prodr., DJ, sales age. WBML Radio, Urbana, 1982—84; prodr., host, DJ, engr., fundraiser, sales rep. WRFG Radio, Atlanta, 1989—96; prodr., host, engr. KPFA/KPFB/KFCF Radio, Berkeley, Calif., 1996—98; prodr., talk show host, copywriter, vocal prodn. talent, sales agt. WIGO Radio, Atlanta, 1993—95; adminstrv. asst., electronic metering technician, accts. payable clk. Pacific Gas & Electric Corp. Inc., San Francisco, 1996—98; sales cons., call ctr. customer svc. agt., acct. rschr. Southwestern Bell Wireless/SBC Inc., Little Rock, 1998—99; substitute tchr. Little Rock Sch. Dist., 1999—2002; instr. Ark. Atty. Gen.'s Office, Little Rock, 2002—04; customer svc., airport svc. agt. Continental Express Airline, Little Rock, 2001; tchr. College Station Elem. Sch., Ark., 2004—; instr. U. Phoenix, Little Rock, 2007; tchr. Geyer Springs Elem. Sch., Little Rock, 2007—. Webmaster, columnist Eloquent Fury Website, 1994—; guest talk show host WGST Radio, Atlanta, 1995—96; instr. U. Phoenix, 2007—. Columnist: Hues Mag., 1996—97, Friends Mag., 1994—96. Named an Outstanding Young Woman Am., 1986. Address: PO Box 55596 Little Rock AR 72215 Personal E-mail: ambwww@yahoo.com.

BANKS, ALLAN RICHARD, artist, art historian, researcher; b. Dearborn, Mich., Feb. 15, 1948; s. Henry Selman and Lillian Margaret (Radovic) B.; children: Christine Marie, Aaron Richard; m. Holly Hope Tumblin, Jan. 1997. Ind. pvt. study, Soc. Arts and Crafts, Detroit, 1966-69; student, Atelier Lack, Inc., Mpls., 1970-73, R.H. Ives Gammell Studio, Williamstown, Mass., 1976. Artist, with studio in, Newburg, N.Y., 1979-81, Huron, Ohio, 1981-87; portrait artist, with studio in Spring Hill, Fla., 1987-93; dir. Atelier of Plein Air, Safety Harbor, Fla., 1993—. Lectr./demonstrator Portraits South, Inc., Raleigh, N.C., 1993, Atelier LeSueur, Mpls., 1995. Exhibited in group shows Sotheby's, N.Y.C., 1997, Guild of Boston Artists, 1996, 20th Century Exhbn., Amarillo Tex.-Springville, Utah, 1982, Butler Inst. Am. Art, Vixseboxse Art Galleries, Cleve., Salmagundi Club, Amarillo (Tex.) Art Ctr., Maryhill Mus. Art, Goldendale, Wash., Historic East-West Russia Exhibit, 1996, others; represented in collections at Wadsworth Athenaeum, Newark Art Mus., Montclair (N.J.) Mus., Hamilton Fish Meml. Libr., Nat. Portrait Gallery/Smithsonian. Trustee Mus. Natural History, Safety Harbor, 1995—; mem. bd. advisors Art Renewal Ctr., N.Y.C.; mem. Downtown Bus. Assn., Inc., Safety Harbor, 1994—. Elizabeth T. Greenshields Found. fellow, Montreal, 1972, 73; John and Anna Stacey Found. grantee, N.Mex., 1979, Ohio Arts Coun. grantee. Mem. Am. Soc. Portrait Artists (vice chmn. 2000-01), Am. Soc. Classical Realism (pres. 1997—), Met. Mus. Art, Appleton Mus. Art (Ocala, Fla.), Salmagundi Club, New Am. Acad. Ard. Lutheran. Avocations: travel, museums. Home: PO Box 233 Safety Harbor FL 34695-0233

BANKS, BRITT D., lawyer; b. Ft. Collins, Colo., Aug. 21, 1961; BS cum laude, U. Denver, 1983; JD, U. Colo., 1988. Bar: Colo. 1989, US Dist. Ct. Dist. Colo. 1991, US Ct. Appeals 10th Cir. 1991. Law clerk to Hon. Oliver Seth US Ct. Appeals 10th Cir., 1988—89; atty. Holland & Hart, 1989—93; joined Newmont Mining Corp., Denver, 1993, assoc. gen. counsel, 1996—2001, sec., 2001—04, v.p., gen. counsel, 2001—06, exec. v.p. legal and external matters, 2006—. Mem.: Colo. State Bar. Office: Newmont Mining Corp 1700 Lincoln St Denver CO 80203*

BANKS, CAROLYN DUTY, retired history educator; b. Rogers, Ark., May 11, 1932; d. Jeff Davis and Lois White Duty; m. Warren Eugene Banks (dec.); children: Karen Marie, Keith Randolph(dec.). BA, U. Ark., 1960, postgrad., 1961—63. Cert. tchr. Ark. Tchr. Washington (Ark.) secondary schs., 1961—80; mem. fine arts staff U. Ark., 1967—69; self employed rschr., editor Ark., 1987—97; staff writer Hist. Soc. Jour., Fayetteville, Ark., 2000—. Rschr., editor: geneal. book In the Line of Duty, 1997; contbr. articles to profl. jours. Mem. Dem. Women's Club Washington County, Ark.; bd. dirs. U. Ark. Retirement Assn., Fayetteville, 1996—2000. Mem.: DAR, NWA Scottish Soc., Washington County Hist. Soc., Third Order of St. Francis, 20th Century Club (pres. 1992), Scottish Knights Templar (dame 2004), Phi Beta Kappa, Delta Delta Delta. Episcopalian. Avocations: historical research and writing, raising skye terriers, gardening, exercise.

BANKS, CHARLES AUGUSTUS, III, distribution executive; b. 1940; BA in Internat. Rels., Brown U., 1962. With Cameron Brown Co., 1965-67, Ferguson Enterprises Inc., Newport News, Va., 1967—2001, pres., COO, 1989-93, pres., CEO, 1993—2001; group chief exec. Wolseley PLC, 2001—06; ptnr. Clayton, Dubilier & Rice Inc., NYC, 2006—. With USN, 1962—64.

BANKS, DAVID RUSSELL, former health care executive; b. Arcadia, Wis., Feb. 15, 1937; s. J. R. and Cleone Banks; married; children: Melissa, Michael. BA, U. Ark., 1959. Vice pres. Dabbs, Sullivan, Trulock, Ark., 1963—74; chmn., chief exec. officer Leisure Lodges, Ft. Smith, Ark., 1974—77; registered rep. Stephens Inc., Little Rock, 1974—79; pres., CEO Beverly Enterprises, Ft. Smith, Ark., 1989—2001, chmn. bd., dir., 1990—2001. Dir. Nat. Coun. Health Ctrs., Pulaski Bank, Little Rock. With US Army. Home: PO Box 4520 Fayetteville AR 72702-4520

BANKS, DEIRDRE MARGARET, retired church organization administrator; b. Melbourne, Australia, May 9, 1934; came to U.S., 1975; d. Haldane Stuart and Vera Avice (Fisher) B. MA, Simpson Coll., 1980. Missionary nurse Leprosy Mission, Kathmandu, Nepal, 1960-69; dean of women Melbourne Bible Inst., 1970-75; asst. to dir. Bible Study Fellowship, Oakland, Calif., 1975-79; dir. adult ministries First Covenant Ch., Oakland, 1980-87, assoc. pastor for adults, St. Paul, 1987-89; exec. dir. Covenant Women Ministries, Chgo., 1989-99; interim pastor Bowie Ch. of the Redeemer Covenant, Md., 2005; ret. Spkr. in field. Chair ch. edn. bd. Pacific S.W. Conf. Evang. Ch., 1985-87, Gilead Group, Oakland, 1985-87; bd. dirs., chair Gilead Group Housing for Abused and Homeless Women and Children; bd. chmn. Barnabas Project for Abused and Homeless Women and Children, 1990-93; mem. bd. world mission Evang. Covenant Ch., 1986-89; bd. Covenant Enabling Residences Inc. for Developmentally Disabled Adults, pres., 1996-98; pastor Mission Covenant Ch., Orange, Mass., 2000-04, 07—. Mem. Evangel. Covenant Ch. Home Phone: 978-544-7550. Personal E-mail: dmbanks7@aol.com.

BANKS, DONNA JO, food products executive; b. Ft. McClellan, Ala., Sept. 6, 1956; d. Walter Dow and Joanne (Phelps) Cox; m. Bobby Dennis Banks, Dec. 27, 1983; children: Cynthia Marie, Elizabeth Anne, Sarah Diane. BS, U. Tenn., 1979, MS, 1980; PhD, Mich. State U., 1984. Assoc. statistician Kellogg Co., Battle Creek, Mich., 1983-84, mgr. product evaluation and stats., 1984-87, dir. cereal product devel., 1987-91, v.p. rsch. and devel., 1991-97, sr. v.p. rsch. and devel., 1997—99, sr. v.p. global innovation, 1999—2000, sr. v.p. rsch., quality and tech., 2000—04, sr. v.p., worldwide innovation and operations, 2004—. Bd. mem. Mich. Life Scis. Corridor. Bd. mem. Mich. State U. Found. Named Disting. Alumni, Mich. State U. Coll. Agr. and Natural Resources, 2000; named one of 25 Masters of Innovation, BusinessWeek, 2006; named to Acad. Women Achievers, YWCA N.Y.C., 1998. Mem.: Product Devel. Mgmt. Assn., Am. Assn. Cereal Chemists, Internat. Food Techs., Am. Statis. Assn., Sigma Xi. Democrat. Baptist. Avocations: racquetball, tennis, needlecrafts, sewing. Office: Kellogg Co 1 Kellogg Sq Battle Creek MI 49016-3599

BANKS, FRED LEE, JR., former state supreme court justice, lawyer; b. Jackson, Miss., Sept. 1, 1942; s. Fred L. and Violet (Mabry) B.; m. Taunya Lovell, June 5, 1967 (div. 1975); children: Rachel R., Jonathan L.; m. Pamela Gipson, Jan. 28, 1978; 1 child, Gabrielle G. BA, Howard U., 1965, JD cum laude, 1968. Bar: Miss. 1968, U.S. Dist. Ct. (no. and so. dists.) Miss. 1968, U.S. Ct. Appeals (5th cir.) 1968, D.C. 1969, U.S. Supreme Ct. 1971. Ptnr. Banks, Owens & Byrd and predecessor firms Anderson, Banks, Nichols & Stewart; Anderson, Banks, Nichols & Leventhal; Anderson & Banks, Jackson, 1968—85; rep. Miss. Ho. of Reps., 1975—85; judge Miss. 7th Cir. Ct., Hinds County and Yazoo County, 1985—91; assoc. justice Miss. Supreme Ct, Jackson, 1991—2000; presiding justice Miss. Supreme Ct., Miss., 2000—01; ptnr. Phelps Dunbar, LLP, 2001—. Chair Spl. Com. on Jud. Campaign Intervention, 2002, 04; mem. Miss. Bd. Bar Admissions, 1978-81; pres. State Mut. Fed. Savs. and Loan, Jackson, 1976-89; mem. minority adv. com. U. Miss. Sch. of Law. Bd. dirs. NAACP, 1981—; mem. Nat. Adv. Com. for the Edn. of Disadvantaged Children, 1978-80; del. Dem. Nat. Conv., 1976, 1980; co-mgr. Miss. Carter-Mondale presidl. campaign, 1976; legislator Miss. Ho. of Reps., Jackson, 1976-85; bd. visitors Miss. Coll. Sch. of Law. Mem. ABA, Magnolia Bar Assn., Nat. Bar Assn., Hinds County Bar Assn., Am. Inns of Ct., Charles Clark Inn, Miss. Bar Assn., D.C. Bar Assn., Sigma Pi Phi. Roman Catholic. Home: 976 Metairie Rd Jackson MS 39209-6948 Office: 200 S Lamar St Ste 500 Jackson MS 39201

BANKS, HENRY H., orthopedist, educator, dean; b. Boston, Mar. 9, 1921; s. Isaac and Bessie B.; m. Judith Epstein, June 1945; children: Nancy (Mrs. Curt Civin), Betsy (Mrs. David Epstein), Steven. AB cum laude, Harvard U., 1942; MD, Tufts U., 1945. Diplomate Am. Bd. Orthopedic Surgery (pres. 1978-79, exec. dir. 1979-86). Surg. intern Beth Israel Hosp., Boston, 1945-46, asst. resident in surgery, 1947-49; asst. resident orthopedic lab. and pathology Children's Hosp., Boston, 1949-50, asst. resident orthopedic surgery, 1950-51, Mass. Gen. Hosp., Boston, 1951-52; chief resident orthopedic surgery Peter Bent Brigham Hosp., Boston, 1952, Children's Hosp. Med. Center, Boston, 1952-53; practice medicine, specializing in orthopedic surgery Boston, 1953—; prof. Tufts U. Sch. Medicine, 1970-90, prof. emeritus, 1990—, chmn. dept. orthopedic surgery, 1970-84, assoc. dean, 1972-82, sr. assoc. dean med. affairs, 1982, acting med. dean, then med. dean, 1983-90, dean emeritus, 1990—; dir. orthopedic surgery Boston City Hosp., 1970-74; orthopedic surgeon-in-chief New Eng. Med. Center Hosps., 1970-84. Orthopedic surgeon children's Hosp. Med. Ctr., 1953-70, Peter Bent Brigham Hosp., 1953-70, chief orthopedic surgery, 1968-70. Author: A Century of Excellence: The History of Tufts University School of Medicine, 1893-1993, 1993, Orthopaedic Surgery at Tufts University School of Medicine, 1893-1998, 1998; editor: The Pediatric Clinics of North America-Musculoskeletal Disorder I, 1967; guest editor: Clinical Orthopedics and Related Research, 1968, Orthopedic Clinics of North America, 1976, 78; contbr. articles to profl. jours. With M.C. AUS, 1945-47. Mem. AMA, ACS, Am. Orthopedic Assn. (v.p. 1986-87), Am. Acad. Orthopedic Surgeons, Am. Acad. Cerebral Palsy (pres.), Eastern Orthopedic Assn., Mass. Med. Soc., Internat. Soc. Orthopedic Surgery and Traumatology, Boston Orthopedic Club (pres.), Pediatric Orthopedic Soc., Am. Bd. Orthopedic Surgery (sec., pres. 1973-79). Home: 54 Commonwealth Ave Boston MA 02116-3043 Office: 136 Harrison Ave Boston MA 02111-1817

BANKS, JAMES ALBERT, research director, educator; b. Marianna, Ark., Sept. 24, 1941; s. Matthew and Lula (Holt) Banks; m. Cherry Ann McGee, Feb. 15, 1969; children: Angela Marie, Patricia Ann. AA, Chgo. City Coll., 1963; BE, Chgo. State U., 1964; MA (NDEA fellow 1966-69), Mich. State U., 1967, PhD, 1969; LHD (hon.), Bank St. Coll. Edn., 1993, U. Alaska, Fairbanks, 2000, U. Wis., Parkside, 2001, DePaul U., 2003, Lewis and Clark Coll., 2004, Grinnell Coll., 2006. Elem. sch. tchr. Joliet, Ill., 1965; tchr. Francis W. Parker Sch., Chgo., 1965—66; asst. prof. edn. U. Wash., Seattle, 1969—71, assoc. prof., 1971—73, prof., 1973—, chmn. curriculum and instrn., 1982—87, Russell F. Stark univ. prof., 2001—06, Kerry and Linda Killinger prof. diversity studies, 2006—; dir. Ctr. Multicultural Edn., Seattle, 1991; Spencer fellow Ctr. Advanced Study Behavioral Scis., Stanford, Calif., 2005—06. Vis. prof. edn. U. Mich., 1975, Monash U., Australia, Australia, 1985, U. Warwick, England, 1988, U. Minn., 1991; vis. lectr. U. Southampton, England, 1989; Harry F. and Alva K. Ganders disting. lectr. Syracuse U., 1989; Tyler eminent scholar chair Fla. State U., 1998; Carl and Alice Daeufer lectr. U. Hawaii, Manoa, 1999; Sachs lectr. Tchrs. Coll. Columbia U., 1996; disting. scholar lectr. Kent State U., 1978; Read disting. lectr. Kent State. U., 2005; 20th ann. faculty lectr. U. Wash., 2004—05; disting. scholar lectr. U. Ariz., 1979, Ind. U., 1983; vis. scholar Brit. Acad., 1983; com. examiners Ednl. Testing Svc., 1974—77; nat. adv. coun. on ethnic heritage studies, U.S. Office Edn., 1975—78, com. on fed. role in ednl. rsch. NAS, 1991-92, mem. com. on developing a rsch. agenda on edn. of ltd. proficient and bilingual students, 1995—97; mem. bd. on children, youth and families NRC and Inst. of Medicine/NAS, 1999—2005; 29th ann. faculty lectr. U. Wash., 2005. Author: Teaching the Black Experience, 1970, Teaching Strategies for the Social Studies, 1973, 5th edit., 1999, Teaching Strategies for Ethnic Studies, 1975, 7th edit., 2003, Multiethnic Education: Practices and Promises, 1977, An Introduction to Multicultural Education, 1994, 3d edit., 2002, Educating Citizens in A Multicultural Soc., 1997, 2d edit., 2007; author: (with Cherry Ann Banks) March Toward Freedom: A History of Black Americans, 1970, 2d edit., 1974, rev. 2d edit., 1978; author: Multiethnic Education: Theory and Practice, 1981, 4th edit., (new title) Cultural Diversity and Education: Foundations, Curriculum, and Teaching, 2001, 5th edit., 2006; author: (with others) Curriculum Guidelines for Multicultural Education, 1976, 5th edit., 2005; author: We Americans: Our History and People, 2 vols., 1982, Race, Culture, and Education: The Selected Works of James A. Banks, 2006, Handbook of Complementary Methods in Education Research, 2006; contbg. author Internat. Ency. of Edn., 1985, Handbook of Research on Teacher Education, 1990, Handbook of Research on Social Studies Teaching and Learning, 1991, Encyclopedia of Ednl. Rsch., 1992, Handbook of Research on the Education of Young Children, 1993, Review of Research in Education, vol. 19, 1993, Encyclopedia of Black Studies, 2005, Preparing Teachers for a Changing World, 2005, Handbook of Complementary Methods in Education Research, 3rd edit., —; editor: Black Self-Concept, 1972, Teaching Ethnic Studies: Concepts and Strategies, 1973; editor: (with William W. Joyce) Teaching Social Studies to Culturally Different Children, 1971; editor: Teaching the Language Arts to Culturally Different Children, 1971, Education in the 80's: Multiethnic Education, 1981; editor: (with James Lynch) Multicultural Education in Western Societies, 1986; editor: (with C. Banks) Multicultural Education: Issues and Perspectives, 1989, 6th edit., 2007; editor: Handbook of Research on Multicultural Education, 1995, 2d edit., 2004, Multicultural Education, Transformative Knowledge, and Action, 1996, Diversity and Citizenship Education: Global Perspectives, 2004; mem. editl. bd. Jour. of Tch. Edn., 1985—89, Coun. Interracial Books for Children Bull., 1982—92, Urban Edn., 1991—96, Race, Ethnicity and Education, 1998—, Tchrs. Coll. Record, 1998—2002, Multicultural Perspectives, 2000—03; contbr. articles to profl. jours. Recipient Outstanding Young Man award, Wash. State Jaycees, 1975, Outstanding Svc. in Edn. award, Seattle U. Black Student Union, 1985, Pres. award, Tchrs. of English to Speakers of Other Languages, 1998, Disting Career Rsch. award, Nat. Coun. for the Social Studies, 2001, Disting. Alumni award, Coll. Edn., Mich. State U., 2004, Mich. State U., 2005, medal, UCLA, 2005; Spencer fellow, Nat. Acad. Edn., 1973—78, Kellogg fellow, 1980—83, Rockefeller Found. fellow, 1980, Ctr. Advanced Studies in Behavioral Sci. fellow, Stanford U., 2005—06. Mem. ASCD (bd dirs. 1976-79, Disting. lectr. 1986, Disting. scholar, lectr. 1994, 97), Nat. Acad. Edn. (bd. dirs. 2003—), Nat. Coun. Social Studies (bd. dirs. 1973-74, 80-85, pres. 1982, Disting. Career Rsch. in Social Studies award 2001), Internat. Assn. Intercultural Edn. (editl. bd.), Social Sci. Edn. Consortium (bd. dirs. 1976-79), Am. Ednl. Rsch. Assn. (com. on role and status of minorities in edn. rsch. 1992-94, publs. com. 1995-96, pres.-elect 1996-97, pres. 1997-98, exec. bd. 1998-99, Disting. scholar/rschr. on minority edn. 1986, Rsch. Review award 1994, Disting. Career Contbn. award 1996, Social Justice in Edn. award 2004), Phi Delta Kappa, Phi Kappa Phi, Golden Key Nat. Honor Soc., Kappa Delta Pi. Office: Ctr for Multicultural Edn Univ Wash Box 353600 110 Miller Hall Seattle WA 98195-3600 Office Phone: 206-543-6636. Office Fax: 206-543-1237. Business E-Mail: jbanks@u.washington.edu. *One of the greatest strengths of our nation is its tremendous ethnic, racial, and cultural diversity. A major goal of my career is to increase understanding and communication across different ethnic, cultural and racial groups and to make it possible for each ethnic, cultural and racial group to make its greatest contribution to the nation. My belief that educational institutions can play a major role in improving race relations in our nation has greatly influenced my life and career.*

BANKS, MCRAE CAVE, II, management educator, consultant; b. Portsmouth, Va., May 8, 1950; s. James W. and Martha Ann (Nemec) B.; m. Lucy D. Hawk, Dec. 22, 1980; children: Caroline D., Margaret S., Elizabeth M., Michael C., Katherine C., John H. BA, Va. Poly. Inst. and State U., 1972, PhD, 1987; MA, Northwestern U., 1973. Pvt. practice, Evanston, Ill., 1973—74; registered rep. IDS, Glenview, Ill., 1974-75; asst. v.p. mktg. Singer Safety Products, Chgo., 1975-78; gen. mgr. Britton Enterprises, Fredericksburg, Va., 1978-79; women's track coach Va. Poly. Inst. and State U., Blacksburg, 1979-82; asst. prof. mgmt. Radford (Va.) U., 1982-87; asst. prof. Miss. State U., Starkville, 1987-90, assoc. prof., 1990-94, prof., 1994-95, acting dir. Agribus. Inst., 1994-95; prof. mgmt., dept. head Worcester (Mass.) Poly. Inst., 1995—. Cons., trainer to over 100 orgns. Editor FOCUS on Mgmt., 1987-97; contbr. articles to profl. jours., also monographs. Mem. com. Va. Gov.'s Conf. on Small Bus., 1986; judge Blue Chip Enterprise Initiative, 1991-93; bd. deacons United Ch. of Christ, 1997-2000. Named Va. Tech Sports Hall of Fame 1999. Fellow Soc. for Advancement Mgmt. (bd. dirs. 1984-99, pres. 1993-94, President's Merit award 1989, Gold Meml. award 1990), Acad. Mgmt. (assoc. dir. placement 1989-92, dir. 1992-95, asst. program chmn. entrepreneurship divsn. 1994-95, program chmn. 1995-96, divsn. chair 1997-98, sponsorship chair 1996-99), So. Mgmt. Assn. (track chmn. 1993-94), Va. C. of C. (chmn. region II task force on small bus. 1985-87, Coalition for Venture Support 1996—, exec. com. WPI Venture forum 1996—), U.S. Assn. Small Bus. and Entrepreneurship, Phi Kappa Phi. Office: Worcester Poly Inst Dept Mgmt 100 Institute Rd Worcester MA 01609-2247

BANKS, PETER MORGAN, physics professor; b. San Diego, May 21, 1937; s. George Willard and Mary Margaret (Morgan) B.; children by previous marriage: Kevin, Michael, Steven, David.; m. Mary E. Stewart, Dec. 28, 2002; 1 child, Mark. MS in E.E, Stanford U., 1960; PhD in Physics, Pa. State U., 1965. Postdoctoral fellow Institut d'Aeronomie Spatiale de Belgique, Brussels, 1965-66; prof. applied physics U. Calif., San Diego, 1966-76; prof. physics Utah State U., 1976-81, head dept. physics, 1976-81; vis. assoc. prof. Stanford U., 1972-73, prof. elec. engring., 1981-90, dir. space, telecommunications and radiosci. lab., 1982-90, dir. ctr. for aeronautics and space info. systems, 1983-90; prof. atmospheres, oceans, and space sci. U. Mich., 1990-95, adj. prof., 1996-2000; dean Coll. Engring., U. Mich., 1990-95; pres. Earth Data Corp., 1985-86; pres., CEO Environ. Rsch. Inst. Mich., 1995-97, ERIM Internat., Inc., 1997-99; ptnr. XR Ventures, LLC, 2000—04; CEO Akonni Biosystems, Inc., 2003; pres. Inst. for the Future, Menlo Park, Calif., 2004—05; gen. ptnr. Red Planet Capital, LP, 2006—. Vis. scientist Max Planck Inst. for Aeronomie, Germany, 1975; pres. La Jolla Scis., Inc., 1973—77, Upper Atmosphere Rsch. Corp., 1978—82; chmn. NASA adv. com. on sci. uses of space sta., 1985—87; prin. investigator space shuttle experiments, 1982, 85, 91; mem. Jason Group, 1983—97; bd. dirs. Tecumseh Products Corp.; chmn. bd. trustees Consortium Internat. Earth Sci. Info. Networks, 1991—94; co-chmn. NRC Commn. on Phys. Scis., Math. and Applications, 1998—2000. Author: (with G. Kockarts) Aeronomy, 1973, (with J.R. Doupnik) Introduction to Computer Science, 1976; assoc. editor: Jour. Geophys. Research, 1974-77; assoc. editor: Planetary and Space Sci, 1977-83, regional editor, 1983-86; contbr. numerous articles in field to profl. jours. Mem. space sci. adv. council

NASA, 1976-80. Served with U.S. Navy, 1960-63. Recipient Appleton prize Royal Soc. London, 1978, Space Sci. award AIAA, 1981, NASA Disting. Service medal, 1986; Alumni fellow Pa. State U., 1982 Fellow Am. Geophys. Union; mem. Internat. Union Radio Sci., Nat. Acad. Engring., Univs. Space Rsch. Assn. (chmn. and trustee 2002—), Cosmos Club. Episcopalian. Home: 5602 Newanga Ave Santa Rosa CA 95405 E-mail: pb2@sonic.net.

BANKS, RELA, sculptor; b. Yaroslav, Poland, Oct. 8, 1933; came to U.S., 1947; d. Jacob and Frieda (Weintraub) Heuberg; m. Stanley Frederic Banks, Aug. 9, 1953; children: Andrew Howard, J. Monica, Gary Mitchell. Student, Mus. Modern Art, 1957, Art Students League, NYC, 1958-61, Summit Art Ctr., NJ, 1966-75. Chmn. nat. juried exhibit Summit Art Ctr., 1976, mem. adminstrv. com., 1977-79, chmn. standing com. spl. events, trustee; mem. exec. com. Phoenix Gallery, N.Y.C., 1983; chmn. membership com. Stone Sculpture Soc. N.Y., 1980-82. One-woman shows include Robins Art Gallery, South Orange, N.J., 1973, Montclair (N.J.) Coll., 1974, Caldwell (N.J.) Coll., 1974, 83, Summit Art Ctr., 1976, Newark Acad., Livingston, N.J., 1976, Douglas Coll., New Brunswick, N.J., 1978, First Women's Bank, N.Y.C., 1979, Phoenix Gallery, 1979, 81, 83, Morris Mus. Arts and Scis., Morristown, N.J., 1983, Ann Leonard Gallery, Woodstock, 1983, NECCA Mus., Bklyn., Conn., 1985, Schiller-Wapner Galleries, N.Y.C., 1985, 87, Ann Norton Sculpture Galleries, West Palm Beach, Fla., 1987, David Gary Ltd, Millburn, N.J., 1988; exhibited in group shows at Phoenix Gallery, 1979, 83, Morris Mus. Art, 1979, 83, Invitational Woodstock Artists Assn., 1980, 84, Eilaine Benson Gallery, Bridgehampton, N.Y., 1980, Searles Art Ctr., Great Barrington, Mass., 1980, Nabisco Art Gallery, 1981, Summit Art Ctr., 1981, First Womens Bank, 1981, Fairleigh Dickinson U., Madison, N.J., 1983, NYU Grad. Sch. Bus., 1983, AT&T Gallery, Basking Ridge, N.J., 1984, Shering Plough Gallery, N.J., 1984, New Orleans Mus. Art, 1986, Gallery Contemporary Art at U. Colorado Springs, Colo., 1986, Schiller-Wapner Galleries, 1986, Lever House, N.Y.C., 1986, Aldrich Mus. Contemporary Art, Ridgefield, Conn., 1986, Okla. Art Ctr., Oklahoma City, 1987, "After Henry Moore", Emily Lowe Mus., Hofstra U., Hempstead, N.Y., 1988, group exhibition , Poland; represented in permanent collections New Orleans Mus. Art, Everson Mus., Syracuse, N.Y., Morris Mus. Sci. and Art, Okla. Art Ctr., Vassar Coll. Gallery, Poughkeepsie, N.Y., Millburn (N.J.) Pub. Library, Minn. Mus. Art, Mpls., Woodstock Hist. Soc., Fordham U., Lincoln Ctr., N.Y.C., Aldrich Mus. Contemporary Art, Warsaw Mus., Poland, various pvt. and corp. collections. Mem. Woodstock Artists Assn. Office: Rela Banks Studio 272 Yerry Hill Rd Woodstock NY 12498 Office Phone: 845-679-2798.

BANKS, RICHARD CHARLES, ornithologist; b. Steubenville, Ohio, Apr. 19, 1931; s. Clinton Seeger and Elizabeth Mae (Harter) B.; m. Gladys Sparks, July 14, 1967; children: Randall C., David R. BS, Ohio State U., 1953; MA, U. Calif., Berkeley, 1957, PhD, 1961. Curator birds and mammals San Diego Natural History Mus., San Diego, 1961-66; zoologist U.S. Fish and Wildlife Svc., Washington, 1966-93, Nat. Biol. Svc., Washington, 1993-97, U.S. Geol. Survey, Washington, 1997—2002. Rsch. assoc. Smithsonian Instn., Washington, 1966—90, 2003—; adj. prof. George Mason U., Fairfax, Va., 1985, 91. Editor: Ornithological Newsletter, 1976-92. 1st lt. U.S. Army, 1953-55, Korea. Fellow: Am. Ornithologists' Union (sec. 1968—72, v.p. 1987—88, pres.-elect 1992—94, pres. 1994—96); mem.: Washington Biologists Field Club (pres. 1990—93), Biol. Soc. Washington (pres. 1979—80, editor 2004—06), Cooper Ornithol. Soc. (hon.), Wilson Ornithol. Soc. (2d and 1st v.p. 1987—91, pres. 1991—93), Am. Assn. Zool. Nomenclature (pres. 2001—03). Home: 3201 Circle Hill Rd Alexandria VA 22305-1609 Office: US Geological Survey-MRC 111 Nat Mus Natural History PO Box 37012 Washington DC 20013-7012 Office Phone: 202-633-0783. Business E-Mail: banksr@si.edu.

BANKS, ROBERT KALEY, real estate and food products executive, lawyer; b. Nampa, Idaho, May 10, 1949; s. Charles C. and Betty F. (Piersal) B.; m. Teresa M. Banks, June 19, 1971; children: Ryan Scott, Andrea Marie. BS in Psychology, USAF Acad., 1971; MA in Psych., St. Mary's U., San Antonio, Tex., 1973, MA in Guidance and Counseling, 1975; MBA, JD cum laude, Ariz. State U., 1980. Bar: Ariz., 1980, Idaho, 1981. Commd. 2d lt. USAF, 1971, advanced through grades to maj., ret. lt. col., 2000; law clk. to presiding justice Idaho Supreme Ct., Boise, 1980-81; atty. Albertson's, Inc., Boise, 1981-84, dir. property mgmt., 1984-87, reg. real estate dir., 1987, v.p., real estate, group v.p., real estate, sr. v.p., real estate, 1987—2000, exec. v.p., development, 2000—05, devel. bus. cons., 2005—. Supt. Sunday sch. USAF Acad., 1970; advisor Explorer post Boy Scouts Am., Phoenix, 1978; founding dir. Eagle (Idaho) Ranch Homeowner's Assn., 1988-89; bd. dirs. United Way, investment coun. chmn., 2002-; mem. adv. bd. ADA County Hwy. Adv. Bd., 2002, Boise City Detox Ctr. Steering Com., 2005-. Mem. A&F Credit Union (vice chmn. 1983-91), Idaho Liaisons Officers (comdr. 1985-00). Avocations: running, basketball, fishing, backpacking. Office Phone: 208-841-2000. Personal E-mail: bobbanks@aol.com.

BANKS, RUSSELL, financial planner, consultant; b. NYC, Aug. 2, 1919; s. Thomas and Fay (Cowen) B.; m. Janice Reed, June 19, 1949; 1 son, Gordon L. BBA, CCNY, 1936-40; JD, N.Y. Law Sch., 1960. Bar: N.Y. 1961. Sr. acct. Selverne, Davis Co., NYC, 1940-45; pvt. practice NYC, 1945-61; exec. v.p. Met. Telecomm. Corp., Plainview, N.Y., 1961-62; pres., former CEO Grow Group, Inc. (formerly Grow Chem. Corp.), NYC, 1962-95, also dir., 1962-95; pres. Russell Banks & Co. Ltd., 1995—. Cons. Imperial Chem. Industries, PLC., 1995-96; adj. prof. bus. adminstrn. Baruch Coll., 1996-98. Editor: Managing the Small Company. Recipient award of achievement Sch. of Bus. Alumni Soc. of CCNY, 1977; Winthrop-Sears medal Chem. Industry Assn., 1980 Mem. Nat. Paint and Coatings Assn. (past pres.), Am. Mgmt. Assn. (gen. mgmt. planning coun. 1966-95, former trustee, exec. com.), Met. Club, Sky Club. Home: 60 Edgewater Dr Apt 14a Coral Gables FL 33134-6975

BANKS, TYRA (TYRA LYNNE BANKS), retired model, television personality; b. LA, Dec. 4, 1973; d. Don Banks and Carolyn London. CEO, TYInc.; founder Tyra Banks Scholarship, 1992, T-Zone summer camp for girls, 2000-; lectr. at UCLA, Johns Hopkins, Georgetown U., others. Appeared on covers of Elle, Essence, Sports Illustrated, GQ Mag., Cosmopolitan, Shape, Harper's Bazaar, Esquire, Arena, Vogue, Victoria's Secret Catalog (contract with mag.). Featured in comml. for Cover Girl, Coors, McDonald's, Nike, Pepsi, Nat. Milk Processor Promotion bd.; writer (book) Tyra's Beauty Inside and Out, 1997; Actor: (films) Higher Learning, 1995, A Woman Like That, 1997, Love Stinks, 1999, Love & Basketball, 2000, Coyote Ugly, 2000, Halloween: Resurrection, 2002, (voice) Eight Crazy Nights, 2002, Larceny, 2004; (TV films) Inferno, 1992, The Apartment Complex, 1999, Life-Size, 2000; (TV series) Fresh Prince of Bel-Air, 1993-94; Creator, writer, prodr., host, judge (TV series) America's Next Top Model, 2003-, host, exec. prodr. The Tyra Banks Show, 2005-; (guest appearances) (TV series) include New York Undercover, 1997, The Oprah Winfrey Show (several appearances), Just Shoot Me, 1999, Mad TV, 2000, 2004, Felicity, 2000, Who Wants to Be a Millionaire, 2000, Soul Food, 2001, American Dreams, 2004 and several others. Named one of 50 Most Beautiful People in the World, People, 1994, 1996, The World's Most Influential People, Time Mag., 2006, 2007; recipient Choice TV: Personality, Teen Choice Awards, 2007. Achievements include being the first African American Woman on the cover of Sports Illustrated Swimsuit Issue. Office: Handprint Entertainment c/o Benny Medina 1100 Glendon Ave Ste 1000 Los Angeles CA 90024*

BANKS, VIRGINIA ANNE (GINGER), association administrator; b. Dallas, Mar. 19, 1949; d. James Houston and Mary Virginia (Bussey) B. B of Journalism, U. Tex., 1971. Traveling cons. Alpha Omicron Pi Fraternity, Indpls., 1971-73, adminstrv. asst. Nashville, 1973-74; pub. info. officer Tex. Dept. of Community Affairs, Austin, 1974-76; asst. dir. of comm. State Bar of Tex., Austin, 1976-78, assoc. editor Tex. Bar Jour., 1977-79, mng. editor Tex. Bar Jour, 1979-91, comm. dir., 1991-99, dir. pub. svcs. divsn., 1992-99, dir. info. tech. divsn., 1999-2000, dir. mem. svcs. divsn., 2000-01; spkr. Campuspeak, Inc., 2003—05; assoc. Law Practice Mgmt. Consulting, 2006—. Internat. rush chmn. Alpha Omicron Pi, Nashville, 1976-77, internat. v.p. ops., 1977-81, internat. pres., 1981-85, v.p. found., 1985-90, fraternity devel. com., 1985-89, pres. Pi Kappa Corp., 1991-95, mem. Austin Alumnae chpt., 1973—, alumnae adv. com. network specialist, 1996-98, del. nat. panhellenic Conf., 1987-93, chmn. Perry award com., 1992-98, rituals, traditions and jewelry com., 1998—, chair rituals, traditions and jewelry com., 1998—; com. to devel. relationship statement, Nat. Panhellenic Conf., 1983, del., 1987-93, area advisor coll. Panhellenics com., 1985-88, chmn. liaison com., 1987-88, Project Future collegiate concerns com., 1987-89, field cons. seminar com., 1987, chmn., 1988, resolutions com., 1988, chmn. pub. rels. com., 1991-93, ednl. devel. com., 1991-93; spkr. in field. Editor Alpha Omicron Pi Centennial History Book, 1995-97; contbr. articles to mags. Bd. dirs. Lone Star Girl Scout Coun., Austin, 1973-75, Nat. Interfraternity Found., 1986-89, M.L. Roller scholarship com., 1988-89, nominations com., 1988-89; mem. Humane Soc. Austin, 1981—; chmn. mag. adv. com. Ex-Students Assn., U. Tex., Austin, 1989-95; active Tarrytown United Meth. Ch. Recipient presdl. citation State Bar of Tex., 1981, 90, 94, presdl. citation Alpha Omicron Pi, 1988, 97. Mem. Am. Soc. Assn. Execs., Assn. Fraternity Advisors, Internat. Assn. Bus. Communicators, Nat. Assn. Bar Execs. (pub. svcs. activities com. 1995-98, vice-chair pub. svc. activities com. 1996-97, chair pub. svcs. activities com. 1997-98, chair awards com. 1995-96, pub. rels. and comms. sect. 1991—, sect.'s comms. audit com. 1994-95, chair sect.'s comms. audit com. 1995-98, sect.'s coun., 1997-2000, sect.'s program com. 1995-98, co-chair sect.'s program com. 1996-98, sect.'s sec. 1998-2000, chair leadership award com. 2002, recipient, Wally Richter Leadership award, 2001), Women in Comms., PEO Sisterhood (chpt. R recording sec. 2002-04, treas. 2004-06), Alpha Omicron Pi (Austin alumnae chpt., Rose award 1991, Adele K. Hinton award 1997). Avocations: gardening, sailing, cooking. Home: 3108 W Terrace Dr Austin TX 78757-4332

BANKS, WEBB FOLLIN, mayor; b. Carnesville, Ga., July 8, 1931; s. John Patterson and Sarah Azille Banks; m. Steva Banks, Nov. 18, 1988; 6 children. BS, Memphis State U., 1954. Commd. 2d lt. USAF, 1955, advanced through grades to lt. col.; chief logistics spl. investigation Washington; chief negotiator wartime agreements; served in Vietnam; ret. USAF, 1977; mayor City of Brownsville, Tenn., 1994—. Pres. Banks R.R. Salvage, Inc., 1977. Decorated Bronze Star, Legion of Merit, Air Commendation medal; named Outstanding Supply Office of Yr., Air Force. Home: 810 Brooks Cove Brownsville TN 38012 Office: City of Brownsville 111 N Washington Ave Brownsville TN 38012

BANKSTON, ARCHIE MOORE, lawyer; b. Memphis, Oct. 12, 1937; s. Archie M. and Elsie Bernice (Shaw) B.; m. Emma Ann Dejan, Apr. 16, 1966; children— Louis, Alice. BA, Fisk U., 1959; LLB, Washington U., St. Louis, 1962, MBA, 1964. Bar: Mo. 1963, N.Y. 1966. Asst. divsn. counsel Gen. Foods Corp., White Plains, NY, 1964-67, product mgr. Maxwell House divsn., 1967-69; asst. sec. and corp. counsel PepsiCo, Inc., Purchase, NY, 1969-72; divsn. counsel Xerox Corp., Stamford, Conn., 1973; sec. and asst. gen. counsel Consol. Edison Co. of N.Y. Inc., NYC, 1974-89, sec., assoc. gen. counsel, 1989—2002. Sec. Consolidated Edison, Inc., NYC, 1998—2002; exec.-in-residence Coll. New Rochelle, NY, 2002—. Mem. 100 Black Men, Inc., NYC; former trustee Beth Israel Med. Ctr.; trustee Hoff-Barthelson Music Sch., Scarsdale, NY; past mem. Westchester County African Am. Adv. Bd.; former trustee Coll. New Rochelle; former bd. dirs. Urban League of Westchester County, Associated Black Charities, Mental Health Assn. Westchester County. Recipient Black Achievers in Industry award, Harlem br. YMCA, 1971, Merit award, Black Exec. Exch. Program Nat. Urban League, 1974, Disting. Svc. Commendation awards, Mental Health Assn., 1987, 1992, Jerome H. Holland Power of Humanity Corp. award, Am. Red Cross, 2001. Mem.: ABA, Am. Soc. Corp. Secs. (mem. audit, edn. and securities industry com., chmn. budget com. and membership com., chmn. 50th anniversary nat. conf. com., bd. dirs., Disting. Svc. award 2000), N.Y. State Bar Assn., Westchester Clubmen (pres.), Alpha Phi Alpha, Sigma Pi Phi, Phi Delta Phi. Office: Consol Edison Co NY Inc 4 Irving Pl New York NY 10003-3502 also: The College of New Rochelle 29 Castle Place New Rochelle NY 10805 E-mail: bankstona@coned.com.

BANKSTON, ELAINE, artist; b. Mar. 8, 1944; Artist-in-residence Art Works, Richmond, Va., 1994—. Exhibited in group shows at Atlanta Hartsfield Airport, Richmond Internat. Airport, Greenbriar Mall, Atlanta, Va. Power, The James Ctr., Crestar, Signet Banks, The Gellman Rm., The Gallery Cafe; rep. by: Uptown Gallery, Lodans Gallery, Richmond, Va., Art Svcs. Network, Richmond, Side Porch Gallery, Fairfax, Va., Poppy Gallery, Columbia, Mo., Markers Gallery, Effingham, Ill., Galeria San Jeronimo, San Juan, P.R., Four Corner of Midlothian, Air, Land and Sea, Alexandria; represented in permanent collections of Pres. Jimmy Carter, Mayor Andrew Young, So. Mus. Flying, Birmingham, Atlanta Hist. Soc. and Mus., Hapeville Hist. Soc. and Mus., U. Aviation Assn., FAA, Glenn Messer, Paul Garber. Recipient 1st place awards: Richmond Parks & Recreations at the Carillon, Chesterfield Towne Ctr., Ea. Airlines Art Show, Gutsy award Chesterfield Towne Ctr., Award of Merit, S.W. Artist League. Mem. S.W. Artist League, Met. Artist Assn., Bon Air Artist Assn. (pres. 1996-98). Personal E-mail: elanesart@msn.com.

BANNARD, WALTER DARBY, artist, art critic; b. New Haven, Sept. 23, 1934; s. Homes and Janet (Darby) B. BA, Princeton U., 1956. Chmn. dept. art and art history U. Miami, Fla., 1989-97. Lectr. in field, 1969—; vis. prof. Princeton (N.J.) U., 1974, also other univs.; mem. grad. faculty Sch. Visual Arts, N.Y.C., 1984-89; curator Hans Hoffman Hirshorn Mus., 1976; mem. internat. exhbn. com., 1976-78; co-chmn. internat. panel for visual arts Nat. Endowment for Arts, 1979-81; founder, editor newcrit.org, 2001—. Contbr. articles and revs. on modern painting to profl. jours.; contbg. editor: Artforum, 1973-74; 75; one-man shows internat. galleries and mus. include retrospective Balt. Mus. Art, 1973, retrospective U. Tampa, 1997, retrospective Lowe Mus., 1999, Retrospective Rauschenberg Gallery, Edison Coll., 2006; numerous internat. group shows; represented in permanent collections at Mus. Modern Art, N.Y.C., Whitney Mus. Am. Art, Met. Mus. Art, N.Y.C., Guggenheim Mus., N.Y.C., others; juror numerous competitions, 1969—; sole juror Australian Bi-Centenary Art Competition, 1988. Recipient Nat. Found. Arts award, 1968-69; Francis J. Greenburger Found. award, 1986; John Simon Guggenheim Meml. Found. fellow, 1968; Richard A. Florsheim Art Fund grantee, 1991. Office: 1540 Levante Ave Miami FL 33124 Home Phone: 305-661-5976; Office Phone: 305-284-2493. Personal E-mail: wbannard@aol.com.

BANNEN, JOHN THOMAS, lawyer; s. James J. and Ruth J. Bannen; m. Carol A. Swanson, Aug. 16, 1975; children: Ryan M., Kelly A., Erin C. BA summa cum laude, Coll. St. Thomas, 1973; JD, Marquette U., 1976; LLM in Taxation, DePaul U., 1989; BA in Spanish, U. Wis., 2003. Bar: Wis. 1976, U.S. Dist. Ct. (ea. and we. dists.) Wis. 1976, U.S. Tax Ct. 1979, U.S. Claims Ct. 1983, U.S. Supreme Ct. 1984. Shareholder Charne, Clancy & Taitelman, S.C., Milw., 1976-91; ptnr. Quarles & Brady, Milw., 1991—. Bd. dirs. Guardianship Svcs. Indigents, Milw., 1983—87; mem. adv. bd. Sch. Sisters Notre Dame, 1993—98, pres., 1995—98; mem. coun. Christ the King Parish, Wauwatosa, Wis., 1989—93, trustee, 1996—98. Fellow: Am. Coll. Trust and Estate Counsel (state law coord. Wis. 1990—95, chmn. com. employee benefits 2001—05, state chair Wis. 2007—); mem.: ABA, Wis. Bar Assn. (bd. dirs. probate sect.), Assn. Advanced Life Underwriters (assoc.). Avocations: reading, gardening, Spanish language, cooking. Office: Quarles and Brady LLP Ste 2040 411 E Wisconsin Ave Milwaukee WI 53202-4497 Office Phone: 414-277-5859. E-mail: jtb@quarles.com.

BANNICK, JANICE CAROL, automotive dealerships executive; b. Clinton, Iowa, Oct. 12, 1938; d. Claus John and Irma Jeanne (Switzer) Greve; m. Robert T. Gallagher, May 21, 1958 (div. Apr. 1967); children: Angela Jeanne, Carol Ellen; m. Mearl G. Bannick, June 24, 1967 (dec. Aug. 1991). Student, Old Dominion Coll., Norfolk, Va., 1956—58, U. Wis., Milw., 1980—83, U. Tex., Arlington, 1983—86, Bradley U., 1992—94. Contr. Kimberly Chrysler-Plymouth, Inc., Davenport, Iowa, 1974-79; cons. Davenport and Milw., 1979-80; contr. Stark Oldsmobile, Inc., Menomonee Falls, Wis., 1980-83; bus. mgr., field rep. Motors Holding divsn. Gen. Motors Corp., Detroit, 1986-89; contr., CFO S&K Chevrolet Pontiac and Oldsmobile, Peoria, Ill., 1989-96; automotive cons. Peoria and Springfield, Ill., 1996-97; contr., dealer acctg. Gen. Acceptance Corp., Bloomington, Ind., 1997-98; CFO Anthony Pontiac, Gurnee, Ill., 1998-2000, Lou Bachrodt Automall & Bachrodt Pontiac, Rockford, Ill., 2000-01; team sales rep. Internat. Teamworks Inc., Vacaville, Calif., 2001—; contr. Magouirk Chevrolet-Olds, Inc., Dodge City, Kans., 2001—02; cons. MSXI, Ford Motor Co. Dealer Devel., Detroit, 2003—05; contr. US Auto Finance & Susuk, Lawrenceville, Ga., 2005—. Bd. dirs., treas. St. Marks Luth. Ch., Chillicothe, Ill., 1994-96, Peoria Art Gild, 1995-96. Republican. Avocations: watercolor painting, reading, running, walking, antique refinishing, gourmet cooking, golf. Home: 307 Tree Creek Pwy Lawrenceville GA 30043-8454 Office Phone: 770-962-9121 ext. 113. Personal E-mail: bannick@bellsouth.net.

BANNICK, MATTHEW, Internet company executive; BA with hons. in Econs. and Internat. Studies, U. Washington, 1991; MBA, Harvard U., 1993. US diplomat, Germany; cons. McKinsey and Co., Europe, 1992, McKinsey and Co., US, 1993—95; with Navigation Techs., 1995—99, pres. N.Am. Divsn., 1997—99; from v.p. product and cmty. to sr. v.p. global online payments eBay Inc., San Jose, Calif., 1999—2003, sr. v.p. global online payments, 2003—. Mem.: Phi Beta Kappa. Office: eBay Inc 2145 Hamilton Ave San Jose CA 95125-5905

BANNIGAN, EUGENE F., lawyer; b. Bklyn., July 1, 1941; BA, Alfred U., 1964; JD cum laude, Bklyn. Law Sch., 1969. Bar: N.Y. 1969. Asst. U.S. atty. S Dist. N.Y., 1972-76, chief narcotics unit, 1975-76; pntr. Lord, Day & Lord, Barrett Smith, NYC; ptnr. Morgan Lewis & Bockius LLP, NYC, mem. mgmt. com. & leader litig. practice group-N.Y. Office. Mem. ABA, Fed. Bar Coun., Assn. Bar City N.Y. Office: Morgan Lewis & Bockius LLP 101 Park Ave New York NY 10178 Office Phone: 212-309-6815. Office Fax: 212-309-3001. Business E-Mail: ebannigan@morganlewis.com.

BANNING, DONNA ROSE, art educator; b. Belle Fourche, SD, July 2, 1934; d. Anzley Meltiah and Rose Helen (Kapsa) Walker; m. Robert Orval Banning (dec.); children: Bruce, Connie, Bernie, Callie. AA, Fullerton Coll., Calif., 1967; BA, Calif. State U., Fullerton, 1969; MA, Calif. State U., Long Beach, 1976. Cert. tchr. Calif., tchr. art K-12 Calif., state adminstr. K-12 Calif. Instr. visual arts El Modena H.S., Orange, Calif., 1970—2003; dist. dept. chair fine arts Orange (Calif.) Unified Sch. Dist., 1974—78, 1982—92; crafts instr. Rancho Santiago Coll., Santa Ana, Calif., 1971—75, ceramics instr., 1974—92; visual arts instr. Calif. State U., Long Beach, 1977—78, 2004; ret., 2003. Instr. art edn. Chapman Coll., Orange; cons. Calif. sch. dists., Orange County, 1991—; mem. Calif. State Framework and Criteria Com., 1994—2006, Legis. Action Com. Arts Edn., 1991—2002, Calif. Arts Assessment Networkcc, 1991—; lectr. art edn. Calif. State U., Long Beach, 2004—; presenter in field. Contbr. Named Tchr. of Yr., Calif. Gifted and Talented Assn., 1998, Disneyland Creativity Tchr. of Yr., Disneyland, 1998. Mem.: Orange County Arts Adminstrs. (Secondary Arts Tchr. of Yr. 2002), So. Calif. Ceramic Design Assn., Calif. Art Edn. Assn. (past pres., Tchr. of Yr. 2000), Nat. Art Edn. Assn. (v.p. pacific region 2004—06, Pacific Region Tchr. of Yr. 2001), Calif. Alliance Arts Edn. Avocations: painting, pottery. Home: 2391 N Waterberry St Orange CA 92865-2851 Home Phone: 714-637-3244; Office Phone: 714-293-4611.

BANNISTER, MICHAEL E., automotive executive; BBA, Memphis State Univ. Held a number of br. and regional mgmt. oper. positions Ford Credit North Am. Region, 1973; mgr. North Atlantic Region Ford Motor Credit Co., Dearborn, Mich., 1991, mgr. Atlantic Region, 1991—93, v.p. mktg., 1993—95; exec. dir. European sales ops. Ford Motor Credit Co. Europe, 1995—97; chmn. Ford Fin. Europe, 1997—2003; pres., COO Ford Motor Credit Co., Dearborn, Mich., 2003—04; group v.p. Ford Motor Co., Dearborn, Mich., 2004—; chmn., CEO Ford Motor Credit Co., Dearborn, Mich., 2004—. Office: Ford Motor Credit Co One American Rd Mail Drop 7440 Dearborn MI 48126-2701*

BANNISTER, ROBERT CORWIN, JR., historian, educator; b. Bklyn., June 4, 1935; s. Robert C. and Ruth (Allen) B.; m. Joan Turner, June 8, 1958; children: Robert Stanley, Emily E., Paul Andrew, James Peter. BA, Yale U., 1955, Oxford U., Eng., 1957, MA, 1961; PhD, Yale U., 1961. Instr. history Yale U., New Haven, 1960-62; asst. to full prof. Swarthmore Coll., Pa., 1962-98, ret., 1998. Bicentennial prof. U. Helsinki, 1977-78; Fulbright prof. U. Rome, 1985, U. Leiden, Netherlands, 1992; mem. advanced placement program Ednl. Testing Service, Princeton, N.J., 1963-79; vis. prof. U. Queensland, Australia, 1988. Author: Ray Stannard Baker, 1966, Social Darwinism: Science and Myth, 1978, Sociology and Scientism, 1987, Jessie Bernard: The Making of a Feminist, 1991; editor: American Values in Transition, 1972, On Liberty, Society and Politics: The Essential Essays of William Graham Sumner, 1992. Mem. Am. Studies Assn., Orgn. Am. Historians Democrat. E-mail: rbannis1@swarthmore.edu.

BANNON, ANTHONY LEO, museum director; b. Hanover, NH, Dec. 6, 1942; s. Robert E. and Frances Ann (Cacioppo) B.; children: Nicholas, Brendan. BS, St. Bonaventure U., NY, 1964; MA, SUNY, Buffalo, 1974, PhD, 1994. Tchr. sci. and English Father Baker H.S., Lackawanna, NY, 1964-66; critic Buffalo News, 1966-85; dir. Burchfield-Penney Art Ctr., asst. v.p. cultural affairs SUNY Coll., Buffalo, 1985-96; dir. George Eastman House Internat. Mus. Photography and Film, Rochester, NY, 1996—. Chmn. visual arts program panel NY State Coun. on Arts, NYC, 1986—88; co-chmn. arts programming com. World Univ. Games, Buffalo, 1991—93; co-chmn. adv. coun. ArtsAction, NY, 1999—2002; vice chmn. Empire State Craft Alliance, Saratoga Springs, NY, 1988—93; chmn. adv. bd. Quick Fine Arts Ctr. St. Bonaventure U., 1996—2002. Author: The Photo-Pictorialists of Buffalo, 1981, The Taking of Niagara, 1983, Arcadia Revisited, 1989, Painterly Photographs: Contemporary Handworked Images, 1980, Grace Woodworth: Photographer Outside the Common Lines, 1984, ArtPark, 1989, Ansel Adams, 2003, Steve McCurry, 2005; organized major exhibits for Albright-Knox Art Gallery, Buscaglia-Castellani Art Gallery, Niagara U., NY, State Mus. of NY, Albany, Washington D.C. Project for the Arts; Burchfield-Penney Art Ctr. and Rockwell Hall Performing Arts Ctr., SUNY Coll., Buffalo, David Anderson Gallery, others. Mem. vestry Ch. Good Shepherd, Buffalo, 1986—89; bd. dirs. Greater Rochester Visitors Assn., 1996—97, Rochester Arts and Cultural Coun., 1998—2003, High Falls Film Festival, 2004—; trustee NY State Alliance of Arts Orgns., 1998—2002, bd. sec., 1999—2001; bd. dirs. Rochester Sch. for the Deaf, 1998—, NY State Coun. on Humanities, 1999—2006; mem. adv. coun. to the sec. Smithsonian Instn., 2001—; mem. adv. coun. Chautauqua Art Ctr., 1998—; bd. dirs. Santa Fe Ctr.

Photography, 2002—06. Recipient Excellence in Writing about Deafness award Gallaudet Coll., 1985, Merit award Am. Photog. Hist. Soc., 1982; Profl. Study Leave grantee NY State/United Univ. Professions, 1993, Outstanding Arts Adminstr. award The Buffalo Partnership, 1995, Arts award, St. Bonaventure U., 2002, Golden Career award Palm Beach Photographic Ctr., 2007. Mem. Am. Assn. Mus., Mus. Assn. NY State (counselor 1994-2003), Gallery Assn. NY State (trustee 1997-2000), Buffalo State Coll. Found. (trustee 1985-91), Soc. Photog. Edn. Assn. Art Mus. Dirs. Office: George Eastman House 900 East Ave Rochester NY 14607-2298 Business E-Mail: tbannon@geh.org. E-mail: tbannon@frontiernet.net.

BANNON, JOHN A., lawyer; BA, U. Va., 1979; MBA, Marymount U., 1988; JD with honors, U. Chgo., 1991. Bar: Ill. 1991, US Dist. Ct. (no. dist. Ill.) 1991. Ptnr. Schiff Hardin, Chgo. Capt. USAF. Office: Schiff Hardin LLP 6600 Sears Tower Chicago IL 60606-6473 Office Phone: 312-258-5597. Office Fax: 312-258-5600. E-mail: jbannon@schiffhardin.com.*

BANOFF, SHELDON IRWIN, lawyer; b. Chgo., July 10, 1949; BSBA in Acctg., U. Ill., 1971; JD, U. Chgo., 1974. Bar: Ill. 1974, U.S. Tax Ct. 1974. Ptnr. Katten Muchin Rosenman LLP, Chgo., 1974—. Chmn. tax conf. planning com. U. Chgo. Law Sch., 1993-94. Co-editor Jour. of Taxation, 1984—; contbr. articles to profl. jours. Mem. ABA, Chgo. Bar Assn. (fed. taxation com., mem. exec. coun. 1980—, chmn. large law firm com., 1999-2000), Am. Coll. Tax Counsel. Office: Katten Muchin Rosenman LLP 525 W Monroe St Chicago IL 60661-3693 Office Phone: 312-902-5200. Business E-Mail: sheldon.banoff@kattenlaw.com.

BANOUN, RAYMOND, lawyer; b. June 1, 1945; BA, CCNY, 1965; JD with honors, George Washington U., 1968. Bar: D.C. 1968, U.S. Supreme Ct. 1980. Law clk. to Hon. Harold H. Green Superior Ct. Washington, 1968-70; asst. atty. gen. Washington, 1970-84; dep. chief and acting chief fraud divsn., 1981-83; sr. litigation counsel, 1983-84; ptnr. Arent, Fox, Kintner, Plotkin & Kahn, Washington, 1984-91; ptnr. bus. fraud practice Cadwalader, Wickersham & Taft, Washington, 1991—, mng. ptnr. Washington office, lead bus. fraud group. Spl. asst. U.S. atty. ctrl. dist. Calif., 1977-80. Contbr. articles to profl. jours. Fellow Am. Coll. Trial Attys.; mem. ABA (vice chmn. white collar crime com. criminal justice sect. 1985-86, chmn. 1986-88, coun. criminal justice 1988-91), Internat. Bar Assn. (vice-chmn. bus. crimes com. sect. bus. law 1988-92, chmn. 1992—). Office: Cadwalader Wickersham & Taft LLP Suite 1100 1201 F St NW Washington DC 20004-1218 Office Phone: 202-862-2426. Office Fax: 202-862-2271. Business E-Mail: ray.banoun@cwt.com.

BANSAK, STEPHEN A., JR., investment banker, financial consultant; b. Bridgeport, Conn., Sept. 19, 1939; s. Stephen A. and Genevieve Bansak; m. Susan Jean Dizon, July 20, 1984; children: Cynthia A., Thomas S., Stephen A. III, Kirk C. BS, Yale U., 1961; MBA, U. Pa., 1968. With Kidder, Peabody & Co., Inc., NYC, 1968-89, v.p., 1971-75, co-mgr. dept. corpl fin., 1975-84; vice chmn. Kidder, Peabody Internat., NYC, 1984—. Bd. dirs. Kidder Peabody P.R., KP Realty Advisers; sr. cons. Concord Internat. Ptnrs., 1990—, bentley Assocs., 1990-92; vice chmn. Myers, Craig, Vallone, Francois, Inc., 1992-93; sr. advisor Universal Tech. inst., 1995-97, Motay Electronics, Inc., 1993-97, Buenavenjura Filamor Echuas (Manila), 1991-94; vis. lectr. Wharton Grad. Sch., U. Pa., 1989; past bd. dirs. Filbrin, Inc., Lighthouse Ptnrs.; bd. dirs. Troy Bioscis., Inc.; bd. dirs., vice chmn. Computerized Med. Sys., Inc.; mem. adv. bd. Global Health Care Ptnrs. (DLJ Mcht. Banking 1998-2001); past adv. com. Manschot Opportunity Fund. Past trustee, v.p. Rumson (N.J.) Country Day Sch. Lt. USN, 1962-66, Vietnam. Mem. Philippine-Am. C. of C. (bd. dirs.), U.S.-Asia inst. (past bd. dirs.), India House (past pres. Broad St. Club), Yale Club N.Y.C., Troon Golf and Country Club, Securities Industry Assn. (chmn. corp. fin. com., rule 415 com.), Am. Stock Exch. (ofcl. 1988-91). Home Phone: 480-585-3202; Office Phone: 480-585-6670. Personal E-mail: pennhavena@aol.com.

BANSAL, ARVIND KUMAR, computer scientist, educator; arrived in U.S., 1984; m. Rekha Gupta. B Tech Elec. Engring., Indian Inst. Tech., Kanpur, 1979, M Tech Computer Sci., 1983; PhD Computer Sci., Case We. Res. U., Cleve., 1988. Asst. exec. engr. Indian Tel. Industries, Allahabad, UP, India, 1979—81; sys. analyst Tata Engring. and Locomotive Co., Pune, Maharashtra, India, 1983—84; grad. rsch. asst. Case We. Res. U., Cleve., 1984—88; asst. prof. Kent State U., Ohio, 1988—93, assoc. prof., 1993—2005, prof., 2005—. Summer rsch. faculty Argonne Nat. Lab., Ill., 1994; vis. scientist European Molecular Biology Lab., Heidelberg, Germany, 1995; rsch. fellow U. Melbourne, Australia, 1996. Contbr. articles to profl. jours. Mem.: AAAS, IEEE (Appreciation award 2001), Internat. Soc. Optical Engring., Assn. Computing Machinery, N.Y. Acad. Sci. Office: Kent State U Kent OH Office Phone: 330-672-9035. Office Fax: 330-672-7824. Business E-Mail: arvind@cs.kent.edu.

BANSE, AMY L., communications executive, lawyer; married; 4 children. BA, Harvard U., Cambridge, Mass., 1982; JD, Temple U., Phila., 1987. Atty. for acquisitions Comcast Corp., Phila., 1991—97, v.p., head of programming investment dept., 1997—2003, exec. v.p. programming investments div., 2003—05, sr. v.p., pres. Comcast Interactive Media, 2005—. Trustee Morris Arboretum, Children's Scholarship Fund Phila. Mem.: Women in Cable & Telecom. (sec. bd. trustees). Office: Comcast 1500 Market St Philadelphia PA 19102*

BANTA, JAMES ELMER, epidemiologist, educator, dean; b. Tucumcari, N.Mex., July 1, 1927; s. James Elmer and Edna Mae (Murnahan) B. MD, Marquette U., 1950; M.P.H., Johns Hopkins U., 1954; diploma, U.S. Naval Med. Sch., 1952. Med. officer USN, 1950-60; capt. med. officer USPHS, 1960-69; dir. med. program Peace Corps, 1963-65; dir. Office Internat. Health, HEW, 1967-68; med. officer WHO, 1968-70; prof. public health U. Hawaii, 1970-73; dep. dir. Office Health, AID, State Dept., Washington, 1973-75; dean, prof. Sch. Public Health and Tropical Medicine, Tulane U., New Orleans, 1975-87; prof. Sch. Pub. Health U. Hawaii, Honolulu, 1987-88; clin. prof. dept. community and family medicine Georgetown U., Washington, 1990-99. Adj. prof. sch. pub. health and health scis. George Washington U., Washington, 1992—. Co-author: How to Travel the World and Stay Healthy, 1969, Year-round Travelers' Health Guide, 1978; Contbr. articles on epidemiology, microbiology and health to profl. jours. Served with USN, 1944-46. Recipient Outstanding Service award Georgetown U., 1965 Fellow AAAS, Am. Coll. Preventive Medicine, Am. Public Health Assn., Am. Heart Assn., Am. Coll. Epidemiology, Coll. Phys. Phila.; mem. ACLU, Common Cause, Environ. Action, Assn. Schs. Public Health (pres. 1979-81), Sigma Xi, Phi Sigma, Delta Omega. Office: George Washington U Med Ctr 2175 K St NW Washington DC 20037-1887 Personal E-mail: jebanta@erols.com.

BANTEL, LINDA MAE, former museum curator, consultant; b. King City, Calif., May 30, 1943; m. David Hollenberg, June 15, 1980; 1 child, Matthew Bantel Hollenberg. MA, NYU, 1973. Rsch. cons. NY Hist. Soc., NYC, 1975—76; guest co-curator Art Mus. of South Tex., Corpus Christi, 1977—79; rsch. assoc. Met. Mus. Art, NYC, 1978—80; curator, dir. Mus. Pa. Acad. Fine Arts, Phila., 1980—95. Co-author (with James Thomas Flexner): The Face of Liberty: Founders of the U.S., 1975; author (with Marcus Burke): Spain and New Spain: Mexican Colonial Arts in Their European Context, 1979; author: The Alice M. Kaplan Collection, 1980, William Rush, American Sculptor, 1982; contbr. American Paintings in the Metropolitan Museum of Art Vol. II: A Catalogue of Works by Artists Born Between 1816-1845, 1985, Raphaelle Peale Still Lifes, 1988, contbr. (with others) Searching Out the Best, 1988, contbr. to Antiques mag., 1989; editor (with Jacolyn A. Mott): American Sculpture in the Museum of American Art of the Pennsylvia Academy of the Fine Arts, 1997. Mem.: Am. Assn. Mus., Coll. Art Assn. Home: 703 W Phil Ellena St Philadelphia PA 19119-3513 Personal E-mail: lindabantel@verizon.net.

BANTHIN, JESSICA S., economist, researcher; children: Emma P. Stevenson, Henry G. Stevenson. AB, Harvard U., Cambridge, 1981; PhD in Econs., U. Md., College Park, 1991. Economist Agy. Healthcare Rsch. & Quality, Rockville, Md., 1991—2003, dir. modeling & simulation rsch., 2003—. Office: Agy Healthcare Rsch Quality 540 Gaither Rd Rockville MD 20850

BANTIVOGLIO, BARBARA, broadcast executive; b. Camden, NJ, May 23, 1949; BA in Polit. Sci., Manhattanvile Coll., 1971; MA in Urban Planning, Hunter Coll., 1974. Dir. downtown svcs. and improvements City of Boston, 1973-76; dir. program planning City of New Rochelle, NY, 1976-78; project mgr. NYC Office of Process & Mgmt. Ctrl., 1978-79; dep. dir. NYC Welfare Mgmt. System, 1973-83; dir. program devel. NYC Bus. Devel., 1983-88; v.p. Mallory Factor Inc., NYC, 1988-89; dir. nat. program mktg. Sta. WQED, NYC, 1989-91; dir. mktg. Sta. WNET, NYC, 1991-92; v.p. mktg. & comm. Liberty Sci. Ctr., Liberty State Park, NJ; with Whitney Mus. Am. Art; v.p. instl. advancement Ednl. Broadcasting Corp., NYC, 2007—. Recipient Silver Anvil award, Pub. Rels. Soc. Am., Award for Pub. Rels. & Mktg., Am. Assn. Museums, 2001, 2003, Roper Starch award, 2000—01, EFFIE award, Am. Mktg. Assn., 2002—03. Mem. Leadership N.Y., Pub. Rels. Soc. Am. (Silver Anvil award 1993, Bronze Anvil award 1996), Am. Assn. Mus. (1st pl. Muse award for Advt. 1993, 2d pl. 1996, Mktg. Instl. Excellence award 1996), Nat. Dance Inst. (bd. dirs., devel. com.). Office: Ednl Broadcasting Corp 450 W 33rd St New York NY 10001*

BANTOM, MICHAEL ALLEN, sports association executive; b. Phila., Dec. 3, 1951; children: Robbie, Misha, Brenda, Alan. BS in Mktg., St. Joseph's U. Draft pick Phoenix Suns, 1973, basketball player, 1973—75, Seattle Supersonics, 1975—77, NY Nets, 1977, Ind. Pacers, 1977—81, Phila. 76ers, 1981—82, Italian Profl. League, 1982—89; licensing mgr. NBA Internat., 1989—92, dir. mktg. progs., 1992; v.p. events & attractions dept. NBA, 1997, sr. v.p. player devel., 1999—. Mem. US Olympic Basketball team, 1972. Named to All-Rookie Team, NBA, 1974. Achievements include winning a silver medal at the 1972 Olympics. Office: NBA Olympic Tower 645 5th Ave Fl 10 New York NY 10022-5986*

BANTON, JULIAN WATTS, banker; b. Gladstone, Va., Aug. 8, 1940; s. John Dorman and Elizabeth (Watts) B.; m. Donna Lea Brown, July 9, 1960; children— Courtney Blair, Stephanie Paige BS, Va. Commonwealth U., 1965; MBA, U. Richmond, 1968; grad. Advanced Mgmt. Program, Harvard U., 1977. Exec. v.p. Bank of Va., Richmond, 1965-77; pres. Bank of Va. Internat., Richmond, 1977-82; exec. v.p. SouthTrust Bank Ala., Birmingham, 1982—, pres., 1986—. Contbr. articles to profl. jours. Bd. dirs., v.p. Sci. Mus. Va.; chmn. ann. fund raiser Ala. Symphony, Birmingham; bd. dirs. Ala. Symphony, Jr. Achievement, Birmingham, Campfire, Grad. Sch. Banking, Washington, Operation New Birmingham; co-chmn. 1986 campaign United Way Central Ala., ann. fund drive; mem. U. Ala. Birmingham Leadership Council. Served with U.S. Army, 1958-61. Mem. Robert Morris Assocs. (com. chmn. 1972-82), Bank Assn. for Fgn. Trade (committeeman 1978), Am. Arbitrators Assn. Clubs: Harvard (N.Y.C.). Lodges: Rotary. Methodist. Office: SouthTrust Bank Ala NA PO Box 2554 420 20th St N Birmingham AL 35203-5200

BANTON, KATHLEEN ARIATTI, artist, educator; b. New Orleans, Dec. 19, 1947; d. Isidore Peter and Evelyn Ruth (Lindenlaub) Ariatti; m. Felix Longsdale Banton, May 3, 1985; children: Andrew, Christopher. BFA, Auburn U., 1969; MFA, Boston U., 1975. Cert. tchr. art, Mass. Graphic artist Ted Drell Art and Design, New Orleans, 1969, Design Ctr., Boston, 1970, T.R. Prodns. Film Co., Boston, 1971; tchr. art Triton Regional H.S., Byfield, Mass., 1971-72; tchr. art, art curriculum coord. Scituate (Mass.) Pub. Schs., 1972-83; art dir., graphic artist Jambalaya Studios, Scituate, 1977-79; artist Wyndy Morehead Fine Arts, New Orleans, 1990-91; chmn. art dept. Metairie Park Country Day Sch., Metairie, La., 1984—98; dir. Colony at Country Day, Metairie, 1991—; artist Sylvia Schmidt Gallery, New Orleans, 1996—. Chmn. fine arts divsn. Ind. Schs. of S.W. Regional Conf., Dallas and Houston, 1991, 92; art fellow in painting Skidmore Coll., Saratoga Springs, N.Y.; presenter dept. edn. NYU, New England Art Edn. Assn., Mass. Art Edn. Assn., Ind. Schs. Assn.; artist with Dance Steps; residencies with Master Artist John Scott, 2001, Master Sculptor Helen Escobedo, Arts Coun. New Orleans, 2002. Designer calendar Coun. for Advancement and Support for Edn. (Silver medal 1989, 1993), designer devel. publ. (Silver medal); painting selected for commemorative stamp, now in permanent collection New Orleans Mus. Fine Arts, 1990; represented in permanent collection Whitney Nat. Bank, New Orleans, New Orleans Mus. Art, City of New Orleans; many pvt. commns.; designer; exhibited in solo shows at Sylvia Schmidt Gallery, New Orleans, Jonathan Ferrarra Gallery, New Orleans, Biggin Gallery, Ala.; in group shows at Staircase Gallery, Hingham, Mass., 1975, Internat. Trade Mart, New Orleans, 1986, 87 (1st pl.), Jewish Cmty. Ctr., New Orleans, 1986, Newcomb Coll., Tulane U., New Orleans, 1987, Wyndy Morehead Fine Arts, New Orleans, 1990, 91, Tex. and Neighbors Regional Juried Exhibit, Irving, Tex., 1991, Miss. Art Colony, 1991, more recently at New City Diner, New Orleans, Zigler Mus. Art, Jennings, La., Miss. Mus. Art, Biloxi, La. Watercolor Invitational, Covington, Sylvia Schmidt Art Gallery, New Orleans, Gallery Contemporary Art, U. Colo., Colorado Springs, 1992—; Red Clay Survey Biennial, Huntsville (Ala.) Mus. Art, 2000, 2002; Julia St. North, Masur Mus. Art, Monroe, La., 2001; Art in Bloom, New Orleans Mus. Art, 2000; Bi-State Art Competition, Meridian (Miss.) Mus. Art., 2003, Grounds for Sculpture, N.J., 2003. Tchr. aide Headstart Program, Somerville, Mass., 1970; staff mem. Office of U.S. V.P. Hubert H. Humphrey, Washington, 1967. RISD honors seminar scholar, 1987; Poet-in-Schs., Arts and Humanities grantee Mass. Dept. Edn., Scituate; recipient visual arts fellowships, residencies, Hambridge (Ga.) Ctr., 2000, Ragdale Found., Lake Forest, Ill., 2002, Va. Ctr. Creative Arts, 2003 Mem. Nat. Art Edn. Assn. (presenter), Miss. Art Colony, La. Watercolor Soc. (signature), Nat. Cum Laude Soc., Delta Kappa Gamma. Democrat. Avocations: travel, reading, hiking. Office: Metairie Park Country Day Sch 300 Park Rd Metairie LA 70005-4142

BANTRY, BRYAN, entrepreneur, air transportation executive; b. Jacksonville, Fla., Oct. 12, 1956; Owner, operator dog-walking svc., 1969-73; photographer's agt. Patrick Demarchelier, 1973—; owner Bryan Bantry Hair-Makeup Agy., NYC, 1973—, Bryan Bantry Celebrity Model Mgmt., NYC, 1992—; chmn., chief exec. officer Royal Atlantic Airways, NYC, 1987—. Co-prodr. (Broadway plays) You Can't Take it With You, 1983, Aren't We All, 1985, (off-Broadway plays) Greater Tuna, 1982, Hey Ma.Kaye Ballard, 1984; creator TV pilot Man's Best Friend, 1983; prodr. (feature documentary) The Cream Will Rise: The Sophie B. Hawkins Story, 1998; theatre prodr. (Broadway musical) Street Corner Symphony, 1997-98; prodr., co-dir. feature short film Eventual Wife, 2000; exec. prodr. (documentary feature film) Pretty Things, 2005. Former chmn. Batoto Yetu inner-city youth program, N.Y.C., 1992-2002; bd. dirs. The Trevor Project, L.A. Mem.: League of Am. Theatres and Prodrs. E-mail: bb@waggingtail.com.

BANTZ, JODY LENORE, psychologist; b. Waukesha, Wis., July 2, 1975; d. Leonard Jerome and Dolores Ethel Bantz. BA, U. Wis., Whitewater, 1997; MA, Calif. Sch. Profl. Psychology, 1999, PhD in Psychology, 2003. Lic. clin. psychologist 2005. Psychology intern Springall Acad., San Diego, 1998—99, The Ctr., San Diego, 1999—2000, Jewish Family Svcs., San Diego, 2000—01; residential counselor Vista Balboa Crisis Ctr., San Diego, 1999—2000; rehab. therapist Telecare San Diego Choices, San Diego, 2000—01; multidisciplinary clinician Desert Regional Med. Ctr., Palm Springs, 2002—03; clinician, lic. clin. psychologist Sharper Future, Palm Desert, 2002—; cons. Fond. for the Retarded, 2005—. Mem. Calif. Coalition on Sexual Offending, 2003—. Recipient Acad. Achievement award, U. Wis., 1997. Mem.: APA, Nat. Register Health Svc. Providers in Psychology, Assn. Treatment Sexual Abusers. Libertarian. Protestant. Avocations: running, reading, hiking, theater. Office: 77-564 Country Club Dr Bldg A Ste 235 Palm Desert CA 92211 Office Phone: 858-344-2668.

BAÑUELOS, ENRIQUE, real estate company executive; b. Valencia, Spain; LLB, Universidad de Valencia. Founder Miel de Luna; chmn., CEO Grupo Astroc, Valencia, Spain. Spkr. in field. Founder Fundación Astroc. Named an World's Richest People, Forbes Mag., 2007. Office: Astroc Paseo Alameda, 35 bis, 4 46023 Valencia Spain also: Paseo de la Castellana, 56 bis 46023 Madrid Spain Office Phone: +34 96 381 25 70.*

BANWART, SIDNEY C., human resources executive; Diploma in Chem. Engring., Iowa State U.; MBA, U. Ill. Various engring. and mgmt. positions including devel. engr. Caterpillar, Inc., Peoria, Ill., 1968—86, mgr. quality control and engring., mgr. tech. svcs. Mexico, 1986—89, quality control mgr., tech. svcs. mgr., motor grade product mgr. Aurora and Decatur, 1989—95, gen. mgr. large engine ctr. Lafayette, Ind., 1995—97, v.p., head tech. svcs. divisn., 1997—2000, head component products divsn., 1998—2000, chief info. officer, head systems and processes divisn., 2000—04, v.p. human svcs. divisn. Peoria, Ill., 2004—. Bd. dirs. Carter Machinery, Salem, Va., Weitz Co., Des Moines. Recipient Ill. 4-H Alumni award, 2004. Mem.: Ill. Manufacturer's Assn., Human Resources Policy Assn. Office: Caterpillar Inc 100 NE Adams St Peoria IL 61629 Office Phone: 309-675-1000. Office Fax: 309-675-1182.

BANYA, SANTONINO KU'CAYA, science educator; b. Gulu, Uganda, July 10, 1957; arrived in U.S., 1989; s. Zakeo Kal Ocaya and Aburijina Ocaya Lapura. Diploma in sci. edn., Kenya Sci. Tchrs/ Coll., 1982; BA in Judaic Studies, U. Judaism, 1993; MS in Edn. in Phys. Sci., Ea. Ill. U., 1998; postgrad., So. Miss. U., 1999—, PhD in Sci. Edn., 2004. Cert. educator Commonwealth of Mass., 1997, Ministry of Higher Edn., Kenya. Tchr. Eng. Amboni HS, Kiganju, Kenya, 1977—78; tchr. Eng. and biology Lirhanda Girl's HS, Kakamega, Kenya, 1978; tchr. chemistry and biology Kangaru HS, Embu, Kenya; tchr. biology and Eng. Kaumoni HS, Makueni, Kenya, 1981—82; tchr. physics and chemistry Nguviu Boy's HS, Embu, Kenya, 1982—89; tchr. world culture S.E. Halifax (N.C.) HS, 1993—94; tchr. physics and chemistry N. Chgo. (Ill.) Cmty. HS, 1994—95; sci. dept. chair St. Martin Poress Acad., Chgo., 1995—97; tchr. chemistry De La Salle Inst., Chgo., 1997—99; instr. sci. Miss Porter's Sch., Farmington, Conn., 1999—2002; tchr. chemistry and physiology Park Tudor Sch., Indpls., 2004—. Author: Sketches of the Soul, 1997, The Best Poems & Poets of 2002, 2002, Study of Factors Affecting Young Females' Attitudes Toward Chemistry in High School, 2005. Mem.: AAAS, N.Y. Acad. Sci., Am. Chem. Soc. Avocations: music, dance, reading, cooking, travel. Home: 5243 Crestview Ave Indianapolis IN 46220 Office: Park Tudor Sch 7200 N College Ave Indianapolis IN 46240 Office Phone: 317-415-2700 3114. E-mail: sbanya@parktudor.org.

BANZHAF, JOHN F., III, legal association administrator, educator; b. NYC, July 2, 1940; s. John F., Jr. and Olga Banzhaf; m. Ursula Maag, 1971. BS in Elec. Engring, MIT, 1962; JD magna cum laude, Columbia U., 1965. Civilian research asst. Signal Corps Engring. Labs., 1957; research engr., cons. Lear Siegler Corp., 1959-62; editor Columbia Law Rev., 1964-65; research fellow Nat. Municipal League, 1965; law clk. to U.S. Dist. Judge Spottswood W. Robinson III, 1965-66; asso. firm Watson, Leavonworth, Kelton & Taggart, NYC, 1967; founder, exec. dir. Action on Smoking and Health, Washington, 1968—, Nat. Inst. Legal Activism, 1980—; prof. law and legal activism Nat. Law Center, George Washington U., 1968—; exec. dir. Action on Safety and Health, 1971-80, Open America, 1975-80; founder Nat. Center for Law and the Deaf, 1975—. Bd. dirs. Consumers Union, 1971. Recipient 17th ann. Sat. Rev. award distinguished TV programming in pub. interest, 1969; Advt. Age award, 1967, 68; those who made advt. news, 1967, 68; Benjamin Franklin Lit. and Med. Soc. award, 1981 Mem. Sigma Xi, Eta Kappa Nu, Tau Beta Pi, World Tech. Network. Office: Action on Smoking and Health 2013 H St NW Washington DC 20006-4207 Home: 104 N Jackson St Arlington VA 22201 Office Phone: 202-659-4311. Business E-Mail: jbanzhaf@law.gwu.edu. *Despite the increasing complexity of society, and the seemingly overwhelming power of large institutions both public and private, one determined individual can still have a significant and beneficial impact on society. (I was responsible, as an individual, for over 200 million dollars worth of free radio and television time for anti-smoking commercials which led to the ban on cigarette commercials.).*

BAO, GANG, biomedical engineer, educator; s. Xicheng Bao and Yuying Sun; m. Bo Fan, Sept. 27, 1978; 1 child, Xiaoyan Robert. PhD, Lehigh U., 1987. Asst. prof. Johns Hopkins U., Balt., 1991—95, assoc. prof., 1995—99, Ga. Inst. of Tech., Atlanta, 1999—2003, prof., 2003—06, disting. prof. Coll. Engring., 2006—, dir. GT-engring. program, 2005—. Co-founder, chief sci officer Vivonetics, Atlanta, 2003—. Editor (editor-in-chief): Molecular and Cellu7lar Biomechanics. Recipient Rsch. Initiation award, NSF of USA, 1992, Cutting Edge Rsch. award, Ga. Inst. of Tech., 2005, Outstanding Achievement in Rsch. Program Devel. award, Ga. Inst. Tech., 2000; Gotshall fellowship, Lehigh U., 1985-1987, Sr. Scientist fellowship, French Govt., 1998, Translational Rsch. grant, Wallace H. Coulter Found., 2001-2003. Mem.: ASME, Soc. Engring. Sci. (bd. dirs.), Biomedical Engring. Soc. Achievements include patents pending for Dual FRET molecular beacons; Peptide-linked molecular beacons; Multi-functional magnetic nanoparticle probes. Office: Georgia Inst Tech 313 Ferst Dr Atlanta GA 30332 Home Phone: 770-745-0166; Office Phone: 404-385-0373. Business E-Mail: gang.bao@bme.gatech.edu.

BAO, KATHERINE SUNG, pediatric cardiologist; b. Soochou, Kiangsu, China, Sept. 7, 1920; came to U.S., 1953; d. Yung H. Bao and Ming King; m. William S. Ting, May 2, 1948; children: Gordon K., Albert C. MD, Nat. Ctrl. Univ. Med. Coll., Nanking, China, 1944. Diplomate Am. Bd. Pediatrics. Intern Mercer Hosp., Trenton, NJ, 1953; resident in pediats. and cardiology Children's Meml. Hosp. Northwestern U., Chgo., 1954-57; fellow in pediatric cardiology Children's Hosp. L.A., Calif., 1957-59, attending cardiologist Calif., 1960—; chief pediatric cardiology City of Hope Med. Ctr., Duarte, Calif., 1965-68; chief heart bd. L.A. Unified Sch. Dist. and PTA Splty. Health Clinics, LA, 1968—90; attending pediatrician, cardiologist Hollywood Presbyn. Med. Ctr., LA, 1970—, UCLA, LA, 1973—. Vis. pediatric cardiologist to univs. in Taipei Nat. Sci. Coun., Republic of China, 1983; U.S. pres.'s appointee Pres.'s Com. on Nat. Medal of Sci., 1983-85; adv. com. on health and med. care svcs. Dept. Health Svcs., Calif., 1988-90; pres. Chinese Physicians Soc. of So. Calif., 1969; speaker in field. Active Rep. Eagle, Rep. Presdl. Task Force, Rep. Presdl. Round Table. Rsch. Fellow Cardiologist, NIH, 1960-63; recipient Physician of Yr., Hon. Svc. award Calif. Congress of PTA, Inc., 1984, U.S. Rep. Senatorial Medal of Freedom, 1994, Lifetime Achievement award United Cultural Convention, 2005; named Internat. Scientist of Yr., IBC, Cambridge, Eng., 2001, Woman of the Yr., ABI, 2002; inducted IBC Hall of Fame, Cambridge, 2005. Fellow Am. Acad. Pediatrics; mem. AMA, AAAS, World Med. Assn., Calif. Med. Assn., L.A. County Med. Assn., Am. Heart Assn., Internat. Cir. of L.A. World Affairs Coun., N.Y. Acad. Scis., Hollywood Acad. Medicine (pres. 1995), Scripps Clinic La Jolla (coun.). Achievements include pioneered research in cardiac arrhythmia in infants and children; research in congenital heart disease in adults. Office: PO Box 10456 Beverly Hills CA 90213-3456

BAO, XUE-MING, librarian, educator; b. Shanghai, People's Republic of China, June 8, 1957; came to U.S., 1985; s. Si-Wen Bao and Xi-Kun Cao; m. Yi-Ping Tao, July 23, 1984; 1 child, David. MEd, U. Victoria, Can., 1983; MLS, No. Ill. U., 1991, EdD, 1989. Cert. profl. libr. Head cmty. learning ctr. Paterson (N.J.) Free Pub. Libr., 1991-94; asst. libr. dir. Belleville (N.J.) Pub. Libr. and Info. Ctr., 1994-97; libr., assoc. prof. Seton Hall U., South Orange, NJ, 1997—. Computer sys. libr. info. ctr. Belleville Pub. Libr., 1997—. Contbr. articles to profl. jours. Grantee numerous fed. and state govts., and pvt. founds., 1991-2000. Mem. ALA, Libr. and Info. Tech. Assn., N.J. Libr. Assn. (mem. coll. and univ. sect.). Avocations: reading, travel, movies. Office: Univ Libr Seton Hall U 400 South Orange Ave South Orange NJ 07079-2671 Home Phone: 973-379-1482; Office Phone: 973-275-2399. Business E-Mail: baoxuemi@shu.edu.

BAPOOJI RYAN, ANITA B., lawyer; BA with distinction, Queen's U., 1994; LLB, U. Toronto, 1997. Bar: Mass., Ontario, US Dist. Ct. (Dist. Mass.), US Ct. Appeals (1st Cir.). Spl. asst. dist. atty. Middlesex County, Mass., 2003; assoc. Litig. Practice Group Testa, Hurwitz & Thibeault, Boston, mem. securities litig. group, mem. ins. risk mgmt. team; assoc. Litig. Dept. Goodwin Procter LLP, Boston, 2005—. Mem.: Boston Bar Assn. (co-chair bus. litig. sect. 2003—05), Boston Lawyers Group (assoc. adv. com.). Office: Goodwin Procter LLP Exchange Place 53 State St Boston MA 02109 Home Phone: 617-227-7278. E-mail: abapooji@goodwinprocter.com.

BAPTIST, ALLWYN J., healthcare consultant; b. India, July 10, 1943; came to U.S., 1971; s. Peter L.G. and Trescilla (Lobo) B.; m. Anita Lobo, Sept. 8, 1973; children: Alan, Andrew, Annabel, Arthur. BCS, U. Calcutta, India, 1962; cert. mgmt., U. Chgo., 1978. CPA, Ill; chartered acct., India. Divisional acct. Rallis India Ltd., Bombay, 1967-71; mgr. Chgo. Blue Cross, 1972-79; sr. mgr. Price Waterhouse, Chgo., 1979-84; v.p., dir. Truman Esmond and Assocs., Barrington, Ill., 1984-86; ptnr. Laventhol and Horwath, Chgo., 1986-90, BDO Seidman, Chgo., 1991-2000; pres. Baptist Cons. Inc., 2000—. Mem. adv. bd. St. Mary of Nazareth Hosp., 1989—, mem. gov. bd., 1992-94, 96-98, lifetime trustee. Contbr. articles to profl. jours. Mem. fin. com. St. James Ch., Arlington Heights, Ill., 1987; mem. AICPA Health Care Com., 1991-94. Mem. Healthcare Fin. Mgmt. Assn. (dir., sec. 1983-85, pres. 1988-89, recipient William J. Follmer award 1984, Reeves award 1989, Muncie Gold award 1992, founders medal of honor 1998), India Cath. Assn. Am. (treas. 1980, 87, pres. 1988). Avocations: travel, reading, tennis, golf. Office: Bapt Cons Inc 126 E Wing St Arlington Heights IL 60004

BAPTISTA, ROBERT CHARLES, JR., federal official, lawyer; b. Buffalo, Sept. 14, 1948; s. Robert C. Sr. and Martha E. (Cole) B.; m. Denise C. Totemeier, June 29, 1974; children: Maria, Robert III. BA, Wheaton Coll., Ill., 1970; MA, No. Ill. U., 1976; JD, U. Ill., 1982. Bar: Ill. 1982. Law clk. to Hon. R. Lanier Anderson U.S. Ct. Appeals (11th cir.), Macon, Ga., 1982-83; assoc. Mayer, Brown & Platt, Chgo., 1983-89, ptnr., 1989—2002; chmn. NLRB, Washington, 2002—.

BAPTISTE, LA VERNE JOHNSON, retired secondary school educator; d. Major Johnson and Emma Louise Richardson. BA in English, Prairie View A&M U., Hempstead, Tex., 1965—69; attended, Calif. State U., San Jose, 1971—77. Cert. tchr. San Francisco State U., 1977. Counselor, recruiter Bill Gates Ednl. Found., San Jose, 2002—04; ret., 2004. Journalism/sch. paper advisor Sequoia HS, Redwood City, Calif., 1980—82; testing proctor Nat. Ednl. Testing Svcs., NJ, 1986—97. Author: (book) The Lonely Mermaid and Other Fish Stories. Mem. Am. Lung Assn., Easter Seals, MADD, NAACP; ret. mem. Calif. Tchrs. Assn., East Side Tchrs. Assn., San Jose, Calif. Mem.: Nat. Ednl. Testing Svcs., Paralyzed Am. Vets., Tri-Schs. Alumni Assn. (assoc.; talent/speech coord. 2006), DAV, VFW. Office Phone: 408-826-9689. Personal E-mail: cochise58@valornet.com, mar06mar@yahoo.com.

BAPTISTE, THOMAS L., career military officer; b. Calif., Mar. 4, 1951; m. Judy Cardoza; 2 children. BSBA in Fin., Calif. State U., 1973; student navigator tng., Mather AFB, Calif., 1973-74; student, MacDill AFB, Fla., 1974-75, 81-82, Williams AFB, Ariz., 1977-78, Squadron Officer Sch., 1977; student F-4 qualification tng., George AFB, Calif., 1978-79; student, Air Command and Staff Coll., 1986; MPA, Golden Gate U., 1987; student, Air War Coll., 1990, Johns Hopkins U., 1997, Syracuse U., 1997. Commd. 2d lt. USAF, 1973, advanced through grades to lt. gen., 2004; weapons sys. officer and instr. 44th Tactical Fighter Squadron, Kadena Air Base, Japan, 1975-77; aircraft comdr., standardization and evaluation officer 334th Tactical Fighter Squadron, Seymour Johnson AFB, NC, 1979-81; stationed at MacDill AFB, Fla., 1982-84, 85-89; F-16 instr. pilot and chief, standardization/evaluation div. 8th Tactical Fighter Wing, Kunsan Air Base, Republic of Korea, 1984-85; asst. dir. nuc. ops. Hdqs. Def. Nuc. Agy., Alexandria, Va., 1990-92; comdr. 52d Ops. Group, Spangdahlem Air Base, Germany, 1992-94; chief weapons tech. control div. Joint Staff, Pentagon, Washington, 1994-96, asst. dep. dir. internat. negotiations, 1994-96, directorate strategic plans and policy, 1994-96; dep. comdr. Can. N. Am. Aerospace Def. Command Region, Winnipeg, Manitoba, 1996-98; comdr. Cheyenne Mountain Ops. Ctr., Cheyenne Mountain Air Sta., Colorado Springs, Colo., 1998-99; asst. chief of staff ops. HQ Allied Air Forces Southern Europe, Naples, Italy, 2000—02; asst. chief of staff ops. div. SHAPE, 2002—04; dir. ops. Joint Forge & Joint Guardian, Mons, Belgium, 2002—04; dep. chmn. mil. com. NATO, Brussels, 2004—. Decorated Def. Superior Svc. medal with two oak leaf clusters, Def. Meritorious Svc. medal, Air medal, Joint Svc. Comendation medal, Air Force Commendation medal, Combat Readiness medal with oak leaf cluster. Office: NATO Blvd Leopold III 1110 Brussels Belgium

BAQUET, CHARLES R., III, former federal agency administrator, international studies educator; b. New Orleans, Dec. 24, 1941; BA, U. Xavier, 1963; MPA, Syracuse U., 1975. With Fgn. Svc., 1968, consular officer Paris, 1969-71; gen. svcs. officer bldg. mgmt. Dept. of State, 1971, adminstrv. officer Bur. Adminstrn., 1971-75, spl. asst. to Asst. Sec. of Adminstrn., 1978-79; gen. svcs. officer U.S. Consulate Gen., Hong Kong, 1975-76; councillor adminstrv. affairs U.S. Embassy, Beirut, 1976-78; dep. Office of Ops., 1979-83; dir. regional mgmt. ctr. U.S. Embassy, Paris, 1983-87; sr. seminar Fgn. Svc. Inst., 1987-88; with U.S. Consul Gen., Cape Town, South Africa, 1988-91; U.S. amb. to Djibouti, 1991-93; dep. dir. Peace Corps, Washington, 1994—2002; dir. Ctr. for Internat. Studies, Xavier U., La., 2002—. Vol. Peace Corps, Somali Republic, 1965-67. Office Phone: 504-520-5490. Business E-Mail: crbaquet@xula.edu.

BAQUET, DEAN PAUL, editor; b. New Orleans, Sept. 21, 1956; s. Edward Joseph and Myrtle (Romano) B.; m. Dylan F. Landis, Sept. 6, 1986; 1 child, Ari Theogene Landis. BA, Columbia U., 1978. Investigative reporter The Times Picayune/The States Item, New Orleans, 1978-84, Chgo. Tribune, 1984-87, assoc. met. editor for investigations, chief investigative reporter, 1987-90; met. reporter NY Times, 1990-92, spl. projects editor bus. desk, 1992—94, spl. project editor exec. editor, 1994—95, deputy met. editor, 1995, nat. editor, 1995—2000, asst. mng. editor & DC bur. chief, 2007—; mng. editor LA Times, 2000—05, exec. v.p., editor, 2005—06. Named Media Mensch of Yr., NY Observer, 2006; recipient Pulitzer Prize for investigative reporting, 1988. Fellow: Acad. Arts and Sciences. Achievements include first African-American editor to run the newsroom for the LA Times. Office: NY Times Washington Bur 1627 I St 7th Fl Washington DC 20006

BAR, ROBERT S., endocrinologist, educator; b. Gainesville, Tex., Dec. 2, 1943; s. Samuel and Emma (Kaplan) B.; m. Laurel Ellen Burns, June 23, 1970; children: Katharine June, Matthew Tomas. BS, Tufts Univ., 1964; MS in Biochemistry, Ohio State U., 1970, MD, 1970. Medicine intern Pa. Hosp., Phila., 1970-71; medicine resident Ohio State Univ., Columbus, 1971-72; asst. prof., dept. medicine Univ. Iowa, Iowa City, 1977-82, assoc. prof., dept. medicine, 1982-86, prof., dept. medicine, 1986. Acting dir. divsn. of endocrinology and metabolism, U. Iowa, 1985-90; dir. diabetes-endocrinology rsch ctr., U. Iowa, 1986—, nat. rsch. svc. award in endocrinology, 1984—, endocrinology fellowship program, 1979—, divsn. of endocrinology and metabolism, 1990—; mem. ad hoc study sect. NIH, 1985, dir. diabetes-endocrinology rsch. ctr. 1986; mem. editorial bd. Jour. of Clin. Endocrinology and Metabolism, 1984-87; mem study sect. Nat. Veterans Adminstrn., 1984-87; v.p. rsch. Nat. Am. Diabetes Assn., 1987-88; mem. orgn. com. Endothelium and Diabetes Symposium, Melbourne, 1988; dir. VA/JDF Diabetes Rsch. Ctr., 1997; mem. study sect. numerous assns. and coms.; guest reviewer numerous jours. Editor Endocrinology, 1987-89, Advances in Endocrinology and Metabolism, 1989—. Mem. Am. Diabetes Assn., Am. Soc. for Clin. Investigation, Assn. Am. Physicians, Endocrine Soc., Ctrl. Soc. for Clin. Rsch., Sigma Xi.

BAR, ROSELYN R., legal association administrator, lawyer, executive secretary; b. 1958; BA, U. Rochester; JD, Bklyn. Law Sch. Bar: NY 1984, Fla. 1984, Calif. 1990. Atty. Skadden, Arps, Slate, Meagher, and Flom, NYC, LA; corp. counsel Sun Am. Inc.; asst. gen. counsel, asst. corp. sec. Martin Marietta Materials, Raleigh, NC, 1994—2001, v.p., gen. counsel, sec., 2001—, sr. v.p., gen. counsel, sec., 2005—. Mem.: Fla. Bar Assn., Calif. Bar Assn., NY Bar Assn. Office: Martin Marietta Materials Inc 2710 Wycliff Rd PO Box 30013 Raleigh NC 27622 Office Phone: 919-783-4603. E-mail: roselyn.bar@martinmarietta.com.

BARA, JEAN MARC, finance and communications executive, artist; b. Roubaix, France, Aug. 22, 1946; came to U.S., 1970; s. Henri and Marie Antoinette (Dousseau) B.; m. Marian Yu, May 8, 1973; 1 child, Patrick Luc. B in Engring., Fed. U. Rio Grande do Sul, Brazil, 1969; MBA, Columbia U., 1972. With Chase Manhattan Bank, 1972-88; assigned Chase's Brazilian affiliate Banco Lar Brasileiro, 1978-80, mng. dir., head corp./retail mktg., planning, product mgr. Rio de Janeiro, 1980; v.p., head Brazil/Argentina/Paraguay liaison office Chase Manhattan Bank, NYC, 1980-82, v.p. corp. banking team, Latin Am. coord. mining and metals, 1983, v.p. nat. positioning group, 1984; corp. fin. exec. Chase Investment Bank, 1985-88; with Young & Rubicam, NYC, 1988—, v.p., corp. treas., 1988-89, sr. v.p., corp. treas., 1989-91; exec. dir., CFO Landor Assocs., NYC, 1992-94; CFO Burson Marsteller, 1997-98; pres. Ams.-Ea. Region, chief learning officer Landor Assocs., 1998—; pres. Americas, 2000—; generative artist, 2001—. Mem. Beta Gamma Sigma. Home and Office: PO Box 4446 Greenwich CT 06831-0408

BARACH, JEFFREY ALVAN, management educator; b. NYC, Aug. 15, 1934; s. Alvan L. and Frederica P. (Barbour) B.; m. Katarina Roth (div. 1982); 1 child, Jeffrey Alvan; m. Barbara J. Howell, Dec. 26, 1997. AB cum laude, Harvard U., 1956, MBA, 1961, DBA, 1967, postgrad. individual studies program, 1977. Tech. writer Honeywell Corp., Phila., 1956-58; account exec., copywriter Renner, Inc., Phila., 1958; tech. writer Teleregister Corp., Stanford, Conn., 1959; rsch. asst. Harvard U. Bus. Sch., 1961-62; asst. prof. Tulane U. Sch. Bus., 1965-68, assoc. prof. mgmt., 1968-86, prof. mgmt., 1986—2004; mktg. and mgmt. cons. New Orleans, 1965—; prof. emeritus Tulane U. Sch. Bus., 2004—. Author: Individual, Business and Society, 1977; co-author: Leadership and the Job of the Executive, 1996; contbr. articles on mktg. and mgmt. to profl. jours. Mem. Met. Crime Commn. of New Orleans. Recipient Extraordinary Svc. award Met. Crime Commn. of New Orleans, 1978, Detur prize Harvard Coll., 1953, Wissner award Tulane U., 1979, 82; Ford Found. grantee, 1962-63. Mem. Krewe d'Etat, Krewe of Bacchus, New Orleans Yacht Club, Bienville Club, Beta Gamma Sigma. Office: Tulane U AB Freeman Sch Bus New Orleans LA 70118 Home Phone: 504-342-7141. E-mail: jbarach@cox.net.

BARAHONA, FRANCISCO, researcher; b. Mar. 5, 1953; Grad. in Math., U. Chile, Santiago, 1975; D of Engring., U. Grenoble, France, 1980. Prof. U. Chile, Santiago, 1980—85, U. Waterloo, Canada, 1985—90; rschr. IBM, NYC, 1990—. Assoc. editor Siam Jour. Optimization, 1985—91, Jour. Ops. Rsch., 2000—05. Mem.: Inst. Ops. Rsch. and Mgmt. Scis., Math. Programming Soc.

BARAKAT, RICHARD, oncologist, gynecological surgeon; b. Kuwait City, Kuwait, July 15, 1959; MD, SUNY, Bklyn Health Sci. Ctr., 1985. Cert. obstetrics and gynecology 1992, gynecologic oncology 1994. Intern NYU-Bellevue Med. Ctr., 1985—86, resident, obstetrics and gynecology, 1986—89; assoc. prof. obstetrics and gynecology Cornell U. Med. Ctr.; fellow, obstetrics and gynecology Meml. Sloan-Kettering Cancer Ctr., NYC, 1989—91, oncologist, gynecology, 1994—, chief, gynecology svc., dept. surgery, 2001—. Vice-chmn. Cancer Prevention Com., Gynecologic Oncology Group; examiner Am. Bd. of Obstetrics and Gynecology. Editl. bd.: Gynecologic Oncology Jour., Oncology, lead editor: MSKCC-MDACC Handbook of Gynecologic Oncology, assoc. editor: Atlas of Procedures in Gynecologic Oncology, Principles and Practice of Gynecology Oncology, 4th edit. Founder and past pres. Met. Gynecological Cancer Soc. of NY. Avocations: golf, tennis. Office: Meml Sloan-Kettering Cancer Ctr 1275 York Ave New York NY 10021-6007 Office Fax: 212-638-9245.

BARAM, MICHAEL S., lawyer, educator; b. 1935; BS, Tufts Univ., 1957; LLB, Columbia Univ., 1960. Bar: Mass. 1962. Ptnr. Bracken & Baram, Boston; prof. Boston Univ. Sch. Law, Boston Univ. Sch. Pub. Health; dir. Ctr. Law & Tech., Boston Univ. Cons. EPA, United Nations, U.S. Congress, Chem. Mfr. Assn. Author: Environmental Law and the siting of facilities, 1976, Alternatives to Regulation: Managing Risks to Health, Safety and the Environment, 1982, Transnational Corporations and Industrial Hazards Disclosure, 1991; co-author: Managing Chemical Risks: Corporate Response to Sara Title III, 1992, Safety Management, 1998. Vol. atty. Conservation Law Found., Mass., 2002—; mem. bd. dir. Belmont Land Trust, Mass. Office: Boston U Sch Law 765 Commonwealth Ave Boston MA 02215-1401 Office Phone: 617-353-5294. E-mail: mbaram@bu.edu.*

BARAMOVA, IRINA ANTONOVA, investment banker; b. Geneva, May 5, 1972; d. Anton Donchev and Eugenia Nedialkova B. BA in Applied Econs., Am. U. in Bulgaria, Bulgaria, 1995, BA in Bus. Adminstrn., 1995; MBA, Duke U., Durham, NC, 1999. Series 7 NASD, 1999, Series 63 NASD, 1999. Client svc. dir. Leo Burnett & Co., Sofia, Bulgaria, 1995—97; tchg. asst. Duke U., Durham, NC, 1998—99; sr. assoc. Merrill Lynch & Co., NYC, 1999—2003; convertible securities analyst trainer Merrill Lynch & Co., NYC, 2000—02, co-head recruiting team to Duke U., 2001—02; assoc. v.p. HSH Nordbank, NYC, 2003; dir. fin. analysis Endo Pharms., Chadds Ford, Pa., 2004—. Founder Marco Polo Global Hedge Fund, Sofia, Bulgaria, 2003—. Translator: confidential documents for the UNDP. Fuqua fellowship, Duke U., 1997, 1998, Ann. Scholarship, Am. U. in Bulgaria, 1991 - 1995. Mem.: PADI (licentiate), BalkanTourist (assoc.; ski instr. 1988—95). Greek Orthodox. Avocations: skiing, jogging, exercise, tennis, rollerblading.

BARAN, JAN WITOLD, lawyer, educator; b. Ingolstadt, Germany, May 14, 1948; came to U.S., 1951; s. Jerzy Leopold and Leonce Sidonie (Vanden Bussche) B.; m. Kathryn Kavanagh, June 16, 1979; children: Brendan Jerzy, Maria Leonce, Elise Jett, Anna Margaret. BA, Ohio Wesleyan U., 1970; JD, Vanderbilt U., 1973. Bar: Tenn. 1973, D.C. 1976, U.S. Dist. Ct. D.C. 1980, U.S. Ct. Appeals D.C. 1980, U.S. Ct. Appeals (10th cir.) 1994, U.S. Supreme Ct. 1980, U.S. Ct. Appeals (5th cir) 2001. Legal counsel Nat. Rep. Congl. Com., Washington, 1975-77; exec. asst. Fed. Election Commn., Washington, 1977-79; assoc. Baker & Hostetler, Washington, 1979-81, ptnr., 1981-85, Wiley Rein LLP, Washington, 1985—. Gen. counsel, George Bush for Pres., Inc., 1987-88; gen. counsel, Bush-Quayle, Inc., 1988; lectr., co-chair Practicing Law Inst., Corp. Polit. Activities, Washington, 1978—. Author: The Election Law Primer for Corporations, 1984, 88, 92, 2000, 02, 04. Chmn. nat. adv. bd. Jour. of Law and Politics, 1983—; gen. counsel Am. Bicentennial Presdl. Inaugural Inc., 1989, Rep. Nat. Com., 1989-92; mem. Pres. Commn. Fed. Ethics Law Reform; amb., head U.S. del. World Adminstrv. Radio Conf. WARC, Malaga, Spain, 1992; mem. Gov.'s Commn. on Govt. Fin. Reform, Va., 2001. Patrick Wilson scholar, 1970-73. Mem. ABA (chmn. com. election law 1981-2000), D.C. Bar Assn., FBA (chmn. polit. campaign and election law com. 1981-83). Roman Catholic. Office: Wiley Rein LLP 1776 K St NW Ste 900 Washington DC 20006-2332 Business E-Mail: jbaran@wileyrein.com.

BARAN, PAUL, computer executive; b. Poland, Apr. 29, 1926; came to U.S., 1928; m. Evelyn Murphy, 1955; 1 child, David. BSEE, Drexel U., 1949; MS in Engring., UCLA, 1959; DSc in Engring. (hon.), Drexel U., 1997; PhD in Policy Analysis (hon.), RAND Grad. Sch., 2000. With Eckert-Mauchley Computer Co., 1949, Rosen Engring. Products Co., 1950-54; systems group Hughes Aircraft Co., 1955-59; with RAND Corp., 1959-64; co-founder Inst. for Future, 1968; founder CableData Assocs., 1972; co-founder Equatorial Comm., 1978-80; founder Packet Techs., 1980, Telebit, 1980, Metricom, Inc., 1985; founder, chmn. bd. Com21, Inc., Milpitas, Calif., 1992—. Trustee IEEE History Ctr., 2000—, Charles Babbage Found., 2000—; bd. dirs. Marconi Internat. Fellowship Found. Named Entrepreneur of Yr. Tech., Silicon Valley Bus. Jour., 1999; named to Nat. Inventors Hall of Fame, 2007; recipient Edwin H. Armstrong award, IEEE Comm. Soc., 1987, 1st Ann. award, ACM Spl. Interest Group in Comm., 1989, Fellowship award, Marconi Internat., 1991, Centennial 100 medal, Drexel U., 1992, Pioneer award, Electronic Frontier Found., 1993, Computers and Comm. Found. award, 1996, award, NAE, 1996, The Economist Innovation award, 2003, Fellow award, Computer History Mus., 2005, Silicon Valley Engring. Hall of Fame award, 2007. Fellow AAAS, IEEE (life, Alexander Graham Bell medal 1990, Centennial medal 2000, Internet award 2000), Franklin Inst. (2001 Bower award and prize achievement in sci. 2001). Achievements include design of first doorway gun detector; inventor digital packet switching; several patents for work on several new communication technologies in part based upon the concept of packets. Home: 83 James Ave Atherton CA 94027-2009 E-mail: paul@baran.com.

BARAN, PHIL S., chemistry professor; AA with honors, Lake Sumter Cmty. Coll., Fla., 1995; BS with honors Chemistry, NYU, 1997; PhD in Chemistry, Scripps Rsch. Inst., La Jolla, Calif., 2001. NIH postdoctoral fellowship Harvard U., Cambridge, Mass., 2001—03; asst. prof. chemistry Scripps Rsch. Inst., La Jolla, Calif., 2003—06, assoc. prof. chemistry with tenure, 2006—. Contbr. articles to profl. jours. Recipient Dean's Undergraduate Rsch. Fund award in Chemistry, NYU, 1996—97, George Granger Brown award for Excellence in Chemistry, 1996—97, NSF Pre-doctoral Fellowship award, Scripps Rsch. Inst., 1998—2001, Lesly Starr Shelton award for Excellence in Chemistry Grad. Studies, 2000, Hoffmann-La Roche award for Excellence in Organic Chemistry, 2000, Nobel Laureate Signature award for Grad. Edn. in Chemistry, Am. Chem. Soc., 2003, Nat. Fresenius award, 2007, GlaxoSmithKline Chemistry Scholar award, 2005—06, Amgen Young Investigator award, 2005, Roche Excellence in Chemistry award, 2005, DuPont Young Prof. award, 2005, AstraZeneca Excellence in Chemistry award, 2005, Eli Lilly Young Investigator award, 2005—06, NSF Career award, 2006—10, Beckman Young Investigator award, Beckman Found. Fellow, 2006—08, Pfizer award for Creativity in Organic Chemistry, 2006; Searle Scholar, 2005, Herman and Margaret Sokol Chemistry Fellowship, NYU, 1995—97, NYU Coll. Art and Sciences Scholarship, 1995—97, William and Sharon Bauce Family Found. Fellowship award, Scripps Rsch. Inst., 1997, BMS Unrestricted "Freedom to Discover" Grant, 2006—10, Alfred P. Sloan Found. Fellow, 2006—08. Achievements include patents in field. Office: Dept Chemistry Mail Drop BCC 169 Scripps Rsch Inst 10550 N Torrey Pines Rd La Jolla CA 92037 Office Phone: 858-784-7373. Office Fax: 858-784-7375. Business E-Mail: pbaran@scripps.edu.

BARAN, XIAOLEI YU, physician, psychiatry professor; d. Tian Shou and Ai Fu (Yang) Yu; m. Mark Richard Baran, Dec. 21, 2002. MD, Shanghai Second Med. Coll., 1983. Med. resident Shanghai Med. Coll., 1983—85, NY Med. Coll., Valhalla, 1991—92; rsch. fellow Am. Health Found., Valhalla, 1990—91; psychiat. resident NY Hosp.-Cornell Med. Ctr., White Plains, 1992—95; psychiat. fellow Cornell Med. Coll., 1995—96, instr. in psychiatry, 1995—98; attending psychiatrist NY Presbyn. Hosp., White Plains, 1996—; asst. prof. psychiatry Weill Cornell Med. Coll., NYC, 1998—2005, asst. prof. clin. psychiatry, 2005—. Mem.: Am. Assn. Geriatric Psychiatry, Am. Psychiat. Assn. (gen. mem. 1992). Office: NY Presbyn Hosp 21 Bloomingdale Rd White Plains NY 10605 Office Phone: 914-997-4358. Office Fax: 914-682-6907. Business E-Mail: xyu@med.cornell.edu.

BARANDES, ROBERT, lawyer; b. Bklyn., May 15, 1947; s. Max and Helen (Berger) B.; m. Joan Noveck, May 28, 1970 (div. Jan. 1981); m. Kathleen Lindsey, Aug. 22, 1982 (div. Jan. 1986). Student, U. Coll., London, 1967-68; BA magna cum laude, Union Coll., Schenectady, NY, 1969; JD, Harvard U., 1972. Bar: N.Y. 1973, U.S. Dist. Ct. (so. and ea. dists.) N.Y. 1976. From assoc. to ptnr. Barandes, Rabbino & Arnold, NYC, 1972-81; ptnr. Roper, Barandes & Fertel, LLP, NYC, 1981-99; of counsel Beckman, Millman & Sanders LLP, NYC, 2000; ptnr. Beckman, Lieberman & Barandes, LLP, NYC, 2001—. Prodr. (on Broadway) The News, 1986, Broadway revival of Damn Yankees, 1994-96, (on Broadway) Epic Proportions, 1999, Broadway revival of Bells Are Ringing, 2001. Assoc. producer: (Broadway Play) On The Waterfront, 1995, Lyricist Musical Etched in Stone, 1984; writer, lyricist, musical Star Crossed Lovers, 1984; bookwriter, lyricist musical Almost Eden, 1990. Mem. ABA, League Am. Theatres and Producers, Phi Beta Kappa. Jewish. Avocations: writing, skiing, golf, tennis. Office: Beckman Lieberman & Barandes LLP 116 John St Rm 1313 New York NY 10038-3303 Home Phone: 631-537-5283. Business E-Mail: RBarandes@BLBLLP.com.

BARANIEWSKI, HENRY M., surgeon; b. Warsaw, Apr. 3, 1943; arrived in US, 1982; s. Franz and Ksawera Baraniewski; m. Anna B. Tarasewicz, July 17, 1983; children: Sylvia, Ursula, Alexander. MD, U. Warsaw, 1967, PhD, 1978. Diplomate Am. Bd. Surgery, Am. Bd. Vascular Surgery, 1990. Resident Albany Med. Ctr., NY, 1987; fellow vascular surgery U. Iowa, 1987—89; assoc. prof. surgery U. Ill., Chgo., 1989—, Northwestern U., Chgo., 2001—; chief vascular surgery T. B. VA Hosp., Chgo., 1993—. Recipient Fogarty Internat. award, NIH, 1981. Fellow: PVSS, ACS, Ill. Surg. Soc. Roman Catholic. Office: 755 S Milwaukee Ave Libertyville IL 60048

BARANKIN, JOSEPH PAUL, director, consultant; b. Berkeley, Calif., June 18, 1945; s. Edward William Barankin and Claire Barankin Wasser, Robert Arden Wasser (Stepfather); m. Catherine Marie Barrett, Sept. 2,

1990; children: Michael David, Nathan Robert, Barrett Allen Sizemore, Phillip Thomas Nails. BA in Psychology, San Francisco State U., 1966, MA in English Lang. Arts, 1968; PhD, US Internat. U., 1975. Dir. pvt. postsecondary edn. divsn. Calif. Dept. Edn., Sacramento, 1986—98; asst. supt. edn. services br. Calif. Dept. Youth Authority, Sacramento, 1998—2003; dir. sch. and dist. accountability divsn. Calif. Dept. Edn., Sacramento, 2003—05; CFO Sacramento Advocacy. Treas. Infant Toddler Commn., No. Calif. Assn. for the Edn. Young Children, Sacramento, 1978—80; western regional v.p. Nat. Assn. State Adminstrs. and Suprs. Pvt. Schs., Sacramento, 1988—89; vice chmn. Boys and Girls Clubs of Greater Sacramento, Sacramento, 1988—2003. Author (with Catherine Barankin): The Advocacy Handbook, 1996, 2000; editor: (handbook) YMCA Public Policy Guide, 1998. Mem.: ASCD. Avocations: travel, music. Office: Sacramento Advocacy 2220 Capitol Ave Sacramento CA 95816 Office Phone: 916-447-7341. Business E-Mail: drj@sacadvocacy.com.

BARANOSKI, JOSEPH THOMAS, music educator; b. Wilkes-Barre, Pa., Jan. 11, 1952; s. Joseph and Mildred (Williams) Baranoski; m. Karen Metzger, July 27, 1974; children: Amy, Kristin, Joseph V. BS in Music Edn., Wilkes U., Wilkes-Barre, 1973; MS in Music Edn., Marywood U., Scranton, Pa., 1978. Tchr. music Hanover Area Sch. Dist., Wilkes-Barre, 1973—, chmn. dept. music, 1993—. Chmn. com. Troop 55 Boy Scouts Am., Wilkes-Barre, 2002—06; coach baseball South Wilkes-Barre Little and Teen League, 2000—02; trustee Firwood United Meth. Ch., Wilkes-Barre, 1990—. Recipient Excellence in Tchg. award, Hanover Area Sch. Dist., 1992. Democrat. Meth. Avocations: gardening, travel. Office: Hanover Area Sch Dist 1600 Sans Souci Pkwy Wilkes Barre PA 18702

BARANY, JAMES WALTER, industrial engineering educator; b. South Bend, Ind., Aug. 24, 1930; s. Emery Peter and Rose Anne Barany; m. Judith Ann Flanigan, Aug. 6, 1960 (div. 1982); 1 child, Cynthia Getty. BSME, Notre Dame U., 1953; MS in Indsl. Engring., Purdue U., 1958, PhD, 1961. Prodn. worker Studebaker Corp., 1949-52; prodn. liaison engr. Bendix Aviation Corp., 1955-56; mem. faculty Sch. Indsl. Engring. Purdue U., West Lafayette, Ind., 1958—, now prof., indsl. engring. Sch. Indsl. Engring. Cons. Taiwan Productivity Ctr., Western Electric, Gleason Gear Works, Am. Oil Co., Timken Co. With US Army, 1954—55. Recipient Best Counselor award Purdue U., 1978, Best Engring. Tchr. award, 1983, 89, Outstanding Indsl. Engring. Tchr. award, 1983, 87, 89, Outstanding Tchr. award Purdue U., 1989, Marion Scott Faculty Exemplary Character award Purdue U., 1993, 2000, NSF and Easter Seal Found. rsch. grantee, 1961, 63, 64, 65; Purdue Tchg. Acad. founding fellow, 1997, Indiana Gov.'s Sagamore of the Wabash award, 1998; named Purdue Book Great Tchrs., 1999. Mem. Inst. Indsl. Engring. (life, Fellows award 1982, Disting. Educator award 1989, Disting. Svc. award 1992, Cert. of Svc. Appreciation 1994, Work Measurement award 2000, Young Engr. Mentoring award 2001), Soc. Mfg. Engr., Am. Soc. Engring. Edn., Methods Time Measurement Rsch. Assn., Human Factors and Ergonomics Soc., Order of Engr., Sigma Xi, Alpha Pi Mu, Tau Beta Pi (Eminent Engr. award 1982). Home: 1120 Northwestern Ave W West Lafayette IN 47906-2503 Office: Purdue U IE GRIS 315 N Grant St West Lafayette IN 47907-2023 Home Phone: 765-743-3308; Office Phone: 765-494-5435. Business E-Mail: jwb@ecn.purdue.edu.

BARANYI, LAJOS, research scientist; b. Novi Sad, Serbia, May 9, 1958; s. Elemer and Erzsebet; m. Katalin Toth, Mar. 12, 1984; 1 child, Timea. PhD, Attila Jozse U. Arts and Scis., Szeged, Hungary, 1986. Rsch. fellow Alder St. Gyorgyi Med., Szeged, 1982—90; vis. scholar Nagoya City. U., Nogoyh, Japan, 1990—99; NRC fellow Walter Reed Army Inst., Silver Spring, Md., 1999—2005; pres. Aspera Biosys. Inc., Gaithersburg, Md., 2005—; exec. v.p. Am. High Tech. Ctr. Inc., Fairfax, Va., 2006—. Contbr. articles to profl. jours. Pvt. US Army, 1986—87. Avocations: fishing, reading.

BARASCH, CLARENCE SYLVAN, lawyer; b. NYC, May 20, 1912; s. Morris and Bertha Lydia (Herschdorfer) B.; m. Naomi Bosniak, July 1, 1957; children: Lionel, Jonathan. AB, Columbia U., 1933, JD, 1935. Bar: N.Y. 1936, U.S. Dist. Ct. (so., ea. and no. dists.) N.Y. 1936, U.S. Ct. Appeals (2d cir.) 1936. Pvt. practice, NYC, 1935—. Lectr. law of real estate brokerage at various real estate bds.; faculty of N.Y. Real Estate Bd. on courses for lic. renewals required by the Dept. of State of N.Y.; chmn. Columbia U. Law Sch. Class of 1935 Ann. Fund 1965—, Columbia Coll. Class of 1933 Ann. Fund, 1977-79; decade chmn. Columbia Coll. Ann. Fund; outside counsel N.Y. Law Jour., 1966-2007. Author: (with Elliot L. Biskind) The Law of Real Estate Brokers, 1969; also cumulative supplements, 1971-83; contbr. articles to profl. jours. Mentor Mt. Sinai Sch. Medicine, NYC, 2006-; mem. adv. bd. to chaplain Columbia U., N.Y.C., 1950-70; dir. Columbia-Barnard Hillel and predecessor, 1946—; pres. Jewish Campus Life Fund, Inc. Columbia U., 1970-87. Capt. Signal Corps AUS, 1942-46. Recipient cert. of appreciation Columbia U., 1981, medal for conspicuous svc. Columbia U., 1984. Mem. ABA, N.Y. State Bar Assn. (real property com.), N.Y. County Lawyers Assn. (com. on real estate brokerage matters), Real Estate Bd. N.Y. (mem. legis and law cms., 1970—, arbitration panel 1989—, rev. ann. Diary and Manual and author of summary of real estate brokerage law and related legal matters 1991—), Am. Arbitration Assn. (arbitration panel 1986—), Men's Club (bd. dirs. 1972-80), Columbia U. Law Sch. Alumni Assn. (bd. dirs. 1985-89). Jewish. Home: 1016 5th Ave New York NY 10028-0132 Office: 425 Park Ave New York NY 10022-3506 Home Phone: 212-988-3466; Office Phone: 212-838-0286. Personal E-mail: csbarasch@aol.com.

BARASCH, DAVID M., lawyer, former prosecutor; BA summa cum laude, SUNY Stony Brook, 1970; JD, Cornell U. Sch. Law, 1974. Consumer adv. Commonwealth Pa., 1983—90; special asst. to Gov. Robert P. Casey, 1990—93; U.S. atty. U.S. Dist. Ct. (mid. dist.) Pa., 1993—2001; mem. McNees Wallace & Nurick, Harrisburg, Pa. Apptd. Atty. General's Advisory Com., 1999. Mem.: Pa. Energy Devel. Authority (bd. dirs. 1983—90), Pa. Bar Assn., Nat. Assn. State Utility Consumer Adv. (v.p. 1985—87, pres. 1987—89). Office: McNees Wallace & Nurick 100 Pine St PO Box 1166 Harrisburg PA 17108-1166 Office Phone: 717-237-5384. Office Fax: 717-237-5300.

BARASCH, EUGENE FRANKLIN, radiologist, physicist, researcher; b. Chgo., Apr. 24, 1945; s. Arthur and Dorothy Barasch. BA in Physics, U. Calif., Berkeley, 1976; MS in Physics, U. Wash., Seattle, 1980; PhD in Physics, U. Calif., Davis, 1985; MD, Technion, Haifa, Israel, 1992. Diplomate Am. Bd. Radiology, 2006. Rsch. scientist dept. physics Tex. A&M U., College Station, 1990—92; intern St. Vincent's Med. Ctr., Staten Island, NY, 1997—98; resident in radiology SUNY, Buffalo, 1998—2002; diagnostic radiologist, 2002—; rsch. diagnostic prof. Touro U., Vallejo, Calif., 2005—. Rsch. adj. prof. dept. phyiscs SUNY, Buffalo, 1999—2004. Grantee, Dept. Edn., 1992, 2001. Mem.: Radiol. Soc. N.Am. (assoc.), Assn. Univ. Radiologists (assoc.), Am. Coll. Radiology (assoc.). Democrat. Jewish. Avocations: music, politics, history. Home: 4225 E St Sacramento CA 95819

BARASCH, MAL LIVINGSTON, lawyer; b. NYC, May 14, 1929; s. Joseph and Ernestine (Livingston) Barasch; m. Ann Beckley, May 19, 1962; children: Amy Pitacairn, Jody Taylor. BS in Econs. with distinction, U. Pa., 1951; LLB, Yale U., 1954. Bar: NY 1957, U.S. Dist. Ct. (so. dist.) NY 1960, U.S. Tax Ct. 1960. Assoc. Mudge Rose Guthrie Alexander & Ferdon, NYC, 1957-62, Rosenman & Colin, NYC, 1962-67; ptnr. Rosenman & Colin, LLC, 1968-2000; counsel Katten Muchin Rosenman LLP and predecessor, 2000—. Mem. exec. com., 2d v.p. libr. NY Law Inst., 1979—2000. Bd. dirs. Lenox Hill Neighborhood Ho., treas., 1995—2006; dist. leader, mem. exec. com. NY County Dem. Com., 1961—65; bd. dirs. Visions, Svcs. for the Blind and Visually Impaired. With US Army, 1954—56. Fellow: Am. Coll. Trust and Estate Counsel, NY Bar Found.; mem.: Internat. Acad. Estate and Trust Law (acamedician, exec. com. 2000—04), Assn. Bar City of NY (chmn. com. trusts, estates and surrogates cts. 2000—03), Univ. Club (N.Y.C.), Beta Gamma Sigma. Home: 1225 Park Ave New York NY 10128-1132 E-mail: mal.barasch@kattenlaw.com.

BARASH, ANTHONY HARLAN, lawyer; b. Galesburg, Ill., Mar. 18, 1943; AB cum laude, Harvard U., 1965; JD, U. Chgo., 1968. Bar: Calif. 1969, S.C. Assoc. Cox, Castle & Nicholson, LA, 1971-74, ptnr., 1975-80, Barash & Hill, LA, 1980-84, Wildman, Harrold, Allen, Dixon, Barash & Hill, LA, 1984-87, Barash & Hill, LA, 1988-93, Seyfarth, Shaw, Fairweather & Geraldson, LA, 1993-96; sr. v.p. corp. affairs, gen. counsel Bowater, Inc., Greenville, SC, 1996—2003; Ctrl. European and Eurasian Law Initiative officer ABA, Uzbekistan, 2003—04; dir. ABA Ctr. Pro Bono, Chgo, 2005—. Fellow Am. Bar Found. (life); mem. ABA (dir. ctr. pro bono 2005—), State Bar Assn. Calif., Beverly Hills Bar Assn. (bd. govs. 1979-81, 88-94, pres. 1992-93) Office Phone: 312-988-5773. Business E-Mail: barasha@staff.abanet.org.

BARASH, PAUL GEORGE, anesthesiologist, educator; b. Bklyn., Feb. 22, 1942; s. Abraham Malcolm and Rose (Shenker) B.; m. Norma Ellen Bernard, Aug. 19, 1967; children: David, Daniel, Jed BA, CCNY, 1963; MD, U. Ky., 1967; MA (hon.), Yale U., 1982. Diplomate Am. Bd. Anesthesiology. Intern SUNY Kings County Hosp., Bklyn., 1967-68; resident Yale-New Haven Hosp., 1970-72, chief resident, 1972-73; asst. prof. anesthesiology Yale U., New Haven, 1973-78, assoc. prof., 1978-82, prof., 1982—, assoc. dean clin. affairs, 1991-94. Chmn. dept. anesthesiology, Yale U., New Haven, 1983-94. Assoc. editor: Advances in Anesthesia, 1984; assoc. editor Jour. Clin. Monitoring, 1984 Surgeon USPHS, 1968-70 Fellow Am. Coll. Anesthesiology, Am. Coll. Chest Physicians; mem. Soc. Cardiovasc. Anesthesiologists (pres. 1984-86), Conn. Soc. Anesthesiologists (pres. 1982-83), Internat. Anesthesia Rsch. Soc., Am. Soc. Anesthesiologists (editor-in-chief Anesthesia Refresher Courses 1985-96). Home: 867 Robert Treat Ext Orange CT 06477-1649 Office: Yale U Sch Medicine 333 Cedar St New Haven CT 06510-3289

BARASH COPPERSMITH, MARIAN UNGAR, magazine publisher; b. Wilkes-Barre, Pa., June 11, 1933; d. Max H. and Tillie (Landau) Ungar; m. Sy Barash, Jan. 31, 1954 (dec. Feb. 1975); children: Carol Lynn, Nan Ruth; m. W. Louis Coppersmith, Apr. 29, 1978 (dec. Jan. 1989). BA in Journalism with honors, Pa. State U., 1953; postgrad., 1953-55. Tech. writer Kling Studios, Chgo., 1951; grad. asst., instr. dept. speech Pa. State U., 1953—55; writer, salesman Friedman & Barash, 1956—59; pub. State College Town-Gown, 1959—. Editl. dir. Daily Collegian Pa. State U., State Coll., 1953, grad. asst., instr. dept. speech, 1961, guest lectr. speech, journalism, mktg. Pa., 1965-, instr. mktg., 1974-75, 78; ptnr. Barash Advt., 1959—60, Morgan Signs, Inc., 1960—75; pres. The Barash Group, 1975—2000, chmn., 2000—; cons. mktg. and pub. rels. fields. Contbr. articles to profl. jours. Chmn. Art Alliance Fund Campaign, 1971, Cancer Crusade, State College, 1973-74; mem. pub. rels. com. Ctrl. Pa. Heart Assn., 1973; mem. Pa. Commn. for Women, 1980-87; bd. govs. Pa. Free Enerprise Week, 1981-85; chmn. bd. govs. Ctr. County Cmty. Found., 1987-89; pres. Nittany Coun. Rep. Women, 1960-61; bd. dirs. United Fund, 1965-70, asst. chmn., 1969; alumni trustee Pa. State U., 1976-97, vice-chmn., 1988-91, chmn., 1991-93; bd. dirs. Pennsylvanians for Effective Govt., 1978, United Way Pa., 1977-82, treas., 1978; bd. dirs. Renaissance Scholarship Fund Pa. State U., 1976—, Capital Blue Cross, 1978-84, Women's Campaign Fund., 1982-85, Pa. Ben Franklin Partnership, 1983-87, Mercy Hosp., Johnstown, Pa., 1983-89, Ctrl. Pa. Festival of the Arts, 1995—2000, Allegheny Highlands Regional Theatre, Pa. Ctr. Stage, Pa. Humanities Coun., Pa. Women's Campaign Fund., Mt. Nittany Med. Ctr. Found., Milton S. Hershey Med. Sch; mem. adv. coun. subcom. small bus. and commerce com. Pa. Ho. of Reps., 1983-86; bd. advs. Palmer Mus. Art, 1994—; mem. leadership coun. Ctr. Performing Arts SUNY, Purchase, 1994—96; chair Women's Resource Ctr, Hemlock Girl Scout Coun.; bd. adv. Palmer Museum Art, 1994-, v.p. bd. adv. 1998-99, pres., 1999-2001; trustee emerita, Pa. State U.; capital campaign coord. Alpha Com. Ambulance, 2001-04; nat. bd. dirs. Girl Scouts US, 2006—. Alumni fellow Pa. State U., 1997; recipient Kiwanis award, 1976, Small buisnessperson of Yr., 1981, Svc. to Soc. award Coll. Liberal Arts Pa. State U., 1984, Lifetime Achievement award Mortar Bd. Alumni, 2007; named Disting. Pennsylvanian, Pa. Gov., 1981, Phila. C. of C. (Disting. Dau. Pa. 1990), One of Pa.'s Best 50 Women in Bus., Pa. Commn. Women, 1996, Crl. Pa. Entrepreneur of Yr., Ctrl. Pa. Bus. Jour., 1996, Disting. Alumna, Pa. State U., 1998; Paul Harris fellow, Rotary, 2004. AAUW, LWV, Mem. Eightsheet Outdoor Adv. Assn., Outdoor Adv. Assn., Outdoor Adv. Inc., Pa. Cable TV Assn. (pub. rels. counsel 1967-75), Pa. Outdoor Adv. Assn., Nat. Cable Assn. (pub. rels. com. 1973-73), Specialties Adv. Assn., Inc., Women in Comms., Friends of Palmer Mus. Art, Pa. State U., Friends of Schlow Libr., Clearwater Conservancy, Mt. Nittany Conservancy, Nittany Lion Club, Delta Sigma Rho, Omicron Delta Kappa. Office: Morgan Signs Inc 403 S Allen St Ste 77 State College PA 16801-5252 Office Phone: 814-238-5051. E-mail: mimi@barashgroup.com.

BARAUSKY, KENNETH P., aerospace company executive; b. White Plains, NY, Apr. 15, 1944; m. Julie Killam; children: Paul, Mark, Amy, adam. BS in aero. Engring., U.S. Naval Acad., 1967. Commd. USN, 1967, advanced through grades to rear admiral; instr. Tng. Squadron Three; comdr. Fleet Logistics Support Squadron Forty; mission comdr., patrol plane comdr., asst. maint. officer Patrol Squadron Forty Four, 1971-73; officer Tng. and Adminstrn. of Res., Hdqr. Navy Recruiting Command, 1973; head Aviation Officer Cand. and Officer Cand. Sch.; ops. officer Patrol squadron Sixty-Four, 1977-80; adminstrv. officer Res. Anti-Submarine Warfare Tng. Ctr., 1980; ret. With USNR, 1980-97. Decorated Navy Commendation medal (3). Address: 212 W Kilbride Williamsburg VA 23188-8926

BARAZANI, MORRIS, artist, educator; b. Highland Park, Mich., June 24, 1924; s. Bencion Barazani and Clara Papo; m. Gail Coningsby Barazani, July 24, 1948; children: David, Alison. Student, Inst. Design, Chgo., 1948—49, Cranbrook Acad., Bloomfield Hills, Mich., 1949—52. Prof. art DePaul U., Chgo., 1959—62, U. Ill., Chgo., 1962—92. With USN, 1943—46. Home: 5340 W Magnolia Chicago IL 60640

BARBA, HARRY, writer, publisher, educator; b. Bristol, Conn., June 17, 1922; s. Michael Hovanessian and Sultone (Mnatsignanian) B.; m. Roberta Ashburn Riley, 1955 (div. 1963); 1 child, Gregory Robert; m. Marian Andrea Homelson, Oct. 29, 1965. AB, Bates Coll., 1944; MA, Harvard U., 1951; MFA, U. Iowa, 1960, PhD with honors, 1963; postgrad., NYU, 1955-56, Boston U., 1950-51, NYU, 1955-56, CCNY, 1956-57, Columbia U., 1957-58, U. Middlebury, 1945. Stringer, feature writer Bristol Press, Conn., 1944-45; instr. English and writing Wilkes Coll., 1947, U. Conn., Hartford, 1947-49; tchr. English Seward Park H.S., NYC, 1955-59; instr. U. Iowa, 1959-63; asst. prof. Skidmore Coll., 1963-68; prof. English, dir. writing Marshall U., Huntington, W.Va., 1968-70, title I writing arts dir., 1969-70; comml. and pub. svcs. radio-TV interviewee, reader, lectr., 1961—; prof. English, dir. writing Marshall U., Huntington, W.Va., 1968-70; Title I Writing Arts dir. W.Va., 1969-70. Vis. prof., Fulbright grantee, vis. Am. specialist Damascus U., 1963-64; disting. vis. lectr. contemporary lit., cons. SUNY, Albany, 1977-78; reader, lectr. USIS Libr., Damascus, Syria, 1963-64; innovator, dir., devel. writers confs. for creative growth in several nat., regional and urban contexts, 1964—; pres., pub., exec. dir. Harian Creative Books, Ballston Spa, N.Y., 1967—; cons. Bantam Books, Random House, 1967, 69-70, Nat. Found. for Arts, Nat. Found. for Humanities, U.S. Dept. Edn., N.Y. State Coun. Arts, N.Y. State Edn. Dept., Poets & Writers, Inc., Harvard U., others; pres. several instns., 1963—, founding pres. and socially functional writer; founder, dir. Skidmore's Writers and Educator's Conf., 1967, Workshop Under the Sky, 1970—. Author: For the Grape Season, 1960, 3 By Harry Barba, 1967, 3 X 3, 1969, The Case for Socially Functional Education, Art and Culture, 1970—74, One of A Kind (The Many Faces and Voices of America), 1976, The Day the World Went Sane, 1979; author: (compiled and co-edited with Marian Barba) (series) What's Cooking in Congress? A Congressional Smorgasbord of Recipes, 1979, 1983; author: Gospel According to Everyman, 1981, Round Trip to Byzantium, 1985 (Pulitzer prize nominee, 1985), When the Deep Purple Falls, a Story (PEN Syndicated Fiction award, 1985), The Nightingale Sings, Mona Lisa Smiles, 1993, The Sword/The Dove, 2007, Haji Baba Says, 2007, The Late Crubby Cox/The Later Gretchen Burfora, 2007; reviewer: plays Three Plays by William Saroyan. Founder, dir. Skidmore Coll. Writers and Educators Conf., 1967, Adirondack-Metroland Writers and Educators Conf., 1967—. Grad. fellow U. Iowa, 1961-62, Yaddo residence fellow, 1950, Macdowell Colony residence fellow, 1970, World's Hall of Fame in Lit., 1997—, Guggenheim fellow, 1989-90; Skidmore Rsch. grant, 1965-68, NY State Coun. Arts grant, 1971, U. Benedeum grantee, 1969; established Harian Creative awards for fiction, poetry, essays, mus. compositions, photography and graphic arts, 1973; chair in his name World Acad. Letters, 2004; named to Am. Hall of Fame for Lit. Mem. MLA, Coll. English Assn., Authors Guild, Writers Union PEN, Academy Am. Poets, Com. Small Press Editors and Pubs., Harvard Grad. Soc. Advanced Study and Rsch., Academy Am. Poets, Harvard Alumni Assn., Harvard Club Ea. N.Y. (dir. 1975-79). Achievements include rsch. in mainstreaming Am.'s multiple ethnic, religious, and racial groups, and for increasing the authority of the UN. Home and Office: 47 Hyde Blvd Ballston Spa NY 12020-1607 Home Phone: 518-885-7397; Office Phone: 518-885-7397.

BARBACHYN, MICHAEL R., chemist; BS in Chemistry, Calvin Coll., Grand Rapids, MI, 1979; PhD in Organic Chemistry, Wayne State Univ., Detroit; postdoctoral studies, Yale Univ., 1985. Assoc. dir. medicinal chemistry Pharmacia Upjohn (merged with Pfizer 2002), Ann Arbor; dir., antibacterial chemistry Pfizer Inc., Ann Arbor. Mem.: Am. Chem. Soc. (Award for Team Innovation 2007, 31st Northeast Regional Indsl. Innovation award 2003). Achievements include recipient of 30 US patents, inc. co-invention of linezolid, which became the basis of Zyvox. Office Phone: 734-622-7000. Business E-Mail: michael.r.barbachyn@pharmacia.com.*

BARBADORO, PAUL JAMES, federal judge; b. Providence, June 4, 1955; s. Donald James and Elizabeth B.; m. Inez E. McDermott, Aug. 16, 1986; children: Katherine E., John James. BA cum laude, Gettysburg Coll., 1977; JD magna cum laude, Boston Coll., 1980. Bar: N.H. 1980. Asst. atty. gen. N.H. Atty. Gen., Concord, 1980-84; legal counsel U.S. Sen. Warren B. Rudman, Washington, 1984-86, Orr & Reno, Concord, 1986-87; dep. chief counsel U.S. Senate Iran-Contra Com., Washington, 1987; dir. Rath, Young, Pignatelli and Oyer, Concord, 1987-92; judge U.S. Dist. Ct., Concord, 1992—, chief judge, 1997—2004. Mem. adv. group for dist. of N.H., Civil Justice Reform Act, Concord, 1992-94; mem. long range planning com. N.H. Supreme Ct., 1989-90; mem. 1st Cir. Jud. Coun., 1994-96, 2005—, jud. conf. com. on automation and tech., 1996-2001; adj. prof. Franklin Pierce Law Ctr., 1997-98. Mem. N.H. Bar Assn. (chmn. unauthorized practice of law com. 1982-84, com. on cooperation with the cts. 1997—), U.S. Dist. Ct. N.H. Bar, 1st Cir. Ct. Appeals Bar, Order of Coif. Office: WB Rudman Courthouse 55 Pleasant St Rm 409 Concord NH 03301-3938

BARBAGALLO, AL T., real estate company executive; children: Shanna, Ricki. BA in Comm., U. Nev., Las Vegas, 1977. Cardiovasc. technician Valley Hosp., Las Vegas; gen. mgr. Am. Ambulance, Las Vegas; officer Met. Police Dept., Las Vegas; salesman, broker Lincoln Nat. Ins. Co., Las Vegas; broker United Comml. Real Estate, Las Vegas; sr. v.p. Grubb & Ellis Real Estate, Las Vegas. Inventor med. pillow. Vol. Sunrise Hosp., Las Vegas, 1970—72, Met. Police Dept., Las Vegas, 1975—79. Named to Cir. of Excellence, Grubb & Ellis, 2005, 2006. Mem.: Internat. Coun. Shopping Ctrs., Nat. Assn. Office and Indsl. Roman Catholic. Avocations: motorcycling, skiing, flying. Office: Grubb & Ellis 3930 Howard Hughes Pky Las Vegas NV 89169 Office Phone: 702-733-7500. Fax: 702-862-8242. Business E-Mail: abarbagallo@gelasvegas.com.

BARBAGELATA, ROBERT DOMINIC, lawyer; b. San Francisco, Jan. 9, 1925; s. Dominic Joseph and Jane Zeffra (Frugoli) B.; m. Doris V. Chatfield, June 8, 1956; children: Patricia Victoria, Robert Norman, Michael Alan. BS, U. San Francisco, 1947, JD, 1950. Bar: Calif. 1950, US Supreme Ct. 1964. Pvt. practice, San Francisco, 1950—; judge pro-tem San Francisco County Superior Ct., 1992-95. Lectr. U. San Francisco Law Sch., Pacific Med. Center. Contbr. to legal jours. Served with USNR, 1943-46. Mem. Calif. State Bar, Calif. Trial Lawyers Assn. (lectr., v.p.), Am. Bd. Trial Advocates (nat. pres. 1981-82, Trial Lawyer of Yr. 1986-87, San Francisco chpt. Pres. Don E. Bailey Professionalism award 2003, Lifetime Achievement award 2004, 05), Assn. Trial Lawyers Am., San Francisco Trial Lawyers Assn. (Lifetime Achievement award 2003), Am. Coll. Trial Lawyers, Internat. Soc. Barristers, San Francisco Lawyers Club. Roman Catholic. Office: 195 Alhambra St San Francisco CA 94123

BARBAN, ARNOLD MELVIN, advertising executive, educator, writer; b. San Antonio, Sept. 17, 1932; s. Sam and Ida Dollie B.; m. Barbara Marie Fox, June 2, 1955; children: Polly Gwen, Pamela Florence. BBA, U. Tex., 1955, MBA, 1959, PhD, 1964. Asst. to v.p. Joske's of Tex., San Antonio, 1955-56; asst. prof. U. Houston, 1959-64; from asst. prof. to prof. in communications U. Ill., Urbana, 1964-83; prof. U. Tex., Austin, 1983-87; prof. advt. U. Ala., Tuscaloosa, 1987-2000, chmn. advt. and pub. rels. dept., 1992-97, prof. emeritus, 2000—. Rsch. prof. communications dept. U. Ill., 1972-83, head advt. dept., 1978-83; cons. Gulf Oil Corp., Houston, 1962, 64, Farm Rsch. Inst., Urbana, 1965-83, Dept. Def., Ft. Sheridan, Ill., 1984; cons. editor Grid Pub. Co., Columbus, Ohio, 1974-84. Author: Readings in Advertising and Promotion Strategy, 1968, Essentials of Media Planning, 1987, 3d edit., 1993, Advertising Media Sourcebook, 4th edit., 1997, Advertising: Its Role in Modern Marketing, 8th edit., 1994, Advertising Media: Strategy and Tactics, 1992, Advertising Campaign Strategy, 1996; editor U. Houston Bus. Rev., 1962-64; cons. editor Jour. Advt., 1979-81; mem. editl. rev. bd. Jour. Current Issues and Rsch. in Advt., 1980-2001, Jour. Advt., 1983-88, 91-94; contbr. articles to profl. jours. Cons. Democratic congl. campaign, Champaign, Ill., 1972. Sgt. U.S. Army, 1956-58. Recipient Outstanding Svc. award Houston Advt. Club, 1964, disting. svc. award Dicionary Internat. Biography, Cambridge, England; fellow U. Tex., Austin, 1960, 1962, Am. Acad. Advt., 1986. Fellow Am. Acad. Advt. (pres. 1981-82, Sandy award 1997). Home: 136 N Stallion Estates Dr Spring Branch TX 78070

BARBARA, PAUL FRANK, chemistry professor; b. Jamaica, NY, Apr. 24, 1953; s. Dominic and Virginia (Bambara) B. BA, Hofstra U., 1974; PhD, Brown U., 1978. Postdoctoral fellow Bell Labs., Murray Hill, NJ, 1978-80; asst. prof. chemistry U. Minn., Mpls., 1980-86, assoc. prof., 1986-90, prof., 1990-95, 3M-Alumni Distg. prof. chemistry, 1995—98; Richard J.V. Johnson Welch chair chemistry U. Tex., Austin, 1998—, dir. Ctr. Nano & Molecular Sci. and Tech., 2000—. Cons. Honeywell, 1983—86, 3M, 1985—98; vis. assoc. prof. Nat. Ctr. Sci. Rsch., France, 1988; exec. com. Inter-Am. Photochemical Soc., 1992—96; vis. prof. Cath. U., Belgium, 1996—97; co-chair Ultrafast Phenomena X Optical Soc. Am., 1996—97; co-chair US-Japan coop. prog. on near-field scanning optical microscopy, 1998; mem. devel. resource for biophysical imaging study grp.

NIH, 1998; chair radiation chemistry workshop US Dept. Energy, Chesterton, Ind., 1998; vice chair Gordon conf. on radiation chemistry, 2002; internat. lectr. Editl. bd. Jour. Phys. Chemistry, 1990-, Jour. Am. Chem. Soc., 1995-, Accounts Chem. Rsch., 1994-1995, Molecular Physics, 1994-, Chem. Physics, 1994-, Rev. of Sci. Instruments, 1994-1997, Jour. Chem. Physics, 1994-1997, Spectroscopy Letters, 1996-, Chem. Physics Letters, 1997-; assoc. editor Advanced Series in Phys. Chemistry, 1994-, accounts of Chem. Rsch., 1995-. Alfred P. Sloan fellow, Sloan Found., 1983-85; recipient Presdl. Young Investigator award, NSF, 1984-89; George Taylor Disting. Rsch. award, 1990; George Taylor Disting. Svc. award, 1997; Creativity award, NSF, 1998. Fellow Am. Phys. Soc., Am. Acad. Arts Scis.; mem. NAS, Am. Chem. Soc. (exec. com. divsn. phys. chemistry, 1992, vice chair, chmn. elect, chmn., 1993-1995, chair centennial issue com., Jour. Phys. Chemistry, 1997), Optical Soc. Am. Office: U Tex Dept Chemistry and Biochem 1 Univ Station A5500 Austin TX 78712

BARBARIN, OSCAR ANTHONY, psychologist; b. New Orleans, July 25, 1945; s. Oscar Anthony and Inez M. (Molison) B. AB, St. Joseph's Sem., Washington, 1968; MA, NYU, 1971; PhD in Psychology, Rutgers U., 1975. Dir. cmty. field sta. U. Md., College Park, 1974-79; prof. U. Mich., Ann Arbor, 1979-2000, dir. family devel. project, 1981-96, prof. psychology and social work, 1990-2000, dir. ctr. for the child and the family, 1992-94, exec. dir. South Africa Initiative, 1996-2000; Preyer disting. prof. social work, fellow Porter Graham Child Devel. Ctr., U. N.C., Chapel Hill, 2000—. Author: Childhood Cancer and the Family, 1987, Mandela's Children, 2000. Fellow APA, Am. Orthopsychiat. Assn. (bd. dirs., pres. 2001-03); mem. Assn. Black Psychologists (life). Office: Frank Porter Granan Child Devel Inst 517 South Greensboro St Carrboro NC 27510-8040

BARBAROSH, CRAIG A., lawyer; b. Bklyn., Aug. 13, 1967; BA, Univ. Calif., Santa Barbara, 1989; JD with distinction, Univ. of the Pacific, 1992. Bar: Calif. 1992, US Ct. Appeals (9th cir.). Extern law clk. Judge James N. Barr, US Bankruptcy Ct, ctrl. dist. Calif.; ptnr., co-chmn. Insolvency & Restructuring practice, office mng. ptnr. Pillsbury Winthrop Shaw Pittman, Orange County, Calif. Editor (articles): Univ. of the Pacific Law Rev. Named an Outstanding Young Bankruptcy Lawyer, Turnarounds & Workouts mag.; named one of Top 20 Lawyers Under Age 40, Daily Jour. Calif. Law Bus.; recipient CLAY Lawyer of the Year award, Calif. Lawyer mag., 2001. Mem.: Am. Bankruptcy Inst., Calif. Bankruptcy Forum, Orange County Bankruptcy Forum, Orange County Bar Assn., Order of the Coif. Office: Pillsbury Winthrop Shaw Pittman 7th Fl 650 Town Center Dr Costa Mesa CA 92626 Office Phone: 714-436-6822. Office Fax: 714-436-2800. Business E-Mail: craig.barbarosh@pillsburylaw.com.

BARBAROSH, MILTON HARVEY, merchant banking executive; b. Montreal, Que., Can., Apr. 22, 1955; came to U.S., 1986; m. Ricki Tucker, June 1, 1980; children: Marli, Lori, Liana. BCom with honours in Acctg., Concordia U., Montreal, 1976; Can. Chartered Acct., McGill U., Montreal, 1977; MBA, York U., Toronto, Ont., Can., 1980. CPA. Sr. staff acct. Thorne, Ernst & Whinney/KPMG Peat Marwick, Montreal, 1976-79; mgr. merger and acquisitions Clarkson Gordon/Ernst Young, Toronto, 1980-84, Royal Bank of Can., Toronto, 1984-86; pres. JW Charles Group, Inc., Boca Raton, Fla., 1987-88, JW Charles Capital Corp., Boca Raton, 1986-89. Pres. Stenton Leigh Group, Inc., Boca Raton, 1989—. Author: (with others) The Acquisition Decision; editor M&A in Canada for Harris-Bentley Ltd. Fellow Can. Inst. Chartered Bankers; mem. Nat. Assn. Cert. Valuation Analysts, Inst. Bus. Apprasers, Can. Inst. Chartered Bus. Valuators, Am. Soc. Appraisers (sr.), Inst. Chartered Accts. Ont., Quebec Order Chartered Accts., McGill U. Alumni, Concordia U. Alumni, York U. Alumni (chpt. exec.), Boca Raton Golf and Country Club. Office: Stenton Leigh Group 101 Plaza Real S Ste 215 Boca Raton FL 33432

BARBAS, STEPHEN MICHAEL, lawyer; b. Tampa, Fla., July 16, 1954; s. Carlos Francis and Gloria F. Barbas; m. Scheznarda Eva Luque, Aug. 2, 1980; children: Terin Marie, Amy Lauren. Student, Stetson U.; BS, Fla. State U., 1976; JD, Loyola U., New Orleans, 1979. Bar: Fla. 1979, US Dist. Ct. (mid. dist.) Fla. 1980, US Ct. Appeals (5th cir.) 1980, US Ct. Appeals (11th cir.) 1981. Asst. city atty. City of Tampa, 1979—; ptnr. Barbas Koenig Nuñez Sanders & Butler, Tampa, 1982—. Contbg. author Loyola Law Rev., 1978. Pres. Bright Horizons of Tampa Bay, Inc., 1979-81, Tampa Day Preschool and Kindergarten, Tampa, 1989-91; pres. bd. trustees Acad. of the Holy Names, 2002-03; mem. bd. trustees Loyola U., New Orleans, pres., chair law vis. com. Sch. Law, 2002-05. Mem. ABA (litigation sect.), Fla. Bar Assn. (workers' compensation sect.), Hillsborough County Bar Assn. Democrat. Roman Catholic. Avocations: golf, fishing, reading, interior designing, antiques. Home: 2916 W Hawthorne Rd Tampa FL 33611-2830 Office: Barbas Koenig Nuñez Sanders & Butler 1802 W Cleveland St Tampa FL 33606-1852 Office Phone: 813-254-6575. Business E-Mail: sbarbas@barbaslaw.com.

BARBASCH, DAN MIHAI, mathematics professor; PhD, Univ. Ill., Urbana-Champaign, 1976. Prof. math., dept. chmn. Cornell Univ. Vis. prof. Hong Kong Univ., 2000. Co-author: (books) The Langlands Classification and Irreducible Characters for Real Reductive Groups, 1992. Achievements include being one of 18 top mathematicians and computer scientists (Atlas of Lie Groups Project) from the US to successfully map E8, one of the largest and most complicated structures in mathematics. Office: 543 Malott Hall Cornell Univ Ithaca NY 14853-4201 Office Phone: 607-255-3685. Office Fax: 607-255-7149. Business E-Mail: barbasch@math.cornell.edu.*

BARBASH, BARRY P., lawyer; b. Lawrence, Mass., 1953; AB summa cum laude, Bowdoin Coll., 1975; JD, Cornell U., 1978. Bar: Mass. 1978, NY 1982, DC 1997. Pvt. practice, NYC, 1980—93; ptnr. Willkie, Farr & Gallagher, LLP, 1987—93, 2006—, Shearman & Sterling, 1998—2005; dir. divsn. investment mgmt. SEC, 1993—98. Mem.: ABA, Mass. Bar Assn., NY Bar Assn. Office: Willkie Farr & Gallagher LLP 1875 K St NW Washington DC 20006-1238 Office Phone: 202-303-1201. Office Fax: 202-303-2201. E-mail: bbarbash@willkie.com.*

BARBATO, ANTHONY L., hospital administrator, medical educator; BA, U. Windsor; MD, Stritch Sch. Medicine, Loyola U. Chgo. Cert. bd. cert. Am. Bd. Internal Medicine, Am. Bd. Endocrinology and Metabolism. Asst. prof. Stritch Sch. Medicine, Loyola U., Maywood, Ill., 1976—81, assoc. prof., 1981—86, prof. medicine, 1986—; dean Stritch Sch. Medicine, Maywood, Ill., exec. dean, asst. chmn., medicine for post-grad. edn., program dir., internal medicine residency; exec. v.p., health affairs Loyola U. Health Sys., Maywood, Ill., provost, health affairs, chief admin. officer, health affairs, v.p., health affairs, pres., CEO, 1995—. Chmn. Assoc. Academic Health Ctrs., 2000; sr. health policy adv. com. Rep. Danny Davis. Office: 2160 S First Ave Maywood IL 60153

BARBE, BETTY CATHERINE, marketing professional, retired financial analyst; b. Chgo., Dec. 24, 1930; d. Norbert Lambert and Helen Weishaar; m. Edward William, Aug. 8, 1953; children: Leonard Walter, Roger Andrew. Student, U. Toledo, 1970-85. Acct. Gorr Printing, Allstate Ins., Muntz TV, Chgo., 1947-53; hostess Welcome Wagon Internat., Maumee, Ohio, 1965-70; v.p. sec., cost acctg. Craftmaster, Toledo, 1970-72; sec., estimator Grinnell Fire Protection, Toledo, 1972-73; exec. sec., payroll Crow, Inc. Aviation, 1973-77; asst. city clk., payroll City of Perrysburg, 1977-83, tax adminstr., 1983-98, ret., 1998; mktg. exec. Melaleuca, Inc. The Wellness Co., 2003—. Sec., vice chair Ohio Women's Policy and Rsch. Commn.; mem. adv. coun. Ohio Bicentennial Commn.; reading coach Evening St. Sch., Park Elem. Sch., Bluffsview Elem. Sch., 2001; active Big Sisters of Toledo, 1979, YWCA; vol. New Albany LPGA Golf Classic, Jamie Farr LPGA Golf Classic, Worthington Rep. Women's Club, 1999, Ptnrs. for Citizenship and Character; tutor Ohio Reads. Paul Harris fellow Dublin-Worthington Rotary, Rookie Rotarian of Yr., 1999-00; honoree Maumee Valley coun. Girl Scouts U.S., 1990; named Woman of Yr., Bus. and Profl. Women Black Swamp Region II. Mem. Internat. Inst., Nat. Notary Assn., Nat. Fedn. Bds. and Profl. Women, Key to the Sea Bus. and Profl. Womens Orgn. (pres. 1982-84), Maumee Bus. and Profl. Women (pres. 1995-97), Maumee Valley Toastmasters (pres. 1989—, area gov.), Toledo Opera Soc. Assn., Two Toledos (sec., 1st v.p.), Christ Child Soc., Maumee C. of C. (sec.), Samagama Club, Zonta II (treas.), Maumee Valley Historical Soc., Rotary (sec. Dublin-Worthington chpt.). Republican. Roman Catholic. Avocations: football, reading, sewing, crafts, travel. Home: 806 Drummond Ct Columbus OH 43214 Office: Melaleuca Inc Wellness Co 3910 So Yellowstone Hwy Idaho Falls ID 83402-6003 Personal E-mail: babybarby4@aol.com.

BARBE, DAVID FRANKLIN, electrical engineer, educator; b. Webster Springs, W.Va., May 26, 1939; s. Damon and Mary K. (Cooper) Barbe; m. Irene Theresa Barbe; children: John David, Jane Suzanne. BSEE with high honors, W.Va. U., 1962, MSEE, 1964; PhD in Elec. Engring., Johns Hopkins U., 1969. Instr. elec. engring. W.Va. U., Morgantown, 1962-65; fellow engr. Westinghouse Advanced Tech. Lab, Balt., 1965-71; head functional devices sect. Electronics divsn. Naval Rsch. Lab., Washington, 1971-74, head microelectronics br., 1974-79, asst. electronics and phys. scis., 1979-83; dir. Submarine and ASW Programs Submarine and ASW Sys., Office Sec. of Navy, 1983-85; prof. elec. and computer engring. U. Md., College Park, 1985—, assoc. dir. Md. Tech. Enterprise Inst., 1985-87, exec. dir. Md. Tech. Enterprise Inst., 1987—, interim dir., assoc. dean engring., 1999—2001, exec. dir., 2001—. Mem. adv. group electron devices Dept. Def., 1971—79, 1987—90; mem. steering com. Internat. Conf. Charge-Coupled Devices, Edinburgh, 1974, Edinburgh, 76, San Diego, 75; lectr. 1st Internat. NATO Congress Charge-Coupled Devices U. Louvain-La Neuve, Belgium, 1975; mem. program com. Internat. Solid State Circuits Conf., 1993—; pres. Elec. Engring. Acad. W.Va. U., 1995—97; faculty dir. Hinman Campus Entrepreneurship Opportunities Program, 2000—05. Contbr. articles on electronics and tech. entrepreneurship to profl. jours. Recipient Dept. Def. award, 1979, Very High Speed Integrated Circuits Pioneer award, 1987, Disting. Alumni award, Elec. and Engring. Acad., W.Va. U., 1990. Fellow: IEEE (assoc. editor Electron Devices Newsletter 1975—79, adminstrv. com. Electron Devices Soc. 1977—83, nat. lectr. 1987—88, awards bd. 1990—94); mem.: Soc. Photog. and Instrumentation Engrs., Am. Soc. Engring. Edn. (Outstanding Entrepreneurship Educator award 2003, pres. entrepreneurship divsn. 2005—06), Eta Kappa Nu (charter mem.), Tau Beta Pi. Home: 6532 Burgundy Ln Clarksville MD 21029-2600 Office: U Md Md Tech Enterprise Inst Potomac Bldg College Park MD 20742-0001 Office Phone: 301-405-3902. Business E-Mail: dbarbe@umd.edu.

BARBE, WALTER BURKE, education educator; b. Miami, Fla., Oct. 30, 1926; s. Victor Elza and Edith (Burris) B.; m. Marilyn E. Wood, Feb. 7, 1967; 1 child, Frederick Walter. BS, Northwestern U., 1949, MA, 1950, PhD, 1953. Tchr. Dade County Bd. Pub. Instrn., 1947; asst. Psycho-Ednl. Clinic Northwestern U., 1949-50; instr. psychology, dir. reading clinic Baylor U., 1950; asst. prof. elementary edn. Kent State U., 1952-53, prof., head spl. edn. dept., 1960-64; adj. prof. U. Pitts., 1964-72, Ohio State U., 1972-89; pub. Modern Learning Press, 1997—; prof. Keystone Coll., 2001—. Editor Highlights for Children, 1964-92, bd. dir.; prof. edn., bd. dir. Jr. League Reading Center, U. Chattanooga, 1953-59; bd. dir. Zaner-Bloser; bd. dirs. internat. council Improvement of Reading Inst.; prof. Keystone Coll., 2001-02. Author: Reading Clinic Directory, 1955, (with Ralph Roberts) Teenage Tales, 1957, (with Dorothy Hinman) We Build Our Words, 1957, Educators Guide to Personalized Reading, 1961, Helping Children Read Better, 1970; sr. author: (with Paul Witty) Creative Growth with Handwriting Series, 1975, Personalized Reading Instruction: New Techniques that Increase Reading Skill and Comprehension, 1975, (with Jerry Abbott) Barbe Reading Skills Check Lists, 1975, (with Swassing and Milone) Teaching through Modality Strengths: Concepts and Practices, 1979; sr. editor: (with Joseph Renzulli) Psychology and Education of the Gifted: Readings, 3d edit, 1980, Basic Skills in Kindergarten, 1980, Resource Book for Kindergarten Teachers, 1980, (with Kurt Reed) The Glass Industry in Wayne County, PA, 1802 to Present, 2003; editor: Teaching of Reading; Selections, 1965, (with Edward Frierson) Educating Children with Learning Disabilities, 1967, Compass Points in Literature, Searchlights in Literature, 1969, Helping Children with Special Needs Series, 1974, A School Year of Poems, 2005; author: (with Francis, Braun) Spelling: Basic Skills for Effective Communication, 1982, (with Lucas, Wasylyk) Basic Skills for Effective Communication, 1984, (with others) Handwriting: Basic Skills and Application Series, 1984, Growing Up Learning, 1985, (with Francis, Gentry, San Jose) Spelling Connections: Words Into Language, 1988, (with others) Reading and Study Skills Mastery, 1996, (with others) Vocabulary, Word Analysis and Comprehension, 1996, Some Folks Like Cats and Other Poems, 2002, I Asked a Tiger to Tea and Other Poems, 2002. Chair exec. com. bd. dirs. Dorflinger-Suydam Wildlife Sanctuary, 1992—. With AUS, 1944-46. Fellow Am. Psychol. Assn.; mem. Nat. Assn. Gifted Children (pres. 1958), Touchstone Applied Sci. Assn. (bd. dirs. 1997—), Internat. Reading Assn. (Disting. Svc. award 1992). Democrat. Presbyterian. Address: 214 9th St Honesdale PA 18431-1911 Personal E-mail: waltco@pdt.net.

BARBEAU, MONIQUE ANDRÉE, chef; Grad., Culinary Inst. Am., 1987; BS in Hospitality Mgmt., Fla. Internat. U., Miami, 1991. Chef The Quilted Giraffe, NYC, 1985, Le Bernardin, NYC, Chanterelle, NYC; exec. chef Fullers, 1992—. Mem. Share Our Strength Benefit, Seattle, 1992, Seattle, 93, Seattle, 94, Seattle, 95; mem., Chef Steering Com. March of Dimes Gala Event, Seattle, 1994, Seattle, 95, Seattle, 96; guest chef James Beard Great Am. Chefs Series, Cambridge, Mass., 1994, James Beard Benefit Dinner, Kansas City, 1995, Real Seattle Dinner, James Beard Found., 1995, Chef's Holiday Series, Ahwahnee Hotel, Yosemite Nat. Park, Calif., 1995, Meals on Wheels, NYC, 1995; participant Club Med Food & Wine Festival, Mexico, 1995. Guest appearances (TV series) In Julia's Kitchen with Master Chefs, PBS, 1995, Ready Set Cook, Cable Food Network, 1995, KIRO, Seattle. Named Best Chef in Pacific Northwest, Pacific Northwest Mag., 1994, James Beard Found., 1994, Seattle's Best Chef, Seattle mag., 1995; recipient Unsung Hero award, March of Dimes, 1995. Mem.: Les Dames D'Esscofier, Cervena Chef Network. Office: Fuller's Restaurant 136 NW 9th Ave Portland OR 97209 Office Phone: 503-222-5608.*

BARBEOSCH, WILLIAM PETER, bank executive, lawyer; b. NYC, Nov. 25, 1954; s. Peter Joseph and Marie Delores (Slesiona) B.; m. Marta B. Varela, Sept. 6, 1986. AB magna cum laude, Brown U., Providence, 1976; JD, Columbia U., NYC, 1979; MBA, Yale U., New Haven, Conn., 1989. Bar: NY 1980, U.S. Tax Ct. 1985. Atty. Casey, Lane and Mittendorf (and successor firms), NYC, 1979—86, Milbank, Tweed, Hadley and McCloy, NYC, 1986—87; mgmt. assoc. Swiss Bank Corp., NYC, 1989—90; v.p. and mng. dir. J.P. Morgan Chase & Co. (and predecessor firms), NYC, 1990—2002; mng. dir. Chase Manhattan Bank & Trust Co. (Bahamas) Ltd., 1999—2002; mng. dir., CFO Citigroup Trust, NYC, 2002—06; CFO Asset Mgmt. Advisors, 2006—; chmn. and dir. Teton Trust Co., 2006—. Bd. advisor The Chase Jour., 1997—2002. Mem. profl. adv. com. Mus. of Arts and Design, NYC, 2002—; mem. Alice Tully Found.; mem. bankers and lawyers adv. com. NY Philharmonic; mem. exec. com. Trust Mgmt. Assoc. Am. Bankers Assn.; v.p. devel. com. Soc. Trust and Estate Practitioners. Mem. NY State Bar Assn., Assn. of the Bar of City of NY, Brown U. Club NY, Stone House Club, Yale Club (NYC), Phi Kappa Psi (sec. RI Alpha chpt. 1974-75), Met. Opera Club (NYC). Republican. Roman Catholic. Avocations: history, politics, travel. Home: 545 W 111th St Apt 7E New York NY 10025-1965 Office: Asset Management Advisors 711 Fifth Ave 14th Fl New York NY 10022

BARBER, BEN BERNARD ANDREW, journalist; b. Warwick, Eng., May 2, 1944; came to U.S., 1948; s. Stephen S. and Miriam (Idler) B.; m. Risa Richman (div. Apr. 1982); children: Karen Cloud, Forest; m. Nognoy Pinsanoa, Apr. 23, 1983 (div. Feb., 2000); children: Stephanie, Natalie. Cert. in French lang. and civilization, Sorbonne U., Paris, 1964; BA, Trinity Coll., Hartford, Conn., 1964; cert. in Asian studies, Gannett fellow, U. Hawaii, 1987; MJ, Boston U., 1979. Reporter Middlesex News, Framingham, Mass., 1979; free-lance reporter Miami (Fla.) Herald, Boston Globe, Balt. Sun, Toledo Blade, San Francisco Examiner, London Observer, Newsweek, Network News Svc., San Diego Union, Omni mag., MacLean's mag., L'Actualite, Atlantic mag.; Miami corr. USA Today, 1983-86; internat. desk editor United Press Internat., 1989-90; policy analyst Refugee Policy Group, 1991-92; correspondent Sunday Age, Melbourne, Australia; state dept. corr. The Washington Times, 1994—2003; sr. writer/editor U.S. AID, 2003—. Trainer journalism workshops U.S. Info. Agy., Africa; adj. prof. Sch. Fgn. Svc., Georgetown U., 1999. Contbr. articles to profl. jours. Jewish. Avocation: international travel. Office: US AID 1300 Pennsylvania Ave NW Washington DC 20523 Office Phone: 202-712-1000.

BARBER, BRUCE JACKSON, II, musician; b. Albany, Ga., May 15, 1960; s. Bruce Jackson Barber and Audrey Clara Hansen; life ptnr. Bernard Francois Zinck, Sept. 23, 2000. BA, Rollins Coll., Winter Park, Fla., 1982; MusM, Yale U., New Haven, 1984. Dir. music Tabor Luth. Ch., Branford, Conn., 1982—84, Christ Holy Trinity Ch., Westport, Conn., 1984—94; dir. cathedral music St. John's Cathedral, Albuquerque, 1994—2004, St. James Cathedral, Chgo., 2004—. Dir.: (CD) To the Creator of Light, 1998, All This Time, 1999. Vol. Habitat for Humanity, Albuquerque, 1998; bd. dirs. Chamber Music Albuquerque, 1998—2004, Bosque Prep. Sch., Albuquerque, 1998—2001, Early Music Now, Milw., 2004—05. Recipient Bravo award in music, City of Albuquerque, 2000. Mem.: Assn. Anglican Musicians, Am. Guild Organists (dean bd. dirs.). Democrat. Episcopalian. Avocations: cooking, tennis, skiing, travel, concerts. Office: St James Episc Cathedral 65 E Huron Chicago IL 60611

BARBER, CHARLES EDWARD, publishing executive, journalist; b. Miami, Fla., Oct. 30, 1939; s. James Plemon and Margaret Katherine (Grimes) B. m. Judith Margaret Tuck, May 28, 1960 (dec.); children: Janet Lynn Wood, Christopher Edward AA, Santa Fe Community Coll., 1971. Prodn. mgr. dept. student publs. U. Fla., Gainesville, 1966-68, ops. mgr., 1968-70, asst. dir., 1970-72, dir. div. publs., 1974; prodn. mgr. State Univ. System Press, Gainesville, 1975-76; pres., gen. mgr. Campus Communications, Inc., Gainesville, 1976—. Pres. The Herald Pub. Co., Inc., 1990—, Tuck Barber & Assocs., 1995—; pub. The High Springs Herald, 1990—; dir. Campus Press; cons. in field. Co-author: (with Judy Barber) screenplay This Small Island, 1989; adv. editor Fla. Quar., 1973-74; contbr. articles to profl. jours. Mem. citizens adv. coun. Stephen Foster Elem. Sch., Gainesville, 1976-77, Santa Fe H.S., 1991, Spring Hill Mid. Sch., 1992; mem. Friends of Five, 1975-77, Friends of Libr., 1975-77; mem. Fla. Newspaper Oral History Project, 1996—; chmn. book com. Fla. State Prison, 1973-85, 89-94; bd. dirs. Gainesville H.S. Band Boosters, 1978-79, 83-84, treas., 1984; key communicator Alachua County Sch. Bd., 1980-91, judge countywide spelling bee, 1997-2004; spl. registered dep. sheriff Alachua County Sheriff's Dept., 1979-92, Monroe County Sheriff's Dept., 1997—; mem. gifted students boosters Howard Bishop Mid. Sch., 1980-82; dir. Howard Bishop Band Boosters, 1980-82; mem. pres.'s coun. U. Fla., 1978—; mem. Leadership Gainesville, 1979, Leadership Fla., 1997—; mentor Coll. Leadership Fla., U. Fla. English Lang. Inst., 1998-2001; mem. steering com. Fla. Alliance for Better Campaigns, chair regional coalition, 1998; mem. Fla. Correct Ct. Com. for 2000 Census, 1998-2000; pack com. chmn. Cub Scouts Am., 1977-78; dir. The Prevention Partnership, 1992-94, Hippodrome State Theatre, 1992-95, bd. advisors. With USCGR, 1957-65. Recipient Nat. 1st pl. for Editl. Writing Hearst Found., 1965, Svc. award Santa Fe C.C., 1982, Cert. of Appreciation Big Bros. and Big Sisters of Gainesville, 1984, Vols. for Internat. Student Affairs, 1986, 88, 89, 90, Fla. Track Club, 1988, U. Fla. Divsn. Housing, 1990, 91, Addy award Gainesville Advt. Fedn., 1986, 87, 2003, Gold Addy, Fla. and Caribbean Dist., 2003; Recognition for Cold War Svc. U.S. Sec. Def.; named to Ind. Fla. Alligator Hall of Fame, 1996. Mem.: Disting. Order of Gator, Soc. Profl. Journalists (treas. No. Fla. chpt. 1972—75, 1986—91, pres.'s club 1994—95, Helen Thomas award for lifetime achievement in journalism 2003), First Amendment Found (trustee 1999—2001), So. Univ. Newspapers (bd. dir. 1980—89), Soc. of News Design, New Media Fedn., Newspaper Assn. Am., Nat. Newspaper Assn. (H.M. for weekly newspaper promotion 1996), Col. Media Advisers, Internat. Newspapers Mktg. Assn., Internat. Newspapers Fin. Execs., Gainesville Advt. Fedn. (bd. dir. 1979—80, Addy award 1986), U. Fla. Coll. Journalism and Comm. (journalism adv. coun. 2000—), Foresight Inst., Fla. Bus. Leadership Network, Fla. Press Found (bd. trustees 2001—, 1st pl. award for newspaper promotion 1992, award for weekly newspaper advt. 1993, 1st pl. award for editl. writing 1994, 1st pl. award for weekly newspaper advt. 1994, Best of Show award weekly newspaper advt. 1994, 1st pl. award weekly newspaper promotion 1995, 1st pl. award for weekly newspaper cmty. svc. 1995, 3rd. pl. award weekly newspaper advt. 1996, 3rd pl. weekly newspaper promotion 1997, award of appreciation,US Census 2000), Fla. Press Assn. (bd. dir. 1992—2001, chmn. continuing edn. com. 1992—2001, v.p. 1997, pres. 1998, chmn. bd. dirs. 1999—2000, Award of Appreciation 1999, Award of Appreciation for 10 years Svc. on Bd. Dirs. 2001, 1st pl. award for Creative Use of Newspaper 2001), Fla. Newspaper Advt. and Mktg. Execs. (chmn. edn. com. 1984—87), Fla. Scholastic Press Assn. (newspaper judge 1981—85, Gold Medallion for svc. 2003), Coll. Newspaper Bus. and Advt. Mgrs. (bd. dir. 1980—81), Am. Advt. Fedn., Am. Collegiate Network (adv. com. 1989—91), Leadership Gainesville Alumni Assn., U. Fla. Nat. Alumni Assn., High Springs C. of C., Alachua C. of C., Gainesville Area C. of C., Alligator Alumni Assn. (bd. dir. 1980—, named Mr. Alligator 1986), Substance Abuse Prevention Partnership (coun. 1992—95), Am. Red Cross (bd. dir., N.Ctrl. Fla. chpt.), Red Herring Club, Nat. Press Club, Rotary Internat. (sustaining, sec. 1993—94, Paul Harris fellow), Alpha Phi Gamma. Office: Campus Comm Inc PO Box 14257 Gainesville FL 32604-2257

BARBER, DONALD GENE, JR., purchasing agent; b. Wimpole Park, Eng., Apr. 7, 1959; s. Donald Gene Barber and Carmel Maxine Adkins; m. Debbie Sue Lee, July 14, 1978; children: Donald Gene III, Debra Lee. Regents degree, Fairmont State Coll., W.Va., 1984. Cert. mgr. Inst. Cert. Profl. Mgrs., 2002, adminstrv. mgr. Inst. Cert. Profl. Mgrs., 2002. With USAF, 1977—89, advanced through grades to 1st lt., inventory mgmt. specialist (munitions) Minot Air Force Base, ND, 1977—81, supr., intercontinental ballistic missile reentry systems maintenance unit Vandenberg Air Force Base, Calif., 1985—87, munitions accountable systems officer, 1987—89; stores foreman Amoco Polymers, Marietta, Ohio, 1990—95; stores supr. James River Corp., Kalamazoo, 1995—95; purchasing mgr. Bosch Braking Systems, Frankfort, Ohio, 1997—98, sr. buyer Clarksville, Tenn., 1998—99; materials mgmt. team leader Potlatch Corp., Warren, Ark., 1999—2000; dir. Indsl. Am. LLC & MROLink Corp., Reston, Va., 2000—01; dir., mem. purchasing programs Packaging Machinery Mfrs. Inst., Arlington, Va., 2001—02; divsn. purchasing mgr. Innertech, a Divsn. of Intier Automotive Interiors of Am. Inc., Nashville, Ill., 2002—. Chmn. Mid-Ohio Valley Supplier Exhbn., Nat. Assn. of Purchasing Mgmt. - Mid-Ohio Valley Inc., Parkersburg, W.Va., 1983—84. Mem.: Am. Purchasing Soc. (cert. purchasing profl. 2002), APICS-The

Ednl. Soc. for Resource Mgmt., Inst. for Supply Mgmt. (accredited purchasing practitioner 1999, cert. purchasing mgr. 2003), Am. Mensa Ltd (life), Air Force Assn. (life). Office: Intier Automotive 18355 Enterprise Ave Nashville IL 62263 Home: 2127 6th St Marinette WI 54143-3610 Home Phone: 618-643-6485; Office Phone: 618-327-5181. Office Fax: 618-327-9441. Personal E-mail: donbarber@donbarber.net. Business E-Mail: don.barber@intier.com.

BARBER, EARL EUGENE, management consultant; b. Dayton, Ohio, Dec. 8, 1939; s. Earl Garnet and Mary Helen (Brown) Barber; m. Sandra Kay Reese, Mar. 11, 1960; children: Steven, Amy, Dana. BS, Ball State U., 1963; MDiv, Asbury Theol. Sem., Wilmore, Ky., 1977. Tchr. Muncie (Ind.) Cmty. Schs, 1963-65; exec. mem. GM, Muncie, 1965-73; pres. Barber Electric, Wilmore, 1973-77; sr. pastor Calvary Temple, Plainview, Tex., 1977-79; exec. Borg Warner Corp., Muncie, 1979-84; COO Barber Cons. Resources, Muncie, 1984—. Author: Statistical Process Control for the Worker, 1985, Statistical Process Control: The Basic Tools, 1986, Team Leader Training, 1989, Problem Solving, 1992, 1996, Understanding SPC for Short Production Runs, 1990, Total Quality Management, 1991, Team Building, 1992, Problem Solving, 1994, Time Management, 1995. Mem. Mayor's Task Force, Muncie, 1980. Mem.: Am. Soc. Quality Control (sustaining mem., Ptnrs. award for Quality 1989), Delaware County Ministerial Assn., Epsilon Pi Tau. Republican. Methodist. Avocations: writing, music, boating. Office: Barber Cons Resources Inc 4501 N Wheeling Ave Unit 9B-2 Muncie IN 47304-6028

BARBER, GARY, motion picture company executive; Chief oper. officer Morgan Creek Prodns., LA; pres. Morgan Creek Internat., LA. Exec. prodr. (films) Midnight Crossing, 1988, Communion, 1989, Young Guns II, 1990, Pacific Heights, 1990, Robin Hood: Prince of Thieves, 1991, Freejack, 1992, White Sands, 1992, Stay Tuned, 1992, The Crush, 1993, Major League II, 1994, Ace Ventura, Pet Detective, 1994, Trial by Jury, 1994, Imaginary Crimes, 1994, Chasers, 1994, Silent Fall, 1994, Ace Ventura, When Nature Calls, 1995, Two if by Sea, 1996, Diabolique, 1996, Bad Moon, 1996, Wild America, 1997, Incognito, 1997, Major League: Back to the Minors, 1998, Wrongfully Accused, 1998, Keeping the Faith, 2000, Unbreakable, 2000, Out Cold, 2001, Bruce Almighty, 2003, 1 Love, 2003, Seabiscuit, 2003, The Legend of Zorro, 2005, Memoirs of a Geisha, 2005, Stick It, 2006; prodr. (films) True Romance, 1993, Shanghai Noon, 2000, The Count of Monte Cristo, 2002, Dragonfly, 2002, Reign of Fire, 2002, Abandon, 2002, Shanghai Knights, 2003, Mr. 3000, 2004, The Pacifier, 2005, The Hitchhiker's Guide to the Galaxy, 2005, Stay Alive, 2006, The Lookout, 2007, The Invisible, 2007.*

BARBER, JAMES ALDEN, navy officer, educator; b. Poplar Bluff, Mo., May 6, 1934; s. James Alden and Ellamay (Morris) B.; m. Beverly June Kingsbury, June 12, 1955; children: Judith Lynn Barber Joyce, Steven Alden, Susan Barber Blackwell. BA in Econs., U. So. Calif., 1955; MA in Econs., Vanderbilt U., 1960; MA in Internat. Rels., Stanford U., 1964, PhD in Polit. Sci., 1965. Commd. ensign USN, 1955, advanced through grades to capt., 1975; comdg. officer USS Hissem, 7th Fleet, Vietnam, 1966-68; Stephen B. Luce Prof. Naval Strategy US Naval War Coll., Newport, RI, 1968-71; comdg. officer USS Schofield, 7th Fleet, Vietnam, 1971-72; exec. asst. under sec. Navy Washington, 1975-76; comdg. officer USS Horne, 7th Fleet, 1977-79; dep. dir. Politico-Mil. Affairs, Navy Dept., Washington, 1979-82; dep. dir., sr. fellow Strategic Concepts Devel. Ctr., Washington, 1982-84; CEO, pub. US Naval Inst., Annapolis, Md., 1984-99; sr. lectr. sys. mgmt. US Naval Postgrad. Sch., Annapolis, 1998—2006. Author: Social Mobility and Voting Behaviour, 1970, Naval Shiphandler's Guide, 2005; co-author: Military and American Society, 1972; contbr. articles to encys. and profl. jours. Decorated Bronze Star with combat V, Legion of Merit, also others; recipient Alfred Thayer Mahan award, US Navy League, 1971, Meritorious Pub. Svc. award USCG, 1999, Dist. Pub. Svc. award Dept. Navy, 2000. Mem. Coun. Fgn. Rels., US Naval Inst., Interuniv. Seminar Armed Forces Soc., Naval Inst. Found., U.S. Naval Acad. Found., U.S. Naval Sailing Assn., NY Yacht Club. Democrat. Presbyterian. Avocations: gardening, book collecting, sailing. E-mail: jaldenb@aol.com.

BARBER, JERRY RANDEL, retired medical device company executive; b. Killarney, W.Va., Sept. 23, 1940; s. Edward Clay and Nora (Mullins) B.; m. Carrolyn Rae Acree, June 9, 1964; 1 child, Alyssa Rae. BSChemE, W.Va. U., 1962; MSChemE, Ohio State U., 1964, PhD, 1968. Rsch. engr. Union Carbide Corp., South Charleston, W.Va., 1968-73, group leader rsch., 1973-77, assoc. dir. rsch., 1977-81, dir. rsch. Tarrytown, NY, 1981-89, dir. new bus. and tech. devel. Danbury, Conn., 1989-93; gen. mgr. Medisyn Techs., Corp., Las Vegas, Nev., 1993-94; mng. dir. Medisyn Techs. Ltd., Arklow, Ireland, 1994-97; exec. v.p. techs. McGhan Med. Corp., Santa Barbara, Calif., 1997-98; v.p. R&D, Mentor Corp., Irving, Tex., 1998-2000, Santa Barbara, Calif., 1999—2000, v.p. advanced devel., 2000—05, v.p. rsch., 2005—06. Mem. AIChE, Am. Acad. Sci., Sigma Xi. Democrat. Methodist. Home: 2785 Poli St Ventura CA 93003-1556 Office: 2785 Poli St Ventura CA 93003 Office Phone: 805-653-7951. Personal E-mail: jrbarber7@aol.com.

BARBER, LEAH ADRIANNE, elementary school educator, literacy educator; b. Searcy, Ark., July 31, 1972; d. Adrian Golden and Paula June Barber. BA, Harding U., 1994, MEd in Reading, 1999. Tchr. aide spl. edn. Searcy-McRae Elem., Ark., 1994—95; 6th grade English tchr. Bald Knob Mid. Sch., Ark., 1995—99; 3d grade tchr. H.L. Lubker Elem. Sch., Bald Knob, 1999—2005, elem. literacy coach, 2005—. Mem. steering com. for devel. of pre-kindergarten and kindergarten Sunday sch. curriculum Coll. Ch. of Christ, Searcy, Ark. Mem.: Internat. Reading Assn. Mem. Ch. Of Christ. Home: 2910 E Moore # 19 Searcy AR 72143 Office: Bald Knob Pub Schs 103 W Park Bald Knob AR 72010 Office Phone: 501-724-3714.

BARBER, LIONEL, journalist; b. London, 1955; married; 2 children. 2d class degree in German/Modern History, Oxford U., Eng., 1978. Journalist The Scotsman, 1978-81; bus. corr. The Sunday Times, 1981-85; financial corr. Financial Times, 1985, Washington corr., 1986-92, Brussels bur. chief, European Cmty. corr. Brussels, 1992—98, news editor, 1998—2000, European edit. editor, 2000—02, US mng. editor NYC, 2002—05, editor London, 2005—. Author: Britain & the New European Agenda, 1998. Office: Financial Times 1330 Ave of the Americas New York NY 10019

BARBER, LLOYD INGRAM, retired university president; b. Regina, Sask., Can., Mar. 8, 1932; s. Lewis Muir and Hildred (Ingram) B.; m. Muriel Pauline MacBean, May 12, 1956; children: Muir, Brian, Kathleen, David, Susan, Patricia. BA, U. Sask., 1953, B in Comm., 1954; MBA, U. Calif., Berkeley, 1955; PhD, U. Wash., 1964; LLD (hon.), U. Alta., 1983, Concordia U., 1984; postgrad., U. Regina, 1993. Hon. chartered acct. Instr. commerce U. Sask., 1955-57, asst. prof., 1957-64, assoc. prof., 1964-65, prof., 1965-68, 74-76, dean commerce, 1965-68, v.p., 1968-74; pres. U. Regina, Sask., prof. adminstrn., 1976-90; dir. Sask. Inst. for Pub. Policy, 2003—. Indian claims commr. Govt. of Can., 1969-76, hon. lt. col.; spl. inquirer for Elder Indian Testimony, 1977-81; bd. dirs. Bank of N.S., 1976-03, The Molson Cos., 1977-2004, Teck-Cominco, N.W. Co. Ltd., 1990-02, Can. West Global Comm. Corp., Greystone Capital Mgmt. Inc.; cons. to bus. and govt.; hon. prof. Shandong U. Trustee Inst. Rsch. on Pub. Policy, 1972-79; bd. dirs. Indian Equity Found., 1978-79, Can. Scholarship Trust Fund, Regina United Way, 1977-79; past bd. dirs. Wascana Centre Authority; bd. dirs. Nat. Mus. Nature, Inst. Sask. Enterprise, Can. Polar Commn.; bd. dirs., past trustee Can. Scheneley Football Awards; adv. com. to Rector on pub. affairs award Concordia U., 1983; past mem. Northwest Territories Legis. Coun., 1967-70, Natural Sci. and Engring. Rsch. Coun. Officer Aboriginal Order of Can.; recipient Vanier medal, 1978; named hon. Sask. Indian Chief Little Eagle. Mem. Am. Inst. Pub. Adminstrn., Nat. Stats. Coun., Assn. Univs. and Colls. Can. (past pres.), Am. Econ. Assn., Can. Econ. Assn., Order of Can. (companion), Sask. Order of Merit, Assn. Commonwealth Univs. (coun.), Assinobia Club, Regina Beach Yacht Club, Masons. Mem. United Ch. Office: PO Box 510 Regina SK Canada S0G 4C0 Office Phone: 306-729-2336. Business E-Mail: barberl@uregina.ca.

BARBER, MARK EDWARD, lawyer; b. Enumclaw, Wash., Dec. 30, 1952; s. Earl Marion Barber and Delila Mae Willis Lontz; m. Pamela Johnson, Aug. 30, 1974; 1 child, Matthew Edward. BA, U. Wash., 1975; JD, Pepperdine U., 1978. Bar: Wash. 1978, U.S. Dist. Ct. Wash. 1978, U.S. Ct. Appeals (9th cir.) 1980, U.S. Supreme Ct. 1985. Atty. Heavey & Woody, Inc. P.S., Seattle, 1978—79; sole practitioner Seattle, 1979—81; atty., prin. shareholder Warren Barber & Fontes, P.S., Renton, Wash., 1981—. Bd. dirs. Justice Polit. Action Com., Tacoma, 1993-95, Sunset Valley Farms Homeowners Assn., Issaquah, Wash., 1991-92, 95-96. Mem.: Wash. State Trial Lawyers Assn. (pres. 1995—96), Wash. State Bar Assn. Office: PO Box 626 Renton WA 98057-0626 Office Phone: 425-255-8678. E-mail: mebarber@seanet.com.

BARBER, MARTHA GAYLE, lawyer; b. High Point, NC, Oct. 7, 1953; BA, Duke Univ., 1975; JD, Wake Forest Univ., 1981. Bar: NC 1982. Ptnr., chair, intellectual property-trademark, copyright group Alston & Bird LLP, Charlotte, NC. Frequent author, spkr. on trademark issues. Mem.: Internat. Trademark Assn. (bd. dir. 2000—03). Office: Alston & Bird LLP Ste 4000 Bank of Am Plz 101 S Tryon St Charlotte NC 28280-4000 Office Phone: 704-444-1018. Office Fax: 704-444-1111. Business E-Mail: mbarber@alston.com.

BARBER, MICHAEL J., cardiologist, educator; b. Gary, Ind., Feb. 3, 1954; s. Joseph W. and Patricia (Remsburg) B. AB cum laude, Wabash Coll., 1976; PhD, Loyola U., Chgo., 1980; MD, Ind. U., Indpls., 1984. Diplomate Am. Bd. Internal Medicine, Am. Bd. Cardiology, Am. Bd. Clin. Cardiac Electrophysiology. Intern U. Va., Charlottesville, 1984-85, resident, 1985-87, asst. prof. of medicine, 1990-93; cardiology fellow Duke U., Durham, N.C., 1987-90; cardiologist Colo. Springs (Colo.) Cardiologists, 1993—. Presenter in field. Contbr. sci. papers to profl. publs., chpts. to book Clinical Electrophysiology. Recipient Nat. Rsch. Svc. award NIH, 1989. Fellow: Heart Rhythm Soc., Am. Heart Assn., Am. Coll. Cardiology (Young Investigator award 1982, scholar 1987); mem.: Biophys. Soc., Am. Physiol. Soc. Office: Colo Springs Cardiologists 2222 N Nev Ave Ste 4007 Colorado Springs CO 80907-6854 Office Phone: 719-634-6671. E-mail: mjb020354@aol.com.

BARBER, PATRICIA LOUISE, clinical specialist; b. St. Paul, Jan. 11, 1953; d. James Bernard and Margaret Mary (Neagle) B. BSN, U. Minn., 1975; cert. nurse practitioner, U. Ill., 1978. RN, Colo., Ill., Minn. Staff nurse U. Minn., Mpls., 1974-75; transplant coord. U. Ill., Chgo., 1978-90; nurse practitioner emergency rm. Denver Presbyn., 1990-93; nurse practitioner in-patient svc. cardiovascular Denver Presbyn. St. Luke's Med. Ctr., 1993-95, nurse practitioner nephrology, 1995-96, nurse practitioner inpatient svc., 1996-99; assoc. prof. of nursing Health Edn. Ctr. C.C. Denver, 1999—2005, assoc. prof. nursing, 2004—06, acting chair nursing, bd. dirs., 2006; nurse practitioner cardiovasc. Cardiovasc. Assocs., Denver, 2003—. Cons. in field, Chgo., 1983—. Editor: Resource Manual for Transplant Coordinators, 1982. Co-chmn. S/A Patient Svcs. Com., 1983-90. Mem. N.Am. Transplant Coords. Orgn. (co-chmn. 1979-90, Honors 1983), Am. Diabetes Assn. (speakers bur. 1982—), Nat. Kidney Found. (bd. dirs. 1983-90). Avocations: fundraiser, volunteering, pet therapy. Office: C C Denver Health Edn Ctr 1070 Yosemite Cir Denver CO 80230-6921 Home Phone: 303-321-6075; Office Phone: 303-365-8372. Business E-Mail: trisha.barber@ccd.edu.

BARBER, TIKI (ATIIM KIAMBU BARBER), sportscaster, retired professional football player; b. Roanoke, Va., Apr. 7, 1975; s. James and Geraldine Barber; m. Virginia (Ginny) Cha, May 15, 1999; children: A.J., Chason. BA in Bus., U. Va., 1997. Running back NY Giants, NYC, 1997—2007; sportscaster WCBS-TV, NYC, 2000—07; corr. The Today Show WNBC-TV, NYC, 2007—, analyst, NBC Sunday Night Football, 2007—. Fill-in host Sta. WFAN-AM-FM. Co-author (with Ronde Barber): Be My Brother's Side, 2004, Game Day, 2005, Teammates, 2006; co-author: (with Gil Reavill) Tiki: My Life in the Game and Beyond, 2007. Named NFL Player of Yr., Sports Illustrated, 2005; named to Nat. Football Conf. Pro-Bowl Team, 2004—06, NFL All-Pro Team, 2005. Office: NBC 30 Rockefeller Plz New York NY 10112*

BARBER, TIMOTHY G., lawyer; b. Elgin, Ill., May 26, 1955; BA, Kenyon Coll., 1977; JD cum laude, Wake Forst U., 1985. Bar: NC 1985, US Supreme Ct., US Dist. Ct. Ea., Mid., & We. Districts NC, US Ct. Appeals Fed. Cir., US Ct. Appeals 4th Cir. Mem. Womble Carlyle Sandridge & Rice PLLC, Charlotte, NC, chair recruiting com., 1993—97, chair bus. litig. practice group, 1998—. Arbitrator Am. Arbitration Assn. Mem.: ABA (litig. sect.), Mecklenburg County Bar Assn., NC Bar Assn. (litig. sect.). Office: Womble Carlyle Sandridge & Rice PLLC One Wachovia Ctr Ste 3500 301 S College St Charlotte NC 28202-6037 Office Phone: 704-331-4937. Office Fax: 704-338-7839. Business E-Mail: tbarber@wcsr.com.

BARBERI, ROBERT OBED, lawyer; b. Chelsea, Mass., July 15, 1945; s. Matthew and Maryhannah Finch (Slingerland) B.; m. Margarita Dominguez Ibarra, Aug. 8, 1981; children: Robert Obed Jr., Jeffery Hayes, Susan Finch. BA cum laude with honors, Amherst Coll., 1967; JD, Columbia U., 1970. Bar: N.Y. 1972, U.S. Ct. Appeals (2d cir.) 1974, U.S. Dist. Ct. (so. and ea. dists.) N.Y. 1975, U.S. Supreme Ct. 1974, Conn. 1988, U.S. Dist. Ct. Conn. 1992. Assoc. Chadbourne & Parke, NYC, 1970-75; counsel Timex Corp., Middlebury, Conn., 1975-77, asst. gen. counsel, 1977-79; v.p., gen. counsel, sec. Risdon Corp., Naugatuck, Conn., 1979-86, Caradon Inc., Westport, Conn., 1986—95. Mem. bd. advisors Jour. Environ. Law and Practice, 1993-2000. Assoc. class agt. alumni fund Amherst (Mass.) Coll., 1978-84, 92—; bd. dirs. Rehab. Ctr. Waterbury (Conn.) Inc., 1983-86; pres. Weston Soccer Club, Inc., 1994-2000. Capt. USAR, 1970-78. Mem. ABA, Assn. Bar City N.Y., Am. Corp. Counsel Assn., Yale Club (N.Y.C.), Phi Delta Phi. Office: Levett Rockwood PC PO Box 5116 Westport CT 06881-5116 Office Phone: 203-222-0885. Business E-Mail: rbarberi@levettrockwood.com.

BARBERIE, JILLIAN, newscaster, meteorologist; b. Ontario, Can., Sept. 26, 1966; m. Bret Barberie (div.). BA in broadcast journalism, Mohawk Coll. of Applied Arts & Tech. Weathercaster The Weather Network, Canada, 1990—92, WSVN, Miami, 1992—93, KTTV Fox 11 10 O'clock news, Los Angeles, 1993—95; co-anchor, weathercaster Morning News and Good Day LA, KTTV Fox 11, 1995—; weathercaster Fox NFL Sunday, 2006—. Newscaster NFL on Fox, 2000—. Actress: (TV series) V.I.P., 1999—2002; guest apperances Clueless, 1996; Live! with Regis and Kathy Lee, 2000; Fastlane, 2002. Office: Fox Broadcasting 10201 Pico Blvd Los Angeles CA 90035*

BARBEZAT, EUGENE LAVAR, computer engineer, retired military officer; b. St. Johns, Ariz., Sept. 28, 1936; s. Fred Eugene Barbezat and Madge (Gibbons) Kindall; m. Karen Elizabeth Leichner, Dec. 22, 1970; children: Michele Lynn, Sean Michael. BS in Sociology, Brigham Young U., 1963; MA in Internat. Rels., U. So. Calif., 1980. Probation officer Ada County Probate Ct., Boise, Idaho, 1963-65; state probation officer 9th Dist. Ct., Ogden, Utah, 1965-66; commd. 2d lt. U.S. Air Force, 1966, advanced through grades to lt. col., 1981; chief Intelligence Report Ctr., 497th Reconaissance Tech. Group, Wiesbaden, Fed. Republic Germany, 1968-73; staff officer 7/13 Air Force, Nakon Phenom, Thailand, Def. Intelligence Agy., Washington, 1973-77, 84-85, Hdqrs. U.S. European Command, Vaihaingen, Fed. Republic Germany, 1977-80; chief Indications and Warning Ctr., Hdqrs. Mil. Airlift Command, Scott AFB, Ill., 1980-84; liaison offer to USCG DIA, 1984—85; staff officer Def. Intelligence Agy., Washington, 1984—85; ret., 1985; staff integration and test software engr. Martin Marietta, Denver, 1985-92; documentation specialist Computer Data Systems Inc., Lakewood, Colo., 1992—98. Staff mem. com. on imagery and exploitation Dept. Def., 1975-77, mem. indications and warning study group, 1980-84. Commr., scoutmaster Boy Scouts Am., Denver, 1986-92; commr., Ft. Collins, 1994-98, 2006-; mem. Operation Santa Claus, Denver, 1987-92; pres. Homeowners Assn., 1994-95. Mem.: DAV (life), Order of Arrow, Am. Legion, Denver Zool. Found., Denver Mus. Natural History, Air Force Assn., Assn. Former Intelligence Officers, Mil. Officer Assn. of Am. (life). Republican. Mem. Lds Ch. Avocations: camping, skiing, fishing, reading, music. Home and Office: 2144 Andrews St Fort Collins CO 80528 Personal E-mail: ebarbezat@earthlink.net.

BARBIAN, OTTO ALFRED, physicist; b. Nagold, Germany, June 4, 1947; s. Alfred Johann and Hermine (Brezing) B.; m. Leonore Elfriede Hauck, June 12, 1968 (div. 1982); children: Janine, Joyce; Klaudia Maria Louis, July 12, 1996, 1 child, Jan Frederik. MS in Physics, U. Saarlands, Saarbruecken, Germany, 1975. Asst. theoretical physics U. Saarland, Saarbruecken, 1972-73, asst. short time physics, 1974; scientist Fraunhofer Inst. for Non-Destructive Testing Inst. fuer Zerstoerungsfreie Pruefverfahren, Saarbruecken, 1974-76, head R&D Automated Inspection with Ultrasonics, 1976-86; head Pipe Mills & Automated Ultrasonic Inspection Plants Salzgitter (Germany) Industriebau, 1986-88, head divsn. phys. engring., 1988-91; mng. dir. Technique Pipetronix, Stutensee, Germany, 1991-2000, NDT Sys. & Svcs., Stutensee, 2000—. Chmn. DGZFP tech. com. Ultrasonic Testing (FAUS), 2003—. Co-author: Dickenmessung Mit Ultraschall, 1991; author: Handbuch Automatische Ultraschallprufsysteme, 2003, Handbook Automated Ultrasonic Testing Systems, 2004. Mem. Dist. Coun., Ballweiler, Germany, 1979-93; vice-mayor, Ballweiler, 1984-89. Achievements include patents in field; inventor in field. Home: Biesingerstrasse 67 D-66440 Blieskastel Saarland Germany Office: NDT Sys & Svcs AG Am Hasenbiel 6 D-76297 Stutensee Germany Business E-Mail: alfred.barbian@ndt-ag.de.

BARBIERI, CHRISTOPHER GEORGE, professional society administrator; b. Bklyn., Jan. 9, 1941; s. Nicholas Joseph and Marie Anne (Bacigalupo) B.; m. Joanne Lee Barnett, Jan. 30, 1965 (div. 1980); children— Matthew, Deborah, Lisa; m. Laurel E. Praet, July 6, 1985 BS, Cornell U., 1962; MS, U. Vt., 1964. Adminstrv. asst., asst. new products mgr., new products mgr., retail sales mgr. H.P. Hood & Sons, Boston, 1964-69; pres. Vt. C. of C., Montpelier, 1969—2003, internat. trade v.p. Shanghai, 2003—. Dir. Vt. World Trade Office, 2001—. Past mem. adv. bd. Congl. Travel and Tourism Caucus; bd. dirs. Union 32 H.S., 1977-80; del. White House Conf. on Better Librs., 1979; mem. Vt. Travel and Recreation Coun., 1988-91; chmn. Vt. Metric Coordinating Coun., past chair Vt. Employer Support for Guard and Res. Com.; past bd. dirs. New Eng. Trade Adjustment Assistance Ctr.; past chmn. New Eng.-USA Found., 1990-92; adv. coun. U. Vt.; former mem. Washington County Rep. Com.; past bd. dirs. Vt. Employers Health Alliance; trustee Ea. States Expdn.; active Vt. State Rep. Exec. Com. With Air N.G., 1964-70; pres. Coun. Am. States, China, 2004—. Mem. Vt. Assn. Execs. (pres. 1972), Vt. Assn. Chamber Execs. (pres. 1971), Small Bus. Adv. Coun. (past chmn.), Vt. Auto Enthusiasts (dirs.), Coun. State C. of C. (chair 1996-98). Lodges: Kiwanis (pres. Burlington 1972-73). Roman Catholic. Office: PO Box 37 Montpelier VT 05601-0037 Office Phone: 802-223-3443. Personal E-mail: chrisvt@granco.com.cn. Business E-Mail: cbarbieri@vtchamber.com.

BARBISCH, DONNA F., retired military officer; d. Jean Feigley; children: Rebecca, Patricia. BS, Calif. U. of Pa., 1984; MPH, U. NC, Chapel Hill, 1993; DHA, Med. U. SC, Charleston, 2000. RN Maine, 1968, cert. registered nurse anesthetist, Am. Assn. Nurse Anesthetists, 1972. Commd. lt. US Army, 1967, advanced through grades to maj. gen., 2001, ret.; pres. Global Deterrence Alternatives, Washington, 2000—. Dir. Inst. Global and Regional Readiness, Washington; cons. in field. Contbr. articles to profl. jours.; mem. editl. bd.: AMA Jour. Disaster Medicine and Pub. Health Preparedness. Mem.: Armed Forces Found. Achievements include research in surge capacity; use of military for domestic response. Home Phone: 202-547-5582; Office Phone: 202-547-0160.

BARBO, DOROTHY MARIE, obstetrician, gynecologist, educator; b. River Falls, Wis., May 28, 1932; d. George William and Marie Lillian (Stelsel) B. BA, Asbury Coll., 1954, DSc (hon.), 1981; MD, U. Wis., 1958. Diplomate Am. Bd. Ob-Gyn. Resident Luth. Hosp. Milw., 1958-62; instr. Sch. Medicine Marquette U., Milw., 1962-66, asst. prof., 1966-67, assoc. prof. Christian Med. Coll. Punjab U., Ludhiana, India, 1968-72; assoc. prof. Med. Coll. Pa., Phila., 1972-87, prof., 1988-91, U. N.Mex., Albuquerque, 1991-99, prof. emerita, 1999—; med. dir. Women's Health Ctr., Albuquerque, 1991-99. Acting dept. chair Christian Med. Coll., Punjab U., 1970; dir. Ctr. for Mature Woman Med. Coll. Pa., 1983-91; examiner Am. Bd. Ob-Gyn, 1984-97; bd. dirs. Ludhiana Christian Med. Coll. Bd., choir mem., 2005—; bd. dirs. Colorado Springs., Colo., chair, 2005, Svc. Master Co. Ltd., Downers Grove, Ill., 1982-91; bd. trustees Asbury Coll., 1996-2006, vice chair bd. trustees, chair acad. com., chair presdl. search com., 2007. Co-author: Care of Post Menopausal Patient, 1985; editor: Medical Clinics of N.A., vol. 71, 1987; assoc. editor, contbg. author: Textbook of Women's Health, 1998; contbr. chpt. to book. Student chpt. sponsor Christian Med. and Dental Soc., Phila., 1973-93, trustee, 1991-95, pres., chair bd. trustees, 1997-99, chair com. for continuing med. and dental edn.; tchr., elder Leverington Presbyn. Ch., Phila., 1988-91; interviewer Readers Digest Internat. fellowships, Brunswick, Ga., 1982—; bd. dirs. Phila. chpt. Am. Cancer Soc., 1980-86, vol., 1984. Named sr. clin. trainee USPHS, HEW, 1963-65, one of Best Woman Drs. in Am. Harper Bazaar, 1985. Fellow ACS (sec. Phila. chpt. 1990), ACOG, Am. Fertility Soc.; mem. Obstet. Soc. Phila. (pres. 1989-90), Phila. Colposcopy Soc. (pres. 1982-84), Philadelphia County Med. Soc. (com. chmn. 1989-90), Alpha Omega Alpha. Avocations: gardening, travel, collecting antiques.

BARBOR, JOHN HOWARD, lawyer; b. Pitts., Mar. 4, 1952; s. Thomas Sharp and Irene (Park) B.; m. Gretchen Suzanne Kunst, Mar. 20, 1982; children: Peter Howard, Katherine Suzanne. AB, Dartmouth Coll., 1974; JD, Boston Coll., 1977. Bar: Pa. 1977. Ptnr. Barbor and Barbor, Indiana, Pa., 1978-89, Barbor & Cicola, Indiana, 1989-93, Barbor, Vaporis & Sottile, P.C., Indiana, 1993—2002, Barbor Sottile & Darr, P.C., Indiana, 2003—. Bd. dirs., solicitor Indiana County YMCA, 1985-94; solicitor Indiana County Red Cross, 1979—; bd. dirs. Indiana Arts Coun., 1986-89; bd. dirs. Indiana County Zoning Appeals Bd., 1995—, chmn., 1998—. Mem. ABA, Pa. Bar Assn., Pa. Bar Inst. (bd. govs. 1995-97), Ind. County Bar Assn. (exec. bd. 1988, 95—), Ind. Country Club, Phi Beta Kappa. Republican. Lutheran. Home: 217 Forest Ridge Rd Indiana PA 15701-7443 Office: Barbor Sottile & Darr PC 917 Philadelphia St Indiana PA 15701-3911 Home Phone: 724-349-8545; Office Phone: 724-465-5618.

BARBOSA, LEANDRO MATEUS, professional basketball player; b. Sao Paulo, Brazil, Nov. 28, 1982; Player Palmieras, Brazil, 1999—2001, Baura Tilibra, Brazil, 2001—03, Phoenix Suns, 2003—; draft pick San Antonio Spurs, 2003. Mem. Brazilian Nat. Team, 2002—03. Named Brazilian League Rookie of Yr., 2002; recipient Sixth Man award, NBA, 2007. Office: Phoenix Suns 201 E Jefferson St Phoenix AZ 85004*

BARBOSA, RUBENS ANTONIO, former ambassador; b. Sao Paulo, June 13, 1938; s. Jose Orlando and Lice (Farina) B.; m. Maria Ignez Correa da Costa, June 13, 1969; children: Joao Bernardo, Mariana. BA in Law, U. Sao Paulo; BA in Diplomacy, Brazil's Fgn. Svc. Acad.; MA in Latin Am. Politics, London Sch. Econs./Polit. Sci. 3rd sec. Brazil's Ministry of Fgn. Rels., Brasilia, Brazil and London, 1962-66; 2d sec. Brazilian Embassy, London, 1966-73, counselor, 1976-79, min., 1979-84; chief of staff to min. of fgn. rels., 1985-86; undersec. gen. for multilateral and spl. polit. affairs Ministry of Fgn. Rels., 1986-87; sec. for internat. affairs Brazilian Fin. Ministry, 1987-88; Brazilian amb. Latin Am. Integration Assn., 1988-91, pres. com. of reps., 1991-92; undersec. gen. for trade, regional integration/econ. affairs Ministry of Fgn. Rels., 1991-93, v.p. permanent com. on fgn. trade, 1992-93; Brazilian amb. to the Ct. of St. James London, 1994-99; Brazilian amb. to the U.S., 1999—2004; sr. dir. Stonebridge International LLC, Washington, 2004—. Brazilian govt. coord. Mercosul Issues, 1991-93; exec. sec. com. on trade with East European Countries, 1976-83. Author: American Latina em Perspectiva: a Integraçao Regional da Retórica à Realidad, 1991, Panorama visto de Londres, 1998, The Mercosur Codes, The British Institute of International and Comparative Law, 2000, O Brasil dos Brasilianistas, Um Guia dos Estudos sobre o Brasil nos Estados Unidos (1945-2000), 2002; contbr. articles to profl. jours. and newspapers. Mem. Assn. of Coffee Producing Countries (pres. 1994-99). Avocations: tennis, classical music. Office: Stonebridge Internat LLC 555 13th St NW Ste 300 W Washington DC 20004 Home Phone: 55-11 3817 5158; Office Phone: 55-11 3039 6330. E-mail: rubens@rbarbesaconsult.com.br.

BARBOUR, ALTON BRADFORD, retired human communication studies educator; b. San Diego, Oct. 13, 1933; s. Ancel Baxter and Mary Jane (Fay) B.; m. Betty Sue Burch, Aug. 19, 1961 (div. 1991); children: Elizabeth, Christopher, Damon, Meagan; m. Jacqueline Moorhead, Feb. 29, 1996. BA, U. No. Colo., 1956; MA, U. Denver, 1961, PhD, 1968; postdoctoral, Moreno Inst., 1976. Diplomate Am. Bd. Psychotherapy; cert. trainer-educator in psychodrama, sociometry and group psychotherapy Am. Bd. Examiners, 1978. Lectr. Colo. Sch. Mines, Golden, 1964-65; instr. U. Denver, 1965-68, asst. prof. human comm. studies Denver, 1968-71, assoc. prof., 1971-77, prof., 1977—, chairperson dept. human comm. studies, 1980—98. Vis. lectr. Swiss Inst. for Group Psychotherapy, Switzerland, 1992, Remin U., China, 1999, Chinese U., Hong Kong. Co-author: Interpersonal Communication: Teaching Resources, 1972, Louder Than Words: Nonverbal Communication, 1974, Assessing Functional Communication, 1978; editor: Free Speech Yearbook, 1974-76; contbg. editor Internat. Jour. Action Methods, Psychodrama, Skill Tng., and Role Playing, Psychodrama Network News; contbr. articles to profl. jours. With USN, 1956-58. Recipient Intellectual Freedom award, Nat. Coun. Tchrs. English, 1997, William McBride Writing award, Colo. Lang. Arts Soc., 1998, William McBride award for Poetry, 2004, Outstanding Alumni award, U. No. Colo., 2003, Outstanding Educator award, 2005, Disting. Alumni in Edn., 2005. Fellow: Counseling and Psychotherapy, Internat. Acad. of Behavorial Medicine, Am. Bd. of Med. Psychotherapists, Am. Soc. for Group Psychotherapy and Psychodrama (Disting. Profl. Svc. award 1998, Outstanding Scholar award 2002, J.L. Moreno Lifetime Achievement award 2007); mem.: Am. Bd. Examiners in Group Psychotherapy (sec. 1983—93, chair 1997—98). Avocation: trapeze artist. Home: 1195 S Vine St Denver CO 80210-1830 Office: Univ Denver Human Comm Studies Denver CO 80208-0001 Business E-Mail: abarbour@du.edu.

BARBOUR, ARTHUR J., artist; b. Paterson, NJ, Aug. 23, 1926; One-man shows include Beumont Mus. Art, Tex., 1965, exhibitions include Nat. Acad. Design, NYC, Am. Watercolor Soc., Am. Artists Profl. League, Wolf Gallery, Franklin, NJ, 1973, Fritchman Galleries, Boise, Idaho, 1974, U.S. Navy Dept., Marietta Coll., Norfolk Mus. Arts and Sci., Prudential Life Ins. Co., others; author: Watercolor: The Wet Technique, 1978, Painting Buildings in Watercolor, 1973, Painting the Seasons in Watercolor, 1980. Recipient Silver Medal Honor, Audubon Artists, 1988. Mem.: Nat. Soc. Painters Casein and Acrylic, Allied Artists, Painters and Sculptors Soc. NJ, NJ Watercolor Soc., Am. Watercolor Soc. (Gold Medal 1965, Mary S. Litt award 1983). Address: 29 Voorhis Pl Ringwood NJ 07456

BARBOUR, CATHERINE JEAN, actress, set designer, director, mime; b. Dover, Del., Nov. 8, 1932; d. Peter Joseph Callovini and Lydia Clara Shane; m. Alan Gregory Barbour, June 18, 1960. Cert., Am. Acad. Dramatic Arts, 1960; BA magna cum laude, Marymount Manhattan Coll., 1987; MFA, NYU, 1991. Tchr., dir. Am. Acad. Dramatic Arts, NYC, 1963-71; asst. dir., performer, tchr., dir. The Am. Mime Theatre, NYC, 1965—. Adminstrv. asst. Internat. Mimes and Pantomimists, N.Y.C., 1973-74; tchr. Am. mime class San Deigo Sch. Creative and Performing Arts, 2006-07. Set piece design for Music Box; performances with The Am. Mime Theatre include Dreams, Evolution, Sludge, Six, Couplings, Abstraction, Peepshow, Unitaur, Pageant; actress (film) Captain Celluloid vs. The Film Pirates, 1968, American Mime Documentary, 2007; appeared on The Today Show, 1975, TV Tokyo-Asayan, 1999; exhibits include Nat. Arts Club, NYC, 2001-07, Sauander-O'Reilly Galleries, NYC, 2001. Recipient Jehlinger award Am. Acad. Dramatic Arts, NYC, 1960, Merit award, Art Students League NY, 2004. Mem. Am. Watercolor Soc. (assoc.), Rehoboth Art League, Inc., Art Students League N.Y. (Merit award 2004—), 1100 Watercolor Soc., Sons of the Desert, Nat. Movement Theater Assn., Drama League of N.Y. Avocations: art, sculpture, writing, set designing. Office: The American Mime Theatre 61 4th Ave New York NY 10003-5204 Office Phone: 212-777-1710. E-mail: AmMime@aol.com, Mimestar@aol.com.

BARBOUR, CLAUDE MARIE, minister, educator; b. Brussels, Oct. 2, 1935; came to U.S., 1969; Diploma d'État d'Infirmières, École d'Infirmières, Paris, 1956; diploma d'Etudes Religieuses, Faculté Libre de Théolog, Paris, 1958; MST, N.Y. Theol. Sem., 1970; DST, Garrett Evang. Theol. Sem., 1973. Ordained to ministry Presbyn. Ch., 1974. Youth counselor Young Women's Christian Assn., Geneva, 1959-61, Edinburgh, 1965-67; missionary Paris Evang. Missionary Soc., So. Africa, 1962-64; deaconess Ch. of Scotland, Edinburgh, 1967-69; from asst. to assoc. pastor First United Presbyn. Ch., Gary, Ind., 1974-80; from asst. to assoc. prof. Cath. Theol. Union, Chgo., 1976-86, prof., 1986—. McCormick Theol. Sem., Chgo., 1990-96. Founder, dir. Shalom Ministries and Community, Chgo., 1975—; parish assoc. First Presbyn. Ch., Evanston, Ill., 1983—. World Coun. Chs. scholar, Geneva, 1969, United Presbyn. Ch. Commn. on Ecumenical Mission and Rels., N.Y., 1972; recipient Laskey award United Meth. Ch. Womens Div. the Bd. Global Ministries, N.Y., 1972, Civic award Ind. Women's Coun., 1976, Challenge of Peace award Chgo. Ctr. for Peace Studies, 1991, Martin P. Wolf O.F.M. award Justice, Peace and Integrity of Creation Coun. of the English-Speaking Conf. of the Order of Friars Minor, 1996, Blessed are the Peacemakers award World Coun. Chs., 2005. Mem. AAUW, Internat. Assn. for Mission Studies, Nat. Assn. Presbyn. Clergywomen, Am. Soc. Missiology, Assn. Prof. Mission, Midwest Fellowship Prof. Mission, Assn. Presbyn. in Cross-Cultural Mission. Home: 1649 E 50th St Apt 21A Chicago IL 60615-6110 Office: Catholic Theological Union 5401 S Cornell Ave Chicago IL 60615-5664 Business E-Mail: barbour@ctu.edu.

BARBOUR, DAVID A., lawyer; b. Austin, Tex., June 17, 1948; Student, Stanford U.; BBA with highest honors, U. Tex., 1971, JD with honors, 1974. Bar: Tex. 1974. Ptnr. Winstead, Sechrest & Minick, PC, Dallas; ptnr., Corp./Securities Practice Andrews Kurth LLP, Dallas, mem. mgmt. com. Del. US Brazil Aspen Global Housing Forum. Fellow: So. Methodist U. Inst. Internat. Banking & Fin. (sr.); mem.: Dallas Bar Assn., State Bar Tex., ABA (Bus. Law Sect., Develop. in Bus. Financing Com., Securitization of Assets Subcom.), Chancellors U. Tex., Order of Coif, Phi Delta Phi, Beta Gamma Sigma, Phi Kappa Phi. Office: Andrews Kurth LLP 1717 Main St Ste 3700 Dallas TX 75201 Office Phone: 214-659-4444. Office Fax: 214-659-4401. Business E-Mail: dbarbour@andrewskurth.com.

BARBOUR, DORIS LAJUNE, editor; d. Claude Bryan Rose and Carrie Yvette Boyd; m. Fred Thomas Ward (dec.); children: Elise, Rose, Ace. BA, Tex. Christian U., Ft. Worth, 1950. Trainee reporter Ft. Worth Star Telegram, 1947—48; pub. rels. US Congress, 1955—59; editor United Cerebral Palsy, Raleigh, NC, 1971—80; state editor Am. Lung Assn., Raleigh, 1980—81; dir. pub. rels. NC Divsn. Aging, Raleigh, 1981—2000; editor Voice Newspaper, Fayetteville, NC, 2000—07. Mem.: DAR, NC Sr. Citizens Assn.

BARBOUR, HALEY REEVES, governor; b. Yazoo City, Miss., Oct. 22, 1947; m. Marsha Dickson; children: Sterling, Reeves. JD, U. Miss., 1973. Bar: Miss. 1973. Exec. dir. Miss. Rep. Party and So. Assn. Rep. State Chairmen, 1973-76; ptnr., of counsel Henry, Barbour and DeCell, 1981-93; spl. asst. to the Pres., Office of Polit. Affairs, Washington, 1985-86, dep. asst. to Pres. for polit. affairs, 1986; sr. Presdl. campaign advisor, 1988; chmn., CEO, founder, ptnr. Barbour, Griffith & Rogers, Washington and Yazoo City, 1986—92; chmn. Republican Nat. Com., Washington, D.C., 1993-97; gov. State of Miss., Jackson, 2004—. Bd. dirs. Deposit Guaranty Nat. Bank, Mobil Telecomms. Techs., Inc. Regular appearances on Crossfire, Larry King Live, Face the Nation, Nightline, The Today Show and The Capitol Gang. Republican nominee U.S. Senate, Miss., 1982; mem. Rep. Nat. Com., Miss., 1984—; exec. dir. Miss. Rep. Party. Republican. Presbyterian. Office: Office of the Gov PO Box 139 Jackson MS 39205 Office Phone: 601-359-3150. Office Fax: 601-359-3741.*

BARBOUR, JOHN, retail executive; b. Scotland; Degree, U. Glasgow. With sales and mktg. Procter and Gamble, M&M Mars; with Universal Matchbox Group; CEO, pres. OddzOn Products; with Satellite Bus. Group Entrepreneurial Divsn. Hasbro, CEO OddzOn Divsn.; from exec. v.p., CEO Toysrus.com to pres. Toys "R" Us Internat. Toys "R" Us, Inc., Wayne, NJ, 1999—2002; pres. Toys R Us Internat. Toys R Us, Inc., 2002—04, pres., Toys R Us US, 2004—. Office: Toys R Us Inc 1 Geoffrey Way Wayne NJ 07470-2030

BARBOUR, LARRY GREGORY, lawyer; b. Brookhaven, Miss., Mar. 25, 1950; s. Russell Clyde Barbour Jr. and Rhoda Ann (Cox) Benson; m. Carol Christine Cronin, June 28, 1980; children: Barrell Christine, Charles Beveridge, Mary Hester. AB in Econs., Princeton U., 1972; MBA, NYU, 1974; JD, U. Tex., 1977. Bar: Tex. 1977, U.S. Ct. Appeals (5th cir.) 1978. Credit analyst Mfrs. Hanover Trust, NYC, 1972-74; assoc. Vinson & Elkins LLP, Houston, 1977-85, ptnr., 1985—. Fellow Houston Bar Found.; mem. ABA, Tex. Bar Assn., Tex. Assn. Bank Counsel, Houston Bar Assn., Order of Coif. Office: Vinson & Elkins LLP First City Tower 1001 Fannin St Ste 3300 Houston TX 77002-6706 E-mail: lbarbour@velaw.com.

BARBOUR, MICHAEL G(EORGE), botanist, educator, ecologist, consultant; b. Jackson, Mich., Feb. 24, 1942; s. George Jerome and Mae (Dater) B.; m. Norma Jean Yourist, Sept. 30, 1963 (div. 1981); m. Valerie Ann Whitworth, Jan. 25, 1987; children: Julie Ann, Alan Benjamin, Steven Allan Whitworth. BS in Botany, Mich. State U., 1963; PhD in Botany, Duke U., 1967. Asst. prof. botany U. Calif., Davis, 1967-71, assoc. prof., 1971-76, prof., 1976—, chmn., 1982-85, prof. environ. horticulture, 1993—; ptnr. Ecolabs Cons., Davis, 1969—. Vis. prof. botany dept. Hebrew U., Jerusalem, 1979-81; vis. prof. marine scis. dept. La. State U., Baton Rouge, 1984; vis. prof. plant biology dept. Complutense U., Madrid, 1999, U. de la Laguna, Canary Islands, 2003. Co-author: Coastal Ecology, Bodega Head, 1973, Botany, Terrestrial Vegetation of California, 1977, 2d edit., 1988, Terrestrial Plant Ecology, 1980, 3d edit., 1998, North American Terrestrial Vegetation, 1988, 2d edit., 2000, California's Changing Landscapes, 1993, Plant Biology, 1998, An Introduction to Plant Biology, 3d edit., 2005. Fulbright Found. fellow Adelaide, Australia 1964, Evora, Portugal, 2005; Guggenheim Found. fellow, 1978; NSF rsch. grantee, 1968-78, MAB/NSF rsch. grantee, 1989-92, USDA rsch. grantee, 1992—. Mem. Ecol. Soc. Am., Brit. Ecol. Soc., Internat. Assn. Vegetation Sci., Sigma Xi. Democrat. Jewish. Office: U Calif Plant Scis Dept Davis CA 95616 Office Phone: 530-752-2956. Business E-Mail: mgbarbour@ucdavis.edu.

BARBOUR, WILLIAM RINEHART, JR., retired book publisher; b. NYC, Mar. 2, 1922; s. William Rinehart and Mary (McKelvey) B.; m. Mary Munsell, Nov. 17, 1951; children: Bruce R., Elizabeth M., Alan W. Student, Mich. State Coll., 1941-42. With Fleming H. Revell Co., 1944-83, pres., 1968-80, chmn., 1980-83. Co-author: (with wife) Trading Places, 1991, Home Exchange Vacationing, 1996, What Kids Say About Life, Love, and God, 2001. Served with USAAF, 1942-44. Named Pub. of Year Religious Heritage Am., 1974. Home: 6810 Turban Ct Shell Point Village Fort Myers FL 33908-1669 Personal E-mail: wbarbour@barbourbooks.com.

BARBUR, PETER T., lawyer; b. Westfield, Mass., Nov. 6, 1960; BA magna cum laude, Dartmouth Coll., 1983; JD cum laude, NYU, 1987. Bar: NY 1989. Law clk., Hon. Hugh H. Bownes U.S. Ct. of Appeals, 1st Cir., 1987—88; assoc. Cravath, Swaine, Moore LLP, NYC, 1988—94, ptnr., litig., 1994—. Articles editor NYU Law Rev. Named a Root-Tilden Scholar. Mem.: Assn. Bar of City of NY (civil rights com.), Order of Coif. Office: Cravath Swaine & Moore LLP Worldwide Plz 825 Eighth Ave New York NY 10019-7475 Office Phone: 212-474-1058. Office Fax: 212-474-3700. Business E-Mail: pbarbur@cravath.com.

BARBUTO, LEAH M., early childhood and technology educator, consultant; d. Mellissa C. and George E. LeSage; m. Robert T. Barbuto, Aug. 5, 1989. BS, Mass. Coll. Liberal Arts, 1973; MS, Ea. Conn. State U., Willimantic, 1997; postgraduate studies, U. Mass., Amherst, 1998—2006. Cert. in K-8 State of Mass., 1973, in N-3, K-6, 7-12 English State of Conn., 1989, Conn. dual cert. in regular and spl. edn., N-K State of Conn., 1997. With alumni office Williams Coll., Williamstown, Mass., 1973—74; faculty mem., preschool to grade 9 Pine Cobble Sch., Williamstown, 1974—89, dir. summer arts, 1982—89; asst. program dir., edn. coord. Windham Area Cmty. Action Program Head Start and Parent Child Ctr., Danielson, Conn., 1989—94; student support and recruitment position Project ACCESS/Violence Prevention and Early Childhood Grant, Willimantic, Conn., 1994—96; coord. Plainfield Intergenerational Family Resource Ctr., Plainfield, Conn., 1994—96; early childhood edn. faculty Ea. Conn. State U., Willimantic, 1997—, early childhood and tech. specialist USN Child and Family Devel. Resource Ctr., 2005—, co-founder Willimantic Pub. Libr. Outreach to Family Child Care Providers Literacy Team Project, 1997—2000, founding mem. Aerospace and Environ. Edn. Resource Ctr., 1997—2000. Child devel. assoc. advisor ACCESS Head Start and Parent Child Ctr., Willimantic, 1989—2000; cons. Sch. Age Child Care Programs NE Conn., Inc., Mansfield Center, 1994—, Sch. Readiness Program, Plainfield, Conn., 1997—, Canterbury Libr. Ladder to Literacy Program, Canterbury, Conn., 2005—. Vol. resource parent Hawkins Ho., Danielson, Conn., 1991—99; co-founder Aldrich Free Pub. Libr. and Plainfield Pub. Schls. Guided Assistance Program Book Buddies Program, Moosup, Conn., 1995—2006; cmty. rep. ACCESS Head Start Policy Coun., Willimantic, 1995—97; mentor Thames River Mentoring Program, Norwich, Conn., 1996—2000; mem. Quinebaug Youth and Family Svcs., Wauregan, Conn., 1996—98, Teen Pregnancy Prevention Program, Wauregan, 1996—98. Named Tchr. of Yr., Pine Cobble Sch. Bd. Trustees, 1980, Child Adv. of Yr., Windham-Norwich Area Family Child Care Assn., 1998; recipient Willie award for Significant Contbn. to Children's Theater, Williamstown Cmty. Theater, 1989, Outstanding Academic Achievement award, Ea. Conn. State U., 1997, Outstanding Cmty. Svc. award, 1997. Mem.: ASCD, AAUW, AAUP, Nat. Assn. Edn. of Young Children, Nat. Assn. Early Childhood Tchr. Educators, Internat. Soc. Tech. in Edn., Am. Ednl. Rsch. Assn., Kappa Delta Pi, Omicron Delta Kappa, Kappa Delta Pi Honor Internat. Soc. Edn. (counselor, epsilon nu chpt. 1997—2002). Avocations: travel, reading, creative arts. Office: Ea Conn State Univ 83 Windham St Willimantic CT 06226 Home Phone: 860-564-1968; Office Phone: 860-465-4530. Office Fax: 860-465-5099. Personal E-mail: barbutolm@juno.com. Business E-Mail: barbutole@easternct.edu.

BARCA, GEORGE GINO, international winery executive, financial investor, consultant; b. Sacramento, Jan. 28, 1937; s. Joseph and Annie (Muschetto) B.; m. Maria Sclafani, Nov. 19, 1960; children: Anna, Joseph, Gina and Nina (twins) AA, Grant Jr. Coll.; student, LaSalle U., 1963. With Italian Swiss Colony of Calif. United Vintners, USA & Italy, St. Helena, Napa Valley, Calif., 1960—. Chmn., pres. Barca Internat., United Arab Emirates, Calif. Grape Growers, United Arab Emirates, Calif. Vintage Wines, United Arab Emirates, Am. Vintners, United Arab Emirates, Barca Internat. Wineries & Vineyards, United Arab Emirates. Named Best Prodr. of Sales, United Vintners, USA. Mem. KC Roman Catholic. Achievements include invention of over 800 international wines and liquors, specialty brands and trademarks and foods. Office Phone: 916-783-0200. Personal E-mail: eginoearthwine@surewest.net. Business E-Mail: e-gino@barcawines.com, barcaintelwines@barcawines.com.

BARCA, KATHLEEN, marketing executive; b. Burbank, Calif., July 26, 1946; d. Frank Allan and Blanch Irene (Griffith) Barnes; m. Gerald Albino Barca, Dec. 8, 1967 (dec. May 1993); children: Patrick Gerald, Stacia Kathleen. Student, Pierce Coll., 1964; B in Bus., Hancock Coll., 1984. Teller Security Pacific Bank, Pasadena, Calif., 1968-69, Bank Am., Santa Maria, Calif., 1972-74; operator Gen. Tel. Co., Santa Maria, 1974-83, supr. operator, 1983-84; account exec. Radio Sta. KRQK/KLLB, Lompoc, Calif., 1985—87; owner Advt. Unlimited, Orcutt, Calif., 1986-88; regional mgr. A.L. Williams Mktg. Co., Los Alamos, Calif., 1988-89; supr. Matol Botanical Internat., 1989-91; account exec. Santa Maria Times, 1989-95; owner a-garagesale.com, 2000—03, Network Mgmt., 2003—. Author numerous local TV and radio commercials, print advt. Activist Citizens Against Dumps in Residential Environments, Polit. Action Com., Orcutt and Santa Maria; chmn. Community Action Com., Santa Maria, Workshop EPA, Calif. Div., Dept. Health Svcs. State of Calif.; vice coord. Toughlove, Santa Maria, 1988-89; parent coord., mem. steering com. ASAP and Friends, 1988-89; mem. Sloco Access, 1997-99; mem. Friends San Luis Obispo Bot. Gardens, 1997-99; v.p. Seneca Hosp. Aux., 1998-2000; active Fire Svcs., 1998-2000. Mem. NAFE, Womens Network-Santa Maria, Ctrl. Coast Ad (recipient numerous awards), Santa Maria C. of C. (amb. representing Santa Maria Times 1990-94, asst. chief amb. 1993-94), Chester Piecemakers Quilt Club, Lake Almaner Womens Club. Democrat. Avocations: raising exotic birds, writing childrens books. Personal E-mail: barcak@ca.rr.com.

BARCAN, STEPHEN EMANUEL, lawyer; b. Buffalo, July 10, 1942; s. Abe and Goldie (Irom) Barcan; m. Bettye Ann Grossman, June 13, 1965; children: Sara Ellen, Daniel Jonathan, Adam Michael. AB, Columbia Coll., 1963; JD cum laude, Rutgers U., 1966. Bar: N.J. 1966, U.S. Dist. Ct. N.J. 1966, U.S. Ct. Appeals (3d cir.) 1971. Law sec. to presiding judge Appellate divsn. N.J. Superior Ct., 1966—67; assoc. Wilentz, Goldman & Spitzer, PA, Woodbridge, NJ, 1967—74, ptnr., 1974—, adminstrv. shareholder, 1999—. Contbg. editor Commercial Real Estate Transactions in N.J., 2003. Pres. Westfield Symphony Orch., 1999—2001, Temple Emanu-El, Westfield, NJ, 1984—86. Mem.: Middlesex County Bar Assn., NJ State Bar Assn. (chmn. land use sect. 1997—98). Democrat. Jewish. Office: Wilentz Goldman & Spitzer PO Box 10 90 Woodbridge Ctr Dr Ste 900 Woodbridge NJ 07095-1142 Office Phone: 732-855-6055. Business E-Mail: sbarcan@wilentz.com.

BARCELLA, ERNEST LAWRENCE, JR., lawyer; b. Washington, May 23, 1945; s. Ernest Lawrence and Louise Marion (Berniere) B.; m. Mary Elizabeth Lashley, June 1, 1970; 1 child, Laura Louise. AB, Dartmouth U., 1967; JD, Vanderbilt U., 1970. Bar: D.C. 1971, U.S. Dist. Ct. D.C. 1971, U.S. Ct. Appeals (D.C. cir.) 1971, U.S. Supreme Ct. 1976. Asst. U.S. atty., Washington, 1970-86; ptnr. Katten, Muchin, Zavis & Dombroff, Washington, 1991-94, Paul, Hastings, Janofsky & Walker LLP, Washington, 1994—, mem. policy com., chmn. white-collar criminal defense practice group. Recipient John Marshall award, U.S. Dept. Justice, 1983; named one of 75 Best Lawyers in Washington, Washigntonian survey mag., 2002. Fellow Am. Coll. Trial Lawyers; mem. ABA (white collar crimes com. criminal justice sect., complex crimes com. litigation sect.), Assn. Trial Lawyers Am., Fed. Bar Assn. (younger lawyer award 1979). Roman Catholic. Office: Paul Hastings Janofsky & Walker LLP 875 15th St NW Washington DC 20005 Office Phone: 202-551-1718. Office Fax: 202-551-0118. Business E-Mail: larrybarcella@paulhastings.com.*

BARCELO, JOHN JAMES, III, law educator; b. New Orleans, Sept. 23, 1940; s. John James Jr. and Elfrida Margaret (Bisso) B.; m. Lucy L. Wood, July 14, 1974; children— Lisa, Amy, Steven. BA, Tulane U., 1962, JD, 1966; SJD, Harvard U., 1977. Bar: La. 1967, D.C. 1974, U.S. Supreme Ct. 1974, N.Y. 1975. Fulbright scholar U. Bonn, Germany, 1966-67; prof. law Cornell U. Law Sch., Ithaca, N.Y., 1969—, A. Robert Noll. prof. of law, 1984-96, William Nelson Cromwell prof. internat. and comprative law, 1996—, Reich dir., Berger internat. legal studies, 1972-88, 90—. Cons. Import Trade Adminstrn., Dept. Commerce Author: (with others) Law: Its Nature, Functions and Limits, 3rd edit., 1986, International Commercial Arbitration, 1999, 3d edit., 2006; co-editor: Lawyers' Practice and Ideals: A Comparative View, 1999, A Global Law of Jurisdiction and Judgments: Lessons from the Hague, 2002; contbr. articles to profl. jours. Mem. Am. Assn. for Comparative Study of Law (bd. dirs.), Am. Soc. Internat. Law, Am. Soc. Comparative Law, Maritime Law Assn. U.S. Office: Cornell U Law Sch Myron Taylor Hall Ithaca NY 14853 Business E-Mail: jjb16@cornell.edu.

BARCEY, HAROLD EDWARD DEAN (HAL), real estate consultant; b. Flint, Mich., Sept. 11, 1949; s. Glen Edward and Joyce Paulene (Dean) B.; children: Allen, Christopher David, David Gregory, Richard, Jackson, Joseph, Christopher Ray, Andrew. BA, U. Fla., 1971, postgrad., 1971-76. Cert. residential mktg. specialist, cert. residential brokerage mgr., cert. residential appraiser, accredited buyer rep., cert. buyer rep. Activist, lectr., fundraiser various environ. orgns. and projects, Fla., Ga., 1970-75; advt. mgr., salesman Towne & Suburban Realty, Salem, Ohio, 1977-87; broker-mgr. Seasons Real Estate Counselors, Salem, 1987—; loan officer Best Rate Fin. Svcs. Artist "Man in Balance with Nature" symbol, 1969. Campaign worker McCarty for Pres., Youngstown, 1967; bd. dirs. adult edn. program Alachua County, Fla., 1969; bd. dirs. Balance Fund Found., Balt., 1970-73, Good Earthkeeping, Inc., Gainesville, Fla., 1971-73; del. Conf. on Population Explosion and the Devel. Profl., Airlie, Va., 1969; solicitor LifeBanc of Ohio, Salem, 1989—; campaign worker Morris Udall for Pres., Gainesville, 1975. Named for Outstanding Citizen Contbn., Village of Canfield, Ohio, 1967. Mem. Nat. Assn. Realtors, Am. Assn. Cert. Appraiser, Realtors Nat. Mktg. Inst., Alpha Gamma Sigma. Independent. Roman Catholic. Avocations: travel, writing, music. Home and Office: 1288 W Perry St Salem OH 44460-3550 Office Phone: 330-332-1598. E-mail: hbarcey@neo.rr.com.

BARCHAS, JACK DAVID, psychiatrist, medical researcher, educator, behavioral molecular neurobiologist; b. LA, Nov. 2, 1935; s. Samuel Isaac and Cecile Margaret (Pasarow) Barchas; m. Patricia Ruth Corbitt, Feb. 9,

1957 (dec.); 1 child, Isaac Doherty; m. Rosemary Anne Stevens, Aug. 9, 1994; stepchildren: Carey T. Stevens, Richard N. Stevens. BA, Pomona Coll., 1956; MD, Yale Med. Sch., 1961. Lic. NY, Va. Med. intern Pritzker Sch. Medicine, Chgo., 1961—62; rsch. assoc. Nat. Inst. Health, Bethesda, Md., 1962—64; resident in psychiatry Stanford Med. Sch., Palo Alto, Calif., 1964—67; dir. lab. behavioral neurochemistry Dept. Psychiatry, Stanford Med. Sch., 1964—76; asst. prof. psychiatry Stanford Med. Sch., Palo Alto, 1967—71, assoc. prof., 1971—76, Nancy Friend Pritzker prof. psychiatry, dir. Nancy Pritzker Lab. Behavioral Neurochemistry, 1976—89, assoc. chair dept. psychiatry, 1982—87; prof. psychiatry UCLA Sch. Medicine, 1990—93, dean neuroscience and rsch. develop., 1990—93; Barklie McKee Henry prof., chair dept. psychiatry, psychiatrist-in-chief Weill Cornell Med. Coll., NY, 1993—, NY Presbyn. Hosp., NY, 1993—. Past chair Stanford Psychiatry Residency Program Stanford Med. Sch., past chair Deanship Search com., past chair Com. on Endowed Chairs; founder, co-chair sci. adv. bd., mem. bd. dirs. NEUREX CORP., Menlo Park, Calif., 1984—90; exec. dir. Pritzker Network on Depression, NY, 1996—2006. Assoc. editor Clinical Neuroscience Research, Elsevier, Amsterdam, 2002—;, author over 300 publ.; co-editor: (numerous monographs and publ. including) Serotonin and Behavior, Psychopharmacology from Theory to Practice, Neuroregulators and Psychiatric Disorders, Biological Aspects of Substance Abuse, Clinical Neuroscience of Depression, Advances in Situ Hybridization Methodolgy; editor: Archives of General Psychiatry, 1994—2001; mem. editl. bd. Jour. of the AMA, 1994—2001. Mem., bd. trustees Hatos Found., Los Angeles, 1993—; mem., sci. adv. bd. Nat. Alliance for Rsch. on Schizophrenia and Depression, 1987—; pres. & chair bd. dirs. Robert J. and Claire Pasarow Found., 2000—; chair Pasarow Med. Rsch. Awards Prog., Los Angeles, 2000—; chair, bd. dirs. Assn. for Rsch. on Nervous and Mental Disorders (ARNMD), New York, 1998—; chair, bd. trustees New York Acad. of Medicine, 2001—. Lt. Comdr. US Public Health Service, 1962—64. Recipient Bennett Rsch. Award and Lifetime Achievement Award, Soc. of Biological Psychiatry, Efron Rsch. Award, Am. Coll. of Neuropsychopharmacology, Career Tchr. Award, Rsch. Scientist Devel. Award & Rsch. Scientist Award, Nat. Inst. of Mental Health, Sachar Award in Psychiatry, Columbia U., Lehmann Award for Psychiatric Rsch., NY State Office of Mental Health, Thomas William Salmon Medal, NY Acad. Medicine; grantee for rsch. on mental illness, drug abuse, and alcohol abuse, Nat. Insts. of Heath, Office of Navel Rsch., NASA, Nat. Sci. Found. Fellow: Am. Psychiatric Assn. (life; past chair Coun. on Rsch., past chair Disting. Service Awards Com., Award for Rsch. in Psychiatry); mem.: AMA (editor Archives of General Psychiatry 1994—2001), Inst. Med. of Nat. Acad. Scis. (chair IOM Bd. of Biobehavioral Scis. and Mental Disorders 1982—94, past mem. Prog. Com. and Mem. Com., past chair Psychiatry-Neurology Sect., past chair for report requested by White House and Executive Branch, Sarnat Prize in Mental Health 2006), Acad. Behavioral Med. Rsch., Am. Assn. for Advancement of Sci., Am. Med. Assn., Am. Soc. for Neurochemistry, Am. Psychopathological Assn., Am. Physiological Soc., Am. Soc. for Pharmacology and Experimental Therapeutics, Am. Psychosomatic Soc., Soc. for Neuroscience, NY Psychiat Soc. (mem. Salmon Awards Com.), Vidonian Club, Phi Beta Kappa. Achievements include research in investigation of neuroregulators (chemicals which act as neurotransmitters or regulate activity of nerve cells) in terms of identification of previously unrecognized substances; study of the formation and inactivation of neuroregulators, and determination of their role in brain, behavior, and mental disorders; compounds studied included serotonin, melatonin, epinephrine, norepinephrine, and dopamine as well as peptides such as the endorphins; findings included the first demonstration of differential changes of neuroregulators in the brain with stress; current research centers about studies of the neurobiology and psychobiology of depressive illness through the Pritzker Network and new projects in sociophysiology; other activities center about public policy in psychiatry and medicine. Avocations: photography, High Haven Music, the Shenandoah Valley, current history. Office: Cornell U Weill Med Coll Dept Psychiatry 1300 York Ave Box 171 Rm F-1231 New York NY 10021*

BARCHET, STEPHEN, obstetrician, gynecologist, retired military officer; b. Annapolis, Md., Oct. 25, 1932; s. Stephen George and Louise (Lankford) B.; m. Marguerite Joan Racek, Aug. 9, 1965. Student, Brown U., 1949—52; MD, U. Md., 1956. Diplomate Am. Bd. Ob-Gyn.; cert. physician exec. Commd. ensign M.C. USN, 1955, advanced through grades to rear adm., 1978; intern Naval Hosp., Chelsea, Mass., 1956-57, resident in ob-gyn., 1958-61, resident in gen. surgery Portsmouth, Va., 1957-58; fellow Harvard Med. Sch., 1959-60; obstetrician-gynecologist Naval Hosp., Naples, Italy, 1961-63, Portsmouth, NH, 1963-64, Beaufort, SC, 1964-66, Bremerton, Wash., 1967-70, chief ob-gyn. Boston, 1970-73; asst. head, tng. br. Bur. Medicine and Surgery, Washington, 1973, head, 1973-75; dep. spl. asst. to surgeon gen. USN, 1975; assoc. dean Sch. Medicine, Uniformed Svcs. U. Health Scis., Bethesda, Md., 1976-77, exec. sec. bd. regents, 1976-77; spl. asst. to surgeon gen. for med. dept. edn. and tng. Bur. Medicine and Surgery, Navy Dept., Washington, 1977-79, insp. gen., 1979-80; comdg. officer Naval Health Scis. and Edn. and Tng. Command, Nat. Naval Med. Ctr., Bethesda, 1977-79; asst. chief planning, resources BUMED, 1980-82; dep. surg. gen., dep. dir. naval medicine Dept. Navy, 1982-83; ret., 1983; with Pacific Med. Ctr., Seattle, 1985-91; cons. Mil. Health Care, Seattle, 1987—; prin. MSA Programs, Seattle, 1995—; mng. ptnr. Benefit Payment $olutions, 1998—; coord. Health Plan for Life, 2003—. Clin. asst. prof. Boston U. Sch. Medicine, 1971—; alt. regent Nat. Libr. Medicine, Bethesda, 1977-79; asst. prof. health care scis. George Washington U. Sch. Medicine and Health Scis., Washington, 1978—; ex officio mem. grad. med. edn. nat. adv. com. HEW, 1978-79; chmn. med.-dental com. Intersvc. Tng. Rev. Orgn., Washington, 1977-79; chmn. Washington Med. Savs. Accounts Project, 1994; bd. dir. Hope Heart Inst., chmn. edn. com. Contbr. articles to med. jours. Sec. The Rainier Club, 1992—93; bd. dir. North Seattle C.C. Found., 1992—95. Decorated Bronze Star, others. Fellow Am. Coll. Obstetricians and Gynecologists, Am. Coll. Physician Execs.; mem. AMA, Assn. Mil. Surgeons U.S., Soc. Med. Cons. Armed Forces, Wash. State Med. Assn., King County Med. Assn., N.W. Mil. Health Benefit Assn. (exec. dir. 1991-94). Home and Office: 18601 SE 64th Way Issaquah WA 98027-8616 *Lasting achievements depend not only upon knowledge well applied but also upon doing what ought to be done.*

BARCHI, ROBERT LAWRENCE, clinical neurologist; b. Phila., Nov. 23, 1946; s. Henry John and Elizabeth (Pesci) B.; children: Jonathan Robert, Jennifer Elizabeth. BS, Georgetown U., 1968, MS, 1969; PhD, U. Pa., 1972, MD, 1973. Diplomate Am. Bd. Neurology and Psychiatry, Am. Bd. Med. Examiners. Resident in neurology U. Pa. Hosp., 1973-75; asst. prof. biochemistry U. Pa. Med. Sch., Phila., 1974-75, asst. prof. neurology and biochemistry, 1975-78, assoc. prof., 1978-81, prof., 1981—99, David Mahoney prof. neurol. scis., 1985—2002, Fairhill prof. medicine emeritus, 2004, chmn. neurosci. grad. program, 1983-89, dir. Mahoney Inst. Neurol. Scis., 1983-96, vice-dean rsch. sch. medicine, 1989-91, chmn. dept. neurosci., 1992-95, chmn. depts. neurology and neurosci., 1995-99; provost and chief acad. officer U. Pa., Phila., 1999—2004; pres. Thomas Jefferson U., Phila., 2004—. Mem. med. adv. bd. Muscular Dystrophy Assn., 1982—94, Soc. To Prevent Blindness, 1999—2001, Cephalon Inc., 1992—2002; mem. sci. adv. bd. Phila. Ventures Inc., 1992—95, TransMolecular, Inc., 1996—; bd. mgrs. The Wistar Inst., 2000—06; bd. dirs., vice chair Pa. BioAdvance, Inc., 2002—; bd. dirs. Covenance, Inc., VWR, Inc.; bd. trustees Ursinus Coll., 2005—. Author: (with R. Lisak) Myasthenia Gravis, 1982; (with Rosenberg, Prusiner, DiMauro) Molecular and Genetic Basis of Neurological Disease, 3 edits.; mem. editorial bd. Muscle and Nerve Jour., 1981-82, 95—, Jour. Neurochemistry, 1981-90, Jour. Neurosci., 1988-91, Ion Channels, 1988—, Current Opinion Neurology and Neurosurgery, 1992—, The Neuroscientist, 1993—, Neurobiology of Disease, 1994—; contbr. chpts. to textbooks, numerous articles to profl. jours. Adv. bd. Ben Franklin Tech. Ptnrs., 1999—2004. Recipient Lindback award U. Pa., 1979, Javits award NIH, 1985, Inst. Med. Nat. Acad. Scis., 1993; Sci. Achievement award Am. Heart Assn., 1997, Disting. Grad. award U. Pa. Med. Sch., 2000. Fellow AAAS, Am. Acad. Neurology, Fellow Am. Neurol. Assn. (bd. councillors 1992-94); mem. Inst. Medicine of the NAS, Biophys. Soc., Soc. for Neurosci. (pub. lectr. 1985), Am. Soc. Clin. Investigation, Assn. Am. Physicians, Phila. Coll. Physicians, Phi Beta Kappa, Alpha Omega Alpha. Avocation: antiquarian horology. Office: Office of the President Thomas Jefferson Univ 1020 Walnut St Philadelphia PA 19107 Business E-Mail: robert.barchi@jefferson.edu.

BARCLAY, DAVID A., lawyer; b. 1962; BA in Mktg., Georgia State U.; MBA in Finance, U. Miami; JD, Nova Southeastern U. Assoc. corp., banking & securities dept. Shutts & Bowen, Miami, Fla.; corp. counsel then sr. corp. counsel Blockbuster Entertainment Corp.; gen. counsel Discovery Zone; v.p., assoc. gen. counsel AutoNation (formerly Republic Industries, Inc.), 1997—98, sr. v.p., gen. counsel solid waste group, 1998; sr. v.p., gen. counsel, sec. Republic Services, Inc., Fort Lauderdale, Fla., 1998—. Mem.: ABA. Office: Republic Services Inc 110 SE 6th St Fort Lauderdale FL 33301

BARCLAY, GEORGE N., lawyer; b. 1951; BA, Brown U.; JD, Boston U., 1977. Bar: DC 1978. Asst. corp. counsel DC Govt., 1978—82; assoc. gen. counsel, personal property Gen. Services Admin., Washington, spl. counsel, FTS2000, asst. gen. counsel., acting gen. counsel, 2004—. Recipient Federal 100 award, Presidential Rank award, 2001. Office: US General Services Admin 1800 F St NW Washington DC 20405 Office Phone: 202-501-2200. E-mail: george.barclay@gsa.gov.*

BARCLAY, H. DOUGLAS (HUGH DOUGLAS BARCLAY), lawyer, legislator, diplomat; b. NYC, July 5, 1932; s. Hugh and Dorothy Barclay; m. Sara Seiter, Aug. 15, 1959. BA, Yale U., 1955; JD, Syracuse U., 1961, LLD (hon.), 1997, St. Lawrence U., 1980, SUNY, 1990, LeMoyne Coll., 2006; ScD (hon.), Clarkson U., 1981. Bar: N.Y. 1962. Ptnr. Hiscock & Barclay and predecessors, Syracuse, NY, 1961—2003, 2007—; US amb. to El Salvador US Dept. State, 2003—07. Sec., gen. counsel KeyCorp and subs., Albany, N.Y., 1971-89; mem. N.Y. State Senate, 1965-84, chmn. Judiciary com., chmn. Select Task Force on Ct. Reorgn., chmn. senate codes com.; dir., chmn. bd. Syracuse Supply Co. Mem. N.Y. State Econ. Power Allocation Bd., N.Y. Racing Assn., former bd. trustees; former pres. Met. Devel. Assn.; former trustee, former chmn. Syracuse U., chair chancellor search com.; vice chmn. N.Y. State George Bush for Pres., 1988; chmn. N.Y. State Bush-Quayle campaign, 1992; mem. policy coun. Gov. Pataki's Transition Team; chmn., bd. trustees, Syracuse U., 1992-98; bd. dirs. Overseas Pvt. Investment Corp., 1990-93; mem. panel of conciliators, Internat. Ctr. of Settlement of Investment Disputes, 2002. Lt. arty. U.S. Army, 1955-57, Korea. Mem. ABA, N.Y. State Bar Assn. Office: Hiscock & Barclay 300 S State St Syracuse NY 13202-1633

BARCLAY, KATHLEEN S., automotive executive; b. Milw. B in Bus., Mich. State U., 1978; MBA, MIT, 1991. With GM, Detroit, 1978—81; retail mgr. Southland Corp., Reno, Chgo.; human resource compensation mgr. Allen-Bradley Co., Milw.; with GM, Warren, Mich., 1985—, mgr. salaried personnel corp. staffs, 1987—88; mgr. labor rels. Chevrolet-Pontiac-GM Can., 1988—91, mgr. exec. compensation, 1991; dir. compensation GM, 1992—95, dir. human resources vehicle sales svc., 1995, gen. dir. human resources mgmt. N.Am. ops., 1996—98, v.p. global human resources, 1998—. Bd. dirs. Cowdrick Group, Mich. Virtual Univ. Bd. govs. MIT; alumni bd. dirs. Mich. State U. Sloan fellow, MIT, 1991. Fellow: Nat. Acad. Human Resources (bd. dirs.); mem.: Detroit Women's Econ. Club. Office: GM Corp 300 Renaissance Ctr Detroit MI 48265-3000 Office Phone: 313-556-5000, 313-556-1988. Fax: 248-696-7300.

BARCLAY, PARIS, television director, television producer; b. Chgo. Heights, Ill., June 30, 1956; BA, Harvard Coll., 1979. Dir.: (TV series) Fastlane, 2002—03, episodes of Angel Street, Moon Over Miami, Silk Stalkings, Diagnosis Murder, Sliders, Second Noah, Clueless, Brooklyn South, NYPD Blue (Emmy award for Outstanding Directing for episode Lost Israel, part II, 1998, Dirs. Guild Am. award for Outstanding Directorial Achievement in a Dramatic Series & Emmy award for Outstanding Directing for episode Hearts & Souls, 1999), City of Angels, ER, American Dreams, The West Wing, Huff, Law & Order, The Shield, Numb3rs, House, Cold Case; supervising prodr. (TV series) NYPD Blue, 1993, co-exec. prodr. Cold Case, 2005—06 (NAACP Image award for Outstanding Directing in a Dramatic Series, 2006); dir.: (TV films) The Cherokee Kid, 1996, America's Dream, 1996, Dead Lawyers, 2004; dir., co-exec. prodr. (TV films) Meet the Changs, 2001, The Big Time, 2002, co-exec. prodr. The Street Lawyer, 2003; dir.: (films) Don't Be a Menace, 1996; author, composer (plays) One Red Flower, 2004; author: (plays) Almost a Man; contbr. to The Advocate. Recipient 2006 Robert B. Aldrich Svc. award, Directors Guild of Am.

BAR-COHEN, AVRAM, mechanical engineering educator; b. Bklyn., Jan. 19, 1946; s. Simon and Dorothy (Halperin) Markowitz; m. Annette Pavony, Sept. 11, 1966; children: Barak, Raanan, Talia Dvora. SB, SM, MIT, 1968, PhD, 1971. Sr. engr. Raytheon Co., Bedford, Mass., 1968-73; lectr. dept. mech. engring. Ben Gurion U., Beer Sheva, Israel, 1973-75, sr. lectr., 1975-77, 79-81; assoc. prof. Ben Gurion U. of the Negev, Beer Sheva, Israel, 1981-84, prof., 1988; vis. assoc. prof. U. Minn., 1984-85, adj. prof., 1985-87, 89, assoc. prof., 1989-91, prof. dept. mech. engring., 1992—2002, dir. Thermodynamics and Heat Transfer divsn., 1992-98, James J. Renier vis. chair Tech. Leadership, 1996-99, exec. dir. Ctr. Devel. Tech. Leadership, 1998—2002, H.W. Sweatt chair in technol. leadership, 2000—02; chair dept. mech. engring. U. Md., 2002—, Disting. Univ. prof., 2005—. Vis. assoc. prof. MIT, Cambridge, 1977-78; adj. prof. Naval Postgrad. Sch., Monterey, Calif., 1982; exec. cons. Control Data Corp., Mpls., 1985-89. Author: (with A.D. Kraus) Thermal Analysis and Control of Electronic Equipment, 1983, Design and Analysis of Heat Sinks, 1995; editor: (with A.D. Kraus) Advances in Thermal Modeling of Electronic Components and Systems, vol. I, 1988, vol. II, 1990, vol. III, 1992, vol. IV, 1998; contbr. articles to profl. jours. Fellow ASME (v.p. rsch. 1998—2001, recipient Edwin F. Church medal 1994, Heat Transfer meml. award 1999, Worcester Reed Warner medal 2000), IEEE (editor-in-chief Transaction on Components and Packaging Technologies 1995—, award 2002); mem. N.Y. Acad. Scis., Sigma Xi, Pi Tau Sigma, Tau Beta Pi. Office Phone: 301-405-3173. Business E-Mail: abc@umd.edu.

BARCUS, ROBERT GENE, retired educational association administrator; b. Oct. 22, 1937; s. Harold Eugene and Marjorie Irene (Dilling) B.; m. Mary Evelyn Shull, Aug. 9, 1959; children: Jennifer Sue, Debra Lynn. BPE, Purdue U., 1959; MA, Ball State U., 1963; postgrad., Ind. U., summer 1966; supts. lic., Butler U., 1967. Tchr., coach Wabash (Ind.) Jr. H.S., 1959-63, Wabash H.S., 1963-64, North Cen. H.S., Indpls., 1964-65; salary cons. Ind. State Tchrs. Assn., Indpls., 1965-67, asst. dir. rsch., 1967-68, dir. spl. svcs., 1968-70, exec. asst., 1971-72, adminstrv. asst., 1972-73, asst. exec. dir. spl. svcs. and tchr. rights, 1973-82, asst. exec. dir. adminstrn., pers. and governance, 1982-85, asst. exec. dir. labor rels. and adminstrn., 1985-93, assoc. exec. dir. labor rels. and adminstrn., 1993—2002, ret., 2003. Clk. Ch. of the Brethren, 1966-74, chmn., 1979-83, 87, 92-96, 97-98, 98-99, fin. sec., 2000; mem. Ind State Libr. and Hist. Bd., 2000, v.p., 2006; trustee Manchester Coll., 2004. Alumni scholar Purdue U., 1959. Mem. NEA, Wabash City Tchr. Assn. (past pres.), Washington Twp. Tchr. Assn. (past pres.), Indpls. Press Club, Nat. Edn. Assn., Ind. State Tchrs. Assn., Phi Delta Kappa Home: 2230 Brewster Rd Indianapolis IN 46260-1521 Personal E-mail: rbarcus@ista-in.org.

BARDACH, JOAN LUCILE, clinical psychologist; b. Albany, NY, Oct. 3, 1919; d. Monroe Lederer and Lucile May (Lowenberg) B. BA, Cornell U., 1940; AM in Psychology, NYU, 1951; PhD in Clin. Psychology, 1957; cert. in psychoanalysis and psychotherapy, NYU, 1970. Supr. clin. psychologist NYU Rusk Inst. Rehab. Medicine, 1959-61; asst. chief and acting chief psychologist Rusk Inst. Rehab. Medicine, 1962-65, dir. psychol. services, 1965-82; research psychologist, mem. faculty N.Y. Med. Coll., 1961-62; clin. prof. rehab. medicine (psychology) NYU Med. Ctr., 1976—; supr. postdoctoral program psychoanalysis and psychotherapy NYU, 1978—; pvt. practice clin. psychology and psychoanalysis NYC, 1957—. Non-govtl. orgn. rep. to UN Internat. Ctr. Sociol., Penal and Penitentiary Rsch. and Studies, Messina, Italy, 1985—; prin. investigator NIMH, 1976-81; mem. adv. bd. Coalition Sexuality and Disability, Planned Parenthood, 1983-89; cons. in field. Contbr. articles to profl. jours., chpt. to books. Recipient 3 awards for ednl. film, Choices: In Sexuality With Physical Disability, Internat. Film Festivals, Pioneer award for Sexual Attitude Reassessment Workshops The Coalition on Sexuality and Disability, 1989; NIMH fellow Inst. Sex Rsch., U. Ind., 1976. Fellow Am. Orthopsychiat. Assn.; mem. APA, Sex Info. and Edn. Council U.S., Nat. Register Health Service Providers in Psychology, NY State Psychol. Assn. Home and Office: 50 E 10th St New York NY 10003-6223 Office Phone: 212-673-2436.

BARDACK, PAUL ROITMAN, cultural organization administrator; b. NYC, Nov. 13, 1953; s. Lawrence Stanley and Charlotte (Sebold) B.; m. Esther Roitman, May 27, 1979; children: David, Avi, Daniella. BA, Yale U., 1975; JD, Am. U., 1978. Bar: D.C. 1980. Atty. U.S. Dept. HUD, Washington, 1978-79; gen. counsel to U.S. congressman Robert Garcia, Washington, 1979-81; atty. Barrett Smith Schapiro Simon & Armstrong, NYC, 1981-83; mgr. econ. devel. dept. City of Cleve., 1983-84; chief exec. officer, gen. counsel Econ. Devel. Resources, Inc., Phila. and Washington, 1984-86; sr. policy advisor Gov. Thomas Kean, Trenton, N.J., 1986-89; dep. asst. sec. for econ. devel. HUD, Washington, 1989-93; v.p. Nat. Mentoring Partnership, Washington, 1993-99; cons. Booz Allen Hamilton, McLean, Va., 1999—2004; CEO My Jewish Learning, Inc., Rockville, Md., 2004—. Mem. ABA, D.C. Bar Assn., U.S. Distance Learning Assn. Jewish. Home: 105 Dunloggin Dr Rockville MD 20850-5615 Office: My Jewish Learning 966 Hungerford Dr Rockville MD 20850 Office Phone: 301-217-0145. Business E-Mail: prbardack@myjewishlearning.com.

BARDACKE, PAUL, lawyer; b. Oakland, Calif., Dec. 16, 1944; s. Theodore Joseph and Frances (Woodward) B.; children: Julie, Brynn, Francheska, Chloe. BA cum laude, U. Calif.-Santa Barbara, 1966; JD, U. Calif.-Berkeley, 1969. Bar: Calif. 1969, N.Mex. 1970. Atty. Legal Aid Soc., Albuquerque, 1969; firm Sutin, Thayer & Browne, Albuquerque, 1970—91; atty. gen. State of N.Mex., Santa Fe, 1983—86; ptnr. Eaves, Bardacke, Baugh, Kierst & Kiernan, P.A., Albuquerque, 1991—2005, Sutin, Thayer & Browne, PC, 2005—. Adj. prof. N.Mex. Law Sch., Albuquerque, 1973—; mem. faculty Nat. Inst. Trial Lawyers Advocacy, 1978—83. Bd. dirs. All Faiths Receiving Home, Albuquerque; bd. dirs. Friends of Art, 1974-76, Artspace Mag., 1970-80; bd. trustees Albuquerque Cmty. Found., 2001-. Reginald Heber Smith fellow, 1969 Fellow Am. Coll. Trial Lawyers; mem. ABA, Calif. Bar Assn., N.Mex. Bar Assn., Am. Bd. Trial Advs. (pres. N.Mex. chpt. 1992-93). Democrat. Office: Sutin, Thayer & Browne PC PO BOX 1945 Albuquerque NM 87103 Office Phone: 505-883-2500.

BARDAGLIO, PETER WINTHROP, humanities educator, former academic administrator; b. Hartford, Conn., Apr. 25, 1953; s. George William and Mary Frances (White) B.; m. Wrexie Anne Lainson, Dec. 21, 1983; children: Sarah Jennings Agan, Jesse Barrett Agan, Anne Winthrop. BA, Brown U., 1975; MA, Stanford U., 1978, PhD, 1987. Vis. lectr. U. Md., College Park, 1981-83; instr. Goucher Coll., Balt., 1983-87, asst. prof., 1987-93, assoc. prof., 1993-95, Elizabeth Conolly Todd disting. assoc. prof., 1995-99, prof., 1999—2002, Elizabeth Connolly Todd disting. prof., 1999-2000, chair History Dept., 1996-98, interim v.p., acad. dean, 2000—02; provost, v.p. acad. affairs, prof. history Ithaca Coll., NY, 2002—07; sr. fellow Second Nature, Inc., Boston, 2007—. Spkr. Md. Humanities Coun. Spkrs. Bur., 1996—99. Author: Reconstructing the Household: Families, Sex, and the Law in the Nineteenth Century South, 1995 (Orgn. Am. Historians James A. Rawley prize 1996); contbr. articles to profl. jours. Mem. Lyman Award Com., 2002—03, 2005, Jameson Fellowship Com., 2002—05; elder Catonsville (Md.) Presbyn. Ch., 1992—2002; bd. trustees Hist. Ctr. Tompkins County, 2004—; bd. dirs. Cayaga Med. Ctr., 2005—. Grantee Nat. Endowment for Humanities, Am. Hist. Assn.; Jesse Ball duPont fellow, Nat. Humanities Ctr., 1999—2000. Mem.: Assn. for Advancement of Sustainability in Higher Edn. (sr. coun. mem.), Associated New Am. Colls. (exec. com. 2004—), Am. Hist. Assn. (Littleton-Griswold rsch. grant 1989), Orgn. Am. Historians, So. Hist. Assn. (membership com. 1991—92, local arrangements com. 2002). Home: 9748 Arden Rd Trumansburg NY 14886 Office: Second Nature, Inc 18 Tremont St, Ste 1120 Boston MA 02108 Office Phone: 617-224-1610.

BARDEEN, WILLIAM ALLAN, research physicist; b. Washington, Pa., Sept. 15, 1941; s. John and F. Jane (Maxwell) B.; m. Marjorie Ann Gaylord; children: Charles Gaylord, Karen Gail. AB in Physics, Cornell U., 1962; PhD in Physics, U. Minn., 1968, DSc (hon.), 2002. Rsch. assoc. SUNY, Stony Brook, 1966-68; mem. Inst. for Advanced Study, Princeton, N.J., 1968-69; asst. prof. Stanford (Calif.) U., 1969-72, assoc. prof., 1972-75; scientist Fermilab, Batavia, Ill., 1975-93, head theoretical physics, 1987-93, scientist, 1994—; head theoretical physics SSC Lab., Dallas, 1993-94. Vis. scientist CERN, Geneva, Switzerland, 1971-72, Max Planck Inst. for Physics, Munich, 1977, 86. Author: Barden-Bardeen Genealogy, 1993; editor: Symp. on Anomalies, Geometry, Topology, 1985; mem. editl. bd. Phys. Rev., 1981-84, 92-94, Jour. Math. Physics, 1986-90, European Physics Jour. C, 1997-2000; contbr. numerous articles to profl. jours. Trustee Aspen Ctr. for Physics, 1987-91. Fellowship Alfred P. Sloan Found., 1971-74, John Simon Guggenheim Found., 1985-86; recipient sr. scientist award Alexander von Humboldt Found., 1977 Fellow Am. Phys. Soc. (exec. com. divsn. of particles and fields 1988-90, J. J. Sajurai prize for theoretical particle physics 1996); mem. Am. Acad. Arts and Scis., NAS. Avocations: genealogy, basketball. Office: Fermilab MS 106 PO Box 500 Batavia IL 60510-0500

BARDELAS, JOSE ANTONIO, allergist; b. Havana, Cuba, Feb. 3, 1948; came to U.S., 1961; s. Jose A. and Georgina (Leyva) B.; m. Sallie Young, July 3, 1971; children: Joseph, Mary. BA in Human Biology, Johns Hopkins U., 1970, MD, 1973. Intern, then resident in pediats. Johns Hopkins Hosp., Balt., 1973-75; fellow in allergy and immunology Nat. Jewish Ctr., Denver, 1975-77; pvt. practice Greensboro, NC, 1977—. Asst. clin. prof. pediats. U. N.C., Chapel Hill, 1979—. Fellow Am. Acad. Allergy and Immunology; mem. AMA, N.C. Soc. Allergy and Immunology (pres. 1982), N.C. Med. Soc. (mem. exec. coun. 1990, 91), High Point Med. Soc. (pres. 1989). Roman Catholic. Avocations: golf, reading. Home: 400 Edgedale Dr High Point NC 27262-2908 Office: 100 Westwood Ave High Point NC 27262-4320 Office Phone: 336-883-1393. E-mail: sybardelas@aol.com.

BARDEN, GEORGE V., county official, watershed specialist; b. Penn Yan, NY, Jan. 20, 1948; s. Gerald and Helen Lou Barden (div.); children: Peter, Thomas. Assoc., Agrl. & Tech. Coll., Canton, NY, 1968. Cert. profl. soil erosion and sediment control specialist. Gen. farm laborer Ej-Lo Farms, Penn Yan, 1963-66; gen. constrn. laborer Penn Yan Builders, 1967-68; designer, design draftsman MRB Group, Rochester, NY, 1969-78, Sear Brown Assocs., Rochester, 1979-83; owner, operator Barden Tech. Svcs., Penn Yan, 1984-90; watershed inspector Canandaigua Lake, Ontario

County Soil & Water Conservation Dist., Canandaigua, NY, 1991—. Rep. Watershed Task Force, Canandaigua Lake Watershed Commn. rep. Watershed Task Force. Pres. Finger Lakes Concert Band, 1984—87. Recipient map competition award N.Y. State Assn. Profl. Land Surveyors, 1980, spl. project award N.Y. State Conservation Dist. Employees Assn., 1994, Merit award N.Y. State Conservation Dist. Employees Assn., 1996, recognition award Canandaigua Lake Watershed Task Force, 1998. Mem.: Finger Lakes Water Works Assn., N.Y. State Bldg. Ofcls. Assn., Am. Water Works Assn., Finger Lakes Bldg. Ofcls. Assn., Am. Design Drafting Assn., Am. Inst. Design and Drafting. Avocations: music, woodworking, furniture refinishing, vegetable gardening. Office: Ontario County Soil & Water Conservation Dist 480 N Main St Canandaigua NY 14424-1049 Office Phone: 585-396-9716. E-mail: ontswcd6@rochester.rr.com.

BARDEN, LARRY A., lawyer; b. 1956; BS, Miami Univ., Ohio, 1978; JD magna cum laude, Washington and Lee Univ., 1982. With Sidley Austin LLP, Chgo., 1982—, ptnr., mergers and acquisitions, 1989—, mem. exec. com., 1999—. Former faculty Northwestern Univ. Garrett Inst. Trustee Hadley Sch. for Blind; rep. Greater Chgo. Food Depository. Fellow: Am. Bar Found.; mem.: ABA, Chgo. Bar Assn., Order of Coif. Office: Sidley Austin LLP One S Dearborn St Chicago IL 60603 Office Phone: 312-853-7785. Office Fax: 312-853-7036. Business E-Mail: lbarden@sidley.com.

BARDEN, ROBERT CHRISTOPHER, lawyer, psychologist, educator, writer; b. Richmond, Va., June 7, 1954; s. Elliott Hatcher and Jane Elizabeth Cole (Ferris) B.; m. Robin Jones, Nov. 14, 1987. BA summa cum laude, U. Minn., 1976, PhD in Clin. Psychology, 1982; postgrad., U. Calif., Berkeley, 1977; JD cum laude, Harvard U., 1992. Lic. cons. psychologist, Minn., Tex.; diplomate Am. Bd. Forensic Examiners. Project asst. NSF, 1978-79; intern in psychology VA Med. Ctr., Stanford Med. Ctr., Palo Alto, Calif., 1979-80; dir. psychology Internat. Craniofacial Surg. Inst., Dallas, 1980-87; corp., civil litigation, family and health law atty. Lindquist and Vennum, Mpls., 1992-96; psychologist, lawyer, expert witness, pub. policy analyst R.C. Barden & Assocs., 1996—. Asst. prof. psychology So. Meth. U., Dallas, 1980—84; asst. prof., coord. child clin. psychology U. Utah, Salt Lake City, 1984—87, rsch. faculty dept. surgery, 1987—93; vis. faculty, asst. prof. psychology Gustavus Adolphus Coll., St. Peter, Minn., 1988; pres. Optimal Performance Sys., Inc., Cambridge, 1989—; mem. Minn. Bd. Psychology, 1993—97; adj. prof. law U. Minn. Law Sch., 1995—97; cons. and spkr. in field. Consulting editor Devel. Psychology, 1989; editor Harvard Jour. Law and Pub. Policy, 1990-91; contbr. to profl. publs. Project dir. ch. cmty. svc. projects, Mpls. and Cambridge, 1988—; mem. Minn. Bd. Psychology, 1993-97, Higher Edn. Coordinating Bd., 1993-94; rep. Minn. Sixth Congl. Dist.; mem. Commn. for Sci. Medicine and Mental Health, 2004—. Recipient Young Scholar award Found. for Child Devel., Faculty Scholar award W.T. Grant Found., 1987-89; NSF fellow, 1978, NIMH fellow, 1976, 77. Mem. ABA, Am. Psychol. Soc., Soc. for Rsch. in Child Devel., Internat. Soc. Clin. Hypnosis, Harvard Law Sch. Soc. Law and Medicine, Lowell House Commons Rm. Harvard U., Nat.Assn. for Consumer Protection in Mental Health Practices (pres. 1995—), Sigma Xi, Phi Beta Kappa. Avocations: church and service work, tennis, martial arts, mountain climbing, music. Home and Office: RC Barden 3605 West 55th St Minneapolis MN 55410 Office Phone: 801-230-8328. Personal E-mail: rcbarden@aol.com, rcbarden@mac.com.

BARDHAN, TRIDIP K., engineering educator, researcher; s. Ranendra N. and Mira K. Bardhan; m. Sarmila D. Datta, Jan. 16, 1991; 1 child, Rishika T. PhD, Wichita State U., Kans., 1996. Cert. mfg. engr., Soc. Mfg. Engrs., 2001. Scientist Nat. Inst. Stds. and Tech., Gaithersburg, Md., 1998—2000; assoc. prof. Morgan State U., Balt., 2000—. Mem.: Inst. Indsl. Engrs. (faculty advisor 2001—). Achievements include research in sequencing of networks. Office: Morgan State Univ 1700 E Cold Spring Ln Baltimore MD 21251-0001 Home Phone: 410-663-3663; Office Phone: 443-885-3152. Office Fax: 443-885-8344. Business E-Mail: bardhan@eng.morgan.edu.

BARDIN, CLYDE WAYNE, biomedical researcher; b. McCamey, Tex., Sept. 18, 1934; s. James A. and Nora Irene (Barnett) Bardin; m. Bonnie Lambdin, June 24, 1958 (div.); children: Charlotte E., Stephanie F.; m. Dorothy Kreiger, Aug. 11, 1978 (dec. Apr. 2, 1985); m. Beatrice MacDonald, June 12, 1987. BA in Biology, Rice U., 1957; MS with honors, MD with honors, Baylor U., 1962; Docteur (hon.), U. de Caen, France, 1990, U. Pierre et Marie Curie, Paris, 1997, U. Helsinki, Finland, 2000. Lic. physician Tex., 1962, N.Y., 1963, Pa., 1970. Resident in medicine N.Y. Hosp., NYC, 1962-64; clin. assoc. NIH, Bethesda, Md., 1964-67; sr. investigator NCI, Bethesda, Md., 1967-70; assoc. prof. Milton S. Hershey Med. Ctr., Pa. State U., Hershey, 1970-72, prof. medicine, 1972—78; v.p. The Population Coun., NYC, 1978-95; pres. Bardin LLC, NYC, 1996—; pres., CEO Thyreos Corp., Newark, 1997—2003. Adj. prof. Rockefeller U., NYC, 1978-2004, Cornell Med. Ctr., NYC, 1985-2004; cons. WHO, 1972-73; chmn. bd. sci. counselors Nat. Inst. Child Health and Human Devel., Bethesda, 1982-83; chmn. endocrine study sect. NIH, Bethesda, 1977-79; nat. prostate cancer task force Nat. Cancer Inst., 1973-78; endocrinologist Nat. Inst. Child Health and Human Devel., NIH, 1996-97; bd. dirs. Harris and Harris Group, Inc. Editor 18 books on medicine and endocrinology; mem. editl. bd. 16 sci. jours.; contbr. over 500 articles to profl. jours. Advisor internat. divsn. Ford Found., NYC, 1975-79; bd. dirs. Internat. Assn. Axel Munthe Awards, 1982-92; chmn. bd. dirs. Hormone Found., 1997-98. Decorated comdr. Order of Lion (Finland); recipient Transatlantic medal Brit. Endocrine Socs., 1988; fellow Josiah Macy Jr. Found., 1976-77; named Disting. Alumnus Rice U., 1994, Disting. Alumnus N.Y. Hosp.-Cornell Med. Ctr., 1992. Mem. Am. Assn. Physicians, Am. Soc. Clin. Investigation, Am. Soc. Andrology (coun., v.p., pres. 1984-89, Serono award 1984, Disting. Andrologist award 1992), Endocrine Soc. (coun. 1976-79, pres. 1993-94, Sidney H. Ingbar Disting. Svc. award 1996), Internat. Soc. Andrology (exec. coun. 1981-85), Internat. Com. Contraception Rsch. (chmn. 1978-95), Inst. Medicine. Democrat. Achievements include studies of male reproduction, hormone action; maturation of germ cells and inhibition of cancer growth as well as direction of a team of scientists that developed seven contraceptives and treatments for menopause and cancer. Home Phone: 212-876-1830. Personal E-mail: cwbardin@aol.com.

BARDIN, DAVID JONAS, lawyer; b. NYC, June 2, 1933; s. Shlomo and Ruth (Jonas) Bardin; m. Livia Goldeen, Mar. 12, 1961; children: Jacob, Matthew, Joseph, Sarah. AB, Columbia U., 1954, JD, 1956. Bar: N.Y. 1956, D.C. 1966, Israel 1970. Atty., dep. gen. counsel FPC, Washington, 1958-69; asst. to atty. gen. Israel, Jerusalem, 1970-72; counsel Israel Environ. Protection Svc., Jerusalem, 1973; commr. N.J. Dept. Environ. Protection, Trenton, 1974-77; dep. adminstr. FEA, Washington, 1977; adminstr. Econ. Regulatory Adminstrn., Dept. Energy, Washington, 1977-80; of counsel, mem. Arent Fox Kintner Plotkin & Kahn PLLC, Washington, 1980-2001, ret., 2001. Lectr. law Bar-Ilan U., Tel Aviv U., U. Va. Ext. Author: Psychological Coercion and Human Rights, 1994, Bakken Crude Oil Resource of the Williston Basin, 2005, Injecting Carbon Dioxide into the Rocks, 2007; co-author: AGA Select Gas Use Handbook: Natural Gas for Environmental Control, 1985; contbr. chapters to books. Mem. Mayor's Coun. on Environment, 1999—2001, D.C. Zoning Adv. Com., 2003—; bd. mgrs. Adas Israel Congregation, 1998—99; trustee The Found. Jewish Studies, 1991—99; moot ct. panel Nat. Assn. Atty. Gens., 1993—; trustee Liberty State Pk. Devel. Corp., 1990—2000, Pinelands Preservation Alliance, 1991—99, Mental Health Liaison Group, 1993—2005; adv. neighborhood commr. of D.C., 1999—2005; mem. Mayor's Com. on Adoption Law, 2000—01; bd. dirs. D.C. Water and Sewer Authority, 2000—; mem. D.C. Bldg. Code Adv. Com., 2002—07. With US Army, 1956—58. Mem.: ABA, Found. for Energy Law Jour. (bd. dirs. 1987—90), Fed. Energy Bar Assn. (bd. dirs. 1985—87), Fed. Bar Assn. Democrat. Jewish. Office: Arent Fox Kintner Plotkin & Kahn 1050 Connecticut Ave NW Ste 400 Washington DC 20036-5339 E-mail: BardinD@arentfox.com. *Combine careful thought with timely action: rely on oneself, work with others, and procrastinate only if there's a very strong reason. Finally, apply this test: How will I explain my acts and omissions to a grandchild?.*

BARDO, JOHN WILLIAM, academic administrator; b. Cin., Oct. 28, 1948; s. John Thomas and Grace Roberta (Day) B.; m. Deborah Joan Davis, Aug. 8, 1975; 1 child, Christopher. Student, U. Southampton, Eng., 1968—69; BA in Econs., U. Cin., 1970; MA in Sociology, Ohio U., 1971; PhD in Sociology, Ohio State U., 1973. Asst. prof. Wichita (Kans.) State U., 1973-79, assoc. prof., 1979-83, chmn. dept. sociology, 1978-83; prof. Southwest Tex. State U., San Marcos, 1983-86, dean Sch. Liberal Arts, 1983-86; prof. U. N. Fla., Jacksonville, 1986-90, provost, v.p., 1986-89; prof. dept. sociology and anthropology Bridgewater (Mass.) State Coll., 1990-95, v.p. acad. affairs, 1990-95, provost, 1993-95; chancellor Western Carolina U., Cullowhee, NC, 1995—. Vis. lectr. Monash U., Clayton, Australia, 1977; vis. prof. Univ. Coll. Wales, Swansea, 1981; cons. various orgns. and govt. agys. Co-author: Urban Sociology: An Integrated Approach, 1982; editor: Defining the Mission of AASCU Institutions, 1990; contbr. articles to profl. jours. and books chpts. Co-chair N.C./Estern Band of Cherokee Indians Econ. Devel. Task Force, 1996—; bd. dirs. N.C. Arboretum, 1995—; trustee N.C. Ctr. for the Advancement of Tchg., 1995—. Recipient Humanities award Kans. Com. for Humanities, 1978; named one of Outstanding Young Men in Am., Jaycees, 1979. Mem. Am. Sociol. Assn., Assn. for Consumer Rsch., Mid-South Sociol. Assn., Am. Assn. Higher Edn., Am. Assn. State Colls. and Univs. (coll. rep. resource ctr.), Soc. Applied Multivariate Rsch. (pres.-elect 1993—), Alpha Kappa Delta, Phi Kappa Phi. Greek Orthodox. Avocations: photography, golf. Home: 10 Chancellor Dr Cullowhee NC 28723-6874 Office: W Carolina Univ Chancellor Cullowhee NC 28723 Office Phone: 828-227-7100. Business E-Mail: jbardo@email.wcu.edu.

BARDSLEY, KAY, historian, archivist, dance professional; b. Port Said, Egypt, Apr. 17, 1921; arrived in U.S., 1929; d. Chris and Helen (Jones) Lanitis; m. James Calvert Bardsley, May 30, 1947 (wid. Sept. 1978); children: Wendy Jane, Amy Kim; m. Donald Marshall Kuhn, Feb. 25, 1990. Student, Duncan Dance Tng./Carnegie Hall, Steinway Hall Studios, NYC, 1931—35; BA in Journalism cum laude, Hunter Coll., NYC, 1942. Dance debut Maria-Theresa Duncan Heliconiades, NYC, 1934; prin. dancer Maria-Theresa Heliconiades, NYC, 1935-42; Duncan tchr. Maria-Theresa Sch., NYC, 1937-46; tchr. Creative Dance for Children, NYC, 1960-66, Isadora Duncan-Maria-Theresa Heritage Group, NYC, 1977-81; fashion editor Woman's Day, NYC, 1943-46; prodr. arts and fashion segments WPIX Gloria Swanson Hour, 1948—49; writer TV Guide, 1949; writer/prodr. culture news and fashion ABC Network/Don Ameche-Langford Show, 1949-50. Syndicated film series prodr., Your Beauty Clin., 1950-60; prodr. video documentation of Duncan Repertory, 1976-80. Writer, lectr. in field:; prodr.: (documentaries) The Last Isadorable, 1988, re-issued, 1997; contbr. to profl. dance jours. and pubs. including Dance Scope, 1977, Ballet Rev., 1991, 1994, staging of ReAnimations of Duncan Masterworks, A Four-year Project, presented at Dance ReConstructed Conf., Rutgers U., 1992; author: numerous conf. presentations and earliest documentation of Isadora Duncan's 1st sch., 1979; resident dancer scholar U. Oreg., Eugene, 1997—98, staging of Duncan solos for Colo. Ballet Dancelab, 1999, Duncan's masterwork to seventh Symphony of Beethoven, U. Colo., 2000; owner, curator Legacy of Isadora Duncan: The Kay Bardsley Collection. Trustee Coun. for the Arts in Westchester, NY, 1973-76; bd. dirs. Bicentennial Com., Chappaqua, NY, 1973-76; co-chmn. Community Day, 1973, 75. Grantee NEA, NYC, 1980; pioneer NYU/Master Tchr. Dance Tng. Inst., 1987; recipient 1997-98 Creativity award in Dance U. Oreg. Mem.: Isadora Duncan Internat. Inst. (dir., founder 1978—), Dance Critics Assn. (bd. dirs. 1997—2000), World Dance Alliance, Am. Dance Guild, Soc. Dance History Scholars. Office: 580 Capp St Ste 809 San Francisco CA 94110 Office Phone: 415-821-0754.

BARDWICK, JUDITH MARCIA, management consultant; b. NYC, Jan. 16, 1933; d. Abraham and Ethel (Krinsky) Hardis; m. John Bardwick, III, Dec. 18, 1954 (div.); children: Jennifer, Peter, Deborah; m. Allen Armstrong, Feb. 10, 1984. BS, Purdue U., 1954; MS, Cornell U., 1955; PhD, U. Mich., 1964. Lectr. U. Mich., Ann Arbor, 1964-67, asst. prof. psychology, 1967-71, assoc. prof., 1971-75, prof., 1975-83, assoc. dean, 1977-83; clin. prof. psychiatry U. Calif., San Diego, 1984—; pres. In Transition, Inc. (name changed to Judith M. Bardwick, PhD, Inc., 1991), La Jolla, Calif., 1983—. Mem. population rsch. study group NIH, 1971—75. Co-author: (book) Feminine Personality and Conflict, 1970; author: Psychology of Women, 1971, In Transition, 1979, The Plateauing Trap, 1986, Danger in the Comfort Zone, 1991, In Praise of Good Business, 1998, Seeking the Calm in the Storm, 2002, One Foot Out the Door, 2007; mem. editl. bd. Women's Studies, 1973—, Psychology Women Quar., 1975—; contbr. articles to profl. jours. Mem. social sci. adv. com. Planned Parenthood Am., 1973. Fellow: APA; mem.: Am. Psychosomatic Soc., N.Y. Acad. Scis., Midwest Psychol. Assn., Phi Beta Kappa. Home and Office: 1389 Caminito Halago La Jolla CA 92037-7165 Home Phone: 858-456-0063; Office Phone: 858-456-1443. Personal E-mail: jmbwick@san.rr.com. *I am particularly grateful to the principle of academic freedom which has allowed me to pursue intellectual questions that I considered important. No other institution would have supported my pursuit of the answers to questions that seemed significant for theoretical or applied reasons before those issues were obviously important to society.*

BARDYGUINE, PATRICIA WILDE, dancer, performing company executive; b. Ottawa, Ont., Can., July 16, 1928; came to U.S., 1943; d. John Herbert and Eileen Lucy (Simpson) White; m. George Bardyguine, Dec. 14, 1953; children: Anya, Youri. Student, Profl. Children's Sch., NYC. Dancer Am. Concert Ballet, NYC, 1943-44, Marquis De Queras Ballet Internat., NYC, 1944-45, Ballet Russe De Monte Carlo, 1945—49; guest artist Roland Petit Ballet De Paris, 1949; prin. ballerina Met. Ballet, 1950, N.Y.C. Ballet, 1950-65; dir. Harkness House, NYC, 1965-67; ballet mistress Am. Ballet Theater, NYC, 1969-82; artistic dir. Pitts. Ballet Theatre, 1982—97, artistic dir. emeritus, 1997—, advisor, tchr., 1997—. Dir. Am. Ballet Theater Sch., 1979-82; dance panelist Nat. Endowment for Arts, N.Y. State Coun. for the Arts; judge Lausanne Internat. Competition; guest tchr., coach N.Y.C. Ballet, Joffrey Ballet, Dance Theater of Harlem, The Royal Ballet of Stockholm, Internat. Summer Seminar, Cologne, Germany, Heinz Bosl Found., Munich, St. Moritz, Japan, Australia, Republic of Korea. Soloist six European tours, also tour of Orient; numerous TV appearances; commd. by N.Y. Philharm. to choreograph ballets Festival, 1964, At the Ball, 1965, Viennese Evening, 1966, Petite Suite, 1967. Adminstr. scholar fund Sch. A. Ballet Group; mem. Nat. Bd. Regional Ballet; Fulbright panelist. Recipient YWCA award for Leadership in Arts and Letters, 1990, Cultural award for Extraordinary Contbns. to Cultural Life in Region, Pitts. Ctr. for Arts, 1997, Cultural award for outstanding contbns. to cultural climate of the region Pitts. Ctr. for Arts, 1997; named Pitts. Woman of Yr. in Arts and Music, 1994. Mem. Am. Guild Mus. Artists, AFTRA, Dance/USA (bd. dirs.). Office: Pitts Ballet Theatre 2900 Liberty Ave Pittsburgh PA 15201-1511

BAREFOOT, ALDOS CORTEZ, JR., retired forester, educator; b. Angier, NC, Feb. 25, 1927; s. Aldos Cortez Barefoot, Sr. and Eva Kathleen (Benson) Barefoot; m. Naomi Gertrude Pugh, 1949; children: Aldos, James, Rebecca. BS, NC State Coll., 1950, Master of Wood Tech., 1951; D Forestry, Duke U., 1958. Registered forester NC, 1981, re-cert. insp. Am. Tree Farm Sys., 2005. Lab. asst. (zoology) NC State Coll., Raleigh, NC, 1948—49, grad. asst. dept. stats., 1952—54, technologist and supt., wood products lab., 1954—55, asst. prof. to assoc. prof. Sch. Forestry, 1955—68; supr. quality control Henry County Plywood Corp., Ridgeway, Va., 1951; statistician Forest Products Lab., US Dept. Agr., 1953; advisor (utilization), forest products rsch. inst. Internat. Cooperation Agy., US State Dept., Chittagong, Bengal, Bangladesh, 1959—61; prof. wood and paper sci. U. NC, Chapel Hill, 1968—86, head divsn. interdisciplinary studies, 1975—82, leader, wood products sect. Coop. Ext. Svc., 1972—75; prof. emeritus of wood and paper sci. and multidisciplinary studies NC State U., Raleigh, 1986—; chief of party, reforestation and watershed mgmt. project, U. Ga., SECID, Chapel Hill, NC, Colombo, Sri Lanka, 1982—84. Owner, forester 300 acres NC Mtn., Piedmont, and Coastal Plain, 1954—; owner, developer, sales Hampton Hills Subdivsn., Raleigh, NC, 1954—; dendrochronologist Winchester Rsch. Unit, Winchester and Oxford, England, 1963—; dir., vis. scientist program, soc. of wood sci. and tech. NSF, Raleigh, 1968—74; ptnr. Southern Pine Mgmt. Co., Indian Ridge Co., Cub Creek Co., 1954—2004, Horseshoe Mtn. Co., 1963—2004, trustee, 1996—2004; vis. fellow Wolfson Coll., Oxford U., 1973—74. Author (with Frank W. Hankins): Identification of Modern and Tertiary Woods, 1982. Chmn. tchr.'s and state employee's benefits study commn. Gen. Assembly NC, Raleigh, 1969—71, mem. commn. on pre-paid health benefits, 1979—81; mem. health adv. com. to the state treas. and bd. of trustees of the tchr. and state employee's retirement sys. The State Treas. Office, State of NC, Raleigh, 1971—81. Served in USN, 1945—46. Recipient Eagle Scout, Boy Scouts Am., 1944, Disting. Leadership Citation, Cubmaster of Yr., Boy Scouts of Am., 1964, Conservation Farmer of the Yr., Wake County, NC, 1960, Second-Mile award, NC Assn. Educators, 1971, Outstanding Contbn. award, State Employees Assn., 1972; grantee Furniture R & D Inst., NSF, 1973—78; Fulbright-Hayes Rsch. scholar, US-UK Ednl. Commn., 1973—74. Fellow: Inst. Wood Sci.; mem.: Tech. Assn. Pulp and Paper Industry (chmn. ann. biology conf. 1966), NC Woodlands (charter mem., mem. bd. dirs.), Soc. Wood Sci. and Tech., Internat. Assn. Wood Anatomists, Soc. Am. Foresters, NC Govtl. Ret. Employees' Assn., NC State U. Club, Tree-Ring Soc., Forest Products Soc., Kiwanis (trustee), Alpha Zeta, Sigma Xi, Xi Sigma Pi, Phi Kappa Phi. Democrat. Baptist. Avocation: hunting, hiking, travel, bridge, dancing.

BAREFOOT, TOMMY DEAN, retired boat captain; b. Pascagoula, Miss., July 23, 1955; s. Dudley Dewey and Lorine Barefoot. Sheet metal worker Ingalls Shipbuilding, Pascagoula, 1973, 1977—79; offshore deck hand John E Graham, Bayou La Batre, Ala., 1980—83, capt., 1982—83, Edison Chouest Offshore, Gallianola, La., 1984—99. E4 US Army, 1973—77. Mem.: All Miss. Airborne, Am. Legion. Republican. Baptist. Avocation: motorcycling.

BARE GROUNDS, PATRICIA KELLY, athletic trainer, small business owner; b. Mt. Holly, NJ, Mar. 3, 1965; d. Darwin B. and Eileen C. Bare; 1 child, Olivia Eileen. BA, DePauw U., 1987; MS, U. Miami, 1996; PhD, U. Fla., 2006. Cert. and lic. athletic trainer NATA. Asst. athletic trainer Fla. Atlantic U., Boca Raton, 1992—93; head athletic trainer Lynn U., Boca Raton, 1993—96; med. coord., med. com. chmn. USA Taekwondo & USTU, Colorado Springs, Colo., 1994—; vis. prof., asst. athletic trainer U. Miami, Coral Gables, Fla., 1996—97; cert. athletic trainer Nat. Spirit Group/NCA/NDA, Dallas, 1997—; doping control officer U.S. Anti-Doping Agy., Colorado Springs, Colo., 2004—; owner, med. coord. Bare Essentials Sports Medicine Co., Navarre, Fla., 2004—. Com. chmn. ASTM, Martial Arts Headgear & Body Padding, Pitts., 2002—; med. com. chmn. USA Tae Kwon Do. Author: Bare Essentials Guide for Martial Art Injury Care & Prevention, (video & dvd). Named Athletic Trainer of the Yr., Nat. Spirit Group, 1997—2006. Mem.: ATAF (licentiate), SEATA (licentiate), ACSM (licentiate), ASTM (licentiate; chmn. martial arts headgear and body padding coms. 2004), Nat. Athletic Trainer Assn. (licentiate). Office: Bare Essentials Sports Medicine Co 2459 Parkridge Dr Navarre FL 32566 Home Phone: 850-939-1762; Office Phone: 850-939-1762. Office Fax: 850-939-1762. Personal E-mail: trish.bare@prodigy.net.

BARENBERG, ERNEST JOHN, engineering educator, consultant; b. Rawlins County, Kans., Apr. 29, 1929; s. John Joseph and Helena (Geerdes) Barenberg; m. Virgie Rawline, Sept. 5, 1953 (dec. Mar. 1983); children: Katherine Ann, Janet Diane, Rita Sue, Michael Eugene, Gena Irene, Myra Lynn; m. Nancy Joan Pogue, Jan. 3, 1984; stepchildren: David Keith Pogue, Stephen Keal Pogue. BCE, Kans. State U., 1953; MCE, Kans. U., 1958; PhD in Civil Engring., U. Ill., 1965. Registered profl. engr. Aircraft designer Cessna Aircraft, Wichita, Kans., 1953; asst. prof. U. Kans., Lawrence, 1955-60; research assoc. U. Ill., Urbana, 1960-65, asst. prof. civil engring., 1965-67, assoc. prof. of civil engring., 1967-71; acting chief, facilities br. system U.S. Army Engrs., CERL, Champaign, Ill., 1971-73; assoc. head civil engring. U. Ill., Urbana, 1981-85, prof. civil engring., 1971—96, prof. emeritus, 1996. Dir. Affiliated Lab. Program Assn. Am. R.R. U. Ill., Urbana, 1983—; cons. in field. Contbr. articles to sci. jours. Served to lt. US Army, 1953—55. Named Educator of Yr., Am. Concrete Paving Assn., 2004. Mem.: ASCE (award Robert Horonjeff Air Transp. Divsn. 1998), ASTM, Pozzolonic Pavement Assn. (award of Merit), Assn. Am. RRs (Outstanding Svc. award), Transp. Rsch. Bd., Nat. Acads. (life), Sigma Xi, Tau Beta Pi, Chi Epsilon (hon.). Republican. Roman Catholic. Achievements include patents for load transfer device. Avocations: swimming, skiing. Office: U of Ill Dept Civil Engring Urbana IL 61801 Home: 3007 Beringer Cir Urbana IL 61802 Office Phone: 217-893-9061. Business E-Mail: ejbm@uiuc.edu.

BARENBOIM, DANIEL, conductor, pianist, music director; b. Buenos Aires, Nov. 15, 1942; s. Enrique and Aida (Schuster) Barenboim; m. Jaqueline DuPre, June 15, 1967 (dec.); m. Elena Bashkirova, Nov. 28, 1988; 2 children. Student, Mozarteum, Salzburg, Austria, Accademia Chigiana, Siena, Italy; grad., Santa Cecilia Acad., Rome, 1956. Music dir. Chgo. Symphony Orch., 1991—2006; gen. music dir. Deutsche Staatsoper Berlin, 1992—. Debut with Israel Philharm. Orch., 1953, Royal Philharm. Orch., 1953, debut as pianist Carnegie Hall, N.Y.C., 1957, Berlin Philharm. Orch., 1963, N.Y. Philharm. Orch., 1964, 1st U.S. solo recital, N.Y.C., 1958, as pianist performed in N.Am., South Am., Europe, Soviet Union, Australia, New Zealand, Near East, condr., 1962—, conducted English Chamber Orch., London Symphony Orch., Israel Philharm. Orch., N.Y. Philharm. Orch., Phila. Symphony, Boston Symphony, Chgo. Symphony Orch., others, musical dir. Orch. de Paris, 1975—89, Staatsoper Berlin, 1992—, artistic advisor Israel Festival, 1971—74, over 100 recs. as pianist and condr., debut as pianist at age 7, Buenos Aires. Named to Legion of Honor, France, 1987; recipient Beethoven medal, 1958, Harriet Cohen Paderewski Centenary prize, 1963, Beethoven Soc. medal, 1982, Prix de la Tolérance, Protestant Acad. of Tutzing, 2002, Wolf Prize in arts, Wolf Found., Israel, 2004. Office: Unter den Linden 7 D-10117 Berlin Germany

BARER, SOL JOSEPH, biotechnology company executive; b. Windsheim, Germany, Apr. 20, 1947; came to U.S., 1949; s. Isaac and Hela Barer; m. Meri I. Barer, Aug. 17, 1969; children: Jennifer, Lori, Ilyssa, Joshua. BS, CUNY, Bklyn., 1968; MS, PhD, Rutgers U., 1974. Sr. rsch. chemist Celanese Co., Summit, NJ, 1974-78, supr. R&D, 1978-82, mgr. chem. R&D, 1982-84; dir. Chem. Systems, Tarrytown, NY, 1984-87; v.p. tech. Celgene Corp., Summit, NJ, 1987-90, sr. v.p.-sci. and tech., v.p., gen. mgr.-Chiral Products, 1990-93, pres., 1993—2006, COO, 1994—2006, CEO, 2006—, also bd. dir., 1994—, mem. exec. com. bd. dirs. Dir. Semorex, Inc. Contbr. articles to profl. jours. Chair Rutgers Grad. Sch. Dean's Adv. Coun. NSF undergrad. fellow NSF, Bklyn., 1968, 70, NDEA grad. fellow Dept. Def., Rutgers U., 1970-72. Mem. Am. Chem. Soc., Am. Soc. Microbiology. Achievements include a wide variety of developments in chemical and biological industries. Office: Celgene Corp 86 Morris Ave Summit NJ 07901

BARETTA, MARSHA MOTYL, elementary school physical education educator; b. Hartford, Conn., July 14, 1950; d. Michael Samuel and Regina McAdoo Motyl; m. John Dominic Baretta, Feb. 17, 1973 (div. June 20, 1984); children: Jason Michael, Kimberly Mary. BS, So. Conn. State U., 1972; MS, Ctrl. Conn. State U., 1979; MEd, Springfield Coll., Mass., 1991. Cert. CPR, first aid Am. Heart Assoc, 1990; profl. educator State of Conn. Dept. Edn., 1972. Phys. edn. tchr. South Windsor Bd. Edn., Conn., 1972—. Test devel. cons. Ednl. Testing Svcs., Princeton, NJ, 1990—94; portfolio scorer Conn. State Dept. Edn., 2000—03; vice-chair Conn. Gov.'s Com. on Phys. Fitness, 2002—; adj. faculty Springfield Coll., 2004—. Head coach Spl. Olympics Conn., Wethersfield, Conn., 1992—2003, Spl. Olympics Conn. Ea. Regional Mgmt. Team, Wethersfield, 2000—03; bd. dirs. Greater Hartford Jaycees, 1986—89; exec., mgmt. com. Canon Greater Hartford Open, 1988—90; bd. dirs. Tri-Town YMCA, Wethersfield, 2000—04. Recipient Governor's Civic Leadership award, Greater Hartford Jaycees, 1983—90, Cmty. Svc. award, Sec. of State, Conn., 2003. Mem.: South Windsor Edn., Conn. (assoc.), Conn. Assn. Health, Phys. Edn., Recreation & Dance (assoc.; exec. officer 1986—88, Profl. Svc. award 1993), Am. Alliance Health, Phys. Edn. Recreation & Dance (assoc.), Amateur Ski Instructor's Assn. (licentiate; cert. instr.), Mt. Laurel Skiers (assoc.). Democrat. Roman Catholic. Avocations: skiing, bicycling, golf. Office: Wapping Elem Sch 91 Ayers Rd South Windsor CT 06074 Home Phone: 860-529-9072; Office Phone: 860-648-5010. Office Fax: 860-684-5802. E-mail: mbaretta@swindsor.k12.ct.us.

BARFIELD, HENRY LEE, II, lawyer; b. Macon, Ga., July 22, 1946; s. L. Bayne and Corinne (Cole) B.; m. Mary Louise Frist, Jan. 31, 1968; children: Mary Lauren, Dorothy, Corinne, Cole. BA, Vanderbilt U., 1968, JD, 1974. Bar: Tenn. 1974, U.S. Dist. Ct. (mid. dist.) 1974, Tenn., U.S. Ct. Appeals (6th cir.) 1982. Assoc. Bass Berry & Sims, Nashville, 1974—78, ptnr. litig., healthcare practices, 1978—, mem. exec. com., 1994—97. Adj. prof. Vanderbilt Law Sch., Bd. Law Examiners, State of Tenn., 1986—2000; mem. adv. commn. on rules of civil procedures Tenn. Supreme Ct., 1982—86. Bd. dirs. Am. Retirement Corp., 1978-2000, Met. Nashville YMCA, 1974—, Ensworth Sch., Nashville, 1980-86, Harpeth Hall Sch., Nashville, 1986—89, Montgomery Bell Acad., 2000—, Frist Visual Arts Ctr., 1998—, WPLN. Served to lt. USNR, 1968-71. Fellow Am. Bar Found., Tenn. Bar Found.; mem. ABA, Tenn. Bar Assn., Nashville Bar Assn. (pres. 1985). Presbyterian. Avocations: golf, skiing, bicycling. Home: 1026 Chancery Ln S Nashville TN 37215-4524 Office: Bass Berry & Sims Ste 2700 315 Deaderick St Nashville TN 37238 Home Phone: 615-665-1563; Office Phone: 615-742-6202. Office Fax: 615-742-2702. Business E-Mail: lbarfield@bassberry.com.

BARFIELD, JON E., employment company executive; b. 1951; BA with honours, Princeton U., 1974; JD, Harvard U., 1977. Assoc. Sidley & Austin; pres. Barfield Mfg. Co., Bartech Group, Livonia, Mich., 1981, chmn., ceo, 1995—. Bd. dirs. Granite Broadcasting Corp., bd. dir. Nat. City Corp., Tecumseh Products Co., Dow Jones & Co., BMC Software, dir. Pantellos Grp. Ltd. Partnership, Inc. Dir. Blue Cross Blue Shield of Mich., Children's Ctr.& Cmty. Found. Southeastern Mich. Mem.: Nat. Tech. Svcs. Assn. (past pres.), Henry Ford Kettering U. and Detroit Renaissance. (bd. of trustees), Emeritus Princeton U. (charter trustee). Office: Baretech Group Inc 17199 N Laurel Park Dr Ste 224 Livonia MI 48152-7903 Office Phone: 734-953-5050. Office Fax: 734-953-5075.

BARFIELD, LOWRY, lawyer; Atty. Larson King, LLP, 1999—2003, Bronis, Kaplan, Miller & Ciresi, 2003—04; pvt. practice Houston, 2004—05; v.p. legal, gen. counsel, sec. Western Refining, Inc., El Paso, Tex., 2005—07, sr. v.p. legal, gen. counsel, 2007—. Office: Western Refining, Inc 6500 Trowbridge Dr El Paso TX 79905 Office Phone: 915-775-3300.*

BARFIELD, ROBERT F., mechanical engineer, educator, retired dean; b. Thomaston, Ga., Feb. 8, 1933; s. Jason Malcome and Nettie Lee Barfield; m. Marion Janelle Neill, June 25, 1953 (div. Jan. 1980); children: Kimberly Faith, Robert Frederick Jr.; m. Sara de Saussure Davis, Nov. 27, 1981 (div. Jan. 1984); m. Leonette Walker, May 1990 (div. June 1994). B.M.E., Ga. Inst. Tech., 1956, MSM.E., 1958, PhD, 1965. Diplomate: registered profl. engr. Preliminary design engr. AiResearch Corp., Los Angeles, 1957-59; asst. prof. mech. engring. Ga. Inst. Tech., Atlanta, 1959-65; corp. mech. engr. Thomaston Mills Corp., Ga., 1965-67; prof. mech. engring. U. Ala., Tuscaloosa, 1967-94, prof. emeritus, 1994, dean of engring., 1982-94, dean emeritus, 1994. Dir., sr. adv. Shiraz Tech. Int., Iran, 1975-77; gen. bd. Assn. Internt. practical Tng., 1980-85; dir. Capstone Engring. Soc., 1982-94; head mech. engring. program, dir. Oil Testing Ctr., U. Petroleum and Minerals, Dhahran, Saudi Arabia, 1971-73; advisor King Saud U., Riyhad, Saudi Arabia, 1982-89, U. Jordan, 1984, Yarmouk U., Jordan, 1986, Birzeit U., Israel, 1985, Kabul U., Afghanistan, 1963; mem. Accreditation Bd. for Engring. and Tech., visitor in Mech. engring., 1982-94; mem. Ala. Commn. High Tech. Bd. dirs. Salvation Army Ala., 1996—, Turning Point, Inc., 1995—. Recipient Disting. Service award Inperial Orgn. for Social Services, Tehran, Iran, 1977, U. Ala. Faculty Senate, 1980, Engr. of Yr. award Ala. Soc. Profl. Engrs., 1987, Liberty Bell award Ala. Law Assn., 1987; inductee Engring. Hall of Fame, 1998. Fellow ASME; mem. Am. Soc. Engring. Edn., Nat. Soc. Profl. Engrs., Ala. Acad. Sci., Tuscaloosa C. of C., Sigma Xi, Tau Beta Pi, Pi Tau Sigma, Phi Kappa Phi, Upsilon Pi Epsilon, Tau Alpha Pi. Presbyterian. Home: 703 Shallow Creek Rd Tuscaloosa AL 35406-2085 Office: Univ Ala PO Box 870200 Tuscaloosa AL 35487-0200

BARFIELD, TIM, manufacturing executive; b. Baton Rouge, La. 4 children. Atty. Vinson & Elkins LLP; Sr. v.p., spl. projects The Shaw Group Inc., Baton Rouge, 1994, asst. to J.M. Bernhard, Jr., sec., gen. counsel, mng. dir. England; pres. The Shaw Group Inc. APP; pres, Shaw Environ. and Infrastructure, Inc., 2002—03; pres., COO The Shaw Group, Inc., 2003—06. Named one of Top 40 Under 40 to Watch, Bus. Report Mag., 2002.*

BARGAGLIOTTI, LILLIAN ANTOINETTE, nursing educator; b. Millington, Tenn., Dec. 29, 1949; d. Benard Wood and Georgeanne (Lowe) McIllwain; m. Ronald M. Prentice, Apr. 24, 1970 (div. 1975); m. bill L. Bargagliotti, July 8, 1978; 1 child, William Benard. RN, Tacoma Gen. Hosp., 1971; BSN, U. Tenn., 1976; MS, U. Calif., San Francisco, 1978; D in Nursing Sci., U. Calif., 1984. Staff nurse Tacoma (Wash.) Gen. Hosp., 1971, St. Joseph's Hosp., Tacoma, 1971-75, City of Memphis Hosp., 1975-76; instr. N.W. Miss. Jr. Coll., Senatobia, 1976-78; inservice coord. Eden Hosp., Castro Valley, Calif., 1978-79; instr. Ohlone Coll., Fremont, Calif., 1979-84; assoc. prof. nursing San Francisco State U., 1984-85; assoc. dean, prof. nursing U. San Francisco, 1985-89, interim dean, prof. nursing, 1989-91; assoc. DON Davies Med. Ctr., 1992; dean, prof. nursing Loewenberg Sch. Nursing, U. Memphis, 1992—2005, prof., 2005—. Clin. evaluator SUNY Western Performance Assessment Ctr., Long Beach and Palo Alto, Calif., 1982-85; program evaluator Collegiate Commn. for Nursing Edn. Contbr. articles to profl. jours. Capt. USAR, 1976-78. Mem. ANA, Tenn. Nurses Assn., Assn. Oper. Rm. Nurses (mem. jour. editl. bd. 1987-90), Nat. League for Nursing (program evaluator, pres.-elect 2003-05, pres., 2005-, bd. govs., trustee found. bd.), Tenn. Assn. Deans/Dirs. Nursing (pres. 1997-99, 99-2001), Sigma Theta Tau. Republican. Mem. Ch. of Christ. Home: 7423 Wood Rail Cv Memphis TN 38119-9007 Office: U Memphis 308 Admin Bldg Memphis TN 38152 Business E-Mail: tbargagl@memphis.edu.

BARGER, AMY J., astronomer, educator; BA in Physics, U. Wis., Madison, 1993; PhD in Astronomy, U. Cambridge King's Coll., 1997. Postdoctoral fellow Inst. Astronomy U. Hawaii; asst. prof. to assoc. prof. astronomy U. Wis., Madison, 2000—. Vis. adj. astronomer dept. physics and astronomy U. Hawaii. Contbr. articles to sci. jours. Named one of Brilliant 10, Popular Sci. mag., 2005; recipient Annie J. Cannon award, Am. Astron. Soc., 2001, Newton Lacy Pierce prize, 2002, Maria Goeppert-Mayer award, Am. Phys. Soc., 2007; Marshall fellow, 1993—2001, Hubble fellow, 1999—2001, Chandra fellow at large, 1999—2001, Sloan fellow, 2002, Packard Found. fellow sci. and engring., 2003. Office: U Wis Madison Dept Astronomy 6512 Sterling Hall 475 N Charter St Madison WI 53706 Office Phone: 608-263-7106. Office Fax: 608-263-6386. E-mail: barger@astro.wisc.edu.

BARGER, DAVID J., air transportation executive; Attended, U. Mich., 1977—81. Mgmt. positions through dir. stations NY Air (subs. Tex. Air Group), 1982—88; dir. positions Continental Airlines, 1988—92, mgmt. positions including staff v.p. ops., regional v.p. ctrl. region, v.p. Newark hub ops., 1992—98; pres., COO JetBlue Airways Corp., Forest Hills, NY, 1998—2007, pres., CEO, 2007—. Bd. dirs. JetBlue Airways, 2001—. Past. chmn. Regional Bus. Partnership, Newark; exec. bd. mem. Prosperity NJ; bd. mem. NJ State C. of C., Newark Econ. Develop. Corp., Gov. Panel of High Edn. in NJ; trustee Newark Mus. Office: JetBlue Airways Corp 118029 Queens Blvd Forest Hills NY 11375*

BARGER, DONALD GORDON, JR., freight company executive; b. Hamilton, Ohio, Feb. 8, 1943; s. Donald Gordon and Mary Elizabeth (Sizemore) B.; m. Linda A. Liveralt, July 25, 1971; children: Neill, Charity, Austin. BS, U.S. Naval Acad., 1965; MBA, U. Pa., 1972. Fin. analyst Irwin Mgmt. Co., Columbus, Ind., 1972-73; various positions The B.F. Goodrich Co., Akron, Ohio, 1973-76; dir. analysis The B.F. Goodrich Co. Tire Group, Akron, 1976-77, dir. product mktg., 1977-78; dir. planning The B.F. Goodrich Co. Chem. Group, Akron, 1978-82, v.p. planning and control, 1982-84, The B.F. Goodrich Co. Tire Group, Akron, 1984-86; v.p., contr. The B.F. Goodrich Co., Akron, 1986—93; v.p., CFO Worthington Industries, Columbus, Ohio, 1993—98, Hillenbrand Industries, Inc., Batesville, Ind., 1998—2000; exec. v.p., CFO YRC Worldwide Inc., Overland park, Kans., 2000—. Served to lt. USN, 1965-70. Office: YRC Worldwide Inc 10990 Roe Ave Overland Park KS 66211*

BARGER, JAMES EDWIN, physicist; b. Manhattan, Kans., Dec. 28, 1934; s. Edgar Lee and Carolyn Marie (Grantham) B.; m. Mary Elizabeth Rupp, Aug. 24, 1957; children: Elaine Marie Fleckenstein, Carolyn Ruth Hanson, James Rupp, Corinne Elizabeth Noordzij. BS, U. Mich., 1957; MS, U. Conn., 1960; MA in Applied Physics, Harvard U., 1962, PhD, 1964. Teaching asst. Harvard U., Cambridge, 1961-64; v.p. BBN Techs. (formerly Bolt Beranek & Newman, Inc.), Cambridge, Mass., 1965-75, chief scientist, 1975—. Trustee Winchester Savs. Bank. Mem. Methods and Procedures Com., Town of Winchester, 1967-71; trustee Winchester Hosp., 1972—; corp. mem. Mt. Vernon House, 1979—. Program officer USN, 1957—60. Recipient Disting. Engring. Alumni award U. Conn., 2002; named to Acad. Disting. Engrs., U. Conn.; NSF fellow, 1960-64. Fellow AAAS, Acoustical Soc. Am.; mem. Marine Tech. Soc., Indsl. Noise Control Engring., Winchester Country Club, Cosmos Club, Tau Beta Pi, Pi Tau Sigma. Congregationalist (deacon). Home: 3 Lakeview Rd Winchester MA 01890-3801 Office: BBN Techs 70 Fawcett St Cambridge MA 02138-1110 Business E-Mail: jbarger@aol.com. E-mail: docobra1@aol.com.

BARGER, RICHARD WILSON, hotel executive; b. Cleve., Aug. 16, 1934; s. Harold Wilson and Blanche (Smith) B.; m. Barbara K. Schroeder, July 20, 1963; children: Scott Wilson, Christopher Armon. BS, Cornell U., Ithaca, NY, 1956. Resident mgr. Sheraton Cleve. Hotel, 1964-67; gen. mgr. Sheraton Biltmore Hotel, Providence, 1967-68, Sheraton Peabody Hotel, Memphis, 1968-69, Sheraton Boston Hotel, 1969-72; v.p., regional mgr. Sheraton Corp., Boston, 1972-79; chmn. Barger Hotel Corp., Boston, 1979—, Conf. Planning Assoc., 1987—. Cons., lectr. hotel adminstrs. Mem. coun. Cornell U. Mem. Boston C. of C., Boston Conv. Bur. (dir.), Cornell U. Alumni Fund, Sigma Chi. Republican. Episcopalian. Home and Office: Barger Hotel Corp 63 Neptune St # A Beverly MA 01915-4746 Office Phone: 978-922-9500. Personal E-mail: bargerhotel@comcast.net.

BARGER, VERNON DUANE, physicist, educator; b. Curllsville, Pa., June 5, 1938; s. Joseph F. and Olive (McCall) Barger; m. M. Annetta McLeod, 1967; children: Victor A., Amy J., Andrew V. BS, Pa. State U., 1960, PhD, 1963. Rsch. assoc. U. Wis., Madison, 1963-65, from asst. prof. to assoc. prof., 1965—67, prof. physics, 1968—, J.H. Van Vleck prof., 1983—, dir. Inst. Elem. Particle Physics Rsch., 1984—, Hilldale prof., 1987-91, Vilas prof., 1991—. Vis. prof. U. Hawaii, 1970, 79, 82, U. Durham, 1983, 84; vis. scientist CERN, 1972, Rutherford Lab., 1972, SLAC, 1975, Kavli Inst. for Theoretical Physics, U. Calif., Santa Barbara, 2003. Co-author: (book) Phenomenological Theories of High Energy Scattering, Classical Mechanics, Classical Electricity and Magnetism, Collider Physics. Recipient Alumni Fellow award, Pa. State U., 1974; Guggenheim fellow, 1972, Fermilab Frontier fellow, 1999. Fellow: Am. Phys. Soc. Methodist. Achievements include research in elementary particle theory and phenomenology; classification of hadrons as Regge recurrences; analyses of neutrino scattering and oscillations; weak boson, Higgs boson and heavy quark production; electroweak models; supersymmetry and grand unification; collider physics; cosmology. Office: U Wis Dept Physics 1150 University Ave Madison WI 53706-1302

BARGER, WILLIAM JAMES, management consultant, educator; b. LA, Nov. 1, 1944; s. James Ray and Aylene M. (Skinner) B.; m. Jane A. Cox, Jan. 30, 1988. BA, U. So. Calif., 1966; MA, Harvard U., 1970, PhD, 1972. Asst. prof econs. U. So. Calif., Los Angeles, 1971-76; v.p. Bank Am., Los Angeles, 1976-81; sr. v.p. Gibraltar Savs. Co., Beverly Hills, Calif., 1981-84, exec. v.p., 1984-88; pres. High Point Acad., Pasadena, Calif., 1995—2001; dir. Maxson Young Assocs., San Francisco, 1995—2004. Mem. Phi Beta Kappa.

BARGER JOHNSON, JENNIFER, law educator, judge; BBA, Cameron U., Lawton, Okla., 1993; JD, U. Ark., Fayetteville, 1997. Bar: Okla., Tex., Ark. Mcpl. judge Apache, Elgin, Fletcher & Sterling, Okla., 2000—; asst. gen. counsel Okla. Corp. Commn., Oklahoma City, 2004—05; legal studies prof. U. Ctrl. Okla., Edmond, 2005—. Named one of 40 Under 40, Oklahoma City Bus. Jour., 2006. Mem.: Cherokee Nation of Okla. (chair compensation com. 2006—). Office Phone: 405-974-2444. Office Fax: 405-793-0083. Personal E-mail: jbarger4@ucok.edu.

BARGFREDE, JAMES ALLEN, lawyer; b. Seguin, Tex., Sept. 10, 1928; s. Herman Fred and Elsie (Vorpahl) B.; m. Virginia Felts, Nov. 27, 1970; 1 child, Charles Allen. BS, Tex. A&M U., 1950; postgrad., Ohio State U., 1952—53; JD, St. Mary's U., 1957. Bar: Tex. 1957, U.S. Patent and Trademark Office 1961; registered profl. engr., Tex. Engr. Signal Corps, San Antonio, 1950-52; elec. engr. San Antonio Pub. Svc. Bd., 1953-58; patent counsel Hubbard & Co., Chgo., 1958-59; pvt. practice law Butler, Binion, Rice, Cook & Knapp, 1960-68, 1968-74, 75—; patent and legal counsel Hydrotech Internat., Inc., 1977-81; ptnr. Bargfrede & Thompson, 1974-75. Subcom. chmn. dist. com. on admissions Supreme Ct. Tex., 1988—. With USAF, 1952—53. Mem. Houston Bar Assn. (chmn. automated equipment com. 1971-75), State Bar Tex., Assn. Former Students Tex. A&M U., Houston Livestock Show and Rodeo (life), Briarcroft Civic Club (pres. 1979-82), Houston A&M Club (treas. 1990, sec. 1991, v.p., 1992, pres. 1993), Delta Theta Phi. Home and Office: 5649 Piping Rock Ln Houston TX 77056-4028

BARGNANI, ANDREA, professional basketball player; b. Rome, Oct. 26, 1985; Player Italian Under-20 Nat. Team, Italian Jr. Nat. Team, Italian Cadets Nat. Team, Monte Paschi Seina jr. team, Italy, 2001—02, Stella Azzurra Roma, Serie B2 divsn., Italy, 2002—03, Benetton Treviso, Lega A, Italy, 2003—06, Toronto Raptors, 2006—. Named Euroleague Rising Star, 2006; named to NBA All-Rookie First Team, 2007. Achievements include being picked first by the Toronto Raptors in the 2006 NBA draft; winner with Benetton Treviso, Italian National Cup, 2004, 2005, Italian National Championship, 2006. Mailing: Toronto Raptors 40 Bay St Toronto ON M5J 2X2 Canada*

BARHAM, CHARLES DEWEY, JR., electric power industry executive, lawyer; b. Goldsboro, NC, July 7, 1930; s. Charles Dewey and Helen Wilkinson (Douglass) Barham Hughes; m. Margaret Wright Crow, June 17, 1960; children: Margaret Douglass, Charles Dewey III. BS, Wake Forest U., 1952, JD, 1954. Bar: N.C. 1954. Asst. atty. gen. N.C. Dept. Justice, Raleigh, 1958-66; assoc. gen. counsel Carolina Power & Light Co., Raleigh, NC, 1966-73; ptnr. Douglass & Barham, Raleigh, 1974-80; v.p., sr. counsel Carolina Power & Light Co., Raleigh, 1981-82, sr. v.p., gen. counsel, 1982-87, sr. v.p., 1982-90, exec. v.p, 1990-95; bd. of dir., 1990—95; ptnr. Douglass & Barham, 1995—. Chmn. bd., pres. Nuclear Mut., Ltd., Hamilton, Bermuda, 1981-86, bd. dirs. 1973-95; bd. dirs. Nuclear Elec. Ins. Ltd., 1987-95 Hamilton; gen. counsel World Nuclear Fuel Mkt., Atlanta, 1974-80; gen. counsel Meredith Coll., Raleigh, 1977-80, trustee, 1984-87, 90-93, 95—2001; mem. regional bd. dirs. Wachovia Bank of N.C., 1990-95. Pres. Raleigh YMCA, 1982-92; bd. vis. Sch. Law Wake Forest U., 1998—. Capt. USNR, 1955-77. Mem.: ABA, N.C. Bar Assn., Glen Forest Club (pres. 1977), Raleigh Civitan Club (dir. 1974—77, 1999—).

BARHAM, WARREN SANDUSKY, horticulturist; b. Prescott, Ark., Feb. 15, 1919; s. Clint A. and Hannah Jane (Sandusky) B.; m. Margaret Alice Kyle, Dec. 27, 1940 (dec. 1997); m. Evelyn M. Csongradi, Dec. 5, 1998 (dec. 2003); children: Barbara E., Juanita S., Margaret Ann, Robert W. BS in Agr., U. Ark., 1941; PhD, Cornell U., 1950. Grad. asst. in plant breeding Cornell U., Ithaca, N.Y., 1942-45; assoc. prof. horticulture N.C. State U., Raleigh, 1949-58; dir. raw material R & D Basic Vegetable Products, Inc., Vacaville, Calif., 1958-76; prof. Tex. A&M U., College Station, 1976-82, head dept., 1976-80; v.p. Castle & Cook Techniculture, Watsonville, Calif., 1982-84; dir. watermelon R & D Tom Castle Seed Co., Morgan Hill, Calif., 1984-86; CEO Barham Seeds Inc., Gilroy, Calif., 1987—; v.p. Kyle and Barham LLC, La Quinta, Calif., 1996—. Cons. Basic Vegetable Products, Inc., Vacaville, 1976-78, U.S. AID, Central Am., 1977, Egypt and U.S., 1980-82, Gentry Foods & Gilroy Foods, 1978-93, Fed. Republic Germany Govt., Ethiopia, 1984; industry rep. adv. com. Onion Rsch. Program USDA, 1960-70. Contbr. articles to profl. jours. Bd. dirs., pres. Vacaville Sch. Bd., 1964-74. Sgt. USAF, 1942-45, ETO. Fellow Am. Soc. Hort. Sci. (pres. 1982, bd. dirs. 1979-83, fellows nominating com. 2002-04, chair 2004); mem. Sons in Retirement (bd. dirs. 1992-95, v.p. 1993, pres. 1994), Rotary Inernat. (bd. dirs. 1964), Elks Club. Achievements include development of 34 varieties and hybrids of processing onions, 15 triploid and 8 diploid hybrid watermelons, 2 cucumber varieties, 13 fresh market hybrid onions and 1 tomato variety. Office Phone: 408-847-3056.

BARI, ROBERT ALLAN, physicist; b. Bklyn., Sept. 3, 1943; s. Dominick and Eleanore B.; m. Angela Maria Schimenti, June 25, 1966; children: Robin, Robert. AB, Rutgers U., 1965; PhD, Brandeis U., 1970. Postdoctoral physicist Lincoln Lab. MIT, Lexington, Mass., 1969-71; asst. physicist, dept. physics Brookhaven Nat. Lab., Upton, NY, 1971-73; asst. prof. physics SUNY, Stony Brook, 1973-74; group leader dept. nuclear energy Brookhaven Nat. Lab., 1975-81, divsn. head dept. nuclear energy, 1981, assoc. chmn. dept. nuclear energy, 1982-88, dep. chmn. dept. nuclear energy, 1988—, chmn. dept. advanced tech., 1995—2000, assoc. lab dir., 1999—. Adj. prof. nuclear engring. Poly. Inst. N.Y., Bklyn., 1979-82; vis. assoc. prof. materials sci. SUNY, Stony Brook, 1990. Assoc. editor Phys. Review, 1979-81; contbr. numerous articles to profl. jours. Recipient Outstanding Scientist award, Brookhaven Nat. Lab., 2004. Fellow Am. Nuclear Soc. (bd. dirs. 1994—; Tommy Thompson award 2003); mem. Am. Phys. Soc., Internat. Assn. for Probabilistic Safety Assessment and Mgmt. (bd. dirs. 1994—, pres. 1996-98), Phi Beta Kappa, Sigma Xi, Sigma Pi Sigma. Achievements include research on assessment of risks from operation of nuclear reactors and related facilities, and proliferation resistance of advanced nuclear systems. Office: Brookhaven Nat Lab Bldg 475B Upton NY 11973

BARIGAR, ELIZABETH GAYLE, painter, art educator; b. Oakland, Calif., Mar. 18, 1936; d. Milton Karl Van Brasch and Winifred Brown Taylor-Van Brasch; m. Robert Eugene Barigar, June 20, 1981 (dec. Jan. 2002); m. Keith Gordon Kading (div.); children: Kelly Brian Kading, Kevin David Kading, Kent Jerome Kading. Student, Trinity U., San Antonio, 1952—53. Cert. tchg. Idaho. Storyboard graphic artist Pacific Tel. Co., Sacramento, 1964—69; route operator Northwestern Bell, Sioux City, Iowa, 1954—58; freelance graphic artist, 1969—89; instr. Coll. So. Idaho, Twin Falls, 1989—96; tchr. Hagerman HS, Idaho, 1967—2006; with Letraset Internat.: Decorative Initials, 1981—2006. Illustrator: Sayings of the Swan, 2002, Nicole, 2002; Exhibited in group shows at 8th Street Ctr., Buhl, Full Moon Gallery, Twin Falls, 2000—, The Lion's Gate, Sun Valley, Idaho, Heirlooms of Tomorrow Gallery, 2007. Supt. Twin Falls County Fair, 1990—96; instr. Magic Valley Art Coun., Twin Falls, 1995. Mem.: Buhl Arts Coun. (founding pres. 1991—96). Avocations: book collecting, languages. Home: 255 Main St Farmington ME 04938

BARIK, SAILEN, biomedical scientist, educator; b. Midnapur, India, June 15, 1954; arrived in US, 1982, naturalized; s. Narayan C. and Promila (Maiti) B.; m. Kumkum Maiti, June 26, 1981; children: Titus, Tiasha. BSc with honors, R.K.M.R. Coll., Calcutta, India, 1972; MSc, Calcutta U., 1975; PhD, Bose Inst., Calcutta, 1982. Rsch. fellow dept. sci. and tech. Govt. India, Calcutta, 1976-81; postdoctoral assoc. U. Conn. Health Ctr., Farmington, 1982-88; project scientist Cleve. Clinic Found., 1989-91, asst. staff, 1992-93; asst. prof. dept. biochemistry and molecular biology U. South Ala., Mobile, 1994—99, assoc. prof., 1999—2003, prof., 2003—. Contbr. articles to profl. jours.; radio host John Carroll U., Cleve., 1992. Soccer coach South Euclid-Lyndhurst Recreation Club, Cleve., 1991-93. Mem. Am. Soc. Virology, Lions Club. Achievements include determination of the mechanism of transcription antitermination; discovery of the role of actin and profilin in respiratory syncytial viral transcription; discovery of bacteriophage protein phosphatase; discovery of RNAi as antiviral. Office: U South Ala Dept Biochem & Mol Biology 307 University Blvd N Mobile AL 36688-0002 Home: 3780 Pelham Dr Mobile AL 36619 Office Phone: 251-460-6860. Business E-Mail: sbarik@jaguar1.usouthal.edu.

BARILLEAUX, RENE PAUL, curator; b. Lafayette, La., June 29, 1958; s. Ira Charles and Joanna Beyt Barilleaux; life ptnr. Timothy Paul Hedgepeth. BFA, U. Southwestern La., Lafayette, 1975—79; MFA, Pratt Inst., Bklyn., 1979—81. Curator for collections & exhibitions Mus. Holography, NYC, 1983—86; exhibitions curator Madison Art Ctr., Wis., 1986—92; gallery dir., asst. prof. Coll. Charleston, SC, 1992—93; chief curator Miss. Mus. Art, Jackson, 1993—2001, dep. dir. programs, 2001—05; chief curator, curator art after 1945 McNay Art Mus., San Antonio, 2005—. Mem. Pub. Art Com., San Antonio, 2006. Mem.: Coll. Art Assn., Assn. Art Mus. Curators, Am. Assn. Museums. Office: McNay Art Mus PO Box 6069 San Antonio TX 78209 Home Phone: 210-323-9145. Office Fax: 210-824-0218. Business E-Mail: rene.barilleaux@mcnayart.org.

BARISH, BARRY C., physics professor, researcher; b. Omaha; BA in physics, U. Calif., Berkeley, 1957; PhD in exptl. high energy physics, Berkeley, 1962. Maxine and Ronald Linde prof. physics Calif. Inst. Tech., Pasadena, 1991—; former chmn. commn. particles and fields Internat. Union Pure and Applied Physics (IUPAP), chmn. US liaison com.; mem. bd. dirs. Nat. Sci. Bd. Spkr. in field. Recipient Klopsteg award, Am. Assn. Physics Tchrs., 2002. Fellow: AAAS, Am. Physics Soc.; mem.: NAS. Achievements include research in high-energy neutrinos important in demonstrating the quark substructure of the nucleon; search for magnetic monopole predicted in theories of Grand Unification. Office: LIGO Lab Calif Inst Tech MS 18 34 Pasadena CA 91125 Office Phone: 626-395-3853. Office Fax: 626-793-9594. Business E-Mail: barish@ligo.caltech.edu.

BARISH, CHARLES FRANKLIN, internist, gastroenterologist, researcher; b. Franklin, NJ, Jan. 5, 1955; s. Philip and Laura (Freedman) Barish; m. Debrah Lee Kaufman, Aug. 13, 1977; children: Philip, Stefanie, Jacob. BS in Chemistry with honors, U. Fla., 1976, MD, 1980. Diplomate in internal medicine and gastroenterology Am. Bd. Internal Medicine. Resident, fellow Wake Forest U. Sch. Medicine, Winston-Salem, NC, 1980-85; physician Wake Internal Medicine Cons., Raleigh, NC, 1985—; pres., founder Wake Rsch. Assocs., Raleigh, 1985—; clin. asst. prof. medicine U. NC Sch. Medicine, Chapel Hill, 1985—. Co-founder Peak Rsch., 1998; chmn. nutritional care com. Rex Hosp., Raleigh, 1987—97. Contbr. numerous articles to med. jours., chapters to books. Pres. Jewish Cmty. Ctr., Raleigh, 1995—97; v.p. Raleigh-Cary Jewish Fedn., 1993—97, bd. dirs., 1990—2006. Fellow: ACP, Am. Gastroenterology Assn., Am. Coll. Gastroenterology; mem.: AMA, Crohn's and Colitis Found. (bd. dirs.), Wake County Med. Soc., N.C. Med. Soc., Am. Liver Found., Am. Soc. Gastrointestinal Endoscopy, Am. Coll. Physician Execs., B'nai Brith, Alpha Epsilon Delta, Phi Kappa Phi, Alpha Omega Alpha. Avocations: gardening, golf, skiing, travel. Office: Wake Internal Medicine Cons 3100 Blue Ridge Rd Ste 300 Raleigh NC 27612-8035 Office Phone: 919-781-7500. Business E-Mail: CFBGastro@aol.com.

BARISH, LAWRENCE STEPHEN, nonpartisan legislative staff administrator; b. Bklyn., Nov. 30, 1945; s. Louis C. and Anna (Sanders) B.; m. Sharon Lee Shapiro, July 2, 1967; 1 child, Lauren. BS in Polit. sci., U. Wis.-Madison, Wis., 1967; MA in Govt., U. Ariz., 1970. Legis. analyst Legis. Reference Bur., Madison, Wis., 1971-87; dir. reference and info. svcs. Wis. Legis. Reference Bur., Madison, 1987—. Chmn. rsch., comm. staff sec. Nat. Conf. State Legislatures, Denver, 1995-97; redistricting cons. Wis. Legis. and Local Govt. units, 1980—. Editor State Almanac, 1987—; contbr. articles to profl. jours. Home: 1429 W Skyline Dr Madison WI 53705-1134 Office: Wis Legis Reference Bur 1 E Main St Ste 200 Madison WI 53701-2037 Business E-Mail: larry.barish@legis.state.wi.us.

BARISH, RANDALL DAVID, application developer; b. Burderop Park, England, Nov. 4, 1955; s. Leo and Joy Bettina Barish; life ptnr. Mari Ann McMahon. BA in Journalism and English, U. Mass., Amherst, 1978. Cert. programming Control Data Inst., 1979. Programmer Q-Comp, Inc., Westwood, Mass., 1984—85; software cons. Various Hi-tech Sites, Mass., 1985—88; programmer analyst Data Gen., Southborough, Mass., 1989—90; sr. systems analyst Cigna Dental, Plantation, Fla., 1991—2006. Musician: (CD) Nostradamus, 1997; actor: (movie) Emma, 1992, (documentary) Vegetarianism Good & Easy, 1991. Buddhist. Avocations: guitar, poetry, song writing. Home: 6320 Pierce St Hollywood FL 33024 Home Phone: 954-989-0707. Personal E-mail: randallbarish0931@yahoo.com.

BARIST, JEFFREY, lawyer; b. Jersey City, Dec. 29, 1941; s. Irving and Lillian (Finkelstein) B.; m. Joan Elaine Travers, Feb. 19, 1967; children: Jessica, Alexis. AB summa cum laude, Rutgers U., 1963; JD cum laude, Harvard U., 1966. Bar: NY 1967, US Ct. Appeals (2d cir.) 1968, US Dist. Ct. (so. dist.) NY 1969, US Supreme Ct. 1975. Law sec. US Dist. Judge Irving Ben Cooper, NYC, 1966-67; ptnr., chmn. nat. litigation group Milbank, Tweed, Hadley & McCloy, NYC, 1996—2006. Author: Commercial Arbitration Law and Clauses, 1994; contbr. articles to profl. jours. Bd. trustees Lawyers Com. for Civil Rights Under Law; mem. NYC Panel of Disting. Neutrals, Ctr. for Public Rsch. Fellow Am. Coll. Trial Lawyers, Am. Bar Found.; mem. Am. Law Inst.; Phi Beta Kappa. Office: Milbank Tweed Hadley McCloy 47th Fl 1 Chase Manhattan Plz Fl 47 New York NY 10005-1413 Home Phone: 860-868-0098; Office Phone: 212-530-5115. Office Fax: 212-822-5115. Business E-Mail: jbarist@milbank.com.

BARITZ, LOREN, history professor; b. Chgo., Dec. 26, 1928; s. Joseph Harry and Helen (Garland) B.; m. Phyllis L. Handelsman, Dec. 26, 1948; children: Tony, Joseph. BA, Roosevelt U., 1953; MA, U. Wis., 1954, PhD, 1956. Asst. prof. history Wesleyan U., Middletown, Conn., 1956-62; assoc. prof. Roosevelt U., Chgo., 1962-63; prof. U. Rochester, 1963-69, chmn. dept. history, 1964-67; leading prof. SUNY, Albany, 1969-71; exec. v.p. Empire State Coll., exec. dir. univ. commn. on purposes and priorities, 1975-76; from exec. v.p. to provost SUNY, 1971-79; dir. N.Y. Inst. Humanities; prof. history NYU, 1979-80; provost, vice chancellor for acad. affairs U. Mass., Amherst, 1980-83, prof. history, 1980-91, prof. emeritus, 1991—. Vis. lectr. U. Wis.-Madison, 1959-60; cultural cons. to UNESCO, Paris, 1968-71; mgmt. cons. Balykchy Inst. of Bus. and Law, Kyrgyzstan, 1997, 99, Slovak U. of Tech., Bratislava, Slovak Republic, 1997, Comenius U., Bratislava, 1998. Author: City on a Hill, 1964, Servants of Power, 1960, Sources of the American Mind, 2 vols., 1966, The Culture of the Twenties, 1970, The American Left, 1971, Backfire, 1985, 98, The Good Life, 1989. Co-chmn. policy coun. rsch. and svc. Assembly Univ. Goals, Am. Acad. Arts and Scis., 1969-70; del. Dem. Nat. Conv., 1968; bd. govs. chmn. com. on acad. affairs Haifa U., 1975-92; mem. exec. bd. Nat. Com. for Labor, Israel, 1984-94; mgmt. cons. Am. Stock Exchange, 1994-95, 97. Rsch. Tng. fellow Social Sci. Rsch. Coun., 1955-56, grantee, 1960; grantee Am. Council Learned Socs., 1963. Home: 266 Hadley Rd Sunderland MA 01375

BARJIS, JOSEPH, computer scientist, educator; b. Kabul, Afghanistan, Sept. 25, 1972; s. Abdulsalam and Rabia Barjis. MSc with honors in Computer Sci., Tashkent Electrotech. U., 1991; PhD in Computer Sci., Moscow Tech. U., 1996; post doctoral in Info. Sys., Delft U. Tech., Netherlands, 1998—2002. Sr. rschr. U. Reading, England, 2002—03; asst. prof. info. tech. Ga. So. U., Statesboro, 2003—07; assoc. prof. info. sys. U. Wis., Stevens Point, 2007—. Vis. prof. Tenn. Tech. U., Cookeville, 2001; organizer profl. and sci. internat. confs., 2002—; lectr. Thames Valley U., England, 2002—03; invited spkr. in field. Contbr. chapters to books, scientific papers and articles to conf. procs. and profl. jours. Adv., organizer Reconstruction of Afghanistan & Restoration of Democracy, 1996—2002; activist various democratic and intellectual org., 1996—2002. Recipient Excellence in Study medal, Govt. of Afghanistan, 1991, Best Paper award, Soc. Computer Simulation Internat.l, San Diego, Calif., 1999, World Order of Sci.-Edn.-Culture, European Acad. Info., Brussels, Belgium, 2001, Award of Excellence, Taekwondo, Black Belt Acad., 2004, First pl. in Forms, Taekwondo Fall Nationals, Orlando, Fla., 2004, Third pl. in Sparing, 2004. Mem.: Assn. Computing Machinery, Assn. for Info. Sys., Am. Taekwondo Assn. Avocations: Tae Kwon Do, philosophy, literature, poetry. Office: Dept Computer Info Sys U Wis Stevens Point Stevens Point WI 54481 Office Phone: 715-346-2078. Personal E-mail: jbarjis@gmail.com.

BARK, NIGEL MARTYN, psychiatrist; b. Tarporley, Eng., July 3, 1941; s. Oliver and Gwen B.; m. Helen (McQuaid) B., OCt. 3, 1970; children: Lesley Bark-Marzec, Philippa Bark-McHugh, Charles. BA in Natural Sci., Cambridge U., 1962, MA, 1986, MB, BChir., 1966; MS in Psychiat. Epidemiology, Columbia U., 1986. Diplomate Am. Bd. Psychiatry and Neurology; cert. in psychopharmacology Am. Soc. Clin. Psychopharmacology, 2000. Surg. intern Worcester Royal Infirmary, England, 1967; med. intern Univ. Coll. Hosp., London, 1967; resident in obstetrics Rotunda Hosp., Dublin, 1968; resident in pediatrics Our Lady's Hosp. for Sick Children, Dublin, 1969; resident in psychiatry St. Patrick's Hosp., Dublin, 1970-73, psychiat. registrar, 1970-75; rsch. assoc. Nathan S. Kline Inst. for Psychiat. Rsch., Orangeburg, 1981-90; pvt. practice psychopharmacology NYC and Rockland County, NY, 1976—; assoc. med. dir. schizophrenia rsch. unit Bronx Psychiat. Ctr., Albert Einstein Coll. Medicine, NY, 1990-95; dir. schizophrenia rsch. unit Bronx Psychiat. Ctr., Albert Einstein Coll. Medicine, 1996—. Cons. psychiatrist Summit Park Hosp. and Robert L. Yeager Health Ctr., Pomona, N.Y., 1982-90; attending psychiatrist Gracie Sq. Hosp., N.Y.C., 1981-90; asst. attending psychiatrist Good Samaritan Hosp., Suffern, N.Y., 1985-89, St. Luke's Roosevelt Hosp., N.Y.C., 1983-86, Harlem Hosp., N.Y.C., 1983-84; med. dir. St. Luke's Day Hosp., N.Y.C., 1982; postdoctoral fellow psychiat. epidemiology tng. program Columbia U., N.Y.C., 1981-82; unit chief in rsch. and rehab. Rockland Psychiat. Ctr., 1978-81; rsch. psychiatrist Rockland Rsch. Inst., 1976-78; adj. psychiatrist Lenox Hill (N.Y.) Hosp., 1985-90. Editor: Internat. Jour. Mental Health on Risk Factors Schizophrenia and Prevention, 2000-01; contbr. about 30 sci. articles to profl. jours.; contbr. chpts. to books. Fellow Am. Psychiat. Assn. (pub. affairs rep. W. Hudson dist. br. 1985-91, pres. 1987-89, organizer, chair Internat. Psychiat. symposia ann. meetings, 2001—, dist. br. rep. 2005—),Royal Coll. Psychiatrists (hon. sec. mental handicap sect. Irish div. 1974-76, organizer, chair Pan Am. session ann. meetings 2001-06, chair N.Am. group, 2000-05, Pan Am. Divsn., 2005—). Home: 117 Constitution Dr Orangeburg NY 10962-2733 Office: Bronx Psychiat Ctr 1500 Waters Pl Bronx NY 10461 also: Pvt Practices 133 E 73rd St New York NY 10021 also: 105 Shad Raw Piermont NY 10968 Office Fax: 718-862-4889. Personal E-mail: nbark1@pol.net. Business E-Mail: brmdnbb@omh.state.ny.us.

BARKAN, JOHN MARTIN, JR., architect; b. Warren, Ohio, Mar. 16, 1945; s. John Martin and Esther (Wagoner) B.; m. Darlene Rose Kast, Oct. 14, 1972 (div. 1992); children: Leilani, John III; m. Alice Faye Byers, Aug. 28, 2004. BArch, Kent State U., 1969. Registered architect, Ohio. Draftsman Mallalieu, Ross & Roberts, Massillon, Ohio, 1968—72, architect, 1972—76; architect capt. Lawrence, Dykes & Goodenberger, Canton, Ohio, 1977—80; project architect Wilson Archtl. Group, North Canton, Ohio, 1982—86; pvt. practice Canton, 1986—89; ptnr. Goodenberger, Dansizen & Barkan Architects, Canton, 1989—95; v.p. L.D. Design Group, Canton, 1995—. Prin. works include Massillon City Hall, McKinley Centre, Ergun residence, Aultman North Med. Ctr., Akron Canton Regional Airport Expansion, NW H.S. Local coord. for Russian med. clinic. adminstr. Ctr. for Citizen Initiatives, 2000, 2003; local coord. Legal Svc. Adminstrn., 2005—. Mem.: AIA (sec. Akron chpt. 1985), Rotary Canton (pres. 2006—07, Paul Harris fellow 2000). Republican. Roman Catholic. Avocations: golf, art, literature. Home: 127 Montrose Ave NW Canton OH 44708

BARKAN, STEVEN M., law librarian, educator; children: Davida, Daniel. AMLS, U. Mich.; JD, Cleve. State U. Reference libr. U. So. Calif. Law Libr.; rsch. libr. Supreme Ct. of US; assoc. law libr. U. Tex. Sch. Law; dir. Law Libr., assoc. dean to interim dean Marquette U. Law Sch.; dir. Law Libr., tchr. tort law U. Wis. Law Sch. Founding editor Perspectives, 1992, contbr. Fundamentals of Legal Rsch.; contbr. articles to profl. jours. Recipient Excellence in Academic Law Librarianship Award, West Pub. Co., 1993. Avocations: movies, music, travel. Office: Law Libr Rm 6358 975 Bascom Mall Madison WI 53706-1399 Office Phone: 608-262-1151. E-mail: smbarkan@wisc.edu.*

BARKEN, BERNARD ALLEN, lawyer; b. St. Louis, July 20, 1924; s. Gottlieb and Hattie E. (Rubin) B.; m. Jocelyn Moss Kopman, Sept. 1, 1948; children: Thomas L., Dale Susan. JD, Washington U., 1947. Bar: Mo. 1947, U.S. Dist. Ct. (ea. dist.) Mo. 1947, U.S. Ct. Appeals (8th cir.) 1954, U.S. Tax Ct. 1966, U.S. Ct. Appeals 2nd cir.) 1985, U.S. Supreme Ct. 1984. Sole practice, St. Louis, 1947-80; ptnr. Shifrin & Treiman, St. Louis, 1980-88; pres. Bernard A. Barken, St. Louis, 1988-91; ptnr. Barken & Bakewell L.L.P., St. Louis, 1991—. With USAAF, 1943-44. Mem. ABA, Bar Assn. Met. St. Louis (v.p. 1958, chmn. young lawyers 1953). Jewish. Avocations: piano, tennis, gardening. Home: 30 Vouga Ln Saint Louis MO 63131-2628 Office: Barken & Bakewell LLP 500 N Broadway Ste 2000 Saint Louis MO 63102-2130 Office Phone: 314-444-1367. Office Fax: 314-444-7892. Personal E-mail: babarken@hotmail.com.

BARKER, BARBARA ANN, ophthalmologist; b. Paterson, NJ, Nov. 10, 1943; d. Earle Louis and Dorothy Louise (Williamson) Barker; m. Joel Ira Papernik, July 28, 1972; children: Deborah Papernik, Ilana Papernik. BA magna cum laude, Conn. Coll., 1965; BS, Yale U., 1967; MA, Rutgers U., 1974; MD, Mt. Sinai Sch. Medicine, 1976. Diplomate Am. Bd. Ophthalmology. Intern Beth Israel Med. Ctr., 1977; resident Mt. Sinai Sch. Medicine/Beth Israel Med. Ctr., 1980, fellow in glaucoma, 1980-81, fellow cornea, refractive surgery, 1981-82; pvt. practice medicine specializing in ophthalmology , NYC, 1983—. Rsch. technician The Rockefeller U., NYC, 1965—66; tchr. Riverdale Country Sch., NYC, 1967—68; rsch. asst. Sloan Kettering Inst., NYC, 1969—72; asst. clin. prof. Mt. Sinai Sch. Medicine, NYC, 1982—; mem. staff N.Y. Eye and Ear Hosp., Beth Israel/St. Luke's/Roosevelt Hosp. Recipient Resident Best Paper award, Beth Israel Med. Ctr., 1989, Honor award, Am. Acad. Ophthalmology, 1995; grantee Beth Israel Rsch. grant, 1983, NSF, 1966. Fellow: ACS, N.Y. Acad. Medicine; mem.: AMA, N.Y. County Med. Assn., Women's Med. Soc. NYC, Am. Med. Women's Assn., Phi Beta Kappa. Home: 11 E 86th St New York NY 10028-0501 Office: 70 E 96th St New York NY 10028 Office Phone: 212-289-2244. Personal E-mail: bbarkermd@aol.com.

BARKER, BEN, chef, restaurant owner; m. Karen Barker; 1 child, Gabriel. Grad., Culinary Inst. Am., 1981. Chef Restaurant Le Residence, Chapel Hill, NC; head chef Fearrington House, Pittsboro, NC; chef, co-owner Magnolia Grill, Durham, NC, 1986—. Featured in (TV series) Americas 1996 - Rising Star Chefs, PBS, 1996, Great Chefs of the South, 1997, NY Times, Washington Post, Food & Wine mag., Bon Appetit, Esquire, Restaurant News, Southern Living. Nominee Best Chef in Southeast, James Beard Found., 1992, 1995, 1996, 1997, 1998, 1999; named Rising Star Chef, Esquire, 1992, Best Chef in Southeast, James Beard Found., 2000; named one of Ten Best New Chefs in Am., Food & Wine mag., 1993; named to Who's Who of Southern Cooking, 1988, Fine Dining Hall of Fame, Nation's Restaurant News, 1996. Achievements include creating southern regional menu for Delta Airlines, 1995. Office: Magnolia Grill 1002 9th St Durham NC 27705 Office Phone: 919-286-3609.*

BARKER, BOB (ROBERT WILLIAM BARKER), television personality; b. Darrington, Wash., Dec. 12, 1923; s. Byron John and Matilda Kent (Tarleton) B.; m. Dorothy Jo Gideon, Jan. 12, 1945 (dec. Oct. 1981). BA in Econs. summa cum laude, Drury Coll., 1947. Founder DJ&T Found., Beverly Hills, Calif., 1995. Host: (radio show) The Bob Barker Show; (TV series) Truth or Consequences, 1956-75, The Price is Right, 1972-2007, Bob Barker Fun and Games Show, 1978; (TV specials) Miss Universe Beauty Pageant, 1966-87, Miss U.S.A. Beauty Pageant, 1966-87, Pillsbury Bake-Off, 1969-85, Rose Parade, CBS, 1969-88; appeared in (TV series) Bonanza, 1960, The Nanny, 1994, Something So Right, 1996, 1997, Martial Law, 1998, Futurama (voice), 2000, Yes Dear, 2001, Family Guy (voice), 2001, The Bold and the Beautiful, 2002; (feature films) Happy Gilmore, 1996. Served to lt. (j.g.) USNR, 1943-45. Recipient Emmy award for Best Audience Participation Host, 1981-82, 83-84, 86-87, 87-88, 89-90, 90-91, 91-92, 93-94, 94-95, 95-96, 99-00, 00-01, Lifetime Achievement Emmy award for Daytime Television, 1999, Carbon Mike award of the Pioneer Broadcasters. Mem. AGVA, AFTRA, Screen Actors Guild. inducted, Acad. of Television and Arts & Sciences Hall of Fame, 2004. Office: The Price is Right care CBS TV 7800 Beverly Blvd Los Angeles CA 90036-2112

BARKER, BRUCE CRICHLOW, barrister, solicitor; b. Chgo., July 19, 1949; s. William Crichlow Lamond Barker and Priscilla Curtis; children: Alison, Andrea, Christopher, Caroline; m. Sonia Basso. Ars Baccalauriat summa cum laude, Dartmouth Coll., 1971; LLB, U. Toronto, Ont., Can., 1975. Rsch. asst. Coun. on Fgn. Rels., NYC, 1971-72; assoc. Tory Tory Des Lauriers & Binnington, Toronto, 1975-83, McMillan Binch, Toronto, 1983—2000, mng. ptnr., 1998—2000; ptnr. Bennett Jones LLP, Toronto, 2000—. Chmn., bd. dirs. Balt. Fin. Svcs. Co., Dublin, Ireland, 1991-1998, SLX Can. Inc., Calgary, Alta., 1989—2006, BayFront Assocs., Toronto, 1993—; sessional instr. Osgoode Hall Law Sch., York U., 1993—; mem. adv. coun. U. We. Ontario Richard Ivey Sch. Bus. Inst. Entrepreneurship, 1998—, chair, 2005-06. Mem. editl. bd. Banking and Fin. Law Rev., 1989—. Mem. Law Soc. Upper Can., Toronto Club.

BARKER, CHRISTOPHER B., lawyer; AB magna cum laude, Brown Univ., 1982; JD, Harvard Univ., 1985. Bar: Mass. 1985. Project mgr. engring., construction firm; atty. Nagashima Ohno & Tsunematsu, Tokyo, 1990—91; ptnr., real estate dept. Goodwin Procter LLP, Boston, chair, real estate group, mem., exec. com. Frequent lectr., writer in field. Mem.: ABA. Office: Goodwin Procter LLP Exchange Pl 53 State St Boston MA 02109 Office Phone: 617-570-1462. Office Fax: 617-523-1231. Business E-Mail: cbarker@goodwinprocter.com.

BARKER, CLIVE, artist, film director and producer, scriptwriter; b. Liverpool, Eng., 1952; s. Len and Joan B. Student, U. Liverpool, Eng. Author: (plays) Incarnations (Frankenstein in Love, History of the Devil, Colossus), Forms of Heaven (Paradise Street, Subtle Bodies, Crazyface); (short story collection) Books of Blood I-VI (books IV, V, and VI released in U.S. as The Inhuman Condition, 1986, In the Flesh, 1986, Cabal; (TV movie) Saint Sinner, 2002; (novels) The Damnation Game, 1985, Weaveworld, 1987, Cabal, 1988, The Great and Secret Show, 1989, Imajica, 1991, The Thief of Always, 1992, Everville, 1994, Sacrament, 1996, A-Z of Horror, 1997, Galilee, 1998, The Essential Clive Barker, 1999, Coldheart Canyon, 2001; prodr. Hellraiser II: Hellbound, 1990, Candyman, 1992, Hellraiser III: Hell on Earth, 1992, Candyman II: Farewell to the Flesh, 1995, Hellraiser: Bloodline, 1996, Gods & Monsters, 1997, (Fox TV) Spirits and Shadows, 1997; writer and dir. (screenplays) Hellraiser, 1987, Nightbreed, 1990, Lord of Illusions, 1995, Art Exhibition, 1998, Clive Barker's Freaks, 1998, Undying, 2001. Home: Los Angeles CA Mailing: PO Box 691829 West Hollywood CA 90069

BARKER, CLYDE FREDERICK, surgeon, educator; b. Salt Lake City, Aug. 16, 1932; s. Frederick George and Jennetta Elizabeth (Stephens) B.; m. Dorothy Joan Bieler, Aug. 11, 1956; children: Frederick George II, John Randolph, William Stephens, Elizabeth Dell. BA, Cornell U., 1954, MD, 1958. Diplomate Am. Bd. Surgery. Intern Hosp. U. Pa., Phila., 1958-59, resident in surgery, 1959-64, fellow in vascular surgery, 1964-65; fellow in med. genetics U. Pa. Sch. Medicine, Phila., 1965-66, assoc. in surgery, 1964-68, assoc. in med. genetics, 1966-72; attending surgeon Hosp. U. Pa., Phila., 1966—; chief div. transplantation U. Pa. Sch. Medicine, Phila., 1966—2001, asst. prof. surgery, 1968-69, assoc. prof. surgery, 1969-73, prof. surgery, 1973—, J. William White prof. surg. research, 1978-82, chief div. vascular surgery, 1982—2001, Guthrie prof. surgery, 1982—, John Rhea Barton prof. surgery, 1983—2001, chmn. dept. surgery, 1983—2001; chief surgery Hosp. U. Pa., Phila., 1983—2001. Dir. Harrison dept. surgery rsch. U. Pa., Phila., 1983-2001; immunobiology study sect. NIH; chmn. clin. practices U. Pa., 1987-89; v.p. United Network for Organ Sharing, 2001-02, pres., 2002-03. Mem. editl. bd. Jour. Transplantation, 1977-2001, Clin. Transplantation, 1988—, Jour. Surg. Rsch., 1979-85, Jour. Diabetes, 1981-86, Archives of Surgery, 1987-96, Transplantation Procs., 1990-2001, Surgery, 1991-95, Cell Transplantation, 1991—, Postgrad. Gen. Surgery, 1991-95, Jour. ACS, 1994—, Annals of Surgery, 1995—; contbr. articles to profl. jours. and textbooks. Markle Found. Scholar, 1968-74; NIH grantee, 1974-2001; recipient Merit award NIH, 1987-95. Fellow AOA, NAS (Inst. Medicine), ACS (com. Forum on Fundamental Surg. Problems 1983-88, vice chmn. 1987-88, bd. govs. 1994-2001, pres. Phila. chpt. 1991-92), Coll. Physicians Phila., Royal Coll. Surgeons Eng. (hon.), Royal Coll. Surgeons Ireland (hon.); mem. AMA, Royal Coll. Surgeons of Ireland (hon.), Assn. Acad. Surgery, Am. Diabetes Assn., Am. Soc. Artificial Internal Organs, Am. Fedn. Clin. Rsch., Juvenile Diabetes Found., Soc. Univ. Surgeons, Am. Surg. Assn. (recorder 1991-96, pres. 1996-97, medallion for sci. achievement 2003), Soc. Clin. Surgery (chmn. membership 1984-85), Halsted Soc. (chmn. membership 1984-85, v.p. 1985-86, pres. 1986-87), Surg. Biology Club II, Soc. Vascular Surgery, Internat. Cardiovascular Soc., Internat. Surg. Group (treas. 1988-94, pres. 1994-95), Internat. Soc. Surgery (v.p. U.S. chpt. 1995-97, pres. 1997-99), Transplantation Soc. (councilman 1978-84, 94—), Am. Soc. Transplant Surgeons (chmn. membership 1980-81, treas. 1988-91, pres. 1992-93), Unitd Network for Organ Sharing (v.p. 2001-02), (pres. 2002-03), Am. Acad. Arts and Scis., Assn. Am. Physicians, Phila. Acad. Surgery (program chmn. 1984-86, v.p. 1986-88, pres. 1988-89), Greater Delaware Valley Soc. Transplant Surgeons (pres. 1978-80), Am. Philos. Soc. (coun. 2003—, v.p. 2005—) Home: 3 Coopertown Rd Haverford PA 19041-1012 Office: Hosp Univ Pa Dept Surgery 3400 Spruce St Philadelphia PA 19104-4206

BARKER, EDWIN BOGUE, musician; b. Tucson, Apr. 14, 1954; s. Francis Hustis and Mary Jeanne (Austin) B.; m. Pamela Paikin, 1980; children: Rachel Leigh, Ilana Michelle. Studies with Henry Portnoi, Peter Mercurio, Angelo LaMariana, Richard Stephan, David Perleman, 1965—76; student, Music Acad. of the West, Santa Barbara, Calif., 1969—71; MusB with honors, New Eng. Conservatory Music, 1976. Prin. bass Lake George Opera Orch., NY, 1971-72; substitute mem. N.Y. Philharm., 1976; mem. Chgo. Symphony Orch., 1976-77; prin. bass Boston Symphony, 1977—; mem. Boston Symphony Chamber Players, 1977—; instr. double bass New Eng. Conservatory Music, 1977-90, 98—, Boston Conservatory Music, 1980-83; instr. double bass and chamber music Tanglewood Music Ctr., 1978—; instr. double bass Boston U., 1983—2002; assoc. prof. Boston U. Coll. Fine Arts, Sch. Music, 2002—. Bass and string clinics Am. String Tchrs. Assn. and U. Mich., Ann Arbor, 1982, 83; instr. double bass Teton Orchestral Tng. Seminar, Wyo., 1984-86; prin. bass and faculty mem. Georg Solti Orchestral Tng. Project, Carnegie Hall, 1994—; prin. bass UN Orch. Musicians of the World, Geneva, 1995—; master classes Nat. Orchestral Inst., U. Md., 1991-, U. Ga., 1997, Juilliard Sch., 1999, New World Symphony, 2003; concert tours in N.Am., Europe, and Asia; chmn. orchestral and instrumental studies Tanglewood Music Ctr., 2005-. Solo appearances with Boston Symphony Orch., Tanglewood, New England Conservatory Symphony Orch., Bergen (Norway) Music Festival, Carnegie Recital Hall, N.Y.C., 1984, 85, others; concerto performance with Boston Symphony, Madrid, 1993; other performances include: Concerto for Double Bass and Chamber Orch. by Gunther Schuller, Boston premiere with Pro Arte Chamber Orch., 1987, Concerto for Double Bass and Chamber Orch. by James Yannatos, premiere performance, 1986, Concerto for Double Bass and Orchestra by Edward Tubin, with Boston Symphony Orch., Boston premiere, 1994, Juilliard Quartet, Libr. of Congress, 1992, Muir Quartet, 1998, 99, premiere performance James Yannatos' Variations for Solo Contrabass, 1998, premier performance with Lydian String Quartet of Serenade in D by Harold Shapiro, for String Quartet and Double bass, 1999, World Premiere of Concertino for Double Bass and Chamber Orch. with Pro Arte Chamber Orch., 2000; soloist with Boston Symphony Orch., 2001; recs. include Three Sonatas for Double Bass, 1998, Variations for Solo Contrabass,

2000, Concerti for Double Bass, 2005. Mem. Am. Youth Symphony, 1961-69, UCLA Symphony, 1968-69; mem. Players com. Boston Symphony, 1988-92, mem. music dir. search com., 2000-. Recipient Benjamin H. Delson award Berkshire Music Ctr., 1975, Chadwick medal New Eng. Conservatory of Music, 1976; named one of Outstanding Young Men of Am., 1986, Most Outstanding Alumni New Eng. Conservatory of Music, 1993. Mem. Am. Fedn. Musicians., Internat. Soc. Bassists (dir. 1983) Office: Symphony Hall Boston MA 02115

BARKER, HAROLD GRANT, surgeon, educator; b. Salt Lake City, June 10, 1917; s. Frederick George and Elizabeth Jennetta (Stephens) B.; m. Kathleen Butler, July 29, 1949; children: Janet Stephens, Douglas Reid. AB, U. Utah, 1939, postgrad., 1939-41; MD, U. Pa., 1943. Diplomate Am. Bd. Surgery. Intern. Hosp. U. Pa., 1943-44, asst. resident in surgery, 1947-51, sr. resident in surgery, 1951-52, asst. attending surgeon, 1952-53; also asst. instr., research fellow U. Pa., 1946-51, instr., research fellow, 1951-52, assoc. in surgery, 1952-53; asst. prof. surgery Columbia U., 1953-57, assoc. prof., 1957-68, prof., 1968-82, prof. emeritus, 1982—. Asst. attending surgeon Presbyn. Hosp., 1953-57, assoc. attending surgeon, 1957-69, attending surgeon, 1969-89, cons. surgeon, 1989—, dir. med. affairs, 1974-82; pvt. practice, Phila., 1952-53, N.Y.C., 1953-88. Contbr. articles med. jours. Served from 1st lt. to capt., M.C. AUS, 1944-46, ETO. Fellow ACS; mem. Soc. U. Surgeons, N.Y. Surg. Soc., Am. Physiol. Soc., Soc. Exptl. Biology and Medicine, AMA, Halsted Soc., N.Y. State (chmn. surg. sect. 1961-62), N.Y. County med. socs., Am. Surg. Assn., N.Y. Gastroent. Assn., Société Internationale de Chirurgie, Soc. Surgery Alimentary Tract, Allen O. Whipple Surg. Soc., Am. Assn. History Medicine, Collegium Internationale Chirurgiae Digestivae, Century Assn., Manursing Island Club, Am. Yacht Club. Home: 5028 Theall Rd Rye NY 10580-1445

BARKER, HAROLD KENNETH, former university dean; b. Louisville, Apr. 14, 1922; s. J.M. and Fannie Mae (Elliott) B.; m. Elizabeth Johns, Mar. 11, 1948 (dec.); children: Leslie Ann, Glenn Lewis.; m. Beverly Williams, Feb. 28, 1984. AB, U. Louisville, 1948, MA, 1949; PhD, U. Mich., 1959. Instr. Gunfire Prep. Sch., Hanau, Germany, 1946; sch. psychologist, vis. tchr. Bay City (Mich.) Pub. Schs., 1949-52; also instr. Bay City Jr. Coll.; sch. psychologist Ypsilanti (Mich.) Pub. Schs., 1952-53; instr. Eastern Mich. U., 1954-58; asst. dir. Bur. Appointments and Occupational Info., U. Mich., 1954-59; assoc. exec. sec. Am. Assn. Colls. Tchr. Edn., Washington, 1959-66, dir., 1972—; dean Coll. Edn., U. Akron, 1966-85, asst. to pres., 1985-87, dean emeritus, 1987. Bd. dirs. World U., San Juan, P.R., 1966— , Joint Council Econ. Edn., 1979 Editor: AACTE Handbook of International Education Programs, 1963; contbr. articles to profl. jours. and periodicals. Chmn. bd. dirs. Edwin Shaw Hosp., 1989; trustee U. Akron Found., 1994—. Recipient award outstanding profl. svc. Am. Assn. Colls. Tchr. Edn., 1966; named Hon. Alumni U. Akron, 1992. Mem. Phi Delta Kappa (internat. commn. 1962-69) Home: 1811 Brookwood Dr Akron OH 44313-5061 Office: Dept Devel Martin Univ Ctr U Akron Akron OH 44325-2603

BARKER, JAMES F., academic administrator; b. Kingsport, Tenn. BArch, Clemson U., 1970; M in Arch. and Urban Design, Washington U., 1973; PhD (hon.), S.C. State U., Mars Hill Coll. Dean Sch. Arch. Miss. State U.; dean Coll. Arch. Clemson U., SC, 1986—95, dean Coll. Arch., Arts and Humanities, 1995—99, pres., 1999—. Fellow: AIA; mem.: Assn. Collegiate Schs. Arch. (past pres., Nat. Disting. Prof. award). Office: Clemson Univ Office of Pres 201 Sikes Hall Clemson SC 29634 Office Phone: 864-656-3413. Business E-Mail: jbarker@clemson.edu.*

BARKER, JAMES REX, water transportation executive, director; b. Cleve., Aug. 3, 1935; s. William Wardel and Elizabeth Ranghild (Wandler) B.; m. Kaye Elizabeth Schumacher, Aug. 3, 1957; children: James Arthur, Karen Elizabeth, Mark William. BA, Columbia U., 1957; MBA with distinction, Harvard U., 1963; DSc (hon.), Maine Maritime Acad., 1978. Planning exec. Pickands Mather & Co., Cleve., 1963-67; v.p. Harbridge House, Boston, 1967-69; founder, exec. v.p. Temple, Barker & Sloane, Wellesley, Mass., 1970-71; chmn. bd. Moore McCormack Resources, Inc., Stamford, Conn., 1971-87, chief exec. officer, 1971-87; vice chmn., founder, co-owner Mormac Marine Group Inc., Stamford, Conn., 1987—; chmn., prin. Interlake Steamship Co., Stamford, 1987—. Vice chmn., prin. owner Moran Towing Co.; owner, chmn. New England Fast Ferry Inc.; bd. dirs. Brink's Co., Verizon. Lt. (j.g.) USCG, 1957-61. Mem. Am. Bur. Shipping (bd. mgrs.) Clubs: Wee Burn Country, Noroton Yacht, N.Y. Yacht, Rolling Rock, Union, Links. Episcopalian. Home: 180 Long Neck Point Rd Darien CT 06820-5816 Office: Mormac Marine Group Inc 1 Landmark Sq Stamford CT 06901-2501

BARKER, JEFF, theater and speech educator; m. Karen Barker; 3 children. Student, Greenville Coll.; BA in Theater, Seattle Pacific U., 1976; MA in Theater Performance, No. Ill. U.; MFA in Directing, U. SD. Mem. faculty to prof. theatre and speech Northwestern Coll., Orange City, Iowa, 1988—, endowed prof., 2006—. Dir. Drama Ministries Ensemble. Co-creator: (musicals) And God Said; author: (plays) Unspoken for Time, 1996 (Meritorious Achievement award, 1995), Kin (Grand Prize New Voices Iowa Playwrights Competition, 2002), That Bamboozler, Scapin!, September Bears, Sioux Center Sudan, David and Goliath, When Scott Comes Home, Elisha, Code Blue, The Final Approach of Flight 232, Word Against Word. Co-recipient Gold Medallion award, Kennedy Ctr. Am. Coll. Theatre Festival, 2003; recipient US Prof. of Yr. award, Carnegie Found. for Advancement of Tchg. and Coun. for Advancement and Support of Edn., 2006. Office: Dept Theatre and Speech Northwestern Coll 101 7th St SW Orange City IA 51041 Office Phone: 712-707-7093. E-mail: barker@nwciowa.edu.*

BARKER, JOHN ROY, lawyer, gas industry executive; b. St. Joseph, Mo., Mar. 9, 1947; s. Frank Otis and Ella Mae (Wiley) B.; m. Mary Lucille Smith, Apr. 17, 1971; children: Sarah J., Kathryn W. Morris, Mary E. BA, U. Mo., 1969; JD, U. Mich., 1974. Bar: US Dist. Ct. (no. dist. Okla.) 1974, Okla. 1974, US Ct. Appeals (10th cir.) 1974. Lawyer Gable Gotwals, Tulsa, Okla., 1974—2004; sr. v.p., gen. counsel ONEOK, Inc., Tulsa, Okla., 2004—; exec. v.p., gen. counsel, sec. ONEOK Ptnrs. LP, Tulsa, Okla., 2006—. Pres. Jenks (Okla.) Pub. Schs. Found., 1989-91; sec. St. Simeon's Episcopal Home, Tulsa, 1991-96, v.p., 1996-98, pres., 1998-2001; pres St. Simeon's Home Found., 2002-04; vice chmn. Sutton Avian Rsch. Ctr., Bartlesville, Okla., 1994-96; pres. Arts and Humanities Coun., Tulsa, 1994-96, pres., 1993-95. With US Army, 1969—71. Mem. ABA, Okla. Bar Assn. (Outstanding Young Lawyer 1978, chair Young Lawyers 1978), Tulsa County Bar Assn., Tulsa Title and Probate (pres. 1987-88). Episcopalian. Avocations: running, bicycling. Office: ONEOK Inc MD 1831 100 W Fifth St Tulsa OK 74103 Office Phone: 918-588-7946. E-mail: jbarker@oneok.com.*

BARKER, JULIE A., school system administrator; b. Rochester, NY, July 30, 1968; d. Philip Noto and Angela Terrell; m. Scott M. Barker; children: Brandon, Colby. BA in History and Secondary Social Studies, SUNY, Cortland, 1990, MA in History, 1995. Cert. tchr. secondary social studies N.Y. State Edn. Dept. Secondary social studies tchr. Maine-Endwell (N.Y.) Ctrl. Sch. Dist., 1991—95, Pittsford (N.Y.) Ctrl. Sch. Dist., 1995—2000, curriculum coord. - social studies, 2000—. Facilitator Franklin Covey Co., Salt Lake City, 2000—; instrnl. coach Pittsford Ctrl. Sch. Dist., 1999—. Bd. dirs. Pittsford Youth Svcs., 1998—2001; dir. vacation Bible sch. Ch. of the Transfiguration, Pittsford, 2003—. Mem.: ASCD, N.Y. State Coun. Social Studies. Office: Pittsford Ctrl Sch Dist 10 Grove St Pittsford NY 14534 Home Phone: 585-249-0164; Office Phone: 585-218-1782. Office Fax: 585-218-1721. E-mail: julie_barker@pittsford.monroe.edu.

BARKER, KAREN, restaurant owner, chef; m. Ben Barker; 1 child, Gabriel. Grad., Culinary Inst. Am., 1981. Pastry chef Restaurant La Residence, Chapel Hill, NC, The Fearrington House; pastry chef, co-owner Magnolia Grill, Durham, NC, 1986—. Featured in (TV series) Americas 1996 - Rising Star Chefs, PBS, 1996, Great Chefs of the South, 1997, NY Times, Washington Post, Food & Wine mag., Bon Appetit, Esquire, Restaurant News, Southern Living. Nominee Outstanding Pastry Chef, James Beard Found., 1997, 1999, 2000; named Best Pastry Chef, Bon Appetit Am. Food and Entertaining awards, 1999; named to Fine Dining Hall of Fame, Nation's Restaurant News, 1996. Achievements include creating a southern regional menu for Delta Airlines, 1995. Office: Magnolia Grill 1002 9th St Durham NC 27701 Office Phone: 919-286-3609.*

BARKER, KEITH RENE, investment banker; b. Elkhart, Ind., July 28, 1928; s. Clifford C. and Edith (Hausmna) B.; children by previous marriage: Bruce C., Lynn K.; m. Elizabeth S. Arrington, Nov. 24, 1965; 1 child, Jennifer Scott. AB, Wabash Coll., 1950; MBA, Ind. U., 1952. Sales rep. Fulton, Reid & Co., Inc., Ft. Wayne, Ind., 1951—55, office, 1955—59, asst. v.p. then v.p., 1960, dir., 1961, asst. sales mgr., 1963, sales mgr., 1964, dir. Ind. ops.; sr. v.p. Fulton, Reid & Co., 1966—75; pres., CEO Fulton, Reid & Staples, Inc., 1975—77; ptnr. William C. Roney & Co., 1977—79; exec. com. Cascade Industries, Inc.; assoc. A.G. Edwards & Sons, Inc., 1984—89, v.p. investments, 1989—. Dir. Fulton, Reid & Staples, Inc., Craft House Corp., Nobility Homes, Inc. Pres. Historic Ft. Wayne, Inc.; cons. to Mus. Historic Ft. Wayne; nominee, trustee Ohio Hist. Soc.; mem. Smithsonian Assocs.; mem. fin. com. E. Tenn. Hist. Soc., dir., treas. collections com.; v.p. Ft. Wayne Hist. Soc.; bd. dirs. Ft. Wayne YMCA, 1963-64; cons. of collections East Tenn. Hist. Soc. Recipient Achievement cert. Inst. Investment Banking, U. Pa., 1959. Mem. Alliance Française, VFW (past comdr.), Co. Mil. Historians, Cleve. Grays, Am. Soc. Arms Collectors, 1st Cleve. Cavalry Assn., Nat. Assn. Securities Dealers (bus. conduct com.), Beaver Creek Hunt Club, Cleve. Athletic Club, Rockwell Springs Club, Hill and Dale Club, Masons, Phi Beta Kappa. Episcopalian. Home: 15812 E 28th Street Ct S Independence MO 64055

BARKER, LARRY LEE, communications educator; b. Wilmington, Ohio, Nov. 22, 1941; s. Milford and Ruth Maxine (Garringer) B.; children: Theodore Allen., Robert Milford. BA, Ohio U., 1962, MA, 1963, Ph. D, 1965. Asst. prof. So. Ill. U., Carbondale, 1965-66, Purdue U., West Lafayette, Ind., 1966-69; assoc. prof. Fla. State U., Tallahassee, 1969-71, prof., 1971—95; prof. emeritus Auburn (Ala.) U., 1995—. Pres. Spectra Inc., New Orleans, 1979—2000. Author: (with R. Kibler) Conceptual Frontiers in Speech Communication, 1969, Behavioral Objectives and Instruction, 1970, Listening Behavior, 1971, Speech Communication Behavior, 1971, Communication Vibrations, 1974, Speech— Interpersonal Communication, 1974, (with R. Edward) Intrapersonal Communication, 1980, (with R. Kibler) Objectives for Instruction and Evaluation, 1981, Communication, 1982, Communication in the Classroom, 1982, (with others) Effective Listening, 1982, (with L. Malandro) Nonverbal Communication, 1983, (with K. Wahlers) Groups in Process, 1983, (with others) Intrapersonal Communication Processes, 1987, (with K. Watson) Interpersonal and Relational Communications, 1989, Listen Up, 2000, Fishing Florida's Top Ten Bass Lakes: Vol. I, 2003, Vol. II, 2004, "F" is for Fishing, 2005, Meditation Techniques for Stress Management, 2006; contbr. articles to profl. jours. Recipient outstanding award in discussion Tau Kappa Alpha, 1962, outstanding tchr. award Ctrl. States Speech Assn., 1969, Robert J. Kibler Meml. award Speech Comm. Assn., 1986. Mem. APA, Internat. Comm. Assn. (v.p. 1972-74), Internat. Listening Assn. (chmn. rsch. com. 1979-82, pres. 1986-87). Methodist. Home: 30617 US Hwy 19 N Ste 630 Palm Harbor FL 34684 Personal E-mail: lbarker933@cs.com.

BARKER, LYNN M., management consultant; BS in Physics, MS in Physics, U. Ariz. Co-founder, pres. Valyn Internat., Albuquerque. Mem. Am. Phys. Soc., Soc. Exptl. Mechanics, Internat. Soc. Optical Enging., Aeriballistoc Range Assn., Sigma Pi Sigma, Pi Mu Epsilon, Phi Beta Kappa, Sigma Xi. Office: 301 Solano Dr SE Albuquerque NM 87108-2649

BARKER, NANCY LEPARD, university official; b. Owosso, Mich., Jan. 22, 1936; d. Cecil L. and Mary Elizabeth (Stuart) Lepard; m. J. Daniel Cline, June 6, 1960 (div. 1971); m. R. William Barker, Nov. 18, 1972; children: Mary Georgia Harker, Mark L. Cline, Richard E., Daniel P., Melissa B. Van Arsdel, John C. Cline MD, Helen Grace Garrett, Wiley D., James G. BS, U. Mich., Ann Arbor, 1957; DHum (hon.), Northwood U., 2001. Spl. edn. instr. Univ. Hosp. U. Mich., Ann Arbor, 1958-61; v.p. Med. Educator, Chgo., 1967-69; asst. to chmn., dir. careers for women Northwood U., Midland, Mich., 1970-77, asst. prof., chmn. dept. fashion mktg. and merchandising, 1972-77, dir. arts programs and external affairs, 1972-77, v.p. univ. rels., 1978-2001, office of the pres., 2001—; dir. Alden B. Dow Creativity Ctr., 2007—. Bd. dirs. Alden B. Dow Creativity Ctr., Midland; cons., lectr. in field. Co-author: (children's books) Wendy Well Series, 1970-72; contbr. chpts. to books, articles to profl. jours. Advisor Mich. Child Study Assn., 1972—; chmn. Matrix: Midland Festival, 1978; bd. dirs. Nat. Coun. of Women, 1971—, pres., 1983-85, chmn. centennial com., 1988; mem. exec. bd. Mich. ACE Network for Women Leaders in Higher Edn., 2001—; bd. dirs. ArtServe, Mich., 2003—, Family and Children's Svcs., Internat. Coun. Women, Paris. Nominee, (3) Mich. Women's Hall of Fame; named 1st ann. Disting. Educator of Yr., Am. Coun. on Edn./MI Network, 2001; named one of Outstanding Young Women in U.S. and Mich., 1974; recipient Hon. award, Ukrainian Nat. Women's League, 1983, Disting. Woman award, Northwood U., 1970, Outstanding Young Woman award, Jr. C. of C., 1974, Athena award, 2007. Mem. Am. Heart Assn.Internat. Coun. Women (bd. dirs. Paris 1991—), The Fashion Group, Internat. Furnishings and Design Assn. (pres. Mich. chpt. 1974-77), Mich. Women's Studies Assn. (founding mem.), Arts Midland Coun. (pres. 2 terms, 25th Anniversary award), Internat. Women's Forum, Mich. Women's Forum, Contemporary Rev. Club, Midland County Lawyers' Wives, Zonta, Phi Beta Kappa, Phi Kappa Phi, Alpha Lambda Delta, Phi Lambda Theta, Phi Gamma Nu, Delta Delta Delta. Office: Northwood Univ 209 Revere Midland MI 48640-4255 Home Phone: 989-631-9864; Office Phone: 989-631-9864. E-mail: barkermid@aol.com.

BARKER, RAY TODD, archivist, writer; b. Akron, Ohio, Sept. 3, 1969; s. Thomas Albert and Cheryl Louise Barker; m. Alexandra Elizabeth Fox, Sept. 4, 2005; 1 child, Beatrice Margaret Mabel. B of English, U. Akron, Ohio, 1994; MLS, Emporia State U., Kans., 2005. Libr. info. specialist Miller Nichols Libr. U. Mo., Kansas City, 2001—05; archivist Combat Studies Inst., Ft. Leavenworth, Kans., 2005—; editor Akros Rev., 1995; freelance writer West Side Leader, Akron, 1995, Akron Mag., 1996, The Pitch, Kansas City, 2005—07, Rev. Revue, 2006. Author: On Looking At A Photograph of My Mother; musician: (compact disc recording) Ray's Drive Inn-Enough Is Not Enough; contbr. poems to mags. Treas. Pendleton Heights Neighborhood Assn., Kansas City, Mo., 2006—, head membership com., 2006—. Scholar, Kans. City Area Archivists, 2005. Mem.: Soc. Am. Archivists (assoc.). Independent. Avocations: travel, reading, writing. Home: 212 Park Ave Kansas City MO 64124 Office: Combat Studies Insitute 201 Sedgwick Fort Leavenworth KS 66027-2345 Home Phone: 816-352-7527; Office Phone: 913-684-2854. Personal E-mail: rayt.barker@gmail.com.

BARKER, RICHARD ALEXANDER, organizational psychologist; b. San Diego, Aug. 11, 1947; s. Alexander Markewich and Donna Lee Barker; m. Barbara Yvonne Schutt, Aug. 1, 1987; children: Jaime Lynn, Cory Richard AB in Psychology, San Diego State U., 1974, MS in Indsl. and Organizational Psychology, 1976; EdD, U. San Diego, 1990. Statis. analyst U.S. Navy Pers. R & D Center, San Diego, 1974-75; pers. and testing analyst City of San Diego, San Diego, 1976, cons. various orgns., 1976-78; employment mgr. Computer Scis. Corp., San Diego, 1978; indsl. psychologist Gen. Dynamics Corp., San Diego, 1978-91; instr. music San Diego City Coll., 1976-91; lectr. psychology, mgmt. sci., stats., orgnl. behavior U. Redlands, 1978-91; asst. prof. bus., chair mgmt. dept. Marist Coll., Poughkeepsie, N.Y., 1991-98; assoc. prof. bus. Clarke Coll., Dubuque, Iowa, 1998-2000, Upper Iowa Univ., Fayette, Iowa, 2000—07. Author: On the Nature of Leadership, 2002, Horses's Hoofs, 2003, At Story Time - The Story of Charles Coleman Parker and Upper Iowa University, 2003, Misplaced Faith, 2005, On Organizational Citizenship, 2006; mem. editl. bd. Jour. Leadership Studies, 1994—; contbr. articles to profl. jours. Bd. dirs. San Diego Youth Svcs., Inc., chmn. pers. com., 1978-81. Served with USNR, 1968-69 Mem. APA, Computer Automated Systems Assn./Soc. Mfg. Engrs., Nat. Mgmt. Assn., Am. Fedn. Musicians, Psi Chi.

BARKER, ROBERT OSBORNE (BOB BARKER), mediator, educator; b. Cleve., June 13, 1932; m. Sharon Ann (div.); children: Debra, Stephen, Dawn, Michael, Colleen. Student, Henry Ford C.C., 1950; BA in Comm. Arts and Sci., Mich. State U., 1954; LLB, LaSalle U., 1969; postgrad. in quality mgmt., U. Wis., 1989; postgrad. in pub. rels., U. Fla., 1996; postgrad. Cert. ct./pvt. mediator alt. dispute resolution/continuing cert. mediator edn., Fla. , 1995-. With pub. rels. dept. Ford Motor Co., Dearborn, Mich., 1953; mgr. Kaiser Aluminum Co., Chgo., 1956-58; advt. mgr. Bastian Blessing Co., Chgo., 1958-59; regional mgr. Sun Oil Co., Ohio and Detroit, 1959-71; mgr. Goodyear Tire & Rubber Co., Detroit, 1971-72; mgr., v.p. Nat. Assn. Mfrs., Washington, Boston and Detroit, 1972-87; pres., CEO Barker Cons. Inc., 1987-96; mgr., v.p. seminars and materials dept. Am. Supplier Inst. (div. of FoMoCo), 1987-90; nat. mdse./mktg. mgr. Costa del Mar Sunglasses, Ormond Beach, Fla., 1990-91; resort mgr. Oceanside 99 Condo, Ormond Beach, Fla., 1992-93, Outrigger Beach Club, Ormond Beach, Fla., 1994-95; mediator Volusia County Mediation Svcs., 1995—. Fed. lobbyist Nat. Assn. Mfrs., 1972—87; owner Dolphin Beach Club Condo, 1981—2001, bd. dirs., 1991—99; adj. prof. pub. rels., advt., retailing, sales fundamentals, global and internat. mktg., quality svc. mgmt. Daytona Beach CC, 1994—2006, Falcon student athlete mentor, 2003—; FACC mem. Fla. Assn. CC's; bd. mem., pub. rels. chair Fla. Hosp. Meml., Ormond Beach, Fla.; jr. achievement advisor, Daytona Beach. Twp. trustee, Findlay, Ohio, 1962; lay min. Episcopal ch., 1960-85, vestry, 1981-1989; mem. exec. bd. dirs. Volusia County Rep., 1991-00; bd. dirs. Am. Cancer Soc., 1991-05; bd. dirs. Dearborn Civic Theatre, 1980-84, Volusia Presdl. forum, 1991-99, Dearborn City Beautiful commr. emeritus, 1970-90; commr. Ormond Beach Quality of Life, Beautification and Planning bds., 1990-99; mem. adv. coun. bd. Habitat Humanity, 1995-99; res. police officer, Dearborn, 1968-88; pres. Dearborn High and Lindbergh Elem. PTA; bd. dirs. Bldg. Assn. Mgrs., 1991-95, Cmty. assoc. Inst., 1993-97, Volusia County Pers. Bd., 1991-93; mem. adv. coun. bd. Coun. of Aging, 1991-00; bd. dirs. Daytona and Ormond Beach Rep. Club, 1991-99, 2006-07, heritage mem. Ormond Meml. Art Mus., 1991-01, 04—; amb. Daytona Internat. Airport, 1996-02; team selection scout Fla. Citrus Sports for New Yr.'s Bowl Capital One Football Game and Champ Sports Bowls, Orlando, Fla., 1997—; mem. elder voice focus group Genesis Elder Care, 2001; asst. publicity dir. bd. dirs. Ormond Sr. Games, 1994-96; mem. City of Daytona Beach Cmty. Rels. Coun., 2006—; mem. pers. bd. City of Daytona Beach, 2006—; mem. visioning com. St. James Episc. Ch., Ormond Beach, Fla., 2006-07; pub. relations chair, Fla. Hosp. Meml. Aux., Ormond Beach; adv. Jr. Achievement, 2007—. Served with USNR, 1949-58, AFROTC, 1951-54. Recipient Vol. of Yr. award Am. Cancer Soc., 1998, Outstanding award for faculty bus. Daytona Beach CC athletic dept. assistance to student athletes Spl. Needs Awareness Program and Svc. Club, 2000-01, Outstanding Adj. Faculty award Daytona Beach CC, 2005-06. Mem.: AARP (asst. state coord., driver safety instr., vol.), Premier Health Srs., Fla. Hosp. Meml. Sys., Mich. State U. Ralph Young Found., Nat. Football Found., Mich. State U. Football Players Assn., Sr. Friends of Volusia/Flagler Counties (pres. 2000—04), Ormond Beach C. of C. (former amb., chmn. pub. rels. Beautification, JazzMatazz, social com. 1990—2002), Fla. Pub. Rels. Soc. Am. (v.p., bd. dirs. Volusia chpt. 1996—98), Assn. Execs., Advt. Fedn., Navy League of U.S., Fla. Sheriffs Assn, Fla. Police Benevolent Assn., Mich. State U. Alumni (life; past pres. 4 alumni clubs), Mich. State Varsity Alumni Club (life), Am. Heart Assn. (bd. dirs. Volusia/Flagler 2002—), U. Fla. Alumni Assn. (bd. dir. 1997—, Gator Club Volusia County, v.p. edn. 1999—2002), Exch. Club, Ormond Shrine Club (pres. 1994—95), Shriners (dir. pub. rels. 1984, provost unit, Fez on Wheels and Vets. unit), Masons, Elks, Am. Legion (life), Rotary (pres. 1987—88), Moose, Delta Tau Delta. Home: Unit 613 229 S Ridgewood Ave Daytona Beach FL 32114-4334 Personal E-mail: bobbarker13_99@yahoo.com. Business E-Mail: Robert_Barker@Falconmail.dbcc.edu.

BARKER, SARAH EVANS, judge; b. Mishawaka, Ind., June 10, 1943; d. James McCall and Sarah (Yarbrough) Evans; m. Kenneth R. Barker, Nov. 25, 1972; 3 children. BS, Ind. U., 1965, LLD (hon.), 1999; JD, Am. U., 1969; LLD (hon.), U. Indpls., 1984; D in Pub. Svc. (hon.), Butler U., 1987; LLD (hon.), Marian Coll., 1991; LHD, U. Evansville, 1993; LLD (hon.), Wabash Coll., 1999, Hanover Coll., 2001; D of Civil Law (hon.), 2003. Bar: Ind. 1969, U.S. Dist. Ct. (so. dist.) Ind., 1969, U.S. Ct. Appeals (7th cir.) 1973, U.S. Supreme Ct., 1978. Legal asst. to senator U.S. Senate, 1969-71; spl. counsel to minority, govt. ops. com. permanent investigations subcom., 1971-72; dir. rsch. scheduling and advance Senator Percy Re-election Campaign, 1972; asst. U.S. atty. So. Dist. Ind., 1972-76, 1st asst. U.S. atty., 1976-77, U.S. atty., 1981-84; judge U.S. Dist. Ct. (so. dist.) Ind., 1984—, chief judge, 1994—2000. Assoc., then ptnr. Bose, McKinney & Evans, Indpls., 1977-81; mem. long range planning com. Jud. Conf. U.S., 1991-96, exec. com., 1989-91, standing com. fed. rules of practice and procedure, 1987-91, dist. judge rep., 1988-91; mem. jud. coun. 7th cir. Ct. Appeals, 1988-2000, jud. fellows commn. U.S. Supreme Ct., 1993-98; jud. adv. com., sentencing commn., 1995-97, bd. advisors, Ind. U., Purdue U., Indpls., 1989—; mem. pres.'s cabinet Ind. U., 1995—; bd. visitors Ind. U. Sch. of Law, Bloomington, 1984—; bd. dirs. Clarian Health Ptnrs., 1996—, Christian Theol. Sem., 1999-2001; bd. dirs. Einstein Inst. for Sci., Health and the Cts., 2001— Recipient Peck award Wabash Coll., 1989, Touchstone award Girls Club of Greater Indpls., 1989, Leach Centennial 1st Woman award Valparaiso Law Sch., 1993, Most Influential Women award Indpls. Bus. Jour., 1996, Paul Buchanan award of excellence Indpls. Bar Found., 1998, Thomas J. Hennessy award Ind. U., 1995, Disting. Citizen fellow Ind. U., 1999-2001; named Ind. Woman of Yr., Women in Comm., 1986, Ind. Univ. Disting. Alumni, 1996, Disting. Citizen fellow Ind. U., 1999-2001, Singing Hoosiers Disting. Alumni award Ind. U., 2000, Man for All Seasons award St. Thomas More Soc., 2000. Mem. ABA, Ind. Bar Assn., Indpls. Bar Assn. (Antoinette Dakin Leach award 1993), Fed. Judges Assn. (exec. com., bd. dirs. 2001—), Com. on Budget (judicial conf. 2001-), Einstein Inst. Sci., Health and Cts. (bd. dirs. 2001-), U.S. Judicial Conf. (spl. redaction rev. panel 2000-), Christian Theol. Sem. (bd. trustees 1999-), Lawyers Club, Kiwanis. Republican. Methodist. Office: US Dist Ct 210 US Courthouse 46 E Ohio St Indianapolis IN 46204-1903

BARKER, STEPHANIE ANNE, middle school mathematics educator; b. Russellville, Ark., July 16, 1971; d. Timothy Ermon and Vickie Jo Hale; m. Stephen Ray Barker, Jan. 16, 1998; children: Rhett Hale, Meredith Grace. BA in Mktg., U. Ctrl. Ark., Conway, 1992. Tour guide Dallas Cowboys, Irving, Tex., 1994—95, travel agent, 1995—96; asst. buyer Zales Corp., Irving, 1996—98; merchandise analyst Bailey Banks & Biddle, Irving, 1998; tchr. Carrolton Montessori Sch., Tex., 1998—99; reading tchr. Bowie Mid. Sch., Irving, 1999—2003; math. tchr. Russellville Mid. Sch., 2003—. Office: Russellville Mid Sch 1203 W 4th Pl Russellville AR 72801

BARKER, TAMARA ELIZABETH, music educator; d. Hugh E. and Barbara A. Northup; m. Scott E. Barker, Mar. 25, 2000; 1 child, Samantha Elizabeth. MusB in Edn., Heidelberg Coll., Tiffin, Ohio, 1992; grad., Perkins Sch. Piano Tuning and Tech., Elyria, Ohio, 1993. Tchr. music grades k-6 Sandusky City Schs., Ohio, 1994; tchr. music grades k-8 SHAPE, Evansville, Ind., 1995—97; tchr. music grades k-12 Marion City Schs., Ohio, 1998—. Owner, tuner and technician Tamara's Tuning and Repair, Sandusky, Ohio, 1992—2003; pvt. piano and voice tchr., Sandusky and Marion, Ohio, 1992—2003. Mem.: Ohio Music Edn. Assn. Avocations: travel, computers, cross stitch. Office: Marion City Schs 910 E Church St Marion OH 43302 Home Phone: 419-927-4095; Office Phone: 740-387-3300. Personal E-mail: tamara91070@yahoo.com.

BARKER, THOMAS B., information technology executive; Grad. in acctg & mgmt., Univ. Dayton, 1976. Sales & mktg. positions Savin, IBM; v.p., div. mgr. Gallup Org.; pres., COO Cue Network Corp.; exec. v.p. West Interactive Corp., 1991—95; pres., COO West Corp., Omaha, 1995—98, pres., CEO, 1998—2004, CEO, 2004—. Bd. mem. Greater Omaha C. of C. Office: West Corp 11808 Miracle Hills Dr Omaha NE 68154*

BARKER, THOMAS CARL, retired health facility administrator; b. Cedar Rapids, Iowa, May 25, 1931; s. Carl Edward and Bertha Olive (Simons) B.; m. Mary Irene Beorkrem, Sept. 1, 1952 (dec. 1995); children: Cheryl Lynn, Thomas Carl Jr. (dec.), Laura Ann, David Edward; m. Patricia Blount Moore, May 2, 1998. Student, Loras Coll., 1949-50, Coe Coll., 1950-51; BS, U. Iowa, 1954, MA, 1960, PhD, 1963. Acct. Wilson & Co., Cedar Rapids, Iowa, 1951-54; contract adminstr. Collins Radio Co., Cedar Rapids, 1956-57; with customer rels. The Cryovac Co., Cedar Rapids, 1957-58; bus. officer Mercy Hosp., Iowa City, Iowa, 1958-59; rsch. asst. U. Iowa, 1959-60, tchg. asst., 1961-63, asst. prof., 1963-64; adminstrv. assoc. U. Iowa Hosp., 1960-62; rsch. assoc. UAW Internat. Union, Detroit, 1964-67; dir. Mich. Health and Social Security Rsch. Inst., Detroit, 1964-67; adj. assoc. prof. health econs. Wayne State U., Detroit, 1966-67; Arthur Graham Glasgow prof., dir. Sch. Hosp. Adminstrn. Med. Coll. Va., Richmond, 1967-71; prof., dean and CEO Sch. Allied Health Professions Va. Commonwealth U., Richmond, 1969-96, dean emeritus, prof. emeritus, 1996—. Mem. com. on allied health edn. and accreditation AMA, chmn. com., 1988-91; served as mem. or cons. to various pub. health svcs., including NIH, Health Resources Adminstrn., VA, HEW agys.; mem. dean's com. VA Med. Ctr., Richmond, 1974-96; mem. Ctrl. Va. Health Sys. Agy., 1976-88, pres., 1979-80; mem. Va. Health Coord. Coun., 1986-88. Contbr. articles to profl. jours. With USN, 1954—56, advanced through ranks to capt. USNR, 1956—85, ret. Named Hon. Alumni, Med. Coll. Va. Fellow APHA, Am. Soc. Allied Health Professions (pres. 1975-76); mem. Am. Health Planning Assn., Assn. Univ. Programs in Health Adminstrn., Soc. Sons. Revolution in State of Va., Va. Assn. Allied Health Professions, Va. Hosp. Assn., Rotary (pres. Richmond club 1991-92), Phi Kappa Phi. Roman Catholic. Home: 2251 Winterfield Rd Midlothian VA 23113-4145 Office: The Grant House PO Box 980203 Richmond VA 23298-0203 Office Phone: 804-828-1892. Office Fax: 804-828-1894. Business E-Mail: tcbarker@hsc.vcu.edu.

BARKER, VIRGINIA LEE, nursing educator; Diploma, Ind. U. Sch. Nursing, 1952, BS, 1955, MS, 1961, EdD, 1969. Dean sch. nursing, prof. Alfred (N.Y.) U., 1969-78; prof., dean nursing U. Louisville, 1978-81; dean Mary Black Sch. Nursing, prof. U. S.C., Spartanburg, 1981-90; dean profl. studies, prof. nursing SUNY, Plattsburg, 1990-98, prof. nursing Plattsburgh, 1990—. Cons. nursing program NY Regents Coll., 1972—91; dir. federally funded telenursing project rural upstate NY, 1993—2005; dir. project to develop virtual reality simulations edn. physicians, nurses, allied health pers. SUNY, Plattsburgh, 1995—; advisor to students in RN-BSN program over no. NY, 2000—. Contbr. articles to profl. jours., papers nat. and internat. confs. Mem. ARC. Grantee Disting. Practitioner, N.Y. State Nurses Assn. Mem.: AAUW, ANA, Internat. Coun. of Nurses, S.C. Deans and Dirs. Nursing Fedn. (chmn. 1989), Am. Assn. Higher Edn., S.C. League Nursing, Nat. League Nurses (com. mem. 1976—77), N.Y. State Nurses Assn. (pres. 1976—77), Ind. U. Sch. Nursing Alumni Assn. (pres. 1960), Kappa Delta Pi, Phi Kappa Phi, Sigma Theta Tau. Business E-Mail: virginia.barker@plattsburgh.edu.

BARKER, WALTER LEE, thoracic surgeon; b. Chgo., Sept. 9, 1928; s. Samuel Robert, M.D., and Esther (Meyerovitz) B.; m. Betty Ruth Wood, Apr. 4, 1967 AB cum laude, Harvard U., 1949, MD, 1953. Diplomate Am. Bd. Surgery, Am. Bd. Thoracic Surgery. Intern, resident in gen. and thoracic surgery Cook County Hosp. and Presbyn. St. Luke's Med. Ctr. and affiliated hosps., Chgo., 1953-62; practice medicine specializing in thoracic surgery Chgo., 1962-95; clin. prof. surgery U. Ill.; prof. emeritus, 1998; head sect. thoracic surgery Cook County Hosp., 1972-93, cons. sect., 1993-98; chmn. dept. surgery St. Joseph Hosp., Chgo., 1982-97. Researcher on tuberculosis, pleural infections, lung cancer Author: The Post Operative Chest, 1977; editl. bd. Chest, 1984-89; cons. to editor, 1989—; contbr. articles to profl. jours. Served with M.C., USNR, 1955-57 Fellow Am. Coll. Chest Physicians (credentials com. 1984-89), ACS; mem. Am. Assn. Thoracic Surgery, AMA (rep. to HS of dels. 1988-94), Boylston Med. Soc., Chgo. Med. Soc., Ill. Med. Soc., Chest Club, Chgo. Surg. Soc. (v.p. 1990-91, chmn. membership com. 1991-92), Ill. Surg. Soc., Central Surg. Soc., Inst. Medicine, Soc. Thoracic Surgeons (founding mem., cons. editor Ann. Thoracic Surgery), Sigma Xi Home: 2912 N Commonwealth Ave Apt 11C Chicago IL 60657-6215 Fax: 773-525-0561. E-mail: b.b.barker@worldnet.att.net.

BARKER, WILLIAM DANIEL, hospital administrator; b. New Orleans, July 21, 1926; s. William Daniel and Ada (Will) B.; m. Nancy Pool, Sept. 23, 1949; children: Nancy Louise, Julia Ann, William Daniel III, Marion DeVilbiss. B in Bus. Adminstrn., Emory U., 1949; M in Hosp. Adminstrn., Ga. State U., 1966. Bus. office mgr. Emory U. Hosp., Atlanta, 1949-50; asst. adminstr. Griffin (Ga.) Spalding County Hosp., 1950-51; adminstr. Winder-Barrow (Ga.) Hosp., 1951-52; hosp. field rep. Ga. Dept. Pub. Health, Atlanta, 1952-54, hosp. cons., 1954-55; asst. adminstr. Tri-County Hosp., Ft. Oglethorpe, Ga., 1955-60; asst. dir. Crawford Long Hosp. Emory U., Atlanta, 1960-73, adminstr., 1973-84, dir. hosps., 1984-90, exec. dir. hosp., 1987-90; ret., 1991; prof. Emory U., Atlanta, 1988-93. Bd. dirs. Ga. Fed. Bank, Atlanta, Blue Cross Blue Shield Ga., Inc.; provider affairs com. Blue Cross Blue Shield Assn., United Network for Organ Sharing, bd. dirs., 1991—; bd. govs. SunHealth, Charlotte, N.C., chmn., 1988-89; bd. commrs. Joint Commn. on Accreditation of Healthcare Orgns., 1981-86; v.p. Greater Atlanta Coalition on Health Care, 1983-84; mem. Gov.'s Coun. Malpractice Ins., 1975-83, Medicaid Adv. Com. Ga. Dept. Human Resources, 1973-77, Health Facilities Planning Com. Met. Atlanta Coun. for Health, 1971-74, Atlanta Regional Commn. Emergency Med. Task Force 1969-73, Gov.'s Commn. on Nursing, 1970-71, adv. commn. Internat. Implant Registry, 1989—, vice-chmn., 1991, chmn., 1992; pres. Health Careers of Ga., Inc., 1969-70, Ga. Coun. Paramed. Edn., 1968. Contbr. articles to profl. jours. With U.S. Army, 1944-46. Recipient R.C. Williams award Ga. State U., 1966, Disting. Alumni award, Ga. State U., 1979, Disting. Svc. award. Ga. Med. Assn. Atlanta, 1980; Disting. Guest Lectr. Ga. State U., 1978. Fellow Am. Coll. Healthcare Execs. (regent 1972-75); mem. Am. Hosp. Assn. (chmn. 1979, Speaker of Ho. 1980, Disting. Svc. award 1987), Ga. Hosp. Assn. (pres. 1966-79, Gold Honor award of Excellence 1980), Ansley Golf Club. Baptist. Home: 50 S Prado NE Atlanta GA 30309-3309 Personal E-mail: dbarker@emory.edu.

BARKER, WILLIAM M., state supreme court justice; b. Chattanooga, Sept. 13, 1941; married; 3 children. BS, U. Chatanooga, 1964; JD, U. Cin., 1967. Bar: Tenn. 1967. Pvt. practice, 1967-83; cir. ct. judge, 1983-95; justice Ct. of Appeals, 1995-98, Tenn. Supreme Ct., 1998—, chief justice, 2005—. Adj. prof. U. Tenn., Chatanooga, 1984—. Chmn. bd. deacons 1st Presbyn. Ch. Chattanooga, 1995-97. Served in USMC, 1967—69. Fellow Tenn. Bar Found., Chattanooga Bar Found.; mem. Am. Legion, Alpha Soc., U. Tenn. Chattanooga Alumni Coun., Chattanooga Rotary Club. Office: Supreme Ct Bldg 401 7th Ave N Ste 321 Nashville TN 37219 Office Phone: 615-741-2484.*

BARKER, WILLIAM THOMAS, lawyer; b. Feb. 28, 1947; s. V. Wayne and Cordelia (Whitten) B.; m. June K. Robinson, Jan. 30, 1981. BS, MS, Mich. State U., 1969; JD, U. Calif., Berkeley, 1974. Bar: Calif. 1975, Ill. 1976. Assoc. programmer-analyst Control Data Corp., Sunnyvale, Calif., 1969-71; law clk. Pa. Supreme Ct., Erie, 1974-75; assoc. Sonnenschein Carlin Nath & Rosenthal, Chgo., 1975-82, ptnr., 1982—. Moderator Ill. Ins. Law Forum, Counsel Connect, 1994-98; co-moderator Nat. Ins. Law gen. forum, 1996-98; moderator Ins. Law Forum, Lexis One, 2001. Bd. editors: Def. Counsel Jour., 1987—; editor Bad Faith Law Report, 1999-2001, contbg. editor 1990-99; mem. editl. bd. Ins. Litigation Reporter, 1987—. editl. dir. and sr. contbg. editor, 2001—; editor Covered Events, 1995-96, editor emeritus, 1996—; ins. law publs. bd. Def. Rsch. Inst., 1992-97; contbr. articles to profl. jours. Fellow Am. Bar Found. (life); mem. ABA (chair-elect com. on appellate advocacy, tort and ins. practice sect. 1994-95, chair 1995-96, chair gen. comm. bd. 1996-97), Internat. Assn. Def. Counsel (Yancey Meml. award for best article 1995, chair spl. com. on Amicus Curie 1996-97, chair ad hoc com. on interstate practice 2000-03), Chgo. Coun. Lawyers (sec. 1987-88, bd. govs. 1989-91, chair com. profl. responsibility 1990-95), Chgo. Bar Assn. (chmn. com. constl. law 1984-85), Def. Rsch. Inst., Assn. Profl. Responsibility Lawyers (chair com. on internat. trade in legal svcs. 2002-03), Am. Law Inst. Home: 132 E Delaware Pl Apt 5806 Chicago IL 60611-4951 Office: Sonnenschein Nath Et Al 8000 Sears Tower 233 S Wacker Dr Ste 8000 Chicago IL 60606-6491 Home Phone: 312-943-3703; Office Phone: 312-876-8140. E-mail: wbarker@sonnenschein.com.

BARKETT, ROSEMARY, federal judge; b. Ciudad Victoria, Tamaulipas, Mex., Aug. 29, 1939; arrived in US, 1946, naturalized, 1958; BS summa cum laude, Spring Hill Coll., 1967; JD, U. Fla., 1970; LLD (hon.), Stetson U., St. Petersburg, Fla., 1987; LHD (hon.), Fla. Internat. U., Miami, 1987; LLD (hon.), John Marshall Law Sch., Chgo., 1990; LHD (hon.), U. So. Fla., Tampa, 1990; DCL (hon.), Spring Hill Coll., Mobile, Ala., 1990; LLD (hon.), Rollins Coll., Orlando, Fla., 1992, Nova U., Ft. Lauderdale, Fla., 1992. Bar: Fla., US Dist. Ct. (so. dist.) Fla., US Ct. Appeals (5th cir.), US Supreme Ct. Pvt. practice, West Palm Beach, Fla., 1971—79; judge 15th Jud. Cir. Ct., Palm Beach County, Fla., 1979—82, administrative judge civil divsn., 1982—83, chief judge, 1983—84; appellate judge 4th Dist. Ct. Appeal, West Palm Beach, Fla., 1984—85; justice Supreme Ct. Fla., Tallahassee, 1985—92, chief justice, 1992—94; cir. judge US Ct. Appeals (11th cir.), Miami, 1994—. Bd. dirs. Lawyers for Children, US Assn. Constl. Law; faculty U. Nev., Reno, Nat. Jud. Coll., Fla. Jud. Coll., Appellate Judges Seminar, Inst. Jud. Adminstrn., NYU; lectr. in field; vis. com. Miami U. Law Sch.; bd. visitors St. Thomas U. Mem. editl. bd.: The Florida Judges Manual. Named Women of Distinction, Crohn's & Colitis Found., 1997; named to Fla. Women's Hall of Fame, 1986, Miami Centennial Hall of Fame, 1996; recipient Woman of Achievement award, Palm Beach County Commn. on Status of Women, 1985, Hannah G. Solomon award, Nat. Coun. Jewish Women, 1991, Lifetime Achievement award, Latin Bus. Profl. Women, 1992, Breaking the Glass Ceiling award, Fla. Fedn. Bus. Profl. Women's Clubs, Inc., 1993, Disting. Jurist award, Miss. State U., 1995, Margaret Brent Women Lawyers of Achievement award, ABA Commn. Women in Profession, 1996, Harriette Glasner Freedom award, ACLU, 1999. Fellow: ABA (Minority Justice Honoree 1992); mem.: Fla. Commn. on Status of Women, Dade Marine Inst., Fed. Judges Assn., Am. Law Inst., Assn. Trial Lawyers Am. (Achievement award 1986), Acad. Fla. Trial Lawyers (Achievement award 1988, Rosemary Barkett award named in her honor 1992), Palm Beach Marine Inst., Nat. Assn. Women Judges (Honoree of Year 1999), Fla. Assn. Women Lawyers (Judge Mattie Belle Davis award 1991, Rosemary Barkett Outstanding Achievement award named in her honor 1999), Am. Acad. Matrimonial Lawyers (award 1984), Palm Beach County Bar Assn., Fla. Bar Assn. Office: US Ct of Appeals (11th cir) Fla 99 NE 4th St Rm 1223 Miami FL 33132-2140*

BARKIN, ELAINE RADOFF, composer; b. NYC, Dec. 15, 1932; m. George J. Barkin, Nov. 28, 1957; 3 children. BA in Music, Queens Coll., 1954, MFA in Composition, 1956; PhD in Composition and Theory, Brandeis U., 1971; Cert. in Composition and Piano, Berlin Hochschule Musik, 1957; studied with Karol Rathaus, Irving Fine, Boris Blacher, Arthur Berger. Lectr. in music Queens Coll., 1964-70, Sarah Lawrence, 1969-70; from asst. to assoc. prof. music theory U. Mich., 1970-74; from asst. prof. to prof. composition and theory U. Calif., LA, 1974-97. Vis. asst. prof. Princeton (N.J.) U., 1974; lectr. in field. Asst. to co-editor: Perspectives of New Music, 1963-85; composer String Quartet, 1969, Sound Play for violin, 1974, String Trio, 1976, Plein Chant, alto flute, 1977, Ebb Tide, 2 vibraphones, 1977,.the Supple Suitor.for soprano and five players, 1978, (chamber mini opera) De Amore, 1980, Impromptu for violin, cello, piano, 1981, (theatre piece) Media Speak, 1981, At the Piano, piano, 1982, For String Quartet, 1982, Quilt Piece graphic score for 7 instruments, 1984, On The Way To Becoming for 4-track Tape Collage, 1985, Demeter and Persephone for violin, tape, chamber ensemble, dancers, 1986, 3 Rhapsodies, flutes and clarinet, 1986, Encore for Javanese Gamelan Ensemble, 1986, Out of the Air for Basset Horn and Tape, 1988, To Whom It May Concern 4 track tape collage, reader and 4 players, 1989, Legong Dreams, oboe, 1990, Gamélange for harp and mixed gamelan band, 1992, Five Tape Collages, Open Space CD #3, 1993, "for my friends' pleasure," soprano and harp, 1994, numerous improvised group and duo sessions on tape; produced cassette and video: New Music in Bali, 1994; "touching all bases" for electronic bass, electronic percussion, and Balinese gamelan, 1996, e: an anthology (music, texts and graphics) 1975-95, "poem" for wind ensemble, 1999, (Chamber Music and Improvisations) Open Space, 2000, (CDs) Song for Sarah for Violin, 2001, Ballade for Violoncello, 2002, Tambellan, 2004, Open Space, 2004, Colors for mixed gamelan, 2004, Four Midi Pieces, 2005. Recipient Fulbright award, 1957, awards NEA, 1975, 79, awards Rockefeller Found., 1980, Meet the Composer award, 1994. Home: 12533 Killion St Valley Village CA 91607-1533

BARKIN, ELLEN, actress; b. NYC, Apr. 16, 1955; m. Gabriel Byrne, 1988 (div. 1993); children: Jack, Romey Marion; m. Ron Perelman, June 28, 2000 (separated Jan. 19, 2006) Student, CUNY; grad., Hunter Coll. Ind. theatrical, film actress, 1980—. Theatrical prodns. include Shout Across the River, 1980, Killings on the Last Line, 1980, Extremities, 1982; appeared on TV soap operas Search for Tomorrow; Actor: Up in Smoke, 1978, Diner, 1982, Daniel, 1983, Tender Mercies, 1983, Enormous Changes at the Last Minute, 1983, Eddie and the Cruisers, 1983, Harry and Son, 1984, The Adventures of Buckaroo Banzai in the Fifth Dimension, 1984, Terminal Choice, 1985, Down by Law, 1986, Desert Bloom, 1986, The Big Easy, 1987, Siesta, 1987, Made in Heaven, 1987, Sea of Love, 1989, Johnny Handsome, 1989, Switch, 1991, Man Trouble, 1992, Mac, 1993, This Boy's Life, 1993, Into the West, 1993, Bad Company, 1995, Wild Bill, 1995, Mad Dog Time, 1996, The Fan, 1996, Fear and Loathing in Las Vegas, 1998, Drop Dead Gorgeous, 1999, the White River Kid, 1999, Crime and Punishment in Suburbia, 2000, Mercy, 2000, Someone Like You, 2001, She Hate Me, 2004, Palindromes, 2004, Trust the Man, 2005, Ocean's Thirteen, 2007; (TV films) Kent State, 1981, We're Fighting Back, 1981, Parole, 1982, The Princess Who Had Never Laughed, 1984, Terrible Joe Moran, 1984, Act of Vengeance, 1986, Clinton and Nadine, 1988, Before Women Had Wings, 1997, Strip Search, 2004 Office: care Creative Artists Agy 9830 Wilshire Blvd Beverly Hills CA 90212-1804*

BARKIN, KENNETH DAVID, history professor; b. Bklyn., July 16, 1939; s. Julius and Mary Barkin; m. Elizabeth Mary Lord, June 19, 1984; children: Noah, Gareth, Matthew. BA in History, Bklyn. Coll., 1960; PhD, Brown U., 1965. Asst. prof. Brandeis U., Waltham, Mass., 1965—68; assoc. full prof. U. Calif., 1968—. Vis. prof. St. Anthony's Coll., Oxford U., England, 1975, U. Gottingen, Germany, 1980. Editor (sr. editor): Ctrl. European History Jour., 1991—2004; contbr. articles to jours. Bd. mem. Conf. Group for Ctrl. European History Bd., 1991—2004. Mem.: Am. Hist. Assn. Home: 151 Broadbent Dr Riverside CA 92507 Office: Univ Calif Riverside History Dept University Ave Riverside CA 92521 Office Phone: 951-827-1994. Business E-Mail: kenneth.barkin@ucr.edu.

BARKIN, MARVIN E., lawyer; b. Winter Haven, Fla., Nov. 9, 1933; s. Isadore and Jean (Epstein) B.; m. Gertrude Parnes, Sept. 20, 1959; children: Thomas I., Michael A., Pamela L. AB, Emory U., 1955; LLB cum laude, Harvard U., 1958. Bar: Fla. 1958, U.S. Dist. Ct. (mid., no. and so. dists.) Fla., U.S. Ct. Appeals (2d, 5th and 11th cirs.), U.S. Supreme Ct. Research aide Dist. Ct. Appeal Fla., Third Dist., Miami, 1958-60; assoc., then ptnr. Fowler, White, Collins, Gillen, Humkey & Trenam, Tampa, 1960-69; mem. Trenam, Kemker, Scharf, Barkin, Frye, O'Neill & Mullis, Tampa, 1970—, Fla. Bd. Bar Examiners, 1979-84, chmn., 1982-83. Chmn. corp., banking and bus. law sect. Fla. Bar, 1974-75, chmn. appellate ct. rules subcom., 1972-73 Mem. Am. Law Inst., Am. Bar Found., Nat. Conf. Bar Examiners (bd. mgrs. 1985-95, chmn. 1993-94, 11th cir. ct. appeal com. on lawyer qualifications and conduct, chair 2001—, spl. counsel Fla. jud. qualification com. 1985-06, in-term gen. counsel 2006—), Fla. Bar, Omicron Delta Kappa. Democrat. Jewish. Home: 1605 Culbreath Isles Dr Tampa FL 33629-4824 Office: Trenam Kemker Scharf Barkin Frye O'Neill & Mullis 101 E Kennedy Blvd Ste 2700 Tampa FL 33602-5179 Home Phone: 813-286-0694; Office Phone: 813-227-7459. Personal E-mail: mebarkin@trenam.com.

BARKLEY, ANDREW PAUL, economics professor; b. Manhattan, Kans., Feb. 5, 1962; s. Paul Weston and Lela Mel (Kelly) B.; m. Mary Ellen Cates, July 14, 1984; children: Katherine Ann, Charles Kelly. BA in Econs., Whitman Coll., 1984; MA in Econs., U. Chgo., 1986, PhD in Econs., 1988. Asst. prof. Kans. State U., Manhattan, 1988-93, assoc. prof., 1993—98, prof., 1998—. Coffman disting. tchg. scholar Kans. State U., 2003—; vis. prof. Quaid-I-Azam U., Islamabad, Pakistan, 1990, U. Ariz., Tucson, 1994—95, U. Cambridge, England, 2002; faculty advisor Pakistan Student Assn., Kans. State U., Agrl. Econs. Club, 1989—94. Assoc. editor Review of Agrl. Econs., 1993—96. Recipient Agrl. and Rural Transp. Rsch. Paper award, 1994; named CASE Kans. Prof. of Yr., 1993. Mem.: Western Agrl. Econs. Assn. (Outstanding Undergrad. Tchg. award 1994), Nat. Agrl. Coll. Tchrs. Assn. (Knight Outstanding Jour. Article award 1992, Ctrl. Region Outstanding Tchr. 1994, Tchr. fellow 1994), Am. Agrl. Econs. Assn. (nat. advisor student sect. 1993—95, Outstanding Undergrad. Tchg. award 1995). Avocations: running, reading, travel. Home: 925 Wildcat Rdg Manhattan KS 66502-2927 Office: Kans State U Dept Agrl Econs Waters Hall Manhattan KS 66506 Office Phone: 785-532-4426. Business E-Mail: barkley@ksu.edu.

BARKLEY, BRIAN EVAN, lawyer, political consultant; b. Teaneck, NJ, Jan. 30, 1945; s. Henry E. and Alice M. (Schultz) Barkley; m. Pamela A. Martin, May 5, 1979; children: Leigh Elizabeth, Christine Elizabeth, Brett Evan. BA, U. Md., 1967; JD with honors, George Washington U., 1970. Bar: Md. 1970, D.C. 1976, U.S. Dist. Ct. Md. 1973. Assoc. Everngam & Goldstein, Silver Spring, Md., 1970—72; pvt. practice Silver Spring, 1972—80, Rockville, Md., 1980—86; spl. asst. Rep. Michael Barnes, Washington, 1981—84; sr. ptnr. Barkley and Kennedy, Chartered, 1987—. Vice chmn. Nat. Capital chpt. Nat. Multiple Sclerosis Com., Washington, 1980—86, Nat. Multiple Sclerosis Soc., Washington, 1998—2001, chmn. chpt. svcs. com., 1985—2001; chmn. Montgomery County Multiple Sclerosis Com., Rockville, Md., 1980; major gifts chmn. Shady Grove Hosp., 1980; chmn. Nat. Capital chpt. Nat. Multiple Sclerosis Com., 2001—03; del. Dem. Nat. Conv., 1984; campaign mgr. Barnes for Congress, Rockville, 1980, campaign chmn., 1982—84; campaign mgr. Montgomery County for Mondale, 1984; vice chmn. Montgomery County for Dukakis, 1988. Recipient Humanitarian award, Nat. Multiple Sclerosis Soc., 1989, Hope award, 2003. Mem.: Montgomery County Bar Assn., Md. Bar Assn., Rockville C. of C. (pres. 1996—97), Bethesda Country Club, Masons. Democrat. Home: 12405 Copenhaver Ter Potomac MD 20854-3028 Office: 51 Monroe St Ste 1407 Rockville MD 20850-2408 Office Phone: 301-251-6600.

BARKLEY, CHARLES WADE, sportscaster, retired professional basketball player; b. Leeds, Ala., Feb. 20, 1963; Student, Auburn U., Ala., 1981—84. Player Phila. 76ers, 1984—92, Phoenix Suns, 1992—96, Houston Rockets, 1996—2000; co-host Inside the NBA, TNT, 2001—; host Listen Up, TNT, 2002—. Mem. US Olympic team, 1992, 96. Co-author (with Roy S. Johnson): Outrageous! The Fine Life and Flagrant Good Times of Basketball's Irresistible Force, 1992; co-author: (with Rick Reilly) Sir Charles: The Wit and Wisdom of Charles Barkley, 1994; author: I May Be Wrong But I Doubt It, 2002, Who's Afraid of a Large Black Man, 2005; actor: (films) Forget Paris, 1995. Named to All-Rookie team, 1985, NBA All-Star team, 1988—93, Basketball Hall of Fame, 2006; recipient Schick Pivotal Player award, 1986—88, IBM award, 1986—88, NBA All-Star Game MVP award, 1991, NBA MVP award, 1993. Achievements include holding single game records for most offensive rebounds in one quarter-11, 1987; holding single game record for most offensive rebounds in one half-13, 1987. Office: Turner Sports One CNN Ctr 13 South Tower Atlanta GA 30303*

BARKLEY, JAMES, artist; b. NYC, Apr. 19, 1941; Fine artist, profl. illustrator; prof. Parson Sch. Design, NYC, U. Bridgeport, Conn. Lectr. in field. Coins, stamps, panels, collections and collectibles, Danbury Mint, exhibitions include Norman Rockwell Mus., 2000, Smithsonian Instn., 2004, UN Touring Artists Exhbns., No. Westchester Ctr. for Arts, Soc. Illustrators, Represented in permanent collections Mus. Am. Illustration, USAF, numerous illustrations for mags., books, various cos., Colubia Performing and Theatrical Artists world opera tours, art, set design, promotions, Brit. Rock Symphony. Recipient Newberry award, Gold medal, Chester Awards. Office: Art Source PO Box 257 Pleasantville NY 10570

BARKLEY, JAMES M., lawyer, real estate company executive; b. 1951; BS, Indiana U., 1974; JD, Indiana U. Sch. of Law, 1977. Staff atty. Melvin Simon & Associates, Inc., Indianapolis, Ind., 1978—84, asst. gen. counsel, 1984—92, gen. counsel, 1992; gen. counsel, sec. Simon Property Group, Inc., Indianapolis, Ind., 1993—. Mem. Am. Coll. of Real Estate Lawyers, 1991—. Bd. dirs. Indiana Chamber of Commerce. Mem.: Indiana State Bar Assn., Indianapolis Bar Assn. Office: Simon Property Group Inc 115 W Wash St Indianapolis IN 46204 Office Phone: 317-636-1600.

BARKLEY, PAUL HALEY, JR., architect; b. Washington, Sept. 24, 1937; Paul Haley Sr. and Mary Barrett (Brewer) B.; m. Jeanette Frances Nickerson, Dec. 20, 1975. Student, Ecole D'Art Americaines, Fontainebleau, France, 1959; BArch, U. Va., 1960. Registered architect, Va., Md., D.C. Archtl. designer Strang & Childers Architects, Annandale, Va., 1960-61; project designer Alan J. Lockman Architect, Washington, 1962-63; design assoc. D.G. Chase & Assocs., Alexandria, Va., 1964; pres. Barkley Pierce Assocs., Falls Church, Va., 1965-94; sole practice Paul H. Barkley, FAIA, Architect, Falls Church, Va., 1994—. Bd. dirs. Hist. Falls Church; lectr. archtl. divsn. continuing edn., 1966-91; mng. ptnr. Village Ctr. Assocs., Falls Church, 1983-99. Prin. works includes Falls Ch. Community Ctr., 1967, Vega Precision Labs., 1972, 1st Va. Bank, Arlington, 1979, Sullyfield Commerce Ctr., 1986, Rigg's Nat. Bank, McLean, Va., 1988; contbr. articles to profl. jours. Chmn. Falls Church Bus. Devel. Commn., 1987—93; mem. exec. com. Citizens for a Better City, Falls Church, 1987—92; mem. Falls Church Econ. Devel. Authority, 2002, Falls Church Pvt. Pub. Partnership, 1991—98, bd. dirs., 1991—98, pres., 1993—94. With USAF, 1960—63. Recipient excellence in design award Falls Church Village Preservation and Improvement Soc., 1979, Indsl. Devel. Vol. of Yr. award So. Indsl. Devel. Coun., 1982, Bus. Person of Yr. award City of Falls Church, 1988; Margaret Thompson Biddle fellow U. Va., 1959. Fellow AIA (bd. dirs. 1986-89, pres. Va. Soc. 1984, regional rep. Coll. of Fellows 1993-95, chair regional reps. 2002-07, numerous other offices, Disting. Svc. award 1983, Outstanding Svc. award No. Va. chpt. 1982, award of recognition of outstanding achievement 1988, Noland award 1991, Leslie N. Boney Spirit of Fellowship award 2005); mem. Falls Church C. of C. (bd. dirs. 1973-75, 99—2006, pres. 1976, 3d v.p. 1977-79, vice chmn. 2003-04 Pillar of the Cmty. award 1977), Va. Found. for Arch. (pres. 1988-89, trustee 1993-99), Fountainbleau Assns. (trustee 1995-2007). Avocations: photography, travel, collecting art. Home and Office: 311 Chestnut St Falls Church VA 22046-2404 Home Phone: 703-534-1474; Office Phone: 703-532-8500. Personal E-mail: pbarkley@cox.net.

BARKLEY, TERRELL WAYNE, archivist, curator, school librarian; b. Tokyo, July 22, 1950; arrived in U.S., 1950; s. Hillard Rhoda and Violet Beatrice (Taylor) Barkley. BS, U. N. Ala., 1973; MA, The Citadel, 1974; MLS, U. Ala., 1987; grad. cert. in mus. studies, Harvard U., 1990; postgrad., Bethany Theol. Sem., Richmond, Ind., 2006, Cert. tchr. Ala., 1975, Va., 1978. Tchr. social studies Randolph Sch., Huntsville, Ala., 1975—78; chmn. Social Studies Dept. Augusta Mil. Acad., Ft. Defiance, Va., 1978—83; tchr. social studies Huntsville City Schs., 1984—86; asst. archivist Birmingham Pub. Libr., Ala., 1988—89; spl. collections libr. Ala. A&M U., Huntsville, 1990—92; archivist, mus. curator Bridgewater Coll., Va., 1993—2005; archivist Marion Mil. Inst., Ala., 2007—. Editl. asst.: The Brethren Encyclopedia, 1996—97, rsch. asst.:, 2001—04; author: One Who Served Brethren Elder Charles Nesselrodt, 1996, 2004; contbr. articles to profl. jours.; musician: Ala. Music Hall Fame (drums), 1999. Mem. com. Valley Brethren Mennonite Cultural Ctr., Harrisonburg, Va., 1998—2001, Shenandoah Valley Battlefields Found., New Market, Va., 2000—02; chmn. Shenandoah Dist. Hist. Com. Ch. of the Brethren, 1996—99; mem. exec. bd. Shenandoah Valley Civil War Roundtable, 1993—98. Advanced Army grad. ROTC, 1973. Mem.: ALA, Am. Assn. Mus., Soc. Am. Archivists, Rockingham Area Hist. Assn., Contemporary Longrifle Assn., Lincoln Soc. Va. (charter), Nat. Soc. Scabbard and Blade, Phi Alpha Theta. Avocations: music, history, travel. Office Phone: 334-302-1038.

BARKMEIER, WAYNE W., dentist, researcher, educator; b. Friend, Nebr., Mar. 29, 1944; m. Carolyn A. Johnsen; children: Kimberly, Jennifer, Wayne Jr. Postgrad., U. Nebr., Lincoln, 1962—65; DDS, U. Nebr. Med. Ctr. Coll. Dentistry, 1965—69; MS, U. Tex. Health Sci. Ctr., Houston, 1973—75. Asst. prof., oral surgery Creighton U., 1978—79; pvt. practice Omaha, 1978—82; asst. prof., operative dentistry Creighton U., 1979—82; rsch. dentist L.D. Caulk Divsn., Dentsply Internat., Milford, Del., 1982—85, intramural rsch. mgr., 1985; asst. dean rsch. and assoc. prof. operative dentistry, Sch. Dentistry Creighton U., 1985—87, dir., Ctr. Oral Health Rsch., 1986—95, assoc. dean rsch., Sch. Dentistry, 1991—94, prof., operative dentistry, Sch. Dentistry, 1991—2000, prof. gen. dentistry, Sch. Dentistry, 2000—, dean, Sch. Dentistry, 1994—2005, dean emeritus, 2006—. Cons. on dental materials Nat. Bd. Test Constrn. Com. for Joint Commn. on Nat. Dental Exams.; past mem. Am. Dental Assn. Coun. on Dental Rsch. Mem. editl. bd. Operative Dentistry, article rev. cons. Jour. Am. Dental Assn., Am. Jour. Dentistry, Dental Materials, Jour. Dentistry, Quintessence Internat., Jour. Dental Edn., Mil. Medicine; contbr. more than 140 articles to profl. jours. Active duty USAF, 1969—78, brig. gen. USAFR, 1991—94. Office Phone: 402-280-5262.

BARKOFF, RUPERT MITCHELL, lawyer; b. New Orleans, May 7, 1948; s. Samuel and Martha B.; m. Susan Joyce Levitt, May 31, 1970; children: Stuart, Jeffrey, Lisa. BA in Econs. with high distinction, U. Mich., 1970, JD magna cum laude, 1973. Bar: Ga. 1973. Assoc. Kilpatrick Stockton LLP, Atlanta, 1973-80, ptnr., 1980—. Contbr. articles to profl. jours. Mem. ABA (bus. law sect., antitrust sect., forum on franchising, panelist ann. forums 1980-92, chmn. 1989-92, assoc. editor Franchise Law Jour. 1981-86), Ga. Bar Assn. (corp. and banking sect.), Atlanta Bar Assn., Phi Beta Kappa. Democrat. Jewish. Home: 5215 Vernon Springs Trl NW Atlanta GA 30327-4511 Office: Kilpatrick Stockton LLP 1100 Peachtree St NE Ste 2800 Atlanta GA 30309-4530 Office Phone: 404-815-6366. Business E-Mail: rbarkoff@kilpatrickstockton.com.

BARKSDALE, CLARENCE CAULFIELD, retired banker; b. St. Louis, June 4, 1932; s. Clarence M. and Elizabeth (Caulfield) B.; m. Emily Catlin Keyes, Apr. 4, 1959; children: John Keyes, Emily Shepley. AB, Brown U., 1954; postgrad., Washington U. Law Sch., St. Louis, 1957-58, Rutgers U., 1964, Columbia U. Grad. Sch. Bus., 1968; LLD (hon.), Maryville Coll., St. Louis, 1976, Westminster Coll., Fulton, Mo., 1982, St. Louis U., 1989. From asst. cashier to chmn. bd., CEO Centerre Bank NA (formerly 1st Nat. Bank), St. Louis, 1960—76, chmn. bd., chief exec. officer, 1976-88; vice chmn. Bank of Am. (formerly Boatmen's Bancshares, Inc.), St. Louis, 1988-89; vice chmn. bd. dirs. Washington U., St. Louis, 1989—2005. Bd. dirs. Mo. Bot. Gardens, Alzheimers Assn., Grand Ctr. Inc., Washington U., Mus. Contemporary Art, St. Louis Boy Scouts, Girls, Inc. With M.I., U.S. Army, 1954-57. Mem. St. Louis Club, St. Louis Country Club, Noonday Club, Bogey Club of St. Louis, Harbor Point Golf Club, Little Harbor Club, Wequetosing Golf Club (Harbor Springs, Mich.), Ocean Club, Gulfstream Golf Club, Gulf Stream Bath and Tennis Club (Delray Beach, Fla.), Alpha Delta Phi. Office: Washington U 7425 Forsyth Blvd Saint Louis MO 63105-2161 Office Phone: 314-935-4389. Business E-Mail: cedgy@wustl.edu.

BARKSDALE, DARYL, historic preservationist; d. Cecil Bruce and Carol Martin Barksdale. BA in Art History, U. SC, 1985; M City Planning, Ga. Inst. Tech., 1994; Cert. in Heritage Preservation, Ga. State U., 1994. Flood recovery coord. hist. preservation divsn. Ga. Dept. Natural Resources, Atlanta, 1994—96, grants coord., 1996—2000; exec. dir. Cobb Landmarks and Hist. Soc., Marietta, Ga., 2001—. Contbr.: chapter Disaster Management Programs for Historic Sites. Mem. steering com. Georgians for Preservation Action, Atlanta. Recipient City Planning award, Am. Planning Assn., 1996, Commendation for Disaster Recovery Efforts, Ga. Dept. Natural Resources, 1997. Mem.: Nat. Trust Hist. Preservation (assoc.), Atlanta Preservation Ctr. (assoc.), Ga. Planning Assn. (assoc.), Am. Mensa (assoc.). Avocations: running, travel, reading. Home: 2870 Pharr Court South NW #302 Atlanta GA 30305 Office: Cobb Landmarks and Historical Soc 145 Denmead St Marietta GA 30060 Home Phone: 404-816-6741; Office Phone: 770-426-4982. Office Fax: 770-499-9540. Personal E-mail: darylbarksdale@mindspring.com. Business E-Mail: clhs2@bellsouth.net.

BARKSDALE, JAMES LOVE, communications executive; b. Jackson, Miss., 1943; married. Grad., U. Miss., 1965. V.p. Cook Industries, Inc., 1973-79; former pres. ISD, Inc.; sr. v.p. info. systems, chief info. officer Fed. Express Corp., Memphis, 1979-83, exec. v.p., COO, 1983-92, also dir.; pres., COO McCaw Cellular Commns.; CEO AT&T Wireless Svcs. (merger McCaw Cellular Comms. and AT&T Wireless Svcs.); pres., CEO Netscape Comms. Corp., Mountain View, Calif., 1995—99, also bd. dirs.; dir. Am. Online, 1999; gen. ptnr. Barksdale Group, LLC, 1999—; pres., CEO Barksdale Mgmt. Corp., 1999—. Bd. dirs. FedEx Corp., Sun Microsystems, Inc., Time Warner, Inc.; spl. advisor Gen. Atlantic Ptnrs. Named one of 50 Most Generous Philanthropists, BusinessWeek, 2005. Office: Time Warner Inc One Time Warner Ctr New York NY 10019

BARKSDALE, MARY ALICE, education educator; b. Roanoke, Va., Feb. 12, 1954; d. Byrd H. and Mary Anne (St. Clair) Barksdale. BA in Elem. Edn., Clemson U., 1976, MEd in Reading Edn., 1979; EdD in Curriculum and Instrn., Va. Tech., 1988. Tchr. Greenville (S.C.) Schs., 1976-81, Bedford (Va.) County Schs., 1981-83; grad. asst. Va. Tech., Blacksburg, 1983-88; prof. W.Va. U., Morgantown, 1988-94, U. South Fla., Tampa, 1994—2001, Va. Tech., Blacksburg, 2001—. Presenter in field. Co-editor Jour. Computing in Childhood Edn., 1995-97; contbr. articles to profl. jours.; reviewer publs. in field. Fulbright scholar 1995. Mem. Internat. Reading Assn. (Albert J. Harris award 1995), Nat. Reading Conf., Coll. Reading Assn., Ea. Ednl. Rsch. Assn., Fulbright Assn., Phi Delta Kappa. Office: 107 War Meml Hall Va Tech Blacksburg VA 24061 Home Phone: 540-818-8620; Office Phone: 540-231-3166. E-mail: mbarksda@vt.edu.

BARKSDALE, RHESA HAWKINS, federal judge; b. Jackson, Miss., Aug. 8, 1944; s. John Woodson Jr. and Mary Bryan (Saunders) Barksdale. BS, U.S. Mil. Acad., 1966; JD, U. Miss., 1972. Law clk. to Hon. Byron R. White US Supreme Ct., 1972—73; assoc., then ptnr. Butler, Snow, O'Mara, Stevens & Cannada, Jackson, 1973—90; judge US Ct. Appeals (5th cir.), Jackson, 1990—. Instr. U. Miss. Sch. Law, Jackson, 1975—76, Miss. Coll. Sch. Law, Jackson, 1976. Chmn. Miss. Vietnam Vets. Leadership Program, Jackson, 1982—85; del. Rep. Nat. Conv., New Orleans, 1988; elector election of Pres. of U.S., Jackson, 1988. Capt. US Army, 1966—70, Vietnam. Decorated Silver Star, Bronze Star for Valor, Purple Heart, Cross of Gallantry with silver star (Republic of Vietnam). Mem.: Phi Delta Phi (Nat. Grad. of Yr. 1972). Episcopalian. Office: US Ct Appeals 5th Cir James O Eastland Courthouse 245 E Capitol St Ste 200 Jackson MS 39201-2414*

BARKUS, BRUCE E., health products executive; BS in Pharmacy, Long Island U.; MBA, Nova Southeastern U., D of Bus. Adminstrn. Mgmt. Pharmacist/mgr. Eckerd Corp., 1978; with Family Dollar Stores, 1999—2005, exec. vice-pres., 2003—05; pres., CEO GNC Corp., 2005—. Office: GNC 300 Sixth Ave Pittsburgh PA 15222 Office Phone: 412-288-4600. Office Fax: 412-288-4764.

BARLAND, SARAH ELIZABETH, secondary school educator; b. College Station, Tex., May 19, 1976; d. David Kenneth Barland and Mary Sue Carter. BA in Exercise Sports Sci., SW Tex. State U., San Marcos, 2001. Std. tchg. cert. SBEC/Tex., 2001. Tchr. Mesquite Ind. Sch. Dist., Tex., 2001—03, Carrollton-Farmers Br. Ind. Sch. Dist., Tex., 2003—. Dance tchr. Am. Dance and Drill Team, Salado, Tex., 2001—. Mem.: Drill Team Dirs. Am. Democrat. Roman Catholic. Avocations: dance, running, travel. Home: 6909 Windhaven Pkwy #35 The Colony TX 75056 Office: R L Turner High School 1600 S Josey Lane Carrollton TX 75006 Home Phone: 512-787-9514; Office Phone: 972-968-5485. Personal E-mail: sbarland@hotmail.com. Business E-Mail: barlands@hotmail.com.

BARLOGA, SCOTT B., lawyer; s. Fred Ross and Sally Barloga; m. Laura Bowland. BS, Fla. State U., Tallahassee, 1990; JD, Mercer U., Macon, Ga., 1994; LLM, U. Fla., Gainesville, 2002. Bar: Fla., Ga., NC. Ptnr. Pope & Barloga, PA, Panama City, 2006—. Office: Pope & Barloga PA 438 N Cove Blvd Panama City FL 32401 Office Phone: 850-784-9174. Office Fax: 850-784-9175.

BARLOW, ANNE JULIA, curator; d. John and Alma Barlow; m. Robert Kloos, Feb. 28, 2005. MA in Art History, U. Glasgow, Scotland, 1986. Registrar, exhibitions asst. Fischer Fine Art Ltd., London, 1987—89; curator contemporary art collection The Scottish Arts Coun., Edinburgh, 1989—94; curator contemporary art and design Glasgow Museums, 1994—99; curator edn. and media programs New Mus. Contemporary Art, NYC, 1999—2006; exec. dir. Art in General, NYC, 2007—. Nominator media arts fellowships (film and video) Program for Media Artists, The Rockefeller Found., NYC, 2003—04; panelist bldg. digital resources Inst. Mus. and Libr. Svcs., Washington, 2003—05; panelist electronic media and film NY State Coun. on the Arts, NYC, 2003—05; retreat cons. Creative Capital Found., NYC, 2005—06. Office: New Mus Contemporary Art 210 11th Ave 2d Fl New York NY 10001 Home Phone: 212-608-6641; Office Phone: 212-219-0473 ext. 36. Business E-Mail: abarlow@newmuseum.org.

BARLOW, ANNE LOUISE, pediatrician, medical researcher; b. Skipton-in-Craven, Eng., Jan. 28, 1925; came to U.S., 1951, naturalized, 1954; m. Howard Cadwell, May 19, 1951; children: Barbara Anne, John James Stewart; m. Alastair Ramsay, Dec. 19, 1969. MB BS, London Sch. Medicine for Women, U. London, 1948; diploma in child health, Royal Colls. Eng., 1950; MPH with honors, Yale U., 1952. House physician North Lonsdale Hosp., Barrow-in-Furness, Lancashire, Eng., 1948-49; house surgeon Royal Infirmary (Glasgow), Scotland, 1949; resident to profl. unit of child health Royal Hosp. for Sick Children, Glasgow, 1949-50; jr. hosp. med. officer Knightswood Infectious Diseases Hosp., Glasgow, 1950; Rotary Found. Internat. fellow U. Toronto Med. Sch., Ont., Canada, 1950-51; research asst. Yale U. Sch. Pub. Health, New Haven, 1952-53; clinic physician in cancer prevention Arlington, Va., part-time 1953-54; resident, staff physician William H. Maybury Tb Sanatorium, Northville, Mich., 1954-56; research dir. Detroit Feeding Study with the Detroit City Health Dept., 1954-56; research asst., instr. sch. health U. Pitts. Grad. Sch. Pub. Health, 1957-62; pvt. practice medicine specializing in pediatrics Pitts., 1959-62; mem. courtesy staff St. Margaret Hosp., Pitts., 1959-62; research assoc. Tice Lab for Tb research, Cook County Hosp., Chgo., 1962; med. writer product info. Abbott Labs., North Chicago, Ill., 1963-66, med. specialist antibiotic medicine, 1966-68; mgr. clin. devel. pharm. products div. Abbott Lab., North Chicago, Ill., 1968-71, asst. med. dir., 1971-72, mgr. parenteral nutrition hosp. products div., 1972-73, med. dir., 1973-80, v.p. med. affairs hosp. products div., 1980-84; pres. Albamed, Inc., 1985—2005; asst. clin. prof. Med.Coll. Pa., 1988. Cons. maternal, child and sch. health, dir. well baby clinic Lake County (Ill.) Health Dept., 1963-76; pres. Tb Sanatorium Bd. Lake County Health Dept., Ill., 1976-79; dir., pres. Lake County Bd. Health, 1979-82; health officer Village of North Barrington, Ill., 1964-67; physician-adviser Head Start Lake County Community Action Project, 1970-84; chmn. profl. adv. com. Lake County Health Dept., 1972-84; preceptor Pediatric Nurse Assoc. Program; chmn. bd. Sutton Place Behavioral Health Inc., 2000-05. Contbr. articles on maternal and infant care, pediatrics and nutrition; patentee high calorie solution of low molecular weight glucose polymer mixtures useful for intravenouse adminstrn. Bd. dirs. Heart Assn. of Lake County, 1979-84, chmn. nutrition com. 1980-82, v.p. 1982-83, pres., 1983-84; mem. sch. bd. Grant Twp. Cmty. H.S. (Ill. Dist. 124), 1973-79; sec. to governing bd. Spl. Edn. Dist. of Lake County, 1977-79; assoc. Nat. Coll. Edn., Evanston, Ill., 1976-84; chmn. Am. Women's Hosp. Svc., 1986-95, 2004-; vol. Guardian ad Litem, 1989-2004. Recipient award of merit for outstanding contbns. to pub. health, Ill. Pub. Health Assn., 1975, award of merit for outstanding cmty. svc., Lake County Cmty. Action Project, 1976, award for outstanding and dedicated svc. as pres., Lake County TB Sanatorium Bd., 1979, TWIN award, YWCA, 1983, Charlotte Danstrom award for excellence, Women in Mgmt., 1984, award for volunteering in medicine, AMA Found., 2006. Mem. AAAS, NOW, LWV, AMA (chair sr. physician gov. com. 1996-2005), Am. Med. Women's Assn. (councilor for orgn. and mgmt. 1977-79, treas. 1980, 1st v.p. 1981, pres. 1983, chair found. 1992-95, chair AWHS com. 2004-, Elizabeth Blackwell medal 1992), Fla. Med. Assn. (vice chair Internat. Med. Grad. sect. 1998-2004, coun. on pub. health 2000-05), Med. Women's Internat. Assn. (v.p. N. Am. 1993-95), Pan-Am. Med. Women's Alliance (pres. 2000), Nassau County Med. Soc. (pres. 2002-03). Home and Office: 20 S 19th St Fernandina Beach FL 32034-2767 Personal E-mail: czardaska@bellsouth.net.

BARLOW, AUGUST RALPH, JR., minister; s. August Ralph and Kathryn Viola (Adams) B.; m. Elizabeth Evone Anderson, Aug. 27, 1960; children: Paul Martin, Andrew Ralph, Ann Kathryn. BA, Haverford Coll., Pa., 1956; BD, Yale U., New Haven, Conn., 1959, STM, 1964. Ordained to ministry Meth. Ch., 1959. Pastor Fox Chapel Meth. Ch., Pitts., 1959—60, Butler St. Meth. Ch., Pitts., 1961—62, Lawrenceville Cmty. Ch., Pitts., 1962—63; intern Cleve. Inner City Protestant Parish, 1960—61; from tchg. min. to pastor Beneficent Congl. Ch., Providence, 1964—97, pastor emeritus, 1997—. Bd. govs. Beneficent House, 1970-97, Beneficent Commons Housing, Providence, sr. min., devel. team, 1991-95; bd. dirs. Pastoral Counseling Ctr., Greater Providence, v.p., 1984-86, pres., 1995-97; pres. Steere House, Providence, 1983-86, past bd. dirs.; bd. dirs. Home Health Svcs. of R.I., 1986-93, chmn. ch. in soc. com., 1985-86; mem. R.I. Conf., United Ch. of Christ, 1964—, mem. com. on ministry, 1981-83, past bd. dirs.; mem. urban divsn. R.I. Coun. Chs., 1979-82. Editor-in-chief: jour. Expanding Horizons, 1996—; contbr. articles to profl. jours., newspapers and mags.; Religious Broadcasting Sta. WEAN, 1964—87. Adv. coun. Providence Pub. Libr., 1968-71; bd. dirs. Mouthpiece Coffee House, Providence, 1969-75, pres., 1974-75; bd. dirs. Citizens United Renewal Enterprises, 1972-77; alumni class agt. for scholarship funds Haverford Coll. and Yale U. Div. Sch., 1979-95; corp. mem. R.I. Hosp. Corp., 1980-95. Rsch. fellow Yale U. Div. Sch., 1979; recipient Alumnal Bd. award Yale U. Div. Sch., 1997. Mem. Providence Intown Chs. Assn., Mins. Assn. R.I. Conf. United Ch. of Christ, Dodeka Symposium, Rotary (trustee Rotary Charities Found. 1977-82, Paul Harris fellow), Beneficent Order of Spike, Phi Beta Kappa. Democrat. Home and Office: 103 Angell Rd Lincoln RI 02865-4710 E-mail: a.r.barlow@att.net.

BARLOW, BARBARA ANN, surgeon; b. Lancaster, Pa., June 20, 1938; d. William Barlow and Esther Stoll Barlow Lowry; m. Andre Zmurek. BA in psychology, Vassar Coll.; MA in psychology, Columbia U.; MD, Albert Einstein Coll. Medicine, 1967. Diplomte Am. Bd. Surgery. Intern Bronx (N.Y.) Mcpl. Hosp., 1967-68, resident in surgery, 1968-73; resident in pediatric surgery Columbia-Presbyn. Med.-Babies Hosp., NYC, 1973-75; chief pediatric surgery Harlem Hosp., NYC, 1975—2000, chief of surgery, 2000—; prof. surgery and epidemiology Columbia U. and Mailman Sch. Pub. Health, NYC; founder, exec. dir. Injury Free Coalition for Kids, 1988—. Recipient Safe Cmty. Award, US Dept. Transp., 1996, David E. Rogers award, Assn. Am. Med. Colleges, 2001, Disting. Career Award, Injury Ctrl. and Health Svcs. Sect., APHA, 2001, Pub. Svc. Award, Alfred P. Sloan Found., 2003. Mem. ACS, Am. Acad. Pediatrics (Injury and Poison Prevention Fellow Achievement Award, 1997), Am. Assn. for Surgery of Trauma, Am. Pediatric Surg. Assn., N.Y. Surgery Soc. Achievements include Featured in the Nat. Libr. Medicine exhibit "Changing the Face of Medicine" honoring women physicians, 2003. Office: Columbia U Mailman Sch Pub Health 722 W 168th St Rm 1709 New York NY 10032

BARLOW, JESSE LOUIS, computer scientist, educator; b. Lawrence, Kans., July 8, 1955; s. Richard Lewis and Elizabeth Marie (McCaffrey) B.; m. Ramsey Stade, Jan. 10, 1981; children: Hilary, Zachary. BA in Computer Sci. and Math., U. Kans., 1977; MS in Computer Sci., Northwestern U., 1979, MS in Stats., 1980, PhD, 1981. Asst. prof. computer sci. Pa. State U., University Park, 1981-87, assoc. prof. computer sci., 1987-92, prof. computer sci., 1992—. Vis. prof. U. Manchester, Eng., 1996, Courant Inst. Math. Sci., 1988, CUNY Grad. Ctr., 2002; vis. Inst. of Math. and It's Applications, Inst. Math. Scis. Contbr. articles to profl. jours. NSF grantee, 1982-84, 84-86, 87, 90-2002, 04—, Air Force Office of Sci. Rsch., grantee, 1988-90; recipient 2d prize L. Prize Meeting, London, 1986. Mem. Soc. Indsl. and Applied Math., IEEE Computer Soc., Assn. for Computing Machinery, Phi Beta Kappa. Office: Pa State U Computer Sci & Engring Dept University Park PA 16802 Home: PO Box 10221 State College PA 16805-0221 Office Phone: 814-863-1705. Business E-Mail: barlow@cse.psu.edu.

BARLOW, JIM B., retired columnist, writer; b. Port Arthur, Tex., Aug. 19, 1936; s. Joseph B. and Goldie (Johnson) B.; m. Karleen Ann Smith, Aug. 24, 1968 (div. Jan. 1974); 1 child, Samantha Lynn; m. Susan Ann Bischoff, June 20, 1975. BA, U. North Tex., Denton, 1972. Newsman KPAC-TV, Port Arthur, Tex., 1959-61; news dir. KPNG-Radio, Port Neches, Tex., 1962-63; reporter Beaumont (Tex.) Enterprise, 1963-64, Denton Record-Chronicle, 1964-66; asst. city mgr. City of Denton, 1967; staff writer U. North Tex., Denton, 1968; newsman AP, Dallas-Houston, 1968-75; dir. info. svcs. Houston Ind. Sch. Dist., 1975-77; reporter Houston Chronicle, 1977-87, columnist, 1987—2002; ret., 2002. Co-author: Big Town, Big Money, 1974, The Woodlands, 2004. With U.S. Army, 1956-59. Avocations: reading, cooking, exercise. Home: # 112 2929 Buffalo Speedway Houston TX 77098 Home Phone: 713-355-8144; Office Phone: 713-303-8874. Personal E-mail: JimB3333@aol.com.

BARLOW, JOHN PERRY, writer, former rancher, advocate; b. Wyo., Oct. 3, 1947; m. Elaine Parker (div. 1996); children: Leah Justine, Anna Winter, Amelia. Degree in comparative religion with honors, Wesleyan U., 1969. Mgr. Bar Cross Land and Livestock Co., Cora, Wyo., 1971-88; co-founder, vice chmn. Electronic Frontier Found., 1990—. Bd. dirs. WELL; cons. Vanguard Group of CSC, Global Bus. Network. Contbg. editor numerous publs. including Comm. of the ACM, Microtimes, Mondo 2000; contbg. writer Wired; co-writer songs for The Grateful Dead, 1971-95. Berkman fellow Harvard Law Sch., 1998—; named Thomas Jefferson of Cyberspace, Yahoo Mag. Internet Life, 1996, one of 25 Most Influential People in Fin. Svcs., Future Banker Mag., 1999. Office: Electronic Frontier Foundation 168 S Franklin Pinedale WY 82941-1009 also: 203 Grand St #2 New York NY 10013 E-mail: barlow@eff.org.

BARLOW, JOHN SUTTON, neuroscientist, lexicographer; b. Raleigh, NC, June 10, 1925; s. David Henry and Anne Mary (Sutton) B.; m. Sibylle E. Jahrreiss, Aug. 5, 1950; children: Thomas Walter, Robert Sutton, Lisa Katharine. BS, U. NC, Chapel Hill, 1944, MS, 1948; MD, Harvard Coll., 1953. Diplomate Am. Bd. EEG. Clin., rsch. fellow, asst. resident neurology Mass. Gen. Hosp., Boston, 1953-57; clin., rsch. fellow Harvard Med. Sch., 1953-57; rsch. assoc. in elec. engring. MIT, Cambridge, 1954-64, rsch. affiliate Rsch. Lab. of Electronics, 1964-99; asst. neurology Mass. Gen. Hosp., Boston, 1957-61, neurophysiologist neurology svc., 1961—2007; rsch. assoc. neurology Harvard Med. Sch., 1961-69, prin. rsch. assoc., 1969-78, sr. rsch. assoc. neurology, neurophysiology, 1979—. Mem. neurology study sect. NIH, Bethesda, Md., 1966-70; mem. rev. panel on neurol. devices FDA, Washington, 1974-76; cons. dept. neurology VA Med. Ctr., Boston, 1979-89, part-time staff, 1989-98; cons. dept. neurology New Eng. Med. Ctr., Boston, 1979-89. Author: The Electroencephalogram: Its Patterns and Origins, 1993, A Chinese-Russian-English Dictionary, 1995, A Pocket Chinese-Russian-English Dictionary, 2000, The Cerebellum and Adaptive Control, 2002; editor: (with Karenina Kollmar-Paulenz) Otto Ottonovich Rosenberg and his Contribution to Buddhology in Russia, 1998; cons. editor EEG Clin. Neurophysiology, 1970-86; translator/editor books from the Russian, Czech, Polish and Chinese; contbr. articles and revs. to profl. jours. Ensign, lt. (j.g.) USN, 1944—46. Recipient Rsch. Career Devel. award NIH, 1962-71, Sr. Scientist award Alexander von Humboldt Found., Göttingen, Germany, 1979, Sr. Scientist Exch. award NAS, USA, USSR Acad. Scis., Moscow, 1982, 83, 88; rsch. grantee NIH, 1962-88; Fogarty Internat. fellow, 1979. Mem. Internat. Brain Rsch. Orgn., Am. EEG Soc. (pres. 1975-76), Am. Neurol. Assn., Am. Acad. Neurology,

Soc. Neurosci., Am. Geophys. Union, Ea. Assn. EEG (pres. 1971-72), Assn. Asian Studies, European Assn. Chinese Studies, Dictionary Soc. North Am., Phi Beta Kappa. Avocations: music, rail travel, languages, international relations.

BARLOW, LOU, painter; b. 1908; Studied, Nat. Acad. Design. Former mil. artist US Army. Prof., dept Art Parsons Sch. Design, ret., 1998. Exhibitions include Assoc. Artists Am. Gallery, Sylvan Cole Gallery, Susan Teller Gallery, Sragow Gallery, NYC, one-man shows include 26 War Paintings, Florence, Italy, Medical Art Paintings, Nat. Arts Club, exhibited in group shows at Met. Mus. Art, Santa Clara Mus., Davidson Gall., NY Watercolor Soc., ACA Gall., Represented in permanent collections Met. Mus. Art, NY Historical Soc., Libr. Congress, Nat. Mus. Art, Mus. City NY, NY Pub. Libr. Mem.: Am. Watercolor Soc., NY Watercolor Club.

BARLOW, MATTHEW, real estate company executive; BS in Biomedical Engring. and Fin., cum laude, Boston U. Exec. v.p., dir. Studley, NYC. Mem. NY Chpt. Fund to Cure Paralysis; chmn. charitable found. bd. Studley, mem. nat. law firm task force. Office: Studley 300 Park Ave 3rd Floor New York NY 10022 Office Phone: 212-326-1079.*

BARLOW, PAULA C., nurse; b. New Albany, Ind., May 27, 1952; d. Chester Joseph and Bonnie Faye Stiller; m. Rick Keith Barlow, Nov. 17, 1984; 1 child, Laura Elise. BSN, U. Louisville, 1982. RN Ga., Ky., Fla. Nurse St. Anthony Hosp., Louisville, 1972—82, St. Vincent's Hosp., Jacksonville, Fla., 1985—97; sch. nurse Camden Bd. Edn., Kingsland, Ga., 1997—. CPR instr. ARC. Mem.: Sight for Students Orgn., Ga. Assn. Sch. Nurses, Nat. Assn. Sch. Nurses. Avocations: reading, cooking, travel. Home: 502 Thrift St Kingsland GA 31548

BARLOW, TANI E., history and women's studies professor; d. Claude Abner Barlow and Alice Voorsanger Barlow; m. Donald M. Lowe, 1993. PhD, U. Calif., Davis, 1985. Asst. prof. history U. Mo., Columbia, 1985—90, assoc. prof. history, 1990—92, San Francisco State U., 1992—94; prof. history and women studies U. Wash., Seattle, 1994—. Co-founder Rockefeller Found. Funded Project for Critical Asian Studies, Seattle, 1996—. Contbr. articles to profl. jours.; founding sr. editor Positions: East Asia Culture Critique, Seattle, 1992—. Office: U Wash PO Box 353650 Seattle WA 98195 Office Phone: 206 616-1769. Fax: 206 616-1566. E-mail: position@u.washington.edu.

BARLOW, WILLIAM PUSEY, JR., accountant; b. Oakland, Calif., Feb. 11, 1934; s. William P. and Muriel (Block) B. Student, Calif. Inst. Tech., 1952-54; AB in Econs., U. Calif., Berkeley, 1956. CPA, Calif. Acct. Barlow, Davis & Wood, San Francisco, 1960-72, ptnr., 1964-72, J.K. Lasser & Co., 1972-77, Touche Ross & Co., San Francisco, 1977-78; self employed acct., 1978-89; ptnr. Barlow & Hughan, 1990—. Co-author: Collectible Books: Some New Paths, 1979, The Grolier Club, 1884-1984, 1984; editor: Book Catalogues: Their Varieties and Uses, 2d edit., 1986, Officially Sealed Notes, 1996-2004; contbr. articles to profl. jours. Fellow Gleeson Libr. Assocs., 1969, pres., 1971-74; mem. coun. Friends Bancroft Libr., 1971-98, chmn., 1974-79; bd. dirs. Oakland Ballet, 1982-99, pres., 1986-89, chmn., 1995-98. Recipient Sir Thomas More medal Gleeson Libr. Assocs., 1989, Herbert Howe Bancroft award Bancroft Libr., U. Calif., 2004; named to Water Ski Hall of Fame, 1993. Mem. Am. Water Ski Assn. (bd. dirs., regional chmn. 1959-63, pres. 1963-66, chmn. bd. 1966-69, 77-79, hon. v.p. 1969—), Machine Cancel Soc. (pres., 2003-06), Internat. Water Ski Fedn. (exec. bd. 1961-71, 75-78), Bibliog. Soc. Am. (coun. 1986-92, pres. 1992-96), Grolier Club (N.Y.C.), Roxburghe Club (San Francisco), Book Club of Calif. (bd. dirs. 1963-76, pres. 1968-69, treas. 1971-83). Home: 1474 Hampel St Oakland CA 94602-1346 Office: 1182 Market St Ste 400 San Francisco CA 94102-4922 Office Phone: 415-522-2490. Business E-Mail: wpbjr@barlowandhughan.com.

BARLOWE, DOROTHEA, art educator, illustrator; b. West Orange, NJ, Jan. 11, 1926; d. Phillip and Laura Kay; m. Sy Barlowe (dec. 2000); children: Amy Louise, Wayne Douglas. Student, Cooper Union Art Sch., NYC, 1942—44, Columbia U., 1948. Sci. illustrator Am. Mus. Natural History, 1945—50; freelance illustrator and writer, 1950—2006. Tchr. Parsons Sch. Design, 1949—51, Massapequa Sch. Sys., 1981—2001. Author, illustrator: Illustrating Nature, 1982, illustrator: Seashores, 1959, Trees of North America, 1952, Amphibians of North American; contbr. illustrator to numerous books, articles to profl. jours. Mem.: Defenders of Wildlife, Nature Conservancy, Sierra Club. Avocations: painting, photography, gardening.

BARLOWE BODMAN, AMY, violinist, composer; b. Copiague, NY, Jan. 20, 1952; d. Sy and Dorothea (Kay) Barlowe; m. Alan Kingsley Bodman, Dec. 27, 1988; children: Alanna, Ariel Rose. BMus, Juilliard Sch. Music, NYC, 1975, MMus, 1976. Violinist Oregon Trio, Salem, 1976-86; assoc. prof. violin Willamette U., Salem, 1976-86; tchr. Bowdoin (Maine) Music Festival, 1983, Estherwood Music Festival, Oneonta, N.Y., 1984, Juilliard Pre-Coll., NYC, 1986-88; faculty Sch. for Strings, NYC, 1986-88; violinist Duo AB2, Akron, Ohio, 1988—; assoc. concertmaster Akron (Ohio) Symphony Orch., 1988—2000; artist/faculty Meadowmount Sch. Music, Westport, NY, 1988—, Ohio Conservatory, Akron, Ohio, 2000—. Violinist, recitalist numerous chamber ensembles, U.S., Can., Mex., 1976—; founder Akron Baroque Chamber Orch., 2006. Author: Guide for Enjoyable Listening, 1983, Happy Listening Guide, 1992, Come Listen With Me, 1993; composer: Reflections from the Edge of the Millennium, 1999, Hebraique Elegie, 2000, Requiem, 2002; violinist recording on Medici label, 1990, Azica label, 1999; numerous violin appearances various radio stas., NY, Oreg., Ohio, Calif., Wash., 1976—; composer (opera, ballet) The Toymaker, 2005, Celebration, 2005, Lullaby and The Lady of Shalott for 2 violas, 2005, Banjo and Fiddle for 2 violins and piano, 2006, Consolation for 2 violins and piano, 2006. Recipient Atkinson award Willamette U., 1983, Helena Rubinstein Found. award, 1975; Willamette U. Northwest Area grantee, 1983; Bach Aria Group fellow. Mem. Am. String Tchrs. Assn., Music Educators Nat. Conf., Music Tchrs. Nat. Assn. Avocation: photography. Home and Office: 338 Castle Blvd Akron OH 44313-6504 Office Fax: 330-873-1174. Personal E-mail: amybarlowe@yahoo.com.

BARLOW-WARE, JACQUELINE SUE, music educator; d. F. John and Dorothy Marx Barlow; m. Michael Brian Ware, Aug. 11, 2001; children: Christopher Barlow Dearing, Brian Michael Ware, Jonathan Edward Ware, Jennifer Christine Ware, David Ray Ware. MusB, Lawrence U. Conservatory, Appleton, Wis., 1978; MusM, MA, Ohio State U., 1982. Cert. Massage Therapist Ohio. Adj. instr. U. Va., Charlottesville, 1973—76; instr. Lawrence U., Appleton, 1976—78; voice instr. Barlow Studio, Columbus, 1978—; mezzo soprano soloist First Cmty. Ch., Columbus, 1982—; instr. Capital U. Cmty. Music Sch., Columbus, 1990—2002; adj. assoc. prof. Capital U. Conservatory Music, Columbus, 1999—. Tchg. assoc. Ohio State U., Columbus, 1978—81. Mem.: Nat. Assn. Tchrs. of Singing (assoc.; v.p. 2005—07, pres. 2007—, bd. dirs. 2003—05). Avocations: travel, languages, reading, decorating. Office: Capital Univ Conservatory Music 1 Main and College Columbus OH 43209 Home Phone: 614-523-1887. Personal E-mail: jackie@barlowstudio.com. Business E-Mail: jbarlow@capital.edu.

BARMANN, BERNARD CHARLES, SR., lawyer; b. Maryville, Mo., Aug. 5, 1932; s. Charles Anselm and Veronica Rose (Fisher) B.; m. Beatrice Margaret Murphy, Sept. 27, 1965; children: Bernard Charles Jr., Brigit. PhD, Stanford U., 1966; JD, U. San Diego, 1974; MPA, Calif. State U., Bakersfield. Bar: Calif. 1974, U.S. Dist. Ct. (so. dist.) Calif. 1974, U.S. Dist. Ct. (ea. dist.) Calif. 1978, U.S. Ct. Appeals (9th cir.) 1984, U.S. Supreme Ct. Asst. prof. Ohio State U., Columbus, 1966-69, U. Toronto, Ont., Can., 1969-71; dep. county counsel Kern County, Bakersfield, Calif., 1974-85, county counsel, 1985—. Adj. prof. Calif. State U., Bakersfield, 1986—. Editor: The Bottom Line, 1991-93, contbr. articles to profl. jours. Mem. exec. bd. So. Sierra coun. Boy Scouts Am., Bakersfield, 1986—; bd. dirs. Kern County Acad. Decathlon, Bakersfield, 1988—. Danforth Found. fellow, 1963-65; grantee Fulbright Found., 1963-65. Mem. Calif. Bar Assn. (law practice mgmt. sect. exec. com., jud. nominees evaluation commn. 1997-2000), County Counsel Assn. Calif. (bd. dirs. 1990—, chair 1993-94), Kern County Bar Assn. (pres. 2001), Rotary. Avocations: golf, skiing, travel, photography. Office: Kern County Office of County Counsel 1115 Truxtun Ave Bakersfield CA 93301-4639 Business E-Mail: bbarmann@co.kern.ca.us.

BARMANN, LAWRENCE FRANCIS, historian, educator; b. Maryville, Mo., June 9, 1932; s. Francis Lawrence and Clary Weber (LaMar) B. BA, St. Louis U., 1956, Ph.L., 1957, S.T.L., 1964; MA, Fordham U., 1960; postgrad., Princeton, 1965-66; PhD, Cambridge U., Eng., 1970. Tchr. history St. Louis U. High Sch., 1957-59; asst. prof. history St. Louis U., 1970-73, asso. prof., 1973-78, prof., 1978—, asst. dir. Am. Studies Program, 1981-83, prof. Am. studies, 1981-01, dir. Am. Studies Program, 1983-88, chair dept. Am. studies, 1999—2000, prof. theol. studies, 1996-01, ret., 2001, prof. emeritus, 2002—. Author: Newman at St. Mary's, 1962, Baron Friedrich von Hügel and the Modernist Crisis in England, 1972, The Letters of Baron Friedrich von Hügel and Professor Norman Kemp Smith, 1982; editor Sanctity and Secularity, 1999; contbr. articles profl. jours. Recipient award Mellon Faculty Devel. Fund, 1987, 92, 94, Emerson Electric Outstanding Tchr. award, 1999; rsch. grantee Am. Philos. Soc. PHila., 1971, Beaumont Fund, 1977, 82; Danforth assoc., 1978—. Mem.: Cambridge Soc. (founding 1977), Am. Cath. Hist. Assn., Phi Beta Kappa. Office: 221 N Grand Blvd Saint Louis MO 63103-2006 Home: 5435 Vicar Ct Saint Louis MO 63119 *I have found for myself that the meaning of life is the joy of continuous discovery in unending intellectual, emotional and spiritual growth, and the satisfaction which comes from sharing my vision and concerns with the young people who will lead the next generation.*

BARNA, LILLIAN CARATTINI, school system administrator; b. NYC, Jan. 18, 1929; d. Juan Carattini and Dolores Elsie Nieves (Alicea); m. Eugene Andrew Barna, July 1, 1951; children: Craig Andrew, Keith Andrew. AB, Hunter Coll., 1950; MA, San Jose State U., 1970. Tchr. N.Y.C. Sch. Dist., 1950—52, Whittier (Calif.) Sch. Dist., 1952—54, tchr. HS, 1954—56; tchr. presch. Long Beach and Los Gatos, Calif., 1958—67; supr. early childhood edn. San Jose (Calif.) Unified Sch. Dist., 1967—72, sch. adminstr., 1972—80, supt. schs., 1980—84, Albuquerque Pub. Schs., 1984—88, Tacoma Sch. Dist. 10, 1988—93; cons. in field; exec. dir. Large City Schs. Supts., 1993—. Named Outstanding Sch. Dist. Supt., Wash. State; named to Hunter Coll. Hall of Fame; recipient Sorptomist Internat. Woman of Yr. award, 1980, Western Region Puertorican Council Achievement award, 1980, Calif. State U. Outstanding Achievement in Edn. award, 1982, Woman of Achievement award, Santa Clara County Commn. on Status of Women/San Jose Mercury News, Disting. Alumni award, San Jose State U., Shero award, Am. Assn. Sch. Adminstrn., 2005. Mem.: LWV, Am. Assn. Sch. Adminstrs. (Disting. Leadership award, Shero award 2006), Assn. Calif. Sch. Adminstrs., Women Leaders in Edn., Pan Am. Round Table, Rotary Club Saratoga, Delta Zeta, Phi Kappa Phi. Office: Large City Schs Supt PO Box 2096 Saratoga CA 95070 Office Phone: 408-867-4190. E-mail: lcbels@aol.com.

BARNARD, DEBORAH E., lawyer; b. Boston, Apr. 8, 1962; BA cum laude, Smith Coll., 1984; JD magna cum laude, Boston U., 1987. Bar: Mass. 1987, Ill. 1991. Ptnr. Holland & Knight LLP, Boston, mem. dir. com., nat. chair, Women's Initiative. Instructor, first year rsch. and writing program Boston U. Sch. Law. Contbr. articles to profl. jours. Participated in LeadBoston Nat. Conf. for Cmty. and Justice; bd. dir. The City Sch.; class agent Milton Acad. Class of 1980. Mem.: ABA. Office: Holland & Knight LLP 10 St James Ave 11th Fl Boston MA 02116 Office Phone: 617-619-9240. Business E-Mail: dbarnard@hklaw.com.

BARNARD, DONALD ROY, medical and veterinary entomologist; b. Santa Ana, Calif., June 7, 1946; s. Alan Whittaker and Ethel Mae (Kennedy) B.; m. Priscilla Margaret Grier, Aug. 12, 1967; children: Jennifer Erin, David Michael; m. Erin Patricia Mullan, Dec. 18, 2006. BS in Zoology, Calif. State U., 1969, MA in Biology, 1972; PhD in Entomology, U. Calif., Riverside, 1977. Postdoctoral fellow Colo. State U., Ft. Collins, 1977-79; rsch. entomologist agrl. rsch. svc. USDA, Poteau, Okla., 1979-85, supervisory rsch. entomologist, 1985-88, rsch. leader agrl. rsch. svc. Gainesville, Fla., 1988—2003. Adj. prof. entomology Okla. State U., 1988—, U. Fla., 1991—; tech. reviewer NIH, 1989-96, NSF, 1995-96, Ctrs. for Disease Control and Prevention, 1990; mem. soybean program operating bd., Ill., 1995-96; mem. USDA, NRI Competitive Grants Program, 1994—, Dept. Def., Def. Logistics Agy., 1995-96; cons., tech. reviewer WHO/FAO, 1980—, USAID, Somali Dem. Republic, 1981-90, Dept. of Def., AFPMB, 1985-2002, Republic South Africa, 1988-1998, State of Fla., DOACS, DAI, DOH, 1992-2000, Unilever Rsch., 1999-2004, Consumers Union, 2000—, USDA, APHIS, 1996—, EPA, 2000—; external reviewer U. Orange Free State, Republic South Africa, 1995-96, Tripura U., India, 1999-2004, Kongunadu Coll., India, 2001-05, Ministry of Health, Brazil, 1988—, Bharathiar U., Coimbatore, India; mem. Coordinating Coun. Mosquito Control, Fla., 1992-2005; rsch. adv. com. Fla. Mosquito Control Assn. Contbr. chpts. to books, articles to profl. jours.; editor Jour. of Med. Entomology, 2000-02; mem. editl. bd. Bull. of the Soc. Vector Ecologists. Mem. Am. Mosquito Control Assn., Internat. Orgn. Biol. Control, Entomol. Soc. Am., Entomol. Soc. Can., Ecol. Soc. Am., Internat. Soc. Travel Medicine, Am. Soc. Tropical Medicine and Hygiene. Home Phone: 352-374-0632; Office Phone: 352-374-5930. Business E-Mail: dbarnard@gainesville.usda.ufl.edu.

BARNARD, GEOFFREY W., judge; b. Batavia, NY, Apr. 4, 1945; Diploma, Univ. of Madrid, Spain, 1965; BA, Alleghany Coll., 1966; JD, Cornell Univ. Sch. of Law, Ithaca, 1969. Magistrate judge for V.I., U.S. Magistrate Ct., Charlotte Amalie, St. Thomas, 1986—. Chair Com. of Bar Examiners. Office: US Magistrate Ct 345 US Courthouse 5500 Veterans Dr Charlotte Amalie VI 00802-6424 also: Territorial Ct Virgin Islands PO Box 70 St Thomas VI 00804*

BARNARD, KEVIN FRANCIS, lawyer; b. NYC, June 1, 1951; s. Frank Louis and Marie Evelyn (Mangin) B.; m. Leigh Elaine Eckmann, Sept. 29, 1979; children: Lorraine, Paul, Maryclaire. BA, Fordham U., 1973; JD, NYU, 1976. Bar: N.Y. 1977. Dep. supt., gen. counsel N.Y. State Banking Dept., NYC, 1982-83; of counsel White & Case, NYC, 1984-85, ptnr., 1985—, global mgmt. bd., 2004—. Spl. counsel Temp. State Commn. on Banking, Ins., and Fin. Svsc., NY, 1984, Supts. Adv. Com. Transnational Banking, NY, 1992; dir. Apple Bank, 2001- Dir. Fgn. Policy Assn., 2007—. Decorated Knight of Malta, Am. Assn. Sovereign Mil. Order. Mem. Assn. of Bar of City of N.Y. Republican. Roman Catholic. Avocations: sailing, woodworking. Office: White & Case LLP 1155 Ave Of The Americas New York NY 10036-2787 E-mail: kbarnard@whitecase.com.

BARNARD, RAY F., engineering and construction management company executive; Exec. v.p. ENSCO Corp., 1988—99; v.p. IBM Corp., 1999—2000; sr. v.p. TradeMC, 2000—02; v.p. ops. Fluor Corp., v.p. global systems, various sr. mgmt. positions in info. tech., engring., mfg. and sales, exec. v.p., chief info. officer, 2002—. Mgmt. cons. DuPont, United Techs. Corp., Englehard, Procter & Gamble, Am. Bd. Achievements include patents in field. Office: Fluor Corp 6700 Las Colinas Blvd Irving TX 75039 Office Phone: 469-398-7000. Office Fax: 469-398-7255.*

BARNARD, ROLLIN DWIGHT, retired financial executive; b. Denver, Apr. 14, 1922; s. George Cooper and Emma (Riggs) B.; m. Patricia Reynolds Bierkamp, Sept. 15, 1943; children: Michael Dana, Rebecca Susan (Mrs. Paul C. Wulfestieg), Laurie Beth (Mrs. Kenneth J. Kostelecky). BA, Pomona Coll., 1943. Clk. Morey Merc. Co., Denver, 1937-40; ptnr. George C. Barnard & Co., Denver, 1946-47; v.p. Foster & Barnard, Inc., 1947-53; instr. Denver U., 1949-53; dir. real estate U.S. P.O. Dept., Washington, 1953-55, dep. asst. postmaster gen., bur. facilities, 1955-59, asst. postmaster gen., 1959-61; pres., dir. Midland Fed. Savs. & Loan Assn., Denver, 1962-84; vice-chmn. Bank Western Fed. Savs. Bank, 1984-87; vice-chmn., pres. Western Capital Investment Corp., 1985-87. Mem. exec. bd. Boy Scouts Am., pres. Denver Area coun., 1970—71, mem. adv. bd., 1973; trustee Mile High United Fund, 1969—72, Denver Symphony Assn., 1973—74; trustee, v.p. and treas. Morris Animal Found., 1969—81, pres. and chmn., 1974—78, trustee emeritus, 1981—; trustee Denver Zool. Found, 1994—2005, hon. life trustee, 2006—, exec. vice chmn., 1996—2000, vice chmn., 2000—01; mem. acquisitions com. Friends Found. Denver Pub. Libr., 1994—2003; treas. Roundup Riders of the Rockies Heritage and Trails Found., Inc., 1988—97, pres., 1997—; chmn. planning and zoning commn. City of Greenwood Village, 1969—73, mem. coun., 1975—77, mayor, 1989—93; bd. dir. Downtown Denver Improvement Assn., pres., 1965; bd. dir. Bethesda Found., Inc., 1973—82, Children's Health Corp., Inc., 1982—93, Children's Hosp., 1979—84, treas, 1983—84; bd. dir. Colo. Coun. Econ. Edn., 1971—80, chmn., 1971—76; dir. Wings over the Rockies Air & Space Mus. Found, 1998—2002. Named one of Ten Outstanding Young Men in Am., U.S. Jaycees, 1955, 57; recipient Disting. Svc. award Postmaster Gen. U.S., 1960; Silver Beaver award Boy Scouts Am., 1969; named Outstanding Citizen of Yr., Sertoma, 1982, Colo. Citizen of Yr., Colo. Assn. Realtors, 1982, Citizen of West, Nat. Western Stockshow, 1994. Mem. Greater Denver C. of C. (pres. 1966-67), U.S. League Savings Instns. (bd. dirs. 1972-77, vice-chmn. 1979-80, chmn. 1980-81, mem. nat. legis. com., exec. com. 1974-77), Savings League Colo. (exec. com. 1969-73, pres. 1971-72), Colo. Assn. Commerce and Industry (dir. 1971-76), Fellowship Christian Athletes (Denver area dir. 1963-76), Western Stock Show Assn. (dir. 1971—, exec. com. 1982-94, 1st v.p. 1985-94, trustee Western Stock Show scholarship trust 2002—), Mountain and Plains Appaloosa Horse Club (pres. 1970-71), Roundup Riders of the Rockies (bd. dirs. 1979-2000, dir. emeritus 2000—, treas. 1980-87, v.p. 1987-89, pres.-elect 1989-91, pres. 1991-93). Republican. Presbyterian. Home: Surrey Ridge Estates 9902 N Heather Dr Castle Rock CO 80108-9133 Personal E-mail: rbarnard01@comcast.net.

BARNARD, SUSAN, literature and language educator; BA, Pomona Coll., 1969. Lang. arts, reading tchr. CHOICE Alternative H.S., Shelton, Wash., 1995—. Vol. Mason County Literacy, 1991—. Finalist Nat. Tchr. of Yr., 2006; named Wash. Tchr. of Yr., 2006. Office: CHOICE Alternative HS 807 W Pine Shelton WA 98584 Business E-Mail: sbarnard@sheltonschools.org.*

BARNARD, TOM, radio personality; b. Minn. Morning Show host 92 KQRS-FM, Mpls. Recipient Marconi Radio award for Large Market Personality of Yr., Nat. Assn. Broadcasters, 2006. Office: 92 KQRS 2000 SE Elm St Minneapolis MN 55414 Office Phone: 612-617-4000. Office Fax: 612-623-9292. E-mail: morningshow@92kqrs.com.*

BARNEA, URI N., rabbi, conductor, musician; b. Petah-Tikvah, Israel, May 29, 1943; came to U.S., 1971; s. Shimon and Miriam Burstein; m. Lizbeth A. Lund, Dec. 15, 1977; 2 children. Tchg. cert., Oranim Music Inst., Israel, 1966; postgrad., Hebrew U., Israel, 1969-71; MusB, Rubin Acad. Music, Israel, 1971; MA, U. Minn., 1974, PhD, 1977; D (hon.), Rocky Mountain Coll., 1999, MAHL, 2007. Music dir. Jewish Cmty. Ctr., Mpls., 1971-73; condr. Youval Chamber Orch., Mpls., 1971-73; asst. condr. U. Minn. Orchs., Mpls., 1972-77; music dir., condr. Unitarian Soc., Mpls., 1973-78, Kenwood Chamber Orch., Mpls., 1974-78, Knox-Galesburg Symphony, 1978-83, Billings (Mont.) Symphony Soc., 1984—2004, Mont. Ballet Co., 1993, 1994, 1998—2005; asst. prof. Knox Coll., Galesburg, Ill., 1978-83; violinist, violist Yellowstone Chamber players, Billings, 1984—2004; violist Tri-City Symphony, Quad-Cities, 1983—84; condr. Cedar Arts Forum String Camp, Cedar Falls, Iowa, 1981—82; rabbi Temple B'nai Israel, Hattiesburg, Miss., 2007—. Guest condr., Ark., Calif., Colo., Fla., Ill., Iowa, Maine, Mich., Minn., Mont., Pa., SD, Va., Wis. European conducting debut, London, Neuchatel and Fribourg, Switzerland, 1986; Can. conducting debut No. Music Festival, North Bay, Ont., 1989; Violin Concerto, 1990; Russian conducting debut Symphony Orch., Kuzbass, Kemerovo, 1993; recordings include: W. Piston's Flute and Clarinet Concertos, Mario Lombardo's Oboe Concerto, two compact discs of Am. music; composer numerous compositions including String Quartet (1st prize Aspen Composition Competition 1976), Sonata for Flute and Piano, 1975 (Diploma of Distinction 26th Viotti Internat. Competition, Italy 1975), Ruth, a ballet, 1974 (1st prize Oberhoffer Composition Contest 1976). Music adv. panel Ill. Arts Coun., 1980-83; v.p. Cmty. Concert Assn., Galesburg, 1980-83; bd. dirs. Knox Coll. Credit Union, Galesburg, 1982-83, Radio Sta. KEMC , Billings, 1984—, Fox Theater Corp., Billings, 1984-86. Recipient Friend of the Arts title Sigma Alpha Iota, 1982, Mont. Gov. Arts award for the arts, 2003, The Tuney award 2004, The Freeman Lacey award 2004; Ill. Arts Coun. grantee, 1979; Hebrew U. Jerusalem scholar, 1972-74, Hebrew U. and Rubin Acad. Mus. scholar, 1969, 70; Individual Artist fellow Mont. Arts Coun., 1986. Mem. NEA (music adv. panel 1990-95), ASCAP, Am. Composers Forum, Condrs. Gukld, Am. String Tchrs. Assn. Home: 1104 Poly Dr Billings MT 59102-1834 Office Phone: 601-545-3871. Personal E-mail: u_barnea@yahoo.com.

BARNEBEY, KENNETH ALAN, food products executive; b. Fremont, Nebr., Apr. 16, 1931; s. Hoyt F. and Mae S. (Mott) B.; m. Faith Price, May 10, 1969; children: Robert, Mark, Holiday, Cindy, Kendra, Valerie, Bonnie, Laurel, Susan. Student, U. Md., 1950, U. Tampa, 1951; BA in Transp., U. Wash., Seattle, 1953; grad. advanced mgmt. program, Harvard U., 1977. With Tropicana Products, Inc., Bradenton, Fla., 1955-80, gen. sales mgr., then v.p. mktg. and sales, 1957-77, exec. v.p., 1977, pres., chief adminstrv. officer, 1977-79, chmn. bd., chief exec. officer, 1979-81, also dir.; corp. v.p. Beatrice Foods, Inc., 1979-81; pres., dir., dep. chmn. Am. Agronomics Corp., Tampa, Fla., 1981-86; bus. acquisition cons. Bradenton, Fla., 1981—. Bd. dirs. Dependable Ins. Group Inc. Am., Exmart, Cmty. Bank Holding Co.; mem. sch. mktg. program Fla. Citrus Dept., 1973—; dir. First Union Bank. Bd. dirs., pres. Am. Acad. Achievement; bd. dirs. Manatee Jr. Coll., Asolo State Theatre, Blowing Rock (N.C.) Hosp., Blowing Rock Stage Co. Theater; mem. Fla. Coun. of 100; adv. coun. Fla. State U.; exec. svc. corp. pres. Manasota Basin Bd. Served with U.S. Army, 1953-55. Mem. Am. Mgmt. Assn. (lectr.), NAM (mktg. adv. com., dir.), Fla. Canners Assn. (mktg. adv. com.), Manatee County C. of C. (dir., chmn. econ. devel. com.) Clubs: Manatee County Exchange (past pres.), Bradenton Country, Blowing Rock Country (past pres.), State of Fla. Govs. Coun. of 100. Home and Office: PO Box 2490 Blowing Rock NC 28605-2490

BARNER, MARK E., minister, consultant; s. Winifred R. Barner. BA, Armstrong State Coll., Savannah, 1984; MDiv, Midwestern Bapt. Theol. Sem., Kansas City, Mo., 1988; MA, Ctrl. Mo. State U., Warrensburg. Cert. pharmacy technician Pharmacy Certification Bd., 2001; med. technician, Mo. Child Care Assn., 1998. Projectionist WSAV-TV, Ga., 1978—84; youth min. First Christian Ch., Butler, Mo., 1985—87; supr., human resource asst. ValueMark Behavioral Healthcare, Kansas City, Mo., 1988—2000; adj. instr. Mo. Western State U., St Joseph, 1994—96; assoc. pastor Gracemor Christian Ch., Kansas City, 2003—. Pres. Kans. City-American Soc. for Tng. & Devel., Kansas City, Mo., 1998—2002. Editor: (newsletter) Mental Notes. Mem.: ASTD (pres. Kansas City chpt. 1998—2002), Mensa (life). Achievements include design of program called Foundations for adult mental health unit assisting patients to understand their psychological processes in terms of faith. Avocations: racquetball, reading, travel. Home Phone: 816-716-5337; Office Phone: 816-454-4919. Personal E-mail: mebarner@cs.com.

BARNES, A. JAMES, dean; b. Napoleon, Ohio, Aug. 30, 1942; s. Albert James and Mary Elizabeth (Morey) Barnes; m. Sarah Jane Hughes, June 19, 1976; children: Morey Elizabeth, Laura LeHardy, Catherine Farrell. BA with high honors, Mich. State U., 1964; JD cum laude, Harvard U., 1967. Asst. prof. bus. adminstrn. Ind. U., 1967—69; trial atty. Dept. Justice, 1969—70, asst. to dep. atty. gen., 1973; asst. to adminstr. EPA, 1970—73; campaign mgr. for Gov. Milliken of Mich., 1974; ptnr. Beveridge, Fairbanks & Diamond, Washington, 1975—81; gen. counsel Dept. Agr., 1981—83; adj. prof. Georgetown U. Sch. Bus. Administrn., Washington, 1978—80; gen. counsel to dep. adminstr. EPA, 1983—85, dep. adminstr., 1985—88; dean Sch. Pub. Environ. Adminstrn., prof. pub. and environ. affairs Ind. U., 1988—2000, prof. pub. and environ. affairs, 1988—, adj. prof. law, 2001—. Spl. counsel Beveridge, Fairbanks & Diamond, Washington, 1988—97; cons., mediator, expert witness Nat. Acad. Pub. Adminstrn., 1988—; adj. prof. law Ind. U., 2001—. Co-author: Essentials of Business Law, 1994, Law of Commercial Transactions and Business Associations, 1995, Bus. Law and the Regulatory Environment, 2000, Law for Bus., 2005, Bus. Law: The Ethical, E-Commerce and Internat. Environ., 12th edit., 2004. Del. Ind. Rep. Conv., 1968, Mich. Rep. Conv., 1974. Named Sagamore of Wabash, 2000; recipient Outstanding Tchg. award, Ind. U., 1969, Trustee Tchg. award, Ind. U., 2005. Fellow: Nat. Acad. Pub. Adminstrn.; mem.: Sagamore of Wabash, Vineyard Haven Yacht Club (Mass.), Edgartown (Mass.) Yacht Club, Met. Club (Washington). Office: Ind U SPEA 418 Bloomington IN 47405 Office Phone: 812-856-2188. Business E-Mail: barnesaj@indiana.edu.

BARNES, ANDREW EARL, former newspaper executive; b. Torrington, Conn., May 15, 1939; s. Joseph and Elizabeth (Brown) B.; m. Marion Otis, Aug. 26, 1960; children: Christopher Joseph, Benjamin Brooks, Elizabeth Cheney. BA, Harvard U., 1961. Reporter, bur. chief Providence Jour., 1961-63; from reporter to edn. editor Washington Post, 1965-73; met. editor, asst. mng. editor St. Petersburg Times, Fla., 1973-75, mng. editor, 1975-84; editor, pres. St. Petersburg (Fla.) Times, 1984-99, CEO, 1988—2004. Chmn. bd. dirs. Congl. Quar., Times Pub. Co., Poynter Inst.; chair Pulitzer prize bd., 2004-05. With USAR, 1963-65. Alicia Patterson fellow, 1969-70 Mem. Newspaper Assn. Am. (chair 2000-01), Am. Soc. Newspaper Editors, Fla. Soc. Newspaper Editors (pres. 1980-81), Internat. Press Inst. Home: 15724 Puckett Rd Dade City FL 33525-7066 Office: Saint Petersburg Times 490 1st Ave S PO Box 1121 Saint Petersburg FL 33731-1121 Home Phone: 727-550-3769; Office Phone: 727-821-9400. E-mail: abarnes@poynter.org.

BARNES, BRENDA C., food products executive; b. Nov. 11, 1953; m. Randall C. Barnes; 3 children. BA in econ., Augustana Coll., 1975, LHD (hon.), 1997; MBA, Loyola U., 1978. With PepsiCo, 1975—98, v.p. mktg. Frito-Lay, bus. mgr. Wilson Spring Sporting Goods; pres. Pepsi-Cola S., 1992; COO Pepsi-Cola N. Am., 1994—96, pres., CEO, 1996—98; interim pres., COO Starwood Hotels & Resorts Worldwide Inc., 1999—2000; COO Sara Lee Corp., Chgo., 2004—05, pres., 2004—05, chmn., CEO, 2005—. Adj. prof. Kellogg Grad. Sch. Mgmt., 2002, N. Central Coll., 2002; bd. dirs. Sara Lee Corp., 2004—, Avon Products Inc., NY Times Co., Sears Roebuck & Co., Staples Inc., Lucas Film, LTD, PepsiAmericas, Inc., Grocery Manufactures Assn. Chair bd. trustees Augustana Coll.; mem. steering com. Kellogg Ctr. for Exec. Women, Northwestern U. Named one of Most Powerful Women, Forbes mag., 2005—06, 50 Women to Watch, Wall Street Journal, 2005, 50 Most Powerful Women in Bus., Fortune mag., 2006. Mem.: Grocery Mfr. Assn. (bd. dir.). Office: Sara Lee Corp 3 First Nat Plz Chicago IL 60602 Office Phone: 312-726-2600.*

BARNES, CARLYLE FULLER, manufacturing executive; b. Bristol, Conn., Feb. 16, 1924; s. Fuller Forbes and Myrtle (Ives) B.; m. Elizabeth Anne May, Oct. 1, 1949; children: Lynne Elizabeth, Janis Lee, Joan Wells, Fuller Forbes. AB, Wesleyan U., 1948. Staff asst. Wallace Barnes Co. div. Barnes Group Inc., 1948-50, gen. mgr., 1951-53, dir., 1951-92, pres., 1953-64, chmn. bd., 1964-77, chmn. exec. com., 1977-94, ret., 1994. Bd. dirs. Bushnell Meml. Hall. Home: Peacedale St Bristol CT 06010

BARNES, CHARLES ANDREW, physicist, researcher; b. Toronto, Ont., Can., Dec. 12, 1921; came to U.S., 1953, naturalized, 1961; m. Phyllis Malcolm, Sept., 1950. BA, McMaster U., Hamilton, Ont., Can., 1943; MA, U. Toronto, 1944; PhD, Cambridge U., Eng., 1950. Physicist Joint Brit.-Canadian Atomic Energy Project, 1944-46; instr. physics U. B.C., 1950-53, 55-56; mem. faculty Calif. Inst. Tech., 1953-55, 56—, prof. physics, 1962-92; prof. emeritus physics, 1992—. Guest prof. Niels Bohr Inst., Copenhagen, 1973-74. Editor, contbr. to profl. books and jours. Recipient medal Inst. d'Astrophysique de Paris, 1986, Alexander von Humboldt U.S. Sr. Scientist award, Fed. Republic of Germany, 1986; NSF sr. fellow Denmark, 1962-63. Fellow AAAS, Am. Phys. Soc. Office: Calif Inst Tech 1201 E California Blvd Pasadena CA 91125-0001

BARNES, CLIVE ALEXANDER, drama and dance critic; b. London, Eng., May 13, 1927; arrived in US, 1965; s. Arthur Lionel and Freda Marguerite (Garratt) Barnes; m. Joyce Elizabeth Tolman (div.); m. Patricia Amy Evelyn Winckley (div.); children: Christopher John Clive, Joanna Rosemary Maya; m. Amy Pagnozzi (div.); m. Valerie Margetson Taylor, July 24, 2004. BA, U. Oxford, Eng., 1951; LittD (hon.), Adelphi U., 1976, Albright Coll., 1982. Co-editor dance mag. Arabesque, 1950; asst. editor Dance and Dancers, 1950-58, assoc. editor, 1958-61, exec. editor, 1961-65, editor NYC, from 1965; writer music, dance, drama, films Daily Express, London, 1956-65; dance critic The Spectator, London, 1959-65, The Times, London, 1962-65, NY Times, NYC, 1965—77, theatre critic, 1967—77; assoc. editor, drama and dance critic NY Post, 1978, dance, opera and sr. theater critic; NY corr. The Evening Standard, London, 1988—91; sr. consulting editor, adv. editor Dance Mag.; contbr. Dance mag., 1956—, reviewer & author, monthly column Attitudes. Adj. prof. dept. journalism NYU, 1968—75. Author: Ballet in Britain Since the War, 1953, Frederick Ashton and His Ballets, 1961, NY Times Directory of the Theatre, 1973, Nureyev, 1982; co-author: Ballet Here and Now, 1961, Dance Scene, USA, 1967, Inside American Ballet Theatre, 1977; co-author: (with Elizabeth Kaye) American Ballet Theatre: A 25 Year Retrospective, 1999; co-author: (with Rose Eichenbaum) Masters of Movement: Portraits of America's Great Choreographers, 2004; co-editor: Best American Plays. With RAF, 1946—48. Decorated Knight Order of Dannebrog Denmark, Comdr. Order Brit. Empire; recipient Dance Mag. award, 2005. Mem.: NY Drama Critics Cir. (pres. 1973—75), Critics Cir. London (past. sec., chmn. ballet sect.), Century Assn. (NY). Office: care NY Post 1211 6th Ave New York NY 10036-8701 Mailing: 241 W 23rd St Apt 4A New York NY 10011-2328 Personal E-mail: clivbar@aol.com.

BARNES, DAVID A., delivery service executive; BBA, U. Mo. Package loader United Parcel Svc., Inc., St. Louis, 1977, various positions UPS Airlines subs., 1986, customer info. mgmt. process mgr., 1998—2001, corp. info. services portfolio coord., 2001—04, sr. v.p., chief info. officer. mem. mgmt. com/, 2005—. Bd. mem. St. Joseph's Mercy Found. Named one of The Premier 100 IT Leaders, Computerworld, 2005. Office: United Parcel Svc Inc 55 Glenlake Pkwy NE Atlanta GA 30328*

BARNES, DONALD MICHAEL, lawyer; b. Hazleton, Pa., June 15, 1943; s. Donald A. and Margaret Barnes; m. Mary Catherine Gibbons, June 3, 1967; children: Donald M., Stephanie A., Susan E. BS in Indsl. Engring., Pa. State U., 1965; JD cum laude, George Washington U., 1970. Bar: D.C. 1970, U.S. Dist. Ct. D.C. 1970, U.S. Ct. Appeals (D.C. cir.) 1970, U.S. Supreme Ct. 1975, U.S. Ct. Appeals (5th cir.) 1980, U.S. Ct. Appeals (4th cir.) 1980, U.S. Ct. Appeals (8th cir.) 1981, U.S. Ct. Appeals (6th cir.) 1993, U.S. Ct. Appeals (10th cir.) 2003. Assoc. Arent, Fox, Kintner, Plotkin & Kahn, Washington, 1970-78, ptnr., 1978-97; mng. shareholder Jenkens & Gilchrist, Washington, 1997-2000; ptnr. Seyfarth Shaw, Washington, 2000—02, Porter Wright Morris & Arthur, LLP, Washington, 2002—. Notes editor: George Washington Law Rev., 1969—70. Mem.: ABA (criminal justice, antitrust, litigation and adminstrv. law sects.), DC Bar Assn., Order of Coif, Phi Delta Phi. Office: Porter Wright Morris & Arthur LLP Ste 500 1919 Pennsylvania Ave NW Washington DC 20006-3434 Office Phone: 202-778-3056. Business E-Mail: dbarnes@porterwright.com.

BARNES, FRANCIS V., school system administrator; BS, Slippery Rock U., 1971; MS, U. Pitts., 1983, PhD, 1986. Dept. chair person, tchr. Pitts. Pub. Bd. of Edn., 1971—85; dean of students Allegheny Middle Sch., 1985—87; asst. HS prin. / dist. staff recruiter North Allegheny Sch. Dist., 1987—88, prin., dist. staff recruiter, 1987—91; supt. Hopewell Area Sch. Dist., 1991—94, Huntingdon Area Sch. Dist., 1994—98, Palisades Sch. Dist., Kintnersville, 1998—2004, 2005—; sec. of edn. Pa. Dept. Edn., 2004—05. Mem. Huntingdon County United Way Edn. Com.; trustee Grandview Hosp. Mem.: AASA (governing bd. mem., membership com.), Pa. Assn. of Sch. Adminstr. (pres. elect 2004, bd. govs.), Phi Delta Kappan. Office: Palisades Sch Dist 39 Short Dr Kintnersville PA 18930 Business E-Mail: fbarnes@palisadessd.org.

BARNES, FRANK STEPHENSON, electrical engineer, educator; b. Pasadena, Calif., July 31, 1932; s. Donald Porter and Thedia (Schellenberg) B.; m. Gay Dirstine, Dec. 17, 1955; children: Stephen, Amy. BS, Princeton U., 1954; MS, Stanford U., 1955, PhD, 1958. Fulbright prof. Coll. Engring., Baghdad, Iraq, 1957-58; rsch. assoc. Colo. Rsch. Corp., Broomfield, 1958-59; assoc. prof. U. Colo., Boulder, 1959-65, prof. dept. elec. engring., 1965—, chmn. dept., 1964-81, faculty rsch. lectr., 1965, acting dean Coll. Engring. and Applied Sci., 1980-81, disting. prof., 1997—, dir. interdisciplinary telecom. program, 1971-75, 88-89, 1996-99; pres. Video Accessory Corp., Boulder, Colo., 2001—. Disting. lectr. IEEE Elec. Device Soc., 1994-01. Regional editor Electronics Letters of Brit. Instn. Elec.Engrs., 1970-75; exec. editor Ann. Rev. Telecom. Bd. dirs. Accreditation Bd. Engring. and Tech., 1980-82. Recipient cert. of merit Internat. Comm. Assn., 1989, Meritorious Svc. award IEEE Edn. Soc., 1993, Leon Montgomery award Internat. Comm. Assn., 1994, Univ. Colo. Centennial Celebration Engring. Recognition award, 1994, Catalyst award Colo. Inst. Tech., 2004, Disting. Rschr. award Internat. Telecomm. Edn. and Rsch. Assn., 2006; fellow Internat. Engring. Consortium, 1995. Fellow AAAS, IEEE (editor Student Jour. 1967-70, mem. G-Ed Adcom 1970-77, v.p. publ. activities 1974-75, pres. device soc. 1974-75, ednl. activities bd. 1976-82, editor IEEE Transactions on Edn. 1988-94, mem. press bd. 1989-90, ednl. activities bd., cert. of merit, Centennial medal, Millennium medal 2000, Edn. Soc. Achievement award 2003); mem. NAE (Bernard M. Gordon prize 2004), Am. Soc. Engring. (Elec. and Computer Engring. Disting. Educator award 2002), Soc. Lasers in Medicine, Engrs. Coun. Profl. Devel. (dir. 1976-82, chmn. com. on advanced level accreditation 1976-78), Biolectromagnetics Soc. (bd. dirs. 1982-84, 96-98, pres. 2000-01), Engring. Info. (bd. dirs. 1984-90). Home: 225 Continental View Dr Boulder CO 80303-4516 Home Phone: 303-499-9144. E-mail: frank.barnes@colorado.edu. *There are always more interesting problems to solve than time to solve them. The trick is to find important problems which can be solved with an effort which is small compared to the value of the results and where one can have a good time learning new ideas at the same time.*

BARNES, FREDERIC WOOD, JR., journalist, political analyst; b. West Point, NY, Feb. 1, 1943; s. Frederic W. and Rosa (Miller) B.; m. Barbara Beatty, Sept. 2, 1967; children: Karen, Sarah, Grace, Frederic W. III. BA in History, U. Va., 1965. Reporter Charleston (S.C.) News Courier, 1965-67, Washington (D.C.) Star, 1967-77, 78-79, Balt. Sun, 1979-85; sr. editor, White House corr. The New Republic, Washington, 1985-95; co-founder, exec. editor The Weekly Standard, Washington, 1995—. Nieman fellow Harvard U., 1977-78; panelist Presdl. debate, Louisville, 1984; regular panelist The McLaughlin Group (TV), Washington, 1988-98; moderator, host Issues in the News on Voice of America, Washington, 1988-; host (syndicated radio show) What's the Story?, 1992-2005; polit. analyst (TV) CBS This Morning, 1990-99; co-host (TV) Beltway Boys, FOX News Channel, 1998-; polit. contbr. FOX News Channel, 1996-; regular contbr. (TV) Special Report with Brit Hume, FOX News Channel; chief corr. (TV Series) National Desk, PBS; nat. polit. corr. Sun; writer "Presspatch", American Spectator. Editor: A Cartoon History of the Reagan Years, 1988; host (syndicated radio show) What's the Story?, 1992-2005; contbr. article to Reader's Digest, NY Times, Wall Street Jour., Spectator, Washingtonian, The Public Interest, Policy Review, Sunday Telegraph and Sunday Times of London; nat. polit. corr. Sun; writer "Presspatch", American Spectator; guest appearances include Nightline, Meet the Press, Face the Nation, and NewsHour with Jim Lehrer; author Rebel-in-Chief, 2006. Bd.dirs. Inst. Religion and Democracy, Fund for Am. Studies. With US Army, 1960—62. Recipient Nat. Fatherhood Initiative award, 2005; named Father of Yr., Father's Day Com., 1994. Mem.: Washington Speakers Bur. Office: The Weekly Standard 1150 17th St NW Ste 505 Washington DC 20036-4617

BARNES, GAIL VANAERNUM, music educator; d. Ronald Lee and Sophia VanAernum; m. Gregory L. Barnes, June 22, 1979; 1 child, Alison Lynn Tisaranni. PhD, Ohio State U., Columbus, 1999. Tchr. Norfolk Pub. Schools, Va., 1978—96; prof. music edn. U. SC Sch. Music, Columbia, 1998—. Dir. String Project U. SC, 1998—. Editor: Applying Research to Teaching and Playing Stringed Instruments. Mem.: Am. String Tchr. Assn. Office: USC Sch Music 813 Assembly St Columbia SC 29204 Home Phone: 803-738-8271; Office Phone: 803-777-3389. Office Fax: 803-777-6508. Business E-Mail: gbarnes@mozart.sc.edu.

BARNES, GREGG, costume designer; Grad., NYU Tisch Sch. Arts, 1983. Resident designer Paper Mill Playhouse, Millburn, NJ. Faculty design dept. NYU Tisch Sch. Arts. Costume designer (tours) On the Record, Ringling Bros. and Barnum and Bailey Circus, Disney's Princess Classics on Ice, Dora the Explorer Live, Anastasia on Ice, Rugrats: A Live Adventure, Blue's Clues Live, Scooby-Doo in Stagefright!, South Pacific, The Wizard of Oz, (Operas) Cinderella, NYC, Merry Widow, (plays) Allegro, Arlington, Va. (Helen Hayes award, 2005), Lucky Duck, San Diego (Craig Noel award, San Diego Theatre Critics Cir., 2004), Pageant, NYC, London's West End, Kathy and Mo Show, NYC, Encores!, Cinderella in a Mirror, Suds, Sweet Release, Dubarry was a Lady, Mame, The Christmas Spectacular, Radio City Music Hall, 1995—2002, Sinatra, (Broadway plays) Sweet Adeline, 1996—97, Side Show, 1997—98, Flower Drum Song, 2002—03 (LA Drama Critics Cir. award, 2002), Dirty Rotten Scoundrels, 2005—, The Drowsy Chaperone, 2006— (Drama Desk award, outstanding costume design, 2006, Tony award, best costume design of a musical, 2006, Outer Critics Cir. award, outstanding costume design, 2006). Recipient Theatre Devel. Fund Irene Sharaff Young Master award, 1994. Office: c/o Marquis Theatre The Drowsy Chaperone 1535 Broadway New York NY 10036

BARNES, HARRY FRANCIS, federal judge; b. Memphis, May 14, 1932; m. Mary Milburn Mann, four children. Student, Vanderbilt U., 1950-52; BS, U.S. Naval Academy, 1956; LLB, U. Ark., 1964. With Pryor & Barnes, Camden, Ark., 1964-66, Barnes & Roberts, Camden, 1966-68, Gaughan, Laney, Barnes & Roberts, Camden, 1968-78, Gaughan, Laney & Barnes, Camden, 1978-82; mcpl. judge Camden and Ouachita Counties, 1975-82; circuit judge 13th jud. dist. State of Ark., 1982-93; judge U.S. Dist. Ct. (we. dist.) Ark., 1993—. Mem. Ark. Jud. Discipline and Disability Commn. With USMC, 1956-86, col. res. ret. Named Outstanding Trial Judge in Ark., Ark. Trial Lawyers Assn., 1986, 2000. Mem. ABA, Ark. Bar Assn., Ark. Jud. Coun. (bd. dirs.). Office: US Dist Ct We Dist PO Box 1735 El Dorado AR 71731-1735 Office Phone: 870-862-1303. Business E-Mail: harry_barnes@arwd.uscourts.com.

BARNES, HARRY G., JR., advocate, consultant; b. St. Paul, June 5, 1926; s. Harry George and Bertha Pauline (Blaul) B.; m. Elizabeth Ann Sibley; children: Pauline, Adrienne, Douglas, Sibley. BA summa cum laude, Amherst Coll., 1949, LLD (hon.), 1984; MA in History, Columbia U., 1968; PhD in Engring. (hon.), Stevens Inst., 1985; LLD (hon.), Monterey Inst. Internat. Studies, 1989. With fgn. service U.S. Dept. State, 1951-88; vice-consul Bombay, 1951-53; vice consul, 2d sec. Prague, Czechoslovakia, 1953-55, Moscow, 1957-59; polit. officer Office of Soviet affairs, Dept. State, Washington, 1959-62; dep. chief mission Kathmandu, Nepal, 1963-67; dep. chief of mission Bucharest, Romania, 1968-71; chief jr. officer program Dept. State, Washington, 1971-72, dep. exec. sec., 1972-74; amb. to Romania Bucharest, 1974-77; dir. gen. fgn. service, dir. pers. Dept. State, Washington, 1977-81; amb. to India, New Delhi, 1981-85, Chile, Santiago, 1985-88; ret.; exec. dir. Critical Langs. and Area Studies Consortium, 1989-94; dir. conflict resolution and human rights programs The Carter Ctr., Atlanta, 1994—2000, chmn. rights com., 1997—2000; sr. advisor Asia Soc., 1999—. Cyrus Vance vis. prof. internat. rels. Mt. Holyoke Coll., spring 1990; Sol Linowitz vis. prof. internat. rels. Hamilton Coll., fall 1990; James and Joan Warburg vis. prof. internat. rels. Simmons Coll., fall 1991-spring 1993; sr. fellow World Wild Life Fund-Conservation Found., 1989-91; interim dir. Human Rights Program Career Ctr., 1993-94, dir. human rights and conflict resolution programs, 1995-2000; chmn. bd. dirs. Romanian-Am. Enterprise Fund, 1996—; pres. Peacham Cmty. Housing, Vt., 2003-. With U.S.Army, 1944-46; pres. Peacham Cmty. Housing, 2002—. Decorated Grand Cross, Order of Bernardo O'Higgins (Chile), 1990; recipient Pres.' Meritorious Svc. award, 1983, 88, Pres.' Disting. Svc. award, 1987. Fellow AAAS. Presbyterian. Home: PO Box 73 Peacham VT 05862-0073 Office Phone: 802-592-3206. Office Fax: 802-592-3046. Personal E-mail: hgbarnes@attglobal.net.

BARNES, HOWARD G., communications executive, film producer; b. NYC, Dec. 27, 1913; m. Joan Lesavoy, Jan. 9, 1949 (div. Nov. 1957); foster children: Marshall Alan (dec.), Denis Joy; m. Mary Ellena Mock, Dec. 7, 1958 (div.); children: Christie Ann, Paul Louis Lloyd; m. Partricia Lee Sills, August 4, 1965 (div.); children: Paxton Louise, Gillian Leigh AB, U. Mich., 1935. Announcer radio sta. WIP, Phila., 1935, KYW, Phila., WHN, NYC, 1936; producer WOR Mut., 1936-38; exec. producer MCA, 1938; producer, writer, exec. CBS, NYC, 1938-46; v.p. in charge network programs CBS Radio, 1955-60; dir. programs CBS-TV, Hollywood, 1960-63; producing independently, 1946-48; v.p. in charge radio and TV Dorland, Inc., NYC, 1948-51; pres. Gen. Entertainment Corp., 1949-60; TV exec. Ashley Famous Agy., Inc., 1963-66; dir. film prodn. Westinghouse Broadcasting Co., NYC, 1966-67, exec. v.p. Group W Films, 1967-73, also dir. parent co.; ind. producer, 1973-89; gen. mgr., dir. advt. The Walking Ctr., Beverly Hills, Calif., 1989-91. Pres. Ragazza Inc., Washington, Conn., 1980-81; bd. govs. Dramalites, Washington, Conn., 1979-89; dir. Trio Films, Ltd., London, 1973-79; ptnr. The Barnes/Sabinson Partnership, 1976-84; exec. dir. Entertainment Hall of Fame Found., 1974-77; cons. film and video Conn. State Dept. Edn., 1985-89; lectr. Sch. Comm., San Diego State U., 1996-97 Lt. USNR, 1942-45 Home and Office: 1930 W San Marcos Blvd Spc 358 San Marcos CA 92078-3930

BARNES, HUBERT LLOYD, geochemistry educator; b. Chelsea, Mass., July 20, 1928; s. George Lloyd and Mary Ellen (MacPherson) B.; m. Mary Talbot Westergaard; children: Roy Malcolm, Catherine Patricia. BS, MIT, 1950; PhD, Columbia U., 1958. Registered Profl. Geologist Pa. Resident geologist Peru Mining Co., Hanover, N.Mex., 1950-52; lectr. geology Columbia U., NYC, 1952-54; postdoctoral fellow Geophys. Lab. Carnegie Inst., Washington, 1956-60; prof. Pa. State U., University Park, 1960-96, dir. ore deposits rsch. sect., 1969-96, emeritus, 1997. Vis. prof. Mineralogy-Petrology Inst., Heidelberg, 1974, Academia Sinica, 1983, U. Sydney, 1987, U. Witwatersrand, 1990; Crosby lectr., MIT, 1983; mem. geophysics rsch. bd. NRC, 1976-80; chmn. US Nat. Com. for Geochemistry, 1976-80; governing bd. Am. Geologic Inst., 1981-83; mem. US Nat. Com. on Geology, 1983-86; gen. chmn. conf., Balt., 1988, co-chmn. Pa. State U., 1995, chmn., sec. symposium, 1985; guest prof. Nanjing U., People's Republic of China, 1996; hon. prof., disting. vis. fellow U. Wales, 1996-2001; pres. Applied Rsch. and Exploration, 1994—2006; cons. Pa. Dept. Transp., 2005-07; cons., lectr. in field. Author: Uranium Prospecting, 1956. Editor: Geochemistry of Hydrothermal Ore Deposits, 1967, 79, 97; co-editor: Hydrothermal Experimental Techniques, 1987; consulting editor Internat. Geol. Rev., 1999-2004. V.p. Pa. chpt. Humboldt Found., 1996-99; cons. Pa. Dept. Transp., 2005—. N.L. Britton scholar, 1955-56; Guggenheim fellow, 1966-67, Japan Soc. Promotion Sci. fellow, 1997; lecturer, World Famous Scientists Forum, Nanjing, 2002; recipient Sr. Humboldt prize Humboldt Found. Germany, 1988; named Disting. Prof. Geochemistry Pa. State U., 1990; Can. Inst. Mining and Metallurgy lectr., 1969, C.F. Davidson lectr., St. Andrews, Scotland, 1971. Fellow Mineral Soc. Am., Geol. Soc. Am., Geochem. Soc. (councillor 1970-73, v.p. 1983, pres. 1984-85, Disting. Svc. award 2003); mem. Soc. Econ. Geologists (councilor 1981-84, Thayer Lindsley lectr. 1980-81, Penrose Gold medal 2002). Democrat. Avocations: skiing, carpentry, classical music, travel. Home: 213 E Mitchell Ave State College PA 16803-3655 Office: Pa State U Dept Geoscis 405 Deike Bldg University Park PA 16802-2711 Home Phone: 814-238-2695; Office Phone: 814-865-7573. Office Fax: 814-238-4327. Business E-Mail: barnes@geosc.psu.edu.

BARNES, JAMES GARLAND, JR., lawyer; b. Ga., Mar. 3, 1940; s. James Garland Sr. and Carolyn L. (Stewart) B.; m. Lucy Curtis Ferguson, Nov. 1976; children: Susan Whitney, David Lawrence, Matthew Martin. BA, Yale U., 1961; LLB, U. Mich., 1966. Bar: Ill. 1967. With firm Baker & McKenzie, Chgo., 1966—, ptnr., 1973—. Co-author: The ABCs of the UCC Article 5: Letters of Credit. Mem. adv. com. Ill. Sec. of State's Corp. Acts, 1981-95; U.S. del. to UN Commn. on Internat. Trade Law, Internat. C. of C., 1994-2000. Mem. ABA (chmn. letter of credit subcom. 1991-96), Ill. Bar Assn. (chmn. corp. and security law sect. 1977-78), Chgo. Bar Assn. (chmn. corp. law com. 1982-83, chmn. profl. responsibility com. 1983-84), Legal Club Chgo. Office: Baker & McKenzie 1 Prudential Pla 130 E Randolph St Ste 3700 Chicago IL 60601-6342 E-mail: james.g.barnes@bakernet.com.

BARNES, JAMES JOHN, historian, educator; b. St. Paul, Nov. 16, 1931; s. Harry George and Bertha (Blaul) B.; m. Patience Rogers Plummer, July 9, 1955; children— Jennifer Chase, Geoffrey Prescott BA, Amherst Coll., 1954, New Coll., Oxford, 1956, MA, 1961; PhD, Harvard U., 1960; DHL,

Coll. of Wooster, 1976, Amherst Coll., 1999. Instr. history Amherst Coll., 1959-62; asst. prof. history Wabash Coll., Crawfordsville, Ind., 1962-67, assoc. prof. history, 1967-76, prof. history, 1976—2006, prof. emeritus, 2006—, chmn. dept. history, Hadley prof., 1979-97. Author: Free Trade in Books: A Study of the London Book Trade since 1800, 1964, Authors, Publishers and Politicians: The Quest for an Anglo-American Copyright Agreement 1815-54, 1974, (with Patience P. Barnes) Hitler's Mein Kampf in Britain and America 1930-39, 1980, (with Patience P. Barnes) James Vincent Murphy: Translator and Interpreter of Fascist Europe, 1880-1946, 1987, (with Patience P. Barnes) Private and Confidential Letters from British Ministers in Washington to the Foreign Secretaries in London, 1849-67, 1993, (with Patience P. Barnes) Nazi Refugee turned Gestapo Spy: The Life of Hans Wesemann, 1895-1971, 2001, (with Patience P. Barnes) The American Civil War through British Eyes: Dispatches from British Diplomats, vol. 1: Nov. 1860-Apr. 1862, 2003, vol. 2: April 1862-February 1863, 2005, vol. 3: February 1863-December 1865, 2005; (with Patience P. Barnes) Nazis in Pre-War London 1930-1939: The Fate and Rule of German Party Members and British Sympathizers, 2005; contbr. articles to profl. jours. Mem. Rhodes Scholar Selection Com. for Ind., 1965-89, Crawfordsville Cmty. Action Coun., 1966-69, Crawfordsville Cmty. Day Care Com., 1966-67; mem. vestry St. John's Episcopal Ch., 1966-69; mem. Ind. Adv. Com. State Rehab. Svcs. for Blind, 1979-81; trustee Ind. Hist. Soc., 1982—. Recipient Disting. Alumni award St. Paul Acad. and Summit Sch., 1989; Rhodes scholar, 1954-56, Fulbright scholar, 1978; Woodrow Wilson fellow, 1956-57, Kent fellow, 1958, Great Lakes Colls. Assn. Teaching fellow, 1958, Great Lakes Colls. Assn. Teaching fellow, 1975; rsch. grantee Amherst Coll., 1960-61, Social Sci. Rsch. Coun., 1962, 70, Wabash Coll., 1962—, Am. Coun. Learned Socs., 1964-65, 80, Am. Philos. Soc., 1964, 68, 76, 91; named Hon. Alumnus, Wabash Coll., 1994. Mem. Am. Hist. Assn., Ouiatenon Literary Soc., Conf. Brit. Studies, Rsch. Soc. Victorian Periodicals, Am. Rhodes Scholars, Soc. Historians Am. Fgn. Rels., Ind. Hist. Soc., Montgomery County Hist. Soc., Midwest Victorian Studies Assn. (pres. 1989-91), Ind. Assn. Historians, N.E. Victorian Studies Assn., Soc. for History of Authorship, Reading and Pub., Am. Coun. of Blind, Royal Over-Seas League (London), United Oxford and Cambridge Club of London, Phi Beta Kappa. Home: 7 Locust Hl Crawfordsville IN 47933-3347 Office: Wabash Coll History Dept Crawfordsville IN 47933 Office Phone: 765-361-6319. Business E-Mail: barnesj@wabash.edu.

BARNES, JAMES MILTON, retired physics and astronomy professor; b. Ypsilanti, Mich., July 5, 1923; s. J. Milton and Elsie (Fischer) B.; m. Marjorie Ruth Petersen, Dec. 17, 1949. BS, Eastern Mich. U., 1948; MS, Mich. State U., 1950, PhD, 1955. Asst. prof. Ea. Mich. U., Ypsilanti, 1955—58, assoc. prof., 1958—61, prof., 1961—88, head, dept. physics and astronomy, 1961—74, prof. emeritus, 1988—. With AUS, 1942—46. Mem. A.A.A.S. (life), Nat. Sci. Tchrs. Assn. (life), Am. Assn. Physics Tchrs., Sigma Xi, Sigma Pi Sigma, Pi Mu Epsilon. Clubs: Ann Arbor (Mich.) Country. Home: 4872 N Whitman Cir Ann Arbor MI 48103-9774 Office: Eastern Mich U Physics Dept Ypsilanti MI 48197

BARNES, JHANE ELIZABETH, fashion design company executive, designer; b. Balt., Mar. 4, 1954; d. Richard Amos and Muriel Florence (Chase) B.; m. Howard Ralph Feinberg, Dec. 12, 1981 (div.); m. 2d, Katsuhiko Kawasaki, Feb. 12, 1988. A.S., Fashion Inst. Tech., 1975. Pres., designer Jhane Barnes for ME, NYC, 1976-78; pres., designer, owner Jhane Barnes Inc., NYC, 1978—; owner Jhane Barnes Textiles, LLC, 1998—. Recipient Coty award Menswear Am. Fashion Critics, 1980, 1984, Contract Textile award Am. Soc. Interior Designers, 1983, 84, Product Design awards Inst. Bus. Designers and Contract Mag., 1983-86, 94, Outstanding Am. Menswear Designer award Woolmark, 1990, Dalmore, 1990, Good Design award 1997, 98, 99, Best of Neo Con award. I.D. 40, 1996, 97, 98, 99, 2000; named Most Promising Designer Cutty Sark, 1980, Outstanding Designer, 1982, Outstanding Menswear Designer, Coun. of Fashion Designers Am., 1982, Design Resources Coun., 1989, 94, Designer of Yr., Neckwear Assn. Am., 1997. Office: Jhane Barnes Inc 119 W 40th St Fl 20 New York NY 10018-2500 Fax: 212-575-2506.

BARNES, JOHN D., health science association administrator; BSBA, Creighton U., 1982. Dir. govt. and pub. affairs Steel Tank Inst.; spl. asst. to US Senator Charles E. Grassley US Senate; chief of staff to US Rep. Greg Ganske US Ho. of Reps.; assoc. exec. dir. govt. rels. and health policy Am. Acad. Dermatology Assn., Am. Acad. Dermatology, 1999—2005, dep. exec. dir., 2005—07; CEO Am. Phys. Therapy Ass., Alexandria, Va., 2007—. Office: Am Physical Therapy Assn 1111 N Fairfax St Alexandria VA 22314-1488 Office Phone: 703-684-2782. Office Fax: 703-684-7343. E-mail: johnbarnes@apta.org.*

BARNES, JOY CHAPPELL, lawyer; b. Talladega, Ala., Aug. 24, 1950; d. George Daniel and Barbara Joyce (Riggleman) Chappell; m. L. Randolph Barnes, May 28, 1969 (dec. Mar. 1970); m. D. Gordon Lewis, Mar. 19, 1983. BA, U. Ala., Birmingham, 1980, JD, 1986. Bar: Ala. 1986, U.S. Dist. Ct. (no. dist.) Ala. 1986, U.S. Dist. Ct. (mid. dist.) Ala. 1987. Br. sec. Stromberg Time Products, Birmingham, 1970-71; sec. Hobbs Trailers/Fruehauf, Birmingham, 1971-72; office mgr. Tidwell Trailer & Equipment, Birmingham, 1972-75; asst. U. Ala., Birmingham, 1978-79; owner, operator Live Wires, Birmingham, 1979-82; assoc. Costello & Stott, Birmingham, 1986-87; ptnr. Livingston & Barnes, Birmingham, 1987-90; sole practitioner Birmingham, 1990—. Tchr. spl. studies U. Ala., Birmingham, 1988. Mem. ABA, State Bar Ala., Birmingham Bar Assn., Assn. Trial Lawyers Am., Ala. Trial Lawyers, Ala. Soc. Blue Tennie Club (pres.), Downtown Dem. Club, Sigma Delta Kappa (alumni advisor 1987-89). Democrat. E-mail: joy.chappell.barnes@gmail.com.

BARNES, JUDITH ANN, real estate company executive; b. Milw., Mar. 10, 1949; d. Einar and Eleanor Svea (Russell) B.; divorced; children: Krista Svea, Erik Leif. BA, Gustavus Adolphus Coll., 1970; grad., Wis. Sch. Real Estate, Milw., 1979; postgrad., Carroll Coll., 1980, U. Wis., 1978—80, postgrad., 1992. Tchr. Oak Grove Mid. Sch., Bloomington, Minn., 1970—71, Mukwonago H.S., Wis., 1971—72; sales mgr. Lincoln Park Homes, West Allis, Wis., 1972—73, v.p., 1973—74, pres., 1974—97, Palm Coast, Fla., 1997—2000; assoc. Coldwell Banker Comml. (Nicholson-Williams), 2000—01; with Hammock Dunes Real Estate Co., 2001—. Chmn. Mfrd. Housing Subdivision S.E. Wisc., Madison, 1978-80; sec. Southeastern Wis. Housing, Milw., 1981-82, treas., 1982-84. Bd. dirs. Waukesha YMCA, 1985-87, v.p. 1987-89; bd. dirs. YMCA Heritage Found., 1994-97, Waukesha County United Way, 1984-87, Hammock Dune Homeowners Assn., 2004-06; coun. pres. Stetson U., 1996-2000; mem. alumni bd. Gustavus Adulphus Coll., St. Peter, Minn., 1974-80; trustee The Cooper Inst., Naples, Fla., 1987-93, mem. adv. bd., 1993—. Recipient Dedicated Svc. award Wis. Mfrd. Housing, 1975-84, 88, Vol. of Yr. award Univ. Lake Sch., 1995. Mem. Wis. Mfrd. Housing Assn. (bd. dirs. 1975-80), Ind. Bus. Assn. Wis. (trustee U. Lake 1991-96), Merrill Hills Country Club (chair golf 1991), Milw. Women's Dist. Golf Assn. (bd. dirs. 1993, v.p. 1994, pres. 1995-96), Vasa Lodge, Hammock Dunes Country Club (adv. bd.). Republican. Lutheran. Avocations: golf, photography. Home: 3 Anastasia Ct Palm Coast FL 32137-2273 Personal E-mail: jbhd@bellsouth.net.

BARNES, JULIAN E., editor; BA, Harvard Coll., 1993. Reporter Ark. Democrat-Gazette, Little Rock, 1993—96; assoc. editor US News & World Report, Washington, 1996—98, sr. editor; with NY Times, 1998—2001. Co-recipient Overseas Press Club award for best mag. reporting, 2006. Office: US News & World Report 1050 Thomas Jefferson St NW Washington DC 20007 Office Phone: 202-955-2304. Office Fax: 202-955-2049. E-mail: jbarnes@usnews.com.

BARNES, KAREN KAY, lawyer; b. June 22, 1950; d. Walter William and Vashti (Greenlee) Sessler; m. James Alan Barnes, Feb. 12, 1972; children: Timothy Matthew, Christopher Michael. BA, Valparaiso U., 1971; JD, DePaul U., 1978, LLM in Taxation, 1980. Bar: Ill. 1978, U.S. Dist. Ct. (no. dist.) Ill. 1978. Ptnr. McDermott, Will & Emory, Chgo., 1978-88; prin. William M. Mercer, Inc. and predecessor firm, Chgo., 1989-93; staff dir. legal dept. McDonald's Corp., Oak Brook, Ill., 1993-95, home office dir. legal dept., 1995-97, mng. counsel, 1998—. Instr. John Marshall Grad. Sch. Law, Chgo., 1986-87; mem. adv. bd. John Marshall Sch. Law, 1996-2004; bd. dirs. Flutes Unlimited; mem. adv. bd. dirs. Plan Sponsor Mag., 2000-; mem. defined contbn. adv. bd. Internat. Bus. Forum, Inc., 2004-. Contbr. case note to DePaul Law Rev., 1976, note and comment editor DePaul Law Rev., 1976-77, editor Taxation For Lawyers, 1986-88; mem. editl. adv. bd. Thompson Pub. Co. retirement plan comms., 2005—. Named one of 50 Most Influential People in 401(k) Industry, 401(k) Wire, 2007. Mem. Am. Coll. Employee Benefit Counsel (bd. dirs. 2006-), Chgo. Bar Assn. (chair employee benefits com. 1991-92, co-chair symphony orch. 1999-2001), Midwest Pension Conf. (name changed to Midwest Benefits Coun.), WEB (pres. Chgo. chpt. 1986-88, v.p. nat. bd. 1988, pres. 1989-90, mem. adv. bd. 2001—), Profit Sharing Coun. Am. (legal and legis. com. 1994—, bd. dirs. 1997-2004, 06-, 2d vice chair 1997-98, 1st vice chair 1998-2000, chair 2000-02). Lutheran. Home: 586 Crescent Blvd # 402 Glen Ellyn IL 60137 Office: McDonald's Corp 2915 Jorie Blvd Oak Brook IL 60523 Business E-Mail: karen.barnes@us.mcd.com.

BARNES, KAY, former mayor; b. Mar. 30, 1938; BS in Secondary Edn., U. Kans.; MS in Secondary Edn. and Pub. Adminstrn., U. Mo., Kansas City. Staff mem. Westport area Cross-Lines Coop. Coun.; pres. Kay Waldo, Inc., human resources devel. co., Kansas City, Mo.; mayor City of Kansas City, Mo., 1999—2007; candidate for U.S. Congress, 2007. Condr. over 400 pub. seminars Nat. Seminars, Inc.; cons., keynote spkr. 14 reginal confs. through U.S., Am. Bus. Women's Assn.; former co-host, prodr. cable TV show Let's Talk; former instr. U. Mo., Kansas City, U. Kans., Ctrl. Mich. U. Author: About Time! A Woman's Guide to Time Management. Co-founder Ctrl. Exch.; vol. Cross-Lines Coop. Coun.; a founder women's resource svc. U. Mo., Kansas City; developer multicultural women's speaking panels through western U.S.; mem. Jackson County (Mo.) Legislature, from 1974; mem. Kansas City City Coun., from 1979; chmn. Tax Increment Financing Commn., 1993-97; pres. bd. dirs. Women's Employment Network; mem. or dir. numerous other orgns., including Women's Found. Greater Kansas City, Greater Kansas City Sports Commn.; mem. chancellor's adv. bd. of Women's Ctr., U. Mo., Kansas City; co-chair of the US Conf. of Mayors Small Business/Partner America Task Force, mem. of the Conference's Community Development and Housing Standing Com.; serves Nat. Adv. Coun. of Fannie Mae. Named One of 7 Outstanding Women in Kansas City, 1977. Mem. Greater Kansas City C. of C. (com.). Home: Kay for Congress PO Box 14194 Kansas City MO 64152 Office Fax: 816-513-3518. Business E-Mail: mayor@kcmo.org.*

BARNES, KEITH LEE, electronics executive; b. San Francisco, Sept. 14, 1951; s. Arch Lee and Charlotte Mae (Sanborn) B.; m. Sharon Ann Tosaw, June 9, 1986; children: Allecia, Alexandra, Wyatt. BS, Calif. State U., San Jose, 1976. Mgr. engring. and mktg. Gould, Inc., Rolling Meadow, Ill., 1976-79; v.p., gen. mgr. Kontron Electronics, Mountain View, Calif., 1979-85; v.p. Valley Data Scis., Mountain View, 1985-86; pres., CEO Integrated Measurement Sys., Beaverton, Oreg., 1986-2000, chmn., CEO, 2000—. Bd. dirs. Data Io Corp., LWG, Inc., Clarity Visual Systems, Inc. Patentee in field. Bd. dirs. Am. Electronics Assn., 1992-93, chmn. Oreg. bd., 1993; trustee Oreg. Grad. Inst. for Sci. and Industry, 1996—; vice chair Oreg. Growth Account, 1998; regent U. Portland, 2000. Mem. IEEE, PGC. Republican. Roman Catholic. Office: Integrated Measurements Systems, Inc 5975 NW Pinefarm Pl Hillsboro OR 97124-8563

BARNES, LILI DARNELLE, music educator, director; b. Cleve., Sept. 5, 1956; d. Johnes Green and Dorothy Mae Bradford; m. Robert Timothy Barnes, Nov. 28, 1998; 1 child, Garrett Paul Bradford. MusB, Heidelberg Coll., 1978; MEd, Trenton State U., 1993; postgrad., Boston U., 2004—. Cert. tchg. Ohio, 1993. Music tchr. Wickliffe Elem., Ohio, 1978—87, vocal music dir., 1987—91, Wickliffe Mid. Sch., 1993—2000; music dept. chair Wickliffe City Schs., 1997—2004; musical dir. Wickliffe HS & Mid. Sch., 1988—91, 1993—; vocal music dir. Wickliffe HS, 2003—, Dhahran Sch., Saudi Arabia, 1991—93, musical dir., 1992. Conf. presenter Ohio Mid. Sch. Assn., Toledo, 1994—95, Cleve., 1994—95. Recipient The Golden Apple Achiever award, Ashland U., 1998; grantee SMARTKids grant, SMARTBoard, 2003. Mem.: Wickliffe Edn. Assn. (pres. 2003—, v.p. 2000—03), Rotary Internat., Wickliffe Chpt. Baptist. Avocations: horseback riding, swimming, computers, poetry, music composition. Home: 1733 E 298th St Wickliffe OH 44092 Office: Wickliffe HS 2255 Rockefeller Rd Wickliffe OH 44092 Office Phone: 440-944-0800.

BARNES, MADGE LOU, physician; b. Clayton, NC, Nov. 30, 1958; BA in Biology & Premed, East Carolina U., Greenville, NC, 1981, MD, 1987. Diplomate Am. Bd. Family Medicine, 2004. Cert. CDL examiner CONCENTRA, Dallas, 2004—; med. dir. Concentra Occupl. Health, Ft. Worth, 2004—05; med. dir. pub. health divsn. Environ. & Health Svcs., Dallas, 2006—; pub. health official Office Emergency Mgmt., Dallas. Bd. pres. Celebrating Life Found., Dallas, 1999—2002; mentor, spkr. debutante program Potter's Ho. Ch., 2001—; mentor, spkr. Tng. for Excellence, 2003. Named one of Am. Top Family Doctors, Consumers' Rsch. Coun. Am., 2007; recipient Mentor Yr. award, Core Debutante Program, 2005. Fellow: Am. Acad. Family Physicians; mem.: Primary Care Network, Lead Coalition, Am. Acad. Family, Tex. Med. Assn., Dallas County Med. Soc., Tex. Acad. Family Physicians, Childhood Obesity Coalition, Am. Heart Assn., African Am. and Hispanic Coalitions. Nondenominational. Avocations: travel, sports, reading, history. Office: 2922 Mlk Blvd B Bldg Ste 301 Dallas TX 75215 Business E-Mail: madge.barnes@dallascityhall.com.

BARNES, MARJORIE, poet, educator; BA, Richard Stockton Coll.; MA, Temple U. Performance poet; toured with Afro-One Dance, Drama and Drum Theatre; assoc. prof. developmental English Union County Coll., 1993—; poet Geraldine R. Dodge Found., 2001—. Founder Sacred Circle Cafe. Performance poet (poetry CD) My Blues Ain't Over Yet, 2006. Grantee, NJ Performing Arts Ctr., 2001, The Puffin Found., 2005, Newark Arts Coun., 2005. Mem.: Cave Canem poetry group. Office: Union County Coll 12 W Jersey St Elizabeth NJ 07201-2314*

BARNES, MARK JAMES, lawyer; b. Oak Park, Ill., Jan. 10, 1957; s. James W. and Lorraine (Brady) B.; m. Ellice Halpern, 1988; children: Julia Elizabeth, Katherine Claire, John Halpern. BS in Polit. Sci. summa cum laude, Ariz. State U., 1978; JD, UCLA, 1981. Staff atty. Senator Ted Stevens U.S. Senate, Washington, 1981-83, chief counsel Senator Ted Stevens, 1983-84; assoc. Davis, Wright & Jones, Anchorage, 1984-86; dep. gen. counsel U.S. Office of Personnel Mgmt., Washington, 1986-87; assoc. dir. adminstrn. U.S. Office Personnel Mgmt., Washington, 1988-89; counsel to sec. for drug abuse policy HHS, Washington, 1989-93; pvt. practice Washington, 1993—. Alaska ambassador organizing com. Anchorage Olympics, 1986; mem. exec. com., World Forum on Future of Sport Shooting Activities, 1998—. Mem. ABA, Alaska Bar Assn., Ariz. Bar Assn., D.C. Bar Assn., Phi Beta Kappa. Republican. Roman Catholic. Avocations: travel, movies, stamps. Office: 1350 Eye St NW Ste 1255 Washington DC 20005-3390 Office Phone: 202-626-0089. Personal E-mail: markb17@aol.com.

BARNES, MARYLOU RIDDLEBERGER, retired academic administrator; b. Bridgewater, Va., Feb. 27, 1930; d. Hensel Dorsey Riddleberger and Ruby Elizabeth Heltzel; children: Tenley Elizabeth, Rachel Patricia. BS, Madison Coll., 1952; MS, Med. Coll. Va., 1957; MA, James Madison U., 1968; EdD, W. Va. U., 1975; DSc (hon.), U. Indpls., 1993. From staff phys. therapist to dir. clin. edn. Woodrow Wilson Rehab. Ctr., Fishersville, Va., 1958-64, dir clin. edn., 1964-67; chief phys. therapy Rockingham Meml. Hosp., Harrisonburg, Va., 1958-59; prof., dir., chair dept. phys. therapy W. Va. U., Morgantown, W. Va., 1968-79; from prof., chair dept. phys. therapy to prof. emeritus Ga. State U., Atlanta, 1979-95, ret., 1995, prof. emeritus, 1995—. Adv. bd. Perry Inst., Strafford, Pa., 1993-95; co-chair program com. Joint Am.-Can. Phys. Therapy Annual Conf. Author: Patient at Home, 1972, Neurophysiological Basis of Physical Therapy Care, vol. I, 1973, vol. II, 1977, Physical Therapy, 1989, Motor Control and Motor Learning in Rehabilitation, 1993; contbr. articles to profl. jours. Vol. Centennial Olympic Games, Atlanta, 1996, Goodwill Industries Book Ctr., Atlanta, 1999. Mem. Am. Phys. Therapy Assn. (nat. survey pool for accreditation of schs. 1974-95, pres. neurology sect. 1985-87, task force on profl. devel. 1994, chair continuing edn. bd. 1994-95, Mary McMillan Lectr. award 1992, Catherine Worthingham fellow 1994, leadership in edn. award 1995, svc. to neurology sect. award 1998, Lucy Blair Svc. award 1988). Presbyterian. Avocations: amateur archaeologist, travel, reading, tree climbers of am. Home: 133 Santolina Park Peachtree City GA 30269-3245 E-mail: mloubarnes@mindspring.com.

BARNES, NANCY, editor-in-chief; b. Cambridge, Mass., 1962; m. Sam Barnes; 3 children. BA, U. Va., 1982; MBA, U. NC, Chapel Hill. Sunday editor Raleigh (NC) News & Observer; asst. mng. editor for bus. Star Tribune, Mpls., 2003—05, dep. mng. editor for enterprise, 2005, dep. mng. editor for content, 2005—07, editor & sr. v.p., 2007—. Office: Star Tribune 425 Portland Ave Minneapolis MN 55488 Office Phone: 612-673-7937. E-mail: nancyb@startribune.com.*

BARNES, NED MACLIN, lawyer; b. Spokane, Wash., Oct. 28, 1936; s. Edwin King and Mary Maclin Barnes; m. Linda Clark Barnes; children: Eric, Mitchel, Katherine Warner. BBA, U. Minn., MN, 1958; JD, U. Wash., Seattle, 1961. Ea. Dist. Ct.: Wash. Lawyer Witherspoon, Kelley, Davenport, Spokane, Wash., 1965—. Dir. Sterling Savs. Bank, Spokane, Wash., 1985—, Sterling Fin. Corp., Spokane, Wash., 1985—2006; sch. advisor Wash. State U. Sch. Bus., Pullman, Wash., 1993—2006. Dir. Spokane Mental Health Assn., Spokane, Wash., 1967—2007; trustee Spokane Libr. Found., Spokane, Wash., 1989—2007; dir. Downtown Spokane Partnership, Spokane, Wash., 1997—2005; mem. Internat. Trade Alliance, Spokane, Wash., 1997—2007. Capt. USAF, 1962—65, New York. Mem.: Pacific Real Estate Inst., Am. Coll. of Real Estate Lawyers, Spokane Athletic Club, Manito Country Club. Avocations: golf, skiing. Office: Witherspoon Kelley Davenport & Toole 422 West Riverside Ste 1100 Spokane WA 99201 Office Phone: 509-624-5265. Office Fax: 509-458-2728. Business E-Mail: nmb@wkdtlaw.com.

BARNES, PETER, federal official; b. Cambridge, Mass., Apr. 13, 1940; s. Tracy Barnes and Janet (White) Lawrence; m. Jan Adair; children from previous marriage: K. Tracy, John E. BA magna cum laude, Yale U., 1962; LLB cum laude, Harvard U., 1965. Bar: DC 1966, Md. 1984. Assoc. Leva, Hawes, Symington, Martin & Oppenheimer, Washington, 1965-71, ptnr., 1971-73, Venable, Baetjer & Howard, Balt., 1983-86; ptnr., shareholder Swidler & Berlin, Chtd., Washington, 1987—98; mem. Swidler Berlin Shereff Friedman, LLP, Washington, 1998-99, counsel, 1999—2001; spl. asst. to gen. counsel US Govt. Printing Office, Washington, 2004—07, project mgr., 2007—. Mem.: Elkridge Club, Met. Club. Home: 4 Deep Run Ct Cockeysville MD 21030-1600 Personal E-mail: peterbarnesc@aol.com.

BARNES, RICHARD GEORGE, physicist, researcher; b. Milw., Dec. 19, 1922; s. George Richard and Irma (Ott) B.; m. Mildred A. Jachens, Sept. 9, 1950; children: Jeffrey R., David G., Christina E., Douglas A. BA, U. Wis., 1948; MA, Dartmouth Coll., 1949; PhD, Harvard U., 1952. Teaching fellow Harvard, 1950-52; asst. prof. U. Del., 1952-55, assoc. prof., 1955-56, Iowa State U., 1956-60, prof., 1960-88, chmn. dept. physics, 1971-75, prof. emeritus, 1988—; sr. physicist Ames Lab., U.S. Dept. Energy, 1960-88; assoc. Ames lab. US Dept. Energy, 1988—; chief physics divsn. Ames lab. AEC, 1971-75. Vis. rsch. prof. Calif. Inst. Tech., 1962-63; guest profl. Tech. U. Darmstadt, Germany, 1975-76; vis. prof. Cornell U., 1982-83; program dir. solid state physics NSF, 1988-89, condensed matter physics NSF, 1995; chmn. Metal Hydrides Gordon Rsch. Conf., 1987. Served with USAAF, 1942-43; C.E. AUS, 1944-46 (Manhattan Project). Recipient U.S. Sr. Scientist award Alexander von Humboldt Found., 1975-76 Fellow Am. Phys. Soc. Office: Iowa State U Physics Dept Ames IA 50011-0001

BARNES, RICK (RICHARD DALE BARNES), men's college basketball coach; b. Hickory, NC, July 17, 1954; m. Candace, July 31, 1976; children: Nicholas, Caroline. Grad. in Health and Phys. Edn., Lenoir-Rhyne Coll., Hickory, NC, 1977, LHD (hon.), 2005. Head coach North State Acad., 1977-78; asst. coach Davidson Coll., 1978-80, George Mason U., 1980-85, U. Ala., 1985-86, Ohio State U., 1986-87; head coach George Mason U., 1987-88, Providence Coll., 1988-94, Clemson U., 1994-98, U. Tex., Austin, 1998—. Named Dist. 1 Coach of Yr., Nat. Assn. Basketball Coaches, 1989, Dist. 9 Coach of Yr., Nat. Assn. Basketball Writers, 1999, 2001, 2003, Dist. 7 Coach of Yr., US Basketball Writers Assn., 1999, 2001, All-S.W. Coach, Basketball Times, 1999, Big 12 Conf. Coach of Yr., 1999, 2003; named to Hall of Fame, Lenoir-Rhyne Coll., 2002; recipient Disting. Alumnus award, 1997. Achievements include being head coach of the 2006 Big 12 champions. Office: Mens Basketball U Tex Intercollegiate Athletics PO Box 7399 Austin TX 78713-7399 Office Phone: 512-471-5816. E-mail: rick.barnes@athletics.utexas.edu.*

BARNES, ROBERT F, agronomist; b. Estherville, Iowa, Feb. 6, 1933; s. Chester Arthur and Pearl Adella (Stoelting) B.; m. Bettye Jeanne Burrell, June 25, 1955; children: Bradley R., Rebecca L. Reinalda, Roberta K. Nixon, Brian L. AA, Estherville Jr. Coll., 1953; BS, Iowa State U., 1957; MS, Rutgers U., 1959; PhD, Purdue U., 1963. Rsch. agronomist USDA-Agrl. Rsch. Svc., West Lafayette, Ind., 1959-70, lab. dir. University Park, Pa., 1970-75, staff scientist nat. program staff Beltsville, Md., 1975-79, assoc. dep. adminstr. So. region New Orleans, 1979-84, dep. adminstr. So. region, 1984-86; exec. v.p. Am. Soc. Agronomy, Madison, Wis., 1986-99; exec. dir. Agronomic Sci. Found., exec. dir. emeritus, 1999—; also fellow Am. Soc. of Agronomy, Madison, Wis. Asst. prof. Purdue U., West Lafayette, 1963-66; assoc. prof., 1966-70; adj. prof. Pa. State U., University Park, 1966-70; adj. prof. agronomy U. Wis., Madison, 1986-99; pres. Internat. Grassland Congress, Lexington, Ky., 1981; cons. Agronomic Sci. Found., Am. Soc. Agronomy. Editor: Forages, 1973, 85, 95, 2003; contbr. articles to profl. jours. With U.S. Army, 1953-55, Germany. Recipient H.S. Stubbs Meml. Lecture award Tropical Grassland Soc., Brisbane, Australia, 1984, Henry A. Wallace award Iowa State U., 1991; Robert F Barnes Grad. Edn. Award for forage and grazing lands established in his name, 2004. Fellow AAAS, Crop Sci. Soc. Am. (pres. 1984-85); mem. Am. Forage and Grassland Coun. (medallion 1981, Disting. Grasslander award 2001), Grazing Lands Forum (pres. 1986-87), Forage and Grassland Found. (pres. 1993-97). Avocations: walking, reading. Personal E-mail: rbarnes0206@sbcglobal.net.

BARNES, ROBERT VERTREESE, JR., construction executive; b. Dallas, Oct. 7, 1946; s. Robert Vertreese and Doris Corinne (Haffen) B.; m. Deborah Dee Brown, May 31, 1968; children: Robert V. III, John David, Leslie Shannon. BS in Indsl. Tech., Tex. A&M U. Commerce, 1976. Registered bldg. contractor, Ariz., 1992; registered and cert. bldg. contractor, Fla., 1994; gen. comml. contractor, Ariz. Salesman Sears, Roebuck and Co., Dallas, 1965-66, dept. mgr., 1967-69; estimator Dee Brown Masonry,

Inc., Dallas, 1969—75, contract adminstr., 1976-77, v.p. Houston, 1980-85, exec. v.p., 1985—89; v.p. Cardinal Masonry Co., Houston, 1978-79; exec. v.p. Dee Brown, Inc., Houston, 1986—89, pres., COO, 1990-99, chmn., pres., CEO, 2000—. V.p., sec./treas., dir. Shiloh Investment Co., 1974-99, chmn., pres., dir. 2000—; mem. exec. com. Contrn. Rsch. Ctr. U. Tex., Arlington, 1992-, vice chmn., 1994, chmn. elect, 1995, chmn., 1996; pres. Stone Erectors, Inc., 1989-93; exec. v.p. Dee Brown Masonry/Hatch, Inc., 1989-90, chmn. 2000—; pres., CEO, dir. Masonry Tech., Inc., 1993-95, chmn., pres., CEO, 1996-2002; dir. Stone Anchors, Inc., 1993-2003; ptnr. Pacific Waterjet, LLC, 1996-2003, Skinner Marble and Granite LLC, 1997-99; mng. ptnr. Kepco & DBI, LLC, 1995-; mng. dir. Salesmanship Club Dallas, 1997—; trustee, chmn. Bricklayers Health and Welfare, 1983-85, Bricklayer Pension Fund, Houston, 1983-85; pres. Youngblood Masonry, Inc., 2000—; mem. arch. and constrn. com. Dallas Arboretum, 2000—, chmn., 2003—, exec. com., 2003—; dir. Innovative Masonry, Inc., 2003-. Coach Katy Youth Soccer Assn., 1978-81, mem., pres., 1980-81, Richardson Youth Soccer Assn., 1976-77; team mgr. Solar "74" Soccer Club, 1986-88, Diggers Soccer Club, 1989-92; mem. bd. White Rock Ch.'s Ath. Assn., 1972-77, commr. baseball, 1976-77; trustee, chmn. Bricklayer Health and Welfare, Houston, 1983-85; bishop warden, com. St. Cuthbert's Episcopal Ch., 1985-86, vestry mem., fin. com., 1999-2001, chmn. fin. com., 2000-2001; bd. dirs. St. John's Episcopal Sch., 1987-93, v.p., 1988-89, sch. fin. com., health, safety and ins. com., bldg. facility com., chmn. bldg. and grounds com., 1988-90, co-chmn. devel. com., vestry mem., fin. com., ath. dir., 1999-2001, co-chmn. bldg. campaign, 2003-; trustee Episcopal Found. Diocese, Dallas, 2000—, Gaston Episcopal Hosp. Found., Dallas, 2000—, John Charles Brown Parish Scholarship Fund, 1996—; exec. adv. bd. mem. Cir. Ten coun. Boy Scouts Am., 2000—, chmn. camping facilities, 2002; mem. exec. com. camp coun. facilities Cir. Ten Coun. BSA, 2002-, chmn., 2003-; mem. bd. Ctr. Brain Health U. tex.-Southwestern Med. Sch., 2004-, East Dallas Young Life, 1990-. Mem. ASTM (mem. C-12, C-15, C-18 coms. 1990—), TPC, Mason Contractors Assn. Am. (contract rsch. com. 1982-83, chmn. labor com., codes and stds. com., 1999-2001, state chmn. Tex. 2002-2004, liaison com., regional v.p. 2004), Tex. Masonry Coun. (bd. dirs. 2003-) Marble Inst. Am., Constrn. Specification Inst., Associated Gen. Contractors (chpt. Dallas 1970-, mem. bd. dirs. 1995-96, subcontractor rels. com. 1988-89, mktg. com. 1990-93, co-chmn. gen. contractor/subcontractor rels. com. 1993-94, bd. dirs. 1995-98, transition com. AGC/ABC 1995-96, nat. assn. bd. dirs. 1995-2000, assoc. mem. AGC 1995-98, Quoin, No. Tex. chpt. bd. dirs. 2002-, sec. exec. com. 2004, vice chmn. exec. com. 2005), Masonry Alliance Codes and Stds. (treas. 1996-2000), Constrn. Edn. Found. (trustee, mem. bd. dirs. 1996-98), Baylor Inst. Rehab. (mem. bd. dirs., trustee 1996-2003, vice chmn. 1998-2000, chmn. 2001-2003, v.p. 1998-2000), Assn. Masonry Contractors Tex. (pres. 1983, sec./treas. 1981-82, v.p. 1990-91), So. Bldg. Congress, Nat. Bldg. Environment and Thermal Envelope Counsel, Assn. Masonry Contractors Houston (pres. 1982-84, v.p. 1981), Am. Subcontractor Assn. (v.p. 1982-83, bd. dirs. chpt. Houston 1982-85, also mem. nat. coms., bd. dir. north Tex. chpt. 1995-97), Bldg. Stone Inst., United Masonry Contractors Dallas (dir. constrn. edn. found. 1996-98, bd. dirs. 2003-, mem. program com. 1996-98, bd. dirs. 2003—, pres. 1982-84), Dallas Exec. Assn., Houston C. of C., N.W. Houston C. of C., Dallas C. of C., East Dallas Younglife (bd. dirs. 1990—), Tex. A&M U. Alumni Assn., Tex. A&M U.-Commerce Found., Tex. A&M U. Commerce (amb. 1999-), John Brown U. Parents' Cabinet (founder, pres. 1989-93), Dallas County Pioneers Assn., Baylor Health Care Sys. Found. (mem. bd. dirs. 2003-), Pine Forest Country Club (Houston), Dallas Athletic Club, Baylor Health Club, Salesmanship Club (Dallas), Tom Landry Ctr., Dallas Country Club, Delta Sigma Pi (life mem. 1967-). Republican. Home: 6531 Meadow Rd Dallas TX 75230

BARNES, ROBERT VINCENT, retired elementary and secondary school art educator; b. Flint, Mich., May 27, 1948; s. Albert J. and Mary Elizabeth (Morey) B.; m. Sandra E. Mathews-Barnes, Dec. 20, 1986; 1 child, Kathryn R. BA, Adrian Coll., 1970; postgrad., U. Mich., 1973-75, Ctrl. Mich. U., 1976-80, Getty Ctr. Edn. Arts, Cin. Art Mus., Cranbrook Acad. Art, Marygrove Coll., Cranbrook Acad. Art, 1995—; MA, Marygrove Coll., 1997. Cert. tchr. art grades kindergarten through 12, Mich. Tchr. art Flushing (Mich.) Cmty. Schs., 1971—2002; instr. Flint Inst. Arts, 1975-76; tchr. genealogy adult edn. program Mott C.C., Flushing, Fenton and Grand Blanc, Mich., 1976-84; pvt. art tchr., 2002—. Tchr. pvt. art lessons. Author: Flushing Area Families, 1981, Fenton Area Families, 1984; editor Flint Geneal. Quar., 1981. Past pres. Flint Geneal. Soc., Fenton Hist. Soc.; bd. dir., past pres. Flushing Area Hist. Soc.; pres. Fenton Mus. Bd., 1984-86; chmn. Fenton 150th Com., 1984; co-chmn. Fenton Civic Com. for New Mus., 1985-86; com. mem. Genesee County Sesquicentennial, Flint, 1986; mentor for jr. HS youth Logas program Fenton United Meth. Ch., mem. edn. commn., 2000—. Recipient 1st prize Flushing Art Fair, Flushing Jr. Women's League, 1975, 78, Orren Hart award Flushing Area Hist. Soc., 1983. Mem. NEA, Mich. Edn. Assn., Nat. Art Edn. Assn., Mich. Art Edn. Assn., Fenton Lions Club (bd. dir. 2006-). Methodist. Avocations: pottery, painting, genealogy. Personal E-mail: bbarnes48@charter.net.

BARNES, SAMUEL HENRY, political science professor; b. Miss, Jan. 20, 1931; s. Eugene Ludlow and Christine (Thompson) B.; m. Annabelle Bivona, Nov. 30, 1954; children: Christopher F.E., Michael Andrew, Catherine Ann. BA, Tulane U., 1952, MA, 1954; PhD, Duke U., 1957; postgrad. (Fulbright scholar), Institut des Hautes Etudes Politiques, Paris, 1956—57. Instr. polit. sci. U. Mich., Ann Arbor, 1957-60, asst. prof. polit. sci., 1960-64, assoc. prof., 1964-68, prof., 1968-91, James Orin Murfin prof. polit. sci., 1982-85, acting chmn. dept. polit. sci., 1968-69, chmn. dept., 1977-82, rsch. assoc. Survey Rsch. Ctr., 1969-70, program dir. Ctr. for Polit. Studies, 1970-91; prof. Comparative European Politics, dir. Ctr. for German and European Studies Georgetown U., Washington, 1991—2003, Graf Goltz emeritus prof. and dir., 2003—. Fulbright lectr. U. Florence, Italy, 1962-63, U. Rome, 1967-68; Ctr. Advanced Study in Behavioral Scis. fellow Stanford U., 1982-83, Hoover Instn. fellow Stanford U., 1989. Author: Party Democracy: Politics in an Italian Socialist Federation, 1967, Representation in Italy: Institutionalized Traditions and Electoral Choice, 1977, (with Max Kaase and others) Political Action: Mass Participation in Five Western Democracies, 1979, Politics and Culture, 1989, (with others) Continuities in Political Action, 1990 (with others) Cultural Dynamics of Democratization in Spain, 1998; contbr. articles to profl. publs., chpts. to books. Trustee Duke U., 1989-2001. Served with USN, 1949-50. Mem. Am. Polit. Sci. Assn. (sec. 1972-74), Conf. Group for Italian Polit. Studies (v.p. 1975-77, pres. 1977-79), Cosmos Club (Washington).

BARNES, SANDRA HENLEY, retired publishing company executive; b. Seymour, Ind., Jan. 15, 1943; d. Ray C. and Barbara Henley; m. Ronald D. Barnes, Sept. 3, 1961; children: Laura, Barrett and Garrett (twins). Student, Ind. State U., 1962-63. Asst. sales mgr. Marquis Who's Who, Indpls., 1973-79, sales, svc. mgr., 1979-82, mktg. ops. mgr., 1982-84, mktg. mgr. Chgo., 1984-86, dir. mktg. Wilmette, Ill., 1986-87; v.p. mktg. Macmillan Directory Div., Wilmette, 1987-88; group v.p. product mgmt. Marquis Who's Who, Wilmette, 1988-89, pres., 1989-92; v.p. Reed Reference Pub., New Providence, N.J., 1992-96; v.p., fulfillment Reed Elsevier-New Providence, 1996-97, LEXIS-NEXIS, Dayton, Ohio, 1997-98, Lexis Law Pub., Charlottesville, Va., 1997-98, Congrl. Info. Svc., Bethesda, Md., 1997-98; sr. v.p. Ednl. Comms., Inc., Lake Forest, Ill., 1998—2001; gen. mgr. Marquis Who's Who, New Providence, NJ, 2002. Republican. Avocation: reading. Office: 121 Chanlon Road New Providence NJ 07974 Home: 2452 N White Pine Dr Flagstaff AZ 86004-7179

BARNES, SANDRA LYNN, special education educator; b. Dearborn, Mich., Dec. 16, 1960; d. Roy Dennis and Selma Francis (Rose) Carnahan; m. Jeffery Monroe Barnes, Feb. 11, 1994; children: Jennifer, Jessica, Andrea, Jody, Anthony, Justin, Janelle, Jarrett. AA, SW Mo. State U., 2002, BA in Edn., 2004; M Edn. Adminstrn., William Woods U., 2006. Aircraft/aviation tech. USMC, 1979—99; tchr. Bakersfield (Mo.) HS, 2004—. Named Female Tchr. of Yr., Mo. State Troops to Tchrs., 2006. Office: Bakersfield Sch 1201 O Hwy Po Box 38 Bakersfield MO 65609 Office Phone: 417-284-7333. E-mail: sandrab@bakersfieldk12.mo.us.

BARNES, THOMAS G., law educator; b. 1930; AB, Harvard U., 1952; DPhil, Oxford U., 1955. From asst. prof. to assoc. prof. Lycoming Coll., Williamsport, Pa., 1956-60; from lectr. to prof. history U. Calif., Berkeley, 1960—, humanities rsch. prof., 1971-72, prof. history and law, 1974—2006, co-chmn. Canadian studies program, 1982—2006, co-dir. Canadian studies program, 2006—, emeritus prof. history and law, 2006—. Dir. legal history project Am. Bar Found., 1965-86; com. mem. on ct. records 9th Cir. Ct. Author: Somerset 1625-1640: A County's Government During the Personal Rule, 1961, List and Index to Star Chamber Procs., James I, 3 vols., 1975, Lawes and Libertyes of Massachusetts, 1975, Hastings College of Law: The First Century, 1978; mem. editl. bd. Gryphon Legal Classics Libr.; editor Pub. Record Office. Huntington Libr. fellow, 1960, Am. Coun. Learned Socs. fellow, 1962-63, John Simon Guggenheim Found. fellow, 1970-71. Fellow Royal Hist. Soc.; mem. Selden Soc. (councillor, state corr.), Assn. Canadian Studies (pres. 2001-03, past pres., 2003-05). Office: U Calif Sch Law 452 Boalt Hl Berkeley CA 94720-7200 Home Phone: 510-524-6602; Office Phone: 510-642-1780. Business E-Mail: barnest@law.berkeley.edu.

BARNES, THOMAS JOHN, lawyer; b. Grand Rapids, Mich., Apr. 1, 1943; s. James and Adeline (Molenda) B.; m. Lynn Marie Owens, Aug. 19, 1967; children: Nicolle, Cynthia. BA in Acctg., Mich. State U., 1965, BA in Polit. Sci., 1966; JD, Wayne State U., 1972. Bar: Mich. 1972, U.S. Dsit. Ct. (ea. and we. dists.) Mich. 1972, U.S. Ct. Appeals (6th cir.) 1974, U.S. Dist. Ct. (no. dist.) Ind. 1994, U.S. Ct. Appeals (7th cir.) 1995. Ptnr. Varnum, Riddering, Schmidt & Howlett, Grand Rapids, 1972—. Arbitrator Mich. Employment Rels. Commn.; spkr. in field. Editor-in-chief Wayne Law Rev.; contbr. articles to profl. jours. Named a Leading Mich. Lawyer, Chambers; named one of Best Lawyers in Am., Michs. 100 Super Lawyers. Fellow Coll. Labor and Employment Lawyers; mem. ABA (nat. labor rels. bd. practice and procedures com.), Mich. Bar Assn. (labor coun., sec., treas. 1987-88, chmn. 1989-90), Grand Rapids Bar Assn. (former chair labor sect.) Roman Catholic. Avocations: reading, horse racing, sports. Office: 333 Bridge St NW Grand Rapids MI 49504 Home Phone: 616-868-6825; Office Phone: 616-336-6621. Business E-Mail: tjbarnes@varnumlaw.com.

BARNES, THOMAS JOSEPH, writer; b. St. Paul, June 18, 1930; s. Ralph Weikert and Helen (O'Connor) B.; m. Mai Tang; children: An, Kim, Kevin; children by previous marriage: Christopher, Ross, Karen, Shannon. BA, U. Minn., 1950, MA, 1951. With fgn. service, 1957-80; vice consul Saigon, Vietnam, 1958—60; prin. officer Am. consulate, Hue, Viet Nam, 1960-61; polit. officer Bangkok, 1962-64, Vientiane, Laos, 1964-67; province sr. adviser Binh Long, Vietnam, 1967-68; country officer for Laos State Dept., 1968-70; prin. officer Am. Consulate, Udorn, Thailand, 1970-71; assoc. dir. AID, Nhatrang, Vietnam, 1971-72; consul gen. Tangier, Morocco, 1972-73, Can Tho, Vietnam, 1973; polit. counselor Bangkok, 1973-75; sr. staff mem. for East Asia Nat. Security Council, 1975-76; student Sr. Seminar in Fgn. Policy, State Dept., 1976-77; regional refugee coordinator Bangkok, 1977-78; diplomat-in-residence U. Hawaii, 1978-79; dir. Interagy. Working Group on Kampuchea, Dept. State, Washington, 1979-80; with UN High Commn. for Refugees, 1980—90, dep. rep. Somalia, 1980—82, chief S.W. Asia sect. Geneva, 1982-86, head supplies and food aid service, 1986-87, head orgn. and mgmt., 1987-90; coord. for ops. and program devel. Internat. Cath. Migration Commn., Geneva, 1991—95. Author: (novel) Tay Son: Rebellion in 18th Century Vietnam, 2000, Coping with Lust and the Colonel: Wartime Korea From Sokchang-ni, 2005, Vietnam When the Tanks Were Elephants, 2005, (memoir) Anecdotes of a Vagabond: The Foreign Service, The UN, and a Volag, 2000, (photographic art book) Southeast Asian Portraits, 2002. Capt. AUS, 1951-56. Decorated UN Svc medal, Korean Svc. medal, Bronze Star with 2 oak leaf clusters, Nat. Def. Svc. medal; recipient Award for Valor, Meritorious Honor award State Dept., Superior Honor awards State Dept, AID. Home: 15005 Solera Drive Austin TX 78717-4449

BARNES, VIRGIL EVERETT, II, physics professor; b. Galveston, Tex., Nov. 2, 1935; s. Virgil Everett and Mildred Louise (Adlof) B.; m. Barbara Ann Green, 1957 (dec. 1964); 1 son, Virgil Everett III; m. Linda Dwight Taylor, 1970; children— Christopher Richard Dwight, Charles Jeffrey, Daniel Woodbridge. AB magna cum laude with highest honors, Harvard U., 1957; PhD, Cambridge U., Eng., 1962. Rsch. assoc. Brookhaven Nat. Lab., Upton, NY, 1962-64, asst. physicist, 1964-66, assoc. physicist, 1966-69; mem. faculty Purdue U., 1969—, prof. physics, 1979—; asst. dean Purdue U. (Sch. Sci.), 1974-78. Cons. in field. Author papers on exptl. high energy particle physics. NSF predoctoral fellow Gonville and Caius Coll., Cambridge U., 1959-62; Marshall scholar Cambridge U., 1957-59; recipient Perkin Elmer prize Harvard U., 1956, Top Ten winner U.S. Westinghouse Sci. Talent Search, 1953. Mem. AAAS, AAUP, Am. Phys. Soc., N.Y. Acad. Scis., Phi Beta Kappa, Sigma Xi. Office: Purdue U Dept Physics West Lafayette IN 47907

BARNES, WALLACE, manufacturing executive; b. Bristol, Conn., Mar. 22, 1926; s. Harry Clarke and Lillian (Houbertz) B.; m. Audrey Kent, June 14, 1947; children: Thomas Oliver, Jarre Ann Betts; m. Mrs. Frederick B. Hollister, Jr.; 1 adopted son, Frederick Hollister; m. Joan C. Fierri, Mar. 3, 1973; m. Barbara Hackman Franklin, Nov. 29, 1986. BA, Williams Coll., 1949; LLB, Yale U., 1952; grad., Advanced Mgmt. Program, Harvard, 1973; LLD (hon.), U. Hartford, 1988; LLD (hon.), Briarwood Coll., 2002. Bar: Conn. 1952. Pres. Nutmeg Air Trans. Inc., 1949-55; asst. to treas. Northeast Airlines Inc., Boston, 1951; assoc. firm Beach, Calder & Barnes (and predecessor), Bristol, 1952-55, partner, 1956-62; exec. v.p. Assoc. Spring Corp. (name changed to Barnes Group Inc.), 1960-64, pres., 1964-77, chmn., chief exec. officer, 1977-91, chmn. bd., 1991-95, ret., 1995; chmn. bd. Rohr Inc., Chula Vista, Calif., 1995-98; chmn. Coun. Employment and Tng. Commn. State of Conn., 1997—; sr. ptnr. Sky Bight Ptnrs. Bd. dirs. TeraBit Comms., LLC, Del Global Techs. Corp.; chmn. bd. Tradewind Turbines Corp., 1994—; ptnr. Green Acres Farm, 1986—. Pres. Bristol Cmty. Chest, 1956; bd. dirs., mem. exec. com. Bristol Boys Club, pres., 1965-68; bd. regents U. Hartford, 1961-94, lifetime regent, 1995, chmn., 1988-93; trustee Bristol Girls' Club Assn.; bd. dirs. New Eng. Legal Found., 1986-90, New Eng. Coun., 1980-83, Jr. Achievement North Ctrl. Conn., 1980-90; nominee for Congress, 1st Congl. Dist. Conn., 1954; Rep. town chmn. Bristol, 1953-55; mem. Conn. Senate from 5th Dist., 1958-62, 8th Dist., 1966-70, minority leader, 1969; Gov.'s Clean Water Task Force, 1966-67; bd. dirs. Cmty. Coun. of Capital Region, 1975-77, Hartford Symphony Soc., 1971-78, Coun. on Employment and Fair Taxation, 1978-80, Bus. Coalition on Health, 1983-88, Conn. Pub. Expenditure Coun., 1979-85; trustee Am. Clock and Watch Mus., Environ. Learning Ctrs. Conn. Inc., The Family Ctr.; bd. trustees New Eng. Air Mus.; corporator Inst. of Living, Hartford, Bristol Hosp., St. Francis Hosp., Hartford Hosp.; co-chair Conn. Children's Med. Cap. Campaign, chmn. CBIA, 1982-93; bd. dirs. Conn. Econ. Devel. Corp. Served as aviation cadet USAAF, 1944-45. Recipient Disting. Svc. award Bristol Jaycees, Keystone award Boys Clubs Am., 1967, Humanitarian award Tunxis C.C., 1982, Human Rels. award Nat. Conf. Christians and Jews, 1985, Hon. Alumnus award U. Hartford, 1985, Salute to Wallace Barnes Bristol C. of C., 1991, Hall of Fame award Jr. Achievement North Ctrl. Conn., 1996, Exec. Philanthropist of Yr. Nat. Soc. Fund Raising Exec., 1996; Bartels fellow U. New Haven, 1992. Mem. ABA, Conn. Bar Assn., Am. Judicature Soc., Am. Arbitration Assn., Bristol Hist. Soc., Newcomen Soc., Conn. Bus. and Industry Assn. (past chmn., dir.), Metro Hartford C. of C. (bd. dirs., exec. com. 1991—), Am. Legion, Elks, Econ. Club N.Y.C., Yale Club, Williams Club, Farmington Country Club, Chippanee Golf Club. Home and Office: Sky Bight 1875 Perkins St Bristol CT 06010-8910

BARNES, WALLACE RAY, retired lawyer; b. Easton, Pa., Nov. 7, 1928; s. Charles Hicks and Erma (Saylor) B.; m. Helen Honey Bartley, July 2, 1958; children: Charles Calvin, Elizabeth McKee, Douglas Wittmer. AB, Duke U., 1950; LLB, Harvard U., 1957. Bar: Pa. 1958, Ohio 1973. Atty. Allegheny Ludlum Steel, Pitts., 1957-62, Columbia Gas, Md., N.Y., Pa., Pitts., 1962-73, sec., gen. counsel Ky., Md., N.Y., Ohio, Pa., Va., W.Va., Columbus, Ohio, 1973-78, sr. counsel, 1978-81, assoc. gen. counsel, 1981-88, dep. gen. counsel, 1988-96, ret., 1996. Corp. dir. Columbia Gas Ohio, 1973-78, N.Y., 1973-78 Bd. dirs. Pitts. Better Bus. Bur., 1972—74. Officer USN, 1947—54, Korea. Mem. FBA (pres. chpt. 1961), ABA, Ohio Bar Assn., Fox Chapel Racquet Club, Racquet Club of Columbus, S&R Club of Columbus, Phi Beta Kappa. Home: 2438 Sandover Rd Columbus OH 43220-2845 Address: Les Deuxoliviers La Fossette France Personal E-mail: wallacerbarnes@hotmail.com.

BARNES, WESLEY EDWARD, energy and environmental executive; b. Chgo., Sept. 11, 1937; s. Donald Edson and Helen Mary (Popovich) B.; m. Constance Arlene Simpson, Nov. 9, 1957; children: Dawn Ellen, Wesley Edward II. Grad., Indsl. Coll. of Armed Forces, 1973; BS, Cen. Mich. U., 1976, MBA, 1981. Chief warrant officer USN, 1955-68; sr. mktg. rep. UNIVAC, Washington, 1968-70; regional mgr. Weismantel Assocs. Inc., Washington, 1970-71; dir. computer ops. U.S. SBA, Washington, 1971-75; asst. dir. legis. affairs U.S. ERDA, Washington, 1975-77; dir. bus. rels. U.S. Dept. Energy, 1977-80, dir. major projects, 1980-83; chief exec. officer Western Rsch. Inst., Laramie, Wyo., 1983-90; pres., chief exec. officer Mktg. Bus. Assocs., Ltd., Washington, 1990-94; project mgr. Dept. of Energy, Yucca Mountain Project, 1995-97; energy and environ. cons. Dagsboro, Del., 1997—. Bd. dirs. Econ. Devel. Corp., Laramie, 1986-90. Mem. Rep. Nat. Com. Mem. Am. Mgmt. Assn. (pres.'s assn.), Cripple Creek Country Club, K. of C. (lector 1981-82). Roman Catholic. E-mail: barnes188@mchsi.com.

BARNES, WILLIAM DAVID, non-profit charities consultant, publisher; b. Gary, Ind., July 14, 1938; s. Frank J. and Marie M. (Jasorka) B.; m. Suzanne Frost Barnes, June 10, 1961 (div. June 1977); children: Adam Frost, Eric Earl. BA in Edn., Ariz. State U., 1960; Cert., Northwestern U., Chgo., 1965. Asst. editor The Arizonian Newspaper, Scottsdale, 1960-61; asst. v.p. First Security Bank, Mesa, Ariz., 1962-65; dir. mktg., v.p. Great Western Bank, Phoenix, 1966-67; dir. alumni fund Ariz. State U., Tempe, 1967-71; pres., sr. editor Barnes Assocs., Inc., Phoenix, Sacramento and Modesto, Calif., 1971—. Mem. editl. bd. Modesto Bee, 2005—. Author: How to Build Your Development Program, 1973, More on How to Build Your Development Program, 1974, Fund Raiser's Planning and Budgeting Guide, 1976. V.p. United Way, Mesa, 1962; Ariz. bus. chmn. Com. to Re-elect Pres., 1972; cons. to 70 local, state and nat. polit. campaigns, 1960-84 (63 victories); chair pub. rels. com. Ariz. Bankers Assn., 1968. Recipient Nat. 1st pl. award in mktg. Chrysler Corp. Young and Rubicam, 1974, Silver Triange award Am. Advt. Assn., 1977, Exec. Leaders Inst. award Lilly Endowment/Assn. Fundraising Profls., 1990, Man of Yr. award for vol. work Rainbow Acres Ranches for Developmentally Challenged, 1982. Mem. Assn. Fundraising Profls. (cert., nat. bd. dirs. 1975-78, One of 25 Authors Worldwide Contributing Most to Profession 1985, Outstanding Fund Raising Exec. No. Calif. 1987, Lifetime Achievement award, 2003). Roman Catholic. Avocations: tennis, gardening. Address: Barnes Associates Inc 1820 Scenic Dr Apt 249 Modesto CA 95355-4999 Office Phone: 209-523-8582. E-mail: barnesnfr@sbcglobal.net.

BARNES, WILLIAM DOUGLAS, advertising executive; b. Washington, Sept. 1, 1953; s. Berry Carter and Virginia Mae (Keeler) Barnes; m. Jeannette Avendano, July 3, 1990; 1 child, Chadsworth. BBA, U. Miami, Coral Gables, 1980, MBA, 1984. Staff acct. Arthur Andersen & Co., Miami, 1980-81; sr. acct. Storer Comm., Miami, 1981-84; pres., personnel cons. Profl. Resources, Miami, 1984-86; acct. exec. Miami Herald, 1986-90; pres. Barnes & Assoc. Advt., Ft. Lauderdale, 1990-97; acct. exec. Sun-Sentinel, 1991—97; CEO Strategic Resource Group, Inc., Ft. Lauderdale, 1997—2004; dir. bus. devel. Am. Home Guides, Hollywood, Fla., 1999—2005; nat. sales mgr. NewHomeGuide.com/Primedia, Hollywood, 2005—06; dir. sales Platt Realty and Mgmt., Hollywood, 2006—; v.p. bus. devel. Personality ID.com, Hollywood, 2007—. Mem. Beta Alpha Psi (chmn. alumni com. 1980). Republican. Home: 1146 Hidden Valley Way Weston FL 33327 Personal E-mail: wjcbarnes@bellsouth.net.

BARNES, WILLIAM WAYNE, geographer, writer; b. Cleve., Apr. 14, 1953; s. William Joseph and Ann Marie Casciato; m. Pamela Rose Hopkins, Sept. 24, 1985 (div. May 1991); m. Mary Ann Traeger, Dec. 7, 1991 (div. Sept. 2006). BA, Cleve. State U., 1975. Cert. Hypnotherapist Internat. Assn. of Regression Rsch. and Therapies, Minn., 2003. Lang. tchr. St. Edward H.S., Cleve., 1975—77; geographer Dept. of Def., Washington, 1979—2005; freelance lectr. Gila Bend, Ariz., 1996—. Author: (book) Thomas Andrews: Voyage Into History, 2000, (newspaper series) In My Viewpoint, 2002, (films) Maledizione, 2003, My Life and Death, 2005. Facilitator, annexation com. Town of Gila Bend, Ariz., 2003. Mem.: Internat. Assn. Regression Rsch. and Therapies (newsletter com. 2002—, scholarship com. 2003), Sigma Delta Pi. Independent. Roman Catholic. Avocation: horseback riding. Office: 263 Lasso Pkwy Oroville CA 95966 Home Phone: 928-683-2019. E-mail: titanicbuilder@hotmail.com.

BARNES-BROWN, PETER NEWTON, lawyer; b. Rutland, Vt., Aug. 22, 1948; s. Rufus Enoch and Julia Pottwin (Morgan) Brown; m. Susan Linda Barnes, Aug. 11, 1974; children: Diana Morgan, David Alexander, Julia Elizabeth. AB, Brown U., 1970; JD, U. Pa., 1976. Bar: Ga. 1978, N.Y. 1979, Mass. 1985. Law clk. Assoc. Justice Alfred H. Joslin R.I. Supreme Ct., Providence, 1977-78; assoc. Olwine, Connelly, Chase, O'Donnell & Weyher, NYC, 1978-84, Goodwin, Procter & Hoar, Boston, 1984-86; internat. counsel Cullinet Software, Inc., Westwood, Mass., 1986-89; co-founder, prin. Van Wert & Zimmer, P.C., Lexington, Mass., 1989-93; co-founder Morse, Barnes-Brown & Pendleton PC, Waltham, Mass., 1993—. Co-founding dir., clk. New Eng.-Latin Am. Bus. Coun., Inc., Boston, 1992-2000. Contbr. articles to profl. jours. Mem.: ABA, Boston Bar Assn., State Bar Ga., NY State Bar Assn., Mass. Bar Assn. Office: Morse Barnes-Brown & Pendleton PC Reservoir Place 1601 Trapelo Rd Waltham MA 02451-7333

BARNES-KEMPTON, ISABEL JANET, retired microbiologist, dean; b. Union City, NJ, Sept. 22, 1936; d. Carl Robert and Isabel Sarah (Cappelletti) B.; m. John D. Bowman, June 15, 1978 (dec. Nov. 1986); m. Arnold J. Kempton, Feb. 5, 2000. BS, Pa. State U., 1958; MS, Cornell U., 1960; PhD, Hahnemann Med. Coll., 1969; postgrad., Inst. Ednl. Mgmt. Harvard U., 1991. Asst. prof. microbiology Hershey Med. Ctr., Pa. State U., 1968-73; asst. prof., then assoc. prof. Sangamon State U., Springfield, Ill., 1973-76; assoc. prof. med. tech. U. Wis., Madison, 1976-85; interim dean Sch. Allied Health Professions, 1981-84; prof. med. tech. Ferris State U., Big Rapids, Mich., 1985-2000; dean Coll. Allied Health Scis., 1985-2000, acting v.p. Acad. Affairs, 1992-93. Mem. Mich. Bd. Podiatric Medicine and Surgery, 1995—2002. Active Mecosta Health Svcs., 1998—2002, Mecosta County Cmty. Found., 2000—, pres., 2005—06; coord. St. Andrews Manna Food Pantry, 2002—; mem. Tamarack Dist. Libr. Bd., 2003—; pres. bd. Tamarack Dist. Libr., 2003—; bd. dirs. Mecosta County Gen. Hosp.,

1988—99, sec., 1991—94, pres., 1996—97, v.p., 1997—99, Alliance for Health, 1993—2002, Mich. Hemophilia Found., 1989—95, 1997—2005, sec., 1991—94. Fellow Assn. of Schs. of Allied Health Professions (bd. dirs. 1989-91); mem. Coll. Health Deans (pres. 1988-90).

BARNESS, LEWIS ABRAHAM, physician; b. Atlantic City, July 31, 1921; s. Joseph and Mary (Silverstein) B.; m. Elaine Berger, June 14, 1953 (dec. Jan. 1985); children: Carol, Laura, Joseph; m. Enid May Fischer Gilbert, July 5, 1987; stepchildren: Mary, Elizabeth, Jennifer, Rebecca. AB, Harvard U., 1941, MD, 1944; MA (hon.), U. Pa., 1971; DS U. Wis. (hon.), 2002. Intern Phila. Gen. Hosp., 1944-45; resident Boston Children's Hosp., 1947-50; asst. chief, then chief dept. pediatrics Phila. Gen. Hosp., 1951-72; vis. physician U. Pa. Hosp., 1952-57, acting chief, then chief, 1957-72. Mem. faculty U. Pa. Sch. Medicine, 1951-72, prof. pediat., 1964-72; chmn. dept. U. So. Fla. Med. Sch., Tampa, 1972-88, prof. pediat., 1988—, Disting. Univ. prof., 2000—; vis. prof. Univ. Wis., 1987-92, prof. emeritus, 1993—. Author: Pediatric Physical Diagnosis Yearbook, edits. 1-6, 1957—; editor: Advances in Pediatrics, 1976-2004, Pediatric Nutrition Handbook, 3d edit., 1991; asst. editor Pediatric Gastroenterology and Nutrition, 1981-91; editl. bd. Cons., 1960-84, Pediatrics, 1978-83, Core Jour. Pediatrics, 1980-96, Contemporary Pediatrics, 1984—, Jour. Clin. Medicine and Nutrition, 1985-95, Nutrition Rev., 1985-87. Served to capt. AUS, 1945-46. Recipient Lindback Teaching award U. Pa., 1963; Borden award nutrition, 1972; Noer Disting. Prof. award, 1980, Joseph B. Goldberger award in clin. nutrition, 1984, Joseph St. Geme Leadership award 7 pediatric socs., 1991, U. So. Fla. Svc. award, 1997, President's Award, U. So. Fla., 2000, Distinguished Prof. award, 2000; inductee Phila. Pediat. Soc. Hall of Fame, 1996. Fellow Am. Inst. Nutrition; mem. AAAS, Am. Pediatric Soc. (recorder-editor 1964-75, pres. 1985-86, John Howland award 1993), Soc. Pediatric Rsch., Am. Acad. Pediatrics (chmn. com. on nutrition 1974-81), Abraham Jacobi award 1991, Hon. Internat. disting. fellow pediatric soc. Thailand, 2004, Med. Edn. Lifetime Achievement award, 1995, Sigma Xi, Alpha Omega Alpha. Home: 3301 Bayshore Blvd Unit 403 Tampa FL 33629-8841 Office: U South Fla Dept Pediat 17 Davis Blvd Tampa FL 33606 Office Phone: 813-259-8711. E-mail: lbarness@hsc.usf.edu. *Most people, when given the opportunity, try to be unselfish and prefer to do good. The human brain is a fantastic instrument, which when exercised, can solve most problems.*

BAR-NESS, YEHESKEL, electrical engineer, educator; b. Baghdad, Iraq, Apr. 28, 1932; arrived in Israel, 1950; came to US, 1978; m. Varda Bar-Ness, Aug. 21, 1952; children: Yael, Yaron, Yegal. BEE, Technion U., Haifa, Israel, 1958, MEE, 1963; PhD, Brown U., Providence, 1969. Chief engr. Elscint Inc., Haifa, 1971-75; assoc. prof. Tel-Aviv U., 1973-78; vis. prof. Brown U., 1978-79, U. Pa., Phila., 1979-81; prof. elec. engring. Drexel U., Phila., 1981-83; tech. staff mem. AT&T Bell Lab., Holmdel, NJ, 1983-85; disting. prof. elec. and computer engring. NJ Inst. Tech., Newark, 1985—, dir. ctr. communication and signal processing rsch., 1985—, found. chair comm. and signal processing, 2000—. Vis. prof. elec. engring. Tech. U. Delft, The Netherlands, 1993-94, Stanford U., 2000-01. Recipient Kaplan Price award Gov. of Israel, 1974. Fellow IEEE (life); mem. Comm. Soc. IEEE (sec. comms. systems engring. com. 1985-87, vice chmn., 1987-89, chmn. 1990-91, editor IEEE transaction on comm., founder and editor-in-chief IEEE Comm. Letters, Pub. Exemplary Svc. award 2005, NJ Inventor of Yr., 2006). Home: 2 Etna Ct Marlboro NJ 07746-1307 Office: NJ Inst of Tech 323 King Blvd Newark NJ 07102-1824

BARNET, ROBERT JOSEPH, cardiologist, philosopher; b. Port Huron, Mich., Apr. 27, 1929; s. John A. and Ruth Elizabeth (Wittliff) B.; children: Benedict, Maria, Antonia, Peter, Elizabeth, Rebecca, Christina, Jacqueline, Ann. Student, Port Huron Jr. Coll., summers 1947, 49; MD, Loyola U., Chgo., 1951; BS in Chemistry magna cum laude, U. Notre Dame, Ind., 1954, MA in Philosophy, 1988; MA in History, U. Nev., Reno, 1986. Diplomate Am. Bd. Internal Medicine, Nat. Bd. Med. Examiners. Intern Boston City Hosp., 1954—55; rotating intern Mercy Hosp., Chgo., 1955; asst. resident in medicine Boston City Hosp., 1958-59; clin. and research fellow in cardiology Children's Med. Center and House of the Good Samaritan, Boston, 1959-60; cons. fellow in rheumatic fever pediatric service Boston City Hosp., 1959-60; research fellow in pediatrics Harvard U., Boston, 1959-60; clin. fellow in cardiology Mass. Meml. Hosps., Boston, 1960-61; physician-in-charge St. Francis Mission Hosp., Solwezi, No. Rhodesia, 1961-62; dir. clinics, assoc. in medicine Stritch Sch. Medicine, Loyola U., Chgo., 1962-65; physician-in-charge Cardiac Clinic, Loyola U., Chgo., Fantus Outpatient dept. Cook County Hosp., Chgo., 1962-65, Hypertension Clinic, Fantus Outpatient dept. Cook County Hosp., 1962-65; assoc. attending physician dept. medicine Cook County Hosp., 1962-63, attending physician, 1963-65; practice medicine specializing in cardiology Reno, 1965-87; med. staff Washoe Med. Center, 1965—2006, St. Mary's Hosp., 1965—2006; assoc. clin. prof. cardiology U. Nev.; also assoc. dir. Lab. Environ. Patho-Physiology, Desert Research Inst., U. Nev., Reno, 1965-68; dir. Cardiac Care unit Washoe Med. Center, 1965-83, exec. com., 1967-71, 73-77, vice chief dept. medicine, 1969, chief, 1970-71, 78, chief dept. emergency services, 1973-77. Vis physician Solwezi Boma Rural Hosp., 1961-62; cons. in cardiology disability determination unit State of Nev., 1966-87, Crippled Children's Svc., 1966-76, Reno VA Hosp., 1967-80; asst. clin. prof. med. edn. U. Utah, 1968-71; cons. Churchill Pub. Hosp., Fallon, Nev., 1969-87, Pershing Gen. Hosp., Lovelock, Nev., 1969-87; clin. assoc. U. Nev., Reno, 1971-72, assoc. clin. prof. medicine, 1973-77, prof., 1978-2006; vis. scholar U. Notre Dame, 1989-90, 96-97; prof. med. ethics St. Louis U., 1993-95; med. reviewer, cons. Nev. State Bd. Med. Examiners, 1994-2007; scholar-in-residence Ctr. Clin. Bioethics, Georgetown U., 2000—; lectr. in electrocardiography and cardiology Loyola U., Chgo., 1962-65. Contbr. articles to profl. jours. Served with US Army, 1955-58. Recipient Clin. Faculty Honor award Loyola U., 1963-64. Fellow A.C.P. (bd. govs. 1980-85), Am. Coll. Cardiology (bd. govs. 1974-77), Am. Coll. Chest Physicians; mem. Nev. Heart Assn. (bd. dirs., exec. com., pres. 1974-75) Office: Georgetown U Ctr Clin Bioethics Box 571409 Washington DC 20057-1409 Office Phone: 202-687-9385. Personal E-mail: phbobmd@aol.com. *I have tried to dedicate my life to the service of all and the betterment of the community while striving for professional excellence without compromise of my moral and religious principles.*

BARNET, WILL, artist, educator; b. Beverly, Mass., May 25, 1911; s. Noah and Sarah (Toahnich) B.; m. Mary Sinclair, Feb., 1935 (div.); children: Peter George, Richard Sinclair, Todd Williams; m. Elena Ona Ciurlys, Mar. 4, 1953; 1 dau., Ona Willa. Student, Boston Mus. Fine Arts Sch., 1927-30, Art Students League, NYC, 1930-33; DFA (hon.), Mass. Coll. Art, 1989. Instr. painting Art Students League, NYC, 1946—; faculty Cooper Union, NYC, 1945—, prof., 1965—; instr., critic Pa. Acad., Phila., 1967—; faculty Famous Artists Painting Course, Westport, Conn., 1954—, Mont. State Coll., summer 1951, Summer Artists Workshop, Regina Coll., U. Sask., Canada, 1957; instr. advanced painting U. Minn. at Duluth, summer 1959, Wash. State U., Spokane, summer 1963, Pa. State U., summer 1965, Des Moines Art Center, summer 1965. Distinguished vis. prof. Pa. State U., 1965-66; vis. critic Yale, 1952-53; vis. prof. Cornell U., 1968-69; condr. grand art tour of, Europe, April, 1959, Ford Found. artist in residence program, 1964 Contbr. to Art Students League Mag; one-man shows, Hudson D. Walker Gallery, 1938, Galerie St. Etienne, 1943, Berthe Schaefer Gallery, Arthur Harlow & Co., Inc., all NYC, 1946, U.S. Nat. Mus., Washington, 1946, Bertha Schaefer Gallery, NYC, 1947, 48, Krasner Gallery, NYC, Gallery Trastevere, Rome, 1960, Terry Dintenfass Gallery, NYC, 1982, Kennedy Galleries, NYC, 1984, 86, 88, retrospective, Inst. Contemporary Art, Boston, 1961, Mary Harriman Gallery, Boston, 1963, 64, Va. Mus., Richmond, 1964, Waddell Gallery, NYC, 1965, 66, 68, 70, Des Moines Art Center, 1965, Pa. Acad. Phila., 1969, Fairweather Hardin Gallery, Chgo., 1971, David and David, Phila., 1972, print retrospective, Asso. Am. Artists, NYC, 1972-79, Hirschl & Adler Galleries, Inc., 1973, 76, 81, Essex Inst., Salem, Mass., 1980, painting retrospective, Neuberger Mus., Purchase, N.Y., 1979, 94, Ringling Mus., Sarasota, Fla., 1980, Wichita Art Mus., Wichita, Kans., 1983, traveling mus. retrospective, Currier Gallery Art, Manchester, N.H., 1984, Huntsville Mus. Art, Ala., 1984, Minn. Mus. Art, St. Paul, 1984-5, Art Gallery of Hamilton, Ont., Can., 1985, Farnsworth Libr. and Art Mus., Maine, 1985, Meek-Harmon Gallery, Naples, Fla., 1990, Terry Dintenfass Gallery, 1991, 94, Butler Inst., Youngstown, Ohio, 1992, Philharm. Ctr. Arts, Naples, Fla., 1994, Ogonquit Mus. Am. Art, Maine, 1994, Worcester Art Mus, Mass., 1995, Nat. Mus. Am. Art, Washington, 1995, Terry Dintenfars Gallery, 1996; drawing retrospective Ark. Art Ctr., Little Rock, 1991—; The Farnsworth Art Mus., Maine, 2002; exhibited, Art USA, 1959, Glenn Horowitz Bookseller, inc., East Hampton, NY, 1997, Nat. Acad. Mus., NYC, 1997, Maine Coast Artists, 1998, Tabor De Nagy Gallery, NYC, 1998, Retrospectives Montclair Art Mus., NJ, 2000, Boca Raton Mus. Art, Fla., 2000, Portland Mus. Art, Maine, 2000, Retrospective Ark. Art Ctr., 2001, Alexandre Gallery, NY, 2002, Harmon-Meek Gallery, Naples, Fla., 2000, Babcock Galleries, 2005; represented in permanent collections, Minn. Inst. Arts, Met., NYC, Fogg Art Mus., Library of Congress, Art Gallery, U. ND, U. Art Gallery, Berkeley, Calif., Cin. Art Mus., Duncan Phillip Meml. Mus., Washington, Phila. Art Mus., Honolulu Acad., Mus. Modern Art, Bklyn. Mus., Mont. State Coll., Whitney Mus. Am. Art, Mus. Fine Arts, Boston, Guggenheim Mus., NYC, Farnsworth Mus. Maine, Butler Inst., Ohio, Ashmolean Mus., Oxford, Eng., Brit. Mus., London, Pulmer Mus. of Art, 2003, Alexander Gallery, 2003, Babcock Gallery, 2005; exhibited in museums throughout, US, including, Art Inst. Chgo., Los Angeles Mus., Portland Mus., John Herron Inst., Carnegie Inst., Virginia Mus. Fine Arts, Columbia (SC) Mus. Art (1st Biennial); pub. Will Barnet 27 Master Prints, 1982; illustrator The World in a Frame; subject of Robert Doty work: Publisher Abrams, 1984. Recipient Bronze medal, 3d prize Corcoran Biennial, 1961, Benjamin Altman 1st prize NAD, 1977, Medal of Honor, Nat. Arts Club, 1990, Winthrop Rockefeller Meml. award, 1992, Life Achievement medal Butler Inst. Am. Art, 1992, Arts & Tourism Coun. Killy Carlisle Hart award, 1999, Disting. Artists Lifetime Achievement award Coll. Art Assn., 2007; named to Gallery of Honors, Art World Mag., 1990. Fellow Royal Soc. Arts; mem. Art Students League (life), NAD (life, Benjamin Altman 1st prize 2007), Am. Abstract Artists, Soc. Am. Graphic Artists, Inc., Fedn. Modern Painters and Sculptors, Century Assn. Liberal, Am. Acad. and Inst. Arts and Letters, NY Acad. Art, Dr. of Fine Arts, Lyme Acad. Coll. Fine Arts. Unitarian Universalist. Home: 15 Gramercy Park S New York NY 10003-1705

BARNETT, AMY DUBOIS, editor-in-chief; m. Nathan Grant. BA, Brown U.; MFA, Columbia U. Mng. editor Fashion Almanac Mag., 1996—98; editor-in-chief Inside NY, 1999; mng. editor Fashion Planet Website; columnist, features editor Total NY Website; editor Essence Mag., 1999—2000; editor-in-chief Honey Mag., 2000—03; mng. editor Teen People, 2003—06. Bd. dir. Lions' Reach. Recipient ALDO award for fashion journalism, 1997.

BARNETT, BENJAMIN LEWIS, JR., retired physician, educator; b. Woodruff, SC, July 22, 1926; s. Benjamin Lewis and Mattie Bernice (Skinner) B.; m. Annalyne Louise Hall, Oct. 25, 1958; children: Benjamin Lewis III, Jane Kristen. BS, Furman U., 1946, LLD, 1978; MD, Med. U. S.C., 1949. Diplomate Am. Bd. Family Practice. Intern Protestant Episcopal Hosp., Phila., 1949-50; pvt. practice Woodruff, 1950-70; from assoc. prof. family practice to asst. dean and prof. Med. U. S.C., Charleston, 1970—75, asst. dean for student affairs, 1975—77; clin. staff Med. U. Hosp., Charleston County Hosp., 1970-77; from prof. to prof. emeritus U. Va. Med. Sch., 1977—2000, prof. emeritus, 2000—; family medicine physician-in-chief U. Va. Med. Ctr. Hosp., 1977-96. Admissions com. U. Va. Med. Sch., 1997-99; Stoneburner lectr. Med. Coll. Va., 1975; Daniel Drake lectr. U. Cin., 1976; Robert P. Walton lectr. Med. U. SC, 1978; Goodlark prof. U. Tenn., 1979; Roy J. Gerard lectr. Mich. State U., 1992; vis. scholar U. Mich. Med. Sch., 1984; vis. lectr. Med. Coll. of Ga., 1982; vis. prof. Case Western Res. Sch. Medicine, 1984, U. Vt., 1988, U. N.Mex., 1991, U. SC Sch. Medicine, 1999; spkr. baccalaureate address U. Va., 1986, 2000; Mack Lipkin vis. prof. U. Oreg., 1987, U. Utah, 1989; Donald J. Welter Meml. lectr. Med. Coll. Wis., 1989; Frederick Lytel Meml. lectr., Abington, Pa., 1989; Bradford Strock lectr. Harrisburg (Pa.) Gen. Hosp., 1989; 7th Leland Blanchard Meml. lectr. Soc. Tchrs. Family Medicine ann. meeting, Nashville, 1985; health officer, Town of Woodruff, 1950-54; keynote speaker Assn. Depts. Family Medicine, Clearwater, Fla., 1991; commencement speaker U. Va. Med. Sch., 1992, 97; Grand Prof. Rounds St. Margaret's Hosp., Pitts., 1993; Julian Keith lectr. Bowman Gray Sch. Medicine, 1993; keynote speaker leadership conf. Fla. Med. Assn., Ponta Vedra, 1994, AHEC conf. SC Family Practice, Myrtle Beach, 1994; B. Leslie Huffman lectr. Med. Coll. Ohio, Toledo, 1994; lectr. Atlanta Med. Ctr., 2000—; grad. speaker McLennan County Med. Edn. and Rsch. Found., Waco, Tex., 1995; Inaugural Buck Crockett lectr., Roanoke, Va., 2000; founder's prof. U. Okla. Health Scis. Ctr., Tulsa, 2000; Harlan Thomas Meml. lectr.; Hiram B. Curry Meml. lectr. MUSC, 1990, 2001; lectr. and cons. in field. Author: Between the Lines (Reflections of a Family Physician), 1989, Pebbles in the Water, 2003; editor: S.C. Family Physician, 1973—74; contbr. articles to med. jours. and chpts. to textbooks. Mem. Spartanburg County Bd. Edn., 1968-70, sec. 1969-70; trustee Bethea Bapt. Home for Aged, Darlington, S.C., 1972-73; mem. bd. trustees Furman U., 1994-99; dir. Marietta-Lost Mtn. Kiwanis, 2003—; mentor character curriculum Kennesaw Mountain HS, 2002-2006. Named Citizen of Year Woodmen of World, 1968; recipient Golden Apple award for clin. teaching Student AMA, 1973; Thomas W. Johnson award Am. Acad. Family Physicians, 1976, Disting. Alumnus award Med. U. S.C., 1993; endowed Barnett Professorship in Family Medicine established U. Va. Bd. Visitors, 1997; Thomas Jefferson award U. Va., 1997. Mem. AMA (mem. residency rev. com. for family practice 1974-79), Am. Bd. Family Practice (exam. bd. 1975-81, dir. 1976-81, exec. com. 1979-81, pres. 1980-81), Va. Med. Soc., Albemarle County Med. Soc., Soc. Tchrs. Family Medicine (v.p. 1974, sec.-treas. 1975, dir. 1981-85, Cert. of Excellence 1983, F. Marian Bishop award 1996), Am. Acad. Family Physicians, S.C. Acad. Family Physicians (v.p. 1973, pres. 1975-76), Spartanburg County Med. Soc. (v.p. 1968), Am. Philatelic Soc., Coun. Acad. Socs., Furman U. Alumni Assn. (dir. 1972-77), U. Va. Raven Soc., Kiwanis (dir.), Alpha Omega Alpha (faculty councilor, vis. prof. U. S.C. Sch. Medicine 1999), Alpha Kappa Kappa (pres. 1948), Kappa Alpha (v.p. 1944), Loyal Order. Baptist (deacon, chmn. bd.). Office Phone: 770-429-1555. Personal E-mail: blbmd@earthlink.net.

BARNETT, BONNIE ALLYN, lawyer; b. Phila., 1958; BA summa cum laude, Temple Univ., 1979, JD summa cum laude, 1982. Bar: Pa. 1982, NJ 1996. Law clerk, Hon. James T. Giles US Dist. Ct. (ea. dist), Pa., 1982—84; joined Drinker Biddle & Reath LLP, Phila., 1984, ptnr., chair, environ. practice group. Articles editor Temple Law Rev., lectr. in field. Named a Pa. Super Lawyer, 2004; recipient, 2005. Office: Drinker Biddle & Reath LLP One Logan Sq 18th & Cherry Sts Philadelphia PA 19103-6996 Office Phone: 215-988-2916. Office Fax: 215-988-2757. Business E-Mail: bonnie.barnett@dbr.com.

BARNETT, BRUCE EDWIN, lawyer; b. Longview, Wash., May 29, 1955; s. David Albert and Betty Jean Barnett; m. Keyte Marie Hladky, July 31, 1982 (div. Feb. 1998); children: Robert Hladky, Markeyta Hladky. MusB, U. Oreg., Eugene, 1978, JD, 1984. Bar: Oreg. Supreme Ct. 1984, Tenn. Supreme Ct. 2003. Dep. dist. atty. Douglas County, Roseburg, Oreg., 1985, Clackamas County, Oregon City, 1985—86; mcpl. ct. clk. City of Eugene, 1986; assoc. atty. Kent Anderson, P.C., Eugene, 1986—88; asst. dist. atty. Lane County, Eugene, 1988—97; child support agt. Oreg. Dept. of Justice, Salem, 1999; staff atty., office of regional counsel Dept. Veterans Affairs, Nashville, 2000—. Chief petitioner Fern Ridge Libr. Dist., Veneta, Oreg., 1993—94, mem. formation com., 1994—95; vol. Eugene Symphony, 1985—87, U. Oreg. Chamber Music Series, Eugene, 1981—87. Recipient Alumni scholarship, U. Oreg. Sch. of Law, 1981. Mem.: Am. Mensa. Independent. Avocations: ham radio, crossword puzzles, reading, piano. Home: 2785 Call Hill Rd Nashville TN 37211 Office: US Dept Veterans Affairs 3322 W End Ave Ste 509 Nashville TN 37203 Home Phone: 615-695-4625; Office Phone: 615-695-4633. Office Fax: 615-695-4634. Personal E-mail: brucebarnett@mac.com. Business E-Mail: bruce.barnett@va.gov.

BARNETT, DANIEL A., sales executive, consultant; s. Kenneth Dale Barnett and Marsha (Krause) Barnett-Krause; m. Deborah Barnett; children: Gabriel, Amanda. BBA in Bus. Mgmt., U. Mich., 1999, BA in Psychology, 1999. Nat. sales mgr. Custom Enterprises, Inc, Fullerton, Calif., 1999—2005; CEO, pres. Promotional Fulfillment Svcs., Inc., Santa Ana, Calif., 2006—. Cons. in field. Vol. Habitat for Humanity, Saddleback Valley Cmty. Ch., Foothill Ranch, Calif. Mem.: U. Mich. Alumni Assn. (assoc.), Delta Sigma Phi (assoc.). Office: Promotional Fulfillment Svcs Inc 2001 E Dyer Rd Ste 400 Santa Ana CA 92705 Office Phone: 800-815-1505. Business E-Mail: dbarnett@promofill.com.

BARNETT, DONALD BLAKE, corporate financial executive; b. Corsicana, Tex., Oct. 2, 1957; s. Donald Wayne and Patricia (Anderson) B.; m. Karen Bryant Tripp; 1 child, Hamilton Chase. BA, Yale U., 1980. Account exec. E.F. Hutton, Houston, 1980-82, Rotan Mosle, Houston, 1982-83, Merrill Lynch, Houston, 1983-84; collections supr. Security Nat. Bank, Nacogdoches, Tex., 1984-85; owner Barnett Investments, Nacogdoches, Tex., 1985-94; pres., CEO, dir. of trading, underwriting Taylor, Pruitt & Sylvester, Houston, 1994; chmn., CEO Blake, Barnett & Co., Inc., Houston, 1996—. Chmn. Pinnacle Advantage Capital, Houston, 1994—, Banita Creek Farms, Nacogdoches, Tex., 1992—; chmn. Money Mgrs. Co., 2000—, The Train Store, Inc., 2001—. Recipient scholarships Yale Alumni Assn. of N.Y., 1976-80, Yale Alumni Assn. of Houston, 1978-80, Philiips Exeter TAD Jones, 1977-80. Mem. NASD, Yale Alumni Assn., Yale Alumni, Houston Soc. Club, Houston Polo Club, Houston Ctr. Club. Presbyterian. Avocations: golf, reading, coaching boys' basketball. Home: 2245 Shakespeare St Houston TX 77030-1112 Office: 2245 Shakespeare St Houston TX 77030-1112 E-mail: bbarnett@moneymanagers.com.

BARNETT, EDWARD WILLIAM, lawyer; b. New Orleans, Jan. 2, 1933; s. Phillip Nelson and Katherine (Wilkinson) B.; m. Margaret Mauk, Apr. 3, 1933; children: Ann Barnett Stern, Edward William. BA, Rice U., 1955; LL.B., U. Tex.-Austin, 1958. Bar: Tex. 1958. Mem. Baker Botts LLP, Houston, 1958—2004, mng. ptnr., 1984-98, sr. counsel, 1998—2004. Chmn. Cen. Houston, Inc., 1989-91; bd. dirs. Reliant Energy, Inc., Enterprise GP, LLC, Westlake Chem. Corp. Trustee Rice U., Houston, 1991-2005, chmn. bd. trustees, 1996-2005; dir. St. Luke's Episcopal Health Sys., 1997—; life trustee U. Tex. Law Sch. Found., 1992—; dirs. Greater Houston Partnership 1989-, chmn., 1992; bd. dirs. Ctr. Houston's Future, 2000-06; bd. dirs. Houston Zoo, 2002—, chmn., 2002-04. Fellow Am. Coll. Trial Lawyers; mem. ABA (chmn. sect. antitrust law 1981-82), State Bar Tex., Houston Bar Assn., Coronado Club (pres. 1989), Houston Country Club, Old Baldy Club. Office: Baker Botts LLP 3000 One Shell Plaza Houston TX 77002

BARNETT, ELIZABETH HALE, organizational consultant; b. Nashville, Mar. 17, 1940; d. Robert Baker and Dorothy (McCarthy) Hale; m. Crawford F. Barnett Jr., June 6, 1964; children: Crawford F. III, Robert H. BA, Vanderbilt U., 1962. Receptionist, sec. U.S. Atty. Gen. Robert F. Kennedy, Washington, 1962-64; free-lance cons. Atlanta, 1973-76; pres. E.H. Barnett & Assocs. orgnl. cons., trainers, Atlanta, 1976-86; trustee The Ga. Conservancy, Atlanta, 1978-92, chmn. bd. trustees, 1986-88, chmn. adv. bd., 1994-98; legis. asst. to Senator Michael J. Egan Ga. State Senate, Atlanta, 1990-93. Bd. dirs. Jr. League Atlanta, 1973-75, Atlanta Mus. Art, High Mus. Art, Atlanta, 1977—; bd. dirs. United Way Met. Atlanta, 1981-84, ARCS Found., Atlanta chpt., found. mem.; bd. dirs. White House Fellows Southeastern Region Selection Panel, 1995-96; chmn., pres. bd. dirs. Vol. Coms. Art Mus. U.S. and Can., 1976-79; chmn. bd. dirs. Met. Atlanta chpt. ARC, 1978-80, hon. bd. dirs., 1980—; cmty. adv. com. NW Ga. Coun. Girl Scouts Am., 1979-83; coun. mem. USO Ga., 1981-1993; bd. sponsors Atlanta Women's Network; apptd. to Ga. Clean and Beautiful Citizens Adv. Com., 1990, Ga. Solid Waste Mgmt. Commn., 1990; appt. sec. to Gov.'s Environ. Edn. Coun., 1992—; sci. coun. Ga. Coalition for Sci. Tech. and Math. Edn., 1993-, Student Aid Found., Atlanta, 2002-(bd. dirs.). Named One of 10 Outstanding Young Women of Am., 1977, Outstanding Young Woman of Ga., 1977; honored by Ga. State Legis., Atlanta, 1978. Mem. LWV. Episcopalian. Avocations: gardening, travel, hiking, snorkeling, politics. E-mail: bethbarne@comcast.net.

BARNETT, GENE HENRY, neurosurgeon; b. Phila., Feb. 2, 1955; s. Edgar Tryon and Anne Shirley (Wenner) B.; m. Kathleen Marie Seng, May 9, 1984 (div. Sept. 1989); 1 child, Alexander; m. Cathy Ann Sila, Dec. 9, 1990; children: Austin, Addison. BA summa cum laude, Case Western Res. U., 1976, MD, 1980. Intern Cleve. Clinic Found., 1980-81, neurosurgery resident, 1981-86, staff neurosurgery, 1987—, co-dir. residency program, 1992-95, vice chmn. dept. neurosurgery, 1993—2002, program dir. dept. neurosurgery, 1995—, dir. Brain Tumor Ctr., 1995—2001, chmn. Brain Tumor Inst., 2001—, dir. Gamma Knife Ctr., 1997—. Hon. registrar U. Edinburgh, Scotland, 1985; fellow Harvard Med. Sch., Mass. Gen. Hosp., 1986-87; cons. in field. Editor: Image Guided Neurosurgery: Clinical Applications of Surgical Navigation Systems, 1998; contbr. over 120 articles to profl. jours., 27 chpts. to books. Grantee Epilesy Found. Am., 1979, NINDS, 1995; clin. and rsch. fellow Harvard Med. Sch., Mass. Gen. Hosp., Boston, 1986-87. Office: Cleve Clinic Found 9500 Euclid Ave Cleveland OH 44195-0001

BARNETT, GUY OCTO, physician, educator; b. Chula Vista, Calif., Sept. 18, 1930; married; 3 children. BA, Vanderbilt U., 1952; MD, Harvard U., 1956. Resident Peter Bent Brigham Hosp., 1956—61; clin. assoc. Nat. Heart Inst., 1958—60; investigator Am. Heart Assn., 1961—67; physician, prof. medicine, dir. computer sci. lab Mass. Gen. Hosp., 1979—; prof. medicine Harvard U., 1980—. Lectr. elec. engring. MIT, 1972—. Recipient Morris F. Collen award. Fellow: Inst. Medicine-NAS; mem.: ACP, Am. Med. Informatics Assn. Office: Mass Gen Hosp Lab Computer Sci 50 Staniford St Boston MA 02114-2517

BARNETT, HELAINE M., lawyer; b. NYC, Nov. 13, 1939; d. Harry and Helen (Chafets) Meresman; m. Victor Jules Barnett, June 28, 1959; children: Craig Edward, Roger Lawrence. Bars: NY 1964, US Dist. Ct. (so. dist.) NY 1970, US Dist. Ct. (ea. dist.) NY 1970, US Ct. Appeals (2nd cir.) 1972, US Supreme Ct. 1967. BA, Barnard Coll., 1960; LLB, NYU, 1964. Assoc. appellate counsel Criminal Appeals Bur., Legal Aid Soc., NYC, 1966-71, Civil Appeals Bur., 1971-74, asst.-atty.-in-charge civil divsn., 1974—94, atty.-in-charge, 1994-2003; adj. prof. law, Benjamin N. Cardozo Sch. Law, 1980-82, 84-85; pres. Legal Svcs. Corp., 2004-. Mem. NY Gov.'s Adv. Com. to Establish Criminal Justice Inst., 1983; bd. dirs. Nat. Equal Justice Libr., Am. U., 2004-; co-chair NY State Commn. to Promote Pub. Confidence in Jud. Elections, 2004-. Recipient Am. Jurisprudence prize NYU Law Sch., 1962. Mem. NY State Bar Assn. (chmn. com. pub. interest law 1984—), Assn. Bar City NY (treas., mem. exec. com.), ABA (mem. com. profession, standing com. ethics and profl. responsibility, bd. gov. ho. del., governance commn.), Am. Law Inst. Contbr. articles to profl. jours. Office: Legal Services Corp 3rd Fl 3333 K St NW Washington DC 20007-3522*

BARNETT, HOYT R. (BARNEY), supermarket company executive; Grad., Fla. So. Coll., 1965. Officer Publix Supermarkets Inc., Lakeland, Fla., 1977—, dir., 1985—, vice chmn., 1999—. Mailing: Publix Supermarkets Inc PO Box 407 Lakeland FL 33802-0407 Office: Publix Super Markets PO Box 407 Lakeland FL 33802-0407*

BARNETT, JONATHAN, urban planner, educator, architect; b. Boston, Jan. 6, 1937; s. David and Josephine Barnett; m. Nory Miller, Mar. 19, 1983. BA magna cum laude, Yale U., 1958, MArch, 1963; MA Mellon fellow, U. Cambridge, Eng., 1960. Designer Haines, Lundberg & Waehler, Archts., NYC, 1963, 64; assoc. editor Archtl. Record, NYC, 1964-67; cons. New City Exhbn. Mus. Modern Art, 1966, 67; prin. urban designer N.Y.C. Planning Dept., 1967-68, dir. urban design group, 1969-71; prof., dir. grad. program in urban design CCNY, 1971-98; prof. city and regional planning, dir. urban design program U. Pa., Phila., 1998—; prin. Wallace, Roberts and Todd, LLC, 2002—. Planning cons., 1971—2002; mem. vis. com. Sch. Architecture Yale U., 1974—80, William Henry Bishop prof., 1983; mem. vis. com. Harvard U. Grad. Sch. Design, 1976—81, UCLA, 1990, MIT Planning Dept., 1999; vis. prof. U. Wis., Milw., 1981; Kea disting. vis. prof. U. Md., 1988, 89; Sam Gibbons eminent scholar U. S. Fla., 1991—94; lectr. in field; cons. in field. Editor: (book) Pespecta 8, 1968; co-author: New Zoning, 1970, Collaborations: Artists and Architects, 1981, The Practice of Local Government Planning, 1988, 3d edit., 2000, Cities in Our Future, 1997, Charter of the New Urbanism, 1999; author: Urban Design as Public Policy, 1974; author: (with John C. Portman, Jr.) The Architect as Developer, 1976; author: Introduction to Urban Design, 1982, The Elusive City, 1986, The Fractured Metropolis, 1995, Planning for the New Century, 2000, Redesigning Cities, 2003, Smart Growth in a Changing World, 2007; editl. cons. Archtl. Record, 1968—90, mem. adv. bd. Jour. Urban Design, 1996—; contbr. articles to profl. jours. Mem. adv. bd. Environment and Behavior, 1968—78; bd. dirs. DC Preservation League, 1996—2000; mem. Com. 100 Fed. City, 1997—2002. Recipient Dale prize, Calif. Polytech. Inst., 2007, Athena medal, Congress NSW Urbanism, 2007. Fellow: AIA, Am. Inst. Cert. Planners; mem.: Congress New Urbanism (bd. dirs. 1995—2005), N.Y. Landmark Conservancy (bd. dirs. 1972—97), Berzelius Soc., Inst. Urban Design (bd. dirs. 1989—99), Mcpl. Art Soc. (bd. dirs. 1970—78, 1981—86), Archtl. League N.Y. (v.p. 1968—70, dir. 1975—98, pres. 1977—81), Century Assn., Elizabethan Club Yale, Yale Club. Unitarian Universalist. Office: Dept of City and Regional Planning Univ Pa Philadelphia PA 19104

BARNETT, MARILYN, advertising executive; b. Detroit; d. Henry and Kate (Boesky) Schiff; children: Rhona, Ken. BA, Wayne State U. Founder, part-owner, pres. Mars Advt. Co., Southfield, Mich. Bd. dirs. Mich. Strategic Fund; apptd. to Mich. bi-lateral trade team with Germany. Named Outstanding Retail Woman of Yr., Outstanding Retail Mktg. Exec., Oakland U., Entrepreneur of Yr., Oakland Exec. of Yr.; named to Mich.'s Top 25 Women Bus. Owners List. Mem. AFTRA (dir.), SAG, Exec. Women Am., Am. Women in Radio & TV (Top Agy. Mgmt. award, Outstanding Woman of Yr.), Internat. Women Forum, Com. of 200, Women's Econ. Club (Ad Woman of Yr.), Adcraft. Office: Mars Advt 25200 Telegraph Rd Southfield MI 48034-7496 Office Phone: 248-936-2234. Business E-Mail: barnettm@marsosa.com.

BARNETT, MARTHA WALTERS, lawyer; b. Dade City, Fla., June 1, 1947; d. William Haywood and Helen (Hancock) Walters; m. Richard Rawls Barnett, Jan. 4, 1969; children: Richard Rawls, Sarah Walters. BA cum laude, Tulane U., 1969; JD cum laude, U. Fla. Coll. Law, 1973; LLD (hon.), Flagler Coll., 1995, Stetson U., 2000, Nova Southwestern U., 2000; LHD (hon.), DePaul U., 2001; LLD (hon.), Wake Forest U., 2003. Bar: Fla. 1973, U.S. Dist. Ct. (mid. and so. dists.) Fla. 1973, U.S. Ct. Appeals (3d, 4th and 11th cirs.) 1975, DC 1989. Assoc. Holland & Knight LLP, Tallahassee, 1973—78, ptnr., 1979—, chair, dirs. com., past chair. pub. law dept. Bd. dirs., v.p. Fla. Lawyers Prepaid Legal Svc. Corp., 1978—80, pres., 1980—82, legis. com., 1983—84, mem. commn. on access to justice, 1984—86, exec. coun. tax sect., 1987—88, exec. coun. pub. interest. sect., 1989—91; active Fla. Commn. Ethics, 1984—87, chairperson, 1986—87, Fla. Taxation and Budget Reform Commn., 1989—; legal adv. bd. Martindale-Hubbell/Lexis-Nexis, 1990—; chair Ho. of Dels., 1994—96; spkr., lectr. in field. Governor's appointee to the Fla. Commn. on Ethics State Fla., 1984—88, chair, Fla. Commn. on Ethics, 1986—87, mem. Governor's Select Com. on Workforce 2000, 1988—89, Governor's appointee to Constitutional Taxation & Budget Reform Commn., 1990—94, Governor's appointee to Constitution Revision Commn., 1997—98; mem. exec. com. Fla. Tax Watch, 2002; bd. dirs. Lawyers Com. Civil Rights Under Law; bd. adminstrs. Tulane Ednl. Fund; mem. Fla. Commn. on Human Rels., 1977—79; bd. trustee Fla. Tax Watch, 1983—; trustee U. Fla. Coll. Law, 1996—; mem. adv. coun. U. Fla. Law Ctr.; mem. Fla. Blue Key; founding mem., bd. dir. Fla. Women's Alliance; founding mem., past pres. Capital Women's Network, 1977—79; vice-chair Fla. Sales Tax on Svcs. Study Commn., 1986—87; mem. Fla. Coun. Econ. Edn., 1989—96, Fla. Edn. Found., 1991—96, Fla. Supreme Ct. Historical Soc.; bd. govs. Fla. Chamber, 2001. Named Nat. Women of Distinction, Girl Scouts U.S.A., 2002; named one of The 50 Most Influential Women Lawyers in Am., Nat. Law Jour., 1998, 2007, 100 Most Influential Lawyers, 2006; recipient Arabella Babb Mansfield award, Nat. Assn. Women Lawyers, 1996, Hillary Clinton Glass Cutter award, 1996, Alumnae of Distinction, U. Fla., 1997, Nat. Assn. Pub. Interest Law award, 1998, Newcomb Coll. Outstanding Alumna, 1999, Kate Stoneman award, Albany Law Sch., 1999, Nat. Legal Aid and Defender Assn. award, 2000, Disting. Alumna award, Tulane U., 2001, Medal of Honor award, Fla. Bar. Found., 2002, Rosemary Barkett award, Fla. Assn. Women Lawyers. Fellow: Am. Bar Found. (life); mem.: ABA (exec. coun. sect. on individual rights and responsibility 1974—86, chair, sect. individual rights and responsibilities 1984—85, task force on minorities in profession 1984—86, House of Delegates 1984—, mem. FJE Resources Com. 1985—89, commn. on legal problems of the elderly 1986—88, bd. govs. 1986—89, 1986—89, consortium on legal svcs and the pub. 1987—89, commn. on women in profession 1987—90, chair bd. govs. fin. com. 1988—89, chair, bd. govs. fin. com. 1988—89, long range planning com. 1988—91, chair commn. on pub. understanding about the law 1990—93, chair, commn. on pub. understanding about the law 1990—93, bd. editors ABA Jour. 1990—94, exec. coun. sect. legal edn. and admission to bar 1990—94, bd. editors, ABA Jour. 1990—96, chair, assembly resolutions com. 1991—94, ex-officio, Am. Bar Endowment 1994—96, ex-officio, Am. Bar Found. 1994—96, bd. govs. 1994—96, chair, Consortium on Legal Services and the Public 1996, exec. coun. sect. legal edn. and admission to bar 1996—99, mem. FJE Coun. 1996—99, Ctrl. European and Eurasian Law Initiative (CEELI) Exec. Bd. 1997—, pres.-elect 1999—2000, bd. govs. 1999—2001, bd. editors ABA Jour. 1999—2001, pres. 2000—01, mem. standing com. on legal aid to indigent defendents, mem. standing com. on prepaid legal svcs.), Tallahassee Women Lawyers Assn., Nat. Assn. Women Lawyers, Am. Judicature Soc. (bd. dir. 1986—89), Bar DC, Tallahassee Bar Assn., Fla. Bar Assn. (exec. coun. pub. interest law sect. 1989—91, mem. legis. com., mem. commn. on access to justice, exec. coun. of the tax sect.), Am. Law Inst., Nat. Inst. Dispute Resolution (sec.-treas. 1988—94, bd. dirs. 1988—94, Gov. appt. Fla. Constitution revision Commn. 1997—98), Phi Delta Phi, Phi Kappa Phi. Office: Holland & Knight LLP 315 S Calhoun St Ste 600 Tallahassee FL 32301 Office Phone: 850-425-5620. Business E-Mail: martha.barnett@hklaw.com.*

BARNETT, MICHAEL, former professional sports team executive; b. Olds, Alta., Can., Oct. 9, 1948; came to U.S., 1988; s. Terence R. and Mary M. Barnett; children: Jesse, Joey, Justin, Janie, Jenna. Student, St. Lawrence U., 1968-70; BS in Health and Phys. Edn., U. Calgary, 1973. Registered agent Nat. Hockey League Players Assn., Sports Lawyers Assn. Profl. hockey player LI Cougars (NAHL), 1973—74, Roanoka-Valley Rebels (SHL), 1974—75; founder, CEO Corpsport Internat. (merged with IMG), 1980—90; pres. hockey divsn. Internat. Mgmt. Group, 1990—2001; gen. mgr., alt. gov. Phoenix Coyotes, 2001—07. Gen. mgr. Ninety-Nine All Stars. Named one of Top 100 Most Powerful in Sports, The Sporting News, 1994, 95, 96, 98, 99, 2000, One of Twelve Most Powerful in Hockey, Hockey News, 1995. Mem. U.S.A. Hockey, U.S. Golf Assn. Achievements include former agent for NHL players such as Wayne Gretzky, Brett Hull, Jaromir Jagr, and Sergei Federov. Avocations: golf, running.

BARNETT, PATRICIA ANN, development professional; b. Culver City, Calif., Jan. 25; d. Howard Taft and Sarah (Ross) B. BJ, U. Tex., 1978; MLA, So. Meth. U., 2002. Program specialist Dallas C. of C., 1978-79, comm. specialist, 1979-81; mgr. pub. rels. Trailways Corp., Dallas, 1981-82, dir. pub. rels., 1982-85; sr. account exec. Keller-Crescent Co., Dallas, 1985-87; dir. comm. Office Pvt. Sector Initiatives The White House, Washington, 1987-89; dir. pub. affairs United Way Am., Alexandria, Va., 1989-91; dir. pub. rels. Dally Advt., Ft. Worth, 1992-94; dir. corp. and found. rels. So. Meth. U., Dallas, 1994-96, dir. major gifts, 1996—2001; exec. dir. devel. Dedman Coll., 2001—07; v.p. donor rels. Baylor Health Care Sys. Found., Dallas, 2007—. Mem.: Jr. League Dallas. Republican. Avocations: history, travel, literature, folk art, bookbinding. Office Phone: 214-820-6144. Business E-Mail: triciaba@baylorhealth.edu.

BARNETT, PRESTON B., lawyer, communications executive; b. Monroeville, Ala., Aug. 4, 1946; m. Billie Barnett. BA in History and Bus. Adminstrn., Birmingham-So. Coll.; JD, U. Ala. CPA; bar: Ala., Ga. Atty. Arthur Andersen & Co., various acctg. firms, Cox Enterprises, Atlanta, 1979—, v.p., gen. tax counsel. Mem.: Broadband Tax Inst. (pres. 2002—04, bd. dirs.), Tax Execs. Inst. (pres. Atlanta chpt. 1991—92, regional v.p. 1996—97), Ga. Bar Assn., Ala. Bar Assn., Birmingham-So. Coll. Nat. Alumni Assn. (pres. 2000—01). Office: Cox Enterprises 6205 Peachtree Dunwoody Rd Atlanta GA 30328*

BARNETT, RICHARD CHAMBERS, historian, educator; b. Davenport, Fla., Apr. 27, 1932; s. Jones Richard and Helen June (Chambers) B.; m. Betty May Tribble, Oct. 18, 1957; children— Amelia Carlton, Colin Warwick BA, Wake Forest Coll., 1953; M.Ed., U. N.C., 1954, PhD, 1963. Instr., acting chmn. dept. social sci. Gardner-Webb Coll., 1956-58; instr. history Wake Forest U., Winston-Salem, NC, 1961-62, asst. prof., 1962-67, assoc. prof., 1967-76, prof., 1976—94, chmn. dept. history, 1968-75, 83-87, acting dean Grad. Sch., 1979; retired. Contbr. articles to profl. jours., chapters to books. Pres Winston-Salem-Forsyth PTA, 1969-71; bd. mgrs. N.C. PTA, 1971-73, exec. com., 1972-73, life mem.; adv. com. N.C. Bd. Edn., 1973-76. Served with CIC, AUS, 1954-56 Southeastern Inst. Medieval and Renaissance Studies fellow, 1974 Mem. Am. Hist. Assn. (pres. elect N.C. conf. 1991-92, pres. 1992-93), AAUP, Carolinas Symposium Brit. Studies (pres. 1979-80), So. Conf. Brit. Studies (pres. 1990-92), N.Am. Conf. Brit. Studies (coun. 1990-92), Danforth Assocs. Home: 2130 Royall Dr Winston Salem NC 27106-5234

BARNETT, ROBERT B., JR., lawyer; b. Cleve., July 24, 1949; s. Robert B. Barnett and Ruth (Woodruff) Lorenz; m. Sally Myers, Apr. 26, 1986. BS, Ohio State U., 1971, JD, 1975. Bar: Ohio 1975. Ptnr. Carlile, Patchen, Murphy & Allison, Columbus, Ohio, 1975—. Sec. Devel. Bd. Children's Hosp., Columbus, 1982—; pres. Encore Group Ballet Met., Columbus, 1983-84; trustee Village Home Inc., Columbus, 1983-85. Mem. ABA, Ohio Bar Assn., Columbus Bar Assn. (chmn. taxation com. 1984-85), Columbus Tax Conf. (chmn. 1985—). Clubs: Athletic (Columbus), Hickory Hills Country. Democrat. Avocations: sports, sailing. Home: 544 S Front St Apt 109 Columbus OH 43215-7611

BARNETT, ROBERT BRUCE, lawyer; b. Waukegan, Ill., Aug. 26, 1946; s. Bernard and Betty Jane (Simon) Barnett; m. Rita Lynn Braver, Apr. 10, 1972; 1 child, Meredith Jane. BA, U. Wis., 1968; JD, U. Chgo., 1971. Bar: D.C. 1971. Law clk. to Hon. John Minor Wisdom U.S. Ct. Appeals (5th cir.), 1971-72; law clk. to Assoc. Justice Byron R. White U.S. Supreme Ct., Washington, 1972-73; legis. asst. to Senator Walter F. Mondale US Senate, Washington, 1973-75; assoc. Williams & Connolly, Washington, 1975-78, ptnr., 1979—. Adj. prof. Georgetown Law Sch., 1973—80. Trustee John F. Kennedy Ctr. Performing Arts, 1994—2004, sr. counsel, 2005—; mem. bd. visitors Sanford Inst. of Pub. Policy, Duke U., 1998—2001, U. Chgo. Law Sch., 2001—04; mem. bd. visitors LaFollette Sch. Pub. Affairs U. Wis., 2004—; mem. bd. trustees Toyota Tech. Inst., U. Chgo., 2006—, bd. mem., 2006—. Named No. 1 of Washington's Best Lawyers, Washingtonian Mag.; named one of 100 Most Influential Lawyers, Nat. Law. Jour., 2006. Mem.: Coun. on Fgn. Rels. Office: Williams & Connolly LLP 725 12th St NW Washington DC 20005-5901 Office Phone: 202-434-5034.

BARNETT, ROBERT JAMES, music educator, musician; b. Erie, Pa., Feb. 12, 1954; s. James Earl and Betty Jo Barnett; m. Arlene Elaine Farmer, Oct. 24, 1954; children: Ryan James, Alexander Earl. MusB, Youngstown State U., 1977; MEd, Ashland U., 1998. Dir. of bands West Br. H.s., Beloit, Ohio, 1977—; prin. timpanist Youngstown Symphony, 1979—, Packard Concert Band, Warren, Ohio, 1986—. Coord. honors band Ohio Music Edn. Assn., 1991—97. Composer, musician: percussion ensemble music Christmas By The Numbers. Mem.: Am. Fedn. Musicians, Music Educators Nat. Conf., Phi Mu Alpha (life; dist. pres. 1975—76). Home: 1193 Hampton Pl Salem OH 44460 Office: West Branch H S 14277 Main St Beloit OH 44609 Home Phone: 330-332-1388; Office Phone: 330-938-2183. Personal E-mail: rbarnett3@neo.rr.com.

BARNETT, SAMUEL TREUTLEN, consultant; m. Rena Harrington, Sept. 22, 2001; children: Elizabeth L., Katharine T., Emily R., Alexander W. BA, Wesleyan U., 1969; MEd, Temple U., 1973, EdD, 1975. Tchr. The Haverford Sch., 1969—74; freelance cons., 1971—76; leadership devel. specialist Phila. Sch. Dist., 1974—75; cons. US Office Personnel Mgmt., 1976—79; founder, mng. ptnr. Barnett Assoc., 1979—90; chief cons. Barnett Internat. subs. PAREXEL Internat., Media, Pa., 1990—99; lead ptnr. N.Am. pharm. sector mgmt. cons. svcs. PricewaterhouseCoopers, Phila., 1999—2002; mem. adv. bd. PharmaStar Ltd., 2003—; lead ptnr. Am. Life Sci. Pharm. Practice IBM Bus. Consultancy Svcs., Phila., 2002—05; ret., 2005; bd. dirs. Astalis Ltd., Fairfield, NJ, 2004—, Medifacts Internat., Rockville, Md., 2005—. Spkr. in field. Contbr. articles to profl. jours. Mem.: Drug Info. Assn. Home: 230 S Ridley Creek Rd Media PA 19063-4216 Personal E-mail: sam.barnett3@verizon.net.

BARNETT, THOMAS O., federal agency administrator; BA summa cum laude, Yale U., 1985; MS, London Sch. Econ., 1986; JD magna cum laude, Harvard Law Sch., 1989. Bar: Md., DC. Law clk. to Hon. Harrison Winter US Ct. Appeals (4th Cir.), Richmond, Va., 1989—90; ptnr., vice chair Antitrust & Consumer Protection practice group Covington & Burling, Washington, 1990—2004; dep. asst. atty. gen. civil enforcement US Dept. Justice, Washington, 2004—05, acting asst. atty. gen., Antitrust Divsn., 2005—06, asst. atty. gen., Antitrust Divsn., 2006—. Adj. prof. Georgetown U. Law Ctr., Washington. Mem.: Antitrust Sect. ABA. Office: US Dept Justice Antitrust Div 950 Pennsylvania Ave Washington DC 20530 Office Phone: 202-514-2401. Office Fax: 202-616-2645.*

BARNETT, VIVIAN ENDICOTT, curator; b. Putnam, Conn., July 8, 1944; d. George and Vivian (Wood) Endicott; m. Peter Herbert Barnett, July 1, 1967; children: Sarah, Alexander. AB magna cum laude, Vassar Coll., Poughkeepsie, NY, 1965; MA, NYU, 1971; postgrad., CUNY, 1979—81. Research asst. Solomon R. Guggenheim Mus., NYC, 1973-77, curatorial assoc., 1978-79, assoc. curator, 1980-81, rsch. curator, 1981-82, curator, 1982-91; dir. Roethel Benjamin Archive at Guggenheim Mus., NYC, 1991—. Author: (book) The Guggenheim Museum: Justin K. Thannhauser Collection, 1978, The Guggenheim Museum Collection 1900-1980, Kandinsky at the Guggenheim, 1983, 100 Works by Modern Masters from the Guggenheim Museum, 1984, Kandinsky and Sweden, 1989, Kandinsky in Major Collections in the West, 1989, Kandinsky Watercolours: Catalogue Raisonnè, vol I 1900-1921, 1992, Kandinsky Watercolours: Catalogue Raisonnè, vol II 1922-1944, 1994, Kleine Freuden, 1992, Das bunte Leben: Kandinsky in Lenbachhaus, 1995, The Blue Four: Feininger, Jawlensky, Kandinsky, Klee in the New World, 1997, The Blue Four Collection at the Norton Simon Museum, 2002, Kandinsky Drawings: Catalogue Raisonne, vol. I, 2006; contbg. author: Kandinsky in Paris: 1934-44, 1985, Kandinsky Drawings: Catalogue Raisonne Vol. II, 2007, Exiles and Emigres: 1933-1945, 1997, The Joy of Color: The Merzbacher Collection, 1998, Mies in America, 2001, Die Brucke in Dresden, 2001, Art of Tomorrow: Hilla Rebay and Solomon Guggenheim, 2005, Klee and America, 2006. Fellow John Simon Guggenheim, 1990, Inst. Advanced Study, Princeton, 2003—04. Mem.: Coll. Art Assn. Am., Internat. Coun. Museums, Soc. Kandinsky (sec. 1992—2001). Office: Solomon R Guggenheim Mus 1071 5th Ave New York NY 10128-0112 Office Phone: 212-423-3612. Personal E-mail: vbarnett@att.net.

BARNETT, WILL, painter; b. 1911; Studied, Sch. Mus. Fine Arts, Boston, Mass. Former instr. Art Students League, Yale Univ., Cooper Union, Cornell Univ., Penn. Acad. Fine Arts; prof., Grad. Sch. Nat. Acad. Sch. Fine Arts. Exhibitions include Babcock Gallery, NYC, Alexander Gallery, Tibor de Nagy Gallery, Susan Teller Gallery, Sylvan Cole Gallery, Montclair Art Mus., Springfield Art Mus., Represented in permanent collections. Mem.: Nat. Acad. (hon. pres.). Office: c/o Babcock Gallery 724 Fifth Ave New York NY 10019-4106

BARNETT, WILLIAM ARNOLD, economics professor; b. Boston, Oct. 30, 1941; s. Marcus Jack and Elizabeth Leah (Forman) B.; m. Melinda Gentry, Sept. 1, 1991. BS, MIT, 1963; MBA, U. Calif., Berkeley, 1965; MS, Carnegie Mellon U., 1972, PhD, 1974. System devel. engr., Apollo Project, Rocketdyne div. Rockwell Internat. Corp., Canoga Park, Calif., 1963-67; research econometrician Bd. Govs., Fed. Reserve System, Washington, 1973-81; Stuart Centennial prof. econs. U. Tex., Austin, 1981-90; prof. econs. Washington U., St. Louis, 1990—; Oswald Disting. prof. macroeconomics U. of Kans., 2002—. Vis. prof. econs. U. Aix-Marseille, Aix-en-Provence, France, 1979, Duke U., Durham, N.C., 1987-88; organizer ann. symposia in econ. theory and econometrics; assoc. dir. Ctr. for Econ. Rsch., U. Tex., Austin, 1981-90. Author: Consumer Demand and Labor Supply, 1981; editor Jour. Econometrics, 1979-80, 85, Cambrige U. Press Monograph series, 1985—, Cambridge U. Press Jour. Macroeconomic Dynamics, 1997—; assoc. editor Jour. Bus. and Econ. Stats., 1982-97; contbr. over 75 articles to profl. jours. Contract selection panel mem. NIH, Washington, 1983; cons. World Bank, Washington, 1985. R.K. Mellon Found. fellow, 1971-73; rsch. grantee NSF, Washington, 1977-89, Hogg Found., Houston, 1983. Fellow ICC Inst. (sr., editor 1983—), Am. Statis. Assn. (assoc. editor 1982—, fellow 1989—, program chair 1992—), Jour. Econometrics (charter fellow 1989—); mem. Inst. Math. Stats., Econometric Soc. (contbr. to jour.), Am. Econ. Assn Home: 1904 Inverness Dr Lawrence KS 66047-1832 Office: U Kans Dept Econs Lawrence KS 66045

BARNETTE, CURTIS HANDLEY, steel company executive, lawyer; b. St. Albans, W.Va., Jan. 9, 1935; s. Curtis Franklin and Garnett Drucella (Robinson) Barnette; m. Loris Joan Harner, Dec. 28, 1957; children: Curtis Kevin, James David. AB with High Honors, W.Va. U., 1956; postgrad. (Fulbright scholar), U. Manchester, 1956—57; JD, Yale U., 1962; grad. advanced mgmt. program, Harvard U., 1974—75; LLD (hon.), W.Va. U., 1995, DeSales U., 1996, U. Charleston, 1998, Lehigh U., 1999, Moravian Coll., 2002. Cert. Conn., 1962, Pa., 1968, D.C., 1988, W.Va., 1990. Atty. Wiggin & Dana, New Haven, 1962—67, Bethlehem (Pa.) Steel Corp., 1967—92, sec., 1976—92, gen. counsel, 1977—92, sr. v.p., 1985—92, chmn., CEO, 1992—2000, also bd. dirs., 1986—2000; of counsel Skadden, Arps, Slate, Meagher & Flom, LLP, 2000—. Lectr. U. Md., 1958—59; law tutor Yale U., 1962—67; chmn. bd. dirs. Am. Iron and Steel Inst., 1997, dir., 1992—2000; bd. dirs. Met Life Ins. Co., Lehigh Valley Partnership; chmn. Internat. Iron and Steel Inst., 1994—95, dir., 1992—2000; Comenius prof., exec. in residence, trustee Moravian Coll., 2000—. Trustee Lehigh U., 1993—2004; Pa. Soc., 1993—; mem. Adminstrv. Conf. U.S., 1988—89; bd. govs. W.Va. U., 2002—, chmn. bd. govs., 2002—04; dir. W.Va. U. Found., 1982—, chair, 1987—88; chmn. Yale Law Sch. Fund; mem. adv. com. Coal Commn., 1990, Pa. 21st Century Environ. Com., 1997—98; bd. mem. pres.'s adv. com. Trade Policy and Negotiation, 1989—2001. With Counterintelligence Corps US Army, 1957—59, maj. USAR, 1959—67. Mem.: ABA, Nat. Ctr. for State Cts. (dir. 2001—07), Pa. Soc. (dir.), Nat. Mus. Indsl. History (chmn.), Pa. Pk. Found., Pa. Bus. Roundtable (dir. 1986—2000, chmn. 1994—95), Bus. Roundtable (policy com. 1992—2000), Bus. Coun., Pa. Chamber Bus. and Industry (dir. 1985—93), Am. Law Inst., Am. Soc. Corp. Secs. (chmn. 1986), Assn. Gen. Counsel (pres. 1988—90), W.Va. Bar Assn., DC Bar Assn., Northampton County Bar Assn., Conn. Bar Assn., Pa. Bar Assn., Met. Club Washington, Blooming Grove Hunting and Fishing Club, Bethlehem Club, Lobolly, Links, Saucon Valley Country Club, Yale Club NYC, Univ. Club Washington, Phi Beta Kappa, Phi Delta Phi, Phi Alpha Theta, Beta Theta Pi. Home: 1112 Prospect Ave Bethlehem PA 18018-4914 also: 1440 New York Ave NW Washington DC 20005-2111 Office: Skadden Arps Slate Meagher & Flom LLP 512 N New St Bethlehem PA 18018 Office Phone: 202-371-7252. E-mail: hbarnett@skadden.com.

BARNETTE, JAMES D., lawyer; b. Sept. 10, 1963; BA, Yale Univ., 1985; JD, Georgetown Univ., 1990. Bar: Pa. 1990, D.C. 1992. Legis. asst. U.S. Senator Arlen Specter, 1985—87; assoc. Weil Gotshal & Manges, Washington, 1990—95; counsel Com. Energy & Commerce, U.S. Ho. Rep., Washington, 1995—98, gen. counsel & dep. staff dir., 1998—2006; ptnr. Collier Shannon Scott PLLC, The Scott Group, Washington, Steptoe & Johnson LLP, Washington, 2007—. Mem.: ABA (vice-chair, Brownfields Task Force), D.C. Bar Assn., Pa. Bar Assn. Office: Committee on Energy & Commerce Room 2125 Rayburn House Office Building Washington DC 20515-6115 also: Steptoe & Johnson LLP 1330 Connecticut Ave Washington DC 20036 Office Phone: 202-429-6207. E-mail: jbarnette@steptoe.com.

BARNEVIK, PERCY NILS, electrical company executive; b. Simrishamn, Sweden, Feb. 13, 1941; s. Einar and Anna Barnevik; m. Aina Orvarsson, 1963; 3 children. MBA, Gothenburg Sch. Econs., Sweden, 1964; postgrad., Stanford U., 1965-66; TechnDr honoris causa, U. Linkoping, Sweden, 1989; Econ. Dr. honoris causa, U. Gothenburg, Sweden, 1991; JD (hon.), Babson Coll., 1995; Sci. Dr. honoris causa, Cranfield U., 1998; D (hon.), U. Manches, 1999. With The Johnson Group, Sweden, 1966-69, Sandvik AB, Sandviken, Sweden, 1969-80, group controller, 1969-75; pres. US affiliate, 1975-79; exec. v.p. Sandvik, Sweden, 1979-80; pres., chief exec. officer ASEA, 1980-87; chmn. Sandvik AB, 1983—2002, hon. chmn., 2002—; pres., CEO Asea Brown Boveri Ltd., 1988-96, chmn.,

CEO, 1996-97; chmn. Investor AB, Sweden, 1997—2002, ABB Ltd., 1997—2001, AstraZeneca PLC, England, 1999—2004. Bd. dirs. GM, Detroit. Advisor Indian Trust Hand in Hand, 2000—. Office: 10 Hill St London W1J 5NQ England

BARNEWALL, MARILYN MACGRUDER, retired banker; b. Indpls. d. Robert Danforth MacGruder and Hester Bruce Wooden Brown; m. Gordon Gouverneur Barnewall, Aug. 1970 (div. Jan. 1973); children: John Clyde, Katherine Barnewall Coomer. Graduate degree, Colo. U., 1978. Reporter Wyoming Eagle, Cheyenne, 1956—57; mgr. Combined Ins. Co., Denver, 1961—65; dir. public relations Nat. Camera, 1966—68; mag. editor, asst. to pub. Bell Publs., 1968—70; v.p. mgr. United Bank, Denver, 1972—79; CEO MacGruder Agy. Inc., Denver, 1979—89, Cin., 1989—93; editorialist Grand Junction Free Press, Colo., 2003—06, World Net Daily, 2004—06, Bus. Reform, 2004—07. Expert witness for equal credit for women Colo. State Legis., 1977. Author: A Banker's Pragmatic Approach to the Upscale, 1982, Profitable Private Banking: The Complete Blueprint, 1986, republished in Europe, 1986, The Warren, Gorham & LaMont 1986 Private Banking Profitability Survey, Cosmic Canines, 1998; sportswriter Wyoming Eagle, Cheyenne, 1957. Bd. mem. Camp Fire Girls, Colo. State U. Family Action Ctr., Am. for Effective Law Enforcement, United Negro Coll. Fund, Metro Denver Urban Coalition, Big Brothers; founder 1st girls' baseball league Denver, 1952; founder NFL Fans Union, Denver, 1985. Sr. fellow, Mt. Vernon Inst., 2007. Mem.: Leukemia Soc. of Am. (chair, fundraiser 1976). Avocations: writing, photography, genealogy, travel, cooking.

BARNEY, AUSTIN DUNHAM, II, real estate developer; b. Hartford, Conn., Apr. 27, 1945; s. Philip Cushman and Elizabeth Cole (Freeman) B.; m. Susan C. Rumney, Aug. 26, 1976 (div. Mar. 1998); children: Austin C. D. III, Amanda Brandegee. BA in Polit. Sci., Yale U., 1967; MPA, Syracuse U., 1969. Lic. real estate broker, Conn., N.Y., Mass.; lic. life/health ins., securities, Conn.; cert. ins. cons., risk profl. Mgmt. asst. U. Hartford, Conn., 1967-68; jr./sr. planner Hartford Police Dept., 1969-70; sr. planner Commn. on City Plan City of Hartford, 1970; sr. adminstrv. analyst fin. dept. City of Hartford Budget and Rsch. Divsn., 1970-71, prin. adminstrv. analyst fin. dept., 1971-72; dir. land use policy planning State of Conn., Dept. Environ. Protection, 1972-73; exec. dir. Environ. Ctrs. Inc., 1973-75; pvt. practice cons., 1975-76; dir. natural resources mgmt. and community design Westledge Ctr. for Edn., 1976-78; sr. cons. corp. citizenship Cigna Corp. (Conn. Gen. Ins. Corp.), 1979-82; dir. contbns. and civic affairs Cigna Corp., Conn. Gen. Ins. Corp., 1982-84; pres., founder Farmvest, Inc., 1984—; prin. Bus. Planning Assocs., 1991-96; pres. Life Legacy Advisors, LLC, West Simsbury, Conn., 1996—. Dir. Spiritus Wines, Inc.; hon. dir. Aid to Artesans; ptnr. Folly Farm Assocs., 1983—90; pres. Folly Farm, Inc., 1983—90. Zoning commr. Town of Simsbury, Conn., 1976—, sec., 1993—, chmn., 2006-; del. People's Republic China, Yale-China Assn., fall 1979, 80; corporator Hartford Pub. Libr., 1981—; corporator The Ctr. Families and Children, 1996—; bd. dirs., exec. com. Riverfront Recapture, Inc., 1981-90; bd. trustees Hartford Art Sch., 1969-03, pres. 1984-86, 96-03, hon. trustee, 2003—; bd. dirs. Conn. Trust for Hist. Preservation, 1982-85, The Nature Conservancy, treas. 1986-89, vice-chmn., 1989-00, Oak Leaf award, 1995; bd. dirs. U. Conn. Found., 1988-92, Ensign-Bickford Found., 1987-93, v.p., 1989-93; bd. dirs. Ea. States Expo., 1989-; chmn. Conn. trustees 1993-96; elector Wadsworth Atheneum, 1983—; bd. dirs., chmn. fin. com. Earth Day 20, Inc., 1990; regent U. Hartford, 1980-86, 90-03; mem. Simsbury Open Space Preservation Commn., 2002—. Recipient Nat. Oak Leaf award Nature Conservancy, 1995, Pubs. Svc. award State of Conn., 2001, Gold medal for outstanding leadership excellence Hartford Art Sch., 2003. Mem. Nat. Assn. Life Underwriters, Am. Assn. Life Underwriters, Conn. Assn. Life Underwriters, Hartford Assn. Life Underwriters, Conn. Life Leaders. Personal E-mail: acdb2@att.net.

BARNEY, CAROL ROSS, architect; b. Chgo., Apr. 12, 1949; d. Chester Albert and Dorothy Valeria (Dusiewicz) Ross; m. Alan Fredrick Barney, Mar. 22, 1970; children: Ross Fredrick, Adam Shafer, John Ross. BArch, U. Ill., 1971. Registered architect, Ill. Assoc. architect Holabird & Root, Chgo., 1972-79; prin. architect Orput Assoc., Inc., Wilmette, Ill., 1979-81; prin. architect, pres. Ross Barney Arch., Chgo., 1981—, also bd. dirs. Studio prof. Ill. Inst. Tech., Chgo., 1993-94; asst. prof. U. Ill., Chgo., 1976-78. Prin. works include Glendale Heights Post Office, Ill., Little Village Acad. Pub. Sch., Fed. Bldg., Oklahoma City, Swenson Sci. Bldg., U. Md. Plan commr. Village of Wilmette, 1986-88, mem. Econ. Devel. Commn., 1988-90, chmn. Appearance Rev. Commn., 1990-2000; trustee Children's Home and Aid Soc. Ill., Chgo., 1986—; mem. adv. bd. Small Bus. Ctr. for Women, Chgo., 1985—. Recipient Fed. Design Achievement award, 1992; Francis J. Plym travelling fellow, 1983. Fellow AIA (bd. dirs. Chgo. chpt. 1978-80, v.p. 1981-82, Disting. Svc. award Chgo. chpt. 1978, Ill. Coun. 1978, Firm award 1995, Honor award 1991, 94, 99, 2002, Thomas Jefferson award for pub. architecture 2005); mem. Nat. Coun. Archtl. Registration Bds. (cert.), Chgo. Women in Architecture (founding pres. 1978-79), Chgo. Network, Cliff Dwellers Club (bd. dirs. 1995). Home: 601 Linden Ave Wilmette IL 60091-2819 Office: Ross Barney Architects 10 W Hubbard St Chicago IL 60610 Office Phone: 312-832-0600 ext. 221. Business E-Mail: crb@r-barc.com.

BARNEY, KLINE PORTER, JR., engineering company executive, consultant; b. Dec. 16, 1934; s. Kline Porter and Doris (Nielsen) B.; m. Cheryl Kathleen Taylor, June 14, 1957; children: Peter, Suzanne, Cathleen, Patrick, Andrew. BS, U. Utah, 1957; MPA, San Diego State U., 1971. Registered profl. engr., 7 states. Asst. engr. Fallbrook (Calif.) Pub. Utility Dist., 1960-63; pres. Engring. Sci., Inc., Arcadia, Calif., 1963-85, Parsons Mcpl. Svcs., Inc., Pasadena, Calif., 1985-89; sr. v.p. Parsons Engring. Sci., Inc., Pasadena, 1989-97; cons., 1997—; owner Kline Barney Engrs., 1999—. Presenter on field of privatization, 1983—; environ. cons. Contbr. articles to profl. jours. Mem. exec. bd. San Gabriel coun. Boy Scouts Am., 1981-96. Capt. USMC, 1957-60. Mem. ASCE, Am. Acad. Environ. Engrs. (diplomate), Am. Acad. Water Resources Engrs. (diplomate), Am. Waterworks Assn., Water Environ. Fedn., Tau Beta Pi, Chi Epsilon, Phi Eta Sigma. Republican. Mem. Lds Ch. Avocations: hiking, astronomy. Home: 800 Juniperpoint Dr Salt Lake City UT 84103-3331 Office Phone: 801-519-0335.

BARNEY, MICHAEL E., lawyer; b. Petersburg, Va., Apr. 20, 1947; s. Jack Hansford and Maxine (Scott) Barney; m. Roslyn Ann Weiner, June 7, 1970; children: Jason Ross, Scott Ryan. BA, U. Va., 1969; JD, U. Richmond, 1972. Bar: Va. 1972. Ptnr. Kaufman & Canoles P.C., Norfolk, Va., 1972—. Lectr. in field. Contbr. articles to profl. jours. Officer, bd. dirs. Jewish Cmty. Ctr. Tidewater, Norfolk, 1980—86, Beth El Congregation, Norfolk, 1988—90. Capt. USAR, 1971—79. Mem.: Am. Coll. Real Estate Lawyers, Norfolk and Portsmouth Bar Assn., Virginia Beach Bar Assn., Va. Bar Assn. (coun. real property sect.), Va. State Bar (bd. govs. real property sect., chairperson real property sect. 1988), Va. Assn. Realtors (assoc.), Tidewater Builders Assn. (assoc.). Avocations: hunting, golf, fishing, boating. Office: Kaufman and Canoles PO Box 626 Virginia Beach VA 23451-0626 Office Phone: 757-491-4040. Business E-Mail: mebarney@kaufcan.com.

BARNHARD, STEVE, travel company executive; BA in Econs., U. Chgo., MBA in Fin. Econ. analyst polyurethanes div. ICI; with Am. Nat. Bank, Chgo.; dir. fin. Pepsi Bottling Group PepsiCo; joined Travelport (formerly Cedant TDS), 2003, CFO consumer travel unit, pres. Orbitz Worldwide, Inc., 2006—07, pres., CEO Orbitz Worldwide, Inc., 2007—. Office: Orbitz Worldwide, Inc 500 W Madison St Ste 1000 Chicago IL 60661*

BARNHARDT, ROBERT ALEXANDER, retired dean; b. Jenkins Township, Pa., Sept. 21, 1937; s. Daniel T. and Janet A. (MacCartney) B.; married. BS in Textile Engring., Phila. Coll. Textiles and Sci., 1959; MS, Inst. Textile Tech., 1961; MEd, U. Va., 1970, EdD, 1974. Assoc. prof. fabric tech. Phila. Coll. Textiles and Sci., 1961-64, chmn. dept. textiles, 1964-66; dir. edn. Inst. Textile Tech., Charlottesville, Va., 1966-69, dean and dir. edn., 1972-76, dir. rsch. and edn., 1977-78, v.p. rsch. and edn., 1978-84, exec. v.p., chief oper. officer, 1984-87; dean Coll. Textiles NC State U., Raleigh, 1987—2004, interim chancellor, 2004. Bd. dirs. Textile/Clothing Tech. Corp., Raleigh, Harriet & Henderson Yarns, Inc., N.C., So. Textile Assn. Mem. Curry Sch. Found., U. Va. Fellow Textile Inst. Gt. Britain (medal 1988); mem. Am. Soc. Engring. Edn., Nat. Coun. for Textile Edn. (pres. 1990—), Internat. Conf. Textile Edn., Phi Kappa Phi. Episcopalian. Avocations: tennis, skiing, singing, golf, gardening. Office: NC State U Coll Textiles Box 8301 4700 Hillsborough St Raleigh NC 27606-1428

BARNHARDT, ZEB ELONZO, JR., lawyer, mediator, arbitrator; b. Winston-Salem, NC, Dec. 28, 1941; s. Zeb Elonzo and Katie Sue (Taylor) B.; m. Pam Hall; children: Daniel Black, Kathleen Martin. AB, Duke U., 1964; JD, Vanderbilt U., 1969. Bar: N.C. 1969; cert. mediator, N.C. Assoc. Womble Carlyle Sandridge & Rice, PLLC, Winston-Salem, 1969-75, mem., 1975-97, of counsel, 1997-98; owner, mgr. Barnhardt & Assocs., Inc., Haw River, NC, 1998—; pvt. practice law Haw River, 1998—; mediator N.C. Superior Ct., 2003—. Arbitrator Nat. Assn. Securities Dealers, 1992—, mediator, 2004—. Alumni admissions adv. com. Duke U., 1970-72; bd. dirs. Industries for Blind, Winston-Salem, 1973-85, vice chmn., 1983-84, chmn., 1985; bd. dirs. Goodwill Industries, Winston-Salem, 1973-80, BarCARES of NC, Inc., 1999-2005, Little Theatre, Winston-Salem, 1979-85, asst. treas., 1980, treas., 1981-82, v.p., 1983-84, pres., 1984-85; adv. bd. Salvation Army, Winston-Salem, 1973-85, chmn., 1979-80, Leadership Winston-Salem, 1984-92, v.p. adminstrn., 1988-89, pres. 1989-90; com. mem. Winston-Salem Found., 1975-84, vice chmn., 1978-80, chmn., 1983-84; trustee High Point U., 1984-96; chmn. Second Journey Inc., 2002-2003, bd. trustees Coastal Horizons Ctr., Inc., Wilmington, NC, 2005-06; bd. dirs. Cmty. Found. Southeastern NC, 2006-07. With USN, 1964—66. Recipient Disting. Service award as Young Man of Yr. Winston-Salem Jaycees, 1974; Disting. Alumni award Duke U., 1979 Mem. ABA (bus. law sect., 1969—, dispute resolution sect., 2003—, Commn. on Lawyer Assistance Programs 2002-05), N.C. Bar Assn. (mem. bus. law. sect., 1969—, chmn. securities regulation com. 1985-87, vice chmn. bus. law sect. 1987-89, chmn. bus. law sect. 1989-91, mem. dispute resolution sect., 2003—, bd. govs. 1991-94, chair membership recruitment and retention com. 1997-2000, chair lawyer effectiveness and quality of life com. 2001—04), Winston-Salem Jaycees (life, pres. 1973-74), N.C. Jaycees (regional dir. 1974-75, legal counsel 1975-77), Greater Winston-Salem C. of C. (bd. dirs. 1973-74), Rotary. Democrat. Methodist.

BARNHART, CHARLES ELMER, zoology educator; b. Windsor, Ill., Jan. 25, 1923; s. Elmer and Irma (Smysor) B.; m. Norma McCarty, Dec. 28, 1946 (dec. Dec. 25, 1970); children: John D., Charles E., Norman R.; m. Jean M. Hutton, Jan. 12, 1973; stepchildren: Mark, David, Bonnie, Beth Hutton. BS in Agr., Purdue U., 1945; MS, Ia. State U., 1948, PhD, 1954. Mem. faculty U. Ky., Lexington, from 1948, assoc. prof. animal sci., 1955-57, prof., 1957-88, prof. emeritus, 1988—, dean, dir. exptl. sta. and coop. extension service, 1969-88, dean emeritus, 1988—. Pres. So. Assn. Agrl. Scientist, 1982-83 Patentee in field. Bd. dirs. Ky. Bd. Agr., 1966-88, Ky. State Fair and Expn. Ctr., 1969-88, Ky. Tobacco Rsch. Bd., Farm Credit Svcs. Mid Am., 1988-93, Ky. Farm Bur., 1969-76; mem. Gov.'s Coun. on Agrl., 1971-80. Named Man of Yr. in Ky. Agr. Progressive Farmer, 1962, Man of Yr. for Ky. Agr. Ky. Agrl. Communicators, 1979; elected to Saddle and Sirloin Portrait Gallery, 1987. Mem. Am. Soc. Animal Sci., Ky. Hist. Soc., Farmhouse Fraternity, Masons (32 deg.), Shriners, Epsilon Sigma Phi, Gamma Sigma Delta., Omicron Delta Kappa, Sigma Xi. Methodist.

BARNHART, CYNTHIA, engineering educator, researcher; BS in Civil Engring., U. Vt., 1981; MS in Transp., MIT, 1985, PhD in Transp. & Civil Engring., 1988. With MIT, 1992—, co-dir. Ctr. for Transp. & Logistics, leader engring. systems group, asst. prof. to prof. civil and environ. engring. Founder Large-Scale Optimization Group Mass. Inst. Tech., 1997; bd. dirs. Inst. Ops. Research Mgmt. Scis. (INFORMS); spkr. in field. Assoc. editor: Operations, Research, and Transportation Science; contbr. articles to profl. jours. Recipient Jr. Faculty Career award, Gen. Electric Found., Presdl. Young Investigator award, NSF. Achievements include research in models and algorithms to improve carrier operations (focusing on airlines). Office: MIT Bldg 1-229/E40-149A 77 Massachusetts Ave Cambridge MA 02139 Office Phone: 617-253-3815. Office Fax: 617-258-5765. Business E-Mail: cbarnhar@mit.edu.

BARNHART, DOROTHY MAY (KOHRS), retired small business owner; b. Des Moines, Apr. 27, 1933; d. Oliver John and Lily Mabel (Smith) Kohrs; children: Jacqueline, Dwaine Jr., Kelly stepchildren: Billy Jo, Jack, Cindy. Attended, Internat. Acctg. Soc., Chgo., Drake U., 1956, Area II C.C., 1987—88. Bookkeeper Iowa Credit Union League, 1954—69, Grand Printing Art-O-Type, 1970—72; office mgr. Am. Bus. Forms & Sys., Inc., 1972—76; forms dept. mgr. Action Forms/Action Printers Co., 1976—77; office mgr. Elliott Beechcraft Flying Svc., 1977—81; tel. selling rep. Coca Cola Co., 1983—84; adminstrv. asst. Coalition for Family and Children's Svc. in Iowa, Des Moines, 1984—97; pres., owner Wellness Games, Ltd., 1985—; ret. Coord. ann. statewide conf. Coalition Family and Children's Svc. in Iowa, 1987—97; coord. Chronic Pain Outreach of Ctrl. Iowa, 1984—, Midwest regional dir., 1985—87; coord. fundraisers, Wellness Game marathons; writer TV show featuring Wellness board game, 2001—04. Mem. Growth Group at Powell III, Iowa Women's Polit. Caucus; mem. choir Grace United Meth. Ch.; mem. disability action com. Des Moines Area Urban Mission Coun. Fellow: Internat. Biographical Ctr. (adv. coun., humanitarian svc. award); mem.: NAFE, Women's C. of C. of Des Moines. Democrat. Achievements include invention of Wellness Game. Home: #15 2525 County Line Rd Des Moines IA 50321 *Think of the things you can do and not the things you can not do. Don't take yourself too seriously. Remember nobody is perfect. Value and be good to yourself and others. Take time for yourself. Be yourself--- you are unique. Learn to enjoy the simple pleasures of life. Learn deep relaxation.Never give up.Never stop learning. Start every day with a positive affirmation such as, "this is going to be a great day because I am going to make it so".*

BARNHART, JO ANNE B., federal agency administrator; b. Memphis, Aug. 26, 1950; d. Nelson Alexander and Betty Jane (Fitzpatrick) Bryant; m. David Lee Ross, Feb. 14, 1976 (div. June 1983); m. David Ray Barnhart, May 24, 1986. Student, U. Tenn., 1968—70; BA, U. Del., 1975. Space and time buyer DeMartin-Marona & Assocs., Wilmington, Del., 1970—73; adminstrv. asst. Mental Health Assn., Wilmington, 1973—75; dir. SERVE nutrition program Wilmington Sr. Ctr., 1975—77; legis. asst. to Sen. William V. Roth, Jr., Washington, 1977—81; dep. assoc. commr. Office Family Assistance, HHS, Washington, 1981—83, assoc. commr., 1983—86; rep. staff dir. U.S. Senate Govt. Affairs Com., 1987—90; asst. sec. for family support US Dept. Health & Human Services, Washington, 1990—91, asst. sec. for children & families, 1991—92; staff mem. to Senator William V. Roth US Senate, Washington, 1993—2001; commr. Social Security Adminstrn., Baltimore, Md., 2001—. Mem. adv. bd. on welfare indicators US Dept. Health & Human Services, 1996—; mem. Social Security adv. bd., 1997—2001. Campaign mgr. U. S. Sen. William V. Roth, 1988, 1994; polit. dir. Nat. Rep. Senatorial Com., 1995—97, polit. and pub. policy cons., 1997—2001; mem. Social Security adv. bd., 1997—2001. Republican. Methodist. Office: Social Security Admin Office of Commr Altmeyer Bldg 6401 Security Blvd Baltimore MD 21235-6401*

BARNHART, MARY C., health facility administrator; b. Milw., Mar. 7, 1951; d. Zenon and Olga Soblewski; m. Clayton F. Barnhart, Feb. 22, 1997 (dec.); children: Clayton D., Lucille. BA, U. Wis. - Milw., 2002; MA in Bioethics, Med. Coll. Wis., 2004. Certified IRB Mgr. Nat. Assn. of IRB Managers, 2001, Certified IRB Profl. Pub. Responsibility in Medicine, 2002. Sec. Milw. County Children's Ct., 1986—96; mgr. instl. revenue bd. programs Oakwood Healthcare Sys., Dearborn, Mich., 1996—2005; coord. instl. rev. bd. St. John Hosp. and Med. Ctr., Detroit, 2005—. Contbr. newsletter articles Nat. Assn. of IRB Managers Newsletter, newsletter articles Med. Ethics Rsch. Network of Mich.; editor: (jour.) Oakwood Healthcare Rsch. Quar., (newsletter) Ch. Newsletter, author short stories, poetry. Ministry leader Twin Oaks Christian Ch., Mich., 1996—. Mem.: Nat. Assn. Internal Rev. Bd. Mgrs. (assoc. program dir. 2001—). Baptist. Avocations: reading, poetry, music, travel, graphic design. Home: 5137 Jackson Rd Trenton MI 48183 Office: St John Hosp and Med Ctr 19251 Mack Ave Ste 34 Grosse Pointe Woods MI 48236 Office Phone: 313-343-8314. Personal E-mail: barnharm@wideopenwest.com. Business E-Mail: mary.barnhart@stjohn.org.

BARNHILL, CHARLES JOSEPH, JR., lawyer; b. Indpls., May 22, 1943; s. Charles J. and Phyllis (Landis) Barnhill; m. Elizabeth Louise Hayek, Aug. 14, 1971; children: Eric Charles, Colin Landis. BS in Econs., U. Pa., 1965; JD, U. Mich., 1968. Bar: Ill. 1968, U.S. Dist. Ct. (no. dist.) Ill. 1968, U.S. Ct. Appeals (7th cir.) 1969, U.S. Supreme Ct. 1972. Assoc. Kirkland & Ellis, Chgo., 1968; Reginald Heber Smith fellow Chgo. Legal Aid, 1968-69; assoc. Katz & Friedman, Chgo., 1969-72; ptnr. Davis, Miner, Barnhill & Galland, P.C. (now Miner, Barnhill & Galland), Madison, Wis., 1972—. Spl. master Fed. Dist. Ct. (no. dist.) Ill. Asst. editor: Mich. Law Rev., 1968. Chmn. Wis. Ctr. Tobacco Rsch. and Intervention, 1996; bd. dirs. Combined Health Appeal, Legal Assistance Found., Chgo., 1972—74, Old Town Triangle Assn., Chgo., 1972—75. Fellow: Am. Coll. Trial Lawers; mem.: ABA (chmn. employment litig. litig. section 1975—78), Order of Coif, Barristers Soc., Chgo. Coun. Lawyers (bd. dirs. 1974—76), Greater Madison Area Tennis Assn. (pres.). Office: Miner Barnhill & Galland 44 E Mifflin St Ste 803 Madison WI 53703-2800 Office Phone: 608-255-5200. Business E-Mail: cbarnhill@lawmbg.com.

BARNHILL, DAVID STAN, lawyer; b. Washington, NC, May 10, 1949; s. Arthur David and Ida Bea (Cox) B.; m. Katherine C. Felger, July 26, 1975; children: Hannah Katherine, Mary Rachel. BS, Va. Poly. Inst., 1971, MS, 1973; doctoral studies, U. Va., 1976-79; JD magna cum laude, Washington and Lee U., 1983. Bar: Va. 1983, U.S. Ct. Appeals (4th cir.) 1983, U.S. Supreme Ct. 1990, Federal Ct. Claims 1994. Asst. prof. social sci. Va. Intermont Coll., Bristol, Va., 1973-76; soc. sci. researcher U. Va., Charlottesville, Va., 1979-80; assoc. Woods, Rogers & Hazlegrove, Roanoke, Va., 1983-88, ptnr., 1989—. Contbr. articles to profl. jours.; lead articles editor Washington & Lee Law Rev., 1982-83. Bd. dirs. Total Action Against Poverty, Roanoke, 1987-90, DePaul Children's Svcs., Roanoke, 1985-95, Legal Aid Roanoke Valley, 1990-92. Sgt. USNG, 1972-78. Named to Legal Elite Litigation, Va. Bus. Mag., 2000, Legal Elite Litigation, 2005, Legal Elite Constrn. Law, 2002—04. Mem.: ABA (forum on constrn. industry, civil litigation sect.), Roanoke Bar Assn. (bd. dirs. 1992—94), Va. Bar Assn. (civil litigation coun. 1994—99, constrn. law coun.), Va. State Bar (chmn. 6th dist. ethics com. 1990—91, bd. govs. constrn. law sect. 1991—99, state bar coun. 1995—2001, state bar disciplinary bd. 1995—2001, vice chair bench-bar and media rels. com. 1996—2000, chair 1998, chmn. bd. govs. constrn. law sect. 1999), Va. Tech. Alumni Assn., Order of the Coif. Democrat. Baptist. Avocations: middle distance running, writing. Home: 5145 Falcon Ridge Rd Roanoke VA 24014-5720 Office: Woods Rogers & Hazlegrove 10 S Jefferson St Ste 1400 Roanoke VA 24011-1319 E-mail: barnhill@woodsrogers.com.

BARNHILL, G. MICHAEL, lawyer; b. Rocky Mount, NC, July 16, 1956; BA cum laude, Davidson Coll., NC, 1978; JD, Wake Forest U. Sch. Law, 1981. Bar: NC 1981, admitted to practice: US Dist. Ct. (We., Mid. & Ea. Dists. NC), US Ct. Appeals (4th Cir.), US Supreme Ct. Jud. clerk to Chief Judge Woodrow W. Jones US Dist. Ct. (We. Dist.), NC, 1981—83; mng. mem., bus. litig. dept. Womble Carlyle Sandridge & Rice, PLLC, Charlotte, NC, mem. mgmt. com. Lectr. Wake Forest U. Sch. Law Ann. Review, 1999—2000. Mem.: NC Assn. of Def. Attys., ABA (mem. litig. sect., mem. tort & litig. sect.), NC Assn. of Police Attys., NC State Bar Assn. (mem. legal svc. planning com. 1987—90), NC Bar Assn. (mem. litig. sect., mem. labor & employment sect.), Mecklenburg County Bar Assn. Office: Womble Carlyle Sandridge & Rice PLLC One Wachovia Center Ste 3500 301 S College St Charlotte NC 28202-6037 Office Phone: 704-331-4960. Office Fax: 704-338-7829. Business E-Mail: mbarnhill@wscr.com.

BARNHILL, GREGORY HURD, investment banker; b. Balt., Feb. 20, 1953; s. Robert Bell and Margaret Katheryn (Hurd) B. Student, Inst. d'Etudes Européenes, 1974, Banque Nat. de Paris, 1974; BA in Econs., Brown U., 1975; postgrad., Inst. Fin., NYC, 1975. Lic. N.Y. Stock Exch./NASD series 7, 9, 10, 63, 65. Mng. dir. internat. investment banking Deutsche Bank Securities Inc., Investment Bankers, Balt., 1975—2003; ptnr. Brown Adv. Securities, LLC, Balt., 2003—, also bd. dirs. Bd. dirs. Agora Press, BTAB-Cook Overseas Ltd., BTAB-Stark Ltd. Partnership/AB-Stark Overseas Ltd., Captel-Nat. Cap. Telesvcs., L.L.C., View Tech., NASA/Goddard Space Flight Ctr. Balt. Incubator, Innovative Med. Svc., Md. Life Mag., Osiris Therapeutics, 2006; corp. co-chair Miss USA, 2005. Mem. adv. bd. Inst. d'Etudes Européenes; affiliate Balt. Mus. Art, Walters Art Gallery; chmn. fundraising com. Balt. Arts Festival, 1980-84; bd. dirs. Palm Beach Maritime Mus., Balt. Heritage Inc., 1981-83, Md. Ballet, 1982-83, Nat. Taxpayers Union Found., 1984-1998, The Netherlands-Am. Amity Trust, Inc., Balt. Columbus 500, Md. Art Place, 1982-90, pres. 1982-86, pres. bd. trustees, 1985-86; co-chmn. Businesspeople for Mayor Schaefer's Re-election, 1982-83; mem. fin. com. Congresswoman Helen Delich Bentley; mem. Balt. Operation Sail (chmn. fin. com., bd. dirs., pres. 1988-93), hon. mem. Christopher Columbus Quincentennary Commn., 1989—; mem. Nat. Rep. Fin. Com., 1991—; vice chmn. bd. dirs. Greater Balt. Med. Ctr., 1992-2002; trustee Md. Internat. Ctr. Md, 1993—; mem. bd. govs. Faberge Arts Found., 1992—; mem. 2000 com. Walters Art Gallery, 1978—; nat. vice-chmn. The Pres.'s Dinner, 1989—; mem. mayor's adv. com. internat. affairs, 1988—; mem. gov's bus. com. for Md.-St. Petersburg, 1993—; trustee St. Paul's Sch., 2000—, Alexander Brown Charitable Found., 2002—; chmn. Found. for Govt. House, 2003—; apptd. to Md. Racing Commn., 2004—; bd. trustees Cystic Fibrosis, 2004-; chmn. bd. UMBC Alex P. Brown Enterprenuership Ctr., 2005—; bd. dirs. Fillmaster Sys., 2006—, By Kids For Kids, 2007—, Econ Inc., 2007—. Named Man of Yr., The Pride II of Balt., 2006, Honoree, Juvenile Diabetes, 2006. Mem. Am. Heart Assn. (co-chair 2007), Bond Club Md., Balt. Hist. Soc. (trustee), Md. Hist. Soc. (trustee 1992-2004, co-chmn. MHS 150 1993—), Md. Soc. Preservation of Antiquities (dir. 1981-83), Mcpl. Arts Soc. (trustee 1985—, dir.), Md. Acad. Scis. (bd. dirs), Brown U. Club of Md. (pres. 1976-81), McDonogh Sch. Alumni Assn. (dir.), Nature Conservancy (bd. dirs.), SAR, Soc. Colonial Wars, Md. Club (bd. govs., treas. exec. com, bd. dirs. 1995), Volvo Ocean Race Chesapeake (formerly Whitbread Ocean Race Chesapeake) (chmn. 1998—), Order of Crown of Charlemagne, Baronial Order of Magna Charta, U.S.A, Soc. War of 1812, Newport Reading Rm. Club, Greenspring Valley Hunt Club, N.Y. Yacht Club, Ocean Reef Club, Rehoboth Country Club, Henlopen Acres Beach Club, Sigma Chi. Republican. Home: 10801 Stevenson Rd Stevenson MD 21153-0679 Office: Brown Adv Securities LLC 901 S Bond St 4th Fl Baltimore MD 21231 Office Phone: 410-537-5527. Business E-Mail: gbarnhill@brownadvisory.com.

BARNHILL, HENRY GRADY, JR., lawyer; b. Buena Vista, Ga., Aug. 24, 1930; s. Henry Grady and Imogene (Hogg) B.; m. Sarah Carolyn Haire, Oct. 29, 1953; children: Grady Michael, Stephen Drew, Kevin Scott, Carol Kelly. JD, Wake Forest U., Winston-Salem, NC, 1958. Bar: N.C. 1958, U.S. Dist. Ct. (ea., mid. and we. dists.) N.C. 1958, U.S. Ct. Appeals (4th cir.) 1961, U.S. Supreme Ct. 1983, U.S. Ct. Appeals (fed. cir.) 1985. Assoc. Womble Carlyle Sandridge & Rice, Winston-Salem, 1958-61, ptnr., 1961—. Bd. visitors Sch. of Law Wake Forest U. Lt. USAF, 1951-55. Fellow Am. Coll. Trial Lawyers (state chmn. 1986-88, Named to Best Lawyers in Am. 1984-); mem. Am. Bd. Trial Advs., N.C. Assn. Def. Attys., N.C. Bar Assn. (litigation sect.), 4th Cir. Jud. Conf., Forsyth County Bar (pres. 1979-80), Inns of Ct. (Chief Justice Joseph Branch). Democrat. Presbyterian. Avocation: tennis. Home: 3121 Robinhood Rd Winston Salem NC 27106-5610 Office: Womble Carlyle Sandridge & Rice PLLC One W 4th St Winston Salem NC 27101 E-mail: gbarnhill@wcsr.com.

BARNHILL, JAMES ORRIS, theater educator; b. Sumner, Miss., May 23, 1922; s. James Arthur and Louise (Sullivan) B BA, Yale U., 1947, MFA, 1954; MA, NYU, 1949; MA (hon.), Brown U., 1956. Instr. English Brown U., Providence, 1954—56, from asst. prof. to assoc. prof., 1956—70, prof., 1970—78, prof. theater arts, 1978—86, prof. emeritus, 1986—. Vis. prof. English R.I. Sch. Design, Providence, 1987-88, 93-94, Tougaloo (Miss.) Coll., 1989; actor Trinity Square Repertory Theatre, Providence, 1971-73 Lt. (j.g.) USNR, 1943-46, PTO Fulbright prof. English M.S. U. Baroda, India, 1984-85, St. Xavier Coll., Ahmedabad, India, 1988-89, Am. Lit. U. Punjab, Pakistan, 1994-96 Mem. Univ. Club, Players Club Baptist. Avocations: hobbies, calligraphy, sculpture. Home: 81 Transit St Providence RI 02906-1022 Office: Brown U Dept Theatre Arts PO Box 1897 Providence RI 02912-1897

BARNHOLT, BRANDON K., retail executive; COO, exec. v.p. mktg. Clark USA Inc. (now Clark Retail Group Inc.); CEO, pres. Clark Retail Group, Inc., Glen Ellyn, Ill., 1999—2005, White Hen Pantry, Inc., 2005—. Office: White Hen Pantry Inc Ste 300 700 E Butterfield Rd Lombard IL 60148

BARNICK, HELEN, retired judicial clerk; b. Max, ND, Mar. 24, 1925; d. John K. and Stacy (Kankovsky) Barnick. BS in Music cum laude, Minot State Coll., 1954; postgrad., Am. Conservatory of Music, Chgo., 1975-76. With Epton, Bohling & Druth, Chgo., 1968-69; sec. Wildman, Harrold, Allen & Dixon, Chgo., 1969-75; part-time assignments for temporary agy. Chgo., 1975-77; sec. Friedman & Koven, Chgo., 1977-78; with Lawrence, Lawrence, Kamin & Saunders, Chgo., 1978-81; sec. Hinshaw, Culbertson et al., Chgo., 1982; sec. to magistrate judge U.S. Dist. Ct. (we. dist.) Wis., Madison, 1985-91; dep. clk., case adminstr. U.S. Bankruptcy Ct. (we. dist.) Wis., Madison, 1992-94; ret., 1994. Chancel choir 1st Bapt. Ch., Mpls., Fourth Presbyn. Ch., Chgo., Covenant Presbyn. Ch., Madison, Wis.; choir, dir. sr. high choir Moody Ch., Chgo.; dir. chancel choir 1st Bapt. Ch., Minot, ND; mem. Festival Choir, Madison; bd. dirs., sec.-treas. Peppertree at Tamarack Owners Assn., Inc., Wisconsin Dells. Mem.: Bus. and Profl. Women Assn., Christian Bus. and Profl. Women (chmn.), Madison Civics Club, Symphony Orch. League, Sigma Sigma Sigma. Home: 7364 Old Sauk Rd Madison WI 53717-1213

BARNICLE, MARY ANNE, music educator, piano accompanist; b. Bridgeport, Conn., Nov. 28, 1946; d. Edward Joseph and Anna Marie (Kolesar) Petrovick; m. Stephan Patrick Barnicle, Aug. 23, 1969; children: Michael, Patricia, Daniel, Kevin. MusB in Music Edn., U. Hartford, 1969, MusB in Piano Pedagogy, 1969; MEd in Fine Arts, Fitchburg State Coll., 1991. Cert. dir. fine arts 1989, music dept. chair Conn., 1994. Vocal music tchr. Avon Middle Sch., Conn., 1969—70; vocal/gen. music tchr. Canton Pub. Schs., Conn., 1981—94, head music tchr., 1989—94, music dept. chair, 1994—2004; vocal music tchr. Canton Jr. HS, HS, 1994—97; vocal music, music theory & tech. Canton HS, 1994—2004. Pvt. piano tchr. Hartt Sch. Studio, Conn., 1970—2004, Simsbury Home, Conn., 1970—2004, home studio, Fayetteville, NC, 2004—. Mem. Canton Creative Arts Coun., Conn., 1982—2002; bd. mem., pres. Simsbury Summer Theater for Youth, Conn., 1985—95; accompanist, orchestra mem. Theater Guild Simsbury, Conn., 1988—94; mem. profl. devel. consortium Farmington Valley Schs., Farmington Valley, Conn., 1989—91; mem., music dept. rep. Canton Parents for Music, Conn., 1990—2004; music dir., accompanist Canton Benefits Productions, Conn., 1993—94; mem. edn. adv. bd. Hartford Symphony Orchestra, Conn., 1990—92; curriculum revision com. mem. Canton Pub. Schs., 1992—2004; organist, accompanist, soloist various chs., Conn., 1970—2004; organ scholar participant Music Ministry of St. Patrick Ch., Fayetteville, NC, 2005—06. Recipient Educator of Yr., Canton C. of C., 1999; grantee Paul Harris fellow, Avon/Canton Rotary Club Internat., 2003. Mem.: NEA, Am. Choral Dirs. Assn., Nat. Assn. Music Edn. Democrat. Avocation: singing. Home: 214 Viking Dr Fayetteville NC 28303 Personal E-mail: mabarnicle@nc.rr.com.

BARNO, DAVID W., retired military officer; b. Endicott, NY, July 5, 1954; Grad., US Mil. Acad., West Point, 1976; MA in Nat. Security Studies, Georgetown U.; Grad., US Army War Coll., 1995. Advanced through grades to lt. gen. US Army, 2003, ret., 2005, asst. divsn. comdr. (ops.), 25th Infantry Divsn. (Light) Schofield Barracks, Hawaii, 1999—2000, dep. dir. ops. U.S. Pacific Command, 2000—02, commanding gen., US Army Training Ctr. Ft. Jackson, SC, 2002—03, commdg. gen. Task Force Warrior Hungary, 2003; comdr. Combined Forces Command, Afghanistan, 2003—05; dir., Near East South Asia Ctr. for Strategic Studies Nat. Def. U., Washington, 2006—. Decorated Def. Disting. Svc. Medal, Disting. Svc. medal with oak leaf cluster, Def. Superior Svc. medal, Legion of Merit with oak leaf cluster, Meritorious Svc. medal with silver and bronze oak leaf clusters, US Army Commendation and Achievement medal; recipient Meritorious Honor award, US Dept. State, NATO Meritorious Svc. medal. Achievements include serving in Operations Urgent Fury (Grenada), Just Cause (Panama) Enduring Freedom (Afghanistan) & Iraqi Freedom (Iraq). Office: Nat Def U Ft Lesley J McNair 300 5th Ave Marshall Hall Washington DC 20319*

BARNOFF, ROBERT MARK, civil engineering educator; b. Punxsutawney, Pa., Aug. 28, 1926; s. Joseph A. and Ruth A. (Morris) B.; m. Norma Gugliemi; children: Joni, Janice, Mark, Joseph. BS, Pa. State U., University Park, 1951; MS, Pa. State U., 1956; PhD, Carnegie Inst. Tech., Pitts., 1966. Steel detailer Am. Bridge Co., 1951-52; constrn. engr. John Mohr & Sons, 1952-53; bridge designer Gannett Fleming Corddry & Capenter, 1953-55; from instr. to prof. civil engring. Pa. State U., University Park, 1955-79, prof., chmn. dept. civil engring., 1979-85. Vis. prof. Bucknell U. Contbr. articles to profl. jours. With USNR, 1944-46. Sci. Faculty fellow NSF, 1965-66. Mem. ASTM, ASCE, Am. Concrete Inst., Sigma Xi, Tau Beta Pi, Chi Epsilon. Achievements include patents on concrete testing device and bridge deck systems. Home and Office: 606 Nimitz Ave State College PA 16801-6415

BARNTHOUSE, CHRIS DAVID, orthopedic surgeon; b. Winfield, Kans., Sept. 9, 1955; MD, U. Kans., Kans. City, 1981. Cert. Am. Bd. Orthop. Surgery, 1989. Intern orthop. surgery U. Kans., 1981—82, resident orthop. surgery, 1982—86; clin. and rsch. fellow sports medicine Harvard Sch. Medicine, 1986—87; team doctor NFL Kans. City Chiefs; staff mem. Orthop. & Sports Medicine Clinic Kans. City, PA; co-dir. Orthop. Sports Medicine Fellowship Program U. Mo., Kans. City, clin. asst. prof. Named one of Golf Digest 2006 Top Golf Doctors in Am. Fellow: Am. Acad. Orthop. Surgery. Office: Kans City Orthop Inst 3651 College Blvd Leawood KS 66211 Office Phone: 913-319-7500.

BARNUM, JOHN WALLACE, lawyer; b. NYC, Aug. 25, 1928; s. William Wallace Atterbury and Frances (Long) Barnum; m. Nancy Russell Grinnell, Sept. 13, 1958; children: Alexander Stone, Sarah Kip, Cameron Long. BA, Yale U., 1949, LLB, Inst. Derecho Internat. Comparativo, Havana, Cuba, 1957. Bar: Conn. 1957, NY 1958, DC 1977; on Brussels fgn. lawyer list, 1995. Adminstrv. asst. Cerro de Pasco Copper Corp., Lima, Peru, 1946; jr. asst. purser Grace Lines, 1946; analyst 1st Banking Corp., Tangier, Morocco, 1950; reg. rep. Bache & Co., London and Paris, 1951-52; assoc. Cravath, Swaine & Moore, NYC, 1957-62, ptnr., 1963-71; gen. counsel U.S. Dept. Transp., Washington, 1971-73, undersec., 1973-74, dep. sec., 1974-77; resident fellow Am. Enterprise Inst. for Pub. Policy Rsch., Washington, 1977-78, vis. fellow, 1978-86; ptnr. White & Case, Washington, 1978-94, McGuireWoods, LLP, Brussels, 1995—; mng. ptnr. McGuireWoods Kazahhstan LLP, Almaty, 1999—. US del. Inter-Am. Comml. Arbitration Commn., 1969—71, NATO Com. Challenges to Modern Soc., 1973—76; adv. mem. Coun. on Wage and Price Stability, 1974—77; mem. Coun. Adminstrv. Conf. U.S., 1973—77. Bd. editors Regulation: AEI Jour. on Govt. and Soc., 1977-86. Chmn. bd. Internat. Play Group, 1962-77; bd. dirs., exec. com. NYC Ctr. Music and Drama, 1969-75; trustee Washington Drama Soc. (Arena Stage), 1983-93; bd. overseers Corcoran Gallery of Art, Washington, 1994-00; pres. US Fedn. Friends Mus., 2002-; v.p. World Fedn. Friends Mus., 2006-. Mem.: Am. Arbitration Assn. (exec. com. 1968—72, bd. dirs. 1968—98), Nat. Def. Transp. Assn. (chmn.mil. airlift com. 1983—94, bd. dirs. 1988—94), Am. Bar Found., D.C. Bar Assn., N.Y. State Bar Assn. (exec. com., chmn. antitrust law sect. 1979—80), Internat. Bar Assn., N.Y. Yacht Club, Amateur Ski Club, Chevy Chase Club, Met. Club, Watersportvereniging Noord-Beveland, Cercle Royal Gaulois Artistique et Litteraire, Am. Club of Brussels (gov., v.p. exec. com.). Home: 182 Ave Franklin Roosevelt 1050 Brussels Belgium also: 2029 Connecticut Ave NW Washington DC 20008-6141 Office: McGuireWoods LLP 250 Ave Louise, Bte 64 1050 Brussels Belgium Office Phone: 011 32-2 629 4230. E-mail: jbarnum@mcguirewoods.com.

BARNUM, MARY ANN MOOK, information management manager; b. Arlington, Va., Apr. 3, 1946; d. Conrad Payne and Barbara Heer (Held) Mook; m. William Douglas Barnum, Aug. 10, 1968. BS in Math., Radford U., 1967. Cert. tchr., Va., N.J., N.Mex. Math. tchr. Prince William County Schs., Woodbridge, Va., 1967-68; mathematician RCA Svc. Co., Andros Island, Bahamas, 1968-70; math. tchr. Cinnaminson (N.J.) Schs., 1970-73, Alamagordo (N.Mex.) Sch. System, 1973-74; data svcs. supr. A.M. Best Co., Oldwick, N.J., 1975-78; assoc. mgr. AT&T Communications, Piscataway, N.J., 1978-86; mgr. AT&T Info. Mgmt. Svcs., Piscataway, N.J., 1986-90, AT&T Bus. Comm. Svcs., Somerset, N.J., 1990-91; mem. tech. staff AT&T Network Systems, Berkeley Heights, N.J., 1991-95, Lucent Techs., Warren, N.J., 1995-96; mgr. AT&T, Morristown, NJ, 1996—98; retired. Sec. Cherry Hill (N.J.) Jaycettes, 1972-73; trustee Friends of Clarence Dillon Libr., Bedminster, N.J., sec., 1989-90, pres., 1990-92, mem., 1986-2000; mem. Far Hills Environ. Commn., 1990-92, chmn., 1992-94; mem. Far Hills Planning Bd., 1994-2000, Wildewood Women's Club, 2000-, Computer Group, 2001-, Wildewood Garden Club, 2000-; mem. Symphony League, Columbia, SC, 2001-. Mem. IEEE, DAR (2d v.p. Columbia chpt. 2006—), Descendants of Washington's Army at Valley Forge (capt. of the guard 1988-90, dep. adjutant gen. 1990-92, adjutant gen. 1992-96), Kappa Delta Pi. Presbyterian. Home: PO Box 23329 Columbia SC 29224

BARNUM, WILLIAM DOUGLAS, retired communications executive; b. Denton, Tex., July 28, 1946; s. Billie Douglas and Leticia Christina Barnum; m. Mary Ann Mook, Aug. 10, 1968. BSBA in Econs. with distinction, Georgetown U., 1967; MBA, Fairleigh Dickinson U., 1985. Acct. RCA Corp., Cherry Hill, NJ, 1967-68, Andros Island, Bahamas, 1968-70, budget and cost analyst Cherry Hill, 1970, adminstr. tel. sys., 1970-73; mgr. project adminstrn. white sands radar project RCA Svc. Co., Holloman AFB, N.Mex., 1973-74; coord. profit ctr. acctg. RCA Global Comms., NYC, 1974-76, adminstr. globcom. sys., 1976-77, mgr. spl. project and accts. payable, 1978-79; mgr. fin. RCA Globcom Sys., Inc., NYC, 1979-81; mgr. gateway ops. RCA Global Comms., Edison, NJ, 1982, dir. field support svcs., 1982-88; sr. mgr. network svcs. MCI Internat., Piscataway, NJ, 1988-90, sr. mgr. sys. support and adminstrn., 1990-92, sr. mgr. messaging and marine ops., 1992-93, sr. staff internat. alliances, 1994; owner, sr. cons. Lake Road Assocs. Consulting, Far Hills, NJ, 1994-99; ret., 1999. Author: Kroodley Made Knife Catalog, 1977. Mem. Security Coun., 1981—92, Far Hills (N.J.) Bd. Health, 1993—99, vice-chmn., 1994—95, chmn., 1996—99; adviser Jr. Achievement, Cherry Hill, NJ, 1968—69, Cherry Hill Jaycees, 1973—74; mem. spl. commn. Far Hills Police Dept., 1993, 1998; bd. dirs. United Cerebral Palsy Somerset/Morris County, 1989. Mem.: NRA (life endowment mem.), Knifemakers Guild (hon.), RCA Commn. Retirees Assn., J. Edgar Hoover Found. (life), Mensa, S.C. Waterfowl Assn., Am. Knife Throwers Alliance (hon.), Mid-Carolina Rifle Club, Woodcreek Country Club, Wildewood Country Club, Delta Mu Delta, Delta Phi Epsilon. Republican. Presbyterian. Home: PO Box 23329 Columbia SC 29224

BARNUM, WILLIAM MILO, architect; b. June 17, 1927; s. Phelps and Catharine (Davis) B.; m. Katharine Miller, Aug. 10, 1971; children: Anne Lyttleton, Catharine Hollerith, William Milo, Nathaniel Phelps, Caleb Townsend; 1 stepchild, Elizabeth Pierce. BA, Yale U., 1950; MArch, U. Pa., 1952. Archtl. asst. job capt. Eggers & Higgins, 1952-54; job capt. W. Stuart Thompson & Phelps Barnum, archs., 1954-58, jr. ptnr., 1958-60; sr. ptnr. Phelps Barnum & Son, NYC, 1960-68; pres. William Milo Barnum Assocs., Inc., NYC, 1968—. Cons. to judges com.; interior designer new U.S. Courthouse Ho., 500 Pearl St., N.Y.C., Scudder Stevens & Clark 5 Fls. Prin. works include Westminster Sch. Chapel, 1961, Westminster Sch. Acad. Ctr., 1964, Howmet Office Bldg., Greenwich, Mfrs. Hanover Bank, Bklyn., Pickwick Pla., Greenwich, R.T. Vanderbilt Corp. Hdqs., Norwalk, Conn., Union Trust Sq., Greenwich, Gen. Host. Corp. Hdqs., Stamford, Conn., Gateway Ctr., Greenwich, The Boatyard Condominium, City Island, N.Y., Gorham Island Office Bldg., Westport, Conn., N.Y. Offices Scudder Stevens and Clark, Mason Place Mixed Use Hist. Restoration, Greenwich, Shawmut Bank offices and Br. Landmark Sq. Bldg., Stamford, Shawmut br., New Canaan, St. Andrews by the Sea Episcopal Ch. Renovation and Reconstruction, Little Compton, R.I. Chmn. Archtl. Rev. Bd., Greenwich, Conn.; mem. selectmen's com. H.S. Property, Greenwich, 1964-68; bd. dirs. Cmty. Chest, Greenwich, 1964-68; mem. alumni coun. Phillips Acad., Andover, Mass., 1965-68; v.p. bd. trustees Putnam Indian Field Sch., vice-chmn.; bd. dirs. Episcopal Ch. at Yale; bd. dirs. Episcopal Ch. Bldg. Fund; sr. warden St. Andrew's By the Sea, 2002-04; With USNR, 1945-46, PTO. Mem. AIA (N.Y. chpt. office practices com.), Concrete Industry Bd. (bd. dir.), Met. Builders Assn. (liaison com.), Andover Alumni Assn. N.Y.C. (pres. 1964-65), Hist. Soc. Greenwich (v.p.), Soc. Colonial Wars, Yale Club (coun. 1958-79, pres. 1970-72) (N.Y.C.), Acoaxet Club, Providence Art Club, St. Andrews-By-The-Sea (vestry), Spindle Rock Club. Office: 150 Chestnut St Providence RI 02903 Office Phone: 401-276-9100. Personal E-mail: wmbarnum@hotmail.com.

BARNWELL, CHARLES BRISON, JR., lawyer; b. York, SC, Jan. 31, 1942; s. Charles Brison Sr. and Susan (Rauch) B.; m. Margaret Ford; Dec. 11, 1971; children: Erin Elizabeth, Brian Montgomery. BA, Presbyn. Coll., Clinton, SC, 1964; JD, U. S.C., 1967. Bar: S.C. 1967, U.S. Dist. Ct. S.C. 1967, U.S. Ct. Appeals (4th cir.) 1974. Page S.C. State Senate, 1964-67; chief clk. Lawyer's Title Ins. Co., Columbia, 1965-67; spl. asst. S.C. Legis. Council, Columbia, 1965-67; sr. ptnr. Horger, Barnwell & Reid, Orangeburg, 1967—. Bd. dirs. Orangeburg County Pub. Defender Corp. Indigent Defendents; mem. adv. bd. S.C. Workers' Compensation Commn., 1980; mem. Orangeburg Human Affairs Comm., 1975-78; mem. Am. Bd. Trial Attys. Author S.C. law rev., 1967. Bd. dirs. Jolley Acres Nursing Home, 1975-88, Orangeburg Assn. Retarded Citizens, 1976-86; mem. Orangeburg City Coun., 2001—. Recipient Outstanding Young Alumnus award Presbyn. Coll., 1977, Dum Vivimus Servimus award, 2004. Mem. ABA, Am. Bd. Trial Attys., S.C. Bar Assn. (cir. v.p. 1972-75, ho. of dels. 1976—, coun. negligence ins. and workers' compensation sect. 1980-86, chmn. fee disputes 1983—), Orangeburg County Bar Assn. (pres. 1974), Southeastern Workers' Compensation Assn., Def. Rsch. Inst., S.C. Trial Lawyers' Assn., S.C. Def. Trial Lawyer's Assn., Kappa Alpha Order (Most Disting. Alumni award, 2004), Blue Key. Home: 727 Brewton St NE Orangeburg SC 29115-4223 Office: Horger Barnwell & Reid 459 Amelia St NE Orangeburg SC 29115-6034 Office Phone: 803-531-3000. E-mail: j.moody@hbrllp.com.

BARNWELL, FRANKLIN HERSHEL, zoology educator; b. Chattanooga, Oct. 4, 1937; s. Columbus Hershel and Esther Bernice (Ireland) B.; m. Adrienne Kay Knox, June 13, 1959; 1 child, Elizabeth Brooks. BA, Northwestern U., 1959, PhD, 1965. Instr. biol. sci. Northwestern U., Evanston, Ill., 1964, research assoc., 1965-67; asst. prof. U. Chgo., 1967-70; from asst. prof. to prof. zoology, ecology and behavioral biology U. Minn., Mpls., 1970—, head dept. ecology, evolution and behavior, 1986-93. Mem. adv. panel NASA, 1963-67, NSF, Washington, 1980; faculty Orgn. for Tropical Studies, San Jose, Costa Rica, 1966-85, bd. dirs.; Nat. Confs. on Underground Rsch., bd. dirs., treas., 1990-96; investigator rsch. R/V Alpha Helix, various locations, 1979, vis. scientist. Contbr. articles on zoology to profl. jours. NSF fellow, 1965; named Minn. Coll. Sci. Tchr. of Yr., Minn. Acad. Sci. and Minn. Sci. Tchrs. Assn., 1997, dist. tchg. prof. of ecology, U. Minn., 1997; recipient Disting. Alumnus award McCallie Sch., Chattanooga, Tenn., 2006. Fellow Linnean Soc. London, AAAS; mem. Soc. Intergrative and Comparative Biology, Soc. for Rsch. on Biol. Rhythms, Assocs. Orgn. for Tropical Studies, Crustacean Soc. (founding and sustaining mem., bd. dirs., sec. 1991-98), Phi Beta Kappa, Sigma Xi. Office: U Minn Dept Ecology Evol & Behav 1987 Upper Buford Cir Saint Paul MN 55108-1051 Business E-Mail: fhb@umn.edu.

BAROFF, GEORGE STANLEY, psychologist, educator; b. Bronx, NY, Nov. 27, 1924; s. Irving and Ida (Herman) B.; m. Rose Kislin, June 15, 1952 (dec. May 1992); children: Marina Binet, Roy James. BS in Zoology, George Washington U., 1948, MA in Psychology, 1950; PhD in Clin. Psychology, NYU, 1955. Research psychologist dept. med. genetics N.Y. State Psychiat. Inst., 1952-60; chief clin. psychologist Vineland (N.J.) Tng. Sch., 1960-63; asso. prof. psychology U. N.C., Chapel Hill, 1963-67, prof., 1967-2000, prof. emeritus, 2000—, dir. devel. disabilties tng. inst., 1964-2000. Forensic psychologist with criminal defendants who may be mentally retarded, 1987—. Author: Mental Retardation: Nature, Cause and Management, 1974, 3d edit. (with J.G. Olley), 1999, Developmental Disabilities: Psychosocial Aspects, 1991; contbr. articles to profl. jours. With US Army, 1943—45. Mem. APA, Assn., Am. Assn. Mental Retardation. Jewish. Home: 417 Granville Rd Chapel Hill NC 27514-2723 Office Phone: 919-942-3044. E-mail: gbaroff@bellsouth.net.

BAROLINI, TEODOLINDA, literary critic; b. Syracuse, NY, Dec. 19, 1951; d. Antonio and Helen (Mollica) B.; m. Douglas Gardner Caverly, June 21, 1980 (dec. Nov. 1993); 1 child: William Douglas; m. James J. Valentini, Feb. 10, 2001. BA, Sarah Lawrence Coll., Bronxville, NY, 1972; MA, Columbia U., NYC, 1973, PhD, 1978. Asst. prof. Italian U. Calif., Berkeley, 1978-83; assoc. prof. Italian NYU, 1983-89; prof., 1989-92; chmn. dept. Italian Columbia U., NYC, 1992—2004, Lorenzo Da Ponte prof. Italian, 1999—. Author: Dante's Poets, 1984, transl. into Italian as Il miglior fabbro 1993, (Howard R. Marraro prize MLA 1986, John Nicholas Brown prize Medieval Acad. Am. 1988), The Undivine Comedy, 1992, transl. into Italian as La Commedia senza Dio, 2003, Dante and the Origins of Italian Literary Culture, 2006; co-editor: (with H.W. Storey) Dante for the New Millennium, 2003; editor: Medieval Constructions in Gender and Identity, 2005; co-editor: (with H.W. Storey) Petrarch and the Textual Origins of Interpretation, 2007; contbr. articles to profl. jours. AAUW fellow, 1977, ACLS fellow, 1981, NEH fellow, 1986, Guggenheim fellow, 1998. Fellow Medieval Acad. Am., Am. Acad. Arts and Scis., Am. Philos. Soc.; mem. MLA, Dante Soc. Am. (v.p. 1983-86, 91-94, 95-97, pres. 1997-2003), Renaissance Soc. Am. Office: Columbia U Dept Italian 510 Hamilton Hall New York NY 10027 Business E-Mail: tb27@columbia.edu.

BARON, ANDREW MICHAEL, blog website producer, educator, composer; BA in Philosophy, Bates Coll.; MFA in Design and Technology, Parsons Sch. Design, NYC, 2003. Short-term contracts for computer related postions, 1992—2000; co-founder, operator Movements Gallery, Austin, Tex., 1997—2000; inventory database mgmt. Motorola, Austin, Utah, 1995; production specialist Tivoli Systems, Austin, Tex., 1996—98; customer support fot AIX RS/6000 IBM, Austin, Tex., 1999—2000; tchg. asst., grad. programming and computation Parsons Master Fine Arts Design and Tech., 2002, helped design curriculum and taught Bootcamp Design, 2002, co-designed curriculum and co-taught Motion Lab, 2003—04; designed curriculum and taught undergraduate Digital Imaging New Sch., NYC, 2002; designed curriculum and taught Sound Design Parsons Digital Design Undergraduate Dept., NYC, 2003; designed curriculum and taught HS Robotics Sch. of the Future, NYC, 2002—04; dir., ID Tec Camp MIT, 2004; co-designed curriculum and co-taught Physical Flocking Parsons Bachelor's Arts and Master Fine Arts Design and Tech., 2005; creator, exec. prodr. Rocketboom.com, 2004—. Mixed arts adv. panalist City of Austin Arts Commn., 2001. Composer: (symphonic songs) Century Plant, 2000, (concerto) Ten Concertos for the Wind, 2001; collaborative performance trio and recording Red, Twenty-Two Records, Austin, Tex., 1997, music composition/recording of digital chamber music The Good Night, 1999, scored music and produced recording Mad About Harry, 2000 (Finalist, Hollywood Film Festival, 2000), composed music set to time-lapse video Sleeveless in Seattle, 2000, music composition/chamber performance Will You Walk In the Park With Me?, 2000, The Magical, Tragical, King Lear Puppet Show, 2001, composed music John Brown's Body, 2001, composed and recorded a score for four dances Midnight Playground, 2001, scored music and produced recordings Repossession, 2001, created digital recording Mass Maximum, 2002. Coach, referee soccer West Austin Youth League, 1997—2000; interfaced a weekly open mike poetry performance reading on-line, 1999. Mailing: Rocketboom PO Box 804 Planetarium Station New York NY 10024-0545 Business E-Mail: andrew@rocketboom.com. E-mail: a@dembot.com.*

BARON, CHARLES HILLEL, lawyer, educator; b. Phila., Aug. 18, 1936; s. Samuel A. and Rose (Balinky) B.; m. Irma Elaine Frankel, June 15, 1958 (dec. 1985); children: Jessica Susan, Ira Benjamin, David Hume; m. Dianne M. Quartarone, Sept. 9, 1988; 1 child, Samuel Guy. AB in Philosophy with honors, U. Pa., 1958, PhD in Philosophy, 1972; LLB, Harvard U., 1961. Bar: Pa. bar 1967, U.S. Supreme Ct. bar 1970, Mass. bar 1972. Asst. prof. law U. Pa., 1965-66; assoc. firm Blank Rome Klaus & Comisky, Phila., 1966-68; chief law reform, consumer's adv. Community Legal Svcs., Inc., Phila., 1968-70; assoc. prof. law Boston Coll., 1970-74, prof., 1974—, assoc. dean, 1972-74. Exec. dir. Resource Ctr. Consumers Legal Svcs., 1975-77. Author: (with M. Saks) The Use, Nonuse, and Misuse of Applied Social Research, 1980, Droit Constitutionnel et Bioéthique: L'Expérience Americaine, 1997; contbr. articles to profl. jours. Chmn. Cheltenham Twp. (Pa.) Dem. Party, 1966-68; mem. Mass. Health Facilities Appeals Bd., 1974-75; chmn. Mass. Gov.'s Adv. Com. on Prepaid

Legal Svcs., 1978-86; bd. dirs. CEPA Found., Death With Dignity Nat. Ctr., Washington, 2001—; mem. bd. overseers Mass. Supreme Jud. Ct. Hist. Soc., 1999—. Recipient various community awards; U. Pa. fellow, 1961-63 Mem. ABA, Am. Assn. Law Schs., Soc. Am. Law Tchrs., Am. Soc. Law and Medicine (bd. editors Am. Jour. Law and Medicine 1978—, bd. dirs.), Civil Liberties Union Mass. (bd. dirs., pres. 1989-91, trustee Mass. Civil Liberties Found.), ACLU. Jewish. Office: Boston Coll Law Sch 885 Centre St Newton MA 02459-1148 Office Phone: 617-552-4376. Business E-Mail: baron@bc.edu.

BARON, DAVID HUME, science journalist; b. Phila., Mar. 31, 1964; s. Charles Hillel and Irma (Frankel) B. BS in Physics and Geology, Yale U., New Haven, 1986. Freelance sci. reporter BBC, CBC, CNN, ABC (Australia), Boston Globe, 1985—; sci. reporter WBUR-FM, Boston, 1987—95; Knight sci. journalism fellow MIT, Boston, 1989—90; sci. writing fellow Marine Biol. Lab., Woods Hole, Mass., 1991; sci. reporter Nat. Pub. Radio, 1996—2000; global devel. editor The World. Mem. adv. bd. Radio and TV News Dirs. Found., Environ. Journalism Ctr., Metcalf Inst. Marine and Environ. Reporting, U. RI. Author: The Beast in the Garden: A Modern Parable of Man and Nature, 2003 (Colo. Book award, 2003). Ted Scripps fellow in environ. journalism, U. Colo., 1998-99; recipient Nat. Sci. Reporting award AAAS-Westinghouse, 1991, 94, 98, Nat. Med. Reporting award AMA, 1992, Pub. Comm. award Am. Soc. Microbiol., 1996, Broadcast Media award Am. Inst. Biol. Scis., 2007; Corp. Pub. Broadcasting grantee, 1990. Mem. Assn. Inds. in Radio, Nat. Assn. Sci. Writers, Soc. Environ. Journalists. Office: The World WGBH Ednl Found 125 Western Ave Boston MA 02134*

BARON, FREDERICK DAVID, lawyer; b. New Haven, 1947; m. Kathryn Green Lazarus; children: Andrew K. Lazarus, Peter D. Lazarus, Charles B. BA, Amherst Coll., 1969; JD, Stanford U., 1974. Bar: Calif. 1974, D.C. 1975, U.S. Supreme Ct. 1978, U.S. Dist. Ct. D.C. 1979, U.S. Ct. Appeals (D.C. cir.) 1979, U.S. Dist. Ct. (no. dist.) Calif. 1982, U.S. Ct. Appeals (9th cir.) 1982. Counsel select com. on intelligence U.S. Senate, Washington, 1975-76; spl. asst. to U.S. atty. gen. Washington, 1977-79; asst. U.S. atty. for D.C., 1980-82; atty. Clark, Baron & Korda, San Jose, Calif., 1982-83; ptnr., chmn. employment practice Cooley, Godward, Palo Alto, Calif., 1983—95, 1997—; assoc. dep. atty. gen., dir. Exec. Office for Nat. Security U.S. Dept. of Justice, 1995-96. Lectr. U.S. Info. Svc., 1979-80; pres. bd. trustees Keys Sch., Palo Alto, 1983-87; bd. dirs. Retail Resources, Inc., 1987-88; mem. bd. vis. Stanford Law Sch., 2003-05; guest lectr. Stanford Bus. Sch., 2000—. Co-author, editor U.S. Senate Select Com. on Intelligence Reports, 1975-76; also articles. Issues dir. election com. U.S. Senator Alan Cranston, 1974, Gov. Edmund G. Brown Jr., 1976; mem. transition team Pres. Carter, 1976-77, Pres. Clinton, 1992; del. Calif. Dem. Conv., 1989-90; mem. credentials com. Nat. Dem. Conv., 2004. Mem. ABA, Calif. Bar Assn., D.C. Bar Assn., Santa Clara County Bar Assn., Univ. Club. Office: Cooley Godward LLP 5 Palo Alto Sq Palo Alto CA 94306-2122

BARON, FREDERICK M., lawyer; b. Cedar Rapids, Iowa, June 20, 1947; m. Lisa Blue. BA, U. Tex., 1968, JD, 1971. Assoc. editor Tex. Law Rev., 1969—71; founder, ptnr. Baron & Budd P.C., Dallas, 1977—. Trustee U. Tex. Law Sch., 2002—04. Named one of 100 Most Influential Lawyers, Nat. Law Jour., 2000, 2006, Dallas' top lawyers, D Mag., 2001, 2005. Mem.: ABA, Am. Law Inst., Trial Lawyers for Pub. Justice (founder, pres. 1997), Dallas Trial Lawyers Assn. (pres. 1980), Tex. Trial Lawyers Assn., Assn. Trial Lawyers of Am. (pres. 2000—01, chmn., environ. law sect. 1981, bd. govs. 1995—98, v.p. 1998—99), Am. Bd. Trial Advocates, State Bar of Tex., Dallas Bar Assn. Office: Baron & Budd PC 3102 Oak Lawn Ave Ste 1100 Dallas TX 75219*

BARON, JEFFREY, retired pharmacologist; b. Bklyn., July 10, 1942; s. Harry Leo and Terry (Goldstein) Baron; m. Judith Carol Rothberg, June 27, 1965; children: Stephanie Ann, Leslie Beth, Melissa Leigh. BS in Pharmacy, U. Conn., 1965; PhD in Pharmacology, U. Mich., 1969. Rsch. fellow in biochemistry U. Tex. Southwestern Med. Sch., Dallas, 1969-71, rsch. asst. prof. biochemistry and pharmacology, 1971-72; from asst. prof. pharmacology to prof. emeritus U. Iowa, Iowa City, 1972—2002, prof. emeritus, 2002—. Mem. chem. pathology study sect. NIH, Bethesda, Md., 1983—87, mem. environ. health scis. rev. com., Nat. Inst. Environ. Health Scis., Research Triangle Park, NC, 1990—94. Contbr. chapters to books, articles to profl. jours. Recipient Rsch. Career Devel. award, NIH, 1975—80. Mem.: Internat. Soc. Study Xenobiotics, Soc. Toxicology, Am. Assn. Cancer Rsch., Am. Soc. Biochem. and Molecular Biology, Am. Soc. Pharmacology and Exptl. Therapeutics. Jewish. Achievements include discovery of of the role of heme synthesis in regulating the induction of cytochrome P450 in liver; participation in the discovery of oxygenated cytochrome P450; research in immunohistochemical localization of cytochromes P450 and other xenobiotic-metabolizing enzymes in liver and extrahepatic tissues. Personal E-mail: jeffrey-baron@uiowa.edu.

BARON, JOSEPH MANDEL, hematologist; b. Oak Park, Ill., 1938; BS in BioChemistry, U. Chgo., 1958; MD, U. Chgo. Pritzker Sch. Medicine, 1962; MS in Pharmacology, U. Chgo., 1962. Diplomate Am. Bd. Internal Medicine, Am. Bd. Hematology, Am. Bd. Med. Oncology. Intern U. Chgo. Hosps., 1962—63, resident internal medicine, 1963—64, 1966—68, fellow hematology, 1967—68, assoc. prof. medicine, hematology and oncology, 1975—. Office: Univ Chgo MC 2115 5841 S Maryland Ave Chicago IL 60637 Office Phone: 773-702-6114.

BARON, LISA ANN, environmental scientist; b. Bethlehem, Pa., Apr. 13, 1967; d. Teresa Connors and Herbert Goldfeder; m. Robert F. Baron, Dec. 14, 1991; children: Jacob, Olivia. BA in Biology and Marine Biology, Bloomsburg U., 1989; MS in Biology, Ind. U. Pa., 1991. Pre-college instr. Wallops Island Marine Sci. Consortium, Wallops Island, Va., 1989; grad. tchg. asst. Ind. U. of Pa., 1989—91; ecol. risk assessor, rsch. scientist Oak Ridge Nat. Lab., Tenn., 1992—95; sr. environ. scientist McLaren Hart, Inc. ChemRisk, Warren, NJ, 1995—99; project mgr. NJ. Dept. of Transp. Maritime Resources, Trenton, NJ, 1999—. Mem.: Soc. Environ. Toxicology and Chemistry (program com. 1998—99, bd. dirs. Hudson chpt. 1996—, editor newsletter 1997—2000, pres. Hudson chpt. 2000—01, sec. N.J. chpt. 2003—, tri-chmn. 2005—, Presdl. citation 2005). Democrat. Roman Catholic. Achievements include initiator of the governmental partnership to remediate and restore the Passaic river. Office: New Jersey Dept Transp Office Maritime Resources 1035 Parkway Ave PO Box 837 Trenton NJ 08625 Home Phone: 908-213-2246; Office Phone: 609-530-4779. Office Fax: 609-530-4860. E-mail: lisa.baron@dot.state.nj.us.

BARON, MARTIN, editor; b. Tampa, Fla. BA, MBA, Lehigh U., 1976. State reporter, bus. writer Miami Herald, 1976—79; with LA Times, 1979—96, bus. editor, 1983—91, asst. mng. editor "column one" polls & spl. projects, 1991—93, editor Orange County Edit., 1993—96; joined NY Times, 1996, assoc. mng. editor nighttime news ops., 1997—99; exec. editor Miami Herald, 1999—2001; editor Boston Globe (NY Times Co.), 2001—. Named Editor of Yr., Editor & Pub. Mag., 2001; recipient Benjamin Bradlee Editor of Yr. award, Nat. Press Found., 2004. Mem.: Phi Beta Kappa. Office: The Boston Globe PO Box 55819 Boston MA 02205-5819*

BARON, MELVIN FARRELL, pharmacy educator; b. LA, July 29, 1932; s. Leo Ben and Sadie (Bauchman) B.; m. Lorraine Ross, Dec. 20, 1953; children: Lynn Baron Friedman, Ross David. PharmD, U. So. Calif., 1957, MPA, 1973. Lic. pharmacist, Calif. Pres. Shield Health Care Ctrs., Van Nuys, Calif., 1957-83; dir. externship program U. So. Calif., LA, 1991—; v.p. Shield Health Care Ctrs., Inc. (C.R. Bard, Inc. subsidiary), 1983-86; pres. Merit Coll., 1988-92, PharmaCom., LA, 1990—; assoc. prof. clin. pharmacy U. So. Calif., LA, 1991—, asst. dean pharm. care programs, 1995—97, dir. PharmD/MBA program, asst. dean programmatic advancement, 1998—; prin. New Horizon Pharmacy Cons. Adj. asst. prof. U. without Walls, Shaw U., Raleigh, NC, 1973; project dir. Haynes Found. Drug Rsch. Ctr., U. So. Calif., LA, 1973; assoc. dir. Calif. Alcoholism Found., 1973—75; adj. asst. prof. clin. pharmacy Sch. Pharmacy, U. So. Calif., 1981—91; cons. Topanga Terr. Convalescent Hosp., 1970—80, Calif. Labor Mgmt. Plan of alcoholism programs and coords., 1974, Office of Alcoholism, State of Calif., Nat. In-Home Health Svc., 1975, Continuity of Life Team, 1975, Triad Med., Longs Drug Stores, HealthTek, others; vis. prof. Tokyo Coll. Pharmacy, 1994, Sandoz Pharm. Co., 1995, Clin Oscar Romero, 2000; lectr. Meijo U., Nagoya U., Japan, 1994; presenter Nat. Pharmacy Dir. Conf., 1995; cons., mem. sci. adv. bd. Leiner Health Products, 1998—; cons. Prime Care Pharmacy, 1998—, Jackson Meml. Hosp., 1998, New Horizon Pharmacy, Avalon Hosp., Queenscare Family Clinics; cons., mem. adv. bd. Medpin, 2001; chair nominating com. CPHA, 1998; co-developer Trends in Healthcare Svcs.; presenter in field. Adv. bd. Pharmacist Newsletter, 1980—. Chmn. Friends of Operation Bootstrap, 1967-77; svc. chmn. tng. coord. Am. Cancer Soc., San Fernando Valley, Calif., 1980; mem. adv. bd. L.A. VNA, 1982; bd. dirs. pres. QSAD, 1987-88; pres. bd. Everywoman's Village, 1988-89; bd. dirs. Life Svcs., 1988-94; pres. bd. counselors, U. So. Calif., 1988-92, co-chmn. good neighborhood campaign Sch. Pharmacy, 1998; mem. Calif. Bd. Pharmacy Com. on Student/Preceptor Manual, 1991-92. Named Disting. Alumnus of Yr., U. So. Calif., Sch. of Pharmacy Alumni Assn. 1983, U. So. Calif. Torchbearer, 1990-91, Hon. Tchr. of Yr. U. So. Calif. Sch. Pharmacy, 1997. Fellow Am. Coll. Apothecaries, Calif. Pharmacist Assn. (chair edn. com.); mem. Am. Pharm. Assn., Am. Soc. Health Sys. Pharmacists, Am. Soc. Pub. Adminstrn., Am. Assn. Colls. of Pharmacy (spkr. ann. meeting 2000), Phi Kappa Phi, Phi Lambda Sigma (hon., faculty advisor), Rho Chi. Home: 1245 Wellesley Ave Apt 201 Los Angeles CA 90025-1170 Office: 1985 Zonal Ave Los Angeles CA 90089-0105 Home Phone: 310-826-6813; Office Phone: 323-442-2686. Business E-Mail: mbaron@usc.edu.

BARON, MITCHELL NEAL, lawyer; b. NYC, Nov. 8, 1947; s. Norman and Ruth (Schliftman) B.; m. Sharon Hefler, Feb. 7, 1971; 1 child, Amanda. BS, Boston U., 1969; JD, Columbia U., 1973. Bar: N.Y. 1974. Assoc. Kaye, Schuler, Fierman, Hays & Handler, NYC, 1973-79; ptnr. Golberg & Abrams, NYC, 1979-87, Morgan, Lewis & Bockius LLP, NYC, 1987—, dep. leader firm real estate group. Mem. N.Y. Bar Assn., N.Y.C. Bar Assn.-property law sect. Office: Morgan Lewis & Bockius LLP 101 Park Ave Fl 44 New York NY 10178-0060 Office Fax: 212-309-6001. Business E-Mail: mbaron@morganlewis.com.

BARON, PATRICIA BURRELL, university director; b. Glen Ridge, NJ, Dec. 16, 1949; d. Leo Duncan and Mollie Amelia (Scard) B.; m. William Robert Baron, June 17, 1972. BA, Allegheny Coll., 1972; MA in Librarianship, U. Denver, 1973; MEd in Ednl. Adminstrn., U. Maine, 1980; EdD in Ednl. Adminstrn., No. Ariz. U., 1987. Reference libr. U. Maine, Orono, 1975, asst. to grad. dean, 1976-80, asst. to acad. v.p., 1980-82; asst. to grad. dean No. Ariz. U., Flagstaff, 1982-87, asst. grad. dean, 1987-93, assoc. grad. dean, dir. grad. admissions, 1993—. Contbr. articles to profl. jours., 1998-. Active commn. on status of women Ariz. Bd. of Regents, Phoenix, 1989-91. Recipient Pres.'s Achievement award No. Ariz. U., 1993, 2005; named Woman of Distinction, Soroptomist Internat., 1993. Mem. AAUW, Nat. Assn. Grad. Admissions (exec. bd. 1998-2004, Pres.'s Achievement award 1995, 2005), Univ. Career Women (founder, chair 1991-92), Phi Kappa Phi. Avocations: needlecrafts, gardening. Office: No Ariz U PO Box 4125 Flagstaff AZ 86011-4125

BARON, ROBERT CHARLES, publishing executive; b. LA, Jan. 26, 1934; s. Leo Francis and Marietta (Schulze) Baron; m. Charlotte Rose Persinger, Nov. 29, 1986; stepchildren: Brett Persinger, Kristen Fochner. BS in Physics, St. Joseph's U., Phila., 1956. Registered profl. engr., Mass. Engr. RCA, Camden, N.J., 1955-57, Computer Control Co., Framingham, Mass., 1959-61, program mgr. Mariner II and IV space computers, 1961-65, engring. mgr., 1965-69; worldwide systems mgr. Honeywell Minicomputer, Framingham, 1970-71; founder, pres., CEO Prime Computer, Framingham, 1971-75; pvt. practice Boston, 1976-83; founder and pres. Fulcrum Pub., Golden, Colo., 1984—. Bd. dirs. Prime Computer, Framingham, Mass., Alling-Lander, Cheshire, Conn., Oxion, Hugoton, Kans., Fulcrum Pub., Golden, Colo. Author: Digital Logic and Computer Operations, 1966, Micropower Electronics, 1970, America in the Twentieth Century, 1995, Footsteps on the Sands of Time, 1999, What Was It Like Orville: The Early Space Program, 2002, Hudson: The Story of a River, 2004, Pioneers and Plodders, 2004, To the Mountaintop, 2007; editor: The Garden and Farm Books of Thomas Jefferson, 1987, Soul of America: Documenting Our Past, 1942-1974, 1989, Colorado Rockies: The Inaugural Season, 1993, Thomas Hornsby Ferrill and the American West, 1996. Vice chmn. bd. dirs. Mass. Audubon Soc., Lincoln, 1980—85; bd. dirs. Rocky Mountain Women's Inst., Denver, 1987—90, Denver Pub. Libr. Friends Found., 1989—96, pres., 1994—96; trustee Lincoln Filene Ctr., Tufts U., Medford, Mass., 1982—84. Mem.: Hakluyt Soc., Western History Assn., Mass. Hist. Soc., Thoreau Soc., Am. Antiquarian Soc. (bd. dirs., chmn. 1993—2003), Internat. Wilderness Leadership Found. (bd. dirs. 1990—, chmn. 1994—2000, 2003—), Explorer's Club, Grolier Club. Avocations: writing, reading, sports, gardening, collecting clocks. Office: Fulcrum Pub 4690 Table Mountain Dr Ste 100 Golden CO 80403 Business E-Mail: bob@fulcrum-books.com.

BARON, ROBERT HOWARD, lawyer; b. Bethpage, NY, Nov. 5, 1957; AB, Princeton U., 1978; JD, Harvard U., 1981. Bar: N.Y. 1982, U.S. Dist. Ct. (so. dist.) N.Y. 1982. Assoc. Cravath, Swaine & Moore, NYC, 1981-88, ptnr., litig., 1988—. Office: Cravath Swaine & Moore 825 8th Ave Fl 38 New York NY 10019-7475 Office Phone: 212-474-1422. Office Fax: 212-474-3700. Business E-Mail: rbaron@cravath.com.

BARON, SAMUEL HASKELL, historian; b. NYC, May 24, 1921; s. James and Dinah (Bader) B.; m. Virginia Wilson, Dec. 22, 1949; children—Sheila, Carla, Laura. BS, Cornell U., 1942; MA, Columbia U., 1948; PhD, 1952. Instr. history U. Tenn., 1948-53; vis. lectr. Northwestern U., 1953-54, U. Mo., 1954-55, U. Nebr., 1955-56; from asst. prof. to prof. Grinnell (Iowa) Coll., 1956-66; prof. U. Calif.-San Diego, 1966-72; Alumni Disting. prof. history U. N.C., Chapel Hill, 1972-91, prof. emeritus, 1991—; chmn. Conf. Slavic and Ea. European History, 1976. Author: Plekhanov: The Father of Russian Marxism, 1963, The Travels of Olearius in Seventeenth Century Russia, 1967, Muscovite Russia: Collected Essays, 1980, Explorations in Muscovite History, 1991, Plekhanov in Russian History and Soviet Historiography, 1994, Bloody Saturday in the Soviet Union: Novocherkassk, 1962, 2001; co-editor: Windows on The Russian Past: Essays on Soviet Historiography since Stalin, 1977, Introspection in Biography: The Biographer's Quest for Self-Awareness, 1985, Religion and Culture in Early Modern Russia and Ukraine, 1997, Adventures in Russian Historical Research, 2003. Served from pvt. to capt. AUS, 1942-46. Ford Found. fellow, 1958-59, Guggenheim Found. fellow, 1970-71, Nat. Endowment Humanities fellow, 1976; chair named in his honor U. N.C., 1994. Mem. AAUP (council 1962-65), Am. Hist. Assn., Am. Assn. Advancement Slavic Studies, Early Slavic Studies Assn. (pres. 1991). Office: U NC Dept History Chapel Hill NC 27599-0001 E-mail: shbaron@email.unc.edu.

BARON, SHELDON, research and development company executive; b. Bklyn., May 13, 1934; s. Harry and Edna (Schleifer) B.; m. Doris Earl Rudd, Aug. 11, 1961; 1 son, David. BS, Bklyn. Coll., 1955; MA, Coll. William and Mary, 1961; PhD, Harvard U., 1966. Simulation engr. USAF-NACA, Hampton, Va., 1955-57; aerospace technologist NASA, Hampton, 1958-65, Cambridge, Mass., 1965-67; mgr., researcher Bolt Beranek & Newman, Cambridge, 1967-71, mgr., prin. scientist, 1971-79, v.p., 1979-94, sr. v.p., 1994-98; ind. cons. Lexington, Mass., 1999—2007; ret., 2007. Mem. sci. adv. bd. U.S. Army Missile Command, Huntsville, Ala., 1975-77; mem. working group on simulation, 1982-84; chmn. working group on human performance modelling Nat. Acad. Scis.-NRC, 1983-87; bd. vistors BBN Techs., 1998-2000; bd. councillors U. S.C. Integrated Media Systems Ctr., 1998—; cons. U.S. Army Sci. Bd., 2000-02. Assoc. editor: Jour. Cybernetics and Info. Scis., Washington, 1976-81. Served to 1st lt. USAF, 1955-57. Fellow (life) IEEE; mem. Control Systems Soc. (sec., treas. 1982-84), AIAA, Harvard Soc. Engrs. and Scientists (pres. 1976-78) Home: 7 Birch Hill Ln Lexington MA 02421-7445

BARON, SHERI, advertising agency executive; b. Bklyn., Sept. 3, 1955; d. Irwin Murray Glaser and Rosalind (Mendelson) Krasik; m. Peter T. Colonel, Sept. 20, 1981 (dec.); m. Alan R. Baron, Dec. 14, 1996. BA in Psychology, SUNY, Courtland, 1977. Account exec. Ted Bates Co., NYC, 1978-80, SSC&B Advt. (name now Lowe), NYC, 1980-82, v.p. acct. supr., 1983-84, sr. v.p mgmt. supr., 1984-88, exec. v.p., 1988-94, bd. dirs., 1990-94; pres., COO, chief strategic officer Gotham Inc., 1994—. Named to Am. Advt. Fedn. Hall of Achievement, 1993, 40 Under 40 List, Crain's N.Y. bus., 1994. Mem. Advt. Women N.Y., Cosmetic Exec. Women, Fashion Group Internat. Office: Gotham Inc 100 5th Ave Fl 16 New York NY 10011-6996 Home: 4 Glendcare Rd Upper Saddle River NJ 07458 Business E-Mail: sherib@gothaminc.com.

BARON, STANLEY N., retired electrical engineer; b. Norwalk, Conn., 1939; s. Albert I. Baron and Beatrice Frances Gaynor; m. Constance Marmins (div.); children: Matthew, Jonathan, Andrew. BSEE, NYU, NYC, 1961, MSEE, 1971. Engr. GE Co., Utica and Syracuse, NY, 1961—64; sr. engr. Sylvania Amherst Lab., NY, 1964—65; sect. mgr. CBS Labs., Stamford, Conn., 1965—72; mgr. Wiltek, Inc., Norwalk, 1972—75; v.p. Comtrend, Inc., Stamford, 1975—77; mgr. product devel. MicroTime, Inc., Bloomfield, Conn., 1977—79; mng. engr. Thomson-CSF Labs., Stamford, 1979—85; mng. dir. TV tech. NBC, NYC, 1985—98; ret., 1998. Mem. working party new tech. European Broadcasting Union, Geneva, 1985—95, NBC rep. to tech. com., 1985—97; mem. adv. com. Internat. Broadcasting Convention, London, 1987—97; mem. steering com. internat. workshop on signal processing HDTV, Turin, Italy, 1988—92; mem. US delegation Internat. Telecomms. Union, Geneva, 1987—98, chmn. task group 11/3 on digital TV, 1992—97; vice chmn., sec. FCC Adv. Com. on Advanced TV Svcs. - Working Party 1, Washington, 1987—95; sec. FCC Adv. Com. on Advanced TV Svcs., Washington, 1993—94; chmn. tech. com. Advanced TV Sys. Com., Washington, 1994—98; presenter in field. Co-author (with M.I. Krivocheev): Digital Image and Audio Communications: Toward a Global Information Infrastructure; contbr. numerous articles to profl. publs. Chmn. Stamford Police Commn., 1983—85. Recipient EMMY Tech. award, 1983, 1990, Mayor's award for excellence in sci. and tech., NY Acad. Scis. and Mayor of NYC, 1993, John Tucker award, Internat. Broadcasting Convention, 1995, cert. recognition, Australian Broadcasting Authority, 1996. Fellow: IEEE (Steinmetz medal 2001), Brit. Kineomatic Sound and TV Soc., Soc. Motion Picture and TV Engrs. (mem. stds. com. 1986—96, bd. govs. 1986—98, bd. editors 1986—, engring. v.p. 1988—91, mem. long range planning com. 1988—98, exec. v.p. 1993—94, pres. 1995—96, David Sarnoff Gold medal 1991, Progress Gold medal 2003), Royal TV Soc. (hon.). Achievements include invention of Vidifont digital graphic gen; digital TV imaging; patents for enhancement of fluroscopically enhanced images.

BARON, STUART, artist, art educator, director; b. New Castle, Pa., July 20, 1947; s. Samuel and Ann (Stein) Baron; m. Judith Goldsmith, June 18, 1972. BFA, Boston U., 1970, MFA, 1972. Prof. art Boston U., 1972—2003; lectr. art Harvard U., Cambridge, Mass., 2002—03; dir., prof. art La. State U., Baton Rouge, 2003—. Initiator, nat. appeal art supplies children, students, and profl. artists displaced by hurricane Katrina La. State U., Baton Rouge, 2005—06. Mass. Artists' fellowship, 1989. Master: Gold Key (hon.; faculty 1992—). Democrat. Home: 628 Audubon Ave Baton Rouge LA 70806 Office: La State U Sch of Art 123 Art Bldg Baton Rouge LA 70803 Office Phone: 225.578.5414. Office Fax: 225.578.5424. Personal E-mail: sbaron1@mac.com.

BARON, SUSAN, former publishing executive; BA, Carnegie Mellon Univ. Sr. leadership positions Reader's Digest, Pleasantville, NY, Family Circle, NYC, McCalls Mag.; sr. leadership positions, Integrated Mktg., Am. Baby Group, Hispanic Ventures Meredith Corp., 2002—06, pub., Parents Mag., 2006—07.

BARON COHEN, SACHA (ALI G, BORAT), actor, comedian; b. London, Oct. 13, 1971; s. Gerald and Daniella Baron Cohen. Studied, Christ's Coll., Cambridge. Actor: (films) Jack and Jeremy's Police 4, 1995, The Jolly Boys' Last Stand, 2000, Madagascar (voice), 2005, Talladega Nights: The Ballad of Ricky Bobby, 2006; actor, writer, prodr.: Borat: Cultural Learnings of America for Make Benefit Glorious Nation of Kazakhstan, 2006 (Best Actor award, LA Film Critics Assn.(Tie), 2006, Best Performance by an Actor in a Motion Picture-Musical or Comedy, Golden Globe award, Hollywood Fgn. Press Assn., 2007, Best Comedic Performance, MTV Movie Awards, 2007); actor: (TV specials) Comic Relief: Say Pants to Poverty, 2001; actor, exec. prodr., writer (films) Ali G Indahouse, 2002, Spyz, 2003, (TV series) Da Ali G Show, 2003, actor, writer The 11 O'Clock Show, 1998, Da Ali G Show, 2000 (BAFTA TV Award for Best Comedy, 2001), (videos) Ali G, Innit, 1999, Ali G, Aiii, 2000, Ali G: Bling Bling, 2002; guest appearance: (TV series) Curb Your Enthusiasm, 2005; host: MTV European Music Awards, 2005. Named one of Barbara Walters-10 Most Fascinating People of 2006, The World's Most Influential People, TIME mag., 2007.

BARONDES, SAMUEL HERBERT, psychiatrist, educator; b. Bklyn., Dec. 21, 1933; s. Solomon and Yetta (Kaplow) B.; m. Ellen Slater, Sept. 1, 1963 (dec. Nov. 22, 1971); children: Elizabeth Francesca, Jessica Gabrielle; m. Louann Brizendine, Sept. 14, 2002. AB, Columbia U., 1954, MD, 1958. Intern, then asst. resident in medicine Peter Bent Brigham Hosp., Boston, 1958-60; sr. asst. surgeon USPHS, NIH, Bethesda, Md., 1960-63; resident in psychiatry McLean and Mass. Gen. hosps., Boston, 1963-66; asst. prof., then assoc. prof. psychiatry and molecular biology Albert Einstein Coll. Medicine., Bronx, NY, 1966-69; prof. psychiatry U. Calif., San Diego, 1969-86, prof., chmn. dept. psychiatry, dir. Langley Porter Psychiat. Inst. San Francisco, 1986-94, dir. Ctr. Neurobiology and Psychiatry, 1994—, Jeanne and Sanford Robertson Prof. Neurobiol. and Psychiatry, 1996—. Pres. McKnight Endowment Fund for Neurosci., 1989-98; sci. adv. com. Rsch. Am.; governing coun. Internat. Brain Rsch. Orgn., 1994-2000; bd. sci. counselors NIMH, 1997-2002, chair, 2000-02. Author: Molecules and Mental Illness, 1993, Mood Genes, 1998, Better Than Prozac, 2003; mem. editl. bd. profl. jours.; contbr. articles to profl. jours. Recipient Rsch. Career Devel. award USPHS, 1967, Elliott Royer award, 1989, P.H. Stillmark medal Estonia, 1989; Fogarty Internat. scholar NIH, 1979; J. Robert Oppenheimer lectr., 2000. Fellow AAAS, Am. Psychiat. Assn., Am. Coll. Neuropsychopharmacology; mem. Inst. Medicine Nat. Acad. Sci. Office: U Calif-San Francisco Langley Porter Psychiat Ins 401 Parnassus Ave San Francisco CA 94143-0984 Business E-Mail: barondes@cgl.ucsf.edu.

BARONDESS, JEREMIAH ABRAHAM, physician; b. NYC, June 6, 1924; s. Benjamin and Dora (Greenberg) B.; m. Sue Kaufman, Nov. 22,

1953 (dec. 1977); 1 child, James Joseph; m. Linda Hiddemen, Dec. 10, 1982. MD, Johns Hopkins U., Balt., 1949; DSc (hon.), Albany Med. Coll., Union U., 1978; LittD (hon.), NY Inst. Tech., Old Westbury, 1992; DMedSci (hon.), Med. Coll. Pa., 1993; DSc (hon.), NY Med. Coll., 1998. Diplomate Am. Bd. Internal Medicine (bd. govs., council gen. internal medicine 1975-81). Intern, then asst. resident in medicine Osler Med. Svc. Johns Hopkins Hosp., 1949-51; asst. medicine Johns Hopkins U. Med. Sch., 1950-51; staff virology sect., rsch. divsn. Children's Hosp., Phila.; rsch. fellow virology U. Pa. Med. Sch., 1951-53; asst. resident, then chief resident in medicine NY Hosp.-Cornell U. Med. Center, 1953-55; faculty Cornell U. Med. Coll., 1953—, clin. prof. medicine, 1971-78, prof. clin. medicine, 1978-87, Irene F. and I. Roy Psaty disting. prof. clin. medicine, 1987-89, William T. Foley Disting.prof. clin. medicine, 1989-90, adj. prof. clin. medicine, 1990, prof. emeritus, 1993—, prof. clin. pub. health, 2006—; staff NY Hosp., 1953—, attending physician, 1971—, chief pvt. med. svc., 1971-92, hon. staff mem., 1992—, assoc. chmn. dept. medicine, 1983-90; asst. vis. physician Bellevue Hosp., 1960-67; cons. medicine Meml. Hosp. Cancer and Allied Diseases, 1972-90; Alpha Omega Alpha vis. prof. U. P.R. Med. Sch., 1972; Meyerowitz meml. lectr. U. Rochester Sch. Medicine, 1980. Disting. lectr. U. NC, 1982; vis. prof. medicine U. Ill. Med. Sch., 1974, U. Va. Med. Sch., 1976, Mayo Clinic and Med. Sch., 1978, U. Iowa Sch. Medicine, 1979, U. Tex. Med. Ctr., 1986, 90, U. Pa., 1986, U. Va., 1989, NY Med. Coll., 1990, Alpha Omega Alpha vis. prof. medicine, 2006; vis. prof. medicine SUNY Health Sci. Ctr., Bklyn., 1992; mem. nat. resources com. Johns Hopkins U., 1965—, trustee, 1977—94, trustee emeritus, 1994—, chmn. vis. com. Sch. Medicine, 1978—92. Author: (with A.M. Harvey and J. Bordley) Differential Diagnosis, (with J. McGovern and C. Roland) The Persisting Osler, 1985, (with A.H. Samiy and R.G. Douglas) Textbook of Diagnostic Medicine, 1987, (with C. Roland) The Persisting Osler II, 1994, (with C. Roland) The Persisting Osler III, 2002; editor: Diagnostic Approaches to Presenting Syndromes, 1971; co-editor Differential Diagnosis, 1994; mem. editl. bd. Forum on Medicine, Pharos, Internat. Jour. Technol. Assessment in Health Care, Jour. Royal Soc. Med.; contbr. articles to profl. jours. Bd. dirs. Am. Fedn. Aging Rsch., 1996-2001. With AUS, 1943-46, USPHS, 1951-53 Recipient Wiggers award Albany Med. Coll. Union U., 1978, Alfred Stengel award ACP, 1983; named Hon. Alumnus Cornell U. Med. Coll., 1974. Fellow AAAS, Am. Acad. Arts and Scis., Royal Coll. Physicians London, ACP (chmn. bd. govs. 1973-75, bd. regents 1975—, pres. 1978-79, pres. emeritus 1988), Federated Coun. Internal Medicine, Royal Soc. Medicine (hon. 2005), Royal Soc. Health, Royal Coll. Physicians Ireland (hon.); mem. Am. Clin. and Climatol. Assn. (coun. 1975-78, pres. 1994), Am. Osler Soc. (pres. 1983-84), Am. Fedn. Clin. Rsch., APHA, Assn. Am. Physicians, Harvey Soc., NY Heart Assn., Inst. Medicine NAS (coun. 1979-81, co-chair coun. on health care tech., chair com. on managed care and chronic disease 1996, chair com. on musculoskeletal disorders and the workplace 1999-01, mem. com. on spinal cord injury, 2004-05), The NY Acad. Scis., The NY Acad. Medicine (pres. 1990-2006, pres. emeritus 2006—), Internat. Soc. Internal Medicine, Phi Beta Kappa, Alpha Omega Alpha (dir. 1978-79, pres. 1987-89), Century Assn.(NYC), Cosmos Club (Washington). Jewish. Home: 544 E 86th St New York NY 10028-7536 Office: NY Acad Medicine 1216 5th Ave New York NY 10029-5202 Business E-Mail: jbaronde@nyam.org.

BARONE, TONY, SR., professional basketball coach; s. Corinne Barone. B in English, Duke U., 1968. Asst. coach Duke U., 1972—74, Bradley U., Peoria, Ill., 1978—85; head coach Creighton U., Omaha, 1985—91, Tex. A&M U., Lubbock, Tex., 1991—98; Big 12 color commentator ESPN regional, 1998—2000; dir. player pers. Memphis Grizzlies, 2000—, asst. coach, 2002—04, interim head coach, 2006—. Host (basketball videos) Drills to Build a Competitive and Fundamentally Sound Team. Named Mo. Valley Conf. Coach of Yr. (twice), Southwestern Conf. Coach of Yr., 1994. Office: Memphis Grizzlies 191 Beale St Memphis TN 38103*

BARONI, BILL (WILLIAM E. BARONI JR.), state legislator; b. Dec. 10, 1971; BA in Hist., George Washington U.; JD, U. Va. Mem. planning bd. Hamilton Twp., 1998—2000; mem. NJ State Assembly from Dist. 14, 2004—, asst. parliamentarian, 2004—05, mem. edn. com., mem. higher edn. com., mem. joint com. on pub. schs., mem. NJ Citizens' Clean Elections Commn.; atty. Adj. prof. Seton Hall U. Sch. Law. Bd. trustees Mercer County Cmty. Coll., NJ, 1998—2003. Named one of 2007 People to Watch, Sunday Star-Ledger, NJ. Republican. Office: 2239 Whitehorse Mercerville Rd Ste E Trenton NJ 08619-2642*

BARONI, MICHAEL L., lawyer; b. NYC, Dec. 26, 1967; m. Lisa Baroni. BA, Boston Coll., 1990; JD, Hofstra U., 1993. Bar: NY 1994, Calif. 2001. Of counsel Jacobson & Colfin, NYC; in-house counsel Gen. Media, Inc., 1995—97; gen. counsel Henry Holt & Co., 1997—98; sr. atty. Metromedia Fiber Network Svcs., White Plains, NY, and Palo Alto, CA, 1998—2003; gen. counsel, sec. BSH Home Appliances Corp., Huntington Beach, Calif., 2003—. Contbr. articles over 80 to profl. jour. Mem.: ABA (mem. antitrust sect., forum on franchising), Assn. Corp. Counsel, State Bar Calif. (mem. antitrust unfair competition sect., bus. law sect.), NY State Bar Assn. (chair product liability com. literary works and related rights 1995), Orange Co. Bar Assn. (mem. product liability sect., bus. and corp. law sect., corp. counsel). Office: BSH Home Appliances Corp Legal Dept 5551 McFadden Ave Huntington Beach CA 92649 Office Phone: 714-899-3506.

BAROODY, ALBERT JOSEPH, JR., pastoral counselor; b. Columbia, SC, Sept. 8, 1952; s. Albert Joseph and Hazel (Haskin) B.; m. Nancy Dell Weatherford, Jan. 3, 1976; children: Joseph McKinley, Blakely Adelle. BS in Sociology, U. S.C., 1974; MDiv, S.E. Bapt. Theol. Sem., Wake Forest, NC, 1978, D of Ministry, 1984. Ordained to ministry Bapt. Ch., 1977; lic. profl. counselor, S.C., 1992. Chaplain intern and resident Palmetto Bapt. Med. Ctr., Columbia, SC, 1977-79; dir. pastoral svcs. Easley (S.C.) Bapt. Med. Ctr., 1979-80, McLeod Regional Med. Ctr., Florence, 1980-91; pastoral counselor McLeod Counseling Svcs., Florence, 1991-94, Cmty. Care and Counseling, Florence, 1994-2000, Baroody Pastoral Counseling, St. John's Episcopal Ch., Florence, 2000—. Chaplain Lions Club, Florence, 1980-83; interim pastor Florence Bapt. Fellowship, 2003, Westminister Presbyn. Ch., 2006; pastoral cons. Tuomey Hosp., Sumter, SC, 1983, Conway Hosp., SC, 1985-86, 92-94, Williamsburg County Hosp., Kingstree, SC, 1986-88. Author (with others): Ministry to Youth in Crisis, Professional Chaplaincy and Clinical Pastoral Education: Should Become More Scientific? Yes and No, 2002; contbr. articles and revs. to profl. jours. and mags., book reviews to jours. Continuing edn. state rep. Coll. Chaplains, 1983-92; mem. adv. bd. Salvation Army, Florence, 2000—, vice chmn. adv. bd., 2002-06, chmn., 2006—; mem. adv. bd. Hospice, Florence, 1988-94, chmn., 1993-94; mem. exec. com., chmn. devel. com. S.E. Region Assn. for Clin. Pastoral Edn., 1986-90; liason coun. S.C. Organ Procurement Assn., 1988-91; mem. Pee Dee Coalition Against Domestic and Sexual Assault cmty. svcs. adv. coun., 1996-2001; mem. palliative care com., cmty. rep. McLeod Regional Med. Ctr., 2004-05. Fellow Am. Assn. Pastoral Counselors (fin. com. S.E. region, 1996-99, profl. concerns com. 2000-03). Avocations: travel, reading, walking, movies. Office: Baroody Pastoral Counseling St John's Episcopal Ch 252 S Dargan St Florence SC 29506-2534 Office Phone: 843-662-0000. Personal E-mail: Joebaroody@aol.com.

BAROODY, MICHAEL ELIAS, trade association executive; b. Washington, Sept. 14, 1946; s. William J. and Nabeeha (Ashooh) B.; m. Mary Cecilia Patton, Dec. 16, 1967; children— Michael Elias, Timothy, Catherine, Matthew, Peter, Meghan BA in Polit. Sci., U. Notre Dame, 1968. Legis. asst. Senator Roman Hruska, Washington, 1970-71; speech writer, exec. asst. Senator Bob Dole, Washington, 1972-75; congl. liaison FEA, Washington, 1975-77; dir. pub. affairs Republican Nat. Com., Washington, 1977-81; exec. asst. to U.S. trade rep. William Brock, Washington, 1981; dep. asst. to Pres., dir. pub. affairs The White House, Washington, 1981-85; asst. sec. for policy Dept. Labor, Washington, 1985-89; sr. v.p. for policy and comms. Nat. Assn. Mfrs., 1990-93; pres. nat. policy forum A Rep. Ctr. for Exch. of Ideas, 1993-94; v.p. pub. affairs Nat. Assn. Mfrs., Washington, 1994-96, sr. v.p. pub. affairs, 1997-99, sr. v.p. policy comm. and pub. affairs, 1999-2001, exec. v.p., 2001—. Editor-in-chief: Commonsense: A Republican Jour. Thought and Opinion, 1978-80, 94, Rep. Platform, 1980. Chmn. bd. Nat. Ctr. for Neighborhood Enterprise, 1997—2002. Lt. (j.g.) USN, 1968-70 Greek Catholic Home: 4628 Newcomb Pl Alexandria VA 22304-1505

BAROUCH, DAN HUNG, physician, scientist, educator; b. Gottingen, Germany, Feb. 4, 1973; s. Eytan and Winifred Wendy B.; m. Fina Canas, May 15, 1999. BA summa cum laude, Harvard U., Cambridge, Mass., 1993, MD summa cum laude, 1999; PhD, Oxford U., Eng., 1995. Diplomate in internal medicine and infectious diseases Am. Bd. Internal Medicine. Rschr. HIV immunology and vaccines Oxford U., 1993-95; rschr. Beth Israel Deaconess Med. Ctr., Boston, 1995—; resident in internal medicine Mass. Gen. Hosp., Boston, 1999—2001; fellow infectious diseases Mass. Gen. Hosp./Brigham Women's Hosp., Boston, 2001—04; staff physician infectious diseases Brigham and Women's Hosp., Boston, 2004—, Beth Israel Deaconess Med. Ctr., 2004—; clin. fellow in medicine Harvard Med. Sch., Boston, 1999—2002, instr. in medicine, 2002—04, asst. prof., 2004—06, assoc. prof., 2006—. Investigator HIV Vaccine Trials Network, Boston, 2000—. Contbr. rsch. articles to profl. jours. and textbooks. British Marshall scholar Marshall Commn., 1993-95, Barry M. Goldwater scholar U.S. Govt., 1991-93, USA Today Coll. scholar, 1993; recipient Ptnrs. in Excellence award Mass. Gen. Hosp., 2002, Maxwell Finland Investigator award Mass. Infectious Diseases Soc., 2004. Master: Copley Soc. Boston; mem.: AAAS, ACP, AMA, Am. Assn. Immunologists, Am. Soc. for Microbiology, Mass. Med. Soc., Infectious Diseases Soc. Am., Mass. Infectious Diseases Soc. Avocations: calligraphy, violin, skiing, travel. Office: Beth Israel Deaconess Med Ctr Rsch E 213 Divsn Viral Pathogenesis 330 Brookline Ave Boston MA 02215 Home: 2 Saint Paul St Apt# 107 Brookline MA 02446 Office Phone: 617-667-4434. Business E-Mail: dbarouch@bidmc.harvard.edu.

BAROUDY, BAHIGE MOURAD, biochemist, researcher; b. Beirut, July 1, 1950; came to U.S., 1973, naturalized, 1988; s. Mourad Bahige and Ludmila Adelheid (Obermuller-Haddad) BSc, Am. U. of Beirut, 1972; PhD, Georgetown U., 1978. Teaching asst. Wesleyan U., Middletown, Conn., 1973-74; rsch. asst. Georgetown U., Washington, 1974-78, fellow, 1982, rsch. assoc. prof., 1985-89; dir. molecular virology div. James N. Gamble Inst. Med. Rsch., Cin., 1989-95; assoc. dir. antiviral therapy Schering-Plough Rsch. Ins., Kenilworth, NJ, 1996-2000, dir., 2000—01, group dir., 2001—02, group dir. antiviral and antimicrobial therapy, 2002—03; v.p. drug discovery Avance Pharma, Laval, Que., Canada, 2003—05; pres. CSO Millenia Hope Inc., Montreal, Quebec, 2006—; CSO Millenia Hope Biopharma, Kirkland, 2006—, pres., 2007—. Vis. fellow scientist NIH, Bethesda, Md., 1979-81, vis. assoc. scientist, 1982-85. Contbr. articles to profl. jours., chpts. to books. Mem. Am. Assn. for Study of Liver Diseases, Am. Chem. Soc., Am. Soc. Biochemistry and Molecular Biology, Am. Soc. for Microbiology, Am. Soc. for Virology, N.Y. Acad. Scis., NIH Alumni Assn., Sigma Xi. Lutheran. Avocations: fencing, viola, skiing. Office: Millenia Hope Biopharma 16800 Trans Can Hwy Kirkland PQ H9H 4M7 Canada Address: Millenia Hope Inc Ste 2200 1250 Rene Levesque W Montreal PQ H3B 4WB Canada Office Phone: 514-288-8822 x 206. Business E-Mail: bahige.baroudy@mh-b.com.

BARQUERO, PEDRO B., mathematician, researcher; b. Barcelona, Apr. 18, 1973; s. Benjamin Barquero and Maria Carmen Salavert. BSc, U. Bath, Eng., 1996; MA, UCLA, 1998, PhD, 2000. Lectr. Calif. State U., Dominquez Hills, 2001—02; prof. N.Y. Inst. Tech., NYC, 2003—; assoc. prof. Santa Monica Coll., Calif., 2000—03; rsch. scholar CUNY. Textbook reviewer Brooks/Cole Pub., 2003—; spkr. in field. Contbr. articles to profl. jours. Fellow Chancellor's fellow, Dept. Math., UCLA; scholar UCLA scholar, 1996, CUNY, Grad. Ctr., NYC. Mem.: Internat. Assn. Cryptology Rsch., Math. Assn. Am., Am. Math. Soc. Office: NYIT-Manhattan Campus Math Dept 1855 Broadway New York NY 10023 Home Phone: 201-969-2173; Office Phone: 212-261-1623.

BARR, ADAM, biology educator; s. Michael and Pamela Barr; m. Melissa Weiner, Sept. 18, 2005; children: Alexandra Merrill, Zachery Merrill, Rebecca, Avi. BA in Biology, SUNY, Binghamton, 1995, MAT in Biology, 1999. Sr. lab. technician U. Medicine and Dentistry NJ, Piscataway, 1996—98; sci. tchr. Mohonasen HS, Rotterdam, NY, 2000—. Adj. faculty mem. Schenectady CC, NY, 2002—, Hudson Valley C.C., Troy, NY, 2002—; instr. Scuba Too NY, Schenectady, 2004—. Youth group advisor Temple TI's, Schenectady, 1997—2006. Recipient Nat. Star of Tchg. award, US Dept. Edn., 2006. Mem.: PA Diving Instrs., Sci. Teachers Assn. NY State, Nat. Assn. Biology Tchrs. Avocation: scuba diving. Home Phone: 518-424-7267; Office Phone: 518-356-8300.

BARR, CHARLES F., lawyer, insurance company executive; BA, Boston Coll., 1972; JD, Suffolk U., 1976. Bar: Mass. 1977, Conn. 1993; CPCU. Counsel Comml. Union Ins. Cos., 1977-81; asst. gen. counsel Reliance Ins. Cos., 1981-87; v.p., gen. counsel United Pacific Life Ins. Co., 1984-87; gen. counsel Gen. Accident Ins. Co., 1987-89, Gen. Reins. Corp., Stamford, Conn., 1989-94, sr. v.p., gen. counsel, sec., 1994-2000; gen. counsel Benfield Blanch, Inc., Westport, Conn., 2000—. E-mail: charles.barr@benfieldgroup.com.

BARR, DONALD ROY, statistics and operations research educator, statistician; b. Durango, Colo., Dec. 10, 1938; s. Russell Wesely and Elizabeth Joanette B.; m. Loudean Suttle, June 14, 1958; children: Mark Edward, Bryan Michael. BA, Whittier Coll., 1960; MS, Colo. State U., 1962, PhD, 1965. Instr. Colo. State U., 1964-65; asst. prof. math. U. Wis.-Oshkosh, 1965-66; prof. stats. and ops. rsch. Naval Postgrad. Sch., Monterey, Calif., 1966-87; v.p. Evaluation Tech. Inc., 1987-88, pres. Monterey, 1988-89; v.p. VRC Corp., Monterey, 1988-89; prof. math. Naval Postgrad. Sch., Monterey, Calif., 1990-93; prof. systems engring. U.S. Mil. Acad., West Point, NY, 1993-99; ret., 1999—. Liaison scientist London br. Office Naval Rsch., 1982-83; vis. prof. systems engring., U.S. Mil. Acad., West Point, N.Y., 1992-93. Author: College and University Mathematics, 1968, Finite Statistics, 1968, Probability, 1971, Analytic Geometry: A Vector Approach, 1971, Probability: Modeling Uncertainty, 1981, Statistics by Calculator, 1983; contbr. articles to profl. jours. Recipient Rist prize for best paper in mil. ops. rsch. Mil. Ops. Rsch. Soc., 1996, Payne award for ops. rsch. U.S. Army, 1997, Wilks award for Stats., 2004. Mem. Am. Stat. Assn., Ops. Research Soc. Am., Internat. Test and Evaluation Assn., Sigma Xi. Home: PO Box 2071 Paradise CA 95967-2071 Home Phone: 530-877-7290. Personal E-mail: dbarrz@sbcglobal.net.

BARR, EDWARD SHELDON, military officer, writer; b. May 14, 1933; BS in Phys. Sci., Stanford U., Palo Alto, Calif., 1956. V.p., ptnr. NY Stock Exch. Roberts, Scott & Co., 1968—72; ship capt. US Coast Guard, San Diego, 1978—. Mem.: Theatre Organ Soc. (founding mem. 1975), Spreckel's Organ Soc. (historian 1993—, founding mem. 1988, Vol. of Yr. 1996), Am. Guild Organists (historian 1993—). Home: 2390 Shelter Island Dr Ste 215 San Diego CA 92106 Personal E-mail: ebout@worldnet.att.net.

BARR, EMILY L., broadcast executive; BA in Film Studies, Carleton Coll., 1980; MBA in Mktg., George Washington U., 1986. News editor KSTP-TV, St. Paul, Minn., 1980-81, news promotion specialist, 1981-82; writer, prodr. WJLA-TV, Washington, 1983-85; advtg. & promotion mgr. KHOU-TV, Houston, 1985-87, dir. creative svcs., 1987-88; dir. broadcast ops. WMAR-TV, Balt., 1988-93, acting gen. mgr., 1993, asst. gen. mgr., 1993-94; pres., gen. mgr. Sta. WTVD, Raleigh, N.C., 1994-97, Sta. WLS-TV, Chgo., 1997—. Grad. leadership program Greater Balt. Com., 1990; active NAPTE, 1988—, BPME, 1983-93, CBS Promotion Caucus, 1987-88. Vol. Mus. Broadcast Comms.; bd. dirs. United Cerebral Palsy-Chgo., Children's Meml. Hosp. Found.; commr. Chgo. State St. Commn. Recipient Dante award Joint Civic com. for Italian Americans, 1998. Mem. Ill. Broadcast Assn., Chgo./Midwest TV Acad., Chgo. C. of C. (bd. dirs.), Chgo. Cen. Area Com. (bd. dirs.). Office: 190 N State St Chicago IL 60601-3302

BARR, JAMES, III, telecommunications company executive; b. Oak Park, Ill., Mar. 2, 1940; s. James Jr. and Florence Marie (Erichsen) B.; m. Joan Benning, Aug. 12, 1961; children: James IV, Brett Christopher, Heather Kathryn, Stephanie Alexandra. BS in Engring., Iowa State U., 1962; MBA, U. Chgo., 1967. Engr. Ill. Bell Tel. Co., Chgo., 1962-66, staff mgr. for regulatory affairs, 1966-69; dist. mgr. for planning AT&T, NYC, 1969-72, dir. regulatory affairs, 1975-80, dir. product mgmt. Basking Ridge, N.J., 1980-85, sales v.p. NYC, 1985-90; gen. mktg. mgr. Bell Can., Ottawa, Ont., 1972-75; pres., CEO, TDS TELECOM, Madison, Wis., 1990—. Exec. vp., bd. dirs. NY Bd. Trade, 1985—90; bd. dirs. Tel. and Data Sys., Chgo., Ctr. for Telecom. Mgmt., LA, TDS Telecom, Madison, Wis. Mem. dean's adv. coun. Bus. Sch. U. Wis., 1997— Republican. Roman Catholic.

BARR, JAMES HOUSTON, III, lawyer; b. Louisville, Nov. 2, 1941; s. James Houston Jr. and Elizabeth Hamilton (Pope) Barr; m. Sarah Jane Todd, Apr. 16, 1970 (div.); 1 child, Lynn Jamison; m. Cindy Ann Jeffries, May 31, 1997; children: Worden Pope Washington, Augustine Washington Jeffries. Student, U. Va., 1960-63, U. Tenn., 1963-64; BSL, JD, U. Louisville, 1966. Bar: Ky. 1966, U.S. Ct. Appeals (6th cir.) 1969, U.S. Supreme Ct. 1971, U.S. Ct. Mil. Appeals 1978. Law clk. Ky. Ct. Appeals, Frankfort, 1966-67; asst. atty. gen. Ky. Frankfort, 1967-71, 79-82; asst. U.S. atty. U.S. Dept. Justice, Louisville, 1971-79, 83—; 1st asst. U.S. Atty., 1978-79; asst. dist. counsel U.S. Army C.E., Louisville, 1982-83. Lt. comdr. USNR, 1967-81, lt. col. USAR, 1981-91. Mem. FBA (pres. Louisville chpt. 1975-76, Younger Fed. Lawyer award 1975), Ky. Bar Assn., Louisville Bar Assn., Soc. Colonial Wars, SAR, Washington Family Soc., Pendennis Club, Louisville Boat Club (pres. 2004-05), Filson Club, Delta Upsilon. Republican. Episcopalian. Home: 100 Westwind Rd Louisville KY 40207-1520 Office: US Atty 510 W Broadway Ste 1000 Louisville KY 40202-2281

BARR, JAMES NORMAN, retired federal judge; b. Kewanee, Ill, Oct. 21, 1940; s. James Cecil and Dorothy Evelyn (Dorsey) B.; m. Trilla Anne Reeves, Oct. 31, 1964 (div. 1979); 1 child, James N. Jr.; m. Phyllis L. DeMent, May 30, 1986; children: Renae, Michele. BS, Ill. Wesleyan U., 1962; JD, Ill. Inst. Tech., 1971. Bar: Ill. 1972, Calif. 1977. Assoc. Pretzel, Stouffer, Nolan & Rooney, Chgo., 1974-76; claims counsel Safeco Title Ins. Co., LA, 1977-78; assoc. Kamph & Jackman, Santa Ana, Calif., 1978-80; lawyer pvt. practice Law Offices of James N. Barr, Santa Ana, 1980-86; judge U.S Bankruptcy Ct. Ctrl. Dist. Calif., Santa Ana, 1987—2006. Adj. prof. Chapman U. Sch. Law, 1996—2006. Lt. USN, 1962-67, Vietnam. Mem. Fed. Bar Assn. (Orange County chpt. bd. dirs. 1996-2000), Orange County Bar Assn. (cmty. outreach com.), Nat. Conf. Bankruptcy Judges, Orange County Bankruptcy Forum (bd. dirs. 1989—), Peter M. Elliott Inn of Ct. (founder, first pres. 1990-91), Warren J. Ferguson Am. Inn of Ct. (founder). Office: US Bankruptcy Ct 411 W 4th St Santa Ana CA 92701-4500 Office Phone: 714-338-5470.

BARR, JOHN BALDWIN, chemist, research scientist; b. Niagara Falls, NY, Nov. 8, 1932; s. Lorne Haworth and Myra (Baldwin) B.; m. Patricia Jane Kromer, Sept. 18, 1954; children: Mark Kromer, John Robert, Kathryn Jean, Karen Patricia. BA, U. Buffalo, 1954; MS, U. Mich., 1956; PhD, Pa. State U., 1961. Rsch. chemist Corning Glass Works (N.Y.), 1961-62; sr. rsch. chemist Union Carbide Corp., Parma, Ohio, 1962-71, rsch. scientist, 1971-82, sr. rsch. scientist, 1982-86, Amoco Performance Products, Parma, 1986-90, Alpharetta, Ga., 1990-91, assoc. rsch. scientist, 1991-95; cons. Rsch. Opportunities, Inc., Torrance, Calif., 1996—2001; cons. for carbon fiber industry, 2002—. Contbr. articles to profl. jours.; patentee in field. Shell Oil Co. fellow, 1959' recipient Am. Chem. Soc., 2003. Mem.: N. Am. Thermal Analysis Soc., Am. Carbon Soc., Am. Chem. Soc. (award 2003), Pi Lambda Upsilon, Sigma Xi.

BARR, JOHN MICHAEL, investor, management consultant; b. Columbus, Ohio, May 13, 1957; s. William Harvey and Mary Louise (Chesser) B.; m. Mary Elizabeth Mudd, Sept. 4, 1982. BA in History and Polit. Sci., Ohio Dominican Coll., 1979; MA in Polit. Sci., Ohio State U., 1980. Tchr. pub. schs., 1981-88; secondary edn. educator Whitehall City Schs., 1981-83, South Western City Schs., 1983-88; profl. investor, speaker, cons. Westerville, Ohio, 1988—. Active Rep. Nat. 500 Club, Washington, 1991, Franklin County Reps., Columbus, 1990, Rep. Nat. Campaign Coun., 1988—, Ohio Rep. Party, 1993—; mem. Rep. Presdl. Task Force. Mem. ASTD, Am. Assn. Individual Investors (life), Am. Polit. Sci. Assn., NRA (life, chmn. second ammend. task force 1993—), Japan Aikido Assn. (life), Internat. Listening Assn., Soc. for Mil. History, Shingitai Jujitsu Assn., Nat. Guild Hypnotists, Marine Corps Assn., US Naval Inst. Methodist. Avocations: shooting, Aikido, travel, poetry. Office: PO Box 506 Westerville OH 43086-0506

BARR, JOHN MONTE, lawyer; b. Mt. Clemens, Mich., Jan. 1, 1935; s. Merle James and Wilhelmina Marie (Monte) Barr; m. Marlene Joy Bielenberg, Dec. 17, 1954; children: John Monte, Karl Alexander, Elizabeth Marie. Student, Mexico City Coll., 1955; BA, Mich. State U., 1956; JD, U. Mich., 1959. Bar: Mich. 1959. Mem. Ellis B. Freatman, Jr., Ypsilanti, Mich., 1959—61; ptnr., chief trial atty. Freatman, Barr, Anhut & Moir and predecessor firm, Ypsilanti, Mich., 1961—63; pres. Barr, Anhut, Assoc. PC, Ypsilanti, Mich., 1963—2001, Barr, Anhut, Gilbreath, Ypsilanti, Mich., 2001—. City atty. City of Ypsilanti, 1981—, City of Belleville, 2000—06; lectr. bus. law Eastern Mich. U., 1968—70. Contbr. articles to boating mags. Pres. Ypsilanti Family Svc., 1967; mem. Ypsilanti Pub. Housing Com., 1980—84, State Boundry Commrs., 2000—; sr. adviser Explorer law post Portage Trail coun. Boy Scouts Am., 1969—71, commr. Potawatomi dist., 1973—74, commr. Washtenong dist., 1974—75, dist. committeeman, 1984, wolverine coun. v.p., 1992, v.p. Great Saulk Trail coun., 1995—97, dist. chair Huron Trails, 2005—06; sec. High/Scope Ednl. Rsch. Found., 1998—2004; mem. Ypsilanti Election Commn., 1981—; pres. Ypsilanti Emmanuel Luth. Ch., 2002—03; bd. dirs. Mich. Mcpl. League Legal Def. Fund, pres., 1989—90; past pres. Washtenaw 100 Club, 1980—; mem. Mich. State Boundary Commn., 2003—. With AUS, 1959—60. Named to Mich. Super Lawyers, Law and Politics, 2006; recipient Silver Beaver award, Boy Scouts Am., 1992, Mich. Mcpl. League award of merit, Mcpl. League Legal Def., 1992. Mem.: ABA, Mich. Mcpl. Attys. Assn. (pres. 1989—90, dist. mcpl. atty. award 1993), Washtenaw County Trial Lawyers Assn., Washtenaw County Bar Assn. (pres. 1975—76, profl. and civility award 1998), Ypsilanti Bar Assn., State Bar Mich. (grievance bd. hearing panel 1969—97, state rep. assembly 1977—82, bd. commrs. 1993—2003, grievance bd. hearing panel 2005—, chair grievance bd. hearing panel 2006—), Ann Arbor Power Squadron (comdr. 1972—73), U.S. Power Squadron (instr. piloting, seamanship, sail), Washtenaw Country Club. Lutheran. Home: 1200 Whittier Rd Ypsilanti MI 48197-2152 Office: 105 Pearl St Ypsilanti MI 48197-2611 Office Phone: 734-481-1234. Business E-Mail: jmbarr@barrlawfirm.com.

BARR, JOHN ROBERT, retired lawyer; b. Gary, Ind., Apr. 10, 1936; s. John Andrew and Louise (Stentz) Barr; m. Patricia A. Ferris, July 30, 1988; children: Mary Louise, John Mills, Jennifer Susan, Anne Elizabeth Ferris. BA, Grinnell Coll., 1957; LLB cum laude, Harvard U., 1960. Bar: Ill. 1960. Assoc. Sidley Austin LLP, Chgo., 1960—69, ptnr., 1970—99, sr. counsel, 2000—02; ret., 2002. Mem. Commn. Presdl. Scholars, Washington, 1975—77, Ill. Ho. of Reps., 1981—83, Ill. Electric Utility Property Assessment Task Force, 1998—99. Chmn. Ill. Student Assistance Commn., 1985—2005; trustee Steppenwolf Theatre Co., Chgo., 1992—, mem. exec. com., 2005—; chmn. Rep. Ctrl. Com. Cook County, Chgo., 1978—85; mem. Rep. state ctrl. com. 9th Congl. Dist. Ill., 1986—93; chmn. Ill. Bd. Regents, 1971—77; mem. Ill. Bd. Higher Edn., 1971—77, 1986—2005; trustee Grinnell Coll., 1996—, mem. exec. com., 2004—. Mem.: ABA (chmn. task force utility deregulation state and local tax com. 1996—2003), Ill. Tax Found. (dir.), Ill. State Bar Assn. (chmn. state tax sect. coun. 1986—87, sec. com. on legislation 2006—), Nat. Assn. State Bar Tax Sects. (sec-treas. 1989—90, vice chmn. 1990—91, chmn. 1991—92), Civic Fedn. (bd. dirs. 1993—97), Taxpayers Fedn. Ill. (mem. exec. com. 1983—2007, treas. 1990—92, vice chmn. 1992—95, chmn. 1995—97), Chgo. Bar Assn. (chmn. com. state and mcpl. taxation 1974—75), Emil Verban Soc., Evanston (Ill.) Hist. Soc. (trustee 2001—07, pres. 2006—07), Chgo. Club, Lawyer's Club Chgo., Phi Beta Kappa. Episcopalian. Home: 1144 Asbury Ave Evanston IL 60202-1137 Office: Sidley Austin LLP One S Dearborn St Chicago IL 60603 Office Phone: 312-853-7447. Business E-Mail: jrbarr@sidley.com. E-mail: barrbob@comcast.net.

BARR, JOHN W., investment company executive, foundation administrator; b. Omaha, Jan. 28, 1943; s. Robert Edward and Lois (Kurtz) B.; m. Penny Glassman, July 13, 1968; children: Nathan, Christian, Jenny BA with honors, Harvard U., 1965, MBA (Baker scholar), 1972. Assoc. Morgan Stanley & Co., NYC, 1972-76, v.p., 1977-80, prin., 1981-83, mng. dir., 1984—90; founder, chmn. U.S. Natural Gas Clearinghouse (now Dynegy Corp.), Houston, 1983—89; co-founder, mng. dir SG Barr Devlin, 1990—. Bd. dirs. Yaddo, 1987—2005. Author: The Hundred Fathom Curve, 1997, Grace, 1999. Chmn. Bennington Coll. Mem. Poetry Soc. Am. (bd. trustees 1984-2004, chmn. 1987-99, bd. govs. 1986-2000, pres. 1996-2000), Century Assn., Union League Club, Chgo. Yacht Club, Grolier Club, Arts Club of Chgo., Poetry Found. (pres. 2004-). Office: SG Barr Devlin 1221 Ave of Americas New York NY 10020

BARR, JON-HENRY, lawyer; b. Livingston, NJ, Sept. 1, 1970; s. Gary and Susan Barr. BA, Lehigh U., 1992; JD, Seton Hall U., 1995. Bar: N.J. 1996, D.C. 1998, U.S. Dist. Ct. N.J. 1996, U.S. Ct. Appeals (3d cir.) 1997, U.S. Supreme Ct. 2006. Jud. law clk. Superior Ct. N.J., Freehold, N.J., 1995-96; assoc. Law Offices of Robert Blackman, Edison, N.J., 1996-98; ptnr. Barr & Canada, LLC, Clark, N.J., 1998—. Mem. Clark Vol. Emergency Squad, N.J. (pres. 2006); councilman Twp. of Clark, 1993-94; mem. Clark Rep. Civic Assn., 1996—. Named one of Outstanding Young Men of Am., 1998. Mem. N.J. State Bar Assn., Union County Bar Assn. (young lawyer trustee 2000-2001), Union County Mcpl. Prosecutors' Assn. (pres. 2001-). Jewish. Avocations: politics, travel. Home: 69 Fairview Rd Clark NJ 07066-2904 Office: Barr and Canada LLC 21 Brant Ave Clark NJ 07066-1512 Mailing: 48 Skyline Dr Clark NJ 07066 Personal E-mail: barrcanada@aol.com.

BARR, MARTIN, science educator, academic administrator; b. Phila., Nov. 11, 1925; s. Louis and Bella (Moskowitz) B.; m. Nancy Lipschutz, July 15, 1951; children: Lawrence Allen, Richard Andrew, Debra Ann, Steven Bruce. B.Sc. in Pharmacy, Temple U., 1946; M.Sc. in Pharmacy, Phila. Coll. Pharmacy and Scis., 1947; PhD, Ohio State U., 1950. Grad. asst., then instr. Ohio State U. Coll. Pharmacy, 1947-50; from asst. prof. pharmacy to prof. phys. pharmacy and pharm. research Phila. Coll. Pharmacy and Sci., 1950-61; prof. pharmaceutics Wayne State U. Coll. Pharmacy, 1961-87, prof. emeritus, 1987—, chmn. dept., 1961-63, dean, 1963-72, v.p. spl. assignments, 1972-76, v.p., sec. to bd. govs., 1976-78, sec. to bd. govs., acting v.p. for health affairs, 1978-80, v.p., dep. provost, 1980-82, dean Coll. Pharmacy and Allied Health Professions, 1982-87; exec. v.p. corp. bus. and med. devel. Mich. Health Care Corp., Detroit, 1987-90, v.p. bd., profl. rels., 1990-92, v.p. continuous quality improvement, 1992-95. Cons. HEW, 1964-69 Contbg. author: Pharmacy, Compounding and Dispensing, 2d edit, 1956, Remington's Practice of Pharmacy, 11th edit., 1956, 12th edit., 1965; Profl. editor: Mid-Atlantic Apothecary, 1953-64, Apothecary, 1953-64, Central Pharm. Jour, 1961-64. Chmn. Mayor's Com. Rehab. Narcotics Addicts, Detroit, 1971-73; pres. Oakland County unit Mich. Heart Assn., 1970-72; chmn. Spectrum Cmty. Svcs., 2003-04; chmn. task force health care costs, del. pers. health svcs. Comprehensive Health Planning Adv. Coun., Mich., 1971. Recipient Disting. Service award, Disitng. Alumnus award Alumni Assn. Coll. Pharmacy, Temple U., 1957, Disting. Alumnus award Temple U., 1964, Alpha Zeta Omega award, 1979, Meritorious Service award Wayne State U. Pharm. Alumni Assn., Ann. Alumus award Phila. Coll. Pharmacy and Sci., 1983, John H. Webster award Met. Detroit Pharmacist Assn., 1985, Disting. alumnus award Pharmacy Alumni Assn., 1987, Jack L. Beal Postbaccalaureate award Ohio State U. Coll. Pharmacy Alumni Assn., 1989, Disting. Svc. award Wayne State U. Pharmacy Alumni Assn., 1993, Advocate award Detroit Occupl. Therapy Assn., 1995; named Mich. Med. Assistance Program Counselor of Yr., 2006. Fellow Am. Coll. Apothecaries, Acad. Pharm. Scis.; mem. Am. Pharm. Assn. (pres. Phila. br. 1954-55, chmn. sci. sect. 1959-60, Ebert medal 1956), Am. Soc. Hosp. Pharmacists, Mich. State Pharm. Assn. (pharmacist of yr. 1971), Am. Assn. Colls. Pharmacy (chmn. sect. tchrs. pharmacy 1959-60, chmn. conf. tchrs. pharmacy 1961-62), Vis. Nurse Assn. S.E. Mich. (chmn. 1999-2002), Vis. Nurse Assn. Inc. (chmn. 2004-06), Sigma Xi, Rho Chi. Home: 7430 Tall Timbers West Bloomfield MI 48322-1082 Office Phone: 248-624-7974. Personal E-mail: mbarr@nshore.net.

BARR, M.E. See BIGELOW, MARGARET

BARR, MICHAEL CHARLES, research director, lawyer; b. White Plains, NY, Nov. 2, 1947; s. Charles Yerger and Joan Tames (Biggar) B.; m. Helen June Rumsey, Mar. 17, 1973. Student, Washington and Lee U.; BA summa cum laude, Rutgers U., 1969; JD, Columbia U., 1972, MBA, 1980. Bar: NJ 1976, NY 1978, US Supreme Ct. 1976. Assoc. McCarter & English, Newark, 1976-77, Conboy, Hewitt, O'Brien & Boardman, NYC, 1977-78; investment banker Kidder, Peabody & Co., Inc., NYC, 1980-82; v.p. Mfrs. Hanover Trust Co., NYC, 1982-90, A-L Assocs., NYC, 1990-92; corp. sec., dir. H. Rivkin & Co., Inc., NYC, 1992-93; securities analyst Standard & Poor's Corp., NYC, 1993-98; Russian securities specialist H. Rivkin & Co., Inc., NYC, 1998-99; emerging markets specialist HP Capital Mkts. Group, NYC, 1999-2000; fin. cons. AXA Advisors, Inc., NYC, 2000; corp. bond cons. Dow Jones and Co., NYC, 2001—03; prin. Barr & Co., Far Hills, NJ, 2003—06; rsch. dir. H. Rivkin & Co., Inc., Princeton, NJ, 2006—. Guest commentator on Russia CNN, 1998—2000. Actor: (films) The Interpreter, 2004; (TV series) Law & Order: Trial By Jury, 2005. Adv. bd. Washington and Lee Alumni Coll., 1996-98; 30th Reunion planning com. Columbia Law Sch. Class of 1972, 2002. Lt. USN, 1972-76. Recipient Loyal Son award, Rutgers Alumni Assn., 1976. Mem.: U.S. Polo Assn., Phi Beta Kappa.

BARR, ROBERT, lawyer, educator; SB, MIT; JD, Boston U. V.p. intellectual property and worldwide patent counsel Cisco Sys., San Jose, Calif.; tchr. Berkeley Sch. Law, U. Calif., exec. dir. Berkeley Ctr. for Law and Tech. Adj. prof. law Hastings College of Law, U. Calif., San Francisco, 1994—99; spkr. in field. Named one of top 25 intellectual property lawyers in Calif., Daily Jour., 2003. Office: Berkeley Ctr for Law & Tech U Calif Sch Law Rm 355 Berkeley CA 94720-7200 Office Phone: 510-643-6960. E-mail: rbarr@law.berkeley.edu.

BARR, ROBERT LAURENCE, JR., lawyer; b. Iowa City, Iowa, Nov. 5, 1948; s. Robert Laurence and Beatrice Emily (Radenhausen) B.; children: Adrian Robert, Derek Ryan; m. Jerilyn Dobbin, Dec. 31, 1986. BA in Internat. Rels., U. So. Calif., 1970; JD, Georgetown U., 1977; MA, George Wash. Univ., 1972. Bar: Ga. 1977, Fla. 1979. Analyst, atty., chief legis. staff CIA, Washington, 1970-78; assoc. Law Offices of Edwin Marger, Atlanta, 1979-81; pvt. practice Marietta, Ga., 1981-85, 91-94; ptnr. Brock & Barr, Marietta, 1985-86; U.S. atty. for No. Ga., 1986-90; mem. U.S. Congress from 7th Ga. dist., Washington, 1995—2003; pres. Liberty Strategies, LLC, Atlanta, 2006—, CEO, 2006—. Mem. banking and fin. svcs., govt. reform and oversight, and judiciary coms., chmn. subcom. on Comml. and Adminstrv. Law, 2001-02; gen. counsel Cobb County Rep. Com., 1981-83, 1st vice-chmn., 1983-85, chmn., 1985-86; pres. Southeastern Legal Found., Atlanta, 1990-91; mem. long-term strategy project for preserving security and democratic norms in the war on terrorism Kennedy Sch. Govt. Harvard U.; bd. dirs. Met. Atlanta Coun. Alcohol and Drugs, 1989-91. Mem. editl. staff Am. Criminal Law Rev., 1974-77; host weekly radio show on Radio Am. network Bob Barr's Laws of the Universe; contbg. editor Am. Spectator; contbr. CNN; contbr. articles to profl. jours. Chmn. youth leadership tng. Leadership Inst., Arlington, Va., 2004—; 21st century liberties chair for freedom and privacy Am. Conservative Union; bd. dirs. Patrick Henry Ctr. Disting. fellow, Freedom Alliance, 2003. Mem. NRA (bd. dirs.), Ga. Bar Assn., Fla. Bar Assn., Kiwanis, Phi Alpha Delta, Delta Phi Epsilon, Tau Kappa Epsilon. Republican. Methodist. Home: 2256 Parkwood Pl Smyrna GA 30080 Office: Liberty Strategies LLC 4401 Northside Pky Ste 100 Atlanta GA 30327 Office Phone: 770-836-1776.

BARR, RONALD JEFFREY, dermatologist, pathologist; b. Mpls., Jan. 5, 1945; s. Maxwell Michael and Ethel Deana (Ring) B.; m. Ulla Elisabet Edstam; children: Anna, Jessica, Sara. BA, Johns Hopkins U., 1967, MD, 1970. Diplomate Am. Bd. Pathology, Am. Bd. Dermatology. Intern U. Calif., San Diego, 1970-71, resident in pathology, 1971-75, resident in dermatology Irvine, 1975-78, fellow in dermatopathology, 1975-78, asst. prof. dermatology, 1977-83, assoc. prof. dermatology and pathology, 1983-86, prof. dermatology and pathology, 1987—, dir. Dermatopathology Lab., 1979—, prof., chmn. dept. dermatology Davis, 1986-87. Bd. dirs. Am. Bd. Dermatology, 1989—, pres., 1997. Contbr. more than 10 chpts. to books. more than 130 articles to profl. jours. Lt. USN, 1971-73. Fellow Am. Soc. Dermatopathology (pres. 1988-89); mem. Internat. Soc. Dermatopathology, Internat. Com. for Dermatopathology (sec.-treas. 1987-91, pres. 1992-93). Office: U Calif Irvine Med Ctr Dermatopathology Lab 101 The City Dr S Orange CA 92868-3201

BARR, ROSEANNE See ROSEANNE

BARR, SANFORD LEE, dentist; b. Chgo., Jan. 18, 1952; s. Mike and Bernice (Kaplan) B.; m. Randy Joyce Briskman, Dec. 24, 1973; children: Shelby Paige, Blake Jared, Taylor Ashley. BS, U. Ill., 1972; DDS, Northwestern U., 1976. Resident gen. practice VA Hosp., Chgo., 1976-77; gen. practice dentistry Chgo., 1977—. Attending dentist Rush Med. Coll., Chgo., 1977—; asst. prof. Presbyn.-St. Luke's Hosp., Chgo., 1977—, Northwestern U. Sch. Dentistry, Chgo., 1977-83; cons. VA Hosp., Chgo., 1978—. Mem. adv. bd. Homehealth of Ill. Chgo., 1984—. Fellow Acad. Gen. Dentistry, Acad. Facial Aesthetics; mem. ADA, Acad. Hosp. Dentistry, Chgo. Dental Soc., Alpha Omega (treas. 1984, pres. elect 1988), Tau Delta Phi. Lodges: B'nai B'rith (v.p. Chgo. chpt. 1984—). Jewish. Avocations: computers, photography, golf, baseball. Home: 632 Dauphine Ct Northbrook IL 60062-2256 Office: 25 E Washington St Chicago IL 60602-1708 Business E-Mail: drsbarr@sanfordbarr.dds.com.

BARR, WILLIAM PELHAM, telecommunications industry executive, lawyer, former United States attorney general; b. NYC, May 23, 1950; s. Donald and Mary (Ahern) B.; m. Christine Moynihan, June 23, 1973; 3 children. AB, Columbia U., 1971, MA, 1973; JD, George Washington U., 1977. Bar: Va. 1977, DC 1978, NY. Staff officer CIA, Washington, 1973-77; law clk. to presiding judge Cir. Ct., Washington, 1977-78; assoc. Shaw, Pittman, Potts & Trowbridge, Washington, 1978-82, 83-84, ptnr., 1985-89, 93-94; dep. asst. dir. domestic policy staff The White House, Washington, 1982-83; asst. atty. gen. Office Legal Counsel, US Dept. Justice, Washington, 1989-90, dep. atty. gen., 1990-91, atty. gen., 1991-93; sr. v.p., gen. counsel GTE Corp., Washington, 1994—97, exec. v.p. govt. & regulatory advocacy, gen. counsel, 1997—2000; exec v.p., gen. counsel Verizon Comm., NYC, 2000—. Mem. bd. Davis Selected Advisers. Vice chmn. bd. dirs. The Coll. of William and Mary. Mem. ABA, Va. State Bar Assn., DC Bar Assn., KC. Republican. Roman Catholic. Office: Verizon Communications Legal Dept 38th Fl 1095 Avenue of the Americas New York NY 10036*

BARRACANO, HENRY RALPH, retired oil company executive, management consultant; b. Bklyn., Apr. 8, 1926; s. Ralph Henry and Josephine (Chianese) B.; m. Dorothy Sue Bartlow, Aug. 19, 1945; children: Ralph Robert, Susan Jo Barracano Ratterree, Linda Joyce Barracano Swartz. BSEE, Pa. State U., 1948. Registered profl. engr., Okla. Distbn. engr. Pub. Svc. Co. Okla., Tulsa, 1948-51; elec. engr. W.R. Holway & Assocs., Tulsa, 1951-56; from staff engr. to asst. to sr. v.p. engrng. and constrn. Arabian Am. Oil Co., 1956-83; ind. cons., 1983-89; sr. project mgr. Hudson Engrng. and Project Mgmt. Corp., 1990-91; ind. cons., 1992—. Mem. grievance com. State Bar Tex., 1994-99; arbitrator NASD, 1994-2007. Precinct chair Dem. Party, Harris County, Tex., 1984-98; precinct judge Harris County, 1984-90; bd. dirs. The Pinemont Apts., 2002-2003. 1st Lt. Signal Corps U.S. Army, 1943-59. Named Outstanding Engrng. Alumnus, Pa. State U., 1993, Alumni Fellow award, 1997, Pa. State Pioneer, 1998. Mem. IEEE (life sr. mem., various offices held), Petroleum Club Houston (resident mem.), Northgate Country Club. Avocation: travel. Home and Office: 7723 Allegro Dr Houston TX 77040-2508 E-mail: barracano@ieee.org.

BARRACK, THOMAS J., JR., real estate investor, lawyer; BA, U. So. Calif., 1969; JD, U. San Diego Law Sch., 1972; LLD (hon.), Pepperdine U. Internat. fin. lawyer; pres. Dunn Internat. Corp., 1976; dep. under sec. US Dept. Interior, Washington; sr. v.p. E.F. Hutton & Co., NY; pres. Oxford Devel. Ventures Inc.; prin. Robert M. Bass Grp.; founder Colony Capital LLC, LA, 1991, chmn., CEO, 1991—. Bd. dirs. Continental Airlines Inc., Accor, First Republic Bank, Pub. Storage Inc. Named one of 400 Richest Ams., Forbes mag., 2006. Office: Colony Capital LLC 1999 Avenue of the Stars Ste 1200 Los Angeles CA 90067

BARRACO, ROBERT DON, surgeon; s. George Samuel and Mary Josephine Barraco; m. Cheryl Ann Durrwachter, Nov. 6, 1999; children: Victoria Lee Buser, Christian Samuel, Gabrielle Marie, Matthew Robert. BA with High Honors, Rutgers U., New Brunswick, NJ, 1985; MPH, Johns Hopkins Bloomberg Sch. Pub. Health, Balt., 1999; MD, Rutgers U., Piscataway, NJ, 1989. Cert. in Surgery and Surgical Critical Care Am. Bd. Surgery, Am. Bd. Hospice and Palliative Medicine. Chief health programs USPHS/Bur. Prisons, Otisville, NY, 1991—92; clin. instr. R. Adams Cowley Shock Trauma Ctr., Balt., 1998—99; assoc. chief trauma Stony Brook U. Hosp., NY, 1999; chief geriatric and pediatric trauma Lehigh Valley Hosp., Allentown, Pa., 2003—. Cons. palliative medicine Lehigh Valley Hosp., Allentown, 2006—, chair ethics com. Chair staff parish rels. com. North Shore United Meth. Ch., Wading River, NY, 2001—03; Bible Study group leader Asbury United Methodist Ch., Allentown, Pa., 2005—, contemporary choir, 2005—. Lt. USPHS, 1990—92. Decorated Unit Commendation US Public Health Svc., Hazardous Duty Ribbon; fellow, Lehigh Valley Hosp. Inst. Physician Leadership, 2005—. Fellow: ACS, Am. Coll. Chest Physicians; mem.: Internat. Trauma, Anesthesia and Critical Care Soc., Am. Geriat. Soc., Soc. Critical Care Medicine, Ea. Assn. Surgery Trauma (vice-chair PMG com. 2005—06), Phi Beta Kappa. Achievements include development of first Section of Geriatric Trauma; research in diagnosis and management of injury in the pregnant patient; development of practice management guidelines; research in interdisciplinary resident palliative care education; true outcomes of eldertrauma. Office: Surgical Specialists of Lehigh Valley 1240 S Cedar Crest Blvd Allentown PA 18103 Office Phone: 610-402-1350. Business E-Mail: robert_d.barraco@lvh.com.

BARRAGÃN, CELIA SILGUERO, elementary school educator; b. Corcoran, Calif., Feb. 4, 1955; d. Frutoso Silguero and Olinda Gonzalez S.; m. Mario Barragãn Jr., Nov. 12, 1977; children: Maricela Aimē, Mario Armando. BS, S.W. Tex. State U., 1976, MA, 1977. 3rd grade tchr. Crockett Elem. Sch., San Marcos, Tex., 1977—78, Bowie Elem. Sch., San Marcos, 1978—84; 5th grade tchr. Travis Elem. Sch., San Marcos, 1984—94, Hernandez Intermediate Sch., San Marcos, 1994—99; asst. prin., bilingual coord. Bonham Elem. Sch., San Marcos, 1985—86, title I reading tchr., trainer, cons., 1995—99; coord., tchr. AVID Miller Jr. H.S., San Marcos, Tex., 1999—2000; ESL/Dyslexia tchr. Miller Jr. High, 2000—01; ESL/dyslexia tchr. Goodnight Jr. H.S., 2001—04; 4th grade bilingual tchr. Comal Intermediate Sch., New Braunfels, Tex., 2004—, 5th/6th grade bilingual/ESL tchr., 2005—06; 5th grade bilingual tchr. Frazier Elem., 2006—. Winter High ability program tchr. S.W. Tex. State U.; project math trainer, migrant tchr., Princeville, Ill.; mem. Tomas Rivera Mex. Am. Children's Book award com. Tex. State U., San Marcos; cons., nat. trainer Lang. Cir. Project Read, Minn. Recipient Latino award for cmty. recognition S.W. Tex. State U.; named Tchr. of Yr., Canyon Intermediate Sch., 2005; Comal Pub. Sch. Found. digital storytelling grantee. Mem. Internat. Reading Assn., Tex. Reading Assn., Tex. State Tchrs. Assn., Tex. Assn. Bilingual Edn., Tex. Classroom Tchrs. Assn., San Marcos (Tex.) Assn. Bilingual Edn. (v.p. 1990-91, 94—, pres. 1995—, Bilingual Tchr. of Yr. 1991, Travis Elem. Tchr. of Yr. 1993, Hernandez Intermediate Tchr. of Yr. 1995, Secondary Tchr. of Yr. 1995, Canyon Intermediate Tchr. of Yr. 2005, KENS 5 ExCel Tchr. of Yr. nominee, 2005), Orton Dyslexia Soc., Nat. Coun. Tchrs. Math., Nat. Assn. Bilingual Educators, Ill. Migrant Edn. Assn., Tex. Assn. Gifted and Talented, N.J. Writing Project, Assn. Comprehensive Edn. in Tex. Roman Catholic. Office: Frazier Elem New Braunfels TX 78130 Office Phone: 830-221-2275. Business E-Mail: celia.barragan@comalisd.org.

BARRAM, DAVID J., federal agency administrator; BA, Wheaton Coll., 1965; MBA, Santa Clara Univ., 1973. Staff acct. Price Waterhouse and Co., Boston, 1965-66; various fin. and mktg. positions Hewlett-Packard, 1970-83, contr. computer products group; v.p. fin. and adminstrn., CFO Silicon Graphics, Inc., 1983-85; v.p. fin., CFO, and v.p. corp. comm. Apple Computer, Inc., 1985-93; dep. sec. Dept. Commerce, Washington, 1993-95; adminstr. GSA, Washington, 1996—2001; bd. dir. Net IQ, 2002, lead ind. dir., 2003. Chair Calif. Commn. Pub. Sch. Adminstrn. and Leadership; bd. dir. Nat. Ctr. Edn. and Economy. Served in USN, 1966-69. Recipient Disting. Svc. Award Assn. Calif. Sch. Adminstr.

BARRAN, THOMAS PAUL, language educator; b. Warren, Ohio, July 8, 1946; s. Paul Thomas and Sophia Catherine Barran; m. Barbara Caplan, June 5, 1983. AB, Columbia Coll., 1968; PhD, Columbia U., 1984. Preceptor Columbia U., NYC, 1978—79; prof. Russian Bklyn. Coll., NYC, 1986—. Vis. prof. Hunter Coll., NYC, 1991; bd. dirs. Classic Rug Collection, Inc., NYC; cons. in field; expert witness in field; lectr. in field. Author: Russia Reads Rousseau 1762-1825, 2002; contbr. articles to profl. jours. Bd. dirs. ROSAS Neighborhood Assn., Bklyn., 1998—2002. Fellow, U.S. State Dept., 1972—74, Internat. Rsch. & Exchanges Bd., 1976—77. Mem.: N.Y. Pub. Libr., Slavic Lang. Profl. Assn., Modern Lang. Assn. Am., Bigelow Soc. Avocations: deep sea fishing, archaeology. Home: 417 16th Street Brooklyn NY 11215 Office: Brooklyn College CUNY Bedford Ave at Ave H Brooklyn NY 11210

BARRANGER, MILLY SLATER, theater educator, writer; b. Birmingham, Ala., Feb. 12, 1937; d. C. C. Slater and Mildred (Hilliard) Hinson; m. G. K. Barranger, 1961 (div. 1984); 1 child, Heather Dalton Barranger Case. BA, U. Montevallo, 1958; MA, Tulane U., 1959, PhD, 1964. Lectr. La. State U., New Orleans, 1964-69; asst. to assoc. prof. Tulane U., New Orleans, 1969-82, chmn. dept. theatre, 1971-82, Alumni disting. prof., 1997—2003, Alumni disting. prof. emerita, 2003—; prof. U. N.C., Chapel Hill, 1982—2003, chmn. dramatic art, 1982-99; producing dir. PlayMakers Repertory Co., Chapel Hill, 1982-99. Pres. Am. Theatre Assn., 1978-79; disting. vis. assoc. prof. U. Tulsa, 1981; vis. young prof. in humanities U. Tenn., Knoxville, 1981-82; scholar-in-residence Yale Sch. Drama, New Haven, Conn., 1982. Author: Theatre: A Way of Seeing, 1980, 1986, 1991, 1995, 2002, 2006, Theatre: Past and Present, 1984, rev. edit., 2001, Understanding Plays, 1990, 1994, 2004, Jessica Tandy, 1991, Margaret Webster, 1994, Margaret Webster: A Life in the Theater, 2004; co-editor: Generations: An Introduction to Drama, 1971, Notable Women in American Theatre, 1989; contbr. articles to profl. jours. Trustee The Paul Green Found., 1982—. Recipient New Orleans Bicentennial award for achievement in the arts, 1976, award for profl. achievement S.W. Theatre Conf., 1978, Pres.'s award U. Montevallo, 1979. Mem. Coll. of Fellows of the Am. Theatre (bd. dirs. 1998-2001); Nat. Theatre Conf. (pres. 1991-93), League Profl. Theatre Women. Avocations: films, travel.

BARRASSO, JOHN ANTHONY, senator, orthopedic surgeon; b. Reading, Pa., July 21, 1952; s. John A. and Louise M. (DeCisco) B.; m. Linda D. Nix, May 6, 1978 (div.); children: Peter, Emma. BS, Georgetown U., 1974, MD, 1978. Diplomate Am. Bd. Orthopaedic Surgeons. Resident Yale-New Haven Hosp., 1978-83; orthopedic surgeon Casper (Wyo.) Orthopaedic Assocs., 1983—; chief of staff Wyo. Med. Ctr., 2003—05; mem. Wyo. State Senate from Dist 27, 2002—07, mem. minerals, bus. & econ. devel. com., labor, health & social services com., 2003—05, chmn. transp., highways & mil. affairs com., 2005—07; US Senator from Wyo., 2007—. Del., Rep. Nat. Convention, 1992, 2004; leader, delegation to Rep. of China, RNC, 1994; fin. chair, Enzi for Senate, 1996, Health reporter on radio and TV, 1984—; health reporter for newspapers, 1991—. Pres. United Way of Natrona County, Wyo. Health Fairs.; emcee Jerry Lewis Labor Day Telethon, Wyo.'s K-2 TV. Recipient Wyo. Physician of the Yr. award, Medal of Excellence, Wyo. Nat. Guard, Legis. Svc. award, Veterans Fgn. Wars. Mem. Wyo. Med. Soc. (pres.), Nat. Assn. Physician Broadcasters (pres. 1988-89), Rep. Nat. Com.(treas. 1991-92) Republican. Office: US Congress 307 Dirksen Senate Office Bldg Washington DC 20510 also: 100 E B St Ste 2201 Casper WY 82601*

BARRATT, DONNA LEE, elementary school educator; b. Westwood, NJ, Nov. 23, 1965; d. Robert Roy B. and Arlene Rose (Solar) Landwehr. BA in English Edn. cum laude, Trenton St. Coll., 1988; MA in Edn., Georgian Ct. Coll., 1998, supervisory cert., 1999, instrnl. tech. cert., 2000; MA in Instrnl. Tech., Georgian Ct. U., 2004. Cert. tchr. English, NJ, Pa., elem. tchr., NJ. Tchr. English St. Mary H.S., South Amboy, NJ, 1989-92; mid. sch. lang. arts tchr. Joyce Kilmer Sch., Milltown, NJ, 1992-94; lang. arts tchr. Manalapan-Englishtown (NJ) Mid. Sch., 1994—. Presenter inservice writing workshop Manalapan-Englishtown Bd. Edn., Manalapan, NJ, 1997; presenter interdisciplinary instr. NJ ASCD state conf., East Windsor, 1999, NJ Ednl. Assn. Good Ideas Forum, 2000, NJ Sch. Bd. Assn., 2000, presenter NJAET, 2004, 05. Recipient Outstanding Ednl. Program award

NJ ASCD, 1998; named Tchr. of Yr., Gov. State of N.J., 2005. Mem.: Nat. Coun. Tchrs. English, Kappa Delta Pi. Roman Catholic. Avocations: reading, music, bike riding, hiking. Office: Manalapan Englishtown Middle Sch 155 Millhurst Rd Manalapan NJ 07726-4002

BARRÉ, LAURA, finance company executive; b. 1973; With Smith Barney Unit Citigroup Inc., 1999; analyst Bank One Corp., 2000; CFO, private client svcs. J.P. Morgan Chase & Co., Chgo. Bd. dirs. Arts of Life, 2004—. Named one of 40 Under Foty, Crain's Bus. Chgo., 2005. Office: Bank One Private Client Svcs IL-0291 300 S Riversidde Plz Chicago IL 60606*

BARRE, STEVEN CRAIG, lawyer; b. NYC, Nov. 11, 1959; s. Gerald J. and Roslyn P. B.; m. Rachel Brody, Aug. 21, 1983; 3 children. BS, Cornell U., 1981; JD, Columbia U., 1984. Bar: NY 1985. Assoc. Weil Gotshal & Manges, NYC, 1984-88; asst. gen. counsel Hanson Industries, Iselin, NJ, 1988-92, assoc. gen. counsel, 1993-95, U.S. Industries Inc., 1995-2000, v.p., gen. counsel, sec., 2000—01, sr. v.p., gen. counsel, sec., 2001—03, Jacuzzi Brands Inc. (U.S. Industries Inc.), West Palm Beach, Fla., 2003—. Pub. jour. Bus. Law Today, 1993. Book rev. editor Columbia Jour. of Environ. Law, 1983-84. Com. mem. Cornell U. Alumni Ambassadors, Ithaca, N.Y., 1981—. Harlan Fiske Stone scholar, 1984, Cornell Nat. scholar, 1977. Mem. ABA, N.Y. State Bar Assn. Avocation: bicycling. Office: Jacuzzi Brands Inc 777 S Flagler Dr Ste 1100W West Palm Beach FL 33401

BARRECA, CHRISTOPHER ANTHONY, lawyer; b. Pittsfield, Mass., Sept. 15, 1928; s. Christopher Joseph and Jennie (Cannici) B.; m. Alice Hazlehurst, Sept. 5, 1953. AA, Boston U., 1950, JD, 1953; LLM, Northwestern U., 1968. Bar: Mass. 1954, Ky. 1969, U.S. Dist. Ct. Ky. 1970, U.S. Dist. Ct. Mass. 1995, U.S. Ct. Appeals (6th cir.) 1970, Conn. 1988. With Gen. Electric Co., Fairfield, Conn., 1953-93, labor arbitration and litigation counsel, 1971-80, sr. labor and employment law counsel, 1980-93; ptnr., office chair Paul, Hastings, Janolsky & Walker LLP, Stamford, Conn., 1993-99, sr. counsel, 1999—. Mem. arbitration services adv. com. Fed Mediation and Conciliation Service, 1973—; adj. prof. U. Louisville, 1970-71, U. Bridgeport (Conn.) Sch. of Law, 1986-90; selectman Weston, 1997-00. Co-author, editor: Labor Arbitrator Development, 1983, A Practical Guide for Advocates, 1990; contbr. articles to profl. jours. Chmn. Weston (Conn.) Bd. Edn., 1977-82; trustee, vice chair exec. com., chmn. com. legal affairs, sec. bd., 2001, vice chair bd., 2002-2003, chmn. bd., Boston U., 2003-2004. Served with AUS, 1946-47. Mem. ABA (chmn. labor and employment law sect. com. labor arbitration advocacy, elected to governing council of labor and employment law sect. 1986—, chair 1996-97, elected to governing coun. dispute resolution sect. 2001-2002), Boston U. Sch. Law Alumni Assn. (Silver Shingle award 1982), Aspetuck Valley Country Club (Weston, pres. 1995-96). Home: 6 Aspetuck Hill Ln Weston CT 06883-2601 Office: Paul Hastings Janolsky & Walker LLP 1055 Washington Blvd Stamford CT 06901-2216 Office Phone: 203-961-7466. Business E-Mail: christopherbarreca@paulhastings.com.

BARREDO, RITA M., auditor; b. Torrington, Conn., June 24, 1953; d. Avelino and Josephine (DiNoia) B. BA, U. Conn., 1975; BS, Post Coll., 1981; MS in Acctg., U. Hartford, 1984, MBA, 1990. CPA Conn.; cert. info. sys. auditor; internal auditor, mgmt. acct., govt. auditing profl., cert. in homeland security, cert. info. tech. profl., diplomate Am. Bd. Forensic Accts., Am. Bd. Forensic Examiners. Timekeeper Timex Corp., Waterbury, Conn., 1976-85; auditor Def. Contract Audit Agy., Lowell, Mass., 1985—. Mem. AICPA, Am. Coll. Forensic Examiners, Am. Womens Soc. CPAs, Conn. Soc. CPA (continuing profl. edn. com. 1989-95, 97— social and recreation com. 1996-97), Inst. Mgmt. Accts. (sec. Waterbury chpt. 1994—), Inst. Internal Auditors, Info. Sys. Audit and Control Assn. Home: 130 Dawes Ave Torrington CT 06790-3627 Office: Def Contract Audit Agy 400 Main St East Hartford CT 06108-0968 Personal E-mail: rbarredo01@snet.net.

BARREDO, RONALD DE VERA, physical therapist, educator; b. Quezon City, Philippines, Apr. 24, 1969; s. Rodolfo Garcia and Josefina De Vera Barredo; m. Maria Adora Simpas, Aug. 7, 2001; children: Rubric Michael children: Ryan Christopher. BS in Phys. Therapy, U. of the Philippines, Manila, 1990; MA in Orgnl. Mgmt., Trevecca Nazarene U., Nashville, 1995, EdD in profl. Practics, 2002. Diplomate Am. Bd. Phys. Therapy Specialties; lic. physical therapist Tenn., Okla., Ark. Program dir., phys. therapist asst. and massage therapy programs Kaskaskia Coll., Centralia, Ill., 2000—05; assoc. prof. grad. program in physical therapy Ark. State U., State University, 2005—. Vis. faculty mem. phys. therapy program Langston (Okla.) U., 2003—; bd. dirs. Fgn. Credentialing Commn. in Phys. Therapy, Alexandria, Va., 2002—, Christian Phys. Therapists Internat., NJ, 2000—. Recipient President's Disting. Pub. Svc. Award, Tenn. State U., 1999. Mem.: Am. Phys. Therapy Assn. (chmn. awards com. 2003—04), Toastmasters Internat. (dist. gov. 1999—2000, Select Disting. Dist. Gov. 2000, Disting. Toastmaster award 1997). Office: Ark State Univ Grad Program in Phys Therapy PO Box 910 State University AR 72467 Home Phone: 615-889-5329; Office Phone: 870-972-3610. Business E-Mail: rbarredo@nstate.edu.

BARREN DE SERRES, BRUCE WILLARD (H.R.H. THE DUKE BRUCE WILLARD BARREN DE SERRES), merchant banker; b. Olean, NY, Jan. 28, 1942; s. James Lee and Marion Frances (Willard) Barren; children: James Lee, Christina Roseanne. Student, Hun Sch. of Princeton, 1959; BS, Babson Coll., 1962; MS, Bucknell U., 1963; grad. cert., Harvard U., 1967, Cambridge U., 1968. Exec. v.p. Am. Extract Co., 1960—62; sr. cons. Price Waterhouse, NY, 1963—67; v.p. Walston & Co., Inc., NY, 1967—70; sr. v.p. Delafield Childs, Inc., NY, 1970—71; chmn. EMCO/Hanover Group Ltd., LA, 1971—; sr. v.p. Goodway, Inc., 1972—73; pres. Park West Med. Group, Inc., 1980—81; CEO First Pacific Bank, 1984—85; exec. editor Mgmt. Gazette, 1988—98. CEO Four Winds Enterprises Inc., San Diego 1985-87, F.W. Myers & Co., Rouses Point, N.Y., 1990-91; vice chmn., CEO Hydro-Mill Co., Chatsworth, Calif., 1996-98; bd. dirs. various U.S. and internat. cos., 1978-95; author, instr. CPA, CPE courses, Tex., Calif. and N.Y.; mem. editl. adv. bd. Prentice-Hall, 2001-02; U.S. rep. Transatlantic Bio-scis. Fund, London, 1988-91; instr. loan documentation and valuation procedures Sanwa Bank, 1995-96; CEO, dir. Potomac Worldwide, 1998-00; chmn. Tech. Asset Mgmt. Ltd., Eng., 2000-01; chmn. exec. com. Sunnylife Global, Inc., 2005-06; lectr. exec. MBA program UCLA, 1988-98, U. S.C. Grad. Sch., Pepperdine Exec. MBA Program. Whittier Sch. Law, Chapman U. Sch. Law; mem. Calif. Small Bus. Adv. Com., 1990-92. Contbr. over 135 articles to profl. jours. including CFO, Contr. Alert, KPMG Banking Insider. Decorated Grand Cross Order of the Cross of Constantinople; recipient numerous Disting. Svc. awards various govt. offcls., including govt. of China, 1984-2007, Disting. Alumni award, Hun, Princeton, 2005, named to Athletic Hall of Fame, 1999. Mem.: Am. Mgmt. Assn. (author, instr. 1991—92), L'Assn. des Familles D'Amours, Byzantine Heraldic Soc., Blue Book Social Registry (LA and S.W.), Order of Constantinople (dep. grand chancellor), St. Andrews Soc., Ordo Supremus Militaris Templi Hierosolymitani (a.k.a. Templars) (chevalier), Grand Sovereign Dynastic Hospitalier Order St. John Knights of Malta (knight comdr.), Mil. and Hospitalier Order St. Lazarus of Jerusalem (comdr.). Roman Catholic. Avocation: writing. Office: 11740-11 West Sunset Los Angeles CA 90049 Office Phone: 310-471-3735. Business E-Mail: bbarren@verizon.net.

BARRERA, ELVIRA PUIG, retired counselor, academic administrator; b. Alice, Tex., Dec. 11, 1943; d. Carlos Rogers and Delia Rebecca (Puig) B.; 1 child, Dennis Lee Jr BA, Incarnate Word Coll., 1971; M Counseling and Guidance, St. Mary's U., San Antonio, 1978; specialist degree marriage and family therapy, St. Mary's U., 1989. Lic. profl. counselor, marriage & family therapist, lic. chem. dependency counselor. Tchr. Edgewood Ind. Sch. Dist., San Antonio, 1965—74, Dallas Ind. Sch. Dist., 1971—72, Northside Ind. Sch. Dist., San Antonio, 1974; ednl. cons. Region 20-Edn. Svc. Ctr., San Antonio, 1974—79; coord. career edn. San Antonio Ind. Sch. Dist., 1979—84, counselor, 1984—91, vice prin., 1998—2005; ret., 2005; program evaluator AOC Solutions, Inc., Chantilly, Va., 2006—. Cons. SBA, 1981, U.S. Office Edn., Washington, 1981-82, Tex. Edn. Agy., Austin, 1979-80; cons., writer San Antonio Ind. Sch. Dist. and Tex. Edn. Agy., 1985; cons. various edn. publs.; family coord. CATCH project U. Tex. Health Sci. Ctr., Houston, 1991-94; counselor Austin Ind. Sch. Dist., 1994-97, dist. transition counselor, 1997-98 Chairperson career awareness exploring divsn. Boy Scouts Am., 1982-87 Named Disting. Alumna, Incarnate Word Coll., 1983, Hall of Fame Internat. Profl. and Bus. Women, 1995; recipient Spurgeon award Boy Scouts Am., 1985, Merit award, 1986, Growth award, 1986 Mem. Am. Assn. Marriage and Family Therapy, San Antonio Hash House Harriers (treas. 1990-91), Incarnate Word Coll. Alumni Assn. (adv. bd. 1990—), St. Mary's U. Alumni Assn. (v.p. Austin alumni chpt. 2003—), The Harp and Shamrock Soc. Tex., Delta Kappa Gamma (Kappa Beta chpt. 2d v.p. 1982-84, 1st v.p. 1986-88, sec. 2005-06, pres. 2006-) Roman Catholic. Avocation: running. Home: 907 Aurora Cir Austin TX 78757-3415

BARRERE, CLEM ADOLPH, business brokerage company executive; b. Bradford, Pa., Jan. 5, 1939; s. Clem A. and Ruth Eleanore (Brauner) B.; m. Jamie Elizabeth Newton, Aug. 30, 1969; 1 child, John Coleman Barrere. B Engring., Yale U., 1960; PhD in Chem. Engring., Rice U., 1965; postgrad., Emory U., 1975. Registered profl. engr., Tex., Okla.; bd. cert. broker; cert. bus. intermediary. Group leader rsch. dept. Conoco, Inc., Ponca City, Okla., 1965-69, dir. gas engring. Houston, 1969-72, dir. gas ops., 1972-77, mgr. loss control, 1977-81; mgr. Dupont-Transp. Svc., Houston, 1981-87, Dupont-Safety and Environ., Houston, 1987-89; pres. Barrere & Co. Ventures, Houston, 1989—. Dir. Barrere & Co. Realtors, Houston, 1978—; pres. Bus. Intermediary Edn. Found., 2006—. Contbr. articles to profl. jours.; 7 patents in field. Mem. Mus. Fine Arts, Houston, Zool. Soc., Houston, Mus. Natural Sci., Houston, 1970-07. Recipient Citations for Svc., Am. Petroleum Inst., 1988, Gas Processors Assn., 1989; NSF rsch. grantee, 1963-65. Fellow Internat. Bus. Brokers Assn. (dir. 1998-03, 06-, Pres. award 2002); mem. Tex. Bus. Brokers Assn., Houston Gas Processors Assn. (pres. 1981-82), Tex. Rolls-Royce Assn. (dir. 1987-96, Spl. award 1991), Houston Gun Collectors (pres. 1964), Houston Area Realtors, Petroleum Club, Lakeside Country Club, Phi Lambda Upsilon, Alpha Chi Sigma. Republican. Methodist. Avocations: golf, travel, sailing, genealogy, car restorations. Office: Barrere & Co Ventures 5652 Doliver Dr Houston TX 77056-2322 Office Phone: 832-452-5652. E-mail: clembarrere@earthlink.net.

BARRERE, JAMIE NEWTON, real estate company executive; b. Russellville, Ark., June 7, 1946; d. James Edward Jr. and Martha (Spillers) Newton; m. Clement Adolph Barrere Jr., Aug. 30, 1969; 1 child, John Coleman. BA in Math., U. Ark., 1968; grad., Realtor Inst., 1984. Cert. real estate brokerage mgr.; grad. Realtor Inst.; accredited relocation coord. Asst. programmer, analyst Conoco, Ponca City, Okla., 1968-69; programmer, analyst Bonner & Moore Assocs., Houston, 1969-70; tchr. math. Lamar Consol. H.S., Rosenberg, Tex., 1970-72; assoc. broker Betty James, Realtors, Houston, 1972-78; pres. Barrere & Co., Realtors, Houston, 1978-96, Barrere Relocation Svcs. affiliate Heritage Tex. Properties, Houston, 1996—2002; assoc. broker Heritage Tex. Properties, Houston, 2002—. Adv. bd. Western Bank-Westheimer, Houston. Active Tex. Real Estate Polit. Action Com., Harris County Heritage Soc., Houston, Houston Jr. Forum, Am. Heart Assn. Guild, Houston Zool. Soc.; guild mem. Mus. Fine Arts, Houston, Covenant House; trustee St. Luke's United Meth. Ch.; bd. dirs., adv. bd. children's dept., tchr. and pianist Moores Sch. Music Soc. U. Houston; past cub scout leader Boy Scouts Am. Mem. Nat. Assn. Realtors (past equal opportunity com.), Tex. Assn. Realtors (bd. dirs. 1989-98, chmn. Multiple Listing Svc. com. 1985-90, named Top Prodr., Star Achiever 2003-06), Houston Assn. Realtors (bd. dirs. 1986-89, 93-95, v.p. 1993), Houston C. of C. (amb.), DAR, U. Ark. Alumnae Assn. (life, v.p. Houston chpt.), RELO Internat. Relocation Network, Lakeside Country Club, Petroleum Club, Tanglewood Garden Club (officer), Delta Delta Delta (past pres. Houston alumnae), Tri Delta Art Show for Charity (past pres., adv. bd.). Office: Heritage Tex Properties 1177 West Loop South Ste 1200 Houston TX 77027 Office Phone: 713-965-0812. Business E-Mail: jbarrere@heritagetexas.com.

BARRETO, HECTOR V., JR., not-for-profit organization executive, former federal agency administrator; b. Kansas City, Mo., May 13, 1961; s. Hector and Mary Louise Barreto; m. Robin Barreto; 3 children. BSBA, Rockhurst U., Kansas City, 1983. South Tex. area mgr. Miller Brewing Co.; founder Barreto Ins. and Fin. Services, Calif., 1986; adminstr. US Small Bus. Adminstrn., Washington, 2001—06; nat. chmn. The Latino Coalition, Washington, 2006—. Past chmn. bd. Latino Bus. Assn., LA. Past vice chmn. bd. US Hispanic C. of C. Named Alumnus of Yr. for Outstanding Achievement, Rockhurst U., 2002; named one of 50 Most Important Hispanics in Govt., Edn., Hispanic Engineer and Info. Tech. mag., 2005. Office: The Latino Coalition 707 Fifth St SE Washington DC 20003

BARRETT, BARBARA MCCONNELL, ranch owner, lawyer; b. Indiana County, Pa., Dec. 26, 1950; d. Robert Harvey and Betty (Dornheim) McC.; m. Craig R. Barrett, Jan. 19, 1985. BS, Ariz. State U., 1972, MPA, 1975, JD, 1978, LHD (hon.), 2000. Bar: Ariz. 1978, U.S. Dist. Ct. Ariz. 1979, U.S. Supreme Ct. Ariz. 1979. Atty. The Dial Corp., Phoenix, 1976-80; assoc. gen. counsel, asst. sec. Southwest Forest Industries, Inc., Phoenix, 1980-82; vice chmn. CAB, Washington, 1982-83, mem., 1983-84, vice chmn., 1984-85; ptnr. Evans, Kitchel & Jenckes, P.C., Phoenix, 1985-88, 1989; dep. adminstr. FAA, Washington, 1988-89; pvt. practice internat. bus. and aviation law Paradise Valley, Ariz., 1989—; pres., CEO American Mngmt. Assn., NYC, 1997-98, Triple Creek Ranch, Mont., 1993—; fellow Inst. Politics, Kennedy Sch. Harvard U., 1999. Chmn. bd. dirs. Valley Bank Ariz., 1997-03; chmn. nominating com. The Lovelace Inst., 1995-99, U.S.-Afghan Women's Coun., 2003—, mem., chmn., US Adv. Commn. Pub. Diplomacy, 2003—, past mem. Adv. Com. on Women in the Svcs., nominated as Sec. USAF, 2003; treas. Asia-Pacific Econ. Cooperation Edn. Found., 1995-99; mem. exec. com., vice chairperson career opportunities subcom. US Dept. Def., 1989-93; mem. adv. com. Gov.'s Regional Airport, Pres.'s Adv. Com. on Trade Negotiations; mem. Adminstrv. Coun. US, 1982-85; chmn. US Sec. of Commerce Export Leaders Conf., 1988, Transp. Cluster Gov.'s Strategic Partnership for Econ. Devel., 1992-94; mem. Ariz. Disease Control Rsch. Commn., 1991-93, Bus. Coun., UN, 1997-98, Nat. Ctr. Polit. Analysis, 1997-98, Dean's Coun. of 100, Ariz. State U., 1998—, nat. campaign cabinet mem., Campaign for Leadership, 1999-2002, Def. Bus. Bd., 2003—; v.p. East Valley Partnership, 1992-94; v.p. Internat. Women's Forum, 1991-99, pres., 1999-01, mem. coun. fgn. rels., 1994—; mem. Phoenix Coun. Fgn. Rels., 1981; mem. steering com. Thunderbird Internat. Symposium, 1992-99; mem. global dispute resolution Global Ctr. Dispute Resolution, 1999—; mem. adv. bd. China Mist Tea Co., 1998-99, Harvard Leadership Bd., 1999-02; mem. corp. adv. bd., Pacific Coun. Internat. Policy, 1999-2001; bd. trustees, Irish Cultural and Learning Found., 2002—; mem. exec. com., heritage Found. Pres.'s Club, 2004—; sr. advisor 61st Session of UN Gen. Assembly, 2006—; trustee Mayo Clinic, 2006—; bd. trustees Aerospace Corp., 2006—; bd. dirs. Exponent, Inc., Ctr. Internat. Pvt. Enterprise, Ratheon, Horatio Alger Assn., Freedom House, Smithsonian Instn., Space Found. Chmn. Ariz. Dist. Export Coun., 1985-92, Ronald W. Reagan Scholarship Program, mentor, 1984-86, Airshow Can. Symposium, 1989, 91; chmn. World Trade Ctr. Ariz., 1992-94, chmn. emerita; dir. class 11 program, 1979, United Way Valley of Sun, charter participant, 1979-80, alumni bd. dirs., bd. dirs. Bronze Soc., cabinet mem., co-chmn., 1990-93; bd. dirs. Samaritan Med. Found., 1981-83, grants and contracts com. chmn., 1985-98; bd. dirs. Nat. Air and Space Mus. Smithsonian Inst., 1988-89, Palms Clinic and Hosp. Corp., 1987-2000, Goldwater Inst., 1991-02; trustee, devel. com., chairperson Thunderbird Garvin Sch. Internat. Mgmt., Glendale, Ariz.; trustee, nominating and devel. com. Embry-Riddle Aeronaut. U., Prescott, Ariz., Daytona Beach, Fla., 1989-97; pres. World Affairs Ariz., 1987-88; vice chmn. Kid's Voting USA, 1991-98; dir., nominating com. chmn dir., ARC, 1993-98, past nominating com. chmn., 1994-96, past pub. support vice-chmn., 1996-98; candidate Gov. Ariz., 1994; trustee Lovelace Inst., 1995-99; vice regent, trustee George Washington's Fredericksburg Found., 1997—; pres. bd. Maricopa Colls. Found., 1997-98; adv. coun. mem., St. Mary's Food Bank, 1997-98; mem. Gov.'s Task Force Canamex Corridor, 1998-01; sr. adv. com. Inst. Politics, Harvard, 1999—; emeritus bd. mem., Maricopa Cmty. CC's Found., 2002-; adv. bd. mem., Boys Hope Girls Hope, 1999-, Our Mil. Kids, Inc., 2005-; global coun. mem., Internat. Mus. Women, 2004-. Named Woman of Yr., Ariz. State U., 1971, named to Hall of Fame, Coll. Pub. Programs, 1989, Coll. Liberal Arts, 1997; recipient Disting. Achievement award Ariz. State U., 1987, Coll. Bus., 1994, Woman Who Made a Difference award Internat. Women's Forum, 1988, Dick Cheney citation U.S. Sec. of Def., 1992, FAA Adminstr.'s award, 1989, Woman of the Yr. Network of Women in Hospitality, 1998, Horatio Alger award, 1999, Beta Gamma Nationwide Achievement award, 2000, Girl Scouts Today and Tomorrow award, 2000, Homeroom Hero award Teach for Am., 2002, Disting. Women's award Northwood U., 2001, Medal of Hon. DAR, 2003; named to Internat. Forest Friendship Hall of Fame, 2003; named one of 100 Women Who Made A Difference in Aviation, 2003; Dubois scholar, 1977. Mem. Am. Mgmt. Assn. (truste, chmn. exec. com., pres. N.Y.C. 1997-98, Lifetime Achievement award, 2002), Nat. Assn. Corp. Dirs. (faculty 1999, bd. dirs. 2000-02), Ariz. State U. Law Soc. (bd. govs. 1990-93), Ariz. State U. Found. (bd. dirs., program chair 1996—), Ariz. Women in Internat. Trade (bd. dirs., exec. com. 1987-93), Phoenix C. of C. (bd. dirs. 1987-93), Reagan Alumni Assn., Nat. Policy Forum, mem., Internat. Women's Forum (pres. 1982-), Nat. Assn. Women Judges (resource bd. mem. 2000-), Ariz. Women's Forum, Charter 100, Circumnavigators, Lewis and Clark Trail Heritage Found., Ariz. Acad., Ariz. State U. Alumni Assn., Network exec. Women in Hospitality, Women in Aviation, Internat., Women's Fgn. Policy Group, Women in Mil. Aviation, Econ. Club of Phoenix (past pres. 1990—).

BARRETT, BERNARD MORRIS, JR., plastic and reconstructive surgeon; b. Pensacola, Fla., May 3, 1944; s. Bernard Morris and Blanche (Lischkoff) B.; m. Sandra Neal Barrett; children: Beverly Frances, Julie Blaine, Audrey Blake, Bernard Joseph. BS, Tulane U., 1965; MD, U. Miami, 1969. Diplomate Am. Bd. Plastic Surgery. Surg. intern Meth. Hosp. and Ben Taub Hosp., Houston, 1969-70; resident in gen. surgery Baylor Coll. Medicine, Houston, 1970-71, UCLA, 1971-73; resident in plastic surgery U. Miami (Fla.) Affilated Hosps., 1973-75, chief resident in plastic surgery, 1975; fellow in plastic surgery Clinica Ivo Pitanguy, Rio de Janeiro, 1973; instr. surgery Baylor Coll. Medicine, 1970-71, clin. instr. plastic surgery, 1977-80, clin. asst. prof., 1980-90, clin. assoc. prof., 1991-97, clin. prof. surgery, 1997—; instr. surg. emergencies L.A. County Paramedics, 1972-73; plastic surgery coord. for jr. med. students Sch. Medicine U. Miami, 1975; practice medicine specializing in plastic and reconstructive surgery Houston, 1976—. Pres., chmn. bd. dirs. Plastic and Reconstructive Surgeons, P.A., 1978—; chmn. Tex. Inst. Plastic Surgery, Houston; assoc. chief plastic surgery St. Luke's Episcopal Hosp., Houston, 1991—; attending physician Jr. League Clinic, Tex. Children's Hosp., Houston, 1977—; active staff St. Luke's Hosp., Houston, Meth. Hosp., Houston; clin. assoc. in plastic surgery U. Tex. Med. Sch., Houston, 1976—; instr. surg. emergencies Harris County C.C.; dir. Am. Physicians Ins. Exch., Austin, 1976-2003, vice chmn., bd. dirs., 1995—; bd. dirs. Advocate M.D. Ins., Austin, 2004—; past chief of staff, chief plastic surgery Travis Centre Hosp., Houston, 1985—; dir. Physicians for Peace, Norfolk, Va., 1991—; cons. physician Houston Oilers, 1978-97; attending physician Ontario Motor Speedway, Calif., 1972-73. Author: Patient Care in Plastic Surgery, 1982, 2d edit., 1996, Manuel de Ciudados en Cirugia Plastica, 1985, Atencion al Paciente de Cirugia Plastica, 1998; contbr. articles to med. publs., presentations to profl. confs.; inventor Barrett sterling surgigrip. Bd. dirs. Plastic Surgery Ednl. Found., Chgo.; mem. Fed. Coun. on Aging, Washington, 1991-93, Pres.'s Coun. U. Miami, 1997—; adv. bd. Johnson & Johnson, New Brunswick, N.J. Lt. comdr. M.C., USNR, 1969-74. Recipient Outstanding Tchg. Plastic Surgeon award Baylor Coll. Medicine, 2003; Surg. exch. scholar to Royal Coll. Surgeons, London, 1968; hon. dep. sheriff Harris County, Tex. Fellow ACS; mem. Am. Assn. Plastic Surgery, Am. Soc. Plastic Surgeons, Royal Soc. Medicine, Michael E. DeBakey Internat. Cardiovascular Surg. Soc., Am. Soc. for Aesthetic Plastic Surgery, Denton A. Cooley Cardiovascular Surg. Soc., Tex. Med. Assn., Tex. Soc. Plastic Surgery, Harris County Med. Soc., Houston Soc. Plastic Surgery, D. Ralph Millard Plastic Surg. Soc. (pres. 1993-94, v.p. 1977-79, sec., treas. 1975-77, historian 1980—), U. Miami Sch. Medicine Nat. Alumni Assn. (bd. dirs. 1975-77, pres. coun. 1997—), Houston City Club, Houstonian Club, Royal Biscayne Racquet Club, Commodore Club, Coral Beach and Tennis Club, Sweetwater Country Club, Alpha Kappa Kappa (pres. 1968-69). Office: 6624 Fannin St Ste 2200 Houston TX 77030-2334 Home Phone: 713-626-4747; Office Phone: 713-790-9000. Personal E-mail: bmb-tips@swbell.net.

BARRETT, BEVERLY FRANCES, public relations specialist; d. Bernard Morris and Julia Prokop Barrett. BS cum laude in Human and Orgnl. Devel., Vanderbilt U., 1997; MA in Internat. Rels., Johns Hopkins U., 2001. Intern Peggy Guggenheim Collection, Venice, Italy, 1997, CNN & CNN Español, Miami, Fla., 2001; spl. asst. for cabinet affairs The White Ho., Washington, 2003—04; press asst., legis. corr. U.S. Ho. of Reps., Washington, 2002; asst. to Nat. Security Coun. The White Ho., Washington, 2004; asst. to amb. U.S. Embassy, Helsinki, Finland, 2004—05. Program dir. Tex. Assn. Adult Literacy Couns., 2006—07. Gov.'s fellow, Tex. Film Commn., Austin, 2000. Personal E-mail: beverly.barrett@jhu.edu.

BARRETT, BRUCE RICHARD, physics professor; b. Kansas City, Aug. 19, 1939; s. Buford Russell and Miriam Aileen (Adams) B.; m. Gail Louise Geiger, Sept. 3, 1961 (div. Aug. 1969); m. Joan Frances Livermore, May 21, 1979. BS, U. Kans., 1961; postgrad., Swiss Poly., Zurich, 1961-62; MS, Stanford U., 1964, PhD, 1967. Rsch. fellow Weizmann Inst. Sci., Rehovot, Israel, 1967—68; postdoctoral rsch. fellow, rsch. assoc. U. Pitts., 1968—70; asst. prof. physics U. Ariz., Tucson, 1970—72, assoc. prof., 1972—76, prof., 1976—, assoc. chmn. dept., 1977—83, mem. faculty senate, 1979—83, 1988—90, 1991—97, mem. tech. transfer com., 1996—97, 1998—99, mem. grad. coun., 1998—2000. Chmn. adv. com. Internat. Scholars, Tucson, 1985-96; program dir. nuc. theory Nat. Sci. Found., 1985-87; chmn. rsch. policy com. U. Ariz. Faculty Senate, 1993-94, 95-96; affiliate prof. U. Wash.-Seattle, 2000—; mem. adv. com. Nat. Inst. Nuc. Theory, 2005—, chair adv. com., 2007—. Woodrow Wilson fellow, 1961-62; NSF fellow, 1962-66; Weizmann Inst. fellow, 1967-68; Andrew Mellon fellow, 1968-69; Alfred P. Sloan Found. research fellow, 1972-74; Alexander von Humboldt fellow, 1976-77; Japan Soc. for Promotion of Sci. rsch. fellow, 1998; NSF grantee, 1971-85, 87—; Netherlands F.O.M. research fellow Groningen, 1980; recipient sr. U.S. scientist award (Humboldt prize) Alexander von Humboldt Found., 1983-85, 2007. Fellow Am. Phys. Soc. (publs. com. divsn. nuclear physics 1983-86, program com. 1993-94, 2002-03, chmn. steering com. nuc. physics summer sch. 1996-98, mem. exec. com. four corners sect. 1998-2004, chair 2003, chmn. forum on internat. physics 2002, chmn. com.

internat. sci. affairs 2003, mem. com. 2001-04, mem. Bonner prize selection com. 2006—, membership com. 2007-), Phi Beta Kappa (pres. Alpha Ariz. chpt. 1992, 2000-02, nat. senate 2000—), Sigma Pi Sigma, Omicron Delta Kappa, Beta Theta Pi. Office: U Ariz Dept Physics PO Box 210081 Tucson AZ 85721-0081 Office Phone: 520-621-2979. Business E-Mail: bbarrett@physics.arizona.edu.

BARRETT, COLLEEN CROTTY, air transportation executive; b. Bellows Falls, Vt., Sept. 14, 1944; AA with highest honors, Becker Jr. Coll., 1964. Legal sec. Oppenheimer Rosenberg Kelleher & Wheatley, San Antonio, 1968—72, adminstrv. asst., paralegal, 1972—78; corp. sec. Southwest Airlines, Dallas, 1978—, exec. asst. to pres. and chmn., 1980—85, v.p. adminstrn., 1985—90, exec. v.p. customs, 1990—2001, pres., 2001—, COO, 2001—04. Bd. dirs. JC Penney Co., Southwest Airlines. Named one of Most Powerful Women, Forbes mag., 2005; recipient Horachio Alger award, 2004. Mem.: Leadership Tex. Roman Catholic. Office: SW Airlines Co PO Box 36611 Dallas TX 75235-1611 Home Phone: 214-956-7565; Office Phone: 214-792-4112. Business E-Mail: vickie.shuler@wnco.com.

BARRETT, CRAIG R., electronics company executive; b. San Francisco, Aug. 29, 1939; m. Barbara Barrett, 1985; 2 children. BS, Stanford U., Palo Alto; MS in Materials sci., PhD in Materials sci., Stanford U. NATO postdoctoral fellow Nat. Physical Lab., 1964—65; assoc. prof., dept. materials sci. and engring. Stanford U., 1965-74; with Intel Corp., Chandler, Ariz., 1974—, tech. develop mgr., 1974—84, v.p. components tech. and mfg. group, 1984—87, sr. v.p., gen. mgr. components tech. and mfg. group, 1987—90, exec. v.p., mgr. components tech., 1990—93, COO, 1993—97, pres., 1997—98, CEO, 1998—2005, bd. chmn., 2005—. Bd. dirs. Intel, 1992—, Qwest Comms. Internat. Inc., US Semiconductor Industry Assn., Silicon Valley Mfg. Group, TechNet; co-chmn. Bus. Coalition for Excellence in Edn., Nat. Innovation Initiative Leadership Coun.; chmn. Computer Systems Policy Project; bd. trustee US Coun. for Internat. Bus.; appointee to President's Adv. Com. for Trade Policy and Negotiations and the the Am. Health Information Cmty.; mem. Nat. Academies Com. on Prospering in the Global Economy of the 21st Century: An Agenda for Am. Sci. and Tech. Author: Principles of Engineering Materials, of over 40 tech. papers dealing with the influences of microstructure on the properties of materials. Bd. dirs. Nat. Forest Found., Achieve. Grantee Fulbright Fellow, Danish Tech. U., Denmark, 1972. Mem.: NAE (chair 2004—). Office: Intel 2200 Mission College Blvd Santa Clara CA 95054-1537*

BARRETT, DAVID A., lawyer; b. Altoona, Pa., Aug. 12, 1950; s. Arthur L. and Mary (Bell) B.; m. Diane DeWitt, May 23, 1981; children: Alexander, Annabel. AB, Harvard U., Cambridge, Mass., 1971; JD, Columbia Law Sch., NYC, 1974. Bar: NY 1975, US Dist. Ct. (so. dist.) NY 1975, US Ct. Appeals (2d cir.) 1975, US Supreme Ct. 1979. Law clk. to Hon. Wilfred Feinberg U.S. Ct. Appeals (2d Cir.), NYC, 1974-75; Karpatkin fellow ACLU, NYC, 1975-76; law clk. to Hon. Thurgood Marshall U.S. Supreme Ct., Washington, 1976-77; spl. counsel U.S. Dept. Justice, Office Legis. Affairs, Washington, 1977-79; assoc. Cravath, Swaine & Moore, NYC, 1979-85; assoc. prof. Rutgers U. Law Sch., Newark, 1985-87; ptnr. Barrett Gravante Carpinello & Stern LLP, NYC, Albany, 1987-2000, Boies, Schiller & Flexner LLP, NYC, 2000—. Author: (with others) NYU Inst. State and Local Taxation, 1987, Reforming Libel Law, 1992. Mem. Senator Charles Schumer's Judicial Screening Comm., 1999—, Spence-Chapin Services for Children & Families (bd. dir., 2000—). Mem. Columbia Law Sch. Bd. Vis., 1996—. Office: 575 Lexington Ave New York NY 10022 Office Phone: 212-446-2300. Business E-Mail: dbarrett@bsfllp.com.

BARRETT, DAVID EUGENE, judge; b. Hiawassee, Ga., June 25, 1955; s. Homer and Laura Arispah (Wilson) B.; m. Donna L. Barrett; children: Laura Elizabeth, Thomas Jeffrey. BA summa cum laude, U. Ga., 1977, JD cum laude, 1980. Assoc. Erwin, Epting, et al, Athens, Ga., 1980-84, Blasingame, Burch, et al, Athens, 1984; pvt. practice Hiawassee, 1984-92; judge Recorders Ct., 1986-92, Superior Ct., Enotah Cir., 1992—. Counsel Towns County Humane Soc., Hiawassee, 1985-92; counselor Alzheimer Support, Hiawassee, 1985; instr. Family Law Inst. Mem. ABA, Ga. Bar Assn., Mountain Bar Assn. (sec. 1987-88, v.p. 1988-89, pres. 1989-90), Western Bar Assn. (sec. 1983-84), Enotah Bar Assn., Ga. Assn. Drug Ct. Profls. (treas. 2003-05), Towns County C. of C. (bd. dirs. 1986-87, 90-92, pres. 1988), Demosthenian Lit. Soc. (bd. dirs., sec. bd. trustees 1978-89, chmn. bd. 1986-89), Athens Jaycees (v.p. 1983-84). Home: 924 Mining Gap Ln Young Harris GA 30582-2324 Office: Superior Ct Enotah Cir 114 Courthouse St Box 2 Blairsville GA 30512 Office Phone: 706-439-6100.

BARRETT, ELIZABETH ANN MANHART, psychotherapist, consultant, nursing educator; b. Hume, Ill., July 11, 1934; d. Francis J. and Grace C. (Manhart) Fridy; children: Joseph B., Jeffrey F., Paula G. Brown, Pamela M. Temple, Scott D. BSN summa cum laude, U. Evansville, 1970, MA, 1973, MSN, 1976; grad., Gestalt Assocs. Psychotherapy, 1982; PhD in Nursing, NYU, 1983; grad., Am. Inst. for Mental Imagery, 1995. From instr. to asst. prof. nursing U. Evansville, Ind., 1970-76; staff nurse Welborn Bapt. Hosp., Evansville, 1975-76, Bellevue Psychiat. Hosp., NYC, 1976-79; clin. tchr. CUNY, 1977-82; asst. prof. Adelphi U., 1979-80; group practice Nurse Healers, 1979-82; pvt. practice psychotherapy, 1980—. Nurse rschr. Mt. Sinai Med. Ctr., N.Y.C., 1982-86, asst. dir. nursing, 1983-86; assoc. prof. Hunter Coll., N.Y.C., 1986-89, prof., 1994-2001, prof. emerita, 2001—, dir. grad. studies, 1989-92, coord. Ctr. for Nursing Rsch., 1993-2001; cons. Internat. Soc. Univ. Nurses; co-chair adv. com. Martha E. Rogers Ctr. for Study of Nursing Svc., 1994-96; sec., treas. Am. Inst. for Mental Imagery, 2002—; com. mem. Regional Health Planning Coun., Evansville, 1974-77. Mem. editl. bd. Alt. Therapies in Health and Medicine, 1995—. Recipient Disting. Nursing Alumnus award NYU, 1994, Disting. Nurse Rschr. award Found. N.Y. State Nurses Assn., 1995. Fellow Am. Acad. Nursing; mem. ANA (cert. psychiat.-mental health), NOW, Nat. League Nursing, Ea. Nursing Rsch. Assn. (charter), Ea. Nursing Rsch. Soc., Soc. Rogerian Scholars (co-founder, 1st pres. 1988-90), Phi Kappa Phi, Sigma Theta Tau (Upsilon chpt. pres. 1986-88), Alpha Tau Delta, Sigma Xi. Home: 415 E 85th St Apt 9E New York NY 10028-6358 Office: 16 E 96th St Ste 1 A New York NY 10128 Office Phone: 917-371-7269. E-mail: eambarrett@nyc.rr.com.

BARRETT, FRANK JOSEPH, lawyer, insurance company executive; b. Greeley, Nebr., Mar. 2, 1932; s. Patrick J. and Irene L. (Printy) B.; m. Ruth Ann Nealon, Aug. 20, 1956; children: Patrick, Mary, Anne, Karen, Thomas. BS in Law, U. Nebr., 1957; LLB, Nebr. Coll. Law, 1959. Bar: Nebr. 1959, U.S. Supreme Ct. 1976, arbitrator. Asst. gen. counsel, asst. sec. Nebr. Nat. Life Co., 1957—61; dir. ins. State of Nebr., Lincoln, 1961—67; exec. v.p., sec., gen. counsel Ctrl. Nat. Ins. Group Omaha, 1967—75; exec. v.p., chief counsel Mut. Omaha (and Affiliates), 1975—81; pres., CEO Ctrl. Nat. Ins. Co. Omaha, 1981—89, Ins. Rsch. Svc. Co., Omaha, 1989—; of counsel Lamson, Dugan & Murray, Omaha, 1990—. Bd. dir. Am. Family Life Assurance Co. State organizational chmn. 3 Nebr. gubernatorial campaigns. Served in U.S. Army, 1953-55, Korea. Recipient service citation Am. Nat. Red Cross, 1964, 65 Mem. ABA, Am. Arbitration Assn., Fedn. Ins. Counsels, Nebr. Bar Assn., Omaha Bar Assn., Consumer Credit Ins. Assn. (past pres. and dir.), Nat. Assn. Ind. Insurers (gov., past chmn.), Nat. Assn. Ins. Commrs. (past pres.), Am. Legion, Irish-Am. Cultural Soc., KC., ARIAS-U.S. (cert. arbitrator, cert. umpire) Democrat. Roman Catholic. Home: 516 S 119th St Omaha NE 68154-3115 Office Phone: 402-397-7300. Office Fax: 402-397-8450. Business E-Mail: fbarrett@ldmlaw.com.

BARRETT, GEORGE EDWARD, lawyer; b. Nashville, Oct. 19, 1927; s. George E. and Annie (Conroy) B.; m. Eloise McBride Barrett, Sept. 14, 1957; (div. 1988); children: Anne-Louise Barrett Thompson, Mary Eloise Barrett Brewer, Kathryn Conroy Barrett Cain. BS, Spring Hill Coll., 1952; diploma, Oxford U., Eng., 1953; JD, Vanderbilt U., Nashville, 1957. Bar: Tenn., U.S. Ct. Appeals (6th cir.), U.S. Supreme Ct. Atty. Barrett, Johnston & Parsley, Nashville. Office: Barrett Johnston & Parsley 217 2nd Ave N Nashville TN 37201-1601 Office Phone: 615-244-2202. Business E-Mail: gbarrett@barrettjohnston.com.

BARRETT, J. CARL, medical researcher, molecular biologist; b. Portsmouth, Va., Dec. 28, 1946; s. Jacob Weaver and Dixie Wike (Ring) B.; m. Roberta Mick, June 8, 1968; children: James, Paul, Lia. BS in Chemistry, Coll. of William and Mary, 1969; PhD in Biophysical Chemistry, Johns Hopkins U., 1974. Postdoctoral fellow divsn. biophysics Johns Hopkins U., Balt., 1974-77; sr. staff fellow lab. pulmonary function and toxicology Nat. Inst. Environ. Health Sciences, Rsch. Triangle Park, NC, 1977-82, group leader environ. carcinogenesis group, 1977-87, rsch. chemist, 1982-87, chief lab. molecular carcinogenesis, 1987-2000, dir. program environ. carcinogenesis Divsn. Intramural Rsch., 1992-96, sci. dir. Divsn. Intramural Rsch., 1995-2000; dir. divsn. basic sciences Nat. Cancer Inst., Bethesda, Md., 2000—01, dir. Ctr. Cancer Rsch., 2001—05; global head oncology biomarkers Novartis Institutes Biomedical Rsch., Cambridge, Mass., 2005—. Adj. prof. dept. pathology U. N.C., 1978—, dept. epidemiology, 1992—; adj. mem. genetics curriculum U. N.C., 1979—, toxicology curriculum, 1985—; adj. sr. fellow Ctr. Study of Aging and Human Devel. Duke U. Med. Ctr., 1993—; mem. study sections NIH, Nat. Cancer Inst., Nat. Cancer Inst. Can.; ad hoc reviewer; vis. prof. Sun Yat-Sen U., People's Rep. China, 1987, Inst. Zoology Academia Sinica, Taiwan, 1992, NYU, 1992; keynote speaker, organizer, chair numerous symposia, conferences, workshops; invited speaker more than 125 symposia, conferences, univs. worl dwide, 1986—; mem. Task Force Health Effects of Synthetic Fuels Dept. Energy, 1980; mem. workshop Internat. Program Chem. Safety, 1982; mem. working group WHO, 1983, Internat. Agy. Rsch. Cancer, France, 1985, 86, peer rev. com. sci. coun., 1988; mem. adv. panel Calif. Biotech., Inc., 1990, Greenwall Found., 1989; mem. various adv. bds., coms. Nat. Coun. Radiation Protection & Measurements, Am. Health Found., Nat. Cancer Inst., U.S. EPA, Health Effects Inst.-Asbestos Rsch. Com., Chem. Industry Inst. Toxicology, also external expert, ad hoc mem.; cons. Abbott Labs., 1989-91, Chem. Industry Inst. Toxicology, 1991-92; chmn. sci. coun. Internat. Agy. for Rsch. on Cancer, 1998. Author: Mechanisms of Environmental Carcinogenesis: Volume I-Role of Genetic and Epigenetic Changes, 1987, Vol. II-Multistep Models of Carcinogenesis, 1987; co-author: Carcinogenesis-A Comprehensive Survey: Volume 9, Mammalian Cell Transformation: Mechanisms of Carcinogenesis and Assays for Carcinogens, 1985, Comparative Molecular Carcinogenesis: Volume 376-Progress in Clinical and Biological Research, 1992; editor-in-chief Molecular Carcinogenesis, 1992—, mem. editl. bd., 1988—; assoc. editor Cancer Rsch., 1984—, Mutagenesis, 1985-88, Toxicology in Vitro, 1986-90; mem. editl. bds. profl. jours., 1988—; contbr. over 405 articles to profl. jours. Recipient merit awards NIH, 1989, 94, 97, Dir.'s award, 1995, 96, Ramazzini award Collegium Ramazzini, Italy, 1995, Secretary's award for Disting. Svc., Dept. Health and Human Svcs., 1996; NSF grantee, 1966; Dow Chem. Co. fellow, 1968. Mem. AAAS, Am. Chem. Soc., Am. Assn. Cancer Rsch. (program com., Rhodes award com., chair spl. membership com., bd. dirs. 1998—), Internat. Soc. Diffrentiation (bd. dirs. 1998—). Office: Novartis Institutes Biomedical Rsch 250 Massachusetts Ave Cambridge MA 02139 E-mail: barrett@mail.nih.gov.

BARRETT, J. PATRICK, manufacturing executive; b. Malone, NY, Feb. 5, 1937; s. John Edward and Evelyn (Flanagan) Barrett; m. Christine Robb, Apr. 25, 1980; 7 children. BS, Siena Coll., 1959; postgrad., NYU. With Chase Manhattan and Grace Nat. Bank, NYC, 1959—64; asst. treas., internat. chmn Carrier Distbn. Credit Corp.; pres. Carrier Overseas Fin. Corp. Carrier Corp., Syracuse, NY, 1964—72; v.p., CFO parent co., 1972—75, v.p., 1975—77, group v.p., 1978—79; exec. v.p. Carrier Internat., Syracuse, 1975—77, pres., 1977—79; exec. v.p., CFO, bd. dirs. Norton Simon, Inc., NYC, 1979—83; CEO Avis Rent A Car Inc. (subs. Norton Simon), 1981—83, chmn., CEO, 1983—87; pres. Telergy, 1998—2001; chmn. Syracuse Exec. Air Service, Bennington Ironworks, Whiteface Club Companies; chmn., CEO CARPAT Investments, 1987—; chmn. Lincoln Fin. Group, Phila., 2007—. Bd. dir. Savs. Bank & Trust Co., NYC, Lincoln Fin. Group, 1990—, Lincoln Life & Annuity of NY, Coyne Internat. Enterprises Corp., Syracuse Skychiefs Baseball Club. Mem. Pres. Reagan's bd. adv. on private initiatives, 1987; delegate Rep. Nat. Convention, 1988, 2004; chmn. NY Rep. State Com., 1989—91; bd. visitors Georgetown U. Sch. Fgn. Svc., Washington; bd. dirs. Vote Am. Found. Inc.; chmn. Vote Am. Youth Initiative; trustee Siena Coll.; trustee emeritus Syracuse Univ. Mem.: Eagles of Rep. Nat. Com., Sky, N.Y. Athletic. Office: Lincoln Fin Group 1500 Market St Philadelphia PA 19102-2112*

BARRETT, JALMA *See* **BOERSMA, JUNE**

BARRETT, JAMES BRUCE, systems engineer; b. Houston, Tex., June 24, 1948; s. Lloyd N/A and Catherine Delbert Barrett; m. Elizabeth Ann Comer, Apr. 3, 1970; children: Kristina Ann Martin, Joshua Brandon. BS, U. Houston, Tex., 1974. Engring., design Brown & Root, Inc., Houston, 1973—74; v.p. engring. and mktg. Houston Fire and Safety Equipment Co., Houston, 1974—80; cons. Fire Internat., Houston, 1980—81; control sys. engring. supr. Bechtel Corp., Houston, 1981—84; dir. maintenance and ops. Uvalde Consol. Ind. Sch. Dist., Uvalde, Tex., 1998—; sys. engring. and sales mgr. Tackaberry Co., Houston, 1984—85; ops. mgr. Honeywell, Houston, 1985—86; control sys. divsn. mgr., engring. mgr. Offshore Control Sys., Inc., Humble, 1986—87; project engr., mgr., i&e mgr., cons. engr. Douglass Engring., Inc., Humble, 1987—96; prin. instrument engr. ABB Randall Corp., Houston, 1996—98. Mem.: Tex. Farm Bur., Am. Soc. Heating, Refrigerating and Air Conditioning Engrs, Inc., Tex. Assn. Sch. Bus. Officials. Home: P O Box 5418 Uvalde TX 78802 Office: Uvalde CISD 1000 N Getty Uvalde TX 78801 Home Phone: 830-278-4217; Office Phone: 830-591-4960. Office Fax: 830-591-4963; Home Fax: 830-591-4963. Business E-Mail: bruce@ucisd.net.

BARRETT, JAMES GRESHAM, congressman; b. Oconee, SC, Feb. 14, 1961; s. Charles G. and Del M. Barrett; m. Natalie Barrett; 3 children. BS in Bus. Adminstrn., The Citadel, 1983. Operator Barrett's Furniture, 1987—2002; mem. SC State Ho. Reps., 1996—2002, US Congress from 3rd SC dist., 2004—, mem. budget com., mem. fin. svcs. com., mem. fgn. affairs com., mem. stds. of ofcl. conduct com. SME chair Oconee Boy Scouts, 1995, chmn.; mem. SC GOP steering com. Bush for Pres., 2000. Positions to capt. US Army, 1983—87. Mem.: Oconee County C. of C. (pres.), Westminster Rotary Club (pres.). Republican. Baptist. Office: 303 W Beltline Blvd Anderson SC 29625 Office Phone: 202-225-5301, 864-224-7401. Office Fax: 864-225-7049.*

BARRETT, JANE FRANCES, lawyer; b. Monterey, Calif., Sept. 13, 1952; d. Harle V. Barrett and Lucille M. Richstatter. BA in Polit. Sci., Loyola Coll., Balt., 1973; JD, U. Md., 1976. Bar: Md. 1976, DC 1979, US Dist. Ct. (dist. Md.) 1986, US Ct. Appeals (4th cir.) 1987, US Dist. Ct. (dist. DC) 1998. With US EPA, Washington, 1976—81; asst. atty. gen. State of Md., Balt., 1981-86; asst. US atty. US Atty. Office Dist. Md., Balt., 1986—98; ptnr., head white collar & corp. def. practice Dyer, Ellis & Joseph, Washington, 1998—2003; ptnr., chair white collar internal and govt. investigative grp. Blank Rome, LLP, Washington, 2003—. Adj. prof. U. Md., Balt., 1990-97. Contbr. articles to profl. jours. Mem. adv. working grp. environ. sanctions US Sentencing Commn., Washington, 1992-93; bd. dirs. Women's Housing Coalition, Balt., 1998-99. Recipient Bronze medal US EPA, 1997, Commdrs. award Army Corps. Engrs., 1998. Mem. ABA (vice-chair environ. crimes enforcement subcommittee 1995), Women's Internat. Shipping & Trading Assn., Fed. Bar Assn. Md. (bd. govs.), Assn. Trial Lawyers of Am., Nat. Assn. Women Lawyers, Nat. Assn. Criminal Def. Lawyers, Maritime Law Assn. Office: Blank Rome LLP Watergate 600 New Hampshire Ave NW Washington DC 20037 Office Phone: 202-772-5907. Office Fax: 202-772-5908. E-mail: barrett@BlankRome.com.*

BARRETT, JANE HAYES, lawyer; b. Dayton, Ohio, Dec. 13, 1947; d. Walter J. and Jane H. Barrett BA, Calif. State U.-Long Beach, 1969; JD, U. So. Calif., 1972. Bar: Calif. 1972, US Dist. Ct. (cen. dist.) Calif. 1972, US Ct. Appeals (9th cir.) 1982, US Supreme Ct. Assoc. Lawler, Felix & Hall, LA, 1972—84; ptnr. Arter & Hadden, 1984—94, DLA Piper, 2002—06, Morrison Foerster, 2006—; mng. ptnr. Preston, Gates & Ellis, 1994—2002. Lectr. bus. law Calif. State U., 1973-75. Mem. adv. bd. Harriet Buhai Legal Aid Ctr., 1991-96, mem. bd. pub. counsel, 1996-98; pres. Pilgrim Parents Orgn. 1990-91; chmn. fin. Our Mother Good Counsel Sch.; bd. regents Loyola, HS, 2000—; mem. adv. coun. Ctr. on Ethnic and Racial Diversity. Named Outstanding Grad. Calif. State U., Long Beach, 1988, Outstanding Alumnae Polit. Sci., 1993, So. Calif. Super Lawyer, LA Mag., 2003, 04, Best Lawyer in Am., 2006. Fellow Am. Bar Found.; mem. ABA (bd. govs. 1980-84, chmn. young lawyers divsn. 1980-81, com. on delivery of legal svcs. 1985-89, exec. coun. legal edn. and admissions sects. 1985-89, fin. sec. torts and ins. practice 1982-83, adv. mem. fed. judiciary com. 9th circuit rep. 2000-05, mem. minority and ethnic diversity bd., v.p. 1997—, Am. Bar Endowment 1999, bd. dirs. 1990—, sec. 1993-95, v.p. 1998-99, pres., 1999-00, bd. fellows young lawyers divsn. 1992—, del 9th cir. jud. conf., atty. del. US Dist. Ct. ctrl. dist. Calif. Atty. Conf. 2002-05, US Dist. Ct. Ctrl. Dist. Calif. (discipline com. 2004-07, chair sect. com., admissions com. 2005-07), 9th Cir. Atty. Conf. (del. 2005), Calif. State Bar (com. adminstrn. of justice, editl. bd. Calif. Lawyers 1981-84), Legion Lex (bd. dirs. 1990-93), Los Feliz Homeowners Assn. (bd. dirs.). Democrat. Office: Morrison Foerster 555 W 5th St Los Angeles CA 90013 Home Phone: 213-253-8659. Business E-Mail: jbarrett@mofo.com.

BARRETT, JOHN ANTHONY, publishing and printing company financial executive; b. Phila., Aug. 12, 1942; s. Stephen Francis and Margaret (Walsh) B.; m. Joan Victoria Lyncheski, Oct. 21, 1967; children: John Anthony Jr., Stephanie Lea. BSBA, Mt. St. Mary's Coll., Emmitsburg, Md., 1964; postgrad., Drexel U., 1980. Mgr. mfg. acctg. Scott Paper Co., Phila., 1968-77; contr. W.B. Saunders Co. div. CBS Inc., Phila., 1977-82; v.p., contr., chief fin. officer Diversified Printing Corp., Atglen, Pa., 1982-87; v.p. sales ops. Maxwell Communication Corp., Greenwich, Conn., 1987-89; v.p. fin. planning and control Arcata Graphics Co., Balt., 1989-94; bus. cons. Washington, 1994-95; sr. v.p., CFO Univ. Press Am., Inc., Lanham, Md., 1995-97, Nat. Book Network, Inc., 1995-97; bus. cons., 1997—; v.p., CFO BDP Internat., Inc. Global Logistics and Transp., Phila., 1997—. Lt. USN, 1964-68; Vietnam. Mem. Fin. Execs. Inst. Roman Catholic. Office: Gepapeak Bay Business Park 141 Log Canoe Cir Stevensville MD 21666-2127

BARRETT, JOHN F., insurance company executive; BBA, U. Cin. Coll. Bus. Adminstrn., 1971. Pres., CEO Bank NY; with Western & Southern Life Ins. Co., Cin., 1987—, exec. v.p., CFO, 1987—89, pres., COO, 1989—94, pres., CEO, 1994—, chmn., 2002—; pres., CEO Western & Southern Fin. Group, Cin., 2000—, chmn., 2002—. Dir. Fifth Third Bancorp, The Andersons Inc. Associated with Am. Coun. Life Ins., Catholic Inner City Schools, Cin., Cin. Bus. Com., Downtown Cin., Nat. Underground R.R. Freedom Ctr., Young President's Orgn. Mem.: Am. Bus. Roundtable. Office: Western & So Life Ins Co 400 E 4th St Cincinnati OH 45202*

BARRETT, JOHN GILCHRIST, retired historian; b. Gastonia, NC, Aug. 24, 1921; s. William Charles and Ruby (McKay) Barrett; m. Lottie Mae Buie; children: Rebecca Anne, Margaret McKay. BA, Wake Forest Coll., 1943; MA, U. N.C., 1950, PhD, 1954; LLD (hon.), Wake Forest U., 1982. Prof. history Va. Mil. Inst., Lexington, 1953—87; ret., 1987. Author: Sherman's March Thru the Carolinas, 1956, The Civil War in North Carolina, 1963, So Much Water, So Little Land, 2001; editor (jour.): Yankee Rebel, 1966. Pres. So. Athletic Conf., 1969—72. Lt. USN, 1942—46, Pacific. Recipient Barrett-Bonner acad. award, So. Athletic Conf.; fellow, John Simon Guggenheim Found., 1958. Mem.: So. Hist. Assn., Phi Beta Kappa. Democrat. Baptist. Avocations: reading, sports, swimming. Home: 6 Junkin Pl Lexington VA 24450

BARRETT, JOHN J(AMES), JR., lawyer; b. Phila., May 19, 1948; s. John J. and Carmela (DiJohn) B.; m. Rosemary A. Campagna, Aug. 23, 1969; children: Jeffrey, Kristin, Jacqueline. BA, Temple U., 1970, JD, 1973. Bar: Pa. 1973, N.J. 1987, U.S. Dist. Ct. (ea. dist.) Pa. 1973, U.S. Ct. Appeals (3rd cir.) 1975, U.S. Dist. Ct. (mid. dist.) Pa. 1986, U.S. Supreme Ct. 1986, U.S. Dist. Ct. N.J. 1987. Ptnr. Saul Ewing LLP, Phila., 1980—2005, Buchanan Ingersoll & Rooney, PC (and predecessor firm), Phila., 2005—. Mem. Nat. Assn. R.R. Trial Counsel, Phila. Assn. Def. Counsel. Office: Buchanan Ingersoll and Rooney PC 14th Fl 1835 Market St Philadelphia PA 19103 Office Phone: 215-665-3854. Business E-Mail: john.barrett@bipc.com.

BARRETT, KATHERINE, writer, columnist; b. NYC, May 24, 1954; d. Herbert and Betty (Palash) B.; m. Richard H. Greene, Feb. 21, 1982; children: Benjamin, Sandra. BS in Journalism, Northwestern U., 1976. Reporter Comml. Appeal, Memphis, 1976-78; assoc. editor, sr. writer, sr. editor Ladies' Home Jour., NYC, 1980-84, contbg. editor, 1984-98; freelance writer, columnist numerous publs., 1984—; prodr. Walt Disney Family Edn. Found., San Francisco, 1996—; corr. Governing mag., Washington. Spkr. on state and city mgmt., 1992—; mem. adv. bd. Govtl. Acctg. Stds. Bd., Norwalk, Conn., 1996—; curator Walt Disney Family Mus. web site; cons. Pew Ctr. on the States, 2005— Author: The Man Behind the Magic, 1991, Frankly, My Dear, 1996, Powering Up, 2000, Inside the Dream, 2001; co-author: The B&G Report, 2006—; co-prodr.: (CD-ROM) Walt Disney: An Intimate History, 1998; co-prodr., writer (TV documentary) Walt: The Man Behind the Myth, 2001; contbr. articles to Redbook, Reader's Digest, Glamour, Ladies Home Jour., Newsweek., others. Recipient award for excellence N.Y. Soc. CPA's, 1991, Children's Choice award Internat. Reading Assn., 1992, Washington Monthly Journalism award, 1999, Folio Editorial Excellence award, Folio Mag., 2002, Excellence in Health Care Reporting award Nat. Inst. Health Care Mgmt., 2004

BARRETT, LIDA KITTRELL, mathematics professor; b. Houston, May 21, 1927; d. Pleasant Williams and Maidel (Baker) Kittrell; m. John Herbert Barrett, June 2, 1950 (dec. Jan. 1969); children: John Kittrell, Maidel Horn, Mary Louise. BA, Rice U., Houston, 1946; MA, U. Tex., Austin, 1949; PhD, U. Pa., Phila., 1954. Instr. math. U. Conn., Waterbury, 1955-56; vis. appointment U. Wis., Madison, 1959-60; lectr. U. Utah, Salt Lake City, 1956-61; assoc. prof. U. Tenn., Knoxville, 1961-70, prof., 1970-80, head math. dept., 1973-80; assoc. provost No. Ill. U., DeKalb, 1980-87; dean, arts and scis. Miss. State U., Mississippi State, 1987-91; sr. assoc. Edn. and Human Resources Directorate NSF, Washington, 1991-95; prof. math. US Mil. Acad., West Point, NY, 1995-98; adj. prof. U. Tenn., 1998—2001. Math. and math. edn. cons., Knoxville, Tenn., 1964-80, 98—. Contbr. articles on topology, applied math. and math. edn. to profl. jours. Mem. Math. Assn. Am. (pres. 1989, 90), Am. Math. Soc., Soc. Indsl. and Applied Math., Nat. Coun. Tchrs. Math., Am. Assn. Higher Edn., Phi Kappa Phi, Sigma Xi. Episcopalian. E-mail: lidak@bellsouth.net.

BARRETT, MICHAEL BAKER, historian, educator; b. Honolulu, Oct. 12, 1946; s. John P. and Bernice (Baker) B.; m. Sara Harriet McKerley, Sept. 20, 1969; 1 child, Michael M. AB, The Citadel, 1968; MA, U. Mass., 1969, PhD, 1977; graduate, US Army Command and Gen. Staff Coll., 1980—81, US Army War Coll., Carlisle, PA, 1991. Lectr. history U. Mass., Amherst, 1973-74, 75-76; instr. history The Citadel, Charleston, SC, 1976-78, asst. prof., 1978-82, assoc. prof., 1982—, prof., 2005—, dean of grad. studies, 1985—. Author: Operation Albion: The German Conquest of the Baltic Islands, 2007; Editor: (Rowman and Littlefield series) Total War: New Perspectives on World War II, 2005-; contbr. articles to profl. jours. Brig. gen. US Army, 1969—2001, comdr. 941st TC Co. US Army, comdr. 812th TC bn. US Army, comdr. 1182d TC Brigade US Army, comdr. 1186th TC Brigade US Army. Recipient Legion of Merit, U.S. Army, others; Fulbright fellow, 1974-75, Citadel Devel. Found. fellow, 1977, 82, NDEA fellow, 1977. Mem. Am. Hist. Assn., Am. Mil. Inst., So. History Assn., SC History Assn., Soc. Mil. History, Hibernian Soc., SC Agrl. Assn., US Army Armor Assn., Transp. Corps. Officers Assn., Fulbright Alumni Assn., Phi Alpha Theta, Phi Kappa Phi, Delta Phi Alpha. Office: The Citadel Grad Studies Office Of The Dean Charleston SC 29409-0001 Mailing: 1170 Chersonese Rd Mount Pleasant SC 29464-9506 Office Phone: 843-953-4855. Business E-Mail: barrettm@citadel.edu.

BARRETT, MICHAEL HENRY, civil engineer; b. Dove Creek, Colo., June 20, 1932; s. Frank Ace and Carrie Ethel (Snyder) B.; m. Barbara Jane Kreutz, Aug. 7, 1954; children: Robert, Mary, Bonnie, William. BS in Civil Engring, U. Colo., 1955, postgrad., 1955-64; MBA, U. Denver, 1979. Registered profl. engr., Colo., Calif., Fla., Wis., N.C., Minn., N.Mex., Utah. Design engr., then partner Ketchum & Konkel, Denver, 1955-69; pres. Ketchum, Konkel, Barrett, Nickel, Austin, Denver, 1969-79, chmn. bd., 1979-85, pres., chmn., 1986-88; prin., cons. Martin/Martin, 1988—2003, prin. emeritus, 2003—; pres. Gold Creek Devel. Corp., 2006—. Bd. dirs. Testing Cons., Inc., Martin Assoc. Group, Restruction Corp., Smart Skyways, Inc.; faculty U. Colo., 1963-64, U. Denver, 1968-69; lectr. Civil Def., 1962-68; cons. MMFX Steel Co., 2000—. Patentee in field. Exec. bd. Denver Area coun. Boy Scouts Am., 1970-, pres., 1974-75, area v.p., 1976-82, area pres., 1982; mem. Westminster Planning Commn., Colo., 1971-72; chmn. bd. dirs. Denver Boys, Inc. Served with USNR, 1951-54, USAR, 1955-63. Recipient Lincoln Arc Welding award, 1966, 68, award Am. Inst. Steel Constrn., 1969, Disting. Engring. Alumnus award U. Colo., 1984, Honor award Colo. Engring. Coun., 1984, Silver Beaver award Boy Scouts Am., 1977, Silver Antelope award, 1983. Fellow ASCE (life); mem. NSPE, Am. Concrete Inst., Soc. Exptl. Stress Analysis, Profl. Engrs. Colo. (pres. 1970), Am. Cons. Engrs. Coun. (life; 1st place award 1973, pres. Colo. chpt. 1982, Orley Phillips award 1992, com. of fellows 1993, peer reviewer 1984—, George Washington Leadership award 1998), Cert. Cons. Engrs. of Colo. (life), Structural Engrs. Assn. Colo., Am. Arbitration Assn., Harvard Bus. Sch. Club, Denver C. of C., Rotary (hon., bd. dirs. 1976-78). Office: Martin & Martin Inc 12499 W Colfax Ave Lakewood CO 80215 Home Phone: 303-429-3408; Office Phone: 303-431-6100. Business E-Mail: mbarrett@martinmartin.com.

BARRETT, MICHAEL JOHN, anesthesiologist; b. Milw., Feb. 27, 1954; s. Walter Joseph and Valerie Clara (Wisniewski) Baclawski; m. Joan Marie Rowley, May 28, 1983; children: Michael J. Jr., Jessica Marie, Monica Jane. BS in Math. with honors, U. Wis., 1974; MD, Med. Coll. Wis., 1981; MBA, U. Toledo, 1998. Diplomate Am. Bd. Anesthesiology, Nat. Bd. Medicine and Surgery, Nat. Bd. Med. Examiners, Am. Acad. Pain Mgmt., Am. Bd. Anesthesiology Pain Mgmt. Intern Med. Coll. Wis. Affiliated Hosps., Milw., 1981, resident in anesthesiology, 1982—84; dir. anesthesiology Putnam Cmty. Hosp., Palatka, Fla., 1984—92, dir. Putnam Pain Ctr., 1985—92; clin. asst. prof. anesthesiology Ohio U. Coll. Osteo. Medicine; chief dept. anesthesia Putnam Cmty. Hosp., Palatka, 1984—92. Pres. Putnam Anesthesia Assocs., Palatka, 1985-92, Associated Anesthesiologists Toledo, 2005—; staff anesthesiologist St. Vincent Med. Ctr., Toledo, 1992—, vice chmn. dept. anesthesia, 2001-05 dir. Pain Mgmt. Ctr., 1994—; ptnr. Assn. Anestheseologists of Toledo, 1993—, fiduciary pension plan, 1999—, pres., 2005—. Bd. dirs. Round Lake Park Homeowners Assn., Palatka, 1986-88. Walter Zeit fellow; recipient St. Vincents Physician Excellence award, 1996. Mem. AMA, Internat. Anesthesia Rsch. Soc., Am. Soc. Anesthesiologists, Am. Soc. Regional Anesthesiologists, Ohio Med. Assn., Acad. Medicine of Toledo and Lucas County, Am. Neuromodulation Soc., Ohio Soc. Anesthesiologists, Assoc. Anesthesiologists Toledo, Putnam County Med. Soc. (pres. 1989-91), Phi Beta Kappa, Phi Kappa Phi. Republican. Avocations: boating, private pilot, swimming. Home: 8646 Plum Hollow Pt Holland OH 43528-8487 Office: Assoc Anesthesiologists 2409 Cherry St Ste 305 Toledo OH 43608-2600 Office Phone: 419-251-4715. Business E-Mail: mjbjmb@ameritech.net.

BARRETT, MICHAEL RYAN, federal judge; b. Cin., Jan. 14, 1951; BA, U. Cin., 1974; JD, U. Cin. Coll. Law, 1977. Bar: Ohio 1977. Adminstrv. hearing officer State of Ohio, 1977—78; asst. pros. atty., chief asst. pros. atty. Hamilton County Prosecutor's Office, 1978—84; assoc., ptnr. Graydon, Head & Ritchey, 1984—94; ptnr. Barrett & Weber, LPA, 1995—2006; judge US Dist. Ct. (So. dist.) Ohio, 2006—. Office: Potter Stewart US Courthouse Rm 815 100 E 5th St Cincinnati OH 45202 Office Phone: 513-564-7660.*

BARRETT, NANCY SMITH, academic administrator; b. Balt., Sept. 12, 1942; d. James Brady and Katherine (Pollard) Smith; children: Clark, Christopher. BA, Goucher Coll., 1963; MA, Harvard U., 1965, PhD, PhD, Harvard U., 1968. Dep. asst. dir. Congl. Budget Office, Washington, 1975-76; sr. staff Council of Econ. Advisors, Washington, 1977; prin. research assoc. The Urban Inst., Washington, 1977-79; dep. asst. sec. U.S. Dept. Labor, Washington, 1979-81; instr. Am. U., Washington, 1966-67, asst. prof. econs., 1967-70, assoc. prof., 1970-74, prof., 1974-89; dean Coll. of Bus. Adminstrn. Fairleigh Dickinson U., Teaneck, NJ, 1989-91; provost, v.p. acad. affairs Western Mich. U., Kalamazoo, 1991-96, U. Ala., Tuscaloosa, 1996—2003, Wayne State U., Detroit, 2003—. Author: Theory of Macroeconomic Policy, 1972, 2d rev. edit., 1975, Theory of Microeconomic Policy, 1974, (with G. Gerardi and T. Hart) Prices and Wages in U.S., 1974; contbr. articles on econs. to profl. jours. Woodrow Wilson fellow, 1963-64; Fulbright scholar, 1973. Mem.: Am. Econs. Assn., Phi Beta Kappa. Office: Wayne State Univ 4092 Faculty Adminstrn Bldg Detroit MI 48202 Home: 2033 Shorepointe Grosse Pointe Woods MI 48236 Office Phone: 313-577-2200. E-mail: nancy.barrett@wayne.edu.

BARRETT, REGINALD HAUGHTON, wildlife management educator; b. San Francisco, June 11, 1942; s. Paul Hutchison and Mary Lambert (Hodgkin) Barrett; m. Katharine Lawrence Ditmars, July 15, 1967; children: Wade Lawrence, Heather Elizabeth. BS in Game Mgmt., Humboldt State U., 1965; MS in Wildlife Mgmt., U. Mich., 1966; PhD in Zoology, U. Calif., Berkeley, 1971. Rsch. biologist U. Calif., Berkeley, 1970—71, acting asst. prof., 1971—72; rsch. scientist divsn. wildlife rsch. Commonwealth Scientific and Indsl. Rsch. Orgn., Darwin, Australia, 1972—75; from asst. prof. to prof. U. Calif., Berkeley, 1975—, George and Wilhelmina Goertz disting. prof. wildlife mgmt., 2002—. Author (with others): Report on the Use of Fire in National Parks and Reserves, 1977, Research and Management of Wild Hog Populations, Proceedings of a Symposium, 1977, Sitka Deer Symposium, 1979, Symposium on Ecology and Management of Barbary Sheep, 1980, Handbook of Census Methods for Birds and Mammals, 1981, Wildlife 2001: Populations, 1992; contbr. abstracts, reports to profl. jours. Recipient Outstanding Achievement award, Humboldt State U. Alumni Assn., 1986, Bruce R. Dodd award, 1965, Howard M. Wight award, 1966; Undergrad. scholar, Nat. Wildlife Fedn., 1964, NSF Grad. fellow, 1965—70, Union Found. Wildlife Rsch. grantee, 1968—70. Fellow: Calif. Acad. Sci., Explorers Club; mem.: AAAS, Orgn. Wildlife Planners, Calif. Bot. Soc., Am. Inst. Biol. Scis., Internat. Union Conservation Nature (life), Am. Soc. Mammalogists (life), Soc. Range Mgmt. (life), Australian Mammal Soc., Soc. Am. Foresters, Ecol. Soc. Am. (cert. sr. ecologist), Wildlife Soc. (pres. Bay Area chpt. 1978—79, pres. western sect. 1997—98, cert. wildlife biologist, R. F. Dasmann Profl. of the Yr. award western sect. 1989), Sigma Xi, Xi Sigma Pi. Episcopalian. Avocations: hunting, fishing, photography, camping, backpacking. Office: U Calif 137 Mulford Hall Berkeley CA 94720-3114 Office Phone: 510-642-7261. Business E-Mail: rbarrett@nature.berkeley.edu.

BARRETT, RICHARD DAVID, university director, consultant, retired bank executive; b. Cin., Sept. 27, 1931; s. Oscar Slack and Helen Rust (Kaiper) B.; m. Pamela P. Soldwedel, Feb. 25, 1971; children: David, Kimball, Randall. Grad., Choate Sch.; BA, Yale U., 1953; postgrad., George Washington U., NYU. Prodn. control Reynolds Metals Co., 1954—56; v.p. ops. Nat. Bank Washington, 1956—66; officer Irving Trust Co., NYC, 1966—70; v.p. mktg. First Am. Bank, N.A., Washington, 1970—74, sr. v.p., 1974—, head internat. divsn., head retail ops. and mktg. group, v.p. internat. and pvt. banking group, exec. v.p. mktg. and cmty. rels.; dir. planned giving Georgetown U., Washington; pres. Barrett Planned Giving, Inc., Washington. Past mem. Bankers Assn. Fgn. Trade, Greater Washington Area Bd. Trade Internat. Com. Author: (with Molly E. Ware) Planned Giving Essentials: A Step-by-Step Guide to Success, 2d edit., 2002. Past trustee Meridian House Internat.; past bd. dirs., treas. Hospice Care of D.C., Watergate South Inc.; past trustee Washington Hosp. Ctr.; past chmn., past mem. bd. dirs. Nat. Capitol Area Health Care Coalition Lt. (j.g.) USNR, 1953-54 Mem. Assn. Fundraising Profls., Nat. Com. on Planned Giving, Yale Club, Met. Club, Chevy Chase Club (Md.). Home: 700 New Hampshire Ave NW # 906 Washington DC 20037-2406 Office Phone: 202-349-3812. E-mail: richard@barretplannedgiving.com.

BARRETT, ROBERT JAMES, III, investment banker; b. Bangor, Maine, July 23, 1944; s. Robert James and Catherine Pauline (Rogan) B.; m. Susan Hopkins Vander Poel, July 26, 1975 (div.); children: Robert James IV, Graham Halsted; m. Catherine Moore Tankoos, Apr. 22, 1995. BA cum laude, Georgetown U., 1966; JD, Columbia U., 1969; MBA with honors, Harvard U., 1971. Bar: N.Y., 1969, Maine 1970. Assoc. Morgan Stanley, NYC, 1971-76; sr. v.p. E.F. Hutton & Co. Inc., NYC, 1976-83; dir. Prudential-Bache Securities, NYC, 1983-90; ptnr. Barrett & Whitman., NYC, 1991-92; sr. fin. cons. Merrill Lynch, 1992-95; vice chmn. Apex Ptnrs., 2002—. Dir. Senator George Mitchell Inst.; founder Bar Harbor Preservation Trust; trustee Husson Coll., Bangor, 1989—96, U. Maine, R.J. Barrett, Beatrix J. Farrand Fund, Landscape Hort. Mem.: Beach Club (Palm Beach, Fla.), Bear Lakes Club (West Palm Beach, Fla.), Northeast Harbor Club(Bar Harbor, Maine), Union Club (N.Y.C.). Republican. Roman Catholic. Avocations: tennis, squash, hunting, fishing, golf. Home: 913 S Lakeside Place Lantana FL 33462-1777 E-mail: bob@barrett3.com.

BARRETT, ROLIN FARRAR, JR., mechanical engineer, consultant; b. Raleigh, NC, May 18, 1962; s. Rolin Farrar and Dixie Hobbs Barrett; m. Petra Arabaszova Barrett, Feb. 27, 2001. BSEE, N.C. State U., 1986, BS in Mech. Engring., 1991; MS in Mech. Engring., La. Tech. U., 1996; PhD in Mech. Engring., N.C. State U., 2005. Registered profl. engr., N.C. Engr. Barrett Engring., Raleigh, 1986—. Rschr. N.C. State U., Raleigh, 2001—. Author: Mechanical Engineering Capstone Senior Design Textbook, 2005. V.p. bd. dirs. Ruston (La.) Symphony, 1992—94; mem., fundraiser Krewe of Janus, Monroe, La., 1994—97. Named Duke, Krewe of Janus, Monroe, 1997. Mem.: Triangle Soc., Cardinal Club, Sir Walter Gun Club (bd. dirs.). Achievements include patents for guided bullet and firearm bolt assembly; patents pending for electronic aid for visually impaired; gun sight. Office: Barrett Engring Ste 280 3141 John Humphries Wynd Raleigh NC 27612

BARRETT, RONALD W., biopharmaceutical executive; PhD in Pharmacology, Rutgers U. Various positions to sr. v.p. Affymax Rsch. Inst., Palo Alto, Calif., 1989—99; co-founder, chief scientist XenoPort, 1999, CEO, 2001—. Recipient Newcomb-Cleve. prize, 1996-97. Office: XenoPort 3410 Central Expressway Santa Clara CA 95051 Office Phone: 408-616-7200. Office Fax: 408-616-7210.

BARRETT, THOMAS J., federal agency administrator, retired military officer; b. Lynbrook, NY, 1947; m. Sheila Walker; children: Tom, Matt, Becky, Paul. BS in Biology, LeMoyne Coll., 1968; JD (with hons.), George Washington U., 1976; grad., Army War Coll., Carlisle, Pa., 1989. Advanced through grades to vice admiral US Coast Guard, 2002, deck officer, US Coast Guard Cutter Chase, staff mem., 13th Coast Guard Dist., staff mem., Claims & Litig. Divsn., Office Chief Counsel, project staff mem., Outer Continental Shelf Safety, Office Marine Safety, Security & Environ. Protection, commdg. officer, Coast Guard Support Ctr., dep. chief, Office of Personnel & Training, 1994—96, dep. comdr., Maintenance & Logistics Command Atlantic Norfolk, Va., 1996—97, dir., reserve & training Washington, 1997—99, comdr., 17th Coast Guard Dist., 1999—2002, vice comdt., 2002—04; COO, v.p. Potomac Inst. for Policy Studies, Washington, 2004—06; adminstr., Pipeline & Hazardous Materials Safety Adminstrn. US Dept. Transp., Washington, 2006—07, acting dep. sec., 2007, dep. sec., 2007—. Decorated 5 Legion of Merit, Meritorious Svc. medal, 2 Coast Guard Commendation medal, Coast Guard Achievement medal, Vietnam Svc. medal. Office: US Dept Transp 400 Seventh St SW Rm 8410 Washington DC 20590 Office Phone: 202-366-4433. Business E-Mail: Thomas.Barrett@dot.gov.*

BARRETT, THOMAS M., mayor, former congressman; b. Milw., Dec. 8, 1953; m. Kristine Barrett; children: Thomas John, Anne Elizabeth, Erin, Kate. BA in Economics, U. Wis., 1976, JD with honors, 1980. Atty. Smith & O'Neill, Milw., 1982-84; mem. Wis. State Assembly, 1984-89, Wis. State Senate from 5th Dist., 1989-92, U.S. Congress from 5th Wis. dist., Washington, 1993—2002; mem. energy and commerce com.; mayor City of Milwaukee, 2004—. Bd. dirs. Sojourner Truth House, Shalom High Sch., Transcenter Home for Youth. Recipient Circle of Friends award Milw. Advocates for Retarded Citizens, 1989, Health Leadership award State Med. Soc., Govt. Leadership award Rehab. for Wis.; named to Clean Sixteen list for environ. voting record by Wis. Environ. Decade, 1987, 89, 90. Mem. Wis. Bar Assn., Phi Beta Kappa. Democrat. Office: 200 E Wells St City Hall Rm 201 Milwaukee WI 53202*

BARRETT, WILLIAM GARY, advertising and marketing executive; b. NYC, Oct. 24, 1943; s. Herbert Mark and Toni Eileen (Craig) B.; m. Christina Louise Sjogren, Sept. 11, 1977 (div. 1980); m. Donna Lou Barnes, May 11, 1984; 1 child, Daniel Martin. BA, U. Buffalo, 1964. Sr. media planner Grey Advt., NYC, 1966-69; v.p., supr. network rels. Batten, Barton, Durstine & Osborn Advt., NYC, 1969-71; v.p., media dir. Martin Landey, Arlow, NYC, 1971-74; v.p. media and mktg. Shaller-Rubin Assocs., NYC, 1974-77; sr. v.p., dir. media and mktg. svcs. Young & Rubicam and Dentsu, Young & Rubicam, NYC, 1977-86; exec. v.p., dir. communications svcs. Earle Palmer Brown, Washington, 1986-88; exec. v.p., COO S.F.M./Havas Media, MPG, LLC, Real Time Direct, NYC, 1988-2000; founding ptnr., specialist in mktg./comm. Barrett Consulting LLC, 2001—. Bd. dirs. Price Compare website, MC Networks; mem. adv. bd. Zango Solutions. Lt. U.S. Army, 1964-66 Avocations: skiing, golf, photography, scuba diving, wine collecting. Home: 297 Miller Rd Hudson NY 12534 Office: PO Box 249 Claverack NY 12513-0249 Home Phone: 518-851-2671. Personal E-mail: barrettllc@cs.com.

BARRETTE, JEAN, physicist, researcher; b. Montreal, May 1, 1946; s. Bertrand and Marguerite Ducharme B. BSc, U. Montréal, 1967, MSc, 1968, PhD, 1974. Postdoctoral fellow Max-Planck Inst., Heidelberg, Germany, 1974-76; physicist Brookhaven Nat. Lab., Upton, NY, 1976-82; engring. physicist Commissariat a l'energie Atomique, Saclay, France, 1982-87; prof. McGill U., Montréal, 1987—, chair dept. physics, 1997—2002; dir Foster Radiation Lab., Montréal, 1988-97. Mem.: Can. Assn. of Physicists, Am. Physical Soc. Achievements include research in nucleus-nucleus reactions and heavy-ion physics with particular interest in the study of reaction mechanism at intermediate and relativistic bombarding energies. Office: McGill U Dept Physics 3600 University St Montreal PQ Canada H3A 2T8 Office Phone: 514-398-7030. Business E-Mail: jean.barrette@mcgill.ca.

BARRETTE-MOZES, SUSAN JEAN, counselor, psychotherapist; b. Tucson, Oct. 20, 1966; d. Thomas Marvin and Kathleen Marie Barrette; 1 child from previous marriage, Hannah Mozes. BA cum laude, U. Ariz., Tucson, 1989; MA in Anthropology, Carleton U., Ottawa, Can., 1993; MA in Mental Health Counseling with distinction, Webster U., Merritt Island, Fla., 2000. Nat. bd. cert. counselor, lic. assoc. counselor Ariz. Bd. Behavioral Health Examiners; cert. guidance counselor Ariz. Dept. Edn. Rschr. Dept. Nat. Def. Hdqs., Ottawa, 1993—98; program dir. Mil. Family Response Ctr. Def. Hdqs. Can., 1995—98; registered mental health therapist Brevard Counseling Ctr., Dept. Disability Determinations Social Security, Devereux Mental Health Agy., 2000—01; profl. counselor Sunnyside Unified Sch. Dist., Tucson, 2001—. Mem. Animal Cruelty Task Force Pima County, Tucson, 2005—06, Animal Welfare Alliance So. Ariz., 2005—06, Tucson Zool. Soc. Mem.: Am. Counseling Assn., Soc. Applied Anthropology, So. Poverty Law Ctr. Avocations: ballet, jazz, tap, modern dance. Home: 7257 E Montecito Dr Tucson AZ 85710 Office: Sunnyside Unified Sch Dist # 12 5093 S Liberty Ave Tucson AZ 85706 E-mail: suzyjeanb@cs.com.

BARRETTO, ANJALI, education educator; d. Noel and Maria Luiza Barretto. PhD, U. Iowa, Iowa City, 2001. Cert. spl. edn. tchr. Dilkhush, 1993. Spl. edn. tchr. Caritas, Goa, India, 1993—95; assoc. prof. Gonzaga U., Spokane, Wash., 2001—. Cons. Gonzaga U., Spokane, Wash. Office Phone: 509-323-3492.

BARRIE, DENNIS RAY, museum director; b. Cleve., July 9, 1947; s. David Ray and Evelyn (Vild) B.; m. Dianne Hester, Sept. 28, 1977; children: Ian Michael, Kevin James. BS, Oberlin Coll., 1969, MS, 1970; PhD, Wayne State U., 1983. Midwest area dir. Archives of Am. Art Smithsonian Inst., Washington and Detroit, 1972—83; dir. Contemporary Arts Ctr., Cinn., 1983—92; pres. Dennis Barrie & Assocs., 1992—93; dir. Rock & Roll Hall of Fame & Mus., 1993—98; pres. Barrie Cons., Cleveland Heights, Ohio, 1996—98, Malrite Co., 1998—2005; dir. cult. planning Westlake Reed Leskosky Archs., Cleve., 2005—; prin. Barrie Project, 2005—. Active internat. arts panel NEA/USIA, Washington, 1984-86, art in pub. pls. and visual arts panel Ohio Arts Council, Columbus, 1986-90; panelist Cinn. Bicentennial Commn. Mem. Assn. Art Mus. Dirs., Am. Assn. Mus., Ohio Mus. Assn., Coll. Art Assn. Democrat. Office: Westlake Reed Leskosky Ste 1900 925 Euclid Ave Cleveland OH 44115 Office Phone: 216-522-1350. Office Fax: 216-522-1357.

BARRIE, JOHN PAUL, lawyer, educator; b. Burbank, Calif., Oct. 7, 1947; s. John and Virginia (Feagans) Barrie; m. Betsy Smith; children: Sean, Tyler. AB in Pol. Sci., UCLA, 1969; JD, U. Calif., San Francisco, 1972; LLM in Tax, NYU, 1973. Bar: Calif. 1972, DC 1975, Mo. 1977, NY 2001. Atty. advisor to judge U.S. Tax Ct., Washington, 1973-75; atty. office of gen. counsel Renegotiation Bd., Washington, 1975-77; assoc. Lewis & Rice, St. Louis, 1977-82, ptnr., 1982-86, Gallop, Johnson & Neuman, St. Louis, 1986-93, Bryan Cave L.L.P., St. Louis, 1993-98, Washington and NYC, 1998—. Adj. prof. Washington U. Sch. Law, St. Louis, 1979—99, Georgetown Law Ctr., 1999—, NY Law Sch., 2006—; past mem. IRS Dist. Dir.'s Liaison Group, Mo. Dept. Rev. Adv. Group, past chmn. Editor: Mo. Bar Ct. and CLE Bull.; editl. advisor Jour. Multistate Taxation; contbr. articles to profl. jours. Commr. Commn. Bot. Garden Subdistrict, St. Louis, 1989—99. Recipient Dir.'s award, IRS, 1993. Fellow: St. Louis Internat. Tax Group, St. Louis Corp. Tax Group (chmn.), St. Louis Tax Lawyers Group (past chmn.), Am. Coll. Tax Counsel, Exec. Inst. Advanced Study Washington U.; mem.: ABA (mem. coun. 2007—, tax sect., past chmn. com. govtl. submissions, past chmn. com. affiliated corps.), Nat. Assn. State Bar Tax Sects. (chmn. 1983—84), Bar Assn. Met. St. Louis (tax sect.), Am. Tax Policy Inst. (life; sponsor), NY Bar Assn. (tax sect.), DC Bar Assn. (tax sec., mem. steering com. 2001—, chmn. 2006—07), Calif. Bar Assn. (tax sect.), Mo. Bar Assn. (tax sect., past chmn. tax com., Pres.'s award 1983), NY Athletic Club, City Club (Washington), Noonday Club. Episcopalian. Office: Bryan Cave LLP 700 13th NW Ste 700 Washington DC 20005 also: 1290 Ave of the Americans 35th Flr New York NY 10104 Office Phone: 212-541-1184. Business E-Mail: jbarrie@bryancave.com.

BARRINGER, JOAN MARIE, counselor, educator, artist, writer; b. Washington, Sept. 30, 1955; d. John Thomas and Maria Reginia Barringer. BA in Latin Am. Studies, George Mason U., 1981; grad. in Creating and Selling Short Stories, Inst. Childrens Lit., 1995; MA in Edn. and Counseling, George Mason U., 1999. Translator and receptionist Brazilian Embassy, Cultural Inst., Washington, 1975—83; dir. and founder day care Rainbow City Army-Navy Country Club, Arlington, Va., 1983—87; visitors svcs. Nat. Gallery Art, Washington, 1991—94; workshop and leadership conf. asst. Women's Ctr., Vienna, Va., 1996—2000; career counselor Dept. Rehab. Svcs., Alexandria, Va., 1998—99, Ind. Art. Bus. Studio of Nat. Arts, 2002—. Presenter in field. Author: (poetry) Metronome, 1979; designer CD cover, singer Gift of Love; Fairfax (Va.) Jour., 1992, Montgomery (Va.) Jour., 1992, one-woman shows include Vienna Arts Soc., 2006, exhibitions include Graffiti Gallery, 2002, Greenbelt Cmty. Ctr., 2003, Joanne Rose Gallery, 2003, Rehoboth Art League, 2004, Angel Eyes, 2004, Mimi's American Bistro, 2004—05, Represented in permanent collections Inova Hosp.;, author numerous poems. Pres. Hampton Roadrunners, 2004—06; leader Internat. Essential Tremor Found. support group Georgetown Hosp., Washington, 2005—; election officer U.S. Govt., Va., 2001; fundraiser Unity Ch. Recipient award, Vienna Photo Show, 2004, 2005. Mem.: Vienna Photog. Soc., Assn. Rsch. and Enlightenment (wayshower 2001—), Women's Caucus for Art (editor, lay out designer, writer, photographer newsletter 1999—2001), Sigma Pi Alpha. Avocations: genealogy, travel, interior decorating, yoga, photography, Oceanography. Home: 11107 Hampton Rd Fairfax Station VA 22039 Personal E-mail: joanmarie5@aol.com.

BARRINGER, PAUL BRANDON, II, lumber company executive; b. Sumter, SC, Aug. 22, 1930; s. Victor Clay and Gertrude (Hampton) B.; m. Merrill Underwood, May 27, 1957; children: Merrill U., Victor Clay, Ann Hampton. BS, U. Va., 1952; postgrad., George Washington U., 1954. With Human Relations Lab., Washington, 1954; with Coastal Forest ResouLces Co., Weldon, NC, 1954—, chmn. bd., CEO, 1967—. Bd. dirs. BB&T Corp., Sea Pines Co., Inc.; mem. Pres.'s Task Force on Internat. Pvt. Enterprise, Industry Policy Adv. Com. for trade policy matters. Mem. coll. bd. trustees U. Va., 1995-96; trustee U. Va. Found. With USAF, 1952-54. Mem.: NAM (bd. dirs.), Chief Execs. Orgn. (dir.), Farmington Country Coub, Sea Pines Country Club, Chockoyotte Country Club, Lamda Chi, Sigma Delta Psi, Zeta Psi. Episcopalian. Home: 14 S Calibogue Cay Rd Hilton Head Island SC 29928-2912 Office: Coastal Lumber Co PO Box 829 Weldon NC 27890-0829

BARRINGER, WILLIAM CHARLES, retired chemist; b. Cleve., Feb. 28, 1934; s. Donald Frederick and Elsa (Smith) Barringer; m. Vera Evelyn

Dodge, July 8, 1955; children: Laura Elizabeth, Donna Lee, Mary Jane, Judy Lynn. BS in Chemistry, Denison U., Granville, Ohio, 1956; MS in Chemistry, NYU, NYC, 1964, PhD of Chemistry, 1968. Devel. chemist, group leader Lederle Labs., Pearl River, NY, 1957—95; sr. rsch. scientist Wyeth-Ayerest Rsch., Pearl River, 1995—2000; ret., 2000. Adj. prof. King's Coll., Briarcliff Manor, NY, 1969—71. Contbr. articles to profl. jours. Mem.: NY Acad. Scis., Am. Chem. Soc. Achievements include patents in field. Avocations: gardening, sports, travel, photography. Home: 155 Pearce Pkwy Pearl River NY 10965

BARRINO, FANTASIA MONIQUE See FANTASIA

BARRITT, EVELYN RUTH BERRYMAN, nurse, educator, dean; b. Detroit, Sept. 4, 1929; d. George C. and Ruby (Mathews) Berryman; m. Ward LeRoy Barritt, Oct. 28, 1951; 1 dau., Kelli Jo. AA, Graceland Coll., 1949; diploma, Independence Sanitarium and Hosp. Sch. Nursing, Mo., 1952; BSN., Ohio State U., 1956, MA, 1962, PhD, 1971. Asst. instr. nursing Atlantic City Hosp., 1952-53; staff nurse Shore Meml. Hosp., Somers Point, NJ, 1953-54, Ohio State U. Hosp., Columbus, 1954-55; instr. White Cross Hosp., Columbus, 1955-57; asso. dir. nursing service Riverside Meth. Hosp., Columbus, 1957-64; asst. exec. dir. Ohio Nurses Assn., Columbus, 1964-65; dean Capital U. Sch. Nursing, Columbus, 1965-72, Coll. Nursing, U. Iowa, Iowa City, 1972-79, prof. nursing, 1972-80; prof. Sch. Nursing U. Miami, Fla., 1980—, dean Fla., 1980-85. Bd. dirs. Health Coun. South Fla., 1988—, pres., 1990-92; bd. dirs. So. Fla. Perinatal Network, Inc., 1980-89, pres., 1984-86; mem. Fla. Bd. Ind. and Pvt. Colls. and Univs., 1980; co-chmn. Dade County Indigent Care Task Force, 1991-93. Author: Florence Nightingale: Her Wit and Wisdom, 1975; author, editor: Thoughts on CareGiving, 1998; contbr. articles to profl. jours. Mem. ANA, Ohio Nurses Assn. (pres. dist. 1966-68), Iowa Nurses Assn., Fla. Nurses Assn., Graceland Univ. Alumni Assn., Am. Assn. Higher Edn., Am. Assn. Colls. Nursing (pres. 1976-78). Home: 416 Park Blvd N Venice FL 34285-1332

BARRON, ARNOLD S., retail executive; Various store operation positions TJX Cos., Inc., 1979—84, sr. v.p., dir. stores, 1984—93, sr. v.p., gen. mdse. mgr. TJ Maxx divsn., 1993—96, sr. v.p., group exec., 1996—2000, exec. v.p., COO Marmaxx Group, 2000—04, sr. exec. v.p., group pres., 2004—. Office: TJX Cos Inc 770 Cochituate Rd Framingham MA 01701 Office Phone: 508-390-1000. Office Fax: 508-390-2091.*

BARRON, BRIGID, education educator; BS in Psychology, U. Calif., Santa Cruz, 1984; MA in Psychology, Vanderbilt U., 1989, PhD in Clin. Developmental Psychology, 1992. Intern in child clin. psychology U. Wash., 1991—92; instr. Peabody Coll., Vanderbilt U., 1992—93; sr. rsch. assoc. Learning Tech. Ctr., Vanderbilt U., 1993—95; asst. prof. edn. Stanford (Calif.) U., 1996—. Mem. adv. bd. tech. task force SPEAK-UP! Leadership Program for Girls; cons. Plugged-In Tech. Access Ctr., Comty. Kids Children's Program. Office: Stanford U Sch Edn 485 Lasuen Mall Stanford CA 94305-3096

BARRON, DAVID JEREMIAH, law educator; b. Washington, July 7, 1967; AB in History, Harvard U., 1989, JD, 1994. Bar: NY 1996. Law clk. to Judge Stephen Reinhardt US Ct. Appeals 9th Cir.; law clk. to Justice John Paul Stevens US Supreme Ct.; atty.-advisor Office Legal Counsel US Dept. Justice; asst. prof. law Harvard Law Sch., Cambridge, Mass., 1999—2004, prof., 2004—. Office: Harvard Law Sch 1563 Massachusetts Ave Cambridge MA 02138 Office Phone: 617-495-8218. Office Fax: 617-495-4863. Business E-Mail: dbarron@law.harvard.edu.

BARRON, HAL S., historian, history professor; b. Louisville, Dec. 29, 1951; m. Katherine T. Kobayashi, June 23, 1977; 1 child, Maya K. BA, Oberlin Coll., Ohio, 1973; MA, U. Pa., Phila., 1976, PhD, 1980. Asst. prof. history Harvey Mudd Coll., Claremont, Calif., 1980—85, assoc. prof. history, 1985—91, prof. history, 1991—, Louisa and Robert Miller prof. humanities, 2005—; mem. grad. history faculty Claremont (Calif.) Grad. U., 1980—. Author: Those Who Stayed Behind: Rural Society in Nineteenth-Century New England, 1984, Mixed Harvest: The Second Great Transformation in the Rural North, 1870-1930, 1997. Recipient Vernon Carstensen award, Agrl. History Soc., 1981, Odyssey award, Mellon Found., 2005—06; Sr. Fellowship, NEH, 1993—94, Fellowship, Huntington Library-Haynes Found., 1988, Newberry Library-NEH, 1986—87. Mem.: Am. Hist. Assn., Agrl. History Soc. (pres. 2005—06), Orgn. of Am. Historians (life). Office: Harvey Mudd Coll 301 Platt Blvd Claremont CA 91711 Home Phone: 626-791-5184; Office Phone: 909-607-3295.

BARRON, HAROLD SHELDON, lawyer; b. Detroit, July 4, 1936; s. George Leslie and Rose (Weinstein) B.; m. Roberta Yellin, Nov. 17, 1963; children: Lawrence Ira, Jean Louise. AB, U. Mich., 1958, JD, 1961. Bar: N.Y. 1963, Mich. 1961, Ill. 1983, Pa. 1992. Pvt. practice, NYC, 1962-68; practice in Southfield, Mich., 1968-83, Chgo., 1983-93, Pa., 1991—2002; atty. Hughes Hubbard & Reed, 1962-68; corp. counsel Bendix Corp., 1968-69, sec., assoc. gen. counsel, 1969-72, sec., gen. counsel, 1972-83, v.p., 1974-83; ptnr. Arnstein, Gluck, Lehr, Barron & Milligan, Chgo., 1983-86, Seyfarth, Shaw, Fairweather & Geraldson, Chgo., 1986-91; v.p., gen. counsel Unisys Corp., Blue Bell, Pa., 1991-92, sr. v.p., gen. counsel, 1992-94, sr. v.p., gen. counsel, sec., 1994-99, sr. v.p., gen. counsel, 1999-2001, vice chmn., 2001—02; counsel McDermott, Will & Emery, 2002—04; gen. counsel Pro-Build Holdings, Inc., 2006—07. Mem. nat. adv. coun. and faculty Practising Law Inst., NYC; bd. dirs. Royal Maccabees Life Ins. Co., Southfield, 1983—94; chmn. bd. F.A. Tucker Group, Inc., 1991—95. Editor: The Business Lawyer. Com. visitors U. Mich. Law Sch.; trustee Children's Hosp. Mich., Detroit, 1976-84; mem. Census Adv. Com. on Privacy and Confidentiality, 1975-76; mem. governing bd., adv. coun. Purdue U. Info. Privacy Rsch. Ctr.; bd. dirs. Citizens Rsch. Coun. of Mich., 1982-83, Greater Phila. Econ. Devel. Coalition. Served with AUS, 1961-62. Mem. ABA (coun. bus. law sect., bus. law sect., chmn. 2002-03, standing com. on fed. judiciary 2003-06, editor The Bus. Lawyer, Latin Am. legal initiatives coun., chmn. com. of corp. gen. counsel, sect. bus. law coun., com. corp. law and taxation, internat. bus. law com., com. devels. in investment svcs., com. long-range issues affecting bus. law practice, com. on corp. laws, commn. on asbestos litigation), Am. Arbitration Assn., Am. Soc. Corp. Secs. (securities law com.), Internat. Inst. Conflict Prevention and Resolution (exec. com., nat. panel disting. neutrals), Am. Law Inst., Mich. Bar Assn., Assn. Bar City NY (com. corp. law depts.), Carlton Club, Chgo. Club, Bryn Mawr Country Club (Chgo.), The Reserve (Indian Wells, Calif.). Office: 980 N Michigan Ave Ste 1400 Chicago IL 60611 Home Phone: 312-337-5642; Office Phone: 312-214-3908. Business E-Mail: hal@barronadr.com.

BARRON, HENRY B., JR., (BREW), energy executive; b. 1950; m. Jacqueline Barron; 2 children. BS in Nuc. Engring., U. Va. Registered profl. engr., NC, SC. Engr. Oconee Nuc. Sta. Duke Energy (Duke Power Co.), SC, 1972, plant engring. and ops. mgmt. positions McGuire Nuc. Sta. NC, supt. ops. Catawba Nuc. Sta. SC, 1986, sta. mgr. Oconee Nuc. Sta., 1990, mgr. nuc. assessment and issues divsn. Nuc. Generation Dept., 1994, v.p. McGuire Nuc. Sta., 1996, sr. v.p. nuc. ops., 2002, chief nuc. officer, 2004—, group exec., 2006—; v.p., gen. mgr. nuc. ops. Idaho Nat. Engring. Lab. Dept. Energy, 1994—96. Chmn. bd. govs. Duke, Cogema and Stone & Webster, LLC, 2002—03. Office: Duke Energy 526 S Church St Charlotte NC 28202-1904 Office Phone: 704-594-6200.*

BARRON, HOWARD ROBERT, lawyer; b. Chgo., Feb. 17, 1930; s. Irwin P. and Ada (Astrahan) B.; m. Marjorie Shapira, Aug. 12, 1953; children: Ellen Barron Feldman, Laurie A. PhB, U. Chgo., 1948; BA, Stanford U., 1950; LLB, Yale U., 1953. Bar: Ill. 1953. Assoc. Jenner & Block, Chgo., 1957-63, ptnr., 1964-97; assoc. Schiff Hardin, Chgo., 1953, of counsel, 1997—. Contbr. articles to profl. jours. and books. Mem., then pres. Lake County Sch. Dist. 107 (now Dist. 112) Bd. Edn., Highland Park, 1964-71; pres. Lake County Sch. Bd. Assn., 1970-71; mem. Lake County High Sch. Dist. 113 Bd. Edn., Highland Park, 1973-77; mem. Highland Park Zoning Bd. Appeals, 1984-89. Lt. (j.g.) USNR, 1953-57. Mem.: ABA (com. corp. counsel litigation sect. 1983—2002, co-chmn. subcom. labor and employment law), Yale Club (N.Y.C.), Met. Club, Internat. Bar Assn., Yale Law Sch. Assn. of Ill. (pres. 1962), Yale Law Sch. Assn. (v.p. 1978—81), Chgo. Bar Assn., Fed. Bar Assn., Ill. State Bar Assn. (chmn. antitrust sect. 1968—69, sr. counselor 2003), Standard Club. Democrat. Home: 1366 Sheridan Rd Highland Park IL 60035-3407 Office: Schiff Hardin LLP 6600 Sears Tower Chicago IL 60606 Home Phone: 847-433-1288; Office Phone: 312-258-5558. Personal E-mail: hrb1366@aol.com. Business E-Mail: hbarron@schiffhardin.com.

BARRON, ILONA ELEANOR, elementary school educator, consultant; b. Sept. 19, 1929; m. George Barron; 1 child, Fred. Cert. elem. tchg., No. Mich. U., 1951; BS in Elem. Edn., Ctrl. Mich. U., 1961; MA in Edn., U. Mich., 1966; postgrad., Mich. State U. Cert. reading specialist. Tchr. Elem. Schs., 1952—67; dir. Title I reading Saginaw Twp. Cmty. Schs., Mich., 1967—68, reading cons., 1971—. Cons. elem. intern Mich. State U., East Lansing, 1968—71; cons. elem. reading Saginaw Twp. Pub. Schs., 1972—. Mem.: NEA, Saginaw Area Reading Coun., Saginaw Twp. Edn. Assn., Mich. Edn. Assn. Achievements include development of methods of teaching developmental reading skills and enrichment. Home (Winter): 35702 Clubber Ct Zephyrhills FL 33541 Home (Summer): 25366 W State Hwy M 64 Ontonagon MI 49953

BARRON, JAMES TURMAN, journalist; b. Washington, Dec. 25, 1954; s. James Pressley and Leirona Faith (Turman) B.; m. Jane-Iris Farhi, Apr. 1, 1995. AB cum laude, Princeton U., 1977. Copy person NY Times, NYC, 1977-78, rsch. asst., 1978-79, reporter, 1979—, acting editor, The Living Sect., 1996-97; broadcast corespondent Sta. WQXR-FM, NYC, 1987—; broadcast corr. Sta. WQEW-AM, NYC, 1992-98; writer Pub. Lives column NY Times, 1998—2001; writer Boldface Names column, 2001—02; writer, narrator Page One Discovery Times Channel, 2005—06. Author: Piano: The Making of a Steinway Concert Grand, 2006. Mem. Princeton Club of NY, Deadline Club NY (asst. treas. 1993-95, v.p. 1995-99) Methodist. Office: 620 Eighth Ave New York NY 10018-1405

BARRON, JOHN, editor; BA in Journalism, Marquette U. Asst. editor Crain's Chgo. Bus., 1980—84; with Detroit Monthly, 1984—95, editor, 1991—94; positions including reporter, Sunday Showcase editor, dep. features editor, features editor Chgo. Sun-Times, 1995—2003, exec. mng. editor, 2003—05, editor-in-chief, 2005—06; exec. editor Sun-Times News Group, Chgo., 2006—. Office: Chgo Sun Times 350 N Orleans Chicago IL 60654 Office Phone: 312-321-3000. Business E-Mail: jbarron@suntimes.com.

BARRON, MICHAEL K., lawyer; BA, Northwestern U., 1982; JD, Boston U. Sch. Law, 1985. Bar: Mass. 1985. Ptnr. Nixon Peabody LLP, DLA Piper US LLP, Boston, 2006—. Founder Mass. Innovation & Tech. Exch., 1995—, gen. counsel, mem. exec. com.; mem. Mass. Biotechnology Coun., MIT Enterprise Forum. Named Mass. Super Lawyer, Boston Mag., 2005. Mem.: Licensing Exec. Soc., Internat. Trademark Assn., Boston Bar Assn. Office: DLA Piper US LLP 33 Arch st 26th Fl Boston MA 02110-1447 Office Phone: 617-406-6006. Office Fax: 617-406-6106.*

BARRON, MYRA HYMOVICH, lawyer; b. July 5, 1938; d. Leo and Lillian Estelle (Berman) Hymovich; m. Jerome Aure Barron, June 18, 1961; children: Jonathan Nathaniel, David Jeremiah, Jennifer Leah. AB cum laude, Smith Coll., 1959; student, L'Institut des Hautes Etudes, Geneva, 1957—58; MA, Johns Hopkins U., 1961; JD, Georgetown U., 1970. Bar: Va. 70, DC 72, NY. Instr. econs. U. ND, Grand Forks, 1962—64; econ. rsch. asst. U. N.Mex., Albuquerque, 1964—65; legal aid staff atty. Fairfax County, Va., 1971—72, asst. county atty. Va., 1974—81; counsel Fairfax County Redevel. and Housing Authority, Fairfax, Va., 1981—88; assoc. Melvin & Melvin, Syracuse, NY, 1973; ptnr. Sprenger & Lang (formerly Weissbrodt, Swiss & Mc Grew), 1989—98, Weinberg & Jacobs, Rockville, Md., 1998—2000, of counsel, 2001—04. Dep. gen. counsel Housing and Devel. Law Inst., 1988—94, of counsel, 1994—2000. Editor: Jour. Affordable Housing and Cmty. Devel. Law, ABA, 1993—99; contbr. articles to housing jours.; mem.: Georgetown Law Jour., 1967—68. Recipient Samuel Bowles award, Smith Coll., 1959. Mem.: LWV (local chmn. nat. events 1962—64), ABA (mem. governing com. 1994—99, co-chmn. profit practice group 2000—03, mem. forum on affordable housing and cmty. devel. law). Home: 3231 Ellicott St NW Washington DC 20008-2061 Personal E-mail: mhbarron@earthlink.net.

BARRON, PATRICK KENNETH, bank executive; b. Atlanta, Aug. 10, 1945; s. Seward Golden and Azzie Lee (Wilson) B.; m. Martha Ann Morgan, Sept. 3, 1965; children: Christina Lee, Deborah Ann, John Patrick. BBA cum laude, Miami U., Fla., 1975; postgrad., Harvard U., 1984. Supr. Fed. Res. Bank, Atlanta, 1967-71, asst. v.p. Miami, 1974—82, branch mgr., 1982—87, sr. v.p., 1987—91, first v.p. San Francisco, 1991—96, 1st v.p., COO Atlanta, 1996—, interim pres., 2006—. Mem. adv. coun. Fla. Internat. U., Miami, 1988-89; vice chmn., exec. com. Greater Miami C. of C., 1985-88; mem. fin. com. United Way of Dade County, Miami, 1984-88; rep. United Way, Atlanta, 1989; mem. Leadership Atlanta, 1989-90; mem. pres.'s coun. U. Miami, 1992—. Mem. Am. Inst. Banking, Beta Gamma Sigma. Republican. Lutheran. Avocations: tennis, running, gardening, reading. Office: Fed Res Bank 1000 Peachtree St NE Atlanta GA 30309

BARRON, ROS, artist; b. Boston, July 4, 1933; d. Louis and Ida (Titel) Myers; m. Harris Barron, Apr. 19, 1953; children: Matt Lewis, Nina Rebecca. B.F.A., Mass. Coll. Art, 1954. Fellow Bunting Inst., Harvard U., 1966-68; co-dir. Zone Visual Theater Co., 1970; assoc. prof. art U. Mass.-Harbor Campus, Boston, 1974—. Vis. artist U. Colo., Boulder, 1983; presenter Arts at the Bunting, 1997. Producer numerous video performance tapes.; one-woman shows include North Hall Gallery, Mass. Coll. Art, Boston, 1988, Watson Gallery, Wheaton Coll., Norton, Mass., 1989, Harbor Gallery U. Mass., Boston, 1990, Mobius, Boston, 1993, Brick Bottom Gallery, Boston, 1996; exhbns. include Whitney Mus. Am. Art, 1967-68, Helen Shlien Gallery, Boston, 1979, 82, Mus. Modern Art, NYC, 1980, 84, Le Nouveau Musee, Lyon, France, 1979, Montevideo Gallery, Amsterdam, Holland, 1979, World Wide Video Festival, Kijkhuis, Holland, 1984, Hirschhorn Mus., Washington, 1984, North Hall Gallery; travelling group exhbns. include Project Rembrandt Biennial, 1991-92, Women's Caucus for Art, 1992; represented in permanent collections Mus. Fine Arts, Boston, Harvard U., Smith Coll. Collection, Worcester Art Mus., Addison Gallery Am. Art., Inst. Contemporary Art, Boston, Samuel P. Harn Mus. Art, U. Fla., Gainesville, Mus. Modern Art, NYC; performance Art: (with Harris Barron) Mr. & Mrs. Zone: Art Life Art, Mobius Theatre, Boston, 1987, Performance Art: (with Harris Barron) Mr. & Mrs. Zone Again, Mobius Theatre, Boston, 1997, Eartheart and other video works, Mobius Theatre, Boston, 1999, Eagle Air, The Life and Work of Harris Barron, 2001, Magritte Meets Descartes, 2007; (exhibitions) Magritte Quartet, Mus. Fine Arts, Boston, 2007. Bd. dirs. Boston Performance Artists. Recipient Design award HUD, 1968; grantee NY Found. for Arts, 1972, Guggenheim Found., 1972, Nat. Endowment Arts, 1975, Rockefeller Found., 1978-80, Mass. Council Arts, 1981-83, Mass. Cultural Coun., 2007, LEF Found., West, 2007, Mass. Cultural Coun., LLC, Brookline, 2007. Address: 30 Webster Pl Brookline MA 02445-7937 Office Phone: 617-232-9544. *I am a visual artist. As a painter and video artist, my work involves how I see and transform reality. My life force feels the ontological mystery, an intense state of wonder, and the endlessness of seeing. Strategies of surrealism and the transformational process provide emotional, intellectual, and metaphysical coherence to my work.*

BARRON, (MARY LOU) SLATER, artist, retired educator; b. East Orange, NJ, July 2, 1930; d. Louis and Williamina Fullerton Slater; m. Thurston B. Barron, July 7, 1950 (div. 1976); children: Janet, J. Scott, Jennifer, Maribeth. BA in Sociology and Psychology, Susquehanna U., 1951; postgrad., Orange Coast Coll., 1972—74; BA in Studio Art, U. Calif., Irvine, 1975; MFA in Drawing and Painting, Calif. State U., Long Beach, 1978. Lifetime C.C. credential Calif. Instr. design Brooks Coll., Long Beach, 1978—2000; instr. art Calif. State U., Long Beach, 1978, 1984; instr. design Fashion Inst. Design and Merchandising, LA, Interior Design Inst., Irvine, Calif., U. Calif., Irvine. Pres. artists' coun. Long Beach Mus. Art, 1993; mem. adv. bd. for pub. art Pub. Corp. Arts, Long Beach, 1995—98. One-woman shows include Four Wall Studio, Santa Ana, Calif., 1974, The Floating Wall, Santa Ana, 1975, Orange Coast Coll., Costa Mesa, Calif., 1976, Calif. State U., Long Beach, 1978, Stage One Gallery, Orange, Calif., 1981, Fiberworks Gallery, Berkeley, Calif., 1981, Loyola Marymount U., L.A., 1983, Long Beach City Coll., 1984, Mus. Ariz. State U., Tempe, 1986, Mendenhall Gallery, Whittier (Calif.) Coll., 1988, Guggenheim Gallery, Chapman Coll., Orange, 1992, Watkins Gallery, Queens Coll., Charlotte, N.C., 1992, Pacific Place, San Pedro, Calif., 1998, Chez Shaw Gallery, Long Beach, Calif., 2005, Utopia, Long Beach, 2005, IGM Gallery, U. So. Calif., LA, 2007, exhibited in group shows at El Camino Coll. Gallery, Torrance, Calif., 1997, 2003, 2005, Orange County Ctr. for Contemporary Art, Santa Ana, 1998, Commune di Orzinuovia, Brescia, Italy, 1999, Main Libr., Long Beach, 1999, Eleven Seven Gallery, 1999, Long Beach Mus. Art, 2000, Long Beach City Coll., 2001, Furlong Art Gallery, U. Wis., Stout, 2001—02, many others, Represented in permanent collections Long Beach Mus. Art, Laguna Beach Mus. Art, L.A. County Mus. Art, Smithsonian White House Collection, Ripley's Believe It or Not!, many others; author: Remembering the Forgetting, 2007. Lt. (j.g.) USN, 1953—55. Named Visual Artist of Yr., Pub. Corp. Arts, 1987—88. Home: 2299 Oregon Ave Long Beach CA 90806

BARRON, STEPHANIE, curator; AB, Barnard Coll., Columbia U., 1972; student, Harvard Inst. Arts Adminstrn., 1973; MA, Columbia U., 1974; postgrad., CUNY, 1975-76. Intern, curatorial asst. Solomon R. Guggenheim Mus., 1971-72; Nat. Endowment Arts intern in edn. Toledo Mus. Art, 1973-74; exhbn. coord. Jewish Mus., NYC, 1975-76; assoc. curator modern art L.A. County Mus. Art, 1976-80, curator Twentieth Century art, 1980-94, coord. curatorial affairs, 1993-96, sr. curator Twentieth Century art, 1995—, v.p. edn. and pub. programs, 1996—2003; chief curator Modern and Contemporary Art, 2002—. Lectr., panelist in field. Contbr. articles to profl. jours. Mem. art adv. panel IRS, 1996—; advisor U.S. Holocaust Mus., 1996—; trustee Scripps Coll., 1996—; mem. steering com. Villa Aurora, 1994—; mem. bd. Stiftung Mortizburg, Halle, Germany, 2005-, Magritte Assn., 2005-. Decorated comdr.'s cross Fed. Republic of Germany, Order of Merit (Germany); recipient George L. Wittenborn award ARLIS, 1991, award for best Am. exhbn. of yr. Assn. Internat. Critics Art, 1991, 97, Theo Wormland Kunstpreis, 1992, George L. Wittenborn award, 1992, Alfred H. Barr Jr. award Coll. Art Assn., 1992, E.L. Kirchner prize, Switzerland, 1997, First Pl. award Am. Assn. Art Mus., 1998, Hon. Mention, ARLIS, 1998; named Woman of Yr., Bus. and Profl. Women of UJA, Jewish Fedn., 1991, Friends of Tel Hashomer, 1991; Nat. Endowment of Arts fellow, 1986-87; John J. McCloy fellow in art, 1981. Fellow Am. Acad. Arts and Scis.; mem. Am. Assn. Mus., Internat. Mus. Modern Art (internat. com. mus.), Internat. Coun. Mus., Internat. Com. for Mus. and Collections of Modern Art, Art Table. Office: LA County Mus Art 5905 Wilshire Blvd Los Angeles CA 90036-4597 Business E-Mail: sbarron@lacma.org.

BARRON, SUSAN, clinical psychologist; b. Chgo., May 13, 1940; d. Earl and Trixie (Chernoff) B.; m. Eugene Pratt, Jan. 18, 1975 (div. 1983). BBA, CCNY, 1960, MA, 1963; PhD, CUNY, 1973. Lic. psychologist, diplomate Am. Bd. Psychol. Specialties, bd. cert. fellow Am. Coll. Advanced Practice Psychologists, cert. alcohol and related substance abuse APA Coll. Profl. Psychology. Intern psychologist Bellevue Psychiat. Hosp., NYC, 1964-65, psychologist, 1966-67; tchg. fellow CUNY, 1965-66; staff psychologist Lighthouse, N.Y. Assn. for the Blind, NYC, 1968-71, sr. clin. psychologist, 1971-74; dir. psychol. counseling svcs. Peninsula Ctr. for the Blind, Palo Alto, Calif., 1974-75; cons. psychologist N.Y. State Commn. for Blind and Visually Handicapped, NYC, 1975-78, 86—; dir. psychol. svcs. Thoms Rehab. Hosp., Asheville, NC, 1978-79; state coord. psychol. svcs. N.Y. State Office Vocat. Rehab., Albany, 1979-85; founder, dir. Family Support Program ICU N.Y. Infirmary-Beekman Downtown Hosp., NYC, 1982-84; cons. clin. psychologist N.Y. Hosp. Cornell U. Med. Ctr., 1987—; pvt. practice, 1987—; behavioral scientist diabetes control/complications trial NIH Cornell U. Med. Ctr., NYC, 1987—; cons. clin. psychologist Joslin Ctr. for Diabetes St. Luke's-Roosevelt Hosp. Ctr./Columbia U. Phys. and Surg., NYC, 1994-95. Cons. clin. psychologist Joslin Ctr. Diabetes, St. Lukes-Roosevelt Hosp. Ctr., U. Hosp. of Columbia U. Coll. of Physicians and Surgeons, N.Y.C., 1994-95, Health Psychology Assocs., Calif., 1997—, N.Y.C., 1997—; mem. Nat. Human Svcs. Adv. Bd.-Retinitis Pigmentosa Found., Balt., 1975-82; cons. Del. State Commn. for Blind, 1975-78, Am. Found. Blind, 1974-82, Calif. Dept. Rehab., 1974-82, Hawaii State Svcs. Blind, 1974-82, Ariz. State Svcs. Blind, 1974-82, Nev. State Svcs. Blind, 1974-82; spkr. Nat. Multiple Disabilities Conf., 1982, NAS, 1981; mem. adv. bd. doctoral psychology internship program Rusk Inst. of Rehab. Medicine, NYU Med. Ctr., 1979-84; behavioral scientist Diabetes Control and Complications Trial NIH-Cornell U. Med. Ctr., 1987—; mem. mended hearts NYU Med. Ctr., Cardiac Prevention and Rehab. Ctr.; group leader nat. tele-support network Parents of Blind and Visually Impaired Children, Jewish Guild for Blind, NYC, 2006—. Contbr. articles to profl. jours. Recipient Leadership award Alumni Assn. CCNY, 1960, 62, Rsch. award Retinal Dystrophy Soc., Australia, 1975, Charles H. Best medal for disting. svc. Am. Diabetes Assn., 1994. Fellow Am. Coll. Advanced Practice Psychologists (bd. cert.), Am. Orthopsychiat. Assn. (life); mem. APA, AAAS, Am. Coll. Forensic Examiners, Calif. State Psychol. Assn., N.Y. Acad. Scis., Mended Hearts. Office: 347 5th Ave Rm 603 New York NY 10016-5010 Office Phone: 212-686-7270.

BARRON, THOMAS WILLIS, real estate broker; b. Newnan, Ga., Apr. 9, 1949; s. Lindsey Hand and Genet Louise (Heery) B.; m. Margaret Rose MacLennan, Aug. 17, 1973; children: Catharine Lindsey, Thomas Willis Jr., John Taliaferro Gaines. BA, Emory U., 1971; JD, Mercer U., 1974. Assoc. Sanders, Mottola, Haugen, Wood, Goodson and Odom, Newnan, 1974-77; v.p. Lindsey's, Inc., Newnan, 1977—; pres. Coweta Developers, Inc., Newnan, 1977—. Dir., mem. local adv. bd., past chmn. BB&T (formerly First Citizens Bank); dir., mem. exec. com. Ga. MLS, Inc., Atlanta. Dir., sec.-treas. Newnan Hosp., 1992—2005, chmn. bd., 1997—2002, past chmn.; trustee Mercer U., Macon, Ga., 1990—95, 1996—97, 2002—06, Coweta Cmty. Found., 1999; past pres. Newnan-Coweta United Way, 1982—; past pres. Newnan Coweta chpt. ARC, 1980—; chmn. deacons Bapt. Ch., 1988—89, 1995—96, 2004—05. Mem. Newnan-Coweta Bd. Realtors (past pres. 1984—, Realtor of Yr. 1991, Million Dollar Club 1989—, Phoenix award 1999), Newnan Country Club (past dir.), Newnan Kiwanis Club (past pres.), Sigma Chi (life, past consul), Newnan-Coweta C. of C. (chmn. bd. 1994). Baptist. Avocations:

sports, history, historical autographs. Office: Lindseys Inc Realtors 14 Jackson St Newnan GA 30263-1929 Office Phone: 770-253-6990. Business E-Mail: chipb@lindseysrealtors.com.

BARROS, COLLEEN, federal agency administrator; BS, U. Md.; MPA, Am. U. With NIH, 1979—, budget analyst, 1979, sr. adminstrv. officer Office of Dir.; assoc. dir. adminstrn. Nat. Inst. Aging, 1995—2004; acting dep. dir. mgmt. NIH, 2004, dep. dir. mgmt., CFO, 2004—. Recipient PHS Superior Svc. Award, 1995, Presdl. Rank Award, 2003, 4 NIH Dir.'s Awards.

BARROS, PAULINO R., JR., communications executive; b. Sao Paulo, Brazil; Degrees in mech. and elec. engring.; MBA, Wash. U., 1991. Several positions Nutrasweet Co., Chgo., Monsanto Co., St. Louis & Brazil; corp. v.p. Latin Am. group personal comm. Motorola, 1996—2000; pres. BellSouth Latin Am. group BellSouth, 2000—04, chief product officer, 2005—06; pres. global ops. AT&T Corp., 2007—. Named one of 50 Most Important Hispanics in Tech. & Bus., Hispanic Engr. & Info. Tech. mag., 2005. Office: BellSouth 2180 Lake Blvd Ste 1237 Atlanta GA 30319

BARROW, CHARLES HERBERT, investment banker; b. Evanston, Ill., July 23, 1930; m. Patricia Wandelt, Dec. 27, 1952; children: Paula, Carla, Barbara. AB, Princeton U., 1952; MBA, U. Chgo., 1956. With No. Trust Co., Chgo., 1952-86, v.p., 1962-68, sr. v.p., 1968-74, exec. v.p., 1974-78, sr. exec. v.p., 1978-81, pres., 1981-86, also dir.; with Blunt Ellis & Loewi, Inc. Kemper Securities, Inc., Chgo., 1987-91, sr. dir., 1987-91; mng. dir. Everen Securities, Inc. (formerly Kemper Securities, Inc.), 1991-99; sr. advisor Howe Barnes Investments, 1999—. Sr. advisor Sumitomo Trust and Banking Co., 1989-93; life mem. adv. coun. J.L. Kellogg Grad. Sch. of Mgmt., Northwestern U. Bd. dirs. Planned Parenthood Assn., Chgo., 1965-81, pres., 1972-73; bd. dirs. Rehab. Inst. Chgo., 1974—, chmn., 1982-83; trustee McCormick Theol. Sem., Chgo., 1984-95, treas., 1988-92, chmn., 1992-95, nat. trustee, 1995-96, trustee, 1996-2004, life trustee, 2004—. Mem. Comml. Club, Univ. Club, Commonwealth Club, Econ. Club, Bankers Club (pres. 1979-80), Bond Club, Glen View Club (Ill.), Michigan Shores Club (Wilmette, Ill.), Ocean Reef Club (Key Largo, Fla.), Pentwater (Mich.) Yacht Club. Presbyterian. Office Phone: 312-655-2976.

BARROW, CLYDE WAYNE, social sciences educator; b. Alice, Tex., Feb. 15, 1956; s. Floyd Smith and Wanda Ruth (Conner) B. BA in Polit. Sci., Tex. A&I U., 1977; MA in Polit. Sci., UCLA, 1979, PhD in Polit. Sci., 1984. Teaching fellow UCLA, 1978-82, dir. instrnl. devel., 1982-84; vis. asst. prof. U. Tex., San Antonio, 1984-85, Tex. A&M U., College Station, 1985-87; from asst. prof. to prof. polit. sci. U. Mass. at Dartmouth, North Dartmouth, 1987-96, prof., 1996—2003, acting chmn. dept., 1992-93, 95, sr. rsch. assoc. Ctr. for Policy Analysis, 1993-94, dir. Ctr. for Policy Analysis, 1994—, chancellor prof. policy studies, 2004—. Mem. adv. bd. Arnold Dubin Labor Edn. Ctr., North Dartmouth, 1988—; policy cons. Office of Mayor, City of Fall River, Mass., 1993—, New Bedford CEO Club, 1994—99, Fall River Sch. Dept., 1995—, Sandwich Sch. Dept., 1996—2004, New Bedford Housing Authority, 1999—2004, Lowell Sch. Dept., 2003—04; exec. staff analyst Gov.'s Commn. on Commonwealth Port Devel., Mass., 1994, Gov.'s Regional Econ. Devel. Strategies Project, 1996, 2000—01; regional analyst Mass. Benchmark Project, 1997—; pub. mem. Cranberry Mktg. Com., 2003—06; chmn., bd. dirs. Fund Higher Edn. Rsch., 2003—06. Author: Universities and the Capitalist State, 1990, Critical Theories of the State, 1993, More Than a Historian: The Political and Economic Thought of Charles A. Beard, 2000, Economic Impacts of the Textile and Apparel Industries in Massachusetts, 2000, Portuguese-Americans and Contemporary Civic Culture in Massachusetts, 2002; co-author: Globalisation Trade Liberalisation and Higher Education in North America, 2003; co-editor Class, Power, and the State in Capitalist Society, 2007; assoc. editor New Polit. Sci., 2005—; mem. bd. editors Am. Academic, 2003-05, Sociol. Inquiry, 1992-95, Jour. Politics, 1993-97; mng. editor New England Jour. Pub. Policy, 1994-97; also articles. Recipient Fontera Meml. award Arnold Dubin Labor Edn. Ctr., 1991, Disting. Svc. award Mass. Fedn. Tchrs., 2001. Mem. Am. Polit. Sci. Assn., Western Polit. Sci. Assn., Caucus for a New Polit. Sci., Policy Studies Orgn., U. Mass. Faculty Fedn. (treas. 1991-96, 2002-03, pres. 1998-2000). Office: U Mass Ctr Policy Analysis 285 Old Westport Rd North Dartmouth MA 02747-2356 Office Phone: 508-999-9265. Business E-Mail: cbarrow@umassd.edu.

BARROW, IRENE MARIE, speech pathology educator; d. Robert Earl and Gloria Ceclia Dziesinski; m. Richard Dowell Barrow, II; children: Rachel Marie, Olivia Anne. BS in Comm. Disorders, Ctrl. Mich. U., Mt. Pleasant, 1982; MA in Speech Lang. Pathology, Ctrl. Mich. U., 1983; PhD in Comm. Scis. and Disorders, E.Carolina U., Greenville, NC, 2001. Cert. clinical competence-speech-lang. pathologist Am. Speech-Lang.-Hearing Assn., 1984. Lectr., supr. Tex. A&M U., Kingsville, 1991—93, dir. comm. disorders clinic, lectr., supr., 1995—97; speech-lang. pathologist Dianne Epplien & Assocs., Va. Beach, 1993—95, Pitt County Meml. Hosp., Greenville, 1997—99; pvt. practice Greenville, 1998—2001; assoc. prof. Hampton U., Va., 2001—. Contbr. articles to profl. jours. Grantee Rsch. grant, Hampton U., 2004—05. Mem.: Gt. Bridge Band Parents Assn. (hospitality co-chair 2005—07), Speech-Lang.-Hearing Assn. Va. (licentiate; v.p. speech pathology 2005—, coord. call for papers 2005—07), Am. Speech-Lang.-Hearing Assn. (licentiate). Achievements include research in confrontation naming following a mild traumatic brain injury; naming following a mild traumatic brain injury; the longitudinal effects of an auditory distraction following a mild traumatic brain injury; filtered auditory feedback and reading disabilties; the effect of color on picture naming in children; the effect of dimension on picture naming in children; discriptive discourse following brain injury; the influence of pause length on the comprehension of phrases. Avocations: basketry, candy making. Office: Hampton Univ Dept Communicative Scis and Disorders 201 Sci & Tech Hampton VA 23668 Office Fax: 767-727-5765; Home Fax: 757-727-5765. Business E-Mail: irene.barrow@hamptonu.edu.

BARROW, JOHN JENKINS, congressman, lawyer; b. Athens, Ga., Oct. 31, 1955; s. James and Phyllis (Jenkins) B.; m. Victoria Pentlarge, Dec. 19, 1953; children: James, Ruth. AB, U. Ga., 1976; JD, Harvard U., 1979. Bar: Ga., US Dist. Ct. (no. and mid. dists.) Ga., US Ct. Appeals (11th cir.), US Ct. Appeals (5th cir.). Clk. to Hon. Tom Clark US Ct. Appeals, Tampa, Fla., 1979-81; assoc. Winburn & Assocs., Athens, Ga., 1981-83; ptnr. Winburn, Lewis Barrow & Stolz, PC, Athens, Ga., 1983—2004; mem. US Congress from 12th Ga. dist., 2005—, mem. edu. and workforce com., agriculture com. & small bus. com., ranking mem. subcom. on rural enterprise, agriculture, and tech. Mem. rev. panel State Bar Disciplinary Bd., 1997-99; mem. Ga. Com. on Continuing Lawyer Competency, 1984-87. Commr. Athens-Clarke County Commn., Athens, 1990-2004. Mem. Ga. Trial Lawyers Assn., Assn. Trial Lawyers Am. Democrat. Baptist. Avocations: politics, tennis, backpacking, sports. Office: US Ho Reps 226 Cannon Ho Office Bldg Washington DC 20515-1012 also: Dist Office Ste G 400 Mall Blvd Savannah GA 31406 Office Phone: 202-225-2823. Office Fax: 202-225-3377.*

BARROW, LIONEL CEON, JR., communications and marketing consultant; b. NYC, Dec. 17, 1926; s. Lionel Ceon and Wilhelmina Barrow; m. Frederica Harrison; children: Lia, Kirsten Erin; stepchildren: Brenda Marie Feliciano, Aurea Nellie (dec.), Rhonda Patricia (dec.), Emily Harrison Smith, Laura Harrison. BA in English, Morehouse Coll., 1948; MA in Journalism, U. Wis., 1958, PhD in Mass Communications, 1960. Reporter Richmond Afro-Am., Va., 1953-54; teaching and research asst. U. Wis., Madison, 1954-60; asst. prof. dept. communication Mich. State U., Lansing, 1960-61; research project dir. Bur. Advt., NYC, 1961-63; research project supr. Kenyon & Eckhardt Advt. Agy., NYC, 1963-64; research group head Foote Cone & Belding, NYC, 1964-68, assoc. research dir., v.p., 1968-71; chmn. dept. Afro-Am. studies U. Wis., Milw., 1971-72, 74-75, prof. mass comms. and Afro-Am. studies, 1971-75; dean Sch. Communications Howard U., Washington, 1975-85, prof. communications, 1975-86; pres. The Barrow Info. Group, Columbia, Md., 1986—. Vis. prof. Stanford U., 1971, Ohio State U., 1986; pres. Journalism Coun. Inc., 1971-79; sec. elected advs. Md. Conf. on Small Bus., 1987-89. Contbr. articles to profl. jours. Active Higher Edn. Group Washington, 1985-92. Served with AUS, 1945-47, 50-53. Recipient media citation Journalism Edn. Assn., 1974; recipient radio pioneer award Medgar Evers Coll., 1979 Mem. Assn. for Edn. in Journalism and Mass Comms. (founder, first head minorities and comm. divsn. 2003, chair commn. on the status of minorities 2003-05), Nat. Assn. Black Journalists, Soc. Profl. Journalists, Capitol Press Club, NAACP (life), 24th Inf. Regimental Combat Team Assn. (life, Combat Inf. badge). Home: 17842 Arbor Greene Dr Tampa FL 33647-3136

BARROW, RICHARD EDWARD, architect; b. Birmingham, Ala., Feb. 3, 1940; s. Ralph A. and Hazel C. (McElroy) B.; m. Sylvia Ann Scherl, Sept. 28, 1963; children: Lisa Dawn, Kathryn Heather. BArch, Auburn U., 1963; postgrad., U. Utah, 1967-69. Reg. architect Ala., Utah. Draftsman Edward M. Paul Architects, Birmingham, 1960-63, Paul Lemoine Architects, Salt Lake City, 1967-68, Dean Gustavson, FAIA, Salt Lake City, 1968-69; project mgr. Marcellous Wright & Ptnrs., Richmond, Va., 1969-71; project architect Cobb, Adams, & Benton, Birmingham, 1971-77; ptnr. Arnold & Barrow Architects, Birmingham, 1977-84, Waters, Barrow & Assocs., Inc., Birmingham, 1984-89; pvt. practice Birmingham, 1989-93; pres. Richard E. Barrow Architects, Inc., Birmingham, 1994—. Mem. Ala. Bd. for Registration of Architects, Montgomery, 1988-2000, chair, 1992-93, 99; mem. archtl. adv. com. Auburn U., 1982-89, chair, 1988, 95-96; bldg. com. Wesley Student Ctr. Jacksonville (Ala.) State U., 1991; R&D subcom. Nat. Coun. Archtl. Registration Bds., Washington, 1992-95, coord. graphics, 1995, archtl. registration exam. subcom., 1996-98, coord., 1997, profl. devel. program com., 1999-2000, mem. interior design task force, 2000; renovations include Women's Pavillion, U. Ala. at Birmingham Hosp., 1985, Cahaba Heights United Meth. Ch., 1989; architect new facilities including Asbury United Meth. Ch., 1986, Sumatanga Retreat Ctr., 1992, Green Acres Mid. Sch., 2000. Bd. dirs. So. region Nat. Coun. Archtl. Registration Bds., 1996-99, New Life Harvest Mission, Birmingham, 1990-96, Blue Lake (Ala.) Emmaus Cmty., 1990-91, Ala. Young Adult Chrysalis, treas. 1995-97; mem. adv. bd. WBHM Pub. Radio, 1996-98. Capt. USAF, 1963-67. NIH fellow, 1967. Fellow AIA (Richard Upjohn fellow 1992, Pres.'s award 1979, 81, 82, Henry Adams Book award). Republican. Methodist. Avocations: flying, golf. Home: 1800 International Park Dr Ste 250 Birmingham AL 35243-4240 E-mail: reb@rebarrow.com.

BARROW, ROBERT EARL, retired agricultural fraternal executive; b. Swansea, Mass., Jan. 30, 1930; s. Charles H. and Etta (Campbell) B.; m. Dolores A. Pannoni, Jan. 30, 1954; children: Kyle A. Kawa, Susan E. Gregory. Grad. high sch., Swansea, 1948. Sr. v.p. 1st Fed. Savs. & Loan Assn., Providence, 1949-77; mgr. Old Red Bank, Fall River, Mass., 1978-79; mgr. bookkeeping Uncle Matty's Tropical Gardens, Warwick, RI, 1980-87; sec. Nat. Grange, Washington, 1983-85, lectr., program dir., 1985-87, pres., 1987-95; sec. Mass. State Grange, 1997—2001; ret., 2001. Master Swansea Grange #148, 1959-60, Bay State Pomona #33, 1965-66, Mass. State, 1981-85. Mem. Bretton Woods Com., 1988—, Agrl. Policy Adv. Com., 1988-94, transp. alternatives group Transp. 2020, 1988, 4-H Coun., 1988—, Bd. Hwy. Users Fedn., 1988—, Nat. Farm Coalition, 1988—, Coalition for Fiscal Restraint, 1988—. With U.S. Army, 1951-53. Avocations: singing, gardening, bell collecting.

BARROW, SALLY SETTLE, retired media specialist, retired librarian; b. Moore Haven, Fla. m. John Guy Barrow, III, June 15, 1969 (div. Jan. 19, 2001); children: Mollie Susan Barrow-Huggins, John Daniel. BA, Fla. State U., Tallahassee, FL, 1969; MSLS, Fla. State U., Tallahassee, FL, 1987. Cert. in Mental Retardation Fla. State U., 1974. Tchr. Duval County Sch. Bd., Duval County, Fla., 1970—72, media specialist, 1970—72; educator Jefferson County Sch. Bd., Jefferson County, Fla., 1974—88; media specialist Duval County Sch. Bd., Long Br. Elem., Jacksonville, Fla., 1988—93, Duval County Sch. Bd., Ctrl. Riverside Elem., Jacksonville, Fla., 1993—2007. Tchr. rep. Demse Title III. Contbr. co-author for curriculum guide; author: In the Shadow of the Lone Cypress, 2003. County coord. Fla. Spl. Olympics, 1982—86, Fla. Big Bend Spl. Arts Festival, 1983—88; educator First Nazarene Ch., Monticello, Fla., 1984—88, libr., 1984—88; active, libr. First Presbyn. Ch., Fernandina Beach, Fla., 2000—04; vacation bible sch. tchr. and coord. First United Meth. Ch., Monticello, 1970—89; tchr. Nassau Nazarene Ch., Yulee, Fla., 1984—88, coord. social teas, 1993—99. Recipient Outstanding Young Women Award, Outstanding Young Women Award, 1982, Selected Participant, Teachers' Seminar Fla. Humanities Coun., 1996. Mem.: Duval County Media Educators In Action, Fla. Humanities Coun., Duval County Reading Coun., Alpha Delta Kappa, Beta Phi Mu Libr. Sci. Honor Frat. D-Liberal. Presbyterian. Avocation: studying Florida history. Office: Central Riverside Elementary School 2555 Gilmore Street Jacksonville FL 32204 Home: PO Box 2362 Yulee FL 32041-2362 Personal E-mail: barrows2@net-magic.net, barrows2@adelphia.net.

BARROW, THOMAS DAVIES, retired oil and mining company executive, consultant; b. San Antonio, Dec. 27, 1924; s. Leonidas Theodore and Laura Editha (Thomson) B.; m. Janice Meredith Hood, Sept. 16, 1950; children: Theodore Hood, Kenneth Thomson, Barbara Loyd, Elizabeth Ann BS, U. Tex., 1945, MA, 1948; PhD, Stanford U., 1953; grad. advanced mgmt. program, Harvard U., 1963. With Humble Oil & Refining Co., 1951-72, regional exploration mgr. New Orleans, 1962-64, sr. v.p., 1966—70, pres., 1970-72, also bd. dirs.; exec. v.p. Esso Exploration, Inc., 1964-65; sr. v.p. Exxon Corp., NYC, 1972-78; chmn., CEO Kennecott Corp., Stamford, Conn., 1978-81; vice chmn. Std. Oil Co., Ohio, 1981-85; investment cons. Houston, 1985-89; chmn. GX Tech., Houston, 1990—2004; pres. Thomson-Barrow, 1989—2005; sr. chmn., bd. dir. GeoQuest Internat. Holdings, Inc., Houston, 1990-97; pres. Tecolotita, Inc., 1991—2005, T-BAR-X, Houston, 1995—2005; ret. Chmn. bd. dirs. GPS Tech. Corp., Houston, 1986—98, Petroleum Info./Dwights, 1994—97, Tobin Internat., 1998—2003; mem. commn. on natural resources NRC, 1973—78, commn. on phys. sci., math. and natural resources, 1984—87, bd. on earth scis., 1982—84; trustee Woods Hole Oceanog. Instn., 20th Century Fund-Task Force on U.S. Energy Policy. Pres. Houston Grand Opera, 1985-87, chmn., 1987-91; trustee Am. Mus. Natural History, 1972-82, Stanford U., 1980-90, Tex. Med. Ctr., 1983—, Geol. Soc. Am. Found., 1982-87; trustee Baylor Coll. Medicine, 1984—, vice chmn bd. trustees, 1991-99. Served to ensign USNR, 1943—46. Recipient Disting. Achievement award Offshore Tech. Conf., 1973, Disting. Engring. Grad. award U. Tex., 1970, Disting. Alumnus, 1982, Disting. Geology Grad., 1985, Disting. Natural Sci. Grad., 1990; named Chief Exec. of Yr. in Mining Industry, Fin. World, 1979. Fellow NY Acad. Scis.; mem. NAE, Am. Mining Congress (bd. dirs. 1979-85, vice chmn. 1983-85), Am. Assn. Petroleum Geologists, Geol. Soc. Am., Internat. Copper Rsch. Assn. (bd. dirs. 1979-85), Nat. Ocean Industry Assn. (bd. dirs. 1982-85), AAAS, Am. Soc. Oceanography (pres. 1970-71), Am. Geophys. Union, Am. Petroleum Inst., Am. Geog. Soc., Houston Country Club, The Hills Club, Petroleum Club, River Oaks Country Club, Houston Club, Sigma Xi, Tau Beta Pi, Sigma Gamma Epsilon, Phi Eta Sigma, Alpha Tau Omega Episcopalian.

BARROW, THOMAS FRANCIS, artist, educator; b. Kansas City, Mo., Sept. 24, 1938; s. Luther Hopkins and Cleo Naomi (Francis) Barrow; m. Laurie Anderson, Nov. 30, 1974; children: Melissa, Timothy, Andrew. BFA, Kansas City Art Inst., 1963; MS, Ill. Inst. Tech., 1965. With George Eastman House, Rochester, NY, 1966-72, asst. dir., 1971-72; assoc. dir. Art Mus. U. N.Mex., Albuquerque, 1973-76, assoc. prof., 1976-81, prof., 1981—2001, Presdl. prof., 1985-90. Author: The Art of Photography, 1971; sr. editor: Reading into Photography, 1982; contbr. to Brit. Ency. Am. Art, 1973, A Hundred Years of Photographic History: Essays in Honor of Beaumont Newhall, 1975, Experimental Vision, 1994; forward The Valiant Knights of Daguerre, 1978; contbr. articles to profl. jours.; one-man shows include Light Gallery, N.Y.C., 1974-76, 79, 82, Amarillo Art Ctr., 1990, Andrew Smith Gallery, Santa Fe, 1992, Laurence Miller Gallery, N.Y.C., 1996, U. N.Mex. Art Mus., 1997, Richard Levy Gallery, Albuquerque, 2000; exhibited in group shows including Pace Gallery, N.Y.C., 1973, Hudson River Mus., Yonkers, N.Y., 1973, Internat. Mus. Photography, Rochester, 1975, Seattle Art Mus., 1976, Mus. Fine Arts, Houston, 1977, Retrospective exhbn. L.A. County Mus. Art, 1987—; represented in permanent collections Nat. Gallery Can., Mus. Modern Art, Getty Ctr. for Arts and Humanities, Ctr. for Creative Photography U. Ariz. Nat. Endowment for Arts fellow, 1971, 78. Business E-Mail: tfbarrow@unm.edu.

BARROWS, FRANK CLEMENCE, journalist; b. Lewes, Del., Nov. 2, 1946; m. Mary S. Newsom, Nov. 16, 1985; 1 child, Margaret S. BA, St. Andrews Coll., 1968. Reporter, columnist Charlotte Observer, NC, 1969-72, 76-81, asst. sports editor, 1981-82, asst. met. editor, 1982-83, exec. sports editor, 1983-84, 86, dep. features editor, 1985, dep. met. editor, 1986-87, asst. mng. editor, 1987-88, dep. mng. editor, 1988-92, mng. editor, 1992—2005; exec. editor Bus. NC, 2006—07; affiliate Neiman Found. Harvard U., 2007—. Contbr. articles to mags. Bd. dirs. Charlotte Trolley, 2006—. Recipient Ethel Fortner Writer and Cmty. award, 2000, reporting awards, NC Press Assn., 1972—80. Mem.: NC Open Govt. Coalition (pres. 2004—05, exec. dir. 2006), Investigative Reporters and Editors, Soc. News Design, Am. Soc. Newspaper Editors. Home: 1810 Shoreham Dr Charlotte NC 28211-2134 E-mail: fcbarrows@aol.com.

BARROWS, RONALD THOMAS, lawyer; b. Detroit, Jan. 19, 1954; s. Harland Wayne and Jeanette Edith (Authier) B. BA in English and Polit. Sci. magna cum laude, Oakland U., 1976; JD, Wayne State U., 1979. Bar: Mich. 1979, U.S. Dist. Ct. (ea. dist.) Mich. 1979, U.S. Ct. Appeals (6th cir.) 1983, U.S. Tax Ct. 1986; lic. real estate broker, Mich. Assoc. Abbott, Nicholson, Quilter, Esshaki & Youngblood, P.C., Detroit, 1979-80; counsel Lindon Land Co., Inc., Harper Woods, Mich., 1980-82; pvt. practice St. Clair Shores, Mich., 1981-87, Grosse Pointe, Mich., 1990—2005, Washington, 2005—; ptnr. Barrows & Alt, P.C., Troy, Mich., 1987-90. Cons./counselor to corp. and pvt. real estate investors and developers; adj. prof. investment banking and venture capital formation, asset protection planning, assoc. prof. Oakland U. Paralegal Program, 1989-90. Contbr. articles to profl. jours. Mem. Mich. Comml. Investment Coun.; chmn. adv. com. Mich. chpt. Nat. Multiple Sclerosis Soc. 1996-2002, co-chair coun. adv. com., 1997-2002, mem. client programs com., 1998—. Mem. ABA, ATLA, Mich. Bar Assn. (land title stds. com. 1985—, real property coun. 1987-97, treas. 1994-97, chmn. Water Law Com. 1985-90), Nat. Assn. Realtors, Mich. Assn. Realtors (sr. instr. 1980-91), Macomb County Assn. Realtors (lawyer realtor com. 1984-88), Nat. Order Barristers. Republican. Presbyterian. Avocations: sailing, billiards, theater, photography. Home: PO Box 817 Washington MI 48094-0817 Home Phone: 586-677-0522; Office Phone: 586-677-0521. Personal E-mail: rtbarrows@sbcglobal.net.

BARRUS, CHARLES LAMAR, JR., music educator; b. Sugar City, Idaho, July 22, 1935; s. Charles LaMar and Ruth Hammond Barrus; m. Carol Ruth Walters, Sept. 12, 1958; children: Connie Barrus Barton, Katherine Barrus Kesler, Deborah Barrus Stoddard, Kent LaMar. BA, MusM, U. Utah, PhD, 1968. Violinist Utah Symphony Orch., Salt Lake City, 1953—65; prof. music Ricks Coll., Rexburg, Idaho, 1960—99; mgr., program dir. Pub. Radio Sta. KRIC-FM, 1982—99. Condr. Rexburg Tabernacle Orch., 2004—, Idaho Falls Symphony Orch., 1965—70. Musician: (choral symphony) Ode to Libertad (Award of Merit, Idaho Fedn. of Music Clubs, 1969). Commr. Idaho Commn. on Arts, 1972—80; patriarch LDS Ch., Rexburg, 2002—. Recipient Exemplary Faculty award, Ricks Coll. Faculty Assn., 1983—84, Eliza R. Snow award in Arts, Ricks Coll. Alumni Assn., 1991, Support Arts Govs. award, Gov. of Idaho, 1992, Exemplary Employee award, Ricks Coll., 1996, Disting. Tchg. award, 1998, Lifetime Achievement award, Rexburg C. of C., 2000. Home: 260 S 3rd E Rexburg ID 83440 Home Phone: 208-356-5793. Personal E-mail: lamarb@cableone.net.

BARRY, ALAN H., consumer products company executive; m. Karen Barry. Contr. brass craft mfg. unit Masco Corp., Taylor, Mich., 1972, pres. divsn., 1988, group pres., 1996, pres., COO, 2003—. Bd. dirs. H.W. Kaufman Fin. Group, Arch Aluminum & Glass Co., Inc.; exec. bd. mem. Plumbing Mfg. Inst., 1985—2000, chmn., 1994; exec. bd., assoc. mem. divsn. Am. Supply Assn., 1995—96. Office: Masco Corp 21001 Van Born Rd Taylor MI 48180*

BARRY, ANNE M., public health officer; BA in Occupl. Therapy, Coll. St. Catherine; JD, William Mitchell Coll. Law; MPH, U. Minn. Dep. commr. health Minn. Dept. Health, Mpls., commr. health, 1995—99; dep. fin. commr. Minn., 1999—; acting commr. fin. Minn., 2002. Office: Dept Fin 400 Centennial Bldg 658 Cedar St Saint Paul MN 55155

BARRY, DAN, columnist; m. Mary Trinity; children: Nora, Grace. BA, St. Bonaventure U., 1980; MA in Journalism, NYU. Reporter Jour. Inquirer, Manchester, Conn., Providence Jour. Bulletin, RI, NY Times, 1995—, columnist, About NY. Author: Pull Me Up: A Memoir, 2004. Co-recipient George Polk award; recipient Pulitzer prize for investigative reporting, 1994, Am. Soc. of Newspapers Editors award for deadline reporting. Office: NY Times 229 West 43rd St New York NY 10036 Office Phone: 212-556-1533. Office Fax: 212-556-3690.

BARRY, DAVE, columnist, writer; b. Armonk, NY, July 3, 1947; m. Beth (div.), 1 child, Robert, m. Michelle Kaufman, 1996, 1 child, Sophie. BA in English, Haverford Coll., 1969. Reporter, editor Daily Local News, West Chester, Pa., 1971-75; with AP, instr. bus. writing Phila., 1975-83; columnist The Miami (Fla.) Herald, 1983—2004. Author: Taming of the Screw: Several Million Homeowners' Problems Sidestepped, 1983, Babies and Other Hazards of Sex, 1984, Bad Habits: A One Hundred Percent Fact Free Book, 1985, Stay Fit and Healthy Until You're Dead, 1985, Dave Barry's Guide to Marriage and/or Sex, 1987, Claw Your Way to the Top, 1987, Dave Barry's Greatest Hits, 1988, Homes and Other Black Holes, 1988, Dave Barry Slept Here, 1989, Dave Barry Turns 40, 1990, Dave Barry Talks Back, 1991, Dave Barry's Only Travel Guide You'll Ever Need, 1991, Dave Barry Does Japan, 1992, Dave Barry Is Not Making This Up, 1994, Dave Barry's Gift Guide to End All Gift Guides, 1994, Dave Barry's Complete Guide to Guys, 1995, Dave Barry in Cyberspace, 1996, Dave Barry is from Mars and Venus, 1997, Dave Barry's Book of Bad Songs, 1997, Dave Barry Turns 50, 1998, Dave Barry is Not Taking This Sitting Down, 2000, My Teenage Son's Goal in Life is to Make Me Feel 3,500 Years Old' and Other Thoughts on Parenting from Dave Barry, 2001, Dave Barry Hits Below the Beltway, 2001, The Greatest Invention in the History of Mankind is Beer And Other Manly Insights From Dave Barry, 2001, Boogers Are My Beat, 2003, Dave Barry's Money Secrets: Like: Why Is There a Giant Eyeball on the Dollar?, 2006, Dave Barry's History of the Millennium (So Far), (novels) Big Trouble, 1999, Tricky Business, 2002; co-author (with others): Mid-Life Confidential, 1994, Naked Came the Manatee, 1996; co-author: (with Ridley Pearson) Peter and the

Starcatchers, 2004, Peter and the Shadow Thieves, 2006, Escape from the Carnivale, 2006, Peter and the Secret of Rundoon. Recipient Disting. Writing award, Soc. Newspaper Editors, 1987, Pulitzer prize for commentary, 1988.

BARRY, DENNIS M., lawyer; b. Washington, Jan. 16, 1951; BA, Ohio Wesleyan U., 1972; JD, U. Va., 1975. Bar: Tex. 1976, DC 1983. Ptnr., head health sect. Vinson & Elkins LLP, DC, 1991—. Mem.: Am. Health Lawyers Assn. (bd. dirs. 2006—). Office: Vinson & Elkins LLP Willard Office Bldg 1455 Pennsylvania Ave NW, Ste 600 Washington DC 20004 E-mail: dbarry@velaw.com.

BARRY, DESMOND THOMAS, JR., lawyer; b. NYC, Mar. 26, 1945; s. Desmond Thomas and Kathryn (O'Connor) B.; m. Patricia Mellicker, Aug. 28, 1971; children: Kathryn, Desmond Todd. AB, Princeton U., 1967; JD, Fordham U., 1973. Bar: N.Y. 1974, U.S. Dist. Ct. (so. and ea. dist.) N.Y. 1974, U.S. Ct. Appeals (2d cir.) 1974, U.S. Ct. Appeals (9th cir.) 1980, U.S. Ct. Appeals (5th cir.) 1983, U.S. Ct. Appeals (3d cir.) 1984, U.S. Supreme Ct. 1985. Assoc. Condon & Forsyth, NYC, 1973-79, ptnr., 1979—. Trustee Canterbury Sch., New Milford, Conn., 1970-80. Capt. USMC, 1967-70, Vietnam. Decorated Navy Commendation medal with combat V, Combat Action medal, 1969, Vietnamese Cross of Gallantry, 1969. Fellow: Am. Coll. Trial Lawyers; mem.: ABA (chmn. aviation and space law com. 1996—97), Internat. Assn. Def. Counsel (exec. com.), Assn. Bar City NY, NY State Bar Assn., US. Srs. Golf Assn., Queenwood Golf Club (London), Hawk's Nest Golf Club (Vero Beach, Fla.), Winged Foot Golf Club (bd. govs. 1999—2001), Univ. Club N.Y.C. Republican. Roman Catholic. Home: 40 Charter Oak Ln New Canaan CT 06840-6705 Office: Condon & Forsyth LLP Times Sq Tower 7 Times Sq New York NY 10036 Office Phone: 212-894-6770. Business E-Mail: dbarry@condonlaw.com.

BARRY, ESSIE MARILYN, elementary school educator, writer; b. Greenwood, Miss., June 9, 1913; d. Otho and Lula Hill (Montgomery) Thurmond; m. Essie Marilyn Thurmond, June 17, 1934; children: Gloria, Francine, Carlita. BA, CUNY, 1971. Lic. practical nurse, N.Y., 1964. Lic. practical nurse Bklyn. Hosp., 1963—64; social svc. investigator Dept. Social Svc., NYC, 1971—72; tchr. State Edn. Dept., NYC, 1972—85; nursery and grades K-6 tchr. Mich. State Dept. Edn., Lansing; lic. tchr. NYU and Columbia U., 1975—, ednl. adminstr., 1975—2005; pres. Barryelectronics, Farmington Hills, Mich. Internet cons. Am. Assn. of On-line Ad Agys., San Francisco, 1996. Author: Deep Dark Secrets of a Preacher's Daughter. Mem. Better Bu. Bur., 2004; founder Essie Barry Scholarship fund Steinhart Sch. Edn., NYU, 2003. Recipient Internet Recognition award, Am. On-Line Ad Agys., 1999, Jefferson cup, Steinhart Sch. Edn., NYU, 2004. Mem.: NYU Alumni Group, So. Poverty Law Ctr. Democrat. Roman Catholic. Achievements include patents for scouring gloves. Avocations: quilting, crafts, tutoring children. Home: 29606 Middlebelt Rd Unit 2801 Farmington Hills MI 48334 Office: Info Express Ad Agy 29606 Middlebelt Rd #2801 Farmington Hills MI 48334 Home Phone: 248-539-7734. Personal E-mail: e4115@aol.com.

BARRY, FRANCIS JULIAN, JR., lawyer; b. New Orleans, Oct. 7, 1949; s. Francis Julian and Bertha Anna (Lion) B.; m. Janice Leigh Gonzales, May 8, 1976; children: Francis III, Marianna. BA, Tulane U., 1970, JD, 1973. Bar: La. 1973, U.S. Dist. Ct. (ea. dist.) La. 1973, U.S. Ct. Appeals (5th cir.) 1973, U.S. Dist. Ct. (we. dist.) La. 1978, U.S. Ct. Appeals (11th cir.) 1982, U.S. Supreme Ct. 1991. Assoc. Deutsch, Kerrigan & Stiles, New Orleans, 1973-78, ptnr., 1978—. Editor Admiralty Law Inst. Symposium Tulane U., New Orleans, 1973. Adv. editor Tulane Maritime Law Jour. (formerly The Maritime Lawyer), 1975—. Served to capt. USAR. Mem. Fed. Bar Assn., La. Bar Assn., New Orleans Bar Assn., Maritime Law Assn. U.S. (proctor, carriage of goods com. 1982-87, com. offshore industries 2004—, com. marine ins. and gen. average 2004—), Admiralty Law Inst. New Orleans (mem. planning com. 1998—, mem. program com. 2000—, chmn. program com. 2004—), U.S. Naval Inst., Southeastern Admiralty Law Inst., La. Assn. Def. Counsel, Def. Rsch. Inst., Assn. Average Adjusters London, Assn. Average Adjusters U.S., Am. Legion, Navy League U.S., Army-Navy Club (Washington), La. Landmarks Soc., Bienville Club, Univ. Club (N.Y.C.), Plimsoll Club, Mariners Club, The Round Table Club. Republican. Roman Catholic. Home: 4301 Dumaine St New Orleans LA 70119-3617 Home Phone: 504-488-2842.

BARRY, HENRY FORD, chemicals executive; b. Detroit, June 25, 1923; s. William H. and Antoinette (Griese) B.; m. Helen A. Sasso, Aug. 27, 1947 (dec. Dec. 1983); children: Henry V., John M., Robert C., Christine M., Elizabeth M., Catherine A. BS in Chemistry, Stanford U., Palo Alto, Calif., 1950; MS in Chem. Engring., U. Mich., 1952, MBA in Mktg., 1978. Registered profl. engr., Ind., Colo. Researcher Amoco Oil Co., Whiting, Ind., 1952-59; tech. dir. Haviland Products Co., Grand Rapids, Mich., 1960-62; supr. Climax Molybdenum Co., Detroit, 1962-66, mgr. chem. rsch. Ann Arbor, Mich., 1967-76, dir. chem. devel., 1977-82; v.p. tech. Shattuck Chem. Co., Denver, 1983—. Editor: Chemistry/Uses of Mo., Vol. III, 1979, Vol. IV, 1982. With U.S. Army, 1943-46. Mem. Am. Chem. Soc., Nat. Assn. Corrosion Engrs., Soc. Tribology and Lubrication Engrs. Achievements include 6 U.S. and 4 foreign patents. Home: 3519 Meadow Grove Trl Ann Arbor MI 48108-9313 Office: SW Shattuck Chemical PO Box 18039 Denver CO 80218-0039

BARRY, HERBERT, III, psychologist, educator; b. NYC, June 2, 1930; s. Herbert and Lucy Manning (Brown) Barry. BA, Harvard U., 1952; MS, Yale U., 1953, PhD, 1957. USPHS-NIMH rsch. fellow Yale U., 1957-59, asst. prof. psychology, 1960-61, U. Conn., Storrs, 1961-63; rsch. assoc. prof. pharmacology Sch. Pharmacy U. Pitts., 1963-70, prof., 1970-87, prof. pharm. scis., 1995—2001, prof. emeritus, 2001—, prof. pharmacology and physiology Sch. Dental Medicine, 1987-94. Mem. alcohol rsch. rev. com. Nat. Inst. Alcohol Abuse and Alcoholism, 1972—76; mem. sociobehavioral subcom. AIDS rsch. rev. com. Nat. Inst. Drug Abuse, 1988—89. Author (with H. Wallgren): (book) Actions of Alcohol, 1970; author: (with A. Schlegel) Adolescence: An Anthropological Inquiry, 1991; field editor: jour. Psychopharmacology, 1974—91; contbr. articles to profl. jours. Bd. dirs. Schalkenbach Found., 1996—, Ctr. Study Econs., 1988—; mem. Allegheny County Dem. Com., 1984—. Recipient Rsch. Scientist Devel. award, NIMH, 1967—77. Fellow: APA (coun. reps. 1975—76, pres. divsn. psychopharmacology 1980—81), AAAS; mem.: Am. Coll. Neuropsychopharmacology, Psychonomic Soc., Am. Name Soc. (mem. exec. com. 2000—03), Sigma Xi, Phi Beta Kappa. Unitarian Universalist. Home: 552 N Neville St Apt 83 Pittsburgh PA 15213-2830 Office: Univ Pitts 534 Salk Hall Pittsburgh PA 15261-1905 Office Phone: 412-648-8551. Business E-Mail: barryh@pitt.edu. *I believe that the contrasting behaviors of persistence and innovation both contribute to effective learning and creativity. Awareness of the need for both contrasting behaviors may help people to avoid the failures caused by overemphasis of either one.*

BARRY, JAMES P(OTVIN), editor, writer; b. Alton, Ill., Oct. 23, 1918; s. Paul Augustine and Elder (Potvin) B.; m. Anne Elizabeth Jackson, Apr. 16, 1966 BA cum laude, Ohio State U., 1940. Commd. 2d. lt. Arty. U.S. Army, 1940, advanced through grades to col., served ETO, 1944-46; adviser to Turkish Army, 1951-53; detailed Army Gen. Staff, Washington, 1953-56; ret., 1966; adminstr. Capital U., Columbus, Ohio, 1967-71; freelance writer, editor Columbus, 1971-77; dir. Ohioana Library Assn., 1977-88; editor Ohioana Quar., 1977-88; sr. editor Inland Seas, 1984—; photographer, documentary and book illustrator, 1968—. Author: Georgian Bay: The Sixth Great Lake, 1968, 3rd edit., 1995, The Battle of Lake Erie, 1970, Bloody Kansas, 1972, The Noble Experiment, 1972, The Fate of the Lakes, 1972, The Louisiana Purchase, 1973, Henry Ford and Mass Production, 1973, Ships of the Great Lakes, 1973 (Dolphin Book Club selection), Ships of the Great Lakes, rev. edit., 1996, The Berlin Olympics, 1975, The Great Lakes: A First Book, 1976, Wrecks and Rescues of the Great Lakes, 1981 (Dolphin Book Club selection), Georgian Bay: An Illustrated History, 1992, Old Forts of the Great Lakes, 1994, Hackercraft, 2002, American Powerboats, 2003; contbr. articles to mags. and jours.; over 300 photographs accepted for permanent collection Inst. Gt. Lakes Rsch. Recipient award Am. Soc. State and Local History, 1974, Nonfiction History award Soc. Midland Authors, 1982; named Gt. Lakes Historian of Yr., Marine Hist. Soc. Detroit, 1995. Mem. Internat. Assn. Gt. Lakes Rsch., Assn. Gt. Lakes Maritime History, Can. Nautical Rsch. Soc., Gt. Lakes Hist. Soc., Marine Hist. Soc., Ohio Hist. Soc., World Ship Soc., Antique and Classic Boat Soc., Royal Can. Yacht Club, Columbus Country Club, Capital Club, Phi Beta Kappa. Home: 353 Fairway Blvd Columbus OH 43213-2507

BARRY, JOHN MAYNARD, urologist; b. Winona, Minn., Mar. 14, 1940; MD, U. Minn., 1965. Intern SUNY, Syracuse, 1965-66; resident U. Oreg. Med. Sch., Portland, 1969-73; prof., chmn. urology Oreg. Health Sci. U., Portland, 1980—, dir. renal transplantation, 1976—, chmn. abdominal organ transplantation, 2000—02. Office: Oreg Health Sci U Divsn Urology 3303 SW Bond Ave Portland OR 97293

BARRY, JOYCE ALICE, dietician, consultant; b. Chgo., Apr. 27, 1932; d. Walter Stephen and Ethel Myrtle (Paetow) B. Student, Iowa State Coll., 1950—52, Loyola U., 1952—58; BS, Mundelein Coll., 1955; postgrad., Simmons Coll., 1963—64, U. Ga., 1979, Calif. We. U., 1980. Registered dietitian. Prodn. supr. Marshall Field & Co., Chgo., 1955-59; dir. food svcs. Women's Ednl. and Indsl. Union, Boston, 1959-62, Wellesley Pub. Schs., Mass., 1962-70; regional dietitian Canteen Corp., Chgo., 1970-83; gen. mgr. bus. devel. Plantation-Sysco, Orlando, Fla., 1983-87; dir. product devel., corp. quality assurance, procurement Marriott Internat. Hdqrs., Washington, 1987-95; owner food svc. cons. svc., 1995—. Cons. Stokes Food Svcs., Newton, Mass., 1960-70; vis. lectr. Affiliate Produce for Better Health Found. Mem.: AAUW, Nutrition in Complementary Care, Nat. Assn. Female Execs., Nat. Hist. Trust, Sch. Nutrition Svcs., Am. Dietetics Assn. (career adv. cons.), Food and Culinary Profls., Dietitians in Bus. and Comm., Smithsonian Instn. (assoc.), Washington Opera Guild, Met. Opera Guild. Republican. Roman Catholic. Home and Office: 1009 Pearce Dr Apt 101 Clearwater FL 33764-1107 Office Phone: 727-669-6454. Personal E-mail: joyce4374@yahoo.com.

BARRY, LANCE LEONARD, judge; b. Boston, Dec. 18, 1965; s. Leonard and Theodora Ann Pawlak. BEE, Cath. U. Am., 1988; MS, Johns Hopkins U., 1991; JD, George Mason U., 1995. Bar: Va. 1995, U.S. Ct. Appeals (fed. cir.) 1995, bar: D.C. 1998. Engring. analyst RCI Internat., Vienna, Va., 1987; engring. aide MPR Assocs., Washington, 1987; engring. technician BBN Labs., Arlington, Va., 1988; cons. Booz, Allen & Hamilton, Bethesda, Md., 1988-90, sr. cons., 1990—91; patent examiner U.S. Patent and Trademark Office, Arlington, Va., 1991-95, primary examiner, 1996-99, adminstrv. patent judge, 1999—. Pub. adv. com. mem. Lawyers Coop. Pub., Raleigh, NC, 1995; spkr. Va. State Bar, Richmond, 1998—; instr. US Patent and Trademark Office, Arlington, 1996—97, curriculum com., 1999—2005, law lectr., 1997—99, 2005—. EEO counselor, 1999; substitute law prof. George Mason U., 2005—06. Contbr. articles to profl. jours. Head tutor St. Francis Xavier Sch., Washington, 1997-2001; cmty. svc. v.p. St. Mary's Ch., Alexandria, Va., 2001; vol. Greater DC Cares, Washington, 1999-2002; social officer Holy Trinity Ch., Washington, 1997-98; tutor kids and chemistry program Am. Chem. Soc., 2002-; lector Our Lady of Lourdes Ch., 2002-03; vol. Alexandria Christmas in April, 2000-, house capt., 2003, Camp Invention, 2004; judge sci. fairs, 2003—. Mem. IEEE (manuscript referee Potentials mag. 1989-93), Am. Intellectual Property Law Assn., Patent and Trademark Office Soc. (rep. 1996-98), Mensa, Phi Theta Kappa, Tau Beta Pi. Avocations: volunteering, Italian, birdwatching, travel, skiing. Office: US Patent and Trademark Office PO Box 1450 Alexandria VA 22313-1450

BARRY, MARYANNE TRUMP, federal judge; b. NYC, Apr. 5, 1937; d. Fred C. and Mary Trump; m. John J. Barry, Dec. 26, 1982; 1 child, David W. Desmond. BA, Mt. Holyoke Coll., 1958; MA, Columbia U., 1962; JD, Hofstra U., 1974, LLD (hon.), Seton Hall U.; LLD (hon.), Caldwell Coll.; LLD (hon.), Kean Coll. Bar: NJ 1974, NY 1975, US Ct. Appeals (3d cir.), US Supreme Ct. Asst. US Atty., 1974-75; dep. chief appeals div., 1976-77; chief appeals div., 1977-82; exec. asst. US Atty., 1981-82; 1st asst., 1981-83; judge US Dist. Ct., NJ, 1983-99, US Ct. Appeals (3d cir.), Newark, 1999—. Chmn. Com. on Criminal Law Jud. Conf. of US, 1994-96. Recipient Sandra Day O'Connor Medal of Honor, 2004. Fellow Am. Bar Found.; mem. ABA, NJ Bar Assn., Am. Judicature Soc. (bd. dirs.), Assn. Fed. Bar of NJ (pres. 1982-83); mem. NY Bar Assn. Office: US Ct Appeals PO Box 999 Newark NJ 07101*

BARRY, MILDRED CASTILLE, artist; b. Sunset, La., Feb. 23, 1924; d. Joseph Hippomene and Beatrice Victoria (Tinney) Castille; m. Francis Xavier Barry, Aug. 16, 1947; children: Christopher, Kevin, Maureen, Robin, Shane, Kim. BA in Edn., Sam Houston U., 1958; student, U. La., Lafayette, 1995—96. Cert. tchr., Tex. Tchr. Sacred Heart Elem., Conroe, Tex., 1959-67, Conroe Sam Houston Elem., 1967-68, Houston Ind. Sch. Dist. Elem., 1968-69. Tchr., stuent of Ernest Gaines, author-in-residence U. So. La., Lafayette, 1985-87. Exhibited in group shows Opelonsas, La., 1973 (1st pl.). With WAC, 1944-45. Recipient 1st pl. award, Miss. Festival of Arts, 1958. Mem. Writers Guild. Roman Catholic. Avocations: reading, writing, painting, sewing, travel. Home: 309 Beverly Dr Lafayette LA 70503-3109 Personal E-mail: mimsyfan@yahoo.com.

BARRY, NANCY MARIE, bank executive; b. Kansas City, Kans., Aug. 2, 1949; d. John Joseph and Lorna Marie Barry. BA in Econs., Stanford U., 1971; MBA, Harvard U., 1975. Divsn. chief pub. sector mgmt. World Bank, Washington, 1986-87, divsn. chief indsl. devel., 1987-90; pres. Women's World Banking, NYC, 1990—2006. Founding mem. World Bank Consultative Group to Assist the Poorest-Policy Advisory Group, Washington; adv. com. Harvard Social Enterprise, Mass. Named Woman of the Yr., Fin. Women's Assn., 2006; named one of 100 Most Powerful Women in World, Forbes mag., 2005. Mem. Harvard Club. Office: Women's World Banking 8 W 40th St Fl 9 New York NY 10018-3993 Office Fax: 212-768-8519. E-mail: nmbarry@swwb.org.

BARRY, PAUL H., utilities executive; BS magna cum laude in Fin., Northeastern U., Boston; MBA, Harvad U. Fin. mgmt. position GE, 1983, v.p. bus. devel. Capital Svcs. Structured Fin. Group; fin. mgr., sr. analyst Amoco Prodn. Co., dir. acquisitions and divestitures; dir. corp. fin. CBS Corp. (formerly Westinghouse Electric Corp.); v.p. mergers & acquisitions Duke Energy, Charlotte, 2002—05, group exec., pres. Duke Energy Ams., 2005—06, sr. v.p., chief devel. officer, 2006—07; sr. v.p., CFO Pepco Holdings Inc., Washington, 2007—. Office: Pepco Holdings Inc 701 9th St NW Washington DC 20068 Office Phone: 704-594-6200.*

BARRY, PHILLIP OWEN, college president; b. Chgo., May 24, 1951; m. April Lee Rank, Nov. 21, 1971; children: Patrick, Collin. Diploma, Edgewater Hosp., 1971; AAS, Morraine Valley Community Coll., 1973; BS, Chgo. Med. Sch., 1975; M. Edn. Adminstrn., Wichita State U., 1978; PhD, Kans. State U., 1983. Registered radiologic technologist Am. Registry Radiologic Technologists. With health care Med. Ctrs., Chgo., 1971-75; with faculty Hutchinson (Kans.) C.C., 1975-80; dir. Labette C.C., Parsons, Kans., 1980-83, assoc. dean, 1983-85, dean, 1985-87; pres. Salem C.C., Carneys Point, N.J., 1987-92, Hawkeye C.C., Waterloo, Iowa, 1992-95, Mesalands C. C., Tucumcari, N.Mex. Mem. grad. faculty Kans. State U., Manhattan, 1984-87, Glassboro (N.J.) State U., 1989-92, Small/Rural Coll. commn., Washington, 1989-92, mem. editorial bd., 1989—. Author: Radiography of Facial Bones, 1979; contbr. articles to profl. jours.; researcher in field. Mem. multiple positions Boy Scouts Am., Kans. N.J., 1975-91, Salem County Youth Commn., 1989-91, Coun. County Colls., 1987—; chmn. Ducks Unltd., Parsons, 1981-86; vice chmn. Econs. Devel. Com., Salem County, N.J., 1988-91; mem. exec. com. Healthy Heart Coalition, Salem County, 1990-91; bd. dirs. Waterloo C. of C., 1993-95, Cedar Valley Econ. Devel. Corp., 1993-95; trustee Silos and Smokestacks, 1992-95. Recipient Disting. Svc. award Ducks Unltd., 1985. Mem. Am. Assn. Community and Jr. Colls. (Outstanding Community Coll. Alumni 1991), Greater Salem C. of C., Rotary, Kiwanis (exec. 1985-87), Jaycees (Outstanding Young Men of Am. 1981). Avocations: horticulture, pomology.

BARRY, R. MICHAEL, lawyer; b. Savannah, Ga., Apr. 24, 1971; BBA cum laude in Fin., Univ. Ga., 1993, JD, 1996, MBA in Fin. Leadership, 2005. Bar: State of Ga. 1996. Mem. atty., corp., healthcare groups Epstein, Becker & Green, PC, Atlanta, 1997—. Mem.: ABA, State Bar Ga., Atlanta Bar Assn., Am. Health Lawyers Assn., Am. Coll. Healthcare Execs. Office: Epstein Becker Green PC Resurgens Plz Ste 945 East Paces Ferry Rd Atlanta GA 30326

BARRY, RICHARD FRANCIS, III, media executive; b. Norfolk, Va., Jan. 18, 1943; s. Richard F. and Mary Margaret (Perry) B.; m. Carolyn Ann Kennett, Aug. 7, 1965; children: Carolyn Michelle, Christopher David. BA, LaSalle Coll., 1964; JD, U. Va., 1967. Bar: Va. 1967. Assoc. Kaufman, Oberndorfer & Spainhour (now Kaufman and Canoles), Norfolk, 1967-71, ptnr., 1972-73; corp. sec. Landmark Comm., Inc., Norfolk, 1973—74, pres., COO, dir., 1978—84, CEO, 1984-91, vice chmn., 1991—; pres. Roanoke Times & World-News, Va., 1974-76, The Virginian-Pilot and The Ledger-Star, Norfolk, 1976-78, pub., 1983-90. Bd. dirs. Dominion Enterprises, The Weather Channel, Greensboro News and Record, Inc., Times World Corp., Capital Gazette Newspapers Inc. Trustee or past trustee Norfolk Acad., Chrysler Mus., U. Va. Colgate Darden Bus. Sch. Found., Cath. H.S. Found., Old Dominion Univ. Ednl. Found., Suffolk Ctr. for Cultural Arts, Mariners' Museum, Obici Healthcare Found.; bd. dirs., past pres., campaign chmn. United Way of South Hampton Rds.; bd. visitors, past rector Old Dominion U., co-chmn. capital campaign; chmn. biography com. Norfolk Hist. Soc. Office: Landmark Comm Inc 150 W Brambleton Ave Norfolk VA 23510-2018

BARRY, SANDRA, school system administrator; Degree, Neb.-Wesleyan U., Calif. State U., Fullerton. Educator and adminstr. Buena Pk. Sch. Dist., 1968—97; supt. Anaheim (Calif.) City Sch. Dist., 2000—. Office: Anaheim City Sch Dist 1001 South East St Anaheim CA 92805 Office Phone: 714-517-7510.

BARRY, STEVE, sculptor, educator; b. Jersey City, June 22, 1956; s. Thomas Daniel and Lorraine (Lowery) B. BFA, Sch. Visual Arts, NYC, 1980; MFA, Hunter Coll., NYC, 1984. Adj. lectr. Hunter Coll., 1984-89; assoc. prof. U. N.Mex., Albuquerque, 1989—. Kohler Arts and Industry Residency, 1996; bd. dir. Albuquerque Ctr. Contemporary Arts. Exhbns. include Bklyn. Army Terminal, NYC, 1983, City Gallery, NYC, 1986, 90, Storefront for Art and Architecture, 1988, Artists Space, NYC, 1989, Santa Barbara Art Mus., 1990, Kohler Arts Ctr., Sheboygan, Wis., 1991, Hirshhorn Mus., Washington, 1990, Fla. State U., 1992, Contemporary Art Mus., Houston, 1992, CAFE Gallery, Albuquerque, 1993, Charolette Jackson, Santa Fe, 1993, Ctr. for Contemporary Arts, Santa Fe, 1994, U. Wyo. Art Mus., 1995, Site Santa Fe, 1996, Sheldon Art Mus., Lincoln, Nebr., 1997, U. N.Mex. Art Mus., Albuquerque, 1997, 2006, Cedar Rapids Mus. of Art, Iowa, 1998, Albuquerque Contemporary Art Ctr., 2000, Plan B, Santa Fe, 2000, Donkey Gallery, Albuquerque, 2004, U. N.Mex. Art Mus., 2006. Rsch. grantee Coll. Fine Arts N.Mex., 2002; grantee Clocktower Nat. Studio, 1985, NEA, 1986, 88, 90, NY State Coun. Arts, 1987, NY Found. Arts, 1988; recipient AVA award, 1990, Regents Lectureship award U. N.Mex., 2006. Home: PO Box 1046 Corrales NM 87048-1046 Office: U NMex Dept Art & Art History Albuquerque NM 87131-0001 Home Phone: 505-897-3902; Office Phone: 505-277-5861. Business E-Mail: sbarry@unm.edu.

BARRY, THOMAS CORCORAN, investment advisor; b. Cleve., Feb. 9, 1944; s. Willard Corcoran and Harriet (Mullin) Barry; m. Patricia Ryan, Feb. 14, 1976; children: Hannah McGrath(dec.) , Ryan Nichols(dec.) , Oliver Mullin, Lillian Nicholson, Michael Corcoran. BA in Latin Am. Studies, Yale U., 1966; MBA, Harvard U., 1969. Chartered fin. analyst. Market research analyst Corning Glass Works, Brazil and Japan, 1966-67; investment analyst T. Rowe Price Assos., Inc., Balt., 1969-70; partner Cole, Thompson and Barry, Inc., Cleve., 1971-73; pres. Rowe Price New Horizons Fund, Balt., 1973-81, Saratoga Assocs., 1981-83; pres., CEO Rockefeller and Co. Inc., 1983-93; pres. Zephyr Mgmt., L.P., 1994—. Dir. numerous cos. Mem. Yale Pres.'s Coun. on Internat. Activities; mem. dean's coun. Harvard U.-Kennedy Sch. Govt.; chair NYC Summer Search; trustee Hotchkiss Sch., 2003—, Univ. Sch., Cleve., 1998—; bd. dirs. Harvard Bus. Sch. Alumni Assn. Office: 320 Park Ave New York NY 10022-6815 Office Phone: 212-508-9410.

BARRY, WILLIAM ANTHONY, priest, writer; b. Worcester, Mass., Nov. 22, 1930; s. William and Catherine (McKenna) B. AB, Boston Coll., 1956, STL, 1963; MA, Fordham U., 1960; PhD, U. Mich., 1968. Joined S.J., Roman Cath. Ch., 1950, ordained priest, 1962. Tchr. high sch. Fairfield (Conn.) Prep., 1956-58; lectr. U. Mich., Ann Arbor, 1968-69; from asst. to assoc. prof. Weston Jesuit Sch. of Theology, Cambridge, Mass., 1969-78; rector Jesuit community Boston Coll., Chestnut Hill, Mass., 1988-91; vice provincial S.J. of New Eng., Boston, 1978-84, asst. novice dir., 1985-88, provincial, 1991-97; co-dir. S.J. Tertianship, 1997—. Dir. staff Ctr. for Religious Devel., Cambridge, 1971-78; trustee Boston Coll., Chestnut Hill, 1988-91, adj. assoc. prof., 1989-91. Co-author: Communication, Conflict, Marriage, 1974, The Practice of Spiritual Direction, 1982, Contemplatives in Action, 2002; author: God and You, 1987, Seek My Face, 1989, Now Choose Life, 1990, Paying Attention to God, 1990, Finding God in All Things, 1991, Spiritual Direction and the Encounter with God, 1992, 2d, rev. edit., 2004, God's Passionate Desire and Our Response, 1993, Allowing the Creator to Deal with the Creature, 1994, What Do I Want in Prayer?, 1994, Who Do You Say I Am?, 1996, Our Way of Proceeding, 1997, With an Everlasting Love, 1999, Letting God Come Close, 2001; editor-in-chief (quar. jour.) Human Development, 2003—. Mem. Phi Beta Kappa, Phi Kappa Phi. Democrat. Roman Catholic. Avocations: reading, writing. Home and Office: Campion Ctr 319 Concord Rd Weston MA 02493-1310 Office Phone: 781-788-6800. Business E-Mail: wbarry@sjnen.org.

BARRY, WILLIAM GARRETT, III, publishing company executive; b. NYC, Aug. 16, 1955; s. William Garrett Jr. and Mary Theresa (Harrington) B.; m. Jeanne Maureen Sweet, Oct. 10, 1981; children: Emily Katherine, Maura Regina, Liam Sun-Ho. BA, Cathedral Coll., 1977. Editorial sec. Doubleday Pub. Co., NYC, 1979-80; corp. research analyst Doubleday & Co., Inc., NYC, 1980-83, bus. assoc., 1983-84, mng. editor, 1984-87, assoc. pub., 1987-90, v.p., 1989-96, dep. pub., 1990-95; dir. pub. ops. Bantam Doubleday Dell Pub. Group, Inc., 1995-96, sr. v.p. ops., 1996; pres. Hungry Minds, DK Publishing; v.p., pub. Doubleday Religion, NYC, 2005—. Mem.: Conn. Beekeepers' Assn. Office: Doubleday Religion Random House 1745 Broadway New York NY 10019

BARRYMORE, DREW, actress; b. Culver City, Calif., Feb. 22, 1975; d. John and Jaid Barrymore; m. Jeremy Thomas, Mar. 20, 1994 (div. Feb. 1995); m. Tom Green, July 7, 2001 (div. Oct. 15, 2002). Co-owner Flower Films, 1995—; amb. against hunger UN World Food Programme, 2007—. Model, spokesperson Covergirl, 2007—. Actor: (films) Altered States, 1980, E.T.: The Extra-Terrestrial, 1982, Irreconcilable Differences, 1984, Firestarter, 1984, Stephen King's Cat's Eye, 1985, See you in the Morning, 1989, Far From Home, 1989, Motorama, 1991, Waxwork II: Lost in Time, 1992, Poison Ivy, 1992, Gun Crazy, 1992, No Place to Hide, 1993, Doppelganger, 1993, Wayne's World 2, 1993, Inside the Goldmine, 1994, Bad Girls, 1994, Boys on the Side, 1995, Batman Forever, 1995, Mad Love, 1995, Wishful Thinking, 1996, Scream, 1996, Like a Lady, 1996, Everyone Says I Love You, 1996, All She Wanted, 1997, Best Men, 1997, Home Fries, 1998, The Wedding Singer, 1998, Ever After: A Cinderella Story, 1998, (voice only) Olive, the Other Reindeer, 1999, Skipped Parts, 2000, (voice only) Titan A.E., 2000, Freddy Got Fingered, 2001, Riding in Cars With Boys, 2001, Confessions of a Dangerous Mind, 2002, 50 First Dates, 2004, (voice only) Curious George, 2006, Music and Lyrics, 2007, Lucky You, 2007; actor, prodr.: (films) Never Been Kissed, 1999, Charlie's Angels, 2000, Donnie Darko, 2001, Charlie's Angels: Full Throttle, 2003, Fever Pitch, 2005; actor: (TV movies) Suddenly Love, 1978, Bogie, 1980, The Adventures of Con Sawyer and Hucklemary Finn, 1985, The Screaming Woman, 1986, Babes in Toyland, 1986, Conspiracy of Love, 1987, Beyond Control: The Amy Fisher Story, 1993; (TV appearances) Amazing Stories, 1985, 2000 Malibu Road, 1992, (voice only) The Simpsons, 2000, (voice only) Family Guy, 2005-06; (host) Hansel and Gretel, 1986; co-author (with Todd Gold), Little Girl Lost, 1989. Named one of 50 Most Powerful People in Hollywood, Premiere mag., 2004—05; recipient Star, Hollywood's Walk of Fame, 2004. Office: Creative Artist Agency 9830 Wilshire Blvd Beverly Hills CA 90212*

BARSALONA, FRANK SAMUEL, retired theatrical agent; b. SI, NY, Mar. 31, 1938; s. Peter and Mary (Rotunno) B.; m. June Harris, Sept. 1, 1966; 1 dau., Nicole. BA, Wagner Coll., SI, 1958; postgrad., Herbert Berghof Sch., NYC, 1959-60. Agt. Gen. Artists Corp., NYC, 1960-64; founder, since pres. Premier Talent Agy. (merged with William Morris Agy.), NYC, 1964—2002, ret., 2002; co-founder, pres. Phila. Fury, 1977-80. Lectr., moderator music industry; founding ptnr. Precision Media Corp., 1984-97. Bd. govs., trustee Rock & Roll Hall of Fame Mus., Cleve. Named to Performance Mag. Hall of Fame, 1988; recipient numerous awards (cover subject spl. issue), Billboard Publs., 1984, Silver Clef award, Nordoff Robbins, 2002, Inducted into the Rock & Roll Hall of Fame Life Time Achievement award, 2005. Mem. Mus. Am. Folk Art. (internat. adv. bd.).

BARSAMIAN, HARUT, computer scientist, consultant; b. Aleppo, Syria, Aug. 21, 1933; s. Sahag Barsamiam and Mayrene Elanjian; m. Tamara Aroushanian, June 19, 1994. PhD, Acad. Sci., Moscow, 1966; grad., Poly. Inst., Yerevan, Armenia, 1956. Sr. rschr., lectr. Poly. Inst., Yerevan, 1956—66; prin. engr. Raytheon Co., Santa Ana, Calif., 1967—69; head advanced studies dept. NCR Corp., San Diego, 1969—77; dir. advanced sys. Sperry Univac, Irvine, Calif., 1977—84; prof. elect. engring. and computer sci. U. Calif., Irvine, 1984—. Owner, prin. Artificial Intelligence Tech., Mission Viejo, Calif., 1984—. Contbr. articles to profl. jours., chapters to books. Founding mem., dir. Armenian Nat. Sci. and Edn. Fund, NY, 1998; founding pres. Yerpi Alumni Assn., LA, 1992, Armenian Engrs. and Scientists Am., LA, 1983; trustee Engring. U. Armenia, 1998. Named Hon. Prof., State Engring. U. Armenia, 2000; recipient Jubilee Gold medal, Internat. Engring. Acad., Poland, 2000. Fellow: IEEE (life); mem.: Am. Acad. Engring., NY Acad. Scis., IEEE Computer Soc. (Meritorious Svc. award 1990, Golden Core mem. 1996). Achievements include patents in field. Avocations: chess, backgammon, classical music. Office: Univ Calif Elect Engring and Computer Sci Irvine CA 92697

BARSAMIAN, JOHN ALBERT, lawyer, arbitrator, criminologist, judge, educator; b. Troy, NY, May 1, 1934; s. John and Virginia Barsamian; m. Alice Missirlian, Apr. 21, 1963; children: Bonnie, Tamara. BS in Psychology with honors, Union Coll., 1956; JD, 1968; LLB, Albany Law Sch., 1959; postgrad., SUNY, Albany, 1964, Nat. Jud. Coll., 1997. Bar: N.Y. 1961, U.S. Dist. Ct. (no. dist.) N.Y. 1961, U.S. Supreme Ct. 1967; advanced arbitration tng. cert., Fla.; fire tng. cert. N.Y. State Exec. Dept.; qualified arbitrator Fla. Supreme Ct., 2006. Spl. investigator Rensselaer County (NY) Dist. Atty.'s Office, 1959—61; pvt. practice, 1961—; dir. criminal sci., chmn. dept. Russell Sage Coll., 1970-88, assoc. prof. criminal sci., 1977-82, prof., 1982-87, prof. emeritus, 1987—. Spl. investigator Rensselaer County Dist. Atty., 1959—61; mem. com. on police selection and tng. ABA, 1967—69; mem. mediation panel N.Y. State Pub. Employment Rels. Bd., 1968—73; counsel Cohoes Police Assn., 1967—74, Colonie Police Assn., 1977—80, Troy Police Command Officers Assn., 1981—85, North Greenbush Police Assn., 1985—90, Office of the Police Chief, Syracuse, NY, 1985—90, Fire Dept. Union, Albany, NY, 1986, Watervliet Police Assn., 1967—74, Shenectady Fire Fighters Union, 1992—95; mem. law guardian panel N.Y. State Family Ct., 1967—77; gen. counsel Troy Uniformed Firefighters Assn., 1977—97, Internat. Narcotic Enforcement Officers Assn., 1982—84; faculty, pub. affairs, policy pub. svc. tng. program Sch. Labor Rels. Ext., Divsn. Cornell U., 1986, Nelson A. Rockefeller Coll., 1986—91; spl. counsel Office of Police Chief, Cohoes, NY, 1986—92; gaming cons. NY State Gov.'s Office Indian Rels., NY, 1991—92; spl. counsel to city mgr., Troy, NY, 1993; judge adminstrv. law N.Y. State Pub. Employment Rels. Bd., 1996—2001, supervising judge, asst. dir. pub. employment practice and representation, 2001—05; supervising judge, asst. dir. Pub. Employment Practices and Representation, 2001—05; qualified arbitrator Fla. State Supreme Ct., 2006; lectr. in field. Founder, chmn. dept. police sci. Hudson Valley C.C., 1961-69; mem. adv. bd. History Ctr. Skidmore Coll., 1993-96; bd. dirs. Rensselaer County ARC, 1966-70; mem. alumni coun. Union Coll., 1981-86; mem. parish coun. St. Peter Armenian Ch., Watervliet, N.Y., 1979-83, chmn., 1981-83, vice chmn., 1984; evaluator office of non-collegiate programs N.Y. State Dept. Edn., 1985-91; hon. dep. sheriff St. Mary Parish (La.); mem. Rensselaer County Criminal Justice Coordinating Coun., 1976-78. Decorated chevalier, knight comdr. Sovereign Order of Cyprus; recipient Lawyers Coop. Pub. Co. prize in criminal law, 1957, Police Sci. Students award to Faculty, Hudson Valley C.C., 1968, meritorious svc. to law enforcement award, Law Enforcement Officers Soc., 1969, Archbishop's cert. merit, Armenian Ch. Am., 1973, Svc. award, Am. Arbitration Assn., 1983, Gabrielli Meml. award, Albany Law Sch., 2003; scholar Tarzian, Union Coll., 1952—56, Porter, Albany Law Sch., 1954—56, Saxton, 1956—59. Fellow: Am. Assn. Criminology; mem.: Internat. Coll. Master Advocates (sr. counsel), N.Y. State Assn. Adminstrv. Law Judges (bd. dirs. 1999, 2001), Am. Coll. Barristers, N.Y. State Trial Lawyers Assn., Union Coll. Alumni Assn. (Silver medal 1956), N.Y. Vet. Police Assn. (life), Acad. Criminal Justice Scis., Nat. Assn. Adminstrv. Law Judges, N.Y. Bar Assn. (chmn. com. on police 1970—72, trial lawyers sect. com. contg. legal edn. 1977—97, subcom. on adminstrv. law judges 2000—04), ATLA, Rose Croix (most wise master Delta chpt. 1986), Les Amis d'Escoffier Soc., Masonic Vet. Assn. Troy (life), Lambda Epsilon Chi, Alpha Phi Sigma, Phi Delta Theta. Home and Office: 5 Sage Hill Ln Albany NY 12204-1315

BARSAN, ROBERT BLAKE, dentist; b. Akron, Ohio, Apr. 7, 1948; s. Emil O. and Letitia (Dobrin) B.; m. Cheryl Lee Adams, Dec. 16, 1972; children: Erin Lee, Kathleen Letitia. BS, U. Cin., 1970; DDS, Ohio State U., 1974. Resident U. Chgo., 1976; gen. practice dentistry Cuyahoga Falls, Ohio, 1976—. Contbr. editor Modern Dental mag., 1984-89. Bd. dirs. Akron Civic Theatre, 1996-2004. Fellow Acad. Gen. Dentistry (v.p. Ohio chpt. 2004—); mem. ADA (chmn. CPR 1984-90), Akron Gnathological Soc. (pres. 1986), Am. Acad. Cosmetic Dentistry, Canton Akron Cleve. Orthodontic Study Club (pres. 1994-98). Home: 3084 Silver Lake Blvd Silver Lake OH 44224-3033 Office: 330 Stow Ave Cuyahoga Falls OH 44221-2516 Office Phone: 330-928-5575.

BARSAN, WILLIAM GEORGE, emergency physician; b. Akron, Aug. 1950; m. Mary Barsan. MD, Ohio State U., 1975. Diplomate Am. Bd. Emergency Medicine. Intern U. Va. Hosp., Charlottesville, 1975-76, resident in radiology, 1976-77; resident in emergency medicine U. Cin. Hosp., 1977-79; resident coordinator U. Cincinnati, 1981—92; prof., chair dept. emergency medicine U. Mich., Ann Arbor, 1992—, dir. surgery, 1992—. Mem. AMA, Soc. Tchrs. Emergency Medicine, U. Assn. Emergency Medicine, Am. Bd. Emergency Medicine (pres. 1998), Am. Coll. Emergency Physicians, Assn. Acad. Chairs of Emergency Medicine (pres. 2005-2006), Inst. Medicine. Office: Taubman Health Care Ctr Rm B1 354 1500 E Med Ctr Dr Ann Arbor MI 48109-0303 Office Phone: 734-936-6020. Office Fax: 734-763-7228.

BARSANO, CHARLES PAUL, medical educator, dean; BS in Biology, Loyola U., Chgo., 1969; PhD in Pathology, U. Chgo., 1974, MD, 1975. Diplomate Am. Bd. Internal Medicine. Resident internal medicine Barnes Hosp./Washington U., St. Louis, 1975-77; fellow endocrinology U. Chgo. Sch. Medicine, 1977-79, rsch. assoc. endocrinology, 1979-80; asst. prof. medicine Northwestern U. and Lakeside VA Med. Ctr., 1980-85, U. Health Scis./Chgo. Med. Sch. and North Chgo. VA Med. Ctr., 1985-87, assoc. prof., 1987-92, prof. medicine, 1992-98, assoc. prof. pharmacology and molecular biology, 1992-94, prof. pharmacology and molecular biology, 1994-98, acting dean Med. Sch., 1998—99, sr. assoc. dean for clin. affairs, vice-chmn. dept. medicine, 1999—2001, interim dean, 2001—03; staff physician med. svc./endocrinology sect. North Chgo. VA Med. Ctr.; with clin. affairs Chgo. Med. Sch. Rosalind Franklin U. Medicine and Sci., 2005—. Mem. editl. bd. Thyroid, 1990-95; mem. adv. bd. Toxic Substance Mechanisms, 1993-99. Recipient Bausch and Lomb Nat. Sci. award, 1965, Individual Nat. Rsch. Svc. award, 1979-80. Mem. Internat. Coun. for Control of Iodine Deficiency Disorders, Assn. Am. Med. Colls. (group on ednl. affairs sect. on resident edn.), Am. Assn. Clin. Endocrinologists, Am. Thyroid Assn. (fiscal com. 1982-85, pub. health com. 1986-88, membership com. 1990-93, chmn. membership com. 1993, local organizing com. 1994, bylaws com. 1995—), Endocrine Soc., Chgo. Endocrine Club (pres. 1984-85), Sigma Xi, Alpha Omega Alpha. Office: Clin Affairs Chgo Med Sch Rosalind Franklin U Medicine and Sci North Chicago IL 60064 E-mail: charles.barsano@rosalindfranklin.edu, cbflyer@aol.com.

BARSHAY, SCOTT A., lawyer; b. Manhasset, NY, Dec. 12, 1965; BA in Polit. Sci, magna cum laude, Colgate Univ., 1988; JD, Columbia Univ., 1991. Bar: NY 1992. Assoc. Cravath, Swaine, & Moore LLP, NYC, 1991—99, ptnr., corp., 1999—. Assoc. editor Journ. Transnational Law, Columbia Univ. Named a Stone Scholar; named one of Top 40 Under 40 Lawyers, Nat. Law. Jour., 2005. Mem.: ABA, Bar Assn. of City of NY, NY Bar Assn., Phi Beta Kappa. Office: Cravath, Swaine & Moore LLP Worldwide Plz 825 Eighth Ave New York NY 10019-7475 Office Phone: 212-474-1009. Office Fax: 212-474-3700. Business E-Mail: sbarshay@cravath.com.

BARSHEFSKY, CHARLENE, lawyer, former federal official; b. Aug. 11, 1950; BA with honors, U. Wis., 1972; JD, Catholic U., 1975. Ptnr. Steptoe & Johnson LLP, Washington, 1975-93; dep. US trade rep. Exec. Office of the Pres., Washington, 1993-96, US trade rep., 1996—2001; pub. policy scholar Woodrow Wilson Internat. Ctr., Washington, 2001; sr. internat. ptnr. Wilmer, Cutler, Pickering, Hale & Dorr LLP, Washington, 2001—. Named one of The 50 Most Influential Women Lawyers in Am., Nat. Law Jour., 2007. Mem.: bd. dirs., Intel Corp., 2004-. Office: Wilmer Cutler Pickering Hale & Dorr LLP 2445 M St Washington DC 20037-1420 Office Phone: 202-663-6130. Office Fax: 202-663-6363.*

BARSNESS, RICHARD WEBSTER, management educator, academic administrator; b. Elbow Lake, Minn., Apr. 26, 1935; s. Russel E. and Joanna (Warga) B.; m. Dorothea L. Gother, Aug. 22, 1964; children: Karen Louise, Erik Richard. BS, U. Minn., 1957, MA, 1958, MAP.A., 1960, PhD, 1963. Budget analyst U.S. Bur. Budget, Washington, 1960-61; instr., asst. prof. Northwestern U., Evanston, Ill., 1962-69, assoc. prof., 1969-78, assoc. dean, 1972-78; dean, prof. Lehigh U., Bethlehem, Pa., 1978-92, prof., 1978—, Iacocca prof. bus., 1992-93, exec. dir. Iacocca Inst., 1992-95, Univ. disting. svc. prof. mgmt., 1995—2005, emeritus prof., 2005. Exec. sec. Lexington Group in Transport History, 1969-89; pres. Bus. History Conf., 1981-82, Lexington Group, Inc., 1997-2005; lectr. Transp. Ctr., Evanston, Ill., 1964-86; editl. cons. Contbr.: articles to profl. jours.; editor: Lexington Newsletter. Mem. Gov.'s Adv. Coun. State of Ill., 1969—72; gen. chmn. United Way Lehigh U., 1981; v.p., bd. dirs. Episcopal House, Allentown, Pa., 1999—, pres., 2003—05. Recipient R.R. and E.C. Hillman award, Lehigh U., 1991. Mem.: Acad. Internat. Bus., Internat. Assn. for Bus. and Soc., Bus. History Conf. (trustee 1978—81, pres. 1981—82), Transp. Rsch. Forum, Acad. Mgmt., Phi Beta Kappa, Beta Gamma Sigma. Republican. Episcopalian. Home: 769 Apollo Dr Bethlehem PA 18017-2556 Office: Lehigh U Coll Bus 621 Taylor St Bethlehem PA 18015-3117 Home Phone: 610-865-1399; Office Phone: 610-758-4355. Business E-Mail: rwb0@lehigh.edu.

BARSUN, HANS FREDERICK, engineer; b. Bloomington, Ind., Feb. 27, 1969; s. H. Fred and Rita M. Barsun; m. Bonnie Dawn MacKenzie, Dec. 31, 1993; children: Heidi, Solomon, Liesl, Stasia. BS in Aero. Engring., Purdue U., West Lafayette, Ind., 1992; MSME, U. N.Mex., Albuquerque, 1995. Facilities engr. INTEL, Rio Rancho, N.Mex., 1995—2006, U. N.Mex., Albuquerque, 2006—. Mem.: N.Mex. Mt. Club (leader 1994—). Democrat. Lutheran. Avocations: bicycling, rock climbing, travel, trombone, woodworking.

BART, PETER BENTON, editor, film producer, writer; b. NYC, July 24, 1932; m. Leslie Cox; children: Colby, Dilys. BA, Swarthmore Coll., 1954; MA, London Sch. Econs., 1956. Staff reporter The Wall Street Jour., NYC, 1956-57, The N.Y. Times, NYC, 1957-67; v.p. Paramount Pictures, Los Angeles, 1967-74; pres. Bart Palevsky Prodn., LA, 1974-77, Lorimar Film Co., Los Angeles, 1977-82; sr. v.p., film producer Metro Goldwyn Mayer/United Artists, LA, 1982-85; v.p., editorial dir. Variety and Daily Variety, LA, 1989—, editor-in-chief. Author: Destinies, 1980, Thy Kingdom Come, 1983, Fade Out: The Calamitous Final Days of MGM, 1990; prodr.: (films) Fun with Dick and Jane, Islands in the Stream, Youngblood. Office: Variety 5700 Wilshire Blvd Ste 120 Los Angeles CA 90036-3644

BART, ROGER, actor; b. Norfolk, Conn., Sept. 29, 1962; children: Alexandra, Eller. BFA, Rutgers U., 1985. Actor(with Broadway/first nat. tour credits including:): You're a Good Man, Charlie Brown (Tony award, Drama Desk award), The Producers, 2001, 2005, 2006, Triumph of Love, The Who's Tommy, (London's West End, U.S. Tour, German prodns. of:): King David, How to Succeed in Business, The Secret Garden, Big River, (off-Broadway) Henry IV, Parts I and II, Up Against It, role of Whizzer in Falsettos; singing voice title role of Walt Disney's animated feature Hercules, other canine credits include singing voice of Scamp in Disney's Lady and the Tramp Part II, acting role in The George Carlin Show, Fox TV; actor: (George St. prodn.) Ancestral Voices, 2002; (TV series) Bram and Alice, 2002, Law & Order: Special Victims Unit, 1999, Desperate Housewives, 2005 (Outstanding Performance by an Ensemble in a Comedy Series, Screen Actors Guild award, 2006); (films) The Insider, 1999, The Stepford Wives, 2004, The Producers, 2005. Office: c/o SAG 360 Madison Ave #12 New York NY 10017-7111

BART, SUSAN THERESE, lawyer; b. Chgo., June 6, 1961; BA, Grinnell Coll., 1982; JD, U. Mich., 1985. Bar: Ill. 1985, U.S. Ct. Appeals (7th cir.) 1985. Law clk. to Hon. Richard D. Cudahy, Fed. Ct. Appeals (7th cir.), 1985—86; with Hopkins & Sutter, 1986—94, ptnr., 1992—94, Sidley Austin LLP, 1994—. Articles editor U. Mich. Law Review, Ann Arbor, 1984-85. Author: Education Planning and Gifts to Minors, 2004; co-author: Illinois Estate Planning: Forms and Commentary, 1997 (Outstanding Achievement award Assn. for Continuing Legal Edn., 1998), rev., 2005. Mem. bd. dirs., exec. com. Ill. Inst. Continuing Legal Edn.; sec., bd. dirs. The Next Theatre; mem. bd. trustees Roosevelt U.; mem. bd. dirs. Domestic Violence Legal Clinic. Mem. Phi Beta Kappa, Order of the Coif. Avocations: classics, literature, theater. Office: Sidley Austin LLP One S Dearborn St Chicago IL 60603

BARTALINI, C. RICHARD, judge; b. Kincaid, Ill., Sept. 25, 1931; s. Chester Richard and Florinda (Galli) B.; m. Anne M. Evanoff, June 4, 1955; children: Robert Charles, Denise Anne, David Chester. BA, U. Calif., Berkeley, 1954; JD, U. Calif, San Francisco, 1957. Bar: Calif. 1957. Practice law, Oakland, 1957-66, Alameda, 1966-77; dep. dist. atty. Alameda County, 1957-59; chief def. counsel Transit Casualty Co., 1959-60; chief trial atty. Alameda/Contra Costa Transit Co., 1960-61; asso. Nichols, Williams, Morgan & Digardi, 1961-66; partner Davis, Craig & Bartalini, 1966-77; judge Superior Ct. Calif., 1977-93; ret., 1993. Atty., counselor Supreme Ct. US; del. Calif. Bar Conf., 1963-68; cons. US Dept. Justice, US Dept. Edn.; faculty Nat. Inst. for Trial Advocacy, Ctr. for Trial and Appellate Advocacy, Hastings Coll. Law, Calif. Ctr. for Jud. Edn. and Rsch. Chmn. Alameda Youth Activities Com., 1958-63, Nat. Coun. on Mental Health and Retardation, 1965-69; mem. President's Coun. on Youth Opportunity, 1965-70; pres. Alameda Bd. Edn.; pres., v.p., bd. dirs. Alameda Boys Club; bd. dirs. Alameda Develop. Corp.; mem. exec. com. Nat. Found. March of Dimes; chmn. No. Calif. Area coun., mem. Nat. Commn. for Constl. Revision and mem. nat. area coun. com. Boys Clubs Am.; chmn. bd. dirs. Moreau High Sch., Hayward, Calif., Alameda Hosp. Found.; mem. adv. bd. Partners Program, The Close-Up Found., CY Press Mandela Wist Tng. Ctr.; mem. civil svc. bd. City of Alameda, 1992-96, mem. housing authority, 1996—; mem. Alameda County Grand Jury, 1997-98, chair Measure A oversight com., superintendents edn. adv. com.; bd. dirs. Alameda Devel. Corp., Alameda Friendly Visitors, chair Measure C oversight com.; mem. Alamed Friendly Visitors, Assistance Parking Patrol. Recipient Svc. award Nat. Congress Parents and Tchrs., 1972, Disting. Svc. award Alameda Unified Sch. Dist., 1972, Man and Boy award Boys Clubs Am., 1975, Bronze Keystone award Boys Club Am., 1979, Bronze Keystone and Svc. Bar awards Boys and Girls Clubs of Am., 1989, Cross and Anchors award Moreau Cath. HS, 2005; named Young Man of Yr. City of Alameda, 1965, Outstanding Civic Leader of Am., 1967. Mem. ATLA, ABA, Calif. Bar Assn., Alameda County Bar Assn. (dir.), Criminal Cts. Bar Assn., Com. for Advancement and Support of Edn., Nat. Assn. Ind. Schs., Alameda Collaborative for Children, Youth and Their Families, Alameda County Lawyers Club (past pres.), Calif. C. of C. (past dir.), Alameda Jaycees (past pres.), US Jaycees (past legal counsel), Elks, Eagles, Kiwanis, Alameda Rod and Gun Club, Commonwealth Club, Chabot Gun Club, Phi Alpha Delta. Home: 1224 Bay St Alameda CA 94501-3914 Home Phone: 510-523-9398. Office Fax: 510-523-1952. Personal E-mail: judgealceste@aol.com.

BARTEAU, MARK ALAN, chemical engineering and chemistry educator; b. St. Louis, Sept. 8, 1956; s. Dallas Frank and Charlotte Jean (Shelker) B.; m. Diane Viola Jorgensen, June 25, 1983; children: Katherine Pearl, Alexander Bradford. BSChemE, Washington U., 1976; MSChemE, Stanford U., 1977, PhD, 1981. Postdoctoral fellow Tech. U. Munich, 1981-82; asst. prof. U. Del., Newark, 1982-87, assoc. prof., 1987-90, prof. chem. engring. and chemistry, 1990-94, Robert L. Pigford prof., 1994—, dir. Ctr. for Catalytic Sci. and Tech., 1996-2000, chmn. dept. chem. engring., 2000—. NSF Postdoctoral fellow, 1981; recipient Presdl. Young Investigator award NSF, 1985, Ipatieff prize Am. Chem. Soc., 1995, Internat. Catalysis award Internat. Assn. Catalysis Socs., 1998, Alpha Chi Sigma award, 2001. Mem. AAAS, AIChE (Allan P. Colburn award 1991, assoc. editor jour.), NAE, Am. Chem. Soc. (Ipatieff prize 1994, Victor K. LaMer award 1982), Catalysis Soc. (Paul H. Emmett award 1993), Materials Rsch. Soc., Am. Vacuum Soc. Democrat. Office: Univ of Del Dept Chem Engring Newark DE 19716 Home Phone: 302-998-6248; Office Phone: 302-831-8905. Business E-Mail: barteau@udel.edu.

BARTEE, NEALE, music educator, musician, conductor; b. Springfield, Mo., Feb. 23, 1947; s. Josephus Christian and Thelma Ruby Bartee; m. Debra Elaine Austin. BS in Edn., U. Ill., 1969, MEd, 1970, PhD, 1977. Tchr. instrumental music pub. schs., Norman, Okla., 1972—73; prof. music Ark. State U., Jonesboro, 1973—. Condr. Delta Symphony Orch., Jonesboro, 1975—; trombonist ch. music programs, Ark., Mo., Tenn., 1973—. Condr. Internat. Trombone Festivals, 1997, 2001. Condr. Clinician fellow, Coll. Band Dirs. Nat. Assn., Austin, Tex., 1989, Bapt. Nat. Music Conf., Glorietta, N.Mex., 1992, Friend of the Arts fellow, Sigma Alpha Iota, Epsilon Gamma chpt., 1999. Mem.: Music Edn. Nat. Conf. (Ark. state pres. 1997—98). Baptist. Home: 3713 Burdyshaw Jonesboro AR 72401 Personal E-mail: enbartee@cox.net.

BARTEE, ROSUSAN D., educational leadership educator; b. Meridan, Miss., Oct. 20, 1974; d. Howard Bartee Sr. and Dorothy K. Bartee. BA in English, Tongaloo Coll., Jackson, Miss., 1997; MS in Liberal Studies, Northwestern U., Evanston, Ill., 1998; PhD in Ednl. Policy Studies, U. Ill., Urbana, 2003. Project coord. U. Ill., Urbana, 2001—03; sr. rsch. assoc., program mgr. Frederick D. Patterson Rsch. Inst., United Negro Coll. Fund, Fairfax, Va., 2003—04, interim exec. dir., 2004—05; assoc. project dir. Nat. Cound. Accrediation of Tchr. Edn., Washington, 2005—06; assoc. prof. U. Miss., University, 2006—. Cons. Quitran County Sch., Marks, Miss., 2006—; grant reviewer US Dept. of Edn., Washington, 2006—; mem. nat. and state bd. examiners Nat. Coun. for Accrediation of Tchr. Edn., 2006—. Author: School Matters: Why African American Students Need Multiple Forms of Capital, 2007. Fellow, Inst. Govtl. Pub. Affairs, Urbana, 2000—01, DC Ctr. for Internatships. Mem.: Am. Ednl. Rsch. Assn., AAUP, Phi Delta Kappa (pres. 2001—02). Avocations: reading, Tae Kwon Do, films, cultural activities. Office: Univ Miss 106 Guyton Hall PO Box 1848 University MS 38677-1848

BARTEE, THOMAS CRESON, computer scientist, educator; b. Moberly, Mo., Dec. 18, 1926; s. Thomas Monroe and Verna Miller (Tippett) B.; m. Mildred Higdon, Sept. 5, 1953; 1 child, Thomas Quentin. BA, Westminster Coll., 1949. Mem. staff computer research M.I.T.-Lincoln Lab., Lexington, Mass., 1955-63; Gordon MacKay lectr. in computer engring. Harvard U., Cambridge, Mass., 1963-69, dir. electronic design center, 1969-72, Gordon MacKay prof. computer engring., 1970—. Cons. Nat. Acad. Scis., IDA, IBM, Honeywell, Raytheon; IEEE disting. computer sci. lectr., 1972-74 Author: (with G. Birkhoff) Modern Applied Algebra, 1971, Introduction to Computer Science, 1972, Digital Computer Fundamentals, 7th edit., 1989, Basic Computer Programming, 1981, 2d edit., 1985, Data Communications, Networks and Systems, 1985, 2d edit., 1992, Digital Communications, 1986, Expert Systems in AI, 1987, ISDN, SNA AND DECNET, 1989; editor: IEEE-IRE Computer Jour., 1963-66. Recipient Disting. contbn. in computer sci. award Westminster Coll., 1980 Mem. IEEE (chmn. N.E. computer group 1973-74), Am. Math. Soc. Office: Aiken Computation Lab Harvard Univ Cambridge MA 02138 Home: 2534 S Walter Reed Dr Apt A Arlington VA 22206-1287 Personal E-mail: tcbartee@hotmail.com.

BARTEE, WAYNE C., retired history professor; b. Springfield, Mo., Jan. 11, 1936; s. Josephus Christian and Thelma Ruby (Clark) Bartee; m. Alice Fleetwood; children: Wayne Clark II, George Fleetwood. BA cum laude, SW Mo. State U., 1958; MA, Columbia U., 1959, PhD, 1966. Asst. prof. history Okla. Bapt. U., Shawnee, 1964—67; head dept. history SW Mo. State U., Springfield, 1976—91; prof. history Mo. State U., Springfield, 1997—2006. Contbr. articles to profl. jours.; author: Litigating Morality, 1992, A Time to Speak Out, 2000. Pres. County Hist. Soc., 1973—76; trustee Judson Coll., Elgin, Ill., 2002—; sec., exec. com. Dem. Ctrl. Com., Greene County, 2002—; bd. dirs. Hist. Preservation Soc., Greene County, Mo., 1970—78. Capt. US Army, 1961—62. Recipient Heritage award, Heritage Coun., 1988; fellow, Woodrow Wilson Found., 1958—59; Fulbright fellow, US Govt., 1962—63. Democrat. Baptist. Avocations: reading, gardening. Home: 3033 E Carlisle Cir Springfield MO 65804

BARTEL, ARTHUR GABRIEL, retired principal, alderman, culinary arts instructor; b. San Francisco, Oct. 20, 1934; s. Irving Peter and Elian Leah (Barker) B.; m. Dottie Lu Smith, Dec. 14, 1963 (dec. Apr. 1972); children: Brian Blake, Scott Michael; m. Suzane M. Loftis, Feb. 14, 1989. Student, San Jose State Coll., 1952-54; BS, U. Calif., Berkeley, 1957; postgrad., U. So. Calif., 1968-70; MA, Pepperdine U., 1973, Calif. State U., Fresno, 1995; AA in Culinary Arts, Art Inst. Seattle, 2004. Cert. FAA air traffic controller, 1957-77, naval flight officer, 1965; lic. standard tchr., life standard svc., life chief coll. adminstrv. officer, life C.C. supr., life C.C. instr., spl. edn. svcs. credential, Calif.; cert. culinary specialist. Enlisted USMC, 1954, commd. 2d lt., 1957, advanced through grades to maj., 1967, comdg. officer VMFA-314 Fighter-Attack Squadron El Toro, Calif., 1970-72, ret., 1977; gen. mgr. Nieuport 17 Restaurant, Santa Ana, Calif., 1977-78; pres., CEO High Flight Inc., Hanford, San Diego, Calif., 1978-81; tchg. vice-prin. Armona Union Elem. Sch., Calif., 1982-84, tchr. sci. and lang. arts. Calif., 1981-84; curriculum cons. Kings County Office Edn., Hanford, 1984-86; program specialist Kings County Supt. Schs., Hanford, 1986-91; prin. Kings County Cmty. Sch., Hanford, 1994-98, ret., 1998; supr. directed tchg. Chapman U., 1999—2002; instr. culinary arts Art Inst. Seattle, 2004—05. Councilman City of Hanford, 1986-90, mayor, 1988-90; mem. adv. bd. San Joaquin Valley Writing Project, 1984-86, 92-99. Vice-chmn. Hanford Planning Commn., 1982-86; vice-chmn. bd. trustees Sacred Heart Hosp., 1987-93; bd. dirs. Navy League, 1992-2002. Decorated Air medal (9), Vietnam Cross of Gallantry, Meritorious Svc. medal, Joint Svc. Commendation medal; fellow internat. writing project U. Calif., Irvine, 1985. Mem. Assn. Calif. Sch. Adminstrs., Calif. Soc. Program Specialists, Hanford C. of C., DAV (life), Ret. Officers Assn., Navy League (v.p. 1993-95), Delta Upsilon (life). Avocations: hunting, fishing, coin collecting/numismatics, gun and knife collecting, travel. Personal E-mail: artbartel@msn.com.

BARTEL, DAVID, biology professor, researcher; PhD, Harvard U., 1993. Whitehead fellow Whitehead Inst., 1994, assoc. mem., 1996, current mem.; asst. prof. biology MIT, 1996, prof. biology; investigator Howard Hughes Med. Inst. Contbr. articles to profl. jours. Named Searle Scholar, 1997; recipient Newcomb Cleveland prize, AAAS, 2002, Molecular Biology award, NAS, 2005, Institut de France's Louis-D. prize, 2005. Achievements include made major contributions to the discovery and understanding of microRNAs, small RNS molecules that are important in gene regulation; created ribozyme (RNA enzyme) that synthesizes pieces of RNA, bolstering the "RNA world" theory; designed RNA sequence that can fold into either of two ribozymes; aided early work in RNAi, including moving the technique to mammalian cells. Office: Whitehead Inst Nine Cambridge Center Room WI 601B Cambridge MA 02142-1479 Office Phone: 617-258-5287. E-mail: dbartel@wi.mit.edu.

BARTELL, ANGELA GINA BALDI, judge; b. Milw., Jan. 25, 1946; d. John Batiste and Marie Alma (Rank) Baldi; m. Jeffrey Bruce Bartell, Aug. 31, 1968; children: Jessica Marie, Carey Laurel, Chad Gerald, Dana Joyce, Nicholas John. BA, U. Wis., 1969, JD, 1971. Bar: Wis. 1972, U.S. Dist. Ct. (we. dist.) Wis. 1972. Intern Wis. Dept. Justice, Madison, 1970; law clk. to Hon. James E. Doyle U.S. Dist. Ct. (we. dist.) Wis., Madison, 1971-72; assoc., then ptnr. LaFollette Sinykin Law Firm, Madison, 1973-78; county judge Dane County Ct., Madison, 1978-79; chief judge Wis. Fifth Jud. Dist., 1982-88; cir. judge Dane County Cir. Ct., Madison, 1979—. Mem. Professionalism Commn., Madison, 1990-93; mem. Legal Edn. Commn., 1994-95; mem. adv. bd. Scan Child Abuse Prevention Project, Madison, 1988-90; assoc. dean Wis. Jud. Coll., 1999—2005. Jud. editor Wisconsin Jud. Benchbooks, 3 vols., 1980-92 (Supreme Ct. award 1992), Wisconsin Jury Handbook, 1983; contbr.: State Bar Civil Forms Manual, 1992—, Wisconsin Jury Instructions-Criminal, 1992-2002. Pres. Young Lawyers divsn. Wis. State Bar, Madision, 1974; bd. dirs. Dane County United Way, 1995-2001, chair bd., 2000-01. Recipient Marygold Melli Legal Achievement award, Dane County Legal Assn. for Women, 2004. Fellow: Am. Bar Found.; mem.: Nat. Assn. Women Judges, Am. Law Inst., Wis. Hist. Soc. (bd. of curators), Rotary Club Madison (pres. 2003—04), Phi Beta Kappa. Office: Dane County Cir Ct 215 S Hamilton St Madison WI 53703-3109 Office Phone: 608-266-4460.

BARTELL, ERNEST, economist, educator, priest; b. Chgo., Jan. 22, 1932; PhB, U. Notre Dame, 1953; AM, U. Chgo., 1954; MA, Coll. Holy Cross, 1961; PhD, Princeton U., 1966; LLD (hon.), China Acad., Taipei, Taiwan, 1975, St. Joseph's Coll., 1983, King's Coll., 1984, Stonehill Coll., 1992. Ordained priest Roman Cath. Ch., 1961. Instr. econs. Princeton U., NJ, 1965—66; asst. prof. econs. U. Notre Dame, Ind., 1966—68, assoc. prof., 1968—71, chmn. dept. econs., 1968—71, dir. Ctr. Study of Man in Contemporary Soc., 1969—71, prof. econs., 1981—2003, prof. emeritus, 2003—; exec. dir. Helen Kellogg Inst. Internat. Studies, 1981—97, fellow, 1997—; pres. Stonehill Coll., North Easton, Mass., 1971—77; dir. Fund for Improvement Post Secondary Edn. U.S. Dept. Health, Edn. and Welfare, Washington, 1977—79; dir. Project 80 Assn. Cath. Colls. and Univs., Washington, 1979—80; coord. overseas mission Priests of Holy Cross, Ind. Province, 1980—84, assoc. dir. Holy Cross Mission Ctr., 1984—95; asst. to pastor St. Anthony Ch., Ft. Lauderdale, Fla., 1993—2003. Active Inst. East-West Securities Studies Working Group on Sources in Instability, 1989-90, Internat. Ctr. Devel. Policy Commn. on U.S.-Soviet Rels., 1988-89, Overseas Devel. Coun., 1988-2000, The Bretton Woods Com., 1992-2002; mem. policy planning commn. Nat. Inst. Ind. Colls. and Univs., 1982-85; bd. dirs. Ctr. for Health Promotion, Internat. Life Scis. Inst. Author; Costs and Benefits of Catholic Elementary and Secondary Schools, 1969; co-editor: Business and Democracy in Latin America, 1995, The Child in Latin America, 2000; contbr. articles to profl. jours. Bd. regents U. Portland, Oreg., 1984-2004; bd. dirs. Missionary Vehicle Assn. Am., 1981-88, Big Bros. and Big Sisters Am., 1978-80, Brockton Cmty. Housing Corp., 1974-77, The Brighter Day, 1974-77, Brockton Hosp., 1973-77, King's Coll., Wilkes-Barre, Pa., 1969-82; trustee Emmanuel Coll., 1977-78, trustee emeritus Stonehill Coll., 2002—; trustee U. Notre Dame, 1974-2002, bd. fellows, 1974-2002, trustee emeritus 2002-; bd. regents U. Portland 1984-2004; trustee Regis Coll., 2002—; adv. bd. Brockton Art Ctr., 1974-77; exec. com. Opera New Eng., 1977. Recipient Fenwick Alumni Recognition award, 1974; named to Fenwick Hall of Fame, 1990; faculty fellow Kellogg Inst., 1997—. Fellow Soc. Values in Higher Edn.; mem. Am. Econ. Assn., Am. Assn. Higher Edn., Nat. Cath. Ednl. Assn. (chmn. govtl. rels. com. 1976-77, vice chmn. exec. com. 1976-77, chmn. mgmt. and planning com. 1974-76), Assn. Soc. Econs., Latin Am. Studies Assn., Young Pres. Orgn. (sec. 1974-77), Delta Mu Delta (hon.). Home: 211 Corby Hall Notre Dame IN 46556-5680 Office: U Notre Dame Kellogg Inst 211 Hesburgh Ctr Notre Dame IN 46556-5677 Office Phone: 574-631-7816. Business E-Mail: ebartell@nd.edu.

BARTELL, LAWRENCE SIMS, chemist, educator; b. Ann Arbor, Mich., Feb. 23, 1923; s. Floyd Earl and Lawrence (Sims) B.; m. Joy Hilda Keer, Aug. 16, 1952; 1 son, Michael Keer. BS, U. Mich., 1944, MS, 1947, PhD, 1951. Research asst. Manhattan project U. Chgo., 1944-45; mem. faculty Iowa State U., 1953-65, prof. chemistry, 1959-65, U. Mich., 1965—, Philip J. Elving prof. chemistry, 1987-94, prof. emeritus, 1994—. Vis. prof. Moscow State U., 1972, U. Paris XI, Orsay, France, 1973, U. Tex., 1978, 86; cons. Gillette Co., Chgo., 1956-62, Mobil Oil Corp., Paulsboro, NJ, 1960-84; mem. commn. on electron diffraction Internat. Union Crystallography, 1966-75 Assoc. editor: Jour. Chem. Physics, 1963-66; mem. editorial bd.: Jour. Computational Chemistry, 1979-90, Chem. Physics Letters, 1981-84. Served with USNR, 1945. Recipient Disting. Faculty Achievement award U. Mich., 1981, Disting. Faculty award Mich. Assn. Governing Bds., 1982, Creativity award NSF, 1982, Metz-Stark award, 2004. Mem. Am. Chem. Soc. (petroleum rsch. fund adv. bd. 1970-73), Am. Phys. Soc. (chmn. divsn. chem. physics 1977-78), Am. Crystallographic Assn., AAAS, Phi Beta Kappa, Sigma Xi, Phi Kappa Phi, Phi Lambda Upsilon, Alpha Chi Sigma. Home: 381 Riverview Dr Ann Arbor MI 48104-1847 Home Phone: 734-663-6120; Office Phone: 734-764-7375. Business E-Mail: lbart@umich.edu.

BARTELS, BRUCE MICHAEL, health facility administrator; b. Chgo., Oct. 13, 1946; s. John Phillip Frederick and Margaret Florine (Michael) B.; children: Sarah, Jennifer, Rebecca. BA, U. Wis., 1969; MBA, U. Chgo., 1975. Adminstrv. asst. U. Chgo. Hosp., 1975-77; asst. adminstr. Meth. Hosp., Indpls., 1977-81; exec. v.p. Med. Ctr. Hosp. Vt., Burlington, 1981-88; pres. York (Pa.) Hosp. and Found., 1988-95, York Health Sys., 1995-99, WellSpan Health, York, 1999—. Contbr. articles to profl. jours. Bd. dirs. York County chpt. YMCA, York, 1989-98, chmn., 1994-96; bd. dirs. ARC, 1990-96, 2003—, United Way, 1991-96, WITF, Inc., Ctrl. Pa. Pub. Broadcasting, 1994-2002, chmn., 1999-2001; bd. dirs. Pa. Trauma Systems Found., Mechanicsburg, 1990-2003, chmn., 1997-99; bd. dirs. Novation, Inc., 2003—, Alliance Ind. Acad. Med. Ctrs., 2005—. With U.S. Army, Korea. Fellow Am. Coll. Healthcare Execs. (membership com. 1990-93); mem. Am. Hosp. Assn., Hosp. Assn. Pa. (bd. dirs., chmn.), York C. of C., U. Chgo. Health Adminstrn. Alumni Assn. (exec. com. 1991-95), Rotary. Avocations: reading, running, travel. Office: WellSpan Health 45 Monument Dr Ste 200 York PA 17403-3676 Office Phone: 717-851-2121. Business E-Mail: bbartels@wellspan.org.

BARTELS, JEAN ELLEN, nursing educator; b. Two Rivers, Wis., July 15, 1949; m. Terry D. Bartels, Aug. 14, 1971; children: Justin Dean, Ashlee Jill. Diploma, Columbia Hosp. Sch. Nursing, 1970; BSN with honors, Alverno Coll., Milw., 1981; MSN, Marquette U., Milw., 1983; PhD in Nursing, U. Wis., Milw., 1990. Staff nurse ICU Columbia Hosp., Milw., 1970-76; prof. nursing Alverno Coll., Milw., 1983-99, dean nursing, 1990-99; chair Sch. Nursing Ga. So. U., Statesboro, 1999—. Contbr. articles to profl. jours. Mem.: AACN (past pres.), ANA, Am. Ednl. Rsch. Assn., Am. Assn. Colls. Nursing, Internat. Soc. for Sci. Study Subjectivity, Mu Kappa, Sigma Theta Tau. Home: 912 Brittany Ln Statesboro GA 30461-4499 Office: Ga So U PO Box 8158 Statesboro GA 30460-1000 Office Phone: 912-681-5455. E-mail: jbartels@georgiasouthern.edu.

BARTELS, ROBERT EDWIN, aerospace engineer; b. Des Moines, May 24, 1955; s. Everett M. and Iola J. (Van Wyck) B. BS, Iowa State U., 1977; MDiv cum laude, N.W. Baptist Sem., Tacoma, Wash., 1983; MS, Iowa State U., 1992, PhD, 1994. Sr. engr. Boeing Comml. Airplane Co., Seattle, 1984—87; teaching asst. Iowa State U., Ames, 1987—92, grad. rsch. fellow NASA, 1992—94; NRC rsch. assoc. NASA Langley Rsch. Ctr., Hampton, Va., 1994—97, aerospace engr., 1997—2003, sr. rsch. engr., 2003—. Adj. prof. Tidewater C.C., 1998; adj. assoc. prof. Old Dominion U., 2005—. Bd. dirs., treas. Second Wind Contemporary Dance Co., 1996-98. Recipient Grad. Student Tchg. Excellence award Iowa State U., 1991. Mem. ASME, Phi Kappa Phi. Office: Nasa Langley Rsch Ctr Hampton VA 23681-0001

BARTELS, ROBERT LOUIS, retired physical education educator, coach; b. Gettysburg, S.D., Nov. 14, 1928; s. Adolph Walter and Ruth Mills Bartels; m. Janet Cowl Redman, June 9, 1951; children: Janet Ruth, Robin Bartels Lucas, Robert Redman. BS, Ohio State U., Columbus, 1951, MA, 1952, PhD, 1962. Swimming/tennis coach and asst. athletic dir. Kenyon Coll., Gambier, Ohio, 1952—54; swimming/tennis coach and asst. prof. Ohio U., Athens, 1954—59; instr. Ohio State U., Columbus, 1959—62, asst. prof., 1962—67, asst. swim coach, 1962—63, head swim coach, 1963—67, assoc. prof., 1968—72, prof., 1972—89. Pres. Coll. Swim Coaches Assn. Am., 1971—72, Ohio State U. Faculty Club, Columbus, Ohio, 1981, Ohio State U. Retirees Assn., 1991—92. Contbr. chapters to books, articles to profl. jours. Vol. dir. safety svcs. Columbus Area Red Cross, Ohio, 1963—86; mem. med. adv. bd. Columbus YMCA, 1970—80. Named to Ohio State U. Athletic Hall of Fame, 1998, Ohio State U. Coll. of Edn. Hall of Fame, 2002; recipient Disting. Coach award, Coll. Swim Coaches Assn. Am., 1972, Honor award, 1980. Fellow: Am. Coll. Sports Medicine. Office: Ohio State Univ Columbus OH 43210

BARTELS, STANLEY LEONARD, investment banker; b. NYC, Sept. 1, 1927; s. Abraham and Anna (Schultz) B.; m. Linda Lauretz; children: Jonathan Scott, Nancy Merrill, Diane Brooke, Elizabeth Cara. BS, NYU, 1954, MBA, 1956; grad., NY State Maritime Acad., 1947. Examiner Mfrs. Hanover Bank, NYC, 1948-50; security analyst Standard & Poor's Corp., NYC, 1950-53; sr. financial analyst internat. div. Ford Motor Co., NYC, 1953-56; asst. treas. W.R. Grace, Inc., NYC, 1956-57; v.p. Tex. McCrary, Inc.; also controller, asst. to pres. NYC, 1957-60; gen. partner, mem. mgmt. com., mem. N.Y. Stock Exchange J.R. Williston & Beane, NYC, 1960-63; pres., dir. Electrocopy Corp., 1963-66; sr. v.p., dir. Shaskan & Co., Inc.; mem. NY Stock Exchange, 1966—75; pres. J.D. Winer & Co., Inc.; v.p. L.M. Rosenthal & Co., Inc.; sr. v.p. Weinrich Zitzmann Whitehead, St. Louis, 1981-82; sr. v.p., prin. investment banking Laidlaw Adams & Peck, Inc., NYC, 1982-84; exec. v.p., founding dir. Yorke McCarter Owen & Bartels, Inc., NYC, 1984-91; exec. v.p., dir. Hampshire Securities Corp., NYC, 1991-94; exec. v.p. Coleman and Co. Securities, Inc., 1995-2000; sr. v.p. Auerbach, Pollak & Richardson, Inc., 2000—02, Gilford Securities Inc., 2003—. Trustee, chair fin. com. Maritime Industry Mus. NY State Maritime Coll., 1994—. Served to lt. comdr. USNR. Mem. Chartered Fin. Analysts Inst., Securities Industry Assn. (mem. nat. investment banking com. 1993-96), Bond Club of NY, Naval Order of the US, Phi Alpha Kappa. Clubs: U. of NY Home: Farley Rd Short Hills NJ 07078 *Only those projects that are of a beneficial nature to society have the tendency to survive.*

BARTELS, TERESA HALL, non-profit organization administrator; m. Chuck Bartels; 5 children. BS, No. Ariz. U. Assoc. regional dir., Mid-Am. region United Way Am., 1982; assoc. campaign and comm. dir. United Way, Lake County, Ill.; owner Manpower Inc.; owner, pres. Hallbert Holdings, LLC., Mundelein, Ill.; pres., CEO United Way Internat., 2007—. Vol. United Way, 1985—; vice chair of bd., chair personnel com. United Way Internat. Vice chair of bd., chair devel. com., mem. capital campaign com. Carmel High Sch.; bd. dirs. Univ. Ctr. Lake County. Office: United Way Internat HQ 701 N Fairfax St Alexandria VA 22314-2045*

BARTELT, WILLIAM E., historian, educator; b. Huntingburg, Ind., Mar. 9, 1946; s. Melvin W. and Mabel Bartelt; m. Kathryn R. Lawson, Apr. 2, 1983. BS, Ind. State U., Terre Haute, 1968. Cert. tchr. Ind., 1972. Adj. instr. history U. So. Ind., Evansville, 1986—2007; tchr., dept. chair Harrison H.S., Evansville, Ind., 1999—2005. Seasonal pk. ranger/historian Nat. Pk. Svc.-Lincoln Boyhood Nat. Meml., Lincoln City, Ind., 1979—92; vice chair Indiana A. Lincoln Bicentennial Commn., 2007—. Co-author: (book) At the Bend in the River: The Story of Evansville, 2004. Trustee Ind. Hist. Soc., Indpls., 2006—. Recipient Hoosier Historian award, Ind. Hist. Soc., 2003, Nat. History Tchr. of Yr., Colonial Dames of the 17th Century, 2004. Home Phone: 812-853-6136.

BARTER, MARY F., academic administrator; BA, U. Minn., 1964; MS, U. Wis., Milw., 1969, PhD, 1975. Supt. Three Village Cen. Sch. Dist., LI, NY, 1992—99, Durango (Colo.) Sch. Dist. 9-R, 1999—. Recipient Disting. Supt. and Outstanding Supt. awards, Suffolk County and N.Y. Coun. Sch. Supts. Mem.: Horace Mann League, N.Y. Assn. for Women in Adminstrn. (bd. dirs.), Wis. Elem. Kindergarten Nursery Educators (pres.), N.Y. Coun. Sch. Supts. (pres.), Am. Assn. Sch. Adminstrs. (exec. com., women adminstrs. adv. com., fed. policy and legis. com., exec. dir.'s adv. com., del. assembly). Office: Durango Sch Dist 9-R 201 E 12th St Durango CO 81301

BARTFELD, DANIEL D., lawyer; b. Washington, 1968; BA, Univ. Mich., 1990; JD, George Washington Univ., 1993. Bar: N.Y. 1994. Ptnr. Global Project Fin. Dept. & mem. recruiting com. Milbank Tweed Hadley & McCloy, NYC. Office: Milbank Tweed Hadley & McCloy 1 Chase Manhattan Plz New York NY 10005-1413 Office Phone: 212-530-5185. Office Fax: 212-530-5219. Business E-Mail: dbartfeld@milbank.com.

BARTH, DANNY, professional sports team executive; married; 2 children. Grad., Seattle U. With audit divsn. Price Waterhouse, LLC, Seattle and NYC; dir. fin. and acctg. Cinnabon, Inc.; v.p. fin., contr. Seattle SuperSonics, 1996—2000, exec. v.p., CFO, 2000—06; interim pres., CEO The Profl. Basketball Club, LLC (parent co. of NBA SuperSonics and WNBA Storm), Seattle, 2006—. Office: The Profl Basketball Club LLC 351 Elliott Ave W Ste 500 Seattle WA 98119*

BARTH, DAVID KECK, retired wholesale distribution executive, consultant; b. Springfield, Ill., Dec. 7, 1943; s. David Klenk and Edna Margaret (Keck) B.; m. Dian Oldemeyer, Nov. 21, 1970; children— David, Michael, John. BA cum laude, Knox Coll., Galesburg, Ill., 1965; MBA, U. Calif., Berkeley, 1971. With data processing div. IBM Corp., Chgo., 1966; with No. Trust Co., Chgo., 1971-72; mgr. treasury ops., then treas. fin. services group Borg-Warner Corp., Chgo., 1972-79; treas. W.W. Grainger, Inc., Skokie, Ill., 1979-83, v.p., 1984-90; pres. Barth Smith Co., 1991—2001. Mem. faculty Lake Forest Grad. Sch. Mgmt., Ill., 1994—2006; bd. dirs. Indsl. Distbn. Group Inc., Atlanta. Served to lt. USNR, 1966-69. Mem. Econ. Club Chgo., Beta Gamma Sigma, Phi Delta Theta. Lutheran. Personal E-mail: davidbarth@sbcglobal.net.

BARTH, FRANCES, artist; b. NYC, July 31, 1946; BFA, Hunter Coll., 1968, MA, 1970. Instr. Princeton U., 1975—79, Sarah Lawrence Coll., Bronxville, NY, 1979—85; prof. Yale U., New Haven, 1986—2004; dir. Mt. Royal Sch. of Art, Md. Inst. Coll. of Art, 2004—. One-woman shows include, N.Y.C., 1974—, Jan Cicero Gallery, Chgo., 1981, 1985, U. Mass. Amherst, 1994, E.M. Donahue Gallery, N.Y.C., 1994, 1997, 2000, Millersville Coll., Pa., 1995, Marcia Wood Gallery, Atlanta, 1998, 2001, 2002, Moravian Coll., Pa., 1999, Donahue Sosinski, N.Y.C., 2000, Dartmouth Coll., N.H., 2005, NY Studio Sch., NYC, 2006, exhibited in group shows at Moore Coll. Art, 1970, Whitney Mus. Am. Art, N.Y.C., 1972—73, Houston Mus. Contemporary Art, 1972, Corcoran Gallery Art, Washington, Bard Coll., Annandale-on-Hudson, N.Y.C., 1973, Trenton State Coll., 1974, Princeton U. Art Mus., 1975, High Mus. Art, Atlanta, 1976, Bennington Coll., 1976, San Francisco Art Inst., 1978, U. Pa., 1978, MIT, 1978, Jan Cicero, CHI, 1995, Moravia Coll., Pa., 1999, William Patterson Coll., Wayne, N.J., 1979, NYU, 1979, Va. Commonwealth U., Richmond, 1980, Sarah Lawrence Coll., 1981, Mus. Modern Art, 1981, Cleve. Mus. Art, 1983, Indpls. Mus., 1984, 1985, Princeton U., 1985, Hunter Coll., 1986, Yale U., 1987, Bennington Coll., 1991, Am. Acad. Arts and Letters, 1988 (Purchase award, 2004), Met. Mus. Art, 1990, Andre Emmerich Gallery, 1991, La Viglie, Nimes, France, 1995, Charles Cowles Gallery, N.Y.C., 1996, Am. Acad. Arts and Letters, 1999, 2004, Tucson Mus. Art, 2003, Am. Acad. Arts and Letters, 2004, Represented in permanent collections New 20th Century Wing, Met. Mus. Art, N.Y.C., Mus. Modern Art, Akron Art Inst., Albright-Knox Gallery, Am. Can Co., Greenwich, Conn., Amerada Hess Corp., N.Y.C., Chase Manhattan Bank, Cornell U., IBM Corp., N.Y.C., Mobil Oil Corp., Prudential Inst. Co., N.J., Whitney Mus. Am. Art, Lehman Bros., N.Y.C. and Chgo., Isham, Lincoln & Beale, Chgo., Security Pacific Nat. Bank, L.A., Swiss Bank Corp., N.Y.C., Cameron Iron Works, Houston, Mus. Modern Art, N.Y.C., Paul Haim Found., Paris, Humana, Inc., Louisville, Coudert Bros., N.Y.C., Dallas Mus. Art, Tucson (Ariz.) Art Mus. Grantee Creative Artists Pub. Svc., 1973, NEA, 1974, 82, N.J. State Coun. on Arts, 1987, Adolph and Esther Gottlieb Ind. Support, 1993; John Guggenheim fellow, 1977; recipient Joan Mitchell Found. award, 1995.

BARTH, JOHN M., manufacturing executive; With Johnson Controls, Inc., Milw., 1969—, exec. v.p., 1992—98, bd. dir., 1997—, pres., COO, 1998—2002, pres., CEO, 2002—04, chmn., pres., CEO, 2004—06, chmn., CEO, 2006—07, chmn., 2007—. Office: Johnson Controls Inc 5757 N Green Bay Ave Milwaukee WI 53209-4408 Office Phone: 414-524-1200. Office Fax: 414-524-2077.*

BARTH, JOHN SIMMONS, writer, educator; b. Cambridge, Md., May 27, 1930; s. John Jacob and Georgia (Simmons) B.; m. Harriette Anne Strickland, Jan. 11, 1950 (div. 1969); children: Christine Anne, John Strickland, Daniel Stephen; m. Shelly I. Rosenberg, Dec. 27, 1970. BA, Johns Hopkins U., 1951, MA, 1952; LittD (hon.), Univ. Md., 1969; DHL (hon.), Pa. State U., 1996. Instr. English Pa. State U., 1953-56, asst. prof. English, 1957-60, assoc. prof. English, 1960-65; prof. English SUNY, Buffalo, 1965-73; prof. creative writing Johns Hopkins U., Balt., 1973-91, prof. emeritus creative writing, 1991—. Author: The Floating Opera, 1956 (Nat. Book award nomination 1956), The End of the Road, 1958, The Sot-Weed Factor, 1960, Giles Goat-Boy, 1966, Lost in the Funhouse, 1968 (Nat. Book award nomination 1968), Chimera, 1972 (Nat. Book award 1973), Letters, 1979, Sabbatical: A Romance, 1982, The Literature of Exhaustion, and The Literature of Replenishment, 1982, The Friday Book: Essays and Other Nonfiction, 1984, Don't Count on It: A Note on the Number of the 1001 Nights, 1984, The Tidewater Tales: A Novel, 1987, The Last Voyage of Somebody the Sailor, 1991, Once Upon a Time: A Floating Opera, 1994, Further Fridays: Essays, Lectures, and Other Non-fiction, 1984-94, 1995, On with the Story, 1996, Coming Soon!!!, 2001, The Book of Ten Nights and a Night, 2004, Where 3 Roads Meet, 2005. Recipient Brandeis Univ. Creative Arts award, 1965, F. Scott Fitzgerald award, 1997, PEN/Malamud award, 1998, Lifetime Achievement award Lannan Found., 1998, Lifetime Achievement in Letters award Enoch Pratt Soc., 1999; Rockefeller Found. grantee, 1965-66, Nat. Inst. Arts and Letters grantee, 1966. Mem. AAAL, Am. Acad. Arts and Scis. Office: Writing Seminars Johns Hopkins U Baltimore MD 21218

BARTH, KARL LUTHER, retired seminary president; b. Milw., Nov. 7, 1924; s. G. Christian and Louise A. (Schneemann) B.; m. Jean L. Kelly, June 8, 1947; children: Linda, Karl, Laurel, Kurt, Lisa. BA, Concordia Sem., 1945, M.Div., 1947; D.D. (hon.), Concordia Theol. Sem., 1975. Ordained to ministry, Luthern Ch., 1947. Asst. pastor First English Lutheran Ch., New Orleans, 1947-50; pastor Trinity Evan. Lutheran Ch., Centralia, Ill., 1950-52, St. Paul's Lutheran Ch., West Allis, Wis., 1956-70; pres. So. Wis. Dist. Luth. Ch. Mo. Synod, Milw., 1970-82, bd. for mission svcs., 1982-90, bd. dirs., 1992—2004; pres. Concordia Sem., St. Louis, 1982-90. Contbr. articles to profl. jours. Vice pres. So. Wis. dist. Lutheran Ch., Mo. Synod, 1966-70, exec. dir. 150th Anniversary; chmn. Com. on Theology and Ch. Relations, St. Louis, 1974-82; denominational rep. Div.

Theol. Studies Lutheran Council U.S.A., NYC, 1975-81; adv. bd. Wis. Citizens Concerned for Life, 1976-82. Mem. Badger Assn. of the Blind (adv. coun. 2000-03), Luth. Blind Mission Soc. (bd. dirs. 2004-05). Republican. Home: Apt 208 8220 Harwood Ave Milwaukee WI 53213

BARTH, MICHAEL CARL, economist; b. Newark, Apr. 3, 1941; s. Abe and Frances (Keller) B.; m. Marilyn Levy, Dec. 11, 1966; children: Christopher Jay, Karen Barth Simon. BA, Harpur Coll., Binghamton, NY, 1962; MA, U. Ill., Champaign, 1963; PhD, CUNY, 1971. Rsch. assoc. CCNY Rsch. Found., NYC, 1965-67; lectr. econs. CCNY, 1966-68; economist Pres's. Commn. on Income Maintenance, Washington, 1968-69, Office Econ. Opportunity, Washington, 1969-73; dir. income sec. policy/analysis U.S. Dept. HEW, Washington, 1973-75; vis. assoc. prof. econs. U. Wis., Madison, 1975-76; dep. asst. sec. U.S. Dept. HHS, Washington, 1976-80; prin. ICF Inc., Washington, 1980-87, sr. v.p., 1987—; pres. ICF Info. Tech. Inc., Washington, 1992-95; exec. v.p. ICF Internat., Fairfax, Va., 1995—. Bd. dirs. ICF Info. Tech., Inc, ICF Resources. Author: (with G. Carcagno and J. Palmer) Toward an Effective Income Support System: Problems, Prospects and Choices, 1974; editor: Greenhouse Effect and Sea Level Rise, 1984 contbr. articles to profl. jours. Recipient Sec.'s Spl. citation HEW, 1975, Sec.'s Outstanding Achievement award, 1977 Mem. Am. Econ. Assn., Am. Evaluation Assn. Home: 3818 Military Rd NW Washington DC 20015-2704 Office: ICF Internat 9300 Lee Hwy Fairfax VA 22031-1207 Home Phone: 202-686-6518; Office Phone: 703-934-3090. Business E-Mail: mbarth@icfi.com.

BARTH, ROLF FREDERICK, pathologist, educator; b. NYC, Apr. 4, 1937; s. Rolf L. and Josephine Barth; m. Christine Ferguson, Oct. 30, 1965; children: Suzanna, Alison, Rolf, Christofer. AB, Cornell U., 1959; MD, Columbia U., 1964. Diplomate Am. Bd. Pathology. Surg. intern Columbia-Presbyn. Med. Ctr., NYC, 1964-65; postdoctoral fellow Karolinska Inst., Stockholm, 1965-66; rsch. assoc. Nat. Inst. Allergy and Infectious Diseases, NIH, Bethesda, Md., 1966-68; resident pathology br. Nat. Cancer Inst., 1966-68, Nat. Inst. Health, 1968-70; Prof. dept. pathology and oncology U. Kans. Med. Ctr., Kansas City, 1970-77; clin. prof. dept. pathology Med. Coll. Wis. and U. Wis., Madison, 1977-79; prof. dept. pathology Ohio State U., Columbus, 1979—. Contbr. articles to profl. jours. Sr. asst. surgeon USPHS, 1966-70, inactive Res., 1970-2007. Grantee NIH. Mem. Am. Assn. Immunologists, Am. Assn. Cancer Rsch., Internat. Soc. for Neutron Capture Therapy, Sigma Xi, Phi Kappa Phi. Office: Ohio State U Dept Pathology 165 Hamilton Hall 1645 Neil Ave Columbus OH 43210-1218 Office Phone: 614-292-2177. Business E-Mail: rolf.barth@osumc.edu.

BARTHELMAS, NED KELTON, brokerage house executive; b. Circleville, Ohio, Oct. 22, 1927; s. Arthur and Mary Bernice (Riffel) B.; m. Marjorie Jane Livezey, May 23, 1953; children: Brooke Ann, Richard Thomas. BS in Bus. Adminstrn., Ohio State U., 1950. Stockbroker Ohio Co., Columbus, 1953-58; pres. First Columbus Securities Corp., 1958—; pres., dir. Ohio Fin. Corp., Columbus, 1960—; pres. Thwirs, Inc., Columbus, 1986—. Trustee, chmn. Am. Guardian Fin., Republic Fin.; bd. dirs. Nat. Foods, Midwest Capital Corp., Capital Equity Corp., Midwest Nat. Corp., 1st Columbus Realty Corp., Dublin Nat. Corp. (all Columbus). Served with Adj. Gen.'s Dept., AUS, 1944-47. Recipient Merit award, State of Ohio, 2001. Mem. Nat. Assn. Securities Dealers (past vice chmn. dist. bd. govs.), Investment Bankers Assn. (exec. com. 1973), Investment Dealers Ohio (sec., treas. 1956-72, pres. 1973), Nat. Stock Traders Assn., Young Pres.'s Orgn. (pres. 1971), World Bus. Coun., Columbus Pres.'s Assn., Nat. Investment Bankers (pres. 1973), Internat. Real Estate Inst., Columbus Jr. C. of C. (pres. 1956), Ohio C. of C. (trustee 1957-58), World's Pres.'s Assn. (Exec. Hall of Fame award 1993), Columbus Area C. of C. (dir. 1956, named an Outstanding Young Man of Columbus 1962), Newcomen Soc., Coun. for Ethics in Econs., Coun. of Orgn. of Am. States, Winston Churchill's Wisdom Hall of Fame, Internat. Soc. Financiers, Oxford Club, Nat. Assn. Appraisers Execs. Club, Pres.' Club (Ohio State U.), Internat. Platform Assn., Stock and Bond Club (past pres.), named top 25 corp. Dirs. (1984-90), Columbus Club, Scioto Country Club, Crystal Downs Country Club, Ohio State U. Faculty Club, Kiwanis (legion of honor 1992), Am. Legion, Columbus Admirals Club, Alpha Kappa Psi, Phi Delta Theta (Golden Legion award). Office: 1241 Dublin Rd Columbus OH 43215-7000 Office Phone: 614-486-0681.

BARTHLOW, MICHELLE JONES, science educator; d. Carey E. and Myrtle Jones; m. Steven D. Barthlow, June 21, 2003; children: Wesley Phelps, Derrick A. Phelps. BS in sci. edn., U. Fla., 1984, MA in edn., 1985. Edn. specialist Piedmont Coll., Ga., 2005, cert. sci. tchr. 7-12, math. 7-12 Ga., advanced placement chemistry tchr. Ga. Math. tchr. Newberry HS, Fla., 1985—90, Gainesville HS, Fla., 1990—93; sci. dept. chair Wayne County HS, Jesup, Ga., 1999—2003; instrnl. lead sci. tchr. Etowah HS, Woodstock, Ga., 2003—. Vol. Ga. Bapt. Children's Home, Baxley, Ga., 1996; com. mem. Anna Keith Meml. Scholarship, Jesup, Ga., 1998—2003; vol. City of Refuge Urban Homeless Outreach, Atlanta, 2004, Faith Luth. Sch. Fundraiser, Marietta, Ga., 2006. Mem.: Nat. Sci. Tchrs. Assn. Avocations: walking, travel, reading, sports. Office: Etowah HS 6565 Putnam Ford Rd Woodstock GA 30189 Home: 650 Briarleigh Way Woodstock GA 30189 Business E-Mail: michelle.barthlow@cherokee.k12.ga.us.

BARTH MENZIES, KAREN, lawyer; b. Dubuque, Iowa, Dec. 8, 1966; d. Henry Victor and Janet Marie Barth. BA, Colo. State U., 1989; JD, U. Calif., Davis, 1995. Bar: Calif. 1995, U.S. Dist. Ct. (ctrl. dist.) Calif. 1995, U.S. Dist. Ct. (so. dist.) Calif. 1999, U.S. Dist. Ct. (ea. and western dists.) Ark. 2003, U.S. Dist. Ct. (so. dist.) Ill. 2003, U.S. Dist. Ct. (ctrl. dist.) Ill. 2006, U.S. Dist. Ct. Colo. 2003, U.S. Dist. Ct. (ea. and no. dists.) Calif. 2006, U.S. Ct. Appeals (9th cir.) 1999, U.S. Ct. Appeals (5th cir.) 2005. Legal intern Colo. Atty. Gen.'s Office, Denver, 1993, Calif. Atty. Gen.'s Office, Sacramento, 1994; legal intern to Justice Davis, Calif. 3d Dist. Appellate Ct., Sacramento, 1994; legal intern Sacramento Dist. Atty.'s Office, Sacramento, 1995; shareholder Baum, Hedlund, Aristei, Goldman & Menzies and predecessor firms, LA, 1995—. Lectr. in field; lead coun., plaintiff's steering com. MDL 1574 Paxil Products liability litig. Contbr. articles to profl. jours. Finalist Consumer Atty. of Yr., CAOC, 2006; named Calif. Lawyer of Yr., Calif. Mag., 2004, Lawyer of Yr., Lawyer's Weekly, 2004, So. Calif. Super Lawyer, 2005—07; named one of Top 40 Lawyers Under 40, Nat. Law Jour., 2005. Mem. AAJ (step-toxic, environ., pharmacol. sect.), ABA (litig. sect., tort, trial and ins. sect.), State Bar of Calif., Nat. Assn. Women Lawyers, Consumer Attys. Calif., Trial Lawyers for Public Justice, LA Women Lawyers Assn., George McBurney Complex Litigation Inn of Ct. Avocations: rock climbing, diving, skiing, basketball, volleyball. Office: Baum Hedlund Anstei Goldman & Menzies 12100 Wilshire Blvd Ste 950 Los Angeles CA 90025-7107 Office Phone: 310-207-3233. Business E-Mail: kbmenzies@baumhedlundlaw.com.

BARTHOLD, JULIA SPENCER, urologist, researcher; b. Parkersburg, W.Va., Apr. 6, 1957; d. R. Donald and Janina R. Spencer; m. Steve Jensen Barthold, July 3, 1993; children: Christopher, Laura. BA, Northwestern U., 1979, MD, 1981. Resident in surgery McGaw Med. Ctr. Northwestern U., 1981—84, resident in urology McGaw Med. Ctr., 1984—88; fellow pediat. urology Children's Hosp. Mich., 1988—89; fellow rsch. Med. Coll. Cornell U., 1989—91, asst. prof. Med. Coll. NY, 1991—92; attending urologist N.Y. Hosp., 1991—92; pediat. urologist Ark. Children's Hosp., Little Rock, 1992—95, Children's Hosp. Mich., Detroit, 1995—99; assoc. chief urology A. I. duPont Hosp., Wilmington, Del., 2000—. Asst. prof. U. Ark. for Med. Scis., Little Rock, 1992—95; assoc. prof. Wayne State U., Detroit, 1995—99, Thomas Jefferson U., Phila., 2000—. Contbr. articles to profl. jours. Fellow: Soc. for Pediat. Urology, Am. acad. Pediat. (exec. com. Mid-Atlantic sect. 2002—); mem.: Am. Urol. Assn. Avocations: swimming, skiing, music. Office: A I duPont Hosp for Children Box 269 1600 Rockland Rd Wilmington DE 19899

BARTHOLET, ELIZABETH, law educator; b. NYC, Sept. 9, 1940; d. Paul and Elizabeth (Ives) Bartholet; divorced; children: Derek DuBois, Christopher, Michael. BA in English Lit., cum laude, Radcliffe Coll., 1962; JD magna cum laude, Harvard U., 1965. Bar: US Supreme Ct. 1969, Mass. 1978. Staff counsel Pres.'s Commn. on Law Enforcement and Adminstrn. of Justice, Washington, 1966—67; staff atty. NAACP Legal Def. & Ednl. Fund, Inc., NYC, 1968-72; counsel VERA Inst. of Justice, NYC, 1972-73; pres., dir. Legal Action Ctr., NYC, 1973-77; asst. prof. law Harvard Law Sch., Cambridge, Mass., 1977-83, prof., 1983—, Morris Wasserstein pub. interest prof. law, 1996—, faculty dir. child advocacy program, 2004—. Civil Rights Reviewing Authority US Dept. Edn., 1979—81; adv com. on intercountry adoption US Dept. State, 1990—2000. Author: Family Bonds: Adoption and the Politics of Parenting, 1993, pub. in 1999 as Family Bonds: Adoption, Infertility, and the New World of Child Production; contbr. articles to profl. journals. Mem. overseers com. to visit Harvard Law Sch., 1971-77; bd. overseers Harvard Coll., 1973-77; mem. assisted reproductive tech. ethics com. Brigham and Women's Hosp., 1990—; mem. IVF ethics com. Boston Fertility & Gynecology Assn., 1991—; mem. adv. com. Internat. Concerns Com. for Children, 1993-; mem New Eng. com. NAACP Legal Def. & Ednl. Fund, Inc., 1994-98; mem. adv. coun. Appleseed Found., 1996-; bd. dirs. Legal Action Ctr., 1977—, vice chair bd., 1998-. Recipient Friends of Adoption Award for Adoption Lit., Adoptive Parents Com., 1993, Media Achievement Award, Cath. Adoptive Parents Assn., 1994, Friends of Adoption Award, Open Door Soc., 1994, Alumnae Recognition Award, Radcliffe Coll., 1997, Award for Advocacy on Behalf of Foster Children, Mass. Appleseed Ctr., 1998. Mem. Assn. Bar City of NY (exec. com. 1973-77), Am. Arbitration Assn. (labor panel 1980-, comml. panel 1995-), Soc. Am. Law Teachers (bd. dirs. 1977-89), Fed. Mediation and Conciliation Svc. Roster Arbitrators, Am. Acad. Adoption Attorneys (hon.), Harvard Club. Democrat. Office: Harvard Law Sch 1563 Massachusetts Ave Cambridge MA 02138 Office Phone: 617-495-3128. Office Fax: 617-496-4947. Business E-Mail: ebarthol@law.harvard.edu.

BARTHOLAMAUS, BRETT WILLIAM, small business owner; b. Milw., Wis., Jan. 19, 1944; s. Weber and Beatrice (Elmergreen) B.; m. Joan Anne Cavosi, Feb. 19, 1977 (dec.); children: Laura, Thomas, Eric. Student, Milw. tech. Coll. Lic. pvt. security Wis. Motorcycle sales rep. Vic Panetti & Sons, Milw., 1963-75; maint. supr. U. Wis., Milw., 1977; owner North Trail Inn Supper Club, Tigerton, Wis., 1978-82; security supr. Sentinal Detective agy., Wausau, Wis., 1988—. Author: (poetry book) Moments Beautiful, Moments Bright, 1993, (novel) Reflection of Evil, 1998; poetry pub. various pubs.; numerous poetry readings. Vol. numerous charitable orgns. Recipient Golden Poets award World of Poetry, 1988, 89, 90, 92. Democrat. Mem. Lds Ch. Avocations: motorcycling, backpacking, weightlifting. Address: Wildwood Apts 100 Wall St Apt 1 Bowler WI 54416 E-mail: brett_bartholomaur@yahoo.com.

BARTHOLOMAY, WILLIAM C., insurance brokerage company and professional sports team executive; b. Evanston, Ill., Aug. 11, 1928; s. Henry C. and Virginia (Graves) B.; m. Sara Taylor, 1950, (div. 1964); children: Virginia, William T., Jamie, Elizabeth, Sara; m. Gail Dillingham, May 1968 (div. Apr. 1980). Student, Oberlin Coll., 1946-49, Northwestern U., 1949-50; BA, Lake Forest Coll., 1955. Ptnr. Bartholomay & Clarkson, Chgo., 1951-63; v.p. Alexander & Alexander, Chgo., 1963-65; pres. Olson & Bartholomay, Chgo. and Atlanta, 1965-69; sr. v.p. Frank B. Hall & Co. Inc., NYC and Chgo., 1969-72, exec. v.p., 1972-73, pres., 1973-74, vice chmn., 1974-90; chmn. bd., dir. Atlanta Braves, 1966—2004, chmn. emeritus, chmn. exec. com., 2004—; pvt. practice Chgo., 1990—91; pres. Near North Nat. Group, 1991—2003; vice chmn., chmn. exec. com. Turner Broadcasting Sys., Inc., Atlanta, 2001—; vice chmn. Willis Group Holdings (NYSE), Chgo., 2003—. Bd. dirs. Midway Games, Inc., Exec. Coun. Maj. League Baseball, Maj. League Baseball Players Pension Plan; dir. Internat. Steel, 2002—05; dir. emeritus WMS Industries, Inc., Chgo., 2005—. Commr. Chgo. Park Dist., 1980-2002, Chgo. Pub. Bldg. Commn., 1989-2003; bd. dirs. Chgo. Maternity Ctr., Lincoln Park Zool. Soc.; trustee Adler Planetarium, Mus. Sci. and Industry, Roosevelt U., Chgo., Ill. Inst. of Tech.; past trustee Lake Forest (Ill.) Coll., Ogelthorpe Coll., Atlanta, Marymount Manhattan Coll., NY With USNR, 1951-54. Mem. Chief Execs. Orgn., World Pres.'s Orgn., Chgo. Pres.'s Orgn., Nat. Assn. CLU, Chgo. Assn. CLU, Chgo. Club, Racquet Club, Saddle and Cycle Club, Econ. Club, Onwentsia Club, Shoreacres Club (Lake Forest), Brook Club, Links Club, Racquet & Tennis Club, Doubles Club (N.Y.C.), Piedmont Driving Club, Atlanta Country Club, Peachtree Golf Club, Commerce Club. Episcopalian. Home: 180 E Pearson St Chicago IL 60611-2130 Office: Willis Group Holdings 10 S LaSalle St Ste 3000 Chicago IL 60603 also: Atlanta Braves PO Box 4064 Atlanta GA 30302-4064 Business E-Mail: bartholomay_wi@willis.com.

BARTHOLOMEW, ARTHUR PECK, JR., accountant; b. Rochester, NY, Nov. 20, 1918; s. Arthur Peck and Abbie West (Dawson) B.; m. Mary Elizabeth Meyer, Oct. 4, 1941(wid. Oct. 1992); children: Susan B. Hall, Arthur Peck III, James M., Virginia B. Keyser. AB, U. Mich., 1939, MBA, 1940. With Ernst & Whinney (name now Ernst & Young), 1940-79, successively jr. accountant, partner charge Eastern dist., Detroit office, 1940-64; nat. office, Cleve. Ernst & Whinney, 1964-65, NY office, 1965-79, also mem. mng. com. Instr. accounting U. Mich., 1940, George Washington U., 1945-46 Mem. Mich. Gov.'s Task Force for Expenditure Mgmt., 1963-64; mem. 2d Regional Plan Commn. NY; bd. dirs. Detroit League for Handicapped, 1952-64; bd. dirs., dir., treas. Bethesda Hosp. Found.; treas. Grosse Pointe War Meml. Assn., 1961; life trustee Greater NY council Boy Scouts Am. Served from pvt. to capt. AUS, 1942-46. Mem. AICPA, Inst. Mgmt. Accts. (pres. Detroit 1963-64, nat. pres. 1974-75), The Conf. Bd., Mich. Soc. CPAs, NY Soc. CPAs, Detroit Country Club, Gulf Stream Golf Club, Wall St. Club (pres. 1976-78), Ocean Club Fla. (pres. 1993-94), Little Club (pres. 1989-91), Phi Beta Kappa, Phi Kappa Phi, Beta Gamma Sigma, Phi Eta Sigma, Beta Alpha Psi, Phi Kappa Sigma. Republican. Presbyn. Home: 6665 N Ocean Blvd Boynton Beach FL 33435-3312

BARTHOLOMEW, DEBRA LEE, publishing executive; b. Cobleskill, NY, Sept. 11, 1958; d. Donald Walter Mochrie, Sr. and Jean Marie (Hamm) Mochrie; m. Richard Ray Bartholomew, July 8, 2001; children: Robert Wayne Kucienski, Jr., Kerry Hartung, Kris Manchester. Author: Hope: Discovering the Power of 'No' (Merit from the Writer's Digest, 2001), Who Am I? My Tree of Hope, 2003, Who Am I? My Tree of Konwledge, 2003; composer: (song) Believing in Myself, 2002, Angel in the Sky, 2003; contbr. poetry to lit. publs. Organizer fundraiser poster contest War against Terrorism, 2001, For the children, boost the moral of the soldiers, Richmondville, NY, 1991. Recipient Dirs. award of merit, 2002—03. Mem.: Internat. Soc. Poets (Silver Cup, Bronze Medallion, Outstanding Achievement award 2003). Home: PO Box 150 Richmondville NY 12149 Office Phone: 518-294-8660. Personal E-mail: rbarthol@nycap.rr.com.

BARTHOLOMEW, GILBERT ALFRED, retired physicist; b. Nelson, Can., Apr. 8, 1922; s. Alfred and Anna (Lenzman) B.; m. Rosalie May Dinzey, Apr. 19, 1952 (dec. Dec. 10, 1990); m. Anna Lubicz-Luba, July 24, 1992. BA, U. B.C., 1943; PhD, McGill U., 1948. With Atomic Energy of Can., Ltd., 1948-83, head neutron physics br., 1962-71, dir. physics div., 1971-83. Contbr. articles to profl. jours. Fellow AAAS, Royal Soc. Can., Am. Phys. Soc.; mem. Can. Assn. Physicists, Can. Nuclear Soc., Assn. for Baha'i Studies, Sigma Xi. Home: PO Box 150 Lions Bay BC Canada V0N 2E0 E-mail: gabarth@telus.net.

BARTHOLOMEW, LINCOLN EDWIN, physician; b. Oct. 12, 1954; MD, U. Pa., 1981; MPH, Columbia U., 1999. Dir. primary care St. Albans (N.Y.) VA Med. Ctr.; med. dir. Montefiore Rikers Island Health Svcs. Home: 401 E 74th St # 8 New York NY 10021-3919 Office Phone: 718-526-1000.

BARTHOLOMEW, LLOYD GIBSON, physician; b. Whitehall, NY, Sept. 15, 1921; s. Emerson F. and Minnie (Swinton) B.; m. Elisabeth Thrall, Dec. 27, 1943; children: Suzanne, Lynne, Lloyd Gibson, Deborah, Douglass Thrall. AA, Green Mountain Jr. Coll., 1939; BA, Union Coll., Schenectady, 1941; MD, U. Vt., 1944; MS in Internal Medicine (fellow), U. Minn., 1952; LHD (hon.), Green Mountain Coll., 1984. Diplomate Am. Bd. Internal Medicine, subsplty. bd. gastroenterology. Intern Mary Hitchcock Meml. Hosp., Hanover, NH, 1944-45, resident, 1945-46, 48-49; asst. internal medicine Dartmouth, 1948-49; 1st asst. div. internal medicine Mayo Clinic, Rochester, Minn., 1949-52, asst. to staff div. internal medicine, 1952-53; practice medicine, specializing in gastroenterology Rochester, 1952—; instr. internal medicine Mayo Found., U. Minn., 1952-58, asst. prof., 1958-63, assoc. prof. internal medicine, 1963-67, prof. medicine, 1967—, Mayo Med. Sch., 1973—. Attending physician St. Mary's, Meth. hosps., Rochester, 1952; mem. adv. bd. to surgeons gen. of armed forces and asst. sec. def., 1978-86; mem. policy bd. Bush Found., 1978-87. Contbr. articles profl. publs. Trustee Green Mountain Coll. Poultney, Vt., 1991—, chmn. bd. trustees, 1997-2003, trustee emeritus, 2003—. Capt. M.C. AUS, 1946-47; col. M.C., 1960-86, ret. Recipient Woodbury prize in medicine, 1944, Carbee prize in obstetrics, 1994, disting. svc. award U. Vt. Coll. Medicine, 1977, Henry J. Plummer disting. clinician award Mayo Found. Internal Medicine, 1992, disting. svc. award Green Mtn. Coll. Alumni Assn., 1995; named to Green Mtn. Coll. Athletic Hall of Fame, 2006. Mem. AMA (sec. gastroenterology sect. 1962-68, vice chmn. gastroenterology sect. 1968-69, chmn. 1969-70, mem. council sci. assembly 1969, chmn. program planning com. 1971-75, chmn. council sci. assembly 1974-76, chmn. council continuing physician edn. 1976-77), Minn. Med. Assn. (del. ho. dels. 1964—, chmn. scholarship and loan com. 1967—, alt. del. to AMA 1974-77, 85—, del. to AMA 1978-83, Pres.'s award 1983, Disting. Service award 1987), So. Minn. Med. Assn. (pres. 1963-64), Zumbro Valley Med. Soc. (sec.-treas. 1969-70, v.p. 1970-71, pres. 1971-72), Soc. Med. Cons. to Armed Forces (mem. governing council 1980-86, pres. 1984, del. to AMA 1984-92), Am. Gastroent. Assn. (com. on procedures 1970-72, presdl. commn. on future of assn. 1973-74, com. on constn. and by-laws 1980-85), Minn. Soc. Internal Medicine, Sigma Xi. Mailing: 211 2nd St NW Apt 1214 Rochester MN 55901-2897

BARTILUCCI, ANDREW JOSEPH, university administrator; b. NYC, Nov. 29, 1922; s. Rocco and Philomena (Innello) B.; m. Lucy Ann Fulvio, June 10, 1950; children— Mary Ann, Phyllis, Eugenie. BS, St. John's U., 1944; MS, Rutgers U., 1949; PhD, U. Md., 1953. Analytical chemist Armed Services Med. Procurement Lab., War Dept., 1947-48; assoc. research pharmacist, research and devel. div. Merck & Co., 1949-50; prof. pharmacy, asst. dean Coll. Pharmacy St. John's U., 1952-56, dean, 1956-88, v.p. for health professions, clin. svc. and rsch., 1979-91; acting dean St. John's Coll. Liberal Arts & Scis., 1989-91, exec. v.p., 1991-96, spl. asst. to pres., 1996—2002. Fellow Am. Found. Pharm. Edn., 1950-52 Served as pharmacist's mate USNR, 1944-46; ensign 1949-57; Pharmacist dir. USPHS(R), 1957-98. Fellow AAAS; mem. Am. Coll. Apothecaries, N.Y. Acad. Scis., N.Y. Acad. Pharmacy, Am. Pharm. Assn., N.Y. State Bd. Pharmacy, Sigma Xi, Rho Chi, Phi Delta Chi. Home: 115 Roosevelt St Garden City NY 11530-2309 Office: Saint Johns Univ 8000 Utopia Pkwy Jamaica NY 11432-1343 E-mail: bartilua@stjohns.edu.

BARTIROMO, MARIA SARA, financial news correspondent; b. Bklyn., Sept. 11, 1967; d. Vincent and Josephine Bartiromo; m. Jonathan Steinberg, June 13, 1999. BA, NYU, 1989, cert. in screenwriting, 1990. Assoc. prodr. Barry Farber Show, NYC; prodr. CNN Bus. News, NYC, 1989-93; freelance columnist Ind. Investor Mag., NYC, 1991—; corr. CNBC, NYC, 1993-97, fin. anchor, 1997—; host CNBC's Wall Street Journal Report, 2000—; anchor CNBC's Closing Bell with Maria Bartiromo, 2006—. Columnist Reader's Digest Mag.; contr. Newsweek, Town & Country, Registered Rep, NY Post. Author: Use the News: How to Separate the Noise from the Investment Nuggets and Make Money in Any Economy, 2001. Bd. dirs. NY City Ballet, Public Ed. Needs Civic Involvement and Leadership. Recipient Excellence in Broadcast Journalism award, Coalition of Italo-Am. Assn., 1997, Lincoln Statue award, Union League of Phila., 2004. Mem. N.Y. Fin. Writers Assn. Office: CNBC 1 CNBC Plz Englewood Cliffs NJ 07632-3313

BARTKOWSKI, KATHLEEN SUSAN, musician; b. New London, Conn., Nov. 29, 1967; d. Brent Gates and Donna Lee Smith Weimer; m. Douglas Robert Bartkowski, May 20, 1995. MusB in Piano Performance, U. of Conn., 1989; MusM, in Piano Accompanying, U. of Mass., 2004; postgrad., U. of Conn., 1991—93. Lectr./accompanist U. of Conn., Storrs, Conn., 1989—91; organist/choir dir. Ch. of the Resurrection, Norwich, Conn., 1991—93; music tchr., k-12 Cabot Sch., Cabot, Vt., 1993—94; dir. of music Ctr. Congl. Ch., Manchester, Conn., 1995—2002; organist Second Congl. Ch., Middle Haddam, Conn., 2002—06; accompanist Mak'hela (Jewish Chorus of Western Mass.), Northampton, Mass., 2003—04, Mystic River Chorale, Conn., 2000—02, 2004—, Vernon Chorale, Conn., 2005—; staff accompanist Ledyard H.S., Ledyard, Conn., 2004—. Accompanist various local schs. and orgns. Musician: (performance accompanist) At Last, The Moment, Claire Mailhot vocal recital, Keene State College, Vocal Recital with Jung-Jin Choi, A Night of Italian Opera with Silk City Opera Quartet, An Afternoon of Classical and Contemporary Music with Peter Perron and Meredith Hansen, Mud Season Gala, Vermont Opera Theater, Montpelier, Vermont, (choral tour accompanist) European Magical History Tour with U. Mass.-Amherst choirs, solo piano recital, Mohegan C.C.; singer: Renaissance Revival; musician: Conn. All-State HS Hon. Choir, 2006, Woodland Scholars, 2006—; musician: (pianist) World Premiere of Mozart Remixed. Organist St. Luke Luth. Ch., Gales Ferry, Conn., 2006—. Recipient Eugenie M. May Award for Piano Performance, U. of Mass., Amherst, 2003; grantee, DAR, 1985, Betty Sonier grantee, Delta Kappa Gamma, 1985; scholar, Mystic River Chorale, 2002, Victor Borge scholar, U. of Conn., 1985—88, U. String scholar, 1985—86. Mem.: Am. Guild of Organists, Am. Choral Dirs. Assn. (repertoire and standards chair, music and worship, Conn. chpt. 2004—06). Avocations: camping, hiking, jigsaw puzzles, sewing, gardening. Home: 48 Gem Dr Colchester CT 06415 Home Phone: 860-537-9668.

BARTKUS, RICHARD ANTHONY, magazine publisher; b. Chgo., Mar. 14, 1931; s. Anthony J. and Mary (Petraitis) B.; m. Betty Ann Luetke, Jan. 2, 1954; children: Susan Kimberly, David Richard. Student, U. Ill., 1949-55. Circulation trainee Chgo. Tribune, 1955-58; asst. advt. mgr. Kilner Pub. Co., Chgo., 1958-59; advt. mgr. Cox Publs., Arcadia, Calif., 1959-60, Bond Pub. Co., 1960, western advt. mgr., advt. dir., 1969-75; pub. Road & Track mag., Newport Beach, Calif., 1975-91; v.p. CBS Publs., 1977-91. With USMC, 1951-53. Mem. Univ. Athletic Club. Home: 18681 Via Torino Irvine CA 92603-3438 E-mail: bartkusra@sbcglobal.net.

BARTKUS, ROBERT EDWARD, lawyer; b. Kearny, NJ, Sept. 30, 1946; s. Edward Charles and Dorothy Agnes (Konschott) B.; m. Mary Bartkus. BA with honors, Swarthmore Coll, 1968; JD, Stanford U., 1976. Bar: Calif. 1976, N.J. 1977, N.Y. 1977, U.S. Supreme Ct (3d, 2d cirs.), U.S. Dist. Ct.

N.J., U.S. Dist. Ct. (so. and ea. dist.) N.Y., U.S. Dist. Ct. (ctrl. and north dist.) Calif. Spl. counsel Schulte, Roth & Zabel, NYC, 1985-88; ptnr. Dillon, Bitar, & Luther, LLC. Tchg. asst. Stanford U. Law Sch., 1976; mem. Dist. X Ethics Com., 1992-97, chair, 2002-03; lectr. N.J. Inst. for Continuing Edn., 1988—; master John J. Gibbons Intellectual Property Inn of Ct. Articles co-editor Stanford Law Rev., 1974-76; author Innovation Competition 28 Stanford Law Rev. 1976; author, editor: New Jersey Federal Civil Practice, 1992, N.J. Federal Civil Procedure, 1999; mem. editl. bd. N.J. Law Jour. (Alfred C. Clapp award 1995). Atty. Community Law Offfice, 1976-79, Legal Aid Soc., 1979-87; mem. alumni coun. Swarthmore Coll., 1977-78. Lt. USNR, 1968-73. Mem. ABA (ethics com. Dist. X), Nat. Assn. Securities Dealers (arbitrator), N.J. Bar Assn. (chair fed. practice com.), Assn. Fed. Bar of State of N.J., Am. Arbitration Assn. (arbitrator), Delta Upsilon. Home: 6 Terrill Dr Califon NJ 07830-3443 Office: Dillon Bitar & Luther LLC 53 Maple Ave Morristown NJ 07963-0398 Home Phone: 908-832-6550; Office Phone: 973-539-3100. Business E-Mail: rbartkus@dbl-law.com.

BARTLEMAN, JAMES K., lieutenant governor; b. Orillia, Ont., Dec. 24, 1939; m. Marie-Jeanne Rosillon, 1975; children: Anne-Pascale, Laurent, Alain. BA in History with honors, U. Western Ont., 1963, LLD (hon.); DLitt, DEd. Lt. gov., Ont., 2002—; amb. to Cuba, 1981—83; amb. to Israel, 1986—90; high commr. to Cyprus, 1986—90; amb. to North Atlantic Coun. NATO, 1990—94; fgn. policy advisor to prime min., 1994—98; high commr. to South Africa, 1998—99; high commr. to Australia, 1999—2000; Can.'s amb. to European Union, 2000—02. Author: (memoirs) Out of Muskoka, 2002, On Six Continents, 2004, Rollercoaster, 2005. Named Knight of Justice in Order of St. John, hon. chief, Toronto Police Svc.; named to Order of Ont.; recipient Golden Jubilee Medal in Commemoration of Queen Elizabeth II, Nat. Aboriginal Achievement award, 1999, Anishinabek Lifetime Achievement award, 2002, Dr. Hugh Lefave award, 2003, Courage to Come Back award, 2004, DAREarts Cultural award, 2004, Jane Chamberlin award, 2006, Mood Disorders Hero award, 2006, award of merit, Social Work Doctors Colloquium, 2006. Office: Lt Gov of Ont Queen's Park Toronto ON Canada M7A 1A1

BARTLETT, ALEX, lawyer; b. Warrensburg, Mo., Aug. 7, 1937; s. George Vest and May (Woolery) B.; m. Sue Gloyd, June 5, 1961 (div. June 1978); children: Ashley R., Nathan G.; m. Eleanor M. Veltrop, Oct. 27, 1978. BA, Cen. Mo. State U., 1959; LLB, U. Mo., 1961. Bar: Mo. 1962, U.S. Ct. Mil. Appeals 1963, U.S. Supreme Ct. 1965, U.S. Dist. Ct. (we. dist.) Mo. 1966, U.S. Ct. Appeals (8th cir.) 1968. From assoc. to ptnr. Hendren & Andrae, Jefferson City, Mo., 1965-79; mem. Bartlett, Venters, Pletz & Toppins, P.C., Jefferson City, 1980-87; pvt. practice Jefferson City, 1987-90; mem. Husch & Eppenberger, LLC, Jefferson City, 1990—. With Transit Casualty Co. Receivership, 1986-90, commr. claims, 1986-87, spl. claims counsel, 1987-89, dir. legal affairs dept., 1989-90; lectr. law U. Mo., Columbia, 1965-66. Contbr. editor Mo. Law Rev., 1960-61. Served to capt. JAGC, U.S. Army, 1962-65. Mem. ABA, FBA, Mo. Bar Assn. (chmn. young lawyers sect. 1972-73, ct. modernization com. 1972-74, jud. reform com. 1974-76, chmn. cts. and jud. com. 1978-79, legis. com. 1981-84, President's award 1976, Smithson award 1976), Cole County Bar Assn., Am. Coll. Trial Lawyers (chmn. Mo. 1994-96), Order of Coif. Democrat. Office: Husch and Eppenberger PO Box 1251 235 E High St Jefferson City MO 65102-3236 Office Phone: 573-635-9118. Business E-Mail: alex.bartlett@husch.com.

BARTLETT, ALLEN LYMAN, JR., retired bishop; b. Birmingham, Ala., Sept. 22, 1929; s. Allen Lyman and Edith Buell (West) B.; m. Jerriette L. Kohlmeier, Dec. 28, 1957; children: Christopher, Stephen, Catherine. BA, U. of South, 1951, D.D. (hon.), 1988; M.Div., Va. Theol. Sem., 1958, D.Min., 1980, D.D. (hon.), 1986. Ordained to ministry Episcopal Ch. 1958, ordained priest 1959. Vicar St. James' Ch., Alexander City, Ala., 1958-61, St. Barnabas Ch., Roanoke, Ala., 1958-61; rector Zion Ch., Charles Town, W.Va., 1961-70; dean Christ Ch. Cathedral, Louisville, 1970-85; ordained bishop, 1986; bishop coadjutor Diocese of Pa., Phila., 1986-87, bishop, 1987-98; assisting bishop Diocese of Washington, 2001—04. Dep. Episcopal Gen. Convention, 1964-67, 73-85; mem. exec. coun. Episcopal Ch., 1979-85. Lt. (j.g.) USN, 1952-55. Mem.: Union League, Phi Beta Kappa. Democrat. Episcopalian. Avocations: tennis, hiking. Home: 316 S 10th St Philadelphia PA 19107-6149

BARTLETT, ARTHUR EUGENE, real estate company executive; b. Glens Falls, NY, Nov. 26, 1933; s. Raymond Ernest and Thelma (Williams) Bartlett; m. Collette R. Bartlett, Jan. 9, 1955 (dec.); 1 child, Stacy Lynn; m. Nancy Sanders Bartlett, Feb. 12, 2005. Sales mgr. Forest E. Olson, Inc., 1960-64; co-founder, v.p. Four Star Realty, Inc., Santa Ana, Calif., 1964-71, v.p., sec., 1964-71; founder, pres. Comps, Inc., Tustin, Calif., 1971-81; co-founder, chmn. of bd., pres., CEO Century 21 Real Estate Corp., Tustin, 1980—; pres. Larwin Sq. LLC Shopping Ctr, Tustin, 1979—2002. Chmn. bd. dirs. United Western Med. Ctrs., 1981—87. Mem.: Internat. Franchise Assn. (v.p., bd. dirs. 1975—80, Hall of Fame 1987), Masons.

BARTLETT, BRUCE REEVES, economist, columnist; b. Ann Arbor, Oct. 11, 1951; s. Frank and Marjorie (Stern) B.d BA, Rutgers U., 1973; MA, Georgetown U., 1976. Spl. asst. to Congressman Jack F. Kemp, Washington, 1977-78; chief legis. asst. to U.S. Senator Roger Jepsen, Washington, 1979-80; dep. dir. Joint Econ. Com., U.S. Congress, Washington, 1981-83, exec. dir., 1983-84; v.p. Polyconomics, Inc., Morristown, NJ, 1984-85; sr. fellow Heritage Found., Washington, 1985-87; sr. policy analyst The White House, Washington, 1987-88; dep. asst. sec. for econ. policy Dept. Treasury, 1988-93; sr. fellow CATO Inst., Washington, 1993, Alexis de Tocqueville Instn., 1993-94, Nat. Ctr. for Policy Analysis, 1995—. Author: Impostor: How George W. Bush bankrupted America and Betrayed the American Legacy, 2006. Author: Coverup: The Politics of Pearl Harbor, 1941-46, 1978, Reaganomics: Supply Side Economics in Action, 1981; co-editor: The Supply Side Solution, 1983; syndicated columnist Creators Syndicate, L.A., 1997—; contbr. articles to Washington Post, N.Y. Times, Wall Street Jour., numerous others. Served with USAF, 1973. Mem. Am. Econ. Assn. Republican. Office: Nat Ctr Policy Analysis 601 Pennsylvania Ave NW Ste 9005 Washington DC 20004-3615 E-mail: bartlettb@cox.net.

BARTLETT, CHARLES LEFFINGWELL, foundation executive; b. Chgo., Aug. 14, 1921; s. Valentine C. and Marie (Frost) B.; m. Josephine Martha Buck, Dec. 16, 1950; children: Peter B., Michael V., Robert S., Helen B. Student, St. Mark's Sch., Southboro, Mass., 1934-39; AB, Yale U., 1943. Reporter Chattanooga Times, 1946-62, Washington corr., 1948-63; editor News Focus Service, 1958-63; columnist Field Syndicate, 1962-80, Chgo. Sun-Times, 1963-75, Chgo. Daily News, 1975-78, Field Syndicate, 1978-81; pres. Jefferson Found., 1982—; editor Coleman/Bartlett's Washington Focus, 1988—. Author: (with Edward Weintal) Facing the Brink, 1957. Served as lt. USNR, 1943-46. Recipient Pulitizer prize for nat. reporting, 1955 Mem.: Gridiron, Federal City. Roman Catholic. Home: 4615 W St NW Washington DC 20007-1515 Office: Washington Focus 2208 46th St NW Washington DC 20007-1031 Office Phone: 202-234-3681.

BARTLETT, CLIFFORD ADAMS, JR., lawyer; b. NYC, Mar. 17, 1937; s. Clifford Adams and Frances (Burke) B.; m. Eileen Marie McCarthy; children: Elizabeth, Kathleen, Clifford III, Christopher, Karen, Charles, Eileen, Kevin, Jamison. BA, St. Francis Coll., NYC, 1959; JD, St. John's U., NYC, 1962. Bar: N.Y. 1963, U.S. Dist. Ct. (so. dist.) N.Y. 1964, U.S. Supreme Ct. 1966. Ptnr. Bartlett, McDonough, Bastone & Monaghan, Mineola, NY, 1992—. Mem. faculty Nassau Acad. Law, Mineola, N.Y. & N.Y.C., 1984—. Mem. ABA, N.Y. State Bar Assn., Nassau County Bar Assn., Nassau-Suffolk Trial Lawyers Assn., Suffolk County Bar Assn. Avocations: golf, skiing, swimming. Office: 300 Old Country Rd Mineola NY 11501-4198 Address: 237 Park Ave New York NY 10169 also: 81 Main St White Plains NY 10601-1711 Office Phone: 516-877-2900. Business E-Mail: clifford.bartlett@bmbm.com.

BARTLETT, CODY BLAKE, retired lawyer; b. Syracuse, NY, Apr. 21, 1939; s. Stanley Jay and Izora Elizabeth (Blake) B.; m. Claudine Germaine Bouthillette, Dec. 27, 1968; 1 child, Cody Blake. AAS, Auburn C.C., 1960; BA with high honors, Mich. State U., 1963; JD, Harvard U., 1966. Bar: Mich. 1967, N.Y. 1967, Colo. 1993, U.S. Dist. Ct. (ea. dist.) Mich. 1967, U.S. Dist. Ct. (no. dist.) N.Y. 1967, U.S. Supreme Ct. 1984, U.S. Dist. Ct. (we. dist.) N.Y. 1985, U.S. Ct. Appeals (2d cir.) 2002, U.S. Tax Ct. 1999, U.S. Ct. Fed. Claims 1999. Law clk. Onondaga County Dist. Atty.'s Office, Syracuse, 1965; assoc. Touche, Ross, Bailey & Smart, Detroit, 1966; law clk. Onondaga County Family Ct., Syracuse, 1967; assoc. Melvin & Melvin, Syracuse, 1967; budget and accounts officer Appellate Divsn., 4th Dept., Rochester, NY, 1967-69, dep. dir. adminstrn., 1969-72, dir. adminstrn., 1972-80; chief atty. State Commn. on Jud. Conduct, 1980-84; ptnr. Newman, Kehoe, Wunder and Bartlett, Lyons, NY, 1984-91, Kehoe, Bartlett & Kehoe, Wolcott, NY, 1992-94, Bartlett Law Offices, Wolcott, 1994—2005; ret., 2005. Spl. adminstr. N.Y. State Dangerous Drug Program, Western N.Y., 1973-75; adj. prof. polit. sci. dept. SUNY, Brockport, 1983-85, Grad. Sch. Pub. Adminstrn., 1985-90; adj. prof. Syracuse U. Coll. Law, 1980-84, Coll. Criminal Justice, Rochester Inst. Tech., 1979-80; grad. asst. polit. sci. dept. Mich. State U., 1962-63; lectr. jud. ethics and discipline Office Ct. Adminstrn., 1990. Author: Staying Fit Past Fifty, 1992; contbr. articles on legal issues and sports and fitness to publs.; drafter numerous legis. bills that became law. Mem. adv. com. Regional Criminal Justice Edn. and Tng. Ctr., Monroe C.C., Rochester, 1974-80; divsn. leader YMCA, Midtown Rochester membership drive, 1976; mem. East Bloomfield Planning Bd., 1984-87, chmn., 1985-87; trustee Village of East Bloomfield, 1985-87; mem. Sodus Point (N.Y.) Zoning Bd. Appeals, 1986-87; mem. adv. bd. Sodus Bay Hist. Soc., 1992; justice Sodus Point Village, 1994-95; mem. adv. bd. Wolcott C. of C., 1993; mem. Circuit of Reebok Profls. and Specialists, 1992-94. Recipient Disting. Alumni award Assn. Bds. Trustees SUNY, 1980; named nat., regional and state powerlifting and bench press champion, 1982, 83, 96-2007; N.Y. State and Am. nat. and world bench press record holder, 1996-2007, world bench press champion, 2004, 06. Mem. N.Y. State Bar Assn. (spl. com. on jud. conduct 1984-90, profl. sports com. 1988-90), Wayne County Bar Assn., Onondaga County Bar Assn. (chmn. Syracuse City Ct. com. 1968-72), Nat. Strength and Conditioning Assn. (cert. strength and conditioning specialist, bd. dirs., lectr. 1989-96), Phi Kappa Phi, Pi Sigma Alpha. Home: 54 Little Spring Run Fairport NY 14450

BARTLETT, DAN (DANIEL JOSEPH BARTLETT), former federal official; b. Jan. 6, 1971; m. Allyson Elizabeth Sikes, 2000; 3 children. BA in Polit. Sci., U. Tex., 1993. With Karl Rove & Assocs., Austin, Tex.; dep. to policy dir. Office of Gov., State of Tex., Austin, Tex., 1994—98, issues dir. gov.'s re-election campaign, 1998; sr. spokesman, dir. Rapid Response Bush for Pres. campaign; dep. asst. to Pres., dep. to counselor to Pres. The White House, 2001—02, comm. dir., 2001—05, counselor to Pres., 2005—07.*

BARTLETT, DAVID, management consultant; b. Bethlehem, Pa., Mar. 23, 1946; s. Bertram Francis and Sally Caroline (Lewis) Bartlett; m. Joan Carol Benevelli, Dec. 27, 1975. BA, Trinity Coll., Hartford, Conn., 1969. News dir. WRC Radio, Washington, 1979-81; mng. editor Metromedia TV news, Washington, 1981-83; dir. news and English broadcasts Voice of Am., Washington, 1984-85; program dir. NBC Radio Networks, NYC, 1986-88, v.p., 1988-89; pres. Radio-TV News Dirs. Assn., Washington, 1989-97; dir. global news svcs. Worldspace Corp., Washington, 1998-2000; ptnr. Rowan & Blewitt, Washington, 2000—06, Weber Merritt, Washington, 2006—. Office Phone: 202-974-8294.

BARTLETT, DAVID CARSON, state legislator; b. New London, Conn., Feb. 2, 1944; s. Neil Riley and Susan Marion (Carson) B.; m. Barbara Hunting, July 14, 1973 (div. 1974); m. Janice Anne Wezelman, Feb. 11, 1979; children: Daniel Wezelman (dec.), Elizabeth Anne. Student, Wesleyan U., Middletown, Conn., 1962-64; BA, U. Ariz., 1966, MA, 1970; JD, Georgetown U., 1976. Teaching asst. U. Ariz., Tucson, 1967-69; program analyst U.S. Dept. Labor, Washington, 1970-76; assoc. Snell & Wilmer, Tucson, 1976-77; pvt. practice Tucson, 1976-79; assoc. Davis, Eppstein & Hall, Tucson, 1979-85; mem. Ariz. Ho. of Reps., Tucson, 1983-88, Ariz. State Senate, 1989-92; chief counsel for civil rights Ariz. Atty. Gen.'s Office, Tucson, 1993-99, spl. couns., 1999—2002. Democrat. Home: 3236 E Via Palos Verdes Tucson AZ 85716-5854

BARTLETT, DEDE THOMPSON, association executive; m. James Wesley Bartlett; children: Katherine, John. BA, Vassar Coll.; MA, NYU. V.p., corp. sec. Philip Morris Cos. Inc., 1991-94, v.p. corp. affairs programs, 1995—2002; comms. cons., 2002—. Lectr. in field. Chair adv. bd. Nat. Domestic Violence Hotline; bd. dirs. Corp. Alliance to Edn Ptnr. Violence, Am. U. Ctr. Asia. Recipient honors, YWCA, N.Y.C., Nat. Ctr. for Victims of Crime, Plays for Living, Nat. Coun. Jewish Women, Ctr. Against Domestic Violence, Lifetime TV. Mem.: Women in Mgmt., Internat. Women's Forum.

BARTLETT, DESMOND WILLIAM, engineering company executive; b. Southampton, Eng., Feb. 11, 1931; came to U.S., 1971; s. Walter Hayward and Gladys (Akerman) B.; m. Joan Margaret Mitchell, July 19, 1952; children: Jennie Claire. Grad. Marine Engring., U. Coll., Southampton, 1951; diploma, Shippingport Nuclear Sch., Pitts., 1961; exec. devel. diploma, Cornell U., 1978. Registered profl. engr., Europe; chartered engr. U.K.; lic. chief engr., U.K. Ministry of Transport, nuclear power plant operator, U.K. Ministry of Def. Engr. officer Cunard Steamship Co., Liverpool, Eng., 1952-57; engr. Vickers Armstrong Ltd., Southampton, 1957-59; project mgr. Rolls Royce & Assocs., Derby, Eng., 1959-65; chief engr. Cammell Laird Shipbuilders & Engrs., Birkenhead, Eng., 1965-71; cons. Gibbs & Hill, Inc., NYC, 1971-72; project dir. Westinghouse Electric Co., Pitts., 1972-79; pres. Dravo Engrs. Inc., Pitts., 1979-85, C.F. Braun, Inc., Alhambra, Calif., 1986-89; v.p. bus. devel. Raytheon Engrs. and Constructors, Inc., Phila., 1991-95; v.p. Corp. Ventures Flour Daniel, Irvine, Calif., 1995-98, Bartlett Consulting Ltd., Sewickley, Pa., 1998—. Bd. dirs. Dravotec spa, Milan, Italy, F.C. de Weger Bv, Rotterdam, Dravo-Still, Inc., Pitts., Worley Santa Fe Ltd., London, Santa Fe Braun (UK) Ltd, London, Biomechanics Corp. Am. Melville, N.Y., Badger Catlytic Ltd., New Malden, England, Catalytic Svcs., Caracas, Venequela, Cosa United C.A., Caracas, United Yemen, Sana Yemen. Decorated officer Order Brit. Empire (Eng.). Fellow Inst. Marine Engring. Sci. and Tech.; mem. ASME, Am. Nuclear Soc., Am. Mgmt. Assn., Project Mgmt. Inst., Am. Petroleum Inst., Coun. on Fgn. Rels. (L.A. com. on fgn. relations). Clubs: Duqesne. Home Phone: 412-749-7838; Office Phone: 412-749-0313. E-mail: bartlettobe@aol.com.

BARTLETT, ELIZABETH EASTON, interior designer; b. Cleve., Apr. 1, 1937; d. Walter James Easton and Elizabeth (Scott) Easton Sullivan; m. Peter B. Bartlett, Nov. 24, 1956 (div. Sept. 1987); children: Elizabeth Kimberley Bartlett Kernan, Christopher, Katherine Bartlett Lieder. Grad., Skidmore Coll., 1959. Model Cluett, Peabody & Co., NYC, 1958-65; pvt. practice NYC, 1978—. Buyer, bd. dirs. Boutique de Noël, N.Y.C., 1976-87. Trustee, vice chmn. St. Barnabas Hosp., Bronx, N.Y., 1978—; v.p. N.Y. Soc. for Prevention of Cruelty to Children, N.Y.C., 1979; trustee, bd. dirs. Youth Counseling League, N.Y.C., 1974—. Mem. Rolling Rock Club. Episcopalian. Home and Office: 30 E 72nd St Apt 12B New York NY 10021-4265

BARTLETT, ELIZABETH SUSAN, audio-visual specialist; b. Bloomington, Ind., Sept. 11, 1927; d. Cecil Vernon and Nell (Helfrich) Bartlett; m. Frederick E. Sherman, July 8, 1955 (div. 1978). Student, Ind. U., 1946—48. Traffic-continuity dir. WTTS-Radio, Bloomington, Ind., 1947—48; traffic continuity dir. WTTV-TV, Indpls., 1949—57, program dir., 1958—59; creative dir. Venus Advt. Agy., Indpls., 1960—68; prodn. mgr. Nat. TV News, Detroit, 1968—71; owner, prodr. Susan Sherman Prodns., Greenwich, Conn., 1971—73; audiovisual officer NSF, Arlington, 1973—2001. Cons. NSF, 2001—; lectr. in field. Concept writer/prodr. film: The Observatories, 1981; prodr.: Science: Woman's Work, 1982, Keyhole of Eternity, 1975, What About Tomorrow?, 1978, The American Island, 1970, The New Engineers, 1986, Discover Science, 1988, A Brain, Books and a Curiosity, 1992, Radio Astronomy: Observing the Invisible Universe, 1999, Breaking the Code: The Arabidopsis Genome, 2000, others. Recipient Silver award Internat. Film and TV Festival of N.Y., 1970, 74, 2001, Gold medal Nat. Ednl. Film Festival, 1982, 89, Chris Bronze plaque Columbus Film Festival, 1982, Bronze award Internat. Film & TV Festival of N.Y., 1982, Gold award 1976, Gold Camera award U.S. Indsl. Film Festival, 1982, Silver Cindy award, Info. Film Prodrs. Assn., 1982, award for creative excellence U.S. Indsl. Film Festival, 1975, Techfilm Festival award, 1979, 80, 88, Gold award Houston Internat. Film Festival, 1987, Art Direction Mag. Creativity award, 1988, Videographer award of Distinction, 2001, Silver award, 2001, Aurora Festival Gold award, 2001; named Outstanding Woman for Contbn. in Arts, Federally Employed Women, 1984, named to Ind. Broadcast Pioneers Hall Fame., 2007. Mem.: Am. Women in Radio and TV (chpt. pres. 1953—56, 1969—70), Coun. on Internat. Non-Theatrical Events (adv. bd., Golden Eagle award 1970, 1974, 1976—79, 1982, 1987, 1999), Washington Film and Video Coun. (pres. 1978—79). Home: 809 S Columbus St Alexandria VA 22314-4206 Office Phone: 703-292-7726.

BARTLETT, JAMES LOWELL, III, investment company executive; b. Boston, May 26, 1945; s. James Lowell and Shirley Victoria (Wyatt) B.; m. Shannon Mara McMillion, May 4, 1979; children: James Lowell IV, Zachary Morgan, Matthew Wyatt. BS, U. Calif., Berkeley, 1967, MBA, 1968. Loan officer nat. div. Bank of Am., Los Angeles, 1968; fin. mgr. Psychology Today mag., Del Mar, Calif., 1969; pres. Forum Communications Corp.; pub. Cuisine, Politics Today, Volleyball mags., NYC, 1970-82; pres. Bartlett & Co., Santa Barbara, Calif., 1982—. Commr. Internat. Volleyball Assn., 1977-80 Mem. Lds Ch. Office: 5662 Calle Real Santa Barbara CA 93117-2317

BARTLETT, JAMES WILSON, III, lawyer; b. Pasadena, Calif., Mar. 21, 1946; s. James Wilson Jr. and Helen (Archbold) B.; m. Jane Edmunds Graves; children: Matthew Archbold, Polly Graves. BA, Washington & Lee U., 1968; JD, Vanderbilt U., 1975. Bar: Md. 1975, U.S. Dist. Ct. Md. 1975, U.S. Dist. Ct. (no. dist.) Ohio, 1992, U.S. Ct. Claims 1984, U.S. Ct. Appeals (4th cir.) 1976, U.S. Ct. Appeals (6th cir.) 1992, U.S. Supreme Ct. 1995. Assoc. Semmes, Bowen & Semmes, Balt., 1975-85; pvt. practice Balt., 1985-86; ptnr. Kroll & Tract, Balt., 1986-87, Wilson, Elser, Moskowitz, Edelman & Dicker, Balt., 1987-98, mng. ptnr., 1998-2001; ptnr. Semmes, Bowen & Semmes, Balt., 2001—, vice chmn., 2006—. Permanent mem. jud. conf. 4th Cir.; bd. dirs. Balt. Maritime Exch., 2001—. Assoc. editor: Am. Maritime Cases, 1997—; contbr. articles to profl. jours. Chmn. law firm campaign United Fund, Balt., 1979; bd. dirs. Roland Park Civic League, 1987-90, Balt. (Md.) Maritime Exchange, 2001—. 1st lt. U.S. Army, 1969-71. Mem.: ABA (vice chmn. 1985—88, 1992—95, 1999—, chmn. admiralty and maritime law tort and ins. practice sect. 1990—91, chmn. admiralty and maritime litig. com. litig. sect. 1997—99), Assn. Average Adjusters U.S., Assn. Average Adjusters (Eng.), Md. Def. Counsel Inc., Def. Rsch. Inst., Maritime Law Assn. U.S. (proctor, bd. dirs. 1998—2001, chair practice and proc. com. 2000—04, sec. 2004—), Balt. City Bar Assn., Md. Bar Assn., St. Andrews Soc., Am. Boat and Yacht Coun., Tupenny Club, Propeller Club U.S. (gov. Balt. chpt. 1984—87, v.p. 1987—88, exec. v.p. 1988—89, pres. 1989—90, nat. regional v.p. 1991—92, nat. 3d v.p. 1995—96, gov. Balt. chpt. 1997—2003, dir. Charitable Trust 2003—). Republican. Presbyterian. Home: 307 Edgevale Rd Baltimore MD 21210-1913 Office: Semmes Bowen & Semmes 250 W Pratt St Baltimore MD 21201 Office Phone: 410-576-4833. E-mail: jbartlett@semmes.com.

BARTLETT, JENNIFER LOSCH, artist; b. Long Beach, Calif., Mar. 14, 1941; BA, Mills Coll., 1963; B.F.A., Yale U., 1964, M.F.A., 1965; studied with Jack Tworkvov, James Rosenquist, Al Held, Jim Dire. Instr. Sch. Visual Arts, NYC. One-woman shows include Mills Coll., Oakland, Calif., 1963, Reese Paley Gallery, N.Y.C., 1972, Paula Cooper Gallery, N.Y.C., 1974, 76, 77, 79, 81, 82, 83, 85, 87, 88, 90, 91, 92, 94, Saman Gallery, Genoa, Italy, 1974, 78, John Doyle Gallery, Chgo., 1975, Contemporary Art Ctr., Cin., 1975, Dartmouth Coll., 1975, Wadsworth Atheneum, Hartford, Conn., 1977, San Francisco Mus. Modern Art, 1978, U. Calif., Irvine, 1978, Hansen-Fuller Gallery, San Francisco, 1978, Balt. Art Mus., 1978, Art Mus. South Tex., Corpus Christi, 1978, Margo Leavin Gallery, Los Angeles, 1979, 81, 83, U. Akron, 1979, Carleton Coll., 1979, Heath Gallery, Atlanta, 1979, 83, Galerie Mukai, Tokyo, 1980, Akron Art Inst., 1980, 89, 92, Albright-Knox Art Gallery, Buffalo, 1980, Joslyn Art Mus., Omaha, 1982, Tate Gallery, London, 1982, McIntosh/Drysdale Gallery, Houston, 1982, Gloria Luria Gallery, Bay Harbor Islands, Fla., 1983, Rose Art Mus., Brandeis U., Waltham, Mass., 1984, Long Beach Mus. Art., Calif., 1984, Univ. Art Mus., U. Calif.-Berkeley, 1984, Knight Gallery, Charlotte, N.C., 1985, Walker Arts Ctr., Mpls., 1985, Nelson-Atkins Mus. of Art, Kansas City, Mo., 1985, Bklyn. Mus., 1985, La Jolla Mus. Coll. Art, Calif., 1986, Mus. of Art, Carnegie Inst., Pitts., 1986, Whitechapel Art Gallery, London, 1986, Cleve. Mus. Art, 1986, Greg Kucera Gallery, Seattle, 1986, 92, Harvard U. Grad. Sch. of Design, Cambridge, Mass., 1987, Milw. Art Mus., 1988, John Berggruen Gallery, San Francisco, 1988, 90, 93, Knoedler Gallery, London, 1989, 90, Richard Gray Gallery, Chgo., 1991, 93, 96, Maier Mus. Randolph-Macon Women's Coll., Lynchburg, Va., 1992, Nancy Drysdale Gallery, Washington, 1992, Santa Fe Inst. Fine Arts, 1993, Gallery Camino Real, Boca Raton, Fla., 1994, Orlando (Fla.) Mus. Art, 1994, Locks Gallery, Phila., 1995, Gagosian Gallery, Beverly Hills, Calif., 1996, 97, others; group exbhns. include Mus. Modern Art, N.Y.C., 1971, 77, 78, 79, 80, 81, 83, 85, Whitney Mus. Am. Art, N.Y.C., 1972, 73, 77, 78, 79, 81, 82, 83, 86, 89, 91, Walker Art Ctr., Mpls., 1972, Kunsthaus, Hamburg, Fed. Republic Germany, 1972, Paula Cooper Gallery, N.Y.C., 1972, 73, 74, 76, 77, 78, 81, 83, 84, 85, 86, 87, 88, 90, 93, Corcoran Gallery Art, Washington, 1975, Art Inst. Chgo., 1975, 76, 86, Kunstmuseum, Dusseldorf, Fed. Republic Germany, 1976, Kassel, Fed. Republic Germany, 1977, Contemporary Arts Mus., Houston, 1980, Am. Acad. Arts and Letters, N.Y.C., 1981, 83, 85, 92, Sarah Lawrence Art Gallery, Bronxville, N.Y., 1984, Archer M. Hunting Art Gallery, U. Tex.-Austin, 1984, Hudson River Mus., Yonkers, N.Y., 1984, Tucson Mus. Art, 1984, Leo Castelli Gallery, N.Y.C., 1984, Gerald Peters Gallery, Dallas, 1994, Numark Gallery, Washington, 1995, others; represented in permanent collections, Mus. Modern Art, N.Y.C., Met. Mus. Art, N.Y.C., Whitney Mus. Am. Art, N.Y.C., Phila. Mus. Art, Walker Art Ctr., Mpls., Yale U. Art Gallery, New Haven, Art Mus. S.Tex., Corpus Christi, R.I. Sch. Design, Providence, Art Gallery S. Australia, Adelaide, Goucher Coll., Balt., Amerada Hess, Woodbridge, N.J., Dallas Mus. Fine Arts, Modern Art Mus. Fort Worth, Tex., Richard B. Russell Fed. Bldg. and U.S. Courthouse, Atlanta, others. Recipient Harris prize Art Inst. Chgo., 1976, 86; recipient Creative Arts award Brandeis U., 1983, award Am. Acad. Arts and Letters, 1983, AIA award, 1986; Creative Artists Public Services fellow, 1974;

Lucas vis. lectr. award Carleton Coll., 1979 Address: 134 Charles St # 114 New York NY 10014-2538 also: Paula Cooper Inc 534 W 21st St New York NY 10011-2812 also: c/o Gagosian Gallery 456 N Camden Dr Beverly Hills CA 90210

BARTLETT, JOHN, fashion designer; b. Columbus, Ohio, 1963; BS in Sociology, Harvard U., 1986; grad., FIT, 1988. Men's clothing designer Willi Wear, NYC; men's design dir. Ronaldus Shamask, NYC; prin. John Bartlett Menswear, NYC, 1992—. Recipient Woolmark Cutting Edge award, 1992, New Fashion Talent in Menswear Perry Ellis award Coun. Fgn. Designers Am., 1993.

BARTLETT, JOSEPH WARREN, lawyer; b. Boston, June 14, 1933; s. Charles W. and Barbara (Hastings) B.; m. May Parish, Apr. 28, 1956 (div.); children: Charles, Susan, Henry; m. Barbara Bemis, Sept. 20, 1980. AB, Harvard U., 1955; LLB, Stanford U., 1960. Bar: Mass. 1962, D.C. 1969, N.Y. 1981. Law clk. Chief Justice Warren, U.S. Supreme Ct., 1960-61; pvt. practice Boston, 1961-66; ptnr. Gaston & Snow, Boston, 1966-80, Gaston & Snow (formerly Gaston Snow Beekman & Bogue), NYC, 1980-90, of counsel, 1990-91; ptnr. Mayer, Brown & Platt, 1991-96, Morrison & Foerster, NYC, 1996—2002; of counsel Fish & Richardson P.C., NYC. Counsel Mass. Commn. Adminstrn., 1964-65; gen. counsel, under sec. Dept. Commerce, Washington, 1967-69; prin. adviser on universal social security coverage Sec. of HEW, Washington, 1978-79; acting prof. Stanford U., 1978; trustee, mem. fin. com. Montefiore Med. Ctr.; mem. Council on Fgn. Relations; adj. prof. NYU Law Sch. Served to 1st lt. US Army, 1956—57. Fellow Am. Bar Found.; mem. Am. Law Inst., Am. Bar Assn., Boston Bar Assn. (pres. 1977-78) Democrat. Episcopalian. Office: Fish and Richardson PC Citi Group Ctr 153 E 53rd St 52nd Fl New York NY 10022 Home: 300 E 77th St Apt 21b New York NY 10021-2490 Office Phone: 212-641-2285. E-mail: bartlett@fr.com.

BARTLETT, KATHARINE TIFFANY, dean, law educator; b. New Haven, Feb. 16, 1947; d. Edgar Parmelee and Elizabeth (Clark) B.; m. Christopher H. Schroeder, Aug. 13, 1975; children: Emily, Ted, Elizabeth. BA magna cum laude, Wheaton Coll., 1968; MA, Harvard U., 1969; JD, U. Calif., Berkeley, 1975. Bar: Calif. 1975, N.C. 1980, U.S. Dist. Ct. (no. dist.) Calif. 1975, U.S. Dist. Ct. (mid. dist.) N.C. Law clk. Childhood and Govt. Project Earl Warren Legal Inst. UC Berkeley, Calif., 1973—74; law clk. to presiding justice Alaska Supreme Ct., Alaska, 1974; law clk. Legal Aid Soc. of Alameda County, Oakland, Calif.; law clk. to presiding justice Calif. Supreme Ct., San Francisco, 1975-76; atty. Legal Aid Soc. of Alameda County, Oakland, Calif., 1976-79; A. Kenneth Pye prof. of law Duke U., Durham, NC, 1979—; dean, 2000—. Vis. prof. UCLA, 1985-86, Boston U., 1990. Grad. prize fellow Harvard U., 1968-69, fellow Nat. Humanities Ctr., 1992-93, Woodrow Wilson. Mem. Am. Law Inst., Soc. Am. Law Tchrs., N.C. Women Attys., N.C. Bar Assn., Am. Law Inst. (reporter for principles of family dissolution), Phi Beta Kappa. Democrat. Office: Duke Univ Law Sch Sci Dr and Towerview Rd Box 90362 Durham NC 27708-0362 Office Phone: 919-613-7001. E-mail: bartlett@law.duke.edu.

BARTLETT, LEONARD LEE, retired communications educator, advertising executive; b. Mountain Home, Idaho, May 31, 1930; s. Harold Roberts and Alma Martina (Nixon) B.; m. Sue Ann Kipfer, Nov. 5, 1966; children: Jennifer, Deborah; children by previous marriage: Linda Lee, Cynthia, Nancy, Pamela, William Charles. BA, Brigham Young U., Provo, Utah, 1957, MA, 1989. Advt. mgr. Steiner Co., Chgo., 1957-59; sr. v.p. Marsteller Inc., Chgo., 1959-67; vice chmn. Cole & Weber, Inc., Seattle, 1966-84; chmn. Cole & Weber Calif., San Francisco, 1984-86, Los Angeles, 1986-87; assoc. prof. communications Brigham Young U., Provo, 1989-2000; ret., 2000. Acting chmn. dept. comms. Brigham Young U., Provo, 1995—96, chmn. dept. comm., 1996—97, asst. to pres. univ. comms., 1997—2000. Mem. Am. Assn. Advt. Agys. (chmn. Western region 1980, nat. bd. 1980-81). Republican. Mem. Ch. Jesus Christ of Latter-day Saints. Home: 1211 East 2080 North Provo UT 84604-2123 Personal E-mail: leebar30@comcast.net.

BARTLETT, LYNN CONANT, English literature educator; b. Bethlehem, Pa., Dec. 14, 1921; s. Fay Conant and Marie Agnes (McGuiness) B.; m. Margaret Emma Johnson, June 29, 1946; 1 dau., Anne Elston. BA, Lehigh U., 1943; A.M., Harvard, 1947, PhD, 1957; B. Litt., Oxford U., Eng., 1952. Instr. English Lehigh U., 1946; teaching fellow Harvard, 1948-50; instr. Vassar Coll., 1952-57; asst. prof., 1957-62; asso. prof., 1962-70; prof., 1970-92; prof. emeritus, 1992—; asst. dean coll., 1958-61; sec. coll., 1966-76. Editor: (with W.R. Sherwood) The English Novel, Background Readings, 1967. Served with AUS, 1943-46. Decorated Bronze Star. Mem. Phi Beta Kappa, Sigma Phi Epsilon. Clubs: Harvard (N.Y.C.), Circumnavigators Club. Home: 170 College Ave Poughkeepsie NY 12603-2806 Personal E-mail: Lcbartlett6@aol.com.

BARTLETT, NEIL, chemist, emeritus educator; b. Newcastle-upon-Tyne, Eng., Sept. 15, 1932; s. Norman and Ann Willins (Vock) B.; m. Christina Isabel Cross, Dec. 26, 1957; children: Jeremy John, Jane Ann, Christopher, Robin. BSc, U. Durham, Eng., 1954, PhD in Inorganic Chemistry, 1957; DSc (hon.), U. Waterloo, Can., 1968, Colby Coll., 1972, U. Newcastle-upon-Tyne, 1981, McMaster U., Can., 1992, U. B.C., 2006; D.Univ. (hon.), U. Bordeaux, France, 1976, U. Ljubljana, Slovenia, 1989, U. Nantes, France, 1990; LLD, Simon Fraser U., Can., 1993; Dr. rer. nat. (hon.), Freie U., Berlin, 1998. Lectr. chemistry U. B.C., Vancouver, Canada, 1958—63, prof., 1963—66; prof. chemistry Princeton U., NJ, 1966—69, U. Calif., Berkeley, 1969—99; guest sr. scientist chem. sci. divsn. LBNL, Berkeley, 1999—. Mem. adv. bd. on inorganic reactions and methods Verlag Chemie, 1978—; mem. adv. panel Nat. Measurement Lab., Nat. Bur. Stds., 1974-80; E.W.R. Steacie Meml. fellow NRC, Can., 1964-66; Miller vis. prof. U. Calif., Berkeley, 1967-68; 20th G.N. Lewis Meml. lectr., 1973; William Lloyd Evans Meml. lectr. Ohio State U., 1966; A.D. Little lectr. Northeastern U., 1969; Phi Beta Upsilon lectr. U. Nebr., 1975; Henry Werner lectr. U. Kans., 1977; Jeremy Musher Meml. lectr., Israel, 1980, Randolph T. Major Meml. lectr. U. Conn., 1985, J.C. Karcher lectr. U. Okla., 1988; Brotherton vis. prof. U. Leeds, Eng., 1981; Erskine vis. lectr. U. Canterbury, New Zealand, 1983; Wilsmore fellow Melbourne U., Australia, 1983; vis. fellow All Souls Coll., Oxford U., 1984; Miller prof. U. Calif.-Berkeley, 1986-87; George H. Cady lectr. U. Wash., Seattle, 1994; Leermakers lectr. Wesleyan U., 1995; Davis Meml. lectr. U. New Orleans, 1997, Pierre Duhem seminaires, U. Bordeaux, 1998. Bd. editors Inorganic Chemistry, 1967-79, Jour. Fluorine Chemistry, 1971-80, Synthetic Metals, Revue Chimie Minerale; mem. adv. bd. McGraw-Hill Ency. Sci. and Tech. Recipient Rsch. Corp. prize; E.W.R. Steacie prize, 1965; Elliott Cresson medal Franklin Inst., 1968; Kirkwood medal Yale U. and Am. Chem. Soc. (New Haven sect.), 1969; Dannie-Heinemann prize The Gottingen acad. 1971; Robert A. Welch award in chemistry, 1976; Alexander von Humboldt Found. award, 1977; medal Jozef Stefan Inst., Slovenia, 1980; Moissan medal, 1986; Prix Moissan, Paris, 1988; Grand Prix de la Fondation de la Maison de la Chimie, 2004; fellow Alfred P. Sloan Found., 1964-66; Bonner Chemieprries, Bonn, 1991; Berkeley citation, 1993. Fellow Royal Soc. (Davy medal, 2002), Royal Soc. Chemistry (U.K., hon.), Am. Acad. Arts and Scis., Chem. Inst. Can. (1st Noranda lectr. 1963), Royal Soc. Can.; mem. NAS (fgn. assoc.), Leopoldina Acad. (Halle, Salle), Akademie der Wissenschaften in Gottingen, Associé Etranger, Academia Europaea, Académie des Sciences, Institut de France, Am. Chem. Soc. (chmn. divs. fluorine chemistry 1972, inorganic chemistry 1977, award in inorganic chemistry 1970, W.H. Nichols award N.Y. sect. 1983, Pauling medal of Pacific N.W. sects. 1989, Disting. Svc. award 1989, award for Creative Work in Fluorine Chemistry 1992), Phi Lambda Upsilon (hon.) Home: 6 Oak Dr Orinda CA 94563-3912 Office: Bldg 70A c/o Rm 3307 LBNL Berkeley CA 94720 Business E-Mail: nbartlett@lbl.gov.

BARTLETT, NORMA THYRA, retired administrative assistant; b. Raymond, SD, June 7, 1922; d. Wilhelm Emil and Olga Sophie (Mailand) Claussen; m. Fred Otis Metcalf, Mar. 29, 1941 (dec. Apr. 1963); children: Linda E. Lepak, Barry Otis (dec. Feb. 2000); m. Francis Grindal Bartlett, Dec. 27, 1963 (dec. Jan. 2004). BA, U. Wash., Seattle, 1969; Diploma, Inst. of Children's Lit., 1997. Cert. profl. sec. Office mgr. Fed. Old Line Ins. Co., Everett, Wash., 1949-55; supr. office svc. Scott Paper Co., Everett, Wash., 1958-63; tchr. bus. edn. Canyon Park Jr. H.S., Seattle, 1969, Bellevue (Wash.) C.C., 1969; exec. asst. Peoples Bank, Starkville, Miss., 1970-76; prin. Satellite Steno Svc., Starkville, Miss., 1976-77; office mgr. Donald Wiley & Assocs., Sydney, Australia, 1977-80. Bd. dirs. United Cmty. Fund Snohomish County, Everett, Wash., 1961-62; pres. Scott Paper Co. Fellowship Fund, Everett, 1961, TLRC Helping Hands, 2005-. Hon. life mem. United Luth. Ch. Women, Everett, Wash., 1958—; organizer, charter pres. Starkville Bus. and Profl. Women, 1972-74; pres. Welcome Wagon Club, Ocean Springs, Miss., 1982-83; tutor Jackson County Literacy, Ocean Springs, 1985-88; organizer Discourse, Ocean Springs, 1985-86. Norma T. Bartlett scholarship named in her honor Starkville Area Bus. and Profl. Women, 1978. Mem.: AAUW (Gig Harbor br. media rep. 1997—99), Intertel, Mensa (local sec. 1989—91, editor newsletter 1987—89), U. Wash. Alumni Assn. Democrat. Lutheran. Avocations: needlecrafts, reading, writing, travel, organist. Home: 1305 N Highlands Pkwy Apt C1 Tacoma WA 98406-2171 E-mail: fgbart@comcast.net.

BARTLETT, RICHARD ADAMS, historian, writer, retired history professor; b. Boulder, Colo., Nov. 23, 1920; s. John Thomas and Margaret Emily (Abbott) Bartlett; m. Marie Regina Cosgrove, Dec. 26, 1945; children: Richard, Margaret, Thomas, Mary. BA, U. Colo., 1942, PhD, 1953; MA, U. Chgo., 1947. Instr. Tex. A&M U., 1945—51; asst. prof. Fla. State U., 1955—63, assoc. prof., 1963—67, prof., 1968—89, prof. emeritus, 1989—. Author: Great Surveys of the American West, 1962, 1966, paperback, 1993, The Wilderness and the Indians: Challenges in the New World, 1970, Nature's Yellowstone, 1974, The New Country: A Social History of the American Frontier, 1776-1890, 1974, paperback, 1976, Freedom's Trail, 1979, 2d edit., 1981, Yellowstone: A Wilderness Besieged, 1985;: paperback, 1989, From Cody to the World: The First Seventy-Five Years of the Buffalo Bill Memorial Association, 1992, Troubled Waters: Champion International and the Pigeon River Controversy, 1995, Yellowstone Holiday, 1998, The World of Ham Radio, 1901-1950; A Social History, 2007; editor: Rolling Rivers: An Encyclopedia of America's Rivers, 1984; contbr. articles and book revs. to profl. jours. Fellow, Am. Philos. Soc., 1967; grantee, Fla. State U.; Hungtington Libr. fellow, 1967, Woodrow Wilson fellow, Smithsonian Inst., 1979—80. Mem.: Fla. Coll. Tchrs. History (pres. 1974—75), Western History Assn. (governing coun. 1976—79, mem. editl. bd. The Am. West 1980—82), Phi Alpha Theta. Episcopalian. Home: 2205 Mendoza Ave Tallahassee FL 32304-1319 Personal E-mail: rbartlet@mailer.fsu.edu.

BARTLETT, RICHARD ALLAN, finance company executive; b. NYC, July 6, 1957; s. Thomas Alva and Mary Louise (Bixby) B. BA, Princeton U., 1979; JD, Yale U., 1982. Law clerk to Hon. David L. Bazelon U.S. Ct. Appeals, Washington, 1982-83; law clerk to assoc. justice Harry A. Blackmun U.S. Supreme Ct., Washington, 1983-84; mng. dir. Resource Holdings Ltd., NYC, 1984—. Bd. dirs. US Airways Group, 2005—. Mem.: NY State Bar, Princeton. Episcopalian.

BARTLETT, RICHARD CHALKLEY, writer, conservationist; b. LA, May 23, 1935; s. Theodore Lester Bartlett and Maud (Colley) Newsom; m. Joanne Krieger; children: Lisa, Christopher. BS in Communications, U. Fla., 1956. With advt. sales dept. The Miami (Fla.) Herald, 1958; internat. sales and mgmt. exec. for home parties div. Tupperware Inc., Orlando, 1959-65; v.p. advt. and sales promotion Vanda Beauty Counselor div. Dart Industries, Orlando, Fla., 1965-71; exec. v.p. mktg. Dynasty Industries Inc., Dallas, 1971-73; dir. mktg. svcs. Mary Kay Inc., Dallas, 1973-76, v.p. mktg., 1976-85, exec. v.p. mktg., 1986-87, pres., COO, 1987-93, vice-chmn., 1993—. Chmn. U.S. Direct Selling Assn., Washington, 1991-93, U.S. Direct Selling Edn. Found., Washington, 1993-94, bd. dirs.; vice chmn. edn. World Fedn. Direct Selling, 1997-99; bd. dirs. Vital Voice Global Partnership, 2001-03; adv. bd. U. Fla. Ctr. for Retailing Edn. and Rsch., Gainesville; adv. coun., bd. dirs. mem. adv. coun. U. Tex. Press; mem. adv. com. Coll. Agrl. Sci. and Natural Resources, Tex. Tech. U.; hon. mem. bd. dirs. Nat. Environ. Edn. and Tng. Found.; bd. dirs. Nat. Coun. Sci. and the Environment. Author: The Direct Option, 1994, Saving the Best of Texas: A Partnership Approach to Conservation, 1995; co-author: The Sportsman's Guide to Texas, 1988. Chmn. Tex. Environ. Edn. Partnership Fund Bd.; bd. dirs. Better Bus. Bur. Met. Dallas, The Aldo Leopold Found.; hon. trustee The Nature Conservancy of Tex.; chmn. edn. and outreach adv. com. Tex. Parks and Wildlife Dept., mem. Gov.'s Adv. Com. Environ. Flows. With U.S. Army, 1957. Named Outstanding Marketer of Yr., Southwestern Mktg. Assn., 1991, Chief of Exec. of Yr., Internat. TV Assn., 1992; named to U.S. Direct Selling Assn. Hall of Fame, 1994, U.S. Direct Selling Edn. Found. Circle of Honor, 1995, Pi Kappa Phi Nat. Hall of Fame, 1996; recipient Oak Leaf award Nature Conservancy, 1997. Mem. Acad. Mktg. Sci. (Disting. Marketer of Yr. 1995). Avocations: conservation work, performing arts. Office: Mary Kay PO Box 799045 Dallas TX 75379-7045

BARTLETT, RICHARD JAMES, lawyer; b. Glens Falls, NY, Feb. 15, 1926; s. George Willard and Kathryn M. (McCarthy) Bartlett; m. Claire E. Kennedy, Aug. 18, 1951; children: Michael, Amy. BS, Georgetown U., 1945; LLB, Harvard U., 1949; LLD (hon.), Union Coll., 1974; ScD (hon.), Albany Med. Coll., 1986. Bar: N.Y. 1949. Pvt. practice, Glens Falls, 1949—73; mem. NY Assembly, 1959—66, Clark Bartlett & Caffry, 1962—73; justice N.Y. State Supreme Ct., 1973-79; chief adminstr. cts. N.Y. State, 1974-79; dean Albany (N.Y.) Law Sch., Union U., 1979-86; mem. Bartlett, Pontiff, Stewart, & Rhodes P.C., Glens Falls, 1986—. Chair N.Y. Pend Law Commn., 1961—70; mem. N.Y. Bd. Law Examiners, 1986—2001, chair, 1998—2001; chmn. N.Y. Jud. Commn. Justice for Children, 1988—90; trustee Nat. Conf. Bd. Examiners, 1987—97, chair, 1996; dir. Nat. Conf. Bar Founds., 2001—03; del. N.Y. Constl. Conv., 1967. Trustee Hyde Collection, Glens Falls, 1967—98. Capt. USAF, 1951—53. Fellow: Am. Bar Found.; mem.: ABA (ho. dels. 1997—2001), N.Y. State Bar Assn. (ho. dels. 2002—, Gold medal 2004), N.Y. Bar Found. (bd. dirs. 1989—, pres. 2000—03), Am. Law Inst. (life), Warren County Bar, Assn. Bar City of N.Y. Republican. Roman Catholic. Office: 1 Washington St PO Box 2168 Glens Falls NY 12801-2168 Office Phone: 518-792-2117. Business E-Mail: rjb@bpsrlaw.com.

BARTLETT, ROBERT HAWES, surgeon; b. Ann Arbor, Mich., May 8, 1939; BA, Albion Coll., Mich., 1960; MD cum laude, U. Mich., 1963. Diplomate Nat. Bd. Med. Examiners, Am. Bd. Surgery (examination cons. 1989-90), Am. Bd. Thoracic Surgery. Intern in surgery Peter Bent Brigham Hosp., Boston, 1963-64, asst. resident/sr. asst. resident, 1964-67, chief resident in thoracic surgery, 1968, chief resident surgeon, 1969; rsch. fellow in surgery Harvard Med. Sch., Boston, 1968, Arthur Tracy Cabot Teaching fellow in surgery, 1969; Harvey Cushing fellow and rsch. fellow in surgery Peter Bent Brigham Hosp./Harvard Med. Sch., Boston, 1969-70; asst. prof. surgery U. Calif., Irvine, 1970-73, assoc. prof. surgery, 1973-77, prof. surgery, 1977-80, U. Mich., Ann Arbor, 1980—2005, prof. emeritus, 2005—. Asst. in surgery Peter Bent Brigham Hosp., 1969-70; attending staff U. Calif.-Irvine/Orange County Med. Ctr., 1970-80, asst. dir. surg. svcs., 1970-80, dir. burn ctr., 1971-80; attending staff St. Joseph Hosp., Orange, Calif., 1970-80, Children's Hosp. of Orange County, 1970-80, VA Hosp., Long Beach, 1970-80, Wayne County Gen. Hosp., 1980-84, Westland Med. Ctr., 1984-85; attending staff U. Mich. Med. Ctr., 1980—, dir. SICU, 1980—, gen. surgery sect. head, 1981-87, dir. grad. edn., 1980-91, trauma/critical care divsn. chief, 1980-91, critical care divsn. chief, 1991—, program dir. surg. critical care fellowship, 1991—, dir. extracorporeal life support program, 1980—; lectr. in field; cons. in field to NIH, Nat. Heart and Lun Inst., Calif. Heart Assn., March of Dimes Found., numerous others. Editl. bd. Perfusion, 1985—, Critical Care, 1985—, Trans ASAIQ, 1986—, Internat. Jour. Biomaterials, Artificial Cells and Artificial Organs, 1987, Jour. Thoracic and Cardiovascular Surgery, 1992-94, SESATS; reviewer Sci., 1974, Chest, 1974-79, 83—. Jour. Applied Physiology, 1977, Heart and Lung, 1978—, New Eng. Jour. Medicine, 1981, 87-88, Surgery, 1984—, Am. Rev. Respiratory Disease, 1985—, Jour. Thoracic and CArdiovascular Surgery, 1987—, Artificial Organs, 1987—, Pediatrics, 1987—, Intensive Care Medicine, 1987—, Jour. Parenteral and Enteral Nutrition, 1988—, Jour. Critical Care, 1989—, Jour. AMA, 1993—, Am. Jour. Respiratory and Critical Care Medicine, 1993—; patentee in field; contbr. over 243 articles to profl. jours., chpts. to books; author: Mechanical Devices for Cardiopulmonary Assistance, Advances in Cardiology, Vol. 6, 1971, Hematological Analysis of extracorporeal Membrane Oxygenation, 1974, Extracorporeal Circulation for Cardiopulmonary Failure, Current Problems in Surgery, Vol. 15, 1978, Extracorporeal Life Support for Cardiopulmonary Failure, Current Problems in Surgery, Vol. 27, 1990; co-editor: Biologic and Synthetic Vascular Protheses, 1982, Life Support Systems in Invensive Care, 1984, Medical Education: A Surgical Perspective, 1986; editor: Respiratory Care of the Surgical Patient, 1980. Rsch. grantee Orange County Heart Assn., 1971, Donald E. Baxter Found., 1970-71, Calif. TB and Respiratory Disease Assn., 1971-72, NIH, 1972-75, 74-77, 76-79, 78-80, 81-84, 84-85, 84-85, 85-90, 90-92, Hearst Found., 1976-78, 79-80, 89-93, Thoratec Inc., 1983, Mead-Johnson, 1983, GM Corp., 1984-85, others; recipient Gibbon award Am. Soc. Extra-Corporeal Tech., 1992, Dwight E. Harken award Temple U., 1992, Kaiser Permanente Excellence in Teaching award, 1993, Medallion for Scientific Achievement, Am. Surg. Assn., 2002, Ladd Medal, Am. Acad. Pediatrics, 2003, Jacobson award, Am. Coll. Surgeons, 2003. Mem. ACS, Am. Surg. Assn., Am. Assn. Thoracic Surgery, Am. Assn. for Surgery of Trauma, Assn. for Acad. Surgery, Ctrl. Surg. Soc., Coller Surg. Soc., Soc. Univ. Surgeons, Surg. Biology Club II, Surg. Infection Soc., Western Thoracic Surg. Assn., Am. Burn Assn., Am. Assn. History of Medicine, Am. Physiol. Soc., Am. Coll. Chest Physicians, Am. Soc. for Artificial Internal Organs (bd. trustees 1986-87, regulatory affairs com. 1985—, pres. 1984, others), Am. Thoracic Soc., Am. Trauma Soc., Extracorporeal Life Support Orgn., Internat. Soc. Artificial Organs, Mich. Soc. Critical Care, Perinatal Assn. Mich., Soc. Critical Care Medicine, Am. Inst. for Med. and Biol. Engring. (charter mem.), Beta Beta Beta, Alpha Omega Alpha, Galens Hon. Med. Soc., Inst. Medicine, 2003. Office: U Mich 1500 E Medical Ctr Dr #2920 Ann Arbor MI 48109-0999

BARTLETT, ROBERT WATKINS, metallurgist, educator, consultant; b. Salt Lake City, Jan. 8, 1933; s. Charles E. and Phyllis (Watkins) B.; m. Betty Cameron, Dec. 3, 1954; children: John C., Robin Parmley, Bruce R., Susanne. BS, U. Utah, 1953, PhD, 1961. Registered profl. engr., Calif. Group leader ceramics SRI Internat., Menlo Park, Calif., 1964-67; assoc. prof. metallurgy Stanford U., Palo Alto, Calif., 1967-74; mgr. hydrometallurgy Kennecott Minerals Co., Salt Lake City, 1974-77; dir. materials lab. SRI Internat., Menlo Park, Calif., 1977-80; v.p. rsch. Anaconda Minerals Co., Tucson, 1980-85; mgr. materials tech. Idaho Sci. and Tech. Dept., Idaho Falls, 1985-87; dean Coll. Mines and Earth Resources, U. Idaho, Moscow, 1987-97. Dir. Idaho Geol. Survey, Moscow. Author approximately 100 rsch. publs. in metallurgy; 12 patents in field; 1 textbook. Served to lt. (j.g.) USN, 1953-56. Recipient Turner award Electrochem. Soc., 1965, McConnell award AIME, 1985. Mem. Nat. Acad. Engring., Metall. Soc. (pres. 1989, EPD lecturer 1997), Soc. Mining Engrs. (disting. mem., Wadsworth award 1996), Sigma Xi, Tau Beta Pi. Office: 2505 Loch Way El Dorado Hills CA 95762 Personal E-mail: bobnbettybartlett@sbcglobal.net.

BARTLETT, ROBERT WILLIAM, lawyer; b. Chgo., Nov. 11, 1941; s. Robert C. and Rita E. Bartlett; m. Mary Lou Holtzman, Mar. 8, 1988; 1 child, Brooke Ann. AB, Stanford U., 1963; LLB, U. Va., 1966. Bar: Ill. 1966. Assoc. counsel U.S. League Savs. Instns., Chgo., 1970-77, assoc. gen. counsel, editor legal bull., 1977-81, sr. v.p., 1981-91; exec. editor bus. and fin. group Commerce Clearing House, Riverwoods, Ill., 1991-2000. Avocation: running. Home: 1945 Maple Pl Riverwoods IL 60015

BARTLETT, RODNEY J., chemistry and physics educator; b. Memphis, Mar. 31, 1944; s. Robert Henry and Sue Anne (Payne) B.; m. Beverly Jean Featherston, Aug. 17, 1966; children: Robert Darron and Ronald Eric. BS in Chemistry and Math., Millsaps Coll.; 1966; PhD in Quantum Chemistry, U. Fla., 1971. NDEA Title IV predoctoral fellow U. Fla., 1966—69, IBM predoctoral fellow, 1969—71; NSF postdoctoral fellow Aarhus U., Denmark, 1971-72; assoc. rsch. scientist John Hopkins U., Balt., 1972-74; prin. rsch. scientist Battelle Pacific NW Labs., Richland, Wash., 1974-76, sr. rsch. scientist, 1976-77, Battelle Meml. Inst., Richland, 1977-79, group leader, chem. physics, 1979-81; prof. Chemistry & Physics U. Fla., Gainesville, 1981-87, grad. rsch. prof., 1988—. Adj. asst. prof. Washington State U., 1975—77; vis. scientist Max Planck Institut fur Astrophysik, Garching bei Munchen, Germany, 1983. Mem. editl. bd. Theoretica Chimica Acta, 1985-89, Internat. Jour. Quantum Chemistry, 1988-91, Jour. Chemical Physics, 1991-92, Molecular Physics, 1992-98, adv. bd. 1999-; mem. adv. bd. Theoretical Chemistry Accounts, 1989-; contbr. articles to profl. jours. Fellow Guggenheim Harvard, U. Calif. (Berkeley), 1986-87, E.T.S. Walton Fellow, Sci. Found. Ireland, Univ. Cork, Ireland. Fellow Internat. Acad. Quantum Molecular Sci., Am. Physical Soc.; mem. Am. Chemical Soc. (chmn.-elect-designate, subdivision Theoretical Chemistry, 1983, chmn.-elect 1984, chmn. 1985, award in theoretical chemistry, 2007). Office: University of Florida Quantum Theory Project PO Box 118435 Gainesville FL 32611-8435 Office Phone: 352-392-6974 (voice). Business E-Mail: bartlett@qtp.ufl.edu.*

BARTLETT, ROSCOE G., congressman; b. Moreland, Ky., June 3, 1926; married; 10 children. BA, Columbia Union, 1947; MS, U. Md., 1948, PhD, 1952. Asst. prof. Loma Linda Med. Sch., 1952-54, Howard Med Sch., 1954-56; rschr. NIH, 1956-59; engr. Naval Aerospace Med. Inst., 1959—67; dir. Space Life Scis. Divsn. Johns Hopkins U., 1968-74; dir. rsch. devel. IBM, 1975-87; owner Roscoe Bartlett & Assocs.; mem. US Congress from 6th Md. dist., 1993—, mem. armed svcs. com., sci. com., vice chmn. small bus. com. Republican. Office: US Ho Reps 2412 Rayburn Ho Office Bldg Washington DC 20515-2006*

BARTLETT, SCOTT PAUL, plastic surgeon; m. Kimberly Ruhanen, Feb. 26, 1983; children: Alexandra Wright, Natalie Paxton. MD, Wash. U., St Louis, 1975. Cert. Am. Bd. Surgery, 1985, Am. Bd. Plastic Surgery, 1987. Assoc prof of surgery Univ. Pa. Sch. Medicine, Phila., 1986—, surgeon, 1986—, dir. craniofacial program, and assoc. prof., plastic surgery; also, chief, divsn. plastic surgery Children's Hosp. Phila. Dir. craniofacial program U. Of Pa, Phila., 2001—; past pres. Northeastern Soc. of Plastic Surgeons; assoc. editor Jour. Named a Top Doc, Phila. mag., 2002, 2004—. Mem.: Northeastern Soc. Plastic Surgeons (past pres. 2001), Am. Soc. Of Plastics Surgeons (licentiate; com. chmn. 2003—). Achievements include research in craniofacial biology. Office: U Pa 10 Penn Tower 3400 Spruce St Philadelphia PA 19104 also: Children's Hosp Phila Wood Bldg 34th E Civic Ctr Blvd Philadelphia PA 19104 E-mail: scott.bartlett@uphs.upenn.edu.*

BARTLETT, SHIRLEY ANNE, accountant; b. Gladwin, Mich., Mar. 28, 1933; d. Dewey J. and Ruth Elizabeth (Wright) Frye; m. Charles Duane Bartlett, Aug. 16, 1952 (div. Sept. 1982); children: Jeanne, Michelle, John, Yvonne Student, Mich. State U., 1952—53, Rutgers U., 1972—74. Auditor State of Mich., Lansing, 1951—66; cost acct. Templar Co., South River, NJ, 1968—75; staff acct. Franco Mfg. Co., Metuchen, NJ, 1975—78; contr. Thomas Creative Apparel, New London, Ohio, 1978—80; mgr. gen. acctg. Ideal Electric Co., Mansfield, Ohio, 1980—85; staff acct. Logangate Homes, Inc., Girard, Ohio, 1985—88; pvt. practice acctg. Youngstown, Ohio, 1985—; acct. Universal Devel. Enterprises, Liberty Twp., Ohio, 1987—88. V.p. Lang Industries, Inc., Youngstown, 1984-93 Author: (play) Our Bicentennial-A Celebration, 1976; mem., soloist various orchs. Mem. Human Rels. Commn., Franklin Twp., 1971—77, Friends of Am. Art; treas. Heritage Found., New Brunswick, NJ, 1973—74, New London Proceeds Corp., 1979—83; commr. Huron Pk. Commn., Ohio, 1979—83; vol. IRS for small bus., 1988—94, Children's Mus., 2005—; mem. planning com. Youngstown State U. Tax Insts., 1990—95, presenter, 1990—98; mem. planning com. for Children's Miracle Network Telethon Tod's Children's Hosp., Youngstown, 1985—2001; mem. citizens adv. bd. Mahoning County Juvenile Ct., 2004—; founder Youngstown Farmer's Market, 2003—; mem. Mahoning Valley Children's Mus., 2004—; elected Dem. com. mem., NJ, Ohio, 1970—82; bd. dirs., treas. Discovery Place, Inc., 1991—95; bd. dirs. First Night Youngstown, 2006—, treas., 2004—07. Mem.: NOW (treas. Youngstown chpt. 1986—93), NAFE, Am. Soc. Notaries, Am. Soc. Women Accts. (bd. dirs. 1986—88, v.p. 1988—89, pres. 1989—91, scholarship com. 1991—2001, chair chpt. devel. 1995—96, bd. dirs. 1996—2001, chair program com. 1997—2001), First Night Youngstown (bd. mem.), Youngstown Arts & Entertainment Dist. Assn. (treas. 2007—, bd. dirs. 2007—), Youngstown Opera Guild, Internat. Platform Assn., Women's Jour. Network, Nat. Women's Polit. Caucus, Bus. and Profl. Women (v.p. 1980—2001), Citizen's League Greater Youngstown, Friends of Am. Art, Chataqua Lit. and Sci. Cir., Sci. Cir. Club (pres. 1979—), Chataqua Lit. Club, Franklin JFK Club (treas. 1970—72, v.p. 1973—78), Investment Club (pres. 1997—99, treas. 1999—2001). Democrat. Unitarian Universalist. Avocations: music, knitting, needlecrafts. Office Phone: 330-398-5347. Personal E-mail: sbartlett328@hotmail.com.

BARTLETT, THOMAS A., telecommunications industry executive; B of Engring., Lehigh U., 1980; BA, Rutgers U., 1981. CPA. With Deloitte Hastins & Sells (now Deloitte Touche), NYC, 1981—84; CFO European ops. Bell Atlantic Bus. Systems Svcs., 1984; pres., CEO Bell Atlantic Internat. Wireless; pres. Global Solutions, Inc.; sr. v.p. investor rels. Verizon Comm., Inc., NYC, 2003—05, sr. v.p., treas., 2005—. Mem.: Bd. Adv. Rutgers School of Mngmnt., Bd. Dir. Prevention Education Inc. Office: Verizon Comm Inc 1095 Ave of Americas New York NY 10036-6797

BARTLETT, THOMAS ALVA, retired educational administrator; b. Salem, Oreg., Aug. 20, 1930; s. Cleave Wines and Alma (Hanson) B.; m. Mary Louise Bixby, Mar. 20, 1954; children: Thomas Glenn, Richard A., Paul H. Student, Willamette U., 1947—49, DCL (hon.), 1986; AB, Stanford U., 1951, PhD, 1959; MA, Oxford U., 1953; LHD (hon.), Colgate U., 1977, Mich. State U., 1978, Union Coll., 1979; DCL (hon.), Pusan Nat. U., 1985, U. Ala., 1983, U. North Ala., 2001; DHL (hon.), Am. U. Cairo, 2004. Mem. U.S. Permanent Mission to UN, 1956—63; advisor Gen. Assembly Dels., 1956—63; pres. Am. U., Cairo, 1963—69, Colgate U., Hamilton, NY, 1969—77, Assn. Am. Univs., Washington, 1977—82; chancellor U. Ala. Sys., 1982—89, Oreg. State Sys. of Higher Edn. Office, Eugene, 1989—94, SUNY, 1994—96; ret., 1996; interim pres. Am. U., Cairo, 2002—03. Mem. UAR-U.S. Ednl. Exch. Commn., 1966-69; mem. Task Force on Financing Higher Edn. in N.Y. State (Keppel Commn.), 1972-73; chmn. Commn. Ind. Colls. and Univs. N.Y., 1974-76; bd. dirs. Nat. Assn. Ind. Colls. and Univs., 1975-76; trustee Univs. Field Staff Internat., 1985-87; mem. NASA Comml. Space Adv. Com., 1988-90. Mem. nat. bd. examining Chaplains Episcopal Ch., 1978-91; trustee Gen. Theol. Sem., 1977-82, Am. U., Cairo, 1978-2002, vice chair 1998-2002; trustee U.S.-Japan Found., 1988-2001, chmn. 1996-2001; bd. mem. Internat. Assn. of Univs., 1995-2000; trustee Am. U. Kuwait, 2004—. Rhodes scholar, Oxford U., 1953. Mem. Coun. Fgn. Rels., Century Assn., Phi Beta Kappa. Home: 1209 SW 6th Ave Apt 904 Portland OR 97204 Personal E-mail: t-mbartlett@att.net.

BARTLEY, ABEL ALPHONSO, history professor; b. Nov. 21, 1965; BA in History and Polit. Sci., Fla. State U., Tallahassee, 1987, MA in US History, 1990, PhD in US History, 1994. Assoc. prof. U. Akron, Ohio, 1994—2004, Clemson U., SC, 2004—. Author: (books) Keeping the Faith: Race, Politics and Social Development, 2000 (Best Local History Book award, 2000), Akron's Black Heritage, 2004. Office: Clemson U History Dept Hardin 108 Clemson SC 29634

BARTLEY, BURNETT GRAHAM, JR., oil industry executive; b. Pitts., Nov. 10, 1924; s. Burnett Graham and Helen (McKee) McKenney B.; m. Mary Lou Gilbert, Aug. 7, 1947; children: Burnett III, Davison Wittmer, Richard McKenney, Parker Bowen, Heather Swinston, Tiffany Gilbert; m. Wendy K. Keyes, May 12, 2001; 1 child, Timothy Lee Vogler. BA, Yale U., 1949; grad. advanced mgmt. program, Harvard U., 1967. Rep. sales Koppers Co. Inc., Pitts., 1949-52, dist. mgr. sales, 1952-56, v.p. sales, 1956-58, v.p., gen. mgr. forest products, 1958-69, dep. chmn. bd., 1969-79, exec. v.p., 1979-88; chmn., chief exec. officer chems. and coatings Kop-coat, Inc., Pitts., 1988-90; chmn., chief exec. officer Anegada Group, Inc., Pitts., 1990—. Chmn., CEO Ameritex Chem. and Coatings Co., Irving, Tex.; chmn. Bridgewater Steel Corp., NJ, Trans-Ocean Trading Corp., Ltd.; chmn. bd. Edgewater Marine Corp., Morgantown, W.Va. Dir. World Affairs Coun., Pitts., 1987; Trustee Rehab. Ctr. Pitts., 1989, Children's Hosp., Pitts., 1989, Mich. Inst. Tech., 1989; chmn. bd. trustees Point Park Coll., Pitts., 1989; bd. dirs. Penn. Economy League, 1989; pres. Health Rsch. and Svcs. Found., Pitts., 1989. Lt. inf. U.S. Army, 1943-45, ETO. Mem. Am. Wood Preservers Inst. (pres. 1970), Am. Wood Preserver's Assn. (pres. 1975), So. Pressure Treaters Assn. (pres. 1974), 35th Infantry Divsn. Assn. (mem. exec. com.), Harvard-Yale-Princeton Club, Duquesne Club, Fox Chapel Golf Club, Annapolis Yacht Club, Buffalo Launch Club, Rolling Rock Club, Laurel Valley Golf Club, Pitts. Athletic Club, St. John (V.I.) Yacht Club, St. Thomas (V.I.) Yacht Club, Chautauqua Lake Yacht Club (Lakewood, NY). Republican. Presbyterian. Avocations: hydroplanes, flying, sailing, fishing, motorcycling. Office: Anegada Group Inc 2335 Koppers Bldg Pittsburgh PA 15219 also: Fairwinds Estate 4072 West Lake Rd Mayville NY 14757-0248 also: Villa 4113 PO Box 1662 Virgin Grand Great Cruz Bay St John VI 00831 Office Phone: 412-232-3270.

BARTLEY, DEE GRAY, information technology executive; b. Lytle, Tex. d. William McMurrian Gray and Velma Gladys McNiel; m. William Call Bartley, July 14, 1956; children: Carol Sue Bartley-Gourlas, Gregory William, Christopher Gray. MusB, San Antonio Coll., 1955; grad., Mich. State U., East Lansing, 1960. Adminstrv. asst. procurement 17th Air Force, Tripoli, Libya, 1956—58; adminstrv. asst. to dir. Office Naval Intelligence, Dallas, 1960—63; asst. to pres. Grad. Rsch. Ctr., U. Tex., Richardson, 1963—66; personal asst. Senator A. Bible, U.S. Senate, Washington, 1967—74; appointments asst. Senator H. Jackson, U.S. Senate, Washington, 1975—82; protocol asst. to U.S. rep. UN/U.S. Mission, Geneva, 1982—88; protocol coord. Dept. State Arms Control U.S. Mission, Geneva, 1984—87; profl. staff Spkr. House Reps., 1989, Senate Majority Leader, Washington, 1990—93; assoc. Bartley Technologies Inc., Bandera, Tex., 1995—. Coord. U.S. Mex. Inter-Parliamentary Group, U.S. Senate Leadership, San Antonio, Boston, Cabo San Lucas, 1990—93; coord. nat. hist. site Tor House U.S. Senate Interior Com., Carmel, Calif., 1972—73; coord. land acquisition Einstein sculpture Nat. Acad. Sci., Washington, 1975—76. Editor: Science in Space, 1967. Fundraising coord. Internat. Red Cross Hdqrs., Geneva, 1987; fundraiser Bandera H.S. Chorale Group, 2005; mem. exec. com., bd. trustees, sec. Frontier Times Mus., 1998—2007; mem., fundraiser chair Friends Kronkosky Libr. Bandera County, 2001—; co-organizer music fund St. Christopher's Episc. Ch., Bandera, 2005; mem. Altar Guild St. Christopher's Parish, 1999; fundraising coord. Frontier Times Mus., Bandera County, 2006—. Recipient Cert. of Appreciation for svc. 1984-86, U.S. Dept. State, 1986, Grateful Recognition honors, U.S. Senate, 1979, Outstanding Svc. award, U. Tex. System, 1966. Mem.: Bandera Fine Arts Club (nominating com. 1996). Episcopalian. Avocations: gardening, music. Home: PO Box 2246 Bandera TX 78003-2246 Office: Bartley Technologies Inc PO Box 821 2628 Bottlesprings Rd Bandera TX 78003-0821 Office Phone: 830-796-7643. Personal E-mail: dee_bartley@yahoo.com.

BARTLEY, GEORGE B., ophthalmologist, surgeon; b. Warren, Ohio, Nov. 12, 1955; B in Zoology, Miami U., Oxford, OH; MD, Ohio State U., 1981. Intern Riverside Methodist Hosp., Columbus, Ohio, 1981—82; resident in ophthalmology Mayo Clinic, Rochester, Minn., 1982—85, staff mem., 1986—2003, chmn. ophthalmology, 1992—2001, prof. ophthalmology Coll. Medicine, 1996—; fellow in ophthal. plastic and orbital surgery Wright State U. Sch. Med., Dayton, 1985—86. CEO Mayo Clinic, Jacksonville, Fla., 2002—; mem. bd. trustees Mayo Found., Rochester, Minn.; dir. Am. Bd. Ophthalmology. Mem.: Am. Acad. Ophthalmology (Senior Achievement award 2003). Office: Mayo Clinic 4500 San Pablo Rd Jacksonville FL 32224 Office Phone: 904-953-2100.

BARTLEY, LINDA L., musician, music educator; b. Amarillo, Tex., 1948; MusB in Edn., Mich. State U., MusM, D of Musical Arts. Asst. prof. clarinet SUNY, Fredonia, NY, 1974—75, Ark. Tech U., Russellville, 1981—83; assoc. prof. clarinet Ctrl. Mich. U., Mt. Pleasant, 1987—92; prof. clarinet U. Wis., Madison, 1992—. Vis. prof. clarinet U. Western Ont., London, 1975—81; prin. clarinet London Symphony Orch., 1975—81, Madison Symphony Orch.; clarinetist Grand Teton Music Festival, Jackson Hole, Wyo., 1989—2001, Powers Woodwind Quintet, Mt. Pleasant, 1987—92, Wingra Woodwind Quintet, Madison, 1992—. Musician (soloist/recitalist): Internat. Clarinet Assn.; contbr. articles to profl. jours. Mem.: Chamber Music Am., Coll. Music Soc., Internat. Clarinet Assn. (state chair, grants com. mem., young artist competition judge). Office: School of Music University of Wisconsin 455 N Park St Madison WI 53706-1483 Office Phone: 608-263-1910. Business E-Mail: lbartley@wisc.edu.

BARTLEY, MATTHEW B., insurance company executive; b. Oct. 28, 1956; BA, U. Pa.; MA, Yale U.; JD, Columbia U. Tax atty. Morgan, Lewis and Bockius, Phila.; v.p. taxes Engelhard Corp.; sr. internat. treasury and tax positions PepsiCo, Inc.; v.p., treas. Marsh and McLennan Companies, Inc., 2001—06, CFO, 2006—. Office: Marsh and McLennan Companies 1166 Avenue of the Americas New York NY 10036 Office Phone: 212-345-5000. Office Fax: 212-345-4808.*

BARTLEY, SHAWN, lawyer; JD, Valparaiso U., Ind., 2000. Bar: US Ct. Appeals Md. 2002. Atty. Goozman, Bernstein & Markuski, Laurel, Md., 2005—. Mem.: Md. State Bar Assn. Office: Goozman Bernstein Markuski 9101 Cherry Ln Ste 207 Laurel MD 20708 Office Phone: 301-953-7480.

BARTLIT, FRED HOLCOMB, JR., lawyer; b. Harvey, Ill., Aug. 1, 1932; s. Fred Holcomb and Agnes Marie (Rahn) Bartlit; m. Jana Cockrell, Feb. 28, 1987. BS in Engring., US Mil. Acad., 1954; JD, U. Ill., 1960. Bar: Ill. 1960, US Ct. Appeals 7th cir. 1962, US Ct. Appeals 6th cir. 1969, US Ct. Appeals 10th cir. 1970, US Supreme Ct. 1970, US Ct. Appeals 8th cir. 1971, US Ct. Appeals 3rd cir. 1973, US Ct. Appeals 5th cir. 1978. Assoc. Kirkland & Ellis, Chgo., 1960—64, ptnr., 1964—93, Bartlit Beck Herman Palenchar & Scott LLP, Chgo., Denver, 1993—. Lectr. in field; mem. faculty Nat. Inst. Trial Advocacy, 1975—. Served US Army, 1954—58. Named one of America's Top Trial Lawyers -- Who They Are & Why They Win, Glasser LegalWorks, 1996, 100 Most Influential Lawyers, Nat. Law Mag., 1997, 2006. Fellow: Internat. Acad. Trial Lawyers, Am. Coll. Trial Lawyers; mem.: Chgo. Bar Assn., Ill. Bar Assn., Castle Pines Golf, Mid-Am., Glen View. Republican. Presbyterian. Office: Bartlit Beck Herman Palenchar & Scott LLP 1899 W Ynkoop St 8th Fl Denver CO 80202*

BARTLO, SAM D., lawyer; b. Cleve., Oct. 5, 1919; BBA, Case Western Res. U., 1941; JD, Cleve.-Marshall Law Sch., 1950. Bar: Ohio, 1950, U.S. Supreme Ct., 1958. Mem. firm Buckingham, Doolittle & Burroughs, Akron, Ohio, 1971-90. Capt. U.S. Army, 1942-46. Fellow Am. Bar Found. (life), Ohio Bar Found. (life, pres. 1981-82, trustee 1976-81); mem. ABA (bd. govs. 1989-92, ho. of dels. 1977-94, state del. 1981-89, exec. com. 1990-92, chair ops. com. 1991-92, trustee FJE resource coun. 1992-94), Akron Bar Assn. (pres. 1967-68, exec. com. 1968-7), Ohio State Bar Assn. (coun. dels. 1970-86, pres. 1977-78, exec. com. 1973-79), Am. Judicature Soc., Nat. Conf. Bar Presidents (trustee 1979-82), Ohio Legal Ctr. Inst. (pres. 1979-81, trustee 1977-81). Office: Buckingham Doolittle Burroughs PO Box 1500 Akron OH 44309-1500

BARTLOW, GENE STEVEN, professional society executive, retired military officer; b. Alva, Okla., Dec. 19, 1939; s. C. Merle and Mildred Violet (Stevens) B.; m. Carolyn F. Strickland, Dec. 31, 1960 (div. Apr. 4, 1962); 1 child, Karie Jean Bartlow Parsons; m. Karin C. Jacobsen, Jan. 13, 1967; children: Christina K., Erik K. BA in Ednl. Comm., N.W. Okla. State U., 1962; disting. grad., Indsl. Coll. Armed Forces, Washington, 1972; MPA, Ball State U., 1978; grad., Air War Coll., Maxwell AFB, Ala., 1984; MS in Computers and Info. Mgmt., Webster U., St. Louis, 1995. Cert. assn. exec. Am. Soc. Assn. Execs. Tchr. speech, debate coach Liberal (Kans.) Pub. H.S., 1962-63; commd. 2d lt. USAF, 1964, advanced through grades to full col.; chief logistics plans divsn. 68th tactical air support group Tactical Air Command, Shaw AFB, SC, 1971-73; chief logistics plans inspection br. Hdqs. Tactical Air Command, Langley AFB, Va., 1973-76; chief NATO logistics plans br. Hdqs. USAF in Europe, Ramstein Air Base, Germany, 1976-80; dep. comdr. for resource mgmt. 474th tactical fighter wing Tactical Air Command, Nellis AFB, Nev., 1980-83; chief congl. activities divsn. Office Asst. Sec. Air Force (Acquisition), Washington, 1984-87; dean adminstrn., prof. sys. acquisition mgmt. Indsl. Coll. Armed Forces, Nat. Def. U., 1987-90; ret., 1990; asst. exec. dir., CFO, Assoc. Cath. Charities, Archdiocese of Washington, 1990-91; dep. exec. dir. Internat. Assn. for Dental Rsch.-Am. Assn. for Dental Rsch., Washington, 1991-94; pres., CEO, Am. Wood Preservers Inst., Fairfax, Va., 1995-97; exec. v.p., COO, Painting and Decorating Contractors Am., 1998-2000; exec. dir., COO Assn. Old Crows, Alexandria, Va., 2002—05. Adj. prof. mgmt. Nat.-Louis U., McLean, Va., 1989-97, U. Md. U. Coll., 1998-99; lectr. congl. liaison activities exec. mgmt. course Def. Sys. Mgmt. Coll., Ft. Belvoir, 1986-92. Contbr. articles to profl. jours. Decorated Legion of Merit, others. Mem.: Greater Washington Soc. Assn. Execs., Air Force Assn., Mil. Officers Assn. Republican. Congregationalist. Avocations: Am. Civil War history, photography, music, politics. Home: 6501 Tiburon Ct Springfield VA 22152-2824 E-mail: eagle85@cox.net.

BARTNICKI, KAREN JO, social services administrator; b. Beverly, Mass., May 2, 1958; d. Edward W. and Ruth B. Bartnicki. BA in Sociology, Regis Coll., 1980; MA in Psychology, Calif. State U., Sacramento, 1997. Cert. Coun. on Social Work Edn., Meeting Planners Internat. Activities dir. Redwood Villa Retirement Residence, Mountain View, Calif., 1989-90; dir. social svcs., admissions and mktg. Southpark Cmty. Hosp., Sacramento, 1990-91, Gold Country Health Ctr., Placerville, Calif., 1991-92; social worker, social work cons. Vital Care Am., Gardena, Calif., 1993-94, Mediplex, Lowell, Mass., 1994-95; adminstr. John Bertram House Assisted Living, Salem, Mass., 1995-96; event cons. Interface Found., Newton, Mass., 1997; mgr. social svcs. Vencor Hosp., Boston-North Shore, Peabody, Mass., 1998-99; exec. dir. Valley Terrace, Terrace Cmtys., Hartford, Vt., 1999-2000; dir. social svcs. Danvers (Mass.) Nursing and Rehab. Ctr., 2000—02; exec. dir. WebAdventures, 2003—. Mem. adv. bd. City of Santa Clara-Silicon Valley 1986 Conv., Santa Clara, Calif., 1986; exec. dir. Meetings Plus, Fremont, Calif., 1986-89; program cons., event planner Computer Faire Inc./The Interface Group, Needham, Mass., 1984-86; program mgr., conf. dir. CW Comms., Inc., Framingham, Mass., 1981-84; mem. adv. bd. West Coast Computer Faire, San Francisco, 1987, 88. Author: (book) An Exploration of Life Experiences, Personality Traits and Sleep Habits in Relation to Dream Recall and Dream Content, 1997; prodr., author: (videotape) Microcomputer Application Spotlight: Desktop Publishing, 1987. Mem. Inst. Noetic Scis., Assn. Rsch. and Enlightenment, Am. Soc. Psychical Rschrs., Assn. for Study of Dreams, Psi Chi, Pi Gamma Mu. Avocations: sleep and dream research, philosophy and religion, poetry, creative writing, outdoor recreation. Address: PO Box 156 Amesbury MA 01913 E-mail: KJ.Bartnicki@verizon.net.

BARTNICKI-GARCIA, SALOMON, microbiologist, educator; b. Mexico City, May 18, 1935; came to U.S., 1957; s. Israel Bartnicki and Refugio Garcia; m. Ildiko Nagy, Aug. 10, 1975; children— Linda Laura, David Daniel. Bacteriological Chemist, Inst. Politecnico Nacional, Mexico City, 1957; PhD, Rutgers U., 1961. Rsch. assoc. microbiology Rutgers U., 1961-62; mem. faculty U. Calif., Riverside, 1962—, prof. plant pathology and microbiology, 1971-94, prof. emeritus, 1994, rsch. prof., 1994-2000, chmn. dept. plant pathology, 1989-92, dir. grad. program in microbiology, 1997-2000; sci. rschr. Ctr. Scientific Investigation and Higher Studies Ensenada, Ensenada, Mexico, 2000—. Vis. prof. Organic Chemistry Inst., U. Stockholm, 1969-70; selected faculty rsch. lectr. U. Calif., Riverside, 1989. Author research and rev. papers. Grantee NIH, 1963-96, NSF, 1971-96. Fellow AAAS, Am. Phytopathol. Soc. (Ruth Allen award 1983); mem. Am. Soc. Microbiology, Mycol. Soc. Am. (Disting. Mycologist award 1994), Brit. Soc. Gen. Microbiology, Brit. Mycol. Soc. (hon.), Am. Soc. Biol. Chemists. Home: 3787 Elliott St San Diego CA 92106-1235 Office: U Calif Dept Plant Pathology Riverside CA 92521-0001 also: CICESE Ensenada Mexico Office Phone: 52-646-175-0513. E-mail: bart@citrus.ucr.edu.

BARTNIKAS, RAYMOND, electrical engineer, educator; b. Kaunas, Lithuania, Jan. 25, 1936; s. Andrius and Eugenia (Kanisauskas) B.; m. Margaret McLachlan, Aug. 19, 1967; children: Andrea Marie, Thomas Benedict. BASc, U. Toronto, 1958; M in Engring., McGill U., Montreal, 1962, PhD, 1964; D in Engring. (hon.), U. Waterloo, 2002. Rsch. engr. No. Electric Co. (now Nortel), Lachine, Que., Canada, 1958—63; mem. sci. staff phys. scis. divsn. No. Electric R&D Labs. (now Nortel Techs.), Ottawa, Ont., Canada, 1963—68; research scientist, sci. dir. materials sci. research div., Disting. Sr. Scientist Hydro-Quebec Inst. Rsch., Varennes, Que., 1968-98; rschr. emeritus Hydro-Quebec Inst. Research, 1998—. Adj. prof., lectr. theory of dielectrics McGill U., 1968—; adj. prof. Fleming Found., visitor dept. elec. and computer engring. U. Waterloo, Ont., 1969—; adj. prof. dept. engring. physics Ecole Poly. U. Montreal, 1982—; vis. prof. U. Rome, 1994—; cons. Cepel Inst. Rsch., Rio de Janeiro, 1973-84; mem. Task Force on Long Term Performance of Insulating Materials Nat. Acad. Scis., 1976-77; mem. elec. engring. com. Nat. Scis. and Engring. Rsch. Coun. Can., 1987-90; mem. Commn. de la recherche universitaire Conseil des Universites, Que., 1989-93. Author, editor: ASTM book series on Engring. Dielectrics, 1979, Elements of Cable Engineering, 1980, Power Cable Engineering, 1987, Power and Communication Cables, 1999; contbr. articles on dielectric and discharge loss mechanisms in elec. insulating systems to profl. jours. Decorated officer Order of Can.; recipient Golden Jubilee medal Can. Fellow IEEE (mem. energy com. 1978—, mem. insulated condrs. com. 1966—, mem. awards and recognition com. 1984-88, mem. electric machinery materials com. 1993—, mem. transformers coms. 2006—, IEEE Thomas Dakin Disting. Sci. Achievement award 1980, Centennial medal 1984, Whitehead Meml. award 1987, Morris Leeds award 1989, MacNaughton Gold medal 1993, 3d Millennium medal 2000), ASTM (chmn. elec. insulation com. 1979-85, mem. editl. bd. Jour. Testing and Evaluation 1985-2004, award of merit 1985, Charles Dudley medal, appreciation award, Arnold Scott award), Can. Acad. of Engring., Inst. Elec. Engrs. Japan (Disting. hon. lectr. symposium on elec. insulating materials 1983), Inst. Physics (U.K.), Royal Soc. Can. Acad. Scis. (Thomas W. Eadie medal 1994); mem. Dielectrics and Elec. Insulation Soc. of IEEE (pres. 1976-78, mem. editl. bd. Elec. Insulation Mag. 1984-91), Internat. Electrotech. Commn. (mem. com. insulation materials, chmn. subcommittee on tests 1993-2006, chmn. com. on elec. insulating liquids 2007—), Order Engrs. Que., Can. Stds. Assn. (Merit award 1986, John Jenkins award 1989), Can. Elec. Assn., Can. Stds. Coun. (J.P. Carrière award 1992), French-Can. Assn. for Advancement of Scis. (Urgel Archambault award 1993), U. Toronto Engring. Alumni Assn. (engring. medal 1993). Roman Catholic. Office: Hydro-Québec Inst Rsch 1800 Boul Lionel-Boulet CP 1000 Varennes PQ Canada J3X 1S1

BARTNOFF, JUDITH, judge; b. Boston, Apr. 14, 1949; d. Shepard and Irene F. (Tennenbaum) B.; m. Eugene F. Sofer, Sept. 10, 1978; 1 child, Nelson Bartnoff Sofer. BA magna cum laude, Radcliffe Coll., 1971; JD (Harlan Fiske Stone scholar), Columbia U., 1974; LLM, Georgetown U., 1975. Bar: DC 1975, US Dist. Ct. DC 1975, US Ct. Appeals (DC cir.) 1980, US Ct. Appeals (fed. cir.) 1985, US Ct. Appeals (11th cir.) 1988, US Ct. Appeals (3d cir.) 1989, US Claims Ct. 1991. Fellow Inst. Pub. Interest Representation Georgetown Law Ctr., Washington, 1974—75; staff atty. Coun. Pub. Interest Law, Washington, 1975—77; spl. asst. to asst. atty. gen. criminal divsn. Dept. Justice, Washington, 1977—78, assoc. dep. atty. gen., 1978—80; spl. asst. U.S. atty. Office of US Atty., Washington, 1980—81, asst. U.S. atty., 1982—85; assoc. Patton, Boggs & Blow, 1987—87, ptnr., 1988—94, assoc. ind. counsel, 1993—94; assoc. judge Superior Ct. of DC, Washington, 1994—, presiding judge domestic violence unit, 2006—07. Mediator US Dist. Ct. DC, 1991-94; mem. com. on pro se litig. US Dist. Ct., 1991-94. Mem. DC Bar Task Force on Children at Risk, 1997—98, DC Child Support Guidelines Commn., 2003—, DC Domestic Violence Fatality Rev. Bd., 2006—. Fellow Am. Bar Found.; mem. Nat. Assn. Women Judges, DC Bar, Women's Bar Assn. Office: 500 Indiana Ave NW Washington DC 20001-2131 Office Phone: 202-879-1988. Business E-Mail: judith.bartnoff@dcsc.gov.

BARTO, DEBORAH ANN, physician; b. West Chester, Pa., July 27, 1948; d. Charles Guy and Jeannette Victoria (Golder) B. BA, Oberlin Coll., Ohio, 1970; MD, Hahnemann U., Phila., 1974; Reiki III, N.W. Sch. Healing, Redmond, Wash., 2003. Cert. Reiki master. Intern, resident Kaiser Permanente Hosp., San Francisco, 1974-77; dir. med. oncology Evergreen Hosp., Kirkland, Wash., 1980-85, head oncology quality assurance, 1992-94; med. dir. Cmty. Home Health Care Hospice, Seattle, 1981-84. Hosp. ethics com. Evergreen Hosp., 1995-98, integrative care com., 1996-2001. Mem. Evergreen Women's Physicians, Reiki III. Democrat. Buddhist. Avocation: horseback riding. Office: 13115 121st Way NE Ste C Kirkland WA 98034

BARTOES, RICHARD ALAN, agricultural products executive; b. Norwich, Conn., July 29, 1928; s. Francis Florian and Katherine Brown Bartoes; m. Nancy Pettice Smith, June 22, 1952; children: Daniel Ryland, Janet Elizabeth, Karen Francis, Marilyn Pettice, Richard Smith. BS in Geology, Trinity Coll., Hartford, Conn., 1951. Plant expediter Charles C. Hart Seed Co., Wethersfield, Conn., 1951—91, sales mgr., 1960—91,

prodn. mgr.; purchasing dir. Helen's Greenhouses, Aquebogue, NY, 1980—; owner, v.p. Blue Ridge Garden Ctr. INc., Charlottesville, Va., 1992—99. Justice of Peace Town of Rocky Hill, Conn., 1960—62; spkr. in field. Scoutmaster Boy Scouts Am.; exec. bd. Stonwall Jackson BSA. Recipient Silver Beaver, Boy Scouts Am., 1989. Mem.: Lions Club (pres. Rocky Hill chpt. 1988). Episcopalian. Avocations: collecting ships and lighthouses, gardening, running, swimming. Home: 1050 Earlysville Forest Dr Earlysville VA 22936-9550

BARTOL, ERNEST THOMAS, lawyer; b. Mineola, NY, Feb. 2, 1946; s. Frank Henry and Mary Ann (Kretlein) Bartol; m. Christine Ann Pillis; children: Jacqueline Marie, Aimee Elizabeth, Suzanne Melissa. BS in Acctg., Fordham U., Bronx, NY, 1967; JD, Villanova U., Pa., 1970. Bar: NY 1971, US Dist. Ct. (ea. and so. dists.) NY 1973, US Ct. Appeals (2d cir.) 1975, US Supreme Ct. 1974, US Tax Ct. Washington, DC 2005. Tax specialist Arthur Young & Co., Phila., 1970; acct. Arthur Andersen & Co., NYC, 1970—71; assoc. Gehrig, Ritter, Coffey et al, Hempstead, NY, 1971—78; founder, mng. ptnr., sr. ptnr. Murphy, Bartol & O'Brien, LLP, Mineola, 1978—. Mem. com. on civil litigation US Dist. Ct. (ea. dist.) NY. Presiding trustee United Cerebral Palsy Assn. Nassau County, 2004—, chmn. forget-me-not-ball, 1987—92; pres., founder cmty. adv. coun. Syosset Cmty. Hosp., 1987—92; bd. dirs. LI Children's Mus., 1996—99; exec. leader Oyster Bay Rep. Com., 1978—2003; vice chmn. Nassau County Rep. Com., 2003—05; sec., mem. parish coun. and spl. sch. com. St. Edward Roman Cath. Ch., Syosset, NY, 1978—80; trustee N.Y. Inst. Tech., 1997—99; bd. dirs. Fair Media Coun., LI, 2001—. Named Man of Yr., United Cerebral Palsy Assn. Nassau County, 1993, Heart Coun. LI, Inc., 2001. Mem.: ABA, Cath. Lawyers Guild Diocese Rockville Centre, NY State Trial Lawyers Assn., Fed. Bar Coun. NY, Nassau Lawyers Assn. LI (bd. dirs. 1977—, chmn. 1992—93, rec. sec. 1993—94, corr. sec. 1994—95, 1st v.p. 1995—97, pres. 1997—98), Criminal Cts. Bar Assn., Nassau County Bar Assn. (estates and trusts law com. 1975—, mem. profl. ethics com. 1980—86, 1989—93), NY State Bar Assn. (trusts and estates law com. 1983—, lectr. estate topics), Chaminade H.S. Alumni Assn. (class rep. 1971, class dir. 1971—72, 1st v.p. 1972—74, pres. 1974—76), Rotary (sec.-treas. Syosset Club 1980—90), Alpha Kappa Psi. Roman Catholic. Avocations: racquetball, tennis, fishing, stamp collecting/philately, sailing. Office: Murphy Bartol & O'Brien LLP 22 Jericho Tpke Ste 103 Mineola NY 11501-2976 Office Phone: 516-294-5100. Personal E-mail: etbartol@aol.com.

BARTOLI, JILL SUNDAY, reading and language arts educator; b. Carlisle, May 17, 1945; d. Harvey Preston and Helen Elizabeth (Hershey) Sunday; m. James Carl Bartoli, June 26, 1971; children: David Carl, Daniel Joseph, Stephen Mario, Catherine Elizabeth, Patrick Preston. BA in English and Speech, U. Ky., 1966, MA in English, 1967; MEd in Reading, Shippensburg U., 1977; PhD in Lang. Arts and Family Literacy, U. Pa., 1986. Cert. supr. comm., cert. reading specialist, Pa. Tchr. English and speech Cumberland Valley H.S., Mechanicsburg, Pa., 1969-73; lectr. English Pa. State U., York, 1968-69; rsch. assoc. U. Pa., Phila., 1988-89, lectr., 1987-89; assoc. prof. Elizabethtown (Pa.) Coll., 1990—. Dir. coll.-sch. partnership Elizabethtown and Steelton Sch. Dist., 1989—, Lancaster Sch. Dist., 1998-2003; dir. rsch. grant, writer, 1992—, partnership with Harrisburg Sch. Dist., 2002—. Author: Unequal Opportunity, 1995, Celebrating City Teachers, 2001; co-author: Reading/Learning Disability, 1988; contbr. articles to profl. jours.; rschr. on successful inner-city schs. Organizer, mem. Social Justice Coalition, Carlisle, Pa., 1990—; mem. cmty. svc. com. Elizabethtown Coll., 1992—. Mem. NAACP, Nat. Coun. Tchrs. of English (mem. nominating com. 1980-92, presenter), Nat. Assn. for Edn. of Young Children, Am. Ednl. Rsch. Assn. (session chairperson 1985-96), Internat. Reading Assn., Kappa Delta Pi (counselor 1992—), Phi Delta Kappa. Home: 316 Garland Dr Carlisle PA 17013-4229 Office: Elizabethtown Coll 1 Alpha Dr Elizabethtown PA 17022-2298 Home Phone: 717-249-7591. Business E-Mail: bartoljs@etown.edu.

BARTOLINI, ROBERT ALFRED, electrical engineer, researcher; b. Waterbury, Conn., Apr. 4, 1942; s. Alfred N. and Maria D. (Cartoceti) B.; m. Janice M. Daly, June 13, 1964; children: Jill C., Ellen G., Robin M. BSEE, Villanova U., 1964; MSEE, Case Western Res. U., 1966; PhD, U. Pa., 1972. Rsch. scientist RCA Labs., Princeton, N.J., 1966-79, leader optical sys., 1979-83, head optoelectronic rsch., 1983-87; head laser diode rsch. David Sarnoff Rsch. Ctr., Princeton, 1987-89, dir. integrated cir., 1989-96, sr. dir. inegrated cir. lab., 1996-97; v.p. integrated cir. lab. Sarnoff Corp., Princeton, 1997—2001, v.p. internat. ops., 2001—02, sr. v.p. comm. ops., 2002—. Chmn. elect. engring. dept. LaSalle U., 1982-90. Contbr. 35 articles to jours. in field; presenter 65 profl. presentations. Chmn. Sewer Oper. Com., West Windsor, N.J., 1974-82, chmn. assessment bd., West Windsor, N.J., 1984; vice chmn. Stony Brook Regional Sewerage Authority, Princeton, N.J., 1980-96, chmn., 1997—. Recipient 3 labs. achievement awards RCA Labs., 1970, 76, 80, Outstanding Paper award Soc. Internat. Display, 1979, Engring. Alumni award Villanova U., 1986, Sarnoff award RCA Corp., 1986, Career Engring. award Villanova U., 2002. Fellow IEEE (Centennial medal 1984), Optical Soc. Am. (chmn. laser conf. 1987-91); mem. Sigma Xi (nat. lectr. 1983-84), Tau Beta Pi, Eta Kappa Nu. Achievements include patents in field; research in embossable holographic devel., optical data storage media devel., optical data storage system devel., surface emitting diode laser devel. Office: Sarnoff Corp 201 Washington Rd Princeton NJ 08540-6449 Business E-Mail: rbartolini@sarnoff.com.

BARTON, ALAN JOEL, lawyer; b. NYC, Sept. 2, 1938; s. Sidney and Claire (Greenfield) B.; m. Ann Rena Beral, Jan. 29, 1961; children: Donna Frieda Olsen, Brian Joseph. AB, U. Calif., Berkeley, 1960, JD, 1963. Assoc. Nossaman, Krueger & Mash, LA, 1963—70, ptnr., 1970—80, Paul, Hastings, Janofsky & Walker, LLP, LA, 1980—2002, sr. counsel, 2002—. Lectr. UCLA Sch. Law, 2001—; lectr. corp. and securities law U. Calif. Continuing Edn. Bar, 1980—; lectr. venture capital and securities law Practicing Law Inst., 1986—. Assoc. editor U. Calif. Law Rev., 1963. Dir. Ctr. for Study of Young People in Groups, L.A., 1988-2004, Planned Parenthood, L.A., 1999-2004; trustee Dubnoff Ctr. for Ednl. Therapy, North Hollywood, Calif., 1976-80. Mem. ABA (com. on fed. regulation of securities), Calif. Bar Assn. (com. on corps.), Order of Coif, The Calif. Club. Republican. Jewish. Avocations: movies, Torah study, contemporary art, tennis, travel. Office: Paul Hastings Janofsky & Walker LLP 515 S Flower St Fl 25 Los Angeles CA 90071-2300

BARTON, BERNARD ALAN, JR., lawyer; b. Glens Falls, NY, Aug. 13, 1948; s. Bernard A. Sr. and Geraldine (Bushey) B.; children: Lindsey, Kylie. BA, U. Fla., 1969, JD, 1975, LLM, 1976. Bd. cert. tax lawyer. Ptnr. Holland & Knight, Tampa, Fla., 1976—. Editor, contbg. author Florida Taxation, State Taxation Series, 1994. Mem. ABA, Nat. Assn. Bond Attys., Fla. Bar Assn. (exec. coun. tax sect., chmn. various coms. 1980-99). Republican. Episcopalian. Office: Holland & Knight PO Box 1288 Tampa FL 33601-1288 Home Phone: 813-223-6972, 727-577-6916; Office Phone: 813-227-6539. Business E-Mail: bernie.barton@hklaw.com.

BARTON, DAVID, activist organization administrator, writer; m. Cheryl Barton; children: Damaris, Timothy, Stephen. BA, Oral Roberts U., Tulsa; LittD (hon.), Pensacola Christian Coll., Fla. Educator, sch. adminstr.; founder, pres. WallBuilders, Aledo, Tex. Bd. advisors Providence Found., Charlottesville, Va.; cons. Rep. Nat. Com.; former vice chmn. Tex. Rep. Party; mem. adv. bd. Nat. Coun. on Bible Curriculum in Pub. Schs. Named one of 25 Most Influential Evangelicals in Am., Time mag., 2005; recipient George Washington Honor medal. Office: WallBuilders PO Box 397 Aledo TX 76008*

BARTON, GERALD LEE, food products executive; b. Modesto, Calif., Feb. 24, 1934; s. Robert Paul and Alice Lee (Hall) B.; m. Janet Murray, June 24, 1955; children: Donald Lee, Gary Michael, Brent Richard. BA with distinction, Stanford U., 1955. Owner, pres. Barton Ranch, Escalon, Calif., 1961—; v.p. R.P. Barton Mfg. Co., Escalon, 1963—86; chmn. bd. Diamond Walnut Growers Inc., 1976-81, chmn. emeritus, 1981—, pres., 1986-90; chmn. GoldRiver Orchards, 2004—. Chmn. Growers Harvesting Com., Modesto, 1976-77, Diamond-Sunsweet Co., Stockton, Calif., 1978-80, Sun Diamond Growers, Inc., 1980-81; bd. dirs. Calif. Fin. Holding Co., Stockton, Stockton Savs. Bank; vice-chmn. Fed. Land Bank, Modesto, 1976-81; pomology rsch. adv. bd. U. Calif., Davis, 1968-74, Walnut Mktg. Bd., Sacramento, 1971-73, 77-2000; mem. Calif. Walnut Commn., 1987-99; agribus. adv. bd. U. Santa Clara, 1979-89; dir. Ross Hort. Found., Union Safe Deposit Bank, 2000-04; ext. adv. bd. San Joaquin County U. Calif. Chmn. bd. edn. Escalon Unified Sch. Dist., 1963—75; vice chmn. San Joaquin County Sch. Bds. Assn., 1965; trustee Yosemite Assn., 1999—2005, The Cortopassi Inst., 2004—; elder Trinity United Presbyn. Ch., Modesto, 2002—05; bd. dirs. St. Joseph's Healthcare Corp., 1991—95; bd. dirs., v.p. Stanislaus River Flood Control Assn., 1965—. With US Army, 1956—58. Decorated Order of the Golden Walnut, 1990; named Outstanding Young Farmer in San Joaquin County C. of C., 1965, Farmer of Yr. Escalon C. of C., 1979; recipient U. Calif. Friend of Ext. award, 1992; named to San Joaquin County Agrl. Hall of Fame, 1993, Escalon Unified Sch. Dist. Hall Fame, 2006; recipient Disting. Svc. award Calif. Walnut Commn., 1998; named Co-op Farmer Yr. Agrl. Coun. Calif., 2001. Mem. Stanford U. Alumni Assn., Delta Chi. Republican. Presbyterian. Office: 22398 McBride Rd Escalon CA 95320-9637

BARTON, GREGORY MARK, Olympic athlete; b. Jackson, Mich., Dec. 2, 1959; BS in Mech. Engring., U. Mich., 1983. Olympic kayak racer, 1000 meter singles, LA, 1984; Olympic kayak racer, 1000 meter singles and doubles Seoul, Korea, 1988; Olympic kayak racer, 1000 meter singles Barcelona, Spain, 1992. Recipient Bronze medal 1000 meter kayak singles Olympics, L.A., 1984, Gold medal 1000 meter kayak singles Olympics, Seoul, 1988, Gold medal 1000 meter kayak doubles Olympics, Seoul, 1988, Bronze medal 1000 meter kayak singles Olympics, Barcelona, 1992.

BARTON, HUGH PERRY, bank executive; b. Modesto, Calif., Apr. 6, 1932; s. Robert Paul and Alice B.; m. Sheila Grieve, Dec. 29, 1954; children: Elizabeth, James. BS, U. Calif., Berkeley, 1954. Pres., CEO R.P. Barton & Co., Escalon, Calif., 1955-91; chair bd. Modesto (Calif.) Banking Co., 1977-94, Barton McLean & Waters, San Francisco, 1992-97; dir. Bank of Los Altos, Calif., 1994—, Heritage Commerce Corp., San Jose, Calif., 2000—02; chmn., dir. Pvt. Bank of the Peninsula, Palo Alto, Calif., 2003—. Recipient Salvation Army Order of Disting. Aux. award, 2005. Mem. Carmel Valley Ranch Golf Club, Pebble Beach Tennis Club, Old Capitol Club. Republican. Episcopalian. Home: 9906 Club Place Ln Carmel CA 93923-8507 Office: PO Box 222097 Carmel CA 93922-2097 Personal E-mail: pawpawbear@sbcglobal.net.

BARTON, JAMES CARY, lawyer; b. Raymondville, Tex., Sept. 1, 1940; s. Dewey Albert and Dorothy Marie (Keene) B.; m. Isabel Pattee Critz, Sept. 12, 1964 (div. June 1975); children: Hamilton Keene, James Albert, John Franklin; m. Carolyn Ann Cox, Dec. 20, 1975; stepchildren: Holly Ann Adams, Laura Lee Adams, Jennifer Adams Krumins. BA, Baylor U., 1962; LLB, Harvard U., 1965. Bar: Tex. 1965, U.S. Dist. Ct. (so. dist.) Tex. 1972, U.S. Tax Ct. 1977. Trial atty. FPC, Washington, 1965-67; atty.-advisor U.S. Tax Ct., Washington, 1967-68; from assoc. to ptnr. Kleberg, Mobley, Lockett & Weil, Corpus Christi, Tex., 1969-75, Brown, Maroney, Rose, Baker & Barber, Austin, Tex., 1975-82; from ptnr. to of counsel Johnson & Swanson, Austin, 1982-88; dir. Smith, Barshop, Stoffer & Millsap, Inc., San Antonio, 1988-91; prin. J. Cary Barton, P.C., San Antonio, 1991-93, Barton & Schneider, L.L.P., San Antonio, 1993—2003, Barton, Schneider & Russell, L.L.P., 2003—04, Barton, Schneider, Russell & East, L.L.P., 2004—06, Barton, Schneider & East, L.L.P., 2006—. Spkr. in field. Author: Tex. Practice Guide: Bus. Entities vols. 1-4, 2007. Sgt. USAF, 1968-69. Named a Super Lawyer, Tex. Monthly and Law & Politics mag., 2003—06; named one of Top 50 in Ctrl. and South Tex., 2006; recipient Tex. Real Estate Lawyer Fourth Ann. Lifetime Achievement award, Real Estate, Probate and Trust sec. State Bar of Tex., 2003. Mem. ABA, State Bar Tex. (mem. coun. of real estate probate and trust law sect. 1982-85, 2006—, mem. real estate forms com. 1986—), Am. Coll. Real Estate Lawyers, Tex. Bd. Legal Specialization (cert. in comml. real estate law; mem. real estate legal assts. divsn. 2006—), Tex. Coll. Real Estate Attys. Democrat. Episcopalian. Office: Barton Schneider & East LLP 700 N Saint Marys St Ste 1825 San Antonio TX 78205-3596 Office Phone: 210-225-1655. Business E-Mail: cbarton@bselegal.com.

BARTON, JEAN MARIE, psychologist, educator; b. Pitts., Mar. 24, 1945; d. Joseph Paul and Jean Marie (Anderson) Adamchic; m. Robert L. Barton, Jr., Aug. 14, 1965; children: Robert Joseph, Katherine Anne. BS summa cum laude, U. Pitts., 1965; MEd, Boston U., 1969; CAGS, Cath. U. Am., 1985, PhD in Ednl. Psychology, 1988. Cert. sch. psychologist, Md., nationally cert. sch. psychologist. Tchr./curriculum Wellesley Pub. Schs., Mass., 1965—69; lectr. U. R.I./R.I. Coll., Providence, 1969—72; curriculum specialist/tchr. St. Jane DeChantal Sch., Bethesda, Md., 1977—83, dir. computer prog., 1982—84; psychology assoc. Long Assocs., Bethesda, 1988—; psychol. cons. gifted unit Montgomery County Pub. Schs., Rockville, Md., 1985—99; sch. psychologist various schs. Archdiocese Washington, Md., 1987—; adj. mem. faculty Cath. U. Am., Washington, 1989—2004. Mem. evaluation team Cath. Schs. Studies, 1987-92; dir. Profl. Devel. Inst., Cath. U. Am., 1985-86; mem. adv. com., chairperson identification com. Jacob Javits Grant, Montgomery County Pub. Schs., 1989-92, project coord. Jacob Javitz grant, 1992-95, supt. adv. com. on Edn. of Gifted, 1992-96, on Spl. Edn.; assoc. dir. Ctr. for Advancement Cath. Edn. at Cath. U. Am., 1998-2004; mem. adv. com. on gifted edn. Md. State Dept. Edn., 1999-2000. Contbr. articles to profl. jours. U. Pitts. scholar, 1962-65. Mem. APA, NASP, Md. Sch. Psychologists Assn. Home: 5008 Benton Ave Bethesda MD 20814-2804 Personal E-mail: docjeanbarton@cs.com. *Meaningful achievements consist of recognizing one's unique talents, working hard to develop them to the fullest, and then striving to seize opportunities to use them so that in some small way humanity is better for one's having lived.*

BARTON, JOE LINUS, congressman; b. Waco, Tex., Sept. 15, 1949; s. Larry Linus and Bess Wynell (Buice) Barton; m. Terri Barton; 4 children; 2 stepchildren. BS in Indsl. Engring., Tex. A&M U., 1972; MS in Indsl. Adminstrn., Purdue U., 1973. Mem. staff to asst. to the v.p. Ennis Bus. Forms, Tex., 1973-81; White House fellow, aide Staff of Energy Sec. James B. Edwards, Washington, 1981-82; natural gas decontrol cons. Atlantic Richfield Oil and Gas Co., Dallas, 1982-84; mem. US Congress from 6th Tex. dist., 1985—, chmn. energy and commerce com., 2004—. Mem. Assn. Former Students Tex. A&M U. (councilman at large 1985—) Republican. Methodist. Office: US Ho Reps 2109 Rayburn Ho Office Bldg Washington DC 20515-4306 Office Phone: 202-225-2002.*

BARTON, JOHN JOSEPH, obstetrician, gynecologist, administrator, educator, researcher; b. Rockford, Ill., Mar. 19, 1933; s. L. David and Helen M. (Fox) B.; m. Lois Maltby, 1959 (div. 1965); children: Mary Katherine, Karen Ann. BA in History, U. Ill., 1957; BS in Medicine, U. Ill., Chgo., 1959, MD, 1961; student Law, Loyola U., Chgo., 1966-69. Diplomate Am. Bd. Ob.-Gyn.; cert. Advanced Cardiac Life Support. Rotating intern Cook County Hosp., Chgo., 1961-62, resident in ob.-gyn., 1962-65; fellow gynecologic pathology Northwestern U., Chgo., 1963, clin. asst. ob.-gyn., 1963-64, clin. instr. ob.-gyn., 1964-65, assoc. in ob.-gyn., 1965-71; prof. ob.-gyn. Cook County Grad. Sch. of Medicine, Chgo., 1965—; dir. ob.-gyn. rsch. and edn. Cook County Hosp., Chgo., 1965-69; chmn. ob.-gyn. Ill. Masonic Med. Ctr., Chgo., 1970—2001; assoc. prof. ob.-gyn. U. Ill. Coll. Medicine, Chgo., 1971-83, prof., 1983-93, lectr. in ob.-gyn., 1993—; prof. ob.-gyn. Rush Med. Coll., Chgo., 1993—; chmn. emeritus ob-gyn Ill. Masonic Med. Ctr., 2002—. Clin. clerkship subcom. U. Ill. Coll. Medicine, 1974-90, acad. senate 1977-91, 85-87, perinatal steering com., 1977-92, admissions com. 1985-91, screening subcom. 1988-89; ad hoc com. on rules for governance, Rush Med. Coll., Chgo., 1993—, curriculum com. 1993, com. on student evaluation and promotions, 1994—, core ckerkship subcom. of curriculum com. 1995—; editl. bd. Jour. Obstetrics and Gynecology, Am. Jour. Obstetrics and Gynecology, Internat. Jour. Obstetrics and Gynecology Contbr. numerous articles to profl. jours., chpts. to books. including Laparoscopy in Gynecologic Practice, 1972, Guidelines for Perinatal Care, 1983, Antepartum HIV Screenings: A Comparison of Methodologies, 1990. Vol. cons. Ob.-Gyn. Claremore (Okla.) Indian Hosp., 1979-80, 86, Fort Defiance (Ariz.) Indian Hosp., 1981, Red Crescent Soc., Heliopolis, Cairo, Egypt, 1987; vol. surgeon Internat. Red Cross and Red Crescent Soc. Vols., West Beirut, Lebanon, 1982; mem. Ill. Gov.'s AIDS adv. coun.; advisor, expert witness Atty. Gen. State of Ill. on Standards of Practice in Ob.-Gyn.; mem. com. formation of outcome-oriented surveillance systems for Ill. Dept. of Pub. Health, adv. com. to Health Planning Com. for Chgo., perinatal adv. com. Ill. Dept. Health, steering com. Mayor Washington's Infant Mortality Reduction Initiative and others. Sgt. USMC, 1950-55, Korea. Fellow Am. Coll. Obstetricians and Gynecologists (adv. coun. 1977-81, adv. coun. dist. VI 1977-81, chmn. Ill. sect. 1977-78, com. on profl. liability 1989-92, Jr. Fellow Rsch. prize award 1991), Ctrl. Assn. Obstetricians nd Gynecologists (ctrl. travel club, sci. awards com. 1985-89. chmn. 1987-89, Ann. prize award 1988), Chgo. Gynecol. Soc. (exec. com. 1994—, pres. 1995-96), Am. Coll. Surgeons, Soc. Contemporary Medicine and Surgery, Am. Soc. Clin. Hypnosis, Chgo. Inst. Medicine, Royal Soc. Medicine (London); mem. Ill. Assn. Maternal and Child Health, Assn. Profs. Gynecology and Obstetrics, Am. Pub. Health Assn., Phi Kappa Phi, Nu Sigma Nu. Avocations: rancher quarter horses, exotic animals, hounds, harleys. Home: Bar T Ranch 20516 Bunker Hill Rd Marengo IL 60152-8003 Office: Ill Masonic Med Ctr 836 W Wellington Ave Chicago IL 60657-9224 Personal E-mail: barthandz@aol.com.

BARTON, LEWIS, food products executive, consultant; b. NYC, Mar. 9, 1940; s. Louis and Mary (Mosca) Bologna; m. Barbara Joan Hummell, Sept. 6, 1964; children: Glenn Scott, Gregory Jon. Student, Adelphi U., Garden City, NY, 1957-59. Sales rep. Olivetti Corp., NYC, 1962-64, W. Ralston Co., Chgo., 1964-65, Milprint Co., NYC, 1965-66; pres., founder Sigma Quality Foods, Farmingdale, NY, 1966-88, Sigma Star Food Corp., NYC, 1993-98; pres. The Barton Group, Inc., NYC, 1998—. Lectr. various confs. Patentee several package design constructions and methods. With USAF, 1961-62. Named to Pres. Coun. for Ednl. Distinction, Adelphi U. Mem. Nat. Single Svc. Food Assn. (charter, chmn. 1977-79, Svc. award 1982), Assn. Dressings and Sauces, Dwight D. Eisenhower Soc. (founder), Columbus Citizen's Found., Internat. Orgn. Packaging Profls., NY Athletic Club. Home: 45 Sutton Pl S New York NY 10022-2444 Office Phone: 212-588-1043. E-mail: lb@consultbarton.com.

BARTON, MISCHA, actress; b. London, Eng., Jan. 24, 1986; Actor: (films) Polio Water, 1995, Lawn Dogs, 1997, Pups, 1999, Notting Hill, 1999, The Sixth Sense, 1999, Paranoid, 2000, Skipped Parts, 2000, Lost and Delirious, 2001, Julie Johnson, 2001, Tart, 2001, Octane, 2003, The OH in Ohio, 2006; (TV films) New York Crossing, 1996, Fankie & Hazel, 2000, A Ring of Endless Light, 2002; (TV series) Kablam, 1996, All My Children, 1996, The O.C., 2003—06 (TV Choice Actress, Teen Choice Awards, 2006), (TV appearances) Once and Again, 2001, Fastlane, 2003.

BARTON, R. GREGORY, lawyer, investment company executive; b. 1951; BA, Colgate Univ.; JD, Coll. of William & Mary; LLM in taxation, Temple Univ. Atty. Vanguard Group, Valley Forge, Pa., 1982—, mng. dir. & gen. counsel; sec. Vanguard Fiduciary Trust Co., mng. dir. advice, brokerage, and retirement services. Office: Vanguard Group PO Box 2600 Valley Forge PA 19482

BARTON, RICHARD N., computer company executive; BS in Indsl. Engring., Stanford U., 1989. Strategy cons. Alliance Consulting Group, 1989-91; with Microsoft Corp., Redmond, Wash., 1991-94; gen. mgr. traveler bus. unit, founder Expedia, a div. Microsoft Corp., Redmond, Wash., 1994—99; pres. CEO, dir. Expedia, Inc., Bellevue, Wash., 1999—2003; chmn., CEO Zillow, Seattle. Bd. dirs. Netflix, Ticketmaster, InterActiveCorp (formerly USA Interactive), AtomShockwave, Inc., Avvo Inc.; venture ptnr. Benchmark Capital. Office: InterActiveCorp 152 W 57th St 42nd Fl New York NY 10019 also: Zillow 999 3rd Ave Ste 4600 Seattle WA 98104*

BARTON, ROBERT H., III, automotive executive; BS in Civil and Elec. Engring., Lehigh U.; postgrad., Carnegie Mellon U. With Alcoa, 1955—96, various mktg. mgmt. positions including industry mgr.-bldg. constrn., N.Y. dist. sales mgr., gen. mgr. Alcoa Export, Alcoa gen. mgr. mktg. sales and distbn. European region, pres. Alcoa Conductor Products Co.; pres. Alcoa Fujikura Ltd., Mexico; non-exec. chmn. J.L. French Holdings, 1996—99; CEO Meridian Automotive Sys. Inc., Dearborn, Mich., chmn., pres., CEO, chmn., 2002—. Mem. internat. supplier adv. coun. Ford Motor Co.; bd. dirs. U.S. Alumweld Co., Outlook Nashville, Japan-Tenn. Soc.; chmn. Tenn. Del. S.E. Govs. U.S.-Japan Orgn. Capt., flight examiner USAF. Mem.: ASCE, Soc. Automotive Engrs.

BARTON, ROBERT LEROY, JR., judge, educator; b. Ballston Spa, NY, June 19, 1943; s. Robert L. Sr. and Bertha (Di Pasquale) B.; m. Jean M. Adamchic, Aug. 14, 1965; children: Robert Joseph, Katherine Anne. BA, U. Pitts., 1965; JD, Boston Coll., 1969. Bar: Mass. 1969, RI 1970, DC 1972, US Ct. Appeals (1st cir.) 1970, US Ct. Appeals (DC cir.) 1973, US Dist. Ct. RI, 1971, US Dist. Ct. DC 1973, US Ct. Cl. Md. 1973. Law clk. US Dist. Ct. RI, Providence, 1969-70; staff atty. RI Legal Svcs., Providence, 1970-71; spl. asst. to solicitor US Dept. Labor, Washington, 1971-72; assoc. Sherman, Dunn, Cohen & Leifer, Washington, 1972-75; trial atty. FTC, Washington, 1975-88; judge Pa. Office of Hearing & Appeals, Pitts., 1988-90, Office of Hearings, Washington, 1990-95, Office of Chief Adminstv. Hearing Officer, U.S. Dept. Justice, Falls Church, 1995—2005, Office of Adminstrv. Law Judges, U.S. Internat. Trade Commn., Falls Church, 2005—. Trial instr. Nat. Inst. Trial Advocacy, Washington, 1982-86, US Dept. Justice, Washington, 1986-96. Chair com. Cath. League for Religious Rights, Milw., 1983-84. Master Am. Inn of Ct.; Fed. Adminstrn. Law Judges Assn. (exec. com.), Nat. Lawyers Assn. Roman Catholic. Avocations: travel tennis, swimming. Office: Office Adminstrv Law Judges 500 E St SW Ste 317 Washington DC 20436 Office Phone: 240-876-4259. Business E-Mail: robert.barton@usitc.gov.

BARTON, SARAH MURIEL, lawyer; b. London, Mar. 23, 1958; d. Russell William Andrew Charles and Katherine Grizel (Maitland-Makgill-Crichton) B.; children: Daniel Russell Bernard, Caroline Sarah Katherine. BA, U. Toronto, Ont., Can., 1978; JD, Union U., Albany, 1981; LLM in Admiralty, Tulane U., 1982. Bar: N.Y. 1982, La. 1983, U.S. Dist. Ct. (ea. dist.) La. 1983, N.J. 1985, U.S. Dist. Ct. (we. dist.) La. 1985, U.S. Dist. Ct. (so. dist.) N.Y., U.S. Ct. Appeals (5th cir.) 1986. Assoc. Law Offices Frederick Gisevius, New Orleans, 1982-83, James Hanemann and Assocs., New Orleans, 1983-85; assoc. counsel Am. Bur. Shipping, NYC and London, 1985-96; gen. counsel ABS Group of Cos., Inc., Houston, 1997—, v.p., 1998—. Spkr. Maritime Cyprus Legal Forum, 1993, Nat. Inst. and Royal Inst. Naval Archs., London, 1994. Mem. Am. Corp. Counsel Assn., Maritime Law Assn. (proctor). Home: 1511 Potomac Dr Houston TX

77057-1925 Office: ABS Group of Cos Inc ABS Plaza 16855 N Chase Dr Houston TX 77060-6008 Home Phone: 713-789-4826; Office Phone: 281-673-2898. Personal E-mail: sbarton@abs-group.com.

BARTON, STANLEY FAULKNER, retired management consultant; b. Halesowen, Worcestershire, Eng., Dec. 30, 1927; came to U.S., 1957, naturalized, 1963; s. Lazarus and Alice (Faulkner) B.; m. Marion Brittain, Dec. 20, 1952; children: Carolyn Francesca, Andrea Elizabeth. B.Sc. (hons.), U. Birmingham, Eng., 1949; PhD, U. Birmingham, 1952. Group leader Naval Rsch. Establishment, Halifax, N.S., Can., 1953-56; project coord. Def. Rsch. Chem. Labs., Ottawa, Ont., Can., 1956-57; devel. engr. Procter & Gamble, Cin., 1957-58, R & D group leader, 1958-59, R & D sect. head, 1959-69; tech. dir. food products-natural resources ITT, NYC, 1969-76; sr. v.p. tech. and quality ITT Rayonier, Inc., Stamford, Conn., 1976-90; v.p., dir. Spectrum Internat. Assocs., Inc., Tucson, 1990-92; ret., 1992. Pres. Catalina Cons., 1990—. Mem. Am. Theater Organ Soc. Home and Office: Catalina Cons 4051 N Circulo Manzanillo Tucson AZ 85750-1879 Personal E-mail: stanb@prodigy.net.

BARTON, THOMAS J., lawyer; b. Allentown, Pa., 1962; BA, Coll. William & Mary, 1984; JD, Boston Coll., 1987. Bar: Pa. 1987, NJ 1991. Ptnr., co-chair, labor, employment practice group Drinker Biddle & Reath LLP, Phila. and Princeton. Office: Drinker Biddle & Reath LLP One Logan Sq 18th & Cherry Sts Philadelphia PA 19103-6996 Office Phone: 215-988-2834. Office Fax: 215-988-2757. Business E-Mail: thomas.barton@dbr.com.

BARTON, THOMAS JACKSON J., chemistry professor, researcher; b. Dallas, Nov. 5, 1940; s. Ralph and Florence (Whitfield) Barton; m. Elizabeth Burton, Oct. 1, 1966; children: Ralph, Brett. BS, Lamar U., 1962; PhD in Organic Chemistry (hon.), U. Fla., 1967. NIH postdoctoral fellow Ohio State U., 1967; mem. faculty Iowa State U., Ames, 1967—, prof. chemistry, 1978—, disting. prof., liberal arts and scis., 1984—, program dir. Ames Lab., 1986—88, dir. Ames Lab (US Dept. Energy), 1988—, dir. Inst. for Phys. Rsch. and Tech., 1998—. Assoc. prof. U. Montpellier, France; exch. scientist NAS, Former Soviet Union, 1975, NATO, France; mem. coun. on materials scis. Dept. Energy, 1992—97; lectr. Japan Society for the Promotion of Science. Contbr. rsch. papers to profl. publs., editl. bd. Organometallics. Recipient Fredric Stanley Kipping award in organosilicon chemistry, 1982, Gov.'s medal for sci. tchg., 1983, Excellence in Tchg. faculty achievement award, Burlington No. Found., 1988, Outstanding Sci. Accomplishment in Materials Chem. award, Dept. Energy, Materials Sci. Rsch. Competition, 1989, Lab. Dir. of Yr. for Tech. Transfer, Fed. Lab. Consortium, 2003. Fellow: Japan Soc. Promotion of Sci.; mem.: Am. Chem. Soc. (Midwest award 1995). Methodist. Home: 815 Onyx Cir Ames IA 50010-8429 Office: Iowa State Univ Dept Chemistry 1605 Gilman Hall Ames IA 50011-3111 E-mail: barton@ameslab.gov.

BARTON-COLLINGS, NELDA ANN, retired political organization worker, retired bank executive, entrepreneur; b. Providence, Ky., May 12, 1929; m. Harold Bryan Barton, May 11, 1951 (dec. Nov. 1977); children: William Grant (dec.), Barbara Lynn, Harold Bryan, Stephen Lambert, Suzanne; m. Jack C. Collings, Mar. 28, 1992 (dec. Feb. 2000). Student, Western Ky. U., 1947-49; grad., Norton Meml. Infirmary Sch. Med. Tech., 1950; student, Cumberland Coll., 1978, LLD (hon.), 1991. Lic. nursing home adminstr.; registered med. technician. Pres. Barton & Assocs. Inc., Corbin, Ky., 1977—2002, ret., 2002; past pres., now chmn. Hazard Nursing Home Inc., Ky., 1977—2002, Health Sys. Inc., Corbin, Ky., 1978—2002, Corbin Nursing Home Inc., 1978—2002, Williamsburg Nursing Home, Inc., 1978—2002; pres. Key Distbg. Inc., 1980—2002, pres., chmn. bd., 1981-97; past pres., now chmn. The Whitley Whiz Inc., Williamsburg, 1983—2002; chmn. bd. dirs., now dir. Tri-County Nat. Bank., 1985-97; bd. dirs., now chmn. Harlan Nursing Home, Inc., 1986—2002; chmn. bd. dirs. Knott Co. Nursing Home, Inc., 1986; pres. Tri-County Bancorp, Inc., 1987—2002; chmn. bd. Instl. Pharmacy, Corbin, Ky., 1990—2002; past pres., now chmn. bd. Wolfe County Health Care Ctr., 1990—2002; pres. Bretors, LLC, 2004—; chmn. Tri-County Cineplex, LLC, 2004—. Mem. exec. com. Corbin Deposit Bank, 1982-84; bd. dirs. Greensburg (Ky.) Deposit Bank, Williamsburg (Ky.) Nat. Bank, Campbellsville Nat. Bank, McCreary Nat. Bank, Tri County Nat. Bank, Somerset Nat. Bank, Laurel Nat. Bank; chmn., organizer, dir. Green County Bancorp Inc., 1987—2002; organizer, dir. Laurel Nat. Bank, 1996—2002; mem. nat. adv. com. SBA, 1990-92; active Nat. Policy Forum, 1994—96. Mem. Fedn. Coun. on Aging, 1982-87; bd. dirs. Leadership Ky., 1984-88, adv. com., 1987—92; bd. dirs. Cumberland Coll. Found., 1995, mem. devel. bd., 1981—; v.p. Southeastern Ky. Rehab. Com., 1981-93; mem. Fair Housing Task Force, Corbin, 1981-84, Ky. Mansions Preservation Found. Inc., 1970-2004, Corbin Comty. Devel. Com., 1970-83; cub scout den mother, 1965-67; pres. Corbin Cen. Elem PTA, 1963-65; vice chmn. 9th dist. PTA, 1958-59; Rep. nat. committeewoman for Ky., 1968-96, sec., 1993-96; del. Rep. Nat. Conv., 1976, 88, 96, 2000, 04; vice-chmn. Rep. Nat. Com., 1984-93; sec.-treas. Nat. Rep. Inst. Internat. Affairs, 1984-86; bd. mem. Ky. Econ. Devel. Fin. Auth., 2000-03, Ky. Econ. Devel. Partnership Bd., 2003-; active numerous other polit. orgns. Recipient Ky. Woman of Achievement award Ky. Bus. and Profl. Women, 1983, Recognition award Joint Rep. Leadership, U.S. Congress, Dwight David Eisenhower award, 1970, John Sherman Cooper Disting. Svc. award Ky. Young Reps. Fedn., 1987, Outstanding Layperson award Ky. Med. Assn., 1992, Nelda Barton Comty. Svc. award Ky. Assn. Health Care Facilities, 1992, 5th Dist. Rep. Party Recognition award, 1996, Tribute to Nelda Barton-Collings Rep. Party of Ky. and 5th Dist. Lincoln Club, 1997, Disting. Recognition award Ky. State Senate, 2002, Hon. Lifetime award Ky. Mansion Preservation Found., 2004; Nelda Barton Collings Rep. internship award established by Rep. Party of Ky., 1997, Jefferson County Ky. Office for Women Hall of Fame, 1999, Ky. State Senate Cert. for Outstanding Women in Bus. and Leadership, 1999, Moral Leadership award U. Cumberlands, 2006, Ky. Woman Remembered award Ky. Com. Women, 2007; named Ky. Col., 1968, Ky. Rep. Woman of Yr., Ky. Fedn. Rep. Women, 1969; named to 5th Dist. Lincoln Club Hall of Fame, 1996; Nelda Barton Day proclaimed by Mayor of Corbin, 1973; Western Ky. U. Acad. scholar, 1947-49. Mem. Am. Coll. Nursing Home Adminstrs., Ky. Assn. Health Care Facilities (legis. com. 1980-97, Ira O. Wallace award 2002), Ky. Assn. Nursing Home Adminstrs. (bd. dirs., polit. action com. 1979—), Ky. Med. Aux. (chmn. health edn. com. 1975-77), Ky. Commn. on Women, Women's Aux. So. Med. Assn. (Ky. counselor), Whitley County Med. Aux. (pres. 1959-60), Aux. Ky. Med. Assn., Ky. Mothers Assn. (parliamentarian 1970—, hon. Mother of Ky. award 1983), Ky. C. of C. (bd. dirs. 1983—, v.p. Region 5 1985—, 1st vice chmn. 1989, chmn. 1990-91). Avocations: fishing, ballroom dancing. Home: 1311 7th Street Rd Corbin KY 40701-2207

BARTOSHUK, LINDA M., otolaryngologist, educator; BA in Psychology, minors in Astronomy and Math., Carleton Coll., 1960; MS in Psychology, Brown U., 1963, PhD in Psychology, 1965; DSc (hon.), Carleton Coll., 2001. Pre-doctoral fellow PHS, 1960—64, NSF, 1960—64; lectr. Brown U., 1966—68; affiliate asst. prof. Clark U., 1966—69; rsch. psychologist Natick Labs, 1966—70; asst. John B. Pierce Found., 1970—73, assoc., 1974—85, fellow, 1985—89; asst. prof. dept. epidemiology and pub. health Yale U., 1971—76, assoc. prof. depts. epidemiology and pub. health and psychology, 1976—85, prof. depts. epidemiology and pub. health and psychology, 1985—88, prof. sect. otolaryngology dept. surgery and prof. dept. psychology, 1989—. Chair Gordon Conf. on Chem. Senses, 1978; mem. various coms. NIH, NRC. Editor: Chem. Senses, 1982—84; cons. editor: Perception and Psychophysics, 1972—86, Sensory Processes, 1976—79; contbr. articles to profl. jours. Recipient Pepper Neuroscience Investigator award, 1984—92, Manheimer award, Monell Chem. Senses Inst., 1990, Kreshover award, Nat. Inst. Dental Rsch., 1990, Disting. Contbn. award, New Eng. Psychol. Assn., 2000. Fellow: AAAS; mem.: APA (mem. at large exec. com. div. 6 1984—87, mem. NSF working group for com. on rsch. support 1985—87, program chair div. 6 1987, pres. div. 6 1988—89, pres. elect div. 1 2001, fellow div. 6 comparative and physiol. psychology, Neal Miller Lectr. 2000), NAS, Am. Assn. Dental Schs. (mem. women's affairs adv. com.), Soc. Exptl. Psychologists, Soc. for Study of Ingestive Behavior (bd. govs. 1987—89, 2000—03), Psychonomic Soc. (mem. publ. com. 1987—92), Ea. Psychol. Assn. (mem. program com. 1983—86, bd. govs. 1987—90, pres. 1990—91), Assn. Chemoreception Scis. (exec. chair 1980—81, Award for Outstanding Achievement in chem. senses 1998), Am. Psychol. Soc. (bd. dirs. 2001—03), Phi Beta Kappa, Sigma Xi. Office: Dept Surgery Yale Univ 333 Cedar St PO Box 208041 New Haven CT 06520-8041 Office Phone: 203-785-2587. Fax: 203-737-3290. E-mail: linda.bartoshuk@yale.edu.

BARTOSIAK, STAN THEODORE, secondary school educator; b. Cambridge, Mass., Nov. 23, 1947; s. Stanley Theodore Bartosiak and Isabell Blanche Goreski. BA, Boston Coll., 1969, MA, 1972, Jagiellonian U., Cracow, Poland, 1974; PhD, UCLA, 1976. Lectr. Calif. State U., Northridge, 1975—79, Orange Coast Coll., Costa Mesa, 1979—81; tchr. Roosevelt Mid. Sch., Glendale, Calif., 1989—2000, Glendale HS, 2000—.

BARTOSIC, FLORIAN, lawyer, educator; b. Danville, Pa., Sept. 15, 1926; s. Florian W. and Elsie (Woodring) B.; m. Eileen M. Payne, 1952 (div. 1969); children: Florian, Ellen, Thomas, Stephen; m. Alberta C. Chew, 1990. BA, Pontifical Coll., 1948; B.C.L., Coll. William and Mary, 1956; LL.M., Yale U., 1957. Bar: Va. 1956, U.S. Supreme Ct. 1959. Asst. instr. Yale U., 1956-57; assoc. prof. law Coll. William and Mary, 1957, Villanova U., 1957-59; atty. NLRB, Washington, 1956, 57, 59; counsel Internat. Brotherhood of Teamsters, Washington, 1959-71; prof. law Wayne State U., 1971-80, U. Calif., Davis, 1980-92; recalled to tchg., 1994-99; prof. emeritus law U. Calif., Davis, 1993—, dean law, 1980-90. Adj. prof. George Washington U., 1966-71, Cath. U. Am., 1960-71; mem. panel arbitrators Fed. Mediation and Conciliation Service, 1972—; hearing officer Mich. Employment Relations Commn., 1972-80, Mich. Civil Rights Commn., 1974-80; bd. dirs. Mich. Legal Services Corp., 1973-80, Inst. Labor and Indsl. Relations, U. Mich., Wayne State U., 1976-80; mem. steering com. Inst. on Global Conflict and Cooperation, 1982-83; mem. adv. bd. Assn. for Union Democracy Inc., 1980—, adv. coms. Calif. Jud. Council, 1984-85, 87; vis. scholar Harvard Law Sch., 1987, Stanford Law Sch., 1987; sr. rsch. scholar ILO, 1990-91; acad. visitor Oxford U., London Sch. Econs., 1991; mem. exec. bd. Pub. Interest Clearinghouse, 1988-90. Co-author: Labor Relations Law in the Private Sector, 1977, 2d edit., 1986; contbr. articles to law jours. Mem. ABA (sec. labor rels. law sect. 1974-75), Fed. Bar Assn., Am. Law Inst. (acad. mem. labor law adv. com. on continuing profl. edn.), Soc. Profls. in Dispute Resolution (regional v.p. 1979-80), Indsl. Rels. Rsch. Assn., Internat. Soc. Labor Law and Social Legis., Internat. Indsl. Rels. Assn., Lawyers Guild, ACLU (dir. Detroit chpt. 1976-77), Order of Coif (hon.), Scribes. Home: 235 Ipanema Pl Davis CA 95616-0253 Office: U Calif Sch Law Mrak Hall Dr Davis CA 95616 Home Phone: 530-752-2889; Office Phone: 530-756-7615. Business E-Mail: fbartosic@ucdavis.edu.

BARTOW, DIANE GRACE, marketing professional, sales executive; b. Maspeth, NY, Apr. 20, 1948; d. Alfred Otto and Charlotte Florence (Bronnenkant) Bruggeman; m. Eugene A. Bartow, aug. 29, 1992; children: Jason, Trudi. AAS, Queensborough C.C., Bayside, NY, 1967; BS, Nova Southeastern U., Ft. Lauderdale, Fla., 1979. Jr. acct. Exxon, NYC, 1967-69; acct. BRM Assocs., NYC, 1969, Texaco, NYC, 1969-74; supr. Eutectic, Flushing, NY, 1974-76; regional industry dir. Am. Express, NYC, 1976-83; v.p. Eastern Exclusives, Boston, 1983-85; pres. The Mktg. Dept., 1985-86; sr. v.p., gen. mgr. Rogers Merchandising Inc., 1986-92; exec. v.p., COO Bartow Ins. Agy., Inc., 1992—. Seminars Marketing to Win. Author tng. manual, travel newsletter, 1982, Ins. Update, 1992. Trustee, v.p. Murray Hill Neighborhood Assn., 1982, pres., 1997—; trustee 7 E 35th Corp., 1983; chmn. judging Promotion and Advt. awards, 1990, awards chair, 2001-02. Mem. Nat. Assn. Advt. and Promotional Allowances (judging chair 1996-00), Am. Soc. Travel Agts. (tour rels. com. 1983), Am. Hotel and Motel Mgmt. Assn., Am. Film Assn., Am. Mgmt. Assn., Life Underwriters, Sigma Mu Omega (pres. Bayside (NY) 1966-67). Home: 325 Fifth Ave New York NY 10016 Office Phone: 631-242-4745.

BARTRAM, RALPH HERBERT, physicist; b. NYC, Aug. 16, 1929; s. Herbert L. and Grace L. Bartram; m. Ellen Anderson Devlin, Oct. 9, 1953; children: Ellen Ruth, Robert Arthur. Student, Northwestern U., 1948-49; BA cum laude, NYU, 1953, MS, 1956, PhD, 1960. Engr. Sylvania Electric Products Inc., Kew Gardens, NY, 1953-56; advanced rsch. physicist GTE Labs., Inc., Bayside, NY, 1956-61, cons., 1961-85; mem. faculty U. Conn., Storrs, 1961—, prof. physics, 1971-92, dept. head, 1986-92, prof. emeritus, 1992—. Rsch. assoc. Atomic Energy Rsch. Establishment, Harwell, England, 1967—68; vis. prof. U. Oxford, England, 1978; sr. vis. fellow U. Strathclyde, Scotland, 1993; cons. U.S. Army, 1966—71, Am. Optical Co., 1966—78, Brookhaven Nat. Lab., 1971—85, Timex Corp., 1981—82, Polaroid Corp., 1987—88, Boston U., 1993—99, ALEM Assocs., 1996—, Photonics Materials Ltd., 2002—03. Author (with J. M. Spaeth and J. R. Niklas): (book) Structural Analysis of Point Defects in Solids, 1992; author: (with B. Henderson) Crystal-Field Engineering of Solid-State Laser Materials, 2000; contbr. articles to profl. jours. With USN, 1946—48. Grantee, U.S. AEC, 1963—69, U.S. Army Rsch. Office, 1971—78, 1982—92, NSF, 1974—77, 1983—91, NATO, 1985—90. Fellow: Am. Phys. Soc.; mem.: AAUP, Conn. Acad. Sci. Engring., Optical Soc. Am., Phi Beta Kappa, Phi Eta Sigma, Sigma Pi Sigma, Phi Kappa Phi, Sigma Xi. Achievements include patents in field. Home: 67 Independence Dr Mansfield Center CT 06250-3259 Office: U Conn Dept Physics Storrs Mansfield CT 06269-3046 Personal E-mail: RHBartram2@aol.com.

BARTREM, DUANE HARVEY, retired military officer, residential designer, consultant; b. Lansing, Mich., June 4, 1928; s. Harvey Theodore and Ruby Leola (Thomas) B.; m. Frances Lillie Bushee, Sept. 12, 1948 (dec. Jan.19, 2000); children: Lawrence Duane, Jeffrey Earl. BA in Bus. Adminstrn., Columbia Coll., Mo., 1976. Enlisted U.S. Army N.G., Lansing, 1948, commd. 2d lt., 1951, advanced through grades to col., 1951-76, comdr. battery, 1956-60; facilities engr. Mich. Nat. Guard, Lansing, 1960-69, chief engr., 1969-76, comdr. 119 FA Bn., 1971-75, comdr. 46th Brigade, 1975-76, comptr., 1976-83, ret., 1983; prin. residential design office Lansing, 1955-60, Grand Ledge, Mich., 1967—. Leader local and regional levels Boy Scouts of Am.; chmn. congregation Bretton Woods Covenant Ch., Mich., 1986—89, v.p. congregation, 1995—. With USNR, 1946—48. Decorated Army Commendation with 3 clusters, Meritorious Svc. medal with 2 clusters, Legion of Merit. Mem. Mil. Officers Assn. (life), Mil. Order Fgn. Wars (sr. vice comdr. gen., 2003-05, comdr. gen. 2005—07, past comdr. gen. 2007-), Assn. of the U.S. Army (life, mem. resolutions com. 1973, 74, chair resolutions com. 1975, area v.p. 1976—, mem. adv. bd. 1978—, chair by-laws com. 1978—, past state pres., past region pres. 1988-92, coun. of trustees 1992-96, Pres.'s medal 1998), Grand Lodge Rotary (pres. 1989-90, Paul Harris award 1992), Boy Scouts Am. (pres. 1973-79, exec. bd. 1970—; disting. Eagle Scout 1989, Silver Beaver award 1969, Silver Antelope 1983, God and Svc. award 1992, James E. West fellow, 1910 Soc., Ernest Thompson Seton Mem. 1999). Avocation: golf. Home Phone: 517-627-9072; Office Phone: 517-627-9072. Personal E-mail: dhbartrem@aol.com.

BARTRUFF, JIM, theater educator, director; b. McCook, Nebr., Aug. 11, 1952; s. Wayne Louis and Phyllis Irene Bartruff; m. Lindy Burkhardt, Aug. 14, 1982. BA, U. Nebr., Kearney, 1974; MS, U. Oreg., Eugene, 1977; MFA, U. Mont., Missoula, 1988. Dir. theatre Carroll Coll., Helena, Mont., 1978—88; asst prof. and dir. Mont. Repertory Theatre U. Mont., Missoula, 1988—90; dir. theatre Minn. State U. Moorhead, 1990—2004, Emporia State U., Kans., 2004—. Bd. mem. FM Communiversity, Moorhead, Minn., 1995—2004; mem. region 5 selection team Kennedy Ctr. Am. Coll. Theatre Festival, Washington, 1998—2006. Named CASE Minn. Prof. of Yr., 2001. Mem.: Actors Equity, Phi Kappa Phi. Methodist. Avocations: travel, baseball. Office: Emporia State Univ King Hall 201G 1200 Commercial St Emporia KS 66801 Home Phone: 620-341-9193; Office Phone: 620-341-5704. Office Fax: 620-341-6031. E-mail: jbartuf@emporia.edu.

BARTSCHAT, KLAUS RICHARD WILHELM, physics professor; b. Steinfurt, Westfalen, Germany, June 17, 1956; s. Richard Ewald and Helmine Angela Käthe (Busch) Bartschat; m. Teresa Elisabeth Zweerman, Aug. 13, 1988; children: Nicholas, Erika. Diploma in physics, U. Münster, Germany, 1981; PhD, U. Münster, 1984, Habilitation, 1989. Rsch. scientist U. Münster, 1984-88; asst. prof. physics Drake U., Des Moines, 1988-91, assoc. prof. physics, 1991-94, prof. physics, 1994-2000, Ellis and Nelle Levitt Disting. prof. physics, 2000—. Author: Computational Atomic Physics, 1996, Polarization, Alignment, and Orientation in Atomic Collisions, 2000; contbr. over 250 articles to profl. jours. Grantee NSF, 1991—, NATO, 1990, 93, 2000, Rsch. Corp., 1989. Fellow Am. Phys. Soc.; mem. Deutsche Physikalische Gesellschaft, Theoretical Atomic, Molecular and Optical Cmty. (chair 1998-2000), Internat. Conf. Photonic, Electronic, and Atomic Collisions (sec. 2001-07), Gaseous Electronics Conf. (treas. 2006—). Am. Baptist. Avocations: exercise, travel. Office: Drake U Dept Physics and Astronomy Des Moines IA 50311 Home: 3714 132d Cir Urbandale IA 50323 Office Phone: 515-271-3750. E-mail: klaus.bartschat@drake.edu.

BARTTER, BRIT JEFFREY, investment banker; b. Berea, Ohio, Dec. 27, 1949; s. Lynn Martin Bartter and Scharlie Ellen (Watson) Handlan; m. Marilyn McCullough, Aug. 25, 1973; children: Bryndl Lynn and Blake McCullough (twins). AB in Econs., Duke U., 1972; MS in Fin., Cornell U., 1976, PhD in Fin., 1977. Asst. prof. computer sci. Grad. Sch. Bus. Cornell U., Ithaca, NY, 1976; asst. prof. fin. Grad. Sch. Mgmt. Kellogg Grad. Sch. Mgmt., Northwestern U., Evanston, Ill.; 1977-79; assoc., then v.p. Merrill Lynch Capital Markets, Chgo., 1979-83; v.p. The First Boston Corp., Chgo., 1983-87, dir., 1988-89, mng. dir., 1989-94, Merrill Lynch Investment Banking, Chgo., 1995—2004, vice chmn., 2004—05, JP Morgan Investment Banking, 2005—. Bd. dirs. Coun. for Young Profls., Chgo., 1985-87. Contbr. articles to Jour. of Fin., Fin. Mgmt. Bd. dirs. Cornell Coun. Chgo., 1987-88, Duke Campaign Chgo., 1987-88. Mem. Econ. Club Chgo., Northwestern U. Assocs., Glen View Golf Club, Chgo. Club, Naples Nat. Golf Club, Merit Club. Home: 221 Apple Tree Rd Winnetka IL 60093-3703 Office: JP Morgan Investment Banking 227 W Monroe St Ste 2800 Chicago IL 60606 Home Phone: 847-446-4196; Office Phone: 312-541-4216. Business E-Mail: brit.j.bartter@jpmorgan.com.

BARTUNEK, ROBERT R(ICHARD), JR., lawyer; b. Cleve., July 2, 1946; s. Robert Richard and Clare Elizabeth (Lonsway) B.; 1 child, Kathryn Elizabeth. BS, Bucknell U., 1968; MBA, Ohio State U., 1974, JD, 1975; LLM, U. Mo., Kansas City, 1986. Bar: Mo. 1975, Kans. 1997, U.S. Dist. Ct. (we. dist.) Mo. 1975, U.S. Tax Ct. 1981, U.S. Dist. Ct. Kans. 1997. Ptnr. Beckett, Lolli & Bartunek, Kansas City, 1975-96, Swanson Midgley, LLC, Kansas City, 1997—2003, Seigfreid, Bingham, Levy, Selzer & Gee, Kansas City, 2003—. Mem. Men's Sr. Baseball League. Decorated Bronze Star. Mem. ABA, Lawyers Assn. Greater Kansas City, Kansas City Met. Bar Assn. (former chmn. tax law com.). Roman Catholic. Office: Seigfreid Bingham Levy Selzer & Gee 2800 Commerce Tower 911 Main St Kansas City MO 64105 Home: 10314 Howe Ln Leawood KS 66206-2517 Office Phone: 816-421-4460. Business E-Mail: rbartunek@sblsg.com.

BARTUS, RAYMOND THOMAS, neuroscientist, writer, pharmaceutical executive; b. Chgo., May 19, 1947; s. Frank A. and Katherine (Bogus) B.; m. Cheryl Marie Gyure, Feb. 11, 1967; children: Raymond T., Kristin Marie. BA, California State U. Pa., 1968; MS, N.C. State U., 1970, PhD, 1972. NRC postdoctoral fellow, research assoc. Naval Med. Rsch. Lab., Groton, Conn., 1972; scientist Parke-Davis Rsch. Labs., Ann Arbor, Mich., 1973-75, sr. scientist, 1975-78, Lederle Labs., Am. Cyanamid Co., Pearl River, NY, 1978-79, group leader neuroscience, dir. geriatric discovery program, 1979-88; sr. v.p. R & D, chief sci. officer Cortex Pharms. Inc., Irvine, Calif., 1988-91, interim pres., 1990, exec. v.p., chief oper. officer, 1991-92, chief sci. officer, 1988-92; sr. v.p. neurobiology Alkermes Inc., Cambridge, Mass., 1992-96, sr. v.p. preclin. R&D, 1996—2001; sr. v.p. Worldwide Life Sci. R&D, 2001—02; v.p., rsch. and devel. Ceregene Inc., San Diego, 2002—04, sr. v.p., COO, 2004—. Bd. dir. Net Met; prof. N.Y.U. Med. Ctr., 1979—; adj. prof. Tulane U., 1978—87, U. Calif., Irvine, Calif., 1988—92, Tufts U., 1992—. Editor-in-chief, founder, Neurobiology of Aging, 1980-89; contbr. articles on neurosci. to profl. jours. Fellow Am. Coll. Neuropsychopharmacology; mem. Alzheimers Assn. (sci. med. bd. 1986-92), Soc. Neurosci., N.Y. Acad. Sci., Brain Tumor Soc., Am. Assn. Pharm. Sci., Am. Soc. Pharmacology and Exptl. Biology. Office: Ceregene Inc 9381 Judicial Dr #130 San Diego CA 92121 Business E-Mail: rtbartus@ceregene.com.

BARTUSKA, ANN, government official, biologist; b. Phila. BS in Biology, Wilkes Coll., 1975; MS in Botany, Ohio U.; PhD in Biology, W.Va. U. Program mgr. nat. acid precipitation assessment program N.C. State U., Raleigh; asst. dir. Southeastern Forest Expt. Sta., Forest Svc., USDA, Asheville, N.C., acting dir. ecosys. mgmt. Washington, spl. asst. chief, liaison to Nat. Biol. Survey, dir. forest health protection state and pvt. forestry orgn., dir. forest mgmt., 1998—2001, dep. chief rsch. and devel., 2004—; exec. dir. Invasive Species Initiative The Nature Conservancy, Va., 2001—04. Mem. Ecol. Soc. Am. (v.p. for pub. affairs). Office: USDA Forest Svc Auditors Bldg 201 14th St SW Washington DC 20250-0001 Fax: 202-205-1045. E-mail: fm.wo@fs.fed.us.

BARTZ, CAROL A., computer software company executive; b. Winona, Minn., Aug. 29, 1948; m. William (Bill) Marr; children: Bill, Meredith, Layne BS in Computer Sci. with honors, U. Wis., 1971; DSc (hon.), Worcester Poly. Inst.; LittD (hon.), William Woods U.; LittD, NJ Inst. Tech. With sales mgmt. dept. 3M Corp., Digital Equipment Corp., 1976-83; mgr. customer mktg. Sun Microsys., 1983-84, v.p. mktg., 1984-87, v.p. customer svc., 1987-90, v.p. worldwide field ops., exec. officer, 1990-92; chmn., pres., CEO Autodesk, Inc., San Rafael, Calif., 1992—2006, exec. chmn., 2006—. Pres. Sun Fed., from 1987; bd. dirs. AirTouch Comm., Bea Sys., Cadence Design Sys., Cisco Sys., Inc., 1994-, Network Appliance; mem. President's Export Coun., 1994, President's Coun. Advisors on Sci. and Tech.; adv. coun. bus. sch. Stanford U. Bd. dirs. U. Wis. Sch. Bus., Nat. Breast Cancer Rsch. Found., Found. for Nat. Medals Sci. and Tech.; mem. adv. coun. Stanford U. Bus. Sch.; mem. Com. of 200; adv. for women's health issues; former mem. Ark. of Gov.'s Econ. Summit, Little Rock; mem. Sec. of Edn.'s Commn. on Future of Edn., 2005. Recipient Donald C. Burnham Mfg. Mgmt. award Soc. Mfg. Engrs., 1994, Horatio Alger Award, 2000, named one of 100 Most Influential Women in Business, San Francisco Bus. Times, 2004, 100 Most Powerful Women in World, Forbes mag., 2005, World's 30 Most Respected CEOs, Barron's mag., 2005. Mem. Calif. C. of C. (bd. dirs.). Avocations: gardening, tennis. Office: Autodesk Inc 111 McInnis Pkwy San Rafael CA 94903-2700*

BARTZ, DAVID JOHN, lawyer; b. Appleton, Wis., Feb. 15, 1955; BA, U. Wis., 1976; MA in Pub. Affairs, U. Minn., 1979; JD, Ariz. State U., 1985. Bar: Ariz. 1985, US Dist. Ct. Ariz. 1985, US Ct. Appeals (9th cir.) 1985, Wis. 1989, US Dist. Ct. (we. dist.) Wis. 1996, US Dist. Ct. (ea. dist.) Wis.

1997. Policy analyst Minn. Dept. Transp., St. Paul, 1978-79; office dir. Wis. Senate, Madison, 1979-82, 86; pvt. practice, Phoenix, 1985-86; adminstr. Wis. Dept. Justice, Madison, 1987-91; pvt. practice, Madison, 1991—. Mem. ASPA (sec. Wis. Capital chpt. 1981-82), ACLU, Ariz. Bar Assn., Wis. Bar Assn., Dane County Bar Assn., Dane County Criminal Defense Lawyers Assn. Office Phone: 608-256-5500.

BARTZATT, RONALD LEE, research biochemist, consultant; b. Lincoln, Nebr., Dec. 18, 1953; s. Frank Wright and Lorretta (Warta) B.; m. Patricia Ann Dockham, July 30, 1979 (div. Oct. 1983). BS, U. Nebr., 1978, MS, 1980, PhD, 1982. Cert. med. lab. technician. Research biochemist U. Nebr., Lincoln, 1983-84, Eppley Cancer Ctr., Omaha, 1984-85, Theodor Gildore Ctr., San Diego, 1985, U. Calif., San Diego, 1985-88; rsch. biochemist Eppley Cancer Ctr., 1988—. Cons. IRCS Med. Sci., Lancaster, England, 1985—. Author: Proceedings of ACS Symposia on Computer Data Analysis and Optimization; contbr. articles to profl. jours. Deacon Luth. Ch., San Diego. Served with U.S. Army, 1973-76. Towle Scholar U. Nebr., 1973; NIH fellow, 1984; grantee Nebr. Water Co., 1981. Mem. Am. Soc. Clin. Pathologists, Phi Lambda Upsilon. Republican. Avocations: kayaking, ice skating, skiing, music. Business E-Mail: bartzatt@mail.unomaha.edu.

BARUAH, SANDY K. (SANTANU KUMAR BARUAH), federal agency administrator; s. Dhrien and Ranee Baruah; m. Lisa Baruah; 1 child, Issac. BS, U. Oregon; MS, Willamette U. Sr. mgmt. cons. Performance Consulting Group, Portland, Oreg., 1994—2001; sr. advisor, dir. policy planning for econ. devel Econ. Devel. Adminstrn., US Dept. Commerce, Washington, dep. asst. sec. for program ops., chief of staff, 2004—05, acting asst. sec for econ. devel, 2005, asst. sec. for econ. devel., 2005—. Office: US Dept Commerce Econ Devel Adminstrn Herbert Clark Hoover Bldg 14th St & Constitution Ave NW Rm 7800 Washington DC 20230 Office Phone: 202-482-5081. Office Fax: 202-482-4781. E-mail: sbaruah@eda.doc.gov.

BARUCH, HURD, retired lawyer; b. NYC, Nov. 29, 1937; s. Eduard and Dorothy (Hurd) B.; m. Mary Ellen Kinney, July 8, 1964; children: Edward, Michael, Amy. BA, Hamilton Coll., 1957; LLB, Yale U., 1960; MBA, Columbia U., 1961. Bar: Conn. 1960, N.Y. 1966, D.C. 1971, Pa. 1972, Ill. 1988, U.S. Supreme Ct. 1964. Ptnr. Winston & Strawn, Chgo.; ret. Spl. counsel divsn. trading and markets, SEC, 1969-72. Author: Wall Street Security Risk, 1971, Light on Light, 2004. Bd. dirs., treas. St. Thomas the Apostle Roman Cath. Parish. Capt. USAF, 1961—64. Mem.: Ventana Canyon Golf Club, Beta Gamma Sigma, Phi Beta Kappa, Order Coif.

BARUCH, JORDAN JAY, retired management consultant; b. NYC, Aug. 21, 1923; s. Solomon L. and Minnie (Kessner) B.; m. Rhoda Wasserman, June 3, 1944; children: Roberta, Marjory, Lawrence. BS, MS, Mass. Inst. Tech., 1948, Sc.D., 1950. Registered profl. engr., Mass., NH, Prince Edward Island, Can. V.p., dir. Bolt, Beranek & Newman, Inc., Cambridge, Mass., 1949-66, dir., 1949-77, Boston Broadcasters, 1963-77, 81-83, Inst. for Mental Health Initiatives, Washington, 1982—2005, treas., 1982-98; dir. Gould Corp., 1985-88, Baupost Group, Cambridge, Mass., 1984-98; asst. prof. elec. engring. MIT, Cambridge, 1950-53, lectr., 1954-70; lectr. bus. adminstrn. grad. sch. bus. adminstrn. Harvard U., Boston, 1970-74; prof. Amos Tuck Sch. Bus. Adminstrn., Thayer Sch. Engring., Dartmouth Coll., Hanover, NH, 1974-77; asst. sec. sci. and tech. Dept. Commerce, Washington, 1977-81; pres. Jordan Baruch Assocs., Washington, 1981—84; ret., 1984. Mem. bd. sci. and tech. for internat. devel. Nat. Rsch. Coun.; advisor to U.S./Israel Hightech Commn.; founder Nat. Ctr. Indsl. Sci. & Tech., Dalian, China; founder, U.S. advisor U.S./Israel Bianational Indsl. R&D Found., 1978—2005; regent Nat. Libr. Medicine, Washington, 1998-2001. Contbr. articles to books and profl. jours.; patentee loudspeakers, acoustical treatments, automotive mufflers. Bd. dirs. Inst. Mental Health Initiatives, Washington. Served with AUS, 1942-46. Named Outstanding Young Elec. Engr. Eta Kappa Nu, 1956 Fellow Acoustical Soc. Am., IEEE, AAAS, Nat. Acad. Engring. (Augustine sr. scholar 2001-), Am. Acad. Arts and Scis. Patentee loudspeakers, acoustical treatments, automotive mufflers. Home and Office: 5630 Wisconsin Ave Apt 905 Chevy Chase MD 20815-4456 Office Phone: 301-907-3601. Personal E-mail: jbaruch@alum.mit.edu.

BARUCH, RALPH M., communications executive; came to U.S., 1940, naturalized, 1944; s. Bernard and Alice B.; m. Jean Ursell de Mountford, June 9, 1963; children by previous marriage: Eve, Renee, Alice, Michele. Student, Sorbonne, U. Paris. Account exec. SESAC, 1947—50, Dumont TV, 1950—54; with CBS, Eastern Sales Mgr. Enterprises, NYC, 1954—59, v.p. internat. sales, 1959—67, v.p., gen. mgr., 1967—70; group pres. CBS, 1970-71; pres., chief exec. officer Viacom Internat. Inc., NYC, 1971-78, chmn. bd., mem. office chief exec., 1987; sr. fellow Gannett Ctr. for Media Studies Columbia U., 1988. Cons. Adv. Commn. on Comm., USIA, 1979-86. Bd. dirs., vice chmn. exec. com. Internat. Rescue Com., N.Y.C., 1975-88; mem. Pres.'s Coun. for Internat. Youth Exch., 1982; trustee Mus. of TV and Radio, Carnegie Hall, Lenox Hill Hosp., 1980-94, Thirteen-WNET, Carnegie Hall; adv. Mayor's Coun. on Cultural Affairs, N.Y.C., 1994. Named to Cable Hall of Fame, Denver, 2006. Fellow Internat. Council TV Acad. Arts and Scis. (pres. 1973-76, 85-87, dir. 1976—); mem. Internat. Radio and TV Soc. (pres., past pres. Found.), Nat. Acad. Cable Programming (chmn. emeritus), Nat. Assn. Broadcasters (task force on pub. broadcasting, chmn. program producers and distbrs. com.), Cable TV Edn. Found. (chmn.). Office: Viacom Inc 1633 Broadway New York NY 10019-6708

BARUD, STEPHANIE, pharmacist, educator; d. John and Judith Barud. PharmD, St Louis Coll. Pharmacy, 2003. Clin. asst. prof. U. Okla. Coll. Pharmacy, Oklahoma City, 2004—. Mem.: Am. Soc. Health Sys. Pharmacists, Am. Coll. Clin. Pharmacists. Home Phone: 405-286-5440; Office Phone: 405-271-6878.

BARUFFI, KUMI YAMAMOTO, lawyer; BA, Wellesley Coll.; JD, Boston U. Bar: Wash. 1996. Assoc. Graham & Dunn, PC, Seattle, 1995—2003, ptnr., 2004—. Named Rising Star, Wash. Law & Politics Mag., 2003—06; recipient Justice League award, Wash. CEO Mag., 2006. Mem.: ABA, Japanese Am. C. of C. (bd. dirs., sec. 2002—). Office: Graham & Dunn PC Pier 70 2801 Alaskan Way Ste 300 Seattle WA 98121 Office Phone: 206-340-9676. Office Fax: 206-340-9599.

BARUSCH, LAWRENCE ROOS, lawyer; b. Oakland, Calif., Aug. 23, 1949; s. Maurice Radston and Phyllis (Rose) B.; m. Susan Amanda Smith, Aug. 7, 1983; children: Nathaniel M., Ariana G. BA summa cum laude, Harvard U., 1971, JD cum laude, 1975. Bar: Calif. 1975. Assoc. Cotton, Seligman & Ray, San Francisco, 1975-77; gen. counsel Jones & Guerrero Co., Inc., Agana, Guam, 1977-82; ptnr. Klemm, Blair & Barusch, PC, Agana, Guam, 1982-85; assoc. Davis, Graham & Stubbs, Salt Lake City, 1986-87; counsel Parsons, Behl & Latimer, Salt Lake City, 1987-89, shareholder, 1989—; counsel Guam Tax Code Commn., 1990-94. Adj. prof. U. Utah Coll. Law, 1998-99, 2000—, vis. assoc. prof., 1999-2000; mem. com. U.S. activities of foreigners and tax treaties, tax sect. ABA, 1994—; mem. tax rev. commn. Utah, 2000—. Contbr. articles to profl. jours. including Guam Bar Jour., Utah Bar Jour., Offshore Investment, Tax Management Internat. Jour., Tax Notes. Chmn. Dem. Party, Davis County, Utah, 1997-99; mem. bd. dirs. The Road Home, 2002—. Recipient Billings prize, U. Utah S.J. Quinney Coll. Law, 2004; Sheldon fellow, Harvard U., 1971. Mem. Guam Bar Assn. (pres. 1982-84), No. Marianas Bar Assn., Utah Bar Assn. (chmn. tax sect. 1994-95), Calif. Bar Assn., Utah Tax Review Comm., Phi Beta Kappa. Office: Parsons Behle & Latimer 201 S Main St Ste 1800 Salt Lake City UT 84111-2218 Home Phone: 801-596-8670; Office Phone: 801-532-1234. Business E-Mail: lbarusch@pblutah.com.

BARUSCH, RONALD CHARLES, lawyer; b. Oakland, Calif., Sept. 6, 1953; s. Maurice Radston and Phyllis Rose (Roos) B.; m. Cynthia Jean Dahlin, May 28, 1977; children: Margaret Camilla Dahlin Barusch, Christopher Charles Barusch Dahlin, Julia Rose Barusch Dahlin. AB, Harvard U., 1974, JD, 1978; M in Pub. Policy, J.F. Kennedy Sch. Govt., 1978. Bar: Mass. 1978, U.S. Ct. Appeals (1st cir.) 1979, U.S. Dist. Ct. Mass. 1979, U.S. Ct. Appeals (D.C. cir.) 1981, U.S. Dist. Ct. D.C. 1982, Va. 2000. From assoc. to ptnr. Skadden, Arps, Slate, Meagher & Flom LLP, Boston, 1978-81, Skadden, Arps, Slate, Meagher & Flom, Washington, 1981-96, ptnr. Sydney, Australia, 1996-99, Skadden Arps Slate Meaghen & Flom, Washington, 1999-2000, Skadden, Arps, Slate, Meaghen & Flom, Reston, Va., 2000—03, Skadden, Arps, Slate, Meaghen & Flom LLP, Washington, 2003—. Democrat. Office: Skadden Arps Slate Meagher & Flom 1440 New York Ave NW Washington DC 20005 Home Phone: 703-526-9521; Office Phone: 202-371-7990. E-mail: rbarusch@skadden.com.

BARVE, KUMAR P., state legislator; b. Schenectady, NY, Sept. 8, 1958; s. Prabhakar R. and Neera S. (Gokhale) B. BS, Georgetown U., 1980. Precinct chmn. Dist. 17 Dem. Caucus; del. Dist. 17 State of Md., Annapolis, 1991—, majority leader, 2003—. Campaign mem. Robert Hacken for Del., 1974, Barnes for Congress, 1980-84, Bruce Adams and Ike Leggett for County Coun., 1986, Barnes for Senate, 1986, Franchot for Congress, 1988, Dukakis for Pres., 1988; treas. Montgomery County Young Dem.; mem. house facility and econ. matters coms., workers compensation subcom.; vice chair Montgomery County del., 1993—. Treas., bd. dirs. Md. Nat. Abortion Rights Action League; del. GCI Consumer Coop.; fin. analyst. Mem. Md. Citizen Action, Washingtonian Towns Civic Assn., Sierra Club, Indian Culture Coord. Com., Gaithersburg and Upper Montgomery County C. of C. Office: Md Ho of Deleg Lowe Ho Off Bldg 84 Coll Ave Annapolis MD 21401

BARWIG, REGIS NORBERT JAMES, priest; b. Chgo., Jan. 16, 1932; s. Ladislas-Joseph and Josepha Agnes (Neugebauer) B. AB, St. Procopius Coll., 1954; postgrad., Georgetown U., 1957, Pontifical Lateran U., Rome, 1959-61. Ordained priest Roman Cath. Ch., 1959. Sec. to abbot of Lisle, 1955-61; sec. gen. Christian Unity Apostolate, 1961-64; founding prior Claremont Priory, Cedarburg, Wis., 1964-67; prior Community of Our Lady, Oshkosh, Wis., 1968—. Co-chmn. 1st Festival Faith, Milw., 1966; chmn. Ecumenical Conf. Spiritual and Liturgical Renewal Religious Life, 1969—; mem. Green Bay Diocese Ecumenical Commn., 1970-73; theol. cons. Consortium Perfectae Caritatis, 1974—; preacher, U.S. and Europe; U.S. liaison for beatification of Pope Pius IX, 1975—; assoc. Wanda Landowska Music Ctr., Lakeville, Conn., 1969; bd. dirs. Inter-Cath. Press Agy., N.Y., 1967-72. Author: Changing Habits, 1971, Waiting for Rain, 1975, Reflections on Spiritual Life for Order of Malta, 1982; translator: His Will Alone, 1971, Wanda Landowska Diaries, 1971, Pius XI-A Close-up, 1975, Pius IX-More than a Prophet, 1977, Writings of Blessed Maximilian Maria Kolbe, 1977, Evaluations of the Possibility of Constructing a Christian Ethic on the Assumptions of the Philosophy of Max Scheler, 1982, Above and Beyond, 2004; editor: Conferences of Mother Mary of Jesus, 1968; contbr. articles to religious publs. Decorated Bruderschaft, Collegio Teutonico, Vatican City, Knight Comdr., Order Isabel la Catolica, Spain, Grand Cross of Merit, Sovereign Mil. Order of Malta, Magistral Chaplain, Conventual Grand Cross Chaplain of Honor, Prelatial Councillor, Chief of Chaplains, Polish Assn., Sovereign Mil. Order of Malta, knight comdr. Ecclesiastical Grace, Gold Benementi medal Sacred Mil. Constantinian Order of St. George-Bourbon Two Sicilies, Chaplain Am. Del., knight Order of Francis I, Bourbon-Two Sicilies, Knight Comdr. Equestrian Order Holy Sepulcher of Jerusalem, Grand Priory of Poland, Comdr., Order of Merit, Republic of Poland, Gold Cross Merit Primate of Poland, hon. Canon, Royal Coll. Chpt., Wilanow-Warsaw, St. Victoria Cross Diocese of Lowicz, Archbishop Weber HS Madonna award, Skowyrow Found. award Pastoral Inst. Cath. U. Lublin, Spl. Fgn. award Warsaw Soc. Civitas Christiana, Person of Yr. award St. John Cantius Soc. Chgo., Gold Cross Merit Polish Cath. Mission Eng. and Wales, Meml. medal Cardinal Stefan Wyszynski, Merit medal Arch. Warsaw. Mem. Selden Soc., Queen Mary Coll., Polish-Am. Assn. Wis. (chaplain 1979—), Polish Arts Club. Home and Office: 2804 Oakwood Ln Oshkosh WI 54904-8406 *From my Roman Catholic faith and my Polish heritage I imbibed early a sense of the importance of Divine Providence in one's life. In this context, then, regret and disappointment are both futile and destructive emotions. Everything can be redeemed. Radical eternalism makes one look Above and Beyond.*

BARZA, HAROLD A., lawyer; b. Montreal, Que., Can., July 28, 1952; came to U.S., 1969; s. Solomon A. and Evelyn (Elkin) B. BA, Boston U., 1973; JD, Columbia U., 1976. Bar: N.Y. 1977, Calif. 1978, U.S. Dist. Ct. (ctrl. dist.) Calif. 1978. Law clk. to Hon. Milton Pollack U.S. Dist. Ct. (so. dist.) N.Y., 1976-77; assoc. Munger, Tolles & Rickershauser, LA, 1978-81; ptnr. Gelles, Singer & Johnson, LA, 1982-83, Gelles, Lawrence & Barza, LA, 1983-87, Loeb & Loeb, LA, 1987-99, Quinn, Emanuel, Urquehart, Oliver and Hedges, LA, 1999—. Adj. prof. mass comm. law Southwestern U. Sch. Law, L.A., 1979-82; judge pro tem., L.A. Mcpl. Ct., 1985—. Mem. bd. editors Columbia Law Rev., 1975-76. Mem. steering com. Jewish Nat. Fund, L.A., 1983. James Kent scholar, 1974-76, Harlan Fiske Stone scholar, 1973-74. Mem. ABA (mem. com. on antitrust litigation), Los Angeles County Bar Assn. (trial lawyers, litigation and intellectual property sects.). Office: Quinn Emanuel Urquhart Oliver and Hedges 865 S Figueroa St Los Angeles CA 90017-2543 E-mail: hab@qeuo.com.

BARZELATTO, JOSE S., social welfare organization executive; b. Santiago, Chile, Apr. 6, 1926; arrived in U.S., 1989; s. Jose Q. Barzelatto and Veronica G. Sanchez; m. Juanita Ramirez Barzelatto, Jan. 8, 1950 (dec. Nov. 21, 1999); children: Veronica, Ana Maria, Jovan, Marcos, Cristina, Virginia. MD, U. Chile, 1949. Lic. physician Fla. Mem. faculty U. Chile, Santiago, 1950—68; postgrad. trainee Mass. Gen. Hosp., Boston, 1951—53, rsch. fellow, 1959—60; spl. advisor OAS, Washington, 1968—75; med. officer, dir. WHO, Geneva, 1975—89; dir. reproductive health The Ford Found., NYC, 1989—97; v.p. Ctr. for Health & Social Policy, NYC and San Francisco, 1997—. Founder, exec. sec. Chile's Nat. Coun. Sci. and Tech., Santiago, 1967—68; mem. coun. Pugwash Conf. Sci. and World Affairs, 1971—82; mem. ethics com. Internat. Fedn. Ob-Gyn., London, 1997—2004; pres. directive coun. Civil Soc. Forum of the Ams., Rio de Janeiro, 2000—05. Author (with Anibal Faundes): The Drama of Abortion Seeking a Consensus, 2004; co-editor: Ethics and Human Values in Family Planning, 1989; contbr. articles to profl. jours., chapters to books. Mem.: Latin Am. Assn. Rsch. in Human Reprodn. (hon.). Avocation: politics. Home: 5800 Nicholson Ln Apt 1201 Rockville MD 20852 Office: Ctr Health & Social Policy 847 25th St San Francisco CA 94121 E-mail: josebarzel@aol.com.

BARZILAY, ZVI, real estate developer; BArch, U. Md.; M in Urban Design/Real Estate Devel., Harvard U. Chief ctr. city planner Phila. City Planning Comm.; with Toll Bros., Inc., Huntingdon Valley, Pa., 1980—, pres., COO, also bd. dirs. Mem. Urban Land Inst., Phila. Dist. Coun. Avocations: sailing, fishing, outdoors. Office: Toll Bros 250 Gibraltar Rd Horsham PA 19044 Office Phone: 215-938-8228.*

BARZUN, JACQUES, writer, literary agent; b. Créteil, France, Nov. 30, 1907; came to U.S., 1920, naturalized, 1933; s. Henri Martin and Anna-Rose B.; m. Mariana Lowell, Aug. 1936 (dec. 1979); children: James Lowell, Roger Martin, Isabel; m. Marguerite Davenport, June 1980. Student, Lycée Janson de Sailly, Paris; AB, Columbia U., 1927, MA, 1928, PhD, 1932. From lectr. history to assoc. prof. Columbia U., NYC, 1927-45, prof., 1945, dean grad. faculties, 1955-58, dean faculties and provost, 1958-67, prof. emeritus, spl. adviser on arts, 1967-75; lit. adviser Scribner's, NYC, 1975-93. Author: The French Race, 1932, Teacher in America, 1945, Berlioz and the Romantic Century, 1950, 3d edit., 1969, Pleasures of Music, 1951, 2d edit., 1977, God's Country and Mine, 1954, Music in American Life, 1956, Darwin, Marx, Wagner, 1941, The Energies of Art, 1956, Of Human Freedom, 2d edit, 1964, Race: A Study in Superstition, 1937, The Modern Researcher, 1957, 6th edit., 2003, The House of Intellect, 2d edit, 1975, Classic, Romantic and Modern, 1961, Science: The Glorious Entertainment, 1964, The American University, 1968, 2d edit., 1995, A Catalogue of Crime, 1971, 2d edit., 1986, On Writing, Editing and Publishing, 1971, The Use and Abuse of Art, 1974, Clio and the Doctors, 1974, Simple and Direct, 1975, 2d edit., 1993, Critical Questions, 1982, A Stroll With William James, 1983, A Word or Two Before You Go, 1986, The Culture We Deserve, 1989, Begin Here: On Teaching and Learning, 1990, An Essay on French Verse, 1991, From Dawn to Decadence: 1500 Years of Western Cultural Life, 2000, A Jacques Barzun Reader, 2001, What Is a School?, 2002; mem. editl. bd. The American Scholar, 1946-76, Ency. Brit, 1979—; editor: Selected Letters of Lord Byron, 1953, Nouvelles Lettres de Berlioz, 1954, The Selected Writings of John Jay Chapman, 1957, Follett's Modern American Usage, 1966. Trustee NY Soc. Libr., 1968-97; adv. coun. U. Buckingham. Decorated Legion of Honor; recipient Presdl. medal of Freedom; Extraordinary fellow Churchill Coll., U. Cambridge (Eng.). Fellow Royal Soc. Arts, Royal Soc. Lit.; mem. Soc. Am. Historians, Mass. Hist. Soc. (corr.), AAAL (pres. 1972-75, 77-78), Am. Philos. Soc., Am. Acad. for Liberal Edn. (hon. pres.), Acad. Delphinale (Grenoble), Century Assn., Phi Beta Kappa.

BASA, ENIKÖ MOLNÁR, retired librarian; b. Huszt, Hungary, Sept. 7, 1939; came to the U.S., 1950; d. Julius Valentine and Terézia (Fejér) Molnár; m. Péter Basa, Nov. 19, 1966. BA, Trinity Coll., 1962; MA, U. N.C., 1965, PhD, 1972. Instr. U. Md., College Park, 1965-69; asst. prof. Dunbarton Coll., Washington, 1970-72; lectr. Am. U., Washington, 1972-75, Hood Coll., Frederick, Md., 1975-76; editor, serials cataloger Libr. of Congress, Washington, 1977—2003; ret., 2004. Mem. symposium Libr. Congress, 1996; lectr. U. Debrecen, Hungary, 2004, vis. lectr. U. Szeged, 2004 Author: Sandor Petőfi, 1980; editor: Twayne World Authors, 1974—, Hungarian Literature, 1993; translator: (play) Screenplay from Örkény, 1983; assoc. editor The Comparatist, 1976-82, editorial bd., 1992—; jour. rev. editor: Hungarian Studies Newsletter, 1975-82; guest editor: Rev. Nat. Lits., 1992; contbr. chpts. to books and articles and book revs. to profl. jours. Recipient Gold medal Pres. of Republic of Hungary, 1997; Kluge Staff fellow Libr. of Congress, 2002-03. Mem. MLA (Hungarian sect. chair 1980, 90), So. Comparative Lit. Assn. (founding v.p. 1977-79, 89—, sec.-treas. 1985-89, pres. 1992-94), Am. Hungarian Educators Assn. (pres. 1974-80, 88-92, exec. dir. 1980—), Internat. Assn. Hungarian Studies, Libr. Congress Profl. Assn. (v.p. 1991, pres. 1996). Avocations: reading, travel, needlecrafts. Home: 4515 Willard Ave Apt 2210 Chevy Chase MD 20815-3685 E-mail: eniko.basa@verizon.net.

BASAGNI, STEFANO, computer engineer, educator; arrived in U.S., 1996; s. Paolo Basagni and Renata Belloni. BS in Computer Sci., U. Pisa, Italy, 1991; PhD in Computer Sci., U. Milan, Milan, Italy, 1998; PhD in Elec. Engring., U. Tex., Dallas, Richardson, 2001. Asst. prof. computer sci. The U. Tex., Dallas, Richardson, Tex., 2000—01; asst. prof. computer engring. Northeastern U., Boston, 2002—. Mem.: IEEE (sr.), Am. Soc. for Engring. Edn., Assn. for Computing Machinery (sr.). Achievements include research in geo-based routing. Office: Northeastern University 312 Dana 360 Huntington Ave Boston MA 02115 Office Phone: 617-373-3061. Business E-Mail: basagni@acm.org.

BASÁÑEZ, MIGUEL EBERGENYI, political scientist, educator; b. Tuxpan, Ver, Mex., Oct. 24, 1947; came to U.S., 1995; s. Miguel Sorcini and Magdalena Ebergenyi Basáñez; m. Tatiana Beltran, Feb. 7, 1970; children: Tatiana, Alejandro, Pamela, Nicolas. BA in Law, UNAM, Mexico City, 1969; MA in Adminstrn., U. Warwick, Coventry, Eng., 1974; PhD in Polit. Sci., London Sch. Econs., 1991. Prof. U Nat. Autonoma Mex., U. Autonoma Estado Mex., Inst. Tech., Mexico City and Toluca, 1975-95; atty. gen. State of Mex., Toluca, 1985-86; chief of staff Ministry of Energy, Mexico City, 1986-88; pres. Mori-Mexico, Mexico City, 1988—2002; vis. prof. U. Mich., Ann Arbor, 1995-96; sr. v.p. MORI-Internat., Princeton, NJ, 1996—98; CEO MORI-USA, Princeton, 1998-2000; CEO, Global Quality Rsch. Corp., Princeton, 2000—. Pub. Este Pais mag., Mexico City, 1990-95; bd. dirs. Serfin Bank, Mexico City, 1986-88, Mexican-Am. Binat. Found., Mexico City/Washington D.C., 2002. Co-author: Human Beliefs and Values, 2004, North American Trajectories, 1996; author: El Pulso de Los Sexenios, 1990, La Lucha por La Hegemonia, 1981, Asia Barometer, 2005. Pres. Acude-Alianza Democratica, Mexico City, 1992-93, LSE Alumnai in Mex., Mexico City, 1980-83; del. PRI, Mex., 1970-72. Recipient Nat. prize Nat. Pub. Adminstrn. Inst., 1982. Mem. World Assn. for Pub. Opinion Rsch. (pres. 1999-2000, Nelson award 1993), Am. Polit. Sci. Assn., Am. Assn. for Pub. Opinion Rsch., Latin Am. Studies Assn. Avocations: photography, water-skiing, computers, films. Office: Global Quality Rsch Corp 116 Village Blvd Ste 200 Princeton NJ 08540-5740 Home Phone: 917-225-7282; Office Phone: 609-818-1531.

BASAVAPPA, RAVI, biophysical science educator; b. Bangalore, India, Feb. 7, 1961; arrived in U.S., 1968; BS, Duke U., 1980; MS, Clemson U., 1983; PhD, U. Chgo., 1991. Postdoctoral fellow Harvard Med. Sch., Boston, 1991—95; asst. prof. dept. biochemistry and biophysics U. Rochester (N.Y.) Med. Ctr., 1995—2002, assoc. prof., 2002—04; program dir. NIH, 2004—. Rsch. scholar Leukemia and Lymphoma Soc. Am. Contbr. articles to sci. jours. Postdoctoral fellow NIH, 1992-95, rsch. grantee, 1998—. Mem. Am. Crystallograpers Assn. Achievements include research in biochemistry and biophysics. Office: NIH Gen Scis 2AS 19C 45 Center Dr Bethesda MD 20892

BASBAUM, ALLAN I., medical educator, researcher; PhD, U. Penn., 1972. Prof. anatomy & physiology U. Calif. San Francisco, 1977—; chair anatomy dept. U. Calif. San Francisco Sch. Medicine, 1997—. Former bd. dirs., treas. Internat. Assoc. for the Study of Pain (IASP); editor-in-chief PAIN, 2003—. Contbr. scientific papers; co-author: Towards a New Pharmacotherapy of Pain, 1990. Pub. lectr. Soc. Neuroscience, 1986; John J. Bonica Lectr. IASP Congress, San Diego, 2002. Recipient Career Devel. award, NIH, 1978—83, Jacob Javits Investigator award, 1985—99, Alfred P. Sloan Fellow, 1979—81, Frederick W. L. Kerr Meml. award, Am. Pain Soc., 1993, Bristol-Myers Squibb prize, 1994. Fellow: Am. Acad. Arts & Sciences; mem.: W.M. Keck Found.Ctr. Integrative Neuroscience, Inst. Medicine. Mailing: UCSF Dept of Anatomy Box 0452 513 Parnassus Ave San Francisco CA 94143-0452 Office Phone: 415-476-5270, 415-476-4311. E-mail: aib@phy.ucsf.edu.

BASCH, RICHARD VENNARD, photographer, producer, writer, director; b. Inpls., Jan. 22, 1945; s. Richard and Helen Louise (Vennard) B.; m. Meredith Baker, Feb. 12, 1966; 1 child, Nicholas; m. Vicki Sylvester, Aug. 15, 1977. Cert., U. Fine Arts, Perugia, Italy, 1965, London Film Sch., 1966; BA, Antioch Coll., 1968; DFA, London Inst. for Applied Rsch., 1995. Dir. filmmaker tng. Am. Film Inst., Washington, 1968-69; instr. film history R.I. Sch. Design, Providence, 1970-73; cons. in theatre Antioch Coll., Yellow Springs, Ohio, 1976-77; prin., photographer Richard Basch Studio, Washington, 1979—2005. Dir. film programs Brown U., 1972-73; cons. Smithsonian Instn., Washington, 1979—. Author: Faces of Fairmont Heights,

1970; producer (films) The Burning Issue, 1984, Notes from the Future, 1996. Mem. Am. Soc. Mag. Photographers. Episcopalian. Office Phone: 520-829-4606. Business E-Mail: watchthebirdie@baschstudio.com.

BASCOM, C. PERRY, retired foundation administrator; b. Boston, July 30, 1936; s. William Richardson and Jean Ames (Hall) B.; m. Sally Cissel Greenwood, July 18, 1995; children: Elisabeth Brooke, Heather Ames, Sarah Duff Greenwood, Amy Greenwood Dunaway. BA, Yale U., 1958; LLB, Harvard U., 1961. Assoc. Bryan Cave, St. Louis, 1962-72, ptnr., 1972-95; adminstr. Gateway Found., St. Louis, 1995—2001, ret., 2001. Judge St. Louis Night Housing Ct., 1970-72; lectr. on various topics, including Truth in Lending, Real Estate Settlement Procedures Act, techniques in comml. bank lending, devels. in Mo. banking law, electronic funds transfers. Sr. warden Trinity Ch., St. Louis, 1974-78. Served with USAR, 1961-68. Mem. Mo. Bar Assn. Home: 4650 Pershing Pl Saint Louis MO 63108-1908 Personal E-mail: scgcpb@earthlink.net.

BASCOM, RUTH F., retired mayor; b. Ames, Iowa, Feb. 4, 1926; d. Frederick Charles and Doris Hays Fenton; m. John U. Bascom, June 14, 1950; children: Lucinda, Rebecca, Ellen, Thomas, Paul, Mary. BS, Kans. State U., Manhattan, 1946; MA, Cornell U., 1949. Tchr. Dickinson County Cmty. H.S., Kans., 1946-48, Nat. Coll. Edn., Chgo., 1949-51. Co-chair Cascadia High Speed Rail, 1995-98. Chair City and State Bicycle Com., 1971-83; chair Met. Park Bd., Eugene, 1972-82; bd. pres. Youth Symphony, 1962-68; city councilor City of Eugene, Oreg., 1984-92, coun. v.p., pres., 1988-90, mayor, 1993-97; v.p., pres. LWV, Eugene, 1967-69; chair Oreg. Passenger Rail Com., 2000-05; state bd. 1000 Friends of Oreg., 1999-05. Recipient Gold Leaf award Internat. Soc. Arboriculture, 1993, Parks Heroes award, 2007; dedicated Ruth Bascom Riverbank Trail Sys., 2003, Disting. Svc. award U. Oreg., 2007. Democrat. Congregationalist. Avocations: music, tree farm, bicycling. Home: 2114 University St Eugene OR 97403-1542 E-mail: jbascomr@pacinfo.com.

BASDEN, CAMERON, dancer; b. Dallas; Student, Joffrey Ballet Sch., 1976-77. Dancer Dallas Ballet, 1975-76, Joffrey II Dancers, NYC, 1977-79, Joffrey Ballet, NYC, 1979—, asst. ballet mistress, 1990-93, ballet mistress NYC, Chgo.; 1993—. Prof. dance Manhattanville Coll. Actor: (films) The Company, 2003. Office: Joffrey Ballet 70 E Lake St Fl 1300 Chicago IL 60601-5917

BASDEO, SAHADEO, government official, educator, politician; b. Rousillac, Trinidad and Tobago, Sept. 10, 1945; s. Basdeo and Ramrajie (Mongru) Seusaran; m. Beverley Shirleen, Aug. 14, 1971; children: William Shastri Narin, Deven Marshall, Kristen Gene Santosh. BA in History and Polit. Sci., Brandon U., Manitoba, Can., 1970; MA in Caribbean Labor and Brit. Imperial History, U. Calgary, Alberta, Can., 1972; PhD in Caribbean Labor History, Dalhousie U., Halifax, NS, 1975. Lectr. in history St. Benedict's Coll., La Romaine, Trinidad and Tobago, 1964-67; teaching asst. U. Calgary, Alberta, Canada, 1970—72; analyst ednl. program Ministry of Edn., Manitoba, Canada, 1975-76; dir. rsch. in edn. Provincial Govt. Manitoba, 1976-78; cons. to sch. divs. Manitoba, Canada, 1976-78; lectr. in history and contemporary politics U. W.I., Trinidad and Tobago, 1978-88; senator Parliament of Trinidad and Tobago, 1981-86, Govt. of Trinidad and Tobago, 1986—91, min. of external affairs and internat. trade, 1988-91; sr. lectr. inst. internat. rels. U. of The West Indies, 1992—94; prof. history and internat. rels. U. BC Okanagan, Kelowna, Canada, 1994—. Mem. pub. accountr com., pub. accounts enterprises com., Parliament of Trinidad and Tobago, 1981-86; mem. exec. com. Commonwealth Parliamentary Assn., Trinidad and Tobago, 1986—89; chmn. standing ocm. Carribean Fgn. Mins., 1988-89; chmn. Carribean Community Coun. Trade Mins., 1989-90; leader nat. dels., internat. confs. on trade and polit. co-operation; participant spl. internat. peace assignments Orgn. of Am. States, Caribbean Community, Grenada, 1983, Panama, Haiti, 1989. Author: Labour Organization and Labour Reform in Trinidad, 1919-1939, 2003, The Foreign Relations of Trinidad and Tobago, 1962-2000, 2001, The Case of the Small State in the Global Arena, 2001, Canada, the United States and Cuba: An Evolving Relationship, 2002; contbr. articles to profl. jours. Chmn. Nat. Alliance for Reconstruction Party. Recipient Lions Club award Brandon U., 1968, Rotary Club award Brandon U., 1968, Meritorious and Yeoman Svc. to the Cause of the Sch., Community and Country award St. Benedict's Coll. Past Students' Assn., 1986, rsch. grant U. Calgary, 1971; grad. teaching fellow U. Calgary, 1970-72; recipient numerous scholarships, Brandon U., Dalhousie U., 1967-75. Mem. Assn. Caribbean Historians, Trinidad Country Club, Trinidad Golf Club. Mem. Nat. Alliance for Reconstruction Party. Hindu. Avocations: golf, swimming, cricket. Office: U BC Okanagan 3333 College Way Kelowna BC Canada V1V 1V7 Office Phone: 250-807-9352. Business E-Mail: sahadeo.basdeo@ubc.ca.

BASE, GRAEME ROWLAND, illustrator, author; b. Amersham, Eng., Apr. 6, 1958; s. Geoffrey Donald and Elizabeth Enid (Philips) B.; m. Robyn Anne Paterson, Aug. 1, 1981; children: James Geoffrey, Katherine Gabrielle, William Alexander. Art diploma, Swinburne Inst. Tech., 1978. Author (illustrator): My Grandma Lived in Gooliguich, 1983, Animalia, 1983 (Australian Children's Book award Children's Book Coun. Australia, 1987, Kids Own Australia Literature award, 1988), The Eleventh Hour: A Curious Mystery, 1988 (Australian Children's Book award Children's Book Coun. Australia, 1989, Book Design award Australian Book Pub. Assn., 1988, Young Australian Best Book award, 1989, Kids Own Australia Literature award, 1989), The Sign of the Seahorse, 1992, The Disovery of Dragons, 1996, The Worst Band in the Universe, 1999, The Water Hole, 2001, Truckdogs, 2003, Jungle Drums, 2004, Uno's Garden, 2006; illustrator Adventures with My Best Worst Friend, 1982, The Island Bike Business, 1982, Jabberwocky From "Through the Looking Glass", 1985, Jabberwocky: A Book of Brillig Dioramas, 1996. Office: Penguin Australia 250 Camberwell Rd Camberwell VIC 3124 Australia

BASERGA, RENATO LUIGI, pathology educator; b. Meda, Milan, Italy, Apr. 11, 1925; came to U.S., 1949; s. Alessandro and Giuseppina (Annoni) B.; m. Jane Conrad, Dec. 23, 1954 (div. Sept. 1974); children: Susan Jane, Janice Rene; m. Beverly Lange, Oct. 12, 1974. MD, U. Milan, 1949. Diplomate Am. Bd. Pathology. Resident U. Milan, 1949-51; intern Columbus Hosp., Chgo., 1952-53; assoc. in oncology Chgo. Med. Sch., 1953-54; resident pathology St. Luke's Hosp., Chgo., 1955-58; instr. pathology Northwestern U., Chgo., 1958-60, asst. prof., 1960-64, assoc. prof., 1964-65; prof. Temple U., Phila., 1965-91, chmn. dept. pathology, 1980-91; prof. microbiology Thomas Jefferson Univ., Phila, 1991—2000, disting. prof., 2000—; dep. dir. Kimmel Cancer Ctr., 1991—2004, interim dir., 2004—. Cons. Argonne (Ill.) Nat. Lab., 1959-65; sr. investigator Fels Rsch. Inst., Temple U., 1965-91; Louis Gross Meml. lectr. NYU, 1974; Searle lectr. Brit. Soc. Cell Biology, 1976; Wellcome vis. prof., 1984. Author: Autoradiography Techniques and Applications, 1969, Multiplication and Division in Mammalian Cells, 1976, The Biology of Cell Reproduction, 1985; editor: The Cell Cycle and Cancer, 1971. Served with vol. forces, 1943-45, Italy. Recipient rsch. career devel. award USPHS, 1964-65, Samuel Noble Found. award, 1989, Rous-Whipple award, 1990, Fred Stewart award, 1990; Maria Antoinetta Della Casa scholar, Milan, 1951; sr. rsch. fellow USPHS, 1958-60, Schiffer Meml. Lectr. Internat. Cell Soc. award, 1992, Susan Swerling lectureship Dana-Farber Cancer Ctr., 1993. Fellow AAAS. Office: Kimmel Cancer Inst Bluemle Life Scis Bldg 233 S 10th St Fl 6 Philadelphia PA 19107-5541

BASFAR, HASSAN OMAR, communications educator; PhD, U. Ill., 1996. Prof. King Abdulaziz U., Jeddah, Saudi Arabia, 1996—. Recipient Outstanding award, King Abdulaziz U., 1998—2000. Mem.: Saudi Assn. Media and Communication (gen. sec. Makkah region 2005—). Office: King Abdulaziz U PO Box 118333 Western Province Jeddah 21312 Saudi Arabia Office Phone: 009662-6121272. Office Fax: 009662-6121272. Business E-Mail: hassanbasfar@yahoo.com.

BASH, FRANK NESS, astronomer, educator; b. Medford, Oreg., May 3, 1937; s. Frank Cozad and Kathleen Jane (Ness) B.; m. Susan Martin Fay, Sept. 10, 1960; children: Kathryn Fay, Francis Lee BA, Willamette U., 1959; MA in Astronomy, Harvard U., 1962; PhD, U. Va., 1967; DSc (hon.), Willamette U., 2000. Staff scientist Lincoln Lab. MIT, 1962; assoc. astronomer Nat. Radio Astronomy Obs., Green Bank, W.Va., 1962-64; rsch. asst. U. Va., 1965-67; postdoctoral faculty assoc. U. Tex., Austin, 1967-69, asst. prof. astronomy, 1969-73, assoc. prof., 1973-81, prof., 1981—, Frank N. Edmonds Regents prof., 1985—2006, Edmonds Regents prof. emeritus, 2006—, chmn. dept. astronomy, 1983-86, dir. W.J. McDonald Obs., 1989—2003. Mem. astronomy adv. panel NSF, 1988-91; chmn. vis. com. Nat. Radio Astronomy Obs., 1990, mem., 1990-93; mem. vis. com. Arecibo Obs., 1990-95, chmn., 1994; mem. planning com. NASA Astrophys. Data Systems, 1991-95; bd. dirs., mem. rep. Assoc. Univs. for Rsch. in Astronomy, 1995-2000; chmn. bd. dirs. Hobby-Eberly Telescope, So. African Large Telescope. Author: (with Daniel Schiller and Dilip Balamore) Astronomy, 1977; contbr. articles to profl. jours. Grantee NSF, 1967—, The Netherlands NSF, 1979, W.M. Keck Found., 1988. Mem. Am. Astron. Soc. (councillor 1996-98), Astron. Soc. Pacific (bd. dirs. 1995-97, v.p. 1997-99, pres. 1999-2000), Internat. Astron. Union, Internat. Sci. Radio Union, Tex. Assn. Coll. Tchrs. (pres. U. Tex. chpt. 1980-82), Tex. Philos. Soc., Town and Gown Club (Austin). Office: U Tex McDonald Obs Mail Code C1402 Austin TX 78712 Home Phone: 512-327-3720; Office Phone: 512-471-3373. Business E-Mail: FNB@astro.as.utexas.edu.

BASHA, EDWARD N., JR., grocery chain owner; CEO Bashas Inc., Chandler, Ariz., chmn. Dir. Pinnacle West Capital Corp. Recipient Disting. Svc. award, Nat. Art Edn. Assn., 1992. Office: Bashas Inc 22402 S Basha Rd Chandler AZ 85248

BASHAM, W. RALPH, federal agency administrator; b. Owensboro, Ky. m. Judith A. O'Bryan; 3 children. BA in Bus. Adminstrn., Southeastern U. Various positions to deputy asst. dir. for trng. US Secret Svc., US Dept. Treasury, Washington, 1993-94, spl. agent in charge Office of Investigations Washington, Louisville, 1970-74, 76-79, 86-87, 90-92, spl. agt. of Protective support divsn. Washington, 1974-76, spl. agt., asst. spl. agt. in charge Vice Presdl. Protective Svc., 1979-83, dep. chief Fin. Mgmt. Divsn., 1983-85, spl. agt. in charge of Vice Presdl. Protective Svc. Washington, Cleve., 87-89, 92-93, spl. agt. in charge of Dignitary Protective Divsn. Washington, 1989-90, asst. dir. for adminstrn., 1994-98, insp. Office of Inspections, 1985-86; dir. Fed. Law Enforcement Tng. Ctr. US Dept. Treasury, Glynco, 1998—2001; dir. US Secret Svc. US Dept. Homeland Security, Washington, 2003—06, chief of staff, Transp. Security Adminstrn., 2002—03, commr. US Customs & Border Protection, 2006—. Recipient Meritorious Presidential Rank award, 1992, 2000. Mem. Sr. Exec. Svc.

BASHAW, DANIEL JAMES, investigator; s. Gerald Arthur and Elinor June Bashaw; 1 child, Daniel J. Jr. 1 stepchild, John S. Barton. BS, SUNY, Oswego, 1971. Investigator-in-charge Office Fed. Investigations, Norfolk, Va., 1978—89; spl. investigator US Investigation Svcs., Malone, 1989—. Mem.: Sons of Am. Legion, Elks. Avocations: reading, billiards, exercise, hiking. Office Phone: 518-483-8625. Office Fax: 518-483-1884.

BASHI, VILNA FRANCINE, sociology professor; d. Frank George Simmons and Vilna Joanetta Welch; m. Christian Treitler, Aug. 17, 2004; 1 child, Jannik Vincent Bashi Treitler. BA, U. South Fla., Tampa, 1982; MA, Columbia U., NYC, 1985; MS, U. Wis., Madison, 1991, PhD, 1997. Asst. prof. Northwestern U., Evanston, Ill., 1997—2000, Rutgers U., New Brunswick, NJ, 2000—07; assoc. prof. Baruch Coll. and CUNY Grad. Ctr., N.Y.C., 2007—. Author: Survival of the Knitted: Immigrant Social Networks in a Stratified World, 2007. Grantee Sociology Panel award, NSF, 2006—. Mem.: Soc. Advancement Socio-Econs., Internat. Sociol. Assn., Am. Sociol. Assn. (sec. sect. racial and ethnic minorities 2004—), Assn. Black Sociologists (life).

BASHIR, MARTIN, news correspondent; b. London, Jan. 19, 1963; BA in English, King's Coll., London. Journalist BBC, London; corr. ITV, London, 1999—2004; corr. 20/20 ABC News, NYC, 2004—, co-anchor Nightline, 2005—. Presenter (documentary film series) Serial Killer Dr. Harold Shipman, Soho Bomber David Copeland, Loyalist Terrorist Johnny Adair, Norfolk Farmer Tony Martin, 1999, (3-part documentary series) The Organ Farm, 2001, (documentary) Living with Michael Jackson, 2003, featured in (movie) Mike Bassett-England Manager, 2001; author: (publs. including) The Financial Times, The Sunday Times, The Standard, The Sunday Express, The Tatler, The Observer. Vol. various charitable insts. for children with physical disabilities and mental illnesses. Nominee BAFTA award; named Journalist of Yr. award, Royal Television Soc., 1996; recipient, BBC's Internat. Awards, 1998. Fellow: Royal Soc. London. Office: ABC News 77 W 66th St New York NY 10023

BASHIRI, IRAJ, Central Asian studies educator; b. Behbahan, Iran, July 31, 1940; arrived in U.S., 1966; s. Muhammad and Robab Bashiri; m. Carol L. Sayers, Apr. 18, 1968; children: Mariam, Manuchehr, Mehrdad. BA cum laude, Pahlavi U., Shiraz, Iran, 1963; MA, U. Mich., 1968, PhD, 1972; PhD in History and Culture (hon.), Tajikstan State U., 1996. Coord., tchr. Peace Corps, Brattleboro, Vt., 1967—68; asst. prof. Iranian studies U. Minn., Mpls., 1972—77, coord. Mid. East studies program, 1975—77, assoc. prof. Iranian studies, 1977—87, acting chair South Asian studies, 1990—91, assoc. chair Russian and Ea. European studies, 1987—90, acting chair Russian and Ea. European studies, 1990—91, assoc. prof. Ctrl. Asian studies, 1987—96, prof. Ctrl. Asian studies, 1996—, interim dir. Inst. of Linguistics, ESL, Slavic lang. and lits., 2005—07, prof. history, 2007—. Rev. bd. Internat. Rsch. and Exch. Bd. for Tajikistan, Princeton, NJ, 1991—; editor bilingual series Mazda Pub., Encino, Calif., 1985-90; selection com. MacArthur Found., Mpls., 1990-91, internat. seminar, 1990; prof. internat. rels. Kyrgyz State Nat. U., 1998-99; assoc. prof. Iranian studies U. Tex., Austin, Tex., 1982, chmn. Slavic and Ctrl. Asia langs. and lit., 1997-98; hon. internat. academician Acad. Sci. Tajikistan, 1996—. Author: Fiction of Sadeq Hedayat, 1984, The Black Tulip (English, Persian), 1985, Firdowsi's Shahname: 1000 Yrs. After, 1994, 2d edit., 2003, Kamal Khujandi: Epoch and its Importance in the History of Ctrl. Asian Civilization, 1996, The Samanids and the Revival of the Civilization of Iranian Peoples, 1998, 2002, The Nowruz Scrolls, 2001; editor: The Pearl Canon, 1986, History of a Nat. Catastrophe, 1996, Tajikistan in the 20th Century, 2002, Beginnings to AD 2000: A Comprehensive Chronology of Ctrl. Asia, Afghanistan and Iran, 2001, The Nowruz Scrolls (English, Russian, Tajiki, Persian), 2002, Prominent Tajik Figures of the 20th Century, 2003;: From the Hymns of Zarathustra to the Songs of Borbad, 1995, 2003; contbr. articles to profl. jours. Recipient: Disting. Tchg. award, Coll. Liberal Arts, 1980; Internat. Edn. Travel grant U. Minn., 1990-92; IREX resident scholar, Tajikistan, 1993-94. Fellow Mid. East Studies Assn.; mem. Am. Inst. Iranian Studies (trustee 1975-79), Assn. for Ctrl. Asian Studies, Assn. Advancement Ctrl. Asian Rsch. (chair devel. com. 1990—), Am. Assn. Tchrs. of Slavic and Ea. European Langs. Avocations: writing realist fiction, painting, fishing, travel. Home: 518 8th St SE Minneapolis MN 55414-1208 Office Phone: 612-624-3314. Business E-Mail: bashi001@umn.edu.

BASHKOW, JACK SIMON, musician; b. Bklyn., Dec. 7, 1954; s. David and Sylvia Bashkow; m. Lorraine Shemesh, Sept. 12, 1993. Student, Queens Coll., 1972—74, Columbia U., 1991—93. Mem. orch. West Side Story traveling road co., 1978—79, Richard III with Kevin Kline, NYC, 1984, Big River Broadway co., NYC, 1985, Grease Broad co., NYC, 1997—98, Footloose Broad co., NYC, 1999, Fosse Broadway co., NYC, 2000, Annie Get Your Gun Broadway co. with Reba McEntire, NYC, 2001, Hairspray -Broadway co., NYC, 2002—03, Laughing Room Only - Broadway co., 2003—, Bklyn. - The Musical - Broadway Co., 2004—05, The Wedding Singer Broadway Co., 2006, Jersey Boys Broadway Co., 2006. Music prodr. Moo Music Prodns.; performed Tony Awards Show in Jersey Boys, N.Y.C., 2006, Kennedy Ctr. in Mark Twain Awards Honoring Neil Simon, Washington, 2006, Westport Playhouse, Conn., 2007, Curtains Broadway Co., NYC, 2007, Grease Broadway Co., NYC, 2007. Recording credits include albums with: Jane Olivor, 1982, Keith Richards, 1992, Lionel Hampton, 1999, performed with: Aretha Franklin, The Temptations, The Four Tops, Cyndi Lauper, Natalie Cole, Manhattan Transfer, Michael Bolton, Darlene Love, Peter Allen, others, musician for numerous TV comms.;. Nominee Helen Hayes award for Outstanding Musical Direction. Home and Office: 22 W 30th St # 4-5 New York NY 10001-4423 Office Phone: 212-517-1000. Personal E-mail: JBashkow@aol.com.

BASHKOW, THEODORE ROBERT, electrical engineering consultant, former educator; b. St. Louis, Nov. 16, 1921; s. Maurice Louis and Caroline (Davidson) B.; m. Delphina Brownlee, Sept. 12, 1960; 1 stepdau., Lynn Michele. BS, Washington U., St. Louis, 1943; MS, Stanford U., 1947, PhD, 1950. Mem. tech. staff David Sarnoff Research Labs., RCA, 1950-52, Bell Telephone Labs., 1952-58; mem. faculty Columbia U., 1958-91, prof. elec. engring., 1967-79, prof. computer sci., 1979-91, chmn. dept. elec. engring., 1968-71, mgr. Sch. Engring. Computing Center, 1961-64. Cons. to industry, 1959—; dir. MSI Inc., Woodside, N.Y., 1961—; chmn. tech. program 1968 Spring Joint Computer Conf.; chmn. sci. sect. Internat. Fedn. Info. Processing Congress, 1965 Author articles, chpts. in books. Served to 1st lt. USAAF, 1943-45. Mem. Assn. Computing Machinery, IEEE, Profl. Group Circuit Theory and Electronic Computers. Home: 92 Jay St Katonah NY 10536-3729

BASHSHUR, RASHID L., health facility administrator, educator; arrived in U.S., 1956; s. Lutfallah M. and Yamna D. Bashshur; m. Naziha S. Sima'an, Sept. 15, 1957; children: Ramona R., Noura R. PhD, U. Mich., 1962. Prof. health mgmt. and policy U. Mich., Ann Arbor, 1977—; dir. telemedicine U. Mich. Health Sys., Ann Arbor, Mich., 1998—. Staff assoc. Inst. of Medicine, NAS, Washington, 1970—72. Editor in chief: eHealth Internat. Jour. Pres. Am. Telemedicine Assn., Washington, 2000—02, pres. emeritus. Grantee Effects of Telemedicine on Cost, Quality and Access, Health Care Financing Adminstrn., 1996—98. Achievements include first original evaluation of telemedicine in the U.S. Avocations: watercolor painting, swimming. Office: Telemedicine Resource Ctr 300 N Ingalls 8B07 Ann Arbor MI 48109-0402

BASHWINER, STEVEN LACELLE, lawyer; b. Cin., Aug. 3, 1941; s. Carl Thomas and Ruth Marie (Burlis) B.; m. Arden J. Lang, Apr. 24, 1966 (div. 1978); children: Heather, David; m. Donna Lee Gerber, Sept. 13, 1981; children: Margaret, Matthew. AB, Holy Cross Coll., 1963; JD, U. Chgo., 1966. Bar: Ill. 1966, U.S. Dist. Ct. (no. dist.) Ill. 1967, U.S. Dist. Ct. (ea. dist.) Wis. 1988, U.S. Dist. Ct. (no. dist.) Calif. 1994, U.S. Dist. Ct. (ea. dist.) Mich. 2003, U.S. Ct. Appeals (7th cir.) 1968, U.S. Ct. Appeals (4th cir.) 1990, U.S. Supreme Ct. 1970. Assoc. Kirkland & Ellis, Chgo., 1966-72, ptnr., 1972-76, Friedman & Koven, Chgo., 1976-86, Katten Muchin Rosenman LLP, Chgo., 1986—. Bd. dirs. Constl. Rights Found., Chgo. Served to sgt. USAFR, 1966-72. Mem. ABA, 7th Cir. Bar Assn., Chgo. Bar Assn., Chgo. Inn of Ct. (pres. 2004-05), Lawyers Club Chgo. Home: 834 Green Bay Rd Highland Park IL 60035-4630 Office: Katten Muchin Rosenman LLP 525 W Monroe St Ste 1900 Chicago IL 60661-3693 Home Phone: 847-432-0671; Office Phone: 312-902-5330. Business E-Mail: steven.bashwiner@kattenlaw.com.

BASICH, RICHARD B., mathematics professor; b. Sewickley, Pa., Jan. 21, 1952; s. Rudolph and Pauline Basich; m. Cheryl G. Goll, June 26, 1976; children: Christopher W., Jonathan M. BS in Edn., Clarion U., 1973; MA in Math., John Carroll U., 1979. Tchr. Thomas W. Harvey H.S., Painesville, Ohio, 1973—90; prof. Lakeland C.C., Kirtland, Ohio, 1990—. Math. cons. Sci., Engring., Math., and Aerospace Acad., Cleve., 1996—2002. Recipient Disting. Svc. award for Faculty, Lakeland C.C., 1999, Excellence in Tchg. award, 2001. Mem.: Ohio Coun. Tchrs. Math., Am. Math. Assn. Two-Yr. Colls., Math. Assn. Am., Nat. Coun. Tchrs. Math. Avocation: music. Home: 1230 Dorothea Dr Painesville OH 44077 Office: Lakeland Community College 7700 Clocktower Dr Kirtland OH 44094 Personal E-mail: rbasich@hotmail.com. Business E-Mail: rbasich@lakelandcc.edu.

BASICHIS, GORDON ALLEN, writer, scriptwriter, novelist, marketing consultant, media consultant; b. Phila., Aug. 23, 1947; s. Martin and Ruth (Gordon) B.; m. Marcia Hammond; 1 child, Casey James. BS, Temple U., 1969. Reporter Phila. Bull., 1969; writer, reporter Santa Fe News, 1971-72; with advt., pub. rels. Jay Bernstein Pub. Rels., LA, 1978-80; screenwriter MGM Feature Films, Culver City, Calif., 1982—83; exec. dir. media and mktg. Laclede, Inc., 2002—04. Exec. v.p. Antigua Rd. Prodns., 1996; sr. v.p. market Nextworld Entertainment Zone; pres. Big Venus Entertainment, 2003; co-founder CorraGroup, 2005. Author: Constant Travelers, 1978, Beautiful Bad Girl: The Vicki Morgan Story, 1985, Chinese Takeout, 2007, Sleeping with Snakes, Notes from the Los Angeles Underbelly, 2007; screenwriter: Breach of Trust, 1995; exec. prodr.: Land of Dreams, 2001. Mem. ASCAP, Writers Guild Am. West, Am. Film Inst., Simon Wiesenthal Inst., Ellis Island Found., Authors' Guild. Office: PO Box 1511 Beverly Hills CA 90213-1511 Office Phone: 310-966-1556. Business E-Mail: gordonb@corragroup.com. E-mail: gabasichis@vzavenue.net.

BASIL, DOUGLAS CONSTANTINE, writer, educator; b. Vancouver, BC, Can., May 30, 1923; s. William and Christina (Findlay) B.; m. Evelyn Margaret Pitcairn, 1950; 1 child Wendy Patricia. B.Commerce, U. B.C., 1949; BA, 1949; PhD, Northwestern U., 1954; postgrad., London Sch. Econs., 1950. Instr. Marquette U., 1951-54; asst. prof. Northwestern U., 1954-57; asso. prof. U. Minn., 1957-61; prof. mgmt. U. So. Calif., 1961-88, prof. emeritus, 1988—. Cons. mgmt. devel.; lectr., Brussels, Caracas, Bogota, Paris, London, others. Author: Executive Development, 1964, (Paul Cone, John Fleming) Effective Decision Making Through Simulation, 1972, Organacao E Controls Da Pequena Empresa, 1968, La Direccion de la Pequena Empresa, 1969, Managerial Skills for Executive Action, 1970, Leadership Skills for Executive Action, 1971, Women in Management: Performance, Prejudice, Promotion, 1972, Autorite Personnelle et Efficacite des Cadres, 1972, Conduccion y Liderazgo, 1973, Developing Tomorrow's Managers, 1973, Management of Change, 1974, others.; Contbr. (Paul Cone, John Fleming) articles to profl. jours. Served to capt. Canadian Army, 1943-46. Home: 636 Nuttal St Westfield IN 46074

BASILE, PAUL LOUIS, JR., lawyer; b. Oakland, Calif., Dec. 27, 1945; s. Paul Louis and Roma Florence (Paris) B.; m. Linda Lou Paige, June 20, 1970; m. 2d Diane Chierichetti, Sept. 2, 1977. BA, Occidental Coll., 1968; postgrad., U. Wash., 1969; JD, UCLA, 1971. Bar: Calif. 1972, U.S. Dist. Ct. (ctrl. dist.) Calif. 1972, U.S. Dist. Ct. (no. dist.) Calif. 1985, U.S. Ct. Appeals (9th cir.) 1972, U.S. Tax Ct. 1977, U.S. Ct. Claims. 1978, U.S. Customs Ct. 1979, U.S. Ct. Customs and Patent Appeals 1979, U.S. Ct. Internat. Trade 1981, U.S. Supreme Ct. 1977; cert. specialist in taxation law Bd. of Legal Specialization, State Bar of Calif. Assoc. Parker, Milliken, Kohlmeier, Clark & O'Hara, LA, 1971-72; corp. counsel TFI Cos., Inc.,

Irvine, Calif., 1972-73; pvt. practice LA, 1973-80, 90-96, 98-99; mem. Basile & Siener, LA, 1980-86, Clark & Trevithick, LA, 1986-90, Tyre Kamins Katz & Granof, LA, 2004—; ptnr. Wolf, Rifkin & Shapiro, LA, 1990, Basile & Lane, LLP, LA, 1996-97; of counsel Wolf, Rifkin & Shapiro, LA, 1990-92, Shaffer, Gold & Rubaum, L.L.P., LA, 1996—2004; sr. ptnr. Basile & Assocs., LA and Pasadena, Calif., 1999—2004; pres., CEO, dir. 765 Inc., Cliffside Park, NJ, 1997—. Gen. counsel J.W. Brown, Inc., LA, 1980—, asst. sec., 1984—92; sec., gen. counsel Souriau, Inc., Valencia, Calif., 1981—90; v.p., sec., dir., gen. counsel Pvt. Fin. Assocs., LA, 1983—94; gen. counsel Quest Relocation Group, LA, 1994—97, v.p. real estate, 1996—2004. Trustee, sec. Nat. Repertory Theatre Found., 1975-94, mem. exec. com., 1976-94, chmn. bd. dirs., 1991-94; mem. fin. com., bd. dirs. Calif. Music Theatre, 1988-92; bd. dirs. March of Dimes Birth Defects Found., Los Angeles County, 1982-87, mem. exec. com., 1983-86, sec., 1985-86; dist. fin. chmn. L.A. Area coun. Boy Scouts Am., 1982-83; trustee Occidental Coll., L.A., 1989-94; active L.A. Olympic Organizing Com., Ketchum Downtown YMCA, Vols. Am. L.A., others; mem. Kenyon Coll. Parents Adv. Coun., 2003-05, regional parents chmn., 2004—. Fellow: Am. Coll. Tax Counsel; mem.: ABA (chmn. subcom. on continuing legal edn. 1990—94, chmn. subcom. on estate planning 1992, taxation sect., corp. tax. com., vice chmn. closely held bus. com. 1992—94, chair 1994—96, sec. 1996—97, small firm lawyers com., bus. law sect., real property sect., estate planning and drafting, pre-death planning issues com., probate and trust law sect., spl. problems of bus. owners com.), State Bar Calif. (bus. law sect., non profit and unincorporated orgns. com. 1989—92, taxation law adv. commmn. 1994—97, vice chmn. 1995—96, chair 1996—97, mem. bd. legal specialization 1996—97, taxation sect., estate planning, trust and probate sect.), L.A. County Bar Assn. (law sect., sole practitioner sect. exec. com. 1995—99, taxation sect., com. on closely-geld and pass-through entities, bus. and corps.), Beverly Hills Bar Assn. (vice chmn. Estate and Gift Tax Com. 1998—99, exec. com. trust and estates planning sect. 2004—, exec. com. taxation sect. 2004—, law practice mgmt. sect.), Can. Calif. C. of C. (dir. 1980—89, 2d v.p. 1983—84, 1st v.p. 1984—85, pres. 1985—87), Occidental Coll. Alumni Assn. (alumni bd. govs. 1977—81, v.p. 1978—79, pres. 1979—80, chmn. ann. fund campaign 1990—91), Small Bus. Coun. of Am., Inc. (legal adv. bd. 1989—2004, dir. 2004—), Attys. for Family Held Enterprises, Estate Counselors Forum L.A. (sec.-treas. 2003—04, pres. 2004—05, 2006—), The Group, Inc, (dir. 2003—), Grand People (bd. dirs. 1985—92, chmn. bd. 1986—92), L.A. Area C. of C. (dir. 1980—81), L.A.-Vancouver Sister City Assn. (treas. 1987—89, dir., exec. c om. 1987—92, pres. 1989—92), French-Am. C. of C. (councilor 1979—84, v.p. 1980, 1982—84), Rotary Club of L.A. (vice-chmn. pres. com. 1985—86, sgt.-at-arms 1986—87, chmn. golf com. 1986—87, chmn. vols. Am. of L.A. com. 1989—90, chmn. world cmty. svc. com. 1991—93, chmn. gateway com. 1993—94, dir. 1994—96), Rotary Internat. (chmn. gift of life com. 1992—93, cmty. svc. dir. 1993—95, chmn. club extension com. 1995—96). Democrat. Baptist. Home: 3937 Beverly Glen Blvd Sherman Oaks CA 91423-4404 Office: Tyre Kamins Katz Granof 1880 Century Pk E Ste 300 Los Angeles CA 90067-1666 Office Phone: 310-553-6822. Business E-Mail: pbasile@tyrekamins.com.

BASINGER, KIM (KIMILA ANN BASINGER), actress; b. Athens, Ga., Dec. 8, 1953; d. Don Basinger; m. Ron Snyder-Britton, Oct. 1980 (div. Dec. 1988); m. Alec Baldwin, August 19, 1993 (div. Feb. 2002), child, Ireland. Student, Neighborhood Playhouse, NYC. Model Eileen Ford Agy., NYC, 1972-77; ind. actress, 1977—. (feature films) Hard Country, 1981, Mother Lode, 1982, Never Say Never Again, 1983, The Man Who Loved Women, 1983, The Natural, 1984, Fool for Love, 1985, 9 1/2 Weeks, 1986, No Mercy, 1986, Blind Date, 1987, Nadine, 1987, My Stepmother Is an Alien, 1988, Batman, 1989, The Marrying Man, 1991, Final Analysis, 1992, Cool World, 1992, The Real McCoy, 1993, Wayne's World 2, 1993, The Getaway, 1994, Ready to Wear (Prêt-à-Porter), 1994, L.A. Confidential (Golden Globe award for best supporting actress, 1998) (Academy Award for best supporting actress, 1998), 1997, I Dreamed of Africa, 2000, Bless the Child, 2000, 8 Mile, 2002, People I Know, 2002, The Door in the Floor, 2004, Elvis Has Left the Building, 2004, Cellular, 2004, The Sentinel, 2006, Even Money, 2006; (TV series) Dog and Cat, 1977; TV films include Katie-Portrait of a Centerfold, 1978, The Ghost of Flight 401, 1978, Killjoy, 1981, The Mermaid Chair, 2006; (TV miniseries) From Here to Eternity, 1980; (TV appearances) Gemini Man, 1976, Charlie's Angels, 1976, The Six Million Dollar Man, 1977, McMillan and Wife, 1977, Vega$, 1978, The Simpsons (voice only), 1998, 2002.

BASINGER, RICHARD LEE, lawyer; b. Canton, Ohio, Nov. 24, 1941; s. Eldon R. and Alice M. (Bartholomew) B.; m. Rita Evelyn Gover, May 14, 1965; children: David A., Darron M. BA in Edn., Ariz. State U., 1963; postgrad. Macalester Coll., 1968-69; JD, U. Ariz., 1973. Bar: Ariz. 1973, US Dist. Ct. Ariz. 1973, US Tax Ct. 1977, US Ct. Appeals (6th cir.) 1975, US Ct. Appeals (9th cir.) 1976, US Supreme Ct. 1977; cert. arbitrator, Assoc. law offices, Phoenix, 1973-74; pvt. practice, Scottsdale, Ariz. 1974-75; pres. Basinger & Assocs., P.C., Scottsdale, 1975—, also bd. dirs. Contbr. articles to profl. jours. Bd. dirs. Masters Trail Ventures, Scottsdale, 1984-85, Here's Life, Ariz., Scottsdale, 1976-84; precinct committeeman Rep. Party, Phoenix, 1983-85, Kingman, 2003—; bd. dirs. Ariz. Coll. of Bible, 1992-93. NSF grantee, 1968-69. Mem. ABA, Ariz. Bar Assn., Ariz. State Horseman's Assn. (bd. dirs. 1984-86, 1st v.p. 1986), Mohave County Bar Assn., Kingman Mohave Lions Club (pres. 2004-05), Mohave Rep. Forum (v.p. 2003-07), Western Saddle Club (bd. dirs. 1983-86, pres. 1985-86). Home and Office: Basinger Legal Svcs PLC 441 Astor Ave Kingman AZ 86409-3514 Home Phone: 928-692-9458; Office Phone: 928-692-4771. Office Fax: 928-692-7663.

BASINGER, WILLIAM DANIEL, computer programmer; b. Washington, Feb. 14, 1952; s. James Samuel and Eleanor (Freeburger) B.; m. Martha Kecskes, July 1, 1978 (div. 1983); m. Mary Teresa Richardson, June 11, 1988. BA in Linguistics, U. Md., 1974; MS in Linguistics, Georgetown U., 1977; MS in Computer Sci., Johns Hopkins U., 1989; PhD in Computer Sci. (hon.), Yorker Internat. U., Milan, Italy, 2006. Programmer Evaluation Techs., Arlington, Va., 1977—78; programmer, analyst, cons. Vitro Corp., Silver Spring, Md., 1978—84, 1987—88; programmer, analyst Tracor Applied Scis., Rockville, Md., 1984—88, PRC, Inc., McLean, Va., 1988—89; sr. programmer, analyst Sys. & Computer Tech. group George Washington U., Washington, 1989—95; sr. programmer, statistician PRC, Inc., Reston, 1996—97; sr. sys. analyst, Yr. 2000 Assessment Project M-Cubed Info. Sys., Rockville, 1997—2000; sr. computer specialist, statistician VGS, Fairfax, Va., 2000—01; statistician U.S. Dept. Transp., 2001—02; sr. computer specialist Ajilon Cons., Rockville, 2002—03, Sci. Applications Internat. Corp. (formerly VGS Inc.), San Diego, 2003—06; cons. in applications software Montgomery Public Schs., 2007—, tutor in math. and stats., instr., 2007—. Cons. applications software dept. geology George Washington U., Washington, 1990-91, 1993-04. Contbr. articles to profl. jours. Contbr., sponsor Statue of Liberty/Ellis Island Found., N.Y.C., 1985—. Md. State Sen. scholar U. Md., 1970-74. Mem. Assn. Computing Machinery, Am. Geophys. Union, Am. Statis. Assn., NY Acad. Scis., Math. Assn. Am., Nat. Assn. Pastoral Musicians, Am. Chem. Soc., Friends of Dresden Soc. Republican. Roman Catholic. Avocations: viola, violin, bridge, poetry, philosophy. Home: Apt 203 11342 Cherry Hill Rd Beltsville MD 20705-3735 Office Phone: 301-890-0524. Personal E-mail: wdbasinger@hotmail.com.

BASINSKI, ANTHONY JOSEPH, lawyer; b. Pitts., Apr. 11, 1947; s. Anthony F. and Emily C. (Klocko) B.; m. Elisabeth Fawcett, Oct. 4, 1980; children: Ann Elisabeth, Robert Anthony. BA, U. Pitts., 1969, JD, 1974. Bar: Pa. 1974, U.S. Dist. Ct. (we. dist.) Pa. 1974, U.S. Ct. Appeals (3d cir.) 1981, U.S. Ct. Appeals (4th cir.) 1992, U.S. Ct. Appeals (fed. cir.) 1995. Law clk. to presiding justice Pa. Supreme Ct., Pitts., 1974-76; ptnr. Reed, Smith, Shaw and McClay, Pitts., 1976—2004; spec. counsel Pietragallo, Bosick & Gordon, Pitts., 2004—. Served with U.S. Army, 1969-71, Vietnam. Mem. Allegheny County Bar Assn., Pa. Bar Assn., Am. Arbitration Assn. (arbitrator 1983—). Democratic. Roman Catholic. Home: 1749 Tupper Dr Pittsburgh PA 15241-2623 Office: Pietragallo Bosick & Gordon One Oxford Centre 38th Fl Pittsburgh PA 15219 Office Phone: 412-263-4346. Business E-Mail: ajb@pbandg.com.

BASKA, JAMES LOUIS, wholesale grocery company executive; b. Kansas City, Kans., Apr. 3, 1927; s. John James and Stella Marie (Wilson) B.; m. Juanita Louise Carlson, Oct. 14, 1950; children: Steven James, Scott David. BSBA, U. Kans., 1949; JD, U. Mo., 1960. Bar: Kans. 1960. Pres., chief exec. officer Baska Laundry Co., Kansas City, 1951-62; ptnr. Rice & Baska, Kansas City, 1962-76; corporate sec., gen. counsel Assoc. Wholesale Grocers Inc., Kansas City, 1976-77, v.p., sec., gen. counsel, 1977-79, exec. v.p., chief fin. officer, sec., gen. counsel, 1979-84, pres., chief exec. officer, 1984-92; pres. emeritus, 1992. Mem. SDC com. Wakefern Food Corp., 1998-2005; bd. dirs. Raley's, Riverwood Homes, Inc. Served as staff sgt. U.S. Army, 1944-46. Mem. Nat. Grocers Assn. (bd. dirs. 1980-89, chmn. 1987-88), Food Mktg. Inst. (bd. dirs. 1988-93). Republican. Roman Catholic. Avocations: hunting, golf. Office: Assoc Wholesale Grocers Inc PO Box 2932 5000 Kansas Ave Kansas City KS 66106-1135 *There is always room at the top and my objectives whatever they may be and no matter how big or wild, are always attainable. The only questions are— am I ready to make the move and willing to pay the price?.*

BASKAKOV, ILIA V., biotechnologist, researcher; b. Vladimir, Russia, Oct. 4, 1969; arrived in US, 1996; s. Vladimir I. Baskakov and Zinaida V. Baskakova. MS (hon.), Lomonosov Moscow State U., 1992; PhD (hon.), Shemyakin Inst. Bioorganic Chemistry, Moscow, 1996. Postdoctoral fellow U. Tex. Med. Br., Galveston, 1996—98, U. Calif., San Francisco, 1999—2001; asst. prof. U. Md. Biotechnology Inst., Balt., 2001—06, assoc. prof., 2006—. Mem. study sect. NDGB, NIH, Bethesda, Md., 2006—. Contbr. more than 50 articles to profl. jours. Recipient Grad. award, George Soros Internat. Sci. Found., 1995; grantee, NIH, 2003—; postdoctoral fellow, John Douglas French Alzheimer's Found., 1999—2000. Achievements include first to generated first synthetic mammalian prions, which proved the protein-only hypothesis of prion propagation; patents for composition and method for monitoring in vitro conversion of full-length mammalian prion protein to amyloid form with physical properties of PrPSc. Office: U Md Biotechnology Inst 725 W Lombard St Baltimore MD 21201 Home Phone: 410-739-5490; Office Phone: 410-706-4562. Office Fax: 410-706-8184. Business E-Mail: baskakov@umbi.umd.edu.

BASKERVILL, CHARLES THORNTON, lawyer; b. South Boston, Va., May 26, 1953; s. William Nelson and Julia Alice (Moore) B.; m. Pamela Temple Shell, July 17, 1976; children: Ann Cabell, Susannah Thornton. BA, Hampden-Sydney Coll., 1975; JD, U. Richmond, 1978. Bar: Va. 1978, U.S. Dist. Ct. (ea. dist.) Va. 1978. Assoc. White, Hamilton, Wyche & Shell, P.C., Petersburg, Va., 1978-96; asst. commonwealth's atty Petersburg, Va., 1985—2005; assoc. Shell, Johnson, Andrews, Baskervill & Baskervill, P.C., Petersburg, Va., 1996-2001, Shell, Johnson, Andrews & Baskervill, P.C., Petersburg, Va., 2001—. Commr. of accts. City of Petersburg, Va., 1996—. Former dir. Petersburg Crime Prevention Found.; bd. trustees Mary Baldwin Coll., 2003—; bd. dirs. Va. Conf. Commrs. of Accounts, 2007-. Named to Athletic Hall of Fame, Hampden-Sydney Coll., 1988. Mem. Prince George County Bar Assn. (sec.-treas. 1990-91, pres. 1991-92), Petersburg Bar Assn. (pres. 2001-02). Methodist. Avocations: golf, tennis. Office: Shell Johnson Andrews Baskervill PC 43 Rives Rd Petersburg VA 23805-9255 Office Phone: 804-732-8384.

BASKERVILLE, LEZLI, educational association administrator; BA, Douglass Coll.; JD cum laude, Howard U. Law Sch. Law clk. DC Ct. Appeals; staffer US Congress; mem. appellate team Lawyers Com. Civil Rights Under Law; exec. dir. Nat. Black Leadership Roundtable; nat. legis. counsel NAACP; adminstrv. appeals judge employee appeals Washington; founding mem. The Baskerville Group; v.p. govt. relations The Coll. Bd., 1999—2003; outside counsel Nat. Assn. for Equal Opportunity in Higher Edn., prog. dir., legal rsch. assoc. for prof. Herbert O. Reid, Sr. Silver Spring, Md., interim pres., 2004, pres., CEO, 2004—; mem. brief writing team in Bakke, Weber and Fullilove cases. Named one of nation's top 10 black women in higher edn., AOL Black Voices, 100 Most Influential Black Ams., Ebony mag., 2006; named to The Ebony Power 150, 2007. Achievements include being first female president of the National Association for Equal Opportunity in Higher Education. Office: Nat Assn for Equal Opportunity in Higher Edn 209 Third St SE Washington DC 20003 Office Phone: 202-552-3300. Office Fax: 202-552-3330.*

BASKETT, MARY WELSH, art dealer, consultant; b. Binghamton, NY, Sept. 2, 1940; d. Frank Hughes Welsh Jr. and Mary Duyckinck VanDerbeek; m. William Denny Baskett III, Aug. 31, 1963; 1 child, Frank Burcham. BA, Wellesley Coll., Mass., 1962; MA, U. Hawaii, Honolulu, 1966. Curator of prints Cin. Art Mus., 1965—71; cons. Japanese prints Phila. Mus. Art, 1970—80; cons. prints Sotheby Parke Bernet, NYC, 1975—77; curator Japanese paper Mus. Contemporary Crafts, NYC, 1975—77; cons. spl. exhbns. Isetan Dept. Store, Tokyo, 1977—78; owner, dir. Mary Baskett Gallery, Cin., 1977—. Adj. prof. U. Cin., 1969—88; lectr. Japanese art history Cln. Art Acad., 1965—71; curator of prints Columbus Gallery Fine Art, Ohio, 1972—75; vis. scholar Calif. State U., Sacramento, 1990. Author: The Art of June Wayne, 1968, Footprints of the Buddha., 1980, John Henry Twachtman, Etchings, 1999; contbr. articles to profl. jours.; exhbn. collection contemporary Japanese clothes Cin. Art Mus., 2007. Bd. dirs. Warwick Found., Salvisa, Ky., 1987—, Cin. Opera, 1999—2003. Mem.: Taft Art Mus., Contemporary Art Ctr. (Cin.), Cin. Art Mus. Republican. Presbyterian. Avocations: swimming, walking. Home and Office: Mary Baskett Gallery 1002 St Gregory St Cincinnati OH 45202 Office Phone: 513-421-0460. Office Fax: 513-421-0466. Personal E-mail: baskett@fuse.net.

BASKIES, JEFFREY ALAN, lawyer; b. Malden, Mass., Feb. 6, 1966; s. Jack Steven and Bethann (Kravetz) B.; m. Nancy Lynn Alpern, Feb. 29, 1992; children: Jessica Marie, Jon Douglas. BA with highest honors, Trinity Coll., 1988; JD cum laude, Harvard U., 1991. Bar: Fla. 1991, Mass. 1991. Ptnr. Ruden, McClosky, Smith, Schuster & Russell, P.A., Ft. Lauderdale, Fla., 1991, Ruden McClosky, Ft. Lauderdale, Fla. Contbr. articles to profl. jours. Residential campaign chairperson United Way South Palm Beach County, Boca Raton, Fla., 1993-97, Kids in Distress (adv. coun.), Palm Beach County (chair, planned gifts com.) Named a Fla. Super Lawyer, 2006; named one of Top 100 Attys., Worth mag., 2005—06, Legal Elite Fla., Trend mag., 2006. Mem. ABA (chair probate and trust law com. young lawyers divsn. 1994-96), Am. Cancer Soc. (chair planned gifts com. 1993-97, bd. dirs. 1994-97, v.p. 1996-97, pres. 1998—), Fla. Bar Assn., Broward County Bar Assn., Boca Raton C. of C. (chair west area com. 1995-96), Jewish Fedn. Greater Ft. Lauderdale (chair profl. adv. com. found. 1998—, bd. trustees 1998—), Anti-Defamation League (chair planned gifts com. 1994-97), Coun. Villages, Inc., Broken Sound Country Club (bd. dirs. 1994-96, sec. 1994-97, treas. 1995-96), Phi Beta Kappa, Pi Gamma Mu, Broward County Estate Planning Coun. (treas., bd. dirs.), Alzheimers Assn., Planned Giving Coun. Broward County (bd. dirs.). Office: Ruden McClosky 200 E Broward Blvd PO Box 1900 Fort Lauderdale FL 33301 Office Phone: 954-527-2488. Office Fax: 954-333-4088. E-mail: Jeff.Baskies@Ruden.com.*

BASKIN, C. R., civil engineer; b. Houston, Mar. 6, 1926; s. Charles Todd and Bessie Emma (Heilig) B.; m. Peggy June Holden, Dec. 31, 1952; children: Richard Karl, Sheila Frances. BSCE, La. State U., 1953. Design engr. City-Parish Dept. Pub. Works, Baton Rouge, 1953-57; city engr. City of Plaquemine, La., 1957-58; sect. head, asst. chief engr. Tex. Bd. Water Engrs., Austin, 1958-62; asst. chief engr. Tex. Water Commn., Austin, 1962-65; asst. chief engr., chief engr. Tex. Water Devel. Bd., Austin, 1965-77; dir. data and engring. svcs. divsn. Tex. Dept. Water Resources, Austin, 1977-83; spl. asst. Office of Asst. Dir. Info. Sys./U.S. Geol. Survey, Reston, Va., 1983-92; ret., 1992. Chmn. Tex. Mapping Adv. Com., 1968-83; chmn. water oriented data programs sect. Tex. Interagy. Coun. on Natural Resources and the Environment, 1968-72, Tex. Natural Resources Info. System Task Force, 1972-83; mem. Non-Fed. Adv. Com. on Water Data for Public Use, 1970-83; chmn. Water Data Coordination Task Force, Interstate Conf. on Water Problems, 1975-83. Contbr. articles to profl. jours. With U.S. Army, 1944-47, POW; commd. Adm. Tex. Navy, 1961. Recipient John Wesley Powell award U.S. Geol. Survey, 1972, Combat Inf. badge. Mem.: Am. Ex-POWs, Sigma Tau Sigma (pres. 1950), Phi Eta Sigma, Chi Epsilon, Tau Beta Pi (chpt. pres. 1950), Phi Kappa Phi. Adventist (elder). Avocations: photography, walking. Home: 304 N Woodlake Dr Columbia SC 29229-8932

BASKIN, MAURICE, lawyer; b. Miami, Fla., June 25, 1954; BA magna cum laude, Harvard U., 1975; JD with honors, U. Fla., 1978. Bar: DC, Md., Fla., US Dist. Ct. Md., US Dist. Ct. DC, US Ct. Appeals (1st, 3d, 4th, 6th, 7th, 9th cirs.), US Supreme Ct., US Ct. Appeals (8th cir.), US Ct. Appeals (DC cir.). Assoc. Pierson, Ball & Dowd, Washington, 1978-81, Venable LLP, Washington, 1981-87, ptnr. Labor & Employment Dept., 1987—. Mem. Labor & Employment Lawyers Adv. Com., Nat. Assn. Mfrs.; legal sect. governing coun. ASAE; adj. prof. labor law Georgetown U. Law Ctr., 1981—87; moderator labor and employment law Counsel Connect. Mem. ABA (chmn. labor rels. divsn. constrn. industry forum 1992-95, chm. constrn. labor com. pub. contract law sect.), U.S. C. of C. (labor rels. com.). Office: Venable LLP 575 7th St NW Washington DC 20004 Office Phone: 202-344-4823. Office Fax: 202-344-8300. E-mail: mnbaskin@venable.com.

BASKIN, OTIS WAYNE, business educator; b. Houston, Oct. 26, 1945; s. Samuel and Ollie Estell (Key) B.; m. Maryan Kay Patrick, Dec. 26, 1970. BA, Okla. Christian Coll., 1968; MA, U. Houston, 1970; PhD, U. Tex., 1975. Asst. prof. Tex. Luth. Coll., Seguin, 1970-75; prof. U. Houston, 1975-87; prof., acad. dir. Ariz. State U., Phoenix, 1987-91; prof., dean Memphis State U., 1991-92, prof., dir. family bus., 1992-95; dean George L. Graziadio Sch. Bus. and Mgmt. Pepperdine U., Malibu, Calif., 1995-2001, prof. mgmt., 1995—. Vis. faculty U. Md., London, 1979, Oxford U., 1994; ons. Ministry Trade, Sophia, Bulgaria, 1990, Utara U., Malaysia, 1992; spl. advisor to the pres. AACSB Internat.; bd. dirs. Emrise, Corp. Author: Guidelines for Research in Business Communication, 1977, (with Craig Aronoff) Interpersonal Communication in Organizations, 1980, Getting Your Message Across, 1981, Public Relations: The Profession and the practice, 1983, (with Grover Starling) Issues in Business and Society: Capitalism and Public Purpose, 1985, (with Craig Aronoff) Effective Leadership in the Family Business, 2005; contbr. articles to profl. jours. Bd. dirs. Jr. Achievement Memphis, 1991-92, Econ. Club Memphis, 1991-94, Margurite Piazza Gala for St. Jude's Hosp., Memphis, 1992-95, Durham Found., Memphis, 1992-95, World Affairs Coun. Ventura County, 2001, L.A. Econ. Devel. Corp., 2000-02, EMRISE Corp., 2004-. Recipient Advancing Pub. Rels. Through Rsch. award Tex. Pub. Rels. Soc., Houston, 1983. Mem. Acad. Mgmt. (divsn. chair 1985), Rotary, Sigma Iota Epsilon (bd. dirs. 1986—), Beta Gamma Sigma. Mem. Ch. of Christ. Avocations: reading, travel. Office: George L Graziadio Sch Bus & Mgmt Pepperdine Univ Malibu CA 90263 Home Phone: 310-506-7321; Office Phone: 310-506-8541. Business E-Mail: Otis.Baskin@pepperdine.edu.

BASKIN, RONALD JOSEPH, biophysicist educator, dean; b. Joliet, Ill., Nov. 25, 1935; s. Mack Robert and Evelyn Josephine (Rudzinski) B.; m. Lydia Olga Lendl, Mar. 29, 1957; children— Ronald James, Thomas William. AB, UCLA, 1957; MA, 1959, PhD, 1960. Asst. prof. biology Rensselaer Poly. Inst., Troy, NY, 1961-64; asst. prof. zoology U. Calif., Davis, 1964-67, assoc. prof., 1967-71, prof., 1971—, chmn. dept. zoology, 1971-78, assoc. dean coll. letters and sci., 1986-90. Mem. editorial bd. U. Calif. Press. Contbr. articles to sci. publs. Nat. Heart Inst. predoctoral fellow, 1957-60 Mem. Biophys. Soc., Soc. Cell Biology, Am. Physiol. Soc., N.Y. Acad. Scis., Sigma Xi. Office: Molecular & Cellular Biology Sect U Calif Davis CA 95616 Office Phone: 530-752-1554. E-mail: rjbaskin@ucdavis.edu.

BASKIN, SCOTT DAVID, lawyer; b. NYC, Oct. 24, 1953; s. George and Anne (Strauss) B.; m. Sherry Nahmias, Mar. 13, 1982; children: Jonathan, Felicia. BA, Stanford U., 1975; JD, Yale U., 1978. Bar: Calif. 1978, U.S. Dist. Ct. (ctrl., ea., so. and no. dists.) Calif. 1979, U.S. Appeals (2d and 9th cirs.) 1979. Law clk. Hon. Herbert Choy, 9th Cir. Ct., Honolulu, 1978-79; ptnr. Irell & Manella, Newport Beach, Calif., 1979—. Lectr. Calif. Continuing Edn. of the Bar, 1985—. Contbr. articles to profl. publs. Office: Irell & Manella 840 Newport Center Dr Ste 400 Newport Beach CA 92660-6323 Home Phone: 949-760-5139; Office Phone: 949-760-5239, 949-760-0991. Business E-Mail: sbaskin@irell.com.

BASKIN, VICTORIA, child and adolescent psychiatrist; b. Kaliningrad, Russia, Aug. 31, 1952; arrived in US, 1993; d. Mark Monin and Bertha Umantseva; m. Simon Baskin, Apr. 23, 1971; 1 child, Anna. MD with honors, Dnepropetrovskaja Medicinskaja Academija, Ukraine, 1975. Intern Children's Hosp. #3, Dnepropetrovsk, Ukraine, 1975—76; pediatrician Children's Hosp. #2, Dnepropetrovsk, Ukraine, 1976—87, child and adolescent psychiatrist, 1987—93; adult psychiatrist Wayne State U., Detroit, 2001—04, child and adolescent psychiatrist, 2004—. Clin. dir. Children's Hosp. #2, Dnepropetrovsk, 1982—87. Family edn. and counseling group Univ. Psychiat. Ctr., Livonia, Mich., 2004—05. Mem.: AMA, Am. Acad. Child and Adolescent Psychiatry (resident award 2004), Am. Psychiat. Assn. Avocations: reading, travel, exercise, cooking. Home: 29557 Sierra Pointe Cir Farmington Hills MI 48331 Office: Univ Psychiat Ctr-Livonia 16836 Newburgh Rd Livonia MI 48154 Office Phone: 734-464-7660 ext. 107. Office Fax: 734-464-5885. E-mail: victoriabaskin@hotmail.com.

BASKIND, SAMANTHA, art historian; b. Pitts., May 26, 1970; BA, U. Pa., 1992; MA, U. NC, 1996, PhD, 2001. Asst. prof. Cleve. State U., 2004—07, assoc. prof., 2007—. Vis. asst. prof. James Madison U., Harrisonburg, Va., 2001—02, U. Miami, Coral Gables, 2003—04. Author: Raphael Soyer and the Search for Modern Jewish Art, Encyclopedia of Jewish American Artists; contbr. more than 60 articles and revs. to jours. and encys.; editor: (U.S. art) Encyclopaedia Judaica. Active Jewish Cmty. Fedn. Cleve. Fellow, Am. Coun. Learned Socs., Terra Found. Arts, 2000—01, Meml. Found. Jewish Culture, 2004, Soc. Preservation Am. Modernists, 2005. Mem.: Am. Acad. Religion, Assn. Historians Am. Art, Assn. Jewish Studies, Coll. Art Assn. Office: Cleve State U 2307 Chester Ave Cleveland OH 44114 Office Phone: 216-687-2096. E-mail: s.baskind@csuohio.edu.

BASKINS, ANN O'NEIL, lawyer, former computer company executive; b. Red Bluff, Calif., Aug. 5, 1955; m. Thomas C. DeFilipps. AB in Hist., Stanford U., 1977; JD, UCLA, 1980. Bar: Calif. 1980. Assoc. Crosby, Heafey, Roach & May, 1980—81; atty. Hewlett-Packard Co., Palo Alto, Calif., 1982—85, sr. atty., 1985—86, asst. sec., 1985—99, corp. counsel, 1986—99, corp. sec., 1999—2006, sr. v.p., gen. counsel, 2000—06. Mem.: ABA, Assn. Gen. Counsel, Am. Soc. Corp. Secs., Am. Corp. Counsel Assn.

BASKIR, LAWRENCE M., federal judge; b. Bklyn., Jan. 10, 1938; s. Philip and Florence B.; m. Marna S. Tucker, May 13, 1973. AB magna cum laude, Princeton U., 1959; LLB, Harvard U., 1962. Bar: N.Y. 1963, D.C. 1964, U.S. Supreme Ct. 1968. Assoc. Weaver and Glassie, 1963-65; counsel Ho. Reps. Judiciary Com., 1965-66; chief counsel Constl. Rights Subcommittee, US Senate, 1968-74; dir. Presdl. Clemency Bd., 1974-75; faculty fellow U. Notre Dame, 1975-77; dep. asst. sec. US Dept. Treasury, Washington, 1977-79; legis. dir. Senator Bill Bradley, 1979-80; sole practice Washington, 1981-93; prin. dep. gen. counsel US Army, 1994-98; judge US Ct. Fed. Claims, Washington, 1998—, chief judge, 2000—02. Adj. prof. Georgetown Law Center, Cath. U. Law Sch.; cons. US Senate Intelligence Com., ABA Contbr. articles to profl. jours.; author: Reconciliation After Vietnam, 1977, Chance and Circumstance: The Draft, the War and the Vietnam Generation, 1978. Grantee, Ford Found., 1975—77. Office: US Ct Fed Claims 717 Madison Pl NW Washington DC 20439-0002 Office Phone: 202-357-6500.

BASLAW-FINGER, ANNETTE, education educator, consultant; b. Paris, Oct. 11, 1929; arrived in U.S., 1943; d. David and Shulamit Notik Szer; m. Seymour Maxwell Finger, June 12, 1988 (dec. July 2005); m. Alfred A. Baslaw, Feb. 11, 1951 (dec. July 6, 1978); children: Robin, Michele Friedman, David. BA, Bklyn. Coll., 1951; MA, Hofstra U., NYC, 1965; PhD (with distinction), NYU, 1969. Exec. sec. L.R. Dooley, Inc., NYC, 1951—52; French copywriter Morse Internat., NYC, 1952—54; French tchr. Glen Cove (N.Y.) HS, 1958—65, Roslyn (N.Y.) HS, 1969; dir. French edn. Columbia Tchrs. Coll., NYC, 1969—73; chairperson fgn. lang. and internat. edn. NYU, 1973—77, dir. fgn. lang. and bilingual edn., 1977—94; ret., 1994. Contbr. articles to profl. jours. Ann. spkr. Long Island and N.J. Schs., 1995—2003, Temple Sholom, Pompano Beach, Fla., 1998—2006. Decorated Order Palmes Academiques France; Danforth fellow, 1965—69. Mem.: MLA (bd. dirs.), N.Y. State Assn. Fgn. Lang. Tchrs. (bd. dirs.), Am. Assn. Tchrs. of French (pres. LI chpt.), Mus. Jewish Heritage, Inst. on Mediterranean Affairs at UN (dep. to pres.), Pi Delta Phi, Kappa Delta Pi (pres.), Phi Beta Kappa, Pi Lambda Theta (pres. Rho chpt.). Avocations: travel, ballet, theater, art, books. Home: 133 N Pompano Beach Blvd Pompano Beach FL 33062

BASLER, LINDA GERBER, retired elementary school educator; b. Harrisburg, Pa., Oct. 10, 1942; d. Boyd Bushey and Evelyn Romaine (Coulson) Gerber; m. Lawrence Edward Basler, Aug. 14, 1965; children: Elizabeth Wilson, Anne Marie. BS, Shippensburg U., 1964, MS. Tchr. Shippensburg Area Schs., 1964—99. Sch. bd. mem. (facilities, athletic, transp., budget, student rels. coms.) Shippensburg Area Schs., 2001—05, after sch. program, 2004—06, pres. after sch. program, 2006—07; bd. mem. Shippensburg Pub. Libr., 2001—06, sec. bd. trustees; 1964 reunion com. mem. Shippensburg U., alumni bd. mem., 2006—; lectr. and greeter Meml. Luth. Ch., Shippensburg, 1969—2005, building com. Mem.: PSERS, Shippensburg Area Edn. Assn., Pa. State Edn. Assn., NEA, Red Hat Soc. Republican. Lutheran. Avocations: reading, travel. Home: 11 Wooded Dr Shippensburg PA 17257 Personal E-mail: lelgb@supernet.com.

BASMAJIAN, JOHN VAROUJAN, medical researcher, educator; b. Constantinople, Turkey, June 21, 1921; came to Can., 1923, naturalized, 1927; s. Mihran and Mary (Evelian) B.; m. Dora Belle Lucas, Oct. 4, 1947; children: Haig, Nancy, Sally. MD with honors, U. Toronto, 1945; LLD (hon.), Queen's U., 1999; DSc (hon.), McMaster U., 2001. Intern Toronto Gen. Hosp., 1945; surg. resident Sunnybrook Hosp. and Hosp. for Sick Children, Toronto, 1946-48; from lectr. to prof. U. Toronto, 1949-57; prof. anatomy, chmn. dept. anatomy Queen's U., Kingston, Ont., 1957-69; prof., dir. regional rehab. rsch. and tng. ctr. Emory U., Atlanta, 1969-77; prof. medicine McMaster U., Hamilton, Ont., 1977-86, prof. emeritus, 1986—2004; dir. rehab. ctr. Chedoke-McMaster Hosps., 1977-86; ret. Exec. sec. Banting Rsch. Found., Toronto, 1954-57; chmn. rsch. com. Fitness Coun. Can., Ottawa, Ont., 1965-69; spl. cons. med. rsch. Ga. Inst. Tech., Atlanta, 1984-90; dir. rsch. and tng. grants Ea. Seal Rsch. Inst., Toronto, 1990-95; bd. dirs. Can. Physiotherapy Found., Toronto, 1984-89; lectureships in Europe, Asia, South Am., Australia, Japan, others. Author 11 med. sci. and clin. books in multiple edits. and transls., 1953—; editor 9 med. clin. books in multiple edits., and transls., 1977—; series editor: Rehabilitation Medicine Library, 24 vols., 1977—; editl. bd. Am. Jour. Phys. Medicine, 1968-90, Am. Jour. Anatomy, 1971-74, Electromyography and Clin. Neurophysiology, 1966-85, Electro-diagnostic-therapy, Physiotherapy Can., 1979-84, Jour. Motor Behavior, 1980—, Med Post; assoc. editor Anat. Record, 1970-73, 77—, BMA Audiotape Series, 1970-77; contbr. articles to profl. jours.; prodr. several motion pictures; inventor sci. and med. devices and techniques. Mem. and chmn. Bd. Edn., Kingston, Ont., 1960-68; founding chmn. bd. govs. St. Lawrence Coll. Applied Arts and Tech., Ont., 1964-69. Served to capt. M.C., Can. Army, 1943-46 Decorated officer Order of Ont., officer Order of Can.; recipient awards including Starr Gold medal U. Toronto, 1957, Kabakjian award Armenian Youth Fedn., 1967; NRC (Can.) vis. scientist Soviet Acad. Scis., 1963, Henry Gray Laureate, 1991,. Fellow Am. Acad. Angiology, Royal Coll. Physicians (Can.), Royal Coll. Physicians and Surgeons (Glasgow, hon.), Royal Coll. Physicians (Edinburgh, hon.), Physicians Coll. Rehabilitative Medicine (Australia, hon., Edinburgh, hon.); mem. Am. Assn. Anatomists (pres. 1985-86, Henry Gray Laureate award 1991), Can. Assn. Anatomists (founding, sec. 1965-69, J.C.B. Grant award 1985), Am. Congress Rehab. Medicine (Gold Key award 1977, Coulter lectr. 1988), Biofeedback Soc. Am. (founding, pres. 1978-79), Internat. Soc. Electromyographic Kinesiology (founding, pres. 1955-60), Order St. John of Jerusalem (hon. life mem.), Am. Orthopedic Foot Soc. (hon. life), Australian Biofeedback Soc. (hon. life), Venezuelan Biofeedback Soc. (hon. life), Mex. Soc. Anatomy (hon. life), Columbian Assn. Phys. Medicine (hon. life), Physiotherapy Assn. North Greece (hon. pres. 1995—). Avocations: travel, music, gardening, writing.

BASOMBRIO, JUAN C., lawyer; b. 1964; BA in Polit. Sci., Univ. Houston, 1986; JD, Ind. Univ., 1989. Bar: Minn. 1989, Calif. 1991, US Supreme Ct. 1992. Ptnr.-in-charge So. Calif. office Dorsey & Whitney LLP, Irvine, Calif., 2001—03, ptnr. trial dept., 1998—, mem. policy com., 2003—05. Office: Dorsey & Whitney LLP 38 Technology Dr Irvine CA 92618-5310 Office Phone: 949-932-3650. Office Fax: 949-932-3601. Business E-Mail: basombrio.juan@dorsey.com.

BASON, GEORGE R., JR., lawyer; b. NYC, 1954; AB magna cum laude, Harvard U., 1975, JD cum laude, 1978. Bar: N.Y. 1979, U.S. Dist. Ct. (so. and ea. dists.) N.Y. 1979; cert. Avocat à la Cour de Paris 1992. Assoc. Davis Polk & Wardwell, NYC, 1978-85, assoc.-Paris Office, 1980—83, ptnr. NYC, 1986—, head mergers and acquisitions practice group. Trustee Collegiate Sch. Mem.: ABA, Bar Assn. City NY, Phi Beta Kappa. Office: Davis Polk & Wardwell 450 Lexington Ave New York NY 10017-3982 Office Phone: 212-450-4340. Office Fax: 212-450-3340.

BASOVA, YULIA, chemical engineer, researcher; permanent resident, USA, 2005; d. Vitaly P. Basov and Valeriya V. Chelikidi; married; 1 child, Egor Palchyk. MS in Chem. Engring., Kiev Poly. Inst., Ukraine, 1988; PhD in Chem. Engring., Aichi Inst. Tech., Japan, 2000. Scientist Inst. Sorption and Problems of Endoecology, Kiev, 1991—2001; vis. scientist Nat. Inst. Metals, Tsukuba, Japan, 1997, Advanced Indsl. Sci. and Tech. Inst., Tsukuba, 1998—2000, Inst. Advanced Indsl. Sci. and Tech., Takamatsu, Japan, 2000—02; vis. asst. prof. Ctr. Advanced Engring. Fibers and Films, Clemson U., SC, 2002—05, vis. asst. prof. environ. engring. and sci., 2005—; vis. asst. prof. NC A&T U, 2007—. HS and undergraduate mentor Rsch. Experience Undergraduates, 2003—05. Recipient Certificate of Excellence, Clemson U. Rsch. Found., 2006; fellowship, Sci. Tech. Agy., Japan, 1997, grant, 1998—2000, fellowship, Agy. Indsl. Sci. and Tech., Japan, 2000—02. Mem.: Am. Chem. Soc., Am. Carbon Soc., Internat. Soc. Electrochemistry. Achievements include research in activated carbon and method of producing same; invention of electrochemical device for purification of water and biological fluids; research in hydrogen storage and mechanistic studies of carbon modulaion. Avocations: photography, alpine skiing, tennis, music. Personal E-mail: ybasova@yahoo.com.

BASQUIN, MARY SMYTH (KIT BASQUIN), museum administrator; b. NYC, July 3, 1941; d. Joseph Percy and Virginia Sandford (Gibbs) Smyth; m. Maurice Hanson Basquin, Feb. 4, 1967 (div. Feb. 1984); children: Susan, Peter Lee, William. BA, Goucher Coll., Balt., 1963; MA, Ind. U., 1970; postgrad., Union Inst. and U., Cin., 2003—. Asst. dir. pub. rels. Indpls. Mus. Art, 1971-72; dir. Washington Gallery, Frankfort, Ind., 1972-79, Indpls., 1977-79, Kit Basquin Gallery, Milw., 1981-83; curator edn. Haggerty Mus. Marquette U., Milw., 1988-95; dir. outreach Milw. Wis. Humanities Coun., 1995-98; curator Marvin Lowe Retrospective, Ind. U. Art Mus., 1998; mktg. William Doyle Galleries, NYC, 1999, exhbn. mgr., 2000; rsch. assoc. Bklyn. Mus. Art, 2000; asst. print study rm. Met. Mus. Art, NYC, 2000—. Instr. art history Concordia U., Mequon, Wis., 1991, instr. Marquette U., Gaza, 1996; pres. contemporary art soc. Milw. Art Mus., 1986-87, prints and drawings subcom., 1991-99, pres. Print Forum, 1996-97; mem. program com. Midwest Mus. conf., Milw., 1992. Wis. editor: New Art Examiner, 1980—81; mem. St. Barts Singers, 1999—; contbr. articles to profl. jours. Trustee Ten Chimneys Found., Genesee Depot, Wis., 1997-99; mem. adv. bd. Ten Chimneys Found., 2000-01; mem. alumnae bd. The Spence Sch., N.Y., 2005—. Mem. Univ. Club NY, Univ. Club Milw., Coll. Art Assn, James Joyce Soc. Episcopalian. Avocations: singing, fashion, theater, swimming. Home: 1675 York Ave Apt 19A New York NY 10128-6756

BASRI, GIBOR, astronomy educator, academic administrator; b. NYC, May 3, 1951; s. Saul and Phyllis Basri; m. Jessica Broitman, June 21, 1981; 1 child, Jacob. BSc in Physics, Stanford U., 1973; PhD in Astrophysics, U. Colo., 1979. Chancellor's postdoctoral fellow U. Calif., Berkeley, 1979-81, asst. prof., 1982-88, assoc. prof. astronomy, 1988—94, prof., 1994—, acting chair Astronomy Dept., 2006—07, vice chancellor for equity and inclusion, 2007—. Bd. mem. Chabot Space and Sci. Ctr., 1998—; co-investigator Kepler Mission, NASA, 2001—. Contbr. articles to astrophys. jours. Bd. mem. I Have a Dream Found., Oakland, 1998—2006. Recipient Bausch and Lomb Sci. Medal, 1969, Chancellor's Award for Advancing Institutional Excellence, 2006. Mem.: Nat. Soc. Black Physicists, Internat. Astron. Union, Astron. Soc. Pacific, Am. Astron. Soc. Office: U Calif MC3411 Astronomy Dept Berkeley CA 94720-0001 Office Phone: 510-642-8198. E-mail: basri@berkeley.edu.*

BASS, AARON, school system administrator; b. Phila., May 26, 1950; arrived in France, 1965, arrived in U.S., 1967; m. Jade King, July 3, 1999; children: Naja Killebrew, Clyde Killebrew, Aaron III, Jared, Sharita. BA in Psychology, Lincoln U., 1972; MA in Social Psychology, Temple U., 1974; AA in Data Processing, Phila. C.C., 1982; MDiv, Luth. Theol. Sem., 1998. Learning specialist Urban Career Edn. Ctr., Phila., 1974; rsch. asst. Sch. Dist. Phila., 1974—94, rsch. assoc., 1994—96, rsch. asst., 1996—2000, analyst pupil data, 2000—05; rsch. and assessment specialist William Penn Sch. Dist., 2005—. Author numerous studies and evaluations, (screenplays) Ashenden's Adventures as British Agent During World War I, 2005. Tchr. Germantown Cmty. Photography Workshop, Phila., 1972-74; elder Eagles Nest Christian Fellowship, Phila., 1999-2001, Mt. Airy Ch. of God in Christ, 2001—; mem. Phila. Interfaith Action; mem. Germantown 1st Presbyn. Ch. Recipient award for Most Unique Reporting Technique for Career Edn. Accumulative Report, Nat. Edn. Resource Info. Ctr., 1980; Temple U. scholar, 1972. Mem.: ASCD, Am. Ednl. Rsch. Assn., Evang. Tng. Assn., Phi Delta Kappa, Omega Psi Phi. Avocations: running, biking, swimming, reading, travel. Home: 6025 Morton St Philadelphia PA 19144 Office Phone: 212-473-4918. Personal E-mail: abass@voicenet.com. Business E-Mail: abass@wpsd.k12.pa.us.

BASS, BILL, apparel executive; b. 1963; With US Dept. Edn., formerly; sr. v.p., e-commerce Land's End; gen. mgr., direct to customer divsn. Sears; co-founder, CEO Fair Indigo, 2006—. Bd. mem. Marc Ecko Enterprises, England. Achievements include co-founding one of first US fair-trade apparel brands. Office: Fair Indigo 2140 W Greenview Dr Ste 7 Middleton WI 53562 Office Phone: 800-520-1806. Office Fax: 608-831-1359.*

BASS, BRENDA L., biochemist, educator; BA, Colo. Coll., 1977; PhD, Univ. Colo., 1985; postdoctoral fellow, Fred Hutchison Cancer Ctr., Seattle, 1985—89. Prof., biochemistry Univ. Utah; and investigator Howard Hughes Med. Inst. Fellow: Am. Acad. Arts & Scis. Office: Dept Biochemistry/HHMI Univ Utah 15 N Medical Dr E Salt Lake City UT 84112-5650 Office Phone: 801-581-4884 801-581-4884. Business E-Mail: bbass@biochem.utah.edu.*

BASS, CARL, computer software company executive; BA, Cornell U., 1978. Co-founder Ithaca Software; v.p. AECAD group, chief tech. officer, exec. v.p. Autodesk Ventures Autodesk Inc., San Rafael, Calif., 1994—99; chmn., pres., CEO buzzsaw.com, 1999—2001; exec. v.p. emerging bus. & chief strategy officer Autodesk Inc., 2001—02, sr. v.p. design solutions group, 2002—04, COO, 2004—06, pres., CEO, 2006—. Bd. dir. Serena Software, PowerLight Corp., iRise. Office: Autodesk Inc 111 McInnis Pkwy San Rafael CA 94903*

BASS, CHARLES FOSTER, former congressman; b. Boston, Jan. 8, 1952; s. Perkins and Katharine J. Bass; m. Lisa A. Levesque; children: Lucy, Jonathan. AB, Dartmouth Coll., NH, 1974. Field worker to US Rep. William S. Cohen US Congress, Maine, 1974, legis. asst. to US Rep. David F. Emery Maine, 1975-76, chief of staff, 1976-79; v.p. High Std., Inc., Dublin, NH, 1980-94; mem. NH Gen. Ct., 1982—88; del. NH Constl. Conv., 1984; chair Columbia Archtl. Products, Beltsville, Md., 1984—94; mem. NH State Senate, 1988—92, US Congress from 2d NH dist., 1995—2007. Mem. energy and commerce com. US Congress. Bd. trustees NH Higher Edn. Assistance Found., Monadnock Conservancy, Monadnock Worksource, NH Humanities Coun. Named Humane Legislator of Yr., Am. Humane Assn., 2000; recipient Legis. Svc. award, Northeastern Econ. Developers Assn., 2000, Friend of Nat. Pks. award, Nat. Pks. Conservation Assn., 2001. Mem. Monadnock Rotary (pres. 1992-93), Amoskeag Vets., Masons. Republican. Episcopalian. Office Phone: 202-225-5206.*

BASS, DAVID STEVEN, law educator, arbitrator, mediator; b. Bklyn., Dec. 10, 1946; s. Joseph and Thelma Bass; m. Carol W. Palevsky, Aug. 17, 1969; children: Adam Brett, Wayne Jonathan. BA, Bklyn. Coll., 1967; JD, NYU, 1971, LLM in Labor Rels., 1975. Bar: NY 1972, US Dist. Ct. (ea. dist.) NY 1975. Atty. Office Labor Rels. and Collective Bargaining NYC Bd. Edn., 1973-80, dep. dir., 1980-84, dep. exec. dir., 1984—2002. Adj. prof. edn. law, fin. and pers. adminstrn. City Coll. CUNY, 1992—, Touro Coll., 2001—; apptd. to various arbitration panels, NY, NJ; apptd. to FMCS and NMB panel. Mem.: NY State Bar Assn. (labor and employment law sect.). Jewish. Home and Office: 31 Whitney Dr Marlboro NJ 07746-1249 Office Phone: 732-972-1114.

BASS, EVELYN ELIZABETH, elementary school educator; b. Magnolia, Ark., Sept. 28, 1948; d. Marvin and Catherine (Grissom) Scott; m. Burlin Lee Hughes, July 17, 1971 (div. Aug. 1984); children: Tionna Latrice, Lee Otis Williams Jr.; m. John W. Bass Sr., July 23, 2000, (dec.) BA, Ark. Bapt. Coll., 1971; MS in Edn., Ouachita Bapt. Coll., Arkadelphia, Ark., 1988; degree, U. Little Rock, 2000—02. Tchr. Pulaski County Spl. Sch. Dist., Little Rock, 1971-97; exec. dir. Lenea's Children's Cottage, Little Rock, 1997—; advisor Choice Care Inc., Little Rock, 1998—; owner, pres. Evelyn's Tutoring Svc., Little Rock, 1998—; presch. tchr. Graceland Kids' Educare Ctr., 2000—. Child devel. assoc. instr., advisor Grace Holiness Christian Acad., 1999—, head instr., prin., 2004—; cons. in field; vocalist of praise/hymn. Author, composer: (poetry and songs) The Printed Word, 1993; (CDs) The Printed Word, 2003, (sound track and children's music book) Never Say Never, 2003; author: The Printed Word/Woman of God, 1995, (poetry) Listen! The Lord is Speaking, 2004. Traffic judge Willard Proctor, Jr. Campaign, 1996, cir. ct. judge, 2000. Democrat. Apostolic. Avocations: singing, songwriting, writing. Home: 5505 Western Ln Little Rock AR 72209 Office Phone: 501-562-6155. Personal E-mail: evelynbass@sbcglobal.net.

BASS, FRANKLIN F., lawyer; b. NYC, Mar. 9, 1951; BA, NYU, 1972; JD, Bklyn. Law Sch., 1976. Bar: NY 1977, US Dist. Ct. So. Dist. NY, US Dist. Ct. Ea. Dist. NY, US Ct. Appeals 2nd Cir., US Ct. Appeals 3rd Cir., US Supreme Ct. Ptnr. Wilson, Elser, Moskowitz, Edelman & Dicker LLP, NYC. Assoc. prof. real estate inst. Sch. Continuing & Profl. Studies, NYU, 1980—87. Mem.: ABA, NY State Trial Lawyers Assn., NY State Bar Assn. (chmn. aviation law com. of torts, ins. & compensation law sect.), Aircraft Owners and Pilots Assn., Warbirds of Am., Exptl. Aircraft Assn., Wings Club, Aviation Ins. Assn. Office: Wilson Elser Moskowitz Edelman & Dicker LLP 23rd Fl 150 E 42nd St New York NY 10017-5639 Office Phone: 212-490-3000 ext. 2405. Office Fax: 212-490-3038. Business E-Mail: bassf@wemed.com.

BASS, GARY D., advocate, director; PhD in Psychology and Education, U. Mich. Pres. Human Svcs. Info. Ctr.; dir. liaison Internat. Yr. Disabled Persons; founder, exec. dir. OMB Watch, Washington, 1983—; creator RTK NET (the Right to Know Network), 1989—. Spl. asst. task force on investigation and prevention of abuse in residential instns. Mich. Gov. Office: OMB Watch 1742 Connecticut Ave NW Washington DC 20009

BASS, GEORGE FLETCHER, retired archaeology educator; b. Columbia, SC, Dec. 9, 1932; s. Robert Duncan and Virginia (Wauchope) B.; m. Ann Singletary, Mar. 19, 1960; children: Gordon Wauchope, Alan Joseph. MA, Johns Hopkins U., 1955; PhD, U. Pa., 1964; PhD (hon.), Bogazici U., Istanbul, Turkey, 1987, U. Liverpool, 1998. Asst. prof. U. Pa., Phila., 1964-68, assoc. prof., 1968-73; prof. archaeology Tex. A&M U., College Station, 1976-80, disting. prof., 1980-2000, George T. and Gladys H. Abell prof. nautical archaeology, 1986-2000, Yamini Family prof., 1994-2000, prof. emeritus, 2001—. Dir. excavations of ancient shipwrecks off Turkish coast, 1960-2003; pres. Inst. Nautical Archaeology, 1972-82, 96-98; chmn. Inst. Nautical Archaeology Found., 2005-07. Author: Archaeology Under Water, 1966, Cape Gelidonya, 1967, History of Seafaring, 1972, Archaeology Beneath the Sea, 1975, Yassi Ada I, 1982, Ships and Shipwrecks of the Americas, 1988, Serce Limani I, 2004, Beneath the Seven Seas, 2005; adv. editor Am. Jour. Archaeology, 1987-99, Archaeology, 1987—, Internat. Jour. Nautical Archaeology, 1987-2007, Nat. Geog. Rsch., 1987-94. Lt. U.S. Army, 1957-59, Korea. Recipient Centennial award Nat. Geog. Soc., 1988, La Gorce Gold medal, 1979, Lowell Thomas award Explorers Club, 1986, Nat. Medal of Sci., 2002 (presented by Pres. George W. Bush); named one of Outstanding Young Men of Yr., Jaycees, 1967. Mem. Inst. Nautical Archaeology (pres. 1973-82), Archaeol. Inst. Am. (Gold medal for disting. archaeol. achievement 1986), Soc. for Hist. Archaeology (J.C. Harrington medal 1999), Nat. Maritime Hist. Soc., Mothers Against Drunk Driving. Presbyterian. Avocation: classical music. Home: 1600 Dominik Dr College Station TX 77840-3623 Office: Tex A&M U Nautical Archaeology College Station TX 77843-4352 Business E-Mail: gfbass@neo.tamu.edu.

BASS, HAROLD NEAL, pediatrician, medical geneticist; b. Chgo., Apr. 14, 1939; s. Louis A. and Minnie (Schachter) B.; m. Phyllis Appell, June 25, 1961; children: Laura Renee, Alana Suzanne. Student, U. Ill., 1956—59; MS in Pharmacology, U. Chgo., 1963, MD, 1963. Diplomate Am. Bd. Pediat., Am. Bd. Med. Genetics, Nat. Bd. Med. Examiners. Intern Children's Meml. Hosp., Chgo., 1963-64, resident, 1964-65, chief resident, 1965-66, fellow in med. genetics, 1965-66; chief pediat. and profl. svcs. Norton AFB Hosp., Calif., 1966-68; attending pediatrician/med. geneticist Kaiser Permanente Med. Ctr., Panorama City, Calif., 1968—; dir. med. genetics prog. Kaiser Permanente Med. Care Program So. Calif., 1987—2003; clin. prof. pediat. and human genetics UCLA Med. Sch., 1970—. Pres. med. staff Kaiser Permanente Med. Ctr., 1989-2004; bd. dirs. So. Calif. Permanente Med. Group, 1998-04; adj. prof. biology Calif. State U., Northridge, 1995—. Contbr. articles to profl. jours. Mem. mayor's adv. com. San Fernando Valley, City of L.A., 1973-78. Capt. USAF, 1966—68. Founding Fellow Am. Coll. Med. Genetics, Western Soc. Pediat. Rsch., Brady Handgun Control, ACLU, Am. Soc. Human Genetics, Amnesty Internat. Democrat. Jewish. Avocations: civic affairs, music, writing. Home: 11922 Dunnicliffe Ct Porter Ranch CA 91326-1324 Office: Kaiser Permanente Med Ctr 13652 Cantara St Panorama City CA 91402-5497 Home Phone: 818-360-0154; Office Phone: 818-375-2073. Business E-Mail: harold.n.bass@kp.org.

BASS, HYMAN, mathematician, educator; b. Houston, Oct. 5, 1932; s. Isador and Fanny (Weiss) B.; m. Mary Ellen Popkin, June 9, 1957 (div. 1978); children: Anne Ruth, Ivan Philip; m. Dorothea Henriette Goldys, Nov. 1, 1979; 1 dau., Gabriella Sierra. BA, Princeton U., 1955; MS, U. Chgo., 1956, PhD (NSF grad. fellow), 1959. With Columbia U., 1959—98, Ritt instr. math., 1959-62, asst. prof., 1963-64, Adrain prof., math dept., chmn. dept. math., 1975; assoc. prof., chmn. Barnard Coll., 1964-65, prof., 1965; prof. math. U. Mich., Ann Arbor, 1999—, Roger C. Lyndon Collegiate prof. math., 2004—. Vis. mem. Inst. Advanced Study, Princeton, 1964, 65-66, Inst. de Hautes Etudes Scientifiques, Paris, 1968-69; vis. prof. Universidad Nacional Autónoma de Mex., 1965, Tata Inst. Fundamental Research, Bombay, 1965-66, 69, 76, 80, U. Paris, 1968, 73, 81, Cambridge U., 1973, Instituto de Matematica Pura e Applicada, Rio de Janeiro, 1977, Bar Ilan U., Israel, 1980; chmn. adv. com. pure math. NRC, 1970-71; adv. panel, div. math. NSF, 1973-75; vis. coms. various math. depts. colls., univs.; disting. lectr. Kans. State U., U. Ind., 1982; Karcher lectr. U. Okla., 1979; Barrett Meml. lectr. U. Tenn., 1978, others; spkr. in field. Editorial bd.: Jour. Indian Math. Soc, 1968— , Cambridge Tracts in Pure and Applied Math.; 968: Jour. Pure and Applied Algebra, 1970— , Am. Jour. Mathematics, 1971— , North-Holland Math. Library, 1971— , Acad. Press Series in Pure and Applied Math, 1974—. NSF fellow Coll. de France, 1962-63; Sloan fellow, 1964-66; Guggenheim fellow, 1968-69; recipient Van Amridge book prize Columbia, 1969, Cole prize Am. Math. Soc., 1975; Phi Beta Kappa Nat. Vis. scholar, 1991-92.; named 2006 Nat. Medal Sci. Laureate, 2007. Fellow AAAS; mem. NAS (chair math. scis. edn. bd. 1992-2000), Am. Math Soc. (editorial bd. 1969— , coun. 1969-72, former pres., mem. com. on edu.), London Math. Socs., Société Mathématique de France, Soc. Collaborateurs N. Bourbaki, Math. Assn. Am., Am. Acad. Arts and Scis., Third World Acad. Scis. Home: 435 Riverside Dr New York NY 10025-7743 Office: U Mich Room 2413 Department Mathematics Ann Arbor MI 48109-1259 Office Phone: 734-615-4043. Business E-Mail: hybass@umich.edu.*

BASS, JAMES ORIN, SR., lawyer; b. Sumner County, Tenn., July 12, 1910; s. Francis Marion and Sadie (Dunn) B.; m. Susanne Warner, June 9, 1937; children: James Orin, Edwin Warner, Francis Marion II, Susan Richardson. BA, U. of the South, 1931, DCL (hon.), 2007; LLB, Harvard U., 1934. Bar: Tenn. 1934. Ptnr. Bass, Berry & Sims, Nashville, 1937—. Mem. Tenn. Ho. of Reps. from Davidson County, 1936-38, Tenn. Senate,

1940-42. Served to lt. col. AUS, 1942-45, ETO. Mem. ABA, Tenn. Bar Assn., Nashville Bar Assn. (pres. 1952), Am. Coll. Trial Lawyers. Presbyterian. Home: 4412 Georgian Pl Nashville TN 37215-4528 E-mail: jbasssr@bassberry.com.

BASS, LEE MARSHALL, food products company executive; b. 1950; s. Perry R. Bass and Nancy Lee; m. Ramona Bass. BA/BS, Yale U., 1979; MBA, U. Pa. Wharton Sch. Bus. With Bass Enterprises Prodn. Co., Ft. Worth, 1970—; chmn. bd. Nat. Farms, Inc., Kansas City, Mo., 1992—, also bd. dirs.; pres. Lee M. Bass Inc., Ft. Worth. Named one of Forbes' Richest Americans, 1999—, World's Richest People, Forbes mag., 1999—. Office: Nat Farms Inc 4800 Main St Kansas City MO 64112-2510 also: Bass Bros Enterprises 201 Main St Fort Worth TX 76102-3105 also: Lee M Bass Inc 201 Main St Fort Worth TX 76102-3105 Office: Modern Art Museum 3200 Darnell St Fort Worth TX 76107-2872*

BASS, LYNDA D., retired medical/surgical nurse, nursing educator; b. Suffolk, Va. d. H.M. and Katie Lea Bass. BSN, NC Agrl. and Tech. State U., Greensboro, 1968; MSN, Cath. U. Am., Washington, 1974. Med.-surg. nurse Kenner Army Hosp., Ft. Lee, Va., 1968—71, Walter Reed Army Med. Ctr., Washington, 1968—71; staff nurse Providence Hosp., Washington, 1971—73, clin. educator, 1988—94; gen. surgery clin. specialist George Washington U. Hosp., Washington, 1974—77; clin. nurse specialist Walter Reed Army Hosp., Washington, 1977—78; coord. clin. staff devel. Mt. Vernon Hosp., Alexandria, Va., 1978—79; clin. nurse preceptor Greater SE Cmty. Hosp., Washington, 1979—81; instr. clin. nursing edn. Suburban Hosp., Bethesda, Md., 1980—83; edn./tng. quality assurance coord. Howard U. Hosp., Washington, 1983—88; edn. specialist Vets. Affairs Md. Healthcare Sys., Balt., 1995—2002. Adj. faculty Cath. U. Am., 1975—76. Active Women in Mil. Svc. for Am. Meml. Found. Capt. USAR, 1967—71, Vietnam. Mem.: Nat. Nursing Staff Devel. Assn., Vietnam Vets. Am., Chi Eta Phi.

BASS, MICHAEL A., lawyer; b. Springfield, Mass., Sept. 22, 1965; BA, U. Vt., 1987; JD, New Eng. Sch. Law, 1990; LLM in Taxation, Boston U. Sch. Law, 1994. Bar: Mass. 1990, Fla. 1991, US Tax Ct. Atty. Bass, Doherty & Finks, P.C., Boston. Named a Mass. Super Lawyer, Law & Politics mag., 2006; named one of Top 100 Attys., Worth mag., 2006. Mem.: Boston Estate Planning Coun. (bd. dirs.), Nat. Acad. Elder Law Attys., Mass. Bar Assn. (mem. Medicaid com. in probate sect.). Office: Bass Doherty & Finks PC 40 Soldiers Field Pl Boston MA 02135-1104 Office Phone: 617-787-6113. Office Fax: 617-787-4963. E-mail: mbass@bassdoherty.com.*

BASS, NORMAN HERBERT, neurologist, educator, research scientist, hospital administrator, academic administrator; b. NYC, July 10, 1936; s. Julius and Celia (Annex) B.; m. Kathleen Bass; children: Joel Martin, Rebecca Pier, Robert Farrell. BS (Ford Found. scholar 1953, N.Y. State Regents scholar 1954), Swarthmore Coll., Pa., 1958; MD, Yale U., 1962. Diplomate: Am. Bd. Psychiatry and Neurology. Intern Med. U. Wash. Hosp., Seattle, 1962-63; resident in neurology U. Va. Hosp., Charlottesville, 1963-65; clin. fellow in neurology Mass. Gen. Hosp., Boston, 1965-67; NIH fellow Harvard U. Med. Sch., 1965-67; from asst. prof. to prof. neurology U. Va. Med. Sch., Charlottesville, 1967-79, dir. Clinic Neurosci. Rsch. Ctr., 1973-79; prof. neurology, chmn. dept. Albert B. Chandler Med. Center, U. Ky., Lexington, 1979-85; neurologist in chief Univ. Hosp., 1979-85; dir. lab. neurochemistry Sanders-Brown Ky. Rsch. Ctr. Aging, 1979-85; dean Sch. Medicine, prof. dept. Neurology Med. Coll. Ga., 1985-86; prof. neurology, rehab. medicine, chief div. rehab. medicine U. Md. Sch. Medicine, Balt., 1986-89; prof. neurology, rehab. medicine U. Pitts., 1989-92; sr. v.p., chief med. officer Harmarville Rehab. Ctr. Inc., Pitts., 1989-92; prof. pediatrics and neurology Sch. Medicine, Boston U., 1992—; sr. v.p. med. affairs Franciscan Childrens Hosp. and Rehab Ctr., 1992-94; pvt. practice Cape and Islands, 1994—. Cons. neurology VA Med. Ctr., Lexington, Augusta, Balt., Pitts., Boston; chmn. nat. rsch. program merit rev. bd. in neurobiology VA, 1978-81; mem. bd. sci. advisers Delta Regional Primate Ctr., Tulane U., 1978-81, chmn., 1979-81; chmn. profl. adv. bd. Epilepsy Assn. VA Ky., 1978-82; chmn. study sect. Nat. Inst. Disability and Rehab. Rsch., 1986-89; program surveyor Commn. on Accreditation of Rehab. Facilities, 1987-92; mem. panel co-chari Task Force Med. Rehab. Rsch. Office Sci. Policy, NIH, 1990; vis. prof. pharmacology U. Goteborg, Sweden, 1972-73. Assoc. editor Neurochem. Rsch. Jour., Jour. Neurol. Rehab.; mem. editorial bd. Stroke jour.; contbr. numerous articles to med. jours. Served to maj. M.C. USAR, 1963-69. Recipient Rsch. Career Devel. award NIH, 1971-75, Nat. Inst. Neurologic Disease rsch. fellow in neurochemistry, 1965-67; Markle scholar in acad. medicine, 1969-74 Fellow Am. Acad. Neurology (S. Weir Mitchell rsch. award 1967, chmn. sect. on geriatrics 1986, sect. on neurol. rehab. 1987), AAAS, Stroke Coun. of Am. Heart Assn., Am. Acad. Cerebral Palsy and Devel. Medicine; mem. Am. Assn. U. Profs. Neurology (v.p. 1980-81), Am. Assn. Anatomists, Am. Soc. Neurochemistry, Am. Soc. Neuro. Rehab., Soc. Neurosci., Internat. Soc. Neurochemistry, Child Neurology Soc., Am. Neurol. Assn., Assn. Rsch. Nervous and Mental Disease, Nat. Head Injury Found., Inc., AMA, Am. Congress Rehab. Medicine, Nat. Assn. Rehab. Facilities Inc., Nat. Multiple Sclerosis Soc., Nat. Head Injury Found., Alpha Omega Alpha. Office: PO Box 1050 West Falmouth MA 02574

BASS, PERKINS, retired lawyer, congressman; b. East Walpole, Mass., Oct. 6, 1912; s. Robert P. and Edith (Bird) Bass; m. Katherine Jackson (dec.); children: Alexander, Katherine, William J., Charles F., Roberta, Roberta; m. Rosaly S. Riley, Sept. 30, 1973. AB, Dartmouth Coll., 1934; LLB, Harvard U. Law Sch., 1938. Bar: N.H. 1938. Lawyer Sheehan, Phinney, Bass & Green PLC, Manchester, NH, 1938—95, of counsel, 1995—2005; rep. N.H. Gen. Ct., Concord, 1949—63; mem. U.S. Ho. Reps., Washington, 1954—63. Trustee New Hampshire Savings Bank, Concord, 1950—80; bd. dirs. Bird & Son, Inc., East Walpole, Mass., 1946—84. Trustee Franklin Pierce Coll., Rindge, NH, 1972—87; trustee, pres. Monadnock Cmty. Hosp., 1948—54; Rep. Nat. Committeeman from N.H., 1964—68; selectman Peterborough, 1972—75. Major USAF, 1942—45, Far Eastern Theater. Decorated Bronze Star USAF, Yun Ma medal Disting. and Meritorious Svc. Nat. Govt. China (now Taiwan). Home: PO Box 210 Peterborough NH 03458 Office: Peterborough Hist Bldg Grove St Peterborough NH 03458 Office Phone: 603-924-3303.

BASS, ROBERT MUSE, financier; b. Ft. Worth, 1948; s. Perry Richardson and Nancy Lee (Muse) B.; m. Anne Thaxton Bass, 1970; 3 children. BA, Yale U., 1970; MBA, Stanford U., 1974. V.p., bd. dirs. Bass Bros. Enterprises Inc., Ft. Worth, until 1985; pres. Robert M. Bass Group Inc. (now The Keystone Group), Ft. Worth, 1985—; founder Oak Hill Capital Partners. Chmn. Aerion Corp. Mem. collector's com. Nat. Gallery, Washington; chmn. emeritus Nat. Trust Historic Preservation; bd. trustees Stanford U. (chmn., 1996-), 1989—, Rockefeller U., Groton Sch., Middlesex Sch., Amon Carter Mus.; commr. Tex. State Hwy. and Pub. Transp. Commn., 1986—87. Named one of Forbes Richest Americans, 1999—, World's Richest People, Forbes Mag., 2000—. Office: Keystone Inc 201 Main St Ste 3100 Fort Worth TX 76102*

BASS, RONALD, screenwriter; b. LA, 1943; Screenplays include Code Name: Emerald, 1985, Black Widow, 1987, Gardens of Stone, 1987, (with Barry Morrow) Rainman, 1988 (Academy award best original screenplay 1988), Sleeping with the Enemy, 1991, (with Amy Tan) The Joy Luck Club, 1993; screenwriter, exec. prodr.: (with Al Franken) When a Man Loves a Woman, 1994, Dangerous Minds, 1995, (with Terry McMillan) Waiting to Exhale, 1995, My Best Friend's Wedding, 1997, What Dreams May Come, 1998, Stepmom, 1998, How Stella Got Her Groove Back, 1998, Entrapment, 1999, Snow Falling on Cedars, 1999, Passion of Mind, 1999, The Lazarus Child, 2004. Office: Creative Artists Agency care Beth Swofford 9830 Wilshire Blvd Beverly Hills CA 90212-1825

BASS, SID RICHARDSON, investment company executive; b. 1943; s. Perry R. Bass and Nancy Lee; m. Anne Bass (div. 1986); 2 children; m. Mercedes Bass. BA, Yale Univ., 1965; MBA, Stanford Univ., 1969. Co-founder Idanta Partners, 1971; founder Buena Venture Associates, 1998—. V.p. & dir. Sid. W. Richardson Found. Former sr. fellow of the corp. Yale Univ.; vice chmn. bd. trustees Mus. Modern Art, NYC. Named one of Forbes' Richest Americans, 2000—, World's Richest People, Forbes mag., 2000—. Mailing: Buena Venture Associates 1201 Washington Terrace Fort Worth TX 76107*

BASS, STEVEN CRAIG, computer science educator; b. Indpls., July 29, 1943; s. Leland Ellsworth and Isabelle Frances (Ross) B.; m. Sara Ann Hiday, Sept. 4, 1965 (div. Apr. 1988); children: Leland Kai, Marshall Lynn; m. Kevyn Anne Salsburg, Jan. 2, 1989. BSEE, Purdue U., 1966, MSEE, 1968, PhD in Elec. Engring., 1971. Prof. elec. engring. Purdue U., Lafayette, Ind., 1971-88; prof. elec. and computer engring. George Mason U., Fairfax, Va., 1988-91; prin. engr. Mitre Corp., McLean, Va., 1988-91; prof. computer sci. and engring., chmn. dept. U. Notre Dame, Notre Dame, Ind., 1991-2000; co-owner St. John Condos, LLC, Notre Dame, Ind., 2007—. Cons. Magnovox Co., Ft. Wayne, Ind., 1971-73, Admiral Corp., Chgo., 1973-76, Kimball Internat., Jasper, Ind., 1978-84, Tektronix Corp., Wilsonville, Oreg., 1987-88. Contbr. over 25 articles to profl. jours., delievered over 35 papers at sci. confs. Rescue officer Stockwell (Ind.) Vol. Fire Dept., 1985-88. Recipient numerous grants from NSF, USAF, IBM, Mitre Corp., others. Fellow IEEE (v.p. circuits and sys. soc. 1981, 91-93, mem. audio engring. soc.); mem. Tau Beta Pi. Roman Catholic. Achievements include 3 U.S. and 6 fgn. patents in the field of digital signal processing. Office Phone: 340-779-4218. Personal E-mail: stevenbass@earthlink.net. Business E-Mail: bass@cse.nd.edu.

BASS, WILLIAM MARVIN, III, anthropology educator; b. Staunton, Va., Aug. 30, 1928; s. William Marvin II and Jennie Britton (Hicks) B.; m. Mary Anna Owen, Aug. 8, 1953; children— Charles E., William Marvin IV, James O. BA, U. Va., 1951; MS, U. Ky., 1956; PhD, U. Pa., 1961. Diplomate: Am. Bd. Forensic Anthropology. Instr. phys. anthropology Grad. Sch. Medicine, U. Pa., 1956-59; instr. U. Nebr., 1959-60; mem. faculty anthropology dept. U. Kans., 1960-71, prof., 1967-71; prof., head dept. anthropology U. Tenn., Knoxville, 1971-92, founder, Anthropology Forensic Ctr.--The Body Farm, 1988, former dir. Anthropology Forensic Ctr., Alumni Disting. prof., 1978, prof. emeritus. Serves Tenn. State Forensic Anthropologist; active in consultations and lectures across the country. Author: Human Osteology: A Laboratory and Field Manual of the Human Skeleton, 1971, 5th edit., 2005, The Leavenworth Site Cemetery: Archaeology and Physical Anthropology, 1971, (with Jon Jefferson as Jefferson Bass) Carved in Bone, 2006, Flesh and Bone, 2007; co-author: Death's Acre, 2003; contbr. numerous articles. Served with AUS, 1951-53. Named Hill Tchr. U. Kans., 1964; recipient H. Bernerd Fink award for excellence in classroom teaching U. Kans., 1965; Alumni Public Service award U. Tenn., 1975; Nat. Prof. of Year award Council Advancement and Support of Edn., 1985. Fellow Am. Assn. Phys. Anthropologists, Am. Acad. Forensic Scis. (Phys. Anthropology award 1985); mem. Am. Anthrop. Assn. Office: Univ Tenn Anthropology Forensic Ctr Dept 250 S Stadium Hall Knoxville TN 37996-0760 Office Phone: 865-974-4408. Office Fax: 865-974-2686. Business E-Mail: wbass@utk.edu.

BASSANO, C. LOUIS, state legislator, fuel oil company executive; b. Newark, Oct. 29, 1942; s. Charles and Mildred (Tortoriello) B.; m. Joan DeFlores, May 25, 1984; children: Charles Louis II, Jennifer Ann, Kimberly Claire, Jeffrey Alan. Student, Bloomfield Coll., 1961-63. V.p. H & I Bassano Fuel Oil, Kennilworth, N.J.; mem. N.J. Gen. Assembly, 1972-74, 76-81, N.J. Senate, Dist. 21, Trenton, 1981—; asst. minority whip, 1987-88; minority whip, 1989; asst. senate minority leader, 1990-91. Mem. senate law, pub. safety and def. com., senate instns., health and welfare com.; chmn. senate health and human svcs. com.; mem. senate family svcs. com. (vice chmn.), senate law and pub. safety com., 1994; chmn. senate sr. citizens, vet. affairs and human svcs. com., 1994—; mem. health com., 1996—, women's issues, children and family svcs. com., 1996—; chmn. legis. caucus on Israel; co-chmn. joint legis. task force to study adult diagnostic and treatment ctr., vice chair women's issues, children and family svcs. com., 1994—, health com., 1996—; active N.J. Intergovtl. Rels. Commn. Chmn. Sammy Davis, Jr. Liver Inst.; past mem. N.J. Monorail Legislation Commn., Senate Rep. Task Force on Liability Ins. Reform, Hazardous Waste Minimization Task Force, Law Enforcement Tng. Acad. Study Commn., Nat. Com. for Treatment of Intractable Pain; bd. dirs. Children's Specialized Hosp.; past chmn. fund drive Meml. Gen. Hosp.; past chmn. Union Township Epilepsy Fund; past co-chmn. Cancer Crusade; mem. bd, dirs. NJ Mental Health Assn.; bd. dirs. Bridgeway Found. for Mental Health Assn. Recipient cert. of recognition Bd. Dirs. Home Health Agy. Assembly N.J./N.J. Home Care Coun., Outstanding Community Svc. award Cancer Care, Inc./Nat. Cancer Found., PTA Safety award State PTA, B'nai B'rith Youth Svc. award, Pub. Safety award N.J. Tire Dealers Assn., Good Govt. award Township of Union Gov. Body, Disting. Svc. award Jr. Achievement, certs. of appreciation Union County March of Dimes, LWV of Cranford, Pres. award N.J. Assn. Rehab. Facilities, 1994; named Unico Man of Yr. by Union chpt. Unico, Senator of Yr. by N.J. Builders Assn., Outstanding Rep. Legislator, Legislator of Yr., Assn. Schs. and Agens. for Handicapped, 1994, N.J. Organ and Tissue Sharing Network, 1994; honored by N.J. State Nurses Assn., N.J. Psychol. Assn., 1996; recipent legis. svc. award Union County C. of C., 1994, outstanding svc. award ARC, 1994, pub. svc. award COSAC, 1995, spl. distinction award Mental Health Assn., legis. recognition award N.J. Alliance for Mentally Ill, 1996, Cmty. Access Unltd. Humanitarian award 1996, Legislator of Yr. Crohn's and Colitis Found. of Ams. N.J. chpt. 1997; named senator of yr. 1996 Garden State Pharmacy Owners. Mem. Elks, K.C.

BASS DE MARTINEZ, BERNICE, academic administrator, consultant; b. Denver, Sept. 23, 1948; d. Arthur and Beatrice Bass. BA, U. No. Colo., 1970, MA, 1972; PhD, U. Fla., 1975. Dept. chair Calif. State U., Fresno, 1987—91; dean edn. and human svcs. Seton Hall U., South Orange, NJ, 1991—93; assoc. provost Mills Coll., Oakland, Calif., 1993—96; sr. assoc. v.p., dean grad. sch. Ind. State U., Terre Haute, 1996—2000; spl. asst. pres., prof. Calif. State U., Sacramento, 2000—. Interim exec. dir., CEO Leadership Am., Alexandria, Va., 2002—02; rschr. Women of Color Rsch., Phoenix, 2003—. Editor: (educational text/book) Prespectives in Multicultural Education. Supporter Nat. Found. for Women Legislators, 2002; chair, recruitment com. Leadership Am., Dallas, 2000; state liaison ACE/OWHE Women's Network, Washington, 1999; dir. internat. edn. euro-American Women's Coun., Athens, 2002. Fellow: Assn. Am. Colls. and Univs.; mem.: Alpha Kappa Alpha (chpt. pres. 1996—2000). Democrat. Roman Catholic. Avocations: walking, travel, reading, networking. Office: Calif State U 6000 J St Sacramento CA 95819-6016 Home Phone: 916-928-2440; Office Phone: 916-928-2440. Home Fax: 916-928-8478. Personal E-mail: babed4sure@aol.com. E-mail: bbdem@csus.edu.

BASSECHES, ROBERT TREINIS, lawyer; b. NYC, Jan. 24, 1934; s. Jacob Thomas and Paula (Treinis) B.; m. Harriet Itkin, July 6, 1958; children: K.B., Joshua, Jessica. BA, Amherst Coll., 1955; LLB, Yale U., 1958. Bar: D.C. 1962, U.S. Ct. Appeals (D.C. cir.) 1962, U.S. Ct. Appeals (2d cir.) 1978, U.S. Ct. Appeals (4th cir.) 1998. Law clk. to judge David L. Bazelon U.S. Ct. Appeals (D.C. cir.), Washington, 1958-59; law clk. to justice Hugo L. Black U.S. Supreme Ct., Washington, 1959; assoc. Shea & Gardner, Washington, 1959-63, ptnr., 1963—2004, adminstrv. ptnr., 1980-86, chmn., exec. com., 1988-93; sr. counsel Goodwin Procter LLP, Washington, 2004—. Trustee Green Acres Sch., Rockville, Md., 1971-76, pres., chmn. bd. trustees, 1973-75; pres. Chevy Chase (Md.) Village Citizens Assn., 1976. Mem. Maritime Adminstrv. Bar Assn. (pres. 1969-71, sec. 1967-69), Phi Beta Kappa. Office: Goodwin Procter LLP 901 New York Ave NW Washington DC 20001

BASSEN, NED HENRY, lawyer; b. NYC, June 8, 1948; s. Harold Russell and Annette (Frankfeldt) B.; m. Susan Millington Campbell, July 2, 1999; children: Amanda Lee, Susannah Spence. BS, Cornell U., 1970, JD, 1973. Bar: NY 1974, US Dist. Ct. (so. and ea. dists.) NY 1974, US Dist. Ct. (ea. dist.) Mich. 1990, US Dist. Ct. (we. dist.) NY 1999, US Dist Ct. (no. dist.) NY 2004, US Ct. Appeals (11th cir.) 1984, US Ct. Appeals (2d cir.) 2001. Assoc. Baer Marks & Upham, NYC, 1975-80, Kelley Drye & Warren, NYC, 1973-75, 80-83, ptnr., 1983-92; ptnr., labor group head Mudge Rose Guthrie Alexander & Ferdon, NYC, 1993-95; ptnr., chair labor and employment dept. Hughes Hubbard & Reed LLP, NYC, 1995—. Note and comment editor Cornell Law Rev., 1972—73. Named one of NY Super Lawyers; named to The Best Lawyers in America; The Legal Media Group Guide to the World's Leading Labour and Employment Lawyers. Fellow Coll. Labor and Employment Lawyers; mem. ABA (labor and employment law sect., com. devel. of law under the nat. legal rels. act), US Coun. Internat. Bus., Indsl. Rels. Com., Indsl. Rels. Rsch. Assn., NY State Bar Assn. (labor law sect., com. on equal employment opportunity law), NY State Mgmt. Attys. Conf. Office: Hughes Hubbard & Reed LLP 1 Battery Park Plz Fl 12 New York NY 10004-1482 Home Phone: 718-875-7918; Office Phone: 212-837-6090. Business E-Mail: bassen@hugheshubbard.com.

BASSETT, ANGELA, actress; b. NYC, Aug. 16, 1958; m. Courtney B. Vance, Oct. 12, 1997; children: Bronwyn Golden, Slater Josiah. BA in African-Am. studies, Yale U., 1980; MFA, Yale Sch. of Drama, 1983. Appeared in (plays) Colored People's Time, 1982, The Mystery Plays, 1984-85, The Painful Adventures of Pericles, Prince of Tyre, 1986-87, Joe Turner's Come and Gone, 1986-87, (Broadway) Ma Rainey's Black Bottom, Fences, 2006, (Broadway) Joe Turner's Come and Gone, 1988, King Henry IV Part I, 1987; (TV films) Line of Fire: The Morris Dees Story, 1991, The Jacksons: An American Dream, 1992, A Century of Women, 1994, Ruby's Bucket of Blood, 2001 (also prodr.), The Rosa Parks Story, 2002 (also exec. prodr.); guest appearances (TV series) The Cosby Show, 1985, 1988, Spenser: For Hire, 1985, A Man Called Hawk, 1989, Tour of Duty, 1989, 227, 1989, thirtysomething, 1989, Alien Nation, 1990, The Flash, 1991, Nightmare Café, 1992, The Bernie Mac Show, 2003; (films) F/X, 1986, Kindergarten Cop, 1990, Boyz N the Hood, 1991, City of Hope, 1991, Innocent Blood, 1992, Malcolm X, 1992, Passion Fish, 1992, What's Love Got to Do with It, 1993 (Acad. award nominee for best actress 1993, Golden Globe award best actress in a musical or comedy 1994), Strange Days, 1995, Panther, 1995, Waiting to Exhale, 1995, A Vampire in Brooklyn, 1995, Contact, 1997, How Stella Got Her Groove Back, 1998, Wings Against the Wind, 1999, 50 Violins, 1999, Music of the Heart, 1999, Supernova, 2000, (voice) Whispers: An Elephant's Tale, 2000, Boesman and Lena, 2000, The Score, 2001, Sunshine State, 2002, Masked and Anonymous, 2003, The Lazarus Child, 2004, Mr. 3000, 2004, Akeelah and the Bee, 2006, Time Bomb, 2006, (voice) Meet the Robinsons, 2007; exec. prodr. Our America, 2002; co-author: (with Counrtney B. Vance & Hilary Beard) Friends: A Love Story, 2007. Recipient Lena Horne award for Outstanding Career Achievement in the Field of Entertainment, 2002.*

BASSETT, CHARLES WALKER, literature and language professor; b. Aberdeen, SD, July 7, 1932; s. Wilfred Walker and Angela (Jewett) B.; m. Carol Hoffer, Sept. 15, 1956 (dec. Feb. 5, 1995); children— David, Elizabeth. BA, U. S.D., 1954, MA, 1956; PhD, U. Kans., 1964; LHD (hon.), U. S.D., 2000. Asst. instr. English U. S.D., 1954-56, U. Kans., 1958-64; instr. U. Pa., Phila., 1964-66, asst. prof., 1966-69; asst. prof. English Colby Coll., Waterville, Maine, 1969-74, assoc. prof., 1974-80, prof., 1980-83, Charles A. Dana prof. Am. studies and English, 1983-93, Lee Family prof. Am. studies and English, 1993-99, dir. Am. studies, 1971-87, 89-96, chmn. dept. English, 1987-89, Lee family prof. Am. Studies & English emeritus, 1999—. Book rev. editor Am. Quar., 1983—91, assoc. editor Ency. of Polit. Parties and Elections in the U.S., 1991; contbr. articles to profl. jours. Recipient Charles Bassett/Sr. Class Tchg. award, 1993, Charles Bassett award for dedicated svc. Colby Alumni Assn., 1997, Student Assn. award for outstanding dedication to the students of Colby Coll., 1981; S.L. Whitcomb fellow, 1961-62, U. Kans. fellow, 1962-63; U. Pa. Faculty Rsch. grantee, 1966-68; Humanities and Mellon grantee, 1973-96. Mem. MLA (New Eng. rep. del. assembly), Am. Studies Assn. (Mary C. Turpie award 1994). Democrat. Roman Catholic. Home: 9 Martin Ave Waterville ME 04901-4625 Office: Colby Coll Dept English Waterville ME 04901 Office Phone: 207-859-5250. E-mail: cwbasset@colby.edu.

BASSETT, DEBRA LYN, lawyer, educator; d. James Arthur and Shirley Ann Bassett. BA, U. Vt., Burlington, 1977; MS, San Diego State U., 1982; JD, U. Calif., Davis, 1987. Bar: Calif. 1987, DC 1990, US Dist. Ct. (no. and ea. dists.) Calif. 1988, US Ct. Appeals (9th cir.) 1988, US Supreme Ct. 1991. Guidance counselor Addison Cen. Supr. Union, Middlebury, Vt., 1982-83, Milton Elem. Sch., Vt., 1983-84; assoc. Morrison & Foerster, San Francisco, 1986; jud. clk. US Ct. Appeals (9th cir.), Phoenix, 1987-88; assoc. Morrison & Foerster, San Francisco and Walnut Creek, Calif., 1988-92; sr. atty. Calif. Ct. Appeal (3d appellate dist.), Sacramento, 1992-99; assoc. prof. Mich. State U., East Lansing, 2002—04, Fla. State U. Coll. Law, Tallahassee, 2004—07, Loula Fuller and Dan Myers prof. law, 2004—07; prof. law, Judge Frank Johnson Jr. scholar U. Ala. Sch. Law, 2007—. Tutor civil procedure, rsch. asst. U. Calif., Davis, 1985—87, instr., 1998, lectr., 1998—2002; adj. prof. McGeorge Sch. Law, 1998—99, dir. legal process, 1999—2000, vis. prof., 2000—01; vis. prof. law U. Calif., Davis, 2005—06. Editor: U. Calif. Law Rev., 1985—86; sr. articles editor:, 1986—87. Mem.: ABA (vice chmn. ethics com. young lawyers divsn. 1989—91, exec. com. labor and employment law com. 1989—90), APA (assoc.), Am. Law Inst., Order of the Coif. Democrat. Avocations: music, tennis, travel, hiking. Home: 801 Middlebrooks Cir Tallahassee FL 32312 Office: U Ala Sch Law Box 870382 Tuscaloosa AL 35487

BASSETT, ELIZABETH EWING (LIBBY BASSETT), writer, editor, consultant; b. Cleve., July 22, 1937; d. Ben and Eileen Grace (Ewing) B.; m. Robert Richter, Feb. 20, 1994. AA, Bradford Jr. Coll., Mass., 1957. Girl Friday Time-Life, animated film cos., others, 1957-63; asst. producer, stage mgr. N.Y. State Pavilion at N.Y. World's Fair, 1963-64; writer, reporter, editor AP, NYC, 1965-72; free-lance corr. AP, Newsweek, Voice of America, UNICEF, ABC Radio, Africa, 1972-74; resident corr. ABC News, Cairo, 1974-77; dir. publs. and comm. World Environment Ctr., NYC, 1978-85; cons. writer, editor, editorial designer Women's Environ. and Devel. Orgn., 1989—98, UN orgns. and others, 1985—2000; co-organizer Project on Religion and Human Rights, 1994-95. Guest lectr. Am. U. Cairo, Rutgers U., Columbia U., L.I. U., Hunter Coll., CUNY; press officer Global Survival Conf., Oxford, Eng., 1988; press coord. Global Forum on Environ. and Devel., Moscow, 1990, Parliamentary Earth Summit, Rio de Janeiro, 1992; info. officer Internat. Green Cross/Global Forum, Kyoto, Japan, 1993; comm. coord. World Women's Congress for a Healthy Planet, Miami, 1991; press. coord. WEDO Web, NGO Forum on Women, China, 1995. Author: The Growth of Environment in the World Bank, World Environment Center, 1982, UNEP N.Am. News, 1986-91, Shared Vision, 1988-92, The Global Forum Decade, 1995, Earth and Faith: A Book of Reflection for Action, 2000, also others; editor, designer: Women in African Economies--From Burning Sun to Boardroom, 2000, Liberian

Women Peacemakers, 2004; assoc. editor, designer: The Bella Abzug Reader, 2003; coord. Wharton Pvt. Wealth Mgmt. Program; cons. writer, editor Inst. for Pvt. Investors, 1999—. Mem.: Soc. Profl. Journalists, Soc. Environ. Journalists.

BASSETT, JOHN E., academic administrator, language educator; b. Washington, May 12, 1942; s. J. Earl and Frances E. (Walker) B.; m. Kay E. Hobart, Sept. 5, 1964; children: Laura, Gregory. BA in History, Ohio Wesleyan U., Delaware, 1963, MA in English, 1966; PhD in English, U. Rochester, NY, 1970. Instr. U. Rochester, NY, 1969-70; asst. prof. Wayne State U., Detroit, 1970-75, assoc. prof., 1975-84; prof., head dept. English No. Carolina State U., Raleigh, 1984-93; dean Coll. Arts and Scis., prof. English Case Western Res. U., Cleve., 1993-2000; pres. Clark U., Worcester, 2000—. Author: William Faulkner: An Annotated Checklist of Criticism, 1972, Faulkner: The Critical Heritage, 1975, Faulkner: A Checklist of Recent Criticism, 1983, Vision and Revisions: Essays on Faulkner, 1989, Faulkner in the Nineties: A Bibliography of Criticism, 1991, A Heart of Ideality in My Realism and Other Essays on Howells and Twain, 1991, Harlem in Review: Critical Reactions to Black American Writers 1917-1939, 1992, Defining Southern Literature, 1997, Thomas Wolfe: An Annotated Bibliography of Criticism, 1996, Sherwood Anderson, 2005; contbr. articles to profl. jours. Bd. dirs. NAICU. Mem. MLA, Thomas Wolfe Soc., Soc. for Study of So. Lit., Assn. Depts. of English (pres. 1990-91), Phi Beta Kappa, Phi Kappa Phi, Phi Alpha Theta. Office: Clark U 950 Main St Worcester MA 01610-1477 Business E-Mail: jbassett@clarku.edu.

BASSETT, JOHN WALDEN, JR., lawyer; b. Roswell, N.Mex., Mar. 21, 1938; s. John Walden Sr. and Evelyn (Thompson) B.; m. Patricia Lubben, May 22, 1965 (dec. Apr. 1995); children: John Walden III, Loren Patricia; m. Nolana Knight, May 2, 1998. AB in Econs., Stanford U., Calif., 1960; LLB with honors, U. Tex., 1964. Bar: Tex. 1964, N.Mex. 1964. Assoc. Atwood & Malone, Roswell, 1964-66; White House fellow, spl. asst. to U.S. Atty. Gen., Washington, 1966-67; ptnr. Atwood, Malone, Mann & Turner and predecessors, Roswell, 1967-95, Bassett & Copple, LLP, Roswell, 1995—. Bd. dir. AMMA Found., Washington. Assoc. editor U. Tex. Law Rev., 1962. Mem. N.Mex. State Bd. Edn., 1987-91; pres., chmn. bd. United Way of Chaves County, N.Mex., 1973; bd. dirs. Ednl. Achievement Found., Roswell, 1992—; pres. Roswell Mus. Found., 2004-07. 1st lt. U.S. Army, 1961-68. Named one of Best Lawyers in Am. Trusts and Estates, 2007; recipient Lifetime Achievement award, United Way, 2007. Mem. ABA, Tex. Bar Assn., N.Mex. Bar Assn., Chaves County Bar Assn., Order of Coif, Rotary (pres. 1976), N.Mex. Amigos, Phi Delta Phi. Republican. Episcopalian. Home: 5060 Bright Sky Rd Roswell NM 88201-8800 Office: Bassett & Copple 400 N Pennsylvania Ave Ste 250 Roswell NM 88201-4788 Office Phone: 505-622-3100. Business E-Mail: bandc@dfn.com.

BASSETT, LAWRENCE C., management consultant; b. NYC, Dec. 11, 1931; s. David Isaac and Genia Esther Bassett; m. Charlotte Corinne Margolis, Jan. 24, 1960; children: Wendy Jill, Craig Henrid, Heidi Jill, Evan Henrid. BA, NYU, 1953, MBA, 1958. Pers. mgr. Republic Carloading & Distbg. Co., NYC, 1956-61; dir. pers. Clay Adams Inc., NYC, 1961-63; asst. dir. pers. Montefiore Hosp. and Med. Ctr., NYC, 1963-65; dir. pers. Hosp. for Joint Diseases and Med. Ctr., NYC, 1965-67; sr. cons. Orgn. Resources Counselors Inc., NYC, 1967-76; pres. Applied Leadership Tech. Inc., Bloomfield, NJ, 1976-86, The Bassett Cons. Group Inc., Thornwood, NY, 1986—. Adj. prof. NYU, 1978—, N.Y. Med. Coll., 1992, Fairleigh Dickenson U., Teaneck, N.J., 1964-86; instr. Helene Fuld Sch. for RN's, N.Y.C., 1966-67. Author: Achieving Excellence, 1986; producer & presenter audio & video tape tng. albums; contbr. articles to profl. jours. Pres., v.p. Mt. Pleasant Bd. Edn., Thornwood, N.Y., 1973-76, 81-87; docent Am. Mus. Natural History. With U.S. Army, 1953-55. Mem. ASTD, Soc. Profl. Mgmt. Cons. (bd. dirs., v.p.), Inst. Mgmt. Cons. (cert. mgmt. cons.), Am. Hosp. Assn., NY Geneal. and Biog. Soc. (vice chmn., trustee 2006—), Masons. Avocations: clock making, baking, beekeeping, skiing, orchid growing. Home and Office: The Bassett Cons Group Inc 1 Ilana Ln Thornwood NY 10594-2001

BASSETT, LESLIE RAYMOND, composer, educator; b. Hanford, Calif., Jan. 22, 1923; s. Archibald Leslie and Vera (Starr) B.; m. Anita Elizabeth Denniston, Aug. 21, 1949; children— Wendy Lynn (Mrs. Lee Bratton), Noel Leslie, Ralph (dec.). BA in Music, Fresno State Coll., 1947; M.Music in Composition, U. Mich., 1949, A.Mus.D., 1956; student, Ecole Normale de Musique, Paris, France, 1950-51. Tchr. music pub. schs., Fresno, 1951-52; mem. faculty U. Mich., 1952—, prof. music, 1965—, Albert A. Stanley disting univ. prof., 1977—, chmn. composition dept., 1970, Henry Russel lectr., 1984, emeritus, 1992. Guest composer Berkshire Music Center, Tanglewood, Mass., 1973 Served with AUS, 1942- 46. Fulbright fellow, 1950-51; recipient Rome prize Am. Acad. in Rome, 1961-63; grantee Soc. Pub. Am. Music, 1960, Nat. Inst. Arts and Letters, 1964, Nat. Council Arts, 1966; Guggenheim fellow, 1973-74, 80-81; recipient Pulitzer prize in music for Variations for Orch., 1966; citation U. Mich. regents, 1966; Walter Naumburg Found. rec. award for Sextet, 1974; Disting. Alumnus award Calif. State U., Fresno, 1978; Disting. Artist award Mich. Council Arts, 1981; Citation of Merit, U. Mich. Sch. Music Alumni, 1980 Mem. Am. Composers Alliance, Mich. Soc. Fellows, Am. Acad. of Arts and Letters, Pi Kappa Lambda, Phi Kappa Phi, Phi Mu Alpha. Methodist.

BASSETT, ROBERT ANDREWS, lawyer; b. Pitts., Dec. 7, 1946; s. Ralph Harris and Mary (Andrews) B.; m. Victoria Ann Panettiere, June 15, 1969; children: Robert Anthony, Christopher James. Student, San Diego State U., 1964-65; BS in Engring., U.S. Mil. Acad., 1969; postgrad., MIT, 1974-75; JD, Quinnipiac Sch. Law, 1991. Bar: Conn. 1991. Commd. 2d lt. U.S. Army, 1969, advanced through grades to capt., 1971; assigned to Air Def. Arty., El Paso, Tex., 1969, Ansbach, Germany, 1969-72, Kunsan and Osan, Republic of Korea, 1972-73, Stewart AFB, N.Y., 1973-74; resigned, 1974; mktg. mgr., product mgr. Linde divsn. Union Carbide Corp., NYC, 1975-82, bus. mgr. Danbury, Conn., 1982-92; corp. counsel, asst. sec. Praxair, Inc., Danbury, 1992—. Mem. proxy fees adv. com. N.Y. Stock Exch., 1995. Contbr. articles on corp. governance to law jours. Chmn. goals com. Newtown (Conn.) Bd. Edn., 1986; chmn. music devel. adv. com. C.H. Booth Pub. Libr., Newtown, 1998—. Mem.: Am. Soc. Corp. Secs. (dir., mem. exec. com., corp. practices com. 1993—, chmn. publs. subcom. 1994—). Home: 10 Monitor Hill Rd Newtown CT 06470-2243 Office: Praxair Inc 39 Old Ridgebury Rd Ste M-1 Danbury CT 06810-5103 E-mail: bob_bassett@praxair.com.

BASSETT, TINA, communications executive; b. Detroit; m. Leland Kinsey Bassett; children: Joshua, Robert. Student, U. Mich., 1974, 76-78, 81, Wayne State U., 1979-80. Advt. dir. Greenfield's Restaurant, Mich. and Ohio, 1972-73; dir. advt. and pub. rels. Kresco, Inc., Detroit, 1973-74; pub's. rep. The Detroiter mag., 1974-75; pub. rels. dir. Detroit Bicentennial Commn., 1975-77; prin. Leland K. Bassett & Assocs., Detroit, 1976-86; intermediate job devel. specialist Detroit Coun. of the Arts, 1977; project dir. Detroit image campaign dept. pub. info. City of Detroit, 1975, spl. events dir., 1978, dep. dir. dept. pub. info., 1978-83, dir. dept. pub. info., 1983-86; pres., prin. Bassett & Bassett, Inc., Detroit, 1986—. Publicity chmn. Under the Stars IV, V, VI, VII, VIII, IX and X, Benefit Balls, Detroit Inst. Arts Founders Soc., 1983-88, Mich. Opera Theater, Opera Ball, 1987, Grand Prix Ball, 1989; bd. dirs., co-chair, prodr. Music Hall Ctr. for Performing Arts, pub. chmn., 1996, bd. dirs., 2007—; bd. dirs. Weizman Inst. Sci., 1996-97, Detroit Inst. Arts, 2006—; mem. Cinema Arts Coun., 1996—. Named Outstanding Woman in Agy. Top Mgmt., Detroit chpt. Am. Women in Radio and TV, 1989, one of Most Powerful Women in Mich., CORP Mag., 2002. Mem. AIA (hon., pub. dir. 1990-91, bd. dirs., Richard Upjohn fellowship 1991), Detroit Hist. Soc., Internat. Women's Forum, Music Hall Assn., Pub. Rels. Soc. Am. (Advt. Woman of Yr. 1989), Woman's Advt. Club Detroit. Home: 30751 Cedar Creek Dr Farmington Hills MI 48336-4989 Office: Bassett & Bassett Inc 1400 First National Bldg 660 Woodward Av Detroit MI 48226-3581 Office Phone: 313-965-3010. Office Fax: 313-965-3016.

BASSETT, WILLIAM, JR., geospatial intelligence officer; b. St. Louis, July 4, 1956; s. William Bassett and Lois Mae (Vincent) Valentine, Edgar Laurence Valentine (Stepfather). BA, U. Ctrl. Mo., 1983; MA, Tchrs. Coll. Columbia U., 1988; diploma, U. Dijon, France, 1982; M in Liberal Arts, Johns Hopkins U., 2005. Math. sci. tchr. US Peace Corps, Moabi, Gabon, 1983—85; peace corps fellow NYC Bd. of Edn. and Tchrs. Coll., Columbia U., 1986—88; cartographer Def. Mapping Agy. Dept. of Def., Bethesda, Md., 1988—92; database mgr. Def. Mapping Agy., Nat. Imagery and Mapping Agy., 1992—2000; regional analyst NIMA Nat. Geospatial-Intelligence Agy., Washington, 2000; staff officer Pentagon, Arlington, Va., 2003—04. Sgt. USMC, 1974—78, US., Republic of Philippines, sgt. US Army N.G., 1982—83. Recipient Letter of Appreciation, Def. Mapping Agency, 1990, 1991, 1992, Spl. Act award, Def. Mapping Agency, NIMA, 1993, 1996, 1997, 1998, 1999, 2000, Quality Improvement award, Def. Mapping Agency, 1994, Editor's Choice award, Nat. Libr. Poetry, 1995, Tradecraft award - For Excellence in Current Intelligence, Nat. Geospatial Intelligence Agy., 2004, Nat. Intelligence Meritorious Unit Citation, Nat. Fgn. Intelligence Cmty., 2003, Brick award For Outstanding Svc. and Dedication, Alliance of the Guardian Angels, 2001, 2002, Performance award, Dept. Def., 1991, 1992, 1993, 1994. Mem.: Assn. Symbolic Logic, Mensa, Internat. High IQ Soc., Kappa Delta Pi, Alpha Mu Gamma, Phi Theta Kappa. Avocations: reading, martial arts (black belt). Home: 1131 University Blvd W 515A Silver Spring MD 20902 Home Phone: 301-593-4348. Personal E-mail: lefty21@earthlink.net.

BASSETT, WILLIAM AKERS, retired geologist, educator; b. Bklyn., Aug. 3, 1931; s. Preston Rogers and Jeanne Reed (Mordorf) B.; m. Jane Ann Kermes, Sept. 8, 1962; children: Kari Nicalo, Jeffrey Kermes, Penelope North. BA, Amherst Coll., 1954; MA, Columbia U., 1956, PhD, 1959. Research assoc. Brookhaven Nat. Lab., 1960-61; Asst. prof. U. Rochester, NY, 1961-65, asso. prof., 1965-69, prof. geology, 1969-77, Cornell U., Ithaca, NY, 1978—99, ret., 1999. Vis. prof. Brigham Young U., 1967-68; Crosby vis. prof. MIT, 1974 Research, publs. on the devel. of techniques for investigation of properties of minerals at pressures and temperatures within the earth's interior Recipient Bridgman award Internat. Assn. for Rsch. at High Pressure and Temperature, 1997; NSF grantee; Guggenheim fellow, 1985. Fellow Geol. Soc. Am., Mineral. Soc. Am. (Roebling medal 1994, Bridgman award 1997), Am. Geophys. Union, AAAS; mem. Sigma Xi (pres. Rochester chpt. 1977-78). Home: 765 Bostwick Rd Ithaca NY 14850-9310 Office Phone: 607-272-5387. E-mail: bassett@geology.cornell.edu.

BASSETT, WOODSON WILLIAM, JR., lawyer; b. Okmulgee, Okla., Nov. 7, 1926; s. Woodson William and Bee Irene (Knerr) B.; m. Marynm Shaw, Dec. 16, 1950; children: Woodson William III, Beverly M., Tod Corbett. JD, U. Ark., 1949. Bar: Ark. 1949. Employed in New Orleans and Monroe, La., 1949-51; claims examiner Employers Group Ins. Cos., 1949-51; mgr. Light Adjustment Co., 1951-56; v.p. legal dept. Preferred Ins. Cos., 1957-62; sr. partner Bassett Law Firm, 1962—. Spl. chief justice Ark. Supreme Ct., 1991—; mem. Ark. Bd. Law Examiners Mem. editorial staff: Ark. Law Review, 9. Pres. Sherman Lollar Boys Baseball League, 1962; v.p. Babe Ruth Baseball Assn., 1968; chmn. bd. dirs. Fayetteville Public Library, 1975-79. Served with AUS, 1950-51. Fellow Am. Coll. Trial Lawyers; mem. ABA, Ark. Bar Assn., Washington County Bar Assn. (pres. 1973-74), Am. Bd. Trial Advs., Delta Theta Phi, Kappa Sigma. Home: 2210 E Manor Dr Fayetteville AR 72701-2640 Office: Bassett Law Firm 221 N College Ave Fayetteville AR 72701-4238 Business E-Mail: b.bassett@bassettlawfirm.com.

BASSEY, RONALD D., tax attorney; b. Detroit, Mich., Feb. 15, 1939; s. Charles Isaac and Mae G. Bassey; m. Joan Rosenberg Bassey, June 7, 1964; children: Kenneth Q., Eric R. BA, U. Mich., 1961; JD, Harvard Law Sch., 1964. Staff supr. Touche Ross and Co., Mich., 1964—71; sr. mgr. Bassey and Selesko PLC, Southfield, Mich., 1971—. Contbr. articles to profl. jours. Legal adv. bd. mem. Small Bus. Coun. of Am., Wash., DC, 1990—. Mem.: Am.Soc. for Technion, Detroit Econ. Club. Avocation: stamp collecting/philately. Office: Bassey and Selesko PLC 27777 Franklin Rd #1400 Southfield MI 48034 Office Phone: 248-355-5000.

BASSFORD, LYNN FOSTER, physicist, engineer manager; b. Webster, Mass., Jan. 23, 1969; d. George E. and Carolyn M. BS in Physics, U. Lowell, Lowell, 1991. NASA cert. for Hubble Space Telescope's Flight Ops. sci. instruments, data mgmt., instrumentation and comms., elec. power, shift supr., and thermal control subsystems. Satellite flight contr. Lockheed Martin Mission Svcs., GSFC, NASA, Greenbelt, Md., 1991-95; Hubble Space Telescope satellite shift supervisor flight ops Lockheed Martin Tech. Ops., NASA, Goddard Space Flight Ctr., Greenbelt, Md., 1995-99, HST sci. instrument systems engr., 1999-2000, sci. instruments sys. engr. group leader, 2000—04; ops. mgr. Moses HST Missions & Flight, 2005—; flight ops. branch head Johns Hopkins Space Sci. Inst., 2005—07. Mem. Nat. Soc. Physics Students. Business E-Mail: lbassford@hst.nasa.gov.

BASS-HOLLIS, CYNTHIA GIBSON, environmental services administrator; b. Charlotte, NC, May 19, 1958; d. John Harold and Virgina Lee Gibson; m. Lawrence Thomas Hollis, Aug. 4, 2000; children: Sean Matthew Bass, Adam Michael Bass, Kathryn Bateman, Joseph Paul Hollis, Amanda Raye Hollis, James Hollis, Eileen Hollis, Joshua Anthony Hollis, Jacob Allen Hollis. BS in Microbiology, U. N.C., Charlotte, 1980. Registered environ. health specialist NC, 1981, Nat. Environ. Health Assn., 2005. Quality control specialist Heinz Inc, Charlotte, 1980—81; environ. health specialist Mecklenburg County Health Dept, Charlotte, 1981—. Cert. milk/water analyst Mecklenburg County, Charlotte, 1981—84. Sch. vol. Charlotte-Mecklenburg Sch. Systems, 1989—2006; pres. PTA Idlewild Elem., Charlotte, 1994—96; voting precinct judge Mecklenburg County Bd. Elections, Charlotte, 1995—2006. Named Employee of Yr., Mecklenburg County Health Dept, 1990. Mem.: Nat. Environ. Health Assn., West Piedmont Environ. Health Assn., NC Pub. Health Assn. Independent. Presbyterian. Avocations: gardening, sports, crossword puzzles, reading, travel. Office: Mecklenburg County 700 N Tryon St Charlotte NC 28202 Home Phone: 704-544-0429; Office Phone: 704-621-0124. Personal E-mail: chs0867@hotmail.com.

BASSI, SUZANNE HOWARD, retired secondary school educator, volunteer; b. Santa Ana, Calif., Feb. 26, 1945; d. David Gould and Marian (Matthews) H.; Roger Joseph Bassi, Aug. 25, 1973; children: Carrie, Steven, Gregory. BA, Rosary Coll., River Forest, Ill., 1966; MA in Teaching, U. Ill., Champaign, 1973. Tchr. Resurrection HS, Chgo., 1966-67, Proviso Twp. HS, Hillside, Ill., 1967-76; home day care operator Palatine, Ill., 1980-84; mem. bd. Palatine Elem. Sch. Dist. # 15, 1987-95. Vice chmn. Ed-Red, Park Ridge, Ill., 1993, chmn., 1994-96; legis. chmn. Ill. Assn. Sch. Bds., North Cook divsn., Lombard, Ill., 1994-96; Rep. candidate dist. 54 Ill. Gen. Assembly, 1996, state rep. dist. 54, 1998—. Named Those Who Excel, Ill. State Bd. Edn., 1992. Mem. LWV (former bd. dir., legis. chair), Rep. Women's Roundtable. Republican. Roman Catholic. Home: 1272 S Falcon Dr Palatine IL 60067

BASSIN, JULES, foreign service officer; b. NYC, Apr. 16, 1914; s. Abe and Bessie (Brooks) B.; m. Beatrice M. Kellner, Dec. 25, 1938; children: Arthur Jay, Nelson Jay. BS, CCNY, 1936; JD, N.Y.U., 1938; student, Criminal Investigation Sch., U.S. Army, 1943, Security Intelligence Sch., 1944, Mil. Govt. Sch., U. Va., 1944, Far East Civil Affairs, Harvard, 1945; grad., Armed Forces Staff Coll., 1960. Bar: N.Y. bar 1939. Dir. law div. Gen. Hdqrs., Supreme Comdr. Allied Powers, Tokyo, Japan, 1945-51; legal attache Am. embassy, Tokyo, 1951-56; also spl. asst. to ambassador for politico-mil. affairs; spl. asst. to ambassador for mut. security affairs Am. Embassy, Karachi, 1956-59; State Dept. faculty adviser Armed Forces Staff Coll., Norfolk, Va., 1960-62; chief titles and rank br. Dept. State, 1962-63, chief functional assignments br., 1963-65, dir. functional personnel program, 1965-67, spl. asst. to dep. undersec. state for adminstrn., 1967-69, exec. sec. Bd. Fgn. Service, 1967-69; dep. rep. of U.S. to European office UN and other internat. orgns.; also dep. chief U.S. mission with personal rank of minister, Geneva, Switzerland, 1969-74; cons. on refugee and migration affairs Dept. State, 1974—; cons. USIA, 1975-76. Served from 2d lt. to col., Judge Adv. Gen. Corps. AUS, 1942-46; col. Res. Mem. Am. Fgn. Service Assn. Clubs: American Internat. (Geneva) (exec. com.).

BASSINGTHWAIGHTE, JAMES BUCKLIN, physiologist, educator, medical researcher; b. Toronto, Sept. 10, 1929; s. Ewart MacQuarrie and Velma Emeline B.; m. Joan Elizabeth Graham, June 18, 1955; children: Elizabeth Anne, Mary, Alan, Sarah, Rebecca. BA, U. Toronto, 1951, MD, 1955; postgrad., Med. Sch. London, 1957-58; PhD, Mayo Grad. Sch. Medicine U. Minn., Rochester, 1964. Intern Toronto Gen. Hosp., 1955-56; physician Internat. Nickel Co., Sudbury and Matheson, Ont., 1956-57; house physician Hammersmith Hosp., London; postgrad. Med. Sch. London, 1957-58; teaching asst. physiology U. Minn., Mpls., 1961-62; fellow Mayo Grad. Sch. Medicine, Rochester, Minn., 1958-64, instr., 1964-67, asst. prof., 1967-69, assoc. prof., 1969-72; vis. prof. Pharmacology Inst., U. Bern, Switzerland, 1970-71; asso. prof. bioengring. U. Minn., 1972-75; prof. physiology Mayo Grad. Sch. Medicine, 1973-75, prof. medicine, 1975; prof. bioengring., radiology and biomath U. Wash., Seattle, 1975—; dir. Ctr. for Bioengring., 1975-80; vis. prof. medicine and physiology McGill U., 1979-81; affiliate prof. physiology Limburg U., Maastricht, Netherlands, 1990—. Mem. study sect. NIH, 1970-74, 80-83, chmn., 2004; chmn. Biotech. Resources Adv. Com., 1977-79, chmn. 1st Gordon Rsch. Conf. on Water and Solute Transport in Microvasculature, 1976; chmn. workshop on metabolic imaging Nat. Heart, Lung and Blood Inst., 1985; bd. dirs. Nat. Space Biomed. Rsch. Inst., NASA, 2002—; adv. bd. mem. Burroughs Wellcome Fund, 2004—, co-chmn. interface in sci. program, 2006—; Lewellen-Thomas lectr., U. Toronto, 1991; Coulter lectr. U. N.C., 1995; Oxford lectr. Internat. Soc. Magnetic Resonance Medicine, 1996; mem. ednl. materials com. Whitaker Found., 1995-2005; CASI award com. Burrough Wellcome Fund, 2004—, chair, 2007—. Author: (with L.S. Liebovitch and B.J. West) Fractal Physiology, 1994; contbr. over 270 articles to profl. publs. Recipient NIH Rsch. Career Devel. award, 1964-74, Louis and Artur Lucian award McGill U., 1979, Witzig award Cardiovasc. Sys. Dyamics Soc., 1982, Faculty Achievement award for outstanding rsch. U. Wash. Coll. Engring., 1993; Edmund Hustinx chair Maastricht U., 1999. Fellow Biomed. Engring. Soc. (dir. 1971-74, pres. 1977-78, Alza award 1986, editor-in-chief Annals of Biomed. Engring. 1993-2001, assoc. editor 2002—, Disting. Svc. award 1999); mem. AAAS, NAE, Am. Heart Assn. (coun. on circulation 1976—), Biophys. Soc. (assoc. editor Biophys. Jour. 1980-83), Microcirculatory Soc. (mem. coun. 1975-78, 80-83, pres. 1990-91, Landis award 1995), Am. Physiol. Soc. (mem. circulation group, editl. bd. 1972-76, 79-83, mem. edn. com., chair cardiovasc. sect. 1995-96, Wiggers award 2005), Internat. Union Physiol. Scis. (U.S.A. nat. com. 1978-86, U.S. del. to assembly 1980, 83, 86, chmn. 1983-86, chmn. Commn. on Bioengring. and Clin. Physiology 1986-97, chmn. satellite to 30th Congress on Endothelial Transport 1986, co-chmn. satellite on microvascular networks 1989, chmn. satellite on Physiome Project 1997, com. on physiome 1997—), Nat. Acad. Engring. (mem. peer com. 2005—, chair 2006—, Russ award com. 2006-07). Achievements include research in cardiovascular physiology and bioengineering, biomathematics and computer simulation with emphasis on ion and substrate exchange in heart, fractals in physiology, integrative biology and originator of the Physiome Project. Home: 3150 E Laurelhurst Dr NE Seattle WA 98105-5333 Office: U Wash Dept Bioengring PO Box 35-5061 Seattle WA 98195-5061 Office Phone: 206-685-2005. Business E-Mail: jbb2@u.washington.edu.

BASSIS, MICHAEL STEVEN, academic administrator; b. NYC, Sept. 8, 1944; s. Lewis and Barbara (Fay) B.; m. Mary Suzanne Wilson, Dec. 27, 1977; children: Anne Elizabeth, Christina, Jessica, Nicholas. BA with honors, Brown U., 1967; MA, U. Chgo., 1968, PhD, 1974. Asst. dir. acad. potential project Brown U., 1966-67; rsch. assoc. Ctr. for the Study of the Acts of Man U. Pa., 1968; instr., asst. prof.-assoc. prof. dept. sociology and anthropology U. R.I., 1971-81, acting asst. dean Coll. Arts and Scis., 1977-78; assoc. Harvard U. Grad. Sch. Edn., 1980-81; assoc. dean faculty U. Wis., Parkside, 1981-85, assoc. prof. sociology, 1981-86, interim asst. chancellor ednl. svcs., 1985-86; v.p. acad. affairs Ea. Conn. State U., 1986-89; exec. v.p., univ. provost Antioch U., Yellow Springs, Ohio, 1989-93; pres. Olivet (Mich.) Coll., 1993-98; dean, warden New Coll., U. South Fla., Sarasota, 1998—2001; president Westminster Coll. of Salt Lake City, 2002—. Presenter in field. Author (with W.R. Rosengren) The Social Organization of Nautical Education: The U.S., Great Britain and Spain, 1976, (with R.J. Gelles and A. Levine) Sociology: An Introduction, 4th edit., 1991, Social Problems, 1982; editor Teaching Sociology, 1982-85; contbr. articles to profl. jours. NIMH grantee, 1967-71, Exxon Edn. Found. grantee, N.Y.C., 1975, Fund for Improvement of Post-Secondary Edn. grantee, Washington, 1978. Mem. Am. Sociol. Assn. (undergrad. edn. sect., membership com. 1979-81, coun. 1980, 82, 86-89, teaching resources group 1984-86, publs. com. 1985, chair 1987-88), Am. Assn. Higher Edn., Nat. Soc. Experiential Edn. Office: Office of the President Westminster College 1840 South 1300 East Salt Lake City UT 84105 E-mail: mbassis@westminstercollege.edu.

BASSLER, BONNIE L., molecular biologist; BS with high honors, U. Calif., Davis, 1984; PhD, Johns Hopkins U., 1990. Head tchg. asst. Johns Hopkins U, 1985—86; postdoctoral fellow Agouron Inst., La Jolla, Calif., 1990—93, rsch. scientist, 1993—94; asst. prof. dept. molecular biology Princeton U., NJ, 1994—2000, assoc. prof., 2000—03, prof., 2003—. Assoc. faculty mem. Princeton Environ. Inst., 1996—; mem. com. academic standing Princeton U., 1996—99; instr. Cold Spring Harbor Lab., NY, 1996—2000; mem. sci. adv. bd. Quorex Pharms., 1999—, Cumbre, 2002—, Damon Runyon Cancer Rsch. Found., 2003; Burroughs Wellcome Fund vis. prof. La. State U., 2001; dir. grad. studies dept. molecular biology Princeton U., 2003—; investigator Howard Hughes Med. Inst., 2005—; internat. lectr. Contbr. articles to profl. jours.; mem. (editl. bd.) Molecular and Cellular Proteomics, 2001—, Jour. Bacteriology, 2001—, assoc. editor Genetics, 2001—04; editor: Molecular Microbiol., 2003—. Recipient Thomas Edison Patent award, NJ Rsch. & Devel. Coun., 2003, Waksman award, Theobald Smith Soc., 2003, Inventor of the Yr., New York Intellectual Property Law Assn., 2004; fellow, Am. Acad. Microbiol., 2002, MacArthur Found., 2002; grantee W.R. Grace & Co. fellowship, 1988. Fellow: Am. Acad. Arts & Scis.; mem.: Internat. Union of Microbiological Socs., Am. Soc. Cell Biology, Am. Soc. Biochemistry and Molecular Biology, Soc. Bioluminescence and Chemiluminescence, NAS (planning com. 2005), Am. Soc. Microbiology (conferences com. 2002—), Phi Kappa Phi, Phi Beta Kappa. Achievements include research in quorum sensing. Office: Princeton U Dept Molecular Biology 329 Lewis Thomas Lab Princeton NJ 08544*

BASSLER, ROBERT COVEY, artist, educator; b. NYC, Nov. 9, 1935; s. Robert Stein and Joan (Covey) B.; m. Linda Marie Allen, June 14, 1964. BA, Bard Coll., 1957; MFA, U. So. Calif., 1960. Instr. sculpture Occidental Coll., 1960-64; prof. sculpture Calif. State U., Northridge, 1964-97, prof. emeritus, 1998—. Artist in residence Calif. Inst. Tech., 1970-71; art film tour Arts Coun. Gt. Britain. Solo exhbns. include Comara Gallery, L.A., 1961, 63, Occidental Coll., L.A., 1961, 70, Calif. State U. Bakersfield, 1964, L.A. Mcpl. Art Gallery, Barnsdall Park, 1965, 81, Calif. State U., Northridge, 1965, Santa Barbara (Calif.) Mus. Art, 1968, Molly Barnes Gallery, L.A., 1969, Baxter Art Gallery, Calif. Inst. Tech., 1971, Galerie La Demeure, Paris, 1972, Amerika-Haus, West Berlin, 1972, Wenger Gallery, L.A., 1988, Security Pacific Pla., L.A., 1989-90, Calif. State U., Northridge, 1997, Orlando Gallery, Sherman Oaks, Calif., 1997; exhibited in group shows at Jewish Mus., N.Y.C., Milw. Art Ctr., San Francisco Mus. of Art, Los Angeles County Mus. of Art, Pasadena Mus. of Art, Long Beach (Calif.) Mus. of Art, LaJolla (Calif.) Mus. of Art, San Francisco Mus. of Art, Newport Harbor Art Mus., Oakland Mus. of Art, Esther Bear Gallery, Santa Barbara, Houston Mus. of Art, Ackland Meml. Art Ctr., Chapel Hill, N.C., Mus. Fine Arts, St. Petersburg, Fla., Jacksonville (Fla.) Art Mus., Musée d'Art Moderne, Paris, Galerie La Demeure, Paris, Redfern Gallery, London, U.S. Embassy, London, Wenger Gallery, L.A., Calif. Inst. Tech., Amerika Haus, Berlin, Century City, Calif., Fine Arts Gallery, San Diego, Art Park, L.A., Design Ctr., L.A., Washington Sq., Washington, Fine Arts Bldg., L.A., Valerie Miller Gallery, Palm Desert, Calif., Tom Bradley Terminal, L.A. Internat. Airport, Finegood Art Gallery, West Hills, Calif., Pacific Design Ctr., L.A., L.A. Contemporary Exhibitions; represented in permanent collections including Atlantic Richfield Corp., Container Corp. Am., Quinn & Assocs., L.A., Security Pacific Nat. Bank, Carter Hawley Hale Stores Inc., Home Savs. & Loan, The Ahmanson Collection, Chgo. Convention Ctr., Arts Coun. of Gt. Britain, U. So. Calif., Bard Coll., N.Y., Kirk O' The Valley, Reseda, Calif., Calif. State U., Northridge. With AUS, 1959-62. Recipient Pres.'s Creativity award Calif. State U., Northridge, 1978, Meritorious Performance award, 1989, 96. Achievements include developing technique for casting clear polyester resin. Address: 8329 Melvin Ave Northridge CA 91324-4132 Home Phone: 818-349-7710. Business E-Mail: robert.c.bassler@csun.edu. *My current work explores visual phenomena created by light and structural juxtapositions and their resulting effects upon one's concept of reality. Most recently painted interpretations of our planet's atmospheric patterns have been incorporated as provocative elements of beauty, fragility, order and chaos.*

BASSUK, ELLEN LINDA, psychiatrist; b. NYC, Feb. 8, 1945; d. Irving and Molly (Pakarow) B.; children: Daniel, Sarah. BA, Brandeis U., 1964; MD, Tufts U., 1968; Dr.P.S. (hon.), Northeastern U., 1993. Diplomate Am. Bd. Psychiatry. Intern Mt. Auburn Hosp., Cambridge, Mass., 1968-69; resident psychiatry Univ. Hosp., Boston, 1969-70, Boston State Hosp., Boston, 1970-71, Beth Israel Hosp., Boston, 1971-73, dir. psychiat. emergency svcs., 1974-82; fellow Bunting Inst., Cambridge, Mass., 1982-84; assoc. prof. psychiatry Harvard Med. Sch., Boston, 1983—. Founder, pres. Nat. Ctr. on Family Homelessness, Newton, Mass., 1988—, Manger Inst. Homelessness and Trauma, Newton, Mass.; mem. Com. on Health Care of Homeless Persons Inst. of Medicine, Washington, 1986-88. Editor: The Practitioners Guide to Psychoactive Drugs, 1977, 83, 91, 97; editor-in-chief Am. Jour. Orthopsychiatry, 1994-98; contbr. numerous articles to profl. jours. Fellow Am. Psychiat. Assn.; mem. Mass. Psychiat. Soc. Office: Nat Ctr Family Homelessness 181 Wells Ave Newton MA 02459-3332 Home: 70 Montvale Rd Newton MA 02459 Office Phone: 617-964-3834 14. E-mail: ellen.bassuk@familyhomelessness.org.

BAST, KENNETH GEORGE, healthcare executive; b. Milw., Oct. 31, 1949; s. George H. and Genevieve (Zimmel) B.; m. Patricia A. Hogan, Nov. 17, 1973. BSBA, Marquette U., 1971; MBA, U. Wis., 1977. Personnel asst. St. Joseph Hosp., Warren, Ohio, 1972-74; v.p. ops. Meml. Hosp., Burlington, Wis., 1974-80; pres. No. Ill. Med. Ctr., McHenry, Ill., 1980-82; v.p. TW3 Corp., Downer's Grove, Ill., 1982-84; v.p. health svcs. John Knox Village, Lee's Summit, Mo., 1984-89; cons. Hamilton/KSA, Mpls., 1989-97; v.p. health care consulting Benedictine Health System, St. Paul, 1998-2000; with Mgmt. Cons. in Healthcare, 2000—. Project dir. Mobile Intensive Care program Emergency Med. Services, McHenry, 1981-82; instr. Cen. Mo. State U., Kansas City, 1986-89; adj. faculty Master of Healthcare Adminstrn. program U. Minn., 1995-97; mem. review bd. of Swedish long term care health facilities, Jonkoping, Sweden, 1987; bd. dirs. Multi Hosp. Mut. Ins., Hamilton, Bermuda; cons. in field. Active McHenry Econ. Commn., 1982, Govs. Adv. Council on Aging, Mo., 1985-88. Mem. Am. Hosp. Assn., Nat. Council on Aging, Am. Coll. Health Care Execs. Roman Catholic. Avocation: photography. Office Phone: 952-953-3684. E-mail: bast@consultant.com.

BAST, KIMBERLY ANN, social studies educator; b. Raleigh, NC, May 15, 1971; d. Kenneth William and Carole Dillon Chapple; m. David Eric Bast, June 10, 1995; children: David John, Derek Michael. BS in Secondary Edn., Bloomsburg U., Pa., 1993; MS in Ednl. Devel. Strategies, Wilkes U., Wilkes-Barr, Pa., 2004. Cert. level II instr. Pa. Tchr. social studies Nazareth Sch. Dist., Pa., 1998—. Team mem. Student Assistance Program, Nazareth H.S., Pa., 1999—. Huddle coach Fellowship of Christian Athletes, 2007—. Mem.: Pa. State Edn. Assn., Nazareth Area Edn. Assn. Avocations: reading, walking, writing, time with family, helping at church. Office: Nazareth HS East Center St Nazareth PA 18064 E-mail: kbast@nazarethasd.org.

BASTIAANSE, GERARD C., lawyer; b. Holyoke, Mass., Oct. 21, 1935; s. Gerard C. and Margaret (Lally) B.; m. Paula E. Paliska, June 1, 1963; children: Elizabeth, Gerard. BSBA, Boston U., 1960; JD, U. Va., 1964. Bar: Mass. 1964, Calif. 1970. Assoc. Nutter, McClennen & Fish, Boston, 1964-65; counsel Campbell Soup Co., Camden, NJ, 1965-67; gen. counsel A&W Internat. (United Fruit Co.), Santa Monica, Calif., 1968-70; ptnr. Kindel & Anderson, Los Angeles, 1970—. Mem. ABA, Calif. Bar Assn., Mass. Bar Assn., Japan Am. Soc., Asia Soc., World Trade Ctr. Assn. Clubs: California (Los Angeles); Big Canyon Country (Newport Beach, Calif.). Home: 2 San Sebastian Newport Beach CA 92660-6828 Office: Kindel & Anderson 2030 Main St Ste 1300 Irvine CA 92614-7220

BASTIAN, DONALD NOEL, retired bishop; b. Estevan, Sask., Can., Dec. 25, 1925; s. Josiah and Esther Jane (Millington) B.; m. Kathleen Grace Swallow, Dec. 20, 1947; children: Carolyn Dawn, Donald Gregory, Robert Wilfrid, John David. BA, Greenville Coll., 1953, DST (hon.), 1974; BD, Asbury Theol. Sem., 1956, DD (hon.), 1991, Seattle Pacific U., 1965; DHL (hon.), Roberts Wesleyan Coll., 1990. Ordained to ministry Free Meth. Ch. N.Am., 1954; pastor chs. Lexington, Ky., 1953-56, New Westminster, B.C., Canada, 1956-61; pastor College Free Meth. Ch., Greenville, Ill., 1961-74; bishop Free Meth. Ch. N.Am., Toronto, Ont., Canada, 1974-90, mem. bd. adminstrn., 1964-90, exec. editor Light and Life mag., 1974-84, chmn. editorial adv. com. Light and Life mag., 1980-86; bishop Free Meth. Ch. in Can., 1990-93. Author: The Mature Church Member, 1960, Along the Way, 1974, Belonging, 1974; editor: The Joy of Christian Fathering: Five First Person Accounts, 1979, Counterfeit: The Lie of Living Together Unmarried, 1988. Recipient Disting. Svc. award Asbury Theol. Sem., 1974; Presdl. award Greenville Coll., 1972; Donald N. and Kathleen G. Bastian chair Wesley studies established at Tyndale Sem., Toronto, 2000. Mem. Can. Holiness Fedn. (pres. 1977, 78), Christian Holiness Assn. (v.p. 1977-78), Evang. Fellowship of Can. (pres. 1989-91). Mem. Free Methodist Ch. Home: 63 Adirondack Cres Brampton ON Canada L6R 1E5 Personal E-mail: dnbasti@aol.com. *I live by the conviction that, however durable it may seem, evil is by nature unstable. Righteousness, by contrast, gives stability to life in the long pull.*

BASTIAN, EDWARD H., air transportation executive; b. 1957; m. Anna Bastian; 1 child; 3 children from previous marriage. BBA, St. Bonaventure U., NY, 1979. CPA. Strategic planning ptnr. Price Waterhouse, NY, ptnr. audit practice; v.p. fin., contr. Frito Lay Internat. PepsiCo, Dallas, v.p. bus. process reengineering Frito-Lay; v.p. fin., contr. Delta Air Lines, Inc., Atlanta, 1998—2000, sr. v.p. fin., contr., 2000—05, exec. v.p., CFO, 2005—07, pres., CFO, 2007—; sr. v.p., CFO Acuity Brands, 2005. Internat. bd. dirs. Habitat for Humanity; bd. dirs. Woodruff Arts Ctr., Atlanta. Avocations: golf, travel, reading. Office: Delta Air Lines Inc PO Box 20706 Atlanta GA 30320-6001 Office Phone: 404-715-2600.*

BASTIAN, STANLEY A., lawyer; b. Seattle, Apr. 3, 1958; BS, U. Oreg., 1980; JD, U. Washington, 1983. Bar: Washington 1983, Oreg. Law clk. to Hon. Ward Williams Washington State Ct. Appeals Divsn. I, 1984—85; asst. city atty. Criminal Divsn. Office of City Atty., Seattle, 1985—88; atty. Jeffers Danielson Sonn & Aylward PS, 1988—. Mem.: Am. Acad. Trial Attys., Oreg. State Bar, ABA, Washington State Bar Assn. (pres.-elect 2006—07, bd. gov. 2004—06), Chelan-Douglas County Bar Assn. (pres. 2004—05). Avocation: travel. Office: Jeffers Danielson Sonn & Aylward PS 2600 Chester Kim Rd Wenatchee WA 98801 Office Phone: 509-662-3685. Office Fax: 509-662-2452. E-mail: stanb@jdsalaw.com.

BASTIANICH, LIDIA MATTICCHIO (LIDIA MOTIKA), chef, food service executive; b. Pula, Croatia, Oct. 11, 1947; m. Felice Bastianich (div.); 2 children. Owner Buonavia Restaurant, Forest Hills, NY, 1972—81, Villa Secondo, Fresh Meadows, NY, 1979—81, Felidia Restaurant, NY, 1981—; co-owner Becco Restaurant, NY, 1993—, Lidia's Restaurant, Kansas City, Mo., 1998—, Pitts., 2001—; founder, pres. Esperienze Italiane Travel, 1996—. Founder, owner Lidia's Flavors of Italy, 1988—; host, chef Lidia's Italian Table, 1998—2001, Lidia's Italian Am. Kitchen, 2001—, Lidia's Family Table, PBS Series. Author: (montly syndicated column) on Italian food, (cookbooks) La Cucina di Lidia, 1990, Lidia's Italian Table, 1998, Lidia's Italian American Kitchen (and host of PBS series of same name), 2001, Lidia's Family Table, 2004, Lidia's Italy, 2007. Established Lidia Matticchio Bastianich Found., 1999. Office: Felidia Restaurant 243 E 58th St New York NY 10022 Office Phone: 212-758-1479. Business E-Mail: info@lidiasitaly.com.*

BASTIN, CLINTON, retired chemical engineer, nuclear scientist; b. Lancaster, Ky., June 4, 1927; s. Clinton Bowen and Adelaide Klingman Bastin; m. Barbara Spencer Bastin; children: Clinton Bowen III, Nancy Bastin Perry, Anna Bastin McKee, Herbert Spencer. BSChemE, Ga. Inst. Tech., 1950. Chemistry instr, US Marine Corps Inst., Washington, 1945—46; fire protection engr. Southeastern Underwriters Assn., Atlanta, 1950—55; mgr. heavy water prodn., distbn., quality assurance tritium weapon components, plutonium 238 prodn., used nuc. fuel disposition US AEC, Aiken, SC, 1955—62, mgr. nuc. fuel reprocessing, nuclear waste, related programs, 1962—72, mem. steering com. gas centrifuge devel., 1966—72, tech. leader fuel reprocessing problems resolution Washington, 1972—74; cons. nuc. proliferation threats US Nat. Security Agys., Washington, 1972—96; chief light water fuel reprocessing br. US ERDA, Washington, 1975—76; lead tech. cons. Internat. Atomic Energy Agy., Vienna, 1976; tech. leader, us nonproliferation initiative with govt. of India US NSC Task Force, US Dept. State, Washington, 1977—79; mgr. fuel reprocessing devel. US Dept. Energy, Washington, 1979—82, coord. with Japan for nuc. fuel cycle devel., 1982—93; pres. Dept. Energy hdqs. employees union Nat. Treasury Employees Union, Washington, 1983—96; ret., 1997. V.p. US sect. World Coun. Nuc. Workers, Paris, 2000—; instr. Emory U. Lifelong Learning Ctr., Atlanta; spkr. in field; cons. in field. Author: (worldwide nuc. programs) US Nuclear Technology: Need for a New Approach, 1996, US Nuclear Technology: Need For New Vision, 1999. Pres. Kiwanis Club of Northlake Golden K, Decatur, Ga., 2004—. Named US Authority on Nuc. Fuel Processing, Dept. Energy, 1997; recipient Disting. Career Svc. award, 1997. Mem.: Am. Nuc. Soc. (chmn. Ga. sect. 2005—). Achievements include adoption by Russian Ministry for Atomic Energy and Russian Nuclear Workers Union of ideas for partnerships for improved safety of nuclear facilities and safeguards of nuclear materials, 1997. Avocations: walking, gardening, writing. Home: 987 Viscount Ct Avondale Estates GA 30002 Home Phone: 404-297-2005; Office Phone: 404-297-2005. Personal E-mail: clintonbastin@bellsouth.net.

BASTIN, THOMA, educational consultant; d. Donald Ray and Joanna Hamrick; m. William Donald Bastin, June 6, 1980; 1 child, Chelsea. BA, Ind. State U., Terre Haute, 1979; MS, Ind. U. Purdue U., Indpls., 1986. French and Spanish instr. Shelbyville Sr. H.S., Ind., 1979—98; French and mid. sch. careers instr. Waldron Jr./Sr. H.S., Ind., 1998—99; sr. ednl. cons. Holt, Rinehart and Winston Pubs., Austin, Tex., 1999—. Adj. faculty French dept. Ind. U. Purdue U., Indpls., 1988—92; presenter and spkr. in field. Contbr. state curriculum proficiency guides, curriculum guidelines, articles to publs. Vol. Salvation Army, Shelbyville, Ind., 1995—96. Named Cons. of Yr., Holt Rinehart and Winston, 2003; recipient Corp. Values award: Boundarylessness, Holt, Rinehart and Winston, 2003; grantee, NEH, 1993; Tchr. Creativity grantee, Eli Lilly Found., 1995. Mem.: Am. Coun. Fgn. Lang. Tchrs. Avocations: travel, volleyball, host parent for foreign exchange students. Home Phone: 317-861-4905.

BASTING, THOMAS J., SR., lawyer; Founding ptnr. Brennan Steil & Basting SC; ret., 2006. Mem.: Wis. Bar Assn. (pres.-elect 2006—07).: PO Box 1766 Madison WI 53701 Office Phone: 608-251-7770. Office Fax: 608-251-6626. E-mail: bastingconsult@tds.net.

BASTRENTA, BRIGITTE ELISABETH, school administrator; b. Moutiers, Savoie, France, Jan. 7, 1952; came to U.S., 1979; d. Marcel Rinaldo and Jeanne Eulalie (Chaville) B.; m. Rudolph Andrew Walter, Dec. 27, 1979; children: Laurie Nicole Walter, Julian Thomas Walter. BA, U. Paul Valéry, Montpellier, France, 1973, MA, 1974. Tchr. French Marin Acad., San Rafael, Calif., 1980-83, Arrowsmith Acad., Berkeley, Calif., 1989-96, dir. admission and devel., 1996—2004; devel. assoc. Katherine Delman Burke Sch., San Francisco, 2004—; admissions dir. Ecole Bilingue, Berkeley, Calif., 2005—. Tchr. French Diablo Valley Coll., Pleasant Hill, Calif., 1990-95; mem. WASC Accreditation Commn., 1998—. Editor (newsletter) Arrowsmith in Action, 1999—. Co-pres. East Bay French-Am. Sch. PTA, Berkeley, 1991-93; mem. Natural Resources Def. Coun. Mem. Amnesty Internat., Doctors Without Borders, So. Poverty Law Ctr., The Carter Ctr. Democrat. Avocations: swimming, skiing, hiking, travel, cooking. Home: 333 Scottsdale Rd Pleasant Hill CA 94523

BASU, ABHIJIT, geologist, educator; b. Calcutta, India; BSc in Geology, Presidency Coll., Calcutta, India, 1959; MSc, Calcutta U., India, 1961; PhD, Ind. U., 1975. Geologist Geol. Survey India; postdoctoral rschr. Harvard U., NASA; Class of 1948 Herman B Wells Endowed prof. Ind. U. Vis. scientist Lunar and Planetary Inst., Houston; mem. sci. bd. Internat. Rsch. Sch. Planetary Scis. U. Gabriele D'Annunzio, 1999—, vis. prof., Italy, 2001, U. Parma, Italy; chair dept. geol. scis. Ind. U. Contbr. articles to sci. jours.; assoc. editor: Jour. Sedimentary Petrology/Rsch., 1993—99, sci. editor: Geol. Soc. Am. Books, 1996—, mem. publs. com.: Geol. Soc. Am., 1996—; co-editor: Quantitative Provenance Studies in Italy, Memoir of the Geol. Survey of Italy, 2004. Recipient Disting. Svc. award, Cultural Assn. Bengal, N.Am., 1994, Geol. Soc. Am., 2006. Office: Dept Geol Scis Ind U 1001 E 10th St Bloomington IN 47405-1405 E-mail: basu@indiana.edu.

BASU, SHABARI, research scientist; b. Germany; d. Bishan and Malabika Basu; m. Raktim Bhattacharya. PhD, Calif. Inst. Tech., Pasadena, 2006. Rsch. asst. Calif. Inst. Tech., Pasadena, 2000—05; rsch. scientist Tex. A&M U., College Station, 2005—. Rsch. scientist Geophys. Fluid Dynamics Lab., Princeton, Pa., 2003—04; composer fusion music. Recipient postdoctoral rsch. fellowship, NASA, 2005; fellow, Nehru Cambridge Trust, 2000. Mem.: IEICO (hon.), Aggie Women in Leadership (assoc.; mentor 2006—). Achievements include discovery of mechanism behind the catastrophic dust storms on Mars and successfully simulated these using a Martian General Circulation Model. Office: Texas A&M U Dept Atmospheric Sci 3150 TAMU College Station TX 77843 Home Phone: 860-670-7974; Office Phone: 979-845-1482. Personal E-mail: shabari_bau@yahoo.com.

BATA, RUDOLPH ANDREW, JR., lawyer; b. Akron, Ohio, Jan. 9, 1947; s. Rudolph Andrew and Margaret Eleanor (Ellis) Bata; m. Genevieve Ruth Brannan, Aug. 25, 1968 (div. May 1985); 1 child, Seth Andrew; m. Linda Lee Waldo, Apr. 7, 1985; 1 child, Sarah Ariel. BS, So. Coll., Collegedale, Tenn., 1969; JD, Emory U., 1972. Bar: D.C. 1973, N.C. 1978, U.S. Dist. Ct. N.C. 1991, U.S. Ct. Appeals (4th cir.) 1991, U.S. Supreme Ct. 2004, cert.: Adminstrv. Office of Cts. (arbitrator, mediator). Assoc. ICC, Washington, 1972-73; in house counsel B.F. Saul Real Estate Investment Trust, Chevy Chase, Md., 1973-74; staff atty. Martha, Cafferky, Powers & Jordan, Washington, 1974-75; asst. corp. counsel Hardee's Food Systems, Inc., Rocky Mount, NC, 1975-78; ptnr. Bata & Blomeley, Murphy, NC, 1978-87, 88-90, Bata & Sumpter, Murphy, 1987-88; sole practice, 1990—. Arbitrator NASD; bd. dirs. Cherokee County United Fund, Murphy, 1981—83. Mem. ABA, NASD (bd. arbitrators), NC Bar Assn., DC Bar Assn., 30th Jud. Dist. Bar Assn., So. Soc. Adventist Attys. (pres. 1984-85), Cherokee County C. of C. (bd. dirs. 1980-82). Avocations: golf, tennis, hiking. Office: 225 Valley River Ave Ste A Murphy NC 28906-3000 Office Phone: 828-837-8684. Personal E-mail: batalaw@yahoo.com.

BATAILLE, GRETCHEN, academic administrator; B of English, Calif. Polytech. State U., M of English Edn.; DA, Drake U. Chair dept. English Ariz. State U., assoc. dean acad. personnel, until 1994; provost U. Calif., Santa Barbara, 1994-97; provost, acad. v.p. Wash. State U., Pullman, 1997-2000; sr. v.p., v.p. acad. affairs U. NC Sys., Chapel Hill, 2000—06; interim chancellor NC Sch. Arts, Winston-Salem, 2005—06; pres. U. No. Tex., Denton, 2006—. Author: Living the Dream in Arizona: The Legacy of Martin Luther King, Jr., 1992, Native American Women: A Biographical Dictionary, 1994, Ethnic Studies in the United States, 1998, others. Office: U N Tex PO Box 311277 Denton TX 76203-1277 Home Phone: 940-387-1940; Office Phone: 940-565-4307. Business E-Mail: gbataille@unt.edu.

BATALDEN, PAUL BENNETT, pediatrician, educator; b. Mpls., Dec. 4, 1941; s. Abner Bennett and Martha (Bjornstad) B.; m. LaVonne Marie Olson; children: Maren, Sonja. BA, Augsburg Coll., 1963; MD, BS, U. Minn., 1967. Diplomate Am. Bd. Pediatrics. Clin. assoc. Nat. Cancer Inst., Bethesda, Md., 1969; med. dir. Job Corps, Washington, 1970-72; dir. Community Health Svc., Rockville, Md., 1972-73; dir., Bur. Community Health Svc., Rockville, 1973-75; pediatrician Park Nicollet Med. Ctr., Mpls., 1975-86, quality assurance dir., 1976-84, chief oper. officer, 1984-86; v.p. med. care, head quality resource group Hosp. Corp. of Am., Nashville, 1986-94; Breech chmn. Dept. Health Care Quality Improvement Edn. and Rsch. Henry Ford Health Sci. Ctr., 1990—2000; prof. pediatrics and cmty. family medicine Dartmouth Med. Sch., prof., dir. Ctr. Healthcare Improvement Leadership Devel. Founding chmn., bd. dirs., sr. v.p. health profl. development Inst. for Healthcare Improvement; dir. leadership preventive medicine residency Dartmouth Hitchcock Med. Ctr.; cons. Accreditation Coun. Grad. Med. Edn. Author: Quality Assurance in Ambulatory Care, 1980, Clinical Improvement Action Guide, 1998; contbr. articles on quality improvement of healthcare, health professional development, and aspects of pediatric practice to profl. jours. Regent Augsburg Coll., Mpls., 1978-90. Recipient Guild of Honor, 1963, Pub. Svc. award Nat. Med. Assn., 1974, Disting. Alumnus award Augsburg Coll., 1984, Award of Honor, Am. Hosp. Assn., 1997, Codman award, 1998, Nemours Found. award for improving quality, 2002. Mem. Inst. of Medicine of NAS, Am. Acad. Pediatrics, Minn. Med. Assn., Tenn. Med. Assn., N.H. Med. Assn., Alpha Omega Alpha Office Phone: 603-650-6513.

BATALHA DA CONCEICAO, JOSE JOAO, chemistry professor, researcher; s. Joao Haracio Maria and Beatriz Berta Batalha da Conceicao. M, Yale U.; PhD, Rice U. Asst. prof. chemistry St. Gregory's U., Shawnee, Okla.; assoc. prof. Northwestern Okla. State U., Alva. Chair, co-chair phys. scis. Okla. Acad. Sci., Edmond, 2003—05; referee Chem. Educator, Boise, Idaho. Co-author: Progress in the Physics of Clusters. Named Outstanding Sr. in Chemistry, Am. Inst. Chemists, 1984; Robert A. Welch Pre-doctorate fellow, 1987—92. Mem.: Am. Chem. Soc., Phi Beta Kappa. Achievements include research in ion beam studies of the reactions of Cr_n^+ ($n = 2$ — 14) with D2: cluster — deuteride bond energies as a chemical probe of cluster electronic structure; photoelectron spectroscopy of anionic iron, cobalt & nickel clusters: correlation of electronic structure to reactivity; efficient production of C_{60} (Buckminsterfullerene), $C_{60}H_{36}$, and the solvated Buckide Ion. Home: 415 12th St Alva OK 73717 Office: Northwestern Okla State U 709 Oklahoma Blvd Alva OK 73717 Home Phone: 580-327-2118; Office Phone: 580-327-8560. Business E-Mail: jjconceicao@nwosu.edu.

BATALI, MARIO FRANCIS, chef; b. Yakima, Wash., Sept. 19, 1960; s. Armandino and Marilyn Batali; m. Susan Cahn; children: Benno, Leo. Student, Rutgers U., Le Cordon Bleu, London. Co-owner, chef Po, NYC, 1993, Lupa, NYC, Otto Enoteca Pizzeria, NYC, 2003—, Bistro du Vent, NYC, 2005; owner, chef Babbo Ristorante e Enoteca, NYC, 1998—, Esca, NYC, 2000—, Del Posto, NYC; owner Italian Wine Merchants, NYC, Bar Jamon, NYC, Casa Mono, NYC, OTTO Enoteca Pizzeria, NYC, Osteria Mozza, LA, Pizzeria Mozza, LA. Challenger Iron Chef TV cooking series; co-owner La Mozza, Tuscany. Author: Simple Italian Food, 1998, Mario Batali Holiday Food, 2000, The Babbo Cookbook, 2002, Molto Italiano: Simple Italian Recipes for Cooking at Home, 2005 (Best Internat. Cookbook award, James Beard Found., 2006), Mario Tailgates NASCAR Style, 2006; host Molto Mario, Food Network, Mario Batali's Italy. Named Man of Yr. in chef category, GQ Mag., 1999; recipient Best New Restaurant award for Babbo, James Beard Found., 1998, Who's Who in Food & Beverage award, D'Artagnan Cervena, 2001, Best Chef: NYC award, James Beard Found., 2002, Outstanding Chef award, 2005. Office: Babbo Ristorante e Enoteca 110 Waverly Pl New York NY 10011-9109*

BATALOV, LEO, lawyer; b. Krasnoturinsk, Russia, June 29, 1971; BA summa cum laude, Whitman Coll., 1996; JD highest honors, Univ. Wash., 1999. Bar: Wash. 1999. Assoc. atty., asset securitization, secured lending, mergers & acquisitions, securities law Heller Ehrman LLP, Seattle, 2000—. Contbr. articles to numerous profl. jours. Named Seattle Rising Star, SuperLawyer Mag., 2006. Mem.: ABA, Seattle Bar Assn., Wash. Bar Assn. Office: Heller Ehrman LLP Ste 6100 701 Fifth Ave Seattle WA 98104-7098

BATARSEH, AMANI MUSA, chemist, researcher; b. Amman, Jordan, Dec. 26, 1981; d. Musa Salameh and Montaha Batarseh. BS in Chemistry magna cum laude, La Roche Coll., Pitts., 2003; BA in Biology, La Roche Coll., 2003. Rschr. Georgetown U., DC, 2003—. Contbr. articles to profl. jours. Recipient Sci. & Tech. Rsch. award, Assn. Arab-Am. Scientists Am., 1999. Fellow: CHEMSOLVE (assoc.; sr. scientist 2002—03); mem.: Am. Chem. Soc. (corr.), Nat. Scholar's Honor Soc. (life). Personal E-mail: batarseha@gmail.com.

BATAVIA, MITCHELL, physical therapist, educator; b. Bklyn., Nov. 8, 1959; s. Gabriel and Renée (Hyman) Batavia; m. Evgenia Yakovleva, Aug. 12, 2001; 1 child, Michael Andrew. BS, U. of Del., 1978—81; MA, Columbia U., 1986; PhD, N.Y. U, 1994—97. Lic. Physical Therapist N.Y. State, 1981. Staff phys. therapist Inst. for Rehab. Medicine, NY U. Med. Ctr., 1981—84; home care phys. therapist Vis. Nurse Svc. of NY, 1984—86; pediatric phys. therapist NY Foundling Hosp., 1986—91; phys. therapy cons. Terence Cardinal Cooke Health Care Ctr., NYC, 1989—97; adj. lectr. Hunter Coll. Phys. Therapy Program, NYC, 1992—93, 1996; asst. prof. of phys. therapy NYU, 1998—2004, assoc. prof. phys. therapy, 2004—. Manuscript reviewer Neurology Sect., Am. Phys. Therapy Assn., Alexandria, Va., 2000—; manuscript reviewer for book submissions Butterworth-Heinemann, Boston, 1999—2001. Author: The Wheelchair Evaluation: A Practical Guide, 1998, Clinical Research for Health Professionals: A User Friendly Guide, 2001, Contraindications in Physical Rehabilitation, 2006; manuscript reviewer: Perceptual-Motor Skills, 2006; contbr. articles to profl. jours. Vol., food distbr. Coalition for the Homeless, NYC, 2002. Recipient NY U. Arch award, NY U., 1997; DeWitt Wallace Reader's Digest fellow, Inst. for Rehab. Medicine; NY U. Med. Ctr., 1978, Trainee for Phys. Therapy Clin. Rsch. in Doctoral Studies, Nat. Inst. for Disabilities Rsch. in Rehab., NY U., 1993—97, Robert Salant Post Doctoral fellow, Dept. of Phys. Therapy, NY U., The Inst. for Rehab., NY U. Med. Ctr., 1997—98, Rsch. Challenge fund, NY U., Sch. of Edn., 2000. Mem.: Neurology Sect. of the Am. Phys. Therapy Assn., Am. Phys. Therapy Assn. Avocation: music. Office: New York U 380 Second Ave 4th floor New York NY 10010 Office Phone: 212-998-9409. Business E-Mail: mitchell.batavia@nyu.edu.

BATCHELDER, ALICE M., federal judge; b. Wilmington, Del., Aug. 15, 1944; m. William G. Batchelder III; children: William G. IV, Elisabeth. BA, Ohio Wesleyan U., 1964; JD, Akron U., 1971; LLM, U. Va., 1988; LHD (hon.), Lake Erie Coll., 1993; LLD (hon.), U. Akron Sch. of Law, 2001. Tchr. Plain Local Sch. Dist., Franklin County, Ohio, 1965—66, Jones Jr. High Sch., 1966-67, Buckeye High Sch., Medina County, 1967-68; assoc. Williams & Batchelder, Medina, Ohio, 1971-83; judge US Bankruptcy Ct., Ohio, 1983-85, US Dist. Ct. (no. dist.) Ohio, Cleve., 1985-91, US Ct. of Appeals (6th cir.), Cleveland, 1991—. Mem. Com. on Bankruptcy Edn., Fed. Jud. Ctr., 1988—91, Jud. Conf. Adv. Com. on Bankruptcy Rules, 1993—96, Jud. Conf. on US Com. on Automation and Tech., 2000—03. Editor-in-chief Univ. Akron Law Rev., 1971. Recipient Outstanding Alumni award, U. Akron Sch. of Law, 1993, Hon. award, 1996, Women of Distinction award, Medina County YWCA, 1997. Mem. Fed. Judge's Assn., Fed. Bar Assn., Medina County Bar Assn.*

BATCHELDER, ANNE STUART, retired publishing executive, political organization worker; b. Lake Forest, Ill., Jan. 11, 1920; d. Robert Douglas and Harriet (McClure) Stuart; m. Clifton Brooks Batchelder, May 26, 1945; children: Edward, Anne Stuart, Mary Clifton, Lucia Brooks Student Lake Forest Coll., 1941-43. Clubmobile driver ARC, Eng., Belgium, France, Holland and Germany, 1943-45; pub., editor Douglas County Gazette, 1970-75, 79-90. Bd. dirs. Firstier Bank Omaha; dir., treas. U.S. Checkbook Com. Mem. Rep. Ctrl. Com. Nebr., 1955-62, 70-83, vice chmn. Ctrl. Com., 1959-64, chmn., 1975-79, mem. fin. com., 1957-64; chmn. women's sect. Douglas County Rep. Fin. Com., 1995, vice chmn. com., 1958-60; v.p. Omaha Woman's Rep. Club, 1957-58, pres., 1959-60; alt. del. Nat. Conv., 1956, 72, del., 1980, 84, 88; mem. Rep. Nat. Com. for Nebr., 1964-70; asst. chmn. Douglas County Rep. Ctrl. Com., 1971-74; 1st v.p. Nebr. Fedn. Rep. Women, 1971-72, pres., 1972-74; chmn. Nebr. Rep. Com., 1975-79; vice-chmn. Bldg. Fedn. Rep. Women, 1998—; mem. Nebr. State Bldg. Commn., 1979-83; Rep. candidate for lt. gov., 1974. Sr. v.p. Nebr. Founders Day, 1958; trustee Hastings Coll., 1977—; bd. dirs. YWCA, 1983-89, Omaha Libr. Found., 1991-2000, Libr. Found., 2000—; past trustee Brownell Hall, Vis. Nurse Assn.; past pres. Nebr. chpt. Freedoms Found. at Valley Forge; chmn. fin. George Bush for Pres., Nebr., 1987-88; apptd. Kennedy Ctr. Performing Arts, 1989, 94, Pres.' Adv. Com. on the Arts, 1990-92, Nat. Com. for the Performing Arts, 1992—; mem. Nebr. Rep. State Fin. Com., 1990, Nat. Fin. Com. Bush-Quayle, 1992; active Omaha Meth. Hosp. Found., Brownell-Talbot Sch. Found.; mem. Uta Halee Home for Girls, 1980—. Elected to Nebr. Rep. Hall of Fame, 1984; named Citizen of the Yr. Midlands Coun. Boy Scouts Am., 1997; recipient Silver Beaver, Boy Scouts Am., Spirit award Uta Halee Home for Girls, 1999. Mem. Mayflower Soc., Colonial Dames, P.E.O., Nat. League Pen Women Omaha Country, Omaha, Halee Spirit of Youth. Presbyterian. Home: 6875 State St Omaha NE 68152-1633

BATCHELDER, DAVID H., investment advisory firm executive; b. Bartlesville, Okla. m. Mary Batchelder; 3 adopted children. BS in Acctg., Okla. State U., Stillwater, 1971. CPA. Audit mgr. Deloitte Haskins and Sells, Denver; asst. to the v.p., treas. Mesa Petroleum Co., 1978—80, corp. controller, 1980, v.p. finance, 1983, v.p. fin., treas., bd. dirs., 1984—87, exec. v.p., CFO, pres., COO, 1986—88; founder, principal Batchelder & Partners, Inc. (now Relational Investors LLC), San Diego, 1988—. Bd. dirs. Apria Healthcare Group Inc., 1998—2003, ICN Pharmaceuticals, Inc., 1999—2000, Nuevo Energy Co., 1999—2002, Washington Group International, 2002—, Con Agra Foods, 2002—, Home Depot, 2007—. Mem.: Am. Inst. Certified Public Accountants. Office: Relational Investors LLC 12400 High Bluff Dr Ste 600 San Diego CA 92130*

BATCHELDER, SAMUEL LAWRENCE, JR., retired corporate lawyer; b. Boston, Apr. 3, 1932; s. Samuel L. and May W. (Read) B.; m. Jane B. Borden, 1955 (div. 1965); children: John H., Benjamin A.; m. Marion C. Thomas, 1967; children: Timothy C., Lily L. AB, Harvard U., 1954, LLB, 1960. Bar: Mass., 1960, U.S. Dist. Mass. 1961. Assoc. Goodwin, Procter LLP, Boston, 1960-67, ptnr., 1968-97, of counsel, 1997—. Active ARC, bd. dirs. local orgns., Boston, 1966-2003, chmn. Mass. Bay unit, 1979-83, mem. various nat. coms., 1981-98, chmn. resolutions com., 1998, NE Blood Svcs., 1981-92; mem. grad. coun. Milton Acad., 1986-91, chmn., 1989-91, trustee, 1989-92; trustee Mass. Continuing Legal Edn., 1995-2004; dir. Exec. Svc. Corps. N.E., 1998—, chair, 2003-05. 1st lt. US Army, 1954—57. Mem. ABA, Mass. Bar Assn., Boston Bar Assn. (chmn. corp. law com. 1985-88, mem. gov. coun. 1988-91, legal edn. com. 1995-2000), Brookline Cmty. Fund (trustee 1998-2004). Clubs: The Country Club (Brookline, Mass.). Democrat. Avocations: tennis, skiing, gardening, music, art. Office: 66 Laurel Rd Chestnut Hill MA 02467-2211 Home Phone: 617-566-5752; Office Phone: 617-566-5752.

BATCHELLER, JOE ANN, entrepreneur; b. Jacksonville, Fla., Dec. 11, 1932; d. Osmer St. Clair and Lorena (Jones) Deming; m.David Springsteen Batcheller, Aug. 8, 1957; children: Elizabeth Batcheller Whalen, Osmer Deming, John Alden. AA, Stephens Coll., Columbia, Mo., 1952; BA, U. N.C., 1955. Sec. Seminole Oil Co., Miami, Fla., 1957-61, pres., bd. dirs., 1961-65; pres., chmn. Blue Water Mobile Home Sales, Inc., Tavernier, Fla., 1967-76; dir. Miami Heart Inst., Miami Beach, 1973—, v.p., 1975—, exec. v.p., 1986-89, pres., chief exec. officer, 1989-93. Sec., bd. dirs. Bluegrass Plant Foods, Inc., Cynthiana, Ky., 1958-72; chmn. Superior Plant Foods, Inc., Lakeland, Fla., 1958-60; v.p., bd. dirs. Pensacola Petroleum Co., Inc., Miami, 1961-65, Top Power Stas., Miami, 1961-65, Atico Savs. Bank, Miami, 1987-88, Pan Am. Bank, Miami, 1984-87; bd. dirs. Intercontinental Bank; vice chmn. Miami Heart Rsch. Inst., Inc., 1993—. Bd. dirs. Am. Heart Assn., Miami, 1989-91; mem. adv. bd. Convent of Sacred Heart, Miami, 1973-77; mem. parents adv. bd. Furman U., Greenville, S.C., 1979-83. Mem. Surf Club on Miami Beach (pres. bd. govs. 1993-97, vice chmn. 1997-99), Surf Club Debutante Com. (chmn. 1976-82, 86, 87), Bay Point Property Owners Assn. (pres. 1991-96), Young Patronesses of Opera, English Speaking Union, DAR. Episcopalian. Avocations: reading, boating, Beaux Arts. Home: 4595 Sabal Palm Rd Miami FL 33137-3363

BATCHELOR, BARRINGTON DE VERE, civil engineer, educator; b. Lucea, Jamaica, W.I., July 2, 1928; s. Reginald Augustus and Vera Louise (O'Connor) B.; m. Alison Yvonnie Johnston, Sept. 14, 1960; children: Roger, Nicola, Wayne. BSc with honors (Elias Issa scholar), U. Edinburgh, 1956; PhD (Commonwealth scholar), U. London, 1963; student, Nat. Def. Coll. Can., 1982—83. Registered profl. engr., Ont. Asst. engr. Sir William Halcrow & Ptnrs., London, 1956—58; exec. engr. Ministry Edn., Jamaica, 1958—63, sr. exec. engr., 1963—64; ptnr. Franks & Batchelor, cons. engrs., Kingston, Jamaica, 1964—66; asst. prof. civil engring. Queen's U., Kingston, Ont., Canada, 1966—68, assoc. prof., 1968—72, prof., 1972—93, prof. emeritus, 1993—. Bd. govs. Kingston Gen. Hosp. Fellow Engring. Inst. Can., Can. Soc. Civil Engrs.; mem. ASCE, Instn. Engrs. Jamaica, Instn. Engrs. Ont. Home: 150 Collingwood St Kingston ON Canada K7L 3X5 Office: Queen's U Dept Civil Engring Kingston ON Canada K7L 3N6 Personal E-mail: drdevb@aol.com.

BATCHELOR, JAMES KENT, lawyer; b. Long Beach, Calif., Oct. 4, 1934; s. Jack Morrell and Edith Marie (Ottinger) Batchelor; m. Jeanette Lou Dyer, Mar. 27, 1959 (div.); children: John, Suzanne; m. Susan Mary Leonard, Dec. 4, 1976 (div.). AA, Sacramento City Coll., 1954; BA, Calif. State U., Long Beach, 1956; JD, U. Calif., 1959. Bar: Calif. 1960, U.S. Dist. Ct. (ctrl. dist.) Calif. 1960, U.S. Supreme Ct. 1968, cert.: Calif. Bd. Legal Specialization (family law specialist) 1980. Dep. dist. atty., Orange County, Calif., 1960-62; assoc. Miller, Nisson, Kogler & Wenke, Santa Ana, Calif., 1962-64; ptnr. Batchelor, Cohen & Oster, Santa Ana, Calif., 1964-67, Kurilich, Ballard, Batchelor, Fullerton, Calif., 1967-72; pres. James K. Batchelor, Inc., 1972—. Instr. paralegal sect. Santa Ana City Coll.; lectr. family law Calif. Continuing Edn. Bar, 1973—; judge pro-tem Superior Ct., 1974—. Contbr. articles to profl. jours. Named one of Best Lawyers in Am., 1989—. Fellow: Am. Acad. Matrimonial Lawyers (pres. So. Calif. chpt. 1989—90); mem.: ABA, Orange County Bar Assn. (pres. family law sect. 1968—71, plaque sec. 1977), Calif. State Barristers (v.p., plaque 1964), Orange County Barristers (founder, pres. plaque 1963), Calif. State Bar (plaque chmn. family law sect. 1975—76, advisor 1976—78). Republican. Methodist. Office: 765 The City Dr S Ste 270 Orange CA 92868-6908 Home Phone: 714-542-2333; Office Phone: 714-750-8388. Personal E-mail: batchelorlaw@aol.com.

BATCHELOR, KAREN SUE, music educator; b. Lake Charles, La., Sept. 22, 1961; d. James W. and Maxyne Harris Batchelor. MusB in Piano Pedagogy, McNeese State U., Lake Charles, La., 1985. Cert. elem. tchr. La. Choir dir., organist Westminister Presbyn. Ch., Lake Charles, 1984—92, Wesley United Meth. Ch., Lake Charles, 1992—93; classroom tchr. First Meth. Sch., Lake Charles, 1988—97; organist St. Luke-Simpson United Meth. Ch., Lake Charles, 1993—2001; music tchr. D.A. Combre Elem. Sch., Lake Charles, 1997—2000, Ralph Wilson Elem. Sch., Lake Charles, 2000—01, J.D.Clifton Elem. Sch., Lake Charles, 1997—2004, A.A. Nelson Elem. Sch., Lake Charles, La., 2004—; music dir. Sweetlake United Meth. Ch., La., 2002—. Recipient KPLC Class Act award, KPLC TV, 2004. Mem.: Vocal Music Tchrs. Orgn. (HS honor choir accompanist 2001—), Sigma Alpha Iota (chpt. treas. 1998—2002, chpt. pres. 2002—). Office: A A Nelson Elem Sch 1001 Country Club Rd Lake Charles LA 70605 Home Phone: 337-439-0999; Office Phone: 337-477-1775.

BATCHVAROVA, MADLEN TODOROVA, music educator, conductor; d. Todor Bachvarov and Stefka Bachvarova. MusB, Acad. for Music and Dance Art, Bulgaria, 1991; MusM in Choral Conducting, Ga. state U., 1997; Mus D, U. of Ala., 2000. Condr. Plovdiv Choral Soc., Bulgaria, 1992—94; piano accompanist Secondary Music Sch., Plovdiv, Bulgaria, 1992—94; grad. tchg. asst. U. of Ala., Tuscaloosa, 1997—2000; asst. prof. music Columbus State U., Ga., 2000—01; asst. prof. music, dir. choral programs Hanover Coll., Ind., 2001—. Mem. internat. jury Internat. Choral Festival, Preveza, Greece, 2002. Singer: (CD recording) John Adams (GRAMMY for Best Choral Performance, 1997); singer: (chorus) (music performance at carnegie hall) Brahms, Requiem. Mem.: Am. Choral Dirs. Assn., NARAS, Pi Kappa Lambda. Office: Hanover Coll POBox 890 Hanover IN 47243 E-mail: batchvarova@hanover.edu.

BATE, BRIAN R., retired psychologist; b. Cleve., July 4, 1940; s. Paul A. and Claire N. B.; children: Jennifer Bate Tyler, Julia L. Bate-Poxon. BA in English, Western Res. U., 1963, MS in Psychology, 1965; PhD in Psychology, Case Western Res. U., 1972. Instr. Cuyahoga C.C. Western Campus, Parma, Ohio, 1969, from asst. prof. to prof. of psychology, 1970—2004; pvt. practice, Cleve., 1972-96. Contbr. articles to profl. jours. Nat. Merit Scholar Princeton U., 1958-61, Western Res. U., 1962-63; USPHS fellow, 1963-67. Mem. APA, Am. Fedn. Musicians, Edelweiss Ski Club, Cleve. Buddhist Temple. Achievements include devel. and tchg. of the first underclass-level behavior modification course in the world, 1970-1977. Avocations: trumpet, trombone. Home: 201 The Apartelle N Escario St 6000 Cebu City Philippines also: 8498 Vera Dr Cleveland OH 44147-2204

BATE, MARILYN ANNE, psychologist; b. Dillonvale, Ohio, May 23, 1939; d. Louis Edward and Veronica (Koval) Dezera; m. Brian Richard Bate, Sept. 7, 1968 (div. Apr. 1976); children: Jennifer, Julia. BSc, Ohio State U., 1961; MA, Case Western Res. U., Cleve., 1965, PhD, 1974. Lic. psychologist. Elem. tchr., sch. psychologist Cleve. City Schs., 1961-67; sch. psychologist, spl. edn. coord. Cleveland Heights, U. Heights, Ohio City Schs., Ohio, 1967-70; sch. psychologist Mayfield City Schs., Ohio, 1970-71, Cleve. City Schs., 1971-79, North Olmsted Schs., Ohio, 1979-82; instr. Cuyahoga C.C., Cleve., 1967-82; pvt. practice Cleve., 1967-82; psychologist Dept. Def. Dependent Schs., Aviano, Italy, 1982-86; pvt. practice Columbus, Ohio, 1986—2000; ct. psychologist Franklin County Ct. Common Pleas, Columbus, 1987—2000; sch. psychologist Montgomery County Pub. Schools, Silver Spring, Md., 2000—. Mem. adv. bd. Eastpark Elem. Sch., Middleburg Heights, Ohio, 1985; vol. Son of Heaven, Columbus, 1989; mem. bd. Cameron Homeowners Assn., 2005-. Mem. APA, Am. Correctional Assn., Nat. Sch. Psychology Assn. (charter mem.), Ohio Psychol. Assn. (mem. ethics com. 1986-92, exec. bd. 1992—), Ctrl. Ohio Psychol. Assn. (exec. bd. 1986-2000, treas. 1990-92, pres. 1993), European Sch. Psychology Assn. (treas. 1985), Ohio Sch. Psychology Assn. (co-chmn. ethics com. 1976-86, exec. bd. 1992-2000), Cleve. Sch. Psychology Assn. (pres. 1969-71), Md. Sch. Psycology Assn. Avocations: skiing, gardening, crafts. Home: 8706 Ramsey Ave Silver Spring MD 20910-3469 Office: Spring Mill Field Office 11721 Kemp Mill Rd Silver Spring MD 20902 Office Phone: 301-649-8003. Business E-Mail: marilyn_a_bate@mcpsmd.org.

BATEMAN, ANGELA ANDERSON, anesthetist; b. Raleigh, NC, Nov. 14, 1952; d. Samuel Garland and Joy Brown Anderson; m. Ronald Bruce Bateman, Apr. 27, 1986. BSN, Atlantic Christian Coll., 1974; student, Southwestern Sem., 2004—. Staff nurse Wake Med. Ctr., Raleigh, 1974—75, Durham Regional Sch. Anesthesia, 1975—77; cert. registered nurse anesthetist Alamance County Hosp., Burlington, NC, 1977—85, Iredell County Meml. Hosp., Statesville, NC, 1986—87, Critical Health Sys., Raleigh, 1987—. Instr. clin. anesthesia Raleigh Sch. Nurse Anesthesia, NC, 1995—. Named Outstanding Clin. Educator, Critical Health Sys., 2003. Mem.: Am. Assn. Nurse Anesthetists. Avocations: camping, needlepoint, beading. Office: Critical Health Sys Raleigh NC Personal E-mail: abateman@earthlink.net.

BATEMAN, DAVID ALFRED, lawyer; b. Pitts., Jan. 28, 1946; s. Alfred V. and Ruth G. (Howe) B.; m. Trudy A. Heath, Mar. 13, 1948; children: Devin C., Mark C. AB in Geology, U. Calif., Riverside, 1966; JD, U. San Diego, 1969; LLM, Georgetown U., 1978. Bar: Calif. 1970, U.S. Dist. Ct. (so. dist.) Calif. 1970, U.S. Ct. Mil. Appeals 1972, Wash. 1973, U.S. Dist. Ct. (we. dist.) Wash. 1973, U.S. Supreme Ct. 1974, D.C. 1976, U.S. Dist. Ct. Appeals (9th cir.) 1981. Assoc. Daubney, Banche, Patterson & Nares, Oceanside, Calif., 1969-72; asst. atty. gen. State of Wash., Olympia, 1977-81; ptnr. Bateman & Woodring, Olympia, 1981-85, Woodring, Bateman & Westbrook, Olympia, 1985-89, Hanemann & Batemann, Olympia, 1989-92, Hanemann, Bateman & Jones, Olympia, 1992—; owner Heavenly Hawaiian Farms-Coffee Farm, Honolulu, 2005—. Instr. Am. Inst. Banking, San Diego, 1972, U. Puget Sound, Olympia campus, spring, 1979; assoc. brokerRealConnections.net, Tacoma, Wash.; owner Heavenly Hawaiian Farms, Holualoa. Served to capt. JAGC, USAF, 1972-77; col. JAGC, USAFR, 1977-97. Mem.: Nat. Assn. Realtors, Wash. State Bar Assn., D.C. Bar Assn., Calif. State Bar Assn., Rotary (past chmn. internat. svcs. com.). Roman Catholic. Office Phone: 360-786-0601, 808-322-7720. Personal E-mail: dbateman@orcalink.com. Business E-Mail: coffee@heavenlyhawaiian.com.

BATEMAN, JASON, actor; b. Rye, NY, Jan. 14, 1969; s. Kent Bateman; m. Amanda Anka, July 3, 2001; 1 child, Francesca Noras. Actor: (films) Teen Wolf Too, 1987, Necessary Roughness, 1991, Love Stinks, 1999, The Sweetest Thing, 2002, Starsky & Hutch, 2004, Dodgeball, 2004, The Break-Up, 2006, (voice) Arthur and the Invisibles, 2006, Smokin' Aces, 2006, The Ex, 2007; (TV films) Just a Little More Love, 1983, The Fantastic World of D.C. Collins, 1984, Poison Ivy, 1985, The Thanksgiving Promise, 1986, Bates Motel, 1987, Moving Target, 1988, Crossing the Mob, 1988, A Taste for Killing, 1992, Black Sheep, 1994, Confessions: Two Faces of Evil, 1994, This Can't Be Love, 1994, Hart to Hart: Secrets of the Hart, 1995; (TV miniseries) Robert Kennedy and His Times, 1985; (TV series) Little House on the Prairie, 1981—82, Silver Spoons, 1982—84, It's Your Move, 1984—85, The Hogan Family, 1988—91, Simon, 1995—96, Chicago Sons, 1997, George & Leo, 1997—98, Some of My Best Friends, 2001, Arrested Development, 2003—06 (Golden Globe for best actor in musical or comedy, 2005); actor, dir.: Valerie, 1986—88; dir.: Family Matters, 1989—98, For Your Love, 1998—2002, Brother's Keeper, 1998—99; TV appearances Knight Rider, 1984, Mr. Belevdere, 1986, St. Elsewhere, 1986, Matlock, 1987, Burke's Law, 1995, Rude Awakening, 2000. Office: Internat Creative Mgmt Inc 8942 WilshireBlvd Beverly Hills CA 90211-1934*

BATEMAN, JOHN JAY, classics educator; b. Elmira, NY, Feb. 17, 1931; s. Joseph Earl and Etha M. (Edwards) B.; m. Patricia Ann Hageman, July 5, 1952; children: Kristine M., Kathleen A., John Eric. BA, U. Toronto, 1953; MA, Cornell U., 1954, PhD, 1958. Lectr. Univ. Coll., U. Toronto, 1956-57; lectr., then asst. prof. U. Ottawa, 1957-60; mem. faculty U. Ill., Urbana, 1960—, prof. classics and speech, 1968-93; prof. emeritus, 1993—; head dept. classics U. Ill., 1966-73, chmn., 1988-92, acting dir. Sch. Humanities, 1973-74. Author, editor books and articles. Mem.: Am. Philol. Assn. (sec.-treas. 1968—73), Renaissance Soc. Am.

BATEMAN, MAUREEN SCANNELL, lawyer; b. NYC, July 27, 1943; d. Daniel Thomas and Gertrude Rose (Lally) Scannell; m. Frank Coffroth Bateman, June 26, 1971; 1 child: Daniel Frank. AB, Manhattanville Coll., 1964; JD, Fordham U., 1968. Bar: N.Y. 1969, Mass. 1998. Assoc. attorney Willkie Farr & Gallagher, NYC, 1968-69, Davis Polk & Wardwell, NYC, 1969-78; asst. resident counsel Morgan Guaranty Trust Co., NYC, 1978-80; v.p., counsel Bankers Trust Co., NYC, 1980-90; mng. dir., gen. counsel U.S. Trust Corp. N.Y., NYC, 1990-97; exec. v.p., gen. counsel State St. Bank & Trust Co., Boston, 1997—2003; ptnr. Holland & Knight, NYC, 2004—. Office: Holland & Knight 195 Broadway 24th Fl New York NY 10007 Business E-Mail: maureen.bateman@hklaw.com.

BATEMAN, PAUL, diversified financial services company executive; With Robert Fleming Holdings, 1967—88, dir., 1988—95; chief exec. Save & Prosper Grp., 1988—95; exec. chmn. Robert Fleming Asset Mgmt., 1995—2000; global head Fleming Asset Mgmt. Chase, 2000; head Fleming Asset Mgmt. for Europe, Asia and Japan J.P. Morgan Chase & Co., CEO Fleming Asset Mgmt. worldwide, 2002—. Office: JP Morgan Chase and Co 270 Park Ave New York NY 10017-2070

BATEMAN, PAUL WILLIAM, federal agency administrator; b. Whittier, Calif., Feb. 28, 1957; s. John William and Glenus Bernice (Redman) B.; m. Marguerite (Cameron); children: Ellen Ryan, Nancy Cameron, Greer Aidan. BA, Whittier Coll., 1979. Asst. to former pres. Office of Richard Nixon, NYC and San Clemente, Calif., 1979—81; dep. dir. adminstrv. ops. div. The White House, Washington, 1981—82; exec. asst. to asst. sec. econ. devel. U.S. Dept. Commerce, Washington, 1982—84, dep. asst. sec. econ. devel., 1984—85; dep. treas. U.S. Dept. Treasury, Washington, 1985—88; sr. v.p. New Eng. Coun., Inc., Boston, 1988—89; dep. asst. to Pres. The White House, Washington, 1989—93; dir. pub. affairs Gold Inst., Washington, 1994—95; v.p. Klein and Saks, Inc., 1995—96; exec. v.p. Gold Inst., Washington, 1995—99; pres. Klein and Saks, Inc., 1996—2002, Gold Inst., Washington, 2000—02, KSG, LLC, 2003—. V.p. George Washington Boyhood Home Found., 1994-96; exec. dir. Silver Inst., 1996-2003. Trustee Whittier Coll., 2000-05; mem. Adv. Coun. Hist. Preservation, 1989-93; chmn. bd. dirs. Internat. Cyanide Mgmt. Inst., 2002—; bd. dirs., treas. U.S. Landcare Initiative, Inc., 2004-07. Mem.: Econ. Club NY (pres. 2004—07). Republican. Episcopalian. Home: 490 Ft Williams Pky Alexandria VA 22304-1810 Office: 1200 G St NW Ste 800 Washington DC 20005-4818 Office Phone: 202-835-0952.

BATEMAN, ROBERT MCLELLAN, artist; b. Toronto, Ont., Can., May 24, 1930; s. Joseph Wilbur and Ann (McLellan) Bateman; m. Suzanne Bowerman, June 1961; children: Alan, Sarah, John; m. Birgit Freybe, Aug. 1975; children: Christopher, Rob. BA in Geography with honors, U. Toronto, 1954; postgrad., Ont. Coll. Edn., 1955; DSc (hon.), Carleton U., Ottawa, 1982, McGill U., Montreal, 1995; LLD (hon.), Brock U., St. Catherine, Ont., 1982, U. Guelph, Ont., 1984, Laurentian U., Sudbury, Ont., 1987, U. Victoria, B.C., 2003; D Letters for Fine Arts (hon.), McMaster U., Hamilton, Ont., Can., 1983; LittD (hon.), Lakehead U., Thunder Bay, Ont., 1986; DFA (hon.), Colby Coll., 1989, Northeastern U., 1991. Tchr. Nelson H.S., Burlington, Ont., 1958-63, 65-69; tchr. geography Nigeria, 1963-65; tchr. art Lord Elgin H.S., Burlington, Ont., 1970-76. One-man shows include Tryon Gallery, London, 1975, 79, Smithsonian Instn., 1987, Nat. Mus. Natural Sci., Ottawa, 1981-82, Everard Read Gallery, Johannesburg, South Africa, 2000, Retrospective Tour, USA, 2002-03, Gerald Peters Gallery, Santa Fe, 2004, Masters Gallery, Calgary, 2006, also touring U.S. and Can., Can. Embassy, Tokyo, 1992; represented in permanent collections Govt. Ont. Art Collection, Toronto Bd. Trade, Hamilton Art Gallery, Leigh Yawkey Woodson Art Mus., Wausau, Wis., H.R.H. The Prince of Wales, H.R.H. Prince Phillip, The Late Princess of Monaco, Am. Artists Collection, Gilcrease Mus., Tulsa, Art Gallery of Greater Victoria; commd. World Wildlife Fund, 1971, Endangered Species Silver Bowl, 1971, Endangered Species Postage Stamp Series, 1976-81, Northern Reflections - Loon Family, 1981, Govt. Can. wedding gift to Prince of Wales, 1981, Can. Post Office, Royal Can. Mint-Platinum Polar Bear series, 1990, Nat. Capital commn. Canadiana Fund; subject of the Art of Robert Bateman, 1981, The World of Robert Bateman, 1985, Robert Bateman An Artist in Nature, 1990, Natural Worlds: Robert Bateman, 1996, Safari, 1998, Thinking Like a Mountain, 2000, Birds, 2002, Backyard Birds, 2005. Bd. dirs. Elsa Wild Animal Appeal, Toronto, 1975—; hon. dir. Long Point Bird Obs., Ont.; hon. chmn. Harmony Found., Ottawa. Decorated Queen Elizabeth Silver Jubilee medal Govt. of Can., 1977, Officer of Order of Can., 1984; recipient award of excellence Soc. Animal Artists, 1979, 80, 86, 90, Gov. Gen. award for conservation, Quebec City, Can., 1987, Lescarbot award Can. Govt., 1992, Rachel Carson award, 1996, Golden Plate award Am. Acad. Achievement, 1998; named Artist of Yr., Am. Artist Collection, 1980, Master Artist, Leigh

Yawkey Woodson Mus., Wausau, Wis., 1982, Environ. Hero, Nat. Aububon Soc., 1998, others. Mem. Order B.C., Jane Goodall Inst. (bd. dirs.), Audubon Soc. (hon. life), Royal Can. Acad. Arts, Can. Wildlife Fedn. (hon. life), Sierra Club (hon. life), Kenya Wildlife Fund (hon. dir.), Sierra Legal Def. Fund (hon. dir.), Ecotrust (adv. coun.), Pollution Probe (adv. coun.). Personal E-mail: rb@gulfislands.com.

BATEMAN, SHARON LOUISE, public relations executive; b. St. Louis, Oct. 18, 1949; d. Frank Hamilton and Charlotte Elizabeth (Hogan) Bateman. Student, Drury Coll., 1967-69; BJ, U. Mo., 1971. Asst. dir. pub. rels. Cardinal Glennon Hosp. Children, St. Louis, 1971-76; staff asst. pub. rels. Ozark Air Lines, St. Louis, 1976-80; mgr. corp. rels. Kellwood Co., St. Louis, 1980-83; mgr. corp. comm. May Dept. Stores Co., St. Louis, 1983-86, dir. corp. comm., 1986-94, v.p. corp. comms., 2000—06; mgr. comm. Arthur Andersen, St. Louis, 1995-96; mgr. editl. and adminstrv. svcs. Falk Design Group, St. Louis, 1996—2000; oper. v.p. corp. comms. and corp. giving Macy's, Inc., Cin., 2006—. Bd. dirs. St. Michael's Houses, 1996—97, Gateway Greening, 1999—2001, The Wellness Cmty., 2004—06, Cin. Ballet, 2007—. Recipient Best Regional Airline Employee Publ. award, Editor's Assn. Am. Transp. Assn., 1978. Mem.: Pub. Rels. Soc. Am. (sec.St. Louis chpt. 1983, bd. dirs. 1988—90, v.p. 1991), Internat. Assn. Bus. Comms. (pres. St. Louis chpt. 1977). Office: Federated Dept Stores Inc 7 W Seventh St Cincinnati OH 45202

BATEMAN, THOMAS ROBERT, lawyer; b. Winchester, Mass., Dec. 9, 1944; s. Richard Holt and Phyllis (Brown) B.; m. Katherine Elizabeth Elliott, Sept. 9, 1972; children: Kyra Elizabeth, Richard Holt, Robert Elliott. BA, Harvard U., 1967; JD, NYU, 1971. Bar: N.Y. 1972, U.S. Dist. Ct. (so. dist.) N.Y. 1973, U.S. Ct. Appeals (2d cir.) 1974, Mass. 1978, U.S. Dist. Ct. Mass. 1978, U.S. Ct. Appeals (1st cir.) 1978. Assoc. Winthrop, Stimson, Putnam & Roberts, NYC, 1971-77, Skadden, Arps, Slate, Meagher & Flom, Boston, 1977-79, ptnr., 1980—. Class agent Phillips Exeter Acad., N.H., 1969—; class steering com. Harvard U., Cambridge, Mass. 1985—. Mem.: ABA, Assn. of Bar of City of N.Y., N.Y. State Bar Assn., Somerset Club, Harvard Club (Boston). Episcopalian. Home: 33 Bullard Rd Weston MA 02493-2203

BATES, BARBARA J. NEUNER, retired municipal official; b. Mt. Vernon, NY, Apr. 8, 1927; d. John Joseph William and Elsie May (Flint) Neuner; m. Herman Martin Bates, Jr., Mar. 25, 1950; children: Roberta Jean Bates Jamin, Herman Martin III, Jon Neuner. BA, Barnard Coll., 1947. Confidential clk. to supr. Town of Ossining, N.Y., 1960-63, receiver of taxes N.Y., 1971-90; ret.; pres. BNB Assocs., Briarcliff Manor, N.Y., 1963-83, Upper Nyack Realty Co., Inc., Briarcliff Manor, 1966-71. V.p. Ossining (N.Y.) Young Rep. Club, 1958; pres. Young Womens Rep. Club Westchester County (N.Y.), 1959-61; regional committeewoman N.Y. State Assn. Young Rep. Clubs, 1960-62; mem. Westchester County Rep. Com., 1963-95; mem. Ossining Women's Rep. Club, 1960-92, pres., 1984-85; mem. Westchester County Women's Rep. Club, 1957-92. Mem. DAR, Jr. League Westchester-on-Hudson, Receivers Taxes Assn. Westchester County (legis. liaison, v.p., pres. 1984-85), Hackley Sch. Mothers Assn. (pres. 1968), R.I. Hist. Soc., Ossining Hist. Soc., Westchester County Hist. Soc., Landmark Preservation Soc. S.E., Ossining Woman's Club, Brewster/Carmel Garden Club. E-mail: cmajvkb@yahoo.com.

BATES, BEVERLY JO-ANNE, artist, educator; b. Pitts., Jan. 29, 1938; d. Joseph Whitfield and Thelma Alease (McMullen) Loftin; divorced; children: Roy F. Jr., Brian Whitfield, Stephen Jeffrey. BS in Art Edn., W.Va. State Coll., 1959; MEd in Art Edn., U. Pitts., 1973, postgrad., 1985-88, Temple U., 1963-64, RISD, 1984. Art tchr. Pitts. Pub. Sch. System, 1959, 70-75, print tchr. Brashear High Sch., 1975-78, coord. art dept., printmaking tchr. Pitts. High Sch., 1970—; art tchr. N.J. Pub. Schs., Camden, N.J., 1961; print instr. Selma Burke Art Ctr., Pitts., 1971, Pitts. Arts and Crafts Ctr., 1972; panel mem. visual arts Pa. Coun. on Arts, Harrisburg, 1979—. Com. mem. Links Inc. Nat. Art Com., Washington, 1992—; mem. adv. bd. Manchester Craftsman's Guild, Pitts., 1985—, Visions, 1990—. Author: (catalogues) Black American Art, 1977 (Meade award 1977), 1978 (W. Pa. Prize 1978); one-person shows include Westmoreland Mus., 1991, Visual Arts Gallery, C.C. of Allegheny County, 1991, Kipp Gallery, Indiana U. Pa., 1991, Westminster Coll. Art Gallery, 1991, others; exhibited in group shows at Pitts. Ctr. for Arts, 1982, 83, 84, 85, 87, 88, 90, 91, 92, Carnegie Mus., 1982, 86, 90, 92, S.G. Galleries, 1992, LaTeste, France, 1992, U. Pitts. Kimbo Gallery, 1990, 91, 92, Carson St. Gallery, 1991, others. Bd. trustees Pitts. Ctr. for Arts, 1989—; bd. dirs. Soc. Contemporary, Pitts., 1990—, Soc. Arts and Crafts. Honors fellow R.I. Sch., Providence, 1984; recipient Frick Fellowship award Pitts. Bd. Edn., 1975, Outstanding Art Edn. award Pitts. Bd. Edn., 1984, Youth Arts award Pa. Art Edn. Assn., Pitts., 1988, Outstanding Art Edn. award Pratt Inst., Bklyn., 1989, Jurors award Pitts. Print Group, 1991, Images show U. Pitts., 1992. Mem. The Links Inc. (bd. mem. nat. arts com.), Nat. Art Edn. Assn., Pa. Art Edn. Assn., Pa. Coun. on Arts (past panel mem.), Pitts. Print Group (past bd. mem.), Associated Artists Pitts. (past bd. mem.), Nat. Conf. Artists, Pa. Alliance for Art Edn. (bd. mem.). Avocations: art, printmaking, reading, travel. Home: 6922 Meade St Pittsburgh PA 15208-2402 Office: Pitts High Sch 925 Brushton Ave Pittsburgh PA 15208-1613 Personal E-mail: jbates6220@aol.com.

BATES, CHARLES WALTER, human resources executive, lawyer; b. Detroit, June 28, 1953; s. E. Frederick and Virginia Marion (Nunneley) B. BA in Psychology and Econs. cum laude, Mich. State U., 1975, M in Labor and Indsl. Rels., 1977; postgrad., DePaul U., 1979-80; JD, William Mitchell Coll. Law, 1984. Bar: Wash. 1990, US Dist. Ct. (we. dist.) Wash. 1992, US Ct. Appeals (9th cir.) 2002; cert. sr. profl. in human resources. Job analyst Gen. Mills, Inc., Mpls., 1977—78, plant pers. asst. II Chgo., 1978—80, plant asst. pers. mgr., 1980—81, pers. mgr. consumer foods mktg. Mpls., 1981—82, pers. mgr. consumer foods mktg. divsns. and Saluto Pizza, 1982—84; mgr. human resources We. divsn. Godfather's Pizza, Inc., Costa Mesa, Calif., 1984—85, mgr. human resources we. U.S. and Can. Bellevue, Wash., 1985—91; dir. human resources Royal Seafoods, Inc., Seattle, 1991—92, dir. human resources and employee rels. counsel, 1992—94, dir. human resources and counsel, 1994—95; sr. internal auditor PACCAR, Inc, Bellevue, Wash., 1995—97; dir. field human resources PACCAR Automotive, Inc., Renton, 1997; dir. human resources, 1997—2000; dir. human resources Centralia ops. TransAlta Corp., Wash., 2000—02; dir. adminstrn., corp. sec. TransAlta USA, Inc., Centralia, 2002—04; dir. human resources Wash. State Ferries Washington State Dept. Transp., 2005—. Instr. employee labor rels. Lake Washington Tech. Coll., Kirkland, Wash., 1992-94; instr. staffing Key Bank Profl. Devel. Ctr. U. Wash., Tacoma, 2005; bd. dirs., TransAlta USA Inc., 2000-01, TransAlta Investments LLC, 2000-01, Olympia Symphony Orch., 2001-02. Candidate for lt. gov. of Minn., 1982; mem. East Bellevue (Wash.) Transp. Study Adv. Com., 1989-92, Sammamish Cmty. Coun., Bellevue, 1990-93, Bellevue Civil Svc. Commn., 1997-2000, vice chmn., 1999, chmn., 2000; commr. Scott Lake Drainage Dist., 2002-05; asst. scoutmaster Boy Scouts Am., 1971-. Recipient Scouter's Tng. award Boy Scouts Am., 1979, Vantage Recruiting award Recruitment Today mag., 1989, Vigil Honor award Order of the Arrow, Boy Scouts Am., 1990, Dist. Award of Merit, Boy Scouts Am., 1991; finalist Wash. Atty. Award of Excellence Butch Blum/Wash. Law and Politics mag., 2003. Mem. Wash. State Bar Assn., Soc. Human Resource Mgmt., Nat. Eagle Scout Assn. Office: Wash State Ferries 2901 3d Ave Ste 500 Seattle WA 98121-3014 Personal E-mail: charlie_bates@hotmail.com.

BATES, CLYDE THOMAS, retired economics professor; b. Sadieville, Ky., June 6, 1933; s. Thomas Marion and Carrie Josephine Bates; m. Frances Ruth Phillips, July 10, 1956; children: Bobby Gene, Calvin Thomas. BS, U. Ky., Lexington, 1960, MS, 1962, PhD, 1969. Asst. prof. Western Ky. U., Bowling Green, Ky., 1961—63; prof. Georgetown Coll., 1964—95; ret., 1995. Quality control statistician Allied Signal, Frankfort, Ky., 1980—89. Pres. Royal Springs Credit Union. With intelligence US Army, 1954—56, Germany. Named Tchr. of Yr., Georgetown Coll., 1969. Mem.: Ky. Econ. Assn. (pres. 1984), Optimist Club. Democrat. Avocations: reading, gardening. Home: 1112 Inca Trail Georgetown KY 40324

BATES, DAVID WESTFALL, internist, educator, medical researcher; b. Madison, Wis., June 5, 1957; s. Robert and Patricia Bates; m. Carol Kurtz; children: Michael, Sarah. BS, Stanford U., 1979; MD, Johns Hopkins U., 1983; MSc, Harvard U., 1990. Diplomate Am. Bd. Internal Medicine. Intern and resident internal medicine Oreg. Health Scis. U., Portland, 1983-86; house physician Vancouver (Wash.) Vets. Hosp., 1984-87, Kaiser Sunnyside Hosp., Portland, 1984-86; assoc. physician Oreg. Health Scis. U. Hosp., Portland, 1986-87; rsch. fellow medicine Harvard Med. Sch., Boston, 1988-90; rsch./clin. fellow medicine Brigham and Women's Hosp., Boston, 1988-90, assoc. physician, 1989-91, attending physician holding unit, 1990-95, attending physician med. consultation svc., 1990-97, attending physician Brigham Internal Medicine Assocs., 1990—, mem. Ctr. for Applied Med. Info. Sys. Rsch., 1993—. Physician Wallace Med. Concern, Portland, 1985-87, Tumu-Tumu Hosp., Karatina, Kenya, 1987-88; instr. medicine Oreg. Health Scis. U., 1986-87, Harvard Med. Sch., 1990-93, asst. prof. medicine, 1993-97, assoc. prof. medicine, 1997—; joint appt. Harvard Sch. Pub. Health, Dept. Health Policy and Mgmt., 2000—; house physician St. Luke's Hosp., New Bedford, 1989-91; mem. program project grant com. Nat. Cancer Inst. Can., 1996; mem. quality care coun. Ptnrs. Cmty. Health Care Inc., 1996—, mem. coronary disease prevention task force, 1996-98, mem. drug therapy team, 1996-98, mem. med. mgmt. com., 1996—; med. dir. Brigham and Women's Physician Hosp. Orgn., 1996-97, Ptnrs. Clin. Data Warehouse, 1997-99; med. dir. clin. and quality analysis Ptnrs. Healthcare Sys., 1997—; mem. Nat. Acad. Clin. Biochemistry, Stds. for Lab. Practice, 1997, Improving Prescribing Practices Initiative, Inst. for Health Care Improvement, 1997-98; chief divsn. Gen. Internal Medicine, 1998—; sci. advisor SCRIPT project Health Care Financing Adminstrn. and Joint Commn. for Accreditation of Healthcare Orgns., 1998—; chair abstract selection com. SGIM N.E. Region, 1999; mem. Consensus Devel. Panel on the Safety of Intravenous Drug Delivery Sys., Latiolais Leaderhip Program, 1999; trustee Inst. for Safe Medication Practices, 2000; mem. steering com. Nat. Quality Forum, 2000—; mem. safe medication use expert com. U.S. Pharmacopeia, 2000—; mem. Harkness Fellows in Health Care Policy, The Commonwealth Fund, 2000—, Inst. Medicine, 2005; presenter in field; many others. Mem. editl. bd. Jour. Evaluation in Clin. Practice, 1997—, The Joint Commn. Jour. on Quality Improvement, 1997—; contbr. numerous articles to profl. jours. Recipient Nat. Rsch. Svc. award Agy. for Health Care Policy and Rsch., 1990, Young Investigator of the Yr. award Soc. for Med. Decision-Making, 1993. Fellow ACP; mem. AMA (mem. medication error reducation initiative 1996-98), Am. Soc. for Clin. Pharmacology and Therapeutics, Am. Med. Informatics Assn. (mem. editl. bd. jour. 1997—, awards com. 2000—), Am. Fedn. Clin. Rsch. (Henry Christian award for excellence in rsch. 1992), Assn. for Health Svcs. Rsch., Soc. for Med. Decision Making, Soc. for Gen. Internal Medicine (Clin. Investigator of Yr. award N.E. region 1993), Inst. Medicine. Office: Brigham and Womens Hosp 75 Francis St Boston MA 02115

BATES, DOUG, editor; b. McMinnville, Oreg. m. Gloria Bates; children: Steven, Lynn, Michael, Liska. BA, U. Oreg., 1968. Mng. editor Register-Guard, Eugene, Oreg.; news editor Seattle Times, Wash.; asst. mng. editor San Diego Union-Tribune, Calif.; assoc. editor The Oregonian, Portland, Oreg., 1993—. Mem. editl. bd. The Oregonian, 1993—. Author: The Pulitzer Prize: The Inside Story of America's Most Prestigious Award, 1991, Gift Children: A Story of Race, Family, and Adoption in a Divided America, 1993. Recipient Pulitzer Prize for editl. writing, 2006. Office: The Oregonian 1320 SW Broadway Portland OR 97201 Office Phone: 503-221-8174. Personal E-mail: dugbates1@aol.com. Business E-Mail: dougbates@news.oregonian.com.

BATES, GEORGE WILLIAM, obstetrician, gynecologist, educator; b. Durham, NC, Feb. 15, 1940; s. George W. and Lillian M. (Streete) B.; m. Susanne Rayburn, Oct. 18, 1969; children: Jonathan Rayburn, Jeffrey William, Robert Wiser. BS, U. N.C., 1962, MD, 1965; SM, MIT, 1984. Diplomate Am. Bd. Ob-Gyn. (examiner 1984-93). Intern U. Ala., Birmingham, 1965-66; resident ob-gyn U. N.C., Chapel Hill, 1966-70; prof., chmn. ob-gyn U. Tenn., Knoxville, 1972-76; fellow reproductive endocrinology U. Tex., Dallas, 1976-78; prof., dir. reproductive endocrinology U. Miss. Med. Ctr., Jackson, 1978-86; prof. ob.-gyn. Coll. Medicine, Med. U. S.C., Charleston, 1986-90, dean, 1986-89; v.p. med. edn. Greenville (S.C.) Hosp. System, 1990-96; exec. v.p., chief med. officer Prin.Care, Inc., Brentwood, Tenn., 1996-98; v.p. devel. Vanderbilt U. Med. Ctr., Nashville, 1998—. CEO digiChart, Inc. Co-author: Obstetrics and Gynecology for Medical Students, 1992, 95; editor: Manual of Clinical Problems in Obstetrics and Gynecology, 1982, 86, 90; contbr. numerous articles to profl. publs. Commr. coun. Boy Scouts Am., 1989-90, v.p. adminstrn., 1992, pres., 1993-94, bd. dirs. Mid. Tenn. Coun., 2002--; elder Mt. Pleasant Presbyn. Ch., Westminster Presbyn. Ch.; mem. pres.'s adv. coun. Mars Hill Coll., Presbyn. Coll., Nat. Devel. Coun., U. N.C. Maj. USAF, 1970-72. Morehead scholar, 1958; NIH rsch. trainee, 1976-78; Sloan fellow, 1983; recipient Eagle Scout award, 1955, Henry Fordham award, 1966, Golden Apple award, 1987, Silver Beaver award, 1989, Hon. Alumnus award Med. U. S.C., 1990, Disting. Eagle Scout award, 1991; named Prof. of Yr., U. Miss., 1980, Top 100 Healthcare Exec., 2002. Mem. ACOG (chmn. fin. com. 1990-94, health care commn. 1994-97, Jr. Fellow Profl. of Y. award dist. IV 1991), AMA, AAAS, Assn. Profs. Ob-Gyn. Found. (bd. dirs. 1993), Am. Gyn.-Ob. Soc., Nat. Bd. Med. Examiners, Gynecol. Investigation, Am. Fertility Soc. (bd. dirs. 1991-94, treas. 1994-96), Soc. Gynecol. Surgeons, Accreditation Coun. Grad. Med. Edn., So. Atlantic Assn. Obstetricians and Gynecologists, Ctrl. Assn. Obstetricians and Gynecologists, Endocrine Soc., Rotary, Alpha Omega Alpha. Office: digiChart Inc 102 Woodmont Blvd Ste 500 Nashville TN 37205-5254 Office Phone: 615-777-2727.

BATES, GERALD EARL, retired bishop; b. Caldwell, Ohio, Sept. 12, 1933; s. Earl and Lillian Inez (Merritt) Bates; m. Marlene Rachel Parsons, Aug. 21, 1954; children: David Earl, William Randall, Elizabeth Ann. AA, Spring Arbor Coll., 1953; AB, Greenville Coll., 1955, DD (hon.), 1998; MDiv, Asbury Theol. Sem., 1958; ThM, Western Theol. Sem., 1964; PhD, Mich. State U., 1975; DD (hon.), Roberts Wesleyan Coll., 1986. Missionary with gen. missionary bd. Free Meth. Ch. N.Am., Winona Lake, Ind., 1957-85, area adminstrv. asst. Ctrl. Africa, 1973-85, bishop Indpls., 1985-99, bishop emeritus, 1999—; interim pres. Spring Arbor U., Mich., 2007. Adj. prof. Union Inst. U., Cin., W. Africa Theol. Sem., Nigeria, Wabash Inst. Author: Soul Afire, 1981, 2d edit., 1993; chmn. bd. editors Book of Discipline, 1985. Pres. Friends of Hope Africa U. Inc., Free Meth. World Fellowship, 1989—95; bd. dirs. India Missionary Tng. Bd. Ctr. Study Wesley and Soc.; mem. governing bd. Hope Africa U., Burundi. Recipient Alumnus of the Yr. award, Spring Arbor Coll., 1974, Goodwill Amb. award, Noble County C. of C., 1988, Alumnus of the Yr. award, Asbury Theol. Sem., 1991, Disting. Alumnus, Greenville Coll., 2005. Mem.: Am. Soc. Missiology, Phi Kappa Phi. Republican. Mem. Free Methodist Ch. Avocations: reading, travel, photography. Office: Spring Arbor Univ 106 E Main St Spring Arbor MI 49283 Home: 218 W Spring Arbor Heights Spring Arbor MI 49283 E-mail: batesgerald@sbcglobal.net.

BATES, GWEN LEE, health facility administrator, consultant; d. Marion Luther and Jennie V. Purcell; children: Ruth Denice Decker, Timothy James. Cert. tech. Sr. ops. tech. Stauffer Chem., Baytown, Tex.; supr. safety & environ. Waste Control Svcs., Channelview, Tex.; tech. writer, tng. specialist Myers Tng. Svc., Galena Park, Tex.; cons., tech. writer, editor Enron Global Asset Ops., Houston; compliance trainer Compliance Solutions Occupations, Denver; mgr. quality HS&E Spar Tec, Inc., Houston; mgr. corp. HS&E J. Ray McDermott, S.A., Houston. Mem. Greater Houston Partnership Clean Air, Clean Water & Wetlands Coms. Mem.: Nat. Fire Protection Assn. Avocations: gardening, bowling, drawing, poetry. Office: J Ray McDermott SA 757 N Eldridge Pky Houston TX

BATES, HAROLD MARTIN, lawyer; b. Wise County, Va., Mar. 11, 1928; s. William Jennings and Reba (Williams) B.; m. Audrey Rose Doll, Nov. 1, 1952 (div. Mar. 1978); children: Linda, Carl; m. Judith Lee Farmer, June 23, 1978 (div. Feb. 2002); m. Helen H. Herndon, May 1, 2004. BA in Econs., Coll. William and Mary, 1952; LLB, Washington and Lee U., 1961. Bar: Va. 1961, Ky. 1961. Spl. agt. FBI, Newark and NYC, 1952-56; tech. sales rep. Hercules Powder Co., Wilmington, Del., 1956-58; investigator US Def. Dept., Lexington, Va., 1959-62, Louisville, 1959-62; practice law Louisville, 1961-62; sec.-treas., dir., house counsel Life Ins. Co. of Ky., Louisville, 1962-66; practice law Roanoke, Va., 1966—2007; ret., 2007; sec., dir. James River Limestone Co., Buchanan, Va., 1970-96; sec. Eastern Ins. Co., Roanoke, 1984-87. Pres., Skil, Inc., orgn. for rehab. Vietnam vets., Salem, Va., 1972-75; freshman football coach Washington and Lee U., 1958-60. With airborne US Army, 1946—47. Mem. Va. Bar Assn., Roanoke Bar Assn., William and Mary Alumni Assn. (bd. dirs. 1972-76), Soc. Former Spl. Agts. of FBI (chmn. Blue Ridge chpt. 1971-72). Republican. Home: 8705 Shadwell Dr Roanoke VA 24019 E-mail: hbates@aol.com.

BATES, JAMES EARL, academic administrator; b. Ligonier, Pa., Aug. 10, 1923; s. Earl Barrington and Margaret (Kinsey) B.; m. Lauralou Courtney, Apr. 15, 1950; children: Susan Bates Jaren, Sara Bates Hudson, James Barrington, Willa Bates Leitten. DSc, Temple U., 1946; DPM, Pa. Coll. Podiatric Medicine, 1970, LHD (hon.), 1996; EdD (hon.), Franklin Pierce Coll., 1972; DSc (hon.), Calif. Coll. Podiatric Med., 1995; LLD, Barry U., 1995; LHD (hon.), Pa. Coll. Podiatric Medicine, 1996. Practice podiatric medicine, Phila., 1946-71; assoc. prof. roentgenology Temple U., Phila., 1948-60; prof., pres. Pa. Coll. Podiatric Medicine, Phila., 1962-95, chancellor, 1995-96, chancellor, CEO, 1997-98; cons. to dean Sch. Podiatric Medicine Temple U., 1998—; chancellor Temple Sch. Podiatric Medicine. Cons. BHRD Region IX, HEW, San Francisco, 1973-74, Region V, Chgo., 1974-75; del. Nat. Commn. on Certifying Health Manpower; mem. health adv. com. HEW, 1972-73; adv. panel for podiatry Inst. Medicine, Nat. Acad. Scis., 1972-74; adv. council for comprehensive health planning Pa. Dept. Health, 1972-75, health manpower task force edn. com., 1976; task force on health manpower distbn. Nat. Health Council, 1973, com. on manpower, 1976-83; mem. Nat. Adv. Council on Health Professions Edn., 1983-87; cons. team So. Regional Ednl. Bd. Feasibility Study for So. Podiatry Sch., 1975-76; mem. Statewide Profl. Standards Rev. Council, 1976-82, Greater Phila. Com. for Med.-Pharm. Scis. Contbr. articles to profl. jours. Trustee First United Meth. Ch. of Germantown, 1965-72, past chmn. fin. com.; v.p. bd. Germantown Businessmen's Assn., Disting. Service award, 1964; chmn. 277th and 278th Ann. Germantown Week, 1958-59; dep. service dir. Phila. CD Council, 1966-73; mem. Health Adv. Commn., Phila., 1976; past pres., bd. mgrs. Germantown YMCA; v.p. Phila. Boosters Assn.; trustee Univ. City Sci. Center, Phila. Served with M.C. AUS, WWII. Recipient citation, Pa. Coll. Podiatric Medicine, 1970, Gov. Pa., 1973, Lifetime Achievement award, Podiatric Mgmt. Mag., 1993, Disting. Svc. citation, Am. Podiatric Med. Assn., 2004, Cert. of Honor, Temple U., 2007. Fellow Internat. Acad. Preventive Medicine (dir. 1973-78), Brit. Soc. Podiatric Medicine (hon.), Royal Soc. Health (Eng.), Am. Coll. Foot Roentgenologists (pres. 1958-59), Coll. Physicians Phila.; mem. Am. Podiatry Assn. (Merit award 1962, gen. chmn. Region Three Ann. Conv. 1975—), Pa. Podiatry Assn. (pres. 1959-60, Man of Yr. award 1961, Spl. citation 1973), Greater Phila. Podiatry Soc. (pres. 1955-56), Fedn. Assns. Schs. of Health Professions (pres. 1975-76), Am. Assn. Colls. Podiatric Medicine (pres. 1969-72), Pi Epsilon Delta, Pi Delta. Clubs: Great Bay Country, Union League, Pyramid Club. Republican. Office: Pa Coll Podiatric Medicine 810 N Race St Philadelphia PA 19107-2496

BATES, JAMES T., chief of staff; b. Jan. 4, 1958; BA magna cum laude, Pepperdine U., 1981; MPP, Claremont Grad. U., 1984. Mgmt. sys. analyst, adminstrv. asst. 1 dept. water and power City of LA, 1985; budget analyst, adminstrv. asst. II Dept. Gen. Svcs., 1986—87; budget analyst US Ho. Reps., Com. on Budget, 1988—90, counsel Washington, 1990—94, chief counsel, 1995—2000, dep. staff dir., chief counsel, 2001—04, chief of staff, 2005—. Office: Committee on Budget 309 Cannon HOB Washington DC 20515-6065

BATES, JOHN CECIL, JR., lawyer; b. Buffalo, May 27, 1936; s. John C. and Geraldine K. Bates; m. Ellen Clare Eyler, June 28, 1964; children: Andrew, Jeremy, Eliot, Emily. AB magna cum laude, Harvard U., 1958; JD, U. Mich., 1961; LLM, NYU, 1962. Bar: N.Y. 1962, D.C. 1977. Assoc. Milbank, Tweed, Hadley & McCloy, NYC, 1963-72; spl. asst. tax policy Treasury Dept., Washington, 1973-76; ptnr. Squire, Sanders & Dempsey, Washington, 1977-84, Reid & Priest, Washington, 1984-91, Foley & Lardner, Washington, 1992-94; tax policy advisor Dept. Treas. Tech. Assistance Program, 1995—98, 2007—; cons. to fgn. govts. on taxation and decentralization, 1998—. Tax and fin. cons. state and local govts., also others, 1977—; adj. prof. Fordham U. Grad. Sch. Bus. Adminstrn., 1992. Co-author: Federal Law of Public Finance, 1988; contbr. numerous articles on tax, energy and fin. to profl. jours. Fellow: Internat. Law Inst. (sr.); mem.: ABA (chmn. com. tax sect. 1981—83), DC Bar Assn., Taxpayers for Improved Procedures (founder). Avocations: historic preservation, environmental protection, music. Home: PO Box 293 Tenants Harbor ME 04860-0293 Office Phone: 207-372-8815. E-mail: bateseeb@aol.com.

BATES, JOHN D., federal judge; b. Elizabeth, NJ, Oct. 11, 1946; married; 3 children. BA, Wesleyan U., 1968; JD, U. Md., 1976. Bar: DC 1976, Md. 1976. Law clk. to Hon. Roszel C. Thomsen US Dist. Ct., Md., 1976—77; assoc. Steptoe & Johnson, Washington, 1977—80; asst. US atty. (DC dist.) US Dept. Justice, 1980—97, chief Civil Divsn., 1987—97, dep. ind. counsel for Whitewater Investigation, 1995—97; chartered ptnr., chair Govt. Contracts/Litig. Dept. Miller & Chevalier, 1998—2001; judge US Dist. Ct. (DC dist.), 2001—, Fgn. Intelligence Surveillance Ct., 2006—. Mem. US Judicial Conf. Com. on Ct. Adminstrn. and Case Mgmt., 2005—. Mem. bd. dirs. Washington Lawyers Com. for Civil Rights and Urban Affairs. 1st lt. US Army, 1968—71. Mem.: FBA (past chmn. Litig. Sect.), DC Bar (past treasurer, chmn. Publs. Com.), Order of Coif. Office: US Dist Ct E Barrett Prettman US Courthouse 333 Constitution Ave, NW Washington DC 20001 Office Phone: 202-354-3430. Office Fax: 202-354-3433.*

BATES, JOHN WYTHE, III, lawyer; b. Richmond, Va., Aug. 22, 1941; s. John Wythe, Jr. and Virginia (Wellington) B.; m. Beverly Jane Estes, June 20, 1964; children: Elizabeth Puller, Kathryn Wellington. BS, Va. Tech., 1963; LLB, U. Va., 1966. Assoc. McGuire Woods Battle & Boothe, L.L.P., Richmond, 1966-71, pntr., 1971—2005, mng. ptnr., 1989-96. Mem. Va. Racing Commn., 1997-2000; chmn. Richmond Renaissance, Inc., 1998—2001. Chmn. United Way Gtr. Richmond, 1975-76; pres. Family and Children's Svc. Richmond, 1978-80; trustee St. Paul's Coll., 1989-96, Va. Found. Ind. Colls., 1994—; sr. warden St. Stephen's Ch., 1985-86, 2002*05; mem. exec. com. Va. Tech. Found. Bd., 1994-2000. Va. Law Found. fellow, 1997. Mem. Am. Coll. Real Estate Lawyers, Richmond Real Estate Group, Forum Club, River Rd. Citizens Assn. (pres. 1983-84), Country Club Va. (pres. 1987-88), Bull and Bear Club (pres. 1980-81),

Commonwealth Club. Episcopalian. Avocations: golf, waterfowl hunting. Office: McGuire Woods LLP One James Ctr 901 E Cary St Richmond VA 23219-4057 Office Phone: 804-775-4302. Business E-Mail: jbates@mcguirewoods.com.

BATES, KATHY, actress; b. Memphis, June 28, 1948; d. Langdon Doyle and Bertye Kathleen (Talbot) Bates; m. Anthony Campisi, 1991 (div. 1997). BFA, So. Meth. U., 1969. Actor: (plays) Vanities, 1976, Semmelweiss, Crimes of the Heart, The Art of Dining, Goodbye Fidel, 1980, Chocolate Cake and Final Placement, 1981, 5th of July, 'night, Mother, 1983 (Tony nomination, Outer Critics Circle award), Two Masters: The Rain of Terror, 1985, Curse of the Starving Class, Frankie and Johnny in the Clair de Lune (OBIE award 1988), The Road to Mecca; (films) Taking Off, 1971, Straight Time, Come Back to the Five and Dime, Jimmy Dean, Jimmy Dean, Summer Heat, Arthur 2: On the Rocks, Signs of Life, High Stakes, Men Don't Leave, Dick Tracy, White Palace, Misery, 1990 (Acad. award for Best Actress 1990, Golden Globe award), At Play in the Fields of the Lord, 1991, Fried Green Tomatoes, 1991 (Golden Globe nomination, BAFTA nomination), The Road to Mecca, 1992, Prelude to a Kiss, 1992, Used People, 1992, A Home of Our Own, 1993, North, 1994, Curse of the Starving Class, 1994, Dolores Claiborne, 1994, Angus, 1995, Diabolique, 1996, The War at Home, 1996, Primary Colors, 1998, Swept from the Sea, 1998, Titanic, 1998, The Waterboy, 1998, Baby Steps, 1999, Dash and Lilly, 1999, My Life as a Dog, 1999, Bruno, 2000, Rat Race, 2001, American Outlaws, 2001, About Schmidt, 2002, Love Liza, 2002, Dragonfly, 2002, Around the World in 80 Days, 2004, The Bridge of San Luis Rey, 2004, 3 & 3, 2005, Rumor Has It, 2005, Failure to Launch, 2006, Relative Strangers, 2006, Bonneville, 2006, (voice) Charlotte's Web, 2006; (TV series) The Doctors, 1977, All My Children, 1984; (TV films) Johnny Bull, 1986, Murder Ordained, 1987, Roe vs. Wade, 1989, No Place Like Home, 1989, Hostages, 1993, Talking with, 1995, The West Side Waltz, 1995, The Late Shift, 1996, Annie, 1999, My Sister's Keeper, 2002, Warm Springs, 2005; dir. (TV films) Fargo, 2003, (films) Have Mercy, 2006; actor, dir. Ambulance Girl, 2005; actor, exec. prodr. The Ingrate, 2004; TV guest appearances include The Love Boat, 1978, St. Elsewhere, 1986, 87, China Beach, 1989, LA Law, 1989, 3rd Rock from the Sun, 1999, (voice) King of the Hill, 2001, Six Feet Under, 2003-05.*

BATES, MARCIA JEANNE, information scientist educator; b. Terre Haute, Ind., July 30, 1942; d. Robert Joseph and Martha Jane B. BA, Pomona Coll., 1963; MLS, U. Calif., Berkeley, 1967; PhD, U. Calif., 1972. Peace corps vol., Saraburi, Thailand, 1963-64, Nongkhai, Thailand, 1964-65; jr. specialist Inst. Libr. Rsch., U. Calif., Berkeley, 1968; acting instr. U. Calif., Berkeley, 1969-70; asst. prof. U. Md., College Park, 1972-76, U. Wash., Seattle, 1976-80, assoc. prof., 1980-81, U. Calif., Los Angeles, 1981-91, prof., 1991—2004, prof. and dept. chmn. libr. and info. sci., 1993—95, prof. emeritus, 2004—. Cons. U.S. Libr. Congress, Washington, 1986, 91, 2002-03, Getty Art Hist. Info. Program, Santa Monica, Calif., 1988-91, Info. Access Co., Foster City, Calif., 1992-95; mem. editl. bd. Jour. of Asis &T, 1989—, Libr. Quar., 1993-2001. Co-author: For Information Specialists, 1992; editor (with M.N. Maack): Encyclopedia of Library and Information Sciences; contbr. articles to profl. jours. and pubs. Recipient Distinguished Lectureship award N.J. Am. Soc. for Info. Sci., New Brunswick, 1991. Fellow AAAS (sect. T electorate nominating com. 1980-84, chmn. 1983-84, sect. T com. mem.-at-large, 2001-04), mem. ALA (Frederick G. Kilgour award, 2001), Am. Soc. Info. Sci. and Tech. (bd. dirs. 1973-74, Best Jour. Article Yr. award, 1980, 99, Rsch. award 1998, award of Merit 2005), Assn. Records Mgrs. Adminstrs., Calif. Libr. Assn. (mem. task force on future of Libr. profession, 1993-95), Phi Beta Kappa. Achievements include design of information systems and interfaces for search and subject access in information retrieval systems. Office: Grad Sch Edn & Info Studies UCLA 405 Hilgard Ave Los Angeles CA 90095-1520

BATES, MARGARET P., historian; BA, Barnard Coll.; MA, Wash. U., St. Louis. Dir. Coun. Basic Edn., Washington. Internat. bd. advisors Monterey Inst. Internat. Studies; bd. trustees York Sch., Carmel/Monterey, Calif.; mem. pres.'s coun. Calif. State U. Monterey Bay; former trustee Barnard Coll.; former mem. Calif. State Bd. Edn.

BATES, MARTHA COPENHAVER, elementary school educator; b. Abilene, Tex., Dec. 22, 1933; d. Robert Madison Copenhaver and Mildred Ailene Manton; m. Charles Benjamin Bates, Apr. 9, 1960; children: Benjamin Madison, Lelia Ann, William Andrew. BS in Psychology, Coll. William and Mary, 1956; MEd in guidance and counseling, Loyola Coll. of Balt., 1974. 1st grade tchr. Montgomery(Md.) County Pub. Schs., 1956—57; mem. staff subscriber svc. and enrollment dept. Group Hospitalization, Inc., Wash., DC, 1957—59; 1st grade tchr. Balt. County Pub. Schs., 1958—61, 2d & 3d grade tchr., 1962—64, elem. sch. guidance counselor, 1973—96; ret., 1996. Chmn., bd. dirs. Noah's Ark Preschool, Upper Falls, Md., 2001—. Methodist. Home: 202 Frazier Ct Joppa MD 21085-4434 Personal E-mail: mpcbates@aol.com.

BATES, ROBERT C., academic administrator; m. Wendy Bates. BS in Biology, Lewis & Clark Coll., 1966; MS in Bacteriology and Pub. Health, Wash. State U., 1969; PhD in Virology, Colo. State U., 1972. Asst. prof. Va. Poly. Inst. and State U., 1972—78, assoc. prof., 1978—85, prof., 1985—2002, assoc. dean for rsch., facilities and grad. studies, 1987—94, dean Coll. Arts and Scis., 1994—2002; provost, exec. v.p. Wash. State U., Pullman, 2002—. Contbr. chapters to books, articles to profl. jours. Mem.: AAAS, Am. Soc. for Virology, Am. Soc. Biol. Chemists, Sigma Xi. Office: Office of Provost Wash State Univ PO Box 641046 Pullman WA 99164-1046 Home Phone: 509-334-6652; Office Phone: 509-335-5582. Business E-Mail: bates@wsu.edu.

BATES, WALTER ALAN, retired lawyer; b. Wadsworth, Ohio, Oct. 27, 1925; s. Edwin Clinton and Gertrude (Connor) B.; m. Aloise Grasselli O'Brien, Feb. 9, 1957; children: Charles, Aloise, Walter Alan Jr., Thomas, David. BS cum laude, Harvard U., 1945, LLB, 1950. Bar: Ohio 1950, U.S. Dist. Ct. (no. dist.) Ohio 1954, U.S. Ct. Appeals (6th cir.) 1965, U.S. Ct. Appeals (7th cir.) 1966, U.S. Dist. Ct. Conn. 1976, U.S. Ct. Appeals (2nd cir.) 1977, U.S. Dist. Ct. Minn. 1978, U.S. Ct. Appeals (8th cir.) 1980, U.S. Ct. Appeals (5th cir.) 1984, U.S. Dist. Ct. (no. dist.) Tex. 1988, U.S. Supreme Ct. 1989. Assoc. McKeehan, Merrick, Arter & Stewart, Cleve., 1950-60; ptnr. Arter & Hadden, Cleve., 1960-94; ret., 1994. Chmn. bd. trustees Cleve. Inst. Music, 1980-85, hon. trustee, 1985—; assoc. v.p., chmn. new programs com. United Way Svcs., Cleve., 1982-85, trustee, 1985-88; mem. Cleve. panel Ctr. for Pub. Resources; trustee Apollo's Fire, 1998—2005. Lt. USN, 1945—46, lt. USN, 1951—53. Mem. ABA (antitrust sect.), Ohio State Bar Assn. (chmn. bd. govs. antitrust sect. 1987-91), Cleve. Bar Assn. (joint com. on bar admissions 1990-97, cert. grievance com. 1992-95), Skyline Country Club, Kirtland Country Club (sec., bd. dirs. 1981-86), Mentor Harbor Yachting Club (emeritus, bd. dirs. 1980-89, commodore 1988), Tavern Club, Harvard Club (Cleve. pres. 1968-69). Republican. Roman Catholic. Avocations: sailing, golf, travel. Home: 2684 Sulgrave Rd Shaker Heights OH 44122 Home Phone: 216-292-7511. E-mail: sailor74@adelphia.net.

BATES, WILLIAM, III, lawyer; b. Phila., May 1, 1949; s. William and Elizabeth (Martin) B. BA, Yale U., 1971; JD, Stanford U., 1974. Bar: Calif. 1974, U.S. Dist. Ct. (no. dist.) Calif. 1976, U.S. Dist. Ct. (ea. dist.) Calif. 1978, U.S. Dist. Ct. (ctrl. dist.) Calif. 1984, U.S. Ct. Appeals (9th cir.) 1986, U.S. Dist. Ct. (so. dist.) Calif. 1987, U.S. Supreme Ct. Law clk. to chief judge U.S. Dist. Ct. Conn., Hartford, 1974—75; assoc. McCutchen, Doyle, Brown & Enersen, San Francisco, 1975—81; ptnr. Bingham, McCutchen (formerly McCutchen, Doyle, Brown & Enersen), 1981—. Mem. bd. visitors Stanford Law Sch., 2003—06. Mem. ABA (mem. bus. bankruptcy com.), State Bar Calif. (chair rules of ct. com. 1979-80, mem. uniform comml. code com. 1985-88, mem. debtor/creditor rels. com. 1989-92), San Francisco Bar Assn. (chair comml. law and bankruptcy sect. 1991-92). Democrat. Episcopalian. Avocations: wine tasting, bicycling, travel. Office: Bingham McCutchen 1900 University Ave East Palo Alto CA 94303-2223 Office Phone: 650-849-4400. E-mail: bill.bates@bingham.com.

BATES, WILLIAM HUBERT, lawyer; b. Lexington, Mo., Apr. 14, 1926; s. George Hubert and E. Norma (Comer) B.; m. Joy LoRue Godbehere, Oct. 20, 1956; children: William Brand, Joy Ann. BA, U. Mo., 1949; JD, U. Mich., 1952. Bar: Mo. 1952. With Lathrop & Gage L.C., Kansas City, Mo., 1952—, chmn., 1988-95. Mem., pres. bd. curators U. Mo. Multi-Campus U., 1983-89. Sgt. U.S. Army, 1943-46, ETO. Recipient Brotherhood award NCCJ, 1984; Disting. Alumni award U. Mo., 1989, Geyer award for pub. svc., 1991. Fellow Am. Bar Found. (state chmn. 1990-97); mem. ABA (ho. of dels. 1990-93), Mo. Bar Assn. (bd. dirs. 1982-91, v.p., pres. 1988-89), Kansas City Bar Assn. (pres. Found. 1985-87), Lawyers Assn. Kansas City (Charles Evans Whittaker award 1990), Mo. C. of C. (chmn., bd. dirs. 1983-85), Greater Kansas City C. of C. (bd. dirs., chmn. 1975-92), Van Guard Club, Mercury Club, Beta Theta Pi (Man of Yr. award Kansas City 1985, Oxford Cup 1996). Democrat. Methodist. Avocations: golf, swimming, music. Home: 310 W 49th St Apt 1002 Kansas City MO 64112-3400 Office: Lathrop & Gage L C 2345 Grand Blvd Ste 2600 Kansas City MO 64108-2617 Home Phone: 816-756-3898; Office Phone: 816-292-2000. Business E-Mail: bbates@lathropgage.com.

BATESON, MARY CATHERINE, retired anthropology educator, writer, lecturer; b. NYC, Dec. 8, 1939; d. Gregory and Margaret (Mead) B.; m. J. Barkev Kassarjian, June 4, 1960; 1 child, Sevanne Margaret. BA, Radcliffe Coll., 1960; PhD, Harvard U., 1963; DHL (hon.), Fordham U., 1994, U. Redlands, 1996, DePaul U., 1998, Marygrove Coll., 1999, Mills Coll., 2000. Instr. Arabic Harvard U., 1963-66; assoc. prof. anthropology Ateneo de Manila U., 1966-68; sr. rsch. fellow psychology and philosophy Brandeis U., 1968-69; assoc. prof. anthropology Northeastern U., Boston, 1969-71; rschr. U. Tehran, 1972-74; vis. prof. Northeastern U., 1974-75; prof. anthropology, dean grad. studies Damavand Coll., 1975-77; prof. anthropology, dean social sci. and humanities U. No. Iran, 1977-79; vis. scholar Harvard U., 1979-80; dean faculty, prof. anthropology Amherst Coll., 1980-87; Clarence J. Robinson prof. anthropology and English George Mason U., 1987—2002, prof. emerita, 2002—. Pres. Inst. Intercultural Studies, 1979—; vis. prof. Spelman Coll., 1996; scholar in residence, Radcliffe Inst. Advanced Studies, Harvard U., 2000-01; vis. prof. Harvard Grad. Sch. Edn., 2001-04; vis. scholar Ctr. on Aging and Work/Work Place Flexibility, Boston Coll. Soc. Work, 2006-; cons. Americans for Libr. Coun. on Lifelong Access Program, 2006-. Author: Arabic Language Handbook, 1967, 2d edit., 2003, Structural Continuity in Poetry: A Linguistic Study of Five Early Arabic Odes, 1970, Our Own Metaphor: A Personal Account of a Conference on Consciousness and Human Adaption, 1972, 3d edit., 2004, With a Daughter's Eye: A Memoir of Margaret Mead and Gregory Bateson, 1984, 3d edit., 2001, Composing a Life, 1989, 3d edit., 2001, Peripheral Visions: Learning Along the Way, 1994, Full Circles, Overlapping Lives: Culture and Generation in Transition, 2000, Willing to Learn: Passages of Personal Discovery, 2004; co-author: Angels Fear: Towards an Epistemology of the Sacred, 1987, 2d edit., 2005, Thinking AIDS, 1988; co-editor: Approaches to Semiotics: Anthropology, Education, Linquistics, Psychiatry and Psychology, 1964. Mem. adv. bd. Cities at Peace Nat. Fellow Ford Found., 1961-63, NSF, 1968-69, Wenner-Gren Found., 1972, Bunting Inst., 1983-84, Guggenheim Found., 1987-88. Mem. Am. Anthrop. Assn., Lindisfarne Assn., Nat. Ctrs. Atmospheric Rsch. (adv. bd.), Phi Beta Kappa. Business E-Mail: mcatb@attglobal.net.

BATES-ROMEO, DELORES ALVENIA, music educator, consultant; b. LA, June 9, 1928; d. Albert and Athaliah Lydia (Crone) Bates; m. Nick Romeo, Dec. 4, 1986. BS, Emporia State U., Kans., 1956; cert., Empire Sch. Piano Tuning, 1960. Tchr. music Emporia Pub. Schs., Kans., 1950—55; supr. music Junction City Pub. Schs., Kans., 1955—59; tchr. music, 4th grade, organist Episcopal Ch., LaMesa, Calif., 1959—60; dir. music, tchr. classroom Lakeside Pub. Schs., Calif., 1960—86; owner, tchr. Bates Music Studios, LaMesa, Spring Valley, El Cajon, San Diego, Calif., 1962—; instr. music US Sch. Music, NYC, 1963—; music dir., coord. pvt. schs. La Mesa, 1970—72. Organist, choir dir. various chs.; cons. elem. tchrs. Junction City Pub. Sch., 1955—59; counselor tchr., students and future tchrs. various pub. and pvt. schs. Mem.: NEA (life), Music Educators Nat. Conf. (life). Avocations: art, reading, herbs, exercise, cooking. Home and Office: Bates Romeo Music and Arts Ctr 3295 Greyling DR #B San Diego CA 92123-2229 Office Phone: 858-277-4442.

BATHRICK, DAVID, foreign language educator, academic administrator; b. NYC, Apr. 17, 1936; s. John Northrup and Margaret (Holmes) B.; m. Serafina Kent, July 1, 1960 (div. 1980); children: Jason, Brendan, Simon; m. Ulrike Liebert, Aug. 8, 1997. BA, Dartmouth Coll., 1959; MA, U. Chgo., 1962, PhD, 1970. Instr. Lab. Sch. U. Chgo., 1961-67; asst. prof. St. Xavier Coll., Chgo., 1969-70; prof. U. Wis., Madison, 1970-87, Free U. of Berlin, 1982-83, Cornell U., Ithaca, NY, 1987—, Jacob Gould Schurman prof. theatre, film and dance and German studies, 1998—, chmn. dept. German, 1991-94, chmn. dept. theatre arts, 1995—. Cons., reader in field; bd. dirs. Internat. Rsch. Exch. Bd., Princeton, NJ, 1986-92. Author: Dialectic and Early Brecht, 1976, The Powers of Speech: The Politics of Culture in the GDR, 1995; author, editor: Modernity and the Text, 1989, Visualizing the Holocaust, 2007; editor, founder Jour. New German Critique, 1973—; contbr. articles to profl. jours. Fulbright grantee, 1967-68; Internat. Rsch. Exch. Bd. fellow, 1982-83, Inst. German Studies Bremen U. fellow, 1998—. Mem. Am. Assn. German Tchrs., Am. Assn. Slavic Studies, Modern Lang. Assn., Internat. Brecht Soc. (v.p. 1980-81). Democrat. Avocations: music, sports, hiking. Home: 111 Stewart Ave Ithaca NY 14850-4550 Office: Cornell U Dept of German 183 Goldwin Smith Hall Ithaca NY 14853-3201 Office Phone: 607-255-5265. Business E-Mail: db17@cornell.edu.

BATIUK, THOMAS MARTIN, cartoonist; b. Akron, Ohio, Mar. 14, 1947; s. Martin and Verna (Greskovics) B.; m. Catherine L. Wesemeyer, June 26, 1971; 1 child, Brian. B.F.A., Kent State U., Ohio, 1969, cert. edn., 1969. Tchr. art Eastern Heights Jr. High Sch., 1969-72; syndicated cartoonist, 1972—. Cartoonist: comic strip Funky Winkerbean, 1972—, John Darling, 1979—, Crankshaft, 1987—; collections include Funky Winkerbean, 1973, Funky Winkerbean, Play It Again Funky, 1975, Funky Winkerbean, Closed Out, 1977, Yearbook, 1979, You Know You've Got Trouble When Your Mascot is a Scpaegoat, 1984, Football Fields are for Band Practice, 1986, Sunday Concert, 1987, Henry C. Dinkle-Live at Carnegie Hall, 1988, A Pizza Pilgrim's Progress, 1990, Funky Winkerbean: Gone with the Woodwinds, 1992, Would the Ushers Please Lock the Doors, 1994, Crankshaft: I've Still Got It, 1995; co-author: And One Slice With Anchovies!, 1993, Crankshaft, 1992; forward: A PArent's Guide to Band and ORchestra, 1991, Attack of the Band Moms, 1996. Recipient 46th Annual Ohio Gov.'s award-Journalism, 1995. Mem. Nat. Cartoonists Soc., Newspaper Features Coun. Office: care Universal Press Syndicate 4520 Main St Ste 700 Kansas City MO 64111-1816

BATLA, RAYMOND JOHN, JR., lawyer; b. Cameron, Tex., Sept. 1, 1947; s. Raymond John and Della Alvina (Jezek) B.; m. Susan Marie Clark, Oct. 1, 1983; children: Sara, Charles, Michael, Traci. BS with highest honors, U. Tex., 1970, JD with honors, 1973. Bar: Tex. 1973, D.C. 1973, N.Y. 2004, U.S. Dist. Ct. (so. dist.) Tex. 1982, U.S. Ct. Appeals (D.C. cir.) 1974, U.S. Ct. Appeals (5th cir.) 1982, U.S. Ct. Appeals (10th cir.) 1978, U.S. Supreme Ct. 1977; registered Fgn. Lawyer, Law Soc. of Eng. and Wales, 2000. Structural engr. Tex. Hwy. Dept., Austin, 1970; assoc. Hogan & Hatson, Washington, 1973-82, gen. ptnr., 1983—, mng. ptnr. internat. offices, 2001—06. Mem. Am. Endowment for Democracy Internat. Observer Del. to Czechoslovakia, 1990; sec. Coun. on Alt. Fuels, 1987-97. Author: Petroleum Regulation Handbook, 1980, Natural Gas Yearbook, 1991; columnist, mem. editorial bd. Natural Gas mag., 1984-91, Energy Law Jour., 1991-93; contbr. articles to profl. jours. Mem. ABA (mem. spl. com. for energy fin., vice chmn. energy com. 1981), Fed. Energy Bar Assn. (chmn. internat. energy transactions com. 1993-94), Fed. Bar Assn., D.C. Bar Assn., State Bar Tex., N.Y. State Bar Assn., City Club of Wash., London Capital Club, Order of Coif, Chi Epsilon, Tau Beta Pi. Home: 12406 Shari Hunt Grv Clifton VA 20124-2056 also: 5 Half Moon St London W1Y 7RA England Office: Hogan & Hartson Juxon House 100 St Pauls Churchyard London EC4M 8BU England also: Hogan & Hartson 555 13th St NW Ste 800W Washington DC 20004-1109 Office Phone: 202-637-5745, 44 (0)20 7367 0200. E-mail: rjbatla@hhlaw.com.

BATLIN, ROBERT ALFRED, retired newspaper editor; b. San Francisco, Aug. 24, 1930; s. Philip Alfred and Lavenia Mary (Barnes) B.; m. Diane Elise Giblin, July 4, 1956; children— Lisa, Philippa. BA, Stanford U., 1952, MA, 1954. Reporter San Bruno Herald, 1952-53; copy editor, then dept. editor San Francisco News, 1956-59; dept. editor San Francisco News-Call Bull., 1959-65; feature editor San Francisco Examiner, 1965-74, arts editor, 1974-85, asst. style editor, 1985-2001; copy editor San Francisco Chronicle mag., 2001—02, ret., 2002. Served with AUS, 1954-56. Mem. Soc. of Profl. Journalists. Home: 91 Fairway Dr Daly City CA 94015-1215

BATLIVALA, ROBERT BOMI D., oil industry executive, economics professor; b. Bombay, Feb. 17, 1940; came to U.S., 1962, naturalized, 1968; s. Dean Shaw and Rose (Engineer) B.; m. Carole Gretchen Feustel, May 9, 1964; children: Amy, Dina. BS in Geology, Chemistry, St. Xavier Coll., Bombay, Ind., 1960; MBA in Bus., Econs., Loyola U., Chgo., 1970; PhD in Bus., Econs., Ill. Inst. Tech., 1971; postgrad., U. Chgo., 1972-73. Rsch. chemist Reynolds Metals Co., McCook, Ill., 1962-64; from sales engr. to staff dir. econs. Amoco Corp., Chgo., 1964-1988, dir. antitrust econs., 1988-93, dir. regulatory econs., 1993-99. Adj. prof. bus. and econs. Rosary Coll., Dominican U., River Forest, Ill., 1976—, Graduate Sch. Bus., 1980-99; bd. dirs. Vesta Ins. Group, Inc., Ill. Ins. Exch. (INEX), Parsee Internat. Ltd. Contbr. articles to profl. jours. Bd. dirs. Ctr. for Conflict Resolution, 1991—96. Stuart Tuition scholar Ill. Inst. Tech., 1970-71; recipient Recognition award Rosary Coll. Grad. Sch. Bus. Alumni Assn., River Forest, 1986. Mem. ABA (assoc.), Nat. Assn. Mfrs. (corp. fin., mgmt. & competition com., regulation, transp. com. 1980-99), Am. Econ. Assn., Assn. of Energy Economists, Loyola U. Grad. Bus. Alumni Assn. (pres., sr. v.p. 1971-73, Disting. Alumni award 1975), Oak Park Country Club. Avocations: ancient history, reading, writing, travel, languages. Home and Office: 1106 Keystone Ave River Forest IL 60305-1326

BATNIJI, RAMI K., facial plastic surgeon; b. LA, Oct. 11, 1973; s. Kamal A. and Turkya S. Batniji. Degree, Williams Coll., 1995; MD, Albany Med. Coll., NY, 2000. Diplomate Am. Bd. Otolaryngology, 2006. Residency in otolaryngology-head and neck surgery Batniji Facial Plastic Surgery, Newport Beach, Calif., 2005, fellowship in facial plastic and reconstructive surgery, 2006, plastic surgeon, 2006—. Mem. com. Am. Acad. Facial Plastic and Reconstructive Surgery. Mem.: Am. Acad. Otolaryngology-Head and Neck Surgery, Am. Acad. Facial Plastic and Reconstructive Surgery, Alpha Omega Alpha. Office: Batniji Facial Plastic Surgery 361 Hosp Rd Ste 329 Newport Beach CA 92663 Office Phone: 949-650-8882. Personal E-mail: ramikbatniji@hotmail.com.

BATOR, FRANCIS MICHEL, economist, educator; b. Budapest, Hungary, Aug. 10, 1925; came to U.S., 1939, naturalized, 1944; s. Victor and Franciska Elisabeth (Sichermann) B.; m. Micheline Charlotte Martin, June 30, 1949; children: Nina, Christopher Francis. Grad., Groton Sch., 1943; BS, MIT, 1949, PhD, 1956; MA (hon.), Harvard U., 1967. Exec. asst. to dir. Center Internat. Studies, MIT, 1951-54; sr. research staff Center Internat. Studies, Mass. Inst. Tech., 1954-63, asst. prof. econs., 1957-60, assoc. prof., 1960-63; sr. econ. adviser AID, Dept. State, 1963-64; sr. staff NSC, 1964-65; dep. asst. to Pres. for nat. security affairs White House, 1965-67; prof. polit. economy John F. Kennedy Sch. Govt. Harvard U., 1967-87, Ford Found. prof. internat. polit. economy John F. Kennedy Sch. Govt., 1987-92; Lucius N. Littauer prof. polit. economy John F. Kennedy Sch. Govt., Harvard U., 1992-96, emeritus Lucius N. Littauer prof. polit. economy, 1996—. Cons. Rand Corp., Inst. Def. Analysis, Office Sec. Treasury, 1961-63, under sec. state for econ. affairs, 1961; U.S. mem. consultative group on econ. projections UN, 1962, on internat. monetary arrangements, 1969; spl. cons. sec. treasury, 1967-69; mem. Pres.'s Adv. Com. Internat. Monetary Arrangements, 1967-69; vis. fellow Collegium Budapest Inst. Advanced Study, 1993. Author: The Question of Government Spending, 1960; co-author: Energy, the Next Twenty Years, 1979; contbr. Agenda for the Nation, 1968, Employment and Growth, 1987, The Theory of Market Failure, 1998; contbr. articles to profl. jours. Fgn. affairs task force Dem. Adv. Coun. Elected Ofcls., 1974-76; nat. adv. bd. Ctr. Nat. Policy, 1981-90; adv. bd. Scudder New Europe Fund, 1990-92, McKinsey and Co. Global Inst., 1991-95; bd. dirs. Hungarian-Am. Enterprise Fund, 1994—. 1st lt. inf. AUS, 1944-46. Recipient Disting. Service award Treasury Dept., 1968; Guggenheim fellow, 1959; named to US Army Officer Candidate Sch. Hall of Fame. Fellow Am. Acad. Arts and Scis.; mem. Coun. Fgn. Rels., Am. Econ. Assn., Century Assn. (NYC). Home: 17 Farrar St Cambridge MA 02138-2007 Office: Harvard U 79 Jfk St Cambridge MA 02138-5801 Business E-Mail: Francis_Bator@Harvard.edu.

BATORY, RONALD LOUIS, rail transportation executive; b. Detroit, Jan. 25, 1950; s. Louis Frank and Bonita Faye (Hall) B.; m. Barbara Ellen Berger, Apr. 19, 1975; 1 child, Erin Faye. BA, Adrian Coll., 1971; MA, Ea. Mich. U., 1975. Adminstrn. asst. to v.p. ops. Detroit, Toledo & Ironton R.R., Dearborn, Mich., 1971—75, asst. engr. track Flat Rock, Mich., 1975—76, mgr. indsl. engr. Dearborn, 1976—77, dir. material procurement and planning, 1977—81; transp. supr. Grand Trunk We. R.R., Pontiac, Mich., 1981—82, trainmaster Toledo, 1982—84, terminal mgr. Chgo., 1984—86, dist. mgr. ops, 1986—87, dir. transp. planning Detroit, 1997; v.p., gen. mgr. Chgo. Mo. & We. Rlwy., Springfield, Ill., 1987—89; asst. gen. mgr. ea. region So. Pacific Transp., Lisle, Ill., 1989—92, gen. mgr. Midwest region, 1992—94; pres. The Belt Railway Co. of Chgo., 1994—98; sr. v.p., COO Conrail, Mt. Laurel, NJ, 1998—2003, pres., COO Phila., 2004—. Bd. dirs. Kansas City Terminal Rlwy., Terminal R.R. Assn. St. Louis. Author: Purchasing Perspective, 1979, Econs. of Planning, 1980. Mem. R.R. Tie Assn., Am. Rlwy. Engr. Assn., Rlwy. Ops. Officers, Inc., Am. Short Line R.R. Assn. (bd. dirs.), Am. Assn. R.R. Supts. (bd. dirs.), Fairlane Club, Laurel Creek Country Club, Union League Club Chgo. Republican. Methodist. Avocations: photography, historical transportation readings. Home: 13 Leeds Rd Moorestown NJ 08057-1887 Office: Consol Rail Corp 1000 Howard Blvd Mount Laurel NJ 08054-2371 Office Phone: 856-231-2003.

BATRA, ROMESH CHANDER, engineering educator, researcher; b. Dherowal, Panjab, India, Aug. 16, 1947; came to U.S., 1969; s. Amir Chand and Dewki Bai (Dhamija) B.; m. Manju Dhamija, June 26, 1972; children: Monica, Meenakshi. BSME, Panjabi U., Patiala, India, 1968; MASc, U. Waterloo, Ont., Can., 1969; PhD, Johns Hopkins U., 1972; DSc (hon.), Thapar U., Patiala, India, 2006. Postdoctoral rsch. assoc. Johns Hopkins U., Balt., 1972-73; rsch. assoc. McMaster U., Hamilton, Ont.,

1973-74; asst. prof. U. Ala., Tuscaloosa, 1976-77; asst. prof. engring. mechanics U. Mo., Rolla, 1974-76, assoc. prof., 1977-81, prof., 1981-94; Clifton C. Garvin prof. Va. Poly. Inst. and State U., Blacksburg, 1994—. Bd. dirs. Midwestern Mechanics Conf., 1989—93, mem. editor procs., 1991; mem. NRC Panel on Armaments, 1996—99, NRC Panel on Survivability and Lethality, 2001—; organizer, co-chair Mechs. and Mats. Conf., 1999; lectr. S.W. Mechanics Series, 2000; Michael L. Sadowski mechanics lectr. Rensselaer Poly. Inst., 2000; hon. prof. Nanjing U. Sci. and Tech., China, 2004—, Lanzhou U. Tech., 2005—; co-chair 1st internat. conf. Mechanical Engring. and Mechanics; co-chair, organizer 14th US Nat. Conf. Theoretical and Applied Mechanics, 2002. Co-editor-in-chief: Internat. Jour. Computater Methods, 2004-; editor: Contemporary Research in Engineering Science, Springer Verlag, 1995; co-editor: Contemporary Research in the Mechanics and Mathematics of Materials, Internat. Ctr. for Numerical Methods in Engring., 1996, Constitutive Laws, Experiments and Numerical Implementation, Internat. Ctr. for Numerical Methods in Engring., 1995, Material Instabilities, Theory and Applications, 1994, Impact, Waves and Fracture, 1994, Contemporary Research in Mechanics, 2002; mem. editl. bd. Internat. Jour. Plasticity, 1989-2003, Internat. Jour. Engring. Design and Analysis, 1992—, Continuum Mechanics and Thermodynamics, 1993-2004, Computational Mechanics, 1994-2006, Jour. Engring. Materials and Tech., 1996-2001, Polish Jour. Theoretical and Applied Mechanics, 2000—, Computer Modeling in Engring. and Sci., 2003-04; editor: Mathematics and Mechanics of Solids, 1995—; author: Elements of Continuum Mechanics, AIAA Publ., 2005; reviewer for various jours. in field; contbr. articles to profl. jours. Grantee NSF, 1980-83, 87—, Army Rsch. Office, 1985—, Office of Naval Rsch., 1994—; recipient Alexander von Humboldt award for sr. scientists, 1992, Jai Krishna award Indian Geotech. Soc., 1994, Eric Reissner medal Internat. Congress in Computational Engrg. Sci., 2000; inducted into Hopkins Soc. Scholars, 1993. Fellow ASME (chair elasticity com. 1995-2000, co-editor symposium procs. 1991, 94-95, co-editor meeting procs. 1999, awards nominating com. 1997-2006, organizer, co-chair mechanics and materials conf. 1999), Am. Acad. Mechanics (awards nominating com. 2002-2006, sec. 2003-05), Am. Soc. Engring. Edn. (Centennial award 1993), Soc. Engring. Sci. (bd. dirs. 1991-96, editor meeting procs. 1982, v.p. 1995, pres. 1996); Soc. Natural Philosophy (treas. 1987-89, editor meeting procs. 1981), U.S. Nat. Congress Theoret. and Applied Mechs. (organizer, co-chmn. 2002), Internat. Soc. Interaction Between Mechanics and Math. Office: Va Polytech Inst & State U Dept Engring Sci & Mechanics 220 Norris Hall Blacksburg VA 24061-0219 Office Phone: 540-231-6051. Business E-Mail: rbatra@vt.edu.

BATROUNEY, CLIVE M., finance company executive; Chmn., dir. Telstra Superannuation Fund, Melbourne, 2003—. Office: Telstra Super Pty Ltd 215 Spring St Level 3 Melbourne VIC 3000 Australia Office Phone: 03-96536000.

BATSAKIS, JOHN GEORGE, pathology educator; b. Petoskey, Mich., Aug. 14, 1929; s. George John and Stella (Vlahkis) B.; m. Mary Janet Savage, Dec. 28, 1957; children: Laura, Sharon, George. Student, Va. Mil. Inst., 1947, Albion Coll., Mich., 1948-50; MD, U. Mich., 1954. Diplomate Am. Bd. Pathology. Intern George Washington Univ. Hosp., Washington, 1954-55; resident in pathology U. Mich. Hosp., Ann Arbor, 1955-59; prof. pathology U. Mich., Ann Arbor, 1969-79; chmn. dept. pathology M.D. Anderson Hosp. U. Tex., Houston, 1981-96, chm. and prof. emeritus dept pathology, 1996—. Ruth Legett Jones prof. U. Tex., Austin, 1982-96; adj. prof. oral pathology U. Tex. Dental Br., Houston; cons. Armed Forces Inst. Pathology, 1972—, VA Hosp., Ann Arbor, 1968-79; Hayes Martin lectr. Am. Soc. for Head and Neck Surgery, 1994; Gunnar Holmgren lectr. Swedish Nat. Ear, Nose, Throat Meeting, 1994; William Christopherson lectr. U. Louisville Dept. of Pathology, 1995; external examiner U. Hong Kong Dental Sch., 1995—; Francis A. Sooy lectr. dept. otolaryngology, head and neck surgery U. Calif., San Francisco, 1997; 2d Matthews lectr. dept. pathology Emory U., 1997; spkr. in field. Author: Tumors of the Head and Neck, 2d edit., 1979; co-author: Surgical Pathology of the Head and Neck, 2000; editor: Clin. Lab. Ann., 1981—86; co-editor: Advances in Anatomic Pathology, 1994—98; editor-in-chief Advances in Anatomic Pathology, 1998—2000; co-editor: Oral Cancer, 2003, Comprehensive Management of Head and Neck Tumors, 1999; mem. editl. bd. 13 jours., 1974—; contbr. articles to profl. jours. Bd. trustees, v.p. Mike Hogg Found., Houston, 1991—; trustee George C. Marshall Found., Lexington, Va., 1995-00, emeritus trustee, 2000—. Capt. U.S. Army, 1959-61. Recipient William H. Rorer award Am. Coll. Gastroenterology, 1972, Disting. Alumnus award Albion Coll., 1987, Reviewer of the Decade award AMA Archives Orolaryngology Head Neck Surgery, 1990, Presdl. award Am. Soc. Head and Neck Surgery, 1991, Harlan Spjut award Houston Soc. Clin. Pathologists, 1992, Honor award Am. Laryngologic Assn., 1995; Spl. Honored Guest of Am. Soc. for Head and Neck Surgery, 1993. Fellow ACP, Am. Soc. Clin. Pathologists, Coll. Am. Pathologists (Disting. Svc. award 2002), Am. Acad. Otolaryngology (assoc., honor award 1994), Royal Soc. Medicine. Republican. Episcopalian. Home: 1701 Hermann Dr Unit 1401 Houston TX 77004-7373

BATSHAW, MARK LEVITT, pediatrician; b. Montreal, Que., Can., Sept. 19, 1945; s. Manuel G. and Rachel (Levitt) B.; m. Karen N. Korman, June 29, 1969; children: Elissa, Michael, Andrew. BA, U. Pa., 1967; MD, U. Chgo., 1971. Diplomate Am. Bd. Pediatrics. Resident in pediatrics Hosp. for Sick Children, Toronto, 1971-73; fellow in developmental pediatrics Kennedy Kreiger Inst., Johns Hopkins U. Sch. Medicine, 1973-75; instr. Johns Hopkins U. Sch. Medicine, Balt., 1975-76, asst. prof., 1976-80, assoc. prof. pediatrics, 1980-88; W.T. Grant prof. pediatrics and neurology U. Pa. Sch. Medicine, Phila., 1988-98; chief div. child devel. and rehab. Children's Hosp. of Phila., 1988-98; physician-in-chief Children's Seashore House, Phila., 1988-98; chief acad. officer Children's Nat. Med. Ctr., Washington, 1998—; chmn. pediats. George Washington U. Med. Ctr., Washington, 1998—; and vice dean, pediat. academic affairs George Washington U., Washington, 2001—; dir. Children's Rsch. Inst., Washington, 1998—. Mem. NIH study NICHD, 1991-95. Author: Children with Disabilities, 4th edit., 1997, Your Child Has a Disability, 1991. Johns Hopkins U. fellow, 1973-75; Kennedy scholar, Kennedy Inst., 1983-86. Fellow Royal Coll. Physicians; mem. Am. Pediatric Soc. Office: Children's Nat Med Ctr 111 Michigan Ave NW Washington DC 20010-2916

BATSON, JONATHON KINGSLEY, composer, singer; b. Washington, Dec. 10, 1944; s. Clifton Jenks and Linda Verrill Batson; m. Eileen Lana Drillick, Oct. 22, 1994; 1 child, Jeremy. Panelist Nashville New Music Conf., 2004; judge Wilmington Songwriters Competition, Wilmington, 2005; panelist Write to Pub. Confs., 2007. Composer (actor, singer): (plays) The Jonathon Who? Revue, 1977; composer: A Special Step to Hollywood, 1978, The Way To Happiness, 1989, Young Jenny Scrooge, 1992, 1994; composer: (singer) (albums) Just Can't Lose, 1966; composer: (actor, singer) (plays) Batson in the Belfry, 1986; composer: (TV series) Off Hollywood, 1982, Murder She Wrote - Ship of Thieves Episode, 1993; composer: (author, musical director) Hollywood Arcade, 1975; singer (songwriter): (albums) Live at the Coffee Gallery Backstage, 2000, (Mostly) Live at McCabe's, 2002, The Ballad of San Jacinto (Ofcl. Town Song, 1988), Crusader (Gt. Humanitarian Award - Religious Freedom Crusade, 1986), Theta Sound Coffee House Live, 2004, Awaken the Dreamer, 2000, (songs) Hey, Bud Clark/ Battle of Portland (Religious Freedom Award, 1985); musician: Tucumcari, 2002, China Friendship Tour (Beijing Appreciation Award, 1987), (Hunan Appreciation Award, 1987); author: (short stories) The Powder Monkey of Cape Fear (Lower Cafe Fear Hist. Soc. 2nd Pl. Short Story Award, 2005), Gaston's Last Run (Lower Cape Fear Hist. Soc. 1st Pl. Short Story award, 2006), Friendship is Something to Share (Artists Helping Artists Poetry Award, 2001), The Rands Conspiracy, 2002, The Songwriter's Hook Book, 2002, Love at the Lumina Pavillion (1st Pl. Short Story award Lower Cape Fear Hist. Soc., 2007), The Trasaron Chronicles, 2007. Recipient award, Artists for New Civilization, 1989. Mem.: ASCAP, Write to Pub. Group, N.C. Songwriters Coooperative (bd. dirs. 2002—, cons. 2007), Songsalive! (seminarist 2004), Ind. Writers So. Calif. Avocations: reading, travel, theater. Home: 3220 Shore View Rd 22 Raleigh NC 27613 Office Phone: 866-696-0587. Home Fax: 866-696-0587. Personal E-mail: jon@jonbatson.com.

BATSON, RICHARD NEAL, lawyer; b. Nashville, May 1, 1941; s. John H. and Mildred (Neal) B.; m. Jean Elizabeth Flanagan; children: John Hayes, Richard Davis. BA cum laude, Vanderbilt U., 1963, JD, 1966. Bar: Ga. 1967. Law clk. to Judge Griffin B. Bell U.S. Ct. Appeals (5th cir.), Atlanta, 1966—67; assoc. Alston & Bird (formerly Alston, Miller & Gaines), 1967—71, ptnr., 1971—2005, spl. counsel, 2006—. Spkr. Nat. Conf. Bankruptcy Judges, 1982, 86, 87, 88, 94, 96, Bank Lending Inst., 1986-87, also other instns. and assns.; adj. prof. Emory U. Sch. Law, 1994-95; co-lectr. Ga. State U., fall 1984; mem. bankruptcy rules com. Jud. Conf. U.S., 1993-99. Co-author: Problem Loan Strategies, 1985, rev. 1998; contbg. author Bankruptcy Litigation Manual, 1990—; contbg. editor Norton Bankruptcy Law and Practice, 1990—. Sgt. USAF, 1967-73. Fellow Am. Coll. Trial Lawyers, Am. Coll. Bankruptcy (bd. dirs., pres. 1997-2001, chmn. bd. dirs. 2001-03); mem. Atlanta Bar Assn. (pres. 1979-80), Am. Law Inst., Southeastern Bankruptcy Law Inst. (bd. dirs., pres. 1986-87), Nat. Bankruptcy Conf. Avocations: hiking, outdoor activities. Office: Alston & Bird One Atlantic Ctr 1201 W Peachtree St Atlanta GA 30309-3400 Home Phone: 970-923-0122; Office Phone: 404-881-7267. Business E-Mail: neal.batson@alston.com.

BATSTONE, JOANNA LOUISE, physicist; BSc in Chem. Physics, U. Bristol, 1982, PhD in Physics, 1985. Computer scientist IBM Thomas J. Watson Rsch. Ctr., Hawthorne, NY, 1989—2000, sr. tech. staff mem., sr. mgr., 2000—05, sr. tech. staff mem., software group, 2005—06; dir. distributed computing IBM Rsch., 2006—. Mem. adv. bd. Bio IT Coalition, 2005. Recipient Robert Lansing Hardy Gold Medal award Minerals, Metals & Materials Soc., 1991, Cosslett award Microbeam Analysis Soc., 1989, Burton award Microscopy Soc. Am., 1995. Mem.: NY Acad. Scis. Womens Investigators Network. Office: IBM TJ Watson Rsch Ctr 19 Skyline Dr Hawthorne NY 10532 Business E-Mail: batstone@us.ibm.com.

BATT, JAMES MURRAY, retired financial consultant; b. Phila., June 28, 1958; s. James Henry and Margaret Kelly Batt. BA, Boston Coll., Chestnut Hill, Mass., 1980; MBA, Rollins Coll., Winter Park, Fla., 1986; MA, U. Miss., Oxford, 1995. Registered rep. Tucker Anthony & R.L. Day, Boston, 1980—81, Drexel Burnham Lambert, Boston, 1981—83, Rose & Co., Chgo., 1983; mktg. specialist GE Capital, Chgo., 1987—88; instr. Erie CC, Buffalo, 1990—93, Canisius Coll., Buffalo, 1991—93. Cons. Nat. Fuel Gas, Buffalo, 1992. Republican. Roman Catholic. Avocations: literature, art history.

BATT, NICK, property and investment executive; b. Defiance, Ohio, May 6, 1952; s. Dan and Zenith (Dreher) B. BS, Purdue U., 1972; JD, U. Toledo, 1976. Asst. prosecutor Lucas County, Toledo, 1976-80, civil divsn. chief, 1980-83; village atty. Village of Holland, Ohio, 1980-91; law dir. City of Oregon, Ohio, 1984-91; spl. counsel State of Ohio, 1983-93; pres. Property & Mgmt. Connection, Inc., Toledo, 1993—2002, All Rental Property Mgmt. Co., 2002—. Mem. Maumee Valley Girl Scout Coun., Toledo, 1977-80; bd. mem. Bd. Cmty. Rels., Toledo, 1975-76; mem. Lucas County Dem. Exec. Com., 1981-83. Named One of Toledo's Outstanding Young Men, Toledo Jaycees, 1979. Mem. KC, Elks. Democrat. Roman Catholic. Home Phone: 419-867-7838. Personal E-mail: nickbatt@toast.net.

BATT, RONALD ELMER, gynecologist, historian, biomedical research scientist; b. Buffalo, Sept. 24, 1933; s. Elmer Lawrence and Mary Catherine (Roll) B.; m. Carol Mary Schaab, Dec. 28, 1957; children: Paula, Douglas, Thomas, Neil, Jennifer, John; m. 2d, Kathleen Over Cansdale, May 19, 1982; stepchildren: William, James, Suzanne, Timothy, John, Mark. BS in Biology, Niagara U., 1954; MD, U. Buffalo, 1958; MA in History, SUNY Buffalo, 2002. Intern Millard Fillmore Hosp., Buffalo, 1958—59; resident in ob-gyn SUNY, Buffalo, 1959—60, 1962—66; rsch. fellow Harvard U. Med. Sch., 1963—64; asst. in surgery Peter Bent Brigham Hosp., Boston, 1963—64; fellow in gynecologic surgery Mayo Clinic, 1965; practice gynecology specializing in endometriosis and reproductive surgery Buffalo, 1966—98; rschr., 1966—. Prof. clin. gynecology, clin. prof. social and preventive medicine SUNY Buffalo. Co-author: Another Era: A Pictorial History of the School of Medicine and Biomedical Sciences, State University of New York at Buffalo 1846-1996; contbr. chpts. to books, articles to profl. jours. With M.C., USN, 1960-62. Recipient Lifetime Career Achievement award Med. Alumni Assn. Sch. Medicine and Biomed. Scis. SUNY, 1998, ACOG-Ortho/McNeil fellow in the history of Am. Obstetrics and Gynecology, 2004. Fellow ACS, Royal Coll. Surgeons Can., Am. Coll. Obstetricians and Gynecologists; mem. Am. Soc. Reproductive Medicine, Soc. Reproductive Surgeons, Am. Assn. History Medicine, Internat. Soc. History Medicine, Am. Assn. Gynecol-.Laparoscopists. Office: Women and Childrens Hosp 219 Bryant St Buffalo NY 14222

BATTAGLIA, ALEX, air transportation executive; Various positions including mgr. baggage dept. Dallas/Fort Worth Internat. Delta Air Lines Inc., 1983—2005, dir. ops., John F. Kennedy Internat Airport NY, 2005—07; v.p. ops., John F. Kennedy Internat Airport JetBlue Airways Corp., NY, 2007—. Office: JetBlue Airways Corp 118-29 Queens Blvd Forest Hills NY 11375

BATTAGLIA, ANTHONY SYLVESTER, lawyer; b. Binghamton, NY, Aug. 21, 1927; s. Sylvester Anthony and Helen B.; m. Catherine Jean, Oct. 1, 1972; children: Christina, Marc Anthony; children by previous marriage— Anthony, Sandra, Brian, Brenda Lee. AA, U. Fla., 1948, BA, 1949, LLB, 1953, JD, 1967. Bar: Fla. 1953, U.S. Dist. Ct. (mid. and so. dists.) Fla., U.S. Ct. Appeals (5th, 11th cirs.), U.S. Tax Ct., U.S. Ct. Appeals (D.C. cir.), U.S. Ct. Mil. Appeals; cert. ct. approved abritrator U.S. Dist. Ct., U.S. Supreme Ct. 1966. Asst. to U.S. dist. atty., So. Dist. Fla., 1953-56; ptnr. Parker, Parker & Battaglia, St. Petersburg, Fla., 1953-56, Parker, Battaglia & Ross, St. Petersburg, 1965-73, Parker, Battaglia, Parker, Ross & Ross, St. Petersburg, 1973-75, Battaglia, Parker, Ross, Parker & Stolba, St. Petersburg, 1975-76, Battaglia, Ross & Stolba, 1976-77, Battaglia, Ross, Stolba & Forlizzo, 1977-78, Battaglia, Ross & Forlizzo, 1978-80, Battaglia, Ross, Hastings, Dicus & Andrews, 1980-93, Battaglia, Ross, Dicus & Wein PA, 1993—. Mem. Fla. Pub. Svc. Commn., 1971; chmn. bd. Metrocare, Inc., 1975-78; mem. grievance com. U.S. Dist. Ct., 1985-88; pres. Asst. U.S. Attys. Assn. for Mid. Dist. Fla., 1994; guest lectr. Stetson U., 1994; bd. dirs. Intervest Bank, 1st Bankers Tampa Bay, N.A., St. Petersburg, Nat. Bank Fla., St. Petersburg, Operation PAR, Inc.; chmn. adv. bd. 1st Union Nat. Bank, South Pinellas, Fla. Republican nat. committeeman, Fla., 1956-64, bd. dirs., Tampa div.; bd. dirs. San Carlo Opera Fla., 1972-74, pres., chmn. bd. dirs., Pinellas County div., 1974-76; bd. dirs. St. Petersburg Opera Co., 1976-77; chmn. bd. Pinellas County Arthritis Found., 1985; founding sponsor Civil Justice Found.; trustee Ctr. Against Spouse Abuse, 1999. Recipient Jack Edmund award for Herbert G. Goldburg Criminal Law Am. Inn of Ct., 2004; named to U. Fla. Hall of Fame and Fla. Blue Key, 1951. Master Ferguson-White Am. Inn of Ct.; fellow Am. Coll. Mortgage Attys.; mem. ABA, ATLA (sustaining), Fla. Bar Assn. (bd. govs. 1993-99, George C. Carr Meml. award, 2004), St. Petersburg Bar Assn. (pres. 1990), Fed. Bar Assn. (v.p. Mid. Fla. dist., Geroge C. Carr Meml. award 2004), U.S. Attys. Assn. for Mid. Dist. Fla. (pres. 2001), Internat. Bar Assn., Hillsborough County Bar Assn., Acad. Fla. Trial Lawyers (judge student competition 1985), Am. Judicature Soc. (Supreme Ct. Hist. Soc. 1985-89), Nat. Assn. Criminal Def. Lawyers, Acad. Criminal Justice Scis., Fla. Criminal Def. Trial Lawyers, Criminal Def. Lawyers Hillsborough County, Pinellas County Trial Lawyers Assn. Roscoe Pound Am., Trial Lawyers Found. (judicial nominating com.), U. Fla. Nat. Alumni Assn., St. Petersburg C. of C. (gov.), Pinellas Inns Ct. (master bench), Herbert G. Goldberg Criminal Law Am. Inn Ct., Fla. Bar Bd. of Govs. Clubs: Treasure Island Tennis and Yacht (bd. dirs.), Suncoast Tiger Bay, St. Petersburg Yacht, Nat. Italian Am. Found., Italian-Am. Unico Internat., K.C. Roman Catholic. Office: 980 Tyrone Blvd N Saint Petersburg FL 33710-6333 Business E-Mail: abatt@brdwlaw.com.

BATTAGLIA, FREDERICK CAMILLO, physician; b. Weehawken, NJ, Feb. 15, 1932; m. Jane B. Donohue; children: Susan Kate, Thomas Frederick. BA, Cornell U., 1953; MD, Yale U., 1957; DSc (hon.), U. Ind. Diplomate Am. Bd. Pediat. Intern in pediat. Johns Hopkins Hosp., 1957—58; USPHS postdoctoral fellow biochemistry Cambridge (Eng.) U., 1958—59; Josiah Macy Found. fellow in physiology Yale U. Med. Sch., 1959—60; asst. resident, fellow in pediat. Johns Hopkins Hosp., 1960—61, resident, fellow, 1961—62; USPHS surgeon lab. perinatal physiology NIH, San Juan, 1962—64; asst. prof. Johns Hopkins Med. Sch., 1963—65; mem. faculty U. Colo. Med. Sch., Denver, 1965—, prof. pediat., prof. ob-gyn., 1969—2003, prof. pediat., ob-gyn. emeritus, 2003—, dir. divsn. perinatal medicine, 1970—74, chmn. dept. pediat., 1974—89. Attending pediatrician Children's, Denver Gen., Fitzsimons Gen. Hosps. Editor (assoc.): Pediatrics; med. progress contbg. editor Jour. Pediat., 1966—74, editl. bd. European Jour. Ob-Gybn., 1971—, assoc. Jour Perinatal, med. editor Biol. Neonate, 1979—; contbr. numerous articles to med. jours. Mem.: Inst. Medicine NAS, Soc. Exptl. Biology and Medicine, Internat. Congress Perinatal Medicine (pres. 1996), Am. Pediatric Soc. (pres. 1996, John Howland medal 2004), Soc. Gynecol. Investigation (coun. 1969—72), We. Soc. Pediatric Rsch. (pres. 1987—), Perinatal Rsch. Soc. (pres. 1974—75), Soc. Pediatric Rsch. (pres. 1976—77), Am. Gynecologic and Obstetric Soc., Am. Acad. Pediat. (E. Mead Johns award 1969), Assn. Am. Physicians, Sigma Xi, Phi Beta Kappa. Home: 2975 E Cedar Ave Denver CO 80209-3211 Office: Fitzsimons Bldg 260 MS F441 PO Box 6508 Aurora CO 80010 Office Phone: 303-724-0546. Business E-Mail: fred.battaglia@uchsc.edu.

BATTAGLIA, LYNNE ANN, judge; b. Buffalo, 1946; BA in Internat. Relations, Am. U., 1967, MA, 1968; JD, U. Md., 1974; JD (hon.), U. Balt., 2001. Asst. US atty. Dist. Md., 1978—82, US atty., 1993-2001; sr. trial atty. special litigation US Dept. of Justice, 1984—88; chief criminal investigations div. Office of Atty. Gen., 1988—91; chief staff Office US Sen. Barbara A. Mikulski, 1991—93; judge Md. Ct. Appeals, 2001—. Adj. prof. U. Md. Sch. Law, 1981—; mem. Task Force Sentencing & Intermediate Sanctions, 1995—96, Md. Alternative Dispute Resolution Commn., 1998—2000; chair Jud. Commn. Professionalism, 2004—. Author: Obeisance to the Separation of Powers, and Protection of Individuals' Rights and Liberties: The Honorable John C. Eldridge's Approach to Constitutional Analysis in the Court of Appeals of Maryland, 2003. Co-chair Women's Health Promotion Council, 1999—2001; mem. Safe Schools Interagency Steering Com., 1999—2001; vice-chair Md. Commn. for Women, 2000—01. Named one of Maryland's Top 100 Women, Daily Record, 1996, 1999, 2001; recipient Dorothy Beatty Memorial award, Women's Law Ctr. of Md., 1994, Margaret Brent-Juanita Jackson Mitchell award, 2002—03, Md. Leadership in Law award, Daily Record, 2003, Professional Legal Excellence award, Md. Bar Foundation, 2004, Lifetime Achievement award, U. Balt., 2006. Mem.: James MacGill Am. Inns of Ct., Howard County Bar Assn., Baltimore City Bar Assn. (chair gender issues subcom., former chair jud. administration com.), Md. State Bar Assn. (chair jud. administration council 2006—, mem. gender equality com., mem. civility task force). Office: Robert C Murphy Ct Appeals Bldg 361 Rowe Blvd Annapolis MD 21401 Office Phone: 410-260-1565.

BATTAH, HAMMAM JAMIL, civil engineer, utilities executive; b. Kirkuk, Nov. 11, 1939; arrived in US, 1994; s. Jamil Gergies and Nadene Joseph (Massa) Battah; m. Haifa Jecob Battah, June 26, 1969; children: Hani, Basil. BSCE, Coll. Engring., Baghdad, 1962, MSCE, 1968. Registered profl. engr., Mich. Field civil engr. Modern Constrn. Co., Lebanon, Iraq, 1964—70; from head engr. to tech. mgr., v.p. Orient Engring. Co., Iraq, 1970—79; owner, pres. Hammam Modern Constrn. Co., Iraq, 1980—92; field engr. Henessy Engrs. and SBG Constrn. Co., Mich., 1994—97; assoc. civil engr. City of Detroit, 1998—2007; ret., 2007. CEO, pres. Solar Water Energy LLC, Mich., 2004—. Achievements include patents for solar distillation system; solar thermal energy conversion system; patents pending for wave breaker. Office: Solar Water Energy LLC 12801 Auburn St Detroit MI 48223 Office Phone: 313-544-7117. Business E-Mail: hammam@solarwaterenergy.net. E-mail: hammambattah@yahoo.com.

BATTELLE, JOHN, journalist, educator, writer, entrepreneur; B, Univ. Calif., B, M, Univ. Calif., Berkeley. Co-founder editor Wired Magazine and Wired Ventures; founder, former chair, CEO Standard Media Internat. (SMI); band mgr. BoingBoing.net; publisher The Industry Standard and Standard.com; monthly columnist, Titans of Technology Business 2.0; founder, chmn. Federated Media Publishing Inc.; maintains daily Searchblog battellemedia.com. Vis. prof. Univ. Calif., Grad. Sch. Journalism, Berkeley, dir., bus. reporting program; founding exec. prodr. Foursquare Conf.; founder, exec. prodr. Web 2.0 conf.; cons. in field. Author: The Search: How Google and Its Rivals Rewrote the Rules of Business and Transformed Our Culture, 2005. Finalist Entrepreneur of Yr., Ernst & Young; named Global Leader for Tomorrow, World Econ. Forum, Davos, Switzerland. Office: Federated Media 123 Second St Sausalito CA 94965 E-mail: jbat@battellemedia.com.

BATTEN, ALAN HENRY, astronomer; b. Tankerton, Kent, England, Jan. 21, 1933; emigrated to Can., 1959, naturalized, 1975; s. George Cuthbert and Gladys (Greenwood) B.; m. Lois Eleanor Dewis, July 30, 1960; children: Michael Henry John, Margaret Eleanor. BSc with 1st class honors, U. St. Andrews, Scotland, 1955, DSc, 1974; PhD, U. Manchester, Eng., 1958. Rsch. asst. in astronomy, jr. tutor St. Anselm Residence Hall, U. Manchester, 1958-59; postdoctoral fellow Dominion Astrophys. Obs., Victoria, B.C., Canada, 1959-61, mem. staff, 1961-91, assoc. rsch. officer, 1970-76, sr. rsch. officer, 1976-91, guest scientist, 1991—. Lectr. astronomy U. Victoria, 1961-64; guest investigator Vatican Obs., 1970, Inst. Astronomia y Fisica del Espacio, Buenos Aires, 1972; lectr. history U. Victoria, 2004-05; rsch. awards com. Craigdarroch, 2003—. Author: Binary and Multiple Systems of Stars, 1973, Resolute and Undertaking Characters: The Lives of Wilhelm and Otto Struve, 1988; editor: Extended Atmospheres and Circumstellar Matter in Spectroscopic Binary Systems, 1973, Algols, 1989, Astronomy for Developing Countries, 2001; sr. author: Eighth Catalogue of the Orbital Elements of Spectroscopic Binary Systems, 1989; co-editor: The Determination of Radial Velocities and Their Applications, 1967; translator: L'Observation des Etoiles Doubles Visuelles par P. Couteau, 1981; contbr. articles to profl. jours. Pres. Willows Elem. Sch. PTA, Victoria, 1971-73; active Anglican Ch. Can. Diocesan Synod, B.C., 1966-68, 74; adv. coun. Ctr. Advanced Studies Religion and Soc., U. Victoria, 1993-2002, 2006-, chmn., 1997-2000. Recipient Queen's Silver Jubilee medal, Can., 1977; Erskine Vis. fellow, U. Canterbury, New Zealand, 1995. Fellow Royal Soc. Can. (convenor interdisciplinary sect. 1980-81, mem. coun. 1980-81), Royal Astron. Soc., Explorers Club; mem. Internat. Astron. Union (v.p. 1985-91, pres. commn. 30 1976-79, pres. commn. 42 1982-85, chmn. nat. orgn. com. XVII Gen. Assembly 1975-79), Royal Astron. Soc. Can. (pres. 1976-78, hon. pres. 1993-98, editor jour. 1981-88), Astron. Soc. Pacific (v.p. 1965-68), Can.

Astron. Soc. (pres. 1972-74), Am. Astron. Socs., Ancient Soc. Coll. Youths. Anglican. Home: 2987 Westdowne Rd Victoria BC Canada V8R 5G1 Office: Dominion Astrophys Obs 5071 W Saanich Rd Victoria BC Canada V9E 2E7 Business E-Mail: alan.batten@nrc.gc.ca.

BATTEN, FRANK, newspaper publisher, cable broadcaster; b. Norfolk, Va., Feb. 11, 1927; s. Frank and Dorothy (Martin) B.; m. Jane Neal Parke; children: Frank, Mary, Dorothy. Grad., Culver Mil. Acad., 1945; AB, U. Va., 1950; MBA, Harvard U., 1952; LittD (hon.), Washington and Lee U., 1996. Reporter The Norfolk Ledger-Star; with advt. and circulation depts. The Virginian-Pilot and Norfolk Ledger-Star newspapers; v.p. The Norfolk Virginian-Pilot and Norfolk Ledger-Star newspapers, 1953, pub., 1954—; chmn. bd. Landmark Comm., Norfolk, 1967-97, chmn. exec. com., 1998—; also chmn. Greensboro News & Record, NC; chmn. Roanoke Times, KLAS-TV, Va.; dir. Capital-Gazette Communications Inc., Annapolis, Md.; 2d vice chmn. AP, 1977-79, 1st vice chmn., 1979-81, chmn. bd., 1982-87; founder The Weather Channel, 1982. Formerly chmn. AP Pension, Tech., Fgn. ops. coms.; past chmn. AP Nominating Com., Va. AP Members; former dir. So. Newspapers Pubs. Assn.; former chmn. bd. Newspaper Advt. Bur. Trustee Culver Ednl. Found., U.S. Naval Acad. Found., So. Newspaper Pubs. Found., U. Va. Grad. Bus. Sch. Sponsors, Hollins Coll.; past chmn. bd. Old Dominion U.; past vice chmn. State Coun. Higher Edn. for Va.; past pres. and campaign chmn. Norfolk Area United Fund; chmn. com. for Internat. Naval Rev., 1957; mem. bd. visitors Coll. William and Mary. With U.S. Merchant Marine, World War II, also USNR. Recipient Norfolk's First Citizen award, 1966, Alumni Achievement award Harvard Bus. Sch., 1998. Mem. Newspaper Assn. of Am. (dir., Katherine Graham Lifetime Achievement award), Delta Kappa Epsilon. Episcopalian. Office: Landmark Communications Inc 150 W Brambleton Ave Norfolk VA 23510-2018

BATTEN, SONJA VICTORIA, psychologist, educator; d. Wesley Alvin and Marlen Batten. BA, U. Ga., Athens, 1994; PhD, U. Nev., Reno, 2000. Lic. psychologist State of Conn., 2002. Predoctoral fellow Med. U. S.C., Nat. Crime Victims Ctr., Charleston, 1999—2000; postdoctoral fellow Nat. Ctr. for PTSD, VA Boston Health Care Sys., 2000—02; assoc. dir. Women's Health Rsch. Yale U., New Haven, 2002—03; assoc. rsch. scientist Yale U. Sch. Medicine, New Haven, 2002—03; coord., trauma recovery programs VA Md. Health Care Sys., Balt., 2003—; asst. prof. psychiatry U. Md. Sch. Medicine, Balt., 2003—. Mem. editl. bd. Jour. of Traumatic Stress, 2002—; inst. dir. Acceptance and Commitment Therapy Summer Inst., Phila., 2005. Recipient New Investigator award, Am. Assn. Behavioral and Cognitive Therapies Women's Spl. Interest Group, 2004, Early Career Psychologist award, Md. Psychol. Assn., 2007; fellow, U. Ga., 1991—94; grantee, U. Nev. Reno Grad. Student Assn., 1999, Woodrow Wilson Found., 2000; scholar, Gov. State Ga., 1991—94, Nev. Women's Fund, 1997—2000; Dean William Tate Jr. scholar, U. Ga. Phi Beta Kappa, 1993, Outstanding Doctoral Student scholar, U. Nev. Reno, 1998-2000, Grad. Student scholar, Soroptimist Nev., 1998, Excellence and Diversity fellow, U. Nev. Reno, 1994—95, Wilson fellow, 1995—97. Mem.: Soc. Sci. Clin. Psychology, Assn. Contextual Behavioral Sci. (charter mem., mem. at large), Assn. Behavioral and Cognitive Therapies (program com. 1998—2007). Office: VA Maryland Health Care System 10 N Greene St (116PTSD) Baltimore MD 21201 Office Phone: 410-605-7422. Personal E-mail: svbatten@earthlink.net.

BATTENBERG, J. T., III, automotive company executive; BS in Indsl. Engring., Kettering U.; MBA Columbia U.; grad. advanced mgmt. program, Harvard U. With GM, 1986, mng. dir. GM Continental divsn. Belgium, gen. mgr. overseas truck ops. Eng., v.p. Buick-Oldsmobile-Cadillac group, 1986, v.p., group exec. Buick-Oldsmobile-Cadillac, v.p., group exec. automotive components group, 1992, sr. v.p., pres. group, 1992-95, exec. v.p., 1995; pres., CEO, chmn. bd. Delphi Corp. (formerly ACG Worldwide), Troy, Mich., 1995—2005. Mem. GM's Pres. Coun.; nat. adv. bd. Chase Manhattan Corp.; bd. dir. Sara Lee Corp., 2002-. Bd. trustees Kettering U.; bd. overseers Columbia U. Bus. Sch.; exec. bd. Detroit area Coun. of Boy Scouts Am.; exec. bd. Oakland County Automation Alley; bd. dirs. For Inspiration and Recognition of Sci. and Tech.; mem. Coun. on Competitiveness; adv. bd. Covisint; mem. Bus. Roundtable and Bus. Coun. Named Internat. Bus. Coun. World Trader of the Yr. Detroit Regional Chamber, 1998. Mem. Soc. of Automotive Engrs., Soc. of Body Engrs., Engring. Soc. of Detroit, Exec. Leadership Coun., Automobile Nat. Heritage Area, Econ. Club of Detroit (mem. exec. com.). Office: Delphi Corp 5725 Delphi Dr Troy MI 48098-2815

BATTERMAN, BORIS WILLIAM, physicist, educator, academic administrator; b. NYC, Aug. 25, 1930; children: Robert W., William E., Thomas A. Student, Cooper Union Coll., 1949-50, Technische Hochschule, Stuttgart, Germany; SB, MIT, 1952, PhD, 1956. Mem. tech. staff Bell Tel. Labs., Murray Hill, NJ, 1956-65; assoc. prof. Cornell U., Ithaca, NY, 1965-67, prof. applied and engring. physics, 1967—, dir. Sch. Applied and Engring. Physics, 1974-78, dir. Synchrotron Radiation Lab. (CHESS), 1978-97, Walter S. Carpenter Jr. prof. engring., 1985—2001, Walter S. Carpenter Jr. prof. emeritus, 2002—. Mem. staff Lawrence Berkeley Lab., 1998—, Stanford Linear Accelerator Ctr., 1999—; mem. U.S.A. Nat. Com. Crystallography, NAS, 1969—72. Assoc. editor Jour. Crystal Growth, 1964—74. Fulbright scholar, 1953-54; Guggenheim fellow, 1971, Fulbright Hayes fellow, 1971, Alexander von Humboldt fellow, 1983. Fellow: AAAS, Am. Phys. Soc. Office: 150 Lombard St #603 San Francisco CA 94111 E-mail: bwb1@cornell.edu.

BATTERMAN, STEVEN CHARLES, engineering mechanics and bioengineering professor, consultant; b. Bklyn., Aug. 15, 1937; s. Jacob and Anna (Abramowitz) B.; m. Judith Wilpon, Mar. 29, 1959; children: Scott David, Risa Karen, Daniel Adam. BCE, Cooper Union, 1959; ScM (NSF fellow), Brown U., 1961, PhD, 1964; MA (hon.), U. Pa., 1971. Bd. cert. diplomate Internat. Inst. Forensic Engring. Scis. Mem. faculty U. Pa., 1964-97, prof. mech. engring. and applied mechanics, 1974-79; assoc. prof. orthopaedic surgery rsch. U. Pa. Sch. Medicine, 1972-74, prof. orthopaedic surgery rsch., 1974-97; prof. biomechanics in vet. medicine U. Pa Sch. Vet Medicine, 1975-84, prof. bioengring., 1974-97; emeritus prof. Sch. Engring. and Applied Sci., Sch. Medicine U. Pa., 1997—; mng. ptnr. Batterman Engring., LLC, Cherry Hill. Forensic enring. and biomechanics cons. to govt., industry, ins. cos., attys.; mem. adv. bd. Cyril H. Wecht Inst. Forensic Sci. and Law, Duquesne U.; adj. prof. Coll. Medicine, Drexel U., 2006—. Contbr. numerous articles to profl. jours. Recipient S.R. Warren Disting. Teaching award, U. Pa., 1982. Fellow ASME; mem. ASCE, Am. Acad. Mechanics, Am. Soc. Engring. Edn., Biomed. Engring. Soc., Soc. Exptl. Mech., Soc. Automotive Engrs., Am. Soc. Safety Engrs., Am. Acad. Forensic Scis. (Founder's award 1992, 2004, pres.-elect 1993-94, pres. 1994-95, Disting. Fellow 2001), Assn. for Advancement Automotive Medicine, Sigma Xi, Tau Beta Pi, Chi Epsilon. Jewish. Achievements include patents for apparatus for acoustically determining periodontal health; method and system for determining occurrence of slips leading to falls. Home: 109 Charlann Cir Cherry Hill NJ 08003-2906 Home Phone: 856-424-3781; Office Phone: 856-795-3993. E-mail: batterman@aol.com.

BATTERSBY, HAROLD RONALD, retired anthropologist, archaeologist, linguist; b. Guildford, Surrey, Eng., Nov. 16, 1922; arrived in US, 1960, naturalized, 1972; s. Eric and Lillian (Darnell) B.; m. Betty Yertchenig O'Hannesian, Apr. 22, 1944. BA in Modern Near Ea. Studies, U. Toronto, 1960; PhD in Altaic Studies-Anthropology Linguistics, Ind. U., 1969. Corr. Surrey Times, London-Guildford, 1947—55; adv. dir. Turkish Post, Istanbul, 1949—53; instr. English Istanbul Med. Faculty, 1948—49, Amerikan Lisan ve San'at Dersanesi, Istanbul, 1948—54, Pangalti Ermeni Orta Okulu, Istanbul, 1949—56; coord. athletic events USO, Istanbul, 1948—54; asst. Royal Ont. Mus., Toronto, 1957—59; asst. mgr. City of Toronto, 1957—59; rsch. asst. in med. anthropology U. Pitts., 1960—62; asst. Ind. U., Bloomington, 1962—69; assoc. prof. anthropology SUNY-Geneseo, 1970—98, dir. linguistics program, 1978—98, adj. prof., 1999—2001; ret., 1998. Author: Anatolian Archaeology: A Comprehensive Bibliograph, 2 vols., 1976; sect. editor: Altaic and Uralic Studies, Ultimate Reality and Meaning, 1982—; contbr. articles to profl. jours., translations, proofreading and editing of Biblical ethnographic and linguistic texts into Altaic langs. and from Altaic langs. into English. With RAF Vol. Res., 1939—46. NDEA fellow; Ind. U. grantee; Geneseo Found. grantee, 1973, 77— Fellow Royal Anthrop. Inst. Gt. Brit. and Ireland, Am. Anthrop. Assn., Royal Asiatic soc.; mem. Am. Oriental Soc., Royal Ctrl. Asian Soc., Royal Soc. Asian Affairs, Hakluyt Soc., Internat. Soc. Oriental Rsch., Middle East Inst., Chgo. Anthrop. Soc., Inst. Ency. of Human Ideas on Ultimate Reality and Meaning, Brit. Inst. Archaeology at Ankara, Am. Oriental Soc., Am. Soc. Study People of Ea. Europe and No. and Ctrl. Asia, Linguistic Soc. Am., Niagara Linguistic Soc., N.Y. State Coun. Linguistics, Soc. Armenian Studies, Zoryan Inst., Ind. U. Alumni Assn., The Smithsonian Assocs., The Wilson Ctr. Assocs., Lambda Alpha. Clubs: Ind. U. Linguistics. Republican. Episcopalian. Avocations: reservation birds, cats, ducks, ethnolinguistics. Home: PO Box 80 Groveland NY 14462

BATTERSBY, JAMES LYONS, JR., language educator; b. Pawtucket, RI, Aug. 24, 1936; s. James Lyons and Hazel Irene (Deuel) B.; m. Lisa J. Kiser, Aug. 6, 1990; 1 child, Julie Ann. BS magna cum laude, U. Vt., Burlington, 1961; MA, Cornell U., Ithaca, NY, 1962, PhD, 1965. Asst. prof. U. Calif., Berkeley, 1965—70; assoc. prof. English Ohio State U., Columbus, 1970—82, prof., 1982—. Cons. Ohio State U. Press, U. Ky. Press, U. Calif. Press, Prentice-Hall, McGraw Hill, Fairleigh Dickinson U. Press, U. Mich. Press, U. Ala. Press. Author: Typical Folly: Evaluating Student Performance in Higher Education, 1973, Rational Praise and Natural Lamentation: Johnson, Lycidas and Principles of Criticism, 1980, Elder Olson: An Annotated Bibliography, 1983, Paradigms Regained: Pluralism and the Practice of Criticism, 1991, Reason and the Nature of Texts, 1996, Unorthodox Views: Reflections on Reality, Truth, and Meaning in Current Social, Cultural, and Critical Discourse, 2002, 7 Poets, 2005; contbg. author: Domestick Privacies: Samuel Johnson and the Art of Biography, 1987, Fresh Reflections on Samuel Johnson: Essays in Criticism, 1987, Criticism, History and Intertextuality, 1988, Beyond Poststructuralism: The Speculations of Theory and the Experience of Reading, 1996; contbr. articles to profl. jours. With US Army, 1954—57. Woodrow Wilson fellow, 1961-62, 64-65, Samuel S. Fels fellow, 1964-65, U. Calif. Summer Faculty fellow, 1966, Humanities Research fellow, 1969; recipient Kidder Medal U. Vt., 1961. Mem. MLA, Am. Soc. 18th Century Studies, Midwest Soc. 18th Century Studies, Royal Oak Found., Phi Beta Kappa, Phi Kappa Phi, Kappa Delta Pi. Home: 472 Clinton Heights Ave Columbus OH 43202-1277 Personal E-mail: batterjay@msn.com.

BATTESTIN, MARTIN CAREY, retired literature and language professor; b. NYC, Mar. 25, 1930; s. Martin Augustus and Marion (Kirkland) B.; m. Ruthe Rootes, June 14, 1963; children: David (dec. 1999), Catherine. BA summa cum laude, Princeton U., 1952, PhD, 1958. English master Westminster Sch., Simsbury, Conn., 1952-53; instr. Wesleyan U., Middletown, Conn., 1956-58, asst. prof., 1958-61, U. Va., Charlottesville, 1961-63, assoc. prof., 1963-67, prof., 1967-75, William R. Kenan, Jr. prof. English, 1975-98, emeritus prof., 1998—, chmn. dept. English, 1983-86. Vis. prof. Rice U., Houston, 1967—68; assoc. Clare Hall, Cambridge (Eng.) U., 1972. Author: The Moral Basis of Fielding's Art, 1959, The Providence of Wit, 1974, 2d edit., 1989, Henry Fielding: A Life, 1989, 2d edit., 1993, New Essays by Henry Fielding, 1989, 1993, A Henry Fielding Companion, 2000; editor: Joseph Andrews (Henry Fielding), 1961, 2d edit., 1967, Shamela (Henry Fielding), 1961, Tom Jones (Henry Fielding), 1974;: 2d edit., 1975, Amelia (Henry Fielding), 1983, Tom Jones: A Collection of Critical Essays, 1968, British Novelists, 1660-1800, 1985, Tobias Smollett, translator Cervantes' Don Quixote, 2003, The Journal of a Voyage to Lisbon, Shamela and Occasional Writings (Henry Fielding), 2007; co-editor: The Correspondence of Henry and Sarah Fielding, 1993. Am. Coun. Learned Socs. fellow, 1960-61, 72; Guggenheim fellow, 1964-65; Sr. fellow Coun. Humanities, Princeton U., 1971; Ctr. for Advanced Studies fellow U. Va., 1974-75; NEH Bicentennial Rsch. fellow, 1975-76. Mem. MLA (chmn. sec. VII 1967, adv. editor publs. 1982-86), South Atlantic Modern Lang. Assn., Internat. Assn. Univ. Profs. English (chmn. sect. V 1990-92), Assn. Lit. Scholars and Critics, East Ctrl. Am. Soc. Eighteenth Century Studies, Nat. Assn. Scholars, The Johnsonians. Mem. Ch. of England. Home: 1832 Westview Rd Charlottesville VA 22903-1648 E-mail: mcb9g@virginia.edu.

BATTEY, JAMES F., JR., federal agency administrator, neurologist; BS in Physics with honors, Calif. Inst. Tech.; MD, PhD, Stanford U. Resident in pediatrics Stanford U.; postdoctoral fellow Harvard Med. Sch.; sr. staff fellow then sr. investigator Nat. Cancer Inst., NIH, 1983—88, head molecular structure sect. lab biol. chemistry, 1992—95; chief molecular neuroscience sect. lab. neurochemistry Nat. Inst. Neurol. Disorders and Stroke, NIH, 1988—92; dir. intramural rsch. Nat. Inst. Deafness and Other Communication Disorders, NIH, Bethesda, Md., 1995—98, chief lab molecular biology, 1996, dir., 1998—. Chmn., Stem Cell Task Force, NIH, 2002-; adj. prof. George Washington U. Sch. Medicine Author: (with Leonard Davis and Michael Kuehl) Basic Methods in Molecular Biology; contbr., co-contbr. over 120 rsch. articles to profl. jours. Recipient Commendation medal Pub. Health Svc., 1990, Outstanding Svc. medal, 1994. Office: Nat Inst Deafness & Other Communication Disorders 31 Center Dr Msc 2320 Bethesda MD 20892-2320 Office Phone: 301-402-0900. Office Fax: 301-402-1590. E-mail: batteyj@nidcd.nih.gov.*

BATTIE, DAVID ANTHONY, art appraiser; b. Oct. 22, 1942; s. Donald Charleson and Peggy Joan Battie; m. Sarah Battie; children: Henrietta Victoria, Eleanor Harriet. Attended, King James I Sch., Knaresborough, UK. Dir. Sotheby's, NYC, 1976—99; expert BBC-TV; appraiser Antiques Roadshow, 1977—. Lectr. in field. Author: Price Guide to 19th & 20th Century British Procelain, 1975, Sotheby's Concise Encyclopedia of Porcelain, 1990, Sotheby's Concise Encyclopedia of Glass, 1991, Treasures In Your Home, 1994, Pottery & Porcelain, Antiques Roadshow Pocket Guides, 1995.

BATTIER, SHANE, professional basketball player; b. Sept. 9, 1978; s. Ed, Sandee; m. Heidi Ufer, 2004. Graduate, Duke Univ., 2001. Profl. basketball player Memphis Grizzlies, 2001—. Mem. bd. St. Jude, Memphis Zoo. Named NABC Def. Player Yr., 1999—2001, Co-Player Yr., ACC, 2001, First Team All-Am., AP, 2001, USBWA, 2001, The Sporting News, 2001; named to First Team All-ACC, 2000—01, All-Rookie Team, NBA, 2002; recipient Naismith award Best Coll. Player, 2001, Wooden award Best Coll. Player, 2001. Office: Memphis Grizzlies FedEx Forum 191 Beale St Memphis TN 38103

BATTILEGA, JOHN A., research and development company executive; b. Portland, Oreg., Nov. 25, 1941; s. Ercole Anthony and Odelia Francis Battilega; m. Nancy Ann Scott, May 2, 1964; children: Catherine, Edward, Michael, David. BS, Gonzaga U., 1963; PhD, Oreg. State U., 1967. Rsch. asst. Tektronix, Beaverton, Oreg., 1961—62, Sandia Nat. Lab., Livermore, Calif., 1965; staff engr. Martin Marietta Corp., Denver, 1971—73; corp. v.p., gen. mgr., rsch. dir. Sci. Applications Internat. Corp., Englewood, Colo., 1973—99; pres. John Battilega Assocs., Littleton, Colo., 1999—. Adj. prof., sr. lectr. Grad. Sch. Internat. Studies U. Denver, 2000—; mem. U.S. Def. Sci. Bd., Washington, 1984—85; dir. Fgn. Sys. Rsch. Ctr., Sci. Applications Internat. Corp., Englewood, Colo., 1978—99; dir. strategic rsch. on def. policy and planning and internat. issues U.S. govt. nat. security orgns., Washington, 1973—; mem. modeling and simulation rev. com. U.S. Space Command, Colorado Springs, Colo., 1986; mem. U.S. strategic def. initiative Soviet red team Dept. Def., Washington, 1985—90; sr. cons. various U.S. govt. agys., Washington, 1973—; adj. prof. U.S. Def. Intelligence Coll., Washington; mem. several adv. panels U.S. govt., Washington, 1980—; seminar developer over 20 seminars on def. planning topics, Washington, 1973—; lectr. def. and intelligence colls., 1978—; mem. AirLand Battle Future Spl. Study Group U.S. Army, Ft. Leavenworth, Kans., 1988; mem. select com. on computer tech. Nat. Def. U., Washington, 1983. Author, editor: book The Military Applications of Modeling, 1984; contbr. book chpts., articles, rsch. monographs. Coach youth baseball, Lakewood and Littlewood, Colo., 1975—98; Pres. parish coun. St. Jude Cath. Ch., Lakewood, Colo., 1972—74. Maj. US Army, 1963—71. Decorated Meritorious Svc. medal, Bronze star, Vietnamese Cross of Gallantry. Mem.: AIAA, IEEE, Denver Coun. Fgn. Rels., U.S. Mil. Ops. Rsch. Soc. (bd. dirs. 1983—85), Inst. for Ops. Rsch. and Mgmt. Sci., Internat. Inst. Strategic Studies. Roman Catholic. Avocations: travel, reading, fishing, baseball, bridge. Home: 7706 S Forest St Littleton CO 80122 E-mail: j.battilega@worldnet.att.net.

BATTIN, PATRICIA MEYER, librarian; b. Gettysburg, Pa., June 2, 1929; d. Emanuel Albert and Josephine (Lehman) Meyer; m. William Thomas Battin, June 16, 1951 (div. 1975); children: Laura, Joanna, Thomas BA, Swarthmore Coll., 1951; MS in LS, Syracuse U., 1967. Asst. libr. SUNY-Binghamton, 1967-69, asst. dir. for reader svcs., 1969-74; dir. libr. svcs. Columbia U., NYC, 1974-78, v.p., univ. libr., 1978-87; interim pres. Research Libraries Group, Palo Alto, Calif., 1982, also dir., 1974-87; pres. Commn. on Preservation and Access, Washington, 1987-94. Trustee Coun. on Libr. Resources, Washington, 1984-94, EDUCOM, Princeton, N.J., 1982-88, Lehigh U., 1989-98, CAUSE, Boulder, Colo., 1993-96; mem. adv. com. on coun. on libr. and info. resources Frye Leadership Inst. Contbr. articles to profl. jours., Co-author: The Mirage of Continuity: Reconfiguring Academic Information Resources for the 21st Century, 1998. Recipient Nat. Medal for the Humanities, 1999. Mem. ALA, Assn. Rsch. Librs. (trustee 1982-85), Phi Beta Kappa, Beta Phi Mu.

BATTIN, R. RAY (ROSABELL HARRIET RAY), audiologist, neuropsychologist; b. Rock Creek, Ohio; d. Harry Walter and Sophia (Boldt) Ray; m. Tom C. Battin, Aug. 27, 1949. AB, U. Denver, 1948; MS, U. Mich., 1950; PhD, U. Fla., 1959; postgrad., U. Miami Sch. Medicine, Fla., 1957, U. Iowa, 1958. Diplomate Am. Bd. Forensic Medicine, Am. Bd. Profl. Disability Cons., Am. Bd. Psychol. Specialties, Am. Bd. Forensic Examiners (cert. forensic examiner, cert. med. examiner), forensic neuropsychology, devel. psychology, psychol. assessment, lic. psychologist Tex., audiologist Tex., speech pathologist Tex. Instr. in speech pathology U. Denver, 1949-50; audiologist Ann Arbor (Mich.) Sch., 1950-51, Houston Speech and Hearing Ctr., 1954-56; clin. fellow divsn. Clin. Svcs. U. Fla., Gainesville, 1952-54; dir. speech pathology/psychology Hedgecroft Hosp. and Rehab. Ctr., Houston, 1956-59; audiologist Drs. Guilford, Wright and Draper, Houston, 1959-63; pvt. practice psychology, audiology, and neuropsychology Houston, 1959—. Clin. instr. dept. otolaryngology U. Tex. Sch. Medicine, Galveston, 1964-80; dir. of audiology vestibulography and speech pathology lab. Houston Ear, Nose and Throat Hosp. Clinic, 1963-73; adj. clin. instr. U. Houston, 1981-86; lectr. The First Word program Sta. KUHT-TV, 1959; v.p. Behavioral Perceptual Ctr., 1986-90; neuropsychol. cons. edn. divsn. Environ. Health Screening Lab., 1989-99, adv. bd., 1989-99; lectr. in field in U.S., So. Am., and Europe. Author: (with C. Olaf Haug) Speech and Language Delay, 1964, Vestibulography, 1974, Private Practice: Guidelines for Speech Pathology and Audiology, 1971; editor (with Donna R. Fox) Private Practice in Audiology and Speech and Language Pathology, 1978; contbg. author: Seminars in Speech, Language, Hearing (Northern), Auditory Disorders in School Children (4th edit. Roeser and Downs), Current Therapy of Communications Disorder (Perkins); editor Jour. Acad. Pvt. Practice in Speech Pathology and Audiology, 1981-84; contbr. articles in field to profl. jours.; author: (with Irvin A. Kraft) The Dysynchronous Child (film), 1971, Symposium Brain Plasticity As it Relates to the Remediation of Attention, Auditory Processing, Language and Reading Disorders, 1999; The Battin Clinic Language Learning Screening Test for Preschool Children, 1985, The Battin Scale of Parent's Attitude Toward Family Experience and Need for Child Cochlear Implant Candidates. Bd. dirs. Juvenile Ct. Vols., 1980—83, Children's Resource and Info. Ctr., 1981—85, Dyslexic Adult Support Svcs., 1986—90, Musicfest, 1990—2002, Houston Repretory Theater, 1993—98; mem. adv. bd. Caring Adoptions, 1993—, HISD for the Performing and Visual Arts Friends, 1998—, Bayou City Concert Musicals, 2006—. Recipient Gold award for Ednl. Exhibit, Am. Acad. Pediats., 1969, Lifetime Achievement award Houston Psychol. Assn., 1996, Leadership award Sci. Learning Corp., 2000. Fellow: Am. Acad. Audiology, World Acad. Inc., Am. Speech and Hearing Assn. (profl. svcs. bd. 1967—70, com. on pvt. practice 1971—74); mem.: APA, Soc. Ear Nose and Throat Advances in Children, Tex. Biofeedback Soc., Internat. Assn. Logopedics and Phoniatrics, Acad. of Aphasia, Harris County Biofeedback Soc. (pres. 1984), Houston Psychol. Assn., Tex. Acad. Audiology, Tex. Psychol. Assn., Tex. Speech and Hearing Assn. (v.p. 1968), Am. Acad. Pvt. Practice in Speech Pathology and Audiology (pres. 1968—70), Am. Coll. Forensic Examiners, Internat. Assn. Applied Psychology. Home: 3837 Meadow Lake Ln Houston TX 77027-4029 Office: Battin Clinic Inc 4545 Post Oak Place Dr Ste 375 Houston TX 77027-3121 Office Phone: 713-621-3072. Personal E-mail: rhrb@pdq.net.

BATTIN, RICHARD HORACE, aeronautical engineer; b. Atlantic City, Mar. 3, 1925; s. Horace Leslie and Martha Esther (Scheu) B.; m. Margery Katheryn Milne, Aug. 25, 1947; children: Thomas, Pamela, Jeffrey. BS, MIT, 1945, PhD, 1951; DSc (hon.), Tex. A&M U., 1999. Instr. math. MIT, Cambridge, 1946-51, research mathematician Instrumentation Lab., 1951-56, adj. prof. aero. and astronautics, 1979-95, sr. lectr., 1995—. Sr. staff mem. Ops. Research Group, Arthur D. Little, Inc., Cambridge, 1956-58; tech. dir. Apollo Mission Devel.; assoc. dir. Instrumentation Lab., 1958-73; assoc. head NASA program dept. Charles Stark Draper Lab., Inc., 1973-87, mem. aerospace safety adv. panel, 1980-86. Author: (with J.H. Laning, Jr.) Random Processes in Automatic Control, 1956, Astronautical Guidance, 1964, An Introduction to the Mathematics and Methods of Astrodynamics, 1987; Mem. editorial com.: Celestial Mechanics, 1968-74. Pres. Project Impact, 1981-90; Mem. Lexington (Mass.) Town Meeting, 1956—; mem. Lexington Appropriations Com., 1958-64. Lt. (j.g.) Supply Corps USNR, 1945-46. Recipient Superior Achievement award, Inst. of Navigation, 1980, 1st Tycho Brahe award, 2000, Tchg. award, dept. aeros. and astronautics MIT, 1981. Fellow: AIAA (hon.; assoc. editor jour. 1967—87, chmn. astrodynamics tech. com. 1978—80, dir. tech. 1979—82, Louis W. Hill Space Transp. award 1972, Mechanics and Control of Flight award 1978, Pendray Aerospace Lit. award 1987, von Karman Disting. Lectureship award in astronautics 1989, Summerfield Book award 2002, Aerospace Guidance, Nav. and Control award 2002), Am. Astronautical Soc. (Dirk Brouwer award 1996); mem.: Celestial Mechanics Inst., Internat. Acad. Astronautics, Nat. Acad. Engring., Hancock Men's Club (pres. 1974—76), Sigma Xi. Home: 15 Paul Revere Rd Lexington MA 02421-6632 Office: MIT' 9-335 77 Massachusetts Ave Cambridge MA 02139-4307 Office Phone: 781-862-3639. Business E-Mail: battin@alum.mit.edu.

BATTINO, RUBIN, retired chemistry professor; b. NYC, June 22, 1931; s. Sadik and Anna (Decastro) B.; m. Charlotte Alice Ridinger, Jan. 30, 1960; children— David Rubin, Benjamin Sadik BA, CCNY, 1953; MA, Duke U., 1954, PhD, 1957; MS, Wright State U., 1978. Lic. profl. clin. counselor, Ohio. Research chemist Leeds & Northrup Co., Phila., 1956-57; asst. prof. Ill. Inst. Tech., Chgo., 1957-66; prof. Wright State U., Dayton, Ohio, 1966-95, ret., 1995, prof. emeritus, 1995—. Vis. prof. U. Vienna,

Austria, Oxford U., Eng., Hebrew U. Jerusalem, Ben Gurion U., U. New Eng., Australia, U. Canterbury, N.Z., Okayama U. Sci., Japan, Rhodes U., U. Turku, Finland. Author: (with S.E. Wood) Thermodynamics-An Introduction, 1968; Oxygen and Ozone, 1981, Nitrogen and Air, 1982, (with S.E. Wood) The Thermodynamics of Chemical Systems, 1990, (with T.L. South) Ericksonian Approaches, A Comprehensive Manual, 1999, 2d edit., 2005, Guided Imagery and other Approaches to Healing, 2000, Coping: A Practical Guide for People Who Have Life-Challenging Diseases and Their Caregivers, 2001, Meaning: The Life of Viktor E. Frankl, 2002, Metaphoria: Metaphor and Guided Metaphor for Psychotherapy and Healing, 2002, Expectation. The Very Brief Therapy Book, 2006; mem. editl. bd. Solubility Data Series, Jour. Chem. and Engring. Data; contbr. tech. papers to profl. jours. Fulbright fellow, 1979; recipient Outstanding Tchr. award Wright State U., 1979, 93, Outstanding Engr. award Engring. and Sci. Found., Dayton, 1985, Bd. Trustees award Wright State U., 1985. Mem. AAAS, Am. Chem. Soc., Internat. Union Pure and Applied Chemistry (commn.), Sigma Xi, Phi Lambda Upsilon Democrat. Jewish. Office: Wright State U Chemistry Dept Dayton OH 45435 Personal E-mail: rubin.battino@wright.edu.

BATTISTA, RICHARD, entertainment company executive; m. Brenda Battista. BS in bus. adminstrn., Georgetown U.; MBA, Harvard Bus. Sch. Fin. analyst Morgan Stanley; with Fox Entertainment Group (formerly Fox, Inc.), 1990—99, 2001—04; v.p. fin. and adminstrn. Morning Studies (sub. Fox Circle Prodn.); sr. v.p. fin. and ops. Fox Circle Prodn.; exec. v.p. Fox/Liberty Networks, 1997—98; head Fox Sports Internat., 1997—98; exec. v.p. Fox Channels Group, 1998—99, Fox TV, 2001—03, Fox Networks Group, 2003—04; exec. v.p. bus. devel. and strategy Fox Entertainment Group, 2004; co-founder, CEO iFUSE, 1999—2001; CEO Gemstar-TV Guide International Inc., LA, 2004—. Bd. dirs. Nat. Geographic Channel US, Nat. Geographic Channels Internat.; founder, chmn. Georgetown Entertainment and Media Alliance. Bd. gov. Georgetown U.; bd. dirs. Hands of Change. Office: Gemstar-TV Guide Internat Inc 6922 Hollywood Blvd 12th Fl Los Angeles CA 90028

BATTISTA, RICHARD, chef, educator; Degree in Fin., Burdett Coll. Cert. Exec. Chef, Exec. Pastry Chef, Culinary Educator. Exec. chef LaBrioche Restaurant chain; chef instr. Watertown Sch. System; dir. food and beverage Fairmont Hotel chain; exec. pastry chef Sheraton Corp., Ritz-Carlton Hotels; dir. colleges of food Calif. Culinary Acad.; dean LA Culinary Inst.; dir. culinary arts Inst. Calif.-LA; pres. Profl. Culinary Inst., Campbell. Former pres., bd. chmn. Am. Culinary Fedn.-LA. Recipient Grand prize, Culinaire Philanthropique of NY. Office: Professional Culinary Inst 700 W Hamilton Ave Ste 300 Campbell CA 95008*

BATTISTA, ROBERT JAMES, federal agency administrator, lawyer; b. Detroit, July 25, 1939; s. Theodore and Marguerite (Dalton) B.; m. Judith Ann Judnich, Oct. 5, 1985; children: Lauren Nicole, Robert James Jr. BA, U. Notre Dame, 1961; JD, U. Mich., 1964. Bar: Mich. Assoc., then ptnr. Butzel Long, Detroit, 1965—2002, v.p., 1989—2002; chmn. NLRB, Washington, 2002—. Mem. rep. assembly State Bar Mich., 1977-80, mem. council labor relations law sect., 1975-78, sec.-treas., 1978-79, vice-chmn., 1979-80, chmn., 1980-81 Mem. Founders Soc., Detroit. Served to 1st lt. U.S. Army, 1964-65. Recipient Disting. Svc. award, State Bar of Mich. Labor & Employment section, 2006. Mem. ABA (com. devel. of law under Nat. Labor Relations Act), Detroit Bar Assn., Mich. Bar Assn., Indsl. Relations Research Assn., Mich. State Bar Assn. Clubs: Detroit Athletic. Roman Catholic. Office: NLRB 1099 14th St NW Washington DC 20570 Office Phone: 202-273-1770.

BATTISTI, PAUL ORESTE, retired municipal official; b. Herkimer, NY, Mar. 16, 1922; s. Oreste and Ida (Fiore) B.; m. Constance Muth Drais, May 18, 1985; children— Paul J., Kate, Deborah, Thomas, Daniel, Melora, Stephen, Valeri. Student, Cornell U., Ithaca, NY, 1947-48, U. Neb., 1951-52. With VA, 1946-75; dir. VA Hosp., Martinez, Calif., 1969-73; western region dir. San Francisco, 1973-75; adminstr. State Vets. Home Calif., 1976-86; supr. County of Napa, 1989-97. Chmn., CEO Medam., Inc.; dir. Med. Am. Corp.; health care cons. 1975-88; chmn. Bay Area Air Quality Mgmt. Dist.; mem. exec. bd. Assoc. Bay Area Govts.; chmn. Bay Area Regional Planning Com.; mem. exec. bd. Bay Area Econ. Forum; chmn. Napa River Flood Control Dist. Fellow Am. Coll. Hosp. Adminstrs.; mem. Hosp. Conf. No. Calif. (pres.), Nat. Assn. State Vets. Homes (pres.). Home: Silverado Country Club 117 Milliken Creek Dr Napa CA 94558-1240

BATTLE, ALLEN OVERTON, JR., psychologist, educator; b. Memphis, Nov. 19, 1927; s. Allen Overton and Florence Louise (Castelvecchi) B.; m. Mary Madeline Vroman, June 14, 1952; 1 son, Allen Overton, III. BS, Siena Coll., 1949; MA, Cath. U. Am., 1953, PhD, 1961; certificate in clin. psychology, U. Tenn. Coll. Medicine, 1953. Diplomate: in clin. psychology Am. Bd. Profl. Psychology, 1971. Instr. dept. psychiatry U. Tenn. Coll. Medicine, 1956-61, asst. prof., 1961-67, asso. prof., 1966-72, prof., 1972—; chief clin. psychologist U. Tenn. Mental Health Center, 1971-78, chief div. clin. psychology, 1974—. Vis. lectr. Southwestern U. at Memphis, 1962-84; vis. prof. Rhodes Coll., 1984—2001. Author: Clinical Psychology for Physical Therapists, 1975, Suicide and Crisis Intervention Training Manuals, 1978, The Psychology of Patient Care: A Humanistic Approach, 1979; contbr. articles to profl. jours. Cons. USPHS, Suicide and Crisis Intervention Svc.; mem. Mayor's Commn. on Alcohol and Drug Abuse, 1974-77; bd. dirs. Runaway House, St. Peter's Home for Children, De Neuville Heights Sch. Family Svc. Decorated knight Russian Imperial Order; knight Order St. John of Jerusalem; recipient Disting. Svc. award Tenn. Dept. Mental Health, 1971, Jefferson award, Am. Inst. for Pub. Svc., 2001. Mem. Am., Tenn. psychol. assns., Am. Anthrop. Assn., N.Y. Acad. Sci., AAAS, Brit. Soc. Projective Techniques, Sigma Xi. Home: 2220 Washington Ave Memphis TN 38104-3025 Office: 135 N Pauline St Memphis TN 38105-4619 Home Phone: 901-726-5641; Office Phone: 901-448-4556. Business E-Mail: abattle@utmem.edu.

BATTLE, LEONARD CARROLL, lawyer; b. Toronto, Ont., Can., Oct. 25, 1929; s. Leonard Conlon and Beatrice Hester Battle; m. Marjory Estelle Holland, Dec. 28, 1953; children: David, Tracy, Thomas, Patricia, John, Mary. AB, U. Mich., 1950; JD, Ind. U., 1958. Bar: Mich. 1961, Ind. 1961, U.S. Ct. Mil. Appeals 1964, U.S. Supreme Ct. 1964. Claims adjuster State Farm Ins. Co., 1959-61; asst. pros. atty. Midland County, Mich., 1961-67; pvt. practice, Midland, Mich., 1967—. Lt. col. JAG, USAFR, 1950-84. Mem. ATLA, Mich. Bar Assn. (mil. law com.), Midland County Bar Assn. (pres.), Air Force Ret. Judge Advs. Assn. Home: 408 Harper Ln Midland MI 48640-7321 Office: 200 E Main St Midland MI 48640-6510 Personal E-mail: afjag05ret@webtv.net.

BATTLE, MICHAEL A., lawyer, former federal agency administrator, prosecutor; b. Oct. 15, 1955; m. Sheila Battle; children: Elisse, Nicole, Michael II. Grad., Ithaca Coll., 1977; JD, SUNY, Buffalo, 1981. Asst. U.S. atty. (we. dist.) NY US Dept. Justice, 1985—92; asst. pub. defender Fed. Pub. Defender's Office, (we. dist.) NY, 1992—95; asst. atty. gen. State of NY, 1995—96; judge Erie County Family Ct., Buffalo, 1996—2002; US atty. (we. dist.) NY US Dept. Justice, 2002—05, dir., Exec. Office US Attys. (EOUSA), 2005—07; ptnr. Fulbright & Jaworski L.L.P., Washington, 2007—. Bd. dir. YMCA Greater Buffalo, NY, Greater Niagara Frontier Council of Boy Scouts of Am., NY; dean's adv. council SUNYat Buffalo Law Sch., NY. Mem.: Minority Bar Assn. We. NY (pres.). Office: Fulbright & Jaworski LLP Market Sq 801 Pennsylvania NW Washington DC 20004*

BATTLE, VINCENT M., former ambassador; b. Teaneck, NJ, Sept. 1940; MA, Columbia U., 1967, PhD, 1974. Consular officer U.S. Fgn. Svc., Manama, Bahrain, 1977—79; head of Immigrant Visa sect., Port-au-Prince, Haiti, 1985—88; polit. officer Muscat, Oman, 1983—85; consular officer Bur. of Near East Affairs, Damascus, Syria, 1980—83; various to dep. chief of mission U.S. Embassy, Cairo, 1996—99; U.S. amb. to Lebanon US Dept. State, Beirut, 2001—04.

BATTLE, WILLIAM ROBERT (BOB), retired publishing executive; b. Nolensville, Tenn., Dec. 25, 1927; s. William Robert and Cleo (Smith) B.; m. Elizabeth Ogilvie, Dec. 23, 1948; children: Valerie Elizabeth Kienzle, William Robert III. Student, George Peabody Coll., 1946-49. Exec. offcl. Nashville Banner, 1943-98, police beat, county polit. beat, 1943-53, city editor, 1953-64, movie columnist, 1955-72, mng. editor, 1964-71, exec. editor, 1971-75, asst. to editor, 1975-78, regional editor, 1978-80, sr. editor, 1980-84, v.p., bus. editor, 1984-89, v.p., sr. bus. editor, 1989-98; staff writer Country Style mag., Livin Country. Columnist Williamson A.M., Tennessean; mem. exec. bd. Tenn. Dept. Agr. Agrl. Mus., 2002—06. Appeared as newspaperman in: film Teacher's Pet, 1957, also in Country Music on Broadway, 1963; contbr. articles to profl. jours.; chpts. to books. Supt. gates and admissions Tenn. State Fair, 1953-64; pub. rels. chmn. Davidson County Coun. for Retarded Children, 1961-66; exec. bd. Mid. Tenn. coun. Boy Scouts Am.; active 4-H Club Found.; exec. bd. dirs., past sec. Nashville Boys Club, life bd. dirs.; bd. dirs. College Grove Sr. Enrichment Ctr., 2002-06; exec. coun. Coll. Grove Sr. Recreational Ctr., 2002-05; bd. dirs. Tenn. Agricultural Mus., 2002-05. Recipient Big Story award NBC-TV, 1956; named Man of Yr., 4-H Club, 1974, Man of Yr., Future Farmers Am., 1975, Silver Beaver award Boy Scouts Am., 1997; Robert Battle scholarship established in his honor Belmont U. Sch. Bus., By Opryland, U.S.A., 1989. Mem. Tenn. Press Assn., Nat. Screen Coun., Country Music Assn., Masons (33d deg., knights commdr. ct. of honor), Shriners (potentate 1976), Royal Order of Jesters (former dir.), Elks (former chmn. scholarship com.), Sigma Delta Chi (former chmn. scholarship com., former pres.). Methodist. Home: 8889 Horton Hwy College Grove TN 37046-9280 Office Phone: 615-368-2353. Personal E-mail: bobbattle11@aol.com.

BATTLES, ROXY EDITH, novelist, consultant, educator; b. Spokane, Wash., Mar. 29, 1921; d. Rosco Jirah and Lucile Zilpha (Jacques) Baker; m. Willis Ralph Dawe Battles, May 2, 1941 (dec. 2000); children: Margaret Battles Holmes, Ralph, Lara. AA, Bakersfield Coll., Calif., 1940; BA, Calif. State U., Long Beach, 1959; MA, Pepperdine U., 1976. Cert. tchr. English, adult basic edn. and elem. edn., Calif. Freelance writer 50 nat. and regional mags., 1940—; tchr. elem. Torrance (Calif.) Unified Schs., 1959-85; tchr. adult edn. Pepperdine U., Torrance, 1969-79, 88-89; freelance children's author, 1966—; mystery novelist Pinnacle Publs., NYC, 1980; with Tex. A&M U., 1988. Instr. Mary Mount Coll., Harbor Coll., 1995; author-in-residence Young Authors Festival, Am. Sch. Madrid, 1991; participant First Educators to Japan Exch., 1973; lectr. in field. Author: Over the Rickety Fence, 1967, The Terrible Trick or Treat, 1970, 501 Balloons Sail East, 1971, The Terrible Terrier, 1972, One to Teeter-Totter, 1973, 2d edit., 1975, Eddie Couldn't Find the Elephants, 1974, reprints, 1982, 84, 88, What Does the Rooster Say, Yoshio?, 1978, reprinted in Swedish, German, French, 1980, The Secret of Castle Drai, 1980, The Witch in Room 6, 1987, 3d edit., 1989, The Chemistry of Whispering Caves, 1988, rev. edit., 1997, Computer Encryptions in Whispering Caves, 1997; playwright: Roxy, 1995, The Lavender Castle, 1996, mus. version, 1997, Sacred Submarine, 2000, Embarking on Rebellion, 2001. Active So. Calif. Coun. on Lit. for Children and Young People, 1973-80, 87—. Recipient Commendation UN, 1979. Mem. S.W. Manuscripters (founder), Surfwriters. Home: Sunrise Senior Living 1837 Pacific Coast Hwy # 225 Hermosa Beach CA 90254 also: 417 N Maria Redondo Beach CA 90277 Office Phone: 310-318-2545. Personal E-mail: groxy@aol.com. *However I rail at prejudice, some prejudgment is inevitable and, except in extremity, foreseeable. Whether caused by neglect or studied plan, negatives are noticed. When the fixable remains unfixed, I deserve to be judged for my part, however I blame my adjudicator.*

BATTOCCHI, RONALD SILVIO, lawyer; b. Hartford, Conn., Sept. 28, 1947; s. Silvio Romano and Elda (Ferrari) B.; m. Mary Therese Bell, June 18, 1977; children: Keith, Scott, Julia. BA, Amherst Coll., 1970; JD, U. Maine, 1974. Bar: Maine 1974, D.C. 1983, U.S. Supreme Ct. 1987. Spl. asst. to chmn. Nat. Transp. Safety Bd., Washington, 1974-76, atty. advisor, 1976-80, spl. asst. and counsel to chmn., 1980-81, atty. advisor, 1981-90, dep. gen. counsel, 1990-94, dep. mng. dir., 1994-99, gen. counsel, 1999—2005. Recipient Presdl. Rank award for disting. svc., 2004, Trans. Atty. of Year, Fed. Bar Assn., 2005.*

BATTS, BARBARA JEAN, academic administrator, director; b. Bloomsburg, Pa., Nov. 18, 1962; d. Kenneth Philip abd Mary Barbara (Sock) Wiest; m. Pierre Louis Batts, Feb. 26, 1988; children: Pierre Louis II, Patrick Rian, Camille Mari, Keira Lynaé. Diploma, Nat. Corr. Schs., Scranton, Pa., 1984; BS in Edn., Bloomsburg U., 1984; MEd in Ednl. Leadership, Tchg., and Learning, Millersville U., 2002. Cert. elem. prin., elem. supr., elem., nursery and kindergarten tchr. Pa. Substitute tchr. various sch. dists., Lancaster, Pa., 1984-86; resident advisor Community Svcs., Mountville, Pa., 1985-86, residential program supr., 1986-87; tchr. Millersville (Pa.) U., 1986; program dir. Provident Enterprises, Hellam, Pa., 1987; behavior specialist Community Found., Sellersville, Pa., 1987; presch. supr., tchr. Learning Ladder, Lancaster, 1988-89; sales assoc. Lane Bryant, Lancaster, 1990-90, co-mgr., 1990—; classroom facilitator Lancaster City Sch. Dist., 1996—2002; instrnl. facilitator Harrisburg City Sch. Dist., 2002—05, coord. math., sci. and tech. curriculum, 2005—. Recipient various pub. speaking awards Collegiate Forensic Assn., 1981-84. Mem. ASCD. Non Denominational. Home: 810 N Duke St Lancaster PA 17602-2022 Office: 2101 N Front St Bldg #2 Harrisburg PA 17110 Office Phone: 717-703-4046. Business E-Mail: bbatts@hbgsd.k12.pa.us.

BATTS, DEBORAH A., federal judge; b. Phila., Apr. 13, 1947; d. James A., Jr. and Ruth Violet (Silas) Batts; 2 children. BA, Radcliffe Coll., 1969; JD, Harvard U., 1972. Summer atty. Foley, Hoag & Eliot, Boston, Mass., 1970, Kaye, Scholer, Fierman, Hays & Handler, NYC, 1971; law clerk to Hon. Lawrence W. Pierce U.S. Dist. Ct. (so. dist.) N.Y., NYC, 1972-73; assoc. atty. Cravath, Swaine & Moore, NYC, 1973-79; asst. U.S. atty. criminal divsn. U.S. Dist. Ct. (so. dist.) N.Y., NYC, 1979-84; assoc. prof. law Fordham U., 1984-94, adj. prof. law, 1994—; spl. assoc. counsel dept. investigation N.Y.C., 1990-91; commr. law revision com. State of N.Y., 1990-94; judge U.S. Dist. Ct. (so. dist.) N.Y., NYC, 1994—. Bd. trustees Cathedral Sch., N.Y.C., 1990-96; mem. faculty Corp. Counsel Trial Advocacy Program, 1988-94. Contbr. articles to legal jours. Trustee Spence Sch., 1987-95. Mem. ABA, Second Cir. Fed. Bar Coun., Assn. Bar. City N.Y., Lesbian and Gay Law Assn. Greater N.Y., Met. Black Bar Assn. Office: US Courthouse 500 Pearl St Rm 2510 New York NY 10007-1316

BATTS, DOROTHY MARIE, clergywoman, educator, writer; b. Elm, NC, Dec. 22, 1942; d. Randolph Hall and Mattie Gear; m. Jesse Lee Batts Jr., Oct. 14, 1961; children: Terrance Christopher, Timothy Connell, Tonnetta Caressia, Tabitha Cynthia, Travis Carlos; adopted children: Renee, Aja, Tamatha, LeDell, Alice. B in Bibl. Studies, Bethel Bible Coll. and Sem., 1999, MA in Theology, PhD in Theology, Bethel Bible Coll. and Sem., 2001, A in Bibl. Studies, 2006. Ordained minister Sprit-fill Christian Ch., 1977; cert. chaplain, Hawaii; cert. counselor Armed Forces; CNA. Christian minister, travelling counselor, South Africa, 1968—; Red Cross vol. Womack Army Hosp., Ft. Bragg, NC, 1981; nurses asst. Fayetteville, NC, 1982; pastor Revivals for Jesus Ch., Southern Pines, NC, 1980-88, Fayetteville, NC, 1981-89; pastor, tchr. Outreach for Jesus Ch., Hope Mills, 1989—; founder., pres. Outreach for Jesus Ch. and Christian Edn. Ctr., Inc.; Christian minister, traveling Christian Word of God counselor Korea, Europe, Hawaii, throughout the US. Spkr. in field. Author Christian books, 1987-93, Bible college study guides, 1987-93, The Book of Exodus, 2000, Between the Old and New Testament, Mathew Study Guide, 2001, The Book of Acts (Power of Holy Spirit), 2001, The Christians Consitutes (The Book of Romans, 1st and 2nd Corinthians, 2002, Doctrin of the Tabernacle, 2002, Developing Into His Image in Difficult Times, 1990, Galatian, 2001, Women in Leadership and Ministry Fan the Flames, 2002, (children and youth book) Prayers for Personal Conflict, 2006, Daily Bread of Poratic Encouragement and Enlightment, 2006. Drug abuse support counselor Cape Fear Med. Ctr., Fayetteville, 1984, support and prayer counselor mentally disturbed, 1984; prayer support counselor, visitor VA Hosp., Fayetteville, 1993; vol. ct. counselor Fayetteville Ct. System, 1974-75, prison telephone counselor. Recipient Soldiers for Christ award US Mil., 2d Mile award Revivals for Jesus, Asheboro, 1984, awards WIDU Radio Sta., 1989. Avocations: writing, travel, bowling, reading, playing scrabble. Office: Outreach for Jesus Ch PO Box 65088 Fayetteville NC 28306-1088 Home: 334 Waterdown Dr Apt 7 Fayetteville NC 28314-4407 Office Phone: 910-423-2999.

BATTS, MICHAEL STANLEY, retired language educator; b. Mitcham, Eng., Aug. 2, 1929; s. Stanley George and Alixe Kathleen (Watson) B.; m. Misao Yoshida, Mar. 19, 1959; 1 dau., Anna. BA, U. London, 1952, BA with honors, 1953, LittD, 1973; PhD, U. Freiburg, Germany, 1957; MLS, U. Toronto, 1974. Mem. faculty U. Mainz, Germany, 1953-54, U. Basel, Switzerland, 1954-56; Mem. faculty U. Wurzburg, Germany, 1956-58; instr. German U. Calif., Berkeley, 1958-60; mem. faculty dept. German U. B.C., Canada, 1960-91, prof., 1967-91, head dept., 1968-80; ret., 1992. Author: Die Form der Aventiuren im Nibelungenlied, 1961, Bruder Hansens Marienlieder, 1964, Studien zu Bruder Hansens Marienliedern, 1964, Das Hohe Mittelalter, 1969, Das Nibelungenlied-Synoptische Ausgabe, 1971, Gottfried von Strasburg, 1971, A Checklist of German Literature, 1945-75, 1977, The Bibliography of German Literature: An Historical and Critical Survey, 1978, A History of Histories of German Literature, 1835-1914, 1993, Germanic Studies at Canadian Universities From the Beginning to 1995, 1998; editor: Seminar, 1970-80. Served with Brit. Army, 1947-49. Alexander von Humboldt fellow, 1964-65, 83; Can. Coun. Sr. fellow, 1964-65, 71-72; Killam fellow, 1981-82. Fellow Royal Soc. Can.; mem. Can. Assn. Univ. Tchrs. German (pres. 1982-84), Modern Humanities Rsch. Assn., Alcuin Soc. (exec. v.p. 1972-79, pres. 1979-80), Internat. Assn. for Germanic Studies (pres. 1990-95). Office: U BC Ctrl Ea and No European Studies Vancouver BC Canada V6T 1Z1 Personal E-mail: msb@interchange.ubc.ca.

BATTS, WARREN LEIGHTON, retired manufacturing executive; b. Norfolk, Va., Sept. 4, 1932; s. John Leighton and Allie Belle (Johnson) B.; m. Eloise Pitts, Dec. 24, 1957; 1 dau., Terri Allison. BEE, Ga. Inst. Tech., 1961; MBA, Harvard U., 1963. With Kendall Co., Charlotte, NC, 1963-64; exec. v.p. Fashion Devel. Co., Santa Paula, Calif., 1964-66; dir. mfg. Olga Co., Van Nuys, Calif., 1964-66; v.p. Douglas Williams Assocs., NYC, 1966-67; co-founder Triangle Corp., Orangeburg, SC, 1967, pres., chief exec. officer, 1967-71; v.p. Mead Corp., Dayton, Ohio, 1971-73, pres., 1973-80, chief exec. officer, 1978-80; pres., chief operating officer Dart Industries, Inc., LA, 1980-81, Dart & Kraft, Inc., Northbrook, Ill., 1981-86; chmn., chief exec. officer Premark Internat. Inc., Deerfield, 1986-96, chmn., 1996-97; chmn., CEO Tupperware Corp., Orlando, Fla., 1996-97.

BATULE, ROBERT JOHN, priest, writer; b. Bklyn., May 23, 1958; s. Robert Philip and Ann Marie (Reilly) B. BA in Sociology, Cathedral Coll., 1980; MDiv, Immaculate Conception, 1985; MA in Sociology summa cum laude, Adelphi U., 1990; MA in Theology summa cum laude, St. Johns U., 1996. Ordained priest Roman Cath. Ch., 1985. Parish priest St. Boniface Roman Cath. Ch., Elmont, NY, 1985-90, St. Martha Roman Cath. Ch., Uniondale, NY, 1990-93, Corpus Christi Roman Cath. Ch., Mineola, NY, 1993—2002, adminstr., 2001—, 2001—02; Monsignor, 2004—; pastor Holy Family Roman Cath. Ch., Hicksville, NY, 2004—06, Sts. Philip and James Roman Cath. Ch., St. James, NY, 2006—. Del. for Pastoral Intervention, 2002—, chmn., moderator Cath. Youth Orgn. Nassau and Suffolk, Hicksville, NY, 1997-2000; adj. faculty St. Vincent's Coll. divsn. humanities, dept. theology, St. John's U., 1996-99. Contbr. Cath. Ency., 1991, 98, Cath. Dictionary, 1993; columnist, The Catholic Answer, 1987-96, The Catholic Transcript, 1993-95, The Long Island Cath. Newspaper; contbr. numerous homilies, revs. and articles to profl. jour. 2d lt. USAF, 1981-82. Mem. Fellowship of Cath. Scholars, Soc. Cath. Social Scientists, Nat. Assn. of Scholars. Roman Catholic. Avocations: athletics, reading. Home and Office: Sts Philip and James RC Ch 1 Carow Pl Saint James NY 11780-1707 Office Phone: 631-584-5454.

BATZLI, GEORGE OLIVER, ecology educator; b. Mpls., Sept. 23, 1936; s. Oscar H. and Bertha M. B.; m. Sandra Lou Scharf, Jan. 2, 1959; children— Jeffrey, Samuel. BS in Psychology, U. Minn., 1959; MA in Biology, San Francisco State U., 1965; PhD in Zoology (Ecology), U. Calif., Berkeley, 1969. Rsch. assoc. U. Calif., Davis, 1969-71, lectr. biology Santa Cruz, 1971; asst. prof. zoology U. Ill., Urbana, 1971-76, assoc. prof. ecology, 1976-80, prof. ecology, 1980—2004, prof. emeritus, 2004—, head dept. ecology, ethology and evolution, 1983-88, 95-97. Sr. scientist rsch. in arctic environs., 1976-78, mem. ecology program adv. panel NSF, 1984-87, 2003, long term ecol. rsch. adv. panel alpine tundra, 1988, arctic tundra, 1992, tall grass prairie, 1999; rsch. scientist DSIR, N.Z., 1979; chmn. ecology program U. Ill., 1976-82. Contbr. articles on ecology to profl. jours.; spl. issue editor Arctic and Alpine Research, 1980, Oikos, 1983; mem. editorial bd. Ecology, Ecol. Monographs, 1981-84. Fellow NSF, 1962-63, NIH, 1967-69, 69-71, Zool. Inst. U. Oslo, Norway, 1982. Fellow AAAS; mem. Am. Inst. Biol. Scis., Am. Soc. Mammalogy (C. Hart Merriam award 2002), Ecol. Soc. Am. Office: U Ill Shelford Vivarium 606 E Healey St Champaign IL 61820-5502 Business E-Mail: g-batzli@life.uiuc.edu.

BATZLI, TERRENCE RAYMOND, lawyer; b. Dec. 28, 1946; s. Marion Raymond and Kathryn Velma (Hudran) Batzli; m. Sharon Lee Heinatz, Aug. 2, 1969; children: Catherine Barrett, Jonathan Raymond. BS, U. Richmond, 1974, JD, 1975. Bar: Va. 1975, U.S. Dist. Ct. (ea. dist.) Va. 1975, U.S. Dist. Ct. (we. dist.) Va. 1983, U.S. Ct. Appeals (4th cir.) 1984. Ptnr. Mays & Valentine and predecessor firms, Richmond, 1982-93, Durrette & Bradshaw, Richmond, Va., 1993-96; prin. Barnes & Batzli, PC, 1996—2004, Batzli Wood & Stiles, 2004—. Mediator McCammon Group, 1997—2006; adj. prof. law Reynolds C.C., Richmond, 1980—82; lectr. in field. Mem. adv. bd. Nat. Head Injury Found., 1988—, VA Head Injury Found., 1990—91. Capt. US Army, 1966—70. Fellow: Internat. Acad. Matrimonial Lawyers, Am. Acad. Matrimonial Lawyers; mem.: Hanover Assn. Bus. (pres. 1989, bd. dirs.), Va. State Bar (bd. govs. family law sect. 1996—, sec. 1997, vice-chair 1999, chair 2000—), Metro Richmond Family Law Bar Assn. (founding pres. 1994), Hanover County Bar Assn. (treas. 1997, sec. 1998, pres.-elect 1999, pres. 2000), Richmond Bar Assn. (chmn. family law sect. 1982—83, exec. com. 1982—83), Ruritan Club (pres., zone gov., dist. sec.), Rotary (bd.dirs. 1980—84). Republican. Methodist. Home: 11910 Aberdeen Landing Ter Midlothian VA 23113-1394 Office: Batzli Wood & Stiles Ste 200 10900 Nuckols Rd Glen Allen VA 23060 Office Phone: 804-545-9800.

BAUCH, THOMAS JAY, financial consultant, retired lawyer, apparel executive; b. Indpls., May 24, 1943; s. Thomas and Violet (Smith) B.; m. Ellen L. Burstein, Oct. 31, 1982; children: Chelsea Sara, Elizabeth Tree. BS with honors, U. Wis., 1964, JD with highest honors, 1966. Bar: Ill. 1966, Calif. 1978. Assoc. Lord, Bissell & Brook, Chgo., 1966-72; lawyer, asst. sec. Marcor-Montgomery Ward, Chgo., 1973-75; spl. asst. to solicitor Dept. Labor, Washington, 1975-77; dep. gen. counsel Levi Strauss & Co., 1977-81, sr. v.p., gen. counsel, 1981-96, of counsel, 1996-2000; pvt. practice, Tiburon, Calif., 1996-2000; mng. dir. Offit Hall Capital Mgmt. LLC, San Francisco, 2000—. Cons. prof. Stanford U. Law Sch., Calif., 1997-04. Mem. U. Wis. Law Rev., 1964-66. Bd. dirs. Urban Sch., San Francisco, 1986-91, Gateway H.S., San Francisco, Charles Armstrong Sch., Belmont, Calif., 1998-2001, San Francisco Opera Assn., 1998-2001, Telluride Acad., 1996-2000, Corinthian Acad.; bd. visitors U. Wis. Law Sch., 1991-95. Mem. Am. Assn. Corp. Counsel (founding mem., bd. dirs. 1984-87), Bay Area Gen. Counsel Assn. (founding mem., chmn. 1994), Univ. Club, Villa Taverna Club, Corinthian Yacht Club, Order of Coif, San Francisco Yacht Club. Office: Offit Hall Capital Mgmt One Maritime Plz Ste 500 San Francisco CA 94111 Office Phone: 415-288-0544. Business E-Mail: tbauch@offithall.com.

BAUCOM, SIDNEY GEORGE, lawyer; b. Salt Lake City, Oct. 21, 1930; s. Sidney and Nora (Palfreyman) B.; m. Mary B., Mar. 5, 1954; children: Sidney, George, John JD, U. Utah, 1953. Bar: Utah 1953. Pvt. practice, Salt Lake City, 1953-55; asst. city atty. Salt Lake City Corp., 1955-56; asst. atty. Utah Power and Light Co., Salt Lake City, 1956-60, asst. atty., asst. sec., 1960-62, atty., asst. sec., 1962-68, v.p., gen. counsel, 1968-75, sr. v.p., gen. counsel, 1975-79, exec. v.p., gen. counsel, 1979-89, dir., 1979-89; of counsel Jones, Waldo, Holbrook & McDonough, Salt Lake City, 1989—. Past chmn. Utah Coordinating Coun. Devel. Svcs., Utah Taxpayers Assn.; past pres. Utah State Fair Found.; past dir. Utah Power & Light Co., El Paso Electric Co., vice chmn. Mem. Alta Club, Lions, Phi Delta Phi Mem. Lds Ch. Home: 2248 Logan Ave Salt Lake City UT 84108-2715 Office: Jones Waldo Holbrook & McDonough 1500 Wells Fargo Bank Bldg 170 S Main St Salt Lake City UT 84101-1605 Home Phone: 801-583-1221; Office Phone: 801-521-3200. Business E-Mail: sbaucom@joneswaldo.com.

BAUCUS, MAX SIEBEN, senator; b. Helena, Mont., Dec. 11, 1941; s. John and Jean (Sheriff) Baucus; m. Wanda Minge, Apr. 23, 1983; 1 child, Zeno. BA in economics, Stanford U., 1964, LLB, 1967. Bar: DC 1969, Mont. 1972. Staff atty. Civil Aeronautics Bd., Washington, 1967-68; atty. SEC, Washington, 1968-71, legal asst. to chmn., 1970-71; atty. George and Baucus, Missoula, Mont., 1971—74; mem. Mont. Ho. of Reps., 1973-74; rep. from 1st Dist. Mont. US Ho. of Reps., 1975-79; US Senator from Mont., 1979—. Mem. com. appropriations US Ho. of Reps.; joint com. taxation ranking minority mem US Senate, joint com. taxation sr. mem., congressional-exec. commn. China ranking minority mem., com. fin. ranking minority mem, com. fin. chmn., 2007—, com. environment and pub. works, com. agr., nutrition and forestry. Bd. dirs. Congressional Award Found. Recipient Guardian of Small Bus. award, Nat. Fedn. Independent Bus., 1983—84, Bronze Symbol Svc. award, Nat. Pork Producers Coun., 1997, Legis. award, Nat. Rural Health Assn., 1999, Am. Fin. Leadership award, Fin. Services Roundtable, 2001, Wheat Leader of Yr. award, Nat. Assn. Wheat Growers, 2003, Cyber Champion award, Bus. Software Alliance, 2005. Mem.: Mont. Bar Assn., DC Bar Assn. Democrat. Avocation: motorcycling. Office: US Senate 511 Hart Senate Bldg Washington DC 20510-0001 also: District Office Ste 100 222 North 32nd St Billings MT 59101 Office Phone: 202-224-2651, 406-657-6790. Office Fax: 202-224-0515.*

BAUDE, PATRICK LOUIS, law educator; b. Independence, Kans., Apr. 7, 1943; s. E.L. Andre and Jane (O'Brien) B.; m. Deborah Robinson, June 1, 1963 (div. Oct. 1977); children: Virginia, Leora; m. Julia Lamber, Feb. 27, 1981; children: William, Jonathan. AB, U. Kans., 1964, JD, 1966; LLM, Harvard U., 1968. Bar: Wis. 1966, Ind. 1990, U.S. Supreme Ct. 1969. Assoc. Foley & Lardner, Milw., 1966-67; fellow Harvard Law Sch., Cambridge, Mass., 1967-68; prof. law Ind. U., Bloomington, 1968-2001, Ralph F. Fuchs prof. law, 2001—. Vis. prof. U. Warsaw, Poland, 1993, U. Paris, 2000; mem. Ind. Bd. Law Examiners, Indpls., 1990-01, pres., 1997-99. Author: Judicial Jurisdiction, 2007. Office: Indiana Univ Law Sch Bloomington IN 47465 E-mail: baude@indiana.edu.

BAUE, ARTHUR EDWARD, retired surgeon, educator, health facility administrator; b. St. Louis, Oct. 7, 1929; s. Arthur Christian and Viola (Wegener) B.; m. Rosemary Dysart, Nov. 24, 1956; children: Patricia Sage Baue Nizen, Arthur Christian II, William Dysart. AB summa cum laude, Westminster Coll., 1950; MD cum laude, Harvard, 1954; M Honoris Privatum, Yale U., 1975; MD honoris causa, Ludwig Maxmillian U., Munich, Germany, 2000. Diplomate Am. Bd. Surgery (dir.), Am. Bd. Thoracic Surgery (dir.). Cpt. asst. chief of surgery USAF Hosp., Philippine Islands, 1955-57; from intern to chief resident surgery Mass. Gen. Hosp., Boston, 1954-61; asst. prof. surgery U. Mo. Sch. Medicine, 1962-64; sr. registrar in thoracic surgery Bristol, Eng., 1961-62; from asst. prof. to assoc. prof. surgery U. Pa. Sch. Medicine, Phila., 1964-67; Harry Edison prof. surgery Washington U. Sch. Medicine, St. Louis, 1967-75; surgeon-in-chief, dir. dept. surgery Jewish Hosp., St. Louis, 1967-75; chief of surgery Yale-New Haven Hosp., 1975-85; prof., chmn. dept. surgery Yale U., 1975-85, Donald Guthrie prof. surgery, 1977-85; assoc. dean for clin. affairs St. Louis U. Sch. Medicine, 1985-86; v.p. for the med. ctr. St. Louis U., 1986-90, prof. surgery, 1986-97, prof. emeritus, v.p. emeritus for the med. ctr., 1997. Dir. surg. edn. St. Mary's Health Ctr., 1990-97; cons. surgery Nat. Bd. Med. Examiners; cons. to chief of staff VAMC, St. Louis, 1994-97; chmn. NIH surgery B study sect., 1978-82; bd. dirs., med. dir. Healthcare Mgmt., Inc.; vis. prof. various colls.; hon. pres., Internat. Symposium Critical Care Medicine, Trieste, 2003, 04, 05; honored chmn. emeritus dept. surgery Yale U. Sch. Medicine, 2007; lectr., spkr. in field. Author: Doctor, Can I Ask You A Question? 2005; chief editor: Archives of Surgery, 1977-88, sr. cons. editor, 1989-93; editor: Thoracic and Cardiovascular Surgery, 4th edit., 1983, The Pathophysiology and Clinical Management of Shock, 1984, Parameters of Health Care, 1986-90, Multiple Organ Failure, Patient Care and Prevention, 1990, Glenn's Thoracic and Cardiovascular Surgery, 5th edit., 1990, 6th edit., 1996, Multiple Organ Failure, 2000, Sepsis and Organ Dysfuntion-Epidemiology and Scoring Systems, 1009, Sepsis and Organ Dysfunction-From Basics to Clinical Approaches, 1999, Sepsis and Organ Dysfunction: The Challenge Continues, 2000, Sepsis and Organ Dysunction-Bad and Good News on Prevention and Management, 2000, Sepsis and Organ Dysfunction-From Chaos to Rationale, 2002; mem. editl. bd. JAMA, 1977-88, Circulatory Shock, Am. Jour. Physiology, 1975-87, Postgrad. Gen. Surgery, Jour. Shock, 1994—; sr. editor: Glenn's Thoracic and Cardiovascular Surgery; contbr. over 630 articles to profl. jours. Life trustee Westminster Coll.; trustee Nat. Commn. for Quality Health Care, 1986-92, Health Care Leadership Coun.; bd. dirs. United Way; chmn. bd. deacons Union Chapel F.I. Capt. USAF, 1959-69. John and Mary R. Markle scholar, 1963; recipient Rsch. Career Devel. award USPHS, 1965-68, Arthur E. Baue award, Munich, 2007; named Scientist of Yr., Sigma Xi, 1991, Honored Chmn. award, Yale Surg. Soc., 2007, Internat. Health Prof. of Yr., 2005. Mem. ACS, AMA (trustee jour., editl. bd. jour.), Assn. Am. Med. Colls. (coun. acad. socs.), Am. Assn. Thoracic Surgery, Am. Coll. Cardiology, Am. Coll. Chest Physicians (Pres.'s citation), Assn. Acad. Surgery, New Eng. Surg. Soc., New Eng. Vascular Soc., Internat. Cardiovasc. Soc., Soc. Thoracic Surgeons, Soc. Univ. Surgeons, Soc. Vascular Surgery, Shock Soc. (Scientific Achievement award 2003), Internat. Fedn. Shock Socs. (pres. 1992-95), Internat. Vascular Soc. Surgery, Am. Assn. for Surgery Trauma, Am. Assn. Artificial Internal Organs, Organ Failure Acad. (Trieste, Italy, hon. pres. 1983-2005), Surg. Biol. Club, Soc. U. Surgeons, Am. Physiol. Soc., Sr. Physiol. Commn., Soc. Critical Care Medicine (Lifetime Achievement award 2007), Am. Surg. Assn., Ctrl. Surg. Assn., Halsted Soc., Soc. Internat. Surgery, Soc. Clin. Surgery, Surg. Infection Soc., James IV Assn. of Surgeons, Southern Thoracic Surg. Soc., Soc. for Surgery Alimentary Tract, St. Louis Surg. Soc. (hon.), Soc. Grad. Surgeons LA County-U. SC Med. Ctr. (hon.), Assn. VA Surgeons (hon.), Colombia Surg. Soc. (hon.), Chgo. Surg. Soc. (hon.), LA Surg. Soc. (hon.), Mpls. Surg. Soc. (hon.), Fla. Assn. Gen. Surgeons, (hon.), Indonesian Shock Soc. (hon.), Organ Failure Soc. (hon. pres.), Alpha Omega Alpha. Home and Office: PO Box 396 Fishers Island NY 06390

BAUER, A. ROBERT, JR., (AUGUST ROBERT BAUER JR.), surgeon; b. Dec. 23, 1928; s. A(ugust) Robert and Jessie Martha-Maynard (Monie) Bauer; m. Charmaine Louise Studer, June 28, 1957; children: Robert, John, William, Anne, Charles, James. BS, U. Mich., 1949, MS, 1950, MD, 1954; M in Med. Sci.-Surgery, Ohio State U., 1960. Diplomate Am. Bd. Surgery. Intern Walter Reed Army Med. Ctr., 1954—55; resident in surgery Univ. Hosp., Ohio State U., Columbus, also instr., 1957—61; pvt. practice medicine, specializing in surgery Mt. Pleasant, Mich., 1962—74; chief surgery Ctrl. Mich. Cmty. Hosp., Mt. Pleasant, 1964—65, vice chief of staff, 1967, chief of staff, 1968; clin. faculty Mich. State Med. Sch., East Lansing, 1974; mem. staff St. Mark's Hosp., Salt Lake City, 1974—91; pvt. practice surgery Salt Lake City, 1974—91. Clin. instr. surgery U. Utah, 1975—91; rschr. surg. immunology. Contbr. articles to profl. publs. Trustee Rowland Hall, St. Mark's Sch., Salt Lake City, 1978—84; mem. Utah Health Planning Coun., 1979—81. With M.C. US Army, 1954—57. Fellow: ACS, Southwestern Surg. Congress; mem.: AAAS (affiliate), AMA, Zollinger Surg. Soc., Pan Am. Med. Assn. (affiliate), Salt Lake Surg. Soc., Utah Med. Assn. (various coms.), Salt Lake County Med. Soc., Phi Rho Sigma, Sigma Phi Epsilon. Episcopalian. Office: PO Box 17533 Salt Lake City UT 84117-0533 Address: 1366 Murray Holladay Rd Salt Lake City UT 84117-5050

BAUER, BARBARA ANN, marketing consultant; b. Fairfield, Ohio, Dec. 4, 1944; d. Charles P. and Grace J. (Peteka) B.; m. Joseph J. Strojnowski. AA, So. Sem. Jr. Coll., Buena Vista, Va., 1964; BA, Am. U., 1966. Pub. relations, advt. specialist Sta. WOR-AM-FM-TV, NYC, 1966-67; pub. relations mgr. Continental Corp., NYC, 1967-68; dir. corp. communications Am. Internat. Group, NYC, 1968-80; dir. mktg. mgmt. infos. CIGNA Corp., Phila., NYC, 1980-83; asst. v.p. Citicorp Credit Services Inc., NYC, 1983-87; v.p., dir. mktg. Skandia Am. Group, NYC, 1987-88, v.p. corp. communications, 1988-89; pres. Bauer Mktg. and Communications, Goshen, NY, 1989—. Mem. Reinsurance Cons. Network. Lifetime mem. Girl Scouts U.S. Mem.: Ins. Media Assn. (adv. bd.), Assn. Profl. Ins. Women (chair pub. rels., advisor bd. dirs.), Pub. Rels. Soc. Am. (accredited, counselors' acad.). Home Phone: 845-294-8791; Office Phone: 845-294-3550. Business E-Mail: bauermarketing@gmail.com.

BAUER, CHRIS MICHAEL, banker; b. Milw., Sept. 2, 1948; s. Heinz Gerald and Maria (Weber) B.; m. Susan Marie Branton, June 28, 1969. BBA, U. Wis., 1970; MBA, Marquette U., 1976. Mgmt. trainee 1st Wis. Nat. Bank, Milw., 1970-72, spl. enterprise officer, 1972-74, asst. mgr., 1974-75; v.p. 1st Wis.-Racine, 1976-78; pres. 1st Wis.-Brookfield, 1978-84; 1st v.p. Firstar Corp. (formerly 1st Wis. Corp.), Milw., 1984-86, sr. v.p., 1986-89; pres., COO Firstar Bank Milw. (formerly 1st Wis. Nat. Bank), Milw., 1989-91, chmn., CEO, 1991-99, 1999—; chmn, CEO Business Banc Group Ltd.; also bd. dirs. Firstar Bank Milw. (formerly 1st Wis. Nat. Bank). Bd. dirs. Aurora Health Care Metro Region, Milw. Pub. Libr. Found., J.A. of Wisconsin, Inc., Next Door Found., Siebert Lutheran Found., The Auto Club Group Inc., AAA Wisconsin; mem. Greater Milw. Com. Mem. Milw. Country Club, Univ. Club, Westmoor Country Club. Lutheran. Office: Bus Banc Group Ltd 18500 W Corporate Dr Ste 170 Brookfield WI 53045-6309

BAUER, CYNTHIA RENAE, nurse; b. Sacramento, Sept. 13, 1958; d. James Russell and Lois Ann Lawson; 1 child, Richard Gregory. BS in Nursing cum laude, U. San Francisco, 1980; MSN, Sacramento State U., 2005. Cert. pub. health nurse, U. San Francisco, 1980, RN Calif., 1980, health svcs. credential, Sacramento State U., 2004. Nurse Woodland (Calif.) Meml. Hosp., 1980—85; charge nurse hemodialysis Bapt. Hosp., Pensacola, Fla., 1986—88, U. West Fla., Milton, 1988—91, St. Vincent Medical Ctr., Jacksonville, Fla., 1991—94, DePaul Medical Ctr., Norfolk, Va., 1994—96, Vacaville Dialysis, Calif., 1998—99; sch. nurse Yolo County Office Edn., Woodland, Calif., 1999—. Den leader Cubscouts, Woodland, 1998—2001; sponsor African child Christian Children, 2003—. Recipient Nurse of Distinction award, DePaul Medical Ctr., 1995, award, Spl. Edn. Adv. Com., 2005. Mem.: Nat. Assn. Sch. Nurses, Calif. Sch. Nurse Orgn. (chair spl. edn. 2004—), Sigma Theta Tau. Avocations: reading, travel. Home: 6 Darby Ct Woodland CA 95776 Office: Yolo County Office Edn Greengate Sch 285 W Beamer St Woodland CA 95695 Office Phone: 530-668-3852.

BAUER, DOUGLAS F., retired lawyer; b. Lackawanna, NY, Nov. 20, 1942; s. Ellsworth W. and Gloria G. (Fakler) B. AB magna cum laude, Princeton U., 1964; JD cum laude, Harvard U., 1967. Bar: N.Y. 1967, D.C. 1979, U.S. Supreme Ct. 1979. Assoc. Chadbourne & Parke, NYC, 1967—71; assoc. counsel Gulf & Western Industries, Inc. (Paramount Communications, Inc.), NYC, 1971—75; gen. counsel Amerace Corp., NYC, 1975—86; gen. counsel, corp. sec. Bowne & Co., Inc., NYC, 1986—2002; ret., 2002. Author: The Grolier Club 1884-1984, 1984; editor: The Bowne Family of Flushing, N.Y., 1987; contbr. articles to profl. jours. Mem. Fellows of the Morgan Libr. and Mus., N.Y.C., 1984—; trustee Bowne House Hist. Soc., Flushing, N.Y., 1986-2003, pres., 1996-2002; sec.-treas., trustee Robert Bowne Found., N.Y.C., 1986-2002; coun. Friends of the Princeton U. Libr., 1980—; chmn. bd. trustees Am. Printing History Assn., 1991-94. Mem. ABA, Assn. of Bar of City of N.Y. (non-profit com. 1997-2001), N.Y. State Bar Assn. (corp. law com. 1982—), Nat. Assn. Corp. Dirs., Am. Soc. Corp. Secs. Clubs: Princeton, Grolier. Republican. Lutheran. Home: 300 Rector Pl New York NY 10280-1416

BAUER, ERNST GEORG, physicist, researcher; b. Schoenberg, Germany, Feb. 27, 1928; MS, U. Munich, 1953, PhD in Physics, 1955. Rsch. asst. U. Munich, 1955-58; head crystal physics br. Michelson Lab., China Lake, Calif., 1958-69; prof. Tech. U. Clausthal, Germany, 1969-96. Disting. rsch. prof. Ariz. State U., Tempe, 1993—. Author: (book) Elektronenbeugung, 1958. Recipient Gaede prize, German Vacuum Soc., 1988, Niedersachsenpreis, 1994, Innovation award, Berliner Elektronenspeicherring-Gesellschaft für Synchrotronstrahlung MBH, 2004. Fellow: Am. Vacuum Soc. (Welch award 1992), Am. Phys. Soc. (Davisson-Germer prize 2005); mem.: German Electron Microscopy Soc., Materials Rsch. Soc., Goettingen Acad. Sci. Office: Ariz State Univ Dept Phys Astronomy Tempe AZ 85287-1504 Office Phone: 480-965-2993. Business E-Mail: ernst.bauer@asu.edu.

BAUER, EUGENE ANDREW, dermatologist, educator; b. Mattoon, Ill., June 17, 1942; s. Eugene C. and Madge L. (Armer) B.; m. Gloria Anne Hehman, Feb. 19, 1966; childen: Marc A., Christine A., J. Michael, Amanda F. BS, Northwestern U., 1964, MD, 1967. Diplomate Am. Bd. Dermatology, Nat. Bd. Med. Examiners. Intern Barnes Hosp., St. Louis, 1967-68; resident, fellow divsn. dermatology Washington U. Med. Ctr., St. Louis, 1968-70; instr. Washington U., St. Louis, 1971-72, asst. prof. dermatology, 1974-78, assoc. prof., 1978-82, prof., 1982-88; prof., chmn. Stanford (Calif.) U. Sch. Medicine, 1988-95, dean, 1995-2001; program dir. Gen. Clin. Rsch. Ctr., 1990-93; v.p. med. affairs Stanford U., 1997-2000, v.p. Med. Ctr., 2000—01. Mem. adv. coun. Nat. Inst. Arthritis and Musculoskeletal and Skin Diseases, 1997—2000; bd. dirs. U. Calif. San Francisco-Stanford Health Care, Connetics Corp., Reconstructive Techs., Arbor Vita Corp., Medgenics. Contbr. numerous articles to profl. jours. Served to lt. comdr. USNR, 1972-74. Recipient Alumni Merit award Northwestern U., 1999. Fellow Am. Acad. Dermatology; mem. Am. Fedn. Clin. Rsch., Am Soc. Clin. Investigation, Am. Dermatol. Assn., Soc. Investigative Dermatology (bd. dirs. 1981-86, assoc. editor Jour. Investigative Dermatology 1982-87, pres.-elect 1994-95, pres. 1995-96), Ctrl. Soc. Clin. Rsch., Assn. Am. Physicians, Inst. Medicine of NAS, Am. Clin. and Climatol. Assn. Office: Stanford U Sch Medicine Office of the Dean M121 Stanford CA 94305 Office Phone: 310-226-6378. E-mail: eugene.bauer@stanford.edu.

BAUER, HENRY HERMANN, chemistry and science educator; b. Vienna, Nov. 16, 1931; came to U.S., 1965, naturalized, 1969; s. Martin Josef and Anne (Rafael) B.; m. Barbara Bush, Aug. 25, 1986; children from previous marriage: Helen Suzanne, Judith Ann. B.Sc., U. Sydney, 1952, M.Sc., 1953, PhD, 1956. Rsch. assoc. U. Mich., 1956-58, vis. scientist, 1965-66; lectr., sr. lectr. U. Sydney, 1958-66; assoc. prof., prof. U. Ky., 1966-78; vis. prof. Southampton (Eng.) U., 1972-73; dean Coll. Arts and Scis. Va. Poly. Inst. and State U., Blacksburg, 1978-86, prof. chemistry and science studies Coll. Arts and Scis., 1986-99. Author: Alternating Current Polarography and Tensammetry, 1963, Electrodics, 1973, Instrumental Analysis, 1978, Beyond Velikovsky, 1984, Enigma of Loch Ness, 1986, (under pseudonym Josef Martin) To Rise Above Principle, 1988, Scientific Literacy and the Myth of the Scientific Method, 1992, Science or Pseudoscience, 2001, Fatal Attractions: The Troubles with Science, 2001, The Origins, Persistence, and Failings of HIV/AIDS Theory, 2007; editor-in-chief Jour. Sci. Exploration, 2000—. Fulbright fellow, 1956-58; Japan Soc. fellow for promotion of sci., 1974 Mem. Soc. Sci. Exploration (founding mem.), Internat. Soc. Cryptozoology. Unitarian Universalist. E-mail: hhbauer@vt.edu.

BAUER, JAMES MONIE, aerospace scientist; s. August Robert Bauer, Jr. and Charmaine L. Bauer; m. Chija Kirsten Skala, 2002. PhD, U. Hawaii, Manoa, 1996—2003. Nrc postdoctoral rschr., 2003—05; scientist jet propulsion lab. Calif. Inst. Tech., Pasadena, 2005—. Achievements include research in outer solar system small bodies.

BAUER, JEAN WARNER, family economics educator; b. Highland, Ill., Oct. 20, 1944; d. Howard E. and Mary Ann Warner; m. Marvin E. Bauer, June 28, 1969. BS, Ind. State U., 1966; MS, Purdue U., 1969; PhD, U. Ill., Champaign-Urbana, 1980. Assoc. prof. U. Minn., St Paul, 1983—94, prof., 1994—2006. Named Invited Keynoter Women's World, Interdisciplinary Congress on Women, Seoul Korea, 2005, Best Dir. Grad. Studies, U. Minn., 2004; recipient Dean and Director's Disting. Diversity and Inclusion award, U. Minn. Ext. Svc., 2005, 2005 Mary W. Wells Diversity award, Nat. Ext. Assn. Family and Consumer Sci., 2005, Excellence in Academic Advising award, U. Minn., 2006; fellow, Nat. Coun. on Family Rels., 2005. Mem.: Am. Coun. Consumer Interests, Am. Assn. Family and Consumer Sci., Nat. Coun. Family Rels. (chai pub. policy com. 2003—04). Office: U Minn 275 McNeal Hall 1985 Buford Ave Saint Paul MN 55108-6140 Home Phone: 651-731-6216; Office Phone: 612-625-1763. E-mail: jbauer@umn.edu.

BAUER, JOANNE B., health products executive; b. Neenah, Wis., 1955; 2 children. Grad. in English, Lawrence U., Appleton, Wis., 1977; MBA, U. Wis., Oshkosh, 1986. With mktg. Adult Care Kimberly-Clark Corp., 1981, various mktg. and mgmt. positions Adult Care and Health Care, v.p. KimFibers, Ltd., 1996, v.p. global mktg. Health Care, 1998—2001, pres. Health Care, 2001—06, pres. global health care, 2006—. Bd. dirs. ContiCare Med., Inc., Medivance, Inc. Office: Kimberly Clark Corp 1400 Holcomb Bridge Rd Roswell GA 30076*

BAUER, JOEL J., surgeon, educator; b. NYC, Aug. 16, 1942; s. David W. and Toby B.; m. Judy Bauer (Siegel), Dec. 3, 1967; children: Dana, Ross, BS, U. Vt., 1963; MD, NYU, 1967. Lic. physician, N.Y.; cert. Am. Bd. Surgery. Intern in surgery Mt. Sinai Hosp., NYC, 1967-68, resident in surgery, 1968-72, chief resident in surgery, 1972-73, clin. asst. surgery, 1973-77, asst. attending surgeon, 1977-81, assoc. attending surgeon, 1981-88, attending surgeon, 1988—; instr. surgery to asst. clin. prof. to clin. prof. surgery Mt. Sinai Sch. Medicine, NYC, 1972—; vice chmn., dept. surgery Mt. Sinai Hosp., 2001—. Presenter in field. Contbr. articles to profl. jours. Named Physician of Yr., Crohn's and Colitis Found., 2003. Fellow Am. Coll. Surgeons; mem. AMA, Assn. Acad. Surgery, Am. Coll. Gastroenterology, Am. Coll. Colon & Rectal Surgery, Soc. for Surgery for the Alimentary Tract, N.Y. Acad. Scis., N.Y. County Med. Soc., N.Y. Acad. Gastroenterology, N.Y. Soc. Colon & Rectal Surgeons, N.Y. Surg. Soc., N.Y. Acad. Medicine (sec. surg. sect. 1986-87, pres. surg. sect. 1987-88), Soc. Pelvic Surgeons, Soc. Laparoscopic Surgeons, Soc. Am. Gastrointestinal Endoscopic Surgeons Office: 25 E 69th St New York NY 10021-4925 Office Phone: 212-517-8600. Business E-Mail: joel.bauer@mssm.edu.

BAUER, JOSEPH W., lawyer, chemicals executive; b. Toledo, July 22, 1953; BA, U. Toledo, 1975, JD, 1981. Bar: Ohio 1981. Atty. Jones, Day, Reavis & Pogue; various positions in legal dept. Lubrizol Corp., Wickliffe, Ohio, 1985—91, v.p., gen. counsel, 1992—. Office: Lubrizol Corp 29400 Lakeland Blvd Wickliffe OH 44092

BAUER, KRIS, air transportation executive; married. BS in Aerospace Engring., U. Kans., Lawrence; MBA, Cornell U., Ithaca, NY. Various fin. positions United Airlines; engring. position Boeing; with NW Airlines Corp., Minn., 1996—, mng. dir. tech. ops. fin., v.p. aircraft maintenance ops., 2003—04, sr. v.p. tech. ops., 2004—. Office: NW Airlines Corp 2700 Lone Oak Pky Eagan MN 55121 Office Phone: 612-726-2111.*

BAUER, MARION DANE, writer; b. Oglesby, Ill., Nov. 20, 1938; d. Chester and Elsie (Hempstead) Dane; m. Ronald C. Bauer, June 25, 1959 (div. Dec. 1988); children: Peter Dane, Elisabeth Alison. AA, LaSalle-Peru-Oglesby Jr. Coll., 1958; student, U. Mo., 1958—59; BA in Lang. Arts, U. Okla., 1961, postgrad., 1961—62. Author: Shelter from the Wind, 1976 (Notable Children's Book ALA, 1976), Foster Child (Golden Kite Honor Book award Soc. Children's Book Writers, 1977), Tangled Butterfly, 1980, Rain of Fire, 1983 (Tchrs.' Choices award Nat. Coun. Tchrs. of English, 1984, Revs. Choice award ALA Booklist, 1983, Children's Book award Jane Addams Peace Assn., 1984), Like Mother, Like Daughter, 1985, On My Honor, 1986 (Newbery Honor Book, 1987, Notable Children's Book ALA, 1986, Best Books of 1986 Sch. Libr. Jour., Editors' Choice Booklist, 1986, Pub.'s Weekly Choice the Yrs.'s Best Books, 1986, Flicker Tale Children's Book award, N.D., 1989, Golden Archer award, Wis., 1989, William Allen White Children's Book award, Kans., 1989, BBY, IRA selection for Janusc Korczak Lit. Competition Poland, 1990), Touch the Moon, 1987, A Dream of Queens and Castles, 1990, (drama) God's Tears: A Woman's Journey, Face to Face, 1991 (Children's Book of Distinction, Hungry Mind Rev., 1992), What's Your Story? A Young Person's Guide to Writing Fiction, 1992 (Notable Children's Book ALA, 1992), Ghost Eye, 1992, A Taste of Smoke, 1993, A Question of Trust, 1994; editor: Am I Blue? Coming Out from the Silence, 1994, When I Go Camping With Grandma, 1995, A Writer's Story, From Life to Fiction, 1995, Alison's Wings, 1996, Our Stories, A Fiction Workshop for Young Authors, 1996, Alison's Puppy, 1997, If You Were Born a Kitten, 1997, Turtle Dreams, 1997, Alison's Fierce and Ugly Halloween, 1997, Bear's Hiccups, 1998, Christmas in the Forest, 1998, An Early Winter, 1999, Sleep, Little One, Sleep, 1999, Jason's Bears, 2000, Grandmother's Song, 2000, My Mother is Mine, 2001, If You Had a Nose Like an Elephant's Trunk, 2001, Frog's Best Friend, 2002, Love Song for a Baby, 2003, Runt, 2002, Land of the Buffalo Bones, 2003, Toes, Ears and Nose, 2003, Why Do Kittens Purr, 2003, Wind, 2003, Snow, 2003, Rain, 2004, Clouds, 2004, The Double-Digit Club, 2004 (CBC Best Books award, 2004), The Very Best Daddy of

All, 2004, A Recipe for Valentine's Day, 2004, Easter is Coming, 2005, The Blue Ghost, 2005, A Bear Named Trouble, 2005, If Frogs Made Weather, 2005, Waiting for Christmas, 2005, Niagara Falls, 2005, The Mississippi River, 2006, The Grand Canyon, 2006, A Mama for Owen, 2006, Christmas Lights, 2006, Baby Bear Discovers the World, 2007, Killing Miss Kitty and Other Sins, 2007, The Secret of the Painted House, 2007; contbr. short stories to mags. and books in field. Mem.: Soc. Children's Book Writers and Illustrators, Authors League Am., Authors Guild. Democrat. Home: 8861 Basswood Rd Eden Prairie MN 55344-7407 Office: Clarion 215 Park Ave S New York NY 10003-1603 Office Phone: 952-941-3102. Personal E-mail: mdanebauer@aol.com. *Children are our future, of course, but they are also the touchstone for our present. To discover who we are and how we are doing we need only check our reflections in our children's eyes.*

BAUER, MARVIN AGATHER, retired lawyer; b. Milw., June 28, 1940; m. Gray Bauer; children: Laura, Andrew BS, U. Wis., 1962; JD, U. Chgo., 1965. Bar: Calif. 1966. Dep. atty. gen. State of Calif., Los Angeles, 1965-69; ptnr. Archbald & Spray, Santa Barbara, Calif., 1969-82, Bauer, Harris Clinkenbeard & Ramsey, Santa Barbara, 1982—2006, ret., 2006. Lectr. U. Calif., 1975—77; instr. Santa Barbara Coll. Law, 2004—05; bd. dir. Summerland Citizens Assn. Bd. dirs. Carpinteria Valley Assn., Calif., 1980-83, Carpinteria Boys Club, 1983-84 Mem. Am. Coll. Trial Lawyers, Am. Bd. Trial Advocates, Santa Barbara Bar Assn. (pres. 1978-79, bd. dirs. 1974-80), Calif. Med.-Legal Com. (pres. 2003-2005), Santa Barbara Med. Legal Com Home: PO Box 1307 Summerland CA 93067-1307

BAUER, MICHAEL ANTHONY, computer scientist, educator; b. Dayton, Ohio, Feb. 18, 1948; married; 2 children. BSc, U. Dayton, 1970; MSc, U. Toronto, 1971, PhD in Computer Sci., 1978. Rschr. artificial intelligence Edinburgh U., 1974-75; prof. computer sci. U. Western Ont., 1975—, chmn. dept., 1991-96, 2002—, assoc. v.p. IT, 1996—2001. Cons. Geac Computers Internat., 1984—88, IBM, 1991—94; advisor IBM Ctr. Advanced Studies, 1990—91, vis. scientist, 1991—2007. Mem.: IEEE, Assn. Computing Machinery (bd. dirs. 1989—94), Can. Info. Processing Soc. (bd. dirs. 1984—88). Achievements include research in in distributed computing, especially distributed systems and applications management, distributed algorithms, correctness, languages for distributed computing, verfication; software engineering, including methodologies, testing, formal specifications, development environments. Office: University of Western Ontario Middlesex College Rm 355 London ON Canada N6A 5B7 Office Phone: 519-661-3562. Business E-Mail: bauer@csd.uwo.ca.

BAUER, NORMAN JAMES, retired education educator; b. Milw., June 13, 1929; s. Hugo Andrew and Erna Theresa (Gocker) B.; m. Betty Jane Zwicky, Dec. 26, 1953 (dec. May 8, 1999); children: Michael James, Barbara Ann; m. Stephanie Burns Crissman, April 21, 2001. BS, Wis. State Coll., 1953; MA, Northwestern U., 1956; EdD, Ind. U., 1964. Cert. elem., secondary tchr., Wis., sch. adminstr., Wis. Tchr. English, world history jr. and sr. high schs., Ripon, Wis., 1953; tchr. sci., math. Horace Mann Jr. High Sch., West Allis, Wis., 1954-57; instr. then asst. prof. Lab. Sch. Ea. Ill. U., Charleston, 1957-62; teaching assoc. Sch. Edn. Ind. U., Bloomington, 1962-64; dir. Lab. Sch. U. Wis., Oshkosh, 1964-67; prof., chmn. dept. curriculum and instrn. SUNY, Geneseo, 1967-71, prof. social foundation of end., 1971—95, v.p. faculty United Univ. Profls., 1982-84, pres. bd. dirs. campus auxilary svcs., 1982-84, dir. video studies ednl. theory and practice, 1985—95, emeritus prof. social found. edn., 1995. Adj. prof. SUNY, Buffalo, 1974-77; pres. NY State Social Found. of Edn., 1986-87; pres. cmty. bd. Rochester Sch. Without Walls, 2000-07. Contbr. numerous articles to profl. jours. V.p. program Rochester chpt. Americans United for Separation Ch. and State, 1982-, mem. nat. adv. coun., 1985-90, pres., 1994-97; bd. dirs. Monroe County Citizens for Pub. Edn. and Religious Liberty, 1991-95; active mem. Dem. Party. Recipient Meritorious Svc. award United U. Profs., Albany, NY, 1983, Eric Steele Meml. award Americans United, 1988, Cert. of Recognition NY State Assn. Tchr. Educators, 1998; named one of Two Outstanding Profs. on Geneseo campus, SUNY, 1976. Mem. Am. Humanist Assn., Metro Justice (Rochester, NY), Am. Ednl. Studies Assn., John Dewey Soc., NY State Found. Edn. Assn. (pres. 1986-87), Phi Lambda Chi (hon.), Phi Delta Kappa (pres. 1984-85, Chpt. Leadership award 1988). Democrat. Avocations: reading, collecting art, classical music. Home: 28 Westview Cres Geneseo NY 14454-1012 Personal E-mail: nbauer@rochester.rr.com, normanbauer@mac.com.

BAUER, PETER F., publishing executive; Degree, U. Colo. Advertising sales rep. People Mag., Boston, 1986—88, NYC, 1988—90, advertising sales mgr., 1990, advertising dir., head, Eastern advertising sales ops., 1994—96, assoc. pub., 1996—98, pub., 1998—2002, pres., 2002—05; pub. Life Mag., 2004—05. Office: People/Time Inc 1271 Ave of Americas New York NY 10020-1393 Office Phone: 212-627-0222. Office Fax: 212-522-0076.

BAUER, R. ANDRE, lieutenant governor; b. Charleston, SC, Mar. 20, 1969; s. William R. and Saundrea J. Bauer. BS, U. S.C., 1991. Rep. SC House of Reps., Columbia, 1997—99; senator SC State Senate, Columbia, 1999—2002; lt. gov. State of SC, Columbia, 2003—. Sec.-treas. freshman caucus SC Ho. of Reps., 1997; with SC State Senate. Mem. Union Meth. Ch. Mem. SAR, TKE. Republican. Office: State House 1st Fl PO Box 142 Columbia SC 29202 Office Phone: 803-734-2080. E-mail: ltgov@scsenate.org.

BAUER, RAYMOND GALE, sales professional; b. Merchantville, NJ, June 19, 1934; s. Robert Irwin and Florence Winifred (Guyer) B.; m. Jayne Whitehead, Feb. 15, 1955; 1 child, Linda Joan. AA, Monmouth Coll., 1955; BBA, U. Miami, 1958. Divsn. mgr. R.J. Reynolds Tobacco Co., Winston-Salem, NC, 1959-68; mgr. Mid-Atlantic U.S. Envelope Co., Springfield, Mass., 1968-74; divsn. sales mgr. Eastern Tablet Corp., Albany, NY, 1974-75; owner Ray Bauer Assocs., mfrs. reps., Haddonfield, NJ, 1975—. With USAFR, 1959-64; officer USAF Aux. Mem. Friends of Haddonfield Libr., Haddonfield Civic Assn., Smithsonian Assn., U. Miami Alumni Assn., Monmouth U. Alumni Assn., Nat. Philatelic Soc., Am. Security Coun., Air Force Assn., Am. Conservative Union, Am. Mgmt. Assn., Internat. Platform Assn., Sch. and Home Office Products Assn., Am. Legion, Rep. Club Haddonfield, U.S. Senatorial Club, Arrowhead Racquet Club, Iron Rock Swim and Country Club, Lambda Sigma Tau, Lambda Chi Alpha. Home and Office: 132 Maple Ave Haddonfield NJ 08033-1432 Home Phone: 856-428-6358; Office Phone: 856-428-6371. E-mail: RayGBauer@aol.com, raygbauer@hotmail.com.

BAUER, RICHARD CARLTON, nuclear engineer; b. Batavia, NY, July 15, 1944; s. Willard Ronald and Ethel Bauer; m. Madeline Joy Amreich, June 28, 1969; children: Jason Todd, Cheryl Robyn. BS in Chem. Engring., Clarkson Coll. Tech., 1966; M in Engring., Cornell U., 1968; PhD in Nuclear Sci., Engring., Carnegie-Mellon U., 1974. cert. in bus. mgmt. Am. Mgmt. Assn. Extension Inst., 1989; registered profl. engr., Pa.; cert. fallout shelter analyst, multiprotection designer. Technician Graham Mfg. Co., Batavia, summer 1965; engr. Linde divsn. Union Carbide Corp., Tonawanda, N.Y., summer 1966; hot cell operator asst. Cornell U., Ithaca, N.Y., 1967; engr. Bettis Atomic Power Lab, Inc., West Mifflin, Pa., 1968-73, sr. engr., 1973-78, staff engr., 1978, mgr. AIW performance analysis, 1979-82, AIW/S5G performance analysis, 1982-86, mgr. centralized safety and plant analysis support, 1986-93, mgr. centralized thermal hydraulic devel. group, 1994—2002, mgr. centralized thermal hydraulic advanced analysis methods devel. group, 2002—. Employee tng. lectr. reactor safety, mem. and sec. lab. reactor ops. safety com. Contbr. articles to sci. jours. Chmn. Cornell Secondary Schs., Pitts., PEI Pitts. Clarkson Trustee scholar; Regents fellow, 1962, Bettis Doctoral Program fellow, AEC spl. fellow, 1967. Mem. Nat. Soc. Profl. Engrs., Pa. Soc. Profl. Engrs. (chmn. sustaining assocs. com., dir. chpt. 1981-83, 2d v.p. 1984, 1st v.p. 1985, chpt. pres. 1987, chpt. past pres. 1988, alt. state dir. 1989, state dir. 1990-94, Mathcounts com. 1984, chpt. award for meritorious svc. 1984, restructuring task force 1992-93, chpt. award dedicated svc. 2000), Cornell Soc. Engrs. (regional v.p. 1970-83), Am. Nuclear Soc., N.Y. Acad. Scis., Am. Inst. Chem. Engrs., Tau Beta Pi, Sigma Xi, Omega Chi Epsilon, Triangle Fraternity.

BAUER, RICHARD P., lawyer; b. Pitts., Nov. 17, 1951; BS, US Mil. Acad., 1973; JD, Cath. U., 1984. Bar: Va. 1984, DC 1985. Ptnr. Katten Muchin Zavis Rosenman, Washington, DC. Mem.: DC Bar Assn., Va. Bar Assn., Am. Intellectual Property Law. Office: Katten Muchin Zavis Rosenman East Lobby, Ste 700 1025 Thomas Jefferson St, NW Washington DC 20007 Office Phone: 202-625-3507. Office Fax: 202-298-7570. E-mail: richard.bauer@kmzr.com.

BAUER, ROBERT F., lawyer; b. NYC, Feb. 22, 1952; BA magna cum laude, Harvard U., 1973; JD, U. Va., 1976. Bar: Pa. 1976, DC 1977. Ptnr. polit. law practice area Perkins Coie LLP, Washington. Author: US Federal Election Law, 1982, Soft Money Hard Law — A Guide To The New Campaign Finance Law, 2002, More Soft Money Hard Law: The Second Edition Of The Guide To The New Campaign Finance Law, 2004. Nat. adv. bd. Jour. Law & Polit., U. Va. Named one of 100 Most Influential Lawyers, Nat. Law Mag., 2006. Mem.: ABA. Democrat. Office: Perkins Coie LLP 607 Fourteenth St NW Washington DC 20005-2011 Office Phone: 202-434-1602. Office Fax: 202-434-1690. Business E-Mail: rbauer@perkinscoie.com.

BAUER, ROGER DUANE, chemistry professor, consultant; b. Oxford, Nebr., Jan. 17, 1932; s. Albert Carl and Minnie (Lueking) B.; m. Jacquelyn True, Aug. 10, 1956; children— Lisa, Scott, Robert. BS, Beloit Coll., 1953; MS, Kans. State U., 1957, PhD, 1959. Asst. prof. chemistry Calif. State U., Long Beach, 1959-64, assoc. prof., 1964-69, prof., 1969-92; dean Calif. State U. (Sch. Natural Scis.), 1975-88. Served with U.S. Army, 1954-56. USPHS fellow, 1966; Am. Coun. on Edn. fellow, 1971 Mem. Am. Chem. Soc., Radiation Rsch. Soc., Sigma Xi, Phi Lambda Upsilon. Home: 6320 E Colorado St Long Beach CA 90803-2202 Office: Calif State U Coll Natural Sci Long Beach CA 90840-0001 Office Phone: 562-985-8640. Business E-Mail: rdbauer@csulb.edu.

BAUER, ROSS, composer, music educator; b. Ithaca, NY, Nov. 19, 1951; s. Simon H. and Miriam R. Bauer; children: Nicholas Wilson, Isaac Benjamin. PhD, Brandeis U., 1984. Lectr. music Stanford (Calif.) U., 1986—88; prof. music U. Calif., Davis, 1988—. Founder and dir. Empyrean Ensemble, Davis, 1988—2002; rec. with New World, GM, and Centaur Recordings; condr. more than 100 performances including numerous world premieres; rec. conductor with Empyrean Ensemble in the music of Mario Davidovsky and David Rakowski; guest composer Wellesley Composers Conf., 2001. Composer: (chamber concerto, cello and 14 players) Thin Ice (Commd. by Sequitur, 2004), (concerto for bassoon and orchestra) Icons (Commd. by the Berkeley Symphony, Kent Nagano, Music Dir., 1997), (orchestral piece) Romanza for Violin and Orchestra (Commd. by the Santa Cruz Symphony, John Larry Granger, Music Dir., 1996), (song cycle) Eskimo Songs (Written for Christine Schadeberg, 1996), (chamber music) Stone Soup (Commd. by the NY New Music Ensemble, 1995), (song cycle) Ritual Fragments (Commd. by the Fromm Found. at Harvard U., 1991), (chamber music) Octet (Written for Empyrean Ensemble, 1994), (orchestral) Halycon Birds (Commd. by the Serge Koussevitzky Music Found. in the Libr. of Congress, 1993), (chamber music) Aplomb (for violin and piano) (Commd. by Dan Kobialka), Tributaries (for cello, percussion, piano) (Commd. by the Core Ensemble, 1992), Anaphora (flute, string trio, piano) (Commd. by the Earplay Ensemble, 1990), Piano Quartet (Commd. by SUNY Stony Brook, 2004), (concerto) Concerto for Piano and Chamber Orchestra (Commd. by Wellesley Coll., 1990), (chamber music) Chimera (Commd. by Alea III, Theodore Antoniou, Music Dir., 1987), (solo piano) Tonarten (Commd. by Christopher Keyes, 1982), (orchestral) Dusk (Commd., Calif. Youth Symphony, 2002), (concerto, saxophone, winds, percussion) This, That, and the Other (Commd. by Nat. Assn. of Coll. Wind and Percussion Instructors, 2001), (chamber concerto, flute and 8 players) Fast and Loose (Fromm Found., Harvard U., 2001), (chamber music for solo flute) Nimbus (Commd. by Perspectives of New Music, 2000), (chamber music) String Quartet No. 3 (Commd. by Stanford Lively Arts for the Alexander Quartet, 2000), Pulse (Commd. by the Left Coast Ensemble, 1999), Motion (for piano trio) (Commd. by the Triple Helix Trio, 1998). Mem. exec. bd. Griffin Music Ensemble, Boston, 1984—90. Recipient award, Am. Acad. Arts and Letters, 2005, Speculum Musicae's Third Annual Composition Competition, Walter Hinrichsen award, Am. Acad. Arts and Letters, 1984, prizes, Internat. Soc. Contemporary Music; fellow, Wellesley Composer Conf., Djerassi Found., Wurlitzer Found., Guggenheim Found., 1988, MacDowell Colony, 1984, 1985, 1987, 1989, 1996; composition fellow, Nat. Endowment Arts, 1986. Democrat. Avocations: hiking, reading, coaching baseball. Office: U Calif Davis Dept Music Davis CA 95616 Home Phone: 510-526-5532; Office Phone: 530-752-4487. Personal E-mail: rmbauer@ucdavis.edu.

BAUER, STEVEN M., lawyer; b. Colorado Springs, Colo., July 3, 1961; BA, Duke U., 1983; JD, Stanford Law Sch., 1986. Bar: Calif. Bar Assn. 1988. Law clk. US Dist. Ct., Los Angeles, 1986—87; assoc. Latham & Watkins, Los Angeles, 1987—89; asst. us atty. Dept. of Justice, Los Angeles, 1989—93; ptnr. Latham & Watkins, San Francisco, 1993—; spl. prosecutor Office of Ind. Counsel, Washington, 1996. Recipient Spl. Achievement award, Dept. of Justice, 1992. Mem.: Assn. Bus. Trial Lawyers. Office: Latham & Watkins 505 Montgomery St Ste 2000 San Francisco CA 94111 Office Phone: 415-395-8083. Office Fax: 415-395-8095. E-mail: steve.bauer@lw.com.

BAUER, VIRGINIA SAMARAS, state agency administrator; b. May 4, 1956; m. W. David Bauer, 1980 (dec. Sept. 11, 2001); children: David, Stephen, Jackie. BA in Psychology, Rosemount Coll., 1978. With Merrill Lynch, Red Bank and Westfield, NJ; dir. NJ Lottery Commn., Trenton, 2003—04; CEO, sec. NJ Commerce, Econ. Growth & Tourism Commn., Trenton, NJ, 2004—. Bd. mem. The Port Authority of NY & NJ, 2007—. Bd. dirs. Family and Children's Services, Monmouth County, NJ; advocate for 9/11 victims.*

BAUER, WILLIAM JOSEPH, federal judge; b. Chgo., Sept. 15, 1926; s. William Francis and Lucille (Gleason) Bauer; m. Mary Nicol, Jan. 28, 1950; children: Patricia, Linda. AB, Elmhurst Coll., 1949, LLD, 1969; JD, DePaul U., 1952, LLD (hon.), 1993; LLD, John Marshall Law Sch., 1987; LLD (hon.), Roosevelt U., 1994. Bar: Ill. 1951. Ptnr. Erlenborn, Bauer & Hotte, Elmhurst, Ill., 1953—64; asst. state's atty. Du Page County, Ill., 1952—56; 1st asst. state's atty., 1956—58; state's atty., 1959—64; judge 18th Jud. Cir. Ct., 1964—70; US dist. atty. No. Ill. Chgo., 1970—71; judge US Dist. Ct. (no. dist.), Chgo., 1971—75, US Ct. Appeals (7th cir.), 1975—86, chief judge, 1986—93, sr. judge Chicago, 1994—. Instr. bus law. Elmhurst Coll., 1952—59; adj. prof. law DePaul U., 1978—91; former mem. Ill. Supreme Ct. Com. on Pattern Criminal Jury Instrns.; chmn. Fed. Criminal Jury Instrn. Com. 7th Cir.; mem. Am. Judicature Soc., Ill. Assn. of Cir. and Appellate Ct. Judges, Ill. States Attys. Assn., Nat. Dist. Attys. Assn. Trustee Elmhurst Coll., 1979—, DePaul U., 1984—, DuPage Meml. Hosp.; bd. advisors Mercy Hosp. With US Army, 1945—47. Mem.: FBA (former bd. dirs.), ABA, Chgo. Bar Assn., DuPage County Bar Assn. (past pres.), Ill. Bar Assn., Legal Club (Chgo.), Law Club, Union League Club. Roman Catholic. Office: US Ct Appeals 219 S Dearborn St Ste 2754 Chicago IL 60604*

BAUERLY, RONALD JOHN, marketing educator; b. Monroe, Wis., Oct. 31, 1953; s. Jack Leroy and Josephine (Wiegel) B.; m. Robin Rochelle Kramer, Aug. 8, 1981; children: Shannon Marie, Thomas Joseph. BBA, U. Iowa, 1975, MBA, 1977; DBA, Southern Ill. U., Carbondale, 1989. Asst. mgr. K-Mart Corp., Racine, Wis., 1977-78; instr. Metropolitan Tech. Community Coll., Omaha, 1978, Loras Coll., Dubuque, Iowa, 1979-81, Northwest Mo. State U., Maryville, 1981-82; asst. prof. Brescia Coll., Owensboro, Ky., 1983-86; asst. prof. mktg. Western Ill. U., Macomb, 1987-91, assoc. prof., 1991-96, prof., 1996—. Editor Jour. of Contemporary Business Issues; contbr. articles to jours. Mem. Am. Acad. Advt., Am. Mktg. Assn., Assn. for Consumer Rsch., Acad. Mktg. Sci., Mktg. Mgmt. Assn., Phi Kappa Phi, Beta Gamma Sigma. Office: Western Ill U 424 Stipes Macomb IL 61455 Office Phone: 309-298-1592. Business E-Mail: rj-bauerly@wiu.edu.

BAUER-SANDERS, KATHERINE ANN, primary school educator; b. Yankton, SD, Mar. 6, 1953; d. James M. and Jean E. (Kennedy) Bauer; m. Steven L. Sanders, July 10, 1971; children: David L., William J., James B. BS in Elem. Edn., U. S.D., 1990, MA, 1996, EdD in Curriculum and Instrn., 2003. Cert. K-12 tchr. Presch. dir. Rhymes and Rainbows Presch., North Sioux City, SD, 1981—88; houseparent St. Anthony's Boys Home, Sioux City, Iowa, 1985-89; substitute tchr. Sioux City (Iowa) Pub. Schs., 1991; kindergarten tchr. Winnebago (Nebr.) Pub. Sch., 1991—98; Title VII project dir. Little Priest Tribal Coll., Winnebago, 1998—99; tchr. St. Augustine Mission Sch., Winnebago, Nebr., 1999—. Adj. ECE faculty Little Priest Tribal Coll., Winnebago, 1996—; soccer coach Sioux City YMCA; softball coach Siouxland Youth Athletics, coach, bd. dirs., t-ball dir.; t-ball coach Youth Devel. Ctr., Winnebago, Nebr.; participant Jr. Class Learning, Auckland, New Zealand, 1995; mem. alcohol prevention program com. Winnebago Pub. Sch., 2003—; assessor trainer Nat. Bd. Profl. Tchg. Stds., 2004—; mem. exec. com. Anti-Drug, Alcohol and Bullying Coaltion, Winnebogo Tribal Project, 2005; curriculum dir. St. Augustine Mission Sch., 2004—. Author: NEA Pub., 2000. Puppeteer, Kids on the Block, Jr. League, Sioux City, 1988-92; camp dir., troop leader Boy Scouts Am., Sioux City, 1976-80; steering com. McCook Lake United Meth. Ch. Ringley Arts and Sci. scholar, U. S.D., 1984-85. Mem. NEA, Nat. Am. Edn. Assn., Nebr. Indian Edn. Assn., Internat. Reading Coun., Nat. Assn. for the Edn. of Young Children, Assn. for Childhood Edn. Internat. Avocations: coaching, writing, puppeteering, music. Home: PO Box 320 152 Suncoast Dr North Sioux City SD 57049-4016 Office: St Augustine Mission Sch PO Box GG #1 Mission Rd Winnebago NE 68071 Office Phone: 402-878-2291.

BAUERSFELD, CARL FREDERICK, lawyer; b. Balt., June 9, 1916; s. Emil George and Irene Marie (Hulse) B.; m. Ann Yancey, Mar. 3, 1944 (div.); children: Elizabeth Bauersfeld Garnett, Carl F. Student, George Washington U., 1937-42; LLB, Am. U., 1937. Bar: D.C. 1937, U.S. Dist. Ct. D.C. 1937, U.S. Ct. Appeals (D.C. cir.) 1937, U.S. Supreme Ct. 1941, U.S. Ct. Claims 1946, U.S. Tax Ct. 1946, Md. Ct. Appeals 1957, U.S. Ct. Appeals (5th cir.) 1947, (9th cir.) 1956, (3d cir.) 1958, (8th cir.) 1960, (4th cir.) 1966, (2d cir.) 1970. Practiced in, Washington, 1937—; ptnr. Bauersfeld, Burton, Hendricks & Vanderhoof, L.L.C., 1956—. Lectr. on fed. taxation at various univs. Lt. comdr. USNR, 1942-46. Mem. ABA, Md. Bar Assn., Bar Assn. D.C., Congl. Country Club, Burning Tree Club, Sigma Nu Phi, Phi Sigma Kappa. Lutheran. Office: 7101 Wisconsin Ave Bethesda MD 20814-4805 Office Phone: 301-986-8600. Business E-Mail: c.bauersfeld@bbhv.net.

BAUGH, BRADFORD HAMILTON, occupational and environmental health advisor; b. Seattle, Jan. 18, 1943; s. Sheppard McReynolds and Naomi Emma (Hugel) B.; m. Karyl Eileen Onstad, June 8, 1974; children: Taggart, Darin, Robyn, Patrick, Tracy. BS in Zoology, BS in Psychology, Wash. State U., 1972; MS in Biology, Ea. Wash. State U., 1976, BSN, 1983, MS in Devel. Psychology, 1992; PhD in Environ. Engring., Kennedy-Western U., 2002; M in Vet. Med. Sci., U. Fla., 2006—. Cert. med. lab. technician, cmty. health nurse, safety specialist. Environ. chemist, research and devel. USCG, Groton, Conn., 1975-76, occupational health advisor Alameda, Calif., 1983—; adj. prof. Whitworth Coll., Spokane, Wash., 1973-82; counselor Morning Star Ranch, Spokane, 1982-83; instr. Chapman Coll., Alameda, 1983—2005; indsl. hygienist, fire chief VA, American Lake, Wash., 1986-87; child mental health specialist Tamarack Ctr., Spokane, Wash., 1987-92; occupational and environ. health cons., Nine Mile Falls, Wash., 1987—; indsl. hygienist Wash. State U., Pullman, 1990-93; environ. protection specialist no. cluster USDA Agr. Rsch. Svc., Pullman, 1993—2005; environ. health and safety coord. Wash. State U., Spokane, 2005—. With USCGR, 1961-93. Mem. Nat. Environ. Health Assn. (registered environ. health specialist and sanitarian), Assn. Profl. Indsl. Hygeinists Mem. Lds Ch. Home: PO Box 209 Nine Mile Falls WA 99026-0209 Office: Washington State Univ 412 E Spokane Falls Blvd Spokane WA 99202 Home Phone: 509-466-5410; Office Phone: 509-468-6699, 509-368-6699. Business E-Mail: bhbaugh@wsu.edu. E-mail: conquest@sisna.com.

BAUGHAM, SAMUEL MCCOY, actor, painter; s. Samuel Glenn and Margaret (McCoy) Baugham. BFA in Drama, NC Sch. Arts, 1968; BA in Arts Mgmt., E. Carolina U., 1983; grad., Columbia Sch. Broadcasting, spl. cert. of completion in radio announcing, 1969. Cert. tchr. of theatre arts NC Dept. Public Instrn. Prin. actor Berkshire Regional Ednl. Theatre, Pittsfield, Mass., 1968, CBS T.V., NYC, 1970, Theatre Ctr. Miss., Jackson, 1971, Theatre Four, NYC, 1971; tchr. theatre arts Hertford County Schs., Ahoskie, NC, 1987—90, Warren County Schs., Warrenton, 1990—92; portrait & landscape painter Baugham Art Studio, Rich Square, 1992—. Fine arts announcer/prodr. WTEB Pub. Radio, New Bern, NC, 1985—87; asst. dir. devel. Brevard Music Ctr., 1983—85. Organist Rich Square United Meth. Ch., NC, 1987—; choir dir. Rich Square United Methodist Ch., 1987—; bd. dirs. Northampton Co. Mus., Jackson, NC, 1987—. Mem.: Actors' Equity Assn. Home and Office: 209 Bryantown Rd Rich Square NC 27869 Office Phone: 252-578-5716.

BAUGHER, PETER V., lawyer; b. Chgo., Oct. 2, 1948; s. William and Marilyn (Sill) Baugher; m. Robin Stickney, Nov. 25, 1978; children: Julia Allison, Britton William Herbert. AB, Princeton U., 1970; JD, Yale U., 1973. Bar: Ill. 1974, U.S. Dist. Ct. (no. dist.) Ill. 1974, U.S. Ct. Appeals (7th cir.) 1974, U.S. Supreme Ct. 1987. Law clk. to judge U.S. Ct. Appeals (7th cir.), Chgo., 1973-74; from assoc. to ptnr. Schiff Hardin & Waite, Chgo., 1974-85; ptnr. Adams, Fox, Adelstein & Rosen, Chgo., 1985-89, Schopf & Weiss, LLP, Chgo., 1989—. Trustee Sta. WTTW Channel 11, Chgo., 1976—81, Kendall Coll., Evanston, 1980—92, WBEZ, Chgo. Pub. Radio, 1992—98, Ill. Humanities Coun., 1997—2003; pres. Chgo. Internat. Dispute Resolution Assn., 1997—. Mem. adv. com. Rep. Nat. Conv., Detroit, 1980; bd. dirs. Protestants for the Common Good, 2001—; mem. adv. com. Northwestern U. Sch. Law Ctr. Internat. Human Rights; bd. dirs. Sabre Found.; pres. Chgo. Lincoln Inn of Ct., 1994—96. Mem.: ABA, Chgo. Coun. Global Affairs, Am. Law Inst., Chgo. Bar Assn. (chair internat. and fgn. law com., chair fed civil practice com.), Ripon Soc. (chmn. 1975—76), Am. Coun. Germany, Mich. Shores Club, Econ. Club Chgo., Univ. Club. Home: 1310 Sheridan Rd Wilmette IL 60091-1834 Office: Schopf & Weiss LLP One S Wacker Dr Chicago IL 60606 Office Phone: 312-701-9300. E-mail: baugher@sw.com.

BAUGHMAN, BRUCE PRENTISS, state agency administrator; b. Oceanside, Calif., July 22, 1948; s. Prentiss H. and Eleanor G. (Klein) B.; children: Shannon D., Heather G.; m. F. Carolyn Weaver. BA, Belhaven Coll., 1971; MS in Edn., Jackson State U., 1978. Area coord. Miss. Emergency Mgmt. Agy., Jackson, 1975-79; program specialist Fed. Emergency Mgmt. Agy. (FEMA), Atlanta, 1979-83, program officer Washington, 1983-89, chief, hazard mitigation br., 1989—92, dir. ops. & planning, 1992—2000, dir., planning & readiness divsn., Readiness, Response & Recovery Directorate, 2000—02; dir. Office Nat. Preparedness, Fed. Emergency Mgmt. Agy (FEMA) US Dept. Homeland Security, Washington, 2002—03; dir. Ala. Emergency Mgmt. Agy., Clanton, Ala., 2003—; asst. dir. Ala. Dept. Homeland Security for Emergency Preparedness & Response, Clanton, Ala., 2003—. Chmn. Interagency Hazard Mitigation Team, Washington, 1989— Mem. Montclair Property Owners Assn., Dumfries, Va., 1985—, Friends of the Kennedy Ctr., Washington, 1988—. Capt. USMC, 1971-75. Named Hon. Col., Gov. of Ala., 1978, Outstanding Young Man in Am., U.S. Jaycees, 1982, 1984; Recipient Disting. Svc. award, Fed. Emergency Mgmt. Agy. (FEMA), Spl. Achievement awards (5), Outstanding Achievement award, Nat. Disaster Med. System, Conversion Gold medal, Pres. Coun. on the Yr., 2000, Disting. Svc. award, Miss. Emergency Mgmt. Agy., Disting. Svc. award, Nat. Hurricane Conf., 2005 Mem. Assn. State Floodplain Mgrs., U.S. Jaycees, Am. Legion, Marine Corps League, Nat. Emergency Mgmt. Assn.(v.p., 2004-05, pres., 2005-06) Office: Ala Emgy Mgmt Agy 5898 County Rd 41 PO Drawer 2160 Clanton AL 35046

BAUGHMAN, JAMES CARSON, minister, sports official; b. Stanford, Ky., July 12, 1938; s. William Henry Baughman and Mary Elizabeth Carson; m. Katherine Ann Roach, Nov. 27, 1994; children: James Carson Jr., Helen Elizabeth Lewis, William Graham. BA, U. of Ky., Lexington, 1960; BD, Coll. of the Bible, Lexington, 1963; MDiv, Lexington Theological Sem., 1967, D of Ministry, 1972. Ordained min. Ravenna Christian Ch., Ky., 1963—65; sr. min. Middletown Christian Ch., Ky., 1965—88; cert. tennis official US Tennis Assn., White Plains, NY, 1966—. Nat. workshop leader Christian Ch. (Disciples of Christ), 1975—90. Author: Keeping Your Worms Warm, 1976, Behind the Pulpit, 1996, From the Pulpit, 1998. Bd. mem. Net Results, Sr. Citizen, Middletown Adv., Louisville, 1973—80; chaplain Ky. Colonels basketball team, Louisville, 1974—75. Pvt. US Army, 1960, Ft. Knox, Ky. and San Antonio, Tex. Recipient Ky. Tennis Hall of Fame, 1998. Mem.: Logan's Fort Restoration Bd. (v.p. 2002—). Disciples Of Christ. Achievements include founding pres. of Louisville area KA Alum. Assn. Avocations: tennis, bridge. Home: 985 US Highway 27 South Stanford KY 40484

BAUGHMAN, KENNETH LEE, cardiologist, educator; b. Kansas City, Mo., Oct. 8, 1946; m. Cheryl Jean Cain, Aug. 10, 1968; children: Matthew Tyler, Christopher Rolle. AB in Chemistry, U. Mo., 1968, MD, 1972; MA (hon.), Harvard U., 2003. Diplomate in internal medicine and cardiovasc. disease Am. Bd. Internal Medicine. Resident in internal medicine Johns Hopkins Hosp., Balt., 1972—75, asst. chief Osler Med. Svc., 1975—77; clin. and rsch. fellow divsn. cardiology Mass. Gen. Hosp., Boston, 1977—79; asst. prof. Johns Hopkins U. Sch. Medicine, Balt., 1979—84, assoc. prof., 1984—94, prof., 1994—2002, asst. dean postdoctoral programs and faculty devel., 1985—91; dir. cardiology divsn. Johns Hopkins Hosp., 1992—2001; sr. physician Brigham and Women's Hosp., Boston, 2002—, dir., adv. heart disease sect., 2003; prof. medicine Harvard Med Sch., Boston, 2003—. Various com. assignments Johns Hopkins Hosp., 1979—2001, bd. mem., 1985—91, chmn., joint com. house staff and postdoctoral program, 1985—91; leadership devel. for Physicians in Academic Health Ctrs. Harvard Sch. Pub. Health, 2001; lectr. in field. Author: Treatment of Advanced Heart Disease, 2006; mem. editl. bd. New Eng. Jour. Medicine, 2003—; reviewer: profl. jours.; contbr. chapters to books, articles to profl. jours. Mem.: Assn. Univ. Cardiologists, Assn. Profs. Cardiology, Am. Fedn. Clin. Rsch., Assn. Subsplty. Profs. (sec.-treas. 2001), Heart Failure Soc., Am. Clin. and Climatologic Assn., Internat. Soc. Heart Transplantation, Paul Dudley White Soc., Am. Coll. Cardiology (nat. program com. 1992—93, gov. 1994—97, bd. govs. steering com., chmn. bd. govs. working group on acad. issues 1995—97, co-chmn. Bethesda conf. 1998, editl. bd. 1999—2003), Am. Heart Assn. (fellow coun. clin. cardiology 1980—, program com. 1995—98). Office: Brigham and Women's Hosp Divsn Cardiology 75 Francis St Bldg A 3rd Fl AB 362 Boston MA 02115 Home: 83 Beethoven Ave Waban MA 02468 Office Phone: 617-732-8970. Business E-Mail: kbaughman@partners.org.

BAUGHMAN, R(OBERT) PATRICK, lawyer; b. Zanesville, Ohio, Nov. 18, 1938; s. Robert G. and Kathryn E. B.; m. Joyce Hall, June 17, 1959; 1 child, Patricia. BS, Ohio State U., 1960, JD, 1963. Bar: Ohio 1963. Assoc. firm Sindell & Sindell, Cleve., 1964-71, Jones, Day, Reavis & Pogue, Cleve., 1972-73; asst. atty. gen. State of Ohio, Columbus, 1971-72; pres., prin. firm Baughman & Assocs., Cleve., 1973—. Mem. ABA, Ohio Bar Assn., Cuyahoga County Bar Assn., Nat. Coun. Self-Insurers, Internat. Assn. Indsl. Accident Bds. and Commns., Internat. Platform Assn., Columbia Hills Country Club. Episcopalian. E-mail: rpaf38@aol.com.

BAUGHMAN, ROBERT WILLIAM, neuroscientist, director; m. Hidemi Tanaka, June 22, 1974; children: Kenneth William, Amy Wisteria. BA, New Coll., Sarasota, Fla., 1968; MA, PhD, Harvard U., Cambridge, Mass., 1975. Assoc. prof. med. sch. Harvard U., Boston, 1975—95; assoc. dir. Nat. Inst. Neurol. Disorders and Stroke, Bethesda, Md., 1995—. Mem.: Soc. Neuroscience. Office: Natl Inst Neurol Disorders & Stroke 6001 Executive Blvd Rockville MD 20892 Home Phone: 301-896-0475; Office Phone: 301-496-1779.

BAUHAN, HOBART BAKER, retired mining engineer, retired farmer; b. Princeton, NJ, Apr. 15, 1930; s. Rolf William and Elizabeth (Lathrop) Bauhan; m. Sheila Kiikpatrick, Dec. 3, 1962; children: Thomas, Elizabeth. BS in Mining Engrng., Ariz. Mines, Tuscon, 1958. Shift boss Climax Molybdenum Co., Colo., 1954—59; petroleum engr. El Paso Natural Gas Co., Farmingion, N.Mex., 1957—59; mining engr. Phelps Dodge Corp., Ajo, Ariz., 1959—62; owner Strasburg Ag-Lime Co., Va., 1962—68, Power Tech. Engrng. Co., Winchester, Va., 1968—99; ret. Contbr. articles to profl. jours. Bd. mem. Clarke County Sanitary Authority, Boyce, Va., 1976—86. 1st lt. US Army, 1954—56, Germany. Republican. Episcopalian. Avocations: sailing, hunting, painting.

BAUKNECHT, BARBARA BELLE, retired pre-school educator; b. Gleason, Wis, Apr. 21, 1933; d. William John and Jessie Marie (Fox) Beyer; m. Ross Eugene Bauknecht, Aug. 11, 1956; children: JoDee Ann Moran, Shelley Marie Courter, Wanda Jean Pace, Todd Randall. Tchr. cert., Lincoln County Normal, Merrill, Wis., 1953; BS, U. Wis., Stevens Point, 1964, M, 1974. Lic. tchr. grades 1-8, reading tchr. K-12, reading specialist K-12. Tchr. grades 5 and 6, Crandon, Wis., 1953-57; tchr. grades 7 and 8 Elcho, Wis., 1957-59; pub. libr. Three Lakes, Wis., 1963-66; tchr. Title 1, reading tchr., 1966-74; tchr., reading specialist, 1974—95; ret., 1995; tchr. caregiver classes, 2002—. Tchr., founder Story Hour - Presch. Program, Three Lakes and Sugar Camp, Wis., 1964—95; reading coord. Three Lakes Sch. Dist., Three Lakes and Sugar Camp, 1978—95; mem., chmn. read com. Three Lakes Dist., 1978—. Chmn. bd. Ed U. Demmer Meml. Libr., Three Lakes, 1989—96; local organizer, leader Campfire Girls, 1970—75; leadership coun. Alzheimers, 2000—; mem. com. Memory Walk com., 2001—, Motorcycle Rally, 2002—03, Golf Tournament, 2002, co-chair, 2004—; mem. com. Support Group Facilitator, 2002—; mem. Edith Reiter Trust Found., 2005—, Oneida Co. Long Term Support Com., 2005; co-facilitator Memory Loss Support Group; coord. Food for the Mind Program Three Lakes Food Panty, 2006; co-founder Ecumenical Vacation Bible Sch., 1978—; Sunday sch. supt. Union Congl. Ch., Three Lakes, 1977—95, moderator, 1988—93, 2001—, pres. women's fellowship, 2006. Recipient Ind. Celebrate Lit. award Headwaters Reading Coun., Rhinelander, Wis., 1990, Spl. Svc. award Alzheimer's Assn., Wis., 2004; Kohl scholarship/fellowship CESA Dist. Winner, 1992. Mem.: Delta Kappa Gamma (treas., pres. Alpha Eta chpt). Mem. Ch. of Christ. Avocations: crocheting, reading. Home: 6653 Schoenfeldt Rd Three Lakes WI 54562-9703 Office: Sch Dist Three Lakes PO Box 280 Three Lakes WI 54562-0280

BAUKNIGHT, CLARENCE BROCK, construction and retail executive, consultant; b. Anderson, SC, May 14, 1936; s. John Edward and Theodosia (Brock) B.; m. Harriet League, June 29, 1959; children: Harriet League, Clarence Brock. BS, Ga. Inst. Tech., 1958. Exec. v.p. Builder Marts Am., Inc., Greenville, SC, 1965-87, pres., chief exec. officer, 1970—88, chmn. bd. dirs., 1987—2003. Chmn. bd. dirs. Enterprise Computer Sys., Inc. Mem. policy adv. bd. Joint Ctr. Urban Studies Harvard U., 1982-87; trustee Bumcombe St. United Meth. Ch., 1985-90, chmn., 1989-90, Greenville Hosp. System, 1987-93, chmn., 1991-92; bd. dirs. Greenville Health Corp., 1994-97. Mem. Chief Exec. Orgn., Greenville Country Club, Cullasaja and Highlands, Masons, Shriners, Phi Delta Theta. Methodist. Home: 111 Rockingham Rd Greenville SC 29607

BAULCOMBE, DAVID C., virologist; BS in Botany, Leeds U., 1973; PhD, U. Edinburgh, 1977. Postdoctoral fellow McGill U., Montreal, U. Ga.; joined Sainsbury Lab. John Innes Centre, 1998, head, 1990—93, 1999—2003, head Plant Molecular Biology Dept. Recipient Prix des Cerealiers de France, 1990, Kumbo Sci. Internat. award in plant molecular biology and biotechnology, 2002, Ruth Allen award, Am. Phytopathology Soc., 2002, Wiley prize biomedical rsch., 2003. Fellow: Royal Soc. London; mem.: European Molecular Biology Orgn., NAS (fgn. assoc. 2005), Internat. Soc. Plant Molecular Biology (pres.). Office: John Innes Centre Norwich Rsch Park Colney Lane Norwich NR4 7UH England

BAUM, AXEL HELMUTH, lawyer; b. Berlin, July 14, 1930; came to U.S., 1933; s. Stefan H. and Gertrud (Goette) B.; m. Elisabeth K. Nordwall, Dec. 11, 1982; children: Nicholas S., Andreas S. BA cum laude, Amherst Coll., 1952; LL.B., Yale U., 1957. Bar: Conn. 1957, N.Y. 1958, U.S. Supreme Ct. 1976; Conseil Juridique, France, 1971; Avocat à la Cour (Paris) 1992. Assoc. Hughes, Hubbard & Reed, NYC, 1957-64; fgn. atty. Lovell, White & King, London, 1959-60; ptnr. Hughes, Hubbard & Reed, NYC, 1964—2002, ptnr.-in-charge European office Paris, 1966—2002, counsel, 2002—. Lectr., spkr. various internat. forums and seminars, France, Germany, U.S., Mid. East, 1970—; arbitrator, U.S. mem. Internat. Ct. of Arbitration of ICC, Paris, 2000-2005; CPR Panel of Disting. Internatl. Mediators. Mng. editor Yale Law Jour., 1957; contbr. articles to profl. jours. Bd. dirs. Am. Aid Soc., France, 1981, chmn. 1995—, Am. Ch. Com. France, 1991-96, World Monuments Fund France, 1989-; trustee Am. Libr. of Paris, 1999-2002. Served to lt. USNR, 1952-54. Mem. Am. Arbitration Assn., U.S. Coun. Internat. Bus., ICC Commn. Internat. Arbitration, Coll. Comml. Arbitrators, London Ct. Internat. Arbitration, German Inst. Arbitration, Swiss Arbitration Assn., French Comite Arbitrage, Internat. Arbitration Inst., Polo Club (Paris), Yacht Club de France, Swedish Cruising Club, Yale Club of N.Y.C. Avocations: sailing, tennis, swimming. Home: 8 Rue des Dames Augustines 92200 Neuilly-sur-Seine France Office: Hughes Hubbard & Reed 47 Ave Georges Mandel 75116 Paris France Office Phone: 33-1-44058000. Business E-Mail: baum@hugheshubbard.com.

BAUM, BERNARD HELMUT, sociologist, educator; b. Giessen, Germany, Apr. 18, 1926; arrived in U.S., 1933, naturalized, 1934; s. Theodor and Beatrice (Klee) Baum; m. Barbara B. Eisendrath, June 13, 1953; children: David Michael, Jonathan Klee, Victoria, Lisa Baum Kritz. PhB, U. Chgo., 1948, MA, 1953, PhD, 1959. Qualifications rating examiner, bd. adviser U.S. CSC, Chgo., 1952-54; instr. human relations, psychology Chgo. Police Officers' Coll. Edn. Program, 1955-59; dir. orgnl. analysis CNA Ins., Chgo., 1960-66; assoc. prof. mgmt. and sociology U. Ill., Chgo., 1966-69, assoc. dean Coll. Bus. Adminstrn., 1967-68, prof. mgmt. and sociology, 1969—2002, prof. mgmt. and sociology emeritus, 2002—, prof. health policy and adminstrn. Sch. Pub. Health, 1973—2002, prof. emeritus, 2002—, dir. health policy and adminstrn. Sch. Pub. Health, 1977-92. Lectr. Roosevelt U., 1955—66, U. Chgo., 1961—68, Northwestern U., 1968—70, U. Colo., 1971—76; mem. spkr.'s bur. Adult Edn. Coun. Greater Chgo., 1963—76; team leader joint evaluation mission UN devel. program WHO primary health care and health mgmt. devel. projects in South Pacific, 1985; vis. scholar Chiang Mai U., Thailand, 1988. Author: Decentralization of Authority in a Bureaucracy, 1961, As If People Mattered: Dignity in Organizations, 2005; co-author: Basics for Business, 1968; co-editor: Intervention: the Management Use of Organizational Research, 1975; contbr. articles to profl. jours. Bd. dirs. Selfhelp Home for Aged, Chgo. With AUS, 1944—46, brig. gen. Ill. Army N.G., ret. Decorated Legion of Merit, Bronze Star; recipient Bus. Adminstrn. and Social Sci. Doctoral Dissertaion award, Ford Found., 1960. Mem.: APHA, AAAS, Acad. Mgmt., Am. Acad. Polit. and Social Sci., Am. Sociol. Assn., Sigma Xi. Office: U Ill Sch Pub Health M/C 923 Chicago IL 60680 Home: Apt 3B 2610 Central St Evanston IL 60201-1354 Home Phone: 847-864-7171; Office Phone: 312-996-5760. Business E-Mail: bhbaum@uic.edu.

BAUM, BERNARD RENE, research scientist; b. Paris, Feb. 14, 1937; s. Kurt and Martha (Berl) Baum; m. Danielle Habib, May 24, 1961; 1 child, Anat. BS, MS, Hebrew U., Jerusalem, 1963, PhD, 1966. Rsch. scientist Agr. Can., Ottawa, Ont., 1966-74, sr. rsch. scientist, 1974-80, prin. rsch. scientist, 1980—, chief vascular plants sect. Biosystematics Research Inst., 1981—89. Author: Oats: Wild and Cultivated, 1977, Monograph of Tamarix, 1978, World Registry of Avena Cultivars, 1972, World Registry of Barley Cultivars, 1985, World Registry of Triticale, (on Internet), 1994; assoc. editor Can. Jour. Botany, 1986-2004, Euphytica, 1987-2007, Plant System Evolution, 1992-2000, Genetic Resources and Plant Evolution, 1992—, Kurtziana, 1999-2007, Natural History Jour. Chulalongkorn U., 2005—. Fellow Acad. Sci.-Royal Soc. Can.; mem. Can. Bot. Assn. (Lawson medal 1979), Bot. Soc. Am., Am. Soc. Plant Taxonomists, Internat. Assn. Plant Taxonomists, Classification Soc., Linnean Soc. London, Orgn. Plant Taxonomy of the Mediterranean Area Home: 15 Murray St Ste 408 Ottawa ON Canada K1N 9M5 Office: Ea Cereal & Oil Seed Rsch Ctr Agrl Food Can Rsch Br Cen Exptl Farm Ottawa ON Canada K1A 0C6 Office Phone: 613-759-1821. Business E-Mail: baumbr@agr.gc.ca. E-mail: baumbd@allstream.net.

BAUM, BRANDON, lawyer, educator; AB, U. Calif., Berkeley, 1982; UC, Hastings, 1985. Bar: Calif., U.S. Internat. Trade Commn., U.S. Ct. Appeals (5th, 9th and Fed. Cirs.). Ptnr. Cooley Godward LLP, Palo Alto, Calif., 1996—2004, Mayer Brown, LLP, Palo Alto, Calif., 2005—. Adj. prof. U. Calif. Hastings Law, San Francisco, 2001—. Pub. adv. Calif. Child Advocates, Martinez, 1985—90. Avocation: horology. Office: Mayer Brown 2 Palo Alto Square 3000 El Camino Real Palo Alto CA 94306-2112 Office Phone: 650-331-2080. Business E-Mail: baum@mayerbrown.com.

BAUM, CARL EDWARD, electrical engineer, researcher; b. Binghamton, NY, Feb. 6, 1940; s. George Theodore and Evelyn Monica (Bliven) B. BS with honors, Calif. Inst. Tech., 1962, MS, 1963, PhD, 1969; Dr.-Ing.E.h. (hon.), Otto-von-Guericke U., 2004. Commd. 2d lt. USAF, 1962, advanced through grades to capt., 1967, resigned, 1971; project officer Air Force Rsch. Lab. (formerly Phillips Lab.), Kirtland AFB, N.Mex., 1963-71, sr. scientist for electromagnetics, 1971—2005; disting. rsch. prof. dept. elect. and computer engrng. U. N.Mex., Albuquerque, 2005—. Pres. SUMMA Found.; US del. to gen. assembly Internat. Union Radio Sci., Lima, Peru, 1975, Helsinki, Finland, 78, Washington, 81, Florence, Italy, 84, Tel Aviv, 87, Prague, Czech Republic, 90, Kyoto, 93, Lille, France, 96, Toronto, Canada, 99, Maastricht, Netherlands, 2002, Delhi, India, 05; mem. Commn. B US Nat. Com., 1975—, Commn. E, 1982—, Commn. A, 1990—. Author: (with others) Transient Electromagnetic Fields, 1976, Electromagnetic Scattering, 1978, Acoustic, Electromagnetic and Elastic Wave Scattering, 1980, Fast Electrical and Optical Measurements, 1986, EMP Interaction: Principles, Techniques and Reference Data, 1986, Lightning Electromagnetics, 1990, Modern Radio Science, 1990, Recent Advances in Electromagnetic Theory, 1990, Scattering, 1992, Direct and Inverse Methods in Radar Polarimetry, 1992, (with A.P. Stone) Transient Lens Synthesis: Differential Geometry in Electromagnetic Theory, 1991; editor: (with H.N. Kritikos) Electromagnetic Symmetry, 1995, (with L. Carin and A.P. Stone) Ultra-Wideband, Short-Pulse Electromagnetics 3, 1997, Detection and Identification of Visually Obscured Targets, 1998, Scattering, 2002; contbr. articles to profl. jours. Recipient award Honeywell Corp., 1962, R & D award USAF, 1970, Harold Brown award Air Force Systems Command, 1990; Air Force Rsch. Lab. fellow, 1996; Electromagnetic pulse fellow. Fellow IEEE (Harry Diamond Meml. award 1987, Richard R. Stoddart award 1984, John Kraus Antenna award 2006, Electromagnetics Field award, 2007); mem. Electromagnetics Soc. (pres. 1983-85), Electromagnetics Acad., Sigma Xi, Tau Beta Pi. Roman Catholic. Home: 5116 Eastern Ave SE Apt D Albuquerque NM 87108-5618 Office: Univ New Mexico Dept Electrical and Computer Engineering MSC01 1100 1 Univ New Mexico Albuquerque NM 87131-0001 Personal E-mail: carl.e.baum@ieee.org.

BAUM, GORDON LEE, lawyer, non-profit organization administrator; b. St. Louis, Aug. 24, 1940; s. James Paul and Johnnie Thelma (Thompson) B.; m. Georgia Dee Thompson, Sept. 12, 1959 (div. 1977); children: Gordon Lee II, Mark Evans Sterling, Duane Russell Stuart; m. Linda Gaye Gulledge, Feb. 10, 1978; children: Laura Leigh, Renee Gabrielle. Grad., U. Mo., 1965; JD, St. Louis U., 1969. Bar: Mo. 1969, U.S. Dist. Ct. Mo. 1969. Sr. inspection clk. Chevrolet Divsn. GM Corp., St. Louis, 1961-65, work standards engr., 1965-69; field dir. mid-west Citizens Coun. Am., Jackson, Miss., 1969-84; pvt. practice civil law St. Louis, 1969—2005. CEO, Coun. Conservative Citizens, St. Louis, 1985—, Conservative Citizens Found., St. Louis, 1985—; dir. St. Louis Met. Area Citizens Coun. Assoc. editor (newspaper) Citizens Informer, 1971—; talk show host WGNU Radio, St. Louis, 1995-2005. State Coord. Wallace Presdl. Campaign, Mo., 1972, 76; del. Dem. Party State Conv., 1976. Yeoman 2d class petty officer USN, 1958-61. Mem. Mo. Bar Assn., Phi Alpha Delta, MENSA, NRA, Sons of Confederate Vets., Hist. Soc. Berks County, Pa., Ger.-Am. Heritage Soc., Am. Legion. Lutheran. Avocations: politics, history, hunting, gardening, travel. Home: 2412 Park Ave Saint Charles MO 63301 Office: Coun of Conservative Citizens PO Box 221683 Saint Louis MO 63122-8683 Office Phone: 636-940-8474. Personal E-mail: lindabaum1951@yahoo.com.

BAUM, HERBERT MERRILL, consumer products company executive; b. Chgo., Dec. 6, 1936; s. Jack William and Ruth Frances (Ginsburg) Baum; m. Diane Jean Kale, Nov. 1, 1975 (div. Sept. 1977); m. Karen Rochelle Oberman, Dec. 22, 1983. BSBA, Drake U., 1958. Account exec. Stern, Walters & Simmons, Chgo., 1962-66, Doyle, Dane & Bernbach, Chgo., 1966-69; v.p., account dir. Needham, Harper & Steers, Chgo., 1969-78; assoc. dir., dir. new products Campbell Soup Co., Camden, NJ, 1978, v.p. mktg., gen. mgr. soup div., 1978-84, exec. v.p. U.S. divsn., 1984-85; pres. Campbell USA, Camden, NJ, 1985-90, sr. v.p., 1986-89, exec. v.p., 1989-93; pres. Campbell N.Am., Camden, NJ, 1990-92, Campbell North & South Am., Camden, NJ, 1992-93; chmn., CEO Quaker State Corp., Irving, Tex., 1993-98; pres., COO Hasbro Inc., Providence, 1999-2000; chmn., CEO Dial Corp., Scottsdale, Ariz., 2000—05. Bd. dirs. Meredith Corp., Pepsi Ams. Inc., US Airways, Playtex Products Co., Inc. With US Army, 1958—59. Mem.: Am. Mktg. Assn. Home: 5223 Center St Jupiter FL 33458 Office Phone: 561-747-2321. Personal E-mail: basilhb@bellsouth.net.

BAUM, INGEBORG RUTH, librarian; b. Berlin, Sept. 20; d. Ella Koch; Oberlyceum (scholar), Kassel, Germany, 1926-33; postgrad. Georgetown U., 1963-70; m. Albert Baum, Feb. 16, 1938 (div. 1960); children: Harro Siegward, Helma Sigrun (Mrs. George Meadows). Came to U.S., 1951, naturalized, 1957. Export corr. Bitter-Polar, Germany, 1933-35, Henschel Locs, Germany, 1936; exec. sec. Fieseler Airplane Mfrs., Germany, 1936-38; interpreter, sec. UNRRA, Germany, 1946-48; payroll supr., civilian dept. U.S. Army, Wetzlar PX, Germany, 1948-51; asst. librarian Supreme Council, Ancient and Accepted Scottish Rite, Washington, 1951-70, librarian and museums curator, 1970-93, ret., 1993; appraiser rare books and documents; v.p. Merical Elec. Contractors, Inc., Forestville, Md., 1974-83. Mem. Am. Soc. Appraisers, Calligraphers Guild. Mem. Ch. Jesus Christ of Latter-day Saints. Free-lance contbr. to Pabelverlag, Rastatt, Germany, Harle, Ofcl. Publs., Inc., Soc. for Contemporary Am. Lit. in German, others. Avocations: travel, art. Office: 1733 16th St NW Washington DC 20009-3103

BAUM, JOHN, physician; b. NYC, June 2, 1927; s. Louis Israel and Lilian (Treitman) B.; m. Erna Rose Bailis, Jan. 28, 1950; children: Nina, Jane, Carl, Antonia, Theodore. BA, NYU, 1949, MD, 1954. Intern Baltimore City Hosp., 1954-55; resident in medicine Lenox Hill Hosp., NYC, 1955-56, VA Hosp., NYC, 1956-57; NIH clin. trainee N.Y.U.-Bellevue Hosp., 1957-58; NIH research fellow Rheumatism Research Unit, Taplow, Eng., 1958-59; asst. prof. medicine U. Tex. Southwestern Med. Sch., 1962-68; dir. arthritis clinic Parkland Meml. Hosp., Dallas, 1959-68, dir. med. clinics, 1965-67; co-dir. pediatric arthritis clinic Scottish Rite Hosp., Dallas, 1960-68; mem. faculty U. Rochester (N.Y.) Med. Sch., 1968—, prof. medicine pediatrics and rehab., 1972-93, prof. medicine emeritus, 1993—, chmn. rsch. subjects rev. bd., 1987-96, prof. orthopedics (rehabilitation), 1991-93, prof. pediatrics, 1997—. Vis. prof. rheumatology, hon. sr. rsch. fellow U. Birmingham, Eng., 1988-89; vis. prof. U. Kiev Med. Sch., 1995; dir. arthritis and clin. immunology unit Monroe Cmty. Hosp., 1968-93; dir. pediatric arthritis clinic Strong Meml. Hosp., 1970—; mem. drug efficacy panel NRC-NAS, 1960-65; mem. rsch. rev. bd. immunology VA, 1970-76; adv. panel U.S. Pharmacopeia, 1975—; coord. therapeutics U.S.-USSR Program Rheumatology, 1974—; mem. test com. for rheumatology Am. Bd. Internal Medicine, 1971-76; locum pediat. rheumatologist Princess Margaret Hosp. for Children, Perth, Australia, 1999-2000. Mem. editl. bd. Clin. Rheumatology (Brussels), Jour. Rheumatology (Can.), Japanese Rheumatology, 1984-93; contbr. articles to profl. jours., chpts. to books. Served with AUS, 1944-46. Recipient award of merit Rochester Acad. Medicine, 1999, Sr. Role Model award, 2000, Earl Brewer award, Am. Juvenile Arthritis Orgn., 2002; Fulbright scholar, 1958; clin. scholar rheumatology Arthritis Found., 1964-69. Mem. Am. Coll. Rheumatology (master 1993, coun. pediat. rheumatology 1975-80, 85-00), Heberden Soc., Am. Fedn. Clin. Rsch., Am. Soc. Human Genetics, Am. Assn. Immunologists, Reticuloendothelial Soc., So. Soc. Clin. Investigation, Tex. Rheumatism Assn., Brit. Soc. Rheumatology, Midlands Rheumatology Soc. (Eng.), Polish Rheumatol. Soc. (hon.), La Found. Rheum Argentina (Dr. Oswaldo Garcia Morteo int. sci. com. 1997—), Great Lakes Interurban Club, Sigma Xi. Office: Strong Meml Hosp 601 Elmwood Ave Rochester NY 14642-0002 Office Phone: 585-275-0236. Business E-Mail: john_baum@urmc.rochester.edu. *If what I have achieved is called success, it is not because it has been my goal. As a clinician, teacher and researcher, I realize that success comes mostly with the latter, but my greatest satisfaction, which must have been my "secret goal," has been with the personal contacts that come through taking care of people and sharing my knowledge with students. The lagniappe of a supportive wife and fascinating children makes achieving the goals more worthwhile.*

BAUM, JOSEPH THOMAS, lawyer; b. Amsterdam, NY, May 25, 1944; s. Joseph W. and Margaret M. (Wilt) B.; children: Jason, Daniel. BA, Siena Coll., 1966; JD, Albany Law Sch., 1972. Bar: N.Y. 1973, U.S. Dist. Ct. (no. dist.) N.Y. 1973. Instr. Alfred U., N.Y., 1973-74; assigned counsel Allegany County, Belmont, N.Y., 1973-74, law sec. Family Ct., 1974; asst. atty. gen. N.Y. State, Albany, 1974-79; clin. dir. Albany Law Sch., 1981—. Town atty. Town of Sand Lake, N.Y., 1980-82, 84, 98-2000, town councilman, 1992-96; bd. dirs. YMCA, Albany, 1984-87. Recipient Disting. Pro Bono Svc. award Legal Aid Northeastern N.Y., 1987, 98. Mem. ABA, N.Y. State Bar Assn., Rensselaer County Bar Assn., Am. Assn. Law Schs. (clin. sect.), Adirondack Mountain Club. Office: Albany Law Sch 80 New Scotland Ave Albany NY 12208-3434

BAUM, JULES LEONARD, ophthalmologist, educator; b. NYC, Mar. 13, 1931; children from previous marriage: Jeffrey Stuart, Alison Rachel; m. Laura Klabin, 1990; stepchildren: Alexander Matthew, Samantha Merrill. AB, Dartmouth Coll., 1952; MD, Tufts U., 1956. NIH fellow in rsch. in ophthalmology NYU, 1958-59, rschr. in ophthalmology, 1961-62; asst. prof. NYU Med. Sch., 1965-68; resident in ophthalmology Bellevue Hosp., NYC, 1962-64; mem. faculty Tufts U. Med. Sch., 1968—, prof. ophthalmology, 1974-91; sr. surgeon New Eng. Med. Ctr. Hosp., Boston, 1973-91; rsch. prof. Tufts U. Med. Sch., 1991—2002, prof. ophthalmology emeritus, 2002—. Assoc. editor Ophthalmic Lit., 1967-85; mem. editl. bd. Investigative Ophthalmology and Vision Sci., 1978-82, Survey of Ophthalmology, 1970-79, Am. Jour. Ophthalmology, 1985-91, Ophthalmic Surgery, 1985-95, Cornea Jour., 1989-98; contbr. articles to profl. jours. Served to capt. M.C. AUS, 1959-61. Recipient William Warner Hoppin award N.Y. Acad. Medicine; Alcon Rsch. Inst. award, 1991; NIH fellow, 1958-59, 64-65; Nat. Eye Inst. grantee. Fellow: Royal Coll. Ophthalmologists; mem.: Ocular Microbiology Immunology Group (pres. 1990—91, Thygeson lecture 2001), Mass. Ophthalmology Soc. (sec. 1974—76), Cornea Soc. (exec. sec., treas. 1979—87, v.p. 1987—89, pres. 1989—91, Castroviejo Corneal medalist 1997), Assn. Rsch. in Vision and Ophthalmology (trustee 1981—86, v.p. 1986), Am. Acad. Ophthalmology (bd. councillors 1981—83, honor award 1979, sr. honor award 1990), Confrerie des Chevaliers du Tastevin, Internat. Wine and Food Soc., Phi Beta Kappa. Jewish. Home Phone: 781-237-5558. Personal E-mail: julesbaum@verizon.net.

BAUM, KERRY ROBERT, retired military officer, director; b. LaGrande, Oreg., May 25, 1939; s. Guy Hiatt Baum and Niola (Anderson) Jones; m. Lynda Sue Christian, Dec. 18, 1964; children: Kerry Jr., Tatia D., Christian H., Buffy Jo, Patrick H., Britta Sue, Natalie A. BA in History, Brigham Young U., Provo, Utah, 1967; MBA in Mktg., Murray State U., Ky., 1978; postgrad., Webster Coll., St. Louis, 1979-80; MA in Nat. Security & Strategic Studies, U.S. Naval War Coll., 1986. Cert. bus. continuity planner Disaster Recovery Inst. Internat., recovery planner Harris Recovery Group. Commd. 2d lt. US Army, 1957, advanced through grades to col., 1990; mgr. emergency preparedness Brigham Young U., 1993—. Joint staff rep. LIVE OAK, 1986—90; U.S. rep. Maj. NATO Comdrs. Alert Com., 1987—90. Author, editor: book NATO Alert Procedures for Joint Staff, 1988, Focal Point Procedures Manual, 1989. Mem., past pres. Utah Campus Safety Assn.; apptd. mem. Utah Seismic Safety Commn., 2001, vice chair, 2006—; bishop Mormon Ch., Hopkinsville, Ky., 1974—78, councilor, bishopric Newport, RI, 1985—86; bishop Mormon Ch. BYU 185th Ward, 1996—99. Decorated Bronze Star, Army Commendation medal, Air Force Commendation medal, Def. Superior Svc. medal; named Mem. of the Yr., Utah Emergency Mgmt. Assn., 2000. Mem.: Internat. Assn. Emergency Mgrs. (cert. emergency mgr., cert. bus. continuity planner Disaster Recovery Inst.), Assn. Contingency Planners (Utah chpt. past treas.), Res. Officers Assn. Home: 10938 N 5870 W Highland UT 84003-9487 Office: Brigham Young U 200 TOMH Provo UT 84602-0100 Office Phone: 801-422-8142. Business E-Mail: kerry_baum@byu.edu.

BAUM, M(ARY) CAROLYN, occupational therapist; b. Chgo., Mar. 26, 1943; d. Gibson Henry and Nelle (Curry) Manville; 1 child, Kirstin Carol. BS, U. Kans., Lawrence, 1966; MA, Webster Coll., 1979; PhD, Washington U., St. Louis, 1993. Occupl. therapist U. Kans. Med. Ctr., 1966-67; staff occupl. therapist Rsch. Med. Ctr., Kansas City, Mo., 1967, dir. occupl. therapy, 1967-73, dir. phys. medicine and rehab., 1973-76; dir. occupl. therapy and clin. svcs. Washington U. Sch. Medicine, St. Louis, 1976—88, from assoc. prof. to prof. occupl. therapy and neurology, 1988—, dir. program on occupl. therapy, 1988—. Vis. prof. NYU, U. Mo., 1985—87; mem. adv. com. Nat. Ctr. Med. Rehab. Rsch. NIH; allied health rep. AMA Health Policy Agenda for Am. People; mem. com. on assessing rehab. sci. and engring. Inst. Medicine; bd. dirs. Rehab. Inst. St. Louis; pres. Occupl. Therapy Certification Bd., 1986—93. Author: Understanding the Prospective Payment System: A Business Perspective, 1986, Occupational Therapy: Overcoming Human Performance Deficits, 1991, Occupational Therapy: Enabling Function and Well Being, 1997, Occupational Therapy: Performance, Participation and Wellbeing, 2005, Measuring Occupational Performance: Supporting Best Practice in Occupational Therapy, 2001, Occupation-Based Practice: Fostering Performance and Participation, 2001, 2nd edit., 2005, Occupational Therapy; Performance, Participation and Well-Being; editor Jour. OTJR; Occupation, Participation and Health; contbr. articles to profl. jours. Coord. St. Louis Ind. Living Coun., 1980-81; mem. nominating com. Greater Kansas City Health Sys. Agy.; vice-chmn. Village Ch. Accessibility Task Force, 1974-76; bd. dirs. Rehab. Inst. St. Louis. Named Employee of Yr., Rsch. Hosp., 1974, Kans. Occupl. Therapist of Yr., 1975, Outstanding Alumni Sch. Allied Health U. Kans., 1999. Fellow Am. Occupl. Therapy Assn. (chmn. stds. and ethics commn. 1973-77, nat. v.p. 1978-82, pres. 1982-83, pres. 2004-07, acad. rsch. 2006, Eleanor Clarke Slagel Lectureship award 1980, award of Merit 1984); mem. Mo. Occupl. Therapy Assn. (Occupl. Therapy Clinician of Yr. 1985), Mo. Assn. Rehab. Facilities (bd. dirs.), St. Louis Med. Rehab. Soc. (pres. 1987). Office: Program Occupl Therapy Wash U Sch Medicine 4444 Forest Park Ave Saint Louis MO 63108-2212 Business E-Mail: baumc@wustl.edu.

BAUM, MICHAEL LIN, lawyer; b. Clinton, Okla., Apr. 10, 1952; s. William Eldon and Patricia (Schumacher) B.; m. Colleen Margaret Condon, Apr. 6, 1991; children: Elizabeth, Alexandra, Kevin. BA summa cum laude, UCLA, 1982, JD, 1985. Bar: Calif. 1985, D.C. 1993, U.S. Dist. Ct. (ctrl. dist.) Calif. 1986, U.S. Dist. Ct. (ea. and no. dists.) Calif. 1989, U.S. Dist. Ct. (we. dist.) Mich. 1991, U.S. Dist. Ct. (no. dist.) Ohio 1993, U.S. Dist. Ct. (no. dist.) N.Y. 1996, U.S. Ct. Appeals (9th cir.) 1990, U.S. Ct. Appeals (4th cir.) 1996, U.S. Ct. Appeals (7th cir.) 1997, U.S. Supreme Ct. 1991. Assoc. Kananack, Murgatroyd, Baum & Hedlund,and predecessors, LA, 1985-87; ptnr., shareholder Baum, Hedlund, Aristei, Goldman & Menzies, PC, LA, 1987—. Discovery and trial teams MDL 817 United Airlines 1989 aircrash at Sioux City, Iowa, Chgo.; plaintiffs' steering com. MDL 891 Northwest Airlines 1990 aircrash at Detroit Met. Airport, Ill. State Ct. procs. for USAir 427 crash, Pa., 1994, MDL 1041 USAir crash at Charlotte, NC, 1994; trial team for consolidated hemophilia-AIDS cases, New Orleans, 1999; plaintiffs' steering com. Paxil products liability litig. MDL-1574. Named So. Calif. Super Lawyer, LA Mag., 2005; recipient Safety award, Nat. Air Disaster Found., 2002. Mem. State Bar Calif., D.C. Bar, Bar Assn. D.C., Consumer Attys. Calif., Consumer Attys. L.A. Office: Baum Hedlund Aristei Goldman & Menzies PC 12100 Wilshire Blvd Ste 950 Los Angeles CA 90025-7107 Office Phone: 310-207-3233. Business E-Mail: mbaum@baumhedlundlaw.com.

BAUM, PETER ALAN, lawyer; b. Jamaica, NY, Sept. 22, 1947; s. Morris and Elsa (Sturtz) B.; m. Barbara Hartman, Nov. 29, 1969; children: Benjamin, Lisa, Alexander. BA, Colgate U., 1969; JD, Syracuse U., 1972. Bar: N.Y. 1973, U.S. Dist. Ct. (no. dist.) N.Y. 1974. House counsel William Porter Real Estate Co., Syracuse, N.Y., 1972-73; pvt. practice Syracuse, 1973-82; ptnr. DiStefano and Baum, Syracuse, 1983-85, Baum and Woodard, Syracuse, 1985-90; prin. Peter A. Baum Law Offices, Chittenango, N.Y., 1990-96; ptnr. Iaconis, Iaconis and Baum, Chittenango, 1997—. Lectr. Onondaga C.C., Syracuse, 1976-79. Chmn. bd. dirs. Syracuse Area Landmark Theater, 1982-83; bd. dirs. Syracuse Opera Co., 1979-85. Mem. N.Y. State Bar Assn. (ho. of dels. 1992-93), Madison County Bar Assn. (pres. 1993), Onondaga County Bar Assn. (continuing edn. chmn. 1977-78), Onondaga Title Assn. Home: 8231 Verbeck Dr Manlius NY 13104-9811 Office: Iaconis Iaconis Baum PO Box 250 Chittenango NY 13037-0250 Home Phone: 315-682-8876; Office Phone: 315-687-7215.

BAUM, RICHARD DAVID, urologist; b. Passaic, NJ, Nov. 30, 1955; s. Samuel and Ethel Baum; m. Ellen Stephanie Dweck, July 11, 1993; children: Lauren, Harrison. BA, Dartmouth Coll., Hanover, NH, 1977; MD, Tulane Med. Sch., New Orleans, 1981. Lic. urology Am. Bd. Urology. Assoc. ptnr. dept. urology The Valley Hosp., Ridgewood, NJ, 1996—2004; vice pres., ptnr. Urology Group P.A., Midland Park, NJ, 1987—. Avocation: weightlifting. Office: Urology Group PA 4 Godwin Ave Midland Park NJ 07432

BAUM, ROGER S., writer; b. LA, Mar. 21, 1938; s. Joslyn S. and Elizabeth Baum; m. Charlene S. Baum. Author: Lion of Oz and The Badge of Courage, 1997, Dorothy of Oz, 1990, Green Star of Oz, 2001, (short stories) SillyOZbul Trilogy, 1991—93, Rewolf of Oz, 1998, Toto in Candy Land of Oz, 2002, Wizard of Oz and The Magic Merry Go Round, 2003, ToTo of Oz and the Surprise Party, 2004, The Oz Odyssey, 2005, (novella) Longears and Tailspins Adventure, 1962, (musical) Lion of Oz, 2001. Schools/hospitals. Po 3 U.S. Navy, 1958—61. Achievements include Animated Musical - Lion of Oz/ Sony Wonder; Legends of Oz / CD Rom. Business E-Mail: roger_baum@tototooinc.com.

BAUM, STANLEY, radiologist, educator; b. NYC, Dec. 26, 1929; s. Herman and Fannie (Harris) B.; m. Jeanne Masch, June 29, 1958; children: Richard Arthur, Laura Dianne, Carol Lisa. BA, NYU, 1951; MD, U. Utrecht, Holland, 1957. Intern Kings County Hosp., NYC, 1957-58; resident in radiology Grad. Hosp., U. Pa., Phila., 1958-61; trainee Nat. Cancer Inst., Bethesda, Md., 1958-61; fellow cardiovascular radiology Stanford (Calif.) U., 1961-62; instr. radiology U. Pa., Phila., 1962-63, asst. prof., 1963-66, assoc. prof., 1966-70, prof., 1970—, Eugene P. Pendergrass prof. radiology, 1977-96, chmn. dept. radiology, 1975-96; chmn. med. bd. Hosp. of U. Pa., 1983-86; chief cardiovascular radiology Mass. Gen. Hosp., Boston, 1971-75; prof. radiology Harvard Med. Sch., Boston, 1971-75. Cons. Radiation Effects Research Found., Hiroshima, Japan, 1975-76; mem. cardiovasc. rev. bd. Am. Heart Assn., 1970-90. Editorial bd.: Investigative Radiology, 1970-80, New Eng. Jour. Medicine, 1975-76, Radiology, 1975-85, Gastrointestinal Radiology, 1975-79, Jour. Continuing Edn., 1978-80, Postgrad. Radiology, 1980-90; editor-in-chief: Acad. Radiology, 2000—. Fellow Am. Coll. Radiology, Am. Coll. Cardiology; mem. Inst. Medicine Nat. Acad. Sci., Soc. Cardiovascular Radiology (pres. 1974-76), Soc. Chmn. Acad. Radiology Depts. (pres. elect 1985-86, pres. 1986), Acad. Radiol. Rsch. (pres. 1997-2000, editor-in-chief Acad. Radiology 2000—). Home: 401 W Moreland Ave Philadelphia PA 19118-4207 Office: U Pa 3400 Spruce St Philadelphia PA 19104-4206 Home Phone: 215-242-2367; Office Phone: 215-662-2028. Business E-Mail: baum@oasis.rad.upenn.edu.

BAUM, STANLEY DAVID, lawyer; b. Bklyn., Feb. 22, 1954; s. Irwin and Muriel A. (Margolis) B.; m. Ilyne Rhona Fried, June 9, 1979; children: Andrew, Miranda. BS, U. Pa., Phila., 1976, JD, 1980; LLM, NYU, 1984. Bar: NY 1981, US Tax Ct. 1993. Lawyer Carter, Ledyard & Milburn, NYC, 1988-98; of counsel Swidler, Berlin, Shereff, Friedman, LLP, NYC, 1998—2004; counsel Dechert LLP, NYC, 2005—. Contbr. articles to profl. jours. Mem. Nassau County Bar Assn. (com. on labor, employment and taxation). Office Phone: 212-698-3838. Business E-Mail: stanley.baum@dechert.com.

BAUM, STANLEY M., lawyer; b. Bronx, NY, Mar. 6, 1944; s. Abraham S. and Mae (Weiner) B.; m. Louise Rae Iteld, Aug. 30, 1970; children: Rachel Jennifer, Lauren Amy. BS in Commerce, Rider Coll., 1966; JD summa cum laude, John Marshall Law Sch., 1969. Bar: Ga. 1970, US Dist. Ct. (no. dist.) Ga. 1970, US Supreme Ct. 1973, US Ct. Appeals (11th cir.) 1981, US Tax Ct. 1983. Law clk. to US atty. No. Dist. Ga., 1969; legal aide Ga. Gen. Assembly, 1970-71; asst. US atty. No. Dist. Ga., 1971-74; ptnr. Bates & Baum, 1974—. Pres. Congregation Shearith Israel, 1976-78; chmn. Rep. Party of DeKalb County, 1983-85, 4th Dist. Rep. Party, 1985-89; pres. Resurgens, Atlanta, 1987-88, Electoral Coll., 1988; del. Rep. Nat. Conv., 1992; mem. DeKalb County Bd. Ethics, 1991—, chair, 1993-95, 2001; mem. Met. Atlanta Rapid Transit Authority Bd. Ethics, 1993—. Mem. ABA (criminal justice sect. white collar com.), Ga. Bar Assn., Atlanta Bar Assn. (chmn. criminal law sect. 1985-86, bd. dirs. 1986-87), Fed. Bar Assn. (pres. Atlanta chpt. 1976-77, nat. council 1974-77), DeKalb Bar Assn. (pres. 1989-90), Am. Judicature Soc., Atlanta Lawyers Club, Masons. Office: 3151 Maple Dr NE Atlanta GA 30305-2503 Office Phone: 404-262-6272. Personal E-mail: stanbaum1@aol.com.

BAUM, WILLIAM ALVIN, astronomer, educator; b. Toledo, Jan. 18, 1924; s. Earle Fayette and Mable (Teachout) B.; m. Ester Bru, June 27, 1961. BA summa cum laude, U. Rochester, 1943; PhD magna cum laude, Calif. Inst. Tech., 1950. Physicist U.S. Naval Rsch. Lab., Washington, 1946-49; astronomer Mt. Wilson and Palomar observatories, Pasadena, Calif., 1950-65; dir. Planetary Rsch. Ctr., Lowell Obs., Flagstaff, Ariz., 1965-90; rsch. prof. astronomy dept. U. Wash., Seattle, 1990—97, rsch. prof. emeritus, 1998—. Adj. prof. astronomy Ohio State U., 1969-91; adj. prof. physics No. Ariz. U., 1973-91; rsch. prof. astronomy U. Wash., Seattle, 1990-97, prof. emeritus, 1998—; cons. physics, astronomy, optics; cons. U.S. Army Research Office, Durham, N.C., 1967-74; vis. prof. Am. Astronom. Soc., 1961-98; adv. com. Nat. Acad. Sci., 19 58-67; mem. optical instrumentation panel adv. Air Force, 1967-76; coms. and panels NSF and NASA Office Space Scis., 1967-91; mem. NASA Viking Orbiter Imaging Team, 1970-79, Hubble Space Telescope Camera Team, 1977-96. *In 1946, Baum was a member of the team that made the very first successful astrophysical observation above the earth's atmosphere by installing an ultraviolet spectrograph in a German V2 rocket. Later, he designed and used a photoelectric "Photon counter" at Palomar Observatory to extend reliable photometry of stars and galaxies about 4 magnitudes fainter than previously possible. Over the years, Baum's publications have dealt with topics ranging from planetary science to cosmology. In the 1990s, he used the Hubble Space Telescope to investigate globular star clusters, the cosmic distance scale, and the age of the universe.* Contbr. articles to tech. publs. Served to lt., jr. grade USNR, 1943-46. Guggenheim fellow, 1960-61; Asteroid 4175 named Billbaum, 1990. Mem. Am. Astron. Soc. (chmn. div. planetary scis. 1976-77), Royal Astron. Soc., Astron. Soc. Pacific, Internat. Astron. Union, Phi Beta Kappa, Sigma Xi, Theta Delta Chi. Achievements include asteroid 4175 named "Billbaum" in his honor, 1990. Home: 2124 NE Park Rd Seattle WA 98105-2422 Office: U Wash Dept Astronomy Seattle WA 98195-1580 Business E-Mail: baum@astro.washington.edu.

BAUMAN, DALE ELTON, nutritional biochemistry professor; b. Detroit, Dec. 26, 1942; s. Elton Blaine and Waneta Mary (Taylor) B.; m. L. Marie Vinande, Aug. 28, 1965; children: Rebecca, Todd, Jeffrey. BS, Mich. State U., 1964, MS, 1968; PhD, U. Ill., Urbana, 1969; D of Agr. (hon.), Mich. State U., 2005. Asst. prof., assoc. prof. U. Ill.-Urbana, 1969-78; vis. prof. Mich. State U., East Lansing, 1978; assoc. prof., then prof. Cornell U., Ithaca, NY, 1979—, Liberty Hyde Bailey prof., 1987. Chmn. NAS/NRC Bd. Agr., 1990-97. Contbr. articles to profl. jours. Recipient N.Y. Farmers award, 1982, Alexander von Humboldt award, 1985, USDA Superior Svc. award, 1986, U. Ill. Alumni award, 1995, Cornell Alumni Faculty award, 2000, Disting. Scientist, U.S. Libr. of Congress, 2001, Outstanding Alumni award Mich. State U., 2003, Disting. Alumni award, 2004. Mem. NAS, Am. Dairy Sci. Assn. (Nat. Student award 1967, Nutrition Rsch. award 1982, Biotech. award 1987, Physiology Rsch. award 1994), Am. Soc. Animal Sci. (Young Scientist award 1977, Growth Biology award 1996, Fellow Rsch. award 1999, Morrison award 2004), Am. Soc. Nutritional Sci. (pres-elect 2002, pres. 2003, past pres. 2004), Coun. Agr. Sci. Tech. (Black award 1995), Fed. Animal Sci. Soc. (New Frontiers award 2004). Methodist. Home: 2 Eagleshead Rd Ithaca NY 14850-9659 Office: Cornell U 262 Morrison Hall Ithaca NY 14853-4801 Office Phone: 607-255-2262. Business E-Mail: deb6@cornell.edu.

BAUMAN, FREDERICK CARL, lawyer; b. Harrisburg, Pa., July 31, 1952; s. Carl Frederick Jr. and June Edna (Roeder) B.; married; 4 children. BA, U. Del., 1974; JD, Harvard U., 1977. Bar: N.Y. 1978, Pa. 1985, Tex. 1988, N.J. 1989, Ariz. 1996, Calif. 2000, Nev. 2003. Assoc. Davis Polk & Wardwell, NYC, 1977-81, Hawkins Delafield & Wood, NYC, 1981-83; atty. Bell Atlantic Corp., Phila., 1983-86; v.p., counsel Bell Atlantic Compushop, Dallas, 1986-88; v.p., spl. counsel Bell Atlantic Capital Corp., Paramus, N.J., 1988; v.p., counsel, sec. Bell Atlantic TriCon Leasing Corp., Paramus, 1989, sr. v.p., gen. counsel, sec., 1990-94, TriCon Capital Corp., Paramus, 1993-94; v.p., assoc. gen. counsel FINOVA Capital Corp. (f/k/a Greyhound Fin. Corp.), Phoenix, 1994—2000; ptnr. Brown & Bain, Phoenix, 2000—03; v.p., gen. counsel Sunterra Corp., Las Vegas, 2003—. Mgr., controlling shareholder McIntyre & Bauman Group, 1998—, Mid. Verde Devel. Co., 1998—, Searchlight Exploration, 1998—, Anaconda Exploration, LLC, 2006—, Am. Molygold, 2007—; chmn. Searchlight West Inc., 1998—. Vice chmn. U.S. Olympic Com., Ariz., 1998—2000. C. Rodney Sharp scholar, 1970, Harvard Club of Del. scholar, 1976. Mem. ABA, Assn. Corp. Counsel (Ariz. chpt. bd. dirs.), Tex. Bar Assn., Ariz. Bar Assn., Calif. Bar Assn., Nev. Bar Assn., Phi Beta Kappa. Republican. Presbyterian. Avocations: piano, classical music. Office Phone: 702-304-7057, 702-804-8600. Personal E-mail: frederickcbauman@aol.com. Business E-Mail: fbauman@sunterra.com.

BAUMAN, JOHN DUANE, lawyer; b. Kaskaskia, Ill., Aug. 22, 1930; s. Louis Wells and Veronica Genevieve (Schmerbauch) B.; m. Avis Crysella Moore, Sept. 15, 1956; children: Mark Duane, Thomas Jon, Jeffery Paul. BA, SE Mo. U., 1952; JD, Washington U., St. Louis, 1957. Bar: Mo. 1957, Ill. 1957. Assoc. Baker, Kagy & Wagner, East Saint Louis, Ill., 1957-62; ptnr. Wagner, Bertrand, Bauman & Schmieder, Belleville, Ill., 1962-86, Hinshaw & Culbertson, Chgo. and Belleville, 1986—. Gen. counsel Okaw Valley coun. Boy Scouts Am., 1980—90; adv. bd. Ill. Dept. Agr., 1999—. With US Army, 1952—54. Mem. ABA, Ill. Bar Assn., Internat. Assn. Ins. Counsel (state membership chmn.), Assn. of Def. Trial Counsel (pres. 1975-76), St. Clair County Bar Assn. (pres. 1972-73), Horsemen's Benevolent and Protective Assn. (v.p. 1989-98), Ill. Thoroughbred Breeders and Owners Found. (bd. dirs. 1999-2002, v.p. 1996-99, sec.-treas. 1999-2000, pres. 2000-07), Bradenton Country Club, St. Clair Country Club (pres. 1982-84), Paducah Country Club, Elks, Mo. Athletic Club (emeritus 1998). Roman Catholic. Avocations: horse racing, golf. Office: Hinshaw & Culbertson PO Box 509 521 W Main St Belleville IL 62220-1533 Office Phone: 618-277-2400. Personal E-mail: jb222555@aol.com.

BAUMAN, JOHN E., JR., chemistry professor; b. Kalamazoo, Jan. 18, 1933; s. John E. and Teresa A. (Wauchek) B.; m. Barbara Curry, June 6, 1964; children— John, Catherine, Amy BS, U. Mich., 1955, MS, 1960, PhD, 1962. Chemist Midwest Research Inst., Kansas City, Mo., 1955-58; research assoc. U. Mich., Ann Arbor, 1958-61; prof. chemistry U. Mo., Columbia, 1961-97, prof. emeritus, 1997—. Active Mo. Symphony Soc. Recipient Faculty Alumni award, 1969, Amoco Teaching award, 1975, Purple Chalk award, 1980, all U. Mo. Mem. Am. Chem. Soc. (nat. lectr.), Mo. Acad. Sci., U. Mo. Retirees Assn. (pres. 2000—), Kiwanis, Sigma Xi, Alpha Chi Sigma. Roman Catholic. Home: 3703 S Woods Edge Rd Columbia MO 65203-6607 Office: Univ Mo 125 Chemistry Building Columbia MO 65211-7600 Personal E-mail: jbauman@centurytel.net. Business E-Mail: baumanj@missouri.edu.

BAUMAN, JON WARD, retired music educator; b. Big Rapids, Mich., June 7, 1939; s. Alvin Henry and Hilda (Nordberg) Bauman; m. Carole Diane Folk, June 21, 1980. MusB, U. Colo., 1961; MusM, U. Ill., 1963, Doctor in Musical Arts, 1972. Instr. Chgo. (Ill.) Pub. Schs., 1969—70; prof. music Frostburg (Md.) State U., 1970—2003; prof. compositon Conservatorio Statale di Musica, Adria, Italy, 2002, 2004, 2005; conductor Western Md. Symphony, Penn. Alps Chamber Orch., Potomac Highlands Symphony. Bd. dirs. Young Audiences of Md., Balt., 1998. Composer (arranger): over 100 compositions and arrangements; six CDs produced. Founder Music at Penn. Alps, Grantsville, Md. Named Outstanding Mentor, Frostburg State U., 1992; Fulbright scholar, U.S. Gov., 1965. Mem.: ASCAP, Am. Composers Forum, Rotary Club Frostburg (Paul Harris fellow 1999). Democrat. Roman Catholic. Avocation: fishing. Home: One Caroles Ln Frostburg MD 21532

BAUMAN, JONATHAN HUGH, psychiatrist; b. Bklyn., June 28, 1948; s. Morris and Rachel Bauman; m. Carol Ann Weiss, Dec. 22, 1973; children: Emily, Jacob. BA, U. Rochester, NY, 1970; MD, Georgetown U., Washington, DC, 1974. Diplomate Am. Bd. Psychiatry and Neurology, Am. Bd. Adolescent Psychiatry, Am. Bd. Med. Examiners. Resident U. Va. Hosp., Charlottesville, 1974-75, Georgetown U. Hosp., Washington, 1975-77; acting clin. dir. Upper Montgomery Cmty. Mental Health Ctr., Olney, Md., 1977-79, cons. psychiatrist, 1977-84; clin. asst. prof. Georgetown U. Sch. of Medicine, Washington, 1977-84; med. staff Montgomery Gen. Hosp., Olney, 1977-84; staff psychiatrist Four Winds Hosp., Katonah, NY, 1984-85, program dir., 1985-92, med. dir., 1992—; asst. prof. Albert Einstein Coll. Medicine, NYC, 1997—. Fellow Am. Psychiat. Assn. Jewish. Avocations: bicycling, skiing, hiking, photography. Office: Four Winds Hosp 800 Cross River Rd Katonah NY 10536-3549 Office Phone: 914-763-8151. Business E-Mail: jbauman@fourwindshospital.com.

BAUMAN, SUSAN JOAN MAYER, mayor, lawyer, commissioner; b. NYC, Mar. 2, 1945; d. Curt H. J. and Carola (Rosenau) Mayer; m. Ellis A. Bauman, Dec. 29, 1968. BS, U. Wis., 1965, JD, MS, 1981; MS, U. Chgo., 1966. Bar: Wis. 1981, U.S. Dist. Ct. (we. dist.) Wis. 1981, U.S. Ct. Appeals (7th cir.) 1983, U.S. Dist. Ct. (ea. dist.) Wis. 1985. Tchr. Madison (Wis.) Pub. Sch., 1970-78; research asst. U. Wis. Law Sch., Madison, 1981; ptnr. Thomas, Parsons, Schaefer & Bauman, Madison, 1981-84; sole practice Madison, 1984-85; ptnr. Bauman & Massing, Madison, 1985-87; pvt. practice, Madison, 1987-97; mayor City of Madison, 1997—2003; mem. Wis. Employment Rels. Commn., 2003—. Alderman Madison Common Coun., 1985-97, coun. pres., 1989-90; commr. equal opportunities com. City of Madison, 1985-89; mem. Econ. Devel. Commn., 1986-87, chmn. human resources com., 1987-90, mem. affirmative action com., 1988-93; mem. Cmty. Action Commn., 1988-97, pres., 1991-96; mem. Pub. Health Commn., 1991-97, Monona Terr. Conv. and Cmty. Ctr. Bd., 1993-97; pres. South Madison Health and Family Ctr., Inc., 1993-97; bd. visitors U. Wis. Coll. Letters and Scis., Madison, 1997—2003; mem. exec. com. Wis. Alliance Cities, 1996-2003; mem. adv. bd. U.S. Conf. Mayors, 1999—2003; dir. Safe Cmtys. Coalition Madison County. Mem. Wis. Bar Assn., Dane County Bar Assn., Wis. Indsl. Rels. Alumni Assn. (pres. 1985-86), Madison Civics Club. Democrat. Avocations: knitting, reading, backpacking, cross country skiing. Home: 125 N Hamilton St 407 Madison WI 53703 Office: Wis Employment Rels Commn 18 S Thornton Ave Madison WI 53707-7870 Office Phone: 608-266-3297. Personal E-mail: sjmbauman@aol.com.

BAUMAN, WILLIAM ALLEN, pediatrician, educator, health systems consultant; b. NYC, Nov. 23, 1923; s. Louis and Stella (Kraus) B.; m. Joan Carlsen, June 28, 1952; children: William Carlsen, Phillip Allen, Pamela Joan. Student, Harvard U., 1942-43, 46; MD, Columbia U., 1947; postgrad. in biostats., Sch. Pub. Health, 1960-63. Intern L.I. divsn. Kings County Hosp., Bklyn., 1947-48; resident The Babies Hosp., NYC, 1948-50, practice medicine specializing in pediatrics, 1953-75; chief pediatric clinic Vanderbilt Clinic, NYC, 1954-65; dir. med. data processing Presbyn. Hosp., NYC, 1966-74, assoc. attending pediatrician, 1973-93, emeritus staff, 1994—. V.p. med. adminstrv. svcs. Group Health Inc., N.Y.C., 1974-77; chmn. bd. govs. Hillcrest Gen. Hosp.-Group Health Inc., 1975-79, attending pediatrician, 1975-79; sr. v.p. Health Svcs. Group Health Inc., 1977-79; v.p. med. affairs Danbury Hosp., Conn., 1979-90; mem. faculty dept. pediatrics Columbia U., 1952-73, assoc. clin. prof. pediatrics, 1973—; mem. med. bd. Maternity Ctr. Assn., 1969-95; chmn. faculty-student adv. bd. P&S Club, Coll. Physicians and Surgeons, Columbia U., 1970-90; chmn. com. on data processing N.Y. County Health Rev. Orgn., 1976-79; mem. exec. com. Babies Hosp. Alumni Assn., 1998—. Contbr. articles to profl. jours. Mem. data protection rev. bd. N.Y. State Dept. Health, 1993—. With M.C. USAF, 1951-52. Fellow Am. Coll. Med. Informatics, N.Y. Acad. Medicine; mem. Am. Acad. Pediatrics, N.Y. County Med. Soc., AMA, Med. Soc. State N.Y. (chmn. com. info. tech. in medicine 1967-93), Assn. Ambulatory Pediatrics, Assn. Computing Machinery, Soc. Computer Medicine (bd. dirs.), Bioengring. Inst., Am. Soc. Info. Scis., N.Y. Acad. Scis., N.Y. State Assn. Professions, Am. Assn. Med. Systems and Infomatics (pres. 1983). Home and Office: 887 Heritage Hls Somers NY 10589-4053 Office Phone: 914-806-3071. Personal E-mail: drgmd@aol.com.

BAUMANN, CAROL EDLER, retired political scientist; b. Plymouth, Wis., Aug. 11, 1932; d. Clarence Henry and Beulah Hanetta (Weinhold) E.; m. Richard Joseph Baumann, Feb. 28, 1959; children: Dawn Carol, Wendy Katherine. BA in Internat. Rels., U. Wis., Madison, 1954; PhD in Internat. Rels., London Sch. Econs./Polit. Sci., 1957. Chmn. internat. rels. major U. Wis., Milw., 1962-79; dep. asst. sec. Bur. of Intelligence and Rsch./Dept. of State, Washington, 1979-81; prof. U. Wis., Milw., 1972-95, dir. internat. studies and programs, 1982-88, prof. emeritus, 1995—; dir. Inst. of World Affairs, Milw., 1964-97, dir. emeritus, 1997—. Internat. edn. adv. coun. U. Wis. Milw., 2000—. Author: Program Planning About World Affairs, 1991, The Diplomatic Kidnappings, 1973; editor: Europe in NATO: Deterrence, Defense, and Arms Control, 1987, Western Europe: What Path to Integration?, 1967. Mem. Gov.'s Commn. on the UN, 1964-79, 82-89, 2004—; Dem. candidate 9th Congl. Dist., 1968; mem. World Affairs Coun. of Milw., 1964-75; bd. dirs. Wis. World Trade Ctr., 1987-2001, Wis. Dist. Export Coun., 1987-2003, Ea. Shores Libr. Sys., 1999—, Inst. World Affairs, U. Wis., Milw., 2000—. Recipient Pub. Svc. Achievement award Common Cause, Wis., 1991, World Citizen of Yr. award Internat. Inst. Wis, 2004; Marshall scholar, 1954-57. Mem. Fgn. Policy Assn. (bd. dirs. 1990—, editl. adv. com. 1977-79, 82-88), Nat. Coun. World Affairs Orgns. (pres. 1977-79, bd. dirs. 1992-96), UN Assn. of USA (bd. dirs. 1977-79, 82-89), Soc. for Citizen Edn. in world Affairs (pres. 1977-79), Phi Kappa Phi, Phi Beta Kappa. Democrat. Lutheran. Avocations: walking, swimming, reading, travel, creative writing. Home: W6248 Lake Ellen Dr Cascade WI 53011-1322 Personal E-mail: rbaumann4@wi.rr.com.

BAUMANN, DANIEL E., publishing executive; b. Milw., Apr. 10, 1937; s. Herbert F. and Agnes V. (Byrne) B.; m. Karen R. Weinkauf, Apr, 29, 1961; children: James W., Jennifer R., Colin D. BJ, U. Wis., 1958, MA in Polit. Sci., 1962, Cert. in Russian Area Studies, 1962. Reporter South Milwaukee (Wis.) Voice Jour., 1958-59, East St. Louis (Ill.) Jour., 1959-60; pub. rels. rep. Credit Union Nat. Assn., Washington, 1962-64; reporter Paddock Publs., Inc., Arlington Heights, Ill., 1964-66, mng. editor, 1966-68, exec. editor, 1968-70, editor and pub. Paddock Circle newspapers, 1970-75, v.p., editor, 1975-83, sr. v.p., gen. mgr., editor, 1983-86, pres., editor, 1986-90, dir., 1986—, pres., COO, 1990—2002, chmn., pub., 2002—. Recipient William Alan White award U. Kans., 1976. Avocation: travel. Office: Paddock Publs Daily Herald 155 E Algonquin Rd Arlington Heights IL 60005-4617

BAUMANN, EDWARD ROBERT, environmental engineering educator; b. Rochester, NY, May 12, 1921; s. John Carl and Lillie Minnie (Roth) B.; m. Mary A. Massey, June 15, 1946; children: Betsy Louise, Philip Robert. BSCE, U. Mich., 1944; BS in San. Engring, U. Ill., 1945, MS, 1947, PhD, 1954; NSF faculty fellow, U. Durham, Eng., 1959-60. Research assoc. U. Ill., 1947-53; assoc. prof. civil engring. Iowa State U., 1953-56, prof., 1956-91, Anson Marston Disting. prof. engring., 1972-91, emeritus Disting. prof., 1991—. Cons. Water Quality Office of EPA, Culligan Internat., Lakeside Engring. Co., Bolton & Menk, many cities and industries. Author: Sewerage and Sewage Treatment, 1958; mem. editorial bd.: Internat. Jour. Air and Water Pollution, London, 1960-67; asst. editor: San. Engr. Newsletter of ASCE, 1962-74; contbr. articles to profl. jours. V.p., treas. Water Found., Inc., 1978-83; mem. Iowa Bd. Health, 1975-76, Iowa State U. Rsch. Found., 1975-78, 83-91. With C.E., AUS, 1944-46. Recipient George B. Gascoigne medal Water Pollution Control Fedn., 1962, 80, Publs. award, 1963, Purification divsn. award Am. Water Works Assn., 1965, Anson Marston medal Iowa Engring. Soc., 1966, Disting. Svc. award, 1968, Gold medal Filtration Soc. Eng., 1970, Bedell award, 1977, Rsch. award, 1978, Philip F. Morgan award Water Pollution Control Fedn., 1986; named Water Works Man of Yr., 1972, Disting. Alumni award U. Ill. Alumni Assn., 1992. Fellow ASCE (life), Iowa Acad. Scis. (disting. sci. 1990), Am. Filtration Separations Soc. (F.M. Tiller award 1994); mem. NSPE (nat. bd. dirs.), AAUP, Am. Water Works Assn. (hon., life, internat. bd. dirs. 1978-80), Assn. Environ. Engring. Profs. (pres. 1967-70, 86-87, Nalco award, Founders award 1991), Am. Soc. Engring. Edn., Am. Inst. Chem. Engrs., Am. Acad. Environ. Engring. (diplomate), Filtration Soc. (Eng., bd. dirs., tech. editor, vice chmn. 1993, chmn. 1994, Fluid/Particle Separation Jour.), Rotary, Sigma Xi, Phi Kappa Phi (Centennial medal 1997), Chi Epsilon. Home: 1627 Crestwood Cir Ames IA 50010-5520 Office Phone: 515-233-6100. Business E-mail: rbaumann13@mchsi.com. E-mail: robertba@bolton-menk.com. *It isn't enough to build a "big pie"; we must also protect its quality and learn how to cut it fairly.*

BAUMANN, HANS D., engineering executive; PhD, Columbia Pacific U. Registered profl. engr. Internat. cons., corp. v.p. Masoneilan Internat. Inc.; mgr. R&D Worthington S/A; dir. engring. CASHCO Inc.; chief engr. W & T Co.; founder H. D. Baumann Assoc. Ltd.; sr. v.p. Fisher Controls Internat., St. Louis. Bd. dirs. E&J Cating Inc., H.D. Baumann Inc. Author 4 books; co-author 5 books; contbr. numerous articles to profl. jours.; patentee 140 patents in field. Bd. govs. Palm Beach Opera Co. Fellow ASME, ISA (life); mem. Abenaqui Country Club, Govs. Club (Palm Beach). Office: HD Baumann Inc 130 International Dr Portsmouth NH 03801-6809

BAUMANN, JULIAN HENRY, JR., lawyer; b. Ft. Leavenworth, Kans., Feb. 20, 1943; s. Julian Henry and Helene (Claiborne) B.; m. Karen Ann Hofmann, July 14, 1973; children: Andrew H., Allison C. BS, Clemson U., 1965; postgrad., U. Tenn., 1966; JD, U. S.C., 1968; LLM in Taxation, NYU, 1975. Bar: S.C. 1968, Del. 1976. Assoc. Richards, Layton & Finger, Wilmington, Del., 1975-80, dir., 1980—. Served to capt., JAGC, U.S. Army, 1969-74. Fellow Am. Coll. Tax Counsel; mem. ABA, S.C. Bar Assn., Del. State Bar (chmn., sec. taxation 1990-91), Wilmington Tax Group (chmn. 1988-89), The Com. of 100 (pres. 1994-96), Bd. of Mgrs., The Nemours Found., Wilmington Club. Democrat. Roman Catholic. Home: 8 Brendle Ln Wilmington DE 19807-1300 Office: Richards Layton & Finger One Rodney Sq 10th & King Sts Wilmington DE 19801 Office Phone: 302-651-7774. Business E-Mail: baumann@rlf.com.

BAUMANN, KARSTEN, engineer, researcher; D of Engring., U. Stuttgart, Germany, 1992. Sr. rsch. engr. Ga. Tech., Atlanta, 1998—2005, RTI Internat., Research Triangle Park, NC, 2005—07; sr. scientist Atmospheric Rsch. and Analysis, Cary, NC, 2007—. Air quality mgmt. expert RTI Internat., 2005—07; dir. analytical lab. Ga. Tech., 1998—2005; cons. in field. Contbr. articles to profl. jours. Fellow, Noaa-cires, Ncar, 1993, 1996. Mem.: AAAS, Environ. Def., Nat. Resources Def. Coun., Am. Assn. Aerosol Rsch., Am. Geophysical Union. Office: ARA Inc 113 Bigbee Trail Morrisville NC 27560 Home Phone: 919-460-7823. Office Fax: 919-678-1159. Personal E-mail: kabau@earthlink.net. E-mail: kbaumann@ncrrbiz.com.

BAUMANN, LINDA ADRIENE, lawyer; d. Richard Baumann and Frances Madeline Rosen; children: Gregory Faron, Douglas Faron, Daniel Faron. BA magna cum laude, Brown U., Providence, RI, 1972; JD, Columbia U. Law Sch., NYC, 1975, Parker cert. in internat., fgn. law with honors, 1975. Bar: Washington 1975, NJ 1997, US Dist Ct., NJ 1997. Atty.-advisor US Dept. Health Edn. and Welfare, Rockville, Md., 1975—76; fgn. svc. officer US Dept. State, Washington, 1976—77, atty-advisor Legal Adviser's Office, 1977—81; assoc. Swidler & Berlin, 1984—87, Fox, Weinberg & Bennett, 1988—93; adj. faculty Princeton U., 1994—96; of counsel Reed Smith LLP, Princeton, Wash. DC, 1997—2002, ptnr., 2003—06, Arent Fox LLP, Washington, 2006—. Editor: (law rev.) Columbia U. Law Sch., 1974—75; editor-in-chief Health Care Fraud & Abuse: Practical Perspectives, 2002, mem. adv. bd. The Health Lawyer, 2000—02, Rehab Report, 2002—, Physician Practice Compliance Alert, 2003—. Mem. Princeton U. Standing Com. Status Women, 1994—96; mem. bd. McCarter Theatre Assoc. Bd., Princeton, 1995—99, Princeton U. Friends Internat. Ctr., 1995—99, Appleseed Found, Pub. Interest Law Ctr. NJ, 1998—. Named an Outstanding Fraud and Compliance Lawyer, Nightingale's Healthcare News, 2004—07. Fellow: Am. Bar Found.; mem.: ABA (vice chair health law sect. pub. 2001—02, vice-chair programs 2002—03, co-chair Washington Healthcare Summit 2003—05, gov. coun. health law sect. 2003—, liaison to commn. women in profession 2005—, co-chair breast cancer task force 2006—, officer health law sect. 2006—, 2006—), Am. Health Lawyers Assn. (chair part D task force 2006—). Office: Arent Fox LLP 1050 Conn Ave NW Washington DC 20036 Office Phone: 202-857-6239. Business E-Mail: baumann.linda@arentfox.com.

BAUMANN, MARK, minister, director; b. Monticello, Iowa, Jan. 24, 1957; s. Harrry and Barbara Baumann; m. Marcia Edwards, May 29, 1982; children: Maria Michelle, Meghann Gabrielle, Meredith Julianna. BA, Ctrl. Coll., Pella, Iowa, 1975—79; MA, U. Iowa, Iowa City, 1981—84, PhD, 1984—97. Dir. Christian edn., assoc. organist First Presbyn. Ch., Marion, Iowa, 1988—90; dir. music & edn. First Luth. Ch., Decorah, Iowa, 1990—93, dir. Christian edn., assoc. organist Cedar Rapids, Iowa, 1993—2000; Saturday organist/cantor Our Savior's Luth. Ch., Cedar Rapids, 1998—; organist, dir. music Temple Judah, Cedar Rapids, 1999—; min. faith formation Zion Luth. Ch., Iowa City, 2000—. Coord., tchr. Leadership Program Musicians, Iowa City, 2004—. Composer: (musical composition) The Creator, (concertato) I Sing the Almighty Power of God; writer (hymnal companion) Rejoice with Understanding: Hymnal Companion to Rejoice in the Lord, 1985. Mem.: Hymn Soc. US & Can., Am. Guild Organists (dean 1995—98). Evangelical Luth. Home: 2795 18th Ave Marion IA 52302 Office: Zion Luth Ch 310 N Johnson St Iowa City IA 52245 Home Phone: 319-377-5707; Office Phone: 319-338-0944. Office Fax: 319-338-5313. Business E-Mail: mark@zionlutheran-ic.org.

BAUMANN, MARTIN F., former finance company executive; BA in Acctg., Queens Coll.; MBA in Fin., Baruch Coll.; degree in Bus. Adminstrn., Columbia U. CPA. With PricewaterhouseCoopers, 1969—2003, ptnr., 1980—2003, World Fin. Svcs. Practice, dep. chmn.; exec. v.p. for fin. Fed. Home Loan Mortgage Corp. (Freddie Mac), McLean, Va., 2003—06, CFO, 2003—06. Recipient Humanitarian of the Year award, Catholic Community Services of Newark, NJ, 2001.

BAUMANN, NANCY, school librarian; m. James F. Baumann; 2 children. MLS. Former elementary sch. tchr.; media specialist, ctr. dir. Barnett Shoals Elementary Sch., Athens, Ga., 2000—. Recipient Giant Step award, Sch. Libr. Jour./Thompson Gale, 2005, Innovative Reading grant, Am. Assn. Sch. Librs., 2007. Office: Barnett Shoals Elementary Sch 3220 Barnett Shoals Rd Athens GA 30605 Office Phone: 706-357-5334.

BAUMANN, RICHARD GORDON, lawyer; b. Chgo., Apr. 7, 1938; s. Martin M. and Harriet May (Granof) B.; m. Terrie Bemel, Dec. 18, 1971; children: Michelle, Alison. BS cum laude, U. Wis., 1960, JD, 1964. Bar: Wis. 1964, Calif. 1970, US Supreme Ct. 1973; bd. cert. creditors rights specialist. Congressional intern U.S. Senator Hubert H. Humphrey, 1959; assoc. firm Kohner, Mann & Kailas, Milw., 1964-69, Sulmeyer, Kupetz & Alberts, LA, 1969-73; mem. firm Sulmeyer, Kupetz, Baumann & Rothman, LA, 1973—2003, SulmeyerKupetz, LA, 2003—. Judge pro tem LA Superior Ct., 1980—. Assoc. editor Comml. Law Jour., 1991—. Fellow Comml. Law Found. (bd. dirs.); mem. Nat. Inst. on Credit Mgmt. (bd. dirs.), Am. Bd. Cert. (bd. dirs.), Acad. Comml. and Bankruptcy Law Specialists (bd. dirs.), Comml. Law League (pres. 1990-91, bd. govs. 1986-92, chmn. Western Region Mem. Assn. 1982-83). Office: 333 S Hope St 35th Fl Los Angeles CA 90071 Office Phone: 213-626-2311. Business E-Mail: rbaumann@sulmeyerlaw.com.

BAUMBACH, JOYCE, library director; d. Marion; m. Klaus Baumbach. Grad., U. North Tex. Sch. Libr. and Info. Scis., Denton. Dir. librs. Plano Pub. Libr. Sys., Tex., 1999—. Mem. Tex. State Libr. and Archives Commn./Tex. Libr. Assn. Task Force on Libr. Dists. Co-chair City of Plano United Way, 2005. Mem.: ALA (coun. mem.), Tex. Libr. Assn. (chair publs. com., ALA councilor 2007—). Avocations: reading, gardening. Office: Plano Pub Libr Sys 2501 Coit Rd Plano TX 75075 Office Phone: 972-769-4209. E-mail: joyceb@plano.gov.

BAUMBACH, NOAH, screenwriter; b. Brooklyn, 1969; Actor(Dir., and Screenwriter): (films) Kicking and Screaming, 1995, Highball, 1997, Mr. Jealousy, 1997, The Life Aquatic, 2004; screenwriter: The Squid and the Whale, 2005 (Best Original Screenplay. Nat. Bd. Review, 2005, Best Screenplay, Nat. Soc. Film Critic award, 2006). Named one of 100 People in Hollywood You Need to Know, Fade In Mag., 2005. Office: Sanford Gross and Assoc 1015 Gayley Ave #301 Los Angeles CA 90024

BAUMBERGER, CHARLES HENRY, lawyer; b. Port Huron, Mich., Sept. 13, 1941; s. Peter Julius and Evelyn Margaret (Jackson) B.; m. Martha Carolyn Megathlin, Aug. 8, 1969; children: Peter Scott, Charles Henry Jr. BA, Vanderbilt U., 1963; JD, U. Fla., 1966. Bar: Fla. 1966, U.S. Dist. Ct. (so. dist.) Fla. 1967; cert. civil trial lawyer. Atty. Stephens, Demos & Magill, Miami, Fla., 1967-68; ptnr. Hastings, Goldman & Baumberger, Miami, Fla., 1969-74; founding ptnr. Rossman & Baumberger P.A., Miami, Fla., 1974—. Lectr. in field. Contbr. articles to profl. jours. Mem. Gov's. Task Force on Emergency Room and Trauma Care, 1987; So. Fla. Health Action Coalition, Inc., 1984; task force on trauma and trauma systems Dept. Transp., 1987—. Served to 1st lt. U.S. Army Res., 1966-72. Named Fla. Trial Lawyer of Yr., 2005. Mem. ABA, ATLA (past chair of Profl. Negligence Sect.), Dade County Bar Assn. (bd. dirs. 1977-88, pres. 1989-90), Fla. Bar (exec. coun. trial lawyers sect. 1983-89, chmn. 1990-91), Acad. Fla. Trial Lawyers (bd. dirs. 1980-89, Jon Krupnick award 2006), Dade County Trial Lawyers Assn. (founding mem. bd. dirs. 1981-84), Am. Bd. Trial Advocates (past pres. Miami chpt., Trial Lawyer of Yr. 2006), So. Trial Lawyers Assn., Trial Lawyers for Pub. Justice (founding mem. 1982—), Am. Coll. Trial Lawyers, Am. Bd. Trial Lawyers, Internat. Soc. Barristers, Coral Reef Yacht Club. Democrat. Methodist. Home: 5755 Suncrest Dr Miami FL 33156-5704 Office: Rossman Baumberger Reboso & Spier 44 W Flagler St Fl 23 Miami FL 33130-1808 Office Phone: 305-373-0708. Business E-Mail: Baumberger@rbrlaw.com.

BAUMEL, HERBERT, violinist, conductor; b. NYC, Sept. 30, 1919; s. Leon and Fannie (Beckerman) B; m. Rachael Bail, Oct. 17, 1949 (div. Nov. 1970); children: Susan, Samuel, Mary Elizabeth (dec.); m. Joan Patricia French, July 11, 1971. Student, Mannes Sch. Music, NYC, 1932-34; diploma, Curtis Inst. Music, Phila., 1937-42; postgrad., Santa Cecilia, Accademia Chigiana, Rome and Siena, 1954-56. Violinist, concertmaster, conductor with orchs., chamber groups, Broadway shows, jazz ensembles, ballets, operas worldwide, 1939—. Baumel-Booth-Smith Trio (1st integrated classical trio to tour deep south), 1968-71; Baumel-Booth Duo, 1968-96; violinist/storyteller, 1970—, co-dir., Baumel Assocs., Yonkers, N.Y., 1984—; judge Fulbright Nat. Screening Com., 1965-67; guest artist Sponsors' Concerts of Dallas Chamber Music Soc., 1991, Internat. Piano Archives U. Md., College Park, Beveridge Webster Celebration Concert, 1991; lectr. and violinist with Dr. Joan French Baumel, 1991—, Yonkers Pub. Libr., 1992, Greenburgh (N.Y.) Pub. Libr., 1992, Waverly Heights, Gladwyne, Pa., 1993, 94, 95, Alliance Francaise, Westchester, N.Y., 1993, 94, 95, 96, 1st Unitarian Soc. Westchester, 1994, Workmen's Circle Lodge, Sylvan Lake, N.Y., 1994, Thomas Paine/Huguenot/New Rochelle (N.Y.) Hist. Soc., 1995, 96, others; commentator All Things Considered, Nat. Pub. Radio, 1999—; contbr. (mag.) Opera News, 2000—. Violinist Phila. Orch. with Ormandy, Toscanini, Walter, Monteux, Mitropoulos, Szell; first to play Samuel Barber's Violin Concerto with Curtis Symphony (Reiner), 1939 and Phila. Orch. (Ormandy); concert artist with: Stokowski, Stravinsky, Copland, Bernstein, Benny Goodman; concertmaster Phila. Opera, N.Y.C. Opera, N.Y.C. Ballet, Joe Bushkin Jazz Ensembles, (original Broadway musicals) New Girl in Town, Fiorello!, She Loves Me, Fiddler on the Roof, A Little Night Music, Rex, Dancin', also three Presdl. galas with Marilyn Monroe, Bill Cosby, Woody Allen, Jack Benny, Johnny Carson, Rudolph Nureyev, Margot Fonteyn; recs. with Heifetz, Horowitz, Rubinstein, Leonard Warren, Frank Sinatra, Edith Piaf, Tallulah Bankhead, many others; writer script and music ednl. audio-visual program The Art of Listening, 1972—; composer: Fiddlers Two, 1976, Caprice #48 1/2, 1978, Sentiment America, 1984, arranger selections from Fiddler on the Roof, 1971, 2001. Mem. adv. bd. Mark Brent Dolinsky Found., White Plains, N.Y., 1982—; played benefits for Westchester Assn. Retarded Citizens, 1982—, Coalition for the Homeless,Westchester County, N.Y., 1986—. Recipient Silver medal New York Music Week Assn., 1928, Gold medal New York Music Week Assn., 1929; 2-time Fulbright scholar to Rome, 1954-56; chosen for both Stokowski All-American Youth Orch. tours, S.Am., U.S., 1940, 41; chosen to organize, present and play concerts for U.S. Embassy and Cultural Offices throughout Italy with Anna Moffo, Ezio Flagello, Ivan Davis, Gimi Beni, and in honor of Queen Elisabeth of Belgium, 1954-56, Phila. Drama Guild Lectr. Series, 1978. Mem. Am. Fedn. Musicians, Curtis Inst. of Music Alumni Assn., Phila. Orch. Retirees and Friends. Democrat. Jewish. Avocations: tennis, gardening, reading, photography, chess. Home and Office: Baumel Assocs 86 Rosedale Rd Yonkers NY 10710-3033

BAUMEL, JOAN PATRICIA FRENCH, writer, educator; b. Winona, Minn., Mar. 12, 1930; d. William Oswald and Gertrude Marie (Fitzgerald) French; m. Herbert Baumel, July 11, 1971. Student, l'Ecole du Louvre, Paris, 1950-51; student with high honors, Inst. Phonétique Sorbonne, Paris, 1950-51; BA magna cum laude, Douglass Coll., New Brunswick, NJ, 1952; postgrad., U. Detroit, 1952-55, Case Western Reserve U., Cleve., 1960, U. Akron, 1962, U. Notre Dame, South Bend, Ind., 1963, Manhattanville Coll., Purchase, NY, 1971; MA in French, Rutgers U., New Brunswick, NJ, 1965; PhD in Modern Langs., Fordham U., Bronx, NY, 1985. Tchr. French lang. and culture, elem. and coll. levels various schs. including Mother House of Religious of the Sacred Heart, Kenwood, Albany, N.Y., Ohio, Mich., 1955-66; tchr. French White Plains (N.Y.) Pub. High Sch., 1966-86; curricula creator Akron (Ohio) Pub. Schs., 1962-63; co-dir. Baumel Assocs., Yonkers, N.Y., 1984—, Concerts and Lectures with Herbert Baumel, 1991—, Words and Music Programs with Herbert Baumel, 1991—, Yonkers Pub. Libr., 1992, Waverly Heights, Gladwyne, Pa., 1993-95, Workmen's Circle Lodge, Sylvan Lake, N.Y., 1994, Thomas Paine/Huguenot Hist. Soc., New Rochelle, N.Y., 1995—. Lectr. French lang. and culture Yonkers (N.Y.) Pub. Libr., 1992, Greenburgh (N.Y.) Pub. Libr., 1992; lectr. anti-semitism CUNY Grad. Ctr., 1988—, B'nai B'rith Internat. Mus., Washington, 1st Unitarian Soc., Westchester, N.Y., Rockland (N.Y.) Ctr. for Holocaust Studies, Unitarian Ch. of All Souls, N.Y.C., Temple Beth Israel, Port Washington, N.Y., Holocaust Resource Ctr. and Archives, Queensborough C.C., CUNY, 1991, Women's Am. ORT, Midchester Jewish Ctr., Yonkers, 1992, 2000, Ctrl. Queens YM & YWCA, N.Y.C., 1992, 2000, Jewish Cmty. Ctr., Scarsdale, N.Y., 2001. Author: Paul Claudel and the Jews: A Study in Ambivalence, 1985; lectr. topics include French Anti-Semitism; The Gallic Road to the Concentration Camp; Klaus Barbie and the Children of Izieu, Kristallnacht Remembered, numerous others. Mem. adv. bd. Mark Brent Dolinsky Meml. Found. Recipient Woodrow Wilson fellowship, 1958-59, Yearbook Dedication award White Plains (N.Y.) Pub. H.S., 1980. Mem. Am. Assn. Tchrs. French, White Plains Tchrs. Assn., N.Y. State Assn. Fgn. Lang. Tchrs., French Inst./Alliance Francaise, Alliance Francaise Westchester, Phi Beta Kappa. Avocations: tennis, gardening, music, reading. Home and Office: Baumel Assocs 86 Rosedale Rd Yonkers NY 10710-3033 Office Phone: 914-793-0299. Personal E-mail: fiddlerplusj@att.net.

BAUMER, BEVERLY BELLE, journalist; b. Hays, Kans., Sept. 23, 1926; d. Charles Arthur and Maryme Mae (Lord) Baumer. BS, U. Kans., 1948. Summer intern reporter Hutchison (Kans.) News, 1946—47; continuity writer, women's program dir. Sta. KWBW, Hutchison, 1948—49; dist. editor Salina (Kans.) Jours., 1950—57; commd. writer State of Kans. Centennial Yr., 1961; contbg. writer Ford Times, Kansas City Star, Wichita (Kans.) Eagle, Ojibway Publs., Billboard, Modern Jeweler, Floor Covering Weekly, other bus. mags., 1962—69; owner, mgr. apts. Hutchison, 1970—; broadcaster Reading Radio Rm., Sta. KHCC-FM, Hutchison, 1982—; columnist Hutchison Record, 1983—86. Author: book of poems, 1941; editor: A Simple Bedside Book for People Who are Kinda, Sorta Interested in Genealogy, 1983. Participant People to People Citizen Amb. Program, China, 1988; mem. Rep. Presdl. Task Force. Info. officer, maj. Kans. Wing Hdqurs. CAP, 1969—72. Recipient News Photo award, AP, 1952, Human Interest Photo award, Nat. Press Women, 1956. Mem.: Nat. Geneal. Soc., Am. Film Inst., Am. Soc. Profl. and Exec. Women, Kans. Press Women, Nat. Fedn. Press Women, Suffolk County Hist. Soc., Fellows Menninger Found., U. Kans. Alumni Assn., Internat. Platform Soc., Daus. Am. Colonists (organizing regent Dr. Thomas Lord chpt., state chmn. insignia com.), Plantagenet Soc., Colonial Dames 17th Century (chaplain, charter mem. Henry Woodhouse chpt.), Order Descs. Colonial Physicians and Chirugiens, Daus. Colonial Wars, Ben Franklin Soc. (nat. adv. bd.), DAR, Nat. Soc. Sons and Daus. Pilgrims (elder Kans. br.), Kans. Soc. Daus. Am. Colonists, Nat. Soc. Daus. Am. Colonists, Nat. Soc. Daus. Founder and Patriots Am., Nat. Soc. Magna Charta Dames. Home and Office: 122 Downing Rd Hutchinson KS 67502-4453 *Kindness belongs in business, the professions and the trades. It is the most sincere form of good will and leaves no one uncomfortable.*

BAUMER, EDWARD FERDINAND, finance company executive; b. Irvington, NJ, Dec. 5, 1913; s. Ferdinand Fred and Augusta Baumer (Wagemann) B.; m. Elizabeth Karl, Feb. 10, 1940 (dec. June 2002); children: Edward K. (dec.), Richard Eaton, Jane Elizabeth Woodman. B in Liberal Arts, Rutgers U., 1934, JSD, LLB, 1937. Bar: N.J. Advanced through grades to brig. gen. U.S. Army, 1973, commd., 1934, ret., 1973; dir. advt., pub. rels. Prudential Ins. Co. Am., LA, 1934-55; v.p. McCann Erickson Comm., NYC, 1955-59, Union Bank, LA, 1959-61; sr. v.p. Great Western Fin. Corp., Beverly Hills, Calif., 1961-65; pres., CEO, E.F. Baumer & Co., LA, 1965-87; chmn. Baumer Fin. Publ., LA, 1987; chmn., pres., CEO, World-Wide Super Sr. Sports, LA, 1999—. Chmn. emeritus Baumer Fin. Publ., L.A., 1997— (affiliate Imagination Publ. Chgo.); v.p. Union Bank, L.A. Named capt., USA's Billy Talbert Cup Tennis Team, 2004—; named to All-Am. Water Polo Team, 1934. Mem. Calif. Club, La Jolla Beach & Tennis Club, Internat. Lawn Tennis Club of U.S.A. Republican. Achievements include winning 15 sr. European Tennis Championships, 2 USTA Natl. Championships and 3 World ITF Tennis Championship (doubles), 1997-99. Home and Office: # 1504 1820 Avenida Del Mundo Coronado CA 92118-4039 Office Phone: 619-435-1444. Office Fax: 619-435-2156.

BAUMER, MARTHA ANN, minister; b. Cleve., Sept. 12, 1938; d. Harry William and Olga Erna (Zenk) B. BA, Lakeland Coll., 1960; MA, U. Wyo., 1963; MDiv, United Theol. Sem., 1973; D Ministry, Eden Theol. Sem., 1990. Parish minister Congl. United Ch. of Christ, Amery, Wis., 1973-79; organizing minister United Ch. of Santa Fe (N.Mex.), 1979-85; conf. minister Ill. South Conf. United Ch. of Christ, Highland, Ill., 1985-93; pastor Windsor (Wis.) United Ch. of Christ, 1993-99; vis. prof. pastoral studies Eden Theol. Sem., St. Louis, 1999—. Trustee pension bds. United Ch. of Christ, N.Y.C., 1983—, mem., chair exec. coun., 1977-83; del. World Coun. Chs., 1961, 83; trustee Eden Theol. Sem., St. Louis, 1990-99. Contbr. articles to profl. publs. Vice chair Pensions Boards United Church of Christ, 2004—05. Mem. Coun. of Conf. Ministers United Ch. of Christ (sec.-treas. 1989-93). Office: Eden Theol Sem 475 E Lockwood Ave Saint Louis MO 63119-3124 E-mail: mbaumer@eden.edu.

BAUMGARDNER, DENNIS J., physician, researcher, educator; b. Springfield, Ill., July 13, 1957; s. Jack and Jean Baumgardner; m. Mary K. Baumgardner, June 20, 1980; children: Mark, Anne, Katie, Jean, John, Nicholas, Andrew. A, Springfield Coll., Ill., 1977; BS in Microbiology, U. Ill., Urbana, 1979; MD, U. Ill., Urbana, 1983. Resident in family medicine Rockford Med. Found., U. Ill., 1986; family medicine residency dir. U. Wis., Milw., 1994—2001, assoc. chair dept. family medicine, 2001—06; dir. campus rsch. Aurora U. Wis. Med. Group, Milw., 2006—. Prof. family medicine U. Wis., Sch. Medicine and Pub. Health, Milw., 2000—. Named Family Practice Educator of Yr., Wis. Acad. Family Physicians, 1993; recipient William Pickles Rsch. award, Wis. Rsch. Network, 2001. Roman Catholic. Achievements include research in epidemiology and ecology of blastomycosis. Office: Ctr Urban Population Health 1020 N 12th St Ste 4180 Milwaukee WI 53233 Office Phone: 414-219-5191.

BAUMGARDNER, JAMES LEWIS, history professor; b. Bristol, Va., Jan. 26, 1938; s. John Richard and Roxie Katherine (Lewis) B.; children: Ellen Lorena, James Michael; m. Paula Louise Jones; stepchildren: Joseph Branscome, Sarah Elizabeth Brock. AA, Bluefield Jr. Coll., 1957; BA, Carson-Newman Coll., 1959; MA, U. Tenn., Knoxville, 1964, PhD, 1968. Ordained to ministry Baptist Ch., 1955. Asst. prof. history Carson-Newman Coll., Jefferson City, Tenn., 1964-67, assoc. prof., 1967-73, prof., 1973—, chmn. history-polit. sci,. dept., 1974-95. Contbr. articles to learned jours. Interim mem. Jefferson County (Tenn.) Bd. Sch. Commrs., 1978; mem. Anderson County (Tenn.) Bd. Edn., 1990-94; active interim, bivocation pastor. Served with U.S. Army, 1959-62. Named Bivocational Pastor of the Yr., Tenn. Bapt. Conv., 1997. Mem. Am. Hist. Assn., Acad. Polit. Sci., Orgn. Am. Historians, So. Hist. Assn., Bapt. History & Heritage Soc., Phi Alpha Theta. Office: Carson-Newman Coll PO Box 71929 Jefferson City TN 37760-7001

BAUMGARDNER, JOHN ELLWOOD, JR., lawyer; b. Balt., Jan. 6, 1951; s. John Ellwood and Nancy G. (Brandenburg) B.; m. Astrid Rehl, Sept. 7, 1974; children: Jeffrey Mark, Julia Alexis. AB, Princeton Univ., 1973; JD, Columbia Univ., 1975. Bar: NY 1976. Assoc. Sullivan & Cromwell, NYC, 1975-83, ptnr., 1983—, also coord. investment mgmt. practice area and mem. Fin. Institutions, Investment Mgmt. Broker-Dealer and Commodities, Futures and Derivatives Groups. Supervisory dir. The Turkish Pvt. Equity Investment Co., 1991-93; trustee JPM Advisor Funds, 1996. Dir. NYC Opera, 2005—. Mem.: ABA, NYC Bar Assn. (chair com. on investment mgmt. regulation 2000—03), NY State Bar Assn., Nat. Dance Inst. (bd. dirs. 1988—89), Princeton Club. Office: Sullivan & Cromwell LLP 125 Broad St Fl 32 New York NY 10004-2498 Office Phone: 212-558-4000. Office Fax: 212-558-3588. E-mail: baumgardnerj@sullcrom.com.

BAUMGARDT, BILLY RAY, professional society administrator, agriculturist; b. Lafayette, Ind., Jan. 17, 1933; s. Raymond P. and Mildred L. Baumgardt; m. D. Elaine Blain, June 8, 1952; children: Pamela K. Baumgardt Farley, Teresa Jo Baumgardt Adolfsen, Donald Ray. BS in Agr., Purdue U., 1955, MS, 1956; PhD, Rutgers U., 1959. From asst. to assoc. prof. U. Wis., Madison, 1959-67; prof. animal nutrition Pa. State U., University Park, 1967-70, head dept. dairy and animal sci., 1970-79, assoc. dir. agrl. expt. sta., 1979-80; dir. agrl. research, assoc. dean Purdue U., West Lafayette, Ind., 1980-98; exec. v.p. Am. Registry Profl. Animal Scientists, Savoy, Ill., 1998—2003; coord. DISCOVER conf. series Am. Dairy Sci. Assn., Savoy, 1998—2007. Contbr. chapters to books, articles to profl. sci. jours. Recipient Wilkinson award, Pa. State U., 1979. Fellow: AAAS, Am. Soc. Nutritional Sci., Am. Dairy Sci. Assn. (pres. 1984—85, Nutrition Rsch. award 1966, award of Honor 1993, Disting. Svc. award 2003); mem.: Nat. Agrl. Biotech. Coun. (chair 1993—94), Am. Soc. Animal Sci., Am. Soc. Nutrition, Rotary, Sigma Xi. Home and Office: 2741 N Salisbury St West Lafayette IN 47906-1431 E-mail: baumgardt@purdue.edu.

BAUMGARDT, GEORGE FRANCIS, bank executive, musician, director; b. Racine, Wis., Apr. 23, 1950; s. Richard Bernard and Blanche Marie Baumgardt; m. Mary Anne Braun, Aug. 3, 1974; children: Gretchen Marie, Erika Ann Slater, Richard Joseph, George Thomas, Gregory John. BA in Music Edn., U. Wis., Kenosha, Wis., 1974; student in Banking and Lending, Am. Banking Assn., 1988—89. 1st v.p. Bank Elmwood, Racine, Wis., 1969—. Pres. Am. Inst. Banking, Racine, 1978—88, instr., 1982—94; bd. dir. Cmty. Econ. Devel. Corp, Racine; pres. Ctr. Cmty. Concerns, Racine, 1986—95; dir. liturgical music St. Paul the Apostle Cath. Ch., Racine, 1965—80, Sacred Heart Cath. Ch., Racine, Wis., 1980—. Composer: (songs) Liturgical Music; dir.: (choir) Salzburg Mozart Music Festival, 2002, Sacred Heart Church Choir, 1999. Sec. Cmty. Econ. Devel. Corp, Racine; bd. dir. Alliance Mentally Ill, Racine, 2001—, United Way, Racine, 1994—96, Ctr. Cmty. Concerns, Racine, 1986—2004. Named Ch. Musician of Yr., Racine County, 1996, Loan Officer of Year, Racine County Economic Devel. Corp., 1996, 1997, 1998, 1999. Mem.: Nat. Assn. Pastoral Musicians, Am. Liturgical Musicians Am. (assoc.), Kenosha Country Club. Roman Catholic. Avocations: golf, travel, music. Home: 5310 Lathrop Ave Racine WI 53403 Office: Bank of Elmwood 2704 Lathrop Ave Racine WI 53405 Home Phone: 262-552-7527; Office Phone: 262-554-5814. Personal E-mail: gbaumgardt@bankofelmwood.com.

BAUMGARTEN, BARBARA, human resources specialist; Mgr. newsroom staffing NY Times. Office: Newsroom Staffing NY Times 229 W 43rd St New York NY 10036 Business E-Mail: baumgba@nytimes.com.

BAUMGARTEN, JON A., lawyer; b. NYC, Oct. 26, 1942; m. Jodi Rush, Jan. 1, 1983. BA, CCNY, 1964; LLB, NYU, 1967. Bar: N.Y. 1968, U.S. Ct Appeals (4th cir.) 1977, D.C. 1980, U.S. Supreme Ct. 1982, U.S. Dist. Ct. D.C. 1983, U.S. Ct. of Appeals, Sixth Circuit, 1994. Assoc. Parker Chapin Flattau, NYC, 1968-70, Linden & Deutsch, NYC, 1970-75; gen. counsel U.S. Copyright Office, Washington, 1976-79; ptnr. Paskus Gordon & Mandel, Washington, 1979-86; ptnr., intellectual property dept. Proskauer Rose LLP, Washington, 1986—. Mem. Internat. Copyright Panel of Adv. Com. to Dept. of State on Internat. Intellectual Property, Adv. Com. to U.S. Copyright Office, Ad Hoc Working Group on Adherence to Berne Convention, Nat. Adv. Com. to U.S. Copyright Office, Internat. Copyright Panel, U.S. State Dept. Author: U.S.-U.S.S.R. Copyright Relations Under the Universal Copyright Convention, 1973; contbr. articles to profl. jours.; mem. editorial bd. Jour. Copyright Soc. U.S.A., Patent, Trademark and Copyright Jour., World Intellectual Property Report, Computer Lawyer, Jour. Proprietary Rights. Named one of Best Lawyers in Am., Best Lawyers in Washington. Mem. ABA Patent Trademark and Copyright Law Sect. (chair various coms.), Copyright Soc. of the U.S.A. (trustee 1975-78, 1992—).

BAUMGARTEN, RONALD NEAL, lawyer; b. Chgo., May 13, 1942; s. Albert and Beatrice (Loseff) B.; m. Aloha Herman, Aug. 27, 1966; children: Brett, Reed, Jaclyn, Blake. BA, U. Ill., 1964, JD, 1966. Bar: Calif. 1970, U.S. Dist. Ct. (cen. dist.) Calif. 1970, U.S. Ct. Appeals (9th cir.) 1973, U.S. Supreme Ct. 1975. Gen. counsel, chief ops. officer Elgin Jewelry Distbrs. Inc., LA, 1967-72, also bd. dirs.; assoc. Grobe, Rinestein, Freid & Katz P.L.C., Beverly Hills, Calif., 1972-75; ptnr. Jacobs & Baumgarten P.L.C., Beverly Hills, 1975-80; CEO Baumgarten & Greene P.L.C., Santa Monica, Calif., 1980-88; pvt. practice Santa Monica, 1988—89, LA, 1989—; sr. v.p. Comml. Fin. Ctr., 1991-95, also bd. dirs.; pres. Occidental Svcs., Inc., 1992-95; pres., CEO, sole shareholder Holmby Investments, Inc., 1994—; pres., CEO Baumgarten Property Mgmt. Svcs., Inc., 1994—; v.p., sec. Sierra Crest Equities, LLC, 1997—, Corner Stone Real Estate Investment, Inc., 1997—; CEO Sierra Sr. Cmtys. LLC, 2001—; mem. Coastal Ptnrs., LLC, 2004—. Chmn., CEO, COO, J.D. Alexander & Assocs., Inc., LA, 1980-92; asst. prof. law U. San Fernando Valley, Calif., 1974. Mem. L.A. World Affairs Coun., 1974—, L.A. Olympic Citizens Adv. Commn., 1982-84, Town Hall, 1983—; exec. v.p., gen. counsel, bd. dirs. Variety-The Children's Charity, 1974-2000, Variety Boy's and Girl's Club, L.A., pres., 1996-99, bd. dirs., 1981—; founder 1st Bus. Bank, L.A., 1981. Mem. ABA, Calif. Bar Assn., LA County Bar Assn., Beverly Hills Bar Assn., Phi Delta Phi, Auburn Rotary Club. Office: 10590 Wilshire Blvd Ste 201 Los Angeles CA 90024 also: Ste 130 2237 Douglas Blvd Roseville CA 95661 Home Phone: 916-660-0201; Office Phone: 916-773-0550. Personal E-mail: rbpacpal@aol.com. Business E-Mail: rbaumgarten@coastalpartners.net.

BAUMGARTEN, SIDNEY, lawyer; b. NYC, July 30, 1933; s. Abraham and Doris (Kanarick) B.; children: Douglas, Frederick, Roger, Julia. AB, Brown U., 1954; JD, NYU, 1960. Bar: N.Y. 1961, U.S. Dist. Ct. (ea. and so. dists.) N.Y. 1961, U.S. Ct. Claims 1961, U.S. Ct. Appeals (2d cir.) 1961. Asst. mgmt., field underwriter Home Life Ins. Co., 1957-61; sole practice, 1961-67; asst. dist. atty. Queens County, NY, 1967-68; law sec. to presiding justice State of N.Y., Queens, 1968-73; asst. to Mayor City of N.Y., 1974-77; gen. counsel Phoenix House Found., 1978-80; sr. ptnr. Baumgarten, Swiedler & Waxman, NYC, 1980-88; pvt. practice NYC, 1989-94; pres., CEO Spectral Biosci. Corp., 1994—. Lectr. various seminars, assns. and ednl. instns; adj. prof. law N.Y. Inst. Tech.; vis. prof. Found. U. Cardiology, Brazil, 1996. Pres. bd. dirs., chmn. N.Y. Therapeutic Communities, Inc.; trustee Lawrence Country Day Sch. (pres. 1985-87). With US Army, 1954—56, with Res., 1956—73, brig. gen. Army Div., 2001—04, N.Y. Guard. Decorated Companion Order of Merit SMOTJ, N.Y. State Conspicuous Svc. medal. Mem.: NAHC, VFW, NRA (life), East Side C. of C. (pres. 1983—86, chmn. 1987—2004), Am. Legion. Office: 355 South End Ave Ste 31J New York NY 10280 Office Phone: 646-781-9587.

BAUMGARTNER, ANDREW C., retired elementary school educator; b. Anniston, Ala., Aug. 21, 1952; BS in Edn., Univ. Ga., 1976; MS in Early Childhood Edn., N. Ga. Coll. Speech therapist Gilmer County (Ga.) Pub. Sch. Sys., 1976—78; kindergarten tchr. Chatham County/Savannah City Pub. Sch. Sys., 1978—82; tchr. Richmond County (Ga.) Pub. Sch. Sys., 1982—95, A. Brian Merry Elem. Sch., Richmond County, 1995—2006; ret., 2006. Early childhood cons. Middle Georgia Coop. Ednl. Svcs. Agy., 1981—82; former chmn. Richmond County Task Force on Kindergarten Assessment. Author: Helping Your Child At Home.with Mathematics. Named Nat. Tchr. of Yr., 1999.*

BAUMGARTNER, ANTON EDWARD, automotive sales professional; b. NYC, May 18, 1948; s. Hans and Carmen Maria (Figueroa) B.; m. Brenda Lee Lemmon, May 24, 1969 (div. 1990); 1 child, Anton Nicholaus; m. Virginia Thiele, 1992 (div. 2003); 1 child, Bree Alexandra; m. Christine Stieber, 2007. BS, Woodbury U., 1970. Sales mgr. Maywood Bell Ford, Bell, Calif., 1966-69, O.R. Haan, Inc., Santa Ana, Calif., 1969-72; pres. Parkinson Volkswagen, Placentia, Calif., 1972-77; exec. v.p. United Moped, Fountain Valley, Calif., 1975-82; pres. Automobili Intermeccanica, Fountain Valley, 1975-82; gen. mgr. Bishop (Calif.) Volkswagen-Bishop Motors, 1982-85, Beach Imports-Irvine Imports, Newport Beach, Calif., 1985-88; chmn. bd. Stan and Ollie Ins. Co., Santa Ana, Calif., 1989—92; exec. v.p. Asterism, Inc., 1992-96; chmn. Marich Acceptance Inland Empire, 1996—98; gen. mgr. Saturn Retail Enterprises, Anaheim, Calif., 1999—2005, Swedish Cars of Orange County, 2005—. Mem. faculty, Automotive World Congress, Detroit, 1980. Contbr. articles to weekly serial publs. Mem. Coachbuilders Assn. N.Am. (sec. 1975-78). Home: 29401 Port Royal Way Laguna Niguel CA 92677-7945 Office: Swedish Motorcars Orange County Santa Ana CA 92705 Personal E-mail: tbaumgartner@cox.net.

BAUMGARTNER, BRIAN, actor; b. Atlanta, Ga., Nov. 29, 1972; married; 1 child. BFA in Acting, Southern Methodist U., 1995. Artist dir. Hidden Theatre, Minneapolis. Actor: (TV series) The Office, 2005— (SAG award outstanding performance by an ensemble in a comedy series, 2007); (films) Herman USA, 2001—, Moosecock, 2006—, No. 6, 2006—, License to Wed, 2007—, (appeared on) CSI: Crime Scene Investigation, 2003, LAX, 2004, Arrested Development, 2005, Jake in Progress, 2005, Everwood, 2005.*

BAUMGARTNER, JOHN H., gas industry executive; b. 1936; married. With Clark Oil & Refining Corp., Milw., 1956-82, retail sales rep., 1960-65, dist. mgr., 1965-72, regional mgr., 1972-74, v.p. retail mktg., asst. gen. sales mgr., 1974-75, sr. v.p. mktg., 1975-78, exec. v.p., 1978-82; pres. J.H. Baumgartner Enterprises, Brookfield, Wis., 1982—; v.p., owner Robert Kidd & Assocs. Inc., 1990—. Served with USMC, 1954-56. Office Phone: 651-210-4018.

BAUMGARTNER, ROBERT, investment company executive, consultant; b. Dallas, Aug. 20, 1934; s. Oren Floyd and Jessie Elizabeth (Seale) B.; m. Sabina Jumatayeva, Aug. 1, 1998; children: Janet, Cathy, Diane, Mitchell. BBA, So. Meth. U., 1956. V.p. Rep. Nat. Bank, Dallas, 1958-70, Bank of Southwest, Houston, 1970-71; v.p., treas. Marathon Mfg. Co., Inc., Houston, 1971-78; CEO Amistad Well Svc., Houston, 1978-79; treas. Anderson Clayton & Co., Inc., Houston, 1980-82; pres. Baumgartner Capital, Austin, Tex., 1982—. Mem. Assn. Corp. Growth, Fin. Execs. Inst., Beta Gamma Sigma. Republican. Methodist. Avocations: golf, travel. Home and Office: Tex Bus Svcs 12400 Wycliff Ln Austin TX 78727-5219 Business E-Mail: bb@onr.com.

BAUMGARTNER, WILLIAM ANTHONY, cardiac surgeon; b. Covington, Ky., Apr. 18, 1947; s. Nicholas Raymond Baumgartner and Rosemary Jones; m. Betsy Reik; children: Bill Jr., Amy, Mark. BS, Xavier U., 1969; MD, U. Ky., 1973. Cert. Am. Bd. Thoracic Surg. Intern surgery Stanford (Calif.) U. Med. Ctr., 1973—74, asst. resident gen. surgery, 1974—75, asst. resident cardiothoracic surgery, 1975—76, asst. resident cardiovasc. surgery, 1976—77, chief resident cardiovasc. surgery, 1977—78, chief resident thoracic surgery, 1978, asst. resident gen. surgery, 1978—80, chief resident, 1980—81; cardiac surgeon-in-charge Johns Hopkins U. Sch. Medicine, Balt., 1993—, Vincent L. Gott prof. Editor: (book) Heart and Heart Lung Transplantation, 1990, 2001. Grantee, NIH, 1988, 1992, 1995, 2000; Javits Neurosci. Rsch. Investigator awardee, 2000. Mem.: ACS, Clin. Practice Assn. (pres., vice dean clin. practice 1999—), Soc. Univ. Surgeons, Am. Assn. Thoracic Surgery, Am. Soc. Transplant Surgeons, Internat. Soc. Heart and Lung Transplantation, Soc. Thoracic Surgeons (pres. 2002—03), Am. Surg. Assn. Avocation: golf. Office: Johns Hopkins Hosp 600 N Wolfe St # 618 Baltimore MD 21287-0005 Office Phone: 410-955-5248. Business E-Mail: wbaumgar@csurg.jhmi.jhu.edu.

BAUMGARTNER, WILLIAM HANS, JR., lawyer; b. Chgo., July 24, 1955; s. William H. and Charlotte Burnette (Lange) B.; m. Andrea Jean Coath, Oct. 6, 1984. BA, U. Chgo., 1976; JD magna cum laude, Harvard U., 1979. Bar: Ill. 1979, US Dist. Ct. (no. dist. Ill.) 1979, US Dist. Ct. (ea. dist. Wis.) 1994, US Ct. Appeals (3rd cir.) 1996, US Ct. Appeals (6th cir.) 1988, US Ct. Appeals (7th cir.) 1992, US Ct. Appeals (8th cir.) 1998, US Ct. Appeals (11th cir.) 1994, US Ct. Appeals (fed. cir.) 1991. Assoc. Sidley & Austin, Chgo., 1979-86, ptnr., 1986—. Mem. ABA, Chgo. Bar Assn., Phi Beta Kappa. Office: Sidley Austin LLP 1 S Dearborn St Chicago IL 60603 Office Phone: 312-853-7250. E-mail: wbaumgar@sidley.com.*

BAUMHART, RAYMOND CHARLES, religious organization administrator; b. Chgo., Dec. 22, 1923; s. Emil and Florence (Weidner) B. BS, Northwestern U., 1945; PhL, Loyola U., 1952, STL, 1958; MBA, Harvard U., 1953; DBA, Harvard, 1963; LLD (hon.), Ill. Coll., 1977; DHL (hon.), Scholl Coll. Podiatric Medicine, 1983, Rush U., Chgo., 1987, Northwestern U., 1993, Xavier U., Cin., 1994, Ill. Benedictine Coll., 1994; DHL (hon.), Loyola U., 2007. Joined Jesuit Order, 1946; ordained priest Roman Cath. Ch., 1957. Asst. prof. mgmt. Loyola U., Chgo., 1962-64, dean Sch. Bus. Adminstrn., 1964-66, exec. v.p., acting v.p. Med. Ctr., 1968-70, pres., 1970-93; cons. to Cardinal George, Cath. Archdiocese of Chgo., 2000—. Alfred Ring lectr. U. Fla., 1988; John and Mildred Wright lectr. Fairfield U., 1992; D. B. Reinhart lectr. Viterbo Coll., 2000; bd. dirs. Ceres Food Group, Inc. Author: An Honest Profit, 1968, (with Thomas Garrett) Cases in Business Ethics, 1968, (with Thomas McMahon) The Brewer-Wholesaler Relationship, 1969; corr. editor: America, 1965-70. Trustee St. Louis U., 1967-72, Boston Coll., 1968-71; bd. dirs. Coun. Better Bus. Burs., 1971-77, Cath. Health Alliance Met. Chgo., 1986-93; mem. U.S. Bishops and Pres.'s Com. on Higher Edn., 1980-84, Jobs for Met. Chgo., 1984-85, Chgo. Health Care Industry, 1990-94. Recipient Gutenberg award, Chgo. Bible Soc., 2006; decorated cavalier Order of Merit, Italy, 1971, commendatore, 1994; recipient Rale medallion Boston Coll., 1976, Daniel Lord S.J. award Loyola Acad., Wilmette, Ill., 1992, Mary Potter Humanitarian award Little Company of Mary Hosp., Ill., 1993, Sword of Loyola Loyola U., Chgo., 1993, Theodore Hesburgh award Assn. Cath. Colls. and Univs., 1995; John W. Hill fellow Harvard U., 1961-62, Cambridge Ctr. for Social Studies Rsch. fellow, 1966-68. Mem. Comml. Club, Mid-Am. Club, Tavern Club. Roman Catholic. Business E-Mail: rbaumhart@archchgo.org.

BAUMKEL, MARK S., lawyer; b. Flint, Mich., Feb. 17, 1951; s. Sherwood and Marilyn (Schiff) B.; m. Julie A. Kimbrell, Oct. 20, 1978; 1 child, Molly. BA cum laude, Oakland U., Rochester,Mich., 1973; JD cum laude, Wayne State U., 1977. Bar: Mich. 1977, U.S. Dist. Ct. Mich. 1977, U.S. Ct. Appeals (6th cir.) 1985. Assoc. dist. counsel U.S. SBA, Detroit, 1977-78; asst. pros. atty. Ingham County Prosecutor's Office, Lansing, Mich., 1978-79; assoc. atty. Shifman & Goodman, P.C., Southfield, Mich., 1979-81, Kaufman & Friedman, Southfield, 1981-84; sole practitioner Troy, Mich., 1984-94; ptnr. Provizer & Phillips, P.C., Southfield, 1994—. Mem. Assn. Trial Lawyers Am. (sustaining), Mich. Trial Lawyers Assn. (PAC contbr.), Oakland County Bar Assn., Wayne County Mediation Tribunal (mediator), Am. Arbitration Assn. (arbitrator), Oakland County Mediation (mediator). Avocations: running, bicycling, guitar. Home: 3826 Lakecrest Dr Bloomfield Hills MI 48304-3040 Office: 30200 Telegraph RD #200 Bingham Farms MI 48025-4510 Office Phone: 248-642-0444. E-mail: m.baumkelm@p-ppclawfirm.org.

BAUMRIN, BERNARD STEFAN HERBERT, lawyer, educator; b. NYC, Jan. 7, 1934; s. David and Regina (Zuckerburg) B.; m. Judith Anne Marti, Dec. 20, 1953; children: Seth, Jeanne, Rachel. Student, Marietta Coll., 1951-52, NYU, 1952-53; BA, Ohio State U., 1956; PhD, Johns Hopkins U., 1960; postgrad., Washington U., St. Louis, 1965-67; JD, Columbia U., 1970. Dir. forensics Johns Hopkins U., Balt., 1957—59; vis. asst. prof. philosophy Butler U., 1960—61, Antioch Coll., 1961; asst. prof. philosophy U. Del., Newark, 1961—64, Washington U., 1964—67; assoc. prof. philosophy Hunter Coll., CUNY, 1967—68, assoc. prof. philosophy Grad. Sch. and Lehman Coll., 1968—72, prof., 1972—, treas. univ. faculty senate, 1978—81, 1990, exec. com., 1976—84, 1987—91, 1992—93, 1998—99, 2002—; ptnr. Baumrin, Galub & Volkomer, 1979—. Adj. prof. med. edn. Mt. Sinai Sch. of Medicine, 1988—; bd. dirs. CUNY Acad. for the Humanities and Scis. Author: Philosophy of Science, 2 vols., 1963, British Moralists, 1964, Hobbes's Leviathan, 1968, Moral Responsibility and the Professions, 1983; U.S. editor: Jour. Applied Philosophy, 1986—2001, mem. adv. bd.: Jour. Philosophy Psychiatry and Psychology, 1995—2005; cons. editor Metaphilosophy, 1968—; contbr. articles to profl. jours. AEC fellow, 1963, U. Del. fellow, 1962, Washington U. Forsyth fellow, 1964-67; CUNY grantee, 1968, 70, 89, 91, 93, N.Y. Council for Humanities grantee, 1976, NEH grantee, 1977-79, 91, Mellon Found. grantee, 1980-84, Am. Council Learned Socs. grantee, 1987. Mem. AAAS, AAUP, ACLU, N.Y. State Bar Assn. (chmn. ethics subcom., com. on legal edn. and admission to bar 1986-2004, 05-), Mind Assn., Am. Philos. Assn. (chmn. standing com. on philosophy and medicine 1988-92, chmn. standing com. on philosophy and law 1998-2001), Soc. for Philosophy and Pub. Affairs, Internat. Assn. Philosophy of Law and Social Philosophy, Conf. on Methods in Philosophy and the Scis. (chmn. 1988-90), Internat. Hobbes Assn. (exec. com. 1986—), Internat. Soc. Econs. and Philosophy (treas. 1994—). Office: CUNY Grad Sch 365 5th Ave New York NY 10016-4334 also: Lehman Coll Philosophy Dept Bronx NY 10468 Home Phone: 212-787-5638; Office Phone: 718-960-8292.

BAUMRIND, DIANA, research psychologist; b. NYC, Aug. 23, 1927; AB, Hunter Coll., 1948; MA, U. Calif., Berkeley, 1951, PhD, 1955. Cert. and lic. psychologist, Calif. Project dir. psychology dept. U. Calif., Berkeley, 1955-58; project dir. Inst. of Human Devel., 1960—, also rsch. psychologist and prin. investigator family socialization and devel. competence project. Lectr. and cons. in field; referee for rsch. proposals Grant Found., NIH, 1970—, NSF, 1970—. Contbr. numerous articles to profl. jours. and books; author 2 monographs; mem. editorial bd. Devel. Psychology, 1986-90, Parenting: Science and Practice, 2000—. Recipient Rsch. Scientist award, NIMH; grantee NIMH, 1955-58, 60-66, Nat. Inst. Child Health and Human Devel., 1967-74, MacArthur Found., Grant Found., 1967—. Fellow Am. Psychol. Assn., Am. Psychol. Soc. (G. Stanley Hall award 1988), Soc. Research in Child Devel. Office: U Calif Inst of Human Devel 1217 Tolman Hall Berkeley CA 94720-1691 Office Phone: 510-642-3603.

BAUM-VILLAVICENCIO, LYNNE MIRIAM, lawyer; b. Waukesha, Wis., Oct. 7, 1972; d. Bernard and Julie Ann Baum. BA, U. Wis., 1994; JD, Georgetown U., 1999. Bar: (N.Y.) 2000, U.S. Dist. Ct. PR 2001, D.C. 2002. Law clk. to Hon. Jaime Pieras Jr. U.S. Dist. Ct. PR, San Juan, 1999—2001; assoc. Hogan & Hartson LLP, Washington, 2001—. Mem.: ABA, DC Bar Assn., Phi Beta Kappa. Office: Hogan & Hartson LLP 555 13th St NW Washington DC 20004 Home: 1452 Ogden St NW Washington DC 20010 Office Phone: 202-637-6636. Business E-Mail: lmbaum@hhlaw.com.

BAUNER, RUTH ELIZABETH, library director; b. Quincy, Ill. d. John Carl and M. Irene (Nutt) B. BS in Edn., Western Ill. U., 1950; MS, U. Ill., 1956; postgrad., So. Ill. U., 1974, PhD, 1978. Asst. res. libr. Western Ill. U., Macomb, 1950; tchr., libr. Sandwich (Ill.) Twp. High Sch., 1950-54; circulation dept. asst. U. Ill. Libr., Urbana, 1955; asst. edn. libr. So. Ill. U., Carbondale, 1956-63, acting edn. libr., 1963-64, edn. and psychology libr., 1965-93, assoc. prof. curriculum and instrn. dept., 1971-93; coord. freshman yr. experience program, vis. assoc. prof. Coll. of Liberal Arts, Carbondale, 1994-96. Dir. Grad. Residence Ctr. Librs., So. Ill. U., 1973-79; subject matter expert Learning Resources Svc. Interactive Video, Carbondale, 1990-91, also scriptwriter; faculty emeritus So. Ill. U., 2004—. Co-author: The Teacher's Library, 1966; contbr. articles to profl. jours. Pres. alumni constituency bd. Coll. Edn., Carbondale, 1988—89; mem. Carbondale Bd. Ethics, 1989—2001; tchr. I Can Read Program, 2001—03; mem. Carbondale Citizens Adv. Commn., 1999—2001; bd. dirs. So. Ill. U. chpt. UN, 1985—86, 1994—97; mem. faculty bd. So. Ill. Learning in Retirement, So. Ill. U. Emeritus Assn.; bd. dirs. Jackson County AARP, 1997—99, 2001—03, 2006—, So. Ill. U. Emeritus Faculty Assn., 2004—; mem. friends bd. Mcleod Playhouse, 2005—. Recipient Luck Has Nothing To Do With It award, Oryx Press, 1993. Mem.: AAUW (univ. rep. Carbondale br. 1988—89), ALA, Ill. Libr. Assn., Assn. Coll. and Rsch. Librs. (chmn. edn. and behavioral scis. sect. 1976—77, Most Active Mem. award 1968—93), AAUP (v.p. So. Ill. U. chpt. 1972—73), Delta Kappa Gamma, Phi Kappa Phi, Phi Delta Kappa (Women of Distinction award 1999). Office: 1206 W Freeman St Carbondale IL 62901-2351

BAUR, MICHAEL L., information technology executive; Product mgr. Gates Corp., 1989—90, merchandising dir., 1990—91; pres., gen. mgr. Argent Technologies Inc., 1991—92; pres. ScanSource Inc., Greenville, SC, 1992—2000, bd. dir., 1995—, pres., CEO, 2000—07, CEO, 2007—. Bd. mem. Assn. Automatic identification & Data Capture Technologies. Office: ScanSource Inc 6 Logue Ct Greenville SC 29615*

BAUROTH, NANCY ANN, journalist, former marketing executive; b. Phila., Oct. 12, 1949; d. Harry William and Mary Octavia (Coffman) B. Dir. advt. and pub. rels. Doubleday & Co., NYC, 1974-80; dir. product advt. Merrill Lynch & Co., NYC, 1989-82, dir. mktg. comm. and cash mgmt., 1982-84; v.p., dir. mktg. direct access electronic banking Citibank, 1984-86; op-ed columnist Charlotte (N.C.) Observer, 1998—. Lectr. advt. writing CUNY, 1978, 79. Honoree Boston Soc. Fin. Analysts, 1982, creative workshop honoree Advt. Age, 1983. Mem. Fin. Comm. Soc. (honoree 1982), Pubs. Advt. Club (v.p. 1976-80). Republican. Presbyterian. Home: 10305 Threatt Woods Dr Charlotte NC 28277-2428 Personal E-mail: nbauroth@carolina.rr.com.

BAUSCH, CLAIRE, library director; Dir. librs. Nicholson Meml. Libr. Sys., Garland, Tex. Ex officio mem. libr. adv. bd. Nicholson Meml. Libr. Sys. Office: Nicholson Meml Libr Sys 625 Austin St Garland TX 75040 Office Phone: 972-205-2543. Office Fax: 972-205-2523. E-mail: cbausch@ci.garland.tx.us.

BAUSHER, VERNE C(HARLES), retired bank executive; b. Reading, Pa. s. La Verne H. and Helen M. (Dornes) B.; m. Sandra Stamm Bausher, May 22, 1965; children: Christopher S., Gretchen S., Samantha A., Andrew P. BS, Drexel U., 1961; MBA, Northwestern U., 1962. Asst. v.p. Cen. Nat. Bank of Cleve., 1962-69; v.p. Meridian Bank (formerly American Bank and Trust Co. of Pa.), Reading, 1969-83; exec. v.p. Penn Savs. Bank, Wyomissing, 1983-87; exec. v.p., chief lending officer Germantown Savs. Bank, Bala Cynwyd, Pa., 1987—2004, ret., 2004. Trustee, v.p. Pub. Edn. Found. for Berks County, 1986—; bd. dirs. Wilson Sch. Dist., West Lawn, Pa., 1977—, pres., 1989-90; bd. dirs. Berks County Intermediate Unit, Reading, 1977—, YMCA of Reading, 1987-89. Republican. Lutheran. Avocations: reading, swimming, diving. Home: 4152 Hill Terrace Dr Sinking Spring PA 19608-9384

BAUTISTA, MARIETA PASCUAL, psychiatrist; b. Manila, Apr. 10, 1947; came to U.S., 1974; d. Amado and Amparo (Pascual) B. BS, U. Santo Tomas, 1966, MD, 1971. Diplomate Am. Bd. Psychiatry and Neurology with subspecialty in child and adolescent psychiatry (bd. examiner). Intern Meriden (Conn.)-Wallingford Hosp., 1974-75; resident psychiatry Fairfield Hills Hosp., Newtown, Conn., 1975-78; resident child psychiatry Lafayette Clinic, Detroit, 1978-79, Fairlawn Ctr., Pontiac, Mich., 1979-81, staff psychiatrist/unit chief Birchwood Hall, 1981-85, dir. young adolescent div., 1985-87; dir. gen. psychiatry tng. program Fairlawn Ctr., Mich. State U./Wayne State U., Pontiac, 1987—; dep. dir. in charge residency tng. program Wayne State U./Fairlawn Ctr.; dir. div. grad. edn. and tng. and dir. pre-adolescent div. Fairlawn Ctr., Wayne State U., Pontiac, 1991—; asst. prof. psychiatry Wayne State U., Detroit, 1992—; chief admission/ cts. Clinton Valley Ctr., Pontiac, 1995—. Cons. in field; supr. Residents in Tng., 1989—, cons. Oakland Intermediate Sch. Dist.; instr. dept. psychiatry Mich. State U., 1980-81, assoc. clin. prof. dept. psychiatry, 1983—. Recipient Five Yr. Svc. award State of Mich., Ten. Yr. Svc. award State of Mich. Mem. Am. Acad. Child and Adolescent Psychiatry, Mich. Coun. Child Psychiatry, Philippine Med. Assn. Mich., U. Santo Tomas Med. Assn. Midwest, Am. Assn. Dirs. Psychiat. Residency Tng. Roman Catholic. Avocations: tennis, walking, cooking. Home: 4046 Hanover Ct West Bloomfield MI 48323-1815 Office: Cmty Network Svcs 35 W Huron Pontiac MI 48342 Office Phone: 248-745-4900. E-mail: mbautista@cnsmi.org.

BAVASI, PETER JOSEPH, sports management executive; b. Bronxville, NY, Oct. 31, 1942; s. Emil Joseph and Evit E. (Rice) B.; m. Judith Marzonie, June 13, 1964; children: Patrick, Cristina. BA in Philosophy, St. Mary's Coll., Moraga, Calif., 1964. Minor league gen. mgr. L.A. Dodgers, 1964-68; dir. minor league ops. San Diego Padres, 1968-73, v.p., gen. mgr., 1973-76; pres., CEO Toronto Blue Jays, 1976-81; pres. Peter Bavasi Sports, Inc., Tampa, Fla., 1981-84; pres., COO Cleve. Indians, 1984-87; pres., CEO Telerate Sports and SportsTicker, Jersey City, 1987-94; pres. ESPN/SportsTicker, Jersey City, 1995-96; prin. Bavasi Sports Ptnrs., LLP, La Jolla, 2001—. Office: Bavasi Sports Ptnrs LLP 1001 Genter St Unit 3G La Jolla CA 92037-5531

BAVEJA, ALOK, finance educator; b. New Delhi, Oct. 7, 1965; s. Ved Parkash and Ramesh Baveja; m. Kalyani Kailasamoni, Nov. 16, 1969; 1 child, Rishi Dev. B in Tech., Indian Inst. Tech., New Delhi, 1987; MS, SUNY, Buffalo, 1987, PhD, 1993. Asst. prof. mgmt. Rutgers U., Camden, NJ, 1994—2000, assoc. prof. info. and mgmt. sci, 2000. Contbr. articles to profl. jours. Founder Indo-American Inst. for Rural Empowerment, South Plainfield, NJ, 2000. Named Prof. of Yr., Inst. Indsl. Engrs., Buffalo Chpt., 1994; recipient Tchg. award, Rutgers U., Sch. Bus., 1996, 2000, 2002, 2006, Award of Honor, Indian Inst. Tech., 2003; grantee, Nat. Inst. Justice, 1998—2001, NJ. Dept. Health and Sr. Svcs., 2003. Mem.: Inst. Ops. Rsch. and Mgmt. Sci. (assoc.). Achievements include research in area of core competencies. Office: Rutgers Univ Sch Bus 227 Penn St Camden NJ 08102 Home Phone: 610-421-8191; Office Phone: 856-225-6694. Office Fax: 856-225-6231. Business E-Mail: baveja@crab.rutgers.edu.

BAWA, KAMALJIT SINGH, biologist, educator; b. Kapurthala, Punjab, India, Apr. 7, 1939; came to US, 1967; s. Rajinder Singh and Dwarki (Ohri) B.; m. Tshering Wangdi, Sept. 22, 1969; children: Sonia, Ranjit. BS, Panjab U., Chandigarh, India, 1958, BS with honors, 1960, MS with honors, 1962, PhD, 1967. Postdoctoral rsch. assoc., instr. U. Wash. Coll. Forest Resources, Seattle, 1967-72; rsch. fellow Harvard U. Gray Herbarium, Cambridge, Mass., 1973-74; asst. prof. biology dept. U. Mass., Boston, 1974—77, assoc. prof., 1977-81, prof., 1981—96, disting. prof., 1996—; pres. Ashoka Trust for Rsch. in Ecology and the Environment, Bangalore, India, 1996—. Mem. La Selva adv. com. Orgn. Tropical Studies, 1978—85; chmn. biology dept. U. Mass., Boston, 1989—92; bd. dirs. New Eng. Forestry Found., Groton, Mass., 2000—04; founder, trustee Ctr. Interdisciplinary Studies in Environment and Devel., Bangalore, India, 2000—. Contbr. articles to profl. jours., chapters to books; mem. editl. bd.: Jour. Arnold Arboretum, 1986—90, Jour. Tree Scis., 1986—91, Evolutionary Trends in Plants, 1987—92, Jour. Sustainable Forestry, 1992—, assoc. editor: Conservation Biology, 1987—93, Econ. Botany, 1997—; co-editor: Reproductive Ecology of Tropical Forest Plants, 1990, La Selva: Ecology and Natural Hist. of a Neotropical Rain Forest, 1994, Forest Genetic Resources: Status, Threats and Conservation Strategies, 2001, Tropical Ecosystems: Structure, Diversity and Human Welfare, 2001; mem. editl. adv. bd.: Plant Systematics and Evolution, 1993—98, editor-in-chief: Conservation and Soc., 2001—. Mem. exec. bd. Found. for Rehabilitation of Local Health Traditions, Bangalore, India, 1998—2000, mem. adv. com., 1998—. Named Pew scholar, Conservation and the Environment, Pew Charitable Trusts, 1991—96; grantee, NSF, Smithsonian Instn., Maria Moors Cabot and Charles Bullard Rsch. fellowship, Harvard U., 1972, Guggenheim fellowship, 1987—88. Fellow: NAS, India, AAAS; mem.: Soc. Conservation Biology, New Eng. Bot. Club, Ecol. Soc. Am., Soc. Am. Naturalists, Soc. for Study of Evolution, Assn. Tropical Biology (councilor 1985—87, pres. 2000), Am. Inst. Biol Scis., Soc. Econ. Botany (councilor 2000—). Office: Dept Biology U Mass Boston MA 02125 also: Ashoka Trust Rsch in Ecology and the Environment 659 5th A Main Rd Hebbal Bangalore 560 024 India

BAWA, RAJ, biotechnology educator, nanotechnologist; s. Sukhdev Raj and Sudesh (Bhalla) B. BSc in Microbiology with honors, Panjab U., 1985; MS in Biology, Rensselaer Poly. Inst., Troy, NY, 1987, PhD in Biology, 1990. Registered patent agent. Rsch. and tchg. asst. biology dept. Rensselaer Poly. Inst., 1985-90, adv. office tech. commercialization, 2003—; patent examiner Patent and Trademark Office, US Dept. Commerce, Washington, 1990-96, primary examiner, supervisory patent examiner (acting), Patent and Trademark Office, 1996—2002; instr. US Patent Acad., 1995—2002; pres. Bawa Biotech. Consulting, LLC, Ashburn, Va., 2002—, Schenectady, NY, 2002—; adj. prof. natural and applied scis. Extended Learning Inst. No. Va. CC, Annandale, Va., 2004—. Nanotech. and biodef. expert; vis. guest lectr. Sch. Sci. Rensselaer Polytechnic Inst., 1998—99, vis. asst. prof., 1999—2002, adj. asst. prof., 2002—04; adv. bd. UN's Online Living Hist. Initiative for HIV/AIDS; review panel NIH, Bethesda, Md., 2005, NSF, Arlington, 2007; bd. dirs. RAA Rensselaer Polytechnic Inst., Troy, NY; spkr. in field. Mem. editl. bd.: Internat. Jour. Nanomedicine, Nanotech. Law and Bus., assoc. editor: Nanomedicine; contbr. articles to profl. jours., chapters to books. Recipient Talbot award US Biophys. Soc., Bethesda, Md., 1988, Cert. Appreciation, US Dept. Commerce, 2001, Rensselaer Alumni Assn. Dir.'s award, 2001, Rensselaer Key award, 2005. Fellow: Am. Acad. Nanomedicine; mem.: Am. Intellectual Property Law Assn., Am. Chem. Soc., World Future Soc. (life; global adv. coun.), Am. Soc. Microbiology, Sigma Xi (life Travel award 1988, 1990). Achievements include research in isolation and biochemical characterization of a new potassium transport protein from mammalian mitochondria, research on membrane transport of cationic anticancer drugs and polyamines in mammalian mitochondria, electron microscopy of animal sperm cells. Office: 21005 Starflower Way Ashburn VA 20147 Home Phone: 703-723-0034; Office Phone: 703-582-1745. Business E-Mail: bawabio@aol.com.

BAWDEN, NINA (MARY BAWDEN), author; b. Eng., 1925; Author: Who Calls the Tune (in U.S. as Eyes of Green), 1953, The Odd Flamingo, 1954, Change Here for Babylon, 1955, The Solitary Child, 1956, Devil by the Sea, 1957, Just Like a Lady (in U.S. as Glass Slippers Always Pinch), 1960, In Honour Bound, 1961, Tortoise by Candlelight, 1963, The Secret Passage (in U.S. as The House of Secrets), 1963, On the Run (in U.S. as Three on the Run), 1964, Under the Skin, 1964, A Little Love, A Little Learning, 1966, The White Horse Gang, 1966, The Witch's Daughter, 1966, A Handful of Thieves, 1967, A Woman of My Age, 1967, The Grain of Truth, 1968, The Runaway Summer, 1969, The Birds on the Trees, 1970, Squib, 1971, Anna Apparent, 1972, Carrie's War, George Beneath a Paper Moon, 1974, The Peppermint Pig, 1975, Afternoon of a Good Woman, 1976, Rebel on a Rock, 1978, Familiar Passions, 1979, Walking Naked, 1981, Kept in the Dark, 1982, The Ice House, 1983, The Finding, 1985, Finding, 1985, Circles of Deceit, 1987, Keeping Henry, 1988, The Outside Child, 1989, Family Money, 1991, Humbug, 1992, The Real Plato Jones, 1993, In My Own Time, 1994, A Nice Change, 1997, Off the Road, 1998, Ruffian on the Stair, 2001, Dear Austen, 2005. Recipient S.T. DuPont Golden Pen award for alifetime's svc. to lit., 2004. Address: care Curtis Brown Ltd 10 Astor Pl New York NY 10003-6935 also: 22 Noel Rd London NI 8HA England also: 19 Kapodistriou Nauplion 21100 Greece Personal E-mail: ninakrak@btinternet.com.

BAWENDI, MOUNGI G., chemist, educator; b. 1961; AB, Harvard U., 1982, AM, 1983; PhD in Chem., U. Chgo., 1988. Postdoctoral rsch. Bell Labs., 1988—90; asst. prof. chem. MIT, Cambridge, 1990—95, assoc. prof. chem., 1995—96, prof. chem., Keck Prof. Energy, 1996—. Contbr. articles to sci. jours. Recipient David & Lucile Packard Sci. & Engring. Fellowship, 1991-96, Coblentz award, 1997, NSF Presdl. Young Investigator award, 1991-96, Alfred P. Sloan Rsch. Fellowship, 1994-96, Raymond & Beverly Sackler prize in phys. sci., 2001; co-recipient Ernest Orlando Lawrence award for Materials Rsch. Dept. Energy, 2007. Fellow: AAAS, Am. Acad. Arts & Scis.; mem.: NAS, Am. Chem. Soc. (Nobel Laureate Signature award for grad. edn. 1997). Office: MIT Dept Chemistry 77 Massachusetts Ave Rm 6-221 Cambridge MA 02139-4307 Office Phone: 617-253-9796. Office Fax: 617-253-7030. E-mail: mgb@mit.edu.*

BAXENDALE, SONIA A., diversified financial services company executive; Grad., U. Toronto. Various positions American Express Canada, Saatchi & Saatchi; joined Canadian Imperial Bank of Commerce, Toronto, 1992—, former mng. dir., former exec. v.p., asset mgmt., card products and collections, former exec. v.p., global private banking and investment mgmt., 2000—02, sr. exec. v.p., wealth mgmt., 2002—05, sr. exec. v.p., retail markets, 2005—. Bd. chmn. CIBC Securities Inc., CIBC Trust Corp., TAL Private Mgmt. Ltd., CIBC Asset Mgmt. Inc.; bd. dirs. CIBC Trust Co. Bahamas Ltd., CIBC Bank & Trust Co. Cayman Ltd., CIBC Investor Services Inc., TAL Global Asset Mgmt. Inc. Named one of Canada's Top 40 Under 40, 2000, 25 Women to Watch, US Banker mag., 2005. Office: Canadian Imperial Bank of Commerce 5650 Yonge St Toronto ON M2M 4G3 Canada

BAXLEY, LUCY, former lieutenant governor; b. Ala., Dec. 21, 1937; m. James Lee Smith, 1996; children: Becky, Louis. Licensed realtor; state treas. State of Ala., Montgomery, 1994—2002, lt. gov., 2002—07. Former spokesperson Senior Promise; Women's Philanthropy Bd. Auburn U. Recipient Senior Citizens' Golden Eagle Statesman of Yr., Outstanding Woman Leader, Am. Assn. of U. Women. Mem.: Nat. Assn. Lt. Govs., Ala. Fedn. of Dem. Women (chair adv. coun.), U. Ala. XXXI. Democrat. Methodist.

BAXLEY, WADE H., lawyer; b. Dothan, Ala., Nov. 1, 1943; BS, Univ. Ala., 1965, JD, 1968. Bar: Ala. 1968, U.S. Dist. Ct. Mid. Ala. Dist. 1969, U.S. Ct. Appeals 5th Cir. 1977, U.S. Ct. Appeals 11th Cir. 1983, U.S. Dist. Ct. No. Ala. Dist. 1991. Law clerk Ala. Ct. Appeals, 1968—69; asst. city atty. Dothan, Ala., 1969—73; city atty., 1973—81; atty. Ramsey Baxley & McDougle, Dothan, Ala., 1981—. Mem.: So. Conf. Bar Pres., Assn. Def. Trial Attys., Def. Rsch. Inst., Ala. State Bar (v.p. 1991—92, pres. 1999—2000), Houston County Bar Assn. (pres. 1978—79), ABA (bd. gov. 2003—05), Ala. Def. Lawyers Assn. (pres. 1996—97). Office: Ramsey Baxley & McDougle PO Drawer 1486 212 W Troy St Dothan AL 36302

BAXT, WILLIAM GORDON, medical educator; b. Mar. 31, 1941; BA, Brown U., 1963; MD, Yale U., 1967. Diplomate Am. Bd. Internal Medicine, Am. Bd. Emergency Medicine. Intern Columbia-Presbyn. Hosp., NYC, 1967-68, resident in internal medicine, 1970-71, fellow in hematology, 1971-73; from asst. prof. medicine to prof. clin. medicine & surgery U. Calif., San Diego, 1973-94; prof., chmn. dept. emergency medicine U. Pa. Med. Ctr., Phila., 1994—. Rsch. biologist U. Calif., La Jolla, 1976-77; med. dir. life flight aeromed. program U. Calif. Med. Ctr., San Diego, 1980-89, assoc. dir. divsn. emergency med. svcs., 1978-80, dir. dept. emergency medicine, 1980-94; chmn. dept. emergency medicine U. Pa. Med. Ctr., 1994—. Co-author: (with others) Cellular Modifiction and Genetic Transformation by Exogenous Nucleic Acids, 1973, The Leukemia Cell, 1979, Systems Approach to Emergency Medical Care, 1983, Trauma: The First Hour, 1985; mem. editl. bd. Emergency Care Quar., Annals of Emergency Medicine; contbr. articles to profl. jours. Surgeon USPHS, 1968-70. Leukemia Soc. Am. scholar, 1976; recipient Physicians Recognition award AMA, 1985, Best Oral Clin. Sci. Paper U. Assn. for Emergency Medicine, 1988, Best Oral Methodology Paper Soc. for Acad. Emergency Medicine, 1990. Mem. Nat. Acad. Scis., Soc. for Acad. Emergency Medicine, Phi Beta Kappa. Office: Hosp U Pa Dept Emergency Med Ground Ravdin 3400 Spruce St Philadelphia PA 19104-4206 E-mail: baxtw@uphs.epenn.edu.

BAXTER, BETTY CARPENTER, academic administrator; b. Sherman, Tex., Oct. 10, 1937; d. Granville E. and Elizabeth (Caston) Carpenter; m. Cash Baxter; children: Stephen Barrington, Catherine Elaine. AA in Music, Christian Coll., Columbia, Mo., 1957; MusB in Voice and Piano, So. Meth. U., Dallas, 1959; MA in Early Childhood Edn., Tchrs. Coll., Columbia, 1972, MEd, 1979, EdD, 1988. Cert. life coach, cons. Acad. Coaching Excellence, Sacramento, Calif., 2004, grief recovery specialist Grief Recovery Inst., LA, 2006. Tchr. Riverside Ch. Day Sch., NYC, 1966—71; head mistress Episcopal Sch., NYC, 1972—87, head mistress, emeritus, 1987—; founding head Presbyn. Sch., Houston, 1988—94; dir. Chadwick Village Sch., Palos Verdes Peninsula, Calif., 1995—; head sch. St. Margaret's Episcopal Sch., Palm Desert, 2001—02; cert. life coach Baxter Coaching and Consulting, 2004—. Author: The Relationship of Early Tested Intelligence on the WPPSI to Later Tested Aptitude on the SAT. Mem.: ACA, ASCD, Nat. Notary Assn., Internat. Coach Fedn. Republican. Episcopalian. Office: 72-828 Joshua Tree St Palm Desert CA 92260 Home Phone: 760-773-1980; Office Phone: 760-424-9980. Business E-Mail: bettybaxtercoach@earthlink.net.

BAXTER, BEVERLEY VELORIS, economic association administrator, educator; b. Eugene, Oreg., July 5, 1943; d. J. Clifford Baxter and O. Veloris Crenshaw; m. Doyle R. Dobbins, July 7, 1962; children: Kendall Reé Baxter Dobbins, Kalen Dobbins, Konlee Baxter Dobbins. Certificate, Graduate Sch. Ecumenical Studies, Bossey, Switzerland, 1965, William Temple Coll., Rugby, Eng., 1965; BS, Phillips U., 1966, MEd, 1967; MA, U. Del., 1971, PhD, 1976. Tchg. asst. U. Del., Newark, 1971—76; asst. prof. dept. English Temple U., Phila., 1977—79; real estate investor Wilmington, Del., 1979—83; dir. edn. programs First Unitarian Ch., Wilmington, 1983; exec. asst. to county exec. New Castle County, Wilmington, 1983—84; v.p. Blue Ball Properties, Wilmington, 1985—93; exec. dir. The Com. of 100, Wilmington, 1993—. Dir. Del. Bus. Pub. Edn. Coun., Wilmington, 1988—2003, Wilmington Area Planning Coun. Wilmington Initiatives Steering Com., 1995—; mem. Gov.'s State Planning Citizens Adv. Coun., Del., 1995—, Del. State C. of C. Small Bus. Alliance Legis. Com., 1997—; mem. working group De. Dept. Transportation; mem. Del. Dept. Natural Resources & Environ. Control Regulatory Adv. com.; bd. dirs., treas. Wiley Coll., Marshall, Tex. Author: Diaries and Journals of Americans Held Prisoner During the Revolutionary War, 1976; editor: For Your Info., 1995. Pres. bd. dir. Montessori Cmty. Sch., Wilmington, 1996—2000; mem. Task Force on Early Childhood Edn., 2004—; bd. dir. Unitarian Universalist Svc. Com., Cambridge, Mass., 1985—91; pres. First Unitarian Ch., Wilmington, 1979—82, bd. dir., 1979—82, Friends of Rockwood Mus., Wilmington, 1986—88. Recipient Disting. Svc. award, Unitarian Universalist Svc. Com., 1991, Economic Turnaround Cert. of Appreciation, Wilmington 2000, 1995, Liveable Cmty. award, Wilmington Area Planning Coun., 1998. Mem.: The Associates, The Bus. Group, New Castle County C. of C. (state affairs coun., county govt. coun.). Unitarian Universalist. Avocations: music, reading, gardening, skiing. Office: The Com of 100 704 King St Ste 5/2 Wilmington DE 19801

BAXTER, CECIL WILLIAM, JR., retired academic administrator; b. Stockton, Kans., Aug. 11, 1923; s. Cecil William and Marjorie LaVerne (Fitzpatrick) B.; m. Pat Ann Layman, June 6, 1951; children: Cecil William, Michael Kent, Patrick Alan. BA, Kans. Wesleyan U., 1950; MBA, U. Denver, 1954; PhD, U. Tex., 1967. Secondary edn. tchr., then secondary sch. prin., 1951-60; bus. mgr. Cottey Coll., Nevada, Mo., 1960-65; dean instrn. Kansas City Community Jr. Coll., Kans., 1967-68, Forest Park Community Coll., St. Louis, 1968-70; pres. North Seattle Community Coll., 1970-85, pres. emeritus, 1985—; exec. dir. Coun. on Naturopathic Med. Edn., 1989-92. Mem. faculty U. Wash., 1971; mem. Comm. on Colls. N.W. Assn. Schs. and Colls., 1981-85 Bd. dirs. Sr. Citizens Orgn., Seattle, 1972. Served with AUS, 1944-46. Ford Found. fellow U. Okla.; Kellogg Found. fellow U. Tex. Mem. Phi Delta Kappa Lodges: Rotary.

BAXTER, DONALD LEON MURRAY, education educator; BA, Oberlin Coll., 1976; MA, U. Pitts., 1980, PhD, 1984. Asst. prof. Princeton U., NJ, 1983—90; prof. U. Conn., Storrs, Conn., 1990—. Author: (monograph) Hume's Difficulty: Time and Identity in the Treatise. Co-recipient Essay Competition, North Am. Leibniz Soc., 1994. Mem.: Hume Soc., Am. Philosophy Assn., Conn. Acad. of Arts and Sciences. Office: Univ of Conn Philosophy Dept Storrs Mansfield CT 06269-2054 Office Phone: 860-486-4419. Business E-Mail: donald.baxter@uconn.edu.

BAXTER, GENE FRANCIS, chemical researcher, consultant; b. Sanish, ND, July 25, 1922; s. Leslie Valentine and Frances (Ellertson) Baxter; m. Elizabeth Rose Turner, Feb. 14, 1970; children: Marsha Lynn, Michael James, Anthony Frederick. BS Chem., Univ. Wash., Seattle, WA, 1944. Rsch. chemist Adhesive Products Co., Seattle, Wash., 1944—46, Martin-Marietta Corp., Seattle, 1946—53; group leader Weyerhaeuser Co., Seattle, 1953—62, rsch. scientist, 1962—73, Georgia-Pacific Corp., Decatur, 1973—83, sr. scientist, 1983—85, cons., 1985—99. Recipient Disting. Scientist Award, Georgia-Pacific Resins Corp., 1986. Achievements include patents for 22 US patents granted between 1940-1990. Avocation: playing cards. Home: 195 Tiburon Drive Lithonia GA 30038

BAXTER, JOHN DARLING, internist, endocrinologist, educator, health facility administrator; b. Lexington, Ky., June 11, 1940; s. William Elbert and Genevive Lockhart (Wilson) B.; m. Ethelee Davidson Baxter, Aug. 10, 1963; children: Leslie Lockhart, Gillian Booth. BA in Chemistry, U. Ky., 1962; MD, Yale U., 1966; DSc (hon.), U. Ky, 2004. Intern, then resident in internal medicine Yale-New Haven Hosp., 1966-68; USPHS research assoc. Nat. Inst. Arthritis and Metabolic Diseases, NIH, 1968-70; Dernham sr. fellow oncology U. Calif. Med. Sch., San Francisco, 1970-72, mem. faculty, 1972—, prof. medicine and biochemistry and biophysics, 1979—, dir., Metabolic Rsch. Unit, 1981—2000. Attending physician U. Calif. Med. Center, 1972-; dir. endocrine research Howard Hughes Med. Inst., 1976-81, investigator, 1975-81; chief div. endocrinology Moffitt Hosp., 1980-97; founder, dir. Calif. Biotechnology, Inc., 1982-1992, dir., chmn. SciClone scientific adv. bd., 1991-. Editor textbook of endocrinology and metabolism; Author research papers in field; mem. editorial bd. profl. jours. Recipient George W. Thorn Outstanding Investigator award, Howard Hughes Med. Inst., 1978, Disting. Alumni award U. Ky., 1980, Dautrebande prize for research in cellular and molecular biology, Belgium, 1985, Albion Bernstein award N.Y. Med. Soc., 1987, Edwin B. Astook award, US Endocrine Society, 1997; grantee NIH, Am. Cancer Soc., others. Mem. Am. Chem. Soc., Am. Soc. Hypertension, Am. Soc. Clin. Investigation, Am. Thyroid Assn., Assn. Am. Physicians, Am. Fedn. Clin. Research, Endocrine Soc., pres., 2002-2003, Western Assn. Physicians, Western Soc. Clin. Research, Inst. Medicine, NAS.

BAXTER, MARVIN RAY, state supreme court justice; b. Fowler, Calif., Jan. 9, 1940; m. Jane Pippert, June 22, 1963; children: Laura, Brent. BA in Economics, Calif. State U., 1962; JD, Hastings Coll. of Law, 1966. Bar: Calif. 1966. Dep. dist. atty. Fresno County, Calif., 1967-68; assoc. Andrews, Andrews, Thaxter & Jones, 1968-70, ptnr., 1971-82; apptd. sec. to Gov. George Deukmejian, 1983-88; assoc. justice Calif. Ct. Appeal (5th dist.), 1988-90, Calif. Supreme Ct., 1991—. Mem. Jud. Coun. of Calif., chmn. policy coord. and liaison com., 1996-; dir. emeritus Hastings Coll. of Law. Recipient Man of the Yr. award, Armenian Nat. Com., 1991, Armenian Professional Soc., 1993, Mentor award, Fresno County Young Lawyers Assn., 1996. Mem. Fresno County Bar Assn. (bd. dirs. 1977-82, pres. 1981), Calif. Young Lawyers Assn. (bd. gov. 1973-76, sec.-treas. 1974-75), Fresno County Young Lawyers Assn. (pres. 1973-74), Fresno County Legal Svcs., Inc. (bd. dirs. 1973-74), Fresno State U. Alumni Assn. (pres. 1970-71), Fresno State U. Alumni Trust Coun. (pres. 1970-75). Office: Calif Supreme Ct 350 Mcallister St San Francisco CA 94102-4712

BAXTER, NANCY, medical writer; b. Grand Rapids, Mich., Oct. 3, 1950; d. Robert Emerson and Mary (Knoblauch) B. BA in Journalism, Am. U., 1972. Asst. dir. publs. Am. Speech, Lang. & Hearing Assn., Washington, 1973-77; mng. editor Biomedia, Inc., Princeton, N.J., 1977-79, Continuing Profl. Edn. Ctr., Inc., Princeton, 1981-82; editor A.M. Best Co., Oldwick, N.J., 1979-81; med. writer, editor Biomed Info. Corp., NYC, 1982-83; pres. Baxter Med. Comms. Co., Warren, N.J., 1983—. Mem.: Am. Med. Writers Assn. Home and Office: 18 Stiles Rd Warren NJ 07059-5413 Office Phone: 908-755-4589. Personal E-mail: baxmedcomm@aol.com.

BAXTER, NATHAN DWIGHT, dean; b. Coatesville, Pa., Nov. 16, 1948; s. Beigium Nathan and Augusta Ruth (Byrd) Baxter; m. Mary Ellen Walker, June 10, 1969; children: Timika Ann, Harrison David. MDiv with honors, Lancaster Theol. Sem., 1976, DMin, 1984; STD (hon.), Dickinson Coll., Carlisle, Pa., 1990; DD (hon.), St. Paul's Coll., Lawrenceville, Va., 2000; DST (hon.), Messiah Coll., Grantham, Pa., 2001; DHL (hon.), York Coll., Pa., 2002; DD (hon.), Colgate U., Hamilton, NY, 2003. Ordained Episcopal Ch., 1977. Curate St. John's Episcopal Ch., Carlisle, Pa., 1976—78; rector St. Cypman's Episcopal Ch., Hampton, Va., 1978—84; chaplain, prof. religious studies St. Paul's Coll., Lawrenceville, Va., 1984—86; dean, assoc. prof. church and ministry Lancaster Theol. Sem., Pa., 1986—90; adminstrv. dean, assoc. prof. pastoral theology Episcopal Div. Sch., Cambridge, Mass., 1990—91; dean Washington Nat. Cathedral, 1991—. Bd. dirs. Faith and Politics Inst., Washington, 1996; lectr., Medina Seminar Princeton U., NJ, 1997—2002; preacher Chautaugua Inst., NY, 1997—2002; bd. mem. U. Va. Ctr. on Religion & Democracy, 2002; bd. dirs. Riggs Nat. Bank, Washington, 2002. Author: Visions for the Millennium: Thoughts on Christian Living. E-5 US Army, 1968—70. Decorated Vietnam Cross of Gallantry with Palm U.S. Army; fellow, Coll. of Preachers, 1990; Charles E. Merrill fellow, Harvard Div. Sch., 1998. Mem.: NAACP (life), Cosmo Club. Episcopalian. Avocations: black poetry, walking, jazz. Office: Washington Nat Cathedral Massachusetts and Wisconsin Aves NW Washington DC 20016-5098

BAXTER, NEVINS DENNIS, bank consultant; b. NYC, June 29, 1941; s. Sol and Beatrice B.; m. Anne Susan Hatow, July 30, 1972; children: S.J., Keith. BA, Columbia Coll., 1961; MA, Princeton U., 1962, PhD in Econs., 1964. Asst. prof. fin. U. Pa., 1965-69; v.p. Mathematica, Princeton, NJ, 1969-71; pres. Baxter & Co., Washington, 1971-75, Golembe Assocs., Inc., Washington, 1975-89; chmn. BEI Golembe Cons., Washington, 1989-90; vice chmn. BEI Holdings Ltd., Washington, 1990-93; prin. Baxter & Co., Washington. Contbr. articles to numerous profl. jours. E-mail: nevindbaxter@comcast.net.

BAXTER, RALPH H., JR., lawyer; b. San Francisco, 1946; AB, Stanford U., 1968; MA, Cath. U. Am., 1970; JD, U. Va., 1974. Bar: Calif. 1974. Chmn. Orrick, Herrington & Sutcliffe LLP, San Francisco, 1990—, ptnr., CEO, 1990—. Mem. adv. bd. Nat. Employment Law Inst.; spkr. in field. Author: Sexual Harassment in the Workplace: A Guide to the Law, 1981, Sexual Harassment in the Workplace: A Guide to the Law, 2d rev. edit., 1989, 1994, Manager's Guide to Lawful Terminations, 1983, Manager's Guide to Lawful Terminations, rev. edit., 1991; mem. editl. bd.: Va. Law Rev., 1973—74, mem. editl. adv. bd.: Employee Rels. Law Jour. Named one of 100 most influential lawyers, Nat. Law Jour., 1997, 2000, Calif. Lawyers of Yr., Calif. Lawyer Mag., 2003. Mem.: ABA-labor & employment law sect. (mgmt. co-chmn. com. employment rights & responsibilities in workplace 1987—90, com. EEO), Nat. Employment Law Inst. (adv. bd.), State Bar Calif., Employee Relations Law Jour. (editl. adv. bd.). Office: Orrick Herrington & Sutcliffe LLP The Orrick Building 405 Howard St San Francisco CA 94105 Office Phone: 415-773-5650. Office Fax: 415-773-5759. Business E-Mail: ralphbaxter@orrick.com.

BAXTER, RICHARD HENRY GEOFFREY, research scientist; b. Hobart, Tasmania, Australia, Sept. 24, 1975; arrived in US, 1998, permanent resident, 2006; s. Geoffrey Robert and Valerie Joan Baxter; m. Agata Monika Bogusz, Oct. 22, 2005. BSc in Chemistry, with honors, Australian Nat. U., Canberra, 1998; MS, U. Chgo., Ill., 1999, PhD, 2004. Tech. asst. Australian Nat. U., 1998; postdoctoral fellow U. Chgo., 2004; rsch. assoc. Howard Hughes Med. Inst. Southwe. Med. Ctr., Dallas, 2004—. Author: 5 peer-reviewed jour. articles. Mem.: Am. Crystallographic Assn., Royal Australian Chem. Soc., Biophysical Soc., Am. Chem. Soc. Office: Univ Tex Southwestern Med Ctr 6001 Forest Park Rd Dallas TX 75390-9050 Office Phone: 214-645-5943. Business E-Mail: richard.baxter@utsouthwestern.edu.

BAXTER, ROBERT BANNING, insurance company executive; b. Rochester, NY, Aug. 26, 1946; s. Robert Clarkson and Flora Corinne (Banning) B.; m. Sandra Anne Weber, Apr. 21, 1973; children: Matthew Hamilton, Darcy Colson, Jeffrey Ford. BA, U. Rochester, 1968. Chartered property casualty underwriter; cert. ins. counselor. Personal lines account underwriter Allstate Ins. Co., Rochester, 1973-77; asst. personal lines underwriting mgr. Reliance Ins. Co., Pitts., 1977-78, personal lines underwriting mgr. Canandaigua, N.Y., 1978-79, regional personal lines underwriting mgr. Cin., 1979-81, mktg. mgr., 1981-84, Hartford Ins. Group, Cleve., 1984-85; regional mktg. mgr. Nat. Grange Mut. Ins. Co., Syracuse, N.Y., 1985-88; asst. br. mgr., mktg. mgr. Gen. Accident Ins., Syracuse, 1988-90, br. mgr., 1990-93; CEO, gen. mgr. Dryden Mut. Ins. Co., Dryden, N.Y., 1994—. Capt. USAF, 1968—73, Thailand, West Germany. Decorated Air Force Commendation medal (2). Mem. Soc. Chartered Property Casualty Underwriters, Soc. Cert. Ins. Counselors, Am. Numismatic Assn., Ind. Ins. Agts. Assn. NY (assoc.), Profl. Ins. Agts. NY (assoc.), Honorable Order of Blue Goose Internat., NY Ins. Assn. (bd. dirs.), Ind. Ins. Agts. and Brokers Assn. (nat. bd. dirs. Ins. vocat. student tng. program 2007—), Air Force Assn., DeWitt Hist. Soc. (trustee 2003—), SAR Soc. Republican. Unitarian Universalist. Avocation: coin collecting/numismatics. Home: 29 Forest Acres Dr Ithaca NY 14850-9782 Office: Dryden Mut Ins Co PO Box 635 12 Ellis Dr Dryden NY 13053 Office Phone: 607-844-8106. Business E-Mail: rbaxter@drydenmutual.com.

BAXTER, ROBERT HAMPTON, insurance company executive; b. Glassport, Pa., Mar. 27, 1931; m. Barbara Miller, Aug. 4, 1956. Student, Carnegie Inst. Tech., 1949-50; AB, U.S.C., 1954, JD, 1958. Bar: S.C. bar 1959. Trust officer Citizens & So. Nat. Bank, Charleston, SC, 1958-60, First Citizens Bank & Trust Co., Charlotte, NC, 1960-68; with Aetna Life & Casualty Co., Atlanta, 1968-91. Comdr. USNR, 1954—77. Mem.: Bernardo Heights C. of C., Phi Delta Phi. Presbyterian. Home: 12143 Caminito Corriente San Diego CA 92128-4569

BAXTER, RUTH HOWELL, educational administrator, psychologist; b. Washington; d. Robert R. and Georgie (Murray) Lassiter; m. Edward A. Howell; children: Robert, Astrid, Mova, Mava, Josephine. BS, D.C. Tchrs. Coll.; MA in Edn., George Washington U.; cert. (N.Am. Com. of Oslo scholar), Oslo U.; grad. Adminstr.'s Acad. Class, D.C. Public Schs. Founder, dir., propr. Jewels of Ann. Pvt. Day Sch., Washington, 1970—; tchr. Newlands Infant, Southampton, Eng.; instr. math. demonstration lessons dept. edn. Howard U. Dir. early childhood edn. workshop Brent Elem. Sch., Washington; tchr. adult edn. Bel Air Sch., Woodbridge, Va.; founder, cons. Ask Dr. Ruth Rdnl. Cons. Group; mem. Ednl. Instn. Licensure Commn. Task Forces; mem. Mayor's Pre-White House Conf. on Libraries and Info. Services; exec. high sch. internship program D.C. Public Schs. Author: A Norwegian Birthday Party; contbr. children's stories to various publs. Mem. planning com. Eastern region Jr. Red Cross, Washington; cons. coll. youth motivation task force program Nat. Alliance for Bus.; bd. dirs. Ctr. Ednl. Change D.C. Pub. Schs. Fulbright scholar; North Atlantic scholar; named Outstanding Tchr. of Yr., Future Tchrs. Am.; recipient Outstanding Contbn. award Nat. Assn. Negro Women, Commemorative Medal of Honor. Mem. APA, EVa. Psychol. Assn., English Speaking Union, Columbia Women (sec.), Zeta Phi Beta (life), Phi Delta Kappa. Home: 13349 Delaney Rd Dale City VA 22193

BAXTER, SANDRA L., government agency administrator; BA in English, Howard U.; M in Education, Loyola Coll.; EdD in Social Policy, Harvard Grad. Sch. of Education, 1995. Sr. evaluator US Gen. Acctg. Office; exec. dir. Nat. Inst. Literacy, 2001—. Office: Nat Inst for Literacy 1775 I Street NW Ste 730 Washington DC 20006 Office Phone: 202-233-2025.

BAXTER, SHEILA R., career military officer; b. Franklin, Va., Apr. 4, 1955; B in Health and Phys. Edn., Va. State Coll., 1977; disting. mil. grad., Reserve Officer's Training Corps; M in Health Svcs. Mgmt., Webster U. Med. svcs. offficer U.S. Army, 1978, advanced through grades to brigadier gen., 2004, asst. surgeon gen., dep. chief of staff for force sustainment med. command US Army Med. Services Corp. Ft. Sam Houston, Tex., 2004—05; comdr. Madigan Army Med. Ctr., Tacoma, 2005—. Evangelist Ch. of God and Christ. Decorated Legion of Merit, Bronze Star, Meritorious Svc. Medal with four oak leaf clusters, Army Commendation Medal with two oak leaf clusters, Army Achievement Medal with two oak leaf clusters, Kuwait Liberation Medal, Expert Field Med. Badge, others; recipient Hon. Silver award for excellence in cmty svc., Lord Mayor of Pirmasens, Germany. Office: Madigan Army Med Ctr Bldg 9040 Fitzsimmons Dr Tacoma WA 98431

BAXTER, STEPHEN BARTOW, retired historian; b. Boston, Mar. 8, 1929; s. James Phinney 3d and Anne (Strang) B.; m. Ann Sweeney, Aug. 22, 1953; children: Clare, Persis Baxter Andrews, James, Nicholas, Stephen, Michael. AB in Econs. with honors, Harvard U., 1950; PhD, Cambridge U., 1955. Instr. history Dartmouth Coll., Hanover, NH, 1954-57; asst. prof. U. N.C., Chapel Hill, 1958-62, assoc. prof., 1962-66, prof. history, 1966-91, Kenan prof. history, 1975-91. Vis. asst. prof. U. Mo., Columbia, 1957-58; dir. post-doctoral summer seminars Clark Meml. Libr. UCLA, 1973, 88, Clark libr. prof., 1977-78; dir. summer seminars NEH, Chapel Hill, 1974, post-doctoral seminar, 1978-79. Author: The Development of the Treasury, 1660-1702, 1957, William III and the Defense of European Liberty, 1650-1702, 1966; (with Paul R. Sellin) Anglo-Dutch Cross Currents in the Seventeenth and Eighteenth Centuries, 1976; (with others) Major Crises in Western Civilization, vol. 1, 1965, Eighteenth Century Studies Presented to Arthur M. Wilson, 1973, The Revolution of 1688 and the Birth of the English Political Nation, 1973, Biography in the Eighteenth Century, 1980, Changing Views on British History, 1984; editor: Basic Documents of English History, 1968, England's Rise to Greatness, 1660-1763, 1983; mem. editorial bd. Jour. Modern. History, 1971-77, Albion, 1982-92. Guggenheim fellow, 1959-60, 73-74; Charles Henry Fiske III scholar Trinity Coll., 1950-51.

BAXTER, WARNER L., electric power industry executive; BS in Acctg., U. Mo. Cert. CPA. Sr. mgr. Price WaterhouseCooper, LLC, Acctg. Auditing Svcs. Dept., St. Louis, 1983—93, Price WaterhouseCooper, LLC, SEC Svcs. Dept., NYC; asst. contr. Union Electric, 1995—96, contr., 1996—97; v.p., contr. Ameren Corp. and Ameren Svcs. (following Union Electric and CIPSCO merger), 1997—2001; sr. v.p., fin. Ameren, St. Louis, 2001—03, exec. v.p., CFO, 2003—. Mem.: Mo. Soc. CPA's, Am. Inst. CPA's, Coll. of Bus., Dean's Adv. Bd., Chancellor's Coun., U. Mo. (v.p.), Mo. Energy Policy Coun., Wyman Ctr. (bd. of trustees). Office: Ameren 1901 Chouteau Saint Louis MO 63166-6149*

BAXTER-LOWE, LEE ANN, science educator; b. Oshkosh, Wis., June 28, 1950; d. James Paul and Jane G. Matejowec; m. Kenneth N. Lowe, Nov. 12, 1983; children: Ashley, Lindsay. BS, U. Wis., 1972, PhD, 1976. Lab. investigator Blood Rsch. Inst., Milw., 1987-94; dir. DNA diagnostics Blood Ctr. Southeast Wis., Milw., 1987-94; dir. molecular genetics program Richland Meml. Hosp., Columbia, S.C., 1994-98; prof. U. Calif., San Francisco, 1998—. Cons., reviewer NIH, Bethesda, Md., 1990—. Contbr. articles to profl. jours.; inventor/patentee in field. Bd. dirs. Calif. Transplant Donor Network. Rsch. grantee NIH, 1988—. Mem. AAAS, Am. Soc. Immunologists, Am. Soc. Histocompatibility & Immunologenetics, Am. Soc. Hematology, Transplantation Soc. Office: U Calif San Francisco PO Box 0508 San Francisco CA 94143-0508

BAXTER-SMITH, GREGORY JOHN, lawyer; b. Davenport, Iowa, Sept. 27, 1949; s. James Sanford Baxter and Doris Arlene (Olson) Smith; m. Carolyn Imes, June 10, 1975 (div. Oct. 1980); children: Bradley Imes, Brian McBride; m. Karen Ruth Thomas, Dec. 12, 1986. BA in English, Bucknell U., 1971; JD, U. Mo., 1974. Bar: Mo. 1974, U.S. Dist. Ct. (we. dist.) Mo. 1975, U.S. Tax Ct. 1975. Clk. Hon. Charles Shangler Mo. Ct. Appeals, Kansas City, 1974-75; assoc. Miller & Poole, Springfield, Mo., 1975-76; shareholder Poole & Smith, P.C., Springfield, 1976-78, Gregory J. Smith, P.C., Springfield, 1978-86, Poole, Smith & Wieland, P.C., Springfield, 1986-90, Smith & Fels, P.C., Springfield, 1990—2004, Gregory J. Smith P.C., Springfield, 2004—. Mem. Springfield Met. Bar Assn., Greene County Estate Planning Coun., Mo. Bar Assn., Elks, Delta Upsilon, Phi Delta Phi. Republican. Lutheran. Avocation: golf. Home and Office: 3950 Bridgend Springfield MO 65809 Office Phone: 417-887-6413. Personal E-mail: gjbkrt@sbcglobal.net.

BAY, MICHAEL BENJAMIN, film director; b. LA, Feb. 17, 1965; Grad., Wesleyan U. Dir. Got Milk/Aaron Burr TV commerical (Grand Prix Clio award for Commerical Dir. of Yr., Mus. of Modern Art award for Best Campaign of Yr.), various other TV commericals; (films) Bad Boys, 1995, The Rock, 1996, Bad Boys II, 2003; dir., prodr.: (films) Armageddon, 1998, Pearl Harbor, 2001, The Island, 2005, The Transformers, 2007; prodr. (films) The Texas Chainsaw Massacre, 2003, The Amityville Horror, 2005, The Texas Chainsaw Massacre: The Beginning, 2006, The Hitcher, 2007. Named Commerical Dir. of Yr., Directors Guild Am., 1995; named one of 50 Most Powerful People in Hollywood, Premiere mag., 2005. Address: c/o Rob Carlson William Morris Agency One William Morris Pl Beverly Hills CA 90212*

BAYDA, EDWARD DMYTRO, retired chief justice; b. Alvena, Sask, Can., Sept. 9, 1931; s. Dmytro Andrew and Mary (Bilinski) B. BA, U. Sask., 1951, LLB cum laude, 1953; LLD (hon.), 1989, LLD (hon.) (hon.), 2006. Bar: Sask. 1954; apptd. Queen's Counsel, 1966. Barrister, solicitor, Regina, Sask., 1953-72; sr. ptnr. Bayda, Halvorson, Scheibel & Thompson, 1966-72; justice Ct. Queen's Bench for Sask., Regina, 1972-74, Ct. Appeal for Sask., Regina, 1974-81; chief justice Sask., Regina, 1981—2006; ret., 2006. Roman Catholic. Home: 3000 Albert St Regina SK Canada S4S 3N7

BAYER, ROBERT EDWARD, retired federal agency administrator; b. Cleve., Oct. 26, 1941; s. Charles and Pauline (Kamuf) B.; m. Mary Ellen Horrigan, Dec. 27, 1965 (div. 1981); m. Rozanne Deane Oliver, Jan. 29, 1983; children: Sylvia M., Laura A., Anne M., John C. BS in Social Sci. magna cum laude, John Carroll U., 1962; postgrad., Loyola U., 1962-63. Commd. 2nd lt. USAF, 1963, advanced through grades to lt. col., 1979, ret., 1983; mem. profl. staff Office of Sen. Sam Nunn U.S. Senate, Washington, 1983-86; mem. profl. staff Senate Com. on Armed Svcs., Washington, 1986-93; dep. asst. sec. of def. installations U.S. Dept. Def., Washington, 1993-97, ret., 1997. Pastor, spiritual dir. The Seeker Ch., Washington, 1989-93; co-chair Bridge Builders Fund, 1998-2000; mem. Mt. Olivet United Meth. Ch., Arlington, Va.; bd. dirs. Arlington Interfaith Coun., Kirkridge Retreat Ctr. Nat. Def. fellow Loyola U., 1962-63. Mem.: Va. Interfaith Ctr. for Pub. Policy, Meth. Fedn. for Social Action, Nat. Alliance for the Mentally Ill, Parents, Families and Friends of Lesbians and Gays. Methodist. Avocations: bicycling, swimming, travel, teaching. Office Phone: 703-276-2829. Personal E-mail: roliver52@comcast.net.

BAYERL, SCOTT LEE, animal welfare organization administrator, web programmer; b. Marshfield, Wis., Dec. 21, 1968; s. LeRoy James and Jane Marie Bayerl; m. Karen Margaret Kimpfbeck, May 6, 2006. Grad., Marshfield Sr. HS, 1987. Founder, dir. Midwest Horse Welfare Found., Inc., Pittsville, Wis., 2001—; pvt. web developer. Home: 10990 Hwy 73 Pittsville WI 54466 Office: Midwest Horse Welfare Found Inc 10990 Hwy 73 Pittsville WI 54466 Home Phone: 715-884-2215; Office Phone: 715-884-2215.

BAYES, BEVERLEY JOAN, retired pediatrician; b. Regina, Can., Nov. 1, 1937; came to U.S., 1988; d. Frederick Charles and Sylvia Mae (Hickling) B.; m. Edgar Gibson Merson, May 25, 1988; children: Jennifer Alice Merson Hersberg, Andrew Charles Merson, Keith Graham Merson. MD, U. Toronto, 1961. Diplomate Am. Bd. Pediat. Intern Toronto (Can.) Gen., 1961-63; resident Hosp. for Sick Children, Toronto, 1963-64, 65-68, Royal Hosp. for Sick Children, Glasgow, Scotland, 1964-65, Children's Hosp. Nat. Med. Ctr., Washington, 1968-69; pediat. Fairfax County (Va.) Health Dept., 1972-82, North Va. Pediat. Assoc., Falls Church, 1982-99, ret., 1999. Family life edn. com. Fairfax County Coun. PTAs, 1982-84. Fellow ACP, Am. Acad. Pediat. (program chair Va. chpt. 1992-93). Presbyterian. Avocations: singing, pottery, reading, travel, painting.

BAYH, BIRCH EVANS, JR., lawyer, former senator; b. Terre Haute, Ind., Jan. 22, 1928; s. Birch Evans and Leah (Hollingsworth) B.; m. Marvella Hern, Aug. 24, 1952 (dec. Apr. 1979); 1 son, Birch Evans III; m. Katherine Halpin, 1981; 1 son, Christopher John. BA, Purdue U., 1951; JD, Ind. U., 1960. Bar: Ind. 1961, DC 1978. Engaged in farming, Vigo County, 1952-57; mem. Ind. Ho. of Reps. from Vigo County, 1954-62, minority leader, 1957-58, 61-62, speaker, 1959-60; U.S. senator from Ind., 1962-81; chmn. intelligence com., mem. appropriations, jud. coms.; sr. ptnr. Bayh, Connaughton & Malone PC, Washington; ptnr. Legis. and Regulatory Group, Govt. Div. Venable LLP, Washington. Mem. U. Va. Commn on Presdl. Disability & the Twenty-Fifth Amendment. Mem. Nat. Inst. Against Prejudice and Violence, Fullbright Foreign Scholarship Bd. Named Outstanding Young Man in Ind. Ind. Jr. C. of C., 1959; one of 10 outstanding Reps. in Ind. Gen. Assembly Ind. Newspaper Men and Women Vets., 1961 Mem.: Mental Health Assn. (mem. Nat. Commn. on Insanity Defense). Democrat. Office: Venable LLP 575 7th St NW Washington DC 20004 Office Phone: 202-344-4705. Office Fax: 202-344-8300. E-mail: bbayh@venable.com.

BAYH, EVAN (BIRCH EVAN BAYH III), senator, former governor; b. Terre Haute, Ind., Dec. 26, 1955; s. Birch Evans Jr. and Marvella (Hern) B.; m. Susan; two children. BS in Bus. Economics, Ind. U., 1978; JD, U. Va., 1981. Bar: DC 1982, Ind. 1983. Atty. Bingham, Summers, Welsh & Spilman, Indianapolis; sec. of state State of Ind., Indpls., 1987-89, gov., 1989-96; ptnr. Baker & Daniel Assocs., Indpls., 1997-98; US Senator from Ind., 1999—. Chmn. Democratic Leadership Coun., 2001—05; mem. com. armed svc. US Senate, com. banking, housing and urban affairs. Author: From Father to Son: A Private Life in the Public Eye, 2003. Recipient Carolyn Mosby Above and Beyond award, Indiana Black Exposition, 1995, Breaking the Glass Ceiling award, Women Executives in State Govt., 1996, Good Govt. award, Cato Inst., 1996, Henry M. Jackson award, Jewish Inst. Nat. Security Affairs, 2004, Friend of Zion award, The Jerusalem Fund, 2004. Democrat. Episcopalian. Office: US Senate 463 Russell Senate Office Bldg Washington DC 20510-0001 also: Market Tower Ste 1650 10 W Market St Indianapolis IN 46204-2934 Office Phone: 317-554-0750, 202-224-5623. Office Fax: 202-228-1377, 317-554-0760.*

BAYKAN, MARY CATHERINE, library administrator; b. Detroit, Nov. 1, 1946; d. Edward Charles and Margaret Ester (Lutes) Jones; m. Yalcin Nafiz Baykan, Feb. 27, 1972; children: Deniz Mary, Peri Catherine. BA in Polit. Sci., U. Houston, 1969; MA in Libr. and Info. Sci., U. South Fla., 1980; MBA, Frostburg State U. Libr. II U. Tex., Houston, 1972-77; libr. assoc. Palm Beach County Libr. System, 1977-81, br. mgr., 1981-87, ctrl. libr. adminstr., 1987; dir. West Palm Beach Central Library, Washington County Free Library, 1995—. Bd. dirs. BookFest of the Palm Beaches, 1990, exec. bd. dirs., 1992; exec. dir. Western Md. Public Library. Named Nat. Libr. of Yr., Libr. Jour., 2007; recipient Delray Beach Brotherhood award, B'nai B'rith, 1987. Mem. S.E. Fla. Libr. Info. Network (com. mem.), Fla. Libr. Assn., Palm Beach County Libr. Assn. (pres. 1993-94), Md. Library Assn. (chair legislative panel), Phi Kappa Phi, Beta Phi Mu. Office: Washington County Free Library 100 South Potomac St Hagerstown MD 21740*

BAYKO, EMIL THOMAS, lawyer; b. Pitts., Mar. 5, 1947; s. Emil and Ruth (Alberti) B.; m. Ruth Ann Loucks, Nov. 5, 1967; children: Anthony M., Keith C., Paul S. BA in Polit. Sci., Kent State U., 1970; JD cum laude, U. Ill., Urbana-Champaign, 1973. Bar: Ill. 1973, U.S. Dist. Ct. (no. dist.) Ill. 1973, U.S. Ct. Appeals (7th cir.) 1974, D.C. 1975, N.Y. 1975, U.S. Ct. Appeals (2d cir.) 1975, U.S. Ct. Claims 1976, U.S. Dist. Ct. (so. dist.) N.Y. 1976, U.S. Ct. Appeals (D.C. cir.) 1976, U.S. Supreme Ct. 1976, U.S. Dist. Ct. (ea dist.) Pa. 1978, U.S. Ct. Appeals (3d cir.) 1978, Tex. 1980, U.S. Dist. Ct. (so. dist., no. dist., ea. dist., we. dist.) Tex. 1981, U.S. Ct. Appeals (5th cir.) 1981. Assoc. Chapman & Cutler, Chgo., 1973-74, White & Case,

NYC, 1975-80; ptnr. Liddell, Sapp, Zivley, Hill & LaBoon, Houston, 1981, Holtzman Urquhart Bayko & Moore, Houston, 1982-95, Bayko Gibson Carnegie & Hagan, Houston, 1995-2000, Jones Day, Houston, 2001—. Co-author: Essays on American Law, 1971, Home Rule, 1972. Harno fellow U. Ill., 1971-73. Mem. ABA, Assn. of Bar of City of N.Y., Houston Bar Assn., Chgo. Bar Assn., Tex. Bar Assn., D.C. Bar Assn., Order of Coif. Clubs: Tex., Houston. Democrat. Presbyterian. Home Phone: 832-287-8928; Office Phone: 832-239-3700. Business E-Mail: tbayko@jonesday.com.

BAYLES, JENNIFER LUCENE, museum program director, educator; b. Tokyo, May 26, 1953; d. Lewis Allen Bayles and Rosemary (Buehler) Fraser; m. Robert Steinfeld, July 4, 1992; children: Noah Isaac Steinfeld, Ezra Milton Steinfeld. BA in Art History with honors, Ind. U., Bloomington, 1976; MA in Art History, U. Mich., 1984, cert. in mus. practice, 1984. Curatorial apprentice Indpls. Mus. Art, 1976; mus. apprentice Portland (Oreg.) Art Mus., 1976-78, asst. curator edn., 1978-81; asst. curator photographic collection dept. art history U. Mich., Ann Arbor, 1981-83, rsch. and editl. asst. Mus. Art, 1982-83; intern dept. mus. edn. Art Inst. Chgo., 1983-84; curator edn. Albright-Knox Art Gallery, Buffalo, 1984—2001, educator spl. projects, 2001—04, grants mgr., 2003—. Mem. leadership teams Amherst Ctrl. Sch. Dist., 2000—. Recipient annual arts educator award, Young Audiences of Western NY, 2001; Horace H. Rackman Grad. scholar, 1981—83, Acad. scholar, U. Mich., 1982. Mem.: Am. Assn. Mus. (regional rep. edn. com. 1979—81). Office: Albright-Knox Art Gallery 1285 Elmwood Ave Buffalo NY 14222-1096 Office Phone: 716-270-8252. E-mail: jbayles@albrightknox.org.

BAYLESS, RICK, chef; b. Oklahoma City, 1953; m. Deann Bayless. Host PBS TV series Cooking Mexican, 1978—79; owner, chef Frontera Grill, Chgo., 1987—, Topolombampo, Chgo., 1989—; host PBS series Mexico One Plate at a Time With Rick Bayless, 2000—. N. Cheffs Collaborative 2000; ptnr. Frontera Foods, 1995; chef's coun. Chefs for Humanity. Author: Authentic Mexican, 1987, Rick Bayless's Mexican Kitchen, 1996, Salsas That Cook, 1999; co-author (with daughter Lanie Bayless): Rick & Lanie's Excellent Kitchen Adventures, 2004; co-author: (with Deann Groen Bayless) Mexican Everyday, 2005; appeared on TV programs: Today, Good Morning Am., This Morning, Martha Stewart Living, Cooking Live, In Julia's Kitchen with Master Chefs, Great Chefs of Am., others; contbr. to numerous food and cooking publs.; contbg. editor: Saveur. Named Best New Chef of 1988, Food and Wine mag., Best Am. Chef: Midwest, James Beard Found., 1991; recipient Nat. Chef of Yr. award, 1995, Chef of Yr. award, Internat. Assn. Culinary Professionals, 1995, Humanitarian award, 2007, Humanitarian of Yr., James Beard Found., 1998, Outstanding Restaurant award for Frontera Grill, 2007. Office: Frontera Grill 445 N Clark St Chicago IL 60610*

BAYLEY, SUZANNE LUDEY, civic volunteer; b. Vienna, W.Va., Apr. 14, 1920; d. Charles Addison and Patty (Spence) Ludey; m. Thomas Way Bayley, Feb. 7, 1942 (dec.); children: Patty Ruth Bayley Dhondt, Thomas Way Bayley III, Charlotte Ann Bayley Schindelholz. Attended, Rollins Studio of Acting, 1938-1939; BA, Finch Coll., 1940. Founder Children's Theatre Bur., Parkersburg, W.Va., 1946—48; actress, dir., adminstr. Actors Guild of Parkersburg, 1956—57; pres. Actors Guild At Theatre Group, 1962, play reading chair, 1963—65, bldg. chair, 1975—76; mem. founding com. Artsbridge Fine Arts Coun., Parkersburg, 1977. Prodr. Eden on the River, Blennerhassett Drama Assn., 1987. Mem. Jr. League, Parkersburg, 1942-62; v.p. Friends of Blennerhassett, 1975; commr. Blennerhassett Island project, 1988-91, docent, 1988-95. Recipient Lifetime Achievement award Altrusa Club and YWCA, 1992, Lifetime Achievement award for arts Finch Coll., 1996; Cmty. Svc. award named in her honor Actors Guild, 1976. Mem.: Nat. Soc. Arts and Letters, Serra Club Internat. Republican. Roman Catholic.

BAYLIS, ROBERT MONTAGUE, investment banker; b. NYC, Aug. 20, 1938; s. Chester, Jr. and Dorothy Montague (Smith) B.; m. Lois Margaret Wells, Apr. 6, 1963; children: Robert Wells, David Martin, John Chester. AB, Princeton U., 1960; MBA, Harvard U., 1962. CFA. Chartered fin. analyst CS First Boston, NYC, 1963-96, vice chmn., 1992-96; chmn. CS First Boston Pacific, Hong Kong, 1993-94. Bd. dirs. Covance, Inc., Host Hotels and Resorts, N.Y. Life Ins. Co., Gildan Activewear, Ptnr. Re Inc. Served with M.C. U.S. Army, 1962-63. Mem. N.Y. Soc. Security Analysts, Nat. Assn. Bus. Economists, Weeburn Country Club, Univ. Club, Nassau Club, Cap and Gown Club, Ocean Reef Club. Home: 116 Delafield Island Rd Darien CT 06820-6017 Office: 119 Rowayton Ave Norwalk CT 06853

BAYLOR, DENIS ARISTIDE, neuroscientist, educator; b. Oskaloosa, Iowa, Jan. 30, 1940; s. Hugh Murray and Elisabeth Anne (Barbou) B.; m. Eileen Margaret Steele, Aug. 12, 1983; children: Denis Murray, Michael Randel; 1 stepchild, Michele Gonelli. BA in Chemistry magna cum laude, Knox Coll., 1961, DS (hon.), 1989; MD cum laude, Yale U., 1965. Post-doctoral fellow Yale Med. Sch., New Haven, 1965-68; staff assoc. NINDS, Bethesda, Md., 1968-70; USPHS spl. fellow Physiol. Lab. Cambridge U., England, 1970-72; assoc. prof. physiology U. Colo. Med. Sch., Denver, 1972—74, Stanford U., 1974-75, assoc. prof. neurobiology, 1975-78, prof. neurobiology, 1978—2001, chmn. dept. neurobiology, 1992-95; sr. sci. officer Howard Hughes Med. Inst., 2004—05; First Annual W.S. Stiles lecturer U. Coll., London, 1989; Jonathan Magnes lecturer Hebrew U., Jerusalem, 1990; Woolsey lectr. U. Wis., 1992; E. Hille lectr. U. Wash., 1995. Mem. NIH Visual Scis. Study Sect., 1984-88, chmn., 1986-88; vis. com. med. scis. Harvard U., 1987-93; chmn. Summer conf. on Vision FASEB, 1989; Wellcome vis. prof. U. Miami, 1995; mem. sci. adv. com. Alcon Rsch. Inst., 1994-99; mem. HHMI Sci. adv. bd. 1997-2003, Med. adv. bd. 1998-01; mem. sci. adv. bd. Found. Fighting Blindness, 1998—; trustee The Grass Found., 1995-99. Mem. editorial bd. Jour. Physiology, 1977-84, Neuron, 1988-93, Jour. Neurophysiology, 1989—, Visual Neurosci., 1990-93, Jour. Neurosci., 1991—; contbr. articles to profl. jours. Recipient Sinsheimer Found. award, 1975, Mathilde Solowey award, 1978, Kayser Internat. award Retina Rsch. Found., 1988, Golden Brain award Minerva Found., 1988, Merit award Nat. Eye Inst., 1990, Alcon Rsch. Inst. award, 1991; Rank Optoelectronics prize Rank Orgn., Eng., 1980; Proctor medal Assn. Rsch. Vision & Ophthalmology, 1986, Von Sallman prize in eye rsch., 1998. Fellow Am. Acad. Arts and Scis.; mem. NAS, Royal Soc. London, Phi Beta Kappa, Alpha Omega Alpha. Avocations: golf, woodworking. Office: 835 Esplanada Way Stanford CA 94305

BAYLOR, ELGIN GAY, professional sports team executive and retired basketball player; b. Washington, Sept. 16, 1934; m. Elaine; 1 child, Krystle. Student, Albertson Coll. Idaho, Caldwell, 1954—55, Seattle U., 1955—57. Player LA (formerly Mpls.) Lakers, 1958—71; asst. coach New Orleans Jazz, 1974—76, head coach, 1976—79; exec. v.p., gen. mgr. LA Clippers, 1986—94, v.p. basketball ops., 1994—. Named MVP, NCAA Tournament, 1958, NBA Rookie of Yr., 1959, co-MVP, NBA All-Star Game, 1959; named to NBA All-Star Team, 1959-65, 67-70, All-NBA First Team, 1959-65, 67-69, Naismith Meml. Basketball Hall of Fame, 1977, NBA 35th Anniversary All-Time Team, 1980, NBA 50th Anniversary All-Time Team, 1996. Office: LA Clippers 1111 S Figueroa St Ste 1100 Los Angeles CA 90015-1300*

BAYLY, JOHN HENRY, JR., judge; b. Washington, Jan. 26, 1944; s. John Henry and Salome Carole (Winters) B.; m. Barbara Jean Downey, Feb. 16, 1974 (dec. Jan. 1977); 1 child, Anne Louise; m. Katherine Bridget Kenny, Dec. 1, 1979; children: Johanna, Georgia. AB, Fordham U., 1966; JD, Harvard U., 1969. Bar: U.S. Dist. Ct. D.C. 1969, U.S. Ct. Appeals (D.C. cir.) 1969, D.C. 1971, U.S. Supreme Ct. 1974. Atty., advisor FCC, Washington, 1969-71; asst. atty. Office of U.S. Atty., Washington, 1971-75, 78-85; dep. minority counsel Senate Select Com. on Intelligence, Washington, 1975-76; acting asst. gen. counsel Corp. for Pub. Broadcasting, Washington, 1976-78; gen. counsel Legal Services Corp., Washington, 1985-87, pres., 1987-88; of counsel Stein, Mitchell & Mezines, Washington, 1988-90; judge D.C. Superior Ct., 1990—. Mem. D.C. Bar Assn., John Carroll Soc., Counsellors, Bryant Inn of Ct., Lawyers Club Washington, Phi Beta Kappa. Republican. Roman Catholic. Home: 3512 Runnymede Pl NW Washington DC 20015-2420 Office: DC Superior Ct 500 Indiana Ave NW Ste 1 Washington DC 20001-2131 Business E-Mail: baylyjh@dcsc.gov.

BAYM (STILLINGER), NINA, literature educator, researcher, writer; b. Princeton, NJ, June 14, 1936; d. Leo and Frances (Levinson) Zippin; m. Gordon Baym, June 1, 1958; children— Nancy, Geoffrey; m. Jack Stillinger, May 21, 1971 BA, Cornell U., 1957; MA, Harvard U., 1958, PhD, 1963. Asst. U. Calif.-Berkeley, 1962-63; instr. U. Ill., Urbana, 1963-67, asst. prof. English, 1967-69, assoc. prof., 1969-72, prof., 1972—, Jubilee prof. liberal arts and scis., 1989—, dir. Sch. Humanities Urbana, 1976-87, sr. Univ. scholar, 1985, assoc. Ctr. Advanced Study, 1989-90, permanent prof. Ctr. Advanced Study, 1997—2004, Swanlund Endowed chair, 1997—2004. Author: The Shape of Hawthorne's Career, 1976, Woman's Fiction: A Guide to Novels By and About Women in America, 1978, 2d rev. edit., 1993, Novels, Readers and Reviewers: Responses to Fiction in Antebellum America, 1984, The Scarlet Letter: A Reading, 1986, Feminism and American Literary History, 1992, American Women Writers and the Work of History, 1790-1860, 1995, American Women of Letters and the 19th Century Sciences, 2002; gen. editor: Norton Anthology of American Literature; sr. editor Am. Nat. Biography; also author essays, edits., revs.; mem. editl. bd. Am. Quar., New Eng. Quar., Legacy, A Jour. of 19th Century Am. Women Writers, Jour. Aesthetic Edn. Am. Lit., Tulsa Studies in Women's Lit., Am. Studies, Studies Am. Fiction, Am. Periodicals, Hemingway Rev., Resources for Am. Lit. Study, Am. Lit. History, Cambridge U.P. Studies in Am. Lit. and Culture; mem. editl. adv. bd. PMLA. Guggenheim fellow, 1975-76, AAUW hon. fellow, 1975-76, NEH fellow, 1982-83; rec pient Arnold O. Beckman award U. Ill., 1992-93, Hubbell Lifetime Achievement medal, Am. Let. Sect., 2000. Mem. MLA (exec. com. 19th century Am. Lit. divsn., chmn. 1984, chmn. Am. Lit. sect. 1984, Hubbell Lifetime Achievement medal 2000), Am. Studies Assn. (exec. com. 1982-84, nominating com. 1991-93), Am. Lit. Assn., Am. Antiquarian Soc., Mass. Hist. Soc., Nathaniel Hawthorne Soc. (adv. bd.), Western Lit. Assn., Mortar Bd., Phi Kappa Phi, Phi Beta Kappa. Office Phone: 217-333-2390. Business E-Mail: baymnina@uiuc.edu.

BAYMILLER, LYNDA DOERN, social worker; b. Milw., July 6, 1943; d. Ronald Oliver and Marian Elizabeth (Doern) Baymiller. Student, U. Hawaii, 1962, Mich. State U., 1965; BA, U. Wis., 1965, MSW, 1969. Vol. Peace Corps, Chile, 1965—67; social worker Luth. Social Svcs. Wis. and Upper Mich., Milw., 1969—77, contract social worker, 1978—79; dist. supr. Childrens Svc. Soc. Wis., Kenosha, 1977—78; supr. social work Sauk County Dept. Human Svcs., Baraboo, Wis., 1979—90; mgr. sales and relief -trainee Wal-Mart, 1992—93, cashier, 1993—. Author: (with Clara Amelia Hess) Now-Won, A Collection of Feeling Poetry, 1973. Bd. dirs. Sauk County Mental Health Assn., 1979-84; mem. Harmony chpt. Sweet Adelines, West Allis, Wis., 1970-75, pres. chpt., 1971; pres. bd. dirs. Growing Place Day Care Ctr., Kenosha, 1977-78; mem. Baraboo Centennial Com., 1982; pres. bd. dirs. Laubach Lit. Coun., Baraboo, 1986-88; mem. Sauk County Humane Soc., 1987—2006, sec., 1988-90. Mem. NASW, Acad. Cert. Social Workers, AAUW (br. sec. 1982-84), U. Wis. Alumni Assn. (life), Am. Legion Aux., DAR, Nat. Soc. Magna Carta Dames, Eddy Family Assn. (life), Nat. Soc. Ancient and Hon. Arty. Co. Mass. (life), Wis. Soc. Daus. of 1812 (rec. sec. 1994-96), Internat. Crane Found. (patron), Daus. Colonial Wars, Daus. Am. Colonists, Zool. Soc. Milwaukee County (life, bd. dirs. Zoo Pride 1975-77), Am. Bus. Women's Assn. (charter mem. 1984-), Order Ea. Star (grad. rep. Miss. in Wis. 1988-90), Order White Shrine of Jerusalem, Cameo Club, Baraboo Citizens, Police and Fire Acad. Alumni Assn., Alpha Xi Delta.

BAYNE, DAVID COWAN, priest, educator, lawyer; b. Detroit, Jan. 11, 1918; s. David Cowan and Myrtle (Murray) B. AB, U. Detroit, 1939; LLB, Georgetown U., 1947, LLM, 1948; MA, Loyola U., Chgo., 1946, STL, 1953; SJD (grad. fellow), Yale, 1949; LLD (hon.), Creighton U., 1980. Bar: Fed. and D.C. 1948, Mich. 1960, Mo. 1963. Joined Soc. of Jesus, 1941; ordained priest Roman Catholic Ch., 1952; asst. prof. law U. Detroit, 1954-60; acting dean U. Detroit (Law Sch.), 1955-59, dean, 1959-60; research assoc. Nat. Jesuit Research Orgn., Inst. Social Order, St. Louis, 1960-63; vis. lectr. St. Louis U. Law Sch., 1960-63, prof. law, 1963-67; vis. prof. Mich. Law Sch., 1967, Inst. fur Auslandisches und Internationales Wirtschaftrecht, Frankfurt, 1967; prof. U. Iowa Coll. Law, Iowa City, 1967-88, prof. emeritus, 1988—. Vis. prof. U. Koln, Germany, 1970, 74 Author: Conscience, Obligation and the Law, 1966, 2d edit., 1988; The Philosophy of Corporate Control, 1986; editor legal materials; contbr. articles to profl. jours. Achievements include research in corp. law. E-mail: dcbsj@netzero.net, dcbsj@buckeye-express.com.

BAYNE, JAMES ELWOOD, investor; b. Detroit, May 6, 1940; s. John David and Alice Angie (Davis) Bayne; children: James E. Jr., Laura Lee Poe. BA, Yale U., 1962; MBA, Columbia U., 1967. Investment adminstr. Bankers Trust, NYC, 1962-65; fin analyst Std. Oil, NYC, 1967; sr. fin. analyst Esso Internat., NYC, 1967-70; asst. treas. Esso S.A.P.A., Buenos Aires, 1970-71; treas. Intercol, Bogota, Colombia, 1971-74; asst. treas. Esso InterAm., Coral Gables, Fla., 1974-77; asst. gen. mgr. Esso Ctrl. Am., Coral Gables, 1977-80; mgr. Mexican Bus. Opportunity, Coral Gables, 1980-81; treas. Exxon Chem. Europe, Brussels, 1981-86; mgr., benefits fin. and investment Exxon, Dallas, 1986-99; mgr. benefits fin. and investment Exxon Mobil, Dallas, 1999-2000, ret., 2001; cons., advisor to fin. svcs. industry, 2001—; pres., CEO 1st & 5th Dance Ctr. Inc., 2002—05. Exec. com. CIEBA, Washington, 1994—, vice chmn., 1995—96, chmn., 1996—98; pension adv. com. N.Y. Stock Exch., NYC, 1995—99; mem. adv. bd. Wharton Trading Sys., 1993—96; mem. adv. com. Aslan Capital, 2001—; mem. Nat. Commn. on Retirement Policy, 1997—99. Del. 1st White Ho. Summit Retirement Savs., Washington, 1998; v.p. Incarnation Found., 1996—2003; pres. secretariat Dallas-Ft. Worth Cursillo Movement, 1992—96; dir. Dallas-Ft. Worth Episcopal Renewal Ctr., 1994—2002; chair Episcopal Renewal Ctr., 1996—2002; mem. investment com. Episcopal Found. Dallas, 1998—2003; trustee Ch. Pension Fund, NYC, 1999—, chair fin. com.; mem. steering com. Interforum, 1993—96; bd. dir. Fin. Execs. Inst., 1996—98, Ch. Life Ins., 1999—. Mem.: Yale Club N.Y., Yale Club Dallas, Order St. John. Episcopalian. Avocations: church work, walking, reading, travel. Home: 3831 Turtle Creek Blvd #18C Dallas TX 75219 Home Phone: 214-356-3454. E-mail: venturejim@msn.com.

BAYNE, KATIE J. (KATHERINE), marketing executive; b. Perth, Australia, 1967; BA, Duke U., MBA, 1989. Joined Coca-Cola Co., 1989; sr. v.p. Coca-Cola brands Coca-Cola N. Am., Coca-Cola Co., chief mktg. officer, 2007—. Bd. dirs. Beazer Homes USA, Inc., 2003—, Imagine It! The Children's Mus. of Atlanta. Named a Woman to Watch, Advt. Age, 2007. Office: The Coca-Cola Co PO Box 1734 Atlanta GA 30310

BAYNES, RONALD EDWARD, pharmacologist, educator; b. St.John's, Antigua and Barbuda, Dec. 20, 1960; m. Deborah Rita Younglao, July 30, 1990. BSc with honors, U. Wis., Barbados, 1984; DVM with honors, Tuskegee U., Ala., 1990; MS, U. Ga., Athens, 1992; PhD, NC State U., Raleigh, 1997. Assoc. prof. NC State U., asst. prof., 1998—2004; toxicologist Syracuse Rsch. Corp., Atlanta, 1992—93. Mem.: AVMA, Am. Chem. Soc., Sigma Xi (exec. com.), Soc. Toxicology. Achievements include patents for methods, systems, and products for determining drug withdrawal intervals. Home: 104 Canterstone Ct Cary NC 27518 Office: NC State Univ 4700 Hillsborough St Raleigh NC 27606 Home Phone: 919-363-9413; Office Phone: 919-513-6261. Personal E-mail: rebdry@yahoo.com. Business E-Mail: ronald_baynes@ncsu.edu.

BAYNHAM, G. CLAY, surgeon; b. Augusta, Ga., July 7, 1957; s. Ronald O'Niel and Nancy Fulmer Baynham; m. Carolyn Marie Tuell Baynham, Aug. 3, 1985; 1 child, Jake. Student, Fla. State U., Tallahassee, 1975—79; BS, U. Fla., Gainesville, 1983. Diplomate Am. Bd. Orthop. Surgery, 92. Intern U. Fla., Jacksonville, 1983—84, resident, 1984—88; fellow Lakewood Orthopaedics, Denver, 1988—89, Kerlan Jobe Clinic, LA, 1989—90; spinal surgeon Palm Beach Orthop. Inst., Palm Beach Gardens, Fla., 1990—2007. Cons. Zimmer Spine, 1997—2007; founder Atlas Spine, Jupiter, Fla., 2002—07. Recipient Resident Rsch. award, Fla. Orthop. Soc., 1988, Profl. Liability award, Fla. Med. Assn., 2000; grantee, Upjohn Pharm., 1988. Mem.: AMA, Palm Beach. County Med. Soc. (past pres.), Fla. Med. Assn., Mensa. Achievements include patents in field. Avocation: golf. Office: Palm Beach Orthop Inst 3401 PGA Blvd Ste 500 Palm Beach Gardens FL 33410

BAYS, JAMES C., lawyer; b. Denton, Tex., July 23, 1949; BA magna cum laude, Dartmouth Coll., 1971; JD, U. Va., 1974. Bar: Ohio 1974. Assoc. Jones, Day, Reavis & Pogue, 1974—78; counsel TRW, Inc., 1978—81, sr. counsel, 1981—85, v.p., asst. gen. counsel, 1985—92; v.p., asst. gen. counsel GenCorp, Inc., 1993—96; sr. v.p., gen. counsel, chief legal officer Invensys plc, London, 1996—2001; v.p., gen. counsel Ferro Corp., Cleve., 2001—. Mem. editl. bd.: Va. Law Review, 1972—74. Mem.: ABA, Ohio State Bar Assn., Cleve. State Bar Assn. Office: Ferro Corp 1000 Lakeside Ave Cleveland OH 44114-7000 Office Phone: 216-875-6122. Office Fax: 216-875-7275. E-mail: baysj@ferro.com.

BAYS, JOHN THEOPHANIS, consulting engineer; b. Bklyn., July 17, 1947; s. Theophanis A. and Mildred Bays; m. Mindy Giardina, July 8, 1973; 1 dau., Nina. BS, N.Y. Inst. Tech., 1972; BArch, CCNY, 1974; cert. in solar design, Ohio State U., 1975. Cert. energy mgr., energy auditor, asbestos investigator, N.Y. Project mgr., head sys. designer Wormser Sci. Corp., Stamford, Conn., 1975-82, v.p. engring., 1982-85; pres. E.E. Linden Assocs., Cons. Engrs., Norwalk, Conn., 1985—. Recipient awards in solar design. Mem.: ASHRAE. Home: 18 Marion Rd Westport CT 06880-2919 Office: 110 Richards Ave Norwalk CT 06854-1622 Home Phone: 203-454-4178; Office Phone: 203-299-1600. E-mail: j.t.bays@eelinden.com.

BAYSAL, OKTAY, dean, educator; s. Selim and Servet Baysal; m. Figen Dinckaya, July 11, 1992; children: Celine M., Sarah I. Diploma engring., Istanbul Tech. U., Turkey, 1977; MS, U. Birmingham, England, 1978; PhD, La. State U., Baton Rouge, 1982. Registered profl. engr., Va., 1984. Asst. prof. dept. mech. engring. and mechanics Old Dominion U., Norfolk, Va., 1982—87, assoc. prof. dept. mech. engring. and mechanics, 1988—92, prof. dept. mech. engring. and mechanics, 1992—93, prof. dept. aerospace engring., 1993—, assoc. dean Frank Batten Coll. Engring. and Tech., 1999—2002, interim dean Frank Batten Coll. Engring. and Tech., 2002—04, dean Frank Batten Coll. Engring. and Tech., 2004—. Design, quality control engr. SEBA Dis Ticaret ve Insaat Ltd., Istanbul, 1976—77; tech. dir. SEBA Internat., Inc., Houston, 1982—95, SEBA Dis Ticaret ve Insaat Ltd., Istanbul, 1982—90; tech. cons. Lockheed Missiles and Space Co., Inc., Sunnyvale, Calif., 1989—90, Sci. and Tech. Corp., Hampton, Va., 1998; cons. ICASE, NASA Langley Rsch. Ctr., Hampton, Va., 1997—2002, Bayshore Concrete Products, Cape Charles, Va., 1998—99, Controls Corp. Am., Virginia Beach, Va., 1999—2000. Guest editor Am. Soc. Civil Engrs. Jour. Aerospace Engring., associate technical editor Am. Soc. Mech. Engrs. Jour. Fluids Engring. Bd. dirs. Va. Air and Space Ctr., Hampton, 2005—06. Recipient Pub. Svc. medal, NASA, 1993; fellow, NASA Langley Rsch. Ctr., Am. Soc. Engring. Edn. Program, 1999; Eminent scholar, Old Dominion U., 1996—. Mem.: NSPE, ASME, AIAA, Va. Acad. Sci., US Assn. Computational Mechanics, Va. Soc. Profl. Engrs., Soc. Indsl. and Applied Math., Soc. Automotive Engineers, Am. Soc. Engring. Edn., Chamber Mech. Engrs. Turkey, Phi Eta Sigma, Phi Kappa Phi, Tau Beta Pi, Epsilon Mu Eta. Office: Old Dominion University 102 Kaufman Hall Norfolk VA 23529 Office Phone: 757-683-3789. Office Fax: 757-683-4898. E-mail: obaysal@odu.edu.

BAYSINGER, KARA, lawyer; b. St. Cloud, Minn., Aug. 26, 1966; BA in Polit. Sci., U. Mich., 1988; JD, Loyola U., 1994. Bar: Ill. 1994, Calif. 1999. Asst. to gen. counsel Provident Ins. Co., Waukegan, Ill., 1988—90; compliance analyst Benefit Trust Life Ins. Co., Lake Forest, Ill.; asst. v.p. legal and regulatory affairs Celtic Life Ins. Co.; dir.-counsel product approval & compliance Bankers Life and Casualty Co., 1994—97; spl. counsel ins. regulatory practice group Long & Levit LLP, 1997; ptnr. Sonnenschein Nath & Rosenthal LLP, San Francisco, vice chair Ins. Practice Group. Co-chair Calif. adv. bd. BizWorld. Mem.: Calif. Bar Assn., Ill. Bar Assn. Office: Sonnenschein Nath & Rosenthal LLP 685 Market St, 6th Fl San Francisco CA 94105 Office Phone: 415-882-2475. Office Fax: 415-543-5472. Business E-Mail: kbaysinger@sonnenschein.com.

BAYTARIAN, P. JEFFREY, not-for-profit fundraiser; b. Pontiac, Mich., Sept. 3, 1955; s. Paul and Lois Jean (Leighton) Baytarian. B, Oakland U., Rochester, Mich., 1986. Freelance writer, Pontiac, 1994—95; fundraiser March of Dimes, Southfield, Mich., 1996; unit dir. United Way Cmty. Svcs., Detroit, 1997—2004; campaign mgr. United Way Southea. Mich., Detroit, 2005—. Coach Dale Carnegie Tng., Livonia, Mich., 1989—91, 2005—06; mem. mktg. com. United Way of Oakland, Pontiac, 1988—95; officer Toastmasters, Rochester, 1992—95; mentor, coach Art of Leadership Found., Birmingham, Mich., 2007—; mem. leadership com. Kensington Cmty. Ch., Troy, Mich., 1996—2000. Mem.: Assn. Fundraising Profls., Golden Key. Avocations: skiing, bowling, acting. Office: United Way Southeastern Mich 1212 Griswold Detroit MI 48226 Office Phone: 313-226-9250. Office Fax: 313-226-9211. Business E-Mail: jeff.baytarian@uwsem.org.

BAYUK, THOMAS M., SR., restaurant owner, writer; b. Plainfield, NJ, June 6, 1942; s. Max and Stella A. (Sulewski) B.; m. Joyce A. Biondi, Apr. 27, 1962; children: Patricia, Thomas Jr., John, Jennifer. Student, Rutgers U., 1960-61, LeCordon Bleu, Paris, 1987-88. Owner Tom's Luncheonette, Flemington, NJ, 1970—74; real estate broker Weichert Realtors, Clinton, NJ, 1974—78; project mgr. Forest City Enterprises, Cleveland, Ohio, 1978—80; ceo West Dennis Village Deli, Inc., West Dennis, Mass., 1981—96, J & T Corp, West Dennis, Mass., 1996—; real estate broker Robert J. Bayuk Assoc., Inc., Clinton, NJ. Author: (book) Coping and Prevailing, 2002, Still Coping and Prevailing, 2004, What We Don't Talk About, 2005. With U.S. Army, 1960-61. Specialist 4th class U. S. Army N.G., 1960—63, Summit, N. J. Mem. Nat. Assn. Realtors, Nat. Restaurant Assn., Mass. Right to Life, Mus. Fine Arts, Boston Ballet. Republican. Catholic. Achievements include Founder- MS2therescue. Avocations: writing, cooking, wine tasting, travel. Home and Office: 19868 Cypres Woods Ct North Fort Myers FL 33903 Office Phone: 239-543-4105. Personal E-mail: tbayuk@comcast.net.

BAZ, MAHER AFIF, internist, educator, medical director lung transplant program; b. Monrovia, Liberia, Aug. 3, 1964; s. Afif Salem and Sana Baz. MD, Am. U. of Beirut, 1989. Resident internal medicine Duke U., Durham, NC, 1989—92, pulmonary fellow, 1992—95; asst. prof. of medicine U. of Fla., Gainesville, 1996—2002, assoc. prof. of medicine, 2002—. Med. dir. lung transplant program U. of Fla., Gainesville, 1996—; thoracic com.

United Network for Organ Sharing. Named one of Young Leaders in Pulmonary Medicine, Boehringer-Ingelheim Pharmaceuticals, 2001. Mem.: Internat. Soc. of Heart and Lung Transplantation, Am. Thoracic Soc. Achievements include research in biology and immunosuppressive therapy of airway rejection. Office: U Fla 1600 SW Archer Rd PO Box 100395 Gainesville FL 32610 Office Phone: 352-265-8940. Business E-Mail: bazma@medicine.ufl.edu.

BAZAN, GUILLERMO C., chemistry and materials professor; BSc in Chemistry, summa cum laude, Univ. Ottawa, 1986; PhD in Inorganic Chemistry, MIT, 1991; postdoctoral studies, Calif. Inst. Tech., 1991—92. Asst. prof., chemistry Univ. Rochester, 1992—97, assoc. prof., 1997—98; prof., chemistry Univ. Calif., Santa Barbara, 1998—, prof., Dept. Materials (Engring.), 1999—, dir., Ctr. Polymers and Organic Solids, 2000—. Recipient Innovation award, Union Carbide, 1998, 1999, Spl. Creativity award, NSF, 2003, Bessel award, Humboldt Found., 2005. Mem.: Am. Chem. Soc. (Arthur C. Cope Scholar award 2007). Office: Dept Materials Engring & Chemistry Univ California Santa Barbara CA 93106-9510 Office Fax: 805-893-4120. Business E-Mail: bazan@chem.ucsb.edu.

BAZANT, ZDENEK PAVEL, engineering educator; b. Prague, Czechoslovakia, Dec. 10, 1937; came to U.S., 1968, naturalized, 1976; s. Zdenek and Stepanka (Curikova) B.; m. Iva Marie Krasna, Sept. 27, 1967; children: Martin Zdenek, Eva Stephanie. Civil Engr., Tech. U., Prague, 1960; PhD in Mechanics, Czechoslovak Acad. Sci., 1963; postgrad. diploma in theoretical physics, Charles U., Prague, 1966; doctorate (hon.), Czech Tech. U., Prague, 1991, Karlsruhe U., Germany, 1998, U. Colo., 2000, Poly. Milan, 2001, Institut Nat. des Scis. Appliques, Lyon, 2004, Vienna U. Tech., 2005. Registered structural engr., Ill. Scientist, adj. prof. Bldg. Rsch. Inst., Tech. U., Prague, 1963-67; docent habilitation Tech. U., Prague, 1967; vis. rsch. engr. Centre d'Étude et de Recherche du Bâtiment et des Travaux Publics, Paris, 1967, U. Toronto, 1967—68, U. Calif., Berkeley, 1969; assoc. prof. civil engring. Northwestern U., Evanston, Ill., 1969-73, prof., 1973-90, Walter P. Murphy prof., 1990—, coord. structural engring. program, 1974-78, 92—; founding dir. Ctr. for Concrete and Geomaterials, 1981-86. Cons. Argonne Nat. Lab., many other orgns. Author: Creep of Concrete in Structural Analysis, 1966, Stability of Structures: Elastic, Inelastic, Fracture and Damage Theories, 1991, Concrete at High Temperatures, 1996, Fracture and Size Effect, 1997, Scaling of Structural Strength, 2002, Inelastic Analysis of Structures, 2002; editor 16 books; editor in chief Jour. Engring. Mechanics, 1989-94; regional editor Internat. Jour. Fracture, 1991—; assoc. editor Applied Mechanics Rev., 1987—, Cement and Concrete Research Internat. Jour, 1970—, Materials and Structures, 1979— Solid Mechanics Archives, 1980-91, Materials and Structures, 1981—; mem. editl. bds. of 16 hours.; contbr. (with others) over 350 articles to profl. jours.; patentee in field. Recipient Best Engring. Book of Yr. award Soc. Am. Pubs., 1992, Outstanding New Citizen award Chgo. Citizenship Coun., 1976, A. von Humboldt award, 1990, Šolín medal Czech Tech. U., Prague, 1998, Stodola gold medal Slovak Acad. Scis., 1999, Highly Cited Scientist award Internat. Sci. Index, 2001; grantee NSF, 1970—, Air Force Office Scientific Rsch., 1975—, Los Alamos Sci. Lab., 1978-80, European Power Rsch. Inst., 1980—, Office Naval Rsch., 1990—, Dept. Energy, 1984—; Ford Found. fellow, 1967-68, Guggenheim fellow, 1978-79, Kajima Found. fellow U. Tokyo, 1987, NATO fellow, Paris, 1988, Japan Soc. Promotion of Sci. fellow U. Tokyo, 1995-96. Fellow ASME (Worcester Reed Warner medal 1997), Am. Acad. Mechanics, ASCE (chmn. com. properties of materials 1976-78, 82-84, editor in chief Jour. Engring. Mechanics 1988-94, Walter L. Huber rsch. prize 1976, T.Y. Lin Prestressed Concrete award 1977, Newmark medal 1996, Croes medal 1997, Lifetime Achievement Award, 2003, von Kármán medal 2005), Am. Concrete Inst. (chmn. fracture mechanics com. 1985-92), Internat. Assn. for Fracture Mechanics of Concrete Structures (pres. 1991-93), Internat. Union Testing and Rsch. Labs. Materials Structures (chmn. com. on creep, L'Hermite gold medal 1975), Soc. Engring. Sci. (pres. 1993, Prager medal 1996); mem. NAS, NAE, Italian Nat. acad dei Lincei Rome, Lombard Acad. Milan, Engring. Acad. Czech Republic (fgn. mem.), Austrian Acad. Scis., U.S. Nat. Com. on Theoretical and Applied Mechanics, Internat. Assn. Structural Mechanics Reactor Tech. (coord. concrete structures divsn.), ASTM (mem. concrete com., skiing com.), Prestressed Concrete Inst., Am. Ceramic Soc. (D.M. Roy award 2001), Internat. Assn. Soil Mech. Found. Engring., Internat. Assn. Bridge and Structural Engring., Soc. Exptl. Mechanics, Am. Soc. Engring. Edn., Bldg. Rsch. Inst. Spain (hon., Torroja Gold medal 1990), Czech Soc. Civil Engring. (hon.), Czech Soc. Mechanics (award of merit 1993), Structural Engrs. Assn. Ill. (Meritorious Paper award 1992). Home: 707 Roslyn Ter Evanston IL 60201-1721 Office: Northwestern Univ Dept Civil Engring Evanston IL 60208-0001

BAZAR, JILL A., music educator; d. Andrew and Mary T. Bazar. MusB, SUNY, Fredonia, 1999; MusM, East Carolina U., 2002. Piano instr. Music Acad. Ea. Carolina, Greenville, NC, 2002—06; lectr. class piano East Carolina U., Greenville, 2005—; ind. piano instr., 2005—. Musician (solo and collaborative performer) piano and chamber music. Grad. scholar, East Carolina U., 2000—02. Mem.: Coll. Music Soc., NC State Music Tchrs. Assn., Music Tchrs. Nat. Assn. (cert.), Greenville Piano Tchrs. Assn. (pres. 2003—). Avocations: painting, hiking, travel. Business E-Mail: bazarj@ecu.edu.

BAZELL, ROBERT JOSEPH, science correspondent; b. Pitts., Aug. 21, 1945; s. Irving and Beatrice (Robb) B.; m. Ilene Tanz, Sept. 11, 1966 (div.); children: Rebecca, Joshua; m. Margot Weinshel, July 31, 1979. BA, U. Calif., Berkeley, 1967; student, U. Sussex, Eng., 1968-69; postgrad., U. Calif., 1971. Writer Sci. Mag., Washington, 1971-72; reporter N.Y. Post, NYC, 1972-76; network corr. NBC News, NYC, 1976—. Contbr. articles to mags. Recipient over 2000 various journalistic awards. Mem. Phi Beta Kappa Office: NBC News 30 Rockefeller Plz Fl 3 New York NY 10112-0002

BAZEMORE, TRUDY MCCONNELL, librarian; d. Charlie Arthur and Elizabeth Bruns McConnell; m. John Everett Bazemore, Jr., Nov. 5, 1983. BA in Interdisciplinary studies magna cum laude, Coastal Carolina U., Conway, SC, 2001. Libr., tech. svcs. Georgetown Pub. Libr., SC, 1978—89, libr., reference svcs., 1989—93, head, pub. svcs., 1993—2001, asst. dir., 2001—. Mem.: Nat. Geneal. Soc., Founding Families of S.C., S.C. Hist. Soc., Interagency Coun., Am. Libr. Assn., Ribbon Club of Georgetown, Phi Theta Kappa, Alpha Sigma Lambda, Phi Sigma Tau. Methodist. Avocations: genealogy, gemology, photography, travel, art. Office: Georgetown County Pub Libr 405 Cleland St Georgetown SC 29440

BAZLER, FRANK ELLIS, retired lawyer; b. Columbus, Ohio, Jan. 17, 1930; s. Frank Hayes and Minnie Maybrum (Rucker) B.; m. Virginia Ann Hutchison, Oct. 17, 1954. BSBA, Ohio State U., 1951, JD, 1953. Bar: Ohio 1953, U.S. Dist. Ct. (we. dist.) Ohio 1956, U.S. Ct. Mil. Appeals 1957, U.S. Supreme Ct. 1957, U.S. Ct. Appeals (6th cir.) 1964. Assoc. Robert S. Miller, Atty., Troy, Ohio, 1955-57; ptnr. Miller, Bazler & Schlemmer, Troy, 1957-71; asst. corp. counsel Hobart Mfg. Co., Troy, 1971-74; corp. atty., asst. sec. Hobart Corp., Troy, 1974—95; ret., 1995; of counsel Dungan & LeFevre, Troy, 1995—2006. V.p. Bazler Transfer & Storage, Inc., Columbus, Ohio, 1950-58; sec., bd. dir. Golden Triangle Farms, Inc., Troy, 1972-2001. Pres. Troy United Fund, Inc., 1960, Troy Mus. Corp., 1990; chmn. Miami County chpt. ARC, 1955-59, Miami County (Ohio) Rep. Fin. Com., 1981-84; mem. Miami County Gen. Bd. Health, 1992-2004, pres. pro-tem, 1998-2001, pres., 2001-04; commn. on cert. of Attys. as Specialists of Supreme Ct. of Ohio, 1994-99, chmn., 1994-96. Capt. JAG, USAFR, 1953-61. Named one of Outstanding Young Men in Troy and Ohio, Troy Jaycees, 1957, Ohio Jaycees, 1961; recipient Disting. Citizen award Troy C. of C., 1985, Citizenship award Ohio State U., 1993, Disting. Svc. award, 2004. Fellow: Ohio State Bar Found. (pres. 1992), Am. Bar Found. (Ohio chmn. 1995—2004); mem.: ABA (mem. gen. practice sect. 1967—, coun. 1976—80, ho. of dels. 1984—2000, mem. standing com. on specialization 1999—2002), Nat. Conf. Bar Pres. (exec. coun. 1988—91), Miami County Bar Assn. (pres. 1966, Meritorious Svc. award 1985), Ohio State Bar Assn. (coun. of dels. 1979—88, pres. 1984—85, Ohio Bar medal 1990), Nat. Caucus State Bar Assns. (Ohio rep. 1993—2002, exec com. 1997—2002, pres. 2000—01), Overfield Tavern Mus. (bd. trustees 2000—, pres. 2001—04), Indsl. Heritage Mus. of Miami County (trustee, sec. 1997—), Brukner Nature Ctr. (trustee 1998—2004, pres. 1999—2002), Kiwanis (pres. 1964), Scottish Rite, Masons. Republican. Presbyterian. Avocations: photography, travel, golf. Home: 1156 Premwood Dr Troy OH 45373

BAZZAZ, FAKHRI A., plant biology educator, administrator; b. Baghdad, Iraq, June 16, 1933; came to U.S., 1958; s. Abdul-Latif and Munifa Bazzaz; m. Maarib D.L. Bakri, Aug. 25, 1958; children: Sahar, Ammar. BS, U. Baghdad, 1953; MS, U. Ill., 1960, PhD, 1963; A.M. (hon.), Harvard U., 1984. Prof. U. Ill., Urbana, 1977-84, head dept. plant biology, acting dir. Sch. Life Scis., 1983-84; prof. Harvard U., Cambridge, Mass., 1984—, Mallinckrodt prof. biology, 1997—. Editor: Oecologia, 1983—; co-editor: Response of Agroecosystem to Climate Change, 1996, Community, Population, Evolutionary Responses to Elevated CO2, 1997, Resource Allocation in Plants and Animals, 2005; author: Plants Changing Environments Linking Physiological, Population and Community Ecology, 1996; contbr. articles to profl. jours. Guggenheim fellow; fellow Clare Hall, Cambridge (Eng.) U., 1981—, Imperial Coll., London, 2002, World Innovation Found., 2004; recipient Nev. medal, 2004. Fellow AAAS, Am. Acad. Arts and Scis.; mem. Ecol. Soc. Am., Brit. Ecol. Soc, Humboldt Forschungspreise, Germany (award 1997), Phi Beta Kappa (hon.). Home: 464 Concord Ave Lexington MA 02421-8040 Personal E-mail: maaribbazzaz@comcast.net.

BAZZI, SAMER, software developer, consultant; arrived in USA, 1987, naturalized, 1994; s. Mohamad Bazzi and Sana Osseiran; 1 child, Moses. BS in Computer sci., Am. U., Washington, 1993. Software devel. cons. Arcs Tech. Solutions, Daly City, Calif., 2001—03, Sun Microsystems, Sunnyvale, Calif., 2003—04. Activist Zahra Ctr., Milpitas, Calif., 2002—06, SABA, San Jose, Calif., 2003—04, Rasool Ctr., Campbell, Calif., 2005—06. Fin. specialist US Army NG, 1989—91. Mem.: Commonwealth Club. Achievements include development of legal discovery software that allowed Sun to detect and submit millions of emails and documents to Microsoft by the court-imposed deadline. Avocations: metaphysics, travel, writing, bicycling, hiking. Home: PO Box 60723 Sunnyvale CA 94088 Personal E-mail: sambazzi@gmail.com.

BEA, CARLOS TIBURCIO, federal judge; b. San Sebastian, Spain, Apr. 18, 1934; Student, Menlo Jr. Coll., 1950—51; BA, Stanford U., 1956, JD, 1958. Bar: Calif. 1959. Assoc. Dunne, Phelps & Mills, 1959—66, ptnr., 1967—75; prin., owner Carlos Bea Law Corp., 1975—90; judge San Francisco (Calif.) Superior Ct., 1990—2003, US Ct. Appeals, (9th cir.), San Francisco, 2003—. Office: US Ct Appeals 95 Seventh St San Francisco CA 94103 Office Phone: 415-355-8180.*

BEA, ROBERT G., civil engineering educator; BS, U. Fla., 1959, MS, 1960. Sr. staff civl engr. Shell Oil Co., 1959-76; chief engr., v.p. Ocean Engring. Divsn., Woodward-Clyde Cons., 1976-81; v.p. PMB Sys. Engring., Inc., 1981-88; prof. dept. civil engring., naval arch. and offshore engring U. Calif., Berkeley, 1988—. Cons. prof. engring Stanford U., 1985-89. Recipient J. Hillis Miller Engring. award. Mem. ASCE (Croes medal, 1959), Nat. Acad. Engring. Achievements include projects and research in coastal, offshore and ocean engineering; development of methods to define design criteria for fixed and mobile offshor structures; development of guidelines for the requalifications and rehabilitation of marine structures and ships; evaluation of forces due to waves, currents, earthquakes, ice and sea floor slides; development of technology for evaluation of the dynamic response characteristics of marine foundations and structures. Office: U Calif 215 Mclaughlin Hall Berkeley CA 94720-1712

BEACH, ARTHUR O'NEAL, lawyer; b. Albuquerque, Feb. 8, 1945; s. William Pearce and Vivian Lucille (Kronig) B.; m. Alex Clark Doyle, Sept. 12, 1970; 1 child, Eric Kronig. BBA, U. N.Mex., 1967, JD, 1970. Bar: N.Mex. 1970. Assoc. Smith & Ransom, Albuquerque, 1970-74, Keleher & McLeod, Albuquerque, 1974-75, ptnr., 1976-78; shareholder Keleher & McLeod, P.A., Albuquerque, 1978—. Tchg. asst. U. N.Mex., 1970. Bd. editors Natural Resources Jour., 1968-70. Mem. ABA, State Bar N.Mex. (unauthorized practice of law com., adv. opinions com., med.-legal panel, legal-dental-osteo.-podiatry com., jud. selection com., specialization bd.), Albuquerque Bar Assn. (dir. 1978-82). Democrat. Mem. Christian Sci. Ch. Home: 2015 Dietz Pl NW Albuquerque NM 87107-3240 Office: Keleher & McLeod PA PO Box AA Albuquerque NM 87103 Office Phone: 505-346-9107. E-mail: aob@keleher-law.com.

BEACH, BARBARA PURSE, lawyer; b. Washington, June 12, 1947; d. Clifford John and Lillian (Natarus) B. BA, U. Ky., 1968; MSW, U. Md., 1972; JD, Am. U., 1980. Bar: D.C. 1980, Va. 1980. Law clk. to presiding justice benefit rev. bd. U.S. Dept. Labor, Washington, 1980; asst. city atty. City of Alexandria, Va., 1981-85; atty. Ross, Marsh, Foster, Myers & Quiggle, Alexandria, 1985-90, Beach, Butt & Assocs., PC, Alexandria, 1990-92; prin. Beach & Assocs., Alexandria, 1992—2005; town atty. Town of Herndon, Va., 1992-94, Va., 2005—. Substitute judge 18th Jud. Cir., 1989-05; 4th dist. com. disciplinary bd. dirs. Va. State Bd., 1998-2004, chmn., 2000-01. Vice-chmn. Va. Health Svcs. Cost Rev. Coun., 1989-92; mem. Va. Commn. on Women and Minorities, 1990-92; bd. dirs. Am. Heart Assn., Alexandria, 1996-2000, divsn. pres., 1998-99. Alexandria Bar Assn. (pres. 1987-88), Kiwanis. Office: Town Atty Town of Leesburg 25 W Market St Leesburg VA 20176 Personal E-mail: bpbeach@aol.com.

BEACH, BERT BEVERLY, clergyman; b. Gland, Vaud, Switzerland, June 15, 1928; s. Walter Raymond and Gladys (Corley) B.; m. Eliane Marguerite Palange, Apr. 8, 1954; children: Danielle, Michele. BA, Pacific Union Coll., 1948; postgrad., Stanford U., 1948-49, 51; PhD, U. Paris, 1958; ThD, Christian Theol. Acad., 1986. Prin. West Liberty Union Intermediate Sch., Gridley, Calif., 1949-50, Italian Jr. Coll., Florence, Italy, 1952-58; chmn. history dept. Columbia Union Coll., Takoma Pk., Md., 1958-60; dir. edn. No. Europe-West Africa Div. of SDA, St. Albans, Eng., 1960-75, gen. sec., 1973-80; sec. Conf. of Secs. Christian World Communions, Silver Spring, Md., 1970—2002; dir. pub. affairs Gen. Conf. of Seventh-day Adventists, Silver Spring, Md., 1980-95; gen. sec. Coun. on Inter-Ch. Rels., 1980—2005; sec. gen. Internat. Religious Liberty Assn., Silver Spring, Md., 1980-95, pres., 1996, 2000. Sec. Internat. Acad. for Freedom of Religion, 1985—; v.p. Internat. Commn. for Prevention of Alcoholism and Drug Dependency, 1980—, pres., 1991, 1997—; editl. dir., panelist Am. Religious Townhall Meeting Telecast, 1995—. Chmn. bd. John H. Weidner Found. Altruism, 1996—2005; sec. bd. Bridging Boundaries Internat., 2002—. Recipient Citation, Senate of State of Md., 1984; named Paul Harris fellow Rotary Internat., 1984, Order of Bishop Hodura, Polish Nat. Cath. Ch., 1986, Order of St. Magdalene, Polish Orthodox Ch., 1987, Honored Alumnus of Yr. Pacific Union Coll., 1997, Knight's Cross of Order of Merit of Polish Republic, 1998, Human Rights Leadership award Freedom Mag., 1998, Pres. Leadership medallion Andrews U., 1999, Distinction medal Gen. Conf. Health Ministries, 2004, Medallion of Distinction Gen. Conf. Edn. Dept., 2005, Bridge award Gen. Conf. Com. Dept., 2005. Mem. Rotary Club (pres. 2005-06), Cosmos Club, SAR, Md. Assn. Founders and Patriots of Am. (gov. 1998-2000), Polish Bible Soc. (hon.). Adventist. Avocation: prestidigitation. Home: 14508 Cutstone Way Silver Spring MD 20905-7430 Office: 12501 Old Columbia Pike Silver Spring MD 20904-6601 Home Phone: 301-384-2271; Office Phone: 301-680-6680. Personal E-mail: bertbbeach@msn.com.

BEACH, CECIL PRENTICE, librarian; b. Knoxville, Tenn., July 12, 1927; s. Frank Alfred and Lillie Maude (Sims) B.; m. Doris Jean Pardue, Apr. 17, 1949; children: Steven Prentice, Rex Arthur, Keven Sanders, Kyle Alfred, Quentin Anthony; m. Marcia Gibson Buckley, June 20, 1969; children: Stephanie Lynn, Shannon Sue. AB, U. Chattanooga, 1950; MA, Fla. State U., 1952. Bookmobile libr. Chattanooga Pub. Libr., 1948-51; extension libr. Decatur (Ga.)-DeKalb Regional Libr., 1952-54; dir. Piedmont Regional Libr., Winder, Ga., 1954-60, Gadsden (Ala.) Pub. Libr., 1960-64, Tampa (Fla.)-Hillsborough Libr. System, 1965-72; state libr. State of Fla., Tallahassee, 1972-77; dir. div. librs. Broward County, Ft. Lauderdale, Fla., 1977-89, dir. pub. svcs. dept., 1989-93, ret., 1993; appt. bond project coord., 1999—; ptnr. Beach/Willey Cons., Tallahassee, 1993—; prof. Fla. State U. Sch. of Libr. and Infr. Studies, 1993—. Instr. dept. libr. sci. U. South Fla.; chmn. Fla. Libr. Study Commn., 1970-72; chmn. bd. dirs. Southeastern Libr. Network; chmn. S.E. Fla. Libr. Info. network; chmn. Fla. del. to The White House Conf. on Libr. and Info. Svcs., 1991; cons. libr. bldgs. and svc. Pres., Gadsden Community Coun., 1963; bd. govs. Nova U.; chmn. adv. coun. Seagull Sch. for Exceptional Children; mem. Fla. Endowment Humanities, 1972—, Ft. Lauderdale Downtown Coun.; bd. dirs. Easter Seal Soc., 1975—, Ft. Lauderdale Art Mus., Multiple Sclerosis Soc., Broward Pub. Libr. Found., Ft. Lauderdale Children's Theater. With USNR, 1944-46. Mem. ALA, Southeastern Libr. Assn. (pres. 1972—), Ala. Libr. Assn., Ga. Libr. Assn., Fla. Libr. Assn. (pres. 1969), Pub. Libr. Assn. (Allie Beth Martin award 1984), Adult Edn. Assn., Tampa C. of C., Greater Ft. Lauderdale C. of C., Fla. State U. Alumni Assn. (pres. 1967, Disting. Alumni award 1985). Lodges: Masons, Rotary. Democrat. Presbyterian. Home and Office: Apt 715 3100 NE 48th St Fort Lauderdale FL 33308-4948 Personal E-mail: cbeach0712@bellsouth.net.

BEACH, CHARLES ADDISON, lawyer; b. Albany, NY, Apr. 21, 1945; s. Charles A.W. and Eleanor (Johnston) B.; m. Jane L. Shlionsky, June 8, 1968; children: James E. and Jonathan M. BA, Hamilton Coll., 1967; JD, Cornell U., 1973. Bar: N.Y. 1974, U.S. Dist. Ct. (no., ea., we. and so. dists.) N.Y. 1974, U.S. Ct. Appeals (2d and 10th cirs.) 1975, U.S. Supreme Ct. 1982, Tex. 1991, U.S. Dist. Ct. (no. dist.) Tex. 1993, U.S. Ct. Appeals (5th cir.) 1995, U.S. Ct. Appeals (6th cir.) 1998. Assoc. Shearman & Sterling, NYC, 1973-77, 79-81, Paris, 1977-79; sr. counsel, coord. corp. litigation Exxon Mobil Corp., NYC, 1981—90, Irving, Tex., 1990—. Mng. editor: Cornell Internat. Law Jour. Vol. Peace Corps., Libya and Tunisia, 1968-71; adv. coun. Cornell Law Sch.; bd. dirs. Irving Symphony Orch., 2006-. Fellow Tex. Bar Found. (sustaining life); mem. ABA, N.Y. State Bar Assn., Assn. of Bar of City of N.Y., Dallas Bar Assn., Irving Bar Assn., Am. Arbitration Assn. (adv. coun. Dallas chpt.), U.S. Coun. Internat. Bus./Internat. C. of C. (arbitration com., S.W. com. on arbitration), Inst. for Trasnational Arbitration Ctr. for Am. and Internat. Law (adv. bd.), Coll. State Bar Tex. Home: 1431 N Travis Cir Irving TX 75038-6238 Office: Exxon Mobil Corp 5959 Las Colinas Blvd Irving TX 75039-2298 Business E-Mail: charles.a.beach@exxonmobil.com.

BEACH, HARRY LEE, JR., mechanical engineer, aerospace engineer; b. Richmond, Va., Aug. 16, 1944; married, 1966; 3 children. BS, N.C. State U., 1966, MS, 1968, PhD in Mech. Engring., 1970. Rsch. engr. Langley Rsch. Ctr., NASA, Hampton, Va., 1970-75, head combustion sect., 1975-77, leader performance analysis group, 1977-80, asst., 1980-81, head hypersonic propulsion br., 1981-89, head nat. aerospace plane, 1989-92, dep. dir., 1992-98; prof. dept. physics, computer sci. and engring. Christopher Newport U., 1998—2002; exec. dir. Hampton Roads Rsch. Partnership, 2002—. Asst. prof. Joint Inst. Advanced Flight Sci., George Washington U., 1977—; adj. prof. Christopher Newport Coll., 1980—. Fellow AIAA (Air Breathing Propulsion award 1997). Achievements include research in supersonic combustion ramjet propulsion, combustion fundamentals, computational fluid dynamics, combustion diagnostics, inlet and combuster conceptual design and testing, inlet-combustor component integration.

BEACH, MARCIA ELLEN, judge; b. St. Petersberg, Fla., Oct. 23, 1944; d. John Milton and Nancy Zetta Gibson; m. Cecil Prentice Beach, June 20, 1969; children: Stephanie Lynn Stone, Steven Prentice, Rex Arthur, Shannon Sue Buckley, Keven Sanders, Kyle Alfred, Quentin Anthony; m. Bill Buckley (div.). BA, Barry U., Miami, 1985; JD, Nova Southeastern, Ft. Lauderdale, 1988. Bar: Am. Bar, Fla. 1988. Exec. sec. Hillsborough County Govt., Tampa, 1962—69; asst. to pres. Tele-Data, Lakeland, Fla., 1969—72; exec. dir. Grandpeople Inc., Tallahassee, 1975—77, Broward Legislative Del., Ft. Lauderdale, 1977—78; legislative aide U.S. Congressman: 12th Dist., Ft. Lauderdale, 1978—80; county commr. Broward County, Fla., Ft. Lauderdale, 1980—86; atty. Holland and Knight, Ft. Lauderdale, 1988—92; atty., dir. Advocacy Ctr. for Persons with Disabilities, Tallahassee, 1992—98; spl. counsel Fla. Attorney Gen., Tallahassee, 1998—2000; circuit ct. judge 17th Jud. Dist., Ft. Lauderdale, 2001—. Chair Fla. Human Rights Advocay Commn., Tallahassee; v.p. legis. adv. Fla. Assn. for Retarded Citizens, Tallahassee; chair Gov. Commn. on Protection and Advocacy, Tallahassee; dir. Spl. Olympics, Dist. III, Tallahassee; pres. Leon County Assn. for Retarded Citizens, Tallahassee; atty. Josias and Goren, Ft. Lauderdale, 1988—99. Author: (publ. law review) No Tears for Corey Greer; a review of Foster Care in Florida. Chair Broward County Planning Coun., Ft. Lauderdale, 1980—88, Broward County Criminal Justice Coun., Ft. Lauderdale, 1980—86, Met. Planning Coun., Ft. Lauderdale, 1980—86, Broward County Tourist Devel. Coun., Ft. Lauderdale, 1980—86. Recipient Svc. to Mankind award, Brandon Sertoma Club, 1971, Leadership award, Broward Legislative Del., 1978, Woman of the Yr., Women in Communication, 1981, Outstanding Legislator award, Early Childhood Devel. Assn., 1984, Humanitarian award, City of Hope, 1985, Legislative Appreciation award, Friends of the Broward County Libr., 1985. Mem.: Nat. Assn. of Drug Ct. Profls., Stephen Boher Inns of Ct., Am., Fla., Broward Bar Assns. (assoc.). Presbyterian. Avocations: reading, travel, genealogy. Home: 3100 NE 48th St #715 Fort Lauderdale FL 33308 Office: Florida 17th Circuit Ct 201 SE 6th St Fort Lauderdale FL 33301 Home Fax: 954-489-0372. Personal E-mail: cbeach0712@bellsouth.net.

BEACH, MARGARET SMITH, retired language educator; b. Decaturville, Tenn., Dec. 9, 1937; d. Luther Grant and Eva Irene Mallard; m. James Edward Smith (dec. 1960); children: James Edward III(dec.) , John Fitzgerald; m. John D. Beach, July 26, 1975; stepchildren: John D. Jr., Michael Jerome. BA in English, Agrl. and Indsl. State U., Tenn., 1961; MS in Psychology, Tenn. State U., 1982. English and French tchr. Townsend HS, Winchester, Tenn., 1959—61, Nashville Christian Inst., 1961—63; part-time English tchr. Burt HS, Clarksville, Tenn., 1963—64; tchr. Cobb Elem. Sch., Clarksville, Tenn., 1963—69; English and French tchr. Wharton HS, Nashville, 1969—70, Neely's Bend Jr. HS, Madison, Tenn., 1970—91; ret., 1991. Chairperson English dept. Neely's Bend Jr. Mid. Sch., Madison, Tenn., 1974—76; cheerleader co-sponsor Neely's Bend Jr. HS, Madison, Tenn., 1975—76; English accreditation chairperson Neely's Bend Mid. Sch., Madison, Tenn., 1978—79, sch. newspaper sponsor, 1980—81; faculty rep. Tchrs. Union, Nashville, 1978—80; writer proficiency test items Metro. Nashville Schs., 1984—85. Author: (book) Creative Poems, 1974, Ethnic Poetry for All, 1998, Religious Poems of Faith, 2001; poet Our World's Best Loved Poems, 1983. Recipient Cert. of Appreciation, Met. Bd. of Edn., 1991, Award of Appreciation, Alumni

Assn., 1992, 1996, 2002, Award of Dedication, 1996, Cert. of Appreciation, Nat. Coun. of Tchrs. of English, 1998, Cert. of Merit, Tenn. Ret. Tchrs. Assn., 2000—01. Mem.: Ret. Tchrs. Assn. Avocations: writing, reading, storytelling, poetry, performing. Office: Agape Pearl Publ PO Box 280653 Nashville TN 37228 Office Phone: 615-242-2307. E-mail: mrgrtmlmsb@aol.com.

BEACH, SANDRA MARIE YUDICHAK, secondary school educator; b. Niagara Falls, NY, Jan. 21, 1946; d. Thomas Stephen and Helen (Kosko) Yudichak; m. Fred Ellsworth Beach, Aug. 28, 1965 (div., May, 1994); 1 child, Gary Nathan. BA, SUNY, Buffalo, 1969; MA in Tchg., Niagara U., 1973. Cert. secondary English tchr., NY. Tchr. Grand Island Mid. Sch., NY, 1969—77, 1983—89, Grand Island H.S., 1977—83, 1999—2002. Tutor, Lewiston, N.Y., 1969—; supt.'s adv. com., Lewiston-Porter H.S., 1994-95, mem. decision making team; tchr. stakeholder Grand Island Mid. Sch. Shared Decision Making, 1992-94. Named del. to Spain, ASCD, 1995; recipient Celebration of Inspiration award, PTA, 2001, 2002. Mem. ASCD (assoc.), Power of Positive Students, N.Y. State United Tchrs. Avocations: writing, needle crafts, travel. Home and Office: 861 Sun Valley North Tonawanda NY 14120 Office Phone: 716-694-0037. Personal E-mail: sandeyb@gmail.com.

BEACH, STEPHEN HOLBROOK, lawyer; b. Highland Park, Mich., June 3, 1915; s. Stephen Holbrook and Katherine Jean (Campbell) B.; m. Mary Frances Mulvihill, July 6, 1951; children: Jennifer Katherine Beach Buda, Stephen Holbrook III. AB with honors in Polit. Sci, Kalamazoo Coll., 1936; LLB cum laude, U. Detroit, 1941; postgrad., Georgetown U., 1945, Columbia U., 1970. Bar: Mich. 1941, U.S. Dist. Ct. (ea. dist.) Mich., 1941, U.S. Supreme Ct. 1944, N.Y. 1947, U.S. Dist. Ct. (so. dist.) N.Y. 1947, U.S. Dist. Ct. (ea. dist.) N.Y. 1949, D.C. 1949, Conn. 1975. Assoc. Winthrop, Stimson, Putnam & Roberts, NYC, 1946-48, Cann, Lamb & Kittelle, NYC, 1948-56, Willkie, Farr, Gallagher, Walton and Fitzgibbon, NYC, 1956-60; staff atty. IBM Corp., NYC, 1960-61, of counsel supplies div. NYC and Dayton, N.J., 1961-65; v.p., gen. counsel, sec. The Svc. Bur. Corp., NYC, 1965-75; v.p., gen. counsel Data Svcs. Control Data Corp., Greenwich, Conn., 1976-78, gen. counsel Computer Co. Mpls., 1979-80, v.p., assoc., gen. counsel, 1980-82, sr. v.p. telecommunications policy, corp. sec., 1983-85; of counsel Rogers, Hoge & Hills, White Plains, N.Y., 1985-86; pvt. practice law Greenwich and Stamford, Conn., 1986—. Bd. dirs., corp. sec. Dataware Techs., Inc. Editor-in-chief U. Detroit Law Jour., 1937-41. Capt. US Army, 1943—46. Mem. ABA (sci. and tech. sect., banking and bus. law sect.), Conn. Bar Assn (intellectual property and computer law sects.), N.Y. State Bar Assn. (banking and bus. law sect.), D.C. Bar Assn., Assn. of Data Processing Svcs. Orgns. (v.p. govt. rels., bd. dirs. 1978-84), The Wee Burn Country Club, Ocean Club of Fla. Republican. Episcopalian. Avocation: golf. Home: 52 Brushy Hill Rd Darien CT 06820-6007 Office Phone: 203-655-7630.

BEACHLEY, MICHAEL CHARLES, radiologist; b. Harrisburg, Pa., Nov. 14, 1940; s. Kenneth Gumbert and Carolyn Elizabeth (Jones) B.; m. Deborah Rowe Samson, July 27, 1963; children: Kenneth, Barbara, William. AB, Dartmouth Coll., 1962, B.MS, 1963; MD, Harvard U., 1965. Diplomate Am. Bd. Radiology. Intern in surgery Med. Coll. Va., Richmond, 1965-66, resident in radiology, 1966-69, instr. radiology, 1970, faculty, 1972—, acting chmn. dept. radiology, 1976, prof., 1977-87, chmn. dept. radiology, 1977-82, prof. radiation scis., 1981-87, prof. biophysics, 1980-82, prof. physiology and biophysics, 1982-87, clin. prof., 1987—; clin. prof. radiology U. Pitts., 1988—; chmn. Dept. Radiology St. Margaret Meml. Hosp., Pitts., 1987-97; pres. Three Rivers Imaging Cons., Ltd., 1993-94, Duquesne Imaging Ltd., 1994-2001; med. dir. Radiology Ptnrs.; chmn. dept. radiology U. Pitts. Med. Ctr., Saint Margaret, 1997-99. Cons. McGuire VA Hosp., 1977—; fellow in radiol. pathology Armed Forces Inst. Pathology, Washington, 1969. Contbr. articles to profl. jours., chapters to books. Vice-pres. College Hills Civic Assn., 1975-77. Served as maj. M.C. U.S. Army, 1970-72. Fellow Am. Coll. Radiology (pres. Va. chpt. 1982-83, chmn. com. on stds. and accreditation 1998-2004); mem. AMA, Am. Heart Assn., Radiol. Soc. N.Am. (chmn. bylaws com. 1994-96), Am. Roentgen Ray Soc., Pitts. Roentgen Soc. (chmn. com on fellowship nomination 1998-99), Pa. Radiol. Soc., Pa. Med. Soc. (alt. del., mem. med.-legal com.), Allegheny Med. Soc. (peer rev. bd. 1997-99), Pa. Radiol. MSO (chmn. by-laws com., exec. com.), Dartmouth Club Western Pa. (exec. com.), Harvard Club Western Pa. (treas.), Pitts. Field Club. Home: PO Box 331 Bakerstown PA 15007-0331 Business E-Mail: beachleymc@upmc.edu.

BEACHLEY, NORMAN HENRY, mechanical engineer, educator; b. Washington, Jan. 13, 1933; s. Albert Henry and Anna Garnet (Eiring) B.; m. Marion Ruth Iglehart, July 18, 1959; children: Brenda Ruth, Rebecca Sue, Barbara Joan. B.M.E., Cornell U., 1956, PhD, 1966. Mem. tech. staff Hughes Aircraft Co., Culver City, Calif., 1956-57; mem. tech. staff Space Tech. Labs., Redondo Beach, Calif., 1959-63; mem. faculty U. Wis., Madison, 1966—, prof. mech. engring., 1978-94, prof. emeritus, 1994—. Cons. numerous orgns., 1967— Co-author: Introduction to Dynamic System Analysis, 1978. Served with USAF, 1957-59. Sci. and Engring. Research Council Gt. Britain fellow, 1981-82 Fellow Soc. Automotive Engrs.; mem. ASME, Sigma Xi. Achievements include research in field of energy storage powerplants for motor vehicles, 1970—. Home: 2332 Fitchburg Rd Verona WI 53593-9278 Office: U Wis 1513 University Ave Madison WI 53706-1539 Business E-Mail: beachley@wisc.edu.

BEACHY, PHILIP ARDEN, molecular biology educator; b. Red Lake, Ont., Oct. 25, 1958; s. Moses Andrew and Ada Barbara (Miller) B.; m. Katrin Ingrid Andreasson, May 21, 1988. BA in Natural Scis., Goshen Coll., 1979; PhD in Biochemistry, Stanford U., 1986. Staff assoc. dept. embryology Carnegie Instn., Balt., 1986-88; asst. prof. dept. molecular biology and genetics Johns Hopkins U. Sch. Medicine, Balt., 1988—93; assoc. prof. molecular biology and genetics Johns Hopkins U., Balt., 1993—98, prof., 1998—; asst. investigator Howard Hughes Med. Inst., Balt., 1988—2000, full investigator, 2000—. Contbr. articles to sci. jours. Sloan Found. fellow, 1987-90; recipient Outstanding Young Sci. award Md., 1998. Fellow AAAS; mem. NAS (Molecular biology award 1998), Genetics Soc. Am., AAAS. Achievements include research in developmental morphogen, its processing and structure, and its covalent attachment to cholesterol; the hedgehog gene and protein, advancing the understanding of embryo development, cell differentiation and cancer development. Office Fax: 410-955-9124. Business E-Mail: pbeachy@jhmi.edu.

BEADEL, STEPHEN JAY, author; b. Sharpsburg, Iowa, Aug. 5, 1949; s. Walter Reldon and Katherine Margaret (Repplinger) B. BS, Iowa State U., 1971. Owner, mgr. Beadel Lumber, Lenox, Iowa, 1976-83; author, 1985—. Guest on numerous talk shows, 1990. Author: The Prophetic Beast, The Predicted Fall of Berlin Wall, 1989, What the Church Won't Tell You About Christmas, 1989, The Four Horseman of the Apocalypse, 1989, What Do You Mean "Born Again"?, 1990, The Pagan Rituals of Easter, 1990, Where is the True Church, 1990, The Reward for Salvation, 1990. Avocations: photography, painting. Home: 1230 70th St Windsor Heights IA 50311

BEADLE, ELIZABETH AHRENS, retired elementary school educator; b. Queens County, NY, Jan. 27, 1927; d. William Henry Ahrens and Marie Esta Strong-Ahrens; m. Harold Kenneth Beadle, Dec. 2, 1950; children: Carol Beadle Shelley, Richard Kenneth, Robert Thomas. BA in Child Study, St. Joseph Coll. for Women, Bklyn., 1948; student, Queens Coll., 1949, Hunter Coll., 1949, St. Leo Coll., Fla., 1968, U. South Fla., 1968—75; student reading improvement, Psychotechnics, Inc., 1968. Cert. tchr. NY, Fla. Tchr. kindergarten P.S. 109, Queens Village, NY, 1948—50; office mgr. Beadle Excavation/Instant Shade Inc., Zephyrhills, Fla., 1951—2000; tchr. 1st grade Pasco Elem. Sch., Dade City, Fla., 1969—70, home-sch. coord., 1974—75, tchr. kindergarten, 1970—72, tchr. 3d grade, 1975—88; tchr. kindergarten Dade City Grammar Sch. (now Cox Elem.), 1972—74; ret., 1988. Organizer Reading is Fundamental program Pasco Elem. Sch., 1974. Pres., sec., treas. Intertown Pvt. Sch. Transp., Inc., Zephyrhills, 1966—69. Mem.: DAV Aux. (organizer, pres. 1958—60), Alpha Delta Kappa. Republican. Roman Catholic. Avocations: reading, travel, birdwatching, mechanical drawing.

BEAGRIE, GEORGE SIMPSON, dentist, educator, retired dean; b. Peterhead, Scotland, Sept. 14, 1925; emigrated to Can., 1968, naturalized, 1973; s. George and Eliza Lawson (Simpson) B.; m. Marjorie McVie, Sept. 30, 1950; children: Jennifer, Lesley, Ailsa, Elspeth. LDS, Royal Coll. Surgeons, Edinburgh, Scotland, 1947; DDS, U. Edinburgh, 1966; DSc (hon.), McGill U., Can., 1985; DDS (hon.), U. Edinburgh, 1987; D, U. Montreal, Can., 1991. Prof., chmn. dept. restorative dentistry U. Edinburgh Dental Sch., 1963-68; prof., chmn. dept. clin. scis. U. Toronto Dental Sch., 1968-78, dir. postgrad. div., 1974-78; dean faculty dentistry U. B.C., Vancouver, Canada, 1978—88, dean emeritus, 1989—. Sci. officer grants com. dental scis. Med. Rsch. Coun. Can., 1971-76, dir. dental tng. grants programme, 1971-78; mem. Nat. Dental Examining Bd. Can.; chmn. written exams com. Nat. Dental Examining Bd., Can., 1984-93; cons. WHO, 1976-1996, in field. Contbr. over 100 articles to dental jours. Mem. United Ch. Can. Served to flight lt. RAF, 1948-50. Fellow Nuffield Found., 1957-58; grantee Med. Research Council U.K., 1962-64; grantee Med. Research Council Can., 1968; grantee Commonwealth Found., 1973 Fellow Royal Coll. Dentists Can. (pres. 1977-79), Am. Coll. Dentists, Internat. Coll. Dentists; fellow in dental surgery Royal Coll. Surgeons Edinburgh and Eng.; mem. ADA (hon.), Internat. Assn. Dental Research (pres. 1977-78), Fedn. Dentaire Internat. (chmn. commn. on dental edn. and practice 1981-87), Can. Dental Assn. (editor tape cassette program 1972-76, coord. Self-Learning, Self-Appt. C-E program for gen. practitioners, 1986-), Omicron Kappa Upsilon.

BEAHM, FRANKLIN D., lawyer; b. Independence, Kans., Jan. 18, 1953; s. Edgar Hiram and Dorothy S.; m. Tawny L. McIntyre, Jan. 7, 1994; children: F. David, Patrick Stuart, Kristin Sanders, Stephen McWilliams. BBA, So. Methodist U., 1975; JD, Tulane U., 1977. Bar: La. 1977, Colo. 1993, Tex. 2000, U.S. Dist. Ct. (ea. dist.) La. 1977, U.S. Dist. Ct. (mid. dist.) La. 1980, U.S. Dist. Ct. (we. dist.) La. 1985, U.S. Ct. Appeals (5th cir.), U.S. Tax Ct. 1989, U.S. Supreme Ct. 1993. Assoc. Manard & Schoenberger, New Orleans, 1977-80, Bourgeois, Bennett, Metairie, La., 1980, Hammett, Leake & Hammett, New Orleans, 1980-83, ptnr., 1983-85, Thomas, Hayes & Beahm, New Orleans, 1985-95, Chehardy, Sherman, Ellis, Breslin, Murray, Metairie, 1995-97, Beahm & Green, New Orleans, 1997—. Mem. Am. Health Lawyers Assn., Am. Soc. Law and Medicine, La. Assn. Def. Counsel, La. Bar Assn. (Interprofl. com. 1997-98, professionalism com. 1999—), La. Med. Soc. (Interprofl. com. 1997-98), La. Soc. Hosp. Attys. of the La. Hosp. Assn., Denver Bar Assn., Def. Rsch. Inst. (med. malpractice com., product liability com.), Beta Alpha Psi. Office: 145 Robert E Lee Blvd Ste 408 New Orleans LA 70124-2581 Office Phone: 504-288-2000. Business E-Mail: frank@beahm.com.

BEAIRD, JAMES RALPH, law educator, dean; b. 1925. BS, U. Ala., 1949, LLB, 1951; LLM, George Washington U., 1953. Bar: Ala. 1951, D.C. 1973. Atty. U.S. Dept. Labor, 1951-56, asst. solicitor, 1956-59; assoc. gen. counsel NLRB, 1959-60; assoc. solicitor U.S. Dept. Labor, 1960-65; vis. prof. U. Ga., 1965-66, prof. law, 1967-89, prof. emeritus, dean, 1976-87, dean emeritus; John Sparkman Vis. Disting. Prof., U. Ala., 1988—; mem. Sec. Labor's Adv. Council on Welfare and Pension Plans, 1968—. Mem. adv. com. for Ga. SBA, 1969—. Mem. Farrah Order Jurisprudence. Office: U Ga Sch Law Athens GA 30602 Personal E-mail: jrb@aol.com. Business E-Mail: jrb@bbgbalaw.com.

BEAK, PETER ANDREW, chemistry professor; b. Syracuse, NY, Jan. 12, 1936; s. Ralph E. and Belva (Edinger) B.; m. Sandra J. Burns, July 25, 1959; children: Bryan A., Stacia W. BA, Harvard U., 1957; PhD, Iowa State U., 1961. From instr. to prof. chemistry U. Ill., Urbana, 1961—, Roger Adams prof. chemistry, 1997—2003, Jubille prof. liberal arts and sci., 1990—, James R. Eiszner chair chemistry, 2003, CAS prof. chemistry. Cons. Abbott Labs., North Chicago, Ill., 1964—, Monsanto Co., St. Louis, 1969-99, G.D. Searle Co., Ill., 1987-2001, Pharmacia, 2001-02, Pfizer, 2003—05. Contbr. articles to profl. jours. A.P. Sloan Found. fellow, 1967-69; Guggenheim fellow, 1968-69 Fellow AAAS (chmn. chemistry sect. 1999), Am. Acad. Arts and Scis.; mem. NAS, Am. Chem. Soc. (editl. and adv. bds., sec. and divsn. officer, A.C. Cope scholar 1993, Mosher award 1994, Gilman award 1997, Gassman award 2000). Home: 304 E Sherwin Ave Urbana IL 61802 Home Phone: 217-344-6856. Business E-Mail: beak@scs.uiuc.edu.

BEAL, GRAHAM WILLIAM JOHN, museum director; b. Stratford-on-Avon, Eng., Apr. 22, 1947; came to U.S., 1973; s. Cecil John Beal and Annie Gladys (Barton) Tunbridge; m. Nancy Jane Andrews, Apr. 21, 1973: children: Priscilla Jane, Julian William John. BA, Manchester U., Eng., 1969; MA, U. London, 1972. Acad. asst. to dir. Sheffield City (Eng.) Art Galleries, 1972-73; gallery dir. U. S.D., Vermillion, 1973-74, Washington U., St. Louis, 1974-77; chief curator Walker Art Ctr., Mpls., 1977-83; dir. Sainsbury Ctr. for Visual Arts, Norwich, Eng., 1983-84; chief curator San Francisco Mus. Modern Art, 1984-89; dir. Joslyn Art Mus., Omaha, 1989-96, Los Angeles County Mus. Art, 1996-99, Detroit Inst. Arts, 1999—. Mem. Fed. Adv. Com. on Internat. Exhbns., 1991-94. Author: (book, exhbn. catalog) Jim Dine: Five Themes, 1984; co-author: (book, exhbn. catalog) A Quiet Revolution, 1987, David Nash: Voyages and Vessels, 1994, Sainsbury Collection Catalogue, vol. I, 1997, Joslyn Art Museum: Fifty Favorities, 1994, Joslyn Art Museum: A Building History, 1998, American Beauty: American Paintings and Sculpture from the Detroit Institute of Arts, 2002; contbg. to Apollo Mag., London, 1989-91. Trustee Djerassi Found., Woodside, Calif., 1987-89. Mem.: Am. Assn. Museums (trustee 2002—05), Assn. Art Mus. Dirs. (trustee 2004), Detroit Athletic Club, Century Club. Avocations: history, cooking, music. Office: Detroit Inst Arts 5200 Woodward Ave Detroit MI 48202 Office Phone: 313-833-7895. Business E-Mail: gbeal@dir.org.

BEAL, JOHN M., surgeon, medical educator; b. Starkville, Miss., 1915; m. Mary Lucinda Phemister, Feb. 20, 1943 (dec. July 2005); children: John M., Bruce Phemister, Margaret Anne MD, U. Chgo., 1941. Diplomate Am. Bd. Surgery. Intern N.Y. Hosp., NYC, 1941-42, asst. resident surgery, 1942-44, 46-47, surgeon, 1947-48, attending surgeon, 1953-63; chmn. tumor bd. and staff surgeon Wadsworth Gen. Hosp., West Los Angeles, 1949-50, chief surg. service, 1950-53; cons. staff St. John's Hosp., Santa Monica, Calif., 1950-53; instr. surgery Cornell U., Ithaca, N.Y., 1948-49, assoc. prof. clin. surgery, 1953-63; instr. surgery UCLA, 1949-50, asst. prof., 1950-53; J. Roscoe Miller disting. prof. Northwestern U., 1981-84, prof. emeritus, 1984—, chmn. dep. surgery, 1963-82; clin. prof. surgery U. N.C., Chapel Hill, 1984-88; chmn. dept. surgery Chgo. Wesley Meml. Hosp., 1963-69, Northwestern Meml. Hosp., 1973-82; chief surgery Passavant Meml. Hosp., Chgo., 1963-73. Chmn. Am. Bd. Surgery, 1970-71. Served to capt. M.C. AUS, 1944-46. Fellow ACS (bd. regents 1973-83, pres. 1982-83); mem. Council of Med. Splty. Socs. (sec. 1978-80), Soc. Univ. Surgeons, Soc. Clin. Surgery, AMA, Am. Surg. Assn. Address: 432 Georgetown Cir Valdosta GA 31602-4114

BEAL, JON G., lawyer; b. Rapid City, SD, Jan. 3, 1965; s. George and Marjorie Beal; m. Kristine J. Rausch, June 22, 1996. BS in Land Resources, Mont. State U., Bozeman, 1987; JD, U. SD, Vermilion, 1992. Bar: Mont. 1993, SD 1992. Law clk. 7th Jud. Ct., Rapid City, 1992—94; pvt. practice Datsopolos, MacDonald & Lind, PC, 1994—99; lawyer Beal Law Firm, PLLC, Missoula, Mont., 2003—. Pres. bd. dirs. U. Mont. Rodeo Team, Missoula. Mem.: FBA, Western Mont. Bar Assn. (v.p.), Def. Rsch. Inst., Mont. Def. Trial Lawyers, Mont. Trial Lawyers Assn., Am. Assn. Justice, State Bar SD (licentiate), State Bar Mont. (licentiate). Office: Beal Law Firm PLLC 121 Hickory St Ste 4 PO Box 8898 Missoula MT 59807-8898 Office Phone: 406-728-2911. Office Fax: 406-728-2912.

BEAL, M. FLINT, neurologist; b. London, Nov. 6, 1950; s. Myron C. and Esther (Delong) B.; m. Judy A. Ahlheim, June 12, 1976; children: Bradley, Emily. BA, Colgate U., 1972; MA, U. Va., 1976. Med. resident N.Y. Hosp. Cornell, NYC, 1976—78; neurology resident Mass. Gen. Hosp., Boston, 1978—81, neurology fellow, 1981—83, asst. prof. neurology, 1983—87, assoc. prof. neurology, 1987—95, prof., 1995—98; Ann Parrish Titzell prof., chmn. dept. neurology Cornell U. Weill Med. Coll., NYC, 1998—; neurologist-in-chief N.Y. Presbyn. Hosp., NYC, 1998—. Editl. bd.: Annals of Neurology and Jour. of Neurochemistry; contbr. articles to profl. jours. Fellow Stroke Coun. Am. Heart Assn., Am. Acad. Neurology, NY Acad. Sci., Soc. Neurosci., Internat. Soc. Cerebral Blood Flow and Metabolism, Alpha Omega Alpha; mem. AAAS, Inst. Medicine, Am. Neurol. Assn. (v.p., Derek Denny-Brown award). Achievements include delineation of postmortem neurochemistry of neurodegenerative diseases improved animal models of neurodegenerative diseases and new therapy for neuro protection in neurodegenerative diseases. Office: NY Hosp-Weill Cornell Med Ctr Dept Neurology and Neurosci 525 E 68th St New York NY 10021 Office Phone: 212-746-6575.

BEAL, MERRILL DAVID, conservationist, museum director; b. Richfield, Utah, June 26, 1926; s. Merrill Dee and Bessy (Neill) B.; m. Jean Lorraine Wood, Feb. 24, 1947; children: John David, James Merrill. BA, Idaho State Coll., 1950; MS, Utah State U., 1952. Park ranger, naturalist Yellowstone Nat. Park, 1953-60; chief park naturalist Grand Canyon Nat. Park, 1960-69; asst. supt. Great Smoky Mountains Nat. Park, Gatlinburg, Tenn., 1969-72; assoc. regional dir. Midwest region Nat. Park Service, Omaha, 1972-75, regional dir., 1975-78; supt. Gt. Smoky Mountains Nat. Park, Gatlinburg, Tenn., 1978-83; asst. dir. Ariz.-Sonora Desert Mus., Tucson, 1983-91. Author: Grand Canyon, the Story Behind the Scenery, 1967. Mem. bd. Grand Canyon Sch., 1964-69. Served with USN, 1944-46. Recipient Meritorious Svc. award US Dept. Interior, 1975. Mem. Wildlife Soc., Gt. Smoky Mountains Natural History Assn. (bd. dirs. 1993-95), S.W. Parks and Monument Assn., Ea. Nat. Park and Monument Assn. (bd. dirs. 1989-95), Sigma Xi.

BEAL, MYRON CLARENCE, osteopath; b. NYC, Dec. 4, 1920; s. Clarence Joseph and Birdice Elvira (Flint) Beal; m. Esther Naomi DeLong, Sept. 11, 1948; children: Rebecca Johnson, Myron Flint, Shelley Rees, Julie Wilson, Christina Beal Bailey. AB, U. Rochester, 1942; D.O., Chgo. Coll. Osteo. Medicine, 1945; MS in Physiology, U. Chgo., 1949. Asst. dir. clinics Chgo. Coll. Osteo. Medicine, 1946-49; instr. London Coll. Osteopathy, 1949-51; pvt. practice osteo. medicine Rochester, N.Y., 1951-74; prof. biomechanics Coll. Osteo. Medicine, Mich. State U., East Lansing, 1974-81, prof. family medicine, 1981-89, prof. emeritus, 1989—, acting chmn. biomechanics, 1975-77. Mem. Nat. Bd. Examiners Osteo. Physicians and Surgeons, 1960—84, cons., 1984—89; mem. N.Y. State Bd. Medicine, 1961—73. Trustee Chgo. Coll. Osteo. Medicine, 1969—93, chmn. bd. dirs., 1985—91. Fellow: Am. Acad. Osteopathy (editor 1987—2005); mem.: Chgo. Osteo. Health Sys. (bd. dirs. 1986—90), Mich. Assn. Osteo. Physicians and Surgeons, N.Y. State Osteo. Soc., Am. Osteo. Assn. Congregationalist. Office: 110 Ferris Hills Canandaigua NY 14424-3202

BEAL, ROBERT LAWRENCE, real estate executive; b. Boston, Sept. 10, 1941; s. Alexander Simpson and Leona M. (Rothstein) B. BS cum laude, Harvard U., 1963, MBA, 1965. Vice pres., ptnr. Beacon Cos., Boston, 1965-76; ptnr. The Beal Cos., Boston; pres. Beal and Co., Inc., Boston, 1976—. Corporator, dir., mem. exec. com., lending com. Provident Instn. Savs., 1975-86; chmn. bd. dirs. Mass. Devel. Fin. Agy., 1976—; instr. real estate Northeastern U., 1969-75; mem. East Cambridge rezoning adv. com., 1989—; dir. Artery Bus. Com., 1989—, chmn., 1995-99, treas., 1989-95. Bd. dirs. Boston Zool. Soc., 1972-86, pres., 1980, chmn., 1981-84, hon. chmn., 1985; mem. vis. com. Sch. Mus. Fine Arts, Boston, 1974-76, 88-89; overseer Boys Club Boston, 1975-93; mem. corp. Belmont Hill Sch.; trustee, overseer Beth Israel Deaconess Med. Ctr., 1981-2001, mem. bldg. and grounds com., 1976-82, 86-90; dir. Harvard Coll. Fund Coun., 1972-73, capital fund dir. Class '63, 1979-85, co-chmn. 25th reunion, co-chmn. 35th and 40th reunions, class gift, class sec., 2000—; exec. bd. Boston chpt. Am. Jewish Com., 1987-96, mem. bd. govs., 1989-92; bd. dirs. Boston Mcpl. Rsch. Bur., 1978—, treas., 1988-89, 92, vice chmn., 1990-93, chmn., 1994-96; bd. dirs. Met. Boston Housing Partnership, Inc., 1983-95; trustee The Partnership, Inc., 1981-89, New Eng. Aquarium, 1987—, bd. govs., 1993-98, 2002—, mem. exec. comm., 2002—, co-chair campaign steering com., 2001—; mem. adv. task force John F. Kennedy Libr., 1982; bd. overseers Mus. Fine Arts, Boston, 1988-97, 98-2001, overseer for life, 2001—; mem. vis. com. Harvard Div. Sch., 1989—, adv. com. Taubman Ctr., John F. Kennedy Sch. Govt., Harvard U., 1989—, chair, 2003—, co-chair campaign steering com., 2001—; co-chair United Way of Massachusetts Bay's Alexis de Tocqueville Soc., 2000, mem. cabinet, 2000, co-chair 2003 campaign; bd. overseers Mass. Soc. Prevention Cruelty to Animals, 1988—; chair coun. fellows Angell Meml. Animal Hosp., 1999—. Mem. Nat. Realty Com. (dir., past sec., mem. exec. com. 1974-99, v.p., vice chmn.), Mass. Assn. Realtors (dir. 1979-81), Greater Boston Real Estate Bd. (bd. dir. 1970-72, 76-90, pres. 1978-79), Am. Soc. Real Estate Counselors, Bldg. Owners-Mgrs. Assn. Boston (dir. 1970-72), Ripon Soc. (co-founder, nat. treas. 1968-73, nat. governing bd. 1979-85), Nat. Assn. Real Estate Appraiser (cert.), Mass. Taxpayers Found. (dir. 1980-86), Inst. Property Taxation (affliate), Internat. Assn. Assessing Officers (primary subscribing mem. 1982—), Beacon Hill Civic Assn. (bd. dir. 1975-79), Bostonian Soc. (life), Greater Boston C. of C. (bd. dirs.), The Vault (coord. com. 1978-97), Combined Jewish Philanthropies Greater Boston (exec. com. 1989—, vice chmn. 1992-93, chmn. com. on endowment fund 1999—, chair devel. com. 2001—, chair cmty. capital campaign 2002—, chmn. 2004—), Greater Boston C. of C. (bd. dirs. 1992—). Republican. Jewish. Home: 21 Brimmer St Boston MA 02108-1001 Office: Beal and Co Inc 177 Milk St Ste 2A Boston MA 02109-3410

BEALE, SUSAN YATES, social worker; b. Saginaw, Mich., Nov. 17, 1943; d. William Miller and Dorothy LaVerne (Langdon) Yates; m. Henry B.R. Beale, Aug. 27, 1966; children: Andrew, Nathaniel. AB cum laude, Oberlin Coll., 1966; MA, U. Chgo., 1969. Social worker West Side VA Hosp., Chgo., 1969-70, DC Dept. Human Resources, Washington, 1970-72, DC Pub. Schs., Washington, 1972-73; pvt. practice Washington, 1973-74; dir. social svc. Capitol Hill Hosp., Washington, 1974-80; social worker No. Va. Dialysis Ctr., Alexandria, 1982-87, Vis. Nurse Assn., Rockville, Md., 1987-89; sr. social worker Hospice of Washington, 1989-95; sr. social svcs. analyst Microeconomic Applications, 1982—; pres. Coping Ptnrs., Washington, 1996—2004; social worker Capital Hospice, Falls Church, Va., 1999—2007, Washington, 2007—. Tchr. Royal Scottish Country Dance Soc. Mem.: NASW. Avocations: singing, gardening. Office: Capital Hospice 4401 Connecticut Ave NW Ste 700 Washington DC 20008 Office Phone: 202-244-8300.

BEALES, RANDOLPH A., lawyer, former state attorney general; m. Julie Leftwich; 3 children. BA in Govt. with high honors, Coll. William and Mary; JD, U. Va. Assoc. Williams Mullen Christian & Dobbins, 1986—87; various pos. U.S. Dept. Education, 1987—92; dep. assoc. dir. policy devel. The White House, 1992—93; assoc. Peterson & Basha, P.C., 1993—94;

exec. dir. commn. champion schs. Gov.'s Office State of Va., 1994—96; exec. dir. Va. Bus.-Edn. Partnership, 1995—98; chief dep. atty. gen. Commonwealth of Va., 1998—2001; atty. gen. Commonwealth Va., 2001—02; ptnr. Christian & Barton, LLP, 2002—. Episcopalian. Office: Christian & Barton LLP 909 E Main St Richmond VA 23219 Office Phone: 804-697-4100.

BEALKE, LINN HEMINGWAY, banker; b. St. Louis, Nov. 14, 1944; s. Charles Francis and Miriam Frances (Hemingway) B.; m. Jean Long Wells, Sept. 6, 1969; children: David Q.W., Emily R., Linn H. BA, U. Ark., 1966; MBA, Washington U., 1969. Fin. analyst Edison Brothers Stores, St. Louis, 1969-74; sr. v.p. Commerce Bank of St. Louis, 1975-78; v.p. fin. and adminstrn. Curlee Clothing Co., Lexington, Ky., 1978-80; vice chmn. County Bank of St. Louis, 1980-84, Southwest Bank of St. Louis, 1984—2004. Bd. dirs. Zoltek Cos., Inc.; bd. dirs. Miss. Valley Bancshares, pres., 1984-2002. Treas. Forsyth Sch., St. Louis, 1980-87; pres. Edgewood Childrens Ctr., Webster Groves, Mo., 1986-88; dir. Mo. Colls. Fund, Jefferson City, Mo., 1990-93. Mem. Mo. Bankers Assn. (dir. 1988-90, 99-2002), Fin. Execs. Inst. (pres. St. Louis chpt. 1989-90, dir. 1991-94), Am. Bankers Assn. Leadership Conf. (del. 1990-92), Racquet Club (v.p. 1987-89), Bellerive Country Club, St. Louis Country Club, Old Baldy Club, John's Island Club. Office: SW Bank St Louis PO Box 790178 Saint Louis MO 63179-0178 Personal E-mail: linnbealke@yahoo.com.

BEALL, BURTCH W., JR., architect; b. Columbus, Ohio, Sept. 27, 1925; s. Burtch W. and Etta (Beheler) B.; m. Susan Jane Hunter, June 6, 1949; children: Brent Hunter, Brook Waite. Student, John Carroll U., 1943; BArch, Ohio State U., 1949. Draftsman Brooks & Coddington, Architects, Columbus, 1949-51, William J. Monroe, Architects, Salt Lake City, 1951-53, Lorenzo Young, Architect, Salt Lake City, 1953-54; prin. Burtch W. Beall, Jr., Architect, Salt Lake City, 1954—. Vis. lectr. Westminster Coll., 1955; adj. prof. U. Utah, 1955-85, 92-97; treas. Nat. Coun. Archtl. Registration Bds., 1982-84. Restoration architect Salt Lake City and County Bldg; contbr. projects to: A Pictorial History of Architecture in America, America Restored, This Before Architecture. Trustee Utah Found. for Arch., 1985, pres., 1987-91; mem. Utah State Bd. Fine Arts, 1987-95, chmn., 1991-93; chmn. Utah State Capitol Adv. Com., 1986-90, Western States Art Fedn., Bd. trustees, 1991-94; mem. exec. residence com. State of Utah, 1991-97; mem. Utah: A Guide to the State Found. With USN, 1943-45. Recipient several merit and honor awards; Found. fellow Utah Heritage Found., 1985. Fellow AIA (jury mem. 2000-02); mem. Masons, Sigma Alpha Epsilon. Methodist. Home and Office: 4644 Brookwood Cir Salt Lake City UT 84117-4908

BEALL, CHARLES DONALD, former special education educator; b. Lumpkin, Ga., Oct. 7, 1932; s. Charlie Will and Margaret Louise (Williams) B.; m. Donna C. Ross, June 12, 1960 (div.). BS, Tougaloo Coll., 1953; MA, U. Mich., 1957, sch. diagnostician and reading clinician, 1959; spl. edn. cert., Wayne State U., 1961. Substitute tchr. Detroit Pub. Schs., 1959; reading clinician Oakland County Reading Clinic, Pontiac, Mich., 1959; spl. edn. tchr. Pontiac State Hosp., 1959-62; tchr. children's svc. Lafayette Clinic, Detroit, 1962-68, head spl. edn. dept., 1968-92. Assoc. prof. spl. edn. dept. Va. State Coll., Petersbury, 1968; lectr. U. Detroit, Marygrove Coll.; instr. Wayne State U., 1968; cons. Mich. Edn. Assn. Conf. for Tchrs./Counselors for Physically Handicapped, Tustin, 1967, Detroit Pub. Schs., 1972, St. Joseph Mercy Hosp., Pontiac, 1982; judge regional/state competitions Nat. History Day, 2000—. Contbr. articles to profl. jours. Named Alumnus of Yr., Tougaloo Coll., 1990; recipient Spl. award All-Class Reunion Black Grads., U. Mich., 1991, Cmty. Svc. award, Green Grobe Bapt. Ch., 1998, Preservation Achievement award, Hist. Preservation Divsn., State of Georgia, 2002, Govs. award in humanities, State of Ga., 2003. Mem. NAACP (life), Coun. Exceptional Children, Am. Orthopsychiatric Assn., Mich. Assn. for Tchrs. of Emotionally Disturbed Children (pres. 1963-64, 66-67), Mich. State Employee's Spl. Edn. Com., Tougaloo Coll. Alumni Assn. (Detroit pres. 1960-92, nat. treas. 1988-91), U. Mich. Alumni Assn. (chmn. Martin Luther King Scholarship com. 1990-91), United Negro Coll. Fund, Inc. (treas., chmn. publicity 1984-90), Plymouth Congregational Ch. (treas. scholarship com., bd. trustees), Alpha Phi Alpha. Home: 4811 Yosemite Dr Columbus GA 31907-1753

BEALL, CYNTHIA, anthropologist, educator; b. Urbana, Ill., Aug. 21, 1949; d. John Wood and J. Alene (Beachler) Beall. BA in Biology, U. Pa., 1970; MA in Anthropology, Pa. State U., 1972, PhD in Anthropology, 1976. Asst. prof. Case Western Res. U., Cleve., 1976—82, assoc. prof. of anthropology, 1982—87, prof. anthropology, 1987—. Co-editor: Jour. of Cross-Cultural Gerontology, 1986—95; contbr. articles to profl. jours. Active Internat. Rsch. Exch. Program, 1990, 1991. Fellow Nat. Program for Advanced Study and Rsch. in China, NAS, 1986—87, 1997; Rsch. grantee, NSF, 1981, 1983, 1986—87, 1993—95, 1997, 2000, 2002, 2005, Am. Fedn. for Aging Rsch., 1983, 1986, Nat. Geog. Soc., 1983, 1986—87, 1993, 1995. Fellow: AAAS; mem.: NAS (coun. 2002—05), Internat. Coun. Sci. (exec. bd. 2005—), Assn. Anthropology and Gerontology, Soc. Study Human Biology, Human Biology Coun. (exec. com. 1989—92, pres. 1992—94), Am. Assn. Phys. Anthropology (exec. com. 1989—92), Am. Anthrop. Assn., Am. Philo. Soc. Achievements include research in human adaptation to high altitude. Office: Case Western Res U Dept Anthropology 238 Mather Meml Bldg Cleveland OH 44106-7125 Business E-Mail: cmb2@case.edu.

BEALL, DENNIS RAY, artist, educator; b. Chickasha, Okla., Mar. 13, 1929; s. Roy A. and Lois O. (Phillips) B.; 1 son, Garm. Student, Okla. City U., 1950-52; BA, San Francisco State U., 1956, MA, 1958. Registrar Oakland (Calif.) Art Mus., 1958; curator Achenbach Found. for Graphic Arts, Calif. Palace of the Legion of Honor, San Francisco, 1958-1965; asst. prof. art San Francisco State U., 1965-69, assoc. prof., 1969-76, prof. art, 1976-92; prof. emeritus, 1992—. Numerous one-man shows of prints, 1957—, including: Award Exhbn. of San Francisco Art Commn., Calif. Coll. Arts and Crafts, 1978, San Francisco U. Art Gallery, 1978, Los Robles Galleries, Palo Alto, Calif.; numerous group shows 1960— including Mills Coll. Art Gallery, Oakland, Calif., Univ. Gallery of Calif. State U., Hayward, 1979, Marshall-Meyers Gallery, 1979, 80, Marin Civic Ctr. Art Galleries, San Rafael, Calif., 1980, San Francisco Mus. Modern Art, 1985; touring exhibit U. Mont., 1987-91, An Inner Vision, Oysterponds Hist. Soc., Orient, N.Y., 1998, Modernism in Calif. Printmaking, Annex Gallery, Santa Rosa, Calif., 1998, The Stamp of Impulse, Worcester (Mass.) Art Mus., 2001, Haverford Coll., 2001, Palm Springs (Calif.) Desert Mus., 2003, Internat. Print Ctr., N.Y.C., 2003, Cummer Mus. Art and Gardens, Jacksonville, Fla., 2003, Tweed Mus. Art, U. Minn., Duluth, 2006, Pollock-Krasner House, East Hampton, NY, 2006; represented in numerous permanent collections including Libr. of Congress, Washington, Mus. Modern Art, N.Y.C., Nat. Libr. of Medicine, Washington, Cleve. Mus., Whitney Mus., Phila. Mus., U.S. embassy collections, Tokyo, London and other major cities, Victoria and Albert Mus., London, Achenbach Found. for graphic Arts, Calif. Palace of Legion of Honor, San Francisco, Oakland Art Mus., Phila. Free Libr., Roanoke (Va.) Art Ctr., Worcester (Mass.) Art Mus., Whitney Mus. Am. Art, Cleve. Mus., various colls. and univs. in U.S. Served with USN, 1947-50, PTO. Office: San Francisco State Univ Art Dept 1600 Holloway Ave San Francisco CA 94132-1722 Office Phone: 707-632-5124. E-mail: chu2kar@comcast.net.

BEALL, J. C., philosopher, educator; s. Charles Edwin and Beverly Long Beall. PhD, U. Mass., Amherst, 1998. Assoc. fellow Arche Ctr. Philosophy Lang., Logic, Math., and Mind, St Andrews, Scotland, 2005—07; prof. U. Conn., Storrs, 2007—. Office: Philosophy Dept Univ Conn Storrs Mansfield CT 06269-2054 Home Phone: 860-455-9232. Office Fax: 860-486-3775. Business E-Mail: jc.beall@uconn.edu.

BEALL, JAMES ROBERT, toxicologist, consultant; b. Stillwater, Okla., June 29, 1940; s. James Arthur and Annabel (Hess) B.; m. Sandra L. Morseth, Aug. 31, 1985; children by previous marriage: Jimmie Karlene, Sidney Sharleen, Tracy Darlene. AAS, Amarillo Coll., 1960; BS, Okla. State U., 1963; MS, U. Okla., 1965, PhD, 1970. Diplomate Am. Bd. Toxicology. Sect. leader toxicology Schering Corp., Lafayette, NJ, 1969-77; biol. sci. adminstr. EPA, Washington, 1977-79; spl. asst. OSHA, Washington, 1979-80; sr. policy advisor, toxicologist U.S. Dept. Energy, Washington, 1980-97. Cons. in toxicology Specialized Tech. Resources, Inc., 1997—; dir. Cytomed. Lab., 1970-71, Am. Bd. Toxicology, Washington, 1981-85, Toxicology Lab. Accreditation Bd., Washington, 1983-87; cons. in field. Author: Uterine Lipid Biosynthesis During Reproductive Cycles, 1970, The Keen Edge of Perfection-A history of the Morseth Knife, 2007; contbr. articles to profl. jours. Mem. Ambulance Squad, N.J., 1974-76. Recipient award of appreciation Consumer Product Safety Commn., 1981, plaque of appreciation Am. Bd. Toxicology, 1985, Md. Govt. award, 1992, Mem. Soc. Toxicology, Teratology Soc., Assn. Govt. Toxicologists (pres. 1983-88, bd. dirs. 1983-88), N.Y. Acad. Scis., Sigma Xi. Avocations: backpacking, photography, writing. Office: 4804 Old Middletown Rd Jefferson MD 21755-8315 Office Phone: 301-473-5967. Personal E-mail: jbeall@fred.net.

BEALL, JULIANNE, librarian; b. Portland, Oreg., July 16, 1946; d. Marsh Flagg and Ruth Gildersleeve (Large) B.; m. William Tobin Amatruda, Jan. 6, 1979. BA, Lewis & Clark Coll., 1967; PhD in English Lit., UCLA, 1974, MLS, 1977. Decimal classification specialist Libr. of Congress, Washington, 1977-86, asst. editor Dewey decimal classification, 1986—. Prin. author: DDC 004-006 Data Processing and Computer Science, 1985; asst. editor: Dewey Decimal Classification, 22d edit., 2003, Abridged Dewey Decimal Classification, 14th edit., 2004. UCLA fellow, 1967-70. Mem. ALA, Spl. Librs. Assn., Internat. Fedn. Libr. Assns. and Instns. (affiliate), Beta Phi Mu. Office: Libr of Congress Decimal Classification Dv Washington DC 20540-4330 Office Phone: 202-707-5715. E-mail: jbea@loc.gov.

BEALL, KENNETH SUTTER, JR., lawyer; b. Evanston, Ill., Aug. 9, 1938; s. Kenneth Sutter and Helen Cantlon (Koenig) B.; m. Blair Hamilton Bissett, May 25, 1975; children: Kevina Anne, Hunter Bissett, Baret Bissett. BA, Washington and Lee U., 1961, LLB, 1963. Bar: Fla. 1964. With Gunster, Yoakley & Stewart, P.A., West Palm Beach, Fla., 1964—, ptnr., 1970—, pres., 1994—2004. Bd. dirs. The Whitehall Found., The Wells Family Found., The Island Sch.; chmn. Palm Beach County Environ. Control Hearing Bd., 1970-92; mem. law coun. Washington and Lee U., 1997-2001; trustee, sec. Caribbean/Latin Am. Action, 2000-03. Served with USMCR, 1963-68. Mem. ABA, Fla. Bar (Pres.'s Pro Bono Svc. award 1983), Palm Beach County Bar Assn., Fed. Bar Assn. (pres. Palm Beach County chpt. 1981). Democrat. Roman Catholic. Office: 777 S Flagler Dr Ste 500E West Palm Beach FL 33401-6121 E-mail: kbeall@gunster.com.

BEALL, ROBERT JOSEPH, foundation executive; b. Washington, May 19, 1943; s. William Joseph and Louise Rachel (Tayman) B.; m. Mary Ellen O'Connor, June 24, 1967; children: Thomas Joseph, Robert Andrew. BS, Albright Coll., 1965; MA, PhD, SUNY, Buffalo, 1970. Asst. prof. dept. physiology Case-Western Reserve U., Cleve., 1971-74; asst. prof. Case-Western Reserve U. (Sch. Dentistry), 1972-74; grants asso. div. research grants NIH, 1974-75; program dir. metabolic diseases program Nat. Inst. Arthritis, Metabolism & Digestive Diseases, 1975-79; med. dir. Cystic Fibrosis Found., Rockville, Md., 1980-93, nat. dir. Bethesda, Md., 1981-84, exec. v.p., 1984-93, pres., CEO, 1994—. Bd. trustees Albright Coll.; bd. dirs. Multiple Myeloma Rsch. Consortium, New Eng. Health Inst. Recipient Merit award NIH, 1980 Mem. AAAS, N.Y. Acad. Scis., Am. Soc. Human Genetics, Sigma Xi. Presbyterian. Office: Cystic Fibrosis Found 6931 Arlington Rd Bethesda MD 20814-5231

BEALL, ROBERT MATTHEWS, II, retail executive; b. Fresno, Calif., Aug. 7, 1943; s. Egbert Ruffin and Lynda Topp (Matthews) B.; m. Aldona Louise Kupchella, June 15, 1943; children: Jennifer, Lydia, Alexis, Robert. BSBA, U. Fla., 1965; MBA with distinction, NYU, 1969. Asst. buyer Bloomingdale's, NYC, 1969-70; mgr. to exec. chmn. Beall's, Inc., Bradenton, Fla., 1970—. Bd. Fla. Power & Light Corp., Blue Cross Blue Shield Fla., SunTrust Bank, Inc. Divsn. chmn. United Way, Bradenton, 1991; bd. dirs. St. Stephens Sch., Bradenton, 1977-80, Tilton Sch., NH, 1988-92. Capt. U.S. Army, 1965-67. Mem. Nat. Retail Fedn. (bd. dirs. 1982—), Fla. C. of C. (chmn. 1994), Fla. Coun. 100 (bd. dirs., exec. com.), Pi Kappa Phi. Episcopalian. Office: Beall's Inc PO Box 9285 Bradenton FL 34206-9285

BEALS, HERBERT KYLE, urban planner, historian, consultant; b. Portland, Oreg., July 26, 1934; s. James Herbert and Mae Adelia (Thompson) B.; m. Barbara Carol Brown, Mar. 22, 1957; children: Patricia Louise, Cheryl Ann, Steven Kyle. BA in Social Sci., Portland State U., Oreg., 1958, MA in History, 1983. Planner, asst. dir. Clackamas County Planning Dept., Oregon City, 1957-65; planning cons. Bur. of Govt. Rsch., U. Oreg., Eugene, 1965-70; prin. planner Columbia Region Assn. of Govs., Portland, 1970-79; housing planner Met. Svc. Dist., Portland, 1979-80; with spl. projects Oreg. Hist. Soc., Portland, 1983-90; hist. cons. Gladstone, Oreg., 1990-96; ret., 1996. Author: Gladstone, Oregon, Part One, 1992, Part Two, 1998; editor, translator: For Honor and Country, 1985, Juan Pérez on the NW Coast, 1989; editor: Seeking Western Waters, 1995; co-editor: The Americas, Antarctica, Africa, 2007, travel jours.; contbr. articles various profl. jours. Vol. Nat. Park Svc., Ft. Vancouver, 1974, USDA Forest Svc., Portland, 1981; commr. City Planning Commn., Gladstone, 1964-67, 72-76, Portland Metro Area Boundary Commn., 1985-88, vice chair 1988; mem. Pub. Libr. Bd., Gladstone, Oreg., 1996-2004, chair 1999-2003; mem. County Hist. Rev. Bd., Clackamas, Oreg., 1990-94, 96-2003, co-chair 1999-2003; bd. dir. Columbia Gorge Interpretive Ctr., 2004—. Recipient John Lyman Book award N.Am. Soc. for Oceanic History, 1990. Mem. Oreg. Archaeol. Soc. (life; pres. 1971, 77), Oreg. Hist. Soc., Hakluyt Soc., Soc. for the History of Discoveries (bd. dirs. 1993), Phi Alpha Theta. Avocation: coin collecting/numismatics. Home: 7005 Valley View Dr Gladstone OR 97027 Personal E-mail: barbherb@aol.com.

BEALS, NANCY FARWELL, former state legislator; b. El Paso, July 21, 1938; d. Fred Whitcomb and Katharine Doane (Pier) Farwell; m. Richard William Beals, June 30, 1962; children: Katharine, Robert, Susannah. BA in Polit. Sci., Bryn Mawr Coll., 1960; MA in Teaching, Harvard U., 1961. Group leader Exptl. Internat. Living, Putney, Vt.; jr. high sch. tchr. Wincehster (Mass.) Pub. Schs., 1961-62; high sch. tchr. Hamden (Conn.) Pub. Schs., 1962-64; state rep. Conn. Gen. Assembly, Hartford, 1993—2003; mem. adv. bd. Parenting Support Programs Yale-New Haven (Conn.) Hosp., 2003—, chairperson adv. bd. Parenting Support Programs, 2005—07, mem. adv. bd., 2007—. Mem. state adv. coun. on spl. edn., 2000-02. Mem. various local and regional offices PTA, Chgo. and Hamden, 1970-83; local pres., state bd. dirs. LWV, Conn., 1979-92; mem., sec., chmn. Hamden Bd. Edn., 1983-92; mem. citizen's adv. bd. High Meadows Residential Treatment Facility, 1993—; treas. Spring Glen Civic Assn., 2003—; bd. dirs. Hamden Edn. Found., 2001-04. Recipient Citizenship award for Conn. Philip Morris Corp., 1992, Hamden Notable award Friends of Hamden Libr., 1986, Children's Hero award Children's Trust Fund, 1995, Disting. Legislator award Conn. Assn. Bds. of Edn., 1998, Master Builder award Habitat for Humanity of Greater New Haven, 2002; named Legislator of Yr. Conn. Libr. Assn., 1994, Caucus of Conn. Dems., 1997, Conn. Coalition on Aging, 2002; Flemming fellow Ctr. for Policy Alternatives, 1995. Democrat.

BEALS, PAUL ARCHER, religious studies educator; b. Russell, Iowa, Feb. 18, 1924; s. Archer Edwin and Myrtle Mae (Kelsey) B.; m. Vivian Brown, Sept. 29, 1945; children: Lois Ruth, Stephen Paul, Samuel Archer, Timothy Joel. AB, Wheaton Coll., Ill., 1945; diploma, Moody Bible Inst., Chgo., 1948; ThM with high honors, Dallas Theol. Seminary, 1952, ThD, 1964. Missionary in Cen. African Republic Bapt. Mid-Missions, Cleve., 1952-64; prof. of missiology Grand Rapids (Mich.) Bapt. Seminary, 1964-97, prof. emeritus missiology, 1998—, dir. continuing edn., 1977-90. Theol. cons. Bapt. Mid-Missions, 1969-72, missionary emeritus, 2002--; conf. speaker. Author: A People for His Name, 1985, rev. edit., 1995; contbr. articles to profl. jours. Mem. Evang. Theol. Soc., Evang. Missiological Soc. (pres. 1990-93), Am. Soc. Missiology, Pi Gamma Mu. Home: 2111 Audley Dr NE Grand Rapids MI 49525-1517

BEALS, VAUGHN LE ROY, JR., retired motorcycle manufacturing executive; b. Cambridge, Mass., Jan. 2, 1928; s. Vaughn Le Roy and Pearl Uela (Wilmarth) B.; m. Eleanore May Woods, July 15, 1951; children: Susan Lynn, Laurie Jean. BS, M.I.T., 1948, MS, 1954. Research engr. Cornell Aero. Lab., Buffalo, 1948-52, MIT Aero Elastic and Structures Research Lab., 1952-55; dir. research and tech. N.Am. Aviation, Inc., Columbus, Ohio, 1955-65; exec. v.p. Cummins Engine Co., Columbus, Ind., 1965-70, also dir.; chmn. bd., chief exec. officer Formac Internat., Inc., Seattle, 1970-75; dep. group exec. Motorcycle Products Group, AMF Inc., Milw., 1975-77, v.p. and group exec. Stamford, Conn., 1977-81; chief exec. officer Harley-Davidson, Inc., Milw., 1981-89, chmn., 1981-96, chmn. emeritus, 1996—. Mem. Desert Mountain Club, Desert Forest Golf Club, Forest Highlands Golf Club. Home: PO Box 3260 Carefree AZ 85377-3260 Office: Harley-Davidson Inc Box 653 3700 W Juneau Ave Milwaukee WI 53208-2865

BEAM, CLARENCE ARLEN, federal judge; b. Stapleton, Nebr., Jan. 14, 1930; s. Clarence Wilson and Cecile Mary (Harvey) Beam; m. Betty Lou Fletcher, July 22, 1951; children: Randal, James, Thomas, Bradley, Gregory. BS, U. Nebr., 1951, JD, 1965. Feature writer Nebr. Farmer Mag., Lincoln, 1951; with sales dept. Steckley Seed Co., Mount Sterling, Ill., 1954—58, advt. mgr., 1958—63; from assoc. to ptnr. Chambers, Holland, Dudgeon & Knudsen, Berkheimer, Beam, et al, Lincoln, 1965—82; judge US Dist. Ct. Nebr., Omaha, 1982—87, chief judge, 1986—87; cir. judge US Ct. Appeals (8th cir.), 1987—. Mem. com. on lawyer discipline Nebr. Supreme Ct., 1974—82; mem. Conf. Commrs. on Uniform State Laws, 1979—, chmn. Nebr. sect., 1980—82; mem. jud. conf. com. on ct. and jud. security, 1989—93; chmn., 1992—93. Contbr. articles to profl. jours. Mem. Nebr. Rep. Ctrl. Com., 1970—78. Capt. US Army, 1951—53, Korea. Scholar Roscoe Pound scholar, U. Nebr., Lincoln, 1964; Regents scholar, 1947. Mem.: Nebr. State Bar Assn. Office: US Ct Appeals 8th Cir 435 Federal Bldg 100 Centennial Mall N Lincoln NE 68508-3859 Office Phone: 402-437-5420.*

BEAM, JAMES CARROLL (JIM BEAM), retired newspaper editor; b. Cameron, La., Oct. 7, 1933; s. Charles Cleveland and Carrie (Welch) B.; m. Jo Ann Drachenberg, Aug. 20, 1954; children: Jamie Lynn Meek, Bryan Carroll. BA, McNeese State, 1955; MA, La. State, 1962. Tchr. Calcasieu Sch. Bd., Lake Charles, La., 1958-62; reporter Lake Charles (La.) Am. Press, 1962-65, city editor, 1965-81, co-editor, 1981-92, editor, 1992-98, dir. polit. and pub. affairs, 1998-99. Lt. U.S. Army, 1955-57. Recipient 1st place column La. Press Assn., 1979, Hal Boyle award La. Miss AP Assn., 1985-86, 1st place Personal Column, 1997. Mem.: Phi Kappa Phi. Democrat. Methodist. Home: 4824 Gentilly St Lake Charles LA 70607-6341

BEAM, JUSTIN, chef; b. McKinney, Tex. Beverage dir. M Crowd Restaurant Grp., Dallas; bar chef Craft, Dallas, The Living Room, Dallas, Pool Bar, Dallas. Named one of Dallas' Rising Stars, StarChefs.com, 2007. Office: Craft W Hotel 2440 Victory Park Ln Ste 100 Dallas TX 75219 Office Phone: 214-397-4111.*

BEAM, RICHARD SQUIRES, theater educator; b. Evanston, Ill., Oct. 12, 1944; s. Robert Edwin and Hope Squires Beam; m. Marilyn Bonnie Jordan, Dec. 27, 1966; children: Katherine, Margaret. AB, Ind. U., 1966, AM, 1969; PhD, U. Ga., 1984. Designer, tech. dir. Theater 65 children's theater, Evanston, 1969—71; instr. Western Carolina U., Cullowhee, NC, 1971—74, asst. prof., 1974—85, assoc. prof., 1985—. Faculty fellow for instrnl. tech., Coulter Faculty Ctr. Western Carolina U., 1993—95, chair faculty, 2006—. Dir., scenery designer and lighting: (more than 250 theatrical prodns.). Mem.: NC Theater Conf., Southeastern Theater Conf., US Inst. Theater Tech. Home: 52 Smoke Rise Tr Sylva NC 28779 Office: Western Carolina U Dept Stage and Screen Cullowhee NC 28723 Office Phone: 828-227-3800. Business E-Mail: beamr@email.wcu.edu.

BEAM, STEPHEN D., lawyer; b. Pampa, Tex., May 10, 1958; BA, Okla. State U., 1979; JD, U. Okla., 1982. Bar: Okla. 1982, US Dist. Ct. (We. Dist. Okla.), US Dist. Ct. (No. Dist. Tex.), US Ct. Appeals (5th Cir.), US Supreme Ct. Solo pvt. practice, Okla. Bd. editors Okla. Bar Jour., 1997—2003. Recipient Solo Lawyer of Yr. award, 2003. Mem.: Okla. Criminal Def. Lawyers Assn., Okla. Trial Lawyers Assn., ABA, Okla. State Bar Assn. (bd. gov. 0195—1997, chmn. solo and small firm com. 1999—2002, v.p. 2003, bd. gov. 2004—, pres. 2006—07, mem. gen. practice sect., profl. responsibility tribunal 2000), Custer County Bar Assn. (pres. 1992). Office: Atty at Law PO Box 31 Weatherford OK 73096 Office Phone: 580-772-2900. Office Fax: 580-772-6879. E-mail: sbeam@ionet.net.

BEAMER, FRANK, college football coach; b. Mt. Airy, NC; m. Cheryl Oakley; 1 child, Shane; 1 child, Casey. BS in Distributive Edn., Va. Tech., 1969; MS in Guidance, Radford, 1972. Grad. asst. Univ. Md., 1972; defensive coord. The Citadel, 1976, Murray State, 1979—80, head football coach, 1981—86, Va. Tech., 1987—. Recipient Nat. Coach Yr., Assoc. Press, 1999, Coach of the Decade, Big East, 1999. Office: Va Tech 359 Jamerson Athletic Ctr Blacksburg VA 24060

BEAN, BENNETT, artist; b. Cin., Mar. 25, 1941; s. William Bennett and Abigail (Shepard) B.; m. Cathy Bao, Dec. 17, 1966; 1 child, William Bao. Student, Grinnell Coll., 1959-62; postgrad., U. Iowa, 1963, U. Wash., 1963; MFA, Claremont Grad. Sch., 1966. Asst. prof. art Wagner Coll., SI, NY, 1966-79. Trustee Am. Craft Enterprises, New Paltz, N.Y., 1982-85, Am. Craft Coun., N.Y.C., 1980-84; former chmn. bd. dirs. Peters Valley, Layton, N.J. One-man show Royal Marks Gallery, N.Y.C., 1969, Henri Gallery, Washington, 1969; one-person retrospective exhbn. lifetime work Ark. Arts Ctr. Decorative Arts Mus.; exhibited in numerous groups show, including Whitney Mus. Am. Art, 1968-69, Newark Mus., 1968, 80, 89, 91, Am. Craft Mus. II, 1982, 86, N.J. State Mus., 19i4, Newport Art Mus., 1984, Hunter Mus., Chattanooga, 1990; represented in permanent collections Whitney Mus. Am. Art, The White House, Washington, Boston Mus. Fine Arts, Newark Mus., N.J. State Mus., St. Louis Mus. Art, Royal Ont. Mus., Ariz. State U., Grinnell Coll., Milw. Art Mus., Crocker Art Mus., Calif., Toledo Mus. Art, Cin. Art Mus., J.P. Speed Art Mus., Ky., others. Recipient editorial award Met. Home mag., 1990; rsch. grantee Wagner Coll., 1968, 70, 77, 78; fellow N.J. Coun. on Arts, 1978, 88, Nat. Endowment for Arts, 1980. Tibetan Buddhist. Studio: 357 County Road 661 Blairstown NJ 07825-4054 E-mail: bennettbean@bennettbean.com.

BEAN, BRUCE WINFIELD, lawyer; b. Albany, NY, Dec. 19, 1941; s. William Joseph and Ruth Elizabeth (Lafferty) B.; m. Barbara Bryant Hunting; children: Austin Bryant, Ashley Elizabeth. AB, Brown U., Providence, 1964; JD, Columbia U., NYC, 1972. Bar: NY 1973, Calif. 1981. Law clk. to judge US Ct. Appeals (2d cir.), 1972-73; assoc. Simpson Thacher & Bartlett, NYC, 1973-76, Patterson, Belknap, Webb & Tyler,

NYC, 1976-80; counsel fin. and planning Atlantic Richfield, LA, 1980-85; exec. v.p., gen. counsel AmBase Corp. (formerly The Home Group Inc.), NYC, 1985-91; ptnr. Coudert Bros., Moscow, 1995—98; ptnr., head corp. dept. Clifford Chance, Moscow, 1998—2002, counsel, 2002—04; prof. Mich. State U. Law Coll., 2005—. Col. USAFR, 1964-86. Mem. ABA (co-chmn. com. Russian-Eurasian Law Com.), Am. C. of C. in Russia (bd. dirs. 1996-03, chmn. bd. 1998-00), Russian Inst. of Corp. Law and Governance (dir. 2001-03). Personal E-mail: beanmoscow@gmail.com. Business E-Mail: beanb@law.msu.edu.

BEAN, EDWIN TEMPLE, JR., lawyer; b. Washington, Feb. 17, 1926; s. Edwin Temple and Mary (a'Becket) B.; m. Susan Roberts, May 22, 1952; children: Douglas C., Philip O., Emelie R. Bean Ventling. BS, MIT, Cambridge, 1946; LLB, Georgetown U., Washington, DC, 1950. Bar: DC 1950, NY 1951, US Dist. Ct. (we. dist.) NY 1952, US Ct. Appeals (2nd cir.) 1975, US Supreme Ct. 1978, US Ct. Appeals (fed. cir.) 1982. Examiner US Patent Office, Washington, 1946-50; assoc. Bean, Brooks, Buckley & Bean, Buffalo, 1950-61; ptnr. Christel & Bean, Buffalo, 1961-78, Christel, Bean & Linihan, Buffalo, 1978-85; pres. Christel, Bean & Linihan, PC, Buffalo, 1985-89; ptnr. Hodgson Russ LLP (formerly known as Hodgson, Russ, Andrews, Woods & Goodyear), Buffalo, 1989—. Lectr., adj. prof. Law Sch., SUNY, Buffalo, 1987—. Pres. Children's Aid, Buffalo, 1968-70; bd. dirs. Child and Family Svcs., Buffalo, 1982—; trustee emeritus Gow Sch., South Wales, NY, chmn., 1991-95. Mem. ABA, Erie County Bar Assn., Am. Intellectual Property Law Assn., Buffalo Tennis and Squash Club (pres. 1974), Buffalo Yacht Club, Mid-Day Club (pres. 1972). Republican. Presbyterian. Office: Hodgson Russ LLP The Guaranty Bldg 140 Pearl St Ste 100 Buffalo NY 14202-4040 Office Phone: 716-856-4000. Business E-Mail: ebean@hodgsonruss.com.

BEAN, GLEN ATHERTON, entrepreneur; b. Mpls., Aug. 30, 1962; s. Douglas Atherton Bean and Eleanor Green (Caswell) Nolan; m. Mary Catherine Slingsby, June 16, 1990. BS, Ariz. State U., 1988. Promotion specialist John Deere & Co., Waterloo, Iowa, 1987; regional mgr. Elliott Meat Co., Duluth, Minn., 1989—90; gen. ptnr. No. Star Food Brokerage, Savage, Minn., 1990—92; pres. Rochester Bus. Group, Ltd., Minn., 1993—98, Hunter Holdings Ltd., Savage, 1998—. Dir. McGab Agribus. Scholar., Ariz. State Univ., 1989—; ann. fund class corod., campus chair Blake Sch., 2006—. Media coord. U.S. Olympic Festival, Mpls. 1990; vol. Multiple Sclerosis Soc., 1989-2000; founder Ariz. State Univ. Agribus. Spkrs. Bur., 1987; bd. mem. alumni assn. Phoenix County Day Sch., Phoenix, 1983-89; guarantor Minn. Orch. Mem. Nat. Cattlemens Assn., Ariz. Cattle Growers Assn., Clan MacBean in N.Am., Universidad Iberoamericana (assoc.), Ducks Unltd. (publicity chmn. Phoenix 1986-88, dinner chmn. Burnsville 1990, 91, zone chmn. 1992-99, dist. chmn. 2000—, state conv. chmn. 1998-99), State Feather Soc. (chair 1999—), Trout Unltd., T.C. Pub. TV, U.S.A. Shooting, Nat. Geog. Soc., Minn. Waterfowl Assn., Izaak Walton League, Nat. Devel. Com., Nat. Wild Turkey Fedn., Nat. Sporting Clays Assn., Nat. Skeet Shooting Assn., NRA, PGA Tour/Ptnrs. Club. U.S. Golf Assn., Pheasants Forever, Ducks Unltd. Can. (life), Ariz. State U. Alumni Assn., Mpls. Inst. Arts, Minn. Hist. Soc., Bell Mus. Natural History, Sci. Mus. Minn., Minn. Zoo, Mustang Club Am., Sigma Nu. Republican. Episcopalian. Avocations: hunting, camping, conservation, international travel. Office: Hunter Holdings Ltd PO Box 1426 Minnetonka MN 55345-1426 Home Phone: 952-942-5127; Office Phone: 952-882-9400.

BEAN, MELISSA, congresswoman; b. Chgo., Jan. 22, 1962; m. Alan Bean; children: Victoria, Michelle. AA in Bus., Oakton Cmty. Coll., 1982; BA in Polit. Sci., Roosevelt U., 2002. Dist. sales mgr. DJC Corp., 1982—85; br. mgr. MTI Systems Inc. Arrow Electronics, 1985—89; dist. mgr. UDS Motorola, 1989—91; area mgr. SynOptics Comm. Inc., 1991—94; v.p. sales Dataflex Corp., 1994—95; pres. Sales Resources Inc., 1995—2004; mem. US Congress from Ill. Dist. 8, 2005—; mem. Fin. Svcs. com., Small Bus. com. Mem. Palatine C. of C.; past pres. Deer Lake Homeowners Assn. Mem.: Nat. Assn Women Bus. Owners, Barrington Area Profl. Women. Democrat. Serbian Orthodox. Office: 512 Cannon House Office Bldg Washington DC 20005 Office Phone: 202-225-3711. Office Fax: 202-225-7830.*

BEAN, PHILIP ALBERT, dean, historian; s. Albert Carville Bean and Gertrude Therese Bonomo. BA in History, Union Coll., 1986; BA/MA in Modern History, Oxford U., Eng., 1989; MA in Am. History, U. Rochester, 1990, PhD in Am. History, 1994. Lectr. history Hamilton Coll., Clinton, NY, 1993—96; exec. asst. to the dean Harvard Coll., Cambridge, Mass., 1997—99, asst. dean freshmen, 1999—2002, lectr. history and lit., 2001—02; assoc. dean and dir. acad. resources Haverford (Pa.) Coll., 2002—06, dean for acad. affairs, 2006—. Assoc. editor: Encyclopedia of New York State. Trustee Landmarks Soc. Greater Utica, NY, 1995—96; sec. Phi Beta Kappa, Haverford Coll., 2005. Recipient Larry J. Hackman Rsch. residency, N.Y. State Archives, 2006; grantee, Agnelli Found., 1992; Wilkinson Fund grantee, Worcester Coll., Oxford, 1987, Gilder-Lehrman fellow, Gilder-Lehrman Inst. for Am. History, 2002. Mem.: Phi Beta Kappa (sec. Haverford Coll. chpt. 2005—). Office: Haverford College 370 Lancaster Ave Haverford PA 19041 Home Phone: 610-642-0982. Business E-Mail: pbean@haverford.edu.

BEAN, S. CRAIG, minister, consultant; b. Racine, Wis., Sept. 27, 1960; s. William H and Josephine (Wheeler) Bean; m. Tami G. Sasser, Aug. 15, 1981; children: Lauren Michael Gonzalez, Kailey Elizabeth, S. Kyle, William Hunter. AA in Liberal Arts, Fla. Coll., Temple Terrace, 1980; BS in Landscape Horticulture, Colo. State U., Fort Collins, 1982; MA in NT Studies, Johnson Bible Coll., Knoxville, Tenn., 1998; PhD in Biblical Studies, Trinity Theol. Seminary, Newburgh, Ind., 2007. Min. Smoky Hill Ch. of Christ, Aurora, Colo., 1992—2000, Kirkland Ch. of Christ, Kirkland, Wash., 2000—02, Spring St. Ch. of Christ, Racine, 2002—. Instr. Fla. Coll., Temple Terrace, 1983—85. Mem. nat. coun. to pres. Fla. Coll.; vol. Rep. Party, Racine, 2002—07. Home: 4711 White Oak Ln Racine WI 53403 Office: Spring Street Church of Christ 6200 Spring St Racine WI 53406 Home Phone: 262-344-4513; Office Phone: 262-886-0475. Personal E-mail: beanfamily6@aol.com.

BEAN, SHARON LOUISE, music educator; d. Frank Allen Rawls and Iris Clair Whitby; m. Michael Allen Bean, June 3, 1972; children: Merry Melody, Erica Ann. B of Music Edn., Coll. Emporia, Kans., 1971. Tchr. music Kans. Sch. Sys., Hope, 1971—73; substitute tchr. music Douglas County Schs., Castle Rock, Colo., 1973—75; model Am. United Guild Models, Denver, 1974—77; sec Brotherhood White Temple, Castle Rock, 1974—2002; tchr. music pvt. practice, Castle Rock, 1975—. V.p. exec. bd. Brotherhood White Temple, 1978—83, 1990. Mem.: Am. Guild Organists (sec. models 1974—77). Republican. Avocation: reading. Home: 8127 W Jackson Creek Rd Sedalia CO 80135

BEANE, BILLY (WILLIAM LAMAR), professional sports team executive; b. Orlando, Fla., Mar. 29, 1962; m. Tara Beane; 1 child, Casey. Student, U. Calif., San Diego. Draft pick NY Mets, 1980, profl. baseball player, 1984—86, Minn. Twins, 1986—88, Detroit Tigers, 1988, Oakland Athletics, Calif., 1988—89, maj. league advance scout, 1990—93, asst. gen. mgr., 1993—97, v.p., gen. mgr., 1997—. Bd. dirs. Riddell, NetSuite, PROTRADE. Named Exec. of Yr., The Sporting News, 1999, Maj. League Baseball's Exec. of Yr., Baseball Am. mag., 2002; named one of 40 Under 40, St. & Smith's Sports Bus. Jour., 2001, Baseball's Heavy Hitters, 2004. Office: Oakland Athletics 7000 Coliseum Way Oakland CA 94621 Office Phone: 510-638-4900.*

BEANE, CLYDE EARL, reporter, political organization worker; b. Little Rock, Ark., Oct. 3, 1929; s. Claude Earl Beane and Minnie Viola Hamlin; m. Zoë Angela Ferris, June 13, 1970; children: Mark David, Jason Anthony, Lisa Marie. Studio engr. KARK Radio, Little Rock, 1935—37; relief transmission chief program dept. ABC, Hollywood, Calif.; with Paine Webber (now UBS), Beverly Hills; disk jockey, newscaster KUTE Radio, LA; writer to cycle editor UPI, LA; Calif. press rep. Sen. Barry Goldwater, 1964; LA beat reporter Orange County Register, 1965—68; pub. rels. specialist Gov. Ronald Reagan, 1968. Paine Webber reporter Wall Street Today. Republican. Roman Catholic.

BEAR, GERALDINE M., nursing assistant, poet; b. Spartanburg, SC, Mar. 6, 1926; d. Clarence Lee and Lucy Bell Hayes; m. Samuel Sidney Bear, Apr. 8, 1945; children: Diana L., Russell M., Joseph J. Student, Edgecombe Acad., 1943. Cert. nursing asst., CPR, RN home health aide. Author: (poems) Dedications of Love, 1974, The Poetry Seed, 1991. Deacon, mem. choir Grace Presbyn. Ch., Springhill, Fla., 1975—79. Avocations: painting, sewing, decorating.

BEAR, GREGORY DALE, writer, illustrator; b. San Diego, Aug. 20, 1951; s. Dale Franklin and Wilma (Merriman) B.; m. Astrid May Anderson, June 18, 1983; children: Erik William, Alexandra. AB in English, San Diego State U., 1973. Tech. writer, host Reuben H. Fleet Space Theater, 1973; freelance writer, 1975—. Author: Hegira, 1979, Psychlone, 1979, Beyond Heaven's River, 1980, Strength of Stones, 1981, The Wind From a Burning Woman, 1983, The Infinity Concerto, 1984, Blood Music, 1985, Eon, 1985, The Serpent Mage, 1986, The Forge of God, 1987, Eternity, 1988, Tangents, 1989, Heads, 1990, Queen of Angels, 1990, Anvil of Stars, 1992, Moving Mars, 1993 (Nebula award 1994), Songs of Earth and Power, 1993, Legacy, 1995, Slant, 1997, Dinosaur Summer, 1998 (Endeavor award 1999), Foundation and Chaos, 1998, Darwin's Radio, 1999 (Endeavor award 2000, Nebula award 2001), Rogue Planet, 2000, Vitals, 2002, Darwin's Children, 2003, Collected Short Stories of Greg Bear, 2003, Dead Lines, 2004; short stories: Blood Music (Hugo and Nebula awards), 1983, Hardfought (Nebula award), 1993, Tangents (Hugo and Nebula awards), 1987; editor: New Legends, 1995. Cons. Citizen's Adv. Council on Nat. Space Policy, Tarzana, Calif. Mem. Sci. Fiction Writers of Am. (editor Forum 1983-84, chmn. grievance com. 1985-86, v.p. 1987, pres. 1988-90). Avocations: book collecting, science, music, movies, history. Home: 506 Lakeview Rd Lynnwood WA 98037-2141

BEAR, LARRY ALAN, retired lawyer, educator; b. Melrose, Mass., Feb. 28, 1928; s. Joseph E. and Pearl Florence B.; m. Rita Maldonado, Mar. 29, 1975; children: Peter, Jonathan, Steven. BA, Duke U., 1949; JD, Harvard U., 1953; LLM, Columbia U., 1967. Bar: Mass. 1953, PR 1963, NY 1967. Trial lawyer Bear & Bear, Boston, 1953-60; cons. legal medicine PR Dept. Justice, 1960-65; prof. law sch. U. PR, 1960-65; legal counsel, then commr. addiction svcs. City of NY, 1967-70; dir. Nat. Action Com. Drug Edn. U. Rochester, NY, 1970-77; pvt. practice NYC, 1970-82; pub. affairs radio broadcaster Sta. WABC, NYC, 1970-82; US legal counsel Master Enterprises of PR, 1982-90. Vis. prof. legal medicine Rutgers U. Law Sch., 1969; mem. alcohol and drug com. Nat. Safety Coun., 1972—82; cons. in field of substance abuse prevention, edn. programming, 1980—; adj. prof. markets, ethics and law Stern Sch. Bus. NYU, 1986—99, vis. prof. bus. ethics, 1999—2003; pres. Found. for a Drug Free Pa., 1991—92; mem. Atty. Gen.'s Med./Legal Adv. Bd. on Drug Abuse, Pa., 1992; lectr. in legis. and ethics Wharton Sch. exec. program U. Pa., 1996—2000; vis. prof. legal, social and ethical context of bus. Athens Lab. Bus. Adminstrn., 1996. Author: Law, Medicine, Science and Justice, 1964, The Glass House Revolution: Inner City War for Interdependence, 1990, Free Markets, Finance, Ethics, and Law, 1994, Descent Into Danger, 2006; contbr. articles to profl. jours. Adv. com. on pub. issues Advt. Coun., 1972-95; mem.-at-large Nat. coun. Boy Scouts Am., 1972-85; chmn. Bd. Ethics, Twp. of Mahwah (NJ), 1990-91; alumni admissions adv. com. Duke U., 1987—. James Kent doctoral fellow, Columbia U., 1966—67. Mem. ABA, NY State Bar Assn., Forensic Sci. Soc. Great Britain, Acad. Colombiana de Ciencias Medico-Forenses, Harvard Club (N.Y.C.). Home: 95 Tam Oshanter Dr Mahwah NJ 07430-1526 Business E-Mail: rmaldona@stern-nyu.edu.

BEAR, MARK FIRMAN, neuroscientist, educator; BS in Psychology, Duke U., 1979; PhD in Neurobiology, Brown U., 1984. Max-Planck fellow Max Planck Inst. for Brain Rsch., Frankfurt, Germany, 1984; rsch. assoc. Brown U., 1985, asst. prof., rsch., 1986, asst. prof., neural sci., 1987—91, assoc. prof., dept. neuroscience, 1991—94, co-dir. neuroscience grad. program, 1991—99, prof., neuroscience, 1995—2003; Picower prof. neuroscience, Picower Ctr. for Learning and Memory MIT, 2003—; dir. Picower Inst. for Learning and Memory, MIT, 2007—. Prin. investigator Neuroscience Grad. Program Tng. Grant, 1991—99; assoc. investigator Howard Hughes Med. Inst., 1994—99, investigator, 1999—; mem. Dana Alliance for Brain Initiatives, Neuroscience Rsch. Prog. Neurosciences Inst., San Diego. Co-author (with Barry W. Connors, Michael A. Paradiso): Neuroscience: Exploring the Brain, 2000; contbr. articles to profl. jours. Recipient Young investigator award, Office of Naval Rsch., 1988, Soc. for Neuroscience, 1993, Sidney A. Fox and Dorothea Doctors Fox Prof. Ophthalmology and Visual Scis., 1995, Elizabeth H. Leduc Award for Teaching Excellence in the Elizabeth H. Leduc award for Tchg. Excellence in the Life Scis., 2000, Class of 2000 Barrett Hazeltine Citation for Tchg. Excellence, 2000; Alfred P. Sloan Rsch. Fellow, 1987, Fogarty Sr. Internat. Fellowship, 1994. Fellow: Am. Coll. Neuropsychopharmacology, AAAS, Am. Acad. Arts and Scis. Achievements include research in disorders ranging from mental retardation and autism to Alzheimer's disease. Office: MIT Dept Brain & Cognitive Sciences 77 Massachusetts Ave Bldg 46-3301 Cambridge MA 02139 Business E-Mail: mbear@mit.edu.*

BEAR, STEPHEN E., pharmaceutical executive; BA, Duke U., Durham, NC; MBA, Harvard U. With Bristol-Myers Squibb, 1985—99, 2001—, exec. v.p. strategy US consumer products group, pres. worldwide consumer medicines bus., sr. v.p. human resources, 2002—; head mktg. and bus. devel. NY Bot. Gardens, 1999—2001. Office: Bristol-Myers Squibb Co 345 Park Ave New York NY 10154-0037*

BEARD, AMANDA, swimmer, Olympic athlete; b. Irvine, Calif., Oct. 29, 1981; Student, U. Ariz., Tucson. Mem. Pan Pac Team, 1995; swimmer U.S. Olympic Team, Atlanta, 1996, Sydney, 2000, Athens, 2004. Holder Am. record for 100 meter breastroke, 1996. Achievements include winning gold medal in 4x100m medley, silver medal in 100m, 200m breast, Atlanta Olympic games, 1996; being the second youngest gold medalist in USA swimming history, Atlanta Olympic games, 1996; winning bronze medal in 200m breast, Sydney Olympic games, 2000; winning gold medal in 100m, 200m breast, Pan Pacific games, 2002; winning gold medal, 200m breast, World Championships, 2003; winning gold medal in 100m, 200m breast, 200m IM, US National Championships, 2004, 200m IM, 2003; winning gold medal in 200m breast, silver medal in 200m IM, 4x100m medley relay, Athens Olympic games, 2004. Office: US Swimming Inc One Olympic Plz Colorado Springs CO 80909

BEARD, ANN SOUTHARD, diplomat, oil industry executive; b. Denver, Jan. 13, 1948; d. William Harvey and Cora Alice Cornelia (Caldwell) Southard; m. Terrill Leon Beard, Dec. 20, 1970 (div. Oct. 1980); 1 son, Jeffery Leon; m. Rainer G. Froehlich, Feb. 12, 1988 (div. 1992). BA, Willamette U., 1970; postgrad., U. Calif., San Diego, 1981-82. Exec. asst. Kidder Peabody & Co., San Francisco, 1970-72; adminstrv. aide Arthur Anderson & Co., Portland, Oreg., 1972-73; owner, mgr. Beard's Frame Shoppes, Inc., Portland, 1973-80; dir. mktg. Multnomah County Fair, Portland, 1979; owner, CEO Ann Beard Spl. Events, San Diego, 1980-82, Frame Affair, Inc., San Diego, 1982-86; pres. Jack Oil Co., Inc., Greeley, 1982—; chancellor, v.p. programs Consular Corps. Coll., Phila., 2002—05. Mem. Pres.'s Small Bus. Adv. Coun.; co-owner, v.p. Froehlich Internat. Travel, La Jolla, Calif., 1987-92; chief of protocol Mayor Susan Golding's Office, City of San Diego, 1993-2001; pres., CEO, Diplomacy & Internat. Protocol, San Diego, 2001—; chmn. 1st Nat. Protocol Officers Assn. conf. U.S. Dept. State, Washington; chmn. 1st Internat. Protocol Conf., Ottawa, Can.; pres. 146 Co., Inc., Greeley, 1970-88; mem. San Diego Consular Corps; cons. SBA, San Diego, 1980-85; prof. San Diego State U., 2002—, Palomar Coll., 2004-05, SAIC U., 2004-05, Smithsonian Inst. Assocs. Program, 2004—; internat protocol advisor Molecular Pictures.com.; VIP ceremonies Presdl. Inauguration, 2005; lectr., presenter in field Bd. dirs. San Diego Master Chorale, 1981-92, La Jolla Rep. Women Fedn., 1992-96; mem. state bd. Miss. Calif. Pageant/Miss. Am., 1982-87; citizens adv. bd. Drug Abuse Task Force/Crime Prevention Task Force, San Diego, 1983-87; campaign coord. Bill Mitchell for City Coun., 1985; candidate for Congress; staff aide to dep. mayor, 1987; active Lead San Diego Alumni, 1988, Scripps Hosp. Aux., 1992—. Internat. Vis. Coun., 1993-2003, San Diego County Commn. on the Status of Women, 1993-96; active Internat. Affairs Bd., San Diego, 1993-2001; chancellor, Consular Corps Coll., Phila., 2001-05; founder, nat. chmn. Nat. Protocol Resource Bd., USA, 2002—, founder, internat. pres. Protocol and Diplomacy Internat., U.S., 2002-04. Mem. Am. Mktg. Assn., World Affairs Coun., San Diego C. of C., Save Our Heritage Orgn., Charter 100 San Diego, San Diego 1970 Alumna Willamette U., 1909 Univ. Club (bd. dirs. 1992-2003, pres. 1996-98), Univ. Club San Diego (mktg., devel. and social dir. 1987-88), Pres., Protocol and Diplomacy Internat., Delta Gamma. Home Phone: 858-735-6673; Office Phone: 858-481-5661. Personal E-mail: bearddiplomacy@yahoo.com.

BEARD, BRUCE H., retired psychiatrist; b. Ft. Worth, May 15, 1921; m. Mary Ann Beard, Sept. 7, 2003. BA, Texas Tech. U., Lubbock, 1940; MD, U. Tex. Med. Br., Galveston, 1944. Cert. Am. Bd. Psychiatry and Neurology in Psychiatry, 1951, lic. Tex., Okla., Colo. Internship Ind. U. Med. Ctr., Indpls., 1944—45; residency in psychiatry U. Tex. Med. Br., John Sealy Hosp., 1945—48; pvt. practice psychiatry Ft. Worth, 1948—66; assoc. prof. psychiatry Okla. U. Sch. Medicine, 1966—69, U. Tex. Southwestern Med. Sch., 1970—73; chief psychiatry Okla. City VA Hosp., 1966—69; clin. dir. psychiatry Presbyn. Hosp. at Dallas, 1970—73; prof. psychiatry Tex. Tech. U. Sch. Medicine, 1974—76, assoc. chmn. Dept. Psychiatry, 1974—76; cli. prof. psychiatry U. Tex. Southwestern Med. Sch., 1977—81; pvt. practice psychiatry Dallas, 1982—92; ret., 1992. Contbr. articles to profl. sci. jours. Maj. USAF, 1955—57. Fellow: Am. Psychiat. Assn. (life Disting.); mem.: AMA, Ctrl. Neuropsychiatric Physicians, North Tex. Soc. Psychiat. Physicians (pres. 1965—66), Tex. Assn. Psychiat. Physicians (sec. 1954—56, treas. 1954—56, pres. 1957—58), Dallas County Med. Soc., Tex. Med. Assn. (life), Sigma XI-Rsch. Soc. of N.Am. Achievements include research in quality of life with hemodialysis renal transplantation. Avocations: amateur radio, dog training. Address: 10199 Vistadale Dr Dallas TX 75238-1636 Home Phone: 214-349-3029; Office Phone: 214-349-3029. Personal E-mail: bruceandmary@sbcglobal.net.

BEARD, CRAIG WYETH, librarian; b. Memphis, Dec. 21, 1954; s. Frank Stanley Beard and Lyta Jean Hancock; children: Jason, Jessica. AA, Fla. Coll., 1975; BA, Harding U., 1977, MA in Religion, 1980; MLS, Fla. State U., 1982. Reference libr. Harding U., Searcy, Ark., 1982—90; head reference svcs. Sterne Libr. U. Ala., Birmingham, 1990—94, reference libr. for engrng. Sterne Libr., 1994—. Adj. instr. U. Ala. Sch. Libr. and Info. Studies, Tuscaloosa, 1992—94, 2004—, U. Ala., Birmingham, 2003—. Contbr. (reference book) Topical Reference Books, 1991, American Reference Books Annual, (index) Restoration Serials Index, 1994—, tech. editor (restoration serials index), 2007—. Vol. So. Bapt. Disaster Relief, Alpharetta, Ga., 1999—2004; lay worker The Ch. at Brook Hills, Birmingham, 1997—. Mem.: Ala. Assn. Coll. and Rsch. Librs. (pres. elect/pres./past pres. 1997—2000), Christian Coll. Librs. (pres. elect/pres./past pres. 1992—98), Am. Soc. for Engrng. Edn. (chair, pub. com. Engrng Libr. Divsn. 2004—). Office: Sterne Library U Ala B'ham 917 13th St South Birmingham AL 35294 Office Phone: 205-934-6364.

BEARD, ELIZABETH LETITIA, physiologist, educator; b. New Orleans, Apr. 2, 1932; d. Howard Horace and Irene (Handley) Beard. BA in Biology, Tex. Christian U., Ft. Worth, 1952, BS in Med. Tech., 1953, MS in Med. Tech., 1955; postgrad., Smith Coll., Northampton, Mass., 1953-54, Vanderbilt U., Nashville, 1954-55; PhD in Animal Physiology, Tulane U., New Orleans, 1961. Instr. dept. biol. scis. Loyola U., New Orleans, 1955-58, asst. prof., 1958-62, assoc. prof., 1962-68, prof., 1969—, chmn. premed. com., 1978—; rsch. assoc. dept. physiology Sch. Medicine Tulane U., New Orleans, 1960-63, prof. biology med. reinforcement and enrichment program, 1968-94. Vis. prof. dept. physiology and biophysics Med. Sch. Harvard U., 1983-84, dept. neuropharmacology Scripps Rsch. Inst., La Jolla, Calif., spring 2001; vis. scientist Am. Indian Rsch. Opportunities Programs at Mont. State U., 1994. Contbr. articles on rsch. in physiology to profl. publs. Project rev. com. New Orleans Health Planning Coun., 1974-77, bd. dirs., 1975-78; soprano soloist Holy Name of Jesus Ch., 1978—, pres. sch. bd., 1976-79; grad. rsch. com. La. chpt. Am. Heart Assn., 1970-72, 81-83, undergrad. rsch. com., 1978-81, 89-93; active Met. Mus. Art, New Orleans Mus. Art. NIH grantee, 1962-64, 67-69, La. Heart Assn. grantee, 1966-67, Edward Schleider Found. grantee, 1974-77, New Orleans Cancer Assn. grantee, 1962-63; Libby Rsch. fellow Sch. Medicine Tulane U., 1961. Mem. AAUP, AAAS, Am. Physiol. Soc., Soc. Exptl. Biology and Medicine, Christian Med. and Dental Soc. (participant internat. med. missions 1993—), Sigma Xi. Office: 6363 St Charles Ave New Orleans LA 70118-6143 Home: # 22 6363 Saint Charles Ave New Orleans LA 70118-6143 Office Phone: 504-865-2768. Business E-Mail: Beard@Loyno.edu.

BEARD, JANET MARIE, health facility administrator; b. Olean, NY, Feb. 18, 1930; d. Paul Claude and Virginia Marie (Mahaney) B. Grad. in nursing, St. Catherine's Hosp., 1951; BS in Clin. Nursing, St. John's U., 1959, MS in Nursing Adminstrn., 1961; MS in Adminstrv. Medicine, Columbia U., 1968. RN, N.Y.; lic. nursing home adminstr. Adminstrv. supr. Mary Immaculate Hosp., Jamaica, N.Y., 1957-66; asst. adminstr. Cath. Med. Ctr. Bklyn. and Queens, Jamaica, 1968-70; asst. dir. Yale-New Haven Med. Ctr., 1971-72, St. Barnabas Hosp., Bronx, N.Y., 1972-78, v.p., 1978-83; chief exec. officer Bethel Nursing and Rehab. Ctr., Croton on Hudson, N.Y., 1983—. Contbr. articles to profl. jours. Active Bronx Cmty. Bd. 6, 1977-83; active Fedn. Protestant Welfare Agys., N.Y.C., 1978-88; planning com. Div. on Aging, N.Y.C., 1978-88; adv. com. Aging in Am., Bronx, 1978-87; treas. Ft. Schuyler House, Bronx, 1977-83; pres.-elect alumni assn. Columbia U. Sch. Pub. Health, 1987-88, pres., 1988-89; mem. longterm planning com. Hudson Valley Health Systems Agy., 1989—; mem. planning coun., task force on AIDS Westchester County Health Dept., 1987-89, Westchester Health Planning Coun., 1992—; exec. adv. bd. health care mgmt. Iona Coll., 1987-92. Fellow Am. Coll. Health Care Execs.; mem. Am. Coll. Health Care Adminstrs., N.Y. State Pub. Health Assn. (Lower Hudson Valley chpt.), N.Y. Assn. Homes and Svcs. for the Aging (housing com. 1985-87), Ossining C. of C. (bd. dirs. 1987-92), Rotary (pres. Croton-on-Hudson 1992-93, Paul Harris fellow 1994), Princeton Club. Office: Exec Dir The Bethel Homes 19 Narragansett Ave Ossining NY 10562-2899 also: Bethel Nursing and Rehab Ctr 67 Springvale Rd Croton On Hudson NY 10520-1343

BEARD, LEO ROY, retired civil engineer; b. West Baden, Ind., Apr. 6, 1917; s. Leonard Roy and Barbara Katherine (Frederick) B.; m. Marian Janet Wagar, Oct. 21, 1939 (dec.); children: Patricia Beard Huntzicker, Thomas Edward, James Robert; m. Marjorie Elizabeth Pierce Wood, Aug.

30, 1974. AA, Pasadena City Coll., 1937; BS, Calif. Inst. Tech., 1939. Engr. U.S. Army C.E., Los Angeles, 1939-49; engr. Office Chief of Engrs., Washington, 1949-52; chief of Reservoir Regulation, Sacramento, 1952-64; dir. Hydrologic Engring. Center, Davis, Calif., 1964-72; prof. civil engring. U. Tex., Austin, 1972-87, prof. emeritus, 1987—. Cons. Espey, Huston & Assos., Austin, 1980-92; v.p. Internat. Commn. of Water Resource Sys.; water sci. and tech. bd. NRC. Editor-in-chief: Water International; Editor: Jour. of Hydrology. Served with USNR, 1945-46. Recipient Meritorious Civilian Service award U.S. Army C.E., 1972. Fellow AAAS,. Internat. Water Resources Assn. (exec. bd.), ASCE (water resources exec. com., Julian Hinds award 1981, hon. mem. 1987, Hunter Rouse award 1993, Lifetime Achievement award 2001); mem. Am. Water Resources Assn. (hon.), Am. Geophys. Union (pres. hydrology sect.), Nat. Soc. Profl. Engrs., Internat. Assn. Hydrol. Scis., World Meteorol. Orgn. (chmn. com. on hydrol. design data), U.S. Com. on Irrigation, Drainage and Flood Control, Univs. Council on Water Resources (exec. bd.), Nat. Acad. Engring. *As you spend most waking hours at your work, choose to love it. The key is to select an occupation that serves others.*

BEARD, LILLIAN B. MCLEAN, pediatrician, consultant; b. NY; d. Johnie Wilson and Woodie (Durden) McLean; m. Delawrence Beard. BS, Howard U., 1965, MD, 1970. MD, 1970. Pvt. practice pediat. Lillian M. Beard, Washington, 1973—; assoc. prof. pediat. George Washington U., 1983—; asst. prof. cmty. medicine Howard U., 1983—; contbg. editor Good Housekeeping Mag., NYC, 1989-95; health adv. WUSA-TV, Washington, 1993-95; health and med. contbr. ABC-TV, Washington, 2000—04. Comm. cons. to industry including: Nestle Nutritional Products; mem. bd. dirs. Nat. Women's Econ. Alliance, 1993-2000, Children's Hosp., 1993-2002. Recipient Disting. Leadership award Nat. Assn. Equal Opportunity in Higher Edn., 1993, Disting. Svc. award Nat. Med. Assn., 1990, Hall of Fame in Medicine award, 1994, Healthy Babies Project "Making a Difference" award, 1995, Howard U. Alumni Achievement award, 1996. Fellow Am. Acad. Pediat.; mem. Nat. Med. Assn., Am. Acad. Pediat. (physician recognition awards 1993—). Home: 10517 Alloway Dr Potomac MD 20854-1662 Office: 10801 Lockwood Dr Ste 260 Silver Spring MD 20901

BEARD, RICK, cultural organization administrator; b. Harrisburg, Pa., Mar. 27, 1947; s. Richard B. and Peggy Ann (O'Gorman) B.; m. Susan Elliott, July 11, 1992; 1 child, Nora. BA in History with honors, Juniata Coll., 1969; MA, Emory U., 1972, PhD in Am. Studies, 1981. Rsch. historian Office of Small Exhibits Nat. Portrait Gallery, Smithsonian Instn., Washington, 1974-77; coord. Yale Ctr. Am. Art and Material Culture, 1977-80; sr. exhibit planner Design and Prodn. Inc., Alexandria, Va., 1981-82; assoc. dir. The Hudson River Mus., Yonkers, NY, 1982-85, dir., 1985-86; assoc. dir. programs, collections, and publs. Mus. of the City of NY, 1986-92; exec. dir. Atlanta Hist. Soc., 1992—2002; COO NY Hist. Soc., 2002—04; dir. Abraham Lincoln Presdl. Libr. & Mus., Springfield, Ill., 2006—. Cons. in field; pres. Civil War 150: The Sesquicentennial Initiative. Author: (with Frederick S. Voss) Packaging Presidents: Memorabilia from Campaigns Past, 1984; editor: On Being Homeless: Historical Perspectives, 1987, A Common Purpose and Shared Commitment: One Hundred Years of Medicine at Beth Israel Medical Center, 1990, Greenwich Village: Culture and Counterculture, 1992; contbr. articles to profl. jours. Mem. Am. Assn. Mus., Am. Studies Assn., Soc. Am. Historians. Office: Abraham Lincoln Presdl Library & Mus 112 N 6th St Springfield IL 62701 Office Phone: 217-558-8879. E-mail: Rick.Beard@illinois.gov.

BEARD, RONALD STRATTON, lawyer; b. Flushing, NY, Feb. 13, 1939; s. Charles Henry and Ethel Mary (Stratton) Beard; m. Karin Paridee, Jan. 24, 1991; children: D. Karen, Jonathan D., Dana K. BA, Denison U., 1961; LLB, Yale U., 1964. Bar: Calif. 1964, U.S. Ct. Appeals (9th cir.) 1980, U.S. Dist. Ct. (ctrl. dist.) Calif. 1964. Ptnr. Gibson, Dunn & Crutcher, LA, 1964—2001, mng. ptnr., 1991—97, chmn., 1991—2001. Bd. dir. Callaway Golf, Javo Beverage Co., Document Sci. Corp. Trustee Denison U., Granville, Ohio, 1975—, chmn., 1998—2003; mem. Constl. Rights Found., 1994—2006; mem. steering com. Calif. Minority Coun. Program, 1991—2001; bd. dir. Gov.'s Coun. Physical Fitness and Sports, 2005—. Mem.: Calif. Bar Assn., Coto de Caza Golf Club, Chancery Club, City Club. Avocations: sports, travel, golf. Home: 27442 Hidden Trail Rd Laguna Hills CA 92653-5876 Office: Gibson Dunn & Crutcher 4 Park Plz Ste 1700 Irvine CA 92614-8560 Office Phone: 949-451-4089. Business E-Mail: rbeard@gibsondunn.com.

BEARDEN, JAMES HUDSON, university official; b. Marion, Ala., Sept. 1933; s. Joseph N. and Lula B.; m. Pauline Larkins, Mar. 31, 1961; children: James Hudson, Jr., Pauline B. Simonowich. BS, Centenary Coll. La., 1956; MA, East Carolina U., 1959; PhD, U. Ala., 1966. Bus. mgr. Marion Inst., 1959; mem. faculty East Carolina U., Greenville, NC, 1959—, prof. bus. adminstrn., 1964—, dir. bur. bus. research, 1964, dean, 1968-83, dir. BB&T Ctr. for Leadership Devel., 1983—. Author articles in field. Former trustee Campbell U.; pres., trustee N.C. Council Econ. Edn. Served with AUS, 1956-58. Mem. Newcomen Soc. N.Am., Assn. Leadership Educators, Fedn. Bus. Honor Socs. (pres. 1991—), Rotary, Beta Gamma Sigma (pres. 1986-1990), Sigma Beta Delta (pres. 1994-2000). Home: 106 Crown Point Rd Greenville NC 27858-5718 Office: BB&T Ctr for Leadership Devel East Carolina U 1100 Bate Bldg Greenville NC 27858-4353

BEARDEN, THOMAS EUGENE, research scientist; b. Cheniere, La., Dec. 17, 1930; m. Doris Faye McDonald, 1964. BS in Math., NE La. U., 1953; MS in Nuc. Engring., Ga. Inst. Tech., 1971; PhD in Sci. (hon.), Trinity Coll., UK, 1999. Commd. US Army, 1954, advanced through grades to lt. col., intelligence specialist air def. and ABM def., 1960—75, ret.; dir. Assn. Disting. Am. Scientists, Huntsville, Ala., 1995—; CEO CTEC, Inc., Huntsville, 1995—. Fellow emeritus Alpha Found.'s Inst. for Advanced Study, 1998—2004. Author: Oblivion: America at the Brink, 2005, (scientific book) Energy from the Vacuum: Concepts and Principles, 2002; contbr. articles to profl. jours. Mem.: Ala. Acad. Sci., Am. Assn. Physics Tchrs. Achievements include discovery of solution to the problem of the source charge and its associated EM fields and potentials; extension to Becker's model of the cellular regenerative system; thermodynamics of permissible COP over 1.0 electrical power systems; corrected flaw in 3-law Aristotelian logic to 5-law logic; design of proposed mechanism for excess antigravity accelerating expansion of the universe; co-inventor of Motionless Electromagnetic Generator; discovery of mechanism for practical antigravity; correction of Second Law of Thermodynamics to include negentropic systems; EM epigenetic reprogramming mechanism in the Prioré effect; mechanisms used in advanced Soviet energetics weapons; negative resonance absorption of the medium in circuits using the nondiverged Heaviside energy flow component arbitrarily discarded by Lorentz; proposed testable mechanism for excess gravity holding the arms of spiral galaxies together; extension and correction of second law of thermodynamics to include asymmetric regauging; co-invention of environmental amplification of Dirac negative energy in circuits; discovery of precursor force-free field structuring; proposed Dirac Sea hole currents produced in sharp strong gradients in cosmological processes as what dark matter is, and negative energy EM fields from dark matter as constituting dark energy; design of proposed mechanism for dark energy, dark matter effects, and anomalous drag on NASA pioneer spacecraft; proposed models for mind dynamics; mind/body coupling mechanism; proposed mechanism for precursor engineering of spacetime. Avocation: aikido (retired, sandan). Office: Assn Distinguished Am Scientists PO Box 1472 Huntsville AL 35807 Personal E-mail: soliton@bellsouth.net.

BEARDSLEY, CHARLES MITCHELL, retired insurance company executive; b. Chgo., Jan. 13, 1921; s. Richard Stanley and Maude Clarice (Mitchell) B.; m. Marjorie Helen Gahan, Feb. 27, 1943; children: Helen Charlene, Karen Jeannette. AB, Depauw U., 1942; MA, U. Wis., 1947. From actuarial student to assoc. actuary Paul Revere Life Ins. Co., Worcester, Mass., 1947-55; from actuary to v.p. Security Life and Trust Co., Winston-Salem, NC, 1955-63; actuary sr. v.p. H.W. Satchwell & Co., Columbus, Ohio, 1963-67; actuary chmn., chief exec. officer Charles M. Beardsley & Assocs., Columbus, 1967-68; from exec. v.p. to chmn. Booke and Co., Winston-Salem, 1968-85, vice chmn., 1985-91. Author Life Company Annual Statement Handbook and New Items in the Annual Statement for Life Insurance Companies, 1959-2005; contbr. articles to profl. jours. Pres. Wachovia Hist. Soc., Winston-Salem, 1981, Huguenot Soc. N.C., 1987-89; bd. dirs. Moravian Music Found., Winston-Salem. Served to lt. (j.g.) USN, 1943-46. Fellow Conf. of Cons. Actuaries (v.p. 1980-82), Soc. Actuaries (dir. 1983-86); mem. Am. Acad. Actuaries, Internat. Actuarial Assn., Internat. Assn. Cons. Actuaries (bd. dirs. 1980-89), Founders and Patriots Am. Democratic. Clubs: Forsyth Country, Twin City, Piedmont (Winston-Salem). Lodges: Masons, Kiwanis (local pres.). Avocation: music. Home: 341 Muirfield Dr Winston Salem NC 27104-3952 Office Phone: 336-748-1120. Personal E-mail: cmb2743@yahoo.com.

BEARE, MURIEL ANITA NIKKI, public relations executive, author; b. Detroit, Mar. 7, 1928; d. Elbert Stanley and Dorothy Margaret (Welch) Brink; m. Richard Austin Beare, June 15, 1946; 1 child, Sandra Lee. AA, Miami Dade C.C., 1974; BA, Skidmore coll., 1979. Writer Key West (Fla.) Citizen, 1959; Miami News, 1967; field dir. Fla. Project HOPE, 1967-68; southeastern area dir., 1968-69; asst. v.p. pub. rels. I/D Assocs., Inc., Miami, 1969-70; pres. Nikki Beare & Assocs., Miami, 1971—; v.p. South Fla. office Cherenson, Carroll & Holzer, Livingston, NJ, 1973; sr. v.p. D.J. Edelman, Inc., 1981-83. Co-owner South Miami Travel Svc., 1976-78; pres. Gov.'s Sq. Travel, Inc., Tallahassee, 1979-85, Travel Is Fun, Miami, 1985-90; owner Silver Beare Travel, Inc., 1995-99; bd. dirs. corp. sec. Imperial Bank; reporter Tallahassee Dem., Focus Gadsden, Bus. Matters Mag. Author: Pirates, Pineapples and People: Tales and Legends of the Florida Keys, 1961, From Turtle Soup to Coconuts, 1964, Bottle Bonanza, A Handbook for Antique Bottle Collectors, 1965; prodr. cable TV program Traveler's Digest, 1986-92; moderator, prodr. Women's Powerline, Sta. WIOD, Miami, 1972-77; reporter Tallahassee Dem., 2005—, Tortoise, 2005—, Bus. Matters, 2005—. Chmn. adv. bd. Met. Dade County Libr., 1964; active Greater Miami Host Com., Met. Dade County Com. Status Women, 1971-76; former chmn. City of Miami Commn. Status Women, 1985-92; active Met. Gen. Land Use Master Planning Com. Employment Handicapped, 1970-72; chmn. Met. Dade Fair Housing and Employment Appeals Bd., 1975-78; active Miami YWCA's; chmn. Handicapped and Elderly subcom. Met. Dade Transit Devel. Com.; mem. Fla. Ins. Commn. Task force, 1975, Dade County Dem. Exec. Com., 1972-76, South Fla. Health Planning coun., 1972-74; founding mem. Nat. Women's Polit. Caucus, 1971—; pres. Capitol Women's Polit. Caucus; v.p. Fla. Women's Polit. Caucus, NWPC, Fla.; v.p. Herstory, 1971—; candidate Fla. Senate, 1974, Fla. Ho. of Reps., 1976; past pres. adv. bd. Inst. for Women, Fla. Internat. U.; pres. Fla. Feminist Credit Union, 1975-78; bd. dirs. Cmty. Health Inst., South Dade County, 1975-77; mem. Jobs for Miami, 1980-88; chmn. Fla. Gov.'s Small Bus. Adv. Coun., 1981-83, Greater Miami Tourism Coalition, 1983-85; del. White House Conf. on Small Bus., 1980, 86; chmn. publicity com. Asta World Congress, 1989,chmn. com. travel persons with disabilities; co-chmn. Fla. Internat. U. Sch. Journalism and Mass Comms. adv. bd., 1984-92; v.p. Havana Learning Ctr., Inc., 1995—; mem. consumer svcs. bd. Fla. Dept. Agr., 1998—. Recipient Silver Image award Pub. Rels. Assn., 1967-68; named to Fla. Women's Hall of Fame, 1994. Mem. AAUW, LWV, NOW, Hist. Assn. So. Fla., Friends of Everglades, Women's C. of C. So. Fla., Am. Soc. Travel Agts., Women in Comms., Nat. Assn. Women Bus. Owners, Pub. Rels. Soc. Am., Fla. Pub. Rels. Assn., Her Story of Fla., Inc., Women's Inst. Freedom of the Press, Antique Bottle Collectors Assn. Fla., Caribbean Tourism Orgn., South by Southeast Profl. Women In Travel, Vet. Feminists Am. Democrat. Office: Nikki Beare & Assocs Inc 7858 Havana Hwy Havana FL 32333-9594 E-mail: nikkibeare@aol.com.

BEARE-ROGERS, JOYCE LOUISE, retired research and development executive; b. nr. Pickering, Ont., Can., Sept. 8, 1927; d. Frederick John and Sarah May (Michell) Beare; m. Charles Graham Rogers, Dec. 30, 1961; 1 child, Anne Catherine. BA, U. Toronto, Ont., 1951, MA, 1952; PhD, Carleton U., Ottawa, Ont., 1966; DSc (hon.), U. Man., Winnipeg, Can., 1985, U. Guelph, Ont., 1993. Rsch. assoc. U. Toronto, 1952-54; instr. Vassar Coll., Poughkeepsie, 1954-56; chemist Food, Drug Directorate, Ottawa, 1956-65; rsch. scientist Health Can., Ottawa, 1965-75; rsch. mgr. Bur. Nutritional Scis., Ottawa, 1975-91. Adj. prof. U. Ottawa, 1980-92; cons. Food and Agrl. Orgn. UN, 1992-94; Hilditch lectr. U.K., 1994; trustee Nat. Inst. Nutrition (Can.), 1997-99. Editor: Methods for Nutritional Assessment of Fats, 1985, Fat Requirements for Development and Health, 1988; contbr. articles on dietary fats to profl. jours. Decorated Order of Can.; recipient Queen's Jubilee medal Govt. of Can., 1977, Medaille Chevreul award Inst. Corps Gras, 1984, Crompton award McGill U., 1986, Normann medal German Assn. for Fat Rsch., 1987, Commemorative medal for 125th Anniversary of Fedn. of Can., 1992, Queen's Golden Jubilee medal 2002. Fellow: Am. Inst. Nutrition, Royal Soc. Can. (panelist on food biotechnology 2000—01, hon. treas. 2000—04, chair com. awards and medals 2004—); mem.: Can. Biochem. Soc., Can. Soc. for Nutrition Scis. (pres. 1984—85, Bordon award 1971, McHenry award 1993), Internat. Soc. Fat Rsch. (pres. 1991—92), Am. Oil Chemists Soc. (pres. 1985—86, Lifetime Achievement award Can. sect. 1995). Avocations: hiking, canoeing, cross country skiing, reading. Home: 41 Okanagan Dr Ottawa ON Canada K2H 7E9 E-mail: jbrogers@sympatico.ca.

BEARMAN, TONI CARBO See CARBO, TONI

BEA ROBERTS, BARBARA ANN, legal secretary; b. Richmond, Va., Nov. 26, 1957; d. Arthur and Edith (Thompson) B.; m. Alan Roberts; 1 child, Michael T. Sec. IEEE, Washington, 1981-83, Greenhoot, Inc., Washington, 1983-85; legal sec. Friedlander, Misler, Friedlander, Sloan & Herz, Washington, 1985-88, Arnold & Porter, Washington, 1988-97, Dickstein, Shapiro, Morin & Olshinsky, Washington, 1997-99, Hale and Dorr, Washington, 1999-00, Littler, Mendelson PC, 2000—01, Katten Muchin Rosenman LLP, Washington, 2001—. Democrat. Mem. Seventh-Day Adventist Ch. Office: Katten Muchin Rosenman LLP 1025 Thomas Jefferson St NW # 700E Washington DC 20007

BEARSCH, LEE PALMER, architect, urban planner; b. Binghamton, NY, July 5, 1942; s. Frederick James and Mildred Jane (Palmer) B.; m. Christine Cromer, Dec. 31, 1972; children: Frederick Cromer, Benjamin Palmer, Peter Furlong. BArch, Clemson U., 1965; M in Planning, Leverhulme Sch. Archtl. Assn., London, 1970. Registered profl. arch., N.Y., Pa., Md., Mass., Wis. Project dir. Llewelyn-Davies Assocs., London, NY, and Racine, Wis., 1970-75; pres. Bearsch Compeau Knudson, Archs. and Engrs., P.C., Binghamton, 1976—. Mem. N.Y. State Edn. Dept. Bd. for Arch. Lic. Bd., 1997—. Mem. Broome County Planning Adv. Bd., Binghamton, 1978-90, sec., 1986-88; bd. dirs. Broome County Small Bus. Coun., 1979-84, vice chmn., 1981-83; vestryman Christ Episcopal Ch., 1981-84; bd. dirs. Family and Childrens Soc. Broome County Inc., 1982—, pres., 1985-86; bd. dirs. Binghamton Symphony Orch., Binghamton U. Found., 2002—; mem. adv. bd. Endicott Trust divsn. Mfrs. and Traders Bank; mem. Binghamton U. Coun., 1993-98; mem. N.Y. State Bd. for Arch. State Licensing Bd., 1995-2005, chmn., 2002, 03, peer panelist, 2005—. Fellow AIA (area dir. 1978-79, v.p. 1979-81, chpt. pres. 1981-82, state conv. chmn. 1983, state pres. 1990, nat. bd. dirs. 1990-93, nat. documents com. 1994-2002, chmn., 1998-2000, nat. conv. chmn. 1996); mem. Am. Inst. Cert. Planners, N.Y. State Assn. Archs. (bd. dirs. 1985—, exec. com. 1987—, pres. 1990, mem. bd. archtl. registration 1995—), Archtl. Assn. (Eng.), Broome County C. of C. (bd. dirs. 1986—, chmn. 1990-91), Leadership Broome (adv. bd. 1988-90), Binghamton City Club (bd. govs. 1995-2000), Binghamton Country Club (bd. govs. 1999-2002, pres. 2002), Live Wire Club, Nat. Coun. Archtl. Registration Bds. (chmn. profl. program devel. com. 2002-05, com. edn. 2005—). Office: Bearsch Compeau Knndson A&E PC 41 Chenango St Binghamton NY 13901-2901 Home: 1312 Robinson Hill Rd Endwell NY 13760 Home Phone: 607-798-0857.

BEARSE, CAROL IRENE, education educator; BS, Boston U., 1967; MS, U. So. Conn., New Haven, 1973; postgrad., UCLA, 1995, Fitchburg State Coll., Mass., 1997; PhD, Lesley U., Cambridge, Mass., 2003. Cert. tchr. K-8, K-12, reading cons. K-12. Writing curriculum coord. Kane Magnet Sch., Lawrence, Mass., 1991—94; bilingual curriculum coord. Walsh Middle Sch., Framingham, Mass., 2000—06; assoc. prof. edn. Touro Coll., NYC, 2006—. Mem. editl. adv. bd. Reading Tchr., 1992—93. Author: The Sky in My Hands, 2005. Recipient award of honor, VFW Post # 292, 1997; grantee, Framingham Edn. Found., 1996—98, 2001—02, 2004; scholar, Boston U.; Fulbright scholar, Tchr. Exch. Program, Brazil, 2000, CMty. Svc. Learning grantee, 1997, creative schs. grantee, Mass. Cultural Coun., 2003. Mem.: ASCD, Am. Ednl. Rsch. Assn., Mass. Reading Assn., Mass. Assn. Bilingual Edn., Nat. Assn. Bilingual Edn., Internat. Reading Assn., Nat. Coun. Tchrs. English, Pi Lambda Theta. Office: Touro Coll Lander Ctr Educational Rsch 43 W 23rd St 8th Fl New York NY 10010 Office Phone: 212-463-0400 ext. 282. Business E-Mail: carol.bearse@touro.edu. E-mail: carolbearse@aol.com.

BEART, ROBERT W., JR., colon and rectal surgeon, educator; b. Kansas City, Mo., Mar. 3, 1945; s. Robert Woodward and Helen Elizabeth (Wamsley) B.; m. Cynthia Anne, Jan. 23, 1971; children: Jennifer, Kristina, Amy. AB, Princeton U., 1967; MD, Harvard U., 1971. Diplomate Am. Bd. Surgery, Am. Bd. Colon and Rectal Surgery. Intern U. Colo., 1971-72, resident, 1972-76; prof. surgery Mayo Clinic, Scottsdale, Ariz., 1976—87, U. So. Calif., LA, 1992—. Maj. USMC, 1972-83. Fellow Am. Soc. Colon and Rectal Surgery (pres. 1994). Office: 1441 Eastlake Ave Ste 7418 Los Angeles CA 90033 Office Phone: 323-865-3690.

BEARY, JOHN FRANCIS, III, rheumatologist, pharmaceutical executive, medical researcher; b. Melrose, Iowa, 1946; s. John F. and Dorothy (McGrath) B.; m. Bianca E. Mason, 1972; children: John Daniel, Vanessa, Webster, Nina. BS summa cum laude, U. Notre Dame, Ind., 1969; MD, Harvard U., Cambridge, Mass., 1973; MBA, Georgetown U., Washington, DC, 1988. Diplomate Am Bd. Internal Medicine, Am. Bd. Rheumatology, Am. Bd. Clin. Pharmacology. Flight surgeon 89th Mil. Airlift Wing (Air Force One), 1974—77; Osler medicine resident Johns Hopkins Hosp., Balt., 1977—78; rsch. fellow Cornell Hosp. Spl. Surgery, NYC, 1978—80; from asst. prof. to clin. prof. Sch. Medicine Georgetown U., Washington, 1980—2005; prin. dept. asst. sec. health affairs Dept. Def., Washington, 1981—83, appropriations task force for USNS Mercy and USNS Comfort, 1982; assoc. dean strategic planning Georgetown U. Sch. Medicine, Washington, 1984—87; sr. v.p. regulatory and sci. affairs Pharm. Rsch. and Mfg. Assn., Washington, 1988—97; sr. med. dir. bone and arthritis rsch. Procter and Gamble Pharma, Cin., 1997—. Steering com. Internat. Conf. on Harmonization of Pharm. Stds., 1990-97; clin. prof. rheumatology and immunology U. Cin., 1997—; mem. OMERACT Rheumatology Rsch. Com., 1998-2003; sci. com. Arthritis Found., Ohio, 1998-. Editor: Manual of Rheumatology, 1981, 5th edit., 2005; mem. editl. bd. Jour. Pharm. Medicine, 1990—, Drug Devel. Rsch., 1992-2000. Bd. dirs. Scleroderma Found., Washington, 1982—92. Served to capt. USNR, 1984—99. Recipient Disting. Mil. Grad. award, 1969, Rsch. award NY Arthritis Found., 1979, Disting. Pub. Svc. medal Dept. Def., 1983, Albia H.S. Career Achievement award, 1992, Navy and Marine Corps Commendation medal, 1997, Georgetown Med. Vicennial medal, 2003, 6th Naval Beach Bn. Normandy award, 2004. Fellow: ACP, Am. Coll. Rheumatology; mem.: Am. Soc. for Bone and Mineral Rsch., Osteoarthritis Rsch. Soc., Am. Soc. Clin. Pharmacology and Therapeutics, Am. Geriat. Soc., Weller-Brown Assn., Mil. Officers Assn., Johns Hopkins Med. and Surg. Assn., US Naval Inst., Harvard Club, Notre Dame Monogram Club, Chevy Chase Club. Office: Procter & Gamble Pharma 8700 Mason Montgomery Rd Mason OH 45040-8006 Office Phone: 513-622-3245.

BEASLEY, BARBARA STARIN, sales executive, marketing professional; b. Nashville, Dec. 31, 1955; d. Donald Francis and Martha Murry (Bridges) S.; m. Johnny Mark Beasley, Oct. 22, 1983; children: John Thomas, Cara Nicole. BFA, So. Meth. U., 1976. Cert. strategic mktg. mgmt., Harvard Bus. Sch. Producer Bill Stokes Assn., Dallas, 1976-80; Mary Kay Cosmetics, Inc., Dallas, 1980-93, sr. v.p. mktg., 1987-89, exec. v.p. sales, 1990-93; sr. v.p. mktg. Nest Entertainment, Dallas, 1994-99, sr. v.p. sales and mktg., 1999-2000; freelance writer, comms. cons., 2000—. Mem. Leadership Tex., 1986. Avocation: birdwatching.

BEASLEY, BRUCE MILLER, sculptor; b. LA, May 20, 1939; s. Robert Seth and Bernice (Palmer) B.; m. Laurence Leaute, May 21, 1973; children: Julian Bernard, Celia Beranice. Student, Dartmouth Coll., 1957-59; BA, U. Calif., Berkeley, 1962. One-man shows include Everett Ellin Gallery, L.A., 1963, Kornblee Gallery, N.Y.C., 1964, Hansen Gallery, San Francisco, 1965, David Stuart Gallery, L.A., 1966, Andre Emmerich Gallery, N.Y.C., 1971, DeYoung Mus., San Francisco, 1972, Santa Barbara Mus. Art, 1973, San Diego Mus. Art, 1973, Fuller-Goldeen Gallery, San Francisco, 1981, Hooks-Epstein Gallery, Houston, 1990, 93, 95, 98, Pepperdine U., L.A., 1990, So. Oreg. State U., 1991, Sonoma State U., Rhonert Park, Calif., 1991, Fresno Art Mus., 1992, Oakland Mus., 1992, Utermann Gallery, Dortmund, Germany, 1993, Scheffel Gallery, Bad Homberg, Germany, 1993, Galerie Rudolfinum, Prague, 1994, Kunsthalle Mannheim, Germany, 1994, Harcourts Gallery, San Francisco, 1994, Galerie Wirth, Zurich, Switzerland, 1995, Yorkshire Sculpture Park, Eng., 1995, City Ctr., Dortmund, Germany, 1996, Atrium Gallery, St. Louis, 1997, Purdue U., West Lafayette, Ind., 1997, Solomon-Dubnick Gallery, Sacramento, 1997, Gwenda Jay Gallery, Chgo., 1998, Kouros Gall., N.Y.C., 1999, Math. Scis. Rsch. Inst., Berkeley, Calif., 2000, Gail Severn Gallery, Ketchum, Idaho, 2001, Silicon Valley Art Mus., Belmont, Calif., 2001, Solomon-Dubnick Gallery, Sacramento, 2002, Atrium Gallery, St. Louis, 2004, 45 Yr. Retrospective, Oakland Mus. Calif., 2005; exhibited in group shows at San Francisco Mus. of Modern Art, 1961, Mus. of Modern Art, N.Y.C., 1961,62, Dallas Mus. Contemporary Art, 1962, Musee d'Art Moderne, Paris, 1963, U. Art Mus., Berkeley, 1964, Fine Arts Museums, San Francisco, 1965, Guggenheim Mus., 1966, Krannert Art Mus., Ill., 1969, Jewish Mus., N.Y.C., 1970, Milw. Art Ctr., 1970, Expo '70, Osaka, Japan, Stanford Art Mus., 1972, Musee d'Art Moderne, Paris, 1973, Nat. Mus. Am. Art, 1980, Musee d'Art Contemporain Bordeaux, France, 1984, Kunsthalle Mannheim, 1984, Palace of Exhbns., Budapest, Hungary, 1987, Middleheim Sculpture Park, Belgium, 1987, Yorkshire Sculpture Park, Eng., 1984, 87, Hakone Open-Air Mus., Japan, 1993, 95, Landesgartenschau, Germany, 1994, Sculpture '97, Bad Homberg, Germany, Pier Walk '97, 98, 99, 2000, 01, Chgo., Galerie Wirth, Zurich, Switzerland, 1997, Darmstadt (Germany) Sculpture Biennale, 1998, Cairo Biennale, Egypt, 1998, Mus. Modern Art, San Francisco, 2000, Grounds for Sculpture, Hamilton, N.J., 2001, Solomon-Dubnick Gallery, Sacramento, 2002, Sigurjon Olafsson Mus., Reykjavik Iceland, 2003, U. Hawaii Art Gallery, 2003, Galleri Dionisi, Hollywood Calif., 2004, Sculpturesite Gallery, San Francisco, 2005, Calif. State U., Fresno, 2006, others; represented in permanent collections Mus. Modern Art, N.Y.C., Guggenheim Mus.,

N.Y.C., Musee d'Art, Paris, Nat. Mus. Am. Art, Washington, Kunsthalle Mannheim, Germany, San Francisco Mus. Modern Art, L.A. County Mus. Art, Sheldon Mem. Art Gallery, Lincoln, Nebr., Hood Mus. Art-Dartmouth Coll., Spencer Mus. Art, Lawrence, Kans., Laguna Art Mus., Franklin D. Murphy Sculpture Garden, UCLA, Crocker Art Mus., Sacramento, Seattle Art Mus., Fresno Art Mus., Xantus Janos Mus., Hungary, Fine Art Muss., San Francisco, Oakland Mus. Calif., Santa Barbara Mus. Art, San Jose (Calif.) Mus. Art, Grounds for Sculpture, Hamilton, N.J., Nora Eccles Harrison Mus., Utah State U., Logan, Sculpture Park, Isla Mujeres, Mex.; commissions include State of Calif., Oakland Mus., City San Francisco, Miami Internat. Airport, San Francisco Internat. Airport, Fed. Home Loan Bank, San Francisco, Stanford U., City Anchorage, City Salinas, Calif., Fresno Art Mus., Gateway Ctr., Walnut Creek, Calif., Village of Flossmoor, Ill., City Oakland, Calif., City of Brea, Calif., U. Oreg. Art Mus., Eugene, Miami U., Oxford, Ohio, La Jolla Crossroads, San Diego, City So. San Francisco. Home: 322 Lewis St Oakland CA 94607-1236

BEASLEY, DAMARCUS LAMONT, professional soccer player; b. Ft. Wayne, Ind., May 24, 1982; Midfielder Chgo. Fire, 2000—04, PSV Eindhoven, Netherlands, 2004—. 58 caps, 12 goals U.S. Nat. Soccer team, 2001—; mem. U.S. World Cup team, 2006. Named All-Am. H.S. co-Player of the Yr., Parade Mag., 1999; named to All-Star team, Major League Soccer, 2003. Mailing: US Soccer Fedn 1801 S Prairie Ave Chicago IL 60616

BEASLEY, DAVID MULDROW, former governor, consultant; b. Lamar, SC, Feb. 26, 1957; s. Richard Lee and Jacqueline Adele (Blackwell) B.; m. Mary Wood Payne; children Mary Hunter, Sarah Catherine, David Jr., and Samuel Ross. Student, Clemson U., 1976-78; BA, U. S.C., 1979, JD. Mem. Dist. 56 S.C. Ho. Reps., 1979-92, majority leader, 1987, mem. joint legis. com. on edn., vice chmn. joint legis. com. on children, 1987-88; atty., 1992-94; gov. State of S.C., 1995—99; fellow Inst. Politics Kennedy Sch. Govt. Harvard U., 1999; prin. Bingham Cons. Group, 1999—2001; partner Beasley, Ervin & Warr; chmn. Nat. Advisory Com. on Rural Health & Human Svcs., 2001—. Recipient Profile in Courage award, John F. Kennedy Libr. Found., 2003.*

BEASLEY, DIANA F., biology educator; BS in Sci. Edn., Univ. Va. Biology tchr. Hickory (NC) H.S., 1989—. Named NC Tchr. of Yr., 2007, NW Region Tchr. of Yr., 2006—07, Hickory Pub. Sch. Tchr. of Yr., 2005—06. Mem.: NC Sci. Tchr. Assn., Nat. Sci. Tchrs. Assn., So. Assn. Coll. and Schs. State Accreditation Team, Alpha Delta Kappa. Office: Hickory High Sch 1234 Third St NE Hickory NC 28601 Business E-Mail: beasleydi@hickory.k12.nc.us.*

BEASLEY, ED, retail executive; m. Bonnie Beasley; 1 child, Lauren. Clk. to dir. human resources People's, 1968; regional dir. store ops. Revco Pharmacy, 1990—97; dist. mgr. Rite Aid Corp., Conn., 1998, regional v.p. so. Calif., 1998—2000, v.p. store ops. NE region, 2000—01, sr. v.p. ea. divsn. Camp Hill, Pa., 2001—. Office: Rite Aid Corp 30 Hunter Lane Camp Hill PA 17011*

BEASLEY, JAMES BARNIE, JR., utilities executive; b. 1951; Coop. edn. student Ga. Power, 1969; various elec. distbn. positions Southern Co., with Alvin W. Vogtle Electric Generating Plant, 1980, v.p. Southern Nuc. Oper. Co., 1998—2003, exec. v.p. Southern Nuc. Oper. Co., 2004, pres., CEO Southern Nuc. Oper. Co., 2004—, chmn. Southern Nuc. Oper. Co., 2005—. Office: Southern Nuc 40 Inverness Center Pky Birmingham AL 35242-4809*

BEASLEY, JAMES W., JR., lawyer; b. Atlanta, July 13, 1943; s. James W. and Sara Capal (Tucker) Beasley; m. Elizabeth Barno Marshall, Nov. 28, 1986. AB cum laude, Davidson Coll., 1965; LLB cum laude, Harvard U., 1968. Bar: N.Y. 1969, DC 1971, Fla. 1972, U.S. Supreme Ct. 1973. Assoc. Sullivan & Cromwell, NYC, 1968, Wilmer, Cutler & Pickering, Washington, 1970-72; assoc., then ptnr. Paul & Thomson, Miami, Fla., 1972-78; mng. ptnr. Beasley, Olle & Downs, Miami, 1978-88; ptnr. Tew, Jordan, Schulte & Beasley, Miami, 1988-89, Cadwalader, Wickersham & Taft, Palm Beach, Fla., 1989-94, Tew & Beasley LLP, Palm Beach, 1994-97, Beasley Hauser Kramer Leonard & Galardi P.A., West Palm Beach, Fla., 1997—. Author: Florida Corporations, 1985; contbr. articles to profl. jours. Chmn. County Conv. Ctr. Adv. Bd., 1994—95, Palm Beach Opera, 2005—. Capt. US Army, 1968—70. Mem.: ATLA, ABA, Acad. Fla. Trial Lawyers, Fla. Bar Assn. Office: Beasley Hauser Kramer Leonard & Galardi PA 505 S Flagler Dr Ste 1500 West Palm Beach FL 33401-5923 Office Phone: 561-835-0900.

BEASLEY, JIM SANDERS See LEE, JACK

BEASLEY, MARK V., lawyer; b. Jackson, Mich., Feb. 13, 1954; m. Linda Beasley. AB with high distinction, U. Mich., 1976, JD cum laude, 1979. Bar: Texas 1979. Assoc. Johnson & Swanson, Dallas, 1979—84; counsel Zale Corp., Dallas, 1984—87; sr. v.p., gen. counsel, sec. Michaels Stores, Inc., Irving, Tex., 1987—. Mem.: ABA, State Bar of Tex. (mem. section on Bus. Law, Corp. Counsel, Labor & Employment Law), Dallas Bar Assn. (mem. sections on Corp. Counsel, Employment Law, Securities). Avocations: stargazing, piano. Office: Michaels Stores Inc Legal Dept 8000 Bent Branch Dr Irving TX 75063 Business E-Mail: beasleym@michaels.com.*

BEASLEY, MAURINE HOFFMAN, journalism educator, historian; b. Jan. 28, 1936; d. Dimmitt Heard and Maurine (Hieronymus) Hoffman; m. William C. McLaughlin, May 20, 1966 (div. 1969); m. Henry R. Beasley, Dec. 24, 1970; 1 child, Susan Sook BA in History, U. Mo., Columbia, 1958; MS in Journalism, Columbia U., N.Y.C., 1963; PhD in Am. Civilization, George Washington U., Washington, 1974. Edn. editor Kansas City Star, Mo., 1959—62; staff writer Washington Post, 1963—73; from asst. prof journalism to prof. U. Md., College Park, 1975—87, prof., 1987—, grad. dir. Coll. Journalism, 2000—02; sr. lectr. Fulbright Jinan U., Guangzhou, China, 2000. Author: Eleanor Roosevelt and the Media: A Public Quest for Self-Fulfillment, 1987, First Ladies and the Press: The Unfinished Partnership of the Media Age, 2005; author: (with others) Women in Media, 1977, The New Majority, 1988, Taking Their Place! Documentary History of Women and Journalism, rev., 2002 (Outstanding Acad. Books Choice, 1994, award Text and Academic Authors Assn., 2004); editor: White House Press Conferences of Eleanor Roosevelt, 1983; co-editor: Voices of Change: Southern Pulitzer Winners, 1978, One Third of a Nation, 1981 (hon. mention Washington Monthly Book award, 1982), Eleanor Roosevelt Encyclopedia, 2000 (Editor's Choice award Booklist, 2001); mem. adv. bd. Am. Journalism, 1983—, Jour. Mass Media Ethics, 1981—, Journalism and Comm. Monographs, 2002—; corr. editor: Journalism History, 1995—; contbr. articles to profl. jours. Violinist Washington Conservatory Orch., 2001—; pres. Little Falls Swimming Club, Inc. 1988-89; pub. mem. Forgeign Svc. Selection Bd. US Dept. State ,2007; bd. dirs. Nat. Capital Area Fulbright Assn., 2007-. Recipient Haiman award Speech Comm. Assn., 1995, Founders Disting. Sr. Scholar award AAUW Ednl. Found., 1999, Columbia U. Sch. Journalism Alumni award, 2000, Smith-Cotton H.S. Hall Fame award, Sedalia, Mo., 2000, Alumni award U. Mo., 2004; named One of Nation's Outstanding Tchrs. of Writing and Editing Modern Media Inst. (Poynter) and Am. Soc. Newspaper Editors, 1981, Most Outstanding Woman U. Md. College Park, Pres. Commn. on Women's Affairs, 1993; Eleanor Roosevelt studies grantee Eleanor Roosevelt Inst., 1979-80, Arthur Schlesinger rsch. fellow and grantee Roosevelt Inst., 1998; fellow Gannett Tchg. Program, 1977, Pulitzer Traveling fellow Columbia U., 1963. Mem.: AAUW (v.p. Coll. Pk. br. 2002—04), Women in Comm., Am. Journalism Historians Assn. (pres.-elect 1988—89, pres. 1989—90, Kobre award for lifetime achievement 1997, Rsch. Paper award named in her honor 1998), Internat. Assn. Mass. Comm. Rsch., Soc. Profl. Journalists (chair nat. hist. site com. 1986—87, bd. dirs. Washington chpt. 1988—90, pres. 1990—91, dir. region 2, nat. bd. dirs. 1991—92, Disting. Local Svc. award 1994, First Amendment award (with others) 1998), Assn. Edn. in Journalism and Mass Comm. (sec. history divsn. 1986—87, vice-head 1987—88, head history divsn. 1988—89, chair profl. freedom and responsibility 1990—91, exec. com. 1990—91, nat. pres. elect 1992, pres. 1993—94, leader People-to-People delegation to China and Hong Kong 1994, exec. com. 1994—95, Outstanding Contbn. to Journalism Edn. award 1994, Disting. Leadership award 2001), Nat. Press Club, Am. News Women's Club (bd. govs. 2001—03), Am. Hist. Assn., Orgn. Am. Historians, Omicron Delta Kappa, Phi Beta Kappa (pres. Gamma chpt. 2007—). Democrat. Unitarian Universalist. Home: 4920 Flint Dr Bethesda MD 20816-1746 Office: U Md Coll Journalism College Park MD 20742-7111 Home Phone: 301-320-3469; Office Phone: 301-405-2413. Business E-Mail: mbeasley@jmail.umd.edu.

BEASLEY, WILLIAM H., meteorology professor; BS, Rice U., 1967, MS, 1969; PhD, U. Tex., Dallas, 1974. Sr. staff officer, bd. on atmospheric sciences and climate NRC; assoc. prog. dir. for meteorology, program mgr., divsn. atmospheric sciences, NSF Nat. Ctr. for Atmospheric Rsch.; with U. Oklahoma, 1989—, dep. dir., Ctr. for Analysis and Prediction of Storms, 1986—91, dir., sch. meteorology, 1991—96, grad. liaison, chmn. and mem. grad. studies com., prof. meteorology. Worked with researchers Los Alamos Nat. Lab., 2004. Contbr. articles to profl. jours.; creator (radio series) WeatherWhys. Organizer, participator in summer youth academies and tchr. institutes in the Coll. Geosciences. Mem.: AAAS (sec., atmospheric and hydrospheric sciences sect.), Am. Meteorol. Soc. (mem., chmn. scientific & tech. affairs com. on atmospheric electricity), Am. Geophysical Union (mem., com. on atmospheric and space electricity, sec. & mem. program com. of the atmospheric sciences sect., editor, search committees, mem., com. on edn. and human resources). Achievements include being co-inventor Campbell Scientific CS-110 Electric Field Meter. This meter has capabilities of detecting when lightning will strike. Avocations: music, photography, gardening. Office: U Oklahoma Dept Meterology 666 Parrington Oval Norman OK 73019-0390 Office Phone: 405-325-3440. E-mail: whb@ou.edu.

BEATO, CRISTINA V., government agency administrator; b. Cuba, 1958; BS, U. N.Mex., MD, 1984. Diplomate Am. Bd. Family Practice. Assoc. dean clin. affairs, chief med. officer U. N.Mex. Health Sci. Ctr., 1999—2001; med. dir. Youth Diagnostic and Devel. Ctr., 1999—2001; dep. asst. sec. health office pub. health and sci. U.S. Dept. Health and Human Svcs., 2001—02, prin. dep. sec. health, 2002—03, acting asst. sec. health, 2003—. Rear adm. USPHS. Office: US Dept Health and Human Svcs 200 Independence Ave SW Washington DC 20201 Home: 5200 W Cedar Ln Bethesda MD 20814 Office Phone: 202-690-7694. Business E-Mail: cristina.beato@hhs.gov.

BEATON, ALBERT EUGENE, education educator; b. Boston, Aug. 9, 1931; s. Albert E. and Annie E. Beaton; m. Joan G. Flaherty; children: Albert E., Douglas L. BS, State Tchr.'s Coll., Boston, 1955; EdM, Harvard U., Cambridge, Mass., 1956, EdD, 1964. Dir. statis. lab. Harvard U., 1957—62, IBM rsch. fellow, 1962—64; rsch., sr. rsch. scientist ETS, Princeton, NJ, 1964—91; prof. Sch. Edn. Boston Coll., Mass., 1990—2002, Augustus Long prof. edn., 2002—05, Augustus Long prof. emeritus, 2005—. Vis. lectr. Princeton U., 1966—78, Trinity Coll., Dublin (Ireland) U., 1980, Stanford (Calif.) U., 1988; vis. rsch. scientist Ednl. Rsch. Ctr., Dublin, 1979—80. Co-author: The NAEP Primer, 1995, Science Achievement in the Middle School Years: IEA's Third International Mathematics and Science Study, 1996, Mathematics Achievement in the Middle School Years: IEA's Third International Mathematics and Science Study, 1996, An Overview of the Third International Mathematics and Science Study, 1999, The Benefits and Limitations of International Educational Achievement Studies, 1999, The Impact of TIMSS on the Teaching and Learning of Mathematics and Science, 2000, Secondary Analysis of the TIMSS Data, 2002; contbr. articles to profl. jours. Recipient Wilcoxon award, Technometrics, 1974, Sr. Scientist award, Ednl. Testing Svc., 1987. Mem.: Am. Statis. Assn., Psychometric Soc., Am. Ednl. Rsch. Assn., Internat. Assn. for Evaluation of Ednl. Achievement (hon.). Home: 308 Main St Norfolk MA 02056 Office: Boston Coll Chestnut Hill MA 02467

BEATRICE, RUTH HADFIELD, hypnotherapist, retired elementary school educator, financial administrator; b. Phila., Feb. 6, 1931; d. Claude and Alice Elizabeth (Smith) Hadfield; m. Michael Joseph Beatrice, May 29, 1954 BS, West Chester State U., 1953; MS, Marywood Coll., 1978; postgrad., Temple U., Pa. State U., 1978-80; cert. clinl. hypnotherapist, Phila. Hypnosis Union Inst., 1980. Cert. hypno-anaesthesia therapist Nat. Bd. Hypnotherapy and Hypnotic Anaesthesiology, 1991. Educator Bristol Twp. (Pa.) Sch. Dist., 1953-54, Phila. Sch. Dist., 1954-55; recreation dir. Phila. Dept. Recreation, 1953-57; educator Worcester (Pa.) Sch. Dist., 1958-59, Springford (Pa.) Joint Sch. Dist., 1960-61, Souderton (Pa.) Sch. Dist., 1961-63, Ctrl. Bucks Sch. Dist., Doylestown, Pa., 1970-1993; ret., 1993; clin. hypnotherapist in pvt. practice Perkasie, Pa., 1980—; clin. hypnotherapist, pvt. practice Avalon, NJ, 1980—, Port St. Lucie, Fla., Perkasie, Pa. Bus. adminstr. Beatrice Adminstrs. Co-author books on tutoring for Ptnrs. at Learning Series, 1978, 1979, 1983. Bd. mem. Pierce Free Libr., Hilltown, Pa., 1970-75; union del. Office and Profl. Employees Internat. Union Internat. Conv., Vancouver, B.C., Can., 1995; treas. Newcomers Civic Assn., Perkasie, 1964-85; me. Avalon (N.J.) Civic Assn., avalon Sr. Assn. Mem. NEA (life), AAUW, Nat. Assn. Profl. Therapists, Am. Legion Aux., Pa. State Edn. Assn. (life), Hypnotism Soc. of Pa. (v.p. Phila. br. 1993-95), Phila. Hypnosis Union Local 476 (v.p. 1993-95), Nat. Guild of Hypnotists, Nat. Bd. for Hypnotherapy and Hypnotic Anaesthesiology, Womens Assn., Ballanlfae's Angler Assn., Ballanlfrae Gulf & Yacht Club. Democrat. Presbyterian. Avocations: biking, fishing, golf, tennis, walking. Home and Office: 3192 Carrick Green Ct Port Saint Lucie FL 34952 also: 273 52d St Avalon NJ 08202 Home Phone: 772-337-1469; Office Phone: 772-337-1469, 609-368-3256. Personal E-mail: rudibea@yahoo.com.

BEATSON, LEGRANDE GUERRY, environmental health specialist; b. Lafayette, La., Oct. 23, 1950; s. LeGrande Guerry Beatson, Sr. and Ethel B. Beatson; m. Amy Wilson Beatson, Aug. 26. AS, Tidewater CC, Hampton Roads, Va., 1973; BS, U. NC, Pembroke, 1975; MS, Old Dominion U., Norfolk, Va., 1997. Registered environ. health specialist Nat. Environ. Health Assn., lic. pvt. pilot. V.p, Miracote of Va., Inc., Valsoh, 1977—97; sr. environ. health specialist Va. Dept. Health, Appomattox, 1998—. Farm owner-operator, Meherrin, Va., 1983—. Named winner, Worrell 1000 Multi-Hull Sailing Race. Mem.: Va. Environ. Health Assn. (del. 1998—2000, v.p. profl. advancement 2000—02, pres. 2002—04, immediate past pres. 2005—). Achievements include 25 years service as NCAA wrestling official. Avocations: private pilot, sailing, hunting, hiking, swimming. Home: 316 Riverside Dr Lynchburg VA 24503 Office: Va Dept Health PO Box 355 401 Court St Appomattox VA 24522 Office Phone: 434-352-2313. Office Fax: 434-352-0232. Business E-Mail: guerry.beatson@vdh.virginia.gov.

BEATT, BRUCE H., lawyer, metal products executive; b. Mpls., 1952; AB, Vassar Coll., 1974; JD, Temple U. Law Sch., 1978. Gen. counsel, sec. Jet Aviation Holdings, Inc., Teterboro, NJ, 1989—90, gen. counsel, sec., gen. mgr. fixed-base operation, 1990—91; v.p., gen. counsel, sec. Dexter Corp., 1991—2000, Stanley Works, New Britain, Conn., 2000—. Office: Stanley Works 1000 Stanley Dr New Britain CT 06053

BEATTIE, ANN, writer, educator; b. Washington, Sept. 8, 1947; d. James and Charlotte (Crosby) B.; m. Lincoln Perry. BA, Am. U., 1969; MA, U. Conn., 1970; L.H.D. (hon.), Am. U., 1983. Vis. asst. prof. U. Va., Charlottesville, 1976-77, vis. writer, 1980, Edgar Allan Poe prof., 2001—; Briggs Copeland lectr. English Harvard U., Cambridge, Mass., 1977. Author: Chilly Scenes of Winter, 1976, Distortions, 1976, Secrets and Surprises, 1979, Falling In Place, 1980, Jacklighting, 1981, The Burning House, 1982, Love Always, 1985, Where You'll Find Me, 1986, Alex Katz, 1987, Picturing Will, 1990, What Was Mine, 1991, My Life, Starring Dara Falcon, 1997, Park City: New & Selected Stories, 1998, Perfect Recall, 2000, The Doctor's House, 2002, Follies: And New Stories, 2005. Recipient Disting. Alumnae award Am. U., 1980, award in lit. Am. Acad. and Inst. Arts and Letters, 1980, PEN/Malamud award for excellence in short fiction, 2000; Guggenheim fellow, 1977. Mem. PEN, Am. Acad. Arts and Letters (v.p. lit., 1989-99), Am. Acad. Arts and Scis., Authors Guild. Office: care Janklow and Nesbit 445 Park Ave New York NY 10022-2606

BEATTIE, DONALD A., aerospace scientist, consultant; b. NYC, Oct. 30, 1929; s. James Francis and Evelyn Margaret (Hickey) B.; m. Ann Mary Kean, Mar. 27, 1973; children: Thomas James, Bruce Andrew. AB, Columbia U., 1951; MS, Colo. Sch. Mines, 1958. Regional geologist Mobil Oil Co., 1958-63; Apollo lunar expts. program mgr. NASA, 1963-72, dir. NASA energy systems div. Washington, 1978-82; v.p. Houston ops. BDM Corp., 1983-84; cons. on energy and space tech., 1984—; pres. Endosat Inc., 1991-96. Dir. advanced energy research and tech. NSF, 1973-75; dep. asst. adminstr. ERDA, 1975-77; acting asst. sec. Dept. Energy, Washington, 1977-78; solar energy coordinator U.S./USSR Coop. in Sci. and Tech.; U.S. rep. Vienna Inst. for Comparative Econ. Studies Workshop on Energy. Author, editor: History and Overview of Solar Heat Technologies, 1997; author: Taking Science to the Moon, 2001, Isscapades: The Crippling of America's Space Program, 2006; contbr. numerous articles on lunar sci., energy to profl. jours. Active Boy Scouts Am., 1958-71. Served with AC USN, 1951-56. Recipient Exceptional Service medal NASA, 1971, Sr. Exec. Service and Outstanding Performance award, 1980; Superior Achievement award Dept. Energy, 1978. Fellow AAAS; mem. Geol. Soc. Am., Am. Astronautical Soc., Nat. Space Club. Home and Office: 808 Mill Pond Ct Jacksonville FL 32259-3027 Home Phone: 904-287-0222.

BEATTIE, ELISE MEREDITH, artist; d. Albert Plaut and Virginia Woodruff; m. Gordon Richard Beattie, Sept. 6, 1986. Cert., Kauai C.C., Hawaii, 1984; student, Skidmore Coll., Saratoga Springs, NY, 1976—79; cert., Bellingham Tech. Coll., Wash., 2000. Educator Whatcom C.C., Bellingham, Wash., 2001—03, Maricopa C.C. Sys., Scottsdale, Ariz., 2003—04; juror, educator Mont. Watercolor Soc., Lewiston, 2007—. Educator Kaiser Art Ctr., Oreg., 2000—02, Daniel Smith Art Materials, Seattle, 2001—03, Spokane Art Supplies, Wash., 2005—. Exhibitions include Dunedin Mus. Fine Arts, Fla., 1999, Whatcom Mus. Art & History, Bellingham, Wash., 2000, Banana Factory Art Ctr., Bethlehem, Pa., 2002, Von Leibig Art Ctr., Naples, Fla., 2002, Lt. Gov. Bradowens Legis. Office, Olympia, Wash., 2003, Tang Art Mus., Saratoga Springs, NY, 2005, Nat. Arts Club, Catherine Lorillard Wolfe Nat. Juried Exhibit, NYC, 2005, Ronald McDonald House & City of Spokane, Wash., 2006, Nat. Assn. Women Artists, NYC, 2006, D. Samuel Neil Gallery, Watercolor Soc. NC, Hendersonville, 2007, Longview Mus. of Art, Tex., 2007. Chairperson exhbns. Charlotte County Art Guild, Punta Gorda, Fla., 1997—99. Recipient Grumbacher Gold award, 2002, Elizabeth Erlanger Meml. award, 2002; grantee Blanchette Hooker Rockefeller Found., Nat. Assn. Women Artists, 2006. Mem.: Nat. Assn. Women Artist (hon.; signature mem. 2000, award 2002), Watercolor Soc. NC (assoc.), NW Water Color Soc. (assoc.), Am. Water Color Soc. (assoc.), Nat. Water Color Soc. (assoc.), Catherine Loriilard Wolfe Art Club (assoc.), Mont. Water Color Soc. (life; signature mem. 2002, award 2002, 2003, 2004, 2005, Merchandise Merit award 2004, 2005, Nancy Beelman Meml. award 2002), Fla. Water Color Soc. (life), Salmagundi Art Club (juried artist mem. 2007). Avocations: art education, holistic health and nutrition, raising and breeding great danes. Home and Office: PO Box 1139 Morehead City NC 28557 Personal E-mail: artist@embart.com.

BEATTIE, GEORGE CHAPIN, retired orthopedist, surgeon; b. Bowling Green, Ohio, Sept. 24, 1919; s. George Wilson and Mary Turner B.; m. Nancy U. Fant, Mar. 1, 1947; children: Michael, Suzanne, Eric. BA, Bowling Green State U., 1939; MD, U. Chgo., 1943. Diplomate Am. Bd. Orthopaedic Surgery. Commd. lt. (j.g.) MC USN, 1943, advanced through grades to lt. comdr., 1951; med. officer, intern U.S. Naval Hosp., Great Lakes, Ill., 1943-44; resident, fellow in orthopaedic surgery Lahey Clinic, Boston, 1944; ward med. officer orthopaedic services Naval Hosp., Guam, 1944-46; sr. med. officer USN, Manus Island, Papua New Guinea, 1946; resident tng. in orthopaedic surgery U.S. Naval Hosp. St. Albans, NYC, 1947-48; resident in orthopaedic surgery Children's Hosp., Boston, 1949; asst. chief orthopaedic surgery U.S. Naval Hosp. Oak Knoll, Oakland, Calif., 1950-52; comdg. officer med. co. 1st Marine Div. Med. Bn., Republic of Korea, 1952-53; chief orthopaedic service Dept. Phys. Medicine and Navy Amputee Ctr. U.S. Naval Hosp., Phila., 1954; resigned USN, 1954; practice medicine specializing in orthopaedic surgery San Francisco, 1954-99; ret., 1999. Co-chmn. handicapping conditions com. Health Action Study San Mateo County, 1965; 1st chmn. orthopaedic sect. surg. dept. Peninsula Hosp. and Med. Ctr., Burlingame, Calif., 1967, chmn. rehab. service, 1967-71, chmn. phys. therapy and rehab. com., 1956—, vice chmn. orthopaedic dept., 1973-76, chmn., 1977-79; med. dir. research and rehab. ctr. San Mateo (Calif.) County Soc. Crippled Children and Adults, 1958-63; mem. exec. com. Harold D. Chope Community Hosp., San Mateo, 1971-76, chief, co-chmn. orthopaedic sect., 1971-76; chief orthopaedic surg. sect. Mills Meml. Hosp., San Mateo, 1976-78; others. Contbr. articles to profl. jours. Active Indian Guides, 1972-77; pres. Calif. Easter Seal Soc., 1969-71. Decorated Bronze Star. Fellow Am. Acad. Orthopaedic Surgeons (exhibit com. 1979-86); mem. AMA (Billings Bronze medal 1954), Internat. Soc. for Prosthetics and Orthotics, Western Orthopaedic Assn. (pres., bd. dirs. 1986), Leroy Abbott Orthopaedic Soc. U. Calif. San Francisco (assoc. clin. prof.), Alpha Omega Alpha.

BEATTIE, RICHARD IRWIN, lawyer; b. NYC, Mar. 24, 1939; s. Richard I. Beattie and Ruth (Fisher) McCarthy; m. Diana Lewis, Dec. 21, 1963; children: Lisa C., Nina M. BA, Dartmouth Coll., 1961; LLB, U. Pa., 1968; EdD, Bank Street Coll. Bar: N.Y. 1968, U.S. Dist. Ct. (so. and ea. dists.) N.Y. 1972, U.S. Ct. Appeals (2d cir.) 1975, U.S. Ct. Appeals (D.C. cir.) 1977, U.S. Supreme Ct. 1978, U.S. Ct. Appeals (5th cir.) 1979. Dep. gen. counsel US Dept. Health, Edn. & Welfare, Washington, 1977-78, exec. asst. to sec., 1978-79, gen. counsel, 1978-79; spl. counsel to sec., dir. transition US Dept. Edn., Washington, 1980; assoc. Simpson, Thacher & Bartlett LLP, NYC, 1968-75, ptnr., 1975-77, 80—, chmn. firm & mem. exec. com., 1991; non-exec. chmn. Heidrick & Struggles Internat. Inc., NYC, 2007—. Teaching fellow Harvard U., 1979-81; chmn. Commn. Reorgn. of Human Resources Adminstrn., N.Y.C., 1984-85, Commn. on Spl. Edn., N.Y.C., 1984-85; Mem. Mayor's Coun. Fgn. Rels., N.Y.C. Mem. Bd. Edn., N.Y.C., 1986-87.; bd. trustees WNET/Channel 13, N.Y.C., 1983—, Natural Resources Def. Counsel, N.Y.C., 1984-86, Carnegie Corp., 1988—; chmn. fund N.Y.C. Pub. Edn, 1989—; bd. dirs. Nat. Women's Law Ctr., Am. Ditchley Found., Am. Restaurant Group, Inst. Internat. Edn., Am.-Israel Friendship League; mem. Mayor's Task Force on AIDS. Capt. USMC, 1961-65; Mem. Hosp. Cancer & Allied Diseases; Meml. Sloan-Kettering Cancer Ctr., chmn.; New Visions Pub. Sch., founder & chmn. bd. Jet pilot USMC. Mem.: Bar Assn. City NY.

Avocations: skiing, mountain climbing. Office: Simpson Thacher & Bartlett LLP 425 Lexington Ave Fl 15 New York NY 10017-3954 Office Phone: 212-455-2635. Office Fax: 212-455-2502. Business E-Mail: rbeatie@stblaw.com.*

BEATTLE, E. SCOTT, cosmetics executive; MBA, Univ. Western Ont. Mgr. Accenture Consulting; v.p mergers and acquisitions grp. Merrill Lynch, Inc.; co-founder, mng. dir. Bedford Capital Corp., 1990; chmn., pres., CEO Elizabeth Arden Inc., NYC, 1992—. Mem. bd. dirs. The Fragrance Found., Bedford Capital Corp., Object Video, Inc., Ivy Sch. Bus. Finalist Ernst & Young Entrepreneur of Yr., 2003; named Most Innovative Marketer of Yr., WWD Beauty Biz, 2006. Mem.: Cosmetic, Toiletry, Fragrance Assn. (bd. mem., mem. exec. com., honored exec. 2005). Office: Elizabeth Arden Inc 200 Park Ave S 7th Fl New York NY 10003*

BEATTS, ANNE PATRICIA, writer; b. Buffalo, Feb. 25, 1947; d. Patrick Murray Threipland and Sheila Elizabeth Jean (Sherriff Scott) B. BA with honors, McGill U., Montreal, Que., Can., 1966. Contbg. editor National Lampoon mag., NYC, 1970-74; writer Saturday Night Live NBC, NYC, 1975-80; creator, prodr. Square Pegs CBS, Los Angeles, 1982-83; co-exec. prodr. A Different World NBC, Los Angeles, 1987-88; exec. prodr. The Stephanie Miller Show, 1994-95. Writer, creative cons. Saturday Night Live 25th Ann. Spl., 1999; exec. story cons. (WETV) Committed, 2000-01; head writer WGA Awards, 2004; co-exec. prodr., co-dir. John Waters Presents Movies That Will Corrupt You, Here! TV, 2006; adj. prof. writing divsn. Sch. Cinema-TV, U. So. Calif., 2003-07. Co-editor: (humorous books) Titters, 1976, Saturday Night, 1977; co-author: (humorous books) Titters 101, 1984, The Mom Book, 1986; author book for Broadway mus. Leader of the Pack, 1985; humor columnist L.A. Times, 1997-98. Mem. AFTRA, SAG, Writers Guild Am. (award 1976, 77, 2000), Dirs. Guild Am., Women in Film, Dramatists Guild, NATAS (2 Emmy awards, 6 Emmy award nominations 1975-80, 2000). Office Phone: 310-550-4525. Personal E-mail: beattsclass@aol.com.

BEATTY, FRANCES, civic worker; b. Chgo., Apr. 17, 1940; d. Pasquale and Rose (Brunetti) Calomeni; m. Robert Alfred Beatty, Aug. 24, 1963; children: Bradford, Roxanna Beatty Goebel. BA, Northwestern U., 1961; MA, U. Chgo., 1967. Tchr. math. Proviso West High Sch., Hillside, Ill., 1961-66. Active Oak Brook Dist. 53 Sch. Bd., 1979-85; women's bd. Field Mus. Natural History, Chgo., 1985—, founders coun., 1988—, treas. women's bd., 1991-93; governing bd. Chgo. Symphony, 1985-92; trustee Chgo. Symphony Orch., 1992-96, life trustee, 2005—; women's bd. Ravinia Festival, Highland Park, Ill., 1987—, Northwestern U., Evanston, Ill., sec. women's bd., 1999-2001, libr. bd., 1990-95; women's bd. U. Chgo.; mem. coun. Wellness House, Hinsdale, Ill., 1994; com. mem. Chgo. Humanities Festival, 1999-2003; treas. 626 Landmark Found., 2005—, v.p. Mem.: 626 Found. (sec., treas. 2005—), Merit Sch. Music, Alumnae of Northwestern U. (pres. 1996—98), The Antiquarian Soc. Art Inst. Chgo., John Evans Club, Woman's Athletic Club Chgo. (3d v.p. 1985—87, 1st v.p. 1992—94, pres. 1994—96).

BEATTY, JAMETHA ANN, communications educator; b. Lawton, Okla., Dec. 10, 1945; d. J. T. and Lou Ann Noel; m. Gregory Alan Beatty, Aug. 11, 1978; children: William, James. BA in English Edn., U. Ariz., Tucson, 1974; MA in ESL, San Francisco State U., 1980; PhD in Rhetoric and Linguistics, Ind. U. Pa., 2003. Assoc. prof., chair humanities and comm. dept. Embry-Riddle Aero. U., Prescott, Ariz., 1982—. Founding pres. Prescott Poets, 1989; featured reader Pantry Poetry Series, Prescott, 1990, Prescott Libr. Program, 1990; marshall faculty senate Embry-Riddle Aero. U., 1999. Contbr. poetry to anthologies. Recipient Poetry in Motion Silver award, Ariz. State Poetry Soc., 1991, Merit award, 1994. Mem.: Coll. English Assn., Western States Comm. Assn., Delta Kappa Gamma, Phi Kappa Phi. Office: Embry-Riddle Aero U 3700 Willow Creek Rd Prescott AZ 86301 Office Phone: 928-777-6967.

BEATTY, JOHN CABEEN, JR., judge; b. Washington, Apr. 13, 1919; s. John Cabeen and Jean (Morrison) B.; m. Clarissa Hager, Feb. 8, 1943 (dec. Apr. 4 1996); children: John Cabeen III, Clarissa Jean; m. Virginia R. Campbell, May 10, 1997. AB, Princeton U., 1941; JD, Columbia U., 1948. Bar: Oreg. 1948. Pvt. practice law, Portland, Oreg., 1948-70; ptnr. Dusenbery, Martin, Beatty, Bischoff & Templeton, 1956-70, of counsel, 1985-96; judge Cir. Ct., Oreg., 1970-85, sr. judge Oreg., 1985—. Mem. Oreg. Bd. Bar Examiners, 1953-54; chmn. legis. com. Oreg. Jud. Conf., 1976-82; mem. Oreg. CSC, 1962-64, Oreg. Law Enforcement Coun., 1974-77; vice chmn. Oreg. Commn. Jud. Br., 1979-85; vice chmn. Oreg. Criminal Justice Coun., 1985-90. Author: D Day to VE Day, 1946, The Fourth Part of Gaul, 2004. Mem. legis. com. Nat. Sch. Bds. Assn., 1966-68, chmn. coun. large city sch. bds., 1967-68; counsel Dem. Party Oreg., 1956-58; co-chmn. Oreg. for Kennedy Com., 1968; bd. dirs. Portland Pub. Schs., 1964-70, chmn., 1967, 69; chmn. policy adv. com. on hazardous waste Dept. Environ. Quality, 1985-86; mem. Mayor's Spl. Rev. Commn., 1986; chmn. various adv. coms. Dept. Environ. Quality, 1987-89; chmn. tech. adv. com. Willamette River Basin Water Quality Study, 1990-94; chmn. city club study Oreg. Initiative and Referendum, 1994-95; chmn. Oreg. Initiative Com., 1996-2000. Capt. AUS, 1941-46, ETO. Decorated Bronze Star medal; recipient City Club of Portland award, 1967. Mem.: ABA, Oreg. Bar Assn., Oreg. Hist. Soc. (dir. 1973—92), City Club (past pres., bd. govs.), Racquet Club. Home and Office: 3331 SW Mitchell St Portland OR 07239-1260 Home Phone: 503-452-3358. Personal E-mail: jcbeatty@comcast.net.

BEATTY, JUDY IOLA SPENCER, library director; b. McAllen, Tex., Oct. 12, 1954; d. Wayne Ellsworth and Vivian Ruth (Comer) S.; children: Amanda Marie, Emily Renee, Matthew Spencer. Student, Iowa Ctrl. C.C., 1973-75, LaSalle U. Libr. dir. Gentry County Libr., Stanberry, Mo. Mem. ALA, AAUW, Mo. Libr. Assn., Mo. Pub. Libr. Dirs. (pres. 2004-05), Grand River Libr. Assn., Am. Legion Aux. Avocations: music, reading, gardening.

BEATTY, KENNETH ORION, JR., chemical engineer, educator; b. East Lansdowne, Pa., Dec. 18, 1913; s. Kenneth Orion and Ada Pearl (Marshall) B.; m. Mary Catharine Carter, Aug. 8, 1936; children: Susan Jennifer, Prudence Carter, Lucy Margaret. BS, Lehigh U., 1935, MS, 1937; PhD, U. Mich., 1946. Registered profl. engr., N.C. Raybestos-Manhattan fellow Lehigh U., 1935-37; chem. engr. Dow Chem. Co., Midland, Mich., 1937-39; asst. prof. chem. engring. U. R.I., Kingston, 1939-44; rsch. assoc. U. Mich., 1944-46; assoc. prof. N.C. State U., Raleigh, 1946-48, prof., 1948—, acting head dept. chem. engring., 1959-60, R.J. Reynolds Industries prof. chem. engring., 1961—, spl. cons. in forensic engring., 1982—. Dir. Carolina Cons. Scientists and Engrs., 1979-87; vis. prof. chem. engring. Ohio State U., summer 1949; vis. engr. Pratt & Whitney Co., Middletown, Conn., summer 1957; resident cons. engr. Nat. Lead Co. of Ohio, Fernald, summer 1959; mem. Max Jakob Award Com., 1963-67, chmn., 1966; mem. Nat. Heat Transfer Conf. Coordinating Com., 1965-71, chmn., 1967; coordinating chmn. 9th Nat. Heat Transfer Conf., Seattle, 1967; U.S. founding del. Assembly for Internat. Heat Transfer Conf., 1967-72; mem. sci. council Internat. Center for Heat and Mass Transfer, Yugoslavia, 1971-90. Contbr. articles to profl. jours. Mem. N.C. Gov.'s Sci. Adv. Com. Rsch. grantee NASA, NSF, Wright Air Devel. Center, AEC, Am. Soc. Refrigerating Engrs.; Princeton U. fellow, 1967-68. Fellow AIChE; mem. Am. Chem. Soc., University Park Homeowners Assn. Home: 323 Shepherd St Raleigh NC 27607-4031 Office Phone: 919-833-7626. E-mail: kennethbeatty@toast.net.

BEATTY, MARK A., librarian; Automation libr. Wis. Interlibr. Svc. Mem. Librarians Assembly, U. Wis.-Madison. Mem.: Wis. Libr. Assn., Libr. and Info. Tech. Assn. (mem. bd. dirs. 2003—, mem. exec. com. 2005—, bd. liaison to top tech. trends com., pres. 2007—). Office: Wis Interlibrary Svc 728 State St Rm 464 & B106B Madison WI 53706 Office Phone: 608-265-5719. Office Fax: 608-262-6067. Business E-Mail: mbeatty@wils.wisc.edu.*

BEATTY, MICHAEL L., lawyer; b. 1947; s. Herbert Francis and Lola (Stuewe) B.; m. Kathleen Murphy; children: Erin, Piper. BA, U. Calif., 1969; JD, Harvard U., 1972. Bar: Tex. 1972. Assoc. mem. Vinson and Elkins, 1972-74; prof. U. Idaho, 1974-79; vis. prof. law U. Wyo., 1980-81; atty. Colo. Interstate Gas Co., 1981-84, gen. counsel, 1984-85; with The Coastal Corp., Houston, 1985-93, exec. v.p., gen. counsel, 1989-93; with Akin, Gump, Strauss, Hauer & Feld LLP, Houston, 1993-98; prin. Michael L. Beatty & Assocs., P.C., Denver, 1998; ptnr. Beatty & Wozniak, P.C., Denver. Chief of staff Colo. Gov. Roy Romer, 1993—95. Office: Beatty & Wozniak PC 216 16th Str Ste 1100 Columbine Plc Denver CO 80202 Office Phone: 303-294-4499. Office Fax: 303-407-4494. Business E-Mail: mbeatty@bwenergylaw.com.

BEATTY, NED, actor; b. Louisville, July 6, 1937; s. Charles William and Margaret (Lennis) B.; m. Walta Addott, 1959 (div. 1968); m. Belinda Beatty, 1971 (div.); m. Dorothy Tinker Lindsay, June 28, 1979 (div. Mar. 1998); m. Sandra Johnson, Nov. 20, 1999; children: Douglas, Charlie and Lennis (twins), Wally, John, Blossom, Thomas, Dorothy. Student pub. schs., Ky. Actor: Barter Theatre, Abingdon, Va., 1957-66, Arena Stage, Washington, 1963-71, (films) include Deliverance, 1972, The Thief Who Came to Dinner, 1972, The Front Page, 1974, Nashville, 1975, W.W. and The Dixie Dancekings, 1975, Network, 1976, All the Presidents' Men, 1976, The Big Bus, 1976, Micky and Nicky, 1976, Silver Streak, 1976, Exorcist II: The Heretic, 1977, Superman, 1978, Gray Lady Down, 1978, The Great Georgia Bank Hoax, 1978, The Passage, 1979, Promises in the Dark, 1979, The Incredible Shrinking Woman, 1981, Superman II, 1981, The Toy, Hopscotch, Touched, 1983, Stroker Ace, 1983, Back to School, 1986, Restless Natives, 1986, The Big Easy, 1987, The Fourth Protocol, 1987, The Unholy, Switching Channels, 1988, Physical Evidence, 1989, A Cry In the Wilderness, 1990, Angel Square, 1990, Hear My Song, 1991, Prelude To A Kiss, 1992, Ed and his Dead Mother, 1993, Rudy, 1993, Radioland Murders, 1994, The Legend of O.B. Taggart, 1995, Just Cause, 1995, Cookie's Fortune, 1998, He Got Game, 1998, Spring Forward, 1999, Life, 1999, The Beautiful Life, 2002, Where the Red Fern Grows, 2003, Sweet Land, 2005, The Walker, 2007, Shooter, 2007; TV films include: The Execution of Private Slovik, 1974, The FBI Story: The FBI Versus The Ku Klux Klan, 1975, The Deadly Tower, 1975, Hunter, 1976, Friendly Fire, 1979, The Last Days of Pompeii, 1984, Celebrity, 1984, Robert Kennedy and His Times, The Last Train Home, 1990, Lockerbie, 1990, Back to Hannibal, 1990, T. Bone and Weasel, 1992, The Affair, 1995, Gulliver's Travels, 1996, Crazy Horse, 1996, Homicide: The Movie, 2000, Roughing It, 2002, The Wool Cap, 2004; (miniseries) Trial, Larry McMurtry's Streets of Laredo, 1995, I Was a Rat, 2001; star: (TV series) Szysznyk, 1977, Homicide, 1993-95. Office: Miller & Co Mgmt 10850 Wilshire Blvd Ste 400 Los Angeles CA 90024-4316*

BEATTY, PERRIN, business association executive; b. Toronto; married; 2 children. Student, Upper Can. Coll., Toronto, U. Western Ont. Elected mem. Parliament, 1972; cabinet min. Min. of State-Treasury Bd., 1979, Min. of Nat. Revenue, 1984; solicitor gen., 1985; min. of nat. def., 1986; min. of health, 1989; min. of comms., 1991; min. external affairs, 1993; pres., CEO Can. Broadcasting Corp., 1995-1999, Canadian Mfrs. & Exporters, Ottawa, Ont., 1999—. Former hon. vis. prof. dept. polit. sci. U. We. Ont.; former columnist Toronto Sun. Office: CME 1 Nicholas St Ste 1500 Ottawa ON Canada K1N 7B7

BEATTY, VIRGINIA LEWIS, librarian, archivist, consultant; b. Quirigua, Guatemala, Mar. 8, 1930; (parents Am. citizens); d. Bevan Blau and Margaret Julia (Ward) Lewis; m. William Kaye Beatty, June 14, 1952 (dec. Dec. 2002); children: Margaret M., William B.K.(dec.) , Carol E. BS, Purdue U., 1951; MS in Libr. Sci., Columbia U., NYC, 1953; postgrad., Northwestern U., Evanston, Ill., 1983—86. Cert. arborist Ill. Lit. rschr. Atomic Energy Commn. Savannah River project DuPont, Wilmington, Del., 1952—53; founder., dir. Med. Lit. Svc. Coll. Physicians, Phila., 1953—56; cons. med. lit. Beatty and Beatty, Columbia, Mo., 1956—64, cons. environ. edn. and urban horticulture Evanston, 1964—; libr., archivist emeritus Frances E. Willard Meml. Libr., Evanston, 1990—; chmn. restoration Evanston soldiers Meml. Movement Patriots Park, 2006—07. Coord. ednl. and amateur exhibits Chgo. World Flower and Garden Show, 1970—74. Author: Rating and Raising Indoor Plants, 1975, Rating and Raising Vegetables, 1977, Annie Wittenmyer, Mentor to Millions, 2002, Anna Adams Gordon, The Can Do President, 2006. Vol. Chgo. Pub. Schs., 1968—2001, Chgo. Housing Authority, 1973—91, Field Mus., Chgo., 1975—90. Recipient Gov. award, Chgo. World Flower and Garden Show, 1972, Mayor's award, 1973, Conservation medal, Nat. Soc. DAR, 1976, Mag. Editor award, Nat. Arbor Day Fond., 1981, Omohundro Environ. Svc. award, Evanston Environ. Assn., 2000; scholar, Med. Libr. Assn., 1952. Fellow: Garden Writers Assn.; mem.: Med. Libr. Assn. (co-archivist 1979—86). Avocations: gardening, travel, ceramics. Office: Frances E Willard Meml Libr 1730 Chicago Ave Evanston IL 60201 Personal E-mail: urbanhort@earthlink.net.

BEATTY, WARREN, actor, film director, film producer; b. Richmond, Va., Mar. 30, 1937; s. Ira O. and Kathlyn (MacLean) Beaty; m. Annette Bening, Mar.12, 1992; children: Kathlyn, Benjamin, Isabel, Ella Corrine. Student, Northwestern U., 1956, Stella Adler Theatre Sch., NYC, 1957. Actor: (films) Splendor in the Grass, 1961, The Roman Spring of Mrs. Stone, 1962, All Fall Down, 1962, Lilith, 1963, Mickey One, 1965, Promise Her Anything, 1965, Kaleidoscope, 1966, The Only Game in Town, 1969, McCabe and Mrs. Miller, 1971, $(Dollars), 1971, The Parallax View, 1974, The Fortune, 1975, Town and Country, 2001; actor, prodr. Bonnie and Clyde, 1967 (Acad. award nomination for Best Actor), Ishtar, 1987; actor, prodr., co-screenwriter Shampoo, 1975 (Acad. award nomination for best screenplay); actor, prodr., co-dir., co-screenwriter, Heaven Can Wait, 1978 (Acad. award nominations for Best Actor, Best Dir. and Best Screenplay); actor, dir., prodr., co-screenwriter, Reds, 1981 (Acad. award for Best Dir., 1981); actor, dir. Dick Tracy, 1990; actor, co-prodr., Bugsy, 1991; actor, prodr., writer Love Affair, 1994, Bulworth, 1998; exec. prodr. The Pick-Up Artist, 1987; actor: (TV appearances) Studio One, 1948, What's My Line, 1950, Vibe, 1997; appeared in Broadway play A Loss of Roses, 1960 Recipient Irving G. Thalberg Memorial award, Acad. Motion Picture Arts & Sciences, 1999, American Soc. of Cinematographers Bd. of Governors award, 2000, BAFTA Fellowship, 2002, Kennedy Ctr. Honors, John F. Kennedy Ctr. Performing Arts, 2004, Cecil B. DeMille award, Hollywood Fgn. Press Assn., 2007. Mem. Dirs. Guild Am. Democrat. Office: Creative Artists Agy care Risa Gertner 9830 Wilshire Blvd Beverly Hills CA 90212-1804

BEATUS, BRIAN J., lawyer; b. Queens, NY, Jan. 17, 1967; BSEE cum laude, Boston Univ., 1989, JD, 1993. Bar: NY 1992, DC 1992, Calif. 1999, Pa. (inactive), US Dist. Ct. (no. & ctrl. dist. Calif., ea. dist. Tex.), US Ct. Appeals (Fed., DC, 9th cir.). Ptnr., head Silicon Valley Intellectual Property dept. Pillsbury Winthrop Shaw Pittman, Palo Alto, Calif. Named one of Silicon Valley's Top 300 Lawyers, San Jose mag., 2003, Silicon Valley's Top Legal Eagles, 2004. Mem.: ABA, Am. Intellectual Property Law Assn. Office: Pillsbury Winthrop Shaw Pittman 2475 Hanover St Palo Alto CA 94304-1114 Office Phone: 650-233-4683. Office Fax: 650-233-4545. Business E-Mail: brian.beatus@pillsburylaw.com.

BEATY, JAMES ARTHUR, JR., federal judge; b. 1949; m. Toyoko Christine Beaty; 1 child. BA cum laude, Western Carolina U., 1971; JD, U. N.C., 1974; postgrad., U. Nev., 1985—91; LHD (hon.), Western Carolina U., 2002. With Richard C. Erwin, Winston-Salem, NC, 1974—77; atty. at law Ewrin and Beaty, Winston-Salem, 1977—78, Beaty and Friende, Winston-Salem, 1980—81; pvt. practice Winston-Salem, 1978—79; judge N.C. Superior Ct., 1981—94; dist. judge U.S. Dist. Ct. (mid. dist.) N.C., 1994—. Recipient Disting. Alumni award, Western Carolina U., 1994. Mem.: ABA, NAACP (life), N.C. Assn. Black Lawyers (sec. 1976, v.p. 1978), N.C. Acad. Trial Lawyers (named outstanding trial ct. judge of yr. 1990), Winston-Salem Bar Assn., Forsyth County and 21st Jud. Dist. Bar, N.C. State Bar, Rotary Club, Sigma Pi Phi, Alpha Phi Alpha. Office: 251 N Main St Rm 248 Winston Salem NC 27101-3914

BEAUBIEN, ANNE KATHLEEN, librarian; b. Detroit, Sept. 15, 1947; d. Richard Parker and Edith Mildred Beaubien; m. Philip Conway Berry, Feb. 7, 2004. Student, Western Mich. U., 1965-67; BA, Mich. State U., 1969; MLS, U. Mich., 1970. Reference libr., bibliographic instr. U. Mich. Libr., Ann Arbor, 1971-80, dir. MITS, 1980-85, dir. coop. access svc., 1985—, head bus. and fin. office, 1995—2000, grants officer, 2000—. Author: Psychology Bibliography, 1980; co-author: Learning the Library, 1982; contbg. articles to profl. jour., editor, conf. proc., 1987. Mem. vestry St. Clare's Episcopal Ch., Ann Arbor, 1986—89, 2002—03; pres. Ann Arbor Ski Club, 1978—79. Recipient Woman of Yr. Award, Ann Arbor Bus. and Profl. Women's Club, 1982, Disting. Alumnus Award Sch. Info. and Libr. Studies, U. Mich., 1987, Virginia Boucher OCLC Disting. ILL Libr. award, 2007. Mem. ALA (Virginia Boucher-OCLC Disting. Interlibrary Loan Libr. award, 2007), Assn. Coll. and Rsch. Librs. (pres. 1991-92). Avocations: skiing, bicycling, ballroom dancing. Office: U Mich Libr 106 Hatcher Grad Libr Ann Arbor MI 48109 Office Phone: 734-936-2322. Business E-Mail: beaubien@umich.edu.

BEAUCHAMP, E(DWARD) WILLIAM, priest, lawyer, university administrator, management educator; b. Detroit, Mich., May 17, 1942; s. Edward F. and Marion K. Beauchamp. BS in Acctg., U. Detroit, 1964, MBA, 1966; postgrad., Mich. State U., 1966-71; JD, U. Notre Dame, 1975, MDiv, 1981; D (hon.), U. Notre Dame Australia, 2005. Bar: Mich. 1975; ordained priest Roman Cath. Ch., Holy Cross Order, 1982. Tchr., assoc. dir. admissions Alma (Mich.) Coll., 1966-71; ptnr. Goggin, Baker and Beauchamp, Alma, 1975-77; asst. prof. mgmt., adminstrv. asst. to exec. v.p. U. Notre Dame, South Bend, Ind., 1980-84, exec. asst. to pres., 1984-87, exec. v.p., 1987—2002; sr. v.p. Univ. Portland, Oreg., 2002—03, pres., 2003—. Bd. dirs. Lumina Found. Recipient Wall St. Jour. award, 1964, Bernstein, Bernstein, Wile and Gordon award, 1963. Office: Univ of Portland 5000 N Willamette Blvd Portland OR 97203-5798*

BEAUCHAMP, JESSE LEE (JACK BEAUCHAMP), chemistry professor; b. Glendale, Calif., Nov. 1, 1942; m. Patricia Margaret Beauchamp; children: Melissa Ann, Thomas Alton, Amanda Jane, Ryan Howell, Michael Andrew. BS with honors in Chemistry, Calif. Inst. Tech., 1964; PhD in Chemistry, Harvard U., 1967. Arthur Amos Noyes instr. in Chemistry Calif. Inst Tech., Pasadena, 1967-69, asst. prof. chemistry, 1969-71, assoc. prof. chemistry, 1971-74, prof. chemistry, 1974—2000, Mary and Charles Ferkel prof. chemistry, 2000—. Panelist chem. rsch. evaluation Directorate of Chem. Scis. Air Force Office of Sci. Rsch., 1978-81, adv. panelist high energy density materials, 1988-92; exec. com. advanced light source users, LBL, 1984-87; exptl. evaluation com. TRIUMPH, U. B.C., 1985-88; grad. fellow selection panel, NSF, 1986-89; postdoctoral selection panel NATO, 1987-89; mem. com. critical techs.: role of Chemistry and Chem. Enging. Nat. Rsch. Coun., 1991-92; chmn. com. on comml. aviation security Nat. Materials Adv. Bd., Nat. Rsch. Coun., 1994-97; mem. Nat. Materials Adv. Bd. (NRC), 1997-00; commr. White House commn. on aviation safety and security, 1996-97; mem. adv. bd. Inst. Atomic and Molecular Scis., Academica Sinica, Taiwan, 2004-. Mem. editl. adv. bd. Chemical Physics Letters, 1981-87, Jour. Am. Chem. Soc., 1984-87, Jour Physical Chemistry, 1984-87, Organometallics, 1989-92, Interat. Jour. Chemical Kinetics, 1990—, The Ency. Mass Spectrometry, 2000-. Woodrow Wilson fellow Harvard U., 1964-65, NSF grad. fellow, 1965-67; fellow Alfred P. Sloan Found., 1967-70; tchr.-scholar Camille and Henry Dreyfus, 1971-76; meml. fellow John Simon Guggenheim, 1976-77. Fellow AAAS; mem. NAS (com. chem. scis., chem. kinetics subgroup 1980-83), Am. Chem. Soc. (award in pure chemistry 1978, exec. com. divsn. physical chem., 1980-82, Peter Debye award in phys. chemistry 1999, Frank H. Field and Joe L. Franklin award 2003), Am. Assn. Mas. Spectometry, Aircraft Owners and Pilots Assn., Soc. Fellows Harvard U. Office: Calif Inst Tech Dept of Chemistry Noyes Lab 127 # 72 Pasadena CA 91125-0001

BEAUCHAMP, MILES PHILIP, editor, columnist, consultant; b. LA, Apr. 17, 1953; s. Henry and Kathrinjo (Shelton) B.; m. Michelle Colleen Ryan, July 1, 1989. BA, San Diego State U., 1993, MA, 1994; PhD, Warnborough U. V.p. Beauchamp Co. Hotels, San Diego, 1972-84; editor, columnist Asian Jour. newspaper, San Diego, 1985—; instr. U.S. Internat. U., San Diego, 1996—. Asst. Alliant Internat. U., 1996—; instr. Nat. Univ., 1996—; cons. The Writing Ctr., San Diego, 1992—96, Main Street mag., San Diego, 1994—95. Co-author: The Exquisite Cadaver, 1993; author: A New Way of Looking, 1996; editor: Filipinos in America, 1992; columnist Still Amazed, 1985-96. Profl. devel. facilitator Grossmont Coll., San Diego, 1990—; tchr. writing St. Vincent De Paul Shelter, San Diego, 1992; tchr., facilitator Profls. in Schs., San Diego, 1990—. Recipient award of appreciation San Diego Journalism Edn. Assn., 1992, San Diego Pub. Libr., 1994, Georgi awards Writers Fedn. Am., 1993. Mem. Film and Video Artists Assn., Writers Haven, San Diego Press Club. Avocations: travel, boating, photography. Office: Asian Jour Newspaper 550 E 8th St Ste 6 National City CA 91950 E-mail: milespb@cox.net.

BEAUCHAMP, ROBERT E., information technology executive; BBA, Univ. Tex. Austin; MS in Mgmt., Houston Baptist Univ., 2001. Various positions in R&D, strategic marketing and corp. develop. BMC Software, Inc., 1988—2001, pres., CEO, 2001—. Mem. bd. dir. Nat. Oilwell Varco, Inc., Memorial Herman Hospital Sys., Tex. Med. Ctr., NYSE Listed Co. Adv. Bd. With Greater Houston Partnership, Ctr. Houston's Future; adv. Houston Tech. Ctr., Indo-Am.C. of C. Greater Houston. Recipient Distinguished Alumnus, Houston Baptist Univ. Office: BMC Software Inc 2101 City West Blvd Houston TX 77042-2827 Office Phone: 713-918-8800. Office Fax: 713-918-8000.

BEAUDET, ARTHUR L., medical genetics researcher; b. Woonsocket, RI, July 4, 1942; s. Louis George and Sylvia Mary (Lareau) B.; m. Marjorie Adelynn Miller, June 10, 1967; m. Nicole, Alissa. BS in Biology magna cum laude, Holy Cross Coll., Worcester, 1963; MD cum laude, Yale U., 1967. Diplomate Nat. Bd. Med. Examiners, 1968, Am. Bd. Pediatrics, 1973, Am. Bd. Med. Genetics, 1982, 93. Pediatric resident John Hopkins Hosp., Balt., 1967-69; rsch. assoc. NIH, Bethesda, Md., 1969-71; instr. Baylor Coll. Medicine, Houston, 1971-73; active staff Harris County Hosp. Dist., 1973—; active staff, chief of genetic svc. Tex. Children's Hosp., 1973—; cons. staff Methodist Hosp., 1976—; asst. prof. Baylor Coll. Medicine, Houston, 1973-77, assoc. prof., 1977-81, prof., 1981—; investigator Howard Hughes Med. Inst., Houston, 1973-80, 85—; acting chmn. dept. moledular and human genetics Baylor Coll. Medicine, Houston, 1994-95, chmn. dep. molecular and human genetics, 1995—. Mem. bd. dirs. Am. Soc. Human Genetics, Rockville, Md., 1987-90; mem. founding bd. dirs. Am. Coll. Med. Genetics, 1990-94; mem. editl. bds. Human Molecular Genetics, 1991—, Human Mutation, 1991—, Human Gene Therapy, 1994—, Gene Therapy, 1994—, Human Genetics, 1994—. Co-author: (book) The Metabolic and Molecular Bases of Inherited

Disease, 7th edit., 1995; editor: (books) The Metabolic Basis of Inherited Disease, 6th edit., 1989, The Metabolic and Molecular Bases of Inherited Disease, 1995; contbr. chpts. to books, articles to profl. jours. Recipient Med. award Alpha Omega Alpha, 1966; grantee numerous orgns. including NIH, March of Dimes, Cystic Fibrosis Found., others. Mem. Am. Acad. Pediatrics, Am. Pediatrics, Am. Pediatric Soc., Am. Soc. Human Genetics (program com. 1984-86, bd. dirs. 1987-90), Am. Soc. Microbiology, Assn. Am. Physicians, Genetics Soc. Am., Tex. Pediatric Soc., Houston Pediatric Soc., Harris County med. Soc., Soc. Inherited Metabolic Disease, Soc. Pediatric Rsch., NAS Inst. Medicine. Achievements include research in the fields of molecular and human genetics, cystic fibrosis, gene therapy, inborn errors of metabolism and gene targeting; discovery of the unipa-rental disomy in humans. Office: Baylor Coll Med Dept Molecular/Human Genetics 1 Baylor Plz # T619 Houston TX 77030-3411

BEAUDOIN, LAURENT, train manufacturing company executive; b. Laurier Station, Que., Can., May 13, 1938; s. P.A. and Yvonne (Rodrigue) B.; m. Claire Bombardier, Aug. 29, 1959; children— Nicole, Pierre, Elaine, Denise. BA, Ste. Anne U., NS, Can., 1957; M. Commerce, Sherbrooke U., 1960, D. Bus. Adminstrn. (hon.), 1971. Partner firm Beaudoin, Morin, Dufresne & Assos., Quebec, Que., 1961-63; comptroller Bombardier Ltd., Valcourt, Que., 1963-64, gen. mgr. Montreal, Que., 1964-66; pres. Bombardier, Inc., Montreal, Que., 1966-86, chmn., CEO, 1979—99, chmn. bd. exec. com., 1999—2004, chmn., CEO, 2005—. Bd. govs. Faculté d'Adminstrn., U. Sherbrooke, Que. Decorated companion Order Can., Ordre National du Québec; comdr. de l'Ordre de Léopold II, Can. Bus. Leader award, U. Alberta, 1991. Fellow Inst. Chartered Accts.; mem. C. of C. Que. (gov.). Office: Bombardier Inc 800 Rene-Levesque Blvd W Montreal PQ Canada H3B 1Y8

BEAUDOIN, ROBERT LAWRENCE, small business owner; b. Newberry, Mich., Nov. 22, 1933; s. Leo Joseph and Edith Wilhelmina (Graunstadt) B.; m. Margaret Cecelia Linck, June 20, 1953; children: Eugene Robert, Kathleen Therese, Annette Marie, Suzanne Margaret. Student, Marquette U., 1952—53. With Fisher plant GM, 1953; dock hand State of Mich., St. Ignace, 1953; sch. bus driver Engadine (Mich.) Consol. Schs., 1957-96; owner, operator Beaudoin's Texaco, Beaudoin's Cafe, Naubinway, Mich., 1956-82, Beaudoin's Cafe and Marathon, Naubinway, 1982-83, Beaudoin's Cafe, Naubinway, 1956—. Mem. Naubinway July 4th Com., 1954—; past mem. Naubinway Port Commn., Garfield Twp. Planning and Zoning Commn.; vol. fireman Garfield Twp. Fire Dept., Naubinway, 1980-94; mem. recreation com. Garfield Twp. Bd., Engadine, 1983; support fellow N.G. and Res., support mem. U.S. Army Recruiting Main Sta., Detroit; mem. USAF Ground Observer Corps. Recipient Cert. of Appreciation, U.S. Army Recruiting Main Sta., Detroit, 1971, Statement of Support, N.G. and Res., 1976. Mem. NRA (life; endowment mem.); mem. Internat. Platform Assn., West Mackinac C. of C., Nat. Fedn. Ind. Bus. (adv. bd. 1971—, 20 Yr. award 1985), Am. Farmland Trust, Heritage Found., Hiawatha Sportsmans Club (bd. govs. Engadine 1965-67, 89-95, apptd. security officer 1996-98, treas. coun. 7472 1998-99), Curtis C. of C., N.Am. Hunting Club (life), Engadine Trap Shooting Club, KC (grand knight 1979-83, 99-2001, coun. 7472 Naubiway membership and program dir. East Marquette diocese 1984-88, 96-98, 2002—, dist. dep. 1988-92, supreme coun. dist. dep. 1988-92, state dir. coun. activities 1992-94, dep. grand knight coun. 7472 1995-96, 2001-2003), Handyman Club Am. (life), Nat. Home Gardening Club (life), NRA Whitttington Ctr. Founders Club, N.Am. Fishing Club (life), NRA Golden Eagles, Lions (3d v.p. Engadine club 1970-71), Hiawatha Sportsmans Club, Cooking Club Am. (life), Creative Home Arts Club (life), Mich. Upper Peninsula Travel and Recreation Assn Roman Catholic. Avocations: hunting, fishing. Home: PO Box 143 Naubinway MI 49762-0143 Office: Beaudoins Cafe PO Box 143 US Hwy 2 Naubinway MI 49762 Office Phone: 906-477-6292.

BEAUFAIT, FREDERICK W(ILLIAM), retired engineering educator; b. Vicksburg, Miss., Nov. 28, 1936; s. Frank W. and Eleanor Chambliss (Haynes) B.; m. Lois Mary Erdman, Nov. 27, 1964; children: Paul Frederick, Nicole. BSc, Miss. State U., 1958; MSc, U. Ky., 1961; PhD, Va. Poly. Inst., 1965. Structural engr. U.S. Army C.E., Vicksburg, 1958-59; engr. L. E. Gregg & Assocs., Lexington, Ky., 1959-60; vis. lectr. civil engring. U. Liverpool, England, 1960-61; prof. civil engring. Vanderbilt U., Nashville, 1965-79; prof., chmn. dept. civil engring. W.Va. U., Morgantown, 1979-83, assoc. dean Coll. Engring., 1983-86; dean Coll. Engring. Wayne State U., Detroit, 1986-95; dir. NSF Greenfield Engring. Edn. Coalition, 1996-98; pres. NYC Coll. Tech. of the CUNY, 1999—2004; ret., 2004. Vis. prof. civil and structural engring. U. Wales, Cardiff, 1975-76; cons. in field; mem. Engring. Accreditation Commn. Accreditation Bd. for Engring. and Tech., 1988-93, Engring. Manpower Commn., 1988-92; bd. dirs. Ford (Motor) Design Inst., 1991-96. Co-author: Computer Methods of Structural Analysis, 1970; author: Basic Concepts in Structural Analysis, 1977; also over 40 articles to profl. jours. Vice chmn. stewardship com. 1st Presbyn. Ch., Morgantown, 1982, elder, 1983-85, mem. long-range planning com., 1985-86; deacon Southminster Presbyn. Ch., Nashville, 1968-69, elder, 1971-73, 78-79, clk. of session, 1971-73; bd. dirs. Presbyn. Campus Ministry, Nashville, 1972-78, treas., 1972-75, pres., 1976-78; mem. citizens adv. com. Met. Sch. System, Nashville, 1978-79; bd. dirs. Independence Cmty. Found., 2001-04; active Lewes Presbyn. Ch., 2006-, co-chair sanctuary restoration com., 2006-. Decorated chevalier Ordre des Palmes Academiques (France); named Outstanding Vol. of Yr. Mich. Ctr. for High Tech., 1991; Disting. Engring. fellow Miss. State U., 1992; named to Acad. Disting. Alumni, Dept. Civil and Environ. Engring., Va. Tech, 2004. Mem. ASCE, NSPE, Mich. Soc. Profl. Engrs. (bd. dirs. Detroit metro chpt. 1987-90, vice chmn. 1991, chmn.-elect 1992, chmn. 1993, pres. profls. in engring. edn. divsn. 1990-93, state bd. dirs., treas. 1995-97, v.p. 1997-98, Outstanding Engr. in Edn. 1994), Am. Soc. Engring. Edn. (chmn. civil engring. divsn. 1992-93, Centennial medallion 1993, George K. Wadlin award of Civil Engring. Divsn. 1994), Engring. Soc. Detroit (Coll. of Fellows 1994, gold award 1997), Order of Engrs. (bd. governance 1989-97), Chi Epsilon, Tau Alpha Pi, Tau Beta Pi. Avocations: painting, reading, travel. Home: 6 Blue Heron Dr Lewes DE 19958 Business E-Mail: fbeaufait@citytech.cuny.edu.

BEAULIEU, NORMAN C., engineering educator, writer; BSc, U. BC, Vancouver, 1980, MSc, 1983, PhD, 1986. Prof. elec. and computer engring. U. Alta., Canada; rsch. chair Alta. Informatics Cir. Rsch. Excellence. Can. rsch. chair iCORE. Recipient K.Y. Lo medal, Engring. Inst. Can., 2004, Thomas W. Eadie medal, Royal Soc. Can., 2005, Leadership award, Alta. Sci. and Tech., 2005, J. Gordin Kaplan award for excellence in rsch., U. Alberta, 2006; NSERC E.W.R. Steacie Meml. Fellowship, 1999. Fellow: Can. Acad. Engring., Engring. Inst. Can., Royal Soc. Can., IEEE (editor-in-chief Transactions on Comm. Theory 2000—03, editor Wireless Comm. Theory, Transactions on Comm., assoc. editor WIreless Comm., Comm. Letters). Office: U Alberta Dept Elec and Computer Engring Edmonton AB T6G 2V4 Canada Office Phone: 780-492-5558. Business E-Mail: beaulieu@icoremail.ee.ualberta.ca.

BEAUPRE, TIMOTHY, lawyer; b. Dover, NH, Nov. 9, 1977; BA, Boston Coll., Chestnut Hill, Mass., 2000; JD, Suffolk U., Boston, 2005. Bar: NH 2005, Mass. 2005. Atty. Shaheen & Gordon, Dover, 2006—. Office: Shaheen & Gordon 140 Washington St Dover NH 03821-0977 Office Phone: 603-749-5000.

BEAUPREZ, BOB (ROBERT L. BEAUPREZ), former congressman; b. Lafayette, Colo., Sept. 22, 1948; m. Claudia Beauprez; children: Joe, Jim, Melanie, John. BS, U. Colo., 1970. Ptnr. Boulder Valley Holsteins, Lafayette, Colo., 1970-89; pres. Indian Peaks, Inc., Lafayette, Colo., 1989—; pres., CEO, chmn. Heritage Bank, Louisville, 1990—; state chmn. Rep. State Ctrl. Com. of Colo., 1999—2002; mem. US Congress from 7th Colo. dist., 2003—07, mem. ways & means com. Pres. Ind. Bankers Colo., 1997-98, chmn. 1998, bd. dirs. 1993-99; vice chmn. , policy devel. com. Ind. Com. Bankers Am., 2000-; mem. Rep. Nat. Com. Western State Chmn. Assn., 1999—. Republican.

BEAUREGARD, JOHN, college librarian, consultant; b. Boston, Jan. 6, 1932; s. Louis D. and Dorothy May (Randall) Beauregard; children: Paul Calvin, Andrew Hudson, Sharon Elizabeth Nichols, Mark Roger. BA, Gordon Coll., Boston, 1953; MDiv, Gordon Div. Sch., Mass., 1956; MLS, U. of Maine, 1969. Prof. Glen Cove Bible Coll. Christian Sch. Inc., Glen Cove, Maine, 1958—69; prof. bibliography, dir. libr. Gordon Coll., Wenham, Mass., 1969—2003; dir. Halle Libr., Endicott Coll., Beverly, Mass., 2003—06. Dir. Fair Haven Camps, Brooks, Maine, 1959—68; archivist Gordon Coll., Wenham, Mass., 1972—; pres. bd., v.p., treas. North of Boston Libr. Exch., Danvers, 1985—91. Author: William Wilberforce, 1789-1833/An Annotated Author and Subject Bibliography, 2003, (book index) Nathan R. Wood, 1963, A School of Christ, 1978; editor: Journal of Our Journey by Maria H. Gordon, 1989. Pastor Appleton Bapt. Ch., Maine, 1956—58; interm pastor 37 Chs. in Maine, Mass., R.I., 1958—2002; elder Calvary Bapt. Ch., Peabody, Mass., 1998—2007. Avocations: hockey, book conserver. Home: 132 Burley St Danvers MA 01923-2366 Home Phone: 978-774-5585; Office Phone: 978-867-4140. Business E-Mail: john.beauregard@gordon.edu.

BEAUREGARD, LUC, public relations executive; b. Montreal, Que., Can., Aug. 4, 1941; s. Francois and Gertrude Beauregard; m. Michelle Beauregard; children: Valérie, Stéphanie, Francois, Philippe. BA, Coll. Stanislas, Montreal. Reporter, parliamentary corr. in Ottawa, city editor Montreal (Que.) Daily La Presse, Canada, 1961-68; press sec. Que. Minister Edn., Quebec City, Que., 1968-69; founding ptnr. Beauregard, Landry, Nantel & Assocs. Pub. Rels. Cons., Montreal; pres., pub. Montreal-Matin Daily Newspaper, 1973-76; chmn., CEO Nat. Pub. Rels., Inc., Montreal, 1976—. Chmn. Amarc, City of Montreal Corp. managing Man and His World (formerly Expo '67), 1982-86. Chmn. Montreal Better Bus. Bur., 1983—84; mem. exec. com. Montreal Mus. Contemporary Art, 1986—97, chmn., 1987—90, Found. Montreal Island Sch. Coun., 1991—97; gov. Conseil du Patronat du Que., 1992—; sec. info. commn. Que. Liberal Party, 1978—79; bd. dirs. Can. C. of C., Nouvelle Compagnie Theatrale, 1984—94, Que. Heart Found., 1983—85; bd. dirs., adv. bd. Montreal Neurological Inst. Decorated mem. Order of Can.; recipient Philip A. Novikoff award Can. Pub. Rels. Soc., Attainment award. Fellow Can. Pub. Rels. Soc. (pres. 1984-85, chmn. Cons. Inst. 1982-83); mem. Am. Pub. Rels. Coun. (chmn. 1985-86), Can. C. of C. (bd. dirs., exec. com. 2003-05), Club des Quinze, Mt. Royal Club, Knowlton Golf Club. Avocation: golf. Office: Nat Pub Rels 2001 McGill Coll Ave Ste 800 Montreal PQ Canada H3A 1G1 E-mail: lbeauregard@national.ca.

BEAUSOLEIL, DORIS MAE, retired federal agency housing specialist; b. Chelmsford, Mass., Jan. 9, 1932; d. Joseph Honorious and Beatrice Pearl (Smith) Beausoleil. Student, State Tchrs. Coll., Lowell, Mass., 1949-51; BA in Sociology and Psychology, Goddard Coll., Plainfield, Vt., 1954; MA in Human Rels., NYU, 1957; postgrad., CUNY, NYC, 1988-97. With divsn. human rights State of NY, NYC, 1960-69, housing dir., 1966-68; housing cons. Nat. Com. Against Discrimination Housing, NYC, 1969—70, Edwin Gould Found., NYC, 1970—71; human resources cons. interfaith housing strategy com., housing cons. Fedn. Prot. Welfare Agys., Inc., NYC, 1971—72; housing cons., 1972—74; equal opportunity compliance specialist NY/NJ Dept. Housing and Urban Devel., NYC, 1975—2000, fed. women's program coord., 1975—79, br. chief Title VI sect. 109 compliance divsn. fair housing and equal opportunity region II, 1979—84, coord. sect. III, 1998—2006, pub. trust specialist, 2000—06. Mem. adv. panel Housing Mag., 1979. Founding mem. N.Y. State HUD Com.; cons., examiner N.Y. State Civil Svc. Commn., 1970—93; bd. dirs. Nat. Assn. Human Rights Workers, 1974—77. Mem.: Citizens Housing and Planning Coun., Goddard Coll. Alumni Assn. (sec. 1988—90), Rep. Bus. Women's Club (pres. 1985—88, bd. dirs. 1989—91). Unitarian Universalist. Avocations: painting, animal rights activism. Home: 392 Central Park W Apt 14N New York NY 10025-5868 Personal E-mail: d_beausoleil@verizon.net.

BEAVER, BARBARA LEANN, elementary school educator, writer; b. Dallas, Dec. 1, 1963; d. Ronald A. Williams and Barbara L. Vines, Marta Williams (Stepmother); m. Franklin D. Beaver, May 30, 1997; 1 child, Amber M.; m. Raymond P. Mullen, June 29, 1984 (div.); children: Joshua D. Mullen, Jacqueline A. Mullen. BS, Tex. A&M, Commerce, 1989; M of Liberal Arts, So. Meth. U., Dallas, 2001. Cert. tchr. Tex., 1989. Math tchr. Waxahachie Jr. H.S., Tex., 1989—91; elem. tchr. Jefferson Davis Elem. Sch., Dallas, 1991—93; math and sci. tchr. A. C. New Mid. Sch., Balch Springs, 1993—97; advanced placement tchr. Met. Christian Sch., Dallas, 1997—2000; info. tech. lead tchr. Ed Vanston Mid. Sch., Mesquite, 2001—. Mentor tchr. Ed Vanston Mid. Sch., Mesquite, Tex., 2001—. Author: (magazine and newsletter articles) A Love and Logic Funny Moment. Victim responder Victim Relief Ministries, Dallas. Recipient Mesquite Apple Corps award, Vanston Mid. Sch., 2006. Mem.: Alpha Delta Kappa (assoc.). Mem. Evang. Ch. Avocations: writing, photography, soccer. Home Phone: 972-289-4643; Office Phone: 972-882-5801.

BEAVER, BONNIE VERYLE, veterinarian, educator; b. Mpls., Oct. 26, 1944; d. Crawford F. and Gladys I. Gustafson; m. Larry J. Beaver, Nov. 25, 1972 (dec. Nov. 1995). BS, U. Minn., 1966, DVM, 1968; MS, Tex. A&M U., 1972. Instr. vet. surgery and radiology U. Minn., 1968-69; instr. vet. anatomy Tex. A&M U., College Station, 1969-72, asst. prof., 1972-76, assoc. prof., 1976-82; prof. Tex A&M U., College Station, 1982-86, prof. vet. small animal medicine and surgery, 1986—, chief medicine, 1990-99. Mem. vet. medicine adv. com. HEW, 1972-74, nat. adv. food and drug com., HEW, 1975, com. on animal models and genetic stocks NAS, 1984-86, 87-89, panel on microlivestock NRC, 1986-87, task force on animal use study Inst. Lab. Animal Resources, 1986, adv. com. for Pew Nat. Vet. Edn. Program, Pew Charitable Trusts, 1987-92, 10th symposium on Vet. Med. Edn. Com., 1988-89; Frank K. Ramsey lects. Iowa State U., 2004; T.S. Williams lectr. Tuskegee U., 2006. Mem. editl. bd. Applied Animal Ethology, 1981-82, 83-84, VM/SAC, 1982-85, Applied Animal Behavior Sci., 1982-84, 84-86, 86-88, 88-2000, Bull. on Vet. Clin. Ethology, 1994-1999, Jour. Am. Animal Hosp. Assn., 1995—, Jour. Vet. Behavior: Clin. Applications and Rsch., 2005—; contbr. articles to profl. jours. V.p. Brazos Valley Regional Sci. and Engring. Fair, 1974—83, dir., 1983—85; bd. dirs. Brazos Valley unit Am. Cancer Soc., 1976—83, v.p., 1976—83. Named Citizen of Week, The Press, 1981, Outstanding Woman Vet. of 1982, Disting. Practitioner, Nat. Acads. Practice; recipient Friskies PetCare award Am. Animal Hosp. Assn., 2001, Bustad Human-Animal Bond award, 2001, Elanco Disting. Lectr. award, 2002, Frank K. Ramsey Lectr. award, 2004. Mem.: AVMA (exec. bd. 1997—2006, chair exec. bd. 2001—02, pres.-elect 2003—04, pres. 2004—05, Animal Welfare award 1996), AAAS, Am. Soc. Lab. Animal Practitioners, Am. Assn. Human-Animal Bond Veterinarians, Am. Assn. Food Hygiene Veterinarians, Am. Horse Coun., Ark. Med. Vet. Assn., Am. Quarter Horse Assn., Tex. Palomino Exhibitors Assn., Palomino Horse Breeders Am. (v.p. 1983—88, treas. 1984—85, pres.-elect 1988—89, pres. 1989—90), Nat. Acad. Practice, Am. Coll. Vet. Behaviorists (chair organizing com. 1976—91, pres. 1991—96, charter diplomate 1993—, exec. dir. 1996—), Animal Behavior Soc., Am. Assn. Bovine Practitioners, Am. Assn. Equine Practitioners, La. Vet. Med. Assn., Am. Vet. Soc. Animal Behavior (pres. 1975—80), Am. Animal Hosp. Assn., Brazos Valley Vet. Med. Assn., Tex. Vet. Med. Assn. (3d v.p. 1990, 2d v.p. 1991, 1st v.p. 1992, pres.-elect 1993, pres. 1994, spkr. com. Southwest Vet. Symposium 2006—, Legacy of Svc. award 2005), Phi Delta Gamma (pres. 1974—75), Phi Zeta (nat. pres. 1979—81), Sigma Epsilon Sigma, Phi Sigma, Delta Soc. Office: Tex A&M Univ Coll Vet Medicine Vet Small Animal Medicine & Surgery College Station TX 77843-4474

BEAVER, FRANK EUGENE, critic, historian; b. Cleve., NC, July 26, 1938; s. John Whitfield and Mary Louise (Shell) B.; m. Gail Frances Place, June 30, 1962; children: Julia Clare, John Francis, Johanna Louise. BA, U. N.C., 1960, MA, 1966; PhD, U. Mich., 1970. Instr. speech Memphis State U., 1965-66; instr. radio-TV-motion pictures U. N.C., Chapel Hill, 1966-68; asst. prof. speech comm. U. Mich., Ann Arbor, 1969-74, assoc. prof., 1974-79, assoc. prof. comm., 1979-84, dir. grad. program in telecom. arts and film, 1981—86, prof., chmn. dept. comm., 1987-91, Arthur F. Thurnau prof., 1989—. Advisor Muskegon (Mich.) Film Festival, 2001. Film critic radio Stas. WUOM, WVGR, WFUM, Ann Arbor, Grand Rapids, Mich., 1975-97; author: Bosley Crowther, 1974, On Film, 1983, Dictionary of Film Terms, 1983, 94 (Mandarin-Chinese translation 1993), 3d edit., 2006, Oliver Stone: Wakeup Cinema, 1994, 100 Years of American Film, 2001; writer, dir. documentary film Under One Roof, 1967; editor (book series) Framing Film, Peter Lang, Pub., N.Y., 1998—; commentator Mich. Today-News-e, 2004—. Advisor Ann Arbor Film Festival, 1975—; bd. dirs. Mich. Theater Found., Ann Arbor, 1977-79, 86—, Ann Arbor Summer Festival, 2005—; alumni adv. bd. Lambda Chi Alpha, Ann Arbor, 1989-94. With M.I. Corps, U.S. Army, 1962-65, Vietnam. Recipient Playwriting award Carolina Playmakers, 1962, Major Hopwood writing awards for drama and essays U. Mich., 1969, Outstanding Tchg. award Amoco Found., Ann Arbor, 1985; fellow NEH, 1975. Mem.: Speech Comm. Assn., Soc. Cinema Scholars, Azazels Club, Phi Kappa Phi, Kappa Tau Alpha. Home: 1050 Wall St #2F Ann Arbor MI 48105 Office: U Mich Screen Arts and Cultures 6525 Haven Hall Ann Arbor MI 48109-1045 Business E-Mail: fbeaver@umich.edu.

BEAVER, HILARY A., medical educator, ophthalmologist; BS in Biology, Coll. William and Mary, Williamsburg, Va., 1987; MD, U. Va., Charlottesville, 1991. Cert. Am. Bd. Ophthalmology, 1997. Intern Baylor Coll. Medicine, Houston, 1991—92, resident in ophthalmology, 1992—95, clin. instr. dept. ophthamology, 1995—98, clin. asst. prof., 1998—2000; asst. prof. U. Iowa Hosps. and Clinics, Iowa City, 2000—06, assoc. prof., 2006—. Dir. med. student edn. U. Iowa Dept. Ophthlmology, 2001—, mem. resident edn. com., 2005—; mem. task force on competencies U. Iowa Dept. Ophthlamology, 2005—. Contbr. articles to profl. jours. Recipient Janet M. Glasgow Meml. Achievement citation, U. Va. Sch. Medicine, 1991, Physicians Recognition award, AMA, 1997—2000. Mem.: Am. Acad. Ophthalmology (mem. task force on aging com. 2001—03, subcom. basic and clin. sci. course sect. 2 2003—, cataract specialty info. team 2005—, Achievement award 2006), Am. Soc. Cataract and Refractive Surgery, Iowa Med. Soc., Iowa Acad. Ophthalmology, Alpha Omega Alpha, Phi Sigma Soc. Office: Univ Iowa Hosps and Clinics Dept Ophthalmology 200 Hawkins Dr Iowa City IA 52242 Office Phone: 319-356-8118. Office Fax: 319-353-7699.

BEAVER, JAMES NORMAN, JR., (JIM BEAVER), actor, writer; b. Laramie, Wyo., Aug. 12, 1950; s. James Norman and Dorothy Adell (Crawford) B.; m. Deborah S. Young, Aug. 10, 1973 (div. Oct. 1, 1976); m. Cecily April Adams, May 7, 1989 (dec. Mar. 3, 2004). Student, Ft. Worth Christian Coll., 1967-68, Okla. Christian Coll., 1971-72; BA in Oral Communications, Cen. State U., Edmond, Okla. Actor, 1971—; critic, columnist Films in Review mag., NYC, 1977-84; film archives dir. Variety Arts Ctr., Los Angeles, 1983-84; TV and screenwriter various studios, Los Angeles, 1985—. Lectr. Okla. Christian Coll., Oklahoma City, 1980. Author: John Garfield: His Life and Films, 1978; (with others) Movie Blockbusters, 1983, 2d rev. edit., 1984; playwright numerous prodns. including Sidekick, 1981, Semper Fi, 1982, Truth, Justice and the Texican Way, 1982, Verdigris, 1985 (Los Angeles Dramalogue Critics award 1985), Pressing Engagements, 1990; screenwriter: (with others) Sweet Revenge, 1987; writer: Vietnam War Story, 1987, Tour of Duty, 1987, Longarm, 1987, (episode for Alfred Hitchcock Presents) The Initiation (Award for Cable Excellence nomination 1987); appeared in stage prodns. including Macbeth, King Lear, One Flew Over the Cuckoo's Nest, The Rainmaker, Sidekick, 1986 (Los Angeles Dramalogue Critics award); films include Semi-Tough, 1977, Nighthawks, 1981, Silkwood, 1983, Hollywood Shuffle, 1987, Two Idiots in Hollywood, 1988, Defense Play, 1988, In Country, 1989, Turner and Hooch, 1989, Little Secrets, 1991, Sister Act, 1992, Silver, 1993, Geronimo: An American Legend, 1993, Twogether, 1994, Blue Chips, 1994, Bad Girls, 1994, Wounded, 1997, At Sachem Farm, 1998, Impala, 1999, Ah! Silenciosa, 1999, Magnolia, 1999, Fraud, 2000, Where the Heart Is, 2000, Joy Ride, 2001, Wheelmen, 2002, Adaptation, 2002, The Life of David Gale, 2003, The Commission, Reflections, 2006, Next, 2007; TV series include Thunder Alley, 1994-95, Days of Our Lives, 1996-2003, Deadwood, 2004-06, Day Break, 2007; TV film Girls of the White Orchid, 1983, El Diablo, 1990, Follow Your Heart, 1990, Court Martial of Jackie Robinso, 1990, Gunsmoke: The Long Ride, 1993, Divided by Hate, 1997, Mr. Murder, 1998, Warden of Red Rock, 2001, (voice) The Valley of Light, 2007. Served as cpl. USMC, 1968-71, Vietnam. Mem. Writers Guild Am. (West chpt.), Screen Actors Guild, AFTRA, Actors Equity Assn., The Actors Fund (life), Theatre West (bd. dirs. 1985-87, chmn. bd. dirs. 1987-88). Mem. Ch. of Christ. Avocations: motorcycling, fencing, baseball, film history. Office: Triad Artists Inc 1173 N Ardmore Ave Apt 2 Los Angeles CA 90029-1443*

BEAVER, WILLIAM HENRY, accounting educator; b. Peoria, Ill., Apr. 13, 1940; s. John W. and Ethel M. (Kostka) B.; m. Suzanne Marie Hutton, May 22, 1965; children: Marie, Sarah, David. BBA, U. Notre Dame, 1962, D (hon.), 1998; MBA, PhD, U. Chgo., 1965; D (hon.), Norwegian Sch. Econs., 1996. CPA, Ill. Asst. prof. U. Chgo., 1965—69; assoc. prof. acctg. Stanford U., 1969—72, prof., 1972—, Joan E. Horngren prof., 1977—. Adv. com. on corp. disclosure SEC, 1976-77; cons. Fin. Acctg. Stds. Bd., 1980-86 Author: Financial Reporting: An Accounting Revolution, 1981, 3d edit., 1998; editl. bd.: The Acctg. Rev., 1977-80, Jour. Acctg. Rsch., 1968—, Jour. Acctg. and Econs., 1978—, Fin. Analysts Jour., 1979-98; contbr. articles to profl. jours Recipient Lit. award Jour. Accountancy, 1978, Faculty Excellence award Calif. Soc. CPA, 1978, Graham and Dodd award Fin. Analysts Fedn., 1979, Notable Contbn. to Acct. Lit. award, 1969, 79, 83, Outstanding Rsch. award Inst. Quantitative Rsch. in Fin., 1981, Nat. Acctg. award Alpha Kappa Psi Found., 1982, Disting. Tchg. award Stanford U., 1985, Seminal Contbn. to Acctg. Lit. award, 1989, Outstanding Doctoral Tchg. award, 2005; named to Acctg. Hall of Fame, 1996 Mem. AICPA, Am. Fin. Assn., Am. Acctg. Assn. (v.p. 1981-83, pres. elect 1986-87, pres. 1987-88, disting. internat. lectr. in acct. award 1979, outstanding educator award 1990, Wildman award 1985), Fin. Acctg. Found. (trustee 1993-96), Fin. Svcs. Rsch. Initiative (co-dir. 1992-95) Home: 949 Wing Pl Palo Alto CA 94305-1028 Office: Stanford U Grad Sch Bus Stanford CA 94305

BEAVER, WILLIAM R., sociology professor; b. Connellsville, Pa., July 10, 1948; s. William A. and Caroline R. Beaver; m. L. Susan McNair, Oct. 19, 1973; children: Michael P., Christopher W. PhD, Carnegie-Mellon U., Pitts., 1986. Prof. Robert Morris U., Coraopolis, Pa., 1972—. Author: Nuclear Power Goes On-Line; contbr. articles to profl. jours. Vol., spokesperson Arthritis Found., Greensburg, Pa., 1999—2005. Recipient Outstanding Paper Presentation award, Lilly Conf. Coll. Tchg. West. Mem.: Am. Sociol. Assn., Pa. Sociol. Assn. (corr.). Democrat. Avocations: triathlons, skiing. Home: 136 Elm Dr Acme PA 15610 Office: Robert Morris University Blvd Coraopolis PA 15108 Home Phone: 724-547-4844; Office Phone: 412-397-5415. Business E-Mail: beaver@rmu.edu.

BEAVERS, JAMES EARL, engineer, director, consultant; b. Quincy, Ill., May 31, 1944; s. A. V. and Virginia (Turner) Beavers; m. Beverly Sue Haden, Aug. 22, 1964; children: Brandon Cash, Justin James. BS in Civil Engring., U. Mo, Rolla, 1962—66; MS in Civil Engring., Vanderbilt U., Nashville, 1966—68, PhD in Civil Engring., 1968—72. Lic. engr.-in-tng., Mo., 1966, profl. engr., Tenn., 1973, Ky., 2001. Dep. dir. Mid-Am. Earthquake Ctr. U. Ill., Urbana, 1998—2003; dir. Constrn. Industry Rsch. & Policy Ctr. U. Tenn., Knoxville, 2004—. Cons. James E. Beavers Cons., Knoxville, 1997—. Contbr. articles to profl. jours. Specialist 5 US Army, 1968—70, Vicksburg, Miss. Decorated Commendation medal US Army; recipient Young Engr. of Yr. award, Nat. Soc. Profl. Engrs., 1978, Tech. Achievement award, Martin Marietta Energy Sys., Inc., 1987, Excellence award, US Dept. Energy, 1994; grantee Corp. fellow, Martin Marietta Energy Sys., 1990. Fellow: ASCE (Tenn. pres. 1988—89); mem.: NSPE, Earthquake Engring. Rsch. Inst. (earthquake spectra editor 1988—93), Am. Concrete Inst., Seismol. Soc. Am. Home: 6318 Beaver Ridge Rd Knoxville TN 37931 Office: Univ Tenn 2000 Lake Ave Knoxville TN 37966-4150 Home Phone: 865-691-7416; Office Phone: 865-974-4955. Office Fax: 865-545-4193; Home Fax: 865-690-8936. Personal E-mail: jbeavers@jebconsultants.com. Business E-Mail: jbeavers@utk.edu.

BEAVERS, KAREN MARJORIE, small business owner; b. Laurel, Md., Nov. 2, 1947; d. James Walter and Marjorie Lois (Fullerton) McQuaid; m. George Edward Kowalski, Aug. 30, 1969 (div.); children: Eddie, Charlie, Bill; m. Edward George Beavers Jr., Feb. 14, 1991; stepchild, Edward. Student, Art Instrn. Sch., 1970; BS in Behavioral Sci., U. Md., 1994; postgrad., Loyola Coll., 1995. Receptionist Capitol Software, Laurel, 1988-89; new accounts devel. staff Focus Telecom., Burtonsville, Md., 1989-90; CSR & tng. asst. Encore Mktg. Internat., Lanham, Md., 1990-91; office mgr. Computer Image Svc., Laurel, 1991-94; pres., owner Gifts & More, Laurel, 1994-95, Gifts & More, Inc., Laurel, 1993-2000. Author: Tippy and Freckles Great Adventures, 1996; The Development of Children's Behavior, several theories of parenting, author of poetry. Hot-line counselor Domestic Violence Ctr., Howard County, Md., 1993-94; vol. art tchr., playground and lunchroom staff St. Marys of the Mills, Laurel; team mother Prince George Gymnastics, Beltsville, Md.; actress Ann Martin's Drama Guild, Laurel. Mem. APA (grad. affiliate), AAUW, Internat. Soc. Poets, Psi Chi. Roman Catholic. Avocations: gardening, doll collecting, antique shopping.

BEAVERS, ROY LACKEY, retired utilities executive, volunteer, writer; b. Joplin, Mo., Apr. 24, 1930; s. Roy L. Sr. and Margarette Nellie (Loughlin) B.; m. Valerie Evelyn Gurney; children: Leslie Anne, Brendan G. BS in Bus., U. Mo., 1952; MA in Polit. Sci., U. Md., 1970. Commd. ens. USN, 1952, advanced through grades to comdr., 1966, retired, 1972; agt., broker ins. agy., Lebanon, Mo., 1972-77; field rep. Nat. Rural Electric Coop. Assn., Washington, 1977-84; mgr. pub. info. and legis. liaison wholesale power coop. KAMO Power, Vinita, Okla., 1984-93. With SALT I strategic arms negotiations U.S. Arms Control Disarmament Agy., 1970—72; cons. in field. Contbr. articles to profl. jours. State hdqrs. dir. Va. Com. to Re-elect Nixon, Richmond, Va., 1972; mem. Bd. Mo. Cmty. Betterment Edn. Fund, 1990-93, Bd. Okla. Acad. for State Goals, 1990-93. Decorated Bronze, Silver, and Gold medals U.S. Naval Inst., Pres. Merit Svc. medal, Navy Commendation medal Mem. U.S. Naval Inst. Achievements include research in electromagnetic fields.

BEAZER, BRIAN C., construction executive; CEO Beazer Plc, 1968-91, chmn., 1983-91; non-exec. chmn. Beazer Homes USA, Atlanta. Dir. Beazer Japan, Ltd., Seal Mint Ltd., Jade Holdings Pte Ltd., Jade Technologies Singapore Pte Ltd., FSM Europe B.V., United Pacific Industries Ltd., U.S. Industries, Inc. Office: Beazer Homes USA Ste 1200 1000 Abernathy Rd Atlanta GA 30328*

BEAZLEY, HAMILTON, writer, educator; b. Houston, Dec. 21, 1943; s. Hamilton and Marjorie Beazley. BA, Yale U., 1966; MBA, So. Meth. U., 1977; PhD, George Washington U., 1998. Founder/exec. con. DyChem Internat. (U.K.) Ltd., Dallas, London, 1970-73; oil and gas industry exec., 1970—80; strategic planning cons. Houston, 1980-88; pres. Nat. Coun. on Alcoholism and Drug Dependence, NYC, 1988-90; assoc. prof. orgnl. scis. George Washington U., 1999—2002; scholar-in-residence St. Edward's U., Austin, Tex., 2003—. Co-creator TV series, BBC, Secrets Out, 1984-87; co-author: (with Bishop Payne) Reclaiming the Great Commission, 2000; author: No Regrets, 2004; co-author: Continuity Management, 2002; co-editor: The Servant-Leader Within, 2003; mem. editl. bd. Internat. Jour. Servant-Leadership. Bd. dirs. Total World Corp., Houston, 1985-97; trustee Ednl. Advancement Found., 1996—; mem. adv. bd. divsn. on addictions Harvard Med. Sch., 1994-98. Mem. APA, Acad. of Mgmt., Yale Club of N.Y.C. Republican. Episcopalian. Avocation: sailing. Home: 411 W St Elmo # 24 Austin TX 78745

BEBCHICK, LEONARD NORMAN, lawyer; b. New Bedford, Dec. 11, 1932; s. Samuel and Frances (Hait) B.; m. Gabriela Meyerhoff, Aug. 31, 1968; children: Ilana, Baruch. AB, Cornell U., Ithaca, NY, 1955; LLB, Yale U., New Haven, Conn., 1958. Bar: Mass. 1958, DC 1960, Md. 1989. Atty. CAB, Washington, 1958—59; assoc. Ginsburg & Leventhal, Washington, 1960-64; ptnr. Bebchick, Sher & Kushnick, Washington, 1964-74, Martin, Whitfield, Smith & Bebchick, Washington, 1974-82; pres. Leonard N. Bebchick P.C., Washington, 1982-88; ptnr. Leva, Hawes, Mason, Martin & Bebchick, Washington, 1988-89; pvt. practice Washington, 1989—. Joint co. sec. Brit. Caledonian Airways, Eng., 1963-88; bd. dirs. Brit. Caledonian Group, Eng., 1978-88, London Transport Internat. Cons., U.S., 1990-92; spl. counsel DC Pub. Svc. Commn., Washington, 1965-66, V.I. Pub. Utilities Commn., 1967-70. Bd. dirs. Partnership for Jewish Life and Learning, 2005—, Jewish Found. Group Homes, 1992—; pres. Congregation Beth El of Montgomery County, 1993—95; bd. dirs. United Synagogue of Conservative Judaism, 1993—2005, Jewish Fedn. Greater Washington, 1996—2002; bd. govs. coms. Jewish Agy. Israel, 1998—2002; bd. dirs., vice chair, exec. com. Muss H.S. Israel, 1997—; mem. nat. coun. Am. Jewish Com., 2002—. Mem.: ABA (chmn. adv. com. on aero. law 1982—83), Am. Assn. Jewish Lawyers and Jurists (bd. dirs. 2005—), Inst. of Dirs. (London), U.S. Nat. Student Assn. (v.p. internat. affairs 1953—54). Democrat. Jewish. Home: 6321 Lenox Rd Bethesda MD 20817-6023 Office Phone: 301-229-7726. Personal E-mail: beblaw@verizon.net.

BEBCHUK, LUCIAN ARYE, law and finance educator; b. Dec. 4, 1955; m. Alma Cohen; children: Alon, Yonatan. BA in Math. and Economics, summa cum laude, U. Haifa, Israel, 1977; LLB magna cumlaude, U. Tel-Aviv Sch. Law, 1979; LLM, Harvard Law Sch., 1980, SJD, 1984; MA in Economics, Harvard U., 1992, PhD in Economics, 1993. Asst. prof. Harvard Law Sch., Cambridge, 1986—88, prof. law, 1988—94, prof. law, economics, and fin., 1994—98, William J. Friedman & Alicia Townsend Friedman prof. law, economics, and fin., 1998—, dir. program on corp. governance, 2003—. Vis. sr. prof. by spl. appointment Tel-Aviv U., 1994—; rsch. assoc. Nat. Bur. Econ. Rsch., Cambridge, 1995—; vis. prof. Tilburg U., Netherlands, 2001; bd. dirs. John M. Olin Ctr. for Law, Economics, and Bus. Harvard Law Sch. Co-author (with Jesse Fried): Pay Without Performance, 2004. Guggenheim Found. Fellow, 2004—05. Fellow: European Corp. Goverance Inst. (inaugural), Centre for Econ. Policy Rsch.; mem.: Am. Assn Law and Economics (bd. dirs. 1997—99), Am. Assn. Law Schools (chair bus. associations sect. 1999—2000), Am. Acad. Arts and Sciences. Office: Harvard Law Sch 1545 Massachusetts Ave Cambridge MA 02138 Office Phone: 617-495-3138. Office Fax: 617-496-3119. Business E-Mail: bebchuk@law.harvard.edu.

BEBER, ROBERT H., lawyer, diversified financial services company executive; b. NYC, Aug. 17, 1933; s. Morris and Martha (Pollock) B.; m. Joan Parsons, June 14, 1957; children: Andrea, Judith, Deborah. AB in Econs, Duke U., 1955, JD, 1957. Bar: N.Y., N.C. With Everett, Everett & Everett, NC, 1957—58; atty. SBA, Washington, 1961—63; with RCA, 1963—81; sr. v.p., gen. counsel, sec. GAF Corp., NYC, 1981—83, exec. v.p., dir., 1983—84, dir. subs.; sr. v.p., gen. counsel, sec. Phlcorp, Inc. (formerly Baldwin United Corp.), Phila., 1984—88; asst. gen. counsel litig. W.R. Grace & Co., NYC, 1988—89, v.p., dir. litig., 1988—91, sr. v.p., gen. counsel, 1991—93, exec. v.p., 1993—98, ret., 1999, cons., 1999—. Bd. vis. Sch. Law, Duke U., 1996—; chmn. bd. Health Care Plan N.J., 1975-78; v.p. South Jersey C. of C., 1974-77; dir. Advantage Bank, Palm Beach, Fla., 1999-2003. Served with U.S. Army, 1958-61. Mem. ABA. Republican. Jewish. Office: WR Grace & Co 5400 Broken Sound Blvd NW Boca Raton FL 33487-3511 Personal E-mail: rhb11682@yahoo.com.

BEBOUT, ELI DANIEL, oil industry executive; b. Rawlings, Wyo., Oct. 14, 1946; s. Hugh and Dessie Bebout; m. Lorraine J. Tavares; children: Jordan, Jentry, Reagen, Taggert. BSEE, U. Wyo., 1969. With U.S. Energy Co., Riverton, Wyo., 1974-75; field engr. Am. Bechtel Corp., Green River, Wyo., 1975-76; pres. NUPEC Resources, Inc., Riverton, 1976-83, Smith-Collins Pharm. Inc., Riverton, 1983—88; cons. Nucor Inc., Riverton, 1984—2006; v.p. Nucor Drilling, Inc., Riverton, 1987—2001; state legislator Wyo. Assembly; pres. Nucor Oil & Gas, 1993—2006. Bd. dirs. Wyo. Bank Corp.; bd. mem. United Bancorporation Wyo. Past chmn. Wyo. Bus. Alliance; Wyo. Heritage Found.; former mem., mem. rules com. mgmt. coun., majority floor leader, spkr. Wyo. Ho. of Reps.; past chmn. Energy Coun.; senator Wyo. State Senate, 2007—. Republican. Office: Nucor Inc PO Box 112 Riverton WY 82501-0112

BECCALLI-FALCO, FERDINANDO, manufacturing executive; b. Italy; M in Chem. Engring., Polytechnic Torino, Italy; student in bus. admin., Xavier U., Cin. Joined G.E.'s strategic planning group GE European Hdqs., Bergen op Zoom, Netherlands, 1977; mgmt. positions in splty. plastics, NORYL ® resin, LEXAN ® resin and mktg. div. GE Plastics Hdqs., Pittsfield, Mass., 1981; dir. of GE European Hdqs., Bergen op Zoom, Netherlands, 1987; mng. dir. SPE, 1990; pres. GE Plastics, Japan Ltd., 1993—96; v.p. gen. mgr. GE Plastics, Am., 1997—2001; exec. v.p. GE Capital Svc., 2001—02; pres., CEO, GE Europe GE, 2002—05, pres., CEO Internat., 2005—. Office: General Electric Co 3135 Easton Turnpike Fairfield CT 06828-0001*

BECCHETTI, FREDERICK DANIEL, JR., physicist, researcher; b. Mpls., Mar. 3, 1943; s. Frederick Daniel and Olga Maxine Becchetti. BS, U. Minn., 1965, MS, 1968, PhD, 1969. Research assoc. Niels Bohr Inst., Copenhagen, 1969-71; research assoc. Lawrence Berkeley Lab., Calif., 1971-73; asst. prof. U. Mich., Ann Arbor, 1973-76, assoc. prof., 1976-82, prof. physics, 1982—. Contbr. articles to profl. jours. NSF fellow, 1970-71. Fellow Am. Phys. Soc.; mem. IEEE, Am. Assn. Physicists Tchrs., Am. Assn. Physicists in Medicine. Democrat. Roman Catholic.

BECERRA, ROBERT JOHN, lawyer; b. Jersey City, Jan. 26, 1962; s. Joseph Hercules and Blanche (Rosado) B.; m. Christiana Marie Carroll, Oct. 30, 1993. BBA, U. Miami, 1986, JD, 1990. Bar: Fla. 1990, U.S. Dist. Ct. (so. and mid dists.) Fla. 1991, U.S. Ct. Appeals (11th cir.) 1991, U.S. Dist. Ct. (ea. dist.) Mich. 1994, U.S. Ct. Appeals (3d cir.) 1997, U.S. Supreme Ct. 1994, U.S. Ct. Appeals (2d cir.) 2003. Assoc. Raskin & Raskin, Miami, Fla., 1990-96, ptnr., 1997—2004; sr. assoc. Sandler, Travis & Rosenberg, Miami, 2004—. Mem. Fed. Bar Assn., Dade County Bar Assn. (fed. cts. com., Certificate of Merit 1993), Phi Kappa Phi. Democrat. Roman Catholic. Avocations: sailplane pilot, scuba diving, boating, skiing. Office: Sandler Travis & Rosenberg 5200 Blue Lagoon Dr 600 Miami FL 33126 Office Phone: 305-267-9200. Personal E-mail: rbecerra@strtrade.com.

BECERRA, ROSINA MADELINE, social welfare educator; b. San Diego, Mar. 6, 1939; d. Ray and Ruth (Albanez) B. BA, San Diego State U., 1961, MSW, 1971; PhD, Brandeis U., 1975; MBA, Pepperdine U., 1981. Mathematician United Tech. Corp., Sunnyvale, Calif., 1962-63; with Peace Corps, Washington, 1963-65; probation officer San Diego County Probation Office, 1965-69; research assoc. Brandeis U., Waltham, Mass., 1973-75; assoc. prof. UCLA, 1975-81, prof., 1981—, acting dean, 1989-90, assoc. dean, 1986-89, 92, dean, 1992—, assoc. vice chancellor faculty diversity, 2002—. Author: Defining Child Abuse, 1979, Hispanic Veterans Seek Health Care, 1982, The Hispanic Elderly, 1984 (Choice Mag. Book award 1986); editor: Hispanic Mental Health, 1981; contbr. articles to profl. jours. Ford Found. award, 1980.

BECERRA, XAVIER, congressman, lawyer; b. Sacramento, Jan. 26, 1958; s. Manuel and Maria Teresa B.; m. Carolina Reyes, 1987. BA in Economics, Stanford U., 1980, JD, 1984. Atty., 1984—; dir. dist. office State Senator Art Torres, LA; dep. atty. gen. dept. justice, Calif., 1987-90; assemblyman, 59th dist. State of Calif., 1990-93; mem. U.S. Congress from 31st Calif. dist. (formerly 30th), 1993—. Mem. Ways and Means com.; chmn. Congl. Hispanic Caucus. Mem. Mexican-Am. Bar Assn., Calif. Bar Assn., Assn. Calif. State Attys. and Administrv. Law Judges. Democrat. Avocations: reading, carpentry, golf. Office: US Ho Reps 1119 Longworth Ho Office Bldg Washington DC 20515-0531 also: Dist Office Ste 560 1910 Sunset Blvd Los Angeles CA 90026*

BECERRA IBANEZ PELLIZA, JULIO C., psychologist, consultant; s. Matias Becerra y Bustos and Irma Soledad Ibanez de Pelliza; m. Elida Elena Vivot, Nov. 27, 2004. Licenciate in Psychology, U. Buenos Aires, 1985; MA in Psychology, Sierra U., Costa Mesa, Calif., 1992; D in Psychology, Calif. Coast U., Santa Ana, 1998. Lic. psychologist Ministry Pub. Health, Argentina, 1985. Cons. dept. medicine Hosp. and Clinic Jose de San Martin U. Buenos Aires, 1985—88; master facilitator batteries intervention dept. criminal justice sys. PrPeil Probation Dept., Calif., 1989—; psychotherapist and counsellor El Nido Family Ctr., Mission Hills, 1990—. Mem. San Fernando Child Abuse Coun. & Batterers Intervention Programs, San Fernando & Long Beach, Calif., 1990. Pilot cadet Argentine Navy, 1964—66. Mem.: Am. Coll. Heraldry, Assn. Batterers Intervention Programs (long beach, calif.), Nat. Shrine Basilica, DC, KC. Roman Catholic. Achievements include research in toxic psychosis of Cushing Syndrome. Avocations: history, genealogy, heraldry.

BECH, DOUGLAS YORK, retired lawyer, resort executive; b. Seattle, Aug. 18, 1945; s. Albert Richard and Vera Evelyn (Peterson) B.; m. Sheryl Annette Tucker, Aug. 9, 1968; children: Kristen Elizabeth, Allison York. BA, Baylor U., 1967; JD, U. Tex., 1970. Bar: Tex. 1970, N.Y. 1993. Ptnr. Andrews & Kurth, Houston, 1970-93, Akin, Gump, Strauss, Hauer & Feld, 1994-97; mng. dir. Raintree Capital Co., Houston, 1994—. Chmn., CEO Raintree Resorts Internat., Inc., Club Regina Resorts, Inc.; bd. dirs. Frontier Oil, Pride Cos., J2 Global Comm. Sgt. USAR, 1968-74. Republican. Baptist. Avocations: running, snowskiing, travel, big game hunting, golf. Office: Raintree Resorts Internat 10000 Memorial Dr Ste 480 Houston TX 77024-3409 E-mail: dybech@raintreeresotrs.com.

BECHAMPS, GERALD JOSEPH, surgeon; b. Flushing, NY, 1937; MD, Georgetown U., 1963. Diplomate Am. Bd. Surgery. Intern Meadowbrook Hosp., East Meadow, NY, 1963-64, resident in surgery, 1964-65; fellow surgery Mayo Clinic-Found., Rochester, 1965-69; clin. instr. U. Va. Sch. Medicine, 1971—; pvt. practice Winchester Surg. Clinic, Ltd., 1971—; asst. clin. prof. Va. Commonwealth U., 2003—. Past pres. Fedn. State Med. Bds. of U.S.; surgeon Winchester Med. Ctr., Surgi-Ctr. of Winchester; mem. Va. State Bd. Medicine, pres., 1985-86, 87-88. Mem. ACS (past pres. Va. chpt.), So. Soc. Clin. Surgeons. Office: Winchester Surg Clinic Ltd 20 S Stewart St Ste 100 Winchester VA 22601 Home Phone: 540-662-8025; Office Phone: 540-662-0377. Office Fax: 540-722-4515.

BECHER, WILLIAM DON, retired electrical engineer, educator, writer; b. Bolivar, Ohio, Nov. 26, 1929; s. William and Eva Vernette (Richardson) Becher; m. Helen Norma Hager, Aug. 31, 1950; children: Eric Alan, Patricia Lynn. BS in Radio Engring., Tri-State U., 1950; MSEE, U. Mich., 1961, PhD, 1968. Registered profl. engr., Mich., N.J. Project engr. Bogue Electric, Paterson, NJ, 1950-53; sr. devel. engr. Goodyear Aircraft Corp., Akron, Ohio, 1953-57; sr. systems engr. Beckman Instruments, Fullerton, Calif., 1957-58; engring. supr. Bendix Aerospace Systems, Ann Arbor, Mich., 1958-63; rsch. engr. U. Mich., Ann Arbor, 1963-68, adj. prof. elec. engring., 1978-79, 81-94, lectr. elec. engring. Dearborn, 1964-68, prof. elec. engring., 1968-78, chmn., 1971-76; engring. dept. mgr. Environ. Rsch. Inst. Mich., Ann Arbor, 1977-79, assoc. dir., 1981-87, tech. cons., 1988-90, engr. emeritus, 1990—; dean engring. Coll. Engring. N.J. Inst. Tech., Newark, 1979-81; cons. Widbec Engr, Ann Arbor, 1978—. Pres. Mich. Computers & Instrumentation, Inc., Ann Arbor, 1983—87; prof., chmn. elec. engring. Calif. State U., Fresno, 1988. Author: (book) Courses in Continuing Education for Electronics Engineers, 1975, 1976, Logical Design Using Integrated Circuits, 1977, An Ocean Between, 2000. With US Army, 1953—55. Fellow GE, 1962—63. Mem.: IEEE (life; sr. mem.), Order of Engrs., Am. Soc. Engring. Edn., Tau Beta Pi, Sigma Xi, Eta Kappa Nu. Achievements include patents in field. Home and Office: Widbec Engring 691 Spring Valley Rd Ann Arbor MI 48105-1060

BECHERER, RICHARD JOHN, architecture educator; b. East St. Louis, Ill., Nov. 8, 1951; s. Adam Jacob and Agnes Evelyn (Baker) B.; m. Charlene Castellano, Aug. 13, 1982. Student Courtauld Inst., U. London, 1973; BA, BArch, Rice U., Houston, 1974; MA, Cornell U., Ithaca, NY, 1977, PhD, 1981. Archtl. asst. Colin St. John Wilson and Ptnr., London, 1972-73; designer The Brooks Assn., Houston, 1973-74; grad. asst. Cornell U., 1974-80, asst. prof. architecture, 1981, assoc. prof., 1996; asst. prof. Auburn U., Ala., 1980-82, U. Va., Charlottesville, 1982-86; head grad. architecture program Carnegie Mellon U., Pitts., 1986-90, assoc. prof. architecture, 1987-96; assoc. prof. Am. U. Beirut, 1999—2001, Iowa State U., 2001—06, So. Polytechnic State U., 2007—. Presenter seminars NEH, 1982, 88, 89, Am. Collegiate Schs. Architecture, 1988, 93, 97, 2002; lectr. Centre Canadien d'Architecture, Montreal, Carnegie Mus., Pitts., and various colls., univs. and nat. confs.; vis. assoc. prof. U. Pitts., 1997-99; assoc. prof. Am. U. Beirut, 1999-2001, Iowa State U., 2001-06, So. Poly. State U., 2007—; mem. Fulbright Fellowship selection com. Author: Science Plus Sentiment; César Daly's Formula for Modern Architecture, 1984, (mus. catalogue and display) Urban Theory and Transformation, 1976, (tourist guidebook) Canandaigua: A Walking Tour, 1977; contbr. articles to profl. jours.; prin. works include interiors Michael P. Keeley House, Belleville, Ill., 1978, Robert Becherer House, Stonybrook, 1990; selected exhibitor Venice Biennale, Prato della Valle, Padua, 1985; exhibitor Heart of the Park, Houston, 1992; exhibitor installation Sioux City Ghosts, Sioux City, Iowa, 2004. Recipient Design Arts award Nat. Endowment for Arts, 1989-90, Graham Found. award, 1993; grad. fellow Cornell U., 1975-79, Eidlitz fellow, 1978, Soc. for Humanities and Mellon Found. fellow, 1984-85, NEH fellow, 1986, Paul Mellon vis. sr. fellow Ctr. for Advanced Study in Visual Arts, Nat. Gallery of Art; Travel to Collections grantee NEH, 1985. Mem. AAUP, Soc. Archtl. Historians (session chmn. ann. meeting 1989), Coll. Art Assn., Rice U. Alumni Assn. Democrat. Roman Catholic. Avocations: free-hand drawing, ballroom dancing, films. Home and Office: 207 W Swissvale Ave Pittsburgh PA 15218-1337 Personal E-mail: richardbecherer@yahoo.com.

BECHKOFF, JENNIFER "KAT", business educator; b. Fresno, Calif., Aug. 28, 1974; d. Robert "Buddy" Bechkoff and Carol Jacobi. BS, Calif. State U., Fresno, 1996, MBA, 1998; postgrad., U. Cin., 2004—. Single Subject Tchg. Credential, Bus. Edn. Calif., 2003. Export mgr., Fresno, 1999—2000; tchr. Citrus Mid. Sch., Orange Cove, 2002—03, Reedley H.S., Calif., 2003—04; rsch. asst. U. Cin., 2004—. Grad. Scholarship, U. Cin., 2004. R-Consevative.

BECHT, LAWRENCE JOHN, elementary school educator; b. Jamaica, NY, May 7, 1927; s. Frederick Joseph and Margaret Mary Becht; m. Joan Molnar Nizzari, Sept. 10, 1994; 1 child, Daniel Frederick; children: Lawrence J., Joan Marie Willette, James Joseph, Michael Charles, Patricia Judith D'Amico, Frederick Joseph children: Mary Ann Montgomery. BA, St. John's Coll., Bklyn., 1950; MA, Columbia U., NYC, 1954; PhD, St. John's U., Jamaica, 1964; JD, Touro Law Sch., East Islip, NY, 1988. Tchr. Levittown Pub. Schs., NY, 1950—58; sch. prin. Half Hollow Hills Schs., Dix Hills, NY, 1958—64; tchr. Old Westbury Sch. of Holy Child, Old Westbury, NY, 1987—92, Collier County Schs., Naples, Fla., 2003—. Pvt. Army Air Force, 1945—47. NY State War Svc. scholar, 1951. Mem.: Phi Delta Kappa. Home Phone: 239-774-3218.

BECHTEL, RILEY PEART, engineering company executive; s. Stephen D. Jr. Bechtel. BA in Polit. Sci., Psychology, U. Calif., Davis, 1974; JD, Stanford U., 1979, MBA, 1979. Bar: Calif. 1979. With Bechtel Group, Inc., San Francisco, 1966—79, Thelen, Marrin, Johnson & Bridges, San Francisco, 1979—81; from exec. v.p. to chmn., CEO, dir. Bechtel Corp., 1987—96, chmn., 1996—, CEO, 1996—, dir., 1996—. Mem. Bus. Coun., Bus. Roundtable policy com; bd. dirs. Bechtel Corp., 1987—; bd. dirs., mem. internat. coun. J.P. Morgan Chase; adv. com. Stanford U. Grad. Sch. of Bus.; dean's adv. coun. Stanford Law Sch. Trustee Jason Found. for Edn. Named one of Forbes' Richest Americans, 2006. Fellow: Am. Acad. Arts and Scis.; mem.: Am. Soc. Corp. Execs. (conservation fund corp. coun.), Am. Soc. Civil Engrs. (hon.). Office: Bechtel Corp 50 Beale St PO Box 193965 San Francisco CA 94119-3965*

BECHTEL, STEPHEN DAVISON, JR., retired engineering company executive; b. Oakland, Calif., May 10, 1925; s. Stephen Davison and Laura (Peart) Bechtel; m. Elizabeth Mead Hogan, June 5, 1946; 5 children. Student, U. Colo., 1943—44, DSc (hon.), 1981; BS, Purdue U., 1946, D (hon.) in Engring., 1972; MBA, Stanford U., 1948. Registered profl. engr., N.Y., Mich., Alaska, Calif., Md., Hawaii, Ohio, D.C., Va., Ill. Engring. and mgmt. positions Bechtel Corp., San Francisco, 1941-60, pres., 1960-73, chmn. of cos. in Bechtel group, 1973-80; chmn. Bechtel Group, Inc., 1980-90, chmn. emeritus, 1990—, Fremont Group, 1995—. Former chmn., mem. Bus. Coun., life-term counselor, past chmn. Conf. Bd. Trustee, mem., past chmn. bldg. and grounds com. Calif. Inst. Tech.; mem. pres.'s coun. Purdue U.; mem. adv. coun., bd. visitors Inst. Internat. Studies, Stanford; former charter mem. adv. coun. Stanford U. Grad. Sch. Bus. With USMC, 1943-46. Decorated officer French Legion Honor; named Man Yr. Engring., News-Record, 1974; named one of Forbes' Richest Americans, 2006; recipient Disting. Alumnus award, Purdue U., 1964, Ernest C. Arbuckle Disting. Alumnus award, Stanford Grad. Sch. Bus., 1974, Outstanding Achievement in Constrn. award, Moles, 1977, Disting. Engring. Alumnus award, U. Colo., 1979, Chmn.'s award, Am. Assn. Engring. Soc., 1982, Kenneth Andrew Roe award, 2003, Washington award, Western Soc. Engrs., 1985, Herbert Hoover medal, 1980, Nat. Medal Tech., Pres. Bush, 1991, Golden Beaver award, 1992, Oxford Cup award, Beta Theta Pi, 1997, Engr. Distinction award, U. Colo., 2000. Fellow AAAS; mem. ASCE (hon., engring. mgmt. award 1979, pres. award 1985, OPAL award for outstanding lifetime achievement in constrn. 2000), Inst. Chem. Engrs. (U.K., hon.); mem. AIME, NSPE (hon. chmn. Nat. Engrs. Week 1990), NAE (past chmn., Founder's award 1999), Calif. Acad. Scis. (hon. trustee), Am. Soc. French Legion Honor (bd. dirs., Disting. Achievement medal 1994), Royal Acad. Engring. (U.K., fgn.), Pacific Union Club, Bohemian

Club, San Francisco Golf Club, Claremont Country Club, Cypress Point Club, Bear River Club (Utah), Wild Goose Club (Calif.), Chi Epsilon, Tau Beta Pi. Office: PO Box 193965 San Francisco CA 94119-3965

BECHTEL, STEPHEN E., mechanical engineer, educator; BS in Engring. summa cum laude, U. Mich., 1979; PhD in Engring., U. Calif., Berkeley, 1983. Prof. dept. mech. engring. Ohio State U., Columbus, 1983—. Reviewer design, mfg. and computer-integrated engring. divsn., fluid dynamics and hydraulics directorate, thermal transport and thermal processing directorate NSF, 1985—. USDA food characterization, process, product rsch. program; cons. Hoechst Celanese Corp., Los Alamos Nat. Lab., Battelle Meml. Inst., Corning, Inc., Proctor & Gamble. Referee Jour. Rheology, Jour. Applied Mechanics, Jour. Non-Newtonian Fluid Mechanics, others. James B. Angell scholar U. Mich., 1976-79. Fellow ASME (mem. fluid mechanics com., elasticity com., applied mechanics divsn. 1989—, rec. sec. gen. com. 1991-92, rec. sec. exec. com. 1992-93, textile engring. divsn, exec. com., 2002-, Henry Hess award 1990); mem. Am. Acad. Mechanics, Soc. Rheology, Tau Beta Pi. Achievements include research in modeling of industrial polymer processing and fiber manufacturing, viscoelastic fluid flows, free surface flows and instability mechanisms, fundamental modeling of thermal expansion, material characterization, transducer characterization in non-destructive evaluation.

BECHTLE, ROBERT ALAN, artist, educator; b. San Francisco, May 14, 1932; m. Nancy Elizabeth Dalton, 1963 (div. 1982); children: Max Robert, Anne Elizabeth; m. Whitney Chadwick, 1982. BA, Calif. Coll. Arts and Crafts, Oakland, 1954, M.F.A., 1958; postgrad., U. Calif.-Berkeley, 1960-61. Graphic designer Kaiser Industries, Oakland, 1956-59; instr. Calif. Coll. Arts and Crafts, 1957-61, assoc. prof. to prof.; lectr. U. Calif.-Berkeley, 1965-66; vis. artist U. Calif.-Davis, 1966-68; assoc. prof. San Francisco State U., 1968-76, prof., 1976-99, prof. emeritus, 1999—. One-man shows Mus. of Art, San Francisco, 1959, 64, Berkeley Gallery, 1965, Richmond Art Ctr. (Calif.), 1965, U. Calif.-Davis, 1967, O.K. Harris Gallery, N.Y.C., 1971, 74, 76, 81, 84, 87, 92, 96, Berggruen Gallery, San Francisco, 1972, E.B. Crocker Art Mus., Sacramento, 1973, Univ. Art Mus., U. Calif.-Berkeley, 1979, O.K Harris Works of Art, N.Y.C., 1981, 84, 87; Daniel Weinberg Gallery, Santa Monica, 1991, Gallery Paul Anglim, San Francisco, 1991, San Francisco Mus. Modern Art, 1991, others; exhibited in group shows San Francisco Art Inst., 1966, Whitney Mus. N.Y.C., 1967, Milw. Art Ctr., 1969, Mus. Contemporary Art, Chgo., 1971, Serpentine Gallery, London, 1973, Toledo Mus. Art, 1975, San Francisco Mus. Modern Art, 1976, 1985, 2005, Pushkin Fine Arts Mus., Moscow, 1978, Pa. Acad. Fine Arts, Phila., 1981, San Antonio Mus. Art, 1981, Pa. Acad. Fine Arts, Phila, 1981, Calif. Palace of Legion of Honor, San Francisco, 1983, Mus. Contemporary Art, L.A., 1984, Univ. Art Mus., U. Calif., Berkeley, 1987, Whitney Mus., N.Y.C., 1991, Fine Arts Mus. San Francisco, 1995, Jaffe Baker Gallery, Boca Raton, Fla., 1997, Young U., Provo, Utah, others; represented in permanent collections Achenbach Found. for Graphic Arts, San Francisco, Chase Manhattan Bank, N.Y.C., E.B. Crocker Art Mus., Sacramento, Gibbes Art Gallery, S.C., High Mus. Art, Atlanta, Hunter Art Mus., Chattanooga, Library of Congress, Washington, Lowe Art Mus.-U. Miami, Coral Gables, Fla., Mills Coll., Oakland, Mus. Modern Art, N.Y.C., Met. Mus., N.Y.C., Neue Gal der Stadt Aachen, West Germany, Oakland Mus., San Francisco Mus. Modern Art, Univ. Art Mus.-U. Calif-Berkeley, Fine Arts Mus. of San Diego, Rose Art Mus., Brandeis U., Waltham, Mass., U. Nebr.-Lincoln, Whitney Mus., N.Y.C., Guggenheim Mus., N.Y.C. Served with U.S. Army, 1954-56. Recipient James D. Phelan award, 1965, Acad. award Am. Acad. Arts and Letters, 1995; named Nat. Academician, Nat. Acad. Design, 1993; Nat. Endowment for Arts grantee, 1977, 83, 89, Guggenheim grantee, 1986. Office: San Francisco State U 1600 Holloway Ave Dept Art San Francisco CA 94132-1722

BECHTOL, J. CURRIE, lawyer, oil industry executive; b. 1941; BBA, LLB, U. Tex., Austin. Bar: Tex. 1968. Atty. priv. practice, 1970—84, Hutcheson & Grundy LLP, 1984—98; v.p., gen. counsel Frontier Oil Corp., 1998—, sec., 2000—. Office: Frontier Oil Corp 10000 Memorial Dr Ste 600 Houston TX 77024-3411 Office Phone: 713-688-9600. Office Fax: 713-688-0616.

BECHTOLSHEIM, ANDY (ANDREAS), information technology executive; b. Germany, 1956; Grad., U. Germany; MS in Computer Engring., Carnegie Mellon U., Pitts., 1976; PhD student in Computer Sci. and Elec. Engring., Stanford U., Calif., 1977—82. Co-founder Sun Microsystems, Inc., Santa Clara, Calif., 1982, various roles including v.p. tech., chief arch., workstation product line, 1982—95, sr. v.p., chief arch. Network Sys., 2004—; founder Granite Systems (acquired by Cisco Sys.), 1995—96; various positions including v.p. engring., v.p., gen. mgr., Gigabit Sys. Bus. Unit Cisco Sys., 1996—2003; co-founder Kealia, Inc. (acquired by Sun Microsystems), Palo Alto, Calif., 2001, head, 2003—04. Co-founder HighBAR Ventures, 1999. Co-founder Carnegie Mellon U. West Coast Campus, Mountain View, Calif. Recipient Stanford Entrepreneur Co. of Yr. award, Smithsonian Leadership award for Innovation; Fulbright Scholarship, German Nat. Merit Found. Scholarship. Mem.: NAE. Achievements include inventing the "Stanford University Network workstation" which eventually became the Sun-1 Workstation and was instrumental in launching other successful Sun products, including the SparcStation 1; the latest design will be a supercomputer to be named the Sun Constellation System that will compete for the title as the world's fastest when installation is completed in 2007. Office: Sun Microsystems Inc 4150 Network Cir Santa Clara CA 95054 Office Phone: 650-960-1300. Office Fax: 405-276-3804.*

BECK, AARON TEMKIN, psychiatrist, educator; b. Providence, July 18, 1921; s. Harry S. and Elizabeth (Temkin) B.; m. Phyllis Whitman, June 4, 1950; children: Judith, Daniel, Alice, Roy. BA, Brown U., 1942, Dr.Med.-Sci. (hon.), 1982; MD, Yale U., 1946; LHD (hon.), Assumption Coll., 1995; DSc (hon.), U. Pa., 2007. Mem. faculty U. Pa. Med. Sch., 1954—, prof. psychiatry, 1971—, Univ. prof. (now prof. emeritus), 1983—, dir. Ctr. for Treatment and Prevention of Suicide; dir. Center Cognitive Therapy, 1965-94; pres. Beck Found. for Cognitive Therapy, 1995—. Mem. rev. panel NIMH, 1965-80, chmn. task force suicide prevention , 1969-80; bd. dirs. West Philadelphia Community Mental Health Consortium, 1975-77. Author: Depression: Causes and Treatment, 1967, Diagnosis and Management of Depression, 1973, Prediction of Suicide, 1973, Cognitive Therapy and the Emotional Disorders, 1976, Cognitive Theory of Depression, 1979, Anxiety Disorders and Phobias: A Cognitive Perspective, 1985, Love is Never Enough, 1988, Cognitive Therapy of Personality Disorders, 1990; co-author: Cognitive Therapy in Clinical Practice, 1989, Cognitive Therapy with Inpatients, 1992, Cognitive Therapy of Substance Abuse, 1993, The Integrative Power of Cognitive Therapy, 1997, Scientific Foundations of Cognitive Theory and Therapy of Depression, 1999, Prisoners of Hate, 1999, Bipolar Disorder: A Cognitive Perspective, 2001, Cognitive Therapy for Chronic Pain, 2003. Served as officer M.C. U.S. Army, 1952-54. Recipient rsch. award, R.I. Med. Soc., 1948, ann. award, Phila. Soc. Clin. Psychologists, 1978, Am. Psychopathol. Assn., 1983, Soc. for Psychotherapy Rsch., 1995, Calif. Psychol. Soc., 1996, Belmont Hosp. award, 1996, Disting. Sci. award, APA, 1989, rsch. award, Am. Assn. Suicidology, 1985, Am. Suicide Found., 1991, Albert Einstein Sch. Medicine award, 1992, Nathaniel Winkelman award, 1996, Heinz Found. award, 2001, Grawemeyer award, 2004, Albert Lasker Clin. Med. Rsch. award, Lasker Found., 2006. Fellow Royal Coll. Psychiatry, NY Acad. Medicine (Thomas Salmon award 1992), APA (rsch. award 1993), fellow Am. Acad. Arts & Scis.; mem. Calif. Psychol. Assn. (lifetime svc. award 1996), So. Psychotherapy Rsch. (pres. 1975-76), Am. Psychiat. Assn. (prize rsch. psychiatry 1979), Am. Assn. Suicidology (rsch. prize 1985), Assn. Advancement of Behavior Therapy (Lifetime Contbn. award 2001), Inst. Medicine (Rhoda and Bernard Sarnat Internat. Prize in Mental Health, 2003, Gustav O. Lienhard award, 2006). Office: 3535 Market St Rm 2022 Philadelphia PA 19104-2641 Office Phone: 215-898-4102. Business E-Mail: abeck@mail.med.upenn.edu.*

BECK, ALBERT, manufacturing executive; b. NYC, Jan. 14, 1928; s. Albert Christian and Mabel Agnes (Dunn) B.; m. Jean Norma Russ, June 16, 1951; children— Nancy, Richard, Douglas BS, Fairleigh Dickinson U., 1950; MS, Rutgers U., 1956. Product line mgr. Tung Sol Electric Inc. div. Wagner Electric, Bloomfield, NJ, 1951-66; dir. quality control IT&T, Brussels, 1966-69, asst. dir. product ops. NYC, 1969-72, dir. N.Am. staff, 1972-73; v.p. ops. Grinnell Fire Protection Co., Providence, 1973-79, exec. v.p., 1979, Grinnell Corp., 1986—2002. Mem. bd. edn. curriculum com. Wayne, N.J., 1964. Served with A.C., USN, 1945-47 Mem. Nat. Fire Sprinkler Assn. (bd. dirs. 1990), Sigma Xi. Republican. Avocations: golf, bridge, travel.

BECK, ANATOLE, mathematician, educator; b. Bronx, NY, Mar. 19, 1930; s. Morris and Minnie (Rosenblum) B.; m. Evelyn Torton, Apr. 10, 1954 (div.); children— Nina Rachel, Micah Daniel; m. Eve-Lynn Siegel, Nov. 30, 2003. BA, Bklyn. Coll., 1951; MS, Yale U., 1953, PhD, 1956. Instr. math. Williams Coll., Williamstown, Mass., 1955-56; Office Naval Rsch. rsch. assoc. Tulane U., New Orleans, 1956-57; traveling fellow Yale U., 1957—58; from asst. to assoc. prof. U. Wis., Madison, 1958—66, prof. math., 1966—; chair of math. London Sch. Econ./U. London, 1973—75. Vis. prof. Cornell U., 1960, Hebrew U., Jerusalem, 1964-65, U. Göttingen, Fed. Republic Germany, 1965, U. Warwick, 1968, Imperial Coll., U. London, 1969, U. Erlangen, Fed. Republic Germany, 1969, U. Md., 1971, Tech. U. Munich, Fed. Republic Germany, 1973, London Sch. Econs. and Univ. Coll., U. London, 1985, 91-92, 94-97, 99—; v.p. Wis. Fedn. Tchrs., 1975-83; co-founder Wis. U. Union, 1984, pres., 1988-91. Author: Continuous Flows in the Plane, 1974, (with M.N. Bleicher and D.W. Crowe) Excursions into Mathematics, 1969, 2d edit., 2000, The Knowledge Business, 1997; contbr. articles to profl. jours. Recipient Disting. Alumnus award, Bklyn. Coll., 1976. Mem. Am. Math. Soc. (council 1973-75), Math. Assn. Am., AAUP, Sigma Xi, Phi Beta Kappa, Pi Mu Epsilon. Office: U Wis 480 Lincoln Dr 721 Van Vleck Hall Madison WI 53706-1329 Business E-Mail: abeck@wisc.edu.

BECK, ANDREW JAMES, lawyer; b. Washington, Feb. 19, 1948; s. Leonard Norman and Frances (Greif) B.; m. Carol Beck, Oct. 13, 2002; children: Carter, Lowell, Justin. BA, Carleton Coll., 1969; JD, Stanford U., 1972; MBA, L.I. U., 1975. Bar: VA. 1972, NY 1973, Pa. 1992. Assoc. Casey, Lane & Mittendorf, NYC, 1972-80, ptnr., 1980-82, Haythe & Curley, NYC, 1982-99, Torys LLP, NYC, 1999—, exec. com., 2000—03. Trustee Bklyn. Heights Synagogue, 1980-81, Bklyn. Heights Montessori Sch., 1988-92, treas., 1990-92. Mem. ABA, Va. State Bar Assn., NY State Bar Assn., Pa. Bar Assn., Assn. Bar City of NY, Nat. Stroke Assn. (gen. counsel 1992—, sec., bd. dirs. 2000—). Avocation: bridge. Home: 525 E 80th St Apt 6A New York NY 10075-0789 Office: Torys LLP 237 Park Ave New York NY 10017-3142 Home Phone: 212-628-2850; Office Phone: 212-880-6010. Business E-Mail: abeck@torys.com.

BECK, BARBARA J., employment services executive; BS with honors, U. Colo., Boulder, 1982. Area v.p., gen. mgr. US-West Sprint, 1996—2000; ind. cons., 2000—02; exec. v.p. US and Can. ops. Manpower, Inc., Milw., 2002—05, exec. v.p., pres. Europe, Mid. East and Africa, 2006—. Bd. trustees Boys and Girls Clubs Greater Milw., co-chair fundraising campaign, 2003; chmn.-elect Big Bros. Big Sisters Metro Milw.; co-chair Women's Initiative United Way Greater Milw.; mem. adv. coun. U. Wis. Sch. of Bus., Milw. Named one of Women of Influence, Milw. Bus. Jour., 2003. Office: Manpower Inc 5301 N Ironwood Rd Milwaukee WI 53217 Office Phone: 414-961-1000.*

BECK, BARBARA NELL, elementary school educator; b. Corpus Christi, Tex., Oct. 25, 1940; d. Marshall Joseph and Madie Ann (Spence) Robertson; m. Joel J. Beck, June 23, 1973. BA, Baylor U., 1964. Tchr. Killeen (Tex.) Ind. Sch. Dist., 1964-2001. Sunday sch. tchr. First Bapt. Ch. of Nolanville, 1967—, co-treas., 2000—. Mem. NEA, Tex. State Tchrs. Assn. (life), Tex. Assn. for the Gifted and Talented, Killeen Edn. Assn. (treas., past pres., bd. dirs.), Clifton Park PTA (past treas.). Personal E-mail: jbeck1@hot.rr.com.

BECK, CHARLES WESLEY, II, lawyer; b. Ft. Worth, June 26, 1933; s. Charles Wesley and Evelyn Virginia Beck; m. Shirley Ann Trowbridge, July 21, 1978; children: Gary N. Trowbridge, Peggy A. Thomas, Julia A. Kenner. BS in Aero Engring., U. Tex., Austin, 1954, BSEE, 1961, MSEE, 1962; JD, Baylor U., Waco, Tex., 1986. Registered prof. engr., Tex., 1973; bar: Tex. 1986. Rsch. engr. defense rsch. lab. U. Tex., Austin, 1959—61; engr. LTV, Dallas, 1961—62; rsch. engr., group leader NASA Ames Rsch. Ctr., Mountain View, Calif., 1962—67; program mgr., mgr. elec. sys. Tracor, Inc., Austin, 1967—73; sub contract mgr. E-Sys., Garland, 1973—75; pres., founder Internat. Avionics, Inc., Addison, 1970—; atty. pvt.pvt. practice, 1986—. Lt. USN, 1954—58. Mem.: Tex. Bar Assn., Mensa. Republican. Achievements include invention of liquid level measurement; computer for liquid level measurement; fuel transmitter. Avocation: old cars. Home: 3405 Haversham Plano TX 75023 Office: Internat Avionics Inc 3782 Arapaho Rd Addison TX 75001 E-mail: charles@beck.name.

BECK, CYNTHIA MARIE, archivist, researcher; b. Chgo., Sept. 8, 1956; d. Albert Edmond DeBock and Joan Elizabeth Farley; m. William Randall Beck, Nov. 6, 1994. AAS, Triton Coll., River Grove, Illinois, 1981; BA, Nat. Lewis U., 1982; MSLS, Chgo. State U., 1994. Cert. Acad. Cert. Archivists. Intern Newberry Libr., Chgo., 1993—94; libr. Underwriters Labs, Inc., Northbrook, Ill., 1995—96; libr. coord. Daily Herald/Paddock Publs., Arlington Heights, Ill., 1996—98; reference archivist Rotary Internat., Evanston, Ill., 1999—2005, order mgmt. supr., 2005—. Mem. archives com. Episcopal Diocese of Chgo., 2005—. Researcher (history book) A Century of Service: The Story of Rotary International, (web page) Global History of Rotary. Pres. NW Suburban Coun. Genealogists, Cook County, Ill., 2000—02. Paul Harris fellow, Rotary Found. of Rotary Internat., 2003. Mem.: Soc. Am. Archivists, Midwest Archives Conf., Chgo. Area Archivists. Democrat. Episcopalian. Avocations: theology, genealogy, singing. Office: Rotary Internat 7100 N Lawndale Ave Lincolnwood IL 60712 Home Phone: 847-593-6409; Office Phone: 847-866-4470. Business E-Mail: cyndi.beck@rotary.org.

BECK, DAVID EDWARD, surgeon; b. Geneva, Ill., May 1, 1953; s. George R. and Gloria M. (Zesch) B.; m. Sharon Mieir, Aug. 30, 1983; children: Allison, Lauren, John. BS, USAF Acad., 1975; MD, U. Miami, Fla., 1979; postgrad., USAF Aerospace Medicine Primary Course, Brooks AFB, Tex., 1978, Combat Casualty Care Course, Ft. Sam Houston, Tex., 1980, Hyperbaric Oxygen CourseB, Brooks AFB, 1982, ATLS Instr. Course, Ft. Sam Houston, 1986, Squadon Officers Sch., 1987-88, Mgmt. for Chief of Hosp. Svcs., Sheppard AFB, Tex., 1988, Sch. Pub. Health, Harvard U., 1990. Diplomate Am. Bd. Colon and Rectal Surgery. Lt. Col. USAF, 1975-93; resident in gen. surgery Wilford Hall USAF Med. Ctr., Lackland AFB, Tex., 1979-84, chief colorectal surgery, 1986-92, staff surgeon, chief colorectal surgery svc., 1986-92, asst. chmn. dept. gen. surgery, 1988, chmn. dept. gen. surgery, residency program dir., 1988-92; staff gen. surgeon Patrick AFB Hosp., Fla., 1984-85; fellow in colorectal surgery Cleve. Clinic Found., 1985-86; residency program dir. gen. surgery Joint Mil. Med. Command, San Antonio, 1989-91; clin. assoc. prof. surgery U. Tex. Health Sci. Ctr., San Antonio, 1990-92, F. Edward Herbert Sch. Medicine, U. Health Scis., Bethesda, Md., 1992—; chief surgery 870 USAF Contingency Hosp., RAF Little Rissington, England, 1993; staff colorectal surgeon Ochsner Clinic, New Orleans, 1993—, chmn. dept. colon and rectal surgery, 1994—; med. dir. Ochsner Endoscopy Ambulatory Surgery Ctr., 2003—06. Cons. USAF Surgeon Gen., Washington, 1986-92. Author chpts. to books; co-editor (textbooks); (with David R. Welling) Patient Care in Colorectal Surgery, 1991, (with Steven D. Wexner) Fundamentals of Anorectal Surgery, 1992, 2nd edit., 1998, (with T.C. Hicks, F.E. Opelka, A.E., Timmcke) Complications of Colon and Rectal Surgery, 1996; editor: Handbook of Colorectol Surgery, 1997, 2d edit., 2002; mem. editl. bd. Current Surgery, 1990-2006; reviewer Diseases of the Colon and Rectum, 1990—, mem. editl. bd., 1992-98, So. Me. Jour., 1988-92; mem. editl. bd. Perspectives in Colon and Rectal Surgery, 1997-2000; editor-in-chief Clinics in Colon and Rectal Surgery, 2001—, Ochsner Jour.; contbr. articles to profl. jours. Decorated Air Force Achievement medal with oak leaf cluster, Air Force Meritorious Svc. medal with oak leaf cluster; recipient Pres. award United Ostomy Assn., 2000. Fellow ACS; mem. AMA, Am. Soc. Colon and Rectal Surgeons (mem. socioecon./legis. com. 1991-94, pub. rels. com. 1993-99, chmn. 1996-99, mem.-at-large exec. coun. 2004—, Outstanding Young Investigator award, 1992), Assn. Mil. Surgeons U.S., La. State Med. Soc., Soc. Air Force Clin. Surgeons (treas. 1989-90, v.p. 1990-92, pres. 1992-93, Excalibur award 1992), Soc. Surgery of Alimentary Tract, So. Med. Assn. (mem. colon and rectal sect., sec. 1988-91, v.p. 1990-91, pres. 1991-92), Soc. Med. Cons. to Armed forces, St. Tamminy Parish Med. Soc., Tex. Soc. Colon and Rectal Surgeons (sec. 1991-93), Air force Assn., USAF Acad. Assn. Grads. Avocations: fishing, wood working, gardening. Home: 127 Deloaks Rd Madisonville LA 70447-9597 Office: Oschner Clin Found 1514 Jefferson Hwy New Orleans LA 70121-2429 Home Phone: 985-845-1063; Office Phone: 504-842-4060. Personal E-mail: dbeckmd@aol.com. Business E-Mail: dbeck@oschner.org.

BECK, EDWARD WILLIAM, lawyer; b. Atchison, Kans., Aug. 19, 1944; s. Russell Niles and Lucille Mae (Leighton) B.; m. Marshia Ablon, June 24, 1966; children: Michael Adam, David Gordon, Stephen Jared BA cum laude, Yale U., 1967; JD cum laude, Harvard U., 1972. Bar: Calif. 1972. Assoc. firm Pillsbury, Madison & Sutro, San Francisco, 1972-77; gen. counsel Pacific Lumber Co., San Francisco, 1977-86, sec., 1978-86, v.p., 1980-86, dir., 1985-86; v.p., gen. counsel, sec. Yamamouchi Consumer Inc. (formerly Shaklee Corp.), San Franciso, Pleasanton, Calif., 1986-87, sr. v.p., gen. counsel, sec., 1987—2004, exec. v.p., gen. counsel, sec., 2004; sr. v.p., gen. counsel, sec. Mervyn's LLC, 2005—. Bd. dirs. Yamanouchi Consumer Inc. (formerly Shaklee Corp.), mem. audit com., 2001—04. Trustee, mem. exec. com. San Francisco Conservatory Music, 1988—, co-chmn. acad. affairs com., 1989—91, chmn. presdl. search com., 1991, chair trustees and officers com., 1993—96, exec. vice chair, 1994—, chair conservatory 2006 com., 1996—99, chmn. maj. gifts com., 1999—2001, co-chmn. instl. advancement com., 1999—2001, mem. bldg. com., 2000—05, chair new conservatory com., 2004—06; mem. law com. United Way of Bay Area Campaign, 1991—2000, chmn., 1992. Mem. ABA, Calif. Bar Assn., San Francisco Bar Assn. (bd. dirs. 1991-94, nominating com. 1993), Bay Area Gen. Counsels Group (chmn. 1991), San Francisco C. of C. (leadership coun. 1987—, gen. coun., bd. dirs., exec. com. 1993-96), San Francisco Yale Alumni Assn. (schs. com.). Office: Mervyns LLC 22301 Foothill Blvd MS 4135 Hayward CA 94541-2771

BECK, GEORGE PRESTON, anesthesiologist, educator; b. Wichita Falls, Tex., Oct. 21, 1930; s. George P. and Amanda (Wilbanks) Beck; m. Constance Carolyn Krog, Dec. 22, 1953; children: Carla Elizabeth, George P., Howard W. BS, Midwestern U., 1951; MD, U. Tex., 1955. Diplomate Am. Bd. Anesthesiology. Intern John Sealy Hosp., 1955—56; resident in anesthesiology Parkland Meml. Hosp., Dallas, 1959—62, vis. staff, 1964—; pvt. practice Lubbock, Tex., 1964—. Asst. prof. anesthesiology U. Tex. Southwestern Med. Sch., Dallas, 1962—64, asst. clin. prof., 1964—71, prof., 1996—; assoc. clin. prof. anesthesiology U. Tex. Med. Br., Galveston, 1971—; pres. Gt. Plains Ballistics Corp., 1967—; clin. prof. Tex. Tech U. Sch. Medicine, Lubbock, 1986—. Pres. coun. Luth. Ch., 1965—66. With USAF, 1956—59. Fellow: Am. Coll. Anesthesiologists; mem.: Lubbock Surg. Soc., Lubbock County Med. Soc., Tex. Soc. Anesthesiologists (pres. 1974), Tex. Med. Soc., Am. Soc. Anesthesiologists. Achievements include invention of Beck Airway Airflow Monitor. Home: 4601 18th St Lubbock TX 79416-5713 Office: PO Box 16385 Lubbock TX 79490-6385

BECK, GEORGE WILLIAM, retired industrial engineer; b. Dayton, Ohio, Aug. 31, 1921; s. George A. and Florence I. (Hosket) B.; m. Elizabeth A. Thatcher, Apr. 14, 1945 (died Nov. 8, 1992); children: Bruce, Christine, William. B of Indsl. Engring., Kettering U., Flint, Mich., 1946. Registered profl. engr., Ohio. Sales rep. Inland Mfg. div. Gen. Motors Corp., Dayton, 1946-53, sr. project engr., 1953-56, staff engr., 1956, asst. chief engr., 1956-62, chief engr., 1962-80, dir. engring., 1980-85; ret., 1985. Trustee Met. YMCA, 1964-71; chmn. bd. mgmt. Kettering YMCA, 1966-70; mem. Centerville City Sch. Dist. bd. edn., 1968-74, v.p., 1973-74. Served to lt. (j.g.) USNR, 1943-45. Mem. Soc. Automotive Engrs., Dayton C. of C., Aircraft Owners and Pilots Assn. (lic. pilot). Clubs: MVMA, Sycamore Creek Country, Mission Valley Country. Lutheran. Achievements include the invention of automotive products; holder of 10 patents in field. Home: 2120 Timucua Trl Nokomis FL 34275-5306

BECK, GLENN, radio personality; b. Feb. 10, 1964; m. Tania Beck; 4 children. Disc jockey WKCI-FM (KC101), Hamden, Conn.; talk radio host WELI, Hamden, Conn., WFLA-AM, The Glenn Beck Program, Tampa, Fla., 2000—02, The Glenn Beck Program, Nat. Radio, 2002—; TV show host CNN Headline News, Glenn Beck on Headline News, 2006—. Founder Fusion Mag., 2005. Author: The Real America.: Messages from the Heart and Heartland, 2003, An Inconvenient Book, 2007; contbg. writer/host (Morning Talk Show) ABC's Good Morning Am., 2006—. Church Of The Latter Day Saints. Office: Premier Radio Networks 15260 Ventura Blvd Sherman Oaks CA 91403 E-mail: me@glennbeck.com.*

BECK, GLENN E., information technology executive; b. Quakertown, Pa., 1952; BS in Mgmt. sci., Lehigh Univ., 1974; grad. mgmt. info. resource program, Harvard Univ., 1990. Joined Air Products and Chem., Allentown, Pa., 1974—, various positions in info. tech. ops, application devel. and project mgmt., 1974—93, dir. of IT, chem. group, 1993—2000, dir., IT bus. process, 2000—01, v.p., global info. tech., 2001—. Bd. dir. Chem. Industry Data Exchange; former bd. dir. Chem. Process Dir. Group. Mem.: Phila. Chapter, Soc. for Info. Mgmt., Lehigh County Conf. of Churches (bd. dir.). Office: VP Global Info Tech Air Products & Chem Inc 7201 Hamilton Blvd Allentown PA 18195-1501

BECK, JAN SCOTT, lawyer; b. Newark, May 5, 1955; s. Robert William and Dorothy (Warhaftig) B.; m. Marla Terri Klein, Sept. 27, 1981; children: Jamie Kyle, Bryan Michael, Sean Jason. BA in Acctg., Rider U., 1977; JD, Villanova U., 1980, LLM in Taxation, 1985. Bar: N.J. 1980, U.S. Dist. Ct. N.J. 1980, N.Y. 1981, U.S. Tax Ct. 1981, D.C. 1985, U.S. Supreme Ct. 1986. Pvt. practice, Westfield, N.J., 1980-86; atty. Inspiration Resources Corp., NYC, 1986-88; dir. taxation ADT Inc., Boca Raton, Fla., 1988-89, v.p., gen. counsel, 1989-96; sr. v.p., dir. ADT Security Svcs., Inc., 1996-97; mng. dir., CEO The Turbary Group, Boca Raton, Fla., 1997—2002; pres., COO StarCapital Corp., 2002—. Atty. Laventhol & Horwath, Phila., 1979-80, Touche Ross & Co., N.Y.C., 1980-86; dir. taxation Inspiration Resources Corp., N.Y.C., Monsoon Internat. LLC, 2000-02. Author: The Strike: Student Involvement, 1975. Mem. ABA, N.Y. State Bar Assn., N.J. Bar Assn., AICPA, N.J. Soc. CPAs, Tax Exec. Inst., Omicron Delta Epsilon,

Delta Epsilon Kappa. Avocations: camping, backpacking, mountain climbing, writing, skiing. Home: 20988 Solano Way Boca Raton FL 33433-1621 Office: Frederick House Frederick St PO Box SS-19392 Nassau The Bahamas Office Phone: 561-795-9200. E-mail: jbeck@starcapital.net.

BECK, JANE, dance educator, choreographer; b. Newark, May 18, 1959; d. David and Beatrice G. Beck; m. Frederick B. Meltzer, Aug. 18, 1991 (div. May 28, 1998); 1 child, Brea Beck Meltzer. BFA, Boston Conservatory, 1981; MEd, Temple U., Phila., 1988. Cert. tchr. Pa., Temple U., 1988, Fla., 2000. Actress, choreographer Green Mt. Guild Summer Stock, White River Junction, Mt. Snow, Stowe and Killington, Vt., 1981; dance dir. Pine Crest Sch., Boca Raton, Fla., 1990—92; actress local and nat. TV commls. and infommercials West Palm Beach, Fla., 1992—95; co-host entertainment TV program Palm Beach County Channel 20, West Palm Beach, 1994—95; performing arts dir. Poinciana Day Sch., West Palm Beach, 1998—2000; dance dir. U.B. Kinsey/Palmview Elem. Sch. Arts, West Palm Beach, 2000—. Asst. to prodr., choreographer: (Off Broadway) Hello, I'm Not In Right Now, 1983; prodr., choreographer: Jane Beck Presents, Inner City Rhythm, Kravis Ctr. for Performing Arts, 2005. Office Phone: 561-802-2145.

BECK, JILL, academic administrator, dance educator; b. Worcester, Mass., Aug. 10, 1949; d. John Jacob and Helen Bernadette (Provost) Lindberg; m. Robert Joel Beck, Apr. 21, 1973. BA, Clark U., 1970; MA, McGill U., 1976; PhD, CUNY, 1985. Cert. tchr. and profl. reconstructor in Labanotation. Dir. edn. Dance Notation Bur., NYC, 1980-83; sr. lectr. S. Australian Coll. Advanced Edn., Adelaide, 1983-85; guest faculty U. Mich., 1985, U. Colo, 1986, Denison U., 1987; faculty Am. Dance Festival, Durham, N.C., 1985, The Juilliard Sch., NYC, 1985, asst. dir. dance div., 1988-89; chmn. theatre and dance dept., CUNY, 1985-87, dir. grad. studies dept. dance, 1987; faculty, cons. Hartford Ballet, Conn., 1983, chmn. dance dept. Southern Meth. U., CUNY, dean, Sch. of Arts, U. Calif. Irvine, 1995-03, pres. Lawrence U., Wis., 2004-. Project dir. Ct. Coun. on the Humanities and Arts, 1989-90; cons. Universal Ballet Co. of Korea, 1988-89; project dir. Fund for Improvement Post-Secondary Edn., Washington, 1982-85, NEH, 1983-85, CUNY Research Found., 1981-82; dance dir., cons. Dance Notation Bur., NYC, 1983, mem. profl. adv. com., 1982-84, 85-88; mem. Internat. Conf. Kinetography Laban, 1982—; mem. exec. com. Internat. Movement Notators Alliance, 1984-85; co-chmn. Soc. Dance History Scholars Conf., NYC, 1985-86; dir. program in advanced studies Am. Dance Festival, 1986; stage dir. Lincoln Ctr. student programs, 1987; Dir. dance revivals Doris Humphrey choregraphy, 1981—, Anna Sokolow choreography, 1982—, founder and dir. ArtsBridge Am., 1996, daVinci Ctr. Learning through Arts, 2001. Editor Dance Notation Jour., 1983-85; author several monographs, dance textbooks, and instructional videotapes. Recipient Exhibit award CUNY, 1982, Jack Linquist award, Clara Barton award, Learning for Life award. Democrat. Avocations: travel, art collecting. Office: Off of Pres Lawrence Univ PO Box 599 Appleton WI 54912*

BECK, JOHN CHRISTIAN, physician, educator; b. Audubon, Iowa, Jan. 4, 1924; s. Wilhelm and Marie (Brandt) Beck. MD, McGill U., 1947, MSc, 1951, DSc (hon.), 1994; PhD (hon.), Ben Gurion U. of Negev, 1981. Diplomate Am. Bd. Internal Medicine (chmn., dir.). Intern Royal Victoria Hosp., Montreal, 1947—48, sr. asst. resident, 1948—49, physician-in-chief, endocrinologist, 1964—74; chmn. dept. medicine and dir. Univ. Clinic McGill U., 1964—74; prof. medicine U. Calif., San Francisco, 1974—79; dir. Robert Wood Johnson Clin. Scholars Program, 1973—78; prof. geriat. medicine and gerontology UCLA, 1979—, dir. academic geriat. resource ctr., 1984—90; dir. long term car gerontology ctr. UCLA/U. So. Calif., 1980—85; dir. Calif. Geriatric Edn. Ctr., 1987—97, emeritus dir., 1993—; dir. multicampus program in geriat. medicine and gerontology UCLA, 1979—93. Pres. Am. Bd. Med. Spltys.; vis. prof. numerous univs.; Simeone lectr. Brown U., 1977; John McCreary Meml. lectr. U. B.C., 1985; Bruce Hall Meml. lectr. Garvan Inst. Med. Rsch., U. NSW, Sydney, 1989; Allen T. Bailey Meml. lectr. U. Sask., Canada, 1989; delivered Chaikin Oration, Australian Acad. Tech. Scis. and Engring., 2004—; Froehlich vis. prof. Royal Soc. Medcine, England, 2007. Editl. bd. Jour. Clin. Endocrinology and Metabolism, Current Topics in Exptl. Endocrinology, Psychiatry in Medicine, Health Policy and Edn., Jour. Am. Bd. Family Practice, cons. editor Roche Lab. Series on Geriatrics and Gerontology. Recipient Lifetime award, Ben Gurion U. of Negev, Israel, 1985, Ann. Gerontology award in edn., Jewish Homes for the Aging, 1994, commendation, City of L.A., 1994. Master: ACP (Philips award 2003); fellow: AAAS, Am. Fedn. on Aging Rsch. (Irving S. Wright award 1991), Gerontol. Soc. Am. (mem. editl. bd. jour., Joseph T. Freeman award 1990, Donald P. Kent award 2001), Am. Geriat. Soc. (Milo F. Leavitt Meml. award 1988), Western Assn. Physicians, Internat. Soc. Neuroendocrinology, Assn. Am. Med. Colls., Can. Assn. Profs. Medicine (Ronald V. Christie award 1987), Can. Physiol. Soc., McGill Osler Reporting Soc. (sec.), Royal Soc. Can., Inst. Medicine, Internat. Soc. Endocrinology (sec.-gen.), Can. Soc. Clin. Investigation (pres.), Endocrine Soc. (v.p., chmn. postgrad. assembly), Am. Fedn. Clin. Rsch. (coun. East divsn.), Can. Med. Assn. (postgrad. edn. com.), Am. Diabetes Assn., Can. Diabetes Assn., Royal Coll. Physicians Can. (mem. coun., Duncan Graham award 1990), Royal Coll. Physicians London, Montreal Physiol. Soc., Laurentian Hormone Conf. (bd. dirs.), Am. Clin. and Climatol. Assn., Can. Med. Protective Assn., Soc. Exptl. Biology and Medicine (mem. editl. bd. jour.), Alpha Omega Alpha, Sigma Xi; mem.: Australian Acad. Technol. Scis. and Engring. (Chaikin Oration 2004), Assn. for Gerontology in Higher Edn. (Disting. Svc. Recognition award 2001). Office: 1562 Casale Rd Pacific Palisades CA 90272-2714 Fax: 310-454-1944. Business E-Mail: egebjcb@ucla.edu.

BECK, JOHN ROBERT, pathologist, information scientist; b. Cleve., Sept. 8, 1953; s. John Edward and Maralyn Janet (Smith) Beck; children: John Benjamin, Stefan Andrew, Meredith Louise; m. Marjorie Callahan Ritchie, July 20, 2002. AB, Dartmouth Coll., 1974; MD, Johns Hopkins U., 1978. Diplomate Am. Bd. Pathology. Intern, then resident in pathology Dartmouth-Hitchcock Med. Ctr., Hanover, NH, 1978-80, dir. bloodbank, 1984-89, dir. clin. pathology, 1987-89; fellow, clin. decision making New Eng. Med. Ctr., Boston, 1981; from asst. to assoc. prof. pathology Dartmouth Med. Sch., Hanover, 1982-89; prof., dir. biomed. info. communication ctr. Oreg. Health Scis. U., Portland, 1989-92; prof., v.p. info. tech. Baylor Coll. Medicine, Houston, 1992—2001; exec. dir. Houston Acad. Medicine-Tex. Med. Ctr. Libr., 1999—2001; sr. mem., v.p. Infotech Fox Chase Cancer Ctr., Phila., 2001—, dep. dir. population scis. divsn., 2006—. Mem. healthcare tech. and decision scis. rev. panel Agy. Healthcare Rsch. and Quality, 2005—; bd. dirs. IDM, Inc. Editor-in-chief Med. Decision Making, 1989-94. Elder First Presbyn. Ch., Moorestown, NJ, 2005—. Recipient Rsch. Career Devel. award, Nat. Libr. Medicine, 1986, Cancer Biomed. Informatics Grid award, Nat. Cancer Inst., 2006. Fellow: Coll. Am. Pathologists (com. vice-chair 1997—2000), Am. Coll. Med. Informatics; mem.: Leadership of Phila., Group on Info. Resources (exec. com. 1997—2000), Am. Assn. Med. Colls., Soc. for Med. Decision Making (sec.-treas. 1985—87, v.p. 1987—88, pres. 1995—96). Republican. Avocations: golf, bridge, trumpet, scuba diving. Office: 333 Cottman Ave Philadelphia PA 19111 Office Phone: 215-214-1490. Business E-Mail: robert.beck@fccc.edu.

BECK, JOSHUA JAMES, information technology executive; b. Columbus, Ohio, Jan. 22, 1973; s. James O. and Patricia L. Beck. Student in Nuc. Engring., U. Cinn., 1991—93; student in Computer Sci., Ohio State U., 1993—95. Pres. Beck Discovery Labs., Powell, Ohio, 1993—99; dir. info. tech. Nat. Auto Care, Westerville, 1996—2000; cons. info. tech. Forte Data Systems, Cumming, Ga., 2000—01; mgr. online svcs., sr. arch. APCO, Norcross, 2001—06; tech. architect Target Corp., Mpls., 2006—. Mem.: Multiple Data Security Pro (key mem.), Assn. Computer Machinery, Mensa. Achievements include design of Multiple complete Vehicle Service Contract core business applications. Avocation: music. Office: Target Corp 33 S 6th St CC-0935 Minneapolis MN 55402 Office Phone: 612-304-3988.

BECK, LOIS GRANT, anthropologist, educator, author; b. Bogota, Colombia, Nov. 5, 1944; d. Martin Lawrence and Dorothy (Sweet) Grant; m. Henry Huang; 1 dau., Julia Huang. BA, Portland State U., 1967; MA, U. Chgo., 1969, PhD, 1977. Asst. prof. Amherst (Mass.) Coll., 1973-76, Univ. Utah, Salt Lake City, 1976-80; from asst. to assoc. prof. Washington U., St. Louis, 1980-92, prof., 1992—. Author: Qashqa'i of Iran, 1986, Nomad, 1991; co-editor Women in the Muslim World, 1978, Women in Iran from the Rise of Islam to 1800, 2003, Women in Iran from 1800 to the Islamic Republic, 2004. Grantee Social Sci. Rsch. Coun., 1990, NEH, 1990-92, 98, Am. Philos. Soc., 1998. Mem. Mid. East Studies Assn. (bd. dirs. 1981-84), Soc. Iranian Studies (exec. sec. 1979-82, edit. bd. 1982-91, coun. 1996-98). Office: Washington U Dept Anthropology CB1114 1 Brookings Dr Saint Louis MO 63130-4899 Office Phone: 314-935-5252. Business E-Mail: lbeck@artsci.wustl.edu.

BECK, MARILYN MOHR, columnist; b. Chgo., Dec. 17, 1928; d. Max and Rose (Lieberman) Mohr; m. Roger Beck, Jan. 8, 1949 (div. 1974); children: Mark Elliott, Andrea; m. Arthur Levine, Oct. 12, 1980. AA, U. So. Calif., 1950. Freelance writer nat. mag. and newspapers, Hollywood, Calif., 1959-63; Hollywood columnist Valley Times and Citizen News, Hollywood, Calif., 1963-65; West Coast editor Sterling Mag., Hollywood, Calif., 1963-74; free-lance entertainment writer LA Times, Calif., 1965-67; Hollywood columnist Bell-McClure Syndicate, 1967-72; chief Bell-McClure Syndicate (West Coast bur.), 1967-72; Hollywood columnist NANA Syndicate, 1967-72; syndicated Hollywood columnist NY Times Spl. Features, 1972-78, NY Times Spl. Features (United Feature Syndicate), 1978-80, United Press abroad, 1978-80, Internat. Editors News and Features, Chgo. Tribune/NY Daily News Syndicate, 1980-97; columnist TV Guide, 1989—92, Creators Syndicate, 1997—. Creator, host Marilyn Beck's Hollywood Outtakes spls. NBC, 1977, 78; host Marilyn Beck's Hollywood Hotline, Sta. KFI, LA, 1975-77; Hollywood reporter Eyewitness News, Sta. KABC-TV, LA, 1981, (TV program) PM Mag., 1983-88; on-air corr. E! TV, 1993-99, CompuServe Entertainment Authority, 1994-96, eDrive Internet Authority, 1996-97, e!online Internet Hollywood Authority, 1997-2000, Compuserve, Netscape, 2000—, aeNTV.com, 2001-02; author: (non-fiction) Marilyn Beck's Hollywood, 1973, (novel) Only Make Believe, 1988; co-author: Unfinished Lives, What If.?, 1996. Recipient Citation of Merit LA City Coun., 1973, Press award Pub. Guild Am., 1974, Bronze Halo award So. Calif. Motion Picture Coun., 1982. Address: 4926 Delos way Oceanside CA 92056 *Being the best isn't everything; it's the only thing. "Life is too short to be little" (Disraeli).*

BECK, MARTHA ANN, curator, director; BA in English Lit., Vassar Coll., 1960; postgrad., NYU, 1963-67. Editor, writer, rschr. The Frick Collection, 1962-64; curatorial asst. drawings dept. The Mus. Modern Art, 1968-75; founder, dir. The Drawing Ctr., 1975-90, The Ctr. for Internat. Exhbns., 1992—. Served on numerous juries and panels including Nat. Endowment for the Arts, SUNY Thayer Family Fellowships, The Westchester Coun. on the Arts and the Jerome Found. Fellowships; lectr. in field. Author: (screenplays) Ashenden's Adventures as British Agent During World War I, 2005—06, Mami, 2006, Los Niños Héroes, 2007. Recipient NYU scholarship, 1964-65. Home: 9 Gramercy Park S New York NY 10003-1742 Office Phone: 212-473-4918.

BECK, NATHANIEL L., political science professor; BA in Mathematics and Polit. Sci., U. Rochester, 1967; MA in Polit. Sci., Yale U., 1969, MPhil in Polit. Sci., PhD, 1977. Asst. prof. Washington State U., 1973—78, U. Calif. San Diego, 1978—86, assoc. prof., 1986—93, prof., 1993—2003, NYU, 2003—. Vis. assoc. prof. Harvard U., 1986—87; lectr., summer program, European Consortium for Polit. Rsch. Essex U., England, 1988—96; lectr., summer program, Interuniversity Consortium for Polit. Rsch. U. Mich., 1990—2001; NSF review panel, Human-Spatial Dynamics Program, 2004; dir., grad. studies, dept. polit. sci. U. Calif. San Diego, 1989—94, grad. council, 1995—98, chair, grad. coun., 1997—98, mem. steering com. CREATE (ORU related to rsch. on edn.), 1998—, chair, com. to review urban studies program, 1999, mem., Com. on Academic Personnel (CAP), 2001—02; dir. grad. studies NYU, 2004—05, vice-chair, 2005—06, chair, 2006—. Editor: Polit. Analysis, 1999—2003; co-editor Analytic Methods for Social Research, 2003—, mem. editl. bd. World Politics, Encyclopedia of Social Science Methods, American Political Science Review, American Journal of Political Science, Public Opinion Quarterly. Recipient Gosnell prize (Best Paper presented in Polit. methodology), 1997, 1999. Fellow: Am. Acad. Arts & Sciences; mem.: Am. Polit. Sci. Assn. (v.p., polit. methodology subfield 1997—99, mem. publications com. 1999—2002, chair, publications com. 2001—02). Office: Dept Politics NYU 726 Broadway Room 758 7th Fl New York NY 10003 Office Phone: 212-998-8535. Office Fax: 212-995-4184. Business E-Mail: nathaniel.beck@nyu.edu.

BECK, PAUL A., lawyer; m. Nancy Flaherty; children: Jennifer, Bradford, Michael. BS, Carnegie-Mellon U., 1957; LLB, Duquesne U., 1962. Bar: Pa. 1962, U.S. Ct. Appeals (4th cir.) 1963, U.S. Supreme Ct. 1966, U.S. Ct. Appeals (2d and 3d cirs.) 1971, U.S. Ct. Appeals (7th cir.) 1974, U.S. Ct. Appeals (Fed. cir.) 1982. Ptnr. Buell, Ziesenheim, Beck & Alstadt, Pitts., 1962-88, Buchanan Ingersoll, Pitts., 1988-95; propr. Paul A. Beck & Assocs. P.C., Pitts., 1995—. Del. U.S. Ct. Appeals (3d cir.) Jud. Conf., 1983. Chmn. alumni forum com. Carnegie-Mellon U., Pitts., 1966-67. Capt. U.S. Army, 1957-59. Mem. ABA, Pa. Bar Assn., Nat. Coun. Pat. Law Assn., Allegheny County Bar Assn. (gov. 1977-79, chmn. intellectual property law sect. 1979-84), Pitts. Intellectual Property Law Assn. (bd. dirs., pres. 1989-90), Duquesne U. Law Sch. Alumni Assn. (v.p. 1997-98, pres. 1999—). Office: Beck & Thomas PC Ste 100 1575 McFarland Rd Pittsburgh PA 15216-1808 Office Phone: 412-343-9700. Business E-Mail: pbeck@beckthomas.com. *Man must set principles as guided by his conscience under which he will live. He will then be accountable to mankind and God in meeting that standard.*

BECK, PAUL ALLEN, dean, political science professor; b. Logansport, Ind., Mar. 15, 1944; s. Frank Paul and Mary Elizabeth (Flanegin) B.; m. Maria Teresa Marcano, June 10, 1967; children: Daniel Lee, David Andrew. AB, Ind. U., 1966; MA, U. Mich., 1968, PhD, 1971. Asst. prof. U. Pitts., 1970-75, assoc. prof., 1976-79; prof. Fla. State U., Tallahassee, 1979-87, chmn. dept., 1981-87; prof. Ohio State U., Columbus, 1987—, chmn. dept., 1991—2004; dean Coll. Social and Behavioral Scis. Ohio State U., Columbus, 2004—. Co-author: Political Socialization Across the Generations, 1975, Individual Energy Conservation Behaviors, 1980, Electoral Change in Advanced Industrial Democracies, 1984, Party Politics in America, 10th edit., 2003. Chmn. coun. Inter-Univ. Consortium for Polit. and Social Research, 1982-83, mem., 1980-83; mem. NSF polit. sci. panel, 1988-89. Recipient Disting. Svc. award Ohio State U., 2000, Disting. Scholar award Ohio State U., 2004. Mem. Am. Polit. Sci. Assn. (exec. coun. 1981-82, 93-94, book rev. editor 1976-79, program chair 1994, chair strategic planning com. 1999-2000, Goodnow award 2005, Eldersveld award, 2007), Midwest Polit. Sci. Assn. (exec. coun. 1987-90, mem. editl. bd. 1988-90, program chair 1991, v.p. 1996-98), So. Polit. Sci. Assn. (mem. editl. bd. 1982-87), Phi Beta Kappa, Pi Sigma Alpha (exec. coun.), Phi Kappa Phi. Democrat. Home: 7003 Perry Dr Columbus OH 43085-2815 Office: Ohio State U Coll Social and Behavioral Scis Columbus OH 43210-1341 Home Phone: 614-436-3978. E-mail: beck.9@osu.edu.

BECK, PETER, marketing executive, minister; b. Cin., July 5, 1965; s. Melvin E. and Janet L. Beck; m. Melanie B. Gundler, Dec. 8, 1984; children: Alexander, Karis. Cert. graphic arts, Ctrl. Acad., Cin., 1989; BA, Boyce Coll., 2001; MDiv, So. Bapt. Theol. Sem., 2003, postgrad., 2004—. Art dir. Foote Cone & Belding, Chgo., 1984—87, TBWA Chiat Day, St. Louis, 1992—94, Hughes Group, St. Louis, 1994—98; pastor Van Buren Bapt. Ch., Louisville, 1999—2005, Kenwood Bapt. Ch., Louisville, 2004—; dir. mktg. So. Sem., Louisville, 2000—. Editor: So. Sem. Mag., 2001—; contbr. articles to profl. jours. With US Army, 1984—87. Recipient Nat. Leadership award, Nat. Rep. Congl. Com., 2003. Mem.: Am. Soc. Ch. History, Am. Hist. Assn., Evang. Theol. Soc. Republican. Baptist. Avocations: reading, writing, illustrating, skiing. Home: 2115 Challedon Way Louisville KY 40223 Office: So Bapt Theol Sem 2825 Lexington Rd Louisville KY 40280

BECK, PHILIP S., lawyer; b. Chgo., Apr. 30, 1951; BA with academic distinction, U. Wis., 1973; JD magna cum laude, Boston U., 1976. Bar: Ill. 1977. Clerk U.S. Ct. Appeals DC Cir., 1976-77; ptnr. Kirkland & Ellis, 1977—93; founding ptnr. Bartlit Beck Herman Palenchar & Scott LLP, Chgo., 1993—. Editor-in-chief Boston U. Law Review. Bd. visitors Boston U. Sch. Law; bd. dir. Northwestern U. Settlement House. Named one of Top 10 Litigators, Nat. Law Jour., 2003. Fellow: Am. Bar Found., Internat. Acad. Trial Lawyers, Am. Coll. of Trial Lawyers. Office: Bartlit Beck Herman et al Courthouse Pl 54 W Hubbard St Chicago IL 60610-4645 Office Phone: 312-494-4400. Office Fax: 312-494-4440. Business E-Mail: philip.beck@bartlit-beck.com.

BECK, ROBERT ALFRED, hotel executive, educator; b. Boston, Nov. 1, 1920; s. Alfred and Laura Martha (Reissman) Beck; m. Mary Kathryn Murray, Nov. 5, 1944; children: Susan Jane, Janice Barbara, Robin Maria. BS, Cornell U., 1942, MS in Edn., 1952, PhD, 1954. Food technologist, pers. mgr. Quincy Market Co., Boston, 1945-50; mem. faculty Sch. Hotel Adminstrn., Cornell U., 1954-84, prof., 1960-84, dean, 1961-81; dir. Internat. Inst. Hotel Mgmt., Cergy-Pontoise, France, 1981-84; prof., disting. scholar in residence Fla. Internat. U., 1984—. Vis. lectr. USAF, PTO and ETO, US Army, Europe, USN, Govt. of Jamaica, Govt. of Barbados, Govt. of Bahama Is., Nat. Restaurant Assn., others. Contbr. articles to trade publs. Trustee, v.p. Ednl. Inst. Am. Hotel and Motel Assn.; v.p. Nat. Inst. Foodservice Industry; trustee Caribbean Hotel Tng. Inst., Ithaca Coll., NY; mem. bd. advisors Nova U., Ft. Lauderdale, Fla.; bd. dirs. Culinary Inst. Am., Internat. Hotel and Tourism Tng. Inst., Basel, Switzerland; mem. governing bd. East-West Coll. Natural Medicine, Sarasota, Fla., 2000—; mem. adv. bd. Atlantic Philanthropies, U. S. Fla. 1st lt. F.A. US Army, 1942—45, ETO. Decorated Purple Heart. Mem.: AAUP, Croix de Guerre, Phi Delta Kappa, Phi Kappa Phi. Home: 1255 N Gulfstream Ave Apt 805 Sarasota FL 34236-8929 Personal E-mail: beckab805@aol.com.

BECK, ROBERT BERYL, real estate executive; b. Dalton, Ga., Feb. 25, 1935; s. Carson W. and Gladys (Gray) B.; m. Martha Lucinda Cone, June 14, 1957; children: Perkie Cone Beck Cannon, Robert B. Jr., Carson W. Student, Vanderbilt U., 1953-57; LLB, JD, Nashville Sch. Law, 1964. Salesman Southeastern Inc., Nashville, 1957-64; purchasing agt. Nashville Bd. Edn., 1965-66; pres. Beck & Beck Realty, Nashville, 1967—, Beck & Beck Ins. Co., Nashville, 1967-78, v.p., 1978—; pres. Tri-County Builders, Nashville, 1974—. Editor Grace Bapt. Monthly, 1985, real estate newsletter, 1986-87. Mem. Tenn. Assn. Realtors, Nat. Assn. Realtors, Nashville Bd. Realtors, Madison C. of C., Masons. Democrat. Avocations: fishing, hiking, bicycling. Office: Beck & Beck 4205 Gallatin Rd Nashville TN 37216-2111 Home: 100 Stonewall Ct Hendersonville TN 37075 Home Phone: 615-826-8377; Office Phone: 615-226-9900. Personal E-mail: robertbecksr@msn.com.

BECK, ROBERT EDWARD, computer scientist, educator; b. Denver, June 7, 1941; s. Arthur Walter and Caroline Adelheid (Petrie) B.; m. Barbara Ruth Pennell, Aug. 21, 1965; children: Philip Arthur, Christopher William, Jennifer Grove. BS in Math., Harvey Mudd Coll., Claremont, Calif., 1963; PhD in Math., U. Pa., 1969. Instr. Villanova (Pa.) U., 1966-69, asst. prof., 1969-74, assoc. prof., 1974-78, prof. computer sci., 1978—, dept. chair, 1992—. Team chair computing accreditation commn. ABET, 1986—. Author: Elementary Linear Programming, 2d edit., 1995; editor: Computers in Nonassociative Rings and Algebras, 1978. Fulbright Exchange fellow, 1981-82. Mem. AAUP, Assn. for Computing Machinery (chair computer sci. conf. 1995, 96, chair preparing future faculty program 1998-2002), Sigma Xi. Office: Villanova U Dept Computing Sci Villanova PA 19085 Office Phone: 610-519-7307. E-mail: robert.beck@villanova.edu.

BECK, ROBERT JAMES, editor, writer, economist, consultant; b. Milw., Nov. 21, 1938; s. Walter John and Evelyn Barbara (Bigus) Beck; m. Mary Ellen Drew, Jan. 20, 1968 (div. Aug. 1978); m. Connie Sue Sparling, Aug. 2, 1988 (div. May 1994). BS in Econs. with honors, U. Wis., Milw., 1961; MS in Internat. Econs., U. Wis., 1965; postgrad., Wharton Sch., U. Pa., 1967, U. Okla., 1981. Actuarial asst. Milliman & Robertson, Milw., 1963-64; rsch. asst. U. Wis., Milw., 1964-65; economist, statistician Wis. Telephone Co., Milw., 1965-68; dir. econ. rsch. Mackay Shields Econs., NYC, 1968-69; head oper. planning Oil Svc. Co. Iran, Ahwaz, 1969-79; econs. editor Oil & Gas Jour., Tulsa, 1979-2000; developer, mgr. Oil & Gas Jour. Energy Database, Tulsa, 1984—; cons. Oil & Gas Jour., 2000—, Robert J. Beck & Assocs., 2000—; contract mgr. Oil & Gas Jour. Online Rsch. Ctr., 2001—. Cons. Oil and Gas Jour. Online Rsch. Ctr., 1994—, Altec Energy, Centralia, Ill., 1986—90, Rainbow Petroleum, NYC, 1986, Farrar and Assocs., Tulsa, 1985—86, Internat. Soc. Energy Advs., 2002—. Author: Oil Industry Outlook, 1983, 20th edit., 2003; developer Energy Statistics Sourcebook, 1986—; editor: Company Performance Statistics Sourcebook, 1966—, International Energy Statistics Sourcebook, 1991—, Natural Gas Statistics Sourcebook, 1993—, Refining Statistics Sourcebook, 1993—, Price Statistics Sourcebook, —; contbr. articles to mags. and newspapers. Active Wis. Gov.'s Commn. Econ. Indicators, 1967, Nature Conservancy, Tulsa, 1988—, Philbrook Mus. Art, Tulsa, 1989—, Tulsa Zoo, 1991—, Mus. Fine Arts, Houston, 1999—, Gilcrease Mus., Philbrook Art Mus., Tulsa Mayor's Energy Adv. Com., 2002—, Tulsa Com. Fgn. Rels., 2002—; bd. dirs., pres. Energy Literacy Project, 1996—; pres. Young Dems., West Allis, Wis., 1960—62. Mem.: Ind. Petroleum Assn. Am. (mem. supply and demand com., mem. cost study com.), U.S. Assn. Energy Econs., Assn. Petroleum Writers, Nat. Assn. Bus. Econs., Internat. Assn. Energy Advs., Internat. Assn. Energy Econs. (coun.). Avocations: bicycling, hiking, movies, tennis, golf. Office Phone: 918-831-9488. Personal E-mail: rbeck1@cox.net. E-mail: bobb@pennwell.com.

BECK, ROBERT N., nuclear medicine educator; b. San Angelo, Tex., Mar. 26, 1928; married, 1958. AB, U. Chgo., 1954, BS, 1955. Chief scientist Argonne Cancer Rsch. Hosp., 1957-67, assoc. prof., 1967-76; prof. radiol. sci. U. Chgo., 1976; dir. Franklin McLean Inst., 1977-94, dir. Ctr. Imaging Sci., 1986-98; prof. emeritus U. Chgo., 1998—. Cons. Internat. Atomic Energy Agency, 1966-68; mem. Internat. Com. on Radiation Units, 1968—, Nat. Coun. on Radiation, Protection & Measurements, 1970—. Recipient Aebersold award FDR, 1991. Mem. IEEE (Med. Imaging Sci. award 1996), Soc. Nuclear Med., Am. Assn. Physicists in Medicine, Soc. Magnetic Resonance. Achievements include research in development of a theory of the process by which images can be formed of the distribution of radioactive material in a patient in order to diagnose his disease. Office: U Chgo MC 2026 5841 S Maryland Ave Chicago IL 60637-1463 Business E-Mail: r-beck@uchicago.edu.

BECK, STEPHANIE G., lawyer; b. Endicott, NY, Jan. 10, 1964; d. Ray A. and Donna E. (Geesey) B. BA with honors, SUNY, Binghamton, 1986;

JD, Syracuse U., 1989. Bar: N.Y. 1990, U.S. Dist. Ct. (no. dist.) N.Y. 1990. Atty. Young & Paniccia, Binghamton, 1990—2003, Paniccia & Beck, LLP, Binghamton, 2004—. Advisor/vol. Drama Club for Mentally and Physically Impaired, Binghamton, 1992—96; asst. coach Boys and Girls Club, Endwell, 1986—91; mem. ch. coun. Our Saviour Luth. Ch., Endwell, NY, 1990—94, 1996, Our Savior Luth. Ch., Endwell, NY, 2003—; mem. pers. com. Broome County Coun. Chs. Mem. N.Y. State Bar Assn., Broome County Bar Assn. (bd. dirs.). Democrat. Lutheran. Avocations: softball, volleyball. Office: Paniccia & Beck LLP Ctr Plz Ste 400 53 Chenango St Binghamton NY 13901 Home Phone: 607-785-1467; Office Phone: 607-724-2385. E-mail: sbeck@pblawllp.com.

BECK, STUART EDWIN, lawyer; b. Phila., Aug. 12, 1940; s. Louis M. Beck and (Cooper) Anna; m. Elaine Kushner, June 20, 1964; children: Adam, Barry, Caroline. BSME, Drexel U., 1964; JD, George Washington U., 1968. Bar: Va. 1968, U.S. Dist. Ct. D.C. 1969, Pa. 1970, U.S. Dist. Ct. (ea. dist.) Pa. 1971, U.S. Ct. Appeals (3d cir.) 1971, U.S. Supreme Ct. 1980, U.S. Ct. Appeals (4th cir.) 1989, U.S. Patent and Trademark Office. Assoc. Seidel, Gonda & Goldhammer, Phila., 1969-73; atty. pvt. practice, Phila., 1974-79, 91—; ptnr. Trachman, Jacobs & Beck, Phila., 1979-88, Weinstein, Trachtman, Beck & Kimmelman, Phila., 1988-91. Adj. prof. patent law Rutgers U. Law Sch., Camden, N.J.; instr. patent, trademark and copyright law The Phila. Inst.; lectr. patent, trademark and copyright law Newmann Coll., 1999, lectr. U.S. trademark prosecution, seminar on U.S. trademark practice for paralegals, Phila., 2003; lectr. trademark law Halfmoon LLC, 2003, internat. patent law, 2005 Capt. Am. Cancer Soc., 1974, 75; bd. dirs. Jewish Family and Children Svc. Phila., 1973-89, legal, fin. and budget com., 1979—, spkrs. com., 1979—, bldg. and grounds com., 1980-82, trustee, 1989; bd. dirs., by-laws revision com., bldgs. and grounds com., edn. com. Temple Beth Hillel; bd. dirs. Phila. Vol. Lawyers for Arts, 1980-84, treas., 1980-82. Mem. ABA (patent trademark and copyright law sect., litigation sect., antitrust law sect.), Am. Intellectual Property Law Assn. (com. patent contracts other than govt. 1971-75), Pa. Bar Assn., Phila. Bar Assn. (com. profl. responsibility 1975-93, com. election procedures 1976-84, com. law and arts 1976-80), Phila. Patent Law Assn. (com. ethics 1977-83, com. pub. rels. 1974-77, com. profl. responsibility 1975-79). Avocations: sailing, travel. Office: The Beck Law Firm 1429 Walnut St Ste 900 Philadelphia PA 19102 Office Phone: 215-568-6000. Personal E-mail: beckemail@aol.com, beckpatent@aol.com.

BECK, SUSAN J., academic librarian; b. Norwalk, Ohio, Nov. 4, 1953; d. Kenneth Ricahrd Beck and Patricia Nabring Brady; m. James Allen Benson, 1984. AB, Ea. Ky. U., 1976; MA, Miami U., 1977; MLS, Kent State U., 1980. Reference libr., instr. U. Ala., Tuscaloosa, 1980—83; reference libr., head pub. svcs. Rutgers U., Camden, NJ, 1983—, coord. libr. LibQual+(TM). Vis. program officer Assn. of Rsch. Libraries, Washington, 2002—; vis. prof. U. Ala. Grad. Sch. Libr. Svc., Tuscaloosa, 1986, Rutgers U. Sch. Comm., Info. & Libr. Studies, New Brunswick, NJ, 1998—2000. Recipient More Than 500 Hours Svc. award, ARC, 1976; fellow, Kent State U., 1979—80, Miami U., 1976—77, 1977, Assn. of Rsch. Libraries, 2002; grantee Rsch. Coun. grantee, Rutgers U., 2001—02. Mem.: ALA (com. mem. in RUSA 1981—, chair measurement & evaluation com. 1986—87, fee-based reference services & rsch. & stats. com. 1996—2002, Mudge RR Bowker award com. 2002—04, exec. bd. 2006—07, chmn. awards, elected chair RUSA reference svcs. sect. 2006—07), Virtual Libr. Environment NJ (chair assessment com. 2004—06), Mgmt. and Operation User Svcs., Assn. Coll. and Rsch. Librs., Reference and User Svcs. Assn. (mgmt. reference com. 2002—06, reference svcs. sect. vice-chair 2005—06, exec. com. 2005—, reference svcs. sect. chair 2006—07, orgn. and palnning com. 2007—, mem. machine assisted reference sect.). Presbyterian. Achievements include research in Impact on Assessment in Decision Making in Academic Libraries in the United States and Canada. Avocations: gardening, swimming, travel. Home: One Hanover Ct Princeton NJ 08540 Office: Paul Robeson Library Rutgers University 300 North 4th Street Camden NJ 08102 Home Phone: 609-419-1304; Office Phone: 856-225-2831. Business E-Mail: susan.beck@rutgers.edu.

BECK, TIMOTHY DANIEL, human resources specialist, consultant; b. Santa Monica, Calif., Mar. 21, 1953; s. James Daniel and Bettye June (Cisler) B.; m. Marcia Ann Smith, Jan. 16, 1977; children: Tracy Beth and Erica Brandy (twins), Jenna Michelle. AA, El Camino Community Coll., 1974; BA, Calif. State U., Northridge, 1979. Registered health underwriter, registered employee benefits cons. Candidate cert. employee benefit specialist, group claims supr. Prudential Ins. Co. Am., LA, 1973-79; employee benefits cons. Olanie, Hurst & Hemrich, LA, 1979-81; v.p. policyholder svc. dept. Health Maintenance Life Ins. Co., Fountain Valley, Calif., 1981; v.p. Robert E. French Ins. Svcs., Inc., Huntington Beach, Calif., 1981-85; v.p., mng. cons. employee benefits Warren, McVeigh & Griffin, Inc., Newport Beach, Calif., 1985-91; mng. cons. employee benefits A. Foster Higgins and Co., Inc., 1991-96; prin. Mellon Cons., Inc., LA, 1996—, Buck Cons., LLC, LA, 2005—. Mem. Kaiser Permanente Orange County Consumer Coun., 1987—; mem. pub. edn. com. Calif. Health Decision, 1988—; mem. bus. and health adv. panel Am. Health Pub.; speaker to confs. and profl. socs.; cons. Healthnet Adv. Coun., 1996—, Orange County Bus. Coun., Town Hall, 1996—; mem. Healthnet Cons. Adv. Coun., 1997—. Creator, contbg. editor Employee Benefits Mgmt. Letter, 1985-91; contbr. articles to profl. publs. Mem. Internat. Found. Employee Benefits, Nat. Assn. Health Underwriters, Calif. Assn. Health Underwriters, Employee Benefit Planning Assn. So. Calif. (bd. dirs. 1992-93), So. Calif. Assn. Benefit Plan Adminstrs., Orange County Assn. Health Underwriters (founder, 1st v.p. 1987-88), Orange County Bus. Coun., Orange County Employee Benefit Coun., Calif. State U. Northridge Alumni Assn. Avocations: fishing, hiking, backpacking, rock climbing.

BECK, VAUGHN PETER, lawyer; b. Eureka, SD, Nov. 13, 1966; s. Floyd and Gladys M. (Zimmerman) B.; m. Julie I. Meier, Jan. 2, 1993; children: Emily I., Philip F. BS, U. S.D., 1989, JD, 1992. Bar: S.D. 1992, U.S. Dist. Ct. S.D. 1993. Legal intern Governmental Rsch. Bureau, Vermillion, SD, 1990, S.D. Pub. Utilities, Pierre, SD, 1991, Freiberg, Rudolf & Peterson, Beresford, SD, 1992; staff atty. Pub. Defenders Office, Deadwood, SD, 1992; atty. Beck Law Office, Ipswich, SD, 1993—. Bd. dirs. Ipswich Devel. Corp., 1993—, Ipswich Comml. Club, 1993—; com. mem. Consumer Protection S.D., 1994—. Mem. Ipswich Vol. Fire Dept., 1993—; trustee, officer United Church of Christ, 1993—. Republican. Office: Beck Law Office P O Box 326 509 Bloemendaal Dr Ipswich SD 57451 Office Phone: 605-426-6319. Business E-Mail: becklaw@valleytel.net.

BECK, WARREN RANDALL, retired glass technologist; b. Bethlehem, Pa., Feb. 14, 1918; s. Stewart Elbert and Lottie (Horn) B.; m. Lois K. Jones, Sept. 1, 1939 (div. 1964); children: Dianne Evelyn Blankenship, Kathryn Lynn Thostenson, Vicki Allison Martin, Constance Rae Stiles; m. Carol J. Anderson, Mar. 14, 1970. BS in Ceramics, Pa. State U., 1942; MS in Mineralogy, U. Minn., 1948. Staff Pa. State U., 1942-43; glass technologist 3M Co., St. Paul, 1943-48, sect. leader, 1948-55, mgr. rsch. and devel., 1955-64, corp. scientist, 1964-86, ret., 1986. Patentee in field; contbr. articles to profl. publs. Recipient Samuel Geijsbeek award for Innovation in Ceramics Am. Ceramics Soc., 1995. Fellow Am. Ceramic Soc. Home: 942 Winterberry Dr Woodbury MN 55125-9122 Office Phone: 651-739-8474. Personal E-mail: beckwdbry@aol.com.

BECK, WILLIAM G., lawyer; b. Kansas City, Mo., Mar. 4, 1954; s. Raymond W. Beck and Wanda Williams; m. Cheryl A. Beck; children: Collin M., Sergei M., Valentina M., Kseniya M., Ekaterina K. BA in Econs., U. Mo., Kansas City, 1974, JD, 1978. Bar: Mo. 1978, U.S. Dist. Ct. (we. dist.) Mo. 1978, U.S. Ct. Appeals (5th cir.) 1988, U.S. Dist. Ct. (ea. dist.) Mich. 1991, U.S. Dist. Ct. (no. dist.) Ill. 1992, U.S. Ct. Appeals (6th cir.) 1992, U.S. Dist. Ct. (ea. dist.) Wis. 1997, U.S. Ct. Appeals (2d cir.) 1997, U.S. Ct. Appeals (10th cir.) 1997, U.S. Supreme Ct. 1997, U.S. Ct. Appeals (1st cir.) 1998, U.S. Ct. Appeals (7th cir.) 1999, U.S. Dist. Ct. Colo. 2000, U.S. Dist. Ct. Rhode Island 2002, U.S. Dist. Ct. Mass. 2002, U.S. Dist. Ct. Kans. 2005. Shareholder Field, Gentry, Benjamin & Robertson, P.C., Kansas City, 1978-89; ptnr. Lathrop & Norquist, Kansas City, 1989-95, Lathrop & Gage, L.C., Kansas City, 1996—. Commr. Human Rels. Commn., Jackson County, Mo., 1985-89; chmn. Citizens Assn., Kansas City, 1991-92, 95-96; mem. Pub. Improvement Adv. Com., Kansas City, 1991-2001, vice chmn., 1995-98, chmn. 1998-2001, fin. chmn. cmty. infrastructure com., 1996-1997; mem. Waste Minimization Com., Kansas City, 1990-91; bd. mem. Regional Transit Alliance, 2001-03. Named a Mo.-Kans. Super Lawyer; named one of Best Lawyers in Am., Chambers Leading Lawyers for Bus. Office: Lathrop & Gage LC 2345 Grand Blvd Ste 2800 Kansas City MO 64108-2684 Office Phone: 816-460-5811. Business E-Mail: bbeck@lathropgage.com.

BECK, WILLIAM HAROLD, JR., lawyer; b. Clarksdale, Miss., Aug. 18, 1928; s. William Harold and Mary (McGaha) Beck; m. Nancy Cassity House, Jan. 30, 1954; children: Mary, Nancy, Katherine. BA, Vanderbilt U., 1950; JD, U. Miss., 1954. Bar: Miss. 1954, La. 1960. Atty., Clarksdale, 1954—57; asst. prof. Tulane U., New Orleans, 1957—59; ptnr. Foley & Judell, New Orleans, 1959—88, of counsel, 1988—2007. Capt. US Army, 1951—53. Mem.: SAR, Miss. Bar Assn., La. Bar Assn., Mil. Order Fgn. Wars, Huguenot Soc., Mil. and Hospitalier Order St. Lazarus of Jerusalem, S.R., Soc. Colonial Wars. Personal E-mail: wandnbeck@suddenlink.net.

BECK, (BECK HANSEN), musician, songwriter; b. LA, July 8, 1970; s. David Campbell and Bibbe Hansen; m. Marissa Ribisi, Apr. 2004; 1 child, Cosimo Henry. Musician: (albums) The Banjo Story, 1988, Golden Feelings, 1993, A Western Harvest Field by Moonlight, 1994, Mellow Gold, 1994, Stereopathic Soul Manure, 1994, One Foot in the Grave, 1994, Odelay, 1996 (Grammy award, best alternative music album, 1997, named best album of yr., Village Voice, 1997), Mutations, 1998 (Grammy award, best alternative music album, 1999), Midnite Vultures, 1999, Sea Change, 2002, Guero, 2005 (NY Times critic's choice), Guerolito, 2005, The Information, 2006, (singles) Loser, 1994, Where It's At, 1996 (Grammy award, best male rock vocal performance, 1996); performer: (tours) Lollapalooza, 1995; exhibitions include Beck & Al Hansen: Playing with Matches, 1998. Named Artist of Yr., Spin Mag., 1996. Scientologist. also: care Bongload Records PO Box 931538 Los Angeles CA 90093-1538

BECKENSTEIN, MYRON, journalist; b. Cleve., Mar. 11, 1938; s. Irwin and Rachel (Miller) B.; 1 child: Amanda Mbuvi. BS, Northwestern U., 1959, MS, 1960. Mem. staff Chgo. Daily News, 1959—78, Balt. Sun, 1978—2002. With US Army, 1961—64. Mem. Upper Patuxent Archeol. Group, Archeol. Soc. Md., Soc. Profl. Journalists. Home: 6817 Pineway University Park MD 20782 Personal E-mail: myronbeck@verizon.net.

BECKER, ALLIENNE R., education educator, writer; b. Dubois, Pa. d. Harold Raymond and Anne Williams Rimer; m. Isidore H. Becker; m. William Sterling Hopwood, June 9, 1947 (div. Jan. 1, 1969); children: William Hopwood, Carolyn Hopwood Blick, Richard B. Hopwood. AB, Duke Univ., Durham, NC, 1947; MA, W.Va. Univ., Morgantown, 1970, MA, 1971; PhD, Pa. State Univ., College Park, 1984. Assoc. prof. Lock Haven (Pa.) Univ., 1970—97. Author: The Lost Worlds Romance, 1992, Visions of The Fantastic, 1996, Divine & Human Comedy of Andrew Greeley, 2000, I, Paul: The Life of the Apostle to the Gentiles, 2002, Andrew M. Greeley: The Mysteries of Grace, 2002, Eagle in Flight: The Life of Athanasius the Apostle of the Trinity, 2002; author: (with Ricardo C. Castellanos) All You Need is Love: The Way of Joy, 2003, Be Free! The Gift of Freedom, 2003; author: (with Ricardo Castellanos) Peace! Be Still: The Gift of Peace, 2004. Avocation: travel.

BECKER, BENJAMIN, professional tennis player; b. Merzig, Germany, June 16, 1981; Grad., Baylor U., 2002—05. Profl. tennis player ATP, 2005—. Named Sportsman of Yr., Germany, Newcomer of Yr., 2006 ATP Awards. Office: Renaissance Tennis Mgmt Ltd 3111 University Dr Ste 601 Coral Springs FL 33065*

BECKER, BRANDON, lawyer; b. Berwyn, Ill., Mar. 19, 1954; BA summa cum laude, U. Minn., 1974; JD magna cum laude, U. San Diego, 1977; LLM, Columbia U., 1979. Bar: Calif. 1978, DC 1978, NY 2002. Atty. SEC, Washington, 1978-80, br. chief, 1980, legal asst., 1981-82, asst. dir., 1982-86, assoc. dir., 1986-91, dep. dir., 1991-93, dir. divsn. mkt. regulation, 1993-95, spl. advisor to the chmn. for internat. derivatives, 1995-96; ptnr. Wilmer Hale, Washington, 1996—, co-chmn. Securities dept. Mem. bd. adv. Ctr. for Study of Securities Markets; instr. Am. Univ., George Mason Univ., Georgetown Univ. Editor (articles): San Diego Law Rev.; contbr. articles to profl. jours.; mem. editl. adv. bd. Internat. Finance, wallstreetlawyer.com. Avocation: chess. Office: Wilmer Cutler Pickering Hale and Dorr LLP 2445 M St NW Washington DC 20037-1435 Home Phone: 301-681-6808; Office Phone: 202-663-6979. Office Fax: 202-663-6363. Business E-Mail: brandon.becker@wilmerhale.com.

BECKER, BRENDA L., medical products executive, former federal official; b. Oct. 1959; m. Jeffrey G. Becker; children: Megan, Max. BA in Polit. Sci. & Pub. Adminstrn., Mich. State U., 1981; MBA, Ctrl. Mich. U., 1985. Staff asst. Mich. Rep. State Com.; legis. analyst, sr. project coord. Blue Cross Blue Shield Assoc., 1981—85, state services rep., 1985—88, blue pac dir., 1988—91, dir. congl. comm., 1991—95, exec. dir. congl. comm, 1995—98, v.p. congl. comm., 1998—2001; asst. sec. for legis. & intergovernmental affairs US Dept. Commerce, Washington, 2004—05; asst. to the v.p. for legis. affairs The White House, Washington, 2005—06; sr. v.p. for global affairs Boston Scientific Corp., 2007—. Office: Boston Scientific Corp 1331 Pennsylvania Ave NW Ste 550 S Washington DC 20004*

BECKER, BRUCE CLARE, clinical psychologist, neuropsychologist, administrator; b. Seattle, Dec. 9, 1929; s. Eugene J. and Hedwig (Gottschalk) B.; m. Margaret Carol Peddle, Nov. 26, 1955; children: Cheryl, Cecilia, Bruce Jr., Gregory, Kurt, Christopher, Lise. AB, St. Ambrose U., 1950; AM, St. Louis U., 1954; PhD, Loyola U., Chgo., 1962. Cert. clin. psychologist, clin. neuropsychologist Am. Bd. Profl. Psychology. Commd. ensign USN, 1954, advanced through grades to capt., 1975, clin. psychologist Tng. Ctr. Great Lakes, Ill., 1975, dir. clin. psychology tng., 1964-84; clin. psychologist U.S. Naval Hosp., Great Lakes, 1958-65; clin. neuropsychologist VA Hosp., Downey, Ill., 1965-68, chief of psychology svc., 1968-69; ret., USN, 1989; pres. Neuropsychology Assocs. Ltd., Bethesda, 1984—; ret. USN, 1989. Cons. in neuropsychology U.S. Dept. State, Washington, 1975—, CIA, 1975—, Peace Corps, 1975—, U.S. Capitol Physician, 1988—. Cons. editor (jour.) The Clin. Neuropsychologist, 1988-90; contbr. chpts. to books and articles to profl. jours. Fellow APA; mem. Internat. Neuropsychol. Soc. Avocations: tennis, scuba diving, sailing. Home and Office: 9508 Newbold Pl Bethesda MD 20817-2226

BECKER, CHARLES A., adult education educator; b. Spring Grove, Minn., Mar. 27, 1944; s. R. L. and Cora T. Becker; m. Ann Buchanan, July 16, 1983. BS in Edn., Winona State U., Minn., 1966. Mgr. Greyhound Food Mgmt., Rock Springs, Wyo., 1977—85; faculty mem. hospitality studies and culinary arts Pueblo C.C., Colo., 1985—. Mem.: Nat. Restaurant Assn. Ednl. Found. (cert. food mgmt. profl. 1997, nat. cert. exam writer 2006—, nat. cert. exam reviewer 2006—, mem. com. for examination excellence 2006—). Home: 615 Tyler St Pueblo CO 81004 Office: Pueblo Community College 900 West Orman Ave Pueblo CO 81004 Home Phone: 719-544-2951; Office Phone: 719-549-3095. Business E-Mail: chuck.becker@pueblocc.edu.

BECKER, CHRISTOPHER, educator, chef; Profl. chef; founder Calif. Sch. Culinary Arts, Pasadena, 1994—, Kitchen Acad., Hollywood, 2005—, Sacramento, 2006—. Mem.: Calif. Assn. Pvt. Postsecondary Schools (treas.). Office: Kitchen Academy Divsn Career Education Corp 521 E Green St Pasadena CA 91101-5221 Office Phone: 626-484-1652. Office Fax: 626-441-0592.*

BECKER, DAVID, artist, retired educator; b. Milw., Aug. 16, 1937; s. Walter Gustav and Fern Bertha (Raddatz) B.; m. Catherine Claytor, Aug. 27, 1960 (div. 1981); children: Sarah Lynne, Amelia Elisabeth; m. Patricia Ann Fennell, Nov. 13, 1988; 1 child, Sloane Fennell. Student, Layton Sch. Art, 1956-58; BS, U. Wis., Milw., 1961; MFA, U. Ill., 1965. Asst. prof. Wayne State U., Detroit, 1965-71, assoc. prof., 1971-80, prof., 1980-85; assoc. prof. U. Wis., Madison, 1985—87, prof., 1987—2006, prof. emeritus, 2006—. Vis. prof. U. Wis., Madison, 1985—87; vis. artist Utah State U., Logan, 1981; art lectr. in field; rep. by Ann Nathan Gallery, Chgo. Exhbns. include Mus. Fine Arts, Boston, 1965, 75, Butler Inst. Am. Art, Youngstown, Ohio, 1967, 68, 72, Lawrence Stevens Gallery, Detroit, 1968, Detroit Inst. Arts, 1971, 77, 86, 91, Richard Nash Gallery, Seattle, 1974, Franz Bader Gallery, Washington, 1974, 77, 80, Madison (Wis.) Art Ctr., 1975, 79, Libr. of Congress, Washington, 1975, Honolulu Acad. Arts, 1975, 83, ADI Gallery, San Francisco, 1975, London Arts Gallery, Detroit, 1976, Boston Ctr. Arts, 1976, 78, Museo de Arte Moderno, Cali, Colombia, 1976, 77, 81, Bawag Found., Vienna, Austria, 1976, Bklyn. Mus., 1976, 84, Met. Mus., Miami, Fla., 1977, 80, Habatat Galleries, Dearborn, Mich., 1977, Visual Arts Ctr. Alaska, Anchorage, 1978, 86, Cranbrook Acad. Art, Bloomfield Hills, Mich., 1980, Associated Am. Artists Gallery, Phila., 1980, Phila. Art Alliance/Phila. Print Club, 1980, Kalamazoo (Mich.) Inst. Arts, 1980, 86, Nat. Mus. Am. Art, Washington, 1982, DeCordova Mus., Lincoln, Mass., 1982, 86, USIA, 1983, Saginaw (Mich.) Mus. Art, 1984, Brockton (Mass.) Mus. Art, 1984, Mich. Gallery, Detroit, 1986, Neville-Sargent Gallery, Chgo., 1986, Intergrafic, East Berlin, 1984, 87, 9th Brit. Internat. Print Biennale, Bradford, 1986, Jane Haslem Gallery, Washington, 1987, 90, 92-93, John Szoke Graphics, N.Y.C., 1988, Silvermine Gallery, Stamford, Conn., 1988, Elvehjem Mus. Art, Madison, 1989, Boston Printmakers 42d and 43d Nat. Print Exhbn., 1993, Fitchburg (Mass.) Mus. Art, 1990, New Orleans Mus. Art, 1990, NAD, N.Y.C., 1986-87, 90-94, Hoyt Inst. Fine Arts, New Castle, Pa., 1992, Sodarco Gallery, Montreal, 1993, Davidson Galleries, Seattle, 1993, Galleria Mesa, Mesa, Ariz., 1993, Intergrafia, Katowice, Poland, 1994, Sapporo Internat. Print Biennale, Japan, 1993, Maastricht Internat. Print Biennale, The Netherlands, 1993, Outside Art Fair, N.Y.C., 2002, Art Chgo., 2002, 03, 04, 05, 06, 07; permanent collections include: Libr. of Congress, Washington, Art Inst. Chgo., Rose Art Mus., Waltham, Mass., Chazen Mus. Art, Madison, Wis., Butler Inst. Am. Art, Minot (N.D.) Art Assn., Silvermine Guild Arts, New Canaan, Conn., Honolulu Acad. Arts, NY Pub. Libr., Detroit Inst. Art, Museo de Arte Moderno, Bklyn. Mus., Met. Mus., Miami, Nat. Mus. Am. Art, Washington, Portland (Oreg.) Art Mus., Art Ctr., South Bend, Ind., USIA, Prague, Czech Republic, Ann Nathan Gallery, Chgo., others. 1st lt. U.S. Army, 1961-63. Creative Artist grantee Mich. Coun. Arts, 1982; NEA Visual Arts fellow, 1993-94. Fellow The MacDowell Colony; mem. NAD (nat. academician). Home: 2512 Lunde Ln Mount Horeb WI 53572-2440 E-mail: dhbecker@wisc.edu.

BECKER, DAVID M., lawyer; married. JD, U. Iowa, 1986. Bar: Iowa 1986, Mo. 1987, Kans. 1988. Dir. legal affairs Seaboard Corp., Shawnee Mission, Kans., 1994—98, gen. counsel., 1998—, v.p., 2001—. Office: Seaboard Corp 9000 W 67th St Shawnee Mission KS 66201 Office Phone: 913-676-8925. E-mail: david_becker@seaboardcorp.com.

BECKER, DOREEN DORIS, medical/surgical nurse; b. Elgin, ND, May 22, 1944; d. Carl Ruff and Dorothy Buttmann; m. Glenn Alan Watson, Jan. 19, 2002; m. Roy Ernest Becker, June 5, 1964 (dec. Sept. 6, 1993); 1 child, Allen Roy. Degree in Nursing, U. Chgo., 1963. Nurse Columbia Hosp., Grand Forks, ND, 1976—77, surg. nurse, 1977—90; surg. nurse supr. Columbia HCA, Plano, Tex., 1990—92, med. records coder, 1993—2001, Baylor Hosp., Richardson, Tex., 2001—02, Med. City, Dallas, 2002—05, Med. Ctr., Rowlett, Tex., 2005—. Instr. HCA Med. Ctr., Plano, 1990—92. Instr. Red Cross, Braddock, ND, 1966. Recipient Medicorp award, Mott HS, 1962. Methodist. Avocations: marathon running, bicycling, fishing, fossils, rocks. Home: 616 Buffalo Bend Plano TX 75023

BECKER, EDWIN DEMUTH, chemist, director; b. Columbia, Pa., May 3, 1930; married, 1953; 2 children. BS, U. Rochester, 1952; PhD in Chemistry, U. Calif., 1955. Instr. U. Calif., 1955; phys. chemist NIH, Bethesda, Md., 1955—, chief sect. molecular biophysics, 1962-72, chief lab. chem. physics, 1972-80, acting dir. Fogarty Internat. Ctr., 1979-80, assoc. dir. for research services, 1980-88, chief sect. NMR, 1972-98, scientist emeritus, 1998—, mem. faculty Grad. Sch., 1963-99; sec. gen. Internat. Union Pure and Applied Chemistry, 1996—2003. Lectr. Georgetown U., 1958-97. Bd. dirs. Chem. Heritage Found., 2003—; treas. Found. for Advanced Edn. in the Scis., 2003—. NSF fellow U. Calif. Fellow AAAS; mem. Am. Chem. Soc., The Nat. Acads. (nat. assoc.), World Innovation Found. (hon.). Achievements include research in nuclear magnetic resonance, hydrogen bonding, molecular structure, infrared spectroscopy. Office: NIH Rm 128 Bldg 5 Bethesda MD 20892-0520 Office Phone: 301-496-1024. Business E-Mail: tbecker@nih.gov.

BECKER, FRANKLIN, chef; b. Brooklyn, NY; Grad., Culinary Inst. Am. Chef Mesa Grill, NYC, Penn Club, NYC; personal chef for Ron Perelman, Revlon Exec.; demonstration chef James Beard House, NYC; exec. chef Local, NYC, 2000, Capitale, NYC, 2003, Tribeca Grand Hotel, NYC, 2003—05, Soho Grand Hotel, NYC, Washington Square, Phila., Brasserie, NYC, 2005—. Author: The Diabetic Chef; featured on (TV series) dLifeTV. Named one of NYC's Rising Stars, StarChefs.com, 2006. Office: Brasserie Seagram Bldg 100 E 53rd St New York NY 10022 Office Phone: 212-751-4840.*

BECKER, FRAWLEY, writer, dialogue director, location manager; s. Arthur A. and Mildred (Cohen) Becker. BA, U. Pa., 1950; postgrad., Oxford U., Eng., 1956. Asst. entertainment dir. Spl. Svcs. Hdqrs. Dept. of Army, Paris, 1958—61; dialogue coach, dialogue dir. various film cos., Paris, 1964—72; asst. to prodr. (film) Weingarten Prodns., LA, 1973—74; rsch. writer (t.v.) Columbia Pictures, Burbank, Calif., 1974—75; location mgr. (film) various film cos., Calif., 1976—; prodn. exec. (film) Disney Studios, Burbank, 1990—91. Founder, dir. Studio 128, Paris, 1957—61, Harlequin Guild, Paris, 1959—61; founder, dir., mng. dir. Paris Playhouse, 1961—63; French interpreter Olympic Games, 1984. Author: (screenplays) But Not A Drop to Drink, 1973, Columbo Stories, 1975, On The Way Out, 1976, The Strike, 1976, Behold the Evening Spider, 1980, The Gang's All Where?, 1989, Bonjour Homicide, 1995, (plays) Dreamhouse, 1987, The Picture They Never Made, 1987, Bashing, 1990, 411 Joseph, 1998, Never Fall in Love with A Fireman, 2001, Tiger by the Tail, 2003, short stories, (novel) Tittyboo For President, 1984, (memoirs) And the Stars Spoke Back, 2004. Cpl. US Army, 1951—53, Korea. Avocations: cooking, travel. Home: 15016 Archwood St Van Nuys CA 91405

BECKER, FRED RONALD, lawyer; b. Phila., Apr. 7, 1937; s. Samuel and Molly (Cletter) B.; m. Judith Ellen Ettlinger, June 5, 1961 BA, U. Pa., 1958; JD magna cum laude, Harvard U., 1961. Bar: D.C. 1963. Law clk.

U.S. Ct. Appeals (9th cir.), 1961-62; asst. Stanford U. Law Sch., 1962-63; atty. tax div. U.S. Dept. Justice, 1963-65; atty. Office Tax Legis. Counsel U.S. Treasury, 1965-69; ptnr. Ropes & Gray, Boston, 1969. Office: Ropes & Gray 1 International Pl Fl 4 Boston MA 02110-2624

BECKER, GAIL ROSELYN, museum director; b. Long Branch, NJ, Oct. 22, 1942; d. Joseph and Adele (Michelsohn) B. BA, Vassar Coll., 1964. Exhibit project officer U.S. Info. Agy., Washington, 1967-87, chief devel. and prodn. exhibits, 1987-91; exec. dir. Louisville Sci. Ctr. (formerly Mus. History and Sci.), 1991—. Bd. dirs. Louisville Advanced Tech. Coun., 1993-2000, Louisville Com. Fgn. Rels., Main St. Assn., 1998—, Arts and Cultural Attractions Coun., 1999—; active Leadership Louisville. Recipient Presdl. Design awards Nat. Endowment for the Arts, Washington, 1984, 88, 92, Special Achievement award U.S. Info. Agy., Washington, 1988. Mem. Am. Assn. Mus. (bd. dirs. 1994-97), Assn. Sci.-Tech. Ctrs. (bd. dirs. 1992—2003, pres. 1999-2001), Vassar Coll. Alumnae Assn., Rotary. Office: Louisville Sci Ctr 727 W Main St Louisville KY 40202-2681

BECKER, GARY STANLEY, economist, educator; b. Pottsville, Pa., Dec. 2, 1930; s. Louis William and Anna (Siskind) Becker; m. Doria Slote, Sept. 19, 1954 (dec.); children: Judith Sarah, Catherine Jean; m. Guity Nashat, Oct. 31, 1979; children: Michael Claffey, Cyrus Claffey. AB summa cum laude, Princeton U., 1951, PhD (hon.), 1991; AM, U. Chgo., 1953, PhD, 1955; PhD (hon.), Hebrew U., Jerusalem, 1985, Knox Coll., 1985, U. Ill., Chgo., 1988, SUNY, 1990, U. Palermo, Buenos Aires, 1993, Columbia U., 1993, Warsaw Sch. Econs., 1995, U. Econs., Prague, Czech Republic, 1995, U. Miami, 1995, U. Rochester, 1995; PhD, Hofstra U., 1997, U. d'Aix-Marseilles, 1999, U. Athens, 2002; PhD (hon.), Harvard U., 2003, Hitotsubashi., 2005. Asst. prof. U. Chgo., 1954—57; from asst. prof. to assoc. prof. Columbia U., NYC, 1957—60, prof. econs., 1960—68, Arthur Lehman prof. econs., 1968—70; prof. econs. U. Chgo., 1970—83, univ. prof. econs. and sociology, 1983—, chmn. dept. econs., 1984—85, prof. Grad Sch. Bus., 2002—. Ford Found. vis. prof. econs. U. Chgo., 1969—70; assoc. Econs. Rsch. Ctr. Nat. Opinion Rsch. Ctr., Chgo., 1980—; mem. domestic adv. bd. Hoover Instn., Stanford, Calif., 1973—91, sr. fellow, 1990—; mem. acad. adv. bd. Am. Enterprise Inst., 1987—91; rsch. policy advisor Ctr. for Econ. Analysis Human Behavior Nat. Bur. Econ. Rsch., 1972—78; mem. and sr. rsch. assoc. Monetary Policy, Min. Fin., Japan, 1988—; bd. dirs. Unext.com, 1999—2003; affiliate Lexecon Corp., 1990—2002, LEAF, Inc., 2003—07. Author: The Economics of Discrimination, 1957, 2d edit., 1971, Human Capital, 1964, 3d edit., 1993, (Japanese transl.) Human Capital, 1975, (Spanish transl.), 1984, (Chinese transl.), 1987, (Romanian transl.), 1997, Human Capital and the Personal Distribution of Income: An Analytical Approach, 1967, Economic Theory, 1971, (Japanese transl.), 1976, 2nd edit., 2007; author: (with Gilbert Ghez) The Allocation of Time and Goods Over the Life Cycle, 1975; author: The Economic Approach to Human Behavior, 1976, (German transl.), 1982, (Polish transl.), 1990, (Chinese transl.), 1993, (Romanian transl.), 1994, (Italian transl.), 1998, A Treatise on the Family, 1981, expanded edit., 1991, (Spanish transl.) A Treatise on the Family, 1987, (Chinese transl.), 1988, 2000, Accounting for Tastes, 1996, (Czech transl.), 1998, (Chinese transl.), 1999, (Italian transl.), 2000; author: (with Guity Nashat Becker) The Economics of Life, 1996, (Chinese transl.), 1997, with Guity Nashat Becker: The Economics of Life, 1998, (Spanish transl.), 2002; author: (in German) Family, Society and State, 1996; author: (in Italian) L'approccio Economico al Comportamento Umano, 1998; author: (with Kevin M. Murphy) Social Economics, 2000; co-author: Becker-Posner Blog, 2005; editor: Essays in Labor Economics in Honor of H. Gregg Lewis, 1976; co-editor (with William M. Landes): Essays in the Economics of Crime and Punishment, 1974; columnist: Bus. Week, 1985—2004; contbr. articles to profl. jours. Named to Hall of Honor, Nat. Inst. Child Health and Devel., 2003; recipient W.S. Woytinsky award, U. Mich., 1964, Profl. Achievement award, U. Chgo. Alumni Assn., 1968, Frank E. Seidman Disting. award in Polit. Economy, 1985, Merit award, NIH, 1986, John R. Commons award, Omicron Delta Epsilon, 1987, Nobel prize in Econ. Sci., 1992, award, Lord Found., 1995, Irene Taueber award, 1997, Nat. medal Sci., 2000, Phoenix award, U. Chgo., 2000, award, Am. Acad. Achievement, 2001, Heartland prize, 2002, Hayek award, 2003, John Neumann Lecture award, Rojk Coll., Corvinus U., Budapest, 2004, medal Italian Presidency, 2004, Arrow award, 2005, Provost's Tchg. award, U. Chgo., 2006. Fellow: Am. Econ. Assn. (Disting., v.p. 1974, pres. 1987, John Bates Clark medal 1967), Am. Acad. Arts and Scis., Nat. Assn. Bus. Economists, Econometic Soc., Am. Statis. Assn.; mem.: NAE, NAS, Nat. Assn. Bus. Economists, Econ. History Assn., Pontifical Acad. Scis., Western Econ. Assn. (v.p. 1995—96, pres. 1996—97), Mont Pelerin Soc. (exec. bd. dirs. 1985—96, v.p. 1989—90, pres. 1990—92), Internat. Union for Sci. Study Population, Am. Philos. Soc., Nat. Assn. Bus. Economists, Phi Beta Kappa. Office: U Chgo Dept Econs 1126 E 59th St Chicago IL 60637-1580 Office Phone: 773-702-8168. Business E-Mail: gbecker@uchicago.edu.

BECKER, JAMES MURDOCH, surgeon, educator; b. Cleve., Jan. 7, 1949; s. Norman O. and Mildred Edith (Murdoch) B.; m. Christine Louise Lohmann, Dec. 30, 1972; children: Alexander, Selby, Catherine, Anne. BA in Biology, Yale U., 1971; MD, Case Western Res. U., 1975. Diplomate Nat. Bd. Med. Examiners, Am. Bd. Surgery; lic. surgeon, Minn., Utah, Mo., Mass. Intern in surgery U. Utah Hosps., Salt Lake City, 1975-76, resident in gen. surgery, 1976-79, chief resident in surgery, 1979—80; research fellow in surgery U. Utah Sch. Medicine, 1977-78, asst. prof. surgery, 1982-86; NIH rsch. fellow digestive diseases Mayo Clinic, 1980-82; mem. surg. staff VA Hosp., Salt Lake City, 1982-86, chief green service, 1983-86, head nutritional support team, 1983-86; mem. cons. staff Intermountain Unit Shriners Hosps. for Crippled Children, Salt Lake City, 1984-86; assoc. prof. surgery, dir. gastrointestinal surgery Washington U. Sch. Medicine, 1986-89; assoc. prof surgery, chief divsn. gen. and gastroint. surg. Harvard Med. Sch./Brigham and Women's Hosp., Boston, 1989-94; James Utley prof. and chmn. surgeon-in-chief Boston U. Sch. Medicine/Boston Med. Ctr., 1994—. Contbr. articles to profl. jours., chpts. to books. NIH fellow, Mayo Clinic, 1980-82; grantee Johnson & Johnson Products, Inc., 1985, NIH, 1985—, Sandoz Corp., 1985-87, Ethicon, Inc., 1985-86. Mem. ACS, AMA, Am. Gastroenterol. Assn., Am. Motility Soc., Am. Pancreatic Assn., Assn. Acad. Surgery, Am. Soc. Parenteral and Enteral Nutrition, Internat. Biliary Assn., Collegium Internat. Chirurgiae Digestivae (Grassi prize 8th World Congress 1984), Soc. for Surgery Alimentary Tract, Soc. Univ. Surgeons, Yale U. Alumni Assn., Am. coll. Surgeons, Am. Surg. Assn., We. Surg. Assn., Cen. Surg. Assn., New Eng. Surg. Assn., Am. Soc. Colorectal Surgeons, Soc. Internat. Chirugiae, Soc. Surg. Oncology, Alpha Omega Alpha. Office: Boston Med Ctr 88 E Newton St Boston MA 02118-2308 Office Phone: 617-638-8600.

BECKER, JAMES RICHARD, lawyer; b. San Juan, Sept. 25, 1954; s. John Joseph and Patricia (Doherty) Becker; m. Mary E. McGurk; children: Colette Anne, Robert Charles II. BA in English, Va. Tech., 1977; JD, George Mason Law Sch., 1982. Bar: Va. 1982, US Dist. Ct. (ea. and we. dists.) Va. 1982, US Ct. Appeals (4th cir.) 1982. Pvt. practice, Middleburg, Chantilly, Va., 1982-93, Chantilly, 2000, 2003—; assoc. atty. Nichols, Bergere & Zauzig, PC, Woodbridge, Va., 1993-94, Joel Atlas Skirble and Assocs., Falls Church, Va., 1994-98, Anderson & Corrie, Fairfax, Va., 1998-2000; assoc. John A. Boneta & Assocs., Falls Church, 2001—03; atty. Law Offices of James R. Becker, Chantilly, Va., 2003—06, Fairfax, 2006—. Editor: Law Rev., 1980—82. Mem.: Fairfax Bar Assn. Avocations: computers, software development. Home: 4515 Fillingame Dr Chantilly VA 20151-2820 Personal E-mail: JamesRBecker@juno.com.

BECKER, JEFFREY M., lawyer; b. San Angelo, Tex., Mar. 15, 1965; BSME with high honors, U. Tex. at Austin, 1987, JD with honors, 1990. Bar: Tex. 1990, admitted to practice: US Dist. Ct. (No. Dist.) Tex. 1990, US Ct. Appeals (Fed. Cir.) 1991, registered: US Patent and Trademark Office. Ptnr., intellectual property law Haynes and Boone LLP, Dallas. Named one of Best Lawyers in Dallas, DMagazine, 2003. Mem.: Coll. of State Bar Tex., DFW Intellectual Property Law Assn., Am. Intellectual Property Law Assn., Internat. Trademark Assn., State Bar Tex. (Intellectual Property Law Sect.), Dallas Bar Assn. (Intellectual Property Sect.), Order of Coif, Tau Beta Pi. Office: Haynes and Boone LLP 901 Main St Ste 3100 Dallas TX 75202-3789 Office Phone: 214-651-5066. Office Fax: 214-200-0558. Business E-Mail: jeff.becker@haynesboone.com.

BECKER, JOANN ELIZABETH, retired insurance company executive; b. Chester, Pa., Oct. 29, 1948; d. James Thomas and Elizabeth Theresa (Barnett) Clark; m. David Norbert Becker, June 7, 1969. BA, Washington U., St. Louis, 1970, MA, 1971. CLU, ChFC, FLMI/M, CFA. Tchr. Kirkwood (Mo.) Sch. Dist., 1971-73; devel. and sr. devel. analyst Lincoln Nat. Life Ins. Co., Ft. Wayne, Ind., 1973-77, systems programming specialist, 1977-79, sr. project mgr., 1979-81, asst. v.p., 1981-85, 2d v.p., 1985-88, v.p., 1988-91; pres., CEO The Richard Leahy Corp., Ft. Wayne, 1991-93; pres. Lincoln Nat. Corp. Equity Sales Corp, Ft. Wayne, 1993-94; v.p. portfolio mgmt. group Lincoln Nat. Investment Mgmt. Co., Ft. Wayne, 1994-97, dir. investment mgmt., sr. v.p., 1997—2000, ret., 2000. Contbr. articles to profl. jours. Bd. dirs. Ind. Humanities Coun., Indpls., 1991-96, treas., exec. com., 1994-95, devel. com., 1995-96; bd. dirs. Auburn Cord Duesenberg Mus., Ind., 1995-2000, devel. and exec. com., 1997-2000; bd. dirs. Priest Lake Mus., 2005—; pres. Priest Lake Mus. Assn., 2006—. Named Women of Achievement, YWCA, Ft. Wayne, 1986, Sagamore of Wabash, Gov. State of Ind., 1990. Fellow Life Mgmt. Inst. Soc. Ft. Wayne (pres. 1983-84, honors designation 1980); mem. Life Ins. Mktg. Rsch. Assn. (Leadership Inst. fellow, exec. com. 1993-94, fin. svcs. com. 1993-94), Am. Mgmt. Assn., So. Ariz. Watercolor Guild (chair fundraising com. 2006—), Ft. Wayne C. of C. (chmn. audit-fin. com. 1989-2000).

BECKER, JOHN ALPHONSIS, retired bank executive; b. Kenosha, Wis., Jan. 26, 1942; s. Paul Joseph and Hedwig (Hammacke) B.; m. Bonny J. Anderson, July 4, 1963; children: Danial, Todd, Kathryn, Erik BS, Marquette U., 1963, MBA, 1965. Asst. v.p. 1st Wis. Nat. Bank of Milw., 1970-73, v.p., 1973-76, 1st v.p., 1976-79; pres. 1st Wis. Nat. Bank of Madison, 1979-86; exec. v.p. 1st Wis. Nat. Bank of Milw., 1986-87, pres., chief oper. officer, 1987-89, also chief exec. officer, 1988-89, chmn., chief exec. officer, 1989-91; pres. Firstar Corp., Milw., 1990-99; ret., 1999. Div. chmn. United Way, Madison, 1984; trustee Edgewood Coll., Madison, 1980—; mem. fin. com. Madison Republican Com. Served to 1st lt. U.S. Army, 1965-67. Mem. Wis. Bankers Assn. (exec. com.), Greater Madison C. of C. (chmn. bd. 1983). Clubs: Madison, Maple Bluff Country. Roman Catholic.

BECKER, JOHN RAYMOND, pharmacist; b. Garden City, Mich., Oct. 22, 1965; s. Raymond Charles and Dian Louise Becker; m. Denise Lynn Knowles, Nov. 8, 2004. Degree with honors, Schoolcraft C.C., 1992; PharmD, U. Mich., Ann Arbor, 1996. Staff pharmacist Providence Hosp., Southfield, Mich., 1996—. Clin. pharmacist USN, Portsmouth, Va., 1996—99; specialist pharmacist William Beaumont Hosp., Royal Oak, Mich., 2000—02; med. sci. liaison Genentech BioOncology, San Francisco, 2003, Wyeth Pharms., Collegeville, Pa., 2002, 2004—. Eucharistic min. St. James Cath. Ch., Novi, Mich., 2005—07. Lt USN, 1996—99. Decorated Commendation medal USN, Air Force Commendation medal USAF, Commendation medal; scholar, Shering-Plough, 1993. Mem.: KC, Am. Pharmacist Assn., N.G. Assn. US. Roman Catholic. Avocations: piano, woodworking. Home and Office: Wyeth Pharmaceuticals 50290 Helfer Blvd Wixom MI 48393 Home Phone: 248-449-3290; Office Phone: 248-449-3290. Personal E-mail: jrb2305@comcast.net. Business E-Mail: beckerjr@wyeth.com.

BECKER, JONATHAN, photographer; b. NY, 1954; Contbg. photographer Vanity Fair, Vogue. Co-author (with Brooke De Ocampo): Bright Young Things, 2000; co-author: (with Bob Colacello) Studios by the Sea, Artists of Long Island's East End, 2002. Office: Vanity Fair 4 Times Sq 17th Fl New York NY 10036 E-mail: office@jonathanbecker.net.

BECKER, KARL MARTIN, retired lawyer; b. Glenridge, NJ, May 30, 1943; s. Alfred Martin and Helen K. (Gramse) B.; m. Barbara A. Benton, Feb. 19, 1966; children— Glenn M., Mark W. AB, Yale U., 1965; JD, U. Chgo., 1968. Bar: Ill. 1968, S.C. 1994. Assoc. Vedder Price Kaufman Kammholz, Chgo., 1968-75, ptnr., 1975-78; asst. gen. counsel Esmark, Inc., Chgo., 1978-83, assoc. gen. counsel, 1983-84; v.p., gen. counsel, sec. Swift Ind. Corp., Chgo., 1985-86, sr. v.p., gen. counsel, sec., 1986; sr. v.p., gen. counsel Beatrice Cos., Inc. and BCI Holdings Corp., Chgo., 1986-87, E-II Holdings, Inc., Beatrice Co., Chgo., 1987-88, Beatrice Co., Chgo., 1988-90; ret., 1990. Dir. Mathers Fund, Inc., Bannockburn, Ill., 1991—98. Mem. S.C. Bar Assn. Avocations: skiing, sailing. Home: 31 Hearthwood Dr Hilton Head Island SC 29928-2906 Personal E-mail: KBecker1@aol.com.

BECKER, LANCE B., medical educator; Bachelor of General Studies, U. Mich., 1972; MA Biochemistry, U. Ill., 1977; MD, U. Ill. Sch. of Medicine, 1981. Cert. internal medicine, emergency medicine, critical care medicine. Founder, dir. Emergency Resuscitation Ctr. at U. Chicago in Chicago and Argonne Nat. Lab; prof. U. Chicago Dept. of Medicine; prof. emergency medicine U. Pa. Nat. Conf. dir. Am. Heart Assn. Emergency Cardiac Care Evidence Evaluation Conf., 1999; past chmn. Cardiopulmonary, Perioperative, and Critical Care Coun. of Am. Heart Assn., Basic Life Support Com.; chmn. Internat. AHA Guidelines Conf. for daily Controversial Topics", 2005; co-direct Resuscitation Sci. Symposium of Am. Heart Assn.; rep. Internat. Liaison Com. on Resuscitation; mem. Food and Drug Adminstrn. Device Evaluation panels, Nat. Am. Heart Assn. Basic Life Support Com. and Advanced Life Support subcommittees. Co-author numerous scientific publications. Named Attending Physician of Yr., Emergency Medicine, 1997; recipient Time, Feeling, and Focus award, Am. Heart Assn., leadership awards, Nat. Emergency Cardiac Care Com. of American Heart Assn. Office: Translational Research Laboratory 125 South 31st Street Suite 1200 Philadelphia PA 19104-3403 Office Phone: 215-746-3625. Office Fax: 215-746-1224. E-mail: lance.becker@uphs.upenn.edu.*

BECKER, LAWRENCE WILFRED, headmaster; b. Albany, NY, Nov. 16, 1941; s. Randall Damas and Hilda (Meuser) B.; m. Grace Marianne Zelinka, Aug. 23, 1969. BA, Amherst Coll., 1963; MA in Teaching, Harvard U., 1964. Math. instr. Hotchkiss Sch., Lakeville, Conn., 1964-86, dir. coll. counseling, 1969-80, dean admission and coll. counseling, 1980-82, dean faculty, 1982-86, asst. headmaster, 1983-86; headmaster Brooks Sch., North Andover, Mass., 1986—. Co-author: Relevant Mathematics/Algebra, 1970, Relevant Mathematics/Geometry, 1971, Relevant Mathematics/Advanced Algebra and Trigonometry, 1971. Trustee Brooks Sch., 1986—, Pike Sch., Andover, Mass., 1988-94. Mem. Univ. Club, Lanam Club, North Andover Country Club. Avocations: reading, jogging, music, musical theater, photography. Home and Office: Brooks School 1160 Great Pond Rd North Andover MA 01845-1206*

BECKER, LORNE ARTHUR, family physician; b. Kitchener, Ont., Can., Mar. 6, 1945; s. Percy Lorne Becker and Katie Klassen; m. Elizabeth Joy Wonnacott, June 1, 1968; children: Andrew James, Doug Scott, Lynn Marie. MD, U. We. Ont., 1969. Diplomate Am. Bd. Family Practice. Asst. prof. U. Rochester, NY, 1977—79; assoc. prof. Temple U., Phila., 1979—83, U. Okla., Oklahoma City, 1983—88, dir. family health program, 1983—88; assoc. prof. U. Toronto, Ont., 1988—94, chief family medicine, 1988—93; prof. dept. family medicine SUNY, Syracuse, 1994—2004, chair dept. family medicine, 1997—2004; prof. emeritus family medicine SUNY Upstate Med. U., Syracuse, 2004—. Founding bd. mem. Family Practice Inquiries Network; mem. steering group Cochrane Collaboration, 2004—, co-chair steering group, coord. pub. policy group, 2006—, chair pub. policy group, 2006—; mem. panel Gulf war and health Inst. Medicine, 2002—03; mem. working group on hearing loss in children US Dept. HHS, 2004—; coord. Cochrane Primary Health Care Field, 1998—2006; mem. rsch. com. World Orgn. Nat. Acads. and Colls. of Gen. Practice/Family Medicine, 2004—. Assoc. editor: Family Practice, 2004—06, mem. editl. bd.: Evidence Based Child Health, 2005—; contbr. chapters to books. Fellow Coll. Family Physicians Can., Am. Acad. Family Physicians; mem. Soc. Tchrs. Family Medicine (chair rsch. com. 1985-89, Curtis Hames Rsch. award 2001), Ambulatory Sentinel Practice Network (bd. dirs. 1979-93). Avocations: sailing, handheld computers. Office: SUNY Dept Family Medicine 475 Irving Ave Ste 200 Syracuse NY 13210-1529 Business E-Mail: beckerla@upstate.edu.

BECKER, MARY LOUISE, political scientist; b. St. Louis; d. W. R. and Evelyn (Thompson) Becker; divorced; children: James, John. BS, Washington U., St. Louis, 1949, MA, 1951; PhD, Radcliffe Coll., Cambridge, Mass., 1957; postgrad., U. Karachi, Pakistan, 1953—54. Intelligence rsch. analyst Dept. State, Washington, 1957—59; internat. rels. officer AID, Washington, 1959—64, cmty. rels. officer, 1964—66, sci. rsch. officer, 1966—71, UN rels. officer, 1971—91; pres. Internat. Devel. Enterprises, Washington, 1992—. Adviser U.S. dels. 19th, 21st, 23d, 24th, 26th, 28th, 30th, 32d, 34th Governing Coun. sessions UN Devel. Program; adv. U.S. del. 3d prep. com. meeting World Conf. UN Decade for Women; adviser U.S. dels. UNICEF exec. bd. sessions, 1987—91; mem. U.S. Com. for UN Fund for Women; lectr. internat. rels. civic orgns., student groups, 1954—. Author: Muhammed Iqbal, 1965; contbg. editor: Concise Ency. of Mid. East, 1973; contbr. articles to profl. jours. Mem. adv. bd. chmn. internat. student placement Washington Citizenship Seminar Nat. YMCA-YWCA, Washington, 1961—71. Blewett fellow, Washington U., 1951, resident fellow, Radcliffe Coll., 1952—56, Fulbright scholar, U. Karachi, 1953—54. Mem.: AAUW, Nat. Press Club, Mo. Soc. Washington (sec. 1959—60), S. Asian Muslim Studies Assn. (v.p. 1992—), UN Assn. (bd. dirs. Nat. Capital area 1991—), Mid. East Inst., Asia Soc., Assn. Asian Studies, Soc. Internat. Devel., Am. Polit. Sci. Assn., Harvard Club (Washington), Chimes, Mortar Bd., Pi Sigma Alpha, Eta Mu Phi, Beta Gamma Sigma, Alpha Lambda Delta. Presbyterian. Home: 2301 E St NW Washington DC 20037-2829

BECKER, MICHAEL ALLEN, internist, rheumatologist, educator; b. NYC, Oct. 3, 1940; s. David S. and Sylvia M. (Salomon) B.; m. Mary E. Baim; children: David, Jonathan, Abigail, Arielle, Daniel. BA, U. Pa., Phila., 1961, MD, 1965. Diplomate Am. Bd. Internal Medicine, Am. Bd. Rheumatology. Intern Barnes Hosp., Washington U., St. Louis, 1965-66, resident, 1969-70; asst. prof. U. Calif., San Diego, 1972-77, assoc. prof., 1977-80; prof. medicine U. Chgo. Pritzker Sch. Medicine, 1980—. Mem. biochemistry study sect. NIH, Bethesda, Md., 1991-95. Contbr. numerous rsch. articles to med. publs. Sr. asst. surgeon USPHS, 1966-69. Fellow, John Simon Guggenheim Meml. Found., 1978—80. Master Am. Coll. Rheumatology; mem. Am. Soc. Clin. Investigation, Assn. Am. Physicians. Office: U Chgo Med Ctr MC0930 Chicago IL 60637 Home Phone: 312-640-8801; Office Phone: 773-702-6899. Business E-Mail: mbecker@medicine.bsd.uchicago.edu.

BECKER, MICHAEL J., air transportation executive; married. BSBA, St. John's U.; M in Human Resources and Indsl. Rels., U. Minn. Various human resources, compensation and planning positions Dow Chem. Co.; with NW Airlines Corp., Minn., 1993—, mng. dir. corp. human resources, v.p. internat., sr. v.p. human resources and labor rels., 2001—. Office: NW Airlines Corp 2700 Lone Oak Pky Eagan MN 55121 Office Phone: 612-726-2111.*

BECKER, MURRAY LEONARD, corporate financial consultant, actuary; b. Phila., July 30, 1933; s. Simon and Bertha B. (Berlin) B.; m. Anita Goodman, Apr. 3, 1955; children: Mark, Lynn, Donna (dec.). BS in Econs., U. Pa., 1955. Actuary Mutual of N.Y., NYC, 1955—70; v.p., cons. actuary Johnson & Higgins, NYC, 1970—88; pres. Becker & Rooney, Inc., Teaneck, NJ, 1988—95; pres. Becker & Rooney divsn. Kwasha Lipton, Ft. Lee, NJ, 1995—97; v.p. J.P. Morgan Investment Mgmt., NYC, 1997—98. Mem. actuarial adv. com. N.Y.C. Retirement System, 1990. Named Advisor of Yr., Pension World Mag., 1986; voted by his peers for the Investment Mgmt. Inst.'s 1996 most respected GIC/Stable Value profl. award. Fellow Soc. of Actuaries; mem. Am. Acad. Actuaries, Actuarial Soc. N.Y. (pres. 1982-83). Home: 631 James Ln Rivervale NJ 07675

BECKER, NANCY ANNE, former state supreme court justice; b. Las Vegas, May 23, 1955; d. Arthur William and Margaret Mary (McLoughlin) Becker. BA, U.S. Internat. U., 1976; JD, George Washington U., 1979. Bar: Nev. 1979, D.C. 1980, Md. 1982, U.S. Dist. Ct. Nev. 1987, U.S. Ct. Appeals (9th cir.) 1987. Legis. cons. D.C. Office on Aging, Washington, 1979—83; assoc. Goldstein & Ahalt, College Park, Md., 1980—82; pvt. practice Washington, 1982—87; dep. city atty., prosecutor criminal div. City of Las Vegas, 1983; judge Las Vegas Mcpl. Ct., 1987—89, Clark County Dist. Ct., Las Vegas, 1989—99, chief judge, 1993—94; assoc. justice Nev. Supreme Ct., 1999—2006. Cons. MADD, Las Vegas, 1983—87. Contbr. articles to profl. jours. Pres. Clark County Pro Bono Project, Las Vegas, 1984—95. Mem.: NCCJ, Am. Businesswomen's Assn. (treas. Las Vegas chpt. 1985—86), Southern Nev. Assn. Women Attys. (past officer), Soroptimist Internat., Vietnam Vets. Am., Las Vegas and Latin C. of C. Mailing: PO Box 80332 Las Vegas NV 89180*

BECKER, NANCY MAY, nursing educator; b. Reading, Pa., July 28, 1949; d. Theodore R. and Minerva M. (Deiseroth) B. Diploma, Reading Hosp. Sch. Nursing, 1970; BS, Albright Coll., 1979; MS, U. Del., 1981. RN Pa., Del. Nurse mgr. Cmty. Gen. Hosp., Reading, 1974-76; nurse educator Albright Coll., Reading, 1980-87; clin. nurse specialist Polyclinic Med. Ctr., Harrisburg, Pa., 1987-89; asst. prof. Lehigh Carbon C.C., Schnecksville, Pa., 1989-95, dir. nursing programs, 1995-97, dean allied health/dir. nursing, 1998—2001, dean profl. accreditation and curriculum, dir. nursing, 2001—06, interim v.p. acad. and student affairs, 2001—02, v.p. academic and student affairs, DON, 2006—. Mem. ANA, Nat. League Nursing, Sigma Theta Tau.

BECKER, NANCY WOOLVERTON, public relations executive, event planner; b. San Antonio, July 31, 1947; d. Tillman Louis and Enid Maxine (Woolverton) Brown; m. William F. Pry II, Mar. 7, 1998 (div. July 31, 2003); m. Lawrence Becker, June 2, 2007; 1 child from previous marriage, Christina Elizabeth Woolverton Jones. Student, Ecole Nouvelle de la Suisse, Romande, Lausanne, Switzerland, 1962, Vanderbilt U., 1964; BA, So. Meth. U., 1968, postgrad., 1969-70. Cert. S.E. Paralegal Inst., Ancien Regime Christie's (London), antiques and residential contents. Tchr. spl. edn. Hot Springs Sch. Dist. (Ark.), 1970-72; reporter, soc. editor Dallas Morning News, 1974-82; soc./celebrity columnist Dallas Times Herald, 1982-91; owner, pub. High Society, Society Fax; bus.editor DFW Cmty. Newspapers divsn. Lionheart Newspapers Inc., Plano, Tex., 1999—2003; co-founder Decorative Arts Soc. Dallas, For Worth; pub. Decorative Arts Mag.; owner Personal Property Appraisal Svc., 2005—; realtor Keller Williams. Realtor, Ebby Halliday Realtors; stringer Washington Post, 1978; owner Nancy Smith Pub. Rels. Contbg. editor Ultra mag., Houston, 1981-82, Tex. Woman mag., Dallas, 1979-80, Profl. Woman mag., Dallas, 1979-80; mem. bd. advisors Ultra Mag., 1985—; columnist North Dallas People; appeared on TV series Jocelyn's Weekend, Sta. KDFI-TV, 1985. Bd. dirs. TACA arts support orgn., Dallas, 1980—, asst. chmn. custom auction, 1978-83; judge Miss Tex. USA Contest, 1984; bd. dirs. Am. Parkinson Disease Assn. (Dallas chpt.), mem. adv. bd. Cattle Baron's Ball Com., Dallas Symphony Debutante presentations; mem. bd. dirs. Dallas Opera Women's Bd., Northwood Inst. Women's Bd., Dallas Symphony League; mem. Friends of Winston Churchill Meml. and libr., Dallas Theatre Ctr. Women's Guild, Childrens' Med. Ctr. Aux.; mem. women's com. Dallas Theatre Ctr.; hon. mem. Crystal Charity Ball Com.; mem. Cmty. Coun. Greater Dallas Cmty. Awareness Goals Com. Impact '88, 1985—; com. mem. Dallas Arboretum, Preservation Dallas; co-chmn. Multiple Sclerosis San Simeon Gala, 1988; celebrity co-chmn. Greer Garson Gala of Hope 1990-91; gala chmn. Greer Garson Gala of Hope for Am. Parkinson's Disease Assn., 1991-93; chmn. gala benefit Northwood U., 1994; co-chmn. star-studded stomp Mar. Dimes, 1994; mem. Femmes du Monde spl. activities com., 1999 luncheon com., com. Dallas Coun. World Affairs; bd. dirs. Dallas Ballet's Lone Star Adagio; pub. rels. vol. Habitat for Humanity, 2005. Mem.: DAR, Internat. Soc. Appraisers (accredited; antiques and residential contents cert.), Nat. Press Club, Soc. Profl. Journalists (v.p. coms. 1978—79), Winterthur, Mes Amis (1st v.p. 2007), Preservation Soc. Newport County, Flagler Mus., City of Plano Sister Cities Com., Daus. of Republic of Tex. (registrar 1972), Dallas So. Meml. Assn., Dallas County Heritage Soc. (bd. dirs.), Dallas Mus. Art League, Dallas Opera Guild, Lancaster Hist. Soc., French Heritage Soc., Decorative Arts Soc. Dallas/Ft. Worth (CEO, appraiser, co-founder), Dallas Glass Club, Bent Tree Country Club, Dallas Knife and Fork Club, S'Amuser, Kermis Club, Coterie Club, Thalia Club, Rondo/Carrousel Club, The 500 Club (Dallas), Argyle Club (sec. 1983—84, 1st v.p. 2005—, pres.-elect 2007), Pub. Affairs Luncheon Club, Trippers Club, Tower Club, Rotary (gala chmn. 2007). Home: 5727 Covehaven Dr Dallas TX 75252-4934 Home Phone: 972-381-0418; Office Phone: 214-625-1162. Personal E-mail: nancywoolvertonsmith@tx.rr.com, nancysmithpry@aol.com. E-mail: decorativeartssociety@gmail.com.

BECKER, PHYLLIS, information technology manager; b. Plainfield, NJ, Nov. 9, 1963; d. Stephen and Jean Mae Potasky; div.; 1 child, Samuel. BS in Computer Sci., Kean U., Union, NJ, 1986; MS, Stevens Inst., Hoboken, NJ, 1998. Programmer ITT Def. Comms., Nutley, N.J.; sys. analyst AT&T, Somerset, N.J., CSC, Somerset. Republican. Jewish. Avocations: dog care, sewing, gardening. Office: CSC 500 Atrium Dr Somerset NJ 08873 Personal E-mail: pbecker@csc.com.

BECKER, QUINN HENDERSON, orthopedic surgeon, military officer; b. Kirksville, Mo., June 11, 1930; s. Quinn Henry B. and Sarah Lucille (Henderson) Finley; m. Gladys Marie Roussell, Aug. 11, 1951; children: Quinn E., Terri K., Paul Eric. Grad., N.E. La. State Coll., 1952; MD, La. State U., 1956; student, Armed Forces Staff Coll., 1969-70, Command and Gen. Staff Coll., 1971, U.S. Army War Coll., 1974-75. Diplomate Am. Bd. Orthop. Surgery. Commd. 2d lt. U.S. Army, advanced through grades to lt. gen., 1985; intern Tripler Gen. Hosp., 1956-57; resident in orthopedic surgery Confederate Meml. Med. Ctr., Shreveport, La., 1958-61; orthopedic surgeon Ft. Gordon, Ga., 1962-63; chief orthopedic service Ft. Rucker, Ala., 1963-64; comdg. officer 5th Surg. Hosp. (Mobile Army), Heidelberg, W. Ger., 1964-65; surgeon 3d Inf. Div., Wurzburg, W. Ger., 1965-66; chief orthpedic surgery 33d Field Hosp., Wurzburg, 1965; asst. chief orthopedic service Walter Reed Gen. Hosp., 1966-69; chief profl. services 85th Evacuation Hosp., Vietnam, 1970; div. surgeon and bn. comdr. 15th Med. Bn. 1st Cavalry Div., Vietnam, 1970-71; chief orthopedic service and orthopedic residency tng. Tripler Army Med. Ctr., 1971-74; surgeon 18th Airborne Corps., Ft. Bragg, 1975-77; comdr. Med. Activity Womack Army Hosp., Ft. Bragg, 1976-77; dir. health care ops. Office Surgeon Gen., 1977-80; comdt. Acad. Health Scis., U.S. Army, Ft. Sam Houston, Tex., 1980-81; dep. surgeon gen. Washington, 1981-83; comdr. 7th Med. Command, Heidelberg, 1983-85; Surgeon Gen. Dept. Army, 1985-88, ret., 1988. Asst. prof. orthopedic surgery Howard U., Washington, 1967-69; clin. assoc. prof. Sch. Medicine U. Hawaii, Honolulu, 1973-74; chief of staff VA Hosp., Asheville, N.C., 1989-92, ret. 1992; mem. Congl. Commn. on Svc. Mems. and Vets. Transition Assistance, 1998. Contbr. papers to publs. and confs. in field. Chmn. bd. Army Med. Mus. Found. Ft. Sam, Houston, 2005—. Decorated Legion of Merit, Meritorious Service medal, Bronze Star, Air medal, Disting. Service medal. Fellow Am. Acad. Orthopedic Surgeons (chmn. mil. affairs com. 1981-85), ACS, Am. Coll. Physician Execs. (disting.); mem. AMA (ho. of dels.), Am. Orthopaedic Assn., Masons (33d degree, Grand Cross 1993), Civitan (pres. Asheville club 1992, chmn. internat. rsch. com. 1996-98). Home: 2111 Peninsula Dr San Antonio TX 78239-3085 E-mail: mqbecker@armyresidence.net.

BECKER, RALPH EDWARD, broadcast executive, consultant; b. Carbondale, Ill., Sept. 18, 1931; s. Ralph Walter and Ola (Goetz) B.; m. Jane Mulholland, May 9, 1959; children: Susan B. McDermott, Nancy B. Gunzenhauser. BS, So. Ill. U., 1955. Gen. sales mgr. Sta. KPLR-TV, St. Louis, 1966-68, Sta. KNEW-TV Metromedia, Inc., San Francisco, 1968-70, Sta. KBHK-TV Kaiser Broadcasting, 1970-72; v.p., gen. mgr. Sta. WJKS-TV Rust Craft Broadcasting, Jacksonville, Fla., 1972-73; exec. v.p. Rust Craft Broadcasting Co., Pitts., 1973-79; pres. Ziff-Davis Broadcasting Co., NYC, 1979-83; pres., COO Toledo TV Investors, 1986-97, TV Sta. Ptnrs. L.P., Greenwich, Conn., 1983—93; pres., CEO, WHP TV L.P., Darien, Conn., 1993—95; pres., owner Saluki Investors Corp., Darien, 1983—, Becker TV, Inc., 1993—. Mem. tech. adv. coun. Grad. Sch. Edn., Harvard U., 1996—; pres., CEO, bd. dirs. Catamount Holdings Inc., Norwalk, Conn., 2002-. Mem. So. Ill. U., Carbondale, 1985—; bd. dirs. So. Ill. U. Found., 1986-2003. Capt. USAF, 1956—59. Recipient Profl. Achievement award So. Ill. U. Alumni Assn., 1985, 95, Radio-TV Dept. Alumnus of Yr. award, 1985. Mem. Broadcast Foundation, Mus. TV and Radio. Republican. Presbyn. Avocations: foreign travel, audio and video recording. Home and Office: 219 Old Kings Hwy S Darien CT 06820-5931 Home Phone: 203-655-6153; Office Phone: 203-852-7164.

BECKER, REX LOUIS, architect; b. St. Louis, May 20, 1913; s. Louis Herman and Elsie (Schroeder) B.; m. Ada Sylva Schmidt, Nov. 20, 1937; children: Susan (Mrs. Robert L. Barley), Kathryn (Mrs. Russell Kisling), Rex Louis, Roger G. B.Arch., Washington U., St. Louis, 1934, M.Arch., 1935. With archtl. firm Johnson & Maack, St. Louis, 1935-42; ptnr. Froese, Maack & Becker, St. Louis, 1946-73; pres. Becker & Flowers, St. Louis, 1973-81. Cons., mem. architects com. Luth. Ch.-Mo. Synod, 1980-96, chmn. 1986-87. Works include: Luth. Hosp., St. Louis, Civil Engring. Bldg., Math & Computer Bldg U. Mo. at Rolla, over 150 ch. projects. Pres. Council Luth. Chs. Greater St. Louis, 1960-61. Served with C.E. U.S. Army, 1942-45. Recipient Disting. Alumni award Washington U., 1995. Fellow AIA (pres. St. Louis 1956, regional dir. 1966-69, treas. 1969-71, Gold Medal award St. Louis chpt. 1998), Mo. Assn. Registered Architects (pres. 1955), Guild Religious Architecture, Scarab. Clubs: Mo. Athletic (St. Louis) (gov. 1973-76, treas. 1975-76), Engrs. (St. Louis). Home: Apt G02 701 S Laclede Station Rd Webster Groves MO 53119

BECKER, RICHARD CHARLES, retired college president; b. Chgo., Mar. 1, 1931; s. Charles Beno and Rose Mildred (Zak) B.; m. Magdalene Marie Kypry, June 19, 1954; children: Richard J., Daniel P., Douglas F., Steven G., Pamela J. BS in Elec. Engring, Fournier Inst. Tech., 1953; MS in Elec. Engring, U. Ill., 1954, MS in Math., 1956, PhD in Elec. Engring, 1959; postgrad., Harvard Inst. Ednl. Mgmt., 1976. Engr. Ill. Bell Tel. Co., Chgo., 1952, Andrew Corp., Chgo., 1953; rsch. asst. U. Ill., Urbana, 1954-58, asst. prof., 1959; sr. staff engr. Amphenol Corp., Chgo., 1959-60, sr. rsch. scientist, 1961-64, dir. program mgmt., 1965-67; dir. Amphenol Corp. (Far Eastern ops.), 1968; group v.p., corporate dir. adminstrn. Bunker Ramo Corp., Oak Brook, Ill., 1968-73; chief exec. officer and chmn. bd. Fortune Internat. Enterprises, Inc., Oak Brook, 1973-76; pres. Benedictine Univ. (formerly Ill. Benedictine Coll.), Lisle, 1976-95, pres. emeritus, 1995—. Trustee, prof. Midwest Coll. Engring., Lombard, Ill., 1968—86; trustee Ill. Benedictine Coll., Lisle, 1973—76; bd. dirs. Amphenol Tyree Proprietary, Ltd., Australia, Amphetronix, Ltd., India, Oxbow Resources, Ltd., Canada; v.p. Bonita Springs Incorporation Com., Inc., 1998—99, pres., 1999—2000; bd. dirs. Arthur J. Schmitt Found., 1970—, pres., 1995—; mem. exec. adv. bd. Internat. Engring. Consortium, 2000—. Contbr. articles and chpts. to profl. jours. and books. Gov. Brook Forest Community Assn., 1971-74; del. Oak Brook Caucus, 1970; trustee, pres. Arthur J. Schmitt Found., Ill. Benedictine Coll.; chmn. Coun. West Suburban Colls., Chgo. Met. Higher Edn. Coun., officer Fedn. Ind. Ill. Colls. and Univs.; chmn. Associated Colls. of Ill., West Suburban Regional Acad. Consortium. Named Disting. Eagle Scout, 1989, Regent, Nat. Eagles Scout Assn., Disting. Alumnus, U. Ill.; Arthur J. Schmitt fellow, 1953—56. Mem. Am. Phys. Soc., Nat. Assn. Ind. Colls. and Univs. (bd. dirs.), Albertus Magnus Guild, Rotary (Paul Harris fellow), Equestrian Order of the Holy Sepulchre of Jerusalem (knight commdr. with star), KC (4th deg. color corps), Sigma Xi, Eta Kappa Nu, Tau Beta Pi. Home: 25761 Creek Bend Dr Bonita Springs FL 34135-9523 Personal E-mail: papinani2@aol.com.

BECKER, RICHARD STANLEY, music publisher; b. Hillside, NJ, Nov. 9, 1934; s. Nat Edward and Hattie Adele (Perkel) B. Student, U. Miami, Fla., 1953. Pres. Richie Becker's Music, Inc. Pub. Music pub.: Moody River (No. 1 song in nation), Pat Boone, 1961, Anna, Beatles, 1963 (million selling album), You Better Move On, Rolling Stones, 1966 (Gold Record award), December's Children album, Moody River, Frank Sinatra, 1969 (Gold Record award), Cycles album, You Better Move On, Dean Martin, 1974, Moody River, Readers Digest, 1975, mgr., Alex Bradford, star of Broadway show, Don't Bother Me, I Can't Cope, 1975; pub.: musical Your Arm's Too Short to Box with God, 1975; dir. first country music show in history, Madison Sq. Garden, 1964, The Alex Bradford Collection, Rock and Roll Hall of Fame and Museum, 2003; contbr.: Moody River to, Colliers Yearbook, 1961, Anna to, Ency. Brit., 1963; Richard S. Becker Collection housed at Bienecke Libr., Yale U., 2005. Recipient Broadcast Music award, 1961, Key to City Memphis, 1973, Ark. Traveler award, 1973; named Hon. Citizen Tenn., 1973, Hon. lt. col. aide-de-camp George C. Wallace, 1973; Alex Bradford Meml. Music scholar Spelman Coll., 1996; Richard S. Becker collection of Alex Bradford Gospel. Music Materials Archives Collection at Smithsonian Nat. Mus. Am. History. Mem. Friars Club, Broadcast Music, Inc. Achievements include establishing Richard S. Becker scholarship Juilliard Sch. Music, 1976. Office: PO Box 144 Deal NJ 07723-0144 Office Phone: 212-724-2800.

BECKER, ROBERT A., advertising executive; b. Mar. 3, 1920; s. William and Eva (Kats) B.; m. Pearl Pehr, Aug. 22, 1948; son, David Jonathan; m. Nancy Gibbs, 1977. BS in Mktg., NYU, 1941; BS in Pharmacy, L.I. U., 1949; DCS (hon.), St. John's U., 1989. Copywriter Plough Inc., Memphis, 1941-42, Murray Breese Assocs., NYC, 1944-48; profl. advt. mgr. Squibb, 1949—57; advt. dir. Nepera Pharm. Co., Yonkers, NY, 1953-54; v.p. Burdick & Becker Inc., NYC, 1957-61; pres. Robert A. Becker, Inc., NYC, 1958—88, Hosp. Publs., Inc., 1963-84. Bd. visitors Fordham U. Sch. Law, 1987-90; bd. dirs. Guild Hall Mus., East Hampton, N.Y., 1995-97, Collegiate Chorale, N.Y.C., 2000-; founder, pres. The Beethoven Soc., N.Y.C., 1976-90. Recipient Decoration of honor in Gold, Govt. Austria; officer's cross Order of Merit, Fed. Republic Germany, 1985; Distinction of Merit in Gold, City of Vienna; elected to Med. Advt. Hall of Fame, 1997. Mem. Lotos Club.

BECKER, ROBERT JEROME, allergist, consultant; b. Milw., May 29, 1922; s. Jacob and Sarah (Saxe) B.; m. June Granof, June 25, 1950; children: Scott M., Jill Becker Wilson, Jon G. BS, U. Wis., Milw., 1943; MD, Med. Coll. Wis., 1949. Intern Michael Reese Hosp., Chgo., 1949-50; resident in internal medicine VA Hosp., Wood, Wis., 1950-53; resident in allergy Roosevelt Hosp., NYC, 1955-56; pvt. practice specializing in allergy Joliet, Ill., 1956-82; founder, chmn. bd. dirs. HealthCare COMPARE, 1982-90, chmn. bd. dirs. emeritus, 1990—98; cons. health care utilization co., 1982-90; founder, pres. Becker Cons. Corp., 1990—; founder, chmn. bd. dirs. Healthcare Cmty. Mgmt. Corp., 1990-93. Med. dir. Quad River Found. Med. Care, 1976-84; pres. Am. Assn. Profl. Stds. Rev. Orgns., 1980-82; exec. v.p. Joint Coll. Allergy and Immunology, 1978-86; mem. adv. coun. Nat. Inst. Environ. Health Scis., 1984-88; vice chmn, bd. dirs. Madison Info. Technologies, Inc.; chmn. Utilization Rev. Accreditation Commn., 1991-94, bd. dirs., 1994-96. Author articles in field. Pres. bd. edn. Joliet Twp. H.S. Dist. 204, 1969-70, 75-76; mem. bus. adv. com. U. Ill. Sch. Bus., Chgo., 1987—. Recipient Clemens von Pirquet award Georgetown U. Internat. Interdisciplinary Ctr. Immunology, 1978, Alumni Merit award Marquette U., 2003; named Entrepreneur of Yr. Arthur Young/Venture Mag., 1988. Fellow ACP, Am. Acad. Allergy, Am. Coll. Allergists (pres. 1987), Am. Coll. Chest Physicians; mem. Ill. Soc. Internal Medicine (pres. 1984-86), Asthma and Allergy Assn. Am. (bd. dirs. 1987—), Asthma and Allergy Found. Am. (bd. dirs. 1990-94), Am. Managed Care and Rev. Assn. (bd. dirs. 1989-95), Am. Assn. Preferred Providers Assn. (bd. dirs. 1989—), Utilization Rev. Accreditation Commn. (chmn. 1991-94, bd. dirs. 1991-96), Am. Assn. Preferred Provider Orgns. (bd. dirs. 1988-93), Am. Psychiat. Sys. (bd. dirs. 1994-2003), Alpha Omega Alpha, Alpha Sigma Nu. Office: 1S 045 Spring Rd Oakbrook Terrace IL 60181 Personal E-mail: wsimed@aol.com. *Whatever success I have achieved has occurred with the following rules of my life: 1) Individual and public accountability for decisions made; 2) Kindness to all persons in my sphere of contact; 3) Hard work; 4) Humility, truth, and respect for human dignity have been uppermost elements in my interpersonal relations; and, 5) I have accepted my humanness when I fall short of these rules.*

BECKER, ROBERT JOSEPH, database consultant, application developer, educator, computer science specialist; b. Grand Rapids, Mich., Apr. 22, 1946; s. Leon Joseph and Alfreda Mary (O'Rielly) B.; m. Kathleen Zbikowski, Jan. 16, 1970; children: Steven, Michael, Kimberly, John. BS in Computer Sci., Mich. State U., 1970. Computer sci. specialist Wolverine World Wide, Rockford, Mich., 1970-73; data base adminstr. Foremost Ins. Co., Grand Rapids, 1973-80, with data base, data communications, 1980-86, mgr. data base adminstrn., 1986-88, cons. of tech. directions, 1988—; prin. info. tech. cons., 2000—. Keynote data base performance speaker U.S. and European Software AG Confs., 1973—; tchr. computer basics to elem. sch. students, 1988-93; actor cmty. theater, 1995—. Editor (data base products) Software AG Connections, 1987-98, author performance courses, 1993—; contbr. articles to profl. jours. Community edn. instr., Wyoming, Mich., 1974-80; vol. examiner FCC, Grand Rapids, 1975-85; vol. religious edn. instr., 1980-2003; amateur radio vol. examiner, 1985—; jr. achievement instr. sch. grades 2-5, 2002—. Mem. Software AG Internat. Users Group (cert., chmn. performance spl. interest group 1978—, tech. rep. 1983-85, data base products rep. 1987-94, chmn. data base future directions 1989-99, comm. and client-server software rep. 1994-96, bd. dirs. 1996—, v.p. software exec. bd. 2002—, best presentation award 1978, 82, best speaker award 1979), Am. Radio Relay League, Nat. Train Collectors Assn. Republican. Roman Catholic. Avocations: amateur radio, commercial broadcasting, community and semi-professional theater. Home: 4560 Bremer St SW Grandville MI 49418-2238 Office: Foremost Ins Co PO Box 1233 Grand Rapids MI 49501-1233 Office Phone: 616-954-6128. E-mail: bob.becker@foremost.com, bob.becker@grnet.com.

BECKER, SCOTT, lawyer; b. Chgo., 1964; BS in Fin. & Acctg., U. Ill., 1986; JD, Harvard U., 1989. CPA Ill.; bar: Ill. 1989, Wis. 2000. Ptnr. Ross & Hardies (merged with McGuireWoods in 2003), Chgo., 1996—2003, McGuireWoods LLP, Chgo., 2003—, co-chair health care dept., 2003—. Office: McGuireWoods LLP Ste 4100 77 W Wacker Dr Chicago IL 60601-1815 Office Phone: 312-920-6016. Office Fax: 312-920-6135. Business E-Mail: sbecker@mcguirewoods.com.

BECKER, STEPHAN E., lawyer; b. Chgo., June 29, 1957; BA, Yale Univ., 1979; JD, Columbia Univ., 1982. Bar: DC 1982, US Dist. Ct. (DC), US Ct. Appeals (7th, 9th, Fed., DC cir.), Ct. Internat. Trade, US Supreme Ct. Ptnr., co-chmn. Internat. Trade practice Pillsbury Winthrop Shaw Pittman, Washington. Adj. prof. Georgetown Univ. Law Ctr. Editor (Notes & Comments): Columbia Law Rev.; contbr. articles to profl. jours. Mem.: ABA. Office: Pillsbury Winthrop Shaw Pittman 2300 N St NW Washington DC 20037-1128 Office Phone: 202-663-8277. Office Fax: 202-663-8007. Business E-Mail: stephan.becker@pillsburylaw.com.

BECKER, STEPHEN A., physicist; b. Evanston, Ill., Sept. 11, 1950; s. John N. and Irene A. (Wlodarski) B.; m. Wendee M. Brunish, May 30, 1980. BA, Northwestern U., 1972; MS, Case Western Res. U., 1974; PhD, U. Ill., 1979. Rsch. and teaching assoc. U. Ill., Champaign, Ill., 1979—80; postdoctoral fellow Calif. Inst. Tech., Pasadena, 1980—82; tech. staff mem. Los Alamos Nat. Lab., N.Mex., 1983—. Contbr. articles to Astrophys. Jour. Recipient Recognition of Excellence award U.S. Dept. Energy, 1999, R&D 100 award, 1999, Def. Program Excellence award, 2000, Disting. Performance award, Los Alamos Lab., 2005. Mem. Am. Astron. Soc., Internat. Astron. Union. Roman Catholic. Office: Los Alamos Nat Lab PO Box 1663 Mail Stop T085 Los Alamos NM 87545 Office Phone: 505-667-8964. Business E-Mail: sab@lanl.gov.

BECKER, STEVEN H., lawyer; b. NYC, Nov. 21, 1956; BA, Cornell Univ., 1977; JD, Vanderbilt Univ., 1980. Bar: N.Y. 1981, D.C. 1985, US Dist. Ct. (so. & ea. N.Y.) 1981, US Ct. Internat. Trade 1982. Ptnr., co-head Global Customs & Internat. Trade practice Coudert Bros. LLP, NYC. Mem.: Customs & Internat. Trade Bas Assn. (dir., past treas., mem. Litigation & Customs & Tariffs com.). Office: Coudert Bros LLP 1114 Ave of the Americas New York NY 10036 Office Phone: 212-626-4834. Office Fax: 212-626-4120. Business E-Mail: beckers@coudert.com.

BECKER, STEVEN RICHARD, beverage corporation executive, consultant; b. NYC, Mar. 28, 1952; s. Isidore A. and Adele (Sandler) B.; m. Abbe Dale Kligman, Feb. 27, 1982; chldren: Robert Sandler, Meredith Brooke. BS, Syracuse U., 1973; JD, Boston U., 1976; MBA, U. Pa., 1978. Bar: N.Y. 1977, U.S. Supreme Ct. 1980. Gen. counsel, asst. to pres. Knickerbocker Liquors Corp., Syosset, NY, 1978-85; exec. v.p., dir. Beauvignot Internat., Syosset, 1979-86; v.p. So. Wine and Spirits, Miami, Fla., 1985-91, 1st v.p., treas., 1991—, also bd. dirs. Cons. Ion Technols., Inc., N.Y., 1984-85. Jewish. Office: So Wine and Spirits 1600 NW 163rd St Miami FL 33169

BECKER, SUSAN KAPLAN, management and marketing communication consultant, educator; b. Newark, Jan. 4, 1948; d. Charles and Janet Kaplan; m. William Paul Becker, 1969 (div. 1977). BA in English cum laude, with distinction, U. Pa., 1968, MA, 1969, PhD, 1973, MBA in Fin., 1979. Instr. English Bryn Mawr (Pa.) Coll., 1972-74; assoc. editor U. Pa., Phila., 1975, asst. dir., lectr. urban studies, 1975-77; fin. analyst Phila. Nat. Bank, 1979-82; asst. v.p. Chem. Bank, NYC, 1982-84; v.p. Bankers Trust Co., NYC, 1984-85; prin. Becker Cons. Svcs., NYC, 1985—; adj. assoc. prof. mgmt. comm. Stern Sch. Bus. N.Y.U., 1990—2005. Cons./evaluator Pa. Humanities Council, Phila., 1977-78; mem. editorial bd. Mgmt. Comm. Quar., 1993-97. Author: How to Develop Profitable Financial Products for the Institutional Marketplace, 1988; contbr. articles and revs. to profl. jours. Vol. N.Y. Cares, 1989-92, N.Y.C. affiliate Am. Heart Assn., 1995-97. U. Pa. fellow, 1968-72; E.I. DuPont de Nemours fellow, 1979, N.Y. Regents Coll. Teaching fellow, 1968-70. Mem. Fin. Women's Assn. N.Y. (profl. devel. com. 1995-2006, grad. scholarship com. 2006—, co-chmn. scholarship com. 2007—, bd. dirs. 2007—), The Wharton Club N.Y. (career devel. com. 2003-05). Democrat. Avocations: painting and drawing, swimming. Office: 155 E 29th St New York NY 10016-8173 Office Phone: 212-689-1659. Business E-Mail: skbecker@beckerconsultingsvcs.com.

BECKER, THEODORE MICHAELSON, lawyer; b. Chgo., Feb. 18, 1949; s. Michael and Hazel Becker; m. Tamara B. Kaplan, June 11, 1983; children: Adam Michael, Alex Jordan, Ian David. AB summa cum laude, Washington U., St. Louis, 1970; MA in Sociology, Northwestern U., 1972, JD summa cum laude, 1974, PhD in Sociology, 1981. Bar: Ill. 1975, U.S. Dist. Ct. (no. and so. dist.) Ill. 1975, U.S. Ct. Appeals (7th and 10th cirs.) 1975, U.S. Ct. Appeals (9th cir.) 1976, U.S. Supreme Ct. 1978, U.S. Dist. Ct. (cen. dist.) Ill. 1979, U.S. Dist. Ct. (no. dist. trial bar) Ill. 1982, U.S. Ct. Appeals (Fed. cir.) 1983. Russell Sage fellow, instr. Yale U., New Haven, 1974-75; pvt. practice Chgo., 1975—. Contbr. articles to books and profl. jours. Mem. ABA, Ill. Bar Assn., Chgo. Bar Assn., Phi Beta Kappa, Order of Coif. Office: Morgan Lewis & Bockius LLP Fifth Fl 77 W Wacker Dr Chicago IL 60601 Home Phone: 847-501-3101; Office Phone: 312-324-1190. Personal E-mail: tbecker@morganlewis.com.

BECKER, WILLIAM EDWARD, economist, consultant; s. William and Bernadette Becker; m. Suzanne Rita Holt, Mar. 11, 1967; children: Jennifer, Catherine, Andrea. BA, Coll. St. Thomas, 1967; MA, U. Wis., 1970; PhD, U. Pitts., 1973. Assoc. prof. econ. edn. U. Minn., Mpls., 1973—79; prof. econs. Ind. U., Bloomington, Ind., 1979—. Adj. prof. commerce U. South Australia, Adelaide, Australia, 1996—. Editor: Jour. Econ. Edn., 1989—, Econ. Rsch. Network Educator, 2003—; author: 13 Books; contbr. over 100 articles to profl. jours. Recipient Marvin Bower Leadership and Svc. to Econ. Edn. award, Nat. Coun. Econ. Edn., 2003. Mem.: Am. Econ. Assn. (com. econ. edn. 1989—), Midwest Econ. Assn. (pres. 2005—06). Achievements include research in contributions to the assessment and development of educational practices and valuation of human capital. Office: Indiana University 100 South Woodlawn Bloomington IN 47405

BECKER, WILLIAM WATTERS, theater producer; b. New Orleans, Apr. 1, 1943; s. Ralph Elihu and Ann Marie (Watters) B.; m. Joan A. Alper; children: Kirsten Anne, Gevry Danielle. BA, Dartmouth Coll., 1964, MBA, 1965; LLB, Harvard U., 1968. Staff atty., Reginald Heber Smith fellow Community Legal Assistance Office, Cambridge, Mass., 1968-69; ptnr. Landfield, Becker & Green, Washington, 1969-89, Breed, Abbott & Morgan, 1989-92; prin. William W. Becker, Chtd., Washington, 1993—2001. Gen. counsel, dir. Voice Found., N.Y.C., 1976-2001; assoc. gen. counsel John F. Kennedy Ctr. Performing Arts, Washington, 1977-93, gen. counsel, 1993-2001; gen. counsel Kennedy Ctr. Prodns., Inc., 1972-2001; dir. Greater Washington Bd. Trade, 1978-92, gen. counsel, 1981-85; chmn. ShowOnDemand.com, Inc., 2000—, TheaterDreams, Inc., 2000- , The Chgo. Theatre, 2004—, The Kodak Theatre, 2005—. Prodr.: (plays) The Dinner Party, 2001, Urinetown, 2002, Into the Woods, 2003, Good Vibrations, 2004. Home: 7252 Stagecoach Dr Park City UT 84098 Home Phone: 435-258-6300. E-mail: beckerw@theatredreams.com.

BECKERLEY, ROBERT M., realtor, consultant; b. Shepard AFB, Tex., Oct. 6, 1943; s. James Evans and Susan N. Beckerley; m. Bernice E. Beckerley, June 20, 1969; children: Cynthia Humphrey, Jennifer White, Rhonda Cabrera. BA, Cambridge Internat. U., Cape Town, South Africa, 1992, MA, 1994, PhD, 2004. Lic. realtor Tex. Mgr. F.W. Woolworth Co., 1984—2001, Montgomery Wards, 1984—2001; realtor RE/MAX, Lindale, Tex., 2003—; CEO Bus. Solutions, Lindale, 2003—. Served with USAF,

1966—70. Recipient Air Combat medal, USAF, Accomodation medal, Vietnam Svc. medals. Mem.: VFW (life), Kiwanis Club, Lions (charter), Am. Legion. Republican. Methodist. Home: 317 Crestview Ln Lindale TX 75771

BECKETT, FAYE TRUMBO, school psychologist; b. Baton Rouge, La., Apr. 29, 1943; d. Leslie Orval and Thelma May Trumbo; m. Robert Earl Beckett, Nov. 19, 1994; children: Denisea Lynn Ray, Douglas Tracey Ray, Heather Dean Ray. BS, U. Memphis, 1981, MS, 1983. Cert. sch. psychologist. Sch. psychologist Memphis City Schs., 1983—87, Tipton & Lauderdale Counties, 1987—2004, Tipton County, 1989—. Various ch. positions, 1963—2005. Recipient Key Man Cert., Parkway Village Jaycettes, 1970, Rosetta I. Miller award, Memphis State U., 1982. Mem.: Tenn. Assn. Psychol. Examiners, Tenn. Assn. Sch. Psychologists, Nat. Assn. Sch. Psychologists.

BECKETT, JOSHUA PATRICK, professional baseball player; b. Spring, Tex., May 15, 1980; Draft pick Fla. Marlins, 1999, player, 2001—05, Boston Red Sox, 2005. Named Pitcher of Yr., Sportsticker Minor League, Baseball Weekly Minor League, Player of Yr., USA Today Minor League, Sporting News Minor League, Top Prospect in 1999 Draft, Baseball Weekly, Marlins Rookie of Yr., Baseball Writers Assn. Am., So. Fla. chpt., 2001, Marlins Orgnl. Pitcher of Yr., Baseball Am. Player of Yr., Fla. State League All-Star, Fla. State League Pitcher of Week, Number 3 Overall Prospect, Baseball Am., Ea. League, Fla. State League best pitching prospect, World Series MVP, 2003; named to Am. League All-Star Team, 2007; recipient Babe Ruth award, 2003. Achievements include being youngest pitcher to win two world series starts, 2001; being third Red Sox Pitcher to win first seven decisions, 2007. Avocations: hunting, fishing. Office: Boston Red Sox 4 Yawkey Way Boston MA 02215*

BECKETT, THEODORE CHARLES, lawyer; b. Boonville, Mo., May 6, 1929; s. Theodore Cooper and Gladys (Watson) B.; m. Daysie Margaret Cornwall, 1950; children: Elizabeth Gayle, Theodore Cornwall, Margaret Lynn, William Harrison, Anne Marie. BS, U. Mo., Columbia, 1950, JD, 1957. Bar: Mo. 1957. Of counsel Baker, Sterchi, Cowden & Rice, LLC; instr. polit. sci. U. Mo., Columbia, 1956-57; asst. atty. gen. State of Mo., 1961-64. Mem. City Plan Commn., Kansas City, 1976-80; bd. curators U. Mo., 1995-2001, pres. 1998. 1st lt. U.S. Army, 1950-53. Mem.: ABA, SAR, Kansas City Bar Assn., Mo. Bar Assn., Blue Hills Country Club (Kansas City, Mo.), Order of Coif, Sigma Nu, Phi Alpha Delta. Presbyterian. Office: 2400 Pershing Rd Ste 500 Kansas City MO 64108 Office Phone: 816-471-2121.

BECKETT, VICTORIA LING, physician; m. Peter G.S. Beckett, 1954 (dec. 1974); 1 child, Paul T. (dec.); m. Joseph C. Sharp, 1996. BA, Mt. Holyoke Coll., 1945; MD, U. Mich., 1949; MA, St. Mary's U., 1995. Intern Mpls. Gen. Hosp., 1949-50; fellow Mayo Grad. Sch., 1951-55; clin. instr. Wayne State U. Sch. Medicine, Detroit, 1956-67; staff cons. internal medicine oncology svc. Henry Ford Hosp., Detroit, 1957-60; rsch. physician Darling Meml. Ctr., Detroit, 1965-69; rsch. assoc. rheumatology Trinity Coll. Dublin U., 1970-72, postgrad. tutor, 1972-73, dir., 1973-76; cons. physician in rheumatology Federated Dublin Vol. Hosps., 1973-76; staff cons. rheumatology Mayo Clinic, 1976-90, emeritus staff, 1990—; asst. prof. medicine Mayo Med. Sch., 1976-90; med. dir. Rochester Health Care Ctr., Minn., 1985—90. Author: Living Medicine: Memoir Snap Shots, 2004. Fellow: ACP; mem.: Mayo Med. Alumni Assn., Am. Coll. Rheumatology (ret. mem.), Minn. State Med. Assn., Zumbro Valley Med. Soc., Phi Beta Kappa, Sigma Xi. Methodist. Avocation: teaching exercise class. Office Phone: 507-284-2691.

BECKFORD, OMAR MARIEN, researcher; b. Ft. Wayne, Ind., Dec. 17, 1976; s. Larry Delesea and Joyce Elveretta Beckford. BSCE, Fla. A&M U., 2000, MSCE, 2002. Presdl. fellow Ronald E. McNair Postbaccalaureate Achievement Program, 2000; fellow, rsch. asst. Fla. A&M U., Tallahassee, 2000—. Author: El Negro, 2006. Mem.: ASCE, Nat. Soc. Black Engrs. Avocations: percussion, guitar, keyboard, tennis, basketball. Office Phone: 850-410-6204. Personal E-mail: omarbeckford@hotmail.com.

BECKHAM, DAVID (DAVID ROBERT JOSEPH BECKHAM), professional soccer player; b. Leytonstone, London, May 2, 1975; s. Sandra and Ted; m. Victoria Adams; children: Brooklyn, Romeo, Cruz. Youth player Manchester United, England, 1991—94, profl. soccer player, 1995—2003, Real Madrid Club, Spain, 2003—07, L.A. Galaxy, 2007—. Mem. Eng. Nat. Team, 1996—, capt., 2000—06. Author (with Dean Freeman): David Beckham: My World, 2000; (with Tom Watt) Both Feet on the Ground: An Autobiography, 2003. Decorated Most Excellent Order of the British Empire (OBE) Queen Elizabeth II's 2003 Honours List; named BBC Sports Personality of the Yr., 2001, Sportsman of the Yr., Sports Press Assn., 2001, Man of Match, World Cup, 2006, Sports-Choice Athlete (Male), Teen Choice Awards, 2006; named to FIFA 100, 2004; recipient PFA Players' Young Player of the Yr. Award, 1997, PFA Players' Player of the Yr. Award, 2003. Office: LA Galaxy The Home Depot Ctr 18400 Avalon Blvd Ste 200 Carson CA 90746*

BECKHAM, WALTER HULL, III, lawyer; b. Boston, Feb. 12, 1948; s. Walter Hull Beckham Jr. and Ethel Brooks (Koger) Beckham. BA, Emory U., 1970, JD, 1977; MBA, U. Mich., 1972. Bar: Ga. 1977, U.S. Dist. Ct. (no. dist.) Ga. 1978, U.S. Dist. Ct. (mid. dist.) Ga. 1988, U.S. Ct. Appeals (11th cir.) 1982. Investment analyst, portfolio mgr. Life of Ga., Atlanta, 1972-74; assoc. Jessee, Ritchie & Duncan, P.C., Atlanta, 1977-81, ptnr., 1981-82; pvt. practice, Atlanta, 1982—. Bd. dirs. Cmty. Outreach YMCA, Atlanta, 1973—75; Brookhaven Boys Club Atlanta, 1976; pres. Sr. Hon. Soc. Emory U., Atlanta, 1984—85, mem. Law Sch. Coun., 1993—2001, bd. govs., 2001—05. Mem.: ABA (tort and ins. practice sect., long range planning com. 1986—90, coun. 1990—93, sect. chmn. 1995—96), Ga. Trial Lawyers Assn. (long range planning com. 1982—86), Internat. Acad. Trial Lawyers (state chmn. 2002—, internat. rels. com. 2004—07), Atlanta Bar Assn. (state ct. com. 1985), Ga. Bar Assn. (co-chmn. com. on professionalism 1997—2000, jud. procedure and adminstrn. com. 2000—), Kappa Alpha (Hardeman Province Ct. of Honor). Avocations: hunting, fishing, skiing. Home: 1208 Village Run NE Atlanta GA 30319-5303 Office: Ste 2600 75 14th St Atlanta GA 30309 Office Phone: 404-873-8000.

BECKINGHAM, KATHLEEN MARY, education educator, researcher; b. Sheffield, Yorkshire, Eng., May 8, 1946; arrived in U.S., 1976; d. Philip and Mary Ellen (Flint) B.; m. Alan Edward Smith, Oct. 7, 1967 (div. Oct. 1978); m. Robert Bruce Weisman, July 25, 1986; 1 child, Caroline Mary Weisman. BA, U. Cambridge, Eng., 1967, MA, 1968, PhD, 1972. Grad. student Strangeways Rsch. Lab., Cambridge, 1967-70; postdoctoral Inst. Molecular Biology, Aarhus, Denmark, 1970-72; rsch. assoc. Nat. Inst. Med. Rsch., London, 1972-76; rsch. assoc., instr. U. Mass. Med. Sch., Worcester, 1976-80; asst. prof. Rice U., Houston, 1980-85, assoc. prof. biochemistry, cell biology, molecular biology, 1985-92, prof., 1992—. Recipient award, Camille and Henry Dreyfus Found., 1979. Office: Rice U Dept Biochemistry and Cell Biology PO Box 1892 Ms-140 Houston TX 77251-1892

BECKINSALE, KATE, actress; b. London, July 26, 1973; d. Richard Beckinsale and Judy Loe; m. Len Wiseman, May 9, 2004; 1 child, Lily. Student, Oxford U., Eng. Actor: (films) Much Ado About Nothing, 1993, Prince of Jutland, 1994, Uncovered, 1994, Marie-Louise ou la permission, 1995, Haunted, 1995, Shooting Fish, 1997, The Last Days of Disco, 1998, Brokedown Palace, 1999, The Golden Bowl, 2000, Pearl Harbor, 2001, Serendipity, 2001, Laurel Canyon, 2002, Underworld, 2003, Tiptoes, 2003, Van Helsing, 2004, The Aviator, 2004, Underworld: Evolution, 2006, Click, 2006, Snow Angels, 2007, Vacancy, 2007; (TV films) One Against the Wind, 1991, Rachel's Dream, 1992, Cold Comfort Farm, 1995, Emma, 1997, Alice Through the Looking Glass, 1998; (TV series) Devices and Desires (voice only), 1991, (TV appearances) Anna Lee, 1993. Office: c/o Internat Creative Mgmt 76 Oxford St London W1N 0AX England*

BECKJORD, ERIC STEPHEN, nuclear engineer, researcher; b. Evanston, Ill., Feb. 17, 1929; s. Walter Clarence and Mary Amelia (Hitchcox) B.; m. Caroline Wendell Gardner, Feb. 28, 1953; children: Eric H., Amy W., Charles A., Sarah H. AB cum laude, Harvard U., 1951; MS in Elec. Engring., MIT, 1956; MBA, U. Chgo., 1984. Devel. engr. GE, San Jose, Calif., 1956-60, project engr. Pleasanton, Calif., 1960-63; engring. mgr. Westinghouse Electric Corp., Pitts., 1963-70, project dir., mgr. strategic planning-nuclear, 1973-75; v.p. Westinghouse Nuclear Europe, Brussels, 1970-73; dep. dir. FEA, Washington, 1975; dir. div. reactor devel. and demonstration ERDA, Washington, 1976-77; dir. nuclear power devel. Dept. of Energy, Washington, 1977-78, coordinator internat. nuclear study, 1978-80; dep. dir. Argonne Nat. Lab., Ill., 1980-84; vis. prof. nuclear engring. MIT, Cambridge, 1984-86, exec. dir. nuclear energy study, 2002—03; dir. rsch. U.S. Nuclear Regulatory Commn., Washington, 1986-95, cons., 1995—2003; chmn. com. safety of nuclear installations NEA-DECD, Paris, 1995. Author: Boiling Water Reactor Design, 1962; contbr. articles to profl. jours. Mem. vis. com. for nuclear engring. dept. MIT, 1992-98; mem. bd. visitors dept. materials and nuclear engring. U. Md., 1995—2002. Lt. (j.g.) USNR, 1951-54. Recipient Presdl. Meritorious award, 1992. Fellow Am. Nuclear Soc. (bd. dirs. 1995-98, chair nuclear installations safety divsn. 2000-01); mem. IEEE (sr.), Sigma Xi. Avocation: history.

BECKLEY, DAVID LENARD, academic administrator; b. Shannon, Miss., Mar. 21, 1946; s. George and Georgianna (Fields) B.; m. Gemma Douglas, June 1, 1968; children: Jacqueline, Lisa. BA, Rust Coll., 1967; MEd, U. Miss., 1975, PhD, 1986. Dir. advancement Rust Coll., Holly Springs, Miss., 1967-87; pres. Wiley Coll., Marshall, Tex., 1987-93, Rust Coll., Holly Spring, Miss., 1993—. Mem. NAACP (life). Named Outstanding Alumni, U. Miss., Oxford, 1989; recipient Silver Beaver award, Yocona Area coun. Boy Scouts Am., 2002. Mem. Tex. Assn. Developing Colls. (chmn. 1991-93), Edn. Ins. Assn. (bd. dirs. 1988-93), United Negro Coll. Fund (bd. dirs. 1990—), Omega Psi Phi (Citizen of Yr. award 1986, Man of Yr. award 1984). Democrat. Methodist. Avocations: reading, travel, collecting antiques. Office: Rust Coll 150 E Rust Ave Holly Springs MS 38635-2330 E-mail: dbeckely@rustcollege.edu.

BECKLEY, HARLAN R., religious studies educator; b. 1943; BS, U. Ill., 1966; attended, Wesley Theol. Seminary; MDiv, Vanderbilt U., 1972, MA, 1973, PhD in Christian Theol. Ethics, 1978. Min. United Meth. Charge, Kingston Springs, Tenn., 1971—74; instr., asst. prof., assoc. prof. religion Washington and Lee U., Lexington, Va., 1984—91, adj. prof. Soc. and Professions Program, 1984—91, prof. religion, 1989—99, chair Dept. of Religion, 1989—95, dir. Shepherd Program for Interdisciplinary Study of Poverty, 1997—, Fletcher Otey Thomas prof. religion, 1999—, interim pres., 2005—06. Mem. Pres. Adv. Com. Washington and Lee U., 1990—93, 1994—95, 1996—2001, 2003—05, mem. Faculty Review Com., 1996—97, co-chair, chair Task Force on Inclusiveness, 2000—01, chair Presdl. Search and Screening Com., 2001—02. Author: James M. Gustafson's Theocentric Ethics: Interpretations and Assessments, 1988, Passion for Justice: Retrieving the Legacies of Walter Rauschenbusch, John A. Ryan, and Reinhold Niebuhr, 1992; editor: The Annual of the Society of Christian Ethics, 1991—96, Economic Justice: Selections from Distributive Justice and A Living Wage, 1996; contbr. articles to profl. jours. Tchr. theology class Trinity United Meth. Ch. Recipient Va.'s Outstanding Faculty Award, State Coun. of Higher Edn., 2004; fellow U. Chgo. Div. Sch., 1981—82, Nat. Humanities Ctr., 1995—96; grantee NEH Fellowship for Coll. Tchrs., 1987—88. Mem.: Soc. Christian Ethics, Am. Acad. of Religion, Omicron Delta Kappa (hon.). Meth. Office: Sheperd Program Newcomb Hall N20 Washington and Lee U Lexington VA 24450 Home: 503 Jackson Ave Lexington VA 24450 Home Phone: 540-463-2041; Office Phone: 540-463-8784. E-mail: beckleyh@wlu.edu.

BECKLEY, ROBERT MARK, architect, educator; b. Cleve., Dec. 24, 1934; s. Mark Ezra and Marie Elizabeth (Kuhl) Beckley; m. Jean Dorothy Love, Feb. 26, 1956 (div. May 1988); children: Jeffery, Thomas, James; m. Jytte Dinesen, Oct. 24, 1990. BArch, U. Cin., 1959; MArch, Harvard U., 1961. From asst. to assoc. prof. U. Mich., Ann Arbor, 1963—69, dean, prof., 1987—97, prof., 1997—2002, prof., dean emeritus, 2002—; from assoc. prof. to prof. U. Wis., Milw., 1969—86. Exec. v.p. Genesee Inst., 2004—07; prin. Beckley-Myers, Architects, Milw., 1980—91. Prin. works include Theater Facilities, 1980—81 (award, 1983), Theater Dist., 1981—82 (award, 1984), Bellevue Downtown Park, 1985 (1st place award, 1985). Recipient Distinction award, Milw. Art Mus., 1986. Fellow: AIA (Mich. Pres.'s award 1994), Graham Found., Inst. Urban Design; mem.: Assn. Collegiate Schs. Architecture (bd. dirs. 1987—90, pres. 1988—89, mem. Nat. Archtl. Accreditation Bd. 1990—92). Office: U Mich Coll Arch 2000 Bonisteel Dr Ann Arbor MI 48109-2069 Home: 2200 Fuller Ct Apt 1115 Ann Arbor MI 48105-2307

BECKLEY, ROBERTA ANN, elementary school educator; b. Somerville, NJ, Oct. 20, 1955; d. Ross Andrew and Maureen Dorothy Beckley; children: Kathleen Erin Arnold, Michael Tynan Arnold. M of Edn., Mansfield U., Pa., 1979. Cert. spl. edn. and elem. edn. PA. Grade 3 tchr. Palmerton Sch. Dist., Pa., 1983—; adj. prof. Northampton CC, Bethlehem, Pa., 2002—. Acad. advisor Palmerton Sch. Dist., 1995—. Mem.: NEA. Home: PO Box 7 Kresgeville PA 18333 Home Phone: 610-871-0822; Office Phone: 610-826-7538. Business E-Mail: beckleyr@ptd.net.

BECKMAN, JAMES WALLACE BIM, management consultant, educator; s. Wallace Gerald and Mary Louise (Frissell) B. BA, Princeton U.; PhD, U. Calif., 1973. Ordained elder & deacon Presbyterian Ch. Pvt. practice, Berkeley, Calif., 1962-67; cons. Calif. State Assembly, Sacramento, 1967-68; pvt. practice Laguna Beach, Calif., 1969-77; cons. Calif. State Gov.'s Office, Sacramento, 1977-80; pvt. practice real estate cons. LA, 1980-83; v.p. mktg. Gold-Well Investments, Inc., LA, 1982-83; pres. Beckman Analytics Internat., mgmt. cons. to bus. and govt., LA and Lake Arrowhead, Calif., 1983—, East European/Middle East Bus. and Govt., 1992—; prof. U. Applied Sciences, Fulda, Germany, 2003—. Adj. prof. Calif. State U. Sch. Bus., San Bernardino, 1989-2002, U. Redlands, 1992-97, U. Calif., 1998-2001. Contbr. articles to profl. jours. Maj. USMC, 1958-67; various positions C. of C., Assn. Realtors, So. Calif., 1988-99. NIMH fellow, 1971-72. Fellow Soc. Applied Anthropology; mem. Am. Econs. Assn., Am. Statis. Assn., Am. Mktg. Assn. (officer), European Econ. Assn., Nat. Assn. Bus. Economists (officer). Democrat. Presbyterian. Avocations: running, weightlifting, travel. Home and Office: Fachbereich Wirtschaft Marquartstr 35 Fulda 36039 Germany Office Phone: 00496619640292. E-mail: bimbhappy@aol.com, happybim@hotmail.com.

BECKMAN, MICHAEL, lawyer; b. NYC, Oct. 8, 1945; s. Albert Beckman and Cecille Bronson; m. Susan Liebowitz, June 26, 1970 (separated Dec. 1987); children: Andrew D., Jason D. Bar: N.Y. 1969, U.S. Dist. Ct. (so. dist.) N.Y. 1972. Atty. Gordon Brady Keller & Ballen, NYC, 1969-71; ptnr. Wolkowitz & Beckman, NYC, 1971-74; sr. ptnr. Bell Kalnick Beckman Klee & Green, NYC, 1974-88; sole practice NYC, 1988-92; sr. ptnr. Beckman & Millman PC, NYC, 1992-96, Beckman Millman & Sanders LLP, NYC, 1996—2000, Beckman, Millman, Barandes, & Douglass, LLP, NYC, 2000—. Adj. prof. law NYU, 1981-93. Dir. N.Y. Jr. Tennis League, N.Y.C., 1986-95, Sports & Arts in Schs. Found. Mem. West Side Tennis Club. Avocations: tennis, skiing. Office: Beckman Millman & Sanders LLP 116 John St Rm 1313 New York NY 10038-3303 Home: 200 E 89th St Apt 30b New York NY 10128-4306

BECKMAN, RICHARD DAVID, publishing and advertising executive; b. London, Jan. 26, 1960; came to U.S., 1987; s. John Neville and Margon Lelia (Rosen) B.; m. Jane Cecilia Heaney, Nov. 5, 1983; 1 child, Alana Jane. BS (honors), U. Manchester, Eng., 1980. Sales exec. Thomson Mag., London, 1980-82; acct. mgr. Thames TV, London, 1982-83; bus. devel. mgr. Find Sup, NYC, 1983-85; pub. Conde Nast Traveler, 1994—95, Gentlemen's Quar., 1995—98; European advt. mgr. The New Yorker Mag., NYC; v.p. pub. Vogue, NYC, 1998—2002; exec. v.p., chief mktg. officer Conde Nast Publications, NYC, 2002—; pres. Conde Nast Media Group, NYC, 2004—; exec. v.p. Advance Media Group, NYC, 2004—. Mem. IAA, Foxholes. Office: The Conde Nast Publications 4 Times Sq New York NY 10036

BECKMAN, ROBERT W., pharmacist; s. Rudolph H. and Edith I. (Atherton) Beckman; m. Linda L. Leitzke; children: Bruce, Laura. BS in Pharmacy, State U. Iowa, Iowa City, 1956. Registered pharmacist Iowa Bd. Pharmacy. Pharmacist, mgr. Walgreen Drug Co., Davenport, Council Bluffs, Waterloo, Iowa, 1956—67; co-owner, pharmacist Rockingham Drug Store, Davenport, Iowa, 1968—86; pharmacist, mgr. Hy-Vee Pharmacy, Davenport, 1986—99, semi-ret. pharmacist, 1999—2006. Avocations: stamp collecting/philately, genealogy. Address: 5020 Nobis Ct Davenport IA 52802

BECKMANN, BILL, mortgage company executive; BA in Mathematical Economics, Brown U.; MS in Mgmt., Stanford Sloan Program. Various positions consumer and info. bus. Citibank; v.p. strategy and new bus. develop. IBM, global internet divsn.; pres. specialty lending US consumer assets divsn. Citigroup, chief service and tech. officer real estate servicing and tech. divsn., pres., COO CitiMortgage, 2005—. Bd. trustees Enterprise Cmty. Partners. Office: CitiMortgage 1000 Technology Dr Saint Peters MO 63304

BECKMANN, CHARLES HENRY, cardiologist, educator; b. NYC, July 18, 1930; s. William and Margaret (Wellershaus) Beckmann; m. Ardith Clara Kuehm, June 9, 1956; children: Eric, Eric, Diana. BS, MIT, Cambridge, 1952; MD, Cornell U., Ithaca, NY, 1956. Diplomate Am. Bd. Internal Medicine, Am. Bd. Cardiology. Entered USAF, 1957, advanced through grades to col., 1971; asst. chief cardiology USAF Willford Hall Med. Ctr., San Antonio, 1965-70; chmn. dept. medicine Clark AFB Hosp. USAF, Philippines, 1970-73, chief cardiology Wilford Hall Med. Ctr. San Antonio, 1973-83; dir. med. ctr. San Antonio State Hosp., 1983-84; cardiologist Skinner Clinic, San Antonio, 1984—; clin. prof. medicine U. Tex., San Antonio, 1983—; prof. medicine Uniformed Svcs. U. Health Scis., Bethesda, Md., 1982-83. Nat. cons. to surgeon gen., USAF, 1979-83, chief cardiology Bapt. Meml. Hosp. System, San Antonio, 1992-93, chmn. dept. medicine, mem. exec. bd., 1993-94; chmn. ethics com. Baptist Meml. Hosp., 1993-94,; chmn. dept. cardiology Bapt. Hosps. Sys., San Antonio, 1996-98. Mem. editl. bd. Heart Smart mag., contbr. articles to Am. Jour. Cardiology, Jour. Nuclear Medicine, Archives Internal Medicine, Jour. Cardia Rehab., Circulation, Jour. Allergy and Clin. Immunology. Pres. Helotes Park Civic Assn., Tex., 1965-67, Helotes Elem. PTA, 1968-70; mem. exec. bd. So. Region Boy Scouts Am., Atlanta, 1989—; bd. dirs. San Antonio dvsn. Am. Heart Assn., 1989-92. Recipient Award of Merit Boy Scouts of Am., San Antonio, 1976, Silver Beaver medal, 1977. Fellow ACP, Am. Coll. Cardiology (bd. govs. 1979-83), Am. Coll. Preventive Medicine, Coun. Clin. Cardiology, Am. Heart Assn., N.Y. Acad. Sci., San Antonio Cardiology Soc. (pres. 1989-90), Am. Fed. Clin. Rsch. (sr.), Masons, Shriners. Lutheran. Home: 14802 Circle A Trl Helotes TX 78023-4023 Office: Skinner Clinic 124 Dallas St San Antonio TX 78205-1288

BECKMANN, JON MICHAEL, publishing company executive; b. NYC, Oct. 24, 1936; s. John L. and Grace (Hazelton) B.; m. Barbara Ann Efting, June 26, 1965. BA, U. Pa., 1958; MA, NYU, 1961. Sr. editor Prentice-Hall Inc., Englewood Cliffs, NJ, 1964-68; v.p., editor Barre Pubs., Mass., 1970-73; pub. Sierra Club Books, San Francisco, 1973-94; pres. Beckmann Assocs. and Millennium Press, Sonoma, Calif., 1994—. Author: After-Dinner Drinks, 1998. Mem. Book Club of Calif. Office: Beckmann Assocs & Millennium Press 18185 7th St E Sonoma CA 95476-4797 Office Phone: 707-938-8194. E-mail: jonnytheb@vom.com.

BECKMEYER, HENRY ERNEST, anesthesiologist, pain management specialist, educator; b. Cape Girardeau, Mo., Apr. 13, 1939; s. Henry Ernest Jr. and Margaret Gertrude (Link) B.; m. Deborah Beckmyer; children: Henry IV, James, Martha, Leigh, Hillary. BA, Mich. State U., 1961; DO, Des Moines U., 1965. Diplomate Am. Bd. Med. Examiners, Am. Acad. Pain Mgmt.; cert. Am. Osteo. Bd. Anesthesiology. Chief physician migrant worker program and op. head start Sheridan (Mich.) Community Hosp., 1967-69; resident in anesthesia Bi-County Community Hosp./DOH Corp., Detroit, 1969-71, chief resident, 1968-69; staff anesthesiologist Detroit Osteo. Hosp./BCCH, 1971-75; founding chmn. dept. anesthesia Humana Hosp. of the Palm Beaches, West Palm Beach, Fla., 1975-79; assoc. prof. Mich. State U., East Lansing, 1979-88, prof. anesthesia, 1988—, chmn. dept. osteo. medicine, 1985-96; chmn. dept. osteo. surg. specialities, 1996-97; chief staff Mich. State U. Health Facilities, 1988-90, chmn. med. staff exec. and steering coms., 1988-90; chmn. of anesthesia St. Lawrence Hosp., Lansing, Mich., 1984-90, adminstrv. dir. dept. anesthesia and pain mgmt., 1994-98. Chief of staff Sheridan Cmty. Hosp., 1968-69; adminstrv. coun. Mich. State U., 1988-97, acad. coun., 1992-96, faculty coun., 1992-96, U. hearing bd., 2000-02, bylaws com., 2000-04, clin. practice bd., bd. dirs. sports medicine, athletic coun., 2003-05; internal mgmt. com. Mich. Ctr. for Rural Health; cons. Ministry Health, Belize C.A., 1993-97; amb. Midwestern U. Consortium Internat. Activities, 1993; chmn. com. student performance, 2002-03, com. on acad. policy, 2000-05, admissions com., 2000-, chmn. admissions com., 2003-07, MOA-MSUCOM liaison com. chair 2005-; adv. com. on pain mgmt. State of Mich., 1999-01; program chmn. Am. Russian Med. Exch., 1993-97; bd. dirs. Belize Med. Partnership. Spkr. Sta. WKAR, Mich. State U.; bd. dirs. Boy Scouts Am., W. Bloomfield, Mich., 1973-74, Palm Beach Mental Health, 1977-79, Care Choices HMO, Lansing, 1987-88; mem. adv. com. pain and symptom mgmt. State of Mich., 1999-02; mem. athletic coun. Mich. State U., 2003-05, self study subcom. NCAA, 2004-05. Fellow Am. Coll. Osteo. Anesthesiologists; mem. AMA, Am. Osteo. Coll. Anesthesiology (chmn. commn. on colls. 1988-89), Soc. Critical Care Medicine, Internat. Anesthesiology Rsch. Soc., Am. Coll. Physician Execs., Am. Osteo. Assn. (spkr., mem. evaluators registry), Am. Acad. Pain Mgmt., Am. Arbitration Assn., Mich. State Med. Soc., Mich. Pain Soc., Mich. Peer Rev. Orgn., Mich. Osteo. Assn. (chmn. edn. com. 2002—), Ingham County Med. Soc. (edn. com.), Am. Soc. Regional Anesthesia, Soc. Security Disability Evaluation, Soc. Internat. Scholars, Phi Beta Delta. Office: Mich State U West Fee Hall East Lansing MI 48824 Office Phone: 517-353-8470. Business E-Mail: beckmey1@msu.edu.

BECKNER, CYNTHIA BYRD, music and elementary school educator; d. Wilbur Herman and Virginia Gail (Penniger) Byrd; m. Ben L. Beckner, Aug. 13, 1977; children: Byran Ellis, Lisa Marie. BS, Radford Coll, Va., 1973. Music tchr. Wythe County Pub. Schs., Wytheville, Va., 1973—74, Lake Highland Prep Sch., Orlando, Fla., 1974—76, Sterling Park Elem. Sch., Casselbery, Fla., 1976—77, Ridgewood Park, 1977—85, Orange County Pub. Schs, Ridgewood Park, Kaley, Shenandoah, 1977—, Kaley Elem., 1985—96, Shenandoah Elem., 1996—. Extended day tchr. Orange County Pub. Schs., chorus dir. Vol. Orange County 4H Club. Recipient

Supt. Competitive Grant, Kaley Elem., 1986, Teacherrific award, 1991, 1992, Shenandoah Elem., 2003; grantee Supt. Competitive Grant, Ridgewood Elem., 1982. Mem.: Fla. Elem. Music Edn. Assn., Fla. Music Educators Assn., Music Educators Nat. Conf. Achievements include classes taught sent 6000 letters and over 200 packages to soldiers deployed overseas in 2001; performed for departing and returning solders after 9/11. Avocation: taught Horseback Riding at summer camp 7 yrs. Home: 5535 Lake Mary Jess Shores Ct Orlando FL 32839 Office Phone: 407-858-3180 ext. 236.

BECKNER, WILLIAM, mathematician; b. Kirksville, Mo., Sept. 15, 1941; s. William Horace and Bessie Mae Beckner; m. Chandra Muller; children: Amalia Marise, Chiara Lisa. BS, U. Mo., Columbia, 1963; PhD, Princeton U., NJ, 1975. L.E. Dickson Instr. U. Chgo., 1975-76; lectr. Princeton U., 1975; asst. prof. U. Chgo., 1976-83; assoc. prof. U. Tex., Austin, 1983-90, prof., 1992—. Vis. prof. Columbia U., NYC, 1984-85, U. Chgo., 1990-91, UCLA, 1992; asst. dir. Inst. Computational Engring. and Sci., chair math. dept. Contbr. articles to profl. jours. Recipient Salem prize French Math., 1975; Sloan fellow, 1976-78. Mem.: Tex. Inst. Computational and Applied Math., Am. Math. Soc. Office: U Tex at Austin Dept of Math Austin TX 78712 E-mail: beckner@math.utexas.edu.

BECKSON, MACE, psychiatrist; b. NYC, Aug. 6, 1959; s. Karl and Estelle Beckson; m. Ann Marie Davis, June 16, 1989. AB magna cum laude, Harvard U., 1980; MD, Cornell U., 1985. Diplomate forensic psychiatry and addiction psychiatry Am. Bd. Psychiatry and Neurology, cert. in Addiction Medicine Am. Soc. Addiction Medicine, lic. Physician State of Calif. Intern N.Y. Hosp.-Payne Whitney Clinic, NYC, 1985—86; resident, chief resident UCLA Neuropsychiatric Inst., 1986—89; neurobehavior fellow UCLA Sch. Medicine, 1989—91; rsch. psychiatrist NIDA-VA Med. Devel., LA, 1991—97; program chief alcohol and drug treatment VA Med. Ctr., LA, 1992—95, chief intensive OPT treatment of addictions, 1995—97; med. dir. PICU VA Greater L.A. Healthcare Sys., 1998—, forensic psychiatrist, expert witness, 1998—; forensic faculty mem. UCLA, 1998—, clin. prof. dept. psychiatry, 2005—, tng. supr. psychiatry residents, 1988—. Cons. Sexual Recovery Inst., LA, 1998—2003, Aim Healthcare Found., LA, 1998—2001, Didi Hirsh Cmty. M.H.C., LA, 1988—98; expert reviewer Calif. Med. Bd., 2000—. Contbr. articles and chpts. to profl. jours. Vol. psychiatrist UCLA Student Psychol. Health, 1989—91. Recipient VA Innovations of Care Recognition award, Dept. Vet. Affairs, Oskar Diethelm prize, Cornell U. Med. Coll., 1985. Fellow: Am. Psychiat. Assn. (disting. fellow); mem.: Am. Soc. Adolescent Psychiatry (chmn. task force adolescent substance abuse 2003—05), Assn. Threat Assessment Profls., Am. Assn. Suicidology, Internat. Soc. Traumatic Stress Studies, Assn. Treatment Sexual Abusers, Am. Acad. Psychiatry & Law (chmn. addiction psychiatry com. 2004—). Office Phone: 310-966-1907. Business E-Mail: becksonmd@becksonmd.com.

BECKWITH, BARBARA JEAN, journalist; b. Chgo., Dec. 11, 1948; d. Charles Barnes (dec.) and Elizabeth Ann (Nolan) Beckwith. BA in Journalism, Marquette U., 1970. News editor Lake Geneva (Wis.) Regional News, 1972-74; asst. editor St. Anthony Messenger, Cin., 1974-82, mng. editor, 1982—. Mem. Cath. Conf. Comm. Com., 1990—92. Mem.: Internat. Cath. Union of the Press (1st v.p. 2005—), Cath. Union of the Press, Cath. Journalism Scholarship Fund (bd. dirs. 1993—, v.p. 1995—96, pres. 1996—99, 2001—), Nat. Cath. Assn. for Broadcasters and Communicators (bd. dirs. 1989—96, 1997—98), Fedn. Ch. Press Assns. of Internat. Cath. Union of the Press (3d v.p. 1989—92, pres. 1992—2004, 3d v.p. 2004—, 2d v.p. 2005—), Cath. Press Assn. (bd. dirs. 1986—96, v.p. 1988—90, pres. 1990—92, best interview 1982, best photo story 1985, St. Francis de Sales award for outstanding contbn. to Cath. journalism 1994, best poetry 1997). Office: St Anthony Messenger 28 W Liberty St Cincinnati OH 45202-6498 Office Phone: 513-241-5615 x 170.

BECKWITH, EDWARD JAY, lawyer; b. Paterson, NJ, July 18, 1949; s. David and Beverly Beckwith; m. Iris Kailo; children: Jessica, Jason, Jenna. BS, Pa. State U., 1971; JD, Georgetown U., 1974, ML in Taxation, 1983. Bar: DC, US Supreme Ct., US Ct. Appeals (fed. cir.), US Ct. Appeals (DC cir.), US Dist. Ct. DC, US Tax Ct., US Claims Ct. Staff asst. Coun. on Environ. Quality Exec. Office of Pres., Washington, 1973; assoc. Fried, Frank, Harris, Shriver & Kampelman, Washington, 1974-82, Baker & Hostetler, Washington, 1982-83, ptnr., 1984—. Adj. prof. law Georgetown U. Law Ctr., Washington, 1984—; bd. advisors Jour. Taxation Trusts and Estates, 1989-92; mem. Greater Washington Bd. Trade. Contbr. articles to profl. jours. Steering com. sect. on trusts and probate law DC Bar, 1985-87; chmn. planned giving adv. coun. Pa. State U., 2000—. Alumni fellow honoree Pa. State U., 1998; named one of Top 100 Attys., Worth mag., 2005-06. Fellow: Am. Bar Found., Am. Coll. Trust and Estate Counsel (state chmn. D.C. 1998—2003, chmn. philanthropy study com. 2000—03, chmn. charitable planning and exempt orgns. com. 2001—04, regent 2002—, found. bd. 2006—, found v.p. 2007—); mem.: ABA, DC Estate Planning Coun., Am. Law Inst., Pa. State U. Alumni Assn., Army-Navy Club (Washington), Omicron Delta Kappa. Office: Baker & Hostetler LLP 1050 Connecticut Ave NW Washington DC 20036-5304 Home Phone: 703-522-4747; Office Phone: 202-861-1646. Business E-Mail: beckwith@bakerlaw.com.

BECKWITH, JOHN, musician, composer, educator; b. Victoria, BC, Can., Mar. 9, 1927; BMus, U. Toronto, 1947, MMus, 1961; DMus (hon.), Mt. Allison U., Sackville, NB, 1974, McGill U., Montreal, 1978, U. Guelph, Ont., 1995, U. Victoria, B.C., 1999; LLD (hon.), Queen's U., Kingston, Ont., 1998. Pvt. piano studies Alberto Guerrero, Royal Conservatory of Music, Toronto, 1945-50; pvt. composition studies Nadia Boulanger, Paris, 1950-51; pub. relations dir. Royal Conservatory of Music, Toronto, 1948-50; staff writer for radio music continuity Can. Broadcasting Corp., Toronto, 1953-55; freelance radio programmer and writer, 1955-70; spl. lectr. U. Toronto, 1952-53, lectr., 1954-60, asst. prof. music, 1960-66, assoc. prof., 1966-70, dean, 1970-77, prof., 1977-90, 1st holder Jean A. Chalmers chair in Can. music, 1984-90. Debut: Toronto, 1950; over 130 compositions including 4 operas, works for orch., chorus, etc.; 30 works published including: 4 songs to poems by e.e. cummings, 1950; Fall Scene and Fair Dance, 1956; Music for Dancing, 1959; Jonah, 1963; Sharon Fragments, 1966; Circle, with Tangents, 1967; Gas, 1969; Taking a Stand, 1972; Musical Chairs, 1973, 6 songs to poems by e.e. cummings, 2007, 3 songs to peoems by Miriam Waddington, 2007; 3 Motets on Swan's China, 1981; Sonatina in 2 Movements, 1982; Harp of David, 1985; recorded compositions include: Music for Dancing; The Trumpets of Summer; Sharon Fragments; Circle, with Tangents; Quartet; Keyboard Practice; 3 Motets on Swan's China; Upper Can. Hymn Preludes; Taking a Stand, Etudes, Arctic Dances, Avowals Harp of David, On the Other Hand., A Concert of Myths, Synthetic Trios, Stacey, Round and Round; recordings.: Music at Sharon, 1982; Musical Toronto, 1984, à la claire fontaine, 2000; arranger, dir. of instrumental ensemble; editor: The Modern Composer and His World, 1961; Contemporary Canadian Composers, 1975; Canadian Composer series, 1975-90, Musical Canada, 1988; Canadian Consultant, The New Grove, London, 1980; author: Music Papers, 1997, In Search of Alberto Guerrero, 2006; contbr. articles to profl. jours. Recipient Can. Music Coun. ann. medal, 1972, Arts Found. of Greater Toronto ann. music award, 1994; named to Order of Can., 1987. Mem. Can. League of Composers (former sec.), Ency. of Music in Can. (bd. dirs. 1972-94), Can. Musical Heritage Soc. (editl. bd. 1981-2003). Office: 121 Howland Ave Toronto ON Canada M5R 3B4 E-mail: j.beckwith@utoronto.ca.

BECKWITH, LEWIS DANIEL, lawyer; b. Indpls., Jan. 30, 1948; s. William Frederick and Helen Lorena (Smith) B.; m. Marcia Ellen Ride, June 27, 1970; children: Laura, Gregory. BA, Wabash Coll., 1970; JD, Vanderbilt U., 1973. Bar: Ind. 1973, U.S. Dist. Ct. (so. dist.) Ind. 1973. Assoc. Baker & Daniels, Indpls., 1973-80, ptnr., 1981—. Articles editor Vanderbilt Law Rev., 1972-73. Bd. dirs. Luth. Disabilities Ministries, Inc., 2003—, Luth. Child and Family Svcs. of Ind./Ky., Inc., 2004—. Named to Ind. Superlawyers for Environ. Law, 2004. Mem. ABA (assoc. editor occupational safety & health law 2002), Ind. Bar Assn., Indpls. Bar Assn., Ind. C. of C. (com. occupational safety and health law 1982—), Associated Gen. Contractors of Ind. (com. occupational safety and health 1988—, safety and health counsel), Order of Coif, Eta Sigma Phi, Beta Theta Pi. Republican. Lutheran. Avocation: sports. Office: Baker & Daniels 300 N Meridian St Ste 2700 Indianapolis IN 46204-1782 Home Phone: 317-849-8464; Office Phone: 317-237-1406. Business E-Mail: lew.beckwith@bakerd.com.

BECKWITH, PETER HESS, bishop; b. Battle Creek, Mich., Sept. 8, 1939; s. Robert Edgar Sr. and Florence Catheryn (Hess) Beckwith; m. Melinda Jo Foulke, July 10, 1965; children: Peter H. II, Michael J. AB, Hillsdale Coll., Mich., 1961, ThD (hon.), 1988; MDiv, U. of the South, 1964, DD (hon.), 1999; STM, Nashotah Ho., 1974, LHD (hon.), 1992. Ordained deacon Episc. Ch., 1964, ordained priest Episc. Ch., 1965, ordained bishop Episc. Ch., 1992; cert. marriage counselor Mich. Asst. rector St. John's Episcopal Ch., Plymouth, Mich., 1964—66, St. Paul's Episcopal Ch., Jackson, Mich., 1966—70; rector St. Matthew's Episcopal Ch., Saginaw, Mich., 1970—78, St. John's Episcopal Ch., Worthington, Ohio, 1978—92; bishop Episcopal Diocese of Springfield, Ill., 1992—; mem. Am. Anglican Coun., 1997—, v.p., 2004—; founding mem. Anglican Communion Network, 2003—. Chaplain USNR, 1972—99; instr. Sch. of Theology Diocese of Mich., Saginaw, 1975; res. instr. Navy Chaplains Sch., Newport, RI, 1979; chaplain to Episcopal inmates So. Mich. State Prison, Jackson, 1966—70; nat. chaplain Navy League of U.S., Washington, 1992—; chaplain Marine Corps Res. Assn., Washington, 1994—96, Ill. State Police, 1995—. Chair Jackson County Cancer Crusade, 1967. Rear adm. USNR, 1996—99, dep. chief of chaplain for total force USNR. Named Hon. Seabee, U.S. Naval Constrn. Force, Washington, 1992; named to Hillsdale Coll. Athletic Hall of Fame, 2002; recipient Alumni Achievement award, Hillsdale Coll., 1982. Mem.: Am. Anglican Coun. (bd. dirs. 2000—), Navy League (pres. Columbus coun. 1990), Delta Tau Delta (no. divsn. v.p. 2004—, Alumni Achievement award 2006). Republican. Avocations: golf, skiing, gardening. Home: 400 Clipper Rd Springfield IL 62711-8010 Office: Episcopal Diocese of Springfield 821 S 2d St Springfield IL 62704-2694 Office Phone: 217-525-1876. Business E-Mail: bishop@episcopalspringfield.org.

BECKWITH, SANDRA SHANK, federal judge; b. Norfolk, Va., Dec. 4, 1943; BA, U. Cin., 1965, JD, 1968. Bar: Ohio 1969, Ind. 1976, Fla. 1979, U.S. Dist. Ct. (so. dist.) Ohio 1971, U.S. Dist. Ct. Ind. 1976, U.S. Supreme Ct. 1977. Pvt. practice, Harrison, Ohio, 1969—77, 1979—81; judge Hamilton County Mcpl. Ct., Cin., 1977—79, 1981—86, commr., 1989—91; judge Ct. Common Pleas, Hamilton County Divsn. Domestic Rels., 1987—89; assoc. Graydon, Head and Ritchey, 1989—91; judge U.S. Dist. Ct. (so. dist.) Ohio, 1992—2004, chief judge, 2004—. Mem. Ohio Chief Justice's Code of Profl. Responsibility Commn., 1984, Ohio Gov.'s Com. on Prison Crowding, 1984-90, State Fed. Com. on Death Penalty Habeas Corpus, 1995—; pres. 6th Cir. Dist. Judges Assn., 1998-99; chair So. Dist. Ohio Automation Com., 1997—. Mem. advisory bd. Tender Mercies. Mem. Fed. Judges Assn., Fed. Bar Assn. (exec. com.), Judicial Conf. of U.S. (mem. com. on defender svcs.) Office: Potter Stewart US Courthouse Ste 810 Cincinnati OH 45202 Office Phone: 513-564-7610. Business E-Mail: sandra_beckwith@ohsd.uscourts.gov.

BECKWITH, STEVEN VAN WALTER, astronomy educator; b. Madison, Wis., Nov. 20, 1951; m. Susan McCormick; 2 children. BS in Engring. Physics, Cornell U., 1973; PhD in Physics, Calif. Inst. Tech., Pasadena, 1978. Asst. prof. astronomy Cornell U., Ithaca, NY, 1978-84, assoc. prof., 1984-89, prof., 1989-94; dir. Max Planck Inst. for Astronomy, Heidelberg, Germany, 1994-98, Space Telescope Sci. Inst., Baltimore, Md., 1998—2005; prof. physics and astronomy Johns Hopkins U., Baltimore, 1999—. Mem. adv. com. for large telescope mirrors NSF, 1989; mem. decade report astronomy in 1990's and working group for priorities in space scis., NAS, 1989-90; Volwiler lectr. in chemistry Lake Forest (Ill.) Coll., 1985. Alfred P. Sloan Found. fellow, 1982-85; recipient Fullam award Dudley Obs., 1983. Fellow Am. Acad. Arts and Scis.; mem. AAAS, Am. Astron. Soc., Internat. Astron. Union.

BECKWITT, RICHARD, construction executive; Mem. Mergers & Acquisitions Dept. and Corp. Fin. Depts. Lehman Brothers Inc., 1986—93; exec. v.p. D.R. Horton, Inc., 1993—98, bd. dirs., 1993—2003, pres. investments divsn., 1996—98, pres., 1998—2000; owner EVP Capital, L.P., 2000—02; exec. v.p. Lennar Corp., Miami, Fla., 2006—. Office: Lennar Corp 700 NW 107th Ave Miami FL 33172 Office Phone: 305-559-4000.*

BECOFSKY, ARTHUR LUKE, arts administrator, writer; b. NYC, Sept. 17, 1950; s. Arthur and Frances (Oliva) B. BA in Polit. Sci., Duke U., 1972; MA in Polit. Sci., Columbia U., 1974. Adminstr. Cunningham Dance Found., NYC, 1974-79, exec. dir., 1980-94; pres. Art Becofsky Associates, 1994—. World booking agt. Merce Cunningham Dance Co., N.Y.C., 1976-94; cons. Found. for Ext. and Devel. of Am. Profl. Theatre, NYC, 1985, Found. for Dance Promotion, 1995-2000, Ringside/Elizabeth Streb, 1995-2001, The Armitage Found., 1995, 2002-05, Cross Performance, Inc., 1995-98, Stephen Petronio Dance Co., 1995-2002, Gotham Dance, Inc., 1995, ODC/San Francisco, 1995—, Twyla Tharp, 1996, David Dorfman Dance, 1996-2001, Ballet Hispanico, 1996-2001, David Rousseve/Reality, 1996-2001, Susan Marshall Dance Co., 1996-2001, Rena Shagan Assocs., 1996-2001, Margaret Jenkins Dance Co., 1997—, Bill Young and Dancers, 1997—, Bridgehampton Chamber Music Assocs., 1997, Ananda Shankar Dance Co., Calcutta, 1997—, Nest/Tokyo, 1997—, Garth Fagan Dance, 1998—, Moving Education, 1998—, Richard Alston Dance Co., London, 1998-2004, Grupo Corpo/Brazil, 1998—, Rosy Co./Tokyo, 1998—, Siobhan Davies Dance Co., London, 1998-99, Lines Contemporary Ballet, 1998-2000, Joe Goode Performance Group, 1999-2001, Compagnie Jant-Bi, 1999—, Pentacle Help Desk, 1999-2003, Art Plus Care to Dance, 1999—, Expressions Dance Co., Brisbane, 1999-2002, Uno Man, Tokyo, 1999—, Kazco Takemoto, Tokyo, 1999—, Kenichi Tanno & Numbering Machine, Tokyo, 1999—, Jose Limon Dance Co., 1999-2002, Daniel Yeung, Hong Kong, 1999—, Compagnie Marie Chouinard, 2001—, Chunky Move, 2001-, Dance Works Rotterdam, 2002—, Compagnie Flak/Jose Navas, 2002—, Pappa Tarahumara, Tokyo, 2002—, Choreographers in Mentorship Exchange, 2004—, Compagnie Ea Sola, 2005—; dance panel NEA, 1983-94. Guitarist Rhys Chatham & The Din, 1981; composer: Secretarial Suite, 1980, Track, 1983, Get Real, Cassandra, 1985, Space Into Action, 1986; author: The Road Show Abroad, 1985, On Commissioning New Art, 1989, MMerce, 1991, Lar Lubovitch: The Company We Keep, 1999. Bd. dirs. Dancing for Life, 1987; U.S. Performing Arts subcom. CULCON for U.S.-Japan cultural exch., 1989-93. Mem. Dance/U.S.A. (bd. dirs. 1983-88, 91-98, treas. 1983-86, vice chair 1993-96), World Dance Alliance (bd. dirs. 1993-97), Am. Arts Alliance (bd. dirs. 1983-87). Democrat. Avocation: photography. Home and Office: 46 Barkit Kennel Rd Pleasant Valley NY 12569 Office Phone: 845-635-9311. Personal E-mail: ckdance@aol.com.

BECTON, HENRY PRENTISS, JR., broadcast executive; b. Englewood, NJ, Oct. 16, 1943; s. Henry Prentiss and Jean Sprague (Coggan) B.; m. Jean Campbell Redpath, Sept. 28, 1968; children: Sara Campbell, Wilson Prentiss, Elizabeth Campbell BA magna cum laude, Yale U., New Haven, Conn., 1965; JD cum laude, Harvard U., Cambridge, Mass., 1968. Tchr. Cambridge Sch., Weston, Mass., 1968-69; tel. producer WGBH Ednl. Found., Boston, 1970-73, program mgr., 1974-78, v.p., gen. mgr., 1978-84, pres., 1984—. Bd. dirs. Becton, Dickinson & Co., Belo Corp., Pub. Broadcasting Svc., 1988—2001, Banff Internat., TV Festival, Pub. Radio Internat., 2003—; bd. dir. Am. Pub. TV, 1997—2003; trustee DWS Scudder Funds, Conn. Coll., 1992—97; mem. Com. for Econ. Devel., 1992—2002; with Ethics Resource Ctr., 1994—97; dir. PBS Found., 2007—. Bd. dirs. Mass. Com. for Prevention of Child Abuse, 1979-81; trustee Boston Ballet, 1976-78, Met. Cultural Alliance, Boston, 1974-76, New Eng. Aquarium, 1981-2003, Boston Mus. Sci., 1984—, Wang Ctr. for Performing Arts, 1985-93, 99, Concord Acad., 1993-2006, v.p., 1994-2002, pres., 2002-06; bd. overseers Boston Mus. Fine Arts, 1990-2003, New Eng. Aquarium, 2003—. Mem. NATAS (bd. dir. New Eng. chpt. 1980-84), Assn. Public TV Stas (bd. dirs. 2005—, vice chmn. 2007—), Mass. Bar Assn., Kollegewidgwok Yacht Club (commodore 2006—), Phi Beta Kappa. Office: Sta WGBH-TV and WGBH-FM 1 Guest St Brighton MA 02135

BEDARD, PATRICK JOSEPH, editor, writer, consultant; b. Waterloo, Iowa, Aug. 20, 1941; s. Gerald Joseph and Pearl Leona (Brown) B. BS in Mech. Engring, Iowa State U., 1963; M.Automotive Engring., Chrysler Inst. Engring., 1965. Product engr. Chrysler Corp., Highland Park, Mich., 1963-67; tech. editor Car and Driver mag., NYC, 1967-69, exec. editor, 1969-78, editor-at-large, 1978—. Race driver, cons. in field; freelance writer mags. and TV films. Author: Expert Driving, 1987. Mem. Soc. Automotive Engrs., U.S. Ultralight Assn., Aero Sports Connection, Sports Car Club Am., Pi Tau Sigma. Roman Catholic. Achievements include first driver to win profl. road race in N.Am. in Wankel-powered car, 1973; raced at Indpls. 500, 1983-84; 1st driver to go 200 miles per hour at Indpls. in Stockblock-powered car, 1984. Home: Rt 1 Box 779 Port Saint Joe FL 32456 Office: Car and Driver 2002 Hogback Rd Ann Arbor MI 48105-9795

BEDAU, HUGO ADAM, philosophy educator; b. Portland, Oreg., Sept. 23, 1926; s. Hugo Adam and Laura (Romeis) B.; m. Jan Lisbeth Peterson Mastin, 1952 (div. 1988); children: Lauren, Mark Adam, Paul Hugo, Guy Antony; m. Constance Elizabeth Putnam, 1990. Student, U. So. Calif., 1944-45; BA summa cum laude, U. Redlands, 1949; MA, Boston U., 1951, Harvard, 1953, PhD, 1961. Instr. Dartmouth, 1953-54; instr. Princeton, 1954-57, lectr., 1958-61; assoc. prof. Reed Coll., 1962-66; prof. philosophy Tufts U., 1967—97, prof. emeritus, 1997—. Vis. prof. law faculty U. Natal, South Africa, 1981, U. Westminster, London, 1994—; vis. life fellow Clare Hall, Cambridge U., 1980; vis. fellow Wolfson Coll., Oxford, 1988; hon. rsch. fellow Bentham Project, U. London, 1997-99, 2003-04. Author: The Courts, The Constitution and Capital Punishment, 1977, Death is Different, 1987, Making Mortal Choices, 1997, Thinking and Writing About Philosophy, 2d edit., 2002, Killing as Punishment, 2004; co-author: Victimless Crimes, 1974, Current Issues and Enduring Questions, 1987, 7th edit., 2004, In Spite of Innocence, 1992, Critical Thinking, Reading, and Writing, 5th edit., 2004; editor: Death Penalty in America, 1964, 4th edit., 1997, Civil Disobedience, 1969, Justice and Equality, 1971, Civil Disobedience in Focus, 1991; co-editor: Capital Punishment in the US, 1976, Debating the Death Penalty, 2004; contbr. articles and essays on social, polit., and legal philosophy to books and profl. jours. Bd. dirs. Am. League to Abolish Capital Punishment, 1959—72, pres., 1969—72; bd. dirs. ACLU, Mass., 1984—87, 1988—93, 1995—98, v.p., 1987; chmn. Nat. Coalition Against Death Penalty, 1990—93. Danforth fellow, 1957-58, Liberal Arts fellow in law and philosophy Harvard U. Law Sch., 1961-62. Mem. Am. Philos. Assn., AAUP, Am. Soc. Polit. and Legal Philosophy (v.p. 1981), Phi Beta Kappa. Office: Tufts U Dept Of Philosophy Medford MA 02155 Personal E-mail: habedau@aol.com.

BEDDALL, THOMAS HENRY, lawyer; b. Pottsville, Pa., Apr. 24, 1922; s. Thomas and Martha Roberta (Gallagher) B.; m. Priscilla Kimball, July 26, 1956 (dec.); children: Laurence, Frederic, Margaret, and Katherine; m. Catherine C. Larmore, May 2, 1994. AB, Yale U., 1943; LL.B., U. Va., 1950. Bar: N.Y. 1951, D.C. 1968. Assoc. Sullivan & Cromwell, NYC, 1950-57, Paul Mellon Interests, Washington, 1957-89. Dir. Carborundum Co., Niagara Falls, N.Y., 1960-78; lectr. U. Va., 1976-79 Chmn. bd. trustees Sheridan Sch., Washington, 1972-74; trustee Va. Mus. and Found., 1984-99, Nat. Mus. of Racing, 1988-2001, The Textile Mus., 1990-92, Va. State Parks Found., 1992-96; chmn. VA Tech. Equine Rsch. Sta., 2000-07. Mem. Bar Assn. City N.Y., Mil. Order World Wars, Order of Coif, Raven Soc., Metropolitan Club, Phi Delta Phi, Omicron Delta Kappa, Pi Delta Epsilon, Chi Psi. Office: PO Box 914 Middleburg VA 20118-0914

BEDDOW, RICHARD HAROLD, retired judge; b. Springfield, Mass., Jan. 3, 1932; s. Richard Harold and Elizabeth Christine (Geehern) Beddow; m. Trudy C. Howells, Jan. 14, 1967; children: Catherine Elizabeth Almand, Elissa Christine Myers. BS, U. Mass., 1953; LLB, Boston Coll, 1959. Bar: Mass. 1960. Atty. ICC, Washington, 1959-69, mem. rev. bd., 1969-73, adminstrv. law judge, 1973-81, NLRB, Washington, 1981—2002; ret., 2002. With USN, 1953—55. Roman Catholic. Avocation: landscape gardening. Home: 2406 Rockwood Rd Accokeek MD 20607-9584

BEDEIAN, ARTHUR GEORGE, business educator; b. Davenport, Iowa, Dec. 22, 1946; s. Arthur and Varsenick B.; m. Lynda, June 29, 1968; children: Katherine Nicole Kingsmill, Thomas Arthur. BBA, U. Iowa, 1967; MBA, Memphis U., 1968; DBA, Miss. State U., 1973. Instr. mgr. Miss. State U., Mississippi State, 1969-71; asst. prof. Ga. So. Coll., Statesboro, 1971-73; adj. asst. prof. Boston U., 1973-74; Edward L. Lowder prof. mgmt. Auburn (Ala.) U., 1974-85; Ralph and Kacoo G. Olinde Disting. prof. mgmt. La. State U., Baton Rouge, 1985-96, Boyd prof., 1997—. Dir. Found. for Adminstrv. Rsch., 1982-93, pres., 1989-90; cons. in field. Author: Organizations: Theory and Design, 1991, Management Laureates, 1992, 6th edit., 2002; Standardization of Selected Management Concepts, 1986, Management, 3d edit., 1993, Management in Extension, 3d edit., 1995; editor Jour. of Mgmt., 1977-79. With USAR, 1968—73. Recipient Ronald G. Greenwood Lifetime Achievement award, 2003, Disting. Faculty award, LSU, 2006, Richard M. Hodgetts Disting. Career award, 2007. Fellow Acad. Mgmt. (pres. 1987-89, dean 1997-99), Internat. Acad. Mgmt., So. Mgmt. Assn.; mem. APA, Inst. Decision Scis. (nat. coun. 1976-79), Southeastern Inst. Decision Scis. (pres. 1978-79), So. Mgmt. Assn. (pres. 1982-83), Am. Sociol. Assn., Soc. Organizational Behavior, Beta Gamma Sigma, Delta Mu Delta, Phi Kappa Phi, Sigma Iota Epsilon. Armenian Orthodox. Home: 838 High Plains Ave Baton Rouge LA 70810-4349 Office: La State U Dept Mgmt Baton Rouge LA 70803-6312 Office Phone: 225-578-6141. Business E-Mail: abede@lsu.edu.

BEDELL, BARBARA LEE, journalist; b. Annapolis, Md., July 10, 1936; d. Royal Lee and Kathryn Rosalee (Alton) Sweeney; m. Raymond Lester Bedell, July 1, 1955 (div. 1979); children: Patricia Bedell Pulito, Barbara Ann Bedell Porrini, Raymond, Robert. DHL (hon.), Mt. St. Mary Coll., 2000. Dir. woman's programming, host daily talk show Sta. KLME, Laramie, Wyo., 1962-68, Sta. WKIP, Poughkeepsie, NY, 1968-70; asst. soc. editor, feature writer Poughkeepsie Jour., 1968-70; dir. comm. and publs. Spackenkill Sch. Dist., Poughkeepsie, 1970-73; columnist, reporter Times Herald-Record Newspaper, Middletown, NY, 1973—. Bd. dirs. Middletown Day Nursery, 1988—; mem. steering com. Dr. Martin Luther King Jr. Cmty. Wide Celebration, 1992—; lectr. on various topics to civic, polit., religious, social orgns., 1961—. Mem. 75th Anniversary Com., Cheyenne, Wyo., 1965; mem. Rep. Precinct Com., 1961-68, Albany County Bd. Electors, 1966-68; mem. com. history and heritage collection

Orange County C.C., Middletown, 1984; mem. 100th Anniversary Com., Middletown, 1983-88; bd. dirs. divsn. marshal 1988 Parade; apptd. del. Gov. Mario Cuomo's N.Y. State Conf. on Librs., 1981; campaign chair United Way, 1996; bd. dirs. Literacy Vols. of Am.; kettle chmn. Salvation Army, 1999. Recipient 1st in N.Y. feature writing award Am. Cancer Soc., 1973, Disting. Svc. award NAACP, 1980, 96, Hadassah Myrtle Wreath award, 1979, Cmty. Svc. award Boy Scouts Am., 1990, Humanitarian award Human Rights Commn., 1997, Lions Knight of the Blind award, 1999, Orange County Agr. Soc. award, Pinnacle award U.S. Harness Racing Hall of Fame, 2002, Masonic DeWitt Clinton award, 2002, Spirit of Caring award Hospice Orange and Sullivan Counties, 2005, Coop. Ext. Friend of Ext. award Cornell U., 2005, Martha Washington Woman of History award, 2006, Presdl. citation Hudson Valley Leisure Svcs. Assn., 2007; named Mrs. Wyo., Mrs. Am. Pageant, 1967, N.Y. State All-Am. Family, 1972, NY State SEnate Woman of Distinction, 2007. Mem. Nat. Fedn. Press Women (8 awards for feature writing 1967-70, top Wyo. state award for radio script writing 1966), Elks (Mother of Yr. award 1989), SAR (Woman of Yr. award 1991), US Harness Writers' Assn. (Good Gal award 2005), Kiwanis, Lions, Rotary. Home: PO Box 458 Walker Valley NY 12588-0458 Office: Times Herald-Record PO Box 2046 Middletown NY 10940-0558 E-mail: bbedell@th-record.com.

BEDELL, ELIZABETH SNYDER (BETTY BEDELL), editor-in-chief, marketing professional; b. Jacksonville, Fla., Mar. 26, 1940; d. Ralph Edward and Elizabeth Follin Snyder; m. David Thorpe Bedell, June 16, 1961 (div. Aug. 1974); children: Charles, Elizabeth Bedell Coyle, George. Student, Hollins U.; BA, U. North Fla. Founding editor Kalliope, A Jour. of Women's Lit. and Art, 1978—81; tchr. Stanton Coll. Prep., Venetia Elem., 1981—84; freelance writer, editor, 1984—93, 1997—; program developer St. Vincent's Found., Inc., 1993—98; editor Betty Snyder Bedell Editl. Svcs., Jacksonville, 1999—. Chmn. garden and grounds Ximenez-Fatio Mus. House, St. Augustine, Fla.; bd. dirs. Jr. League, Jacksonville. Mem.: Colonial Dames, Fla. Yacht Club Jacksonville. Home and Office: 4242 Ortega Blvd # 21 Jacksonville FL 32210 Personal E-mail: ebedell@bellsouth.net.

BEDELL, GEORGE NOBLE, internist, educator; b. Harrisburg, Pa., May 1, 1922; s. George Harold and Elsie Clair (Noble) B.; m. Betty Jane Goldzier, Nov. 4, 1950 (dec. Mar. 1970); children: David, Mark, Barbara, Bruce; m. Mirriel Shields Hummel, Oct. 17, 1970; step-children: Judy, Jeffrey, Eric, Deborah, Andrew. BA, DePauw U., 1944; MD, U. Cin., 1946. Intern U. Iowa, 1946-47, resident in pathology, 1947-48, resident in internal medicine, 1950-52, research fellow in internal medicine, specializing in cardiology, 1952-54; research fellow physiology Postgrad. Sch. Medicine, U., Pa., 1954-55; asst. prof. dept. medicine Coll. Medicine, U. Iowa, 1955-59, asso. prof. dept. medicine, 1959-68, prof., 1968—; dir. Pulmonary Disease div. Dept. Medicine, 1968-81. Cons. VA Hosp., Iowa City, 1954—; mem. staff U. Hosps., Iowa City Contbr. articles to profl. jours. Mem. Johnson County Democratic Central Com., 1956-69, treas., 1958-64. Served with AUS, 1948-50. NIH Spl. fellow, 1954-55; recipient Career Devel. award, 1960-70, Walter L. Bierring award Am. Lung Assn. Iowa, 1973 Mem. ACP, Am. Lung Assn. (dir. 1972-80), Am. Lung Assn. Iowa (dir. 1971-81), Am. Fedn. Clin. Research, Am. Thoracic Soc., Iowa Thoracic Soc. (v.p. 1960-61, pres. 1962-63), Iowa Tb and Health Assn. (dir. 1961-65, 67-71), AMA (vice chmn. sect. council on diseases of chest 1971-73, chmn. sec. council diseases of chest 1974-76, Am. Thoracic Soc. del. to AMA 1979-85), Iowa, Johnson County med. socs., Soc. Exptl. Biology and Medicine, Iowa Clin. Soc. Internal Medicine, Central Soc. Clin. Research, Am. Coll. Chest Physicians, Am. Physiol. Soc., Am. Soc. Clin. Investigation, A.C.P., Central Clin. Research Club. Democrat. Unitarian Universalist. Home: 903 Highwood St Iowa City IA 52246-3807 Office Phone: 319-356-2755. E-mail: george-bedell@uiowa.edu.

BEDELL, JAY DEE, small business owner, writer; b. Monterey, Calif., Oct. 20, 1946; s. John Dewhirst and Lucille (Huffman) Bedell. BA, U. Calif., Davis, 1968. Tchr. Antioch Schs., Calif., 1969—84; v.p., dir. Credit Union, 1979—81; owner Bedell Enterprises, 1986—; supr. security Chevron U.S.A., 1988—90. Mem. Adv. Coun. for Spl. Edn., Antioch, Calif., 1979-81; mem. State Dept. Conf. on Spl. Edn., 1978; staff devel. com. Office of Supt. of Schs., Contra Costa County, Calif., 1979-81; cons. in field. Author numerous poems. Deacon Adventist Ch., Antioch, Calif.; sch. bd. Hilltop Christian Sch., Antioch; honor guard Vets. Home Calif. With US Army, 1971-75. Recipient Golden Poet award, World of Poetry Press, 1985—92. Fellow Am. Biog. Inst. Rsch. Assn. (life); mem. NRA (cert. asst. rifle instr.), Sierra Club, Nature Conservancy, Internat. Platform Assn., Wilderness Soc., Libr. of Congress (assoc.), Smithsonian (assoc.), Commonwealth Club Calif. (assoc.), Marines Mem. Club San Francisco, Knight Sovereign Mil. Templar Order, Delta Upsilon. Democrat. Address: Vets Home of Calif PO Box 1200 Yountville CA 94599 Personal E-mail: jaydbedell@yahoo.com.

BEDENBAUGH, ALLYN PURVIS, retired elementary school educator; b. Columbia, SC, Aug. 22, 1951; d. Morris James and Ellen P. Purvis; m. Don E. Bedenbaugh, June 2, 1979 (dec.); children: John Elliott, James Adam. BA, U. SC, 1973, MA in Tchg., 1976. Cert. tchr. SC. Elem. tchr. Richland County Sch. Dist., Columbia, 1973—85, Lexington (SC) County Sch. Dist., 1985—2003; ret., 2003. Vol. Sharing God's Love, Irmo, SC, 2003—; treas. SC chpt. Aux. Luth. Theol. So. Sem., Columbia, 2004—. Named Tchr. of Yr., Wardlaw Elem. Sch., Columbia, 1982, Lexington Intermediate Sch., 1990. Mem.: Internat. Reading Assn., SC Reading Assn., Columbia Area Reading Coun. (sec. bd. dirs. 1992—2002, Dist. Disting. Tchr. of Reading 1990). Avocations: reading, painting, yardwork. Home: 127 Sheath Dr Columbia SC 29212-2212

BEDENBAUGH, ANGELA LEA OWEN, chemistry educator, researcher; b. Seguin, Tex., Oct. 6, 1939; d. Wintford Henry and Nelia Melanie (Fischer) Owen; m. John Holcombe Bedenbaugh, Dec. 27, 1961; 1 child, Melanie Celeste. BS cum laude, U. Tex., 1961; PhD in Organic Chemistry, U. S.C., 1967. Instr. chemistry lab. U. Tex., Austin, 1960—61; rsch. assoc. chemistry U. So. Miss., Hattiesburg, 1966—80, rsch. assoc. prof. chemistry and biochemistry, 1980—, bd. mem. women's studies program, 1996—97. Co-prin. investigator Bell South Found. grant, 1998; dir. website NASA grant, 1999-00; project dir. math. and sci. ptnr. program U.S. Dept. Edn., 2004-06. Author: Nomenplayture, 1998; co-author: (with John H. Bedenbaugh) Handbook for High School Chemistry Teachers, 1985, Teaching First Year Chemistry, 4th edit., 1993, Teaching Physical Science, Vols. 1 and 2, 2003; patentee in field. Adminstrv. bd. Parkway Heights United Meth. Ch., 1974-75, women's unit leader, 1973-75, women's unit treas., 1977, Wesleyan Svc. Guild v.p., 1970, Sunday Sch. tchr., 1973-74; bd. dirs. Forrest Stone Area Opportunity Inc., 1970-72, bd. dirs. exec. com., 1972, com. to rewrite pers. policies and procedures, 1971, Headstart monitoring com., 1971-72, pers. screening com., 1971; nat. Women's Polit. Caucus, 1976—; mem. Toastmasters Internat., 1986—, club. pres., 1993, area gov., 1994; adminstr., dir. Tchr. Mentoring Initiative through Bell South Found. Grant, 1998-2000; Miss. state coord. Bldg. a Presence for Sci., 2002-; mem. Gov.'s Edn. Summit, 2004; mem. U.S. Dept. Edn. Math. and Sci. Partnership, 2004-06, 07—; Arbor Day Found.; mem. Comdr.'s Club, Disabled Am. Vets., Common Cause, Cystic Fibrosis Found., Defenders of Wildlife, Habitat for Humanity, Environ. Def. Action Fund, Oxfam, Nat. Osteoporosis Found., Nat. Park Trust, Ocean Conservancy, various other orgns. Recipient John and Angela Bedenbaugh award Coastal Miss. Assn. H.S. Chemistry Tchrs., 1996—; rsch. grantee U.S. Dept. Energy, U. So. Miss., 1979-80, NSF, U. So. Miss., 1985, Adminstrv. Dir. Rsch. grant, 1988-91, 1993-96, 2001-04, NSF, 2000-05, grantee Miss.-NASA Space Consortium, 1999-2000, 2000-01, Miss. State Achievement award, Delta Kappa Gamma Soc. Internat., 2007. Mem. NSTA (nat. resource rev. panel for rev. of instrnl. materials), LWV, AAUW, Am. Chem. Soc. (chmn. 1984-85, program chmn. 1983-84, exec. bd. 1983—, grantee 2002, Chemist of Yr. award 1991, Johnnie Marie Whitfield Svc. award 2004), Miss. Sci. Tchrs. Assn. (exec. bd. 1994—, pres.-elect 1998-2000, pres. 2000-02, state bldg. a presence for sci. coord. 2002—, rep., coord. continuing edn. credit units, Disting. Sci. Tchr. award 1994, legis. liason, coll. and univ. rep. on exec. bd.), Nat. Wildlife Fedn., Wilderness Soc., Union of Concerned Scientists, Nat. Resources Def. Coun., Nat. Women's History Mus. (charter), Delta Kappa Gamma (pres. Miss. br. 1989-91, chmn. internat. rsch. com. 1980-82, chmn. internat. computer share fair at internat. conv. 1994, editor U.S. Forum Connection 2000—, State Achievement award 2007), Nat. Audubon Soc., Sierra Club, Commonwealth Club, Sigma Xi (charter, sec.-treas. 1967-69, treas. 1970, pres. 1973-74, program chmn. 1972-73), Nature Conservancy, Smithsonian Instn., Nat. Geog. Soc., Nat. Parks Conservation Assn., Humane Soc. U.S., MADD, ASPCA, The Wings, Order of the Magnolia. Democrat. Methodist. Home: 63 Suggs Rd Hattiesburg MS 39402-3639 Office: Univ So Miss 118 College Dr 8466 Hattiesburg MS 39406-1000 Business E-Mail: angela.bedenbaugh@usm.edu.

BEDERSON, BENJAMIN, physicist, researcher; b. NYC, Nov. 15, 1921; s. Abraham Michael and Lena (Waxlowsky) B.; m. Betty Weintraub, Jan. 20, 1956; children: Joshua Benjamin, Geoffrey Adam, Aron Gregory, Benjamin Boris. BS, CCNY, 1946; MS, Columbia U., 1948; PhD, NYU, 1950. Rsch. scientist MIT, Cambridge, 1950-52; faculty dept. physics NYU, 1952-92, prof., 1967-92, prof. emeritus, 1992—, chmn. dept., 1973-76, spl. advisor for sci. to dean Faculty Arts and Scis., 1983-86, dean Grad. Sch. Arts and Scis., 1986-89. Chmn. Internat. Conf. Physics of Electronic and Atomic Collisions, 1983-85; chmn. vis. panel Ctr. for Absolute Phys. Quantities, Nat. Bur. Standards, 1980-83. Editor-in-chief Am. Phys. Soc., 1992-96; editor Phys. Rev. A, 1978-91; assoc. editor Atomic Data and Nuclear Data Jour., 1969-98; editor (with Herbert Walther) Advances in Atomic, Molecular, and Optical Physics, 1974—2004; editor Forum on History of Physics, 2003-06; contbr. articles to profl. jours.; patentee in field. With U.S. Army, 1942-46, Manhattan Project, Los Alamos, 1944-46, PTO. Fellow: APS (chair forum history physics 2001—02), AAAS. Home: 60 E 8th St Apt 24K New York NY 10003-6522 Office: NYU Physics Dept 4 Washington Pl New York NY 10003-6621 Home Phone: 212-529-8687; Office Phone: 212-998-7695. Business E-Mail: ben.bederson@nyu.edu.

BEDGOOD, ALVIN J., information technology manager, director; b. New Orleans, Dec. 21, 1956; s. Alvin P. and Pierrine C. Bedgood. AS cum laude, Mt. Wachusett CC, Gardner, Mass., 1979; BA, Loyola U., New Orleans, 1981; MS, Troy U., Ala., 1985; ednl. specialist, Nat.-Louis U., Evanston, Ill., 1994; diploma, US Army Command and Gen. Staff Coll., Fort Leavenworth, Kans., 1997. MCSE 2000, cert. profl. & internet Microsoft, 2000; cert. bus. mgr. Assn. Profls. Bus. Mgmt., 2002, level III, IV & V Am. Bd. Cert. Homeland Security, 2005, Profl. Project Mgmt. Inst., 2006, quality mgmt. sys. prin. auditor RABQSA Internat. Registrar Accreditation Bd., 2006. Dep. G2 5th Signal Command US Army, Worms, Germany, 1993—94, exec. officer ops. bn., 66th M.I. Group Augsburg, Germany, 1995—96; dep. group comdr. 93rd ops. group US Army Joint STARS, Robins Air Force Base, Ga., 1996—98; program mgr. sys. integration Titan Corp., Tampa, 1998—2001; dir. quality and process improvement L-3 Titan, Global Mission Solutions, Tampa, 2001—. Quality assurance auditor L-3 Titan, 2002—, info. tech. svc. mgmt. instr., 2004—; dir. curriculum and instrn. SE Region Staff Coll., CAP, Alcoa, Tenn., 2004—; mem. drug demand reduction com. CAP, Maxwell Air Force Base, Ala., 2003—04, mem. nat. profl. devel. com., 2004—, mem. nat. info. tech. com., 2006—. Editor: (regional newsletter) Southwind, 1988—90, (reference book) Known World Handbook, 3d edit., 1992; artist, designer Ops. Bn. Distinctive Unit Insignia, 1995. Certifying ofcl. Pres.'s Vol. Svc. Awards, Tampa, 2004—; founding mem. Ramstein Cadet Squadron, CAP, Ramstein Air Base, Germany, 1985; city vol. Cmty. Ctr., Sierra Vista, Ariz., 1988—92; vol. Spl. Olympics, Hillsborough County, Fla., 2003—07; Katrina search & rescue ground team leader Miss. Gulf Coast, 2005; com. chair US Vol. Cavalry Assn., The Rough Rider's, 2005—; com. mem. Armed Forces Comm. and Elec. Assn., 1993—94, 2006—; coun. sec. St. Mary's Ch., Augsburg Military Cmty., Germany, 1994—96, lay min., 1995—96; mem. pres.'s adv. com. Loyola U., New Orleans, 1980—81; amb. US Army Freedom Team Salute, Tampa, 2006—. Maj. US Army, 1981—97, ret. Decorated Legion of Merit; recipient Outstanding Vol. Svc. award, City of Sierra Vista, 1990, Knowlton award, M.I. Corps Assn., 1995, Army Achievement medal, 1995, Gold Vol. Svc. award, Augsburg Mil. Cmty., 1996, Mayor's cert. of merit, City of New Orleans, 1998, Key to City award, Warner Robins, Ga., 1998, Gov.'s Cert. Merit award, NY, 1998, Gov.'s citation, La., 1998, Mass., 1998, Va., 1998, Freedom Team Salute Commendation award, US Army, 2004, Lifetime Vol. Achievement award, Pres.'s Coun. Svc. & Civic Participation, 2005, Gold Vol. Svc. award, 2005. Fellow: Upsilon Beta Lamda (life; pres. 1981—82, Bro. of Yr. award 1981); mem.: CAP (wing spl. advisor, group comdr., dep. squadron comdr. 1995—2006, artist heraldic insignia, chief of staff, southeast region 2007—, vice chief of staff, southeast region 2006, deputy dir., southeast region staff coll. 2006—, mem. nat. profl. devel. com. 2004—, Squadron Mem. of Yr. award 1985, 1986, Comdrs. Commendation award 1986, Brig. Gen. Charles E. Chuck Yeager Aerospace Edn. Achievement award 1988, A. Scott Crossfield Aerospace Edn. Master Educator award 1989, Comdrs. Commendation award 1989, Gil Robb Wilson Meritorious Achievement award 1990, Comdrs. Commendation award 1990, Meritorious Svc. award 1994, Comdrs. Commendation award 1994, 2 Exceptional Svc. awards 2005, Meritorious Svc. award 2006, Nat. Commanders Commendation award 2006), VFW (life), Mil. Officers Assn. of Am., Mil. Intelligence Corps Assn., Am. Soc. Quality, 361st Infantry Regimental Assn WWII (life), Res. Officers Assn. (life), Korea Def. Vets. Am. (life), Armed Forces Comm.-Electronics Assn. (life; com. mem. 1993—94, 2006—), Spl. Forces Assn. (life), Air Force Assn. (life), Assn. US Army (life; chpt. pres. 1980—81), Regtl. Signal Corps Assn. (life), York Rite Bodies, Free Masonry, 32 Degree Scottish Rite of Free Masonry, Huguenot Soc. of New Orleans, Ind. Order of Saint Stanislaus, Knight Companion, Am. MENSA, Assn. Old Crows (life), Soc. Creative Anachronism, Inc. (corp. chronicler, dir. comm. 1990—91, founding pres. Korea chpt., co-founder, Pacific Rim regional area, Master of Order of Pelican award 1989), Am. Coll. Heraldry (life), 1st US Vol. Cav. Rough Riders of Tampa, Fla. (com. chmn. 2005—, Spl. Achievement award 2004), Osiris, Trowel and Fidelity Lodge #300, La. Free Masons (life), Masons (life), Scabbard and Blade Soc., Blue Key, Alpha Sigma Nu, Phi Alpha Theta. Avocations: reading, hiking, history, horseback riding. Home: PO Box 18264 Tampa FL 33679-8264 Personal E-mail: alvin.bedgood@yahoo.com.

BEDKE, MICHAEL A., lawyer; b. Oct. 19, 1960; BA with high honors, Univ. Fla., 1981, JD with honors, 1984. Bar: Fla. 1984. Ptnr. DLA Piper Rudnick, Tampa, Fla. Adj. prof. Stetson Coll. Law, Fla.; bd. dirs., past pres. Bay Area Legal Svcs., Fla. Recipient William Reece Smith Jr. Public Svc. award, 1994. Mem.: Hillsborough County Bar Assn., ABA (bd. govs. 2004—), Fla. Bar Assn. (Outstanding Young Lawyer, Pres. Pro Bono award). Office: DLA Piper Rudnick US LLP Suite 2000 101 E Kennedy Blvd Tampa FL 33602-5149 Office Phone: 813-222-5924.

BEDNAR, CHARLES SOKOL, political science professor; b. NYC, Nov. 3, 1930; s. Karel and Anna (Tomcala) B.; m. Beluse Alzbeta Pokorny, Aug. 31, 1959. AB, Rutgers U., 1951, MA, 1952; PhD, Columbia, 1960. Asso. prof. Lynchburg Coll., 1958-62; prof., chmn. dept. polit. sci., asso. dean of coll. Muhlenberg Coll., 1962-99, Eve Elizabeth Muhlenberg Disting. Svc. prof., 1989-99, prof. emeritus; adj. prof. grad. program in gen. edn., chmn. social sci. panel Temple U., 1963-86. Author: Transforming the Dream: Ecologism and the Shaping of an Alternative American Vision, 2003; contbr. articles to profl. jours. Chmn. Lehigh Valley Citizens for Progress, 1972-75; pres. Allentown YMCA, 1979-80. Recipient award Lindback Found., 1965, Paul E. Empie Meml. award, 1983. Mem. Czechoslovak Acad. Arts and Scis., Phi Beta Kappa, Delta Phi Alpha, Tau Kappa Alpha, Omicron Delta Kappa, Pi Sigma Alpha. Home: 1285 Sheridan Rd Coopersburg PA 18036-1816

BEDNAR, MICHAEL JOHN, architecture educator; b. Cleve., Mar. 19, 1942; s. Peter and Mary (Rohal) B.; m. Mary Kathryn Gillman; children: Richard Earl, Matthew Scott, Rachel Catherine; m. Elizabeth Waddel Lawson. BArch, U. Mich., 1964; MArch, U. Pa., Phila., 1967. Registered architect, Pa., NY, Va. Jr. designer I.M. Pei & Ptnrs., NYC, 1965-66; project architect Geddes, Brecher, Qualls, Cunningham, Phila., 1967-68; asst. prof. Renselaer Polytech. Inst., Troy, 1968-72; assoc. prof. U. Va., Charlottesville, 1972—, co-chmn. div. of architecture, 1976-81, assoc. dean for academics, 1992-95, assoc. dean for students, 2006, prof. arch., 2007, dir. advising, 2007. Prin. Michael Bednar, FAIA Architect, Charlottesville, 1973-90, Bednar Lawson Architects, 1990—. Author: Architecture for Handicapped, 1973, The New Atrium, 1986; Interior Pedestrian Places, 1989, L'Enfant's Legacy, 2006; editor: Barrier-Free Environment, 1977. Mem., chair City Planning Commn., Charlottesville, 1982—; chmn. Urban Design Task Force, Charlottesville, 1985-88; mem. Bd. of Architectural Review, Charlottesville, 1983-86; bd. dirs. Charlottesville Habitat for Humanity, 2006. Booth fellow U. Mich., 1972, NEA fellow, 1984, Graham Found. fellow, 1988-2003; recipient Nat. Book award Am. Assn. of Publ., 1986, Nichols award Preservation Alliance Va., 1997, Cmty. Svc. award AIA Ctrl. Va., 1997. Fellow Am. Inst. Architects (Disting. Achievemnt award 1997), Assn. for the Preservation of Va. Antiquities (bd. dirs. Jefferson chpt. 1999-2000). Avocations: jazz music, tennis, travel. photography. Home: 1201 E Jefferson St Charlottesville VA 22902-5414 Business E-Mail: mjb6g@virginia.edu.

BEDNAR, RUDY, television producer, director; b. Palmerton, Pa., May 31, 1951; s. Rudolph and Rita (Colan) Bednar. BA, Marquette U., 1973. Producer, dir. various TV stas., 1973—79; prodr., dir. ABC, NYC, 1980—84, Good Morning Am., ABC, NYC, 1984—88, 20/20 ABC, NYC, 1989; prodr. Prime Time Live ABC, NYC, 1990—92; sr. prodr. Turning Point ABC News, NYC, 1993—98; exec. prodr. ABC News Long Form Unit, 1999—. Recipient 10 Emmy awards, Monitor award, Investigative Reports & Editors award, 4 Dupont awards. Mem.: Dirs. Guild Am. Office: ABC News 147 Columbus Ave New York NY 10023-5999

BEDNAR, SUSAN GAIL, social worker, mediator, consultant, social sciences educator; b. Chgo., Ill., May 28, 1949; d. Charles and Evelyn Bednar; m. Bruce Kevin Barnard, Nov. 15, 1988. BA in Sociology, U. Ill., 1973, MSW, 1996. Ct. approved mediator; LCSW Ill., cert. Domestic Violence Counselor III Nat. Assn. Forensic Counselors. Addictions therapist Prairie Ctr. Health Systems, Danville, Ill., 1997—98; clin. dir. DeWitt County Human Resource Ctr., Clinton, Ill., 1998—99; program coord. Shelby County Cmty. Svcs., Shelbyville, Ill.; clin. assoc. Dovetail Consulting, Crystal Lake, Ill., 2000—01; rsch. asst. Ind. U., Indpls., 2000—02; cons. Champaign, Ill., 2001—; clin. social worker in pvt. practice, 2003—; mediator, cons., 2003—. Dir. Mental Health Assn., Champaign, Ill., 1996—97; adj. faculty Richland CC, 2006—. Contbr. Counseling Female Offenders and Victims, articles to profl. jours. Mem.: NASW, Assn. Family and Conciliation Cts., Ill. Soc. Clin. Social Work, Am. Sociol. Assn., Assn. for Conflict Resolution, Nat. Assn. of Forensic Counselors. Avocation: horse owner. Office: Susan G Bednar LCSW 6 Dunlap Ct Savoy IL 61874 Office Phone: 217-352-8502.

BEDNASH, GERALDINE, educational association administrator; b. San Antonio, May 6, 1943; d. David Anthony and Bernice (Brewer) Parrott; m. Thomas Francis Bednash, June 24, 1967; children: Thomas F. Jr., Joseph Andrew. B of Nursing, Tex. Women's U., 1965; M of Nursing, Cath. U. Am., 1977; PhD, U. Md., 1989. Cert. nurse practitioner. Nurse Binghamton Gen. Hosp., NY, 1967—69; instr. Broome County Cmty. Coll., Binghamton, 1967—71; asst. prof. No. Va. Cmty. Coll., Annandale, 1977—78, George Mason U., Fairfax, Va., 1978—86; dir. govt. rels. Am. Assn. Colls. Nursing, Washington, 1986—89, exec. dir., 1989—. Co-chmn. Nat. Com. Nursing Implementation Project, Washington, 1990-91; cons. in field. Contbr. articles to profl. jours. Polit. action chmn. Va. Nurses Assn., 1979-83; nurse clinician So Others Might Eat, Washington, 1981-83. Capt. US Army, 1963—67. Primary Care fellow Robert Wood Johnson Found., U. Md., 1981-82, Nat. Rsch. Svc. fellow, Washington, 1983-87. Fellow Am. Acad. Nursing; mem. ANA, Sigma Theta Tau. Roman Catholic. Avocations: skiing, horticulture. Office: Am Assn Colls Nursing One Dupont Cir NW Ste 530 Washington DC 20036-1135 Office Phone: 202-463-6930 ext. 222. E-mail: pbednash@aacn.nche.edu.*

BEDOS-REZAK, BRIGITTE MIRIAM, historian, educator; b. Paris, June 3, 1953; came to U.S., 1980; d. Jacques and Anne (Labatcahn) Bedos; m. Ira Loeb Rezak; Sept. 6, 1980. PhD, Ecole Nationale des Chartes, France, 1977. Archival and curatorial trainee Nat. Archives of France, Paris, 1977, head Ctrl. Dept. of Seals, 1978-80; fellow Dept. Medieval Art Met. Mus. of Art, NYC, 1982-87; adj. assoc. prof. history SUNY, Stony Brook, 1985-87; dir. summer seminar for coll. tchrs. NEH, 1987; vis. assoc. prof. history U. Md., College Park, 1987-89, assoc. prof. history, 1989-94, dir. grad. studies dept. history, 1990-93, prof. history, 1994—, 1994—. Reviewer and panelist NEH Fellowships for Univ. Tchrs.: Panels on European History, 1988, 89, 90; NEH grant reveiwer; dir. Internat. Ctr. for Medieval Art, 1990-93; mentor for 1991 NEH/Reader's Digest Tchrs.-Scholar from D.C., 1991-92; external reviewer Medieval Inst.'s Grad. Program, U. Notre Dame, 1993. Author: Histoire de Montmorency, Le Moyen Age, 1979, Corpus des sceaux français du Moyen Age, tome Ier: Les sceaux des villes, 1980, La Châtellenie de Montmorency des origines à 1368, 1980, Anne de Montmorency, seigneur de la Renaissance, 1990, Polity and Place: Regionalism in Medieval France, 1993, Form and Order in Medieval France, Studies in Social and Quantitative Sigillography, 1993; contbr. articles and revs. to profl. publs.; mem. editorial bd. Hist. Reflections, 1993—. Recipient Fellowship for Ind. Study and Rsch., NEH, 1984, Mellon fellowship Met. Mus. of Art, 1985, Directorship of Summer Seminar for Coll. Tchrs., NEH, 1986, Semester Rsch. award U. Md. Grad. Rsch. Bd., 1995. Mem. Am. Hist. Assn., Assn. of French Archivists, Internat. Ctr. for Medieval Art, Majestas, Medieval Acad. of Am., Soc. for French Hist. Studies, Société de l'Ecole des Chartes, Société française d'héraldique et de sigillographie, Société Nationale des Antiquaires de France. Jewish. Avocations; writing, photography, travel, sailing. Home: 5 Shore Dr Setauket NY 11733-1619 Office: U of Maryland Dept Of History College Park MD 20742-0001

BEDRIJ, OREST, physicist, investment banker; b. Ukraine, 1933; arrived in U.S., 1949, naturalized, 1955; s. Eustachy and Olha Bedrij; m. Oksana Cymbalista, 1956; children: Orest W., Roksana Bedrij Arpa, Chrystyna Bedrij Stecyk. BSEE, Rochester Inst. Tech., 1956, MS in Humanities; PhD in Physics, Columbia Pacific U., 1986. Various positions IBM Corp., Poughkeepsie, NY and LA, 1956-68; IBM tech. dir. Space Flight Ops. facility Jet Propulsion Lab., Calif. Inst. Tech., 1962—63; founder, pres., dir. Securities Coun., Inc., 1965-83, Profit Tech., Inc., 1983-89, Griffin Capital Mgmt. Corp., NYC, 1989—98; with Griffin Securities, Inc., NYC, 1998—. Co-founder, dir. Advance Memory Sys. Inc. (merged with GE) as Intersil, Inc., Sunnyvale, Calif., 1968—72, Inst. Math. Physics, 1972—, Inst. for Advanced Study of '1', 2001—, Jour. Nonlinear Math. Physics, Kiev, 1992; mem. exec. com., treas., dir. Ukranian Studies Fund Harvard U., 1959—72. Author: Yes, It's Love: Your Life can be a Miracle, 1974, One,

1977, You, 1988, La preuve scientifique de l'existence de Dieu, 2000, Seeing God Face to Face, 2005, Celebrate Your Divinity: The Nature of God and the Theory of Everything, 2007; contbr. articles to profl. jours. Trustee, treas. John E. Fetzer Found., 1987—89. With USAR, 1954—60. Mem.: Am. Inst. Physics, Metanexus Inst., Sci. and Med. Network London, Shevchenko Sci. Soc., N.Y. Acad. Arts and Scis., Internat. Soc. Study Human Ideas Ultimate Reality and Meaning (dir.). Achievements include patents in field; research in physics and philosophy of ultimate reality and meaning.

BEDROSIAN, EDWARD, retired electrical engineer; b. Chgo., May 22, 1922; s. Charles and Hazel (Najarian) B.; m. Evelyn Patricia Gardner, Apr. 16, 1971; children— William C., Barbara A., Charles E., Edward G., Victoria G. BS, Northwestern U., 1949, MS, 1950, PhD, 1953. Aero. engr. Convair, San Diego, 1942, Hughes Aircraft Co., Culver City, Calif., 1943-44; elec. engr. Motorola, Chgo., 1953-57; sr. scientist Rand Corp., Santa Monica, Calif., 1957-98. Adj. prof. U. So. Calif., 1968-71 Contbr. articles to profl. jours. Served with USMC, 1944-46. Fellow IEEE, Inst. Advancement Engring.; mem. Sigma Xi, Eta Kappa Nu, Tau Beta Pi. Home: 3923 Sierks Way Malibu CA 90265-5214 E-mail: bedrosian@charter.com.

BEDROSIAN, GREGORY RONALD, investment banker; b. Phila., Sept. 14, 1966; s. Samuel D. and Agnes Bedrosian; m. Elena V. Mayorova; 1 child, Nicholas G. BS in Econs., U. Pa., 1988; MBA, Harvard U., 1992. Investment banker Salomon Bros., Inc., NYC, 1988-90; investment banker Credit Suisse First Boston Ltd., London, Moscow, 1992-95; co-founder, mng. dir. Sputnik Funds (Renaissance Capital), Moscow, 1995-99; CEO Redwood Capital Group, NYC and London, 2000—. Mem.: Royal Inst. Internat. Affairs, Inst. Dirs. (London), Coun. on Fgn. Rels., Indian Harbor Yacht Club, Penn Club N.Y., Met. Club, Harvard Club of N.Y. Republican. Home: 25 Pecksland Rd Greenwich CT 06831

BEDSWORTH, WILLIAM W., judge; b. Long Beach, Calif., Nov. 21, 1947; m. Carolyn Kelly McCourt, Mar. 28, 1999. BA cum laude, Loyola U., LA, 1968; JD, U. Calif., Berkeley, 1971. Felony trial deputy, appellate atty., mng. atty. Orange County Dist. Atty.'s Office, Calif.; judge Orange County Superior Ct., 1986-97; assoc. justice 4th Appellate Dist., Calif. Ct. of Appeals, Santa Ana, 1997—. Adj. prof. Western State U. Coll. of Law, Chapman U. Sch. of Law, Orange, Calif., Calif. Jud. Coll., Berkeley. Author: What I Saw and Heard, 1996, A Criminal Waste of Time, 2003; author nationally syndicated column A Criminal Waste of Space; contbr. articles to profl. publs. Former bd. dirs. NCCJ, Orange County Bar Assn.; bd. dirs. Fair Share 502; goal judge Nat. Hockey League, 1993—. Named Judge of Yr., Hispanic Bar Assn., 1997. Mem. Assn. Orange County Dep. Dist. Atty. (past pres.). Avocations: softball, country music, ice hockey.

BEDWORTH, DAVID ALBERT, health educator; b. Cortland, NY, Mar. 31, 1949; s. Albert Ernest and Agnes Sheldon (Franklin) B.; children: Jodi Michele, Michael David. BS, Butler U., 1971; MS, U. Ill., 1972, PhD, 1976. Instr. Russell Sage Coll., Troy, NY, 1973-75; asst. prof. SUNY, Brockport, 1976-78; program coord. Heart Health Edn. R.I., Pawtucket, 1978-79; prof. SUNY, Plattsburgh, 1979—. Cmty. edn. cons. STOP Ctr. for Domestic Violence, Plattsburgh, 1982; drug edn. cons. Federal Correction Instn., Ray Brook, N.Y., 1982, Ticonderoga (N.Y.) Ctrl. Sch. Dist., 1985. Author: (with Albert E. Bedworth) Health Education: A Process for Human Effectivess, 1978, Health for Human Effectiveness, 1982, The Profession and Practice of Health Education, 1992; contbr. articles to profl. jours., chpts. to books. Task force on youthful alcohol abuse N.Y. State Dept. Mental Hygiene, 1977; profl. edn. com. Am. Lung Assn., 1980-84, exec. com., 1981-82. Mem. APHA, ASCD, N.Y. State Fedn. Profl. Health Educators (pres. 1977). Democrat. Avocations: antiques, travel. Office: SUNY Plattsburgh NY 12901 Home Phone: 518-293-7228. Business E-Mail: david.bedworth@plattsburgh.edu.

BEE, ROBERT NORMAN, banker; b. Milw., Mar. 4, 1925; s. Clarence Olson and Norma Pern (Pitt) B.; m. Dolores Marie Cappelletti, Apr. 23, 1955; children: Diane, John, Leslie. PhB, Marquette U., 1949; BS in Fgn. Svc., Georgetown U., 1950, MA, 1955. With Dept. Treasury, various locations, 1950—65; fin. attache Stockholm, 1952—54, Ankara, Turkey, 1956—60; chief fin. affairs Am. embassy, Bonn, Germany, 1960—65; dep. dir. AID, Karachi, Pakistan, 1965—67; 1st. v.p. 1st Wis. Nat. Bank, 1967—71; sr. v.p. Wells Fargo Bank; also pres. Wells Fargo Internat. Investment Corp., San Francisco, 1971—78; mng. dir., CEO London (England) Interstate Bank Ltd., 1978—87; mng. dir. TSB Pvt. Bank Internat. SA, London, 1987—90; chmn. U.S. Fin. Adv. Svc., London, 1990—92, SAJ Investments Ltd., London, 1991—95; sr. advisor Porvenir Inc., San Francisco, 1998—2000. Sr. fellow Ctr. Internat. Banking Studies, Charlottesville, Va. Chmn. World Affairs Coun. Milw., 1970-71; bd. dirs. Adam Smith Inst., London, chmn., 1985-87; chmn. Am. Soc. in London, 1986-87. With AUS, 1943-46. Recipient Bronze Star, 1945. Mem. Bankers Assn. for Fgn. Trade (pres. 1977-78). Home and Office: 1940 Vallejo St Apt 5 San Francisco CA 94123-4918 Office Phone: 415-931-7520. Personal E-mail: robnbee@comcast.net.

BEE, SAMANTHA, comedian, actress; b. Toronto, Can., 1969; m. Jason Jones, 2001; 1 child, Piper Bee-Jones. Grad., U. Ottawa, Can. Mem. sketch comedy troupe The Atomic Fireballs. Actor: (films) Ham & Cheese, 2004; (TV films) Ham I Am, 2001, Jasper, Texas, 2003; (TV series) The Endless Grind, 2001, The Daily Show with Jon Stewart, 2003—. Office: The Daily Show 604R W 52nd St New York NY 10019-5013

BEEBE, MARY LIVINGSTONE, curator; b. Portland, Oreg., Nov. 5, 1940; d. Robert and Alice Beebe; m. Charles J. Reilly. BA, Bryn Mawr Coll., Pa., 1962; postgrad., Sorbonne, U. Paris, 1962—63. Apprentice Portland Art Mus., 1962—64, Boston Mus. Art, 1964—66; curatorial asst. dept. drawing Fogg Art Mus., Harvard U., Cambridge, Mass., 1966-68; prodr. Am. Theatre Co., Portland State U., Oreg., 1969—72; exec. dir. Portland Ctr. for Visual Arts, 1972—81; dir. Stuart Collection U. Calif., San Diego, 1981—. Cons. in field; lectr. in field; mem. art steering com. Portland Devel. Commn., 1977-80, New Denver Internat. Airport, 1990-97; bd. dirs. Henry Gallery, U. Wash., Seattle, 1977-80; project cons. Nat. Rsch. Ctr. for Arts, N.Y.C., 1978-79; bd. dirs. Western Assn. Art Museums, Art Mus. Assn. San Francisco, 1978-84; bd. dirs., trustee Art Matters Inc., N.Y.C., 1984-, Balboa Art Conservation Ctr., San Diego, 2001-; trustee Russell Found., 1982-94, bd. dirs., 1983-85; hon. mem. bd. dirs. Portland Ctr. for Visual Arts, 1981-88; mem. arts adv. bd. Centre City Devel. Corp., San Diego, 1982-94, U. Calif. San Francisco Mission Bay, 1999—, Indpls. Mus. Art, Art and Nature Pk. adv. bd., 2003-05, nat. adv. bd. Headlands Ctr. for the Arts, San Francisco; panel mem., cons. Nat. Endowment Arts; mem. adv. com. Port of San Diego, 1983-88, San Diego Design Ctr., 1987-88, ART/LA, 1987-94, Pearl Art Found., Portland, 1998-2000, inSITE94, inSITE97, inSITE00, inSITE03 and 05, San Diego, 1993-, Friends of Art and Preservation in Embassies Profl. Sculpture adv. com., Wash., 2003-; mem. pub. art adv. com. Harvard and Radcliffe, 1989-93, U. Wash., Seattle, 1989-96, Commn. for Arts and Culture, San Diego, 2003-; juror numerous art exhbns. Nat. Endowment Arts fellow, 1979. Author: Landmarks: Sculpture Commissions for the Stuart Collection at the University of California, San Diego, 2001; contbr. articles to profl. jours. Recipient Allied Professions award AIA, 1992, Nat. Honors award, 1994. Achievements include having the Stuart Collection featured on CBS Sunday Morning with Charles Kuralt, 1993. Office: U Calif San Diego Stuart Collection 9500 Gilman Dr La Jolla CA 92093-0010 Office Phone: 858-534-2117. Business E-Mail: mbeebe@ucsd.edu.

BEEBE, MIKE (MICHAEL DALE BEEBE), governor, former state attorney general, lawyer; b. Amagon, Ark., Dec. 28, 1946; s. Lester Kendall and Meadean Louise (Quattlebaum) Beebe; m. Ginger Croom, Mar. 2, 1979; 3 children, Kyle, David, Tammy. BA in Polit. Sci., Ark. State U., 1968; JD, U. Ark. Sch. Law, Fayetteville, 1972. Bar: Ark. 1972. Ptnr. Lightle, Beebe, Raney, Bell & Simpson, Searcy, Ark., 1972—2003; mem. Ark. Senate from Dist. 21, Little Rock, 1983—2003, pres., 2001—03; atty. gen. State of Ark., Little Rock, 2003—07, gov., 2007—. Editor-in-chief: U. Ark. Sch. Law, 1972. Trustee Ark. State U., Jonesboro, 1974-79, chmn. bd. trustees, 1977-79; chmn. Ctrl. Ark. Gen. Hosp., Searcy, 1985-93. Served in USAR, 1968—74. Named Outstanding Trial Lawyer, Ark., 1982. Mem. Ark. Mcpl. League (dist. svc. award 1985), Searcy C. of C. Democrat. Episcopalian. Avocation: golf. Office: Office Gov State Capitol Rm 250 Little Rock AR 72201

BEECHER, LEE HEWITT, psychiatrist; b. Mpls., Feb. 18, 1939; s. James Morrison and Ruth Eleanor (Borgendale) Beecher; m. Mary Jane Heinen, June 10, 1978; children: James Arthur, Lynn Ruth. BA, Carleton Coll., 1961; MD, U. Minn., 1965. Lic. md State of Minn.; cert. in psychiatry ABPN, 1971, in addiction psychiatry ABPN, 1994. Resident U. Chgo., 1966—69; psychiatrist Mpls. Clin. Psychiatry and Neurology, Golden Valley, Minn., 1972—73; self employed Lee H. Beecher, St. Louis Park, Minn., 1973—. Bd. dir. Alliance for the Mentally Ill, Minn., 1982—91; assoc. med. dir. Preferred One, Golden Valley, Minn., 1991—95; adj. prof. U. Minn., Dept. Psychiatry, 2006. Contbr. articles numerous profl. jours. Lcdr USN, 1969—72, Hawaii. Named one of Top 100 Minn. Healthcare Leaders, Minn. Physician, 2004; recipient Pres. award, Minn. Med. Assn., 2004; Dist. Life fellow, Am. Psychiatric Assn., 2001. Mem.: Clin. Psychiatry News (edtl. adv. bd.), Minn. Physician Patient Alliance (pres. 1998—2005), Minn. Psychiatric Soc. (pres. 1987—89), Minn. Med. Assn. (trustee 1998—2005). Avocations: philosophy, swimming, sci. and nature, cosmology. Home: 7574 Mariner Pt Maple Grove MN 55311-2617 Office: Lee H Beecher MD PA 6600 Excelsior Blvd Ste 121 Saint Louis Park MN 55426-4746 Office Phone: 952-935-7116. Office Fax: 952-935-0687. E-mail: leebeecher@aol.com.

BEECHER, WILLIAM MANUEL, management consultant; b. Framingham, Mass., May 27, 1933; s. Samuel and Gertrude (Kradelman) B.; m. Eileen Brick, June 8, 1958; children: Debbie, Diane, Lori, Nancy. BA, Harvard U., 1955; MS, Columbia U., 1956. Reporter St. Louis Globe-Democrat, 1956-59; corr. Fairchild Pubs., Washington, 1959-60, Wall Street Jour., Washington, 1960-66, N.Y. Times, Washington, 1966-73; asst. sec. def. U.S. Dept. Def., Washington, 1973-75; corr. Boston Globe, Washington, 1975-87; Washington bur. chief Mpls. Star Tribune, Washington, 1987-92; pub. affairs dir. U.S. Nuclear Regulatory Commn., Washington, 1993—2003; mem. U.S. Sr. Exec. Svc., 1993—2003; pres. Strategic Vision LLC, 2004—; prin. The Dilenschneider Group, NYC, 2004—. Author: Mayday Man, 1990, Submerged Rage: The Hidden Grievance, 2005; co-author: (newspaper study) U.S.-Soviet Relations, 1983 (Pulitzer prize 1983); bd. of editors Foreign Svc. Jour. 2d lt. U.S. Army, 1956. Recipient Disting. Pub. Svc. medal Dept. of Def., 1975, Excellence awards Overseas Press Club, N.Y.C., 1975, 79, 86, Weintal award Georgetown U., Washington, 1983, Presdl. medal Y2K conversion, 2000; named Knight, Order of St. John of Medina, 2003. Mem. Internat. Inst. for Strategic Studies, State Dept. Corrs. Assn. (pres. 1982), Overseas Writers Assn. (pres. 1978-79), Aviation/Space Writers Assn. (pres. 1970-71), Coun. Fgn. Rels., Gridiron Club, Army and Navy Club. Home and Office: 7911 Robison Rd Bethesda MD 20817-6928 Office: The Dilenschneider Group MetLife Bldg 200 Park Ave 26th Fl New York NY 10166

BEEDLES, WILLIAM LEROY, finance educator, consultant; b. Independence, Kans., Apr. 9, 1948; s. Roy William Beedles and Opal Irene (Connor) Hunter; m. Margaret Ann Vanderlip, Dec. 21, 1974; children: Margaret Micaela, Patricia Opal, Cyrus Dean. BS, Kans. State U., 1970, MS, 1971; PhD, U. Tex., 1975. Asst. prof. Ind. U., Bloomington, 1975-78; vis. prof. Monash U., Melbourne, Victoria, Australia, 1984, U. NSW, Sydney, Australia, 1985; assoc. prof. to prof., dir. Masters program U. Kans., Lawrence, 1978—. Vis. rsch. fellow Pub. Utilities Commn., Austin, Tex., 1981 Contbr. articles to profl. jours. Capt. U.S. Army, 1970-78 Mem. Am. Fin. Assn., Western Fin. Assn., So. Fin. Assn. (assoc. editor jour. 1979-84), Fin. Mgmt. Assn. Congregationalist. Avocation: racquetball. Office: U Kans Summerfield Hall Lawrence KS 66045-7585 E-mail: wbeedles@ku.edu.

BEEGLE, AMY, music educator, researcher; b. Albuquerque, Jan. 20, 1968; d. Richard W. Beegle and Joyce A. Bonteaux; m. Michael J. Hawrylycz, Aug. 21, 1999. B in Music Edn., U. N.Mex., Albuquerque, 1991; MA in Music Edn., St. Paul, 2001; PhD in Music, U. Wash., Seattle, 2006. Piano instr. Ednl. Svcs., Inc., Albuquerque, 1984—92; tchr. music Los Alamos Pub. Schs., 1992—98; piano, saxaphone, percussion instr. Mahogany Music Studio, Los Alamos, 1993—98; asst. prof. music Nat. Louis U., Evanston, Ill., 1998—2000; tchr. music Seattle Pub. Schs., 2001—04; instr., tchg. asst. U. Wash., Seattle, 2001—05; asst. prof. music Pacific Luth. U., Tacoma, 2006—. Northwest rep. Music Educators Nat. Conf. Soc. Gen. Music, 2003—06. Contbr. articles to profl. jours. Recipient John Batcheller award, N.Mex. Music Educators Assn., 1998; Demar-Irvine fellow, U. Wash. Sch. Music, 2003—04. Mem.: Soc. Ethnomusicology, Orgn. Am. Kodaly Educators, A. Orff Schulwerk Assn. (pres. N.Mex. chpt., Gunild Keetman grant 1995).

BEEHLER, BRUCE MCPHERSON, research zoologist, ornithologist, conservationist; b. Balt., Oct. 11, 1951; s. William Henry Jr. and Cary (Baxter) B.; m. Carol Hare, June 7, 1982; children: Grace Bryant, Andrew McPherson, Cary Elizabeth Selden. BA, Williams Coll., 1974; MA, Princeton U., 1978, PhD, 1983. Sci. asst. to sec. Smithsonian Instn., Washington, 1981-84, sci. asst. to sec. emeritus, 1984-88, zoologist, 1988-91; assoc. rsch. zoologist N.Y. Zool. Soc., Washington, 1991-93; sr. ecologist Conservation Internat., 1993-95; natural resource mgmt. officer U.S. Dept. State, Washington, 1995-97; dir. environ. conservation Counterpart Internat., 1997-99, v.p. environ. and nat. resources, 1999-2001; sr. rep. Melanesia Conservation Internat., 2001—02, sen. dir. Melanesia, 2002—03, v.p. Melanesia, 2003—. Leader expdns. to Papua New Guinea, 1975-76, 78-84, 86-87, 89, 91-93, 2005, to India, 1983, 85-86, 88; rsch. assoc. dept. vertebrate zoology Nat. Mus. Natural History, 1985—. Author: Birdlife of the Adirondack Park, 1978, Upland Birds of Northeastern New Guinea, 1978, A Naturalist in New Guinea, 1991; sr. co-author: Birds of New Guinea; jr. co-author: The Birds of Paradise, 1998; contbr. articles to sci. jours. Thomas J. Watson Found. fellow, 1974; rsch. grantee Nat. Geog. Soc., 1980, 86, 89, 94, N.Y. Zool. Soc., 1986. Fellow Am. Ornithologists Union (elective). Democrat. Co-discoverer with John P. Dumbacher of toxicity in the Pitohui, a genus of bird that uses as a chemical defense the alkaloid homobatrachotoxin. Office: Conservation Internat 1919 M St NW Ste 600 Washington DC 20036 Office Phone: 703-341-2434.

BEEHLER, TOBI LORRAINE, elementary school educator, education educator; b. Montebello, Calif., Nov. 1, 1950; d. Robert Thomas and Helen Gore; m. Patrick Alan Beehler, Jan. 21, 1995; children: Courtney Helaine Klems, Tyler James. BS in Phys. Edn., Calif. State U., Fullerton, 1972, MS in Ednl. Adminstrn., 1980. Continuing tchg. cert. Wash. Elem. tchr. Yakima (Wash.) Sch. Dist., 1989—. Stakeholder Wash. State U. CO-TEACH Grant, Pullman, 1999—2005; state-wide sci. assessment revision developer Ednl. Svc. Dist. 105, Yakima, 2000; mem. strategic planning com., outcomes subcom. Yakima Sch. Dist., 1994; adj. prof. Heritage U., Toppenish, Wash., 1991—94, Ctrl. Wash. U., Ellensburg, 2001—, mem. profl. edn. adv. bd., 2002—. Mem. Yakima Schs. Found., 2001—03. Nominee, KCTS Golden Apple award, 1993; named Best Supporting Actress, Warehouse Theatre, Yakima; recipient cert. of appreciation, Yakima Sch. Dist., 1989, 1994; grantee, Yakima Ret. Tchrs. Assn., 2006. Mem.: NEA, Nat. Sci. Tchrs. Assn., Yakima Edn. Assn., Wash. Edn. Assn. Avocations: singing, flower arranging, gardening. Office: Yakima Sch Dist 104 N 4th Ave Yakima WA 98902 Home Phone: 509-453-3941.

BEEHR, TERRY A., psychology professor; s. Elmer and Allice Beehr; children: Dana, Matthew, Alison. BS, Ctrl. Mich. U., 1968; PhD, U. Mich., Ann Arbor, 1974. Rsch. investigator Inst. for Social Rsch., Ann Arbor, Mich., 1974—75; asst. prof. Ill. State U., Normal, 1975—78; from asst. prof. to prof. Ctrl. Mich. U., Mount Pleasant, 1978—. US Army, 1968—70. Office: Ctrl Mich Univ Psychology Dept Mount Pleasant MI 48859 Business E-Mail: beehr1ta@cmich.edu.

BEEKE, JOEL ROBERT, minister, educator, writer; b. Kalamazoo, Dec. 9, 1952; s. John and Johanna Lucy (Van Strein) B.; m. Mary Ann Kamp, Aug. 21, 1989; children: Calvin James, Esther Idelette, Lydia Ruth. Student, Western Mich. U., 1971-73; BA, Thomas A. Edison Coll.; MDiv, Netherlands Reformed Theol. Sch., St. Catharines, Ont., Can., 1978; PhD in Reformation and Post-Reformation Theology, Westminster Theol. Sem., 1988. Ordained to ministry The Netherlands Ref. Congregations, 1978. Pastor The Netherlands Ref. Congregation, Sioux Center, Iowa, 1978-81, Ebenezer Netherlands Ref. Ch., Franklin Lakes, NJ, 1981-86, Heritage Netherlands Ref. Congregation, Grand Rapids, Mich., 1986—; instr. theology Netherlands Ref. Theol. Sch., 1986-92. Clk. The Netherlands Ref. Synod, 1980-92; v.p. The Netherlands Ref. Gen. Mission, 1980-82; pres. The Netherlands Ref. Book and Pub., 1980-93; v.p. The Netherlands Ref. Synodical Edn., 1986-93; pres. Interitance Pubs., 1987—, Macedonia Mission Soc., sermon divsn., 1990-93; v.p. Dutch Reformed Translation Soc., 1994—; lectr. Ctr. for Urban Theol. Studies, 1984-86; lectr. Westminster Theol. Sem., Phila., 1985-86, adj. prof., 1993—; pres. Stitching Studie der Nadere Reformatie, 1992-2003; editl. dir. Reformation Heritage Books, 1994—; pres., prof. systematic theology and homiletics Puritan Reformed Theol. Sem., 1995—; lectr. Westminster Theol. Sem., Calif., 1995—, The Puritan Project, Brazil, 1995—, Reformed Theol. Sem., 1995—. Author: Jehovah Shepherding His Sheep, 1982 (Korean edit. 2001), Backsliding: Disease and Cure, 1982 (Korean edit. 2004), Student Workbook on the Reformed Faith: Based on Rev. Hellenbroek's "A Specimen of Divine Truths", vol. I, 1985, Verachtering in de Genade: Kwaal en Genezing, 1989, Assurance of Faith: Calvin, English Puratinism and the Dutch Second Reformation, 1991, Holiness: God's Call to Sanctification, 1994 (Spanish, Portguese and Chinese edits. 2000), Justification by Faith: Selected Bibliography, 1995, A Tocha dos Puritanos: Evangelizacao Biblica, 1996, Heidelberg Cutechism, 5 vols., 1998, Truth that Frees, 1998, Reformed Confessions Harmonized, 1998, A Reader's Guide to Reformed Literature, 1999, The Quest for Full Assurance: Calvin and the Legacy of His Successors, 1999, Porguese edit., 2003, Puritan Evangelism, 1999, Chinese edit. 2001, Korean edit. 2002, Portguese edit. 2003, Gisbertus Voetius, 1999, Bringing the Gospel to Covenant Children, 2001 (Portguese edit. 2004), Family Worship, 2002, Puritan Reformed Spirituality, 2004, The Family at Church, 2004, Portraits of Faith, 2004, Overcoming the World: Grace to Win the Daily Battle, 2005, Calvin's Passion for the Lost and the Puritans on Adoption and Meditation, 2006, Striving Against Satan, 2006, The Epistles of John, 2006, Walking as He Walked, 2007, others; contbr. over 1500 articles to profl. jours.; co-author: (with J.W. Beeke) Bible Doctrine Student Workbook, 1982, (with J.W. Beeke and Diane Kleyn) Building on the Rock, Book 1, 1989, Book 2, 1990, Book 3, 1993, (with J.D. Greendyk) Knowing and Living the Christian Life, 1997, (with D. Patrick Ramsey) An Analysis of Human Witsins's "Economy of the Covenants", 2002, (with J.W. Beeke and Diane Kleyn) Book 4, 2000, Chinese edit., 2000, (with Randall Pederson) Meet the Puritans, 2006; co-translator: (with J.C. Weststrate) Reformed Dogmatics, vol. I, 1980, vol. II, 1983; editor: Religious Stories for the Young and Old, vol. 4, 1983, The Twenty-fifth Mission Day, 1984, Sovereign Grace in Life and Ministry, 1984, Experiential Grace in Dutch Biography, 1985, Collected Writings of Rev. William C. Lamain, vol. I, 1986, Doctrinal Standards, Liturgy and Ch. Order, 1992, Heaven Taken By Storm, 1992, The Pearl of Christian Comfort, 1997, (with H. Boorsma) God's Alphabet for Life, 2000, (with D. Kleyn) The Truths of God's Word, 2002, Daily Devotional for Children, 5 vols., 2003; gen. editor: The Poor Man's Morning and Evening Portions, 1995, Memoirs of Thomas Halyburton, 1996; co-editor (with B. Elshout) The Christian's Reasonable Service, 4 vols., 1992-95, Forerunner of the Great Awakening, 2000, The Path of True Godliness, 2003; editor: (periodicals) Banner of Truth, 1985-93, Paul, 1984-93, Banner of Sovereign Grace Truth, 1993—, Christian Observer, 1994—, Gospel Trumpet, 1995—; radio pastor, 1995-. With U.S. Army, 1971-74. Mem. Evang. Theol. Soc., Soc. for Reformation Rsch., Calvin Studies Soc., 16th Century Studies Conf. Soc., Am. Soc. Ch. History, Colloquium on Calvin Studies, Conf. on Faith and History. Republican. Home and Office: 2965 Leonard St NE Grand Rapids MI 49525-5828 Office Phone: 616-977-0599 123. Personal E-mail: jrbeeke@aol.com.

BEEKEN, TIMOTHY K., lawyer; b. Apr. 2, 1959; BA with honors, Haverford Coll., 1983; JD, Columbia U., 1991. Assoc. Debevoise & Plimpton LLP, NYC, 1991—2002, mng. atty., 2002—. Mem.: Mng. Attys. and Clks. Assn. (exec. com. 2004—, newsletter com. 2002—), Assn. of Bar of City of NY (consumer affairs com. mem. 1999—2001), NY State Bar Assn., NY County Lawyers Assn. Office: Debevoise & Plimpton LLP 919 Third Ave New York NY 10022 Office Phone: 212-909-6518. Fax: 212-909-6836. E-mail: tkbeeken@debevoise.com.

BEEKLEY, ALEC C., surgeon, researcher; s. David C. and Cynthia X. Beekley; m. Melodie M. Icasiano, Apr. 11, 2003; 1 child, Alexandra P. MD, Case Western Res. U. Sch. Medicine, Cleve., 1996. Med. Diplomate Am. Bd. Surgery, 2003. Staff gen. surgeon Madigan Army Med. Ctr., Ft. Lewis, Wash., 2002—07, trauma med. dir., 2004—, 2005—; staff gen. surgeon Blanchfield Army Cmty. Hosp., Ft. Campbell, Ky., 2001—02, 102nd Forward Surg. Team, Kandahar, Afghanistan, 2002—03; med. dir. 912th Forward Surg. Team, Al Mussayib, Iraq, 2004; staff gen. surgeon 31st Combat Support Hosp., Baghdad, Iraq, 2004; dir., deployed combat casualty care rsch. team 28th Combat Support Hosp., 2007. Maj. US Army, 1996—2007, Ft. Lewis. Mem.: ACS. Achievements include research in combat casualty care. Office: Madigan Army Med Ctr 9040A Fitzsimmons Rd Fort Lewis WA 98431 Office Phone: 253-968-2200. Office Fax: 253-968-0232. Business E-Mail: alec.beekley@us.army.mil.

BEEKMAN, MARVIN LEE, lawyer; b. 1969; BSEE, Dordt Coll., Sioux Ctr., Iowa, 1991; JD, Hamline U. Sch. Law, St. Paul, 1994. Bar: Minn. 1994. Assoc. small intellectual property law firm; dir. ops. engring. co.; atty. Schwegman, Lundberg, Woessner & Kluth, P.A., Mpls. Named a Rising Star, Minn. Super Lawyers mag., 2006. Mem.: Minn. Intellectual Property Law Assn., Am. Intellectual Property Law Assn. Office: Schwegman Lundber Woessner & Kluth PA 1600 TCF Tower 121 S 8th St Minneapolis MN 55402 Office Phone: 612-373-6960. E-mail: mbeekman@slwk.com.*

BEEKMAN, WILLIAM BEDLOE, lawyer; b. NYC, July 8, 1949; s. Robert S. and Mary M. Beekman; m. Helen Hinckley, June 7, 1980; children: Izaak, Hugo. BA magna cum laude, Harvard U., 1971; JD, Yale U., 1980. Bar: N.Y. 1981. Assoc. Debevoise & Plimpton LLP, NYC, 1980-89, ptnr., 1989—. Bd. dirs. Lafayette Studios Corp., N.Y.C. Bd. dirs. Romanian Am. Enterprise Fund. Mem. ABA, Assn. Bar City NY, Am. Coll. Investment Counsel, NY Hist. Soc. (bd. dirs.), Libr. Coun. for Mus. Modern Art, Century Assn. Grolier Club (bd. dirs.). Democrat. Episcopalian. Home: 284 Lafayette St Apt 4B New York NY 10012-3303 Office: Debevoise & Plimpton LLP 919 3rd Ave 2d fl New York NY 10022-6225 Office Phone: 212-909-6215. Business E-Mail: wbbeekman@debevoise.com.

BEELER, CHARLES ALAN, retired music educator; b. St. Louis, Feb. 10, 1939; s. Charles Franklin and Eleanor (Jones) B. BMus in Theory/Composition, Ill. Wesleyan, 1961; MA in Music Theory/Composition, Washington U., St. Louis, 1965, PhD in Music Theory/Composition, 1973. Instr. Washington U., St. Louis, 1963-64; from instr. to asst. prof. Wis. State U., Stevens Point, 1967-70; from assoc. prof. to prof. Ea. Ky. U., Richmond, 1970—2007; ret., 2007. Oboist St. Louis Symphony/Gateway Festival Orch., 1962-66, Stevens Point Symphony/Woodwind Quintet, 1967-68, Ea. Ky. U. Orch./Faculty Woodwind Quartet, 1970-89, 92—. Co-author: Music Theory and Musicanship, 1981; composer, arranger Orchestral, piano, chamber works, 1962—. Mem. AAUP, Internat. Double Reed Soc., Coll. Music Soc., Soc. Composers Inc. Avocations: record collecting, stamp collecting/philately, chamber music performing. Business E-Mail: alan.beeler@eku.edu.

BEELER, CHARLOTTE JEAN, oil and supply company executive, interior design business executive; b. Normal, Ill., Dec. 9, 1928; d. John William and Viola Maude (Walters) Geske; m. Charles Gilbert Beeler, Feb. 12, 1949; children: Judy Ann Kjellander, Mark Geske, David William. Student, Ill. Wesleyan U., 1946-48, Ill. State U., 1962-75; degree in interior design, Ray Coll. of Design, Chgo., 1991. Lic. interior designer Ill. Gift buyer Dixie Truckers, McLean, Ill., 1967-78, gift buyer, mgr. Tuscola, Ill., 1978-80; adminstrv. mgr. travel stores Dixie Truckers Home, dba Shirley Oil and Supply Co., McLean and Tuscola, 1983-91; sec. bd. dirs. Dixie Truckers, McLean and Tuscola, 1985—. Owner, designer Creative Interiors, 1987—. Rep. precinct committeewoman, McLean, 1960-76; mem. bd. visitors Ill. Wesleyan U., 1980; trustee Wesley United Meth., Bloomington, 1986—, vice chmn., 1989; bd. dirs. YWCA, 1980-85, treas. bd. dirs., 1983-85; bd. dirs. Centrillio coun. Girl Scouts U.S.A., 1990-91, Route 66 Assn., 1994—, mem., 1990—, mem. Hall of Fame com., 1991—; mem. McLean County Greenways Adv. Com., 1999. Mem.: PEO, Am. Soc. Interior Designers, Sigma Kappa, Ill. Wesleyan U. Alumni Assn. Avocations: reading, bridge, sculpture. Home: Creative Interiors 124 Hawthorne Lake Rd Bloomington IL 61704-8530 also: 3500 Gulf Of Mexico Dr # 102 Longboat Key FL 34228-2828 Personal E-mail: cj.beeler@verizon.net.

BEELER, SANDRA GILLESPIE, realtor; b. Knoxville, Jan. 27, 1946; d. Robert Burl and Dorothy Aileen Warren; m. William Gene Beeler, Aug. 19; m. James Stephen, Sr. Gillespie (div.); 1 child, James Stephen Gillespie Jr. Lic. realtor Tenn., 1987. Collections supr. General Motors Accept Corp., Knoxville, 1966—82; mgr., buyer MS Apropos, Knoxville, 1983—86; realtor Re/max Preferred Properties, Knoxville, 1987—. Chair numerous coms. Knoxville Area Assn. Realtors, Knoxville, 1995—2003, pres., 2000, State Chpt. of Cert. Residential Specialists, Tenn., 2000. Recipient Realtor of Yr., Knoxville Area Assn. of Realtors, 2001, Hall of Fame award, Knoxville, 2003, Hall of Fame, Re/max Internat., 1998, Lifetime Achievement award, 2004. Mem.: CRS of Tenn. (state pres. 2000, CRS of Yr. 2001), Women's Council of Realtors, SRES, REBAC. Avocations: travel, entertaining. Office: Re/max Preferred Properties 117 Center Park Dr Knoxville TN 37922

BEEM, JACK DARREL, retired lawyer; b. Chgo., Nov. 17, 1931; AB, U. Chgo., 1952, JD, 1955. Bar: Ill. 1955. Assoc. firm Wilson & McIlvaine, Chgo., 1958-63; ptnr. firm Baker & McKenzie, Chgo., 1963—2004; ret., 2004. Decorated Order of the Sacred Treasure gold rays with rosette Japan. Mem. ABA, Chgo. Bar Assn., Japan-Am. Soc. Chgo. (pres. 1988-92), Am. Fgn. Law Assn. (chmn. Chgo. br.), Am. Law Inst., Univ. Club of Chgo., Tokyo Club, Tokyo Am. Club, Sons Am. Revolution, Phi Beta Kappa, Alpha Delta Phi. Home: 175 E Delaware Pl Apt 8104 Chicago IL 60611-7746 Personal E-mail: abojdb@comcast.net.

BEEM, JOHN KELLY, retired mathematician, educator; b. Detroit, Jan. 24, 1942; s. William Richard and June Ellen (Kelly) B.; m. Eloise Masako Yamamoto, Mar. 24, 1964; 1 child, Thomas Kelly. AB in Math., U. So. Calif., 1963, MA in Math., 1965, PhD in Math., 1968. Asst. prof. math. U. Mo., Columbia, 1968-71, assoc. prof., 1971-79, prof., 1979—2002; ret., 2002. Author: (with P. Y. Woo) Doubly Timelike Surfaces, 1969, (with P. E. Ehrlich) Global Lorentzian Geometry, 1981, (with P.E. Ehrlich and K.L. Easley), 2d edit., 96, Geometry Connections, 2006; condr. research in differential geometry and gen. relativity. Recipient Kemper Tchg. award, 1996; NSF fellow, 1965, 68. Mem.: Am. Math. Soc., Math. Assn. Am., Phi Beta Kappa. Home: 5204 E Tayside Cir Columbia MO 65203-5191

BEEMAN, RICHARD ROY, historian, educator; b. Seattle, May 16, 1942; m. Pamela Jane Butler, Dec. 26, 1964; children: Kristin Dowds, Joshua Douglas. AB in History, U. Calif., Berkeley, 1964; MA in History, Coll. of William and Mary, 1965; PhD in History, U. Chgo., 1968. Asst. prof. history U. Pa., 1968-73, assoc. prof., 1973-82, prof., 1982—, acting chmn. dept., 1986-87, chmn., 1987-91, assoc. dean, 1991-96; vis. prof. Am. studies U. Hull, Eng., 1976-77; dean Coll. Arts and Scis. U. Pa., 1998—2003; William R. Kenan prof. history, chmn. Colby Coll., 1979-80; Vyvian Harmsworth prof. Am. history Oxford U., 2003—. Dir. Phila. Ctr. for Early Am. Studies, 1980-85. Author: The Old Dominion and the New Nation, 1788-1801, 1972, Patrick Henry: A Biography, 1974, The Evolution of the Southern Backcountry, 1984; editor: Beyond Confederation: The Origins of the American Constituion and National Identity, 1987, The Varieties of Political Experience in Eighteenth Century America, 2003; also articles and book revs. Dept. of History fellow Coll. William and Mary, 1964, Univ. fellow U. Chgo., 1966-67, Newberry Library jr. fellow, Chgo., 1967-68, U. Pa. summer research grants, 1969, 71, Am. Philos. Soc. research grants, 1971, 76, 89, Social Sci. Research Council post-doctoral fellowship, 1972-73, Nat. Book Award nominee, 1974, Fulbright sr. lectr., U.K., 1976-77, NEH basic research grant, 1983-84, summer seminar grant, 1986, sr. fellow, 1989—; fellow Inst. Advanced Study, 1989-90, Huntington Libr., 1997. Office: U Pa 213 College Hall Philadelphia PA 19104 Home Phone: 610-566-3773; Office Phone: 215-848-5801. E-mail: rbeeman@sas.upenn.edu.

BEEMER, JOHN BARRY, lawyer; b. Scranton, Pa., Sept. 4, 1941; s. Ellis T. and Rose Mary (Costello) B.; m. Diane Montgomery Fletcher, July 18, 1964 (dec. July 1999); children: David, Bruce. BS, U. Scranton, 1963; LLB, George Washington U., 1966. Bar: Pa. 1966, U.S. Supreme Ct. 1980; cert. civil trial adv. Nat. Bd. Trial Advocacy. Law clk. U.S. Ct. Claims, 1966-67; clk. to judge U.S. Dist. Ct. (mid. dist.) Pa., 1967-68; assoc. Warren, Hill, Henkelman & McMenamin, Scranton, 1968-72; ptnr. Beemer, Brier, Rinaldi & Fendrick, 1972-77; pres. Beemer, Rinaldi, Fendrick & Mellody, P.C., Scranton, 1977-83; ptnr. Beemer & Beemer, Scranton, 1984—. Lectr. in law U. Scranton, 1969-70. Chmn. com. constn. and by-laws revision Lackawanna (county Pa.) United Fund., 1971; nat. chmn. U. Scranton Alumni Fund Drive, 1972; chmn. profl. divsn. Am. Cancer Soc. Drive, Lackawanna County, Pa., 1976. Mem. ABA, Pa. Bar Assn., Lackawanna Bar Assn. (bd. dirs. 1988—), Assn. Trial Lawyers Am., Pa. Trial Lawyers Assn., Phi Delta Phi. Office: 114-116 N Abington Rd Clarks Summit PA 18411 Home Phone: 570-587-0744; Office Phone: 570-587-0188. Personal E-mail: bbeemer123@aol.com.

BEEMSTER, JOSEPH ROBERT, risk management consultant; b. Chgo., Nov. 11, 1941; s. Joseph Z. and Emily (Dehaus) B.; m. Judith L. Scheffers, Sept. 7, 1963; children: David, Susan. BA, DePaul U., 1962; postgrad., Ill. Inst. Tech., 1976, postgrad., 1977, U. Minn., 1979, postgrad., 1980. Mfg. mgr. Johnson & Johnson, Chgo., 1967—71, mgr. safety and security, 1971—78; corp. dir. safety and health Pacific Dunlop GNB Inc., St. Paul, 1978—88; v.p. loss control Willis of Ill., 1988—. Author: Safe Work Practices for Workers Exposed to Lead; prodr. videotapes on health and safety tng. Chmn. Bolingbrook (Ill.) Human Rels. Commn., 1971-77. Mem. Am. Soc. Safety Engrs., Am. Indsl. Hygiene Assn. Home: 1606 Hadley Ct Wheeling IL 60090-6916 Personal E-mail: jbeemster@aol.com.

BEER, BARRETT LYNN, historian; b. Goshen, Indiana, July 4, 1936; s. Peter J. and Mabel M. B.; m. Jill (Parker), 1965. BA, DePauw U., Greencastle, Ind., 1958; MA, U. Cin., 1959; PhD, Northwestern U., Evanston, Ill., 1965. Instr. history Kent State U., Ohio, 1962—65; asst. prof. U. N.Mex., Albuquerque, 1965—68; assoc. prof. Kent State U., Ohio, 1968—76, prof., 1976—2002, prof. emeritus, 2002—; asst. dean Coll. Arts and Sci. U. N. Mex., Albuquerque, 1966—68; Fulbright prof. U. Tromso, Norway, 1983. Author: Northumberland: The Political Career of John Dudley, Earl of Warwick and Duke of Northumberland, 1973, Rebellion and Riot: Popular Disorder in Eng. during the Reign of Edward VI, 1982, 2nd edit., 2005; (with others) Recent Historians of Great Britain, 1990, Tudor England Observed: The World of John Stow, 1998; editor: (with S.M. Jack) The Letters of William, Lord Paget of Beaudesert, 1547-1563, 1974, The Life and Raigne of King Edward the Sixth (John Hayward), 1993, contbr., Oxford Dictionary of Nat. Biography, 2004. Am. Philos. Soc. grantee, 1966; Am. Coun. Learned Soc. grantee, 1973; fellow Newberry Libr., 1991, Folger Shakespeare Libr., 1997. Fellow Royal Hist. Soc.; mem. Conf. on Brit. Studies, Phi Beta Kappa. Episcopalian. Home: 445 Dansel St Kent OH 44240-2626 Office: Kent State U Dept History Kent OH 44242-0001 Business E-Mail: bbeer@kent.edu.

BEER, CLARA LOUISE JOHNSON, retired electronics executive; b. Bisbee, Ariz., Jan. 14, 1918; d. Franklin Fayette and Marie (Sturm) Johnson; m. Philip James McElmurry, May 15, 1937 (div. July 1944); children— Leonard Franklin, Philip James Jr.; m. William Sigvard Beer, July 15, 1945 (dec. Aug. 1977); 1 son, Douglas Lee; m. Kenneth Christy Huntwork, May 1, 1982 (dec. Jan. 2003). Student, Merritt Bus. Sch., Oakland, Calif., 1935, Bus. Instrn. Sch., Palo Alto, Calif., 1955. Sec., artist M.R. Fisher Studios, Oakland, 1936-40; piano, organ instr. Anna May Studios, Palo Alto, 1948-50; pvt. piano, organ instr. Palo Alto, 1949-56; sec. Stanford Electronics Labs., Stanford U., 1955-58; corporate sec. and exec. sec. to chmn. bd. Watkins-Johnson Co., Palo Alto, 1958-88. Dir., sec. Watkins-Johnson Internat., 1968-88, Watkins-Johnson Ltd., 1971-88, Watkins-Johnson Assocs., 1977-88. Mem. Nat. Secs. Assn., Christian Bus. and Profl. Women's Coun. (sec. 1966-67, adviser 1968) Home: 24157 Hillview Rd Los Altos CA 94024-5222

BEER, FRANCIS ANTHONY, political science professor emeritus; b. NYC, Feb. 5, 1939; s. William Joseph and Anne (Benedikt) B.; m. Diana Darnall, June 12, 1965; children: Omar, Marie, Jeremy. AB cum laude, Harvard U., 1960; MA, U. Calif., Berkeley, 1963, PhD, 1967. Asst. prof. dept. govt. U. Tex., Austin, 1967-70, assoc. prof. dept. govt., 1970-75; prof. dept. polit. sci. U. Colo., Boulder, 1975—2005, prof. emeritus, 2006—. Author: Integration and Disintegration in NATO: Processes of Alliance Cohesion and Prospects for Atlantic Community, 1969, Peace Against War: The Ecology of International Violence, 1981, Meanings of War and Peace, 2001; editor Alliances: Latent War Communities in the Contemporary World, 1970; co-editor: (with Ted. R. Gurr) Conflict, Violence, Peace: An International Series of Books, 1990-93, (with R. Hariman) Post-Realism: The Rhetorical Turn in International Relations, 1996, (with C. DeLandtsheer) Metaphorical World Politics, 2004; asst. editor Jour. Politics, 1968-71; contbr. articles to profl. jours. Lt. USNR, 1960-62. Fulbright fellow, 1965-66, 71, Mershon fellow, 1966-67, NEH fellow, 1990; grantee Earhart Found., 1972, Inst. World Order, 1974-77. Mem. Internat. Polit. Sci. Assn., Internat. Soc. Polit. Psychology, Am. Polit. Sci. Assn., Internat. Studies. Assn. Office: U Colo Polit Sci Dept PO Box 333 Boulder CO 80309-0333

BEER, JAMES A., information technology executive, former air transportation executive; b. London; BS in Aero. Engring., London U.; MBA, Harvard U. With Anderson Consulting; fin. analyst Am. Airlines, 1991, mng. dir. corp. devel., mng. dir. internat. planning, v.p. fin. analysis and fleet planning, 1998—2000, treas., v.p. corp. devel., 2000—02, v.p. for Europe and Asia, 2002—03; sr. v.p., CFO AMR Corp. and Am. Airlines, 2003—06; CFO Symantec, Cupertino, Calif., 2006—. Office: PO Box 619616 Dallas TX 75261-9616 also: Symantec 20330 Stevens Creek Blvd Cupertino CA 95014*

BEÉR, JÁNOS MIKLÓS, engineering educator; b. Budapest, Hungary, Feb. 27, 1923; s. Sandor and Gizella (Trismai) B.; m. Marta Gabriella Csato, Oct. 27, 1944. Dipl. Ing., Jozsef Nador U. Tech., Budapest, 1950; PhD, U. Sheffield, Eng., 1960, DSc, 1968; Dr honoris causa, U. Miskolc, Hungary, 1987, U. Tech. Scis., Budapest, Hungary, 1997. Research engr. Heat Research Inst., Budapest, 1949-56, head combustion div., 1952-56; prin. lectr. combustion Budapest Tech. U., 1953-56; research engr. Babcock & Wilcox Ltd., Renfrew, Scotland, 1956-57; head research sta. Internat. Flame Research Found., Ijmuiden, Holland, 1960-63; prof. fuel sci. Pa. State U., 1963-65; Newton Drew prof., head dept. chem. engring. and fuel tech. U. Sheffield, 1965-76, dean engring., 1973-75; prof. chem. and fuel engring., sci. dir. MIT Combustion Rsch. Facility MIT, Cambridge, Mass., 1976-93, prof. emeritus dept. chem. engring., 1993—. Vis. fellow Australian Commonwealth, 1972; joint com. Internat. Flame Rsch. Found., 1972-89 , supt. rsch., 1972-89; adv. coun. rsch. and devel. fuel and power U.K. Dept. Energy, 1973-76; mem. Clean Air Coun., Dept. Environ., U.K., 1974-76; chem. tech. com. U.K. Sci. Rsch. Coun., 1972-75; combustion sci. com. Italian Nat. Rsch. Coun., 1974—; chmn. clean coal utilization project NAS, 1987-88; adv. coun. U.S. Sec. Energy Nat. Coal Coun., 1992—. Co-author: Combustion Aerodynamics, 1972; editor: Fuel and Energy Science Monograph Series, 1972; co-editor: Heat Transfer in Flames, 1972, Industrial Flames, 1972, Combustion Technology, 1974; author articles; patentee in field. Recipient BCURA Coal Sci. Gold medal, 1986, Alfred Egerton Gold medal Combustion Inst., 1986, Axel Axelson Johnson medal Swedish Acad. Engring. Scis., 1995, AIAA Energy Sys. award, 1998, George Westinghouse Gold medal ASME Internat., 2001, Homer Lowry Gold medal, US Dept. of Energy, 2003; named Hon. Supt. Rsch., Internat. Flame Rsch. Found., 1991. Fellow ASME (Moody award 1964, Percy Nicholls award 1988, Internat. George Westinghouse Gold medal 2001), Inst. Energy (sr., Melchett medal 1985), Royal Acad. Engring. U.K.; mem. Am. Inst. Chem. Engrs., Hungarian Acad. Scis. (hon.), Hungarian Nat. Acad. Engring. (hon.), Finnish Acad. Tech. (fgn.). Office: MIT 66-301 Dept Chem Engring Cambridge MA 02139 Office Phone: 617-253-6661. Business E-Mail: jmbeer@mit.edu.

BEER, MICHAEL, biophysicist, educator, environmentalist; b. Budapest, Hungary, Feb. 20, 1926; came to U.S., 1958, naturalized, 1965; s. Paul and Lidia (Pap-Kovacs) B.; m. Margaret Terry Peters, Jan. 22, 1954; children: Nicholas, Suzanne, Wendy. MA, U. Toronto, 1950; PhD, U. Manchester, Eng., 1953. Rsch. assoc. U. Mich., Ann Arbor, 1953-56; rsch. fellow Nat. Rsch. Coun. Can., 1956-58; mem. faculty Johns Hopkins U., Balt., 1958—, prof. biophysics, 1964-96, prof. emeritus, 1996—, chmn. dept. biophysics, 1974-80, assoc. dean arts and scis., 1989-92. Mem. Biophys. Soc. (pres. 1975-76), Electron Microscopy Soc. Am. (pres. 1980), Chesapeake Bay Trust (Ellen Fraites Wagner award, 1999). Home: 4623 Wilmslow Rd Baltimore MD 21210-2549

BEER, PAUL MARIUS, ophthalmologist, educator; b. Lupeni, Romania, Mar. 28, 1955; s. Idel and Emilia Beer; m. Cynthia Ann Simon, Feb. 8, 1986; children: Jonathan Sebastian, Emily Anna. BS, Columbia U., NYC, 1978; MD, SUNY, 1982. Lic. dr. Am. Bd. Ophthalmology, 1987. Founder, pres. Retina Office, PLLC, Slingerlands, NY, 2000—02; clin. prof. ophthalmology Albany Med. Ctr., NY, 2000—; pres. Retina Consultants, PLLC, Slingerlands, NY, 2002—, Retina Rsch. Found., Inc., Albany, 2004—. Protocol concept rev. com. Nat. Eye Inst., DRCR, Balt., 2005—; prin. investigator Retina Rsch. Ctr., Slingerlands. Lead faculty Eye Mission to Belize, San Pedro, 2007; bd. chmn. Retina Rsch. Found., Inc., Albany, 2004. Recipient Tchr. of Yr. award, Luisiana State U., 1987, Golden Apple award, Albany Med. Coll., 1998—99, Merit award, Am. Soc. Retinal Specialists, 2002, Sr. Merit award, 2005. Fellow: Am. Acad. Ophthalmology (life); mem.: Am. Soc. Vitreoretina Specialists, European Soc. Retinal Specialists (assoc.). Avocations: windsurfing, scuba diving. Office: Retina Cons PLLC 1220 New Scotland Rd Ste 201 Slingerlands NY 12159 Office Fax: 518-533-6556.

BEER, PETER HILL, federal judge; b. New Orleans, Apr. 12, 1928; s. Mose Haas and Henret (Lowenburg) B.; children: Kimberly Beer Bailes, Kenneth, Dana Beer Long-Innes; m. Marjorie Barry, July 14, 1985. BBA, Tulane U., 1949, LLB, 1952; LLM, U. Va., 1986. Bar: La. 1952. Successively assoc., ptnr., sr. ptnr. Montgomery, Barnett, Brown & Read, New Orleans, 1955-74; judge La. Ct. Appeal, 1974-79, U.S. Dist. Ct. (ea. dist.) La., New Orleans, 1979—. Vice chmn. La. Appellate Judges Conf.; apptd. by chief justice of U.S. to state-fed. com. Jud. Conf. U.S., 1985-89; apptd. by chief justice of U.S. to Nat. Jud. Coun. State and Fed. Cts., 1993—. Mem. bd. mgrs. Touro Infirmary, New Orleans, 1969-74; mem. exec. com. Bur. Govtl. Rsch., 1965-69; chmn. profl. divsn. United Fund New Orleans, 1966-69; mem. New Orleans City Coun., 1969-74, v.p., 1972-74. Capt. USAF, 1952-55. Decorated Bronze Star, Air Force Commendation medal; recipient Justice William Brennan award U. Va. Sch. Law, 2005. Mem. ABA (mem. ho. dels.), Am. Judicature Soc., Fed. Bar Assn., La. Bar Assn., Nat. Lawyers Club, So. Yacht Club, St. John Golf Club. Jewish. Home: 133 Bellaire Dr New Orleans LA 70124-1008 Office: US Dist Ct US Courthouse 500 Poydras St New Orleans LA 70130-3313 Home Phone: 504-482-8745; Office Phone: 504-589-7510.

BEER, REINHARD, atmospheric scientist; b. Berlin, Nov. 5, 1935; came to U.S., 1963, naturalized, 1979; s. Harry Joseph and Elizabet Maria (Meister) B.; m. Margaret Ann Taylor, Aug. 11, 1960. B.Sc. with Honors, U. Manchester, Eng., 1956, PhD, 1960. Rsch. asst. physics U. Manchester, 1956-60, sr. asst. astronomy, 1960-63; sr. scientist Jet Propulsion Lab., Pasadena, Calif., 1963-70, group supr. tropospheric sci., 1970—2005, sr. rsch. scientist, 1985—, mgr. atmospheric and oceanographic scis. sect., 1990-92, flight team leader, 1997—, prin. scientist, 1999—. Vis. assoc. prof. astronomy U. Tex., Austin, 1974; vis. astronomer Kitt Peak Nat. Obs., 1979-81, Mauna Kea Obs., 1982-86; prin. investigator Tropospheric Emission Spectrometer NASA Earth Observing System, 1989—, airborne emission spectrometer program NASA, 1992-2003, group supr. Tropospheric Emission Spectrometry, 2005—06; co-investigator NASA Atlas 1 mission, 1992, Atlas 2, 1993. Author: Remote Sensing by Fourier Transform Spectrometry, 1992; contbr. articles to profl. jours. Hon. Turner and Newall fellow, 1961; recipient medal for exceptional sci. achievement NASA, 1974, NASA group achievement award for Pioneer Venus, 1980, Spacelab 3 ATMOS experiment and sci., 1986, group achievement award Tropospheric Emission Spectrometry, 2005 Mem. AAAS, Am. Geophys. Union, Optical Soc. Am. Achievements include discovery of extraterrestrial deuterium (heavy hydrogen), 1972, of carbon monoxide in Jupiter, 1975. Office: 183-601 Jet Propulsion Lab Pasadena CA 91109

BEER, TOMASZ M., physician; b. Warsaw, 1965; MD, Johns Hopkins U., 1991. Diplomate Am. Bd. Internal Medicine. Intern Oreg. Health Scis. U., Portland, 1991-92, resident internal medicine, 1992-94, chief resident internal medicine, 1995-96, fellow hematology, oncology, 1996—99, assoc. prof. medicine/oncology, and dir., prostate cancer program, Grover C. Bagby Endowed Chair for Prostate Cancer Rsch. Mem. ACP, Oreg. Med. Assn., Am. Soc. Clin. Oncology, Am. Soc. Hematology, Am. Assn. Cancer Rsch., SW Oncology Group. Office: Oreg Health Scis U 3181 SW Sam Jackson Park Rd Portland OR 97201-3011 Office Phone: 503-494-6594. Business E-Mail: beert@ohsu.edu.*

BEERBOWER, CYNTHIA GIBSON, lawyer; b. Dayton, Ohio, June 25, 1949; d. Charles Augustus and Sarah (Rittenhouse) Gibson; m. John Edwin Beerbower, Aug. 28, 1971; children: John Eliot, Sarah Rittenhouse. BA, Mt. Holyoke Coll., 1971; JD, Boston U., 1974; LLB, Cambridge U., Eng., 1976. Bar: N.Y. 1975. Assoc. Cadwalader, Wickersham & Taft, NYC, 1975-76, Simpson, Thacher & Bartlett, NYC, 1977-81, ptnr., 1981-93; internat. tax counsel, dept. asst. sec. Dept. Treasury, Washington, 1993-96; chmn., CEO Reeve Ct. Ins. Ltd., 1997—2001; prin. Quellos Group, 2001—04; mng. dir. XE Capital, 2004—05, Paget LLC, 2005. Mem. ABA, Assn. Bar City N.Y., N.Y. State Bar Assn. (com. co-chmn. 1987-93). Presbyterian. Home: 720 Park Ave New York NY 10021-4954

BEERBOWER, JOHN EDWIN, lawyer; b. Columbus, Ohio, Jan. 7, 1948; m. Cynthia Gibson, Aug. 28, 1971; children: John Eliot, Sarah Rittenhouse. BA, Amherst Coll., 1970; JD, Harvard U., 1973; student, Trinity Coll., Eng. Bar: N.Y. 1975. Mem. Cravath, Swaine & Moore, LLP, NYC, 1980—, ptnr., litig. Bd. govs. Mannes Coll. Music, 1993—, vice chmn., 2000—02, chmn., 2002—; com. on instl. policy New Sch. U., 2003—; trustee Madison Ave. Presbyn. Ch., 1995—2001, pres. bd. trustees, 2000—01. Mem. ABA, N.Y. State Bar Assn., N.Y. Law Inst. (mem. nominating com.), Assn. of Bar of City of N.Y. (chmn. profl. and jud. ethics com. 1990-93), Soc. of Alumni Amherst Coll. (pres. 1994-95), Union Internat. Advocats, Am. Econ Assn., Phi Beta Kappa. Office: Cravath Swaine & Moore LLP Worldwide Plz 825 8th Ave Fl 40 New York NY 10019-7416 Office Phone: 212-474-1864. Office Fax: 212-474-3700. Business E-Mail: jbeerbower@cravath.com.

BEERING, STEVEN CLAUS, academic administrator, medical educator; b. Berlin, Aug. 20, 1932; arrived in U.S., 1948, naturalized, 1953; s. Steven and Alice (Friedrichs) Beering; m. Catherine Jane Pickering, Dec. 27, 1956; children: Peter, David, John. BS summa cum laude, U. Pitts., 1954, MD, 1958, ScD (hon.), 1998; DSc (hon.), Ind. Cen. U., 1983, U. Evansville, Ind., 1984, Ramapo Coll., 1986, Anderson Coll., 1987, Purdue U., 2000; ScD (hon.), Ind. U., 1988; LLD (hon.), Hanover Coll., 1986, Tex. Wesleyan, 2001. Intern Walter Reed Gen. Hosp., Washington, 1958—59; resident Wilford Hall Med. Center, San Antonio, 1959—62, chief internal medicine, edn. coordinator, 1967—69; prof. medicine Ind. U. Sch. Medicine, Indpls., 1969—, asst. dean, 1969—70, assoc. dean, dir. postgrad. edn., 1970—74, dir. statewide med. edn. system, 1970-83, dean, 1974—83; chief exec. officer Ind. U. Med. Center, Indpls., 1974—83; pres. Purdue U. and Purdue U. Rsch. Found., West Lafayette, Ind., 1983—2000, pres. emeritus, 2000—; dir. emeritus Purdue Rsch. Found., West Lafayette, 2006—. Prof. pharmacology and toxicology Purdue U.; bd. dirs. NISource, Inc.; chmn. Med. Edn. Bd. Ind., 1974—83, Liaison Com. Med. Edn., 1976—81, Ind. Commn. Med. Edn., 1978—83. Contbr. articles to sci. jours. Sec. Ind. Atty. Gen.'s Trust, 1974—83; regent Nat. Libr. Medicine, 1987—91; trustee U. Pitts., 2000—. Lt. col. M.C. USAF, 1957—69. Fellow: ACP, Royal Soc. Medicine; mem.: Nat. Sci. Bd. (chmn.), Ind. Acad., Nat. Acad. Sci. Inst. of Medicine, Assn. Am. Univs. (chair 1995—96), Coun. Med. Deans (chmn. 1980—81), Assn. Am. Med. Colls. (chmn. 1982—83), Endocrine Soc., Am. Diabetes Assn., Am. Fedn. Med. Rsch., Meridian Hills Club, Skyline Club, Phi Rho Sigma (U.S. v.p. 1976—85), Alpha Omega Alpha, Sigma Xi, Phi Beta Kappa. Presbyterian. Home: 10487 Windemere Dr Carmel IN 46032 Office: Purdue U Office Pres Emeritus Rm 218 Memorial Union West Lafayette IN 47906-3584 Office Phone: 765-496-7555. Personal E-mail: sbeering@indy.rr.com. Business E-Mail: scb@purdue.edu.

BEERITS, JANET PENROSE ROBINSON, sculptor; b. Abington, Pa., Apr. 24, 1917; d. Otho Ernest Cox Robinson and Florence Gillingham Willard; m. Henry Christopher Beerits, Aug. 14, 1943; children: Christopher John, Susan Willard, Peter Cox. BA, Wellesley Coll., Mass., 1938, MA, 1940; student in Sculpture, Pa. Acad. Fine Arts, Phila., 1962—66; MFA in Sculpture, U. Pa., Phila., 1971. Tchr. Dept. Art Wellesley (Mass.) Coll., 1938—42. Recipient Stimson prize, award, Pa. Acad. Fine Arts, 1964; Durant scholar, Phi Beta Kappa Wellesley (Mass.) Coll., 1938. Mem.: Maine Women in Fine and Performing Arts (pres. 1980—82), Deer Isle Artsts Assn. (exhibn. chmn. 1975—78, v.p., pres.). Democrat. Mem. Soc. Friends. Avocation: gardening. Home: 108 Sheepscot Rd Alna ME 04535

BEERMAN, JOEL I., lawyer, chemical manufacturing company executive; b. Johnstown, Pa., 1950; BA, Boston U., 1972; JD, Seattle U., 1974. Bar: Wash. 1975, Oreg. 1975, Ga. 1983. Assoc. counsel Zidell Explorations, Inc., 1975—77; assoc. atty. Fellows, McCarthy, Zikes & Kayser, 1977—79; sr. counsel Ga. Gulf Corp., Atlanta, 1979—84, gen. counsel, 1985—, v.p., sec., 1994—. Office: Ga Gulf Corp Ste 460 115 Perimeter Ctr Place Atlanta GA 30346 Office Fax: 770-395-4529.*

BEERMANN, ALLEN J., former state official; b. Sioux City, Iowa, Jan. 14, 1940; BA, Midland Lutheran Coll., Fremont, Nebr., 1962; JD, Creighton U., Omaha, 1965; LLD (hon.), Midland Luth. Coll., 1995. Bar: Nebr. 1965. Legal counsel, adminstrv. asst. to sec. state, Nebr., 1965-67; dep. sec. state Nebr., 1967-71; sec. of state, 1971-95. Mem. Fed. Election Commn. adv. panel. Bd. dirs. NebraskaLand Found.; exec. bd. Cornhusker coun. Boy Scouts Am.; state chair N.E. Commn. Employer Support for Guard and Res., 1997-2002. Lt. col. U.S. Army, ret. Recipient Disting. Svc. plaque Omaha Legal Aid Soc., 1964, Silver Beaver award Boy Scouts Am., 1979, Fgn. Svc. Medallion Rep. of China, 2001, Homeland Def. Ribbon, 2001; named Outstanding Young Man Lincoln Jaycees, 1975, Outstanding Young Man Nebr. Jaycees, 1975 Mem. ABA, Nat. Assn. Secs. State (pres. 1976-77), Nebr. Bar Assn. (exec. dir. 1995—), Nebr. Press Assn., Am. Legion (fed. election commn. adv. panel, Cert. Appreciation). Republican. Lutheran. Office: Nebr Press Assn 845 S St Lincoln NE 68508-1226 Home Phone: 412-488-7624; Office Phone: 402-476-2851. Business E-Mail: nebpress@nebpress.com.

BEERS, BURTON FLOYD, historian, educator; b. Chemung, NY, Sept. 13, 1927; s. Franklyn McDowell and Alice (Wood) Beers; m. Pauline Elizabeth Cone, Sept. 6, 1952; children: Martha McDowell Beers Williams, Burton Floyd Jr. BA cum laude, Hobart Coll., Geneva, NY, 1950; MA, Duke U., Durham, NC, 1952; PhD, Duke U., 1956. Instr., asst. prof. history N.C. State Coll., Raleigh, 1955—61; assoc. prof., prof. N.C. State U., Raleigh, 1963—96, prof. emeritus, 1996—. Head history dept. N.C. State U., 1981—85; post-doctoral studies Japanese Civilization Asia Soc. Duke U., 1957; post-doctoral fellow East Asian Studies Ford Found. Harvard U., Cambridge, Mass., 1959—60; Fulbright vis. prof. Am. Studies Nat. Taiwan U., Taipei, 1966—67; cons. Nat. Humanities Ctr., Research Triangle Park, NC, 1984; cons. East Asia N.C. Dept. Pub. Instrn., 1970—74. Author: Vain Endeavor: Robert Lansing's Attempts to End the American-Japanese Rivalry, 1961, China in Old Photographs, 1978; editor-in-chief: Living in Our World. Mem. adv. bd. China Coun., NYC, 1977—81. Named Alumni Disting. Prof., N.C. State U. Alumni Assn., 1970—72; recipient Disting. Contbns. award, N.C. State U. Bd. Trustees, 1998, Alexander Quarles Holladay Excellence medal, 1992, Excellence medal, Hobart Coll. Bd. Trustees, 1994. Mem.: Assn. Asian Studies (SE Regional Conf.), World History Assn., Assn. Historians of Am. Fgn. Rels. Democrat. Home: 201 John Wesley Rd Greenville NC 27858 Personal E-mail: burtbeers@aol.com.

BEERS, NATHANIEL BRITTINGHAM SAVIO, pediatrician; s. Rand Brittingham and Marian Alice Brittingham Beers; m. Lee Ann Savio, June 9, 2001; 1 child, Charlotte Savio. MD, George Wash. U., 1995; Cert. in Leadership in Human Resource Devel., George Wash. U. Sch. of Edn., 2004; MPA, Harvard U., 2001, Cert. in Clin. Effectiveness, 1999. Diplomate Am. Bd. of Pediat. Pediatric intern and resident Children's Nat. Med. Ctr., Washington, 1995—98; Anne Dyson fellow in child advocacy The Children's Hosp. Boston, 1998—2000, chief fellow divsn. gen. pediat., 1999—2000, clin. instr. pediat., 2000—01; asst. prof. pediat. Children's Nat. Med. Ctr., Washington, 2001—, continuity clinic dir., 2003—05; med. dir. Children's Health Ctr., 2005—. Bd. dirs. Syrentha Savio Endowment, Washington, 2003—, Neighbors Consejo, Washington, 2005—. Contbr. articles to profl. jours. Recipient Mel Levine Award for Devel. Behavioral Pediat., The Children's Hosp. of Boston, 2000; grantee Master Tchr., Children's Nat. Med. Ctr., 2003—. Fellow: Am. Acad. Pediat. (chair sect. on residents 1999—2000, rep. on membership com. 2002—, DC chpt. sec., treas. 2004—06, v.p. 2006—); mem.: Ambulatory Pediatric Assn. Democrat. Office: Children's Natl Med Ctr 111 Michigan Ave NW Washington DC 20010 Office Phone: 202-884-3948.

BEERY-POLGLASE, PENELOPE (PIXIE), education educator; d. Jack and Margaret Beery-Polglase; m. Jack Beery, Sept. 6, 1987; children: Rhea Beery-Fox, Kaya Winter Beery. BA, Western Mich. U., Kalamazoo, 1965; MS, Pepperdine U., Malibu, Calif., 1985; EdD, Nova Southeastern U., Ft. Lauderdale, Fla., 2006. Landscape arch. cert. of completion, UCLA; sch. adminstrn. clear credential Calif. Commn. for Tchr. Credentialing, gen. tchg. life credential Calif. Commn. for Tchr. Credentialing, profl. devel. cert. L.A. Unified Sch. Dist., profl. devel. collaborative L.A. Unified Sch. Dist., UCLA sci. project, English lang. devel. and specially designed acad. instrn. in English Senate Bill 1969, State of Calif. Tchr. women's health initiatives UCLA, 1953—2003; tchr. Chgo. Pub. Schs., 1965—69, L.A. Unified Sch. Dist., tchr., Birdielee V. Bright Elem. Sch., ten schs. program, 1987—98, instr., Tchr. Tng. Acad., 1996—98, asst. prin., Victoria Ave. Elem. Sch. South Gate, Calif., 2003—05, coord. year-round programs, 1982—86, coord. categorical programs, 1986—87, instr. new tchr. orientation, 1996—98, tchr., early childhood edn. programs, 1997—99, adviser, dist. intern program, 1998—2000, specialist tchr. coaches dist. J, 2000—03, literacy trainer, 2000—03, instr., beyond the bell intervention program, 2003—05; asst. prin. Independence Elem. Sch., South Gate, Calif., 2005; enrichment tchr., Will Rogers Learning Cmty. Santa Monica Malibu Unified Sch. Dist., Calif., 1994—95; instr., ESL, cmty. adult programs Santa Monica City Coll., 1995—96; trainer of trainers CA Formative and Support Sys. for Tchrs. Calif. Commn. on Tchr. Credentialing, LA, 2000—07, trainer of trainers Towards Equity, 2000—07; external evaluator Calif. State Dept. Edn., Sacramento, 2001—02; CEO Willow Leaf Investments LLC, Venice, Calif., 2007—. Adj. instr. Nova Southeastern U., LA, 2002—03; adj. prof. Loyola Marymount U., LA, 2002—; adj. instr. Pepperdine U., 2004—06; student tchr. supr. U. So. Calif., 2005—06; presenter in field. Commr. for sex equity L.A. Unified Sch. Dist., 1987—90; asst. leader Girl Scout Troop 181, Westchester, Calif.; beautification chair Will Rogers Learning Cmty., Santa Monica, 1994—99. Recipient Math Innovation grant, L.A. Edn. Partnership, 1997, 1998, Cmty. Gardening Program grant, U.S. EPA, 1998, First Pl. award in landscape archtl. design, UCLA Ext., 1989; grantee, Gardening Angeles Partnership, 1995—98, Gardens for Kids, 1996—98, Nat. Youth Gardens, 1997—98. Mem.: Women in Ednl. Leadership (membership chair 2002—04, treas. 2004—06, pres.-elect 2006, pres. 2006—07). Home: PO Box 9416 Venice CA 90295 Business E-Mail: probatebeery@hotmail.com. E-mail: pbeery@hotmail.com.

BEESLEY, H(ORACE) BRENT, bank executive; b. Salt Lake City, Jan. 30, 1946; s. Horace Pratt and Mary (Brazier) B.; m. Bonnie Jean Matheson, Dec. 20, 1980; children: Laura Jean, Sarah Janice, Mary Roslyn, Amy Elizabeth, David Brent, Katherine Ann, Daniel Pratt. BA, Brigham Young U., 1969; MBA, JD, Harvard U., 1973. Bar: Utah 1973. Instr. U. Utah, Salt Lake City, 1973-81; ptnr. Ray, Quinney & Nebeker, Salt Lake City, 1977-81; dir. Fed. Savs. and Loan Ins. Corp., Washington, 1981-83; chmn., chief exec. officer Charter Savs. Corp., Jacksonville, Fla., 1983-86; pres., chief exec. officer Farm Credit Corp. Am., Denver, 1986-88; chmn., chief exec. officer Heritage Bank, St. George, Utah, 1988—. Bd. dirs. Fed. Home Loan Bank, Seattle, 1992-95, Savs. and Cmty. Bankers Am., 1992-96, Utah Heritage Found., 1978-81, Utah Arthritis Found., 1978-81; trustee So. Va. Coll., 1998-2002. Mem. Utah State Bar Assn., Alta Club, Entrada at Snow Canyon Country Club. Home: 1492 Kristianna Cir Salt Lake City UT 84103-4221 Office: 95 E Tabernacle St Saint George UT 84770-2307

BEESON, ANN, lawyer; b. 1964; MA in Anthropology, U. Tex.; JD, Emory U. School Law, 1993. Attorney Human Rights Watch; assoc. legal dir. ACLU, 1995—2007; dir. US programs Open Soc. Inst., NYC, 2007—. Co-chair ACLU Internat. Human Rights Task Force. Named Global Leader for Tomorrow, World Econ. Forum; named one of America's top 50 Women Litigators, Nat. Law Journal, The 50 Most Influential Women Lawyers in Am., 2007, Litigation's Rising Stars, The Am. Lawyer, 2007. Avocations: amateur pilot, singing. Office: Open Society Institute 400 W 59th St New York NY 10019*

BEESON, JACK HAMILTON, composer, educator, writer; b. Muncie, Ind., July 15, 1921; children: Christopher Sigerist (dec.), Miranda. Student, U. Rochester, Columbia U.; studied with, Béla Bartók; Mus D (hon.), Columbia U., 2002. Tchr. Juilliard Sch. Music; former chmn. dept. music, assoc. dir. opera workshop Columbia U., NYC, MacDowell prof. emeritus. Former sec. Alice M. Ditson Fund; former chmn. music publ. com. Columbia U. Press.; bd. dirs. Composers Recs., Inc., others. Composer: (operas) Jonah, Hello Out There, The Sweet Bye and Bye, Lizzie Borden (commd. by Ford Found.), My Heart's in the Highlands (commd. by NET), Captain Jinks of the Horse Marines (commd. by Nat. Endowment of Arts), Dr. Heidegger's Fountain of Youth (commd. Nat. Arts Club), Cyrano, Sorry, Wrong Number, Practice in the Art of Elocution, (for orch.) Hymns and Dances, Symphony in A, Transformations, Interludes and Arias from Cyrano (for baritone and orchestra), Two Concert Arias (for soprano and orch.), (chamber music) Sonata for Viola and Piano, Interlude, Song, 4th and 5th Piano Sonatas, Two Diversions, Round and Round, Sonata Caronica for two alto recorders, Old Hundredth for Organ, (vocal works) Six Lyrics, Five Songs, Eldorado, Piazza Piece, Big Crash Out West, Indiana Homecoming, Margret's Garden Aria, To a Sinister Potato, (cycles) From a Watchtower, (bass-baritone and piano) Two by Betjeman and A Rupert Brooke Cycle, (for bass and piano) Three Viereck Songs, (countertenor and chamber ensemble) The Daring Young Man on the Flying Trapeze, (mezzosoprano and chamber ensemble) Ophelia Sings, (soprano, tenor and chamber ensemble) The Equilibrists, others, works for voice and string quartet, (choral works) Knots, Magicke Pieces, Epitaphs, In Praise of Singing, Summer Rounds and Canons. Recipient Rome prize, City of Rochester prize, Marc Blitstein Mus. Theatre award Nat. Inst. Arts and Letters, Gold medal for music Nat. Arts Club, 1976, Gt. Tchrs. award Columbia U., 1979, Alumni Achievement award U. Rochester, 1985, award for Lifetime Achievement award Nat. Opera Assn., 1998; Guggenheim fellow, Fulbright fellow to Italy. Mem. ASCAP (bd. dirs. 1991-95), AAAL (treas., v.p. for music), Phi Beta Kappa. also: 404 Riverside Dr New York NY 10025-1861 Office: Columbia U Dept Music New York NY 10027

BEESON, STEPHEN CHARLES, physician; b. San Diego, Oct. 21, 1964; s. William and Carole Beeson; m. Deanna Beeson, May 4, 1994; children: Sydney, Nicholas. BA, U. Calif., San Diego; MD, U. Calif., 1991. Physician Sharp-Rees Stealy Medical Grp., San Diego, 1994—2006, physician dir., 2001—06; med. dir. Studer Grp., Pensicola, Fla., 2000—06, Villa Rancho Bernardo Nursing Home, San Diego, 2001—06, Valeocyte, San Diego, 2002—04. Med. advisor Studer Grp. Author: (book) Practicing Excellence: Physicians Manual to Exceptional Healthcare, 2006. Vol. faculty homeless clinic UCSD, San Diego, 2001—06. Named Best Physician, San Diego Mag., 2005—06. Mem.: Am. Acad. Family Practice. Achievements include trained 220 physicians within a medical group on communication and collaboration with patients. Office: Sharp-Rees Stealy Medical Grp 16950 Via Tazon San Diego CA 92192

BEETON, ALFRED MERLE, lab administrator, director, biologist, educator, environmentalist; b. Denver, Aug. 15, 1927; s. Charles Frederick and Edna F. (Smith) B.; m. Mary Eileen Wilcox, July 20, 1945; children: Maureen Ann, Heather Ann, Celeste Nadine; m. Ruth Elizabeth Holland, June 4, 1966; children: Jonathan Eugene, Daniel Paul. BS, U. Mich., 1952, MS, 1954, PhD, 1958; DSc (hon.), U. Wis., Milw., 1996. Fishery biologist U.S. Bur. Comml. Fisheries, Ann Arbor, Mich., 1957—65, chief environ. research, 1960—65; prof. zoology U. Wis.-Milw., 1966—76, asst. dir. Ctr. for Gt. Lakes Studies, 1966—69, assoc. dir. Ctr. for Gt. Lakes Studies, 1969—73; assoc. dean U. Wis.-Milw. (Grad. Sch.), 1973—76; dir. Gt. Lakes and Marine Waters Ctr., Mich. Sea Grant; prof. engrng. and natural resources U. Mich., Ann Arbor, 1976—86; dir. Gt. Lakes Environ. Research Lab., Nat. Oceanic and Atmospheric Adminstrn. Dept. Commerce, Ann Arbor, 1986—96, emeritus, 2002—, acting chief scientist Nat Oceanic & Atmospheric Adminstrn. Washington, 1996—97, sr. sci. advisor, 1998—2002. Instr. biology Wayne State U., 1956—57, lectr. biology, 1957—61; lectr. civil engring. U. Mich., 1961—65; U.S. chmn. Sci. Adv. Bd. Internat. Joint Commn., 1986—91; mem. Mich. Toxic Substance Control Commn., 1987—89; mem. rsch. adv. coun. Wis. Dept. Natural Resources; mem. water quality criteria com. Nat. Acad. Scis.; cons. U.S. Army C.E., 1967—73, Met. San. Dist. Chgo., 1968—76, EPA, 1973—83; adviser on projects in Ghana, Laos and Yugoslavia Smithsonian Instn., 1972—82; adviser WHO/Pan Am. Health Orgn., Venezuela, 1978; mem. environ. program com. NRC, 1976—82, internat. environ. program com., 1977—82, mem. environ. studies bd.; adj. vis. prof. Oreg.State U., 1982; mem. Coun. Great Lakes Rsch. Mgrs., 1995—97; chmn. sci. adv. bd. NOAA, 1998—2002; mem. Ocean Rsch. Adv. Panel/Nat. Oceanographic Partnership Program, 2000—02; adj. prof. Sch. Pub. Health U. Mich., 1999—; bd. dirs. Ecology Ctr., Gt. Lakes Observing Sys., 2006—. Contbr. chpts. to books; articles Ency. Brit. Mem.: Mich. Acad. Sci., Arts and Letters, Internat. Assn. Gt. Lakes Rsch., Am. Soc. Limnology and Oceanography (treas. 1962—81), Internat. Assn. Theoretical and Applied Limnology (nat. rep. for U.S. 1976—95), Detroit Audubon Soc. (bd. dirs. 2002—04), Mich. Sierra Club (exec. com. 2006—). Home: 2761 Oakcleft St Ann Arbor MI 48103-2247 Personal E-mail: abeeton@netzero.net.

BEEVER, ERIK ALAN, ecologist, biologist; b. Lynwood, Calif., Sept. 17, 1971; s. Richard David and Sharon Kay Beever. BS in Biol. Scis., U. Calif., Davis, 1989—93; PhD in Ecology, Evolution & Conservation Biology, U. Nev., Reno, 1994—99. Rsch. intern sect. plant biology U. Calif., Davis, 1991, rsch. intern wildlife, fisheries and conservation biology, 1992—93, GIS intern, 1993—94; environ. edn./urban ecology exch. intern Ptnrs. of the Ams., Calif. Divsn. Forestry, Sacramento, 1993; forest inventory supr. Plumas Nat. Forest USDA Forest Svc., Quincy, Calif., 1993; tech. asst. Calif. Dept. Edn., Sacramento, 1994; prin. investigator, grad. rsch. asst. Biol. Resources Rsch. Ctr., U. Nev., Reno, 1994—99, postdoctoral fellow biology dept., 2000; ecologist biol. rsch. divsn. US Geol. Survey Forest and Rangeland Ecosystem Sci. Ctr., Corvallis, Oreg., 2000—05; ecologist NPS Inventory and Monitoring Program, Ashland, Wis., 2005—. Contbr. articles to profl. jours. Translator, sister city amb., internat. observer & agt. of accompaniment Salvadorean Humanitarian Aid, Rsch. & Edn., Rutilio Grande, El Salvador, 1992—93; translator various humanitarian efforts; private-citizen adv., 1992—2006; lector various religious cmtys., 1987—2006. Named one of Top 5 Finalists, INT Water Skiing Assn., 2004; recipient Humanitarian Effort award, Davis Interfaith Coun., 1993, STAR ward, US Geol. Survey, Biol. Rsch. Divsn., 2001—03; grantee Collaborative Rsch. Program, US Geol. Survey, 2002—03, Innovative Rsch. Program, 2004—05; Theodore Roosevelt Meml. Fund Rsch. grant, Am. Mus. Natural History, 1996, Rsch. grant, Gt. Basin Coop. Ecosystems Studies Unit, 2004—06. Mem.: Am. Inst. Biol. Scis., Am. Soc. Mammalogists, Soc. Conservation Biology, Sigma Xi, The Wildlife Soc. (pres.-elect 2006—). Achievements include research in interactions of free-roaming horses with other ecosystem components; local losses of populations of the American pika during the 20th and 21st centuries. Avocations: soccer, travel, skiing, backpacking, mountain climbing, coin collecting/numismatics. Office: US Nat Pk Svc Great Lakes Inventory & Monitoring Netwk Ashland WI 54806 Home Phone: 715-682-9839. Office Fax: 715-682-6190. Business E-Mail: erik_beever@nps.gov.

BEEVER, JAMES WILLIAM, III, biologist; b. Balt., Aug. 17, 1955; s. James William, Jr. and Virginia Irene (Ruhlmann) Beever; m. Lisa Britt Dodd, May 26, 1990. BS, Fla. State U., 1977, MS, 1979; postgrad., U. Calif., Davis, 1984. Environ. specialist Fla. Dept. Environ. Regulation, Ft. Myers, 1984—88; coord. resource mgmt. and rsch. S.W. Fla. Aquatic Preserves, Bokeelia, 1988—90; biol. scientist III Fla. Game and Fresh Water Fish Commn., Punta Gorda, 1990—98; biol. scientist IV Fla. Fish and Wildlife Conservation Commn., Punta Gorda, 1998—2006; sr. planner S.W. Fla. Regional Planning Coun., 2006—. Mem. tech. adv. bd. Sarasota Bay and Tampa Bay Nat. Estuary Program, Sarasota, 1989—2006; mem. policy com. and tech. adv. com. Charlotte Harbor Nat. Estuary Program; chair sci. com. on Mangrove Tech. Adv. Com. Fla. Dept. Environ. Protection, 1994—95; coord. Conservation Plan Hillsborough River Greenway Area, 1995; founder Frog Listening Network, 1997; chair Estero Bay Agy. on Bay Mgmt., 1999—2006; expert witness in field, 1986—. Author: (book) Lemon Bay Aquatic Preserve Management Plan, 1988, The Cedar Point Study, 1992, Hydric Pine Flatwoods of Southwest Florida, 1994, (database) Resource Inventory of Species in S.W. Fla., Coastal Conservation Corridor Plan; contbr. articles to profl. jours. Recipient Grad. Rsch. award, 1982—83, Outstanding Profl. Achievements award, Fla. DNR, 1989, Spl. Chmn.s award, Fla. Wildlife Fedn./Nat. Wildlife Fedn., 2000, Guy Bradley award, 2001; Regents fellow, U. Calif., 1983—84. Mem.: Ecol. Soc. Am., Soc. Conservation Biology, Soc. Wetland Scientists, Estuarine Rsch. Fedn., Fla. Acad. Sci., Sigma Xi, Phi Beta Kappa. Achievements include research in mangrove tree crab and arboreal folivore; mangrove cutting; endangered species protection; red cockaded woodpeckers; hydric pine flatwoods; xeric oak scrub; regional wildlife habitat/wildlife corridor planning; designation Florida ecosystems; hydrogeomorphic method for the Everglades. Office: SW Fla Regional Planning Coun 1926 Victoria Ave Fort Myers FL 33901 Office Phone: 239-338-2550 ext 224. Personal E-mail: jlbeever@aol.com. Business E-Mail: jbeever@swfrpc.org.

BEEZER, ROBERT RENAUT, federal judge; b. Seattle, July 21, 1928; s. Arnold Roswell and Josephine (May) B.; m. Hazlehurst Plant Smith, June 15, 1957; children: Robert Arnold, John Leighton, Mary Allison. Student, U. Wash., 1946-48, 51; BA, U. Va., 1951, LLB, 1956. Bar: Wash. 1956, U.S. Supreme Ct. 1968. Ptnr. Schweppe, Krug, Tausend & Beezer, P.S., Seattle, 1956-84; judge pro tem Seattle Mcpl. Ct., 1962—76; judge US Ct. Appeals (9th cir.), Seattle, 1984-96, sr. judge, 1996—. Alt. mem. Wash. Jud. Qualifications Commn., Olympia, 1981-84 1st lt. USMCR, 1951-53 Fellow Am. Coll. Trust and Estate Counsel, Am. Bar Found.; mem. ABA, Seattle-King County Bar Assn. (pres. 1975-76), Wash. Bar Assn. (bd. govs. 1980-83) Clubs: Rainier, Tennis (Seattle). Office Phone: 206-553-0384.*

BEEZLEY, WILLIAM H., history professor; b. Albuquerque, N.Mex., Mar. 22, 1942; s. Howard Claude and Lorene Sallee Beezley; m. Cheryle Blue Champion, Aug. 24, 1983; children: Paul Richard, John Sallee, Mark Madrid. BA, Chico State Coll., Calif., 1960; MA, PhD, U. Nebr., Lincoln, 1969. Asst. prof. SUNY, Plattsburgh, 1968—72; prof. history NC State U., Raleigh, 1972—89; Neville G. Penrose endowed chair Tex. Christian U., Ft. Worth, 1989—98; prof. history U. Ariz., Tucson, 1998—; Richard Greenleaf endowed chair Tulane U., New Orleans, 2000. Author: (book) Oxford History of Mexico (named History Book Club Selection, 2000), Judas at the Jockey Club (named History Book Club Selection), (books) 13 others. Recipient 10 Tchg. awards, various Univs. and Regional Orgns.; grantee, Hewlett Found., Dept. Edn., Tinker Found., Am. Philos. Soc., Fulbright Found., 2007, NEH. Office: Univ Arizona Dept History Tucson AZ 85721 Home Phone: 520-621-7107; Office Phone: 520-621-7107.

BEFFORT, SUE WILSON, state legislator; b. Albuquerque; BA, So. Meth. U. Mem. N.Mex. Senate, Dist. 19, Santa Fe, 1996—; mem. fin. com. N.Mex. Senate. Republican. Home: 67 Raindance Rd Sandia Park NM 87047

BEGALA, PAUL EDWARD, television personality, political scientist, consultant; b. Montclair, NJ, May 12, 1961; m. Diane Friday Begala, 1989; children: John Paul, William Travis, Patric Aaron. BA in Govt., U. Tex., Austin, 1983, JD, 1990. Bar: Pa. Ptnr., polit. cons. Carville & Begala; travel aide Lloyd Doggett Campaign for Senate, Tex., 1984; speech writer Congressman Richard Gephardt, 1987—88, speech writer presdl. campaign, 1989—91; cons. Dem. Nat. Com. and Clinton Adminstrn., 1992—95; sr. v.p. Pub. Strategies, Austin, 1995—97; asst. to Pres., counselor to Pres. The White House, 1997—99; rsch. prof. govt. and pub. policy Georgetown U., 1999—; co-host Equal Time, MSNBC, 1999—2000, Crossfire, CNN, 2002—. Lectr. U. Tex., Austin, 1995—97; contbg. editor, columnist Capital Hillbilly George mag. Author: Is Our Children Learning?: The Case Against George W. Bush, 2001, It's Still the Economy Stupid: George W. Bush, The GOP's CEO, 2002; co-author (with James Carville): Buck Up, Suck Up and Come Back When You Foul Up: 12 Winning Secrets from the War Room, 2001; contbr. articles to profl. jours. Office: CNN Crossfire 820 1st St NE Washington DC 20002*

BEGAM, ROBERT GEORGE, lawyer; b. NYC, Apr. 5, 1928; s. George and Hilda M. (Hirt) B.; m. Helen C. Clark, July 24, 1949; children—Richard, Lorinda, Michael. BA, Yale U., 1949, LL.B., 1952. Bar: N.Y. bar 1952, Ariz. bar 1956, U.S. Dist. Ct. Ariz. 1957, U.S. Ct. Appeals (9th cir.) 1958, U.S Supreme Ct. 1973. Assoc. firm Cravath, Swaine & Moore, NYC, 1952-54; spl. counsel State of Ariz., Colorado River Litigation in U.S. Supreme Ct., 1956-58; pres. Begam & Lewis PA, Phoenix. Author: Fireball, 1987. Pres. Ariz. Repertory Theater, 1960—66; trustee Atla Roscoe Pound Found.; bd. dirs. Boys Clubs of Met. Phoenix; bd. govs. Welzmann Inst. Sci., Rehovot, Israel; pres. Am. Com. for Welzmann Inst. of Sci., 1996—98, chmn. fin. resource devel., 2000—; v.p. Ariz. Theatre Co., 2006—07; bd. dirs. Phoenix Theater Ctr., 1955—60, 1987—92, Ariz. Theatre Co., 2001—. 1st lt. USAF, 1954—56. Fellow: Internat. Soc. Barristers; mem.: State Bar Ariz. (cert. specialist in injury and wrongful death litigation), Am. Bd. Trial Advocates (bd. dirs.), Western Trial Lawyers Assn. (pres. 1970), ATLA (pres. 1976—77, chmn. polit. action com. 1979—86), Phoenix Country Club, Yale Club (N.Y.C.). Avocations: writing, theater, golf. Office: Begam Lewis & Marks 111 W Monroe St Ste 1400 Phoenix AZ 85003-1787 Office Phone: 602-254-6071. Business E-Mail: r.begam@begamlaw.com.

BEGELL, WILLIAM, publisher; b. Wilno, Poland, May 18, 1928; came to U.S., 1947, naturalized, 1953; s. Ferdinand and Liza (Kowarski) Beigel; m. Esther Kessler, May 27, 1948; children: Frederick Paul (dec.), Alissa Maya (dec.). BChemE, CCNY, 1953; MChemE, Poly. Inst. Bklyn., 1958; postgrad., Columbia U., 1958-59; DSc, Acad. Sci. BSSR, Minsk, 1984. Engrng. mgr. heat transfer research facility dept. chem. engring. Columbia U., 1953-59; co-founder, exec. v.p. Scripta Technica, Inc., Washington, 1959-74; founder, pres. Hemisphere Publishing Corp., Washington, 1974-

91, Begell House, Inc., Pubs., NYC, 1991—; pres., chief scientist Byelocorp Sci., Inc., 1991—; dir. Supco Internat. Engring. Corp., Milan, 1994—. Lectr. pub. George Washington U., Washington, also NYU; cons. Heat Transfer Research Lab., Columbia U.; cons. in field. Editor 7 books; contbr. numerous articles on heat transfer to profl. jours.; patentee in field. Mem. nat. adv. bd. ctr. for the Book, Libr. of Congress; chmn. exec. coun. Profl. and Scholarly Pubs.; bd. dirs. Am. Fedn. for the Blind. Recipient Benjamin Gomez award book pub. divsn., Anti-Defamation League, 1984. Mem. AAAS, Am. Inst. Chem. Engrs., Am. Soc. for Engring. Edn., ASME (communications bd. Fellow, 1996, Disting. Svc. award 1992), Assn. Am. Publishers (dir.), NY Acad. Scis. (publs. bd.), Internat. Centre for Heat and Mass Transfer, Washington Book Publishers (founder), Am. Assn. Engring. Socs. Jewish. Home: 46 E 91st St New York NY 10128-1350 Office: Begell House Inc Pubs 50 Cross Hwy Redding CT 06896 Office Phone: 203-938-1300. Personal E-mail: billbegell@aol.com. Business E-Mail: bill@begellhouse.com.

BEGGS, HARRY MARK, lawyer; b. LA, Nov. 15, 1941; s. John Edgar and Agnes (Kentro) B.; m. Sandra Lynne Mikal, May 25, 1963; children: Brendan, Sean, Corey, Michael. Student, Ariz. State U., 1959-61, Phoenix Coll., 1961; LLB, U. Ariz., 1964. Bar: Ariz. 1964, US Dist. Ct. Ariz. 1964, US Ct. Appeals (9th cir.) 1973, US Ct. Appeals (fed. cir.) 1995, US Supreme Ct. 1991. Assoc. Carson Messinger Elliott Laughlin & Ragan, Phoenix, 1964-69, ptnr., 1969-93; mem. Carson Messinger Elliott Laughlin & Ragan, P.L.L.C., 1994—2006, of counsel, 2007. Mem. editl. bd. Ariz. Law Rev. 1963-64; contbr. articles profl. jours. Abner S. Lipscomb scholar U. Ariz. Law Sch., 1963.; Fegtly Moot Ct. award, 1963, 64; recipient award highest grade state bar exam. State Bar Ariz., 1964; named to Martindale Hubbell Register Preeminent Lawyers, 2006. Fellow Ariz. Bar Found. (founder); mem. State Bar Ariz., Ariz. Acad., Maricopa County Bar Assn. Office: PO Box 33907 Phoenix AZ 85067-3907 Office Phone: 602-264-2261. Business E-Mail: hbeggs@carsonlawfirm.com.

BEGGS, WILLIAM H., microbiologist, researcher; b. Ft. Dodge, Iowa, Feb. 19, 1935; s. Harold William and Bliss Jewel (Swanstrom) Beggs; m. Nancy Florence Ost, Sept. 14, 1957 (dec. June 1995); children: John W., Margaret B. BA, U. Minn., 1956; PhD, U. Cin., 1964. Rsch. microbiologist Dept. Vets. Affairs Med. Ctr., Mpls., 1965—. Bd. dirs. Minn. Vets. Rsch. Inst., Mpls. Contbr. articles to profl. jours. and conf. procs. 1st lt. US Army, 1956—58, Tex., Kans., La. Mem.: Am. Soc. Microbiology. Achievements include research in chemical properties, biological activities, modes of action and chemotherapeutic potentials of antituberculosis and antifungal drugs. Avocations: tennis, travel, hiking, music.

BEGHE, RENATO, federal judge; b. Chgo., Mar. 12, 1933; s. Bruno and Emmavve (Frymire) B.; m. Bina House, July 10, 1954; children: Eliza Ashley, Francesca Forbes, Adam House, Jason Deneen. BA, U. Chgo., 1951, JD, 1954. Bar: NY 1955. Practiced in, NYC; assoc. Carter, Ledyard & Milburn, 1954-65, ptnr., 1965-83, Morgan, Lewis & Bockius, 1983-89; judge US Tax Ct., Washington, 1991—2003, sr. judge, 2003—. Lectr. NYU Fed. Tax Inst., 1967, 78, U. Chgo. Fed. Tax Conf., 1974, 80, 86, also other profl. confs. Mng. editor U. Chgo. Law Rev., 1953-54; contbr. articles to profl. jours. Mem. ABA, Internat. Bar Assn., NY State Bar Assn. (chmn. tax sect. 1977-78), Assn. of Bar of City of NY (chmn. art law com. 1980-83), Am. Law Inst., Internat. Fiscal Assn., Am. Coll. Tax Counsel, Am.-Italy Soc. Inc. (bd. dirs. 1980-92), Phi Beta Kappa, Order of Coif, Phi Gamma Delta. Office: US Tax Ct 400 2nd St NW Washington DC 20217-0002 Office Phone: 202-521-0638. Business E-Mail: jbeghe@ustaxcourt.gov.

BEGISHEV, ILDAR, electronics engineer; b. Tashkent, Uzbekistan, Sept. 5, 1959; arrived in US, 2000; s. Akhmed Begishev and Asia Khasanova; m. Adelya Begishev, Sept. 2, 1989; children: Ilmar, Erick. MA with highest honors, Poly. Inst., Tashkent, 1981; PhD in Physics and Math., Inst. Electronics Acad. Scis., Tashkent, 1991. Engr. Inst. Electronics, Tashkent, 1980—88, scientist, 1988—91, sr. scientist, 1991—99; scientist Max Born Inst., Berlin, 1999—2001, U. Rochester, NY, 2001. Contbr. articles to profl. jours. Grantee, Am. Phys. Soc., 1993, Internat. Sci. Found., 1994, 1995. Mem.: Optical Soc. Am. Office: U Rochester Lab Laser Energetics 250 E River Rd Rochester NY 14623

BEGLEITER, MARTIN DAVID, law educator, consultant; b. Middletown, Conn., Oct. 31, 1945; s. Walter and Anne Begleiter; m. Ronni Ann Frankel, Aug. 17, 1969; children: Wendy Cara, Hilary Ann. BA, U. Rochester, 1967; JD, Cornell U., 1970. Bar: NY 1970, US Dist. Ct. (ea. dist.) NY 1971, US Ct. Appeals (2d cir.) 1975. Assoc. Kelley Drye & Warren, NYC, 1970—77; assoc. prof. Law Sch., Drake U., Des Moines, 1977—80, prof., 1980—87, 1993—2005, Richard M. and Anita Calkins disting. prof. law, 1987—93, Ellis and Nelle Levitt Disting prof. law, 2005—. Author (with Scoles, Halbach and Roberts): Problems and Materials on Decedents' Estates and Trusts, 7th edit., 2006; contbr. articles to legal jours. Fellow Am. Coll. Trust and Estate Counsel (academic fellow 2005-); mem. ABA (com. on estate and gift taxes, taxation sect. 1980—, com. malpractice, real property, probate and trust law sect. 1999—, com. on tax legislation and regulations, lifetime transfers, real property, probate and trust law sect. 1980-02, study com. law reform 1996-02, chmn. task force on spl. use valuation 1988-93, advisor Nat. Conf. Commns. on Uniform State Laws 1988-93), Iowa Bar Assn. (adviser, resource person, probate, trust sect. 1983-89, 93—), Am. Law Inst. (adviser restatement 3d trusts 1994—). Jewish. Avocations: science fiction, golf. Office: Drake U Sch Law 2507 University Ave Des Moines IA 50311 Home Phone: 515-225-3807; Office Phone: 515-271-2062. Business E-Mail: martin.begleiter@drake.edu.

BEGLEY, CHARLENE, manufacturing executive; b. Oct. 30, 1966; married; 3 children. BS in Bus. Adminstrn. magna cum laude, U. Vt., 1988. With transp. sys. GE, 1988—90, corp. audit staff, 1990—94, v.p. ops. capital mortgage svc., 1994—97, CFO transp., 1997, dir. fin. plastics, 1998—99, v.p. corp. audit staff, 1999—2001, pres., CEO transp. sys., 2001, pres., CEO GE Plastics, 2004—07, pres., CEO GE Enterprise SOlutions, 2007—. Named one of 50 Most Powerful Women in Business, Fortune mag., 2006, 50 Most Powerful Women in Bus., 2006, 50 Women to Watch, Wall St. Jour., 2006. Office: GE Plastics 1 Plastics Ave Pittsfield MA 01201 Office Phone: 413-448-7110.*

BEGLEY, CHRISTOPHER B., pharmaceutical executive; b. Chgo., Apr. 13, 1952; married; 3 children. BBA, Western Ill. U.; MBA, No. Ill. U. V.p. mktg. V. Mueller Divsn., Am. Hosp. Supply Corp.; various positions Abbott Labs., Abbott Park, Ill., 1986—90, divisional v.p., gen. mgr. hosp. products bus. sector, 1990—93, v.p. hosp. products bus. sector, 1993—96, v.p. MediSense, Inc., 1996—98, v.p. Abbott HealthSystems, 1998—99, sr. v.p. chem. and agrl. products, 1999—2000, pres. hospital products div., 2000—04; CEO Hospira Inc. (spin-off from Abbott Labs.), Lake Forest, Ill., 2004—; chmn., CEO Hospira Inc., Lake Forest, Ill., 2007—. Bd. dir. Children's Meml. Hosp., Chgo.; mem. Healthcare Leadership Council, AdvaMed; mem. civic com. Comml. Club Found. Mem.: Econ. Club Chgo., Executives Club Chgo. Office: Hospira Inc 275 North Field Dr Lake Forest IL 60045*

BEGLEY, ED, JR., actor; b. Hollywood, Calif., Sept. 16, 1949; s. Edward James and Allene Jeanne Begley; m. Ingrid Margaret Taylor, Oct. 31, 1976 (div. Oct. 1989); m. Rachelle Carson-Begley, Aug. 23, 2000; children: Amanda, Nicholas, Hayden. Student, Los Angeles Valley Coll. Actor (theatre) Love Letters, The Cryptogram, The Old Neighborhood, (films) including Showdown, 1973, Citizen's Band, Stay Hungry, 1976, Blue Collar, 1978, Goin' South, 1978, The In-Laws, 1979, The One and Only, Airport 79, 1979, TPrivate Lessons, 1981, Buddy Buddy, 1981, Cat People, 1982, Protocol, 1984, Transylvania 6-5000, 1985, The Accidental Tourist, 1988, Scenes from The Class Struggle in Beverly Hills, 1989, She Devil, 1989, Meet The Applegates, 1991, Dark Horse, 1992, Mastergate, 1992, Page Master, 1994, Even Cowgirls get the Blues, 1993, Cooperstown, 1993, Sensations, Renaissance Man, Greedy, 1994, Renaissance Man, 1994, Batman Forever, 1995, Santa With Muscles, 1996, Lay of the Land, 1997, Ms. Bear, 1997, Joey, 1997, I'm Losing You, 1998, Addams Family Reunion, 1998, Best in Show, 2000, Anthrax, 2001, Bug, 2002, Ragged Point, A Mighty Wind, 2003, Going Down, 2003, The Trailer, 2003, Stateside, 2004, Raising Genius, 2004, The First Person, 2004, (voice) Hair High, 2004, Alone in a Crowd, 2005, Desolation Sound, 2005, Welcome to California, 2005, Relative Strangers, 2006, Tripping Forward, 2006, For Your Consideration, 2006, others; (TV films) A Shining Season, Elvis, Amateur Night at the Dixie, Dead of Night, Rascals & Robbers, Hot Rod, An American Love Affair, Spies, Lies and Naked Thighs, The Incredible Ida Early, Roman Holiday, Home, In the Best Interest of the Child, Not a Penny More, Not a Penny Less, 1990, A Change of Heart, Story Lady, Stand Off At Marion, Exclusive, World War II: When the Lions Roared, Jacks, The Late Shift, Alone, Not in This Town, Murder She Purred: A Mrs. Murphy Mystery, 1998, Homicide: The Movie, 2000, Hounded, 2001, War Stories, 2003, Life on Liberty Street, 2004, True, 2005, Spirit Bear: The Simon Jackson Story, 2005; (TV series) Tale of Two Freedoms, The Practice, Mary Hartman, Mary Hartman, Battlestar Galactica, Roll Out, Room 222, St. Elsewhere, Parenthood, Winnetka Road, Todays Environment, Meego, Maggie Day, Meego, 7th Heaven, 1999—2003, The Web, Six Feet Under, 2001, Providence, 2000, Wednesday 9:30 (8:30 Central), 2002, Veronica Mars, 2006; also numerous TV commls., night club performances; dir. Enemies of Laughter, 1999; TV guest appearances include Quincy, The Love Boat, Touched by an Angel, 3rd Rock from the Sun, Star Trek: Voyager, Sabrina, The Teenage Witch, The Drew Carey Show, Ellen, The Simpsons, The Agency Titus, others. Chmn. Santa Monica Mountains Conservancy; commr. environ. affairs, L.A. Mem.: Acad. Motion Picture Arts and Scis. Democrat. Roman Catholic. Avocations: carpentry, organic gardening, environmental concerns. Office: Sterling Winters Co 10900 Wilshire Blvd Ste 1550 Los Angeles CA 90024-6525*

BEGLEY, HEIDI MARIE, nurse, entrepreneur; d. Donald Joseph Stubblefield and Shirley Ann Miller, adopted d. Henry Miller; m. Paul Wyatt Begley, Aug. 21, 1982; children: Brock Paul, Bart Charles, Paul Andrew. ASN, Purdue U. North Ctrl., Westville, Ind, 1989. RN Ind., Ky. Dir. nursing Tioga Pines, Monticello, Ind., 1991—95; asst. dir. nursing Our Lady of Holy Cross, San Pierre, Ind., 1995—98, 2006—; charge nurse pediat. psychology Caritas Peace, Lousiville, 2000—03; staff nurse Bapt. Hosp. East, Louisville, 2003—05. Legal nurse cons. Begley Exec. Svcs. and Tng., Shelbyville, Ky., 2005—. Mem. Orissa Project Inc., Kokomo, Ind., 1997—2006. Mem.: Am. Mensa (assoc.; editor newsletter Kentuckiana group), Alpha Lambda Delta. Baptist. Avocations: writing, missions, travel. Home: 509 S Main St Wanatah IN 46390 Office: Our Lady of Holy Cross 7520 S Hwy 421 San Pierre IN 46374 Home Phone: 219-733-2965; Office Phone: 219-828-4111. Personal E-mail: heidibegley@aol.com.

BEGLEY, LOUIS, writer, lawyer; b. Stryj, Poland, Oct. 6, 1933; came to U.S., 1948, naturalized, 1953; s. Edward David Begley and Frances Hauser; m. Sally Higginson, Feb. 11, 1956 (div. May 1970); children: Peter Higginson, Amey B. Larmore, Adam C.; m. Anne Muhlstein Dujarric de la Riviere, Mar. 30, 1974. AB summa cum laude, Harvard U., 1954, LLB magna cum laude, 1959. Bar: N.Y. 1961. Assoc. Debevoise & Plimpton, NYC, 1959-67, ptnr., 1968—2003, of counsel, 2004—06. Author: Wartime Lies, 1991, The Man Who Was Late, 1993, As Max Saw It, 1994, About Schmidt, 1996, Mistler's Exit, 1998, Schmidt Delivered, 2000, Das Gelobte Land, 2001, Shipwreck, 2003, Matters of Honor, 2007; author: (with Anka Muhlstein) Venedig unter vier Augen, 2003; contbr. articles and revs. to newspapers and periodicals. With U.S. Army, 1954-56. Recipient Irish Times-Aer Lingus Internat. Fiction Prize, 1991, PEN/Hemingway Found. award, 1992, Prix Medicis Etranger, 1992, Harold U. Ribalow prize, 1992, award in Lit., Am. Acad. Arts and Letters, 1995, Jeanette Schocken prize, 1995, Konrad-Adenauer-Stiftung Literaturpreis, 2000, Chevalier de l'Ordre des Arts et Lettres. Mem. Am. Philos. Soc., PEN Am. Ctr. (pres. 1993-95, trustee 1995-2001), Century Assn. Democrat. Office: Debevoise & Plimpton 919 3rd Ave 46th Fl New York NY 10022-3904 Office Phone: 212-909-6273.

BEGUM, KHURSHIDA, zoologist, researcher; b. Cox's Bazar, Bangladesh, Apr. 17, 1967; arrived in US, 2003; d. Sikander Sawdagar and Altaj Begum; m. Muhammad Jahangir Alam, May 7, 1993; children: Ananna Anu, Apurba Apu. BSc with honors, U. Dhaka, Bangladesh, 1990, MSc, 1992; PhD, Okayama U., Japan, 2003. Lectr. zoology Rajuk Uttara Model Coll., Dhaka, Bangladesh, 1995—98; postdoctoral rschr. Kans. State U., Manhattan, 2003—. Rschr. Okayama U., Japan, 1998—2000. Contbr. articles to profl. jours. Yoneyama Meml. Found. fellowship, Rotary Club, Japan, 2001—03. Mem.: Entomol. Soc. Am. Office: Kansas State Univ 123 Waters Hall Entomology Manhattan KS 66506 Home Phone: 415-578-5270. Business E-Mail: begumk@ksu.edu.

BEHAN, KATHLEEN A. (KITTY BEHAN), lawyer; b. Milw., July 28, 1963; BA magna cum laude, Yale U., 1985; JD, Columbia U., 1989. Bar: Md. 1989, DC 1991. Staff counsel Nat. Security Project ACLU, 1989—90; assoc. Arnold & Porter LLP, Washington, 1990—96, ptnr., 1996—, co-chair pro bono com. Bd. dirs. probono.net, So. Ctr. for Human Rights, Atlanta, Am. Assn. People with Disabilities; bd. trustees Metrostage, Alexandria, Va.; bd. advisors Tahirih Justice Ctr., Falls Church, Va. Named one of Washington's Top 40 Lawyer's Under 40, Washingtonian Mag., 1998, The Top 50 Women Litigators, Nat. Law Jour., 2001, The Top 40 Litigators Under 40. Mem.: Women's Bar Assn. DC (bd. dirs.). Office: Arnold & Porter LLP 555 12th St NW Washington DC 20004-1206 Office Phone: 202-942-5533. Office Fax: 202-942-5999.

BEHAR, KEVIN L., neuroscientist; s. Richard C. and Lea J. Behar; m. Barbara I. Gulanski. BS, U. Iowa, 1979; MPhil, Yale U., New Haven, 1983, PhD, 1985. Assoc. rsch. scientist dept. of molecular biophysics and biochemistry Yale U., New Haven, 1986—88, asst. prof. dept. neurology, 1989—94; rsch. scientist dept. neurology Yale U. Sch. of Medicine, 1994—2001, rsch. scientist dept. psychiatry, 2001—06, assoc. prof. dept. psychiatry, 2006—. Dir. neurometabolism rsch. lab., magnetic resonance rsch. ctr. Yale U. Sch. of Medicine, New Haven, 1998—; dir. MRS/MRI core Yale/NIDDK Mouse Metabolic Phenotyping Ctr., 2001—05. Grantee Prin. Investigator, NIH, 1989—94, Prin. Investigator of Project of Program Project, 1994—2004, Prin. Investigator, 1996—2006, Prin. Investigator of MRS/MRI Core Resource within the Ctr., 2001—05, Prin. Investigator, 2005—, Young Investigator award, Nat. Alliance for Rsch. in Schizophrenia and Depression, 2001—03. Mem.: Yale Aviation, Am. Soc. Neurochemistry, Internat. Soc. for Neurochemistry, Soc. for Neuroscience. Achievements include development and application of in vivo proton and carbon-13 nuclear magnetic resonance spectroscopy to studies of brain metabolism. Office: Yale Univ Sch of Medicine PO Box 208043 New Haven CT 06510 Home Phone: 203-481-4714; Office Phone: 203-737-4121. Office Fax: 203-785-6643. Business E-Mail: kevin.behar@yale.edu.

BÉHAR, YVES, industrial designer; b. 1967; Studied indsl. design in Europe and US; BS in Indsl. Design, Art Ctr. Coll. Design. Design leader frogdesign, Calif., Lunar Design, Calif.; design prin., founder fuseproject, San Francisco, 1999—. Designer with team Footprints, Birkenstock Shoes, Jawbone, Aliph, (signature collection of lifestyle products) MINI_motion name,MINI, designer with team for Herman Miller, Nike, Microsoft, Hussein Chalayan, Toshiba, haasprojekt, Hewlett Packard, PUIG, and Philou, work can be found in permanent collections San Francisco Mus. Modern Art, Munich Mus. of Applied Arts, Cooper-Hewitt Nat. Design Mus., NY, Chgo. Athenaeum Mus., designer (one-man shows) San Francisco Mus. Modern Art, Musée de design et d'arts appliqués contemporains in Lausanne; author: Yves Béhar+fuseproject: Concept/Commerce:Commerce/Concept. Nominee Rave award for Technology, WIRED, 2005; recipient Nat. Design award for Product Design. Mem.: Indsl. Design Soc. Am. Office: Fuse Project Inc 528 Folsom St San Francisco CA 94105-3102 Office Phone: 415-908-1493 est. 11. Business E-Mail: yves@fuseproject.com.*

BEHLING, CHARLES FREDERICK, psychologist, educator; b. St. George, SC, Sept. 8, 1940; s. John Henry and Floy (Owings) B.; m. Jennifer Crocker; children: John Charles, Andrew Crocker. BA, U. S.C., 1962, MA, 1964, Vanderbilt U., 1966, PhD, 1969. Asst. dean of students U. S.C., Columbia, 1962-63; asst. state news editor The State Newspaper, Columbia, 1963-64; asst. prof. psychology Lake Forest (Ill.) Coll., 1968-74; assoc. prof. Lake Forest Coll., 1974-88, chmn. dept., 1977-84; pvt. practice psychotherapy Lake Bluff, Ill., 1970-88, Buffalo, 1988-95; clin. assoc. prof. SUNY, Buffalo, 1988-95; dir. of undergraduate studies, 1989-95; adj. prof. U. Mich., Ann Arbor, 1995—; dir. intergroup rels., conflict and cmty., 1995—. Contbr. articles to profl. jours. Bd. dirs. Nat. Abortion Rights Action League, Planned Parenthood; mem. long-range planning com. Lake Bluff Bd. Edn. Named Outstanding Prof., Underground Guide to Colls., 1971, Birnbaum Guide, 1992, Outstanding Tchr., Lake Forest Coll., 1981, SUNY, Buffalo, 1991; NASA fellow. Mem. Am. Psychol. Assn., Soc. Psychol. Study of Social Issues, Assn. Humanistic Psychology, AAUP, Univ. S.C. Alumni Assn., Psi Chi, Sigma Delta Chi. Democrat. Office: U Mich Dept Psychology Ann Arbor MI 48109 Address: 1325 Wynnstone Dr Ann Arbor MI 48105-2894 Office Phone: 734-936-1875. E-mail: cbehling@umich.edu.

BEHLING, PAUL LAWRENCE, lawyer, educator; b. Washington, Feb. 15, 1948; s. John Lawrence Behling and Elizabeth (Freer) Nicholson; m. Cristina Grande, Jan. 13, 1979; children: Cassandra, Catrina, Jonathan. BS cum laude, U. Hartford, 1970; JD with high honors, U. Conn., 1973; LLM in Taxation, NYU, 1974. Bar: Conn. 1973, NY, 2003, US Dist. Ct. (dist. Conn.) 1974, US Tax Ct. 1974, US Ct. Appeals (2nd cir.) 1974, DC 1980, US Supreme Ct. 1980. Assoc. Solomon & Brown, Meriden, Conn., 1974-75, Copelon, Schiff & Zangari, New Haven, 1975-78, ptnr., 1978-86; ptnr. Siegel, O'Connor & Schiff, 1987-88, Wiggin & Dana, New Haven, Conn. 1988-95; prin. Bergman, Horowitz & Reynolds, P.C., 1995-2001, Withers Bergman, 2001-; adj. prof. law Quinnipiac Coll., 1982—, U. New Haven, 1982—. Named one of Top 100 Attys., Worth mag., 2005-06. Author: Taxation of Real Estate, 1984, Taxation of 401(K) and Other Salary Reduction Plans, 1994; contbr. articles to profl. publs. Served to sgt. US Army, 1965-67. Mem. ABA (chmn. sect. taxation closely held corp. 1982-85), Conn. Bar Assn. (chmn. tax sect. 1981-85). Democrat. Roman Catholic. Club: New Haven Lawn. Lodge: Kiwanis (v.p. New Haven 1978-81). Home: 1670 Hartford Turnpike North Haven CT 06473-1247 Office: Withers Bergman 157 Church St 19th Fl New Haven CT 06510-2100 Office Phone: 203-974-0392. E-mail: paul.behling@withers.us.com.*

BEHLKE, MARK AARON, biotechnologist, research scientist; s. Frank and Eleanor Behlke; m. Janet Lynn Waite, Feb. 14, 2003. BS, MIT, Cambridge, Mass., 1981; PhD, MD, Wash. U., St. Louis, Mo., 1988. Resident physician Brigham & Women's Hosp., Boston, 1988—90, endocrinology fellow, 1990—93; postdoctoral fellow Whitehead Inst. Biomedical Rsch., Cambridge, Md., 1991—94; rsch. dir. Integrated DNA Techs., Coralville, Iowa, 1995—96, v.p. molecular genetics & biophysics, 1995—. Bd. dirs. Carver Ctr. Comparative Genomics, U. Iowa, Iowa City, 2002—06. Mem. editl. bd.: Jour. RNAi and Gene Silencing, 2005—; contbr. articles to profl. jours. Bus. rep. seat, bd. dirs. MECCA, Iowa City, 2003—06. Fellow, Whitehead Inst. Biomedical Rsch., Cambridge, 1991—94, Howard Hughes Med. Inst., 1992—94; scholar, Nat. Merit Scholar Corp., 1977. Mem.: Oligonucleotide Therapeutics Soc. Achievements include patents in field. Office: Integrated DNA Technologies 1710 Commercial Pk Coralville IA 52241 Home Phone: 319-354-0264; Office Phone: 319-626-8432. Office Fax: 319-626-9621. Business E-Mail: mbehlke@idtdna.com.

BEHLMAR, CINDY LEE, medical association administrator, management consultant; b. Smyrna, Tenn., July 4, 1959; d. James Wallace and Barbara Ann (Behlmar) Gribble. BBA, Coll. William and Mary, 1981; MBA, Old Dominion U., 1995. Cert. mgmt. acct.; gen. mediator. Adminstrv. extern Hampton Gen. Hosp., Va., 1981-82; from mktg. rep. to supr. mktg. svcs. PruCare of Richmond, Va., 1983-85; exec. dir. PhysicianCare, Inc., Newport News, Va., 1986-89; provider rels. cons. Va. Health Network, Richmond, 1989-91; ind. cons. Tidewater Health Care, Virginia Beach, Va., 1991-92; COO Tidewater Phys. Therapy, Inc., Newport News, 1993-95; ind. cons. Yorktown, Va., 1996-97; contract mgr. Sentara Health Mgmt., Virginia Beach, 1998-99; state mgr. managed care Va. Oncology Assocs., 1999—2004; adminstr. Peninsula Emergency Physicians, Inc., 2004—. Sec., bd. dirs. Greater Peninsula Area Med.-Bus. Coalition, Newport News, 1987-89; symposium faculty mem. Am. Hosp. Assn., Orlando, Fla., 1987, Washington, 1988; profl. spkr. in field. Mem. ch. coun. St. Mark Luth. Ch., Yorktown, Va., 1988-91. Fin. Exec. Inst. scholar, 1993. Mem. Inst. Mgmt. Accts., Toastmasters Internat. (club pres. 1997-98, area gov. 1998-99, Club Toastmaster of Yr. 1997-98, Dist. Spirit Success award 1998, Dist. Area Gov. of Yr. 1998-99, Disting. Toastmaster 1999), Phi Kappa Phi, Beta Gamma Sigma. Avocations: reading, art, fashion, music, piano. Home: 922 Hanson Dr Newport News VA 23602-8910 Office: Peninsula Emergency Physicians Inc Ste E 11828 Canon Blvd Newport News VA 23606-4250 Office Phone: 757-599-4922.

BEHLMER, RUDY H., JR., retired director, writer, film educator, scriptwriter; b. San Francisco, Oct. 13, 1926; s. Rudy H. and Helen Mae (McDonough) B.; 1 child by previous marriage, Curt; m. Stacey Endres, Oct. 1992. Student, Pasadena Playhouse Coll., 1946-49, Los Angeles City Coll., 1949-50. Dir. Sta. KLAC-TV, Hollywood, Calif., 1952—56; network TV dir. ABC-TV, Hollywood, 1956—57; TV comml. prodr.-dir., exec. Grant Advt., Hollywood, 1957—60; exec. prodr.-dir. KCOP-TV, Hollywood, 1960—63; v.p., TV comml. prodr.-dir. Leo Burnett USA, Hollywood, 1963—84; lectr. film Art Ctr. Coll. of Design, Pasadena, Calif., 1967—92, Calif. State U., Northridge, 1984—92, UCLA, 1988. Author: Memo from David O. Selznick, 1972, (with Tony Thomas) Hollywood's Hollywood, 1975, America's Favorite Movies-Behind the Scenes, 1982, Inside Warner Bros., 1985, Behind the Scenes: The Making of., 1990, Memo From Darryl F. Zanuck, 1993, W.S. Van Dyke's Journal-White Shadows in the South Seas, 1996, Henry Hathaway (a Directors Guild of Am. Oral History), 2001; co-author: The Films of Errol Flynn, 1969; text on Warner Bros. Fifty Years of Film Music, 1973; editor: The Adventures of Robin Hood, 1979, The Sea Hawk, 1982 (Wis./Warner Bros. screenplay series), Warner Bros. 75 Years of Film Music, 1998; contbr. articles on film history, booklets for film music CDs; writer, narrator and on camera participant for DVDs, laserdiscs, and video documentaries. Served with AC, USNR, 1944-46. Mem. Dirs. Guild Am.

BEHM, DUTSI, physician; b. Uzhgorod, Ukraine, Aug. 2, 1948; came to U.S., 1978; d. Aron and Rose Akerman; m. Ernest Behm, Aug. 20, 1972; 1 child, Thomas. MD with honors, Uzhgorod State U., 1973. Resident in medicine N.Y. Meth. Hosp., Bklyn., 1980-83; physician in pvt. practice, Bklyn., 1983—. Mem. ACP. Jewish. Avocation: music (opera). Home: 2364 E 66th St Brooklyn NY 11234-6326

BEHM, MARK EDWARD, academic administrator, consultant; b. Balt., Apr. 21, 1945; s. Carl and Margaret Anderson (Weichman) Behm; m. Linda Ann Walker, Oct. 9, 1976; children: Scott Anderson, Craig Redgwick. BS, U. Md., 1967; MBA, Loyola Coll., Balt., 1980. Co-owner Applied Light Tech. Co., Silver Spring, Md., 1968-69; product area adminstr. Singer Co., Link Div., Silver Spring, Md., 1969-73; asst. comptroller U. Md. Balt. County, 1973—75, dir. fin. planning, 1976—85, dir. planning and budget, 1986—88, v.p. for adminstrv. affairs, 1988—2005; interim v.p. adminstrn. Ann Arundel C.C., 2005—. Chmn. bd. dirs. UMBC Tng. Ctrs., LLC. Bd. dirs. Grant-a-Wish Found., Balt., 1979-87, BWI Partnership. Mem.: Assn. Univ. Rsch. Parks, Ea. Assn. Coll. and Univ. Bus. Officers (bd. dirs.). Home: 8983 Glebe Creek Rd Easton MD 21601 Office Phone: 443-552-0260. Personal E-mail: behm.mark@gmail.com.

BEHN, MARK DIETRICH, marine geophysicist, educator; s. Robert Dietrich and Judith Howe Behn; m. Elizabeth Belle Kujawinski, Oct. 29, 1972; 1 child, Alexander Dietrich. PhD, Mass. Inst. Tech., Woods Hole Ocean. Inst. Joint Program, Cambridge, Mass., 1996—2002. Postdoctoral rsch. fellow Carnegie Instn., Washington, 2002—; asst. scientist Woods Hole Oceanog. Instn., Woods Hole, 2004—06. Contbr. papers to profl. jours. and pubs. Grantee, NSF, 2003—05. Mem.: Am. Geophys. Union (Student Presentation award 2000). Republican. Home: Woods Hole MA 02543 Office: Woods Hole Oceanog Inst 360 Woods Hole Rd - MS 22 Woods Hole MA 02543 Home Fax: (508) 539-8725. Personal E-mail: behn@dtm.ciw.edu.

BEHNAVA, SHAHRIYAR, management consultant; b. Tehran, Iran, Sept. 5, 1954; s. Nasrollah Behnava and Gohar Mirfakhraee; m. Belinda Maree Bogsrud, Feb. 27, 1949; 1 child, Saman. Degree in Internat. Banking, City of London Poly., 1980; BA with hon. in Econ., London Guildhall U., 1979; MBA, Clayton U., 1986. Cert. mgmt. acctg., 1980. Mgmt. cons. Shadow Mgmt. cons., Portsmouth, England, 1984—87; CEO S & E Internat., Inc., Newport Beach, Calif., 1988—90, Irvine Analytical Lab., Irvine, Calif., 1988—91; mng. cons., dir. Blue Ocean Shipping Co., Ltd., Tehran, Iran, 1990—. Fellow: Chartered Mgmt. Inst.; mem.: Inst. of Mgmt. Cons. (assoc. mem. 1990), Amer. Acad. of Mgmt. (exec. mem. 1988). Achievements include design and construction of jetties for ro-ro vessels, Nowshahr ro-ro ramp, 1986, designed and engineered Pneumatic Grain Terminals, Caspian Sea Ports, 1998-2002. Office Phone: 9821 8875 8248. E-mail: sbehnava@blueoceanshipping.com.

BEHNEY, CLYDE JOSEPH, health policy researcher; b. Williamstown, Pa., May 19, 1946; s. Clyde J. Behney and Gladys Yvonne (Host) Williams; children: Lindsay, Fletcher, Taylor. BS, Lehigh U., 1968; MBA, U. Md., 1972; postgrad., George Washington U., 1975—82. Staff asst. US Dept. Health, Edn., & Welfare, Washington, 1972-74, mgmt. intern, 1974-77; analyst/project dir. Office Tech. Assessment US Congress, Washington, 1977-81, health program mgr. Office Tech. Assessment, 1981-93, asst. dir. Office Tech. Assessment, 1993-96; dir. divsn. health care svcs. Inst. Medicine, NAS, 1996-97, dep. dir., 1997—, interim exec. officer, 1998, acting dir. healthcare svcs. bd., 2005—06, 2006—07. Exec. dir. Sorcerer's Apprentice Network, Washington, 1981—85, 1998—; mem. steering com. Nat. Health Policy Forum, 1998—2000; mem. quality awards adv. bd. Health Improvement Inst., 1998—; adv. com. mem. George Washington Univ. Pub. Health Program, 1999—; mem. tech. adv. bd. Millbank Meml. Fund, NYC, 1998—2002; liaison mem., bd. dirs. Nat. Quality Forum, 2005—07. Co-author: Toward Rational Technology in Medicine, 1981; editor: (newsletter) The Sorcerer's Apprentice, 1981-85; mem. editl. bd. Internat. Jour. Tech. Assessment in Health Care, 1985-98; contbr. articles to profl. jours.; chpts. to books. Treas. Glebe Elem. PTA, Arlington, Va., 1990—94, Swanson Mid. Sch. PTSA, Arlington, 1994—96, Yorktown H.S. PTA, 2001—02, 2005—06. Sgt. US Army, 1969—71. Home: 2515 N Vermont St Arlington VA 22207-4125 Office: Inst Medicine 500 Fifth St NW Washington DC 20001 Business E-Mail: cbehney@nas.edu.

BEHNIA, ROYA, lawyer; b. Chgo., 1966; Grad., Harvard U., 1987; JD, U. of Chgo. Law Sch., 1991. Litigator Kirkland & Ellis, 1991—97, ptnr., 1997—98; dir. of litigation Brunswick Corp., 1998—2001; grp. gen. counsel SPX Corp., 2001—05; sr. v.p., gen. counsel, sec., and chief privacy officer Rewards Network, Inc. (IRN), 2006—. Avocations: gardening, cooking, hiking, architecture. Office: Rewards Network Inc 2 N Riverside Plz Ste 950 Chicago IL 60606 Office Phone: 800-438-9013.*

BEHNKE, MARYLOU, pediatrician, educator; b. Orlando, Fla., Sept. 1, 1950; d. Ernest Edmund and Elizabeth (Kolb) Behnke. BS in Chemistry, U. Fla., 1972, MD, 1976. Diplomate Am. Bd. Pediatrics, Am. Bd. Neonatology-Perinatology. Intern dept. pediat. Coll. Medicine U. Fla., Gainesville, 1976-77, resident, 1977-79, chief resident, 1979-80, fellow in neonatology, 1981-83, asst. prof., 1979-81, 83-89, assoc. prof., 1989-99, prof., 1999—, adj. asst. prof. Coll. Nursing, 1988-89, adj. assoc. prof., 1989-99, mem. senate-at-large, 1984-89, 2004—07, mem. grad. studies faculty, 1988-2000. Presenter nat. and internat. meetings, 1981—; med. dir. ICU Shands Hosp., Gainesville, 1983—89, neonatal devel. follow-up program, 1989—; ad hoc mem. spl. rev. com. human devel. rsch. NIH, 1991—96, chair, 1993, 94, mem. human devel. and aging-3 study sect., 1998—99; mem. BBBP-6 study sect., 1999—2002. Mem. editl. bd.: Death Studies, 1983—94; mem. editl. bd. Jour. Addiction Medicine, 2007—; contbr. chpts. to books, articles to profl. jours. Grantee, NIH, 1984—87, 1991—, Nat. Inst. Drug Abuse, 1991—, Ctr. Substance Abuse Treatment, 1993—95. Fellow: Am. Acad. Pediat. (sect. perinatal pediat. com. substance abuse); mem.: Am. Pediatric Soc., Fla. Soc. Neonatal Perinatologists, Fla. Interagency Coord. Coun. Infants and Toddlers, Soc. Pediatric Rsch., Nat. Perinatal Assn., Soc. Pediat. Rsch., Alachua County Med. Soc., Fla. Med. Assn. Republican. Mem. Ch. Of Christ. Avocation: reading. Home: 426 SW 40th St Gainesville FL 32607-2749 Office: J Hillis Miller Health Ctr Dept Pediatrics PO Box 100296 Gainesville FL 32610-0296 Office Phone: 352-392-4193. Business E-Mail: behnkem@peds.ufl.edu.

BEHNKE, MICHAEL CLARE, academic administrator; b. Grand Rapids, Mich., May 15, 1943; s. Clarence W. and Norma (Sessink) Behnke; m. Mary Vanleer Hancort; children: Matthew, Margaret; m. Lee Behnke. BA with honors, Amherst Coll., 1966; MA in Am. Civilization, U. Pa., 1971. Tchr. Northamdton Sch. for Girls, Mass., 1966-67; with Peace Corps US Govt., Sierra Leone, 1967-69; assoc. deam of admissions and dean of freshmen Amherst Coll., Mass., 1971-76; dean of admission Tufts U., Medford, Mass., 1976-85; dir. admission MIT, Cambridge, 1985—97; v.p., dean coll. enrollment U. Chgo., 1997—. Trustee Coll. Entrance Examination Bd.; cons. Overseas Schs. Project, US Dept. State, 1989—; higher edn. admissions rep. Nat. Edn. Goals Adv. Group on Standards. Contbr. articles to profl. jours. Mem.: Nat. Assn. Coll. Admissions Counselors (chair Adv. Com. on Enrollment Mgmt.). Democrat. Episcopalian. Avocations: music, reading, gardening, travel. Office: U Chgo 1101 E 58th St Chicago IL 60637 Office Phone: 773-702-8695. E-mail: mbehnke@uchicago.edu.*

BEHNKE, MICHELLE A., lawyer; b. 1961; BA, JD, U. Wis. Bar: Wis. 1988. Pvt. practice. Spkr. in field; mem. bd. attys. profl. responsibility, dist. 9 com., 1994—2002; mem. bd. visitors Wis. Law Alumni Assn., 1995—; treas. Equal Justice Coalition, 1997—98. Contbr. articles to profl. jours. Mem.: ABA, Legal Assn. Women, Dane County Bar Assn., State Bar Wis. (co-chair diversity outreach com. 1994—99, bd. dirs. practice mgmt. sect. 1998—2000, pres.-elect 2003—04, pres. 2004—05), Madison Breakfast Rotary Chpt., Rotary Internat. Office: Atty at Law Ste 1 222 N Midvale Blvd Madison WI 53705 Office Phone: 608-233-9024.

BEHNKEN, WILLIAM JOSEPH, artist, educator; b. NYC, Mar. 29, 1943; s. William Henry and Margaret Mary (Hoolan) Behnken. BA, CCNY, 1968, MA, 1995. Dir. art sch. Provincetown Art Assn. Mus., Mass., 1984-93; prof. art Bronx C.C., NY, 1973-83, CCNY, 1970—; instr. studio art Art Students League, NYC, 1998—; instr. printmaking Sch. Fine Arts Nat. Acad. Design, 2001—. Lectr. History of Landscape, Art Students League NY, 2006; lectr. in field. Artist print edits. lithographs, aquatints, mezzotints, commd. Albany NY Print Club, 2006; represented in permanent collections at Met. Mus. Art, NYC, Fitzwilliam Mus., Cambridge, Eng., Brit. Mus., NY Pub. Libr. Print Divsn., Bklyn. Mus., Bowdoin Coll. Mus., Indpls. Mus. Fine Arts, Mus. Nat. Acad. Design, Jane Voorhees Zimmerli, Mus. Rutgers U., Mus. City NY, New Orleans Mus. Recipient Louis Lozowick awards Audubon Artists Soc., NYC, 1991, 92, 1st Ann. Art Career Achievement award City Coll. Art Alumni Assn., 2004, Silver medal for graphics Audubon Artists Ann., 2005, Emile and Dines Carleson award Nat. Acad. Design, 2005. Mem. Soc. Am. Graphic Artists (pres. 1998-2002), NAD (graphics prize 1992, Ralph Fabri Graphics prize 2003, Silver medal for graphics 2005, instr. 2001—), Boston Printmakers, Phi Beta Kappa (pres. chpt. 2001). Democrat. Home: 3415 Fort Independence St Bronx NY 10463-4507

BEHR, KEN, religious organization administrator; m. Carol Behr; 2 children. With Ford Motor Co.; pres., CEO Ford Fin. Group, Mexico City; COO North Way Christian Cmty.; pres. Evang. Coun. for Fin. Accountability, Winchester, Va., 2006—. Adj. prof. bus. Fla. Atlantic U., Geneva Coll., Beaver Falls, Pa. Office: Evang Coun for Fin Accountability Ste 130 440 W Jubal Early Dr Winchester VA 22601 Office Phone: 540-535-0103.

BEHR, MARION RAY, artist; b. Rochester, NY, Sept. 12, 1939; d. Justin Max and Sophie Gusta (Koffler) Rosenfeld. B.Art Edn., Syracuse U., 1961, M.F.A., 1962; m. Omri Marc Behr, June 24, 1962; children: Dawn Marcy Yael, Darrin Justin Mason, Dana Marisa Jana. Curator, contbr. Internat. Electrotech Print Show World of Electrotech: N.J. Print Coun. Contbr. publs. for stories, crafts, mag. covers and toy designs to nat. mags. including McCall's, Good Housekeeping, Lady's Circle, 1962-77; one-woman shows include Douglas Coll., 1983, Pargot Gallery, 1989, Eldorado Gallery, 1992, Beamsderfer Gallery, 1992, Hunterdon Art Gallery, 1993; Hunterdon Mus. Art, 1998; Inst. Cultural Peruano Norteamericano, 1999, Johnson Gallery, 2002, Discover Jersy Arts (artist of the month 2005); creator MyLyne drawing blog; exhibited in group shows at Contemporary Am. Artists, Scarsdale, N.Y., 1964, Douglass Coll., 1977, John Szoke Gallery, 1989, Kanagawa Prefectual Gallery, Yokohama, Japan, 1989, 80 Washington Sq. East Gallery, N.Y.C., 1990, Juniper Gallery, Napa, Calif., 1991, Eldorado Gallery, Colorado Springs, Colo., 1992, B. Beamsderfer Gallery, Highland Park, N.J., 1992, Artsquad Gallery, Easton, 1993, Lever House, 1995, Audubon Artists, 1995, 97, 99, Cork Gallery, 1996, Cheltenham Ctr. for Arts, 1996, Krasdale Gallery, 1998, Nat. Acad. Mus., 1998, Stark & Stark, 1998, Grounds for Sculpture, 2001, Zimmerli Art Mus., Rutgers U., New Brunswick, 80th Fifth Ave Gallery, 2004, German Archtl. Ctr., Berlin, 2004, Hunteron Mus., 2005, Redbrick Gallery, Beverly, Mass., 2006, Ortho Gallery, Raritan, NJ, 2006; permanent print collection Smithsonian Instn. Nat. Mus. Art History, 1995, Jane Voorhees Zimmerli Art Mus., 1993, 96, 2002, 04, 05, Piero Gallery, 2004, Thai Royal Art Collection, Bangkok, 1995, Inst. Cultural Peruano Norteamericano, Peru, 1999, Bethanien Gallery, Berlin, 2004, World of Electrotech, N.J. Print Coun., 2005, Ben Shahn Galley, 2006, Redbrick Gallery, Beverly, Mass., 2006, Ben Shshn Gallery, 2006, Newark Pub. Libr., 2006; creator survey Women Working Home-the Invisible Workforce, 1978; pres. Women Working Home, Inc., Edison, N.J., 1980—; condr. workshops; author: (with others) Women Working Home: The Homebased Business Guide and Directory, 1981, 2nd edit., 1983; contbr. articles to popular mags., 1988-89, popular art jours., 1991-98, numerous articles to profl. jours.; illustrator Jewish Holiday Book, 1977; inventor (with Omri Behr) acid free, environmentally safe graphic etching process; installed Electrotech processor and taught first non toxic intaglio etching class at Stanford U., 1999; installed electroetch and established non-toxic etching in the Inuit Artists Holman Eskimo Co-op Art Center, Holman Island, NWT, Canada, 1999, U. Al Moutamid IBN Abbad, Asilah, Morocco, 2000, Howard U., Washington, Syracuse U., N.Y., 2001, U. Alaska, Juneau, U. Alaska, Fairbanks, 2001, Druckwerkstatt Bethanien, Berlin, 2001, Christchurch Poly. and UCOL, Wanganui, New Zealand, 2004; extensive radio and TV appearances rep. Nat. Alliance Homebased Businesswomen. Mem. Kean for Gov. campaign, 1981; mem. White House Conf. on Free Enterprise Zones, 1982, Nat. Assn. of Women Artists, 1992, Soc. Am. Graphic Artists, So. Graphics Coun., 1992, Print Coun. N.J., 1993; trustee Women's Bus. Ownership Ednl. Conf., Inc., N.J., 1985; apptd. to N.J. Devel. Authority for Small, Minority and Women's Bus. Commn., 1986; Presdl. del. White House Conf. on Small Bus., 1986. Recipient N.J. Women in Bus. Advocate of the Yr. award SBA, 1984, Merit award Am. Artist Profl. League, Woman of Yr. in Bus. and Industry award, 1985, Audubon Artists Merit award, 1995, Purchase award Am. Impressions Ben Shahn Gallery, William Patterson U., 2006; named Artist of Month (August) Discover Jersey Arts, 2005; Syracuse U. alumni grantee, 1957; Arts and Humanities grantee Charles E. Lindbergh Fund, 1993-94. Mem. Nat. Alliance Homebased Businesswomen (pres. 1980-82, legis. chair 1982-85; originator, founder), Women's Caucus for Art, Audoban Artists. Jewish. E-mail: electroetch@prodigy.net. *Father Justin Rosenfeld, born 1901 in Schopfloch, Bavaria. Studied law and economics, 1926, employed by bankers Wilhelm Vogt & CO., full responsibility for stories, casting, advertising, licensing, production and distribution of films for German speaking and foreign countries, film producer, president Orbis Film, Berlin.1936, very successfully produced film Razzia in St. Pauli and Mademoiselle Josette, Ma Femme. 1937, compelled by Nazi laws to cease operations completely. Fled to United States in 1938 with wife, Sophie Koffler Rosenfeld. Died in 1947 at 47. Mother- Sophie Koffler Rosenfeld Lustik-teacher and translator of fine languages lived to be 92.*

BEHR, OMRI M., lawyer; m. Marion Behr. BA in Chemistry with honors, Oxford U., 1956, BSc in Organic Chemistry, 1958, MA in Chemistry, 1960; PhD in Organic Chemistry, U. Glasgow, 1961; NIH postdoctoral fellow, Columbia U., 1960-61; LLB/JD, Seton Hall U., 1966. Bar: NJ 1967, NY 1968, US Dist. Ct. NJ 1967, US Patent and Trademark Office 1966, US Ct. Customs and Patent Appeals, 1977, US Supreme Ct. 1977; Chartered Chemist UK, European Chemist, Scientist U.K., 2004. Rsch. chemist U.S. Rubber Co., Inc., Wayne, NJ, 1961-63; patent trainee, agent, atty. Merck & Co., Rahway, NJ, 1963-67; assoc. Ostrolenk, Faber, Gerb & Soffen, NYC, 1967-68; ptnr. Lerner, David & Behr, Newark, 1968-69, Cifelli & Behr, Newark, 1969-72, Omri M. Behr, Newark, 1972-74, Behr & Woodbridge, Princeton, NJ, 1974-76, Omri M. Behr, Princeton, 1976-81, Behr & Adams, Edison, NJ, 1981—2000; counsel Selitto, Behr & Kim, Metuchen, NJ, 2000—03, The Behr Office, 2003—. Contbr. articles to profl. jours.; inventor (with Marion Behr) new acid free, environ. safe graphic etching process (patent of week N.Y. Times, May 2, 1992). Del. N.J. White House Confs Small Bus., 1986; moderator N.J. Gov. Conv. Small Bus., 1986; lectr. U.S. Dept. Energy Licensing Seminars, 1983-87; legis. co-chair, mem. nom. com. Nat. Assn. Homebased Bus.; mem. N.J. Small Bus. Devel. Adv. Bd., 1988—93; mem. Edison Twp. Rent Control Bd., 1984-94; committeeman Rep. County Middlesex County, N.J., 1989-94. Charles E. Lindbergh Fund: Arts and Humanities co-grantee, 1993-94. Fellow Royal Soc. Chemistry, Royal Inst. Chemistry (U.S. sect., hon sec. 1968-74); mem. ABA, N.J. Bar Assn., Middlesex County Bar Assn., Internat. Fedn. Counsels in Indsl. Property, Am. Indsl. Property Law Assn., Phi Lambda Upsilon. Office: 325 Pierson Ave Edison NJ 08837-3123 Home Phone: 908-595-1724; Office Phone: 732-603-6006. Personal E-mail: omrib@aol.com.

BEHRE, ROBERT FULLER, journalist; b. Somerville, NJ, Mar. 13, 1963; s. Merrill Clifford and Joan Butler Behre; m. Holly Hamor, Apr. 13, 1991; children: Dorothy Estelle, Henry Hamor, Joseph Butler. B English, Dartmouth Coll., Hanover, NH, 1985. Reporter Greenville Piedmont, SC, 1985—90; reporter, editor, columnist Post and Courier, Charleston, SC, 1990—. Adult leader Boy Scouts Am., Charleston, 1998—2007. Recipient Alliance award, SC chpt. AIA, 2001. Home: 29 Chapel St Charleston SC 29403 Office: Post and Courier 134 Columbus St Charleston SC 29403 Home Phone: 843-722-4825; Office Phone: 843-937-5771. Office Fax: 843-937-5579. Business E-Mail: rbehre@postandcourier.com.

BEHREN, ROBERT ALAN, lawyer, accountant; b. NYC, Dec. 29, 1929; s. Jeremiah E. and Sue (Windman) B.; m. Judith Sandra Morgan, Dec. 20, 1971. BBA, CUNY, 1951, MBA, 1956; JD, NYU, 1956, LLM, 1958. Bar: N.Y.; CPA, N.Y.; cert. flight instr.; lic. airline transport pilot. Prof. CUNY, NYC, 1957-72; pvt. practice NYC, 1958—; pub., CEO, founder Inst. Continuing Profl. Devel., NYC, 1967-87; CEO Behren Fin. Strategies, West Palm Beach, Fla., 1990—; ptnr. Behren & Cohen. Contbr. over 1000 articles to profl. mags., fin. pubs., newsletters. Pres. Musician's Emergency Fund, N.Y.C., 1991—. Maj., jet fighter pilot USAF, 1952-53. Recipient Master Pilot award FAA, numerous scholastic and profl. awards, scholarships and grants. Mem. Mil. Officers Am. Assn., U.S. Polo Assn., Mensa. Avocations: teaching aviation, skiing and sailing. Home: 2417 Golf Brook Dr Wellington FL 33414-7067 Office Phone: 203-557-4366. E-mail: rbehren@aol.com.

BEHREND, DONALD FRASER, academic administrator, educator; b. Manchester, Conn., Aug. 30, 1931; s. Sherwood Martin and Margaret (Fraser) B.; m. Joan Belcher, Nov. 9, 1957; children: Andrew Fraser, Eric Hemingway, David William. BS with honors and distinction, U. Conn., 1958, MS, 1960; PhD in Forest Zoology, SUNY, Syracuse, 1966. Forest game mgmt. specialist Ohio Dept. Natural Resources, Athens, 1960; res. asst. Coll. Forestry, SUNY, Newcomb, 1960-63, res. assoc., 1963-67; dir. Adirondack ecol. ctr. Coll. Environ. Science and Forestry, SUNY, Newcomb, 1968-73; acting dean grad. studies Syracuse, 1973-74; asst. v.p. research programs, exec. dir. Inst. Environ. Program Affairs, 1974-79; v.p. acad. affairs, prof., 1979-85; prof. emeritus, 1987—; asst. prof. wildlife mgmt. U. Maine, Orono, 1967-68; provost, v.p. acad. affairs U. Alaska Statewide System, Fairbanks, 1985-87, exec. v.p., provost, 1988; chancellor U. Alaska, Anchorage, 1988-94, chancellor emeritus, 1994—. Mem. patent policy bd. SUNY, 1983-85, chmn. Res. Found. com. acad. res. devel., 1984-85; chmn. 6-Yr. planning com. U. Alaska, 1985-86; bd. dirs. Commonwealth North, 1991-92, Alaska Internat. Ednl. Found., 1997; mem. selection com. Harry S. Truman Scholarship Found.; mem. Pres.'s Commn., NCAA, 1992-95; chmn. spl. com. on student athlete welfare access and equity, 1993-95; chmn. 20th Great Alaska Shootout, 1997. Contbr. numerous articles and papers to profl. jours. Mem. Newcomb Planning Bd., 1967-69; mem., pres. Bd. Edn. Newcomb Cent. Sch., 1967-73; chmn. governing bd. N.Y. Sea Grant Inst., 1984-85; trustee U. Ala. Found., 1990-94. Served with USN, 1950-54. Mem. Alaska Internat. Edn. Found. (bd. dirs. 1997—), Wildlife Soc., Soc. Am. Foresters, AAAS, Phi Kappa Phi (hon.), Sigma Xi, Gamma Sigma Delta, Sigma Lambda Alpha (hon.). Lodges: Rotary (bd. dirs. Fairbanks club 1985-86), Lions (bd. dirs. Newcomb club 1966-67). Avocations: reading, writing, photography, fly fishing, bagpiping. Home: 8 Wicklow Dr Skaneateles NY 13152

BEHRENDT, DAVID FROGNER, retired journalist; b. Stevens Point, Wis., May 25, 1935; s. Allen Charles and Vivian (Frogner) B.; m. Mary Ann Weber, Feb. 4, 1961 (dec. Sept 1998); children: Lynne, Liza, Sarah. BS, U. Wis., 1957, MS, 1960. Reporter Decatur (Ill.) Review, 1957-58; reporter Milw. Jour., 1960-70, copy editor, 1970-71, editorial writer, 1971-84, editorial page editor, 1984-95; Crossroads sect. editor Milw. Jour. Sentinel, 1995-98. Home: 1522 N Prospect Ave #1402 Milwaukee WI 53202

BEHRENDT, JOHN CHARLES, geophysicist, researcher, writer; b. Stevens Point, Wis., May 18, 1932; s. Allen Charles and Vivian Eulaine B.; m. Donna Ebben, Oct. 6, 1961 (div.); children: Kurt Allen, Marc Russell; m. Laura Backus, May 16, 2004. Student, Cen. State Coll., Stevens Point, 1950-52; BS in Physics, U. Wis., Madison, 1954, MS in Geology, 1956, PhD in Geophysics, 1961. Cert. geophysicist, Calif. Asst. seismologist Arctic Inst. N.Am., Ellsworth Sta., Antarctica, 1956-58; rsch. assoc. U. Wis., Madison, 1958-64; rsch. geophysicist U.S. Geol. Survey, Denver, 1964—68, Liberia, West Africa, 1968-70, Denver, 1970-72; chief br. of Atlantic-Gulf of Mex. marine geology Woods Hole, Mass., 1974-77; research geophysicist, Antarctic coordinator U.S. Geol. Survey, 1977-95, geophysicist emeritus, 1995—; fellow Inst. Arctic and Alpine Rsch U. Colo., Boulder, 1996—, rsch. scientist, 1996—. Frequent pub. spkr. on Antarctica and other rsch.; advisor U.S. Depts. State and Interior, Washington, 1977—; mem. U.S. del. to Antarctic Treaty Meetings, various countries, 1977-95, various working groups NAS-NRC; rsch. on Antarctic, earthquakes in ea. U.S., Rocky Mountain tectonics, Gt. Lakes geologic structure, Atlantic continental margin of N.Am. and West Africa. Author: Innocents on the Ice: A Memoir of Antarctic Exploration, 1957, 1998 (Colo. Book award for non-fiction 1999), The Ninth Circle: A Memoir of LIfe and Death in Antarctica, 1960-1962, 2005; contbr. more than 275 articles to profl. jours. Recipient Antarctic Svc. medal U.S. Dept. Def., 1966, Meritorious Svc. award Dept. Interior, 1992, Filice Ippolito Gold medal for Antarctic Rsch., Italian Antarctic Rsch. Program and Acad. Nazionale dei Linceia, 1999. Fellow: AAAS, Geol. Soc. Am., Explorers Club; mem.: Am. Polar Soc. (pres. 2006—), Soc. Exploration Geophysicists, Am. Geophys. Union. Avocations: photography, outdoor activities, music. Business E-Mail: behrendj@stripe.colorado.edu.

BEHRENS, BEREL LYN, physician, academic and health facility administrator; b. New South Wales, Australia, 1940; MB, BS, Sydney U., Australia, 1964. Diplomate Am. Bd. Pediatrics, Am. Bd. Allergy and Immunology. Intern Royal Prince Alfred Hosp., Australia, 1964; resident Loma Linda (Calif.) U. Med. Ctr., 1966-68, Henrietta Egleston Hosp. for Children, Atlanta, 1968—69, T.C. Thompson Children's Hosp., Chattanooga, 1969—70; faculty pediatrics Loma Linda U., 1970-72, with dept. pediatrics, 1972—, dean Sch. Medicine, 1986-91, pres., 1990—, Loma Linda U. Med. Ctr., 1999—; pres., CEO Loma Linda U. Adventist Health Scis. Ctr., 1997—. Office: 11175 Campus St Loma Linda CA 92354 E-mail: myhanna@ahs.llumc.edu.

BEHRENS, HENRY WILLIAM, international business educator, investment company executive; b. Scheessel, Germany, Aug. 4, 1935; came to U.S., 1955, naturalized, 1960; s. Claude William and Sophie Magdalena (Ellmers) B.; m. Eva Paeslack, June 12, 1960; children: Andrew M., Lawrence H. BS, Columbia U., 1961, MBA, 1962; PhD, New Sch. U., 1969. Economist Exxon Internat., NYC, 1962-65; vis. lectr. econs. Columbia U., NYC, 1965; asst. prof. econs. and fin. Fairleigh Dickinson U., Rutherford, NJ, 1965-68; assoc. prof. econs. and fin. Union Coll. and U., Schenectady, NY, 1968-72; pres. Algonquin Investors Corp., Niskayuna, NY, 1972-78; exec. dir. U.S.A.F.E.C., NYC, 1979-81; prof. world bus. Am. Grad. Sch. Internat. Bus., Phoenix, 1982-84; prof. fin. and internat. bus. Nat. U., San Diego, 1984-96; prin., CEO The McCormack Group, San Diego, 1985—, The Behrens Investment Group, 1994—. Author: The Effects of Monetary Policy on Commercial Banks, Thrift Institutions and the Residential Mortgage Market, 1968; Export Guide, 1985; author various rsch. reports. Mem. U.S. Senate Club, Am. Mgmt. Assns., Am. Fin. Assn., Am. Econ. Assn., Columbia U. Club (N.Y.C.), Alpha Kappa Psi. Office: PO Box 27708 San Diego CA 92198-1708 E-mail: hbehrens@san.rr.com.

BEHRENS, JAMES WILLIAM, physicist, administrator, author; b. Litchfield, Ill., Apr. 29, 1947; s. George William and Norma Clara Marie (Boeker) B.; m. Pamela Jane Breese, July 7, 1973 (div. Jan. 1980); 1 child, Jaime Rhea; m. Linda Sue Lawrence, July 5, 1984. BS in Engring. Physics, U. Ill., 1970; MS in Engring and Applied Sci., U. Calif., Davis, 1976, postgrad., 1976-78. Physicist Lawrence Livermore (Calif.) Nat. Lab., 1969-78, U.S. Dept. Commerce, Nat. Bur. Stas., Gaithersburg, Md., 1978-89; sci. tech. advisor Joint Chiefs of Staff, U.S. Dept. Def. Joint Staff, Washington, 1989-91; asst. exec. program mgr. Office Asst. Sec. Def. U.S. Dept. Def., Washington, 1991-92; sr. spl. projects mgr. U.S. Dept. Def., USN, Indian Head, Md., 1992-93; asst. dir. U.S. Dept. Def., Interagy. Tng. Ctr., Ft. Washington, Md., 1993-95; dep. dir. Interagy. Tng. Ctr. U.S. Dept. Def., Ft. Washington, Md., 1995-97; dir. U.S. Dept. Def. Ft. Washington Facility, 1997-99; sr. rsch. scientist, engr. U.S. Dept. Def., Naval Rsch. Lab., Washington, 1999—2000; sr. analyst Computer Sci. Corp., Alexandria, Va., 2004—06, BAI-Inc., Alexandria, 2006—. Tech. cons., pres. I.Q. in Nuc. Electronics Sys. & Tech., Inc., Rockville, Md., 1983-89; guest scientist Commissariat à l'Energie Atomique (CEA), Bruyere-le-Chatel, France, 1984. Author: Symbols and Fragments, 1993, Record of the House of Braunschweig-Illinois-Hannover, 1995, The 1995 Behrens Chronicle: A Complete Work, 1996, The 1995 Boeker Chronicle: A Complete Work, 1996, The 1996 Behrens-Boeker Chronicles: A Combined Work, 1997; co-editor: Fifty Years with Nuclear Fission, 1989; contbr. tech. articles to profl. pubs. Mem. Nat. Geneal. Soc., Nat. Writers Assn., Internat. Platform Assn., Nat. Audubon Soc., Nat. Wildlife Fedn., Am. Nuc. Soc. (cert. Appreciation 1989). Independent. Lutheran. Achievements include investigation of fast neutron-induced fission cross section measurements of the actinide elements, improvement of accuracy of neutron-induced fission cross section values which are used in broad areas of applied nuclear physics.

BEHRENS, JUNE ADELLE, writer; b. Maricopa, Calif., Apr. 25, 1925; d. Mark H. and Mattie Aline (Stafford) York; m. Henry William Behrens, Aug. 23, 1948; children: Terry Lynne, Denise Noel BA, U. Calif., Santa Barbara, 1947; MA Edn. Adminstrn., U. So. Calif., LA, 1961; postgrad., UCLA, 1964—65, postgrad., 1973—74. Tchr. Hermosa Beach City Schs., Calif., 1947—48, Torrance Schs., Calif., 1950—54, 1956—58, Am. Dep. Schs., France, Germany, 1954—56; tchr., adminstr., reading specialist L.A. City Schs., 1958—80; reading specialsit Carson Sch., Calif., 1968—74; with Park We. Pl. Sch., San Pedro, Calif., 1974—80; writer, 1962—. Author: Soo Ling Finds A Way, 1965, Who Am I?, 1968, Walk in Neighborhood, 1968, Earth is Home, 1971, Farm, 1971, Desert, 1973, Feast of Thanksgiving, 1974, Death Valley, 1980, The Manners Book, 1980, Whalewatch!, 1980, (biography) Ronald Reagon, 1981, Gung Hay Fat Choy, 1982, Hanukkah, 1983, Powwow, 1983, (biography) Sally Ride, 1984, I Can Be An Astronaut, 1984, I Can Be A Truck Driver, 1985, I Can Be A Pilot, 1985, Miss Liberty, First Lady, 1986, Samoans!, 1986, I Can Be A Nurse, 1986, Whales of the World, 1987, Passover, 1987, (biography) Juliette Low, 1988, (biography) George Bush, 1989, Dolphins!, 1989, Sharks!, 1989, (biography) Barbara Bush, 1990, Spanish California and the Mission Trail, 1993 Docent Mus. Natural History Named Disting. Alumni of Yr., U. Calif. Santa Barbara, 1979 Mem. Internat. Reading Assn., So. Calif. Coun. on Lit.-Children & Young People, Soc. Children's Book Writers, Delta Kappa Gamma Democrat. Avocations: tennis, theater, travel. Home: 829 Mission Canyon Rd Santa Barbara CA 93105-2171

BEHRENS, KATHLEEN, sports association executive; Grad., U. Hartford, Conn. Exec. dir. Friends of Cuomo Campaign Com., 1994; positions up to exec. dir. NY Cares, 1995—2000; v.p. cmty. rels. NBA, NYC, 2000—05, sr. v.p. cmty. and player progs., 2005—. Bd. dirs. NY Cares. Office: NBA Olympic Tower 645 5th Ave Fl 10 New York NY 10022-5986*

BEHRENS, KAY S., lawyer; b. 1961; BA, Tex. State Univ., San Marcos; JD, Univ. Tex., Austin. Bar: Tex. 1986. Dir. corp. law H.E. Butt Grocery Co., San Antonio; v.p. corp. compliance, sr. atty. KCI, 2006—. Mailing: HE Butt Grocery Co PO Box 839955 San Antonio TX 78283-3955

BEHRENS, M. KATHLEEN, medical researcher; PhD in Microbiology, U. Calif., Davis. With Robertson Stephens Mgmt. Co., 1983—99, gen. ptnr., 1986-93; mng. dir. RS Investments, San Francisco, 1999—. Bd. dirs. Abgenix Inc., HealthTrio; mem. President's Coun. Advisors on Sci. and Tech. Mem. Nat. Venture Capital Assn. (pres. elect 1999—). Office: RS Investments 388 Market St San Francisco CA 94111 also: Abgenix Inc 7601 Dumbarton Cir Fremont CA 94555-3616

BEHRMAN, BRUCE WARD, social sciences educator; b. Peoria, Ill., Sept. 15, 1934; s. Carl Martin and Elwin Ward Behrman; m. Rileyne Elizabeth Brown; children: Zachary, Matthew, Mark. BA, Bradley U., 1956, MA, 1957; JD, Northwestern U., 1962; PhD, Purdue U., 1967, MA, 1977. Tchg. asst., grad. instr. Purdue U., 1965—66; asst. prof. Calif. State U., Sacramento, 1967—70, assoc. prof., 1970—77, prof., 1978—. Cons. in field, 1980—. Contbr. articles to profl. jours. Mem.: Am. Psychology & Law Soc., Am. Psychol. Soc., Phi Kappa Phi. Independent. Presbyterian. Office: Calif State U Dept Psychology 6000 J St Sacramento CA 95819 Business E-Mail: behrmanbw@csus.edu.

BEHRMAN, EDWARD JOSEPH, biochemistry educator; b. NYC, Dec. 13, 1930; s. Morris Harry and Janet Cahn (Solomons) B.; m. Cynthia Fansler, Aug. 29, 1953; children: David Murray, Elizabeth Colden, Victoria Anne. BS, Yale, 1952; PhD, U. Calif., Berkeley, 1957. Research asso. biochemistry Cancer Research Inst., Boston, 1960-64; bd. tutors biochem. scis. Harvard, 1961-64; asst. prof. chemistry Brown U., Providence, 1964-65; from mem. faculty to prof. emeritus Ohio State U., Columbus, 1965—2006, prof. emeritus, 2006—. Rschr. in peroxydisulfate and nucleotide chemistry. Contbr. articles to profl. jours. USPHS fellow, 1955-56, 57-60; NSF grantee, 1966-73; NIH grantee, 1973-81 Mem. Am. Chem. Soc., Royal Soc. Chemistry, Phi Beta Kappa, Sigma Xi. Home: 6533 Hayden Run Rd Hilliard OH 43026-9642 Office: Ohio State U Dept Biochemistry Columbus OH 43210 Office Phone: 614-292-9485. Business E-Mail: behrman.1@osu.edu.

BEHRMAN, HAROLD RICHARD, endocrinologist, physiologist, educator; b. Sask., Can., Nov. 26, 1939; s. Henry Fred and Minnie Alice (Waslenko) B.; m. Carol Hope O'Rourke, Aug. 8, 1981; children: Tracy Lee, Terri Lynne, Russell Norman, Kevin Michael, Kathleen Hope. BS, U. Man., (Can.), 1962, MA, 1965; PhD, N.C. State U., 1967; MS (hon.), Yale U., 1982. Research fellow Harvard U. Med. Sch., Boston, 1967-71, asst. prof., 1971-72; dir. reproductive biology Merck Inst., Rahway, NJ, 1972-75; assoc. prof. gynecology and pharmacology Yale U., New Haven, 1975-81, prof. ob-gyn. and pharmacology, 1981—, dir. reproductive biology sect., 1975—. Cons. NIH, 1978-83, 91-95, USDA, 1985, NSF, 1985, Med. Rsch. Coun. Can., 1990-91. Fulbright-Hays Disting. prof., 1978; MRC Can. fellow, 1967-70; recipient Rsch. award Lalor Found., 1971-72, Alta. Heritage Vis. Prof. award, 1983 Mem. AAAS, Am. Physiol. Soc., Endocrine Soc., Soc. Study of Reprodn., Soc. Endocrinology, Can. Physiol. Soc. Home: 790 Green Hill Rd Madison CT 06443-2404 Office: Yale U Dept Ob-Gyn 1303A Yale Sta New Haven CT 06520

BEHRMAN, JERE RICHARD, economics professor; b. Indpls., Mar. 2, 1940; s. Robert Wilbur and Mary Jane (Krull) B.; m. Barbara Ann Ventresco; children: Kennedy Robert, Julia Andrea, Emily Louise. Student, Russian Lang. Inst., Ind. U., 1960-61; BA summa cum laude, Williams Coll., Williamstown, Mass., 1962; PhD in Econs., Mass. Inst. Tech., 1966. Asst. prof. econs. U. Pa., Phila., 1965-68, asso. prof., 1968-71, prof., 1971—, chmn. dept. econs., 1973-79, research asso. Center for Population Studies, 1979—, William P. Kenan, Jr. prof. econs., 1983—, assoc. dir. Lauder Inst. Mgmt. and Internat. Studies, 1983-87; co-dir. Ctr. for Analysis Developing Economies, 1982-95; Ctr. for Household and Family Econs., War Cannon, prof. econ, 1982—; South Asian Studies Ctr., 1983-95; acting dir. Population Studies Ctr., 1992-93, dir., 1998—. Faculty assoc. NSF sponsored project, 1965-68; vis. seminar coord. U. Catolica, Santiago, Chile, 1969; vis. lectr. pub. and internat. affairs, Princeton U., 1973; rsch. assoc. Nat. Bur. Econ. Rsch., 1975-79; hon. fellow dept. econs. U. Wis., 1976-77; rsch. assoc. Ctr. Latin Am. Devel. Studies, Boston U., 1978-79; cons. econs. dept. IBRD, Washington, 1966-69, Devel. Rsch. Ctr., 1972-73; rsch. assoc.; cons. MIT-ODEPLAN-Ford project Office Nat. Econ. Planning, Santiago, 1968-71; cons. Wharton Econ. Forecasting Assocs., Inc., 1970-71, U.S. Treasury, 1972, U.S. Treasury Brookings-SIECA-BID project on Cen. Am. Common Market, 1973-78, UN Com. on Trade and Devel. World Commodity Models, 1974, Harvard Inst. Internat. Devel., Cen. Bank Nicaragua Econ. Modeling Project, 1975, ILPES-NBER-UN Project on Short Term Policy in Latin Am. Econs., 1975, AID, 1976-77, Dept. of Treasury, 1977, ECIEL, 1978, Internat. Crops Rsch. Inst. for Semi-Arid Tropics, 1980-87, UN, 1982, Botswana Ministry at Planning, 1982, Ncaer India, 1980, World Bank, 1981—, Thai Devel. Rsch. Inst., 1987-91, Indonesian Ministry of Planning, 1987-88, Internat. Rice Rsch. Inst., 1987-89, Malaysian project ILO, 1989, humanresource and devel. project ILO/ARTEP, 1989-90, World Bank Mellon Brazilian edn. project, 1990, Pakistan rural edn. project Internat. Food Policy Rsch. Inst., 1989-95, World Bank Productivity Project, 1990, HIID Bolivia project on social sectors, 1992-94, World Bank project on Pakistan in 2010, Internat; internat. expert Unido Social Summit, 1994-95, cons. UNPP human resources, 1995; prin. investigator on NSF project, 1972-75, 95—, AID, 1977-80, Ford-Rockefeller, 1977-78, 16 project NIH, 1981—, Population Coun., 1982-86, Pew Charitable Trust, 1988—; vis. scholar NAS, Am. Coun. Learned Socs., Social Sci. Rsch. Coun., People's Republic of China, 1987-88; Arnold Bernhard Disting. vis. prof. econs. Williams Coll., 1990-91. Autor 25 books and monographs; co-editor Jour. Devel. Econs., 1985-95; contbr. more than 240 articles and book revs. to profl. jours. Recipient Benedict prize as outstanding math. student Williams Coll., 1960, Grosvenor Cup as outstanding mem. class of, 1962; award of merit for outstanding research in agrl. econs. Am. Farm Econ. Assn., 1967; Nat. Merit scholar, 1958-62; Tyng Found. fellow, 1958-64; Carnegie fellow, 1961; Danforth Found. fellow, 1962-66; NSF fellow, 1962-63; Mass. Inst. Tech. Center for Internat. Studies fellow, 1964-65; Ford Found. Faculty fellow, 1971-72; Guggenheim Found. Faculty fellow, 1979-80; Compton Found. Population fellow, 1980-81; Fulbright 40th Anniversary Disting. fellow, 1987. Fellow Econometric Soc.; mem. Am. Econ. Assn., L.Am. Studies Assn., Population Assn. Am., Phi Beta Kappa. Home: 320 Mallwyd Rd Merion Station PA 19066-1411 Office: U Pa Dept Econs 3718 Locust Walk Philadelphia PA 19104-6209 E-mail: jbehrman@econ.sas.upenn.edu.

BEHRMAN, MICHAEL J., professional sports team executive; m. Colleen Braun, July 26, 2005; children: Brianne, Cailan. BS in Elec. Engring. and Computer Sci., Princeton U., NJ; MBA in Fin. and Corp. Acctg., U. Rochester, 1992. CFA. With Goldman Sachs, Merrill Lynch Internat., Disney Sports, Disney Internet Grp.; sr. v.p. fin. Charlotte Bobcats, 2005—06, exec. v.p., CFO, 2006—. Mem. exec. adv. com. U. Rochester Simon Sch., 2006—. Office: Charlotte Bobcats 333 E Trade St Charlotte NC 28202*

BEHRMAN, RICHARD ELLIOT, pediatrician, dean; b. Phila., Dec. 13, 1931; s. Robert and Vivian (Keegan) Behrman; m. Ann Nelson, Aug. 14, 1954; children: Amy Jane, Michael Jameson, Carolyn Ann, Hillary. AB, Amherst Coll., 1953; JD, Harvard U., 1956; MD, U. Rochester, 1960; DSc (hon.), Med. Coll. Wisc., 2000. Diplomate Am. Bd. Pediat. (examiner). Intern Johns Hopkins Hosp., Balt., 1960—61, resident in pediat., 1963—65; asst. prof. pediat. U. Oreg. Sch. Medicine, Portland, 1965—67, assoc. prof., 1967—68; prof. U. Ill. Coll. Medicine, Chgo., 1968—71; prof., chmn. dept. pediat. Columbia U. Coll. Physicians and Surgeons, NYC, 1971—76; prof., chmn. dept. Case Western Res. U. Sch. Medicine, Cleve., 1976—81, dean Sch. Medicine, 1980—89; prof. clin. pediat. Stanford U., 1989; v.p. med. affairs Case Western Res. U. Sch. Medicine, Cleve., 1987—89; dir. dept. pediat. Rainbow Babies and Children's Hosp., Cleve., 1976—81; dir. Ctr. for Future of Children, 1989—99; sr. v.p. med. affairs Lucile Packard Found. for Children's Health, Palo Alto, Calif., 1999—2002, chmn. bd., 1996—99; dir. Lucile S. Packard Children's Hosp./Stanford Health Svcs., Stanford, UCSF-Stanford Health Care; exec. chair pediat. edn. steering com. Fedn. Pediat. Orgns., 2002—06; exec. dir. Non-Profit Healthcare and Ednl. Cons., 2006—. Author: Neonatology: Diseases of the Fetus and Infant, 1973, Neonatal-Perinatal Medicine, 1977; editor: Nelson's Textbook of Pediatrics, 1978, 1983, 1987, 1992, 1995, 2000, 2004, Essentials of Pediatrics, 1989, 1993, 1997, 2001, 2005; editor-in-chief: The Future of Children, 1990—2005, mem. editl. bd., sect. editor fetal and neonatal medicine: Jour. Pediat., 1970—85, assoc. editor, mem. editl. bd., cons. editor: Pediat. Rsch. Jour., 1971—80. With USPHS, 1961—63. Fellow, Wyeth pediat., 1963—65; scholar, Whipple, 1960—61, Univ., U. Rochester, 1960. Fellow: Am. Acad. Pediat.; mem.: Soc. Gynecol. Investigation, Perinatal Rsch. Soc. (coun. 1970—73), Inst. Medicine of NAS, Soc. Pediat. Rsch. (v.p. 1976—77), Century Assn., Sigma Xi. Episcopalian. Home: PO Box 4446 Santa Barbara CA 93140 Office Phone: 805-565-2953. Business E-Mail: behrmannon-profitconsult@nphec.org.

BEHRMANN, JOAN GAIL, editor; b. NYC; d. Jerome and Jeanette Metzner; m. Larry Jinks, Oct. 2, 1960 (div. 1970); children: Laura Jinks Kastigar, Daniel Carlton Jinks; m. Nicolas Lee Behrmann, Dec. 21, 1972. BA, Queens Coll., 1956; MS, Columbia U., 1958. Reporter Charlotte Observer, NC, 1958-60, Miami Herald, Fla., 1960-64, Miami News, 1965-66; asst. prof. Miami Dade CC, 1968-72; assoc. prof. Boston U., 1975-78; Sunday editor The Saratogian, Saratoga Springs, NY, 1979-80; editor Gannett Westchester, Westchester County, NY, 1981-83; page one editor, entertainment editor USA Today, Rosslyn, Va., 1983-87; exec. editor Desert Sun, Palm Springs, Calif., 1987-95; arts editor Detroit News, 1996-2000; ret., 2000; freelance writer Trash or Treasure column, theater revs. Detroit News, 2001—05. Co-author: Questioning Media Ethics, 1978. Founder Every Women's Coun., Glens Falls, NY, 1978—80; v.p. edn. Guilds of the Santa Fe Opera, Inc., 2007—; bd. dirs. Coll. of Desert Found., Palm Desert, 1993—95, Jewish Family Svcs., Palm Springs, 1994—95, Palm Springs Opera Guild, 1989—91, Adult Well-Being Svcs., Detroit, 1997—2000, Mich. Opera Theatre, 2000—05, Santa Fe Opera Guild, 2005—. Recipient Athena award, Palm Springs C. of C., 1991. Mem.: Am. Soc. Newspaper Editors, Assn. Press Mng. Editors Orgn. (bd. dirs. 1991—96, com. chair 1996—97). Avocations: travel, reading. Personal E-mail: jbehrmann@aol.com.

BEIDEMAN, PAUL S., bank executive; B in Social Scis., Millersville U., Pa.; M in Fin., Widener U., Wilmington, Del. Chmn. Mid-Atlantic Region Mellon Fin. Corp., Phila.; pres., CEO Associated Banc-Corp., 2003—07, bd. dirs., 2003—, chmn., CEO, 2007—; pres., dir. Associated Bank, Nat. Assn. (affiliated of Associated Banc-Corp.), 2003—. Office: Associated Banc-Corp 1200 Hansen Rd Green Bay WI 54304 Office Phone: 920-491-7000.*

BEIDER, MARLYS ANNA, hotel executive, writer; b. Hannover, Germany, Feb. 7, 1945; d. Walter Schroeder and Elfriede (Ellen) Pallenberg-Schroeder; m. Harold Beider, Apr. 21, 1971 (dec.); children: Jacqueline Lee Shear, Kenneth Harry, Kelly Tema Rubin, Daniel Ayal. Bus., Buhmann Fachschule, 1960—63. V.p. Mid Am. Hotel Corp., Chgo., 1975—90, pres., 1990—. Author: (novels) Fateful Parallels, Continuum. Woman's bd. mem. North Shore Country Day Sch., Winnetka, Ill., 1981—91; adv. bd. The Theatre Sch. DePaul U., Chgo.; v.p. To Protect Our Heritage PAC, Chgo., 1985—90. Mem.: Royal Melbourne. Avocations: writing, opera, golf, hiking.

BEIDLER, MARSHA WOLF, lawyer; b. Bridgeton, NJ, Feb. 29, 1948; d. Benjamin and Esther (Lourie) Wolf; m. John Nathan Beidler, Aug. 18, 1974; children: Dora E., Evan A. BA, Dickinson Coll., Carlisle, Pa., 1969; JD, Rutgers U., Camden, NJ, 1972; LLM in Taxation, NYU, 1979. Bar: Pa. 1972, Fla. 1973, N.J. 1975; Fla. bar bd. cert. tax lawyer. Estate and gift tax atty. IRS, Phila., 1972-74, Trenton, NJ, 1974-76; atty. McCarthy & Hicks, Princeton, NJ, 1976-81; ptnr. Pinto & Beidler, Princeton, 1981-83; prin. Smith, Lambert, Hicks & Miller, Princeton, 1983-88; ptnr. Drinker, Biddle & Reath, Princeton, 1988—2005, of counsel, 2006—. Sec. Mercer County Estate Planning Council, 1977-86; prof. paralegal studies Rider Coll., Trenton, 1982; lectr. estate planning various corps. and univs. Bd. dirs. Birth Alternatives, Princeton, 1980; bd. dirs. Mercer Council on Alcoholism, Trenton, 1985-86. Fellow Am. Coll. Trusts and Estate Counsel; mem. ABA (taxation sect., real property, probate and trust sect.), Fla. Bar Assn., N.J. Bar Assn. (taxation sect.). Office: Drinker Biddle & Reath 105 College Rd E PO Box 627 Princeton NJ 08542-0627 Office Phone: 609-716-6515. Business E-Mail: marsha.beidler@dbr.com.

BEIDLER, PETER GRANT, retired language educator; b. Bethlehem, Pa., Mar. 13, 1940; s. Paul Henry and Margaret (Grant) B.; m. Anne E. Gilbert, June 15, 1963; children: Paul, Kurt, Gretchen, Nora. BA, Earlham Coll., 1962; MA, Lehigh U., 1965, PhD, 1968. Asst. prof. English Lehigh U., Bethlehem, Pa., 1968-72, assoc. prof., 1972—77, prof., 1977—2007, Lucy G. Moses Disting prof. English, 1978—2007, acting v.p. for student affairs, 1982-83; Robert Foster Cherry disting. tchg. prof. Baylor U., 1995-96; ret., 2007. Author: Fig Tree John: An Indian in Fact and Fiction, 1977; co-author: (bibliography) The Indian in American Short Fiction, 1979; editor: John Gower's Literary Transformations, 1982, Ghosts, Demons and Henry James, 1989, Writing Matters, 1992, Henry James's The Turn of the Screw: Case Studies in Contemporary Criticism, 1995, 2d edit., 2004, Geoffrey Chaucer's The Wife of Bath: Case Studies in Contemporary Criticism, 1996, Masculinities in Chaucer, 1998, Chaucer's Wife of Bath: Prologue and Tale: An Annotated Bibliography, 1990-1995, 1998, A Reader's Guide to the Novels of Louise Erdrich, 1999, 2d edit., 2006, Native Americans in the Saturday Evening Post, 2000, The Native American in Short Fiction in the Saturday Evening Post, 2001, Why I Teach, 2002, Approaches to Teaching Henry James's Daisy Miller and the Turn of the Screw, 2005, A Manual of the Writings in Middle English, Vol. II, 2005, The Canterbury Tales, 2006. Served with USAF, 1962-68. Named Nat. Prof. of Yr. Coun. for Advancement and Support of Edn., 1983; Fulbright lectr. Sichuan U., Chengdu, Peoples Republic of China, 1987-88; recipient Robert Foster Cherry Disting. Teaching chair Baylor U., 1995-96. Mem. MLA, New Chaucer Soc., Medieval Soc. Am., Phi Beta Kappa, Phi Beta Delta. Office: Lehigh U English Dept 35 Sayre Dr Bethlehem PA 18015-3116 Personal E-mail: pgb1@lehigh.edu.

BEIER, CAROL ANN, state supreme court justice; b. Kansas City, Kans., Sept. 27, 1958; Student, Benedictine Coll., 1976-77, The Poynter Inst., 1979; BS, U. Kans., 1981, JD, 1982-85; ML in Judicial Process, U. Va. Sch. Law, 2004. Bar: Kans., 1985, D.C., 1988; U.S. Dist. Kans., 1985; U.S. Ct. Appeals (10th cir.) 1986. With Balloun & Bodinson, Olathe, Kans., 1983; jud. clk. U.S. Ct. Appeals (10th cir.), Olathe, 1985-86; staff atty. Nat. Women's Law Ctr., Washington, 1986-87; assoc. Arent, Fox, Kintner, Plotkin & Kahn, Washington, 1987-88, Foulston & Siefkin, Wichita, Kans., 1988-93, ptnr., 1993—2000; judge Kansas Ct. of Appeals, 2000—03; justice Kans. Supreme Ct., 2003—. Dir. Kans. Defender Project, Lawrence, 1989-90, Kans. Appellate Clinic, Lawrence, 1989-90; vis. asst. prof. U. Kans. Sch. of Law, Lawrence, 1989-90, lectr. Wichita State U., 1994; fellow Georgetown Women's Law and Pub. Policy Program, Washington, 1986-87. Articles editor U. Kans. Law Rev., 1984-85. Pres. Wichita Women Atty.'s Assn., 1993-94; bd. dirs. Kans. Civil Liberties Union, Wichita, 1990-94. Recipient Bernard Kilgore award, Soc. Profl. Jours., U. Kans., 1980, Louise Mattox Atty. of Achievement award Wichita Women's Attys. Assn., 2003. Fellow Kans. Bar Found., ABA, Sam A. Crow Inn of Ct. (master); mem. ABA, Kans. Bar Assn., D.C. Bar, Wichita Bar Assn., Women's Atty. Assn. Topeka, Order of the Coif. Office: Kansas Supreme Ct 301 W 10th Topeka KS 66612

BEIER, DAVID, medical products executive; B, Colgate U.; JD, Albany Law Sch. Staff counsel US House Reps.; v.p. govt. affairs and pub. policy Genentech; chief domestic policy advisor Staff of V.P. Al Gore, 1998—2001; ptnr. Hogan & Hartson, Washington; sr. v.p. global govt. affairs Amgen, Inc., Washington, 2003—. Bd. dirs. Nat. Health Coun. Office: Amgen Inc 555 13th St NW Ste 600 West Washington DC 20004 Office Phone: 202-585-9500. Office Fax: 202-585-9729.*

BEIERWALTES, WILLIAM HOWARD, physiologist, educator; b. Ann Arbor, Mich., Oct. 6, 1947; s. William Henry and Mary-Martha (Nichols) B.; m. Patricia Sue Olson, July 11, 1982; children: William N., Peter L., Nora R. BA, Kalamazoo Coll., 1969; PhD, U. N.C., 1978. Instr. Mayo Med. Sch., Rochester, Minn., 1979-81; sr. staff scientist Henry Ford Hosp., Detroit, 1981—. Prof. Wayne State U. Sch. Medicine, Detroit, 2004—. Contbr. articles to profl. jours. With US Army, 1971—72. Mem. Am. Physiol. Soc., Am. Heart Assn. (fellow coun. on high blood pressure 1992, fellow coun. on high blood pressure rsch. 2001, honor roll coun. on kidney 1988, chair rsch. fellowship com. Mich. chpt. 1987-90, 92-94, established investigator 1983-88), Am. Soc. Nephrology, Inter-Am. Soc. Hypertension, Mich. Soc. Med. Rsch. (bd. dirs. 1988-94, pres. 1992-94), Nat. Kidney Found. Mich. (rsch. rev. com. 1984-85, 88, 2004-06). Presbyterian. Avocation: collecting antique toy soldiers. Home: 750 Lakepointe St Grosse Pointe Park MI 48230-1706 Office: Henry Ford Hosp 2799 W Grand Blvd Detroit MI 48202-2689 Office Phone: 313-916-7494. Business E-Mail: wbeierw1@hfhs.org.

BEIGHEY, LAWRENCE JEROME, packaging company executive; b. Akron, Ohio, June 24, 1938; s. Jac Laverne and Martha Rose (Vestal) B.; m. Carole Anne LaFlamme, Dec. 11, 1970; children: Basil, Susan, Thomas, Timothy, Elizabeth, Anne. BS in Indsl. Engring., Pa. State U., 1960. Registered profl. engr., Pa.; cert. data processor. Mgr. internat. div. Brockway (Pa.), Inc., 1968-76, mgr. energy div., 1976-78, project mgr., 1978-79, plant mgr., 1979-81, mgr. mfg. staff and services, 1981-83; exec. v.p. Brockway Standard, Atlanta, 1983-86, pres., 1986-89; v.p. Brockway, Inc., Jacksonville, Fla., 1986-89; pres. Transition Mgmt. Resources, Atlanta, 1989; v.p., gen. mgr. All-Pak, Inc., Decatur, Ga., 1990; pres. Plastite Corp., 1990-95; mfg. cons., 1995—. Bd. dirs. Boy Scouts Am., DuBois, Pa., 1978-80, YMCA, DuBois, 1981-83; mem. sch. bd. Brockway Area Sch. Dist., 1981-83; pres. Jaycees, DuBois, 1964. Mem. Steel Shipping Container Inst. (bd. dirs. 1986), Data Processing Mgmt. Assn. (bd. dirs. 1966-68), Alpena Country Club, Amelia Island (Fla.) Ocean Club. Avocations: golf, tennis. Personal E-mail: LJBeighey@aol.com.

BEIGHLE, DOUGLAS PAUL, aerospace transportation executive; b. Deer Lodge, Mont., June 18, 1932; s. Douglas Paul Beighle and Clarice Janice (Driver) Kiefer; m. Gwendolen Anne Dickson, Oct. 30, 1954 (dec. Jan. 1996); children: Cheryl, Randall, Katherine, Douglas J.; m. Kathleen Pierce, June 26, 2005 BS in Bus. Adminstrn., U. Mont., 1954; JD, U. Mont, 1958; LL.M., Harvard U., 1960. Bar: Mont. 1958, Wash. 1959, U.S. Supreme Ct. 1970. Assoc. Perkins & Coie, Seattle, 1960-67, ptnr., 1967-80; v.p. contracts Boeing Co., Seattle, 1980-81, v.p. contracts, gen. counsel, sec., 1981-86, sr. v.p., 1986-97; chief legal counsel Puget Energy, Inc., Bellevue, Wash., 1970-80, bd. dirs., 1981—2005, chair, 2002—05; exec.

dir. Wash. State, U.S. West Comm., Denver, 1990-95. Bd. dirs. Washington Mut. Inc., Seattle, 1989-05, ret., 2005, Active Voice Corp., Seattle, 1997-01, Simpson Investment Co., Seattle, 1998-05; bd. dirs., chmn. KCTS-9 TV, 1996-05. Nat. bd. dirs. Jr. Achievement, Colorado Springs, 1981-95; bd. dirs. Greater Puget Sound Jr. Achievement, 1983—, Intiman Theatre, Seattle, 1991-93; trustee Mcpl. League Seattle, 1983-88, U. Mont. Found., Missoula, 1983-91, Mansfield Found., Missoula, 1990-95, Pacific Sci. Ctr., Seattle, 1992—, pres. 1996; trustee Arts Fund, Seattle, 1994—, chair, 1995-96. 1st lt. USAF, 1954-56. Harvard U. Law Sch. fellow, 1959 Mem. Wash. State Bar Assn. (chmn. adminstrv. law sect. 1979-80), Nat. Assn. Mfrs. (bd. dirs., regional vice chmn. 1988-93), Greater Seattle C. of C. (chair 1994-95), Rainier Club Seattle, Seattle Yacht Club. Republican. Presbyterian. Office: 1000 2nd Ave Ste 3700 Seattle WA 98104-1053

BEIHL, FREDERICK, retired lawyer; b. St. Joseph, Mo., Jan. 26, 1932; s. Ernst F. and Evelyn E. (Kline) B.; m. Lillis Prater, Mar. 3, 1962. AB, U. Mo., 1953, LLB, 1955. Bar: Mo. 1955, U.S. Supreme Ct. 1968. With Shook Hardy & Bacon, Kansas City, 1955-99, ptnr., 1961-99, shareholder, 1992-99; ret., 1999. Chmn. bd. dirs. UMKC Conservatory of Music, Kansas City, 1988-91, Visiting Nurses Assn., Kansas City, 1977-79; pres. Heart of Am. Family and Children Svcs., Kansas City, 1982-84, Friends of Art Nelson Mus., Kansas City, 1979-81. Avocations: tennis, skiing, art collecting. Office: Shook Hardy & Bacon 2555 Grand Blvd Kansas City MO 64108-2613 Business E-Mail: fbeihl@shb.com.

BEILEIN, JOHN PATRICK, men's college basketball coach; b. Feb. 5, 1953; m. Kathleen Beilein; children: Seana, Patrick, Mark, Andrew. B in Hist., Wheeling Jesuit U., 1975; MEd, Niagara U., 1981; degree (hon.), Wheeling Jesuit U., 2005. Head coach Newfane Ctrl. HS, NY, 1975—78, Erie CC, Buffalo, 1978—82, Nazareth Coll., Rochester, NY, 1982—83, Le Moyne Coll., Syracuse, NY, 1983—92, Canisius Coll., Buffalo, 1992—97, U. Richmond, 1997—2002, W.Va. U., Morgantown, 2002—07, U. Mich., Ann Arbor, 2007—. Co-chair W.Va. U. United Way campaign. Recipient Furfari award for Coll. Coach of Yr., W.Va. Sports Writers Assn., 2005. Achievements include coaching NIT champions, 2007. Office: U Mich Mens Basketball Athletic Dept 1000 S State St Ann Arbor MI 48109-2201*

BEILENSON, PETER LOWELL, former public health official; b. LA, Feb. 6, 1960; s. Anthony Charles and Dolores (Martin) B.; m. Christina Weininger; children: Valerie, Alex, Jane, Jack. AB, Harvard U., 1981; MD, Emory U., 1987; MPH, Johns Hopkins U., 1990. Family practice intern U. Md., Balt., 1987-88; resident in preventive medicine Johns Hopkins U., Balt., 1989-91, chief resident, 1991-92; commr. Balt. City Health Dept., 1992—2005. Mem. AMA, APHA (Milton and Ruth Roemer award for creative pub. health 1996). Avocations: sports, coaching youth sports. Office: 5820 York Rd Ste 205 Baltimore MD 21212 Office Phone: 410-323-1777. Office Fax: 410-323-3889. Business E-Mail: peter@beilensonforcongress.com.

BEILER, ANNE F., food company executive; m. Jonas Beiler; 2 children. Mgr. concession stand Md. Farmers Mkt., 1987; owner concession stand Farmers Mkt., Downingtown, Pa.; owner, chair, CEO Auntie Anne's, Gap, Pa., 1988—. Recipient Entrepreneur of Yr. award Inc. Mag., 1992, 94, Spirit of Achievement award Jr. Achievement Orgn. Ctrl. Pa., 1998; named one of 50 Pa.'s Best 50 Women in Bus., 1998. Office: Auntie Anne's Inc 160A Route 41 Gap PA 17527-9410

BEILER, HOLLY ANNE, education educator; d. George W. and Marilyn T. Beiler; 1 child, Kayla C. Hale. Adminstrv. Licensure, N.Mex Highlands U., Rio Rancho, N. Mex., 2004; M in Secondary Edn., U. N.Mex, Albuquerque, N. Mex., 2002; B of Bus. Edn., Ea. N.Mex U., Portales, N. Mex., 1994. Tech. resource tchr. Albuquerque Pub. Sch., Albuquerque, 1999—2003, tchr., 1995—99, grant project mgr., 2003—. Examiner Quality N.Mex, Albuquerque, 2004; ind. cons., Albuquerque, 2000—04. Contbr. profl. devel. curriculum; presenter Nat. Sch. Bd. Assn., Milken Educator's Conf., New Mex. State Tech. Conf. Grantee Sliver Quality Edn. for All, N.Mex Pub. Edn. Dept., 2004-2005, Enhancing Edn. Through Tech., 2004-2005, IDEA and Tech. Mem.: ASCD (assoc.). Office: Albuquerque Pub Sch 6400 Uptown Blvd NE Ste 220E Albuquerque NM 87110 Home Phone: 505-831-8914; Office Phone: 505-830-8096. Personal E-mail: holly_beiler@yahoo.com. Business E-Mail: beiler@aps.edu.

BEILMAN, TERESA MARIE, artist, poet; d. Carl Joseph Buchholz and Marie Theresa Sigg; m. Lavern Joseph Beilman, Aug. 23, 1958; children: Gregory, Douglas, Elizabeth, Rose Marie, James, Jane. BA Kans. Newman U., Wichita, 1958. Portrait painter, sculpture, Wichita, 1958—2004; ret., 2004. Sculpture, St. Peter, Marie de Mattias, Gaspar de Bufalo, one-man shows include Kansas Newman U., 1978, Ursaline Coll., Louisville, 2004, mag., Birds and Blooms, 2004, Best of Birds and Blooms, 2005. Vol. Habitat for Humanity, Wichita. Mem.: Amnesty Internat. Avocations: reading, gardening.

BEILOCK, SIAN LEAH, psychology professor, psychologist; BS Cognitive Sci., U. of Calif., San Diego, 1997; MA Psychology, Mich. State U., PhD Kinesiology, 2003, PhD Psychology, 2003. Asst. prof. Miami U., Ohio, 2003—05, U. Chgo., 2005—. Contbr. articles to profl. sci. jours.; Spkr. in field. Named one of 25 Women to Watch, Crain's Chgo. Bus., 2007; recipient young investigator award, Internat. Soc. of Sport Psychology, 2005, Early Career Disting. Scholar Award, N. Am. Soc. for the Psychology of Sport and Physical Activity (NASPSPA), 2007. Office: Univ of Chgo Dept of Psychology 5848 South Univ Ave Chicago IL 60637 Office Phone: 773-834-3713. Office Fax: 773-702-0886. E-mail: beilock@uchicago.edu.*

BEIM, DAVID ODELL, investment banker, educator; b. Mpls., June 2, 1940; s. Raymond Nelson and Moana (Odell) B.; m. Elizabeth Lucile Artz, Aug. 29, 1964; children— Amy Marie, Nicholas Frederick. BA with honors, Stanford U., 1963; MPhil (Rhodes scholar), Oxford U., Eng., 1965. With First Boston Corp., NYC, 1966-75, v.p., 1971-75, head project finance, 1973-75; exec. v.p. Export-Import Bank U.S., Washington, 1975-77; head corp. fin. Bankers Trust Co., NYC, 1978-87, sr. v.p., 1978-79, exec. v.p., 1979-86, mem. mgmt. com., 1986-87; mng. dir. Dillon Read & Co., 1987-89; prof. Bus. Sch. Columbia U., NYC, 1990—; dir., audit com. chair, Cluster D Funds Merrill Lynch Investment Mgrs., 2001—. Chmn. Wave Hill, Inc., 1990-2006; trustee Phillips Exeter Acad. Mem. Coun. Fgn. Rels. Office: Columbia U Uris Hall 711 New York NY 10027

BEIM, NORMAN, playwright, actor, theater director, writer; b. Newark; s. Herman and Frieda (Thau) B.; m. Virginia Rapkin (div.). Student, Ohio State U., Hedgerow Theatre Sch., Phila., Inst. Contemporary Art, Washington. Appeared in Broadway play Inherit the Wind, 1956-58, off-Broadway play Coriolanus, 1953, Black Visions, 1973; nat. touring prodn. Tribute, 1980; plays include The Deserter, (Samuel French award) 1979, Success, 1983, Pygmalion and Galatea, 1984, Archie's Comeback, 1986, Jewel Thieves, 1990, On a Darkling Plain (James Ellis Meml. award 1992), Death Amid the Rich and Famous, 1991, Cri de Coeur, 1991, Dreams (No Empty Theater New Play award 1993), Shakespeare Revisited (Maxim Mazumdar New Play award 1993); author: Six Award Winning Plays, Plays at Home and Abroad, My Family, The Jewish Immigrants, 1997, (novel) Hymie and the Angel, 1998, Giants of the Old Testament, 2001, Infamous People, 2004, Comedy Tonite, Woman Laid Bare, 2006. Mem. Bronx Coun. of the Arts. Served with F.A. U.S. Army. Mem. SAG, AFTRA, Dramatists Guild Am., Actors Equity Assn. Home: 425 W 57th St New York NY 10019-1764 Home Phone: 212-265-6284; Office Phone: 212-265-6284. Personal E-mail: normanbeim@aol.com.

BEIN, FREDERICK L., geography educator; BA in geography, U. Colo., 1969; MA in geography, U. Fla., Gainesville, 1971, PhD in geography, 1974. Instr. regional geography U. Catolica do Mato Grosso, Camp Grande, Brazil, 1972; asst. prof. of geography U. N.D., Grand Forks, 1977-78; asst. prof., acting coord. of geography program Ind. U., Purdue U., 1981-93, prof., 1978—2003, dept. chair geography, 1979—96. Coord. State Geography Alliance, 1988—96; dir. Environmental Rsch. and Mgmt. Ctr. Papua New Guinea Univ., 1996—99; Rotary Internat. Acad. Ambassador Dept. Surveying PNG Univ. Tech., 2000. Contbr. articles of profl. jours. Fulbright Scholar, U. Eduardo Mundance Maputo Mocambigur, 2004—05. Office: Indiana Univ Purdue Dept of Geography 425 University Blvd Dept Of Indianapolis IN 46202-5148 Office Phone: 317-274-1100. Business E-Mail: rbein@iugui.edu.

BEINART, PETER ALEXANDER, editor, columnist; b. 1971; s. Julian and Doreen Beinart; m. Diana Robin Hartstein, Oct. 25, 2003; 1 child. BA, Yale U., 1993; MPh, U. Coll, Oxford, England, 1995. Mng. editor The New Republic, 1995—97, sr. editor, 1997—99, editor, 1999—2006, editor-at-large, 2006—. Columnist Washington Post, Time Magazine. Contbr. columns in newspapers THe Washington Post, commentary on CNN, NPR, PBS and other radio & TV programs; author: The Good Fight: Why Liberals--And Only Liberals--Can Win the War on Terror and Make America Great Again, 2006. Named Columnist of Yr., Week mag., 2004; Rhodes scholar, Marshall scholar (declined). Fellow: Coun. Fgn. Rels. Office: The New Republic Suite 700 1331 H St NW Washington DC 20005*

BEINECKE, CANDACE KRUGMAN, lawyer; b. Paterson, NJ, Nov. 26, 1946; d. Martin and Sylvia (Altshuler) Krugman; m. Frederick W. Beinecke II, Oct. 2, 1976; children: Jacob Sperry, Benjamin Barrett. BA, NYU, 1967; JD, Rutgers U., 1970. Bar: NY 1971. Assoc., then ptnr. Hughes, Hubbard & Reed, NYC, 1970—, chair, 1999—. Bd. dirs. First Eagle Funds, NYC, 1996—, chair bd. dirs., 2004—; bd. dirs. Alstom, France, 2001—, Rockefeller Fin. Services, Inc., Rockefeller & Co., Inc. Bd. dirs. Merce Cunningham Found., NYC, Jacob's Pillow Dance Festival, Lee, Mass., The NYC Partnership; mem. vis. com. Met. Mus. Art Watson Libr.,Yale Law Sch. Ctr. for Study of Corp. Law Named one of The 50 Most Influential Women Lawyers in Am., Nat. Law Jour., 2007. Mem. ABA, Assn. Bar City of NY, River Club, Women's Forum. Office: Hughes Hubbard & Reed One Battery Park Plaza New York NY 10004-1466*

BEINECKE, FRANCES G., environmentalist; MS, Yale U. With Natural Resources Def. Coun. (NRDC), NYC, 1973—, exec. dir., 1998—2006, pres., 2006—. Bd. dirs. World Resources Inst.; co-founder NY League of Conservation Voters; lectr. in field. Office: Natural Resources Def Coun 40 W 20th St New York NY 10011 Office Phone: 212-727-2700. Office Fax: 212-727-1773.

BEINECKE, FREDERICK WILLIAM, investment company executive; b. Stamford, Conn., June 3, 1943; s. William S. and Elizabeth (Gillespie) B.; m. Candace Krugman, Oct. 2, 1976; children— Jacob Sperry, Benjamin Barrett. BA, Yale U., 1966; JD, U. Va., 1972; PMD, Harvard U., 1977. Bar: N.Y. 1973. Assoc. firm Hughes Hubbard & Reed, NYC, 1972-73; gen. counsel South Street Seaport Mus., NYC, 1973-75; with Sperry and Hutchinson Co., NYC, 1975-82; pres. Gunlocke Co. subs., 1979-80, corp. v.p., 1977-80, pres., 1980-82, dir., 1977-82; pres. Antaeus Enterprises, Inc., 1982—, also bd. dirs. Chmn. bd. Catalina Mktg. Corp. Trustee Phillips Acad., Andover, Mass., 1980—2000, Wildlife Conservation Soc., 1984—, Outward Bound USA, 1987—2000; mem. trustees' coun. Nat. Gallery of Art, 2004—; trustee Sterling and Francine Clark Art Inst., 2000—, Trudeau Inst., Saranac Lake, NY, 1971—98, chmn., 1984—91, 1995—97, chmn. emeritus, 1998—2004; bd. dir. Close Encounters with Music, 1995—, pres., 1995—2003; bd. dir. Prospect Hill Found., 1962—, Samuel H. Kress Found., 1997—, chmn., 2006—; bd. dir. N.Y.C. Ballet, 1978—88, 1992—2000, 2001—, pres., 2003—; bd. dir. Sperry Fund, 1977—, pres., 1982—; bd. visitors Yale Sch. Music, New Haven, 1997—. Capt. USMC, 1966—69. Decorated Bronze Star. Mem.: Assn. Bar City NY, Knickerbocker Club, Clove Valley Club, Hollenbeck Club, Yale Club. Office: Antaeus Enterprises Rm 2200 99 Park Ave New York NY 10016-1601

BEINECKE, WILLIAM SPERRY, retired consumer products company executive; b. NYC, May 22, 1914; s. Frederick William and Carrie (Sperry) B.; m. Elizabeth Barrett Gillespie, May 24, 1941; children: Frederick W. II, John B., Sarah S., Frances G. BA, Yale U., 1936, MA (hon.), 1971; LL.B., Columbia U., 1940; LL.D. (hon.), Southwestern U., 1967, Cath. U. Am., 1972, Yale U., 1986. Former asso. firm Chadbourne, Wallace, Parke & Whiteside; co-founder firm Casey, Beinecke & Chase; became gen. counsel The Sperry and Hutchinson Co., NYC, 1952, v.p., 1954-60, pres., 1960-67, chmn. bd., chief exec. officer, 1967-80. Bd. dirs. Antaeus Enterprises, Inc. Chmn. bd. dirs. The Prospect Hill Found.; chmn. emeritus Hudson River Found. for Sci. and Environ. Rsch.; bd. dirs. The Sperry Fund; hon. trustee Am. Mus. Natural History, The Pingry Sch.; life trustee Ctrl. Park Conservancy. Served to comdr. USNR, World War II. Recipient Alumni medal Alumni Fedn. Columbia U., 1971, Yale medal, 2000, Frederick Law Olmsted award, 1986. Mem. Yale U. Club, Union League Club, Baltusrol Golf Club, Eastward Ho Country Club, Gulf Stream Golf Club, Ocean Club, Little Club. Home: 21 E 79th St New York NY 10021-0125 Office: Antaeus Enterprises Inc 99 Park Ave #2200 New York NY 10016-1601 Office Phone: 212-370-1144.

BEINEKE, LOWELL WAYNE, mathematics professor; b. Decatur, Ind., Nov. 20, 1939; s. Elmer Henry and Lillie Agnes (Snell) B.; m. Judith Rowena Wooldridge, Dec. 23, 1967; children: Jennifer Elaine, Philip Lennox. BS, Purdue U., 1961; MA, U. Mich., 1962, PhD, 1965. Asst. prof. Purdue U., Ft. Wayne, Ind., 1965-68, assoc. prof., 1968-71, prof., 1971-86, Jack W. Schrey prof., 1986—. Tutor Oxford (Eng.) U., 1974, The Open U., Milton Keynes, England, 1974, 75; vis. lectr. Poly. North London, 1980—81; vis. scholar Wolfson Coll., Oxford U., 1993—94, 2000—01; mem. SCR Keble Coll., 2000—01. Co-author (co-editor): Selected Topics in Graph Theory, 3 vols., 1978, 1983, 1988, Applications of Graph Theory, 1979, Graph Connections, 1997, Topics in Algebraic Graph Theory, 2004; assoc. editor Jour. Graph Theory, 1977—80, mem. editl. bd., 1977—, Internat. Jour. Graph Theory, 1991—95; editor: The Coll. Math. Jour.; co-editor: Congressus Numerantium, Vols., 1963—64, 1988; contbr. numerous articles to profl. jours. Corp. mem. Bd. for Homeland Ministries, United Ch. of Christ, N.Y., 1988-91, del. Gen. Synod, 1989, 91. Recipient Outstanding Tchr. award AMOCO Found., 1978, Friends of the Univ., 1992, Outstanding Rsch. award Ind. U.-Purdue U. Ft. Wayne, 1999; Fulbright Found. grantee London, 1980-81, rsch. grantee Office Naval Rsch., Washington, 1986-89; fellow Inst. Combinatorics and its Applications, 1990—. Mem. Math. Assn. Am. (chairperson Ind. Sect. 1987-88, bd. govs. 1990-93, 2004-, mem. exec. com., 2006-, Disting. Tchg. award Ind. Sect. 1997, Disting. Svc. award Ind. Sect. 1998), Am. Math. Soc., London Math. Soc., Common Cause, Amnesty Internat., Summit Book Club, Internat. Affairs Forum, Sigma Xi (club pres. 1984-86, chpt. pres. 1997-98), Phi Kappa Phi (chpt. pres. 1993), Pi Mu Epsilon. Democrat. United Ch. Of Christ. Achievements include characterization of line graphs and thickness of complete graphs; enumeration of multidimensional trees. Home: 4529 Bradwood Ter Fort Wayne IN 46815-6028 Office: Ind U-Purdue U Dept of Math Scis 2101 E Coliseum Blvd Fort Wayne IN 46805-1445 Home Phone: 260-471-7074; Office Phone: 260-481-6223. Business E-Mail: beineke@ipfw.edu.

BEIRNE, MARTIN DOUGLAS, lawyer; b. NYC, Oct. 24, 1944; s. Martin Douglas and Catherine Anne Beirne; m. Kathleen Harrington; children: Martin, Shannon, Kelley. BS, Spring Hill Coll., 1966; JD with honors, St. Mary's U., 1969. Bar: Tex. 1969, U.S. Dist. Ct. (ea. dist.) Tex. 1972, U.S. Dist. Ct. (so. dist.) Tex., 1971, U.S. Dist. Ct. (no. dist.) Tex., U.S. Dist. Ct. (we. dist.) Tex., U.S. Dist. Ct. DC, U.S. Ct. Appeals (5th and 11th cirs.) 1974, U.S. Dist. Ct. (ea. dist.) Calif., U.S. Supreme Ct. 1975. Ptnr. Fulbright & Jaworski, Houston, 1971-85; mng. ptnr. Beirne, Maynard & Parsons, Houston, 1985—. Editor-in-chief St. Mary's Law Rev. Bd. dirs. St. Thomas U., Houston Law Rev. Found.; bd. trustees St. Mary's U., chmn. law sch. found.; trustee Tex. Day Found.; commr. Tex. Access to Justice Commn. Capt. US Army, 1969—71. Fellow Am. Bar Found., Tex. Bar Found. (bd. dirs.); mem. ABA, Tex. Bar Assn., Houston Bar Assn., Coronado Club, Houstonian Club, Legatus-U. Houston Law Sch. Found. Am. Law Inst., Inst. for Transnat. Arbitration, Houston Bar Found. (bd. dirs.). Roman Catholic. Office: Beirne Maynard & Parsons LLP 1300 Post Oak Blvd Fl 25 Houston TX 77056-3028 Office Phone: 713-623-0887.

BEIRNE, OWEN ROSS, dental educator, researcher; b. Santa Maria, Calif., Jan. 18, 1947; s. Owen and Thelma Beirne; m. Sheryl Martha Schochet; children: Samuel, Deborah. BA, U. Calif., Berkeley, 1968; DMD, Harvard U., 1972; PhD, U. Calif., San Francisco, 1979. Cert. in oral and maxillofacial surgery, diplomate Am. Bd. Oral and Maxillofacial Surgery, Nat. Dental Bd. Anesthesiology. Asst. prof. U. Calif., San Francisco, 1979—85, assoc. prof., 1985—85; assoc. prof. Sch. Dentistry U. Wash., Seattle, 1985—93, prof., 1993—, dir. residency tng. dept. oral and maxillofacial surgery, 1985—99, chmn. dept. oral and maxillofacial surgery, 1999—. Mem. oral biology and medicine II study sect. Nat. Inst. Dental Rsch., Bethesda, Md., 1988—91; abstract reviewer Internat. Jour. Oral and Maxillofacial Implants, 1988—, cons., 1989—, ADA Commn. Dental Accreditation, Chgo., 1997—2003; mem. examination com. Am. Bd. Oral and Maxillofacial Surgery, 1997—2001. Sect. editor Principles of Oral and Maxillofacial Surgery, 1992; contbr. articles to profl. jours., chpts. to books; assoc. editor: Jour. Oral Implantology, 1992—; mem. editl. bd. Jour. Evidence Based Dental Practice, 2001—. Mem. editl. bd. Anesthesia Progress, 2003—; mem. boundary com. Northshore Sch. Dist., Bothell, 1996—98. Recipient Distinction in Tchg. award, U. Calif.-San Francisco, 1984. Fellow: Am. Coll. Dentists, Am. Dental Soc. Anesthesiology (pres. Wash. State 1996—2006); mem.: Nat. Dental Bd. Anesthesia (pres.), Oral Maxillofacial Surgery Found. (rsch. com. 2002—), Am. Assn. Oral and Maxillofacial Surgeons (chmn. adv. com. on rsch. and tech. assessment 1999—2000), Am. Assn. Dental Rsch. (councilor 1992—2007), Phi Beta Kappa, Omicron Kappa Upsilon (pres. Supreme chpt. 2000—01). Office: Univ Washington Oral Maxillofacial Surgery Box 357134 Seattle WA 98195-7134 Office Phone: 206-543-7722. Business E-Mail: slsb@u.washington.edu.

BEISNER, JOHN HERBERT, lawyer; b. Salina, Kans., Feb. 24, 1953; s. Herbert J. and Matilda (Cordel) B.; m. Diane G. Klinke, Apr. 26, 1980; 1 child, Laura Ann. BA with honors, U. Kans., 1975; JD with honors, U. Mich, 1978. Bar: Calif. 1978, U.S. Dist. Ct., Central Dist. Calif., 1978, D.C. 1980, U.S. Dist. Ct., DC 1980, U.S. Supreme Ct., 1985. Assoc. O'Melveny & Myers LLP, Washington, 1978-85, ptnr., 1985—, mng. ptnr., Washington office, 2000—, office head, class action practice, mem. policy com. Mem. Litigation Dept. of Yr. American Lawyer; lectr. in field. Contbr. articles to profl. jours.; adminstrv. editor Mich. Law Review, 1977—78, assoc. editor, 1976—77. Mem. State Colls. Coord. Com. Kans. Bd. Regents, 1974-75. Mem. ABA, DC Bar, State Bar Calif., Am. Law Inst., Fed. Comm. Bar Assn., Phi Beta Kappa. Office: O'Melveny & Myers LLP 1625 Eye St NW Washington DC 20006-4001 Office Phone: 202-383-5370. Office Fax: 202-383-5414. Business E-Mail: jbeisner@omm.com.

BEISTLINE, EARL HOOVER, mining consultant; b. Juneau, Alaska, Nov. 24, 1916; s. Ralph H. and Catherine (Krinach) B.; m. Dorothy Ann Hering, Aug. 24, 1946; children— Ralph Robert, William Calvin, Katherine Noreen, Lynda Marie. B. Mining Engring., U. Alaska, 1939, E.M., 1947, LL.D. (hon.), 1969. Mem. faculty U. Alaska, 1946-82, dean Sch. Mines, 1949-61, dean Coll. Earth Sci. and Mineral Industry, 1961-75, provost Coll. Earth Sci. and Mineral Industry, 1970-75, exec. officer no. region, 1970-73, dean Sch. Mineral Industry, 1975-82, dean emeritus, prof. mining engring. Sch. Mineral Industry, 1982—; mining cons. Served to maj. AUS, 1941-46. Fellow AAAS, Explorers Club; mem. NSPE, Am. Inst. Mining and Metall. Engrs., Mining and Metall. Soc. Am., Arctic Inst. N.Am., Am. Soc. Engring. Edn., N.W. Mining Assn., Alaska Mining Assn., Pioneers of Alaska. Home and Office: PO Box 80148 Fairbanks AK 99708-0148

BEITLER, STEPHEN, investment company executive, venture capitalist; s. Stanley and Arline Beitler; m. Deborah; children: Grace, Elinore. BA, cert. Asian Study, Am. U. Sch. Internat. Studies, 1977; postgrad., U. Chgo., 1977—78; MS, Nat. Def. Intelligence Coll., 1986. Legis. aide U.S. Ho. Reps., Washington, 1975—77; commd. 2d lt. U.S. Army, 1977, advanced through grades to maj., 1989; intelligence briefing officer Sec. Def. and Chmn. Joint Chiefs of Staff, Washington, 1984—86; asst. to asst. sec. of def. Office Sec. Def., Washington, 1987—88, asst. to undersec. of def., 1988—89; resigned U.S. Army, 1989; mgr. ops. devel. Helene Curtis, Inc., Chgo., 1989—90, corp. mgr. strategy and devel., 1990—92, dir. strategy and devel., 1993; nat. mgr. operational planning and info. Sears Merchandise Group, Hoffman Estates, Ill., 1993—95; sr. dir. fin. processes and sys. Sears, Roebuck and Co., Hoffman Estates, 1995—97, asst. corp. contr., 1997—98, v.p. elect, 1998; mng. dir., gen. ptnr. Trident Capital, Chgo., 1998—2002; mng. ptnr., sr. mng. dir. Dunrath Capital, Chgo., 2002—. Comdr. 305th psychol. ops. bn. USAR, Arlington Heights, Ill., 1992-96; comdr. 16th psychol. ops. bn. USAR, Ft. Sheridan, Ill., 1996-98; cons. MGA, Inc., Chgo., 1985—; founding chmn. Conf. Bd. Coun. Competitive Analysis; bd. dirs. Metatomix Inc., bd. adv. ReachMD, Inc., Gichner Inc., ARXAN, Inc.; entrepreneurial adv. bd. Grad. Sch. Bus., U. Chgo., 2003—; mem. security coun. Underwriters Labs. Inc., 2005—. Contbg. author: The Military Intelligence Community, 1986; contbr. articles to profl. publs. Bd. dirs. United Way of Highland Park-Highwood, 1999-2002; vol. Bus. Vols. for Arts, Chgo., 1991-94; bd. dirs. Spl. Ops. Warrior Found., 1999-; mem. adv. bd. Northwestern U. Homeland Security Innovation and Entrepreneurship Ctr., 2005—. Decorated Green Beret for valor and svc. Fellow Inter-univ. Seminar on Armed Forces and Soc., Soc. Competitive Intelligence Profls. (bd. dirs. 1991-94), Ill. Venture Capital Assn. (founding mem., bd. dirs., sec. 2001, vice chmn. 2002, chmn. 2003-2004); mem. Chicagoland C. of C. (bd. dirs. 2003—), Spl. Forces Club, Army and Navy Club, Union League Club Chgo., Execs. Club Chgo., Fin. Execs. Inst., The Birchwood Club, Carlton Club, Met. Club City of Washington DC, Econ.Club Chgo. Office Phone: 888-287-3459. Business E-Mail: steve@dunrath.com.

BEIZER, LANCE KURT, priest, lawyer; b. Hartford, Conn., Sept. 8, 1938; s. Lawrence Sidney and Victoria Merriam (Kaplan) B. BA in Sociology, Brandeis U., 1960; MA in English, San Jose State U., 1967; JD, U. San Diego, 1975; MDiv, Ch. Divinity Sch. Pacific, 2005. Bar: Calif. 1975; Ordained to ministry Episcopal Ch. as priest, 2005. Selective svc. affairs coord. U. Calif., 1969-73, vet. affairs coord., 1973-75; vet. outreach coord. San Diego Community Coll. Dist., 1975-76; dep. dist. atty. Santa Clara County, Calif., 1976—2002; Episcopal priest, 2005—. Bd. mgrs. Santa Clara Valley S.W. YMCA, Saratoga, Calif., 1988—, chmn., 1991-93; bd. dirs. Lumen Found., San Francisco, 1985—; bd. dirs. Fedn. Cmty. Ministries, Calif., 1992—; bd. dirs. Santa Clara County Counc. Chs., 2006—, Santa Clara County Child Abuse Coun., 2007—. Lt. USNR, 1961-65. Mem. Nat. Assn. Counsel for Children, Am. Weil Soc., Mensa, Commonwealth Club. Republican. Episcopalian. Office: Trinity Episcopal Cathedral 81 N 2d St San Jose CA 95113 Home Phone: 408-374-7458; Office Phone: 408-293-7953. Personal E-mail: lbeizer@yahoo.com.

BEJA, MORRIS, English literature educator; b. NYC, July 18, 1935; s. Joseph and Eleanor (Cohen) B.; children: Andrew Lloyd, Eleni Rachel; m. Ellen Carol Jones, 1990. BA, CCNY, 1957; MA, Columbia U., 1958; PhD, Cornell U., 1963. From instr. to prof. English Ohio State U., Columbus, 1961-2000, prof. emeritus, 2001—. Vis. prof. U. Thessaloniki, Greece, 1965-66, Univ. Coll. Dublin, 1972-73, Northwestern U., Evanston, Ill., 2007. Author: Epiphany in the Modern Novel, 1971, Film and Literature, 1979, Joyce the Artist Manqué and Indeterminacy, 1989, James Joyce: A Literary Life, 1992; editor: Virginia Woolf's Mrs. Dalloway, 1996, Joyce in the Hibernian Metropolis, 1996, Perspectives on Orson Welles, 1995, Samuel Beckett: Humanistic Perspectives, 1983, James Joyce Newestlatter, 1977—, James Joyce's Dubliners and Portrait of the Artist, 1973; editor: (with E.C. Jones) Twenty-First Joyce, 2004. Pres. Internat. James Joyce Found., 1982-90, sec. 1990—; dir. Internat. James Joyce Symposia, 1982, 86, 92, 2004. With USAR, 1958-63. Guggenheim fellow, 1972-73; Fulbright lectr., 1965-66, 72-73. Mem. MLA, Internat. Virginia Woolf Soc. (trustee 1976-84), Am. Conf. Irish Studies. Jewish. Avocations: photography, travel, bicycling. Home: 1135 Middleport Dr Columbus OH 43235-4060 Office: Ohio State U Dept of English 164 W 17th Ave Columbus OH 43210-1326 E-mail: beja.1@osu.edu.

BEJAN, ADRIAN, mechanical engineering educator; b. Sept. 24, 1948; married; 3 children. SB in Mech. Engring., SM in Mech. Engring., MIT, 1972, PhD Mech. Engring., 1975; PhD (hon.), Poly. U. Bucharest, 1992, U. Galati, Romania, 1995, U. Constantza, 1997. Engr. Sci. Energy Systems, Inc., Watertown, Mass., 1972; rsch. asst. dept. mech. engring. MIT, 1971-74, lectr., rsch. assoc., dept. mech. engring., 1975-76; fellow Miller Inst. Basic Rsch. Sci., U. Calif., Berkeley, 1976-78; asst. prof., dept. mech. engring. U. Colo., Boulder, 1978-81; Croft prof. U. Colo. Coll. Engring., 1981-82; assoc. prof., dept. mech. engring. U. Colo., Boulder, 1981-84; prof., dept. mech. engring. and materials sci. Duke U., Durham, NC, 1984-89, J.A. Jones prof., dept. mech. engring., 1989—. Author: Entropy Generation Through Heat and Fluid Flow, 1982, Convection Heat Transfer, 1984, 2d edit., 1995, Advanced Engineering Thermodynamics, 1988, Heat Transfer, 1993, Entropy Generation Minimization, 1996; co-author: Convection in Porous Media, 1992, Thermal Design and Optimization, 1996; hon. editorial bd.: International Journal of Heat and Mass Transfer, 1992, International Communications in Heat and Mass Transfer, 1992, Termotehnica, 1993; bd. editors: Internat. Journal for Engineering Analysis and Design; adv. editor: Heat Transfer Japanese Rsch., 1990, Internat. Jour. Heat and Fluid Flow, 1988, Numerical Heat Transfer, 1995, Jour. Non-Equilibrium Thermodynamics, 1996, Energy-The Internat. Jour., 1997, Revue Générale de Thermique, 1997; reviewer manuscrips for numerous jours.; contbr. over 260 articles to profl. jours. Recipient Ralph R. Teetor award Soc. Automotive Engrs., 1980, De Florez award MIT, 1969, Heat Transfer Meml. award, 1994, Worcester Reed Warner medal 1996; Faculty fellow U. Colo., 1984-85; F. Mosey Vis. scholar U. Western Australia. Fellow ASME (Gustus L. Larson award 1988, James Harry Potter Gold medal 1990); mem. Am. Acad. Mechanics, Tau Beta Pi, Pi Tau Sigma. Office: Duke U Box 90300 Dept Mech Engring Sc Durham NC 27708-0300 Office Phone: 919-660-5309. Business E-Mail: dalford@duke.edu.

BEJANISHVILI, SABA, neurologist; b. Tbilisi, Georgia, Mar. 15, 1974; s. Vazha Bejanishvili and Marine Chachkhiani; m. Nino Giorgobiani, June 15, 2006. MD (hon.), Tbilisi State Med. U., 1998. Diplomate Am. Bd. Psychiatry and Neurology, 2005, Am. Bd. Electrodiagnostic Medicine, 2005. Med. intern Emory U., Atlanta, 1999—2000, resident neurology, 2000—03; gen. neurology Kans. Med. Clinic, Topeka, 2005—; fellow movement disorders La. State U., New Orleans, 2004—05, fellow clin. neurophysiology, 2003—04. Mem.: Am. Assn. Neuromuscular and Electrodiagnostic Medicine, Am. Acad. Neurology. Home Phone: 785-271-2452; Office Phone: 785-354-9300. Office Fax: 785-354-0292.

BEKAVAC, NANCY YAVOR, retired academic administrator, lawyer; b. Pitts., Aug. 28, 1947; d. Anthony Joseph and ELvira (Yavor) Bekavac. BA, Swarthmore Coll., 1969; JD, Yale U., 1973. Bar: Calif. 1974, U.S. Dist. Ct. (cen. dist.) Calif. 1974, U.S. Dist. Ct. (no. dist.) Calif. 1975, U.S. Ct. Appeals (9th cir.) 1975, U.S. Dist. Ct. (so. dist.) Calif. 1976, U.S. Surpeme Ct. 1979, U.S. Ct. Appeals (8th cir.) 1981. Law clk. at large U.S. Ct. Appeals (D.C. cir.), Washington, 1973-74; assoc. Munger, Tolles & Rickershauser, LA, 1974-79, ptnr., 1980-85; exec. dir. Thomas J. Watson Found., Providence, 1985-87, cons., 1987-88; counselor to pres. Dartmouth Coll., Hanover, N.H., 1988-90; pres. Scripps Coll., Claremont, Calif., 1990—2007. Adj. prof. law UCLA Law Sch., 1982—83; mem. Calif. Higher Edn. Roundtable, 1996—; trustee Am. Coun. Edn., 1994—97; bd. dir. Electro Rent Corp. Author: (books) Imagining the Real Future, 1996. Bd. mgrs. Swathmore Coll., 1984—; trustee Wenner-Gren Found. Anthrop. Rsch., 1987—94; bd. trustees Am. Coun. Edn., 1994—97; chair Assn. Ind. Colls. and Univs., 1996—97. Recipient Human Rights award, LA County Commn. Civil Rights, 1984; fellow Woodrow Wilson fellow, Thomas J. Watson fellow, 1969. Mem.: WestEd. (bd. dir.), Women's Coll. Coalition, Am. Assn. Ind. Calif. Colls. and Univs. (chair 1996), Commn. on White House Fellowships (chmn., selection com. 1993—94), Seaver Found. (bd. dir.), Sierra Club. Avocations: hiking, reading, travel. Office Phone: 909-621-8148. E-mail: president@scrippscollege.edu.*

BEKENDAM, CAROL HELEN, psychologist; b. Rock Valley, Iowa, Dec. 20, 1933; d. Francis Louis and Annetta Corwin; m. Peter Bekendam, June 15, 1951; children: Randall Scott, Michael Dean(dec.) , Cheryl Ann Dixon, Jeffrey Todd. BA in Behavioral Sci. summa cum lade, Calif. State Poly. U., Pomona, 1977; MA in Marriage and Family Counseling summa cum lade, Azusa Pacific U., Calif., 1979; PhD in Clin. Psychology summa cum lade, Fielding Inst., Santa Barbara, Calif., 1997. Cert. in hypnotherapy Calif., doctoral addictions counselor Calif., criminal justice counselor Calif. State Poly. U., 1976, domestic violence counselor Nat. Assn. Forensic Counselors. Southern Calif. rep. M-2, Chino, Calif., 1972—74; exec. dir. Creative Counseling Ctr., Pomona, 1979—2000, dir., owner Claremont, 1986—. Dir. Am. Friends Prison Program, Claremont, Calif., 1971—72; supr. intern tng. marriage, family therapy Creative Counseling Ctr., Pomona, Calif., 1979—2001, Claremont, 1979—2001. Sponsor prison visiting Am Friends Svc. Com., Claremont, 1966—86, Chino, 1966—86; founder Crossroads, Inc., Claremont, 1974; spkr. caring elderly parents Chino, 2005; foster parent, 1966—86; tchr. LIFT Pomona First Bapt. Ch., 1975—2005. Recipient Women Helping Women award, Soroptomists, 1975, Achievement award, Calif. State Poly U., 1976. Mem.: AAUW, APA, Calif. Assn. Marriage, Family Therapy, Am. Assn. Marriage, Family Therapy, Phi Kappa Phi. Bapt. Avocations: reading, painting, travel, walking, writing. Office: Creative Counseling 250 W 1st St Claremont CA 91711-4743 Home: 2471 Santa Rosa Ct Upland CA 91784 Office Phone: 909-625-3990.

BEKENSTEIN, JOSHUA, venture capital company executive; b. NYC, July 2, 1958; s. Arthur L. and Doris P. Bekenstein; m. Anita S. Bekenstein, Oct. 6, 1985. BA in Econs., Yale U., 1980; MBA, Harvard U., 1984. Cons. Bain & Co., Boston, 1980-82; gen. ptnr. Bain Venture Capital, Boston, 1984—. Office: Bain Capital 111 Huntington Ave Boston MA 02199

BEKEY, GEORGE ALBERT, computer scientist, educator; b. Bratislava, Slovakia, June 19, 1928; arrived in U.S., 1945, naturalized, 1956; s. Andrew and Elizabeth Bekey; m. Shirley White, June 10, 1951; children: Ronald Steven, Michelle Elaine. BS with honors, U. Calif., Berkeley, 1950; MS, UCLA, 1952, PhD, 1962. Rsch. engr. UCLA, 1950-54; mgr. computer ctr. Beckman Instruments, LA and Berkeley, Calif., 1955-58; mem. sr. staff, dir. computer ctr. TRW Systems Group, Redondo Beach, Calif., 1958-62; mem. faculty U. So. Calif., LA, 1962—, prof. elec. and biomed. engring. and computer sci., 1968—2003, chmn. dept. elec. engring. systems, 1978-86, dir. Robotics Lab., 1983-98, chmn. computer sci. dept., 1984-89, dir. Ctr. for Mfg. and Automation Rsch., 1987-94, assoc. dean Sch. Engring., 1996-2001; adj. prof. engring. Calif. Poly. State U., San Luis Obispo, Calif., 2005—. Chair computer sci. Gordon Marshall, 1990—2002; cons. to govt. agys. and indsl. orgns. Author (with W. J. Karplus): Hybrid Computation, 1968; author: (with K. Goldberg) Robotics and Neural Networks, 1994; author: Autonomous Robots, 2005; co-editor: Hospital Information Systems, 1972, System Identification, 1983, Neural Networks and Robotics, 1993, Autonomous Underwater Robots, 1996, Robot Colonies, 1997, Distributed Autonomous Robotic Systems, 2000, Modeling and Simulation, Theory and Practice, 2003; editor-in-chief Autonomous Robots Jour.; founding editor: IEEE Trans. Robotics and Automation, mem. editl. bd.: 3 profl. jours.; contbr. articles to profl. jours. With US Army, 1954—56. Recipient Disting. Faculty award, 1977, Sch. Engring. Svc. award, U. So. Calif., 1990, Presdl. medallion, 2000, Engelberger prize in robotics, 2001, Alumni Achievement Academia, UCLA, 2005; scholar, Calif. Polytech. U. San Luis Obispo, 2005—. Fellow: IEEE (3d Millennium medal 2000), AAAS, Am. Assn. Artificial Intelligence, Am. Inst. Med. and Biol. Engring.; mem.: NAE, Biomed. Engring. Soc., Soc. Computer Simulation, Assn. Computing Machinery, IEEE Robotics and Automation Soc. (pres. 1996—97, Pioneer in Robotics and Automation award 2002, Disting. Svc. award 2004, Nat. Robotics award 2006), Tau Beta Pi, Eta Kappa Nu. Achievements include patents in field. Office: U So Calif Computer Sci Dept Los Angeles CA 90089-0781

BEKKERS, JOHN, former food products executive; b. Arnhem, The Netherlands; arrived in U.S., 1962, naturalized, 1983; Student, The Netherlands, Harbor Jr. Coll., San Pedro, Calif.; grad., Duke U. Dir. Poultry Group Mgmt. Sys., Atlanta, 1985-87; mgr. N.E. Ala. Poultry divsn. Boaz, 1987-94, exec. v.p., 1994-95; exec. v.p., mem. exec. com. Gold Kist Inc., Atlanta, pres., COO, 1995—2001, pres., CEO, 2001—07. With US Army, Vietnam.*

BEKRENEV, ANATOLIY, physicist; b. Shuya, Russia, Feb. 24, 1944; s. Nikolai and Anna Bekrenev; m. Ludmila Kudysh, Sept. 16, 1972; children: Vlada, Sergei. MS, Petrozavodsk State U., Russia, 1966; PhD, Kharkov State U., Ukraine, 1971; DSc, Materials Sci. Inst., Ukraine, 1985. From asst. prof. to 1st v.p. Samara State Tech. U., 1970—96; cons. Phys. Tech. Co., 1996—99; prof. Nat. Am. U., 1999—. Author: Small-angle X-ray Scattering, 1991, Post Deformation Processes, 1992, Physics Problems with Solutions, 1996, Diffusion Along Dislocations, 1996, Phase Transformations and Mass Trnasport Under Pulse Reactions, 2001, Mass Transport Under Pulse Reactions, 2002, Laser Treatment of Materials, 2005. Mem.: Internat. Higher Edn. Acad. Sci., St. Petersburg Acad. Sci. for Strength Problems, NY Acad. Sci. Avocations: gardening, reading, history. Home: 13951 Wellington Dr Eden Prairie MN 55347 Office: Nat Am U Metro Pkwy Bloomington MN 55425 Office Phone: 952-883-0439. Personal E-mail: abekrenev@gmail.com.

BELAFONTE, HARRY (HARRY GEORGE BELAFONTE JR.), singer, concert artist, actor; b. Harlem, NYC, Mar. 1, 1927; s. Harold George and Melvine (Love) B.; m. Margurite Byrd, 1948 (div. 1957); m. Julie Robinson, Mar. 8, 1957; children: Adrienne, Shari, David, Gina. LHD (hon.), Park Coll., Mo., 1968; HHD (hon.), Park Coll.; Doctorate Liberal Arts, Arts (hon.), New Sch. Social Research; MusD (hon.), Morehouse Coll., 1987; DFA (hon.), SUNY, Purchase, 1987, Spelman Coll., 1990; DFA, CCNY, 1990; DSc (hon.), Tufts U., 1991, Brandeis U., 1991, Long Island U., 1991; DHL (hon.), Columbia U., 1993; DA (hon.), Bard Coll., 1993; DLitt (hon.), U. West Indies, Kingston, Jamaica, 1996; degree (hon.), U. Mass., 1996; LLD (hon.), McMaster U., Hamilton, Ont., Can., 1996; D in Civil Law (hon.), U. Newcastle, Britain, 1998; LHD (hon.), Bklyn. Coll., 1998. Pres. Belafonte Enterprises, Inc., NYC. Participant, Voices of the Arts Kennedy Ctr. for Performing Arts, Washington, 2006. Singer, actor in Broadway shows John Murray Anderson's Almanac (Tony award 1953), Three for Tonight, 1955; motion pictures: Bright Road, 1952, Carmen Jones, 1954, Island in the Sun, 1957, The World, the Flesh and the Devil, 1958, Odds Against Tomorrow, 1959, The Angel Levine, 1969, Buck and the Preacher, 1971, Uptown Saturday Night, 1974, White Man's Burden, 1995, Kansas City, 1996, Bobby, 2006; prodr. stage play To Be Young Gifted and Black, 1969; appeared in TV movies Grambling's White Tiger, 1981, Swing Vote, 1999; prodr. TV spls. A Time for Laughter, 1967, Harry and Lena, 1969; TV program Tonight with Belafonte, 1960 (Emmy award); appeared on German TV spl. I Sing What I See, 1980; concert performances in Cuba, Jamaica, Europe, 1980, Australia, N.Z., U.S., Europe, 1981, Can., 1982, U.S., Europe and with Can. symphony orchs., 1983, U.S., 1985, U.S., Can., Japan, Europe, 1986; prodr. Strolling Twenties-TV, Parting the Waters, (miniseries), 2000; co-prodr. Beat Street, 1984; appeared at Golden Nugget, Atlantic City and Las Vegas, 1985, 86; initiator, performer rec. We Are the World, 1985 (Grammy award 1985); performer concert tours, U.S., Can. and Europe including 60 city tour, 1988, concerts in U.S., Europe, Can., 1989, 90, 93, concerts in U.S., Japan and Can., 1991, concert tour U.S., 1992, concerts U.S., Can. and Europe, 1995, U.S., Can., Europe and Far East, 1996, 50-city European tour, 1998; 1st N.Y. appearance in 30 yrs. Avery Fisher Hall, Lincoln Ctr., 1993; albums: The Long Road to Freedom, 2001, Island in the Sun, 2002. Chmn. Martin Luther King., Jr. Holiday Commn., 1987; goodwill amb. UNICEF, 1987; bd. dirs. N.Y. State Martin Luther King, Jr. Inst. for Nonviolence, 1989—; N.Y. State Employees Brotherhood com. (Benjamin Potocker brotherhood award 1993); served with USN. Recipient award of appreciation for initiation of and work for USA for Africa, Am. Music, 1986, Leader for Peace award Peace Corps, 1988, Danny Kaye award US Com. for UNICEF, 1989, Africa's Future award, 1994, Whitney M. Young Jr. Svc. award Boy Scouts Am., 1989, Golden Acorn award Bronx Community Coll., 1989, Kennedy Ctr. honors, 1989, Mandela Courage award (inaugural presentation), 1990, Tribute to a Black Am. award Nat. Conf. Black Mayors, Inc., 1991, Bill of Rights award ACLU So. Calif., 1991, Internat. House Berkeley award, 1994, Food and Hunger Hotline award, 1994, Humanitarian award NY Assn. New Americans, 1994, Brotherhood award 100 Black Men, 1994, Children's Champion award UNICEF Com. Greater Boston-joint award with Julie Belafonte, 1994, Nat. Medal of the Arts, 1994, Letelier-Moffitt Human Rights award, 1994, Best Supporting Actor (Kansas City), 1996, NY Film Critics Cir., Jesse Owens Humanitarian award, 1996, Man of the Yr. award NY chpt. Hadassah, 1996, Hadassah Internat. First Citizen of the World award, 1996, Medal of Distinction, Lenox Hill Hosp., NYC, 1996, South African-Am. Orgn. Leadership award, 1996, Florinda Lasker Civil Liberties award, 1997, Living Landmark award NY Landmarks Conservancy, 1997, Humanitarian of Yr. award WLIW/21, 1997, William Moses Kunstler Racial Justice award, 1997, NY Arts & Bus. Coun. award, 1997, Chmn.'s award NAACP Image Awards, 1999, Ronald H. Brown award Nat. Child Labor Com., 1999, Humanitarian award, Black Entertainment TV, 2006; inducted into Miami Children's Hosp. Internat. Pediat. Hall of Fame, 1996.*

BELAK, MICHAEL JAMES, information technology executive; b. Cleve., Nov. 26, 1961; s. John James and Violet Mae (Yamek) B.; children: Michael James II, Nathaniel Hinds; m. Monica Vidal: children: Nils, Vidal, Jean Paul Vidal BS Computer Engring., Ohio State U., 1985; MBA Info. Systems Mgmt., George Washington U., 1990; PhD Mgmt., U. Md., 2005. Application programmer, office of registrar Ohio State U., Columbus, 1984—85; project leader database adminstrn. IBM, Gaithersburg, Md., 1985—88; mgr. cons. svcs. GE, Rockville, Md., 1988—91; dir. fleet svcs. devel. PHH Corp., Hunt Valley, Md., 1991—94; dir. data quality mgmt. Nat. Assn. Securities Dealers, Rockville, 1994—97; sr. dir. data mgmt. Marriott Internat., Bethesda, Md., 1998—2001; chief info. officer Dept. Pub. Works, Washington, 2001—. Adj. faculty DeVry U., 2005—, Am. U., 2006—, U. Md., 2006—. Contbr. articles to profl. jours Allocation panel United Way, 1993-94; tech. and innovation com. City of Gaithersburg, 2001— Named to Premier 100 IT Leaders Computerworld, 2000 Mem. Internat. DB2 Users Group (conf. com. 1990-92), Washington Case Users Group (sec. 1991), Assn. for Computing Machinery (profl. devel. com. 1989-91), Soc. Info. Mgmt. (East Coast working group on client server tech., bd. dirs. D.C. chpt. 1997) Avocations: motorcycling, weight training, golf, jetskiing. Home: Kentlands 301 Ridgepoint Pl Gaithersburg MD 20878-5704 Office: Dept Pub Works DC 2000 14th St NW Washington DC 20009 Office Phone: 202-671-2814. Business E-Mail: michael.belak@dc.gov.

BELANGER, CHERRY CHURCHILL, elementary school educator; b. Berea, Ky., May 14, 1923; d. David Carroll and Anna Eleanor (Franzen) Churchill; m. Paul Adrien Belanger, Oct. 15, 1950 (dec. Feb. 1987); children: Peter Carroll, Karen Michelle Belanger-Magon. BA, Pomona Coll., Claremont, Calif., 1944; MA in Elem. Edn., Calif. State U., Northridge, 1983. Cert. tchr. early childhood edn. Actress Actor's Equity Assn., 1944-49; retail promotion asst. Bloomingdale's, NYC, 1948-52; editor Living for Young Homemakers, NYC, 1953-54, Bride-To-Be Mag., NYC, 1955; off-camera editor NBC Home Show, NYC, 1955-56; publicist home furnishing Alfred Auerbach, Bell & Stanton, NYC, 1956-61; retail rep. Betsy Ross Martin Assocs., LA, 1961-66; exec. sec. So. Calif. Assn. Bedding Mfrs., LA, 1966-70; retail rep. Hercules Corp., LA, 1971; tchr. early childhood edn. Carthay Nursery, Beverly Hills, Calif., 1971-78, L.A. Unified Sch. Dist., 1976-79, tchr. kindergarten and 1st grade, 1979-99. Den mother, treas., chmn., inst. rep. Boy Scouts Am., Beverly Hills, 1961-85; troop leader Brownies, Girl Scouts U.S., 1968-83. Recipient Silver Fawn award Boy Scouts Am., L.A., 1972, Elizabeth H. Brady Tchr. award So. Calif. Kindergarten Assn., 1997; honored Cherry Belanger Day in Beverly Hills, City Coun., 1976. Mem. DAR, AAUW, United Tchrs. of L.A. Avocations: drama, music, camping.

BELANGER, DEVON TAYLOR, small business owner; b. Weymouth, Dorset, Eng., Aug. 24, 1969; came to U.S., 1997; d. Charles Denison and Helen Joy Bate; m. Michael Trevor Webb, May 31, 1992 (div.); m. William Scott Landman, Aug. 30, 1997 (dec. 2004); m. Yves Belanger, Dec. 29, 2006. Pers. adminstr. RAF, Uxbridge, 1987—92; pres. Bodytalk Fitness, Ltd., Haslemere, England, 1992—97, Elite Retail Leasing, Inc., Parkland, Fla., 1997—2005; owner Journey's End Farm (dressage facility), Gibson Truck World, Sanford, Fla., 2006—. Actress, model, TV presenter. Editor: (other) Flying Changes Publ.; prodr.: (workout video) Bodytalk Step Workout Video, 1992; contbr. articles on fitness to mags. Organizer charity events Starlight Found., 1995. Mem. Aerobics Orgn. Gt. Britain, Fitness Profls. U.K., Nat. Register Personal Trainers, IDEA Fitness Profls. Anglican. Avocations: exercise, horseback riding, dressage, travel, cycling. Home: 233 New Gate Loop Lake Mary FL 32746 Office: Gibson Truck World 3455 Orlando Dr S Sanford FL 32773 Office Phone: 407-321-0660. Office Fax: 407-322-0376. Business E-Mail: devon@gibsontruckworld.com.

BELANGER, GERARD, economics professor; b. St. Hyacinthe, Que., Can., Oct. 23, 1940; s. Georges and Cecile (Girard) B.; 1 child, Marie-Jose. BA, U. Montreal, 1960; B in Social Sci., Laval U., 1961, M in Social Sci., 1967; MA, Princeton U., 1966. Asst. prof. econs. Laval U., 1967-71, assoc. prof., 1971-77, prof. econs., 1977—; rsch. coord. Howe Inst., Montreal, 1977-79; mem. fin. com. Coun. Univs., Que., 1971-73. Co-author: The Price of Health, 1974, Le Prix du Transport au Quebec, 1978; author: L'economique du secteur public, 1981, Croissance du secteur public et fédéralisme, 1988, L' Economique de la santé et l'Etat providence, 2005. Woodrow Wilson scholar, 1964-65; Walter N. Rothchild scholar, 1965-66. Fellow Royal Soc. Can. Office: Université Laval Dept D'eco Pav Desêve Quebec City PQ Canada G1K 7P4 Home Phone: 418-681-3075; Office Phone: 418-656-5363. Business E-Mail: gebe@ecn.ulaval.ca.

BELANGER, LAURA HEWLETTE, environmental scientist, consultant; b. Columbia, SC, Jan. 1, 1977; d. Earl Durant and Sue Swartout Hewlette; m. Matthew David Belanger, Apr. 23, 2005. Student, Evergreen State Coll., 1996; BS in Recreation Mgmt. summa cum laude, Appalachian State U., 1998; MA in Energy and Environ. Analysis, Boston U., 2004. Program dir. Camp Ton-A-Wandah, Hendersonville, NC, 1998—2000, Adventure Treks, Inc., Hendersonville, 2000—03; environ. scientist CR Environ., Falmouth, Mass., 2004; americorps program dir. Carolina Mountain Land Conservancy, Hendersonville, 2004; project mgr. Environ. Permitting Cons., Inc., Greenville, SC, 2005—. Mem. recreation mgmt. adv. coun. Appalachian State U., Boone, NC, 1999—2001. Eric DeGrott scholar, Appalachian State U., 1998. Mem.: Soc. Wetland Scientists, Mensa (life), Alpha Chi (life). Achievements include research in determinants of OPEC production: implications for OPEC behavior. Avocations: travel, photography. Home: 662 Holiday Dr Hendersonville NC 28739 Office: Environmental Permitting Consultants In 125 W Stone Ave Greenville SC 29609 Home Phone: 828-553-9548; Office Phone: 864-271-3040. Personal E-mail: laurabelanger@gmail.com. Business E-Mail: laura@enviropermit.com.

BELANGER, SHARON AMLING, special education educator; b. Berkley, Calif., Apr. 28, 1961; d. Harold Warner and Martha Elizabeth Amling; m. Gregory James Belanger, June 15, 1983; children: Joshua James, Jason Alexander, Joel Gregory, Justin Michael. BA, Calif. State U., 1983; MEd, U. Minn., 2001. Cert. computer, ednl. tech. U. Minn.; lic. emotional behavioral disorders tchng. U. Minn., specific learning disabilities tchng. U. Minn., cert. multiple subjects tchr. Calif. State U. Eighth grade tchr. Fond du Lac Ojibwe Sch., Cloquet, Minn., 1994—95, mid. sch. sci. tchr., 1995—96, spl. edn. tchr., 1996—2002, spl. edn. coord., 2002—. Spl. edn. adv. coun. State Dept. Edn., Minn., 1998—2002; bd. dirs. Minn. Coun. Exceptional Children, 2000—02; adj. prof. U. Minn., 2001—02; adv. bd. exceptional children Bur. Indian Affairs, 2005—; adj. prof. Fond du Lac Tribal, C.C., 2005—06. Mem.: Coun. Exceptional Children. Office: Fond du Lac Ojibwe Sch 49 U Rd Cloquet MN 55720 Home Phone: 218-727-8587; Office Phone: 218-878-7551. Business E-Mail: sharonbelanger@fdlrez.com.

BELANGER, TERRY, historian, educator; b. Hartford, Conn., Mar. 21, 1941; BA, Haverford Coll., 1963; MA, Columbia U., 1964, PhD, 1970. Svc. faculty Columbia U. Sch. Libr., 1971—92; assistant dean Columbia U., 1980—86, founder Book Arts Press bibliog. lab., 1971—92, founder Rare Book Sch., 1983—; moved Book Arts Press and Rare Book Sch. to U. Va., 1992; prof., hon. curator spl. collections U. Va. Named MacArthur fellow, John D. and Catherine T. MacArthur Found., 2005. Mem.: Bibliographical Soc. U. Va. (coun. 1992—), Bibliographical Soc. Am. (chair nominating com. 1995, 2007), Bibliographical Soc. London, Assn. Coll. Rsch. Libr. (bd. dir. 1976—78, chair rare books and manuscripts sect. 1978—79), Am. Antiquarian Soc., Am. Printing History Assn. (trustee 1974—81, pres. NY chpt. 1979—82, Laureate 1994). Office: U Va PO Box 400103 114 Alderman Libr Alderman Libr Charlottesville VA 22904-4103 Office Phone: 434-924-8851. Business E-Mail: belanger@virginia.edu.

BELANGER, WILLIAM JOSEPH, chemist, consultant; b. Chgo., Mar. 20, 1925; m. Keltah Long, Feb. 1, 1947; children: William Joseph, Thomas, Kathryn, Michael, Jeanne, Judith, Elizabeth, John, Anne. BS in Chemistry, St. Louis U., 1948; PhD in Organic Chemistry, Notre Dame U., 1951. Research chemist duPont Co., 1951-53; research chemist, then tech. service mgr. Devoe & Reynolds Co., 1953-60; tech. mgr. resin devel. Celanese Coatings & Specialties Co., Louisville, 1960-69; v.p. tech. and engring. Celanese Polymer Specialities Co., Jeffersontown, Ky., 1970-79; v.p. Specialties Group, Celanese Plastics & Specialties Co., 1979-82; Splty. polymer applications cons., 1982—. Tchr. polymer chemistry U. Louisville, 1957; tchr. organic chemistry Ind. Univ. Southeast, 1986. Patentee in field. Vice chmn. Jefferson County Housing Authority, 1975-78; trustee Audubon Hosp., 1979-82. Served with USNR, 1943-45. Mem. Am. Chem. Soc., Nat. Paint and Coatings Assn. Home and Office: 1208 Creighton Hill Rd Louisville KY 40207-2244 Personal E-mail: billb1208@insightbb.com.

BELASCO, STEVEN RONALD, lawyer; b. Bklyn., Jan. 16, 1947; s. Philip Robert and Edythe (Barbell) B.; m. Claire Belasco, Aug. 14, 1969 (div. Feb. 1984); children: Daniel, Judith; m. Frances Schwartz, May 3, 1987; 1 child, Sara. BS cum laude, Bklyn. Coll., 1967; JD, U. Va., 1970; LLM in Taxation, NYU, 1974. Bar: N.Y. 1971. Assoc. Jackson, Nash, Brophy, Barringer & Brooks, NYC, 1973-76; sr. tax atty. Colgate-Palmolive Co., NYC, 1976-78, v.p. taxation, 1987-95, v.p. taxation and real estate, 1996—2005; pvt. practice Scarsdale, NY, 2005—. Contr. articles to profl. jours. Active Zoning Bd. Appeals, Greenburgh, NY, 1993—, chmn., 2000—. Mem. ABA, N.Y. Bar Assn., Assn. of Bar of the City of N.Y., NYU Tax Soc. (v.p. 1986—2001). Avocation: stamp collecting/philately. Home and Office: 287 Evandale Rd Scarsdale NY 10583-1505 Office Phone: 917-710-2668. Business E-Mail: sbelasco@gmail.com.

BEL BRUNO, JOSEPH JAMES, chemistry professor; b. Passaic, NJ, June 30, 1952; s. Joseph and Carmella (Nicastro) Bel B.; m. Kathleen B. Cassidy, Aug. 10, 1980; children: Joseph Hugh, Elizabeth Kelly. BS, Seton Hall U., South Orange, NJ, 1974; PhD in Phys. Chemistry, Rutgers U., New Brunswick, NJ, 1980. Rsch. assoc. chemistry Princeton U., NJ, 1980—82; asst. prof. chemistry Dartmouth Coll, Hanover, NH, 1982—88; assoc. prof. chemistry Dartmouth Coll., Hanover, 1988—93, prof. chemistry, 1994—. Chair dept. chemistry Dartmouth Coll., Hanover, 1998—2001. Feature editor Jour. Chemistry Edn.; contbr. over 100 articles to profl. jours. Bd. dirs. Cradle and Crayon Child Devel. Ctr., Hanover, 1991-95. Alexander von Humboldt Found. fellow, 1988, Dartmouth Humanities Rsch. Inst. fellow, 1998. Mem. Am. Chem. Soc., Am. Phys. Soc., Inst. for Main Group Chemistry, Material Rsch. Soc., Sigma Xi. Office: Dartmouth Coll Burke Laboratory Hanover NH 03755 Office Phone: 603-646-2270. Business E-Mail: jjbchem@dartmouth.edu.

BELCASTRO, PATRICK FRANK, pharmacist, researcher; b. Italy, June 3, 1920; came to U.S., 1927, naturalized, 1943; s. Samuel and Sarah (Mosca) B.; m. Hanna Vilhelmina Jensen, July 6, 1963; children— Helen Maria, Paul Anthony. BS, Duquesne U., 1942; MS (Am. Found. Pharm. Edn. fellow), Purdue U., 1951, PhD in Pharmacy and Pharm. Chemistry (Am. Found. for Pharm. Edn. fellow), 1953. Instr. pharmacy Duquesne U., 1946-49; asst. prof. pharmacy Ohio State U., 1953-54; prof. indsl. pharmacy Purdue U., 1954-90, prof. emeritus, 1990—. Author: Physical and Technical Pharmacy, 1963; contbg. editor: (with others) Pharm. Tech, 1977—; contbr. to: (with others) Jour. Pharm. Scis. Served with U.S. Army, 1942-46. Mem. Am. Pharm. Assn., Rho Chi, Phi Lambda Upsilon. Roman Catholic. Home: 327 Meridian St West Lafayette IN 47906-2603 Office: Purdue-U Sch Pharmacy and Pharm Scis West Lafayette IN 47907 E-mail: pbelcas1@purdue.edu.

BELCHER, ANGELA, engineering educator; Attended, Santa Barbara City Coll., 1986—88; BA in Creative Studies, U. Calif. Santa Barbara, 1991, PhD in Chemistry, 1997. Intern in gravitational and space biology NASA Kennedy Space Ctr., 1988; undergraduate researcher, Plant Biochemistry Lab., UCLA, 1988—89, undergraduate researcher, Ctr. for Evolution and Origin of Life, 1988—89; undergraduate researcher, plant molecular biology lab U. Calif. Santa Barbara, 1989—91, summer field rsch., 1989—90, postdoctoral fellow, 1997—99; faculty, dept. chem. and biochemistry U. Tex., Austin, Tex., 1999—2002; John Chipman Career Devel. assoc. prof. materials sci. and engring. MIT, Cambridge, Mass., 2002—05, Germehausen prof. material science and engring. and biol. engring., 2005—. Spkr. in field. Author: numerous rsch. articles, including in Science and Nature; research mentioned in Forbes Mag., 2001, Technology Insider, MIT Report, & Technology Review, NY Times, 2004. Named Rsch. Leader of Yr., Scientific Am. mag., 2006; named one of PopSci Brilliant 10, Popular Science Mag.; recipient Army Young Investigator award, 1999, Du Pont Young Investigators award, 1999, Beckman Young Investigator award, 2000, IBM Faculty Partnership award, 2000, Presdl. Early Career award in Sci. and Engring., 2000, Harvard U. Wilson Prize in Chemistry, 2001, World Technology award, 2004; Alfred P. Sloan Rsch. Fellow, 2001, Harrington Faculty Fellow, 2001, MacArthur Fellowship, 2004. Office: Biological Engring 16-244 MIT 77 Mass Ave Cambridge MA 02139-4307 Office Phone: 617-252-1163. Business E-Mail: belcher@mit.edu.*

BELCHER, DENNIS IRL, lawyer; b. Wheeling, W.Va., Aug. 24, 1951; s. Finley Duncan Belcher and Ellen Jane (Huffman) Good; m. Vickie Marie Early, Aug. 2, 1975; children: Sarah Anne, Matthew Irl, Benjamin Scott. BA, Coll. William and Mary, 1973; JD, U. Richmond, 1976. Bar: Va. 1976, U.S. Tax Ct. 1978. Assoc. McGuire, Woods, Battle & Boothe, Richmond, Va., 1976-83, ptnr., 1983—, mem. exec. com., 1996—2001, mem. bd. ptnrs., 2005—. Adj. prof. taxation Va. Commonwealth U., Richmond, 1985-88. Co-author: Business Tax Planning Forms for Businesses and Individuals, 1985. Chmn. Richmond chpt. Am. Heart Assn., 1984-85; trustee St. Christopher's Sch., 1993-2003. Fellow Am. Coll. Trust and Estate Counsel (bd. regents 1999-05, sec. 2005-06, treas. 2006-); mem. ABA (real property and probate sect., sec. 1997-98, chmn. marital deduction com., vice chmn. lifetime transfers com., ho. of dels. 1998-99, vice chair probate divsn. 1999-01, chair 2002-03), Va. Bar Assn. (wills and trusts and taxations sects.), Country Club of Va., Kinloch Golf Club. Presbyterian. Avocations: golf, farming. Office: McGuireWoods LLP One James Ctr 901 East Cary St Richmond VA 23219 Office Phone: 804-775-4304. Business E-Mail: dbelcher@mcguirewoods.com.

BELCHER, DOROTHY S., state correctional department administrator; b. Macon, Ga., Sept. 3, 1954; d. Lawyer B. Stanley and Lena Mae Montgomery; divorced; children: Ayotunde Ronke Ware, Aziza Asha Belcher. BA, U. Wis., Madison, 1976. Cert. correctional probation officer, correctional officer inspector, Fla. Probation and parole officer I State of Fla. Dept. of Corrections, Miami, 1978-80, probation and parole officer II, 1980-83, pub. svc. officer, 1983-87, gold program coord., 1987-89, probation and parole supr., 1989-90, correctional probation sr. supr., 1990-91, correctional officer, sr. inspector, 1991-97, correctional probation sr. supr. Ft. Lauderdale, 1997-98, correctional probation dep. adminstr. Miami, 1998-99, correctional probation sr. cir. adminstr., 1999—. Fellow Eta Phi Beta; mem. 100 Black Women, Fla. Coun. on Crime and Delinquency, Criminal Justice Inst. (hon.). Democrat. Pentecostal. Avocations: reading, writing, singing, playing piano, gardening. Home: 17731 NW 32d Ave Opa Locka FL 33056 Office: State of Fla Dept Corrections Probation and Parole 3552 Okeechobee Rd Fort Pierce FL 34947-4597 Personal E-mail: virtuousone1954@aol.com.

BELCHER, LOUIS DAVID, marketing professional, retired mayor; b. Battle Creek, Mich., June 25, 1939; s. Louis George and Josephine (Johnson) B.; children: Debora Louise, Sheri Lynn, Stacy Elizabeth; m. Jane Elisabeth Dillon, May 8, 1987. Student, Kellogg Community Coll., 1959; BS, Eastern Mich. U., 1962. With GM, Livonia, Mich., 1962; adminstr. U. Mich., Ann Arbor, 1962-63; with NCR, Lansing, Mich., 1963-69, Veda, Inc., Ann Arbor, 1969-72; owner, v.p., treas. First Ann Arbor Corp., 1972-83; owner, chief fin. officer Third Party Services, Inc. and Data Scan, Inc., Ann Arbor, Mich., 1983-84; pres., chief exec. officer Data Scan, Inc., Ann Arbor, 1984-86, Ann Arbor Rod & Gun Co., 1986-88; ptnr. Shipman, Corey, Belcher, Ann Arbor, 1984-86; sr. asst. to pres. and dir. tech. svcs. Environ. Rsch. Inst. Mich., Ann Arbor, 1988-93; owner, prin. L. D. Belcher and Assocs. Mgmt. Cons., Ann Arbor, 1993—; v.p. Cybernet Syss. Corp., Ann Arbor, 1996-97; pres., CEO, owner, dir. Innovative Rsch. Corp., Ann Arbor, 1999—2007. Bd. dirs. Geosat Com., Inc., Washington; corp. dir. M.W. Microwave, Inc., Ann Arbor Environment Tech. Corp., Ann Arbor, Innovative Rsch. & Svcs., Inc.; adv. bd. dirs. Mich. Consol. Gas Co.; exec. com. Ann. Conf. Earth Observations and Decision Making - A National Partnership, Washington, 1988—, Ann. Internat. Symposium on Remote Sensing of Environment, 1990—, Thematic Conf. Geol. Remote Sensing, 1990, Ann. Thematic Conf. Coastal and Marine Environment, 1992—; co-founder, dir. Ann Arbor IT Zone, 1999. Mem. City Coun., Ann Arbor, 1974-78, mayor pro tem, Ann Arbor, 1976-78, mayor, 1978-85; mem. adv. coun. region 5 SBA, Detroit, 1982-86; pres., bd. dirs. U. Mich. Theatre, 1983-85, Marcel Marceau World Ctr. for Mime, Inc., Ann Arbor, 1986-89; bd. dirs. Mich. Theatre Found., Ann Arbor, 1986-92; mem. nat. Rep. campaign team, 1980. Served to capt. Air N.G., 1956-70. Recipient Outstanding Alumni awards Kellogg C.C., Outstanding Alumni awards Ea. Mich. U. Coll. Bus., Silver Elephant award Rep. Party, Commendation Adminstr. Vets. Affairs, Commendation Ann Arbor Vets. Hosp.; Bügermedaille, City of Tübingen, Fed. Republic Germany; elected Mayor's Hall of Fame, 1995. Mem. AIAA, Air Force Assn., U.S. Conf. Mayors (past pres.), Mich. Conf. Mayors (chmn.), Am. Soc. for Photogrammertry and Remote Sensing, Am. Inst. Aeronautics and Astronautics, Ann Arbor Club. Republican. Mem. Ch. of Christ. Home: 1352 Cobblestone Ct Ann Arbor MI 48108-9553 Personal E-mail: belcherld@yahoo.com. *I have had incredible luck - I was born an American and given the opportunity and freedom to chase my dreams.*

BELCHER, MAX, social services administrator, dean; b. East Lynn, W.Va., Mar. 16, 1942; s. George H. and Ella D. (Dickerson) B.; m. Linda L. Frey, Aug. 8, 1964; children: Kipling, Babbette, Andrew, Raleigh, Perry. BA, Berea Coll., Ky., 1969; ThM, Trinity Coll., 1972; ThD, Trinity Theol. Sem., 1973; MA, Liberty (Va.) U., 1994; DD, LLD (hon.), Internat. Free Prof. Episc. U., London, 1966; PhD, U. San Jose, 1996. Cert. cognitive behavorial therapist, rational marriage and family therapist, rational sex therapist. From caseworker to dist. mgr. Mich. Dept. Social Svcs., Flint, 1964-97, dist. mgr., 1992-97; mem. faculty dept. psychology Baker Coll., Flint, 1987-98, 99—, dean for gen. edn., 1998-99. Bd. dirs. Consortium on Child Abuse and Neglect, Flint, 1993-97, 99. Recipient Cert. of Merit in Youth Employment, Genesee Intermediate Sch. Dist., 1979, Cert. of Appreciation, Health Care Access Project, 1990. Mem. Nat. Assn. Cognitive Behavioral Therapists, Am. Assn. Christian Counselors, Intercollegiate Studies Inst. (faculty advocate), Mich. County Social Svcs. Assn. (life). Office: Baker Coll 1050 W Bristol Rd Flint MI 48507-5516 Home: 2100 Crystal Wood Trail Flushing MI 48433-3519 Office Phone: 810-766-4130. Business E-Mail: max.belcher@baker.edu.

BELCK, NANCY GARRISON, dean, educator; b. Montgomery, Ala., Aug. 1, 1943; d. Lester Moffett and Stella Mae (Whaley) Garrison; m. Jack Belck, May 27, 1976; 1 child, Scott Brian. BS, La. Tech. U., 1964; MS, U. Tenn., 1965; PhD, Mich. State U., 1972. Cert. tchr., La. State textile specialist coop. extension svc. U. Ga., Athens, 1965-67, chair, dir. Tucson, 1976-79; asst. prof./instr. Mich. State U., East Lansing, 1967-73; family econ. researcher USDA Agrl. Res. Svcs., Hyatsville, Md., 1973-75, nat. extension evaluation coord. Washington, 1978-79; dean, prof. Coll. Human Ecology U. Tenn., Knoxville, 1979-87; dean, prof. Coll. Edn. Cen. Mich. U., Mt. Pleasant, 1987—91, interim provost, v.p. acad. affairs, 1988-89; provost, vice chancellor academic affairs La. State U., 1991—93; chancellor So. Ill. U., Edwardsville, 1994—97, U. Neb., Omaha, 1997—. Author: Development of Egyptian Universities Linkages, 1985, Mid-Career Administrators, 1986, Textiles for Consumers, 1990. Mem. exec. com. Mich. Milescular Inst., Midland, strategic planning team Pub. Schs., Mt. Pleasant, 1989—; chair Women's Networking Group, Mt. Pleasant, 1990—. Mem. Am. Home Econs. Assn., Am. Assn. for Higher Edn., Am. Assn. for Colls. Tchr. Edn., Am. Home Econs. Assn., Rotary, Sigma Iota Epsilon, Omicron Nu, Phi Delta, Kappa, Omicron Delta Kappa, Phi Kappa Phi. Avocations: gardening, walking, travel, international food tasting. Office: U of Nebraska at Omaha Office of the Chancellor Omaha NE 68182

BELCO, KAREN MARIE, cardiology nurse; b. Cleve., Oct. 24, 1953; d. Arthur W. and Daniella E. (Lokar) Schultz. m. Joseph E. Belco, Nov. 24, 1979. BSN, St. John Coll., 1975. Staff nurse cardiac surgery Cleve. Clinic, 1976-79, 81, clin. instr. cardiac surgery, 1982-85, nurse clinician dept. cardiology, 1985-92, mgr. electro physiology, 1989-92; sr. clin. electrophysiology specialist, mgr. Baylor Coll. Medicine, Houston, 1993—98, rsch. assoc., 1993-98; cardiac electrophysiology and device specialist Houston VA Med. Ctr., Houston, 1995-98; mgr. cardiac electro physiology and device specialist Cardiology Assoc. of Lubbock, Tex., 1998—2002; mgr., cardiac electro physiology and device specialist, practice mgr. Cardiac Arrhythmia Svc., Lubbock, Tex., 2002—. Mem. writing com. NASPEXAM; Medtronic Patient Edn. adv. bd.; Guidant nurse adv. bd.; lectr. in field. Author book chapters and abstracts; contbg. to abstracts and manuscripts. Active in The Woodlands Symphony Chorus. Mem.: North Tex. EP Soc., Am. Heart Assn., Am. Coll. Cardiology (coalition for collaborative cardiology practice 1999—, allied health profls. coms. 2001—), North Am. Soc. Pacing and Electro Physiology (CAP exec. com. 1989—96, trustee 1992—94, CAP chair 1992—94, writing com. 1995—, publs. com. 1996—, credentialing com. 1997—99, data base com. 1998—2000, history com. 1998—). Avocations: boating, golf. E-mail: KBelco@aol.com.

BELDA, ALAIN J. P., metal products executive; b. Meknes, Morocco; Degree in bus. adminstrn., MacKenzie U. With Alcoa Aluminio, Brazil, 1969—79, pres., 1979—94; v.p. Alcoa Inc., 1982—94, pres. Latin Am., 1991, exec. v.p. Pitts., 1994—97, vice chmn., 1995—97, pres., COO, 1997—99, CEO, 1999—, chmn., 2001—. Bd. dirs. Citigroup, Coopers Industries. Office: Alcoa Inc 201 Isabella St Pittsburgh PA 15212-5858*

BELDEN, DAVID LEIGH, professional society administrator, engineering educator; b. Mpls., Jan. 9, 1935; m. Lois Marion Lind, June 14, 1956; children: Richard Alan, Grant David. B in Gen. Edn., U. Omaha, 1961; MS in Indsl. Engring., Stanford U., 1963, PhD, 1969; disting. grad., Indsl. Coll. Armed Forces, 1973; DSc (hon.), Manhattan Coll., 1992. Registered profl. engr., Calif. rated navigator, aviator. Enlisted U.S. Air Force, 1954, commd. 2d lt., 1956, advanced through grades to col., 1973; served Thailand; asst. for procurement mgmt. to Sec. Air Force, Washington; ret., 1976; exec. dir. Inst. Indsl. Engr., Norcross, Ga., 1976-87, ASME, NYC, 1987—2002, United Engring. Found., 2003—. Adj. prof. Far East divsn. U. Md., 1970; asso. prof. George Washington U., 1974 Author articles in field. Bd. dirs. NYC Indsl. Tech. Assistance Corp., ASME Found., 1987—. Decorated Legion of Merit, Meritorious Svc. medal, Commendation medal (3), Air medal; recipient Nat. Engring. Leadership award Ariz. State U., 2000. Fellow ASME, Instn. of Engrs. of Ireland, Hong Kong Instn. of Engrs., Inst. Indsl. Engrs., Inst. Prodn. Engrs. (Eng., life); mem. Am. Assn. Engring. Socs. (bd. govs. 1980-2002, Kenneth Andrew Roe award), Coun. Engring. and Sci. Soc. Execs. (pres. 1984-85, Leadership award), N.Y. Soc. Assn. Execs. (bd. dirs. 1996-2004, vice chair 2000-01, chair 2002-03, Outstanding Assn. Exec. award), Am. Soc. Assn. Execs. (found. bd. 1992-94, bd. dirs. 1994-97), United Engring. Found. (bd. dirs. 1998-2002, pres. 2002), Australian Inst. Indsl. Engrs. (hon.), Japan Mgmt. Soc. (assoc.), Israeli Soc. Mech. Engrs. (hon.), Nat. Eagle Scout Assn. (Disting. Eagle Scout 1987), Alpha Pi Mu, Tau Beta Pi. Republican. Office: United Engring Found PO Box 70 Mount Vernon VA 22121-0070 Office Phone: 973-244-2328. Business E-Mail: beldend@asme.org.

BELDOCK, DONALD TRAVIS, investor; b. NYC, May 29, 1934; s. George and Rosa (Tribus) B.; m. Lucy Geringer, Apr. 23, 1971; children: John Anthony, Gwen Ann, James Geringer. BA, Yale U., 1955. Mdse. and fin. exec. R. H. Macy & Co., NYC, 1955-60; mng. ptnr., fin. cons., chmn. D. T. Beldock & Co., NYC, 1961-66; pres., chief exec. officer, chmn. fin. com. BASIX Corp. (formerly Basic Resources Corp.), NYC, 1966-69, chmn. bd., pres., chief exec. officer, 1970-88; chmn., dir. White Shield Greece Oil Corp., NYC, 1969—98; chmn., chief exec. officer Fundamental Properties, Inc., NYC, 1989—, also bd. dirs.; chmn., pres., chief exec. officer Primavera Labs, 1989—; also bd. dirs. CRA Inc. Phoenix, 1982-89. Chmn., CEO Packard Press Corp., Phila., 1987-88, bd. dirs., 1977-88; founding ptnr. Transp. Infrastructure Adv. Group; mng. dir. Hellenic Oil Co., 1989—; chmn., CEO AGB2, Inc., 1999—; bd. dirs. Amromco Energy, LLC. Patentee in field. Chmn. bd. trustees Strang Cancer Rsch. Ctr.-Preventive Medicine Inst., 1985-89, chmn. emeritus, 1989—, chmn. investment com., 1996-; mem. bd. advisors Chem. Bank, 1983-88; bd. dirs. Renewable Energy Inst., 1981-86; trustee Am. Symphony Orch., 1979-96; chmn. bd. dirs. Teamwork Found., 1980-89, trustee, 1989—; mem. com. Nat. UN Day, 1978-87; mem. N.Y. Gov.'s Commn. on Voluntary Enterprise, 1985-88; chmn. N.Y. Gov.'s Commn. Subcom. on Foster Care, 1986-88, Foster Care Ind. Living, 1986-89; bd. advisers Free Fellowship program U. Hawaii, 1982-86; mem. pvt. sector adv. panel on infrastructure financing of budget com. U.S. Senate, 1984-88; mem. devel. bd. Yale U., 1983-93, mem. exec. com., 1984-88. Honoree testimonial dinner United Jewish Appeal, 1960, Vol. Svc. Leadership award, NY State Gov. Mario Cuomo, 1983, Outstanding Entrepreneur, Pres. Ronald Reagan, 1983, Innovation Leadership award, US Sec. Commerce Malcolm Baldridge, 1984, Outstanding Leadership award, Strang Cancer Rsch. Ctr. & Preventive Medicine Inst., 1989, Lifetime Achievement award, 2005. Mem. Am. Mgmt. Assn., Fgn. Policy Assn., Assn. Yale U. Alumni (nat. class rep. 1983-86, bd. govs. 1986-89), Alumni Assn. N.Y. (hon., bd. dirs.), Westchester Country Club.

BELDOCK, MYRON, lawyer; b. NYC, Mar. 27, 1929; s. George J. and Irene (Goldstein) B.; m. Elizabeth G. Pease, June 28, 1953 (div. 1969); children: David, Jennifer, Hannah, Benjamin, Adam Schmalholz; m. Karen L. Dippold, June 19, 1986. BA, Hamilton Coll., 1950; LLB, Harvard U., 1958. Bar: (N.Y.) 1958, N.Y. (U.S. Dist. Ct. (ea. and so. dists.)) 1960, (U.S. Ct. Appeals (2d cir.)) 1960, (U.S. Supreme Ct.) 1973. Asst. U.S. Atty. U.S. Atty's Office, Eastern Dist., NY, 1958-60; assoc. Geist, Netter & Marx, NYC, 1960-62; sole practice NYC, 1962-64; ptnr. Beldock Levine & Hoffman LLP, NYC, 1964—. Bd. dirs., v.p. Brotherhood-In-Action, N.Y.C., 1972-2006; bd. dirs. Brookdale Revolving Fund., N.Y.C., 1973-76. Served with U.S. Army, 1951-54. Recipient Milton S. Gould award for outstanding oral advocacy, Office of Appellate Defender, 2004. Mem. NY State Bar Assn. (award 2002), Assn. Bar City NY (spl. com. penology 1974-80, com. judiciary 2000-03, com. criminal justice, 2005—), NY County Lawyers Assn., Bklyn. Bar Assn., Kings County Criminal Bar Assn. (Humanitarian of Yr. 1989), NY County Criminal Bar Assn. (award Excellence 2000), NY State Assn. Criminal Def. Lawyers (Pres.'s commendation 2004), Nat. Assn. Criminal Def. Lawyers, Nat. Lawyers Guild.

BELDON, SANFORD T., publisher; b. Scranton, Pa., Nov. 9, 1932; s. Benjamin and Evelyn (Jacobson) B.; m. Jeanne Sherman, June 25, 1967 (dec. Nov. 1992); m. Patricia Wood, Feb. 4, 1995; children: Mary, Kenneth, Emily. BBA, CCNY, 1955; postgrad., NYU Grad. Sch. Bus., 1956—57. Publicist Prentice-Hall, Inc., NYC, 1956-59; publicity dir. Fawcett Publs., Inc., NYC, 1959-62; asst. dir. public relations Crowell-Collier-Macmillan, NYC, 1963-65; dir. advt. and public relations, edn. group Litton Industries, White Plains, NY, 1966-68; dir. promotion Baker & Taylor divsn. W.R. Grace Co., 1968-71; dir. mktg. book div. Rodale Press, Inc., Emmaus, Pa., 1971-74; dir. advt. Organic Gardening mag., Emmaus, 1974-78, v.p., 1974-82, pub., 1978-86, group v.p., 1982-91, sr. v.p., 1991-98. Pub. New Shelter mag., 1984-86, Pub. Prevention Mag., 1986-91, sr. v.p., 1991-99. Pres. ecology adv. com. Allentown (Pa.) City Coun., 1972-75; bd. dirs. Lehigh Valley Child Care, Allentown, 1974-82, pres. bd., 1976-80; bd. dirs. Lehigh Valley Conservancy, Allentown, 1976-77, Planned Parenthood Lehigh County, Pa., 1977-78, Lehigh County Youth and Childrens Office, 1999-2002, Jewish Family Svc. Lehigh Valley, 2000-2003; mem. bd. assocs. Cedar Crest Coll., 1985—; trustee, mem. corp. com., chmn. mktg. coms. Allentown Art Mus., 1992-2005, pres. bd. trustees, 1997-2006, mem. exec. com., 2006—; bd. dirs. Second Harvest Food Bank of Lehigh Valley, 1996—2007, chmn., 2002—07; mem. Pa. Housing Adv. Commn., 1997-2002; trustee Lehigh County Hist. Soc., 2007—. Democrat. Jewish. Personal E-mail: sbeldon@yahoo.com.

BELENCHIA, ELIZABETH C., international corporate realtor; b. Fort Wayne, Indiana, July 19, 1944; d. George P. and Mildred M. (Rawles) Shaffer; m. James F. Carroll, July 24, 1965 (div. May 1985); children: David, Kristin, Stephen, Brian; m. Thomas Alexander Belenchia, Dec. 30, 1989 Cert. comml. investment realtor 1982. Resident realtor, Spartanburg, SC, 1971—75; pres. Carroll Properties Corp., Spartanburg, SC, 1976—. Governor's appointee trustee bd. S.C. Jobs Econ. Devel. Authority, 1999-; expert witness contaminated properties, comml. and indsl. values and market analyses, expert witness, market value/brownfield affects; Spartanburg Teen Ctr., Inc., pres. 1982-84, Presdl. Citation, 1985 Mem. People to People Mission, People's Republic China, 1994; del. Asian Trade Mission, 1981-82; pilot coord. Cowpens Brownfield, 1996-2000; camp dir. Lions Internat. Youth Camp, 1988, Outward Bound Leadership program, 1985, 1993, 94; bd. mem. Spartanburg Little Theatre, Magnolia Debutante Club, 1983-88; USC Upstate Internat., 1976-; bd. dir. off campus, distance and continuing edn. Clemson U.; pres. PTA McCracken Jr. H.S., 1984 Presented Key to Town of Cowpens, 1985; named Leadership Spartanburg Alumni of Yr., 1981-82; named to Soc. Internat. Bus. Fellows, 2006. Mem. MLS (pres. 1980-81), Soc., Indsl., and Office Realtors (ednl. found., IT Chair, 1999 (Internat. RE Fed. v.p. Legis Environ. Forum Reg. Del. United Nations, Internat. Real Estate Fedn.), Investor S.C. Upstate Alliance, Spartanburg County Econ. Devel. Corp., S.C. Econ. Developers Assn., Spartanburg C. of C., Japan Am. Assn., SEUS/Japan Assn. del. 1988-2005, Spartanburg Bd. Realtors (chairperson pub. rels.), Western S.C. Internat. Trade Assn. (pres. 1990, Pres.'s award), Nat. Assn. Realtors (land use, property rights, and environ. com. 1998-), S.C. Assn. Realtors (legis. liaison Wash., bd. dir. 1980), Spartanburg Multiple Listing Svc. (leader S.C. 1985, Spartanburg 1980-81, opportunity Greenville 1983, pres.), German Am. Club Carolinas, Rotary (pres. East Spartanburg, 1999-2000, asst. gov. rotary dist. 7750 2001—, team leader rotary group study exch. Japan 1999), Lions (chmn. state internat. youth exch. United Svs. Coun.), Internat. Environ. Forum (1st v.p. 2005) Democrat. Roman Catholic. Avocations: gardening, decorating with art, reading, travel, music. Home: 1340 Pinecrest Rd Spartanburg SC 29302-3332 Office: Carroll Properties Corp PO Box 2524 Spartanburg SC 29304-1004 Office Phone: 864-949-5250. Fax: 864-949-5251.

BELEW, JOHN SEYMOUR, academic administrator, chemist; b. Waco, Tex., Nov. 3, 1920; s. George H. and Mary (Seymour) B.; m. Ruth Edna McAtee, June 3, 1944; children— James Seymour, Janet Elizabeth. BS, Baylor U., 1941; MS, Wichita State U., 1947; PhD, U. Wis., 1951; LLD, Hong Kong Bapt. U., 1995. Instr. U.S. Army Air Corps Tech. Tng. Command, 1941-43; rsch. assoc. Brown U., Providence, 1951-53; acting. asst. prof. U. Va., 1953-56; asst. prof., then assoc. prof. and prof. chemistry Baylor U., Waco, Tex., 1956-91, prof. emeritus, 1991—, assoc. dean Coll. Arts and Scis., 1973-74, dean Coll. Arts and Scis., 1974-79, chief acad. officer, 1979-91, Jo Murphy chair in internat. edn., 1990-96, provost emeritus, 1991—. Vis. fellow Manchester Coll., Oxford U., summer 1995; mem. team advs. to Tech. U. Liberec, Czech Rep., 1999. Mem. various cmty. bds.; trustee Midway Ind. Sch. Dist., Waco, 1962-72; bd. dirs. Tex. High Speed Rail Authority, 1992-1996; del. Nat. Dem. Conv., 2000. With USAAF, 1943-46. Wilton Park fellow, 1976; recipient Disting. Alumnus award Baylor U., 1993. Mem.: Royal Soc. Chemistry, Am. Chem. Soc., Turner Soc. London, Grolier Club, Sigma Xi. Office: Provost Emeritus Baylor Univ Waco TX 76798-7121 E-mail: seymourbelew@earthlink.net.

BELFER, INNA, research scientist, medical educator; b. Moscow, May 29, 1965; arrived in US, 2001; d. Anatoly Monisov and Isabella Belfer; m. Igor Bengert, July 16, 1988; children: Alina Bengert, Anita Bengert, Amiel Bengert. MD magna cum laude, Moscow Inst. Medicine, 1988; PhD, Hebrew U., Jerusalem, 2001. Nurse Moscow Clin. Rsch. Inst., 1984—87; clin. rsch. asst., attending neurologist Hosp. #6, Moscow, 1988—89; rsch. asst. MMSI, Moscow, 1989—90, Hebrew U., Jerusalem, 1993—2001; clin. fellow NIH, Bethesda, Md., 2001—03, rsch. fellow, 2003—05, staff scientist, 2005—07; assoc. prof. U. Pitts., 2007—. Sci. rep. Ornat Bio Rsch., Inc., Jerusalem, 1992—93; Israel rep. vis. fellows exec. com. NIH, Bethesda, 2005—07; jour. and grant expert referee; spkr. in field. Chief judge HS Sci. Fair, Md., 2004—07; category judge Montgomery Sci. Fair, Md., 2005—07; spl. vol. Nat. Cherry Blossom Festival, Washington, 2005—07. Recipient Spl. Act award, NIDCR, NIH, 2003—07, Fellows award for rsch. excellence, 2006. Mem.: Am. Soc. Human Genetics, Am. Pain Soc. Achievements include patents for diagnostic methods for pain sensitivity. Avocations: travel, reading.

BELFER, ROBERT ALEXANDER, oil and gas company executive; b. Chorzow, Poland, Mar. 27, 1935; s. Arthur B. and Rachelle b. (Anisfeld) B.; m. Rene'e Elissa Kones, Sept. 3, 1960; children: Rachelle Belfer Malkin, Laurence David Belfer, Elizabeth Kones Belfer. AB, Columbia Coll., 1955; JD, Harvard U., 1958; LHD (hon.), Yeshiva Univ., 1986. V.p. Belco Petroleum Corp., NYC, 1958-65, pres., 1965-85, chmn., 1985-86, Belco Oil and Gas Corp., NYC, 1992—. Bd. dirs. Enron Corp., Houston, mem. exec. com. and fin. com., 1983—; bd. dirs. EOTT Energy Corp., Houston; pres. Belfer Found.; mem. fin. com. and exec. com. NACRe Corp. Treas. Albert Einstein Coll. Medicine, NYC, 1981, mem. bd. overseers, 1972—, chmn., 2000, chmn. budget and fin. com. 1981—; trustee Yeshiva U., NYC, 1992—, mem. investment com., 1993—; mem. bd. overseers Cornell U. Med. Coll., NYC, 1990—; bd. dirs. Weizmann Inst., Hebrew U., Jerusalem; mem. vis. com. John F. Kennedy Sch. Govt., Harvard U., Cambridge, Mass., 1984-90, 92—; mem. exec. com. Am. Israel Pub. Com., Washington, 1990—; mem. vis. com. of Greek and Roman art dept. Met. Mus. Art, NYC, 1994—. Recipient Presdl. Recognition award for Outstanding Community Svc. Pres. Ronald reagan, 1987. Mem. Coun. on Fgn. Rels., Harmonie Club, Palm Beach Country Club, Chief Execs. Orgn., Sigma Alpha Nu. Avocations: collecting antiques, tennis, reading. Office: Belco Oil and Gas Corp 767 5th Ave Ste 4600 New York NY 10153-4699

BELFIGLIO, VALENTINE JOHN, political science professor; b. May 28, 1934; s. Edmond Liberato and Mildred Elizabeth (Sherwood) B.; 1 child by previous marriage, Valentine Edmond; m. Ellie K. Belfiglio; stepchildren: Andy, Kevian Navid. BS, Union U., 1956; MA, U. Okla., Norman, 1967; PhD, U. Okla., 1970. Registered pharmacist, Fla., Okla., Tex.; cert. cons. pharmacist. Grad. asst., instr. U. Okla., 1967-70; prof. polit. sci., instr. drug law and policy Tex. Woman's U., Denton, 1970—; cons. pharmacist Whitaker Med., Ltd. Contbr. textbooks in the practice of pharmacy Holbrook Press, Boston, 1973-75. With USAF, 1959—67. Decorated knight Order of Merit, Republic of Italy; recipient Guido Dorso prize U. Naples, 1985, C.K. Chamberlain award East Tex. Hist. Assn., 1990, Cornaro award Tex. Woman's U., 2003, Faculty Devel. leave, Rome, 2001, Cornaro award Tex. Woman's U., 2003, Counseling Excellence award in pharmacy Pharmacy Today, 2006, One-to-One award in pharm. counseling Am. Pharm. Assn., 2006; Instnl. Rsch. grantee Tex. Woman's U., 1973-74, 76-77, NEH grantee, 1978, Internat. Conf., Grenada, Spain, 2007; postdoc. fellow Republic of South Africa, 1976; Faculty Devel. fellow, Rome, 2001. Fellow Am. Soc. Cons. Pharmacists; mem. AAUP, Internat. Studies Assn. (sec.-treas. region 1974-76), Am. Polit. Sci. Assn., Am. Italian Hist. Assn. (col., ret.), Tex. State Def. Forces, Fourth degree Knight of Columbus, Mensa, Kappa Psi Republican. Roman Catholic. Avocations: chess, dance, gourmet cooking. Office: Tex Woman's U PO Box 425889 Denton TX 76204-5889 Home: 11505 Sonnet Dr Dallas TX 75229-2629 Office Phone: 940-898-2144. Business E-Mail: vbelfiglio@twu.edu.

BELFORT, GEORGES, chemical engineering educator, consultant; b. Johannesburg, Transvaal, Republic of South Africa, May 8, 1940; came to U.S., 1964; s. Nathan Leveen and Sophie (Konviser) Belfort; m. Marlene Bertha Stern, Dec. 28, 1967; children: David, Gabriel, Jonathan. BSc-ChemE, U. Capetown, 1963; MS in Engring., U. Calif., Irvine, 1969, PhD in Engring., 1972. Rsch. engr. Astropower Labs., McDonnel Douglas Corp., Newport Beach, Calif., 1964-70; acting instr. U. Calif., Irvine, 1971-72; sr. lectr. Hebrew U., Jerusalem, 1973-77; vis. assoc. prof. Northwestern U., Evanston, Ill., 1977-78; assoc. prof. Rensselaer Poly. Inst., Troy, NY, 1978-82, prof., 1982—, Russell Sage prof. chem. engring, 2003—. Chair Gordon Rsch. Conf. on Membranes, Materials and Processes, 1977; cons. in field. Mem. editl. bd. Jour. Membrane Sci., Biotechnology Progress, Desalination, Bioseparation, Separation Sci. and Tech., internat. editl. bd. North, Ctrl. and South Am. of Jour. Chem Engring. Japan; co-editor (author (with others): Fundamentals of Adsorption, 1984, Advanced Biochemical Engineering, 1987; contbr. articles over 180 articles to profl. jours. Fellow Japanese Soc. for Promotion Sci., 1981, 96; rsch. grantee U.S. Dept. Energy, 1994—, USN, 1990-94, NSF, 1995—; elected Nat. Acad. Engring., 2003; apptd. to Russel Sage Endowed chair chem. engring., 2003. Mem. NAE, AIChE (Sci. and Tech. award 2000), Am. Chem. Soc. (Award in Separations Science and Technology 1995), N.Am. Membrane Soc. (pres. 1995, bd. dirs. 1993—), European Membrane Soc. Office: Rensselaer Poly Inst Chem Engring Dept Troy NY 12180-3590 E-mail: belfog@tpi.edu.

BELFOUR, ED, professional hockey player; b. Carman, Man., Can., Apr. 21, 1965; Student, U. N.D. Goalie Chgo. Blackhawks, 1988—97, San Jose Sharks, 1997, Dallas Stars, 1997—2002, Toronto Maple Leafs, 2002—06, Fla. Panthers, 2006—. Mem. Team Can., Olympic Games, Salt Lake City, 2002; player NHL All-Star Game, 1992, 93, 96, 98, 99, 2003. Co-recipient Garry F. Longman Meml. Trophy, 1988, William M. Jennings Trophy, 1999; named to All-Rookie Team, NHL, 1991, First All-Star Team, 1991, 1993, Second All-Star Team, 1995; recipient Calder Meml. Trophy, 1991, Trico Goaltender award, 1991, Vezina Trophy, 1991, 1993, William M. Jennings Trophy, 1991, 1993, 1995, Roger Crozier Saving Grace Award, 2000. Achievements include being a member of Stanley Cup Champion Dallas Stars, 1999; being a member of gold medal Canadian Hockey team, Salt Lake City Olympic Games, 2002. Office: Fla Panthers Hockey Club One Panther Parkway Sunrise FL 33323

BELGOROD, BARRY MILES, surgeon, educator; b. NYC, Mar. 27, 1953; s. Howard H. and Madeline (Bloom) B. BA summa cum laude, Queens Coll., 1973; MD, U. Pa., 1977. Diplomate Am. Bd. Ophthalmology, Nat. Bd. Med. Examiners. Intern in internal medicine Pa. Hosp., 1977-78; resident in ophthalmology Manhattan Eye, Ear and Throat Hosp., NYC, 1978-81, assoc. attending surgeon, 1981—; asst. attending ophthalmologist N.Y. Hosp., 1982—. Clin. instr. dept. ophthalmology Cornell U. Med. Coll., NYC; pres. BMB Patent Holding Corp.; med. coun. U. Pa., 1973-76; cons. in field. Bd. dirs. Soc. Salk Scholars, 1983—88. Fellow NSF, 1972; recipient Ira M. Goldin award, 1973, Charles A. Oliver Meml. prize in ophthalmology, 1977; scholar N.Y. States Regents, 1969-73, Jonas Salk Found., 1973-77. Fellow ACS, Am. Acad. Ophthalmology, NY Acad. Medicine, NY State Ophthal. Soc.; mem. U. Pa. Alumni Assn., Phi Beta Kappa, Sigma Xi, Beta Delta Chi. Achievements include patents for electronic photocromic lens. laser corneal surgery, analgesics. Office: 115 E 61st St New York NY 10021-8183 Office Phone: 212-753-2020.

BELIAVSKY, NINAH, linguistics professor; b. Moscow, Jan. 31, 1962; d. Yuri and Eleonora Beliavsky; m. Jonathan Twersky, Mar. 27, 1988; children: Michaella Shoshana Twersky, Delilah Lital Twersky. BS in Linguistics, U. Wis., 1982, BS in Psychology, 1983, BPh, 1982; MA in Applied Linguistics, Northwestern U., Evanston, Ill., 1986, PhD. Adj. asst. prof. NYU, 1987—88, Queens Coll., NY, 1987—99; asst. prof. St. John's U., Queens, 1999, assoc. prof., 2005—. Contbr. articles to profl. jours., books. Mem. bd. edn. Congregation Sons of Israel, Woodmere, NY, 2006—, mem. of re-imagine task force, 2004—. Scholarship, Northwestern U., 1984—87. Mem.: TESOL, Nat. Coun. Tchrs. English, Internat. Linguistics Assn. (exec. com. 2003—06), Am. Assn. Applied Linguistics, Am. Ednl. Assn. Achievements include research in child language acquisition and development; an artistic approach to teaching college ESL; the Mozart Effect in the ESL classroom; Vygotsky and Gardner in language learning. Office: St John's U 8000 Utopia Pky Jamaica NY 11439 Home Phone: 516-792-6477; Office Phone: 718-990-1929.

BELICH, JOHN PATRICK, SR., journalist, private investigator; b. Peekskill, NY, Dec. 6, 1938; s. John Andrew and Iris Patricia (Brown) B.; m. Louise Daniel, June 4, 1971; children: Mary Louise, John P. Jr., Andrew J. Student, N.Y. Inst. Photography, St. Petersburg Jr. Coll. Staff news photographer UPI, 1963-69; So. div. photo mgr. Atlanta, 1969-72; photo editor, dir. photography St. Petersburg Times and Evening Independent, 1972-87, mgr. newsroom projects, 1987-94, asst. to pres., 1994—2006; pvt. investigator J. Belich & Assocs., 2006—. V.p., bd. dirs. N.W. Fla. Little Maj. League Assn.; mem. photography adv. com. St. Petersburg Vocat. Tech. Inst.; guardian ad litem 6th Jud. Ctr., Fla.; Skywarn vol. Amateur Radio Emergency Svc. Corp., Nat. Weather Svc.; bd. advisors Coll. Comm., Fla. State U. Recipient Pres.'s medal Nat. Press Photographers Assn., 1978, citation of excellence, 1979. Mem. Nat. Press Photographers Assn. (bd. dirs., chmn. info. com. 1978), Atlanta Press Photographers Assn. (past treas., v.p.), Fla. News Photographers Assn., Nat. Press Photographers Found., Am. Meteorol. Soc., Nat. Weather Assn., Am. Radio Relay League, Amateur Radio Satellite Corp., NRA, Clearwater Amateur Radio Soc., Fla. Assn. Lic. Investigators (bd. dirs. 2004-06, 2007-), Am. Soc. Indsl. Security, Nat. Coun. Investigation and Security Svcs. Computer Security Inst., Info. Sys. Security Assn., Sigma Delta Chi. Office: J Belich & Assoc Inc 6822 22nd Ave N 304 Saint Petersburg FL 33701 Home Phone: 727-345-1021; Office Phone: 877-724-9253. Business E-Mail: jbelich@jbelich.com.

BELICH, KAY S., music educator; d. Robert W. and Lorna O. Schoenfeld; m. Sam M. Belich, Aug. 16, 1975; children: Aaron F., Eva A. MusB, U. Wis., Madison, 1974; MusM, The Juilliard Sch., NYC, 1977. Lic. tchr. Wis., 1991. Singer NYC Opera Co., 1977—90; elem. sch. music tchr. Kenosha Unified Pub. Sch. Dist., Wis., 1991—96, West Allis/West Milw. Pub. Sch. Dist., 1996—; studio vocal and instrumental tchr. freelance, NY and Milw., 1968—, opera and concert singer, 1972—; u. instr. Cardinal Stritch U., Milw., 1999—. Apprentice singer Ctrl. City Opera Co., Colo., 1975; union del. NYC Opera Touring Co., 1990; cooperating tchr. for student tchr. Carthage Coll., Kenosha, Wis., 1993—94; mentor West Allis/West Milw. Pub. Sch. Dist., 2001—02; cooperating tchr. for student tchr. Cardinal Stritch U., Milw., 2002—03. Singer performances include Cami Hall recital. Ch. coun. mem. Grace and St. Paul's Luth. Ch., NYC, 1980—81; various positions Mt. Hope Luth. Ch., West Allis, Wis., 1991—. Recipient First Pl. award, Wis. Fedn. of Music Clubs, 1974; U. Wis. scholar, 1970—74, regional finalist, Met. Opera, 1978. Mem.: Milw. Civic Music Assn., Wis. Sch. Music Assn., Music Educators' Nat. Conf., Take Off Pounds Sensibly (treas. 1998—). Lutheran. Achievements include Solo Debuts: with New York City Opera, 1982; with Music Under the Stars, 1991; with Skylight Opera Theatre, 1993; with Racine Symphony , 1996; with Waukesha Symphony, 1997. Avocation: organic gardening. Home: 2141 South 105 St West Allis WI 53227-1211 Office: Hoover School 12705 West Euclid Ave New Berlin WI 53151-4611 also: Cardinal Stritch Univ 6801 North Yates Rd Milwaukee WI 53217-3985

BELICHICK, BILL (WILLIAM STEPHEN BELICHICK), professional football coach; b. Nashville, Apr. 16, 1952; s. Stephen and Jeannette (Munn) Belichick; m. Debbie Belichick April 30, 1977; children: Amanda, Stephen, Brian. BS in Econ., Wesleyan U., 1975; LHD, Boston U., 2004, New England Inst. Tech., 2004. Spl. asst to the coaching staff Balt. Colts, 1975; asst. spl. teams coach Detroit Lions, 1976—77, tight ends & receivers coach, 1977—78; asst. spl. teams coach & asst. to defensive coord. Denver Broncos, 1978-79; spl. teams coach N.Y. Giants, 1979—81, spl. teams & linebackers coach, 1981—83, linebackers coach, 1983—85, defensive coord., 1985-91, defensive backs coach, 1989—91; head coach Cleve. Browns, 1991-95; asst. head coach, defensive backs coach New England Patriots, Foxboro, Mass., 1996-97, head coach, 2000—; asst. head coach, defensive backs coach N.Y. Jets, 1997-99. Named Coach of the Yr., Dallas Morning News, 2002, 2003, NFL Coach of the Yr., AP, 2003, NFL Alumni, 2003, Coach of the Yr., NFL.com, 2003, The Sporting News, 2003; named one of TIME's 100 Most Powerful & Influential People in the World, TIME mag., 2004; recipient Baldwin medal, Wesleyan U., 2002, Tom Landry award: AFC Coach of the Yr., USA Today, 2002, Amos Alonzo Stagg Coaching award, US Sports Acad., 2004. Defensive coord., Super Bowl Champion New York Giants, 1986, 1990, Head coach, Superbowl Champion New England Patriots, 2002, 2004, 2005. Achievements include holds the NFL record for the best postseason coaching record, 2005. Office: New England Patriots One Patriots Pl Foxboro MA 02035-1388

BELIĆ WEISS, ZORAN, artist, design educator, director; b. Beograd, Srbija, Yugoslavia, Apr. 24, 1955; arrived in U.S., 1989, naturalized, 2000; s. Milan and Ljubinka (Vidosavijevic) B. BFA in Painting/Mixed media, U. Arts, 1981; BA in Philosophy, U. Belgrade, 1985; MFA in Multi-media, Rutgers U., 1991. Pvt. practice, Irvine, Calif.; art dir. D'Arcy, Masius, Benton & Bowles, Inc., NYC, 1991-93; prof. Miss. State U., 1993-96, U. Denver, 1996-97, Laguna Coll. Art Design, 1997—2005, chmn. design program, 2001—05; prof. U. Calif., Irvine, 1997—2005; dir. gen. Imperium Design, Irvine-Cosmopolis, 1998—; chmn. design program Savannah Coll. Art and Design, 2005—. Tchr. Internat. Aikido Fedn., Irvine, 1988—; juror numerous exhbns., art event proposals for art programs; curator, co-curator 17 exhbns.; lectr. in field. Author: Academy of Arts and Sciences Dictionary of Visual Arts, 1989; editor: Mental Space, 1983—87, Dragon Series, 1988—89; one-man shows include SKC, Belgrade, 1977, 1978, 1979, 1980, 1984, 1994, New Gallery, Zagreb, Yugoslavia, 1979, Gallery Rhinoceros, Novi Sad, Yugoslavia, 1984, Collegium Artisticum, Sarajevo, Yugoslavia, 1984, Gallery AUT, Groznjan, Yugoslavia, 1989, Jewish Hist. Mus., Belgrade, 1989, Rutgers U., New Brunswick, NJ, 1990, 1991, Gallery Sebastian, Belgrade, 1994, McCommas Gallery, Miss. State U., 1996, Asbury Gallery, Denver, 1997, OCCCA Gallery, Santa Ana, Calif., 2002, exhibited in group shows at White Palace, Genoa, Italy, 1979, The Apple, Amsterdam, Holland, 1979, Mus. Modern Art, Paris, 1980, Mus. Arch., Wroclaw, Poland, 1981, Bilbao, Spain, 1982, Mus. Modern Art, Brussels, 1982, Mus. Contemporary Art, Belgrade, 1983, Mimar Sinan U., Istanbul, Turkey, 1983, Modern Mus., Stockholm, 1983, Art Space, Hamburg, Germany, 1985, Skenderija, Sarajevo, 1989, Franklin Furnace, N.Y.C., 1989, Mus. Modern Art, Tampere, Finland, 1989, Gallery ULUS, Belgrade, 1990, Zimmerly Mus., New Brunswick, 1991, Gallery V, N.Y.C., 1991, Anthology Film Archives, 1992, Art in Gen., 1993, Sherry Frumkin Gallery, Santa Monica, Calif., 1995, Barutana, Belgrade, 1997, Seven Degrees, Laguna Beach, 2003, others, Represented in permanent collections Mus. Contemporary Art, Belgrade, ULUS, Nat. Mus., Wroclaw, Poznan, Poland, others; contbr. over 55 articles to profl. jours. Recipient 2d award Internat. Drawing Triennial, Wroclaw, Poland, 1981, 4th award Internat. Drawing Biennial, Rijeka, Yugoslavia, 1988; Robert Watts Meml. scholar Rutgers U. 1989; ULUS fellow Beograd, Yugoslavia, 1986-87; rsch. grantee U.S. Dept. Interior, Washington, 1995. Mem. Internat. Assn. Aesthetics, Internat. Assn. Philosophers, Internat. Aikido Fedn., Coll. Art Assn., Udruzenje Likovnih Umetnika Srbije (v.p. 1987-89, pres. expanded media chpt. 1986-89, cons. program bd. 1987-89), Serbian Assn. Aesthetics, Assn. Spacial Rsch. (Belgrade). Avocation: Aikido (2d degree black belt). Home and Office: Imperium Design 3857 Birch St Ste 114 Newport Beach CA 92660 Home Phone: 949-660-1554; Office Phone: 949-280-5029. Business E-Mail: zbelic@imperiumdesign.com.

BELINGER, HARRY ROBERT, retired business executive; b. Phila., Sept. 16, 1927; s. Harry and Florence (McGovern) B.; m. Jean Marie O'Neill, Nov. 30, 1957 (dec. Aug. 1998); 1 child, Lizanne. BS, Temple U., 1957. Reporter UPI, Phila., 1957-62, Phila. Daily News, 1962-63, asst. city editor, 1963-66, city editor, 1966-68, 70-71, Phila. Inquirer, 1968-70; city rep., dir. commerce City of Phila., 1972-76; v.p. pub. affairs ARAMARK Inc., Phila., 1976-95; ret., 1995. Pres. Great Flag Gateway, Inc., 2002. Former ex-officio mem. City Planning Commn.; former v.p. Phila. Indsl. Devel. Corp.; past dir., mem. exec. com. Phila. Port Corp.; former mem. sch. bd. Archdiocese of Phila.; past bd. dirs., mem. exec. com. Conv. and Tourist Bur., Phila.; past bd. dirs. Phila. Civic Ctr., Mercy Fitzgerald Hosp. With inf., AUS, 1950-52. Mem. Phila. Press Assn. (bd. dirs. 1964-66). Home: 830 Strawberry Ln Wynnewood PA 19096-1644

BÉLISLE, PAUL CHARLES, Canadian government official; b. St. Joachim, Ont., Can., Nov. 14, 1950; m. Danielle Parent; children: Ariane, Alexia. B in Social Sci. (hon.), U. Ottawa, Ont., 1974, cert. in pub. adminstrn., 1975, LLL, 1980. Bar: Que. Clk. Coms. and Pvt. Legis. Directorate, 1979-84, asst. dir., 1984-94; sec. gen. Can.-France Interparliamentary Assn., 1989-91; clk. of the Senate, clk. of the Parliaments Senate of Canada, Ottawa, Ont., 1994—. Mem. editl. bd. Can. Parliamentary Rev. Recipient l'Ordre de la Pleiade award, Mem. Assn. Clks.-at-the-Table Can., Commonwealth Parliamentary Assn. (exec. sec. treas.), Assn. of Secs. Gen. of Parliaments. Office: Senate of Canada Parliament Bldgs Centre Block Rm 185-S Ottawa ON Canada K1A 0A4 Office Phone: 613-992-2493. Fax: 613-992-7959.

BELITZ, PAUL EDWARD, lawyer; b. Omaha, July 11, 1951; s. Edward Paul and Jo Anna Beverly (Brown) B.; m. Joanne Deborah Nilson, June 9, 1973; children: Nicholas P., Christopher T. BS with high distinction, U. Nebr., 1973; JD magna cum laude, Creighton U., 1976. Bar: Nebr. 1976, Colo. 1982. Assoc., then ptnr. Kutak Rock LLP, Omaha, 1976-81, ptnr. Denver, 1982—. Bd. dir. Fleischer Found., Scottsdale, Ariz., 1986—. Mem.: ABA, Denver Bar Assn., Colo. Bar Assn., Nebr. Bar Assn., Glenmoor Country Club (Cherry Hills Village, Colo. stategic planning com.). Avocations: reading, skiing, golf. Office: Kutak Rock LLP 1801 California St Ste 3100 Denver CO 80202 Office Phone: 303-297-2400. E-mail: paul.belitz@kutakrock.com.

BELK, JOAN PARDUE, language and literature educator; b. Lancaster, SC, Oct. 4, 1933; d. William Hazel and Alfleda Steele Pardue; m. Joe Harvey Belk, Sr.; children: Joe Harvey Jr., Jennifer Elizabeth White. Degree, Winthrop U., 1954; BA summa cum laude, U. Houston, 1957. Cert. tchr. Tex. Asst. to dir. librs. U. Houston, Houston, 1957—61; tchr. English Galena Park H.S., Galena Park, Tex., 1961—62; tchr. English (advanced placement) Meml. H.S., Houston, 1962—96; instr. English Houston C.C., 1996—2002; copy editor Kaplan Profl. Schs., Houston, 2006—. Musician, piano accompanist, piano tchr. Editor articles for profl. pubs. Mem. Happy Hide-a-Way Civic Assn., Crosby, 1972—, Royal Spring Civic Assn, Houston, 1989—, newsletter editor, 2002—; mem. Cancer Fighters Houston, Inc., 1998—, bd. dirs., 2003—05, 2006—, Woman's Club Houston, 2004—, v.p. comm., 2006—; chmn. evaluations com. Expanding Your Horizons (conf. jr. HS girls), Houston, 1997—2003; mem. chancel choir, accompanist children's choir, elder Spring Branch Presbyn. Ch., Houston. Recipient Excellence in Tchg. award, So. Meth. U., 1992, Mrs. James P. Houstoun Found. award, 1957, Phi Mu Alumnae award, 1957; Friedheim Found. scholar, Winthrop U., 1954. Mem.: AAUW (com. chair 1997—2003), NEA, Nat. Coun. Tchrs. English, Spring Br. Edn. Assn., Tex. State Tchrs. Assn., Spring Branch Ind. Sch. Dist. Minority Lit. Reading and Discussion Group (discussion leader 1990—96), U. Houston Reading and Discussion Group (sec. 1990—), Tex. Coun. Tchrs. English, Spring Br. Coun. Tchrs. English, Outstanding Lit. Book Club, Les Belles Lettres Club (pres. 1967—68), Shadow Oaks Garden Club (v.p. 1958—60, pres. 1960—61), En Amie Book Rev. Club, Kappa Delta Pi (award 1957), Phi Kappa Phi (treas. 1958—60, award 1957), Delta Kappa Gamma (rsch. com. chair 1998—2002, yearbook com. chair 2004—05). Presbyterian. Avocations: piano, bridge, travel, crocheting. Home: 2014 Southwick Dr Houston TX 77080 Home Phone: 713-465-9535. Personal E-mail: joebelksr@aol.com.

BELK, LEOTIS S., language educator; b. Lancaster, SC, Jan. 8, 1934; s. Samuel David and Mabel Cora Belk; m. Johnnie Ruth Alexander (div.); 1 child, Shayila Nicole Adela. BA, Queens Coll., 1955; MDiv, Va. Union U., 1958; MA, U. San Carlos, 1963; PhD, Temple U., 1975. Instr. J.C. Smith U., Charlotte, NC, 1958—63, Bishop Coll., Dallas, 1963—69; chair, philosophy of religion Colgate-Rochester Divsn. Sch., NY, 1969—75; pastor New Hope Bapt. Ch., Niagara Falls, 1977—80; assoc. prof. Shaw U., Raleigh, NC, 1991—93; adj. prof. Campbell U., Buies Creek, NC, 1998—2000; asst. prof. St. Augustines Coll., Raleigh, 2000—05. Bd. mem. Charlotte symposium of World Affairs, NC, 1962—63; chmn. Colgate-Rochester Div. Sch., Philos. Religion Dept., 1971—72; cons. NY State Correctional Sys., Albany, NY, 1974—75; vice-chair Love Canal Revitalization Agy., Niagara Falls, 1980—90; adj. prof. U. Rochester, NY, 1965—69, U. Buffalo, NY, 1977—. Author: A Record of the Carey Mungo Family and Kin Families of SC; contbr. Outstanding Black Sermons. Exec. dir. HUD of Niagara Falls, 1982—83; tchr. cmty., Spanish course Church Spanish; mem. Criminal Justice Task Force, Niagara County, NY, 1978—79. Grantee Study grant for Mex., J.C. Smith U., 1956. Mem.: NAACP, Raleigh Area Theo. Soc., Martin Luther King Fellows Inc. Democrat. Baptist. Avocations: genealogy, badminton, languages, anthropology, second hand books. Home Phone: 919-790-7079. Personal E-mail: belkleo@aol.com. E-mail: lsbelk@nc.rr.com.

BELK, THOMAS MILBURN, JR., (TIM), apparel executive; s. Thomas Milburn and Katherine (McKay) Belk. With Belk Inc., Charlotte, NC, 1981—, pres. store div., 1998—2004, chmn., CEO, 2004—. Trustee NC Blumenthal Performing Arts Ctr.; mem. adv. bd. Kenan-Flagler Bus. Sch., Univ. NC, Chapel Hill, Univ. NC, Charlotte; bd. mem. Carolinas Healthcare Sys., Rsch. Triangle Found. NC. Office: Belk Inc 2801 W Tyvola Rd Charlotte NC 28217*

BELKHARRAZ, ABDERRAZAK IDRISSI, education educator, researcher; s. Mustapha Idrissi Belkharraz and Zoubida Akil. MS (hon.), St. Petersbourg State Tech. U., Russia, 1995; MPhil, CUNY, 2002, PhD, 2003. Cert. Can. Coun. Profl. Engrs., 2002. Elec. engr. Sibelec Electric, Casablanca, 1995—97; grad. asst. CCNY, 1998—2003; asst. prof. LaGuardia Coll., Long Island City, NY, 2003—. Author: articles in field. Recipient Best Paper Presentation, Am. Control Conf., 2003; grantee, CUNY, 2004—06. Mem.: AIAA, IEEE, Sigma Xi. Achievements include development of a simple adaptive control which accomodates the control surface failures during gust conditions. Avocations: reading, travel, swimming. Office: LaGuardia Coll 31-1- Thomson Ave Long Island City NY 11101

Home Phone: 347-254-6552; Office Phone: 718-482-5412. Business E-Mail: abelkharraz@lagcc.cuny.edu.

BELKIN, BORIS DAVID, violinist; b. Sverdlovsk, USSR, Jan. 26, 1948; s. David Boris and Anna Alexander Belkin; children: Alexander, Maïa. Student, Central Music Sch., Moscow, 1969, Moscow Conservatory, 1969-74; studied with, Yankelevitch and Andrievsky. Violinist; appeared with orchs. throughout world, including, N.Y. Philharm., Israel Philharm., Chgo. Symphony Orch., Los Angeles Philharm., Cleve. Symphony Orch., Boston Symphony Orch., Berlin Philharm., Royal Philharm., Phila. Symphony Orch., Paris National, Vienna Symphony, London Philharm., Pitts. Symphony Orch., Concertgebouw, Tokyo Philharm., Phila. Orch.; recs. include Prokofiev Concertos, Brahms, Sibelius, Strauss, Paganini, Shostakovich, Bruch, Glazunov. Recipient 1st prize Nat. Violin Competition USSR, 1973 Office: care Terry Harrison Artists Mgmt The Orchard Market St Charlbury 0X7 3PJ England Office Phone: 0044 1608 810330. Business E-Mail: artists@harrisonturner.co.uk.

BELKIN, STEVEN, professional sports team owner; m. Joan Wolfers Belkin; children: Julie, Amy. B in Indsl. Engring., Cornell U., 1969; MBA, Harvard U., 1971. Founder, chmn. Trans. Nat. Grp., Boston, 1974—; prin. Atlanta Spirit, LLC (parent co. of NBA Atlanta Hawks and NHL Atlanta Thrashers). Bd. trustees Cornell U., Boston Med. Ctr., Sports Mus. New Eng.; mem. vis. com. Harvard Coll., mem. com. on univ. resources; bd. dirs. Hoffman Inst. Mailing: Atlanta Spirit LLC Ste 1900 101 Marietta St NW Atlanta GA 30303*

BELKIND, ELIZABETH, chef; b. Mexico City; Grad., Bard Coll., NY; M in Russian Studies, U. Mich.; grad. Calif. Sch. Culinary Arts. Bartender Houston's Restaurant; extership Campanile, cook, asst. pastry chef; pastry chef Grace, LA, 2003—. Named one of LA's Rising Stars, StarChefs.com, 2006. Office: Grace 7360 Beverly Blvd Los Angeles CA 90036 Office Phone: 323-934-4400.*

BELKNAP, MICHAEL H. P., real estate developer; b. South Bend, Ind., Oct. 27, 1940; s. Paul E. and Mary Elizabeth (Gibb) B.; m. Dorothy Callaway, Aug. 12, 1967 (div. Dec. 1989); children: Michael, Jenny Warner, Matthew Gibb; m. Martha Burke-Hennessy, May 25, 1996; stepchildren: Hélène Lesterlin, Roland Lesterlin. BA, Harvard U., 1963, JD, 1967; LLB, Cambridge U., Eng., 1965. Bar: N.Y. 1969. Assoc. Sullivan & Cromwell, NYC, 1967-70; dir. Coun. on Environment, Office of Mayor City of N.Y., 1970-72; v.p., gen. counsel Corp. Property Investors, NYC, 1972-75; v.p. Levitt & Sons Inc., Greenwich, Conn., 1975-78; pres. Belknap Co. Ltd., Canaan, NY, 1978—. Adj. prof. Western New Eng. Coll. Sch. Law. English Speaking Union fellow, 1963-64. Mem. Berkshire Natural Resources Coun. (trustee), Harvard Club. Democrat. Episcopalian. also: 45 E End Ave New York NY 10028-7953 Office: 41 Warner Crossing Rd Canaan NY 12029-2807 Office Phone: 518-781-4646.

BELKNAP, NORTON, foundation administrator; b. Topeka, June 17, 1925; s. Paul Edward and Twila Norton Belknap; m. Mary Lonam, June 7, 1950; children: Paula Belknap Reynolds, David Barrett, Randall Page. BS, MIT, 1950, MS, 1951. Various tech. and supervisory positions Exxon, 1951-60; v.p., dir. Esso Japan, 1961-65; chmn., mng. dir. Esso Australia, 1966-69; v.p., exec. v.p., dir. Esso Europe, 1969-73; v.p. corporate planning Exxon Corp., NYC, 1973-79; sr. v.p. Exxon Internat., NYC, 1979-82; trustee Carnegie Hall, NYC, 1974—, mng. dir., 1983-88. Petroleum cons., 1982-2003; bd. dirs. So. Pacific Petroleum USA, 1989-2003; dir. So. Pacific Petroleum NL, 1999-2003. Pres., dir. Paul Taylor Dance Co. 1st lt. USAAF, 1943—46. Decorated Air medal with oak leaf cluster. Mem. Union Club, Century Assn., Met. Opera Club. (N.Y.C.), Tau Beta Pi, Alpha Tau Omega. Home: 563 Park Ave New York NY 10021-7314 Office Phone: 212-644-0454.

BELKNAP, ROBERT LAMONT, literature educator; b. NYC, Dec. 23, 1929; s. Chauncey and Dorothy (Lamont) B.; m. Josephine E. Hornor, Aug. 20, 1955 (separated 1992); children: Lydia Duff, Ellen Belknap, Abigail Krueger; m. Cynthia H. Whittaker, Aug. 24, 1997. AB summa cum laude, Princeton U., 1951; postgrad., U. Paris, 1951-52; MA, Columbia U., 1954; cert., Russian Inst., 1957, PhD, 1960; postgrad., Leningrad U., 1963-64; PhD (hon.), Petrozavodsk, 2001. Instr. Russian, Columbia U., 1957-60, asst. prof., 1960-63, chmn. freshman humanities, 1963, 67-68, 88-91, assoc. prof., 1963-68, assoc. dean student affairs, 1968-69, prof., 1968—2001, acting dean of Coll., 1976-77; dir. Russian Inst., 1977-80; prof. emeritus Columbia U., 2001—. Vis. assoc. prof. Russian Ind. U., 1966, 67; adj. prof. Russian Yale U., 1967; vis. foreign scholar, Hokkaido U., 1999-2000; dir. Columbia U. Seminars, 2001—. Author: The Structure of the Brothers Karamazov, 1967, reprint, 1989, Russian translation, 1997, The Genesis of The Brothers Karamazov, 1990, Russian translation, 2003; co-author: General Education and the Reintegration of the University, 1977; editor, Russianness, 1990. Pres. bd. trustees Brearley Sch., N.Y.C., 1981-87; trustee Whiting Found., 1985—, pres. 2001—. With US Army, 1953—55. Fellow, Guggenheim, 1994—95; Woodrow Wilson fellow, 1951—52, Inter Univ. Travel Grant, 1963, IREX fellow, 1966—67, 1973, 1989, NEH fellow, 1980—81, Kennan Inst. fellow, 1988—89, Bellagio Ctr. fellow, 1989. Office: Univ Seminars Columbia Univ New York NY 10027 Office Phone: 212-854-2389. Business E-Mail: rb12@columbia.edu. *Students rarely learn anything they are told. They often learn the things they say themselves. Good teaching wrestles them into saying sensible, verifiable, interesting, and sometimes important things.*

BELL, ALBERT ATWOOD, JR., history professor, writer; b. Laurens, SC, Sept. 23, 1945; s. Albert Atwood and Montine Crisp Bell; m. Bettye Jo Barnes; children: Stephen Thomas, Matthew Alan, Allison K., Jennifer K. MA, Duke U., Durham, NC, 1968; MDiv, Southeastern Sem., Wake Forest, NC, 1973; PhD, U. NC, Chapel Hill, 1977. Prof. history Hope Coll., Holland, Mich., 1978—. Author: (book) Death Goes Dutch, Perfect Game, Imperfect Lives: A Memoir Celebrating the 50th Anniversary of Don Larsen's Perfect Game, The Secret of the Lonely Grave, All Roads Lead to Murder, Exploring the New Testament World. Home Phone: 616-395-7558.

BELL, ALBERT JEROME, lawyer; b. Columbus, Ohio, Apr. 24, 1960; s. Albert Leo and Jean Marie (DeFino) B.; m. Carla Jean Hudak, June 7, 1986; 2 children, Brian Albert, Kristin Elizabeth. BA, Ohio State U., 1982; JD, Capital U., 1985. Bar: Ohio 1985. Writer Battelle Meml. Inst., Columbus, 1982-84; pvt. practice law Columbus, 1985-86; vice-chmn., chief adminstrv. officer Big Lots Inc., Columbus, 1987—2004; CEO Moochie & Co., 2005—. Mem. adv. bd. devel. comm. chair, Annual Fund St. Charles Prep. HS; co-chmn. St. Paul Bldg. Campaign. Mem. ABA, Ohio Bar Assn., Columbus Bar Assn., Assn. Trial Lawyers Am., Internat. Assn. Corp. Real Estate Execs., Ohio State U. Alumni Assn. Roman Catholic. Avocations: golf, skiing, exercising.

BELL, ALEXIS T., chemical engineer, educator; b. NYC, Oct. 16, 1942; BS, MIT, 1964, ScD, 1967. From asst. prof. to prof. U. Calif., Berkeley, 1967-76, prof. chem. engring., 1976-99, asst. dean Coll. Chemistry, 1979-81, chmn. Dept. Chem. Engring., 1981-91, dean Coll. Chemistry, 1994—. Cons. Tracer Labs., Calif., 1967-69, Internat. Plasma Corp., 1969—, Tegal Corp. & Lockheed Space & Missile Co.; sr. scientist Lawrence Berkeley Nat. Lab. Contbr. articles to profl. jours. Recipient Curtis W. McGraw Rsch. award Am. Soc. Engring. Edn., 1981, Paul E. Emmett award Catalysis Soc., 1985; Donald L. Katz lectr. U. Mich., 1984, B. F. Dodge lectr. Yale U., 1988, Langmuir lectr. Am. Chem. Soc., 1992. Fellow Am. Acad. Arts & Scis.; mem. NAE, Am. Chem. Soc. (A. Glenn award 1978), AIChE (R.H. Wilhelm award 1992), Electrochem. Soc., Sigma Xi. Office: Dept Chem Engring 201G Gilman Hall U California Berkeley CA 94720-0001 Fax: 510-642-4778. Business E-Mail: bell@cchem.berkeley.edu.*

BELL, ANDREW C., music educator; b. New Orleans, Oct. 9, 1964; s. Clark B. and Maxine P. Bell; m. Angela W. Bell, June 3, 1989; children: Andee, Alayna. B in Music Edn., Glenville State Coll., W.Va., 1987; M in Music Edn., VanderCook Coll. Music, Chgo., 1997. Band dir. Washington Middle Sch., Cairo, Ga., 1987—93, Screven County H.S., Sylvania, Ga., 1993—2000, Ctrl. H.S., Macon, Ga., 2000—04; prof. Ga. Mil. Coll., Warner Robins; band dir. Crisp County H.S., Cordele, Ga., 2004—. Mem.: Internat. Assn. Jazz Educators, Percussive Arts Soc., Music Educators Nat. Conv., Condrs. Guild, Ga. Music Educators Assn., Nat. Band Assn. (dist. band chair 1997—2000, state rsch. and advocacy chmn. instrumental 1999—2002). Avocations: movies, reading, Star Trek. Office: Crisp County HS Band 2402 Frontage Rd Cordele GA 31015 Home: 2153 Hwy 280 W Cordele GA 31015 Home Phone: 229-276-0213; Office Phone: 229-276-3430 ext. 2209. Business E-Mail: abell@crisp.k12.ga.us. E-mail: 4abell@hughes.net.

BELL, ANGELA, music educator; b. St. Louis, Feb. 1, 1932; d. John Simonds Bell, Jr. and Florence Sippy Bell. MusB, Oberlin Conservatory, Ohio, 1954; MusM, American Conservatory, 1972; studied with Cecile de Horvath, Chgo., 1954—62; student, Great Russian Sch. Piano Playing. Pvt. piano tchr., Chgo., 1955—87, St. Louis, 1987—2007. Mem.: Mo. State Music Tchrs. Assn.

BELL, ANGELA MARIE, accountant; b. Chgo., Aug. 9, 1964; d. Earl and Juanita Bell. BS in Acctg., De Paul U., Chgo., 1999. Acct. Mt. Sinai, Chgo., 1999—2003; clk. Circuit Ct., Chgo., 2004—. Fin. sec. Ladies Aux. Knights Columbus, 2000—. Mem.: Nat. Assn. Female Execs., Nat. Assn. Black Accountants. Democrat. Roman Catholic. Avocations: singing, writing, poetry. Home: 6832 S Evans Ave Chicago IL 60637

BELL, BENJAMIN HARRISON, JR., solicitor; b. Pulaski, Va., May 13, 1960; s. Benjamin Harrison and Barbara Lynch Bell; m. Kristen Kay Heintz, Oct. 18, 1997. BA, Coll. William and Mary, Williamsburg, Va., 1982; JD, Cumberland Sch. Law, Birmingham, Ala., 1986. Bar: SC 1986. Sr. asst. solicitor First Jud. Cir. Solicitor's Office, Summerville, SC, 1987—. Vol. Friends Hunley, North Charleston, 2001—03; congl. coun. Peace Luth. Ch., North Charleston, SC, 2004—06; bd. dirs. Frances R. Willis SPCA, Summerville, SC, 2005—06. Mem.: SC Solcitor's Assn. Lutheran. Office: First Judicial Cir Solicitor's Offic 140 N Main St Ste 102 Summerville SC 29483 Home Phone: 843-207-7519; Office Phone: 843-871-2640. Personal E-mail: bhbelljr@earthlink.net. Business E-Mail: bhbelljr@scsolicitor1.org.

BELL, BRADLEY J., water treatment company executive; b. 1952; BS, U. Ill., 1974; MBA, Harvard U., 1978. Fin. analyst G.E., 1974-76; mgr. treasury analysis Bendix Corp., 1978-80; treas. Bundy Corp., 1983-87, v.p., treas., 1987; treas. Whirlpool Corp., Benton Harbor, Mich., 1987—97, v.p., 1990—97; sr. v.p., CFO Rohm & Haas Co., 1997—2003; exec. v.p., CFO Nalco Co., Naperville, Ill., 2003—. Bd. dirs. Idex Corp., Compass Minerals Internat. Office: Nalco Co 1601 W Diehl Rd Naperville IL 60563-1198

BELL, C. GORDON, computer architect and engineer, entrepreneur, researcher; b. Kirksville, Mo., Aug. 19, 1934; s. Roy Chester and Lola Dolph (Gordon) Bell; m. Gwendolyn Kay Druyor, Jan. 3, 1959; 2 children. BSEE, MIT, 1956, MSEE, 1957; DEng (hon.), Worcester Polytechnic Inst., 1993. With Digital Equipment Corp., 1960—66, v.p., R&D, 1972—83; prof., computer sci. and elec. engring. Carnegie-Mellon U., 1966—72; founder Encore Computer, 1983; first asst. dir. NSF Computing Directorate, 1986—87; founding mem. Ardent Computer, 1986—88; v.p., R&D Ardent Computer (merged with Stellar), 1988—89; advisor Microsoft Corp., 1991—95, sr. researcher, media presence rsch. group San Francisco, 1995—. Led Nat. Rsch. and Edn. Network panel; chairing the cross-agy. govt. panel that led to the formation of the Internet; author First High Performance Computer and Comm Initiative; co-founder Computer Mus., Boston, 1979; founding bd. mem. Computer History Mus., Mountain View, Calif., 1999; bd. dir., tech. adv. bd. Cradle Tech., DiamondCluster Exchange, Dust Networks, Inc., Vanguard Group; founder, dir. Bell-Mason Group. Contbr. articles to profl. jours.; co-author: Computer Structures: Readings and Examples, 1971, Designing Computers and Digital Systems Using PDP-16 Register Transfer Modules, 1972, Computer Engineering, 1978, Computer Structures: Principles and Examples, 1982, High Tech Ventures: The Guide To Entrepreneurial Success, 1991; maintains MyLifeBits. Sponsor Gordon Bell prize (Assn. Computing Machinery/IEEE Conf. on Supercomputing), 1987—. Named Fellow, Computer History Mus., 2003; recipient AEA Inventor award for the greatest economic contribution to the New England region, Nat. Medal Tech., 1991, MCI Comm. Info. Tech. Leadership award for Innovation, 1995; Fulbright Scholar, U. New South Wales, 1957—58. Fellow: IEEE (also Computer Pioneer) (Von Neumann medal 1992, Vladamir Karapetroff Eminent Member's award of Eta Kappa Nu 2001), Assn. for Computing Machinery, AAAS, Am. Acad. Arts and Sciences; mem.: NAS, NAE. Achievements include being the architect of various mini- and time-sharing computers (PDP's) and led the develop. of Digital Equipment Corp. VAX and VAX computing environ; patents in field. Avocations: bicycling, scuba diving, skiing, fishing. Office: Microsoft Corp 455 Market St Ste 1690 San Francisco CA 94105 Office Fax: 415-778-8225, 425-936-7329. Business E-Mail: GBell@microsoft.com.*

BELL, CARL COMPTON, psychiatrist, researcher; b. Chgo., Oct. 28, 1947; s. William Yancy and Pearl Louise (Debnam) Bell; m. Joanne Scott, Jan. 1, 1969 (div. Apr. 1971); 1 child, Cristin Carol; m. Dora Dixie, Dec. 1984 (div. May 1989); m. Tyra Taylor, Mar. 19, 1991 (div. Oct. 2003); children: Briatta Honore, William Yancy Bell IV; m. Phyllis West, Mar. 18, 2005. BS Biology, U. Ill.-Chgo., 1967; MD, Meharry Med. Coll., 1971. Diplomate Am. Bd. Psychiatry and Neurology (examiner). Intern Ill. State Psychiat. Inst., Chgo., 1971—72, resident, 1972—74; pvt. practice medicine specializing in psychiatry Chgo., 1974—; dir. psychiat. emergency svcs. Jackson Park Hosp., Chgo., 1976—77, assoc. dir. divsn. behavioral and psychodynamic medicine, 1979—82, mem. staff, 1972—; staff psychiatrist Human Correctional and Svcs. Inst., Chgo., 1977—78, Chgo. Bd. Edn., 1977—79, Chatham Avalon Mental Health Ctr., Chgo., 1977—79, Cmty. Mental Health Coun., Chgo., 1977—79, med. dir., 1983—87, exec. dir., 1987—; pres., CEO Cmty. Mental Health Coun. and Found., 1993—; assoc. prof. to prof. clin. psychiatry U. Ill., 1983—, prof. pub. health, 1993—. Cons. Cmty. divsn. Lilly Endowment; cons. editl. bd. Jour. Prison and Jail Health, 1990-92, Cmty. Mental Health Jour., 1989—, Jour. Hosp. and Cmty. Psychiatry, 1990-94, Jour. Nat. Med. Assn., 1994-98, Psychiat. Svcs., 1994-98, Jour. Correctional Health Care, 1997-2000, Jour. Health Care to Poor and Underserved, 1991—, Jour. Infant, Child and Adolescent Psychotherapy, 1997—, Clin. Psychiat. News, 2000—; mem. editl. bd. Ill. Child Welfare, 2004; mem. com. prevention mental disorders and substance abuse among children, youth, young adults, rsch. advances and promising intervention NAS, 2007— ons. in field Prodr.(creator animation): Book Worm, 1984; author: Psychiatric Aspects of Violence: Issues in Prevention and Treatment, 2000, Sanity of Survival: Reflections on Community Mental Health and Wellness, 2004; co-author: Suicide and Homicide Among Adolescents, 1994; mem. editl. bd.: Am. Psychiat. Pub., Inc., 2001—; contbr. articles to profl. jours.; prodr.(creator): (video) Eight Pieces of Brocade, 2000—; talk show host: Sta. WVON-AM, 1987—90; Sta. WJPC-FM, 1992—93. Profl. adv. panel Mental Health Assn. Greater Chgo., 1983—; adv. com. funded grant on Aggressors, Victims and Bystanders, 1989-92; bd. dirs. Ill. Coun. Against Handgun Violence, Nat. Commn. on Correctional Health Care, chmn., 1992; lectr. U. Chgo., 1986—, Chgo. Med. Sch., 1987—; co-dir. Interdisciplinary violence Prevention Ctr. U. Ill., 2006—; tchr. martial arts, 1973—; apptd. to violence against women adv. coun., 1995-2000; mem. White House strategy session on Children, Violence and Responsibility, 1999; mem. surgeon gen. report on mental health-Culture, Race and Ethnicity Working Group, 2000; mem. Surgeon Gen. report on youth violence working group, 2000—; mem. Chgo. Bd. Health, 2002—; apptd. adv. group. strengthening families Joint Learning Initiative on Children and HIV/AIDS Human Scis. Rsch. Coun., South Africa, 2007. Lt. comdr. USN, 1974-76 Named Top Doctor, Chgo. mag., 1997, 2001, 2007, Internat. fellow Inst. Philosophy, Diversity and Mental Health, Ctr. Ethnicity and Health U. Ctrl. Lancashire, Eng., 2007; named to Guide To Am.'s Top Psychiatrists, Consumers Rsch. Coun. Am., 2004—05; recipient plaque in recognition and appreciation, Chatham-Avalon Mental Health Ctr., 1979, Div. Behavioral Medicine, 1982, Social Action award, Chgo. chpt. Black Social Workers, 1988, Mental Health award, Englewood Cmty. Health Orgn., 1988, Scholastic Achievement award, Chgo. chpt. Nat. Assn. Black Social Workers, 1980, Ellen Quinn Meml. award, 1986, Monarch award, Alpha Kappa Alpha, 1986, Alumnus of Yr. award, Meharry Med. Coll., 1991, Cmty. Psychiatry award, Am. Assn. Cmty. Psychiatrists, 1992, Lifetime Achievement award, Black Psychiatrists of Am., 1994, Freddye Smith award, Cmty. Mental Health Coun., 1997, Blanche F. Ittleson award Lifetime Contbns., Am. Ortho Psychiatric Assn., 2000, Lifetime Achievement award, Cmty. Behavioral Healthcare Assn. Ill., 2001, Living Legacy award, Provident Found., 2001, Dr. Jeanne Spurlock Lectr. award, Am. Acad. Child and Adolescent Psychiatrists, 2002, George B. Nash, Sr. Pub. Edn. award, Nat. Alliance for Mentally Ill, Chgo., 2003, Disting. Psychiatrist Lecture Award Outstanding Achievement in Psychiatry, Am. Psychiat. Assn., 2003, Minority Mental Health award, Am. Psychiat. Found., 2003, Minority Svcs. award, 2004, Welcome Back award, Eli Lily Co., 2003, From Whence We Came award, Allstate Ins. Co., 2004, Recognition plaque, Ill. Mental Health and Adv. Coun., 2005, Graduating Class of Hyde Pk. Acad., 2005, Health Warriors award, Ga. Doty Mental Health Edn. Fund, 2005, Pub. Svc. award, Inst. Medicine Chgo., 2006; fellow, 2004; grantee, NIMH, 2001—; Goldberger fellow, 1969, Dr. Martin Luther King Jr. fellow, 1970—71. Fellow Am. Coll. Psychiatrists (com. Laughlin fellows 1989-92, fin. com. 1993-96, pub. edn. com. 1994-96, com. membership devel. 1996-00, com. strategic planning 2000—, bd. regents 2006—, Bowis Disting. Svc. award 2002), Am. Psychiat. Assn. (disting.; Falk fellow 1972-73, task force-delivery psychiat. svcs. to proverty areas 1972-73, com. black psychiatrists, 1988-90, chmn. black caucus 1990-92, vice chair task force psychiat. aspects of violence 1997—, joint commn. on pub. affairs 2000—, psychiat. diagnosis and assessment com. 2003—, chair Coun. on Social Issues and Pub. Psychiatry, personality disorders work group task force on the Diagnostic and Statis. Manual of Mental Disorders 5th edit., 2007-, Spl. Presdl. Commendation 1997, Disting. Psychiatrist Lecture award 2003, apptd. to presdl. task force on biopsychosocial consequences of early childhood violence, 2005, vice chair coun. advocacy and pub. policy, 2006-07); mem. Nat. Med. Assn. (local chmn. sect. on neurology and psychiatry 1983, conv., nat. chmn. sect. on psychiatry and behavioral scis. 1985-86, E.Y. Williams Disting. Sr. Clin. scholar psychiatry sect. 1992), Am. Psychiat. Assn. (chmn. coun. social issues and pub. psychiatry 2007—), Black Psychiatrists Am. (editor Bottom Line newsletter 1977-82, v.p. 1980-82), Cook County Physicians Assn., Prairie State Physicians, Ill. Psychiat. Soc., Am. Assn. Cmty. Mental Health Ctr. Psychiatrists (bd. dirs. 1985-89), Am. Coll. Psychiatry, Nat. Coun. Cmty. Health Ctrs. (sec. bd. dirs. 1986, sec., treas. 1987), Underwater Explorers Soc., Shorei Goju Karate Soc. (7th degree Black Belt), Martial Arts Karate Assn., Alpha Omega Alpha. Office: Community Mental Health Coun 8704 S Constance Ave Chicago IL 60617-2756 Office Phone: 773-734-4033 ext. 204. Business E-Mail: carlcbell@pol.net.

BELL, CHARLES EUGENE, JR., retired industrial engineer; b. NYC, Dec. 13, 1932; s. Charles Edward and Constance Elizabeth (Verbella) Bell; m. Doris R. Clifton, Jan. 14, 1967; 1 child, Scott Charles. B in Engring., Johns Hopkins U., 1954, MS in Engring., 1959. Registered Calif. Indsl. engr. Signode Corp., Balt., 1957—61, asst. to plant mgr., 1961—63, plant engr., 1963—64, divsn. indsl. engr. Glenview, Ill., 1964—69, asst. to divsn. mgr., 1969—76, engring. mgr., 1976—93; cons., 1993—2004; ret., 2004. Host committeeman Internat. Indsl. Engring. Conf., Chgo., 1984, Chgo., 92. With US Army, 1955—57. Mem.: NSPE, Soc. Plastics Engrs., Tenn. Soc. Profl. Engrs., Indsl. Mgmt. Club Ctrl. Md. (pres. 1964), Am. Inst. Indsl. Engrs. (pres. 1981), Druid Hills Country Club. Republican. Roman Catholic. Home: 207 Markham Ln Crossville TN 38558

BELL, DAVID ARTHUR, retired advertising agency executive; b. Mpls., May 29, 1943; s. Arthur E. and Frances (Tripp) B.; m. Gail G. Galvani; children: Jennifer L., Jenny L., Jeffrey D., Ashley Tripp, Andrew Joseph. BA in Polit. Sci., Macalester Coll., 1965. Account exec. Leo Burnett, Chgo., 1965—74; pres. Knox Reeves, Mpls., 1972—74; pres. Atlantic div. Bozell & Jacobs, 1974-85; pres. Bozell, Jacobs, Kenyon & Eckhardt, 1986-92; chmn., CEO Bozell Worldwide Inc., 1995—98, True North Comm., Inc., 1998—2001; vice chmn. Interpublic Group of Companies, Inc., NYC, 2001—03, chmn., CEO, 2003—04, co-chmn., 2005—07, chmn. emeritus, 2006—; adv. Pegasus Capital Advisors, L.P., NYC, 2007—. Bd. dir. Primedia, Inc., Warnaco Group Inc.; past chmn. Am. Advt. Fedn., 1988—91. Trustee Macalester Coll., 1986—98, trustee emeritus, 1998—; chmn. Advt. Ednl. Found., Ad Coun., 2002—; bd. dir. Nat. Forest Fedn., 2002—, chmn., 2004—; mem. corp. coun. Interlochen Ctr. Arts, 2003—. Recipient charter centennial medallion Macalester Coll., 1974; named disting. alumnus Macalester Coll., 1978; recipient Minn. Airman of Yr. award, 1967; named to Advertising Hall of Fame, 2007 Mem. Am. Assn. Advt. Agys. (chmn. 1996-97. Republican. Presbyterian. Office: Pegasus Capital Advisors LP 505 Park Ave 21st Fl New York NY 10022*

BELL, DEBBIE MCCULLEY, science educator; b. Heidelburg, Germany, June 26, 1971; d. Arvil Eugene McCulley and Jennifer Manus; m. Ronnie Wayne Bell, June 18, 1993; 1 child, Austin Wayne. B in Gen. Sci. Edn., U. Ark., 1993, M in Sci. Edn., 1997. Cert. tchr. Dept. Edn., Ark. Life and earth sci. educator Ramay Jr. HS, Fayetteville, Ark., 1993—2000; life sci., reading educator Holt Mid. Sch., Fayetteville, 2000—07, Owl Creek Sch., Fayetteville, 2007—. Cheerleading sponsor Ramay Jr. High, Fayetteville, Ark., 1993—95; sci. curriculum com. mem. Holt Mid. Sch., Fayetteville, Ark., 2000—07, math acsip com. mem., 2000—07, recycling club sponsor, 2001—02, student coun. asst. sponsor, 2004—07, developer master schedule, 2005—07, bible club sponsor, 2005—07, hooked on fishing not on drugs asst. sponsor, 2005—07; tchr. to son through Ark. Virtual Sch., Little Rock, 2003—07. Choir mem. First Bapt. Ch., Springdale, Ark., 1996—2004, sec. small group, 2004—05, small group leader of mid. sch. girls, 2000—01; founding mem. Crossroads Cmty. Ch., Hindsville, 2005—. Recipient 10 Yr. Educator award, Fayetteville Pub. Sch., 2003. Mem.: Nat. Sci. Tchr. Assn., Christian Educator Assn. Internat. Conservative. Christian. Avocations: travel, reading, exercise, bicycling, cross stitch. Home: 227 Madison 7025 Hindsville AR 72738 Office: Owl Creek Sch 375 N Rupple Rd Fayetteville AR 72704 Office Phone: 479-718-0200. Office Fax: 479-718-0201. Personal E-mail: dbell@dluxlink.com. Business E-Mail: dbell@fayar.net.

BELL, DELORIS WILEY, physician; b. Solomon, Kans., Sept. 30, 1942; d. Harry A. and Mildren H. (Watt) Wiley; children: Leslie, John. BA, Kans. Wesleyan U., 1964; MD, U. Kans., 1968. Diplomate Am. Bd. Ophthalmology. Intern St. Luke's Hosp., Kansas City, Mo., 1968-69; resident U. Kans. Med. Ctr., Kansas City, 1969-72; practice medicine specializing in ophthalmology Overland Park, Kans., 1973—. Mem. AMA, Kans. Med. Soc. (pres. sect. ophthalmology 1985-86, spkr. house 1994-97), Am. Acad. Ophthalmology (councillor 1988-93, chmn. state govtl. affairs 1993-97, bd. trustees 2000-03), Kans. Soc. Ophthalmology (pres. 1985-86), Kansas City Soc. Ophthalmology and Otolaryngology (sec. 1984-86, pres.-elect 1988, pres. 1989). Avocations: photography, travel. Office: 7000 W 121st St Ste 100 Shawnee Mission KS 66209-2010 Office Phone: 913-498-2015. Personal E-mail: cd2cdb@gmail.com.

BELL, ERNEST LORNE, III, retired lawyer; b. Boston, June 12, 1926; s. Ernest L. and Ellamay (Currier) B.; m. Margaret Van Nostrand Depue, Apr. 14, 1951 (dec. Oct. 1988); children: David E., Robin E., Roseanne Margaret; m. Sally Leavitt Cheney, Nov. 25, 1989. BA cum laude, Harvard Coll., 1949; JD, U. Mich., 1952. Bar: N.H. 1952, U.S. Supreme Ct. 1962. Pvt. practice, Keene, NH, 1952; ptnr. firm Bell & Falk, P.A., 1972-99; sole practice law Keene, NH, 1999—2003; ret., 2003. Author: An Initial View of Ultra as an American Weapon in World War II. Mem. exec. bd. Daniel Webster coun. Boy Scouts Am., 1970-79, 93—; chmn. bd. advisers Colony House Mus., 1984-91; trustee, treas. Keene Pub. Libr.; del. N.H. Constl. Conv., 1964, 74; mem. World War II Studies Assn.; mem. N.H. Aero. Commn., 1980-86. Recipient Silver Beaver award Fellow Am. Bar Found. (N.H. chair 1993-99); mem. ABA, N.H. Bar Assn (pres. 1978-79), N.H. Bar Found. (sec., bd. dirs. 1985-90, chmn. 1991-93), Cheshire County Bar Assn., Lawyer Pilots Bar Assn. (founding dir. 1962-68), Def. Rsch. Inst. (v.p. 1969-73, sec. 1973-76), Am. Kennel Club (del. 1979-81), Std. Schnauzer Club Am., Harvard Club (Boston). Anglican. Home: 35 Felt Rd Keene NH 03431-2103 Personal E-mail: tutt_b@verizon.net.

BELL, FORD WATSON, museum association administrator; b. Minneapolis; m. Amy Bell. BA in Spanish, U. Minn., 1972, DVM, 1982; ed., Walsh Sch. Fgn. Svc., Georgetown U., U. Pacific. Spanish tchr. Blake Sch., Hopkins, Minn.; clin. assoc. prof. oncology, Coll. Veterinary Medicine U. Minn., 1995—; pres. and CEO Minneapolis Heart Inst. Found., 1995—2005; CEO Am. Assn. Museums, Washington, 2007—. Bd. dirs. Spl. Projects Found., Minn. Veterinary Med. Assn. Found., James Ford Bell Mus. Natural Hist.; lectr. in field. Chmn. James Ford Bell Found.; trustee Minneapolis Inst. Arts, 1998—, Conn. Coll. Office: American Association Museums Ste 400 1575 Eye St NW Washington DC 20005*

BELL, FRANCES LOUISE, medical technologist; b. Milton, Pa., Apr. 28, 1926; d. George Earl and Kathryn Robbins (Fairchild) Reichard; m. Edwin Lewis Bell II, Dec. 27, 1950; children: Ernest Michael, Stephen Thomas, Eric Leslie. BS Biology cum laude, Bucknell U., Lewisburg, Pa., 1948; med. technologist, Geisinger Meml. Hosp., 1949. Registered med. technologist. Med. technologist Burlington County Hosp., Mt. Holly, NJ, 1949—50, Robert Packer Hosp., Sayre, Pa., 1950, Carle Hosp./Clinic, Urbana, Ill., 1951—52, St. Joseph Hosp., Reading, Pa., 1972—83. Vol. Crime Watch, City Hall, Reading, 1985-90, Am. Heart Assn., Reading, 1956-2000, March of Dimes, Reading, 1956-72, Am. Cancer Soc., Reading, 1956-71, Multiple Sclerosis, Reading, 1956-72, Reading Musical Found., 1985-90, Hist. Soc. Berks County; corr. sec. women's aux., 1986-90; fin. sec. aux. Albright Coll., 1988-95; hospitality co-chmn. women's com. Reading Symphony Orch., 1985-90, editor yearbook women's com., 1992-96; editor yearbook Reading Symphony Orch. League, 1996-2003; chmn. hospitality Reading-Berks Pub. Librs., 1988-91; mem. Friends Reading Mus., Berks County Conservancy. Mem. AAUW (hon. life, assoc. editor bull. 1961-63, cultural interests rep. 1967-68), Woman's Club Reading (treas. 1986-88, fin. sec. 1991-2004), United Meth. Women, World Affairs Coun. Berks County, Libr. Soc. Albright Coll., Phi Beta Kappa Republican. Methodist. Avocations: music, photography, art. Home: 1454 Oak Ln Reading PA 19604-1865 *Life and grace are cherished gifts to each one of us from our creator. We are spiritual beings, so our nature is to be loving, kind, understanding, forgiving and compasssionate in all our relations with others.*

BELL, FRANK OURAY, JR., lawyer; b. San Francisco, Aug. 13, 1940; s. Frank Ouray Sr. and Clara Belle (McClure) Bell; m. Sherrie A. Levie, Mar. 29, 1981; children: Aimee, David;children from previous marriage: Carin, Laurie. AB, San Francisco State U., 1963; JD, U. Calif., San Francisco, 1966. Bar: Calif. 1966, U.S. Dist. Ct. (no. dist.) Calif. 1967, U.S. Ct. Appeals (9th cir.) 1967, U.S. Supreme Ct. 1973. Dep. atty. gen. Calif. State's Atty.'s Office, Sacramento, 1966-68; ptnr. Goorjian & Bell, San Francisco, 1968-70; chief asst. Fed. Pub. Defender's Office, San Francisco, 1970-82; dir. Calif. State Pub. Defender's Office, 1984-87; pvt. practice law San Francisco, 1982-84; sr. litig. assoc. Olimpia, Whelan & Lively, San Jose, Calif., 1987-89; pvt. practice San Mateo and Redwood City, Calif., 1989—. Mem.: Calif. Pub. Defenders Assn. (bd. dirs. 1986—87), San Mateo County Bar Assn. Democrat. Jewish. Office: 333 Bradford St Ste 270 Redwood City CA 94063 Office Phone: 650-365-8300. Business E-Mail: FrankBell@FrankBellLaw.com.

BELL, GENEVIEVE, anthropologist; Grad., Bryn Mawr Coll., Pa.; PhD in Anthropology, Stanford U. Tchr., anthropology, Native Am. Studies Stanford U.; anthropologist, people and practices rsch. group Intel, Santa Clara, Calif., 1998—. Contbr. articles to profl. jours. Mem.: Nat. Assn. for the Practice of Anthropology. Office: Intel 2200 Mission College Blvd Santa Clara CA 95052 Office Phone: 503-264-7510. Office Fax: 503-264-2225.

BELL, GLADYS SMILEY, university librarian; b. Hamilton, Ohio, Aug. 13, 1949; d. Chainous William Jr. and Margaret Ennis (Dabney) Smiley; m. Howard Anthony Bell, July 25, 1986; children: Dwyte, Gwyndolyn Cathrin. BS, Howard U., 1972; MLS, L.I. U., 1973. Tech. libr. Xerox Corp., Webster, NY, 1973-75; head circulation Howard U., Washington, 1975-77; asst. libr. Case Western Reserve U., Cleve., 1977-90; assoc. prof. libr. & media svcs. Kent (Ohio) State U., 1990; int. libr. dir. Hampton U. William R. & Norma B. Harvey Libr., 2004—05, dir., 2005—. Co-chair Joint Conf. Librs. of Color, 2006. Recipient Scholarly Contbn. award, Kent State U., 1996, Institutional Diversity Cmty. Svc. award, 2000. Mem. ALA (councilor-at-large, mem. governing coun. 2007-, Equality award, 2007), Black Caucus of the ALA (pres. 2000-02, Excellence in Librarianship award, 2005), Afro-Am. Studies & Libr. (chair 1995—), Assn. Coll. & Rsch. Librs. (past chair African Am. Studies & Libr. sect., Harvard Leadership Inst. scholar, 2006), Acad. Libr. Assn., Human Diversity Interest Group (chair 1995—), Southeastern Libr. Network (bd. dirs.) Baptist. Avocations: photography, gardening. Office: William R & Norma B Harvey Libr Hampton U 130 E Tyler St Hampton VA 23668 Office Phone: 757-727-5371. Office Fax: 757-727-5952. E-mail: gladys.bell@hamptonu.edu.

BELL, GREGORY JAMES, information technology manager; b. Kenmore, NY, Oct. 7, 1964; s. James Norman and Sandra Lee Bell; m. Brenda Ann Barrett; children: Christopher Adam, Andrew Earl. BS in Computer Info. Svcs., Medaille Coll., Buffalo, NY, 1996, BSBA, 1996; MBA, Strayer U., Richmond, Va., 2001. CPA internal controls auditor, The IIC, 2007; cert. info. svcs. auditor ISACA, 1996, project mgmt. profl. Project Mgmt. Inst., 1999, cert. profl. Microsoft, 2007, GIAC web application security SANS, 2007. CEO Blue Canary LLC, Richmond, 2002—07; info. tech. audit mgr. Va. Dept. Taxation, Richmond, 2007—. Author: (novels) Managing Remote Resources. Pres.-elect Va. Child Care Resource and Referral Network, Richmond, 2006. With USAR, 1983—89. Decorated Achievement medal USAR. Mem.: ISACA. Democrat. Home: 1401 Olde Sage Ct Glen Allen VA 23059 Office: Blue Canary LLC 12732 Stonebriar Ln Richmond VA 23233 Home Phone: 804-291-6126. Personal E-mail: gregoryjbell@hotmail.com.

BELL, GRIFFIN BOYETTE, lawyer, former United States attorney general; b. Americus, Ga., Oct. 31, 1918; s. A. C. and Thelma (Pilcher) Bell; m. Mary Foy Powell, Feb. 20, 1943 (dec.); 1 child, Griffin; m. Nancy Duckworth Kinnebrew, June 8, 2001. Student, Ga. Southwestern Coll.; LL.B. cum laude, Mercer U., 1948, LL.D., 1967. Bar: Ga. 1947. Pvt. practice law, Savannah, Rome, Ga., 1947-53; ptnr. firm King & Spalding, Atlanta, 1953—58, mng. ptnr., 1959-61, sr. ptnr., 1976—77, 1979—2004, sr. counsel, 2004—; chief of staff to Gov. Ernest Vandiver State of Ga., Atlanta, 1959-61; judge U.S. Ct. Appeals (5th cir.), 1961-76; atty. gen. U.S. Dept. Justice, Washington, 1977-79. Mem. vis. com. Vanderbilt U. Law Sch.; head Am. del. Madrid Conf. Security and Coop. Europe, 1980. Co-chmn. Nat. Task Force Violent Crime, 1981, Pres. Bush's Com. Fed. Ethics Law Reform, 1989; mem. Sec. of State's Adv. Com. South Africa; mem. rev. panel U.S. Office Mil. Commn. for mil. tribunals at Guantanamo Bay, Cuba, 2003—; chmn. Atlanta Commn. Crime Delinquency, 1965—66; bd. dirs. Fed. Jud. Ctr., 1974—76; trustee Mercer U., Ga. Served to maj. US Army, 1941—46. Recipient Thomas Jefferson Meml. Found. award for Excellence in Law, 1984. Mem.: ABA (chmn. divsn. jud. adminstrn. 1975—76), Am. Law Inst., Am. Coll. Trial Lawyers (pres. 1985—86), Order of Coif. Baptist. Office: King & Spalding LLP 1180 Peachtree St NE Atlanta GA 30309-3521 Office Phone: 404-572-4879. Business E-Mail: gbell@kslaw.com.

BELL, HANEY HARDY, III, lawyer; b. Staunton, Va., Aug. 20, 1944; s. Haney Hardy Jr. and Maud (Deekens) B.; m. Alice Tester, Feb. 17, 1968; 1 child, Landon D. BA, U. Va., 1966; JD cum laude, U. Wis., 1973. Bar: Va. 1974. Group ins. rep. Prudential Ins. Co. Am., Milw., 1969-70; assoc. Woods, Rogers & Hazlegrove, Roanoke, Va., 1973-78; assoc. counsel R.J. Reynolds Industries, Inc., Winston-Salem, NC, 1978-79; sec., gen. counsel RJR Foods, Inc., 1979-80; sr. internat. counsel R.J. Reynolds Tobacco Internat., Inc., 1980-87; assoc. gen. counsel Fieldcrest Cannon Inc., Eden, NC, 1987-95, Lorillard Tobacco Co., Greensboro, 1996—2002; v.p., asst. gen. counsel Santa Fe Natural Tobacco Co., 2002—. Lt. AUS, 1967-69. Mem. Va. State Bar, Order of Coif. Office Phone: 505-438-1335. Business E-Mail: hbell@sfntc.com.

BELL, HELEN LAVIN, artist; b. Allentown, Pa. d. Thomas Joseph and Anna Helen Lavin; m. Paul Edward Bell, June 10, 1950; children: Celine Butler, Sharon Neiman, Paul Jr., Christine Schlacter. Student, Western Md. Coll., 1945-47, Md. Inst. Art, 1947-48, Telfair Acad. Arts, 1958-59, U. Calif., Riverside, 1970-71, 80-81. Asst. art dir. Davison's, Atlanta, 1950—. One-woman shows include Riverside Art Mus., Calif., 1980, 2003-04, Rizzoli Internat., Costa Mesa, Calif., 1987, Zola Fine Art, Beverly Hills, Calif., 1990, EOS Gallery, Redlands, Calif., 2003, Mission San Juan Capistrano, Calif., 2005, Sandstone Gallery, Laguna Beach, Calif., 2005, others; group shows include City of Riverside, Calif., 1975, Riverside County Mus., Beaumont, Calif., 1976, 90, Calif. Poly. U., Pomona, 1987, LA County Mus. Art, 1989-95, Calif. Small Works, Santa Rosa, 1992-93, Carte Blanche, 1996, Made in Calif., Brea, 1997, 2006, Echoes and Visions II, V, 2002, Laguna Niguel, Calif., 1998, Millard Sheets Small Works Gallery, 2001, EOS Gallery, Redlands, 2003, Riverside Art Mus., 2003, J. Wayne Stark Gallery, Tex. A&M U. Coll. Station, 2004, NAWA Curated Exhibit Blue Hill Cultural Ctr., Pearl River, NY, 2007 Event chair Nat. Charity League, Riverside, Calif., 1979-83; trustee Riverside Art Mus., 1979-82. Merit scholar Telfair Acad. Arts and Scis., Savannah, Ga., 1958. Mem. Redlands Art Assn. (trustee 1985-87, 91-95, 2005-07), Art Alliance (pres. 1979-80, com. chairs 1978, 81-82, 2000), Nat. Assn. Women Artists, Inc., Calif. Art Club (painting patron), So. Calif. Plein Air Painters Assn. Republican. Roman Catholic. Avocations: swimming, travel. Studio: 6359 Dulcet Pl Riverside CA 92506 Office Phone: 951-682-9289. Personal E-mail: sabrplt@msn.com.

BELL, HILARI, writer, former librarian; b. Denver, 1958; Part-time reference libr. Author: Songs of Power, 2000, Navohar, 2000, Matter of Profit, 2001 (named a Best Book for Young Adults, ALA, named one of Books for the Teen Age, NY Pub. Libr., 2002), The Goblin Wood, 2003 (named a Best Book for Young Adults, ALA, named one of Books for the Teen Age, NY Pub. Libr.), Farsala: Fall of a Kingdom, 2003, Rise of a Hero, 2005, The Wizard Test, 2005, The Prophecy, 2006, Farsala: Forging the Sword, 2006, Shield of Stars, 2007. Mem.: Sci. Fiction and Fantasy Writers Am., Inc. Avocations: board games, fantasy games, camping, hiking. Mailing: c/o HarperCollins Childrens Book 1350 Ave of the Americas New York NY 10019

BELL, JAMES A., aerospace transportation executive; b. LA, 1949; m. Mary Bell. B in Acctg., Calif. State U., LA. Acct. Rockwell, 1972, various positions including corp. sr. internal auditor, mgr. acctg. and mgr. gen. and cost acctg., 1972—86, dir. acctg., Rocketdyne, 1986—92; dir. bus. mgmt., Space Sta. Electric Power Sys., Rocketdyne unit Rockwell (acquired by The Boeing Co.), Chgo., 1992—96; v.p. contracts and pricing Boeing Space and Comm. The Boeing Co., Chgo., 1996—2000, sr. v.p. fin., corp. contr., 2000—03, exec. v.p., CFO, 2004—, interim CEO, pres., 2005. Bd. dirs. New Leaders for New Schs., LA Urban League, Joffrey Ballet; past bd. dirs. Charles Drew U. Medicine and Sci. Mem.: World Bus. Chgo. (bd. dirs.). Office: The Boeing Co 100 N Riverside Plz Chicago IL 60606-2609*

BELL, JAMES A.H., lawyer; b. Knoxville, Tenn., Nov. 10, 1948; BS, East Tenn. State U., 1970; JD, U. Tenn., Knoxville, 1973. Bar: Tenn. 1974, US Dist. Ct. (ea. dist.) Tenn. 1975, US Supreme Ct. 1981, US Ct. Appeals (6th cir.) 1983. Pvt. practice, Knoxville, Tenn. Lectr. in field. Fellow: Am. Bd. Criminal Lawyers; mem.: ABA, Tenn. Trial Lawyers Assn., Assn. Trial Lawyers of Am., Nat. Assn. Criminal Defense Lawyers (chmn. By Laws Com. 1990—), Tenn. Assn. Criminal Defense Lawyers (bd. dirs. 1977, pres. 1983—84). Office: 110 W Summit Hill Dr Knoxville TN 37902 Office Phone: 865-637-2900. Office Fax: 865-971-4298. E-mail: jbell@jamesahbell.com.*

BELL, JAMES L., lawyer; b. Tuscaloosa, Ala., July 8, 1947; s. Archie and Margaret B. BA in Internat. Studies, U. S.C., 1970, JD, 1973. Bar: S.C., U.S. Dist. Ct. S.C., Fla., U.S. Tax Ct., U.S. Ct. Appeals (4th, 5th and 11th cirs.), U.S. Dist. Ct. (no., so. and mid. dists.) Fla., U.S. Supreme Ct. 1980. Sr. ptnr. The Bell Law Firm, P.A., Charleston, S.C. Gen. counsel S.C. Homeowners Assn., Chopstick Theater, Inc., BIROM, Inc.; counsel S.C. Disabled Am. Vets., Tacht Cove, Lowco Concrete Pumping, Inc.; bd. dirs. Fla. Legal Svcs., Inc. Contbr. articles to profl. jours. Mem. S.C. Bar (mem. unauthorized practice of law com. 2000—, mem. access and justice com. 2000—), Phi Delta Phi (life mem.). Office: The Bell Law Firm PA 184 E Bay St Ste 303 Charleston SC 29401-2142 Fax: 843-722-7028. E-mail: jbell@lawyer.com.

BELL, JAMES R., III, bank executive; B in Acctg. and Econs., Duke U., Durham, NC; MBA in Fin., U. Chgo. Corp. mgmt. trainee Nat. City Corp., Cleve., 1982—83, account officer nat. divsn. Corp. Banking, 1983, divsn. head multi-nat. east divsn., 1987—89, sr. v.p., mem. sr. loan com., 1989—90, divsn. head metro/Ohio-East divsn. Corp. Banking, 1990—91, head metro/Ohio group, 1991—92, group head multi-nat. group corp. banking, co-chmn. sr. loan com., 1992—94, exec. v.p. corp. banking Nat. City Bank of Ky., 1994, pres., CEO Nat. City Bank of Ky., exec. v.p., 1996—, head retail sales and distbn., 1998—2000, head Capital Markets Group, chief risk officer, chmn. Corporate Credit Policy and Enterprise Risk Coms. Bd. trustees Cleve. Mus. Natural History. Office: Nat City Corp Nat City Ctr 1900 E Ninth St Cleveland OH 44114-3484 Office Phone: 216-222-2000.*

BELL, JANET S., interior designer, developer, event producer; b. Ft. Campbell, Ky., Feb. 13, 1954; d. Mack Carson Smith and Walburga Maria Franz; Studied, with Joffrey Ballet; studied mime, with Marcel Marceau. Mem. dir. for Jacques Cousteau, NYC; owner Janet Bell, Event Design, Virginia Beach, Va., Mike Bell Inc. Event Prodn. Co., Virginia Beach, Va., 5 cos. dedicated to design and art prodn., Janet Bell Inc. Featured in: Grace Ormonde Wedding Style mag., 2005. Founder Va. Cat Found., Virginia Beach. Recipient Nat. Winner, AIA, 1986, Nat. Home of Yr. and Architects favorite, 1986.

BELL, JERRY ALAN, science education association administrator; b. Davenport, Iowa, June 28, 1936; s. Walter Samuel and Lilah Mae (Mergy) B.; m. Dorothy Alice Rodgers, June 10, 1961 (div. Dec. 1981); children: Allan Tracy (dec.), John Leonard; m. Mary Ann Stepp, Mar. 21, 1984; children: Christina Marie, Allison Rachel. AB, Harvard U., 1958, PhD, 1962. Asst. prof. U. Calif., Riverside, 1962-67; assoc. prof., prof. Simmons Coll., Boston, 1967-92; dir. sci. edn. program AAAS, Washington, 1992—99; sr. scientist Edn. divsn. Am. Chem. Soc., Washington, 1999—. Mem. adv. bd. Merck Inst. for Sci. Edn., Newark, 1993-99. Author: Chemical Explorations, 1993; editor, author: Chemical Principles in Practice, 1967, Chemistry, 2004. Recipient Catalyst award Mfg. Chemists Assn., 1977, John Timm award New Eng. Assn. Chemistry Tchrs., 1986. Fellow AAAS, Am. Chem. Soc. (sec. div. chem. edn. 1977-82, chmn. 1988, vis. scientist western Conn. sect. 1979, Norris award northeastern sect. 1992, George C. Pimentel award in Chem. Edn., 2000). Avocations: carpentry, gardening. Office: Am Chem Soc 1155 16th St NW Washington DC 20036 Business E-Mail: j_bell@acs.org.

BELL, JOHN ALTON, lawyer, judge; b. Greer, SC, Dec. 1, 1958; s. Dallas Frank Sr. and Una Merle (Gay) B.; m. Vida Ivy, June 30, 1984; children: Luke, Meredith. BA, Carson-Newman Coll., 1980; JD, Memphis State U., 1982. Bar: Tenn. 1983, U.S. Dist. Ct. (we. dist.) Tenn. 1983, U.S. Army Ct. Mil. Rev. 1984, U.S. Ct. Mil. Appeals 1987, U.S. Dist. (ea. dist.) Tenn. 1988. Assoc. Litigation Support, Inc., Memphis, 1983; officer ops. and tng. U.S. Army, Ft. Knox, Ky., 1983-84, legal assistance atty., 1984-86, defense counsel, 1986-87, chief Criminal Law Divsn. Fort Campbell, Ky., 2003—04; assoc. King & King, Greeneville, Tenn., 1987-89; ptnr. King, King & Bell, Greeneville and Newport, Tenn., 1989-90, Bell & Bell P.C., Newport, 1990-98; judge Cocke County Sessions and Juvenile Ct., Newport, 1998—; spl. asst. U.S. prosecutor U.S. Dist. Ct. (mid. dist.) Tenn., 2003—04, U.S. Dist. Ct. (we. dist.) Ky., 2003—04; chief No. Iraq Office Jud. Ops., Mosul, 2003. Instr. bus. law Sullivan Jr. Coll., Ft. Knox, 1986-87; adj. prof. bus. law Walter State C.C., 1989-90, 97—. Columnist It's The Law, Newport Plain Talk, 1984-85, 89-98. Bd. dirs. Extended Sch. Program, Greeneville, 1988; co-vice chmn. Rep. Com. Cocke County, Tenn., 1989-95. Lt. comdr. USAR, 1986—. Named Ky. Col., Gov. Ky., 1986. Mem. ABA, Fed. Bar Assn., Tenn. Bar Assn., Assn. Trial Lawyers Am., Judge Advocate Gen.'s Assn. Republican. Baptist. Avocations: sports, church activities. Office: Cocke County Sessions Ct 111 Court Ave Newport TN 37821-3102 Office Phone: 423-623-8619.

BELL, JOHN IRVING, medical researcher, educator; b. July 1, 1952; Student, Ridley Coll., Can., 1966-71; B Med. Sci. with honors, U. Alta., Can., 1975; BA in Physiol. Scis. with honors, Oxford U., Eng., 1976, BM BCh, 1979, DM, 1990. House officer John Radcliffe Hosp., Oxford, 1979-80; sr. house officer dept. clin. cardiology Hammersmith Hosp., London, 1980-81; sr. house officer renal unit Guy's Hosp., London, 1981; sr. house officer in neurology Nat. Hosp. Neurol. Diseases, London, 1982; rsch. fellow Nuffield dept. clin. medicine Oxford U., 1982, univ. lectr. Nuffield dept. clin. medicine, 1989, Nuffield prof. clin. medicine, 1992—, Regius Chair of Medicine, 2002—; clin. fellow medicine, postdoctoral fellow med. microbiology Stanford (Calif.) U., 1982-87; Wellcome sr. clin. fellow, hon. cons. physician John Radcliffe Hosp., Oxford, 1987. Mem. Oxford U. Coun. 2001-; bd. dirs. Isis Innovation; Norbert Freinkel lectr. Am. Diabetes Assn., 1991; dep. chmn. Powderject Pharms., 1998—, Oxagen, 1998—. Editor: Genetics and Human Nutrition, 1990, T Cell Receptor Genes, 1998; mem. editl. bd. Trends in Genetics, Immumogenetics Monitor, 1991, Human Molecular Genetics, 1992, Quar. Jour. Medicine, 1992, Immunological Revs., 1998—; mem. various grant rev. coms.; contbr. numerous articles to profl. publs.; patentee in field. Founder Wellcome Trust Ctr. for Human Genetics. Rhodes scholar, 1975-78; John Radcliffe Rsch. fellow, 1982, Alta. Heritage Trust Fund for Med. Rsch. fellow, 1983-87, fellow Magdalen Coll., 1990, 92; grantee Wellcome Trust, Arthritis and Rheumatism Coun., EEC. Fellow Royal Coll. Physicians, Acad. Med. Sci. (founder); mem. Assn. Physicians Gt. Britain and Ireland, Human Genome Orgn., Brit. Soc. Rheumatology, Internat. T Cell Receptor Nomenclature Com., Oxford Exptl. Medicine Club, Inst. Medicine (fgn. assoc.). Office: John Radcliffe Hosp Nuffield Dept Clin Medicine Headington Oxford England

BELL, JOHN MALCOLM, art educator; s. John and Katherine Bell; 1 child, Meghan. BA, Ind. U. Pa., 1990; MFA, James Madison U., Harrisonburg, Va., 1990. Asst. prof. art Blue Ridge C.C., Weyers Cave, Va., 1990—. Artist in residence Cill Rialaig Project, County Kerry, Ireland, 2005. Pres. Ctrl. Shenandoah Arts, Harrisonburg, Va., 2004—06. Named Outstanding Tchr. of Yr., Blue Ridge C.C., 2006. Avocations: travel, motorcycling. Office: Blue Ridge Cmty Coll Box 80 Weyers Cave VA 24486 Home Phone: 540-879-3624; Office Phone: 540-453-2225.

BELL, JOHN PERRY, minister, religious organization administrator; b. Columbia, La., Feb. 8, 1948; s. John Dixon and Laverne (Beck) B.; m. Gwendolyn Jean McKay, Dec. 18, 1971; children: Felicia, Peter, Rachel. BA, N.E. La. U., 1970, MA, 1971; ThM, So. Meth. U., 1973; DMin, Garrett Evang. Sem., 1989. Ordained to ministry United Meth. Ch., 1974. Min. youth United Meth. Ch., Athens, Tex., 1972, pastor Argyle, Wis., 1973-76, Sheboygan Falls, Wis., 1976-84, Waupaca, Wis., 1984-91; assoc. conf. min. United Ch. of Christ, 1991-97; exec. dir. United Meth. Found., 1998-2000. Bd. dirs. Bell Press, Waupaca, 1990—; sec. Coun. on Fin. Adminstrn., Sun Prairie, Wis., 1984-92; del. World Meth. Conf., Honolulu, 1981, Nairobi, 1986, New World Mission, Bangalore, India, 1989, UNCED, Rio de Janeiro, 1992, UN Conf. on Population, Cairo, Egypt, 1994. Pres. Am. Cancer Soc., Waupaca, 1988-90, Mental Health Assn., Waupaca, 1988-91. Recipient Superior award Am. Cancer Soc., 1989-90. Mem. World Future Soc., Kiwanis (local pres. 1983). Democrat. Home: 2212 Stockton Dr Springfield IL 62703-5268 Office Phone: 815-865-5314. E-mail: gnanny50@aol.com. *Life is both internal and external. We have to place equal emphasis on both. Our internal life needs as much care as any other part of life. How we think and feel will determine what we do and say. Faith, then, is the foundation for life.*

BELL, JOHN WILLIAM, lawyer; b. Chgo., May 3, 1946; s. John and Barbara Bell; m. Deborah Bell, Aug. 25, 1974; children: Jason, Alicia. Student, U. So. Calif., 1964-65; BA, Northwestern U., 1968; JD cum laude, Loyola U., Chgo., 1971. Bar: Ill. 1971. Assoc. Kirkland & Ellis, Chgo., 1972-75; ptnr. Johnson & Bell, Ltd. (formerly Johnson, Cusack & Bell, Ltd.), Chgo., 1975—. Mem. ABA (vice chmn. products, gen. liability and consumer law com. sect. tort and ins. practice 1986-87, 88—, com. on torts and ins. practice sect.), Ill. Bar Assn., Chgo. Bar Assn. (tort liability sect., aviation com. 1982—, chmn. med.-legal rels. com. 1994-95), Internat. Assn. Ins. Def. Counsel, Ill. Def. Coun. (faculty mem. trial acad. 1994), Soc. Trial Lawyers Am., Ill. Trial Lawyers Assn., Am. Coll. Trial Lawyers, Fed. Trial Bar.

BELL, JONATHAN ROBERT, lawyer; b. Bklyn., Oct. 2, 1947; s. Saul A. and Hope R. (Rosenblat) B.; children: Gabriel J., Nicholas R.; m. Catherine Janow, May 5, 1989. BA, Yale U., 1969; JD, Harvard U., 1973. Bar: Mass.

1974, US Tax Ct. 1977, NY 1978, US Dist. Ct. (so. dist.) NY 1980. Assoc. Nutter, McClennen & Fish, Boston, 1973-77, Debevoise & Plimpton, NYC, 1977-83, ptnr., 1984-93, Paul, Weiss, Rifkind, Wharton & Garrison, NYC, 1993—2001, Duane Morris, NYC, 2002—07, Stern, Tannenbaum & Bell, NYC, 2007—. Bd. dirs. United Way, NYC, 1984-95, NYC Ballet, 1995-2003, 04—; bd. dirs. Studio in A Sch., 1988—, vice chair, 2003—. Fellow Am. Coll. Trust and Estate Counsel; mem. NY State Bar Assn. (trusts and estates law sect.), Assn. Bar City NY (chair trusts, estates and surrogate cts. com. 1995-98). Home: 99 Jane St New York NY 10014-7221 Office: Stern Tannenbaum & Bell LLP 380 Lexington Ave New York NY 10168 Home Phone: 212-691-2753; Office Phone: 212-792-8488. Business E-Mail: jrbell@sterntannenbaum.com.

BELL, JOSEPH CHARLES, lawyer; m. Ruth Greenspan, June 9, 1968; children: Samuel Robert, Johanna Rebecca. BA summa cum laude, U. Colo., 1962; AM in econs., Harvard U., 1965; JD, Yale U., 1968. Bar: D.C. 1977, Mass. 1968. Legal asst. Cabinet Task Force on Oil Import Control, Washington, 1969-70; atty. advisor Antitrust divsn., Dept. of Justice, Washington, 1970-72; asst. prof. Duke U., Durham, N.C., 1972-74; asst. gen. counsel Fed. Energy Adminstrn., Washington, 1974-77; assoc. Hogan & Hartson, Washington, 1977-79, ptnr., 1979—, energy practice group dir. Gen. counsel Citizens Energy Corp., 1979-88; advisor on privatization State Ministry of Property and Entrepreneurship, Ukraine Republic, 1991; adv. bd. Program on Econ. Reform in Ukraine, Harvard U., 1990-92; spl. counsel Ministry of Fin., Republic of Poland, 1989-91; resident ptnr. Warsaw, Poland, Hogan and Hartson, 1991-93; economist Office of Tax Analysis, Treasury Dept., summer 1965, Office of Internat. Tax Affairs, summer 1966. Contbr. articles to profl. jours. Mem. Wilson Coun., World Affairs Coun. of Washington. Mem. ABA (internat., adminstrv. and bus. sects.), Am. Econ. Assn., Fed. Energy Bar Assn., Phi Beta Kappa, Harvard Club. Office: Hogan and Hartson Columbia Sq 555 13th St NW Ste 800E Washington DC 20004-1161 Office Phone: 202-637-5780. Office Fax: 202-637-5910. Business E-Mail: jcbell@hhlaw.com.

BELL, JOSHUA, musician; b. Bloomington, Ind., Dec. 9, 1967; violin teacher Josef Gingold, supplemented by additional studies & master classes with Ivan Galamian and Henryk Szeryng. Sr. lectr. Jacobs Sch. Music, Ind. U., Bloomington, 2007—. Vis. prof. Royal Acad. Music. Youngest guest soloist Phila. Orch. Subscription concert, 1982; participant European tour St. Louis Symphony, 1985, German tour Indpls. Symphony, 1987; guest soloist with numerous orchs., USA, Can., Europe; recitalist USA, Europe, Far East; recs. include Mendelssohn and Bruch concertos with Acad. St. Martin-in-the-Fields, Sir Neville Marriner, Tchaikovsky and Wieniawski concertos with Cleve. Orch. and Vladimir Ashkenazy, (recital album) Brahms, Paganini, Sarasate, Wieniawski with Samuel Sanders, Lalo Symphonie Espagnole and Saint-Saens Concerto with Montreal Symphony Orch. and Charles Dutoit, Franck, Fauré and Débussy, Chausson Concerto for violin, piano, string quartet with Thibaudet and Isserlis, Poème with Royal Philharmonic Orch. and Andrew Litton, Mozart Concertos 3 and 5 with English Chamber Orch. and Peter Maag, Prokofiev violin concertos with Montreal Symphony Orch. and Charles Dutoit, Barber and Walton concertos, Bloch Baal Shem, with Balt. Symphony and David Zinman; Sibelius and Goldmark concerti with LA Philharm and Esa-Pekka Salonen; Gershwin Fantasy with London Symphony Orch., others; albums include The Essential Joshua Bell, 2007, Red Violin Concerto, 2007. Named 50 Most Beautiful People, People Mag.; recipient grand prize winner, First annual Seventeen Mag./General Motors Nat. Concerto Competition, Rochester, NY, Avery Fisher prize for Lifetime Achievement, 2007. Avocations: chess, computers, golf, tennis, baseball. Address: care IMG Artists Lovell House 616 Chiswick High Rd Chiswick London W4 5RX England*

BELL, JULIE MARIE, health facility administrator, consultant; b. Mt. Clemens, Mich., Aug. 21, 1974; d. John and Helen Mary Bell. BA in Psychology and Bus., Siena Hts. U., Adrian, Mich., 1997; MS in Psychology, U. Detroit Mercy, 2000; PhD in Psychology. Cert. Baldridge examiner, green belt Six Sigma, master change agt. Constrn. asst. Triangle Elec., Madison Hts., Mich., 1996—98; human resource cons. Aero Svcs., Internat., Troy, Mich., 1998—2000; sr. orgnl. cons. St. John Health, Warren, Mich., 2000—; sr. mgr. orgnl. devel. DaimlerChrysler, internal cons. Auburn Hills, Mich. Cons. in field; mem. adv. bd. U. Detroit-Mercy, 2001—. Girl's athletic coach St. Anne Cath. Sch., Warren, 2004—; care ptnr. Providence Hosp., Southfield, Mich., 2004—; Shoes for Children vol. Little Rock Bapt. Ch., 2003—. Scholar McCracken scholar, McCracken Basketball Camps, Ind., 1999. Democrat. Roman Catholic. Avocations: reading, travel, home decorating, pets. Office: Saint John Health 28000 Dequindre Rd Warren MI Business E-Mail: jmb179@dcx.com.

BELL, KAREN A., dean; BA in Sociol., SUNY, Potsdam; MFA in Dance, Sarah Lawrence Coll. Prof. SUNY Potsdam, Elmira Coll., Wells Coll.; visiting asst. prof. Cornell U.; prof. Ohio State U., 1980—; chairperson Dept. Dance, Ohio State U., 1995—; assoc. dean Coll. Arts. Ohio State U., 1995—2001, interim dean, 2001—02, dean, 2002—. Individual Artist Fellowship, Ohio Arts Coun., Academic Leadership Fellow, Com. Instl. Cooperation, 1991—92. Mem.: Nat. Assn. Sch. Dance (commn. accreditation, evaluator), Am. Coll. Dance Festival Assn. (bd. dirs., northeast regional rep.). Office: Office of Dean OSU Coll Arts 152 Hopkins Hall 128 North Oval Mall Columbus OH 43210 Office Phone: 614-292-5171. Office Fax: 614-292-5218. E-mail: bell.1@osu.edu.

BELL, KENNETH B., state supreme court justice; married; 4 children. BA in History, Davidson Coll., NC, 1978; JD cum laude, Fla. State U., 1982. Pvt. practice, real estate atty., Pensacola, 1982—91; trial judge 1st Jud. Cir. Fla., 1991—2002; justice Fla. Supreme Ct., Tallahassee, 2002—. Mem. cir. com. on professionalism Supreme Ct., 2000—. Founding pres. of bd. dirs. Friends of Children's Hosp. at Sacred Heart, Inc.; bd. dirs. Escambia County 4-H Found., Waterfront Rescue Mission; c-founder Yan-Bian Chinese-Korean Tech. U., China. Mem.: Am. Judicature Soc., AMA (mem. real property, probate and trust law sections), Fla. Bar Assn. (mem. real property, probate and trust law sections), Escambia-Santa Rosa Bar Assn. Office: Supreme Ct Fla 500 Duval St Tallahassee FL 32399*

BELL, KENNETH DAVIS, lawyer; b. Bedford, Ohio, July 22, 1958; s. Richard Gordon and Evalyn (Crawford) B.; m. Gayle Adams, June 21, 1986; children: Kenneth Davis Jr., Gavin Adams. BA in Philosophy and Politics, Wake Forest U., 1980, JD, 1983. Bar: NC 1983, US Dist. Ct. (ea. dist.) NC, US Dist. Ct. (mid. dist.) NC, US Dist. Ct. (we. dist.) NC, US Ct. Appeals (4th cir.). Assoc. Womble, Caryle, Sundridge and Rice, Winston-Salem, NC, 1988-90; asst. US atty. for western dist. NC US Atty.'s Office, Asheville, NC, 1983-88, Charlotte, NC, 1990-93, 1st asst. US atty., 1993—2003; ptnr. Mayer, Brown, Rowe & Maw, LLP, 2003—06, Hunton & Williams, LLP, 2006—. Rep. nominee for NC 5th congl. dist. US Ho. of Reps., 1990. Named one of Best Lawyers in Am., 2007, NC Super Lawyers, 2007; recipient US Atty. Gen. John Marshall award for Trial Litig. Mem.: NC State Bar Assn. Roman Catholic. Office: Hunton & Williams LLP Bank of America Plz Ste 3500 101 S Tryon St Charlotte NC 28280 Office Phone: 704-378-4834. Office Fax: 704-331-4237.*

BELL, KURT ROBERT, archivist; b. Doylestown, Pa., Oct. 15, 1972; s. Gordon Lewis and Helen Jane (Muhly) Bell. BA, Millersville U. Pa., 1995; MA, U. Del., 2004. Cert. museum studies. Editl. asst. Locomotive and Railway Preservation Mag., Richmond, Vt., 1990; program coord. Friends of Railroad Museum Pa., Strasburg, 1995—98; libr., archivist Railroad Museum Pa., Strasburg, 1997—2002; archivist Pa. Hist. and Mus. Commn., Strasburg, 2002—. Cons. archivist, historian Strasburg (Pa.) Rail Road Co., 2004—05. Author: Steel Rails to Stewartstown, 1999. Book reviews various profl. jours. Mem.: Soc. Indsl. Archaeology, Mid-Atlantic Regional Archivist Conf., Railway and Locomotive Hist. Soc. (Railroad Hist. awards 2003). Republican. Presbyn. Avocations: antiques, exercise, mountain biking, indsl. archaeology. Home: 1849 Hans Herr Dr Willow Street PA 17584 Office: Pa Hist and Mus Comm Railroad Mus Pa 300 Gap Rd PO Box 15 Strasburg PA 17579

BELL, LARRY STUART, artist; b. Chgo., Dec. 6, 1939; s. Hyman David and Rebecca Ann (Kriegmont) B.; three children. Student, Chouinard Art Inst., LA, 1957-59. One man exhbns. include Stedelijk Mus., Amsterdam, 1967, Pasadena (Calif.) Art Mus., 1972, Oakland (Calif.) Mus., 1973, Ft. Worth Art Mus., 1975, Santa Barbara (Calif.) Mus. Art, 1976, Washington U., St. Louis, 1976, Art Mus. So. Tex., Corpus Christi, 1976, Erica Williams, Anne Johnson Gallery, Seattle, 1978, Hayden Gallery, MIT, Cambridge, Mass., 1977, Hudson River Mus., Yonkers, N.Y., 1981, Newport Harbor Art Mus., 1982, Marian Goodman Gallery, N.Y.C., 1982, Ruth S. Schaffner Gallery, Santa Barbara, Calif., Arco Ctr. Visual Arts, L.A., 1983, Unicorn Gallery, Aspen, Colo., 1983, Butler Inst. Am. Art, Youngstown, Ohio, 1984, Leigh Yawkey Woodson Art Mus., Wausau, Wis., 1984, Colorado Springs, Colo. Fine Arts Ctr., 1987, Cleve. Ctr. for Contemporary Art, Ohio, 1987, Mus. Contemporary Art, L.A., 1987, Am. Acad. and Inst. Arts and Letters, N.Y.C., 1987, Boise (Idaho) Gallery Art, 1987, Gilbert Brownstone Gallery, Paris, 1987, Braunstein/Quay Gallery, San Francisco, 1987, 89, Fine Arts Gallery, N.Mex. State Fairgrounds, 1987, Laguna Art Mus., Laguna Beach, Calif., 1987, High Mus. Art, Atlanta, 1988, Sena Galleries West, Santa Fe, 1989, Kiyo Higashi Gallery, L.A., 1989, 90, 94, 02, Musee D'Art Contemporain, Lyon, France, 1989, Contemporary Art Ctr., Kansas City, Mo., 1989, San Antonio Art Inst., 1990, New Gallery, Houston, 1990, Braunstein/Quay Gallery, San Francisco, 1990, Galerie Rolf Ricke, Koln, Fed. Republic Germany, 1990, Galerie Montenay, Paris, 1990, 95, The Works Gallery, L.A., 1990, Galerie Kammer, Hamburg, Germany, 1990, Tony Shafrazi Gallery, N.Y.C., 1991, Tucson Mus. Art, 1991, New Gallery, Houston, 1991, Janus Gallery, Santa Fe, 1992, Kiyo Higashi Gallery, L.A., 1992, 93, New Gallery, Houston, 1992, Tampa Mus. Art, 1992, Kiyo Higashi Gallery, L.A., 1993, 94, New Directions Gallery, Taos, N.M., 1993, Dartmouth St. Gallery, Albuquerque, 1994, Braunstein/Quay Gallery, San Francisco, 1994, Leedy/Voulkos Gallery, Kansas City, 1994, Kiyo Higashi Gallery, L.A., 1994, U. Wyo. Art Mus., Laramie, 1995, Denver Art Mus., 1995, Indigo Gallery, Boca Raton, Fla., 1995, Harwood Mus. U. N. Mex., Taos, 1995, Galerie Montenay, Paris, 1995, Joy Tash Gallery, Scottsdale, Ariz., 1996, Kiyo Higashi Gallery, L.A., 1996, Boulder Mus. Contemporary Art, 1996, Braunstein/Quay Gallery, San Francisco, 1996, Art et Industrie Gallery, N.Y.C., 1996, The Albuquerque Mus., 1997, The Reykjavik Mcpl. Art Mus., Iceland, 1997, Bergen (Norway) Kunstmus., 1998, Seljord (Norway) Art Assn., 1998, Wood Street Galleries, Pitts., 1999, Mus. Moderner Kunst Landkreis Cuxhaven, Otterndorf, Germany, 1999, Kiyo Higashi Gallery, 1999, Center Galleries, Detroit, 2000, Larry Bell Studio Annex/New Directions Gallery, Taos, N.Mex., 2000, Mus. Moderner Kunst Landkreis Cuxhaven, Otterndorf, Germany, 2000, New Gallery, Houston, 2001, Gallery Gan, Tokyo, 2001, Skovridder AS , Oslo, Norway, 2001, Roswell Mus. and Art Ctr., 2002, New Gallery, Houston, 2002, Off Main Gallery, Santa Monica, Calif., 2003, St. John's Coll., Santa Fe, 2003, Harwood Art Mus. U. N.Mex., Taos, N.Mex., 2004, Bernard Jacobson Gallery, London, U. Tenn., Chattanooga, 2005, Jacobson Howard Gallery, N.Y.C., 2005, Pace Wildenstein Gallery, N.Y.C., 2005, McClain Gallery, Houston, Alan Koppel Gallery, Chgo.; 2005, Frank Lloyd Gallery, Santa Monica, Calif., 2006, Daniel Templon Gallery, Paris, 2006, Annandale Galleries, Sydney, 2006, Bernard Jacobson Gallery, London, 2007, Danese Gallery, NY, 2007, Maines Gallery, San Francisco, 2007; numerous group exhbns. including most recently Calif., 2000, Peggy Guggenheim Collection, Venice, Italy, 2000, Guggenheim Mus. Bilbao, Spain, 2000, La. Mus. Art, Humlebaek, Denmark, 2000, L.A. County Mus. Art, 2000, Solomon R. Guggenheim Mus., N.Y., 2001, Bernard Jacobson Gallery, London, 2001, Museu Serralves, Porto, Portugal, 2002, The Contemporary Mus., Honolulu, 2002, Yale U. Art Gallery, New Haven, Conn., 2002, Denver Art Mus., 2002, Gagosian Gallery, N.Y.C., 2002, Franklin Parrasch Gallery, N.Y.C., 2003, Gagosian Gallery, N.Y.C., 2002,Stephen Stux Gallery, N.Y.C., 2002, Harwood Mus. U. N.Mex., Taos, 2004, Bernard Jacobson Gallery, London, 2005, Sintra Mus. Modern Art, Portugal, 2003, Contemp.Art Ctr., New Orleans, 2003, Guggenheim Mus. Art, N.Y., 2003, MOCA, L.A., 2004, U. Pa., Phila., 2004, L.A. County Mus. Art, L.A., 2004, Miami Art Mus., , 2004, Mus. Contemporary Art, San Diego, 2004, Marian Goodman Gallery, N.Y., 2004, Jacobson-Howard Gallery, N.Y., 2004, Frederick R. Weisman Art Mus., U. Minn., 2005, McNay Art Mus., San Antonio, 2005, Centro Cultural Belem, Lisboa, Portugal, 2005, Patricia Faure Gallery, Santa Monica, Calif., 2005, Chevron Gallery, Irvine, Calif., 2005, Las Vegas Art Mus., Nev., 2006, Ctr. George Pompidou, Paris, 2006, LACMA, L.A., 2006, Norton Simon Mus., L.A., 2006, Whitney Mus. Am. Art, NYC, 2006, 223 Art, Belgium, 2006, L&M Arts, NYC, 2006, Harwood Mus. ARt, Taos, N.Mex., 2007, Orange County Mus. Art, Newport Beach, Calif., 2007, Smithonisan Inst., Washington, 2007, others; represented in permanent collections including Nat. Collection Fine Arts, Musee de Art Contemporaine, Lyon, France, Mus. of Fine Arts, Santa Fe, N.Mex., Whitney Mus. Am. Art, N.Y.C., Laguna Gloria Mus., Austen, H & W Bechtler Gallery, Charlotte, Calif. Crafts Mus., San Francisco, Parrish Art Mus., Southampton, Tate Gallery, London, Gallery New South Wales, Australia, Albright-Knox Gallery, Buffalo, Art Inst. Chgo., Denver Art Mus., Dallas Mus. Fine Arts, Guggenheim Mus., Houston, L.A. County Mus., Victoria and Albert Mus., London, San Antonio Mus. Art, The Menil Collection, Houston, Mpls. Inst. Arts, Mus. Ludwig, Koln, Albuquerque Mus., Mpls. Inst. Arts, others; instr. sculpture, U. South Fla., Tampa, U. Calif., Berkeley, Irvine, So. Calif. Inst. of Architecture, Taos (N.Mex.) Inst. of Art, City of Albuquerque, Art in Pub. Places, 1999, Myers Devel. Co., 1999, Billingsley Co., Carrolton, Tex., Mus. Abteiberg, Monchengladbach, Germany, Centex Homes, South Coast Divsn., Brea, Calif., MOCA, LA, Calif., Great Eagle Devel. and Mgmt. Ltd., Hong Kong. Copley Found. grantee, 1962; Guggenheim Found. fellow, 1970; Nat. Endowment Arts grantee, 1975; recipient Gov.'s award for excellence in visual arts, N.Mex., 1990. Office Phone: 505-758-3062. Business E-Mail: bell@newmex.com.

BELL, LAWRENCE T., lawyer; b. 1948; BBA, St. Bonaventure U., 1970; JD, William Mitchell Coll. Law, St. Paul, Minn., 1979. Bar: Minn. 1979. Joined Ecolab Inc., St. Paul, 1979, internat. v.p. - adminstrn., 1986—91, named gen. counsel, 1998, now sr. v.p., gen. counsel, sec. Mem. bd. Twin Cities Pub. TV, St. Paul Chamber Orch.; bd. dirs. VocalEssence, 2002—; bd. trustees William Mitchell Coll. Law, 2004—. Office: Ecolab Inc 370 Wabasha St N Saint Paul MN 55102*

BELL, LEE PHILLIP, television personality, producer; b. Chgo. d. James A. and Helen (Novak) P.; m. William Joseph Bell, Oct. 23, 1954; children: William J., Bradley, Lauralee. BS in Microbiology, Northwestern U., Evanston, Ill., 1950. With CBS-TV, Chgo., 1952-86; pres. Bell-Phillip TV Prodns., 1985—. Bd. dirs. William Wrigley, Jr. Co., Chgo. Bank Commerce, Phillips Flowers Inc. TV and radio shows include Lee Phillip Show, Chgo., from 1952, Lady and Tiger Show WBBM Radio, from 1962, WBBM TV from 1964; hostess Noon Break, numerous TV Spls. including Forgotten Children, The Rape of Paulette (nat. Emmy award, duPont Columbia award); Children and Divorce (Chgo. Emmmy award) co-creator: (with William Bell) The Young and the Restless CBS-TV daytime drama, 1973 (Emmy award); co-creator, exec. producer The Bold and the Beautiful, 1987—. Bd. dirs. United Cerebral Palsy, Chgo. Unlimited, Northwestern U. Hosp., Chgo. Heart Assn., Nat. Com. Prevention of Child Abuse, Mental Health Assn., Children's Home and Aid Soc., Salvation Army, Chgo., Family Focus; mem. Chgo. Maternity Ctr.; life mem. Northwestern U. Bd. Trustees. Recipient 16 Chgo. Emmys, Emmy, Achievement award, Nat. Acad. TV and Arts and Sci., 2007; Top Favorite Female award TV Guide mag., 1956, Outstanding Woman of Radio and TV award McCall's mag., 1957-58, 65, bd. govs. award Chgo. chpt. Nat. Acad. TV Arts and Scis., 1977, William Booth award for community svc. Salvation Army, 1990; named Person of Yr. Broadcast Advt. Club, Chgo., 1980. Mem. Am. Women Radio and TV (Golden Mike award 1968, Broadcaster of Yr. 1993), Acad. TV Arts and Scis. (bd. dirs.), Chgo. chpt. Acad. TV Arts and Scis., Women's Athletic Club of Chgo., Comml. Club, Delta Delta Delta. Home: 9955 Beverly Dr Beverly Hills CA 90210 Office: CBS c/o Bold and Beautiful 7800 Beverly Blvd Los Angeles CA 90036-2188 Home Phone: 310-467-1932; Office Phone: 323-575-2812. Business E-Mail: markpinciotti@boldandbeautiful.tv.

BELL, LEWIS CLAY, economics professor, government administrator; b. New Dorp, NY, Mar. 29, 1928; s. Samuel Virgil and Ruth Bell; m. Dolores Eva Bell, Dec. 19, 1951; children: Brent, David, Daniel. BA in Econs., Berea Coll., 1953; postgrad., Emory U., 1953—54; PhD in Econs., U. Ky., 1957. Rsch. asst. Bur. Bus. Rsch. U. Ky., 1954—55, rsch. assoc., 1956—57; asst. dir. purchases Commonwealth of Ky., 1957, dir. purchases, 1957—60; assoc. prof. U. Miss., 1960—63, assoc. prof. econs., econs. rsch. analyst, 1963—64, prof. econs., sr. rsch. analyst, 1964, prof. econs., 1964—65; dir. Tax Rsch. Ctr., prof. econs. Western Ky. U., 1965—66, dir. Tax Rsch. Ctr., Office of Rsch. and Svcs., prof. econs., 1966—68; prof. econs. fiscal cons. to W.Va. Legis., 1968—70; dir. legis. fiscal studies W.Va. U., 1969—70, prof. econs., 1969—88, dir. grad. programs econs., 1978—83, prof. emeritus, 1988—; exec. dir. W.Va. Coun. Econ. Edn., 1985—87; prof. econs. Christian Sci. Practitioner, 1988—. Author (with D.H. McKinney): The Role of Third-Structure Taxes in the Highway-User Tax Family, 1968; contbr. articles to profl. jours., chapters to books. Active Ky. Efficiency Task Force, 1966—68; Ky. col.; treas. Support Our Schs., Morgantown, 1971; chmn. com. on publ. for W.Va. Christian Sci., 1975—91; counsel, advisor Christian Sci. Coll. Orgn. W.Va. U., chmn. bd.; 1st reader, Sunday sch. supt. Christian Sci. Ch.; advisor Sch. Bonds. Com., Morgantown, 1971. Mem.: Mountain State Econ. Assn. (pres. 1980), W.Va. Tax Inst. (pres. 1973), So. Econs. Assn., Tax Inst. Am., Nat. Tax Assn., Am. Econ. Assn., Rotary (pres. 1983—84), Beta Gamma Sigma, Phi Kappa Phi. Democrat. Christian Scientist. Home and Office: 1287 Colonial Dr Morgantown WV 26505-2437 Office Phone: 304-599-1605. Personal E-mail: lou328@aol.com.

BELL, LINDA R., writer, photographer; b. Columbia, Tenn., Nov. 13, 1949; d. William Fleming Jr. and Dorothy Virginia (Cecil) Rainey; m. Dennis L. Bell, Sept. 11, 1971 (div. Dec. 1980); m. Talmadge Martin Warren, Dec. 17, 1983. BSChemE cum laude, U. Tenn., 1971, MS in Engring. magna cum laude, 1972. Process engr. E.I. du Pont de Nemours, Inc., Chattanooga, 1972—75; design engr. Olin Corp., Charleston, Tenn., 1975-78; environ. engr. TVA, Knoxville, 1978—85; instr. writing U. Tenn., Knoxville, Tenn., 1985—88. Freelance writer and photographer, Knoxville, 1982—; speaker Presdl. Mgmt. Interns, Knoxville, 1980; featured guest poet Espirit & Espirit Seminars, Nashville, 1982. One-woman shows include Thompson Photo Products, Knoxville, 1986, 1990, 1991, Farragut Arts Coun., Tenn., 2003, 2004, Meadow View Garden Ctr., Lenoir City, Tenn., 2006, 2007, numerous group shows; author: Environmental Development Plan Ammonia from Coal Project, 1979, vol. of poems Love Puzzles, 1982, January Summers, 1982, Heartprints, 1989, (non-fiction) The Red Butterfly, 1983, What I Remember, 2004; contbr. numerous articles and poems to lit. jours., anthologies and nat. mags., numerous photographs to regional and nat. mags. and calendars. Vol. Girl Scouts US, 1966—69, 2003—, Ijams Nature Ctr., Knoxville, 2003—; swim instr. ARC, 1970—71. Finalist Nat. Wildlife photography competition, 2004, 2006; nominee Pushcart prize, 1985; named one of Outstanding Young Women of Am., 1985; recipient 1st pl. award, Knoxville Zoo Photo Contest, 1983, Winner of the Week Cat Calendar award, Workman Pub. Co., 1989, Stray of the Month Cat Calendar award, 1991, 1993, 1994, 1999, Bad Cat Calendar award, 2007, Best of Photography Annual, 1992, Ann. Writing Competition Poetry award, Writer's Digest, 1992, 1993, Poetry award, Now & Then Appalachian Poetry Competition, 2002. Mem.: NAFE, Knoxville Writers' Guild, Tenn. Writers Alliance, Humane Soc. Tennessee Valley, Nat. Wildlife Fedn. (life; Backyard Habitat award 1986), Lupus Found. Am. (bd. dirs. East Tenn. chpt. 1985—2003), Knoxville Recycling Coalition, Tau Beta Pi (life). Presbyterian. Avocations: swimming, gardening, reading, travel. Office: 10211 Julie Ln Knoxville TN 37932-1620 Office Phone: 865-705-4624.

BELL, LORI (LORELEI JUNOT), library director, library and information scientist; MLIS, U. Ill., Urbana, 1982. Med. libr. OSF St. Francis Med. Ctr., Peoria, Ill.; dir. Mid-Ill. Talking Book Ctr.; dir. innovation Alliance Libr. Sys., East Peoria, Ill.; founder & chief libr. Alliance Second Life Libr. 2.0, 2006—. Co-recipient Leader in Tech. award, ALA, 2004, Libr. of the Future award for Alliance Second Life Libr., 2007, Network Libr. of Yr. award, Libr. of Congress Nat. Libr. Svc. for the Blind & Physically Handicapped, 2005, 2006; recipient Alexander Skryzpek award, Ill. Libr. Assn., 1994, TBS Tech. Svcs. award, 2003, Ill. Cybrarian of Yr. award, MCI, 1998, Mover & Shaker award, Libr. Jour., 2004. Office: Alliance Libr Sys 600 High Point Lane East Peoria IL 61611 Office Phone: 309-694-9200 ext. 2128. Office Fax: 309-694-9230. E-mail: lbell@alliancelibrarysystem.com.

BELL, M. JOY MILLER, financial planner, real estate agent; b. Enid, Okla., Dec. 29, 1934; d. H. Lee and M.E. Madge (Hatfield) Miller; m. Richard L.D. Berlemann, July 21, 1957 (div. Nov. 1974); children: Richard Louis, Randolph Lee; m. Donald R. Bell, Aug. 17, 1996; children: Jeri, Johnna, Nolan, Charles, Mary. BSBA, N.Mex. State U., 1956. CFP; grad. Realtors Inst.; fellow Life Underwriting Tng. Coun. Tchr. bus. and math. Alamogordo (N.Mex.), Las Cruces (N. Mex.) and Omaha Pub. Schs., 1956-63; tchr., dir. Evelyn Wood Reading Dynamics So. N.Mex. Inst., 1967-68; registered rep. Westamerica Fin. Corp., Denver, 1968-76; gen. agt. Security Benefit Life, Topeka, 1969—2001, Delta Life & Annuity, Topeka, 1969—2001; registered rep. World Capital Brokerage, Denver, 1976—; pres., broker Fin. Design Corp. R.E. (name changed to Bell, Inc. 1997), Las Cruces, 1977—; with Allianz L.I. Co. N.Am., 2000—. Mrs. U.S. Savings Bonds ofcl. goodwill amb. U.S. Treasury, U.S. Savs. Bond Divsn., Washington, 1968-70. Contbr. articles to profl. jours. V.p. programs Dona Ana County Fedn. Rep. Women. Recipient Top Sales Person award Investment Trust and Assurance, 1976-77; named Outstanding Young Woman of N.Mex., 1970, Outstanding Young Women of Am., 1970. Mem. Nat. Assn. Realtors, Nat. Assn. Ins. and Fin. Advisors, Nat. Assn. Ret. Fed. Employees (v.p. programs local chpt.), Internat. Assn. Registered Fin. Planners, Fin. Planners Assn., S.W. N.Mex. Assn. of Ins. and Fin. Advisors (treas. 1990-91, pres.-elect 1991-92, pres. 1992-93), Las Cruces Assn. Realtors (bd. dirs.), Multiple Listing and Info.Svcs., Inc. (treas. 2002, pres.-elect 2004, pres. 2005), Las Cruces City Alumnae Panhellenic, Altrusa, Order Ea. Star, Delta Zeta. Presbyterian. Home: 4633 Lamar Rd Las Cruces NM 88005-3558 Office: Bell Inc PO Box 577 Las Cruces NM 88004-0577 Office Phone: 505-526-9166. E-mail: joybell@bellinc.com.

BELL, MARTIN ALLEN, investment company executive; b. NYC, Apr. 29, 1951; s. Bernard B. and Helene (Spiro) Bell; m. Alison D. Brown, Dec. 1, 2002; 1 child, Olivia Joan;children from previous marriage: Daniel Warren, Frances Annelies. BA, U. Mich., 1974; JD, NYU, 1977. Bar: N.Y. 1978. Ptnr. Finley, Kumble, Wagner, Heine, Underberg, Manley & Casey, NYC, 1977-85; pres. Svc. Resources Corp., NYC, 1985-90; gen. counsel D.H. Blair Investment Banking Corp., NYC, 1991—, vice chmn., 1995—. Bd. dirs. Rand Pub. Corp., News Comm., Inc. Democratic. Jewish. Home: 1035 5th Ave New York NY 10028-0135 Office: D H Blair Investment Banking Corp 44 Wall St New York NY 10005-2401 E-mail: mab10355@aol.com.

BELL, MARVIN HARTLEY, poet, language educator; b. NYC, Aug. 3, 1937; s. Saul and Belle (Spector) B.; m. Mary Mammosser, 1958 (div.); m. Dorothy Murphy; children: Nathan Saul, Jason Aaron. BA, Alfred U., 1958, LHD (hon.), 1986; MA, U. Chgo., 1961; MFA, U. Iowa, 1963. Mem. faculty, Writers' Workshop U. Iowa, Iowa City, 1965—2005, Flannery O'Connor prof. letters, 1986—2005, Iowa poet laureate, 2000—04. Vis. lectr. Goddard Coll., 1970; disting. vis. prof. U. Hawaii, 1981; vis. prof. U. Wash., 1982; faculty Pacific U., 2004—, Pacific Luth. U., 2004-05; Lila Wallace-Reader's Digest Writing fellow U. Redlands, 1991-92, 92-93; Woodrow Wilson vis. fellow St. Mary's Coll. of Calif., 1994-95, Nebr. Wesleyan U., 1996-97, Pacific U., 1996-97, Hampden-Sydney Coll., 1998-99, W.Va. Wesleyan Coll., 2000-2001, Birmingham So. U., 2000-2001, Ill. Coll., 2002-03, Bethany Coll., 2003-04, Juanita Coll., 2005—; judge Lamont Award-Acad. Am. Poets, 1989-91, Pushcart Prizes, 1991, 97, Western Book Awards-Western States Arts Fedn., 1991, Nat. Poetry Series, NEA, N.C. Arts Coun., Coordinating Coun. Lit. Mags., Discovery Contest-Poetry Ctr. of 92nd St Y, N.Y.C., Poetry Soc. Am., Hopwood Awards, Tulsa Arts Coun., Anhinga Poetry Prize-Fla. State U. Press, numerous others; disting. poet-in-residence Wichita State U., 2004, Prague Seminar, 2002, 04; disting. vis. prof. Portland State U., 2007. Author: (poems) Things We Dreamt We Died For, 1966, A Probable Volume of Dreams, 1969 (Lamont award Acad. Am. Poets 1969), The Escape into You, 1971, 94, Residue of Song, 1974, Stars Which See, Stars Which Do Not See, 1977 (Nat. Book award finalist 1977), 92, These Green-Going-To-Yellow, 1981, Drawn by Stones, by Earth, by Things That Have Been in the Fire, 1984, New and Selected Poems, 1987, Iris of Creation, 1990, The Book of the Dead Man, 1994, Ardor: The Book of the Dead Man, vol. 2, 1997, Wednesday: Selected Poems, 1998, Poetry for a Midsummer's Night, 1998, Nightworks: Poems 1962-2000, 2000, Ashes Poetica, 2002, Rampant, 2004, Shakespeare's Wages, 2004, Mars Being Red, 2007; (essays) Old Snow Just Melting: Essays and Interviews, 1983; (anthology) A Marvin Bell Reader, 1994; co-author: Segues: A Correspondence in Poetry, 1983, Annie-Over, 1988, editor, pub. Statements, 1959-64; poetry editor The Iowa Rev., 1969-71, guest poetry editor, 1980, 2005; poetry editor The Pushcart Prize, vol. XXI, 1996-97, editor-at-large vol. series, 1994-96, series editor, poetry, 1997—; columnist The Am. Poetry Rev., 1975-78, 90-92; series editor New Poets, Short Books series Lost Horse Press, 2006—; contbr. and commd. poetry to numerous mags. and anthologies. Fellow Guggenheim Found., 1977, NEA, 1978, 84; Sr. Fulbright scholar to Yugoslavia, 1983, Sr. Fulbright scholar to Australia, 1986; recipient Bess Hokin award Poetry, 1969, Emily Clark Balch prize Va. Quar. Rev., 1970, Am. Poetry Rev. prize, 1982, Lit. award Am. Acad. Arts and Letters, 1994, Shestack prize Am. Poetry Rev., 2003; Poet Laureate of Iowa, 2000-04. Home: 1416 E College St Iowa City IA 52245

BELL, MARY E. BENITEAU, accountant; b. San Antonio, Dec. 20, 1937; d. Thomas Alfred and Mary Elizabeth (McMurrain) Beniteau; m. William Woodward Bell, May 31, 1969; children: Susan Elizabeth, Carol Ann. BBA, Baylor U., 1959; MBA, U. Tex., 1960. CPA Tex. Tchg. asst. U. Tex., Austin, 1959-60; prin. Deloitte & Touche CPA, Dallas, 1960-69; county auditor Brown County, Tex., 1972-78; pvt. practice acctg. Brownwood, Tex., 1969-95; ptnr. Bell & Isbell LLP, CPA, 1996—2006; acct. Brownwood Regional Med. Ctr. Aux., 1969—. Bd. dirs., sec. Brownwood Civic Improvement Found., Inc., 1991—2001, pres., 1993—95, treas., 1995—2001; mem. bus. and audit com. Bapt. Gen. Conv., Tex., 1985—90, Tex., 1997—2002, vice chmn. Tex., 1987—88, chmn. Tex., 1988—89. Named Outstanding Woman Over 35, Brownwood Jaycees, 1986, Outstanding Com. Chmn., Dallas chpt. CPA, 1968—69; recipient W. R. White Meritorious Svc. award, Baylor U., 1996. Mem.: AICPA, Brownwood Com. CPA (pres. 1987—88), Abilene chpt. CPA (dir. 1984—85, 1987—88), Tex. Soc. CPAs (dir. 1979—82, trustee found. 1981—89, sec.-treas. 1982—84, pres. 1984—86, chair rels. with AICPA com. 1988—89, mem. peer rev. com. 1993—96, mem. CPA helping schs. com. 1994—95, dir. 1999—2002, 2004—, Kenneth W. Hurst fellow 1990), Baylor U. Alumni Assn., Brownwood C. of C. (dir. 1979—82, sec.-treas. 1981—82), Brownwood Woman's Club (pres. 1980—84), Rotary Ann of Brownwood (pres. 1983—84, 2000—01), DAR (Mary Garland chpt. 1994—, regent 1998—2000, Tex. soc. treas. 2003—06, vice chair nat. fin. com. 2004—, state chaplain 2006—, CPA of Yr. 1984—85), Pi Beta Phi. Baptist. Home: PO Box 1564 Brownwood TX 76804-1564 Office: 115 S Broadway Brownwood TX 76801

BELL, MARY MARGARET, archivist; d. James Eugene and Mary Jane Bell. BA in History, U. Louisville, 1978; MLS, U. Ky., 1980. Field archivist Ky. Dept. Librs. and Archives, Frankfort, Ky., 1981—83; curator manuscripts Ky. Hist. Soc., Frankfort, 1983—94; assoc. archivist U. Louisville, 1994—2002; coord. archives Jefferson County Pub. Schs., Louisville, 2002—. Bd. dirs. Ky. State Hist. Records Bd., Frankfort; mem. commn. Ky. Archives and Records, Frankfort, 1987—94. Author short stories; contbr. articles to profl. jours. Vol. Pub. Radio Partnership, Louisville, 1989—; vol. ofcl. Metro Pks. Track Club, Louisville, 1989—2002; marshall parade various local parades, Ky., 1990—2005; mem. coun. St. Brigid Parish, Louisville, 2002—. Mem.: Ky. Coun. Archives (chmn. 1986—87), Soc. Am. Archivists. Roman Cath. Office: Jefferson County Pub Schs Archives 3001 Crittenden Dr Louisville KY 40209

BELL, MAXINE TOOLSON, state legislator, librarian; b. Logan, Utah, Aug. 6, 1931; d. John Max and Norma (Watson) Toolson; m. H. Jack Bell, Oct. 26, 1949; children: Randy J. (dec.), Jeff M., Scott Alan (dec.). Assocs. in Libr. Sci., Coll. So. Idaho; CSI, Idaho State U., 1975. Librarian Sch. Dist. 261, Jerome, Idaho, 1975-88; mem. Idaho Ho. of Reps., 1988—. Bd. dirs. Idaho Farm Bur., 1976-77; rep. western states Am. Farm Bur. Women, 1990-93, vice chmn., 1993—; vice chmn. Am. Farm Bur., 1993-2005, chmn. appropriations com., 1999—; mem. Jerome County Rep. Precinct Com., 1980-88. Recipient Pres. medallion award, Idaho State U., 2005. Home: 194 S 300 E Jerome ID 83338-6532 Personal E-mail: mbell@magielink.com.

BELL, MICHAEL W., insurance company executive; BS summa cum laude, U. Ill., 1985. Various positions CIGNA Corp., 1984—94; v.p., CFO CIGNA Intracorp, 1994—95; v.p., actuary CIGNA HealthCare, 1995—97; v.p. corp. acctg. and planning CIGNA Corp., 1997—2000, exec. v.p., CFO Phila., 2002—; pres. CIGNA Group Ins., 2000—02. Fellow: Soc. Actuaries. Office: CIGNA Corp Two Liberty Pl 1601 Chestnut St Philadelphia PA 19192-1550 Office Phone: 215-761-1000.*

BELL, NANCY LEE HOYT, real estate investor, middle school educator, volunteer; b. LA, Oct. 25, 1929; d. James and Mabel Ruth (Lockard) Hoyt; m. Ralph Rogers Bell, July 3, 1953; children: Linda Lee, John Curtis, James Hoyt, Martha Chambers, Ralph Rogers II, Nancy Lee II. Student, Whittier Coll., 1948, San Jose State Coll., 1949; BA in Edn., U. Calif., Santa Barbara, 1950; postgrad., San Francisco State Coll., 1952, UCLA, 1953; MS in Edn., U. So. Calif., 1955. Tchr. John Adams Jr. H.S., Santa Monica, Calif., 1950-54; real estate investor. Pres. Santa Clarita Cmty. Concerts, Saugus, Calif., 1968-69; vol. worker USO, YWCA, 1944-45, Cancer Crusade, Calif. and Wash., 1960-90. Mem. AAUW (charter life; pres.), Big Bear Valley Hist. Soc. (life; sec.), DAR (charter life; treas.), Gen. Soc. Mayflower Descs. (life; bd. dirs.), Alpha Delta Pi. Republican. Methodist. Avocations: world travel, collecting antiques, genealogy researcher, music. Home: 615 Main St Apt B Edmonds WA 98020-3804

BELL, NORMAN HOWARD, retired endocrinologist, educator; b. Gainesville, Ga., Feb. 11, 1931; s. Kenneth Rush and Henrietta Maria (Howard Rankin) Bell; m. Claude Handy Bell, June 27, 1959 (dec. 1967); children: Douglas Howard, Julianne Rankin; m. Mary Virginia Baughman, Aug. 24, 1968 (div. July 1927); m. Ledlie Laird Dinsmore, Dec. 16, 1972; 1 child, Bayard Gardiner. AB, Emory U., 1951; MD, Duke U., 1955. Intern Duke U. Med. Ctr., Durham, NC, 1955-56, resident, 1956-57; clin. assoc. Nat. Inst. Allergy and Infectious Diseases, NIH, Bethesda, Md., 1957-59; mem. staff clin. endocrinology br. Nat. Heart, Lung and Blood Inst., NIH, Bethesda, 1959-63, assoc. in medicine, 1963-65; asst. prof. medicine Northwestern U. Sch. Medicine, Chgo., 1965-68; assoc. prof. Ind. U. Med Sch., Indpls., 1968-71, prof., 1971-79; prof. medicine and pharmacology Med. U. SC, Charleston, SC, 1979—2006, disting. univ. prof., 1998—; ret. Mem. gen. medicine B study sect. NIH, Bethesda, 1982—86, chmn., 1985—86, mem. spl. grants rev. com. Nat. Inst. Arthritis, Musculo-Skeletal and Skin Diseases, 1990—95, chmn., 1993—94. Mem. editl. bd. Calcified Tissue Internat., 1978—83, 1994—2002, Jour. Clin. Endocrinology and Metabolism, 1982—87, Jour. Bone and Mineral Rsch., 1989—93, Italian Jour. Mineral and Electrolyte Metabolism, 1990—, Current Drug Targets-Immune, Endocrine and Metabolic Disorders, 2000—06, Reviews in Endocrine & Metabolic Disorders, 2000—05. Trustee Nat. Osteoporosis Found., Washington, 1984—88, chmn. sci. adv. bd., 1985—88. With USPHS, 1957—63. Recipient Career Devel. award, USPHS, 1965—68, VA Med. Investigator award, 1979, 1981—87, Thomas A. Roe Found. award, S.C. Med. Assn., 1982, William S. Middleton VA award, 1983, Frederic C. Bartter award, Am. Soc. Bone and Mineral Rsch., 1992, Career Recognition award, Vitamin D Workshop, 1997. Mem.: Endocrine Soc., Assn. Osteobiology (councillor 1997—98, sec.-treas. 1999, pres. 2000—02), Assn. Am. Physicians, Am. Soc. Pharmacology and Exptl. Therapeutics, Am. Soc. Bone and Mineral Rsch. (sec.-treas. 1978—85, pres. 1986—87, Shirley Hohl Svc. award 1998), Am. Soc. Clin. Investigation, Alpha Omega Alpha. Democrat. Episcopalian. Home: 1 Johnson Rd Charleston SC 29407-7514 Office Phone: 843-876-5162. Business E-Mail: belln@musc.edu.

BELL, PAUL D., computer company executive; BFA, BBA, Pa. State U.; MBA in Pub. and Pvt. Mgmt., Yale U., 1990. Mng. cons. Bain & Co.; joined Dell Inc., 1996, v.p., gen. mgr. home and small bus. group, 1997—98, sr. v.p., gen. mgr. home and small bus. group, 1998—2000, sr. v.p. Europe, Middle East and Africa, 2000—07, sr. v.p., pres. Americas, 2007—. Office: Dell Inc One Dell Way Round Rock TX 78682-2222*

BELL, PHILIP WILKES, accountant, economist, educator; b. NYC, Oct. 24, 1924; s. Samuel Dennis and Miriam Ball (Wilkes) B.; m. Katharine Elizabeth Hubbard, June 16, 1945 (div. May 1980); children: Susan, Geoffrey, Mary Ellen, James; m. Virginia Wood Crozier, June 14, 1980 (dec. Nov. 1998); stepchildren: Thomas, Steven, Peter; m. Jean Grady Wyeth, Oct. 24, 1999. BA, Princeton U., 1947; MA, U. Calif., Berkeley, 1949; PhD, Princeton U., 1954. Instr. Princeton (N.J.) U., 1948-51; rsch. assoc. Inst. for Advanced Study, Princeton, 1951-52; asst. prof. Haverford (Pa.) Coll., 1952-56, assoc. prof., then prof., 1960-68; assoc. prof. U. Calif., Berkeley, 1957-60; prof. Merrill Coll., U. Calif., Santa Cruz, 1968-79, provost, 1968-72; William A. Kirkland prof. Rice U., Houston, 1979-89; prof. acctg. and econs. Boston U., 1989-92; ret. Assoc. dir. Rockefeller Found., 1963-68; chmn., prof. econ. Makerere U. Coll., Uganda, 1963-65; chmn. econ., Fisk U., 1965-66; dir. Edn. Abroad Program U. Calif., Kenya, 1972-74; vis. prof. Univ. Sains Malaysia, Penang, 1976-77, Norges Handelshoyskole, Bergen, Norway, spring 1982, U. Pa., Phila, fall 1982. Author: Sterling Area in the Postwar World, 1956, Toward Greater Logic and Utility in Accounting: The Collected Writings of Philip W. Bell, 1997; co-author: (with Edgar O. Edwards) Theory and Measurement of Business Income, 1961, (with Edgar O. Edwards and L. Todd Johnson) Accounting for Economic Events, 1979, (with Michael H. Granof) Financial Accounting: Principles and Issues, 1992; contbr. articles to profl. jours. 2d lt. USAF, 1943-45. Social Sci. Rsch. Coun. rsch. fellow, London, 1956-57, Ford Found. fellow, Berkeley, 1959. Mem. Am. Acctg. Assn., Brit. Acctg. Assn., European Acctg. Assn., Royal Econ. Soc. (U.K.), Acctg. Assn. Australia and New Zealand (elected to Acctg. Hall of Fame, Columbus, Ohio, 2003). Mem. Soc. Of Friends. Home and Office: 30 Lonsdale Ln Kennett Square PA 19348-2045

BELL, PHILLIP JACKSON, federal agency administrator; b. Portsmouth, Va., Dec. 31, 1941; s. John Henry and Lois Belle (Hendrix) B.; m. Virginia Phillips Inman, Apr. 11, 1981; children by previous marriage: Scarlett Lee Talamantes, Christopher J. Bell, John R. Bradley, Lynda I. Kleene. BSBA, Northwestern U., 1963; MA, U. S.C., 1964. Mgmt. cons. McKinsey & Co., Washington, 1967-73; dir. corp. planning Washington Post Co., 1973-77; asst. to pres. Allegheny Airlines, Washington, 1977-78; v.p.-long range planning USAir Inc, Washington, 1978-83, sr. v.p.-fin., CFO, 1983-86, exec. v.p.-fin., 1986-89; v.p.-fin., chief fin. officer USAir Group, 1984-89; exec. v.p., chief fin. officer Burlington Northern Inc., Ft. Worth, 1989-91; sr. v.p. planning Am. Airlines Inc., Ft. Worth, 1991-92, sr. v.p. strategic programs, 1992-93; exec. v.p., CFO Conner Peripherals Inc., San Jose, Calif., 1993-96; exec. v.p., CFO, chief adminstrv. officer Adobe Systems, Inc., San Jose, 1996-98, venture advisor, 1998—2003; chief staff Afghanistan Reconstruction Group U.S. State Dept., Washington, 2003—04; dep. under sec. Dept. Army, Washington, 2005; dep. under. sec. for logistics & material readiness US Dept. Def., Washington, 2005—. Capt. USMC, 1964—67, Vietnam.

BELL, RAJA, professional basketball player; b. St. Croix, US VI, Sept. 19, 1976; m. Cindy Green, 2004. Student, Boston U., Fla. Internat. U. Guard US Basketball League Tampa Bay Windjammers, 1999, Continental Basketball Assn. Yakima Sun Kings, 1999—2000, Phila. 76ers, 2000—02, Dallas Mavericks, 2002—03, Utah Jazz, Salt Lake City, 2003—05, Phoenix Suns, 2005—. Mem. US VI Nat. Team. Named to Continental Basketball Assn. All-Rookie Team, 2000, NBA All-Defensive First Team, 2007. Achievements include winning a Continental Basketball Association Championship as a member of the Sun Kings, 2000. Mailing: Phoenix Suns 201 E Jefferson St Phoenix AZ 85004*

BELL, RANDALL KEITH, writer; b. South Bend, Ind., Oct. 30, 1949; s. Robert Kent and Mabel Louise (Keefer) Bell; m. Theresa Loretta Roe, Nov. 22, 1970; children: Rebecca Lianne, Lydia Renee, Tabitha Joy, Joanna Ruth, Rachel Christine. Author: A Lion in the Snow, 1999, (short stories) Tales of Us and Others, 2001. Home: 1018 Highland Pk Dr Lexington KY 40505

BELL, RICHARD EUGENE, agricultural products executive, state official; b. Clinton, Ill., Jan. 7, 1934; s. Lloyd Richard and Ina (Oglesby) B.; m. Maria Christina Mendoza, Oct. 22, 1960; children— David Lloyd, Stephen Richard. BS with honors, U. Ill., 1957, MS, 1958. Internat. economist Dept. Agr., Washington, 1959-60, dir. grain div., 1969-72; agrl. attache Am. embassies in Ottawa, Can., Brussels, and Dublin, Ireland, 1961-68; asst. sec. agr. internat. affairs and commodity programs, 1973-77; pres., CEO Riceland Foods Inc., Stuttgart, Ark., 1977—2004; sec. of agr. State of Ark., 2005—. Bd. dirs. First Comml. Corp., GTE S.W. Inc., Fed. Res. Bank St. Louis; pres., dir. Commodity Credit Corp., also Fed. Crop Ins. Corp., 1975-77; exec. sec. Pres.'s Agrl. Policy Com., 1976-77; rep. Internat. Wheat Coun., London, 1970-77; adviser World Food Conf., Rome, 1974; trustee Ark. State U., 1997—2005. Recipient Disting. Service award Dept. Agr., 1975 Mem. Alpha Gamma Rho, Alpha Zeta. Republican. Mem. Christian Ch. (Disciples Of Christ). Office: Ark Agr Dept 1Natural Resources Dr Little Rock AR 72205 Home Phone: 870-673-3022; Office Phone: 870-672-4761. Business E-Mail: secretary@aad.ar.gov.

BELL, ROBERT, literature educator; b. 1946; BA, Dartmouth Coll., 1967; PhD, Harvard U., 1972. Prof. Williams Coll., Williamstown, Mass., 1972—, founder, dir. Project for Effective Tchg., 1994—. William R. Kenan, Jr., Prof. English. Host The Book Show, Northeast Pub. Radio, 1996—98. Author: Jocoserious Joyce: The Fate of Folly in Ulysses, Bertrand Russell and the Eliots, Blushing Like the Morn: Milton's Human Comedy in Paradise Lost, Metamorphoses of Spritual Autobiography, James Boswell's Notes Toward a Supreme Fiction, David Hume's Fables of Identity, Dryden's Aeneid as English Augustan Epic, Sterne's Etristramology, Rousseau: Prophet of Sincerity, Shakespeare in Cyberspace, Critical Essays on Kingsley Amis, Bob Dylan and the Language that He Used, Shakespeare's Anatomy of Folly, A Teacher for All Seasons, Hades Episode: Notes and Annotations; editor-in-chief Berkshire Review. Recipient Exemplary Tchr. award, Am. Assn. Higher Edn., 1994, Robert Foster Cherry Award, 1998, Outstanding Baccalaureate Coll. Prof. of Yr., Coun. for Advancement and Support of Edn. & Carnegie Found. for Advancement of Tchg., 2004; fellow, NEH, 1989; grantee Danforth Found. Fellowship, 1967—72; Woodrow Wilson fellow, 1967—68. Avocations: jazz, theater, films, history. Office: Stetson Hall Williams Coll Williamstown MA 01267 Business E-Mail: Robert.H.Bell@williams.edu.

BELL, ROBERT CECIL, lawyer; b. San Francisco, June 1, 1951; s. Robert Elmer and Lillian Marie (Petrik) B. BJ, U. Nev., 1973; JD, U. Pacific, 1980. Bar: Nev. 1980, Colo. 1993, U.S. Dist. Ct. Nev. 1980, U.S. Bankruptcy Ct. 1981, U.S. Ct. Appeals (9th cir.) 1982, U.S. Supreme Ct., 1988. Investigator, legal asst. Washoe County Dist. Atty.'s Office, Reno, 1975-77; law clk. to presiding justice Washoe County Dist. Ct., Reno, 1980-81; sole practice Reno, 1981—. Judge pro tem Reno Mcpl. Ct., 1985—, Sparks Mcpl. Ct, 1986—; adminstrv. law judge, Reno; bd. dirs. Washoe Legal Svcs., Reno. Bd. dirs. March of Dimes, Reno, 1985—; mem. Supreme Ct. Hist. Soc. Mem. ABA, Washoe County Bar Assn., Assn. Trial Lawyers Am., Nev. Trial Lawyers Assn., Reno Rodeo Assn., Reno Air Races, U. Pacific McGeorge Sch. Law Alumni Assn. (bd. dirs. 1986—). Democrat. Lutheran. Avocations: photography, flying, skiing, golf, guitar. Office: 20 Winter St Reno NV 89503 Office Phone: 775-333-9977.

BELL, ROBERT HOLMES, federal judge; b. Lansing, Mich., Apr. 19, 1944; s. Preston C. and Eileen (Holmes) B.; m. Helen Mortensen, June 28, 1968; children: Robert Holmes Jr., Ruth Eileen, Jonathan Neil. BA, Wheaton Coll., 1966; JD, Wayne State U., 1969. Bar: Mich. 1970, U.S. Dist. Ct. (we. dist.) Mich. 1970. Asst. prosecutor Ingham County Prosecutor's Office, Lansing, Mich., 1969-72; state dist. judge Mich. State Cts., 1973-78, state cir. judge Mason, 1979-87; judge US Dist. Ct. (we. dist.) Mich., Grand Rapids, Mich., 1987-2001, chief judge, 2001—. Office: US Dist Ct 602 Fed Bldg 110 Michigan St NW Grand Rapids MI 49503-2363 E-mail: kim@miwd.uscourts.gov.

BELL, ROBERT JEFFREY, lawyer; b. LA, June 1, 1947; AB, U. Calif., Santa Cruz, 1969; JD summa cum laude, Loyola U., LA, 1976. Bar: Calif. 1976. Ptnr. Luce, Forward, Hamilton & Scripps, San Diego, mng. ptnr., 2004—. Chief note and comment editor: Loyola U. L.A. Law Rev., 1975-76. Mem. ABA, State Bar Calif. Office: Luce Forward Hamilton & Scripps LLP 600 W Broadway Ste 2600 San Diego CA 92101 E-mail: rbell@luce.com.

BELL, ROBERT LLOYD, retired neurosurgeon; b. McKeesport, Pa., Sept. 3, 1923; s. Samuel Lowry and Nellie Pearl Bell; m. Helen Louise Matthews, Oct. 13, 1951; children: Robert Matthews, Louise Helen. BS, Washington and Jefferson Coll., 1944; MD, U. Pitts., 1947. Jr. intern Shady Side Hosp., Pitts., 1945—47; intern Western Pa. Hosp., Pitts., 1947—48; resident in surgery Aspin Wall Pa. Hosp., Pitts., 1948—49; resident in neurosurgery Bklyn. Hosp., 1949—50, Kings County Hosp., Bklyn., 1950—51, chief neurosurg. resident, 1953—54; chief neurosurgery 98th GH Hosp., Munich, 1951—53; from instr. to assoc. prof. SUNY, Bklyn., 1954—59; chief neurosurgery Wadsworth (Kans.) VA Hosp., 1959—64, Coatesville (Pa.) VA Hosp., 1964—69, Chester County Hosp., West Chester, Pa., 1969—83; chair nuc. medicine VA Hosp. Coatesville, 1983—91. 1st lt. col. USMC, 1951—53. Fellow: ACS, Am. Coll. Nuc. Medicine (gold medal 1989); mem.: AMA, SAR (compatriot), Chester County Med. Soc., Pa. Med. Soc., Am. Legion. Presbyterian. Home: 51 S 12th St Coatesville PA 19320

BELL, ROBERT M., judge; b. Rocky Mount, NC, July 6, 1943; AB with honors, Morgan State Coll., 1966; JD, Harvard U., 1969. Bar: Md. 1969. Judge Md. Dist. Ct. Dist. 1, Balt., 1975-79; former judge Cir. Ct. Md. 8th Jud. Cir.; assoc. judge Md. Ct. Spl. Appeals, 1980-91, Md. Ct. Appeals, Balt., 1991-96, chief judge, 1996—. Mem. exec. com. Md. Jud. Conference, 1996—2000, chair, 1996—, mem. jud. compensation com., 1996—; chair Library Com. State Law Library, 1996—; mem. Judges, Masters & Juvenile Justice Com., 1996—; chair Com. on Bldg. Public Trust & Confidence in Justice System, 1998—99, Md. Alternative Dispute Resolution Commn., 1998—2001, Hall of Records Commn., 1998—, Technology Oversight Bd., 1999—; mem. State Commn. on Criminal Sentencing Policy, 1999—2000, Juvenile Justice Coord. Council, 2000—02; chair Public Trust & Confidence Implementation Com., 2000—, Jud. Cabinet, 2000—; chair jud. council Md. Jud. Conference, 2000—; chair advisory bd. Md. Mediation & Conflict Resolution Office, 2001—; mem. Task Force to Study Criminal Offender Monitoring by Global Positioning Systems, 2004—; bd. dirs. Conf. of Chief Justices. Recipient Legal Excellence award, Md. Bar Foundation, 1999, Rosalyn B. Bell award, Women's Law Ctr. of Md., 1999, Louis M. Brown award, ABA, 2000, Access to Justice Tribute award, Pro Bono Resource Ctr., 2001, Md. Top Leadership in Law award, Daily Record, 2001, D'Alemberte/Raven award, ABA, 2003, Medal for Access to Justice, Md. Legal Svc. Corp., 2004. Mem. ABA, Nat. Bar Assn., Md. State Bar Assn. (Special award 1998), Inc., Bar Assn. Balt. City, Monumental City Bar Assn. Office: Court of Appeals 634 Courthouse East 111 N Calvert St Baltimore MD 21202-1904*

BELL, RONALD, secondary school educator; b. Paris, Tex., July 2, 1947; m. Betty Bell, Aug. 1, 1974. BS, Tex. A&M U., Commerce, 1969; MS, Tex. A&M U., 1972. Drafting tchr. H. Grady Spruce H.S., Dallas, 1969—82; CAD tchr. Lakeview Centennial H.S., Garland, Tex., 1987—2004. Avocations: fishing, Bible study. Home: 3401 Oak Trail Dr Rowlett TX

BELL, RONALD A., lawyer; b. Jamaica, 1967; BS in Aerospace and Mech. Engring., Polytechnic U., 1988; MS in Aerospace and Mech. Engring., U. Cin., 1991; JD, Ohio State U., 1994. Bar: Ohio 1994, US Dist. Ct. Southern Dist. Ohio, US Tax Ct.; cert. CFA 2001. Ptnr. Squire, Sanders & Dempsey L.L.P., Cin. Mem., Leadership Cin. Class XXVI Greater Cin. Chamber of Commerce. Mem., Human Resources Com. Nat. Underground Railroad Freedom Ctr. Named one of Ohio's Rising Stars, Super Lawyers, 2006. Office: Squire Sanders & Dempsey LLP 312 Walnut St Ste 3500 Cincinnati OH 45202-4036 Office Phone: 513-361-1200. Office Fax: 513-361-1201.

BELL, RONALD MACK, university foundation administrator, consultant; b. Atlanta, Mar. 4, 1937; m. Deborah Jean Slaton, Dec. 28, 1989. BS in Indsl. Mgmt., Ga. Inst. Tech., 1959; MBA, U. Mich., 1965; attended, Cornell U., 1980. Commd. USN, 1959, advanced through grades to capt., 1979, ret., 1985; assoc. dir. rsch. contracts Ga. Inst. Tech., Atlanta, 1985-88; v.p., gen. mgr. Ga. Tech. Rsch. Corp., Atlanta, 1988-97; exec. dir. S.C. Rsch. Inst., Columbia, 1997-2001; v.p., bd. dirs. Pisgah Astrol. Rsch. Inst., 1999—2003; pres., CEO UCRF Support Assocs., St. Simons Island, Ga., 1998—. Bd. dirs., past pres., now dir. emeritus Nat. Supply Corps. Assn.; cons. Wesvaco/Post, Buckley, Coastal Cons., Inc., also others, 1985—; expert witness ELSCO, U. Tenn., others, 1987-90; nat. chmn. Univ. Connected Rsch. Found., 1990-91. Past chmn., dir. emeritus Naval Supply Corps. Sch. Mus. Com., Athens, mem., 1983—; mem. Exec. Roundtable, Atlanta, 1985-97; resource staff Gov.'s Com. Tech. & Devel.,

Atlanta, 1992-97; bd. dirs. Ga. Tech. Sch. Mgmt., 1995-98; bd. grad. studies advisors Ga. So. U., 2004—. Decorated Legion of Merit (2), Meritorious Svc. medal (2), Navy Commendation medal (2); named to Honor Roll of Mentors, U. Connected Rsch. Found., 2004. Mem. Soc. Rsch. Adminstrs. (nat. coms., chair regional com. 1985-2002), Licensing Execs. Soc., Nat. Coun. Univ. Rsch. Adminstrs. (chair regional com., nat. panelist 1985-2001), Coun. Rsch. and Tech. (dir. workshop, tax com. 1986-92), Ga. Tech. Nat. Alumni Assn. (various coms.), Nat. Conf. on the Advancement of Rsch. (conf. com. 2000), Assn. Univ. Tech. Mgrs., Theta Chi (past chpt. pres.), Phi Kappa Phi, Beta Gamma Sigma. Avocations: golf, woodworking. Home: 113 Thompson Cv Saint Simons Island GA 31522-3768 Office: UCRF Support Assoc PO Box 20272 Saint Simons Island GA 31522 E-mail: bellssi@earthlink.net.

BELL, SAMUEL H., federal judge, educator; b. Rochester, NY, Dec. 31, 1925; s. Samuel H. and Marie C. (Williams) B.; m. Joyce Elaine Shaw, 1948 (dec.): children: Henry W., Steven D.; m. Jennie Lee McCall, 1983. BA, Coll. Wooster, 1947; JD, U. Akron, 1952. Pvt. practice, Cuyahoga Falls, Ohio, 1956-68; asst. pros. atty. Summit County, Ohio, 1956-58; judge Cuyahoga Falls Mcpl. Ct., Ohio, 1968-73, Ct. of Common Pleas, Akron, Ohio, 1973-77, Ohio Ct. Appeals, 9th Jud. Dist., Akron, 1977-82, U.S. Dist. Ct. (no. dist.) Ohio, Akron, 1982-2000, sr. status, 1996; sr. judge. Adj. prof. Coll. Wooster, 1998-2003, Bell disting. lectr. in law, 1998—; adj. prof., adv. bd. U. Akron Sch. Law, past trustee Dean's club; bd. dirs. Jos. R. Miller Found; co-owner Bell Lettres Ltd. Co-author: Federal Practice Guide 6th Cir., 1996. Recipient Disting. Alumni award U. Akron, 1988, St. Thomas More award, 1987. Fellow Akron Bar Found. (trustee 1989-94, pres. 1993-94); mem. Fed. Bar Assn., Akron Bar Assn., Akron U. Sch. Law Alumni Assn. (Disting. Alumni award 1983), Charles F. Scanlon Akron Inn Ct. (pres. 1990-92), Masons, Phi Alpha Delta. Republican. Presbyterian. Office: US Dist Ct 433 US Court House Fed Bldg 2 S Main St Akron OH 44308-5836

BELL, SANDRA ELIZABETH, corporate financial executive; b. Toronto, Ont., Can., Apr. 23, 1957; came to U.S., 1961; d. Alexander James Bell and Marion Ann (Scaysbrook) Robinson. BA in Econs., Ohio State U., 1979; MBA, Harvard U., 1983. Mgmt. trainee, systems analyst First Nat. Bank of Cin., 1979-81; asst. v.p. E.F. Hutton & Co., NYC, 1983-87; v.p. The Deerpath Group, Lake Forest, Ill., 1988-91; mng. dir. Deutsche Bank Securities Inc., NYC, 1991—2004; exec. v.p., CFO Fed. Home Loan Bank of Cin., 2004—. Mem. Phi Beta Kappa. Avocations: skiing, tennis, reading. Office: Fed Home Loan Bank 221 E 4th St Fl 10 Cincinnati OH 45202 Home Phone: 513-474-3443; Office Phone: 513-852-7524. E-mail: bellse@fhlbcin.com.

BELL, SHEILA TRICE, lawyer; b. Aug. 25, 1949; married. BA in Biol. Scis., Wellesley Coll., Mass., 1971; JD, Harvard U., 1974. Bar: Mass. 1974, US Dist. Ct. Mass. 1975, Tenn. 1977, US Dist. Ct. (mid. dist.) Tenn. 1978, US Ct. Appeals (6th cir.) 1980, Ky. 1985. Assoc. Hutchins & Wheeler, Boston, 1973-77; pvt. practice Nashville, 1977-79, 83-84; univ. counsel Fisk U., Nashville, 1979-83; acting univ. counsel, affirmative action officer No. Ky. U., Highland Heights, 1984-85, univ. legal counsel, 1985—; atty. Gurne, Porter and Baulig P.L.L.C., Wash., DC. Spl. asst. atty. gen. Commonwealth of Ky., 1985-87; instr. bus. law Tenn. State U., Nashville, 1979; instr. polit. sci., student advisor Pine Manor Jr. Coll. (now Pine Manor Coll.), Chestnut Hill, Mass., 1972-74; speaker various confs. Mem. editorial bd. Jour. Coll. and Univ. Law, 1982-83. Active blue chip campaign Econ. Devel. Task Force, Cin., 1988, Mayor's Spl. Task Force on Union Sta., Nashville, 1982-83, Mayor's Task Force on Transp., Nashville, 1979-80, Task Force of ERA Commn. Commonwealth of Mass., 1976, adv. bd. Ctr. for Fertility and Reproductive Rsch. Vanderbilt U., Nashville, 1981-83, nominating com. Nashville YWCA, 1980-83; incorporator, mem. organizing com. North Avondale (Tenn.) Montessori Found., 1983-84; bd. dirs. Program for Cin., 1986—, Family and Children's Svcs., Nashville, 1979-83, Hist. Nashville Inc., 1983-83, Nashville Inst. for the Arts, 1980-82. Named Career Women of Achievement YWCA, Cin., 1988, One of Outstanding Young Women Am., 1982. Mem. ABA, Nat. Assn. Coll. and Univ. Attys. (bd. dirs. 1985-88), Links (v.p. Cin. chpt. 1986—), Jack and Jill Inc., Wellesley Club Cin. Office: Gurne Porter and Baulig PLLC 1750 K St NW Ste 350 Washington DC 20006 Office Phone: 202-778-0020. Office Fax: 202-778-0029.

BELL, STEPHEN D., lawyer; b. 1951; AB, Dartmouth Coll., 1974; JD, Univ. SD, 1978. Bar: SD 1978, Minn. 1980, Mont. 1984, Colo. 1993. Ptnr., trial group Dorsey & Whitney LLP, Denver, and mem., policy com. Office: Dorsey & Whitney LLP Ste 4700 Republic Plz Bldg 370 17th St Denver CO 80202-5647 Office Phone: 303-629-3405. Office Fax: 303-629-3450. Business E-Mail: bell.steve@dorsey.com.

BELL, STEPHEN ROBERT, lawyer; b. Menominee, Mich., July 10, 1942; s. John Martin and Catherine Irene (Goodman) B.; m. Linden Tucker, May 22, 1976. AB, Georgetown U., 1964; JD, U. Wis., 1967. Bar: D.C. 1971, Minn. 1967, Wis. 1967, U.S. Ct. Appeals (4th and 5th cirs.), U.S. Supreme Ct. Assoc. Dorsey & Whitney, Mpls., 1967—68; ptnr. Wilkinson, Cragun & Barker, Washington, 1971—82, Squire, Sanders & Dempsey, Washington, 1982—96, Willkie, Farr & Gallagher LLP, Washington, 1996—. Contbr. articles to profl. jours. Lt. USNR, 1968—71. Mem. ABA, D.C. Bar Assn., Fed. Communications Bar Assn., Computer Law Assn. (bd. dirs. 1987-93), Order of Coif. Office: Willkie Farr & Gallagher LLP 1875 K St NW Washington DC 20006-1238 Office Phone: 202-303-1102. Personal E-mail: sbell@willkie.com.

BELL, STEPHEN SCOTT (STEVE BELL), journalist, educator; b. Oskaloosa, Iowa, Dec. 9, 1935; s. Howard Arthur and Florance (Scott) B.; m. Joyce Dillavou, June 16, 1957; children: Allison Kay, Hilary Ann. BA, Central Coll., Pella, Iowa, 1959, PhD (hon.), 1969; MS in Journalism, Northwestern U., 1963. Announcer Radio Sta. KBOE, Oskaloosa, 1955-59; reporter WOI-TV, Ames, Iowa, 1959-60; news writer WGN Radio-TV, Chgo., 1960-61; reporter, anchorman WOW-TV, Omaha, 1962-65; anchorman Radio Sta. WNEW, NYC, 1965-66; corr. ABC News, 1967-86, assignments include Vietnam War corr. Vietnam, 1970-71, polit. corr., 1968, 72, chief Asia corr., 1972-73, White House corr. Washington, 1974-75; news anchorman World News This Morning and Good Morning Am., 1975-86; news anchor KYW-TV, Phila., 1987-91, USA Network Updates, 1989-92; prof. telecomm. Ball State U., Muncie, Ind., 1992—2007, endowed chmn. emeritus in telecomm., 2007—. Recipient Emmy nominations, 1965, 73, Overseas Press Club award, 1969, Headliner award, 1975 Mem. AFTRA, Council Fgn. Relations. Presbyterian (elder). Office: Ball State U Dept Telecommunications Muncie IN 47306-0001 *As a journalist, the older I get, the less inclined I am to "play God.".*

BELL, STEVEN J., school librarian, educator, writer; BA in Liberal Arts cum laude, Temple U., Phila., 1976; MS in Libr. Sci., Drexel U., Phila., 1977; EdD in Higher Edn. Adminstrn., U. Pa., Phila., 1997. Libr. Phila. Corp. Aging, 1978—84; bus. info. specialist Laventhol and Horwath, Phila., 1984—85; reference libr. U. Pa. Lippincott Libr. of Wharton Sch., Phila., 1986—89, head circulation and res., 1989—95, asst. dir., 1995—97; dir. Paul J. Gutman Libr. Phila. U., 1997—2006; assoc. univ. libr. rsch. and instrnl. svcs. Temple U., 2007—. Asst. adj. prof. Drexel U. Coll. Info. Sci. and Tech., 1995—, St. Joseph's U. Sch. Bus., 1997—2001. Contbr. articles to profl. publs. Named one of the Movers & Shakers, Libr. Jour., 2002. Mem.: ALA, Phila. Area Reference Librs. Info. Exch., Libr. Adminstrn. and Mgmt. Assn., Assn. Coll. and Rsch. Librs. Office: Samuel L Paley Libr Temple U 1210 W Berks St Philadelphia PA 19122 Office Phone: 215-204-5023. Office Fax: 215-204-5201. E-mail: bells@temple.edu.

BELL, STOUGHTON, computer scientist, mathematician, educator; b. Waltham, Mass., Dec. 20, 1923; s. Conrad and Florence Emily (Ross) Bell; m. Mary Carroll O'Connell, Feb. 26, 1949 (div. 1960); children: Karen, Mark; m. Laura Joan Bainbridge, May 24, 1963 (div. 1979); children: Nathaniel Stoughton, Joshua Bainbridge; m. Edna Casman, June 25, 2001. Student, Harvard U., 1946-49; AB, U. Calif., Berkeley, 1950, MA, 1953, PhD, 1955. Mem. staff Sandia Corp., Albuquerque, 1955-66, div. supr., 1964-66; vis. lectr. U. N.Mex., 1957-66, dir. computing center, 1966-79, assoc. prof. math., 1966-71, prof. math. and computer sci., 1971-92, prof. emeritus, 1992—. Vis. lectr. N.Mex. Acad. Scis., 1965—. Co-author: (book) Linear Analysis and Generalized Functions, 1965, Introductory Calculus, 1966, Modern University Calculus, 1966, Mathematical Analysis for Modeling, 1999. With AUS, 1943—44. Mem.: Ops. Rsch. Soc. Am., Am. Statis. Assn., Soc. Indsl. and Applied Math., Math. Assn. Am., Am. Math. Soc., Assn. Computing Machinery (nat. lectr. 1972—74). Office: U NMex Computer Sci Dept Albuquerque NM 87131-1386 Home Phone: 505-256-9489. Business E-Mail: sto@cs.unm.edu.

BELL, SUSAN GROAG, historian, researcher; arrived in US, 1957; d. Friedrich and Edith Louise Groag. BA, Stanford U., Calif., 1964; MA, Santa Clara U., Calif., 1970. Lectr. Santa Clara U., 1970—81; sr. scholar Clayman Inst. for Gender Rsch. Stanford U., Calif., 1978—, lectr., 1981—92. Author: Women from the Greeks to the French Revolution, 1973, Medieval Women Book-Owners: Arbiters of Lay Piety and Ambassadors of Culture, 1982, Between Worlds: in Czechoslovakia, England and America, 1991, The Lost Tapestries of the City of Ladies, 2004. Home: 101 Alma St # 503 Palo Alto CA 94301-1006 Office: Clayman Institute Stanford University Stanford CA 94305-8640 Business E-Mail: groagbel@stanford.edu.

BELL, SUSAN JANE, nurse; b. Columbus, Ohio, July 24, 1946; d. Donald Richard Bell and Martha Jane (McDowell) Nichols; m. Robert Earlin Ward, Oct. 24, 1964 (div. 1984); children: Duane Allen Ward, Melissa Jane Ward, Bryan Thomas Ward. Degree in nursing, Columbus Sch. Practical Nursing, 1986; ADRN, Columbus State C.C., 1989; student, Franklin U., 1993, Edn. Direct Nutrition and Fitness; diploma in nutrition and fitness, Penn Foster Coll. RN Ohio; cert. CPR. Nurse's asst. Riverside Meth. Hosp., Columbus, 1970-80, Norworth Convalescent Ctr., Columbus, 1980-86; nurse, charge nurse Heartland Thurber Care Ctr., Columbus, 1986-89; staff nurse Am. Nursing Care, Columbus, 1989—; medicare home visitation, staffing and pvt. duty nurse Telemed, Columbus, 1989—; asst. head nurse Northland Terr., Columbus, 1989; supr. Elmington Manor, Columbus, 1989; staff nurse cardiac step down unit Grant Hosp., Columbus, 1989-92; nurse med. ICU, CCU and pediatric ICU, 1992-93; charge nurse critical-skilled unit First Cmty. Village Health Care Ctr., Columbus, 1992-95; supr., charge nurse St. Rita's Home; charge nurse Mother Angeline McCrory Manor, 2005—, supr., 2005—07. Pvt. duty ALS ventilator patients Med. Pers. Poole. Sponsor Childreach. Mem. NAFE, ASPCA, World Wildlife Found., Nature Conservancy, Ohio Hist. Found. (archives/libr. divsn.), Nat. Audubon Soc., Environ. Def. Fund, Nat. Wildlife Fedn., Humane Soc. U.S., Am. Coun. on Exercise, Columbus Met. Mus. Art (supporting), Internat. Assn. Global Execs., Nat. Notary Assn., Nat. Mus. of Women in the Arts, Ohio Hist. Soc.-Archives Libr., Omtermat/ Exec. Guild, Rotary, Sierra Club. Avocations: bodybuilding, power lifting, swimming, music, crocheting. Personal E-mail: bellcanine@aol.com.

BELL, TAUNJAH PATREASE, research scientist; b. Miami, June 14, 1967; d. Frank Bell Sr. and Cleo Bell. BA, U. South Fla., Sarasota, 1995; MA, U. No. Iowa, Cedar Falls, 1999; PhD in Psychology with honors, So. Ill. U., Carbondale, 2007. Qualified mental retardation profl. Hillsborough County Devel. Ctr., Tampa, Fla., 1999—2001; recruiter, advisor ednl. talent search program U. No. Iowa Ctr. Urban Edn., Waterloo, 2001—02; program evaluator, Spanish tchr. gear up program U. No. Iowa, Cedar Falls, 2001, dir. gear up program, 2001—02. Tutor English students of other langs. program Manatee CC, Bradenton, Fla., 1993—95. Mem. search com. dir. campus computing U. South Fla., 1995. Mem.: APA, AAAS, Soc. for Neurosci., Phi Kappa Phi, U. South Fla. Arts and Scis. Honor Soc., Phi Theta Kappa, Gamma Beta Phi. Democrat. Baptist. Avocations: fishing, hunting, camping, hiking. Home: 2751 NW 174 St Miami Gardens FL 33056-4032 Personal E-mail: taunjah@aol.com.

BELL, THEODORE AUGUSTUS, III, (TED BELL), writer, former advertising executive; b. Tampa, Fla., July 3, 1946; s. Theodore A. and Mary Trice (Howell) B.; m. Evelyn Byrd Lorentzen, Mar. 31, 1978; 1 child, Evelyn Byrd. BA in English, Randolph-Macon Coll., 1969; DFA (hon.), Kendall Coll., 1990. Copywriter Wilson, Haight, Welsh Advt., Hartford, Conn., 1970-71, Tinker, Dodge & Delano, NYC, 1971-72; v.p., creative dir. Doyle Dane Bernbach, NYC, 1972-82; pres., chief creative officer Leo Burnett USA, Chgo., 1982-93; vice-chmn., worldwide creative dir. Young & Rubicam, NYC, 1993—2000. Creative cons. Heart of Am. America's Cup Challenge, Chgo., 1985-86. Author (novels) Nick of Time, 2000, Hawk, 2003, Assassin, 2004, Pirate, 2005. Bd. dirs. Lincoln Park Zoo, 1988—, Prentice Women's Maternity Ctr. Northwestern Meml. Hosp., Chgo., 1981—. Recipient Gold Lion award Cannes (France) Internat. Festival du Film Publicitaire, 1988. Mem. Racquet Club (Chgo. and N.Y.C.), Field Club (Greenwich, Conn.). Republican. Episcopalian. Avocations: sailing, golf, writing, hunting. Office: c/o Atria Books 1230 Av of Am New York NY 10020

BELL, THOMAS DEVEREAUX, JR., real estate company executive; b. Niagara Falls, Nov. 2, 1949; s. Thomas Devereaux and Lenore (Chisholm) B.; m. Margaret McDaniel, Jan. 17, 1975 (div.); 1 child, Thomas Devereaux III; m. Jennifer Holtzman, Dec. 27, 1987; children: Kevin Holtzman Bell, Hannah Holtzman Bell. Student, U. Tenn., 1967-70, George Washington U., 1973, NYU, 1984-88. Exec. dir. Presdl. Inaugural Ball Com., Washington, 1972; dep. div. dir. Com. to Reelect the Pres., Washington, 1971-72; adminstrv. asst. U.S. Senator William Brock, Washington, 1973-75; pres., CEO Bell and McDaniel, Washington, 1975-76, Holder, Kennedy, Dye & Bell, Nashville, 1976-79, Creative Com. Corp., Washington, 1979-82, Hudson Inst., Indpls., 1982-87; exec. v.p. Ball Corp., Muncie, Ind., 1987-89; vice chmn., COO Burson-Marsteller, 1989-94; vice chmn. Gulfstream Aerospace Corp., Savannah, Ga., 1994-95; pres., CEO Burson-Marsteller, NYC, 1995-98; also bd. dirs. Gulfstream Aerospace Corp., Savannah, Ga.; chmn., CEO Young & Rubicam Advt., NYC, 1998-99; pres., COO Young & Rubicam Inc., NYC, 1999—2000, pres., CEO, 2000; vice chmn., pres. Cousins Properties Inc., 2001—, CEO, 2002—, chmn., CEO, 2006—. Regal Entertainment, 2003—, AGL Resources, 2004—. Mem. Transition Team for Pres. Ronald Reagan, Washington, 1981. Mem. Burning Tree Club (Bethesda, Md.), Georgetown Club (Washington), Blind Brook Club (Harrison, N.Y.), Capital Club, Peachtree Golf Club (Atlanta). Republican. Office: Cousins Properties Inc 2500 Windy Way Pkwy Suite 1600 Atlanta GA 30339 Office Phone: 770-955-2200. Office Fax: 770-303-2899.

BELL, W. DONALD, electronics executive; BSEE, U. AL. V.p., sales and mktg. Texas Instruments; pres and CEO Electronic Arrays (now NEC Microelectronics); sr. vp memory & microprocessors, mktg. v.p., exec. v.p. Am. Microsystems Inc.; exec. V.P. Kierulff Electronics, 1980-81, pres., 1981-86; pres and COO Docummun, Inc., 1986-88; pres., CEO, chmn. Bell Microproducts, San Jose, CA, 1988—. Mem. bd. dir. Sand Hill Capital, Eng. Leadership Bd. for the U. of AL. Disting. Eng. Fellow of U. of AL. Office: Bell Microproducts 1941 Ringwood Ave San Jose CA 95131-1721

BELL, WALLACE EDWARD, minister, insurance agent; b. Jackson, Tenn., Feb. 23, 1950; s. William and Marvelyne Eugenia (Wallace) B.; m. Johnnie Mae Mitchell, Sept. 12, 1974; children: Jonathan Edward, Candace Michelle. BS, Union U., 1972. Lic. to ministry Ch. of Christ (Holiness) U.S.A., 1973; ordained, 1979. Engr. I Jet Propulsion Lab., Pasadena, Calif., 1974—77; assoc. minister Christ Temple Ch. of Christ (Holiness) U.S.A., Jackson, 1978—79; bus. tax inspector Madison Cty. Clk., Jackson, 1978—87; pastor Christ Temple Ch. of Christ (Holiness) U.S.A., Jackson, 1979—87, Greater Peace Ch. of Christ, Aurora, Colo., 1987—88, Christ Temple Ch. of Christ (Holiness) U.S.A., Kans. City, Kans., 1988—95; agt. Am. Nat. Life Ins. Co., Shawnee Mission, Kans., 1995—97, Woodmen Accident & Life Ins. Co., Kans. City, Mo., 1997; personal ins. cons. Sitel Corp., Shawnee Mission, 1997—98; pastor First Ch. of Christ, Kans. City, Mo., 1998—2001; ins. lic. trainer Sitel Corp., Shawnee Mission, 1998—2001; pastor Mount Zion Ch. of Christ (Holiness) U.S.A., Inc., Gilbert, La., 2001—. Trustee C.M. & I. Coll. Nat. Bd., Jackson, 1980-92; sec. Northcentral Diocese, St. Louis, 1982-90; dir. comms. Nat. S.S. Congress CoCHUSA, Jackson, 1989-96; career agt. Am. Nat. Life Ins., 1995-97; agt. Woodmen Accident & Life, 1997; personal ins. cons. Sitel, 1997-98; dist. chmn. midwest dist. Ch. of Christ (Holiness) USA, Kansas City, Mo., 1997-2001, dist. pres. 1997-2001, chmn Nat. Bd. Claimants, 2000-; ins. licensing trainer, 1998-2001; lic. trainer Sitel Corp., 1998—. Bd. dirs. Aspell Manor, Jackson, 1985-87. Recipient E.M. Wills award Tenn.-Ky. Dist., 1986. Mem. Jaycees (chaplain 1984-85). Office: Mt Zion Ch of Christ (Holiness) 7140 Hwy 15 Gilbert LA 71336 Home: PO Box 367 Winnsboro LA 71295 Personal E-mail: wallbell@yahoo.com.

BELL, WAYNE S., lawyer, state agency official; b. LA, June 24, 1954; s. Joseph and Jane Barbara (Barsook) B.; m. M. Susan Modzelewski, Apr. 1, 1989; 1 child, Seth Joseph Bell. BA magna cum laude, UCLA, 1976; JD, Loyola U., LA, 1979; Advanced Mgmt. Program, Rutgers U., 1992. Bar: Calif. 1980, U.S. Dist. Ct. (cen. dist.) 1981, U.S. Tax Ct. 1981, U.S. Ct. Appeals (9th cir.) 1981, U.S. Dist. Ct. (so. and no. dists.) Calif. 1983, U.S. Supreme Ct. 1984, D.C. 1986, Tex. 1995; lic. real estate broker, Calif. Intern office of gov. State of Calif., Sacramento, summer 1976; assoc. Levinson, Rowen, Miller, Jacobs & Kabrins, LA, 1980-82; sr. assoc. Montgomery, Gascou, Gemmill & Thornton, LA, 1982-84; counsel, project developer Thomas Safran & Assocs., LA, 1984-85; of counsel Greenspan, Glasser & Medina, Santa Monica, Calif., 1984-86; assoc. gen. counsel Am. Diversified Cos., Costa Mesa, Calif., 1985-88; legal cons. Project Atty., LA, 1988-89; sr. counsel, asst. sec. Ralphs Grocery Co., LA, 1989-99, v.p., sr. counsel, asst. sec., 1999; dep. sec., gen. counsel Calif. Bus., Transp. and Housing Agy., Sacramento, 1999—2003, spl. counsel to Gov.'s Legal Affairs Sec., 1999—2003, provisional undersecretary, 2001—03; dir. Homeownership Calif. Housing Fin. Agy., 2003—06; spl. assignment Office of Gen. Counsel, 2005—06; chief counsel, asst. commr. legal policy & recovery Calif. Dept. Real Estate, 2006—. Judge pro tem Mcpl. Ct. South Bay Jud. Dist., 1987, L.A. Superior Ct., 1991, 94, 97; settlement officer L.A. Mcpl. Ct., Settlement Officer Program, 1990-92; spl. master State Bar Calif., 1991-92; fellow Program Sr. Execs. State & Local Govt., Fannie Mae Found., Harvard. Chief note and comment editor Loyola U. Law Rev., 1978-79; contbr. articles to profl. jours. and gen. pubs. Vol. atty. Westside Legal Svcs., Santa Monica, 1982-87; legal ombudsman Olympics Ombudsman Program L.A. County Bar Assn., 1984; gov. apptd. mem. Calif. adv. coun. Legal Svcs. Corp., 1982-88, Autism Soc. Am., Amnesty Internat.; contbg. mem. Dem. Nat. Com.; mem. leadership coun. So. Poverty Law Ctr.; charter mem. presdl. task force Ams. for Change; bd. dirs. Am. Theatre Arts, Hollywood, Calif., 1983-84; pres., exec. com., bd. dirs. Programs for the Developmentally Handicapped, Inc., L.A., 1987-92; chmn. bd. appeals handicapped accommodations City of Manhattan Beach, 1986-88; bd. dirs. The Foodbank of So. Calif., 1991-94, sec., 1993; legal oversight com. Legal Corps L.A., 1995-97; sec. bd. trustees The Ralphs/Food 4 Less Found., 1995-99; vol. L.A. County Bar Assn., Barristers Homeless Shelter Advocacy Project, 1996-99, exec. com. labor and employment law sect., 1997-99; mem. coordinating com. Calif. Lake Tahoe Interagy Coun., 2001-05; mem. San Francisco Bay Conservation and Devel. Commn., 2002-05. Mem. Calif. Bar Assn. (legal svcs. sect. standing com. legal problems of aging 1983-86, chmn. legis. subcom. 1984-86, conf. dels. alternate 1987), D.C. Bar Assn., Legal Assistance Assn. Calif. (bd. dirs., mem. exec. com., legis. strategy com. 1984-86), Loyola Law Sch. (advocate), Phi Beta Kappa. Democrat. Avocations: sailing, hiking, human behavior study, photography, travel. Office: Calif Dept Real Estate 2201 Broadway Sacramento CA 95818 Office Phone: 916-227-0789. Business E-Mail: wayne_bell@dre.ca.gov.

BELL, WENDELL, sociologist, educator, futurist; b. Chgo., Sept. 27, 1924; s. Wendell and Blanche (Leiferman) B.; m. Lora-Lee Edwards, June 15, 1947; children: Karen Ann, Sharon Lee (dec. 2001), David Howard. BA with highest honors, Calif. State U., Fresno, 1948; MA, UCLA, 1951, PhD, 1952; MA (hon.), Yale U., 1963. Asst. prof. sociology, acting dir. survey rsch. facility Stanford U., 1952-54; assoc. prof. sociology Northwestern U., 1954-57; from assoc. prof. to prof. sociology, dir. West Indies study program UCLA, 1957-63; prof. sociology Yale U., New Haven, 1963-95, chmn. dept., 1965-69, dir. comparative sociology tng. program, 1969-77, dir. undergrad. studies, 1976-83, dir. grad. studies, 1984-89, 94; prof. emeritus, 1995—. Sr. rsch. scientist Yale Ctr. for Comparative Studies, 2000-05; fellow Henry Koerner Ctr., Yale U., 2003—; mem. divsn. behavioral scis. NRC, 1966-69, mem. exec. com., 1968-69; tng. grant dir. in comparative sociology NIMH, 1969-77; vis. fellow Inst. Advanced Studies, The Australian Nat. U., 1985. Author: (with E. Shevky) Social Area Analysis, 1955; (with R.J. Hill and C.R. Wright) Public Leadership, 1961; (with I. Oxaal) Decisions of Nationhood, 1964, Jamaican Leaders, 1964, Foundations of Futures Studies, Vol. I. History, Purposes, and Knowledge, 1997, paperback edit., 2003, Chinese transl., 2004, Vol II Values, Objectivity, and the Good Society, 1997, paperback edit., 2004, Chinese translation, 2007; editor, contbr.: The Democratic Revolution in the West Indies, 1967; (with James A. Mau) The Sociology of the Future, 1971; (with Walter Freeman) Ethnicity and Nation-Building, 1974; editor Internat. Studies in Polit. and Social Change, 1966-76; assoc. editor Am. Sociol. Rev., 1958-61; mem. editl. adv. bd. Sage Profl. Papers in Internat. Studies, 1972-84, Sage Rsch. Papers in Social Sci., Series Social Orgn. of Cmty., U. Iowa, 1974-84, Futurics, 1976—, Cultural Futures Rsch., 1976-87, Technological Forecasting and Social Change, 1995-96; editl. cons. Sociometry, 1959-61; mem. editl. bd. Internat. Studies Quar., 1970-80, Plantation Soc. in the Americas, 1978-90, Political Behavior, 1978-80, Jour. Conflict Resolution, 1980-97, Futures Rsch. Quar., 1992—, The Jour. of Contingencies and Crisis Management, 1992-2004, Jour. Futures Studies, 2000—, Foresight, 1998—; cons. editor D.C. Heath and Co., 1971-84, cons., U.S. Commn. on National Security/21st Century, 1999. Gov.'s appointee Commn. on Conn.'s Future, 1987-89; mem. adv. coun. Inst. for Global Ethics, 1990—2006. Aviator USNR, 1943-46, CBI. Recipient Disting. Alumnus award Calif. State U., Fresno, 1988, W. Bloomberg award for promoting a vision of future based on social justice, 2000; rsch. tng. predoctoral fellow Social Sci. Rsch. Coun., 1951-52, faculty fellow, 1956-59, fellow Ctr. for Advanced Study Behavioral Scis., 1963-64; rsch. grantee, Soc. Sci. Rsch. Coun., 1978, grantee Carnegie Corp. N.Y., 1960-63, NSF, 1969-70. Mem. AAUP, Internat. Sociol. Assn., Am. Sociol. Assn., Eastern Sociol. Soc., Pacific Sociol. Assn. (v.p. 1960-61), Sociol. Rsch. Assn., Internat. Studies Assn. (v.p. 1970-71), Caribbean Studies Assn. (v.p. 1978, pres 1979, Meritorious Service award 1985, mem. coun. 1988-89), World Future Soc., World Futures Studies Fedn. (award for lifetime achievement and contbns. 2005). Avocation: ballroom dancing. Office: Yale U Dept Sociology PO Box 208265 New Haven CT 06520-8265 Business E-Mail: wendell.bell@yale.edu.

BELL, WILLIAM C., foundation administrator; BS in Biology and Behavioral Sci., Delta State U.; MS, Hunter Coll. Sch. Social Work. Former assoc. exec. dir. Miracle Makers, NYC; deputy commissioner of field svcs. and contract agy. case mgmt. NYC Administration for Children's Svcs., 1994—96, deputy commissioner div. of child protection, 1996—2002, commissioner, 2002—04; exec. v.p. child and family svcs. Casey Family Programs, 2004—06, pres., CEO, 2006—. Mem. Pew Commn. on Children in Foster Care; bd. dirs. Council on Social Work Ed.; mem. exec. com. Nat. Assn. of Public Child Welfare Administrators. Recipient Leadership Recognition award, Black Administrators in Child Welfare, Advocacy Merit award for Outstanding Leadership in Children's Svcs., Child Welfare League of Am., 2000, Betsey R. Rosenbaum award for Excellence in Public Child Welfare Admin., Nat. Assn. for Public Child Welfare Administrators, 2003. Office: Casey Family Programs 1300 Dexter Ave N Seattle WA 98109-3542

BELL, WILLIAM J., JR., television producer; b. 1963; s. William Joseph and Lee Phillip Bell; m. Maria Bell. Pres. Bell-Phillip TV Prodns. Inc., LA, Bell Dramatic Serial Co., LA. Trustee LA County Mus. Art, 2005—. Named one of Top 200 Collectors, ARTnews mag., 2006. Office: LA County Mus Art 5905 Wilshire Blvd Los Angeles CA 90036 Office Phone: 323-857-6000. Office Fax: 323-857-4702.

BELL, WILLIAM WOODWARD, lawyer; b. May 15, 1938; s. Charles Smith and Janie Mae (Woodward) B.; m. Mary Elizabeth Beniteau, May 31, 1969; children: Susan Elizabeth, Carol Ann. BBA, Baylor U., 1960, JD, 1965. Bar: U.S. Dist. Ct. (we. dist.) Tex. 1967, U.S. Dist. Ct. (no. dist.) Tex. 1993, U.S. Supreme Ct. 1971. Ptnr. Sleeper, Boynton, Burleson, Williams & Johnson, Waco, Tex., 1965-68, Holloway, Slagle & Bell, Brownwood, 1968-71, Johnson, Slagle & Bell, Brownwood, 1971-74; pvt. practice Brownwood, 1974—. Capt. USMC, 1960-63. Named Vol., 1991, Developer of Yr., Tex. Indsl. Devel. Coun. Fellow Tex. Bar Found.; mem. AAS, ABA, Tex. Bar Assn., Brown County Bar Assn., Am. Judicature Soc., Phi Alpha Delta. Baptist. Home: PO Box 1564 Brownwood TX 76804-1564 Office: PO Box 1726 115 S Broadway Brownwood TX 76804-1726 Office Phone: 325-646-5547.

BELL, WISHART BRYAN, music educator, conductor; b. Collingwood, Can., Dec. 8, 1948; s. Clinton Eric Bell and Elsa Lorraine Carter; m. Mary Hess Bell, July 11, 1983; children: Michael Bryan, Jameson Bradley, Emily Katherine. BA, Trinity Coll., Deerfield, Ill., 1971; MusM, Am. Conservatory Music, Chgo., 1974, D in Musical Arts, 1997. Faculty voice Bethel Coll., Mishawaka, Ind., 1997—. Artistic dir. vesper chorale Vesper Chamber Orch., South Bend, 1993—; dir. Cantus Cathedralis, South Bend, 2004—; dir. music First United Meth. Ch., South Bend, 2000—. Composer: (songs) Ye Watchers and Ye Holy Ones, 1995, O Come O Come Emmanuel, 1995, O Come All Ye Faithful, 1996; contbr. articles to profl. jours. Founder Children's Choir Michiana. Recipient Leo Heim Meml. award, Am. Conservatory Music, 1997; grantee, Elnora Stickley Found., 1999, 2000, Banff Ctr. Arts, 2004. Mem.: Nat. Assn. Tchrs. Singing, Condr.'s Guild, Chorus Am., Am. Choral Dirs. Assn. (life). Office: Vesper Chorale 18211 Kern Rd South Bend IN Home Phone: 574-229-2247. Business E-Mail: wbell@wishartmusicservices.com.

BELL, ZOË, stunt-woman, actress; b. New Zealand, Nov. 17, 1978; d. Andrew and Tish Bell. Attended, Selwyn Coll., New Zealand. Actress, stunt double (TV series) Xena: Warrior Princess, 1995—2001, Cleopatra 2525, 2000, (TV films) The Extreme Team, 2003, (films) Kill Bill: Vol. 1, 2003, Kill Bill: Vol. 2, 2004, Catwoman, 2004, Reflections, 2006, The Devil's Den, 2006, Penny Dreadful, 2006, Grindhouse (Death Proof segment), 2007, appeared in (documentaries) Double Dare, 2004. Office: c/o Paradigm 360 N Crescent Dr N Bldg Beverly Hills CA 90210*

BELLA, JONATHAN N., cardiologist; b. Cotabato City, The Philippines, Apr. 12, 1965; came to U.S., 1991; s. Primitivo Jr. and Patrocinio (Noriega) B. BA in Humanities, U. of Philippines, Manila, 1985; MD, U. of East, Manila, 1989. Cert. Am. Bd. Internal Medicine, Am. Bd. Cardiovasc. Disease. Intern Atlantic City Med. Ctr., NJ, 1991-92; resident Montefiore Med. Ctr., NYC, 1992-94; fellow in cardiology N.Y. Hosp.-Cornell Med. Ctr., 1994-97; instr. medicine Weill Med. Coll. Cornell U.; fellow in echocardiography N.Y. Hosp.-Cornell Med. Ctr., 1997-98; instr. Weill Med. Coll. Cornell U.; dir. echocardiology Louis Stokes Cleve. VA Med. Ctr., 1998-2000; asst. prof. medicine Sch. Medicine Case Western Res. U., Cleve., 1998-2000; dir. echocardiology Bronx-Lebanon Hosp. Ctr., Bronx, NY, 2000—; assoc. prof. medicine Albert Einstein Coll. Medicine, 2000—; chief cardiology Bronx Lebanon Hosp. Ctr., 2005—. Fellow: Am. Soc. Echocardiography., Am. Coll. Cardiology; mem.: Am. Heart Assn. Roman Catholic. Office: Bronx-Lebanon Hosp Ctr 1650 Grand Concourse Bronx NY 10457 E-mail: jbella@bronxleb.org.

BELLAH, ROBERT NEELLY, sociologist, educator; b. Altus, Okla., Feb. 23, 1927; s. Luther Hutton and Lillian Lucille (Neelly); m. Melanie Hyman, Aug. 17, 1949; 4 children BA, Harvard U., 1950, PhD, 1955. Rsch. assoc. Inst. Islamic Studies McGill U., Montreal, Canada, 1955—57; with Harvard U., Cambridge, Mass., 1957—67, prof., 1966—67; mem. faculty dept. sociology U. Calif., Berkeley, 1967—97, Elliott prof. emeritus, 1997—. Author: Tokugawa Religion, 1957, Beyond Belief, 1970, The Broken Covenant, 1975 (Sorokin award Am. Sociol. Assn. 1976), (with Charles Y. Glock) The New Religious Consciousness, 1976, (with Phillip E. Hammond) Varieties of Civil Religion, 1980, (with others) Habits of the Heart, 1985, (with others) The Good Society, 1991, Imagining Japan, 2003, The Robert Bellah Reader, 2006. With U.S. Army, 1945-46 Fulbright fellow, 1960-61; recipient Harbison award Danforth Found., 1971, Nat. Humanities medal, 2000 Mem. Am. Acad. Arts and Scis., Am. Sociol. Assn., Am. Acad. Religion, Am. Philos. Soc Episcopalian. Office: U Calif Dept Sociology Berkeley CA 94720-1980

BELLAMY, CAROL, international organization administrator; b. Plainfield, NJ, Jan. 14, 1942; BA in Psychology, Gettysburg Coll., 1963; JD, NYU, 1968. Asst. commr. Dept. Mental Health and Mental Health Retardation Svc., NYC; with Peace Corps., Guatemala, 1963—65; assoc. Cravath, Swaine & Moore, NYC, 1968—71; mem. NY State Senate, 1973—77; pres. NYC Coun., 1978—85; prin. Morgan Stanley & Co., NYC, 1986—90; mng. dir. Bear Stearns, NYC, 1990—93; dir. Peace Corps., Washington, 1993-95; exec. dir. UNICEF, 1995—2005; pres., CEO World Learning, Brattleboro, Vt., 2005—, pres. Sch. Internat. Training, 2005—. Former trustee, NYC Pension Sys., mem., NY Met. Transit Authority, First v.p. Nat. League of Cities. Fellow, Harvard U. Kennedy Sch. Govt. Mem.: Phi Alpha Alpha. Avocation: Mets baseball fan. Office: World Learning PO Box 676 Kipling Rd Brattleboro VT 05302-0676

BELLAMY, FREDRIC, lawyer; b. Tachikawa USAF Base, Japan, Sept. 30, 1961; s. Frederick Douglas and Ran Kimura Bellamy; m. Margie Lois Shafer, Dec. 28, 2002. AB cum laude, Harvard Coll., Cambridge, Mass., 1983; JD, Harvard Law Sch., Cambridge, 1986. Bar: Ariz. 1986, US Dist. Ct., (no. dist.), Calif. 1986, US Dist. Ct., Ariz. 1987, US Ct. Appeals, (9th cir.) 1987, US Supreme Ct. 1990. Assoc. Brown and Bain, P.A., Phoenix, 1986—90, Horne, Kaplan and Bistrow, P.C., Phoenix, 1990—91, North and Barron, P.C., Phoenix, 1991—93; shareholder Beshears Wallwork Bellamy Chartered, Phoenix, 1993—2005; ptnr. Steptoe and Johnson LLP, Phoenix, 2005—. Mem., bd. dirs. Ariz. Tech. Coun., Phoenix, 2007—; spkr. in field. Pres. Ariz. Consumers Coun., Phoenix. Mem.: Ariz. State Bar Assn. (chmn. intellectual property section 1994—95, chmn. E-commerce and internet section 2001—02, former editor nviron. and natural resources law section). Home: 416 E Tierra Buena Ln Phoenix AZ 85022 Office: Steptoe and Johnson LLP 201 E Washington St Ste 1600 Phoenix AZ 85022 Home Phone: 602-789-0845; Office Phone: 602-257-5204. Office Fax: 602-257-5299. Personal E-mail: bellamy@az-law.com. Business E-Mail: fbellamy@steptoe.com.

BELLAMY, GAIL ANNE GHETIA, magazine editor, author, speaker; b. Lakewood, Ohio, Dec. 19, 1949; f. George and Janice Arlene (Fleming) Ghetia; m. Stephen Paul Bellamy, Nov. 17, 1990. BA, Ohio U., 1971; postgrad., Case Western Res. U., 1971; PhD, The Union Inst. and Univ., 2000. Exec. food editor Restaurant Hospitality mag., Cleve., 1980—. Contbg. columnist Cleve. Free Times newspaper, 1992-98; workshop presenter Dept. Cmty. Svcs., Cleve., 1993—, Lakeland CC, Mentor, Ohio, 1993-2000; dining columnist Am. Online, 1995-98, 2007—; nat. adv. bd. Culinary Arts Inst., Miss. U. for Women; contbg. editor Tableware Today mag., Bloomfield, NJ, 1997—; adj. prof. Ursuline Coll., 2000-05; tutor Empire State Coll./SUNY, 2002, 03; faculty PWLGC Literary Ctr., Cleve., 2002-. Author: Design Spirits, 1995, Victual Reality, 2000, Cleveland Food Memories, 2003; co-editor: Ohio Writer Mag., 2001—03; mem. editl. adv. bd.: Cleve. Clinic Press; contbr. chapters to books, articles to profl. jours. Vol. lectr. Write-on Cleve!, 1993—; vol. examiner Am. Radio Relay League, 1994—; bd. dirs. Ursuline Sophia Ctr., Cleve., 1999—2005. Recipient Communicators award/Merit cert. Women in Comm., 1993. Mem.: Internat. Assn. Culinary Profls., Les Dames D'Escoffier, Press Club of Cleve., Soc. Profl. Journalists, Internat. Foodsvc. Editl. Coun. (bd. dirs. 1994—95, pres. 1996, bd. dirs. 1997, 1999, sec. 2004, bd. dirs. 2004—06, Betty Bastion Outstanding Svc. award 2005), Am. Soc. Bus. Press Editors (1st pl./Editl. Ctrl. Region Competition award 1994), The Poets' and Writers' League of Greater Cleve. (pres. bd. trustees 2000—06), Am. Radio Relay League, Acad. Am. Poets. Avocations: violin, viola, mentor writing programs. Office: 1300 E 9th St Cleveland OH 44114

BELLAMY, IVORY, elementary school educator, consultant; b. Tuscaloosa, Ala., Feb. 21, 1952; d. Iverson Gandy Sr. and Betty Belle Gand; children: Cinnamon Nicole Jones, Cecily Dawn Jones. BA, Stillman Coll., Tuscaloosa, Ala., 1974. Cert. Tchr. Ala. Asst. dir. admissions U. Miami, Coral Gables, Fla., 1984—88; tchr. Fayette County Schs., Fayetteville, Ga., 1990—93, Clayton County Schs., Jonesboro, Ga., 1998—. Author (Book of Poetry): Life Is a Million Good-byes, 2005. Achievements include Founder, CEO Sisters Inc. Avocations: crafts, poetry, writing. Office: Martin Luther King Jr Elem 5745 W Lee and Mill Atlanta GA 30349 E-mail: ivorybellamy@bellsouth.net.

BELLAMY, JAMES CARL, retired insurance company executive; b. Detroit, Oct. 15, 1926; s. Robert Maxwell Belllamy and Mamie (Moery) B.; m. Marie Alice Brakebill, Jan. 20, 1951; children: James Carl, Janet Marie. BS, U. Tenn., 1950. C.L.U. Agt., asst. mgr. Nat. Life & Accident Ins. Co., Chattanooga, Louisville, 1950-58, dist. mgr. Little Rock, Nashville, 1958-73, 2d v.p. Nashville, 1973-78, v.p., 1978-82; sr. v.p., dir. Am. Gen. Life & Accident Ins. Co., Nashville, 1982-87; sr. v.p. mktg. Southlife Holding Co., Nashville, 1987-91, ret., 1991. Exec. v.p. mktg. Pub. Savs. Life Ins. Co., Charleston, S.C.; vice chmn. Security Trust Life Ins. Co., Macon, Ga., bd. dirs.; pres. Southlife Gen. Agys., Nashville; bd. dirs. Pub. Savs. Life Ins. Co., Charleston. Solicitor United Way, Nashville, 1968-74; solicitor Boy Scouts Am., 1968-74. Served with USNR, 1944-46, PTO. Mem. Nat. Assn. Life Underwriters, Nashville Assn. Life Underwriters (pres. 1970-71), Nashville Gen. Agts. and Mgrs. Assn. (pres. 1967), Ins. Mktg. Research Assn. (exec. com.), Hillwood Country Club (bd. dirs.), Univ. Club, Kiwanis, Sigma Chi. Republican. Baptist. E-mail: jasbellamy@aol.com.

BELLAMY, JOHN STARK, II, librarian, historian, writer; b. Cleve. s. Peter and Jean (Dessel) B.; m. Laura A. Serafin, Aug. 9, 1996; children: Sarah, Catherine. BA, Goddard Coll., Plainfield, Vt., 1971; M. History, U. Va., 1977; MLS, Case Western Res. U., 1978. Pub. svcs. libr. Cuyahoga County Pub. Libr., Beachwood, Ohio, 1982-89, subject specialist libr. Fairview Park, Ohio, 1989—2004. Author: Angels on the Heights, 1991, They Died Crawling, 1995, The Maniac in the Bushes, 1997, The Corpse in the Cellar, 1999, By the Neck Until Dead, 2000, The Killer in the Attic, 2002, Death Ride At Euclid Beach, 2004, Women Behaving Badly, 2005, Vintage Vermont Villainies, 2007. Mem.: Samuel Johnson Soc. Vt. Roman Catholic. Home: 135 Towle Hill Ln Corinth VT 05039 Personal E-mail: jstarkbi@tops-tele.com.

BELLAMY, RENEE ADELE, secondary school educator; b. Queens, NY, Feb. 3, 1966; d. Lloyd and Annie Mae Bellamy; 1 child, Chauncey Payne Jr. BS, Howard U., 1988; MS, Queens Coll., 1994; postgrad., Columbia U., 1996—98; advanced cert. in edn., Hunter Coll., 2003. Cert. tchr. NY, sch. adminstr., supr. NY, CPR/Automated Elec. Defibrilator, first aid. Libr. aide Howard U., Washington, 1984—87; tour guide Washington Nat. Zoo, 1985—87; HS tchr. NY Dept. Edn., Bronx, 1988—91, middle sch. tchr. Queens, 1991—, asst. prin., 2001—03. Basketball and cheerleading coach Middle Sch. 72, Queens, 1993—2001, sch. health coord., 1997—2000; coach adaptive phys. edn. NYC Dept. Edn., 2000; coach sports and fitness league Champs Mid. Sch., 2004—; coach girls crew team Middle Sch. 210, Queens, 2006—; sch. health educator facilitator, 2005—06. Cubmaster Boy Scouts Am., Queens, 1998—2001; ptnr. fundraising Spl. Olympics, NY, 2000—05; v.p. St. Peter Claver Parents Assn., Queens, 2001—02. Recipient Cert. Appreciation, Spl. Olympics, 2005. Mem.: ASCD, Am. Fedn. Tchr., Wildlife Conservation Soc., Eastern Star, Phi Delta Kappa. Achievements include creaton of Bellamy Drill and Bellamy Beat fitness routines. Avocations: gardening, dance, interior decorating, reading, coaching. Office: Middle Sch 210 93-11 101 Ave Ozone Park NY 11416

BELLAMY, WALTER, professional basketball player; Student, Ind. U., 1957-61. With Chgo. Packers, 1961-62, Balt. Bullets, 1963-66, N.Y. Knicks, 1966-68, Atlanta Hawks, 1970-74. Mem. U.S. Olympic Basketball Team, 1960. Mem. Atlanta Police Athletic League, Ga.; trustee Gate City Day Nursery Assn.; founder, 1st pres. Men of Tomorrow, Inc., Md.; bd. dirs. S.W. Youth Bus. Orgn.; membership chmn. Campbelltown/Cascade YMCA Men Internat. Club; chmn. Atlanta Labor Day Weekend Football Classic; vice chmn. College Park Bus. and Devel. Authority, Metro Atlanta Respite Svc.; bd. dirs. Gate City Day Nursery Assn., Fulton Atlanta Cmty. Action Authority. Named Rookie of Yr., 1962, Basketball Hall of Fame, 1993; winner Gold medal U.S. Olympics, 1960; named to U.S. Olympic Hall of Fame, N.C. Sports Hall of Fame, 100% Wrong Club Atlanta Hall of Fame, Ind. U. Sports Hall of Fame, NBA Hall of Fame. Mem. NAACOP (mem. exec. bd.), Ind. U. Alumni Club, Alpha Phi Alpha, Alpha Phi Omega. Achievements include mem. gold-medal-winning U.S. Olympic Team, 1960, holds single-season record for most games played-88, 1969. Address: PO Box 42751 Atlanta GA 30311-0751

BELLANCA, JOSEPH PAUL, engineering construction executive; b. Rochester, NY, Nov. 25, 1936; s. Sam and Anna (Cani) B.; m. Joy Eleanor Gaston, Dec. 5, 1964 (dec.); children: Joseph Jr., Victoria Ann Gordon, Lizabeth Ann Wilbur, Lorraine Thacker. BSCE, Purdue U., 1958. Registered profl. engr., D.C. and 10 states. Assoc./project mgr. TAMS Cons., Dallas/Ft. Worth, 1968-73, assoc./resident mgr. Washington, 1973-77; pres. Bellanca Engring. Cons., Atlanta, 1977-85; dir. Schal Assocs., Chgo., 1985-86; v.p. Greiner, Inc., Orlando (Fla.), Denver, 1986-88, Bechtel Internat. Inc., Vienna, Va., 1988-92, Turner Constrn. Co., Atlanta, 1992-98; exec. v.p. Bovis Lend Lease, Atlanta, 1998—2002; v.p. Heery Internat., 2002—. Lobbyist Airport Cons. Coun. Editor Airports--Challenges of the Future, 1973; (design compendium) World Travel Center--Detroit Met. Airport (Design award for $1 billion new air terminal complex). Named Young Engr. Yr. Mid-Cities chpt. Tex. Soc. Profl. Engrs., 1971. Mem. ASCE (sec. 1973, vice-chmn. 1979, exec. com., air transport divsn.), NSPE, Tex. Soc. Profl. Engrs. (pres. Mid-Cities chpt. 1972-73). Achievements include aifield pavement design for future 2 million pound aircraft at Dallas-Ft. Worth airport; executive-level involvement in airport development programs for Dallas-Ft. Worth, Atlanta, Chicago, Denver, Barcelona, 2-Jordan, 4-Saudi Arabia, New Seoul, and Detroit Downtown People Mover. Home: 9295 Heatherton Walk Duluth GA 30097-2492 Office: Heery Internat 999 Peachtree St Atlanta GA 30309 Office Phone: 404-946-2551. E-mail: jbellanca@bellsouth.net.

BELLANDO, JOHN W., publishing executive, accountant; b. Bklyn., May 11, 1956; s. John W. and Mildred Bellando; m. Ellen Linda Runkel, Oct. 16, 1981; children: Joseph, John, Kenneth, Katherine, Rachel. BS in Acctg., Bklyn. Coll., 1978. CPA. Pub. acct. Ernst and Young, NYC, 1978-83; mgr. corp. acctg. Macmillan, Inc., NYC, 1984—85, dir. corp. acctg., 1985-88, asst. corp. contr., 1988-90, v.p. corp. contr. Greenwich, Conn., 1991, v.p., CFO, 1993; contr. Random House, sr. v.p. finance; sr. v.p. acctg. and fin. Conde Nast Publ. Inc., NYC, 1999—2000; CFO Conde Nast Publs. Inc., NYC, 2000—04, exec. v.p., COO, 2004—; exec. v.p., CFO Advance Mag. Group, NYC, 2001—. Mem. AICPA, N.Y. Soc. CPAs. Office: Conde Nast Publications Inc 4 Times Sq New York NY 10036-6561*

BELLANGER, SERGE RENÉ, bank executive; b. Vimoutiers, France, Apr. 30, 1933; s. René Albert and Raymonde Maria (Renard) Bellanger. MBA, Paris Bus. Sch., 1957. With Citibank, 1966-73, mem. Paris br., 1966-69, world corp. rels. officer for Europe NYC, 1969-73, asst. v.p., 1969-71, v.p., 1972-73; sr. v.p., gen. mgr. Crédit Industriel et Commercial, NYC, 1974-79, exec. v.p., gen. mgr., 1979—; US gen. rep. CIC Group, NYC, 1973—, mem. exec. com., 1998—. Prof. banking French Banking Inst., 1961—64; mem. adv. com. French House Columbia U., 1976—, chmn., 1996—, mem. internat. adv. bd. Inst. Study Europe, 2002—; mem. Nat. Com. Fgn. Trade Advisors France, 1978—, exec. v.p. U.S. nat. com., 1985—93, bd. dirs. nat. com., 1987—2002, v.p. U.S. nat. com., 1992—93, mem. Paris exec. com., 1994—95; chmn. internat. banking course New Sch. Social Rsch., NYC, 1981—83; dir. Am. Ctr. Paris, 1985—93; mem. adv. com. Ctr. Study French Civilization and Culture NYU, NYC, 1988—2000; mem. adv. bd. French Inst. Culture and Tech. U. Pa., 1992—, chmn. adv. bd., 1992—95; mem. adv. bd. Lycée Francais, NY, 2000—; mem. Adv. Coun. French Abroad, 2000; mem. exec. com. Fedn. French Vets., 2001—; bd. dirs. Ubifrance, 2002—, French Ctr. Fgn. Trade, Banque Transatlantique, 2002—; pres. Grand Marnier Found., 2004—. With French Air Force, 1958—60. Decorated Algeria Commemorative medal, comdr. Legion of Honor, Nat. Order of Merit. Mem.: Bank Adminstrn. Inst. (mem. editl. bd. World Banking Mag. 1981—87, columnist Banker's Mag. 1986—96), NY Cotton Exch. (bd. dirs. fin. instrument exch. divsn. 1985—95), NY Futures Exch. (dir. 1980—87, chmn. fgn. exch. com. 1981—82), Banque de l'Union Européenne (bd. dirs. 1989—90), Assn. Promotion French Sci., Industry and Tech. (pres. 1986—91), Lyonnaise de Banque (bd. dirs. 1986—89), Inst. Internat. Bankers (trustee 1975—77, v.p. 1977—79, chmn. legis. and regulatory com. 1977—79, chmn. 1979—80), French Overseas Assn., European-Am. Bus. Coun. (bd. dirs. Washington 1991—), Food and Wine France (bd. dirs. 1983—93), FCC Partnership and C. of C. (ptnr. 1991—), Assn. French C. of C. and Industry Abroad (adminstr. 1984—, v.p. 1989—95, 1st v.p. 1995—99, pres. 1999—), NY C. of C. (mem. internat. bus. initiative 1994—95), French-Am. C. of C. (councillor 1973—74, mem. exec. com. 1974—80, v.p. 1980—82, exec. v.p. 1982—83, nat. pres. 1983—, pres. NY chpt. 1983—), European-Am. C. of C. (pres., CEO 1990—96, hon. chmn. 1996—), Automobile Club de France, River Club, Univ. Club. Home: 860 U N Plz Apt 23/24C New York NY 10017-1810 Office: 37th Floor 520 Madison Ave New York NY 10022-4213 Office Phone: 212-715-4444. Business E-Mail: sbellanger@cicny.com.

BELLARDO, LEWIS JOSEPH, JR., archivist; b. 1943; m. Lynn Lady Bellardo. Archivist Ky. Dept. Libraries & Archives, Frankfort, 1980—86; dir. Ctr. for Legis. Archives The Nat. Archives & Records Adminstrn., College Park, Md., 1989—90, dir. preservation policy & svcs. divsn., 1990—95, dep. asst. archivist, 1993—95, acctg. asst. archivist for presdl. libacrs., 1995—96, dep. archivist, chief of staff, 1996—. Fellow: Soc. Am. Archivists; mem.: Nat. Assn. Govt. Archives & Records Administrators (sec. 1981—82, v.p. 1982—84, pres. 1984—86). Office: The Nat Archives & Records Adminstrn 8601 College Pk College Park MD 20740 E-mail: lewis.bellardo@arch1.nara.gov.

BELLAS, ALBERT CONSTANTINE, investment executive; b. Steubenville, Ohio, Sept. 15, 1942; s. Constantine Michael and Kiki (Michalopoulos) B.; m. Kay Mazzo, Dec. 21, 1978; children: Andrew James, Kathryn Kiki. BA, Yale U., New Haven, Conn., 1964; JD, U. Chgo., 1967; MBA, Columbia U., NYC, 1968. Summer intern The White House, Washington, 1963; assoc. Dillon, Read & Co., Inc., NYC, 1968-72; v.p. Goldman Sachs & Co., NYC, 1973-76; gen. ptnr. Loeb Rhoades & Co., NYC, 1976-78; sr. exec. v.p. Shearson Lehman Bros., NYC, 1979—91; bd. dirs. Lehman Bros., NYC, 1981—91; mng. dir. Offitbank, NYC, 1992—2000; chmn., CEO Neuberger Berman Trust Co., NYC, 2000—03; mng. dir. Neuberger Berman, LLC, NYC, 2000—03; CEO The Solaris Group, LLC, 2004—. Allied mem. NY Stock Exch., 1976-92; invest com. Soc. Neurosci., 2005-. Trustee St. Mary's Found. for Children, 1999—2002, Lenfest Found., 2000—03, Statue of Liberty-Ellis Island Found., 2002—, investment com. NYC, 2002—; bd. mgmt. Century Assn., NYC, 2002—06, treas., 2002—06; day sch. com. Brick Ch., NYC, 1985—88; bd. regents Mercersburg Acad., Pa., 1992—, exec. com., 1993—, chmn. fin. com., 1994—; bd. dirs. Lincoln Ctr. Performing Arts, NYC, 1987—, audit com., 1989—; bd. dirs. Sch. Am. Ballet, NYC, 1975—86, chmn., 1987—2004, chmn. emeritus, 2004—; bd. dirs. Guild Hall, 1990—96, 1998—, fin. com., 1998—; bd. dirs. Partnership Children's Rights, 2006—, Pilgrims of US, 2007—. McKinsey scholar, 1968. Mem.: ABA, Ohio Bar Assn., Econs. Club NY, Brook Club, Univ. Club, Maidstone Club. Avocation: tennis. Home: 1130 Park Ave New York NY 10128-1255 Office: 598 Madison Ave 15th Fl New York NY 10022 E-mail: bellas@solarisgroupllc.com.

BELLATTI, LAWRENCE LEE, lawyer; b. Oklahoma City, Apr. 19, 1944; s. Lawrence Fitzhugh and Esther Lee (Swank) Bellatti; m. Barbara Gail Wolfinger, June 25, 1977; children: Julie M., Jenny E., Jill N. BS, Okla. State U., 1966; JD, Okla. U., 1969. Bar: Okla. 1969, Tex. 1974, U.S. Dist. Ct. (so., we, ea. and no. dists.) Tex., U.S. Dist. Ct. (no., we. and ea. dists.) Okla., U.S. Ct. Mil. Appeals, U.S. Ct. Appeals (5th cir., 10th and 11th cirs.). Assoc. Andrews, Kurth, Campbell & Jones, Houston, 1974-80; ptnr. Andrews Kurth LLP, Houston, 1980—. Bd. dirs. Samaritan Counseling Ctrs., Inc., Houston, 1984—2001. Mem. Harris County Flood Control Dist. Task Force, Houston, 1984. Lt. comdr. JAGC USNR, 1969—74. Mem.: Houston Bar Assn., Okla. Bar Assn., State Bar Tex., Order of Coif, Phi Delta Phi, Sigma Chi, Phi Kappa Phi. Republican. Baptist. Office: Andrews Kurth LLP 600 Travis St Ste 4200 Houston TX 77002-2910 Office Phone: 713-220-4196.

BELL BURNELL, S. JOCELYN (SUSAN JOCELYN BELL), astrophysicist, physics professor; b. U.K., July 15, 1943; d. G. Philip and M. Allison (Kennedy) Bell; m. Martin Burnell, Dec. 21, 1989 (div. 1993); 1 child, Gavin. BSc, Glasgow U., Scotland, 1965; PhD, Cambridge U., Eng., 1968; DSc (hon.), Heriot-Watt U., Scotland, 1993; DUniv (hon.), U. York, Eng., 1994; DSc (hon.), U. Warwick, Eng., 1995, U. Newcastle, 1995, U. Cambridge, 1996, U. Glasgow, 1997, U. Sussex., 1997; DSc (hon.), St. Andrews U., 1999, U. London, 1999, Haverford Coll., Pa., 2000, Leeds U., England, 2000, Williams Coll., Mass., 2000, U. Portsmouth, 2001, Queen's U., Belfast, 2001, U. Edinburgh, 2003, Keele U., 2005; MA, U. Oxford,

England, 2006. Fellow U. Southampton, 1968-73; programmer, fellow Mullard Space Sci. Lab., 1974-82; head of James Clerk Maxwell Telescope sect. Royal Observatory Edinburgh, 1982-91; prof., chair physics dept. Open U., Milton Keynes, 1991-99; dean sci. U. Bath, 2001—04; vis. prof. Oxford U., 2004—, fellow Mansfield Coll. Mem. policy making and peer rev. coms. Sci. and Engring., and Particle Physics and Astronomy Rsch. Couns., Eng., 1978—; fgn. mem. Onsala Space Observatory Nat. Bd., Sweden, 1995-2002; chair physics tng. panel European Commn., 1996-98; mem. Open Univ. Coun., 1997-99; vis. prof. Princeton U., NJ, 1999-2000. Author: Broken for Life, 1989; editor: Next Generation Infrared Space Observatory, 1992; contbr. articles to profl. jours. Mem. Quaker rep. Brit. Coun. Chs., 1978-90; mem. planning com. Edinburgh Sci. Festival, 1991-96; role model, spokesperson, rep., promoter Advancement of Women in Sci. Recipient Michelson award Franklin Inst., 1973, J. Robert Oppenheimer Meml. prize Ctr. for Theoretical Studies, 1978, Rennie Taylor award Am. Tentative Soc., 1978, Jansky award, Nat. Radio Astronomy Observatory, 1995, hon. fellowship New Hall, Cambridge, 1996, Comdr. Brit. Empire, 1999, Edinburgh medal, 1999. Fellow Royal Astron. Soc. (coun. 1978-81, 92-95, v.p. 1995-97, award 1969, Herschel medal 1989, pres. 2002-04), Inst. Physics (award 1992), Royal Soc. of Arts London (Herschel medal 1989); mem. Am. Astron. Soc. (Beatrice M. Tinsley prize 1987), Internat. Astron. Union (award 1979), NAS (fgn. assoc.), Am. Philos. Soc. Avocations: swimming, walking, quaker activites, needlecrafts, choral music. Office: Mansfield College Oxford Univ Oxford OX1 3TF England Office Fax: 44 (0) 1865 273390. E-mail: jocelyn@astro.ox.ac.uk.

BELLER, GARY A., lawyer, former insurance company executive; b. NYC, Oct. 16, 1938; s. Charles W. and Jeanne A. B.; m. Carole P. Wrubel, Nov. 22, 1967; 1 child, Jessie Melissa. BA, Cornell U., 1960; LLB, NYU, 1963, LLM, 1971. Bar: N.Y. 1963. Various positions gen. counsel's office Am. Express Co., NYC, 1968-82, exec. v.p., gen. counsel, 1983-94; exec. v.p., chief legal officer Met. Life Ins. Co., NYC, 1995—2003; sr. legal counsel Marsh & McLennan Cos. Inc., NYC, 2004—07; ptnr. fin. services practice Goodwin Procter LLP, NYC, 2007—. Bd. dirs. Lenox Hill Neighborhood Assn.; chmn. Citizens' Crime Commn. N.Y., 1990-2000 Mem. ABA, Assn. Bar City N.Y. Office: Goodwin Procter LLP 599 Lexington Ave New York NY 10022 E-mail: gbeller@goodwinprocter.com.*

BELLER, GEORGE A., cardiologist, educator; b. NYC, Dec. 23, 1940; children: Michael, Amy, Leslie, Ray Wadlow, Jeff Wadlow. MD, U. Va., 1966. Diplomate Am. Bd. Internal Medicine. Chief cardiovasc. divsn., prof. cardiology and internal medicine U. Va. Health Sys., Charlottesville, 1977—2004; pres. clin. staff U. Va. Med. Ctr., 1999—2005. Editor-in-chief: Jour. Nuc. Cardiology, 2003—; contbr. articles to profl. jours. Maj. M.C., U.S. Army, 1970-73. Maj. US Army, 1970—73. Recipient Disting. Achievement award, Am. Heart Assn., Herrick award, 2000. Mem. Am. Soc. Clin. Investigation, Am. Fedn. Clin. Rsch., Assn. Am. Physicians, Am. Coll. Cardiology (chmn. bd. govs. 1994-95, pres. 2000), Assn. Profs. Cardiology (pres. 1995). Home: 714 Rugby Rd Charlottesville VA 22903 Office: U Va Health Sys Box 800158 Charlottesville VA 22908 Business E-Mail: gbeller@virginia.edu.

BELLER, HERBERT N., lawyer; b. Ill., 1943; BSBA, Northwestern U., 1964, JD cum laude, 1967. Bar: Ill. 1967, D.C. 1969; CPA, Ill. Law clk. to Hon. Theodore Tannenwald, Jr. U.S. Tax Ct., 1967-68; ptnr. Sutherland, Asbill & Brennan, Washington. Adj. prof. law Georgetown U., Washington, 1972-81; mem. adv. coun. IRS, 2007—. Editor-in-chief: The Tax Lawyer, 1993-96. Mem. ABA (mem. sect. taxation, vice chair 1993-96, chair 2002-03, mem. coun. 1989-92, liaison to AICPA tax div. 1998-2000, chmn. govt. submissions com. 1988-89, chmn. closely held corps. com. 1981-83), Am. Coll. Tax Counsel (regent 2000-06), D.C. Bar Assn., Ill. State Bar Assn., Nat. Conf. Lawyers and CPAs (co-chair 2003-06), Am. Tax Policy Inst. (trustee 2003-05). Office: Sutherland Asbill & Brennan LLP 1275 Pennsylvania Ave NW Washington DC 20004

BELLER, LUANNE EVELYN, retired accountant; b. Ft. Dodge, Iowa, Feb. 5, 1950; d. Gerald L. and Evelyn E. (Liston) Heyl; m. Stephen M. Beller, June 28, 1970; children: Clancy Dee, Corby Lu. BA, Oreg. State U., 1977; MBA, Rochester Inst. Tech., 1981. CPA, Ill. Plant acct. DuBois Plastic Products, Avon, N.Y., 1977-79; coll. acct. SUNY, Geneseo, 1979-81; gen. acctg. supr. MasterFoods, USA (formerly M&M/Mars, Inc.), Cleveland, Tenn., 1981—83, Hackettstown, NJ, 1983—84, sales rep. Jacksonville, Ill., 1984—86, terr. sales supr., 1986—88; gen. acctg. coord. MasterFoods USA (formerly Kal Kan Foods, Inc.), Columbus, Ohio, 1988-90, fin. info. coord., 1990-92, gen. acctg. supr., 1992-97, site svc. and fin. mgr., 1997—2004; ret., 2004. Vol. Girl Scouts U.S.A., Jacksonville, 1985—88, Bexley, Ohio, 1988—2004, Kid's Inc., Crossville, Tenn., 2006—, Seashore Learning Ctr., Corpus Christi, Tex., 2006—; mem. sound control com. Bexley United Meth. Ch., 1989—2001, chair edn. com., 1998—2001, mem. edn. com., 1996—2004, LOGOS vol., 1996—2002, mem. diversity team, 2001—02; com. mem. Meth. Theol. Sch. Ohio Partnership, 2001—02; vol. children's programs St. John's United Meth. Ch., Corpus Christi, 2005—, Fairfield Glade United Meth. Ch., 2006—. Mem. Phi Kappa Phi, Beta Gamma Sigma, Beta Alpha Psi. Democrat. Avocation: reading.

BELLER, MARTIN LEONARD, retired orthopaedic surgeon; b. NYC, Apr. 30, 1924; s. Abraham Jacob and Ida (Fishkin) B.; m. Wilma Gertrude Kjelgaard, June 29, 1947; children: Alan Lewis, Beatrice Ann Beller Foreman Heck, Peter James. AB with honors, Columbia U., 1944, MD, 1946. Diplomate Am. Bd. Orthopaedic Surgery. Intern Mt. Sinai Hosp., NYC, 1946-47; resident in orthopaedic surgery Hosp. Joint Diseases, NYC, 1949-52; pvt. practice Phila., 1952-87; asst. prof. orthopaedic surgery U. Pa. Sch. Medicine, Phila., 1967-72, assoc. prof., 1972-80, clin. prof., 1980-87; ret., 1987. Attending orthopaedic surgeon Hosp. U. Pa., 1963-87; assoc. attending orthopaedic surgeon Albert Einstein Med. Center, Phila., 1960-70; chmn. dept. orthopaedic surgery Albert Einstein Med. Center (Daroff divsn.), 1970-79. Author (with I. Stein and R. O. Stein): Living Bone in Health and Disease, 1955; author: (with I. Stein) Clinical Densitometry of Bone, 1970. Vestryman Episcopal Ch., 1966—87, 1990—93, 1996—99, 2002—05, 2007—; trustee St. Paul's Episcopal Ch., Wellsboro, Pa., 1999—. Am. Orthopaedic Assn. exchange fellow, Gt. Britain, 1963. Fellow ACS, Am. Acad. Orthopaedic Surgeons (bd. councilors 1978-81, Pa. rep. commn. on trauma 1984-87), Internat. Soc. Orthopaedic Surgery and Traumatology; mem. Am. Orthopaedic Assn., Pa. Orthopaedic Soc. (pres. 1975-77), Orthopaedic Rsch. Soc., Am. Coll. Rheumatology, NY Acad. Sci., Phi Beta Kappa, Alpha Omega Alpha, Phi Delta Epsilon (nat. pres. 1975-76, chmn. bd. trustees 1984-85, assoc. exec. sec. 1991-95, exec. com. 1995—), Union League Phila. (life), Tyoga Country Club (Wellsboro, Pa.). Republican. Home: 2415 Rt 6 Gaines PA 16921-9505

BELLER, STEPHEN MARK, retired academic administrator; b. Chgo., Aug. 14, 1948; s. I.E. and De Vera (Jameson) B.; m. Luanne Evelyn Heyl, June 28, 1970; children: Clancy Dee, Corby Lu. BS, U. Ill., 1970; MS, Western Ill. U., 1972; PhD, Oregon State U., 1977. Asst. head ed. Awards of Rotary Found., Evanston, Ill., 1972-73; asst. dean of students SUNY, Geneseo, N.Y., 1977-81; dean of student svcs. Tenn. Wesleyan Coll., Athens, 1981-83, MacMurray Coll., Jacksonville, Ill., 1984-88, Capital U., Columbus, Ohio, 1988-99, v.p., dean of student svcs., 1999—2003, v.p. emeritus, 2003—. Mem.: Phi Delta Kappa, Phi Kappa Phi. Methodist. Avocations: railroading, photography. Home: PO Box 18268 Corpus Christi TX 78480-8268 Business E-Mail: sbeller@capital.edu.

BELLET, PAUL SANDERS, pediatrician, educator; b. Phila., June 28, 1945; BA, Johns Hopkins U., 1967; MD, U. Rochester, 1971. Diplomate Am. Bd. Pediat. Intern in pediat. Cleve. Met. Gen. Hosp., 1971-72; resident in pediat. Case Western Res., Cleve., 1972-73, fellow in pediat. cardiology, 1973-75; pediatrician USAF/Maxwell AFB Regional Hosp., Montgomery, Ala., 1975-77; asst. prof. pediat. U. Ala., Tuscaloosa, 1977-81, assoc. prof. of pediat., 1981-83; assoc. prof. pediat. Children's Hosp. Med. Ctr./U. Cin. Coll. Medicine, Cin., 1983-94, prof. pediat., 1994—2004, prof. emeritus pediat., 2004—. Author: The Diagnostic Approach to Symptoms and Signs in Pediatrics, 2d edit., 2002. Fellow Am. Acad. Pediat.; mem. Ambulatory Pediat. Assn., Cin. Pediat. Soc. Office: Cin Children's Hosp Med Ctr 3333 Burnet Ave Cincinnati OH 45229-3039 Home Phone: 513-772-8627; Office Phone: 513-636-4506. Business E-Mail: paul.bellet@cchmc.org.

BELLEVILLE, PHILIP FREDERICK, lawyer; b. Flint, Mich., Apr. 24, 1934; s. Frederick Charles and Sarah (Adelaine) B.; m. Geraldean Bickford, Sept. 2, 1953; children: Stacy L., Philip Frederick II, Jeffrey A. BA in Econs. with high distinction and honors, U. Mich., 1956, JD, 1960, MS in Psychology CCU, 1997. Bar: Calif. 1961. Assoc. Latham & Watkins, LA., 1960-68, ptnr. L.A. and Newport Beach, Calif., 1968-98, chmn. litigation dept., 1973-80, ptnr. L.A., Newport Beach, San Diego, Washington, 1980-98, Chgo., 1983-98, NYC, 1985-98, London and San Francisco, 1990-98, Moscow, 1992-98, Hong Kong, 1995-98, Tokyo, 1995-98, Singapore, 1997-98, Silicon Valley, 1997-98. Mem. diversion evaluation com. Calif. Med. Bd., 2006—; mem. evaluation com. State Bar Lawyer's Assistance Program, 2003—06, mem. oversight com., 2006—, vice chmn., 2007—. Past mem. So. Calif. steering com. NAACP Legal Def. Fund, Inc.; cmty. adv. bd. San Pedro Peninsula Hosp., 1980—88; bd. dirs. Harbor Interfaith, 2001—, chmn. bd., 2004—06, pres., 2007; bd. dirs. House of Hope, 2004—, pres., 2006—. James B. Angell scholar U. Mich., 1955-56 Mem. ABA, State Bar Calif., LA County Bar Assn., Order of Coif, Portuguese Bend (Calif.) Club, Palos Verdes (Calif.) Golf Club, Caballeros, Phi Beta Kappa, Phi Kappa Phi, Alpha Kappa Psi Avocations: antique and classic automobiles, sports, art, antiques. Home Phone: 310-541-5256.

BELLIN, HOWARD, management consultant; b. NYC, Oct. 30, 1933; arrived in Australia, 1961; s. Paul and Anna (Sterner); m. Barbara Ann Box, May 12, 1962; children: Sara Lea, Paul. BSMetE, Carnegie Mellon U., Pitts., 1955. Trainee Great Lakes Steel Corp., Detroit, 1955; dept. mgr. Kelsey Hayes Corp., Detroit, 1955-57; from indsl. engr. to dept. mgr. Gillette Co., Boston, 1957-64; factory mgr. Allied Corp., Richmond, Va., 1964-65, Sydney, Australia, 1966-67; mng. dir. Avin Plating, Melbourne, Australia, 1967-69; founder, chmn. IF Cons., Melbourne, 1969—. Presenter in field. Mem. editl. bd. Jour. Mktg. Channels; contbr. articles to profl. jours. Active Franchising Cons. divsn. Australian Consumer and Competition Commn. With US Army, 1957. Mem. Am. Club. Liberal. Jewish. Avocations: exercise, jogging, photography, reading, history. Home: 17 Moule Ave Brighton 3186 Victoria Australia Office: I F Cons PO Box 446 3186 Brighton Victoria Australia Office Phone: 61-3-9596-0074. Business E-Mail: hbellin@i-f.com.

BELLINGER, EDGAR THOMSON, lawyer; b. NYC, Sept. 23, 1929; s. John and Margaret (Thomson) B.; children from previous marriage: Edgar Jr., Robert, Margaret; m. Ann Clark, Feb. 25, 1989. BA, Haverford Coll., 1951; JD with honors, George Washington U., 1955. Bar: DC 55, Md. 1955. Law clk. to chief judge U.S. Dist. Ct. D.C., 1955-57; asst. U.S. aty for Washington, 1957-59; ptnr. Pope, Ballard & Loos, Washington, 1959-81, Zuckert, Scoutt and Rasenberger, Washington, 1981-94, Bellinger & Assocs., Washington and Md., 1995—. Chmn. unauthorized practice com. DC Ct. Appeals, 1972-78, orgn. com., 1972; mem. DC jud. conf., 1972-90; bd. mgrs. Chevy Chase Village, 1983-86 Mem. ABA (fidelity and surety coms., forum on constrn. industry, past chmn. bonds, liens and ins. divsns.), Am. Arbitration Assn. (panel of arbitrators), Md. Bar Assn., Talbot County Bar Assn., Nat. Assn. Securities Dealers (panel of arbitrators), Met. Club, Chevy Chase Club (bd. govs. 1972-77, pres. 1976-77). Home: 4791 Sailors Retreat Rd Oxford MD 21654 Office Phone: 410-819-0023.

BELLINGER, JOHN B., III, lawyer, federal official; b. Paris, Mar. 28, 1960; s. John B., Jr. and Anne Taliaferro (Tynes) Bellinger; m. Caroline Dawn Renzy, June 9, 1984; children: Catharine Meade, Ann Thomson. AB, Princeton U., 1982; JD, Harvard U., 1986; MA, U. Va., 1991. Assoc. Shaw, Pittman, Potts & Trowbridge, Washington, 1986—88; spl. asst. to dir. CIA, Washington, 1988-91; assoc., then spl. counsel Wilmer, Cutler & Pickering, Washington, 1991-95; gen. counsel Commn. Roles and Capabilities US Intelligence Cmty., 1995—96; spl. counsel senate select com. on intelligence U.S. Senate, Washington, 1996; sr. counsel for nat. security matters criminal divsn. US Dept. Justice, Washington, 1997-2001; sr. assoc. counsel to Pres., The White House, Washington, 2001—05, legal adviser to NSC, 2001—05; sr. adviser to sec. US Dept. State, Washington, 2005, legal adviser, 2005—. Bd. govs. St. Albans Sch., Washington, 1997—2004, vice chmn., 2003—04; vestryman St. Mary's Episcopal Ch., Arlington, Va., 1991—94, sr. warden, 1993—94. Fellow, Brit.-Am. Project. Mem.: Am. Coun. Germany, Coun. Fgn. Rels. Office: US Dept State Harrry S Truman Bldg 2201 C St NW Rm 6423 Washington DC 20520 Office Phone: 202-647-9598.

BELLINI, FRANCESCO, chemist; b. Ascoli, Piceno, Italy, Nov. 20, 1947; s. Berardino Bellini; m. Marisa Bellini; children: Roberto, Carlo. Diploma in chem. engring., I.T.I.S., Italy, 1967; BSc in Chemistry, Coll. Loyola, Montreal, Que., Can., 1972; PhD in Organic Chemistry, U. N.B., Can., 1977. Rsch. asst. Ayerst Labs., 1968-74, postdoctoral fellow, 1977-79, sr. scientist, 1979-81, rsch. assoc., 1981-84; dir. biochems. divsn. Institut Armand Frappier, Laval, Que., 1984-86; pres., CEO Biochem Pharma Inc., Laval, Que., Canada, 1986—2001; chmn., CEO Biochem. Pharma Inc., Laval, Que., Canada, 2001—, Picchio Pharma and Picchio Internat., 2001—; chmn., pres., CEO Neurochem, 2002—. Chmn. Adaltis, 1992—, Innodia, 2003—, Virochem, 2004—; bd. dirs. Molson-Coors Inc. Contbr. numerous articles to profl. jours. Achievements include patents on angiotensin conberting enzyme inhibitors; discovery of 6-(lower alkoxy)-5- (trifluorimenthyl) -1-naphtalene -carboxylic acid, known and Tolrestat, used as an aldose reductase inhibitor; co-author of 20 patents.

BELLIS, CARROLL JOSEPH, surgeon, educator; b. Shreveport, La. s. Joseph and Rose (Bloome) B.; m. Mildred Darmody, Dec. 26, 1939; children: Joseph, David. BS summa cum laude, U. Minn., 1930, MS in Physiology, 1932, PhD in Physiology, 1934, MD, 1936, PhD in Surgery, 1941. Diplomate Am. Bd. Surgery, cert. Internat. Bd. Proctology, Internat. Bd. Surgery. Fellow in physiology U. Minn., Mpls., 1930-34; resident in surgery U. Minn. Hosps., Mpls., 1937-41; pvt. practice surgery Long Beach, Calif., 1945-95. Prof., chmn. dept. surgery Calif. Coll. Medicine, 1962—; surg. cons. to surgeon gen. U.S. Army; adj. prof. surgery U. Calif. Author: Fundamentals of Human Physiology, A Critique of Reason, Lectures in Medical Physiology; contbr. numerous articles on surgery and physiology to profl. jours. Served to col. M.C. AUS, 1941-46. Recipient Charles Lyman Green prize in physiology, 1934, prize Mpls. Surg. Soc., 1938, ann. award Mississippi Valley Med. Soc., 1955; Alice Shevlin fellow U. Minn., 1932-34. Fellow: ACS, Peripheral Vascular Soc. Am. (founding), Internat. Acad. Proctology, Nat. Cancer Inst., Phlebology Soc. Am., Gerontol. Soc., Am. Med. Writers Assn., Internat. Coll. Surgeons, Royal Soc. Medicine, Am. Coll. Gastroenterology, Internat. Coll. Angiology (sci. coun.), Am. Soc. Abdominal Surgeons; mem.: AAAS, Pan Am. Med. Assn. (diplomate), Indsl. Med. Assn., Pan Pacific Surg. Assn., Am. Assn. History Medicine, Irish Med. Assn., Am. Geriatrics Soc., Hollywood Acad. Medicine, N.Y. Acad. Scis., Miss. Valley Med. Soc., Am. Assn. Study Neoplastic Diseases, Alpha Omega Alpha, Sigma Xi, Phi Beta Kappa. Home: PMB 808 904 Silver Spur Rd Rolling Hills Estates CA 90274

BELLISARIO, DOMENIC, lawyer; b. Pitts., May 14, 1953; s. Domenic and Mary (Murgia) B. BA, U. Pitts., 1975, JD, 1978. Bar: Pa. 1978, U.S. Dist. Ct. (we. dist.) Pa. 1978, U.S. Dist. Ct. (no. dist.) Ohio 1999, U.S. Ct. Appeals (3d cir.) 1985, U.S. Ct. Appeals (6th cir.) 2002, U.S. Supreme Ct. 2004. Trial atty. Nat. Labor Rels. Bd., Pitts., 1978-83; human resource counsel Western Res. Care Sys., Youngstown, Ohio, 1986-89; ptnr. Bellisario & Pontier, Pitts., 1984-90; pvt. practice Pitts., 1991—. Author: Preventing and Defending Sexual Harassment Claims in Pennsylvania, 1996, Basic Wage and Hour Law in Pennsylvania, 1997. Mem. coun. Nat. Italian Am. Found., Washington, 1991. Mem. ABA, Am. Arbitration Assn. (arbitrator), Nat. Italian Am. Found., Pa. Bar Assn., Allegheny County Bar Assn., Pa. Trial Lawyers Assn., Italian Cultural Heritage Soc. West Pa. Avocations: travel, skiing. Office: 1000 Law & Finance Bldg Pittsburgh PA 15219 Office Phone: 412-471-6463. Business E-Mail: domenic@bellisario.com.

BELLISSIMO, MARY E., art educator; b. Ellwood City, Pa., Oct. 26, 1955; d. James J. and Inese Bellissimo. BSEd Art Edn., Indiana U. of Pa., 1977; MSEd Classroom Tech., Wilkes U., 2004. Long range planner and tchr. of gifted Laurel Sch. Dist., Pa., 1978—79; art tchr. Easton Area Sch. Dist., 1979—. Mem.: Lehigh Valley Arts Coun., Easton Edn. Assn., NEA, St. Jane Frances de Chantal Ch., Pa. State Edn. Assn. Avocations: gardening, travel, social orgns. Home: 2529 Madison Ave Bethlehem PA 18017-3872 Office: Easton Area Sr High Sch 2601 William Penn Hwy Easton PA 18045

BELLIVEAU, GERARD JOSEPH, JR., librarian; b. Waltham, Mass., May 27, 1940; s. Gerard Joseph and Mary Teresa (Reilly) B. BA in English Lit., Boston Coll., 1963; MA in Philosophy, Boston U., 1972; MLS in Libr. Svc., Rutgers U., 1973. Lectr. U. Rouen (France), 1965-66; philosophy bibliographer Boston Pub. Libr., Boston, 1967-68; asst. libr. Racquet & Tennis Club: Libr. of Sport, NYC, 1971-78, head libr., 1979—; libr. gen. rsch. div. N.Y. Pub. Libr., NYC, 1973-79, libr. in charge gen. rsch. div., 1980-81, asst. chief pub. catalog sect. gen. rsch. div., 1981-88, asst. chief libr. gen. rsch., 1988-95. Mem. coop. acquisitions program com. METRO Ref. and Rsch. Libr. Agy., N.Y.C., 1984-88, chair coop. acquisitions program com., 1985-86, mem. resources devel. com., 1986-89. Bd. dirs. Peabody-Mason Music Found., Boston, 1972-87. Mem. Williams Club. Democrat. Avocations: architecture, travel, french medieval history. Office: Racquet & Tennis Club Libr 370 Park Ave New York NY 10022-5968

BELLIZZI, JOHN J., law enforcement association administrator, pharmacist, educator; b. NYC, July 26, 1919; s. Francis X. and Carmela (Bruno) B.; m. Celeste Morga, Sept. 1, 1942; children: John J. Jr., Robert F. PhG, St. John's U., NYC, 1939; LLB, Albany Law Sch., 1960; JD, Union U., 1968; LLD, St. John's U., 1981. Pharmacist St. Luke's Hosp., NYC, 1939-44; police officer N.Y.C. Police Dept., 1944-53; narcotics agt. N.Y. Bur. Narcotics Enforcement, NYC, 1953-59, dir. Albany, 1959-81; exec. dir. N.Y. State Drug Abuse Commn., Albany, 1981-84, Internat. Narcotics Enforcement Assn., Albany, 1984—. Prof. pharmacy law St. John's U., N.Y.C., 1962-76; lectr. in field. Contbr. articles to profl. jours. Recipient Papal medal Vatican, 1965. Mem. Internat. Narcotics Enforcement Officers Assn. (pres. 1960-62, Anslinger medal 1979, chmn. law enforcement com. Paramount Pictures, 1972-75, Svc. award 1975), Ft. Orange Club, Albany Country Club, Univ. Club (Albany), Am. Friends of Law Enforcement Found. (bd. dirs., sec. Japanese), Phi Alpha Delta, Phi Sigma Chi (pres. 1939), Sigma Chi (fellow). Address: 15 Rusfield Dr Glenmont NY 12077 Home Phone: 518-439-5129; Office Phone: 518-463-4569.

BELLM, JOAN, civic worker; b. Alton, Ill., June 20, 1934; d. Harvey Jacob and Alma Lorene (Roberts) Goldsby; m. Earl David Bellm, Oct. 1, 1955; children: David, Lori, Michael. Bd. dirs. Drug Watch Internat., 1991-02, lifetime hon. dir., 1998—; exec. dir. Ctr. for Drug Info., 1998—. Editor Best of IDEA newsletter, 1991-96, Drug Watch World News, 1996-02; chmn. Drug Watch Internat. editl. rev. com., 1996-02; columnist weekly newspaper, 1998—. Organist, dir. jr. choir St. Mary's Cath. Ch., 1958-78; mem. adv. bd. Carlinville (Ill.) Area Hosp., 1981-86; trustee Blackburn Coll., Carlinville, 1983-86; bd. dirs. Cath. Children's Home, Diocese of Springfield, Ill., 1986—; founder, bd. dirs., state networker Ill. Drug Edn. Alliance, 1982-86, pres., 1987-89; bd. dirs., nat. networker Nat. Fedn. Parents for Drug-Free Youth, Washington, 1984-86; mem. Ill. Gov.'s Adv. Coun. on Alcoholism and Substance Abuse, 1989-93; dir. Ctr. for Drug Info., 1998—; founder Drug Watch Internat., 1991, Internat. Drug Strategy Inst., 1993, invited participant Internat. Private Sector Conf. on Drugs, Seville, 1993, advisor U.N. Internat. Drug Ctrl. Program, 1994; numerous others. Recipient letter of endorsement Pres. of U.S., 1981, citation of recognition Ill. Dept., Am. Legion, 1981, Meritorious Svc. award, 1982, award Ill. Drug Edn. Alliance award, 1984, Southwestern Ill. Law Enforcement Commn., 1984, Carlinville Sch. Bd., 1985, Outstanding Svc. award Nat. Fedn. Parents, 1986, award Ill. Alcohol and Drug Dependence Assn., 1986, Optimist Internat., 1987, Ill. Drug Edn. Alliance, 1988, Outstanding Citizen award Blackburn U., 1989, Citizen of Yr. award, Carlinville, 1990; Leadership award Drug Watch Internat., 2001.

BELLO, MARIA ELANA, actress; b. Norristown, Pa., Apr. 18, 1967; 1 child, Jackson Blue McDermott. BS in Polit. Sci., Villanova U. Co-founder Harlem's Dream Yard Drama Project, 1992. Actress: (off-Broadway plays) include The Killer Inside Me, Small Town Gals With Big Problems, Urban Planning; film appearances include Maintenance, 1992, Permanent Midnight, 1998, Payback, 1999, Coyote Ugly, 2000, Duets, 2000, Sam the Man, 2000, China: The Panda Adventure, 2001, Auto Focus, 2002, 100 Mile Rule, 2002, The Cooler, 2003, Nobody's Perfect, 2004, Secret Window, 2004, Silver City, 2004, Assault on Precinct 13, 2005, A History of Violence, 2005, The Sisters, 2005, The Dark, 2005, Thank You for Smoking, 2006, World Trade Center, 2006, Flicka, 2006; (TV films) The Commish: In the Shadow of the Gallows, 1995, Born in Brooklyn, 2001; (TV series) Mr. & Mrs. Smith, 1996, ER, 1997-98 (Screen Actors Guild award for outstanding performance by an ensemble in a drama series, 1997). Co-founder Dream Yard Drama Project for Kids, Harlem, NYC. Office: Creative Artists Agy 9830 Wilshire Blvd Beverly Hills CA 90212*

BELLON, VENETIA ROCHELLE, retired financial consultant; b. Beaufort West, Cape, South Africa, July 24, 1941; arrived in U.S., 1965; d. Michael and Roslyn (Sklaar) Bellon; m. Barry Fenroy Bass, Jan. 17, 1963 (div. Aug. 15, 1977); children: Tracey Hysjulien, Dayana Sebo; m. Andrew Jackson Ponton, III, Oct. 2004. Cert., U. Capetown, South Africa, 1960; BA in History, U. Tex., 1981, MA, LBJ, U. Tex., 1984. Tchr. Ellerton Jr. Sch., Capetown, 1961—63, Girls' HS, Pietermartizburg, South Africa, 1964; mktg. mgr. Austin Mag., 1978; officer corp. Bank Am., Va., 1987—91; mortgage cons. Penn Nat. Bancshares, McLean, Va., 1993—95, Access Nat. Mortgage, Reston, 1995—99, Countrywide Home Loans, Alexandria, Va., 2001—06; ret., 2006. Cert. coord. Third World Militarization, 1984; mem. Amnesty Internat.; mem. task force Gov. State of Tex., 1984. Named Honoree, Wall of Tolerance, 2005. Mem.: NAFE, AAUW, Humane Soc. Ptnrs. Cir., Ptnrs. of Conscience, So. Poverty Law Ctr. (Wall of Tolerance honoree), Tex. Execs., Amnesty Internat., Nat. Yiddish Book Ctr. Democrat. Jewish. Avocations: abstract expressionism, travel, crossword puzzles, politics. Personal E-mail: incomprono@aol.com.

BELLOTTI, MIKE, football coach; b. Concord, Calif. married; 1 child, Luke; children: Keri, Sean. BS with hon. in Phys. Edn., Univ. Calif. Davis, 1973. Wide receivers coach Univ. Calif. Davis; head coach Chico St. Univ.,

1984—88; offensive coord. Univ. Oregon, 1989—95, head coach, 1995—. Achievements include led team to unprecedented 7 consecutive bowl appearances, 1997-2003. Office: Dept Athletics Univ Oregon Eugene OR 97403*

BELLOTTI, ROBERT MICHAEL, coach, educator; b. Sacramento, Dec. 21, 1950; s. Bruno Gene and Carol Joyce (Snider) B.; m. Colleen Fotheringham, Aug. 5, 1978; children: Luke, Keri. BA in Phys. Edn., U. Calif. Davis, 1973; MS in Phys. Edn., Calif. State U., 1982. Dir. phys. edn. Holy Rosary Cath. Sch., Woodland, Calif., 1972—73; asst. track coach, tchr. Woodland HS, 1974—77; asst. football coach U. Calif.-Davis, 1973—77; offensive coord. Calif. State U., Hayward, 1977—79, 1980—84, Weber State Coll., Ogden, Utah, 1979—80; head football coach Calif. State U., Chico, 1984—88; offensive coord. Oregon Univ., 1989—94, head coach, 1995—. CPR instr. ARC, Hayward, 1978—84; lifetime sealbearer Calif. Scholastic Fedn. Named Coach of Yr., No. Calif. Athletic Conf., Nat. Coll. Assn. Coaches, 1986. Mem.: Am. Football Coaches Assn. (rules com.), Sports Med. Fitness Club, Chico Racquet Club, Delta Sigma Phi. Democrat. Roman Catholic.

BELLOVIN, STEVEN M., computer science educator; BA, Columbia U., 1972; MS, U. NC-Chapel Hill, 1977, PhD, 1982. Instructor, dept. computer sci. U. NC-Chapel Hill, 1977—78; mem. technical staff AT&T Bell Lab., 1982—87; Disting. mem. technical staff AT&T Bell Lab. and AT&T Labs-Rsch., 1987—98; AT&T fellow AT&T Labs-Rsch., 1998—2004; prof., computer sci. Columbia U., NY, 2005—. Mem. Internet Engring. Task Force (IETF) IPng Directorate, 1993—95; co-chair Usenix Security Symposium, 1996; mem. Internet Architecture Bd., 1996—2002; mem., study com on info. systems trustworthiness NRC, 1996—98, mem., study com. on authentication technologies and their privacy implications, 2001—03, mem. info. tech. sub-committee, study com. on sci. and tech. against terrorism, 2002, mem., study com. on cybersecurity rsch, needs, 2004—; co-chair Internet Engring. Task Force (IETF) PINT working group, 1997—2001, Internet Engring. Task Force (IETF) SPIRITS working group, 1999—; Internet Engring. Task Force (IETF) rep. Internet Corp. for Assigned Names and Numbers Protocol Supporting Orgn., 1999—2002; co-chair Usenix Security Symposium, 2000; chair Internet Engring. Task Force (IETF) ITRACE working group, 2000—02; vice-chair, program com. IEEE Symposium on Security and Privacy, 2001, chair. program com., 02; mem. adv. com. on security and privacy Assn. Computing Machinery, 2001—03; adj. prof., computer sci. U. Pa., 2002—04; co-dir., security area Internet Engring. Task Force (IETF), 2002—04; mem., security and stability adv. com. Internet Corp. for Assigned Names and Numbers, Domain Name Sys. (ICANN DNS), 2002—04; mem. sci. and tech. adv. com. Dept. Homeland Security, 2005—06; chair Steps Towards Reducing Unwanted Traffic in the Internet (SRUTI), 2006. Contbr. articles to profl. jours., chapters to books; co-author: Firewalls and Internet Secutiry: Repelling the Wily Hacker. Co-recipient Usenix Lifetime Achievement award (The Flame), 1995. Mem.: NAE. Achievements include co-creator of USENET; several patents on cryptographic and network protocols and patents pending. Office: 454 Computer Science Bldg Dept Computer Sci Columbia U 1214 Amsterdam Ave MC 0401 New York NY 10027-7003 Office Phone: 212-939-7149. Office Fax: 212-666-0140. Business E-Mail: smb@cs.columbia.edu.

BELLOWS, CARL D., lawyer; b. Bklyn., Sept. 29, 1944; BA, Columbia U., 1966; JD cum laude, NYU Sch. Law, 1969, LLM in Taxation, 1974. Bar: NY 1969, US Tax Court 1969, US Ct. Fed. Claims 1969. With Weil, Gotshal & Manges LLP, NYC, 1969—, ptnr., co-chair trusts and estate dept. Lectr. NYC Bar Assn., NY State Bar Assn. Contbg. editor Review of Taxation of Individuals, 1978—82; co-author: (treatise) Partnership Buy-Sell Agreements, 1995. Mem.: NY State Bar Assn. (mem. com. on Income Taxation, Estates and Trusts Law Section 1971—), Order of the Coif. Office: Weil Gotshal & Manges LLP 767 Fifth Ave New York NY 10153 Office Phone: 212-310-8134. Office Fax: 212-310-8007. Business E-Mail: carl.bellows@weil.com.

BELLOWS, CHARLES FREDERICK, III, surgeon, educator; b. Auburn, NY, Sept. 12, 1963; s. Charles Frederick Bellows, Jr. and Nancy Jane Bellows; m. Renee Jeanette Rabalais, June 29, 2001. BS, U. R.I., 1986; M in Liberal Arts, Harvard U., 1990; MD, Med. Coll. Pa., Phila., 1995. Diplomate Am. Bd. Gen. Surgery. Resident in surgery Tulane U., New Orleans, 1995—2001; asst. prof. surgery U. Fla., Jacksonville, Fla., 2001—04, Baylor Coll. Medicine, Houston, 2004—; chief laparoscopic surgery Michael E. DeBakey VA Med. Ctr., Houston, 2004—. Editl. bd. Duval County Med. Soc. Journal, Jacksonville, 2001—. Contbr. articles to profl. jours., including Jour. Surg. Rsch. Recipient Krementz Rsch. award, Tulane U., 1999, Rsch. award, Assn. Acad. Surgery, 1995. Mem.: ACS, Soc. Am. Gastrointestinal Endoscopic Surgeons, Soc. Surgery of the Alimentary Tract. Business E-Mail: cbellows@bcm.tmc.edu.

BELLOWS, HOWARD ARTHUR, JR., corporate financial executive; b. NYC, Mar. 10, 1938; s. Howard Arthur and Rita Jennie (Maffitt) B.; m. Mary Josephine Boyd, Sept. 7, 1968; children— Maffitt Vodrey, Alexander Scott, Hillary Newland, Jennifer Pacheteau. BA, Princeton U., 1960; MBA, Harvard U., 1964. Dir. mktg. Olga Co., Van Nuys, Calif., 1964-66; chmn. bd., co-chief exec. officer Triangle Corp., Stamford, Conn., 1967-71, chmn. bd., pres., chief exec. officer, 1971-95; pres. Audits & Surveys Worldwide, Inc., NYC, 1995—99; chmn. The Finance Network, LLC, 2000—. Bd. dirs. Hexcel Corp., Beacon Roofing Supply, Inc., 1st Comms., Inc. Trustee emeritus Western Res. Acad., Hudson, Ohio. Served to lt. (j.g.) USNR, 1960-62. Mem. Links Club, Blind Brook Club, Round Hill Club, Eagle Springs Golf Club, Univ. Cottage Club (bd. govs.), McArthur Golf Club. Home Phone: 203-869-7024; Office Phone: 203-869-6606. E-mail: artbellows@earthlink.net.

BELLOWS, KEITH ADAMS, editor-in-chief, writer; b. Kinshasha, Congo, Oct. 1, 1951; s. Lawrence William and Mavis Doreen (McPherson) B.; m. Shelley Williams, May 5, 1984 (div. Dec. 1998); 1 child, Adam Gordon. BA cum laude, Dartmouth Coll., 1974. Asst. editor Reader's Digest, Montreal, 1974-78; editor Hockey Mag., Southport, Conn., 1978-81; freelance writer NYC, 1982; group editor, editor, exec. prodr. 1330 Corp., Knoxville, Tenn., 1982-88; editor, exec. prodr. Spl. Reports/Whittle Comms., Knoxville, Tenn., 1988-90, pres., creative and sr. ptnr., 1990-93; founder, ptnr. Media Devel. Group, Knoxville, Tenn., 1994; founder, ptnr., creative dir. WestWorld Media, LLC, Knoxville, Tenn., 1995-96; devel. editor Meigher Comms., NYC, 1996-97; editor-in-chief Nat. Geog. Traveler, Washington, 1998—; exec. prodr. Excite, Redwood City, Calif., 1997. V.p. National Geog. Soc. Author: Canuck Book, 1978, 1980 Winter Olympics Access Guide, 1980. Mem.: Am. Soc. Profl. Journalists, Am. Soc. Mag. Editors. Episcopalian. Avocations: skiing, canoeing, photography. Office: Nat Geog Traveler 1145 17th St NW Washington DC 20036-4701*

BELLOWS, LAUREL GORDON, business lawyer; m. Joel J. Bellows. BA, U. Pa., 1969; JD, Loyola U., Chgo., 1974. Bar: Ill. 1974, Fla. 1975, U.S. Dist. Ct. (no. dist.) Ill. 1975, U.S. Dist. Ct. (no. dist.) Ga. 1980, Calif. 1981, U.S. Dist. Ct. (cen. dist.) Calif. 1980. Ptnr. Bellows and Bellows, Chgo., 1975—. Editor Loyola U. Law Rev., 1973-74; co-author: Trial Techniques in Business and Commercial Cases, 1988-2000. Past pres. women's bd. Traveller's Aid Soc., Chgo.; past chmn. Chgo. Network, 1992—; mentor Woman of Destiny program, 1990-91. Mem. ABA (bd. govs. 2001—, sec.-treas. 1991-92, past chmn. commn. on women 1993-95, mem. fed. jud. com. 1999—), Ill. Bar Assn., Chgo. Bar Assn. (bd. mgrs. 1983-85, sec. 1987-89, pres. 1991-92, chair, ho. dels., 2006-), Women's Bar Assn. Ill., Women's Bar Assn. Ill. Found. (bd. dirs. 1988—), Am. Arbitration Assn. (arbitrator 1976—, award 1990). Office: Bellows and Bellows PC 209 S LaSalle St Ste 800 Chicago IL 60604 Office Phone: 312-332-3340. Business E-Mail: lbellows@bellowspc.com.

BELLOWS, THOMAS JOHN, political scientist, educator; s. Charles Everett and Dorothy (Morrison) B.; m. Marilyn Denise Corbell; children: Scott Anthony, Justin Thomas, Trevor Cullen, Ethan Forrest; children by previous marriage: Roderick Alan, Adrienne Marie, Jeannine Louise, Derek John, Marshall Everett. Student, Am. U., 1956, UCLA, 1956-57; BA, Augustana Coll., 1957; MA, U. Fla., 1958, Yale U., 1960, PhD, 1968. From asst. prof. to prof. polit. sci. U. Ark., Fayetteville, 1967-81, chmn. dept., 1971-78; dir. divsn. social policy scis. U. Tex., San Antonio, 1981-88, prof. polit. sci., 1981—. Vis. lectr. depts. history, polit. sci. Nanyang U., Singapore, 1965; vis. prof. Nat. Chengchi U., Taiwan, 1979. Author: The People's Action Party of Singapore: Emergence of a Dominant Party System, 1970; (with S. Erikson and H. Winter) Political Science: Introductory Essays and Readings, 1971, Taiwan's Foreign Policy in the 1970's, 1976, (with H. Winter) People and Politics: An Introduction to Political Science, 1985, Bridging Tradition and Modernization: The Singapore Bureaucracy, 1989, Conflict and Compromise, 1992; Taiwan and Mainland China, 2000, The Republic of China's Legislative Yuan: A Study of Institutional Evolution, 2003; (with Felix Almaraz) Modern Texas: Perspectives on Politics and History, 2006; editor Am. Jour. Chinese Studies, 1999—. Mem.: Am. Assn. for Chinese Studies (pres. 1998—2000), Assn. Asian Studies, S.W. Conf. Asian Studies (pres. 1995), Phi Beta Kappa, Phi Kappa Phi. Methodist. Office: U Tex Dept Polit Sci San Antonio TX 78249 Office Phone: 210-458-4628. Business E-Mail: thomas.bellows@utsa.edu.

BELL SWANSON, KATIE J., music educator; b. Janesville, Wis., June 18, 1979; d. Earl Robert and Judith Marie Bell; m. Kenneth Alan Swanson. MusB in Voice Performance, U. Wis., Whitewater, 2002. Tchr. Ward-Brodt Music Mall, Madison, Wis., 2002—. Mem.: Nat. Assn. Tchrs. Singing. Lutheran. Avocations: performing, kickboxing. Home: 9412 Briar Haven Dr Verona WI 53593

BELLUGI, URSULA, neuropsychologist, educator; b. Jena, Germany, Feb. 21, 1931; d. Max J. and Edith (Kaufmann) Herzberger; m. Edward S. Klima; children: David, Robin. BA, Antioch Coll., 1952; EdD, Harvard U., 1967. Sr. rsch. asst. Harvard U., Cambridge, Mass., 1964-67, asst. prof., 1967-68; mem. Salk Inst. Biol. Studies, San Diego, 1968-69, rsch. assoc., 1969-74, assoc. rsch. prof., 1974-81, prof., 1981—, dir. Lab. for Cognitive Neurosci., 1970—. Adj. prof. U. Calif., San Diego, 1977—; vis. prof. Consiglio Nationale delle Ricerche, Rome, 1981; mem. adv. coun. Nat. Inst. on Deafness and Communicative Disorders, 1989—; mem. panel human devel. study sect. NIH, 1975-79, mem. behavioral and neurosciences fellowship panel, 1981—; mem. gov. bd. Ctr. for cognitive Neuroscience, 1990; trustee Salk Inst., 1980-91. Author: (with E.S. Klima) The Signs of Language, 1979, (with H. Poizner and E.S. Klima) What the Hands Reveal About the Brain, 1987; editor: (with R. Brown) The Acquisition of Language, 1971, (with M. Studdert-Kennedy) Signed and Spoken Language: Biological Constraints on Linguistic Form, 1980, (with J. Stiles-Davis and M. Kritchevsky) Spatial Cognition: Brain Bases and Development, 1988, Journey from Cognition to Brain to Gene: Perspectives from Williams Syndrome, 2001; contbr. numerous articles to profl. jours., chpts. to books; mem. editorial bd. Jour. Child Lang., Contemporary Psychology, Internat. Jour. Human Communication, others. Recipient found. award for rsch. in neuronal plasticity IPSEN, Neurosci. Investigator award NIH, 1989, Merit award NIH, 1989, Distinguished Scientific Contribution Award APA, Distinguished Woman of the Decade Award city of LA; Most Outstanding Book award Assn. Am. Pubs., 1979; named Disting. Woman of Decade, women in bus., 1984; grantee NIH, 1970—, NSF, 1974—. Fellow APA (Disting. Sci. Contbn. award 1992); mem. Acad. Aphasia, Acad. Neurology, European Brain and Behavior Soc., Internat. Brain Rsch. Orgn., Internat. Neuropsychol. Soc., Linguistic Soc. Am., Psychonomic Soc., Am. Psych. Soc., soc. Rsch. in Child Devel., Soc. Neurosci, NAS Office: Salk Inst for Biol Studies 10010 N Torrey Pines Rd La Jolla CA 92037-1099*

BELLUOMINI, FRANK STEPHEN, accountant; b. Healdsburg, Calif., May 19, 1934; s. Francesco and Rose (Giorgi) B.; m. Alta Anita Gifford, Sept. 16, 1967; 1 child, Wendy Ann. AA, Santa Rosa Jr. Coll., 1954; BA with honors, San Jose State U., 1956. CPA, Calif. Staff acct. Hood, Gire & Co., CPA's, San Jose, Calif., 1955-60, ptnr., 1960-66, Touche Ross & Co., CPA's, San Jose, 1967-89, ptnr.-in-charge San Jose office, 1971-85, sr. ptnr., 1985-89; ptnr. Deloitte & Touche, San Jose, 1989-95. Bd. dirs. Santa Clara Valley chpt. ARC, 1993-2000, chmn. bd. dirs. 1995-97; adv. bd. Salvation Army, San Jose, 1979-85, San Jose Children's Coun., 1982-89; citizens adv. coun. Via Rehabiliation Svcs., Inc., 1989-94, bd. dirs., 1995-2002, sec./treas., 1996-98, vice chair, 1998-99, chair, 1999-2000; trustee Santa Clara County (Calif.) United Way, 1979-95, v.p. planning and allocations, 1981-83, vice chmn., 1985-87, chmn. 1987-89; bd. dirs. San Jose Mus. Art, 1984-86; mem. Presentation HS Devel. Bd., 1989-92; dean's adv. coun. San Jose State U. Bus. Schl., 1990-95, adv. bd. Acad. of Fin., 1992-94. Named Disting. Alumnus, San Jose State U. Sch. Bus., 1978. Mem. AICPA (chmn. state and local govt. com. 1976-79), Santa Clara County Estate Planning Coun. (pres. 1979-80), Calif. Soc. CPA's (pres. chpt. 1968-69, state v.p. 1976-77), San Jose State Alumni Assn. (treas. 1960-61, dir. 1961-62, exec. com. 1961-62), San Jose State Acctg. Round Table (bd. dirs., treas. 1982-87, 92-97, pres. 1994-95), Beta Alpha Psi (San Jose State U. Outstanding Alumnus award 1986), Rotary (dir. 1979-81, dir. San Jose Rotary Endowment 1976-83, 2000-01, pres. 2001-03).

BELLUSCHI, ANTHONY C., architect; b. Portland, Oreg., Aug. 2, 1941; s. Pietro and Helen (Hemila) B.; m. Helen Risom, June 25, 1966 (div. 1975); children: Pietro Antonio, Catharine Camilla; m. Martha Mull Page, July 17, 1992. BArch, R.I. Sch. Design, 1966. Lic. arch. 28 states including N.Y., Mass., R.I., Calif., N.J., Oreg., Ill., Fla., Ga. Draftsman Ernest Kump Assocs., San Francisco, 1964; designer Zimmer-Gunsel-Frasca, Portland, 1965; assoc. Jung/Brannen Assocs., Boston, 1968-73; prin., treas. Belluschi/Daskalakis Inc., Boston, 1973-77; sr. v.p. Charles Kober Assocs., LA, 1977-84; mng. ptnr. Kober/Belluschi Assocs., Chgo., 1984-87; pres. Anthony Belluschi Assocs. Inc., 1984-87; founder Anthony Belluschi Archs., Ltd., Chgo., 1988-2000; pres. Belluschi-OWP&P Arch. Inc., Chgo., 2000—03; cons. architect Chgo., 2003—, Strategic Alliance, NYC, Chgo., 2005—, with Perkins Eastman Architects, NYC, Chgo., 2005—. Archtl. cons. U.S. Peace Corps, El Salvador, 1966-68; trustee R.I. Sch. Design, 1986—, vice chmn., 1995-2000, chair bd., 2000-04. Bd. adv. Inland Arch. Mag., 1992-95. Bd. dirs. Friends of the Park, Chgo., 1993—. Recipient First prize sculpture contest RKO & Redevel. Agy., Boston, 1973, award of merit Mass. Commn. Housing, 1975, Alumni of Yr. award RISD, 1982-83. Fellow AIA (award of excellence 1997); mem. Urban Land Inst. (award of excellence 1997), Internat. Coun. Shopping Ctrs. (design awards for Erieview Galleria, Clevel., Bridgewater Commons, N.J., 1989, Sportsgirl Office/Retail Hirise Bldg., Melbourne, Australia, 1991, Park Meadows Retail Resort, Denver, Univ. Retail Ctr., Tampa, Fla., 1996, The Falls, Miami, 1996, Northwood Cafe, Appleton, Wis., 1999), RISD Alumni Assn. (founder Chgo. chpt.). Avocations: travel, automobiles, hunting. Home: The Coach House 119 W Chestnut St Chicago IL 60610-3254

BELLUZZO, RICK E. (RICHARD), information technology and former computer software company executive; BS in Acctg., Golden Gate U. Various positions including gen. mgr. Laser Jet Divsn., Hewlett-Packard Co., exec. v.p.; CEO Silicon Graphics Inc., 1998—99; group v.p. Personal Svcs. and Devices Group, group v.p. consumer group Microsoft Corp., Redmond, Wash., 1999—2001, pres., COO, 2001—02; chmn. bd., CEO Quantum Corp., San Jose, Calif., 2002—. Mem. Sr. Leadership Team, Bus. Leadership Team, Microsoft Corp.; bd. dir. PMC-Sierra, JDS Uniphase. Bd. trustee Golden Gate Univ. Avocations: running, scuba diving, skiing. Office: Quantum Corp 1650 Technology Dr Ste 800 San Jose CA 95110-1382

BELL-WHITE, PATRICIA, photographer, artist, writer; b. Sumter, SC, Oct. 21, 1952; d. Clarence Allen Bell, Jr. and Virgina Mae Verhoeven; m. T.A. White, Dec. 2, 2006; 1 child, Daryl Allen Terry. AAS in Visual Comm. cum laude, Ivy Tech State Coll., Terre Haute, 2000; BFA in Photography, Art History minor magna cum laude, Ind. State U., Terre Haute, 2004. Accounts rep. Gt. Western Unifreight, Compton, Calif., 1978—81; prodn. asst. location/stage layout/ fabrication Renaissance Pleasure Faire, Novato and San Bernardino, Calif., 1989—96; CEO Ann Bell: Photography and Original Art, 2005—. Exhibitions include Granny's Vine (Ind. State U. Permanent Art Collection Purchase award, 2003), A Few of My Favorite Things (Ind. State U. Presdl. Merit award, 2002), Dried Flowers (First Pl./Wabash Valley Art Guild Spring Show at The Meadows, 2000), Rose Hulman Inst. Tech., Terre Haute, 2004—05, Wallflowers (Juried entry/Swope Museum's 57th Ann. Wabash Valley Exhbn.), Starving Artists Bread and Water Art Show (Best of Show, 2000), Rebirth: A Mile In My Shoes. Mem.: Ladies' Aux., VFW, Marine Corps League (assoc.), Phi Kappa Phi. Office Phone: 812-236-4425. Personal E-mail: patriciaa1@hotmail.com.

BELL WILSON, CARLOTTA A., social services specialist, state official, consultant; b. Detroit, Dec. 7, 1944; d. Albert Powell (dec.) and Elfrieda (Bertram) Bell; divorced; children: Lizette C. Wilson, SaMia M. Wilson, Shira M. Ingram. AA, Wayne County C.C., Detroit, 1975; BS, Wayne State U., 1979; MEd, Bowling Green State U., 1983. Dental asst. Fred Colvard, DDS, Detroit, 1968-73; edn. coord. Merrill Palmer Inst., Detroit, 1979-81; head start evaluator Cmty. Devel. Inst., Wayne County, 1981; grad. asst. Bowling Green (Ohio) State U., 1981-83; child care worker Meth. Children's Village, Detroit, 1984-85; tchr. New Calvary Head Start, Detroit, 1985; child welfare specialist Mich. Dept. Social Svcs., Detroit, 1985-93; resource program analyst teen parent program Family Independence Agy., Lansing, Mich., 1993—2002; social svcs. specialist, recipient rights rep. Detroit-Wayne County Cmty. Mental Health Agy. Office Recipient Rights, 2006—. Conf. presenter U. Mich., Ann Arbor, 1995, Mich. Assn. Cmty. and Adult Edn., Bellaire, 1995, Baker Coll., Flint, Mich., 1996. Mem. Mich. Profl. Soc. Abuse of Children, Internat. Assoc. Infant Massage (cert. infant massage instr.). Roman Catholic. Avocations: gardening, pottery, cultural activities, travel. Home: 2110 Chene Detroit MI 48207 Office Phone: 313-833-2162.

BELMONTE, STEVEN JOSEPH, hotel chain executive; b. Oak Park, Ill., Aug. 25, 1952; s. Silvio J. and Vilma (Giannini) B.; m. Dwyonia Conrad; children: Gino Anthony, Kellie Rose, Michael Steven. BA in Hotel Mgmt., Wright Coll., Chgo., 1974; student, Holiday Inn U., Memphis, 1974; BM in Innkeeping, Harper Coll., Rolling Meadows, Ill., 1981; D Applied Pub. Svc. (hon.), Hocking Coll., 1993. Gen. mgr., regional dir. Holiday Inns, Chgo., 1972-84; pres., CEO Equity Hotel Corp., Rolling Meadows, 1984-91, Ramada Franchise Sys., Inc., 1991—. Chmn. Ramada Inns Nat. Assn.; founding sponsor Childreach; speaker Ill. Budget for Tourism, 1978-81. Bd. advisors Wright Jr. Coll.; mem. Joint Civic Com. Italian Ams.; hon. chmn. Childreach Plan Internat., 1996; bd. dirs. Chgo. chpt. Inner City Games, 1998—, chmn., 2000—; active fund raiser for various charities and retirement homes; chmn., lodging chair Am. Hotel Found., 2000—. Recipient citation Italo-Am. War Vets, U.S., 1980, Humanities award PLAN Internat. Charities, 1994, Ambassador of Peace Humanitarian award Am. Friends of Neve Shalom/Wahat-Al-Salam, 1999. Fellow Hotel and Catering Internat. Mgmt. Assn. (hon.); mem. Am. Soc. Travel Agts., Am. Hotel and Motel Assn. (bd. trustees ednl. inst.), Am. Hotel Fedn., Hotel Sales Mgmt. Assn., Soc. Mng. Execs., Chgo. Innkeepers Assn. (v.p. 1979-81), Am. Hotel Found. (exec. com. 1997—, chmn. devel. com. 1997-2000). Office: Ramada Franchise Sys Inc 1 Sylvan Way Parsippany NJ 07054-3878

BELNAP, DAVID F., journalist; b. Ogden, Utah, July 27, 1922; s. Hyrum Adolphus and Lois Ellen B.; m. Barbara Virginia Carlberg, Jan. 17, 1947. Student, Weber Coll., Ogden, 1940. Asst. city editor Seattle Star, 1945-47; bur. chief UP Assns., Helena, Mont., 1947-50, Honolulu, 1950-52; regional exec. Pacific N.W., 1952-55, dir. Latin Am. services, 1955-67; Latin Am. corr. L.A. Times, 1967-80, asst. fgn. news editor, 1980-93. Recipient Overseas Press Club Am. award for best article on Latin Am., 1970, Maria Moors Cabot prize, 1973 Mem. Overseas Press Club Am., LA Press Club, Am. Club of Buenos Aires, Phoenix Club of Lima (Peru). Home and Office: 1134 W Huntington Dr Arcadia CA 91007-6308

BELNICK, MARK ALAN, lawyer; b. Elizabeth, NJ, Oct. 30, 1946; s. Ben B. and Rhoda Helen (Dubrowsky) B.; m. Randy Lee Birer, Mar. 23, 1974; children: Kelly Ann, Cory Frances, Jason Todd. BA cum laude, Cornell U., 1968; JD, Columbia U., 1971. Bar: NY 1972, US Tax Ct., 1972, US Ct. Appeals (2d cir.) 1972, US Dist. Ct. (so. dist.) NY 1973, US Supreme Ct. 1975, US Dist. Ct. (ea. dist.) NY 1978, US Ct. Appeals (9th cir.) 1980, US Ct. Appeals (4th cir.) 1982. Assoc. Marshall, Bratter, Greene et al, NYC, 1971-72, Paul, Weiss, Rifkind, Wharton & Garrison, NYC, 1972-79, ptnr., 1979-98; exec. v.p., chief corp. counsel Tyco Internat. Ltd., NYC, 1998—2002; atty., prin. Law Offices of Mark A. Belnick LLC, NYC, 2005—. Adj. prof. law Benjamin N. Cardozo Sch. Law, NYC, 1982-86; visiting prof. govt. Cornell U., 1999—2005; mem. panel mediators and fact finders NY State Pub. Employment Rels. Bd., Albany, 1972-79; dep. chief counsel US Senate select com. on secret mil. assistance to Iran and Nicaraguan opposition, 1987-88; chief counsel select com. on structure and governance Nat. Assn. Security Dealers, 1994-96; bd. visitors Columbia Law Sch., 1996—; dir., prin. instr. Cornell U. prelaw program, 1999—2005; univ. lectr. Princeton U., 2007-. Mem. com. on alumni trustee nominations Cornell U., 1993—97, mem. Cornell coun., 1992—96, 1998—2002, 2006—, mem. adv. coun. Coll. Arts and Scis., 1993—, dir. prelaw program, 1999—2005; mem. adminstrv. bd. Cornell Coun., 1999—2001; trustee Ethical Fieldston Schs., 1999—2001; bd. trustees Thomas Aquinas Coll., 1999—, Newark Acad., 2001—02; mem. adv. coun. James Madison Inst., Princeton U., 2000—02; bd. dirs. The Legal Aid Soc. N.Y., 2000—05, The Christopher Reeve Paralysis Found., 2001—02. Harlan Fiske Stone scholar, 1971. Fellow Am. Coll. Trial Lawyers; mem. ABA, N.Y. State Bar Assn., Assn. Bar City N.Y., Univ. Club N.Y.C. Home Phone: 212-877-7253; Office Phone: 646-453-2901. Business E-Mail: mbelnick@belnicklaw.com.

BELSHAW, GARY D., music educator, composer; b. Washington, Mar. 17, 1949; s. Walter Dwinnell Belshaw and Virginia Louise Barlow, Robert L. Barlow (Stepfather); m. Renée Reinholt, Aug. 21, 1975; children: Benjamin David, Bethany Louanne Reinecke, Micah Paul. B.M., Tex. Tech U., 1991, MusM, 1994, PhD, 2000. Assoc. prof. piano pedagogy Wayland Bapt. U., Plaiview, Tex., 2000—. Composer: Spirit of the Llano Estacado, A Concerto in One Movement for Piano and Orchestra, 1994, Weekend Stories for Trombone and Piano, 1995, Wind Sculptures for Trombone and Band, 2000, Oldest and Finest Concert March, 2002, At a Lake for Solo Trombone and Trombone Quartet, 2002, Constellations for Solo Trombone and Trombone Choir, 2003. Mem.: ASCAP, Tex. Music Educators Assn., Soc. Composers, Inc., Am. Music Ctr. Home: 513 Raleigh Plainview TX 79072 Office: Wayland Baptist Univ 1900 W Seventh St Plainview TX 79072 Home Phone: 806-293-0799. Personal E-mail: garydbelshaw@yahoo.com. E-mail: belshawg@wbu.edu.

BELSHAW, GEORGE PHELPS MELLICK, bishop; b. Plainfield, NJ, July 14, 1928; s. Harold and Edith (Mellick) B.; m. Elizabeth Wheeler, June 12, 1954; children: Richard, Elizabeth, George. BA, U. of South, 1951; STB, Gen. Theol. Sem., NYC, 1954, STM, 1959, DD (hon.), 1975, U. of South, 1994, Hamilton Coll., 2003. Ordained to ministry, Episcopal Ch., consecrated bishop. Vicar St. Matthew's Ch., Waimanalo, Hawaii, 1954-57; fellow, tutor Gen. Theol. Sem., NYC, 1957-59; rector Christ Ch., Dover, Del., 1959-65, St. George's Ch., Rumson, NJ, 1965-75; suffragan bishop Diocese of N.J., Trenton, 1975-83, bishop of N.J., 1983-94. Vis. lectr. Gen. Theol. Sem., 1969, 70; governing bd. Episc. Urban Caucus, 1982—, pres., 1986-89; mem. Commn. Peace of Episc. Ch., 1979-85, Econ. Justice Implementation Com., Episc. Ch., 1988-95. Editor: Lent with Evelyn Underhill, 1964, Lent with William Temple, 1966; contbr. articles to theol. jours. Trustee Gen. Theol. Sem., 1975—, chmn. 1992-2000, acting dean, pres., 1997-98; trustee Westminister Choir Coll., 1976-82. Mem. Am. Teilhard de Chardin Assn. (bd. dirs. 1976—), N.J. Coalition Religious Leaders (pres. 1986), Bd. Anglican Theol. Rev. (1993—), Coalition for Peace Action (chmn. 1999-2004). Episcopalian. Home: 15 Boudinot St Princeton NJ 08540-3007 E-mail: gpmbelshaw@aol.com.

BELSKI, KEITH CHRISTOPHER, computer technician; b. Bloomsburg, Pa., May 16, 1963; s. Giles James and Donna Lee Belski. BA in Philosophy and Religion, Barton Coll., NC, 1996. Cert. Microsoft, 1998, Tier 2 The Help Desk Inst., 1998. Rep. aide Pa. Ho. Reps., Harrisburgh, 1985; Russian linguist, signal voice intercept US Army, 1985—93; trainer, technician, mgr. Tech Resource Group, Raleigh, 1996—2001; computer technician Bayada Nurses, Langhorne, Pa., 2001—. Mem. Young Democrats, Pa. Decorated Commendation medal with 2 oak leaf clusters US Army, Achievement medal with 2 oak leaf clusters. Mem.: MENSA, Theta Alpha Kappa (life; local pres. 1995—96). Home Phone: 215-785-1868; Office Phone: 215-757-9000. Personal E-mail: k_belski@comcast.net.

BELSKY, MARTIN HENRY, law educator, dean; b. May 29, 1944; s. Abraham and Fannie (Turnoff) Belsky; m. Kathleen Waits, Mar. 9, 1985; children: Allen Frederick, Marcia Elizabeth. BA cum laude, Temple U., 1965; JD cum laude, Columbia U., 1968; cert. of study, Hague Acad. Internat. Law, The Netherlands, 1968; diploma in Criminology, Cambridge U., England, 1969. Bar: Pa. 1969, Fla. 1983, N.Y. 1987, U.S. Dist. Ct. (ea. dist.) Pa. 1969, U.S. Ct. Appeals (3d cir.) 1970, U.S. Supreme Ct. 1973. Chief asst. dist. atty. Phila. Dist. Atty.'s Office, Pa., 1969—74; assoc. Blank, Rome, Klaus & Comisky, Phila., 1975; chief counsel U.S. Ho. of Reps., Washington, 1975—78; asst. adminstr. NOAA, Washington, 1979—82; dir. ctr. for govtl. responsibility, assoc. prof. law U. Fla. Holand Law Ctr., 1982—86; dean Albany Law Sch., 1986—91, dean emeritus, prof. law, 1991—95; dean U. Tulsa Coll. of Law, Okla., 1995—2004, dean emeritus, prof. law, 2004—07; dean U. Akron Sch. Law, 2007—. Chmn. Select Commn. on Disabilities, NY, Spl. Commn. on Fire Svcs.; bd. advs. Ctr. Oceans Law and Policy; mem. corrections task force Pa. Gov.'s Justice Commn., 1971—75; adv. task force on cts. Nat. Adv. Commn. on Criminal Justice Standards and Goals, 1972—74; mem. com. on proposed standard jury instrns. Pa. Supreme Ct., 1974—81; lectr. in law Temple U., 1971—75; mem. faculty Pa. Coll. Judiciary, 1975—77; adj. prof. law Georgetown U., 1977—81; dean-elect U. Akron Sch. Law, Ohio, 2007—. Author (with Steven H. Goldblatt): (non-fiction) Analysis and Commentary to the Pennsylvania Crimes Codes, 1973; author: Handbook for Trial Judges, 1976, Law and Theology, 2005, (non-fiction) Rehnquist Court: A Retrospective, 2002; editor (in chief): (jour.) Jour. Transnat. Law, Columbia Law Sch., 1968; contbr. articles to legal pubs. Chmn. N.Y. region, mem. D.C. bd. Anti-Defamation League, 1977—78, chmn. N.Y. region, mem. nat. leadership coun.; exec. v.p. Urban League Northeastern N.Y. and Tulsa Urgan League; state chair exec. com. Okla. Anti-Defamation League; mem. magnet schs. task force Tulsa Pub. Schs., 2000, mem. woods task force, 2003—04; mem. Okla. Ethics Commn., 2002—04; v.p. Nat. Jewish Coun. on Pub. Affairs; pres. Tulsa Met. Ministry, Jewish Fedn. Tulsa; bd. dirs. Coun. on Aging and Disability; pres. Jewish Fedn.; mem. exec. com Nat. Conf. for Cmty. and Justice. Fellow Intenat., Columbia U. Law Sch.; scholar Stone. Mem.: ABA (del. young lawyers sect. exec. bd. 1973—75), Fund for Modern Cts. (bd. dirs.), Am. Law Inst., Am. Arbitration Assn. (referee N.Y. State Commn. on Jud. Discipline), Am. Soc. Internat. Law, Nat. Dist. Attys. Assn., Am. Judicature Soc. (bd. dirs.), Fed. Bar Assn., Fla. Bar Assn., Pa. Bar Assn. (exec. com. young lawyers sect. 1973—75), Phila. Bar Assn. (chmn. young lawyers sect. 1974—75), Albany County Bar Assn., N.Y. State Bar Assn., United Jewish Fedn. Northeastern N.Y. (v.p., pres. elect), Cardozo Soc., B'nai B'rith (v.p. lodge 1973—75), Sword Soc., Hudson-Mohawk Assn. Coll. and Univs. (v.p.), Temple U. Liberal Arts Alumni Assn. (v.p. 1971—75). Office: U Tulsa Coll Law 3120 E 4th Pl Tulsa OK 74104-2418 Home Phone: 918-645-7837, 918-749-3888; Office Phone: 330-972-6361.

BELSON, JAMES ANTHONY, judge; b. Milw., Sept. 23, 1931; s. Walter W. and Margaret (Taugher) B.; m. Rosemary P. Greenslade, Jan. 11, 1958; children: Anthony James, Marie Taylor, Elizabeth Ann, Stephen Griffin. AB, Georgetown U., 1953, JD, 1956, LLM, 1962. Bar: D.C. 1956, Md. 1962. Law clk. US Ct. Appeals (DC cir.), 1956-57; assoc. Hogan & Hartson, Washington, 1960-67, ptnr., 1967-68; trial judge DC Superior Ct., Washington, 1968-81, chmn. rules com., 1971—81, presiding judge civil divsn., 1978-81, assoc. judge, 1981-91; sr. judge DC Ct. Appeals, Washington, 1991—. Faculty Nat. Jud. Coll., 1973-80; bd. dirs. Coun. for Ct. Excellence, 1981—; bencher Am. Inn of Ct. VI, 1983-90. Bd. editors Georgetown Law Jour., 1955-56. Bd. dirs. Project SHARE D.C., Inc., 1992—, chmn., 1997-99; bd. dirs. Cath. Legal Immigration Network, 1994-98. With JAGC, U.S. Army, 1957-60. Mem. ABA, Bar Assn. of D.C. (bd. dirs. 1966-67, chmn. jr. bar 1965-66), Am. Judicature Soc. (bd. dirs. 1980-85), Am. Bar Found., John Carroll Soc. (bd. govs. 1978-85, 1st v.p. 1989-91), Sovereign Mil. Order of Malta Fed. Assn. (pres. 1991-94, bd. dirs. 1988-95, 97-2003, chmn. task force on Cuba 1994-2000). Home: 12 W Severn Ridge Rd Annapolis MD 21409-5844 Office: DC Ct Appeals 500 Indiana Ave NW Washington DC 20001-2131 Business E-Mail: jbelson@dcca.state.dc.us.

BELSON, KEN, reporter; Freelance journalist, Japan, 1993—96; reporter Bloomberg News, Japan, 1996—98, Reuters Fin. TV, Japan, 1998—2000, Bus. Week, Japan, 2000—01, New York Times, Japan, 2001—04, tech. reporter NYC, 2004—. Co-author: Hello Kitty: The Remarkable Story of Sanrio and the Billion Dollar Feline Phenomenon, 2003. Office: New York Times 229 W 43d St New York NY 10036 Office Phone: 212-556-1474. Office Fax: 212-556-1448. Business E-Mail: belson@nytimes.com.

BELT, BRADLEY DECK, financial services executive; b. Waco, Tex., Oct. 11, 1958; s. Charles Deck and Judith Ann (Skaggs) B. BS in Bus. Adminstrn., Nebr. U., 1980; JD, Georgetown U., 1984; postgrad., Harvard U., 1993. Bar: N.Y.1985, D.C. 1995, U.S. Supreme Ct. 1989. Fin. analyst Fed. Reserve, Kansas City, Mo., 1980-81; spl. counsel U.S. SEC, Washington, 1984-86; counsel SEC Commn. Charles Cox, 1986-88; Rep. chief securities counsel Senate Banking Com., Washington, 1988-93; gen. counsel and legis. dir. Sen. John McCain, Washington, 1993-94; pres. Washington Capital Group, Inc.; mng. dir. The Commonwealth Group, LLP; of counsel Perkins, Smith & Cohen, 1997—99; exec. dir., CEO Pension Benefit Guaranty Corp., Washington, 2004—. Sr. v.p. Ctr. Strategic and Internat. Studies, 1994-00, sr. adv. 2000-; v.p. Strategic Growth FOLIOfn, Inc., 2000-03; mem. social security adv. bd., 2003-04; bd. govs. Securities Traders Assns., 1996-00; exec. dir., mem. Nat. Commn. Retirement Policy, 1996-98. Contbr. articles to profl. jours. Bd. trustees Nat. Cathedral, 2004—. Kennedy Sch. Govt. & Alumni fellow, 1993, Eisenhower fellow, 1997; recipient Manuel F. Cohen award for outstanding younger SEC lawyer, 1987, Masters award U. Nebr., 1989. Office: Pension Benefit Guaranty Corp 1200 K St NW Washington DC 20005-4026 Office Phone: 202-326-4010. Business E-Mail: bradley.belt@rcn.com.

BELTCHEVA (BELCHEVA), MARIANA, research scientist, educator; d. Mantcho Nentcheva and Nadka Nentchev; m. Beltcho Beltchev, July 20, 1979; 1 child, Petya Beltcheva. PhD, Sofia U., Bulgaria. Assoc. rsch. prof. St. Louis U., 2001—. Fellow, Leopold Schepp Found., 1998—99. Home: 330 Camellia Dr Saint Louis MO 63119 Home Phone: 314-962-8359.

BELTH, JOSEPH MORTON, retired business educator; b. Syracuse, NY, Oct. 22, 1929; s. Irving and Helen Rose (Bright) B.; m. Marjorie Helen Lavine, June 12, 1955; children: Ann Irene, Michael Irving, Jeffrey Edward. AAS, Cayuga C.C., 1958; BS summa cum laude, Syracuse U., 1958; PhD, U. Pa., 1961. CLU, CPCU. Asst. purchasing agt. Onondaga Supply Co., Syracuse, NY, 1947-53; agt. Continental Am. Life Ins. Co., Syracuse, 1953-58; asst. dir. continuing edn. Am. Soc. Chartered Life Underwriters, Bryn Mawr, Pa., 1961-62; asst. prof. Ind. U., Bloomington, 1962-65, assoc. prof., 1965-68, prof., 1968-93, prof. emeritus, 1993—. Author: Participating Life Insurance Sold by Stock Companies, 1965, The Retail Price Structure in American Life Insurance, 1966; Life Insurance: a Consumer's Handbook, 1973, 2d edit., 1985, The A.L. Williams Replacement Empire, 1987, 2d edit., 1989, Viatical Transactions, 2000; editor newsletter The Ins. Forum, 1974— (George Polk award 1990). Mem. Am. Risk and Ins. Assn. (pres. 1973-74, Elizur Wright award, 1966, Jour. Risk and Ins. awards 1962,64,65,67,71,79), Huebner Gold medal, 1999, AAUP, Beta Gamma Sigma, Phi Kappa Phi. Democrat. Jewish. Home: 5125 N Starnes Rd Bloomington IN 47404-9358

BELTON, JOHN THOMAS, lawyer; b. Yonkers, NY, Feb. 24, 1947; s. Harry James and Anne Marie (Kupko) B.; m. Linda Susanne Cheugh, jan. 6, 1973; 1 child, Joseph Timothy. BA, Ohio State U., 1972; postgrad. in bus. adminstrn., Xavier U., Cin., 1972-73; JD, Ohio No. U., Ada, 1976. Bar: Ohio 1977, US Ct. of Claims. Sole practice, Columbus, Ohio, 1976-83; ptnr. Belton & Marlin, and predecessor firm Belton, Golowin & Cheugh, Columbus, 1983—; arbitrator Franklin County Ct. Common Pleas, 1983—; dir. Weeks-Finneran Inc. Rep. precinct chmn., 1983; spl. counsel to atty. gen. State of Ohio, 2003. V.p. Far Northwest Coalition, 1984; spl. counsel Ohio Atty. Gen., 2004. Mem. ch. coun. St. Bridgets Parish, 1988—, Dublin Pub. Bd. Zoning Appeals, 1991—; pres. Dublin Youth Athletics, 1985—. With USAF, 1968-71. Mem. ABA, ATLA, Columbus Bar Assn. (com. chmn. 1976—), US Dist. Ct. Fed. Bar, US Supreme Ct. Bar, Ohio Bar Assn. (bd. govs. 1993—), Dublin Jr. C. of C., The Pres. Club. of Ohio State U., Ohio State Alumni, Republican Glee, Columbus Shamrock, KC, Order of Barristers, Omicron Delta Kappa, Phi Alpha Delta (justice 1975). Roman Catholic. Avocations: reading, chess, golf, racquetball, recreational activities. Home: 8649 Dunsinane Dr Dublin OH 43017-8757 Office: Belton & Marlin 2066 Henderson Rd Columbus OH 43220-2452 Office Phone: 614-457-2034. Business E-Mail: beltonlaw@aol.com.

BELTON, ROBERT, law educator; b. 1935; BA, U. Conn., 1961; JD, Boston U., 1965. Bar: N.Y. 1966, N.C. 1970, Tenn. 1980. Asst. counsel legal def. fund NAACP, NYC, 1966-70; ptnr. Chambers, Stein, Ferguson & Lanning, Charlotte, NC, 1970-75; lectr., dir. fair employment clinic Vanderbilt U., Nashville, 1975-77, assoc. prof., 1977-82, prof., 1982—. Vis. prof. Harvard U. Law Sch., Cambridge, Mass., 1986-87, U. No. Car., 1990-91, Charles Hamilton Houston Disting. vis. prof. N.C. Ctrl. Law Sch., 1997. Author: Remedies in Employment Discrimination Law, 1992; co-author Casebook on Employment Discrimination Law, 1999; contbr. articles to profl. jours. Fellow Coll. Labor and Employment Lawyers, Inc.; mem. ABA, Nat. Bar Assn., Am. Assn. Law Schs. (exec. com. 1991-94), Am. Law Inst., Nat. Employment Lawyers' Assn. (exec. bd. 1996—). Office: Vanderbilt U Sch Law 131- 21st Ave S Nashville TN 37203-1181

BELTRAMO, MICHAEL NORMAN, management consultant; b. LA, Feb. 9, 1942; s. Blase and Violette (Murphy) B.; m. Susan Annette Lawton, Dec. 24, 1969 (div. 1980); m. Jane Sinden Spiegel, Apr. 21, 1984; children: Helen Weedon, Anna Sinden, Emily Murphy. AB, UCLA, 1964; MPA, U. So. Calif., 1967; PhD, Rand Grad. Inst., Santa Monica, Calif., 1983. Cert. cost estimator/analyst. Mem. tech. staff The RAND Corp., Santa Monica, 1969-75; dep. mgr. Sci. Applications Internat. Corp., LA, 1975-80; pres. Beltramo and Assocs., LA, 1980—. Author: LA County Economic Adjustment Strategy for Defense Reduction; contbr. articles to profl. publs. Named Ky. Col. Commonwealth of Ky., 1973. Mem. Soc. Cost Estimating and Analysis (cert., bd. dirs. 1987-88). Republican. Avocations: fly fishing, surfing. Home and Office: 13039 Sky Valley Rd Los Angeles CA 90049-1037

BELTRAN, CARLOS, professional baseball player; b. Manati, PR, Apr. 24, 1977; m. Jessica Lugo. Draft pick Kans. City Royals, 1995, player, 1998—2004, Houston Astros, 2004, NY Mets, 2005—. Named Am. League Rookie of Yr., 1999; named to Nat. League All-Star Team, Maj. League Baseball, 2004—07; recipient Nat. League Gold Glove award, 2006, Silver Slugger award, 2006. Office: NY Mets 123-01 Roosevelt Ave Corona NY 11368-1699 also: Sports Placement Service Inc c/o Creed Poulson 5458 Wilshire Blvd Los Angeles CA 90036*

BELTRAN, EUSEBIUS JOSEPH, archbishop; b. Ashley, Pa., Aug. 31, 1934; s. Joseph C. and Helen Rita (Kozlowski) Beltran. Grad., St. Charles Sem., Overbrook, Pa. Ordained priest Roman Cath. Ch., 1960. Consecrated bishop, 1978; pastor various chs., Atlanta and Decatur, Ga., 1960; notary, then vice officialis Atlanta Diocesan Tribunal, 1960—62; vice chancellor Archdiocese Atlanta, 1962; officialis Archdiocesan Tribunal, 1963—74; pastor various chs., Atlanta and Rome, Ga., 1963—66; vicar gen. Archdiocese of Atlanta, 1971—78; pastor St. Anthony's Ch., Atlanta, 1972—78; bishop of Tulsa, 1978—92; archbishop Archdiocese of Okla. City, 1992—. Liturgy com. Nat. Conf. Cath. Bishops; com. mem. Am. Coll., Louvain, Belgium; bd. regents Conception Sem.; bd. dirs. St. Gregory's Coll., Shawnee, Okla. Mem.: NCCJ, Equestrian Order Holy Sepulchre, K.C. Office: Archdiocese of Oklahoma City 7501 NW Espressway Oklahoma City OK 73132-2180

BELTZNER, GAIL ANN, music educator; b. Palmerton, Pa., July 20, 1950; d. Conon Nelson and Lorraine Ann (Carey) Beltzner. BS in Music Edn. summa cum laude, West Chester State U., 1972; postgrad., Kean State Coll., 1972, Temple U., 1972, Westminster Choir Coll., 1972, Lehigh U., 1978. Tchr. music Drexel Hill Jr. H.S., 1972-73; music specialist Allentown (Pa.) Sch. Dist., 1973—; tchr. Corps Sch. and Cmty. Devel. Lab., 1978-80, Corps Cmty. Resource Festival, 1979-81, Corps Cultural Fair, 1980, 81. Mem. bd. assocs. Lehigh Valley Hosp. and Health Network. Mem. Mus. Fine Arts, Boston, aux. Allentown Art Mus., aux. Allentown Hosp.; mem. woman's com. Allentown Symphony, The Lyric Soc. of the Allentown Orch.; mem. Allentown 2nd and 9th Civilian Police Acads.; bd. dirs. Allentown Area Ecumenical Food Bank, Allentown Arts Commn; mem. Growing with Sci. partnership—Air Products and Chems., Inc. and Allentown Sch. Dist., Good Shepherd Home Aux. Decorated Dame Comdr., Ordre Souverain et Militaire de la Milice du St. Sepulcre; recipient Cert. of Appreciation, Lehigh Valley Sertoma Club; Excellence in the Classroom grantee Rider-Pool Found., 1988, 91-92. Mem. AAUW, NAFE, ASCD, Am. String Tchrs. Assn., Am. Viola Soc., Internat. Reading Assn., Internat. Platform Assn., Allentown Edn. Assn., Music Educators Nat. Conf., Pa. Music Educators Assn., Am. Orff-Schulwerk Assn., Orgn. Am. Kodaly Educators, Am. Recorder Soc., Phila. Area Orff-Schulwerk Assn., Soc. Gen. Music, Am. Assn. Music Therapy, Internat. Soc. Music Edn., Internat. Tech. Edn. Assn., Assn. for Tech. in Music Instrn., Civil War Roundtable Ea. Pa., Choristers Guild, Lenni Lenape Hist. Soc., Lehigh Valley Arts Coun., Allentown Symphony Assn., Midi Users Group, Pa.-Del. String Tchrs. Assn., Nat. Sch. Orch. Assn., Lehigh County Hist. Soc., Confedn. Chivalry (life mem. of merit, grand coun.), Maison Internat. des Intellectuels Akademie, Order White Cross Internat. (apptd. dist. comdr. for Pa./U.S.A. dist., nobless of humanity), Airedale Terrier Club of Greater Phila., Kappa Delta Pi, Phi Delta Kappa, Alpha Lambda. Republican. Lutheran. Home: PO Box 4427 Allentown PA 18105-4427

BELUE, JANIE A., music educator; b. Sheffield, Ala., Aug. 25, 1952; d. Alver Kendrick and Lucille Counce Belue. AA, N.E. Miss. C.C., Booneville, 1974; MusB in Edn., Miss. State U., Starkville, 1974, cert. in gifted edn. and adult edn., 1980. Cert. music edn. Nat. Bd., N.C. Adminstrv. dir. Camp Crestridge for Girls, Ridgecrest, NC, 1985—; chorus tchr. Alcorn Cen. H.S., Glen, Miss., 1978—84; tchr. gifted edn. Burnsville (Miss.) Elem. Sch., 1984—91; dir. Montreat (N.C.) Morning Sch., 1991—92; music tchr. Emma and Pisgah Elem. Schs., Asheville, NC, 1992—. Contbr.: (video) The Gift of Flight (Creative Tchr. of Yr. in N.C., 1995). Asst. min. music 1st Bapt. Ch., Black Mountain, NC, 1991—2005. Mem.: Music Educators N.C. Home: 10 E Keesler Ave Apt F Black Mountain NC 28711-3294 Home Phone: 828-669-0686. Personal E-mail: jabelue@aol.com.

BELUSHI, JAMES A., actor; b. Chgo., June 15, 1954; s. Adam and Agnes Belushi; m. Sandra Davenport, May 17, 1980 (div.); 1 child; m. Marjorie Bransfield, Sept. 22, 1990 (div. Apr. 1992); m. Jennifer Sloan, May 2, 1998; 2 children. Student, Coll. DuPage; grad., So. Ill. U. Mem., musician James Belushi & The Sacred Hearts, Blues Brothers Band. Mem. Second City comedy troupe, 1977-78, 80; co-owner (with Dan Aykroyd) House of Blues clubs. Actor: (plays) Under Milkwood, Born Yesterday, Dubwaiter, Sexual Perversity in Chicago, 1979, Baal in the Twenty-first Century, 1980, Pirates of Penzance, 1982, True West, 1983, Moon Over Miami, 1987; (films) About Last Night, 1986—, Little Shop of Horrors, 1986, K-9, 1989, Taking Care of Business, 1990, Mr. Destiny, 1990, Only the Lonely, 1991, Curly Sue, 1991, Diary of a Hitman, 1991, Once Upon a Crime, 1992, Trace of Red, 1992, Separate Lives, 1995, Race the Sun, 1996, Gang Related, 1997, Angel's Dance, 1999, The Florentine, 1999, Made Men, 1999, K-9, 1999, Return to Me, 2000, Joe Somebody, 2001, Easy Six, 2003, Behind the Smile, 2004, DysEnchanted, 2004, Underdog, 2007; voice overs (films) Nuttiest Nutcracker, 1999; voice overs: (TV series) Bad Baby; Mighty Duck's Duckman; Ahh, Monsters; Animaniacs; Superman; Pinky and the Brain; actor, dir. (TV series) According to Jim, 2001—; voice overs: (TV series) 3 Little Pigs; Real Monsters; Looie and Louie; Cow & Chicken; voiceovers (TV series) Legend of the Lost Tribe, 2002; voice overs: (TV series) Life with Louie; (films) The Pebble and the Penguin, 1995; Dog's Best Friend, 1997; Babes In Toyland, 1997; Hey Arnold!, 1997; Gargoyles; Felix the Cat; Timon and Pumbaa; The Tick; Bruno the Kid; Hercules; Greedy Show; voice overs (films) Pinocchio, 2002, Snow Dogs, 2002, Hoodwinked, 2005; actor(voice overs): (films) The Wild, 2006; co-author: (films) Number One With a Bullett; writer: TV series Saturday Night Live, 1983—85, TV films Birthday Boy, 1986, films Greedy Show, 2001. Mem. Actors Equity Assn., Screen Actors Guild, AFTRA, Writers Guild Am., Acad. Motion Picture Arts and Scis., Acad. TV Arts and Scis. Office: care ICM 8942 Wilshire Blvd Beverly Hills CA 90211-1934*

BELVIS, RENEE MAGDALENA, elementary school educator; d. Toni Martha Ramos and Jean Michel Deslandes (Stepfather), Peter and Ana Maria Medina (Stepmother); m. Edwin Belvis, Sept. 22, 1985; children: Kristopher Edwin, Nicholas David. AA, Fiorello LaGuardia C.C., Queens, NY, 1984; BA, York Coll., Queens, NY, 2000. Cert. tchr. ESOL Fla. Dept. Edn., 2003, reading endorsement Fla. Dept. Edn., 2006. Tchr. English Safety Harbor Mid. Sch., Fla., 2003—04, John F. Kennedy Mid. Sch., Clearwater, Fla., 2004—. Site coord. adult ESOL literacy United Meth. Coop. Ministries, Clearwater, Fla., 2006—. Grantee, Pinellas Edn. Found., 2005. Mem.: TESOL, Bay Area Regional TESOL, Sunshine State TESOL, World Langs. Tchrs. Assn. (liaison 2005), Kappa Delta PI. Home Phone: 727-712-9728; Office Phone: 727-298-1609.

BELYTSCHKO, TED, engineering educator; b. Proskurov, Ukraine, Jan. 13, 1943; arrived in U.S.A., 1950; s. Stephan and Maria B.; m. Gail (Eisenhart), Aug. 1967; children: Peter, Nicole, Justine. BS in Engring. Sci., Ill. Inst. Tech., 1965, PhD in Mechanics, 1968; PhD (hon.), U. Liege, 1997; Doctorate (hon.), Ecole Ctrl., Paris, 2004, U. Lyon, 2006. Asst. prof. structural mechanics U. Ill., Chgo., 1968—73, assoc. prof., 1973—76, prof., 1976—77; Walter P. Murphy prof. and McCormick Disting. prof. mech. engring. Northwestern U., Evanston, Ill., 1977—, chair mech. engring., 1998—2002. Editor (assoc.): (jour.) Computer Methods in Applied Mech. and Engring., 1977—, Jour. Applied Mechanics, 1979—85; editor: Nuc. Engring. and Design, 1980—88, Engring. with Computers, 1984—98, Internat. Jour. Numerical Methods in Engring., 1998—; hon. editor: Internat. Jour. Computational Methods. Chmn. U.S. Nat. Com. on Theoretical and Applied Mechanics, 2004—06. NDEA Fellow, 1965-68; recipient Thomas Jaeger prize Internat. Assn. Structural Mechanics in Reactor Tech., 1983; Japanese Soc. Mech. Engr. Computational Mechanics Award, 1993; Gold medal Internat. Conf. on Computational Engring. and Sci., 1996; Computational Mechanics Award, Internat. Assn. for Computational Mechanics, 1998; Gauss Newton medal, 2002. Fellow: ASME (chmn. applied mechanics divsn. 1991, Pi Tau Sigma Gold medal 1975, Timoshenko medal 2001), Am. Acad. Arts and Scis.; mem.: NAE, ASCE (chmn. engring. mechanics divsn. 1982, Walter Huber Rsch. Prize 1977, Structural Dynamics and Materials Award 1990, Theodore von Karman medal 1999), Am. Acad. Mechanics (pres. 2004), Shock and Vibration Inst. (Baron medal 1999), U.S. Assn. Computational Mechanics (pres. 1992—94, von Neumann medal 2001, Computational Structural Mechanics Award 1997). Office: Northwestern Univ Mech Engring Dept 2145 Sheridan Rd Evanston IL 60208-3111 Business E-Mail: tedbelytschko@northwestern.edu.

BELZBERG, ALLAN JOEL, neurosurgery educator; b. Montreal, Que., Can., July 1, 1956; came to U.S., 1990; s. Sam Isadoer and Dorothy (Chetner) B.; m. Lorinda Gayle Sproule, May 29, 1988; children: Micah, Adam. BSc in Physiology with honors, U. B.C., Vancouver, Can., 1978, postgrad., 1978-79; MD, U. Calgary, Alta., Can., 1982. Mixed surg. and med. intern McGill U. Tchg. Hosps., Montreal, 1982-83; jr. resident in neurosurgery Foothills Hosp.-U. Calgary, 1984-85, 86, 87, sr. resident, 1988, resident in neuroradiology, sr. resident in neurology, 1986, resident in neuropathology, 1988; jr. resident, then sr. resident in neurosurgery Calgary Gen. Hosp., 1985, 87, chief resident, 1989; sr. resident Alta. Children's Hosp., 1988; rsch. fellow in neurosurgery U. Calgary, 1989-90, clin. asst. dept. neurosci., 1989-90; tng. in pain dept. neurosurgery, instr. Johns Hopkins U. Sch. Medicine, Balt., 1990-92, asst. prof., 1992, assoc. prof. Attending neurosurgeon Johns Hopkins Hosp., 1990—, Bay View Hosp., Balt., 1990—; lectr., vis. prof., presenter in field. Contbr. articles to med. jours., chpts. to books. Fellow Royal Coll. Surgery Can.; mem. Am. Assn. Neurol. Surgeons, Am. Soc. for Neurosci., Am. Soc. for Peripheral Nerve, Am. Pain Soc., Internat. Assn. for Study Pain, Can. Neurosurg. Soc., Can. Neurosci. Soc., Md. Neurosurg. Soc. Office: Johns Hopkins Sch Medicine Meyer 5-109 600 N Wolfe St Baltimore MD 21287-0005

BELZBERG, EDET, filmmaker; BA, U. Colo., Boulder, 1991; MA, Columbia U. Sch. Internat. and Pub. Affairs, 1997. Tchr., Tisch Sch. Arts NYU, 2001; frequent lectr., Sch. Journalism Columbia U. Assoc. prodr. (documentaries) Anthem, 1997, dir. & prodr. A Master Violinist, 1997 (John M. Patterson Enterprise award, Columbia U. Sch. Journalism, 1997),

Children Underground, 2001 (Spl. Jury prize, Sundance Film Festival, 2001, Best Documentary Film award, Internat. Documentary Assn., 2001), The AMC Project: Lookalikes, 2003, Gymnast, 2005. MacArthur Fellow, John D. and Catherine T. MacArthur Found., 2005.

BELZER, IRVIN V., lawyer; b. Kansas City, Apr. 6, 1948; BA, Oberlin Coll., 1970; JD cum laude, U. Mo., Kansas City, 1976. Bar: Mo. 1976. Atty. Smith, Gill, Fisher & Butts, Kansas City; mng. ptnr., group co-leader comml. litig. Bryan Cave LLP, Kansas City. Mem. bd. editors: U. Mo. at Kansas City Law Rev., 1975-76; cases and statutes editor: The Urban Lawyer, 1975-76. Mem. ABA, Mo. Bar, Lawyers Assn. Kansas City, Comml. Law League Am., Order of Bench and Robe. Office: Bryan Cave LLP One Kansas City Pl 1200 Main St, Ste 3500 Kansas City MO 64105 Office Phone: 816-391-7677. E-mail: ivbelzer@bryancave.com.

BELZER, RICHARD, actor, comedian; b. Bridgeport, Conn., Aug. 4, 1944; s. Charles and Francis B.; m. Gail Susan Ross (div.); m. Dalia Danoch (div.); m. Harlee McBride. Student, Dean Jr. Coll. Appeared in (films) Fame, Author! Author!, The Groove Tube, Night Shift, Scarface, The Puppet Masters, North, 1994, Not of This Earth, 1995, Girl 6, 1996, A Very Brady Sequel, 1996, Get on the Bus, 1996, Species II, 1998, The Bar Channel, 1998, Man on the Moon, 1999, Jump, 1999, (TV films) It's Just a Ride, 1994, Prince for a Day, 1995, Deadly Pursuits, 1996, Homicide: The Movie, 2000, (TV mini-series) The Invaders, 1995; stand-up comedian NYC and LA clubs; host (cable TV show) Hot Properties, Crime Stories, 1998; performer (TV show) Thicke of the Night, The Late Show David Letterman, Tonight Show with Johnny Carson, (voice) South Park, The Beat; TV (series) Homicide: Life on the Street, 1993-99, Lois & Clark/Superman, Law & Order: Special Victims Unit, 1999—; (guest appearances) Law & Order, 1996, 97, 99, 2000, Mad About You, 1999, Law & Order: Trial By Jury, 2005, Arrested Development, 2006; author: (book) How To Be a Standup Comic. Office: c/o NBC 30 Rockefeller Plz New York NY 10112

BEMENT, ARDEN LEE, JR., engineering educator, government agency administrator; b. Pitts., May 22, 1932; s. Arden Lee and Edith Ardelia (Bigelow) B.; m. Mary Ann Baroch, Aug. 24, 1952 (dec.); children: Kristine, Kenneth, Vincent, Cynthia, Mark, David, Paul, Mary; m. Louise Coquestrain, June 15, 2001. Degree of Engr. in Metallurgy, Colo. Sch. Mines, 1954; MSMetE, U. Idaho, 1959; PhD, U. Mich., 1963; PhD honoris causa, Cleve. State U., 1997, Case Western Res. U., 2002. Rsch. metallurgist Hanford Labs., GE, Richland, Wash., 1954-65; sr. rsch. mgr. Pacific N.W. Lab., Battelle Meml. Inst., Richland, 1965-70; prof. nuc. materials MIT, 1970-76; dir. Def. Advanced Rsch. Projects Agy. Office Materials Sci., DARPA, DOD, Washington, 1976-79, dep. undersec. rsch. and advanced tech., 1979-80; v.p. tech. resources TRW, Lyndhurst, Ohio, 1980-89, v.p. sci. and tech., 1990-92; Basil S. Turner disting. prof. engring. Purdue U., West Lafayette, Ind., 1992-98, head sch. nuc. engring., 1998—2001; dir. Nat. Inst. Standards & Tech., Gaithersburg, Md., 2001—04; acting dir. NSF, Arlington, Va., 2004, dir., 2004. Tech. assistance expert to Mexico UNIAEA, 1974-76; cons. NRC, Taiwan, 1975; mem. ex officio Nat. Sci. Bd., 1988-94; mem. sci. adv. com. Electric Power Rsch. Inst., 1987—, Advanced Tech. Inc., 1993—. Author publs. in field; editor: Biomaterials: Structural and Biomedical Bases for Hard Tissue and Soft Tissue Substitutes, 1971; co-editor: Dislocation Dynamics, 1968, Creep of Zirconium Alloys in Nuclear Reactors, 1983; mem. editl. bd. Jour. Nuclear Materials, 1970-77, Materials Tech., 1987-99; contbr. articles to profl. jours. Chmn. bd. health Mental Health/Mental Retardation, Benton-Franklin Counties, Wash., 1968-70; mem. Richland, Wash. city coun., 1968-70; pres. Arts Coun., Richland, Pasco and Kennewick, Wash., 1968-70; bd. dirs. Cleve. Opera Bd., treas., 1982-86, v.p., 1986-91, nat./internat. bd. mem., 1992—; bd. dirs. LaFayette Symphony, 1998—; bd. overseers Fermi Nat. Accelerator Lab., 1999—. Lt. col. USAR, 1954-79. Recipient Outstanding Achievement award Colo. Sch. Mines, 1984, Melville F. Coolbaugh award, 1991, Disting. Engr. award UCLA, 1987, Honor Roll award U. Idaho Alumni Assn., 1991, Engring. Alumnus of Yr. award U. Mich. Alumni Assn. (Cleve. br.), 1992, Merit award U. Mich. Alumni Assn., 1993, Nat. Mats. Adv. award Fedn. of Mats. Socs., 1997. Fellow Am. Nuclear Soc., Am. Soc. Metals (Disting. Life mem. 1998), Am. Inst. Chemists; mem. Nat. Acad. Engrs., ASTM, AIME, NSF, Am. Acad. Arts & Sci., Metals Soc. of AIME (Leadership award 1988, life mem. 2000), Sigma Xi, Tau Beta Pi, Sigma Gamma Epsilon. Republican. Roman Catholic. Office: NSF 4201 Wilson Blvd Arlington VA 22230 Office Phone: 301-975-2300.

BEMIS, MARY FERGUSON, magazine editor; b. NYC, Dec. 28, 1961; d. Edmund Augustus and Anne Adoian (Nalbandian) Bemis. BFA in Writing, Johnson State Coll., 1983. Co-editor, co-pub. Ave. Literary Rev. Ave. Publs. Inc., Burlington, Vt., 1983-85; editor Unique Hair and Beauty Mag., 1994; editor Lady's Circle Mag. Lopez Publs., NYC, 1987-94, editor, 1989-94; freelance editor, writer Mus. Sci., Boston, 1991-93; freelance editor Woman's Day Spl. Interest Publs., 1996—98; sr. editor Am. Salon and Am. Spa Mags., 1988—98; editor-in-chief Am. Spa Mag., 1998—2003; bd. dirs. Internat. Spa Assn., 2003; spa reporter, founder Founder Insider's Guide to Spas, 2004—; contbg. editor Skin Inc. mag., 2004—. Spa adviser Shape mag., 2004. Co-editor: The Green Mountain Rev., 1982—83, Nature Through Her Eyes: Art and Literature by Women, 1994, Journey Into the Wilderness, 1994; sr. editor Am. Salon Mag., 1996—98, editor-in-chief Am. Spa Mag., 1998—2003; contbg. editor: Luxury Spa Finder mag., 2004. Mem.: Am. Soc. of Mag. Editors. Democrat. Unitarian Universalist. Mailing: Allured Publishing 362 S Schmale Rd Carol Stream IL 60188-2787 E-mail: MFBEMIS@aol.com.

BEMIS, MICHAEL B., utility company executive; b. Pascagoula, Miss., Mar. 24, 1947; s. James E. and Mary I. (Rowell) Loris; m. Elizabeth Ann Welfare, May 2, 1982 BS, U. So. Miss., 1969. C.P.A., Ark., La., Miss., N.C. Staff acct. Deloitte Haskins & Sells, New Orleans, 1970-72, sr. acct., 1972-75, mgr., 1975-79, ptnr., 1979-81, ptnr. in charge acctg. and audit services, 1981-82; sr. v.p., sec., asst. treas. Ark. Power & Light Co., Little Rock, 1982—. Vice chmn. Econ. Devel. Council, Little Rock C. of C.; bd. dirs. Ark. Arthritis Found., First Ark. Devel. Fin. Corp., Little Rock. Mem. Am. Inst. C.P.A.s, Ark. Soc. C.P.A.s Avocation: golf. Office: Ark Power & Light Co PO Box 551 Little Rock AR 72203-0551 also: Miss Power & Light Co PO Box 1640 Jackson MS 39215-1640

BENABOU, ROLAND JEAN-MARC, economist, educator; Degree in Engring., Ecole Poly., 1980, Ecole Nat. des Ponts et Chaussées, 1982; PhD, MIT, 1986. Prof. econs. and pub. affairs Princeton (N.J.) U., 1999—; chargé de rsch. Ctr. Nat. de la Rsch. Sci., CEPREMAP, Paris, 1986—88; asst. prof. econs. MIT, Mass., 1988—92, assoc. prof. econs. Mass., 1992—94, NYU, NY, 1994—96, prof. econs. NY, 1996—99; prof. econs. and pub. affairs dept. econs., Woodrow Wilson Sch. Pub. and Internat. Affairs Princeton (N.J.) U., 1999—. Vis. prof. U. Paris X-Nanterre, France, 1995, IDEI, Toulouse, France, 1997—99, CERAS, Paris, 1997—99; mem. Sch. Social Sci., Inst. for Advanced Studies Princeton U., NJ, 2002—03; lectr. in field. Assoc. editor: Jour. Econ. Growth, 1995—, Macroeconomic Dynamics, 1997—, Quarterly Jour. Econs., 1997—2001, QR Jour. Macroeconomics, 2000—, Jour. Pub. Econs., 2000—, Jour. European Econ. Assn., 2003—, fgn. editor: Rev. Econ. Studies, 1993—2001, overseas assoc. editor: European Econ. Rev., 1994—2000, mem. editl. bd.: Annals d'Economie et de Statistique, 1993—. Fellow, Guggenheim Found., 2003; grantee, NSF, 1990—92, 1992—94, 1996—99, 2001—; sr. fellow, Bur. for Rsch. and Econ. Analysis of Devel., 2002—. Fellow: Econometric Soc.; mem.: Inst. for Rsch. on Poverty (assoc.). Office: Woodrow Wilson Sch Pub and Internat Affairs Princeton Univ Princeton NJ 08544

BENACERRAF, BARUJ, pathologist, educator; b. Caracas, Venezuela, Oct. 29, 1920; arrived in US, 1939, naturalized, 1943; s. Abraham and Henriette (Lasry) Benacerraf; m. Annette Dreyfus, Mar. 24, 1943; 1 child, Beryl. B es L, Lycee Janson, 1940; BS, Columbia U., 1942; MD, Med. Sch. Va., 1945; MA, Harvard U., 1970; MD (hon.), U. Geneva, 1980; DSc (hon.), NYU, 1981, Va. Commonwealth U., 1981, Yeshiva U., 1982, U. Aix-Marseille, 1982, Columbia U., 1985, Adelphi U., 1988, Weizmann Inst., 1989, Harvard U., 1992, U. Bordeaux, 1993, U. Vienna, 1995. Intern Queens Gen. Hosp., NYC, 1945—46; rsch. fellow dept. microbiology Med. Sch. Columbia U., 1948—50; charge de recherches Centre Nat. de Recherche Scientique Hosp. Broussais, Paris, 1950—56; asst. prof. pathology Sch. Medicine NYU, 1956—58, assoc. prof. Sch. Medicine, 1958—60, prof. Sch. Medicine, 1960—68; chief immunology Nat. Inst. Allergy and Infectious Diseases NIH, Bethesda, Md., 1968—70; Fabyan prof. comparative pathology, chmn. dept. Med. Sch. Harvard U., 1970—91; ret. Med. Sch., Harvard U., Cambridge, Mass., 1991. Pres, CEO Dana-Farber Cancer Inst, 1980—91, Dana-Farber Inc, 1990—95; mem immunology study sect NIH; pres Fedn Am Socs Experimental Biol, 1974—75; chmn sci adv comt Centre d'Immunologies de Marseille, France. Bd govs Weizmann Inst Med; mem sci adv comt Children's Hosp, Boston; mem award comt GM Cancer Research Found, chmn selection comt Sloan Prize, 1980. Capt MC AUS, 1946—48. Recipient T Duckett Jones Meml Award, Helen Hay Whitney Found, 1976, Rabbi Shai Shacknai Lectr and Prize, Hebrew Univ Jerusalem, 1974, Waterford Award, 1980, Nobel Prize, 1980, Corr, Emerite de l'Institut de la Sante et de la Rcherche Scientifique, Nat Medal Sci, NSF, 1990. Fellow: Am Acad Arts and Scis; mem.: NAS, Int Union Immunology Socs (pres 1980—83), French Soc Biol Chemistry, Brit Asn Immunology, Am Asn Immunologists (pres 1973—74), Nat Inst Med. Office: Dana-Farber Cancer Inst 44 Binney St Boston MA 02115-6084

BENAMATI, DENNIS CHARLES, librarian, editor, consultant; b. Orlando, Fla., Oct. 30, 1948; s. Thomas Guy and Ann (Clements) Benamati; m. Evelina Estella Lemelin, Aug. 19, 1983; children: Suzette, Alicia, Marcus. BA, St. Francis Coll., Loretto, Pa., 1970; MA, Fordham U., 1974; MLS, So. Conn. State U., 1975. Law libr. Conn. State Libr., Stamford, 1976-78; reference libr. U. Bridgeport (Conn.) Sch. Law, 1979; asst. law libr. for tech. svcs. U. Maine Sch. Law, Portland, 1979-83; asst. law libr. Aetna Life & Casualty Co., Hartford, Conn., 1983-84; head cataloging U. Conn. Sch. Law, Hartford, 1984-88; dir. The Dewey Grad. Libr. SUNY, Albany, 1988-93; adj. faculty Sch. Criminal Justice, SUNY, Albany, 1993—95; vis. elec. info. svcs. libr., instr. advanced legal rsch. U. S.C. Sch. Law, 1995—97; asst. libr. dir. Marist Coll., 1997—2002, adj. instr. criminal justice dept., interim libr. dir., adj. instr. Sch. Mgmt., 2000—02; libr. Sacred Heart U., Fairfield, Conn., 2002—. Ptnr. Lemelin & Benamati; cons., Nassau, NY, 1985—, various law firms, Lawyers Coop. Pub. Co., European Inst. Crime Prevention and Control; adj. prof. Coll. Edn. and Health Professions, Sacred Heart U., 2005—. Co-author: Publication Opportunities for Law Librarians, 1995, Criminal Justice Information: How to Find It, How to Use It, 1998; rapporteur World Criminal Justice Libr. Netowrk Conf., 1997, 1999, 2001, 2004, 2006; contbr. articles to profl. jours. Mem.: ALA, Coun. Conn. Acad. Libr. Dirs., Law Librs. New Eng. (bd. dir. 1985—87), Am. Assn. Law Librs., Assn. Coll. and Rsch. Librs. Roman Catholic. Mailing: 358 Kingman Rd Nassau NY 12123 Home Phone: 518-766-0440; Office Phone: 203-371-7700. E-mail: benamatid@sacredheart.edu.

BEN-AMI, LEORA, lawyer; BS, SUNY, Stony Brook; JD cum laude, SUNY, Buffalo. Law clk. to Sr. Circuit Judge Philip Nichols, Jr., US Ct. Appeals Fed. Circuit, 1984—85; ptnr. Clifford Chance, chair Am. Intellectual Property Group; ptnr. Kaye Scholer LLP, 2003—. Spkr. on patent law at conferences and seminars. Contbr. articles in field. Named one of 45 under 45, Am. Lawyer Media, 2003, The Nation's Top Litigators, Nat. Law Jour., 2007. Mem.: Am. Intellectual Property Law Assn., NY Patent, Trademark and Copyright Law Assn., Fed. Circuit Bar Assn., NY State Bar Assn. Office: 425 Park Ave New York NY 10022-3598 Office Phone: 212-836-8000. Office Fax: 212-836-8689. Business E-Mail: lbenami@kayscholer.com.*

BEN-ARIE, RONIT PELEG, elementary school educator; arrived in U.S., 1989; d. Israel and Edith Popovich; m. Jezekiel Ben-Arie, Nov. 17, 1983. BA, Haifa U., Israel, 1985; postgrad., Oranim Tchrs. Sem., Israel, 1986; MA, Lesley Coll., 1988. Music and art therapist in charge of expressive arts rehab. programs Fliman Rehab. Geriatric Hosp., Haifa, 1985—89; music and arts therapist Ill. Masonic Hosp. Ctr., Warren Barr Pavilion, Chgo., 1989—92; instr. tchrs. Jewish Fedn., Chgo., 1998—2000; tchr., kindergarten curriculum developer Solomon Schechter Day Schs., Skokie and Northbrook, 1992—. Composer included in nat. curricula Union of Am. Hebrew Congregations; presenter, spkr. in field. Composer: Songs in Easy Hebrew, 1996, Hebrew in Song, 2000 (No. 1 rating in Jewish and Yiddish music, Amazon.com, 01, No. 1 rating in Israeli style music, Amazon.com, 01), Hello World, 2006, More Hebrew in Song, 2007. Advocacy group organizer, convenor Conf. on Alternatives in Jewish Edn., Chgo., 2002. Lt. Israeli Def. Forces, 1977—80. Recipient songs selected to be part of nat. music curricula, Union Am. Hebrew Congregations. Avocations: ceramic sculpture, painting, reading, ballroom dancing, bicycling. Home: 155 N Harbor Dr Apt 2011 Chicago IL 60601 Office: Solomon Schechter Day Schs 3210 Dundee Rd Northbrook IL 60062 Office Phone: 847-412-5600. E-mail: rbenarie@yahoo.com.

BENARIO, HERBERT WILLIAM, classicist, educator; b. NYC, July 21, 1929; s. Frederick and Ilse (Kessler) Benario; m. Janice M. Martin, Dec. 23, 1957; children: Frederick M., John H. BA, CCNY, 1948; MA, Columbia U., 1949; PhD, Johns Hopkins U., 1951. Instr. Greek and Latin Columbia U., 1953-58; asst. prof. Greek and Latin Sweet Briar Coll., 1958-60; mem. faculty Emory U., Atlanta, 1960—, prof. classics, 1967-87, chmn. dept., 1968-73, 76-78, prof. emeritus, 1987, disting. fellow emeritus, 2001—02. Dir. Vergilian Soc. Summer Sch., Italy, 1963, Italy, 67, Italy, 73, Italy, 81, asst. dir., Italy, 57, Italy, 59; dir. Roman Britain Tour, 1977, 86, Roman Germany Tour, 1981, 88, Rome and North Italy, 1982, Roman Germany Tour Mediterranean Soc., 1998, North Italy Tour Mediterranean Soc., 1999; vis. prof. Intercollegiate Ctr. Classical Studies, Rome, 1967, co-prof. in charge, 1984—85; vis. prof. U. Colo., 1969, Brigham Young U., 1999; Fulbright Sr. prof. U. Passau, Germany, 1990; co-exec. sec. Vergilian Soc., 1992—93; mem. Latin achievement test com. Coll. Entrance Exam. Bd., 1963—66. Author: (book) Tacitus, Agricola, Germany, Dialogue on Orators, 1967, Tacitus, Agricola, Germany, Dialogue on Orators, rev. edit., 1991, 2006, An Introduction to Tacitus, 1975, A Commentary on the Vita Hadriani in the Historia Augusta, 1980, Tacitus Annals 11 and 12, 1983, The Classical Association of the Middle West and South, 1989, Caesaris Augusti Res Gestae et Fragmenta, 1990, Thusnelda: A German Princess in Ancient Rome, 1993, Tacitus Germany, 1999; co-editor: Basil Lanneau Gildersleeve: An American Classicist, 1986. With AUS, 1951—53. Fellow Am. Coun. Learned Soc., 1978, Heilbrun, Emory U., 2002; grantee Fulbright, 1956, Rsch., Am. Philos. Soc. Mem.: Classical Soc. Am. Acad. Rome (pres. 1965), Am. Classical League, Vergilian Soc. Am. (trustee 1960—65, 1969—73, pres. 1980—82), Classical Assn. Midwest and South (pres.so. sect. 1968—70, pres. 1971—72), Am. Philological Assn., Phi Beta Kappa (pres. Emory U. chpt. 1968—69). Home: 1717 N Decatur Rd NE #119 Atlanta GA 30307 Office: Emory U Classics Dept Atlanta GA 30322-0001 Personal E-mail: hwbenario@yahoo.com.

BEN-ASHER, DANIEL LAWRENCE, photojournalist, retired legislative staff member; b. Newark, Apr. 15, 1946; s. Jerry and Florence (Tasoff) Ben-Asher; m. Michele Lauren Cohn, July 16, 1978; children: Sarah, Joshua. AB, Rutgers Coll., 1968; MA, U. Minn., 1970. Plant pers. adminstr. Tanatex Chem. Co. divsn. Sybron Corp., Lyndhurst, NJ, 1970—71; rsch. asst. Office Legis. Svcs. N.J. State Legislature, Trenton, 1971—76, rsch. assoc., 1976—87, sr. rsch. assoc., 1987—98, sr. rsch. analyst, 1999—2003; freelance photojournalist NJ, 2005—. Staff N.J. Assembly Labor Com., 1974—81, Assembly Commerce and Industry Com., 1981—82, Assembly Drug and Alcohol Abuse Policy Com., 1990—91, Assembly Housing Com., 1995; mem. N.J. Tobacco Age-of-Sale Enforcement Task Force, 1994—96; mem. politics and govt. judges panel Best in Am. spl. edit. U.S. News and World Report, 1990. Mem. Ewing Twp. (N.J.) Rent Control Bd., 1976—77; fin. coord. Lawrence Twp. (N.J.) Hist. Preservation Adv. Com., 1985—92; twp. chmn. Guide Lawrenceville's Hist. Landmarks, 1991—93; mem. nat. alumni adv. com. admissions Rutgers U., New Brunswick, alumni admissions rep., 1994—2001, chmn. Mason Gross Presdl. Meml., 1992—94. Recipient Loyal Son award for Extraordinary Svc. to Alma Mater, Rutgers Alumni Assn., 1995. Home: 11 Bennington Dr Lawrenceville NJ 08648-1536 E-mail: Legisdan@aol.com.

BENATAR, PAT (PAT ANDRZEJEWSKI), rock singer; b. Bklyn., Jan. 10, 1953; m. Neil Geraldo; 1 child, Haley. Albums include: In the Heat of the Night, 1979, Crimes of Passion, 1980, Precious Time, 1981, Get Nervous, 1982, Live From Earth, 1983, Tropico, 1984, Seven the Hard Way, 1985, Wide Awake in Dreamland, 1988, Best Shots, 1989, True Love, 1991, Gravity's Rainbow, 1993, All Fired Up: The Very Best of Pat Benatar, 1994, Heartbreaker: 16 Classic Performances, 1996, Innamorata, 1997, 8-15-80, 1998, Synchronistic Wanderings: Recorded Anthology 1979-99, 1999, Live at Electric Ladyland, 2002, Greatest Hits Live, 2003, Go, 2003, The Best of Pat Benatar Vols. I & II, 2004, Greatest Hits, 2005; popular recs. include Treat Me Right, Hit Me With Your Best Shot, Love is a Battlefield, Hell is for Children. Recipient Grammy award for best female rock vocal performance, 1981, 82, 83, 84

BEN-AVI, SIMON STEPHEN, biomedical researcher, educator; s. Harold Barber and Annabelle Cynthia Bevan; m. Nina Ben-Avi (div.); children: Julia Caroline, Emma Hannah. BS with honors, U. Manchester Inst. Sci. and Tech., 1972, MS, 1973; PhD, Queen Victoria U. Manchester, 1979. Prof. computer sci. N.Y. Inst. Tech., NYC; prof. elec. engring. Cooper Union, 1984—, assoc. dean engring., 1998—; ednl. cons. AT&T Bell Labs., Holmdel, 1986—92; biomed. cons. Lenox Hill Hosp., NYC, 1994—. Rschr. Lenox Hill Hosp., 1986—. Musician: (organist) Church Organist; contbr. articles to profl. jours. Bd. dirs. C. W. Starr Rsch. Found. of Cooper Union, NYC, 2000—. Grantee, NSF, 1985—2005. Mem.: IEE, ACM, IEEE, Inst. Elec. and Radio Engineers, Brit. Computer Soc. Achievements include research in biomedical engineering; patents for biometric Internet security. Office: The Cooper Union Sci and Art 51 Astor Pl New York NY 10023 Office Phone: 212-353-4289. Office Fax: 212-353-4341, 212-353-4341. Business E-Mail: benavi@cooper.edu. E-mail: sba490@aol.com.

BENAVIDES, FORTUNATO PEDRO (PETE BENAVIDES), federal judge; b. Mission, Tex., Feb. 3, 1947; BBA, U. Houston, 1968, JD, 1972. Atty. Rankin, Kern & Martinez, McAllen, Tex., 1972—74, Cisneros, Beery & Benavides, McAllen, 1974, Cisneros, Brown & Benavides, McAllen, 1975, Cisneros & Benavides, McAllen, 1976; pvt. practice McAllen, 1977; judge Hidalgo County Ct.-at-Law # 2, Edinburg, Tex., 1977—79; prin. Law Offices of Fortunato P. Benavides, McAllen, 1980—81; judge 92nd Dist. Ct. of Hidalgo County, Tex., 1981—84, 13th Ct. Appeals, Corpus Christi, Tex., 1984—91, Tex. Ct. Criminal Appeals, Austin, 1991—92; atty. Atlas & Hall, McAllen, 1993—94; judge US Ct. Appeals (5th cir.), Austin, 1994—. Commr. Tex. Juvenile Probation Commn., 1983—89; vis. judge to cts. in Tex., 1993. Active Mustangs of Corpus Christi, 1990—91, hon. mem., 1992; active Mex.-Am. Dems. of Tex., 1990—92; mem. St. Michael Episc. Ch., Austin, 1992—. Mem.: ABA, Hidalgo County Bar Assn., State Bar Tex. Office: US Ct Appeals 5th Cir Homer Thornberry Judicial Bldg 903 San Jacinto Blvd Rm 450 Austin TX 78701 Office Phone: 512-916-5796.*

BENBOW, CAMILLA PERSSON, dean, psychology professor; b. Lund, Sweden, Dec. 3, 1956; came to U.S., 1965, naturalized, 1985; m. David Lubinski; children: Wystan R., Bronwen G., Trefor A., Evan M., Lovisa D., G. Byron, Lena C. BA in Psychology with honors, Johns Hopkins U., 1977, MA in Psychology, 1978, MS in Edn. of the Gifted, 1980, EdD with distinction in Edn. of Gifted, 1981. Dir. Office of Precollegiate Programs for Talented & Gifted Iowa State U., 1987-98, Johns Hopkins U., Balt., 1977-79, asst. dir. Study of Mathematically Precocious Youth, 1979-81, assoc. dir., 1981-85, co-dir., 1985-86, dir., 1986—, assoc. rsch. scientist dept. psychology, 1981-86, asst. prof. sociology, part-time, 1983-86; assoc. prof. psychology Iowa State U., Ames, 1985-90, prof. psychology, 1990-95, chair dept. psychology, 1992-98, disting. prof., 1995-98, interim dean coll. edn., 1996-98; dean Peabody Coll. of Edn. and Human Devel., Vanderbilt U., Nashville, 1998—. Mem. Nat. Sci. Bd., 2006—; vice chmn. Nat. Math Panel, 2006—. Sr. editor: Academic Precocity: Aspects of Its Development, 1983, Intellectual Talent: Psychometric and Social Issues, 1996; contbr. articles to profl. jours. Recipient John Curtis Gowan prize Nat. Assn. Gifted Children, 1980, 81, 86, Rsch. award Am. Ednl. Rsch. Assn., 1982; Spencer fellow, alt., 1984, 85, 86, Rsch. paper award Mensa, 1985, 86, 89, 94, 95 Mensa Lifetime Achievement award, 2004; Early Scholar award Nat. Assn. Gifted Children, 1985, Disting. Scholar award 1992, George A. Miller award APA, 1999. Mem. Johns Hopkins Soc. Scholars, Phi Beta Kappa, Sigma Xi. Office: Vanderbilt Univ Peabody Coll Edn/Human Devel Deans Office Box 329 Peabody Sta Nashville TN 37203 Office Phone: 615-322-8407. Business E-Mail: camilla.benbow@vanderbilt.edu.

BENBOW, JOEL JOSHUA, minister; b. Hartley, Iowa, Apr. 28, 1968; s. Joel Rudolph and Patricia Ann Benbow. BA in Theology, Internat. Bible Coll., Independence, Mo., 2004, ThM, 2005, PhD with honors, 2007. Ordained to ministry 2006. Companion dog trainer Friends for Folks, Lexington, Okla., 1993—95; computer graphics designer OCI, Stringtown, Okla., 1995—2004; ministry assoc. Faith Outreach, Pottsboro, Tex., 2005—. Dir. World Vision, Stringtown, 2006—; worship coord. various chs., Stringtown, 1999—. Creator, co-writer: comic book Generic Man, 2004. V.p. Jaycees, Stringtown, 1996—97; facilitator substance abuse edn. for prisoners. Mem.: Peculiar People, Mensa. Avocations: reading, writing, metal fabrication, music, sports.

BENBROOK, CHARLES MALLARD, executive consulting company; b. LA, Nov. 26, 1949; s. Samuel Benbrook and Barbara Arons; m. Donna Mae Benbrook, July 23, 1974; children: Stephen, Rachel, Michael. BS, Harvard U., 1971; MS, U. Wis., 1979, PhD, 1980. Policy analyst President's Coun. on Eviron. Qualty, Washington, 1980-81; staff dir. subcom. on dept. ops., rsch. and fgn. agr. U.S. Ho. of Reps., Washington, 1981-83; exec. dir. Bd. on Agriculture, Nat. Acad. Scis., Washington, 1984-90; pres., prin. Benbrook Consulting Svcs., Washington, 1991—; chief scientist Organic Ctr. Achievements include development of Ag BioTech InfoNet. Avocations: farming, fishing, travel. Home and Office: Benbrook Consulting Svcs 5085 Upper Pack River Rd Sandpoint ID 83864-5938 Business E-Mail: cbenbrook@organic-center.org.*

BENCARDINO, JENNY TERESA, musculoskeletal radiologist; b. Bogota, Colombia, Aug. 6, 1968; d. Libardo and Teresa (Suárez) Bencardino; m. Alvand Hassankhani, Apr. 20, 2002; children: Dario A. Hassankhani, Avan P. Hassankhani. Bachelor's degree, Divine Savior Sch., Bogota, 1985; MD, Xaverian U., Bogota, 1991, specialist in diagnostic imaging with honors, 1996. Diplomate Am. Bd. Radiology, 2000. Resident in diagnostic imaging Albert Einstein Coll. Medicine, New Hyde Pk., NY, 2000; dir. musculoskeletal MRI Mass. Gen. Hosp., Boston, 2000—02,

Med. Arts Radiology P.C., Bay Shore, NY, 2003—06; asst. prof. radiology Harvard Med. Sch., Boston, 2000—03; musculoskeletal radiologist Franklin & Seidelmann Subspecialty Radiology, 2006—. Mem. faculty refresher course Radiol. Soc. N.Am., Chgo., 2006—07. Manuscript reviewer Skeletal Radiology, 2005—; co-author: MRI in Orthopaedics and Sports Medicine, 2007; co-editor: (jour.) Topics in MRI. Recipient Resident/Fellow Rsch. award, Radiol. Soc. N.Am., 1999. Mem.: Radiol. Soc. N.Am., Internat. Soc. MRI, Internat. Skeletal Soc. Avocations: travel, Latin-American literature, swimming. Personal E-mail: jennybencardino@yahoo.com.

BENCH, JOHNNY LEE, retired professional baseball player; b. Oklahoma City, Dec. 7, 1947; s. Ted Bench. Grad. high sch. Catcher Cin. Reds, Nat. League, 1967-83; spl. cons. to gen. mgr. Cin. Reds, 1997-98; speaker Keppler Assocs. Inc., Arlington, Va., 1998—; broadcaster. Propr. bowling alley, Cin.; spokesman, bd. dirs. Interactive Mktg. Tech., Inc., Tarzana, Calif., 1999—. Profl. nightclub singer, from 1970; host TV interview show MVP-Johnny Bench, until 1976; baseball instructional show The Baseball Bunch, 1981, 82, 83; toured Vietnam with Bob Hope Christmas Show, 1970, 71; author: Catch You Later. Named Minor League Player of Yr., Sporting News, 1967, Nat. League Rookie of Yr., Sporting News, 1968, Nat. League Rookie of Yr., Baseball Writers Assn. Am., 1968, Nat. League MVP, 1970, 72, Major League Player of Yr., Sporting News, 1970, Nat. League Player of Yr., Sporting News, 1970, MVP, 1976 World Series; player Nat. League All-Star Fielding Team, 1968-77, 79-80, Nat. League All-Star Team, Sporting News, 1968-70, 72, 73-77; inducted into Baseball Hall of Fame, 1989; recipient Gold Glove award 10 times; named to All-Time Rawlings Gold Glove Team, 2007. Achievements include catching over 100 games a yr. for 13 consecutive seasons. Address: Interactive Mktg Tech Inc 5120 Whitsett Ave Valley Village CA 91607-3016

BENCINI, SARA HALTIWANGER, concert pianist; b. Winston Salem, N.C., Sept. 2, 1926; d. Robert Sydney and Janie Love (Couch) Haltiwanger; m. Robert Emery Bencini, June 26, 1954; children: Robert Emery, III, Constance Bencini Waller, John McGregor. Mus. B., Salem Coll., 1947; postgrad. grad. Juilliard Sch. Music, 1948-50; M.A., Smith Coll., 1951; D In Mus. Arts, U. N.C., Greensboro, 1989. Head piano dept. Mary Burnham Sch. for Girls, Northampton, Mass., 1949-51; pianist, composer dance and drama dept. Smith Coll., 1951-52; head music dept. Walnut Hill Sch. for Girls, Natick, Mass., 1952-54; pvt. piano tchr., High Point, N.C., 1954-66; concert pianist appearing in Am. and Europe, 1948—; duo-piano performances with PBS-TV, Columbia, S.C., 1967, Winston Salem Symphony, N.C., 1964-68, Ea. Mus. Festival, Greensboro, N.C., 1969. Mem. DAR. Democrat. Presbyterian.

BENCLOSKI, JOSEPH W., geography educator; BS in Edn., Ind. U., Pa., 1964, MA, 1970; PhD, Pa. State U., 1976. Grad. teaching asst. dept. geography Pa. State U., University Park, 1970-72; vis. asst. prof. Ohio State U., Columbus, 1976-77; temp. asst. prof. U. Ga., 1978-83, asst. prof., 1983-85; asst. prof. dept. geography and regional planning Indiana (Pa.) U., 1988—. Vis. prof. dept. geoscis. Pa. State U., 1988; vis. assoc. prof. U. N.C., Greensboro, 1985-87; researcher in field. Contbr. articles to profl. jours. Recipient Teaching Excellence award Teaching Excellence Ctr., 1993. Mem. AAAS, Nat. Coun. Geographic Edn. (dep. exec. dir. 1988—, editor Perspective, 1988—, coord. svc. coords. program 1988-91, ad hoc mem. long range planning com. 1989-91, awards com. 1983-86, chair awards com. 1985-86, Disting. Teaching Achievement award 1990), Assn. Am. Geographers (population geography specialty group, climatology specialty group), Nat. Collegiate Honors Coun., Pa. Geographic Soc. (Devel. Exemplary Teaching Materials award 1993), Kappa Delta Pi, Sigma Xi, Phi Delta Kappa, Pi Gamma Mu, Gamma Theta Upsilon. Office: Indiana U Pa Dept Geography & Regional Planning 1011 S Drive 1C Leonard Hall Indiana PA 15705-0001

BENDELAC, ROGER E., investment executive, financial consultant; b. Oct. 5, 1956; s. David and Marie Bendelac; married; 2 children. Diplome, Institut D'Etudes Politiques, Paris, France, 1978; MBA, Columbia U., 1980. Lic. securities and commodities registered rep. Acct. exec. Oppenheimer & Co., Inc., NYC, 1980-83, v.p. retail sales dept., 1983-84, sr. v.p. retail sales dept., 1984-85; sr. v.p. internat. br. Shearson Lehman Hutton, Inc., NYC, 1985-87; pres., CEO REB Futures, Inc., NYC, 1987-90; investment exec. Westminster Securities Corp., NYC, 1988—; CEO Generis Capital Corp., NYC, 1990-91; mng. dir. Genersis Assocs., Inc., NYC, 1991—; mng. dir. internat. instnl. sales Laidlaw Global Securities, NYC, 1997-98; pres., COO, dir. Laidlaw Global Corp., NYC, 1998—, Global Electronic Exch., Inc., NYC, 1998—; chmn., CEO Laidlaw Global Corp., NYC, 2003; mem., mgr. Roger Bendelac Advisors, LLC, Strategic Consultants, NYC, 2003—. Exec. advisor Geo Genesis Group, Inc., 2006—. Editor bus. rev. Columbia U., 1979. Mem. N.Y. Acad. Scis. (elected mem.), Columbia Bus. Sch. Club. Avocations: running, team hand ball, readings in economics and history. Office: Roger Bendelac Advisors LLC 575 Madison Ave New York NY 10022 Office Phone: 212-937-8423. Business E-Mail: roger@rogerbendelac.com.

BENDELIUS, ARTHUR GEORGE, engineering firm executive; b. Passaic, NJ, May 21, 1936; s. Arthur Leopold and Lydia Ella (Flach) B.; m. Virginia Brown, June 21, 1958; children: Linda Ellen Newlin, Bonnie Sue, Heidi Ann Mitchell. BE, Stevens Inst. Tech., 1958, MMS, 1966. Registered profl. engr., NY, NJ, Mich., Minn., Ga., Fla., Tex. Ala., Ky., NC, SC, Miss., Tenn., La., Ohio, Ark., Okla., Md., Utah, Colo., Wyo., W.Va., Pa. Engr. Syska & Hennessey, NYC, 1958-60, Parsons Brinckerhoff Quade & Douglas, Inc., NYC, 1960-62, Nat. Biscuit Co., NYC, 1962—63; asst. dept. head Parsons Brinckerhoff Quade & Douglas, Inc., NYC, 1963-68, dept. head, 1968-70, project mgr., 1970-73, regional mgr. Atlanta, 1973-76, asst. v.p., 1976-78, v.p., 1978-82, sr. v.p., 1982-89; regional mgr. Energy Sys. Group, NYC, 1989-93, prin. profl. assoc., 1991—2004, sr. v.p., 1989—2004, tech. dir., 1992—2004. Divsn. mgr. PBES, NYC, 1994-96, Parsons Brinckerhoff Quade & Douglas, Inc., NYC, 1996-2002, Atlanta, 2002-04; pres. A & G Cons., Inc., 2004—; presenter in field. Co-author: Tunnel Engineering Handbook, 1982, 2d edit., 1996, ASHRAE Handbook Applications, 1978, 5th edit., 2007, Fire Protection Handbook, 20th edit., 2007, Handbook of Tunnel Fire Safety, 2005, Fire & Smoke Contrik in Road Tunnels, 1999; co-editor Equipment and Systems for Fire Smoke Control in Road Tunnels, 2007; contbr. articles to profl. jours. Pres. Brookside Home Sch. Orgn., Westwood, NJ, 1972-73; co-v.p. Dunwoody Band Booster Club, Ga., 1975-76, co-pres., 1976-77. Named Atlanta Engr. of Yr. in Pvt. Practice, 1978; recipient Harold R. Fee Alumni award, 1978. Fellow Soc. Am. Mil. Engrs. (pres. Atlanta chpt. 1978-79, nat. bd. dirs. 1983-86), ASHRAE (life, chmn. tech. com. 1975-79, rsch. promotion com. 1980-82, tech. com. 5.0 1982—, bd. dirs., 2005—); mem. NSPE, ASME (life), Ga. Soc. Profl. Engrs. (bd. dirs. 1976-78), Nat. Coun. Examiners Engring. and Surveying (cert.), Ga. Engring. Found. (life 1983—, bd. dirs. 1977-89, sec. 1979, v.p. 1980, pres. 1982, 83), Steven's Alumni Assn., Brit. Tunneling Soc., Transp. Assn. SC (bd. dirs. 1987, treas. 1987-89), Nat. Fire Protection Assn. (tech. com. 130, 1992-2004, task group ventilation, tech. com. 502 1993—, chair NPPA 502 subcom. 1994-97, chair tech. com. 502, 1996-2004, World Road Assn. (PIARC) (tech. com. C5 and C3.3 on Rd. Tunnel Operation, 1999-, working group Ventilation & Fire Control 1992—, chmn., 1999-2007), Aircraft Owners and Pilots Assn., Tau Beta Pi, Sigma Nu (pres. alumni assn. 1966-70, comdr. 1971-73), Ansley Golf Club, Atlanta Stevens Club (pres. 1974-90, 2002-). Lutheran. Office: A&G Consultants Inc 11391 Big Canoe Big Canoe GA 30143-5108 Office Phone: 706-268-1965. E-mail: bendelius@tds.net.

BENDELIUS, BONNIE SUE, elementary school educator; b. Westwood, NJ, Oct. 28, 1961; d. Arthur George and Virginia Brown Bendelius; m. Brian Vincient Harr, Sept. 22, 1998. BA in Early Childhood Edn., Clemson U., SC, 1983; MA in Early Childhood Edn., Oglethorpe U., Atlanta, 1992. Tchr. The Village Sch., Cheyenne, Wyo., 1983—86, R.D. Head Elem. Sch., Lilburn, Ga., 1987—91, Norcross Elem. Sch., Ga., 1991—98, Knight Elem. Sch., Lilburn, Ga., 1998—2002, Pharr Elem. Sch., Snellville, Ga., 2002—. Costumer, actor: Kaliedoscope Children's Theater; Abracadabra! Children's Theater. Avocations: theater, sewing, football. Home: 5202 Addison Tr SW Lilburn GA 30047-6670

BENDER, BETTY WION, librarian; b. Mt. Ayer, Iowa, Feb. 26, 1925; d. John F. and Sadie A. (Guess) Wion; m. Robert F. Bender, Aug. 24, 1946. BS, N.Tex. State U., Denton, 1946; MA, U. Denver, 1957. Asst. cataloger N. Tex. State U. Library, 1946-49; from cataloger to head acquisitions So. Meth. U., Dallas, 1949-56; reference asst. Ind. State Library, Indpls., 1951-52; librarian Ark. State Coll., 1958-59, Eastern Wash. Hist. Soc., Spokane, 1960-67; reference librarian, then head circulation dept. Spokane (Wash.) Public Library, 1968-73, library dir., 1973-88. Vis. instr. U. Denver, summers 1957-60, 63, fall 1959; instr. Whitworth Coll., Spokane, 1962-64; mem. Gov. Wash. Regional Conf. Libraries, 1968, Wash. Statewide Library Devel. Council, 1970-71 Bd. dirs. N.W. Regional Found., 1973-75, Inland Empire Goodwill Industries, 1975-77, Wash. State Library Commn., 1979-87, Future Spokane, 1983-88, vice chmn., 1986-87, pres., 1987-88. Recipient YWCA Outstanding Achievement award in Govt., 1985 Mem. ALA (mem. library adminstrn. and mgmt. assn. com. on orgn. 1982-83, chmn. nominating com. 1983-85, v.p./pres.-elect. 1985-86, pres. 1986-87), Pacific N.W. Library Assn. (chmn. circulation div. 1972-75, conv. chmn. 1977), Wash. Library Assn. (v.p./pres.-elect 1975-77, pres. 1977-78), AAUW (pres. Spokane br. 1969-71, rec. sec. Wash. br. 1971-73, fellowship named in honor 1972), Spokane and Inland Empire Librarians (dir. 1967-68), Am. Soc. Pub. Adminstrn. Clubs: Zonta (pres. Spokane chpt. 1976-77, dist. conf. treas. 1972). Republican. Lutheran. Home: 221 E Rockwood Blvd Apt 504 Spokane WA 99202-1274

BENDER, BRUCE F., book publishing executive; b. Toledo, Oct. 4, 1949; s. Richard S. and Joan B. Bender; m. Margaret Norris, Sept. 4, 1971; children: Courtney, Meghan. BA, Musklingum Coll., 1971; MBA, Rutgers U., 1972. Supr. Coopers & Lybrand CPA's, NYC, 1972-76; pres. Lyle Stuart, inc., Secaucus, NJ, 1989—; also bd. dirs.; pres. Carol Pub. Group, NYC, 1989-2000; mng. dir. Citadel Press, NYC, from 2000, Kensington Pub. Corp., NYC, 2000—04; CFO Book Club Am., 2004—. Pres. Brightwood Assn.; bd. dirs. Westfield Symphony. Mem. AICPA, Pub. Fin. Round Table, N.J. Inst. CPAs, Echo Lake Club, Royal Poinciana Club. Office: Book Club America 100 Marcus Blvd Hauppauge NY 11788 Office Phone: 631-235-4644. Business E-Mail: brucebender@bookclubusa.com.

BENDER, BYRON WILBUR, linguistics educator; b. Roaring Spring, Pa., Aug. 14, 1929; s. Ezra Clay and Gertrude Magdalene (Kauffman) B.; m. Lois Marie Graber, Aug. 25, 1950; children: Susan Alice, Sarah Marie, Catherine Anne, Judith Lee, John Richard. BA, Goshen Coll., 1949; MA, Ind. U., 1950, PhD, 1963. Edn. specialist Trust Terr. of Pacific Islands, Majuro, Marshall Island, 1953-59, Saipan, Marianas Island, 1962-64; asst. prof. Goshen Coll., Ind., 1960-62; assoc. prof. linguistics U. Hawaii at Manoa, Honolulu, 1964-69, prof., 1969-99, chmn. dept., 1969-95, prof. emeritus, 2000—. Bd. dirs. U. Hawaii Profl. Assembly, Honolulu, 1978-88, 92-98, pres., 1982-88. Author: Spoken Marshallese, 1969, Linguistic Factors in Maori Education, 1971, (with others) Marshallese-English Dictionary, 1976; editor Oceanic Linguistics Spl. Publ., 1965-2007, Studies in Micronesian Linguistics, 1984, Oceanic Linguistics, 1991-2007; mng. editor Oceanic Linguistics, 1965-90. Trustee Hawaii Pub. Employees Health Fund Bd., 1987-95; regent U. Hawaii Bd. of Regents, 2003-. Recipient Merit awards U. Hawaii 1971, 76, 86. Mem. NEA (standing com. higher edn. 1985-89), Linguistic Soc. Am. (dir. Linguistic Inst. summer 1977, program com. 1987-89, parliamentarian 1994-97). Mem. Soc. Of Friends. Home: Apt 1504 6710 Hawaii Kai Dr Honolulu HI 96825-1548 Office: U Hawaii Dept Linguistics 1890 E West Rd Honolulu HI 96822-2318 Home Phone: 808-395-3269; Office Phone: 808-956-8374. Personal E-mail: bender@hawaii.rr.com. Business E-Mail: bender@hawaii.edu.

BENDER, CARL MARTIN, physics professor, consultant; b. Bklyn., Jan. 18, 1943; s. Alfred and Rose (Suberman) B.; m. Jessica Dee Waldbaum, June 18, 1966; children— Michael Anthony, Daniel Eric AB summa cum laude with distinction, Cornell U., 1964; AM, Harvard U., 1965, PhD, 1969. Mem. Inst. for Advanced Study, Princeton, NJ, 1969-70; asst. prof. math. MIT, Cambridge, 1970-73, assoc. prof., 1973-77; prof. physics Washington U., St. Louis, 1977—; research assoc. Imperial Coll., London, 1974. Cons. Los Alamos Nat. Lab., 1979—; vis. prof. Imperial Coll., London, 1986-87, 95-96, 2003-04, 06-, Technion Israel Inst. Tech., Haifa, 1995; vis. prof. dept. math. Imperial Coll, London, 2006-. Author: Advanced Mathematical Methods for Scientists and Engineers, 1978; editor: Am. Inst. Physic series on math. and computational physics; mem. editl. bds. Jour Math. Physics, 1980-83, Advances in Applied Math., 1980-85, Jour. Physics A, 1999-2003; editor-in-chief, Jour. Physics A, 2004—; contbr. more than 230 articles to sci. jours. Trustee Ctr. for Theoretical Study of Phys. Sys., Clark Atlanta U. Recipient Burlington No. Found. Faculty Achievement award, 1985, Fellows award Acad. Sci. St. Louis, 2002; Telluride scholar, 1960-63, NSF fellow, 1964-69, Woodrow Wilson fellow, 1964-65, Sloan Found. fellow, 1973-77, Fulbright fellowship to U.K., 1995-96, Lady Davis fellowship to Israel, 1995, Rockefeller Found. grantee to visit Bellagio Study and Conf. Ctr., 1999; Guggenheim Fellow, 2003-04, fellow Engring. and Phys. Scis. Rsch. Coun., London, 2003-04; Ulam fellow Los Alamos Nat. Lab., 2006—. Fellow: Inst. of Physics (U.K.), St. Louis Acad. Sci., Am. Phys. Soc. (vice chmn. Danny Heineman prize selection com., chmn. Danny Heineman prize selection com.); mem.: Assn. Mems. Inst. Advanced Study (trustee), Phi Kappa Phi, Phi Beta Kappa. Home: 509 Warren Ave Saint Louis MO 63130-4155 Office: Washington U Dept Physics Saint Louis MO 63130 Home Phone: 314-726-2396; Office Phone: 314-935-6216. Business E-Mail: cmb@wustl.edu.

BENDER, CHARLES CHRISTIAN, retail home center executive; b. Bklyn., July 4, 1936; s. Charles C. and Virginia R. (Rahlfs) B.; m. Jean Ann Couper; children: Lori Ann Grenier, Hallie Couper Fivecoat. BA, Hillsdale Coll., 1959; MBA, U. Mich., 1960. Buyer Target, Detroit, 1962-69; v.p., gen. mdse. mgr. Wickes Lumber, Saginaw, Mich., 1969-81; gen. mgr. Wickes B.V., Utrecht, Netherlands, 1981-84; chmn., CEO, owner Busy Beaver Bldg. Ctrs., Pitts., 1984—2007, chmn., owner, 2007—. Mem. adv. bd. Home Ctr. Industry Pres. Coun., 1986—; mem. Coun. of Exec. Officers; chmn. bd. dirs. Home Ctr. Inst., 1998. With US Army, 1960—61. Mem.: Pitts. Field Club, Rotary. Republican. Presbyterian. Avocation: golf. Home: 310 Buckingham Rd Pittsburgh PA 15215-1527 Office: Busy Beaver Bldg Ctrs Inc 3130 William Pitt Way Pittsburgh PA 15238-1360 Home: 23310 Copperleaf Blvd Bonita Springs FL 34135

BENDER, CHARLES WILLIAM, lawyer; b. Cape Girardeau, Mo., Oct. 2, 1935; s. Walter William and Fern Evelyn (Stroud) Bender; m. Carolyn Percy Gavagan, June 20, 1961 (div. 1983); children: Theodore Marten, Christopher Percy; m. Betty Lou Port, May 5, 1983; stepchildren: Courtney Elizabeth, Cameron Ann. AB magna cum laude, Harvard U., 1960, LLB magna cum laude, 1963. Bar: Calif. 1965, U.S. Dist. Ct. (ctrl. dist.) Calif. 1965, U.S. Ct. Appeals (9th cir.) 1969, U.S. Supreme Ct. 1979, DC 1984. Assoc. O'Melveny & Myers, LA, 1965—71, ptnr., 1972—84, mng. ptnr., 1984—92, chmn., 1993—2001. Editor: Harvard U. Law Rev., 1961—62; articles editor., 1962—63. Trustee LA Legal Aid Found., 1971, Lawyers' Com. for Civil Rights Under Law, Washington, 1985—2001; advisor campaign Alan Cranston for Senator, Calif., 1968, Calif., 1974, Calif., 1980; mgr. campaign Jess Unruh for Gov., Calif., 1970. With US Army, 1956—57. Fellow Sheldon Traveling, Harvard U., 1963—64. Democrat. Home: 2831 The Strand Hermosa Beach CA 90254-2400 Office: O'Melveny & Myers 400 S Hope St Los Angeles CA 90071-2899

BENDER, DAVID RAY, retired library association executive; b. Canton, Ohio, June 12, 1942; s. John Ray and Mary Elizabeth (Witmer) B.; children: Robert Ray, Scott David, Lori Jo Ryan. BS, Kent State U., 1964; MS in LS, Case Western Res. U., 1969; PhD, Ohio State U., 1977. Librarian South High Sch., Willoughby, Ohio, 1964-68; cons. sch. library services Ohio Dept. Edn., Columbus, 1969-70; grad. research asso. Ohio State U., Columbus, 1970-72; br. chief sch. library media services Md. Dept. Edn., Balt., 1972-79; exec. dir. Spl. Librs. Assn., Washington, 1979-2001, exec. dir. emeritus, 2001—; ret., 2001. Lectr. Rutgers U., New Brunswick, N.J.; vis. prof. Towson State U., Balt.; cons., project dir. various state depts. edn. and colls. and univs., profl. assns. also internat., state and local orgns.; mem. adv. com. on naval history, USN, 1991-95. Author: Learning Resources and the Instructional Program in Community College, 1980, Library Media Programs and the Special Learner, 1981; co-author (with others): Nat. Information Policies: Strategies for the Future, 1991; contbr. numerous articles to profl. jours. Adv. coun. Kent State U. Sch. Libr. and Info. Sci., Ohio, 1991-99, Washington Nat. Cathedral Fund Com., 1998—; libr. com. Cathedral Coll. Preachers, 2005—; CWRU Libr. ann. gift fund chair, 1999-2002; bd. dirs. Dresden Condominium, 2002—, dir., pres. 2004—; sr. medicare error patrol project AARP, 2002-05; pres. Spanish Steps Preservation Project, DC, 2006—; treas. Kalorma Village, 2007—. Recipient award for outstanding svc. Md. Ednl. Media Orgn., 1980, H.W. Wilson Co. award, 1989. Mem. Spl. Librs. Assn. (President's award 1986, John Cotton Dana award 2001, David R. Bender Endowment Fund for Internat. Devel. 2001), Nat. Libr. and Info. Assns. (chmn. 1990-91), Internat. Fedn. Libr. Assns. and Instns. (chmn. round table for Mgmt. of Libr. Assn. 1993-99), Am. Soc. Assn. Execs. Found. (chmn. 1988), Greater Wash. Soc. Assn. Execs. (chair CEO adv. coun. 2000-2001, Five Smart Assn. CEO's 2001), Kappa Sigma. Republican. Episcopalian. Home: Unit 34 2126 Connecticut Ave NW Washington DC 20008-1701

BENDER, JACK, television producer, television director, actor; Dir.: (films) A Real Naked Lady, 1980, Child's Play 3, 1991, Lone Justice 2, 1995; (TV films) In Love With An Older Woman, 1982, Two Kinds of Love, 1983, Shattered Vows, 1984, Deadly Messages, 1985, Letting Go, 1985, The Midnight Hour, 1985, Side by Side, 1988, Tricks of the Trade, 1988, Charlie, 1989, My Brother's Wife, 1989, The Dreamer of Oz, 1990, The Perfect Tribute, 1991, Love Can Be Murder, 1992, Armed and Innocent, 1994, Gambler V: Playing for Keeps, 1994, Family Album, 1994, A Face to Die For, 1996, Sweet Dreams, 1996, Friends 'Til The End, 1997, Killing Mr. Griffin, 1997, My Little Assassin, 1999, The David Cassidy Story, 2000, The Lone Ranger, 2003; dir. & prodr. (TV films) A Call to Remember, 1997, The Tempest, 1988, dir. prodr. & writer It Came From the Sky, 1999; dir.: (TV series) Eight Is Enough, 1977, Falcon Crest, 1981, Fame, 1982, King's Crossing, 1982, Northern Exposure, 1990, Beverly Hills, 90210, 1990, Ned Blessing: The Story of My Life and Times, 1993, New York News, 1995, Profiler, 1996, Felicity, 1998, The Sopranos, 1999, Judging Amy, 1999, That's Life, 2000, Boston Public, 2000, Alias, 2001, Presidio Med, 2002, Boomtown, 2002, Carnivale, 2003, Joan of Arcadia, 2003, The Lyon's Den, 2003; dir. & prodr. (TV series) Lost, 2004 (best TV series, drama, Producers Guild Am., 2006), writer & dir. The Paper Chase, 1978; actor: (films) The Barefoot Executive, 1971, The Million Dollar Duck, 1971, Now You See Him Now You Don't, 1972, Hot Lead and Cold Feet, 1978; (TV films) Savage, 1973, Columbo: Publish or Perish, 1974, Target Risk, 1975, McNaughton's Daughter, 1976, Sergeant Matlovich vs. the US Air Force, 1978, Naomi & Wynonna: Love Can Build a Bridge, 1995. Mailing: c/o Lost ABC Inc 500 South Buena Vista St Burbank CA 91521-4562

BENDER, JAMES J., lawyer, oil industry executive; b. Aurora, Ill., 1956; m. Kristin Bender; 3 children. BA summa cum laude in Math., St. Olaf Coll., Northfield, Minn.; JD magna cum laude, U. Minn. Law Sch., 1981. Bar: Minn., Colo. Law clk. to Judge Donald D. Alsop Fed. Dist. Ct., St. Paul; assoc. Gibson, Dunn & Crutcher, Denver and London; ptnr. Masion, Edelman, Borman & Brand, 1983—88, Leonard, Street & Deinard, 1993—94; sr. counsel Pfizer, Inc., 1989—93; asst. gen. counsel AlliedSignal, 1996—97; sr. v.p., gen. counsel NRG Energy, 1997—2002, The Williams Companies Inc., Tulsa, 2002—. Spkr. in field. Divsn. chair United Way, Tulsa; bd. trustees Philbrook Mus. Art; bd. mem. YMCA, Minn.; treas., bd. dirs. The Parent Child Ctr. of Tulsa; conducted pro-bono legal work Interfaith Outreach, Minn. Mem.: Colo. Bar Assn., Okla. Bar Assn., Assn. Corp. Counsel, Minn. State Bar Assn., ABA. Office: Williams One Williams Ctr Tulsa OK 74172*

BENDER, JAMES Y., not-for-profit fundraiser; s. Merrill A. and Sally H. Bender; m. Catherine A. Warda-Bender, July 30, 1988; children: Margaret B., Erin G. BA, Washington U., St. Louis, 1984. Cert. fund raising exec. Cert. Fund Raising Exec. Internat./Va., 2004. Mgr. in home supports Heritage Ctrs., Buffalo, 1989—99; coord. planned giving Our Lady of Victory Homes of Charity, Buffalo, 1999—2005; dir. devel. Buffalo Acad. of the Sacred Heart, 2005—06; dir. endowment devel. YMCA Buffalo Niagara, 2006—. Pre cana instr. Our Lady of Victory Parish, Lackawanna, NY, 2004—07. Recipient Father Baker Svc. to Youth award, Baker Victory Svcs., 2004. Mem.: Nat. Com. Planned Giving, Assn. Fundraising Profls. Avocations: swimming, sailing. Home: 1390 McKinley Pkwy Buffalo NY 14218 Office: YMCA Buffalo Niagara 280 Cayuga Rd Buffalo NY 14225 Office Phone: 716-565-6000.

BENDER, JOEL CHARLES, lawyer; b. Bklyn., Dec. 12, 1939; s. Harry and Edna (Bogolowitz) B.; m. Terry Bender; children: Lisa, Andrew, Gary. BA, Cornell U., 1961; JD, NYU, 1964. Bar: N.Y. 1964, U.S. Supreme Ct. 1970, Fla. 1980; diplomate Am. Coll. Family Trial Lawyers. Ptnr. Bender, Jenson & Silverstein, LLP, White Plains, N.Y., 1999—. Councilman Greenburgh, N.Y. 1977-89; dep. supv., police commr. Greenburgh, 1979-89. Fellow Am. Assn. Matrimonial Lawyers, Internat. Acad. Matrimonial Lawyers; mem. ABA (mem. faculty Trial Advocacy Inst.), Am. Acad. Matrimonial Lawyers (pres. N.Y. chpt. 1999-2001, former officer, bd. mgrs.), N.Y. State Bar Assn., Fla. Bar, Westchester County Bar Assn. Democrat. Office: Ste 104 120 Bloomingdale Rd White Plains NY 10605-1518 E-mail: jbender@jcbender.com.

BENDER, JOHN CHARLES, lawyer; b. NYC, May 17, 1940; s. John H. and Cecilia B.; m. Helen Hadjiyannakis; 1 child, Marianna Celene. BSME, Northea. U., 1964; JD, NYU, 1968, LLM, 1971. Bar: N.Y. 1968, U.S. Dist. Ct. (so. dist.) N.Y. 1972, U.S. Supreme Ct. 1997. Atty. Marshall, Bratter, Greene, Allison and Tucker, 1968-69; asst. dir, NYU Ctr. for Internat. Studies, NYC, 1969-71; atty. Poletti Freidin Prashker Feldman & Gartner, NYC, 1971-75; spl. counsel Moreland Act Commn. on Nursing Homes and Residential Facilities, NYC, 1975-76; gen. counsel N.Y. State Fin. Control Bd., NYC, 1976-80; v.p., gen. counsel News Am. Pub. Inc., NYC, 1980-85; group v.p., gen. counsel Simon & Schuster Inc., NYC, 1985-90; sr. v.p., gen. counsel Maxwell Macmillan Group, 1991-95; dir. Black Book Mktg. Group, Inc., 1994-96. Chmn., trustee Trust for Cultural Resources of City of N.Y., 1981-99; chmn., trustee Mary McDowell Ctr. for Learning, 1993—; trustee Univ. Settlement House, 2005—, Oakwood Friends Sch., 2005—. Mem. ABA, Assn. of Bar of City of N.Y. (mem. com. on comm. law 1981-85, mem. spl. com. on edn. and the law 1982-85, mem.

com. on bioethics). Home: 27 W 67th St New York NY 10023-6258 Office: 10 E 40th St New York NY 10016 Home Phone: 212-362-4433; Office Phone: 212-813-0999. Business E-Mail: jcb@benderlaw.net.

BENDER, JOHN HENRY, JR., (JACK), editor, cartoonist; b. Waterloo, Iowa, Mar. 28; s. John Henry and Wilma (Lowe) B.; divorced; children: Thereza, John Henry IV, Anthony; m. Carole R. Suggs, 1995. BA, U. Iowa, 1953; postgrad., Art. Inst. Chgo., 1956, Washington U. St. Louis, 1957; MA, U. Mo., 1962. Art dir., asst. editor Commerce Pub. Co., St. Louis, 1953-54, 56-58; editor Florissant Reporter, 1958-61; editl. cartoonist Waterloo Courier, 1962-84, assoc. editor, 1975-83; art. dir., editor Alpha VII Corp., Tulsa, 1984-87; head dept. prodn. art Platt Coll., Tulsa, 1987-92; cartoonist Don Martin Studio, Miami, Fla., 1989-92; artist Alley Oop comic strip United Media Syndicate, NYC, 1991—. Sports cartoonist Basketball Weekly, Baseball Digest Mag., U. Iowa, others. Author: Pocket Guide to Judging Springboard Diving, (with Dick Smith) Inside Diving, (with Ed Gagnier) Inside Gymnastics; exhibited at Grout Mus., Waterloo, Iowa, 2002. With USAF, 1953-56, col., ret. 1983. Recipient Best Editl. award Mo. Press Assn., 1960, Grenville Clark Editl. Page award, 1968, Freedoms Found. award, 1969, 75, Freedoms Found. Honor medal, 1971, Ignatz award Orlandocon, 1992, Air Force Commendation medal, 1981; named to Hall of Fame East H.S., Waterloo, Iowa, 1972, Names on Main, Cedar Falls, Iowa, 1997, Okla. Cartoonists Hall of Fame, 2005. Mem. Assn. Am. Editl. Cartoonists, Nat. Cartoonists Soc., Comic Art Profl. Soc., Sigma Chi, Kappa Tau Alpha. Office: RR 1 Box 540 Terlton OK 74081-9740 Home: 7424 E 31st Pl Tulsa OK 74145

BENDER, JUDITH, journalist, editor; d. Samuel and Edith Bender. BA, U. Mich., 1954; MS, Columbia U., 1964. Reporter Passaic Herald News, Clifton, NJ, 1964—65, Knickerbocker News, Albany, NY, 1965—69; reporter, editor Newsday, Melville, NY, 1969—2000; freelance writer, 2000—; consulting editor Columbia Journalism Rev., NYC, 2002—. Recipient award for Washington corr., Soc. for Profl. Journalists, 1982, Pub. Svc. award, N.Y. State Pubs. Assn., 1974. Mem.: Alumni Assn. Grad. Sch. Journalism Columbia U. (v.p. 2005—06). Office: Columbia Journalism Rev Grad Sch Journalism 2950 Broadway New York NY 10027

BENDER, MICHAEL LEE, state supreme court justice; b. NYC, Jan. 7, 1942; s. Louis and Jean (Waterman) B.; m. Judith Jones, Feb. 27, 1967 (div. Mar. 1977); children: Jeremy, Aviva; m. Helen H. Hand, Sept. 10, 1977; children: Maryjean Hand-Bender, Tess Hand-Bender, Benjamin Hand-Bender. BA in Philosophy, Dartmouth Coll., 1964; JD, U. Colo., 1967. Bar: Colo. 1967, D.C. 1967, U.S. Supreme Ct. 1980. Pub. defender City and County Denver, 1968-71; assoc. regional atty. EEOC, 1974-75; supr. atty. Jefferson County Pub. Defender, 1975-77; divsn. chief Denver Pub. Defender, Denver, 1977-78; atty. Gibson, Dunn & Crutcher, LA, 1979-80; ptnr. Bender & Treece PC, Denver, 1983-93; pres., shareholder Michael L. Bender PC, 1993-97; justice Colo. Supreme Ct., 1997—. Adj. faculty U. Denver Coll. Law, 1981-86, chair. ABA Criminal Justice sect., Washington, 1990-91, NACD Lawyers Assistant Com., 1989-90, U. Colo. Sch. of Law, 2004; dir. Nat. Assn. Criminal Def. Lawyers, 1984-90; mem. practitioner's adv. com. U.S. Sentencing Com., 1990-91; mem. com. for Criminal Justice Act for Dist. Colo. U.S. Dist. Ct., 1991-93, domestic rels. reform com.; liaison mem. Colo. Pub. Edn. com., Ct. Svcs., 1998—, atty. regulation adv. com., 1998-99; co-chair civil justice com. Supreme Ct., 1998-; liaison Supreme Ct. Standing Com. Colo. Rules Profl. Conduct, 2003-; bd. mem. Int. for Advancement of Am. Legal System, 2006-. Contbr. articles to profl. jours. Bd. govs. Colo. Bar, 1989-91. Recipient Fireman award Colo. State Pub., 1990; Robert C. Heeney Meml. award Nat. Assn. Criminal Def. Lawyers, 1990; Named Vol. of Yr. Denver Bar Assn., 1988. Mem. Colo. Bar Assn. (ethics com. 1980—), ABA (chair criminal justice sect. 1990-91, criminal justice standards com. 1997—). Democrat. Jewish. Avocations: aerobics, skiing, bicycling, camping. Office: Colo Supreme Ct State Jud Bldg 2 E 14th Ave Fl 4 Denver CO 80203-2115*

BENDER, NATHAN EDWARD, librarian, archivist; b. Amherst, Ohio, Sept. 29, 1957; s. George Edward and Pauline Ella (Pike) B. BA with distinction in Anthropology, Ohio State U., 1980; MA in Anthropology, U. Wash., 1983; MLS, Kent State U., 1986. Libr. western history collections U. Okla. Librs., Norman, 1986-89; head spl. collections Mont. State U. Librs., Bozeman, 1989-94; head spl. collections, curator W.Va. and regional history collection W.Va. U. Librs., Morgantown, 1994-97; house curator McCracken Rsch. Libr./Buffalo Bill Hist. Ctr., Cody, Wyo., 1997—. Dir. Piatt Park Archaeol. Project, Woodsfield, Ohio, 1984-85; mem. W.Va. State Hist. Records, Charleston, 1995-97, Mont. Hist. Records Adv. Coun., Helena, 1992-94; reviewer NEH, Washington, 1995. Contbr. articles to profl. jours., chpts. to book. Historian Sweet Pea Festival of the Arts, Bozeman, Mont., 1992-94; advisor Riverfront Mus., Inc., Morgantown, W.Va., 1995-97. Grantee US Dept. Edn., 1992-93. Mem. ALA, Soc. Am. Archivists (W.Va. key contact rep. 1996-97). Avocations: shooting sports, photography, camping, craftwork, writing. Office: WVa U Librs Colson Hall PO Box 6464 Morgantown WV 26506-6464

BENDER, PAUL EDWARD, lawyer; b. Decatur, Ill., Dec. 5, 1951; s. Kenneth Donald and Martha Rosalie (Heinzelmann) B.; m. Anne Marie Scartabello, Dec. 31, 1976 (div. 1978). BA, Millikin U., 1973; JD cum laude, Hamline U., 1976; MBA, U. Phoenix, 1997. Bar: Minn. 1976, Ill 1977, U.S. Dist Ct. (cen. dist.) Ill. 1982. Assoc. Halloran & Alfuby, Mpls., 1976-77; sole practice Bender Law Office, Arthur, Ill., 1977-79; sr. title atty Chgo. Title Ins. Co., Peoria, Ill., 1979-82; ptnr. Cordis & Bender, Princeville, Ill., 1982-84; sr. title atty. Chgo. Title Co., Champaign, Ill., 1984-88, asst. v.p., mgr., 1990-92, resident v.p., Champaign County mgr., 1992-96; mgr. McLean County Title Co., 1996—, Decatur Title, 1997—. Mem. ABA, Peoria Bar Assn. (chmn. real estate com. 1983-84, mem. continuing legal edn. 1981-83), McLean County Bar Assn., Ill. Bar Assn., Optimist Club (Peoria chpt., prs. 1981-82, lt. gov. zone 6 Ill. 1982-83), Champaign C. of C. (zoning com. 1990-96), Mason, Shriners. Republican. Methodist. Home: 303 N Cottage Ave Normal IL 61761-4264 Home Phone: 309-452-3094; Office Phone: 309-828-5097. Business E-Mail: paul.bender@ctt.com.

BENDER, ROSS THOMAS, minister; b. Tavistock, Ont., Can., June 25, 1929; came to U.S., 1960, naturalized, 1966; s. Christian and Katie (Bender) B.; m. Ruth Eileen Steinmann, Dec. 22, 1950 (dec. Dec. 1997); children: Ross Lynn, Elizabeth, Michael, Lenore, Anne. BA, Goshen Coll., 1954, BD, 1956; MA, Yale U., 1961, PhD, 1962. Ordained to ministry Mennonite Ch., 1958. Prin. Rockway Mennonite sch., Kitchener, Ont., 1956-60; prof. Christian edn. Associated Mennonite Bibl. Sem., Elkhart, Ind., 1962-96, dean, 1964-79, dean emeritus, 1996; dir. Inst. Mennonite Studies, 1990-97; ret. Pres. Mennonite World Conf., 1984-90. Author: The People of God, 1969, Christians in Families, 1982, Education for Peoplehood, 1997; co-editor: Baptism, Peace and the State in the Reformed and Mennonite Traditions, 1991. Rockefeller doctoral fellow, 1960-61; Am. Assn. Theol. Schs. fellow, 1961-62; NIMH postdoctoral fellow U. Pa., 1970-71 Mennonite.

BENDER, THOMAS, historian, educator; b. Redwood City, Calif., Apr. 18, 1944; s. Joseph Charles and Catherine Frances (McGuire) B.; m. Sally Hill, June 8, 1966 (div. 1983); 1 child, David William; m. Gwendolyn Wright, Jan. 14, 1984; 1 child, Sophia Wright BA, U. Santa Clara, 1966; MA, U. Calif.-Davis, 1967, PhD, 1971. Asst. prof. history and urban studies U. Wis., Green Bay, 1971-74; asst. prof. history NYU, NYC, 1974-76, assoc. prof. history, 1976-77, prof. history, 1977—, Samuel Rudin prof. humanities, 1977-82, Univ. prof. humanities, 1982—, dean for the humanities, 1995-98, dir. Internat. Ctr. for Advanced Studies, 1996—2007. Rsch. planning com. N.Y.C. Social Sci. Rsch. Coun., 1985-88. Author: Toward an Urban Vision, 1975 (Frederick Jackson Turner prize 1975), Community and Social Change in America, 1978, (with Edwin Rozwenc) The Making of American Society, 1978, New York Intellect, 1987, Intellect and Public Life, 1993, The Unfinished City: New York and the Metropolitan Idea, 2002; co-author: The Education of Historians for the Twenty-First Century, 2004, A Nation Among Nations: America's Place in World History, 2006; editor: Democracy in America, 1981, Intellectual History Group Newsletter, 1978-85, The University and the City, 1988, The Anti-Slavery Debate: Capitalism and Abolitionism as a Problem in Historical Interpretation, 1992; co-editor: (with Carl Schorske) Budapest and New York: Studies in Metropolitan Transformation 1870-1930, 1994, (with Carl Schorske) The Tranformation of American Academic Culture, 1998, (with Michael Peter Smith) City and Nation: Rethinking Identity and Place, 2001, Rethinking American History in a Global Age, 2002, (with Wilson Smith) American Higher Education Transformed, 1945-2000, 2007, (with Alev Çinar) Urban Imaginaries: Locating the Modern City, 2007; cons. editor New Studies in American Intellectual and Cultural History, 1981-94; mem. editl. bd. Readers Encyclopedia of American History, 1988-91, Am. Hist. Rev., 1991-94, Modern Intellectual History, 2002—, Jour. Am. History, 2007—; assoc. editor Am. Nat. Biography, 1990-97. Bd. dirs. Mcpl. Art Soc. N.Y., N.Y.C., 1983-84, N.Y. Coun. for the Humanities, 1989-96, chair, 1992-95; mem. gov. coun. Rockefeller Archives Ctr., Pocantico Hills, N.Y., 1987-92; trustee Grace Sch., N.Y.C., 1987-94. N.Y. Inst. Humanities fellow, 1977-88; Guggenheim fellow, 1980-81; Rockefeller Found. fellow, 1984-85; Getty scholar Getty Ctr. Study of Art and Humanities , 1992-93; Mel and Lois Tukman fellow Cullman Ctr. Scholars and Writers, N.Y. Pub. Libr., 2002-03, Ctr. Advanced Study in the Behavioral Scis. fellow, 2005-06. Fellow Am. Acad. Arts and Scis.; mem. Am. Hist. Assn., Orgn. Am. Historians, Soc. Am. Historians, Am. Antiquarian Soc., Writers Guild, PEN. Democrat. Office: NYU Dept History 53 Washington Sq S New York NY 10012-1098

BENDER, VIRGINIA BEST, computer scientist, educator; b. Rockford, Ill., Feb. 10, 1945; d. Oscar Sheldon and Genevieve Best; m. Robert Keith Bender, July 19, 1969; children: Victoria Ruth, Christopher Keith. BS in Chemistry, Math., No. Ill. U., 1967; postgrad., U. Ill., 1967—69; MBA, Loyola U., Chgo., 1973. Cert. computer profl. Sr. sys. rep. Burroughs Corp., Chgo., 1969-73; sys. analyst Marshall Field & Co., Chgo., 1973-74; project leader Fed. Home Loan Bank, Chgo., 1974-76; sr. sys. analyst United Air Lines, Elk Grove Village, Ill., 1976-78; supr. Kemper Group, Long Grove, Ill., 1978-82; prof. computer info. sys., coord. computer info. sys. William Rainey Harper Coll., Palatine, Ill., 1982—2002, prof. emeritus, 2002—. Spkr. Midwest Computer Conf., DeKalb, Ill., 1988, moderator, 91; exch. prof. Maricopa CC, Mesa, Ariz., 1990, rsch. sabbatical, 93, 98; spkr. conf. info. tech. League for Innovation, Kansas City, Mo., 1995; steering com. Midwest Computer Conf., 1995—99; facilitator ToolBook User's Conf., Colorado Springs, Colo., 2000, presenter, Colo. Springs, 2001—03; adj. prof. SUNY/Westchester C.C., Valhalla, 2003—. Nat. chief mother-dau. group Indian Maidens YMCA, Des Plaines, 1982—83; mem. Vols. Pks. Environ. Edn. Westchester County Dept. Pks., Recreation and Conservation, NY, 2002—; mem. Master Singers of Westchester, 2005—; choir Kingswood United Meth. Ch., Buffalo Grove, Ill., 1982—2002, asst. organist, 1982—89; choir 1st Congl. Ch., Chappaqua, NY, 2002—, bell choir, 2003—, substitute organist, 2003—; bd. dirs. Consumer's Energy Coop., Inc., 2003—06, webmaster, 2004—. Named Tchr. of the Month, Burroughs Corp., Chgo., 1972. Mem.: No. Ill. Computer Soc., Ill. Assn. Data Processing Instrs., Inst. Cert. Computer Profls. (life), Am. Guild Organists (webmaster 2006—, dir. 2006—), No. Ill. Alumni Assn. (life), Mortar Bd., Sigma Zeta, Phi Theta Kappa. Avocations: swimming, needlecrafts, playing piano, organ, and marimba. Personal E-mail: vbender@hotmail.com.

BENDICKSON, MARCUS J., engineering company executive; BS, Iowa State U.; MS, Columbia U.; PhD, U. Ala., 1980. Rschr. signal and com. lab Bell Labs; mgr. radio bulk filtering br. Teledyne Brown Engrng.; pres., CEO Dynetics, Inc., Ala., 1989—. Mem. adv. bd. U. Ala., Colonial Bank; bd. dirs. Huntsville-Madison County C. of C. Address: Dynetics Inc 1000 Explorer Blvd NW Huntsville AL 35806-2806

BENDIDI, RACHID, dean, educator; s. Lahbib and Maria (Ajana) Bendidi; m. Hanane Soufi, Sept. 20, 1974. BSME, U. DC, Washington, 1993; MME, W.Va. U., Morgantown, 1996; PhD, Howard U., Washington, 2002. Dean of arts and sci. Voorhees Coll., Denmark, SC, 2002—. Vis. scientist Nat. Crash Analysis Ctr., Ashburn, Va., 2000—02. Grantee, UNCF, 2003—06; scholar, W.Va. U., 1994—96, Howard U., 1997—2001. Mem.: ASME, AAUP (assoc.), ASCE (assoc.), Soc. Automotive Engrs. (assoc.). Achievements include design of G4-1S guardrail sys., composite bridge; development of practical optimization theory for the advanced composite material that increased the stiffness of the beams; method to reinforce concrete using advanced composite rebar and plate. Avocations: soccer, football, basketball, swimming, fishing. Office: Voorhees Coll PO Box 678 213 Wiggins St Denmark SC 29042 Home: 30 Chase Mill Cir Owings Mills MD 21117 Personal E-mail: rbendidi@hotmail.com. Business E-Mail: bendidi@gmail.com.

BENDIG, WILLIAM CHARLES, editor, artist; b. Corry, Pa., Dec. 1, 1927; s. William Charles and Hazel Grace Mae (Dailey) B. BA with honors, Trinity Coll., 1953; postgrad., U. London, 1955-56. Founding editor Erie (Pa.) Tribune, 1944-48; mgr. Nat. Symphonic Choir, Erie, 1946-49; program mgr. Erie Philharmonic Orch., 1947-49; instr. Cheshire (Conn.) Acad., 1953-54, Brunswick Sch., Greenwich, Conn., 1954-55; editor in chief, pub. theARTgallery Mag., Ivoryton, Conn., 1957-84; prin., pub. Hollycroft. Pubs., Ivoryton, 1987—; editor in chief Botswana Rev., Ivoryton and Gaborone, 1988-90; curator, archivist theARTgallery Archive, 1990—; pres. Hollycroft Found., 1992—; cons. Kuwait Info. Office, Washington, 1993-96; chief curator The Sculpture Mile Exhbns., Madison and Middletown, Conn., 2001—. Cons. Submarine Force Libr. and Nautilus Mus., Groton, Conn., 1994—; dep. dir. U.S.-Africa Arts Found., Gaborone, 1988-93, life trustee; trustee Contemporary Sculptors Guild, 1994-95; dep. dir. Sculptors Guild, N.Y.C., 1997-2000; juror nat. art exhbns.; lectr. univs. and mus. Designer, fabricator Pentecost rose window All Sts.' Episcopal Ch., Ivoryton, 1988; contbr. works in various art exhbns. V.p. Essex Art Assn., 1960-62; founding v.p. Ivoryton Village Assn.; mem. Essex Landmark Commn., 1981-82; trustee Ivoryton Pub. Libr., Ivoryton Playhouse Found. (founding); founding trustee Episcopal Conf. Ctr., Ivoryton, 1979, dir. art seminar program, 1982-92. Recipient award, Greater New Haven Arts Coun., 2003. Mem. Mediaeval Acad. Am., Africa Studies Assn., Friends of Trinity Libr., Naval Submarine League, Trinity Coll. Alumni Assn. (pres. New London chpt. 1963-67), Grad. Club, New Haven Club. Episcopalian (vestryman 1970-92). Home and Office: Hollycroft Found Main St Ivoryton CT 06442-0278

BENDIKSEN, ODDVAR OLAV, aerospace engineer, educator; b. Tennskjer, Troms, Norway, July 7, 1945; s. Albert and Mally Bendiksen; m. Ellen Berit Myklebust, Oct. 24, 1964; children: Lene, Aage. BS, Northrop Inst. Tech., 1968; MS, UCLA, 1975, PhD, 1980. Airframe and power plant lic. FAA, 1968. Engrng. sys. analyst The Fluor Corp., LA, 1968—69; power plant engr. TWA, Kansas City, Mo., 1969—70; engrng. systems analyst Pacific Airmotive Corp., Burbank, Calif., 1970—72, project engr., 1972—75, sr. project engr., 1975—76, dir. engrng., 1976—77, dir. of project engrng., 1977—80; asst. prof. U. So. Calif., LA, 1980—81, Princeton U., 1981—88; assoc. prof. U. Calif., LA, 1988—94, prof., vice chmn., 1994—99, prof., 1999—. Aviation and aerospace engrng. cons.; assoc. editor AIAA Jour., 1983—86. Contbr. numerous articles to profl. jours. Recipient Structures and Materials award, ASME, 1990, 1992. Fellow: AIAA (assoc.). Office: UCLA Mech and Aerospace Engring Los Angeles CA 90095-1597 Office Phone: 310-205-5453.

BENDINER, ROBERT, writer, editor; b. Pitts., Dec. 15, 1909; s. William and Lillian (Schwartz) B.; m. Kathryn Rosenberg, Dec. 24, 1934; children: David, William (dec.), Margaret. Student, CCNY, 1928-33; LHD (hon.), L.I. U., 1994. Mng. editor The Nation, NYC, 1937-44, assoc. editor, 1946-50, free-lance writer, 1951-68, 78—. Lectr., program chmn. Wellesley Summer Inst. Social Progress, 1946-53; mem. faculty Salzburg Sem. in Am. Studies, 1956; vis. lectr. journalism Wesleyan U. (Conn.), 1983 Contbg. editor The Reporter, N.Y.C., 1956-60; U.S. corr. New Statesman, London, 1959-61; mem. editorial bd. N.Y. Times, 1969-77; author: The Riddle of the State Department, 1942, White House Fever, 1960, Obstacle Course on Capitol Hill, 1964, Just Around the Corner, 1967, The Politics of Schools, 1969, The Fall of the Wild, The Rise of the Zoo, 1981, TV documentary NBC White Paper, The Man in the Middle, The State Legislator, 1961. Served with AUS, 1944-45. Guggenheim fellow, 1962-63; grantee Carnegie Fund; recipient Benjamin Franklin Mag. award U. Ill., 1955, NEA award, 1960 Mem. Nat. Press Club. Clubs: Coffee House (N.Y.C.). Home and Office: Southampton Estates 238 Street Rd Apt OBTS Southampton PA 18966-3128 Office Phone: 215-942-9487.

BENDINGER, GARY FREDERICK, lawyer; b. Sioux City, Iowa, Jan. 28, 1950; s. Warren Frederick and Joann (Janssen) B.; m. Christina Ruth Griffith (div.); m. Lorie Jean Carter, Sept. 17, 1981; children: Zelda Fay, Alton Mandel, Bernard Nathaniel. BA, Hastings Coll., 1972; JD, U. San Francisco, 1975. Bar: UT 1975, N.D. 1975, U.S. Ct. Appeals (10th cir.), U.S. Supreme Ct. 1981. Assoc. ptnr. Berman & Giauque, Salt Lake City, 1975-80; v.p. Biauque, Holbrook, Bendinger & Gurmankin, Salt Lake City, 1980-81, Giauque & Williams, Salt Lake City, 1981—, Giauque, Williams, Wilcox & Bendinger, Salt Lake City, 1987; ptnr., litig. practice Bendinger Crockett Peterson Greenwood & Casey, Salt Lake City. Fellow Am. Coll. Trial Lawyers; mem. ABA (litigation and antitrust sects.), State Bar of Utah (litigation sect.), NY Bar Assn. Democrat. Lutheran. Avocation: golf. Office: Howrey LLP Ste 400 170 S Main St Salt Lake City UT 84101 Office Phone: 801-533-8383. Office Fax: 801-531-1486.

BENDIX, HELEN IRENE, lawyer; b. NYC, July 24, 1952; d. Gerhard Max and Eva Gabriela (Sternberger) B.; m. John A. Kronstadt, Nov. 29, 1974. BA, Cornell U., 1973; JD, Yale U., 1976. Bar: Calif. 1976, D.C. 1978, U.S. Dist. Ct. D.C. 1980, U.S. Dist. Ct. (ctrl. dist.) Calif. 1986, U.S. Ct. Appeals (D.C. cir.) 1981, U.S. Ct. Appeals (9th cir.) 1987, U.S. Dist. Ct. (so. dist.) Calif. 1990. Law clk. to Hon. Shirley M. Hufstedler U.S. Ct. Appeals (9th cir.), LA, 1976-77; assoc. Wilmer Cultler & Pickering, Washington, 1977-79; asst. prof. law UCLA, 1979-80; from assoc. to ptnr. Leva Hawes Symington Martin & Oppenheimer, Washington, 1980-85; of counsel Gibson Dunn & Crutcher, LA, 1986-89; ptnr. Heller Ehrman White & McAuliffe, LA, 1989-96; sr. v.p., gen. counsel KCET Cmty. TV of So. Calif., 1996—; judge Mcpl. Ct. L.A. Jud. Dist., 1997-2000, Superior Ct. L.A., 2000—. Vis. prof. law UCLA, 1985-86; chair ADR com. L.A. Superior Ct., 2004-. Co-author: Moore's Federal Practice, Vols. X and XI, 1976, Vols. XII and XIII, 1979; contbr. articles to profl. jours. Violinist Palisades Symphony, Pacific Palisades, Calif., 1989—. Mem. European Union Ctr. of Calif., (mem. exec. adv. bd. 2003-05), Am. Law Inst., DC Bar Assn., Calif. State Bar Assn. (chair internat. law sect. 1990-91), Calif. Judges Assn., L.A. County Bar Assn. (past pres. dispute resolution svcs.), Jud. Coun. Calif. (mem. ad hoc com. on canon 6D 1998, working group on mediator ethics 2000, mem. access and fairness adv. com.), Chancery Club, Phi Beta Kappa. Office: Dept 18 111 N Hill St Los Angeles CA 90012-3014

BENE, STEVEN G., lawyer, game systems company executive; BS, Rice U.; JD, Stanford U. Bar: Calif. Joined Electronic Arts Inc., Redwood City, Calif., 1995, v.p., assoc. gen. counsel, 2003—04, v.p., acting gen. counsel, corp. sec., 2004, sr. v.p., gen. counsel, corp. sec., 2004—. Office: Electronic Arts Inc 209 Redwood Shores Pky Redwood City CA 94065*

BENEDETTO, ANTHONY DOMINICK See **BENNETT, TONY**

BENEDETTO, ANTHONY R., religious mediator; BS in Nuc. Engring., Tex. A&M U., Coll. Station, 1968, M in Nuc. Engring., 1970; MBA, Sul Ross State U., Alpine, Tex., 1976; PhD in Nuc. Engring., Tex. A&M U., Coll. Station, 1984; JD, South Tex. Coll. Law, Houston, 2005. Lic.: Tex. 2005; cert. in nuc. medicine physics and instrumentation Am. Bd. Sci. in Nuc. Medicine, 1979, in med. nuc. physics Am. Bd. Radiology, 1980, in healthcare mgmt. Am. Coll. Healthcare Execs., 1998. Asst. prof. dept. radiology U. Tex. Health Sci. Ctr., San Antonio, 1979—84; assoc. prof. to full prof. dept. radiology U. Tex. Med. Branch, Galveston, 1984—94; sr. sys. engr. ADAC Labs., Inc., Milpitas, Calif., 1994—95; prof., dir. ops. dept. diagnostic radiology U. Ky. Chandler Med. Ctr., Lexington, Ky., 1995—99; film lib. performance improvement project adminstr. M.D. Anderson Cancer Ctr., Houston, 2000—02; med. physicist Guidant Corp., Houston, 2002—03; scripture based conflict resolution conciliator Woodlands Conciliation Ctr., The Woodlands, 2005—. Mem. nuc. sci. com. Am. Coll. Nuc. Physicians, 1983—96, mem. quality assurance and practice cert. com., 1984—96, mem. publs. com., 1984—96, mem. com. single photon emission computed tomography quality control, 1992—96; dir. U. Tex. Med. Branch Diagnostic Radiology and Nuc. Medicine Sci. Lecture Series, 1984—94, instr., 1984—94; mem. sci. com. Nat. Coun. Radiation Protection and Measurements, 1989—2002, chmn. sci. com., 1992—95; cons. to standards com. Health Physics Soc., 1991—99; mem. comml. affairs com. Soc. Nuc. Medicine, 1992—95, chmn. advertising subcom., 1992—95, publs. com., 1992—95, mem. bylaws com., 1993—95, vice chmn. comml. affairs com., 1994—95; com. physics and instrumentation Am. Bd. Sci. in Nuc. Medicine, 1993—97; dir. UK Diagnostic Radiology Sci. Lecture Series, 1995—99, instr., 1995—99; profl. devel. com. Healthcare Info. and Mgmt. Sys. Soc., 1998—2000, ann. meeting proposal reviewer, session coach, 2000—03, chmn. clin. sys. spl. interest group, 2000—01, mem. evaluation task force edn. com., 2001; presenter in field. Contbr. articles to profl. jours., chapters to books; referee: Jour. Nuc. Medicine, 1983—96, reviewer:, 1984—96, mem. editl. bd.:, 1986—96; contbg. editor: Health Physics Soc. Newsletter, 1983—95; referee: Health Physics, 1983—96, book reviewer:, 1984—96, Med. Physics, 1984—96, referee:, 1987—95, RadioGraphics, 1992—98; contbg. editor: Jour. Nuc. Medicine Tech., 1995—97, credits reviewer: Am. Healthcare Radiology Adminstrs., 2000, mem. editl. review bd.:, 2001—03. Named one of Top 100 Vols., Harris County Dispute Resolution Ctr., 2006. Fellow: Am. Coll. Radiology (mem. com. standards and accreditation 1992—97), Am. Coll. Healthcare Execs., Am. Assn. Physicists in Medicine (chmn. publs. com. 1993—96, mem. com. electronic archival and comm. 1993—96); mem.: ABA, Tex. Radiology Soc., Christian Legal Soc., Assn. for Conflict Resolution. Office: Woodlands Conciliation Ctr 2203 Timberloch Pl Ste 100 The Woodlands TX 77380 Office Phone: 281-296-5716. Business E-Mail: tony@thedove.info.

BENEDICK, RICHARD ELLIOT, diplomat; b. NYC, May 10, 1935; s. Lester and Jean (Shamski) B.; m. Hildegard Schulz, 1957 (div.); children: Andreas, Julianna; m. Helen Freeman, 1983 (div.); m. Irene Federwisch, 1997. AB summa cum laude, Columbia U., 1955; MA with honors, Yale U., 1956; DBA, Harvard U., 1962; DSc (hon.), N.C. State U., 2004. Program economist AID U.S. Dept. State, Washington, 1958, Tehran, Iran, 1959-61, Karachi, Pakistan, 1962-64; economist OECD, Paris, 1964-66; 1st sec. Am. Embassy, Bonn, Germany, 1966-71; dir. Office Devel. Fin., Washington, 1971-75; counselor for econ. and comml. affairs Am. Embassy, Athens, Greece, 1975-77; mem. sr. seminar Dept. State, Washington, 1977-78; coord. population affairs with rank amb. U.S. Dept. State, Washington,

1979-84, dep. asst. sec. for environ., health and natural resources, 1984-87; sr. fellow World Wildlife Fund, 1987-98; dep. dir. Battelle Pacific N.W. Nat. Lab., 1998—; sr. adv. Battelle/Joint Global Change Rsch. Inst./U. Md., 2001—. Spl. advisor to sec. gen. UN Conf. on Environ. and Devel., 1990-92, Internat. Conf. on Population and Devel., 1993-94; pres. Nat. Coun. for Sci. and Environ., 1994—; vis. prof. Acad. Internat. l'Environnement, Geneva, 1992-96; lectr. in field; head U.S. del. to confs.; chief U.S. negotiator Montreal Protocol on protection of ozone layer, 1985-87; bd. dirs. Population Resource Ctr., Pacific Inst., Environ. and Energy Study Inst.; internat. adv. bd. Battelle, 1994-97, Environ. Tech. Ctr., Berlin, 1996, Climate Policy Ctr., 2002—; v.p. OECD Environ. Com., 1984-87; v.p. Transboundary Air Pollution Conv., Econ. Commn. for Europe, 1985-87; vis. fellow Nat. Ctr. Atmospheric Rsch., 1988-89, Ostwestwirtschafts Akademie, Berlin, 1991-96, Wissenschaftszentrum Berlin, 1995—; faculty Fgn. Svc. Inst., U.S. Dept. State, 1999—; mem. Nat. Acads. Com. Global Change Assessments, 2005-07; cons. in field. Author: Industrial Finance in Iran, 1964, The High Dam and the Transformation of the Nile, 1979, Ozone Diplomacy, 1991, rev. edit., 1998; contbr. articles to profl. jours. Recipient Presdl. Meritorious Svc. award, 1984, 90, Superior Honor medal Dept. State, 1985, 87, John Jacob Rogers award, 1993, Presdl. Disting. Svc. award, 1988, ann. award Climate Inst., 1988, UN Global Ozone award, 1997; Evans fellow Oxford U., 1956, Population Ref. Bur. hon. fellow, 1986, Stimson fellow Yale U., 2001. Fellow World Acad. of Art and Sci. (elected 1991), Am. Acad. Diplomacy (elected 2002); mem. Toenissteiner Kreis (Germany), Phi Beta Kappa. Home: 4111 27th St N Arlington VA 22207-5211 Office: Joint Global Change Rsch Inst 8400 Baltimore Ave College Park MD 20470 Business E-Mail: richard.benedick@pnl.gov.

BENEDICT, BURTON, retired museum director, anthropologist; b. Balt., May 20, 1923; s. Burton Eli Oppenheim and Helen Blanche (Deiches) B.; m. Marion MacColl Steuber, Sept. 23, 1950; children: Helen, Barbara MacVean AB cum laude, Harvard U., 1949; PhD, U. London, 1954. Sr. rsch. fellow Inst. Islamic Studies, McGill U., Montreal, Que., Can., 1954-55; sociol. rsch. officer Colonial Office, London and Mauritius, 1955-58; sr. lectr. social anthropology London Sch. Econs., 1958-68; prof. anthropology U. Calif., Berkeley, 1968-91, prof. emeritus, 1991—, chmn. dept., 1970-71, dean social scis., 1971-74, dir. Hearst Mus. Anthropology, 1989-94; dir. emeritus Hearst Mus. Anthropology, 1994—. Dir. U. Calif. Study Ctr. for U.K. and Ireland, London, 1986-88 Author: Indians in a Plural Society, 1961; author and editor: Problems of Smaller Territories, 1967, (with M. Benedict) Men, Women & Money in Seychelles, 1982, The Anthropology of World's Fairs, 1983; contbr. numerous articles to profl. jours. Trustee East Bay Zool. Soc. Sgt. USAF, 1942-46. Recipient Western Heritage award Nat. Cowboy Hall of Fame, 1984; rsch. fellow Colonial Office, 1955-58, 60, U. Calif., Berkeley, 1974-75; grantee NEH, 1981-83. Fellow Royal Anthrop. Inst. (mem. coun. 1962-65, 67-68, 86-89), Am. Anthrop. Assn.; mem. Assn. Social Anthropologists of Brit. Commonwealth, Athenaeum Club (London) Avocations: museums, the zoo, birdwatching, collecting postcards, world fairs. Office: U Calif Berkeley Dept Anthropology Berkeley CA 94720-0001

BENEDICT, DOROTHY JONES, genealogist, researcher; b. Bronxville, NY, Mar. 23, 1916; d. Harry Edwin and Katherine Jones; m. Mark Charles Benedict; children: Ann, Sharon, Gail, Faye. BA, Goucher Coll., 1938. Statistician E.W. Axe Co., NYC, 1938; with Nat. Labor Rels. Bd., NYC, 1938-39. Leader Girl Scouts of Am., Glastonbury, Conn., 1957-64; creator convalescent homes Sunday mini-svc. Asbury Ch., Glastonbury, 1960-70. Mem. Nat. Soc. Magna Carta Dames, DAR, Delta Delta Delta, Phi Beta Kappa. Methodist. Avocations: golf, art. Home: 100 S Interlachen Ave Winter Park FL 32789-4438

BENEDICT, JAMES NELSON, lawyer; b. Norwich, NY, Oct. 6, 1949; s. Nelson H. and Helen (Wilson) B.; m. Janet E. Fagal, May 8, 1982. BA magna cum laude, St. Lawrence U., 1971; JD, Albany Law Sch. of Union U., 1974. Bar: N.Y. 1975, U.S. Dist. Ct. (no., ea. and so. dists.) N.Y. 1975, U.S. Ct. Appeals (2d cir.) 1975, U.S. Ct. Appeals (8th cir.) 1977, U.S. Ct. Appeals (10th cir.) 1978, U.S. Ct. Appeals (11th cir.) 1982, U.S. Supreme Ct. 1978. Assoc. Rogers & Wells, NYC, 1974-82; ptnr. Clifford Chance, NYC, 1982—2004, Milbank Tweed, Hadley & McCloy, NYC, 2004—. Mem. bd. contbg. editors and advisors The Corp. Law Rev., 1976-86; contbr. articles to profl. jours. Bd. dirs. Reece Sch., N.Y.C., 1984-89, Stanley Isaacs Neighborhood Ctr., N.Y.C., 1984-89; trustee St. Lawrence U., Canton, N.Y., 1985-91. Mem. ABA (chmn. securities litigation subcom. on 1940 Act matters 1984-86, 96—), Fed. Bar Coun. N.Y. State Bar Assn., Assn. Bar City N.Y. (com. on securities regulaton, fed. legislation com., fed. cts. com.), Am. Soc. Writers on Legal Subjects, Sky Club (N.Y.C.), Scarsdale Golf Club, Phi Beta Kappa. Home: 26 Kensington Rd Scarsdale NY 10583-2217 Office Phone: 212-530-5696. Business E-Mail: jbenedict@milbank.com.

BENEDICT, KENNETTE MARI, foundation executive, researcher; b. NYC, Jan. 19, 1948; d. Donald LaVerne Benedict and Ann Kennette Cnare; m. Jonathan David Casper, Aug. 2, 1980 (div. 2002); 1 child, Sarah Casper. AB, Oberlin Coll., 1971; PhD, Stanford U., 1981. Rschr. Gov.'s Com. Law Enforcement/Adminstrn. Criminal Justice, Boston, 1971; asst. prof. Rutgers U., New Brunswick, NJ, 1980-81, U. Ill., Urbana-Champaign, 1981-85; dep. dir. peace and internat. cooperation MacArthur Found., Chgo., 1989-92, dir. internat. peace and security, 1992—, sr. advisor on philanthropy, 2002—. Cons. Compton Found., Menlo Park, 1998-2000, bd. dirs.; adv. coun. Stanley Found., Muscatine, Iowa, 2001-, Ctr. for Effective Philanthropy, 2003—; advisor Rockefeller Bros. Fund, NYC, 1996-97, com. mem. Leonard Rieser Prize, Chgo., 2000— Contbr. articles to profl. jours. Bd. trustees mem. Oberlin Coll., 2004—; bd. dirs. Compton Found., 2003—. Lena Lake Forrest fellow Bus. and Profl. Women's Found., 1977-78. Mem. Coun. on Fgn. Rels., Internat. Inst. Strategic Studies, Chgo. Coun. on Fgn. Rels. Avocations: hiking, music. Office: MacArthur Found 140 S Dearborn St Chicago IL 60603

BENEDICT, LAWRENCE NEAL, foreign service officer; b. Independence, Mo., Dec. 17, 1942; s. Albert Michael and Audentia Elizabeth (Thomas) B.; m. Gloria Kay Bruning, July 2, 1966. BA, Calif. State U., Long Beach, 1974. V.p. A.M. Benedict & Assocs., Long Beach, 1966-72; vice consul Am. Embassy, Dahka, Bangladesh, 1974-77; comml. officer Am. Consulate Gen., Rio de Janeiro, 1977-79; desk officer for Bangladesh U.S. Dept. State, Washington, 1979-80, desk officer for Turkey, 1980-82, dep. dir. devel. fin., 1986-89; fin., devel. officer Am. Embassy, Ankara, Turkey, 1982-86, counselor econ. affairs Islamabad, Pakistan, 1989-92, dep. chief of mission Khartoum, Sudan, 1992-95, amb. Praia, Cape Verde, 1996—. Staff sgt. U.S. Army N.G., 1963-69. Mem. Am. Fgn. Svc. Assn. Avocations: tennis, reading, collecting books and wine. Home: 358 Falcon Crest Dr Arroyo Grande CA 93420 Personal E-mail: benedict_li@hotmail.com.

BENEDICT, STEPHANIE MICHELLE, purchasing agent, sales consultant; b. North Kansas City, Mo., Aug. 28, 1980; d. Stephen Richard and Hope Marvel Benedict. MusB in Edn., Ctrl. Mo. State U., Warrensburg, 2003. Purchasing agt. Polymeric Imaging, Inc., North Kansas City, 2003—; sales cons. Lemongrass Spa Products, LLC, Bailey, Colo., 2004—. Clarinetist North Star Cmty. Band, Kansas City, 2003—06; vol. State Rep. Silvey Campaign, Kansas City, 2004—05. Scholar, Dept. Music Ctrl. Mo. State U., 2001, 2002; Regents scholar, Ctrl. Mo. State U., 1998—2000, Glenn Bixby Music scholar, Dept. Music Ctrl. Mo. State U., 2001, Merville Meverden Edn. scholar, 2002, Edith Brooks Music scholar, 2002. Mem.: Music Educators Nat. Conf. (assoc.), Collegiate Music Educators Nat. Conf. (assoc.), Mo. State Tchr.'s Assn. (assoc.), Kappa Delta Pi (assoc.), Rho Lambda (assoc.), Alpha Phi (assoc.; v.p. program devel. 1999—2000, chaplain 2000—01, marshall 2000—01, v.p. program devel. 2001—02, founding mem., treas. Kansas City Met. Alumnae chpt. 2003—05). R-Conservative. Disciples Of Christ. Avocations: musical ensembles, travel, photography, crafts, walking. Office: Polymeric Imaging Inc 117 E 14th Ave Kansas City MO 64116 Home Phone: 816-616-5670. Business E-Mail: stephanie@polymericimaging.com.

BENEDICT, STEWART H., writer, playwright; Author (editor): (book) Tales of Terror and Suspense, 1963, Harper's English Grammar, 1964, The Crime Solvers, 1966, A Teacher's Guide to Senior High School Literature, 1966, Famous American Speeches, 1967, A Teacher's Guide to Modern Drama, 1967, A Teacher's Guide to Poetry, 1969, Blacklash: Black Protest in Our Time, 1970, Twelfth Night and Your Own Thing, 1970, Making a Difference, 1971, A Teacher's Guide to Contemporary Teenage Fiction, 1973, A Teacher's Guide to Jonathan Livingston Seagull, 1973, A Teacher's Guide to Fireweed, 1973, A Teacher's Guide to the Faraway Lurs, 1973, The Literary Guide to the United States, 1981, Street Beat, 1982, Curtain Going Up, 2002; contbr. chapters to books; author: (plays) One Day in the Life of Ivy Dennison, 1967, The Puppeteer, 1967, Not Guilty, 1967, Dance of Life, 1981, Bad Guy, 1972, Judgment Day, 1971, Count That Day Lost, 1971, Going Up, 1971, Red, 1972, Busy, Busy, Busy, 1975, A Crime, 1977, Floored, 1979, It's the Rhinoceros Man's Life, 1983, Down Home, 1984, Gift of Tongues, 1984, Dead Center, 1984, City Desk, 1985, The Wild West: A Liberated Look, 1987, St. Patrick's Day, 1987, Frissons, 1989, I Have Seen the Future., 1989, Out of the Frying Pan, 1990, Gone to the Dogs, 1994, Left Face, 1994, Right Face, 1994, Family Values, 1994, Dr. Hyde and Mr. Jekyll, 1994, The Bargain, 1995, The Mother, 1995, The People Store, 1995, Tomorrow the World, 1995, The Robbery, 1996, Absolutely Fabulous Fairy Tales, 1996, Fancy Bread, 1996, Be Still My Liver, 1996, Yuletide Treasure, 1996, The Hero, 1999, Homicidal Murders, 2002, The Gap, 2003, Humanoids Using Goodness, 2003, Monody, 2004, Wow!, 2005, Alcestis, 2007, City Desk, 2007; contbr. to encys., articles to profl. jours. Office Phone: 212-228-1440.

BENEDICT, TIM, lawyer; b. Portland, Ore., Feb. 6, 1972; BS, Univ. Minn., 1995; JD, Univ. Wash., 2000. Bar: Wash. 2000. Assoc. atty. comml. litig. Hillis Clark Martin & Peterson, Seattle, 2001—. Contbr. articles to numerous profl. jours. Named Seattle Rising Star, SuperLawyer Mag., 2006. Mem.: ABA, Seattle Bar Assn. Office: Hillis Clark Martin & Peterson 500 Galland Bldg 1221 Secibd Ave Seattle WA 98101-2925

BENEDICT XVI, HIS HOLINESS POPE (JOSEPH ALOIS RATZINGER), Pope of Roman Catholic Church, Bishop of Rome; b. Marktl am Inn, Bavaria, Germany, Apr. 16, 1927; s. Joseph and Maria (Peintner) Ratzinger. Student, Superior Sch. Philos. and Theology, Freising & U. Munich, 1946—51; PhD in Theology, U. Munich, 1953; laurea in jurisprudence (hon.), Libera Universita Maria Santissima Assunta, 1999. Ordained Priest of Munich, Germany, 1951—77, Archbishop of Munchen und Freising, Germany, 1977—82; elevated Cardinal-Priest of St. Marie Consolatrice al Tiburtino, 1977—2005; Cardinal-Bishop of Velletri-Segni, 1993—2005; Cardinal-Bishop of Ostia, 2002—05; prof. dogma & fundamental theology Superior Sch. Philos. and Theology, Freising, 1952—59, U. Bonn, 1959—63, U. Munster, 1963—66, U. Tubingen, 1966—69; v.p., prof. dogmatic theology & hist. of dogma U. Regensburg, 1969—77; elected Pope, 2005; installed Pope, 2005—. Consultar Vatican Coun. II, 1962; prefect Congregation for Doctrine of the Faith, 1981—; pres. Internat. Theol. Commn., 1981—, Pontifical Bibl. Commn., 1981—; vice dean Coll. Cardinals, 1999—2002, dean, 2002—05; mem. Secretariat of State (2nd sect.), Congregation for Oriental Churches, Congregation for Divine Worship and Sacraments, Congregation for Bishops, Congregation for Evangelization of Peoples, Congregation for Cath. Edn., Pontifical Coun. for Christian Unity, Pontifical Coun. for Culture, Pontifical Commn. for L.Am., Pontifical Commn. Ecclesia Dei. Editor: Principles of Christian Morality, 1986; author: Intro. to Christianity, 1968, Feast of Faith, 1986, The Ratzinger Report, 1987, Behold the Pierced One, 1987, Meaning of the Christian Brotherhood, 1993, A Turning Point for Europe?, 1994, The Nature and Mission of Theology, 1995, A New Song for the Lord, 1996, Called to Communion, 1996, Salt of the Earth, 1997, Milestones: Memoirs 1927-1977, 1998, Many Religions-One Covenant, 1999, The Spirit of the Liturgy, 2000, God and the World, 2002, Truth and Tolerance, 2004, The End of Time?, 2005, John Paul II, My Beloved Predecessor, 2007, others. Aux. anti-aircraft svc., WWII. Named one of Most Influential People, TIME mag., 2005, 100 Most Influential People, 2006. Mem.: Pontifical Acad. Scis. (hon.). Roman Catholic. Office: Congregation for Doctrine of the Faith Piazza del S Uffizio 11 00193 Rome Italy Business E-Mail: benedettoxvi@vatican.va.

BENEFIELD, EMILY ANNE, nurse, human services manager; d. James Henderson and Verla Jane Benefield; children: Kimberly Anne Davis, Jerry Justin Davis. Assoc., Texarkana C.C., 1971; BS in Health Care Adminstrn., Tex. A & M, 1975. RN Bd. of Nurse Examiners State of Tex., 1971, cert. case mgr., Commn. Case Mgr. Cert., 2003, legal nurse cons., Am. Legal Nurse Cons. Cert. Bd. Nursing supr. St. Michaels Hosp., Texarkana, Ark., 1971—72, Wadley Regional Med. Ctr., Texarkana, Tex., 1972—73; don New Boston Gen. Hosp., New Boston, Tex., 1973—75; nursing instr. Texarkana C.C., Texarkana, Tex., 1975—78; co-owner Jerry Davis Farms, Texarkana, Tex., 1975—2000; case mgr. Tex. Assn. Sch. Bds., Austin, Tex., 2000—04; instr. Austin C.C., Austin, Tex., 2003—; owner Legal Nurse Cons. and Case Mgmt. Svcs., Austin, Tex. Advisor Austin C.C. Case Mgmt. Adv. Bd., Austin, Tex., 2003—. Contbr. jour. article TASB Risk Mgmt. Life mem. Presbyn. Women, Texarkana, Tex., 1989; pres., life mem. Parent Tchrs. Assn., Texarkana, Tex., 1990; pres. DAR, Texarkana, Tex., 1992; treas. Pleasant Grove Band Boosters Assn., Texarkana, Tex., 1996; edn. advisor Bowie County Rep. Party, Texarkana, Tex., 1998—99. Nominee Christine Nelson Vol. of Yr. award, Texarkana Tex., 1982. Mem.: Cert. Case Mgrs. (Austin chpt. 2002—05), Am. Assn. Legal Nurse Cons. (assoc.; capital area chpt. 2004—). Presbyterian. Avocations: photography, genealogy.

BENEFIELD, JANIS WILSON, school librarian, media specialist; b. San Angelo, Tex., Apr. 17, 1947; d. Woodrow and Madolynne Bradley Wilson; m. Harry Clayton Reno, Sept. 21, 1968 (dec. Nov. 10, 1968); m. Lester Benefield; 1 child, Bradley Lynn. BA, U. Houston, 1968; MLS, North Tex. State U., 1974. Lic. tchr. secondary english State Bd. Educator Certification, Tex., 1969, tchr. secondary french State Bd. Educator Certification, Tex., 1969, cert. profl. all-level learning resources specialist State Bd. Educator Certification, Tex., 1977. Tchr. Gabbs (Nev.) Sch., 1969—71, Mary S. Black Intermediate Sch., Battle Mountain, Nev., 1971—73; dist. libr. Dolores County Schs., Dove Creek, Colo., 1973—74; children's and young adult libr. Moore Meml. Pub. Libr., Texas City, Tex., 1974; libr. media specialist Westchester Jr. H.S., Houston, 1975—85; libr. resources and media specialist Nottingham Elem. Sch., Houston, 1985—. Freelance storyteller, Houston, 2001—. Tutor Spring Br. Ind. Sch. Dist., Houston, 2000—05; leader Tallowood Bapt. Ch., Houston, 1983—88. Named Tchr. of Yr., Nottingham Elem. Sch., 2002; grantee, Apache Corp., 2003; J. Landon Short Mini grant, Partnerships and Vol. Programs Dept., 1990, 1991, 2003, 2005. Mem.: Tex. Computer Edn. Assn., Tex. Assn. for Gifted and Talented, Tex. Libr. Assn., Pi Delta Phi (sec. 1967—68, award French Cultural Svcs. Houston 1968), Beta Phi Mu. Conservative. Southern Baptist. Avocations: travel, reading, ballet, flute, walking. Home: 14800 Memorial Drive 274 Houston TX 77079 Office: Nottingham Elementary School 570 Nottingham Oaks Trail Houston TX 77079 Home Phone: 281-497-3831; Office Phone: 281-560-7460.

BENENSON, JAMES, JR., manufacturer; b. Moultrie, Ga., Mar. 9, 1936; s. James and Mary (Camp) B.; m. Sharen Statler, Aug. 28, 1966; children: James, Clement. BS, MIT, 1958. With F. Eberstadt & Co., NYC, 1960-65, Walker, Hart & Co., NYC, 1965-68, James Benenson & Co., Inc., NYC, 1968—; CEO Indsl. Mfg. Co., Newtown Square, Pa., 1978—; chmn. bd. Summa Holdings, Inc., Cleve., 1983—. Served with U.S. Army Chem. Corps, 1959. Woodrow Wilson scholar, 1959-60; Andover tchg. fellow, 1958-59 Mem. Hort. Soc. N.Y., N.Y. Bot. Garden (dir.), Soc. of Cincinnati, Century Assn., Racquet Club (Phila.), Buck's Harbor Yacht Club (Brooksville, Maine), N.Y. Yacht Club. Episcopalian. Office: Indsl Mfg Co 3400 W Chester Pike Newtown Square PA 19073-4638

BENENSON, MARK KEITH, lawyer; b. NYC, Oct. 13, 1929; s. Aaron and Luba (Stein) B.; m. Letizia Pitigliani, Dec. 29, 1959; children: Alexander, Daniela. BSS., CCNY, 1951; JD, Columbia U., 1956. Bar: N.Y. 1956. Atty. Dept. Labor, Washington, 1957-58; practiced in NYC, 1958—. Bd. dirs. Amnesty Internat. U.S.A., 1966-80, sec., 1966-67, chmn., 1968-71, vice chmn., 1972-73, gen. counsel, 1972-80; pres. Vanguard Found., Inc., 1962— Contbr. articles to profl. jours., mags. and newspapers. Exec. sec. Nat. Found. for Firearms Edn., 1983-91, Pres. 1991—. With U.S. Army, 1951-53. Recipient John Amber Gun Digest Writing award, 1998. Home and Office: 585 W End Ave New York NY 10024-1715 Personal E-mail: mkbenenson@aol.com.

BENEPE, VIRGINIA LYNN, medical/surgical nurse, oncological nurse, educator; b. Oak Park, Ill., Mar. 30, 1964; d. Irvin Guy and Marilyn Sherwood (Warner) Goodman; m. John Gregory Benepe, Aug. 30, 1986; children: David Irvin, John Wesley. BSN, Tex. Christian U., 1986. RN, Tex.; cert. chemotherapy therapist, nurse med.-surg. nursing, diabetes educator, gerontology nurse, pediatric nurse. Staff nurse Breckenridge Hosp., Austin, Tex., 1986-87; staff nurse, relief charge nurse Harris Hosp. Ft. Worth, 1987—97; staff nurse Cook Children's Hosp., Ft. Worth, 1997—. Bd. dirs. Greater Tarrant County chpt. Juvenile Diabetes Rsch. Found. Mem. Am. Diabetes Assn. (bd. dirs. Greater Tarrant County chpt.), Am. Assn. Diabetes Educators (cert.), Tex. Nurses Assn. Home: 7614 Dijon Lake Dr Corpus Christi TX 78413-5245

BENERIA, LOURDES, economist, educator; b. Boi, Lleida, Spain, Oct. 8, 1939; came to U.S., 1964; d. Agusti Beneria and Josepa Farre; children: Jordi, Marc. Licenciatura, U. Barcelona, Spain, 1961; MPhil, Columbia U., 1974, PhD in Econs., 1975. Coord. program on rural women ILO, Geneva, 1977-79; asst. prof. Rutgers U., New Brunswick, N.J., 1975-81, assoc. prof., 1981-86; prof. city and regional planning and women's studies Cornell U., Ithaca, NY, 1987—, dir. program on gender and global change, 1987—92, 2000—03, dir. Latin Am. studies program, 1993—97, dir. internat. studies in planning, 2003—; pres. Internat. Assn. for Feminist Econs., 2003—. Recipient Narcis Monturiol award, Barcelona. Office: Cornell Univ CRP W Sibley Hall Ithaca NY 14853-2148

BENES, FRANCINE M., neuroscientist, psychiatrist; b. NYC, May 8, 1946; d. Joseph William and Emma Mary B. BA in Biology, St. John's U., 1967; PhD in Cell Biology, Yale U., 1972, MD, 1978. Lectr. in neuroanatomy Yale Sch. of Medicine, New Haven, 1975-77; asst. prof. psychiatry Harvard Med. Sch., Boston, 1982-87, assoc. prof., 1987-97, prof., 1997—; dir. program in structural and molecular neurosci. lab. McLean Hosp., Belmont, Mass., 1992—, dir. Harvard Brain Tissue Resource Ctr., 1996—; dir. clin. neurosci. tng. program in psychiatry Harvard Med. Sch., 1994-99. Mem. bd. sci. counselors Nat. Inst. Mental Health, Bethesda, Md., 1994-98; mem. sci. adv. bd. Internat. Congress Schizophrenia Rsch., 1994—, Schizophrenia Bull., Calif. Neuro-Aids Tissue Network, San Diego, 2000—; cons. WHO, Paris, 1999. Neuropsychiatry editor Current Opinion in Psychiatry, 2000—; mem. editl. bd. Biotechniques, 1990-96, Devel. and Psychopathology, 1991—, Synapse, 1995—, Neuropsychopharmacology, 1997-2001, Schizophrenia Rsch., 1998—; contbr. articles to profl. jours. Bd. dirs. Waldon Pond Reservation Trust, Concord, Mass., 2001—; mem. Nat. Wildlife Fedn., Humane Soc. of U.S.; chair affirmative action com., McLean Hosp., Belmont, 1993-94. Recipient Shervert S. Frazier Lifetime Achievement award, 1999, Merit award NIMH, 2000-02, Lifetime Achievement award in monitoring, 2006, Kempf award Am. Psychiat. Assn. Mem. Inst. Medicine, Soc. for Neurosci., Am. Coll. Neuropsychopharmacology, World Fedn. Socs. of Biol. Psychiatry (co-chair task force on brain pathology 2001—), Nat. Assn. for Rsch. on Schizophrenia and Depression (mem. sci. adv. bd., Lieber prize 2002). Avocations: sailing, reading, creative writing. Office: McLean Hosp 115 Mill St Belmont MA 02478 E-mail: benesf@mclean.harvard.edu.

BENES, SOLOMON, retired biomedical scientist, physician; b. Iasi, Romania, Mar. 28, 1925; came to U.S., 1978; s. Moritz and Cecilia (Abramovici) B.; m. Liudmila Topor, Mar. 27, 1954. MD, U Bucharest, Romania, 1952. Intern microbiology lab. Mil. Hosp., Bucharest, 1949—50, fellow microbiology lab., 1950—51, dir. clin. lab. outpatient dept., 1951—52; dir. rsch. lab. Ctr. Radiobiology Rsch., Bucharest, 1953—57, 1959—66; chief physician microbiology lab. Mil. Hosp., Bucharest, 1967—73; chief physician clin. lab. Ctr. Haematology, Bucharest, 1973—76; assoc. medicine Havard Med. Sch., Boston, 1978—81; asst. rsch. scientist, asst. prof. SUNY Downstate Med. Ctr., Bklyn., 1982—95; sr. rsch. scientist, asst. prof. SUNY Rsch. Found., Bklyn., 1995—98; ret., 1998. Author: (with others) Seminars in Infectious Diseases, 1983; contbr. articles to Sexually Transmitted Diseases, Antimicrobial Agts. and Chemotherapy, Jour. Clin. Microbiology, Proceedings of the 6th Internat. Symposium on Human Chlamydial Infections. Col. Romanian Army Med. Svc., 1946—73. Achievements include discovery that the Trachoma biovar of Chlamydia trachomatis is able to achieve intercellular propagation in cell culture and that, in a proper cell setting, this bacterium spreads from cell to cell in cell culture, contrary to what was generally believed. Home: 2421 Shellpot Dr Wilmington DE 19803-2547

BENESTANTE, VINCENZO, writer; b. Chgo., June 16, 1945; s. Anthony Victor Benestante and Frieda Ann Dobrin; m. Adelheid Engst (div.); 1 child, Adrian; m. Sabina Trooger, Mar. 7, 1997. BA, M Performing Arts, So. Ill. U., 1968. Opera singer various theaters, Switzerland, 1968—70; actor various theaters, TV, Germany, Italy, France, 1970—98; freelance author, translator, 2002—; performance poet Fla., 2002—. Author: (short stories) Anthologie Der Fantasie, 2000, (novels) The Gate of Anki, 1999, The Time of Tipa-We, 2000, The Master's Shadow, 2002, The Nephilim, 2003. Finalist, Miami Grand Slam Spoken Word Poetry. Mem.: Lip, Tongue and Ear Poetry Guild (officer 2003—, lectr. in drama in poetry). Avocations: scuba diving, bicycling, reading. Home and Office: 10725 SW 146th St Miami FL 33176 E-mail: genomm@earthlink.net.

BENET, HELEN CURRY, retired toxicologist, artist; b. Greenwood, SC, May 4, 1939; d. Graham Payne and Ethel (Martin) Curry; m. Richard Ward Benet, Sept. 5, 1959 (dec.); children: Richard, Nancy Clarke, Carmen Downey. PhD, U. Miss., 1983. Analyst Def. Intelligence Agy., Washington, 1983—2002; pres. Benet Biol. Scis., DeLand, Fla., 2002—05; owner Benet Art Studio, DeLand, 2002—. Contbr. chapters to books. Mem.: Nat. Mus. Women in the Arts (sec. Fla. chpt. 2005), Maitland Art Ctr., Fla. Watercolor Soc., Ctrl. Fla. Watercolor Soc. Avocation: painting. Home: 137 Woodward Ave Deland FL 32720-4965 Personal E-mail: beneth@cfl.rr.com.

BENET, JAY S., insurance company executive; Ptnr. Pricewaterhouse-Coopers; sr. v.p., Group Annuity Travelers Life & Annuity, 1996—98, CFO, 1998—2000, exec. v.p., Group Annuity, 1998—2000; CFO, Global

Consumer Europe, Middle East and Africa unit Citigroup, 2000—01; vice chmn., CFO St. Paul Travelers Companies,Inc., 2002—. Office: c/o St Paul Travelers 385 Washington Street Saint Paul MN 55102*

BENET, LESLIE ZACHARY, pharmacologist, educator; b. Cin., May 17, 1937; s. Jonas John and Esther Racie (Hirschfeld) Benet; m. Carol Ann Levin, Sept. 8, 1960; children: Reed Michael, Gillian Vivia. AB in English, U. Mich., 1959, BS in Pharmacy, 1960, MS in Pharm. Chemistry, 1962; PhD in Pharm. Chemistry, U. Calif., San Francisco, 1965; PhD (hon.), Leiden U., Netherlands, 1995, U. Athens, 2005; PharmD (hon.), Uppsala U., Sweden, 1987; DSc (hon.), U. Ill., Chgo., 1997, Phila. Coll. Pharm. and Sci., 1997, LI U., 1999. Asst. prof. pharmacy Wash. State U., Pullman, 1965—69; asst. prof. pharmacy and pharm. chemistry U. Calif., San Francisco, 1969—71, assoc. prof., 1971—76, prof., 1976—, vice chmn. dept. pharmacy, 1973—78, chmn. dept. pharmacy, 1978—96, dir. drug studies unit, 1977—, dir. drug kinetics and dynamics ctr., 1979—98, chmn. dept. biopharm. scis., 1996—98. Mem. pharmacology study sect. NIH, Washington, 1977—81, chmn., 1979—81, mem. pharmacol. scis. rev. com., 1984—88, chmn., 1986—88; mem. generic drugs adv. com. FDA, Washington, 1990—94; mem. Sci. Bd., 1992—98; chair external rev. com. CBER, 1998, chair expert panel on individual equivalence, 1998—2000; mem. sci. adv. bd. SmithKline Beecham Pharms., 1989—92, Pharmetrix, 1989—92, Alteon, Inc., 1993—, TheraTech, Inc., 1993—96, Roche Bio-sci., 1998—2001, Pain Therapeutics, Inc., 1999—, UMD, Inc., 1999—, Silico Insights, Inc., 2000—, InforMedix, 2001—; chmn. bd. AvMax, Inc.; bd. dirs. OxoN Medica, Inc., InforMedix, Inc., Josman Labs., Inc., Impax Pharmas., One World Health. Assoc. editor Pharmacology and Therapeutics, 1995—2000, editor Jour. Pharmacokinetics and Biopharmaceutics, 1976—98, mem. editl. bd. The Effect of Disease States on Drug Pharmacokinetics, 1976, Pharmacology, 1979—, Pharmacy Internat., 1979—82, Pharm. Rsch., 1983—95, Pharmacokinetic Basis for Drug Treatment, 1984, Pharmacokinetics: A Modern View, 1984, ISI Atlas of Sci.: Pharmacology, 1988—89, Integration of Pharmacokinetics, Pharmacodynamics and Toxicokinetics in Rational Drug Development, 1992, Clinical Applications of Mifepristone (RU486) and Other Antiprogestins, 1993, Pharm. News, 1994—98, AAPS Jour., 1999—, Molecular Interventions, 2000—, Chemistry and Pharm. Bull., 2000—, Drug Metabolism and Pharmacokinetics, 2002—, Current Drug Metabolism, 2004—, Giving Full Measure to Counter Measures, 2004, Expert Opinion on Drug Metabolism and Toxicology, 2005—; contbr. more than 470 articles to profl. jours. Apptd. Forum on Drug Devel. and Regulation, 1988. Named ISI Highly Cited Rschr., 2003; recipient Rsch. Achievement award in pharm. scis., Pharm. Sics. World Congress, 2004, Career Achievement award in oral drug delivery, Controlled Release Soc., 2004. Fellow: AAAS (mem.-at-large exec. com. pharm. scis. sect. 1978—81, 1991—95, chair 1996—97), Am. Assn. Pharm. Scientists (pres. 1986, treas. 1987, bd. dirs. 1988—93, Disting. Pharm. Scientist award 1989, Disting. Svc. award 1996, Wurster rsch. award in pharmaceutics 2000), Acad. Pharm. Scis. (chmn. basic pharmaceutics sect. 1976—77, mem.-at-large exec. com. 1979—83, pres. 1985—86, Rsch. Achievement award 1982); mem.: ISSX (councillor 1992—96, treas. 1998—99), AAUP, Pharm. Scis. World Congress (Rsch. Achievement award 2004), Inst. Medicine of NRC (devel. & acquisition med. countermeasures against biol. warfare agts. 2002—, chmn. com. accelerating rsch.), Am. Assn. Colls. Pharmacy (bd. dirs. 1992—95, pres. 1993—94, Volwiler Rsch. Achievement award 1991), Am. Coll. Clin. Pharmacy, Drug Info. Assn., Internat. Pharm. Fedn. (bd. pharm. scis. 1988—, chair 1996—2000, Host-Madsen medal 2001), Generic Pharm. Industry Assn. (mem. blue ribbon com. on generic medicines 1990), Am. Soc. for Pharmacology and Exptl. Therapeutics, Am. Soc. Clin. Pharmacology and Exptl. Therapeutics (Rawls-Palmer award and lectureship 1995), Am. Pharm. Assn. (Higuchi Rsch. prize 2000), Am. Coll. Clin. Pharmacology (Disting. Svc. award 1988), Am. Found. for Pharm. Edn. (bd. dirs. 1987—, Disting. Svc. "Profile" award 1993), Inst. Medicine of NAS (forum on drug devel. and regulation 1988—94, chmn. com. on antiprogestins 1993, membership com. 1994—97, chmn. other health profns. sect. 1995—97, chmn. com. pharmacokinetics and drug interactions in elderly 1996—97, mem. Round Table R & D Drugs, Biologics & Med. Devices 1997—2000, bd. on health scis. policy 1999—2005, mem. forum on drug discovery, devel. and transl. 2005—), Sigma Xi, Phi Lambda Sigma, Rho Chi (Ann. Lecture award 1990). Office: U Calif San Francisco Dept Biopharm Scis 533 Parnassus Rm U68 San Francisco CA 94143-0446 Office Phone: 415-476-3853. Business E-Mail: leslie.benet@ucsf.edu.

BENEZRA, NEAL, museum director, curator; b. Oakland, Calif., Aug. 20, 1953; m. Maria Makela; 1 child, Ava. BA, U. Calif., Berkeley, 1976; MA, Stanford U., 1981, PhD, 1983; postgrad., German Acad. Exch. Svc., 1983. Coord. Anderson Collection, Atherton, Calif., 1980-83; asst. curator Des Moines Art Ctr., 1983-84, curator, 1984-85; assoc. curator The Art Inst. Chgo., 1985-86, curator, 1987-91, asst. dir. art and pub. programs, 1996, dep. dir., Frances and Thomas Dittmer curator modern and contemporary art, 2000—02; chief curator Hirshhorn Mus. and Sculpture Garden, Smithsonian Instn., Washington, DC, 1991—96, asst. dir. art & pub. progs., 1996—99; dir. San Francisco Mus. Modern Art, 2002—. Vis. lectr. U. Ill., Urbana-Champaign, 1988; vis. assoc. prof. U. Chgo., 1990; mem. Smithsonian Coun.; art adv. bd. mem. U. Calif., San Francisco; art adv. panel IRS, Dept. Treasury. Curator exhbn./author catalogue: Robert Arneson: A Retrospective, 1986, Ed Paschke: Paintings, 1989, Affinities and Intuitions: The Gerald S. Elliott Collection of Contemporary Art, 1990, Martin Puryear, 1991, Bruce Nauman, 1993-94, Stephen Balkenhol, 1995-96. Grad. fellow Stanford U., 1978-81, McCloy fellow in German art, 1984-85. Office: San Francisco Mus Modern Art 151 Third St San Francisco CA 94103-3159

BENFER, DAVID WILLIAM, hospital administrator; b. Toledo, May 28, 1946; s. Wilson L. and Marjorie (Baringer) B.; m. Mary Sturner, Sept. 5, 1970; children: Emily, Matthew, Andrew. BA, Wittenberg U., 1968; MBA in Hosp. Adminstrn., Xavier U., 1970. Asst. admintrn. Med. Coll., Ohio Hosp., Toledo, 1971-76, exec. dir., CEO, 1976-81, Bon Secours Hosp., Grosse Pointe, Mich., 1982-84, Henry Ford Hosp., Detroit, 1985-92; pres., CEO, St. Joseph Med. Ctr., Joliet, Ill., 1992-99; CEO St. Raphael Healthcare System, New Haven, 1999—. Dir. Merchants and Mfrs. Bank, Stereotaxis, Inc.; fellow Berkeley Coll. Yale U., 2002—. Co-author: Issues in Health Care Management, 1982; contbg. author: Sisters of Bon Secours Centennial, 1982. Trustee, chmn. Family Svcs., Detroit and Wayne County, 1982-92; chmn. AIDS Consortium Southeastern Mich., Toledo, 1988-92l v.p. Med. Value Plan, Inc., 1986-91; chmn. S.E. Mich. Hosp. Coun.; bd. dirs. U. St. Francis, Joliet, 1993-2002; vice chmn. New Ctr. Area Coun., 1991-92; mem. Mich. Tastefest, 1996; bd. dirs., chmn. Ctr. Econ. Devel., Will County C. of C., Ill., New Haven Symphony, v.p. bd. Recipient Commendation 114th Ohio Gen Assembly, 1981, Torch of Liberty award Anti Defamation League, 2005. Fellow Am. Coll. Health Care Execs. (coun. regents 1989-92, bd. govs. 1992—2000, Robert S. Hudgens award 1982, chair 1998-99); mem. Am. Hosp. Assn. (regional policy bd.), Conn. Hosp. Assn. (bd. dirs.), Cath. Health Assn. (bd. dirs.), Quinnipiack Club (New Haven), Country Club Detroit (Grosse Pointe), New Haven Country Club. Roman Catholic. Avocations: jogging, golf. Office: St Raphael Healthcare System Hosp St Raphael 659 George St New Haven CT 06511-5324

BENFIELD, ANN KOLB, retired lawyer; b. Reading, Pa., May 1, 1946; d. Curtis Kepler and Stella (Kolb) B. BA, George Washington U., 1969, MA, 1974; JD, U. Ky., 1983. Ky. 1983, U.S. Ct. Appeals (6th cir.) 1985, U.S. Supreme Ct. 1987; cert. mental health consumer cons./educator; cert. trained mediator. Probation officer Superior Ct. of D.C., Washington, 1973-78; jud. law clk. to chief judge U.S. Dist. Ct. (we. dist.) Ky., Louisville, 1983-86, jud. atty. to fed. sr. judge, 1989-95; trial atty. Ogden, Welsh and Newell (formerly Ogden & Robertson), Louisville, 1986-89; pvt. practice Louisville, 1995—2001; ret., 2002; pro bono practice, 2002—. Adj. prof. U. Louisville Sch. Law, 1993, pro bono legal svcs., 2001-. Mem. exec. com., bd. dirs. Ky. chpt. ACLU, 1988-89, 91—2005, nat. bd. dirs., 1992-94, sec., 1995-96, treas., 1996-98, mem. legal panel, 1988-2003; mem. Reproductive Freedom Adv. Com., 1994-2001; mem. steering com. Fellowship Reconciliation, Louisville, 1997-2002; mem. governing coun. U. Louisville Women's Ctr., 1998-2001; rape crisis advocate Ctr. for Women and Families, 1997—2005, domestic violence advocate, 1998-2005; bd. dirs., gen. counsel Depressed Self-Help Svcs., Inc., 1998-2000. Fellow: Ky. Bar Found. (bd. dirs. 1994—96, charter mem.); mem.: Louisville Bar Assn., Ky. Alliance Against Racism and Polit. Repression (life), Ky. Bar Assn. (Donated Legal Svcs. Recognition award 2000, 2001, 2003), Ky. Paso Fino Horse Assn. (sec. 2000—01), Amicus Club of ACLU (founder Ky. chpt. 2004), Phi Beta Kappa, Order of Coif. Home Phone: 717-677-0776. Personal E-mail: akbenfield@aol.com.

BENFIELD, JOHN RICHARD, surgeon, educator; b. Vienna, June 24, 1931; arrived in U.S., 1938, naturalized, 1945; s. Richard and Charlotte Lola Benfield; m. Joyce A. Cohler, Dec. 22, 1963; children: Richard L., Robert E., Nancy J. AB, Columbia U., 1952; MD, U. Chgo., 1955. Diplomate Am. Bd. Surgery, Am. Bd. Thoracic Surgery. Intern Columbia-Presbyn. Hosp., NYC, 1955-56; E.H. Andrews fellow in thoracic surgery U. Chgo., 1956-57; chief resident and instr. in surgery U. Chgo. Clinics, 1962-64, resident in surgery, 1956-57, 59-63; asst. prof. surgery U. Wis., 1964-67; asst. prof. UCLA, 1967-69, assoc. prof., 1969-73, prof., 1973-77, clin. prof., 1978-88; prof. surgery, chief cardiothoracic surgery, vice chmn. surgery U. Calif. Davis Med. Ctr., Sacramento, 1988-95, prof. surgery, chief thoracic surgery, 1995-98, prof. emeritus, 1998—; attending surgeon V.A. Martinez Med. Ctr., 1988-98; courtesy staff Kaiser Permanente Med. Ctr., Sacramento, 1988-98. James Utley prof. surgery, chmn. dept. surgery Boston U., 1977; chmn. surgery City of Hope Nat. Med. Ctr., Duarte, Calif., 1978-87; bd. dirs. Am. Bd. Thoracic Surgery, 1982-88; cons. U.S. Naval Med. Ctr., San Diego, 1968-88; mem. sr. staff VA Wadsworth Med. Ctr., LA, 1978-88. Editor Current Problems in Cancer, 1975-86; mem. editl. bd. Annals Thoracic Surgery, 1979-2001, assoc. editor, 1987-2001; mem. editl. bd. Annals Surg. Oncology, 1994-2000; contbr. articles to profl. jours., chpts. to books. Sec., trustee Univ. Synagogue, LA. Served as capt. M.C. U.S. Army, 1957-59, Korea. Grantee Life Ins. Med. Rsch., 1962-66, Am. Heart Assn., 1968-71, USPHS, 1971-92. Mem. ACS (bd. govs. 1982-88, 92-98), Am. Surg. Assn., Am. Assn. Thoracic Surgery, Am. Assn. Cancer Rsch., Am. Med. Writers Assn., Internat. Assn. Study Lung Cancer, Internat. Soc. Surgery, Calif. Med. Soc., Ctrl. Surg. Assn., LA Acad. Medicine, The Royal Soc. Medicine (Gt. Britain), The Transplantation Soc., Soc. Thoracic Surgeons (v.p. 1994-95, pres. 1995-96), Soc. Univ. Surgeons, Pacific Coast Surg. Assn. (v.p. 1995-96), Soc. Surg. Oncology, Am. Coll. Chest Physicians (pres. Calif. chpt. 1996-97), Western Thoracic Surgeons Assn. (pres. 1989-90), Internat. Surg. Soc., Thoracic Surgery Dirs. Assn. (pres. 1995-97), Thoracic Surgery Found. Rsch. and Edn. (pres. 2003-06). Office Phone: 310-294-7333. Personal E-mail: j.benfield@verizon.net.

BENFIELD, MARION WILSON, JR., law educator; b. Belwood, NC, July 26, 1932; s. Marion Wilson and Gazzie Cleo (Martin) B.; m. Dalida Quijada, Feb. 21, 1964; children: Marion, Steve, Robin, Rosalina, Christopher, Jeanette, Antonio, Maria. AA, Gardner-Webb Coll., Boiling Springs, NC, 1951; AB in English, U. N.C., 1953; LLB, Wake Forest U., 1959; LLM, U. Mich., 1965. Bar: N.C. 1959. Asst. dir. Inst. Govt. U. N.C., 1959-61; individual practice law Hickory, NC, 1961-63; asst. prof. law U. Ga., 1963-65; assoc. prof. Case Western Reserve U., 1965-66, U. Ill., 1966-68, prof., 1968-88, Albert E. Jenner, Jr. prof. law, 1988-90, assoc. dean, 1980-85; disting. chair law Wake Forest U., 1990-97, adj. prof., 1997-98. Vis. prof. U. Houston, 1976-77, Duke U., 1979, NYU, 1984, Peking U., 1985, Shenzhen U., China, 1986, Loyola U., L.A., 1995, U. Tex., 1998-2001, U. Ala., 2001; mem. Nat. Conf. Commrs. on Uniform State Laws, 1973—. Reporter, draftsman: The Uniform Land Transactions Act and Uniform Simplification of Land Transfers Act, 1970-77, Revised Uniform Commercial Code, Article 2A, 1995-9, Article 2, 2002-03; author: Social Justice through Law-New Approaches in the Law of Contracts, 1970, (with W.H. Hawkland) Cases and Materials on Sales, 1979, 5th edit. (wth Michael Greatfield), 2006, (with Peter Alces) Commercial Paper and Alternative Payment Systems, 1987, (with Peter Aces) Payment Systems, 1993; mem. editl. bd. Uniform Commercial Code, 1974— , Uniform Land Transactions Act and Uniform Simplification of Land Transactions Act, 1982-93. Served with U.S. Army, 1954-56. Mem.: Am. Law Inst. Home: 10 Overlook Cir New Braunfels TX 78132-4728 E-mail: mbenfield@compuvision.net.

BENFORD, GREGORY ALBERT, physicist, writer; b. Mobile, Jan. 30, 1941; s. James Alton and Mary Eloise (Nelson) Benford; m. Joan Abbe, Aug. 26, 1967; children: Alyson Rhandra, Mark Gregory. BS, U. Okla., 1963; MS, U. Calif., San Diego, 1965, PhD, 1967. Research asst. U. Calif., San Diego, 1964—67; postdoctoral fellow Lawrence (Calif.) Radiation Lab., 1967—69, research physicist, 1969—71; prof. physics U. Calif., Irvine, 1971—. Cons. in field. Author: (novels) If the Stars are Gods, 1977, In the Ocean of Night, 1977, The Stars in Shroud, 1978, Find the Changeling, 1980, Timescape, 1980 (Nebula award), Against Infinity, 1983, Across the Sea of Suns, 1984, Artifact, 1985, Heart of the Comet, 1986, In Alien Flesh, 1986, Great Sky River, 1987, Tides of Light, 1989, Beyond the Fall of Night, 1990, Chiller, 1993, Furious Gulf, 1994, Sailing Bright Eternity, 1995; author: (with Mark O Martin) A Darker Geometry, 1996; author: Foundation's Fear, 1997, Cosm, 1998, The Martian Race, Eater, 2000; author: (collections) Matter's End, 1994; editor: Far Futures, 1995; editor: (with Martin H. Greenburg) The New Hugo Winners Volume IV, 1997; editor: Nebula Awards Showcase 2000: The Year's Best SF and Fantasy Chosen by the Science Fiction and Fantasy Writers of America, 2000; editor: (with George Zebrowski) Skylife: Space Habitats in Story and Science, 2000; editor: Worlds Vast and Various, 2000, Deep Time, 1999, Cosm, 1999, Eater, 2000. Recipient Brit. Sci. Fiction award, 1981, Australian Ditmar award for internat. novel, 1981, John Campbell award for best novel, 1981, UN medal in Lit., 1993, Lord prize in Sci., 1994, Lord Found. prize, 1995; fellow Woodrow Wilson, 1963—64; grantee Office Naval Rsch., 1975—, 1982—, Army Rsch. Orgn., 1977—82, Air Force Office Sci. Rsch., 1982—, Calif. Space Office, 1984—85. Mem.: NASA Sci. Adv. Bd., Soc. Sci. Exploration, Sci. Fiction Writers Am. (Nebula award 1975, 1981), Royal Astron. Soc., Am. Phys. Soc., Phi Beta Kappa. Office: Univ California Physics Dept 4129 Frederick Reines Hall Irvine CA 92697-4575 Business E-Mail: gbenford@uci.edu.

BENFORD, ROBERT DEE, social studies educator, editor; b. Akron, Ohio, July 22, 1951; s. Robert Dee Benford, Sr. and Carolyn Sue Benford; m. Michelle Hughes Miller, Aug. 17, 1990; children: Kiri Elaine Miller, Cambra Rae Benford-Miller. BA, U. Tex., 1981, MA, 1984, PhD, 1987. CEO Benford and Assocs., Inc., Houston, 1969—85; social sci. rsch. assoc. III Hogg Found. for Mental Health U. Tex., Austin, 1986—87; prof. dept. sociology U. Nebr., Lincoln, 1987—2000; prof. So. Ill. U., Carbondale, 2000—, chair dept. sociology, 2000—03. Editor Jour. of Contemporary Ethnography, Thousand Oaks, Calif., 2000—04; series editor Twayne's Social Movements Past and Present, NYC, 1995—99; pres. faculty senate So. Ill. U., 2005—06. Editor: (ency.) Compendium of Social Issues; contbr. articles to profl. jours. Exec. coun. The Drake Group, Des Moines, 1999—2001; peacekeeping coord./trainer Red River Peace Network, Austin, 1984—85; del., peace rsch. del. to Cuba Pastors for Peace, Mpls.; vol. coord. Austin Peace and Justice Coalition, 1983—84; co-founder gun free zone movement U. Nebr., 1994—96. Recipient People Who Inspire award, Black Masque chpt. Mortarboard Nat. Honor Soc., 1998, U. Grad. fellowship, U. of Tex. at Austin, 1982—85. Mem.: So. Sociol. Soc., Soc. for Study of Symbolic Interaction, Soc. for Study of Social Problems, Midwest Sociol. Soc. (pres.-elect 2004—05, pres. 2005—06), Am. Sociol. Assn. (chair peace, war, and social conflict sect. 1998—99), Phi Kappa Phi, Alpha Chi, Alpha Kappa Delta (pres.Gamma chpt. 1984—85). Achievements include research in social movements, peace movements, Chinese democracy movement, environmentalism, nuclear politics, political discourse. Home: 45 Hillcrest Dr Carbondale IL 62901 Office: So Ill U 3426 Faner Hall Carbondale IL 62901-4524 Office Phone: 618-453-7610. Business E-Mail: rbenford@siu.edu.

BENGERT, W. RAYMOND, lawyer, chemical engineer; b. Kansas City, Oct. 15, 1928; s. Harry C. and Lola E. Bengert; m. Penny Ann Bengert, Dec. 27, 1970. BS in Chemistry, U. Mo., 1953, JD, 1956. Bar: Calif. 1975. Profl. baseball player, 1944—46, 1948—49; chmn. Draft Rockefeller for Pres., Denver, 1958—60; pres. Bengert Tire Chains, Denver and Kansas City, 1960—68; founder Baskets-of-Hope, San Carlos, Calif., 1968—74; pres. IGF Container Corp., San Carlos, 1972—83; atty. San Francisco, 1975—. Cons. Bengert Enterprises, La Quinta, Calif., 1998—. Patentee chem. process. Served with USMC, 1946—48. Mem.: Calif. State Bar, Indian Ridge Country Club. Avocations: poetry, tennis. Office: PO Box 1475 Carmel CA 93921 Office Phone: 760-771-5323. Fax: 760-771-2225.

BENGLIAN, BARBARA MASON, music educator; m. David Benglian. BA, West Chester Univ. Music tchr. Upper Darby H.S., Drexel Hill, Pa.; also, dist. music supr. Named a Disting. Alumna, West Chester Univ.; named Pa. Tchr. of Yr., 2006. Office: Upper Darby H S 601 N Lansdowne Ave Drexel Hill PA 19026 Business E-Mail: benglian@udsd.k12.pa.us.

BENGTSON, ROGER DEAN, physicist, department chairman; b. Wausa, Nebr., Apr. 29, 1941; s. Fridolph M. and Edith E. (Pearson) B.; m. Billie A. Spies, June 15, 1963; children— Nissa C., Hans E. BS, U. Nebr., 1962; MS, Va. Poly. Inst. and State U., 1964; PhD, U. Md., 1968. Aerospace engr. NASA-Langley Research Ctr., Hampton, Va., 1962-67; research assoc. U. Tex., Austin, 1968-70, asst. prof. physics, 1970-75, assoc. prof., 1975-81, prof., 1981—, chmn. dept., 1984-88. Mem. Am. Phys. Soc., AAAS, Sigma Xi Home: 411 Honeycomb Rdg Austin TX 78746-5324 Office: U Tex Dept Physics C-1600 Austin TX 78712 Business E-Mail: bengtson@physics.utexas.edu.

BENGTSSON, ERLING BLÖNDAL, musician, educator; b. Copenhagen, Mar. 8, 1932; arrived in U.S., 1990; s. Valdemar and Sigridur (Nielsen) Bengtsson; m. Merete Bloch-Jørgensen, Oct. 19, 1958; children: Henrik Bløndal, Stefan Bløndal. Diploma, Curtis Inst. Music, Phila., 1950. Asst. tchr. cello Curtis Inst. Music, Phila., 1949—50, tchr. cello, 1950—53; prof. music Royal Danish Conservatory Music, Copenhagen, 1953—90; tchr. cello Swedish Radio's Inst. Advanced String Studies, Stockholm, 1958—78; prof. music Staatliche Hochschule für Musik, Cologne, Germany, 1978—82, U. Mich. Sch. Music, Ann Arbor, 1990—2006; ret., 2006. Tchr. cello master classes, Europe and US, 1953—. Performer: (DVD) The Cello and I, 2006, numerous LPs and CDs, 1949—, worldwide concerts, 1950—. Named knight 1st class, Order of Dannebrog, Queen of Denmark, 1972, grand knight, Order of Falcon, Pres. Iceland, 1970, chevalier du violoncello, Ind. U. Eva Janzer Meml. Cello Ctr., 1993, Premier Master Cellist, Detroit Cello Soc., 2005; recipient award of distinction, Manchester (Eng.) Internat. Cello Festival, 2001. Avocation: collecting modern Scandinavian art. Home: 1217 Westmoorland Ypsilanti MI 48197 Personal E-mail: cellist@erlingbb.com.

BENHABIB, JESS, adult education educator; b. Istanbul, Turkey, June 9, 1948; s. Jack and Nelli Benhabib; m. Madeline Jennifer Blum, May 12, 1950; children: Nicole, Michael Eric. PhD, Columbia U., 1976. Paulette Godard prof. polit. economy NYU, 1991—, dean of social scis., 1997—2000, dean of arts and sci., 1998—2000, sr. vice provost, 2006—. Editor: Jour. of Econ. Theory, 1992, (book) Cycles and Chaos in Economic Equilibrium, 1992. 2d lt. Ordinance-Turkish Army, 1974, Balikesir, Turkey. Fellow: Econometric Soc. Home: #16 37 Washington Sq West New York NY 10011 Office: NYU Dept Econs 19 W 4th St New York NY 10003 Office Phone: 212-998-8971. Business E-Mail: jess.benhabib@nyu.edu.

BEN-HAIM, ZIGI, artist; b. Baghdad, Iraq, Nov. 28, 1945; came to U.S., 1970; s. Jacob and Violet (Halawe) B.-H.; m. Tsipi Inberg, July 28, 1980; 1 child, Yori Lee. Diploma, Avni Inst. Fine Arts, Tel Aviv, 1970, Calif. Coll. Arts and Crafts, 1971; MFA, San Francisco State U., 1974. Guest artist fellow Artists Union, Russia, 1992. Prin. works include sculptures and paintings Bklyn. Mus., Buscaglia-Castellani U. Mus., Ghent (Belgium) Mus., Israel Mus., Jerusalem, Malmo Mus., NYC, Jewish Mus., NYC, Tel Aviv Mus., U. Md., College Park, Westminster Bank, NYC, Chelouche Gallery, Tel Aviv, Herbert Johnson Mus., Cornell U., Ithaca, NY, Jewish Mus., NYC, Baumgartner Gallery, Washington, Art Gallery Hamilton, Ont., Can., Munro Gallerie, Hamburg, Germany, Cleve. Mus. Art, Jersey City Mus., Stux Gallery NYC, Las Vegas Art Mus, Grounds for Sculpture. N.J., Stux Gallery, N.Y.C. Recipient Achievement award Israel Ministry Culture, 1971; grantee N.Y. State Coun. on Arts, 1983, NEA, 1984, Pollock Krasner Found., 1990, 96; DAAD fellow, Berlin. Home: 94 Mercer St New York NY 10012-4425 Office Phone: 646-220-4685. Personal E-mail: zigi@zigiland.com.

BENHAM, GRANT, psychologist, researcher; m. Chelse F. Benham. PhD, U. Tenn., Knoxville, 2005. Asst. prof. The U. Tex., Edinburg, Tex., 2002—. Fellow: Soc. Clin. and Exptl. Hypnosis (treas. 2005—). Office: The Univ Texas Pan Am 1201 W University Dr SBS 354 Edinburg TX 78541 Office Phone: 956-292-7342. Business E-Mail: gbenham@utpa.edu.

BENHAM, HELEN, music educator; b. NYC, Dec. 4, 1941; d. Charles Mead and Dorothea Wheaton Benham; m. Samuel S. Kim, June 12, 1965; 1 child, Sonya Wheaton Guardo. MusB, Oberlin Conservatory Music, Ohio, 1962; BA, Oberlin Coll., Ohio, 1963; MS, The Juilliard Sch., NYC, 1965; PhD, Rutgers U., 2001. Music faculty Diller-Quaile Sch. Music, NYC, 1964—75, Mannes Coll. Music, NYC, 1966—82, Monmouth Conservatory Music, Red Bank, NJ, 1967—; prof. music Brookdale C.C., Lincroft, NJ, 1973—. Concert artist, piano and harpsichord. Author: Piano for the Adult Beginner Books I and II, 1977. Trustee, sec. A. Louis Scarmolin Trust. Named Outstanding Young Women of Am., 1978. Mem. Music Tchrs. Nat. Assn., Nat. Guild Piano Tchrs., Am. Musicological Soc., Shore Music Educators Assn. Avocations: swimming, walking. Home: 960 Elberon Ave Long Branch NJ 07740-4709 Office: Brookdale CC Music Dept 765 Newman Springs Rd Lincroft NJ 07738-1597 Office Phone: 732-224-2065.

BENHAM, JAMES H., state official; b. Twin Falls, Idaho, July 14, 1944; s. James Henry and Matilda (Riggs) B.; m. Ann Elizabeth McIntosh, Mar. 27, 1965; 2 children. BA in Polit. Sci., Idaho State U., 1990, MPA, 1992. From police officer to chief of police Pocatello (Idaho) Police Dept., 1988-94; U.S. marshal dept. justice U.S. Dist. Idaho, Boise, 1994—. Contbr. articles to profl. jours. Bd. dirs. Nat. Criminal Justice Assn., 1992-93. Mem. Idaho Peace Officers Assn. (pres. 1986), Idaho Chief of Police Assn. (pres. 1990-91), Pocatello Police Relief Assn., Lions, Phi Kappa Phi. Methodist. Avocations: golf, fishing, hunting, gardening, exercise. Office: US Marshal for Dist Idaho 550 W Fort St # 010 Boise ID 83724-0101

BENHAM, ROBERT, state supreme court justice; m. Nell (Dodson) B.; children: Corey Brevard, Austin Tyler. BS in Polit. sci. (hon.), Tuskegee U., 1967; JD, U. Ga. Lumpkin Sch. of Law, 1970; LLM, U. Va., 1989. Former trial atty. Atlanta Legal Aid Society, Inc.; judge Ga. Ct. Appeals, Ga., 1984-89; justice Supreme Ct., State of Ga., Atlanta, 1989—, presiding justice, former chief justice, 1995. Mem. adv. bd. 1st So. Bank. Chmn. Gov.'s Commn. on Drug Awareness and Prevention, State of Ga.; mem. Ga. Hist. Soc.; trustee Ga. Legal Hist. Found.; bd. dirs. Cartersville (Ga.) Devel. Authority, Cartersville-Bartow C. of C.; deacon, former Sunday Sch. supt. The Greater Mt. Olive Bapt. Ch. Captain USAR. Recipient Ben F. Johnson, Jr. Pub. Svc. award, Ga. State Univ. Sch. Law, 2004. Mem Atlanta Bar Assn. (bd. dirs. jud. sect.), Ga. Bar Found., Lawyers Club Atlanta, Masons, Shriners, Elks. Office: Ga Supreme Ct 244 Washington St SW Rm 572 Atlanta GA 30334-9007 Fax: (404) 657-4329.

BENI, GERARDO, electrical engineer, educator; b. Florence, Italy, Feb. 21, 1946; came to U.S., 1970; s. Edoardo and Tina (Bazzanti) B.; m. Susan Hackwood, May 24, 1986; children: Catherine Elizabeth, Juliet Beatrice. Laurea in Physics, U. Firenze, Florence, Italy, 1970; PhD in Physics, UCLA, 1974. Research scientist AT&T Bell Labs., Murray Hill, NJ, 1974-77, Holmdel, NJ, 1977-82, disting. mem. tech. staff, 1982-84; prof. elec. and computer engring. U. Calif., Santa Barbara, 1984—91, dir. Ctr. for Robotic Systems in Microelectronics, 1985—91, prof. elec. engring. Riverside, 1991—, dir. multimedia lab. and studio, 1991—94, chmn. elec. engring. dept., 1997—98. Dir. Multimedia Lab & Studio, 1991—94. Founder, editor: Jours. Robotic Systems, 1983-2005 (Jour. of Yr. award 1984); editor: Recent Advances in Robotics, 1985, Vacuum Mechatronics, 1990; contbr. more than 170 articles to tech. jours. Fellow AAAS, Am. Physics Soc. Achievements include patents in field. Office: U Calif-Riverside Coll Engring Riverside CA 92521-0001 Business E-Mail: beni@ee.ucr.edu. *Produce in freedom; give in freedom; and in freedom enjoy.*

BENIGNO, THOMAS DANIEL, lawyer; b. Queens, NY, July 29, 1954; s. John Baptiste and Ernesta Mary (Yannaco) B.; m. Maria Angelica Vasquez, Jan. 26, 1980; children: Diana Maria, Laura Michelle, John Frederick. BA with honors, Hofstra U., 1976; JD, Benjamin Cardozo Law Sch., 1979. Bar: NY 1981, US Dist. Ct. (so. and ea. dists.) NY 1985, US Supreme Ct. 2004. Atty. Legal Aid Soc., Bronx, N.Y., 1979-84; ptnr. Benigno, Cassisi & Casissi, Floral Park, N.Y., 1984-87; mng. ptnr., gen. counsel Benigno/Gurrieri Real Estate Mgmt. and Devel., Bklyn., 1984-95. Pres. Gurben Properties, Inc., Floral Park, 1987-88, Movies for Kids Inc., Valley Stream, N.Y., 1989-90; gen. counsel Our Gang Assocs. Inc. (dba Thin White Line), Cedarhurst, N.Y., 1988-90. Mem.: NY Bar Assn., Rotary Internat. (pres. Malverne chpt. 2001—04). Office: 269 Hempstead Ave Ste 2 Malverne NY 11565-1224

BENING, ANNETTE, actress; b. Topeka, May 29, 1958; m. J. Steven White, 1984 (div. 1991); m. Warren Beatty, March 12, 1992; children: Kathlyn Bening Beatty, Benjamin Beatty, Isabel Ashley Ira Beatty, Ella Corinne Beatty. Student, Mesa Coll.; theatre degree, San Francisco State U.; studied at, Am. Conservatory Theatre. Films include The Great Outdoors, 1988, Valmont, 1989, The Grifters, 1990 (Acad. award nomination best supporting actress 1990), Postcards from the Edge, 1990, Guilty by Suspicion, 1991, Regarding Henry, 1991, Bugsy, 1991, Love Affair, 1994, Richard III, 1995, The American President, 1995, Mars Attacks!, 1996, The Siege, 1998, American Beauty, 1999 (Acad. award nom. best actress), In Dreams, 1999, What Planet Are You From, 2000, Open Range, 2003, Being Julia, 2004 (Named Best Actress Nat. Bd. Rev. Motion Pictures 2004, Golden Globe for Best Actress, 2005), Running with Scissors, 2006; stage appearances Coastal Disturbances, 1986, (Tony award nomination 1986, Clarence Derwin award 1987, Theatre World award 1987), Spoils of War, 1988, Hedda Gabler, 1999; TV movies: Manhunt for Claude Dallas, 1986, Hostage, 1988; TV series: Liberty's Kids (voice only); TV appearances: Sesame Street, 1969, Miami Vice, 1987, Wiseguy, 1987, The Sopranos, 2004. Recipient Star, Hollywood Walk of Fame, 2006. Avocation: scuba diving. Office: Creative Artists Agy c/o Kevin Huvane 9830 Wilshire Blvd Beverly Hills CA 90212-1804*

BENIOFF, MARC, Internet company executive; BS in Bus. Admin., U. of Southern Calif., 1986. With Apple Computer; founder Liberty Software; various leadership positions in sales, mktg. and prod. devel. Oracle Corp., 1996—99, sr. v.p. web/workgroup systems div., 1995—96, sr. v.p. mktg., 1996—99; founder, chmn., CEO Salesforce.com, Inc., 1999—, also bd. dir. Apptd. by Pres. George W. Bush as co-chairman President's Information Technology Advisory Com. (PITAC), 2003—; apptd. by Hawaiian Gov. Linda Lingle Citizens to Achieve Reform in Edn., 2003—; bd. dirs. Grand Central Communications, 2003—. Co-author: Compassionate Capitalism, 2004. Founder salesforce.com Found., 2000—. Named Northern Calif. Entrepreneur of Yr., Ernst & Young, 2003, Alumni Entrepreneur of Yr., U. SC Marshall Sch. Bus., 2004, Entrepreneur of Yr., SunBridge, World Class Innovator, DEMO, 2005, Internat. CEO of Yr., Selling Power; named one of Top 10 Entrepreneurs to Watch, Fortune, 25 people responsible for turning e-business around, BusinessWeek, 20 Most Influential People in the Industry, CRM Mag., Agenda Setters, Silicon.com, 50 Who Matter Now, CNNMoney.com Bus. 2.0, 2006; recipient Promise of Peace award, Prime Min. of Israel Benjamin Netanyahu, Bridge award, HEAVEN (Helping Educate, Activate, Volunteer, and Empower via the Net). Created an on-demand hosted Customer Relationship Management (CRM) solution that would replace traditional enterprise software technology which went public in June, 2004. Office: salesforce.com One Market St Ste 300 San Francisco CA 94105*

BENIRSCHKE, KURT, retired pathologist, educator; b. Glueckstadt, Germany, May 26, 1924; arrived in US, 1949, naturalized, 1955; s. Fritz Franz and Marie (Luebcke) B.; m. Marion Elizabeth Waldhausen, May 17, 1952; children: Stephen Kurt, Rolf Joachim, Ingrid Marie. Student, U. Hamburg, Germany, 1942, 45-48, U. Berlin, 1943, U. Wuerzburg, 1943-44; MD, U. Hamburg, 1948; DVM (hon.), U. Zürich, 2004. Resident, Teaneck, NJ, 1950-51, Peter Bent Brigham Hosp., Boston, 1951-52, Boston Lying-in-Hosp., 1952-53, Free Hosp. for Women, Boston, 1953, Children's Hosp., Boston, 1953; pathologist Boston Lying-in-Hosp., 1955-60; tchg. fellow, assoc. Med. Sch. Harvard, 1954-60; prof. pathology, chmn. dept. pathology Med. Sch. Dartmouth, Hanover, NH, 1960-70; prof. reproductive medicine and pathology U. Calif., San Diego, 1970-94, ret., 1994; chmn. dept. pathology U. Calif. at San Diego Sch. Med., La Jolla, 1976-79. Dir. rsch. San Diego Zoo, 1975-86, trustee, 1986-00, pres., 1998-00; cons. NIH, 1957-70. Served with German Army, 1942-45. Mem. Am. Soc. Pathology, Internat. Acad. Pathology, Am. Coll. Pathology, Am. Acad. Arts and Scis., Teratol. Soc., Am. Soc. Zool. Vets. Home: 8457 Prestwick Dr La Jolla CA 92037-2023 Office: Univ Calif San Diego Med Ctr 200 W Arbor Dr San Diego CA 92103-8321 Office Phone: 619-543-2618. Business E-Mail: kbenirsc@ucsd.edu.

BENISSAN, JORDAN MESSAN, music educator; b. Kinshasa, Zaire, Sept. 3, 1958; arrived in U.S., 1987; s. Jacques Barrigah and Nadou Addy Benissan; 1 child, Olivia Dodzi. Degree in bus., Inst. Scis. Commls., Lome, Togo, 1982; master drummer, Sch. African Drumming, Lome, 1983. Instr. U. Okla., Norman, 1986—87, Macalester Coll., St. Paul, 1997—98, St. Catherine Coll., St. Paul, 1997—98; world music tchr. Colby Coll., Waterville, Maine, 1998—. Author: Drumming Through the Spirit of My Ancestors, 1997, Beautiful Music of West Africa, 2003 (nominee Best World Music award Phoenix Mag.), (album) Let Play My Music, 2004. Home: 12 High St Waterville ME 04901 Office: Colby Coll Music Dept 4000 Mayflower Hill Waterville ME 04901 Office Phone: 207-872-9146.

BENITEZ-SILVA, HUGO A., economics professor; arrived in US, 1996; s. Hugo Benitez-Puga and Mabel Silva; m. Anna Vellve, May 29, 1996; 1 child, Albert. BA, Esade Bus. Sch., Barcelona, Spain, MBA, 1996; MA in Econs., Yale U., New Haven, 1998, PhD in Econs., 2000. Prof. SUNY, Stony Brook, 2000—. Contbr. articles to profl. jours. Rsch. grantee, NIH-NIA, 2004—, TIAA-CREF, 2004, Mich. Retirement Rsch. Ctr., 2005—06. Mem.: Econs. Soc., Am. Econs. Assn. Office: SUNY Dept Econs Stony Brook NY 11794-4384

BENJAMIN, ADELAIDE WISDOM, retired lawyer, community volunteer and activist; b. New Orleans, Aug. 23, 1932; d. William Bell and Mary (Freeman) Wisdom; m. Edward Bernard Benjamin Jr., May 11, 1957; children: Edward Wisdom, Mary Dabney, Ann Leith, Stuart Minor Student, Hollins Coll., 1950—52; BA in English, Newcomb Coll., 1954; JD, Tulane U., 1956; student, Loyola U., New Orleans, 1980—81; grad. ext. program Sewanee Theol. Sch., U. South, 1982. Assoc. Wisdom, Stone, Pigman and Benjamin, New Orleans, 1956—58; tchr. ext. courses Sewanee Theol. Sem., 1984—88; ret., 1959. Spkr., panelist on sch. issues various local and nat. groups. Mem. Tulane Law Rev., 1954—56, compiler, editor, pub. Trinity Ch. supplemental songbook, 1980. Trustee RosaMary Charitable Found., sec., 1987—92, pres., 1990—94, 2000—, treas., 1994—; trustee Mary Freeman Wisdom, sec., pres., 1990—94, 2000—, treas., 1994—; sec. bd. dir. YWCA, New Orleans, 1967—68, 1st v.p., 1968—69; bd. dir. Kingsley House, New Orleans, 1971—77; trustee Metairie Pk. Country Day Sch., 1971—79, sec., 1976—79; mem. adv. bd. Tulane Summer Lyric Theatre, Tulane U., 1972—, pres. adv. bd., 1977—79; bd. dir. Children's Hosp., New Orleans, 1976—79; mem. adv. bd. Pub. Radio Sta. WWNO, 1980—; bd. dir. Parenting Ctr., 1981—; pres. E&A Charitable Found., New Orleans, 1983—; pres. bd. New Orleans Symphony, 1984—89; mem. Loving Cup selection com. New Orleans Times Picayune, 1985; bd. dir. La. Mus. Found., New Orleans, 1989—, S.E. La. coun. Girl Scouts US, New Orleans, 1989—97, Loyola U., New Orleans, 1989—99, mem. exec. com., 1996—99, hon. bd. mem., 2003—; bd. dir. Louise S. McGehee Sch., New Orleans, 1990—, v.p., 1991—97, hon. bd. dir., 1991; pres. New Orleans Mus. Art Fellows Forum, 1991—; mem. exec. com. La. Mus. Found., New Orleans, 1991—; bd. dir. Newcomb Children's Ctr., New Orleans, 1991—94; mem. adv. bd. dept. psychiatry La. State U. Med. Ctr., 1992—; mem. exec. bd. La. Philharm. Orch., 1992—; mem. Newcomb Dean's Coun., 1997—, pres., 2002—; bd. dir. Nat. D-Day Mus., New Orleans, 1998—2002; sec. parish coun. Trinity Episc. Ch., New Orleans, 1973—75, sec. vestry, 1975—79, active, leader Trinity Quartet, 1979—84; bd. dir. New Orleans Opera Assn., 2007—. Recipient Weiss Brotherhood award Nat. Conf. Christians and Jews, 1986, Outstanding Philanthropist, Nat. Soc. Fundraising Exec., 1986, Vol. Activist Award, St. Elizabeth Guild, 1986, Jr. League Sustainer award, 1987, Disting. Alumna award McGehee Sch., 1987, George Washington Honor Medal for Individual Achievement, Freedom Found. at Valley Forge, 1988, Living and Giving award Juvenile Diabetes Found. 1991, Outstanding Citizen New Orleans award La. Colonials, 1994, Jacques Yenni award Outstanding Cmty. Svc. Sch. Bus. Adminstrn. Loyola Univ., 1994, Integritas Vitae award for outstanding cmty. svc. Loyola U., 1994, Classical Arts Patron award Tribute to the Classical Arts, 1998, Big Bros./Big Sisters award for cmty. svc., New Orleans, 2004; named Goodwill Amb. for La. Gov.'s Commn. Internat. Trade, Industry and Tourism, 1987, Sweet Art, Contemporary Arts Ctr., 1988, Significant Role Model, Young Leadership Coun., 1988, Woman of Distinction S.E. La. Girl Scout Coun., 1992; named among Outstanding Alumni Class of 1954, Tulane U., 2004 Mem. ABA, LWV, La. Bar Assn., New Orleans Bar Assn., Jr. League New Orleans (exec. com. 1971-72, bd. dir. 1967-72), Ind. Women's Orgn., Com. 21, Am. Symphony Orch. League, Quarante Club (2d v.p. 1978-79), Debutante Club, Le Debut des Jeunes Filles Club, New Orleans Town Gardeners (pres. 1979-80), Thomas Wolfe Soc. (life) Home: 1837 Palmer Ave New Orleans LA 70118-6215

BENJAMIN, ANDRE LAUREN (DRE, ANDRÉ 3000), vocalist, actor; b. Atlanta, Ga., May 24, 1975; 1 child, Seven Sirius. Performer OutKast, 1992—. Singer: (albums) Southernplayalisticadillacmuzik, 1994, ATLiens, 1996, Aquemini, 1998, Stankonia, 2000 (Grammy awards: Best Rap Album, 2001, Best Rap Performance By A Duo Or Group for song "Ms Jackson", 2001), Big Boi and Dre Present.Outkast, 2001 (Grammy award: (with Killer Mike) Best Rap Performance By A Duo Or Group for song "The Whole World", 2002), Speakerboxxx/The Love Below, 2003 (Grammy awards: Album Of The Yr., 2003, Best Urban/Alternative Performance for song "Hey Ya!", 2003, Best Rap Album, 2003, MTV Video Music award Best Hip-Hop Video for song "Hey Ya!", 2004, MTV Video Music award Best Special Effects In a Video for the song "Hey Ya!", 2004, MTV Video Music award for Best Art Direction In a Video for the song "Hey Ya!", 2004, MTV Video Music award Video of Year for the song "Hey Yeah!", 2004, Am. Music Awards Favorite Album Rap/Hip-Hop, 2004), Idlewild, 2006; actor: (films) Be Cool, 2005, Four Brothers, 2005, Revolver, 2005, Idlewild, 2006, (voice only) Charlotte's Web, 2006, (TV appearances) Martin, 1995, Mad TV, 2000, Saturday Night Live, 2003, The Shield, 2004. Recipient Best New Rap Group of Yr., Source awards, 1995, Favorite Band, Duo or Group-Pop or Rock, Am. Music Awards, 2004, Favorite Band, Duo or Group-Rap/Hip-Hop, 2004, Duo/Group Artist of Yr., Billboard Music Awards, 2004, Billboard 200 Duo/Group Album Artist of Yr., 2004, Hot 100 Duo/Group of Yr., 2004, R&B/Hip-Hop Duo/Group of Yr., 2004, Digital Track of Yr., 2004. Address: Arista Records inc 8750 Wilshire Blvd Beverly Hills CA 90211-2713

BENJAMIN, ARLIN JAMES, physicist; b. Guthrie, Okla., Oct. 9, 1933; s. Harold Dinsmore and Lula Martha (Black) Benjamin; m. Patricia Ann Crabb, Oct. 10, 1964; children: Arlin James, Cynthia Denise, Deborah Dawn. BS, Sam Houston State Coll., 1955; MS, Okla. State U., 1957; postgrad., MIT, 1959, Wichita U., 1959-60. Rsch. engr. Boeing Co., Wichita, Kans., 1956-63; lead nuc. engr. LTV Corp., Dallas, 1963-64; ops. rsch. analyst Research Triangle Inst., Research Triangle Park, NC, 1964-66; sr. ops. rsch. analyst Gen. Dynamics Corp., Ft. Worth, 1966-68; mgr. Control Data Corp., Honolulu, 1968-70; sr. scientist S.W. Rsch. Inst., San Antonio, 1970-78; prin. scientist Hittman Assocs. Inc., Sacramento, 1978-81; mgr., sr. staff mem. BDM Corp., Hawthorne, Calif., 1981-86; prin. engr. Northrop Grumman Corp., Pico Rivera, Calif., 1986-95, Midwest City, Okla., 1995—2006; ret., 2006. Contbr. articles to profl. jours. Mem.: Inst. Mgmt. Sci., European Phys. Soc., Inst. of Physics and the Phys. Soc. (London), Am. Phys. Soc., Am. Nuc. Soc., Am. Geophys. Union, Pi Gamma Mu, Alpha Chi.

BENJAMIN, BERNARD EDWARD, school system administrator, director; b. Woonsocket, RI, Dec. 17, 1957; s. Bernard Mathias and Doris B. Benjamin; m. Mary Jane Desjardin, June 3, 1978; children: Christopher Michael, Joshua Edward. BA, Westfield State Coll., Mass., 1979; MA, Fitchburg State Coll., Mass., 2006. Pvt. music instr. Home Studio, Blackstone, Mass., 1979—; EMT Blackstone (Mass.) Fire Dept., 1980—98, rescue lt., 1980—98; specialist music Blackstone-Millville (Mass.) Sch. Dist., 1995—98; dir. fine and performing arts Benjamin Franklin Classical Charter Pub. Sch., Franklin, Mass., 1998—. Clinician smartmusic MakeMusic Inc., Mpls., 2004—. Counselor merit badge Boy Scouts Am., Providence, 1979—. Recipient Merit award, Town Blackstone, 1998, Outstanding Music Achievment award, Zildjian Co., 2005; grantee, Mr. Holland's Opus found., 2003. Mem.: Administrator's in Music Edn., Assn. Suprs.and Curriculum Devel., Tech. Inst. Music Educators, Internat. Assn. Jazz Educators, Nat. Assn. Suprs. Music, Music Educators Nat. Conf., Mass. Music Educators Assn. (life). Roman Catholic. Avocations: camping, fishing, computers. Home: 156 Blackstone Street Blackstone MA 01504 Office: Ben Franklin Classical Charter School 201 Main Street Franklin MA 02038 Home Phone: 508-883-7023 106; Office Phone: 508-541-3434 106. Office Fax: 508-541-5396; Home Fax: 508-541-5396. Business E-Mail: bbenjamin@bfccps.org.

BENJAMIN, BEZALEEL SOLOMON, structural engineer, educator; b. Anand, India, Feb. 21, 1938; came to U.S., 1971; s. Solomon and Penninah (Ellis) B.; m. Nora Jacob David, Feb. 25, 1962; children— Ashley Bezaleel, Jennifer Elana B.E. in Civil Engring., Bombay U., India, 1957; D.I.C., Imperial Coll., London, 1958; MS in Engring., London U., 1959, PhD, 1965. Design engr. M.N. Dastur & Co., Bombay, 1961-63; postdoctoral fellow U. Surrey, Eng., 1965-66; prin. lectr. Hatfield Poly., Eng., 1966-71; asst. prof. archtl. engring. U. Kans., Lawrence, 1971-72, assoc. prof., 1972-76, prof., 1976—. Vis. Fulbright prof. Technion, Haifa, Israel, 1987-88. Author: The Analysis of Braced Domes, 1963, Structural Design with Plastics, 1969, Structures for Architects, 1975, Building Construction for Architects and Engineers, 1978, Structural Evolution: An Illustrated History, 1990, Statics, Strengths and Structures for Architects, 1992; (children's book) Susan Altencroft, 1976; (novels) Rampaging Lovers, 1988, A Nazi Among Jews, 1990, Bene Israel Tales, 1991, The Jewish Amendment, 1992, David Rahabi, 1993. Jewish. Avocation: writing. Office: U Kans Sch Architecture Lawrence KS 66045-0001 Home Phone: 785-843-4080; Office Phone: 785-864-4383. Business E-Mail: sben@ku.edu.

BENJAMIN, BRENT D., state supreme court justice, lawyer; b. Marietta, Ohio, July 3, 1957; m. Janice Benjamin; 5 children. BA in Political sci., Ohio State U., 1981, JD, 1984. Bar: W.Va. 1984, U.S. Fourth Circuit Ct. of Appeals, U.S. Dist. Ct. Southern W.Va., W.Va. Supreme Ct., Ky. Supreme Ct. 2001. Atty. Robinson and McElwee, Charleston, W.Va., 1983—90, ptnr., 1990—2004; justice W.Va. Supreme Ct. of Appeals, 2004—. Mem. Hocking Coll. Archaeological Mission; former treasurer W.Va. Republican Party. Mem.: ABA, Kanawha County Bar Assn., W.Va. State Bar Assn. Office: WVa Supreme Ct Appeals Capitol Complex Bldg 1 Charleston WV 25305*

BENJAMIN, EDWARD BERNARD, JR., lawyer; b. New Orleans, Feb. 11, 1923; s. Edward Bernard and Blanche (Sternberger) B.; m. Adelaide Wisdom, May 11, 1957; children: Edward Wisdom, Mary Dabney, Ann Leith, Stuart Minor. BS, Yale U., 1944; JD, Tulane U., 1952. Bar: La. 1952. Practiced in, New Orleans, since 1952; ptnr. Jones, Walker, Waechter, Poitevent, Carrere & Denegre, New Orleans, 1967—. Pres. Am. Coll. Probate Counsel, 1986-87, Internat. Acad. Estate and Trust Law, 1976-78; vice chmn. bd. trustees Southwestern Legal Found., 1980-88, bd. dirs., 1988-90; chmn. bd. Starmount Co., Greensboro, N.C., 1968-88, chmn. emeritus, 1988—. Editor-in-chief Tulane U. Law Rev., 1951-52; mem. editl. bd. Cmty. Property Jour., 1974-89. Trustee Hollins Coll., 1966-87; chancellor Episcopal Diocese of La., 1984-2003, Trinity Episcopal Ch., New Orleans, 1974-92; mem. adv. bd. CCH Estate & Fin. Planning Svc., 1982-88; chmn. Salvation Army City Commd. Adv. Bd., 1965-68; pres. New Orleans Jr. C. of C., 1953. 1st lt., F.A. pilot, U.S. Army, 1943-46. Mem. Am. Coll. Tax Counsel, Am. Law Inst., ABA (sec. taxation sect. 1967-68, coun. 1976-79, coun. real property, probate and trust law sect. 1978-81), La. Bar Assn. (chmn. taxation sect. 1959-60), La. Law Inst., La. Bar Found. (trustee 1998-99), New Orleans Country Club, Southern Yacht Club, New Orleans Lawn Tennis Clu Home: 1837 Palmer Ave New Orleans LA 70118-6215 Office: Jones Walker Waechter Poitevent Carrere & Denegre 201 Saint Charles Ave Fl 51 New Orleans LA 70170-5100 Office Phone: 504-582-8114. Business E-Mail: ebenjamin@joneswalker.com.

BENJAMIN, ERNST, educational association administrator; b. Washington, Mar. 30, 1937; s. Herbert and Lillian (Gerber) B.; m. Judith McCombs, June 12, 1960; children: Cassandra, Daniel. AB, Ohio Wesleyan U., 1958; MA in Polit. Sci., U. Chgo., 1960; student in African Studies, UCLA, 1962—63; PhD in Polit. Sci., U. Chgo., 1972. Grad. rsch. polit. scientist U. Calif., Berkeley, 1961—62; asst. prof. to assoc. prof. Wayne State U., Detroit, 1965—86; gen. sec. AAUP, Washington, 1984—94, dir. rsch., 1995—2001, sr. cons., 2001, exec. dir., 2006—07, interim gen. sec., 2007—. Dir. Weekend Coll. Prog., Wayne State U., 1981-82, interim dean Lifelong Learning Prog., 1982-84; cons. labor rels., higher edn. Contbr. articles to profl. jours. Vice-chmn. Mich. Dem. Edn. Caucus, 1977-81; adv. panel on post secondary edn. Mich. State Bd. Edn., 1978-79; bd. dirs. Mich. chpt. ACLU, 1973-75. Fellow Woodrow Wilson Found., 1958-59, Com. Comparative Study of New Nations U. Chgo., 1960-61, 64-65, Fgn. Area Tng. Ford Found., LA and Ghana, 1962-64. Mem. AAUP (chmn. Collective Bargaining Congress 1976-80, Marilyn Sternberg award 1981), Am. Polit. Sci. Assn., Indsl. Rels. Rsch. Assn., Phi Beta Kappa. Jewish. Office: AAUP 1012 Fourteenth St NW Ste 500 Washington DC 20005-3465 Office Phone: 202-737-5900. Business E-Mail: ebenjamin@aaup.org.

BENJAMIN, GEORGES CURTIS, emergency physician, consultant; b. Chgo., Sept. 28, 1952; s. George and Tessie Cozie (Edwards) B.; m. Yvette Josphanie Janisse; children: Stephanie, Kali. BS, Ill. Inst. Tech., 1973; MD, U. Ill., 1978. Diplomate Am. Bd. Internal Medicine, Am. Bd. Med. Examiners. Intern and resident internal medicine Brooke Army Med. Ctr., San Antonio, 1978-81; dept. emergency medicine Madigan Army Med. Ctr., Tacoma, 1981-83; chief emergency medicine Walter Reed Army Med. Ctr., Washington, 1983-87; chair. dept. com. health & ambulatory care Dist. Columbia Gen. Hosp., Washington, 1987-90; commr. pub. health Dist. Columbia, Washington, 1990-91; health policy cons., 1992-95; emergency physician Holy Cross Cmty. Hosp., Silver Spring, Md., 1991-95; dep. sec. Pub. Health State of Md., Balt., 1995-99; sec. Dept. Health and Mental Hygiene, Balt., 1999—2002; exec. dir. APHA, 2002—. Emergency physician Patuxent Naval Air Station, Patuxent River, Md., 1989, Nisqually Clinic, Yelm, Wash., 1981-82, Allenmore Com. Hosp., Tacoma, 1981-82; house internist Greater Southeast Com. Hosp., Washington, 1985-87; clin. instr. emergency medicine, Georgetown U., 1988-95; adj. prof. Health Care Scis., 1993, asst. prof. medicine Uniformed Svcs. U. Health Scis., Bethesda, Md., 1984-87. Mem. editl. bd. Jour. Nat. Med. Assn., 1986-93; reviewer Am. Coll. Physician Execs., 1989-2006, Am. Jour. Emergency Medicine, 1986-94, Mil. Medicine, 1983-87; contbr. articles to profl. jours. Bd. dirs. Hosp. Sick Children, Boarder Baby Project, Inc. Whiteman Walker Clinic Inc.; adv. bd. D.C. Comm. Pub. Health Disability and Injury Prevention Program, 1993, Montgomery County HIV/AIDS Citizens, 1992-93; bd. trustees Am. Cancer Soc.; bd. govs. Medico Chirurg. Soc. D.C.; mem. D.C. Emergency Med. Svcs. Com., 1990-91, D.C. State Health Coord. Coun., 1990-91; gov. commn. Welfare Policy State of Md., 1993, mem. adv. com. on pub. health preparedness, US Dept. HHS, adv. com. to Dir. CDC. With M.C. U.S. Army, 1978-87, USAR, 1974-78. Recipient Cert. Recognition, 1993, Coun. Govs. Svc. award, 1991, Disting. Pub. Svc. award, 1991, Cert. Appreciation Best Friends of D.C., 1991, Cert. Appreciation D.C. Pub. Schs., 1991, Svc. award Medico Chirurg. Soc., 1990, Recognition award D.C.G.H. Med./Dental staff, 1990; decorated Army Commendation medal, 1983, Comdrs. award, 1981, Eisenhower Proclamation medal, 1970. Fellow ACP, Am. Coll. Emergency Physicians (Nat. Key Contact 1987-90, 92-95, gov. affairs com. 1993, DC chpt. v.p. 1988-90, DC chpt. pres. 1989-90, liaison rep. emergency nurses assn. 1992-95, nat. health policy com. 1992-93); mem. Inst. Medicine, APHA, AMA, Nat. Med. Assn. (mil. and aerospace medicine sect. sec. 1983, nat. co-chmn. 1985, 86, nat. chmn. 1987, emergency medicine nat. chmn. 1990-93), Medico Chirurg. Soc. (violence task force chmn. 1992-94), Am. Coll. Physicians Execs., Assoc. State Territorial Health Ofcls. (sec.-treas. 1999-2000, pres. 2001-02). Office: APHA 800 I St NW Washington DC 20001-3710 Business E-Mail: georges.benjamin@apha.org.

BENJAMIN, HARVEY E., lawyer, sports association executive; b. NYC, Feb. 16, 1941; s. Morris and Ethel (Mouber) Benjamin; m. Stephanie Talmud, Dec. 25, 1963; children: Julie, Caren. BS, Queens Coll., 1961; LLB cum laude, Columbia U., NYC, 1964. Bar: NY 1964, Fla. 1978. Assoc. Proskauer, Rose, Goetz & Mendelsohn, NYC, 1965-73, ptnr., 1973-92; v.p. internat. bus. affairs NBA, NYC, 1992, exec. counsel bus. and fin. Co-chmn. panel on leveraged acquisitions Practicing Law Inst. Contbr. articles to profl. jours. and legal newspapers; case notes editor Columbia Law Rev. Mem. Jewish Communal Network Commn., UJA/Fedn. of NY. Democrat. Office: NBA 645 5th Ave Fl 10 New York NY 10022-5986

BENJAMIN, JAMES SCOTT, lawyer; b. Miami Beach, Fla., Aug. 28, 1954; s. Julian R. Benjamin and June Lois Garvin; m. Laura Cipolla, Mar. 5, 1989; children: Kaitlyn, Courtney. BS in Advt., U. Fla., 1976; JD, Samford U., 1979. Bar: Fla. 1980, U.S. Dist. Ct. (so. dist.) Fla. 1981, U.S. Dist. Ct. (mid. dist.) Fla. 1989, U.S. Ct. Appeals (11th cir.) 1989, U.S. Dist. Ct. (we. dist.) Tex. 1993, U.S. Supreme Ct. 1994. Asst. state atty. 17th Jud. Cir. Broward County, Ft. Lauderdale, Fla., 1981-84; shareholder Benjamin & Aaronson P.A., Ft. Lauderdale, 1984—. Presenter, lectr. in field. Author, columnist Xcitement Mag., 1990—, Screw Mag., 1998. Bd. dirs. Arthritis Found., Ft. Lauderdale, 1998, treas., 1999. Mem. Fla. Assn. Criminal Def. Attys. (bd. dirs. 1998—), Broward County Assn. Criminal Def. Lawyers (v.p. 1997-98, pres. 1998-99, bd. dirs. 1995—), First Amendment Lawyers Assn. (nat. sec. 2000—, nat. treas. 2001, v.p. 2002-04, pres. 2004—), Free Speech Coalition, Inns of Ct. Avocation: fly fishing. Office: Benjamin & Aaronson PA Ste 1615 One Financial Plaza Fort Lauderdale FL 33394 Office Phone: 954-779-1700.

BENJAMIN, JEFF, lawyer, pharmaceutical executive; b. Bklyn., Dec. 28, 1945; s. Haskell and Lillian (Sikofski) B.; m. Betty Gae Meckler, Mar. 21, 1971; children: Lily Meckler, Ross Meckler. BA, Cornell U., 1967; JD cum laude, NYU, 1971. Bar: N.Y. 1971, U.S. Dist. Cts. (so. and ea. dists.) N.Y. 1972. Assoc. Kronish, Lieb, Shainswit, Weiner & Hellman, NYC, 1971-74; atty. Ciba-Geigy Corp., Ardsley and Tarrytown, NY, 1974—, counsel for regulatory affairs, 1976—, divsn. counsel, 1978—, asst. gen. counsel, 1985—, dir. legal dept., assoc. gen. counsel, 1986-89, v.p., gen. counsel, 1996-97; assoc. gen. counsel Novartis Corp., NYC, 1997—2001, ethics and law compliance officer, 1997—, v.p. dep. gen. counsel, 2004, v.p. gen. counsel, 2005—, v.p. gen. counsel, litigation, ethics and compliance officer, 2006—. Mem. adv. bd. Brennan Ctr. for Justice, 2002—; mem. bd. dirs. Ethics Officer Assn., 2005—; lectr. in field. Contbr. articles to law jours. Mem. Citizens Adv. Com., Ramapo, N.Y. With USAR, 1969—74. Mem. ABA, Antitrust Section, Litigation Section, Cornell U. Alumni Assn. (admissions amb.), Order of Coif. Home: 13 Park Ave New City NY 10956-1107 Office: Novartis Corp 608 Fifth Ave 10th Fl New York NY 10020-2305

BENJAMIN, KARL STANLEY, artist, educator; b. Chgo., Dec. 29, 1925; s. Eustace Lincoln and Marie (Klamsteiner) B.; m. Beverly Jean Paschke, Jan. 29, 1949; children: Beth Marie, Kris Ellen, Bruce Lincoln. Student, Northwestern U., 1943-46; BA, U. Redlands, 1949; MA, Claremont Grad. Sch., 1960. With dept. arts Pomona Coll., Claremont, Calif., 1979-97, Loren Barton Babcock Miller prof., artist-in residence, 1978-94, prof. emeritus, 1997—; prof. art Claremont Grad. Sch. Traveling exhbns. include New Talent, Am. Fedn. Arts, 1959, 4 Abstract Classicists, Los Angeles and San Francisco museums, 1959-61, West Coast Hard Edge, Inst. Contemporary Arts, London, Eng., 1960, Purist Painting, Am. Fedn. Arts, 1960-61, Geometric Abstractions in Am., Whitney Mus., 1962, Paintings of the Pacific, U.S., Japan and Australia, 1961-63, Artists Environment, West Coast, Amon Carter Mus., Houston, 1962-63, Denver annual, 1965, Survey of Contemporary Art, Speed Mus., Louisville, 1965, The Colorists, San Francisco Mus., 1965, Art Across Am, Mead Corp., 1965-67, The Responsive Eye, Mus. Modern Art, 1965-66, 30th Biennial Exhbn. Am. Painting, Corcoran Gallery, 1967, 35th Biennial Exhbn. Am. Painting, 1977, Painting and Sculpture in California: The Modern Era, San Francisco Mus. Modern Art, 1976-77, Smithsonian Nat. Collection Fine Arts, Washington, 1976-77, Los Angeles Hard Edge: The Fifties and Seventies, Los Angeles County Mus. Art, 1977, Corcoran Gallery, Washington, Cheney Cowles Mus., Spokane, 1980, Calif. State U., Bakersfield, 1982, Henry Gallery, U. Wash., 1982, U. Calif., Santa Barbara, 1984, LA Mcpl. Art Galleries, Barnsdall Park, 1986, Turning the Tide: Early Los Angeles Modernists, Santa Barbara Mus. Art, Oakland Mus., others, 1989-91, LA County Mus. Art, 1996, After Geometric Expression, LA Mus. Art, 2004, The Optic Nerve, Columbus, Ohio, Mus. of Art, 2006, Birth of the Cool, Orange County, Calif., Mus. of Art, 2006; rep. permanent collections, Whitney Mus., LA County Mus. Art, San Francisco Mus. Art, Santa Barbara, Calif., Mus. Art, Pasadena, Calif., Art Mus., Long Beach, Calif., Mus. Art, La Jolla, Calif., Mus. Art, Fine Arts Gallery San Diego, U. Redlands, Mus. Modern Art, Israel, Pomona Coll., Scripps Coll., Univ. Mus., Berkeley, Calif., Wadsworth Atheneum, Nat. Collection Fine Arts, Seattle Mus. Modern Art, Newport Harbor Mus., U. N.Mex. Mus. Art, Wash. State U., LA Mus. Contemporary Art, Houston Mus. Contemporary Art, Balt. Mus. Art, Chgo. Art Inst.; retrospective exhbn. covering yrs. 1955-87 Calif State U. at Northridge, 1989, retrospective exhbn. 1979-94, Pomona Coll., 1994, 40 year survey Calif. art Orange County Mus. Art, Newport Beach, 1998-99, LA County Mus., 2004, San Diego Mus. Art, 2004, Riverside Mus. Art, Calif., 2006, Columbus Mus. Art, Ohio, 2007. Served with USNR, 1943-46. Visual Arts grantee NEA, 1983, 89. Office: Pomona Coll Dept Arts 333 N College Way Dept Arts Claremont CA 91711-4429 also: Claremont Grad U Art Dept 251 E 10th St Claremont CA 91711-3913 Office Phone: 909-626-1483.

BENJAMIN, LATANYA T., dermatologist; d. Winston and Elaine Benjamin. BS, U. Fla., Gainesville, Fla., 1996; MD, Drexel U., Phila., Pa., 2001. Lic. physician Pa., 2001. Resident Dept Pediat. U. Miami, Fla., 2001—03, rsch. fellow pediatric dermatology Dept Dermatology and Cutaneous Surgery, 2003—05, resident Dept Dermatology and Cutaneous Surgery, 2005—. Contbr. articles to profl. jours. Tchr. Continued Christian Devel., Hollywood, Fla., 2005—06. Recipient Rsch. Apprenticeship Program award, 1995. Mem.: Com. Interns and Residents (del. 2002—03, chpt. leader 2002—03), Women's Dermatol. Soc., Alumnae and Alumni Assn.MCP Hahnemann (hon.), Dermatology Found. (hon.), Alpha Epsilon Delta. Office: University of Miami Miller School of Med 1600 NW 10th Ave RMSB 2023A Miami FL 33136 Home Phone: 305-904-9292; Office Phone: 305-904-9292. Personal E-mail: godrlt@yahoo.com. Business E-Mail: lbenjamin@med.miami.edu.

BENJAMIN, LLOYD WILLIAM, III, academic administrator; b. Painesville, Ohio, Sept. 2, 1944; s. Lloyd William and Shirley M (Emmett) Benjamin; m. Wieke van der Weijden; children: Saskia Jansje, Lloyd William. BA, Emory U., 1966; PhD, U. N.C., 1973. Prof. art history East Carolina U., Little Rock, 1970-76; prof. U. Ark., Little Rock, 1976—95, dean fine arts, 1983-88, dean arts and humanities, 1988-95; v.p. acad. affairs Valdosta State U., 1995-2000; pres. Ind. State U., 2000—. Pres. ISU Found. Author: History Early Netherlandish Painting, 1977, Art of Designed Environments-Netherlands, 1983; co-author: Drawings from the Collection of Herbert and Dorothy Vogel, 1986; also articles. Mem. Arts and Humanities Commn., 1990-91; pres. Ark. Endowment for Humanities, 1986, Friends of KLRE/KUAR, 1990. Mem.: Am. Assn. State Colls. and Univs. (AASCU) (state rep.). Office: Office of Pres Ind State U 217 N Sixth St Terre Haute IN 47809 Office Phone: 812-237-4000. E-mail: president@indstate.edu.*

BENJAMIN, LORNA SMITH, psychologist; d. Lloyd Albert and Esther Smith; children: Laureen, Linda. AB, Oberlin Coll., 1955; PhD, U. Wis., 1960. Lic. psychologist Utah, Wis. NIMH fellow dept. psychiatry U. Wis., 1958-62, clin. psychology intern, 1960-64, asst. prof., 1966-71, assoc. prof., 1971-77, prof. psychiatry, 1977-88; prof. psychology U. Utah, 1988—; co-dir. Interpersonal Reconstructive Therapy Clinic U. Utah Neuropsychiatric Inst. Adj. prof. psychiatry U. Utah, 1988-; rsch. assoc. Wis. Psychol. Inst., Madison, 1962-66. Author: Interpersonal Diagnosis and Treatment of Personality Disorders, 2003, Interpersonal Reconstructive Therapy: A Peronality Based Treatment Approach for Complex Cases, 2006; contbr. articles to profl. jours. Mem.: APA, Soc. Psychotherapy Rsch., Phi Beta Kappa. Office: Univ Utah Dept Psychology 380 S 1530 E Salt Lake City UT 84112-8934 Home Phone: 801-558-9504; Office Phone: 801-581-4463. Business E-Mail: lsb_3@msn.com. *I attribute my success to a high energy level, and to some teachers and friends who supported me in times and places women were unwelcome.*

BENJAMIN, SUSAN SELTON, elementary school educator; b. NYC, June 3, 1946; m. Robert F. Benjamin, Nov. 30, 1968; children: Joshua, Alana. BS, Cornell U., 1968; MEd, Tufts U., 1969. Tchr. Wakefield (Mass.) Schs., 1969-73, Los Alamos (N.Mex.) Schs., 1973—, Piñon Elem. Sch., Los Alamos, N.Mex. Resource tchr. Montessori Sch. House, San Diego, 1986; tchr. U. N.Mex., Los Alamos, 1989, 90; cons. Activities Integrating Math. and Sci. (AIMS) Nat. Leadership, Fresno, Calif., 1992—. Chair leadership Hadassah, Los Alamos, 1991—. Named Outstanding Women of N.Mex., 1980, N.Mex. State Tchr. of Yr., 2002; recipient Presdl. award for excellence in math. tchg. N.Mex. State, 1990, 92, Leadership award Hadassah, 1996. Mem. Nat. Coun. Math. Tchrs. Avocations: hiking, travel, tennis, aerobics. Office: Piñon Elem Sch 90 Grand Canyon Los Alamos NM 87544*

BENJAMIN, THERESA MARY, retired psychotherapist; b. Boston, July 27, 1926; d. Vincenzo James and Maria (Morelli) Cardinale; children: Richard, Lorri, Denise. PhD, 1982; BA, Internat. Coll., 1978, MA, 1979; PhD, Profl. Sch. for Humanities Studies, 1982. Pvt. practice, Carlsbad, Calif., 1988—. Cons. Mgmt. Plus, Oceanside; lectr. U. So. Calif., LA, Carlsbad (Calif.) HS, Carlsbad. Author: What's The Meta, 1982, I'd Rather Be Right Than Happy, 1995, The Priest is in the Parlor, 2004. Grantee, Social Work Advancement Assn., 1997. Mem.: Sierra Club. Home and Office: 4809 Kelly Drive Carlsbad CA 92008 Office Phone: 760-434-6444. E-mail: drtmbenjamin@msn.com.

BENJAMIN, WILLIAM CHASE, lawyer; b. Glen Cove, NY, Dec. 2, 1947; AB, Princeton U., 1969; postgrad., Grad. Inst. Internat. Affairs, Geneva, 1969-70; JD, Harvard U., 1973. Bar: N.Y. 1974, U.S. Tax Ct. 1978, Mass. 1983. Assoc. Cleary, Gottlieb, Steen & Hamilton, Brussels, 1975-78, NYC, 1978-82; assoc. Hale and Dorr, Boston, 1982-84, jr. ptnr., 1984-86, sr. ptnr., 1986—. Fulbright scholar, 1969-70. Mem. ABA, Internat. Bar Assn., Mass. Bar Assn., Boston Bar Assn., Internat. Fiscal Assn. Avocations: skiing, tennis, swimming, sailing. Office: Wilmer Cutler Pickering Hale and Dorr LLP 60 State St Boston MA 02109-1816 Office Phone: 617-526-6318. E-mail: william.benjamin@wilmerhale.com.

BENKARD, JAMES W. B., lawyer; b. NYC, Apr. 10, 1937; s. Franklin Bartlett and Laura Derby (Dupee) B.; m. Margaret Walker Spofford, Dec. 12, 1964; children: Andrew Minturn, James Robinson, Margaret Mercer. AB, Harvard U., 1959; LLB, Columbia U., 1963. Bar: N.Y. 1963. Assoc. Davis Polk & Wardwell, NYC, 1963-73, ptnr., 1973—, co-chmn. firm pro bono com. Law clk. to Hon. Charles D. Breitel, Appellate Div. First Dept. & N.Y. Ct. Appeals, 1966—67. Trustee Vassar Coll., Poughkeepsie, N.Y., Tchrs. Coll., N.Y.C., Environ. Def. Fund, N.Y.C., St. Mark's Sch., Southborough, Mass, Columbia Law Sch. Alumni Assn., Scenic Am. Mem. Am. Coll. Trial Lawyers, Knickerbocker Club, River Club (N.Y.C.), Fishers Island Country Club. Office: Davis Polk & Wardwell 450 Lexington Ave Fl 31 New York NY 10017-3982 Office Phone: 212-450-4000. Office Fax: 212-450-3800. Business E-Mail: james.benkard@dpw.com.

BENKE, ROBIN PAUL, librarian; b. Trinidad, W.I., Jan. 30, 1953; came to U.S., 1967; s. Albert and Rita A. (Riva) B. BA, Hampden-Sydney Coll., 1975; MLS, Peabody Coll., 1978. Libr., asst. prof. libr. sci. U. Va.'s Coll. Wise, Wise, 1978—. Compiler reference and bibliography workbook, 1987. Bd. dirs. Pro-Art Assn., Wise, 1983-99, 2007-, pres., 1995-97; mem. cultural and humanities com. Mountain Empire CC, 1991—; mem. State Coun. of Higher Edn. for Va.; mem. Libr. Adv. Coun., chair, 2003-05; mem. steering com. Virtual Libr. Va., 2001-07. Recipient Educator of Yr. for Higher Edn. award Va. Ednl. Media Assn., 1996, Outstanding Svc. award Clinch Valley Coll., 1998. Mem. AAUP, ALA, Assn. Coll. Rsch. Librs. (mem. bibliographic instrn. sect. planning com., policy com. 1989-93, nat. adv. coun. 1990-95, coll. libr. sect. stds. com. 1995-97), Southeastern Libr. Assn., Va. Libr. Assn. (intellectual freedom com. 1988-93, mem. coll. and univ. sect., chmn. 1996—, mem. awards and recognition com., 1996-98), Va. Edn./Media Assn., S.W. Info. Network Group (pres. 1994-96), Commn. Colls., So. Assn. Colls. & Schs., Friends of the Pub. Libr. (pres. 1994-96), Wise County C. of C., Beta Phi Mu, Kappa Delta Pi. Republican. Episcopalian. Avocations: travel, reading. Office: U Va's Coll at Wise College Ave Wise VA 24293 Business E-Mail: rbenke@virginia.edu.

BENKLER, YOCHAI, law educator; LLB, Tel-Aviv U. Faculty Law, 1991; JD, Harvard U. Law Sch., 1994. Bar: Mass. 1995. Mem., treas. Kibbutz Shizafon, Israel, 1984—87; tchg. fellow Harvard Coll., 1992—94; assoc. Ropes & Gray, Boston, 1994—95; law clk. to Hon. Stephen G. Breyer US Supreme Ct., 1995—96; asst. prof. law NYU Sch. Law, 1996—99, assoc. prof. law, 1999—2000, prof. law, 2001—03, Yale U. Law Sch., New Haven, 2003—07; prof. law, faculty co-dir. Berkman Ctr. for Internet & Soc. Harvard Law Sch., Cambridge, 2007—. Faculty co-dir., JSD program NYU Sch. Law, 1997—2001, dir., Engleberg Ctr. for Innovation Law and Policy, 2001—03, dir., Info. Law Inst., 2001—03; vis. prof. law Yale Law Sch., 2001—02, Harvard Law Sch., 2002—03; bd. advisors, pub. knowledge BIOS IP Watch. Contbr. articles to law jours.; author: Rules of the Road for the Information Superhighway: Electronic Communications and the Law, 1996, 1997, The Wealth of Networks: How Social Production Transforms Markets and Freedom, 2006. Military svc. Israel Defense Force, 1982—86. Mem.: World Tech. Network (World Tech. Network award (Law) 2005). Office: Harvard Law Sch 1563 Massachusetts Ave Cambridge MA 02138 E-mail: yochai.benkler@yale.edu.*

BENKOWITZ, KEVAN I., lawyer; b. 1975; BBA in Fin., Tex. A&M U., 1998; JD, U. Tex. Sch. Law, Austin, 2002. Bar: Tex. 2002, US Dist. Ct. (no. and ea. dists. Tex.). Law clk. Colbert, Freeman & Stribling, P.C., Austin, Tex., Law Office of Rick Freeman, P.C., Austin, 2001—02; assoc. Touchstone, Bernays, Johnson, Beall & Smith, L.L.P., 2002—06; assoc. def. atty. Walters, Balido & Crain, Dallas, 2006—. Named a Rising Star, Tex. Super Lawyers mag., 2006. Mem.: Dallas Assn. Young Lawyers, Dallas Bar Assn. Office: Walters Balido & Crain 900 Jackson St Founders Sq Ste 600 Dallas TX 75202 Office Phone: 214-347-8372. E-mail: kevan.benkowitz@wbclawfirm.com.*

BENN, CANDACE MARILEA, elementary school educator; b. L.I., NY, Apr. 2, 1980; d. Mervin Leroy and Antoinette Patricia Foster; m. Jason Edward Benn, July 12, 2003; 1 child, Lanai Taylor. BS, Va. State U., Petersburg, 2002. Daycare counselor Chester Child Devel., Chester, Va., 1999—2002; Head Start tchr. Woodlawn Learning Ctr., Dinwiddie, Va., 2003—. Mem.: Am. Counselors Assn., Nat. Urban League, Va. Counseling Assn., Pi Lambda Theta. Home: 4408 Widgeon Ct Petersburg VA 23803

BENN, THEODORE ALEXANDER (ALEC BENN), writer; b. London, July 10, 1918; came to U.S., 1925, naturalized, 1933; s. Theodore and Beatrice Alice (Martin) B.; m. Ethel Borner, June 14, 1940 (div.); 1 child, Theodore A. Jr.; m. Caroline Meredith Whittingham, Dec. 31, 1959; children: Alexander W., Richard R. ScB in Engring., Brown U., 1939; postgrad., NYU, 1939-40, 83-87, Columbia U., 1946-56. Exec. Aluminum Co. Am., Edgewater, N.J., 1939-44, 46-48; writer Merrill Lynch Pierce Fenner and Smith, NYC, 1948-51, McGraw Hill, NYC, 1952; copy dir., v.p., creative dir. Doremus & Co., NYC, 1953-64; v.p. Kudner Agy., NYC, 1964-65, J.M. Mathes, NYC, 1965-66, Bozell & Jacobs, NYC, 1966-67; pres. Benn & MacDonough, Inc., NYC, 1967-87, Short Hills, N.J., 1987-88. Columnist Money and Power, 1988; author: 27 Most Common Mistakes in Advertising, 1978, 23 Most Common Mistakes in Public Relations, 1982, Advertising Financial Products and Services, 1986, The Unseen Wall Street of 1968-1975 and Its Significance For Today, 2000; playwright: Love Game (Nat. Arts Club award 1952); Answer the Sphinx, 1952, The Comedy of Love and Power, 2002, A Tale of Tangled Love, 2003, The Comedy of Love & Power, 2004; contbr. articles to profl. jours. Lt. (s.g.) USN, 1944-46. Recipient awards for advt. Mem.: Deep Canyon Tennis Club, Univ. Club. Avocations: backgammon, duplicate bridge. Home: 73224 Bill Tilden Ln Palm Desert CA 92260 Personal E-mail: cmbenn@aol.com.

BENNACK, FRANK ANTHONY, JR., publishing company executive; b. San Antonio, Feb. 12, 1933; s. Frank Anthony and Lula W. Bennack; m. Luella M. Smith, Sept. 1, 1951; children: Shelley, Laura, Diane, Cynthia, Julie. Student, U. Md., 1954—56, St. Mary's U., 1956—58. Advt. account exec. San Antonio Light, 1950—53, 1956—58, adv. mgr., 1961—65, asst. pub., 1965—67, pub., 1967—74; gen. mgr. newspapers Hearst Corp., NYC, 1974—76, exec. v.p., COO, 1975—78, pres., CEO, 1978—2002, vice chmn. bd. dirs., chmn. exec. com., 2002—. Chmn. Mus. of TV and Radio, NYC, 1991—; dir. Mfrs. Hanover Trust Co., NYC, Am. Home Products Corp. Chmn. bd. San Antonio Symphony, 1973—74; trustee Our Lady of Lake Coll.; hon. trustee Witte Meml. Mus.; bd. govs. N.Y. Hosp., NYC; chmn. Lincoln Ctr., NYC, 2005—. With US Army, 1954—56. Fellow: Am. Acad. Arts & Scis.; mem.: Am. Newspaper Pubs. Assn. (dir.), Tex. Daily Newspaper Assn. (pres. 1973), Greater San Antonio C. of C. (pres. 1971—), Rotary Club (pres. 1974—75). Office: Lincoln Ctr for Performing Arts 140 West 65th St New York NY 10023 also: Hearst 300 W 57th St New York NY 10019-3741*

BENNER, C. JONATHAN, lawyer; b. 1948; BA in Internat. Svc., Am. Univ., 1970; JD, Georgetown Univ., 1973. Bar: DC 1973. Gen. counsel Fed. Maritime Commn., 1981—84; ptnr. Troutman Sanders LLP, Washington, 2001—. Mem.: DC Bar, Maritime Adminstrv. Bar Assn. Office: Troutman Sanders LLP Ste 1000 401 Ninth St NW Washington DC 20004-2134 Office Phone: 202-274-2880. Office Fax: 202-654-5647. Business E-Mail: jonathan.benner@troutmansanders.com.

BENNER, MARY WRIGHT, freelance/self-employed conference director; b. Chgo., Aug. 4, 1956; d. Robert V.L. and Sara Helen (Beeler) W.; children: Sara Eleanor, Robert Fox. BA, Conn. Coll., 1979; MBA, Columbia U., 1983. Rsch. assoc. Acad. for Contemporary Problems, Washington, 1979-81; rating specialist Standard & Poor's, NYC, 1983-84; asst. adminstr. Twp. of Princeton, NJ, 1984-86; v.p. Fin. Guaranty Ins. Co., NYC, 1986-99, mgr. dept. govt. affairs, 1997-99; pres. Wright Benner Assocs., 1999—; program dir. The Conf. Bd., 2002—. Bd. dirs. Nat. Com. for Pub./Pvt. Partnerships, 1997-99; mem. sponsor adv. com. Women Exec. in State Gov., 1998-99; mem. steering com. Rebuild Am. Coalition, 1997-99; co-chair Uniting Citizens for Housing Affordability in Newton, 2000-04; chair out reach commn. Eliot Ch. of Newton, 2001—. Mem. Pub. Works Forum (bd. dirs. 1986-88), Assn. for Govtl. Leasing and Fin. (bd. dirs. 1991-95, treas. 1994-95), Assn. Fin. Guaranty Insurers (chmn. com. govt. affairs 1997-99), Rebuild Am. Coalition (exec. bd. dirs. 1998-88), Cape Cod Chamber Mus. Festival, (v.p., bd. dirs. 2000-03), Can-Do (bd. dirs. 2005-07). Avocations: cooking, tennis. Home and Office: 136 Washington St Newton MA 02458-2250 Personal E-mail: mwbenner@rcn.com.

BENNER, RICHARD EDWARD, JR., marketing consultant, volunteer, investor; b. Jersey City, Dec. 7, 1932; s. Richard E. and Dorothy (Linstead) B.; m. Virginia Hart; children: Linda, Richard III, Christopher. BS, Lehigh U., 1954; postgrad., NYU, 1959-63. Sales exec. IBM Corp, Norwalk, Conn., 1955-58; with Avon Products, Inc., NYC, 1959-78, group v.p. mktg. and internat., 1972-78; divsn. exec. v.p. Sara Lee, Kansas City, Mo., 1979-86; mktg. cons. Kansas City, 1987—. Bd. dirs. Game Hill, Inc., Weston, Mo., exec. com., chmn., bd. dirs., cons. Exec. Svc. Corp., 1993—; LINC, Local Investment commn., 21st Century Initiative; mentor Helzberg Entrepreneurial Mentoring Program, 1998—. Bd. dirs., pres. Northland Homes Partnership for the Homeless, 1988-94; active Eccumedia, 1987-89; maj. corp. com. chmn. United Way, N.Y.C., 1976; Rep. committeeman, Bergan County, 1973; mem. SCORE, 1990—, vice chmn., 1991-92; vice chair cmty. rels. Exec. Svc. Corps, 1990—, chmn., 1993-97, dir., 1997—; trustee Shepherd Ctr. North, 2000—; Stephen minister Luth. Ch., 1998—. With inf. U.S. Army, 1955-56. Named Mentor of Yr. (Kansas City), Helzberg Entrepreneuriel Mentoring Program, 1995—. Mem. Direct Selling Assn. Edn. Found. (bd. dirs. 1982-84). Clubs: Beaverkill Trout (Livingston Manor, N.Y.) (bd. dirs. 1975-78); Old Pike Country (bd. dirs. 1987-90). Lodges: Rotary (bd. dirs., Polio Plus area coord., past pres.). Avocations: fly fishing, investing, gardening. Home and Office: 4404 NW Normandy Ln Kansas City MO 64116-1553

BENNER, RICHARD WALTER, oil industry executive, petroleum engineer, geologist; b. Dayton, Ohio, June 2, 1922; s. Frederick and Edna Marie B.; m. Parnel Gillilan, Mar. 19, 1949 (dec. Apr. 1970); m. Donna Tschappat, Nov. 24, 1978 (dec. Sept. 1995). BS in Geology, U. Mich., 1947, MS in Geology, 1948. Registered profl. engr., Colo. Photo geologist Texaco, Inc., Lewistown, Mont., 1947-48, field geologist, 1948-59, dist. geologist Denver, 1959-66, spl. projects geologist, 1966-77; v.p. Kissinger Petroleum Corp., Englewood, Colo., 1977-81, Kissinger Drilling & Exploration, Englewood, 1981-86; pres. Kissinger Exploration, Inc., Denver, 1981-86; cons. Corpus Christi, Tex., 1987—; ret., 2003. Author, co-author: Ann. Field Book Publs., Rocky Mountain Geol. Soc. and Montana Geol. Soc., 1949-77; co-author Geological Atlas of Rocky Mountain Region, Wind River Basin, Wyo., 1970, U.S. Geol. Bull., Reserves of Oil and Gas in Rocky Mountain Region, 1977. With U.S. Coast Guard, 1943-44, lt. U.S. Navy, 1944-46, ETO, PTO. Named Hon. Alumnus, William Woods U., 2002. Mem. Am. Assn. Petroleum Geologists (50 yr. mem.), Sigma Gamma Upsilon. Home and Office: 5206 Wooldridge Rd Corpus Christi TX 78413-3833

BENNET, DOUGLAS JOSEPH, JR., former academic administrator; b. Orange, NJ, June 23, 1938; s. Douglas Joseph and Phoebe (Benedict) B.; m. Susanne Klejman, June 27, 1959 (div. 1995); children: Michael, James, Holly; m. Midge Bowen Ramsey, July 27, 1996. BA, Wesleyan U., Middletown, Conn., 1959; MA, U. Calif., Berkeley, 1960; PhD, Harvard, 1968. Asst. to econ. adv. AID, New Delhi, 1963—64; spl. asst. to Am. ambassador to India, 1964—66; asst. to Vice Pres. Hubert H. Humphrey, 1967—69; adminstrv. asst. to U.S. Senator Thomas Eagleton, 1969—73, to U.S. Senator Abraham Ribicoff, 1973—73; staff dir. com. budget U.S. Senate, 1974—77; asst. sec. state congressional relations, 1977—79; adminstr. AID, Washington, 1979—81; pres. Roosevelt Ctr. for Am. Policy Studies, 1981—83; pres., CEO Nat. Pub. Radio, Washington, 1983—93; asst. sec. state Internat. Orgnl. Affairs Dept. State, Washington, 1993—95; pres. Wesleyan U., Middletown, Conn., 1995—2007; trustee Wellesley Coll. Mem. Coun. Fgn. Rels., Cosmos Club. Democrat. Office Phone: 203-685-3500.

BENNETT, ALAN HUGH, retired medical educator; b. Boston, June 29, 1937; s. Theodore and Gladys Morrison Bennett; m. Susan McCulloch Bennett, Apr. 15, 1978; children: Gordon Eric, Jeffrey Paul, Jennifer Ellen. BA, U. Va., Charlottesville, 1959; MD, Boston U., 1963. Diplomate Am. Bd. Urology, 1970. Intern surgery U. Fla., 1963—64; resident gen. surgery and urology Peta Bent Bright Hosp. Harvard Med. Sch., Cambridge, Mass., 1966—70, asst. prof. surgery med. sch., 1970—78; assoc. prof. surgery U. Pitts., 1978—79; prof. surgery, divsn. head Albany Med. Coll., NY, 1979—94. Chmn. health policy coun. Am. Urol. Assn., Balt., 1990—95. Author 3 books; contbr. articles to profl. jours., chapters to books. Capt. US Army, 1964—66, Vietnam. Recipient Army Commendation medal, 1966. Fellow: ACS; mem.: NE Sect. Am. Urol. Assn. (pres. 1990—92), Alpha Omega Alpha, Phi Beta Kappa. Avocations: canoe racing, golf, model ship building, opera. Home: 28 Oak Bend West Orange NJ 07052 Office Phone: 201-618-7093.

BENNETT, ALAN JEROME, electronics executive, physicist; b. Phila., June 13, 1941; s. Leon Martin and Reba (Perry) B.; m. Frances Kitey, June 16, 1963; children: Sarah, Rachel, Daniel. BA, U. Pa, 1962; MS, U. Chgo., 1963, PhD, 1965. Physicist R & D ctr. GE, Schenectady, N.Y., 1966-74, br. mgr. R & D ctr., 1975-79; dir. electronics lab. Gould Inc., Rolling Meadows, Ill., 1979-84; v.p. R & D Varian Assocs., Palo Alto, Calif., 1984-91; dir. program devel. Lawrence Livermore Nat. Lab., Livermore, Calif., 1992-96, dir. indsl. partnerships and commercialization, 1997—2003, mgr. program devel., lab. assoc., 2003—. Contbr. articles to profl. jours. Fellow NSF, 1963-65, 66. Mem. Phi Beta Kappa, Sigma Xi. Avocations: linguistics, amateur radio. Home: 233 Tennyson Ave Palo Alto CA 94301-3737 Personal E-mail: alanbennett@sbcglobal.net.

BENNETT, ALAN R., lawyer; b. Greenwich, Conn., Apr. 12, 1948; BA with honors, Univ. Conn., 1969; JD, Columbia Univ., 1972. Bar: D.C. Atty. Office of Gen. Counsel, FDA, Washington, 1972—76; assoc. Weil Gotshal & Manges, 1976—77; spec. counsel U.S. Senate Com. Govt. Affairs, 1977—81; assoc. Kaye Scholer Fierman Hays & Handler, 1981—84, ptnr., 1985—86, Fox Weinberg Bennett, 1986—99, Bennett Turner Coleman, 1999—2002; ptnr. corp. dept. & co-leader life sciences group practice Ropes & Gray, Washington, 2002—. Harlan Fiske Stone scholar. Mem.: ABA, N.Y. State Bar Assn., D.C. Bar, Phi Beta Kappa. Office: Ropes & Gray One Metro Ctr Suite 900 700 12th St NW Washington DC 20005-3948 Office Phone: 202-508-4604. Office Fax: 202-508-4650. Business E-Mail: alan.bennett@ropesgray.com.

BENNETT, ALEXANDER ELLIOT, lawyer; b. Houston, Aug. 9, 1940; s. William Ernest and Verna Evelyn (Donelan) B.; m. Marilyn A. Bennett, June 6, 1960 (div. 1981); children: Andrew, Laura, Peter; m. Brooksley Born, Oct. 9, 1982; children: Nicholas Landau, Ariel Landau. BA, U. Mich., 1961, JD, 1963. Bar: D.C. 1964. Assoc. Arnold & Porter, Washington, 1966-70, ptnr., 1971—2006. Editor U. Mich. Law Rev., 1963. Mem. ABA, D.C. Bar Assn., Order of Coif. Democrat. Avocations: sailing, tennis. Home: 2319 Tracy Pl NW Washington DC 20008-1640 Office: Arnold & Porter Thurman Arnold Bldg 555 12th St NW Washington DC 20004-1206 Office Phone: 202-942-5192. Office Fax: 202-942-5999. Business E-Mail: alexander.bennett@aporter.com.

BENNETT, AMANDA, former editor; b. 1952; m. Terence B. Foley; 2 children. Grad. cum laude, Harvard U., 1975. Auto industry reporter Wall St. Jour., Pentagon & State Dept. reporter, Beijing corr., mgmt. editor/reporter, nat. economics corr., chief Atlanta bur.; mng. editor projects The Oregonian, 1998—2001; editor, v.p. Lexington Herald-Leader, Ky., 2001—03; editor, exec. v.p. Phila. Inquirer, 2003—06; vis. fellow Columbia U., NYC, 2007—. Mem. Pulitzer Prize Bd., 2002—. Author: Death of the Organization Man, 1991; co-author (with Sidney Rittenberg): The Man Who Stayed Behind, 1993; co-author: (with Terence B. Foley) In Memoriam, 1998. Co-recipient Pulitzer Prize for nat. reporting, 1997.

BENNETT, ARLIE JOYCE, clinical social worker; b. Central Lake, Mich., Nov. 22, 1921; d. Charles Herbert and Bernice Evelyn (Miller) B. Student, Alma Coll., Mich., 1946-48; BA, U. Mich., 1950, MSW, 1955. Bd. cert. diplomate emerita Am. Bd. Examiners in Clin. Social Work. Social worker Ypsilanti (Mich.) State Hosp., 1950-54; staff social worker Kalamazoo Child Guidance Clinic, 1955-67, chief social worker, 1967-71; clin. social worker State Tech. Inst. Rehab. Ctr., Plainwell, Mich., 1971-90; pvt. practice, Kalamazoo, 1991-92. Field instr. Mich. State U., 1959-76, Western Mich. U. Sch. Social Work, Kalanazoo, 1971-90, U. Mich., 1967-71. Author: Pie Is in the Eye of the Beholder, 1980, War and Memory, 1991; editor newsletter Late Show Connection, 1993—; contbr. articles to profl. jours. Vol. record reviewer Cath. Family Svcs. Agys., Kalamazoo; bd. dirs. Youth Opportunities Unltd., Kalamazoo, 1968—1980; bd. mem. Juvenile Home Found., 2004—. Tech. sgt. WAC, AUS, 1944-46, ETO. Mem. NASW (past chmn. and officer), AAUW (legis. chmn. Kalamazoo br. 1985-89, 93-95, pres. 1991-93, pub. policy chmn. 1999-2002), Mensa (local coord. 1990—), Loners Am. (pres. Mich. chpt. 1990-92, 97-98), U. Mich. Alumnae Club (past pres. and officer), Phi Kapa Phi. Avocations: poetry, camping, seat weaving. Home: 1110 W Maple St Kalamazoo MI 49008-1846 Office Phone: 269-349-6293.

BENNETT, BRUCE W., retired construction executive, civil engineer; b. St. Joseph, Mo., Dec. 24, 1930; s. Bruce W. and Laura Louella (Clark) B.; m. Barbara Gail Haase, July 26, 1957; children: Stacy Suzanne, Bruce W. BS in Civil Engring., U. So. Calif., 1954. Project mgr. George A. Fuller & Co., Chgo., 1956-61; contract mgr. Huber, Hunt & Nichols, Indpls., 1961-70, v.p., 1970-82, exec. v.p., 1982-84, pres., 1984-95, ret., 1995. Pres. Hunt Corp., 1988-95, bd. dirs. Served to capt. USAF, 1954-57 Mem. Archimedes Circle, David Wilson Assocs., Newcomen Soc. Clubs: Indpls. Athletic, Skyline (Indpls.). Republican. Avocations: tennis, golf. Home: 437 Seville Ave Newport Beach CA 92661-1528

BENNETT, BRYCE HUGH, JR., lawyer; b. Jackson, Mich., Aug. 6, 1953; s. Bryce H. Sr. and Elizabeth Post B.; children: Carolyn, Amy, Rebecca, Molly; m. Donna Dillon, Mar. 20, 1993: children: Bryce III, Dillon, Luke. BS in Fin. with high distinction, Ind. U., 1975; JD magna cum laude, Ind. U., Indpls., 1978. Bar: Ind. 1978, U.S. Dist. Ct. (so. dist.) Ind. 1978, U.S. Ct. Appeals (7th cir.) 1981, U.S. Supreme Ct. 1991. Assoc. Callahan Riley & Hillis, Indpls., 1978-83; ptnr. Riley, Bennett & Egloff, Indpls., 1984—. Bd. chmn. Ind. Better Bus. Bur.; chmn. Indpls. City Market, 2000-01, Historic Indpls. City Market Found., 2005-06; bd. dirs. Arts Coun. Indpls., Indpls. Symphony Orch.; bd. advisors Small Bus. Devel. Ctr. Mem. ABA, Ind. State Bar Assn., Indpls. Bar Assn., Ind. Def. Lawyers Assn., Indpls. Bar Found. (pres. 2001), Indpls. Press Club, Skyline Club, Internat. Assn. Def. Counsel. Office Phone: 317-636-8000. Business E-Mail: bbennett@rbelaw.com.

BENNETT, BYRON LEE, chemistry professor, researcher; s. Charles Maurice IV and Emily Janice Bennett; m. Barbara Anne Hager, May 30, 1998; 1 child, Callisto Moran. BA in Chemistry, Cedarville U., Ohio, 1989; PhD in Chemistry, U. Wyo., Laramie, 1997. Grad. rsch. asst. U. Wyo., Laramie, 1992—97; postdoctoral fellow U. Utah, Salt Lake City, 1997—98, U. Nev., Reno, 1998—2000, asst. prof. chemistry Las Vegas, 2000—06; assoc. prof. chemistry Daytona Beach CC, Fla., 2006—07; asst. prof. chemistry Idaho State U., Pocatello, 2007—. Grant reviewer Rsch. Corp., Tucson, 2001—; tech. sci. reviewer Elsevier-Jour. Fluorine Chemistry, Columbus, Ohio, 2002—, Jour. of Chem. Soc.-Dalton Transactions, London, 2002—, Wiley-VCH; European Jour. Inorganic Chemistry, Weinheim, Germany, 2002—; assoc. scientist Oxysense, Inc., Las Vegas, 2003—07; text reviewer Thomson Learning, Belmont, Calif., 2003—, McGraw Hill, NYC, 2005—. Contbr. articles to profl. jours. Recipient Cottrell Coll. Sci. award, Rsch. Corp., 2003—06, G.E. Coates Tchg. award, U. Wyo., 1002—1993; grantee, Am. Cancer Soc., 2005, Oxysense Inc., 2003—06, Assoc. Provost for Rsch., U. Nev. Las Vegas, 2001, 2002, 2003, Am. Cancer Soc., 2005. Mem.: Am. Chem. Soc. (tech. sci. reviewer organometallics 2001—, grant reviewer petroleum rsch. fund 2005—). Achievements include patents pending for organic materials with tunable electric and electroluminescent properties; Fluorinated 2, 2'-Bipyridine and 1, 10-Phenanthroline Platinum (II) complexes as cisplatin analogs for cancer treatment. Avocations: rock climbing, mountaineering, golf. Office: Idaho State Univ Dept Chemistry 921 S 8th Ave Stop 8023 Pocatello ID 83209-8023

BENNETT, C. LEONARD, electrical engineer; b. Lowell, Mass., Oct. 5, 1939; s. C. Leonard and Ruth E. (Glow) B.; m. Patricia Ann Derival, Aug. 22, 1966; children: Craig, Dawn Marie. BS in Elec. Engring., Lowell Tech. Inst., Mass., 1961; MS, N.C. State U., Raleigh, 1964; PhD, Purdue U., 1968. Registered profl. engr., Mass. Research engr. Purdue U., 1968; mem. tech. staff Sperry Research Ctr., Sudbury, Mass., 1968-73, mgr. systems applications, 1973-83; cons. engr. Raytheon, Marlboro, Mass., 1983—2004, sr. prin. engring. fellow, 2004—; lectr. in field. Contbr. chpts. to books, articles to profl. jours.; patentee field. Chmn. Groton Fin. Com., Mass., 1970-76; treas. Groton Ctr. for the Arts, 1976-78; coach Groton Jr. Hockey, 1979-86, Groton Little League Baseball, 1981-84; mem. com. local troop Boy Scouts Am., 1983—; bd. dirs. Groton Dunstable Soccer Club, 1981-92, Nashoba Valley Youth Soccer League, 1986—; soccer referee U.S. Youth Soccer Assn., 1987—. Fellow IEEE (assoc. editor Trans. on Antennas and Propagation 1983-96); mem. Internat. Union of Radio Scis., Eta Kappa Nu, Tau Beta Pi, Phi Kappa Phi, Sigma Pi Sigma. Home: 304 Reedy Meadow Rd Groton MA 01450-1408 Office: Raytheon 1001 Boston Post Rd E Marlborough MA 01752-3789

BENNETT, CARL, retired discount department store executive; b. Greenwich, Conn., Jan. 27, 1920; s. Mayer and Rebecca (Lipsky) B.; m. Dorothy Becker, June 24, 1951; children: Marc Mitchell, Robin Cheryl Bennett Kanarek, Bruce Kenneth. Student, NYU, 1937-38. Wholesale liquor salesman, Conn., 1940-51; founder, ret. chmn. bd., chief exec. officer Caldor, Inc., Norwalk, Conn., 1951-84; ptnr. DorCal Assocs., Norwalk, Conn., 1984—. Chmn. Bi-Cultural Day Sch., Stamford, Conn., 1965-67, treas., 1967-68; bd. dirs. Stamford Hosp., nat. bd. dirs. NCCJ; mem. Am. com., internat. bd. govs. Weizmann Inst. Served with AUS, 1942-45. Recipient Amudin award outstanding work Hebrew day schs., 1965, disting. service award Prime Minister Israel, 1973; named Retailer of Yr., 1982; named to Retailers Hall of Fame, 1983 Mem. World Bus. Council (charter), Nat. Retail Mchts. Assn. (bd. dirs.) Clubs: Sailfish Point Country (Stuart, Fla.); Quaker Ridge Country (Scarsdale, N.Y.). Office: DorCal Assocs 2001 W Main St Ste 248 Stamford CT 06902

BENNETT, CAROL(INE) ELISE, retired reporter, actress; b. New Orleans, Dec. 27, 1938; d. Gerald Clifford Graham and Edna Doris (Toennies) Kerr; m. Ralph Decker Bennett, Jr., Feb. 27, 1966; children: Ralph Decker III, Katherine Elise. BA, U. BC, Vancouver, Can., 1960; BLS, McGill U., Montreal, Que., Can., 1962. Libr. various locations, 1962-76; reporter TV/radio Washington-Ala. News Report, Washington, 1981-2001; ret., 2001. Actor: (plays) Girl in My Soup, 1978; (films) Kennedy, 1983, Prime Risk, 1984; host (TV series) Modern Maturity, 1986—88; author (with Terese Loeb Kreuzer): How to Move to Canada, A Primer for Americans, 2006. Vol. reader Rec. for Blind, Washington, 1985—. Mem.: AAUW, AFTRA, SAG, Nat. Press Club, Soc. Profl. Journalists. Avocation: tennis. Home: 115 Southwood Ave Silver Spring MD 20901-1918

BENNETT, CHARLES ANDREW, economics professor, department chairman; b. NYC, Feb. 8, 1943; s. Joseph C. and Catherine F. (Gallagher) B.; divorced; 1 child, William C.B. BA in Econs. with honors, St. Francis Coll., Bklyn., 1965; MA in Econs., Fordham U., 1968; postgrad., U. Chgo., 1970, Stanford U., Palo Alto, Calif., 1971, U. NC, Greensboro, 1980, UCLA, 1981, U. Buffalo, NY, 1985. Grad. asst., tchg. fellow Fordham U., Bronx, NY, 1965—68; instr. econs. Gannon U., Erie, Pa., 1968—76, asst. prof., 1976—, dir. Ctr. for Econ. Edn., 1977—, chmn. dept. econs. and fin., 1986—97. Cons., presenter in field. Author: Principles of Microeconomics Manual for External Study Courses, 1977, 12th edit., 2003; mem. editl. bd. Worth Pub., NYC, Harper & Row, NYC, Wadsworth Pubs., NYC, Dryden Press, NYC, McGraw Hill Pub. Co. Mem. Erie Mayor's Office Cmty. Affairs; mem. microcomputer com. Fairview (Pa.) Sch. Dist., mem. resource com. strategic planning action group, mem. tech. edn. task force; mem. steering com. Family Support Svcs., Erie; mem. task force on citizenship Pa. Dept. Edn.; mem. strategic planning com. Dahlkemper Sch. Bus. Adminstrn. Jones Motor Co. fellow, 1970; grantee Commodore Bus. Machines Computer Hardware and Software, 1984; recipient award for meritorious support of free enterprise BP Oil, 1980, Leavey award Freedoms Found., 1984, Internat. Paper award Joint Coun. on Econ. Edn., 1988, Com. to Excellence award in econ. edn., 1989, Gold award Gannon U., 2006; named Man of Achievement, Internat. Biographical Ctr., 1993. Mem. Nat. Fedn. Ind. Bus. (mem. adv. panel), Nat. Assn. Econ. Educators, Nat. Coun. Econ. Edn., Econ. Am., Econs. Pa., Assn. for Pvt. Edn. Avocations: bicycling, swimming. Home: 5570 Sebago Dr Fairview PA 16415-2223 Office: Gannon U 109 Univ Sq Erie PA 16541 Office Phone: 814-871-7585. Personal E-mail: charkswim55@yahoo.com. Business E-Mail: bennett@gannon.edu.

BENNETT, CHARLES FRANKLIN, JR., biogeographer, educator; b. Oakland, Calif., Apr. 10, 1926; s. Charles Franklin and Charlotte Louise (Normand) B.; m. Carole Ann Messenger, Nov. 30, 1947; 1 child, Ashley Lynn. PhD, UCLA, 1959. Instr. UCLA, 1959-60, asst. prof., 1960-65, assoc. prof., 1965-69, prof. biogeography, 1969—; prof. emeritus, 1993—. Cons. in field. Author: Human Influence on Zoogeography of Panama, 1968, Man and Earth's Ecosystems, 1976, Conservation of Natural Resources, 1983; contbr. articles to profl. jours. Guggenheim fellow, 1970-71. Fellow AAAS, Royal Geog. Soc.; mem. Ecol. Soc. Am., Brit. Ecol. Soc., Assn. Tropical Biology, Soc. for Conservation Biology, Fauna and Flora Preservation Soc., Am. Inst. Biol. Scis. Avocation: collecting natural history books. Home: 317 S Anita Ave Los Angeles CA 90049-3805 Office: UCLA Dept Geography 405 Hilgard Ave Los Angeles CA 90095-9000 Business E-Mail: chasben@ucla.edu.

BENNETT, CHARLES LEONARD, astrophysicist, educator; b. New Brunswick, NJ, Nov. 16, 1956; s. Lawrence Herman and Devora Mae (Spintman) B.; m. Renee Elizabeth Marlin, Sept. 2, 1984; 1 child, Andrew. BS cum laude in Astronomy, U. Md., 1978; PhD in Physics, MIT, Cambridge, 1984. Astrophysicist NASA Goddard Space Flight Ctr., Greenbelt, Md., 1984—2004, acting head infrared astrophysics br., 1993, 1994, head infrared astrophysics br., 1994—2000, sr. scientist exptl. cosmology, 2004; prof. physics and astronomy Johns Hopkins U., Balt., 2005—. Dep. prin. investigator Differential Microwave Radiometers (DMR) instrument on Cosmic Background Explorer (COBE), leader of COBE DMR software effort NASA, 1987—96, prin. investigator Wilkinson Microwave Anisotrophy Probe (WMAP) mission, 1996—, co-investigator Legacy Archive for Microwave Background Data Analysis, 2003—. Contbr. articles to profl. jours.; co-editor: After the First Three Minutes, 1991, Dark Matter, 1995. Named Most Highly Cited Rschr. in space sci. worldwide, ISI, 2002, Alumus of Yr., Physics Dept. U. Md., 2003; recipient NASA Outstanding Performance rating, 1985, 1994, GSFC Group Achievement Award for COBE, 1988, NASA/GSFC Performance Award, 1989, NASA Group Achievement Award for COBE, 1990, NASA Exceptional Sci. Achievement Medal for COBE, 1992, GSFC Group Award for MAP Proposal, 1996, NASA/GSFC Performance Award, 1996, 1998, 2002, NASA MIDEX Group Award, 1997, NASA/GSFC Leadership Award, 1999, "Best of What's New" Award in Aviation and Space for WMAP, Popular Sci., 2001, NASA/GSFC Ctr. of Excellence Group Achievement Award for MAP, 2002, NASA/GSFC Group Achievement Award for MAP, 2002, NASA Outstanding Leadership Medal for devel. and success of WMAP, 2003, NASA Performance Award, 2003, "Breakthrough of Yr." Award for WMAP/Sloan proof of Dark Energy, Sci. Mag., 2003, NASA Group Achievement Award to WMAP Sci. Team, 2004, John C. Lindsay Meml. Award for Space Sci., NASA, 2003, NASA Exceptional Sci. Achievement Medal for WMAP, 2004, Mid Career Stellar Award, Rotary Nat. Award for Space Achievement, 2005. Fellow: Am. Phys. Soc., AAAS; mem.: Internat. Astron. Union, Am. Astron. Soc., Am. Inst. Physics, Am. Acad. Arts & Scis., NAS (Henry Draper medal 2005), Sigma Xi. Democrat. Jewish. Achievements include discovery of new gravitational lenses; first detection of atomic and molecular transitions; research on precise measurements of spectrum and anisotropy limits on the cosmic microwave background radiation, large radio astronomy surveys.*

BENNETT, CHRISTOPHER LAWRENCE, hotel executive, lawyer; b. Washington, Nov. 29, 1969; s. Francis Joseph and Beverly Carol (Dailey) B. BS in Acctg. & Fin., Va. Polytechnic Inst., 1991; JD, U. Va., 1995. CPA, Md. Staff acct. Deloitte & Touche, Washington, 1991-92; assoc. Thacher Proffitt & Wood LLP, NYC, Donovan, Leisure, Newton & Irvine LLP, 1997—98; v.p., sec. Interstate & MeriStar Hospitality Corp., 1998—2001; sr. v.p., gen. counsel, sec. Interstate Hotels & Resorts Inc., Arlington, Va., 2001—06, exec. v.p., gen. counsel, sec., 2006—. Vol. Spl. Olympics, Va., 1987-90, Salvation Army, Va., 1992-93. Recipient award Price Waterhouse, 1990. Mem. Beta Alpha Psi, Eta Kappa Nu. Roman Catholic. Avocations: golf, reading. Office: Interstate Hotels & Resorts Inc 4501 N Fairfax Dr Arlington VA 22203

BENNETT, CLAY, cartoonist; b. Clinton, SC, Jan. 20, 1958; m. Cindy Procious; children: Sarah, Matt, Ben. B in Art and History, U. North Ala., 1980. Artist Pitts. Post-Gazette, Fayetteville Times, Fayetteville, NC; editl. cartoonist St. Petersburg Times, 1981—94, Christian Sci. Monitor, Boston, 1998—. Editl. cartoonist King Features Syndicate, 1994—. Named Editl. Cartoonist of Yr., Editor & Pub. Mag., 2001; recipient Nat. Headliner award, 1999, 2000, 2004, John Fischetti award, 2002, 2005, Pulitzer Prize for Editl. Cartooning, 2002, Thomas Nast award, Overseas Press Club, 2006, Robert F. Kennedy Journalism award for Editl. Cartooning, 2007. Office: Christian Sci Monitor One Norway St Boston MA 02115 E-mail: claybennett@earthlink.net.

BENNETT, CLAYTON IKE, professional sports team owner; m. Louise Gaylord; 3 children. Grad., U. Okla. Chmn. Profl. Basketball Club, LLC (owns NBA Seattle SuperSonics and Women's NBA Seattle Storm), 2006—, Dorchester Capital, Oklahoma City. Chmn. emeritus bd. dirs. Okla. Heritage Assn. Office: Seattle Sonics 351 Elliott Ave W Ste 500 Seattle WA 98119 also: Dorchester Capital Okla Tower 210 Park Ave Ste 3121 Oklahoma City OK 73102

BENNETT, DICK, college basketball coach; b. Pitts., Apr. 20, 1943; m. Anne; children: Kathi, Amy, Tony. BS in phys. edn., Ripon Coll., 1965; MEd, UW-Stevens Point. Basketball coach West Bend (Wis.) HS, 1965-66; coach various Wis HS teams, 1966-76, UW-Stevens Point, 1976-85, UW-Green Bay, 1985-95, U. Wis., Madison, 1995—2000, Wash. St. U., Pullman, 2003—06. 1st team at U. Wis. (17-15) appeared in 1996 N.I.T.; 2d team (18-10) made 2d U. Wis. appearance in N.C.A.A. tournament in 50 yrs., put together sch.'s 1st 6-game winning streak since 1951. Named WSUC Coach of Yr., 1982, 1985, NAIA Coach of Yr., 1984, NAIA Area IV Coach of Yr., 1985, Mid-Continent Coach of Yr., 1990, 1992, NABC Dist. 11 Coach of Yr., 1992, 1994, Basketball Times Midwest Coach of Yr., 1994. Achievements include 21-yr. collegiate coaching record, 395-214 (.649). Office: Bohler Athletic Complex Wash State Univ Basketball PO Box 641602 Pullman WA 99164-1602

BENNETT, EDWARD JAMES, lawyer; b. Newton, Iowa, Dec. 27, 1941; s. Erskine Francis and Malvina Esther (Goodhue) B.; m. Virginia Lee Cook, Jan. 30, 1965; children: Susan Elizabeth, Edward James. BA, U. Iowa, 1964, JD, 1966. Bar: Iowa 1966, U.S. Dist. Ct. (so. dist.) Iowa 1967. Atty. Diehl, Clayton & Cleverley, Newton, 1966-70, The Maytag Co., Newton, 1970-74, sr. atty., 1974-80, assoc. counsel, 1980-85, asst. sec., asst. gen. counsel, 1985-86, Maytag Corp. (formerly The Maytag Co.), Newton, 1986-90; sec., asst. gen. counsel Maytag Corp., Newton, 1990-99. Sec. The Hoover Co., 1990-99, Dixie-Narco Inc., 1990-99, Maytag Internat. Inc., 1990-99, Hoover Holdings Inc., 1990-99, Maytag Fin. Svcs. Corp., 1990-99, Maytag Corp. Found., 1990-99; dir. Progress Industries, 1993—, sec., 1994—. Active Civil Svc. Commn., Newton, 1980-86, Newton Zoning Bd. Adjustment, 1978-96, chmn., 1978-85; sec., trustee Newton Cmty. Ctr., Inc., 1976-94; trustee Newton Cmty. Schs. Found., 1994-99, v.p., 1996, pres., 1997; bd. dirs. Des Moines Metro Opera, 1998—, sec. 1998-99, pres. 2001-02; bd. dirs., pres. Des Moines Metro Opera Found., 2000-; bd. dirs. Progress Industries Found., 1998—, Calvin Cmty., 2002—, Friends of Drake Arts, 2003—, Des Moines Pastoral Counseling Ctr., 2004—. Mem. ABA, Iowa State Bar Assn. (trade regulation com. 1981-97, 1999-2003), Iowa Assn. Bus. and Industry (chmn. unemployment compensation com. 1976-94), Assn. Home Appliance Mfrs. (product safety com. 1975-92). Republican. Methodist. Home: 2325 N Wayne Ave Chicago IL 60614-3118 E-mail: vandjbenn@aol.com.

BENNETT, EDWARD VIRDELL, JR., surgeon; b. Nashville, July 17, 1947; s. Edward Virdell and Florence Elaine (Nelson) B. BA in Biology, Fisk U., 1969; MD cum laude, Ohio State U., 1973. Fellow in surgery Johns Hopkins U., Balt., 1973—75; intern, then resident Johns Hopkins Hosp., Balt., 1973—75; resident in surgery and cardiothoracic surgery Albany (N.Y.) Med. Ctr. Hosp., 1975—80, instr. in surgery, 1976—80; asst. prof. surgery Health Ctr. U. Tex.-San Antonio, 1980—83; practice medicine specializing in cardiothoracic surgery Sayre, Pa., 1983—91; mem. staff Robert Packer Hosp., Sayre, 1983—91; mem. Guthrie Clinic, Ltd., Sayre, 1983—91; chief cardiac surgery Guthrie Clinic Ltd., Sayre, 1990—91; cardiac surgeon Albany Cardiothoracic Surgeons, P.C., 1991—, pres., 2000—; mem. staff Albany Med. Ctr. Hosp., 1991—, St. Peters Hosp., Albany, 1991—; chief cardiac surgery St. Peter's Hosp., Albany, 1997—; clin. asst. prof. Albany Med. Coll., 1991—; med. dir. cardiac surgery Champlain Valley Physicians Hosp., 2003—. Bd. dirs. St. Peter's Hosp. Prodr. med. motion picture; contbr. articles to med. jours. Mem. N.Y. State Cardiac Adv. Com., 1994-2006. Named one of Best Drs. in Am., 2001—, Top Surgeons in Am., 2002—. Fellow ACS, Am. Coll. Chest Physicians, Am. Coll. Cardiology; mem. Soc. Thoracic Surgeons, Upstate Soc. Thoracic Surgeons (pres. 2000—), Internat. Soc. for Heart Transplantation, Sigma Xi, Alpha Omega Alpha, Omega Psi Phi. Republican. Episcopalian. Avocations: sailing, scuba diving, skiing. Home Phone: 518-439-1247; Office Phone: 518-591-2240.

BENNETT, SISTER ELSA MARY, retired secondary school educator; b. Muskegon, Mich., Dec. 13, 1930; d. Thomas B. and Elsa (Koelbel) B. BS, Our Lady of Lake Coll., San Antonio, 1955, MEd, 1971. Registered massage therapist, Tex.; Reiki master. Tchr. phys. edn. parochial schs., Abilene, Tex., Tulsa, San Antonio, Houston, Ennis, Tex., Alexandria, La., 1954, tchr., coach San Antonio, 1969—74, 1986—87, pub. schs., Mich., 1974—78; tchr. St. Augustine Sch., Laredo, Tex., 1978—79; adminstr., coach Our Lady of Lake U., 1979—86; phys. therapy aide Warm Springs Rehab., San Antonio, 1989—90; tchr. San Antonio Ind. Sch. Dist., 1990—2000; ret., 2000. With pub. rels. dept. San Antonio City Parks and Recreation Dept., 1987-89; masseuse, Reiki and water aerobics instr.

Retirement Ctr. at Our Lady of the Lake Convent, San Antonio, 2000—. Instr. ARC, San Antonio, 1952. Mem. AAHPER and Dance, Tex. Assn. Health, Phys. Edn., Recreation and Dance. Avocations: golf, swimming, sailing, bowling, travel. Home: 2574 W Patagonia Way Anthem AZ 85086

BENNETT, GARY LEE, physicist, consultant; b. Twin Falls, Idaho, Jan. 17, 1940; s. Joseph Albert and Adelaide Phillipa (Leonard) B.; m. Cleo Sue Guetschow McMurtrie, Sept. 14, 1961. AA, Boise State U., 1960; BS, U. Idaho, 1962, M of Nuclear Sci., 1966; PhD, Wash. State U., 1970. Physicist, engr. Idaho Nat. Lab., Idaho Falls, 1962-66; mgr. project Lewis Rsch. Ctr., Cleve., 1970-71; mgr. safety U.S. Atomic Energy Commn., Germantown, Md., 1971-74; br. chief U.S. Nuclear Regulatory Commn., Silver Spring, Md., 1974-79; dir. nuclear ops. U.S. Dept. Energy, Germantown, 1980-85, dep. office dir., 1985-88; program mgr. advanced technology NASA, Washington, 1988-91, deputy div. dir., 1992-94, aerospace cons., 1994—. Author: The Star Sailors, 1980, 2d edit., 2005; contbr. articles and papers to profl. jours. Served as staff sgt. ANG, 1957-63. Recipient numerous profl. and govt. awards including Dist. Alumnus award Boise State U., 1990, Silver & Gold award U. Idaho Alumni Assn., 1994, Schreiber-Spence Space Achievement award, 1996, Friend of Darwin award Nat. Ctr. Sci. Edn., 2000. Fellow AIAA (Aerospace Power Systems award, 1995), Brit. Interplanetary Soc., Am. Phys. Soc.; mem. AAAS, Fedn. Am. Scientists, Am. Astronaut. Soc., Am. Assn. Physics Tchrs., Planetary Soc., Com. Sci. Investigation Claims Paranormal, Sci. Fictions Writers Am., Nat. Space Soc., Ams. United Separation Ch. and State (mem. nat. adv. bd.), Sigma Xi, Sigma Pi Sigma. Home and Office: 5000 Butte Rd Emmett ID 83617-9500

BENNETT, GENEVIEVE, artist; b. Chgo., Feb. 11, 1927; d. Joseph and Mary Sieczka; m. William A. Bennett, Jan. 31, 1953; children: William George, J. Daniel, Gordon Dean. BA, Calif. State U., Fullerton, 1974; MA, Calif. State U., Long Beach, 1978. Artist, Anaheim, Calif. Tchr. art Ebell Club Anaheim, 1985-97, Whittier and Anaheim, Calif.; lectr. N.Am. temple mound builders. One-woman shows include Calif. Poly. U., Pomona, 1995, Orange County Fair, Calif., 1995, Anaheim Mus., 1997, exhibitions include Hotel-Restaurant La Musardiere, Giverny, France, 2002, Anaheim Arts Coun. Annual Souree, 2004 (Artist Honoree). Recipient Grumbacher Gold medal, 1999, Celebrating Remarkable Women Among Us award Orange County chpt. Nat. Assn. Women Bus. Owners, 1999, Cert. Spl. Congl. Recognition, Loretta Sanchez, 1999, Beyond the Call award Anaheim (Calif.) Arts Coun. and Arts in Pub. Places, 2002. Mem. Am. Internat. Culture and Art Assn., Nat. League Am. Pen Women (state v.p. 1997-98, Am. Internat. Culture and Art Assn., Orange County br. pres. 1997-98, recipient State Women of Achievement award, 1998), Calif. State U. Art Alliance, So. Calif. Women's Caucus for Art, Orange County Fine Arts, Phi Delta Gamma (Phi chpt.). Avocations: archaeology, piano, music, travel, art meetings. Home: 2026 W Judith Ln Anaheim CA 92804-6511

BENNETT, GEORGE FREDERICK, retired investment company executive; b. Quincy, Mass., Aug. 16, 1911; s. Wallace Cherrington and Lois E. (Williams) B.; m. Helen F. Brigham, Oct. 25, 1935; children— Peter C., George Frederick, Robert B. AB cum laude, Harvard, 1933. With First Boston Corp., Boston, 1934-37, Newton, Abbe & Co., Boston, 1937-43; with State Street Research & Mgmt. Co., Boston, 1943—, partner, 1946—. Chmn. State St. Exchange Fund, Boston; pres. State St. Investment Corp., Boston, Fed. St. Fund, Inc., Boston; dir. Campbell Taggert, Inc., Dallas, Middle South Utilities, Inc., N.Y.C., N.E. Electric System, Hewlett Packard Co., Palo Alto, Calif., Fla. Power & Light Co., Miami, Ford Motor Co., Detroit, John Hancock Mut. Life Ins. Co., Boston, Hanna Mining Co., Cleve. Treas. Harvard U., Harvard-Yenching Inst.; trustee Wheaton (Ill.) Coll., Rockefeller U., Gordon Conwell Theol. Sem., Com. Econ. Devel., Washington. Mem. Pi Eta. Clubs: Harvard (Boston and N.Y.C.); Union (Boston); Links (N.Y.C.). Home: 712 Main St Hingham MA 02043-3327 Office: State Street Rsch & Mgmt Co One Financial Ctr Boston MA 02111

BENNETT, G(EORGE) KEMBLE, engineering educator; b. Jacksonville, Fla., Apr. 2, 1940; s. George K. and Murla E. (Weeks) B.; m. Jill Alison McMaster, June 5, 1982; children: Russell William, Paige E., Alison Kemly; BS in math., Fla. State U., 1962; MS in engring. math., San Jose State U., 1968; PhD in indsl. engring., Tex. Tech U., 1970. Profl. engr., Fla., Tex. Assoc. engr. Martin Co., Orlando, Fla., 1962-63; engr. Lockheed Research Labs., Palo Alto, Calif., 1963-64, sr. engr., 1964-66; asst. dir. Computer Ctr., Tex. Tech U., Lubbock, 1966-69; vis. scientist NASA Manned Spacecraft Lab., Houston, 1969-70; asst. prof. indsl. engring. Va. Poly. Inst., Blacksburg, 1970-73; prof., chmn. indsl. and mgmt. systems engring. U. South Fla., Tampa, 1973-86; pres., CEO G. Kemble Bennett & Associates, 1975-79; staff engr. Honeywell Avionics Divsn., 1984-86; prof., head indsl. engring. Tex. A&M U., College Station, 1986—91, assoc. dean engring., 1991-2002, dir. Tex. Engring. Extension Svc., 1992-2002, assoc. vice chancellor engring, 1992-2002, dir. Tex. Engring. Expt. Sta., 2002-, vice chancellor engring., 2002-, dean Dwight Look Coll. Engring., 2002-. Assoc. editor IIE Transactions; mng. editor Logistics Spectrum; contbr. articles to nat. and internat. jours. Fellow Inst. Indsl. Engineers. (Fla. West Coast Engr. of Year 1979, 82, Albert G. Hozlman Disting. Educator Award, 1996), Soc. Logistics Engineers. (bd. referees The Annals; Eccles Medal, 1997); Mem. Am. Soc. Engring. Edn., The Inst. Mgmt. Scis., Tau Beta Pi, Phi Kappa Phi. Republican. Methodist. Office: Dwight Look Coll Engring Texas A&M U 3126 TAMU College Station TX 77845-3126

BENNETT, GRACE, publishing executive; Adminstrv. mgr. Detroit Free Press. Office: Detroit Free Press 600 W Fort St Detroit MI 48226-2706

BENNETT, HAROLD EARL, physicist, optics researcher; b. Missoula, Mont., Feb. 25, 1929; s. Edward Earl and Linda Queen (McCoy) B.; m. Jean Louise McPherson, Aug. 17, 1952 (div. Nov. 1984); m. Dorothy Jean Searles, Nov. 17, 1984; children: Jeanie Nybo, Dorothy Anne Picking BA, U. Mont., 1951; MS, Pa. State U., 1953, PhD, 1955. Instrument-rated pilot. Grad. asst. Pa. State U., State College, 1951—55; physicist Wright Air Devel. Ctr., Dayton, Ohio, 1955—56, Naval Air Warfare Ctr., China Lake, Calif., 1956—62; rsch. physicist Naval Air Warfare Ctr. (name Naval Weapons Ctr. 1964-93), China Lake, 1962—95; ret. Naval Air Warfare Ctr., China Lake, 1995; assoc. head rsch. dept. physics divsn. Naval Air Warfare Ctr. (name Naval Weapons Ctr. 1964-93), China Lake, 1972—91; pres. Bennett Optical Rsch. Inc., Ridgecrest, 1995—. Co-chmn. Laser Induced Damage in Optical Materials Conf., Boulder, Colo., 1979-96 Adv. editor Optics Communications, 1969-86; contbr. over 100 articles on optics to profl. jours., chpts. to books. Pres. Indian Wells Valley Cmty. Concert Assn., Ridgecrest, 1974-75; sr. fellow Naval Weapons Ctr., 1990; former mem. Calif. Rep. State Ctrl. Com Recipient LTE Thompson award Naval Weapons Ctr., 1974, Tech. Dir.'s award, 1983; Capt. Robert Dexter Conrad Rsch. award Dept. Navy, 1979, Disting. Alumnus award U. Mont., 1991, Dep. Comdr.'s award for R&D, 1995, Tech. Leadership award Navy High Energy Laser Project, 1995, Navy Meritorius Civilian Svc. award, 1995, cert. of recognition for creative devel. of tech. innovation NASA, 2004 Fellow Optical Soc. Am. (assoc. editor Jour. 1968-79, bd. dirs. 1972-75), Internat. Soc. for Optical Engring. (bd. dirs. 1985-87, v.p. 1987, pres. 1988, Tech. Achievement award 1983, organizer and chair Laser Power Beaming II Conf. 1995, chair Free Electron Laser Challenges Conf. 1997, chair Free Electron Laser Challenges II 1999), Maturango Mus. (life) Republican. Achievements include development of polishing techniques for reducing scattered light from astronomical mirrors, laser power beaming to space and fabrication of large light weight, low expansion low scatter adaptive optic mirrors; 14 patents on optical instruments. Home: 916 N Randall St Ridgecrest CA 93555-3007 Office: 201 N Sanders St Ridgecrest CA 93555-3867 Home Phone: 760-446-6471; Office Phone: 760-384-1177. E-mail: bennett@hbbor.com.

BENNETT, JACK FRANKLIN, oil industry executive; b. Macon, Ga., Jan. 17, 1924; s. Andrew Jackson and Mary Eloise (Franklin) B.; m. Shirley Elizabeth Goodwin, Sept. 17, 1949; children: Jackson Goodwin, Philip Davies, Hugh Franklin, Elizabeth Fraser. BA, Yale U., 1944; MA, Harvard U., 1949, PhD, 1951. Negotiator Joint U.S.-U.K. Export Import Agy., Berlin, 1946—47; tchg. fellow fin. Harvard U., 1949—51; spl. asst. to adminstr. Tech. Assistance Program, U.S. Dept. State, Washington, 1951—52; economist U.S. Mut. Security Agy., Washington, 1952—53; sr. economist Presdl. Commn. on Fgn. Econ. Policy, 1954; sr. fgn. exch. analyst Exxon Corp., NYC, 1955—58, dep. European fin. rep. London, 1958—60; treas. Esso. Petroleum Co., Ltd., London, 1960—61; asst. treas. Exxon Corp., NYC, 1961—65, mgr. gen. econs. dept., 1965—66, mgr. coordination and planning dept., 1966—67; gen. mgr. supply dept. Exxon Co., U.S.A., Houston, 1967—69; v.p., dir. Exxon Internat., NYC, 1969—71; sr. v.p. Exxon Corp., NYC, 1975—89, also bd. dirs., ret., 1989. Dep. undersec. for monetary affairs U.S. Dept. Treasury, Washington, 1971-74, undersec. for monetary affairs, 1974-75. Contbr. articles to profl. jours. Trustee Com. Econ. Devel. With USNR, 1943-46. Mem. Stanwich Club (Greenwich, Conn.), York (Maine) Club, Blind Brook Club, John's Island Club (Fla.). Republican. Office: 21 Marker Way Vero Beach FL 32963 E-mail: jbnt@aol.com.

BENNETT, JAMES THOMAS, economics professor; b. Memphis, Oct. 19, 1942; m. Sara Ellen Dorman, Sept. 2, 1967. BS in Ops. Research magna cum laude, Case Inst. Tech., 1964, MS in Mgmt. Sci., 1966; PhD in Econs., Case Western Res. U., 1970; student Grad. Sch. Bus., Columbia U., 1964-65. Teaching fellow Case Inst. Tech., 1968-69; instr. bus. Cleve. State U., 1967-68; asst. prof. econs. George Washington U., Washington, 1970-75; assoc. prof. econs. George Mason U., Fairfax, Va., 1975-77, Eminent Scholar and William P. Snavely prof. polit. economy and pub. policy, 1975—. Dir. John M. Olin Inst. for Employment Practice and Policy; chmn. faculty senate George Mason U., 2002-05. Co-author: The Political Economy of Federal Government Growth: 1958-1978, 1980, Better Government at Half the Price, 1981, Deregulating Labor Relations, 1981, Underground Government: The Off-Budget Public Sector, 1983, Destroying Democracy: How Government Funds Partisan Politics, 1985, Unfair Competition: The Profits of Nonprofits, 1989, Patterns of Corporate Philanthropy: Ideas, Advocacy and the Corporation, 1989, Health Research Charities: Image and Reality, 1990, Health Research Charities II: The Politics of Fear, 1991, Official Lies: How Washington Misleads Us, 1992, Unhealthy Charities: Hazardous to Your Health and Wealth, 1994, Cancer Scam: The Diversion of Federal Cancer Funds to Politics, 1998, The Food and Drink Police: America's Nannies, Busybodies and Petty Tyrants, 1999, From Pathology to Politics: Public Health in America, 2000, Public Health Profiteering, 2001, The Future of Private Sector Unionism in the United States, 2002, Tax-Funded Politics, 2004, Information Technology and the World of Work, 2004, Homeland Security Scams, 2006, The Politics of American Feminism: Gender Conflict in Contemporary Society, 2007, What Do Unions Do? A Twenty-Year Perspective, 2007; editor Jour. Labor Rsch., 1980—2007; contbr. chapters to books, articles to profl. jours. Trustee Horowitz Found. Social Policy, 2006—. Ford Found. scholar, 1960-64; Continental Grain Corp. fellow; McKinsey scholar; Case Inst. fellow, 1965-67; Fed. Res. Bank Cleve. fellow, 1969-70 Mem. Am. Econ. Assn., So. Econ. Assn., Pub. Choice Soc., Western Econ. Assn., Am. Statis. Assn., Phila. Soc., Mont Pelerin Soc., Phi Beta Kappa, Sigma Xi, Tau Beta Pi, Alpha Lambda Delta, Phi Theta Kappa. Office: George Mason U Dept Econs Fairfax VA 22030 Business E-Mail: jbennett@gmu.edu.

BENNETT, JAY D., lawyer; children: Summer, Lillian, Sky. BA with honors, U. N.C., 1974; JD cum laude, Harvard U., 1977. Bar: U.S. Dist. Ct. (no. and mid. dist.) Ga., U.S. Ct. Appeals (4th, 5th, 9th and 11th cirs.), U.S. Supreme Ct. Assoc. Alston & Bird, Atlanta, 1977-83, ptnr., 1983—. Morehead scholar Morehead Found. 1970-74. Mem. State Bar Ga., Atlanta Bar Assn., Lawyers Club Atlanta, Trial Attys. Am., Phi Beta Kappa. Avocations: flying, skydiving, motorcycling, fishing. Office: Alston & Bird LLP One Atlantic Ctr 1201 W Peachtree St Atlanta GA 30309-3424 Office Phone: 404-881-7643. E-mail: jbennett@alston.com.

BENNETT, JEAN LOUISE MCPHERSON, physicist, research scientist; b. Kensington, Md., May 9, 1930; d. Archibald Turner and Margaret Fitch (Willcox) McPherson; m. Harold Earl Bennett, Aug. 17, 1952 (div. Nov. 1984). BA summa cum laude, Mt. Holyoke Coll., 1951, DSc (hon.), 1992; MS, Pa. State U., 1953, PhD in Physics, 1955. Physicist Wright Air Devel. Ctr., Dayton, Ohio, 1955—56, Naval Ordnance Test Sta. (now Naval Air Warfare Ctr. Weapons Divsn.), China Lake, Calif., 1956—85; sr. rsch. scientist Naval Air Warfare Ctr. Weapons Divsn., China Lake, 1987—93, 1995; vis. prof. U. Ala., Huntsville, 1986—87, Mt. Holyoke Coll., South Hadley, Mass., 1994—95; ret., 1996. Mem. NRC Evaluation Panel Nat. Bur. Stds., Ctr. for Radiation Rsch., 1979-85, Nat. Inst. Stds. and Tech. Mfg. Engring. Lab., 1988-94, U.S. Nat. Com. for Internat. Commn. for Optics, 1984-85, 88-95; vis. scientist Inst. Optical Rsch., Royal Inst. Tech., Stockholm, Mar.-Sept., 1988, 98, 99, 2000, 01. Author: (with Lars Mattsson) Introduction to Surface Roughness and Scattering, 1989, rev., 1999; author: Surface Finish and Its Measurement, 1992; contbr. sci. articles to profl. jours.; patentee in field. Recipient Tech. Achievement award Soc. Photo-Optical Instrumentation Engrs., 1983, L.T.E. Thompson award Naval Weapons Ctr., 1988, Women in Sci. and Engring. Lifetime Achievement award, 1993, Outstanding Sci. Alumni award Pa. State U., 1999; named sr. fellow Naval Weapons Ctr., 1989, Disting. Fellow, 1994. Fellow Optical Soc. Am. (v.p. 1984, pres.-elect 1985, pres. 1986, past pres. 1987, chmn. book publ. com. 1991-94, David Richardson medal 1990); mem. Am. Inst. Physics (subcom. on books 1990-94), Phi Beta Kappa, Sigma Xi, Sigma Delta Epsilon, Iota Sigma Pi, Pi Mu Epsilon, Sigma Pi Sigma. Achievements include being the first woman to receive PhD in Physics at Pa. State U., 1955; first woman pres. Optical Soc. of Am. Office: Code 4T41A0D Michelson Lab Naval Air Warfare Ctr Stop 6302 1900N Knox Rd Ridgecrest CA 93555 Home Phone: 760-446-4339. E-mail: jbennett@ridgenet.net.

BENNETT, JOAN WENNSTROM, biology educator; b. Bklyn., Sept. 15, 1942; d. John Anton and Kerttu L. (Johnson) Wennstrom; m. David L. Peterson; 3 children. BS, Upsala Coll., 1963; MS, U. Chgo., 1964, PhD, 1967; Litt.D (hon.), Upsala Coll., 1990. NSF postdoctoral rsch. assoc. U. Chgo., 1967-68; NRC rsch. assoc. So. Reg. Rsch. Labs., New Orleans, 1968-70; NSF postdoctoral rsch. assoc. Tulane U., New Orleans, 1970-71, asst. prof. biology, 1971-76, assoc. prof. biology, 1976-81, prof. biology, 1981-89, prof. cell and molecular biology, 1991—2006; prof. II, plant biology and pathology, assoc. v.p. Rutgers U., New Brunswick, NJ, 2006—. Vis. scientist dept. plant molecular biology Leiden (The Netherlands) U., 1991-92; NRC postdoctoral fellow So. Regional Rsch. Lab., 1968-70, collaborator, 1982—. Editor: (with K.I. Abroms) Genetics and Exceptional Children, 1981, (with A. Giegler) Differentiation and Secondary Metabolism in Fungi, 1983, (with L. Lasure) Gene Manipulations in Fungi, 1985, More Gene Manipulations in Fungi, 1991; editl. bd. Mycol. Rsch., 1991-94, Applied and Environ. Microbiology, 1978-85, Jour. Indsl. Microbiology, 1985-89, Mycopathologia, 1984-94, Applied Microbiology and Biotechnology, 1985-94, Ann. Rev. Microbiology, 1996-2001, editor-in-chief Mycologia, 2000-04; contbr. articles to profl. jours. Bd. dirs. Newcomb Found., 1988-89. Recipient Mortar Board award of excellence in Teaching, 1974-75, others; named Honors Prof. of Yr., Tulane U., 1991. Fellow Soc. for Indsl. Microbiology (bd. dirs. 1986-89, pres. 2001-02); mem. AAAS, NAS, Am. Soc. Microbiology (pres. 1990-91, chair biology divsn. 2006-), Brit. Mycol. Soc. (v.p. 1988-89), La. Acad. Sci., Mycol. Soc. Am., Soc. for Gen. Microbiology, Czech Microbiology Soc. (hon.), Torrey Bot. Club, Sigma Xi (pres. Tulane chpt. 1986-89). Avocations: photography, jogging. Office: Dept Plant Biology & Pathology Cook Coll Rutgers U 59 Dudley Rd New Brunswick NJ 08901 Office Phone: 504-865-5546. E-mail: jbennett@tulane.edu.

BENNETT, JOE CLAUDE, pharmaceutical executive; b. Birmingham, Ala., Dec. 12, 1933; s. Claude and Clara Lucille (Clark) B.; m. Nancy Miller, June 17, 1958; children: Katherine Diane, Miller, Clark Barton. AB, Samford U., 1954; MD, Harvard U., 1958; DSc (hon.), U. Ala., 1992. Diplomate Am. Bd. Internal Medicine (governing bd. 1987—, cert. exam. com. for 1989, ind. com. R & D, 1988—), Am. Bd. Rheumatology, Nat. Bd. Med. Examiners. Intern Univ. Ala. Hosp., Birmingham, 1958-59, resident, 1959-60; rsch. assoc. molecuar biology NIH, Bethesda, Md., 1962-64; sr. rsch. fellow div. biology Calif. Inst. Tech., Pasadena, Calif., 1964-65; asst. prof. dept. medicine, assoc. prof. dept. microbiology, asst. dir. div. clin. immunology and rheumatology U. Ala. Med. Sch., Birmingham, 1965-70, dir. div. clin. immunology and rheumatology, 1970-83, prof., chmn. dept. microbiology, 1970-82, prof., chmn. dept. medicine, 1982-92, Spencer Prof. Med. Sci., 1992—, dir. multipurpose arthritis center, 1977-84, disting. faculty lectr., 1979; pres. U. Ala., Birmingham, 1993-96; pres., COO BioCryst Pharms., Birmingham, 1996—. Physician in chief U. Ala. Hosp.; vis. prof. U. Mo.-Columbia Sch. Medicine, 1987, U. Leiden, The Netherlands, 1988, Baylor U. Coll. Medicine, Houston, 1989, others; invited lectr. various univs., confs. including IX Pan-Am. Congress Rheumatology, Buenos Aires, 1986, U. Mo.-Columbia Sch. Medicine, 1987, Cornell Med. Sch., 1986, U. Colo., 1986; mem. sci. adv. bd. Merck Sharp & Dohme Rsch. Labs., 1987-89, Gorgas Meml. Inst. Tropical and Preventive Medicine, 1985—, others; mem. bd. health sci. policies, NIH, NAS, 1988—. Editor: Vistas in Connective Tissue Diseases, 1968; co-editor: Rheumatology and Immunology, 2d edit., 1986, Cecil Textbook of Medicine, 1988—, Cecil Essentials of Medicine; editor-in-chief Am. Jour. Medicine, 1986-97, Arthritis and Rheumatism, 1975-80; mem. editorial bd. Protein and Peptide Revs., 1980—, Current Opinion in Rheumatology, 1988—, Arthritis and Rheumatism, 1969-75; contbr. numerous articles, papers, book revs., abstracts to profl. publs. Recipient Ala. Acad. Honor award, 1987, Seale Harris award So. Med. Assn., 1987; John and Mary R. Markle Found. scholar in acad. medicine, 1965-70; recipient Rsch. Career Devel. award NIH, 1965-75; fellow Arthritis and Rheumatism Found., Harvard Med. Sch., Mass. Gen. Hosp., 1960-62 Fellow AAAS (sec. N. Med. scis. nominating com. 1989—); mem. Am. Bd. Internal Medicine (exec. com. 1992), Federated Coun. of Internatl Medicine, Assn. of Am. Med. Colls. (adv. panel on biomed. rsch. 1991-92), Inst. Medicine NAS, ACP (master 1990), Am. Assn. Immunologists, Am. Fedn. Clin. Rsch., Am. Coll. Rheumatology (pres. 1981-82, bd. dirs. planning group 1986-87), Am. Soc. Biol. Chemists, Am. Soc. Clin. Investigation, Am. Soc. Microbiology, more. Office: BioCryst Pharms 2190 Parkway Lake Dr Birmingham AL 35244-1879 Home: 2920 Redmont Park Cir Apt 400 Birmingham AL 35205-2162

BENNETT, JOEL HERBERT, construction executive; b. Chgo., Nov. 7, 1936; m. Seraphima H. Lamb, 1999; children: Evan Alan, Julie Andrea. BSChemE, U. So. Calif., LA, 1958, MSChemE, 1962; MBA in Ops. Rsch., UCLA, 1960. Chem. process engr. C. F. Braun & Co., Alhambra, Calif., 1960-65, with bus. devel., 1965-73; v.p. Arthur G. McKee & Co., Cleve., 1973-78, Parsons Engring. Sci., Inc., Pasadena, Calif., 1978-81; sr. v.p. Santa Fe Braun Inc., Alhambra, 1981-89; exec. v.p. The Parsons Corp., Pasadena, 1989-92, 96—, 1995-96; pres. Parsons Environ. Svcs. Inc., Pasadena, 1992-96, Harland Bartholomew & Assocs., 1992-95; sr. v.p. Parsons Brinckerhoff, Inc., NYC, 1997—2006; chmn., pres. PB Power Inc., NYC, 1998—2004; bd. dirs. Parsons Brinckerhoff Internat., Inc., 1998—2003, chmn., pres., 2001—05. Bd. dirs. Inst. to Redesign Learning; co-chair environ. mgmt. adv. bd. U.S. Dept. Energy, 1994-2001. Author: (with others) Project Management, 1989. Dir. Calif. State U. L.A. Found.; mem. bd. advisors The Asian Am. Architects/Engrs. Assn. Mem. Am. Inst. Chem. Engrs., Jonathan Club (L.A.). Avocations: skiing, jogging, tennis, music. Home: 128 Outrigger Mall Marina Del Rey CA 90292-5793 Home Phone: 310-577-9321. Personal E-mail: joelhbennett@msn.com.

BENNETT, JOHN CHARLES, former engineering and construction executive; b. Dover, NJ, Jan. 23, 1925; s. John and Therese Adele (Weiss) B.; m. Betty Evelyn Koenig, June 17, 1950; children: John Lance, Stephen Gary. BS in Engring., Swarthmore Coll., 1945. Registered profl. engr., 48 states, D.C., P.R., Venezuela, Greece; registered profl. planner, N.J.; registered land surveyor, La. Field engr., supt., dist. mgr., v.p., engring. ptnr., dir. The Austin Co., NYC, Cleve., Canada, 1946—79, v.p. spl. projects in Greece, Mid. East and North Africa, 1975-79; pres., CEO, Structors, Inc., Chgo., 1979-82, Advanced Tech. Sys., Fairlawn, NJ, 1982-85; chmn. bd. Scandia, Inc., Atlanta, 1979-82; owner, operator Abacus Bennett Farm, Blairstown, NJ, 1985—. Asst. sec. HUD, Washington, 1973. Pres., bd. dirs. N.J. Easter Seal Soc., Morris Plains, 1968-74, Morris County Rehab. Ctr., Morris Plains, 1971-74; bd. dirs. Morris Ctr. YMCA, Morristown, N.J., 1978-92. Lt (j.g.) USN, 1943-46. Mem. Nat. Bd. Engring. Examiners, Newcomen Soc., Loyal Order Ky. Cols., Intrepids Club, Tau Beta Pi. Home and Office: 12 Moraine Rd Morris Plains NJ 07950-2711

BENNETT, JOHN JOSEPH, electronics executive; b. Camden, NJ, Sept. 4, 1923; s. John Henry and Margaret Katherine (Bloxsum) B.; m. Dolores Florence Griffiths, June 17, 1943; children: Jill, T. Robert, T. Richard. Student, Centenary Coll., 1951-55; MBA, Mich. State U., 1961; DBA, George Washington U., 1974. Commd. 2d lt. USAAF, 1943; advanced through grades to col. USAF, officer various operational and mgmt. jobs, 1942-60; asst. comptroller Hdqrs. AFSC, Washington, 1961-66; asst. to Asst. Sec. Air Force and dep. chief staff, Personnel Hdqrs. USAF, Washington, 1967-69; ret. USAF, 1969; exec. dir. Mauchley Edn. Inst., Washington, 1969-70; pres. Sycom, Inc., Washington, 1969-70; mgr. aerospace def. practice Peat, Marwick, Mitchell & Co., Washington, 1970-74; prin. dep. asst. U.S. Sec. of Def., Washington, 1975-76, Asst. Sec. of Navy, Washington, 1976-77; dir., exec. office pres. Fed. Acquisition Inst., Washington, 1977-79; chief exec. officer ANADAC, Inc., Washington, 1979-88, chmn. bd., 1988-92, chmn. emeritus, 1992-96. Lectr. George Washington U., 1979—89; chmn. bd. dirs. TBG Reliance Corp., 1997—. Author: The Next Generation Management Systems for Systems Management, 1967, Department of Defense Systems Acquisition Management, 1974, Program Management Principles and Practices, 1994; author: (with others) Systems Concepts for Human Resources Management, 1968. Decorated Legion of Merit, D.F.C., Air medal with 4 oak leaf clusters; recipient Disting. Civilian Svc. award, 1976, Disting. Pub. Svc. award, 1977. Methodist. Home: 343 Bayshore Dr Palm Harbor FL 34683-5482 Office: TBG Reliance PO Box 69 Ozona FL 34660 Personal E-mail: jaci2ben@gmail.com.

BENNETT, KENNETH ALAN, retired biological anthropologist; b. Butler, Okla., Oct. 3, 1935; s. Kenneth Francis and Lillian Imogene (McDaniel) B.; m. Helen Lucille Maze, Sept. 6, 1959; children: Letitia Arlene, Cheri Lynn. AS, Odessa Coll., 1956; BA, U. Tex., 1961; MA, U. Ariz., 1966, PhD, 1967. Asst. prof. anthropology U. Oreg., 1967-70; assoc. prof. U. Wis., Madison, 1970-75, prof., 1975-97, ret., 1997. Forensic anthropology cons. to Wis. law enforcement agys. and Wis. state crime lab., 1970—98. Author: The Indians of Point of Pines, Arizona, 1973, Fundamentals of Biological Anthropology, 1979, Skeletal Remains from Mesa Verde National Park, 1975, A Field Guide for Human Skeletal Identification, 1987, 2nd edit., 1993; editor Yearbook of Phys. Anthropology, 1976-81; contbg. editor Social Biology, 1981-87; mem. editl. com. Ann. Revs. in Anthropology, 1987-91; editor, reviewer Human Biology, 1981-87; contbr. articles to profl. jours. Mem. Wis. Burial Sites Preservation Bd., 1988. With U.S. Army, 1956-58. NIH fellow, 1964-67 Mem. Am. Assn. Phys. Anthropologists, Am. Soc. Naturalists, Human Biology Council, Soc. for Study Evolution, Am. Acad. Forensic Scis., Soc. for Study Human Biology, Soc. Systematic Zoology, Am. Assn. Physical Anthropologists (exec. com. 1976-81), Sigma Xi. Home: 5718 Hammersley Rd Madison WI 53711-3450 Personal E-mail: kabennet@wisc.edu.

BENNETT, LAWRENCE HERMAN, physicist; b. Bklyn., Oct. 17, 1930; s. Harold and Irene (Kamel) B.; m. Devora Mae Spintman, Mar. 22, 1953; children: Claire Ann Bennett Freeland, Charles Leonard, Craig David. BA cum laude, Bklyn. Coll., 1951; MS, U. Md., 1955; PhD, Rutgers U., 1958. Physicist Naval Ordnance Lab., White Oak, Md., 1950-58, Nat. Bur. Stds., Gaithersburg, Md., 1958-96. Adj. prof. physics U. Md., College Park, 1959-94, rsch. prof. Inst. for Magnetics Rsch. The George Washington U., Washington, 1995—. Author: (with G.C. Carter and D.H. Kahan) Metallic Shifts in NMR, 1977; editor: Theory of Alloy Phase Formation, 1980, Computer Modeling of Alloy Phase Diagrams, 1986, High Temperature Superconductors: Magnetic Interactions, 1989, Magnetic Multilayers, 1994; contbr. articles to profl. jours. Recipient Gold medal Dept. Commerce, 1971. Fellow Am. Phys. Soc. (chair magnetism group 1999-2000), Am. Soc. for Metals (Burgess Meml. award 1964); mem. IEEE Magnetics Soc., AIME Metall. Soc., Phi Beta Kappa, Sigma Xi (pres. bur. of stds. 1987). Achievements include discovery of Bose-Einstein condensation of magnons in nanostructures; patent in magnetic refrigeration; First in vivo nuclear magnetic resonance of cancer; equipment collected by the Smithsonian. Home: 6524 E Halbert Rd Bethesda MD 20817-5414 Office: George Washington U Inst Magnetic Rsch Ashburn VA 20147 Business E-Mail: lbennett@gwu.edu.

BENNETT, LERONE, JR., retired magazine editor, author; b. Clarksdale, Miss., Oct. 17, 1928; s. Lerone and Alma (Reed) Bennett; m. Gloria Sylvester, July 21, 1956; children: Alma Joy, Constance, Courtney; 1 child, Lerone III. BA, Morehouse Coll., 1949, LittD (hon.), 1966; HHD (hon.), Wilberforce U., 1977; DLitt (hon.), Marquette U., 1979, Voorhees Coll., 1981, Morgan State U., 1981; LHD (hon.), U. Ill., 1980, Lincoln Coll., 1980, Dillard U., 1980; LittD (hon.), Howard U., 1982; LHD (hon.), Boston U., 1987; DLitt (hon.), Tuskegee U., 1989. Reporter Atlanta Daily World, 1949—51, city editor, 1952—53; assoc. editor Ebony mag., Chgo., 1953—58, sr. editor, 1958—87, exec. editor, 1987—2003, exec. editor emeritus, 2003—. Vis. prof. hist. Nothwestern U., 1968—69. Author: Before the Mayflower: A History of Black America, 1619-1964, 1962, 3d edit., 1982, The Negro Mood, 1964, What Manner of Man, A Biography of Martin Luther King, Jr., 1964, Confrontation: Black and White, 1965, Black Power U.S.A., 1968, Pioneers in Protest, 1968, The Challenge of Blackness, 1972, The Shaping of Black America, 1975, Wade in the Water, 1979, Forced Into Glory: Abraham Lincoln's White Dream, 2000; contbg. author: New Negro Poets: USA, 1964, American Negro Short Stories, 1966. Trustee Columbia Coll. Named to The Ebony Power 150, Ebony mag., 2007; recipient Patron Saints award, Soc. Midland Authors, 1965, Book of the Yr. award, Capital Press Club, 1963, AAAL Acad./Inst. lit. award, 1978. Mem.: Sigma Delta Chi, Kappa Alpha Psi, Phi Beta Kappa.*

BENNETT, MARC LOGAN, otolaryngologist; b. Morristown, NJ, July 19, 1974; s. Gregory and Paula Bennett; m. Joy Poneros, Nov. 13, 1999; children: Nicholas Angelo, Arthur Jacob. MD, Johns Hopkins U., Balt., 2000. Cert. American Board Otolaryngology, 2006. Asst. prof. Vanderbilt U., Nashville, 2005—. Recipient Travel Award, 2003. Mem.: Nashville Otolaryngology Soc. Office: 300 20th Ave N Nashville TN 37203 Home Phone: 615-309-8156; Office Phone: 615-284-4444. Business E-Mail: marc.bennett@vanderbilt.edu.

BENNETT, MARGARET AIROLA, lawyer; b. San Francisco; AB cum laude, U. Calif., Berkeley, 1972; JD, U. San Francisco and Loyola U., 1976. Bar: Ill.1976, US Dist. Ct. (no. dist.) Ill. 1977, US Ct. Appeals (7th cir.) 1983. Intern Cook County State's Atty.'s Office, Chgo., 1975-76; assoc. Dunlap, Thompson & Boyd, Ltd., Libertyville, Ill., 1977-79; ptnr. Bennett & Bennett, Ltd., Oak Brook, Ill., 1980-96; pvt. practice The Law Offices of Margaret A. Bennett, Oak Brook, Ill., 1997. Atty. rep. McDonald's Corp., Oak Brook, 1982—, County of DuPage, Wheaton, Ill., 1990-95. Counsel fo DuPage Ill. Fair and Exposition Authority, County of DuPage, 1991-95, co-chmn. next generation com.; devel. coun. Good Samaritan Hosp., 1988-92. Mem. DuPage County Bar Assn. (chmn. real estate law com. 1994-95, Cert. of Appreciation 1989, Bd. Dir. award 1998, chmn. profl. responsibility com. 1996-97, chmn. family law com. 1997-98), Ill. State Bar Assn. (assembly mem., 1996-2000, Cert. of Appreciation 1990, real estate sect. counsel 1996-2002, jud evaluation com. 1998—), Womens Bar Assn. DuPage County, Evang. Health Found. (bd. sponsors 1988-92). Republican. Episcopalian. Avocations: golf, reading, skiing, travel. Office: Ste 718 1200 Hanger Rd Oak Brook IL 60523-1908

BENNETT, MARK J., state attorney general; m. Patricia Tomi Ohara. BA summa cum laude in Polit. Sci., Union Coll., 1976; JD magna cum laude, Cornell U., 1979. Law clk. to Hon. Samuel P. King, Chief Judge US Dist. Ct. Hawaii; asst. US atty. Washington, 1980—82, Honolulu, 1982—90; litig. ptnr. McCorriston, Miller, Mukai & MacKinnon, LLP, Honolulu, 1991—2002; pro bono spl. dep. atty. gen., spl. asst. pros. atty. Hawaii State Ct.; atty. gen. State of Hawaii, Honolulu, 2003—. Instr. criminal and civil trial advocacy Atty. Gen.'s Adv. Inst., Washington; instr. U. Hawaii Sch. Law. Recipient Spl. Achievement award, US Atty. Gen., 1986. Mem.: Am. Coll. Trial Lawyers. Republican. Office: Office of Atty Gen 425 Queen St Honolulu HI 96813 Office Phone: 808-586-1500.

BENNETT, MATTHEW DAMON, entrepreneur, researcher; BS, Va. Tech, Blacksburg, 2000, MS, 2002, PhD, 2005. Grad. rsch. asst. Va. Tech, Blacksburg, 2000—05; pres. Discover Techs., Inc., Research Triangle Park, NC, 2005—. Aerospace Grad. Rsch. fellow, Va. Space Grant Consortium, 2003—05. Achievements include two patents pending related to electroactive polymers. Avocations: homebrewing, scuba diving. Office Phone: 919-767-0620.

BENNETT, MICHAEL L., agricultural products executive; Tech. & mgmt. positions with Terra Industries, Sioux City, Iowa, 1973—90, v.p. wholesale fertilizer, 1990—92, v.p. no. div. sales, 1992—94, sr. v.p. no. div. sales, 1994—95, sr. v.p., pres. dist. div., 1995—97, exec. v.p., COO, 1997—2001, pres., CEO, 2001—. Bd. dir. Alliant Energy; bd. mem. Fertilizer Inst.; past. chmn. Methanol Inst., Agribusiness Assn. Iowa. Office: Terra Industries Inc 600 4th St Sioux City IA 51101 Office Phone: 712-277-1340.*

BENNETT, MICHAEL VANDER LAAN, neuroscience educator; b. Madison, Wis., Jan. 7, 1931; s. Martin Toscan and Cornelia (Vanderlaan) B.; m. Ruth Berman, July 19, 1963 (div. 1993); children: Nicholas Toscan, Elena Paula; m. R. Suzanne Zukin Nov. 19, 1997. BS, Yale U., 1952; DPhil, Oxford U., Eng., 1957. Rsch. worker Coll. of Physicians and Surgeons Columbia U., NYC, 1957-58, rsch. assoc., 1958-59, asst. prof. neurology, 1959-61, assoc. prof. neurology, 1961-66; co-dir. neurobiology Marine Biol. Lab., Woods Hole, Mass., 1970-74; prof. anatomy Albert Einstein Coll. Medicine, Bronx, NY, 1967-74, prof. neurosci., 1974—, chmn. neurosci., 1982-96, Sylvia and Robert S. Olnick prof. of neurosci., 1986—2005; disting. prof. neurosci., 2005—. Editor rev. jours.; contbr. articles to profl. jours. Hon. Pepsi Cola scholar, 1948, Rhodes scholar, 1952; Grass Fellow, 1958. Fellow AAAS; mem. NAS, Am. Physiol. Soc., Am. Soc. Cell Biology, Biophys. Soc., Soc. Neurosci., N.Y. Road Runners Club, Phi Beta Kappa. Avocations: running, skiing, scuba, science. Office: Albert Einstein Coll of Medicine Dept Of Neurosci Bronx NY 10461 Office Phone: 718-430-2536. Business E-Mail: mbennett@aecom.yu.edu.

BENNETT, OLGA SALOWICH, civic worker, graphic arts researcher, consultant; b. Detroit, June 30, 1925; d. Nicholas Stefanovich and Maria Elarionovna (Mikuliak) Salowich; m. Robert William Bennett, Dec. 20, 1947 (dec. Aug. 21, 2003); 1 child, Susan Roberta. Student, U. Mich., 1943-45, Parsons Sch. Design, 1948, U. Md., Nagoya, Japan, 1959; BA, NYU, 1975. Graphic artist Silver & Co., NYC, 1948-50; editor, pub. Bull., organizer radio series LWV, Pitts., 1950-55; instr. Nanzan U., Nagoya, 1959; aide, cons. to U.S. hon. consul, Safi, Casablanca, Morocco, 1962-65; chmn. internat. affairs LWV, Montclair, N.J., 1966-73; conf. coord. UN Assn., Madison, N.J., 1974; weekly broadcaster LWV, San Juan, P.R., 1979-81; lectr. color theory Cunard, Ltd., London, Miami, Fla., 1985-88. Bd. dirs., docent Ctr. Fine Arts, Miami, 1990-92; docent Bass Mus. Art, Miami Beach, Fla., 1990-92, Vizcaya Mus. Art, Miami, 1983—; cons. on corp. overseas placement. Author artist brochures, ednl. pamphlets; translator Russian-Am. Conf., Miami, 1990. Mem. panel theater award com. New Theater, Miami, 1991; mem. Nat. Mus. of Women in the Arts; bd. dirs. Kings Creek South Condominium Assn., 1996-99. Mem. AAUW, LWV (life), UN Assn., NYU Alumni Assn., New Sch. Alumni Assn., Fgn. Policy Assn., Great Decisions Program (discussion leader), World Affairs Coun. Houston, League of Women Voters of Houston (life). Democrat. Russian Orthodox. Home: 3811 Audley St Apt 24107 Houston TX 77098-2913

BENNETT, P. TYSON, lawyer; b. Annapolis, Md., Nov. 21, 1947; B, Towson Coll.; JD, Univ. Balt., 1971. Bar: Md. 1972. Ptnr. Reese & Carney, Columbia, Md. Adj. faculty, sch. law, disabilities law Johns Hopkins Univ. Mem.: Edn. Law Assn. (bd. dir. 1996—98, pres. 2004—05), Md. Coun. Local Sch. Bd. Attys (past pres.). Office: Reese & Carney Ste 200 Hawthorne Exec Ctr 10715 Charter Dr Columbia MD 21044-2871 Office Phone: 410-740-4600. Office Fax: 410-730-7729. Business E-Mail: ptb@reese-carney.com.

BENNETT, PAUL B., stock exchange executive; BA in Econs., U. Chgo., 1972; PhD in Econs., Princeton U., 1979. Rsch. economist Fed. Reserve Bank of NY, 1978—79, sr. economist, 1980—81, 1983, mgr. domestic and internat. fin. rsch. and analysis, 1984, asst. v.p., 1986—89, v.p. fin. rsch., 1989—91, v.p. Fedwire Funds and Securities Transfer, 1991—93, sr. v.p. rsch. and statistics, 1993—2001, head capital rsch. divsn., 1993—2001; sr. v.p. and chief economist NY Stock Exch., 2001—. Author publ. numerous papers on fin., econ., and securities markets in both academic and practitioner journ. Mem.: Global Capital Markets Ctr., Duke U. Office: NY Stock Exch 17th Fl 11 Wall St New York NY 10005 Office Phone: 212-656-3257. E-mail: pbennett@nyse.com.

BENNETT, PETER BRIAN, medical researcher, educator; b. Portsmouth, Hampshire, Eng., June 12, 1931; s. Charles Risby and Doris Isobel (Peckham) B.; m. Margaret Camellia Rose, July 7, 1956; children: Caroline Susan, Christopher Charles BSc, U. London, 1951; PhD, U. Southampton, 1964, DSc, 1984; Dr. honoris causa, U. de la Mediterranean, France, 2001. Asst. head surg. sect. Royal Navy Physiol. Lab., Alverstoke, England, 1953-56, head inert gas narcosis sect., 1953-66; dep. dir., prin. sci. officer, head pressure physiology sect. Royal Naval Physiol. Lab., Alverstoke, 1968-72; head pressure physiology group Can. Def. and Civil Inst. for Environ. Rsch., Toronto, Ont., 1966-68; prof. biomed. engring. Duke U., Durham, NC, 1972-75, assoc. prof. physiology, 1975—80, prof. anesthesiology, 1972—, founder, pres. Nat. Divers Alert Network, 1980—2003, dir. rsch. dept. anesthesiology Med. Ctr., 2007; dep. dir. F.G. Hall Lab. Environ. Rsch., 1973-74; co-dir. F.G. Hall Lab. Environ. Research, 1974-77, dir., 1977-88; sr. dir. Hyperbaric Ctr., 1988—2007; exec. dir. Underseas and Hyperbaric Med. Soc., 2007—. Cons. in field Author: The Aetiology of Compressed Air Intoxication and Inert Gas Narcosis, 1966; author, editor: The Physiology and Medicine of Diving and Compressed Air Work, 1969, Russian edit., 1987, 4th edit., 1993; contbr. over 200 articles to profl. jours. With RAF, 1951-53. Recipient Letter of Commendation, Pres. Ronald Reagan, 1981, Sci. award Underwater Soc. Am., 1980, Leonard Greenstone Safety award Nat. Assn. Underwater Instrs., 1985, 1st Prince Tomohito of Mikasa Japan prize, 1990, Craig Hoffman Meml. award, 1992, Dan Seap Mentor award, 1998, Ernst & Young Entrepreneur of Yr. in Life Scis. award, NC and SC, 2002, Reaching Out award Diving Equipment Mfrs., 2002. Fellow Nat. Underwater Explorers Club; mem. Undersea Med. Soc. (pres. 1975-76, mem. exec. com. 1972-75, editor jour. 1976-79, 1st Oceaneering Internat. award 1975, Albert R. Behnke award 1983), Am. Physiol. Soc., European Undersea Biomed. Soc., Russian Acad. Sci. (fgn. mem., Pavlov medal 2001), Aerospace Med. Soc., Marine Tech. Soc., Croatian Undersea and Hyperbaric Med. Soc. (hon.), Nat. Acad. Scuba Educators (Meritorious Svc. award 1997). Avocations: gardening, swimming, boating. Home: 213 Lancaster Dr Chapel Hill NC 27517-3430 Office: Internat Divers Alert Network 21 W Colony Pl Ste 280 Durham NC 27705 Home Phone: 919-932-5879; Office Phone: 919-490-6161. E-mail: pbennett25@nc.rr.com.

BENNETT, PETER DUNNE, retired marketing educator; b. Mt. Pleasant, Tex., Feb. 19, 1933; s. Alvin Lowell and Jessie Lorene (Wintz) B.; m. Mary Lou Sanders, Aug. 23, 1953; children— Bonnie Kathleen, Blythe Allison BBA, U. Tex., Austin, 1955, MBA, 1961, PhD, 1965. Mktg. rep. IBM Corp., Lubbock, Tex., 1957-60; lectr. U. Tex., Austin, 1961-63; vis. rschr. U. Chile, Santiago, 1963-64; prof., chmn. dept. mktg., assoc. dean, bus. Pa. State U., University Park, 1964-97; gen. contractor State College, Pa., 1997—. Bd. dirs. Walshire Asurance; cons. and lectr. in field. Author: Consumer Behavior, 1973, Marketing, 1988, Dictionary of Marketing Terms, 1989, 2d edit. 1995; editor numerous books in field; contbr. chpts. to books. Mem. Habitat for Humanity. Served to capt. USAF, 1955-57 Named Disting. Visitor, U. Tex., 1979. Mem. Assn. Consumer Research, Am. Mktg. Assn. (v.p. mgmt. 1983-85, editor 1982-84) Independent. Baptist And Brethren. Avocations: golf, sailing, water-skiing, house building, wood working. Personal E-mail: pdb1@psu.edu.

BENNETT, PHILIP, editor; b. San Francisco; m. Monica Klien-Samanez; 1 child. Grad., Harvard Univ. Reporter Lima Times, Lima, Peru; with Boston Globe, 1984—97, fgn. correspondent to metro editor, 1984—95, fgn. editor, 1995—97; stringer Washington Post, Peru, 1982—84, nat. sec. editor, 1997—99, asst. mng. editor, fgn. news, 1999—2005, mng. editor, 2005—. Office: Mng Editor Wash Post 1150 15th St NW Washington DC 20071-0002 Office Phone: 202-334-7513. Business E-Mail: bennettp@washpost.com.*

BENNETT, R. MONTY, church organist; b. Santa Clara, Calif., Nov. 4, 1969; s. Raymond John and Nancy Sfreddo Bennett. MusB, U. Calif., Santa Barbara, 1991. Assoc. min. music, organist Calvary Ch., Charlotte, NC, 1995—97; prin. organist Friendship Missionary Bapt. Ch., Charlotte, NC, 2000—. Bd. mem. Cemetery Commn., Rock Hill, SC, 2003—06; mem. exec. com. Am. Guild Organists, Charlotte, NC, 2005—06. Mem.: Am. Guild Organists, Nat. Assn. Negro Musicians. Baptist. Home: 730 Hawthorne Ln Rock Hill SC 29730 Office: Friendship Missionary Baptist Church 3400 Beatties Ford Rd Charlotte NC 28216 Home Phone: 803-328-9504; Office Phone: 704-391-6618. Personal E-mail: rmb10@aol.com. E-mail: mbennett@friendshipcharlotte.org.

BENNETT, RICHARD EDWARD, lawyer; AB, Boston Coll., 1975, JD, 1978. Bar: Mass. 1978, U.S. Dist. Ct. Mass. 1979, U.S. Ct. Appeals (1st cir.) 1979, U.S. Ct. Appeals (fed. cir.) 1989. Atty. Willcox, Pirozzolo & McCarthy, P.C., Boston, 1979—2006, Michienzie & Sawin LLC, Boston, 2007—.

BENNETT, ROBERT F., senator; b. Salt Lake City, 1933; s. Wallace F. Bennett; m. Joyce McKay; 6 children. BS, U. Utah, 1957. Staff positions US House Reps., US Senate, Washington; CEO Franklin Quest, Salt Lake City, 1984-90; senator from Utah, chief dep. whip, counsel to Rep. leader U.S. Senate, Washington, 1993—, ranking mem. agr. appropriations and fin. inst. subcom, 2007—, mem. joint econ. com., 2007—, mem. banking, housing, urban affairs com., appropriations com., ranking mem. rules com., 2007—. Mem. Rep. high tech. task force; lobbyist various orgns., Washington; head Dept. Transp.'s Congl. Liaison. Author: Gaining Control. Chmn. Education Strategic Planning Commn. Utah State Bd. Edn. (mem. Edn. Strategic Planning Com.). Recipient Light of Learning award for Outstanding Contbns. to Utah edn., 1989; named Entrepreneur of Yr. for Rocky Mtn. region INC. magazine, 1989. Republican. Office: US Senate 431 Dirksen Senate Ofc Bldg Washington DC 20510-0001 Office Phone: 202-224-5444.

BENNETT, ROBERT LEROY, computer software development company executive; b. Salt Lake City, May 16, 1937; s. Edward L. and Helen (Hofheins) B.; m. Linda Lou Anderson, Aug. 25, 1961; children: Keri Lynn, Troy, Nicole, Jessica, Candice, Chelsea. BA, Brigham Young U., 1962; JD, UCLA, 1965. Bar: Calif. 1966, U.S. Supreme Ct. 1969. Atty., advisor CIA, Washington, 1965-70; exec. v.p., chief operating officer Mead Data Central, Inc. (now Lexis-Nexis), Washington and NYC, 1970-81; assoc. Heidrick and Struggles, Inc., NYC, 1982-83; pres., chief exec. officer Mirror Systems, Inc., Cambridge, Mass., 1983—93; prin. Bennett, Fisher, Giuliano and Gottsman; The Electronic Publishing Group, NYC, 1993—2000. Mem.: ABA. Mem. Lds Ch. Personal E-mail: rlbllb@comcast.net.

BENNETT, ROBERT R., telecommunications company executive; b. Apr. 19, 1958; BA in Econ. (with Honors), Denison U.; MBA, Columbia U. With The Bank of N.Y.; v.p., dir. fin. Telecom., Inc., 1987-90; prin. fin. officer Liberty Media Corp., Englewood, Colo., 1990, exec. v.p., CFO, exec. v.p. & sec. & treas., 1995—97, CFO, 1996—97, CEO, 1997—2005, pres., 1997—2006, Discovery Holding Co., Englewood, Colo., 2006—. Bd. dirs. OpenTV Corp., UnitedGlobalCom, Inc., Ascent Media Group, Inc., Liberty Satellite & Technology, Inc., IAC/Interactive Corp., 2001—04, Starz Encore Group, Discovery Holding Co., 2006—, Sprint Nextel Corp., 2006—. Office: Discovery Holding Co 12300 Liberty Blvd Englewood CO 80112*

BENNETT, ROBERT ROYCE, engineering and management consultant; b. Spokane, Wash., May 7, 1926; s. Fred Alonzo and Rebecca Jane (Sommerville) B.; m. Margaret Stewart Keyes, Aug. 20, 1950; children: Susan Bennett Olson Nelson, Philip K., Laurie B. Mapes. BS, Calif. Inst. Tech., 1945, MS, 1947, PhD, 1949. Registered profl. engr., Oreg.; lic. surveyor, Oreg. Mem. tech. staff Hughes Aircraft, Culver City, Calif., 1949-54; v.p. TRW Systems, Redondo Beach, Calif., 1954-65; engring. mgmt. cons. Eugene, Oreg., 1965—. Contbr. articles to profl. jours.; patentee in field. Served to lt. (j.g.) USNR, 1944-54. Fellow IEEE. Republican. Home and Office: 85334 S Willamette St Eugene OR 97405-9568 Home Phone: 541-345-3988. Business E-Mail: bennett500@prodigy.net.

BENNETT, ROBERT STEPHEN, lawyer; b. Bklyn., Aug. 2, 1939; s. F. Robert and Nancy (Walsh) Bennett; m. Ellen C. Bennett, Sept. 20, 1969; children: Catherine, Peggy, Sarah. BA, Georgetown U., 1961; LLB, Georgetown Law Ctr., 1964; post grad., U. Va. Law Sch., 1961—62; LLM, Harvard U. Law Sch., 1965. Bar: Va. 1964, DC 1965, US Supreme Ct. 1969, Mont. Law clk. to Hon. Howard F. Corcoran US Dist. Ct., Washington, 1965—67; asst. US atty. DC US Dept. Justice, Washington, 1967—70; assoc. Hogan & Hartson LLP, Washington, 1970—75; founding ptnr. Dunnells, Duvall, Bennett & Porter, Washington, 1975—90; ptnr., civil and criminal enforcement matters and complex civil litigation, white collar crimes Skadden, Arps, Slate Meagher & Flom, LLP, Washington, 1990—. Adj. prof. George Washington U., 1975—79; spl. counsel DC Commn. on Jud. Disabilities and Tenure, 1976—82; legal cons. US Senate Fgn. Rels. Com., 1981, 82; spl. counsel US Senate Select Com. on Ethics, 1981—82; judge Court of Arbitration for Sport. Contbr. articles to publs. Named one of 75 Best Lawyers in Washington, Washingtonian survey mag., America's Leading Lawyers for Bus., Chambers USA, 2000, 100 Most Influential Lawyers, Nat. Law Jour., 2000, 2006; fellow Am. Coll. Trial Lawyers. Fellow: Am. Coll. Trial Lawyers; mem.: Def. Rsch. Inst., Va. Trial Lawyers Assn., DC Bar Assn., Va. State Bar, ABA (co-chmn. several ABA Nat. Inst. programs). Home: 1840 24th St NW Washington DC 20008-4024 Office: Skadden Arps Slate Meagher & Flom LLP 1440 New York Ave NW Ste 600 Washington DC 20005 Office Phone: 202-371-7180. Office Fax: 202-661-8205. Business E-Mail: rbennett@skadden.com.*

BENNETT, ROBERT THOMAS, lawyer, accountant; b. Columbus, Ohio, Feb. 8, 1939; s. Francis Edmund and Mary Catherine (Weiland) B.; B.S., Ohio State U., 1960; J.D., Cleve. Marshall Law Sch., 1967; m. Ruth Ann Dooley, May 30, 1959; children— Robert Thomas, Rose Marie. Admitted to Ohio bar, 1967; C.P.A., Ernst and Ernst, Cleve., 1960-63; with tax assessing dept. Cuyahoga County (Ohio) Auditor's Office, Cleve., 1963-70; mem. firm Bartunek, Bennett, Garofoli and Hill, Cleve., 1975-79; mem. firm Bennett & Klonowski, Cleve., 1979-83; mem. firm Bennett & Harbarger, Cleve., 1983-88. Exec. vice chmn. Cuyahoga County Rep. Orgn., 1974-88; state chmn. Ohio Rep. Orgn., 1988—; mem. Rep. Nat. Com., 1988—; bd. dirs. Univ. Hosp. of Cleve. and S.W. Gen. Health Ctr. Republican. Roman Catholic. Mem. Citizens League Club, Capitol Hill Club (Washington). Contbr. articles to profl. publs. Office: Ohio Rep Party 211 S 5th St Columbus OH 43215-5203 Home: 10810 Edgewater Dr Cleveland OH 44102-6133

BENNETT, ROBERT WILLIAM, law educator; b. Chgo., Mar. 30, 1941; s. Lewis and Henrietta (Schneider) Bennett; m. Harriet Trop, Aug. 19, 1979. BA, Harvard U., 1962, LLB, 1965. Bar: Ill. 1966. Legal asst. FCC commr. Nicholas Johnson, 1966-67; atty. Chgo. Legal Aid Bur., 1967-68; asso. firm Mayer, Brown & Platt, Chgo., 1968-69; faculty Northwestern U. Sch. Law, Chgo., 1969—, prof. law, 1974—, dean, 1985-95, Nathaniel L. Nathanson prof., 2002—. Author (with LaFrance, Schroeder and Boyd): Handbook on Law of the Poor, 1973; author: Talking it Through: Puzzles of American Democracy, 2003, Taming the Electoral College, 2006. Knox Meml. fellow, London Sch. Econs., 1965—66. Fellow: Am. Bar Found. (pres., bd. dirs.); mem.: ABA, Am. Law Inst., Chgo. Coun. Lawyers (pres. 1971—72). Home: 2130 N Racine Ave Chicago IL 60614-4002 Office: Northwestern U Sch Law 357 E Chicago Ave Chicago IL 60611-3059 Office Phone: 312-503-8430. Office Fax: 312-503-5950. Business E-Mail: r-bennett@law.northwestern.edu.

BENNETT, SAMUEL, elementary school educator; BS, Toccoa Falls Coll., 1985; MS in Elem. Edn., Clemson Univ., 1992; PhD student in Organizational Leadership, Nova Southeastern Univ. Tchr., 1985—, Garner Elem. Sch., Winter Haven, Fla., 1992—. Finalist Nat. Tchr. of Yr., 2006; named Fla. Tchr. of Yr., 2006. Office: Garner Elem Sch 2500 Havendale Blvd Winter Haven FL 33881 E-mail: samsrbsam@aol.com.*

BENNETT, SCOTT BOYCE, retired librarian, consultant; b. Kansas City, Mo., July 22, 1939; s. Preston Theodore Bennett and Viola Louise (Scott) Mayberry; m. Carol Jean Glass, June 20, 1960; children: Beth Louise, Theodore David, Myron Richard, Kristellen Anne. AB magna cum laude, Oberlin Coll., 1960; MA in English, Ind. U., 1966, PhD in English, 1967; MS in Libr. Sci., U. Ill., 1976. Woodrow Wilson teaching intern St. Paul's Coll., Lawrenceville, Va., 1964-65; asst. prof. English U. Ill., Urbana-Champaign, 1967-74, from instr. to asst. prof. to assoc. prof. libr. adminstrn., 1974-81; asst. libr. collection mgmt. Northwestern U., Evanston, Ill., 1981-89; dir. Milton S. Eisenhower Libr. Johns Hopkins U., Balt., 1989-94; univ. libr. Yale U., New Haven, 1994-2001; project worker Coun. Ind. Colls. and Coun. on Libr. and Info. Resources, 2001—. Contbr. articles to profl. jours. Adv. panel library and archival preservation Ill. State Libr., adv. bd. Ill. State Archives; rev. panelist NEH; chair project Rsch. Librs. Group; prin. state-wide preservation planning Md. Woodrow Wilson Nat. fellow 1960-61, Ind. U. Dissertation Yr. fellow, Haskell fellow, 1966-67, U. Ill. Faculty fellow, 1969, Hon. Vis. Rsch. fellow Victorian Studies Ctr. U. Leicester, Eng., 1979, Am. Coun. Learned Socs. fellow, 1978-79. Mem. AAUP (pres., sec. Urbana-Champaign chpt. 1975-78, various other offices), Rsch. Soc. Victorian Periodicals (exec. bd. 1971-73, pres. 1977-82). Address: 711 S Race Urbana IL 61801-4132

BENNETT, SCOTT LAWRENCE, lawyer; b. NYC, July 8, 1949; s. Allen J. and Rhoda Bennett. BA with high distinction, U. Mich., 1971; JD, Cornell U., 1974. Bar: NY 1975, U.S. Ct. Appeals (2d cir.) 1975, U.S. Dist. Ct. (so. and ea. dists.) N.Y. 1975, U.S. Supreme Ct. 1976. Assoc. Donovan, Leisure, Newton & Irvine, NYC, 1974—79; sr. v.p., assoc. gen. counsel, sec. The McGraw-Hill Cos., Inc., NYC, 1979—. Mem.: ABA, Assn. Am. Pubs. (lawyers com.), Assn. Bar City N.Y., N.Y. State Bar Assn., Phi Beta Kappa. Office: The McGraw Hill Co Inc Fl 48 1221 Avenue Of Americas New York NY 10020-1095 Business E-Mail: Scott_Bennett@Mcgraw-Hill.com.

BENNETT, STEPHEN M., computer software company executive; b. Madison, Wis., Mar. 8, 1954; BA in Fin. and Real Estate, U. Wis., 1976. Various mgmt. positions GE Appliances, GE Med. and GE Supply; v.p. of Ams. GE Elec. Distbn. and Control; pres., CEO GE Capital Vendor Fin. Svcs., 1996—99, GE Capital e-Bus., 1999; exec. v.p., CEO GE Capital subs. of GE Corp., 1999—2000; CEO, pres. Intuit Inc., Mountain View, Calif., 2000—. Bd. dirs. Sun Microsystems, Inc., 2004—. Office: Intuit Inc 2632 Marine Way Mountain View CA 94043 Office Phone: 650-944-6000.*

BENNETT, STEVEN ALAN, lawyer, insurance company executive; b. Rock Island, Ill., Jan. 15, 1953; s. Ralph O. and Anne E. B.; m. Jeanne Aring; children: Preston, Spencer, Hunter, Whitney. BA in Art History, U. Notre Dame, Ind., 1975; JD, U. Kans., Lawrence, 1982. Bar: Tex. 1983, Ohio 1995, US Dist. Ct. (no. dist. Tex.) 1983, US Ct. Appeals (5th cir.) 1983, US Supreme Ct. 1995. Atty. Freytag, Marshall et al, Dallas, 1982-84, Baker, Mills & Glast, Dallas, 1984-87; ptnr. Shank, Irwin, Conant et al, Dallas, 1987-89; gen. counsel Bank One, Tex., N.A., Dallas, 1989-94; sr. v.p., gen. counsel, sec. Banc One Corp., Columbus, Ohio, 1994-99; exec. v.p., chief legal officer, sec. Cardinal Health, Inc., Dublin, Ohio, 1999-2001; pvt. practice atty. Columbus, 2001—03; sr. v.p., gen. counsel Fed. Savs. Bank USAA (United Svcs. Automobile Assn.), San Antonio, 2003—04, exec. v.p., gen. counsel, sec., 2004—. City councilman, Mesquite, Tex., 1984-86, mayor pro tem, 1985; trustee Meadowview Sch., Mesquite, 1985-92; chair fin. com. St. Brendan Ch., Hilliard, Ohio, 1998-2003; pres., bd. dirs. Dallas Dem. Forum, 1993-94; bd. dirs. Ohio Hunger Task Force, Columbus; trustee Woodrow Wilson Internat. Ctr. for Scholars, Washington, 1996-2002, vice-chmn., 1999-2002; bd. dirs. Capital U. Law Sch., Columbus, 1998-2003, Ctr. Thomas More Studies, Dallas; mem., Citizens Commn. for City-County Svc. Integration, San Antonio, 2003-04. Fellow Am. Bar Found., Ohio State Bar Found.; mem. ABA, Dallas Bar Assn., Ohio State Bar Assn., Columbus Bar Assn., St. Thomas More Soc. (Dallas bd. dirs. 1990-94), Am. Corp. Counsel Assn. (sec. 1999-2000, bd. dirs. 1996-2002, chair policy com. 1997-99), Phi Beta Kappa. Avocation: landscape photography. Office: Gen Counsel C3E USAA 9800 Fredericksburg Rd San Antonio TX 78288 Office Phone: 210-498-1888. E-mail: steven.bennett@usaa.com.*

BENNETT, THOMAS B., federal judge; b. Phila., Jan. 6, 1949; BS, W.Va. U., 1970, MA, 1973, JD, 1976. Bar: W. Va., 1976, Tex., 1979. Instr. econs. W.Va. U., 1971-76; law clk. hon. John R. Brown U.S. Ct. Appeals 5th Cir., 1976-77; assoc. Bowles, Rice, McDavid, Graff & Love, 1977-79, ptnr., 1980-95; judge US Bankruptcy Ct. for Northern Dist. of Alabama, Birmingham, 1995—. Office: 1800 5th Ave N Rm 128 Birmingham AL 35203-2111 Office Phone: 205-714-3880. Office Fax: 205-714-3882.

BENNETT, THOMAS LEROY, JR., clinical neuropsychology educator; b. Norwalk, Conn., Sept. 25, 1942; s. Thomas LeRoy and Gertrude Upson (Richardson) B.; m. Jacqueline Beekman, Aug. 5, 1972; children: Dean, Shannon, Brian, Laurie. BA, U. N. Mex., 1964, MS, 1966, PhD, 1968. Diplomate Am. Bd. Profl. Neuropsychology (examiner, treas. 1993-96, 2001--, pres.-elect 1995-97, pres. 1997-99), Am. Bd. Forensic Examiners, Am. Bd. Profl. Disability Cons., Am. Bd. Profl. Psychology. Asst. prof. Calif. State U., Sacramento, 1968-70; assoc. prof., then prof. psychology and physiology Colo. State U., Ft. Collins, 1970-98, coord. exptl. psychology sect., 1978-81, 92-95, prof. emeritus, 1998—; pvt. practice neuropsychology Ft. Collins, 1981—. Mem. allied health staff Poudre Valley Hosp., Ft. Collins; clin. dir. Ctr. for Neurorehab. Svcs., Ft. Collins. Author: Brain and Behavior, 1977, The Sensory World, 1978, The Psychology of Learning and Memory, 1979, Exploring the Sensory World, 1979, Introduction to Physiological Psychology, 1982, The Neuropsychology of Epilepsy, 1992, Brainwave-R: Cognitive Strategies for Brain Injury Rehabilitation, 1997, Mild Traumatic Brain Injury, 1999, Psychology Video Teaching Modules: The Brain, 2d edit., 1997, Psychology Video Teaching Modules: The Mind, 2000; also articles and book chpts.; assoc. editor Rehab. Psychology, Archives of Clinical Neuropsychology; mem. editl. bd. Cognitive Rehab., Archives Clin. Neuropsychology, Jour. Head Injury, Bull. of Nat. Acad. Neuropsychology, Neuropsychology Rev., others. Elder Timnath Presbyterian Ch. Named Outstanding Grad. Educator for Coll. Natural Scis., 1998. Fellow APA, Nat. Acad. Neuropsychology (editl. bd. Bull., bd. dirs. 1993-95, conv. chmn. 1993, 94), Am. Psychol. Soc., Am. Coll. Profl. Neuropsychology (pres. 1997-99); mem. Am. Coll. Forensic Examiners, Psychonomic Soc., Rocky Mountain Psychol. Assn., Soc. for Cognitive Rehab., Nat. Head Injury Found. (provider's coun.), Colo. Head Injury Found. (provder's coun.), Internat. Neuropsychol. Soc., Colo. Neuropsychol. Soc., Sigma Xi (named Colo. State U. Honored Scientist 1996). Home: 213 Camino Real Fort Collins CO 80524-8907 Office: Ctr Novorehabilitation Svc K145 Robertson St Fort Collins CO 80524 Office Phone: 970-493-6667. *Always look for something good in everyone you meet.*

BENNETT, TONY (ANTHONY DOMINICK BENEDETTO), entertainer; b. Astoria, NY, Aug. 3, 1926; s. John and Anna (Suraci) Benedetto; m. Patricia Beech, Feb. 12, 1952 (div. 1971); children: D'Andrea, Daegal; m. Sandra Grant, Dec. 29, 1971 (div. 1984); children: Joanna, Antonia; life ptnr. Susan Crow. Student, Am. Theatre Wing, NYC; MusD, U. Berkeley. Ofcl. artist Ky. Derby, 2001. Classic pop vocalist, entertainer (frequent appearances on TV, in concert); singer: (albums) Treasure Chest of Songs, 1955, Tony, 1957, Count Basie Swings, Tony Bennett Sings, 1958, Blue Velvet, 1959, To My Wonderful One, 1960, Bennett and Basie Strike Up the Band, 1961, I Left My Heart in San Francisco, 1963 (Grammy award, Album of Yr., 1962), I Wanna Be Around, 1963, Love Story, 1971, Summer of '42, 1972, Sunrise, Sunset, 1973, 16 Most Requested Songs, 1986, The Art of Excellence, 1986, Bennett/Berlin, 1987, The Movie Song Album, 1989, Astoria, 1990, Forty Years: The Artistry of Tony Bennett, 1991, Perfectly Frank, 1992 (Grammy award, Best Traditional Vocal Performance, 1992), Steppin' Out, 1993 (Grammy award, Best Traditional Pop Vocal, 1993), The Essence of Tony Bennett, 1993, In Person! With Count Basie and His Orchestra, 1994, MTV Unplugged, 1994 (Grammy award Album of Yr., Best Traditional Pop Vocal), Here's to the Ladies, 1995, Tony Bennett on Holiday, 1997, Tribute to Billie Holiday, Bennett Sings Ellington-Hot and Cool, 1999, The Ultimate Tony, 2000, Playin' With My Friends: Bennett Sings The Blues, 2001 (Grammy award best traditional pop vocal album, 2003), The Essential Tony Bennett, 2002, A Wonderful World, 2002, The Art of Romance, 2005 (Grammy award Best Traditional Pop Vocal Album 2006), Duets: An American Classic, 2006 (Best Pop Collaboration with Vocals for For Once in My Life, Best Traditional Pop Vocal Album, Grammy awards, 2007); owner, rec. artist Improv Records; appeared in: The Scout, 1994; appeared in (TV films) Men, Movies & Carol, 1994, The Scout, 1994, Sinatra: 80 Years My Way, 1995, (TV series) The Simpsons, 1989, Muppets Tonight, 1996, (TV spl.) Tony Bennett on Holiday: A Tribute to Billy Holiday, 1997, Analyze This, 1999, TV guest appearances The Andy Williams Show, 1966, The Jackie Gleason Show, 1969, Space Ghost Coast to Coast, 1994, Suddenly Susan, 1997; author: The Good Life: The Autobiography of Tony Bennett; painting, Homage to Hockney, hangs permanently in Butler Inst. Am. Art, exhibitions include Butler Inst. of Am. Art, Youngstown, Ohio, 1994, Nat. Arts Club, NYC. Raised millions of dollars for Juvenile Diabetes Found.; co-founder (with Susan Crow) Frank Sinatra Sch. for Arts HS, Queens, NY, 2001. Served with inf. AUS, World War II. Named to Star on Hollywood Walk of Fame; recipient Gold records for recs., Because of You, I Left My Heart in San Francisco, Best Male Vocalist award, Cash Box mag., 1951, Grammy lifetime achievement award, Salute to Greatness award Martin Luther King Ctr., Atlanta, Kennedy Ctr. Honor, John F. Kennedy Ctr. for Performing Arts, 2005, Billboard Century award, 2006. Avocation: painting.

BENNETT, TONY (ANTHONY G. BENNETT), men's college basketball coach; b. 1969; s. Dick Bennett; m. Laurel Bennett; children: Anna, Eli. Student, U. Wis., Green Bay, 1989—92. Profl. basketball player NBA Charlotte Hornets, NC, 1992—95; basketball player North Harbor Kings, Auckland, New Zealand, 1996, player/coach, 1997, head coach, 1998—99; various basketball positions including recruiting and player devel. U. Wis., Madison, 1999—2003; asst. coach Wash. State U., 2003—04, assoc. head coach, 2004—06, head coach, 2006—. Named Pacific-10 Conf. Coach of Yr., 2007, Dist. 9 Coach of Yr., US Basketball Writers Assn., 2007, Coll. Basketball Coach of Yr., AP, 2007; recipient Naismith Men's Coll. Coach of Yr. award, Atlanta Tipoff Club, 2007. Achievements include ranking as the NCAA all-time leader in 3-point percentage (.497). Office: Wash State U Intercollegiate Athletics Bohler Athletic Complex Colorado Ave PO Box 641602 Pullman WA 99164-1602 Office Phone: 509-335-0240. E-mail: coachtony@wsu.edu.*

BENNETT, VELMA JOYCE (JOYCE WILLIAMS), writer, poet; b. Chgo., Mar. 25, 1941; d. Floyd Theodore and Willie Belle (Williams) B. BA in Secondary Edn., Western Mich. U., 1964; MEd, Loyola U., 1975. Cert. secondary and elem. edn., coll. counseling. Tchr. English and social studies Wendell Phillips H.S., Chgo., 1964-65; editor Follett Pub. Co., Chgo., 1965-66; tchr. Bryant Elem. Sch., Chgo., 1966-72; H.S. tchr. Outward Bound, Grand Rapids, Mich., 1979-81; pvt. practice writer, poet Allegan, Mich., 1990—. Author: Everybody's Poetry, 1994. Past pres. NAACP, Allegan. Avocations: reading, listening to music, nature watching, people watching, spirits.

BENNETT, VICTORIA ELIZABETH, rehabilitation nurse, dialysis nurse and technician; b. Ironton, Ohio, Aug. 6, 1949; d. George William and Lorene Ellen (Jones) Bennett. Student, Morehead State U., Ky., 1968—69; LPN, Ashland Vo-Tech. Sch., Ky., 1971. LPN, Ky. LPN Cabell/Huntington Hosp., Huntington, W.Va., 1971—73; staff nurse Huntington Hosp., 1973—77; charge nurse Heartland Health Care, Charleston, W.Va., 1977—86; staff nurse orthop. VA Med. Ctr., Lexington, Ky., 1986—88, rehab staff nurse, 1988—2000, staff nurse, dialysis technician, 2000—. Mem. LPN promotion bd. VAMC, 1996—. Juror Jessamine County Dir./Dist.Cts., Nicholasville, Ky., 1998, 2004. Named Most Valuable Player, Ky. Women State Slow Pitch Tournament, 1971, Ky. Col., 2001; recipient Phoenix award, Am. Heart Assn., 1980. Mem.: AARP. Avocations: softball, bicycling, fishing, hiking, French-style cooking. Home: 1338 Shun Pike Nicholasville KY 40356 Office: VAMC 1100 Veterans Dr Lexington KY 40506

BENNETT, WILLIAM JOHN (BILL BENNETT), radio personality, former secretary of education; b. Bklyn., July 31, 1943; s. F. Robert and Nancy (Walsh) Bennett; m. Mary Elayne Glover, May 29, 1982; children: John, Joseph. BA, Williams Coll., 1965, LLD (hon.), 1983; PhD, U. Tex., 1970; JD, Harvard U., 1971; LittD (hon.), Gonzaga U., 1982; HHD (hon.), Franklin Coll., Ind., 1982, U. N.C., 1984, George Washington U., 1985, Gallaudet Coll., 1985, The Citadel, 1986; LHD (hon.), U. N.H., 1982, Manhattan Coll., 1983, Elon Coll., 1984, Loyola Coll., Md., 1984, Assumption Coll., 1985, Yeshiva U., 1986, Cen. State U., Wilburforce, Ohio, 1987; LD (hon.), Williams Coll., 1983, U. Notre Dame, 1984. Asst. to pres. Boston U., 1972-76; exec. dir. Nat. Humanities Ctr., Research Triangle Park, NC, 1976-79, pres., dir., 1979-81; assoc. prof. NC State U., Raleigh, 1979-81, U. NC, 1979-81; chmn. NEH, Washington, 1981-85; sec. US Dept. Edn., 1985-88; dir. Office Nat. Drug Control Policy, Washington, 1989-90; co-dir. Empower America, Washington, 1993—2004; co-chmn. Nat. Commn. on Civic Renewal, College Park, Md., 1996—98, Partnership for a Drug-Free Am., New York; host Bill Bennett's Morning in America, 2004—. With faculty U. So. Miss., U. Tex., Harvard U., U. Wis.; Wash. Fellow, Claremont Inst., Calif., 2003-, chmn. Americans for Victory Over Terrorism, 2002-; contbr. CNN, 2006-. Author: Schools Without Drugs, 1986; The De-Valuing of America: The Fight for Our Culture and Our Children, 1992, The Book of Virtues: A Treasury of Great Moral Stories, 1993, The Children's Book of Virtues, 1995, The Moral Compass: Stories for a Life's Journey, 1995, The Children's Book of Heroes, 1997, Our Sacred Honor: Words of Advice from the Founders in Stories, Letters, Poems and Speeches, 1997, The Death of Outrage: Bill Clinton and the Assault on American Ideals, 1999, The Broken Hearth: Reversing the Moral Collapse of the American Family, 2001, Virtues of Friendship and Loyalty, 2002, Why We Fight: Moral Clarity and the War on Terrorism, 2003, America: The Last Best Hope, Vol. I:From the Age of Discovery to a World at War, 2006, Vol. II, 2007; co-author (with Cribb John T. E and Chester E. Finn) The Educated Child: A Parents Guide From Preschool Through Eighth Grade, 2000. Republican. Roman Catholic. Office: Claremont Inst Ste E 937 W Foothill Blvd Claremont CA 91711 Office Phone: 909-621-6825. Office Fax: 909-626-8724.*

BENNETT, WILLIAM MICHAEL, internist, educator, nephrologist; b. Chgo., May 6, 1938; s. Harry H. and Helen A. (Kaplan) B.; m. Sandra S. Silen, June 12, 1977; four children. Student, U. Mich., 1956-59; BS, Northwestern U., 1960, MD, 1963. Diplomate Am. Bd. Internal Medicine, Am. Bd. Nephrology, Am. Bd. Clin. Pharmacology. Intern U. Oreg., 1963-64; resident Northwestern U., 1964-66; practice medicine specializing in internal medicine Portland, Oreg., Boston; mem. staff Mass. Gen. Hosp., 1969-70; asst. prof. medicine U. Oreg. Health Scis. Center, 1970-74, assoc. prof., 1974-78, prof. medicine and pharmacology, 1978-2000, ret., 2000. Author: Pharmacology and Management of Hypertension, 1994, Manual of Nephrology, 1990, Drug Therapy in Renal Failure, 1994; contbr. articles to med. jours. Served with USAF, 1967-69. Master ACP; mem. Am. Soc. Nephrology (pres. 1998-99), Transplantation Soc., Internat. Soc. Nephrology, Am. Soc. Pharmacology and Exptl. Therapeutics. Office: Legacy Good Samaritan Hosp Transplant Svcs 1040 NW 22d Ave Ste 480 Portland OR 97210 also: NW Renal Clinic 1130 NW 22d St Ste 640 Portland OR 97210 Office Phone: 503-413-6555. E-mail: bennettw@lhs.org.

BENNETT, WILLIAM RALPH, JR., physicist, researcher; b. Jersey City, Jan. 30, 1930; s. William Ralph and Viola (Schreiber) B.; m. Frances Commins, Dec. 11, 1952; children: Jean, William Robert, Nancy. AB, Princeton U., 1951; MA, PhD, Columbia U., 1957; MA (hon.), Yale U., 1965; D.Sc. (hon.), U. New Haven, 1975. Rsch. asst. physics Columbia Radiation Lab., 1952-54; mem. Pupin Cyclotron Group, 1954-57; mem. faculty Yale U., New Haven, 1957-59, 62—, prof. physics and applied sci., 1965-72, Charles Baldwin Sawyer prof. engring. and applied sci., prof. physics, 1972-98, prof. emeritus, 1998—, fellow Berkeley Coll., 1963-81, master Silliman Coll., 1981-87, life fellow Silliman Coll., 1981—. Tech. staff Bell Telephone Labs., Murray Hill, NJ, 1959—62; cons. Tech. Rsch. Group, Melville, NY, 1962—67, Inst. Def. Analysis, Washington, 1963—70; vis. scientist Am. Inst. Physics Vis. Scientist Program, 1963—64; vis. prof. Brandels Summer Inst. Theoretical Physics, 1969; cons. mem. bd. dirs. Laser Scis. Corp., Bethel, Conn., 1968—71; mem. adv. panels atomic physics and astrophysics Nat. Bur. Stds., 1964—69; cons. CBS Labs., Stamford, Conn., 1967—68, AVCO Corp., 1978—81, Reeves Sci. Co., New Haven, 1989—91, Oak Ridge Assn. Univs., Washington, 1991—92, MCG Internat., New Haven, 1992—93, Kahn Electronics, NY, 1998—2000, Premier Heart, 1999, U. Cin., 2000; mem. lab. adv. bd. for rsch. Naval Rsch. Adv. Com., 1968—78; guest Soviet Acad. Scis., 1967, 69, 79; rschr. gas lasers and atomic physics, gravitational physics, applications of computers to med. diagnostics. Author: Introduction to Computer Applications, 1976, Scientific and Engineering Problem Solving With the Computer, 1976, The Physics of Gas Lasers, 1977, Atomic Gas Laser Transition Data: A Critical Evaluation, 1979, Health and Low Frequency Electromagnetic Fields, 1994, Science of Musical Sound, 2007; guest editor: Applied Optics, 1965; mem. editl. adv. bd. Jour. Quantum Electronics, 1965-69. Recipient Western Electric Fund award for outstanding tchg. Am. Assn. Engring. Educators, 1977, Outstanding Patent award R & D Coun. N.J., 1977, Eli Whitney Patent award Conn. Patent Lawyers Assn., 1994, DeVane medal Phi Beta Kappa, 2000; fellow Alfred P. Sloan Found., 1967, Guggenheim Found., 1967, John Fenders fellow, 1987. Fellow IEEE (life, Morris Liebmann award 1965), Am. Phys. Soc., Optical Soc. Am.; mem. Sigma Xi.

BENNETT SPECTOR GREENFIELD, VERONICA (RONNIE SPECTOR), singer; b. NYC, Aug. 10, 1943; d. Louis Albert and Beatrice (Mobley) Bennett; m. Harvey Phillip Spector, Apr. 14, 1968 (div. Feb. 1974); adopted children: Gary and Lewis (twins), Donté; m. Jonathan Greenfield, Jan. 16, 1982; children: Austin Drew, Jason Charles. Grad. high sch., NYC. Dancer Murray The K's Dancing Girls, NYC, 1962-63; lead singer, choreographer, designer The Ronettes, 1962-67. Singer: (albums) The Ronettes Feat. Veronica, 1965, Siren, 1980, The Ronettes Greatest Hits, 1981, Unfinished Business, 1987, The Best of the Ronettes, 1992, She Talks to Rainbows, 1999, Something's Gonna Happen, 2003, The Last of the Rock Stars, 2006; author: Be My Baby: How I Survived Mascara, Miniskirts, and Madness, 1990. Active mayor John Lindsay campaign. Recipient 16 Mag. Gee-Gee award, 1963, 64, Grammy award, 1964, Grammy Nomination, 1986, NY Music awards nomination, 1987, 1988; named one of Greatest Women of Rock & Roll, VH1; named to NY Music Hall of Fame, 1987, Vocal Group Hall of Fame, 2004, Rock & Roll Hall of Fame, 2007. Mem. Literary Guild.*

BENNETZEN, JEFFREY L., molecular biologist; BA in biology, U. Calif., San Diego, 1974; PhD in biochemistry, U. Wash., 1980; postdoctoral study, Wash. U., 1980—81, Stanford U., 1980—81, U. Calif., Berkeley, 1980—81. Rsch. scientist Internat. Plant Rsch. Inst., 1981—83; asst. to full prof. Purdue U., 1983—99, Umbarger prof. genetics, 1999—2003; Norman Giles Eminent Scholar chair in molecular biology and functional genetics U. Ga., 2003—. Vis. prof. U. Calif., Davis, 1998. Mem. editl. bd. Current Opinion in Plant Biology, Ency. Life Scis. Recipient McKnight Found. award, Plant Biology, 1986, Fulbright award, 1990, Faculty Rsch. award, Sigma Xi, 1995, Nehru Centenary Professorship, U. Hyderabad, 2002. Fellow: AAAS; mem.: NAS. Office: U Ga C426A Life Sci Bldg Athens GA 30602 Business E-Mail: maize@uga.edu.

BENNEY, DOUGLAS MABLEY, direct marketing executive, consultant; b. Cold Spring Harbor, NY, Aug. 7, 1922; s. William Mabley and Wilhelmina (Walters) B.; m. Eugenia Sammis, Sept. 30, 1944 (div. Jan. 1980); children: William Douglas, Barbara Gates, Robert Scott; m. Barbara Mueller, July 8, 1983; stepchildren: Gregory Carmichael, Andrew Carmichael. Navy air cadet, U. N.C.-Chapel Hill, 1943, Cornell U., 1943; student in engring., Purdue U., 1939-41; AB, Colgate U., 1946-49; postgrad., Columbia U., 1951-52. With Curtis Publs., Phila., 1950-63; editor, assoc. pub. Jack & Jill, 1960-63; mktg. mgr. edn. div. Doubleday & Co., NYC, 1963-67; advt. and sales mgr. Hearst Book div., NYC, 1967-68; v.p. creative svcs. Nat. Liberty Corp., Valley Forge, Pa., 1968-72; v.p. mktg. Gerber Life Ins. Co., NYC, Pa., 1972-75; sr. mktg. officer Internat. Group Plans, Washington, Pa., 1975-78; v.p. mktg. Maxon Adminstrs., Inc., Irvington, NY, 1978-89; pres. A&B Advt., Inc., Springdale, Md., 1989—. Lt. (j.g.) AC, USN, 1943-46; PTO. Recipient award Artists Guild Delaware Valley, 1969, Direct Mail Mktg. Assn., 1965, Myasthenia Gravis Found., 1985, Profl. Ins. Mass Marketers Assn., 1992, 94, 96. Mem. Direct Mktg. Assn. Washington, Greater Washington Soc. Assn. Execs., Mt. Vernon Country Club (Alexandria, Va.). Achievements include patents for newspaper inserts, self-mailers. Avocations: woodworking, sailing, photography, scuba diving.

BENNING, JOSEPH RAYMOND, principal; b. Streator, Ill., May 23, 1956; s. Joseph Charles and Shirley Ann (Smith) B.; m. Katherine Marie Turner, Apr. 24, 1976; children: Jennifer Nichole, Joseph Donald. BA, Augustana Coll, 1978; MS in Edn., No. Ill. U., 1988. Cert. state supr., teaching, Ill. Tchr., coach Fulton (Ill.) High Sch., 1978—79; recreation dir. Fulton Recreation Corp., 1979; tchr., coach Streator (Ill.) High Sch., 1979—80, Woodland High Sch., Streator, 1980—83; program dir. Ill. State Bd. Edn., Ottawa, 1983—85; prin. St. Mary Grade Sch., Streator, 1985—89; assoc. supt. schs. Cath. Diocese Peoria, Ill., 1989—91, supt. schs. Ill., 1991—94; prin. St. Bede Acad., Peru, Ill., 1994—99, St. Columba Sch., Ottawa, Ill., 1999—2005, Sacred Heart Sch., Lombard, Ill., 2005—. Pres. Streator Youth Football League, 1984-90; adv. bd. Streator High Sch., 1985-89; prins. adv. bd. Cath. Diocese Peoria, 1987-89. Recipient CJ McDonald award Streator Youth Football League, 1989. Mem. ASCD, Nat. Cath. Edn. Assn., Nat. Assn. Secondary Sch. Prin., Nat. Assn. Elem. Sch. Prin., Ill. Elem. Sch. Assn., Cath. Conf. Ill., KC. Roman Catholic. Avocations: sports, music. Office: Sacred Heart Sch 322 W Maple Lombard IL 60148 Office Phone: 630-629-0536. Personal E-mail: benningjr@hotmail.com.

BENNINGTON, RONALD KENT, lawyer; b. Circleville, Ohio, July 16, 1936; s. Ralph P. and Delorice (Dudley) B.; m. Barbara Schumm, June 19, 1959; children: Scott C., Amy E. BA magna cum laude, Kenyon Coll., 1958; JD summa cum laude, Ohio State U., 1961. Assoc. Black, McCuskey, Souers & Arbaugh, Canton, Ohio, 1961-65, ptnr., 1965—. Sec. Hoover Worldwide Corp., 1969-86; bd. dirs. United Hard Chrome, Inc. Bd. trustees Plain Twp., Canton, 1972-78, Malone Coll., Canton, 1982—, chmn. 1984-86, Timken Mercy Med. Ctr., Canton; adv. com. Kenyon Coll., Gambier, Ohio; mem. Leadership Canton; bd. dirs. ARC, Canton; fundraising United Way Fund Drive; trust com. Hoover Found.; ambassador Ohio Found. Ind. Colls.; steering com. Pro Football Hall of Fame, 1985—;

Big Ten football ofcl., 1984—; trustee The Hoover Found., Canton, Greater Canton C. of C.; bd. assocs. Union Coll., Alliance, Ohio. Fellow Am. Bar Found., Ohio State Bar Found.; mem. ABA, Ohio Bar Assn., Stark County Bar Assn., Greater Canton C. of C. (bd. trustees), Ea. Ohio Football Ofcls. Assn. (pres. 1986—), Stark County Law Libr. Assn. (pres.). Republican. Presbyterian. Home: 3528 Darlington Rd NW Canton OH 44708-1714 Office Phone: 330-458-4220.

BENNINGTON, THOMAS FRANCIS, lawyer, county official; BA, North Ctrl. Coll., 1984; JD, DePaul U., 1987. Bar: Ill. 1987, U.S. Dist. Ct. (no. dist.) Ill. 1987. Ptnr. Chuhak & Tecson, P.C., Chgo., 1987—; commr. DuPage County Bd., Wheaton, Ill., 1998—. Commr. DuPage Cmty. Svc. Block Grant Commn., Wheaton, 1988—88, Forest Preserve Dist. DuPage County, Wheaton, 1998—2002, DuPage Cmty. Devel. Commn., Wheaton, 1998—; bd. dirs. Ill. Prairie Trail Authority, Wheaton. Com. mem. Nat. Assn. Counties Homeland Security Task Force, Washington, 2004—06; bd. mem. United Way Met. Chgo., 2004—; mem. Med. Response Corp, Wheaton; bd. mem. United Way South DuPage, Downers Grove, Ill., 2000—03; trustee North Ctrl. Coll. Bd. Trustees, Naperville, 1998—2000; bd. mem. U. Ill. Coop. Ext. Bd. (DuPage Unit), Wheaton, 2000—; asst. scoutmaster Boy Scouts Am., Downers Grove, 2005—; vol. Conservation Found., Naperville, 2000—05; active FEMA Cmty. Emergency Response Team, Darien, Ill., 2004—; membership chmn. Nat. Conf. Rep. County Ofcls., Washington, 2003—05. Recipient Vol. Leadership award, United Way Met. Chgo., 2003, Vol. of Yr. award, 2006, Pedal Power award, Chicagoland Bicycle Fedn., 2004. Mem.: ABA, DuPage Bar Assn., Chgo. Bar Assn., St. Charles Sportsmen's Club, Phi Alpha Delta (pres. 1986—87). Office: Chuhak & Tecson PC 26th Fl 30 South Wacker Dr Chicago IL 60606 Home Phone: 312-855-4317; Office Phone: 312-855-4317. Office Fax: 312-444-9027; Home Fax: 312-444-9027. Business E-Mail: tbennington@chuhak.com.

BENNINGTON, WILLIAM JAY, management consultant; b. Dayton, Ohio, Apr. 16, 1939; s. Jay G. and Mary Joahnn (Weisner) Kirby; m. Pamela Joan Manus, Oct. 22, 1977; children: J. Bret, J. Brad, J. Brian, J. William; 1 adopted child, Christian LeSuer BA in Journalism, U. Dayton, 1965. Asst. city editor Dayton Jour. Herald, 1964-66; asst. pub. rels. Pickands Mather & Co., Cleve., 1966-67; dir. pub. rels. Bayless-Kerr Co., Cleve., 1967-69; mgr. corp. pub. rels. Eaton Corp., Cleve., 1969-71; v.p. communications The Allen Group, Melville, NY, 1971-77; dir. pub. info. ITT Corp., NYC, 1977-78; sr. v.p. corp. affairs Colonial Penn Group, Phila., 1978-85; pres. SGI Communications, Inc., 1985-90, Laurel Communications, Moorestown, NJ, 1990-96, The Phoenix Partnership, Inc., Moorestown, 1995-97. Dir. pub. rels., comms. and cmty. rels. Blue Cross and Blue Shield NC, 1996-99, v.p. corp. comm., 1999-2000, v.p. tng. and orgnl. devel., 2000-04; pres. Bennington Enterprises, LLC, Moorestown, NJ, 2004—. Mem.: Union League Phila. Home and Office: 201 Laurence Dr Moorestown NJ 08057-2806 Office Phone: 856-235-2952. Personal E-mail: wjbpjb@comcast.net.

BENNINK, JACK RICHARD, microbiologist, researcher; b. Corry, Pa., Feb. 18, 1953; s. Ivan Guy and Mary Lou (Hurlbert) B.; m. Cindi Sue Merkle, May 29, 1976; children: Nathanael Scott, Tara Susanne. BA, Asbury Coll., 1975; PhD, U. Pa., 1978. Staff mem. Basel (Switzerland) Inst. for Immunology, 1980-82; asst. prof., assoc. prof. Wister Inst., Phila., 1982-87; sr. investigator NIH, Bethesda, Md., 1987—. Contbr. articles to profl. jours. Recipient Pub. Health Svc. award, 1990, 94, 95, 96, 99, 2000. Mem.: Am. Soc. Virology, Am. Assn. Immunologists. Office: NIH Rm 213 Bldg 4 Bethesda MD 20892-0440 Business E-Mail: jbennink@nih.gov.

BENNION, DAVID JACOBSEN, lawyer; b. Glendale, Calif., Jan. 29, 1940; s. Donald Clark and Margaret (Jacobsen) Bennion; m. Constance Wilson, Jan. 27, 1966; children: Marian, Margaret, Elizabeth, David, Sarah, Heidi. BA, Stanford U., Calif., 1964, JD, 1966. Bar: Calif. 1966. Ptnr. Boccardo Law Firm, San Jose, Calif., 1966-79; mission pres. LDS Ch., Geneva, 1979-82; ptnr. Packard, Packard and Bennion, Palo Alto, Calif., 1982-90, Bohn, Bennion & Niland, San Jose, 1993-98; pvt. practice San Jose, 1998—. Instr. continuing edn. bar, personal injury trial. Mem.: ABA, ATLA, Am. Inns Ct. (past pres., mem. exec. com. Santa Clara County chpt., nat. trustee at large), Calif. State Bar, Am. Bd. Trial Advs. Republican. Home: 650 Center Dr Palo Alto CA 94301 Office: 95 S Market St Ste 360 San Jose CA 95113-2301 Office Phone: 408-298-1977. Business E-Mail: dbennion@djbennion.com.

BENNION, JOHN WARREN, urban education educator; b. Salt Lake City, Nov. 25; s. M. Lynn and Katherine Bennion; m. Sylvia Lustig; children: Philip, Stanford, David, Bryan, Grant, Andrew. BS in Philosophy, English, U. Utah, 1961, MA in Edn. Adminstrn., 1962; PhD in Edn. Adminstrn., Ohio State U., 1966. Tchr. Granite High Sch., Salt Lake City, 1961-63; asst. instr. Ohio State U., Columbus, 1963-64, adminstrv. asst., 1965-66; adminstrv. intern Parma (Ohio) Sch. Dist., 1964-65; asst. supt. Elgin (Ill.) Pub. Schs., 1966-68; asst. prof. edn. adminstrn. Ind. U., Bloomington, 1968-69; supt. Brighton Cen. Schs., Rochester, N.Y., 1969-79, Bloomington (Minn.) Pub. Schs., 1979-80, Provo (Utah) Sch. Dist., 1980-85, Salt Lake City Schs., 1985-94; prof. urban edn., dir. Utah Edn. Consortium U. Utah, Salt Lake City, 1994—. Dir. Utah Urban Sch. Alliance, Salt Lake City; ednl. cons. Comprehensive Sch. Reform, Salt Lake City. Mem. ASCD, Assn. Early Childhood Edn., Am. Assn. Sch. Adminstrs. (Nat. Superintendent of Yr. award 1992, Disting. Svc. award 2002), Phi Delta Kappa, Rotary. Home: 1837 Harvard Ave Salt Lake City UT 84108-1804 also: 4001 S 700 E Ste 230 Salt Lake City UT 84107-2522

BENNION, SCOTT DESMOND, physician; b. Casper, Wyo., July 26, 1948; s. Desmond and Wanda Bennion; m. Stephanie Dawn Bennion; children: Scott, Beau, Brandon. BS summa cum laude, U. Wyo., 1970, MS, 1972; MD, U. Utah, 1975. Diplomate Nat. Bd. Med. Examiners, Am. Bd. Internal Medicine, Am. Bd. Dermatology, Am. Bd. Dermatologic Immunology/Diagnostic and Lab. Immunology. Intern U. Rutgers Med. Sch., 1975-76, resident in internal medicine, 1976-78, chief resident dept. medicine, 1978; commd. 2d lt. U.S. Army, 1976, advanced through grades to col., 1991; resident in dermatology Fitzsimons Army Med. Sch., Denver, 1981-84, chief resident dermatology svc., 1984, chief dept. clin. investigations, 1994-96, chmn. lab. animal use and care com., 1994-96; asst. chief dermatology svc. 98th Gen. Hosp., Nuremburg, Germany, 1986, chief dept. health clinics, 1987-88; chief immunodermatology sect. dermatology svc. Fitzsimons Army MC, Aurora, Colo., 1989—96; command surgeon AR-TASK, Kuwait, 1992; command surgeon joint task force Kuwait and Army Ctrl. Command-Forward, 1992; dermatology cons. to the Army Surgeon Gen., 1996-99; chief Troop Med. Clin. Fitzsimmons Army Garrison, 1996-99. Asst. clin. prof. dept. dermatology U. Colo. Health Sci. Ctr., 1992—99, assoc. prof. clin. dermatology, 1999—; assoc. prof. clin. medicine U. Wash. Med. Ctr. Contbr. chpts. to books: Military Dermatology, 1994, Secrets of Dermatology, 1996, 2d edit., 2000, 3rd edit., 2007, Dubois Lupus, 1997, also articles to profl. publs. Pres. Nuremburg Elem. Sch. PTSA; asst. cubmaster, cubmaster, chmn. Volksmarch com. Boy Scouts Am., 1986; pres. Foxridge Improvement Assn., 1992-01, pres., 1994-01; bd. dirs. Wyo. Make a Wish Found., 2000-; mem. Alcova Lake Area Bd., 2001-; trustee Casper Coll., 2000-, sec. to bd., 2002-04, treas. to bd., 2004-05, v.p. 2005—; trustee Anam Chara Hospice, Denver, 2001. Named to Order of Mil. Med. Merit, 1987; named Cubmaster of Yr. Bavaria dist. Boy Scouts Am., 1987, Businessman of Yr., Nat. Rep. Congl. Com. Bus. Adv. Coun., 2001; recipient Legion of Merit award, 1999. Fellow: ACP, Am. Acad. Dermatology (mem. govt. medicine task force 1996—2000, Colo. Dermatology Soc. rep. to adv. bd. 1997—, mem. rev. bd. to adv. bd. 2000—, Wyo. Acad. Dermatology rep. to adv. bd.); mem.: Dermatology Found. Leadership Soc. (chmn. Wyo.), Ctrl. Wyo. Skin Clinic, Wyo. Acad. Dermatology (sec. 1999—2003, pres. 2003—), Soc. for Investigative Dermatology, Assn. Mil. Dermatologists (sec.-treas. 1990—96, guest editor jour. 1991, pres. 1998—99, Residents award 1984), Assn. Mil. Surgeons, Phi Kappa Phi. Avocations: skiing, diving. Home: 2800 Garden Creek Rd Casper WY 82601 Office: 2546 E 2nd St #400 Casper WY 82609

BENNIS, WARREN GAMELIEL, business administration educator; b. NYC, Mar. 8, 1925; s. Philip and Rachel (Landau) B.; m. Clurie Williams, Mar. 30, 1962 (div. 1983); children: Katharine, John Leslie, Will Martin; m. Mary Jane O'Donnell, Mar. 8, 1988 (div. 1991); m. Grace Gabe, Nov. 29, 1992. AB, Antioch Coll., 1951; degree in Econ. (hon.), London Sch. Econs., 1952; PhD, MIT, 1955; LLD (hon.), Xavier U., Cin., 1972, George Washington U., 1977; LHD (hon.), Hebrew Union Coll., 1974, Kans. State U., 1979; DSc (hon.), U. Louisville, 1977, Pacific Grad. Sch. Psychology, 1987, Gov.'s State U., 1991; LHD (hon.), Doan Coll., 1993; LLD (hon.), London Bus. Sch., 2004. Diplomate Am. Bd. Profl. Psychology. Asst. prof. psychology MIT, Cambridge, 1953-56, prof., 1959-67; asst. prof. psychology and bus. Boston U., 1956-59; prof. Sloan Sch. Mgmt., 1959-67; provost SUNY-Buffalo, 1967-68, v.p. acad. devel., 1968-71; pres. U. Cin., 1971-77; U.S. prof. corps. and soc. Centre d'Etudes Industrielles, Geneva, Switzerland, 1978-79; exec.-in-residence Pepperdine U., 1978-79; George Miller Disting. prof.-in-residence U. Ill., Champaign-Urbana, 1978; Disting. prof. Bus. Adminstrn. Sch. Bus., U. So. Calif., LA, 1980-88; univ. prof., disting. prof. bus. adminstrn. U. So. Calif., LA, 1988—. Vis. lectr. Harvard U., 1958-59, Indian Mgmt. Inst., Calcutta; vis. prof. U. Lausanne (Switzerland), 1961-62, INSEAD, France, 1983; bd. dirs. The Foothill Group. Author: Planning of Change, 4th edit., 1985, Interpersonal Dynamics, 1963, 3d and 4th edits., 1975, Personal and Organizational Change, 1965, Changing Organizations, 1966, repub. in paperback as Beyond Bureaucracy, 1974, The Temporary Society, 1968, Organization Development, 1969, American Bureaucracy, 1970, Management of Change and Conflict, 1972, The Leaning Ivory Tower, 1973, The Unconscious Conspiracy: Why Leaders Can't Lead, 1976, Essays in Interpersonal Dynamics, 1979; author: (with B. Nanus) Leaders, 1985; author: On Becoming a Leader, 1989; author: (with I. Mitroff) The Unreality Industry, 1989; author: Why Leaders Can't Lead, 1989, Leaders on Leadership, 1992, An Invented Life: Reflections on Leadership and Change, 1993, Beyond Bureaucracy, 1993; author: (with J. Goldsmith) Learning to Lead, 1994; author: (with M. Mische) Reinventing the 21st Century, 1994; author: Beyond Leadership, 1994, Herding Cats: Bennis on Leadership, 1996, Organizing Genius, 1997, The Temporary Society, 1998, Co-Leaders, 1999, Old Dogs, New Tricks, 1999; author: (with G. Heil and D. Stephens) Douglas McGregor Re-Visited, 2000; author: Co-leaders, 1999, Managing the Dream, 2000; co-author: Geeks & Geezers, 2002, On Becoming a Leader, 2003; co-author: (with Bob Townsend) Re-inventing Leadership, 2005; cons. editor: Calif. Mgmt. Rev., Mgmt. Series Jossey-Bass Pubs. Mem. Pres.' White House Task Force on Sci. Policy, 1960-70; mem. FAA study task force U.S. Dept. Transp., 1975; mem. adv. com. N.Y. State Joint Legis. Com. Higher Edn., 1970-71; mem. Ohio Gov.'s Bus. and Employment Coun., 1972-74; mem. panel on alt. approaches to grad. edn. Coun. Grad. Schs. and Grad. Record-Exam Bd., 1971-73; chmn. Nat. Adv. Commn. on Higher Edn. for Police Officers, 1976-78; adv. bd. NIH, 1978-84; trustee Colo. Rocky Mountains Sch., 1978-82; bd. dirs. Am. Leadership Forum, 1984-89; mem. vis. com. for Humanities MIT, 1975-81; trustee Antioch Coll., Salk Inst.; chmn. adv. bd. Harvard U. Ctr. for Pub. Leadership. Capt. AUS, World War II. Decorated Bronze Star, Purple Heart; recipient Dow Jones award, 1987, McKinsey Fedn. award, 1967, 68. Mem. Am. Acad. Arts and Scis. (co-chmn. policy coun. 1969-71), Am. Mgmt. Assn. (dir. 1974-77), U.S. C. of C. (adv. group scholars). Office: U So Calif Sch Bus University Park Los Angeles CA 90089-0001 Office Phone: 213-740-0766. Personal E-mail: wbennis@earthlink.net.

BENNO, JONATHAN, chef; Grad., Culinary Inst. Am., Hyde Park, NY, 1993. Chef Aqua, San Francisco, French Laundry, Yountville, Calif., Daniel, NYC, Les Celebrites, NYC, L'Auberge du Vieux Puits, Corbieres, France, Gramercy Tavern, NYC; sous chef Craft, NYC; chef Per Se, NYC, 2004—. Office: Per Se in c/o Jonathan Benno 10 Columbus cir New York NY 10019 Office Phone: 212-823-9335.

BENNUR, MALLIKARJUNA, automotive executive; arrived in U.S., 1990; s. SiddeGowda and Parvathi Bennur. PhD, Indian Inst. Tech., Bombay, 1989; postgrad., Laval U., Que., Can., 1990, U. Toronto, 1991. Registered profl. engr. Assoc. prof. rsch. Laval U., Que., 1992—94; engring. cons. Que., 1995—97; chief engr. Group NewTech. Internat., Montreal, 1997—99; computer-aided engring. lead N&V prestige and luxury car group GM, Milford, Mich., 1999—. Contbr. articles to profl. jours. Recipient People Make Quality Happen award, GM, 2004; Indsl. Rsch. fellow, Natural Scis. and Engring. Rsch. Coun. of Can., 1996. Fellow: ASME, Soc. of Automotive Engrs. Achievements include invention of A New Full Contact Disc Brake for Automobiles. Office: GM Corp Mail Code 483-344-275 3300 GM Rd Milford MI 48380 Business E-Mail: mbennur@gmail.com.

BENOIST, CHRISTOPHE O., immunologist, educator; MD, Univ. Paris VII, 1981; doctoral degree, Univ. Louis Pasteur, Strasbourg, 1981. Co-head immunology and immunogenetics Joslin Diabetes Ctr.; William T. Young chair in diabetes rsch. Harvard Med. Sch., prof. medicine. Co-chair (with Dr. Mathis) Ctr. on Immunological Tolerance in Type I Diabetes Juvenile Diabetes Rsch. Found., Harvard Med. Sch. Mem.: NAS. Office: Joslin Diabetes Ctr Inc Rm 396 One Joslin Pl Boston MA 02215 Office Phone: 617-732-2400. E-mail: cb@joslin.harvard.edu.

BENOIT, CHRISTOPHER LOUIS, music educator; b. West Palm Beach, Fla., Jan. 18, 1965; s. Harold Pierre and Ann Scarpino Benoit; m. Robin Bailey, May 27, 2000; children: Jeffrey Pierre, Sarah Elizabeth Ware, Philip Andrew, Jack Ryan Ware. MusB in Edn., cert. in music performance, Fla. State U., Tallahassee, 1987. Band dir. Pierce Jr. H.S., Tampa, Fla., 1987—89; adj. instr. of horn U. of Tampa, 1988—91; band and orch. dir. Largo (Fla.) H. S., 1989—. Secondary music content coach Pinellas County Schs., Largo, 2002—05, dir. of all-county h.s. band, 1996, curriculum writer, 1994—; adjudicator for various music performance assessments, Fla. and S.C., 1998—. Cantor St. Catherine of Siena Cath. Ch., Largo, 1990—2005. Mem.: Music Educators Nat. Conf., Fla. Music Educators Assn., Pinellas County Music Educators Assn. (h.s. band chair 1994—96), Nat. Band Assn., Fla. Orch. Assn., Fla. Bandmasters Assn. (dist. chair state exec. bd. 1993—96, mem. state music performance assessment com. 1991—). Office: Largo H S 410 Missouri Ave Largo FL 33770 Home Phone: 727-447-9873; Office Phone: 727-585-4653. E-mail: benoitc@pcsb.org.

BENOIT, MARILYN B., psychiatrist, consultant; b. Trinidad & Tobago, 1943; MD, Georgetown U., 1973; M in Health Svcs. Adminstrn., George Washington U., 1993. Diplomate Am. Bd. Psychiatry and Neurology with subspecialty in child and adolescent psychiatry. Resident in psychiatry Georgetown U., Washington, 1973—75, resident in child psychiatry, fellow in child psychiatry, 1975—77, clin. assoc. prof. psychiatry; med. dir., exec. dir. Devereux Children's Ctr., 1993—98; pvt. practice, cons. Washington, 1998—. Pvt. practice psychiatry. Fellow: Am. Acad. Child and Adolescent Psychiatry (past pres. 2001—03); mem.: AMA, Am. Psychiat. Assn. Office: 1015 33d St NW 115 Washington DC 20007 Office Phone: 202-607-3032. E-mail: bartolom@aol.com.

BENOIT, PHILIP GROSVENOR, communications executive, educator, writer; b. Syracuse, NY, June 11, 1944; s. Paul Grosvenor and Doris Louise (Pond) B.; m. Candace Gail Blohm, Sept. 11, 1971; children: Kimberly Whitney, Marie Suzanne. BA, St. Lawrence U., 1966; MA, SUNY-Oswego, 1973. Asst. prof. comm. SUNY-Oswego, 1971—79; dir. pub. rels. Hartwick Coll., Oneonta, NY, 1979—84; dir. comm. Dickinson Coll., Carlisle, Pa., 1984—96; dir. pub. affairs Middlebury Coll., Vt., 1996—2005; assoc. v.p. coll. comm. Franklin Marshall Coll., Lancaster, Pa., 2005—06; cons. comm., pub. rels. Lancaster, 2006—. Author: (with Carl Hausman) Do Your Own Public Relations, 1983, Radio Station Operations, 1989, Positive Public Relations, 1990, (with O'Donnell and Hausman) Announcing: Broadcast Communicating Today, 6th edit., 2006, Modern Radio Production, 7th edit., 2006. Served to capt. U.S. Army, 1966-69. Decorated Bronze Star. Avocations: photography, music. Office Phone: 717-291-6468. Personal E-mail: pbenoit4@verizon.net.

BENOIT, RICHARD ARMAND, lawyer, retired police chief; s. Oliver Maurice and Delina Marie Benoit; m. Elizabeth Benoit, Nov. 17, 1962; children: Karen Marie, Richard Michael. AS, Bristol CC, Fall River, Mass., 1972; BS, Salve Regina U., 1975, MS, 1979; JD, So. New Eng. Sch. Law, New Bedford, 1989. Bar: Mass. 1990. Police officer New Bedford Police Dept., 1967-71, sgt., 1971-75, lt., 1975-82, capt., 1982-86, chief of police, 1986—; pvt. practice law New Bedford, 1990-97; ret., 1997; pvt. practice law, 1997—. With U.S. Army, 1959-62. Mem. ABA, Mass. Bar Assn., New Bedford Bar Assn., Bristol County Bar Assn. Avocations: swimming, golf, reading. Home: 209 Maywood St New Bedford MA 02745-5108

BENOIT BIRD, KELLY J., science educator; d. Bernard L. and Jane R. Benoit; life ptnr. Chad M. Waluk; m. Christopher E. Bird, June 13, 1998 (div. 2006). BS, Brown U., Providence, 1998; PhD, U. Hawaii, Manoa, 2003. Postdoctoral fellow U. Hawaii, Manoa, 2003—04; asst. prof. biol. oceanography Oreg. State U., Corvallis, 2004—. Contbr. articles to profl. jours. Recipient Best Young Presenter award, European Congress on Underwater Acoustics, 2004, Young Investigator award, Office Naval Rsch., 2005, Presdl. Early Career award for Scientists and Engrs., George W. Bush, 2006. Mem.: Ecol. Soc. Am., Internat. Soc. for Behavioral Ecology, Soc. for Marine Mammalogy (edn. com. 2001—06, Excellence in Sci. Comm. award 2003), Acoustical Soc. Am. (animal bioacoustics tech. com. 2002—06), Am. Soc. for Limnology and Oceanography. Office: Oregon State Univ 104 COAS Admin Bldg Corvallis OR 97331 Office Phone: 541-737-2063.

BENOLIEL, JOEL, lawyer; b. Seattle, June 11, 1945; s. Joseph H. and Rachel (Maimon) B.; m. Maureen Alhadeff, Mar. 1971; 1 child, Joseph D. BA in Polit. Sci., U. Wash., 1967, JD, 1971. Bar: Wash., US Dist. Ct. (we. dist.) Wash., US Ct. Appeals (9th cir.), US Mil. Ct. Appeals. Assoc. atty. MacDonald, Horgue & Bayless, Seattle, 1971-73, ptnr., 1973-78; v.p., gen. counsel Jack A. Benaroya Co., Seattle, 1978-84; ptnr. Trammell Crow Co., Seattle, 1985-87, Spieker Ptnrs., Bellevue, Wash., 1987-92; sr. v.p. law and real estate, gen. counsel Costco Wholesale Corp. (formerly Price Costco, Inc.), Issaquah, Wash., 1992—. Bd. dir. Overlake Sch., Redmond, Wash., 1995—, Congregation Ezra Bessaroth, Seattle, 1992-95. With US Army, 1968-74. Avocations: tennis, boating, skiing, reading fiction. Office: Costco Wholesale Corp 999 Lake Dr Issaquah WA 98027-5367*

BENOR, SARAH BUNIN, language educator, religious studies educator; BA, Columbia U., NYC, 1997; PhD, Stanford U., Calif., 2004. Asst. prof. contemporary jewish studies Hebrew Union Coll., Jewish Inst. Religion, LA, 2004—. Office Phone: 213-749-3424.

BENOSKI, JAMES E., insurance company executive; Sr. v.p. claims Cincinnati Ins. Co., Fairfield, Ohio, CEO, 2006—; chief ins. officer Cincinnati Fin. Corp., Fairfield, Ohio, 2004—, vice-chmn., pres., COO, 2006—. Office: Cincinnati Fin Corp 6200 S Gilmore Rd Fairfield OH 45014*

BENOWITZ, JUNE MELBY, historian, educator; b. Portland, Oreg., Mar. 8, 1949; d. Harold Eugene and Peggy Terry Melby; m. Elliot Benowitz, Sept. 29, 1979. AS in History, Portland C.C., 1979; BA in History, Portland State U., 1981, MA in History, 1988; PhD in History, U. Tex., Austin, 1996. Adj. history instr. Portland State U., 1991—93, Portland C.C., 1994—95, Keiser Coll., Sarasota, Fla., 1997—2002, Manatee C.C., Bradenton, Fla., 2001—02; asst. prof. history U. South Fla., Sarasota/Manatee, 2002—. Faculty adv. Coll. Democrats, Sarasota-Manatee History Club, U. South Fla. Author: Days of Discontent, 2002, Encyclopedia of American Women and Religion, 1998 (Choice Mag. award, 1999); contbr. chapters to books. Bd. dirs. Friends of Sarasota History Ctr. Mem.: Am. Hist. Assn., Orgn. Am. Historians, Phi Alpha Theta, Phi Kappa Phi. Evangelical Lutheran. Avocations: hiking, swimming, bird study and care, reading, theater. Office: Univ South Florida 8350 N Tamiami Trail Sarasota FL 34243-2049

BENSCH, KLAUS GEORGE, pathology educator; b. Miedar, Germany, Sept. 1, 1928; married; 3 children. MD, U. Erlangen, Germany, 1953. Diplomate: Am. Bd. Pathology. Intern U. Hosps. of Erlangen, 1953-54; resident in anat. pathology U. Tex./M.D. Anderson Hosp., Houston, 1954—56; instr. pathology Yale Med. Sch., 1958-61, asst. prof., 1961-64, assoc. prof., 1964-68; prof. pathology Stanford Med. Sch., 1968—, acting chmn. dept. pathology, 1984-85, chmn. dept. pathology, 1985-99, prof. emeritus, 2001—. Office: Stanford U Med Sch Dept Pathology 300 Pasteur Dr Palo Alto CA 94304-2203 E-mail: kbensch@stanford.edu.

BENSELER, DAVID P., foreign language educator; b. Balt., Jan. 10, 1940; s. Ernest Parr and Ellen Hood Escar (Turnbaugh) B.; m. Suzanne Shelton, May 25, 1985; children: James Declan, Derek Justin. BA, West Wash. U., 1964; MA, U. Oreg., 1966, PhD, 1971. From asst. prof. to assoc. prof. Wash. State U., 1969—77; prof. , chair dept. German, Ohio State U., 1977—91; chair dept. modern langs. and lits. Case Western Res. U., 1991-98, Louis D. Beaumont U. prof. humanities, 1991-98, Emile B. de Sauzé prof. modern lang. and lit., 1998—2004, Emile B. de Sauzé prof. emeritus modern lang. and lit., 2004—. Disting. vis. prof. fgn. langs. U.S. Mil. Acad., West Point, N.Y., 1987-88, N.Mex. State U., Las Cruces, 1989; founding dir. German Studies program Case Western Reserve U. and Max Kade Ctr. for German Studies; mem. numerous coms. Case Western Res. U., U.S. Military Acad., U.S. Naval Acad., U. Akron, Ohio State U., Wash. State U., Ind. U., Emory U., U. Md., U. Cin., U. Wis., Pa. State U., U. Va., U. Mich., various others; lectr., panel mem., workshop convr, cons. in field. Compiler, editor: (with Suzanne S. Moore) Comprehensive Index to the Modern Language Journal, 1916-1996, MLJ Electronic Index, 1997—; author/editor more than 75 other books, bibliographies, jours.; contbr. chpts. to books and articles to profl. jours. With USN, 1957—63. Decorated Bundesverdienstkreuz I. Klasse (Germany); recipient Army Commendation medal for disting. civilian svc. U.S. Mil. Acad., 1988; Lilly Found. Faculty Renewal fellow Stanford U., 1975, Fulbright grad. fellow, 1967-68, NDEA fellow, U. Oreg., 1964-67; various other grants, fellowships, scholarships. Mem. MLA, AAUP, Am. Assn. Applied Linguistics, Am. Assn. Tchrs. of German, Am. Coun. on the Tchg. of Fgn. Langs., Am. Goethe Soc., Am. Soc. for 18th Century Studies, German Studies Assn., Lessing Soc., Soc. German-Am. Studies, Phi Sigma Iota, Sigma Kappa Phi, Delta Phi Alpha. Office Phone: 216-368-3071. Business E-Mail: dpb5@case.edu.

BENSEN, ANNETTE WOLF, graphic art company consultant; b. Bklyn., Aug. 7, 1938; d. Isidor and Sylvia Wolf; m. Gene Bensen, Oct. 14, 1979. AAS, NYC C.C., 1958; postgrad., Pratt Inst., 1974-75, Sch. Visual Arts, NYC. With Wagner-Ellsberg, Inc., NYC, 1958-62; art dir. Island Pen Mfg. Inc., Stacie Pen, Curtis Rand Industries, Inc., NYC, 1962-68; with G.S. Lithographers, Inc., NYC, 1968-70; ptnr., pres. Rembrandt's Mother, Inc.,

NYC, 1970-72; co-owner, pres. Film Comp., Inc., NYC, 1972-75; mgr. Expertype, NYC, 1975-90, Expertype & The Graphic Word Co., NYC, 1990-92; sr. v.p. Expertype divsn. JCH Group Ltd., NYC, 1992-93; v.p. prodn. Metro Creative Graphics, Inc., NYC, 1993-97; v.p. ops. Digital Ops. Tech. Svcs., Inc., NYC, 1997-98; owner, mgr. AnGen Svcs., NYC, 1999—. Adj. lectr. NYC CC, 1971—75, 1998—; adv. commn. dept. graphic arts and advtg. tech. Coll. Tech./CUNY, 1994—; adv. commn. HS Graphic Comm. Arts, 1999—, HS Art and Design, NYC, 2002—; adj. lectr. Parsons Sch. Design, 2004—. Chair graphic arts adv. commn. for occupl. edn. NYC Dept. Edn.; adv. commn. Graphic Arts HS of City of NY; bd. dirs. Graphic Arts Edn. Found., 2007—. Recipient Florence B. and Leo H. Joachim award for disting. industry svc., 2004, Gamma Gold Key award Gamma Epsilon Tau, 2001, Bus. and Industry Partnership award HS of Graphic Comm. Arts, 2002, Svc. to Industry award Navigators, 2003, Arthur Meyers Meml. award for recognition of excellence in edn. Assn. Graphic Comms., 2003; NY Club of Printing House Craftsmen fellow, 1996. Mem. Advt. Women NY, Graphic Arts Profls., Women in Prodn., Printing Women NY (pres.), Printing Tchrs. Guild NY (Contbn. to Edn. award 2001), Mid-Hudson Graphic Art Assn. Address: AnGen Svcs 585 C Heritage Hills Dr Somers NY 10589-1908 Office Phone: 914-277-8727. Fax: 914-276-0666. Business E-Mail: angen@comcast.net.

BEN SHAUL, YOCHANAN MENASHSHEH See MISHLER, JOHN

BENSINGER, DAVID AUGUST, dentist, dean; b. St. Louis, May 14, 1926; s. William and Esther (Lissner) B.; m. Myra Blass, Dec. 24, 1944 (div. June 1972); children: Judith Ann (Mrs. William Thomas Haynes), Scott David; m. Susan Cohn Hartman, May 31, 1975. BA, Washington U., 1944; DDS, St. Louis U., 1948; postgrad. health systems mgmt, Harvard U. Sch. Bus. Adminstrn., 1977. Mem. faculty, adminstrn. Sch. Dentistry Washington U., St. Louis, 1949—, assoc. prof. dept. periodontics, 1956-76, prof., 1976-90, assoc. dean, 1970-76, acting dean, 1976-83, exec. assoc. dean, 1983-87; dean Washington U. Sch. Dental Medicine, 1987-90, dean, prof. emeritus, 1990; practice dentistry, specializing in periodontics St. Louis, 1949-90; mem. staff Barnes, Jewish hosps., both St. Louis; mem. deans com. VA Hosp.; mem. nat. adv. com. Dental Edn. Rev. Com., NIH, 1969-72. Cons. Scott AFB, St. Louis, 1956-62; mem. adv. coun. SBA, 1975. Editor: Jour. Greater St. Louis Dental Soc, 1963-70; asso. editor: Jour. Mo. Dental Assn, 1966-73. Mem. exec. bd. Ladue (Mo.) Sch. Sys., 1964-67; chmn. bd. counselors U. Calif. Med. Ctr., San Francisco, 1995-98; chmn. regional cabinet Wash. U., San Francisco, 1996—; elected trustee Coll. of Notre Dame, Belmont, Calif., 1998—, chmn. fin. and investment com. Lt. M.C., U.S. Army, 1948-49, capt. med. dept. USAF, 1955-56. Fellow Am. Coll. Dentists, Internat. Coll. Dentists; mem. ADA (ho. of dels.), Mo. Dental Assn. (pres. 1973-74, jud. coun.), Greater St. Louis Dental Soc. (bd. dirs. 1963-70, Svc. award 1971), Am. Acad. Peridontology, Internat. Assn. Dental Rsch., Midwest Soc. Peridontology (pres. 1972-73), Pierre Fouchard Acad., Royal Soc. Medicine (Eng.), Inst. Internat. Edn. (vice chmn. bd. dirs., chmn. exec. com. 1996-98), Washington U. Alumni Assn. (Alumnus of Yr. 1968), Univ. Club (St. Louis), St. Louis Club, Harvard Club (Boston and N.Y.C.), Omicron Kappa Upsilon. Home: 2100 Pacific Ave San Francisco CA 94115-1585

BENSINGER, PETER BENJAMIN, consulting firm executive; b. Chgo., Mar. 24, 1936; s. Benjamin Edward and Linda Elkus (Galston) B.; m. Judith S. Bensinger; children: Peter Benjamin, Jennifer Anne, Elizabeth Brooke, Virginia Brette. BA, Yale, 1958; degree (hon.), San Marcos U., Peru, 1978; LLD (hon.), Dan Kook U., Seoul, Republic of Korea, 1980. Various mktg. positions Brunswick Corp., Chgo., 1958-65, new products mgr., 1966-68; gen. sales mgr. Brunswick Internat., Europe, 1965-66, spl. products mgr., 1966-68; chmn. Ill. Youth Commn., 1969-70; dir. Ill. Dept. Corrections, Chgo., 1970-73; exec. dir. Chgo. Crime Commn., 1973; adminstr. Drug Enforcement Adminstrn., Washington, 1976-81; pres. Bensinger, DuPont & Assocs., Chicago, 1982—. Chmn. Ill. Criminal Justice Info. Authority, 1991—; cons. various orgns.; del. White House Conf. on Corrections, 1971, Drug Abuse, 1988, U.S. Del. to Interpol, 1978. Pres. Lincoln Park Zool. Soc., Chgo., 1962-63; governing life mem., also mem. men's council Chgo. Art Inst.; mem. Ill. Alcoholism Adv. Council, Ill. Law Enforcement Commn., Ill. Council on Diagnosis and Evaluation Criminal Defendants, Ill. Narcotics Adv. Council; adv. com. Center for Studies in Criminal Justice, So. Ill. U., Center for Studies in Criminal Justice, U. Chgo.; vice chmn. ad hoc adv. com. U.S. Dept. Justice Nat. Inst. Corrections; mem. exec. com. Am. Bar Assn. Nat. Commn. Corrections; chmn. Ill. Task Force on Corrections, 1969; mem. bd. Fed. Prison Industries, Inc., 1973-85; bd. dirs. Jewish Fedn. Met. Chgo., Council Community Services Met. Chgo., Ill. Commn. on Children, Children's Meml. Hosp., Chgo., 1988—; bd. dirs., mem. exec. council Anti-Defamation League; regional bd. dirs. NCCJ; trustee Phillips Exeter Acad.; chmn. nat. law enforcement explorers conf. Boy Scouts Am., 1981, U.S. del. to, Interpol, 1978. Recipient Young Leadership award Jewish Fedn.-Welfare Bds. Met. Chgo., 1969, award for excellence John Howard Assn., 1972, Disting. Svc. award Govt. of Peru, 1978, U.S. Dept. of Justice award, EEO award, 1979, Disting. Svc. medal USCG, 1981, John Phillips award Phillips Exeter Acad., 1990, Lincoln medal Lincoln Acad., 1998, Lifetime Achievement award, Assn. Former Fed. Narcotics Agents, 2006. Mem. Am. Correctional Assn. (bd. dirs.), Assn. State Correctional Adminstrs. (sec. 1971-72, pres. 1972-73), Internat. Assn. Chiefs of Police (mem. exec. com.), Nat. Sheriffs Assn. (life), Chgo. City Club (bd. dirs.), Arts Club, Comml. Club Chgo., Yale Club (N.Y.C.), Shoreacres Club (Lake Bluff), Casino Club (Chgo.). Office: 20 N Wacker Dr Chicago IL 60606-2806

BENSINGER, STEVEN J., insurance company executive; b. NYC, Jan. 12, 1955; m. Karen Bensinger; children: Kaylin, Kyle. BS, NYU, 1976. CPA, NY. Ptnr. Coopers & Lybrand, NYC, 1976-87; exec. v.p., CFO Skandia Am. Group, NYC, 1987-90, pres., COO; exec. v.p., CFO Combined Specialty Group, Inc.; treas. Am. Internat. Group, Inc., NYC, 2002—05, sr. v.p., 2005, exec. v.p., 2005—; CFO, 2005—. Mem. AICPA, Brokers & Reins. Markets Assn., Reins. Assn. Am., Soc. Ins. Accts., NY State Soc. CPAs, NYU Stern Sch. Bus. Alumni Assn. (bd. dirs.). Office: Am Internat Group Inc 70 Pine St New York NY 10270*

BENSMAIA, REDA, French studies educator, researcher; b. Kouba, Algeria, Oct. 15, 1944; arrived in U.S., 1979; s. Kaddour and Saleha (Benouniche) Bensmaia; m. Joelle Proust, Feb. 2, 1947 (div. June 1989); children: Sliman, Djamel; m. Maurizia Natali, Oct. 22, 1995. Licence es-lettres, Facultes des lettres, Aix-En-provence, France, 1969, MPhil, 1971; BA, Ecole Pratique, Paris, France, 1977, PhD, 1981. Asst. prof. Institut d' Etudes Politiques, Algiers, Algeria, 1973-74, U. Algiers, Algeria, 1974-76; prof. philosophy Lycée Français, San Francisco, 1979-81; assoc. prof. U. Minn., Mpls., 1981-85; dir. Paris Ctr. for Critical Studies, 1985-88; assoc. prof. U. Minn., Mpls., 1988-89; prof. U. Va., Charlottesville, 1989—91, Brown U., Providence, 1991—. Author: The Barthes Effect, 1987, The Year of Passages, 1995, Alger ou la maladie de la mémoire, 1997, Experimental Nations or the invention of the Maghreb, 2003; editor: On Gilles Deleuze, 1989; contbr. articles to profl. jours. Decorated chevalier des Palmes Academiques France; recipient award, Am. Inst. for Maghrebi Studies, 1995; grantee, NEH, 1983; EDP grantee, U. Minn., 1989. Mem.: MLA, Coun. for Internat. Ednl. Exch. (steering com., adv. bd. curriculum), Sites (adv. bd.), Lendemains (adv. bd.), Continuum (adv. bd.). Avocations: writing poetry and fiction, music, hiking. Office: Brown U Dept French Studies PO Box 1961 Providence RI 02912-1961 Office Phone: 401-863-2741. E-mail: Reda_Bensmaia@brown.edu.

BENSMAN, STEPHEN J., school librarian, researcher; b. Sheboygan, Wis., Aug. 26, 1938; s. Solomon and Leah Z. Bensman; m. Miriam Roza, July 9, 1936. MLS, U. Wis., 1975, PhD in History, 1977. Fgn. law libr. U. Wis., Madison, 1975—78; libr. La. State U., Baton Rouge, 1978—. Contbr. articles to profl. jours. Specialist 6 US Army, 1963. Mem.: ALA, Am.Soc. Info. Sci. and Tech., Phi Beta Kappa, Beta Phi Mu, Phi Eta Sigma. Home: 724 Shady Lake Pky Baton Rouge LA 70810-4328 Office: LSU Librs La State Univ Baton Rouge LA 70803-3300 Office Phone: 225-578-6932. Personal E-mail: bensmans@bellsouth.net. Business E-Mail: notsjb@lsu.edu.

BENSON, AL BOWEN, III, oncologist, educator; b. Buffalo, Dec. 23, 1950; BA, SUNY, 1972; MD, SUNY, Buffalo, 1976. Diplomate Am. Bd. Internal Medicine, cert. med. oncology Am. Bd. Internal Medicine, diplomate internal medicine 1979, med. oncology 1983. Intern U. Wis. Hosps., Madison, 1976—77, resident medicine, 1977—79; co-dir. medicine Nat. Pub. Health Svc., Ill., 1979—81; fellow oncology U. Wis. Hosps., Madison, 1981—84; attending physician Northwestern Meml. Hosp., Chgo., 1984—, Lakeside VA Med. Ctr., Chgo., 1984—. Prof. medicine U. Ill., 1979—81, Northwestern U., 1984—, assoc. dir. clin. investigations, 1995—. Office: Northwestern Univ 676 N St Clair Ste 850 Chicago IL 60611-2998

BENSON, ALLEN B., chemist, educator, consultant; b. Sioux Rapids, Iowa, Oct. 1, 1936; s. Bennett and Freda (Smith) B.; m. Marian Richter, Aug. 24, 1959; children: Bradley Gerard, Jill Germaine. BS in Secondary Edn. magna cum laude, Western Mont. U., 1960; postgrad., U. Mont., Missoula, 1960-61, Seattle U., 1962-63; M in Natural Sci., Highlands U., 1965; postgrad., Ill. Inst. Tech., 1969; PhD in Chemistry, U. Idaho, 1970. Chemistry instr. U. Wis., Whitewater, 1968-69, Spokane Falls C.C., Wash., 1969—2000. Mem. steering com. Hanford Edn. Action League, Spokane, 1984-86; energy and nuclear cons., 1970-88; mem. Hanford Health Effects Panel, Richland, Wash., 1986; numerous speeches, interviews and pub. articles on energy and nuclear issues, including speaker nat. conv. Physicians for Social Responsibility, Denver, 1990; lead sci. cons. Hanford Radiation Litigation Lawsuit for Hanford Downwinders against GE, DuPont and Rockwell, Wash., 1991-93; sci. conf. leader UNLV on radiation and health effects, 1992; advisor internat. team of experts of contamination and health affects Simultec Ltd., Zurich, 1996-97. Author: Hanford radioactive Fallout: Are There Observable Health Effects?, 1989; co-author: Benson-Nguyen Proposal on Kazakhstan's Nuclear Test Site and the Human Health Effects, 1994, On Practical Application of the Yakima Holistic Concept to Environmental Restoration, 1995. Active Spokane County Dem. Platform Com., 1980, 84; prepared and gave testimony for Yakama Nation to U.S. Pres.'s Risk assessment Com., Seattle, 1995; sr. scientific con. Yakama Nation, 1995-97. With U.S. Army, 1955-57. Roman Catholic. Achievements include designed, invented and experimentally verified a holistic fertilizer Dr. Benson's Natural Mix, being commercialized in Nevada and California, 1999. Home Phone: 702-631-2626; Office Phone: 702-631-0558. E-mail: allenbbenson@earthlink.net.

BENSON, BRUCE ELLIS, philosophy educator; s. Warren Sten and Lenore Evelyn Benson. BA, Wheaton Coll., Ill., 1983; PhD, Leuven U., Belgium, 1993. Asst. prof. philosophy Wheaton Coll., Ill., 1993—2000, assoc. prof. philosophy, 2000—07, prof. philosophy, 2007—. Lectr. in philosophy Union Theol. Sem., NYC, 2003. Author: (books) Graven Ideologies, 2002, The Improvisation of Musical Dialogue, 2003, Pious Nietzsche, 2007; editor: The Phenomenology of Prayer, 2005, Hermeneutics at the Crossroads, 2006. Recipient Sr. Scholarship Achievement award, Wheaton Coll., 2006; Fulbright fellow, 1990. Mem.: Soc. Phenomenology and Existential Philosophy, Soc. Christian Philosophers, Soc. Continental Philosophy and Theol. (mem. exec. com. 1997—), Ctr. Theol. and Philosophy, Am. Soc. Aesthetics, Am. Acad. Religion (co-chair, theol. and continental philosophy group 2005—), Am. Philos. Assn. Avocation: jazz. Office: Wheaton Coll 501 College Ave Wheaton IL 60187 Office Phone: 630-752-5817.

BENSON, CEDRIC, professional football player; b. Midland, Tex., Dec. 28, 1982; Student, Univ. Tex., 2005. Running back Chgo. Bears, 2005—. Named to All-American Team, NCAA, 2005. Office: Chgo Bears 1000 Football Dr Lake Forest IL 60045

BENSON, CRAIG ROBERT, former governor; b. NYC, Oct. 8, 1954; m. Denise Benson; 2 children. B in Fin., Babson Coll., 1977; MBA, Syracuse U., 1979. With Teradyne Inc., Boston, 1979—81, Inetlan, Chelmsford, Mass., 1981—83; co-founder Cabletron, 1983, dir. ops., 1984—89, chmn., COO, treas., 1989—97, pres., CEO, chmn., treas., 1998—99; gov. State of N.H., Concord, 2003—05. Adj. prof. entrepreneurship Babson Coll., 2000. Republican.

BENSON, DEE VANCE, federal judge; b. Salt Lake City, Aug. 25, 1948; s. Gilbert and Beryl Butler (Despain) B.; children: Angela, Natalie, Lucas, Katherine. BA, Brigham Young U., 1973, JD, 1976. Bar: Utah 1976, admitted to practice: US Dist. Ct. Utah 1976, US Ct. Appeals (10th Cir.) 1976, US Supreme Ct. 1984, US Ct. Appeals (5th Cir.) 1988. Ptnr. Snow, Christensen & Martineau, Salt Lake City, 1976-84; legal counsel Senate Judiciary Com., Washington, 1984-86; chief of staff Senator Orrin Hatch's Office, Washington, 1986-88; legal counsel US Senate Select Com., Washington, 1987; assoc. dep. atty. gen. US Dept. Justice, Washington, 1988, US atty. dist. Utah Salt Lake City, 1989-91; judge US Dist. Ct., Salt Lake, 1991—99, chief judge, 1999—; judge Fgn. Intelligence Surveillance Ct., 2004—. Legal counsel Iran-Contra Congl. Investigating Com., Washington, 1987. Contbg. author univ. law rev. Mem. ABA, Utah State Bar (com. on cts. and judges), Salt Lake County Bar Assn., Phi Alpha Delta. Mem. Lds Ch. Avocations: soccer, skiing, bicycling, basketball, running. Office: US Dist Ct 350 S Main St Ste 251 Salt Lake City UT 84101-2106*

BENSON, DONALD ERICK, finance company executive; b. Mpls., June 1, 1930; s. Fritz and Annie (Nordstrom) B.; children: Linda K., Nancy A., Stephen D.; m. Roberta Mann, 1992 BBA in Acctg., U. Minn., 1955. CPA, Minn. From staff to partnership Arthur Andersen & Co., Mpls., 1955-68, MEI Corp., Mpls., 1968-86; pres. MEI Diversified Inc., Mpls., 1986-94; exec. v.p. Marquette Fin. Companies, Mpls., 1992—; also bd. dirs. Bd. dirs. Mair Holdings, Inc., Minn. Twins Baseball Club, Mass. Mut. Corp. Investors, Mass. Mut. Participation Investors, Cargo Holdings Internat., Inc., First Calif. Fin. Group, Inc.; dir. Swedish Coun. Am. and its Royal Round Table Chmn. Bethel U. Found., St. Paul; past chmn. Pk. Nicollet Med. Services, Mpls.; past pres. Boys and Girls Clubs, Mpls., Minn. Mem. AICPA, Minn. CPA Soc., Mpls. Club, Interlachen Country Club

BENSON, EDWIN WELBURN, JR., trade association executive; b. Nashville, Feb. 18, 1945; s. Edwin Welburn and Mildred B.; m. Jamie Suzanne Parks, Aug. 14, 1982; 1 child, Edwin III. BA, Vanderbilt U., 1967. V.p. The Benson Co., Nashville, 1970-78; assoc. exec. dir. Country Music Assn., Nashville, 1979-91, exec. dir., 1992—2005, chief strategic officer, 2006—. Bd. govs. Nashville C. of C., 1994-97; bd. dir. County Music Retirement Cmty., 2001-, Leadership Music, 2004-, Tenn. Repertory Theatre, 2007-; bd. trustees, Country Music Found., 2000-05, Nash. Centennial Hosp., 2007-. With U.S. Army, 1967-70. Decorated Bronze Star for Svc. in Vietnam US Army; named a Tennessean of Yr., Nashville Tennessean newspaper, 2005. Mem. Leadership Music Alumni, Leadership Nashville Alumni, The Rec. Acad., Acad. TV Arts and Scis., Am. Soc. Assn. Execs. Avocations: golf, travel, music. Office: Country Music Assn 1 Music Cir S Nashville TN 37203-4312

BENSON, ELIZABETH POLK, art specialist; b. Washington, May 13, 1924; d. Theodore Booton and Rebecca Dean (Albin) Benson. BA, Wellesley Coll., 1945; MA, Cath. U. Am., 1956. Mus. aide, curator Nat. Gallery of Art, Washington, 1946-60; curator Pre-Columbian Collection Dumbarton Oaks, Washington, 1962-79, dir. Ctr. for Pre-Columbian Studies, 1971-79; rsch. assoc. Inst. Andean Studies, Berkeley, Calif., 1980—. Lectr. Cath. U. Am., Washington, 1968—69; adj. prof. Columbia U., NYC, 1973; sr. lectr. U. Tex., Austin, 1985; Andrew S. Keck disting. vis. prof. Am. U., Washington, 1987; cons. Montreal Mus. Fine Arts, 1980—84, 1990—92; mem. adv. bd. L.Am. Indian Lits. Jour., Pitts., 1989—; co-curator traveling exhbn. Birds and Beasts of Ancient L.Am., 1995—98; mem. exec. com. Peruvian Am. Rsch. Found., 2004—; mem. adv. bd. Found. for the Advancement of Mesoam. Studies, 1994—2000. Author: The Maya World, 1967, 1972, 1977, The Mochica, 1972, Birds and Beasts of Ancient Latin America, 1997; co-editor: Olmec Art of Ancient Mexico, 1996, Ritual Sacrifice in Ancient Peru, 2001. Mem.: Assn. L.Am. Art, L.Am. Indian Lits. Assn. (v.p. 1989—), The Lit. Soc., Soc. Women Geographers (mus. com. 1994—2006). Home and Office: 8314 Old Seven Locks Rd Bethesda MD 20817-2005

BENSON, GEORGE W., lawyer; b. Ottowa, Ill., July 29, 1948; BA, Williams Coll., 1970; JD, Harvard U., 1973. Bar: Ill. 1973, US Tax Ct., US Ct. Fed. Claims, US Ct. of Appeals (fed. & 7th cirs.), US Supreme Ct. Ptnr. McDermott, Will & Emery, Chgo. Contbr. articles to various profl. journs. Mem. Chgo. Bar Assn., Phi Beta Kappa, Nat. Coun. Farmer Coops. (legal, tax and acctg. com.), Nat. Soc. Accts. for Coops. (tax com.). Office: McDermott Will & Emery 227 W Monroe St Ste 3100 Chicago IL 60606-5096 Office Phone: 312-984-7529. Office Fax: 312-984-7700. Business E-Mail: gbenson@mwe.com.

BENSON, HANDE YURTTAN, adult education educator; d. Necdet and Iffet Yurttan; m. Daniel Robert Benson, Aug. 30, 1999. PhD, Princeton U., NJ, 1997—2001. Asst. prof. US Naval Acad., Annapolis, Md., 2002—03, Drexel U., Phila., 2003—. Office: Drexel Univ Dept Decision Sci 3141 Chestnut St Philadelphia PA 08610 Business E-Mail: benson@drexel.edu.

BENSON, JAMES, aerospace transportation executive; BS in Geology, U. Mo., 1971. Founder, pres. ImageFast, McLean, Va., Compusearch Software Systems, McLean, Va., 1984—95; founder, bd. dir. SpaceDev, Inc., Poway, Calif., 1997—, chief tech. officer, chmn. bd., 1997—2006; founder Benson Space Co., Poway, Calif., 2006—. Vice-chmn., private sector repr., Nat. Space Grant Review Panel NASA. Named Alumnus of Yr., U. Mo., 2005. Mem.: Am. Soc. Civil Engr. (mem. subcommittee on Near Earth Object Impact Prevention and Mitigatio), Personal Spaceflight Fedn. (founding dir. 2005—). Achievements include invention of modern text indexing and searching in 1984; SpaceDev designing and producing an innovative satellite for NASA and the hybrid rocket motor technology for Paul Allen's SpaceShipOne; seeking to provide the first, safest and lowest cost astronaut-making spaceflights for the emerging personal suborbital commercial spaceflight market through Benson Space Company; Benson Space Company is working with SpaceDev to develop the SpaceDev Dream Chaser, which will be used to achieve hopefully the first suborbital flight by the end of 2008.*

BENSON, JAMES BRACKEN, lawyer; b. Bloomington, Ill., Mar. 14, 1945; s. Thomas Bracken and Ruth Mabel (Glasener) B.; m. April Lane, June 4, 1972; children: Corey L. Benson, Eric L. AB, Dartmouth Coll., 1967; JD, Harvard U., 1970. Bar: N.Y. 1971, N.J. 1985. Assoc. Strock, Strock & Lavan, NYC, 1970-77; assoc., gen. counsel, corp. v.p. Automatic Data Processing, Inc., Roseland, N.J., 1977—. Office: Automatic Data Processing Inc 1 A D P Blvd Roseland NJ 07068-1786 Office Fax: 973-974-3334.*

BENSON, JAMES M., investment company executive; b. 1945; m. Marlene Benson; 2 children. BA in Econs., U. Ill., 1968; MBA, U. So. Calif., 1972. CLU. With Pacific Mut. Life Inst. Co., 1968-84; ptnr. Mgmt. Compensation Group, 1984-93; former pres., COO Equitable Life Assurance Soc. U.S., NYC, former bd. dirs.; pres., CEO New Eng. Fin., Boston, 1997-98, chmn., CEO, 1998—2002; pres. individual bus. MetLife, Inc., 1999—2002; chmn., pres., and CEO Gen Am. Fin. Corp., 2002; sr. exec. v.p., pres. sales and mktg. John Hancock Fin. Svcs., Inc., 2002—; pres., CEO John Hancock Life Ins. Co., 2002—; dir. John Hancock Subs., LLC. Bd. dirs. Achilles Track Club, The Am. Coll., Christopher Reeve Found., Alliance Francaise, Hosp. for Spl. Surgery, African Wildlife Found.; founder, chmn. World T.E.A.M. Sports.

BENSON, JOANNE E., retired lieutenant governor; b. Jan. 4, 1943; m. Robert Benson; 2 children. BS, St. Cloud State U. Mem. Minn. Senate, St. Paul, 1991-94; lt. gov. State of Minn., St. Paul, 1994-98; CEO, Minn. Bus. Acad., St. Paul, 1999—2005.

BENSON, JOHN ALEXANDER, JR., internist, educator; b. Manchester, Conn., July 23, 1921; s. John A. and Rachel (Patterson) B.; children: Peter M., John Alexander III, Susan Leigh, Jeremy P. BA, Wesleyan U., Middletown, Conn., 1943; MD, Harvard Med. Sch., Boston, 1946. Diplomate Am. Bd. Internal Medicine (mem. 1969-91, sec.-treas. 1972-75, pres. 1975-91, pres. emeritus 1991—), Subsplty. Bd. Gastroenterology (mem. 1961-66, chmn. 1965-66). Intern Univ. Hosps., Cleve., 1946-47; resident Peter Bent Brigham Hosp., Boston, 1949-51; fellow Mass. Gen. Hosp., Boston, 1951-53; rsch. asst. Mayo Clinic, Rochester, Minn., 1953-54; asst. in medicine Mass. Gen. Hosp., 1954-59; instr. medicine Harvard U., 1956-59; head divsn. gastroenterology U. Oreg. Med. Sch., Portland, 1959-75, prof. medicine, 1965-93; prof. emeritus Oreg. Health & Sci. U., Portland, 1993—, interim dean Sch. Medicine, 1991—93, dean emeritus, 1993—, asst. dir. Ctr. for Ethics in Health Care, 1992—2003; prof. internal medicine U. Nebr. Coll. Medicine, Omaha, 2003—. Cons. VA Hosps., Madigan Gen. Army Hosp., John A. Hartford Found. Editorial bd.: Am. Jour. Digestive Diseases, 1966-73, The Pharos, 2000—; contbr. articles to profl. jours. Mem. Oreg. Med. Ednl. Found., 1967-73, dir., 1967-73, pres., 1969-72; bd. dirs. N.W. Ctr. for Physician-Patient Comm., 1994-99, Am. Acad. on Physician and Patient, 1994-99, chmn., 1995-98, Found. Med. Excellence, 1996-2003, pres., 1998-2000; trustee Oreg. Health and Sci. U. Found., 1999-2003. With USNR, 1947-49. Mem. AAS, AMA, ACP (master), Am. Gastroenterol. Assn. (sec. 1970-73, v.p. 1975-76, pres.-elect. 1976-77, pres. 1977-78), Am. Clin. and Climatol. Assn. (v.p. 1997), Am. Soc. Internal Medicine, Western Assn. Physicians, North Pacific Soc. Internal Medicine, Am. Fedn. Clin. Rsch., Federated Coun. for Internal Medicine, Am. Assn. Study Liver Disease, Western Soc. Clin. Investigation, Soc. Health and Human Values, Assn. Health Svcs. Rsch., Inst. Medicine NAS, Phi Beta Kappa, Sigma Xi, Alpha Omega Alpha. Office: 983332 Nebr Med Ctr Omaha NE 68198-3332 Office Phone: 402-559-4887. Business E-Mail: jabenson@unmc.edu.

BENSON, JON H., information technology executive; Grad. in Elec. Engrng. V.p., gen. mgr. StorageTek overall tape bus. Sun Microsystems, Inc., v.p. engrng. for virtual storage and tape solutions bus., sr. v.p. storage, 2007—. Mem. indsl. adv. bd. elec. and computer engrng. Colo. State U., Ft. Collins. Achievements include patents in field. Office: Sun Microsystems Inc 4150 Network Cir Santa Clara CA 95054 Office Phone: 650-960-1300. E-mail: jon.benson@sun.com.*

BENSON, KENNETH VICTOR, manufacturing executive, lawyer; b. New Lisbon, Wis., Aug. 2, 1929; s. Carl W. and Ottilia (Olson) B.; m. Alice May Drewry, June 23, 1951; children: Jennifer, Elizabeth, Kenneth, Jonathan, Nathan. BBA, U. Wis., 1951, JD, 1957. Bar: Wis. 1957. Sales trainee, sales corr. Marathon Corp., Menasha, Wis., 1953-54; practice law with Benson & Day, Marshfield, Wis., 1957-58; sr. v.p., dir., exec. com. Kohler Co., Wis., 1959-81; pres., mem. exec. com., dir. Vollrath Co.,

Sheboygan, Wis., 1982-89; ptnr. Benson, Zufelt & Donohue, Sheboygan, 1990-92. Bd. dirs. Sheboygan United Fund, 1969-75, Wis. 4-H Found., Inc., 1988-92, Sheboygan YMCA, 1971-79, sec., 1975-76, v.p., 1977-79; pres. Sheboygan Comty. Players and Civic Orch., 1967-69, bd. dirs., 1963-76; bd. dirs. Sheboygan Retirement Home, 1976-85, v.p., 1979-80, pres., 1980-81; trustee Lakeland Coll., 1978-92. With AUS, 1951-53. Mem. Home: 3351 S Bridgeport Ln Boise ID 83706

BENSON, KEVIN E., transportation executive; b. South Africa, Feb. 23, 1947; married. Grad., Witwatersrand Univ., Johannesburg, South Africa. CA, 1971. With Coopers & Lybrand, South Africa; joined Trizec-Hahn Corp., 1977, CFO, 1983—86, pres., 1986—95, CEO, 1987—95; CFO Canadian Airlines Internat., 1995—96, pres., CEO, 1996—2000; pres. Jim Pattison Group, 2000—01; pres., CEO Ins. Corp. British Columbia, 2001—02, Laidlaw Inc., 2002—03, Laidlaw Internat., Naperville, Ill., 2003—. Bd. dir. Manulife Financial, 1995—. Office: Laidlaw International Ste 400 55 Shuman Blvd Naperville IL 60563*

BENSON, LUCY WILSON, historian, consultant; b. NYC, Aug. 25, 1927; d. Willard Oliver and Helen (Peters) Wilson; m. Bruce Buzzell Benson, Mar. 30, 1950 (dec. Mar. 1990). BA, Smith Coll., Northampton, Mass., 1949, MA, 1955; LHD (hon.), Wheaton Coll., 1965; LLD (hon.), U. Mass., 1969; LHD (hon.), Bucknell U., Lewisburg, Pa., 1972; LLD (hon.), U. Md., 1972; LHD (hon.), Carleton Coll., Northfield, Minn., 1973; LLD (hon.), Amherst Coll., Mass., 1974, Clark U., Worcester, Mass., 1975; HHD (hon.), Springfield Coll., Mass., 1981; LHD (hon.), Bates Coll., Lewiston, Maine, 1982; LLD (hon.), Lafayette Coll., Easton, Pa., 1999. Mem. jr. exec. tng. program Bloomingdale's, NYC, 1949-50; asst. dir. pub. rels. Smith Coll., 1950-53; rsch. asst. dept. Am. studies Amherst Coll., 1956-57; pres. Amherst LWV, Mass., 1957-61, pres. Mass., 1961-65, nat. pres., 1968-74; mem. Gov.'s cabinet and sec. human svcs. Commonwealth of Mass., 1975; mem. spl. commn. on adminstrv. rev. US Ho. of Reps., Washington, 1976-77; under sec. State Security Assistance, Sci. and Tech. US Dept. State, Washington, 1977-80; cons. US Dept. State and SRI Internat., Washington, 1980-81; pres. Benson and Assocs., Amherst, 1981—. Vice-chair Citizen Network Fgn. Affairs; bd. dirs. Dreyfus Fund, others, Internat. Exec. Svc. Corps., Amherst Cinema Arts Ctr., 2006—. Pub. adv. com. US Trade Policy, 1968; mem. town meeting Amherst, 1957—74, 2000; mem. fin. com., 1960—66; mem. Gov. Mass. Spl. Com. Rev. Sunday Closing Laws, 1961, Mass. Adv. Bd. Higher Ednl. Policy, 1962—65, Gov. Mass. Com. Rev. Salaries State Employees, 1963; adv. com. racial imbalance and edn. Mass. Bd. Edn., 1964—65; Mass. adv. com. US Commn. Civil Rights, 1964—73; vice-chair Mass. Adv. Coun. Edn., 1965—68; Mass. Com. Children and Youth Com. to Study Report by U.S. Children's Bur. Mass. Youth Svc. Divsn., 1967; steering com. Urban Coalition, 1968, exec. com., 1970—75, 1980—84, co-chair, 1973—75; vis. com. John F. Kennedy Sch. Govt., Trilateral commn. Coun. Fgn. Rels.; former bd. govs. Am. Nat. Red Cross, Common Cause, Women's Action Alliance; bd. govs. Internat. Ctr. Election Law and Adminstrn., 1985—87; spl. commn. Mass. Legislature Study Budgetary Powers Trustee U. Mass., 1961—62; trustee Edn. Devel. Ctr., Newton, Mass., 1967—72, Nat. Urban League, 1974—77, Brookings Instn., 1974—77, Smith Coll., 1975—80, Alfred P. Sloan Found., 1975—77, 1981—2000, Bur. Social Sci. Rsch., Inc., 1985—87; bd. dirs. Catalyst, 1972—90, Atlantic Coun. U.S., 1988—, vice-chair, 1993—2000; trustee Lafayette Coll., 1985—2000, vice-chair, 1990—2000, trustee emeritus, 2000—; chmn. bd. Amherst Cinema Arts Ctr., Mass., 2007—. Recipient Achievement award, Bur. Govt. Rsch. U. Mass., 1963, Disting. Svc. award, Boston Coll., 1965, Northfield Mt. Hermon Sch., 1976, Disting. Civil Leadership award, Tufts U., 1965, medal, Smith Coll., 1969; fellow, Radcliffe Inst., 1965—67. Mem.: ACLU, NAACP, Coun. On Fgn. Rels., Internat. Inst. Strategic Studies, Nat. Acad. Pub. Adminstrn., Jersey Wildlife Preservation Trust Channel Islands, E. African Wildlife Soc., Assn. Am. Indian Affairs, Urban League, UN Assn.

BENSON, MICHAEL T., academic administrator; m. Celia Barnes; 2 children. BA in Polit. Sci., Brigham Young U.; PhD in Modern Middle Ea. History, St. Antony's Coll. Mem. staff devel. office U. Utah, 1995—98, assoc. dir. major gifts, spl. asst. to pres. & sec., 1999—2002; pres. Snow Coll., Ephraim, Utah, 2002—06, Southern Utah U., Cedar City, Utah, 2006—. Cons. historian Harry S. Truman Presdl. Libr.; academic adv. Skirball Cultural Ctr., LA; instr. U. Utah; bd. adv. Marriott Libr.; adv. bd. U. Utah Internat. Studies. Author: Harry S. Truman and the Founding of Israel, 1997. Office: Office of President Southern Utah University 351 W University Blvd Cedar City UT 84720 Office Phone: 435-586-7700.*

BENSON, MORGAN, energy engineer, retired military officer; b. Washington, Sept. 20, 1948; s. Wilmer Kersey and Virginia Cabell Benson; m. Elaine Rae Page, Oct. 26, 2000; children: Jennifer R., Jason C. Gaskill, Karen L., Matthew E. Gaskill, Erik P. Gaskill. BS, U. Del., 1972; MBA, U. Scranton, 1984. Cert. energy engr., Assn. Energy Engrs., 2000, registered profl. engr., Ky., 1974. Commd. 2d lt. U.S. Army, 1972, advanced through grades to lt. col., 1994; facilities engr. Scranton (Pa.) Army Ammunition Plant, 1979—86; chief environ. br. U.S. Army Tobyhanna (Pa.) Army Depot, 1986—88; energy mgr. HQs, US Army, Europe / 7A, Heidelberg, Germany, 1988—94; chief of utilities U.S. Army 26th Area Support Group, Heidelberg, 1994—99; project mgr. Walter Reed Army Med. Ctr., Washington, 1999—2000; master planner, installation energy mgr. U.S. Army Dugway (Utah) Proving Ground, 2000—. Ops. officer HQs, U.S. Army 21st TAACOM, Kaiserslautern, Germany, 1988—94, HQs, U.S. Army V Corps, Heidelberg, 1994—96. Assoc. editor: Encyclopedia of World War II. Lt. col. CAP, 1999—. Decorated Meritorious Svc. medal HQs, U.S. Army, Europe /7A, Army Commendation medal, 7th Oak Leaf Cluster; recipient Energy Mgmt. award, Sec. of the Army, 2002, 2006, Fed. Energy and Water Mgmt. award, Dept. of Energy, 1998, 2003. Fellow: Soc. Am. Mil. Engrs. (life; post pres. 1997—99, Silver medal 1994, Paul W. Thompson medal 1996, Regional Vice President's medal 1994); mem.: ASME, Ret. Officers Assn. (life). Avocations: military history, genealogy, travel. Office: US Army Dugway Proving Ground 5330 Valdez Cir Dugway UT 84022 Office Phone: 435-831-3555.

BENSON, P. GEORGE, academic administrator, finance educator; b. Lewisburg, Pa., June 3, 1946; s. Paul Benson and Anna Louise (Stolz) McDowell; m. Jane Alison Oas, July 17, 1982; children: Jeffery George, Laura Jane, Alison Louise. BS in math., Bucknell U., 1968; postgrad., NYU, 1970-71; PhD in decision sciences, U. Fla., 1977. Mgmt. analyst US Army Security Agy., Arlington, Va., 1968-69; computer scientist Bell Telephone Labs., Whippany, NJ, 1969-71; prof. decision sciences Carlson Sch. Mgmt. U. Minn., Mpls., 1977-93, head decision sciences area, 1983—88, dir. Ops. Mgmt. Ctr., 1992—93; dean Rutgers Bus. Sch., Newark and New Brunswick, NJ, 1993—98, Terry Coll. Bus., U. Ga., Athens, 1998—2007, Simon S. Selig, Jr. chair econ. growth; pres. Coll. Charleston, SC, 2007—. Judge Malcolm Baldridge Nat. Quality Award, 1997-2000, bd. overseers 2004-, chmn., 2005-; bd. dirs. AGCO, Inc., Duluth, Ga., Nutrition 21 Inc., Purchase, NY, Crawford & Co., Atlanta, Athens First Bank & Trust Co., Athens, Ga.; bd. advisors Executrack Inc., Atlanta, Preferred Real Estate Funds, LLC. Author: (with James McClave) Statistics for Business and Economics, 6th edit., 1994, A First Course in Business Statistics, 6th edit., 1995; contbr. articles to profl. journals; bi-monthly columnist Ga. Trend mag. Bd. advisors Metro Atlanta C. of C.; bd. governors Buckhead Club, Atlanta. Grantee US Dept. Transp., 1988-90; fellowship Burlington No., 1982-86. Fellow: Decision Sciences Inst. Avocation: golf. Office: Coll Charleston Randolph Hall 66 George St Charleston SC 29424 Office Phone: 843-953-5500. Office Fax: 843-953-5811. E-mail: bensong@cofc.edu.*

BENSON, RICHARD, dean, photographer; Prof. Yale U. Sch. Art, 1979—, dean, 1996—. Co-author: Maritime Album, 100 Photog. & Their Stories, 1997, Lay this Laurel, 1972; author: Face of Lincoln, Work of Atget; author: (photog. by Lee Friedlander) Am. Monument; Represented in permanent collections Mus. Modern Art. Office: Office of the Dean Yale U Sch Art PO Box 208339 New Haven CT 06520

BENSON, ROBERT CRAIG, III, business consultant; b. Waukegan, Ill., May 27, 1944; s. Robert Craig II and Leona (Pollard) B.; m. Ree Ann Christensen, June 3, 1961; children: Bradley, Barry. BA in Bus. Adminstrn. and Math., Dakota Wesleyan U., Mitchell, SD, 1967. CPA, Cert. Mgmt. Cons. Supervising sr. Broeker Hendrickson & Co., St. Paul, 1967-70; ptnr. Sands Benson & Weinberg, St. Paul, 1970-73; mgr. Miller, McCollom & Co., Denver, 1973-74; mng. ptnr. Benson Wells & Co., Denver, 1974-84; pres. Am. Bus. Advisors, Denver, 1984—. Lectr. Ctr. for Leadership Devel., Kiev, Ukraine, 1998—; Opperman disting. alumni lectr. Dakota Wesleyan U., 2002. Contbr. articles to profl. jours. Bd. mem., chair Denver Youth for Christ, 1975-85; elder Cherry Hills Cmty. Ch., Highlands Ranch, Colo., 1982-87; bd. dirs. COMPA Food Bank, Denver, 1986-93, Global Connections Internat., 2000-2003, Project C.U.R.E., 2000-04, Dakota Wesleyan U., 2004—, Loveland Logic Inst., 1999—. Recipient Alumnus of Yr., Dakota Wesleyan U., 2006. Mem.: AICPA, Inst. Mgmt. Cons., Colo. Soc. CPAs (co-chmn. profession practice bd. 1981—82). Avocations: golf, teaching about God. Office: Am Bus Advisors Inc 6635 S Dayton Ste 210 Greenwood Village CO 80111 Business E-Mail: bob@abadvisors.com.

BENSON, ROBERT EUGENE, lawyer; b. Red Oak, Iowa, Apr. 7, 1940; s. Paul J. and Frances (Sever) B.; m. Ann Marie Lucke, July 20, 1968; children: Steven J., Robert J., Katherine A. BA, U. Iowa, 1962; LLB, U. Pa., 1965. Bar: Colo. 1965. Assoc. Holland & Hart, Denver, 1965—71, ptnr., 1971—2006, of counsel, 2007—. Adj. faculty U. Denver Coll. Law, 1992. Author: The Power of Arbitrators and Courts to Order Discovery in Arbitration, 1996, Application of the Pro Rata Liability, Comparative Negligence and Contribution Statues, 1994, Colorado Arbitration and Other ADR Law, 2006, CLE in Colorado, 2006; co-author: How to Prepare For, Take and Use a Deposition, 5th edit., 1994; mng. editor: Colorado Construction Law, 1999, 2003, 05; contbr. articles to profl. jours. Capt. USAF, 1965-73. Mem. ABA, Colo. Bar Assn., Denver Bar Assn., Coll. Comml. Arbitrators. Democrat. Avocations: golf, skiing. Home: 5454 Preserve Pky N Greenwood Village CO 80121-2185 Office: Holland & Hart LLP 555 17th St Ste 3200 Denver CO 80202-3950 Home Phone: 303-770-3571; Office Phone: 303-295-8234. Business E-Mail: rbenson@hollandhart.com.

BENSON, SIDNEY WILLIAM, chemistry researcher; b. NYC, Sept. 26, 1918; m. Anna Bruni, 1986; 2 children. AB, Columbia Coll., 1938; A.M., PhD, Harvard U., 1941; Docteur Honoris Causa, U. Nancy, France, 1989. Rsch. asst. Gen. Electric Co., 1940; rsch. fellow Harvard U., 1941-42; instr. chemistry CCNY, 1942-43; group leader Manhattan Project Kellex Corp., 1943; rsch. scientist, div. 9 Nat. Rsch. Coun., 1944—46; asst. prof. U. So. Calif., 1943-48, assoc. prof., 1948-51, prof. chemistry, 1951-64, 76-89, distng. prof., 1986—, disting. prof. emeritus, 1989—, dir. chem. physics program, 1962-63; rsch. chemist Nat. Rsch. Coun., Divsn. 9, 1944—46; dir. dept. kinetics and thermochemistry Stanford Rsch. Inst., 1963-76; sci. dir. Hydrocarbon Rsch. Inst. U. So. Calif., 1977-90, sci. dir. emeritus, 1991—; rsch. assoc. dept. chemistry and chem. engring. Calif. Inst. Tech., 1957-58; vis. prof. UCLA, 1959, U. Ill., 1959; hon. Glidden lectr. Purdue U., 1961; vis. prof. chemistry Stanford U., 1966-70, 71, 73; mem. adv. panel phys. chemistry Nat. Bur. Standards, 1969-72, chmn., 1970-71; hon. vis. prof. U. Utah, 1971; vis. prof. U. Paris VII and XI, 1971-72, U. St. Andrews, Scotland, 1973, U. Lausanne, Switzerland, 1979. Frank Gucker lectr. U. Ind., 1984—; Brotherton prof. in phys. chemistry U. Leeds, 1984; cons. G.N. Lewis; lectr. U. Calif., Berkeley, 1989. Author: Foundations of Chemical Kinetics, 1960, rev. edit. 1982, Thermochemical Kinetics, 1968, 2d edit., 1976, Critical Survey of the Data of the Kinetics of Gas Phase Unimolecular Reactions, Reactions, 1970, Chemical Calculations, 3d edit., 1971, Atoms, Molecules and Chemical Reactions, 1972; founder, editor-in-chief Internat. Jour. Chem, Kinetics, 1967-83; mem. editl. adv. bd. Combustion Sci. and Tech., 1973-94, Oxidation Comms., 1978—, Revs. of chem. Intermediates, 1979-87, Hydrocarbon Letters, 1980-81, Jour. Phys. Chemistry, 1981-85; sci. adv. coun. Annales Medicales de Nancy, 1993-2002. Recipient cert. of Merit for War Work, NRC, 1946; Polanyi medal Royal Soc. Eng., 1986; faculty rsch. award U. So. Calif., 1984, Presdl. medal, 1986, Peter Kapitsa Gold Medal award Russian Acad. Natural Sci., 1997; Guggenheim fellow, 1950-51, Fulbright fellow, France, 1950-51, fellow NSF, 1957-58, 71-72; recipient citation Chem. Rev., 2000; nominated for Scientist of Yr. Internat. Biog. Ctr., Cambridge, Eng., 2002. Fellow AAAS, Am. Phys. Soc.; mem. NAS, Am. Chem. Soc. (Tolman medal 1977, Hydrocarbon Chem. award 1977, Langmuir award 1986, Orange County award 1986), Faraday Soc., Indian Acad. Sci., Phi Beta Kappa, Sigma Xi, Pi Mu Epsilon, Phi Lambda Upsilon, Phi Kappa Phi Home: 1110 N Bundy Dr Los Angeles CA 90049-1513 Office: U So Calif University Pk Mc 1661 Los Angeles CA 90089-0001

BENSON, STEVEN CLARK, management and engineering executive; b. Chillicothe, Ohio, Sept. 27, 1954; s. Myron Clark and Velma Lucille (Dye) B.; married Barbara B.; children: Michael Lee, Kelly Dawn. BSCE, Ohio U., 1976. Registered profl. engr., Ohio; lic. surveyor, Ohio. Project engr. McNally Pittsburg, Inc., Wellston, Ohio, 1976-87; pres. SBA Cons., Inc., Jackson, Ohio, 1995—97, SBA Assocs., Inc., Jackson, 1989—, also bd. dirs. City engr., svc. dir. City of Jackson, Ohio. Mem. NRA (life), NSPE, Ohio Soc. Profl. Engrs., Profl. Land Surveyors Ohio, Ohio Gun Collectors Assn., Aircraft Owners and Pilots Assn., Cousteau Soc., Exptl. Aircraft Assn. Avocations: flying, scuba diving, camping, travel, hunting. Home: 54399 Benson Rd Ray OH 45672-8947 Office: SBA Inc PO Box 962 Jackson OH 45640-0962

BENSON, STEVEN DONALD, marketing professional, mechanical engineer, writer; b. Longview, Wash., Oct. 11, 1953; s. Steven Hughes Benson and Donna Ruth (Johnson) McKinney; m. Patricia Joyce Krauss, Feb. 14, 1982; children: Steven William, Patricia Ann. AA in Drafting, Merit Davis, 1973; AA in Robotics, AMADA Sch., Buena Park, Calif., 1997. Precision sheet metal mechanic Ariz. Precision Sheet Metal, Phoenix, 1980-86, Neilson Mfg. Inc., Salem, Oreg., 1986—2002; co-owner Time Honored Gifts, Salem, 1988—94; pres. Advanced Sheet Metal Applications, Salem, 1986—; co-owner A-Cab Taxi and Transp. Svcs. LCC, Salem, 2000—05, Gizmo Med. Transport Inc., 2003—05, BACA Safety, 2004—05. Instr. Oreg. Advanced Tech. Consortium, Wilsonville, 1990-1994; sheet metal instr. Clackamas C.C., Oregon City, Oreg., 1997-2003; editor, pub. Precision Sheet Metal Chronicle, electronic mag., 1998—; pres. Brake Tng. & Cons; chmn. Precision Sheet Metal Coun Author: (textbooks) Introduction to Precision Press Brake, 1991, Intermediate Press Brake, 1992, Advanced Precision Press Brake, 1994, Press Brake Technology, 1997, Lasers, Punches, PressBrakes & Shears, 2001, Darkness to Light, 2002, (software) Advanced Sheet Metal Applications (ASMA 4.0), 1982, 1990, 1992, 1996, 1997; contbr. over 60 articles to profl. jours. Sec., treas. Bike PAC of Oreg., Salem, 1988-2001, lobbyist, 1992; mem. A Brotherhood Against Totalitarian Enactments (ABATE), Oreg., Inc.; chief petitioner Statewide Initiative Petition, Oreg. (Road to Freedom award, Bike PAC of Oreg., 1992); hon. chmn. Oreg. chpt. Nat. Rep. Congl. Com., 2002. Named Businessman of Yr., NRCC, 2003; recipient Edn. award, Fabricators and Mfg. Assn. Internat., 1999, Article of the Yr. award, Croydon/FMA, 2001, Congl. Leadership award, 2002, Freedom isn't Free award, Bike PAC of Oreg., 1997, Legends of BikePac award, 2001, Reader's Choice award, TheFabricator.com, 2003, 2004. Master: Masons (worshipful master 2006); mem.: Internat. Sheet Metal Workers (local 16), Soc. Mfg. Engrs., Fabricators and Mfrs. Assn. (adv. com. precision sheet metal 1997—, coun., vice chair 2004—05, chair 2005—). Avocations: politics, indian moto-cycles, british sports cars. Home: 2952 Doaks Ferry Rd NW Salem OR 97304 also: 2952 Doaks Ferry Rd Nw Salem OR 97304-1326 Office Phone: 503-399-7514. E-mail: steve@asmachronicle.com, sbenson37@comcast.net.

BENSON, STUART WELLS, III, lawyer; b. Sewickley, Pa., Jan. 6, 1951; s. Stuart Wells and Rosalie (Sassin) B.; m. Ruthanne Ackerman, July 15, 1978; children: Kate Eileen, Laura Elizabeth, Sarah Wells. BA, Northwestern U., 1972; JD, U. Pitts., 1975. Bar: Pa. 1975, US Dist. Ct. (we. dist.) Pa. 1975, U.S. Supreme Ct. 1982. Assoc. Brandt McManus Brandt & Malone, Pitts., 1975-80; ptnr. Dickie, McCamey & Chilcote, PC, Pitts., 1980—96, Pietragallo, Bosick & Gordon, Pitts., 1996-2002, Dapper, Baldasare, Benson, Behling & Kane PC, Pitts., 2002—. Contbr. articles to profl. jours. Bd. dirs. North Hills YMCA, Pitts., 1981-84. Mem. ABA, Am. Arbitration Assn. (Appreciation award 1980), Pa. Def. Inst., Pa. Claims Assn., Pitts. Claims Assn., Allegheny County Bar Assn., Pa. Bar Assn., Internat. Assn. Indsl. Accident Bds. and Commns., Duquesne Club, Oakmont Country Club, Wildwood Golf Club, Rotary (bd. dirs. 1979-87, pres. 1985, parliamentarian 1985—, found. chmn. 1999—) Republican. Episcopalian. Home: 2116 Grandeur Dr Gibsonia PA 15044-7498 Home Phone: 724-444-4776. Personal E-mail: sbenson@dbbk.com.

BENSON, TERRY, stage manager; Grad., Yale U. Second stage mgr. Sesame St.; staff assoc. WNET, NYC, 1971—2003, lead negotiator, shop steward, 1976—2003. Mem.: AD/SM/PA Coun. (chair, vice-chair, sec.), Directors Guild of Am. (2006 Franklin J. Schaffner Achievement award).*

BENSON, WILLIAM EDWARD (BARNES), geologist; b. West Haven, Conn., May 15, 1919; s. John Edward and Lucia Purdy (Barnes) B.; m. Mary Freda Hill, July 11, 1944; children— Sharon (Mrs. J.G. Rachel), Lynn (Mrs. J.D. Walker), William Edward. BA, Yale U., 1940, MS, 1942, PhD, 1952. Geologist Conn. Geol. and Natural History Survey, 1940-42; geologist U.S. Geol. Survey, 1942-54, br. chief, 1953-54; exec. sec. divsn. earth sci. NAS/NRC, 1954-55; chief geologist Manidon Mining Inc., N.D., 1955-56; program dir., sect. head NSF, 1956-75, chief scientist earth sci. divsn., 1975-79; sci. adv. to Office of Pres., Washington, 1976-77; pvt. cons., 1980—. Vis. prof. U. Hawaii, 1980; sr. staff assoc. NAS, 1980-99; docent Smithsonian Inst., 1996-. Contbr., editor profl. jours. Served with USNR, 1944-45. Yale U. fellow, 1940-42. Fellow Geol. Soc. Am., Am. Geophys. Union, AAAS (sec. sect. E 1969-73, chmn. sect. E 1974-75); mem. Geol. Soc. Washington (v.p. 1958), Pick and Hammer Soc. (chmn. 1970-73), Phi Beta Kappa, Sigma Xi (lectr. 1980-81). Home: Apt 420 7418 Spring Village Dr Springfield VA 22150 E-mail: bilfre@aol.com.

BENSTON, GEORGE JAMES, accountant, economist; b. NYC, Mar. 18, 1932; s. William and Rose L. B.; m. Alice N. Schwartz, July 28, 1951; children: Kimberly Wayne, Randall Craig. BA, Queens Coll., 1952; MBA, NYU, 1953; PhD, U. Chgo., 1963. CPA, N.C. Acct. CPA firms, 1952-53; acctg. and tax specialist 1st Nat. Bank of Atlanta, 1956-57; asst. prof. acctg. Ga. State U., 1957-58, U. Chgo., 1962-66; assoc. prof. acctg. and fin. U. Rochester, 1961-69, prof. fin., acctg. and econs., 1969-87; Harlan prof. fin., acctg. and econs. Emory U., Atlanta, 1987—, assoc. dean faculty rsch. and ctr. devel., 1990-92, area coord. fin., 1988-90, 92-96, area coord. acctg., 1993-96. Vis. prof. U. Calif., Berkeley, Grad. Sch. Bus. Studies, London, London Sch. Econs., Hebrew U., Jerusalem; hon. vis. prof. City U. London, Oxford U.; trustee Coll. Retirement Equities Fund; Disting. Internat. Lectr. Am. Acctg. Assn., 1980. Author: Corporate Accounting Disclosure in the UK and the USA, 1976, Contemporary Cost Accounting and Control, 1970, 77, Analysis of Causes of SLA Failures, 1985, The Separation of Commercial and Investment Banking: The Glass-Steagall Act Revisited and Reconsidered, 1990, Regulating Financial Markets: A Critique and Some Proposals, 1999; assoc. editor, mem. editl. bd. Jour. Money and Credit Banking, Jour. Acctg. Pub. Policy; others; contbr. articles to profl. jours. Ford Found., U.S. Steel and Woodrow Wilson fellow, 1958-59; Olin Disting. fellow Oxford U. Mem. Shadow Fin. Regulation Com., Fin. Economists Roundtable, Am. Acctg. Assn., Am. Fin. Assn., Am. Econ. Assn., Fin. Mgmt. Assn., Phi Beta Kappa, Beta Gamma Sigma. Home: 3572 Knollwood Dr NW Atlanta GA 30305-1022 E-mail: benston@bus.emory.edu.

BENSUSSEN, GALE K., health products company executive; b. 1946; BS, U. So. Calif.; JD, Southwestern U. Sch. Law. Bar: Calif. 1979. Rep. Transatlantic Bus. Partnership; founding exec. Leiner Health Products, Carson, Calif., 1974, pres. Bd. mem. Consumer Healthcare Products Assn.; bd. dir. Ind. Colleges of Southern Calif.; spkr. in field. Office: Leiner Health Products Inc 901 E 233d St Carson CA 90745 Office Phone: 310-835-8400. Office Fax: 310-835-6615.

BENT, ALAN EDWARD, political science professor; b. Shanghai, June 22, 1939; s. Walter J. and Tamara (Rocklin) B.; m. Dawn Bickler, Aug. 13, 1977; 1 son by previous marriage, Ronald Geoffrey. BS, San. Francisco State U., 1963; MA, U. So. Calif., 1968, Claremont Grad. Sch., 1970, PhD, 1971; MBA, Xavier U., 1985. Instr. polit. sci. Chapman Coll., Orange, Calif., 1969-70; research assoc. Mcpl. Systems Research, Claremont Grad. Sch., 1970-71; asst. prof. polit. sci., assoc. dir. Inst. Govtl. Studies and Research Memphis State U., 1971-74; assoc. prof., chmn. dept. pub. adminstrn. Calif. State U., Dominguez Hills, 1974-77; prof. polit. sci. U. Cin., 1977-81, 82-92, head dept. polit. sci., 1977-81, prof. emeritus Dept. Polit. Sci.; dean Coll. Arts and Scis. U. No. Colo., Greeley, 1981-82, prof. polit. sci., 1981-82; prof. pub. adminstr. Troy State U., Europe, 1989-92. Cons. police agys., govtl. and pvt. instns. Author: Escape from Anarchy: A Strategy for Urban Survival, 1972; The Politics of Law Enforcement: Conflict and Power in Urban Communities, 1974, 2d edit., 1976; co-author: Police, Criminal Justice and the Community, 1976, Collective Bargaining in the Public Sector: Labor-Management Relations and Public Policy, 1978; co-editor, contbr. Urban Administration: Management, Politics and Change, 1976, 2d edit. 1977; contbr. articles to profl. jours.; bd. editors: Rev. Pub. Personnel Adminstrn., 1980-89, Spectrum, A Jour. of Comparative Politics and Devel., New Delhi, 1984-92. Served to capt. USAF, 1964—69. NASPAA fellow, 1981-82 Home: 1006 Oro St Laguna Beach CA 92651-3534 Personal E-mail: rory2@cox.net.

BENTAS, LILY HASEOTES, retail executive; Chmn, pres. Cumberland Farms, Canton, Mass., 1989, pres., CEO, 1991—. Office: Cumberland Farms Inc 777 Dedham St Canton MA 02021-1484

BENTEL, FREDERICK RICHARD, architect, educator; b. NYC, Jan. 2, 1928; s. Carl August and Mary (Muller) B.; m. Maria L. R. Azzarone, Aug. 16, 1952 (deceased Nov. 8, 2000); children: Paul Louis, Peter Andreas, Maria Elisabeth. BArch., Pratt Inst., 1949; grad. fellow, Mass. Inst. Tech., MArch., 1950; DArch., Technische Hochschule, Graz, Austria, 1953. Registered architect, N.Y., 1956, N.J., 1960, Va., 1958, Vt., 1970, Conn., 1985, Mo., 2001, Del., 1998, Mass., 2001, profl. planner, N.J., 1967. Architect, partner Bentel & Bentel (AIA), Locust Valley, NY, 1957—; pres. Correlated Designs Inc., Locust Valley, 1961—; ptnr. Old Path Realty, Cobblestone Enterprises. Prof. Sch. Architecture, Pratt Inst., 1955-70; prof. Sch. Architecture, N.Y. Inst. Tech., 1969—. Author publs. in field. Founding mem. com. Locust Valley Bus. Dist. Planning; adv. bd. Oyster Bay Planning and Hist. Preservation Commn., 1970-73; mem. Oyster Bay Hist. Preservation Commn., 1975-91; alt. APD panel N.Y. State Coun. on Arts, 1985-86, St. Joseph's Coll. Libr. Arch., L.I., chpt. AIA, 1990, St. Stephen's Ch., Warwick, N.Y., L.I. chpt. AIA, 1991, Pavilion, Old Westbury, N.Y. Fulbright scholar, 1952-53; recipient awards in field including 1st pl. commn. Islip Bay Shore downtown redevel. competition, 1976. Fellow AIA (task force for archtl. graphic stas., St. Joseph's Coll. Libr. Arch. L.I. chpt. 1990, St. Stephen's Ch., Warwick, N.Y., L.I. chpt. 1991, Pavilion, Old Westbury, N.Y., Gramercy Tavern, N.Y.C., L.I. chpt. 1996, Nat. Design award, 2003); mem. N.Y. Soc. Architects (numerous awards), Am. Italy Soc., MIT Alumni Assn. (ednl. coun.). Home: 23 Frost Creek Dr Locust Valley NY 11560-1029 Office: Bentel & Bentel Architect & Planner 22 Buckram Rd Locust Valley NY 11560-1928 Office Phone: 516-676-2880. Business E-Mail: architecture@bentelandbentel.com.

BENTEL, PAUL LOUIS, architect, educator; m. Carol Rusche, 1987. BA in Visual Studies (magna cum laude), Harvard Coll., 1979, M in Architecture (with hons.), 1982; student, Swiss Fed. Inst. Tech., Zurich, 1981—82; PhD in History Theory, Criticism, MIT, 1992. Ptnr. Bentel & Bentel, Locust Valley, NY, 1985—; prof. history, preservation and design Columbia U., 1993—. Dir. Am. archl. design studio Swiss Fed. Inst. Tech., 1988—90; dir. hist. preservation program Columbia U., 2001—02; reviewer GSA. Mem. U.S. Internat. Commn. on Monuments and Sites. Fellow: AIA; mem.: Soc. for Preservation of L.I. Antiquities (bd. dirs.), Soc. Archl. Historians. Office: Bentel & Bentel 22 Buckram Rd Locust Valley NY 11560

BENTLEY, CAROL LIGON, retired library and information scientist; b. Brownsville, Tenn., Mar. 8, 1927; d. Gavin and Ethel Ligon; m. Harry Bentley, Jan. 11, 1962; children: Patrice, Harry Dion. BE, Chgo. State U., 1969, MS in Edn., 1973, No. Ill. U., Dekalb, 1979, EdS, 1989. Tchr. elem. sch. Oliver Wendell Holmes Sch., Chgo., 1969—72; libr., tchr. Richard Crane H.S., Chgo., 1972—74; from instr. to prof. Chgo. State U., 1974—99; ret., 1999. Vol. Am. Diabetes Assn., Chgo., 2003—06, Am. Heart Assn., Chgo., 2006. Mem.: Nat. Hook-Up Black Women, Assn. Black Women in Higher Edn. (Leadership award 2000), Schamburg Ctr. Rsch. in Black Culture, Chgo. State U. Alumni Assn. (bd. dirs.), Phi Delta Kappa (dir. Chgo. chpt.). Home: 9211 S Halsted St Chicago IL 60620 Personal E-mail: carolbentley1014@hotmail.com.

BENTLEY, CHARLES RAYMOND, geophysics educator; b. Rochester, NY, Dec. 23, 1929; s. Raymond and Janet Cornelia (Everest) B.; m. Marybelle Goode, July 3, 1964 (dec. Oct. 13, 2004); children: Molly Clare, Raymond Alexander. BS, Yale U., 1950; PhD, Columbia U., 1959. Rsch. geophysicist Columbia U., 1952-56; Antarctic traverse leader and seismologist Arctic Inst. N.Am., 1956-59; project assoc. U. Wis., 1959-61, asst. prof., 1961-63, assoc. prof., 1963-68, prof. geophysics, 1968-98, A.P. Crary prof. geophysics, 1987-98, prof. emeritus, 1998—. Recipient Bellingshausen-Lazarev medal for Antarctic rsch. Acad. Scis. USSR, 1971; NSF sr. postdoctoral fellow, 1968-69; NAS-USSR Acad. Sci. exch. fellow, 1977, 90 Fellow AAAS, Am. Geophys. Union, Arctic Inst. N.Am., Am. Polar Soc. (hon., bd. dirs.); mem. AAUP, Soc. Exploration Geophysicists, Internat. Glaciological Soc. (Seligman Crystal award 1990), Am. Quaternary Assn., Oceanography Soc., Am. Geol. Inst., Geol. Soc. Am., Phi Beta Kappa, Sigma Xi. Achievements include research on Antarctic glaciology and geophysics, satellite studies of geomagnetic anomalies, magnetotelluric exploration of Earth structure, satellite radar and laser altimetry, ice coring and drilling services. Office Phone: 608-238-8873. Business E-Mail: bentley@geology.wisc.edu.

BENTLEY, CHARMAINE CLARK O'FALLON, secondary school educator; b. Austin, Tex., Dec. 15, 1954; d. Harold Roy and Maria Rafaela Bentley; m. Charles Oliver Mixon, May 4, 1980; 1 child, Charlotte Farrar Mixon. BA in Anthropology, U. Tex., 1977, BS in Geol. Sci., 1977; MS in Computer Sci., U. Tex., Dallas, 2007; BS in Computer Sci., SW Okla. State U., 1984, MEd in Math., 1988. DATA engr. Dresser Industries, Magcobar DATA, Oklahoma City, 1972-82; tchr. Dallas Ind. Sch. Dist., 1988—, tchr., technologist F.D. Roosevelt H.S., 1992—2003, chmn. computer sci. curriculum com., 1997-98, 2003—04. Presenter in field. Asst. troop leader Girl Scout US, Farmers Branch, Tex., 1992-95, Sunshine Literacy Project Coord., 1989-91; v.p. IB Parent Booster com. Clark HS, Plano, Tex., 1995-96, sec., 1996-97; troop chmn. Boy Scout Am., Elk City, Okla., 1986-87; mem. F.D. Roosevelt HS Site Based Decision Com., 1998-2005, 2007— sec., 1998-2001, sec. student support team, 2005-06, 2007, faculty adv.com, 2005-07, chair 2003-05, dep. chair, 2007—. Recipient Award of Appreciation, City of Farmers Branch, 1990; scholar F.D. Roosevelt HS, 1991, 94. Mem. IEEE, Am. Assn. Petroleum Geologists, Nat. Coun. Tchrs. Math., Internat. Soc. Tech. Edn. (computer sci. spl. interest group), Tex. Computer Edn. Assn., Assn. Tex. Profl. Educators, Tex. Computer Edn. Assn. Computer Sci. (computer sci. spl. interest group, area 5 rep. 2000-02, sec./treas. 2002—), Assn. Computing Machinery, Computer Sci. Tchrs. Assn. (steering com. 2003-04, bd. dirs. 2005-07, chmn. membership com. 2005-07). Episcopalian. Avocations: reading, woodworking, photography, gardening. Home Phone: 972-985-9946; Office Phone: 972-925-6800. Personal E-mail: charmainebentley@acm.org.

BENTLEY, CLARENCE EDWARD, savings and loan association executive; b. Ranger, Tex., Oct. 9, 1921; s. Clarence Edward and Rosa Estelle (Bryant) B.; m. Gloria Gill, Oct. 9, 1943; children: Jon (dec.), Kitty, Perry (dec.). Student, McMurry U., Abilene, Tex., 1939-42. Pres. Abilene Savs. Assn., 1944-77, Southwestern Group Fin. Co., Houston, 1976-77; pres. United Savs. Assn. Tex., Houston, 1977-80, chmn. bd., 1980-85; dir., chmn. bd. Sandia Fed. Savs. & Loan, Albuquerque, 1986-89; dir. Kaneb Pipeline Partners, 1990—. Chmn. bd. dirs. United Fin. Mortgage Co., Dallas, United Fin. Group, Inc., Houston, 1980-86; bd. dirs. Kaneb Services Inc., Investors Mortgage Ins. Co., Boston; adb.bd. FNMA, 1980-81; trustee Thrift Instns. Short Term Liquidity Fund, N.Y.C., N.Y., 1982-83. Contbr. articles to profl. publns. Pres. Abilene Indsl. Found., 1970, United Fund Abilene, 1962, United Way, 1960; mem. bd. Tex. State Hosps., 1962-64; mem. Tex. Fin. Commn., 1964-76, chmn., 1971. Served with USAAF, 1942-43. Recipient Outstanding Citizen award City of Abilene, 1964, Disting. Alumnus award McMurry U., 1971, John T. Mahone award 1981. Mem. Nat. Savs. and Loan League (pres. 1970-71), Tex. Savs. and Loan League (pres. 1970-71), Assn. Thrift Holding Cos. (chmn. bd. 1985-87), Abilene C. of C. (pres. 1964). Clubs: Abilene Country (pres. 1951). Episcopalian. Home: 52 Rue Maison St Abilene TX 79605-4710 Office Phone: 325-670-9237. E-mail: cbent63@yahoo.com.

BENTLEY, DIANNE H. GLOVER, minister, consultant; BA, Drew U., Madison, NJ, 1976; MDiv, Drew Theol. Sch., 1997. LCSW HIV prevention counselor Pa. Dept. Health, 2003. Cons., trainer L.E.A.D., 2004; pastor First United Meth. Ch. of Sayre, 1997—. Dir. Ministry Resource Libr., Madison, NJ, 1994—97; pres. Bridge of Penn-York Valley Churches, Sayre, 1999—2002; chair Poverty Task Group, 2000—05, Teen Pregnancy Prevention Task Force, 2002—. Mentor Prudential Youth Leadership Inst., Wyo. Ann. Conf. United Meth. Ch.; mem. Com. Status and Role Women, Pa.; pres. Valley Clergy Assn., 2006—. Recipient Edwin A. Lewis Theology award, Drew Theol. Sch., 1997, GFWC Short Story award, 1991. Mem.: Binghamton Dist. Pastors' Assn., Lambda Iota Tau. Methodist. Office: PO Box 222 Sayre PA 18840

BENTLEY, DIERKS, country singer, songwriter; b. Phoenix, Nov. 20; Rschr. TNN TV; signed with Dangling Rope Records, 2001, Capitol Records, Nashville, 2002—. Singer: (albums) Don't Leave Me In Love, 2001, Dierks Bentley, 2003, Modern Day Drifter, 2005, (singles) What Was I Thinkin', 2003. Named Top New Artist, Acad. Country Music, 2003; recipient Horizon award, Country Music Assn., 2005. Office: Capitol Records 3322 W End Ave Nashville TN 37203 Office Phone: 615-269-2000. E-mail: dbstreet@dierks.com.

BENTLEY, DONALD LYON, mathematics professor, minister; b. LA, Apr. 25, 1935; s. Byron R. and Clara Viola (Lyon) B.; m. Anne P. Alexander, Aug. 28, 1957; children: James, Jillene, Janet. BS, Stanford U., 1956, MS, 1958, PhD, 1961; MDiv, Claremont Sch. Theology, 1998. Ordained Congl. min. 1998. Asst. prof. math. stats. Colo. State U., Ft. Collins, 1961-64; asst. prof. math. Pomona Coll., Claremont, Calif., 1964-67, assoc. prof., 1967-74, Burkhead prof. math., 1974—2001, ret., 2001. Cons. Allergan Pharm., Irvine, Calif., 1968-80, Intermedics IntraOcular, Pasadena, Calif., 1981-86, Tokos Med. Corp., 1986-90, Cardio Genisis Corp., 1995-2000; consulting minister Pilgrim Congl. Ch., 1998-2005, assoc. minister, 2005-07. Co-author: Linear Algebra with Differential Equations, 1973. Fellow Am. Statis. Assn.; mem. Math. Assn. Am., Nat. Assn. Congrl. Christian Chs. (chair exec. com. 1994-95, moderator-elect 2002-03, moderator 2003-04). Congregationalist. Avocations: music, woodworking, genealogy.

BENTLEY, ERIC, writer, playwright, literature educator; b. Eng., Sept. 14, 1916; s. Fred and Laura (Evelyn) B. BA, Oxford U., Eng., 1938; Litt.B., Oxford U., 1939; PhD, Yale U., 1941; D.F.A., U. Wis., 1975; Litt.D. (hon.), U. East Anglia, 1979; DHL, New Sch. Social Rsch., 1992. Brander Matthews prof. dramatic lit. Columbia U., 1953-69; dramatic critic The New Republic, 1952-56; Norton prof. poetry Harvard U., 1960-61; artist in residence Ford Found., Berlin, 1964-65; Katharine Cornell prof. theatre SUNY-Buffalo, 1974-82; prof. comparative lit. U. Md., College Park, 1982-89. Co-producer of: DMZ, a political Cabaret, 1968 (recipient George Jean Nathan award 1966, Obie award 1978, Pirandello Soc. award, 1991, Robert Lewis award, 1992); author: A Century of Hero-Worship, 1944, The Playwright as Thinker, 1946, Bernard Shaw, 1947, In Search of Theatre, 1953, The Dramatic Event, 1954, What is Theatre?, 1956, The Life of the Drama, 1964, The Theatre of Commitment, 1967, What Is Theatre and Other Reviews, 1968, A Time to Die & A Time to Live, 1970, The Red White and Black, 1970, Are You Now or Have You Ever Been, 1972, The Recantation of Galileo Galilei, 1972, Theatre of War, 1972, Expletive Deleted, 1974, Memoirs of Pilate, 1977, Rallying Cries, 1977, Lord Alfred's Lover, 1978, Wannsee, 1979, The Brecht Commentaries, 1981, Concord, 1981, The Fall of the Amazons, 1982, The Kleist Variations, 1983, The Pirandello Commentaries, 1985-86, Monstrous Martyrdoms, 1985, The Brecht Memoir, 1985, Thinking About the Playwright, 1987, Round 2, 1990; author-editor: Thirty Years of Treason, 1971; editor: The Importance of Scrutiny, 1948, From the Modern Repertoire, 1949-56, The Modern Theatre, 1955-60, The Classic Theatre, 1958-61, The Theory of the Modern Stage, 1968, The Great Playwrights, 1970, Eric Bentley's Dramatic Repertoire, (4 vols.) 1985-86; adapter, translator: plays A Man's a Man, 1962, Mother Courage, 1963, Inspector and Other Plays by Nikolai Gogol, 1987, others. Guggenheim fellow, 1948-49, 67-68; Fulbright scholar in Yugoslavia, 1980; recipient Amoco Gold Medallion of Excellence Am. Coll. Theatre Festival, 1985, Spl. award Pirandello Soc. Am., 1992, OBIE award Lifetime Achievement, Village Voice, 2006, Thalia prize Internat. Critics, 2006; inducted Theatre Hall of Fame, 1997-98 Mem. Am. Acad. Arts and Scis., Am. Acad. Arts and Letters. Subject (book): The Play and Its Critic: Essays for Eric Bentley, U. Press of Am., 1986; entire first issue mag. Theatre Three, Carnegie Mellon U., 1986, dedicated to Eric Bentley. Address: 194 Riverside Dr New York NY 10025-7259 Personal E-mail: ericbentley@verizon.net.

BENTLEY, FRED DOUGLAS, SR., lawyer; b. Marietta, Ga, Oct. 15, 1926; s. Oscar Andrew and Ima Irene (Prather) B.; children from previous marriage: Fred Douglas, Robert Randall; m. Jane Morrill McNeel, Nov. 7, 1997. BA, Presbyn. Coll., 1949; JD, Emory U., 1948; HHD (hon.), PhD (hon.), LHD (hon.), Kennesaw State U., 2000. Bar: Ga. 1948. Sr. mem. Bentley & Dew, Marietta, 1948-51; ptnr. Bentley, Awtrey & Bartlett, Marietta, 1951-56, Edwards, Bentley, Awtrey & Parker, Marietta, 1956-75, Bentley & Schindelar, Marietta, 1975-80, Bentley, Bentley & Bentley, Marietta, 1975—. Pres. Beneficial Investment Co., Newmarket, Inc., Happy Valley, Inc., Bentley & Sons, Inc.; founder, chmn. emeritus bd. Charter Bank and Trust Co.; founder, trustee emeritus Kennesaw State U. Mem. Ga. Ho. Reps., 1951-57, Ga. Senate, 1958; past pres. Cobb County (Ga.) C. of C.; founder, hon. curator Bentley Rare Book Galleries-Brenau U., Kennesaw State U.; mem., past chmn. Ga. Coun. Arts, 1976-89; mem. Gov.'s Fine Arts Com., 1990-92, Cummer Mus. of Art (hon. life); attache Ghana Olympic Com.; founder Cobb Emergency Svc.; fell. US Supreme Ct. Museum Acquisition Com., US Constitution Museum; Served with USN. Recipient Blue Key Cmty. Svc. award, Founder's award, 1992, Clarisse Baqwell award for outstanding svc., Spl. Svc. award Kennesaw State U., Robert Cleveland award for lifetime achievement in law; named Citizen of Yr., C. of C., 1951, Leader of Tomorrow, Time mag., 1953, 1st Golden Cir. award Vol. Citizen of Yr., Atlanta Jour. Constn., 1981, Kennesaw Hist. Soc. Man of Yr., 1996, Brenau U. Man of Yr. award, 1996, President's award Kennesaw State U., 1999, Disting. Alumna Marietta HS, Bus. Assoc. of Yr. award ABWA, 2002, The Extra Mile trophy, 2003, Disting. Alumna, Emory U. Law Sch., 2004; Bridge named in his honor, 2000; Oct. 15th Day named in his honor City and Coun., City of Kennesaw, Kennesaw State U., 2006; fellow J. Pierpont Morgan Libr. Fellow Am. Trust Brit. Libr., Marietta Cobb Mus. Art (founder), U.S. Supreme Ct. Hist. Soc., U.S. Const. Ctr.; mem. Ga. Bar Assn., Ga. Mus. Art (bd. advisors, hon. life), Nat. PTA (hon. life), Cobb Landmarks Soc. (founder), Kennesaw Mountain Jaycees (founder), Rotary (hon. life), Georgian Club (bd. dir.). Republican. Presbyterian. Home: 1441 Beaumont Dr Kennesaw GA 30152-3201 Office: 241 Washington Ave NE Marietta GA 30060-1958 Office Phone: 770-422-2300.

BENTLEY, JAMES LUTHER, former journalist; b. Panama City, Fla., Jan. 24, 1937; s. Thomas Pierce and Sara Pope (Woodruff) B.; m. Patricia Ann Daniel, July 30, 1965. Student Ga. Inst. Tech, Ga. State U., 1958-61, N.C. State U., 1962. Reporter Atlanta Constitution, 1958-64, asst. city editor, 1964-66, night city editor, 1966-71, city editor, 1971-79; corr. Reuters Ltd., 1967-79; dir. info. TVA, 1979; mng. editor Cox News Svc., Washington, 1979-98. Bd. dirs. Friends of Jekyll Island, Hofwyl Plantation. Served with U.S. Army, 1961-63. Mem. Rotary. Lutheran. Home: 317 Old Plantation Rd Jekyll Island GA 31527-0857 E-mail: jimbentley@bellsouth.net.

BENTLEY, KENNETH CHESSAR, oral and maxillofacial surgeon, educator; b. Montreal, Que., Can., Sept. 22, 1935; s. Albert Edwin and Lilian Beatrice (Hoare) B.; m. Jean Wadsworth, Aug. 19, 1961; children: Douglas, Margaret. DDS, McGill U., 1958, MD, CM, 1962. Intern, then resident Montreal Gen. Hosp. and Bellevue Hosp., NY, 1962-66; from asst. prof. to assoc. prof. McGill U., 1966-67, prof. dentistry, 1975-98, prof. emeritus, 1998; dean McGill U. Sch. Dentistry, 1977-87; jr. asst. dental surgeon Montreal Gen. Hosp., 1966, assoc. dental surgeon, assoc. dir. dentistry, 1968, dental surgeon-in-chief, 1970-2000. Pres. Thistle Coun. Quebec; pres., bd dirs. Griffith McConnell Residence Nursing Home. Co-author: Advanced Oral Radiographic Interpretation, 1979. Named Decorated Hospitaller, Order St. John Jerusalem; recipient Queen's Golden Jubilee medal, 2002. Fellow Am. Coll. Dentists, Internat. Coll. Dentists, Royal Coll. Dentists Can., Pierre Fauchard Acad., Academie Dentaire Du Quebec; mem. Assn. Oral and Maxillofacial Surgeons Que., Bellevue Soc. Oral Surgeons, Can. Dental Assn. (hon.; chmn. coun. hosp. svcs. 1971-75, coun. edn. 1982-85), Can. Assn. Oral and Maxillofacial Surgeons (sec.-treas. 1970-71), Internat. Assn. Oral Surgeons, Montreal Dental Club (sec. 1968, pres.1992), Nat. Dental Exam. Bd. Can., Order Dentists Que., St. Andrew's Soc. Montreal (1st v.p.). Avocations: music, pipe organ, scottish country dancing. Home Phone: 450-246-2285. E-mail: kcb@total.net.

BENTLEY, RICHARD NORCROSS, regional planner, writer, educator; b. Chgo., Mar. 17, 1937; s. Richard and Phoebe Wrenn (Norcross) B.; m. Carolyn Stiglic, Sept. 10, 1977; children: Nicholas Northrup, Julia Wrenn. BA, Yale U., 1959; MFA, Norwich U., 1992. Chief project mgr. Kate Maremont Found., 1965-70, Rose Assocs., NYC, 1973-75, Adv. Svcs. for Better Housing, NYC, 1975-78, Mass. Dept. Community Affairs, Boston, 1978-83; chief planner Mayor's Office Housing, Boston, 1983-86; planning dir. Boston Housing Authority, 1986-87; sr. planning mgr. Pioneer Valley Planning Commn., West Springfield, Mass., 1987-88. Instr. Internat. City Mgmt. Assn., Washington, 1982-90; instr. creative writing U. Mass., 1992-2003, Cambridge Coll., 1994-2000, Mass. Coll. Liberal Arts, 1995-99, Holyoke CC, 1997-99; instr. MFA program Vt. Coll., 1997, 99; adj. prof. Western New England Coll., 2000—, Am. Internat. Coll., 2004. Author: Post-Freudian Dreaming, 2002, A General Theory of Desire, 2007; mng. editor Peregrine Mag., 1991-93. Bd. govs. Groton Sch., Mass., 1990-95; gov.'s appointee Mass. Mortgage Rev. Bd., 1984—; del. Dem. State Conv., Mass., 2000. Served with U.S. Army, 1960-62. Recipient Internat. Fiction award Paris Writers' Workshop, 1994. Mem.: Am. Planning Assn., Nat. Assn. Housing and Redevel. Ofcls., Assn. Yale Alumni Assembly (del. 2000—03), Soc. Mayflower Descs., Assn. Personal Historians (founding), Harvard Club (Boston), Yale Club (Conn. Valley), Amherst Yacht Club. Home: 24 N Prospect St Amherst MA 01002-2014 Office Phone: 413-781-1780. E-mail: rbentley@valinet.com.

BENTLEY, THOMAS ROY, retired language educator, writer; b. Belfast, No. Ireland, June 5, 1931; s. Thomas and Anne (Hill) B.; m. Joan M. Williams, Dec. 24, 1955; children: Kimberley, Shannon, Carolyn. BA, U. Toronto, 1960, MA, 1966; EdB, Ont. Coll., 1961; PhD, Meml. U., Nfld., Can., 1970. Assoc. dean edn. U. B.C., Vancouver, Can., 1973-77, head lang. edn., 1978-79, acting dean edn., 1979-81, prof. lang. edn., 1983-96, prof. emeritus, 1996—. Cons. to maj. cos. on comm. and transp. issues; co-founder Internat. Lifewriting Network. Author 4 books on English comms.; editor 12 books on Can. lit.; contbr. articles to profl. jours.; broadcaster numerous programs on radio and TV. Mem. Nat. Assn. Tchrs. English (chmn. internat. assembly 1981), Assn. Profs. Emeriti, Nat. Conf. for Rsch. in English, Can. Coun. Tchrs. English (editor, bd. dirs., 1975-78), Vancouver Club. Office: 5529 University Blvd Vancouver BC Canada V6T 1K5 Business E-Mail: roy.bentley@ubc.ca.

BENTON, ALLEN HAYDON, biology professor; b. Ira, NY, Sept. 4, 1921; s. Haydon Willey and Pearl Amelia (Diddy) B.; m. Marjorie Lois Hall, Aug. 16, 1947; children: Thomas Hall, Christopher Allen, Holly Anne. BS, Cornell U., 1948, MS, 1949, PhD, 1952. Jr. wildlife biologist U.S. Fish and Wildlife Service, 1949; asst. prof. biology SUNY-Albany, 1949-57, assoc. prof., 1957-62; prof. biology SUNY-Fredonia, 1962-73, disting. teaching prof., 1973-84, faculty exchange scholar, 1975-84, prof. emeritus, 1984—. Vis. prof. Stephen F. Austin Coll., 1957, Concord Coll., Athens, W.Va., 1969-70, U. Minn. Biol. Sta., 1970; cons. Nuclear Fuel Services Inc., Fla. Arthropod Collection, Roger Tory Peterson Inst. for the Study of Natural History. Author: (with W.E. Werner Jr.) Field Biology and Ecology, 3rd edit., 1974, Atlas of Fleas of the Eastern United States, 1980, Manual for Field Biology and Ecology, 6th edit., 1983, Wild Worlds, 1988, Light and Natural, 1992, Birding Through Life, 2004, To Walk in Beauty, 2005, (books of poetry) The Nature of Nature, 1976, Sonnets from Nebraska and Beyond, 1984, Slivers of Jade, 1987, Reflections on a Water Lily Pool, 2003, The Wheel of Life, 2004, A Sense of Nonsense, 2004; columnist Dunkirk (N.Y.) Evening Observer, Albany (N.Y.) Knickerbocker News, Jamestown (N.Y.) Post Jour.; freelance writer on nature and sci.; contbr. articles to profl. jours. Served with cav. U.S. Army, 1942-46. Decorated Bronze Star; grantee Research Found. SUNY, 1963, 83; NSF grantee, 1972; E.N. Huyck Found. grantee, 1976-78 Mem. Am. Ornithologists Union, Am. Soc. Mammalogists, Wilson Ornithol. Soc., Fedn. N.Y. State Bird Clubs (pres.), PTA (life), Sigma Xi, Phi Kappa Phi. Home: 292 Water St Fredonia NY 14063-2025 Personal E-mail: marginal@mymailstation.com.

BENTON, ANDREW KEITH, academic administrator, lawyer; b. Hawthorne, Nev., Feb. 4, 1952; s. Darwin Keith and Nelda Lou Benton; m. Deborah Sue Strickland, June 22, 1974; children: Hailey Michelle, Christopher Andrew. BS in Am. Studies, Okla. Christian Coll., 1974; JD, Oklahoma City U., 1979. Bar: Okla. 1979, U.S. Dist. Ct. (we. dist.) Okla. (admitted to) 1982. Sole practice, Edmond, Okla., 1979-81, 83-84; ptnr. Benton & Thomason, Edmond, 1981—83; asst. v.p. Pepperdine U., Malibu, Calif., 1984—85, v.p., 1985—87, v.p. adminstrn., 1987—89, v.p. univ. affairs, 1989—91, exec. v.p., 1991—2000, pres., 2000—. Chmn. precinct, state conv. del. Okla. Reps., 1980. Mem.: Am. Coun. on Edn., Assn. of Ind. Calif. Coll. & Univ., Nat. Assn. Ind. Coll. & Univ., Okla. Bar Assn. (contbr. articles to ednl. community), ABA (chmn. subcom. emerging land use trends 1987—88, chmn. subcom. decisional trends 1988—90), Calif. Club, Jonathan Club. Republican. Mem. Ch. Of Christ. Office: Pepperdine U 24255 Pacific Coast Hwy Malibu CA 90263-0002*

BENTON, AUBURN EDGAR, lawyer; b. Colorado Springs, Colo., July 12, 1926; s. Auburn Edgar and Ella Dot (Heyer) B.; m. Stephanie Marie Jakimowitz, June 8, 1951; children: Margrit Laura, Mary Ellen. BA, Colo. Coll., 1950; LLB, Yale U., 1953. Bar: Colo. 1953, U.S. Dist. Ct. Colo. 1953, U.S. Ct. Appeals (10th cir.) 1954. Assoc. Holme Roberts & Owen LLP, Denver, 1953-57, ptnr., 1957-91, of counsel, 1992—. Mem. Bd. Edn. Denver Pub. Schs., 1961-69; mem. Colo. Commn. Higher Edn., Denver, 1975-85; mem. Colo. Bd. Ethics, Denver, 1975-98; mem. Nat. Common Cause Bd., Washington, 1975-85; dir. soc. sci. found. U. Denver. Mem. Colo. Bar Assn., Denver Bar Assn., Cactus Club (Denver), Phi Beta Kappa. Democrat. Home: 901 Race St Denver CO 80206-3735 Office: Holme Roberts & Owen LLP 1700 Lincoln St Ste 4100 Denver CO 80203-4541

BENTON, DANIEL C., investment company executive; AB, Colgate U., 1980; MBA, Harvard U. Pres. Pequot; founder, chmn. CEO Andor Capital Mgmt., Stamford, Conn., 2001—. V.p of bd. Whitney Mus. Am. Art; trustee Colgate U., James B. Colgate Soc., 2001—. Mailing: c/o Whitney Mus Am Art 945 Madison Ave New York NY 10021 Office: Andor Capital Mgmt 153 East 53 St 58th Floor New York NY 10022

BENTON, DONALD STEWART, publishing company executive, lawyer; b. Marlboro, NY, Jan. 2, 1924; s. Fred Stanton and Agnes (Townsend) B. Student, U. Leeds, Eng., 1945; BA, Columbia U., 1947, JD, 1949; LLM, NYU, 1953. Bar: N.Y. 1953. Practiced in N.Y.C., 1953-56; atty. N.Y. State Banking Dept., 1954-55; v.p. Found. Press, Inc., Bklyn., 1957-60; exec. asst. to exec. v.p. N.Y. Stock Exchange, 1960-61; dir. reference book dept. and spl. projects editor Appleton Century Crofts, NYC, 1962-71; sr. editor Matthew Bender & Co., Inc., NYC, 1974-77; sr. legal editor Warren, Gorham & Lamont, Inc., NYC, 1977-89. Author: Thorndike Encyclopedia of Banking and Financial Tables, 3rd edit., 2000 yearbook, Federal Banking Laws, 3rd edit., 2000, Real Estate Tax Digest, 1984, Criminal Law Digest, 3rd edit., 1983, Modern Real Estate and Mortgage Checklists, 1979. Mem. Cresskill (N.J.) Zoning Bd. Adjustment, 1969-71, 82-83, 86—, Cresskill Planning Bd., 1971-74; councilman City of Cresskill, 1972-74. With AUS, 1943-46, 50-52. Decorated Bronze Star. Mem. Phi Delta Phi. Mem. Reformed Ch. in Am. Home: 117 Heatherhill Rd Cresskill NJ 07626-1020

BENTON, GERALDINE ANN, preschool owner, director; b. Plymouth, NH, Apr. 25, 1960; d. Alton G. and Geraldine (Holecek) B. BS, Plymouth State Coll., 1984; MA in Curriculum and Tech., U. Phoenix, 2005. Cert. bus driver, N.H. Pvt. practice tutor; bus driver Robertson Transit, Campton, N.H., 1986-96; owner, dir. Mad River Learning Ctr. and Daycare, Thornton, N.H., 1996—; sub. tchr., 1982-96. Mem. Interested Citizens in Town

Govt. Mem. Nat. Head Injury Found., Nat. Arbor Day Found., Nat. Audubon Soc., Nat. Wildlife Found. Home: 5 Benton Rd Campton NH 03223 Office Phone: 603-726-3883.

BENTON, JANETTA REBOLD, art historian, professor, writer; b. Phila., July 6, 1945; d. Joseph and Lillie (Frankel) Rebold; m. Elliot Raymond Benton, Feb. 4, 1967; children: Phillips Alexander, Ethan Aubrey, Meredith Rebold, Leland Samuel. BFA, Cornell U., Ithaca, NY, 1967; M, George Washington U., Washington, 1969; PhD, Brown U., Providence, 1981; diploma, Harvard U., Cambridge, Mass., 2000. Mus. curator dept. edn. Nat. Gallery Art, Washington, 1968—69; lectr. art history George Washington U., 1969—70; instr. art history U. Va. No. Va. Ctr., 1969—70, U. Mass., Boston, 1970—71, Boston Coll., Chestnut Hill, Mass., 1973—75; asst. prof. art history Mass. State Coll., Bridgewater and Framingham, 1971—71, 1977—78; instr. art history U. Md. European divsn., 1982—85; instr. Pace U., Pleasantville, NY, 1986—, acting chmn. dept. fine arts, 1997, dir. Pforzheimer Honors Coll., 1998—, disting. prof. art history, 2004—. Lectr. DeCordova Mus., Lincoln, Mass., 1977—78, Cloisters, NYC, 1986—89, Met. Mus. Art, NYC, 1986—89, staff lectr. dept. concerts and lectures, 1988—; chmn. numerous conf. sessions in field; presenter, lectr. in field. Author: The Medieval Menagerie: Animals in the art of the Middle Ages, 1992 (Book of Month Club selection), The Medieval Menagerie: Animals in the Art of the Middle Ages (French edit.), 1992;: Holy Terrors: Gargoyles on Medieval Buildings, 1997, Art of the Middle Ages, 2002, Medieval Mischief: Wit and Humour in the Art of the Middle Ages, 2004; co-author: Art and Culture: An Introduction to the Humanities, 2 vols. combined vol., 1998, 3rd edit., 2007; contbr. articles to profl. publs., chpts. to books; curator (exhibitions) Medieval Monsters: Dragons and Fantastic Creatures, Katonah Mus. Art, NY, 1995. Office: Pace U Pforzheimer Honors Coll 861 Bedford Rd Pleasantville NY 10570 Business E-Mail: jbenton@pace.edu.

BENTON, LEE F., lawyer; b. Springfield, Ohio, Feb. 18, 1944; AB, Oberlin Coll., 1966; JD, U. Chgo., 1969. Bar: Calif. 1970. Sr. counsel Cooley Godward Kronish LLP, Palo Alto, Calif. Teaching fellow Stanford Law Sch., 1969-70. Mem. Order Coif, Phi Beta Kappa. Office: Cooley Godward Kronish LLP 5 Palo Alto Sq 3000 El Camino Real Palo Alto CA 94306-2120 Home Phone: 650-321-8128; Office Phone: 650-843-5017. Business E-Mail: lbenton@cooley.com.

BENTON, NICHOLAS FREDERICK, publisher; b. Ross, Calif., Feb. 9, 1944; s. Frederick C. H. and Jeanne Emma (Brun) B.; m. Donna Carley, Apr. 15, 1979 (div. Oct. 1984); m. Janine Schollnick, Oct. 20, 1985 (div. Apr. 2000). AA, Santa Barbara City Coll., Calif., 1963; BA, Westmont Coll., 1965; MDiv cum laude, Pacific Sch. Religion, Berkeley, Calif., 1969. Reporter Santa Barbara News Press, 1961-66; dir. Christian edn. Plymouth Ch., Oakland, Calif., 1966-69; chief corr. Berkeley Barb, 1970-72; dir. advt. display Syufy Enterprises, San Francisco, 1973-76; regional dir. Exec. Intelligence Rev., San Francisco, LA, Houston, Washington, 1976—87; pres., CEO Benton Comms., Inc., 1987—; founder, owner, editor Falls Church News Press, 1991—. Clk. Emmaus Ch., 1989-92; bd. dirs. Arlington (Va.) Symphony, 1992-93, bd. dirs., mem. Falls Church Edn. Found., 2003-. Recipient Bus. of Yr. award Falls Church City Coun., 1991, Bus. Contbn. to Cmty. award, 1997, Bus. of Yr. award Fall Church City Coun., 2001, Grand Marshall Falls Church Meml. Day Parade, 2001; named to Media Honor Roll, Va. Sch. Bd., 1998, 2005. Mem. Greater Falls Church C. of C. (bd. dir. 1991—, pres. 1993-94, Pillar of Cmty. award 1993, 2003), LWV of Falls Church, mem. Falls Church City Dem. Com., Optimists Club, White House Corr. Assn., Nat. Press Club (Washington), Kennedy Ctr. Cirs. (Washington). Mem. United Ch. Christ. Office: Falls Church News Press 929 W Broad St Ste 200 Falls Church VA 22046-3121 Office Phone: 703-532-3267. Personal E-mail: nfbenton@aol.com. Business E-Mail: nfbenton@fcnp.com.

BENTON, ROBERT, film director, screenwriter; b. Waxahachie, Tex., Sept. 29, 1932; BA, U. Tex. Screenwriter: (with David Newman) There Was A Crooked Man, 1962, Bonnie and Clyde, 1967, What's Up Doc?, 1972, (with Mario Puzo and Tom Mankiewicz) Superman, 1978, The Ice Harvest, 2005; dir., writer: Bad Company, 1972, The Late Show, 1977, Kramer vs. Kramer, 1979 (Best Dir. Acad. award 1979, Best Screenplay Acad. award 1979), Still of the Night, 1982, Places in the Heart, 1984 (Best Screenplay Acad. award 1984), Nadine, 1987, Nobody's Fool, 1994, Twilight, 1998; dir.: Billy Bathgate, 1991, The Human Stain, 2003; co-exec. prodr.: The House on Carroll Street, 1988. Recipient Screen Laurel award, Writers Guild Am., West, 2007. Mem. Dirs. Guild Am.*

BENTON, WILLIAM DUANE, federal judge; b. Springfield, Mo., Sept. 8, 1950; s. William Max and Patricia F. (Nicholson) B.; m. Sandra Snyder, Nov. 15, 1980; children: Megan Blair, William Grant. BA in Polit. Sci. summa cum laude, Northwestern U., 1972; JD, Yale U., 1975; MBA in Accounting, Memphis State U., 1979; student Inst. Jud. Adminstrn., NYU, 1992; LLD (hon.), Ctrl. Mo. State U., 1994; LLM, U. Va., 1995; LLD (hon.), Westminster Coll., 1999. Bar: Mo. 1975; CPA, Mo. Ensign USN, 1972; advanced through grades to capt., 1993; judge advocate USN, Memphis, 1975-79; chief of staff for Congressman Wendell Bailey, Washington, 1980-82; pvt. practice Jefferson City, Mo., 1983-89; dir. revenue Mo. Dept. of Revenue, Jefferson City, 1989-91; judge Mo. Supreme Ct., Jefferson City, 1991—2004, chief justice, 1997-99; judge US Ct. Appeals (8th cir.), Kansas City, Mo., 2004—. Adj. prof. Westminster Coll., 1998-, U. Mo.-Columbia Sch. Law, 1998-. Contbr. articles to profl. jours.; mng. editor Yale Law Jour., 1974-75 Chmn. Multistate Tax Commn. Washington, 1990-91; chmn. Mo. State Employees Retirement System, Jefferson City, 1989-93; regent Ctrl. Mo. State U., 1987-89; dir. Coun. for Drug Free Youth, Jefferson City, 1989-97; mem. Mo. Mil. Adv. Com., 1989-91; mem. Mo. Commn. Intergovernmental Coop., Jefferson City, 1989-91; trustee, deacon 1st Bapt. Ch., Jefferson City. Danforth fellow JFK Sch. Govt. Harvard U., 1990. Mem. AICPA (tax com. 1983—), Mo. Bar Assn. (tax com. 1975—), Mo. Soc. CPA's (tax com. 1983—), Navy League, Mil. Order of World Wars, Vietnam Vets of Am., VFW, Am. Legion, Phi Beta Kappa, Beta Gamma Sigma, Rotary. Baptist. Lt. USN, 1975-80. Capt. JAGC USNR, 1993-2002. Office: 10-20 US Courthouse 400 E 9th St Kansas City MO 64106-2605 Office Phone: 816-512-5815.*

BENTSEN, KENNETH E., JR., trade association administrator, former congressman; b. Houston, June 3, 1959; m. Tamra Bentsen; children: Louise, Meredith. BA, U. St. Thomas, Houston, 1982; M in Pub. Adminstrn., Am. U., 1985. Mem. staff Congressman Ronald D. Coleman, 1983-87; assoc. staff U.S. House Appropriations Com., 1985-87; chair Harris County Dem. Party, 1990-93; investment banker Houston, 1987-94; mem. US Congresses from 25th Tex. dist., 1995—2003; mng. dir. Pub. Strategies Inc., Washington, 2003—; pres. Equipment Leasing Assn., Arlington, Va., 2006—. Democrat. Presbyterian. Office: ELFA 4301 N Fairfax Dr Ste 550 Arlington VA 22203

BENTSEN, KENNETH EDWARD, architect; b. Mission, Tex., Nov. 21, 1926; s. Lloyd Millard and Edna Ruth (Colbath) B.; m. Mary Dorsey Bates, Dec. 3, 1953; children: Molly Bates, Elizabeth Jean, Kenneth Edward Jr., William Lloyd. BS, U. Houston, 1951, BA, 1952. Pvt. practice architecture, prin. Kenneth Bentsen Assocs., Houston, 1958-91. Projects include Baylor Coll. Medicine, Jones and Anderson Med. Research Tower, M.D. Anderson-R. Lee Clark Clinic Bldg., West Tower, Clin. Care Ctr., Tex. Children's Hosp., Houston, Tex. Med. Ctr., Agnes Arnold Hall, Philip Hoffman Hall, U. Houston, M.D. Anderson Library, U. Houston, Pan Am. U., Grad. Sch. Bus., U. Tex, M.D. Anderson Environ. Rsch. Ctr., U. Tex, Learning Ctr., Allied Health Sci. & Nursing, U. Tex. Med. Br., Galveston, Compaq Ctr., Houston State Law Ctr., Austin, Tex., Harris County Adminstrn. Bldg., Houston, Tex. Commerce Bldg. Complex, McAllen, Tex. Bd. dirs. Tex. Children's Hosp., Cultural Trust Coun. Tex.; past bd. dirs. Tex. Commn. on the Arts, Mayor's Com. Bd. Appeals, Mus. Fine Arts, Blaffer Gallery; past mem. adv. coun. U. Tex. Sch. Architecture Pres.'s Adv. Com. Recipient numerous design awards. Mem. AIA, Tex. Soc. Architects, Houston C. of C. Office: Kenneth Bentsen FAIA 12 E Greenway Plz Ste 1100 Houston TX 77046-1201

BENTZ, DALE MONROE, retired librarian; b. York County, Pa., Jan. 3, 1919; s. Solomon Earl and Mary Rebecca (Wonders) B.; m. Mary Gail Menius, June 13, 1942; children: Dale Flynn, Thomas Earl, Mary Carolyn. AB, Gettysburg Coll., 1939; BSL.S., U. N.C. Chapel Hill, 1940; MS, U. Ill., 1951. With Periodicals dept. U. N.C. Library, Chapel Hill, 1940-41, Serials Dept., Duke U. Library, Durham, N.C., 1941-42; asst. librarian E. Carolina Tchrs. Coll., Greenville, N.C., 1946-48; head processing dept. U. Tenn. Library, Knoxville, 1948-53; assoc. dir. libraries U. Iowa, Iowa City, 1953-70, univ. librarian, 1970-86, univ. librarian emeritus, 1986—. Editor U. Tenn. Library Lectures, 1952; contbr. articles to profl. jours. Pres. Iowa City Bd. Edn., 1962-63 Mem. Iowa Library Assn. (pres., 1959-60), ALA (pres. resources and tech. services div. 1975-76), AAUP, Assn. Coll. and Research Libraries, Beta Phi Mu (pres. 1966-67) Clubs: Triangle (pres. 1958-59), Univ. Athletic (sec. 1979-80). Lutheran. Home: 701 Oaknoll Dr # 430 Iowa City IA 52246-5168 Personal E-mail: dalembentz@hotmail.com.

BENVENISTE, LAWRENCE M., dean; 1 child, Jeffrey. BS in math., U. Calif., Irvine, 1972; PhD in math., U. Calif., Berkeley, 1975. Staff economist for bd. governors FRS, Washington; mem. faculty U. Rochester, U. Pa., Northwestern U.; assoc. prof. fin. Wallace E. Carroll Sch. Mgmt., Boston Coll.; US Bancorp prof. fin. Carlson Sch. Mgmt., U. Minn., Twin Cities, 1996—99, chair fin. dept., 1999—2000, assoc. dean faculty and rsch., 2000—01, interim dean, 2001, dean, prof. fin., 2001—05; dean Goizueta Bus. Sch., Emory U., Atlanta, 2005—, Asa Griggs Candler prof. fin. Bd. dirs. Rimage Corp., 2003—, Alliance Data Systems. Office: Emory U Goizueta Bus Sch 1300 Clifton Rd Atlanta GA 30322 Office Phone: 404-727-6377. Business E-Mail: carol_hagins@bus.emory.edu.

BEN-VENISTE, RICHARD, lawyer; b. NYC, Jan. 3, 1943; s. Isaac and Sylvia (Schultz) B.-V. AB magna cum laude, Muhlenberg Coll., 1964, LLD (hon.), 1975; JD, Columbia U., 1967; LLM, Northwestern U., 1968. Bar: N.Y. 1968, U.S. Dist. Ct. (so. dist.) N.Y. 1968, U.S. Ct. Appeals (2nd cir.) 1969, U.S. Supreme Ct. 1974, D.C. 1975, U.S. Ct. Appeals (1st cir.) 1976, U.S. Ct. Appeals (D.C. cir.) 1982, U.S. Dist. Ct. (no. dist.) Calif. 1983, U.S. Dist. Ct. D.C. 1983. Asst. U.S. atty. (so. dist.) N.Y. U.S. Dept. Justice, 1968-73, chief, spl. prosecution sect., 1971—73, chief, Watergate Task Force, Watergate Spl. Prosecution Force, 1973-75; spl. outside counsel Senate Subcom. on Govtl. Ops., Washington, 1976-77; ptnr. Melrod, Redman & Gartlan, 1975-81, Ben-Veniste & Shernoff, 1981-90, Weil, Gotshal & Manges, Washington, 1990—2002, Mayer, Brown, Rowe & Maw LLP, Washington, 2002—. Chmn. D.C. Advisory Com. on Prison Edn. Reform, 1984-86; chief minority counsel Senate Whitewater Com., 1995-96; co-founder Trial Lawyers for Pub. Justice, 1982; presdl. appointment Mem. Interagy. Working Group (to declassify Nazi era documents), 2000—; commr., The Nat. Commn. on Terrorist Attacks Upon the U.S.(The 9-11 Commn.), 2003-04. Co-author: Stonewall, The Real Story of the Watergate Prosecution, 1977. Recipient Outstanding Pub. Svc. award Seymour Assn., 1976; named one of Best Lawyers in Washington, Washingtonian Mag., 1992-2006, Best Lawyers in Am. 1975-2006; Harlan Fiske Stone Scholar. Office: Mayer Brown Rowe & Maw LLP 1909 K St NW Washington DC 20006-1101 Office Phone: 202-263-3000. Office Fax: 202-263-3300. Business E-Mail: rben-veniste@mayerbrownrowe.com.

BENVENUTTI, PETER J., lawyer; b. Gulfport, Miss., June 24, 1949; s. Peter J. and Elizabeth Cullen (Beyer) B.; m. Lise A. Pearlman, May 31, 1974; children: Anna B., Jamie E., Amalia R. AB, Harvard U., 1971; JD, U. Calif., Berkeley, 1974. Bar: Calif. 1974, U.S. Dist. Ct. (no. dist.) Calif. 1974, U.S. Dist. Ct. (ea. dist.) Calif. 1977, U.S. Dist. Ct. (ctrl. and so. dists.) Calif. 1989, U.S. Dist. Ct. Ariz. 1990, U.S. Ct. Appeals (9th cir.) 1984. Assoc. Dinkelspiel & Dinkelspiel, San Francisco, 1974-80, ptnr., 1981-88, Heller, Ehrman, White & McAuliffe, San Francisco, 1988—; mng. ptnr. San Francisco Office, 1995-97. Bd. dirs. ARC, 1981-83. Mem. ABA, Bar Assn. San Francisco (pres. Calif. bankruptcy forum 1993-94, lawyer rep. 9th Cir. Jud. Conf. 1994—). Democrat. Home: 1147 Clarendon Cres Oakland CA 94610-1807 Office: Heller Ehrman White & McAuliffe 333 Bush St San Francisco CA 94104-2806 Office Phone: 415-772-6403. Office Fax: 415-772-6268. E-mail: pbenvenutti@hewm.com.

BENWAY, HEATHER, oceanographer, researcher; d. Richard and Katherine Balow; m. Matthew Arsenault, Sept. 9, 2006. BS, U. Rochester, NY, 1994; MS, U. NH, Durham, 1997; PhD, Oreg. State U., Corvallis, 2005. Grad. rsch. asst. U. NH, 1995—96; with Nat. Oceanic and Atmospheric Adminstrn., Silver Spring, Md., 1997—98, program mgr. office global programs, 1998—2000; rsch. asst. coll. oceanic and atmospheric scis. Oreg. State U., Corvallis, 2000—05; rschr. dept. geology and geophysics Woods Hole Oceanog. Instn., Mass., 2005—. Contbr. articles to profl. jours. Vol. Heartland Humane Soc., Corvallis. Recipient Most Outstanding Student Poster prize, Internat. Marine Global Changes, 2001; Dean John A. Knauss Marine Policy fellowship, Nat. Sea Grant Program, 1997—98, Schlanger Ocean Drilling Program fellowship, US Sci. Support Program, 2002, Comer-Steele Postdoctoral scholarship, Woods Hole Oceanog. Instn., 2005—07. Mem.: Nat. Postdoctoral Assn., Woods Hole Oceanog. Instn. Postdoctoral Assn. (pres. 2006—), Am. Geophysical Union. Office Phone: 508-289-2838. Business E-Mail: hbenway@whoi.edu.

BENYEI, CANDACE REED, psychotherapist; b. NYC, Feb. 25, 1946; d. Harlow John and Jacqueline de la Valtaire (Smyth) Reed; m. Curt Christian Benyei, July 1, 1967; children: Tara Elaine, Christian Harlow. BA in Chemistry, Colo. Coll., 1967; MS in Sch. Psychology, So. Conn. State U., 1985; MS in Marriage and Family Therapy, U. Bridgeport, Conn., 1987; PhD in Clin. Psychology, Union Inst., Cin., 1988; MPS, N.Y. Theol. Sem., 1994. Lic. marriage and family therapist, Conn. Rsch. assoc. Cornell U., Ithaca, N.Y., 1967-68; rsch. asst. Yale-New Haven Hosp., 1968-70, Clairol, Inc., Stamford, Conn., 1970-71; asst. chaplain So. Conn. State U., New Haven, 1984-85; adj. prof. U. Bridgeport, 1988-89; cons. family svcs. div. Danbury (Conn.) Superior Ct., 1990-91; mgr., pres. Whimsy Brook Farm, Ltd., Redding, Conn., 1972—; dir. Inst. for Human Resources, Redding, 1985—. Lectr. So. Conn. State U., 1990—97; adj. prof. Fairfield U., 1990—97; acting exec. dir. Burning Tree, Inc., 1998—; founder, tchg. elder Congregation of the Way, 2000—; adminstr. Schulhof Animal Hosp., 1999—. Author: Called to Be Lonely: A Company of Clowns, 1984, A Cape Cod Journal, 1985, Understanding Clergy Misconduct in Religious Systems: Scapegoating, Family Secrets and the Abuse of Power, 1998, How to Get There From Here: Creating God Among Us, 2002, numerous poems; contbr. chapters to books. Pres. Fairfield Coop. Ext. Coun., 1975-78; mem. Redding Bd. Edn., 1978-86; lic. lay reader Episc. Diocese Conn., 1982-91, mem. diocesan com. on spiritual direction, 1985-87; assoc. Order of Holy Cross, 1986—; mem. adv. com. Ellis Clark Regional Agri-Sci. and Tech. Ctr. Mem.: Nat. Ctr. Homeopathy, Conn. Holistic Health Assn., Conn. Assn. Marriage and Family Therapists (clin mem., approved supr.), Am. Assn. Marriage and Family Therapists (approved supr.), Conn. Psychol. Assn., Conn. Farm Bur. (bd. dirs.), Am. Quarter Horse Assn. Avocations: photography, gardening, poetry. Office: Inst Human Resources 29 Giles Hill Rd Redding CT 06896-2511 Home Phone: 203-938-3414; Office Phone: 203-938-9309. E-mail: drcandace@earthlink.net.

BEN-YOSEPH, MIRIAM, social sciences educator; m. Yoav Ben-Yoseph, Dec. 24, 1974. BA, MA, Hebrew U., Jerusalem; PhD in French Lit., Northwestern U. V.p. market rsch. and tng. Continental Bank; faculty mem. to assoc. prof. Sch. New Learning DePaul U., Chgo., 1991—. Recipient US Prof. of Yr. award, Carnegie Found. for Advancement of Tchg. and Coun. for Advancement and Support of Edn., 2006. Office: Sch New Learning DePaul U 25 E Jackson Chicago IL 60604 Office Phone: 312-362-6560. E-mail: mben@depaul.edu.*

BENYUS, JANINE M., writer; Grad. in Natural Resource Mgmt. and English Lit., Rutgers U., NJ. Mem. Biomimicry Guild; lectr. U. Mont. Author: Field Guide to Wildlife Habitats of the Western US, Field Guide to Wildlife Habitats of the Ea. US, 1989, Northwoods Wildlife: A Watcher's Guide to Habitats, 1989, Biomimicry: Innovation Inspired by Nature, 1997; co-author: Beastly Behaviors: A Zoo Lover's Companion, 1993, Secret Language & Remarkable Behavior of Animals, 1998. Recipient Earth award, Wings WorldQuest Women of Discovery Awards, 2006. Office: Biomimicry Guild PO Box 575 Helena MT 59624

BENZ, EDWARD JOHN, SR., clinical pathologist; b. June 11, 1923; s. Henry John and Gertrude Nora (Heffernan) B.; m. Verna Marie Cuddyre, June 20, 1945; children: Edward John, Thomas James, Gregory Paul, Mary Louise. BS, U. Pitts., 1943, MD, 1946; MS, U. Minn., 1952. Intern St. Joseph's Hosp., Pitts., 1946-47; resident, fellow Mayo Found., Mayo Clinic, 1949-53; pathologist, dir. labs. St. Luke's Hosp., Bethlehem, Pa., 1953-84, v.p. med. affairs, 1984-89; med. dir. utilization rev. Sacred Heart Hosp., Allentown, Pa., 1990-98. Adj. prof. microbiology Lehigh U., Bethlehem, 1956-64; pres. Lab. Clin. Pathology, Bethlehem, 1956-88, ret., 1988; cons. Palmerton (Pa.) Hosp., Allentown (Pa.) State Hosp.; past dir. Miller Meml. Blood Bank, Bethlehem Mem. adv. com. Pa. Sec. Health on Clin. Labs., 1973-89; mem. health sci. adv. com. Lehigh U., 1973-89. Contbr. articles to profl. publs. Trustee St. Luke's Hosp., 1968-71; pres. Pa. Assn. Clin. Pathologists, 1966-67. Capt. M.C., AUS, 1947-49. Fellow Coll. Am. Pathologists (past chmn. anat. path. commn., past del. from Pa.), Am. Soc. Clin. Pathologists; mem. Internat. Acad. Pathology, Am. Assn. Pathologists and Bacteriologists, Am. Assn. Blood Banks, Am. Coll. Physician Execs., Saucon Club, Valley Country Club, Sigma Xi, Alpha Omega Alpha. Home and Office: 10 Devon Dr Apt 314 Acton MA 01720-5859

BENZ, EDWARD JOHN, JR., internist, hematologist, geneticist, educator, health facility administrator; b. Pitts., May 22, 1946; s. Edward John and Verna Marie (Cuddyre) Benz; m. Margaret A. Vettese; children: Timothy Edward, Jennifer Kirsten. AB in Biology cum laude, Princeton U., 1968; MD magna cum laude, Harvard U., 1973. Diplomate Am. Bd. Internal Medicine, Am. Bd. Hematology. Resident Peter Bent Brigham Hosp., Boston, 1973-75; fellow pediatric hematology Children's Hosp. Med. Ctr., Boston, 1974-75; fellow adult hematology Yale U. Sch. Medicine, New Haven, 1978-79, asst. prof. internal medicine, 1979-82, assoc. prof. internal medicine, human genetics, 1982-87, prof. internal medicine, human genetics, 1987-92, chief sect. hematology, 1987-92, chmn. dean's curriculum task force, 1987-88, assoc. chmn. dept. internal medicine, 1988-92; Jack D. Myers prof., chmn. dept. medicine U. Pitts. Sch. Medicine, 1993-95; Sir William Osler prof., dir. dept. medicine Johns Hopkins U. Sch. Medicine., Balt., 1995-2000; prof. molecular biology and genetics Johns Hopkins U. Sch. of Medicine, 1995-2000; physician-in-chief Johns Hopkins Hosp., Balt., 1995-2000; pres., CEO Dana Farber Cancer Inst., Boston, 2000—; Richard & Susan Smith prof. medicine, prof. pediat. and pathology Harvard Med. Sch., Boston, 2000—. CEO Dana Farber Ptnrs. Cancer Care, Boston, 2000—; dir. Dana Farber Harvard Cancer Ctr., Boston, 2000—; rsch. assoc. molecular hematology Nat. Heart, Lung, Blood Inst., Bethesda, Md., 1975—78; chmn. curriculum com. Yale Sch. of Medicine, New Haven, 1985—88; prof. pro-tem, hon. vis. chief svc. Brigham & Women's Hosp., 1997; surgeon USPHS, 1975—78; adj. prof. biol. scis. Carnegie Mellon U., 1993—95; Howard Hiatt vis. prof. Harvard Med. Sch., 1998; Clement Finch prof. U. Wash., 1998; Litchfield lectr. Oxford U., 1999; Bulfinch vis. prof. medicine Mass. Gen. Hosp., Harvard Med. Sch., Boston, 2000; Haynes disting. vis. prof. medicine Duke U., 2000; Franz Inglefinger vis. prof. Boston U., 2001; Farr and Bondy Lecr. Yale U., 2004, 07; lectr. in field. Author: Molecular Genetics Methods, 1987; co-editor: Hematology, Principles and Practice, 1990 (First prize Brit. Med. Soc.), 4th edit., 2004; mem. editl. bd. Blood, 1988—94, New Eng. Jour. Medicine, 2002—; assoc. editor: New Eng. Jour. Medicine; contbr. over 200 articles to profl. jours.; co-editor: Oxford Textbook of Medicine, 2002 (First prize Royal Soc. Authors). Pres. Friends Nat. Inst. Nursing Rsch., 2005—06; mem. governing bd. Dana Farber Children's Hosp. Cancer Care, 2000—; trustee Rockefeller U., 2004—. Recipient Career Devel. award, NIH, 1982, Edward Paradiso Rsch. award, Cooley's Aemia Found., NYC, 1985, Basil O'Connor award, March of Dimes, 1980, Disting. Eagle Scout award, Boy Scouts Am., 2003. Fellow: AAAS, ACP, Am. Acad. Arts and Scis.; mem.: NIH (study sect. 1984—, chmn. 1993—95), Am. Assn. Cancer Inst. (v.p. 2005—06, pres. 2007—), Inst. Medicine, Am. Soc. Human Genetics, Am. Clin. and Climatol. Soc., Am. Soc. Hematology (exec. coun. 1994, v.p. 1998, pres.-elect 1999, pres. 2000), Am. Fedn. Clin. Rsch., Assn. Am. Physicians, Am. Soc. Clin. Investigation (nat. coun. 1987—91, pres. 1991—92), Princeton Elm Club, Interurban Clin. Club, Alpha Omega Alpha, Sigma Xi, Phi Beta Kappa. Office: Dana Farber Cancer Inst 44 Binney St Boston MA 02115 Office Phone: 617-632-4266. Personal E-mail: ebenz@comcast.net. Business E-Mail: edward_benz@dfci.harvard.edu.

BENZ, SUSAN, library and information scientist; MLS, U. Md., 1998. Project mgr. Nat. Digital Libr. NY Hist. Soc.; librarian Goettingen Digitization Ctr., Germany, Brooklyn Pub. Libr., 2002—, mgr. digital libr. services. Mem. collaborative digitization planning com. Met. NY Libr. Coun. Named one of the Movers & Shakers, Libr. Jour., 2007. Avocation: painting. Office: Brooklyn Public Library Grand Army Plaza Brooklyn NY 11238 Office Phone: 718-230-2750.

BENZER, SEYMOUR, neuroscience educator; b. NYC, Oct. 15, 1921; s. Mayer and Eva (Naidorf) Benzer; m. Dorothy Vlosky, Jan. 10, 1942 (dec. 1978); children: Barbara Ann Benzer Freidin, Martha Jane Benzer Goldberg; m. Carol A. Miller, May 11, 1980; 1 child, Alexander Robin. BA in Physics, Bklyn. Coll., 1942; MS, Purdue U., 1943, PhD in Physics, 1947, DSc (hon.), 1968; DSc, Columbia U., 1974, Yale U., 1977, Brandeis U., 1978, CUNY, 1978, U. Paris, 1983, Rockefeller U., NYC, 1993, Cold Spring Harbor Watson Sch. of Biol. Scis., 1999. Mem. faculty Purdue U., 1945—67, prof. biophysics, 1958—61, Stuart disting. prof. biology, 1961—67; prof. biology Calif. Inst. Tech., 1967—75, James G. Boswell prof. neuroscience, emeritus, divsn. biology, 1975—; biophysicist Oak Ridge Nat. Lab., 1948—49; vis. assoc. Calif. Inst. Tech., Pasadena, 1965—67. Contbr. articles to profl. jour. Recipient award of honor, Bklyn. Coll., 1956, Sigma Xi rsch. award, Purdue U., 1957, Ricketts award, U. Chgo., 1961, Gold medal, NY City Coll. Chemistry Alumni Assn., 1962, Gairdner award of merit, 1964, McCoy award, Purdue U., 1965, Lasker award, 1971, T. Duckett Jones award, 1975, prize, Leopold Mayer French Acad. Scis., 1975, Louisa Gross Horwitz award, 1976, Harvey award, Israel, 1977, Warren Triennial prize, Mass. Gen. Hosp., 1977, Dickson award, 1978, Nat. Sci. medal, 1982, Rosenstiel award, 1986, T.H. Morgan medal, Genetics Soc. Am., 1986, Karl Spencer Lashley award, 1988, Gerard award, Soc. Neurosci., 1989, Helmerich award, 1990, Wolf Found. Medicine prize, Israel, 1991, Neurosci. award, Bristol-Myers Squibb, 1992, Crafoord prize, Royal Swedish Acad. Scis., 1993, Mendel award, Brit. Genetical Soc., 1994, Alberto Feltrinelli prize, Accademia dei Lincei, Italy, 1994, Internat. Biology prize, Japan, 2000, Passano award, 2001, Neuroscience award, NAS, 2001, prize, March of Dimes, 2002, Pasarow award,

2002, Bower Achievement in Sci. award, Franklin Inst., 2004, Internat. award, Gairdner Found., 2004, Peter Gruber Found. award, Gruber Found., 2004, Albany Med. Ctr. prize, 2006; fellow, Calif. Inst. Tech., 1949—51, Fulbright Found., 1951—52, NSF, 1957—58. Fellow: Indian Acad. Sci. (hon.); mem.: AAAS, NAS, European Acad. Scis., Acad. des Sci. France (fgn. mem.), Royal Acad. Sci. Spain (fgn. mem.), Royal Soc. London (fgn. mem.), NY Acad. Sci., Harvey Soc., Am. Philos. Soc. (Lashley award 1988), Am. Acad. Arts and Sci. Home: 2075 Robin Rd San Marino CA 91108-2831

BENZING, DAVID HILL, biologist, educator; b. Evanston, Ill., Oct. 13, 1937; s. Frances Hill and Kenneth Benzing; m. Linda Grashoff, Aug. 9, 1989. BA, Miami U., Ohio, 1959; PhD, U. Mich., 1965. Robert S. Danforth prof. biology Oberlin Coll., Ohio, 1965—2006; Jessie Cox chair tropical botany Marie Selby Bot. Gardens, Sarasota, Fla., 2006—. Various bd. offices Oberlin Shansi Meml. Assn., Environ. Design Innovation Ctr., Ohio, 1980—2006. E-4 USAR, 1960—65, Fort Jackson SC, Ann Arbor, Michigan. Grant, US Nat. Pk. Svc., NSF, Nat. Geog. Soc., 0196—1995. Democrat-Npl. Home: 52755 Garfield Rd Wakeman OH 44889 Office: Oberlin Coll Wesr Lorain Oberlin OH 44074 Home Phone: 440-965-5586; Office Phone: 440-775-8120. Office Fax: 440-775-8960; Home Fax: 440-775-8960. Business E-Mail: david.benzing@oberlin.edu.

BENZLE, CURTIS MUNHALL, artist, educator; b. Lakewood, Ohio, Apr. 20, 1949; s. Arthur George and Martha (Munhall) B; m. Wendy Sue Wilson, 2007; children: Elliott, Kyle, Marisa. Student, Hillsdale Coll., 1967-69; BFA, Ohio State U., 1972; postgrad., Rochester Inst. Tech., 1973; MA, No. Ill. U., 1978. Owner, mgr. Oz Crafts, Hilton Head, SC, 1973-76, Benzle Porcelain Co., Columbus, Ohio, 1980—, Benzle Applied Arts, Huntsville, Ohio, 1988—. Owner Creative Spirit Workshop; exec. dir. Ohio Designer Craftsmen, 1996—99; instr. U. SC, Beaufort, 1978—79; prof., chair dept. dimensional studies Columbus Coll. Art and Design, 1982—2007, dir. com. art project; pres. Japan-USA Exch. Exhbn., 1988—92; bd. overseers Am. Crafts Assn., 1991—96; trustee Am. Crafts Coun., 1992—96; chair Ala. Clay Conf., 2007. One-man show U. SC, 1979, Indpls. Mus. Art, 1984, Lawrence Gallery, Portland, Oreg., 1986, Running Ridge Gallery, Santa Fe, 1986, Akasaka/Green Gallery, Tokyo, 1987, 90, Zanesville Art Ctr., 1988, Swidler Gallery, 1990, Tsukushi Gallery, Kitakyushu, Japan, 1991, del Mano Gallery, 1998, Canton Mus. Art, Ohio, 2004-05, Sherrie Gallery, Columbus, 2004-05, also others; exhibited in numerous group shows, 1971—, including Smithsonian Instn., 1980, 83, Leeuwarden, Suntory Art Mus., Tokyo, 1984, Cermaic Nat. Everson Mus., Syracuse, 1988, Internat. Competition of Ceramics, Mino, Japan, 1989, Seto Ceramic and Glass Ctr., Japan, 2003 21st Century Ceramics, Canzani Gallery, Columbus, Ohio, St. Joseph Gallery, Netherlands, 2004-05; represented in numerous permanent collections, including Smithsonian Instn., Everson Mus. Art, LA County Mus. Art, Cleve. Mus. Art., White House Collection Contemporary Craft. Mem. Ohio Citizens Com. for Arts, 1986—. Nat. Endowment for Arts fellow, 1980, Ohio Arts Coun. fellow, 1981, 83, 84, 86, 88, 2005, Greater Columbus Arts Coun. fellow, 1987. Mem. Am. Crafts Coun. (bd. overseers 1991-96, trustee 1992-96), Nat. Coun. on Edn. in Ceramic Art, Ohio Designer Craftsmen (bd. dirs. 1984-88, pres. 1985-87). Avocation: gardening. Personal E-mail: curtisbenzle@gmail.com.

BEPKO, GERALD LEWIS, retired academic administrator, law educator; b. Chgo., Apr. 21, 1940; s. Lewis V. and Geraldine S. (Bernath) B.; m. Jean B. Cougnenc, Feb. 24, 1968; children: Gerald Lewis Jr., Arminda B. BS, No. Ill. U., DeKalb, 1962; JD, Chgo. Kent Coll. Law Ill. Inst. Tech., 1965; LLM, Yale U., New Haven, 1972; D of Juridicial Sci. (hon.), Chgo. Kent Coll. Law Ill. Inst. Tech., 2003; LLD (hon.), Ind. U., Bloomington, 2007. Bar: Ill. 1965, U.S. Supreme Ct. 1968, Ind. 1973. Assoc. Ehrlich, Bundesen, Friedman & Ross, Chgo., 1965; spl. agt. FBI, 1965-69; asst. prof. law Ill. Inst. Tech.-Chgo. Kent Coll. Law, 1969-71; prof. Ind. U., Indpls., 1972-86, assoc. dean acad. affairs, 1979-81, dean, 1981-86, v.p., long-range planning, 1986—2003, chancellor, 1986—2002, interim pres., 2002—03, chancellor emeritus, 2003—, trustees prof., 2003—. Vis. prof. Ind. U.-Bloomington, summers, 1976, 77, 78, 80, U. Ill., 1976—77, Ohio State U., 1978—79; cons. and reporter Fed. Jud. Ctr.; bd. dirs. First Ind. Bank/Corp., Ind. Energy Inc. & Ind. Gas Co., Inc., 1989—97, Lumina Found. for Edn., Indpls. Life Ins. Co., One Am. Ins.; mem. Conf. Commrs. on Uniform State Laws, 1982, mem. permanent editl. bd. for the Uniform Comml. Code, 1993—2004; mem. Ind. Lobby Registration Commn., 1992—2004, vice chair, 1992—96, chair, 1996—2000; mem. Ind. Commn. Higher Edn., 2006—. Author: (with Boshkoff) Sum and Substance of Secured Transactions, 1981; contbr. articles on comml. law to profl. jours. Bd. dirs. Lumina Found. Indpls. Chgo. Title and Trust Co. Found. scholar 1962-65; Ford Urban law fellow, 1971-72. Fellow Am. Bar Found., Ind. State Bar, Indpls. Bar Found.; mem. ABA, Ind. State Bar Assn., Indpls. Bar Assn., Country Club Indpls. Methodist. Office: Ind U Inlow Hall 530 W New York St Indianapolis IN 46202-3225 Office Phone: 317-278-9240.

BERACHA, BARRY HARRIS, food products executive; b. Bronx, NY, Feb. 28, 1942; s. Nissim Macy and Celia Grace (Sides) B.; m. Barbara Marie Capobianco, Dec. 23, 1967; children: Brian, Bradley, Bonnie. BChE, Pratt Inst., 1963; MBA, U. Pa., 1965. Ops. researcher Celanese Corp., 1965-67; tech. economist Sun Oil Co., 1964-65; with Anheuser-Busch Cos., Inc., 1967-96, v.p. corp. planning, 1974-76, v.p., group exec., 1976-96; chmn., CEO Earthgrains Co., Clayton, Mo., 1996—2001; exec. v.p. Sara Lee Corp., Clayton, 2001—03; CEO Sara Lee Bakery Group, Clayton, 2001—03; ret., 2003; non-exec. chmn. Pepsi Bottling Group, Somers, NY, 2007—. Office: Pepsi Bottling Group 1 Pepsi Way Somers NY 10589-2201

BERAKA, GEORGE JOSEPH, plastic surgeon; b. Buenes Aires, Argentina, Nov. 21, 1942; s. David and Esther Rossi Beraka; m. Judith Chestman, Sept. 5, 1980; children: Scott, David, Michael. BS, Columbia U., 1965, MD, 1969. Diplomate plastic surgery Am. Bd. Plastic Surgery. Surgery resident Johns Hopkins Hosp., Balt., 1969—73; plastic surgery resident Cornell NY Hosp., NYC, 1973—75; pvt. practice Princeton, 1975—77, NYC, 1977—. Asst. prof. surgery Rutgers Med. Sch., New Brunswick, NJ, 1975—79, Cornell NY Hosp., 1985—; preceptor cosmetic surgery fellowship Lenox Hill Hosp., 1997—. Author: The Breast, 1977, Aesthetic Facial Surgery, 2002; contbr. articles various profl. jours.; mem. editl. bd.: Plastic Surgery Practice Advisor, 2004—. Tutor E. Harlem Sch., NYC, 2000—. Recipient Annual award, Artists for Breast Cancer, 2001, Outstanding Med. Student Roche award, Columbia U., 1969. Mem.: ACS, Am. Soc. Aesthetic Plastic Surgery, U. Club, Metropolitan Opera Club, Phi Beta Kappa. Republican. Episcopalian. Avocations: sailing, opera, persian rugs, biblical scholarships. Office: 875 Pk Ave New York NY 10021 Office Phone: 212-288-1122.

BERALL, FRANK STEWART, lawyer; b. NYC, Feb. 10, 1929; s. Louis J. and Jeannette F.; m. Christiana Johnson, July 5, 1958 (dec. July 1972); children: Erik Dustin, Elissa Alexandra; m. Jenefer M. Carey, Sept. 1, 1980. BS, Yale U., 1950, JD, 1955; LLM in Tax, NYU, 1959. Bar: N.Y. 1955, Conn. 1960; accredited estate planner. Assoc. firm Mudge, Stern, Baldwin & Todd, NYC, 1955-57, Townley, Updike, Carter & Rodgers, NYC, 1957-60; atty. Conn. Gen. Life Ins. Co., Bloomfield, Conn., 1960-65; atty. trust dept. Hartford Nat. Bank & Trust Co., Conn., 1965-67; assoc. Cooney & Scully, Hartford, Conn., 1968-70; ptnr. Copp & Berall, LLP and predecessors, Hartford, 1970—. Asst. in instrn. Yale U. Law Sch., 1954—55; lectr. U. Conn. Sch. Ins., 1964—72; instr. estate planning Am. Coll. Life Ins., 1968—69; v.p., sec., gen. counsel John M. Blewer, Inc., Essex, Conn., 1969—86; counsel Conn. Gov.'s Strike Force for Full Employment, 1971—72; lectr. U. Conn. Law Sch., 1972—73; counsel Conn. Gov.'s Commn. on Tax Reform, 1972—73, State Tax Commr.'s Commn., 1972—75; adj. asst. prof. grad. tax program U. Hartford, 1973—74; counsel Com. on Tax Law Clarification, 1984—88; lectr., spkr. in field. Co-author: A Practitioners Guide to the Tax Reform Act of 1969, 1970, Estate Planning and the Close Cooperation, 1970, Planning Large Estates, 1970, Revocable Inter Vivos Trusts, 1985, The Migrant Client: Tax, Community Property, and Other Considerations, 1994; sr. editor Conn. Bar Jour., 1969—, mem. editl. bd. Estate Planning mag., 1973—, Practical Tax Lawyer, 1988—, Jour. Taxation of Trusts and Estates, 1988—92, Estate Tax Planning Advisor. Bd. dirs. Bloomfield Interfaith Homes, 1967—71; adv. coun. U. Hartford Tax Inst., 1970—82; co-chmn. adv. coun. Hartford Tax Inst., 1986—94; co-chmn. Notre Dame Estate Planning Inst., 1977—. 1st lt., F.A. US Army, 1951—52. Named one of Top 50 Super Lawyers, Conn. Mag. Fellow: Am. Coll. Trust and Estate Counsel (Conn. chpt. chmn. 1975—81, mem. editl. bd. 1975—87, regent 1977—82); mem.: ABA, Culver Ednl. Found. (trustee 1997—99), Internat. Acad. Estate and Trust Law (exec. councilor 1980—82, 2004—06, v.p. Am. 2006—), Am. Law Inst., Hartford County Bar Assn. (chmn. com. liaison with IRS 1972—74, com. charter and by-laws 1975), Conn. Bar Assn. (chmn. tax sect. 1969—72, exec. com. 1969—, exec. com., estates and probate sect. 1973—, vice chmn. 1984—86), Am. Coll. Tax Counsel, Culver Summer Schs. Alumni Assn. (v.p. 1975—85, bd. dirs. 1985—91, 1993—2001, pres. 1997—99, trustee ednl. fund 1997—99), Yale Club of Harford (dir. 1998—, pres. 1999—2001, 2005—), Culver Club Ctrl. New Eng. (pres. 1996—), Tax Club of Hartford (pres. 1975—76). Office: Copp & Berall LLP 864 Wethersfield Ave Hartford CT 06114-3184 Office Phone: 860-249-5261. Business E-Mail: frank.berall@coppberall.com. *As a tax lawyer, I view my job as helping to keep the system going by seeing to it that my clients pay the government all it is legally entitled to receive in taxes, but no more, and doing pro bono work for the improvement of the entire federal and state tax law system.*

BERAN, DENIS CARL, publisher; b. Apr. 14, 1935; s. Carl Earl and Jessica Mary (Bogue) B.; m. Virginia Martha Knox, Feb. 20, 1960; children: Michael Knox, Elizabeth Virginia. BA in Econs., U. Mich., 1958; postgrad. in mktg. mgmt., Harvard Bus. Sch., 1976; Internat. Strategies Program, Columbia U., 1984. With McGraw-Hill Pubs. Co., NYC, 1962—, advt. sales trainee, 1962, dist. mgr. nucleonics, 1962-65; dist. mgr. Business Week, 1965-70, sales devel. mgr., 1970-72, mktg. dir., 1972-76, asst. pub., 1979, internat. pub. dir., 1980-85, v.p. Europe McGraw-Hill, 1976-79; v.p. advt. Gannett Internat., 1986-87, v.p. mktg., 1988-89. Chmn. New Canaan Am. Cancer Soc., 1973-75; dir. So. Fairfield County Am. Cancer Soc., 1972-76, 80-90, 1st v.p., 1975-76. 1st lt. USMC, 1958-61. Mem. Internat. Periodical Pubs. Assn. (exec. com.), Aircraft Owners and Pilots Assn. (v.p. 1990-00, 00-), Midnight Aviation, Inc. (pres.), New Canaan Country Club, Grand Harbor Club. Republican. Roman Catholic. Home: 5550 N Harbor Village Dr Vero Beach FL 32967-7268 Office Phone: 772-794-1900. Personal E-mail: dbinub@comcast.net.

BERAN, GEORGE WESLEY, veterinary microbiology educator; b. Riceville, Iowa, May 22, 1928; s. John and Elizabeth (Buresh) B.; m. Janice Ann Van Zomeren, Dec. 21, 1954; children: Bruce, Anne, George. DVM, Iowa State U., Ames, 1954; PhD, Kans. U., 1959; LHD, Silliman U., Philippines, 1973. Diplomate Am. Coll. Vet. Preventive Medicine, Am. Coll. Epidemiology. Epidemic intelligence officer USPHS, 1954-56; asst. prof. biology Silliman U., Dumaguete City, Philippines, 1960-63, chmn. dept. agr., 1962-71, assoc. prof. microbiology, 1963-67, prof. microbiology, 1967-73; prof. vet. microbiology and preventive medicine Iowa State U., Ames, 1973-93, disting. prof. vet. microbiology, immunology-preventive med., 1993—, dir. Packer Heritage Mus., 2000—. Rsch. del. USSR/Iowa State U. exch. program, Moscow, 1989-90, Latvia, 1993; rsch. cons., Taiwan, 1983, 96, 98, Hungary, 1988, 90, U. Yucatan, 1989-90, 97, 98, 2003, Ukraine, 1996, Japan, 1998; vis. lectr. Nat. Inst. Vet. Bioproducts and Pharms., Beijing, Faculty Vet. Medicine, Huazhong Agrl. U. Wuhan, Peoples Republic of China, 1988; mem. WHO Expert Panel on Zoonoses, 1980-99; expert panel on risk assessment WHO-FAO; Fulbright prof. Ahmadu Bello U., Zaria, Nigeria, 1980; subcom. on drug use in animals NRC, 1993-98, mem. nat. adv. com. on microbiol. criteria for foods, 1997-99; adv. com. Wellcome Trust, 1998-99; mem. Food Safety and Inspection Svc. Task Force for Veterinarians, 1999-2000; mem. HACCP Based Inspection Models Project, 1999-2000; dir. Packer Heritage Mus., Iowa State U., Ames, WHO Collaborating Ctr. in Food Safety, 1994-2006; cons. in field. Editor: Viral Zoonoses, Vol. I-II, 1981, Bacterial, Rickettsial, Chlamydial and Mycotic, 1984, Sulfonamides and Public Health, 1989, Bacterial, Rickettsial, Chlamydial and Mycotic, 1994, Veterinary Medical Education at Iowa State University, 2007; contbr. articles to profl. jours., chpts. to books. Active Ames Humane League, Ames chpt. Ptnrs. of Ams., UN Assn.; election supr. OSCE, Bosnia, 1998, Kosovo, 2000; mem. adv. com. Nat. Cath. Rural Life Ctr., 2001. Recipient James H. Steele award World Vet. Epidemiology Soc., 1979, Nat. Meritorious Svc. award Livestock Conservation Inst., 1989, Gold Head Cane award Am. Vet. Epidemiology Soc., 1993. Mem. AVMA (mem. coun. pub. health and regulatory vet. medicine, Internat. Svc. award 1996, Pub. Svc. award 1999), Am. Coll. Vet. Preventive Medicine (pres.), Conf. Pub. Health Veterinarians (pres.), Am. Assn. Food Hygiene Veterinarians (Outstanding Tchr. award 1978), Assn. Tchrs. Vet. Pub. Health and Preventive Medicine, Iowa Vet. Med. Assn. (chair pub. health com.), Iowa Pork Producers Assn. (pseudorables com.), Practical Farmers Iowa (Svc. to Agr. award, Sustainable Agr. Achievement award), US Animal Health Assn. (com. on pseudorables, pub. health, food safety, feed safety, chair com. on feral swine), Cardinal Key, Sigma Xi, Phi Beta Delta, Phi Kappa Phi (pres.), Gamma Sigma Delta (Svc. to Agr. Merit award 1995), Phi Zeta, Alpha Zeta, Phi Eta Sigma. Home: 304 24th St Ames IA 50010-4834 Office: Coll Vet Medicine Iowa State U Rm 2280 Ames IA 50011-0001 Office Phone: 515-294-7630. Business E-Mail: gberan@iastate.edu.

BERAN, JOHN R., banker; BS in Indsl. and Sys. Engring., U. Dayton, MS in Mgmt. Sci. Exec. v.p. BancSystems Assn.; chmn., CEO Green Machine Network Corp.; sr. v.p. Electronic Payment Services Group Soc. Corp.; pres., CEO Money Access Svc.; exec. v.p., chief info. officer Comerica Inc., Detroit, 1995—. Bd. dir. WTVS Channel 56, U. Dayton; adv. com. mem. U. Dayton Sch. Engring.; bd. dir. Mich. Virtual U.; steering com. The Clearing House; exec. com. Banking Industry Tech. Secretariat. Office: Comerica Tower 500 Woodward Ave Detroit MI 48226-3416

BERANEK, LEO LEROY, acoustical engineer, consultant; b. Solon, Iowa, Sept. 15, 1914; s. Edward Fred and Beatrice (Stahle) B.; m. Phyllis Knight, Sept. 6, 1941 (dec. Nov. 1982); children: James Knight, Thomas Haynes; m. Gabriella Sohn, Aug. 10, 1985. AB, Cornell Coll., 1936, D.Sc. (hon.), 1946; MS, Harvard U., 1937, D.Sc., 1940; D.Eng. (hon.), Worcester Poly. Inst., 1971; D.Comml. Sci. (hon.), Suffolk U., 1979; LL.D. (hon.), Emerson College, 1982; Dr. Pub. Service (hon.), Northeastern U., 1984. Instr. physics Harvard U., 1941—43, asst. prof., 1941—43; dir. Electro-Acoustics and Systems Rsch. Labs., 1941-46; assoc. prof. communications engring. MIT, 1947-58; pres., dir., chief exec. officer Bolt Beranek & Newman, Cambridge, Mass., 1953-69, dir., 1953-84, chief scientist, 1969—71; pres., chief exec. officer, dir. Boston Broadcasters, Inc., 1963-79, chmn. bd., 1980-83; pres. Am. Acad. Arts and Scis., Cambridge, 1989-94. Part-owner WCVB-TV, Boston, 1972-82; chmn. bd. Mueller-BBM GmbH, Munich, 1962-86. Author: Acoustic Measurements, 1949, 2d edit., 1986, Music, Acoustics and Architecture, 1962, Noise Reduction, 1960, Noise and Vibration Control, 1971, 2d edit., 1988, Noise and Vibration Control Engineering, 1992, 2d edit., 2006, Concert and Opera Halls: How They Sound, 1996, Concert Halls and Opera Houses: Music, Acoustics and Architecture, 2004. Charter mem. bd. overseers Boston Symphony Orch., 1968-80, chmn., 1977-80, trustee, 1977-87, chmn. bd. trustees, 1983-86, hon. chmn., 1987, life trustee 1994-; mem. bd. overseers Harvard U., 1984-90; mem. coun. for arts MIT, 1972—; life trustee Cornell Coll., 1998—. Guggenheim fellow, 1946-47; recipient Presdl. certificate of merit, 1948, Abe Lincoln TV award So. Bapt. Conv., 1976, Lord Rayleigh award Mex. Inst. Acoustics, 2002, Pres.'s Nat. Medal of Science award, 2002, Per Bruel Gold medal ASME, 2004. Fellow NAE (bd. dir, marine bd., com. pub. engring. policy, aeros. and space engring. bd.), AAAS, IEEE (chmn. profl. group audio 1950-51), Am. Phys. Soc., Am. Acad. Arts and Scis. (Scholar-Patriot Disting. Svc. award 2000), Audio Engring. Soc. (pres. 1967-68, Gold medal 1971, gov. 1966-71), Acoustical Soc. Am. (mem. coun. 1944-47, v.p. 1949-50, pres. 1954-55, Bienniel award 1944, Sabine award 1961, Gold medal 1975, Hon. mem. 1994); mem. Inst. Noise Control Engring. (charter pres. 1971-73, dir. 1973-75, 1st Disting. Noise Control Engr. 1997), Internat. Inst. Acoustics (hon. fellow 2000), Am. Inst. Archs. (hon.), Acad. Disting. Bostonians, Greater Boston C. of C. (dir. 1973-79, v.p. 1976-79, Disting. Cmty. Svc. award 1980, 83), Acoustical Soc. Spain (Caracole award 2007), Phi Beta Kappa, Sigma Xi, Eta Kappa Nu (eminent mem. 2000). Episcopalian. Home and Office: 975 Memorial Dr Ste 804 Cambridge MA 02138-5755 Office Phone: 617-576-3141. E-mail: beranekleo@ieee.org.

BERANOVA-GIORGIANNI, SARKA, biomedical researcher, educator; b. Brno, Czech Republic, June 22, 1966; d. Zdenek Beran and Eva Beranova; m. Francesco Giorgianni, Apr. 23, 1963; children: Francesca Eva, Gino Martin. MS, Prague Inst. Chem. Tech., Czech Republic, 1989; PhD, U. Akron, Ohio, 1995. Rsch. assoc. U. Tenn. Health Sci. Ctr., Dental Rsch. Ctr., Memphis, 1996—2000, asst. prof., 2000—02, 2003—. Contbr. over 24 scientific papers. Grantee Rsch. grant, NIH, 2002—06, Dept. of Def., 2003—. Mem.: Am. Assn. Pharm. Scientists, Am. Soc. Mass Spectrometry. Office: Univ Tenn Health Sci Ctr 874 Union Ave Rm 5P Memphis TN 38163 Home Phone: 901-521-9726; Office Phone: 901-448-5433. Office Fax: 901-448-6940. E-mail: sberanova@utmem.edu.

BERBERICH, PATRICIA LOUISE, librarian; b. Norwalk, Conn., Nov. 2, 1928; d. Thomas Edward and Theresa A. (Nesline) B. BS in English Lit., St. Joseph Coll., West Hartford, Conn., 1949; MLS, Rutgers U., New Brunswick, 1966. Contract writer group ins. The Travelers Ins. Co., Hartford, Conn., 1950-55; editorial asst. The Catholic Transcript, Hartford, 1955-59; libr. asst. Pope Pius X Libr. St. Joseph Coll., West Hartford, 1961-65; head libr. Blue Hills br. Hartford Pub. Libr., 1966-69, head libr. Camp Field br., 1969-77, adminstrv. asst. to chief libr., 1977-82, assoc. libr., 1982-91, chief libr., 1991-94. Coord. ext. svcs. Hartford Pub. Libr., 1974-82; bd. dirs. Capitol Region Libr. Coun., 1979-85. Named Disting. Alumna St. Joseph Coll., 1992. Home: 100 Sarah Lane Apt 17B Simsbury CT 06070

BERCE, DANIEL EUGENE, financial services company executive, accountant; b. Milw., Nov. 10, 1953; s. Eugene Daniel and Mary (Mullen) B.; m. Mary Anne Tiger, Oct. 9, 1977; children: Sarah, Emily, Eric. BS in Acctg., Regis U., 1975. CPA. Staff auditor Coopers & Lybrand, Denver, 1975-86, ptnr. Ft. Worth, 1986-90; CFO AmeriCredit Corp., Ft. Worth, 1990—2003, pres., 2003—05, pres., CEO, 2005—. Bd. dir. Cash Am. Internat. Inc., 2006—. Com. chmn. United Way, Ft. Worth, 1987—; bd. dirs. Lena Pope Home, Ft. Worth, 1989—, Cath. Charities, Ft. Worth, 1990—. Mem. AICPA, Tex. Soc. CPAs, Ft. Worth Club (fin. com. 1987—), Ridglea Country Club. Avocations: golf, basketball, bicycling, reading, travel. Office: Americredit Corp 801 Cherry St Fort Worth TX 76102*

BERCH, REBECCA WHITE, state supreme court justice, lawyer; b. Phoenix, June 29, 1955; d. Robert Eugene and Janet Kay (Zimmerman) White; m. Michael Allen Berch, Mar. 9, 1981; 1 child, Jessica. BS summa cum laude, Ariz. State U., 1976, JD, 1979, MA, 1990. Bar: Ariz. 1979, U.S. Dist. Ct. Ariz., U.S. Ct. Appeals (9th cir.), U.S. Supreme Ct. Assoc., ptnr. McGroder, Tryon, Heller, Rayes & Berch, Phoenix, 1979-85; dir. legal rsch. and writing program Ariz. State U. Coll. Law, Tempe, 1986-91, 94-95; solicitor gen. State of Arizona, Phoenix, 1991-94, 1st asst. atty. gen., 1996—98; judge Ariz. Ct. Appeals, 1998—2002; justice Ariz. Supreme Ct., Phoenix, 2002—, vice chief justice, 2005—. Mem. Judicial Ethics Advisory Com., Bd. Certified Ct. Reporters, Arizona Supreme Ct. Com. on Examinations, Arizona Judicial Coll. Bd.; co-chair Arizona Appellate Practice Inst. Co-author: (Book) Introduction to Legal Method and Process, 1985, 2002, Teacher's Manual for Introduction to Legal Method and Process, 1992, 2002, Handling Complex Litigation, 1986; Bd. editors Jour. Legal Writing Inst., 1993—2002; contbr. articles to profl. jours. and newspapers. Bd. dirs. Tempe-Mesa chpt. ACLU, 1984—86, Homeless Legal Assistance Project , Phoenix, 1990—98. Recipient Outstanding Service award, Arizona Atty. General's Office, 1992, 1994, Outstanding Alumnus award, Ariz. State U. Coll. Law, 1999. Mem. Ariz. Women Lawyer's Assn. (Profl. Achievement award 2002), Ariz. State Bar Assn. Republican. Methodist. Avocations: reading, travel. Office: Ariz Supreme Ct 1501 W Washington St Phoenix AZ 85009-3831 Office Phone: 602-542-4535. Business E-Mail: Rberch@Azbar.org.*

BERCHEM, ROBERT LEE, SR., lawyer; b. Milford, Conn., Aug. 17, 1941; s. Robert W. and Barbara (Maher) B.; m. Lee Contrucci, Feb. 19, 1966; children: Kerry, Robert L. Jr., Jonathan. AB, Fairfield U., 1962; LLB, Villanova U., 1965; LLM, U. Mich., 1967. Bar: Conn. 1965. Law clk. U.S. Dist. Ct., Conn., 1965-66; prin. Berchem, Moses & Devlin, P.C., Milford, 1967—. Trustee Fairfield (Conn.) U.; chmn. Milford Hist. Dist. Commn., 1976—. Mem. ABA, Conn. Bar Assn., New Haven County Bar Assn., Milford Bar Assn. Democrat. Roman Catholic. Avocations: golf, skiing. Home: 125 W River St Milford CT 06460-3420 Office: Berchem Moses & Devlin PC 75 Broad St Milford CT 06460-3331

BERCI, MARGARET ELIZABETH, education educator; b. Budapest, Hungary, Jan. 24, 1947; arrived in US, 2002, permanent resident, 2005; d. Bela and Margaret (Kiss) Berci; children: Jason Cory Hidegh, Joseph Christopher Hidegh. BEd in Social Studies, U. Calgary, Can., 1971, MA in Curriculum and Instrn., 1997, PhD in Ednl. Context, 2001. Cert. Permanent Tchr. Alta., Can. Classroom tchr. Calgary Roman Cath. Schs., 1969—75, adult program instr., 1990—92; bus. mgr. Pro-Dent Lab. Ltd., 1975—90; instr. Chinook Coll., 1992—2002; field advisor U. Calgary, 1996—97, sessional instr., 1998—2001; assoc. prof. edn. Coll. S.I., CUNY, 2002—. Presenter in field; peer reviewer Can. Jour. Edn. Contbr. articles, revs. to profl. publs., chapters to books. Social studies curriculum liaison Chinook Coll., 1999—2002; tchr. rep. to leadership team Calgary Bd. Edn., 1994—96, social studies rep. to learning and tchg. com., 1997—98, social studies curriculum leader, 1998—99; team mgr. Team Alta. to Western Can. Summer Games, 1990, Calgary Patriots Swim Club, 1988—89, pres., 1989—91. Recipient award of merit, Alta. Tchrs.' Assn., 2001, Exec. Svc. award, 2002; grantee, Com. on Excellence in Learning Tech., 2003—05, CUNY, 2004; Edn. grantee, Calgary Roman Cath. Schs., 1968—69, grad. rsch. scholar, U. Calgary, 1997—99. Mem.: Soc. Profs. Edn., Rsch. Social Studies Edn., Philosophy of Edn. Soc., Nat. Coun. Social Studies, Can. Philosophy Edn. Soc., Can. Assn. Curriculum Studies, Can. Assn. Founds. of Edn., Can. Soc. Study of Edn., Am. Hungarian Educators' Assn., Am. Ednl. Rsch. Assn. (peer reviewer), Kappa Delta Pi (v.p. 1999—2000, historian 1999—2000, pres. 2000—01). Office: CUNY Coll SI Dept Edn 2800 Victory Blvd Staten Island NY 10314 Office Phone: 718-982-4133. Business E-Mail: berci@mail.csi.cuny.edu.

BERCOVITCH, SACVAN, English language professional, educator; b. Montreal, Que., Can., Oct. 4, 1933; s. Alexander and Brytha (Avrutick) B.; m. Susan L. Mizruchi; children: Eytan, Alexander. BA, Sir George William Coll., 1961; MA, Claremont Grad. Sch., Calif., 1963, PhD, 2965; LittD (hon.), Concordia U., 1993; DHL (hon.), Claremont U., 2005. Asst. prof.

English and Am. lit. Brandeis U., 1966-68; asso. prof. U. Calif., San Diego, 1968-70; prof. English and Am. Lit. Columbia U., 1970-83; Powell M. Cabot rsch. prof. Am. lit. Harvard U., 1983—. Lectr., Kyoto, Tokyo, Shanghai, Beijing, Amsterdam, Frankfurt, Konstanz, Lisbon, Jerusalem, Tel Aviv, Salzburg, Coimbra, Montreal, Rome, Budapest, Paris, Venice, Bologna, Toronto, Oxford, Berlin, Moscow, Prague, Olomouc, Ostrava, Brno, Yale U., Princeton U., U. Pa., U. Calif., Berkeley, L.A., San Diego, Irvine, Cornell U., Dartmouth Coll., Concordia Coll., Claremont Grad. Sch., many others; advisor, cons. in field. Author: Typology and Early American Literature, 1972, The American Puritan Imagination, 1974, The Puritan Origins of the American Self, 1975, The American Jeremiad, 1978, Reconstructing American Literary History, 1986, Ideology and Classic American Literature, 1986, The Office of the Scarlet Letter, 1991, The Rites of Assent: Transformations in the Symbolic Construction of America, 1992; gen. editor: Cambridge History of American Literature (8 vols.); author more than 100 essays and revs.; trans. Yiddish lit. Am. Philos. Soc. fellow, 1968-69, Guggenheim fellow, 1969-70, Am. Coun. Learned Socs. fellow, 1971-72, Nat. Humanities Inst. fellow, 1975-76, Ctr. for Advanced Study in Behavioral Scis. fellow, 1978-79, NEH fellow, 1978-79, 86-87, Woodrow Wilson Ctr. fellow, 1990-91, Time-Life fellow Huntington Libr., 1994—, Cabot fellow for achievement in humanities, Mellon Emeritus fellow, 2004—; recipient James Russell Lowell prize for scholarship, 1992, Disting. Scholar award for extraordinary lifetime contbns. in Early Am. Lit., 2003, Award for Excellency in Tchg. Fellow Am. Acad. Arts and Scis.; mem. MLA (mem. exec. com. Am. sect. 1976-78, Jay B. Hubbell award for lifetime achievement in Am. lit. studies 2004), English Inst., Am. Studies Assn. (pres. 1982-84) Office Phone: 617-495-2511. Business E-Mail: bercovit@fas.harvard.edu.

BERCU, BARRY BERNARD, pediatric endocrinologist; b. Montreal, Aug. 10, 1944; m. Sandra Bercu, 2 children. BS, U. Md., 1965, MD, 1969. Diplomate Nat. Bd. Med. Examiners, Am. Bd. Pediatrics, Am. Bd. Pediatric Endocrinology; lic. physician, Mass., Md., Fla. Med. intern V and VI Med. Svc. Boston City Hosp., 1969—70; asst. and sr. resident pediat. Mass. Gen. Hosp., Boston, 1970—72; clin. and rsch. fellow pediatric endocrinology & metabolism Harvard Med. Sch., Boston, 1974—77; clin. and rsch. fellow endocrinology dept. internal medicine Tufts U. Med. Sch., New Eng. Med. Ctr., Boston, 1974—77; clin. assoc. Nat. Inst. Child Health and Human Devel., NIH, Bethesda, Md., 1977—79, head pediatric endocrine unit neonatal & pediatric med. br., 1979—82, head pediatric endocrine unit, pregnancy rsch. br., 1982—84; assoc. prof. pediat. Uniformed Svcs. U., Bethesda Naval Ctr., 1980—84; assoc. rsch. prof. child health and devel. George Washington U. Sch. Medicine and Health Scis., Washington, 1983—84; prof. pediat., biochemistry and molecular biology, pharmacology and therapeutics U. South Fla. Coll. Medicine, Tampa, 1984, pres. faculty coun., 1998—99. Grant reviewer various orgns.; chmn. U. IRB Com.; mem. Dir.'s Conf. on Uses and Abuses of Growth Hormone in Children, Nat. Inst. Child Health and Human Devel., NIH, 1983-; mem. med. adv. bd. Parent Coun. Growth Normality, 1985—; mem. pediatric clin. oncology group Clin. Oncology Program, 1989—, MAGIC Found., 1995—; mem. staff All Children's Hosp., St. Petersburg, 1984-, Shriner's Hosp. , Tampa, 1985-, Tampa Gen. Hosp., 1986-, others; instr. online courses Bioethical Considerations in Human Subject Rsch., Therapeutic Interventions in Aging-Growth Hormone, 2004; chmn. numerous internat. and nat. symposia, 1985—. Mem. editl. bd. Jour. Clin. Endocrinology and Metabolism, 1986-89, Jour. Anti-Aging Medicine, 1998—, Internat. Jour. Integrative Medicine, 2003—, Jour. Evidence Based Integrative Medicine, 2003—, Jour. Rejuvenation Medicine, 2004—, Jour. Clin. Intervention Into Aging, 2005—; editl. manuscript reviewer Acta Endocrinologica, Am. Jour. Nutrition, Biol. Psychiatry, Biology of Reprodn., Clin. Endocrinology, Clin. Pediatrics, Endocrine Jour., Endocrine Revs., Endocrinology, European Jour. Pediatrics, Hormone and Metabolic Rsch., Jour. AMA, Jour. Clin. Endocrinology and Metabolism, Jour. Clin. Investigation, Metabolism, Advances in Pituitary Disease: Metabolic, New England Jour. Medicine, Neuroendocrine and Psychosocial Issues, 2001, others; contbr. articles to profl. jours.; patentee in field. Bd. dirs. Birth Defects Found., Fla. Bay Area chpt., 1991—, chmn. med. adv. com., 1991; mem. expert divsn. vaccine injury compensation and mem. bd. dirs. USF Divsn. Sponsored Rsch., 1994-95. Grantee NIH, NIDA, BioNebr., Eli Lilly and Co., Genentech Corp., Daniel Pharm. Corp., Serono Labs., Am. Cancer Soc. Fla., ICN Pharms., Merck & Co., Novo Nordisk, Pfizer, Pharmacia Peptides, Inc., Pharmacia & Upjohn, Wyeth-Ayerst, Alkermes, Astra Zeneca, Infimed, BioPtnrs. and LG Bioscis. Mem. AMA, Am. Acad. Pediatrics (endocrinology sect.), Am. Assn. Clin. Endocrinologists, Am. Fedn. Clin. Rsch., Am. Pediatric Soc., Am. Pituitary Assn., Endocrine Soc., Fla. Endocrine Soc., Fla. Med. Assn., Hillsborough County Med. Assn., Hillsborough County Pediatric Soc., Lawson Wilkins Soc. Pediatric Endocrinology, Soc. Pediatric Rsch., So. Soc. Pediatric Rsch., Tampa Bay Area Soc. Neurosci.

BERCZI, ANDREW STEPHEN, academic administrator, educator; b. Budapest, Hungary, Aug. 15, 1934; s. Stephen Andrew and Iren Maria (Bartha) B.; m. Susan Bartok, Aug. 30, 1958; children— Thomas Edgar, Peter Alexander. EE, U. Tech. Scis., Budapest, 1956; BSc, Sir George Williams U., 1961, BA, 1963; MBA, McGill U., 1965, PhD, 1972. Engr. Bell Telephone Co., Montreal, 1956-59, mem. hdqrs. staff acctg., 1959-62, supr. computer systems, 1962-65; prof. quantitative methods, chmn. dept. quantitative methods Sir George Williams U., 1965-71; dean Faculty of Commerce and Adminstrn. Concordia U., Montreal, 1971-77; dean Faculty of Grad. Studies Wilfrid Laurier U., Waterloo, Ont., Canada, 1978-87, v.p. fin. and adminstrn., 1987-98, prof. mgmt. scis. and decisions scis., 1999—. Cons. govtl. agys., pvt. industry; lectr. U. Calif. at Berkeley, U. Va., U. Chgo., U. Waterloo. Author: Exercises in Management Science, 1968, Problems in Managerial Operations Research, Vol. I and II, 1969, The Stock Exchange - A Total System Approach, 1970; contbr. over 80 articles and papers to profl. jours. and assns. McConnell fellow, 1965-66; Canada Council fellow, 1966-67; Quebec Province scholar, 1967-68 Fellow AAAS.; mem. IEEE, Operations Research Soc. Am., Canadian Operations Research Soc., Inst. Mgmt. Scis., Assn. Systems Mgmt., Fin. Execs. Inst., Acad. of Mgmt., Am. Statis. Assn. Home: 76 McCarron Crescent Waterloo ON Canada N2L 5N1 Office: Wilfrid Laurier U 75 University Ave W Waterloo ON Canada N2L 3C5 E-mail: aberczi@wlu.ca.

BERDAHL, ROBERT MAX, history professor, association and former academic administrator; b. Sioux Falls, SD, Mar. 15, 1937; s. Melvin Oliver and Mildred Alberta (Maynard) Berdahl; m. Margaret Lucille Ogle, Aug. 30, 1958; children: Daphne Jean, Jennifer Lynne, Barbara Elizabeth. BA, Augustana Coll., Sioux Falls, SD, 1959; MA, U. Ill., 1961; PhD, U. Minn., 1965, DSc (hon.), 1997. Asst. prof. hist. U. Mass., Boston, 1965—67, U. Oreg., Eugene, 1967—72, assoc. prof., 1972—81, prof., 1981—86, dean Coll. Arts and Scis., 1981—86; prof. U. Ill., 1986—93, vice chancellor academic affairs, 1986—93; pres. U. Tex., Austin, 1993—97; prof. U. Calif., Berkeley, 1997—2006, chancellor, 1997—2004; pres. Assn. Am. Univs., Washington, 2006—. Rsch. assoc. Inst. Advanced Study, Princeton, NJ, 1972—73. Author (with others): (novels) Klassen und Kultur, 1982; author: The Politics of Prussian Nobility, 1988; contbr. articles to profl. jours. Grantee Fulbright fellow, 1975—76, Nat. Endowment Humanities fellow, 1976—77. Mem.: Am. Acad. Arts & Scis. Office: Assn Am Univs 1200 New York Ave NW Ste 550 Washington DC 20005 Office Phone: 202-408-7500. E-mail: robert_berdahl@aau.edu.*

BERDAN, ROBERT J., lawyer, insurance company executive; b. Waukesha, Wis., Aug. 31, 1946; BS with honors, U. Wis., Milw., 1968, MS with honors, 1969; JD cum laude, Marquette Univ., 1975. Bar: Wis. 1975, US Ct. Appeals (7th cir.) 1975. V.p., head compliance and best practices dept. Northwestern Mutual Life Ins., 1996—2000, v.p., gen. counsel, sec., 2000—. Mem.: ABA, Milw. Bar Assn., State Bar Wis., Alpha Sigma Mu. Office: Northwestern Mutual Life Ins Legal Dept 720 E Wisconsin Ave Milwaukee WI 53202*

BERDON, ROBERT IRWIN, judge; b. New Haven, Dec. 24, 1929; s. Louis J. and Jean (Cohen) B.; m. Nancy Tarr, Aug. 30, 1964 (dec. Mar. 1992); 1 child, Peter A. BS, Duke U., 1951; JD, U. Conn., 1957; LLM in Jud. Process, U. Va., 1988. With Bank of Manhattan, 1953-54; pvt. practice New Haven, 1957-73; treas. State of Conn., 1971-73; judge Superior Ct., State of Conn., New Haven, 1973-91; justice Supreme Ct., State of Conn., 1991-99, ret., 1999, judge trial referee, 2000—. Adj. prof. law U. Bridgeport Sch. Law, 1986-91; lectr. in law U. Conn. Sch. of Law, 1993; assoc. fellow Saybrook Coll., Yale U., 1986—; lectr. Am. Bd. Trial Advs., 1986; mem. Conn. Bd. Pardons, 1991-92. Contbr. articles to profl. jours. Recipient Judiciary award Conn. Trial Lawyers Assn., 1976, Disting. Alumni award U. Conn., 1977, Outstanding State Trial Judge in U.S. award ATLA, 1982, Pub. Svc. award U. Conn. Sch. Law Alumni Assn., 1989, Judiciary award Conn. Bar Assn., 1991, Hartford Neighborhood Housing Coalition award, 1992, RosCossi - Koskoff Justice award Conn. Trial Lawyers Assn., 1999, Jud. Recognition award Conn. Def. Lawyers Assn., 1999, citation Conn. Bar Assn., 2000, Lifetime Achievement award New Haven County Bar Assn., 2003. Office: Superior Ct 235 Church St New Haven CT 06510

BERÉ, DAVID L., retail executive; B, Ind. U., B, MBA, Ind. U., Bloomington. White House fellow, 1983; pres. Breakfast divsn. and Golden Grain divsn. Quaker Oats Co.; pres., CEO McCain Foods USA (subs. of McCain Foods Ltd.), 1996—98; pres., CEO, bd. dirs. Bakery Chef, Inc., 1998—2003; bd. dirs. Dollar Gen., 2002—, pres., COO, 2006—, interim chmn., CEO; corp. v.p. Ralcorp Holdings, Inc., 2003—05. Office: Dollar Gen 100 Mission Ridge Goodlettsville TN 37072 Office Phone: 615-855-4000.*

BEREDAY, THADDEUS MATTHEW SIGMUND, lawyer; b. Boston, Mar. 17, 1965; s. George Z.F. and Mary H. (Gillam) B.; m. Margaret S. Russell, Dec. 22, 1992. BA, Brown U., 1987; JD magna cum laude, Case Western Res. U., 1993. Bar: Ohio 1993. Legis. asst. US Rep. Benjamin A. Gilman, Washington, 1987-89, legis. dir., 1989-90; assoc. Jones, Day, Reavis & Pogue, Cleve., 1993; v.p., gen. counsel SmarTalk TeleServices, 1998—99, pres., acting gen. counsel, 1999—2000; ptnr. Morgan, Lewis & Bockius, LLP, 2000—01, Brobeck, Phleger & Harrison, LLP, 2001—02; sr. v.p., gen. counsel WellCare Health Plans, Inc, Tampa, 2002—. Recipient 4 Am. Jurisprudence awards Lawyers Coop., 1990-93; Morris E. Lewis scholar, 1991-93. Mem. ABA, Ohio State Bar Assn., Cleve. Bar Assn., Order of Coif. Office: WellCare Health Plans, Inc Renaissance One 8725 Henderson Rd Tampa FL 33634*

BEREK, PETER, literature and language professor; b. Bklyn., June 20, 1940; s. Leo and Ida (Kantrowitz) B.; m. Ellen H. Stark, June 10, 1962; children— Rachel, Martha, Elizabeth BA, Amherst Coll., 1961; MA, Harvard U., 1963, PhD, 1967. Instr. English, Hamilton Coll., Clinton, NY, 1965-67; asst. prof. English, Williams Coll., Williamstown, Mass., 1967-72, assoc. prof., 1972-77, prof., 1977-90, dept. chmn., 1980-86, Morris prof. rhetoric, 1984-90, dean of coll., 1975-78, spl. asst. to pres., 1987-90; prof. English Mt. Holyoke Coll., South Hadley, Mass., 1990—, dean faculty, provost, 1990-98, interim pres., fall 1995. Cons. NEH, Washington, 1973-76, 86-87, 89. Contbr. articles to profl. jours. Woodrow Wilson Found. fellow, 1961-62; NEH fellow, 1971-72, 82-83. Mem. MLA, Shakespeare Assn. Am. Jewish. Home: 87 Woodlot Rd Amherst MA 01002-3452 Office: Mt Holyoke Coll Dept English South Hadley MA 01075 Home Phone: 413-253-9166; Office Phone: 413-538-2311. E-mail: pberek@mtholyoke.edu.

BERENATO, JOSEPH C., manufacturing executive; b. 1947; BS in Engring., U.S. Naval Acad.; MA in English, U. Va.; MBA in Fin., NYU. Various exec. mgmt. positions Mfrs. Hanover Trust Co.; v.p., CFO, treas. Ducommon Inc., LA, 1991-95, exec. v.p., COO, 1995-96, pres., 1996—, pres., CEO, 1997—, also bd. dirs. Office: Docommun Inc 23301 Wilmington Ave Carson CA 90745

BERENATO, MARK ANTHONY, lawyer, insurance company executive; b. Lansdowne, Pa., Feb. 24, 1958; s. Anthony Francis and Dena Marie (Marchione) B.; m. Linnie Louise Swineford, Sept. 9, 1989. Diploma, Episcopal Acad., 1976; BS in Acctg., Villanova U., 1980; JD, Am. U., 1983; postgrad., Temple U., 1984. Bar: Pa. 1984, U.S. Dist. Ct. (ea. dist.) Pa. 1987. Tax lawyer Deloitte, Haskins & Sells, NYC, 1984-85; pvt. practice Law Offices of Mark A. Berenato, Phila., 1985—. Counsel Custom Art Metals, Inc., Barrington, N.J., 1985-91; pres. Cumberland Devel. Corp., Voorhees, N.J., 1989-95; sec., gen. counsel Sterling Metal Fabricators, Inc., Barrington, N.J., 1985-93; prin. Mark A. Berenato Ins. Agy., Media, Pa., 1993—. Mem. ABA, Pa. Bar Assn., Phila. Bar Assn., Rolling Green Golf Club, Vesper Club, Phi Alpha Delta. Republican. Roman Catholic. Avocations: golf, literature, antiques. Home: 740 Iris Ln Media PA 19063 Office: 2 Penn Ctr Ste 200 Philadelphia PA 19102-1754 Office Phone: 215-854-6381. E-mail: markberenato@earthlink.net.

BERENBAUM, MAY ROBERTA, entomology educator; b. Trenton, NJ, July 22, 1953; BS, Yale U., 1975; PhD, Cornell U., 1980. Asst. prof. entomology U. Ill., Urbana-Champaign, 1980-85, assoc. prof. entomology, 1985-90, prof. entomology, 1990-95, head dept., 1992—, Swanlund prof. entomology, 1996—. Assoc. editor Am. Midland Naturalist, 1982-85; mem. editl. bd. Jour. Chem. Ecology, Chemoecology, Proceedings of the Nat. Acad. Scis. USA. Recipient Presdl. Young Investigator award NSF, 1984, Founder's award Entomol. Soc. Am., 1994. Fellow AAAS, Am. Assn. Arts and Sciences, Encol. Soc. Am. (George Mercer award, Robert MacArthur award); mem. NAS (council mem.), Am. Philos. Soc., Entomol. Soc. Am. (fellow 2002; Founder's award), Phytochem Soc. Am., Internat. Soc. Chem. Ecology, Sigma Xi. Achievements include research in chemical aspects of insect-plant interaction, evolutionary ecology of insects, phototoxicity of plant products, host-plant resistance. Office: U Ill Dept Entomology 286 Morrill Hall 505 S Goodwin Ave Urbana IL 61801-3707 E-mail: maybe@uiuc.edu.

BERENBOM, LOREN DAVID, cardiologist; b. Kansas City, Kans., Mar. 15, 1953; s. Max and Doreen Sybil (Katz) B.; m. Merilyn Kay Krigel, June 17, 1975; children: Anne, Michael, Katie. BS with honors, Northwestern U., 1975, MD with honors, 1977. Diplomate Am. Bd. Internal Medicine, Am. Bd. Cardiology. Intern, resident in internal medicine Barnes Hosp. Wash. U., St. Louis, 1977-80, fellow cardiology, 1980-82, rsch. instr. cardiology, 1982-83; cons. cardiologist Mid Am. Heart Inst., Kansas City, 1983—; clin. assoc. prof. med. U. Mo., Kansas City, 1983—; dir., Bloch Heart Rhythm Ctr. Univ. Kans. Hosp. Named a Kans. City Super Doctor, Kans. City mag., 2007. Fellow Am. Coll. Cardiology; mem. AMA, North Am. Soc. Pacing and Electrophysiology, Alpha Omega Alpha. Office: 4320 Wornall Rd Ste 40 Kansas City MO 64111-3201 also: 3901 Rainbow Blvd Ste G600 Kansas City KS 66160 Office Phone: 913-588-9600.*

BERENDT, JOHN LAWRENCE, writer, editor; b. Syracuse, NY, Dec. 5, 1939; s. Ralph Sidney and Carol (Deschere) B. AB, Harvard U., Cambridge, Mass., 1961. Assoc. editor Esquire mag., NYC, 1961-69; sr. staff editor Holiday mag., NYC, 1969; assoc. prodr. David Frost Show, NYC, 1969-71; writer Dick Cavett Show, NYC, 1973-75; editor N.Y. Mag., NYC, 1977-79; columnist Esquire mag., NYC, 1982-94. Author: Midnight in the Garden of Good and Evil, 1994 (Pulitzer prize finalist for gen. non-fiction 1995), The City of Falling Angels, 2005; contbr. articles to profl. jours Bd. dirs. Theater for a New Audience. Mem. PEN, Century Assn. Office: c/o William Morris Agy 1325 Ave of the Americas New York NY 10019-0002

BERENDZEN, RICHARD, astronomer, educator, author; b. Walters, Okla., Sept. 6, 1938; s. Earl Emmanuel and Florine Adora (Harrison) B.; m. Gail Anita Edgar, Nov. 26, 1964; children: Deborah Carol, Natasha Karina. BS, MIT, 1961; MA, Harvard U., 1967, PhD, 1969; LLD (hon.), W.Va. Wesleyan U., 1979; LHD (hon.), Bridgewater Coll., 1983; LLD (hon.), Kean Coll. of NJ, 1984, Seton Hall U., 1985; DS (hon.), U. Columbo, Sri Lanka, 1985; LLD (hon.), U. Charleston, 1986, U. Balt., 1990. Staff scientist Geophysics Corp. Am., 1959-64, Ling-Temco-Vought, 1961-62; lectr. Harvard U., 1964, 66; mem. staff Project Physics, 1965; mem. faculty Boston U., 1965-73, assoc. prof. astronomy, 1971-73, acting dept. chmn., 1971-72; prof. physics, dean Coll. Arts and Sci., Am. U., Washington, 1974-76; univ. provost Am. U., Washington, 1976-79, pres., 1980-90, prof., 1990—2006, prof. emeritus, 2006—; commentator on edn. and astronomy Stat. WUSA-TV/WTOP, Washington, 1984-90; cons. NASA, 1991, 98; sr. scholar Woodrow Wilson Internat. Ctr. Scholars, 2005—. Commentator on NASA for NBC-TV, 2003; cons. space sci. bd. NAS, 1973-74, mem. panel astron. survey com., 1971-73; cons. acad. affairs Am. Coun. on Edn., 1973-74; cons. to pub. cos.; Am. specialist in Asia Am. Council Edn. and Dept. State; adv. Am. Inst. Physics, Library of Congress, Internat. Comm. Agy., UNESCO, Smithsonian Instn., NSF; univ. evaluator Commn. Higher Edn. Middle States Assn. Colls. and Secondary Schs.; chmn. priorities and planning com. Assn. Am. Colls., 1978-80, chmn. pres.'s adv. com., 1977-79; program evaluator US Armed Forces Inst.; mem. rev. panel human resources NRC; lectr. USIA; host spls. on astronomy and higher edn. NBC-TV, 1976-77; organizer Space 2000 Symposium, 1999; frequent guest radio and TV shows; researcher on cosmology, history of astronomy, sci. and soc., Am. and internat. edn. Author: Education in and History of Modern Astronomy, 1972, Life Beyond Earth and the Mind of Man, 1973, Man Discovers the Galaxies, 1976, Is My Armor Straight? A Year in the Life of a University President, 1986, Come Here: A Man Overcomes the Tragic Aftermath of Childhood Sexual Abuse, 1993, Pulp Physics: Humankind in Space & Time Audio Series, 2000; founding editor Jour. Coll. Sci. Teaching; contbr. numerous articles and revs. to profl. jours. Bd. dirs. Bus. Coun. for Internat. Understanding, 1980-84, Assn. Am. Colls., 1981-83, European Inst., Group Hospitalization Med. Svc. Inc., Nat. Network for Youth, Inc., 1994-97; chmn. Com. on Fng. Students and Instl. Policy, 1981-82; chmn. Employment/Edn. Bur. Greater Washington Bd. Trade, 1989; co-chmn. AIDS project Meyer Found., 1988-90; mem. DC Com. on Pub. Schs., 1988-90; chmn. DC Commn. on Budget and Fin. Priorities, 1989-90, 94; mem. NASA Exploration Adv. Task Force, 1988-91; chmn. bd. dir. Orphan Found. Am., 1996-97; dir. NASA's DC Space Grant Consortium, 2000—. Named one of Top Young Educators Change: Mag. of Learning, 1978; recipient Mortar Bd. Faculty award, 1977, Freedoms Found. Valley Forge award, 1982, Glenn T. Seaborg award Internat. Platform Assn., 1997, Tchr. of Yr. award American U., 2006; fellow Com. Scientists Investigating Claims of the Paranormal, 1977-78. Fellow AAAS; mem. Internat. Astron. Union, Internat. Assn. Univ. Pres., Am. Astron. Soc., Am. Assn. U. Adminstrs., Am. Assn. for Higher Edn., Internat. Assn. Univs., NY Acad. Scis., Am. Assn. Physics Tchr., Astron. Soc. Pacific, History of Sci. Soc., Nat. Sci. Tchrs. Assn., Am. Assn. Higher Edn., Am. Conf. Acad. Deans, Washington Inst. Fgn. Affairs, Cosmos Club, Sigma Xi, Kappa Mu Epsilon, Phi Eta Sigma, Phi Kappa Phi. Home: 1300 Crystal Dr 1402 Arlington VA 22202-3234 Office: Am U Dept Physics Washington DC 20016-8058 Office Phone: 202-885-2798. Personal E-mail: rberendzen@aol.com.

BERENGER, TOM (THOMAS MICHAEL MOORE), actor; b. Chgo., May 31, 1950; m. Lisa Berenger, July 1986 (div. 1997); 3 children; m. Patricia Alvaran, Jan. 23, 1998; m. Barbara Wilson, 1976 (div. Feb. 1984); 2 children. Grad., U. Mo. Actor stage prodns. The Rose Tattoo, Streetcar Named Desire, End as a Man, Electra; motion pictures include Beyond the Door, 1975, The Sentinel, 1977, Looking for Mr. Goodbar, 1977, In Praise of Older Women, 1979, Butch and Sundance: The Early Days, 1979, The Dogs of War, 1981, The Big Chill, 1983, Eddie and the Cruisers, 1983, Firstborn, 1984, Fear City, 1984, Rustler's Rhapsody, 1985, Platoon, 1987 (Oscar nomination), Someone to Watch Over Me, 1987, Betrayed, 1988, Born on the Fourth of July, 1989, Major League, 1989, Love at Large, 1990, At Play in the Fields of the Lord, 1991, Sniper, 1993, Sliver, 1993, Gettysburg, 1993, Major League 2, 1994, Chasers, 1994, Last of the Dogmen, 1995, The Substitute, 1996, An Occasional Hell, 1996, The Gingerbread Man, 1998, Shadow of Doubt, 1998, One Man's Hero, 1999, Diplomatic Siege, 1999, Fear of Flying, 2000, Takedown, 2000, Cutaway, 2000, Watchtower, 2001, Training Day, 2001, The Hollywood Sign, 2001, True Blue, 2001, D-Tox, 2002, (voice) Firedog, 2005; TV films include Johnny We Hardly Knew Ye, 1977, Flesh and Blood, 1979, Body Language, 1995, Avenging Angel, 1995, Body Language, 1995, Rough Riders, 1997, In the Company of Spies, 1999, The Junction Boys, 2002, Capital City, 2004, Detective, 2005, Amy Coyne, 2006; TV series include One Life to Live, 1975-76, Peacemakers, 2003, October Road, 2007; TV miniseries include Detective, 2005, Into the West, 2005, Nightmares and Dreamscapes: From the Stories of Stephen King, 2006. Office: care Creative Artists Agy 9830 Wilshire Blvd Beverly Hills CA 90212-1804*

BERENJI, HAMID REZA, research scientist, educator; s. Javad Berenji and Batool Seddigh; m. Maryam Naghibzadeh, Dec. 31, 2003. PhD, U. So. Calif., LA, 1986. Rsch. scientist NASA Ames Rsch. Ctr., Moffett Field, Calif., 1986—93; chief rsch. scientist IIS Corp, Moffett Field, Calif., 1993—. Chmn. Fuzzy Tech. Com. Recipient Appreciation cert., NASA, 1992, Recognition cert., 1999, Appreciation cert., 1996, Achievement cert., 1999, Group Achievement award, 1998. Fellow: IEEE (life; chmn. neural networks conf. 1993). Islam. Achievements include patents for actor critic based fuzy reinforcement learning. Office: Intelligent Inference Sys Corp MS:566-108 NASA Rsch Park Moffett Field CA 94035 Home Phone: 408-730-1016; Office Phone: 650-965-9365. Business E-Mail: berenji@iiscorp.com.

BERENS, MARK HARRY, lawyer; b. St. Paul, Aug. 4, 1928; s. Harry C. and Gertrude M. (Scherkenbach) B.; m. Barbara Jean Steichen, Nov. 20, 1954; children: Paul J., Joseph F. (dec.), John M., Stephen M., Thomas M., Michael M., Lisa B. Moran, James M., Daniel M. BS in Commerce (Acctg.) magna cum laude, U. Notre Dame, 1950, JD magna cum laude, 1951; postgrad., U. Chgo., 1951-53. Bar: Ill. 1951, D.C. 1955, U.S. Supreme Ct. 1971; CPA, Ill. Assoc. Mayer, Brown and predecessors, Chgo., 1956-61, ptnr., 1961-96; chmn., CEO Attys.' Liability Assurance Soc., Inc., Chgo., 1987-95; ptnr. Altheimer & Gray, Chgo., 1996—2003; of counsel Bell, Boyd & Lloyd LLP, Chgo., 2003—. Nat. chmn. Nat. Assn. Law Rev. Editors, 1950-51; chmn. bd. dirs. Attys. Liability Assurance Soc. (Bermuda) Ltd., 1979-95, bd. dirs. Accts. Liability Assurance Co., 1986-2004 Editor-in-chief Notre Dame Law Rev., 1950-51; contbr. articles to profl. jours. 1st lt. JAGC U.S. Army, 1953-56. Mem. D.C. Bar Assn., Chgo. Bar Assn., Am. Law Inst., The Comml. Bar Assn. (London), Union League Club, Lawyers Club of Chgo., Met. Club, Sunset Ridge Country Club (Northbrook). Republican. Roman Catholic. Home: 1660 North Ln Northbrook IL 60062-4708 Office: Bell Boyd & Lloyd LLP 70 W Madison St Chicago IL 60602 Business E-Mail: mberens@bellboyd.com.

BERENS, WILLIAM JOSEPH, lawyer; b. New Ulm, Minn., Dec. 12, 1952; s. Robert J. and Lorraine M. (O'Brien) B.; m. Janet Christiansen, June 13, 1975; children: Margaret, Elizabeth, Catherine. BA, Coll. St. Thomas, 1975; JD, U. Minn., 1978. Bar: Minn. 1978. Assoc. Dorsey & Whitney, LLP, Mpls., 1978-83, ptnr., estate and trust svcs. group.; chmn., tax, estate planning group, 1984—. Adj. prof. William Mitchell Coll. of Law, St. Paul, 1981-84. Fellow: Am. Coll. Trust and Estate Counsel. Office: Dorsey & Whitney LLP 50 S 6th St Minneapolis MN 55402-1498 Office Phone: 612-340-2621. Office Fax: 612-340-2868. E-mail: berens.bill@dorsey.com.

BERENSON, ABBEY BELINA, gynecologist, educator; b. Nashville, Aug. 19, 1958; d. Leon and Florence (Keiles) B.; m. Steven Mitchell Kornblau, Nov. 24, 1983; children: Ilyse Samantha, Jake Alexander. BA summa cum laude, U. Tex., 1980; MD, Baylor U., 1984. Lic. gynecologist, Tex. Resident in ob-gyn. Baylor Coll. Medicine, Houston, 1984-88; fellow in pediat. gynecology Queen Charlotte's and Chelsea Hosp., London, 1991; asst. prof. U. Tex. Med. Br., Galveston, 1989-93, assoc. prof., chief divsn. pediat. and adolescent gynecology, 1993-98, prof., chief divsn. pediat. and adolescent gynecology, 1998—. Reviewer: Jour. Adolescent Health, Pediats., Obstetrics and Gynecology, Archives of Pediats. and Adolescent Medicine, Jour. Reproductive Medicine; contbr. numerous articles to profl. publs. including Jour. Adolescent Health, Adolescent Pediat. Gynecology, Pediats., Am. Jour. Ob-Gyn. James and Minnie Edmonds scholar. Fellow ACOG (bd. cert.), Ctrl. Assn. Obstetricians and Gynecologists (pres. 2004), Soc. Adolescent Medicine; mem. Internat. Fedn. Gynecologists Obstetricians (expert adv. panel 1997-2000), Soc. Gynecologic Investigation, N.Am. Soc. Pediat. and Adolescent Gynecology (abstract rev. com. 1992-93, com. position statements 1996). Achievements include research on appearance of external genitalia in prepubertal girls; physical abuse in pregnancy; contraceptive compliance in adolescents; drug abuse in pregnancy.

BERENSON, ALEX, reporter; b. 1973; BS in History, Econ., Yale Univ., 1994. Intern Denver (Colo.) Post; reporter TheStreet.com, NYC; fin. investigative reporter NY Times, NYC, 1999—. Author: The Number: How the Quest for Quarterly Earnings Corrupted Wall Street and Corporate America, 2003. Office: Business News NY Times 229 W 43rd St New York NY 10036 Office Phone: 212-556-1474. Office Fax: 212-556-1448.

BERENSON, BRADFORD A., lawyer; BA summa cum laude, Yale U., New Haven, Conn., 1986; JD magna cum laude, Harvard U., Cambridge, Mass., 1991. Bar: DC 1994, US Dist. Ct. DC 1994, US Ct. Appeals (3d cir.) 1995, US Ct. Appeals (4th cir.) 1995, US Ct. Appeals (11th cir.) 1995, US Ct. Appeals (DC cir.) 1995, US Supreme Ct. 1998, US Ct. Appeals (2d cir.) 1998, US Ct. Appeals (5th cir.) 2005, US Dist. Ct. Md. 2000. Law clk. to Judge Laurence H. Silberman US Ct. Appeals (DC Cir.), 1991—92; law clk. to Justice Anthony M. Kennedy US Supreme Ct., 1992—93; assoc. Sidley Austin LLP, 1993—99, ptnr., 1999—2001, 2003—; assoc. counsel to Pres. of U.S. The White House, 2001—03. Cons. to ind. counsel David M. Barrett in the prosecution of former HUD secretary Henry Cisneros; legal commentator various news channels including NBC, CBS, NBC, PBS, NPR, Fox News Channel, CNN; chmn. Federalist Soc. Criminal Law and Pracice group; adj. fellow Am. Enterprise Inst. Contbr. articles to newspapers. Mem.: Edward Bennet Williams Inn of Ct. Office: Sidley Austin LLP 1501 K St NW Washington DC 20005 Office Phone: 202-736-8971.

BERENSON, GERALD SANDERS, physician; b. Bogalusa, La., Sept. 19, 1922; s. Meyer A. and Eva (Singerman) B.; m. Joan Seidenbach, Mar. 7, 1951; children— Leslie, Ann, Robert, Laurie. BS, Tulane U., 1943, MD, 1945. Intern U.S. Navy Hosp., Great Lakes, Ill., 1945-46; practice medicine specializing in cardiology New Orleans; mem. staff Charity Hosp., U. Hosp.; instr. dept. medicine Tulane U., 1949-52, prof. epidemiology Sch. Pub. Health, 1992—; asst. prof. medicine La. State U. Med. Sch., 1954-58, assoc. prof., 1958-63, prof., 1963-92, Boyd prof., 1988-92, prof. emeritus, 1992—; prof. medicine, biochemistry and pediatrics Tulane U. Sch. Medicine, New Orleans, 1992—. Dir. Specialized Ctr. Rsch. Arteriosclerosis, New Orleans, 1972-87, Nat. Rsch. and Demonstration Ctr. in Arteriosclerosis, 1984-87, Nat. Ctr. Cardiovascular Health, Sch. Pub. Health and Tropical Medicine Tulane U., 1992—; sr. vis. physician Charity Hosp. La., New Orleans, 1948—; cons. Touro Infirmary, 1967—. Contbr. articles to profl. jours. Served with USNR, 1945-48. USPHS fellow U. Chgo., 1952-54 Mem. Am. Coll. Cardiology (gov. La. 1985-88, trustee 1988, chmn. prevention com. 1990-93), So. Soc. Clin. Investigation (pres. 1969), La. Heart Assn. (pres. 1971), New Orleans Acad. Internal Medicine (pres. 1966), Musser-Burch Soc. (pres. 1981), Soc. Geriatric Cardiology (pres. 1999-00), Sigma Xi, Alpha Omega Alpha. Office: Tulane Sch Pub Health Nat Ctr Cardiovascular Health 1440 Canal St Ste 1838 New Orleans LA 70112-2750 Office Phone: 504-988-7197. Business E-Mail: berenson@tulane.edu.

BERENSON, RED (GORDON A. BERENSON), hockey coach, retired professional hockey player; b. Regina, Sask., Can., Dec. 8, 1939; m. Joy Berenson; children: Kelly, Sandy, Gordie, Rusty. BS, U. Mich., 1962, MBA, 1966. Left wing Montreal Canadiens, 1961—66, NY Rangers, 1966—67, St. Louis Blues, 1967—71, 1974—78, Detroit Red Wings, 1971—74; asst. coach St. Louis Blues, 1978—79, head coach, 1979—82; asst. coach Buffalo Sabres, 1982—84; head coach U. Mich. Hockey Team, Ann Arbor, 1984—. Player Summit Series, 1972. Named to Mich. Sports Hall of Fame, U. Mich. Athletic Hall of Honor, Dekers Club Hall of Fame, Saskatchewan Sports Hall of Fame, 2000; recipient Jack Adams Award, 1981, Lester Patrick Award, 2006. Office: U Mich 1000 S State St Ann Arbor MI 48109-2202 Office Phone: 734-647-1201. E-mail: redbaron@umich.edu.*

BERENSON, WILLIAM KEITH, lawyer; b. Nashville, Nov. 23, 1954; s. Leon and Lorraine Florence (Keiles) B; m. Mara Lynn Rubinton; 1 child, Marissa Laurel. BA with honors, U. Tex., 1976; JD, So. Meth. U., 1979. Bar: Tex. 1979, U.S. Dist. Ct. (no. dist.) Tex., U.S. Ct. Appeals (5th and 11th cirs.), U.S. Supreme Ct.; cert. personal injury trial law, Tex. Bd. Legal Specialization. Mem. Supreme Ct. Jury Task Force. Author: Evaluating Settlement Offers, 1990, Texas Automobile Injury Guide, 1993, Trying the Automobile Injury Case in Texas: Plaintiff's Perspective, 1995, Automobile Injury Cases in Texas, 1996, Quantification of Personal Injury Claims, 1997; mem. editl. bd. Ins. Settlement and Litigation Reporter, Ins. Issues Annotated. Chmn. Longhorn coun. Boy Scouts Am., Ft. Worth; bd. dirs. So. Meth. U. Alumni Assn., AIDS Interfaith Network; bd. dirs. Regional Coun. Parents and Alumni, So. Meth. U.; vol. atty. Animal Rescue Orgn. Fellow Tarrant County Bar Found.; mem. ABA, Am. Assn. Justice (sustaining mem. pub. interest group com.), State Bar Tex., Tex. Bar Assn., Tarrant County Bar Assn. (jud. evaluation com., fee arbitration com.), Tarrant County Lawyrs Assn. (bd. dirs. 1994—), Tex. Trial Lawyers Assn., Coll. State Bar Tex., Nat. Coll. Advocacy, Roscoe Pound Found., Phi Alpha Delta. Avocations: marathons, bicycling. Office: 900 River Plaza Tower 1701 River Run Fort Worth TX 76107-6579

BERENTSEN, KURTIS GEORGE, music educator, conductor; b. North Hollywood, Calif., Apr. 22, 1953; s. George O. and Eleanor J. (Johnson) B.; m. Jeanette M. Sacco, Aug., 1975 (div. 1977); m. Floy I. Griffiths, March 17, 1984; 1 child, Kendra Irene. MusB, Utah State U., 1975; MA in Music, U. Calif., Santa Barbara, 1986; cert. colloguy, Concordia Coll., 1996. Cert. cmty. coll. tchr., Calif., pub. tchr., Calif.; commd. minister Luth. Ch., Mo. Synod, 1996. Dir. music Hope Luth. Ch., Daly City, Calif., 1975—81; gen. mgr. Ostara Press, Inc., Daly City, 1975—78; condr. U. Calif., Santa Barbara, 1981—86; dir., condr. Santa Barbara Oratorio Chorale, 1983—85; dir. music 1st Presbyn. Ch., Santa Barbara, 1983—84, Goleta Presbyn. Ch., Calif., 1984—85; min. music Trinity Luth. Ch., Ventura, 1985—92, Christ Luth. Ch. & Sch., Little Rock, 1992—98; dir. choral music Concordia U., Portland, Oreg., 1998—; instr. Ventura Coll., 1987—88; music dir., condr. Gold Coast Cmty. Chorus, Ventura, 1988—92. Choir dir. Temple Beth Torah Jewish Community, Ventura, 1982-87; adj. prof. Pepperdine U., Malibu, Calif., 1988; chorus master Ventura Symphony Orch., 1987. Condr. oratorios Christus Am Oelberg, 1983, Elijah, 1984, Hymn of Praise, 1988, cantata Seven Last Words, 1979, 84, Paukenmesse, 1989, Mozart's Requiem, 1990, 05, Requiem-Fauré, 1991, 2002, Judas Messiah-Handel, 2007; soloist 15 major oratorio and opera roles, 1971-92, Nat. Anthem, L.A. Dodgers, 1989; dir. (with John Rutter) Gold Coast Community Chorus, Carnegie Hall, NYC., 1991, Tribute to America, Lincoln Ctr. Concert, NYC, 1991. Min. music, tchr. Christ Luth. Ch. and Sch., Little Rock, 1992—. First place winner baritone vocalist Idaho Fedn. Music Clubs, 1971, recital winner Utah Fedn. Music Clubs, 1974. Mem. Choral Condrs. Guild, Assn. Luth. Ch. Musicians, Am. Guild of English Handbell Ringers, Am. Choral Dirs. Assn., Music Educators Nat. Conf., Sigma Nu (sec., song leader 1973-75). Home and Office: 2811 NE Holman St Portland OR 97211-6067 Home Phone: 503-358-5878. Business E-Mail: kberentsen@cu-portland.edu.

BERENZWEIG, JACK CHARLES, lawyer; b. Bklyn., Sept. 29, 1942; s. Sidney A. and Anne R. (Dubowe) B.; m. Susan J. Berenzweig, Aug. 8, 1968; children: Mindy, Andrew. BEE, Cornell U., 1964; JD, Am. U., 1968. Bar: Va. 1968, Ill. 1969. Examiner U.S. Pat. Off., Washington, 1964-66; pat. adviser U.S. Naval Air Systems Command, Washington, 1966-68; ptnr. Brinks, Hofer, Gilson & Lione and predecessor firm, Chgo., 1968—. Editorial staff Am. U. Law Rev., 1966-68; contbr. articles to profl. jours. Mem. ABA, Chgo. Bar Assn., Ill. State Bar Assn., Bar Assn. 7th Fed. Cir., Va. State Bar, Internat. Trademark Assn. (bd. dirs. 1983-85), Brand Names Edn. Found. (bd. dirs. 1993-2000), Meadow Club (Rolling Meadows, Ill.), Miramar Club (Naples, Fla.), Delta Theta Phi. Home: 127 W Oak St Apt A Chicago IL 60610-5422 Office: Brinks Hofer Gilson & Lione Ltd Ste 3600 455 N Cityfront Plaza Dr Chicago IL 60611-5599 Office Phone: 312-321-4212. Business E-Mail: jcb@brinkshofer.com.

BERESFORD, DOUGLAS LINCOLN, lawyer; b. Washington, June 1, 1956; s. Spencer Moxon and Ann (Lincoln) B.; m. Lori Anne Mainous, Sept. 22, 1990; children: Alexander Gould, Erik Mainous. AB cum laude, Harvard U., 1978; JD, Georgetown U., 1982. Bar: D.C. 1982, U.S. Ct. Appeals (D.C. cir.) 1984, U.S. Supreme Ct. 1986. Assoc. Morgan, Lewis & Bockius, Washington, 1982-83, Newman & Holtzinger, P.C., Washington, 1983-89, ptnr., 1989-94, Long, Aldridge & Norman, Washington, 1994-2000, Hogan & Hartson LLP, Washington, 2000—. Office: Hogan & Hartson LLP 555 13th St NW Ste 700E Washington DC 20004-1161 Office Phone: 202-637-5819. Business E-Mail: dlberesford@hhlaw.com.

BEREUTER, DOUGLAS KENT, foundation administrator, former congressman; b. York, Nebr., Oct. 6, 1939; s. Rupert Wesley and Evelyn Gladys (Tonn) B.; m. Louise Meyer, June 1, 1962; children: Eric David, Kirk Daniel. BA, U. Nebr., 1961; M in City Planning, Harvard U., 1966, MPA, 1973. Urban planner HUD, San Francisco, 1965-66; dir. div. state and urban affairs Nebr. Dept. Econ. Devel., 1967-68, state planning dir., 1968-70; coord. fed.-state relations Nebr. State Govt., 1967-70, urban planning cons., 1971-78; assoc. prof. U. Nebr., 1971—73, Kansas St. U., 1971—78; mem. Nebr. Legislature, 1974-78, US House of Reps. from 1st Nebr. Dist., 1979—2004, mem. fin. svcs. com., mem. and vice chmn. internat. rels. com., vice chmn. intelligence com., mem. transp. and infrastructure com.; pres. The Asia Found., San Francisco, 2004—. Mem. Nebr. State Crime Commn., 1969-71; chmn. standing com. urban devel. Nat. Conf. State Legislatures, 1977-78; mem. Nat. Agrl. Export Commn., 1985-86; pres., CEO The Asia Found.; bd. trustees Nat. Arbor Day Found., Lincoln; pres. NATO Parliamentary Assembly, 2003-04. Served as officer US Army, 1963-65. Mem. Coun. Fgn. Rels., Phi Beta Kappa, Sigma Xi. Republican. Lutheran. Office: The Asia Found PO Box 193223 San Francisco CA 94119

BEREZOVSKY, BORIS ABRAMOVICH (PLATON ELENIN), entrepreneur; b. Moscow, Jan. 23, 1946; m. Elena Berezovsky; 4 children. Grad., Moscow State U. Engr. Rsch. Inst. Testing Machines, Equipment and Measurment Devices, 1968—69, Hydrometeorological Rsch. Ctr., 1969; engr., rschr. divsn. head Isnt. Problems of Man., 1969—87; supr. Togliatti Car Works (VAZ), 1973—91; founder, dir.-gen. LogoVAZ Co., 1991—; dir.-gen. All-Union Automobile Alliance (AVVA), 1993—96. Corres. mem. Russian Acad. Scis., 1991; founder Triumph Charity Found., 1994; dep. chmn. bd. dirs. Pub. Russian TV, 1995—96; dep. sec. security coun. Russian Fedn., 1996—97; exec. sec. CIS, 1998—99; founder Internat. Found. for Civil Liberties, 2000; co-founder Liberal Russia polit. party, 2001. Contbr. articles to profl. jours. Mem. State Duma (Russian Parliament), 1999—2000. Office: c/o Internat Found for Civil Liberties 152 W 57th St 25th Fl New York NY 10019 Office Phone: 212-397-2974.

BERG, ALAN, lawyer, arbitrator; b. Scranton, Pa., June 5, 1947; s. Donald and Lucile (DeLugo) Berg; m. Rita A. Samin, June 15, 1975 (dec. Feb. 20, 2001); children: Thomas M., Matthew P., Andrew J. BA, Hartwick Coll., Oneonta, NY, 1969; JD, St. John's U., 1972; LLM in Labor Law, NYU, 1975. Bar: N.Y. 1973, U.S. Dist. Ct. (dists. N.Y.) 1973, U.S. Ct. Appeals 1973, U.S. Supreme Ct. 1976. Atty. N.Y. State Labor Rels. Bd., 1972—79, adminstrv. law judge, 1979—80, chief judge, 1980—84, gen. counsel, 1984—91, N.Y. State Employment Rels. Bd., 1991—2003, arbitrator, 2003—. Judge N.Y. Law Sch. Wagner Moot Ct.; advisor NYU Law Sch. student adv. program. Trustee Freeport Meml. Lib., NY, 1976—81; coach Freeport H.S. summer basketball team, 1973—; N.Y. all-star team N.Y.-Phila. basketball festival, 1985—86, 1988—97; arbitrator Better Bus. Bur. Recipient George Emma Meml. Sportsmanship award, 1986, Citizen award, Freeport Boosters Club, 1987. Mem.: Indsl. Rels. Rsch. Assn., N.Y. State Bar Assn., St. John's Law Sch. Alumni Assn. Home: 108 Delaware Ave Freeport NY 11520-1313

BERG, AMIE G., lawyer; b. Houston, Feb. 11, 1964; BBA in Finance magna cum laude, U. Houston, 1996, JD, 1999. Bar: US Dist. Ct. (so. dist. Tex.) 1999, US Dist. Ct. (ea. dist. Tex.) 2000, US Dist. Ct. (no. dist. Tex.) 2000, US Dist. Ct. (we. dist. Tex.) 2000, US Supreme Ct. 2003, US Ct. Internat. Trade 2003. Risk mgmt. analyst Hines Interests Ltd. Partnership; intern Staff of US Magistrate Judge Marcia Crone; assoc. atty. litigation sect. Baker Hostetler, Houston, 1999—. Named a Rising Star, Tex. Super Lawyers mag., 2006. Mem.: Risk and Ins. Mgmt. Soc. (Houston chpt.), Tex. Bar Assn., Houston Bar Assn., Woodlands Fit Marathon Tng. Team. Office: Baker Hostetler 1000 Louisiana Ste 2000 Houston TX 77002-5009 Office Phone: 713-646-1361. Office Fax: 713-751-1717. E-mail: aberg@bakerlaw.com.*

BERG, A(NDREW) SCOTT, writer; b. Norwalk, Conn., 1949; Grad., Princeton U., 1971. Author: Lindbergh, 1999 (Pulitzer prize for biography 1999), Goldwyn: A Biography, Max Perkins: Editor of Genius, 1978 (Nat. Book award), Kate Remembered, 2003; (films) Making Love, 1982; co-prodr., co-writer Goldwyn, 2001. Trustee Princeton (NJ) U., 1999—2003, Libr. of Am., 1999—. Guggenheim fellow, 1982. Office: Janklow & Nesbit Assocs 445 Park Ave 13th Fl New York NY 10022

BERG, CARL E., real estate developer; b. 1938; 1 child, Kara. Owner, pres. Internat. Network Svcs., 2002—, Mission West Properties REIT; prin. Berg & Berg Enterprises, LLC. Office: International Network Services Ste 200 1600 Memorex Dr Santa Clara CA 95050-2842

BERG, CHARLES G., insurance company executive; m. Casey Wiggins; 3 children. BA in Polit. Sci., Macalester Coll., St. Paul, MN, 1978; degree in law, Georgetown U. Founder, CEO Health Ptnrs., Inc.; exec. v.p. med. delivery Oxford Health Plans, Inc., 1998—2000, exec. v.p. med. delivery and tech., 2000—01, pres., COO, 2001—02, pres., CEO, 2002—. Bd. dirs. America's Health Ins. Plans. Office: Oxford Health Plans Inc 48 Monroe Turnpike Trumbull CT 06611

BERG, DANIEL, science and technology educator; b. NYC, June 1, 1929; s. Jack and Hattie (Tannenbaum) B.; m. Frances Helena Ely, Aug. 18, 1956; children: Brian, Laura, Meredith. BS, CCNY, 1950; MS, Yale U., 1951, PhD, 1953; grad. execs. program, Carnegie-Mellon U., 1972. With Westinghouse Electric Corp., Pitts., 1953-77, research div. mgr., then tech. dir., 1976-77; prof. sci. and tech. Carnegie-Mellon U., 1977-83, dean Mellon Coll. Sci., 1977-81, univ. provost, 1981-83; v.p. acad. affairs, provost, Inst. prof. sci. and tech. Rensselaer Poly. Inst., Troy, NY, 1983-85, pres., 1985-87, Inst. prof., 1987—. Bd. dirs. Hy-Tech. Machine Co., Inc.; chmn. bd. Crystek Inc.; mem. Pa. Sci. and Engring. Found., 1975-76; mem. vis. coun. sci. and engring. CCNY, 1980-84; mem. vis. coun. Sch. Computer Sci., Carnegie-Mellon U., 1992—; mem. Yale U. Coun., 1981-85; assoc. fellow Jonathan Edwards Coll., 1982—; cons. to industry and govt. Author, editor, patentee in field. Fellow IEEE, AAAS, INFORMS, Am. Inst. Chemists, N.Y. Acad. Scis.; mem. Nat. Acad. Engring. (coun. 1985-88), Am. Chem. Soc., Cosmos Club of Washington, Rivers Club of Pitts., Phi Beta Kappa, Sigma Xi, Alpha Chi Sigma, Tau Beta Pi. Home: 12 The Crossways Troy NY 12180-7263 Office: Rensselaer Poly Inst 5015 CII Troy NY 12180-3522 Home Phone: 518-272-7611; Office Phone: 518-276-2895. Business E-Mail: bergd@rpi.edu.

BERG, DARRELL MATTHEWS, musicologist; b. Marianna, Fla., Oct. 5, 1927; d. John Benjamin Matthews; children: Rebecca Louise, James Emmanuel. BS, The Juilliard Sch., NYC, 1955; MA, Smith Coll., Northampton, Mass., 1957; PhD, SUNY, Buffalo, 1975. Violinist Kansas City Philharm., Mo., 1957—60, Cin. Symphony Orch., 1960—62, Buffalo Philharm., 1963—65; prof. music history St. Louis Conservatory of Music, 1978—90; vis. assoc. prof. Washington U., St. Louis, 1990—2000. Artistic dir. Collegium Vocale of St. Louis, 1997—2006. Contbr. articles to profl. jourss.; gen. editor C.P.E. Bach: The Complete Works, 1999—. Grantee, NEH, 1982, Internat. Rsch. Exch., 1988, German Govt., 1993. Mem.: Am. Bach Soc., Am. Musicological Soc. Episcopalian. Home: 6334 Waterman Ave Saint Louis MO 63138 Personal E-mail: dmberg@wustl.edu.

BERG, DAVID HOWARD, lawyer; b. Springfield, Ohio, Mar. 4, 1942; s. Nathan Stewart Berg and Mildred (Besser) Berg-Filion; children: Geoffrey Alan, Gabriel Adam, Caitlin Hannah; m. Kathryn Page, July 10, 1994. Student, Tulane U., 1963; BA in English, U. Houston, 1964, JD, 1967. Bar: Tex. 1967, NY 1989, US Dist. Ct. (so., no. we., ea. dist. Tex., so., ea. dist. NY, we. dist. Va.), U. Ct. Appeals (2d, 4th, 5th, 8th and 11th cirs.), US Supreme Ct. 1970. Law clk. NLRB, Washington, 1967-68; ptnr. David Berg & Assocs., Houston, 1968-77, Berg & Androphy, 1977—. Mem. fed. ct. lawyers adv. com. U.S. Dist. Ct. (so. dist.) Tex.; spl. counsel commn. on lawyer discipline, Tex. State Bar, 1996—. Author, The Trial Lawyer: What It Takes to Win, 2003; contbr. articles and essays to mags. Adv. Jimmy Carter Transition Govt., Washington, 1976, Mayor Kathy Whitmire Campaign, 1980-91; patron Friends of Menil Collection, 1990-91; adv. campaign Mayor Bob Lanier, 1991; chmn. Imagine Houston, City of Houston; adv. bd. Camp for All; bd. dirs. U. Houston Law Ctr, Law Found., 1996, Houston Shakespeare Festival, 1997, Anti-Defamation League, 2002, Houston Holocaust Mus.; chmn. bd. Houston Area Water Corp., 1999-; mem. Pres. Council Tulane Univ. 2000-. Recipient 1st pl. for best feature article in a scholarly jour. Nat. Assn. Publ., 1991; Theatreworks USA Goodworks award, 2002. Fellow Internat. Acad. Trial Lawyers, Tex. Bar Found., Houston Bar Found.; mem. ATLA, State Bar Tex. (chmn. grievance com. 1984-85), NY State Bar Assn., Tex. Trial Lawyers Assn., Houston Trial Lawyers Assn., Houston Bar Assn., U. Houston Law Alumni Assn. (bd. dirs. 1992-95), Am. Bd. Trial Advocates (assoc.). Democrat. Jewish. Avocations: writing, running, fishing. Home: 16 Sunset Blvd Houston TX 77005-1838 Office: Berg & Androphy 3704 Travis St Houston TX 77002-9550 Office Phone: 713-529-5622. Office Fax: 713-529-3785. Business E-Mail: dberg@bafirm.com.

BERG, HOWARD C., biology professor; b. Iowa City, Mar. 16, 1934; s. Clarence P. and Esther M. (Carlson) B.; m. Mary E. Guyer, Dec. 19, 1964; children— Henry G., Alexander H., Elena C. BS in Chemistry, Calif. Inst. Tech., Pasadena, 1956; AM in Physics, Harvard U., 1960, PhD in Chem. Physics, 1964. Jr. fellow Harvard Soc. Fellows, Cambridge, Mass., 1963-66; asst. prof. dept. biology Harvard U., Cambridge, 1966-69, assoc. prof. dept. biochemistry and molecular biology, 1969-70, prof. dept. molecular and cellular biology, 1986—; prof. physics, 1997—; assoc. prof. to prof. dept. molecular, cellular and developmental biology U. Colo., Boulder, 1970-79; prof. div. biology Calif. Inst. Tech., Pasadena, 1979-86. Mem. Rowland Inst., Cambridge, 1986—. Author: Random Walks in Biology, 1983, revised edit., 1993, E. coli in Motion, 2004; contbr. articles to profl. jours. Fulbright fellow, 1956-57, Guggenheim fellow, 2000-01; NSF Sci. Faculty Devel. awardee, 1978-79. Mem. AAAS, Am. Phys. Soc. (Biol. Physics prize 1984), Biophys. Soc. (Single Molecule Biology prize 2007), Am. Soc. Microbiol., NAS, Am. Acad. Arts and Scis., Am. Philos. Soc. Office: Harvard U Biology Labs 16 Divinity Ave Cambridge MA 02138-2020 also: Rowland Inst 100 Edwin H Land Blvd Cambridge MA 02142 Office Phone: 617-495-0924. Business E-Mail: hberg@mcb.harvard.edu.

BERG, JANICE CAROL, elementary school educator; b. Painesville, Ohio, Feb. 18, 1953; d. Kenneth White Edds and Audrey Helen Nelson; children: Peter James, Steven Alan. BS in Elem. Edn., Slippery Rock State Coll., 1975; MEd, Slippery Rock U., 1987, cert. in early childhood edn., 1995; cert. reading specialist, Clarion U., 1994. Cert. elem. tchr. Pa. 3d grade tchr. Brookville (Pa.) Area Sch. Dist., 1975—76; 5th grade tchr. Seoul (Rep. of Korea) Fgn. Sch. Dist., 1977—78, 1st grade tchr., 1978—79; reading specialist Punxsutawney (Pa.) Area Sch. Dist., 1994, Allegheny-Clarion Valley Sch. Dist., Foxburg, Pa., 1996—. Sub. tchr. Derry Twp. Sch. Dist., Hershey, Pa., 1990; pvt. tutor, Brookville, Pa., 93. Room mother PTO, Elizabethtown, Pa., 1985; den leader, chmn. com. Boy Scouts Am., Elizabethtown, 1987—94; vacation bible sch. dir., tchr., Sunday sch. tchr., chmn. Christian edn. com. Mem.: Pa. State Edn. Assn., Seneca Reading Coun. (pres., corr. sec. 2001—02), Allegheny-Clarion Valley Edn. Assn., Keystone State Reading Assn. (mem. conf. membership com. 2002), Butler Outdoor Club (sec. 2004—05). Avocations: swimming, hiking, bicycling, reading, table tennis. Home: 404 Walnut St Emlenton PA 16373

BERG, JEFFREY SPENCER, talent agency executive; b. LA, May 26, 1947; s. Dick Berg and Barbara Freedman; m. Denise Luria; 2 children. BA in English with honors, U. Calif., Berkeley, 1969. V.p., head lit. divsn. Creative Mgmt. Assocs., Los Angeles, 1969-75; v.p. motion picture dept. Internat. Creative Mgmt., Los Angeles, 1975-80, pres., 1980-85, chmn., CEO, 1985—. Dir. Josephson Internat., Inc., Marshall McLuhan Ctr. of Global Communication; bd. dirs. Oracle Corp., Am. Film Inst. Trustee U. Berkeley Found.; bd. govs. Music Ctr. L.A. County; pres. letters and sci. exec. bd. U. Calif. Berkeley; bd. vis. Anderson Grad. Sch. of Mgmt., UCLA. Named one of 50 Most Powerful People in Hollywood, Premiere mag., 2004—06; recipient Cavaliere Ufficiale Order of Merit, Republic of Italy, 1991. Mem. U. Calif. Berkeley Alumni Assn. Office: Internat Creative Mgmt 8942 Wilshire Blvd Beverly Hills CA 90211-1934

BERG, JEREMY MARK, federal agency administrator, biochemist, researcher; BS in Chemistry, MS in Chemistry, Stanford U., 1980; PhD in Chemistry, Harvard U., 1985. Visiting rsch. assoc. Charles F. Kettering Rsch Lab., Yellow Springs, Ohio, 1979; predoctoral fellow, Nat. Science

Found Harvard U., Cambridge, Mass., 1980—83; Jane Coffin Childs Meml. Fund postdoctoral fellow The Johns Hopkins U. Sch. Med., Balt., 1984—86; asst. prof. chemistry The Johns Hopkins U., 1986—90, prof. chemistry, 1992—2003, co-dir., Keck Ctr. for Rational Design of Biologically Active Molecules, 2001—03; prof., dir. dept. biophysics & biophysical chemistry The Johns Hopkins U. Sch. Med., Balt., 1990—2003, dir., Markey Ctr. for Macromolecular Structure & Function, 1990—2003, dir., Inst. for Basic Biomedical Sciences, 2001—03; dir. Nat. Inst. Gen. Med. Sciences, NIH, Bethesda, Md., 2003—. Recipient Pure Chemistry award Am. Chem. Soc., 1993, Eli Lilly Biological Chemistry award Am. Chem. Soc. 1995. Office: Nat Inst of Gen Med Sciences Natcher Bldg 45 Ctr Dr Bethesda MD 20892 Office Phone: 301-594-2172.

BERG, JOHN TOWNSEND, physiologist, researcher; b. Mpls., July 3, 1945; s. John Wilmer and Jean Townsend Berg; m. Gemma deGuzman, Mar. 23, 1997; children: John Joseph, Melisa deGuzman. PhD, U. Hawaii at Manoa, Honolulu, 1985. Postdoctoral fellow U. Calif. San Diego, La Jolla, 1994—97; sr. rsch. fellow U. Wash., Seattle, 1998—2000; assoc. rsch. prof. U. Hawaii at Manoa, Honolulu, 2001—. Outside mem. animal use com. Oceanic Inst., Waimanalo, Hawaii, 2002—. Contbr. articles to profl. jours. Recipient Geist award, Hawaii Cmty. Found., 2001—04; Summer scholar, Pacific Health Rsch. Inst., 1983, Hawaii Heart Fellowship and Grant-in-Aide, Hawaii Heart Assn., 1985, Parker B. Francis Fellowship in Pulmonary Medicine, Parker B. Francis Found., 1988. Mem.: Am. Physiol. Soc. (life). Achievements include Demonstrated that inhibition of hypoxic pulmonary vasoconstriction prevents high altitude pulmonary edema; discovery of ginkgo biloba prevents high altitude pulmonary edema in rats; carbonic anhydrase is present in mammalian vascular smooth muscle; increased wall stress induced vascular remodeling in lung parenchyma; endotoxin prevents hyperoxic lung injury by induction of manganese superoxide dismutase. Home: 94-125 Pahu St # 29 Waipahu HI 96797 Office: Univ Hawaii at Manoa Rm 122 1951 East-West Rd Honolulu HI 96822 Home Phone: 808-676-2622; Office Phone: 808-956-5381. Office Fax: 808-956-5381; Home Fax: 808-676-2622. Personal E-mail: johnberg@hawaii.edu.

BERG, LORINE MCCOMIS, retired guidance counselor; b. Ashland, Ky., Mar. 28, 1919; d. Oliver Botner and Emma Elizabeth (Eastham) McComis; m. Leslie Thomas Berg, Apr. 27, 1946; children: James Michael, Leslie Jane. BA in Edn., U. Ky., 1965; MA, Xavier U., 1969. Tchr. A.D. Owens Elem. Sch., Newport, Ky., 1963-64, 6th dist. Elementary Schs., Covington, Ky., 1965-69; guidance counselor Twenhofel Jr. H.S., Independence, Ky., 1969-78, Scott H.S., Taylor Mill, Ky., 1978-84. Bd. dirs. Mental Health Assn., Covington, Ky, 1970-76, v.p., 1973 (valuable svc. award 1973); mem. Lakeside Christian Ch., Ft. Mitchell, Ky. Named to Honorable Order of Ky. Colonels, Hon. Admissions Counselor U.S. Naval Acad.; cited by USN Recruiting Command for Valuable Assistance to USN, 1981. Mem. Am. Assn. of Univ. Women, Covington Art Club, Retired Tchrs. Assn., Kappa Delta Pi, Delta Kappa Gamma, Phi Delta Kappa. Democrat. Avocations: painting, dance, reading, arts and crafts. Home: 11 Idaho Ave Covington KY 41017-2925

BERG, LOUIS LESLIE, investment executive; b. Vienna, Austria; s. Gustav and Hedwig B.; came to US, 1938, naturalized, 1943; student U. Vienna, 1937-38, Coll. City NY, 1941-43; m. Minnette, 1959; children: Sharon, Randee, Michel. Pres., Gt. Empire Corp., NYC, 1946-, Bendalou Real Estate Corp., NYC, 1950-60, Netherlands Securities Co., Inc., NYC, 1959-62, Imported Automotive Parts, Ltd., LI City, NY; chmn., bd. dirs. IAP Inc., Avenel, NJ, IAP West Inc., LA; bd. dirs., exec. com. Auto Internat. Assn.; advisor US Congl. Adv. Bd. dir. Internat. Aviation Corp., Cosmos Industries, Kane-Miller Corp., Knickerbocker Toy Co., Inc., Vernitron Corp., Jet Aero Corp., Fidelity Am. Finance Corp., SW Fla. Enterprises, Sulray Inc., US Airlines, Commuter Airlines, Aviation Equipment. Mem. Am. Mgmt. Assn. Club: Wings. Office: IAP Inc 26 Engelhard Ave Avenel NJ 07001-2217 also: IAP West Inc 20036 Via Baron Rancho Dominguez CA 90220 also: IAP West Inc 3820 Delp St Memphis TN 38118

BERG, MADELAINE R., lawyer; b. Bklyn., Aug. 13, 1951; d. Gerald and Lorraine (Nodkin) B. BA, Bklyn. Coll., 1973, MFA, 1975; JD, Bklyn. Law Sch., 1980. Bar: N.Y. 1981, U.S. Dist. Ct. (so. dist.) N.Y. 1981, Pa. 1992, U.S. Dist. Ct. (ea. dist.) Pa. 1992. Spl. counsel, environ. law practice area Stroock & Stroock & Lavan LLP, NYC, 1980—. Contbr. articles to profl. jours. Office: Stroock & Stroock & Lavan LLP 180 Maiden Ln New York NY 10038-4982 Home Phone: 914-834-6817; Office Phone: 212-806-5823. Office Fax: 212-806-6006.

BERG, MARK S., lawyer, oil industry executive; BA magna cum laude, Tulane U., 1980; JD with honors, U. Tex., 1983. Bar: Tex., 1983. Joined Vinson & Elkins LLP, Houston, 1983, ptnr., 1990—97; exec. v.p., gen. counsel, corp. sec. Am. Gen. Corp., Houston, 1997—2002; sr. v.p., gen. counsel, sec. Hanover Compressor Co., 2002—04; exec. v.p., gen. counsel Pioneer Natural Resources Co., Irving, Tex., 2005—. Mem. ABA, Tex. Bar Assn., Houston Bar Assn., Houston Bar Found. (bd. dirs. 2000—), Phi Delta Phi, Phi Beta Kappa, Omicron Delta Kappa. Office: Pioneer Natural Resources Co Ste 200 5205 N O'Connor Blvd Irving TX 75039

BERG, PATRICIA ELENE, molecular biologist; b. Dubuque, Iowa, Sept. 17, 1943; d. Clifford Jay and Dorothy Ruth (McKibben) Emerson; 1 child, Bridget K. Mora; m. Robert S. Weiner. SB in Math., U. Chgo., 1965; PhD in Microbiology, Ill. Inst. Tech., 1973. Postdoctoral fellow U. Chgo., 1973-78; dir. genetic engring. Bethesda Rsch. Labs., Rockville, Md., 1978-80; expert NIH, Bethesda, 1980-82, sr. staff fellow, 1982-85, Nat. Inst. Digestive Diseases and Kidney, 1985-91; assoc. prof. divsn. of pediatric hematology/oncology Sch. Medicine U. Md., Balt., 1991-98; assoc. prof. dept. biochem. and molecular biology George Washington U. Med. Sch., Washington, 1999—. Contbr. articles to profl. jours. and to NY Times, Washington Post, L.A. Times, AP, Reuters; reported on CNN, Fox, CBS, 160 TV stas. , U. Chgo. scholar, 1961—65. Mem. AAAS, Am. Soc. Microbiology, Am. Soc. Hematology, Am. Assn. Cancer Rsch., Sigma Xi. Achievements include discovery of BP1, gene expressed in over 80 percent of breast cancer patients. Office: George Washington U Med Sch Dept Biochem/Molecular Biol 2300 Eye St NW Washington DC 20037-2336 Home Phone: 301-283-0821. Business E-Mail: bcmpeb@gwumc.edu.

BERG, PAUL, biochemist, educator; b. NYC, June 30, 1926; s. Harry and Sarah (Brodsky) Berg; m. Mildred Levy, Sept. 14, 1947; 1 child, John. BS, Pa. State U., 1948; PhD (NIH fellow 1950-52), Western Res. U., 1952; DSc (hon.) (hon.), U. Rochester, 1978, Yale U., 1978, Washington U., St. Louis, 1986, Oreg. State U., 1989, Pa. State U., 1995. Postdoctoral fellow Copenhagen (Denmark) U., 1952—53; postdoctoral fellow Sch. Medicine, Washington U., 1953—54, Am. Cancer Soc. scholar cancer research dept. microbiology sch. medicine, 1954—57, from asst. to assoc. prof. microbiology, 1955—59; prof. biochemistry Sch. Medicine, Stanford (Calif.) U., 1959—, Sam, Lulu and Jack Willson prof. biochemistry, 1970—94, Robert W. Cahill prof. cancer rsch., 1994—2000, chmn. dept. sch. medicine, 1969—74, now Cahill prof. in cancer rsch. emeritus; and dir. emeritus, Beckman Ctr. for Molecular and Genetic Med., 2000—. Dir. Stanford U. Beckman Ctr. for Molecular and Genetic Medicine, 1985—2000, Affymetrix, 1993—, Nat. Found. Biomed. Rsch., 1994—; non-resident fellow Salk Inst., 1973—83; adv. bd. NIH, NSF, MIT; vis. com. dept. biochemistry and molecular biology Harvard U.; bd. sci. advisors Jane Coffin Childs Found. Med. Rsch., 1970—80; chmn. sci. adv. com. Whitehead Inst., 1984—90; bd. sci. adv. DNAX Rsch. Inst., 1981—; internat. adv. bd. Basel Inst. Immunology; chmn. nat. adv. com. Genome Project, 1990—92. Editor: Biochem. and Biophys. Research Communications, 1959—68; editl. bd.: Molecular Biology, 1956—69; contbr. to profl. jours. Trustee Rockefeller U., 1990—92. Lt. (j.g.) USNR, 1943—46. Named Calif. Scientist of Yr., Calif. Museum Sci. and Industry, 1963, Lynen lectr., 1977, Priestly lectrs., Pa. State U., 1978, Dreyfus Disting. lectrs., Northwestern U., 1979, Lawrence Livermore Dir.'s Disting. lectr., 1983, Linus Pauling lectr., 1993; recipient Eli Lilly prize biochemistry, 1959, V.D. Mattia award, Roche Inst. Molecular Biology, 1972, Henry J. Kaiser award for excellence in teaching, 1969, Disting. Alumnus award, Pa. State U., 1972, Sarasota Med. awards for achievement and excellence, 1979, Gairdner Found. annual award, 1980, Lasker Found. award, 1980, Nobel award in chemistry, 1980, NY Acad. Sci. award, 1980, Sci. Freedom and Responsibility award, AAAS, 1982, Nat. Medal of Sci., 1983, 7th Ann. Biotechnology Heritage award, Chem. Heritage Found., 2005, numerous disting. lectureships including Harvey lectr., 1972. Fellow: AAAS; mem.: NAS, Royal Soc. (elected fgn. mem. 1992), French Acad. Sci. (elected fgn. mem. 1981), Japan Biochem. Soc. (elected fgn. mem. 1978), Internat. Soc. Molecular Biology, Am. Philos. Soc., Am. Soc. Microbiology, Am. Soc. Cell Biology (chmn. pub. policy com. 1994—), Am. Soc. Biol. Chemists (pres. 1974—75), Am. Acad. Arts and Scis., Inst. Medicine. Office: Stanford Sch Medicine Beckman Ctr B-062 Stanford CA 94305-5301 E-mail: pberg@cmgm.stanford.edu.

BERG, PETER, actor; b. NYC, Mar. 11, 1964; m. Elizabeth Rogers, 1993 (div. 1996). Film appearances include Demonstrator, 1971, Miracle Mile, 1988, Heart of Dixie, 1989, Never on Tuesday, 1989, Shocker, 1989, Genuine Risk, 1991, Late for Dinner, 1991, Aspen Extreme, 1993, Fire in the Sky, 1993, Across the Moon, 1994, The Last Seduction, 1994, Girl 6, 1996, The Great White Hype, 1996, Cop Land, 1997, Dill Scallion, 1999, Corky Romano, 2001, Collateral, 2004, Smokin' Aces, 2006, others; dir.: (films) Very Bad Things, 1998, The Rundown, 2003, Friday Night Lights, 2004; actor, dir.: (TV series) Chicago Hope, 1994-98.*

BERG, THOMAS KENNETH, lawyer; b. Willmar, Minn., Feb. 10, 1940; s. Kenneth Q. and Esther V. (Westlund) B.; m. Margit Kathryn Larson, July 31, 1965; children: Erik, Jeffrey. BA, U. Minn., 1962, JD, 1965. Bar: Minn. 1965, U.S. Dist. Ct. Minn. 1968, U.S. Ct. Appeals (8th cir.) 1974, U.S. Supreme Ct. 1980. Atty. Dept. Navy, Washington, 1965-67; assoc. Carlsen, Greiner & Law, Mpls., 1967-79; state rep. Minn. Ho. of Reps., St. Paul, 1970-78; U.S. atty. Dept. of Justice, Mpls., 1979-81; ptnr. Popham, Haik, Schnobrich & Kaufman, Mpls., 1981-97, Hinshaw & Culbertson, Mpls., 1997—. Treas. Moe for Gov. com., 2002. Chair Gov.'s Re-election Com., St. Paul, 1984-86, Gov.'s Commn. for Drug Abuse, Mpls., 1989; U.S. Senate candidate for endorsement Dem. Farmer Labor Party, Mpls., 1994; bd. dirs. League Conservative Voters, 2005—; trustee Wolf Ridge Environ. Learning Ctr., 2003—. Recipient Outstanding Narcotics Prosecution award U.S. Drug Enforcement Adminstrn., 1981. Master: Am. Health Lawyers Assn. Office: Hinshaw & Culbertson 333 South 7th St Minneapolis MN 55402

BERG, WALTER LOUIS, retired history professor; b. Tacoma, Wash., Feb. 17, 1922; s. Walter Berg and Elsie Karrenstein; m. Rosemary S. Bell (dec.); m. Eleanor R. Todd Wilson-Berg, Mar. 1, 1986; children: Karen L. Beahm, Melissa B. Mercer, Geoffrey W. BA, U. Puget Sound, 1946; MA, U. Wash., 1948, PhD, 1957. Prof. history Ctrl. Wash. U., Ellensburg, 1955—82, chmn. dept., 1965—69; ret., 1982. Fulbright prof. U. Madrid, 1961—62; vis. prof. history U. Wash., Seattle, 1963—64. Contbr. book revs. to jours., articles to profl. jours. Lt. j.g. USNR, 1943—46. Mem.: Am. Hist. Assn. (grad. com. 1966—69). Avocation: growing rhododendrons. Home: 16550 Agate Pass Rd NE Bainbridge Island WA 98110 E-mail: basanite@donobi.net.

BERG, WARREN STANLEY, retired bank executive; b. Lynn, Mass., Jan. 17, 1922; s. Carl W. and Gladys (Colburn) B.; m. Marjorie E. Coleman, Mar. 25, 1944; children— Peter C., Carolyn (Mrs. John Spengler), Dana S. BS, Harvard U., 1943; grad. exec. devel. program, Cornell U., 1944. Player Boston Red Sox, 1946; farm sys. coach MIT Baseball Team, 1948-50; Dir. pub. relations and sales promotion Arthur D. Little, Inc., Cambridge, Mass., 1951-65; with Shawmut Bank of Boston (N.A.), 1965-87, sr. v.p., 1969-87. Author: History of Harvard Baseball, 1964, History of Massachusetts Institute of Technology Athletics, 1950. Trustee, pres. Mus. Sci.; chmn. bd. dirs. Freedom House, Freedom Trail; pres. Freedom Trail Found.; chmn. Freedom Trail Commn.; exec. com. Wang Ctr. for Performing Arts. Capt. USMCR, 1943-46. Named to Harvard U. Athletic Hall of Fame (baseball). Mem. Pub. Relations Soc. Am. (presdl. citation for meritorious service 1962), Assoc. Grantmakers of Mass. (v.p.) Clubs: Harvard (Boston), Harvard Varsity (Boston); Province Lake Country Club. Home: 635 Witchtrot Rd Sanbornville NH 03872-4224

BERG, WILLIAM JAMES, language educator, writer, translator; b. Dunkirk, NY, Oct. 26, 1942; s. Francis John and Adalyn Huldah (Goodwin) B.; m. Verity Anne Fry, July 2, 1966 (div. 1985); children— Jennifer Anne, Jessica Lyn; m. Laurey Kramer Martin, Feb. 1, 1986; stepchildren: Stirling Brooke Martin, Hunter Kirk Martin. Cert. pratique, Sorbonne, Paris, 1962-63; BA, Hamilton Coll., 1964; MA, Princeton U., 1966, PhD, 1969. NDEA inst. asst. Hamilton Coll., Clinton, NY, 1964; teaching asst. Princeton (N.J.) U., 1966; instr. French U. Wis., 1967-68, asst. prof., 1968-73, assoc. prof., 1973-79, prof., 1979—, assoc. chmn. French dept., 1974-75, 78-79, 79-80, 90-92, 99-2000, chmn. dept. French and Italian, 1982-85, 2002; dir. Acad. Yr. Abroad, Paris and NYC, 1973-74. Outside examiner Swarthmore Coll., 1978, No. Ill. U., 1985, 86; outside program evaluator U. Mich., 1979; tenure reviewer Swarthmore Coll., 1982, Tulane U., 1985, Marquette U., 1992, 2000, U. Calif., Riverside, 2002, U. Wis.-Milw., 2007, U. Ala., 2007; invited lectr. Rice U., 1985, U. Tenn., 1993; full prof. reviewer Georgetown U., 1984, Swarthmore Coll., 1992, U. Mich., 1994, Northwestern U., 1996, U. Colo., 1997, Va. Tech., 1999, U. Mich., 2001, NYU, 200,; U. Oklahoma, 2002, Dartmouth Coll., 2006; editl. bd. Summa Publs., Birmingham, Ala., 1983—; reviewer panel for travel and collections NEH, 1989. Author: (with P. Schofer and D. Rice) Poèmes, Pièces, Prose, 1973, (with G. Moskos and M. Grimaud) Saint/Oedipus. Psychocritical Approaches to Flaubert's Art, 1982; (with L. Martin) Images, 1989, The Visual Novel, 1992, (with L. Martin) Emile Zola Revisited, 1992, Gustave Flaubert, 1997, (with S. Magnan, Y. Ozzello and L. Martin-Berg) Paroles, 1999, 3d edit., 2005, Imagery and Ideology, 2007; author study guides on Twain's Huckleberry Finn, 1986, Tom Sawyer, 1987; (with L. Martin) Flaubert's Madame Bovary, 1989, Zola's Germinal, 1989, Maupassant's Short Stories, 1992; translator: (with P. Scott) Graphics and Graphic Information-Processing, 1981; Semiology of Graphics (design award Midwest Books Competition 1983), 1983-84; mem. editl. bd. Substance, 1971-79; contbr. articles to profl. jours. Travel grant Am. Philos. Soc., 1969, Rsch. grant U. Wis., 1969, 75, 81-82, 86, 87; Vilas assoc., 1991-93, honors fellow, 1994—; Halverson-Bascom professorship, 1995-2000; recipient U. Wis. Chancellor's award for excellence in tchg., 1995. Mem. MLA, Am. Coun. Tchrs. Fgn. Langs., Am. Assn. Tchrs. French, Phi Beta Kappa. Home: 5201 Pepin Pl Madison WI 53705-4724 Office: U Wis Dept French and Italian Madison WI 53706 Office Phone: 608-262-3941. Business E-Mail: wjberg@wisc.edu.

BERG, YEHUDA, rabbi, author, television personality; BA, MHL, Yeshiva Rabbinical Seminary of America, NYC; studied, Yeshivat Shaar Ha Torah. Odeained Rabbi Yeshiva Knesset Israel, Jerusalem. Religious dir. The Kabbalah Children's Acad.; assoc. dir., spiritual advisor The Kabbalah Centre. Editor Kabbalistic Daily and Shabbat Prayer Books. Editor: Kaballistic Chumash; author: Power of Kabbalah, 2002, The 72 Names of God, 2003, The Dreams Book, 2004, The Red String Book, 2004. Named one of The Top 50 Rabbis in America, Newsweek Mag., 2007. Office: Kabbalah Publ 1054 S Robertson Blvd Los Angeles CA 90035*

BERGA, SARAH L., obstetrician, gynecologist, educator; b. San Benito, Tex., May 22, 1954; d. John Orrin and Nancy Estelle (Michael) B.; m. Frederick S. Sherman, Sept. 26, 1981 (div. 1994); children: Alexis Estelle, Nathaniel Abbott; m. Lockwood Hoehl, Oct. 28, 1995. BA, U. Va., Charlottesville, 1976, MD, 1980. Diplomate Am. Bd. Ob-Gyn., Am. Bd. Reproductive Endocrinology and Infertility. From asst. to assoc. prof. U. Pitts., 1988-2001; dir. reproductive endocrinology and infertility divsn. U. Pitts. Sch. Medicine, 2000; prof. U. Pitts., 2001—03; prof., chair, dept. gynecology and obstetrics Emory U., Atlanta, 2003—. Mem.: Am. Soc. Reproductive Medicine (bd. dirs. 2002—04), Soc. Gynecologic Investigation (coun. mem. 1999—2002). Office: Emory U Sch Medicine Dept GYNOB Atlanta GA 30322 Home: 21 Palisades Road NE Atlanta GA 30309 Office Phone: 404-727-8600. Business E-Mail: sberga@emory.edu.

BERGAN, EDMUND PAUL, JR., lawyer; b. NYC, May 6, 1950; s. Edmund Paul and Alice (Gordon) P. B.; m. Patricia Ann Gallagher, Jan. 31, 1987; children: Annabel (dec.), Caroline. BA, Holy Cross Coll., 1971; JD, Fordham U., 1975. Bar: N.Y. 1976. Staff atty. SEC, Washington, D.C., 1975-77; v.p., assoc. gen. counsel Securities Industry Assn., NYC, 1977-81; v.p., asst. gen. counsel Alliance Capital Mgmt. LP, NYC, 1981-88; v.p. gen. counsel Alliance Fund Distbrs., NYC, 1988-94; v.p., gen. counsel Alliance Fund Svc. Subs., NYC, 1988-94; sr. v.p., gen. counsel Alliance Fund Svcs. (now Alliance Global Investor Svcs., Inc.) and Alliance Fund Distbrs. (now Alliance Bernstein Investment Rsch. and Mgmt., Inc.), NYC, 1994—2003; vice chmn., CEO France Growth Fund Inc., NYC, 2004—; sr. regulatory counsel Proskauer Rose LLP, NYC, 2005—06; sr. v.p., gen. counsel, sec., bd. dirs. The Reserve, NYC, 2006—07; gen. counsel, chief compliance officer Westford Asset Mgmt. LLC, NYC, 2007—. Mem. ABA (mem. fed. securities com. 1982—, investment advisers and cos. subcom. 1999—), Investment Co. Inst. (SEC rules com. 1986—2003, closed-end fund com. 1989—2003, chmn. 1992-97, various subcoms.), Assn. Bar City N.Y. (investment mgmt. com. 1999—). Republican. Roman Catholic. Avocations: history, sports. Office Phone: 561-237-2500. Business E-Mail: bergan@westfordfunds.com.

BERGAN, WILLIAM LUKE, lawyer; b. Auburn, NY, Sept. 3, 1939; s. Luke Joseph and Mary Beatrice (Twyne) B.; m. Marilyn Terese Meister, Aug. 8, 1964 (dec. May 1990); children: William Luke, Elizabeth M., Ann G.; m. Frances Maureen West, Jan. 2, 1993. BA summa cum laude, Niagara U., Niagara Falls, NY, 1961; JD magna cum laude, Syracuse U., 1964. Bar: N.Y. 1964, U.S. Dist. Ct. (we. dist.) N.Y. 1977, U.S. Dist. Ct. (no. dist.) N.Y. 1968, U.S. Ct. Appeals (2d cir.) 1970. Sr. ptnr. Bond, Schoeneck & King, Syracuse, 1966—. Trustee, past pres. parish coun. St. John the Evangelist Ch., Syracuse, 1993—. Capt. U.S. Army, 1964-66. Fellow Am. Bar Found., Coll. Labor and Employment Lawyers; mem. ABA, N.Y. State Bar Assn. (chmn. labor and employment law sect. 1981-82, exec. com. 1976—), Onondaga County Bar Assn., Nat. Assn. Coll. and Univ. Attys., Am. Arbitration Assn. (bd. dirs. 1984-2000), Greater Syracuse C. of C. (bd. dirs. 1992-96), Niagara U. Alumni Assn., Century Club Syracuse. Democrat. Roman Catholic. Avocation: tennis. Office Phone: 315-218-8218. E-mail: wbergan@bsk.com.

BERGAU, FRANK CONRAD, real estate, commercial and investment properties executive; b. NYC, Sept. 17, 1926; s. Frank Conrad and Mary Elizabeth (Davie) B.; m. Rita I. Korotkin; children: Mary, Rita, Francis, Theresa, Veronica. BA in English, St. Francis Coll., Loretto, Pa., 1950; MS in Edn. and English, Potsdam State U., NY, 1969. Cert. tchr., supr., adminstr., N.Y.; cert. comml. investment mem. Tchr. English, Gouverneur (N.Y.) Schs., 1962-81, dir. continuing edn., 1968-81, summer prin., 1974-80; project dir. St. Lawrence County (N.Y.) Bd. Co-op Ednl. Svcs., Canton, 1974; pres. Irenicon Assocs., Clermont, Fla. Bd. dirs. St. Lawrence County Assn. Retarded Children, 1965—; pres. bd. dirs. Gouverneur Libr.; mem. Family Care Coun., Fla. Dist. 13. Mem.: KC (fin. sec. coun. 13240), NEA, N.Y. Assn. Continuing Edn. (dir.), South Lake County Devel. Coun. (pres.), Lake County Bd. Realtors, Nat. Assn. Realtors, Gouverneur C. of C. (bd. dirs. 1963—66), Kiwanis (creator Terrific Kids award 1985), Gouverneur Luncheon Club. Personal E-mail: irenicon@verizon.net.

BERGDOLL, BARRY G., architectural historian, educator; b. Apr. 16, 1955; PhD, Columbia U., NYC, 1986. Faculty dept. art history and archaeology Columbia U., 1986—, prof., chmn. dept. art history and archaeology; chief curator arch. and design Mus. Modern Art, 2007—. Contbr. articles to profl. jours., chapters to books; co-author: Friedrich Weinbrenner, 1984, Mies in Berlin, 2001, The Eiffel Tower, 2002; author: Léon Vaudoyer: Historicism in the Age of Industry, 1994, Karl Friedrich Schinkel: An Architecture for Prussia, 1994, European Architecture 1750—1890, 2000; co-curator (exhibitions) Mies in Berlin, curator Le Panthéon: Symbole des Révolutions, 1989, Les Vaudoyers: une dynastie d'architectes, Paris, 1992. Recipient J.P. Morgan Berlin prize, Am. Acad. Berlin, 2005. Mem.: Soc. Archtl. Historians (pres. 2006—). Office: Columbia U 909 Schermerhorn Hall 1190 Amsterdam Ave New York NY 10027 Office Phone: 212-854-4505. E-mail: bgb1@columbia.edu.

BERGE, ANNA CATHARINA BJÖRNSDOTTER, veterinarian, epidemiologist; b. Linköping, Östergötland, Sweden, Oct. 1, 1966; arrived in U.S., 1998; d. Björn Leif and Gunnel Elisabet Berge. DVM, Swedish Agrl. U., Uppsala, 1991; M in Preventive Vet. Medicine, U. Calif., Davis, 2001, PhD in Comparative Pathology, 2004. Lic. vet. Swedish Bd. Agr. State large animal vet. practitioner Swedish Bd. Agr., Östersund, Jämtland, Sweden, 1992, vet. insp. Jönköping, Småland, Sweden, 1992—95; sr. vet. insp. Nat. Food Adminstrn., Uppsala, 1995—98; nat. expert European Commn., Brussels, 1996; assoc. rschr. U. Calif., Davis, 2004—07. Pres. Girls Ultracycling, Visalia, Calif., 2005—06; founder Internat. Coun. for Ultra Cycling, 2006—. Named Ultracyclist of the Yr., Perimeter Bicycling Assn.-Race Across Am., 2005; fellow, Western Inst. Food Safety and Security, 2004—05; Rsch. grant, Elsa och Ivar Sandbergs Fond, 1999. Fellow: Calif. Agrl. Leadership Foun.; mem.: Am. Soc. Microbiology. Office: Field Disease Investigation Unit Wash State U Sch Vet Med Pullman WA 99164 Home Phone: 559-799-1699. Personal E-mail: acbberge@hotmail.com. Business E-Mail: cberge@vetmed.wsu.edu.

BERGÉ, PIERRE, apparel design executive; b. Nov. 14, 1930; Founder, chmn., mng. dir. Yves Saint Laurent, NYC, 1961—. Bd. dirs. C. Mendes SA, Dollfus-Mieg & Cie, DEFI, Fondation Cartier, Parsons Sch. Design, France Libertes-Danielle Mitterrand Found.; pres. Inst. de la Mode, 1986—. Founder La Patrie Mondiale jour., 1949. Founder Lundis Musicaux de l'Athenee, 1977; pres. Chinese House of Democracy, 1989—, Arcat-Sida; chmn. Paris Opera House, 1988; goodwill amb. UNESCO, 1993. Recipient Diploma of Honour and Gold medal Weizmann Inst. Sci.; named Kinght Legion Honour, 1985, Officer Nat. Order Merit, 1987, Officer Legion of Honour, 1992, Commdr. Art and Litterature, 1992, UNESCO Goodwill Amb., 1993. also: Yves Saint Laurent 5 ave Marceau 75116 Paris 16 France

BERGEN, BENJAMIN KARL, research scientist; b. Atlanta, Nov. 19, 1969; s. Dale Lee Bergen and Radine Lee Robinson. B, Emory U., Atlanta, 1993; M in Applied Math., U. Colo., Boulder, 2001; DEng, U. Erlangen-Nuremberg, Germany, 2004. Rsch. asst. U. Erlangen-Nuremberg, 2001—04; rsch. scientist Los Alamos Nat. Lab., N.Mex., 2004—. Contbr.

scientific papers. Home: 2122 D 41st St Los Alamos NM 87544 Office: Los Alamos Nat Lab Los Alamos NM 87545 Home Phone: 505-412-9718; Office Phone: 505-606-1886. Personal E-mail: ben.bergen@gmail.com. Business E-Mail: bergen@lanl.gov.

BERGEN, CANDICE, actress, writer, photojournalist; b. Beverly Hills, Calif., May 9, 1946; d. Edgar and Frances (Westerman) B.; m. Louis Malle, Sept. 27, 1980 (dec. 1995); 1 child, Chloe; m. Marshall Rose, June 15, 2000. Student, U. Pa. Model during coll. Actor (films) The Group, The Sand Pebbles, 1966, The Day the Fish Came Out, Live for Life, 1967, The Magus, 1968, Soldier Blue, The Executioner, The Adventurers, Getting Straight, 1970, The Hunting Party, 1970, Carnal Knowledge, 1970, 19 T.R. Baskin, 1971, 11 Harrowhouse, 1974, Bite the Bullet, The Wind and the Lion, 1975, The Domino Principle, The End of the World in Our Usual Bed in a Night Full of Rain, Oliver's Story, 1978, Starting Over, 1979, Rich and Famous, 1981, Gandhi, 1982, Stick, 1985, Miss Congeniality, 2000, Sweet Home Alabama, 2002, View from the Top, 2003, The In-Laws, 2003; (TV films) Arthur the King, 1985, Murder by Reason of Insanity, 1985, Mayflower Madam, 1987, Shelley Duvall's Bedtime Stories, Vol. 7, 1993, Mary and Tim, 1996 (TV appearances) What's My Line, 1965, Coronet Blue, 1967, The Muppet Show, 1976, The Way They Were, 1981, 2010 (voice), 1984, Trying Times, 1987, Seinfeld, 1990, Images of Life: Photographs that have Changed the World, 1996, The Human Face (miniseries), 2001, Murphy Brown: TV Tales, 2002, Sex and the City, 2002; (TV series) Murphy Brown, 1988-98 (Emmy award, Leading Actress in a Comedy Series, 1989, 90, 92, 94, 95), Boston Legal, 2004-; (TV miniseries) Hollywood Wives, 1985, Trying Times, Moving Day; author Knockwood; photojournalist credits include articles for Life, Playboy; dramatist: (play) The Freezer (included in Best Short Plays of 1968).

BERGEN, DORIS, psychologist, educator; b. St. Louis, Mo., Feb. 11, 1932; m. Joel S. Fink; m. James Sponseller (div.); children: Ellen Creager, Holly Andrecheck, Gail Burnett. Student, Heidelberg Coll., 1949—51; BS, Ohio State U., 1953; MA, Mich. State U., 1970, PhD, 1974. Instr., asst. prof., assoc. prof. Oakland U., Rochester, Minn., 1970—80; dean grad. sch. Wheelock Coll., Boston, 1980—84; dean grad. studies and rsch. Pittsburg State U., Pittsburg, Kans., 1984—88; prof., chair Ednl. Psychology Dept. Miami U., Oxford, Ohio, 1988—98, prof., dir. Ctr. for Human Devel., Learning and Tchg., 1998—. Assoc. dean Oakland U., Rochester, 1979—80; vis. scholar Com. Scholarly Comm. with China NAS, 1989—91; cons. Fisher-Price, Inc., 2000—; trainer Heads Up Network, 1998—99; cons. PBS TV program, Dooley and Pals, 1995—99; cons. Mayerson Found., 1994—95; cons. High/Scope, 1990—91. Author: Assessment Methods for Infants and Toddlers: Transdisciplinary Team Approaches, 1994, 2003, Human Development: Traditional and Contemporary Theories, 2007; co-author (with J.M. Coscia): Brain Research and Childhood Education: Implications for Educators, 2001, 2006; co-author: (with R. Reid, L. Torelli) Educating and Caring for Infants and Toddlers: A Comprehensive Curriculum, 2000; editor: Play as a Learning Medium, 1974, Play as a Learning Medium, 2d printing, 1976, Play as a Learning Medium, 3d printing, 1978, Play as a Learning Medium, 4th printing, 1982, Play as a Medium for Learning and Development: A Handbook of Theory and Practice, 1988, Readings from Play as a Medium for Learning and Development, 1998; co-editor (with D. Fromberg): Play from Birth to Twelve, Perspectives and Meanings, 1998; co-editor:, 2006; contbr. chpts. in books, articles to profl. jours., parent brochures, book reviews, curriculum manuals, govt. booklets; presenter at scholarly meetings. Grantee Rsch. on Rescue Heroes, Laugh and Learning, Fisher-Price, Inc., 2001—02, Evaluation of Dragonfly Sci. Inquiry Tng., Eisenhower Grant, 1996—99, Evaluation of Oxford/Talawanda Family Resource Ctr., Oxford/Talawanda Cmty. Svcs., 1999, Evaluation of RISE Winning Teams Early Childhood Tng., Ohio Dept. Edn., 1996—98, Evaluation of Butler County Early Intervention Tracking Program, Civitan Svc. Club, 1996—98, Instl. Devel. Grant, U.S. Dept. Edn., 1986—89, Birth through Seven: Early Intervention and Preschool Spl. Needs, U.S. Dept. Spl. Edn., 1981—84, Day Care Policy: Views of Parents and Practitioners in Mich., NSF, 1979—80. Fellow: Am. Orthopsychiatric Soc., Assn. Psychological Sci.; mem.: Nat. Assn. Early Childhood Tchr. Educators (sec. 2000—02, Found. bd. dirs.), Jean Piaget Soc., Coun. Exceptional Children (divsn. Early Childhood), Soc. Rsch. Adminstrs., Am. Evaluation Soc., Assn. for Study of Play, Nat. Assn. for Edn. Young Children (governing bd. 1996—), Soc. Rsch. in Child Devel., Am. Ednl. Rsch. Assn. (Early Childhood sect., bd. dirs. 1998—2000), Assn. Childhood Edn. Internat., Internat. Humor Soc., Phi Delta Theta, Phi Kappa Phi. Office: Miami Univ 100G McGuffey Hall Oxford OH 45056 Office Phone: 513-529-6622. Business E-Mail: bergend@mohio.edu.

BERGEN, JEFFREY BRUCE, art gallery owner; b. NYC, Jan. 14, 1953; s. Sidney and Pearl Bergen; m. Dorian Perchik, June 16, 1985; children: Casey, Vaughn. BA, Antioch Coll., Yellow Springs, Ohio, 1977. Pres., dir. ACA Galleries, NYC, 1978—. Office: ACA Galleries 529 W 20th St New York NY 10011 Office Phone: 212-206-8080. Business E-Mail: info@acagalleries.com.

BERGEN, JOHN DONALD, public relations and communications executive; b. Bronx, NY, Sept. 16, 1942; s. John D. and Alice Jean (Almand) B.; m. Linda L. Rosewall, Nov. 21, 1964; children: John M., Michael L. BS in Engring., U.S. Mil. Acad., 1964; MA in English, Ind. U., 1971. Commd. 2d lt. U.S. Army, 1964, advanced through grades to lt. col., 1968; battalion advisor Vietnam, 1968-69; comdr. U.S. Army, Republic of Korea, 1974-76; prof. U.S. Mil. Acad., West Point, N.Y., 1971-74; strategic planner Dept. Def., Washington, 1976-81; dir. speechwriting and issue mgmt. Office of Sec. Def., Washington, 1981-84; v.p., corp. affairs RCA, NYC, 1984-86; mgr. corp. affairs Gen. Electric Corp., Fairfield, Conn., 1986; sr. v.p., chief adminstrv. officer Hill & Knowlton, Inc., NYC, 1987, exec. v.p., gen. mgr. ea. region, 1988-90, also bd. dirs.; pres., COO, Hill and Knowlton USA, NYC, 1990-91; pres., CEO, GCI Group, NYC, 1991-96; sr. v.p. corp. rels. Westinghouse/CBS, NYC, 1996-98; pres. Coun. of PR Firms, 1998—2001; sr. v.p. corp. affairs and mktg. Siemens Corp., 2001—. Author: Military Communications: A Test for Technology, 1987; contbr. articles to profl. and tech. jours. Chmn. Inst. of Pub. Rels. Named Outstanding Young Am., Jaycees, 1973. Mem. Pub. Rels. Soc. Am., Pub. Rels. Seminar, Arthur W. Page Soc. Roman Catholic. Avocations: tennis, soccer, sports officiating. Home: 1789 Wrightstown Rd Newtown PA 18940-2603 Office: Siemens Corp 153 E 53rd St New York NY 10022 E-mail: jack.bergen@siemens.org.

BERGEN, POLLY, actress; b. Bluegrass, Tenn. d. William and Lucy (Lawhorn) Burgin; m. Freddie Fields, Feb. 13, 1956 (div. 1976); children: Kathy, Pamela, Peter. Pres. Polly Bergen Cosmetics, Polly Bergen Jewelry, Polly Bergen Shoes. Author: Fashion and Charm, 1960, Polly's Principles, 1974, I'd Love To, But What'll I Wear, 1977; author, producer for TV: Leave of Absence, 1994; Broadway plays include Champagne Complex, John Murray Andersons' Almanac, First Impression, Plaza Suite, Love Letters, Follies (Best Supporting Actress Tony and Drama Desk nominee), The Vagina Monologues, Cabaret; films include Cape Fear, Move Over Darling, Kisses for My President, At War with the Army, The Stooge, That's My Boy, The Caretakers, A Guide for the Married Man, Making Mr. Right, Cry-Baby, 1990, Dr. Jekyll and Ms. Hyde, When We Were Colored, 1994; performed in one woman shows in Las Vegas, Nev., and Reno; albums: Bergen Sings Morgan, The Party's Over, All Alone By the Telephone, Polly and Her Pop, The Four Seasons of Love, Annie Get Your Gun and Do Re Mi, My Heart Sings, Act One Sing Too; numerous TV appearances including star of The Polly Bergen Show, NBC-TV; other TV appearances include The Helen Morgan Story, 1957 (Emmy award as best actress), To Tell the Truth, The Lightning Field, The Surrogate, For Hope; miniseries include The Winds of War (Emmy nomination), 79 Park Ave, War and Remembrance, 1988 (Emmy nomination); writer, prodr. NBC movie Leave of Absence, 1994. Bd. dirs. Martha Graham Dance Ctr., The Singer Co., Soc. Singers, Calif. Abortion and Reproductive Rights Action League, Show Coalition; hon. canister campaign chairperson Cancer Care, Inc., Nat. Cancer Found.; founder Nat. Bus. Coun. for ERA; mem. Planned Parenthood Fedn., Am. Bd. Advs.; mem. nat. adv. com. NARAL, Hollywood Women's Polit. Com. Recipient Fame award Top Ten in TV, 1957-58, Troupers award Sterling Publs., 1957, Editors and Critics award Radio and TV Daily, 1958, Outstanding Working Woman award Downtown St. Louis, Inc., Golden Plate award Am. Acad. Achievement, 1969, Outstanding Mother's award Nat. Mothers' Day Com., 1984, Best Achievement in New Jewelry Design award, 1986, Cancer Care award, 1989, Woman of Achievement award LWV, 1990, Extraordinary Achievement award Nat. Women's Law Ctr., 1991, Freedom of Choice award Calif. Abortion and Reproductive Rights Action League, 1992; Polly Bergen Cardio-Pulmonary Rsch. Lab., Children's Rsch. Inst. and Hosp., Denver dedicated, 1970. Mem. AFTRA, AGVA, SAG, Actors Equity. Office: 1746 S Britain Rd Southbury CT 06488-3200 E-mail: zimzack@msn.com.

BERGEN, STANLEY SILVERS, JR., retired academic administrator; b. Princeton, NJ, May 2, 1929; s. Stanley Silvers and Leah (Johnson) B.; m. Suzanne E. Miller, Nov. 16, 1965; children: Stephen Richard, Victoria Elizabeth, Stuart Vaughn; children by previous marriage: Stanley Silvers III, Amy Dorle. AB, Princeton U., 1951; MD, Columbia U., 1955; degree (hon.), Bloomfield Coll., 1972, Stevens Inst., 1985; LLD (hon.), Princeton U., 1995; DSc (hon.), Patterson State U., NJ, 1997, Ramapo Coll. NJ, 1997, NJ Inst. Tech., 1998; DHL (hon.), Univ. Medicine Dentistry NJ, 2002. Resident St. Luke's Hosp., NYC, 1955-58, chief resident, Francis Zabriskie fellow, 1958-59, asst. chief dept. medicine, 1959-60, asst. attending physician, 1962-64; med. dir. Convalescent and Research Unit, Greenwich, Conn., 1962-64; chief medicine Cumberland Hosp., Bklyn., 1964-68; asst. dir. dept. medicine Bklyn.-Cumberland Med. Center, 1964-68, chief community medicine, 1968-70; sr. v.p. N.Y.C. Health & Hosps. Corp., 1970-71; instr. medicine Columbia, 1959-64; asso. prof. medicine Downstate Med. Sch., Bklyn., 1964-71; pres. U. Medicine and Dentistry N.J., Newark, 1971-98, founding pres. emeritus, 1998—. Prof. medicine N.J. Med. Sch., Robert Wood Johnson Med. Sch., Sch. Osteo. Medicine; prof. cmty. dentistry N.J. Dental Sch.; attending med. staff Univ. Hosp., Newark, 1971-2004, VA Hosp., East Orange, 1972-98, Robert Wood Johnson U. Hosp., 1981-98; trustee Univ. HealthCare Corp., 1993-99; chair bd. trustees Univ. Health Plans N.J., 1994-99; trustee University Heights Sci. Park, 1995-2004, chmn. bd., 1996-2004. Author articles in field. Mem. Mayor's Commn. Health and Hosps., N.Y.C., 1969-70; mem. N.J. Comprehensive Health Planning Coun., 1971-91; chmn. N.J. Commn. to Study Structure and Function N.J. Dept. Health, 1973, N.J. Abortion Commn., 1975, Adv. Coun. Grad. Edn. N.J., 1978-98; adv. com. mcpl. health svc. program R.W. Johnson, also. Nat. Conf. Mayors, 1980-85; mem. Bd. Comprehensive Health, Newark, 1976-81, treas., 1972-80; bd. dirs. Cancer Inst. N.J., 1974-98; bd. dirs. Ednl. Commn. Fgn. Med. Grads., 1982-91, sec., vice chmn., 1985-86, chmn., 1986-91; bd. dirs., mem. exec. com. Hastings Ctr. on Biomed. Ethics, 1976-2004, chmn. devel. com., 1980-95, mem. governance com., 1995-, chmn. elect, 1997, chmn., 1998-2004; bd. dirs., mem. exec. com. Art Center No. N.J., 1978-82; chmn. N.J. Blood Banks Task Force, 1980-90; trustee Robert Wood Johnson U. Hosp., 1985-98, exec. com. 1987-98; trustee Hackensack Med. Ctr., 1990-99, exec. com., 1992-99; bd. joint mgrs. Cancer Inst. N.J., 1991-98, trustee 1998-2002; trustee Bergen Pines County Hosp., 1994-98, exec. com. 1994-98, trustee Univ. Healthcare Corp. of N.J., 1993-97, Gilda's Club No. N.J., 1997-2000, treas., mem. exec. com., 1998-2000, Kessler Med. Rehab. Rsch. Edn. Corp., 1998-2003, Matheny Sch. and Hosp., 1998-2000, Internat. Ctr. Pub. Health Inc., 1999-2004; treas. Pres.'s Coun. N.J. Commn. Higher Edn., 1996-98; chmn. bd. trustees U. Health Plan N.J., 1997-99; chair bd. mgrs. N.J. Ctr. Biomaterials, 1997-02; bd. dirs. Blue Hill Meml. Hosp., 2000- , vice chmn. bd., 2001-04, chmn. bd. 2004-07; sec. Found. Blue Hill Meml. Hosp., 2007—; chair strategic planning com. Eastern Maine Healthcare Sys., 2002-, nomination com., 2004-, exec. compensation, 2006—, co-chair, CEO search com., 2005-06; chair ad hoc com. on Waterville Jint Venture and New Hosp., 2006-07; chair bd. dirs. MedTower, 2000-04; chair bd. dirs. Opera House Arts, Stonington, Maine, 2003—; mem. sci. adv. bd. Maine Inst. Human Genetics and Health, 2007—. First recipient Woodrow Wilson medal for pub. svc. leadership Gov. of N.J., 1987, Univ. medal UMDNJ, 1995. Fellow ACP, Assn. Am. Med. Colls., Am. Fedn. Clin. Rsch., Endocrine Soc., Clin. Soc. N.Y., Diabetes Assn. (v.p. 1969-70, chmn. clin. soc. 1968-69), N.Y. Acad. Scis., Am. Inst. Nutrition; mem. AMA (ho. dels. sect. on med. schs. 1978-98), Assn. Acad. Health Ctrs., Am. Diabetes Assn. (bd. dirs. N.J. affiliate), Am. Soc. Clin. Nutrition, Am. Coll. Healthcare Execs. (hon. fellow), Essex County Med. Soc., Med. Soc. N.J., Am. Hosp. Assn. (trustee 1992-94, chmn. com. grad. med. edn. 1974-76, mem. coun. profl. svcs. 1973-76, mem. governing coun. sect. met. hosps. 1984-87, com. med. edn. 1984-91, ad hoc com. on AIDS 1987-91, chmn. tech. com. biomed. ethics 1986-91, alt. del. Ho. Dels., 1991, mem. AHA regional policy bd., 1988-94, mem. internat. med. scholars program 1987-92, mem. com. to study single pathway to nat. med. licensure 1987-90, mem. com. to study clin. med. skills assessement 1988-92, trustee 1991-94, trustee regional plan commn. 1995-98), Greater Newark C. of C. (dir. 1978-84), Nat. Assn. Pub. Hosps. (trustee 1982-88), State N.J. Health Coord. Coun., Univ. Health System N.J. (trustee, exec. com. 1987-98), Univ. Hosp. Consortium (trustee 1988-92, exec. com. 1990-92), N.Y. Acad. Scis., Opera House Arts (mem. bd. advisors, 2002-, chair facilities com., 2003-, chmn. bd. 2003—). Home: 44 Greenhead Ln Stonington ME 04681 Office: U Medicine & Dentistry NJ 100 Bergen St Newark NJ 07103-2407 Personal E-mail: sasbergen@aol.com. *My career has taken many significant turns, most of which have improved my ability to lead efforts toward better and more accessible health services. I have been fortunate in the opportunity to lead a variety of activities and to express creativity through institutions and individuals. My successes are due to the extent to which this nation still rewards those willing to work hard and learn from experience, as well as to the many intelligent, compassionate mentors with whose guidance I have been blessed.*

BERGENN, JAMES WALTER, lawyer; b. Bklyn., Nov. 21, 1954; s. Walter R. and V. Patricia B.; children: Kristin, Eric; m. Susan King; stepchildren: Thomas, Christopher. BA in Polit. Philosophy, Cath. U. Am., 1976; JD, Columbia U., 1979. Bar: Conn. 1979, U.S. Dist. Ct. Conn. 1979, U.S. Ct. Appeals (2d cir.) 1981. Law clk. Chief Judge U.S. Dist. Ct. Conn., Hartford, 1979-80; assoc. Shipman & Goodwin, Hartford, 1980-81, 1983-86, ptnr., 1987—; asst. defender Office of the Fed. Pub. Defender, Hartford, 1981-83. Lectr. U. Conn. Sch. Law, 1986—. Editor of daily polit. report to Pres. Carter during Carter-Mondale Reelection Campaign, 1980. Pres. Hartford Apt. Improvement Program, Inc., 1980-86; mem. Glastonbury Conservation Commn., 1985-87, Glastonbury Dem. Town Com., 1988-96, chair 1994-95; lector St. Paul's Roman Cath. Ch., 1986-96, instr., 1988-94; lector St. Patrick-St. Anthony's, 2001—. Mem. ABA, Conn. Bar Assn., Hartford County Bar Assn., Assn. Trial Lawyers Am., Conn. Trial Lawyers Assn., Nat. Assn. Criminal Def. Lawyers, Conn. Criminal Def. Lawyers Assn., Nat. Lawyers for Pub. Justice. Democrat. Roman Catholic. Avocations: basketball, skiing, reading. Home: 50 Castlewood Rd West Hartford CT 06107 Office: Shipman & Goodwin 1 Constitution Plz Hartford CT 06103-2833 E-mail: jbergenn@goodrich.com.

BERGER, ALBERT, film producer; Grad., Tufts U.; student, Columbia U., NYC. Owner, mgr. Sandburg Theatre, Chgo.; script writer Paramount Pictures, v.p. devel. Marvin Worth Prodns.; co-founder Bona Fide Prodns., 1993—. Prodr.: (films) King of the Hill, 1993, Election, 1999, The Wood, 1999, Pumpkin, 2002, Cold Mountain, 2003, The Ice Harvest, 2005, Bee Season, 2005, Little Miss Sunshine, 2006 (Darryl F. Zanuck Prodr. of Yr. award in Theatrical Motion Pictures, Prodrs. Guild of Am., 2007), Little Children, 2006; exec. prodr.: Crumb, 1994, I Am Trying to Break Your Heart, 2002; (TV films) The Spree, 1998. Office: Bona Fide Prodns Ste 804 8899 Beverly Blvd Los Angeles CA 90048*

BERGER, ALLAN SIDNEY, psychiatrist, educator; b. NYC, Nov. 26, 1931; s. Nathan and Ida (Masor) B.; m. Lois Harriet Blumfield, Dec. 27, 1953; children: Karen, Gary, Jonathan. AB magna cum laude, Syracuse U., 1951; MD, SUNY, Bklyn., 1955. Diplomate Am. Bd. Psychiatry and Neurology, 1962; additional qualification in geriatric psychiatry cert., 1991. Intern L.I. Coll. Hosp., NYC, 1955-56; resident Yale U. Sch. Medicine, New Haven, 1956-58, fellow Yale Child Study Ctr., 1958-59; pvt. practice Silver Spring, Md., 1961—; asst. chief D.C. Gen. Hosp., Washington, 1961-62. Clin. prof. Georgetown U. Sch. Medicine, Washington, 1986—; cons. NIH, 1987-88; command cons. Nat. Naval Med. Ctr. Bethesda, 1990-97; mem. physician expert panel VA, 1993-96; mem. peer rev. com. on behalf of Md. Med. Licensing Bd., 1992-2003. Contbr. articles to profl. jours. Cons. Peace Corps, 1962, Hebrew Home for the Aged, Rockville, Md., 1962-72. Recipient Vicennial Medalist award Georgetown U. Sch. Medicine, 1981. Mem. AMA, Mid-Atlantic Group Psychotherapy Soc. (bd. dirs. 1977-78), Metro. Washington Soc. Adolescent Psychiatry (treas. 1979-80, pres. 1982-83), Med. and Chirurgical Faculty Md., B'nai B'rith. Republican. Avocations: tennis, swimming, gardening. Home and Office: 1302 Midwood Pl Silver Spring MD 20910-1645 Office Phone: 301-589-1443.

BERGER, ANDRE, plastic surgeon; m. Tracy Berger; children: Adam, Joshua, Gabrielle. MD, U. Ottawa. Cert. Holistic Medicine, Emergency Medicine. Internal medicine & clin. pharmacology resident McGill U.; co-founder & prin. Managed Provider Networks, Inc., 1993—2000; co-founder, pres./prin., & sr. lead cons. Absolute Health Svcs., Beverly Hills, Calif., 2000—; founder Rejuvalife Vitality Inst., Beverly Hills, Calif., 2003—. Mem.: Am. Acad. Bioenergetic Medicine, Am. Soc. Aesthetic Mesotherapy, Am. Assn. Clin. Endocrinologists, Am. Coll. Nutrition, Am. Holistic Med. Assn., Am. Acad. Anti-Aging Medicine. Office: Rejuvalife Vitality Inst Ste 405 9400 Brighton Way Beverly Hills CA 90210 also: Absolute Health Svcs 333 S Oakhurst Dr Beverly Hills CA 90212 Office Phone: 310-276-4494, 310-285-9910. Office Fax: 310-285-9920. E-mail: info@absolutehs.com, info@rejuvalife.md.*

BERGER, ARTHUR SEYMOUR, organization executive, former city official; b. NYC, Sept. 19, 1920; m. Joyce Berger. JD cum laude, NYU. Bar: NY 1949. Mcpl. atty. State of N.Y., 1963-71; pres. Survival Rsch. Found., Miami, Fla., 1981—; dir. Internat. Inst. for Study of Death, 1985—; instr. Inst. for Ret. Profls., U. Miami, 1999; instr. Lifelong Learning Soc., Fla. Atlantic U.; vice mayor City of Aventura. Instr. Acad. for Lifelong Learning, Fla. Internat. U., adj. prof., 1996-97; instr. Fla. Atlantic U. Lifelong Learning Soc., Inst. for Ret. Profls., U. Miami, Nova Southeastern U.; adj. prof. Broward Coll., 1989-94, Union Inst., 1990-92; cons. Readers Digest; former commr. City of Aventura, Fla. Author: Liberation of the Person, 1964, Aristocracy of the Dead, 1987, Lives and Letters in American Parapsychology, 1988 (outstanding acad. book list), Evidence of Life After Death: Casebook for Tough-Minded, 1988, Dying and Death in Law and Medicine, 1993, When Life Ends, 1995; co-author: The Encyclopedia of Parapsychology and Physical Research, 1991, Fear of the Unknown, 1995; co-editor: Religion and Parapsychology, 1989, Perspectives in Death and Dying, 1989, To Die or Not to Die?, 1990; mem. NYU Law Rev. Mem. Aventura (Fla.) City Commn.; former mem. ethics com. Columbia Aventura Hosp. and Med. Ctr.; narrator reading program for blind Libr. of Congress. 1st lt. U.S. Army, 1942-46, 50-52. Recipient Ashby Meml. award Acad. Religion, grantee, 1985, Phys. Rsch. Found., 1984, Fla. Endowment of the Arts, 1989. Mem. DAV (life), Soc. for Sci. Exploration, Am. Soc. for Psychical Rsch., Soc. for Psychical Rsch., Parapsychol. Assn. Personal E-mail: s5rf@aol.com.

BERGER, BARBARA, special education educator, consultant; b. Bklyn. d. Salvatore and Jean Pisano; m. Charles R. Berger; children: Allison, Rachel. AAS in Merchandising, Fashion Inst. Tech., NYC, 1963; BS in Elem. Edn., Empire State Coll. SUNY, Old Westbury, 1988; MS in Edn., Hofstra U., Hemstead, NY, 1992. Rep. GEICO Ins. Co., Hempstead, NY, 1963—69; tchg. asst. No. Pky. Sch., Uniondale, 1981—89; spl. edn. tchr. Syosset Home Tutoring, 1998—99; tchr. asst. Garden City HS, Garden City, 1989—2001; pres. Exceptional Student Learning Svcs., 2001—. Mem.: Coun. Exceptional Children, Garden City Ret. Tchrs. Assn.

BERGER, BONNIE G., sport psychologist, educator; b. Champaign, Ill., May 20, 1941; d. Bernard G. and Mildred W. Berger; 1 child, Stephen Casher. BS, Wittenberg U., Springfield, Ohio, 1962; MA, Columbia U., NYC, 1965, EdD, 1972. Tchr. George Rogers Clark Jr. H.S., Springfield, Ohio, 1962-64; supr. phys. edn. Agnes Russell Elem. Sch., NYC, 1964-65; asst. prof. SUNY, Geneseo, 1965-66, Dalhousie U., Halifax, N.S., Can., 1969-71, Bklyn. Coll., 1971-77, assoc. prof., 1978-82, prof., 1982-93, dir. Sport Psychology Lab., dep. chair dept. phys. edn., 1989-93; prof., assoc. dean Sch. Phys. and Health Edn. U. Wyo., Laramie, 1993-96, prof., assoc. dean Coll. Health Scis., 1996-99; prof., dir. Sch. Human Movement, Sport and Leisure Studies, Bowling Green State U., Ohio, 1999—. Cons. in field. Author: Free Weights for Women, 1984, Foundations of Exercise Psychology 2d edit., 2007; contbr. chapters to books, articles to profl. jours. Fellow Assn. for Advancement of Applied Sport Psychology (exec. bd.) Am. Acad. Kinesiology and Phys. Edn.; mem. APA, AAHPERD, Internat. Soc. Sports Psychology, N.Am. Soc. Psychology and Phy. Activity. Home: 640 Pine Valley Dr Bowling Green OH 43402 Home Phone: 419-353-1473; Office Phone: 419-372-7234. Business E-Mail: bberger@bgnet.bgsu.edu.

BERGER, CARL BRENDT, art educator; b. Oakland, Calif., July 10, 1940; s. Charles Otto Berger and Gloria Jerrett; m. Giovanna Cocchiarelli, Dec. 16, 2007; children: Sararhenia, Buzz. BFA, U. Hawaii, Honolulu, 1964. Instr. Richmond Art Ctr., Calif., 1964—65, Sch. Visual Arts, NYC, 1967—68, Honolulu Acad. Arts, 1994—2003; pres., founder Mus. of Friends, Walsenburg, 2005—. One-man shows include Kansai Gadai Hawaii Coll., Honolulu, 1996, Chamot Gallery, Jersey City, 2002, exhibited in group shows at US Dept Edn., Washington, 1978, Artists of Hawaii, Acad. of Arts, Honolulu, 1999, SOM Arts, San Francisco, 2001, Mus. of Friends, Walsenburg, Colo., 2007, commissioned, Hawaii State Culture Arts Commn., 1948, Tower Records, 1996, Sheridan Hotel, Poipu, Kauai, 1998. Founder Sunspot Art Cmty., Eastport, Maine, 1969—73. With USAFR, 1958—64. Recipient Weller Trowbridge award, Am. Soc. Graphic Artists, NYC, 1967. Avocations: reading, gardening.

BERGER, CAROLYN, state supreme court justice; BA, U. Rochester, 1969; MA in Elementary Education, Boston U., 1971; JD, Boston U. Sch. of Law, 1976; LLD (hon.), Widener U. Sch. of Law, 1996. Bar: Del. 1976. Dep. atty. gen. Del. Dept. of Justice, 1976—79; assoc. Prickett, Ward, Burt & Sanders, Wilmington, Del., 1979, Skadden, Arps, Slate, Meagher & Flom, Wilmington, Del., 1979—84; vice chancellor Del. Ct. of Chancery, Wilmington, Del., 1984—94; justice Del. Supreme Ct., 1994—. Assoc. mem. Bd. of Bar Examiners. V.p. then pres. Milton & Hattie Kutz Home; mem. Wilmington Community Advisory Council, Junior League of Wilmington; bd. mem. Jewish Federation, Del. Region Nat. Conference of Christians & Jews. Mem.: Del. Bar Assn., Am. Bar Assn., Rodney Inn of Court, Am. Law Inst., Am. Bar Foundation. Office: Del Supreme Ct Carvel State Office Bldg 820 N French St Fl 11 Wilmington DE 19801-3509*

BERGER, CHARLES LEE, lawyer; b. Evansville, Ind., Oct. 14, 1947; s. Sydney L. and Sadelle (Kaplan) B.; m. Leslie Lilly, Apr. 20, 1973; children: Sarah, Rebecca, Leah BA, U. Evansville, 1969; JD cum laude, Ind. U., 1972. Bar: Ind. 1972, U.S. Dist. Ct. (so. dist.) Ind. 1972, U.S. Ct. Appeals (7th cir.) 1972, U.S. Ct. Appeals D.C. 1975, U.S. Supreme Ct. 1977, U.S. Dist. Ct. (we. dist.) Ky. 1981, U.S. Ct. Appeals (6th cir.) 1984. Ptnr. Berger & Berger, Evansville, 1972—. Mem. Ind. Jud. Qualifications Disciplinary Commn., 1998; study com. Rules of Evidence, Ind. Supreme Ct., 1993—, rules com., 2005—. Bd. dirs. Leadership Evansville, 1977 Recipient James Bethel Gresham award, Evansville Bar Assn., 2005. Fellow Ind. Bar Found.; mem. Ind. Bar Assn. (chmn. trial lawyers sect. 1982-83), Am. Bd. Trial Advocates, Ind. Trial Lawyers Assn. (bd. dirs. 1973-77, 77-84, v.p. 1984—) Jewish. Home: 7408 E Sycamore St Evansville IN 47715-3762 Office: Berger & Berger 313 Main St Evansville IN 47708-1485 Home Phone: 812-479-0235; Office Phone: 812-425-8101. Business E-Mail: cberger@bergerlaw.com.

BERGER, DEBORAH KORNBLUTH, educator, consultant, real estate agent; b. Chgo., Oct. 10, 1968; d. Ralph Ross and Anita Dubow Kornbluth; m. Burman Aaron Berger, Mar. 14, 1992; children: Benjamin Adam, Eli Matthew, Ezra Bruce. BA, Emory U., 1990; MEd, Loyola U., Balt., 1993; cert., AMI Assn. Montessori Internat., Washington, 1993. Cert. tchr., Md. Youth advisor B'nai B'rith Youth Orgn., Rockville, Md., 1990—93; spl. asst. ABRH Cons., Washington, 1990—91; dir. youth Kadima Orgn., Rockville, 1991—93; tchr. Hebrew B'nai Shalom, Alexandria, Va., 1991—94, Kehilat Shalom, Gaithersburg, Md., 1992—94; ednl. cons., tchr. Jefferson Montessori, Gaithersburg, 1995—96; elem. directress, tchr. Manor Montessori Internat., Potomac, Md., 1993—98; ednl. tutor, cons., owner Tutoring & Test Preparation by Deborah K. Berger, North Potomac, Md., 1992—; co-owner Acad. Connections LLC, 2005—; real estate agt. Keller Williams Realty, 2005—. Ednl. cons. Flower Hill Sch., Gaithersburg, Butler Sch., 1999-04; mem. adv. bd. B'nai Israel, Rockville, 1998-01; tutor, ednl. cons. Butler Sch., 1999-02. Mem. nursery bd. B'nai Israel, 1998-2001; mem. leadership com. United Jewish Appeal, 1994-95; mem. Jones Cane PTA. Recipient Internat. Gold Star award B'nai B'rith Orgn., 1986, Nat. Leadership Orgn. award of Honor, 1985. Mem. Hadassah, Potomac Chase Women's Assn., Bunco Club, Reading Club. Jewish. Avocations: reading, writing, skiing, dance, volunteering at schools. Office Phone: 301-793-0711. E-mail: tutoringdeb@earthlink.net.

BERGER, FRANK MILAN, biomedical researcher, retired pharmaceutical executive; b. Pilsen, Czech Republic, June 25, 1913; came to U.S., 1947, naturalized, 1953; s. Otto and Martha (Weigner) B.; m. Bozena Jahodova, Mar. 15, 1939 (dec. Nov. 1972); children: Franklin Milan, Thomas Jan; m. A. Christine Spade, May 21, 1975. MD, U. Prague, Czechoslovakia, 1937, SUNY, 1948; D.Sc. (hon.), U. of the Scis. in Phila., 1966. Rsch. fellow physiology U. Prague, 1934-36, rsch. asst. bacteriology, 1936-38; bacteriologist Czechoslovak State Inst. Health, 1938-39; sr. resident Monsall Hosp. Infectious Diseases, Manchester, England, 1941-43; chief pharmacologist Brit. Drug Houses, London, 1945-47; asst. prof. pediatrics U. Rochester, 1947-49; dir. rsch. Carter-Wallace Inc., 1949-55, v.p., 1955-58; pres. Wallace Labs. div. Carter-Wallace Inc., Cranbury, NJ, 1958-73; mem. adv. coun. dept. biology Princeton U., 1961-74, lectr., prof., 1969-74; mem. sci. adv. com. Waksman Inst. Microbiology, Rutgers U., 1960-67; cons. Surgeon Gen., Walter Reed Army Med. Ctr., Washington, 1974-80; pres. Mario Negri Inst. Found. for Biomed. Rsch., Inc., 1973—; prof. psychiatry U. Louisville Med. Sch., 1974-90; hon. prof. microbiology Waksman Inst. Microbiology, Rutgers U., 1982. Chmn. Ad Hoc Study Group on Clin. and Preclin. Pharmacology, 1977-80. Fellow N.Y. Acad. Scis., Am. Coll. Neuropsychopharmacology, AAAS; mem. AMA, AAUP, Am. Pharm. Soc., Brit. Pharm. Soc., Can. Pharm. Soc., Am. Bacteriol. Soc., Soc. Exptl. Biology and Medicine, Am. Chem. Soc., Biometric Soc., Cosmos Club (Washington), N.Y. Athletic Club, Sigma Xi. Achievements include inventing tranquilizer meprobamate, muscle-relaxant mephenesin, pain reliever carisoprodol, antiepileptic felbamate; also method purification penicillin. Office: 200 E 72nd St New York NY 10021-4537 Home Phone: 212-988-1128; Office Phone: 212-794-8520. *Concentrate on the important, rather than the urgent; try not to do what everybody else is doing; and remember that within limits of reason and decency, it is better to do what you like rather than what is expected of you.*

BERGER, FRANK STANLEY, management consultant; b. NYC; s. Ernest A. and Anna Berger; m. Judith Berger; children: Evan, Stacey. BA, Queens Coll.; MBA, NYU; postgrad., N.Y. Law Sch., IBM Edn. Center. Supr. dept. mktg. and fin. analysis Lever Bros.; v.p. fin. and adminstrn. Pacific Enterprises; mem. corp. mktg. staff Joseph E. Seagram & Sons, Inc.; from mktg. asst. to v.p. Calvert Distillers; v.p., gen. sales mgr. Frankfort Distillers, exec. v.p. mktg. and fin., pres., dir.; pres. Gen. Wine & Spirits Co., NYC; pres. and dir. Seagram Distillers Co.; pres., CEO House of Seagram; dir. Joseph E. Seagram & Sons, Inc.; chmn. bd. Quadrillion Investments Inc., 1980-86; chmn. bd., pres. Viceroy Imports, Inc., 1981-86; chmn., CEO Hazel Bishop Cosmetics Inc., 1981-87; dir. Majestic PLC, 1988-89; chmn. bd. dirs., pres. CII, Inc., 1990—; chmn., pres., CEO Naturally Scientific Inc., 1996—. Trustee N.Y. Hall of Sci.; chmn. N.Y. Lunch-o-Ree Boy Scouts Am., United Jewish Appeal, Gaucho Basketball Assn., Cystic Fibrosis Soc.; exec. com. wine and spirits div. Anti-Defamation League, Pro-Am. tennis sponsor Cerebral Palsy; bd. dirs. Bronfman Found. With AUS. Mem. AIM, Nat. Assn. Chain Drug Stores, Am. Mgmt. Assn., Am. Mktg. Assn, NY C. of C., Young Pres.' Orgn., Nat. Nutritional Foods Assn., Quality and Productivity Mgmt. Assn., Conf. Bd. (CEO program), Nat. Nutritional Found., Natural Products Assn., Advt. Club NY, NY Sales Execs. Club.

BERGER, GEORGE, lawyer; b. NYC, Jan. 21, 1936; BA summa cum laude, NYU, 1957, JD, 1960. Bar: N.Y. 1960, U.S. Dist. Ct. (so. dist.) N.Y. 1961, U.S. Ct. Appeals (2nd cir.) 1963, U.S. Supreme Ct. 1971, U.S. Ct. Appeals (5th cir.) 1974, U.S. Dist. Ct. (ea. dist.) N.Y. 1975, U.S. Dist. Ct. (we. dist.) 1980, U.S. Ct. Appeals (D.C. cir.) 1977, U.S. Ct. Appeals (10th cir.) 1985. Assoc. Phillips, Nizer, LLP, NYC, 1960-67, ptnr., 1967—. Disting. neutral, N.Y. panel, Ctr. for Pub. Resources, 1992-93. Editor: Hazardous Waste and Toxic Torts: Law and Strategy, 1987-92. Mem. ABA, Assn. of Bar of City of N.Y. Office: Phillips Nizer LLP 666 5th Ave New York NY 10103-0084 Office Phone: 212-841-0740. E-mail: gberger@phillipsnizer.com.

BERGER, HAROLD, lawyer, electrical engineer; b. Archbald, Pa., June 10, 1925; s. Jonas and Anna (Raker) Berger; m. Renee Margareten, Aug. 26, 1951; children: Jill Ellen, Jonathan David. BSEE, U. Pa., 1948, JD, 1951. Bar: Pa. 1951. Practiced in, Phila.; judge Ct. of Common Pleas, Phila. County, 1971-72; chmn., moderator Internat. Aerospace Meetings Princeton U., 1965-66; chmn. Western Hemisphere Internat. Law Conf., San Jose, Costa Rica, 1967; chmn. internat. Confs. on Aerospace and Internat. Law, Coll. William and Mary; permanent mem. Jud. Conf. 3d Circuit Ct. of Appeals; mem. County Bd. Law Examiners, Phila. County, 1961-71; chmn. World Conf. Internat. Law and Aerospace, Caracas, Venezuela, Internat. Conf. on Environ. and Internat. Law, U. Pa., 1974, Internat. Confs. on Global Interdependence, Princeton U., 1975, 79; mem. Pa. State Conf. Trial Judges, 1972-80, Nat. Conf. State Trial Judges, 1972—; chmn. Pa. Com. for Independent Judiciary, 1973—. Adv. coun. Biddle Law Libr. U. Pa., 1991—2004, bd. overseers Sch. Engring. and Applied Sci., 1998—. Mem. editl. adv. bd.: Jour. Space Law, U. Miss. Sch. Law, 1973—; contbr. articles to profl. jours. Mem. We the People 200 Com. for Constn. Bicentennial, 1991; chair Friends of Biddle Law Libr., 2004—. With inf. and Signal Corps, AUS, 1944—46. Recipient Alumnus of the Yr. award, Thomas McKean Law Club, U. Pa. Law Sch., 1965, Space award, GE, 1966, Nat. Disting. Achievement award, Tau Epsilon Rho, 1972, Spl. Pa. Jud. Conf. award, 1981, Special National Distinguished Svc. Award, Fed. Bar Assn., 1978. Mem.: ABA (past chmn. aerospace law com., mem. state and fed. ct. com., nat. conf. state trial judges, Spl. Presdl. Program award and medal 1975), Internat. Acad. Astronautics, Assn. U.S. Mems. Internat. Inst. Space Law Internat. Astronautical Fedn. (former bd. dirs.), Phila. Bar Assn. (past chmn. jud. liaison com. 1975, chmn. internat. law com. 1977), Fed. Bar Assn. (past nat. chmn. com. aerospace law, pres. Phila. chpt. 1983—84, chmn. class action and complex litig. com. 3d cir. 1990—, nat. chmn., alt. dispute resolution com. 1992—95, pres. eastern dist. Pa. chpt. 1996—2002, mem. nat. exec. coun. 1996—2002, chair spl. bench bar liason com. eastern dist. Pa. chpt. 2001—, nat. com. 1987 bi-centennial of U.S. Constn., past chmn. nat. fed. jud. com., Presdl. award 1970, Spl. Disting. Svc. award ea. dist. chapter 2002), Inter-Am. Bar Assn. (past chmn. aerospace law com.). Office: Berger & Montague PC 1622 Locust St Philadelphia PA 19103-6305

BERGER, HAROLD RICHARD, physician; b. Elizabeth, NJ, Oct. 31, 1914; s. Abraham and Frances (Herfield) B.; m. Minna Constance Wolfson, Aug. 22, 1943; children: Brian, Andrew, Alan, James. AB, Cornell U., Ithaca, NY; MD, NYU Sch. Medicine. Diplomate Am. Bd. Pediatrics. Intern Elizabeth (N.J.) Gen. Hosp., 1940-41; maj. U.S. Med. Corp., 1941-46; resident in pediatrics Jersey City (N.J.) Med. Ctr., 1951-53; pvt. practice, 1946—. Mem. child health program Elizabeth Bd. of Health, Hillside Bd. of Health; sch. physician Elizabeth Bd. Edn. Recipient award Am. Bd. Pediatrics, 1954. Mem. AMA, N.J. Med. Soc., Union County Med. Soc. Avocations: golf, reading, travel. Home and Office: 987 Harding Rd Elizabeth NJ 07208-1047

BERGER, HARVEY JAMES, pharmaceutical executive, physician, educator; b. NYC, June 6, 1950; s. Howard H. and Edith E. (Muskat) B.; children: Eric Michael, Mark Phillip, Nicole Elizabeth Grad., The Hotchkiss Sch., 1968; AB magna cum laude, Colgate U., 1972; MD, Yale U., 1977. Diplomate Am. Bd. Nuclear Medicine. Resident Yale-New Haven (Conn.) Hosp., 1977-81, dir. cardiovascular imaging, 1981-84; asst. prof. radiology and medicine Yale U., New Haven, 1981-83, assoc. prof., 1983-84; prof. radiology and assoc. prof. medicine Emory U., Atlanta, 1984-86; dir. Divsn. Nuclear Medicine Emory U. affiliated hosps., Atlanta, 1984-86; sr. v.p. med. affairs Centocor, Inc., Malvern, Pa., 1986—87; sr. v.p., R&D Centacor, Inc., Malvern, Pa., 1987—89; pres. R&D div., exec. v.p., med. dir. Centocor, Inc., Malvern, Pa., 1989-91; chmn., chief exec. officer, founder ARIAD Pharms., Inc., Cambridge, Mass., 1991—; chmn., CEO, founder ARIAD Gene Therapeutics, Inc., Cambridge, Mass., 1993—; chmn. ARIAD Inst. Biomed. Rsch., 1993—. Bd. dirs. Centocor Devel. Corp. I, PTC Therapeutics, Inc.; lectr. divsn. health scis. and tech. MIT, 1992-97, Harvard Med. Sch., 1992-97; adj. prof. U. Pa., Phila., 1986-92; mem. adv. study sects. Nat. Heart, Lung and Blood Inst., Washington, 1984-90; advisor Office of Dir. NIH, Washington, 1984-87; mem. panel on govt. role in civilian tech. NRC/NAS, 1989-92; mem. Dean's Coun. Yale Sch. Medicine, New Haven, 2007-. Founding editor Am. Jour. of Cardiac Imaging, 1985-89; editor Nuclear Medicine Communications, 1985-88; mem. editl. bd. Investigative Radiology, 1984-88; contbr. numerous articles to profl. jours.; patentee in field. Cline Fixott award Am. Acad. Dental Radiologists, 1984, Symbol of Caring award Sarcoma Found. Am., 2005 Mem. ACP, Soc. Nuclear Medicine (com. chmn., nat. trustee, Tetalman award 1982), Am. Coll. Cardiology (editl. bd. jour. 1983-88), Am. Coll. Chest Physicians, Am. Heart Assn. (established investigator 1981, cardiovascular radiology/circulation couns.), Am. Coll. Radiology, Am. Fedn. Clin. Rsch., Assn. Univ. Radiologists (Young Investigator award 1979), N.Am. Soc. Cardiovascular Radiology, Soc. Thoracic Radiology, Soc. Exptl. Biology and Medicine, Harvard Club of Boston, Yale Club of N.Y., Phi Beta Kappa. Office: ARIAD Pharmaceuticals Inc 26 Landsdowne St Cambridge MA 02139-4216

BERGER, JEROME MORRIS, communications executive; b. Cleve., Dec. 7, 1951; s. Jack and Beatrice Berger; m. Francine Ellis, Oct. 9, 1977. BA, Boston U., 1973; MS in Journalism, Columbia U., 1976. Editor, reporter Marlboro (Mass.) Enterprise, 1977-82; reporter UP Internat., Boston, 1982-87, statehouse bur. chief, 1987-90; asst. prof. Sch Journalism Northeastern U., Boston, 1990-96; comms. dir. com. on ways and means Mass. Senate, Boston, 1996-98; comms. dir. Mass. Cultural Coun., Boston, 1998-2001; dir. media rels. Beth Israel Deaconess Med. Ctr., Boston, 2001—. Developer, cons. Nat. Polit. Awareness Test, Project Vote Smart, Boston, 1993—96. Media columnist The Middlesex News, 1996; editor-in-chief: Insuring American Health for the Year 2000, 1992; contbr. articles to profl. publs. Mem. adv. network State Fiscal Analysis Initiative, Boston, 1993-94; media cons. Graduated Income Tax Campaign, Boston, 1994. Mem. Soc. Profl. Journalists. Avocations: reading, walking. Office: 330 Brookline Ave Boston MA 02215 Home Phone: 617-734-0383. Personal E-mail: jfberger@theworld.com.

BERGER, LAURA ANN, dance studio owner; b. Westland, Mich., Mar. 29, 1979; d. Ann and Randall Stepp (Stepfather). Owner LA Dance, Lake Orion, Mich., 1998—. Nat. competition judge Kids Artistic Revue, South Gate, Calif., 2003—, Halle of Fame, West Bloomfield, Mich., 2006—. Named Top Secondary Studio, Kids Artistic Revue, 2002, Top Prodn., 2002; named one of Top 50 Studios Across the Country, Dance Tchr. and Dance Spirit Mags., 2005; recipient Studio Spirit award, Kids Artistic Revue, 2002, World Fast Dance champion, 2003, Mid-West Invitational Hustle champion, 2003, Best Choreography award, Nexstar, 2005, Hall of Fame, 2006. Office: LA Dance 2651 S Lapeer Rd Lake Orion MI 48360 Home Phone: 248-814-8898; Office Phone: 248-393-1339. E-mail: ladance329@yahoo.com.

BERGER, LAWRENCE DOUGLAS, lawyer; b. Phila., Oct. 2, 1947; s. Milton and Nellie Leah (Kean) B.; m. Caroline Eggerding, Jan. 14, 1984; children: Jonathan Philip, Katherine Eleanor. BA magna cum laude, U. Pa., 1969; JD, Yale U., 1972. Bar: Pa. 1972, U.S. Dist. Ct. (ea. dist.) Pa. 1975, U.S. Ct. Appeals (3d cir.) 1976, U.S. Supreme Ct. 1978, N.J. 1991, U.S. Dist. Ct. N.J. 1991, U.S. Dist. Ct. (mid. dist.) Pa. 1993. Assoc. Dilworth, Paxson, Kalish & Kauffman, Phila., 1972-78, ptnr., 1978-92, Ballard Spahr Andrews & Ingersoll, Phila., 1992—. Mem. bd. Edn. Haddonfield NJ 1996, chair Negotiation Com., chair Bldgs. and Grounds Com. Mem. ABA (litig. sect., bus. law sect., law practice mgmt. sect.), Pa. Bar Assn., Phila. Bar Assn., NJ Bar Assn., Camden County Bar Assn., Phi Beta Kappa. Office: Ballard Spahr Andrews & Ingersoll 1735 Market St 51 Fl Philadelphia PA 19103-7599 Office Phone: 856-761-3400. Office Fax: 215-864-9509. Business E-Mail: berger@ballardspahr.com.

BERGER, LAWRENCE HOWARD, lawyer; b. Phila., May 19, 1947; s. Howard Merrill Berger and Doris Eleanor Cummins; m. Julie Mitchell Collins, Aug. 8, 1970; children: Colby Shaw, Ryan Lawrence, Lindsey Wade. BS, Mich. State U., 1969; JD, U. Va., 1972. Bar: Pa. 1972, U.S. Dist. Ct. (ea. dist.) Pa. 1973, U.S. Ct. Appeals (3d cir.) 1986. Assoc. Morgan, Lewis & Bockius LLP, Phila., 1972-79, ptnr., 1979—2005, sr. counsel, 2006—; gen. counsel Phila. Mus. Art, 2006—. Bd. dirs. US Lacrosse, 2000—06, chmn., 2002—04, vice chmn., 2004—. Trustee Agnes Irwin Sch., 1984—86, Naomi Wood Charitable Trust-Woodford Mansion Mus., 1986—, Fairmount Park Coun. for Hist. Sites, 1989—95, Fairmont Park Hist. Trust, 1993—95; bd. dirs. Phila. Lacrosse Assn., 1992—2000, U.S. Lacrosse Found., 2006—, Found. for Self Taught Am. Artists, 2005—. Recipient Frank Carr Cmty. Svc. award, 1991, Leading Bus. Lawyer award Chambers & Ptnrs, 2004, 05. Fellow Am. Bar Found.; mem. ABA (sec. com. on nonprofit corps. 1980-90), Pa. Bar Assn. (chmn. com. on uniform comml. code 1978-80), Phila. Bar Assn., Pa. Bar Inst., Banking Law Inst. (lectr. 1985), Pa. Bankers Assn. (lectr. 1980, 89), Martins Dam Club, Blue Key, Omicron Delta Kappa. Home: 360 Pond View Rd Devon PA 19333-1732 Office: Morgan Lewis & Bockius LLP 1701 Market St Philadelphia PA 19103-2903 Office Phone: 215-963-5480.

BERGER, LEV ISAAC, physicist, researcher; b. Rostov, USSR, June 23, 1929; came to U.S., 1978; s. Isaac Mark and Sara (Poltevsker) B.; m. Ninelle Rossine, July 2, 1956; 1 child, Yuri. MS in Physics, State U., Moscow, 1955; PhD in Physics, State U., Minsk, USSR, 1959; PhD in Tech. Scis., U. Steel and Alloys, Moscow, 1968. Lectr. physics U. Nonferrous Metals, Moscow, 1956-60; docent Physics U. Metallurgy, Moscow, 1960-62; prof. Poly. Inst., Moscow, 1962-77; sr. scientist New Eng. Research Ctr., Sudbury, Mass., 1979-81; lectr. physics San Diego State U., 1981-89, U. San Diego, 1989-98; pres. Calif. Inst. Electronics & Materials Sci., Hemet, 1981—. Dir. divsn. Inst. Spl. Purity Substances, Moscow, 1962-71, Introscopy Research Inst., Moscow, 1971-77. Author: Ternary Diamond-like Semiconductors, 1969, Semiconductor Materials, 1997; contbr. articles to profl. jours.; patentee in field. San Diego State U. grantee, 1983. Mem. ASTM (com. electronics, thermal measurements), Soc. for Advancement of Material and Process Engring. (exec. bd.), Am. Phys. Soc., Am. Assn. Crystal Growth, Materials Rsch. Soc., Nat. Assn. Scholars. Home: 2115 Flame Tree Way Hemet CA 92545-7803 Office: Calif Inst Electronics & Materials Sci PO Box 832 Hemet CA 92546-0832 Office Phone: 951-929-2659. Business E-Mail: info@ciems.com.

BERGER, MARSHA J., computer scientist, educator; BS, SUNY, Binghamton, 1974; MS, Stanford U., 1978, PhD, 1982. Prof. computer sci. Courant Inst. of Math. Scis., NYU. Contbr. articles to profl. jours. Mem.: NAE. Office: Courant Inst NYU 251 Mercer St New York NY 10012 Office Phone: 212-998-3305. Office Fax: 212-995-4121. E-mail: berger@cims.nyu.edu.

BERGER, MARVIN, medical educator; b. Bronx, NY, July 22, 1936; s. Jack and Hannah Berger; m. Roslynn Berger, June 26, 1965; children: David, Kenneth. BA, Ohio U., 1957; MD, Chgo. Med. Sch., 1961. Diplomate Am. Bd. Internal Medicine, Am. Bd. Cardiovasc. Disease, Am. Bd. Echocardiography. Intern Beth Israel Med. Ctr., NYC, 1961-62, resident in internal medicine, 1962-64, dir. echocardiography lab., 1975—, assoc. chief cardiology, 1981—2003; fellow in cardiology Mt. Sinai Med. Ctr., NYC, 1964-65; asst. prof. clin. medicine Mt. Sinai Sch. Medicine, NYC, 1976-81, assoc. prof., 1982-90, assoc. prof. medicine, 1990-94; assoc. prof. Albert Einstein Coll. Medicine, Bronx, 1994—, prof. clin. medicine, 1999—. Editor: Doppler Echocardiography in Heart Disease, 1987; contbr. articles to profl. jours. Capt. US Army, 1965—67. Fellow: ACP, Am. Soc. Echocardiography, Am. Coll. Cardiology, Am. Coll. Chest Physicians, N.Y. Cardiol. Soc.; mem.: AMA, Am. Heart Assn. Avocations: reading, classical music, dixieland jazz, sports. Office: Beth Israel Med Ctr 1st Ave and 16th St New York NY 10003 E-mail: mberger@bethisraelny.org.

BERGER, MAX W., lawyer; b. Bronx, NY, July 26, 1946; BBA in Acctg., CCNY, 1968; JD, Columbia U., 1971. Bar: NY 1972, US Dist. Ct. (so. dist. NY) 1973, US Ct. Appeals (2nd cir.) 1973, US Dist. Ct. (ea. dist. NY) 1975, US Dist. Ct. (dist. Ariz.) 1992. Founding ptnr., class action litig., securities litig. Bernstein, Litowitz, Berger & Grossmann, LLP, NYC, 1983—. Instr. Columbia U. Law Sch.; lectr. Fed. Jud. Ctr., Practicing Law Inst. Editor: Columbia Survey of Human Rights Law. Trustee Baruch Coll.; mem. bd. vis. & Dean's council Columbia Univ. Law Sch.; advisor Am. Law Inst. Named Trial Lawyer of Yr. finalist, Trial Lawyers for Pub. Justice, 1997; named one of Top 10 Trial Lawyers in Am., Nat. Law Jour., 2005; recipient Idealist of Yr. award, City Yr. NY, 2005, Disting. Alumnus award, Baruch Coll., 2006. Mem.: ABA (chmn. comml. litig. sect. 1983—84), Assn. Trial Lawyers Am., Fed. Bar Coun., NY State Bar Assn. Office: Bernstein Litowitz Berger & Grossmann 1285 Ave of the Americas New York NY 10019 Office Phone: 212-554-1403. Office Fax: 212-554-1444. Business E-Mail: max@blbglaw.com.

BERGER, MELVIN, allergist, immunologist; b. Phila., Mar. 7, 1950; MD, Case Western Res. U., 1976, PhD in Biochemistry, 1976. Intern, resident in pediatrics Children's Hosp. Med. Ctr., Boston, 1976-78; fellow allergy and immunology Nat. Inst. Allergy and Infectious Diseases, Bethesda, Md., 1978-81; pediatrician, chief immunology-allergy divsn. Rainbow Babies and Children's Hosp., Cleve., 1984—. Prof. pediats. and pathology Case Western Res. U. With USPHS, 1978—81, col. USAR, 1981—2004. Fellow Am. Acad. Pediatrics, Am. Acad. Allergy, Asthma & Immunology. Office: Rainbow Babies Hosp Div Pediatrics/Immunology Cleveland OH 44106 Office Phone: 216-844-3237. Business E-Mail: mxb12@po.cwru.edu.

BERGER, MILES LEE, land economist; b. Chgo., Aug. 9, 1930; s. Albert E. and Dorothy (Ginsberg) B.; m. Sally Eileen Diamond, Aug. 27, 1955; children: Albert E., Elizabeth Ann. Student, Brown U., 1948-50. Engaged in real estate and fin. svc. fields, 1950—; mng. chmn. bd. Berger Fin. Svcs. Corp., Chgo., 1950—. Chmn. bd. Mid-Am. Appraisal & Rsch. Corp., Chgo., 1959-80, also dir.; chmn. bd. Real Estate Svcs. Corp., 1969—; vice chmn. bd., trustee Heitman Fin. Ltd., 1970-98; chmn. bd. Mid Town Bank Chgo., 1974-2001; vice chmn. bd., prin. econ. cons. Columbia Nat. Bank, Chgo., 1965-96; bd. dirs. Franklin Corp., Evans Inc., Franklin Capital Corp., Innkeepers USA Trust, Universal Health Svcs., Inc., Medallion Bank; trustee Heitman Mortgage Investors, Innkeepers Am. Mem., chmn. Chgo. Plan Commn., 1980-84; cons. city Chgo. on Ill. Ctrl. Air Rights, 1967—; trustee Latin Sch. Chgo., 1967-73, treas., 1953-55, bd. dirs. Latin Sch. Found.; bd. govs. Met. Planning Coun.; bd. mgrs. James Jordan Boys Club. Mem. Am. Inst. Real Estate Appraisers, Soc. Real Estate Appraisers, Soc. Real Estate Counselors, Am. Right-of-Way Assn., Nat. Assn. Housing and Redevel. Ofcls., Nat. Tax Assn., Internat. Assn. Assessing Officers, Lambda Alpha. Jewish (trustee synagogue). Home: 737 N Michigan Ave Ste 1570 Chicago IL 60611-7017 Home Phone: 312-943-4575; Office Phone: 312-255-0600. Personal E-mail: mberger670@aol.com.

BERGER, MIRIAM ROSKIN, dance therapist, educator; b. NYC, Dec. 9, 1934; d. Israel and Florence Roskin; m. Meir Berger, July 16, 1967; 1 child, Jonathan Israel. Student, Barnard Coll., NYC, 1952—53; BA, Bard Coll., Annandale-on-Hudson, NY, 1956; postgrad., CCNY, 1956—58; D Arts, NYU, 1998. Dir. alumni Bard Coll., Annandale-on-Hudson, NY, 1958—59, bd. govs., 2000—; dance therapist Manhattan Psychiat. Ctr., NYC, 1959—60; performer, educator Jean Erdman Theater of Dance, NYC, 1959—62; dir. adult program Hebrew Arts Sch., NYC, 1981; mem. faculty Dance Notation Bur., NYC, 1974—75, 1977; asst. prof. dance therapy program NYU, 1975—, acting dir. dance therapy program, 1991, dir. dance edn. program, 1993—2002; dir. creative arts therapies Bronx Psychiat. Ctr., NYC, 1970—90; mem. faculty Pratt Inst., 2004—05; dir. dance therapy program Harkness Dance Ctr. 92d St. Y, 2005—. Workshop leader in field; tchr., Sweden, 1981—2004, Netherlands, 1991—2002, Germany, 1993—99, Czech Republic, 1997—2005, Poland, 2000, Republic of Korea, 02, Greece, 2004—, Israel, 2004—, Spain, 2005, Taiwan, 07; keynote spkr. Israel Dance Conf., 2004; mem. adv. coun. Am. Symphony Orch., 2007—. Prodr. off-Broadway The Coach with the Six Insides, 1962-63; author, prodr. Non-Verbal Group Process, 1978; co-editor Am. Jour. Dance Therapy, 1991-94; led dance therapy session Senate hearing on Aging, 1992; contbr. articles to profl. jours.; editl. bd. Arts in Psychotherapy, Jour. Dance Edn., Amer. Jour. Dance Therapy. Chair Nat. Coalition of Creative Arts Therapies Assns., 2002—; bd. dirs. Theater Open Eye, 1978—82, v.p. bd. trustees, 1982—89, pres., 1989—94. Recipient NYU scholarship, 1981, Best Paper award Med Art World Congress on Arts and Medicine, 1992 Mem.: Acad. Registered Dance Therapists, Am. Dance Therapy Assn. (founder, bd. dirs. 1967—76, v.p. 1974—76, credential com.

1976, 1982, keynote speaker at nat. conf. 1991, v.p. 1992, pres. 1994—98, chmn. internat. panel 1995—, Marian Chace award 2002), Dance Libr. Israel (v.p. 1999—, Hall of Fame inductee 2005). Business E-Mail: miriam.berger@nyu.edu.

BERGER, MITCHELL ZACHARY, oncologist; b. Newark, Oct. 15, 1957; MD, Robert Wood Johnson Med. Sch. U. Medicine and Dentistry NJ, 1983; Master's Degree in Med. Mgmt., Tulane U., New Orleans. Cert. Internal Medicine, Med. Oncology, Physician Exec. Resident, internal medicine U. Ala., Birmingham, 1983—86; fellow, hematologic oncology Meml. Sloan-Kettering Cancer Ctr., 1986; med. dir., nat. accounts Roche Lab., Nutley, NJ, med. dir., bone marrow transplantation; nat. dir., regional scientific dirs. Novartis Oncology, Florham Park, NJ; dir. med. oncology Ga. Cancer Ctr. of Excellence, Grady Health Sys., Emory U., Atlanta, 2006—; mem. physician staff Grady and Emory Crawford Hosps., Atlanta, 2006—. Office: Grady Health Sys Georgia Cancer Ctr of Excellence 80 Jesse Hill Jr Dr SE Atlanta GA 30303*

BERGER, NATHAN ALLEN, medical educator, academic administrator; b. Phila., July 8, 1940; s. Meyer and Lillian (Salko) B.; m. Sosamma John, June 23, 1968; children: Joshua S., Ravi B., Sarina H. AB, Temple U., 1962; MD, Hahneman U., 1966. Intern Michael Reese Med. Ctr., Chgo., 1967-68; rsch. assoc. NIH, Balt., 1968-71; assoc. prof. Washington U. Sch. Medicine, St. Louis, 1971-82; prof. medicine, biochemistry, and oncology Case Western Res. U., Cleve., 1983, Hannah-Payne prof. experimental medicine, 1983—95, dir. cancer ctr., 1985-95, interim dean, v.p. med. affairs, 1995-96, dean, v.p. med. affairs, 1996—2002, dir. Ctr. Sci., Health and Soc., 2002—, dir. Sci. Enrichment and Opportunity Program, 2003—; med. dir. Case Mini Med. Sch., 2005—. Bd. trustees Edison Biotech. Am. Cancer Soc., U. Hosp. Cleve., Henry Ford Health System, Montefiore, Ohio Biomed. Rsch. and Tech. Task Force. Contbr. articles to profl. jours.; mem. editl. bd. Jour. Clin. Investigation, Jour. Biol. Chemistry, Cancer Rsch.; others. Lt. comdr. USPHS, 1968—71. Fellow Washington U. Sch. Medicine, 1971-82; Leukemia Soc. Am. scholar; named to Am. Cancer Soc. Hall of Fame, Cleve. Med. Hall of Fame. Mem. Am. Soc. Hematology, Am. Soc. Biol. Chemists, Am. Soc. Clin. Oncology, Am. Soc. Cancer Rsch., Am. Soc. Clin. Investigation, Am. Assn. Physicians, Alpha Omega Alpha. Office: Case Western Res U 10900 Euclid Ave Cleveland OH 44106-4971 Home Phone: 216-371-9811; Office Phone: 216-368-4084. Business E-Mail: nab@case.edu.

BERGER, OTTO, engineer; s. Alois and Paula Berger; m. Elisabeth Berger; children: Torben, Linda, Marco. Diploma in physics, U. Muenster, Germany, 1981, PhD in Exptl. Physics, 1985. Devel. engr. Siemens, Munich, 1985—90, devel. mgr., 1990—98; dir. gas ops. Infineon, Munich, 1998—2002; dir. process devel. TriQuint, Hillsboro, Oreg., 2002—06, dir. advanced devel., 2006—. Office: TriQuint Semiconductor 2300 NE Brookwood Pky Hillsboro OR 97124 Business E-Mail: oberger@tqs.com.

BERGER, PATRICIA WILSON, retired librarian; b. Washington, May 1, 1926; d. Thomas Decatur Wood and Nina Hughes; m. George Hamilton Combs Berger, May 20, 1970. BA, George Washington U., 1965; MSLS, Cath. U. Am., 1974. Asst. libr., ops. rsch. office Johns Hopkins U., Chevy Chase, Md., 1949-51, asst. ops. rsch. analyst, 1951-54; head libr. CEIR, Washington, 1954-55; chief, tech. info. and libr. svcs. Human Rels. Area Files Yale U., Washington, 1955-57; tech. info. officer, chief libr. Inst. for Def. Analyses, Washington, Arlington, Va., 1957-67; dir. tech. info. and security programs Lambda Corp., Arlington, 1967-71; chief libr. U.S. Commn. on Govt. Procurement, Washington, 1971-72; head gen. ref. br., later dep. chief libr. U.S. Patent and Trademark Office, Arlington, 1972-76; chief libr. divsn. U.S. Nat. Bur. Stds., Gaithersburg, Md., 1976-78; dir. info. resources and svcs. U.S. EPA, Washington, 1978-79; chief libr. and info. svcs. U.S. Nat. Bur. Stds., Washington, 1979-83; chief info. resources and svcs. Nat. Inst. Stds. and Tech., 1983-91; dir. Office Info. Svcs. U.S. Nat. Bur. Stds., 1990-92; ret., 1992. Cons. libr., info. and security matters, 1965-95; del. 1st White House Conf. on Librs. and Info. Svc., 1979; bd. dirs. Universal Serial and Book Exch., 1983-84; chmn. Nat. Info. Std. Orgn., Am. Nat. Std. Inst., 1981-83, elected Nat. Info. Std. Orgn. fellow, 1989. Mem. editl. bd. Sci. and Tech. Librs., 1979—92; contbr. articles to profl. jours. Apptd. by Govs. of Va. to Libr. of Va. Bd., 1986-90, 90-95, vice chair, 1992-93, chair, 1993-94; bd. dirs. Va. Commn. for Reenactment of Battle First Bull Run, 1960-61; bd. dirs. Freedom to Read Found., 1988-90, 92-94; apptd. U.S. Postmaster Gen's. Commn. Lit., 1990-92. Recipient Internat. Women's Yr. award Dept. Commerce, 1976, Bronze medal, 1980, Silver medal, 1984, Outstanding Adminstrv. Mgr. award, 1985, H.W. Wilson Pub. Co. award, 1980, Disting. Svc. award U. Richmond Librs., 1989, Cert. of Recognition, Gov. State of Va., 1989, Resolution of Esteem, Va. State Libr. Bd., 1988, award Coun. Libr. and Media Technicians, 1989; named Outstanding Alumnus in Libr. and Info. Sci., Cath. U. Am., 1988, 20th Century Nat. Libr. Adv., Am. Libr. Assn./Am. Libr. Trustees Assn. Nat. Adv. Honor Roll, 2000, Outstanding Scientists, Engrs. and Adminstrs. Nat. Inst. Stds. and Tech./Nat. Bur. Stds., 2006; Cert. of appreciation Martin Luther King Jr. Fed. Holiday Commission, 1996. Fellow AAAS; mem. Spl. Librs. Assn. (exec. bd. Washington chpt. 1970-71, pres. Washington chpt. 1977, elected assn. fellow 1987), ALA (coun. 1984-88, exec. bd. 1986-90, v.p./pres.-elect 1988-89, pres. 1989-90), D.C. Libr. Assn. (Ainsworth Rand Spofford Pres.'s award 2001), Fed. Librs. Roundtable (pres. 1982-83, Achievement award 1985, portrait in the NBS/NIST Gallery of Disting. Scientists, Engrs. and Adminstrators 2006), Cosmos Club, Chi Omega, Beta Phi Mu. Episcopalian. Home: 105 Queen St Alexandria VA 22314-2610 Personal E-mail: pberger@his.com.

BERGER, PAUL ERIC, artist, photographer; b. The Dalles, Oreg., Jan. 20, 1948; s. Charles Glen and Virginia (Nunez) B. BA, UCLA, 1970; M.F.A., SUNY-Buffalo, 1973. Vis. lectr. U. Ill., 1974-78; prof. art U. Wash.-Seattle, 1978—. Exhibited one-man shows of photographs, Art Inst. Chgo., 1975, Light Gallery, N.Y.C., 1977, Seattle Art Mus., 1980, Light Gallery, N.Y.C., 1982, Univ. Art Mus., Santa Barbara, Calif., 1984, Cliff Michel Gallery, 1989, Seattle Art Mus., 1990, Fuel Gallery, 1993, Galerie Lichtblick GFFK, Cologne, Germany, 1996, SOHO Photo, N.Y.C., 1999, Mus. Contemporary Photography, Chgo., 2003. NEA Photographer's fellow, 1979, NEA Visual Artist's fellow, 1986; recipient Artist's Commn., Wash. State Arts Commn., 1990. Mem. Soc. Photographic Edn., Mus. of Contemporary Photography. Office: U Wash Sch Art PO Box 353440 Seattle WA 98195-3440 E-mail: peberger@u.washington.edu.

BERGER, PEARL, librarian, dean; b. NYC, Nov. 30, 1943; d. Baruch Mayer and Tova (Brandwein) Rabinowitz; m. David Berger, June 14, 1965; children: Miriam Esther, Yitzhak, Gedalyah Aaron. B in Religious Edn., Yeshiva U.; BA, Bklyn. Coll., 1965; MLS, Columbia U., 1974. Tchr. Hebrew & Jewish studies Yeshiva of Crown Heights, Bklyn., 1963-65; asst. libr. YIVO Inst. Jewish Rsch., NYC, 1976-80; head tech. services Librs. Yeshiva U., NYC, 1980-81, head libr. Pollack Libr., 1981-83, head libr. main ctr. librs., 1983-85, dean librs., 1985—. V.p. Met. Reference and Rsch. Libr. Orgn., 1996-99, Coun. Archives and Rsch. Librs. in Jewish Studies, 1984-86, pres. 1986-89. Assoc. editor: Jour. Judaica Librarianship, 1983-2004, mem. editl. bd. 2004-; compiler: (catalog) Guide to Yiddish Classics on Microfichecontbr., 1980; articles to profl. jours. Recipient Benjamin Gottesman Libr. Chair Yeshiva U. Mem. ALA, Metro. Reference Rsch. Libr. Agy. (trustee 1991—2002, sec. 1993-99, 1st v.p. 1996-99), Assn. Jewish Librs. (rsch., spl. librs. divsn., v.p. 1982-84, pres. 1984-86, voting rep. Nat. Info. Stds. Orgn. 1995-2000, v.p., pres.-elect 2000-01, pres. 2002-04). Office: Yeshiva U Dean of Libraries 500 W 185th St New York NY 10033-3299 Office Phone: 212-960-5363. Business E-Mail: berger@yu.edu.

BERGER, ROBERT BERTRAM, lawyer; b. NYC, Sept. 1, 1924; s. Edward William and Sophie (Berkowitz) B.; m. Phyllis Ann Korona, June 14, 1947; children: Barry Robert, Mark Alan, Karen Elizabeth Berger Adametz, James Michael; m. 2d, Arlene Kidder Wills, Dec. 27, 1980; 1 stepchild, Kimberly Kidder Wills Campbell. BS, Georgetown U., 1948; JD, U. Conn., 1952. Bar: Conn. 1952, U.S. Dist. Ct. Conn. 1953, U.S. Tax Ct. 1967, U.S. Ct. Appeals (2d cir.) 1968. Sole practice law, 1952-56; ptnr. Berger & Alaimo, Enfield, Conn., 1956-82, Berger, Alaimo, Santy & McGuire, Enfield, Conn., 1982-91, Berger, Santy & McGuire, Enfield, 1991-94, Berger & Santy, Enfield, 1994—2001, Berger, Santy & Barbieri, Enfield, 2001—. Judge Probate Dist. of Enfield, 1989-94; dir. Enfield Vis. Nuses Assn., 1993-96; bd. dirs., mem. exec. com. Conn. Attys. Title Ins. Co., Rocky Hill, 1980-2003; chmn. Enfield Dem. Town Com., 1979-87, Conn. Psychiat. Security Review Bd., 1985—; bd. dirs. Catic Fin. Inc. Contbr. monthly polit. column Enfield Press, 1980-84. Pres. United Way North Ctrl. Conn., 1981-84; trustee St. Bernard's Roman Cath. Ch., 1977-90, 99-2000; trustee, exec. bd. mem. Johnson Meml. Hosp.; chmn. Johnson Meml. Corp., Stafford, Conn.; bd. dirs. United Way of Capitol Area, 1981-85, United Way North Ctrl. Conn., 1977—. With USMCR, 1942-45. Decorated Purple Heart; recipient disting. svc. award Enfield Jr. C. of C., 1955, Clayton Frost award U.S. Jr. C. of C., 1959-60. Mem. ABA, Conn. Bar Assn., Hartford County Bar Assn., Enfield Lawyers Assn. (pres. 1973-74), Am. Judicature Soc., Enfield Rotary (pres. 1970-71, Paul Harris fellow 1984).

BERGER, ROBERT LEWIS, retired biophysicist; b. Omaha, Sept. 2, 1925; BS, Colo. State U., Ft. Collins, 1950; MS, Pa. State U., 1953, PhD, 1956. Instr. Park Coll., Parkville, Mo., 1950-51; postdoctoral fellow Cambridge (Eng.) U., 1956-57; asst. prof. Utah State U., Logan, 1957-60, assoc. prof., 1960-62; sr. investigator Nat. Heart Inst., Bethesda, Md., 1962-77; chief biophysics sect. Nat. Heart, Lung and Blood Inst., NIH, Bethesda, 1977-96; sr. sci. advisor Blood Rsch. Detachment Walter Reed Army Inst. Rsch., Washington, 1994—96; pvt. cons. Bethesda, 1996—; emeritus sr. investigator Walter Reed Army Inst. Rsch., 1998—. On-loan sci. exec. EEG, Inc., Las Vegas, Nev., 1959—60; vis. scientist dept. chemistry U. Calif., San Diego, 1969—71; organizer med. and biol. sect. 4th Internat. Conf. Temperature, Washington, 1971; invention devel. coord. Nat. Heart Lung Blood Inst., 1990—94. Contbr. chapters to books, articles to profl. jours.; mem. editl. bd. Jour. Biochemical and Biophysical Methods, 1982—96. Pres., CEO, fund raiser Karma House, Inc., Rockville, Md., 1974—77; bd. dirs., fund raiser Protestant Student House, Utah State U., Logan, 1958—62; adv. bd. Christian edn. United Presbyn. Ch., 1960—68. Lt. (j.g.) USCG, 1943—46. Recipient Comdrs. award for Pub. Svc., 1994—96, Disting. Svc. award, Eberely Coll. of Sci., Pa. State U. Alumni Soc., 1998. Fellow: AAAS, Am. Phys. Soc.; mem.: Am. Soc. Molecular Biology and Biochemistry, Soc. Gen. Physiology, Biophysical Soc. (chmn. discussions com. 1976—92). Democrat. Episcopalian. Achievements include invention of Berger Ball Mixer; D-B finite element method of analysis; optical-thermal stopped flow mixing machines; diamond-coated thermistors for salt water thermal measurements in the millisecond and sub-millisecond time domain; introduction of Hopkinson pressure bar method of peak pressure in nuclear explosions. Avocation: amateur radio. Home: 4503 Avamere St Bethesda MD 20814-3930 Office Phone: 301-319-7692. Personal E-mail: rlberger@comcast.net.

BERGER, ROBERT MICHAEL, lawyer; b. Chgo., Jan. 29, 1942; s. David B. and Sophia (Mizock) B.; m. Joan B. Israel, Aug. 16, 1964; children: Aliza, Benjamin, David. AB, U. Mich., 1963; JD, U. Chgo., 1966. Bar: Ill. 1966, U.S. Supreme Ct. 1975. Law clk. to cir. judge Henry J. Friendly U.S. Ct. Appeals, 2d Circuit, NYC, 1966-67; atty. Chgo. Legal Aid Bur. Law Reform Unit, 1967-68; mem. firm Mayer Brown, Chgo., 1968-72, ptnr., 1972-2001; exec. v.p., gen. counsel, sec. Capri Capital LP, 2001—04; sr. counsel Krasnow, Saunders & Cornblath, 2001—. Lectr. Northwestern U. Law Sch., 1973, adj. prof., 1997-2007; adj. prof. grad. program in real estate law John Marshall Law Sch., 1995-97; summer inst. faculty Nat. Inst. Law-Focused Edn., Chgo., 1969-74; hearing bd. Ill. Supreme Ct. Atty. Disciplinary Sys., 1973-79; mem. Ill. Sec. State Adv. Com. on Revised Uniform Ltd. Partnership Act, 1984-88, mem. spl. tax adv. commn. to Ill. Dept. Ins., 1972; legal counsel Consumer Fedn. Ill., 1967-71; regional consumer adv. coun. coun. FTC, 1969; bd. dirs., chmn. program com. Legal Assistance Found., Chgo., 1975-78; mem. Highland Park (Ill.) Zoning Bd. Appeals, 1984-86; chmn. blue ribbon com. Cook County Recorder, 1989-92; real estate adv. bd. Dai-Ichi Kangyo Bank, Chgo., 1988-93; lectr. in field. Comment editor: U. Chgo. Law Rev, 1965-66; author: Law and the Consumer, 1969, 74; reporter Revised Uniform Ltd. Partnership Act, 1984-88; adv. com. Restatement of the Law of Property 3d-Mortgages; contbr. articles to profl. jours., chpts. to books. Pres. Am.-Israel C. of C., 2003—05; trustee Am. Friends of Hebrew U.; mem. exec. com. Primo Ctr. for Women and Children, 2001—05; bd. dirs. Am. Friends of Hebrew U. Mem. ABA (chmn. subcom. on rev. uniform ltd. partnership act 1981-85, chmn. com. on partnerships and unincorporated bus. orgns. 1985-88), Am. Law Inst., Am. Coll. Real Estate Lawyers (bd. govs. 1995-98, nominating com., vice chmn. program com.), Chgo. Bar Assn. (bd. mgrs. 1970-72, chmn. com. on real estate fin. 1984-86, chmn. real property law com. 1987-88), Chgo. Coun. Lawyers (founder, bd. govs. 1969-71), Order of Coif, Phi Beta Kappa, Phi Kappa Phi. Office: Krasnow Saunders Cornblath LLP 500 N Dearborn St Chicago IL 60610 Office Phone: 312-832-7894. Business E-Mail: rberger@ksc-law.com.

BERGER, SANDY (SAMUEL R. BERGER), former national security advisor; b. Sharon, Conn., Oct. 28, 1945; m. Susan Harrison; children: Deborah, Sara, Alexander. AB, Cornell U., 1967; JD cum laude, Harvard U., 1971. Bar: D.C. 1971. Legis. asst. to Senator Harold E. Hughes US Senate, Washington, 1971-72; spl. asst. to Mayor John V. Lindsay City of NY, 1972; dep. dir. policy planning staff US Dept. State, Washington, 1977-80; ptnr. Hogan & Hartson LLP, Washington, 1973—77, 1981—92, internat. strategic advisor; asst. dir. nat. security Presdl. Transition Team, 1992; dep. asst. to the Pres. for nat. security affairs NSC, Washington, 1993—96, asst. to the Pres. for nat. security affairs, 1997—2000; chmn. Stonebridge Intl. LLC, Washington, 2001—; sr. advisor Lehman Brothers. Author: Dollar Harvest, 1971, (with others) Manual of Foreign Investment in the United States, 1984. Mem. ABA. Office: Stonebridge Internat Ste 300 W 555 Thirteenth St NW Washington DC 20004

BERGER, SANFORD JASON, retired lawyer, securities dealer, real estate broker; b. Cleve., June 29, 1926; s. Sam and Ida (Solomon) Berger; m. Bertine Mae Benjamin, Aug. 6, 1950 (div. Dec. 1977); children: Bradley Alan, Bonnie Jean; life ptnr. Marcia Saul, 1978. BA, Case Western Res. U., 1950, JD, 1952. Bar: Ohio 52, U.S. Supreme Ct. 79, U.S. Ct. Appeals 81. Field examiner Ohio Dept. Taxation, Cleve., 1952; pvt. practice law Cleve., 1952—. Real estate cons., Cleve., 1960—; investment cons., Cleve., 1970—; lectr. The Art of Conversation and Body Lang. Contbg. author Family Evaluation in Child Custody Litigation, 1982, Child Custody Litigation, 1986, The Parental Alienation Syndrome and the Differentiation Between Fabricated and Genuine Child Sex Abuse, 1987, Family Evaluation in Child Custody Mediation, Arbitration and Litigation, 1989; copyright 10 songs:. Candidate police judge, East Cleveland, 1955; mem. Bd. Edn., Beachwood, Ohio, 1963; judge ct. common pleas Cuyahoga County, Ohio, 1986; judge Ct. Appeals, 1988, 1990, 1992, 1994; mayor Beachwood, 1967. With USMC, 1944—45, PTO. Recipient Cert. Appreciation, Phi Alpha Delta, 1969, Healer award, U.S. Supreme Ct. Chief Justice Warren Burger, 1987, Outstanding Ohio Citizen award, Ohio Gen. Assembly, 1987. Mem.: B'nai B'rith (editor 1968—70). Republican. Jewish. Avocations: poetry, writing lyrics, legal writing, drag racing, scuba diving. Office Phone: 440-461-5777. E-mail: sanlllmar@aol.com.

BERGER, SEYMOUR MAURICE, social psychologist; b. Bklyn., Jan. 7, 1928; s. Leo and Bessie Ida (Okun) Berger; m. Sara Marilyn Nappen, Sept. 7, 1952; children: Evelyn Joyce, Nancy Faith. BS, Okla. A&M Coll., 1949; MA, Columbia U., 1950; PhD, Cornell U., 1959. Instr. Trinity Coll., Hartford, Conn., 1958-59; from instr. to assoc. prof. Ind. U., Bloomington, 1959-69; prof. social psychology U. Mass., Amherst, 1969-95, prof. emeritus, 1995—, acting dean social and behavioral scis., 1991-92, dean social behavioral scis., 1992-95. Contbr. articles on social psychology to profl. jours.; mem. editorial bd. Jour. Personality and Social Psychology. Served with USNR, 1945-46; served with USAF, 1951-55. Fulbright sr. research scholar, 1975-76,83; spl. fellow NIH, 1965-66 Democrat. Jewish. Home: 459 Flat Hills Rd Amherst MA 01002-1219 E-mail: berger@psych.umass.edu.

BERGER, STANLEY ALLAN, mechanical and biomechanical engineering educator; b. Bklyn., Aug. 9, 1934; s. Jack and Esther B.; m. Anna Ofman, Jan. 30, 1966 (div. Aug. 1984); children: Shoshana, Maya. BS, Bklyn. Coll., 1955; PhD, Brown U., 1959. Rsch. assoc. Princeton U., NJ, 1959-60; from lectr. to prof. U. Calif., Berkeley, 1961—2005, Montford G. Cook chair bioengring., 2005—. Cons. IBM, The Rand Corp., Lockheed Missiles and Space Co., Sci. Applications, Inc., Aluminum Co. Am. Author: Laminar Wakes, 1971; editor: Introduction to Bioengineering, 1996; contbr. articles to profl. jours. Fellow: AIAA, ASME (chair applied mechanics divsn. 1997—98), AAAS, Biomed. Engring. Soc., Am. Inst. Med. and Biol. Engring., Am. Phys. Soc. (chair divsn. fluid dynamics 2001—02). Office: U Calif Dept Mech Engring Berkeley CA 94720-1740 Home Phone: 510-526-8682; Office Phone: 510-642-5950. Business E-Mail: saberger@me.berkeley.edu.

BERGER, STEPHEN, finance company executive; b. NYC, July 11, 1939; s. Saul and Paula (Rosenzweig) B.; m. Cynthia C. Wainwright, Sept. 24, 1977. BA, Brandeis U., 1959. Editor Crowell-Collier Publs., NYC, 1961-62; exec. asst. to Rep. Jonathan Bingham NYC, 1964-68; pres. PCM Corp., NYC, 1969-73; exec. dir. N.Y. Study Commn. on N.Y.C., 1972-73; dir. Studies Commn. on Critical Choices for Americans, NYC, 1973-74; commr. N.Y. Dept. Social Svcs., Albany, 1975-76; dir. N.Y. Office Planning Svcs., Albany, 1975; exec. dir. N.Y. Emergency Fin. Control Bd., NYC, 1976; mem. N.Y. Bd. Social Welfare, 1977; dir. corp. devel. Oppenheimer & Co., Inc., NYC, 1981-82; investment banker Odyssey Ptnrs., NYC, 1983-85; chmn. U.S. Ry. Assn., Washington, 1980-87; prof. pub. adminstrn. N.Y.U., 1977-85; bd. dirs., chmn. fin. com. N.Y. Met. Transp. Authority, 1979-85; exec. dir. Port Authority, N.Y., N.J., 1985-90, Intergovtl. Policy Adv. Com. (office U.S. trade rep.), 1988-90; chmn., chief exec. officer Fin. Guaranty Ins. Co., NYC, 1990-92; exec. v.p. GE Capital Corp., 1992-93; ptnr. Odyssey Ptnrs., L.P., NYC, 1993—. Chmn. Odyssey Investment Ptnrs., LLC, 1997—; bd. dirs. Dayton Superior, Pro Mach Inc., York Ins. Svcs. Group, Inc.; chmn. commn. health care facilities in 21st century NY State, 2005—06. Co-chair Gov.'s Com. on Scholastic Achievement; chair Gov.'s Task Force on Health Care Reform, 2003—05; trustee Brandeis U., 1994—2001; chmn. NY State Commn. on Health Care Facilities in the 21st Century, 2005—06. Democrat. Jewish. Office: Odyssey Investment Ptnrs 280 Park Ave Fl 38 New York NY 10017-1216 Home Phone: 212-876-7788; Office Phone: 212-351-7950. Business E-Mail: sberger@odysseyinvestment.com.

BERGER, STEVEN R., retired lawyer, state official; b. Miami, Aug. 23, 1945; s. Jerome J. and Jeanne B. B.; m. Francine Blake, Aug. 20, 1966; children: Amy, Charlie. BS, U. Ala., Tuscaloosa, 1967, JD, 1969. Bar: Fla. 1969, U.S. Dist. Ct. (no. dist.) Fla. 1969, U.S. Dist. Ct. (so. dist.) Fla. 1971, U.S. Ct. Appeals (5th cir.) 1971, U.S. Supreme Ct. 1972, U.S. Ct. Claims 1977, U.S. Ct. Appeals (11th cir.) 1981, U.S. Dist. Ct. (mid. dist.) Fla. 1989, N.Y. 1990, Nev. 1991, U.S. Dist. Ct. Nev. 1991, U.S. Ct. Appeals (2nd and 9th cirs.) 1991; cert. appellate specialist Fla. Bar Bd. Assoc. W. Dexter Douglass, Tallahassee, 1969-71, William R. Dawes, Miami, 1971; ptnr. Carey, Dwyer, Cole Selwood & Bernard, Miami, 1971-81; sole practice Steven R. Berger, P.A., 1981-89; ptnr. Wolpe, Leibowitz, Berger & Brotman, 1989-94, Berger & Chafetz, 1994-99; asst. atty. gen. State of Fla., 1999—2005; ret., 2005. Mem. faculty Nat. Appellate Advocacy Inst., Washington, 1980; vice chmn. bench and bar adv. com. Ct. Appeals. 4th Dist., 1986-92. Mem. steering com. Fla. Appellate Practice Manual, Fla. Bar CLE, 3d, 4th, 5th edits. Chmn. City Miramar Planning Bd., 1975-76. Mem. ABA (vice chmn. app. practice com. litigation sect. 1981-83, chmn. 5th cir. subcom. appellate practice com. 1978-81), Am. Judicature Soc., Am. Arbitration Assn., Nev. Bar Assn. (mem. gaming law sect.), Rep. Nat. Lawyers Assn., Tallahassee Bar Assn.

BERGER, THOMAS LOUIS, author; b. Cin., July 20, 1924; s. Thomas Charles and Mildred (Bubbe) Berger; m. Jeanne Redpath, June 12, 1950. BA with honors, U. Cin., 1948; postgrad., Columbia U., 1950—51; LittD (hon.), L.I.U., 1986. Librarian Rand Sch. Social Sci., NYC, 1948—51; staff mem. N.Y. Times Index, 1951—52; assoc. editor Popular Sci. Monthly, 1952—53. Disting. vis. prof. Southampton Coll., 1975—76; vis. lectr. Yale U., 1981, 82; Regent's lectr. U. Calif., Davis, 1982. Author: Crazy in Berlin, 1958, Reinhart in Love, 1962, Little Big Man, 1964, Killing Time, 1967, Vital Parts, 1970, Regiment of Women, 1973, Sneaky People, 1975, Who Is Teddy Villanova?, 1977, Arthur Rex, 1978, Neighbors, 1980, Reinhart's Women, 1981, The Feud, 1983 (Pulitzer Prize nomination, 1984), Nowhere, 1985, Being Invisible, 1987, The Houseguest, 1988, Changing the Past, 1989, Orrie's Story, 1990, Meeting Evil, 1992, Robert Crews, 1994, Suspects, 1996, The Return of Little Big Man, 1999, Best Friends, 2003, Adventures of the Artificial Woman, 2004, (plays) Other People, 1970. With US Army, 1943—46, ETO. Recipient Rosenthal award, Nat. Inst. Arts and Letters, 1965, Western Heritage award, 1965, Ohioana Book award, 1982; Dial fellow, 1962. Office: c/o Don Congdon Assocs 156 Fifth Ave Ste 625 New York NY 10010-7002 Office Phone: 212-645-1229. Personal E-mail: thosberg@earthlink.net. *In my work I try to compete with that reality to which I must submit in life.*

BERGER, TOBY, electrical engineer, educator; b. Sept. 4, 1940; s. Henry and Doris L. (Goldstein) B.; m. Florence Cohen, Aug. 27, 1961; children: Elizabeth, Lawrence. BS, Yale U., 1962; MS, Harvard U., 1964, PhD, 1966. Assoc. scientist Raytheon Co., Wayland, Mass., 1962—66, sr. scientist, 1966—68, cons., 1968—75; from asst. prof. elec. engring. to prof. engring. Cornell U., Ithaca, NY, 1968—84, Levis prof. engring., 1984—99, acting dir. dept. elec. engring., 1988—, Irwin and Joan Jacobs prof. engring., 2000—06; prof. engring. U. Va., Charlottesville, 2006—. Cons. IBM, Owego, N.Y., 1975-94, Bell Labs., Murray Hill, N.J., 1987-97, TCSI, Berkeley, Calif., 1986-96; co-founder Sight Speed Tech., Berkeley, Calif., 2003—; vis. prof. ENST, Paris, 1986, Princeton U., 1989-90, Northeastern U., 1990, U. Va., 1997, 2003, Harvard U., 2004. Author: Rate-Distortion Theory, 1971, Digital Compression for Multimedia, 1998, Information Measures for Discrete Random Fields, 1998; contbr. articles to profl. jours. Fellow Guggenheim Found., 1975-76, Japan Soc. Promotion of Sci., 1980-81, Peoples Republic of China Ednl. Ministry, 1981, Fulbright Travel fellow, 1987; recipient Shannon award, IEEE Info. Theory Soc., 2002. Fellow: IEEE (pres. info. theory group 1979, editor-in-chief Transactions on Info. Theory 1987—89, Frederick E. Terman award 1982, Leon K. Kirchmayer Grad. Tchg. award 2006); mem.: AAAS, Nat. Acad. Engring., Info. Theory Soc. of IEEE (Shannon award 2002), Am. Soc. Engring. Tech., Tau Beta Pi, Sigma Xi. Home: 810 Gilliams Mountain Ct Charlottesville VA 22903-9756 Office: U Va Elec and Computer Engring Charlottesville VA 22903 Business E-Mail: tb6n@virginia.edu.

BERGER, WILLIAM ERNEST, newspaper publisher; b. Ferris, Ill., June 6, 1918; s. William George and Ethel (Nelson) B.; m. Jerry June Barnes, Feb. 26, 1943; children: William Edward, Barbara, John Jeffrey. Student,

Carthage Coll., 1935-38. Newspaper editor and pub., Hondo, Tex., 1946-65, 81—; commr. Tex Water Rights Commn., Austin, 1965-69; pres. Assoc. Tex. Newspapers, Inc., 1957—, South Tex. Press, Inc., Hondo, 1979—. Owner Sta. KRME, Hondo, 1969—94; newspaper broker, 1980—. Treas. Medina Meml. Hosp., Hondo. 1962-64, del. Tex. Dem. Conv., 1962, 64, 66, 68, Nat. Dem. Conv., 1968. Served with AUS, 1942-46. Mem. Tex. Press Assn. (pres. 1963), South Tex. Press Assn. (pres. 1954), SAR (Patrick Henry chpt.), Headliners Club, Lions (Hondo past pres.). Methodist.

BERGER, WOLFGANG H., oceanographer, educator, geologist; b. Erlangen, Germany; came to U.S., 1961; MS in Geology, U. Colo., 1963; PhD in Oceanography, U. Calif., San Diego, 1968. Asst. prof. Scripps Inst. Oceanography U. Calif., La Jolla, Calif., 1971-74, assoc. prof., 1974-80, prof. oceanography, 1980—. Co-editor: Abrupt Climatic Change, 1987, Ocean Productivity, 1989, co-author: The Sea Floor, 1993. Co-chief scientist, Ocean Drilling Prog., Leg 130 (1990), Leg 175 (1997). Recipient Bigelow medal Woods Hole (Mass.) Oceanographic Inst., 1979, Huntsman medal Bedford Oceanographic Inst., Can., 1984, Humboldt award German Sci. Found., Bonn, Germany, 1986, Lady Davis fellow Hebrew U., 1986, Albert I medal, Paris, 1991, Balzan prize, 1993, Steinmann medal Geol. Vereingung, 1998, Francis P. Shepard medal, Soc. for Sedimentary Geology, 2001. Fellow AAAS, Am. Geophysical Union (Ewing medal 1988), Geol. Soc. Am.; mem. European Geophysical Soc., Academia Europaea (fgn.). Avocation: photography. Office: U Calif San Diego Scripps Inst Oceanography MS 0244 La Jolla CA 92093-0244

BERGERON, ARTHUR WILLIAM, JR., historian, writer; b. Alexandria, La., Dec. 5, 1946; s. Arthur William and Elsie Mae Bergeron; m. Carol Bella Flashenburg, June 6, 1996; m. Phyllis Dianne Martina, June 19, 1969 (div. Mar. 1996); children: Terry Robin Powers, Geoffrey Scott, Kathleen Suzanne. BA, La. State U., Baton Rouge, 1968, MA, 1972, PhD, 1980. Lead archivist La. State Archives, Baton Rouge, 1977—81; curator Port Hudson State Hist. Site, Zachary, 1981—86; chief interpretive svcs. La. State Pks., Baton Rouge, 1987—96; historian Pamplin Hist. Pk., Petersburg, Va., 1996—2003; ref. historian US Army Mil. History Inst., Carlisle, Pa., 2004—. Editor: (non-fiction book) A Thrilling Narrative: The Memoir of a Southern Unionist, The Civil War in Louisiana, Part B: The Home Front, The Civil War in Louisiana, Part A: Military Activity; co-editor (non-fiction book) Louisianians in the Civil War; editor: (non-fiction book) The Civil War Reminiscences of Major Silas T. Grisamore, CSA; author: Confederate Mobile, 1861-1865, Guide to Louisiana Confederate Military Units, 1861-1865; co-author (non-fiction book) Boone's Louisiana Battery: A History and Roster, Miles' Louisiana Legion: A History and Roster; contbr. articles to profl. jours. With US Army, 1969—71. Recipient Charles L. Dufour award, New Orleans Civil War Round Table, 1993. Fellow: La. Hist. Assn. (life; pres. 1995—96); mem.: Soc. Civil War Historians (assoc.), So. Hist. Assn. (assoc.). Conservative. Baptist. Avocations: travel, collect political memorabilia. Office: U S Army Military History Institute 950 Soldiers Dr Carlisle PA 17013-5021 Home Phone: 717-532-5658; Office Phone: 717-245-3601. Office Fax: 717-245-3711. E-mail: arthur.bergeron@carlisle.army.mil.

BERGERON, CLIFTON GEORGE, engineer, educator; b. LA, Jan. 5, 1925; s. Lewis G. and Rose C. (Dengel) B.; m. Laura H. Kaario, June 9, 1950; children— Ann Leija, Louis Kaario. BS, U. Ill., 1950, MS, 1959, PhD, 1961. Sr. ceramic engr. A. O. Smith Corp., Milw., 1950-55; staff engr. Whirlpool Corp., St. Joseph, Mich., 1955-57; research asso. U. Ill., Champaign-Urbana, 1957-61, asst. prof., 1961-63, asso. prof., 1963-67, prof., 1967-78, head dept. ceramic engring., 1978-86, prof. emeritus, 1988—. Cons. A. O. Smith Corp., Whirlpool Corp., Ingraham Richardson, U.S. Steel Corp., Pfaudler Corp., Ferro Corp. Editor, Ann. Conf. on Glass Problems. Served in U.S. Army, 1943-46, ETO. Recipient Everitt award for tchg. excellence U. Ill., 1975; NSF grantee, 1961-82. Fellow: Am. Ceramic Soc. (Outstanding Educator award 1988); mem.: Am. Soc. for Engring. Edn., Am. Assn. for Advancement of Sci., Nat. Inst. Ceramic Engrs. (Friedberg lectr. 1986, Greaves-Walker award for Profl. Achievement 2005), Keramos, Sigma Xi. Achievements include research in crystallization kinetics in glass; high temperature reactions. Home: 208 W Michigan Ave Urbana IL 61801-4944 Office: 105 S Goodwin Ave Urbana IL 61801-2901

BERGERON, EARLEEN FOURNET, actress; b. New Orleans, Aug. 7, 1938; d. Earl Joseph Fournet and Lucia (Cuccia) Wadsworth; m. James Ronald Bergeron Sr., June 17, 1961; children: Blanche Theresa, Michele Yvette, James Ronald Jr. B in Social Sci. in Theatre and Speech, Loyola U., 1960. Actor: (plays) The Secret Affairs of Mildred Wilde, 1977, The Boyfriend, 1977, The Shadow Box, 1979, California Suite, 1980, Hay Fever, 1985, Brighton Beach, 1986, Beyond Therapy, 1987, Steel Magnolias, 1988, 1989, Nunsense, 1990, Broadway Bound, 1991, The Women, 1993, Nunsense II, 1995, Stomping Grounds, 1995, 1996, Angels in America, Part I: Millenium Approaches, Part II: Perestroika, 1997, Spareribs, 1998, Come Back Little Sheba, 1999, The Cripple of Inishmann, 2001, Ancestral Voices, 2002, Our Town, 2002, Morning's At Seven, 2004, The Aristocats, 2005, (comml.) Goodwill, 1988, Schumpert Medical Center, 1991, Cunningham and McDonald, Plastic Surgeons, 1991, JB Cable Ads, 1995, Pierre Bossier Mall, 1996; (films) Man in the Moon, 1990; (TV series) Rescue 911, 1991. Bd. dirs. Port Players, Shreveport, La.; assoc. mem. Co. Repertory Theatre, Inc., Project Shakespeare in Schs.; active Shreveport Med. Aux., 1968—97, mem. exec. bd., 1976—78; mem. Shreveport Opera Guild, 1972—97; area leader fund dr. Am. Cancer Soc., Shreveport, 1985—89. Named one of Outstanding Team Capts., United Way Fund, 1969. Mem.: Shreveport Little Theatre Guild (bd. dirs. 1985—86), Strand Theatre, Majorie Lyons Playhouse, Shreveport Little Theatre. Roman Catholic.

BERGERON, ELMO P., chemical engineer, consultant; b. Gray, La., Dec. 18, 1936; s. Elmo P. and Estelle F. Bergeron; m. Carolyn Gaudet, Nov. 30, 1963; 1 child, Ann Michele. BS in Chem. Engring., La. State U., Baton Rouge, 1960, MS, 1961, PhD, 1963. Registered profl. engr., La. Devel. engr. Allied Chem., Morristown, NJ, 1963-66; sys. engr., process specialist Dow Chem., Plaquemine, La., 1966-74, process cons. Terneuzen, Netherlands, 1974-76, process cons., project mgr. Plaquemine, 1977-93; cons., 1993—. Contbr. articles to profl. jours.; patentee in fields of math. modeling, control of chem. processes and vapor deposition. Named to Outstanding Young Men of Am., 1970. Mem. AIChE, La. Soc. Profl. Engrs. Republican. Roman Catholic. Avocations: reading, photography, woodworking.

BERGERON, PATRICIA ANN, education educator, consultant; b. Bklyn., Oct. 7, 1940; d. Louis Vincent and Viola Helen Fryzell; children: Michael Leo Boulé, Ann Patricia Boulé(dec.). BS in Edn., Castleton State Coll., Vermont, 1962; MEd, Lesley Coll., 1986; cert. in Human Devel., Harvard U., 1987. Cert. tchr. Mass. State Dept. Edn., 1995. Ednl. tech. specialist Boston Pub. Schs., 1987—88; pvt. practice ednl. tech. cons. Burlington, Vt., 1988—89; ednl. tech. specialist IBM Ednl. Sys., Burlington, 1989—90; dir. acad. computing Champlain Coll., Burlington, 1990—94; coord. ednl. tech. Canton Pub. Schs., 1994—98, Belmont Pub. Schs., 1998—99; mgr. Sch. Tech. Svcs. Family Edn. Network, Boston, 1999—2000; mgr. Tech. Evaluation Svcs. Edn. Alliance Brown U., Providence, 2000—01; grants officer Lesley U., Cambridge, Mass., 2002; pvt. edn. cons. Weymouth, Mass., 2003; part-time mus. guide Plymouth Antiquarian Soc., Mass., 2004—06. Edn. cons. Coll. for Lifelong Learning U. Sys. NH, Gorham, 1987—90; tech. plan reviewer Mass. State Dept. Edn., Melrose, 1996—99; judge JFK Profiles in Courage essay contest, 2006—07; vol. coord. bookmobile Americorps VISTA, Franklin-Grand Isle, Vt., 2007—. Judge JFK Profiles in Courage Essay Contest, 2006—07. Personal E-mail: pberge@juno.com.

BERGERON, PAUL ROBERT, city clerk; b. Nashua, NH, 1950; s. Robert Paul and Ann Theresa Bergeron; m. Meghan Brady; children: Jessica, Christine. BA, U. NH, Durham, 1972, MA, 1974; EdM, Cambridge Coll., Mass., 2002. Cert. archivist Acad. Cert. Archivists, 2003, city clk. NH City and Town Clks. Assn., 2002. Reporter Nashua Telegraph, 1972; rep. to the gen. ct. State of NH, Concord, 1973—74; exec. v.p. Retail Merchants Assn. NH, Concord, 1974—76; tchg. asst. dept. English Tex. A&M U., College Station, 1976—77; English tchr. Milford Area H.S., NH, 1977—79; v.p. Bergeron's, Inc., Nashua, 1979—87; sales mgr. Filene's Dept. Stores, Boston, 1987—94; dep. city clk. Office of the City Clk., Manchester, NH, 1994—99, city clk. Nashua, 1999—. Adv. com. NE Document Conservation Ctr., Andover, Mass., 1998—2004; leader Local Govt. Industry Specific Group, ARMA Inc., Lenexa, Kans., 1999—2001; vital records improvement fund adv. com. State of NH, Concord, 2001—05, mcpl. records bd., 2001—03, hist. records adv. bd., 2002—, vital records instl. rev. bd., 2005—, chair vital records instl. rev. bd., 2005; mem. state plan com. NH Help Am. Vote Act, Concord, 2003—. Maj. gifts co-chair NH Pub. TV Network's Auction Com., Durham, 1975; mem. Rivier Coll. Adv. Bd., Nashua, 1975—76, 1982—89; bd. dirs. Heart of Nashua Found., Inc., 1979—87, pres., 1982—84; bd. dirs. Nashua Children's Assn., 1980—83, Bishop Guertin H.S. Alumni Assn., Nashua, 1988—94, vice chmn., 1988—89; pres. Kiwanis Club of Hudson, Inc., Hudson, NH, 1997—98; mem. Ethnic Awareness Com., Nashua, 2003; trustee Hills Meml. Libr., Hudson, NH, 1974—76; del. NH Constl. Conv., Concord, 1974; chmn. Hudson Town Govt. Study Com., NH, 1974; mem. Charter Commn., Hudson, 1984—85, Distributive Edn. Found. NH, Inc., Concord, 1973—76, NH Coun. on Econ. Edn., Concord, 1974—76. Named NH Journalism Tchr. of Yr., NH Scholastic Press Assn., 1979; recipient Sales Mgr. of Yr., Filene's Dept. Stores, Belmont, 1988. Mem.: Soc. Am. Archivists (steering com. and newsletter editor govt. records sect. 2004—, chair govt. records sect. 2002—03, chair local govt. records roundtable 2002—03), Nat. Assn. Govt. Archives and Records Adminstrs. (bd. dirs. 2003—), Internat. Inst. Mcpl. Clks., New Eng. Archivists (program, nominating, local arrangements coms. 2003—07, Richard L. Haas award 1998), New Eng. Assn. City and Town Clks. (chair info. mgmt. com. 2001—02), NH City and Town Clks. Assn., Mensa. Office: City of Nashua 229 Main St Nashua NH 03060 Office Phone: 603-589-3010. Business E-Mail: bergeronp@nashuanh.gov.

BERGERON, PIERRE H., lawyer; b. Knoxville, Tenn., 1974; BA, Centre Coll., 1996; JD, U. Va., 1999. Bar: Ohio 1999, Ky. 2005, US Supreme Ct., US Ct. of Appeals Second Cir., US Ct. of Appeals Fifth Cir., US Ct. of Appeals Sixth Cir., US Ct. of Appeals Ninth Cir., US Ct. of Appeals Eleventh Cir., US Dist. Ct. Eastern Dist. Ky., US Dist. Ct. Western Dist. Ky., US Dist. Ct. Southern Dist. Ohio. Clerk US Ct. of Appeals Sixth Cir.; adj. prof. Sixth Cir. appellate practice, U. Cin.; sr. assoc. Squire, Sanders & Dempsey L.L.P. Editor (editor, contbg. author): Sixth Circuit Practice Manual. Named one of Ohio's Rising Stars, Super Lawyers, 2006. Mem.: Phi Beta Kappa. Office: Squire Sanders & Dempsey LLP 312 Walnut St Ste 3500 Cincinnati OH 45202-4036 Office Phone: 513-361-1200. Office Fax: 513-361-1201.

BERGERSON, DAVID RAYMOND, lawyer; b. Mpls., Nov. 23, 1939; s. Raymond Kenneth and Katherine Cecille (Langworthy) Bergerson; m. Nancy Anne Heeter, Dec. 22, 1962; children: W. Thomas C., Kirsten Finch, David Raymond. BA, Yale U., 1961; JD, U. Minn., 1964. Bar: Minn. 1964. Assoc. Fredrikson Law Firm, Mpls., 1964-67; atty. Honeywell Inc., Mpls., 1967-74, asst. gen. counsel, 1974-82, v.p., asst. gen. counsel, 1983-84, v.p., gen. counsel, 1984-92; pvt. practice law Mpls., 1992-94; v.p., sec. Telcom Sys. Svcs., Inc., Plymouth, Minn., 1994-96, dir., cons., 1996-97; v.p. bd. dirs. Hogan Bergerson, Inc., Mpls., 1997—. Mem. city coun. Minnetonka Beach, Minn., 2001—07; bd. dirs. Pillsbury Neighborhood Svcs., Inc., Mpls., 1983—92. Republican. Avocations: scuba diving, bird-hunting. Office: Hogan Bergerson Inc 4610 IDS Ctr Minneapolis MN 55402 Home: 16215 Holdridge Rd W Wayzata MN 55391 Office Phone: 952-471-9664. Personal E-mail: dbergerson1@mchsi.com.

BERGESEN, ROBERT NELSON, transportation consultant; b. Phila., Nov. 1, 1937; s. Bernhard E. and Carol Pearl (Nelson) B.; m. Jean Nicol, Apr. 23, 1966; children: Susan, Jean, Jeffrey. BA, Cornell U., 1959, MBA, 1961. With Price Waterhouse and Co., NYC, 1961-63; sys. analyst Warner-Lambert, Morris Plains, NJ, 1963-66; asst. contr. C.T.I., NYC, 1970-71; contr. Flexi-Van Leasing, NYC, 1971-75; from controller to gen. mgr. Vt. Transit Co., Inc., Burlington, Vt., 1977-2000. Mem. New Eng. Bus. Assn. (bd. dir. 1993-2000). Lutheran. Home: 182 Morningside Dr Middlebury VT 05753-1074 Personal E-mail: rbergesen@hotmail.com.

BERGESON, DONNA POTTIS, lawyer; b. Warwick, NY, Aug. 21, 1960; BA magna cum laude, U. S.C., 1981, JD, 1984. Bar: Ga. 1984. Ptnr., group leader, health care regulatory group Alston & Bird LLP, Atlanta. Mem. ABA, Atlanta Bar Assn., Gwinnett County Bar Assn., State Bar of Ga., Ga. Acad. Hosp. Attys., Phi Beta Kapa, Phi Eta Sigma. Office: Alston & Bird LLP 1 Atlantic Ctr 1201 W Peachtree St NW Atlanta GA 30309-3424 Office Phone: 404-881-7278. Office Fax: 404-881-7777. Business E-Mail: dbergeson@alston.com.

BERGESON, TERESA, school system administrator; b. Mass. BA in English, Emmanuel Coll., Boston, 1964; M in Counseling and Guidance, Western Mich. U., 1969; PhD in Edn., U. Wash. Tchr., sch. guidance counselor, Mass., Alaska, Wash.; exec. dir. Ctrl. Kitsap Sch. Dist., 1989-92, Wash. State Commn. on Student Learning, 1993—96; state supt. pub. instrn. Olympia, Wash., 1997—. V.p. Wash. Edn. Assn., 1981, pres., 1985—89. Mem.: Wash. Edn. Assn. (v.p. 1981—85, pres. 1985—89). Office: Old Capital Bldg 600 S Washington PO Box 47200 Olympia WA 98504-7200 Office Fax: 360-753-6712. E-mail: bergeson@ospi.wednet.edu.*

BERGESON-DANA, TONYA, psychologist, researcher; BA, Northwestern U., Evanston, IL, 1991—96, MusB, 1996; PhD, U. Toronto, 2002. Asst. prof.m Philip F. Holton investigator Ind. U. Sch. Medicine, Indpls., 2004—. Office Phone: 317-274-8466.

BERGEVIN, V. RÉAL, customer relationship management executive; b. Oshawa, Mar. 9, 1963; Bus. degree Sir Wilfrid Laurier U., 1986. With General Motors, 1984—88; with Wardair Airlines, 1988—90; with Rogers Cablesystems, 1990—92; founder John Moss Assoc., 1992—96; founder, CEO NuComm Internat., 1991—. Pub. (other) 23 Steps to an Effective Call Centre, 2000, Call Centers for Dummies, 2005. Recipient Niagara Entrepreneur Yr. Award. Office: NuComm Internat Corbloc Bldg 80 King St 3d Fl Saint Catharines ON Canada L2R 7G1

BERGGREN, RONALD BERNARD, surgeon, retired educator; b. SI, NY, June 13, 1931; s. Bernard and Florence (Schmidt) B.; m. Mary Beth Griffith, Nov. 25, 1954; children: Karen Berggren Murray, Eric Griffith. BA, Johns Hopkins U., 1953; MD, U. Pa., 1957. Diplomate Am. Bd. Surgery, Nat. Bd. Med. Examiners, Am. Bd. Plastic Surgery (bd. dirs. 1982-88, chmn. 1987-88). Asst. instr. surgery U. Pa., 1958-62, instr., 1962-65; gen. surg. resident Hosp. U. Pa., 1958-62, resident plastic surgery, 1963-64, chief resident plastic surgery, 1964-65; sr. resident surgery Phila. Gen. Hosp., 1962-63; asst. prof. surgery Ohio State U. Sch. Medicine, 1965-68, dir. div. plastic surgery, 1965-85, assoc. prof. surgery, 1968-73, prof. surgery, 1973-86, emeritus prof. surgery, 1986—; attending staff Ohio State U. Hosps., chief of staff, 1983-85, hon. staff, 1986—. Attending staff, dir. div. plastic surgery Children's Hosp., Columbus, Ohio, 1965-90; v.p. Plastic Surgery Ednl. Found., 1984-85, pres., 1986-87; sec. Plastic Surgery Tng. Program Dirs., 1981-83, chmn., 1983-85; mem. med. adv. bd. Ohio Bur. for Children with Med. Handicaps, 1974-2004, mem. emeritus, 2004. Trustee Mid Ohio Health Planning Fedn., 1979-82, 84, PSRO, 1980-84, Scioto Valley Health Systems Agy., 1985-87; del. Coun. Med. Splty. Socs., 1982-90, dir., 1988-90. Recipient Disting. Svc. award Plastic Surgery Edn. Foun., 1990. Fellow: ACS (gov. 1996—2001, chair gov.'s com. on ambulatory surg. care); mem.: AMA, Coun. Plastic Surgical Orgn. (convenor 1996—2000), Coun. Med. Specialty Socs. (dir. 1989—90, sec. 1991—92, pres.-elect 1993, pres. 1994), Accreditation Coun. for Grad. Med. Edn. (rev. com. for plastic surgery 1983—90, mem. exec. com. 1987—90, designate chmn. 1988, chmn. 1989, mem. exec. com. 1994, chmn. 1994, institutional rev. com. 1996—2004, chair 2002—04, John C. Gienapp award 2005), Am. Soc. Maxillofacial Surgery, Am. Soc. Aesthetic Plastic Surgery (parliamentarian 1992—93), Am. Trauma Soc., Am. Burn Assn., Assn. Acad. Surgery, Am. Assn. Surgery Trauma, N.Y. Acad. Scis., Plastic Surg. Rsch. Coun. (chair 1975—76), Franklin County Med. Soc. (pres.-elect 1982—83, pres. 1983—84), Am. Assn. Plastic Surgeons (treas. 1982—85, v.p. 1988—89, pres.-elect 1989—90, pres. 1990—91), Am. Cleft Palate Assn., Ohio Valley Plastic Surg. Soc., Am. Soc. Plastic and Reconstructive Surgeons (spl. hon. citation 1995, Trustees award for spl. achievement in plastic surgery 2000), Columbus Surg. Soc., Ctrl. Surg. Soc., Alpha Kappa Kappa, Phi Kappa Psi, Sigma Xi. Office: 9787 Windale Farms Cir Galena OH 43021-9609 Personal E-mail: rbergg@aol.com.

BERGGREN, WILLIAM ALFRED, geologist, research micropaleontologist, educator; b. NYC, Jan. 15, 1931; s. Wilhelm Fritjof and Lilly Maria (Skog) B.; m. Lois Albee, June 19, 1954 (div. July 1981); children: Erik, Anna Lisa, Anders, Sara Maria; m. Marie Pierre Aubry, June 19, 1982 BS, Dickinson Coll., 1952; M.Sc., U. Houston, 1957; PhD, U. Stockholm, 1960, D.Sc., 1962; doctorate (hon.), U. Utrecht, 2001, U. Athens, 2003. Research micropaleontologist Oasis Oil Co., Tripoli, Libya, 1962-65; asst. scientist Woods Hole Oceanographic Inst., Mass., 1965-68, assoc. scientist, 1968-71, sr. scientist, 1971-98, sr. scientist emeritus, 1998—; Disting. vis. prof. Rutgers U., New Brunswick, N.J., 2001—; Adj. prof. Brown U., Providence, 1968-93. Editor: Catastrophes and Earth History, 1984, Late Eocene-Early Oligocene Climatic and Biotic Change, 1992, Geochronology Time-Scales and Global Stratigraphic Correlation, 1995, Late Paleocene-Early Eocene Climate and Biotic Events, 1998; contbr. articles to sci. jours. Recipient Cushman Found. award for foraminiferal rsch., 1995, Raymond C. Moore medal in paleontology Soc. of Sedimentary Geology, 1997. Fellow Geol. Soc. Am., Geol. Soc. London (hon.); mem. NAS (Mary Clark Thompson medal 1982), Am. Assn. Petroleum Geologists, Soc. Econ. Paleontologists and Mineralogists (hon.), Paleontol. Soc. Am. (co-editor jour. 1980-84), Am. Geophys. Union. Avocation: skiing. Office: Woods Hole Oceanographic Inst 22 Water St Woods Hole MA 02543-1024

BERGHAHN, KLAUS LEO, German and Jewish studies educator; b. Duesseldorf, Germany, Aug. 5, 1937; arrived in U.S., 1967; s. Wilhelm and Anna (Bong) B.; m. Doris E. Beyer, Aug. 10, 1966; 1 child, Marcus J. Student, U. Cologne, Germany, 1957-59; Staatsexamen, U. Muenster, Germany, 1963, Dr phil, 1967. Tutor, asst. U. Muenster, 1963-67; asst. prof. German studies U. Wis., Madison, 1967-71, assoc. prof., 1971-73, prof., 1973—, chmn. German dept., 1994-97, mem. senate, 1974-78, 85-87, dir. Ctr. German and European Studies, 1998—2005, Weinstein-Bascom prof. German and Jewish studies, 1999—2004, DAAD prof., 2004—. Vis. prof. Free U. Berlin, 1978, U. Bielefeld, Germany, 1980-81, U. Giessen, Germany, 1983, 92, U. Mich., Ann Arbor, 1984, U. Calif., Davis, 1989, Hebrew U., Jerusalem, 1993, U. London, 2005; mem. adv. bd. German Am. Art Found., Chgo., 1995-99; mem. German sect. Fulbright Commn., 1995-98; mem. adv. bd. German dept. Harvard U., 1994-95, 96-97; organizer spl. sessions, confs. and symposia, 1983—. Author: Formen der Dialogführung in Schillers klassischen Dramen, 1970, Friedrich Schiller: Vom Pathetischen und Erhabenen, 1970, Friedrich Schiller: Kallias oder über die Schönheit, 1971, Briefwechsel zwischen Schiller und Körner, 1973, Schillers Gedichte, 1980, G.E. Lessing: Hamburgische Dramaturgie, 1981, Schiller Ansichten eines Idealisten, 1986, (with Beate Pinkerneil) Am Beispiel Wilhelm Meister, 2 vols., 1980, Grenzen der Toleranz, 2000; editor: (with Reinhold Grimm) Schiller Zur Theorie und Praxis der Dramen, 1972, Wesen und Formen des Komischen im Drama, 1975, Utopian Vision Technological Innovation Poetic Imagination, 1990, (with Hans Ulrich Seeber) Literarische Utopien von Morus bis zur Gegenwart, 1983, 2d edit., 1985, (with Holub and Scherpe) Responsibility and Committment. Ethische Postulate der Kulturvermittlung. Festschift für Jost Hermand, 1996; editor: Schiller Zur Geschichtlichkeit seines Werkes, 1976, The German-Jewish Dialogue-Reconsidered, 1996, Friedrich Schiller: Ueber die aesthetische Erzhiehung des Menschen, 2000, Goethe in German-Jewish Culture, 2001, Friedrich Schiller: Ueber naire und sentimentalische Dichtung, 2002, Cultural Representations of the Holocaust in Germany and United States, 2002, Unmasking Hitler: Cultural Representation of Hitler from the Weimar Republic to the Present, 2005; mem. editl. bd. Monatshefte, 1975—, Goethe Yearbook, 1985—, German Poltics and Society, 2000—; contbr. articles and revs. to profl. jours., chpts. to book. Recipient Hilldale Career award U. Wis.-Madison, 2007, ILS Tchg. and Svc. award U. Wis.-Madison, 2007, Bundesverdienst-Krenz, 2007; fellow VW-Found., Germany, 1965-67, Am. Philos. Soc., 1969, 73, Inst. Rsch. in Humanities, U. Wis., 1972, 89-94, Ctr. Interdisciplinary Rsch., Bielefeld, 1980-81, German Acad. Exch. Svc., 1990, 99, Rosenzweig Ctr., Jerusalem, 1993; 14 summer rsch. grants U. Wis. Grad. Sch. Mem. MLA (19th and early 20th century German lit. divsn. exec. com. 1974-78, chmn. 1977, mem. 18th and early 19th century German lit. divsn. 1983-88, chmn. 1987, mem. adv. bd. MLA Profession 1997-99), Am. Assn. Tchrs. German (program and selection com. 1990), Internat. Union Germanists (program com. 1995, 2005), Lessing Soc., Schiller Soc. (medal 1984), Goethe Soc Avocations: reading, writing, music, theater, chess. Home: 2908 Oxford Rd Madison WI 53705-2220 Office: U Wis Dept German 860 Van Hise Hall 1220 Linden Dr Madison WI 53706-1525 Office Phone: 608-262-2192. Business E-Mail: klbergha@wisc.edu.

BERGHAHN, VOLKER ROLF, history professor; b. Berlin, Feb. 15, 1938; came to U.S., 1988; s. Alfred and Gisela (Henke) B.; m. Marion Ilse Koop, Dec. 29, 1969; children: Sascha, Vivian, Melvin. MA, U. N.C. Chapel Hill, 1961; PhD, U. London, 1964; Habil., U. Mannheim, 1966-69. Sr. scholar St. Anthony's Coll., Oxford, England, 1964-66; rsch. fellow U. Mannheim, 1966-69; lectr. U. East Anglia, Norwich, 1969-71; reader U. E. Anglia, Norwich, 1971-75; prof. U. Warwick, Coventry, 1975-88, Brown U., Providence, 1988-97, Columbia U., NYC, 1998—. Author: Der Stahlhelm, 1966, Der Tirpitz Plan, 1970, Germany and the Approach of War, 1973, Modern Germany, 1982, The Americanization of West German Industry, 1945-1973, 1986, Otto A. Friedrich, 1902-1975, 1992, Imperial Germany, 19871-1914, 1995, America and the Intellectual Cold Wars in Europe, 2001, Europe in the Era of Two World Wars, 2006. Various grants and fellowships. Fellow Royal Hist. Soc.; mem. German History Soc. (pres. 1986-88), Am. Hist. Assn., German Studies Assn. Avocations: tennis, walking. Office: Columbia U Dept History New York NY 10027 Home Phone: 212-531-1196; Office Phone: 212-854-8604. Business E-Mail: vrb7@columbia.edu.

BERGLEITNER, GEORGE CHARLES, JR., investment banker; b. Bklyn., July 16, 1935; s. George Charles and Marie (Preitz) B.; m. Betty Van Buren, Oct. 29, 1966; children: George Charles III, Michael John,

Stephen William. BBA, St. Francis Coll., Bklyn., 1959; MBA, CCNY, 1961; PhD in Bus. Adminstrn. (hon.), Colo. State Christian Coll. Dir. instl. sales A.T. Brod & Co. , NYC, 1965-66; dir. instl. sales Weis, Voisin & Cannon, Inc., NYC, 1966-67, C.B. Richard, Ellis & Co., NYC, 1967-68; pres. Stamford (N.Y.) Fin. Co., also bd. dirs. Pres. M.J. Manchester & Co., Fashion & Time, Inc., B.J.B. Graphics, Inc., First Coinvestors, Inc., Smart Fit Foundations, Inc., Jay Co., Computer Holdings Corp., Ltd., Delhi Mfg. Corp., Delhi Industries, Delhi Mfg., Inc., Delhi Internat., Inc., Luxemborg; bd. dirs. Alpha Capital Corp., Am. Energy Mgmt. Corp., Stamford Fin., Electronic Tax Ctrs., Inc., L.I.U.G., LI Venture Capital Group, LI Venture Group, Del. County Indsl. Devel., sec.; sponsor NY Venture Group; bd. dirs. Indsl. Devel. Agy., Delaware County, NY. Chmn. Franciscan fathers Devel. Program, 1967-71; mem. Pres.'s Econ. Coun., Franciscan Spirit award, 1959-, Knight of Malta, 2001; pres. South Kortright Ctrl. Sch.; chmn. No. Catskills Econ. Devel. Coun., Econ. Devel. Coun. Stamford, Econ. Devel. Coun. Delaware County; regent St. Francis Coll.; bd. dirs. Econ. Devel. Coun., Printing Trade Sch., Cmty. Hosp. Stamford, N.Y., Stamford Econ. Devel. Coun., Delaware County Indsl. Devel. Authority County, 1999—, ECO Devel. Coun. Delaware County; sec. Delaware County Econ. Devel. Agy., 2000—; co-chair Project Strive, Albany, N.Y.; fin. com. Sacred Heart Roman Cath. Ch.; pres. Otsego Delaware Bd. Realtors, 2000; v.p. bd. dirs. Cath. Charities, 1999-2004, pres., 1999-2000, 2003-; Delaware County Indsl. Devel. sec., 2000—; pres., Stamford Rotary, 2004-. Paul Harris fellow Rotary Internat.; Internat. Rotary Benefactor; recipient St. Francis Coll. Alumni Fund award, 1965, Del. County Youth award, 1991, John F. Kennedy Meml. award, 1972, Internat. award Svc. to Investment Commn., 1982, Youth Bur. award, 1991, St. Francis Prep Sch. Alumni Achievement award, 1993; named Stamford Citizen of Yr., 1992, Realtor of Yr., 1992, Col. Harper Grange Citizen of Yr., 1993. Mem.: Am. Inst. Mgmt., Stamford C. of C. (pres. 1991—92), Otsego- Delaware Bd. Realtors (P.A.F. chmn., bd. dirs., pres.), Assn. Investment Bankers, Venture Assn. NJ (bd. dirs.), Conn. Venture Capital Assn., NY State Realtors Assn. (polit. action dir. 1999, trustee 2000—, bd. dirs., chmn. polit. action), Alumni Assn. CCNY, Honor Legion N.Y.C. Police Dept., Am. Legion, Cath. War Vets., Univ. Club of Albany, Alumni Assn. St. Francis Coll., Stamford Rotary Club (pres. 2004—), KC (4th deg.), Knights of Malta, Moose, Elks. Republican. Home: 1331 Red Rock Rd Stamford NY 12167 Office: Stamford Fin Bldg Off Bd Dirs Stamford NY 12167 Office Phone: 607-652-3311. Office Fax: 607-652-6301. Business E-Mail: dcre@wpe.com. *With all affluence, accomplishment, and success goes the responsibility of assistance; economic, social, and physical to the less fortunate of the world.*

BERGLES, ARTHUR EDWARD, mechanical engineering educator; b. NYC, Aug. 9, 1935; s. Edward H. and Victoria (Winkelmann) B.; m. Priscilla Lou Maule, June 19, 1960; children: Eric, Dwight. SB, SM, MIT, 1958, PhD, 1962; DEng (hon.), U. Porto, Portugal, 1998, Rand Afrikaans U., Johannesburg, S. Africa, 1999. Registered profl. engr., Mass. Research staff Nat. Magnet Lab., Cambridge, Mass., 1962-69; asst. prof. to assoc. prof. mech. engring. MIT, Cambridge, 1963-69, assoc. dir. heat transfer lab., 1966-69; prof. mech. engring. Ga. Inst. Tech., Atlanta, 1970-72; prof., chmn. dept. mech. engring. Iowa State U., Ames, 1972-83, prof., dir. heat transfer lab., 1983-86; Clark and Crossan prof. engring., dir. heat transfer lab. Rensselaer Poly. Inst., Troy, NY, 1986-97, dean of engring., 1989-92, Clark and Crossan prof. emeritus, 1997—; Glenn L. Martin Inst. prof. engring. U. Md., College Park, 1999—; sr. lectr. MIT, 1999—. Chmn. U.S. group heat transfer U.S./USSR Agreement, Washington, 1979-82; cons. to industry, mem. numerous adv. groups.; hon. prof. Beijing U. Tech., St. Petersburg State U., Russia. Co-author: Two-Phase Flow and Heat Transfer in the Power and Process Industries, 1981; co-editor: Two-Phase Heat Exchangers, 1988, Heat Transfer Enhancement of Heat Exchangers, 1999, others; editor: Heat Transfer in Electronic and Microelectronic Equipment, 1990; mem. editl. adv. bd. 13 jours.; contbr. numerous articles to tech. jours. Scoutmaster Boy Scout Am., Ames, 1976-84; bd. dirs. Ames Soc. for Arts, 1975-79. Recipient U.S. Sr. Scientist award Alexander von Humboldt Found., U. Hanover, Fed. Republic Germany, 1979-80, Tech. U., Munich, 1996-97, Faculty Achievement award in research Iowa State U., 1986, Nusselt-Reynolds prize Assembly Internat. Conf. on Exptl. Heat Transfer, 2001; named Anson Marston Disting. prof. engring., Iowa State U., 1981. Fellow AIAA (assoc.), ASHRAE (Edn. and Rsch. award N.E. chpt. 1993, Disting. Svc. award 1996, Anderson award 2000, Holladay award 2002), AAAS, NAE, ASME (hon. mem. 1996, v.p. 1981-85, chmn. heat transfer divsn. 1982-83, bd. govs. 1985-89, pres. 1990-91, Heat Transfer Meml. award 1979, Dedicated Svc. award 1984, Max Jakob Meml. award AIChE and ASME 1995, ASME medal 2000), Internat. Ctr. Heat and Mass Transfer (exec. com. 1984-2000, chmn. exec. com. 1996-98, Luikov medal 1998), Am. Soc. Engring. Edn. (Lamme award 1987, Centennial cert. and medal 1993), AIChE (Donald Q. Kern award 1990); mem. Soc. Automotive Engrs. (Ralph R. Teetor award 1987), Union Mech. and Elec. Engrs. and Technicians Yugoslavia (hon.), Acad. Scis. and Arts Slovenia (fgn.), Italian Nat. Acad. Scis. (fgn.), Polish Soc. Theoretical and Applied Mechanics (fgn.), Royal Acad. Engring. U.K. (fgn.), Rotary (Paul Harris fellow), Theta Chi. Republican. Lutheran. Office: Rensselaer Poly Inst Mech Aeronautical and Nuc Engring Troy NY 12180-3590 E-mail: abergles@aol.com. *My personal philosophy is to do as many things as I can, always striving for excellence and professionalism.*

BERGLUND, LARRY GLENN, mechanical engineer, educator; b. Mpls., Oct. 17, 1938; s. Lawrence Emil and Audrey Martina (Pearson) B.; m. Corinne Kay Swenberg; children: Bret Lawrence, Hans Nicholas. Student, St. Olaf Coll., Northfield, Minn., 1956-59; BME, U. Minn., 1962, MSME, 1965; PhD, Kans. State U., Manhattan, 1971. Registered profl. engr., Minn. Project engr. Trane Co., LaCrosse, Wis., 1965-68; asst. prof. mech. engring. Mich. Tech. U., Houghton, 1972-75; assoc. fellow John B. Pierce Found. Lab.; lectr. Yale U., New Haven, 1975—96; prof. arch. dept. Tohoku U., Sendai, Japan, 1996—99; assoc. rsch. fellow Kimberly Clark Corp., Neenah, Wis., 1999—2000; rsch. biomed. engr. U.S. Army Rsch. Inst. Environ. Medicine, Natick, Mass., 2000—. Mem. ASHRAE (Ralph G. Nevins award 1979), ASME, Japanese. Soc. Heating Air Conditioning and Sanitation Engrs., Eta Kappa Nu, Sigma Xi, Sigma Pi Sigma, Pi Tau Sigma, Phi Kappa Phi, Pine Orchard Yacht Club. Lutheran. Achievements include research in biothermal, environmental sensory, air quality, RFR research, human thermo-physiological response modeling and simulation. Home: 156 Lakeside Dr Lebanon CT 06249-2822 Office: USARIEM Kansas St Natick MA 01760 Home Phone: 860-887-4972; Office Phone: 508-233-4833. Business E-Mail: larry.berglund@na.amedd.army.mil.

BERGLUND, ROBIN G., psychiatrist, management consultant; b. Milw., Oct. 12, 1945; s. Gunnar E. and V. June (Huebsch) B.; children: Victoria S., Christopher F.; m. Akiko Haraguchi, Oct., 2000; 1 child, Liri. BS in Biochemistry magna cum laude, Mich. State U., 1967; MBA, Harvard U., 1971; MD, Med. Univ. S.C., 1995. Engr. Eastman Kodak Co., Rochester, NY, 1967-69; v.p. The First Nat. Bank of Chgo., 1971-75, Wells Fargo Bank, N.A., LA, 1975-77; exec. v.p. Ponderosa Homes, Newport Beach, Calif., 1977-84; chmn., CEO Glenfed Devel. Corp., Encino, Calif., 1984-88; pres. Lowe Enterprises Northwest, Seattle, 1988-89, Met. Homes Inc., Portland, Oreg., 1989-90; pediatrician UCLA-Cedars Sinai Med. Ctr., LA, 1995-96; psychiatrist UCLA Neuropsychiatric Inst. and Hosp., 1996-98, child psychiatrist, 1998-2000; pvt. practice child and adult psychiatry, 2000—. Bd. dirs. United Svc. Orgn., Hollywood, Calif., 1975-80, Am. Youth Soccer Orgn., Newport Beach, Calif., 1980-84, Waring Libr. Soc., Charleston, 1992-95; scoutmaster Boy Scouts of Am., San Marino, Calif., 1984-89; vol. Children's Hosp., Seattle, 1990-91. Nat. Merit and Nat. Honor Soc. scholar, Mich. State U., 1964-67. Mem. Am. Psychiat. Assn., Am. Acad. Child and Adolescent Psychiatry, Young Pres.'s Orgn., Blue Key, Phi Kappa Phi, Phi Eta Sigma, Delta Phi Epsilon, Omicron Delta Kappa. Avocations: travel, sailing. Office Phone: 818-784-4706.

BERGMAN, ANDREW, scriptwriter, film director; b. Queens, NY, Feb. 20, 1945; Grad. magna cum laude, Harpur Coll.; PhD in History, U. Wis., 1970. Publicist United Artists. Author: We're in the Money, The Big Kiss-Off of 1944, Hollywood and Levine, Sleepless Nights; writer: (Broadway comedy) Social Security, (films) Blazing Saddles, 1974, Black Bart, 1975, The In-Laws, 1979, Oh, God! You Devil, 1984, Fletch, 1985, Big Trouble, 1986, Soapdish, 1991, The Scout, 1994, The In-Laws, 2003; writer, dir.: So Fine, 1981, The Freshman, 1990, Honeymoon in Vegas, 1992, Striptease, 1996; dir.: It Could Happen to You, 1994, Isn't She Great, 2000; exec. prodr.: Chances Are, 1989, White Fang, 1991, Undercover Blues, 1993, Little Big League, 1994. Recipient Writers Guild Am. award, 1975, Ian McLellan Hunter Award for Lifetime Achievement in Writing, Writers Guild Am., East, 2007. Office: Creative Artists Agy 9830 Wilshire Blvd Beverly Hills CA 90212-1804*

BERGMAN, ARLENE, lawyer; b. NYC; BS, Adelphi U., 1974, MS, 1975; RN, CUNY, 1984; JD, Yeshiva U., 1990. Bar: NY 1991, US Dist. Ct. So. Dist. NY, US Dist. Ct. Ea. Dist. NY. Tchr. learning disabled; pvt. duty nurse; staff nurse Meml. Sloan Kettering Cancer Ctr.; joined Wilson, Elser, Moskowitz, Edelman & Dicker LLP, NYC, 1997, now ptnr. Office: Wilson Elser Moskowitz Edelman & Dicker LLP 23rd Fl 150 E 42nd St New York NY 10017-5639 Office Phone: 212-490-3000 ext. 2542. Office Fax: 212-490-3038. Business E-Mail: bergmana@wemed.com.

BERGMAN, BARBARA E., law educator; BA, Bradley U., 1973; JD, Stanford Law Sch., 1976. Bar: Calif., DC, N.Mex. Law clk. to Judge Ben C. Duniway, 9th Cir.; atty. Wilmer, Cutler & Pickering, Washington; assoc. counsel Pres. Jimmy Carter; staff atty. Pub. Defender Svc., Washington; practiced labor law Bredhoff & Kaiser; prof. evidence/trial practice, advocacy and criminal procedure U. N.Mex., 1987—. Tchr. Nat. Inst. Trial Advocacy progs., Nat. Criminal Def. Coll., Inst. Criminal Def. Advocacy; team leader Nat. Inst. Trial Advocacy Nat. Prog., Boulder, Colo. Co-author: Every Trial Criminal Defense Resource Book, 1994, Wharton's Criminal Evidence, 15th edit.; editor: New Mexico Criminal Practice Manual, DC Criminal Jury Instructions, 4th edit.; contbr. articles to profl. jours. Recipient Richard S. Jacobson award, Roscoe Pound Found. Mem.: Nat. Assn. Criminal Def. Lawyers (past pres., has served as first v.p., second v.p., treas., sec., and bd. dir., past chair budget and investment coms., past co-chair Amicus Curiae Com., Robert C. Heeney award 2000). Office: UNM Sch Law MSC11 6070 Office 3115 1 University of New Mexico Albuquerque NM 87131-0001 Office Phone: 505-277-3304. Office Fax: 505-277-4594. E-mail: bergman@law.unm.edu.*

BERGMAN, BRUCE E., municipal official; m.; 2 children. BA, Simpson Coll., 1970; JD, U. Houston, 1972. Clk. to Hon. M.E. Rawlings Iowa Supreme Ct., 1973-74; assoc. Williams, Hart, Lavorato & Kirtley, West Des Moines, Iowa, 1974-78, ptnr., 1978-79, Davis, Baker & Bergman, Des Moines, 1980-85, Isaacson, Clarke & Bergman, P.C., Des Moines, 1985-89; asst. city atty. City of Des Moines Legal Dept., 1989-90, solicitor, 1990-91, chief solicitor, 1991-96, corp. counsel, 1996—. Mem.: ABA, Internat. Municipal Lawyers Assn. (regional v.p. 2003—), Iowa Mcpl. Attys. Assn. (bd. dir. 1996—99, 2002—06, sec., treas. 2003, v.p. 2004, pres. 2005), Polk County Bar Assn., Iowa State Bar Assn. Home: 4508 49th St Des Moines IA 50310-2970 Office: Office of the Corp Counsel City of Des Moines City Hall 400 E 1st St Des Moines IA 50309 Office Phone: 515-283-4130. E-mail: bebergman@dmgov.org.

BERGMAN, CHARLES CABE, foundation executive; b. May 1, 1933; s. Sidney Meyer and Esther Rachel (Cabe) B. AB, Harvard U., 1954. Account asst. Ketchum, MacLeod & Grove, Inc., Pitts., 1955-57; assoc. dir. devel. and alumni affairs Browne & Nichols Sch., Cambridge, Mass., 1957-59; assoc. v.p. Lavin Co., Inc., Boston and NYC, 1959-61; v.p. People to People Health Fedn., Washington, 1962-63, Inter-Am. Found. for the Arts, NYC, 1963-65; exec. v.p., treas., trustee Acad. Religion and Mental Health, NYC, 1965-72; exec. v.p., COO, dir. Inst. Religion and Health, 1972-78; sr. assoc. Jeffcoat Schoen & Morrell, 1981-82; exec. v.p., COO Pollock-Krasner Found., Inc., NYC, 1985-99, chmn. bd., CEO, 1999—. Cons. UN Ctr. on Transnat. Corps., 1979-80; dir. George Nelson & Co., N.Y.C. Cons. Adminstrv. Psychiatry Program, Yale Med. Sch., New Haven, 1971, NIMH, Argentina, 1969, Ctr. for Studies Child and Family Mental Health, NIMH, Washington, 1971; spl. adviser Pres.'s Com. on Mental Retardation, Washington, 1971, Maurice Falk Med. Fund, 1971; Presdl. fellow Aspen Inst. Humanistic Studies. Chmn. internat. coun. Am. Field Svc. Internat. Intercultural Programs; bd. dirs. The Alliance Young Artists and Writers, Inc., NY, VSA Arts, Washington, Delfina Studios Trust, London, The Nat. Found. Advancement in the Arts, Miami, Fla.; mem. bd. advisors Fund Arts and Culture in Ctrl. and East Europe; bd. artistic advisors Ctr. Emerging Visual Artists; mem. N.Y. State Coun. on Arts, 1999—; sr. advisor Foursome Investments, Ltd., London; adv. bd. Lucy Daniels Found., Raleigh, NC; former mem. overseers' com. to visit Harvard U. Art Mus.; mem. NYC Cultural Affairs Adv. Com.; bd. dirs. Rubin Mus. Art.; sr. advisor nonprofit sector and philanthropy program Aspen Inst. Home: 24 E 82nd St # 4C New York NY 10028-0344 Office: 863 Park Ave New York NY 10021-0342 Home Phone: 212-472-8601; Office Phone: 212-517-5400. Business E-Mail: cbergman@pkf.org.

BERGMAN, DONALD ARTHUR, endocrinologist, educator; b. Bklyn., Apr. 6, 1946; s. Joseph and Clara Bergman; m. Susan Menin, June 23, 1970; 1 child, Melissa. AB, Dartmouth Coll., 1967; MD, Jefferson Med. Coll., 1971. Diplomate Am. Bd. Internal Medicine, Am. Bd. Internal Medicine. Ob-gyn. resident Mt. Sinai Hosp., NYC, 1971—72; med. intern NYU Hosps., NYC, 1972—73; med. resident Mt. Sinai Hosp., NYC, 1973—75, endocrinology fellow, 1975—77; pvt. practice NYC, 1977—; asst. clin. prof. medicine Mt. Sinai Sch. Medicine, NYC, 1984—97, assoc. clin. prof., 1997—2004, clin. prof., 2004—. Co-author: Mount Sinai Book of Nutrition, Clinical Practice Guidelines for Physicians-Thyroid Cancer, 2000; co-editor: Guide to Physical Activity, 2006; contbr. articles to profl. jours.; assoc. editor: Endocrine Practice, 1996—99. Bd. dirs. N.Y. Menopause Ctr., 1997—99. Capt. USAR, 1971—77. Fellow: ACP, Am. Coll. Endocrinology (sec.-treas. 2000—01, trustee 2000—01, chancellor 2004—05, pres. 2006—07, immediate past pres. 2007—); mem.: Endocrine Soc., Am. Assn. Clin. Endocrinologists (bd. dirs. 1993—, chair practice stds. com. 1995—97, state chpts. chair 1997—2002, sec. 1999—2000, treas. 2000—01, v.p. 2001—02, co-chmn. corp. adv. bd. 2002—03, pres.-elect 2002—03, co-chmn. ann. meeting 2003, pres. 2003—04, chair power prevention com. 2004—). Office: 1199 Park Ave Apt (1f) New York NY 10128-1713

BERGMAN, EDWARD JONATHAN, lawyer, educator; b. Jersey City, Aug. 10, 1942; s. Abe and Ethel (Leitner) B.; m. Jennifer Mullen; children: Peter Jeremy, Jennifer Amy. BA, U. Pa., 1963; JD, Columbia U., 1966. Bar: NJ 1974, US Dist. Ct. NJ 1974, US Supreme Ct. 1989. Ptnr. Bergman & Barrett, Princeton, N.J., 1975—; pub. defender Princeton Borough, 1986—, Princeton Twp., 1988—; fed. mediator U.S. Dist. Ct., N.J., 1992—; mediator N.J. Superior Ct., 1995—. Lectr. Woodrow Wilson Sch., Princeton U., 1990-92, dept. politics, 2003—; affiliated faculty dept. legal studies U. Pa. Wharton Sch. Bus., Phila., 1995—; vis. lectr. U. Calif., Berkeley, St. Petersburg U. Joint Mgmt. Program, Russia, 1995-99; assoc. Ctr. Bioethics U. Pa. Sch. Medicine, 2005—, dir. mediation svcs., 2006—; acad. dir. negotiation workshops IGE Ltd., India, 1999-2000; cert. comml. mediator NJ Assn. Profl. Mediators; complementary dispute resolution com. NJ Supreme Ct., 2005— Author: (with J. Bickerman) Court-Annexed Mediation: Perspectives on Selected State & Federal Programs, 1998; contbr. articles to profl. jours. Trustee Princeton Ballet, 1984-92, Arts Coun. Princeton, 1998-2003. Mem. ABA (sec. on dispute resolution, mediation com., vice-chmn. subcom. on ct.- annexed dispute resolution, mem., sec. dispute resolution publs. bd.), NJ Bar Assn., Mercer County Bar Assn., Princeton Bar Assn. (pres. 1986-87), Penn Basketball Club (exec. bd. 1995—), Penn Club NY, NJ Assn. Profl. Mediators (bd. dirs. 2005—), Inn of Ct. (Master Justice Marie Garibaldi, complementary dispute resolution 2003—) Avocations: wine, travel, sports, art, architecture. Home: 95 Wilson Rd Princeton NJ 08540-2601 Office: Bergman & Barrett PO Box 1273 Princeton NJ 08542-1273 Office Phone: 609-921-1502. Business E-Mail: ejb@gear3.net.

BERGMAN, EMILY ANNE, librarian; b. July 24, 1953; d. Arthur L. and Jean Lucy (Anson) Bergman; m. Mark Andrew Allen, June 20, 1982; children: Philip Isaac Allen, Brian Anson Allen. Student, Wroxton Coll., Banbury, Eng., 1974; BA, Goucher Coll., 1975; MLS, U. Tex., Austin, 1976. Rsch. libr. Tracy-Locke Advt., Dallas, 1977—78; catalog Dallas Pub. Libr., 1978—80, head, spl. collections cataloging, 1980—81; asst. libr. dir. Calif. Sch. Profl. Psychology, LA, 1981—90; catalog libr. Gene Autry Western Heritage Mus., LA, 1990—92, head libr., 1992—96, curator, rare books, 1996—98; head, collections and tech. svcs. Occidental Coll., LA, 1998—. Mem.: ALA (com. mem.), Mental Health Librs. (v.p., pres.-elect 1987—88, pres. 1988—89), Libr. Instruction Round Table (vice treas. 1992—93, treas. 1993—94), Libr. Adminstrn. and Mgmt. Assn. (systems and svcs. sect. vice chair 2003—04, chair 2004—05, sec. 2005—), L.A. Preservation Network (vice chair 1998, chair 1999), Calif. Acad. and Rsch. Librs. Democrat. Jewish. Home: 1001 Geneva St Glendale CA 91207-1709 Office: Occidental Coll 1600 Campus Rd Los Angeles CA 90041

BERGMAN, GEORGE MARK, mathematician, educator; b. Bklyn., July 22, 1943; s. Lester V. and Sylvia G. (Bernstein) B.; m. Mary Frances Anderson, Dec. 26, 1981; stepsons: Jeff Elam, Michael L. Anderson; children: Clifford I. and Rebecca N. Anderson-Bergman (twins). BA, U. Calif., Berkeley, 1963; PhD, Harvard U., 1968. Asst. prof. Dept. Math. U. Calif., Berkeley, 1967-72, assoc. prof., 1972-78, prof., 1978—. Contbr. articles to profl. jours. Mem. AAUP, ACLU, Am. Math. Soc. Democrat. Avocations: linguistics, dance. Office: U Calif Dept Math Berkeley CA 94720-3840

BERGMAN, HERMAS JOHN (JACK), retired college administrator; b. May 3, 1926; s. Ruebin Eric and Esther (Schierman) Bergman; m. Jeanne Louise Culton, 1946 (div. 1961); children: Stephen, Kathleen, Marsha; m. Evelyn Alice Templeman, Apr. 6, 1963; children: Kristin, Robert. BA, Walla Walla Coll., 1948; MA, U. Puget Sound, 1963; PhD, Wash. State U., 1967. Tchr. Wash. Pub. Schs., Wenatchee and Tacoma, 1948—58, 1961—64; bus. mgr. Totem Plywood, Inc., Tacoma, 1958—61; prof. history Western Oreg. U., Monmouth, 1966—79, dean Liberal Arts and Scis., 1980—85; pres. Walla Walla U., College Place, Wash., 1985—90; ret., 1990. Author: The Religious Fringe; contbr. articles to profl. jours. Chmn. bd. commrs. Polk County Parks and Recreation Commn., Dallas, Oreg., 1977—80; nat. adv. coun. Am. United for Separation of Ch. and State, 1992—2001; bd. trustees Walla Walla Gen. Hosp., 1985—2005; chmn. bd. Internat. Children's Care Inc., Vancouver, Wash., 1981—89; bd. dirs. Walla Walla Symphony, 2003—06; exec. com. Oreg. Conf. Seventh-day Adventists, 1981—85; v.p. Wash. State Religious Liberty Assn. of Pacific N.W., 1991—2001; mem. exec. com. North Pacific Conf. Seventh-day Adventists, 1985—90; bd. dirs. Portland Adventist Med. Ctr., 1972—78, 1985—90, Ind. Colls. of Wash., Seattle, 1985—90, United Way of Walla Walla, 1988—91, Wash. Friends of Higher Edn., Seattle, 1985—90. Avocations: photography, geology, stamps, lapidary.

BERGMAN, MARILYN KEITH, lyricist, writer; b. Bklyn. d. Albert A. and Edith (Arkin) Katz; m. Alan Bergman, Feb. 9, 1958; 1 child, Julie Rachel. BA, NYU; MusD (hon.), Berklee Coll. Music, 1995, Trinity Coll., 1997. Lyricist, collaborator (with Alan Bergman) (numerous pop, theatrical and film score songs, TV themes) Bracken's World, 1969—70, The Sandy Duncan Show, 1972, Maude, 1972—78, Good Times, 1974—79, The Nancy Walker Show, 1976, The Dumplings, 1976, Alice, 1976—82, In the Heat of the Night, 1988—94, Brooklyn Bridge, 1991—93, The Powers That Be, 1993, TV film lyrics The Hands of Time (from Brian's Song), 1971, Queen of the Stardust Ballroom, 1975 (Emmy award for best dramatic underscore and best musical material, 1975, score only), Sybil, 1976 (Emmy award for best dramatic underscore 1976, 1976), Too Many Springs (from Hollow Image), 1979, theatrical scores Something More, 1964, Ballroom, 1978 (Grammy award nominee for best cast show album, 1979), The Lady and the Clarinet, 1980, feature film songs The Marriage Go-Round, from The Marriage Go-Round, 1960, Any Wednesday, from Any Wednesday, 1966, Make Me Rainbows, from Fitzwilly, 1967, (score) In the Heat of the Night, 1967, The Windmills of Your Mind, from the Thomas Crown Affair, 1968 (Acad. award for best song, 1968, Golden Globe award best original song, 1969), His Eyes, Her Eyes, from The Thomas Crown Affair, 1968, You Must Believe in Spring, from Young Girls of Rochefort, 1968, Maybe Tomorrow, from John and Mary, 1969, Tomorrow Is My Friend, from Gaily, Gaily, 1969, There's Enough to Go Around, 1969, A Smile, A Mem'ry and an Extra Shirt, from A Man Called Gannon, 1969, Sugar in the Rain, from Stiletto, 1969, What Are You Doing the Rest of You Life?, from The Happy Ending, 1969 (Acad. award nominee for best song, 1969), I Was Born in Love With You, from Wuthering Heights, 1970, Sweet Gingerbread Man, from The Magic Garden of Stanley Sweetheart, 1970, Nobody Knows, 1970, Move, from Move, 1970, Pieces of Dreams (Little Boy Lost), from Pieces of Dreams, 1970 (Academy award nominee for best song, 1970), The Costume Ball, from Doctors' Wives, 1971, All His Children, from Sometimes a Great Notion, 1971 (Acad. award nominee for best song, 1971), Rain Falls Anywhere It Wants To, from the African Elephant, 1971, The Summer Knows, from Summer of '42, 1971 (Grammy award nominee for song of the year 1972, 1972), A Face in the Crowd, from Le Mans, 1971, Marmalade, Molasses and Honey, from The Life and Times of Judge Roy Bean, 1972 (Acad. award nominee for best song, 1972), Love's the Only Game in Town, from Pete and Tillie, 1972, Molly and Lawless John, 1972, The Way We Were, from The Way We Were, 1973 (Grammy award for song of the year, 1973, Acad. award for best song, 1973, Golden Globe award for best original song, 1974, Grammy award for best original score, 1974), Breezy's Song, from Breezy, 1973, In Every Corner of the World, from Forty Carats, 1973, Summer Wishes, Winter Dreams, from Summer Wishes, Winter Dreams, 1973, Easy Baby, from 99 and 44/100%, 1974, There'll Be Time, from Ode to Billy Joe, 1975, Evening Sun, Morning Moon, from The Yakuza, 1975, I Believe in Love, from A Star is Born, 1976 (Grammy award nomination best original score, 1977), I'm Harry, I'm Walter, from Harry and Walter Go to New York, 1976, Hello and Goodbye, from Noon to Three, 1976, Bobby Deerfield, from Bobby Deerfield, 1977, The Last Time I Felt Like This, from Same Time Next Year, 1978 (Acad. award nominee for best song, 1978), The One and Only, from The One and Only, 1978, There's Something Funny Goin' On, from ...And Justice For All, 1979, I'll Never Say Goodbye, from The Promise, 1979 (Acad. award nominee for best song, 1979), Where Do You Catch the Bus for Tomorrow, from A Change of Seasons, 1980, Ask Me No Questions, from Back Roads, 1981, How Do You Keep the Music Playing?, from Best Friends, 1982 (Acad. award nominee for best song, 1982), Think About Love, 1982, Comin' Home to You, from Author! Author!, 1982, Tootsie, from Tootsie, 1982, It Might Be You, 1982 (Acad. award nominee for best song, 1982, Grammy award nominee for best original score, 1983), If We Were in Love, from Yes, Giorgio, 1982 (Acad. award nominee for best song, 1982), Never Say Never Again, from Never Say Never again,

1983, Papa, Can You Hear Me?, from Yentl, 1983 (Academy award nomination best song, 1983), The Way He Makes Me Feel, 1983 (Acad. award nominee for best song, 1983), Will Someone Ever Look at Me That Way?, 1983 (Acad. award best original score and Grammy award nomination for best original score, 1984, Acad. award nominee for best original song, 1983), Yentl, 1983 (Acad. award for best original score, 1983), Little Boys, from The Man Who Loved Women, 1983, Something New in My Life, from Mickey and Maude, 1984, The Music of Goodbye, from Out of Africa, 1985, I Know the Feeling, from The January Man, 1989, The Girl Who Used to Be Me, from Shirley Valentine, 1989 (Acad. award nominee for best song, 1989, Golden Globe nominee for best original song, 1990, Grammy award nominee, 1990), Welcome Home, from Welcome Home, 1989, Most of All You, from Major League, 1989, Dreamland, from For the Boys, 1991, Places That Belong to You, from The Prince of Tides, 1991, It's All There, from Switch, 1991, Moonlight, from Sabrina, 1995 (Acad. award nominee for best original song, 1996, Golden Globe nominee, Grammy nominee), The Best of Friends, from Bogus, 1996, Love is Where You Are, from At First Sight, pop songs You Don't Bring Me Flowers, 1978 (Grammy award nominee for song of the year, 1978), In the Heat of the Night, The Summer Knows, Nice 'N' Easy (Grammy award nominee for song of the year, 1960), Someone in the Dark, L.A. Is My Lady, After the Rain, I Was Born in Love With You, That Face, Look Around, I Love to Dance Like They Used to Dance, What Matters Most, One Day, A Child Is Born, Sleep Warm, Sentimental Baby, Live It Up, If I Close My Eyes, Yellow Bird, Like a Lover, Where Do You Start?, On My Way to You, Ordinary Miracles (Cable Ace award and Emmy award for best original song), A Ticket to Dream (Emmy Awd. for best song), albums Never Be Afraid for Bing Crosby, The Ballad of the Blues for Jo Stafford, 1999, Barbra Streisand: The Concert (Ace nominee for writing of a spl.). Named to songwriters hall of Fame, 1980; recipient singers salute to songwriter award, Clooney Found., 1986, Aggie award, Songwriter's Guild, 1987; grantee Am. Film Inst., 1976. Mem.: ASCAP (pres., chmn. bd. dirs. 1994—). Office: ASCAP 7920 Sunset Blvd Ste 300 Los Angeles CA 90046

BERGMAN, NANCY PALM, real estate investment company executive; b. McKeesport, Pa., Dec. 3, 1938; d. Walter Vaughn and Nellie (Sullivan) Leech; m. Donald Bergman; 1 child, Tiffany Palm Taylor. Student, Mt. San Antonio Coll., 1970, UCLA, 1989—93. Corporate sec. U.S. Filter Corp., Newport Beach, Calif., 1965—. Pres. Jaguar Research Corp., L.A. and Atlanta, 1971-; owner Environ. Designs, L.A., 1976—; pres. Prosher Corp., L.A., 1978-83; now pres., dir. Futura Investments, L.A.; CEO Rescor, Inc. Author: Resident Managers Handbook. Elder Beverly Hills Presbyn. Ch., 2006. Home: 1255 Benedict Canyon Dr Beverly Hills CA 90210 also: 23540 Tapatia Rd Homeland CA 92548 Office: PO Box 15246 Beverly Hills CA 90209

BERGMAN, RICHARD ISAAC, health information executive; b. Bklyn., Jan. 18, 1934; s. Joseph and Clara (Menchel) Bergman; m. Judith Hyman, June 24, 1956 (div. 1974); children: Deborah Jill, Susan Bergman Hackett; m. Victoria Smalley, June 9, 1987. SB, MIT, Cambridge, 1955, SM, 1956. Devel. engr. Exxon Rsch., Linden, NJ, 1956-60; mem. adj. faculty NJ Inst. Tech., Newark, 1957-58; dir. engring. Princeton Chem. Rsch., NJ, 1960-67; exec. v.p. Systemedics, Inc., Princeton, 1967-80; pres. Savant Assocs., Inc., Princeton, 1980-98; exec. dir. White House Task Force on Workplace Safety and Health, Washington, 1977-78; pres. Project Masters, Inc., Princeton, 1980—. Mem. vis. com. med. dept. MIT, Cambridge, 1973—83, Cambridge, 1986—88, Whitaker Coll., 1979—85; dir. Response Analysis Corp., Princeton, 1970—77; pres., dir. CWW, Inc., Princeton, 1998—. Contbr. articles to profl. jours. Mem.: AIChE (past chmn. NJ sect.), NY Acad. Scis., Am. Chem. Soc., MIT Alumni/ae Assn. (bd. dirs. 2000—03). Achievements include patents in field. Home: 134 Leabrook Ln Princeton NJ 08540-3622 Office: Project Masters Inc PO Box AG Princeton NJ 08542-0872 Office Phone: 609-921-0749. Personal E-mail: richard.bergman@verizon.net.

BERGMAN, ROBERT GEORGE, chemist, educator; b. Chgo., May 23, 1942; s. Joseph J. and Stella (Horowitz) Bergman; m. Wendy L. Street, June 17, 1965; children: David R., Michael S. BA in Chemistry cum laude, Carleton Coll., 1963, PhD (hon.), 1995; PhD, U. Wis., 1966. NATO fellow in chemistry Columbia U., NYC, 1966-67; Arthur Amos Noyes instr. chemistry Calif. Inst. Tech., Pasadena, 1967-69, asst. prof. chemistry, 1969-71, assoc. prof. chemistry, 1971-73, prof., 1973-77; prof. chemistry U. Calif., Berkeley, 1977—2002, Gerald E.K. Branch disting. prof. chemistry, 2002—, asst. dean Coll. Chemistry, 1987-91, 96, Miller Rsch. prof., 1982-83, 93, 2003. Sherman Fairchild Disting. scholar Calif. Inst. Tech., 1984; mem. panel bioinorganic and metallobiochemistry study sect. NIH, 1977—80; cons. Union Carbide Corp., 1977—81, 1990—2001, E. I. DuPont de Nemours, 1982—85, Chevron Rsch. Co., 1983—89, Dow Chem. Co., 2001—02; disting. vis. prof. U. NC, Chapel Hill, 1999. Mem. editl. bd.: Chem. Revs., Jour. Am. Chem. Soc., Organometallics, Tetrahedron Pubs., European Jour. Inorganic Chemistry; contbr. articles to profl. jours. Recipient Tchr. Scholar award, Camille and Henry Dreyfus Found., 1970—75, Excellence in Tchg. award, Calif. Inst. Tech., 1978, Merit award, NIH, 1991, E. O. Lawrence award for Chemistry, Dept. Energy, 1993, Chem. Pioneer award, Am. Inst. Chemists, 2000, Technology Transfer award, Lawrence Berkeley Nat. Lab., 2004; NIH fellow, 1964—66, Alfred P. Sloan Found. fellow, 1970—72, Guggenheim fellow, 1999. Mem.: NAS (NAS award in chemical sciences 2007), AAAS, Am. Chem. Soc. (Organometallic Chemistry award 1986, Arthur C. Cope scholar 1987, Edward Fahs Smith award Pa. sect. 1990, Ira Remsen award Balt. sect. 1990, Arthur C. Cope award 1996, Edward Leete award 2001, James Flack Norris award 2003), Phi Beta Kappa, Phi Lambda Upsilon, Sigma Xi (Monie Ferst award 2003). Home: 501 Coventry Rd Kensington CA 94707-1316 Office: U Calif Dept Chemistry Berkeley CA 94720-0001 Home Phone: 510-527-2937. E-mail: bergman@cchem.berkeley.edu.

BERGMAN, STANLEY M., health products executive; CPA. Exec. v.p. Henry Schein, Inc., Melville, NY, 1985-89, bd. dir., 1982—, v.p. fin. and adminstrn., 1980-85, chmn., CEO, pres., 1989—2005, chmn., CEO, 2005—. Office: Henry Schein Inc 135 Duryea Rd Melville NY 11747*

BERGMAN, VICTORIA BESTERMAN, small business owner, consultant; b. Covington, Ky., Aug. 22, 1944; d. John Joseph and Marion Julia (Schlueter) Besterman; m. Ralph D. Smalley, June 6, 1966 (div. Sept. 1975); m. Richard I. Bergman, June 9, 1987. BA in Polit. Sci., U. Cin., 1966, MA in Pub. Adminstrn., 1969. Adminstr., organizer state and local govt., Cin., 1966-72; project coord., planner Health Svcs., Atlantic County, N.J., 1972-73; program and budget analyst, spl. asst. to Asst. Commnr. N.J. State Govt., Trenton, 1973-77; pub. affairs officer, staff spl. reorgn. project, adminstr. U.S. Govt., EOP, Washington, 1977-81; v.p. Savant Assocs., Inc., Princeton, NJ, 1981—98. Adj. faculty in pub. adminstrn. Trenton State Coll., 1973-77; v.p. Project Masters, Inc., 1981—. Founder Princeton Cmty. Without Walls; past co-chair Princeton U. Summer Chamber Concerts Com.; founder Women's PAC of N.J., past co-chair; founder N.J. Women's Network, past trustee; zoning bd. adjustment Princeton Twp., 1989—96, chair zoning bd. adjustment, 1995—96; active Regional Planning Bd. Princeton, 2000—05, chair, 2001—04, vice chair, 2004—05. Mem.: Am. Soc. Pub. Adminstrn. (past bd. dirs. sect. women in pub. adminstrn., regions I and II liaison, coun. and coms. mem. N.J. chpt., natural resources sect. environ. adminstrn. sect.), U. Cin. Alumni Assn. (Outstanding Disting. Alumna award). Avocations: singing, walking, hiking, reading. Office: Project Masters Inc PO Box AG Princeton NJ 08542-0872 Personal E-mail: vicky.bergman@verizon.net. E-mail: vbergman@princeton-township.nj.us.

BERGMANN, ARTHUR M., writer, retired journalist, retired county official; b. NY, Nov. 24, 1927; s. Augustus H. Bergmann. BS in Polit. Sci. and Pub. Adminstrn., Empire State Coll., SUNY, Old Westbury, 1974; M in Pub. and Gen. Adminstrn., L.I.U., 1979. Cert. arbitrator. With N.Y. Herald Tribune, 1945-63; asst. news editor Riverhead News, 1949-50; Suffolk County (N.Y.) corr. for N.Y.C. newspapers, 1949-63; news editor Moriches (N.Y.) Tribune, 1950-51; mem. staff Newsday, 1951-71, Suffolk County polit. editor, columnist, 1965-71; chief dep. Suffolk County Exec., Hauppauge, NY, 1972-79. Chmn. Suffolk Criminal Justice Coordinating Coun., 1975-79, Arson Action Com.-Suffolk Arson Task Force, 1975-77, MTA Permanent Citizens Adv. Com., 1978-79; adv. coun. N.Y. State Crime Victims Compensation Bd., 1978-79; trustee Suffolk Acad. Medicine, 1974. Served with USAAF, 1946-47. Recipient Disting. Svc. award United Jewish Appeal, 1976; Pub. Adminstrn. award C. W. Post Coll., 1977; Disting. Svc. plaque L.I. Assn. Commerce & Industry, 1977; Exemplary Svc. award Empire State Coll., SUNY, 1981; nominated for Pulitzer prize (2). Mem. Acad. Polit. Sci., Soc. Silurians, Am. Legion, Pi Alpha Alpha. Address: 2403 24th Way West Palm Beach FL 33407

BERGMANN, BARBARA ROSE, economics professor; b. NYC, July 20, 1927; d. Martin and Nellie Berman; m. Fred H. Bergmann, July 16, 1965; children: Sarah Nellie, David Martin. BA, Cornell U., 1948; MA, Harvard U., 1955, PhD, 1959; PhD (hon.), De Montford U., 1996, Muhlenberg Coll., 2000. Economist U.S. Bur. Labor Stats., NYC, 1949-53; sr. staff ecomomist, cons. Council Econ. Advisors, Washington, 1961-62; sr. staff Brookings Inst., Washington, 1963-65; sr. econ. advisor AID, Washington, 1966-67; assoc. prof. U. Md., College Park, 1965-71, prof. econs., 1971-88; disting. prof. econs. Am. U., Washington, 1988-97, prof. emeritus, 1997—. Author: (with Chinitz and Hoover) Projection of a Metropolis, 1961; (with George W. Wilson) Impact of Highway Investment on Development, 1966; (with David E. Kaun) Structural Unemployment in the U.S., 1967; (with Robert Bennett) A Microsimulated Transactions Model of the United States Economy, 1985, Saving Our Children from Poverty: What the United States Can Learn from France, 1996, In Defense of Affirmative Action, 1996, Is Social Security Broke? A Cartoon Guide to the Issues, 1999, (with Suzanne W. Helburn) America's Child Care Problem: The Way Out, 2002, The Economic Emergence of Women, 2d edit., 2005; mem. editl. bd. Am. Econ. Rev., 1970-73, Challenge, 1978—, Signs, 1978-85; columnist econ. affairs N.Y. Times, 1981-82. Mem. Economists for McGovern, 1977; mem. panel econ. advisors Congl. Budget Office, Washington, 1977-87; mem. price adv. com. U.S. council on Wage and Price Stability, 1979-80. Fellow: Nat. Acad. Polit. and Social Sci.; mem.: AAUP (coun. 1980—83, pres. 1990—92), Soc. Advancement Socio-Econs. (pres. 1995—96), Internat. Assn. Feminist Econs. (pres. 1999), Ea. Econ. Assn. (pres. 1974), Am. Econ. Assn. (v.p. 1976, adv. com. to US Census Bur. 1977—82). Democrat. Home: 5430 41st Pl NW Washington DC 20015-2911 E-mail: bbergman@umd.edu, bberg@american.edu.

BERGMANN, DONALD GERALD, pharmaceutical company executive; b. Aug. 13, 1949; s. Edgar Frank and Dorothy Bertha Bergmann; m. Kathy Jeanne Dumont, Sept. 4, 1976; children: Karen Ann, Kim Jeanne. BS, Mich. State U., 1972; PhD, Ohio State U., 1978. Rschr. UCLA, 1978-81; project leader Burroughes-Wellcome Co., Kansas City, Kans., 1981-83; scientist Genentech, Inc., South San Francisco, Calif., 1983, ops. mgr., 1983-87, sr. project mgr., 1987-88; dir. biopharm. mfg. SmithKline Beecham Pharms., Phila., 1988-91, group dir. biopharm. tech. ops., 1991-95, gen. mgr. biopharms., 1995-2000; gen. mgr. global biopharms. GlaxoSmithKline Pharms., Phila., 2001—04; sr. v.p. ops. Tengion, Inc., Phila., 2005—. Contbr. articles to profl. jours. and publs. Fellow Nat. Cancer Inst., 1978-80; grantee Nat. Cancer Inst., Am. Cancer Soc. Avocations: skiing, wine collecting.

BERGMANN, PETER GEORGE, lawyer; b. NYC, July 1, 1949; s. Paul and Therese (Greenfield) B.; m. Kay Kirstine Gardiner, Oct. 13, 1991. BA, NYU, 1970; JD with honors, George Washington U., 1973. Law clk to Hon. James T. Foley U.S. Dist. Ct. (no. dist.) N.Y., Albany, 1973-74; ptnr. Cadwalader Wickersham & Taft, NYC, 1974—, chmn., Health Care & Not-for-Profit dept. Recipient Reverend Parks award St. Margaret's House, 1992. Mem. ABA (past chmn. Regional Forum on Health Law), N.Y. State Bar Assn., Fed. Bar Council, N.Y. County Lawyers Assn. (past chmn. com. health svcs.), N.Y. Assn. Homes and Svcs. for Aging (gen. counsel), Am. Assn. Homes for Aging (chmn. legal com. 1998-2000). Office: Cadwalader Wickersham & Taft LLP 1 World Fin Ctr New York NY 10281 Office Phone: 212-504-6595. Office Fax: 212-504-6666. Business E-Mail: peter.bergmann@cwt.com.

BERGMANN, THOMAS E., corporate financial executive; BA, Coll. of St. Thomas, 1987; M mgmt., Kellogg Sch. Northwestern Univ., 1994. CPA. Fin. mgmt. positions Honeywell Internat.; dir. treas. & internat. treas. services Johnson & Johnson; v.p., treas. The St. Paul Companies; v.p., contr. Sears Roebuck & Co., 2002—03, v.p. fin. services, 2003; sr. v.p., CFO USF Corp., 2004, exec. v.p., interim CFO, 2004—05; v.p., CFO Harley-Davidson Inc., Milw., 2006—. Mailing: Harley-Davidson Inc PO Box 653 Milwaukee WI 53201-0653 Office: Harley-Davidson Inc 3700 W Juneau Ave Milwaukee WI 53201*

BERGNER, JANE COHEN, lawyer; d. Louis and Selma (Breslaw) Cohen; m. Alfred P. Bergner, May 30, 1968 (dec. Sept. 24, 2002); children: Lauren, Justin. AB, Vassar Coll., 1964; LLB, Columbia U., 1967. Bar: DC 1968, US Dist. Ct. DC 1968, US Ct. Appeals (DC cir.) 1968, US Ct. Fed. Claims 1969, US Ct. Appeals (fed. cir.) 1969, US Tax Ct. 1979, US Supreme Ct. 1992. Trial atty. tax divsn. U.S. Dept. Justice, Washington, 1967-74; assoc. Arnold & Porter, Washington, 1974-76, Rogovin, Huge & Lenzner, Washington, 1976-83; of counsel Arter & Hadden, 1983-86; ptnr. Spriggs & Hollingsworth, 1986-89, Feith & Zell, P.C., 1989-93; pvt. practice Washington, 1993—. Mem. jud. confs. US Ct. Fed. Claims, US Tax Ct. Author: Tax Court Practice and Court of Federal Claims Practice, West's Federal Forms, 2007, Mertens Law of Federal Income Taxation, Chpt. 50, U.S. Tax Court; contbr. articles to profl. jours. Bd. dirs. Jewish Social Svc. Agy., Washington; former mem. cmty. adv. bd. Sta. WAMU-FM, Washington; former mem., bd. dirs. Jewish Coun. for the Aging. Named one of Best Lawyers in Am., Am.'s Most Influential Women, Forbes Radio Network. Fellow: Am. Coll. Tax Counsel; mem.: ABA (chmn. regional liaison meetings com. 1993—95, sect. taxation, mem. govt. rels. com., mem. civil and criminal penalties com.), Washington DC Estate Planning Coun., Women's Bar Assn. DC, Fed. Bar Assn., DC Bar (chair taxation sect. 1985—90, chair tax audits and litig. com. 1990—93, Outstanding Sect. award 1986, Cmty. Outreach award 1993), Columbia U. Law Sch. Alumni Assn., Women's Tax Luncheon Group, Vassar Coll. Class Alumnae (chair spl. gifts com. 25th reunion), Vassar Club. Avocations: opera, classical music, travel, art collecting, gardening. Office: 1776 K St NW Ste 800 Washington DC 20006 Office Phone: 202-470-5520. Office Fax: 202-719-4031. Business E-Mail: jbergnerlaw@abanet.org.

BERGNER, JEFFREY THOMAS, federal agency administrator; BA, Carleton Coll.; MA, PhD, Princeton U. Staff dir. fgn. rels. com. U.S. Senate; founder, pres. Bergner, Bockorny, Castagnetti, Hawkins & Brain, Inc.; sr. transatlantic fellow German Marshall Fund; asst. sec. legis. affairs US Dept. State, Washington, 2005—. Former adj. prof. U. Pa., U. Mich., Georgetown U.; trustee Asia Found.; bd. dirs. Bus. Execs. for Nat. Security, Hudson Inst. Office: US Dept State 2201 C St NW Washington DC 20520

BERGNER, JOHN F., lawyer; b. Pratt, Kans., Mar. 27, 1957; BBA in Fin., Washburn U., Kans., 1979, JD, 1982; ML in Taxation, Georgetown U., Washington, DC, 1985. Bar: Kans. 1982, Mo. 1982, Tex. 1985, US Dist. Ct. (dist. Kans.) 1982, US Ct. Appeals (DC cir.) 1983, US Tax Ct. 1983. Tax adv. Touche Ross & Co., Kansas City, Mo., 1982-83; tax law clk. Steptoe & Johnson, Washington, 1984; atty. adv. to Daniel J. Dinan US Tax Ct., Washington, 1984-85; atty. Winstead PC, Dallas, 1985—. Mem. Nat. Com. Planned Giving; adv. coun. Tex. Cmty. Found., Children's Med. Ctr. Found., Tex.; bd. dir. Bryan's House, Dallas; mem. Estate Planning Coun. S.W. Med. Found., Tex.; bd. gov. Dallas Estate Planning Coun., 1998—2000. Named one of Best Lawyers in Dallas, D Mag., 2001, 2003, 2005, Best Lawyer in Dallas, 2007, Top 100 Attys., Worth mag., 2005—06. Fellow: Am. Coll. Trust and Estate Counsel; mem.: Tex. Bd. Legal Specialization (bd. cert. Estate Planning & Probate Law), Mo. Bar Assn., DC Bar Assn., Kans. Bar Assn., Tex. Bar Assn., Dallas Bar Assn. (past chmn.), ABA (chmn. Estate Gift & Taxes Com.). Republican. Episcopalian. Avocation: numismatist specializing in early Am. copper coinage. Office: Winstead PC 5400 Renaissance Tower 1201 Elm St Dallas TX 75270-2199 Office Phone: 214-745-5289. Office Fax: 214-745-5390. Business E-Mail: jbergner@winstead.com.

BERGONIA, RAYMOND DAVID, venture capitalist; b. Spring Valley, Ill., May 21, 1951; s. Raymond A. and Elva M. (Bernadini) B.; m. Linda Goble, Dec. 31, 1988; children: Alexandra, Andrew, Caroline, Margot. BBA, U. Notre Dame, 1973; JD, Harvard U., 1976. Bar: Ill. 1976, U.S. Dist. Ct. (no. dist.) Ill. 1976, U.S. Tax Ct. 1977; C.P.A., Ill. Assoc. Winston & Strawn, Chgo., 1976-79; legal counsel, v.p. adminstrn. Heizer Corp., Chgo., 1979-86; v.p. corp. fin. Chgo. Corp., 1986-89; exec. v.p., prin. N.Am. Bus. Devel. Co. L.L.C., Chgo., 1989—. Bd. dirs. numerous pvt. cos. Recipient Elijah Watts Sells award Am. Inst. C.P.A.s, 1973 Mem. ABA, Chgo. Bar Assn. Home: 605 Essex Rd Kenilworth IL 60043-1129 Office: NAM Bus Devel Co LLC 135 S La Salle St Chicago IL 60603-4159 Office Phone: 312-332-4950. Business E-Mail: dbergonia@northamericanfund.com.

BERGQUIST, JAMES MANNING, history professor; b. Council Bluffs, Iowa, Feb. 1, 1934; s. Reuben Neil and Irene Mary (Norton) B.; m. Joan Marie Solon, May 17, 1969; children: John Norton, Charles James. BA, U. Notre Dame, 1955; MA in History, Northwestern U., 1956, PhD in History, 1966. Instr. history Coe Coll., Cedar Rapids, Iowa, 1961-63, Villanova (Pa.) U., 1963-66, asst. prof., 1966-69, assoc. prof., 1969-86, prof., 1986—2002, prof. emeritus, 2002—. Contbr. articles on Am. social history and immigration to profl. jours., chapters to books. Trustee Balch Inst. for Ethnic Studies, Phila., 1988—92, 1994—2001; mem. Pa. Task Force on Diversity in Higher Edn., 1991—94. Fellow, NEH, 1967, 1977, 1980. Mem.: AAUP (pres. Pa. divsn. 1988—90, nat. coun. 1995—2001), Ethnic Studies Assn. Phila. (pres. 1980—82), Hist. Soc. Pa., Am. Assn. State and Local History, Immigration and Ethnic History Soc. (bd. dirs. 1995—), Soc. for History of the Early Am. Republic, Orgn. Am. Historians, Am. Hist. Assn. Democrat. Roman Catholic. Avocations: swimming, travel. Home: 217 Devon Blvd Devon PA 19333-1616 Office: Villanova U History Dept Villanova PA 19085 Business E-Mail: james.bergquist@villanova.edu.

BERGQUIST, PETER, retired music educator; b. Sacramento, Aug. 5, 1930; s. Ed Peter and Margaret (Rogers) B.; m. Dorothy Catherine Clark, June 16, 1956; children: Carolyn, Emily (dec.). Student, Eastman Sch. Music, Rochester, NY, 1948-51; BS, Mannes Coll. Music, NYC, 1958; MA, Columbia U., 1960, PhD, 1964. Asst. prof. Sch. Music, U. Oreg., Eugene, 1964-69, assoc. prof., 1969-73, prof., 1973-95, prof. emeritus, 1995—. Editor: Orlando di Lasso, Samtliche Werke neue Reihe, vol. 22-25, 1992—93, Orlando di Lasso: The Complete Motets, 21 vols. and supplement, 1995—2007, Orlando di Lasso Studies, 1999; music reviewer Eugene Register Guard; contbr. articles to profl. jours. Sr. warden, jr. warden, vestryman St. Mary's Episcopal Ch., Eugene. With USAF, 1951-55. Recipient Ersted award for disting. teaching U. Oreg., 1973; Fulbright sr. rsch. awardee, 1985; Nat. Endowment for Humanities grantee, 1994-98; rsch. and travel awardee DAAD, ACLS. Mem. AAUP, Am. Musicol. Soc., Internat. Musicol. Soc., Soc. for Music Theory, Music Libr. Assn., Coll. Music Soc. Democrat. Home: 3195 Portland St Eugene OR 97405-5140 Office: Sch Music 1225 U Oreg Eugene OR 97403-1225 Business E-Mail: pbergq@uoregon.edu.

BERGQUIST, RICK, software company executive; BS in Computer Sci., Calif. Polytechnic State U.; diploma in Mgmt. Devel. Program, Harvard U. Sch. Bus. With Am. Mgmt. Sys. Inc., 1975—87; joined PeopleSoft Inc., Pleasonton, Calif., 1987, sr. v.p., 1999, chief tech. officer, 1999—. PeopleSoft Fellow award, 2002.

BERGQUIST, SANDRA LEE, medical and legal consultant, nurse; b. Carlton, Minn., Oct. 13, 1944; d. Arthur Vincent and Avis Lorene Portz; m. David Edward Bergquist, June 11, 1966; children: Rion Eric, Taun Erin. BSN, Barry U., 1966; MA in Mgmt., Central Mich. U., 1975; student U. So. Calif., 1980-82. RN, advanced RN practitioner; cert. physician asst. Commd. 2d lt. USAF, 1968, advanced through grades to lt. col., 1985; staff and charge nurse USAF, 1968-76, primary care nurse practitioner, McConnell AFB, Kans., 1976-79, officer in charge Wheeler Med. Facility, Wheeler AFB, Hawaii, 1979-83, supr. ambulatory care services, Elgin AFB, Fla., 1983-84; med.-legal cons., Pensacola, Fla., 1985—; risk mgr., quality assurance coordinator HCA-Twin Cities Hosp., Niceville, 1986-88. Bd. dirs. Elder Svcs. Okaloosa County, Fla., 1984-2003; adv. bd. Gentiva Home Health, 1990—; chair Niceville/Valparaiso Task Force on Child Abuse Prevention, Fla., 1985-88; chair home and family life com. Twin Cities Women's Club, Niceville, 1985-88; chair advancement com. Gulf Coast coun. Boy Scouts Am., 1985-87; instr. advanced and basic cardiac life support Hawaii Heart Assn. and Tripler Army Med. Ctr., 1981-83. Decorated Commendation medal with 1 oak leaf cluster, USAF Meritorious Svc. medal, Air Force Commendation medal. Mem. AACN, Am. Assn. Physician Assts., Assn. Mil. Surgeons U.S., Soc. Ret. Air Force Nurses, Soc. Air Force Physician Assts., Twin Cities Women's Club. Lutheran. Avocations: fused glass art, silver wire wrap jewelry art.

BERGREN, BYRON L., retail executive; Pres. Belk, Inc., Charlotte, NC; CEO Elder-Beerman, Dayton, Ohio; CEO, pres. Bon-Ton Stores, Inc., 2004—. Office: Bon-Ton Stores Inc 2801 E Market St York PA 17402 Office Phone: 717-757-7660.*

BERGREN, SCOTT C., career officer; b. Mineola, NY; BA in Econ., Clemson U., 1970; student navigator tng., Mather AFB, Calif., 1970-71; student, Squadron Officer Sch., 1974; M in Polit. Sci., Auburn U., 1981; student, Air Command and Staff Coll., 1981, Air War Coll., 1990, Harvard U., 1996. Commd. 2d lt. USAF, 1970, advanced through grades to maj. gen., 1999, various F-4 Phantom assignments, 1971-76; air staff ops. officer programs and resources Air Staff Tng. program, Hdqs. USAF, Pentagon, Washington, 1976-77, asst. exec. officer to dep. chief staff programs/resources, 1976-77; instr., navigator and exchange officer 237th Operational Conversion Unit, RAFB Honington, Eng., 1977-80; dir. ops. force analysis div. then spl. asst. comdr. Hdqs. Tactical Air Command, Langley AFB, Va., 1981-85; comdr. 325th Tactical Tng. Wing's Aircraft Generation Squadron, Tyndall AFB, Fla., 1985-87, asst. dep. comdr. maintenance, 1985-87; dep. comdr. maintenance 33rd Tactical Fighter Wing, Eglin AFB, Fla., 1987-89; Air Univ. chair for chief staff of Air Force Maxwell AFB, Ala., 1990-91; various comdr. positions Nellis AFB, Nev., 1991-93; stationed at U.S. Ctrl. Command, MacDill AFB, Fla., 1994-96; vice comdr. San Antonio Air Logistics Ctr., Kelly AFB, Tex., 1996-97; comdr. 82d Tng. Wing, Sheppard AFB, 1997-99; dir. maintenance, dep. chief staff installations & logistics HQ/USAF, 1999-2000; comdr. Ogden Air Logistics Ctr., Hill AFB, Utah, 2000—. Decorated Silver Star, D.F.C. with silver oak leaf cluster, Purple Heart, Air medal with three silver oak leaf clusters and bronze oak leaf cluster, Small Arms Expert Marksmanship Ribbon, Rep. Vietnam Gallantry Cross with Palm, Rep. Vietnam Campaign medal. Office: Hill AFBM OO-ALC/CC 7981 Georgia St Hill AFB UT 84056-5824

BERGRUN, NORMAN RILEY, aerospace executive; b. Green Camp, Ohio, Aug. 4, 1921; s. Theodore and Naomi Ruth (Stemm) B.; m. Claire (Michaelson), May 23, 1943; children: Clark, Jay, Joan. BSME, Cornell U., 1943; grad. student in Aeronautics, Stanford U., Calif., 1947—48; LLB, LaSalle U. Ext., 1955; DSc (hon.), World U., Benson, Ariz., 1983. registered profl. mech. engr., Calif. Thermodynamicist Douglas Aircraft Co., El Segundo, Calif., 1943—44; rsch. scientist NACA Ames Rsch. Lab., Mt. View, Calif., 1944—56; mgr. analysis Lockheed Missile and Space Co., Sunnyvale, Calif., 1956—67, staff scientist, 1967—69; dir. mgmt. systems Nielsen Engring. and Rsch., Mt. View, Calif., 1969—71; CEO, scientist Bergrun Rsch. and Engring., Los Altos, Calif., 1971—. Guest radio and TV programs in the U.S., Can., Australia, and Europe; spkr. Accademia Nazional Del Lincei, 1987; instr. NASA Space Day, 1998; founder Bergrun Rsch., Mt. View, Calif., 1999; lectr. in field Author: Ringmakers of Saturn, 1986, Tomorrow's Technology Today, 1972, A Warming Trend for Icing Research, 1995, Air Travel Safety Forum Attracts Public Media Interest, 1997, The Prospective Impact of Science on Contemporary Culture, 1987, The International Space Station: A Momentous Cultural, Scientific and Societal Undertaking, 1998, Lunar Life Forms Do Exist, 2000, Lunar Life Forms: Revelations of Apollo 14, 2001, Earth's Moon.Why We Never Returned, 2001, Mars Puts on a Good Face: The Masquerade, 2002, Alien Vehicles in the Solar System, 2003; photographer Sir Francis Drake Collection, 1990; contbg. over 90 articles to profl. jours. Co-incorporator Aurora Singers Found., Palo Alto, Calif., 1989; co-founder NSPE Edn. Found., Sacramento, advisor to bd., 1985-92; mem. Steinman Coun., 1988—, steering com. Congressional Visits Day, 1997-2005; active Cornell U. Concert Musician Carnegie Hall, 1989, Presdl. Bus. Commn., 2002-07. Named Man of Yr., Am. Biog. Assn.; recipient Archimedes Award, 1988, Cert. of Appreciation, Eglin AFB, 1961; named charter mem. Nat. Aviation Hall Fame, 1967. Fellow AIAA (life, assoc., sr. judge 7th and 8th grade essay contest 1992-95, 97-2005, chair nat. pub. policy comm. sub-com. 1992-2002, coord. nat. pub. policy com. task force, 1999-2001, regional dep. dir. at large 1995— San Francisco sect. nominating com., 2006-, pub. policy liaison rep. 2000-02, spl. svc. citation 1994, 98, 2002, cert. of recognition 2001, Sustained Svc. Award 2001, advisor Airline Safety Initiative 1997, moderator Internat. Space Sta. Forum 1998), AAAS, NSPE (life), Profl. Engr. Soc. (Calif. pres. 1988-89, Integrity Award 1989, Outstanding Exec. Performance Award 1986, Disting. Contbn. Award 1985-87, 98), Fedn. Am. Scientists, The Planetary Soc. (sec. 1981—). Achievements include discovery of existence of large, mobile cylindrical objects, identified at Saturn, Miranda, Iapetus, Mars, Neptune, Earth's moon, the Sun, and deep space, and life forms on Earth's moon; patents for cyclic electric thermal ice prevention sys. for airplanes. Avocation: photography. Mailing: Bergrun Rsch PO Box 373 Los Altos CA 94023

BERGSCHNEIDER, DAVID PHILIP, legal administrator; b. Springfield, Ill., Nov. 19, 1951; s. Fred J. and Ruby A. (Martin) B.; m. Dawn E. Combes, Sept. 23, 1989; children: Alec, Bryant, Cale. Student, Bradley U., 1969-71; BA, Ill. Coll., 1973; JD, Marquette U., 1976. Bar: Ill. 1976, Wis. 1976, U.S. Ct. Appeals (7th cir.) 1990, U.S. Supreme Ct. 1980. Mem. legis. staff Ill. Gen. Assembly, Springfield, 1976-77; asst. defender Office State Appellate Defender, Springfield, 1977-93, legal dir., 1993—. Mem. governing bd. Ill. Integrated Justice Info. Sys. Co-author: Defending Illinois Criminal Cases, 1988, 3d edit., 2007, Illinois Criminal Practice, 1980, Brief Writing and Oral Argument Handbook, 1988, 4th edit., 2007; author: Illinois Handbook of Criminal Law Decisions, 1993, 2d edit., 1998, supplement, 2003; also articles. Recipient Award of Excellence Ill. Pub. Defender Assn., 1989. Mem. ABA, Ill. Bar Assn. (criminal justice sect. coun. 1987-91, 94-98, sec. 1995-96, chmn. 1996-97, Virgil E. Tipton Jr. Publs. award 2004). Office: Office State Appellate Def PO Box 5240 Springfield IL 62705-5740

BERGSON, HENRY PAUL, professional society administrator; b. Boston, Dec. 22, 1942; s. Harry, Jr. and Elizabeth (Paul) Bergson; m. Jacqueline Hope Wilson, June 11, 1966; children: Susan Elizabeth, Abigail Anne. BS, U. N.H., 1966. Various mgmt. positions Fed. Signal, Blue Island, Ill., 1970-78; dir. mktg. Tork, Mt. Vernon, N.Y., 1978-83; v.p. ops. G.C.S. Svc., Chappaqua, N.Y., 1983-85; exec. v.p. Nat. Elec. Mfrs. Reps. Assn., Tarrytown, NY, 1985-93, pres., 1994—, also bd. dirs. Bd. dirs. Elec. Industry Joint Bus. Productivity Coun. Contbr. articles to profl. jours. Chief Katonah (N.Y.) Vol. Fire Dept., 1980—84, v.p., 1984—87, pres., 1987—90, bd. dirs., 1990—, chmn. bd. dirs., 1995—; mem. Bedford Transp. Com., 1984—86; fire commr. Katonah Fire Dist., 1992—, vice chmn. bd. fire commrs., 1996—; mem. fire adv. bd. Westchester County, NY, 2001—; cmty. adv. bd. Taconic and Bedford Hills Correctional Facilities, N.Y. State Dept. Corrections; elder 1st Presbyn. Ch., Katonah, 1991—94. Capt. US Army, 1967—70. Decorated Bronze Star for Valor with two oak leaf clusters, Purple Heart, Vietnam medal of Honor. Mem.: Nat. Assn. Elec. Distbrs., Nat. Elec. Mfrs. Assn. (assoc.). Republican. Avocation: collecting firematic antiques. Home: PO Box 182 Katonah NY 10536-0182 Office: NEMRA 660 White Plains Rd Fl 6 Tarrytown NY 10591-5147 Office Phone: 914-524-8650.

BERGSRUD, MARK, air transportation executive; married; 2 children. B in Polit. Sci., Augustana Coll., Sioux Falls, SD; MPA, Syracuse U., NY. Schedule planning position NW Airlines, 1992; dir. schedule planning Continental Airlines, Inc., 1994—97, staff v.p. long-range planning, 1997, staff v.p. revenue programs, 1997, v.p. mktg. programs & distbn., 2000, sr. v.p. mktg. programs & distbn. Office: Continental Airlines Inc PO Box 4607 Houston TX 77210*

BERGSTEDT, ROGER ALLEN, biologist, researcher; b. Duluth, Minn., Mar. 31, 1947; s. Roy Axel and Pearl Marie Bergstedt; m. Jocelyn Susan Jacobs, Feb. 7, 1970; children: Christina Marie, Gretchen Ann. BA, U. Minn., Duluth, 1970; BS, U. Minn., St. Paul, 1973; MS, Iowa State U., Ames, 1975. Fishery biologist U.S. Fish and Wildlife Svc., Ann Arbor, Mich., 1976—77, Oswego, Mich., 1977—85; rsch. fishery biologist U.S. Geol. Survey, Hammond Bay Biol. Sta., Millersburg, Mich., 1985—99, field sta. supr., 2000—06. Assoc. editor Am. Fisheries Soc., Bethesda, Md., 1997—99; guest assoc. editor Jour. of Gt. Lakes Rsch., Ann Arbor, Mich., 2001—03. Contbr. over 40 articles to profl. jours. With USNR, 1970—71. Recipient Vernon Applegate award, Gt. Lakes Fishery Commn., 2004. Mem.: Am. Fisheries Soc. Home: 12390 M-68 Hwy Millersburg MI 49759 Office: USGS Hammond Bay Biol Sta 11188 Ray Rd Millersburg MI 49759 Home Phone: 989-733-8337; Office Phone: 989-734-4768.

BERGSTEIN, DANIEL GERARD, lawyer; b. Nice, France, May 1, 1943; came to U.S., 1952; s. Max and Suzanne (Fenigstein) B.; children: Jordan, Elizabeth C. BA, CUNY, 1965; JD, Bklyn. Law Sch., 1968. Bar: N.Y. 1968, Fla. 1974. From assoc. to ptnr. Greenbaum, Wolff & Ernst, NYC, 1982; ptnr. Reavis & McGrath, NYC, 1982-85, Finley, Kumble, Wagner, Heine, Underberg, Manley, Myerson & Casey, NYC, 1985-87, Paul, Hastings, Janofsky & Walker, NYC, 1988—, chmn. telecom. practice group. Mem. ABA, French-Am. C. of C. in U.S. Office Phone: 212-318-6033. Business E-Mail: danielbergstein@paulhastings.com.

BERGSTEIN, JERRY MICHAEL, nephrologist; b. Cleve., June 26, 1939; s. Sol R. and Hilda (Nittscoff) B.; m. Renee M. Hillman, July 7, 1963; children: Stephanie, Michael, Jeffrey. BA, UCLA, 1961; MD, U. Minn., 1965. Diplomate Nat. Bd. Med. Examiners, Am. Bd. Pediat., Am. Bd. Pediat. Nephrology; lic. physician, Ind. Intern in pediat. U. Minn., Mpls., 1965-66, jr. pediat. resident, 1966-67, chief pediat. resident, 1969-70, postdoctoral fellow in pediat. nephrology, 1970-73; asst. prof., head pediat. nephrology UCLA, 1973-77; assoc. prof. Ind. U. Sch. Medicine, Indpls., 1977-82, head pediat. nephrology, 1977—, prof., 1982—. Mem. adv. bd. Nat. Kidney Found. Ind., 1980—; mem. adv. coun. Am. Heart Assn., 1988—. Mem. editl. bd. Child Nephrology and Urology, 1980-90, Pediat. Nephrology, 1995—; contbr. chpts. to books. Lt. comdr. USN, 1967-69. Recipient Fellowship USPHS, Washington, 1970; grantee Thrasher Fund, 1980, Amgen, 1990. Mem. Am. Soc. Nephrology, Am. Soc. Pediat. Nephrology, Am. Soc. Investigative Pathology, Soc. Exptl. Biology and Medicine. Achievements include research on the role of the fibrinolytic inhibitor plasminogen activator inhibitor-1 in the pathogenesis and outcome of the hemolytic-uremic syndrome; development of anti-tubular basement membrane antibody disease; development of radiation nephritis in bone marrow transplant patients. Office: James Whitcomb Riley Hosp for Children 702 Barnhill Dr Indianapolis IN 46202-5128 Business E-Mail: jbergste@iupui.edu.

BERGSTEIN, MELVYN, information technology executive; BS econ., Wharton Sch. Univ. Pa. CPA. With Arthur Andersen, LLP, 1968—89, ptnr., 1977—89, mng. dir., 1985—89; sr. v.p. sys. integration CSC Consulting and Tech., 1989—91; exec. mgmt. roles Tech. Solutions Co., 1991—93; co-found., chmn. Diamond Technology Ptnrs. (now DiamondCluster Internat.), 1994—, CEO, 1994—2005. Bd. dir. New Era of Networks, Inc.; adv. bd. Cross Atlantic Technology Fund; bd. dirs. Simon Property Group. Bd. trustees Chgo. Symphony Orch., Ravinia Festival; bd. overseers U. Pa. Sch. Engring.; bd. dirs. Rehab. Inst. Chgo. Mem.: Chgo. Club, Standard Club, Econ. Club, Comml. Club, Executives' Club Chgo. (bd. dirs.). Office: DiamondCluster Internat John Hancock Ctr Ste 3000 875 N Michigan Ave Chicago IL 60611

BERGSTEN, C. FRED, economist; b. Bklyn., Apr. 23, 1941; s. Carl Alfred and Lois Halkaline (Kirk) Bergsten; m. Virginia Lee Wood, June 16, 1962; 1 child, Mark. AB, Ctrl. Meth. Coll., Fayette, Mo., 1961, LHD, 1995; MA, Fletcher Sch. Law and Diplomacy, Medford, Mass., 1962, MA in Law and Diplomacy, 1963, PhD, 1969. Internat. economist Dept. State, 1963—67; vis. fellow Council Fgn. Relations, 1967—68; asst. for internat. econ. affairs NSC, 1969—71; sr. fellow Brookings Instn., 1972—76; asst. sec. treasury internat. affairs, 1977—81; sr. assoc. Carnegie Endowment Internat. Peace, 1981; dir. Inst. Internat. Econs., 1981—. U.S. coord. U.S.-Saudi Arabia Joint Econ. Commn., 1977—81; mem. def. mgmt. bd. Task Force on Fgn. Ownership and Control, 1989—90, competitiveness policy coun., 1991—97, chmn., 1991—97; mem. panel on pub.-pvt. cooperation in civilian tech. NAS, 1990—91; mem. exec. com. Trilateral Commn., 1991—, Bretton Wood Com., 1989—, Carnegie Endowment, Nat. Commn. Am. and the New World Order, 1992, Commn. Govt. Renewal, 1992; chmn. APEC Eminent Persons Group, 1993—95; vice chmn. adv. com. on fgn. econ. policy Dept. State, 1996—. Author: The Future of the International Economic Order: An Agenda for Research, 1973, Toward a New World Trade Policy, 1975, World Politics and International Economics, 1975, Toward a New International Economic Order: Selected Papers of C. Fred Bergsten, 1972-1974, 1975, The Dilemmas of the Dollar: The Economics and Politics of United State International Monetary Policy, 1976, American Multinationals and American Interests, 1978, Managing International Economic Interdependence: Selected Papers of C. Fred Bergsten, 1975-1976, 1977, The International Economic Policy of the United States: Selected Papers of C. Fred Bergsten, 1977-1979, 1980, The World Economy in the 1980s: Selected Papers of C. Fred Bergsten, 1981, The United State in the World Economy: Selected Papers of C. Fred Bergsten, 1981-82, 1983, Bank Lending to Developing Countries: The Policy Alternatives, 1985, The United States-Japan Economic Problem, 1985, Global Economic Imbalances, 1985, Auction Quotas and United States Trade Policy, 1987, America in the World Economy: A Strategy for the 1990's, 1988, International Adjustment and Financing, 1991, Pacific Dynamism and the International Economic System, 1993, Reconcilable Differences? United States-Japan Economic Conflict, 1993, Global Economic Leadship and the Group of Seven, 1996, Whither APEC?, 1997, No More Bashing, 2002, Dollar Overvaluation and the World Economy, 2003, Dollar Adjustment: How Far? Against What?, 2004, The United States and the World Economy, 2005; mem. editl. bd.: Fgn. Affairs, 1972—77, Internat. Orgn., 1973—77, Jour. Internat. Econs., 1977—80, Fgn. Policy, 1987—99. Recipient Meritorious Honor award, Dept. State, 1965, Disting. Alumnus award, Ctrl. Meth. Coll., 1975, Exceptional Svc. award, Treasury Dept., 1980, French Legion of Honor, 1987. Fellow: Chinese Acad. Social Scis. (hon.); mem.: Coun. Fgn. Rels., Am. Econ. Assn. Personal E-mail: kstewart@iie.com.

BERGSTEN, JAMES ROBERT, computer technology architect; b. NYC, May 21, 1954; s. Robert Frederick and Jean Laura B.; m. Mary Elizabeth, July 20, 1980; children: Sarah Margaret, Carl Alexander. Student, Cooper Union, 1972-74. System developer NASA, NYC, 1974-77; software mgr. Amdahl Corp., Sunnyvale, Calif., 1977-81; founder, pres./CEO Kolinar Corp., Santa Clara, Calif., 1981-90; v.p. engr. Andor Systems, Cupertino, Calif., 1990-94; founder, pres. ARK Rsch. Corp., San Jose, Calif., 1995—2000; dir. LSI Logic, Milpitas, Calif., 2000—05; pres., CEO ARK Systems Corp, 2003—, TraxRx Corp., 2005—. Bd. dirs. Ark Rsch., Kolinar, Santa Clara; owner CTHIA Prodns.; chmn., CEO Ark Storage Systems Corp., 2003—. Author: (operating system) Arts, 1995, (software) Xmenu, 1991 (ICP award 1995); co-author: (software) Kprobe, SQ Lexec, SQ Lmenu, 1995; contbr. articles to profl. jours.; patentee in field. Mem. computer adv. bd. KTEH TV, San Jose, 1985. Mem. IEEE, Assn. Computing Machinery, Audio Engring. Soc. Avocation: composing and producing music. Home: 8 Brightwood Way Danville CA 94506 Personal E-mail: jim@thebergstens.com.

BERGSTRESSER, PAUL RICHARD, dermatologist, educator; b. Ottawa, Kans., Aug. 24, 1941; s. Karl Samuel and May (Holmes) B.; m. Rebecca Louise Baird, Jan. 4, 1969; children: Daniel Baird, Laura Suzanne. AB, Coll. of Wooster, 1963; MD, Stanford U., 1968. Diplomate Am. Bd. Dermatology (bd. dirs. 1996-2005, v.p. 2003-05). Asst. prof. dept. dermatology U. Miami, 1975-76; asst. prof. to prof. Southwestern Med. Ctr. U. Tex., Dallas, 1976—, chmn. dept., 1986—. Mem. dermatologic drugs adv. com., FDA, 1986-88; mem. gen. medicine study sect. GM1A, NIH, 1989-93; mem. adv. coun. Nat. Inst. Arthritis and Musculoskeletal and Skin Disease, 1999-2003. Editor Photodermatology, Photoimmunology and Photomedicine, 1990-99; contbr. numerous articles to profl. jours. Maj. U.S. Army, 1970-72. Fellow AAP, AAAS, ACP, Am. Acad. Dermatology; mem. Am. Assn. Immunologists, Assn. Am. Physicians, Soc. Investigative Dermatology (bd. dirs. 1987-92, sec.-treas. 1999-2004), Am. Assn. Tissue Banks, Am. Dermatol. Assn., Assn. Profs. Dermatology (bd. dirs. 1990-95, pres.-elect 1998-2000, pres. 2000-02). Democrat. Methodist. Avocations: choral music, running. Home: 3758 Pallos Verdas Dr Dallas TX 75229-2740 Office: U Tex Southwestern Med Ctr Dept Dermatology 5323 Harry Hines Blvd Dallas TX 75390-9069 Business E-Mail: paul.bergstresser@utsouthwestern.edu.

BERGSTROM, ALBION ANDREW, retired military officer, educator; b. Salem, Mass., Sept. 2, 1947; s. Eric Hjalmar and Helen Lawrence (Andrew) Bergstrom; m. Angela Jane Feyerabend, May 11, 1997; children: Victoria Helen, John Albion. Student, Boston U., 1965-67; BA, Colo. State U., 1969; MA, Ctrl. Mich. U., 1978; grad., Command and Gen. Staff Coll., 1982; MA, Naval War Coll., 1998. Cert. fed. ofcl. Commd. 2d lt. U.S. Army, 1969, advanced through grades to col., 1991, platoon leader, aide de camp Vietnam, 1970-71, co. comdr. Ft. Hood, Tex., 1974-75; bn. exec. officer I-35 Armor, Erlangen, Germany, 1980—81; assignment officer Armor Br. U.S. Army, 1983-85, bn. comdr. 1-35 Armor, 1986-88, cols. assignment officer Pers. Command Alexandria, Va., 1988-89, chief, officer divsn. DCS pers., The Pentagon Washington, 1990-92; dep. comdr. U.S. Army Phys. Disability Agy., Washington, 1992-96; prof. jt. mil. ops., chief regional contingency planning and war fighting divsn. Naval War Coll., Newport, RI, 1996-99, prof. electives program, CDE, 2000—, prof. joint mil. ops., 2002—. Program chmn. Abrams Ch. Armor Assn., 1982—85. Del. N.H. Rep. Convs., 1966, 1968. Decorated Legion of Merit (3), Bronze Star, Purple Heart, Bronze medal, Silver medal, Order St. George; Nat. Security fellow, John F. Kennedy Sch. Govt., Harvard U., 1988—90. Mem.: VFW, Harvard U. Alumni Assn., 5th Inf. Divsn. Assn., Boston U. Alumni Assn., Naval War Coll. Found., 1st Cav. Divsn. Assn., Armor Assn., Assn. U.S. Army, U.S. Naval Inst., U.S. Army War Coll. Alumni Assn., Colo. State U. Alumni Assn., Ctrl. Mich. U. Alumni Assn., Order Ky. Cols., Mil. Order Purple Heart, Shriners, Masons, Am. Legion, Nat. Sojourners, Zeta Beta Tau, Phi Sigma Delta. Congregationalist. Avocations: photography, cross country skiing. Home: 19 Madison Way Portsmouth RI 02871-2249 Office Phone: 401-841-6484. E-mail: bergstra1@aol.com.

BERGSTROM, SHERYL LINDSEY, jet propulsion administrator; b. Hamilton AFB, Calif., May 12, 1948; d. Gerald Frank and Hazel Loueen Lindsey; 1 child, Joseph Andrew. MS, Clemson U., SC, 1972. Mem. tech. staff Caltech/Jet Propulsion Lab., Pasadena, Calif., 1973—80, group supr., 1980—90, mgr., 1990—. Contbr. articles to procs. and profl. jours. Elder Presbyn. Ch. USA, Fla., 2002—07. Recipient Group Achievement awards, NASA. Mem.: AAAS. Achievements include patents for production of butanol by fermentation in the presence of co-cultures of Clostridium. Home Phone: 321-453-2678.

BERGT, GREGORY PAUL, chemist, consultant; b. West Point, Nebr., Nov. 20, 1948; s. Lowell Duane and Elaine Angela (Schula) B.; m. Diann Helen Stigge, May 6, 1972; children: Matthew, Lisa, Troy, Ross. BS, Nebr. Wesleyan U., 1971; postgrad., U. Minn., 1974. Chemist Wendt Labs., Belle Plaine, Minn., 1971—77, dir. sci. and regulatory affairs, 1978—87; v.p. Eudaemonic Corp., Omaha, 1987—97; dir. regulatory affairs I.D. Russell Co., Longmont, Colo., 1989—95; dir. R&D, Pennfield Animal Health, Omaha, 1995—2006, v.p. regulatory affairs, 2006—. Cons. VA Hosp., Mpls., 1977. Patentee in field. Pres., St. John's Luth. Ch., Belle Plaine, 1981, Bethlehem Luth. Ch., Longmont, 1993-94; sponsoring liaison Boy Scouts Am., Belle Plaine, 1980-84; county del. Republican Party, Scott County, Minn., 1982. Recipient award Chemistry Tng. Program, NSF, 1967. Mem. Parenteral Drug Assn., Generic Pharm. Industry Assn./Animal Drug Alliance (treas., dir. Rocky Mountain Biomed. Devel. Forum 1990-95), Am. Dairy Sci. Assn., Am. Chem Soc., Am. Inst. Chemists, Am. Fedn. Ind. Pharm. Mfrs. (sec.-treas., dir. 1979—), Coun. Agrl. and Sci. Tech., Tiger Booster Club (pres. 1973-75), Rotary (pres. 1984-85). Home: 335 S 124th Cir Omaha NE 68154-2319 Office: Pennfield Animal Health 14040 Industrial Rd Omaha NE 68144 Office Phone: 402-330-6000. Business E-Mail: gbergt@pennfieldanimalhealth.com.

BERGTRAUM, HOWARD MICHAEL, lawyer; b. NYC, Jan. 8, 1946; s. Murry and Edith (Katz) B.; m. Susan Levitan, July 27, 1969; children: Jordan, Matthew, Andrea. BS, Queens Coll., 1966; JD, Cornell U., 1969; LLM, Georgetown Law Ctr., 1972. Bar: N.Y. 1970. Atty. adviser SEC, Washington, 1969-72; ptnr. O'Sullivan LLP, NYC, 1975—2002, O'Melveny & Myers LLP, NYC, 2002—. Mem. ABA, N.Y. State Bar Assn. Home: 10 I U Willets Rd Old Westbury NY 11568-1519 Office: O'Melveny & Myers LLP 7 Time Square Tower New York NY 10036 Office Phone: 212-408-2408. Business E-Mail: hbergtraum@omm.com.

BERHALTER, GREGG, professional soccer player; b. Englewood, NJ, Aug. 1, 1973; m. Rosalind Berhalter; 2 children. Attended, Univ. N.C. Defender FC Zwolle, Netherlands, 1994—96, Sparta Rotterdam, Netherlands, 1996—98, Cambuur Leeuwarden, Netherlands, 1998—2000, Crystal Palace, England, 2001—02, Energie Cottbus, Germany, 2002—06, TSV 1860 Munich, Germany, 2006—. 30 caps U.S. Nat. Soccer team, 1994—; mem. U.S. World Cup team, 2002, 06. Named two time All Am. Mailing: US Soccer Fedn 1801 S Prairie Ave Chicago IL 60616

BERICK, JAMES HERSCHEL, lawyer; b. Cleve., Mar. 30, 1933; s. Morris and Rebecca Alice (Gerdy) B.; m. Christine Berick; children: Michael, Daniel, Robert, Joshua. AB, Columbia U., 1955; JD, Case Western Res. U., 1958. Assoc. Burke, Haber & Berick, Cleve., 1958-60, ptnr., 1960-86, mng. ptnr., 1968-83; chmn. Berick, Pearlman & Mills Co., L.P.A., 1986-99; ptnr. Squire, Sanders & Dempsey, LLP, 2000—02, ret. ptnr., 2003—. Bd. dirs. The Town and Country Trust, The Town and Country Funding Corp.; sec. Cleve. Browns Football Co. LLC; lectr. law Case Western Res. U., 1969—78; mem. dean's adv. coun. Case Western Res. U. Sch. Law, 1998—, mem. bd. visitors, Cleve. Clinic Lerner Coll. Medicine, 2005—. Founding and life trustee Rock and Roll Hall of Fame and Mus.; mem. Shaker Heights (Ohio) Bd. Edn., 1980-83; bd. visitors Columbia Coll., 1981-87, 90-96, emeritus, 2000—2004, member, 2004-; bd. dirs. Univ. Circle Inc., 1994—2004; trustee Arthritis Found. of N.E. Ohio, mem. med. and sci. com. Mem.: Soc. of Benchers, Ct. of Nisi Prius, Seagate Beach Club, Union Club (Cleve.), Shoreby Club, Order of Coif. Home: 1225 S Ocean Blvd #801 Delray Beach FL 33483 Office: Squire Sanders & Dempsey LLP 4900 Key Tower 127 Public Sq Cleveland OH 44114-1216 Office Phone: 216-479-8450. E-mail: jberick@ssd.com.

BERINGER, WILLIAM ERNST, mediator, arbitrator, lawyer, retired manufacturing executive; b. Madison, Wis., Oct. 24, 1928; s. William and Martha M. Beringer; m. Marilyn J. Walter, Aug. 4, 1984; children: Amy, Julia, Barry, Thomas, Maureen. BA summa cum laude, Lawrence Coll., 1950; JD with distinction, U. Mich., 1953. Bar: Mich. 1953, Wis. 1953, Ill. 1955. Assoc. Vedder, Price, Kaufman & Kammholz, Chgo., 1953-56; atty. law dept. Swift & Co., Chgo., 1956-71; dir. gen. law dept. Allis-Chalmers Corp., Milw., 1971-77; v.p., gen. counsel, sec. Siemens Energy & Automation, Inc., Alpharetta, 1978-94; assoc. gen. counsel Siemens Corp., 1987-94. Bd. dirs. corp. banking and bus. law sect. Wis. Bar, 1976-78; mem. antitrust and corp. policy com. U.S. C. of C., 1974-80; mem. panels Am. Arbitration Assn., Resolution Resources Corp., NASD Regulation, N.Y. Stock Exch., EEOC. Editorial bd. Mich. Law Rev. 1952-53. Bd. dirs. Hinsdale (Ill.) Community Concert Assn., 1969-71, Dupage County (Ill.) Girl Scouts U.S., 1969-71, Clarendon Hills (Ill.) Community Chest, 1968-70; vice chmn. Clarendon Hills Human Relations Commn., 1968-70; mem. Chgo. study team Nat. Commn. on Causes and Prevention Violence, 1968; chmn. MAPI Law Coun. II, 1992-94. Mem. ABA, Am. Corp. Counsel Assn. (bd. dirs. Ga. chpt. 1985-88), Atlanta Bar Assn., Lawrence U. Alumni Assn. (bd. dirs. 1998-2002), Order of Coif, Cherokee Town and Country Club, Rotary. Republican. Home Phone: 770-992-5693. Personal E-mail: wberinger@aol.com.

BERIO, BLANCA, editor, writer; b. San Juan, Aug. 26, 1950; d. Gaspar and Blanca (Morales) B.; m. Martin Martino, Nov. 11, 1972; children: Blanca Iris, Martin, Bibiana. BA, U. P.R., 1968, MA, 1985, EdD, 1997. Prof. Guadalajara (Mex.) Autonomus U., 1973-76; tchr. Spanish Colegio de La Salle, Bayamón, P.R., 1980-88; prof. edn. U. Sacred Heart, Santurce, P.R., 1984-91; ednl. editor Editorial Norma, Cataño, 1991-92; chief editor Editorial Rio Ingenio, 1987—2007; dir. grad. program U. Cen. Bayamon, 1998—2000. Cons. Learn Aid, Rio Piedras, P.R., 1990-98, acad. dean U. Central Bayamon, 2000-04, prof., 1997-07. Author: De 13 a 19, 1969, El Paso, 1971, Tapatea, 1987, 2nd edit., 1994, Bibliografía de Literatura Puertorriqueña Para Niños, 1994; editor bull. Algo Nuevo, 1990, (software) Nos Comunicamos: K-3, 1992, Lectoescritura, 20 modulos, 2002, 2003, 2005, Un Murcielago Amigo, 2003, (with audio CD) La Flor de Luz, 2005, (with audio CD) Antenita, 2005, (book, audio CD, puppet) Gluglú, 2007;

contbr. articles to profl. jours. Recipient Excelsa Benjamina Assn. Autores Puertorriqueños San Juan, 1971. Mem. Internat. Reading Assn., Assn. Grads. U. P.R., Alpha Delta Kappa. Roman Catholic. Avocations: reading, stamp collecting/philately, swimming, writing. Home: Rio Hondo 2 Ah14 Calle Rio Ingenio Bayamon PR 00961-3234 Office: Rio Ingenio Bayamon PR 00961 E-mail: blancaberio@gmail.com.

BERIS, ANTONY NICOLAS, chemical engineer, educator; b. Athens, Greece, Jan. 14, 1957; came to U.S., 1980; naturalized, 1991; s. Nicolas Elias and Mary (Lazopoulos) B.; m. Martha Deborah Brown, Apr. 20, 1990 (div. June 1998); m. Sophia Jutzi, Dec. 29, 2001. BSChemE, Nat. Tech. U., Athens, 1980; PhDChemE, MIT, 1985. From asst. prof. chem. engrng. to prof. U. Del., Newark, 1985—2002, Arthur B. Metzner chair prof. chem. engrng., 2002—. Author rsch. monograph (with B.J. Edwards) Thermodynamics of Flowing Systems with Internal Microstructure, 1994; contbr. more than 90 articles to profl. jours.; mem. editl. adv. bd. Jour. Non-Equilibrium Thermodynamics, Jour. Non-Neutonian Fluid Mechanics, Computing in Sci. and Engring. Recipient Dow Outstanding Young Faculty award, Middle Atlantic sect. of ASEE, 1991; Fulbright fgn. scholar, Belgium, 1999-2000. Fellow AAAS; mem. Inst. Chem. Engring. and High Termperature Chem. Processes (affiliated mem.), Inst. Electronic Structure and Laser Found. for Rsch. and Tech.-Hellas, Am. Inst. Chem. Engrs., Soc. Rheology, Am. Phys. Soc., Soc. Indsl. and Applied Math., Am. Soc. Engring. Edn., Sigma Xi. Greek Orthodox. Achievements include development of spectral methods in the numerical simulation of viscoelastic flows; generalization of bracket theory for the modeling of continuum systems; modeling and simulation of complex fluids flows. Office: U Del Dept Chem Engring Newark DE 19716 Home Phone: 302-894-1364; Office Phone: 302-831-8018. Business E-Mail: beris@udel.edu.

BERISFORD, JOHN L., consumer products company executive; B in Polit. Sci., West Liberty Coll.; M in Indsl. Rels., W.Va. U., Morgantown. Various positions including several field human resources assignments Pepsi Bottling Group, Inc., Pitts., 1988—91, human resources mgr., mgr., orgn. capability, sr. labor mgr., 1991—95, dir. human resources heartland bus. unit, 1995—98, v.p. orgn. capability, head N.Am. bottling bus. Somers, NY, 1998—2001, v.p. field human resources, 2001—04, v.p. human resources, 2004—05, sr. v.p. human resources, 2005—. Office: Pepsi Bottling Group 1 Pepsi Way Somers NY 10589-2201 Office Phone: 914-767-6000. Office Fax: 914-767-7761.*

BERISH, BRAD A., lawyer; b. Chicago, Ill., July 1, 1962; m. Audrey A. Solent. BS in Acctg., Ind. U., Bloomington, 1984; JD, Emory U., Atlanta, 1989. Bar: Supreme Ct., Ill. 1989, US Dist. Ct., (no. dist.), Ill. 1989, US Ct. Appeals, (7th cir.) 1991, US Ct. Appeals, (3rd cir.) 2003, US Dist. Ct., (ctrl. dist.), Ill. 2003, US Dist. Ct., Colo. 2006. Ptnr. Adelman & Gettleman, Ltd., Chgo., 1989—. Mem.: Turnaround Mgmt. Assn., Chgo. Bar Assn. Office: Adelman & Gettleman Ltd 53 W Jackson Blvd Chicago IL 60604 Office Phone: 312-435-1050. Office Fax: 312-435-1059. Business E-Mail: bab@ag-ltd.com.

BERK, ADELE L., composer, music educator; d. Sidney Levan and Hattie Pauline Levitt; m. Robert Harris Berk, July 30, 1950; children: Valerie, Mark. BA, Hunter Coll., NYC, 1946; postgrad., Juilliard Sch., 1946—47, Berkshire Music Ctr., 1949; MA, Columbia U., NYC, 1950. Cert. music tchr. NY. Music tchr. Jr. HS, NYC, 1947—54; music instr., choir dir. Temple Bethel, Huntington, NY, 1956—68; instr. theory, piano, composition, music appreciation Nassau Cmty. Coll., Garden City, NY, 1968—71; composer-in-residence Wantagh (NY) Pub. Schs., 1971—73; asst. prof. music Dowling Coll., Oakdale, NY, 1973—81; coord. choral music, composer-in-residence Liberal Jewish Day Sch., West Hempstead, NY, 1986—89. Invited composer Mars Hill Coll. Contemporary Choral Festival, 1980, Internat. Congress on Women in Music, Atlanta, 1986, Charles Ives Ctr. Choral Festival, New Milford, Conn., 1987, Women in Music Symposium, Bklyn. Coll., 1988, Festival New Am. Music, Bates Coll., Maine, 1994, Mostly Women Composers Festival, Bloomingdale House of Music, NYC, 1994. Recipient Libby Van Arsdale Meml. award, 1946, Kappa Mu Epsilon Composition prize, 1949; grantee, Meet the Composer, 1990, 1993, 1999, 2003. Mem.: ASCAP (spl. award in composition 1998, 1999, 2000, 2001—07), Internat. Alliance Women in Music, Am. Music Ctr., LI Composers Alliance (treas. 1985—92, mem. adv. bd. 1993—2007). Home: 254 Twin Lane E Wantagh NY 11793

BERK, ALAN S., accountant; b. NYC, May 11, 1934; s. Phil and Mae (Buchberg) B.; m. Barbara Binder, Dec. 18, 1960; children— Charles M., Peter M., Nancy M. BS in Econs., U. Pa., 1955; MS in Bus., Columbia U., 1956. CPA N.Y., 1960. Staff acct. Arthur Young & Co., NYC, 1956-62, mgr., prin., 1962-67; sr. v.p. Avco Corp., Greenwich, Conn., 1967-75; dir. Arthur Young & Co., 1975—, ptnr., 1976—, chief fin. officer, 1979-89; nat. dir. fin., treas. Ernst & Young, 1989-92; exec. dir. Kelley, Drye & Warren, NYC, 1993-94. Mem. nat. adv. group Nat. Tech. Inst. for the Deaf, Rochester, N.Y.; chmn. bd. dirs. Jewish Home for the Elderly of Fairfield County, Inc., 1997-99, vice chmn., 2002—; 1st v.p., treas. Bruce Mus., Greenwich, Conn.; mem. golf bd. Town of Greenwich, Conn.; commn. on aging Town of Greenwich. With U.S. Army, 1957. Mem. AICPA, N.Y. State Soc. CPAs, Fin. Execs. Inst., Landmark Club, Stockbridge (Mass.) Golf Club, Lake Dr. Homeowners Assn. (pres.), Stockbridge Bowl Assn. (treas.). Home: 41 Doral Greens Dr W Rye Brook NY 10573

BERK, BLAIR, lawyer; b. Fayetteville, NC, May 16, 1964; BA, MA, Boston U., 1987; JD, Harvard Law Sch., 1990. Bar: Calif. 1992. Ptnr. Tarlow & Berk P.C., L.A. Mem.: ABA, Calif. Lawyers for Criminal Justice (co-chair seminars com. 1997—99, bd. govs. 1997—2004), Women Lawyers Assn. LA (co-chair crimnal law section 1996—99), Beverly Hills Bar Assn. (chair. 2001—). Office: Tarlow & Berk PC 9119 Sunset Blvd Los Angeles CA 90069*

BERK, GEORGE ELLIS, cardiologist; b. NYC, May 4, 1942; s. Samuel and Muriel Berkowitz; m. Noel Nelkin, Oct. 7, 1967 (div.); children: Matthew Adam, Bradley Tyler; m. Penelope Susan Smith, Apr. 25, 1998. AB, Princeton U., 1964; MD, Cornell U., 1968. Diplomate Am. Bd. Internal Medicine. Intern Cornell Cooperating Hosps., 1968—69, resident, 1969—70; cardiology fellow North Shore Univ. Hosp., 1973—75; resident Cornell Cooperating Hosps., 1972—73; pvt. practice cardiology No. Westchester Cardiology, Yorktown Heights, NY, 1975—; attending physician Westchester Med. Ctr., 1975—, No. Westchester Hosp. Ctr., 1975—. Chief divsn. cardiology No. Westchester Hosp., Mt. Kisco, NY, 1994—98; med. dir. Imaging for Life, LLC, NYC and White Plains, 1999—. Adv. bd. Free Romania Relief Fund, NYC, 1992—95, Albanian Relief Assn., NYC, 1992—97; bd. dirs. Westchester/Putnam divsn. Am. Heart Assn., Purchase, NY, 1981—; pres. Westchester/Putnam chpt. Am. Heart Assn., 1996—98. Maj. USAF, 1970—72. Decorated Air Force Commendation medal; recipient Congl. Proclamation, Congresswoman Nita Lowey, 2000. Fellow: Am. Coll. Cardiology (assoc.). Avocations: Oriental carpets, collecting vintage photography, art glass, pottery, running, mountain climbing. Home: 181 Hook Rd Bedford NY 10506 Office: Northern Westchester Cardiology 1888 Commerce St Yorktown Heights NY 10506 Home Phone: 914-234-3638; Office Phone: 914-962-4000.

BERK, JACK EDWARD, gastroenterologist, educator; b. Phila. s. Samuel and Esther B.; m. Adeline Elizabeth Alberts, June 26, 1937; children: Philip Howard (dec.), Richard Hanna. BA, U. Pa., 1932, MSc in Medicine, 1939, DSc in Medicine, 1943; MD, Jefferson Med. Coll., 1936; postgrad., Grad. Sch. Medicine, U. Pa., 1937-38. Diplomate Am. Bd. Internal Medicine, Am. Bd. Gastroenterology. Intern Walter Reed Gen. Hosp., Washington, 1936-37; resident in medicine No. divsn. Albert Einstein Med. Ctr., Phila., 1938-39; fellow gastroenterology Grad. Hosp., U. Pa., 1939-40; Ross V. Patterson fellow physiology Jefferson Med. Coll., Phila., 1940-41; instr. gastroenterology U. Pa., 1941-46; asst. prof. medicine Sch. Medicine, Temple U., 1946-54; asst. dir. Fels Research Inst., 1946-54; assoc. prof. clin. medicine Coll. Medicine, Wayne State U., 1954-62, prof. clin. medicine, 1962-63; prof. medicine Coll. Medicine, U. Calif., Irvine, 1963-79, Disting. prof. medicine, 1979—, chmn. dept. medicine, 1963-79, head div. gastroenterology, 1963-79, asst. dean, 1979-90. Cons. VA Hosp., Long Beach, Calif., 1963-97, Cedars-Sinai Med. Ctr., 1963—, Meml. Hosp., Long Beach, 1964-97. Contbg. author: Bockus Gastroenterology, 1st and 2d edits.; assoc. editor: Bockus Gastroenterology 3d edit., 1974, editor-in-chief 4th edit., 1985, cons. editor 5th edit., 1994; editor: Developments in Digestive Diseases, Vol. 1, 1977, Vol. 2, 1979, Vol. 3, 1980; co-editor: Gastrointestinal Symptoms: Clinical Interpretation, 1991; mem. editl. bd. 13 med. jours., various times, 1959—; delivered 14 named lectureships; contbr. 200 articles to med. jours., 108 chpts. in more than 60 books. U.S. Dept. State rep. to S.Am. countries Cultural Exch. Program, 1961. Served to maj. M.C. AUS, 1941-46. Recipient Disting. Svc. award Mich. Med. Soc., 1959, Faculty Cmty. Svc. award U. Calif.-Irvine Alumni Assn., 1971, also Faculty Univ. Svc. award, 1976, Disting. Achievement award Jefferson Med. Coll. Alumni Assn., 1977, Maimonides award Maimonides Soc., 1984, Centennial award N.E. High Sch., Phila., 1990, Aldrich Disting. Univ. Svc. award U. Calif., Irvine, 1993, Bockus medal World Orgn. Gastroenterology, 1994; named Disting. Physician Nat. Found. for Ileitis and Colitis, 1980; J. Edward Berk Lectr. established U. Calif. Irvine Gastroenterology Alumni Assn., Aug., 1991, J. Edward Berk Lectr. established U. Calif. Irvine Vol. Clin. Faculty, 1991, J. Edward Berk Alumni Med. Edn. Ctr. dedicated U. Calif., Irvine, May 30, 1996. Master ACP (gov. So. Calif. region II 1976-80, Laureate award So. Calif. region 1990), Am. Coll. Gastroenterology (pres. 1975-76, Rorer award 1970, 74, 78, 79, Disting. Sci. Achievement award 1982, Clin. Achievement award 1988, Samuel Weiss award 1995); mem. AMA (chmn. sect. gastroenterology 1965-66), Am. Gastroent. Assn. (Disting. Educator award 1992), Am. Soc. Gastrointestinal Endoscopy (pres. 1958-59, Rudolf Schindler award 1966), Am. Fedn. Clin. Rsch. (chmn. Ea. sect.), Bockus Internat. Soc. Gastroenerology (pres. 1967-71), Detroit Gastroent. Soc. (pres. 1960-61), So. Calif. Soc. Gastroenterology (pres. 1967-68), L.A. Acad. Medicine (gov. 1981-84), So. Calif. Soc. Gastrointestinal Endoscopy (hon.), Orange County Acad. Medicine, Orange County Gastroenterology Soc. (founding pres.), Interam. Gastroent. Assn. (life, hon. pres. 1981—), Fgn. Med. Soc., Acad. Med. Ecuador, Peruvian and Cuban Soc. Gastroenterology (hon.), Gastroenterology Socs. Colombia, Gastrointestinal Endoscopy Soc. Colombia, Ecuador, Venezuela and Brazilian Soc. of Gastroenterology and Nutrition, Sigma Xi, Alpha Omega Alpha. Home: 894 Ronda Sevilla Unit C Laguna Woods CA 92653-4796 E-mail: jeberk@uci.edu.

BERK, JONATHAN BRYAN, finance educator; s. Morris Eli and Renate Berk; m. Rebecca Carolyn Schwartz; children: Natasha Samantha, Hannah Isabell. BA, Rice U., Houston, 1984; MSc, MPhil, Yale U., New Haven, 1989, PhD, 1990. Assoc. Goldman Sachs, 1985—87; asst. prof. U. BC, Canada, 1991—96, U. Wash., 1996—98; prof. U. Calif., Berkeley, 1998—2007, Sylvan C. Coleman prof. fin., 2007—. Rsch. assoc. Nat. Bur. Econ. Rsch., Boston, 1998; assoc. editor Jour. Fin., 2000. Author: Corporate Finance, 2007; contbr. articles to profl. jours. Named one of two best papers published, Rev. Fin. Studies, 2006; recipient Best Paper award, 1995, Roger F. Murray prize, 1996, Smith Breeden prize, 1999, Roger F. Murray prize, 2003, Paul A. Samuelson award, TIAA-CREF, 2005. Office: U Calif Berkeley Haas Sch Bus Berkeley CA 94720 Home Phone: 510-666-9588; Office Phone: 510-642-3364. Business E-Mail: berk@haas.berkeley.edu.

BERK, PAUL DAVID, internist, research scientist, educator; b. Bklyn., Apr. 3, 1938; s. Charles and Helen (Goell) B.; m. Aviva Ancona, July 4, 1965 (div. Aug. 1990); children: Claire, Philip, Edward; m. Nicole Polak, 1991; 1 child, David. BA, Swarthmore Coll., 1959; cert., U. St. Andrews, Scotland, 1960; MD, Columbia U., 1964. Diplomate Am. Bd. Internal Medicine, Am. Bd. Hematology. Intern Columbia-Presbyn. Med. Ctr., NYC, 1964-65, resident, 1965-66, fellow in hematology, 1969-70; clin. assoc. metabolism br. Nat. Cancer Inst., Bethesda, Md., 1966-69, sr. investigator, 1970-73; clin. asst. prof. medicine Georgetown U., Washington, 1971-75, clin. assoc. prof., 1975-77; chief sect. on diseases of the liver Nat. Inst. Arthritis, Metabolism and Digestive Diseases, NIH, Bethesda, 1973-77; prof. medicine Mt. Sinai Sch. Medicine, NYC, 1977—2004, Albert and Vera List prof. medicine, 1980-89, prof. biochemistry, 1987-99, Henry and Lillian Stratton prof. molecular medicine, 1989—2004, chief divsn. hematology, 1977-89, acting chief, 1989-90, chief divsn. liver disease, 1989-01; prof. dept. medicine Columbia U. Coll. Physicians and Surgeons, NYC, 2004—. Prof. biochemistry and molecular biology Mt. Sinai Sch. Medicine, 1999-2004; adj. prof. Rockefeller U., 1987-89; cons. in liver disease NIH, 1977-80, mem. adv. coun. Nat. Inst. Diabetes and Digestive and Kidney Diseases, 1990-94. Editor: (with others) Chemistry and Physiology of the Bile Pigments, 1977, Frontiers in Liver Disease, 1981, Myelofibrosis and the Biology of Connective Tissue, 1984, Hans Popper: A Tribute, 1992, Hepatic Transport and Bile Secretion, 1993, Polcythemia Vera, 1994; editor-in-chief Seminars in Liver Disease, 1981-90, 96—, Hepatology, 1991-96; mem. editorial bd. Artificial Organs, 1979-92, Liver, 1980-93; contbr. articles to profl. jours. Served as sr. surgeon USPHS, 1966-69, 75-77. Recipient Merck award Columbia U., 1964; Fulbright scholar, 1959 Fellow ACP, Am. Coll. Gastroenterology; mem. Am. Liver Found. (chmn. bd. dirs. 2000-04), Am. Soc. Clin. Investigation, Assn. Am. Physicians, Am. Assn. Study of Liver Disease (councillor 1985-93, v.p. 1988, pres. 1989), Internat. Assn. Study of Liver (councillor 1988-91), Am. Soc. for Hematology, Am. Clin. and Climatological Assn., Nat. Polycythemia Vera Study Group (vice chmn. 1978-95), Soc. Exptl. Biol. Medicine (councillor 1993-96), N.Y. Soc. Study of Blood (pres. 1982-83), Sigma Xi, Phi Beta Kappa, Alpha Omega Alpha. Office: Columbia Univ Med Ctr Divsn Digestive & Liver Disease 630 W 168th St Box 83 New York NY 10032 Home Phone: 212-860-3728; Office Phone: 212-342-3718. Business E-Mail: pb2158@columbia.edu.

BERK, PHILIP WOOLF, journalist; b. Cape Town, South Africa, Feb. 13, 1933; arrived in U.S., 1952; s. Benjamin and Rebecca (Brenner) Berk; m. Ruth Greenberg, June 20, 1954; children: Benjamin, Alexander, Ann, Melanie. BA, UCLA, 1955; gen. secondary life tchg. credential, Calif. State U., Northridge, 1963—63; MA, Calif. State U., 1965. With The Argus Group, Johannesburg, 1974—83; pres. Hollywood Fgn. Press Assn., 1989—; internat. freelancer. Mem.: Phi Eta Sigma. Home: 6829 Mclennan Ave Van Nuys CA 91406-4530 Office: The Argus Group PO Box 1014 Johannesburg South Africa 2000

BERKA, MARIANNE GUTHRIE, health and physical education educator; b. Queens, NY, Dec. 25, 1944; d. Frank Joseph and Mary (DePaul) Guthrie; m. Jerry George Berka, June 1, 1968; children: Katie, Keri. BS, Ithaca Coll., 1966, MS, 1968; EdD, NYU, 1990. Tchr. Northport H.S., 1966—67; prof. Health, Phys. Edn. and Recreation Nassau C.C., Garden City, NY, 1968—. Adj. assoc. prof. Hofstra U., Hempstead, NY, 1998—. Mem.: AAHPER, AAHPERD, Am. Coll. Sports Medicine (cert. health/fitness instr.), Am. Assn. Sex Educators, Counselors and Therapists (cert. sex educator), N.Y. State Assn. Health, Phys. Edn., Recreation and Dance (J.B. Nash scholarship com. 1983—2000, Nassau Zone Disting. Svc. award 1988, Nassau Zone Higher Edn. Tchr. of Yr. 2003), Assn. Women Phys. Educators N.Y. State (chpt. chmn. 1973—74, chpt. treas. 1980—84). Roman Catholic.

BERKE, BARRY H., lawyer; b. 1964; BA, Duke U., 1986; JD, Harvard Law Sch., 1989. Bar: NY 1989, US Dist. Ct., Southern Dist. NY 1990, US Ct. of Appeals, Second Cir. 1993, US Dist. Ct., Eastern Dist. NY 1995. Clerkship US Dist. Ct., Southern Dist., NY, 1989—90; acting asst. prof. of Law NYU, 1995, adj. asst. prof., 1995—2003, adj. prof., 2003—; ptnr. Kramer Levin Naftalis & Frankel LLP, NYC, 1996—; tchr. Nat. Inst. Trial Adv., Hauppauge, NY, 1997—. Co-author: (textbook) The Practice of Federal Criminal Law: Prosecution and Defense, 2006. Named one of Litigation's Rising Stars, The Am. Lawyer, 2007. Mem.: NY State Assn. Criminal Def. Lawyers, Nat. Assn. Criminal Def. Lawyers, ABA, Assn. of Bar of City of NY. Office: Kramer Levin Naftalis & Frankel LLP 1177 Ave of Americas New York NY 10036 Business E-Mail: bberke@kramerlevin.com.

BERKE, BRETT ALAN, neuroscientist, research scientist; b. Hinsdale, Ill., Sept. 6, 1973; s. James Byron and Eileen Sandra Berke; m. Brett Alan Berke, Sept. 16, 2000; children: Hattie Zoe, Byron Amerson. PhD in Neurosci. and Biol. Sci., U. Iowa, Iowa City, 2004. Postdoctoral rsch. assoc. Yale U., New Haven, 2004—. Home: 25 Rose St Hamden CT 06514 Office: Yale U MCDB Dept Rm 640 KBT New Haven CT 06520-8103 Home Phone: 203-288-5926; Office Phone: 203-432-3479. Business E-Mail: brett.berke@yale.edu.

BERKEBILE, CHARLES ALAN, geology educator, hydrogeology researcher; b. Queens, NY, Mar. 4, 1938; s. Charles Dean and Bernice (Manlove) B.; 1 child, Patricia Berlowe; m. Martha S. Berkebile, May 17, 2003. BS, Allegheny Coll., 1960; MA, Boston U., 1961, PhD, 1964. Mem. rsch. staff MIT, Cambridge, 1963—64; asst. prof. Southampton Coll. L.I. U., NY, 1964—67, assoc. prof., dept. chair Southampton Coll., 1969—75, prof., assoc. dir. Southampton Coll., 1975—81; rsch. mineralogist Corning Glass Works, NY, 1967—69; prof., dept. chair Corpus Christi State U., Tex., 1981—91; prof., dir. Tex. A&M U., Corpus Christi, 1991—2004, prof., asst. dean, 1994—98, Regents prof., 2001—04, prof. emeritus, 2004—. Vis. assoc. chemist Brookhaven Nat. Lab., Upton, N.Y., 1966-67; vis. sr. rsch. geologist Princeton (N.J.) U., 1979-80. Contbr. articles to profl. jours. Mem. Regional Stormwater Master Plan Adv. Com., Corpus Christi, 1989-90, Mayor's Adv. Com. on Water Issues, Corpus Christi, 1991-92; treas., bd. dirs. Rockport (Tex.) Country Club Estates Homeowners Assn., 1991-94. Named Outstanding Educator, Koch Industries, 2001. Fellow Geol. Soc. Am.; mem. Assn. Ground Water Scientists and Engrs., Nat. Ground Water Assn., Nat. Assn. Geology Tchrs., Tex. Ground Water Assn. (hon., life, bd. dirs., v.p. ground water sci. 1994, pres. 1995-96), Corpus Christi Geol. Soc. Avocations: golf, music. Home: 314 Champions Dr Rockport TX 78382-6906 E-mail: alanb@pyramid3.net.

BERKELEY, EDWARD, performing arts association administrator, music educator; b. NYC; Grad, Carleton Coll., Minn., 1966. Artistic dir. Willow Cabin Theater Co.; now dir., undergrad. opera studies Juilliard Sch., NYC, 1987—; and gen. dir. Aspen Opera Theatre Ctr., Colo. Benedict Disting. Vis. Prof. of Theater Carleton Coll., 2003. Office: Office of the Director Aspen Opera Theatre Ctr 2 Music School Rd Aspen CO 81611 also: Opera Studies The Juilliard Sch 60 Lincoln Ctr Plz New York NY 10023-6588*

BERKELHAMER, JAY ELLIS, pediatrician; b. Tuscaloosa, Ala., Apr. 8, 1942; s. Louis H. and Belle F. B.; m. Jacqueline Beth Colman, June 12, 1966; children: Beth Carolyn, Sara Kay, Adam Colman. BS, U. Mich., 1963, MD, 1967. Resident U. Chgo., 1967-70, asst. prof., 1972-78, assoc. prof., 1978-84, prof., 1984-93, assoc. chair, dir. residency program, 1986-93, assoc. dean ambulatory care, 1983-88; chair pediatrics Henry Ford Health Sys., Detroit, 1993-99. Prof. pediatrics Case Western Res. U., Cleve., 1994-99; clin. prof. pediatrics and communicable diseases U. Mich., Ann Arbor, 1994-99; sr. v.p. for med. affairs Children's Healthcare of Atlanta, 1999—; clin. prof. pediats. Emory U., Atlanta, 1999—. Lt. comdr. USPHS, 1970-72. Robert Wood Johnson Health Policy fellow NAS, Washington, 1978-79. Mem. Am. Acad. Pediatrics (pres. Ill. chpt. 1992, pres.-elect 2005), Chgo. Pediatric Soc. (pres. 1987, Archibald L. Hoyne award 1993), Ambulatory Pediatric Assn. (pres. 1986). Office: 1600 Tullie Circle Atlanta GA 30329 Office Phone: 404-785-7005. Office Fax: 404-785-7027.

BERKELHAMMER, ROBERT BRUCE, lawyer; b. Providence, Oct. 27, 1949; s. Cyril Lester and Anne Louise (Rossman) Berkelhammer; m. Miriam June Finkelstein, Mar. 9, 1975; children: Jessi, Max, Abby. BA, U. Rochester, 1971; JD, Boston U., 1974. Bar: RI 1975, US Dist. Ct. RI 1977, Mass. 1998, Conn. 2001. Atty. NLRB, Pitts., 1974—77; ptnr. Licht & Semonoff, Providence, 1977—97, Chace Ruttenberg & Freedman, LLP, Providence, 1997—. Pres. Jewish Family Svc., Inc., Providence, 1988—91. Mem.: ABA, RI Bar Assn., RI Jewish Hist. Assn. (pres. 2000—02). Jewish. Home: 131 Laurel Ave Providence RI 02906-4622 Office: Chace Ruttenberg & Freedman LLP 1 Park Row Ste 300 Providence RI 02903-1235 Home Phone: 401-831-4472; Office Phone: 401-453-6400. Business E-Mail: rberkelhammer@crfllp.com.

BERKELMAN, KARL, retired physics professor; b. Lewiston, Maine, June 7, 1933; s. Robert George and Yvonne (Langlois) Berkelman; m. Mary Bowen Hobbie, Oct. 10, 1959; children: Thomas, James, Peter. BS, U. Rochester, NY, 1955; PhD, Cornell U., 1959. From asst. prof. to prof. physics Cornell U., Ithaca, NY, 1961—2006, dir. lab. nuclear studies, 1985-2000; prof. emeritus, 2006; sci. assoc. DESY, Hamburg, Germany, 1974-75, CERN, Geneva, 1967-68, 81-82, 91-92, 2000-2001. Office: Cornell Univ Newman Lab Ithaca NY 14853

BERKELMAN, RUTH, medical educator; AB, Princeton U., 1973; MD, Harvard U. Med. Sch., 1977. Epidemic intelligence svc. officer CDC, 1980—82, med. epidemiologist, Epidemiology Program Office, 1982—83, chief, epidemiologic studies branch, Epidemiology Program Office, 1983—86, dir., divsn. surveillance & epidemiologic studies, Epidemiology Program Office, 1986—88, chief, surveillance br., Divsn. HIV/AIDS, 1988—92, dep. dir., Nat. Ctr. Infectious Diseases, 1992—97, sr. advisor to Dir., 1998—2000; cons. Nuclear Threat Initiative, 2001; Rollins prof. Emory U., Rollins Sch. Pub. Health, 2002—, dir. Ctr. Pub. Health Preparedness & Rsch., 2002—. Chmn. Pub. and Sci. Affairs Bd. Am. Soc. Microbiology, 2004—. Trustee Princeton U., 2000—04. Recipient Sec.'s award for Disting. Svc., CDC, 1997, Certificate of Recognition, Coun. State & Territorial Epidemiologists, 1995; John Maclean Fellow, Princeton U., 1995. Mem.: Inst. Medicine. Office: Rollins Sch Pub Health 1518 Clifton Rd Mailstop 1518-002-1AA Atlanta GA 30322 Office Phone: 404-727-5409. Office Fax: 404-712-8345. E-mail: rberkel@sph.emory.edu.

BERKENES, JOYCE MARIE POORE, social worker, director; b. Des Moines, Aug. 29, 1953; d. Donald Roy and Thelma Beatrice (Hart) Poore; m. Robert Elliott Berkenes, Jan. 3, 1976; children: Tiffany Noelle, Cory Matthew. BA in Social Work and Biology, Simpson Coll., Indianola, Iowa., 1975. Cons. in field, 1975—76; resident counselor and group home mgr. Chaddock Boys Home, Quincy, Ill., 1976-78; social service dir. North Adams Nursing Home, Mendon, Ill., 1978; home tchr. Head Start, Camp Point, Ill., 1978-79, home tchr. supr./edn. and parent involvement coordinator, 1979-82; family counselor Iowa Children's and Family Services, Des Moines, 1982-85; family counselor and vol. coordinator Luth. Social Services, Des Moines, 1985-89; coordinator/educator/social worker Parent-Infant Nurturing Ctr., Meth. Med. Ctr., Des Moines, 1989-95; social worker The Homestead, 1995-97; state program mgr. Healthy Families Iowa Projects of Home Care Iowa, Des Moines, 1997-01, Healthy Families Am. Trainer, 1998—; program dir. HOPES/ Healthy Families Iowa Prevent

Child Abuse Iowa, 2001—03; rep. State Domestic Violence Response Tng. Team Iowa Dept. Pub. Health, 2003—04; program mgr. for home care Generations Inc., 2004—05; med. social worker oncology Iowa Meth. Med. Ctr., 2005—. Mem. Greater Des Moines Child Abuse and Neglect Coun. Bd. Mem. Prevent Child Abuse Iowa, Prevent Child Abuse Am. Mem. Internat. Assn. Infant Massage, Abbie Gardner Questers. Democrat. United Ch. Christ. Avocations: collecting antiques, reading, piano, ballet. Home: 2901 NE 80th St Altoona IA 50009-9423

BERKENKAMP, FRED JULIUS, management consultant; b. Alma, Wis., Oct. 19, 1925; s. Julius Henry and Elisabeth Helen Berkenkamp; m. Ruth Ethelyn Taylor; children: Linda Birch, Vicki Fitzgerald, Thomas, JoAnne. BS in Electron Engring, U. Wyo., 1948; postgrad., U. Syracuse, 1951. Mgmt. quality control GE, Syracuse, 1948—55, corp. cons. mfg. mgmt. NYC, 1955—65, mgr. planning jet engines Cin., 1966—68, mgr. nuc. fuels mfg. Wilmington, NC, 1969; corp. exec. v.p., pres. Appliance Group, Roper Corp., Kankakee, Ill., 1970—80; pres., CEO, dir. Allied Structural Steel Co. subs. MSL Industries/Alleghany Corp., Chicago Heights, Ill., 1980—83; pres. Berkenkamp & Co. Inc., mgmt. cons., 1984—; pres., CEO FMH, Inc., Newport Beach, Calif., 1988—91. Trustee Community Coll., 1974-80. With USNR, 1944—46. Mem. Assn. Home Appliance Mfrs. (chmn. bd. dirs.), Gas Appliance Mfrs. Assn. (dir.), Rotary, Sigma Chi. Home: 14216 W Cavalcade Dr Sun City West AZ 85375-5624

BERKERY, ROSEMARY THERESA, lawyer, investment company executive; b. Apr. 18, 1953; BA magna cum laude in English, Coll. Mt. St. Vincent, 1975; JD, St. John's U. Sch. Law, Jamaica, NY, 1978. Bar: N.Y. 1980. Corp. and securities lawyer Shearman & Sterling, NYC, 1978—83; atty. Merrill Lynch & Co., Inc., NYC, 1983—95, sr. v.p., assoc. gen. counsel, 1995—97, co-dir. global securities rsch. and econs. grp., 1997—2000, sr. v.p., dir. US pvt. client mktg. and investments, 2000—01, exec. v.p., gen. counsel, 2001—07, vice-chmn., gen. counsel, 2007—. Editor: St. John's Law Rev. Office: Merrill Lynch and Co Inc 4 World Fin Ctr 250 Vesey St New York NY 10080*

BERKETT, NEIL, telecommunications industry executive; Div. mgmt. acct. through fin. contr. ICL Australia, 1978—85; gen. mgr. fin. & adminstrn. Eastwest Airlines, Australia, 1986—87, dir., gen. mgr., 1987—92; sr. gen. mgr. Citibank Ltd. Australia, 1992—95; head retail banking St. George Bank, Australia, 1995—96; dir. integration Advance Bank, Australia, 1996—97; prin. Marsh Mill Consulting Ltd, England, 1997—2002; chief exec. Trek Investco Ltd., England, 1998—2002; COO Prudential Assurance Co. Ltd. (UK), 2002—03; mng. dir. distbn. Lloyds TSB Group plc (UK), 2003—05; COO Virgin Media Inc., NYC, 2005—, acting CEO, 2007—. Non-exec. dir. Sydney Aquarium, Australia, 1995—99. Office: Virgin Media Inc Ste 2863 909 Third Ave New York NY 10022*

BERKEY, DENNIS DALE, academic administrator; b. Wooster, Ohio, May 27, 1947; s. William Bruce and Mary Louise (Schrock) B.; m. Catherine Grooms, Aug. 24, 1974; children: Cristin, Aaron, Jessica. BA, Muskingum Coll., New Concord, Ohio, 1969; MA, Miami U., Oxford, Ohio, 1971; PhD, U. Cin., 1974. Lectr. U. Cin., 1972-73; instr. Miami U., Oxford, Ohio, 1973-74; asst. prof. math. Boston U., 1974-79, assoc. prof. math., 1979-93, prof. math., 1993—, dean Grad. Sch., 1987—2002, dean arts and scis., 1987—2002, provost, 1987—91, 1996—2004; pres. Worcester Poly. Inst., Mass., 2004—. Author: Calculus, 1983, 3d edit., 1992, Applied Calculus, 1986, 3d edit., 1994, Calculus for Management, 1986, 3d edit., 1994. Recipient Metcalf Award for Excellence in Tchg., Boston U., 1978. Mem. Am. Math. Soc., Math. Assn. Am., Soc. for Indsl. and Applied Math. Home: 1 Drury Ln Worcester MA 01609 Office: Worcester Poly Inst 100 Institute Rd Worcester MA 01609 Home Phone: 508-753-2662; Office Phone: 508-831-5200. Business E-Mail: dberkey@wpi.edu.

BERKHOUDT, THOMAS WALTER, director; b. Buffalo, Jan. 22, 1967; s. Herman and Ethel Berkhoudt; m. Kimberly Susan Miller, Sept. 12, 1992; children: Drew Addison, Erika. BS in Acctg., Alfred U., 1989; MBA, U. Rochester, 1994. Jr. acct. U. Rochester, NY, 1989—92, sr. acct., strong meml. hosp., 1992—94, spl. projects adminstr., dept. medicine, 1994—96, sr. cardiology adminstr., cardiology unit, 1996—2000; fin. & reporting specialist Rochester Inst. Tech., 2000—03, asst. dir. sponsored programs fin. mgmt. svcs., 2003—. Sr. assoc. Rochester Chpt. Cert. Football Officials, 2003; treas. Rochester Cardiovasc. Soc., 1996—2000. Mem.: Med. Group Mgmt. Assn. (assoc.), Am. Acad. Med. Adminstrs. (assoc.), Nat. Coun. U. Rsch. Aadminstrs. (assoc.). Avocations: running, gardening, tennis, golf, travel. Home Phone: 585-624-1259.

BERKLAND, JAMES OMER, geologist; b. Glendale, Calif., July 31, 1930; m. Janice Lark Keirstead, Dec. 19, 1966; children: Krista Lynn, Jay Olin. AA, Santa Rosa Jr. Coll., 1951; BA, U. Calif., Berkeley, 1958; MS, San Jose State U., 1964; post grad., U. Calif., Davis, 1969—72. registered engrng. geologist, Calif. Psychiat. tech. Sonoma State Hosp., Calif., 1951—57; with U.S. Geol. Survey, 1958—64; engrng. geologist U.S. Bur. Reclamation, 1964—69, cons. geologist, 1969—72; asst. prof. Appalachian State U., Boone, NC, 1972—73; county geologist Santa Clara County, San Jose, Calif., 1973—94; ret., 1994. Mem. geology tech. adv. com., San Jose, Calif.; adj. prof. San Jose State U., Calif., 1973—75; lectr. gen. edn. conf. Sci. and Tech. Soc., 1985—89, coord. com. Calif. conv., 1978; mem. evening faculty San Jose City Coll., Calif.; mem. West Valley Legis. Com., Calif., 1979—90; lectr. ann. deposit receipt seminar San Jose Real Estate Bd., Calif., 1980—85; discoverer in field; featured spkr. Keynote Speakers, Inc.; geology tchr. Sonoma High Sch. Adult Edn., Calif., 2001—03. Contbg. numerous articles to profl. journals.; originator seismic window theory for earthquake prediction, 1974; TV and radio appearances including PBA, Frontline, Evening Mag., People are Talking, 48 Hours, Sightings, You Bet Your Life, Science Faction, Science Fiction Cable, Two on the Town, In Search of CNN News, WGN, KIRO, KSL, KIEV, KGO, KCBS, KNYV, KOA, KOGO, KVEN, KSCO, KOMO, KPFK, Two at Noon, KPFA-FM Radio, The Other Side, Northwest Afternoon, Art Bell's Coast to Coast, Town Meeting, Ron Owens Show, Laura Lee Show, Art Bell Show, Kathi Gori Show, Extra, Strange Universe; articles on work featured in OMNI, STERN, Wall St. Jour., Bergen's Tidende, San Francisco Examiner, San Francisco Chronicle, L.A. Times, Nat. Geog., Am. Health, The Astrology Ency., Old Farmers Almanac, 1991, Gilroy Dispatch, Bakersfield Californian, San Jose Mercury News, Sonoma Index Tribune, Intuition, Farmers Almanac, others; editor, pub.: SYZYGY An Earthquake Newsletter, 1990—; co-founder Quakeline; author: (biography) Cal Orey: The Man Who Predicts Earthquakes, 2005. Active mem. Statue of Liberty Found., NY; treas. Creekside Pk. Pl. Homeowner's Group, Calif.; mem. various city and county adv. boards Calif.; mem. legis. com. Rt. 85 Task Force, Calif., Earthquake Watch, Calif., 1979—82, New Weather Observer, Calif., Nat. Wildlife Fedn., Calif.; mem. tech. and soc. San Jose Sch. Dist., Calif., 1980—, mem. role model program, 1995—97; mem. Sonoma Land Trust, Calif.; bd. dir. Glen Ellen Cmty. Ch., Calif., 2001—; Nat. Wildlife Fedn.; v.p. West Coast Aquatics, Calif., Creekside Pk. Pl. Swim Team, Calif.; mem. ctr. study early man East Valley WMCA, Calif.; mem. legis. com. West Valley YMCA, Calif., 1980—; mem. Found. for the Study of Cycles, Calif., invited lectr. monthly and ann. meeting, Calif.; mem. The Nature Conservancy, Calif.; charter mem. The Dolphin Inst.; docent Bouverie Nature Preserve, Calif., 1999—; mem. Jack London Found. Recipient Resolution of Commendation Santa Clara Bd. Supervisors, 1994, award of excellence Sonoma League, 2002; Dwight E. Stanford fellow, A.J. Robinson Found. Mem. Smithsonian Inst. (assoc.), Ret. Pub. Employee Assn. Calif., Alumni Assn. San Jose State U., Sons of Norway, Sonoma Hist. Soc., Jack London Reading Group, Lions Club (various offices and awards, including pres. Valley of the Moon Lions, 2002-03, Lion of Yr. Awards 1990,91,93,94). Home: 1175 Chauvet Rd # 1926 Glen Ellen CA 95442-1926 Office Phone: 707-935-6512. Fax: 707-935-6512. Personal E-mail: syzygyjob@aol.com.

BERKLEY, EMILY CAROLAN, lawyer; b. Richmond, Va., Mar. 2, 1950; d. Charles Garvice and Edna Gray (Berkley) Broom; m. Richard E. Bird, Sept. 6, 1969 (div. Mar. 1988); children: Jessica A. Bird, Martel J. Bird. Student, Coll. of William and Mary, 1968—70; BS in Psychology cum laude, Tufts U., 1972; JD magna cum laude, Temple U., 1977. Ptnr. Ballard Spahr Andrews & Ingersoll LLP, Phila., 1977—. Seminar panelist Pa. Bar Inst., 1992, 1998—2003, 2005, 07, Practicing Law Inst., 1993—2005, Phila. Compliance Roundtable, 2004—07. Long range planning com. Performing Arts for Tredyffrin-Easttown Sch. Dist., Berwyn, Pa., 1989, chair subcom. on creativity, futures com., 1990; active United Way, 1989-91; bd. dir. Devon-Strafford Little League, 1992-95. Fellow: Am. Bar Found. (life); mem.: ABA (bus. law sect. chair task force on exporation of Uniform Comml. Code 1995—97, vice chair internat. comml. law subcom. 1997—99, bus. law sect. liaison U.S. Sec. of State's adv. com. on pvt. internat 1997—99, chair legal opinion com. 2004—07, uniform comml. code com., fed. regulation securities com., corp. compliance com.), N.Y. TriBar Opinion Com., Phila. Bar Assn., Pa. Bar Assn. (officer 2003—, bus. law sect., chair legal opinion com., chair article 9 task force, secured trans.), Am. Law Inst. (editl. bd. uniform comml. code), Am. Coll. Comml. Fin. Lawyers (bd. regents 1993—2001, pres. 2000, rep. to permanent editl. bd. on unform comml. code.). Office: Ballard Spahr Andrews et al 1735 Market St Ste 5100 Philadelphia PA 19103-7599 Home Phone: 610-687-1236; Office Phone: 215-864-8611. Business E-Mail: berkley@ballardspahr.com.

BERKLEY, ERMA VAN METER, retired librarian; b. Thayer, Kans., Nov. 18, 1922; d. George William and Elizabeth (Hamill) Van Meter; m. Donald William Berkley, May 28, 1944 (dec. 1980); children: Ann Elizabeth, James Donald. BA in Bus. Edn. magna cum laude, Western Wash. U., 1964; MLS, U. Wash., 1973. Cert. profl. libr., 1976. Sec., bookkeeper Blue Ribbon Growers, Inc., Yakima, Wash., 1941-44; aircraft communicator CAA, Kodiak, Alaska, 1944-47; libr., sec., tchr. Crescent Consol. Sch., Joyce, Wash., 1965-66; asst. libr., reference libr. Port Angeles (Wash.) High Sch., 1966-68, secretarial tchr., 1968-75, head libr., 1975-86; ret., 1986. Bd. dirs. exec. com. Wash. Libr. Network, 1979-81; N.W. rep.-at-large Washington Libr. Media Assn., 1983-84; del. Gov.'s Conf. on Libr. and Info. Svcs., Olympia, 1979; sec. Western Wash. Bus. Edn. Assn., 1973-74. Mem. AAUW (treas. 1966-67, pres. 1982-84, v.p. 1988-90), PEO, Nat. Ret. Tchrs. Assn., Am. Philatelic Soc., Phi Theta Kappa, Beta Phi Mu. Avocations: travel, stamp collecting/philately, golf, hiking, gardening.

BERKLEY, EUGENE BERTRAM (BERT), envelope company executive; b. Kansas City, Mo., May 8, 1923; s. Eugene Bertram (Bert) Berkowitz and Caroline Newman (Newburger) B.; m. Joan Meinrath, Sept. 1, 1948; children: Janet Lynn Berkley Dubrava, William (Bill) Spencer Berkley, Jane Ellen Berkley Levitt. BA, Duke U., 1948; MBA, Harvard U., 1950. Pres., CEO Tension Envelope Corp., Kansas City, Mo., 1962-88, chmn. bd., 1967—. Chmn. Global Envelope Alliance, 2005—. Patentee in field. Mem. Mayor's Prayer Breakfast Com., 1964-84, Kitchen Cabinet, Kansas City, Mo. Sch. Dist., 1990-92; pres. Civic Coun. Greater Kansas City, 1967-68, charter mem., bd. dirs. 1982-83; pres. C. of C. Greater Kansas City, 1968-69; trustee exec. com. Midwest Rsch. Inst., 1969-72; chmn. Comprehensive Needs and Svc. Survey Com., 1971, Ctr. Bus. Innovation, 1987-89, Global Envelope Alliance, 2005-07; bd. dirs. Can. Cellulose Co., Vancouver, BC, 1973-80, Menorah Med. Ctr. Bd., 1980-94, Kansas City Area Health Planning Coun., Inc., 1982-83, Nat. Minority Supplier Devel. Coun., 1989-98, Ctr. Entrepreneurial Leadership, 1991-2002, Nat. Youth Info. Network, 1997-04, Centerpoint for Leaders, Washington, 2001-, Inst. Ednl. Leadership Inc., Washington, Ewing Marion Kauffman Found; mem. exec. com., met. chmn. Nat. Alliance Businessmen Met. Kansas City, 1973; mem. exec. com. Ctr. Mgmt. Assistance, 1980-83; human resources com. Heart Am. United Way, 1983; chmn. bd. dirs. Human Svcs. Testing and Retng. Coun., 1983-90, Minority Supplier Coun., 1986-88; trustee, chmn. U. Kansas City, 1983-85, vice chmn., 1981-83, North Campus Devel. Com., policy bd., charter mem. U. Assocs.; mem. adv. bd. Nat. Parks and Conservation Assn., 1986—, Nat. Coun. Econ. Edn., 1993-95, U. Kans. Natural History Mus., 1994-2000; chmn. adv. com., bd. dirs. Ctr. for Workforce Preparation, U.S. C. of C., 1989-91; active Bus. Roundtable Dept. Social Svcs. State of Mo., 1989-99; founder, LINC, 1992; chmn. local investment commn. LINC Mo. Dept. Social Svcs., 1992-95, exec. comm., 1992—; dir. family and cmty. trust State of Mo., 1999-. Decorated Bronze Star; recipient Brotherhood award NCCJ, 1968, numerous other awards, including Mr. Kansas City award C. of C. of Greater Kansas City, 1972, Disting. Svc. award Johnson County Friends of the Libr. (Johnson County, Kans.), 1982, Chancellor's medal U. Mo.-Kansas City, 1989, Disting. Svc. to State Govt. award Nat. Govs. Assn., 2000. Mem. Envelope Mfrs. Assn. (exec. com. 1960-63, 67-70, 76-79, vice chmn. exec. com. 1981-83, v.p. 1981-83, pres. 1983-85), Flexographic Tech. Assn. (bd. dirs. 1993-97), Oakwood Country Club, Homestead Country Club. Avocations: fly fishing, race walking, camping, white water rafting, backpacking. Office: Tension Envelope Corp 819 E 19th St Kansas City MO 64108-1781 Home Phone: 913-362-6638; Office Phone: 816-471-3800. E-mail: bertberkley@tension.com.

BERKLEY, JAMES DONALD, clergyman; b. Yakima, Wash., May 19, 1950; s. Donald William and Erma Ercile (Van Meter) B.; m. Deborah Milam, Aug. 18, 1974; children: Peter James, Mary Milam. BS, U. Wash., 1972; MDiv, Fuller Theol. Seminary, 1975, D Ministry, 1980. Intern First Presbyn. Ch., Yakima, Wash., 1971-73, Bel Air Presbyn. Ch., LA, 1973-75; asst. pastor Community Presbyn Ch., Ventura, Calif., 1975-78; sr. pastor Dixon (Calif.) Community Ch., 1978-85; sr. assoc. editor Leadership jour. Christianity Today Inc., Carol Stream, Ill., 1985-90, editor Your Church, 1990-94; sr. assoc. pastor First Presbyn. Ch., Bellevue, Wash., 1994—2002; nat. issues ministry dir. Presbyns. for Renewal, Bellevue, 2002—05; dir Presbyn. Action, Bellevue, 2005—. Author: Making the Most of Mistakes, 1987, Called into Crisis, 1988, The Dynamics of Church Finance, 2000, Essential Christianity, 2001; gen. editor: Preaching to Convince, 1986, Leadership Handbooks of Practical Theology, Vol. I, 1992, Vols. II and III, 1994; editor reNEWS, 1999—2005. Recipient 1st place award interview Evangelical Press Assn., 1991, 92. Republican. Avocations: bagpipes, hiking, golf, films, music. Home: 304 128th Ave NE Bellevue WA 98005-3242 Office: Presbyn Action 304 128th Ave NE Bellevue WA 98005 Office Phone: 425-637-7742. E-mail: jimberkley@msn.com.

BERKLEY, PETER LEE, lawyer; b. Newark, Mar. 10, 1939; s. Irving S. and Goldie A. (Karp) Berkley; m. Nancy R. Margolis, Aug. 2, 1964; children: James, Alison Wagonfield, John. BA, Williams Coll., 1960; JD, Harvard U., 1963. Bar: N.J. 1963, U.S. Dist. Ct. N.J. 1963. Assoc. Riker, Danzig, Scherer & Brown, Newark, 1963—68; ptnr. Riker, Danzig, Scherer & Hyland, Newark and Morristown, NJ, 1969-83; mng. ptnr. Riker, Danzig, Scherer, Hyland & Perretti, L.L.P., Morristown, 1984—95; ptnr. Riker, Danzig, Scherer, Hyland & Perretti, LLP, 1996—99, of counsel, 1999—. Trustee Livingston (N.J.) Symphony Orch., 1975-89. Mem. ABA, N.J. State Bar Assn., Am. Coll. Real Estate Lawyers, Harvard Law Sch. Alumni Assn. N.J. (pres. 1980-81), Williams Coll. Alumni Assn. Ctrl. N.J. (pres. 1986-89), Phi Beta Kappa. Office Phone: 973-451-8403. Business E-Mail: pberkley@riker.com.

BERKLEY, SHELLEY (ROCHELLE LEVINE BERKLEY), congresswoman, lawyer; b. NYC, Jan. 20, 1951; m. Lawrence Lehrner; 2 children. BA in Polit. Sci., U. Nev., Las Vegas, 1972; JD, U. San Diego Sch. Law, 1976. Counsel S.W. Gas Corp.; dep. dir. Nev. Commerce Dept.; mem. Nev. State Assembly, 1982—84; vice chair bd. regents Nev. Univ. and Cmty. Coll. Sys., 1990—98; v.p. govt. and legal affairs Sands Hotel, 1996—98; mem. US Congress from 1st Nev. dist., 1999—, mem. ways and means com. and vets.' affairs com. Bd. chair Nev. Hotel and Motel Assn.; nat. dir. Am. Hotel-Motel Assn.; del. White House Conf. on Tourism. Bd. trustees Sunrise-Columbia Hosp. and Med. Ctr., Las Vegas. Recipient Clark County Mother of Yr., 1994, Humane Legislator of Yr. award, Am. Humane Assn., 2000, Medal of Merit, Jewish War Vets. of the U.S.A., 2003, Outstanding Dem. of Yr., Paradise Democratic Club. Mem.: Women's Democratic Club Clark County, Clark County Bar Assn., US Bar Assn., So. Nev. Assn. Women Attys., Nev. State Bar Assn. Democrat. Jewish. Office: US House Reps 405 Cannon House Office Bldg Washington DC 20515 Office Phone: 202-225-5965. Office Fax: 202-225-3119. E-mail: shelley.berkley@mail.house.gov.*

BERKLEY, STEPHEN M., entrepreneur, investor; b. NJ, 1944; s. Irving S. and Goldie A. Berkley; children: David, Michael. Student, London Sch. Econs., 1964-65; BA in Econs., Colgate U., 1966; MBA, Harvard U., 1968. Mgmt. cons. Boston Cons. Group, 1968, 71-73; mgr. strategic planning Potlatch Corp., 1973-77; v.p. bus. devel. Qume Corp. subs. ITT, Hayward, Calif., 1977-80, v.p., gen. mgr. memory products divs., 1980-81; v.p. mktg. Quantum Corp., Milpitas, Calif., 1981-83, chmn., CEO, 1987-92, chmn., 1992-93, 95-98; pres. Plus Devel. Corp. (Quantum subs.), 1983-87, chmn., CEO, 1987-92; pres. The Rosewood Found., 1991—. Bd. dirs. Quantum Corp., Edify Corp.; chmn. Coactive Computing Corp.; instr. bus. and econs. East Carolina U., 1969-71. Bd. dirs. Hidden Harvest, 2005—, v.p. of bd., 2006—; bd. dirs. Splashcast Inc., 2006—. Served to lt. USNR, 1968-71. Mem. Corp. Planners Assn. (dir.), Harvard Bus. Sch. Club No. Calif., Los Altos Golf and Country Club, The Reserve Golf Club, Phi Beta Kappa. Avocations: golf, modern art, travel.

BERKLEY, WILLIAM ROBERT, insurance holding company executive; b. Oct. 31, 1945; m. Marjorie Adnepos, June 19, 1971; children: Lisa A., W. Robert Jr., Lauren E. BS, NYU, 1966; MBA, Harvard U., 1968. Founder, chmn., chief exec. officer W.R. Berkley Corp., 1967—, pres., COO, 2000. Officer and/or dir., chmn. Assoc. Cmty. Bancorp, Inc., Conn. Cmty. Bank, N.A.; officer and/or dir. Interlaken Capital, Inc. and affiliates, Forethought Fin. Group, Inc., The First Marblehead Corp., Kiln plc, Five Mile Capital Ptnrs., LLC, HealthEquity, Inc. Chmn. bd. overseers Stern Sch. Bus., NYU; chmn. bd. Achievement First; vice chmn. bd. trustees, exec. com., fin. com., investment com. NYU. Office: W R Berkley Corp 475 Steamboat Rd Greenwich CT 06830-6608

BERKMAN, LANCE, professional baseball player; b. Waco, Tex., Feb. 10, 1976; Attended, Rice Univ., Houston, Tex. First baseman, outfielder Houston Astros, 1999—. Named to Nat. League All-Star Team, 2001, 2004—05; recipient Silver Slugger award, MLB, 2005. Office: Minute Maid Park 501 Crawford St Houston TX 77002

BERKMAN, LISA F., public health educator; PhD, U. Calif., Berkeley, 1977. Thomas D. Cabot prof. pub. policy Harvard Sch. Pub. Health, Boston, chair Dept. of Soc., Human Develop., and Health. Contbr. articles to profl. jours. Mem.: Inst. of Medicine of NAS. Achievements include research in on psychosocial influences on health outcomes. Office: Harvard Univ Kresge Bldg Rm 709 677 Huntington Ave Boston MA 02115

BERKMAN, LOUIS, steel company executive; b. Canton, Ohio, Jan. 15, 1909; s. Hyman L. and Sarah (Galman) B.; m. Sandra Weiss, Apr. 14, 1935 (dec. Aug. 1983); children: Marshall, Donna Berkman Paul. DBA (hon.), Bethany Coll.; DBus Sci. (hon.), U. Steubenville. Pres., treas. Louis Berkman Co., Steubenville, Ohio, 1931—; pres., chmn. Parkersburg Steel Corp., W.Va., 1946—; pres., treas. Follansbee Steel Corp., W.Va., 1954—. Chmn. bd., pres. First Fin. Group, Inc., Washington, Pa.; dir. Asso. Communications Corp. Pres., trustee Louis and Sandra Berkman Found., Steubenville, 1952— , Ampco-Pitts. Found.; mem. adv. com. Ft. Steuben Area council Boy Scouts Am. Mem. Steubenville C. of C., Pitts. Symphony Soc., Oglebay Inst.; mem. B'nai B'rith. Clubs: Rotarian, Elk, Steubenville Country; Westmoreland Country (Export, Pa.); Downtown (Pitts.), Concordia (Pitts.). Office: Ampco-Pittsburgh Corp 600 Grant St Pittsburgh PA 15219 Office Phone: 740-283-3722.

BERKMAN, MICHAEL G., lawyer; b. Poland, Apr. 4, 1917; came to U.S., 1921; s. Harry and Bertha (Jay) B.; m. Marjorie Edelstein, Nov. 28, 1941; children— Laurel, William BS, U. Chgo., 1937, PhD, 1941; JD, DePaul U., 1958; LLM in Intellectual Property, John Marshall Law Sch., 1962; spl. courses, Harvard U., 1943, MIT, 1943. Bar: U.S. Patent Office 1960. Research chemist Argonne Nat. Lab., 1946-51; assoc. dir., chief chemist Colburn Labs., Chgo., 1951-59; instr. chemistry Roosevelt U., Chgo., 1946-49; patent lawyer Mann, Brown & McWilliams, Chgo., 1959-63; ptnr. Kegan, Kegan & Berkman, Chgo., 1963-84, Trexler, Bushnell, Giangiorgi & Blackstone, Chgo., 1984-91; pvt. practice law Glenview, Ill., 1991—. Chem. cons.; expert witness in patent law. Contbr. articles to profl. jours. Served to 1st lt. Signal Corps, U.S. Army, 1942-46. Mem. Am. Chem. Soc., ABA, Patent Law Assn., Chgo., Sigma Xi. Home and Office: 939 Glenview Rd Glenview IL 60025-3172

BERKMAN, RICHARD LYLE, lawyer; b. Pitts., Sept. 4, 1946; s. Allen H. and Selma (Wiener) B.; m. Toni Seidl, June 7, 1998; children: Benjamin, Lisa, Daniel. AB magna cum laude, Harvard U., 1968, JD cum laude, 1973. Bar: Pa. 1973, U.S. Dist. Ct. (ea. dist.) Pa. 1973, U.S. Ct. Appeals (3d cir.) 1975, U.S. Supreme Ct. 1986. Asst. to dir. Office Emergency Preparedness Exec. Office of US President, Washington, 1970; law clk. to Hon. Edward R. Becker U.S. Dist Ct., Phila., 1973—74; ptnr. Dechert LLP, Phila., 1974—. Adj. prof. Temple Law Sch. Co-author: Damming the West, 1971, Pennsylvania Evidence, 1974; contbr. articles to profl. jours. Bd. govs. Am. Jewish Com., Hebrew Union Coll.; officer, bd. dirs. Congregation Rodeph Shalom; active Salzberg Seminar on AIDS. Lt. (j.g.) USN, 1968-70. Mem. ABA, Phila. Bar Assn., Am. Law Inst. Avocations: reading, charities, sports. Office: Dechert LLP Cira Ctr 2929 Arch St Philadelphia PA 19104-2808 Office Phone: 215-994-2684. Office Fax: 215-994-2222. Business E-Mail: richard.berkman@dechert.com.

BERKMAN, WILLIAM ROGER, lawyer, army reserve officer; b. Chisholm, Minn., Mar. 29, 1928; s. Carl Emil and Millie (Mikkelson) B.; m. Betty Ann Klamt, Dec. 17, 1950. AB, U. Calif., Berkeley, 1950, JD, 1957. Bar: Calif. 1957, D.C. Ct. Appeals 1957, D.C. 1957. Law clk. to judge James Alger Fee, U.S. Ct. Appeals 9th cir., 1957-58; assoc. Morrison & Foerster, San Francisco, 1958-67, mem. firm, 1967-79; comdg. gen. 351st Civil Affairs Command, Mountain View, Calif., 1975-79; chief Army Res., Dept. of Army, Washington, 1979-86; mil. exec., Res. Forces Policy Bd., Office Sec. Def. Dept. of Def., Washington, 1986-92. Mng. editor: Calif. Law Rev, 1956-57. Pres. Sausalito (Calif.) Bd. Libr. Trustees, 1976-78; pres. Civil Affairs Assn., 1979-80, 93-99; bd. dirs. Army Distaff Found., 1988-92; dir. Sausalito-Marin City Sanitary Dist., pres., 2002—. Maj. gen. U.S. Army, 1979—. Decorated DSM with oak leaf cluster, Def. DSM , Def. Superior Svc. medal , S. Order of Calif., U.S. Spl. Ops. command medal U.S. Army, USN, C.G., Legion of Merit medal, Army Commendation medal; named to Hall of Fame Sr. Army Res. Comdrs. Assn.; recipient Meritorious Svc. medal, Army Outstanding Civilian Svc. medal. Mem.: ABA (chmn. standing com. on lawyers in armed svcs. 1988—91), U.S. Army Civil Affairs Corp. (hon. chief civil affairs), Civil

Affairs Assn. (pres. 1992—99, pres. emeritus 1999—), Res. Officers Assn., Assn. U.S. Army, State Bar Calif., Army and Navy Club, Lions (dir. Sausalito Marin City san. dist., past pres.). Home and Office: 33 Atwood Ave Sausalito CA 94965-2245 Personal E-mail: wbaberkman@sbcglobal.net.

BERKOBEN, JOHN PERRI, physician; b. Lakewood, NJ, 1947; BA, Cornell U., 1969; MD, U. Pa., 1973. Intern Montefiore Hosp., Bronx, 1973-74, resident, 1974-76; physician Lahey Clinic, 1992—; pvt. practice internal medicine and cardiology, 1978—. Cardiology fellow Boston U. Med. Ctr., 1976-78. Mem. Am. Coll. Physicians, Am. Coll. Cardiology, N.Am. Soc. Pacing & Electrophysiology, Mass. Med. Soc. Office: Lahey-Arlington 20 Wall St Burlington MA 01803

BERKOFF, ADAM T., lawyer; b. Milw., June 5, 1969; BA with honors & distinction, Univ. Wis., Madison, 1991; JD, Marquette Univ., 1994. Bar: Wis. 1994, Ill. 1994. Ptnr., chmn. Condominium & Complex Mixed-Use Devel. practice group DLA Piper Rudnick Gray Cary, Chgo. Adj. prof. DePaul Univ. Real Estate Ctr. Editor (exec.): Marquette Law Rev. Mem.: Chgo. Bar Assn. (mem. condominium subcom.), State Bar Assn. Wis., Golden Key, Iron Cross Soc. Office: DLA Piper Rudnick Gray Cary Suite 1900 203 N LaSalle St Chicago IL 60601-1293 Office Phone: 312-368-7266. Office Fax: 312-630-5331. Business E-Mail: adam.berkoff@dlapiper.com.

BERKOFF, CHARLES EDWARD, pharmaceutical and biotech consultant; b. London, Sept. 29, 1932; arrived in US, 1963, naturalized, 1975; s. Maurice and Dora (Landy) B.; children: Timothy, David, Kevin; m. Heide-Gisela Triesch, 1997. BS in Chemistry (1st class honors), U. London, 1956; DIC, PhD, Imperial Coll., U. London, 1959. Chartered chemist. Dir. GlaxoSmithKline, Phila., 1964-83; exec. v.p. ImuTech, Inc., Huntingdon Valley, Pa., 1983-84; pres., CEO Antigenics, Inc., Horsham, Pa., 1984-89, Creative Licensing Internat., Inc., Sarasota, Fla., 1987—, CEBRAL, Inc., 1987—. Research fellow Johns Hopkins U., Balt., 1959-60; sr. research fellow Southampton U., Eng., 1960-61; mem. Adv. Council Smithsonian Sci. Info. Exchange, Washington, 1976-82. Contbr. articles to profl. jours.; patentee numerous U.S. and fgn. patents. Monsanto Research fellow Imperial Coll. Sci. and Tech., 1956-59; Fulbright scholar, 1959-60; recipient Statue of Victory World Culture prize Centro Studi e Ricerche Delle Nazioni, 1985. Fellow Am. Chem. Soc., Royal Soc. Chemistry; mem. Am. Arbitration Assn., Entomol. Soc., Am. Inst. Chem. Engrs., Licensing Execs. Soc. Clubs: Engrs. Club of Phila. Republican. Unitarian Universalist. Avocations: writing, tennis, guitar, bridge, swimming. Office: CEBRAL Inc PO Box 5850 Sarasota FL 34277-5850 Office Phone: 941-923-3268. Business E-Mail: cebral@comcast.net.

BERKOFF, MARK ANDREW, lawyer; b. Boston, Aug. 8, 1961; s. Marshall Richard and Bebe R. B.; m. Susan Lynn; children: Alexander, Rachel. BA with honors, U. Wis., 1983; JD, U. Chgo., 1986. Bar: Ill. 1987, U.S. Dist. Ct. (no. dist. Ill., no. dist. Ind.), U.S. Ct. Appeals (7th cir.) 1990. Ptnr. DLA Piper US LLP, Chgo., 1986—2004, co-chmn. fin. restructuring and bankruptcy practice group, 2005—. Contbr. articles to profl. jours. Vol. Am. Cancer Soc., Chgo., 1993-96; mem., past chmn. Corp. Donations Com. Make-A-Wish Found. No. Ill.; gen counsel Bus Products Credit Assn. Mem. ABA, Chgo. Bar Assn., Turnaround Mgmt. Assn., Am. Bankruptcy Inst., Phi Beta Kappa, Phi Kappa Phi. Avocations: sports, coin collecting/numismatics. Office: DLA Piper 203 N LaSalle St Suite 1900 Chicago IL 60601-1293 Office Phone: 312-368-4000. Office Fax: 312-236-7516. Business E-Mail: mark.berkoff@dlapiper.com.

BERKOFF, MARSHALL RICHARD, lawyer; b. Milw., Apr. 10, 1937; s. Louis S. and Edith E. (Cohen) B.; m. Bebe R. Brandwein, June 19, 1960; children: Mark Andrew, Jonathan Hale, Adam Todd. BA, U. Wis., 1959; LLB, Harvard U., 1962. Bar: Wis. 1962, U.S. Dist. Ct. (we. and ea. dists.) Wis. 1962. Ptnr. Michael, Best & Friedrich, Milw., 1962—. Co-author: Employment Law Challenges of 1987, 1987, Labor Relations: The New Rules of the Game, 1984, The Legal Issues of Managing Difficult Employees, 1987; author/editor Currier and Ives "The New Best 50", 1991. Chmn. Charles Allis and Villa Terrace Art Mus., Milw., 1983-96; chmn. Milw. County War Meml. Corp., 1989-94, bd. dirs., 1983; chmn. bd. dirs. St. Michael Hosp., Milw., 1988-89; bd. dirs. Covenant Health Care, 1993-95. Mem. ABA (labor and employment sect., hosp. and health care law sect.), Wis. Bar Assn., (chmn. labor law sect. 1977-78), Milw. Bar Assn., Am. Hist. Print Collector Soc. (pres. 1987-90, bd. dirs. 2002—). Avocations: writing, lithographs, fishing. Office: Michael Best & Friedrich 100 E Wisconsin Ave Ste 3300 Milwaukee WI 53202-4108 Home Phone: 414-352-2942. E-mail: mrberkoff@michaelbest.com.

BERKON, MARTIN, artist; b. Bklyn., Jan. 30, 1932; s. Samuel F. and Sara (Hodes) B.; m. Eileen Phyllis Eichel, July 10, 1960. Student, Pratt Inst., 1952; BA, Bklyn. Coll., 1954; MA, NYU, 1959. Mem. adj. faculty Fairleigh Dickinson U., 1966, Nassau C.C., 1966-67; lectr. City Coll., CUNY, 1968-69; guest lectr. Middlebury Coll., 1977, Nassau C.C., 1982, St. Thomas Aquinas Coll., 1995; interviewed L.I. Art Scene TV, 1986. One-man shows include Smolin Gallery, NYC, 1962, 20th Century West Gallery, NYC, 1967, Soho Ctr. for Visual Artists, NYC, 1974, Genesis Galleries, NYC, 1978, Adelphi U., Garden City, NY, 1983, Blue Hill Cultural Ctr., Pearl River, NY, 1995, Schering Plough Corp. Gallery, Madison, N.J., 2001; exhibited in group shows at Bklyn. Mus., 1958, Silvermine Guild Artists, Conn., 1963, Ohio U. Gallery, 1964, Ball State U., 1965, Wesleyan Coll. at Ga., 1965, Butler Inst. Am. Art, 1965, 67, 69, Aldrich Mus. Contemporary Art, Ridgefield, Conn., 1974, 75, 82, New Britain Mus., Conn., 1974, Am. Fedn. Arts traveling show, 1975-77, Meadowbrook Art Gallery Oakland U., Rochester, Mich., Flint Inst. Art, Flint, 1974-76, Firehouse Gallery, Garden City, 1982, Barbara Walter Gallery, NYC, 1982, Spaceport USA Kennedy Space Ctr., 1985, 87, NASA collection traveling exhbn. Visions of Flight, 1988-91, Vero Beach Mus. Art The Abstract Image, Fla., 1996, Blue Hill Cultural Ctr., Pearl River, 1997-98; represented in permanent collections Aldrich Mus. Contemporary Art, Ridgefield, Texaco Inc., White Plains, NY, Pepsico Inc., Somers, NY, Pfizer Inc., Rye Brook, NY; commd. NASA, 1984, 87, NASA Gallery of Art, Kennedy Space Ctr., Vero Beach Mus. Art. Home: 503 Devries Ct Piermont NY 10968-1068 Personal E-mail: marteil@msn.com.

BERKOW, IRA HARVEY, writer, journalist; b. Chgo., Jan. 7, 1940; s. Harold Grosswald and Shirley (Halperin) B.; m. Dolores Case, Apr. 18, 1978. BA, Miami U., Oxford, Ohio, 1963; MS in Journalism, Northwestern U., 1964. Reporter Mpls. Tribune, 1965-67; sports columnist, sports editor Newspaper Enterprise Assn., NYC, 1967-76; sports columnist, feature writer N.Y. Times, NYC, 1981—. Author: Oscar Robertson The Golden Year, 1971, (with Walt Frazier) Rockin' Steady, 1974 (Am. Libr. Assn. Best Books of Yr. 1975), Beyond the Dream, 1975, Maxwell Street, 1977, The DuSable Panthers, 1978, (with Rod Carew) Carew, 1979, Red: The Biography of Red Smith, 1986, The Man Who Robbed the Pierre, 1987, Pitchers Do Get Lonely and Other Sports Stories, 1988; editor: Hank Greenberg: The Story of My Life, 1989, (with Jackie Mason) How to Talk Jewish, 1991, (with Jim Kaplan) The Gospel According to Casey, 1992, To the Hoop: The Seasons of a Basketball Life, 1997, Court Vision, 2000, The Minority Quarterback, and Other Lives in Sports, 2002, Full Swing, 2006; Playwright: The Shakespeare of the Press Box, 2003. Recipient Page One award Newspaper Guild, Mpls., 1966, Scripps-Howard Feature award N.Y.C., 1969, N.Y. Pub. Libr. commendation, 1978, 2005, AP Sports Editors award, 1982, 93, 94, 95, 96, 2001, Disting. Achievement medal Miami U., 1988, Feature Reporting award Deadline Club, 1994, award N.Y. State Newspaper Pubs., 1990; nominee ACE awards, 1983, Edgar award, 1988; finalist Pulitzer prize for commentary, 1988, Harold Washington Profl. Achievement award Roosevelt U., 2003; named to Hall of Achievement, Northwestern U. Medill Sch. of Journalism, 1997; mem. N.Y. Times Pulitzer-Prize-Winning Team for Nat. Reporting, 2001. Mem. Baseball Writers Assn. Am., Authors Guild, PEN, Mystery Writers Am. Office: NY Times 229 W 43rd St New York NY 10036-3959 Office Phone: 212-556-7371.

BERKOWITZ, BRAD ALAN, portfolio manager; b. Woodmere, NY, May 5, 1964; s. Morton Michael and Barbara Judith Berkowitz. BS in Econs., U. Pa., 1986; MBA in Fin., NYU, 1993. Investment analyst Integrated Resources, NYC, 1986—89; fixed income sales Lehman Bros., NYC, 1989—94; fin. cons., prin. AXA Advisors, NYC, 1995—2000; stock analyst Cramer, Berkowitz, NYC, 2001—; portfolio mgr. Adv. bd. mem. Smartix, Internat., NYC, 2002—. Author: (Book) The 21st Century Guide to Bachelorhood, 1999, The Iran Barkley Story: The Rise and Fall of a Boxing Champion, 2001; co-author: Natural Disaster, 2001. Mem.: AFTRA, Am. Mensa. Jewish. Avocations: golf, sports, movies, theater, acting. Home: Apt 30A 1520 York Ave New York NY 10028 Office: Berkowitz Capital 14th Fl 909 Third Ave New York NY 10022 Personal E-mail: berkathome@aol.com.

BERKOWITZ, HENRY, artist; b. Bklyn., Feb. 5, 1933; s. Abraham and Mary (Pellman) B.; m. Hannah Meyer, Dec. 26, 1954; children: Madeline Lisa, Jared Ian. Student, Bklyn. Mus. Art Sch., Workshop Sch. Editorial and Comml. Art, NYC, Sch. of Visual Art. Art dir. Pyramid Books. Judge Belle Terre East Art Show, Fla., 1978, Hollywood Arts and Crafts Guild, Fla., 1981, 82. One-man shows include Ahda Artzt Gallery, West Islip Libr., NY, Nat. Bank N.Am., NYC, Babylon Libr., NY, Islip Town Gallery, NY, Sunrise Libr., Fla.; exhbn. in group shows at Bklyn. Mus., Berkshire Mus., Mass., Parrish Mus., NY, Guttenberg Mus., Fed. Republic of Germany, Art Festival Tours, France, Le Musee De Luxemberg, Paris, Rotunda Gallery, London, NY Coliseum, Guild Hall, NY, Lever House, NYC, Avanti Gallery, NYC, Union Carbide Bldg., NYC, Salmagundi Club, NYC, Burr Gallery, NYC, Lynn Kottler Gallery, NYC, Ligoa Duncan Gallery, Paris, CAM Gallery, NY, Nat. Arts Club, NYC, Hotel-de-Ville, Paris, Wilkes Gallery, NYC, So. Regional Courthouse, Ft. Lauderdale, others. Recipient Prix de Paris, Ligoa Duncan Gallery, 1974, 76, Palmas D'Oro medal Internat. Art Festival, Paris, 1974, Abstract Work of Art award Am. Vets. Soc. Artists, 1972, Abstract Oil award Guild Hall, 1973, 74, 1st prize Abstract Watercolor, Huntington Art League, 1972, Award of Merit, NY Internat. Art Show, 1970, and others.

BERKOWITZ, LAUREN M., music company executive; b. Nov. 20, 1971; BA Comm., Boston U.; MBA, JD, Suffolk U., Boston. Held posts Bertelsmann AG's CDNOW unit; head bus. devel. Linkedwith GmbH, Berlin; v.p. Sony BMG Music Entertainment, Europe; v.p., global digital bus. Sony ATV Music Pub.; sr. v.p. digital EMI Music N.Am., 2007—. Office: EMI Records Grp N Am 1290 Ave of the Americas 38th Fl New York NY 10104 Office Phone: 212-492-5448.*

BERKOWITZ, LAWRENCE M., lawyer; b. Leavenworth, Kans., Nov. 29, 1941; s. Barney and Sarah (Kramer) B.; m. Ursula Lustenberger, Sept. 2, 1969; children: Lizbeth Berkowitz, Leslie Berkowitz. BA Polit. Sci., U. Mich., 1963, JD, 1966. Bar: Mo. 1966, N. Mex. 1997, US Dist Ct. (ea., we. dist. Mo., Kans., N. Mex.), US Ct. Appeals (8th, 10th DC cir.), US Supreme Ct. Law clerk Judge John W. Oliver, U.S. Dist. Ct., we. dist. Mo., Kansas City, Mo., 1966-68; assoc., ptnr. Stinson, Mag & Fizzell, P.C., Kansas City, Mo., 1968-97; ptnr., litig. & mediation practices Berkowitz Oliver Williams Shaw & Eisenbrandt LLP, Kansas City, Mo., 1997—. Mng. ptnr. Stinson, Mag & Fizzell, Kansas City, 1991-92. Bd. dirs. Nelson Gallery Bus. Coun., Kansas City, 1989—, Downtown coun., Kansas City, 1992-93; trustee Kansas City Art Inst., 1994—. Fellow Am. Coll. Trial Lawyers, Am. Bar Found., Mo. Bar Found.; mem. ABA, Am. Judicature Soc., Kansas City Met. Bar Assn., Lawyers Assn. Kansas City, Mo. Bar Assn., Soc. Profls. Dispute Resolution. Avocations: tennis, hiking, skiing, history, reading. Office: Berkowitz Oliver Williams Shaw & Eisenbrandt Ste 500 Two Emanuel Cleaver Blvd Kansas City MO 64112 Office Phone: 816-627-0211. Office Fax: 816-561-1888. Business E-Mail: lberkowitz@bowse-law.com.

BERKOWITZ, RICHARD LEE, obstetrician, gynecologist, director; b. NYC, July 28, 1940; MD, NYU, 1965. Diplomate Am. Bd. Ob/gyn. Intern Kings County Hosp. Ctr., NYC, 1965-66; resident in ob/gyn. NY Hosp.-Cornell Med. Ctr., NYC, 1968-72; staff Mt. Sinai Hosp., NYC, 1982—2003; prof., chmn. ob/gyn. reproductive sci. Mt. Sinai Med. Ctr., NYC, 1985—2003; staff Presbyn. Hosp., 2003—; prof. ob-gyn., dir. quality improvement Columbia U. Med. Ctr., NYC, 2003—, dir. ob-gyn. residency program, 2005—. Fellow Am. Coll. Obstetricians/Gynecologists; mem. Am. Gynecol. and Obstet. Soc., Am. Inst. Ultrasound Medicine, N.Y. Obstet. Soc., Soc. Gynecol. Investigation, Soc. Maternal-Fetal Medicine (SMFM). Office: Columbia Univ Med Ctr Dept Ob-gyn 622 W 168th St PH 16 New York NY 10032 also: 16 E 60th St New York NY 10022 Office Phone: 212-305-0197.

BERKOWITZ, SEAN M., lawyer; b. May 27, 1967; BS summa cum laude, Tulane U., 1989; JD cum laude, Harvard U., 1992. Bar: Ill. Assoc. Katten Muchin Rosenman LLP, Chgo.; asst. U.S. atty. (no. dist.) Ill. criminal divsn. US Dept. Justice, Chgo., 1998—2003, mem. Enron Task Force, 2003—05, dir. Enron Task Force, 2005—06; ptnr. litigation dept. Latham & Watkins LLP, Chgo., 2006—. Part owner Double Door nightclub, Chgo. Named one of 40 Under Forty, Crain's Bus Chgo., 2005, Litigation's Rising Stars, The Am. Lawyer, 2007. Avocations: running, motorcycling. Office: Latham & Watkins LLP Sears Tower Suite 5800 Chicago IL 60606

BERKSON, JACOB BENJAMIN, lawyer, writer; b. Washington County, Md., Dec. 6, 1925; s. Meyer and Ida Evelyn (Berman) B.; m. Ann Goldstein, June 25, 1955 (dec.); children: Daniel Jeremy (dec.), Susan Kay, James Meyer. BA, U. Va., 1947, LLB, 1949, JD, 1970; grad., US Naval Sch., Naval Justice, Newport, RI, 1952, Fed. Exec. Inst., Charlottesville, Va., 1972, USNR Midshipmen's Sch., Columbia U., NY; attended, Naval Sch. Oriental Langs. Bar: Md. 1949, Va. 1949, U.S. Supreme Ct. 1965, Calif. 1975. Sole practice, Hagerstown, Md., 1949-52, 54-64; ptnr. McCauley, Cooey, Berkson & Wright, Hagerstown, 1964-70; dep. gen. counsel U.S. GSA, Washington, 1970-76; pvt. practice law Hagerstown, 1976—. Instr. Law Hagerstown Bus. Coll., 1986; trial magistrate, Hagerstown and Washington County, Md., 1951-52; mem. Legis. Coun. Md., 1957-58; del. Md. Legislature, 1955-58; trial magistrate, Hagerstown, 1958-59. Recipient commendation for svc. to U.S. Naval Acad. and pub. interest Chief of Naval Personnel, 1956. Author: Shingahi Saburo and Short Stories, 1978, Comin' Home, 1993, A Canary's Tale: The Final Battle: Politics, Poisons and Pollution vs. the Environment and Public Health, 1996; case editor, co-founder Va. Law Weekly, 1948; contbr. articles to profl. jours., address to Congrl. Record. Scoutmaster Boy Scouts Am.; organizer, dir. County Youth Conservation Corps; active Big Bros.; camp sponsor YMCA; advisor Model Youth Legis.; pres. PTA; chmn. Washington County Pk. Commn., 1961—68; bd. dirs. Doub's Woods County Pk., Devil's Backbone County Park, Rachel Carson Coun., Inc., Chevy Chase, Md., 1996—2003; assisted in establishment of C&O Canal Nat. Hist. Pk., 1954—77. WWII USNR V12 program line officer UVA, 1944, Commissioned Ensign, 1945, ordered to staff Comdr. Naval Base, Saipan, Marianas I., staff legal officer, 1945—46, Judge Advocate General Courts Martial, recalled, 1952, Korean War, Lt. USNR, ordered to Pusan, Korea, ordered to Comdr. Naval Forces, Far East, Yokosuka, Japan, staff legal, trial counsel, 1952—53, Defense Counsel before General Courts Martial, ordered to serve as staff legal officer to Comdr. Destroyer Divsn. 322 on Round the World Mission, 1953—54, aboard USS Healey DD 672, Navy JAG duties. Mem. ABA, Calif. Bar Assn., Va. Bar Assn., Md. Assn. County Civil Attys. (pres., award for svc. as pres. 1966), Washington County Bar Assn. (pres.), Am. Legion, Hagerstown Club, Lions (pres.), Speakers Soc., Elks, Torch Club (Hagerstown), Thomas Jefferson Soc. Alumni U. Va., Lile Law Soc U. Va. Republican. Jewish. Home and Office: 1419 Potomac Ave Hagerstown MD 21742-3315

BERKUS, JAMES, talent agent; Founder, pres. Leading Artists Agy. (now United Talent Agy.), 1981—91; pres., chmn. United Talent Agy., Beverly Hills, Calif., 1991—. Bd. advisors IFILM Corp., Hollywood. Mem. Santa Monica Mountains Conservancy, 2005—. Named one of 50 Most Powerful People in Hollywood, Premiere mag., 2004—06. Office: United Talent Agy 9560 Wilshire Blvd Fl 5 Beverly Hills CA 90212-2400 E-mail: berkusj@unitedtalent.com.

BERL, JOSEPH M., lawyer; b. Bklyn., Oct. 1, 1942; AB, Columbia U., 1964; JD with honors, George Washington U., 1967. Bar: N.Y. 1968, D.C. 1972, U.S. Supreme Ct. 1972. Law clk. to Hon. Frank H. Myers D.C. Ct. Appeals, 1967-68; trial atty. Div. Trading and Markets, SEC, Washington, 1968-70, br. chief, 1970-71; ptnr. Fortas & Koven, Washington, 1971-83, Stroock and Stroock and Lavan, Washington, 1984-86, Baker & Hostetler, Washington, 1986-98, Powell Goldstein LLP, Washington, 1998—. Mem. ABA (mem. corp., banking and bus. law sect.), D.C. Bar. Office: Powell Goldstein LLP 3d Fl 901 New York Ave NW Washington DC 20001-4413 Home Phone: 202-337-3374; Office Phone: 202-624-7271. Business E-Mail: jberl@pogolaw.com.

BERLACK, EVAN RADEN, lawyer; b. NYC, Apr. 1, 1934; s. Harris and Edith Ann (Raden) B.; m. Kay Baumler, July 15, 1963 (dec. July 1986); children: Andrew E., Kenneth H.; m. Phyllis Bonanno, Oct. 14, 1989. AB magna cum laude, Harvard U., 1956, LLB, 1962. Bar: NY 1963, DC 1969. Fgn. service officer U.S. Dept. State, Washington and Paris, 1963-66, atty., adviser Office Legal Adviser Washington, 1966-68; assoc. Arent, Fox, Kintner, Plotkin & Kahn, Washington, 1968-73, ptnr., 1974—2001; of counsel Baker Botts LLP, Washington, 2001—. Co-editor: Coping with U.S. Export Controls, 1985-86, 88-06. 1st lt. USAF, 1956-59. Mem. ABA, Am. Soc. Internat. Law, Harvard Club (N.Y.C., Washington). Clubs: Harvard (N.Y.C. and Washington). Avocations: swimming, baseball, classical music, history. Office: Baker Botts LLP 1299 Pennsylvania Ave NW Washington DC 20004 Home Phone: 206-252-2005; Office Phone: 202-639-7771. Office Fax: 202-585-1073. E-mail: evan.berlack@bakerbotts.com.

BERLAGE, GAI INGHAM, sociologist, researcher; b. Washington, Feb. 9, 1943; d. Paul Bowen and Grace (Artz) Ingham; m. Jan Coxe Berlage, Aug. 7, 1965; children: Jan Ingham, Cari Coxe. BA, Smith Coll., 1965; MA, So. Meth. U., 1968; PhD, NYU, 1979. Tchr. math. Piner Jr. High Sch., Sherman, Tex., 1968-69; asst. prof. sociology Iona Coll., New Rochelle, NY, 1971-83, assoc. prof., 1983-88, chmn. dept., 1981—90, 1996—2003, prof., 1988—. Coord. urban studies program, 1984-90, gerontology program, 1984-90, NCAA faculty athletic rep., 1996—. Author: Experience with Sociology: Social Issues in American Society, 1983, Understanding Social Issues: Sociological Fact Finding, 1987, 2d edit., 1990, 3d edit., 1993, Women in Baseball: The Forgotten History, 1994, Understanding Social Issues: Critical Thinking and Analysis, 1996, 6th edit., 2003; mem. editl. bd. Jour. Sport and Social Issues, 1990-94; contbr. articles to profl. jours. Commr. Wilton Commn. on Aging and Social Svcs., 1980-88, chmn., 1982-88; co-chmn. Wilton Task Force on Youth Coun., 1988; chmn. Wilton Task Force Com. for Outreach Program, 1981-82, Wilton Task Force on Day Care, 1983-88; mem. Wilton Task Force for Pub. Health Nursing Assn., 1981-82, Wilton Sport Coun., 1985-88; bd. dirs. Wilton Meals on Wheels, 1983-88; fellow N.Am. Faculty Network of Northeastern Univs. Ctr. for Study of Sport in Soc. Recipient Best Profl. Paper award Third Annual Cooperstown Symposium on Baseball and the Am. Culture; named to Iona Coll. Women of Achievement, 1993. Mem. N.Am. Soc. Sociology of Sport (treas. 1992-93), Wilton Assn. for Gifted Edn. (pres. 1980-81), N.Am. Soc. for Sports History, Soc. for Am. Baseball Rsch., Women's Sport Found. (resources coun.). Office: Iona Coll Dept Sociology New Rochelle NY 10801 Office Phone: 914-633-2594. Business E-Mail: gberlage@iona.edu.

BERLAGE, JAN INGHAM, lawyer; b. Lewiston, NY, Nov. 17, 1969; s. Jan Coxe and Gai Elizabeth (Ingham) Berlage. BA, Wesleyan U., 1992; postgrad., Oxford U., 1992; JD, U. Va., 1995. Law clk. to Hon. E. Stephen Derby U.S. Bankruptcy Ct. Dist. Md., Balt., 1995—96; assoc. Day, Berry & Howard, Hartford, Conn., 1996—2001, Ballard Spahr Andrews & Ingersoll, Balt., 2001—06; ptnr. Gohn Hankey & Stichel LLP, Balt., 2006—. Adj. prof. U. Md. Sch. Law, 2005—. Exec. editor Jour. Law and Politics, Charlottesville, 1994-95, mem. editl. bd., 1993-94; author: Aguilar Expression, 1990; contbr. articles to profl. jours. Deacon Avon Congl. Ch., 1997-2001; active Rep. Town Com., Avon, 1998-2001, Avon Zoning Bd. Appeals, 1999-2001; exec. adv. bd. Heroes-Helping-Heroes, Inc., 2003-05, bd. dirs., 2005—, sec., 2006—, gen. counsel, 2006—. Maj. Md. Def. Force, JAG Corp., 2006—. Fellow Am. Bar Found., Md. Bar Found., ABA; mem. ABA (vice chmn. young lawyers divsn. individual rights and responsibilities sect. 2001-02, chmn. 2002-03, awards judge 2005-06, chmn. young lawyers divsn. bankruptcy com. 2003-05, chmn. ethics and profl. responsibility com. 2005-06), Md. State Bar Assn. (chmn. young lawyers divsn. edn. com. 2003-04, 06—, membership chmn. 2004—05, bd. govs. 2005-07), Federalist Soc. (pres. U. Va. chpt. 1994-95, co-chmn. Hartford chpt. 1997-2001, bd. dirs. Chesapeake chpt. 2001-), Conn. Young Lawyers Assn. (co-chmn. comml. law and bankruptcy sect. 1997-2000, co-chmn. civil rights sect. 2000-01), NY Bar Assn. (comml. law and fed. litig. sects., intellectual property subcom. 1998-2001), Jefferson Lit. and Debating Soc., N.Am. Securities Adminstrn. Assn. (task force 1994), Oxford U. Legal Soc., United Oxford/Cambridge U. Club, Phi Delta Phi, Psi Upsilon, Phi Beta Kappa. Home: 16422 J M Pearce Rd Monkton MD 21111 Office: Gohn Hankey & Stichel LLP 201 N Charles St Ste 2101 Baltimore MD 21201 Office Phone: 410-752-1261. Personal E-mail: Jan_Berlage@msn.com. Business E-Mail: jberlage@ghsllp.com.

BERLAND, DAVID I., psychiatrist, educator; b. St. Louis, Aug. 1, 1947; s. Harry I. and Mildred (Cornblath) B.; m. Elaine Prostak, May 22, 1977; children: Katharine J., Rachel P. BA, U. Pa., 1969; MD, U. Mo., 1973. Diplomate Am. Bd. Psychiatry and Neurology. Resident psychiatry Menninger Found., Topeka, Kans., 1973-78, staff child and adolescent psychiatrist, 1978-83; dir. div. child and adolescent psychiatry St. Louis U. Med. Sch., 1983-93; with dept. adolescent psychiatry St. Luke's Hosp., Chesterfield, Mo., 1993-97; pvt. practice St. Louis, 1997—. Contbr. articles to profl. jours. Fellow Am. Acad. of Child and Adolescent Psychiatry; mem. AMA (rotating seat relative value update com. 1996-99), Soc. of Profs. of Child and Adolescent Psychiatry,. Jewish. Office: 7700 Clayton Rd Ste 103 Saint Louis MO 63117 Office Phone: 314-644-6910.

BERLAND, GRETCHEN K., medical educator, filmmaker; BA, Pomona Coll., 1986; MD, Oreg. Health and Sci. U., 1996. Internship and residency Wash. Univ. Med. Ctr. in St. Louis Barnes Hosp., 1996—99; fellowship UCLA Robert Wood Johnson Clin. Scholars program, 1999—2001; asst. prof., internal med. Yale U. Sch. of Med., New Haven, 2001—. Contbr. articles to profl. jours.; contbr. WGBH TV for PBS Primetime-Condition Critical, MacNeil/Lehrer for PBS & NBC-Hard Choices and A Time For Change, GBH TV for the NOVA Series. Named a MacArthur Fellow, 2004. Office: Yale Univ Med Sch-Internal Med 333 Cedar St PO Box 208033 LMP 87 New Haven CT 06520 Office Phone: 203-737-5157. Office Fax: 203-737-5358. Business E-Mail: gretchen.berland@yale.edu.

BERLEANT, ARNOLD, philosopher; b. Buffalo, Mar. 4, 1932; s. Bernard and Elizabeth (Barkun) B.; m. Riva Schiller, Aug. 1, 1958; children: Daniel, Andrea, Anne Nicole. Student, SUNY, Fredonia, 1949-51; MusB, Eastman Sch. Music; BM, U. Rochester, 1953, MA, 1955; PhD, SUNY, Buffalo, 1962. Teaching fellow SUNY, Buffalo, 1958-60, instr., 1960-61, lectr., 1961-62; asst. prof. philosophy C.W. Post Campus, L.I.U., 1962-65; asso. prof. C.W. Post Center, L.I.U., 1965-70, prof., 1970-92, prof. emeritus, 1992—. Bingham prof. humanities U. Louisville, 1994; vis. assoc. prof. San Diego State Coll., 1966; mem. social sci. faculty Sarah Lawrence Coll., 1966-68 Author: The Aesthetic Field, 1970, Art and Engagement, 1991, The Aesthetics of Environment, 1992, Living in the Landscape: Toward an Aesthetics of Environment, 1997, Re-thinking Aesthetics, 2004, Aesthetics and Environment, 2005; editor: Environment and the Arts, 2002; co-editor: The Aesthetics of Natural Environments, 2004, The Aesthetics of Human Environments, 2007; founding editor online jour. Contemporary Aesthetics, 2003; contbr. articles to profl. jours. Served with U.S. Army, 1954-56. Am. Council Learned Socs. grantee, 1972, 76 Mem. AAUP, Internat. Assn. Aesthetics (sec.-gen. 1987-95, pres. 1995-98), Am. Soc. Aesthetics (sec.-treas. 1978-88), Internat. Inst. Applied Aesthetics (Lahti, Finland), Finnish Soc. Aesthetics (hon.), Sydney Soc. Lit. and Aesthetics (hon.), French Soc. Aesthetics (mem. com. of honor), Internat. Assn. Aesthetics (hon. life). Home: PO Box 52 Castine ME 04421-0052 Home Phone: 207-326-4306. E-mail: ab@contempaesthetics.org.

BERLEKAMP, ELWYN RALPH, mathematics professor; b. Dover, Ohio, Sept. 6, 1940; s. Waldo and Loretta Berlekamp; m. Jennifer Joan Wilson, Aug. 21, 1966; children: Persis, Bronwen, David. BSEE, MSEE, MIT, 1962, PhD in Elec. Engring., 1964. Asst. prof. U. Calif., Berkeley, 1964-66; mem. tech. staff Bell Labs., Murray Hill, NJ, 1966-71; prof. math. U. Calif., Berkeley, 1971—, assoc. chmn. of elec. engring. and computer sci. dept., 1975-77; pres. Cyclotomics, Berkeley, 1981-89, Axcom, Berkeley, 1989-90. Bd. dirs. AK Peters, Ltd.; chmn. bd. Math. Sci. Rsch. Inst., Berkeley, 1994—96, Internat. Computer Sci. Inst., Berkeley, 2000—03. Author: Key Papers in Coding Theory, 1974, Algebraic Coding Theory, 1984; co-author: Winning Ways, vols. 1 and 2, 1982, Mathematical Go, 1994, The Dots and Boxes Game, 2000; contbr. scientific papers, articles to profl. jours. Named Outstanding Young Elec. Engr., Eta Kappa Nu, 1971; fellow, Am. Assn. Advancement Sci., 2004. Fellow: IEEE (Best Rsch. Paper award 1967, Centennial medal 1984, Koji Kobayashi award 1990, Hamming award 1991), Info. Theory Soc. of IEEE (pres. 1973, Shannon award 1993); mem.: NAS, NAE, AAAS, Am. Math. Soc. (bd. govs. 1980—82), Am. Acad. Arts and Scis. Achievements include patents for algorithms and devices which corrects errors, erasures, and missed synchronization in communications and digital memory systems. Avocation: bicycling. Home: 120 Hazel Ln Piedmont CA 94611-4033 Office: 2039 Shattuck Ave 408 Berkeley CA 94704

BERLEY, DAVID RICHARD, lawyer; b. Bklyn., Apr. 9, 1942; s. Alexander and Ruth (Ginsburg) B.; m. Sharon Lee Freeman, Aug. 10, 1964 (div. 1975); children: Steven N., Barbara Robin; m. Katalin Fine, Feb. 14, 1992 (div. 2003) BS, Boston U., 1963; JD, Boston Coll., 1966. Bar: Mass. 1966, U.S. Dist. Ct. Mass. 1966, U.S. Ct. Claims 1970, Fla. 1977, U.S. Dist. Ct. (so. dist.) Fla. 1977, U.S. Tax Ct., U.S. Ct. Appeals (11th cir.). Pvt. practice, 1966-77; gen. counsel Econocar Internat. Inc., Miami, Fla., 1976-77; v.p., gen. counsel Emergency Med. Services Assn., Inc., Miami, 1977-79, pvt. practice, 1979-85; ptnr. Berley & Littman, PA, Miami, 1985-94; pvt. practice Miami, 1994—. Active Greater Miami Heart Assn., Jewish Fedn. Greater Miami, Bus. Vols. for Arts; past chmn. City of Miami Waterfront adv. bd., Coconut Grove Playhouse Soc. of Stars; mem. citizens' adv. bd. Sta.-WLRN Pub. Radio; mem. City of Miami Fin. Com. Mem. Mass. Bar Assn., Fla. Bar Assn. (grievance com.), Fla. Internat. Bankers Assn., Boston Coll. Law Sch. Alumni Assn., Greater Miami C. of C., Coconut Grove C. of C., Coconut Grove Playhouse Soc. Stars. Office: 848 Brickell Ave Ste 200 Miami FL 33131-2981 Address: 1415 Panther Ln Naples FL 34109 Office Phone: 305-373-8000. Business E-Mail: drberley@cs.com.

BERLIN, ALAN DANIEL, lawyer, real estate company officer, consultant; b. Bklyn., Oct. 20, 1939; s. Joseph Jacob and Rose (Smith) B.; m. Renee Wellinger, Dec. 22, 1962; children— Nicole Suzanne, Allison Leigh. BBA, CCNY, 1960; LLB, NYU, 1963, LLM, 1968. Bar: NY 1963. Assoc. Aranow, Brodsky, Bohlinger, Einhorn & Dann, NYC, 1965-68; asst. counsel Gen. Electric Co., NYC, 1968-70; tax counsel Norton Simon Inc., NYC, 1970-77; asst. prof. Pace U. Grad. Sch. Bus., 1977-85; pres. Belco Petroleum Corp., NYC, 1977-88, The Crown Group, White Plains, NY, 1988-95; ptnr. Aitken Berlin LLP, 1995—. Spl. cons. to UN Dept. Tech. Cooperation for Devel., 1989—, UN Ctr. for Transnat. Corps., 1990—; hon. assoc. Ctr. for Petroleum and Mineral Law and Policy, U. Dundee, Scotland, 1993—. Author monographs on fed. income tax. With U.S. Army, 1963-65. Mem. ABA, Internat. Bar Assn., N.Y. State Bar Assn., Assn. of Bar of City of N.Y., Inter-Am. Bar Assn., Assn. Internat. Petroleum Negotiators. Lodges: Masons. Office: Aitken Berlin LLP 2 Gannett Dr White Plains NY 10604-3403 Business E-Mail: adberlin@aibvlaw.com.

BERLIN, ANDREW MARK (ANDY BERLIN), advertising agency executive; Copywriter Ogilvy & Mather; co-founder, prin., mng. dir. Goodby Berlin & Silverstein, San Francisco, 1983-92; pres. DDB Needham NY, NYC, 1992-93; chmn., CEO Berlin Wright Cameron, NYC, 1993—95; founding ptnr. Fallon McElligott Berlin, NYC, 1995—97, Berlin Cameron & Ptnrs., NYC, 1997—2001; chmn. Berlin Cameron/Red Cell, NYC, 2001—05; co-CEO Red Cell, 2001—04, chief creative officer, 2001—04, chmn., CEO, 2004—05, Voluntarily United Group of Creative Agencies, NYC, 2005—. Recipient Agy. of the Yr. for Berlin Cameron/Red Cell, AdAge, 2003. Office: Berlin Cameron United 100 Avenue Of The Americas # 2 New York NY 10013-1689 Office Phone: 212-415-3183. E-mail: andy.berlin@group-united.com.*

BERLIN, HEATHER AYN, neuroscientist, philosopher, educator; b. East Meadow, NY, June 20, 1975; d. Leonard Arthur Berlin and Beth Judy Pardo; m. Michiel Visser, Aug. 28, 2006. BS, SUNY, Stony Brook, 1997; MA, New Sch. for Social Rsch., NYC, 2000; PhD, U. Oxford, Eng., 2003; MPH, Harvard Sch. of Pub. Health, Boston, Mass., 2004. Intern Bellevue Hosp., NYC, 1996—96; rsch. coord. Cornell U. Med. Ctr./N.Y. Presbyn. Hosp., NYC, 1997—97; rsch. asst. Applied Behavioral Medicine Rsch. Inst., SUNY, Stony Brook, 1998—98, project dir. dept. psychiatry and behavioral sci., 1998—99; clin. rsch. NYU Med. Ctr., NYC, 1999—2000, Inst. of Psychiatry/Bethlem Royal Hosp.; Radcliffe Infirmary/John Radcliffe Hosp.; Rivermead Rehab. Centre, London/Oxford, 2001—03; psychiat. mgmt. practicum Harvard U. Health Svcs., Cambridge, Mass., 2004—04; vis. asst. prof. Vassar Coll., Poughkeepsie, NY, 2005—06; nimh post-doctoral fellow Mt. Sinai Sch. of Medicine, NYC, 2004—. Vis. asst. prof. Vassar Coll., 2005—06; vis. lectr. Swiss Fed. Inst. Tech., U. Zurich, 2007, Hebrew U. Jerusalem, 2007; lectr. in field. Contbr. articles to profl. jours. Recipient Young Investigator award, Nat. Edn. Alliance Borderline Personality Disorde, 2005; fellow, New Sch. for Social Rsch., 2000, NY Acad. Scis., 2007; scholar, New Sch. for Social Rsch., 1998—2000, Brit. Coun., 2000-2003; Oppenheim scholarship, Magdalen Coll., Oxford, Eng., 2002-2003. Fellow: NY Acad. Scis.; mem.: APA, Assn. for the Sci. Study of Consciousness, Internat. Soc. for Rsch. on Impulsivity and Impulse Control Disorders, Nat. Acad. of Neuropsychology, Am. Psychopathological Assn., Am. Neuropsychiatric Assn. (Young Investigator award 2005), Brit. Neuropsychological Soc., Internat. Neuropsychological Soc., Psi Chi, Sigma Beta, Golden Key Honor Soc. Office: Mt SInai Sch of Medicine Box 1230 One Gustave L Levy Pl New York NY 10029 Home Phone: 617-519-7217; Office Phone: 212-241-4761.

BERLIN, HOWARD RICHARD, investment company executive, retired portfolio manager; b. White Plains, NY, Dec. 30, 1935; s. Simon and Frances (Held) B.; m. Joy Monte Shortino, June 10, 1961; children: Howard R. Jr., Asa Ward, Carter Franklin. BS in Econs., U. Pa., 1957; postgrad., NYU, 1962-63. Security analyst Merrill Lynch, NYC, 1961-69, v.p. capital markets, 1969-86; sr. portfolio mgr. Neuberger & Berman, NYC, 1986—2001, prin. ptnr., mem. exec. com., 1990—2001; ret., 2001; mng. mem. The Maverick Group, LLC. Pres. Berlin Assocs. Inc. Hon. nat. campaign chmn. Uriah P. Levy Ctr., US Naval Acad.; scholarship co-chmn. Inst. Am. Indian Arts; trustee Heard Mus., Phoenix. Cmdr. USN, 1957—59. Mem. Fin. Analyst Fedn., Naval Res. Assn., Ret. Officers Assn., Boulders Club (Carefree, Ariz.). Avocations: land development, small business development. Personal E-mail: howardandjoyce@hotmail.com.

BERLIN, KENNETH, lawyer; b. NYC, July 9, 1947; s. Joseph and Helen (Cohen) B.; m. Sue Ann Keller, June 27, 1971; children: Jennifer, Theodore. BA, U. Pa., 1969; JD, Columbia U., 1973. Bar: NY 1974, DC 1982, US Ct. Appeals (DC cir.) 1981, US Ct. Appeals (7th cir.) 1984, US Ct. Appeals (6th cir.) 1987, US Dist. Ct. DC 1988. Assoc. Paul, Weiss, Rifkind et al, NYC, 1973-75, Kramer, Levin, Nessin et al, NYC, 1975-78; sect. chief, wildlife and marine resources sect., environ. and nat. resources divsn. US Dept. Justice, Washington, 1979—81; counsel legis. specialist Nat. Audubon Soc., Washington, 1981-82; ptnr. Winston & Strawn, Washington, 1982-87, Winthrop, Stimson, Putnam & Roberts, Washington, 1987-94; ptnr., head environ. practice area Skadden, Arps, Slate, Meagher & Flom, LLP, Washington. Bd. dirs. Ctr. Internat. Environ. Law; chmn. Environ. Law Inst., 2003—05. Asst. editor Columbia U. Law Rev.; contbr. articles in the field. Chmn. Am. Bird Conservancy; bd. dirs. Earth Day Network. Mem. ABA (former vice chmn. environ. quality com. natural resources law sect., former chairperson health environ. rights com. individual rights and responsibilities sect.), Am. Ornithologists Union, Internat. Com. Environ. Law. Office: Skadden Arps Slate Meagher & Flom 1440 New York Ave NW Ste 600 Washington DC 20005 Office Phone: 202-371-7350. Office Fax: 202-661-8207. Business E-Mail: kberlin@skadden.com.

BERLIN, KENNETH DARRELL, chemistry professor, consultant, researcher; b. Quincy, Ill., June 12, 1933; s. Kenneth Marion Fischer and Mary Esther (Beckley) B.; m. Grace Frances Smith, Apr. 3, 1937; children: Grace Esther, James Darrell. BA cum laude, North Ctrl. Coll., Naperville, Ill., 1955; PhD, U. Ill., 1958. Postdoctoral fellow U. Fla., Gainesville, 1958-60; asst. prof. chemistry Okla. State U., Stillwater, 1960-63, assoc. prof., 1963-66, prof., 1966-71, Regents prof., 1971—. Spl. cons. Nat. Cancer Inst., Bethesda, Md., 1969—; cons. E.I. DuPont Co., Wilmington, Del., 1969-70, Am. Heart Assn., Oklahoma City, 1983-86, Ariz. Disease Control Comm., 1989—. Co-author: Organic Chemistry, 1972, Phosphorous Stereochem, 1977; contbr. rsch. Jour. Organic Chemistry, 1960, articles to profl. jours. Recipient Regents Disting. Tchg. award, 1998, Sigma Xi rsch. award Okla. State U., Stillwater, 1969, Okla. Chemist of Yr. award, 1977. Fellow Okla. Acad. Sci. (scientist of yr. 1976), Burlington No. Faculty Achievement award 1988, Eminent Faculty award 1998, Okla. medallion Excellence in Tchg. at Coll./Univ. Regents Disting. Rsch. award 2003); mem. Am. Chem. Soc. (sr.), Internat. Soc. Hetercyclic Chemists, Alpha Chi Sigma. Mem. Assembly Of God Ch. Home Phone: 405-372-7756; Office Phone: 405-744-5950. Business E-Mail: kdb@okstate.edu.

BERLIN, MARK A., lawyer; b. Bklyn., Nov. 1, 1944; s. Roy and Bess (Wolfe) B.; m. Renee D., June 7, 1970; children: Robert, Brian, Steven. BS in Econs., NYU, 1966; LLM, 1973; JD, Bklyn. Law Sch., 1969. Bar: NY 1970, Fla. 1979. With Touche Ross & Co., 1969-73; assoc. Seidman & Seidman, NYC, 1973-75; with Schulman & Berlin PC, NYC, 1975-89, mng. atty.; sole practice, 1990—. Mem. ABA, NY State Bar Assn., Fla. Bar Assn., Am. Inst. CPAs, NY State Soc. CPAs. Home and Office: PO Box 179 Albertson NY 11507-0179 Home Phone: 561-739-5123; Office Phone: 561-736-0487.

BERLIN, NORMAN B., lawyer; b. Wilmington, Del., Mar. 11, 1954; s. Irvin I. and Sylvia (Rosenthal) B.; m. Elizabeth A. Berlin, Sept. 18, 1986; children: Daniel Joseph, Michael, Andrew Ian. BA with honors, U Va., 1976; JD, Harvard U., 1979. Bar: Md. 1979, DC 1980, Pa. 1985. Atty. Weinberg & Green, Balt., 1979-80, Content, Stuart, Tatusko & Patterson, Washington, D.C., 1980-83, Johnson & Swanson, Dallas, 1983-84, Pepper, Hamilton & Scheetz, Phila., 1984-88, ptnr., 1988, Pepper Hamilton LLP, Phila. Author: Rehabilitation Lease, 1991, Practical Aspects of the Sale of Assets in Bankruptcy: A Seller's Approach to Maximizing Value. Mem. ABA, Md. Bar Assn., DC Bar Assn., Pa. Bar Assn. Avocation: sports. Office: Pepper Hamilton LLP 18th & Arch St Philadelphia PA 19103 Office Phone: 215-981-4468. Office Fax: 215-981-4750. Business E-Mail: berlinn@pepperlaw.com.

BERLIN, ROBERT HARRY, historian, educator; b. Pitts., Oct. 24, 1946; s. Abraham Maurice and Betty W. Berlin; children: Jessica Sabrina, Leslie Farrah. BA, Rockford Coll., 1968; PhD in History, U. Calif., Santa Barbara, 1976. Vis. prof. Mansfield (Pa.) State Coll., 1976—77; instr. Allan Hancock C.C., Lompoc, Calif., 1976—79; assoc. prof. U.S. Army Command and Gen. Staff Coll., Ft. Leavenworth, Kans., 1979—90; prof. and dir. academic affairs Sch. of Advanced Mil. Studies, Ft. Leavenworth, 1991—2005, dir. academic affairs, 1991—2004, dir. academic outreach, 2004—06, prof. emeritus, 2006. Exec. dir. Soc. for Mil. History, Lexington, Va., 1999—; vis. prof. summer program Oxford (England) U., 2003—; historian cruise lectr. Author: (history booklet) U.S. Army World War II Corps Commanders (The Journal of Military History, 53), 1989 (Moncado Prize Award, 1990). Decorated Superior Civilian Svc. award Dept. of the Army, Meritorious Civilian Svc. award. Mem.: Soc. for Mil. History (Gendes Meml. Svc. award 2006), Orgn. Am. Historians (life). Jewish. Avocations: travel, hiking, biking, military poetry, oneology. Home Phone: 928-237-1289. Personal E-mail: rhbrlin@aol.com.

BERLIN, STEVEN RITT, oil industry executive; b. Pitts., July 1, 1944; s. Sidney D. and Pauline (Ritt) B.; children: Leslie, Jessica, Loren. BBA, Duquesne U., 1967; MBA, U. Wis., 1969. Prof. U. Houston, 1970—72; various fin. positions Cities Svc. Co., Tulsa, 1973-83; v.p. fin. Citgo Petroleum, Tulsa, 1983-85, gen. mgr., 1985-86, CFO, 1986-97; prof., assoc. dean U. Tulsa, 1997-99; chief fin. officer Kaiser-Francis Oil Co., Tulsa, 1999—. Speaker various industry, profl. seminars; mem. Acctg. Edn. change Commn. Mem. bd. visitors U. Wis.; sec.-treas. Green T Club of Tulsa. Mem. AICPA, Am. Acctg. Assn., Okla. Soc. CPAs, Stanford U. Alumni Assn., Beta Gamma Sigma. Avocations: jogging, reading. Office: Kaiser-Francis Oil Co 6733 S Yale Ave Tulsa OK 74136-3302 Home: 1243 E 32d St Tulsa OK 74105 Business E-Mail: cfo@berlin.com.

BERLIND, BRUCE PETER, poet, educator; b. Bklyn., July 17, 1926; s. Peter Sydney and Mae (Miller) B.; m. Doris Lidz, 1947 (div. 1950); m. Mary Elizabeth Dirlam, 1954 (div. 1983); children: Lise, Anne, John, Paul, Alexandra; m. Jo Anne Pagano, 1985. Student, Mercersburg Acad., 1941-43; AB, Princeton U., 1947; MA, Johns Hopkins U., 1950, PhD, 1958. Instr. English Colgate U., Hamilton, NY, 1954-58, asst. prof., 1958-63, assoc. prof., 1963-66, prof., 1966-80, Charles A. Dana prof. English, 1980-88, prof. emeritus, 1988—, chmn. dept. English, 1967-72, 80-83; poet in residence U. Rochester, 1966. USIS lectr., Germany, 1963, with Hungarian P.E.N. Translation Program, Budapest, 1977, 79, 84, 86, 88, 91. Author: (poems) Ways of Happening, 1959, Companion Pieces, 1971; translator: (poems) Selected Poems of Agnes Nemes Nagy, 1980, Birds and Other Relations: Selected Poetry of Dezso Tandori, 1987, When You Became She by Imre Oravecz, 1994, The Journey of Barbarus by Ottó Orbán, 1997, Charon's Ferry: Fifty Poems of Gyula Illyés, 2000; assoc. editor: (poems) The Hopkins Rev., 1949-53; contbr. poems, essays, revs. to mags. 1st lt. AUS, 1945-46, 50-52. Recipient Meml. medal Hungarian PEN, 1986; Fulbright grantee, Hungary, 1983-84. Mem. PEN Am. Ctr., Poetry Soc. Am., Am. Lit. Translators Assn., AAUP (mem. council, past pres. N.Y. State Conf.) Home: PO Box 237 Hamilton NY 13346-0237 E-mail: bberlind@mail.colgate.edu.

BERLIND, ROBERT ELLIOT, artist, educator; b. NYC, Aug. 20, 1938; s. Peter Sidney Berlind and Mae (Miller) Bach; m. Dorothy Welch, June 1963 (div. 1974); 1 child, Alexey Fuller; m. Nancy Lee Hubbard, June 17, 1978 (div. 1993); 1 child, Gabriel Peter; m. Mary Lucier, June 7, 1997. BA, Columbia U., 1960; BFA, Yale U., 1962, MFA, 1963. Assoc. prof. art N.S. Coll. of Art and Design, Halifax, Can., 1974-76; prof. SUNY, Purchase, 1979—2007, prof. emeritus, 2007—. One man shows include Alexander Milliken Gallery, N.Y.C., 1981-82, Tomasulo Gallery, Union Coll., 1983, Ruth Siegel Gallery, N.Y.C., 1984, 86, 88, 90, Gallery One, Toronto, Can., 1985, Warren Wilson Coll., Swanonoa, N.C., 1986, St. Peter's Ch., N.Y.C., 1988, Delaware Valley Arts Alliance, Narrowsburg, N.Y., 1992, Tibor de Nagy Gallery, N.Y.C., 1994, 96, 98, 01, 05, Hampshire Coll. Main Gallery, Amherst, Mass., 1995, Reynolds Gallery, Richmond, Va., 1996, Wright State U., Dayton, Ohio, 1997, Newberger Mus. Art, Purchase, N.Y., 1998, Alexander Hogue Gallery, Tulsa, 2005; group shows: N.Y. Studio Sch., 1986, Bronx Mus. of the Arts, 1987, Sherry French Gallery, N.Y.C., 1987, One Penn Pla., N.Y.C., 1988, Fay Gold Gallery, 1988, Art Mus. Fla. Internat. U., 1989, Meml. Art Gallery U. Rochester, 1989, Found. Mona Bismarck, Paris, 1991, Am. Acad. and Inst. Arts and Letters, 1992, Neuberger Mus., Purchase, N.Y., 1994, Maier Art Mus., Lynchburg, Va., Ringling Mus. Art, Sarasota, Fla., 2000, Locks Gallery, Phila., 2002, NAD Painting Ctr., N.Y.C., 2004, 05, others. Recipient award in painting Am. Acad. Inst. Arts and Letters, 1992, Pollock-Krasner award, 1997 B. Altman Painting award Nat. Acad., 2007; fellow NEA, 1993. Mem. Coll. Art Assn., Internat. Assn. Art Critics, Nat. Acad. Design. Home: 215 W 20th St Apt 4W New York NY 10011-3552 Personal E-mail: berlind4@aol.com.

BERLIND, ROGER STUART, stage and film producer; b. NYC, June 27, 1930; s. Peter Sydney and Mae (Miller) B.; m. Helen Polk Clark, July 7, 1962 (dec.); 1child, William Polk; m. Brook Wheeler, May 19, 1979. AB, Princeton U., 1952. Account exec. Eastman Dillon, Union Securities & Co., NYC, 1956-60; gen. ptnr. Carter, Berlind & Weill, NYC, 1960-65; chmn. exec. com. Cogan, Berlind, Weill & Levitt, Inc., NYC, 1965-69; chief exec. officer Shearson Lehman Bros., NYC, 1969-73, vice chmn. bd., 1974-75. Bd. dris. Lehman Bros. Prodr.: (films) Beyond Therapy, 1987; (plays) Rex, Music Is, Diversions and Delights, The Merchant, The 1940's Radio Hour, Passione, The Lady from Dubuque, Amadeus, Sophisticated Ladies, Lydie Breeze, Nine, All's Well that Ends Well, The Real Thing, The Rink, Joe Egg, After the Fall, Precious Sons, Big Deal, Long Day's Journey into Night, Ain't Misbehavin', Jerome Robbins's Broadway, City of Angels, Artist Descending a Staircase, Lettice and Lovage, Death and the Maiden, Guys and Dolls, Passion, Indiscretions, Hamlet, Getting Away with Murder, A Funny Thing Happened on the Way to the Forum, Skylight, Steel Pier, The Life, A View from the Bridge, The Judas Kiss, The Blue Room, Closer, Amy's View, Kiss Me Kate (Tony award, 2000), Copenhagen (Tony award, 2000), Proof (Tony award, 2001), Dance of Death, Medea, The Wild Party, Anna in the Tropics, Wonderful Town, Caroline or Change, Who's Afraid of Virginia Woolf, Doubt, Well, Faith Healer and History Boys, The Vertical Hour, The Year of Magical Thinking, Deuce, Curtains, The Caine Mutiny Court Martial, 2007. Hon. trustee Am. Acad. Dramatic Arts. With CIC, U.S. Army, 1952-54. Mem. League Am. Theatres and Producers (gov.), Princeton Club (N.Y.C.), Univ. Club, River Club, Century Assn. Office Phone: 212-888-5220.

BERLINE, JAMES H., advertising and public relations executive; b. Youngstown, Ohio, Aug. 6, 1946; s. James Howard and Eloise Blanche (Smith) Berline; children: Erin Michele, Jess Brandon, Quincy Blaine. BA in Econs., U. Mich., 1968; MS in Advt., U. Ill., 1971. V.p. Campbell-Ewald Co., Detroit, 1971-76; sr. v.p. Batten Barton Durstine & Osborn Inc., Troy, Mich., 1976-78, exec. v.p. Southfield, Mich., 1984-85; pres. Yaffe Berline Inc., Southfield, 1980-82; pres., CEO Berline Group, Birmingham, Mich., 1982—. Bd. dirs. Leadership Detroit Alumni; pres. MAGNET (Mktg. and Advt. Global Network). Program chmn. United Found., Detroit, 1984; mem. adv. bd. Jr. League; founder Winning Futures; trustee Detroit Sci. Ctr., 1985—, Juvenile Diabetes Found., 1994; chmn. comm. com. Leadership Detroit, 1993; bd. dirs. Make-A-Wish Found., chmn., 2001—03; trustee CATCH, mem. exec. com., chmn. bd. dirs.; bd. dirs. Operation Able, Minds, 2003—, Children's Leukemia Found. Mich., 2007—. Mem.: Young Pres. Orgn. (chair office commn. 1994, trustee, com. chmn. Ea. Mich. chpt.), World Pres. orgn., Detroit C. of C. (mktg. com. 1987—88), Greater Detroit Alliance Bus. (bd. dirs. 1984—86), Birmingham Athletic Club (pres.), U. Mich. Grad. M Club (bd. dirs. 1986), U. Mich. Club Detroit (past bd. govs.), Adcraft Club (bd. dirs. 1980—99, pres. 1988). Avocations: squash, travel, golf. Office: 70 E Long Lake Rd Bloomfield Hills MI 48304 Office Phone: 248-593-7402.

BERLINER, ALLEN IRWIN, dermatologist; b. NYC, Apr. 18, 1947; s. Joseph Benjamin and Ruth (Kaplan) B.; m. Edwina BA, Queens Coll., 1967; MD, SUNY, Buffalo, 1971. Diplomate: Am. Bd. Dermatology. Intern Nassau County Med. Ctr., East Meadow, NY, 1971-72; resident in dermatology Boston U. Med. Ctr., 1974-76, chief resident, 1976-77; practice medicine specializing in dermatology Norwood, Mass., 1977—; asst. clin. prof. Tufts U., 1980-90, assoc. clin. prof., 1990—; chief dermatology sect. Caritas Norwood Hosp., 1986—; assoc. staff, Tufts-New Eng. Med. Ctr. Bd. dirs. Mass. Acad. Dermatology. Served as surgeon USPHS, 1972-74. Mem. Am. Acad. Dermatology, New Eng. Dermatol. Soc., Mass. Acad. Dermatology (pres. 1994-95). Office: 95 Chapel St Norwood MA 02062-3161 Home Phone: 508-359-6171; Office Phone: 781-762-5858.

BERLINER, BARBARA, retired librarian, consultant; b. Bklyn., July 14, 1947; d. Robert and Mildred M. (Sklar) Morris; 1 child, Stefanie Lauren. BA in Anthropology, NYU, 1969; MLS, Columbia U., 1970. Libr. N.Y. Pub. Libr., NYC, 1970-81, sr. libr., telephone reference, 1981-86, supervising libr., tele. reference, 1986-92, head libr., Mid-Manhattan sci. and bus., 1992-93; coord. NYPL Express, NYC, 1993—2002. Cons. John Wright, N.Y.C., 1991; bibliographer Collier's Encyclopedia. Author: The Book of Answers, 1990. Mem. ALA, Planetary Soc. Avocations: sports, astronomy. Home: 235 Portside Dr Edgewater NJ 07020

BERLINER, HANS JACK, retired computer scientist; b. Berlin, Jan. 27, 1929; came to U.S., 1937, naturalized, 1943; s. Paul and Theodora (Lehfeld) B.; m. Araxie Yacoubian, Aug. 15, 1969 (dec.). BA, George Washington U., 1954; PhD, Carnegie Mellon U., 1975. Systems analyst U.S. Naval Rsch. Lab., 1954-58; group head systems analysis Martin Co., Denver, 1959-60; adv. systems analyst IBM, Gaithersburg, Md., 1960-69; prin. rsch. scientist Carnegie-Mellon U., Pitts., 1974-98. Mem. editorial bd. Artificial Intelligence, 1976-98, Pitman: Research Notes in Artificial Intelligence, 1984-98, Internat. Jour. Intelligent Sys., 1986, Theoretical Computer Sci., 1990. Served with AUS, 1951-53. Awarded title Internat. Grandmaster Corr. Chess, 1968; inducted into U.S. Chess Hall of Fame, 1990. Fellow Am. Assn. for Artificial Intelligence; mem. Internat. Joint Conf. Artificial Intelligence, U.S. Chess Fedn., Internat. Computer Chess Assn. Achievements include being among the leading chess players in

U.S., 1950-75, N.Y. State champion, 1953, So. Open champion, 1949, U.S. Open Corr. Chess champion, 1955, 56, 59, World Corr. Chess champion, 1968-72; developed first computer program to defeat a world champion at his own game (backgammon), 1979; co-developer Hitech, first chess computer to become a U.S. Chess Fedn. sr. master; among top 0.5% of all registered tournament chess players; discovered B* tree search algorithm, 1975, the method humans use to search trees, SNAC method of constructing polynomial evaluation functions, 1979. Home: 4000 N Ocean Dr Apt 1903 Riviera Beach FL 33404-2849 E-mail: berliner@cs.cmu.edu.

BERLINER, HERMAN ALBERT, academic administrator, economist, educator, dean; BA, CCNY, 1965; PhD, CUNY, 1970. Assoc. prof. econs. Hofstra U., Hempstead, NY, 1970-85, assoc. dean advisement, 1975-76, assoc. provost, 1976-83, dean Sch. Bus., 1980-82, 83-90, prof. econs., 1985—, provost, dean faculties, 1989-2001, Lawrence Herbert disting. prof., 1996—, provost, sr. v.p., 2001—. Mem. Health and Welfare Coun., LI, NY, 1997-2005, bd. dirs., sec. ProjectGrad-Long Island, 2004-. Assoc. editor Am. Economist, 1975-80, 83—. Fellow, TIAA/CREF, 2006—. Home: 93 Plymouth Dr N Glen Head NY 11545-1126 Office: Hofstra U Office of Provost Hempstead NY 11549 Home Phone: 516-759-9117; Office Phone: 516-463-5402. Business E-Mail: herman.berliner@hofstra.edu.

BERLINER, RUTH SHIRLEY, real estate company executive; b. NYC, June 20, 1928; d. Irving William and Florence (Tomback) Blum; m. Arthur Ivan Berliner, Sept. 23, 1948; children: Daniel Scott, Michael Robert, Eric Lance. BA, Empire State Coll., Westbury, NY, 1974; diploma, Wilsey Sch. Interior Design, Hempstead, NY, 1975; MBA, Adelphi U., 1980. Lic. real estate broker, N.Y. Sec. to dir. librs. NYU, NYC, 1948-50; sec. Paragon Mut. Syndicates Inc., NYC, 1958-72; v.p. Paragon Mut. Investors Svcs., NYC, 1972-78; pres. Ruth S. Berliner, Inc., NYC, 1978—. Pres. Irmed Corp., 1983—; cons. E. 59th St. Assocs., N.Y.C., 1962-70, Amrep Corp., N.Y.C., 1968-75, FKBA Assocs., N.Y.C., 1974-78; mem. stores com. Real Estate Bd. N.Y., 1984-96. V.p. NYU Dental Sch. Parents Assn., 1974-76; bd. dirs. Hadassah, Hewlett, N.Y., 1978-87; advisor Citizens for Charter Change, N.Y.C., 1987—. Mem. Nat. Assn. Realtors, Real Estate Bd. N.Y. (store com. 1984-98, econ. devel. com. 1994-99), Inwood Club, Nat. Realty Club, Williams Club, N.Y. Athletic Club. Avocations: tennis, swimming, dance, painting.

BERLINGER, WARREN, actor; b. Bklyn., Aug. 31, 1937; s. Elias and Frieda (Shapkin) B.; m. Betty Lou Keim, Feb. 18, 1960. Student, Profl. Children's Sch., 1952-55, Columbia, 1958. Broadway appearances include Annie Get Your Gun, 1946, Happy Time, 1950, Take a Giant Step, 1951, Anniversary Waltz, 1955, Roomful of Roses, 1957, Blue Denim, 1958 (Theatre World award 1959), Come Blow Your Horn, 1960, Bernardine, 1953; London appearance in How to Succeed in Business Without Really Trying, 1963-64; film appearances include The Long Goodbye, Spinout, The World According to Garp, My African Adventure, Outlaw Force, Hero, 1992, Crime and Punishment, 1994, Feminine Touch, 1994, Dear God, 2000, The Great John Rexx, 2002, Time and Again, 2002, So They Call Him Sasquatch, 2002, Another Pretty Face, 2003; TV appearances on Secret Storm, 1955-57, The Funny Side, 1971-72, Touch of Grace, 1973, My African Adventure, 1986, Take Two, 1987, Agatha Christie's Death on Safari, (TV series) Shades of L.A., 1991, Picket Fences, 1993; films include Hero, That Thing You Do!, Dear God, T.O. Friends, November Conspiracy; plays include Lend Me a Tenor, 4318 Clarindon Road, 2003; prodr., dir. Take A Giant Step, 2006. Named hon. mayor of Chatsworth Calif., 1968, hon. sheriff, 1975; recipient Theatre World award, 1958.

BERLOWITZ, LESLIE, cultural organization administrator; BA in English with honors, NYU, 1965; MA in English, Columbia U., 1967. Mem. dept. English NYU, NYC, 1967-96, asst. dean U. Coll. Arts and Scis., Washington Square Coll. Arts and Scis., 1969-73, dir. acad. program devel., 1973-81, asst. v.p. acad. affairs, 1981-84, assoc. v.p. acad. affairs, 1984-88, dep. v.p. acad. affairs, 1988-91, v.p. instnl. advancement, 1991-96; exec. officer Am. Acad. Arts and Scis., Cambridge, Mass., 1996—. Founder, dir. The Humanities Coun., 1977-96, Faculty Resource Network, 1985-96; nat. dir. AmeriCorps, Project SafetyNet, 1995-96. Editor: (with Denis Donoghue and Louis Menand) America in Theory, 1988, Greenwich Village: Culture and Counterculture, 1990. Bd. dirs. Mass. Inst. Psychoanalysis; panelist Boston Jewish Film Festival; exec. bd. Corp. Yaddo; active Fund for Artists' Colonies, Inc., Coun. Internat. Edn. Exch., Urban Rsch. Ctr., Am. Jewish Congress, Fedn. Jewish Philanthropies, Joseph S. Gruss Found.; panelist NEH. Recipient Pacesetter award Tougaloo Coll., 1993. Fellow N.Y. Inst. Humanities, Am. Acad. Arts & Scis. 2004; mem. MLA, Century Assn. (N.Y.). Office: Am Acad Arts and Scis Norton's Woods 136 Irving St Cambridge MA 02138-1929 Fax: (617) 576-5055.

BERLUSCONI, MARINA, publishing executive; b. Milan, Aug. 10, 1966; d. Silvio Berlusconi. V.p. Fininvest, 1996; chairwoman Arnoldo Mondadori Editore, 2003, Fininvest. Bd. dir. Mediaset S.p.A., Mediolanum S.p.A., Medusa S.p.A., 21 Investimenti S.p.A. Named one of most powerful women, Forbes mag., 2005, 50 Most Powerful Women in Global Bus., Fortune mag., 2005—06. Mailing: via Mondadori 1 20090 Segrate Milan Italy

BERMAN, ALEXIS DANIELLE, elementary school educator; d. John Allen and Judith Ellen Lambert; m. Daniel Karl Berman, July 24, 2004. BEd in Early Childhood, SUNY, Fredonia, 1996—2000, MEd in Reading, 2000—02. Cert. reading tchr. U. State NY Edn. Dept., 2005, PreK, Kindergarten, grades 1-6 tchr. U. State NY Edn. Dept., 2005. Substitute tchr., tchr. aide Ithaca Cmty. Childcare Ctr., 1997—2000; internat. tchg. experience Bassett's Farm Primary Sch., Exmouth, England, 2000; grad. asst. edn. dept. SUNY Coll., 2000—02; reading specialist Lake Shore Ctrl. Schs., Angola, NY, 2002—04, substitute tchr., 2004—05; devel. reading tchr. Brocton Ctrl. Schs., NY, 2005—. Playground com. mem. Brocton Ctrl. Schs., NY, 2005—, compact team mem., 2006—. Recipient Nat. Collegiate Edn. award, 2001, Workshop Presenter, Kappa Delta Pi Convocation, 2001; grantee Future Tchrs. scholarship, Ithaca Tchrs. Assn., 1996. Fellow: We. NY Writing Project; mem.: ASCD, Nat. Coun. Tchrs. English, Internat. Reading Assn., Phi Delta Kappa, Kappa Delta Pi (v.p. 1999—2000), Alpha Phi Omega (life; apo leads presenter 2002—04, sect. 89 staff 2002—06, advisor Epsilon Sigma chpt. 2002—06, Chi Pi chpt. advisor 2006—, Chpt. Disting. Svc. Key 2002, Brother of Yr. award 2002). Office: Brocton Ctrl Schs 138 W Main St Brocton NY 14716 Home Phone: 716-648-8697; Office Phone: 716-792-2132. Business E-Mail: aberman@broc.wnyric.org.

BERMAN, ARIANE R., artist; b. Danzig, Mar. 27, 1937; m. Mario La Rossa, 1965. B.F.A., Hunter Coll., NYC, 1959; M.F.A., Yale, 1962; AAUW and Found. des Etats-Unis fellow, U. Paris, 1962-63. Juror nat. screening com. Fulbright grants, 1976-77, chmn. screening com., 1977-78. One man shows at Center Gallery, Conn., 1963, Harry Salpeter Gallery, N.Y.C., 1966, Brentano's Art Gallery, N.Y.C., 1973, Graphic Art Gallery, Tel Aviv, 1973, Galleria San Sebastianello, Rome, 1973, Eileen Kuhlik Gallery, N.Y.C., 1971, 73, Pub. Mus., Oshkosh, Wis., 1974, Wustum Mus. Fine Arts, Racine, Wis., 1974, Fontana Gallery, Pa., 1963, 71, 74, Galleria d'Arte Helioart, Rome, 1974, Munson Gallery, Conn., 1975, Ward-Nasse Gallery, N.Y.C., 1975, 77, 80, Phila. Art Alliance, 1980, Silvermine Guild Artists, Conn., 1976, Kornblee Gallery, N.Y.C., 1982, Babson Coll., Mass., 1983, Northwood Inst., Mich., 1983, Westenhook Gallery, Mass., 1984, Phoenix Gallery, N.Y.C., 1985, 87, Concordia Coll., Bronxville, N.Y., 1989, Gallery 84 Inc., N.Y.C., 1992, L'Artisanat, Mass., 1992, others; exhibited in group shows at Galerie Atrium Artis, Geneva, Switzerland, 1975, F 15 Gallery, Norway, 1974, Galeries Raymond Duncan, Paris, 1964, Asso. Am. Artists, N.Y.C., 1971, Circle Galleries Ltd., N.Y.C., 1974, Margo Feiden Galleries, N.Y.C., 1972, Gallery 500, Pa., 1973, Van Straaten Gallery, Chgo., 1974, Genesis Gallery, N.Y.C., 1978, Marymount Coll., N.Y.C., 1983, NYU, 1982, Fairleigh Dickenson U., 1982, Allentown Art Mus., Pa., 1982, numerous others; represented in permanent collections at Am. Petroleum Inst., Israel Ministry of Tourism, USIA, McGregor-Doniger, Inc., Shipley Sch., Bryn Mawr, Pa., Readers Digest, N.J. Bd. Edn., Athena Gallery, New Haven, Charles E. Ellis Coll., Newton Square, Pa., Hearst Corp., Met. Mus. Art, Phila. Mus. Art, Phila. Art Alliance, Ms. mag., Seventeen, Redbook, Feminist Press, Duke U., Newspaper Advt. Bur., Purdue U., Phila. Child Guidance Ctr., others. Recipient Yale Painting prize, 1960, Purchase award Purdue U., 1964, Stella Drabkin Meml. award, ACPS Purchase prize, 1973, Catherine Lorillard Wolfe Arts Club Gold medal, 1973, Hon. mention Hudson River Mus., 1974, Artists Equity award, 1985. Mem. Am. Color Print Soc., Nat. Assn. Women Artists, Yonkers Art Assn., Women's Caucus for Art, Met. Painters and Sculptors, Pen and Brush, League of Present Day Artists, Sheffield Art League, Silvermine Guild of Artists, Soc. Women Artists (past corr. sec.), Hunter Coll. Alumni Assn. (Hall of Fame 1974) Home: 161 W 54th St New York NY 10019-5322 Office Phone: 212-765-2030. *I use art as a means of communicating to people. My work is representational and tries to depict life in all its humor, sorrow, satiric aspects, and dream-like qualities of humanity as I see it. I particularly use color for emphasis in everything I do— paintings, graphics, plastics, and sculpture.*

BERMAN, ARTHUR LEONARD, retired state legislator; b. Chgo., May 4, 1935; s. Morris and Jean (Glast) B.; m. Barbara Dombeck; children: Adam, Marcy Padorr. BS in Commerce & Law, U. Ill., 1956; JD, Northwestern U., 1958. Bar: Ill. 1958. Atty. pvt. practice, Chgo.; ptnr. White, White & Berman, Chgo., 1958-74, Maragos, Richter, Berman, Russell & White, Chtd., 1974—81, Chatz, Berman, Maragos, Haber & Fagel, Chgo., 1981-82, Berman, Fagel, Haber, Maragos & Abrams, Chgo., 1982-86, Karlin & Fleisher, Chgo., 1986-99; cons. Chgo. Bd. Edn., 2000—05. Spl. atty. Bur. Liquidations, Ill. Dept. Ins., 1962-67; spl. asst. atty. gen. Ill., 1967-68; mem. Ill. Ho. of Reps., 1969-76, Ill. Senate, 1977-99; legis. policy advisor to Chgo. Bd. Edn., 2000-06. Pres. 50th Ward Young Dems., 1956-60; v.p. Cook County Young Dems., 1956-60, 50th Ward Regular Dem. Orgn., 1955-99; active 48th Ward Regular Dem. Orgn., 1967-99; exec. bd. Dem. Party, Evanston, Ill., 1973-99; bd. govs. State of Israel Bonds. Mem. ABA, Ill. Bar Assn., Chgo. Bar Assn. (bd. mgrs. 1988-89), Nat. Assn. Jewish Legislators (pres. 1987-89), U. Ill. Alumni Assn., Phi Epsilon Pi, Tau Epsilon Rho. Office: 6007 N Sheridan Rd Chicago IL 60660-3039 Office Phone: 773-769-2787. Personal E-mail: senatorart2000@aol.com.

BERMAN, BRUCE, entertainment company executive, television producer; b. NYC, Apr. 25, 1952; Grad., Calif. Inst. Arts Film Sch.; grad. magna cum laude in history, UCLA, 1975; JD, Georgetown U., 1978. Bar: Calif. 1978. Asst. to Jack Valenti Warner Bros., Burbank, Calif.; asst. to Peter Guber Casablanca Filmworks, 1979; asst. to Sean Daniel and Joel Silver Universal Pictures, 1979, v.p. prodn., 1982, Warner Bros., 1984, sr. v.p. prodn., 1988, pres. theatrical prodn., 1991-96, chmn., CEO Village Roadshow Pictures, 1998; pres. Worldwide Prodn., 1991-96. Founder Plan B Entertainment, 1996—. Office: Village Roadshow Pictures care Warner Bros Studios 3400 W Riverside Dr Ste 900 Burbank CA 91505-4639

BERMAN, BRUCE JUDSON, lawyer; b. Roslyn, NY, Oct. 9, 1946; s. Howard M. Berman and Soosha T. (Draizen) Hurwitz; m. Susan Leigh Readinger, Dec. 29, 1991; children: Andrew J., Josie A.;children from previous marriage: Daniel H., Ann N. BA, Williams Coll., 1968; MBA, Columbia U., 1972; JD, Boston U., 1972. Bar: Fla. 1973, U.S. Supreme Ct. 1976, U.S. Dist. Ct. (so. dist.) Fla. 1980, U.S. Ct. Appeals (5th cir.) 1980, U.S. Ct. Appeals (11th cir.) 1981, U.S. Dist. Ct. (mid. dist.) Fla. 1990. Assoc. Guggenheimer & Untermyer, NYC, 1973-79; from assoc. to ptnr. Myers, Kenin, Levinson, Frank & Richards, Miami, Fla., 1979-85; ptnr. Weil, Gotshal & Manges LLP, Miami, 1985-2000, McDermott, Will & Emery LLP, Miami, 2000—. Spl. ad hoc trial com. Dade County Cir. Ct., Fla., 1988—2000; apptd. ct. reporter cert. planning com. Fla. Supreme Ct., 1995; apptd. Workgroup on access to pub. records, Fla. Supreme Ct., 2000, Fla. Supreme Ct. Com. Std. Jury Instrns. Civil Cases, 2000—06. Author: Florida Civil Procedure, West Group, 1998—2007. Mem. New World Symphony Cmty. Bd., Miami Beach, Fla., 1991—2000; bd. dirs., v.p. Daily Bread Food Bank, 2002—. Mem.: Dade County Bar Assn., Fla. Bar Assn. (mem. civil procedure rules com. 1984—2004, chmn. 1988—90, mem. jud. adminstrn. rules com. 1988—2002, chmn. 1993—94), Internat. Bar Assn. Office: McDermott Will & Emery LLP 201 S Biscayne Blvd Ste 2200 Miami FL 33131 Home Phone: 305-665-4211; Office Phone: 305-347-6530. Business E-Mail: bberman@mwe.com.

BERMAN, CAROL, retired commissioner; b. Bklyn., Sept. 21, 1923; d. Hyman and Sarah (Levy) B.; m. Seymour Jerome Berman, May 19, 1944; children: Elizabeth, Charles. BA, U. Mich., 1943. Trustee Bd. Edn., Lawrence, NY, 1973-77; senator State of N.Y., Albany, 1978-84; spl. rep. State Divsn. for Housing, Hempstead, NY, 1985-86; commr. N.Y. State Commn. on Lobbying, Albany, 1988-92, N.Y. State Commn. of Elections, Albany, 1992—2005; ret., 2005. NY co-chair Nat. Jewish Dem. Coun., 1988-05, Met. Airport Noise Mitigation Rev. Commn., 1992; vice-chair Nassau Dem. County Com., Mineola, NY, 1970-72. Mem. Phi Beta Kappa, Phi Kappa Phi. Jewish. Avocation: golf. Home: 42 Lord Ave Lawrence NY 11559-1324

BERMAN, CAROL WENDY, psychiatrist; b. NYC, Sept. 14, 1951; d. Irving and Dora (Adler) B.; m. Martin Farber, Feb. 5, 1994. BA, U. Calif., Berkeley, 1972; MD, NYU, 1981. Diplomate Am. Bd. Psychiatry and Neurology. Intern, resident in psychiatry St. Lukes-Roosevelt Hosp., NYC, 1982-85; rsch. fellow in psychiatry NYU Med. Ctr., NYC, 1986-87, mem. attending staff, 1987—; pvt. practice, NYC, 1988—. Author: (book) 100 Questions and Answers About Panic Disorder, 2005, (plays) Under the Dragon, Sunshine Sally; contbr. numerous articles to med. jours.; patentee device to prevent drunk driving. Active legal problems of mentally ill, Bar Assn. City N.Y., 1993-95. Recipient writing prize Psychiat. Annals, 1987. Mem. Am. Psychiat. Assn. Office: 866 U N Plz Rm 473 New York NY 10017-1822

BERMAN, CHRIS, sportscaster; b. Greenwich, Conn., May 10, 1955; BA in History, Brown U., 1977. Disc jockey WERI, Westerly, RI, 1977-78; broadcaster WNVR Radio, Waterbury, Conn., 1978-79; weekend sports anchor WVIT-TV, Hartford, Conn., 1979; NFL studio host, anchor Sports-Center, baseball commentator ESPN, 1979—; host NFL Gameday, ESPN, 1985—; halftime host Monday Night Football, 1996—99; sports commentator KFRC-Radio, San Francisco, 1986, WFAN-Radio N.Y., 1987. Sunday night NFL telecasts, NFL draft coverage, commentator major league baseball games, host Baseball Tonight, SportsCenter ESPN. Appeared as himself in 10 films, including Little Big League, 1994, Necessary Roughness, 1991, Eddie, 1996, The Garbage Picking Goal Kicking Philadelphia Phenomenon, 1998, Big Daddy, Second String, Even Steven, Kingpin, 1996, The Program, 1993, Celtic Pride, The Longest Yard, 2005, also TV programs, including Spin City, 1999, The Jersey, 1999, and Arli$$, 1997. Named nat. sportscaster of yr. Nat. Sportscasters and Sportswriters Assn., 1989, 90, 93, 94, 96, 2001; named among top stars of the '90's TV Guide, 1990; winner sports Emmys for NFL GameDay, 1989, 91, 94, 95, 2001, CableACE awards, 1989, 92, 93, 94, 95. Office: ESPN ESPN Plz 935 Middle St Bristol CT 06010*

BERMAN, DANIEL LEWIS, lawyer; b. Washington, Dec. 14, 1934; s. Herbert A. and Ruth N. (Abramson) B.; children: Priscilla Decker, Jane, Katherine Ann, Sara Mark, Heather, Melinda. BA, Williams Coll., 1956; LLB, Columbia U., 1959. Bar: N.Y. 1960, Utah 1962, Wyo. 2004. Assoc. Chadbourne, Parke, Whiteside & Wolff, NYC, 1959-60; asst. prof. law U. Utah, 1960-62; pvt. practice Salt Lake City, 1962—; sr. ptnr. Berman & Savage PC, Salt Lake City, 1981—. Vis. prof. U. Utah, 1970, 74, 77; mem. Utah Coordinating Coun. Higher Edn., 1965-68; mem. Salt Lake County Merit Coun., 1974-80; mem. nominating commn. Utah Appellate Ct., 1999—2003. Trustee Salt Lake Art Ctr., 1978-80; Dem. candidate for U.S. Senate from Utah, 1980; mem. Utah Transit Authority, 1992-97. Mem. Am. Law Inst., Salt Lake Area C. of C. (bd. govs. 1976-79). Democrat. Jewish. Office: Berman & Savage PC 170 S Main Ste 500 Salt Lake City UT 84101-1660 Office Phone: 801-328-2200. Personal E-mail: dlb@bermansavage.com.

BERMAN, DAVID, lawyer, poet; b. NYC, Sept. 11, 1934; s. Joseph and Sophie (Hersh) B. BA with honors, U. Fla., 1955; postgrad. Johns Hopkins U., 1955-56; JD, Harvard U., 1963. Bar: Mass. 1963. Tchg. fellow Harvard Coll., 1962-63, 66-67; law clk. to justice Mass. Supreme Ct., 1963-64; asst. atty. gen. Commonwealth of Mass., 1964-67; assoc. Zamparelli & White, 1967, ptnr., 1968-74; pvt. practice, 1974-82, 1990—; ptnr. Berman & Moren, Medford, Mass., 1982-89. Author: Future Imperfect, 1982, Slippage, 1996, Early Mandamus in Massachusetts, Massachusetts Legal History, 1998, David Berman Greatest Hits, 1965-2002, 2003. Trustee Cantata Singers, 1981—. Mem. ABA, Mass. Bar Assn., Mass. Bar Found., Middlesex Bar Assn. (Most Outstanding Trial Lawyer Appelate award, 1998), Harvard Club (Boston), Signet Soc., Confrerie de la Chaine des Rotisseurs, Ordre Mondial, Masons. Republican. Unitarian. Home: 33 Birch Hill Rd Belmont MA 02478-1729 Office: 100 George P Hassett Dr Medford MA 02155-3264 Office Phone: 781-395-7520. E-mail: davidberman2@verizon.net.

BERMAN, DEBBIE L., lawyer; b. 1966; AB in Economics, summa cum laude, Brandeis U., 1987; JD cum laude, Harvard Law Sch., 1990. Bar: Ill., US Ct. (No. Dist. Ill.), US Tax Ct. Ptnr., co-chmn. trade secrets and unfair competition practice Jenner & Block LLP. Mem. alum. admissions coun. Brandeis Univ., 1990—; comm. mem. EZRA Multi-Service Ctr., 1996—; mem. bd. dir. Jewish Cmty. Ctr. Chgo., 1998—2003, Jewish United Fund/Jewish Fedn. Chgo., 2003—; v.p., mem. bd. trustees Temple Anshe Sholom, Chgo., 2001—. Named Ill. Super Lawyer in 1st Amendment and media, 2005, Super Lawyer in bus. litigation, 2006—07; named one of 40 Under Forty, Crain's Bus. Chgo., 2005, New Stars, New Worlds, Lawdragon mag., 2006; recipient Chambers USA award for media and entertainment, 2006, Davis, Gidwitz & Glasser award, Jewish Union Fund/Jewish Fedn. Met. Chgo., 2005; fellow, Leadership Greater Chgo., 2007. Mem.: Chgo. Bar Assn., Ill. Bar Assn., ABA, Intellectual Property Law Assn. Chgo., Am. Intellectual Property Law Assn., Brandeis Univ. Nat. Alum. Assn., Phi Beta Kappa. Office: Jenner & Block LLP 330 N Wabash Ave Chicago IL 60611 Office Phone: 312-923-2764. Office Fax: 312-840-7764. E-mail: dberman@jenner.com.

BERMAN, ELLEN SUE, energy and telecommunications executive, theatre producer; Student, U. N.C., Greensboro, 1960-62, U. N.C., Chapel Hill, summer 1961, U. Calif., Berkeley, summer 1962; BA in Russian, Barnard Coll., 1964. Legis. asst. Senator Joseph Tydings, 1965-66; rsch. assoc. Washington Poverty Program United Planning Orgn., 1966-70; pres. emeritus Consumer Energy Coun. Am. Rsch. Found., Washington, 1973—. Mem. Office Tech. Assessment Residential Energy Conservation Adv. Com., 1976-77, Magnetic Fusion Adv. Com., 1986-87, Aspen Inst. Energy Policy Forum; mem. coun. for the Arts MIT, 1995—; mem. Com. on Energy and Econ. Devel. NAACP; mem. German Marshall Fund Adv. Com. on Energy Efficiency in Swedish Bldgs. Co-author: A Decade of Despair, A Compendium of Utility-Sponsored Appliance Rebate Programs, Transportation, Energy and Environment: Balancing Goals and Identifying Policies, 1995, Restructuring the Electric Utility Industry: A Consumer Perspective; 1998; author: Equity and Energy: Rising Energy Prices and the Living Standards of Lower Income Americans, 1983, Oil, Gas or...? A Guide to Saving Heating Dollars, The Consumer and Energy Impacts of Oil Exports, Operating Costs of Refrigerators/Freezers and Room Air Conditioners, If You Want to Lower Your Heating Bill, It's Time to Raise the Roof, A Comparative Analysis of Utility and Non-Utility Based Energy Services Companies, A State by State Compendium of Energy Efficiency Programs Using Oil Overcharge Funds; (reports) The Consumer and Energy Impacts of Oil Exports, 1984, A Comprehensive Analysis of a Crude Oil Import Fee: Dismantling a Trojan Horse, 1982, A Comparison of Crude Oil Decontrol and Natural Gas Deregulation: An Analysis of the Impract of Immediate Decontrol of Crude Oil and Related Products on End Use Consumers, Natural Gas Deregulation: A Case of Trickle Up Economics, 1982; pub. The Quad Report, 1993—. Bd. dirs. Barnard in Washington, 1994—; bd. trustees Wider Opportunities for Women; bd. mgrs. Adas Israel Congregation, 1996—; chmn. bldgs. and gounds com. Woodley Park Towers condominium. Named Woman of the Eighties, Ladies Home Jour., 1979; grantee German Marshall Fund. Mem. Barnard Coll. Washington Alumnae Assn. (bd. dirs.), Cosmos Club (admissions com., mem. coun. arts, named one of Key Women 2004). Home: 2737 Devonshire Pl NW Washington DC 20008-3479 Office Phone: 202-659-0404.

BERMAN, GAIL, former film company executive; b. Aug. 17, 1956; m. Bill Masters, 1980; 2 children. B in Theater, U. Md., 1978. Former exec. prodr. Comedy Channel, HBO; from v.p. TV to pres. and CEO Sandollar Prodns., 1991—97, advisor, 1997—98; founding pres. Regency TV, 1998—2000; pres. entertainment Fox Broadcasting Co., 2000—05; pres. Paramount Pictures, Hollywood, Calif., 2005—07. Named one of 100 Most Powerful Women in Entertainment, Hollywood Reporter, 2003, 2004, 2005, 2006, 50 Most Powerful Women in Am Bus., Fortune Mag., 2003, 100 Most Powerful Women, Forbes mag., 2005—06; recipient Lucy award, Women in Film, 2003.*

BERMAN, GEOFFREY LOUIS, diversified financial services company executive; b. LA, July 15, 1953; s. Geoffrey M. and Patricia A. (Meyer) B.; m. Autumn Joy Patton, Mar. 26, 1983; children: Arielle Louise, Michelle Elise. BA/BS in Bus. Adminstrn., U. of the Pacific, 1975; JD, Southwestern U., 1985. Loan officer Union Bank, LA, 1975-80; adminstrv. asst. Credit Mgrs. Assn., LA, 1980-82; asst. v.p. Mitsui Mfrs. Bank, LA, 1982-86; asst. sec., mgr. adjustment bur. Credit Mgrs. Assn., Burbank, Calif., 1986-97; v.p. turnaround management Devel. Specialists, Inc., LA, 1997—. Dir. Comml. Fin. Conf. Calif., L.A., 1978-80; co-chair insolvency laws com. Am. Bankruptcy Inst., Alexandria, Va., 1994—, dir., 2002-, v.p. publs., 2007-, mem. exec. com., 2007-; mem. panel of mediators Ctrl. Dist. Bankruptcy Ct., L.A., 1995—, registrar mediators, 2004—; chmn. Task Force on Gen. Assignments for Benefit of Creditors, 1995-2000; mem. register of mediators Dist. Del. Bankrupcy Ct., 2003—. Author: (manual) ABI Creditor's Com. Manual, 1995, 2nd edit., 2006, ABI General Assignments for the Benefit of Creditors, A Practical Guide, 2000; contbg. editor Am. Bankruptcy Inst. Jour., 1996—, Fed. CT Receiver, 1999-2000; exec. editor Am. Bankruptcy Inst. Jour., 2006-07, v.p. publs., 2007—; contbr. articles to profl. jours. Mem. task force City of Buena Park (Calif.) Investment Policy Rev. Com., 1995. Recipient Recognition award Fed. Bar Assn., L.A., 1986. Mem. L.A. Bankruptcy Forum, Bay Area Bankruptcy Forum, Orange County Bankruptcy Forum. Office: Development Specialists Inc 333 S Grand Ave Ste 4070 Los Angeles CA 90071-1544 E-mail: gberman@dsi.biz.

BERMAN, GREG, think-tank executive; BA Wesleyan Univ. Project coord. Red Hook Cmty. Justice Ctr., NYC, 1994—96; dep. dir. Ctr. for Ct. Innovation, NYC, 1996—2002, dir., 2002—. Contbr. articles in law jour.; co-author: Good Courts: The Case for Problem-Solving Justice, 2005.

Mem. bd. Poets House, NYC. Coro fellow in Pub. Affairs. Office: Center for Court Innovation 520 8th Ave New York NY 10018 Office Phone: 212-397-3050. Business E-Mail: bermang@courtinnivation.org.

BERMAN, HOWARD LAWRENCE, congressman, lawyer; b. LA, Apr. 15, 1941; s. Joseph Berman and Eleanor (Schapiro); m. Janis Schwarz Berman, 1979; children: Brinley Ann, Lindsey Rose. BA in Internat. Rels., UCLA, 1962, LLB, 1965. Bar: Calif. 1966. Vol. VISTA, Balt., San Francisco, 1966-67; assoc. Levy, Van Bourg & Hackler, LA, 1967-72; mem. Calif. State Assembly from 43d dist., 1972—82, majority leader, 1974—79; mem. U.S. Congress from 28th Calif. dist., Washington, 1983—. Mem. jud. com., immigration and claims sub com.; ranking mem. on courts, the internet, and intellectual property subcoms.; mem. internat. rels. com., Middle East and Ctrl. Asia subcom.; ranking minority mem. on com. on standards of ofcl. conduct Pres. Calif. Fedn. Young Democrats, 1967-69 (budget com.); mem. adv. bd. Jewish Fund for Justice. Recipient President's award, Nat. Music Pubs.' Assn., 2007. Democrat. Office: US Ho Reps 2221 Rayburn Ho Office Bldg Washington DC 20515-0528 also: Dist Office 14546 Hamlin St Ste 202 Van Nuys CA 91411*

BERMAN, JEFFREY SCOTT, psychology professor; b. Cambridge, Mass., Feb. 14, 1950; s. Morris Lewis and Mae Arlene Berman. BA, Reed Coll., Portland, 1972; AM, Harvard U., Cambridge, Mass., 1976, PhD, 1979. Tchg. asst. Reed Coll., Portland, 1969—72; instr. U. Tex., Austin, 1977—80, asst. prof., 1980—85; assoc. prof. U. Memphis, 1985—90, prof., 1990—. Fellow, NSF, 1972—75, Harvard U., Cambridge, 1974—77. Mem.: APA, Soc. Psychotherapy Rsch., Assn. Psychol. Sci., Soc. Sci. Clin. Psychology, Phi Beta Kappa. Office: University of Memphis Department of Psychology Memphis TN 38152 Office Phone: 901-755-2311. E-mail: jberman@memphis.edu.

BERMAN, JOSHUA G., lawyer; b. Miami, July 14, 1970; BS in Govt. magna cum laude, Cornell U., 1991; JD magna cum laude, U. Mich., 1994. Bar: Ill. 1994, DC, US Dist. Ct. No. Dist. Ill. 1995, US Dist Ct. So. Dist. NY 1998, US Ct. Appeals 2nd Cir., US Ct. Appeals 7th Cir., US Ct. Appeals 9th Cir., US Supreme Ct. Law clk. to Hon. Joel M. Flaum US Ct. Appeals 7th Cir.; with Jenner & Block, Chgo.; asst. US atty. So. Dist. NY; assoc. investigative counsel Webster Commn., 2001; joined pub. integrity sect. US Dept. Justice, 2002; ptnr. Sonnenschein Nath & Rosenthal LLP, Washington, 2004—. Adj. prof. law Georgetown U., Am. U., George Washington U., The Cath. U. of Am. Mem.: ABA (nat. co-chair white collar crime subcom. pub. corruption and extortion). Office: Sonnenschein Nath & Rosenthal Ste 600, E Tower 1301 K St NW Washington DC 20005 Office Phone: 202-408-5208. Office Fax: 202-408-6399. Business E-Mail: jberman@sonnenschein.com.

BERMAN, JOSHUA MORDECAI, lawyer, manufacturing executive; b. Rochester, NY, Aug. 4, 1938; s. Jeremiah Joseph and Rose (Rappaport) B.; m. Ruth Freed, Mar. 17, 1996; children: Marc Ethan, Eve. BBA summa cum laude, CCNY, 1958; JD cum laude, Harvard U., 1961. Bar: Mass. 1961, NY 1984. With Goodwin, Procter & Hoar, Boston, 1961-80, ptnr., 1969-80; pres. Berman Engel P.C., 1980-85; counsel Kramer, Levin, Naftalis & Frankel, 1985—. Chmn. bd. CEO Tyco Internat. Ltd., 1970—73; adviser Fidelity Investments, 1971—, Rank Group Ltd., Auckland, New Zealand, 1996—, Med. Info. Tech., Inc., 1970—. Founder, pres. Boston Children's Sch., 1965-66. Home: Alexandra La Frasse 1660 Chateau d'Oex Switzerland Business E-Mail: jberman@kramerlevin.com.

BERMAN, KEITH, solicitor, lawyer; b. Liverpool, Eng., Dec. 23, 1942; came to U.S., 1980; s. Joseph and Gerty Berman; children; Chloé Jo, Jade Kara, Kate Alexis. LLB with honors, U. Liverpool, 1963. Admitted as solicitor Supreme Ct. Eng. and Wales, 1966; bar: N.Y. 1980, U.S. Dist. Ct. (so. and ea. dists.) N.Y. 1982, U.S. Ct. Internat. Trade 1992, U.S. Ct. Appeals (fed. cir.) 1992. Founding ptnr. Bermans English Solicitors, Liverpool, Manchester, 1970—, NYC, 1980—. Trustee Fifth Ave Synagogue, N.Y.C., 1986—. Mem. ABA, Law Soc. Eng. and Wales, Comml. Law League Am., Internat. Bar Assn. Office: Bermans 1775 Broadway #608 New York NY 10019-1903 E-mail: 3kb@bermans.net.

BERMAN, LAURA, sex therapist; BA in anthropology, U. Vt., 1990; MA in health edn., NYU Sch. Edn., 1992; MSW, NYU, 1994, PhD in philosophy, 1997. Fellow in human sexual therapy NYU Med. Ctr., 1997; former co-dir. (with sister Jennifer) Women's Sexual Health Clinic, Boston U. Med. Ctr.; co-dir. (with sister Jennifer) Network Excellence Women's Sexual Health; clinical asst. prof. ob-gyn. and psychiatry Feinberg Sch. Medicine Northwestern U.; dir. Berman Ctr., Chgo., 2004—; co-host (with sister Jennifer) Berman & Berman: For Women Only, Discovery Health Channel, 2004—. Co-author (with sister Jennifer): For Women Only: A Revolutionary Guide to Overcoming Sexual Dysfunction and Reclaiming Your Sex Life, 2001, Secrets of the Sexually Satisfied Woman, 2005; actor: (TV series) Sexual Healing, 2006. Found. bd. mem. Soc. Sci. Study Sexuality (SSSS). Named one of 40 Under 40, Crains' Chicago Business, 2005; recipient Rising Star Yr., Nat. Assn. Women Bus. Owners, LA, 2002, Women Action award, Israel Cancer Rsch. Fund, 2002. Mem.: Am. Assn. Sex Educators, Counselors, and Therapists, Internat. Soc. Study Women's Sexual Health, Am. Assn. Social Workers. Office: Berman Ctr LLC 211 E Ontario Ste 800 Chicago IL 60611 Office Phone: 800-709-4709, 312-255-8088. Office Fax: 312-255-8007.*

BERMAN, LEONARD KEITH, lawyer; b. Dearborn, Mich., Mar. 30, 1963; s. Hyman Jack and Doris (Grushky) B.; m. Sharon Elizabeth Williams, Oct. 8, 1988; children: Sarah, Rebbeca, Joseph. BA, Mich. State U., 1985; JD cum laude, Wayne State U., 1988. Bar: Mich. 1988, U.S. Dist. Ct. (ea. and we. dists.) Mich. 1988. Assoc. Bodman, Longley & Dahling P.C., Troy, Mich., 1987-91; staff atty. Elias Bros. Restaurants Inc., Warren, Mich., 1991-94; assoc. Hainer & Demorest P.C., Troy, 1994—96; ptnr. Hainer & Berman PC, Bingham Farms, Mich., 1996—. Mem. ABA, State Bar Mich. Republican. Office: Hainer and Berman PC 24255 W 13 Mile Rd Ste 270 Bingham Farms MI 48025-4322 Business E-Mail: lenberman@hainerberman.com.

BERMAN, MARSHALL FOX, lawyer; b. Portsmouth, Va., Aug. 27, 1939; s. Israel and Etta (Fox) B.; m. Barbara Pressner, Aug. 29, 1965 (dec. Feb. 1993); m. Karen Orloff Kaplan, Nov. 18, 1996; children: Richard Joseph, Deborah Lynn. BA, U. Va., 1961, postgrad. in rhetoric, 1961-62; JD, Am. U., 1967; LLM in Labor Law with highest honors, George Washington U., 1970. Bar: Va. 1967, D.C. 1971, U.S. Supreme Ct. 1971. Tchr. reading pub. schs., Washington, 1965-66; staff D.C. Minimum Wage and Indsl. Safety Bd., 1966-67; atty. NLRB, Washington, 1968-71; assoc. Gall, Lane & Powell, Washington, 1971-75; ptnr. Dow, Lohnes & Albertson, Washington, 1975-91, Epstein, Becker and Green, Washington, 1992-98, Hewes, Gelband, Lambert and Dann, Washington, 1999—2000, Ruben & Aronson, Washington, 2000—; spl. master for labor and employment cases U.S. Dist. Ct. D.C., 2001—. Co-author: Aviation Drug Testing Handbook, 1989, Aviation Drug Testing Operating Manual, 1990. Mem. ABA, Fed. Bar Assn., D.C. Bar Assn., Va. Bar Assn. Office: 4800 Montgomery Lane Ste 150 Bethesda MD 20814 also: 1101 30th St NW Ste 500 Washington DC 20007 Home: 1555 Colonial Ter Apt 100 Arlington VA 22209-1426 Home Phone: 703-387-0989; Office Phone: 202-337-4808. Personal E-mail: lawfirmmberman@yahoo.com.

BERMAN, MIRIAM NAOMI, librarian; b. Phila., May 27, 1929; d. Max Isaac and Sonia Leona (Brown) Mosevitzky; m. Aaron Arthur Berman, July 4, 1955; children: David Hirsh, Raphael Judah, Michael Jonah. BA, CUNY, 1950, MA, 1952; MLS, Pratt Inst., 1975. Lic. profl. librarian, N.Y.; lic. elem and secondary tchr., N.Y. Tchr. Crown Heights Yeshiva, Bklyn., 1950-52, Pub. Sch. 26/N.Y.C. Bd. Edn., Bklyn., 1952-64; exec. Aaron Berman Gallery, NYC, 1976-77; librarian Bklyn. Pub. Library, 1977-79, Aviation High Sch., LI, N.Y., 1979-89, Sheepshead Bay High Sch., Bklyn., 1989-96; ret., 1996. Juror Art Auction Com., N.Y.C., 1972-77. Mem. N.Y.C. Library Assn. (treas. 1985-87). Avocations: music, art, theater, ballet.

BERMAN, MONA S., actress, playwright, theater director, theater producer; b. Jersey City, 1925; d. Edward and Mary (Auster) Solomon; m. Caroll Z. Berman (dec.); children: Marcie Berman Ries, Laura Jane. BA, Beaver Coll., 1945; postgrad., Columbia U.; MFA, Boston U., 1957. Tchr. English, drama Jersey City HSs; actress indsl., stage, TV, Valley Players Holyoke, Mass.; actress Millbrook Playhouse, Mill Hall, Pa., 1991; owner, dir. Theater Sch. and Producing Co., Maplewood, NJ. Chmn. drama edn. YM-MWHA Met. N.J. Cons., Clark Ctr. Performing Arts, NYC, 1965—66; instr. South Orange, Maplewood Adult Sch., 1967; artistic dir. Children's Theatre Co. Inc., Maplewood, 1968—70; cons. Whole Theater Co., City Theatre, Miami, Fla., 2000; dir. pub. rels. Co. 3 by 2. Author: (plays) Hello Joe, That Ring in the Center, The Big Show, Interim, Who Can Belong?, Sudden Changes, Without Malice, Interim 2; prodr., dir.: (plays) A Night of Stars; guest theater reviewer: El Paso Herald Post, 1980—82; mem. artistic steering com. Women's Theatre Project. Active Boston United Fund, 1955—59, chmn. Boston residential area, 1957; bd. dirs. Greater Boston Girl Scouts Am., 1956—58; active S. Fla. Theater League, City Theatre, Miami, Fla.; mentor Arts for Learning, Miami-Dade County, Fla., 2006; bd. dirs. Tufts Med. Faculty Wives, 1956—58, Campositions Hybrid Theatre Wks., Miami, 2006—. Mem.: Creative Alliance, Profl. Actors Assn. Fla., Actors Equity Assn., Dramatist Guild.

BERMAN, MYLES LEE, lawyer; b. Chgo., July 11, 1954; s. Jordan and Eunice (Berg) B.; m. Mitra Moghimi, Dec. 19, 1981; children: Elizabeth, Calvin, Justin. BA, U. Ill., 1976; JD, Chgo.- Kent Coll. of Law, 1979. Bar: Ill. 1980, Calif. 1987, U.S. Dist. Ct. (no. dist.) Ill. 1980, U.S. Dist. Ct. (ctrl. dist.) Calif. 1988, U.S. Dist. Ct. (no. and so. dist.) Calif., 2001, U.S. Supreme Ct. 1992. Asst. state's atty. Cook County State's Atty.'s Office, Chgo., 1980-82; pvt. practice Offices of Myles L. Berman, Chgo., 1982-91; pvt. practice, LA, 1988—. Founder Nat. Drunk Driving Def. Task Force; traffic ct. judge pro tem Beverly Hills Mcpl. Ct., 1990—; traffic ct. judge pro tem adminstr. Culver Mcpl. Ct., 1991—; probation monitor State Bar Calif., 1992—; spkr. in field. Mem. editl. com.: Century City Lawyer, 1992—; co-author: Driving Under the Influence Cases, California Criminal Law Procedure and Practice 3d edit.; author: DUI Trial Notebook; contbr. articles to profl. jours. Mem. ABA, NACDL (mem. DUI com.), Santa Monica Bar Assn., Los Angeles County Bar Assn., Calif. Attys. for Criminal Justice, Beverly Hills Bar Assn., Century City Bar Assn. (chmn. criminal law sect. 1989—, bd. govs. 1991—, Outstanding Svc. award 1990, 92, 93, 94, Spl. Recognition 1994, treas. 1994, sec. 1995, v.p. 1996, pres.-elect 1997, pres. 1998-99, criminal law award for excellence 2001-02), Criminal Cts. Bar Assn. (evaluation profl. stds. and state bar com. 1996-97), Orange County Bar Assn., South Orange County Bar Assn., Cyberspace Bar Assn., Assn. Calif. Deuce Defenders (specialist), John M. Langston Bar Assn., Italian Am. Lawyers Assn., San Fernando valley Bar Assn. Avocations: family, sports. Office: 9255 Sunset Blvd Ste 720 Los Angeles CA 90069-3304 also: #9 3075 E Thousand Oaks Blvd Westlake Village CA 91362 also: 4665 MacArthur Ct Ste 240 Newport Beach CA 92660 Office Phone: 310-273-9501. E-mail: duilaw@topgundui.com.*

BERMAN, NEIL SHELDON, retired chemical engineering professor; b. Milw., Sept. 21, 1933; s. Henry and Ella B.; m. Sarah Ayres, June 3, 1962; children: Jenny, Daniel. BS, U. Wis., 1955; MS, MA, U. Tex., 1961, PhD, 1962. Engr. Std. Oil Co. Calif., LA, 1955-62; rsch. engr. E.I. DuPont Co., Wilmington, Del., 1962-64; from asst. prof. to prof. chem. engring. Ariz. State U., 1964-2000, prof. emeritus, 2000—, Grad. Coll. Disting. Rsch. prof., 1984-85; ret., 2000. Cons. air pollution, fluid dynamics; mem. Phoenix Air Quality Maintenance Area Task Force, 1976-77. Contbr. articles on fluid dynamics of polymer solutions, air pollution, thermodynamics and chem. engring. edn. to profl. jours. Served to capt. M.S.C. USAR, 1956-58. Recipient numerous grants for rsch. in fluid dynamics and air pollution. Fellow Am. Inst. Chem. Engrs. (chmn. Ariz. sect. 1978-79), AAAS, Ariz.-Nev. Acad. Sci. (corr. sec. 1981-88, pres.-elect 1988-89, pres. 1989-90); mem. ASME, Am. Chem. Soc., Am. Phys. Soc., Ariz. Coun. Engring. and Sci. Assns. (chmn. 1980-81), Soc. Rheology, Am. Soc. Engring. Edn., Am. Acad. Mechanics, Nat. Assn. State Acads. Sci. (mem.-at-large bd. dirs.), Sigma Xi, Tau Beta Pi, Phi Kappa Phi. Home: 418 E Geneva Dr Tempe AZ 85282-3731 Office: Ariz State U Dept Chem Engring Tempe AZ 85287-6006 Home Phone: 480-966-0290. Business E-Mail: neil.berman@asu.edu.

BERMAN, PAUL JUSTIN, lawyer; b. Chgo., Jan. 7, 1951; s. Barry L. and Judith M. (Mendelsohn) B.; m. Susan Elizabeth Schonberger, June 25, 1972; children: David Benjamin, Michael Jonathan. BA, Harvard U., 1972, JD, 1975. Bar: D.C., U.S. Ct. Appeals (3rd , federal and D.C. cirs.), U.S. Supreme Ct.; reg. U.S. Patent Atty. Assoc. Covington & Burling, Washington, 1975-83, ptnr., 1983—, chmn., Intellectual Property Practice Group. Dir. Harvard Ctr. for Info. Policy Rsch., Cambridge, Mass., 1976—; intellectual property com. mem., MIT. Co-author: High and Low Politics: Information Resources for the 1980's, 1977. V.p. Temple Emanuel, Kensington, Md., 1987—. Mem. Am. Intellectual Property Law Assn. Office: Covington & Burling PO Box 7566 1201 Pennsylvania Ave NW Washington DC 20004-2401 Office Phone: 202-662-5468. Office Fax: 202-778-5468. Business E-Mail: pberman@cov.com.

BERMAN, RICHARD ANGEL, health facility administrator; b. Cin., Jan. 23, 1945; s. Isidore Alexander and Cecilia (Angel) B.; 1 child, Joshua BBA with distinction, U. Mich., 1966, MBA with distinction, 1968, MHA, 1968. Spl. asst., asst. sec. health, dir. health policy Econ. Stblzn. Program, HEW, Washington, 1972-74; sr. program cons. Robert Wood Johnson Found., Princeton, NJ, 1974-77; asst. dean, assoc. hosp. dir. N.Y. Hosp.-Cornell Med. Ctr., NYC, 1974-77; dir. N.Y. State Office Health Sys. Mgmt., Albany, 1977-80; commr. N.Y. State Divsn. Housing and Cmty. Renewal, 1981-83; exec. v.p. NYU Med. Ctr., NYC, 1983-86; prof. health care mgmt. NYU Sch. Medicine, 1983-86; candidate for U.S. Congress, 1986; spl. cons. McKinsey and Co., NYC, 1987-90; v.p. Korn/Ferry Internat., NYC, 1990-91; pres. N.Am. Howe-Lewis Internat., NYC, 1991-92, pres., CEO, 1992-94; pres. Manhattanville Coll., Purchase, NY, 1995—. Cons. in field; bd. dirs. Health Ins. Plan Greater NY, NCAA-Divsn. III Pres.'s Coun., 2002—06. Contbr. articles to profl. jours. Chmn. NY State Bldg. Code Coun., 1981-83; mem. NY State Housing Fin. Agy., 1981-83, NY Statewide Health Coord. Coun.; adv. bd. Ctr. Hosp. Fin. and Mgmt.; bd. dirs. NYC Pub. Devel. Corp., 1985-90; mem. Prospective Payment Assessment Commn., 1989-95; exec. com. NY March of Dimes Bd., 1980-95; mem. Mayor's Mgmt. Adv. Task Force, 1991-93; nat. adv. coun. Nat. Inst. for Nursing Rsch., NIH, 1991-94; trustee SUNY, 1993-95; v.p. Seeds of Peace Orgn., 2004—; bd. dirs. Inst. for Student Achievement, Manhasset, NY, 199-2001, Today's Students Tomorrow's Tchrs., Yorktown Heights, NY, 1998-2005, chmn. bd. dirs., 2005—; bd. dirs. Westchester Med. Ctr., Valhalla, NY. Recipient Horace M. Kallen Disting. Cmty. Svc. award Am. Jewish Congress, 1981, Brotherhood award NCCJ, 1985, Disting. Achievement award B'nai B'rith, 1997, award of honor Westchester Holocaust Edn. Ctr., 2002. Fellow Am. Coll. Health Care Execs., N.Y. Acad. Medicine (assoc.); mem. APHA, Am. Hosp. Assn., Pub. Health Assn. N.Y., Nat. Acad. Sci. Inst. Medicine. Office Phone: 914-323-5230. Business E-Mail: bermanr@mville.edu.

BERMAN, RICHARD BRUCE, lawyer; b. Freeport, NY, Sept. 26, 1951; s. Nathan and Helen Dorothy (Raiden) B.; m. Laurie Michael, Nov. 2, 1985. BA in Speech Communication cum laude, Am. U., Washington, 1973; JD, U. Miami, 1976. Bar: Fla. 1976, U.S. Dist. Ct. (so. dist.) Fla. 1976, D.C. 1978. Atty. Travelers Ins. Co., Ft. Lauderdale, Fla., 1977-84; assoc. Frank & Flaster P.A., Sunrise, Fla., 1984-88, DeCesare & Salerno, Ft. Lauderdale, Fla., 1988-89; pvt. practice, 1989—. Bd. dirs. Frosch Health Care Cons., Inc., Lauderhill, Employers for Ins. Reform, 2002-04—; mem. worker's compensation rules com. Fla. Bar, 1991-94; bd. dirs. Fla. Workers Advs., 1991—, chmn. media rels. com., 2000—. Mem. panel health care Dem. Legis. Task Force, Ft. Lauderdale, 1985-87; mem. adv. bd. Reflex Sympathetic Dystrophy Syndrome Assn. Fla., 1992—94; mem. B'nai Brith; bd. dirs. Mommy & Me Enterprises, 1997-2002. Mem. ABA, ATLA, D.C. Bar, Fla. Bar Assn., Acad. Fla. Trial Lawyers, Broward County Trial Lawyers Assn. Avocations: performing music, theater, writing music. Office Phone: 954-741-7066. Personal E-mail: richardbberman@raol.com.

BERMAN, RICHARD KEITH, television producer, film producer; b. NYC, Dec. 25, 1945; BA in Speech, U. Wis., Madison, 1967. Dir. current programming Paramount, 1984—87. Sr. prodr. Big Blue Marble, 1977-82 (Emmy award); ind. prodr. HBO, PBS, 1982-84; prodr., writer (story): Star Trek: Generations, 1994, Star Trek: First Contact, 1996, Star Trek: IMAX, 1998, Star Trek: Insurrection, 1998; prodr., writer (story), (TV): Star Trek: Deep Space Nine-Emissary/Emissary, 1993, Star Trek: Voyager-Caretaker, 1995; supervising prodr.: Star Trek: The Next Generation-Encounter at Farpoint, 1987, -All Good Things, 1994, (series) Star Trek: The Next Generation, 1987-94, exec. prodr., 1991-94 (also co-creator with Gene Roddenberry); creator (TV series) Star Trek: Deep Space Nine/DS9, 1993-99; co-creator (TV series) Star Trek: Voyager, 1995-2001; creative cons. Star Trek: The Experience, 1998.

BERMAN, RICHARD MILES, judge; m. Elizabeth T. Gildersleeve. BS, Cornell U., 1964; JD, NYU, 1967; diploma in comparative law, U. Stockholm, 1968, diploma in internat. law, 1970; MSW, Fordham U., 1996. Bar: N.Y. 1971. Assoc. Davis, Polk & Wardwell, NYC, 1970-74; exec. asst. Senator Jacob K. Javits, NYC, 1974-78; gen. counsel, exec. v.p., dir. Warner Cable Comm. Inc., NYC, 1978-86; gen. counsel, sec. MTV Networks, Inc., NYC, 1983-86; ptnr. LeBoeuf, Lamb, Greene & MacRae, NYC, 1986-95; mng. ptnr. LA, 1989-91; judge Family Ct. State of N.Y., 1995-98, U.S. Dist. Ct. (so. dist.) N.Y., 1998—. Exec. dir. N.Y. State Alliance Save Energy, Inc., NYC, 1977—78; mem. N.Y.C. Child Abuse Task Force, 1995, N.Y. State Permanent Commn. Justice Children, 1996—2000; chmn. collegiality com. U.S. Dist. Ct. (so. dist.) NY, 2000—06, chmn. media rels. com., 2006—; chmn. 2d US Cir. Jud. Conf., 2005. Judge Valente, Clarence Palitz and Jacob Levy Found. scholar, NYU Sch. Law, 1964—67, Thord-Gray fellow, Am.-Scandinavian Found., 1967—68, Donald Frank Sussman Meml. scholar, Cornell U. Mem.: U.S. Jr. Davis Cup Squad (met. N.Y.C.). Avocations: tennis, horseback riding, house restoration. Office: US Dist Ct 40 Centre St New York NY 10007-1502

BERMAN, RICHARD P., lawyer; b. LA, Oct. 26, 1946; BA, U. Calif., 1968, JD, 1972. Bar: Calif. 1973. Mem. Law Office of Richard P. Berman, Fresno, Calif. Instr. criminal law Fresno City Coll., State Ctr. Peace Officers Acad., 1974—79; mem. adv. coun. sch. scis. Calif. State U., Fresno, 1986—98. Capt. med. svc. corps USAR, 1975—79. Master: Am. Inns of Ct.; mem.: Calif. Attys. Criminal Justice (mem., patron bd. govs. 1983—89, 1992—2001), Fresno Trial Lawyers Assn. (dir. 1979—85), Consumer Attys. Calif., Nat. Assn. Criminal Def. Lawyers (life), State Bar Calif. (mem. pub. affairs com. 1986—89), Fed. Bar Assn., Fresno County Bar Assn. (chmn. criminal law sect. 1982, 1984, mem. bench, bar and media com. 1990, dir. 1992—94, pres. 1994—95, mem. blue ribbon com. ct. coordination), Phi Alpha Delta. Office: 2333 Merced St Fresno CA 93721 Office Phone: 559-438-7425. Office Fax: 559-233-6947.

BERMAN, ROBERT L., imaging company executive; BS, U. Minn.; M in Indsl. and Labor Rels., Cornell U., Ithaca, NY. With Eastman Kodak Co., Rochester, NY, 1983—, human resources dir. Colo. divsn., dir. and divisional v.p. human resources Consumer Imaging Bus., assoc. dir. human resources, dir. and divisional v.p. human resources for global ops., v.p., dir. human resources, 2002—05, sr. v.p., chief human resources officer, 2005—. Office: Eastman Kodak Co 343 State St Rochester NY 14650 Office Phone: 585-724-4000. Office Fax: 585-724-1089.*

BERMAN, ROBERT S., marketing consultant; b. NYC, Apr. 13, 1932; s. Sydney and Beatrice (Lipman) B.; m. Eleanor Rae Greenwald, June 16, 1956 (div. 1973); children: Thomas, Eric, Terry; m. Sherry Rona Frawley, May 29, 1975 (div. 1994); m. Sharon Louise Erbe, Oct. 5, 1996. BA, Cornell U., 1953, MA, 1954; advanced mgmt. certificate, Harvard U., 1964. Vice pres. Marschalk, Inc., NYC, 1962-64; exec. v.p. DeGarmo, Inc., NYC, 1964-70, 1970-80; exec. v.p., gen. mgr. D'Arcy MacManus & Masius, NYC, 1980-83; chmn. exec. com. Margeotes Fertitta & Weiss, 1984-88; ptnr. Ber/Cam Ptnrs., 1987-89; pres. Berman Mktg. Network, Naples, 1983—. Instr. dept. communications Parsons Sch., 1968-70, Pratt Inst., 1974-76; columnist Madison Ave. Mag., N.Y.C., 1968-72. Dir. Collier County Spl. Olympics Internat. Served to 1st lt. U.S. Army, 1954-56. Named Advt. Accountman of the Yr. N.Y. Advt. Council, 1969 Mem. Unity of Naples (bd. dirs.), The Conservancy, Civil War Roundtable N.Y., Komos Aiden Theatrical Assn., Quill and Dagger Club, Cornell Club, The Vineyards Golf Club, Naples Bath and Tennis Club. Office: 4080 Kensington High St Naples FL 34105-5666

BERMAN, RONALD CHARLES, lawyer, accountant; b. Chgo., July 7, 1949; s. Joseph and Helen Berman; m. Kristine K. Topp, May 1, 1993; children: Daniel J. Lohr, Joseph James. BBS with highest honors, U. Ill., 1971, JD with honors, 1974. Bar: Ill. 1974, Wis. 1976; CPA, Wis. Mem. tax staff Grant Thornton, Chgo., 1974-76, tax supr. Madison, Wis., 1976-78, tax mgr., 1978-81, ptnr. tax dept., 1991-94; assoc. Neider & Boucher, Madison, 1995, shareholder, 1996—. Lectr. cont. legal edn. U. Wis., 1999—. Mem. editl. adv. bd. Physician's Tax Advisor Newsletter, 1986-89, Physician's Tax and Investment Advisor, 1989-93. Scoutmaster Boy Scouts Am., Middleton, Wis., 1978—; fin. chmn. Mohawk Dist. Four Lakes Coun., Madison, 1981—85, chmn. endowment fund, 1984—92, v.p. fin., 1992—94, mem. exec. bd., 1982—2006, treas., 1994—96, nat. rep., 1996—2004; cubmaster Boy Scouts Am., Middleton, 2001—02, asst. cubmaster, 2002—05; v.p. Scouts on Stamps Soc. Internat., 1996—2002, bd. dirs., 1986—96; mem. adv. bd. Glacier's Edge Coun., 2006—; bd. dirs. Madison Pension Coun., 1986—98, pres., 1988—89. Recipient Silver Beaver award Boy Scouts Am., 1981, Middleton Good Neighbor award Middleton Good Neighbor Festival, 2000. Mem.: AICPA, ABA, Web Network Profls., Nat. Coun. Planned Giving, Wis. Planned Giving Coun., Madison Estate Coun., Ill. Bar Assn., State Bar. Wis., Wis. Inst. CPAs, Optimists, Order of Coif, Phi Alpha Delta, Phi Kappa Phi, Alpha Pi Omega. Avocations: photogrphy, stamp collecting/philately, camping. Home: 3906 Rolling Hill Dr Middleton WI 53562-1224 Office Phone: 608-661-4500. Business E-Mail: rberman@neiderboucher.com.

BERMAN, RUSSELL SCOTT, oncologist, educator; m. Susan B. Berman. BS, Sophie Davis Sch. Biomed. Edn., 1988; MD, NYU, 1990. Diplomate Am. Bd. Surgery. Fellow in surg. oncology, jr. faculty assoc. M.D. Anderson Cancer Ctr., Houston, 1997—2000; asst. prof. surg. oncology NYU Sch. Medicine, 2000—. Mem. health commn. Village of East Hills, NY, 2001—. Fellow: ACS; mem.: Soc. Surg. Oncology (tng. com. 1997—). Home Phone: 516-316-0652; Office Phone: 212-263-2982.

BERMAN, SANFORD, librarian; b. Chgo., Ill., Oct. 6, 1933; BA with Highest Honors in Polit. Sci., UCLA, 1955; MLS, Catholic U. Am., Washington, DC, 1961. Asst. chief, acquisitions dept., supervisory libr. DC Pub. Libr., 1957—62; adminstrv. libr. US Army Spl. Services Libraries, Germany, 1962—66; coll. libr. Schiller Coll., Kleiningerheim, West Germany, 1966—67; periodicals libr. UCLA Rsch. Libr., 1967—68; asst. libr. periodicals sect., U. Zambia Libr., Lusaka, 1968—70, Inst. Social Rsch., Makerere U, Kampala, Uganda, 1971—72; principal libr., head cataloger Hennepin County Libr., Minn. Co-editor: Alternative Library Literature, 1996/1997: a biennial anthology, 1998. Named Minn. Libr. Yr., 1977; recipient Margaret Mann Citation, 1981, Honeywell Project Anniversary award for Peace and Justice, 1988, ALA Equality award, 1989, Carey McWilliams award, 1994. Mem.: Beta Phi Mu, Phi Beta Kappa.*

BERMAN, SAUL J., rabbi; m. Shellee Berman; 4 children. BA, MHL, Yeshiva U.; MA in Political Sci., U. Calif., Berkeley; JD, NYU; studied mishpat ivri, Hebrew U., Israel, Tel Aviv U. Rabbi Congregation Beth Israel, Berkeley, Calif., 1963—69, Young Israel, Brookline, Mass., 1969—71; chmn. dept. Judaic Studies Stern College for Women, Yeshiva University, 1971—84, assoc. prof. Jewish Studies, 1990—95; sr. rabbi Lincoln Square Synagogue, NYC, 1984—90; rabbi, dir. Edah Modern Orthodox Synagogue, 1997—. Contbr. articles Encyclopedia Judea and other profl. jours. Named one of The Top 50 Rabbis in America, Newsweek Mag., 2007.*

BERMAN, SHARI SPRINGER, film director, scriptwriter; b. NYC, July 1964; m. Robert Pulcini. BA, Wesleyan U., 1985; MFA in Film, Columbia U., 1985. Author: (screenplays) Am. Splendor, 2003 (Grand Jury prize Sundance Film Festival, 2003, Critics award Cannes Film Festival, 2003, Open Palm award IFP, 2003, New Dir.'s award Edinburgh (Scotland) Internat. Film Festival, 2003, Best Film, Montreal's (Can.) Comedia Festival, 2003, Critics award Deauville Film Festival, 2003, nominated Best Adapted Screenplay Acad. Awards, 2003, Best Adapted Screenplay, Writers Guild, 2003, Best Film and Best Screenplay, Nat. Soc. Film Critics and LA Film Critics Assn., 2003, Best First Feature, NY Film Critics Cir., Chgo. Film Critics, Toronto Film Critics and Fla. Film Critics, 2003); co-dir.: (films) Off The Menu: The Last Days of Chasen's, 1997 (One of Ten Best Movies of 1998, USA Today and CNN, 1998, Best Documentary Grand Jury award Hamptons Internat. Film Festival, Spl. Jury award Locarno Internat. Film Festival, Spl. Jury award Newport Film Festival), The Young and the Dead, 2000, Hello, He Lied, 2002.

BERMAN, STANLEY ZISSMAN, allergist, immunologist, educator, internist; b. New Orleans, June 17, 1941; s. Herman Zissman and Golda (Kleinfeldt) Feir; m. Leslie Dale Miller, July 7, 1968; children: Jason Lee, Laura Elizabeth; 1 adopted child, Leo. Student, Tulane U., 1959-62; BSM, Northwestern U., Evanston, Ill., 1963; MD, Northwestern U., Chgo., 1966. Diplomate Am. Bd. Internal Medicine, Am. Bd. Allergy and Immunology. Intern Chgo. Wesley Meml. Hosp., 1966-67; med. resident Mayo Grad. Sch. Medicine, Rochester, Minn., 1969-71; fellow in allergy and immunology Scripps Clinic and Rsch. Found., La Jolla, Calif., 1971-73; chmn. allergy Lovelace Clinic now Lovelace Health Sys., Albuquerque, 1973—99, ret., 1999; clin. asst., assoc. prof. dept. medicine U. N.Mex. Sch. Medicine, Albuquerque, 1973—98, clin. prof. dept. medicine, 1998—2000; adj. prof. U. St. Francis, Albuquerque, 2003—. Spkr. in field. Co-author, reviewer, contbr.: articles to profl. jours. Lt. comdr. M.C. USNR, 1967—73. Fellow: ACP, Asthma and Immunology (emeritus), Am. Acad. Allergy, Am. Coll. Chest Physicians; mem.: Am. Thoracic Soc. (pres. N.Mex. chpt. 1977—78), N.Mex. Lung Assn. (bd. dirs. 1977—78). Avocations: jogging, travel, history. Office: 7416 Vista Del Arroyo Ave NE Albuquerque NM 87109-2941

BERMAN, STEPHEN ALAN, neurologist; b. Oak Park, Ill., Mar. 15, 1948; s. Edward and Esther Ruby Berman; m. Sherry Bursztajn. BS, U. Ill., Champaign-Urbana, 1970. Diplomate Am. Bd. Psychiatry and Neurology, Am. Bd. Clinical Neurophysiology. Intern Greater Balt. Med. Ctr., 1976—77; resident in neurology Baylor Coll. Medicine, Houston, 1977—80, fellow in genetics and muscle disease, 1980—83; asst. prof. neurology U. Chgo., 1983—89, U. Tex. and MD Anderson Cancer Ctr., Houston, 1989—90; instr. neurology Harvard Med. Sch., Boston, 1990—92, asst. prof., 1992—96; prof. neurology La. State U., Shreveport, 1996—2000; prof. medicine neurology Dartmouth Med. Coll., Hanover, NH, 2000—; chief neurology White River Junction Vets. Med. Ctr., White River Junction, Vt., 2000—. Med. dir. lab. clinical neurophysiology La. State U., Shreveport, 1997—2000. Contbr. articles to profl. jours.; mem. editl. bd. E-Medicine, 1999. Med. adv. com. Multiple Sclerosis Soc., Shreveport, La., 1997—2000. Recipient Rsch. award, Clarence A. Hawkinson Meml. Fund, 1983—84, Brain Rsch. Found., 1984—87, Tchr. Investigator Devel. award, NIH, 1985—89, Physician Scientist award, Nat. Inst. Aging, 1992—96; fellow, Muscular Dystrophy Assn., 1981—83; grantee, Alzheimer Found., 1984—85, Louis Bloch Fund grant, 1984—87. Mem.: Soc. for Neurorehabilitation (cert.), Am. Acad. Neurology (quality stds. subcom., therapeutics and tech. assessment subcom. 1998), Alpha Omega Alpha (v.p. Ill. chpt. 1973—74), Phi Beta Kappa. Jewish. Office: Dartmouth Med Sch 215 N Main St White River Junction VT 05009 Office Phone: 802-295-9363 5489. Business E-Mail: stephen.berman@dartmouth.edu.

BERMAN, STEVE WILLIAM, lawyer, author; b. Chgo., Nov. 13, 1954; s. Mert E. and Lois Ann (Eliot) B.; m. Janet S. Friend, June 18, 1979 (dec.); children: Eliot Michael, Jacob Paul, Abby Hannah; m. Katherine Weisfield Berman. BS, U. Mich., 1976; JD, U. Chgo., 1980. Bar: Ill. 1980, Wash. 1982, U.S. Dist. Ct. Ill. 1980, U.S. Ct. Appeals (7th cir.) 1980, Wash. 1982, U.S. Dist. Ct. 1982, U.S. Ct. Appeals (3d and 9th cirs.), U.S. Supreme Ct. 1986. Assoc. Jenner & Block, Chgo., 1980-82, Shidler, McBroom & Gates, Seattle, 1982-85; resident ptnr. Bernstein, Litowitz, Berger & Grossman, Seattle, 1986-89; ptnr. Betts, Patterson & Mines, Seattle, 1989-92; mng. ptnr. Hagens Berman, LLP, Seattle, 1993—. Apptd. spl. asst. atty. gen. State of Wash., 1996-98, State of Ariz., 1996-97, State of Ill., 1996-98; adj. prof. law U. Puget Sound, Tacoma, 1983-84; asst. coach Syracuse U., 1976. Author: A Tarnished Hero, 1988; contbr. articles to profl. jours. Mem. com. Juvenile Conf., Seattle, 1984; apptd. spl. counsel Wash. State Bar, 1988-93. Named one of 100 Most Influential Lawyers, Nat. Law Jour., 2000, 2006. Mem. Nat. Assocs. Securities and Comml. Attys. (bd. dirs. 1991—), Trial Lawyers for Pub. Justice, Mercle Island Boys and Girls Club (bd. dirs.). Jewish. Avocations: running, rowing, hiking, skiing. Office: Hagens & Berman 1301 5th Ave Ste 2929 Seattle WA 98101-2603*

BERMAN, STEVEN RICHARD, computer company executive; b. NYC, Dec. 30, 1947; s. Harold and Norma (Bystock) B.; m. Susan Segall, Aug. 3, 1969; 1 child, Russell T. BS in Meteorology, CCNY, 1968; postgrad., U. Chgo., 1968-69; MS in Tech. Mgmt., Pepperdine U., 1993. Programmer, analyst Logicon, Inc., San Pedro, Calif., 1970-73, 75-78, Hughes Aircraft Co., Culver City, Calif., 1973-75; sr. analyst Argosystems, Inc., Sunnyvale, Calif., 1978-80; mgr. software support Ultrasystems, Inc., Irvine, Calif., 1981-86; sr. rsch. engr. Northrop Grumman Inc., Hawthorne, Calif., 1986-98; software project mgr. TRW Inc., LA, 1998—2003; mgr. sys. engring. Northrop Grumman Info. Tech., Inc., El Segundo, 2003—. Author (computer programs) Recording Input-Output, 1983, Batch Jobs from Fortran, 1988, Marking Files No Backup, 1988. NDEA Title IV fellow, Chgo., 1968. Mem. Am. Contract Bridge League, Mensa. Avocations: bridge, travel. Home: 17336 Flame Tree Cir Fountain Valley CA 92708-3522

BERMAN, TONY, lawyer; s. Murray T. and Lillian L. (Levine) B.; m. Ann Rooke-Ley, 1992; children: Julie A., Nina A. JD cum laude, NYU, 1957. Bar: NY 1958, U.S. Ct. Appeals (2d cir.) 1960, U.S. Dist. Ct. (so. and ea. dists.) NY 1961. Asst. atty. gen. State of NY, NYC, 1957-63; ptnr. Berman Paley Goldstein & Monte LLP, NYC, 1963—2006. Co-author: Construction Business Handbook, 1978, Avoiding Liability in Architecture Design and Construction, 1983. Mem. ABA, NY State Bar Assn., Assn. Bar City NY, The Moles. Home Phone: 212-691-1966; Office Phone: 212-354-9600. Business E-Mail: tberman@bpgk_law.com.

BERMAN, WALTER S., treasurer; With Am. Express, 1965—96, CFO Travel Related Svcs.; CFO, Am. Express Fin. Advisors, NYC; treas. Am. Express, IBM, 1999—2000; sr. v.p. fin. Am. Express, NYC, 2001—02, exec. v.p., corp. treas., 2002—05; exec. v.p., CFO Ameriprise Fin. Inc., Mpls., 2005—. Office: Ameriprise Fin Inc 243 Ameriprise Fin Ctr Minneapolis MN 55474*

BERMAN, WILLIAM H., retired publishing company executive; b. Stamford, Conn., 1936; Grad., U. of Pa., 1959. Exec. v.p. Houghton Mifflin Co., Boston, retired, 1993.

BERMAS, STEPHEN, lawyer; b. NYC, Apr. 27, 1925; BS, Cornell U., 1949, JD, 1950; LLM, NYU, 1957. Bar: N.Y. 1950. Assoc. Wagner, Quillinan, Wagner & Tennant, NYC, 1950-51; law sec. to chief justice U.S. Dist. Ct. (so. dist.) NY, NYC, 1951-55; assoc. Gordon, Brady, Caffrey & Keller, NYC, 1955-59; ptnr. Medine & Bermas, NYC, 1959-63, Feltman & Bermas, NYC, 1964-66; sr. atty. Columbia Gas System Corp., NYC, 1966-69; asst. gen. counsel Continental Group Inc., NYC, 1970-77, assoc. gen. counsel, 1978-82; v.p., gen. counsel Continental Can Co. Inc., Norwalk, Conn., 1982-86, exec. v.p., gen. counsel, 1987-91; v.p., gen. counsel Continental Plastic Containers, Inc., 1991—2001; gen. counsel Lockwood, Kessler and Bartlett, Inc., 1998—. Instr. law Queen's Coll, NYC, 1964-68; adminstrv. law judge Office Profl. Med. Conduct NY State Dept. Health, NYC, 1993—. Mem. ABA. Office: 1 Aerial Way Syosset NY 11791-5501 Office Phone: 516-938-0600.

BERMES, EDWARD WILLIAM, JR., biochemist, educator; s. Edward William and Magdelen Bermes; m. Patricia Anne Skokan, Oct. 19, 1957; children: Kathleen Lynn Onori, Edward William III, Mark Laurence, Alicia Marie Joebgen, Christopher John. BS, St. Mary's Coll., 1950—54; MS, Loyola U., 1954—56, PhD, 1957—59. Asst. prof. Loyola U. Med. Ctr., 1959—69; dir. of biochemistry St. Francis Hosp., Evanston, 1961—69; assoc. prof. Loyola U. Med. Ctr., 1969—74, prof., 1975—99, prof. emeritus, 1999—. Dir. of clin. chemistry Loyola U. Med. Ctr., 1969—97, dir. of clin. lab., 1981—97, acting chmn., pathology, 1982—86, assoc. chmn, pathology, 1986—96; chmn., editl. rev. group Doody's Health Sci. Book Rev., 1993—2000. Author: (exhibition) Effect of Hemolysis on Serum Chemistry Values (Gold Medal: ASCP/CAP Meeting, 1978); contbr. chapters to books; mem. editl. bd. Clin. Chem., 1981—90, Clinical and Applied Hemostasis, 1994—2002, Annals of Clinical Laboratory Science, 1978—82, 1990—2000; author: of over 100 articles published in profl. jours. including the Annals of Clinical Laboratory Science, Blood Coagulation and Fibrinolysis, British Journal of Experimental Pathology, Clinical Chemistry, et. al. Recipient Natelson award, Chgo. Sect. , Am. Assoc. for Clin. Chemistry, 1976, Diploma of Honor, Assn. of Clin. Scientists, 1980, Edn. award;Outstanding Efforts in Edn. and Tng., Am. Assn. for Clin. Chemistry, 1983, Presdl. Citation, 1998, Outstanding Contributions to Clin. Chemistry award, Am. Assn. Clin. Chemistry, 2005. Fellow: Nat. Acad. of Clin. Biochemistry; mem.: Commn. on Accreditation in Clin. Chemistry (bd. dirs. 1981—), Assn. of Clin. Scientists, Am. Assn. of Pathologists, Am. Chem. Soc., Commn. on Edn. in Clin. Chemistry (pres. 1989—96), Am. Assn. for Clin. Chemistry (sec. 1978—80, mem. fin. com, exec. com., bd. dir. 1978—80, chmn., commn. on edn. and science 1985—87, Outstanding Contbns. Clin. Chemistry award 2005), Sigma Xi. Home: 1907 Sunnyside Circle Northbrook IL 60062 Office: Loyola University Medical Center 2160 So First Ave Maywood IL 60153 Personal E-mail: ebermes@sbcglobal.net. Business E-Mail: ebermes@lumc.edu.

BERMUDEZ, EUGENIA M. See DIGNAC, GENY

BERN, DORRIT J., apparel executive; b. Apr. 28, 1950; 3 children. BSc in Bus., U. Wash., 1972. Various positions The Bon Marche, Joske's; v.p. women's apparel Sears, Roebuck & Co., 1987—92, group v.p. women's apparel & home furnishings, 1993—95; vice-chmn., pres., CEO Charming Shoppes, Inc., Bensalem, Pa., 1995—97, chmn., pres., CEO, 1997—. Bd. dirs. So. Co. Atlanta, Charming Shoppes, Inc., 1995—, Office Max Inc., 2006—. Mem. Active Keeping Kids Warm, Bensalem, Pa. Recipient Pa. Best 50 Women in Bus. award, 1997, Women of Distinction award, The Phila. Bus. Jour., Nat. Assn. Women's Bus. Owners, Forum Exec. Women, 1998, Entrepreneur of the Yr., Ernst & Young, 2001, Visionary Woman award, Moore Coll. Art & Design, 2004, H.U.G. award, Intimate Apparel Sq. Club, 2005, Paradigm award, Greater Phila. C. of C., 2006. Mem.: Women Bus. Leaders, Com. of 200, Fashion Group Internat., Atlanta C. of C. (bd. dirs.). Office: Charming Shoppes Inc 450 Winks Ln Bensalem PA 19020-5993*

BERN, MARC JAY, lawyer; b. Milw., June 19, 1950; s. James Ellis and Harriet (Kramer) B.; children: Lindsay, Jesse, Noah, Erica; m. Cathy Anthone; 1 child, Emma. BA with distinction, U. Wis., 1972; JD, Ill. Inst. Tech., 1975. Bar: Wis. 1975, US Dist. Ct. (ea. and we. dists.) Wis., N.Y. 1983, US Dist. Ct. (so. and ea. dists.) N.Y., US Dist. Ct. (we. dist.) N.Y. 1990, US Dist. Ct. Pa., US Dist. Ct. Ariz. Assoc. Habush, Gillick, Habush, Davis & Murphy, Milw., 1975-79; ptnr. Gillick, Murphy, Gillick, Bern & Wicht, Milw., 1979-82; assoc. Lipsig, Sullivan, Liapakis, NYC, 1983-84; sr. trial assoc. Julien & Schlesinger, P.C., NYC, 1984-86, Trolman & Glaser, P.C., NYC, 1986-88; pvt. practice law, 1988-91; counsel Weitz & Luxembourg PC, 1992-95; sr. ptnr. Napoli, Kaiser, Bern & Assocs. LLP, 1995—, Napoli Bern LLP, 2002—. Lectr. Milw. Area Tech. Coll., 1979-80, Continuing Edn. State Bar Wis., 1978—, Melvin Belli Seminar, Am. Trial Lawyers Assn., 1982—, Hahneman Med. Coll., 1980, Practicing Law Inst., 1984—, Wis. Acad. Trial Lawyers, Madison, 1981—, NYU Sch. Continuing Edn., 1985—, Inst. Continuing Profl. Edn., 1981-82, N.Y. State Trial Lawyers Assn., 1986-88, Mealeys Seminars, 1999—, Fen-Phen, Rezulin, Methyl Tertiary Butyl Ether. Mem. Am. Trial Lawyers Assn., State Bar Wis., State Bar N.Y., Am. Judicature Soc., Am. Soc. Law and Medicine, N.Y. State Trial Lawyers Assn., Assn. Trial Lawyers Am. (ann. conv. lectr. 1991), Delta Theta Phi. Home: 65 First Neck Ln Southampton NY 11968 Office: 115 Broadway 12th Fl New York NY 10006 Office Phone: 212-267-3700. E-mail: Lawbern@aol.com, mjbern@napolibern.com.

BERN, RONALD LAWRENCE, management consultant, writer; b. Anderson, SC, Aug. 23, 1936; s. Samuel Harris and Minnie (Siegel) B.; m. Elaine Kay Lefkowitz, Dec. 25, 1960; children: Brett Alan, Melissa Lynn. BA in Journalism, U. S.C., 1958, MA in Journalism, 1961. Writer William Barton Marsh Co., NYC, 1958-59; editor, writer Univac div. Sperry Rand, NYC, 1959-60; editor, mgr. Bell Tel. Labs., NYC, 1961-63; pres. Ronald Bern Co., NYC, 1965—85, 1990—2000; corp. sr. v.p. The LVI Group, Inc., NYC, 1985-90. Cons. AT&T Co., NY, NJ, 1966-85, The LVI Group, Nico Constrn.; bd. dir. Talon Corp., The Bern Cos., Inc., Healing Images Inc., Riverstone Svc., Inc. Author: An American in the Making, 1960, The Successful Salesman, 1972, The Legacy, 1975; Gone Fishin': The 100 Best Spots in New Jersey, 1998, Gone Fishin': The 100 Best Spots in New York, 1999, Mule Maddox, 2005; contbr. articles to profl. publ. Bd. dir. North Brunswick Little League, NJ, 1975-79; mem. North Brunswick Planning Commn., 1984. With US Army, 1958-59, 61-62. Fellow SC Press Assn., 1960. Mem. South Caroliniana Soc. Democrat. Jewish. Avocations: fishing, reading, travel. Home: 37 Hidden Lake Dr North Brunswick NJ 08902 E-mail: mulemaddox@aol.com.

BERNABEI, LYNNE ANN, lawyer; b. Highland Park, Ill., Apr. 11, 1950; d. Guy and Anna (Tamarri) Bernabei. BA, Harvard U., 1972, JD, 1977. Bar: DC 1997, admitted to practice: US Dist. Ct. (DC) 1977, US Ct. Appeals (DC Cir.) 1979, US Ct. Appeals (3rd Cir.) 1985, US Ct. Appeals (Fed. Cir.) 1988, US Supreme Ct. 1988, US Ct. Appeals (4th Cir.) 1992, US Ct. Appeals (6th Cir.). Clk. US Dist. Ct. Judge William Bryant, Washington, 1977-78; assoc. Tigar & Buffone, Washington, 1978-80; clin. instr. Georgetown U., Washington, 1980-81; gen. counsel Govt. Accountability Project, Washington, 1981-85; ptnr. Newman, Sobol, Trister & Owens, Washington, 1985-87, Bernabei & Katz, Washington, 1987—2006, Bernabei & Wachtel, Washington, 2006—. Co-author: The High Citadel: On the Influence of Harvard Law School, 1978; contbr. articles to profl. jours. and revs. Named one of 75 Best Lawyers in Washington, Washingtonian mag., 2002. Fellow: Coll. Labor and Employment Lawyers; mem.: AJA, ABA, Nat. Lawyers Guild, Trial Lawyers for Pub. Justice. Office: Bernabei & Wachtel PLC 1775 T St NW Washington DC 20009-7124 Office Phone: 202-745-1942. Business E-Mail: bernabei@bernabeipllc.com. E-mail: lbernabei@aol.com.

BERNABEI, RAYMOND, management consultant; b. New Castle, Pa., Nov. 26, 1925; s. Leo and Maria Bernabei; m. Rosella E. Taucher, May 4, 1946; children: Raymond L., Alan J., Rosemary, Leo J., Lori J. BS in Math. and Geography, Indiana U. of Pa., 1947; MEd in Ednl. Adminstrn., U. Pitts., 1950; cert. in guidance and counseling, Duquesne U., 1960; DEd, Western Res. U., 1966. Math. tchr., head basketball coach Clymer (Pa.) H.S., 1947-50; math. tchr. Tarentum (Pa.) H.S., 1950-54; dir. guidance and testing, head football coach Tarentum Sch. Dist., 1954-61; asst. jr.-sr. H.S. prin. Hampton Twp. (Pa.), 1961-63; grad. asst. Western Res. U., Cleve., 1963-64; dir. secondary edn. Mentor Pub. Schs., Ohio, 1964-65, asst. supt. Ohio, 1965, supt. Ohio, 1965-67; asst. exec. dir. Bucks County (Pa.) Schs., 1967-80; mgmt. cons. I.E. Banreb Assocs., Longwood, Fla. Vis. tchr. John Carroll U., Cleve., 1965, Bowling Green (Ohio) U., 1966, N.S. Summer Sch./Dalhousie U., Halifax, Can., 1967, Wis. State U., Eau Claire, 1968, U. Ala., University, 1969, 71, U. Nev., Las Vegas, 1970, 72, 93, Cleve. State U., 1970, Laurence U., Sarasota, Fla., 1971, 72, 73; adj. prof. U. Ala., 1974, 75, 76, Lehigh U., Bethlehem, Pa., 1978, 80, 81, 82, Rollins Coll., Winter Park, Fla., 1983—; presenter in field. Recipient Disting. Prof. award Nat. Acad. Sch. Execs., 1973, Recognition award Nat. Soccer Coaches Athletic Assn., 1983, Bill Jeffrey award, 1985, Honor award Nat. Soccer Coaches Assn. Am., 1991, Honor award Nat. Intercollegiate Soccer Ofcls. Assn., 1975, Disting. Svc. award Pa. State Athletic Dirs. Assn., 1987, Nellie DelCamp Excellence in Tchg. award Rollins Coll., 1995, 2002; named to Western Pa. Hall of Fame, 1977, Nat. Soccer Hall of Fame, 1978, Allegheny-Kiski Valley Hall of Fame, 1979, Nat. Assn. Intercollegiate Athletics Hall of Fame, 1994, Ind. U. Pa. Hall of Fame, 1996. Home and Office: 541 Woodview Dr Longwood FL 32779-2614

BERNABEO, GREGORY S., lawyer; b. Bryn Mawr, Pa., 1970; BSME cum laude, Bucknell U., 1993; MBA, JD, Villanova U., 1997. Bar: Pa. 1997, NJ 1997, US Dist. Ct., NJ, US Patent and Trademark Office. Law clk. Synnestvedt & Lechner LLP, Phila., 1995—97, assoc., 1997—2004, ptnr., 2004—. Mem.: Phila. Bar Assn., Pa. Bar Assn., Phila. Intellectual Property Law Assn., Phi Kappa Phi, Beta Gamma Sigma. Office: Synnestvedt & Lechner LLP 2600 Aramark Tower 1101 Market St Philadelphia PA 19107-2950 Office Phone: 215-923-4466, 215-717-2245. Office Fax: 215-923-2189. E-mail: gbernabeo@synnlech.com.

BERNACCHI, RICHARD LLOYD, lawyer; b. LA, Dec. 15, 1938; s. Bernard and Anne B. BS with honors in Commerce (Nat. Merit Found. scholar), U. Santa Clara, 1961; LL.B. with highest honors (Legion Lex scholar, Jerry Geisler Meml. scholar), U. So. Calif., 1964. Bar: Calif. 1964. Assoc. Irell and Manella, LA, 1964-70, ptnr., 1970—; lectr. Am. Law Inst., 1972-73; lectr. data processing contracts and law U. So. Calif., LA, 1972, 78, 81. Co-chmn. Regional Transp. Com., 1970-72; mem. adv. bd. U. So. Calif. Computer Law Inst., 1979—, Ariz. Law and Tech. Inst., 1982-86; U. Santa Clara Computer and High Tech. Law Jour., 1982-90. Author: (with Gerald H. Larsen) Data Processing Contracts and the Law, 1974, (with Frank and Statland) Bernacchi on Computer Laaw, 1986; editor-in-chief U. So. Calif. Law Rev., 1962-64; adv. bd. Computer Negotiations Report, 1983-95, Computer and Tech. Law Jour., 1984-93, Computer Law Strategist, 1984-94. Capt. AUS, 1964—66, PTO. Mem. ABA (mem. adv. com. on edn. 1973-74, chmn. subcom. taxation computer sys. of sect. sci. and tech. 1976-78), L.A. Bar Assn., Computer Law Assn. (bd. dirs. 1973-86, chmn. preconf. symposium on law and computers 1974-75, West Coast v.p. 1976-79, sr. v.p. 1979-81, pres. 1981-83, adv. bd. 1986—), Internat. Bar Assn. (co-chmn. sect. on bus. law mem. com. on internat. tech. and e-commerce law 1995-98, steering com. 1998—), Am. Fedn. Info. Processing Socs. (mem. spl. com. electronic funds transfer sys. 1974-78), Order of Coif, Scabbard and Blade, Tech. Coast Angels, Beta Gamma Sigma, Alpha Sigma Nu. Office: Irell & Manella 1800 Avenue Of The Stars Los Angeles CA 90067-4276 Office Phone: 310-770-5608. Business E-Mail: dbernacchi@irell.com.

BERNANKE, BEN SHALOM, chairman board of governors of the Federal Reserve System; b. Augusta, Ga., Dec. 13, 1953; s. Philip Richard and Edna Rivy (Friedman) Bernanke; m. Anna Friedmann, May 29, 1978; children: Joel, Alyssa. BA summa cum laude in Econs., Harvard U., 1975; PhD in Econs., MIT, 1979. Asst. prof. econ. Grad. Sch. Bus., Stanford U., 1979—83, assoc. prof., 1983—85; prof. econ. & pub. affairs Princeton U., 1985—94, prof. econ. & Woodrow Wilson Sch. Pub. & Internat. Affairs, 1985, Class of 1926 prof. econ. & pub. affairs, 1994—96, chair, dept. econ., 1996—99, 2000—02, Howard Harrison & Gabrielle Snyder Beck prof. econ. and pub. affairs, 1996—2005; mem. bd. govs. Fed. Reserve Sys., Washington, 2002—05, 2006—, chmn. bd. govs., 2006—; mem., chmn., Coun. Econ. Advisors Exec. Office of the Pres., Washington, 2005—06; US alt. gov. IMF, Washington, 2006. Vis. prof. econ. MIT, 1983, 1989—90; Morgenstern vis. prof., dept. econ. NYU, 1993; mem. adv. bd. US Census, 1986—89; vis. scholar Fed. Reserve Banks, Phila., 1987—89, Boston, 1989—90, NYC, 1990—91, NYC, 1994—96, mem. acad. adv. panel, 1990—2002; dir. Bendheim Ctr. for Fin., Princeton, 1997—98; rsch. assoc. Nat. Bur. Econ. Rsch., dir. monetary econ. program, mem. bus. cycle dating com.; lectr., Money, Credit and Banking Lecture Ohio State U., 1994; David H. Steine Lecture Vanderbilt U., 1996. Contbr. articles to profl. jours.; co-editor: Economic Letters, 1993—96, Journal of Business, 1993, National Bureau Economic Research Macroeconomics Annual, 1994; assoc. editor Quarterly Journal of Economics, 1985—92, Journal of Financial Intermediation, 1990, Review of Economics and Statistics, 1993, Journal of Money, Credit, and Banking, 1993, mem. adv. bd., mem. editl. bd. Journal of Macroeconomics, 1998—; editor: American Economic Review, 2001—. Named one of 50 Who Matter Now, CNNMoney.com Bus. 2.0, 2006; Nat. Sci. Found. Grad. Fellow, 1975, Hoover Inst. Nat. fellow, 1982—83, Alfred P. Sloan fellow, 1983—84. Fellow: Am. Acad. Arts and Scis., Econometric Soc. (chmn., program com., ASSA meetings, New Orleans 1992); mem.: Phi Beta Kappa. Office: Fed Res Sys 20th St & Constitution Ave NW Washington DC 20551*

BERNARD, ALEXANDER, protective services official; b. LA, Apr. 23, 1952; s. Louis and Hannah (Bergman) Bernard; m. Diana LoRee Winstead, Dec. 17, 1976; children: Michael Alexander, Andrew Alexander. AA magna cum laude, L.A. Valley Coll., 1976; BS summa cum laude, Calif. State U., LA, 1989. Parking meter collector LA (Calif.) City Clk.'s Office,

1973—79; police officer LA (Calif.) Airport, LA, 1979—95, sgt. police svcs. divsn., 1995—2003; gen. mgr. Kern Law Enforcement Assn., Bakersfield, Calif., 2003—. Adv. com. Calif. Commn. Peace Officer Stds. and Tng., 1999—2004, vice chmn., 2001, chmn., 2007—. Contbr. articles to profl. jours. Active Boy Scouts Am. Mem.: NRA (life), Ret. Peace Officers Assn. Calif. (bd. dirs. 2005—, pres. 2006—), LA Airport Peace Officers Assn. (pres. 1981—89, bd. dirs. 1992—94, pres. 1994—95), Fraternal Order Police, LA Airport Police Suprs. Assn. (v.p. 1997—98, pres. 1999—2003, v.p. 2003, bd. dirs.), Peace Officers Rsch. Assn. Calif. (chpt. pres. 1982—84, state bd. dirs. 1984—85, chpt. pres. 1985—87, state bd. dirs. 1987—2003, 1987—2003, ethnic rels. com. 1993—94, exec. com. 1994—2003, sec. 1999—2003, state bd. dir. 2006—), Calif. Peace Officers Assn., Labor and Employment Rsch. Assn., Law Enforcement Alliance Am. (life), Internat. Police Assn. (life), Calif. Rifle and Pistol Assn. (life), Golden Key (life), Phi Kappa Phi (life). Democrat. Avocations: travel, record collecting. Office: Kern Law Enforcement Assn 3417 Pegasus Dr PO Box 82516 Bakersfield CA 93380 E-mail: kleagm@etcrier.net.

BERNARD, APRIL, poet, literature educator; BA, Harvard U. Former sr. editor Premiere, GQ, Vanity Fair; instr. Amherst Coll., Yale U.; prof. lit., MFA core faculty Bennington Coll., 1998—2003, assoc. dean acad. affairs Vt., 2003—. Author: (novels) Pirate Jenny, (poetry) Blackbird Bye Bye (Walt Whitman prize, Acad. Am. Poets), Psalms: Poems, 1993, Swan Electric: Poems, 2002; contbr. poems, literary essays, and articles to various publs. Guggenheim fellow, 2003. Office: Bennington Coll One College Dr Bennington VT 05201 Office Phone: 802-442-5401. E-mail: aprilbernard@earthlink.net.

BERNARD, CATHY S., management corporation executive; b. Bronx, NY, Nov. 13, 1949; d Burton and Norma (Ebb) B. BBA, George Washington U., 1971, M of Pub. Adminstrn., 1978; MA, U. Miami, 1972. Cert. property mgr. Staff asst. HEW, Washington, 1970-74; evaluation specialist OEO, Washington, 1974; tchr. St. Patrick's Acad., Washington, 1975; staff dir. Dem. Nat. Conv., NYC, 1976; pres., chief exec. officer CSB Assocs. Mgmt. Corp., Riverdale, Md., 1977—. Asst. prof. No. Va. CC, Woodbridge, 1976-78; mem. Housing Opportunities Commn., Kensington, Md., 1979-93, chmn., 1988, vice chair, 1980, 87, chair pro tem, 1986, chair housing honor roll, 1985-88, Moderate Priced Dwelling Unit Commn.; mem. exec. coun. Inst. Real Estate Mgmt., Washington, 1982-87, cert. property mgr.; adj. prof. bus. Prince Georges CC, 2002, 06. Adv. coun. Suburban Hosp., Bethesda, Md., 1984-89; bd. dirs. Ivymount Sch. for Handicapped, Potomac, Md., 1984—, pres. bd. dirs., 2003, chair property com., chair bldg. expansion project, 1999-2002; treas. Jewish Coun. on Aging, 1988; bd. dirs., chair property com. Jewish Found. for Group Homes, Rockville, Md., 1989-91; bd. dirs. Roundhouse Theatre, Wheaton, Md., 1994—, treas., 1995—; bd. dirs. McLean Sch. Md., 2001-06, trustee 2001—04, vice chmn., sec., site com. chair, 2002; v.p. bd. dirs. Bethesda's Imagination State, 2003—; trustee Temple Emanuel, Kensington, Md., 1994-97; candidate Md. State Legislature, 1986; pres. Cmty. Housing Res. Bd., 1985. Recipient Hughes award for property mgmt., 1980, Jewish Coun. award, 1989; named Adj. Faculty of Yr.; named one of 100 Outstanding Women in Md. Mem. Montgomery County C. of C. (bd. dirs., v.p. housing com. 1981-82), Apt. and Office Bldg. Assn. (bd. dirs., chmn. affordable housing com. 1990-99).

BERNARD, DAVID GEORGE, retired management consultant; b. Cambridge, Mass., Oct. 30, 1921; s. Frederick and Fayetta (Smith) B.; m. Edith Barnes, Dec. 10, 1960; 1 child, Andrew; children by prior marriage: Jeffrey, Frederick, Joan, Peter. BS, Harvard U., 1943, MBA, 1947. Gen. sales mgr. Am. Can. Co., NYC, 1958-61; sr. v.p. Medusa Corp., Cleve., 1961-63; v.p. Internat. Paper, NYC, 1968-78, Nat. Can Corp., Chgo., 1978-81; exec. v.p. Fischbach Corp., NYC, 1981-83; pres. Delta Marine Supply Corp., NYC, 1983-84. Bd. dirs. Trojan Techs. Inc. Bd. dirs. S.C.A.N. Served to lt. USN, 1943-46, PTO. Mem. Newcomen Soc., Bay Head Yacht Club (N.J.). Democrat. Episcopalian. Home: 254 E 68th St Apt 27E New York NY 10021-6017

BERNARD, DONALD RAY, retired law educator; b. San Antonio, June 5, 1932; s. Horatio J. and Amber (McDonald) B.; children: Doren, Kevin, Koby; m. Elizabeth Priscilla Gilpin, 1986. Student, U. Mich., 1950-52; JD, U. Tex., 1958, BA, 1954, JD, 1958, LLM, 1964. Bar: Tex. 1958, U.S. Ct. Mil. Appeals, 1959, U.S. Supreme Ct. 1959; lic. comml. pilot. Commd. ensign U.S. Navy, 1954, advanced through grades to commdr., 1956-75, retired, 1975; briefing atty. Supreme Ct. Tex., Austin, 1958-59; asst. atty. gen. State of Tex., Austin, 1959-60; ptnr. Bernard & Bernard, Houston, 1960-80; pvt. practice law Houston, 1980-94; prof. internat. law U. St. Thomas, Houston, 1991-94; guest lectr. Sch. Bus. Mont. State U., 1995-96; mng. dir. Mentat Resources LLC, 2003—. Mem. faculty S.W. Sch. Real Estate, 1968-77; chmn. Glacial-Gen. des Mines au Congo Joint Venture Dem. Republic of Congo, 2006—. Author: Origin of the Special Verdict As Now Practiced in Texas, 1964; co-author: (novel) Bullion, 1982. Bd. dirs. Nat. Kidney Found., Houston, 1960-63; chmn. Bd. Adjustment, Hedwig Village, Houston, 1972-76; bd. regents Angeles U. Found., The Philippines; chmn. of the bd. Metro Verde Devel. Corp., The Philippines; bd. dirs. Gloria Dei Luth. Ch., Endowment Found.; v.p. Estekan Lodges, Inc., 2005-, pres. Glacial Energy LLC, 2005—; chmn. Glacial Gen. Des Mines Congo Joint Venture, Rep. of Congo, 2006—; Comdr. USN, 1950-92; ret., air show pilot Confederate Air Force, 1970-80. Mem. Lawyers Soc. Houston (pres. 1973-74), Houston Bd. Realtors, ABA, Inter-Am. Bar Assn., Tex. Bar Assn. (com. liaison Mex. legal profession), Houston Bar Assn. (chairperson emeritus internat. law sect.), Internat. Bar Assn. (del. to 1st seminar with Assn. Soviet Lawyers, Moscow, 1988), Assn. Soviet Lawyers , Lawyer-Pilot Bar Assn., Sons of the Republic of Tex., Lic. Execs. Soc., St. James's Club, Masons, Shriners, Alpha Tau Omega, Phi Delta Phi. Lutheran. Home: 14 Scenic Dr Whitehall MT 59759-9789 E-mail: donbernard@msn.com.

BERNARD, EDDIE NOLAN, oceanographer; b. Houston, Nov. 23, 1946; s. Edward Nolan and Geraldine Marie (Dempsey) B.; m. Shirley Ann Fielder, May 30, 1970; 1 child, Elizabeth Ann BS, Lamar U., 1969; MS, Tex. A&M U., 1970, PhD, 1976. Geophysicist Pan Am. Petroleum Co., 1969; rsch. asst. oceanographic rsch. Tex. A&M U., College Station, Tex., 1969-70; rschr. NOAA, 1970-73, dep. dir. pacific marine environ. lab. Seattle, 1980-82, dir. hydrothermal vents program, fisheries oceanography program; rschr. Joint Tsunami Rsch. Effort, 1973-77; dir. Nat. Tsunami Warning Ctr., 1977-80, Pacific Marine Environ. Lab., Seattle, 1982—, chmn. Nat. Tsunami Hazard Mitigation Program, 1997—2004. Exec. com. Coop. Inst. for Marine Resource Studies and adv. bd. for Coll. of Oceanic and Atmospheric Sci., Oreg. State U., 2002—; adminstrv. bd. Joint Inst. Marine and Atmospheric Rsch. U. Hawaii; mem. adminstrv. bd. Joint Inst. for the Study Atomsphere and Oceans, U. Wash.; mem. Washington Sea Grant Steering Com., 1987-2003; sci. coun. Joint Inst. for Marine Observations, Scripps Instn. of Oceanography, 1992—; exec. com. Cooperative Inst. Arctic Rsch. U. Alaska; advisor Japan Agy. for Marine-Earth Sci. and Tech., 2000—; head US del. first, second and third meetings internat. coordinating group Indian Ocean Tsunami Warning Sys.; affiliate prof. U. Wash. Editor: Tsunami Hazard: A Practical Guide for Tsunami Hazard Reduction, 1991, Developing Tsunami Resilient Communities, 2005; contbr. articles to profl. jours. Named Best of New Generation award, Esquire Mag., 1984; recipient Meritorious Presdl. Rank award, Pres. Clinton, 1993, Pres. G.W. Bush, 2002, Gold medal, US Dept. Commerce, 2004, 2005, Tsunami Soc. award, 2006. Mem. Am. Meteorological Soc., Internat. Union of Geodesy and Geophysics (chmn. Tsunami commn. 1987-95), Am. Geophys. Union, Oceanography Soc. Office: Pacific Marine Environ Lab 7600 Sand Point Way NE Seattle WA 98115-6349 Business E-Mail: eddie.n.bernard@noaa.gov.

BERNARD, JOHN MARLEY, lawyer, educator; b. Phila., Feb. 6, 1941; s. Edward and Opal (Marley) B.; children: John Marley Jr., Kendall M., Katherine M., James M.; m. Esther L. von Laue, May 31, 1986. BA, Swarthmore Coll., 1963; LLB, Harvard U., 1967. Bar: Pa. 1967. Assoc. Montgomery McCracken Walker & Rhoads, Phila., 1967-73, ptnr., 1973-86, Ballard Spahr Andrews & Ingersoll, LLP, Phila., 1986—. Lectr. Temple U. Law Sch., Phila., 1975-95; instr. Phila. Acad. for Employee Benefits Tng., 1996-99; guest instr. U.S. Dept. Labor, Washington, 1984-96; instr. U. Pa. Wharton Sch., Phila., 1989-90. Contbg. author: Handbook of Employee Benefits, 1989. Mem. ABA, Pa. Bar Assn. Office: Ballard Spahr Andrews & Ingersoll LLP 1735 Market St Fl 51 Philadelphia PA 19103-7599 E-mail: bernard@ballardspahr.com.

BERNARD, LAWRENCE B., lawyer; b. Rockville Centre, NY, June 13, 1948; BA, Cornell U., 1970; JD, Harvard U., 1973. Bar: DC 1973, US Dist. Ct, DC 1979, US Ct. Appeals (2nd cir.) 1987, US Supreme Ct. 1989, Md. 1991, US Ct. Appeals, Fed. Cir. 1992, US Dist. Ct., Md. 1992, US Ct. Appeals (4th cir.) 1994, Va. 1996, US Dist. Ct. 1997, Va. (ea. dist.) 1997. Atty. FTC, 1974—87; ptnr. Comml. Litig. and Advt. Law Depts. Venable LLP, Washington, DC. Instr. FTC-NITA Trial Advocacy and Deposition Prog., 1980—87; assoc. profl. lectr. in law George Washington U., 1989—91. Mem.: ABA, Va. Bar Assn., DC Bar Assn., Md. State Bar Assn. Office: Venable LLP 575 7th St NW Washington DC 20004 Office Phone: 202-344-4854. Office Fax: 202-344-8300. E-mail: lbbernard@venable.com.

BERNARD, LOUIS JOSEPH, surgeon, educator; b. Laplace, La., Aug. 19, 1925; s. Edward and Jeanne (Vinet) B.; m. Lois Jeannette McDonald, Feb. 1, 1976; children: Marie Antonia, Phyllis Elaine. BA magna cum laude, Dillard U., New Orleans, 1946; MD, Meharry Med. Coll., 1950. Diplomate: Am. Bd. Surgery. Instr. surgery Sch. Medicine, Meharry Med. Coll., Nashville, 1958-59, prof., 1973-90, chmn. dept. surgery, 1973-87, dean, 1987-90, v.p. for health svcs., 1988-90; practice medicine specializing in surgery, 1959-69; mem. clin. faculty U. Okla., 1959-69, assoc. prof., vice chmn. dept. surgery, 1969-73, chmn. dept. surgery, 1973-87, disting. prof. emeritus, 1990—. Dir. Drew-Meharry Morehouse Consortium Cancer Ctr., 1990-96. Contbr. articles in field to profl. jours. Mem. Okla. State Bd. Corrections, 1968-69. With M.C. U.S. Army, 1951-53. USPHS research fellow NCI, U. Rochester, 1953-54 Fellow ACS, Southeastern Surg. Congress; mem. Soc. Surg. Oncology, Internat. Surg. Soc., Am. Assn. Cancer Edn., Alpha Omega Alpha. Democrat. Roman Catholic. Home: 156 Queens Ln Nashville TN 37218-1826

BERNARD, LOWELL FRANCIS, retired academic administrator, educator; b. Long Beach, Calif., Dec. 14, 1931; s. Francis Montgomery and Irma Viola (Phillips) B.; m. Diana Gypson, June 15, 1957; children: Deborah Diana Bernard North, Steven Lowell, Jocelyn Dawn Bernard Jablonski. BA in Microbiology, UCLA, 1955, MS in Pub. Health and Pre Medicine, 1959. Registered sanitarian, Calif. Instr. pub. health edn. UCLA, 1955-59; asst. dir. Heart and Tb Assn., Poughkeepsie, NY, 1959-60; instr. Dutchess Community Coll., Poughkeepsie, 1960-66; dir. edn. Cleve. Health Edn. Mus., 1966-69, exec. dir., 1969-88; adj. asst. prof. Med. Sch. Case Western Res. U., Cleve., 1969-83, adj. asst. prof. pediatrics, 1985-89, dir. Cleve. Health Edn. Project, 1989-97, adj. asst. clin. prof. family medicine, 1990-99, rsch. cons., 1997-98; ret., 1999. Adminstr. Case Western Res. U. Urban Area Health Edn. Ctr., 1991-97; internat. cons. to mus., 1969-2000; speaker, media appearances in field. Author profl. publs. Bd. dirs. Cleve. chpt. Epilepsy Found. Am., 1972-76; trustee Doan's Ctr. Inc., Retinal Vascular Found., 1984-89; mem. men's coun. Gibbs Mus.; bd. dirs. Kiawah Naturalist Conservancy. Recipient Outstanding Service to City award City of Cleve., 1972; fellow in pub. health Case Western Res. U. Med. Sch., 1985-97. Mem. WHO (cons. Internat. Union of Health Edn.), Am. Alliance for Health, Phys. Edn., Recreation and Dance, Am. Assn. Health and Med. Mus. (v.p. 1971-73, pres. 1973-75), Assn. Sci. and Tech. Ctrs. (bd. dirs. 1976-83, sec.-treas. 1978-83, program chmn. 1979), Am. Assn. Mus. (program chmn. nat. meeting 1979, mus. assessment program evaluator 1982-89, mem. mus. accreditation team 1983-89), Aesculapian Soc., Am. Pub. Health Assn., Cleve. Acad. Medicine (hon.), Am. Soc. Sex Educators, Therapists and Counselors (cert. sex educator), Mid-West Mus. Conf., Ohio Mus. Assn., Greater Cleve. Growth Assn., Kiawah-Seabrook Exch. Club. Republican. Presbyterian. Avocations: sports, travel. Home: 13102 Muir Dr NW Gig Harbor WA 98332

BERNARD, MICHAEL MARK, lawyer, city planning consultant; b. NYC, Sept. 5, 1926; s. H.L. and Henryetta (Siegel) B.; m. Laura Jane Pincus, Aug. 28, 1958; 1 dau., Daphne Michelle. AB, U. Chgo., 1949; JD, Northwestern U., 1953; MCity Planning, Harvard U., 1959. Bar: Ill. 1952, U.S. Dist. Ct. (no. dist.) Ill. 1953, N.Y. 1955, U.S. Ct. Appeals (1st cir.) 1956. Pvt. practice law, Chgo. and NYC, 1953-55; rsch. asst. Law Sch. Harvard U., 1955-56; city planning cons., atty.-adviser Puerto Rico, 1956-58; rsch. atty. Model Laws Project Am. Bar Found., 1959-60; city planner, legal adviser Chgo. Dept. City Planning, 1960-64; cons. planning and land regulation, 1964—; cons. Chgo. Area Transp. Study, 1964-65; mem. exec. faculty Boston Archtl. Ctr., 1967—. Adv. to Gov.'s Exec. Office on reorgn. Commonwealth Mass., 1968-72; chmn. 1st Nat. Transp. Needs Study Mass.; cons. A.I.A. Rsch. Corp., 1974; cons. Mass. Atty. Gen., 1981—; mem. com. urban devel. and housing World Peace Through Law Ctr., 1965—; mem. com. transp. law transp. research bd. NRC-NAS, 1966—; cons. White House Policy Adv. Com. to D.C., 1966; del. World Congress Housing and Planning, Paris, France, 1962, Tokyo, Japan, 1966; fellow Ctr. Advanced Visual Studies, M.I.T.; prin. investigator Northwestern U. Transp. Ctr.; lectr. in field; vis. prof. urban and regional planning U. Iowa, 1969-70; vis. lectr. Harvard U., MIT, U. Mich.; mem. faculty Am. Law Inst., 1978—. Author: Constitutions, Taxation and Land Policy, 2 vols., 1979-80, Airspace in Urban Development, 1963; co-editor: Policy Studies Jour.; editor, pub.: Reflections on Space; revision project mgr.: Constitutional Uniformity & Equality in State Taxation, 2 vols., 1984, Transformation of Property Rights in the "Space Age", 1993, (U.S. Govt. manual) Transportation Planning for Small Cities, 1973; spl. editor: Urban Law Ann. Washington U. Sch. Law; columnist: Jour. Real Estate Devel.; bd. editors: Real Estate Fin.; contbr. articles to profl. jours. Patron Hull House Assn., Chgo., 1965; v.p., trustee Cambridge Community Art Ctr., 1971-73; mem. standing com. Unitarian Ch.; mem. founding site com. Mus. Contemporary Art, Chgo. With USN, 1944-46. Recipient cert. of commendation for teaching Boston Archtl. Ctr., 1984; grantee NRC-NAS, 1964-66. Fellow Lincoln Inst. Land Policy; mem. ABA (land use, planning and zoning com., chmn. T.D.R. subcom. 1984-89, air and space com.), Internat. Fedn. Housing and Planning, Am. Arbitration Assn. (cert., bldg. and constrn. arbitrator),Am. Soc. Pub. Adminstrn., Policy Studies Orgn., Am. Planning Assn. (chmn. legis. com. Met. Chgo. sect. 1963-65, Mass. state reporter planning and law div. 1990—), Boston Soc. Architects (affiliate), Nat. Space Soc. (bd. dirs., space law com. Boston chpt.), Am. Underground Space Assn., Internat. Ctr. for Land Policy Studies, Urban Affairs Assn. (jour. rev. editor), Am. Crafts Coun., Mass. Assn. Craftsmen (v.p. 1975-78). Boston Visual Artists Union (hon., sec.-gen. 1971-72), New England Poetry Club (life), U. Chgo. Club Boston (bd. dirs.), Boston Athenaeum (life, dir. Poetry program). *It seems to me that man's random, specialized intervention in the universe will prove to be the most constant cause for concern in the future. The problem might be seen not so much as how to keep the earth whole, but as how man may keep whole himself: this remains the role and strength of creative, intuitive endeavor, the source of everything I find of true value. Hopefully, ours will not become the "Age of the Idiot Savant".*

BERNARD, PAMELA JENKS, lawyer; b. Montgomery, Ala., Nov. 27, 1955; d. Harford Perry and Mable (Sawyer) Jenks; m. Geoffrey Pedrick Bernard, Sept. 19, 1981. BA, U. Fla., 1976, JD, 1981. Bar: Fla. 1982, U.S. Dist. Ct. (mid. dist.) Fla. 1983, U.S. Ct. Appeals (11th cir.) 1983. Asst. atty. U. Fla., Gainesville, 1982-83, assoc. gen. counsel, 1983-87, gen. counsel, 1987—2006; v.p., gen. counsel Duke U., Durham, NC, 2006—. Pvt. investment trustee, Gainesville, 1976-83. Mem. Nat. Assn. Coll. and Univ. Attys. (former pres.). Office: Duke U Office of Univ Counsel Box 3024 Med Ctr Durham NC 27710 Office Phone: 919-684-3955. E-mail: pamela.bernard@duke.edu.

BERNARD, RICHARD LAWSON, retired geneticist, educator; b. Detroit, Aug. 12, 1926; s. Clarence Rolla and Ilda Gentry (Lawson) B.; m. Ruth V. Thorne, June 14, 1952 (div. 1975); children: Betty Ruth Marnell, Richard Thorne, Alice Jean, Daniel Lawson. Student, U. Mich., Ann Arbor, 1943—45, Okla. State U., Stillwater, 1947—48; BS, Ohio State U., Columbus, 1949, MS, 1950; PhD, NC State U., Raleigh, 1960. Research geneticist USDA, Urbana, Ill., 1954-88; prof. plant genetics U. Ill., Champaign, 1966-92, prof. emeritus, 1992—. Served with USAF, 1945-47. Baptist. Office: U Ill Crop Scis Dept 1101 Peabody Dr Urbana IL 61801 Office Phone: 217-333-7279. Business E-Mail: rbernard@uiuc.edu.

BERNARD, RICHARD PHILLIP, lawyer; b. Chgo., May 29, 1950; s. Martin Joseph Jr. and Ruth (Hadka) B.; m. Svetlana Shoutova; children: Rachel, Benjamin, Alex. BA, Mich. State U., 1972; JD, NYU, 1976; M of Pub. Affairs, Princeton U., 1976; grad. Advanced Mgmt. Program, Harvard U., 1998. Bar: N.Y. 1977. Assoc. Milbank, Tweed, Hadley & McCloy, NYC, 1976-84, ptnr., 1985-94; exec. v.p., gen. counsel New York Stock Exchange, NYC, 1996—; exec. dir., resource sec. Russian Securities Commn., Moscow, 1995. Participating atty. Legal Aid Soc. Community Law Offices, N.Y.C., 1977-80; mem. internat. legal adv. com. Cairo Stock Exchange, 2001—. Mem. ABA (banking and bus. sects., com. on fed. regulation of securities). Democrat. Avocations: russia, carpentry. Office: New York Stock Exchange 11 Wall St New York NY 10005-1905

BERNARD, ROBERT WILLIAM, plastic surgeon; b. NYC, Aug. 18, 1942; Student, U. Mich., 1959-60; BA in Zoology with honors, U. Vt., 1963, MD cum laude, 1967. Diplomate Am. Bd. Surgery, Am. Bd. Plastic Surgery. Intern U. Pa. Hosp., Phila., 1967-68; resident in gen. surgery NYU Med. Ctr., 1968-72, resident in plastic surgery, 1972-74; asst. prof. plastic surgery NYU Med. Sch., 1972—86; chief plastic surgery No. Westchester Hosp., Mt. Kisco, NY, 1982-87, 96—, White Plains (NY) Hosp., 1979-86, United Hosp., Port Chester, NY, 1986-94. Author, editor: book Aesthetic Restoration of the Aging Face, 1997; editor: Aesthetic Surg. Jour., 1993—98; contbr. articles to profl. jours. Fellow: ACS; mem.: AMA (Recognition award 1983, 1984, 1986, 1988, 1990, 1992, 1995, 1998, 2001, 2004), Am. Cancer Soc., Westchester County Med. Soc., NY Regional Soc. Plastic and Reconstructive Surgery (chair sci. program com. 1984—85, pres. 1986—87, mem. exec. com. 1987—88), NY State Med. Soc. (pres. plastic surgery sect. 1983—84), Am. Soc. Aesthetic Plastic Surgery (pres. 2003—04). Office: 10 Chester Ave White Plains NY 10601-5112 also: 91 Smith Ave Mount Kisco NY 10549-2810 Office Phone: 914-761-8667.

BERNARD, ROBERT WILLIAM, language educator, theology studies educator, humanities educator; m. Mary Ella Gibson, Feb. 12, 1972; 1 child, Helen Margaret. BA, Princeton U., NJ, 1969; MDiv, Princeton Theol. Sem., NJ, 1979; PhD, Princeton U., NJ, 1984. Rsch. asst. Rev. Std. Bible Com., Princeton, 1984—87; scholar in residence Southwestern Bapt. Theol. Sem., Fort Worth, Tex., 1987—88, instr. langs., 1988—91, assoc. prof., 1992—; lectr. philosophy U. North Tex., Denton, 1989—91. Adj. instr. German, French Brite Div. Sch., Ft. Worth, 2000—. Author: (article) Biblical Hermeneutics in Historical Perspective, Biblical Hermeneutics: A Comprehensive Introduction to Interpreting Scripture, 2002. Spl. agt. US Army, 1971—73, Germany. Mem.: Phi Beta Kappa. Home: 4408 Alta Mesa Blvd Fort Worth TX 76133 Office Phone: 817-923-1921 ext.6650. Office Fax: 817-921-8760. Business E-Mail: bbernard@swbts.edu.

BERNARD, STEPHEN ALAN, oncologist; b. High Point, NC, 1947; MD, U. N.C., 1973. Diplomate Am. Bd. Internal Medicine, Am. Acad. Internal Medicine, am. Bd. Oncology. Intern Colum-Presbyn. Med. Ctr., 1973-74, resident in medicine, 1974-76; fellow in hematol. oncology Washington U. Hosps., St. Louis, 1976-78; mem. staff U. N.C. Hosp., Chapel Hill, 1981—; assoc. prof. U. N.C. Sch. Medicine, Chapel Hill, 1990—. Mem. ACP, Am. Soc. Clin. Oncology. Office: U NC Sch Medicine Cb # 7305 Chapel Hill NC 27599-0001

BERNARD, SUSAN SHATTUCK, retired secondary school educator; b. Cambridge, Mass., Sept. 12, 1945; d. Kenneth Elton and Phyllis Shattuck; m. Robert Allen Scott, Dec. 27, 1968 (div. 1973); 1 child, Kenneth Charles Scott; m. Wilbert Bernard, Jr., July 10, 2005. BS in Edn., Boston State Coll., 1967; M in Math., Worcester Poly. Inst., 1990. Cert. secondary math. tchr., Mass. Tchr. South Jr. H.S., Weymouth, Mass., 1967-73; editor Houghton-Mifflin Co., Boston, 1973-74; tchr. Ctrl. Jr. H.S., Weymouth, 1974-81, South H.S., Weymouth, 1981-90, Weymouth H.S./Vocat. Tech. H.S., 1990—2002; ret., 2002. Freelance editor Houghton Mifflin, Boston, 1974-75. Treas. Singles' Group, Duxbury Bapt. Ch., 1976-78, Stone Village Condo. Assn., Wareham, Mass., 1993-. Mem. Nat. Coun. Tchrs. Math. Avocations: walking, swimming, reading, gardening, cooking. Home: PO Box 138 Colebrook NH 03576 Personal E-mail: sspeace@msn.com.

BERNARD, WILBERT AUGUSTER, JR., retired school system administrator; b. Boston, Jan. 21, 1946; s. Wilbert Auguster Bernard and Josephine Edna Patrice; m. Susan Shattuck Scott, July 10, 2005; m. Judith Ann Gaines, July 13, 1974 (dec. Feb. 2004); children: Douglas Matthew, Tamara Angela. BA in Philosophy, St. Joseph's Coll., Washington, 1970; MA in History, Bridgewater State Coll., Mass., 1976. Cert. secondary adminstrn. Mass., 1987. Tchr. history South Jr. HS, Wey. Mass., 1971—87; asst. prin. Wey South HS, 1987—90, Abigail Adams Mid. Sch., Wey, 1991—94; asst. prin. Milton HS, Mass., 1994—2005; ret. Recipient Martin Luther King Citizen of Yr., Town of Wyemouth, 1994, Cmty. Builder Award, Celebrate Milton Orgn., 1998. Mem.: Mass. Ret. Tchrs. Avocations: reading, art, films, weightlifting, martial arts. Home: PO Box 138 Colebrook NH 03576

BERNARDI, ROY A. (ROMOLO ALBERT BERNARDI), federal agency administrator; b. Syracuse, NY; m. Alice Bernardi; children: Dante, Bianca. AA, Onondaga C.C., 1964; B in Internat. Rels., U. Americas, Mexico City, 1966; M in Guidance and Counseling, Syracuse U., 1972. Spanish tchr. Liverpool High Sch., Syracuse, guidance counselor, 1971-73; auditor City of Syracuse, 1973-93, mayor, 1993—2001; asst. sec. community planning & devel. US Dept. H.U.D., Washington, 2001—04, dep. sec., 2004—. Bd. dirs. Eye Rsch. Found. of Ctrl. N.Y.; former trustee Leukemia Soc. of Am., Syracuse chpt.; hon. chmn. Big Brother/Big Sister Orgn., Am. Diabetes Assn. of Ctrl. N.Y.; chmn. exec. com. Syracuse Symphony. Avocations: cooking, reading. Office: US Dept HUD 451 7th St SW Rm 10100 Washington DC 20410-9000

BERNARDIN, JAMIE, information technology executive; BS in Engring. Physics, Applied Math., Brown Univ., MSEE, PhD in Engring. Physics. Rsch. fellow NASA; with Bank of America, Risk Mgmt. Tech.;

adv. strategies, rsch. group Barclays Global Investors; founder DataSynapse Inc., NYC. Named one of Top 25 Chief Tech. Officers, InfoWorld mag., 2007. Office: DataSynapse Inc 632 Broadway New York NY 10012 Office Phone: 212-842-8842.

BERNARDIN, THOMAS L., advertising executive; Grad., Hillsdale Coll. Acct. dir. McCann-Erickson, Detroit, McCann-Erickson Europe; sr. v.p., dir. internat. ops. Campbell-Mithum-Esty Advt., Southfield, Mich., 1988—90, exec. v.p., mgmt. dir., 1990—92, pres., 1992—94, Bozell/North (formerly Campbell-Mithum-Esty Advt.), 1994—97; exec. v.p., gen. mgr. Bozell, NYC, 1997, pres., CEO; pres., COO Lowe US, NYC, 2003, pres., CEO, 2003—04; CEO Leo Burnett USA, 2004—05; pres. Leo Burnett Worldwide, 2004—05, chmn., CEO, 2005—. Bd. dirs. Lake Forest Hosp., Chgo., 2006—. David Rockefeller fellow, 2002. Mem.: Am. Advt. Fedn. (mem. exec. com., chair corp. mems.), Found. Fighting Blindness (trustee). Office: Leo Burnett Worldwide Inc 35 W Wacker Dr Chicago IL 60601 Office Phone: 312-220-5959. Office Fax: 312-220-3299.*

BERNARDINO, CARLO ROBERTO, ophthalmologist, educator; b. Manilla, Philippines, July 15, 1971; s. Vitaliano B. and Evelina Abuel Bernardino. Student, U. Alicante, Spain, 1991—91; BA in Biology, Lehigh U., 1993; MD, Jefferson Med. Coll., 1997. Lic. Ga., 2003, cert. Am. Bd. Ophthalmology, 2003. Intern Crozer-Chester Med. Ctr., Upland, Pa., 1997—98; resident in ophthalmology Wills Eye Hosp., Phila., 1998—2001, chief resident, 2000—01; oculoplastics fellow Mass. Eye and Ear Infirmary, Boston, 2001—03; asst. prof. Emory U. Sch. Medicine, 2003—. Contbr. chapters to books, articles to profl. jours.; reviewer (manuscript) Lippincott, Williams, and Wilkins, 2000—, Am. Jour. Ophthalmology, 2002. Grantee Bausch & Lomb Young Investigator Travel grant, Contact Lens Assn. of Opthamologists, 2000, 2001; Grant, Schepens Eye Rsch. Inst., 2002—03. Fellow: Am. Acad. Ophthalmology; mem.: Am. Med. Assn. (Physician Recognition award 2001—04), Ga. Soc. Ophthalmology. Office: 1365 B Clifton Rd NE Rm 4513 Atlanta GA 30303 Office Phone: 404-778-4144. Business E-Mail: crbernardino@mac.com.

BERNARDO, ANGELITO ALDAY, nephrologist, medical products executive; s. Angel Domingo Bernardo and Leonile Guballa Alday; m. Elnore Manalo Bernardo, Dec. 15, 1982; children: Christian, Carl Emmanuel. BS in Zoology, U. Philippines, Manila, 1976, MD, 1981. Diplomate Am. Bd. Internal Medicine, cert. in internal medicine, in nephrology. Staff physician Cook County Hosp., Chgo., 1991—2005, U. Ill. Hosps., 1991—2006; dir. renal clinic Jesse Brown VA Med. Ctr., 1998—2006, dir. dialysis unit, 1998—2006, dir. nephrology and hypertension, 2001—06; dir. global clinical, med., and sci. affairs Baxter, McGaw Park, 2006—. Asst. prof. medicine, 1995—; cons. Chgo. Cons. Physicians, 1998—2005, Ill. Found. Quality, 2002—05; spkr. and advisor Novartis. Editor profl. publs.; contbr. articles to profl. jours. Mem. adv. bd. Nat. Kidney Found., 2004—; dir. Give Care, Chgo., 2005. Grantee, Hoesct, 1992, Nat. Kidney Found., 1992, Wyeth Ayerst, 1993, Nat. Kidney Found., 1994, 1999, VA Merit, 2001, Merck, 2001—02, NIH, 2004, Am. Heart Assn., 2005, Amgen, 2005. Fellow: ACP, Am. Soc. Nephrology; mem.: Am. Soc. Internal Medicine, Am. Heart Assn., Internat. Soc. Nephrology. Avocations: reading, writing, travel, music. Office: Baxter Internat 1629 Waukegan Rd Mc Gaw Park IL 60085 Business E-Mail: aabernar_@uic.edu, angelito_bernardo@boxter.com.

BERNAT, JAMES LAWRENCE, neurologist, educator; b. Cin., May 23, 1947; s. Mitchell Joseph and Ruth Claire (Betagole) B.; m. Judith Elaine Lenzner, June 8, 1969; children: Deborah Eden, David Clare. BA, U. Mass., Amherst, 1969; MD, Cornell U., NYC, 1973. Diplomate Nat. Bd. Med. Examiners, 1974, Am. Bd. Psychiatry and Neurology., 1978. Resident in medicine Dartmouth-Hitchcock Med. Ctr., Hanover, NH, 1973-74, resident in neurology, 1974-77, staff neurologist Lebanon, 1995—, assoc. chmn. neurology sect., 1999—2002; staff neurologist VA Med. Ctr., White River Junction, Vt., 1977-94; prof. medicine Dartmouth Med. Sch., Hanover, 1991—, asst. dean, 1995—99, dir. program in med. ethics, 1995—. Author: Neurology: Problems in Primary Care, 1987, 2d edit., 1993, Ethical Issues in Neurology, 1994, 2d edit., 2002; editor (editl. bd.): Neurocritical Care; co-editor: Palliative Care in Neurology, 2004. Bd. dirs. Vt. Ethics Network, Montpelier, 1995-2000, New Eng. Organ Bank, 1999-2006, Hospice V.N.H., 1999-2002; mem. Dana Alliance Brain Initiatives. Fellow ACP, Am. Acad. Neurology (chair ethics, law & humanities com. 1993-03, exec. bd. 1993-97), Am. Neurological Assn. Office: Neurology Sect Dartmouth-Hitchcock Med Ctr Lebanon NH 03756 Office Phone: 603-650-5104. Business E-Mail: bernat@dartmouth.edu.

BERNATH, JOHN CHARLES, JR., electronics engineer; b. Pitts., Dec. 20, 1943; s. John Charles Bernath and Ethel Marie Smith; m. Dorothy Marie Lavers, June 4, 1988; children: Carolyn Marie O'Brien, Michael Christopher, Judith Ann Kimmell, John Francis, Laura Jean Becht. AAS in Electronics Tech., DeVry Inst. Tech., Chgo., 1963; BS in Elec. Engring., U. Colo., Colorado Springs, 1971. Registered profl. engr., Colo., 1972, Ariz., 1982, Calif., 1993, cert. quality engr., Am. Soc. Quality, 1993, reliability engr., Am. Soc. Quality, 1994. Sr. tech. aide Bell Tel. Labs. Inc., Columbus, Ohio, 1963—68; test engr. Hewlett-Packard Inc., Colorado Springs, Colo., 1968—76; reliability assurance mgr. TRW Colo. Electronics Inc., Colorado Springs, 1976—81; quality assurance mgr. Motorola Govt. Electronics Group, Scottsdale, Ariz., 1981—92; lead reliability engr. I-Bus PC Technologies Divsn. Maxwell Labs., San Diego, 1992—94, Applied Digital Access Inc., San Diego, 1994—99, JNI Corp., San Diego, 1999—2001; sr. prin. elec. engr. Orbital Sciences Corp., Chandler, Ariz., 2002—05. Mem. profl. engr. exam com. Calif. Bd. Registration Profl. Engrs., Sacramento, 1994—98; cons. reliability specialist; assoc. mem. Com. Skeptical Inquiry. Contbr. scientific papers, articles to profl. jours. Pres., dir. San Diego North County Bluegrass & Folk Music Assn., Escondido, Calif., 1994—98; dir. Ariz. Bluegrass Assn., Phoenix, 1988—91. Named MVP, Del Mar Fair Bluegrass Dobro, 1999; recipient 2d pl., Julian Lions Club Bluegrass Banjo Contest, 1992, 3d pl., 1995. Mem.: NRA, Am. Soc. Quality (edn. com. mem. 1997—2000, mem. certification exam com. 1996—99), Profl. Engrs. Colo. (licentiate; pres. 1975—76), Am. MENSA (corr.), Am. Radio Relay League (licentiate mem. DX Century Club 1999, 2000). Libertarian. Achievements include development of use of Weibull analysis to determine optimum equipment burn-in cycles; design of method to determine IC die bond integrity by measuring thermal resistance; research in highly accelerated life testing of electronic equipment; reliability prediction of electronic and electromechanical equipment using statistical methodology. Avocations: amateur radio, music, fishing, target shooting. Personal E-mail: w6qo@arrl.net.

BERNATOWICZ, FRANK ALLEN, management consultant; b. Chgo., Nov. 3, 1954; s. Chester and Pauline (Maciula) B.; m. Kathleen Ann Carlson, Apr. 29, 1978; children: Amy Elizabeth, Laura Ann. BSEE, U. Ill., 1976; MBA in Fin., Loyola U., Chgo., 1981, postgrad. in acctg., 1982-84. Registered profl. engr., Ill.; CPA, Ill. Engr. Commonwealth Edison Co., Chgo., 1976—79, gen. engr., 1979—82, prin. engr., 1982—84; sr. cons. Brenner Group, Chgo., 1984—85; supr. Ernst & Young (formerly Ernst & Whinney), Chgo., 1985, mgr., 1985—86; sr. mgr. Ernst & Young, Chgo., 1986—88, ptnr., 1989—96; prin. J. Alix & Assoc., Chgo., 1996—99; ptnr. PricewaterhouseCoopers, Chgo., 1999—2001, BDO Seidman, Chgo., 2001—03; mng. prin. FAB Adv. Svcs., LLC, Chgo., 2003—06; mng. dir. Huron Consulting Group, Chgo., 2006—; mng. prin. FAB Group, Inc. Spkr. in field. Mem. bd. regents Mercy Boys Home, 1990—. Mem. ABA (assoc.), AICPA, Am. Bankruptcy Inst., Ill. Soc. CPAs, Nat. Soc. Profl. Engrs., Turnaround Mgmt. Assn., Comml. Law League, Am. Bankruptcy Inst., Chgo. Soc. Clubs (Met.). Avocations: golf, racquetball, computers, investments. Home: 6543 Hillcrest Dr Burr Ridge IL 60527 Office: Huron Consulting Group 550 W Van Buren St Chicago IL 60607 Home Phone: 630-654-2179; Office Phone: 630-655-3474, 312-880-3075. Business E-Mail: fbernatowicz@huronconsultinggroup.com.

BERNBACH, JOHN LINCOLN, marketing professional; b. 1944; s. William Bernbach. Grad. polit. sci., Georgetown U. Trainee account mgmt., then v.p. account services Gilbert Advt., 1966-72; with DDB Needham Worldwide, Inc. (formerly Doyle Dane Bernbach), Paris, 1972-79, London, 1979-84, pres., chief exec. officer internat. div. NYC, 1984-86, pres., 1986-93, vice chmn., 1993-94; chmn., CEO The Bernbach Group, Inc., NYC, 1994—; gen. ptnr. Barnet-Bernbach-Carduner LLC, NYC, 2000—03; pres., COO, NTM, Inc., NYC, 2003—. Office: NTM Inc 32 E 57th St 10th Fl New York NY 10022

BERNDT, ELLEN GERMAN, lawyer; b. Schenectady, NY, 1953; BS, Denison U., 1975; JD, Capital U., 1984. Bar: Ohio 1984. Legal asst. Borden Chem. Inc., Columbus, Ohio, 1978-84, corp. atty., 1984-90, asst. sec., corp. atty., 1990-96; corp. sec., asst. gen. counsel Hexion Specialty Chem., Inc. (formerly known as Borden Chem. Inc.), 1996—. Mem.: Ctrl. Ohio Corp. Counsel Assn. (pres. 1997), Soc. Corp. Sec. and Goverance Profls., Assn. Corp. Coun. Office: Hexion Specialty Chemicals Inc 180 E Broad St Columbus OH 43215-3799

BERNDT, ERNST RUDOLF, economist, educator; b. Crespo, Entre Rios, Argentina, Apr. 13, 1946; came to U.S., 1949; s. Markus William and Charlotte Marie (Zimmerman) B.; m. Martha Ann Mirly, June 10, 1967 (div. 1982); children: Jeffery, Nathan; m. Joan Margaret Curran, May 15, 1994. BA with honors, Valparaiso U., 1968; MS., U. Wis., 1971, PhD, 1972; PhD (hon.), Uppsala U., 1991. Staff economist Exec. Office of the Pres. U.S. Govt., Washington, 1971-72; asst. prof. U. (Vancouver) B.C., Can., 1973-78, assoc. prof., 1978-80; prof. applied econs. MIT, Cambridge, Mass., 1980—. Dir. program on technol. progress and productivity measurement Nat. Bur. Econ. Rsch., Cambridge; rsch. assoc. Nat. Bur. Econ. Rsch., Cambridge, 1980—; acad. affiliate Analysis Group, Inc., Belmont, Mass., 1985—. Contbr. profl. articles. Most cited economist under age 40 in 1985. Mem. Am. Econ. Assn., Econometric Soc., Conf. Rsch. in Income and Wealth. Independent. Lutheran. Office: MIT Sloan Sch of Mgmt 50 Memorial Dr # E52 452 Cambridge MA 02142-1347 E-mail: eberndt@mit.edu.

BERNE, BRUCE J., chemistry professor; BS, Bklyn. Coll., 1961; PhD (NASA fellow, NSF fellow), U. Chgo., 1964. NATO postdoctoral fellow U. Brussels, 1964-65; asst. prof. chemistry Columbia U., NYC, 1966—69, assoc. prof., 1969—72, prof., 1972—98, Higgins prof. chemistry, 1998—, chmn. dept. chemistry, 2002—05. Vis. prof. U. Tel Aviv, 1972-73, Sackler Disting. lectr., 1985, Miller Inst. U. Calif., Berkeley, 1993-94; vis. scientist IBM Thomas J. Watson Rsch. Labs., Yorktown, N.Y., 1990-92, 2000—; Reilly lectr. U. Notre Dame, 1998; Davidson lectr. U. Kans., 1998; Albert K. Moscowitz lectr. U. Minn., 2000; Moses Gomberg lectr. U. Mich., 2000; Joseph Hirschfelder lectr. U. Wis., Madison, 2001; Joe L. Franklin Meml. lectr. Rice U., 2003, W.E. Palke Lectr. U. Calif., Santa Barbara, 2007. Mem. editl. bd. Jour. Statis. Physics, 1976-79, Advances in Chem. Physics, 1984—, Jour. Phys. Chemistry, 1985-88, Jour. Chem. Physics, 1985-88, Chem. Physics Letters, 2000-02; assoc. editor Phys. Rev. Letters, 2000-03, Procs. of NAS, 2001-06, Jour. Chem. Theory and Computation. Recipient Alexander von Humboldt Found. award 1998, award in theoretical chemistry Am. Chem. Soc., 1995, Joseph O. Hirschfelder prize U. Wis., Joel Henry Hildebrand award Am. Chem. Soc., 2002; Alfred P. Sloan Found. fellow, 1968-71, John Simon Guggenheim Found. fellow, 1972-73. Fellow: AAAS, Am. Acad. Arts and Scis., Am. Phys. Soc.; mem.: Nat. Acad. Scis. Office: Dept Chemistry Columbia U MC 3103 3000 Broadway New York NY 10027-6941 Business E-Mail: bb8@columbia.edu.

BERNE, PATRICIA HIGGINS, psychologist, writer, educator; b. Indpls., Feb. 21, 1934; d. Edward Robert and Esther Josephine (Maschino) Higgins; m. John Henry Berne, June 19, 1957 (div. May 1979); children: Suzanne, Eve, Serena; m. Louis M. Savary, Oct. 11, 1992. Student, Am. U., 1970-72, George Washington U., 1974; MA, Goddard Coll., 1976; PhD, Union Inst., Cin., 1978. Lic. clin. psychologist, Washington. Counselor Campus Ministry Georgetown U., 1978-80; dir. Counseling Ctr. Trinity Coll., Washington, 1979-81; pvt. practice Washington, 1982—; pvt. practice, therapist The Life Ctr., Tampa, Fla., 1992—. Co-dir. Inner Devel. Assocs., Washington, 1990—, adj. prof., 1981—; adj. faculty at several colls. and univs., 1978—; lectr. at confs. internationally, 1980—; cons. DMA, Salem, Mass., 1984-89. Co-author: Prayerways, 1980, Building Self-Esteem in Children, 1981, Dreams and Spiritual Growth, 1984, Prayer Medicine, 1986, Kything, 1988, Dream Symbol Work, 1991. Mem. APA, ACA, Eye Movement Desentization and Reprocessing Internat. Assn., Assn. for Transpersonal Psychology, Inst. for Noetic Sci., DC Psychol. Assn., Am. Soc. Clin. Hypnosis. Roman Catholic. Avocations: travel, theater, mentoring, kayaking. Office: Inner Devel Assocs 3404 Ellenwood Ln Tampa FL 33618-3425 Office Phone: 813-494-0220. Personal E-mail: lousavary@yahoo.com.

BERNE, SUZANNE, writer, educator; b. Washington, 1961; married; children: Avery, Louisa. BA, Wesleyan Univ., Conn., 1982; grad., Iowa Writers' Workshop. Reporter New Haven Advocate; lectr., English, Am. History Harvard Univ. Author: (novels) A Crime in the Neighborhood, 1997 (Orange prize for fiction, Great Britain, 1999), A Perfect Arrangement, 2001, The Ghost at the Table, 2006. Recipient Nat. Endowment for Arts fellowship. Mailing: c/o Algonquin Books of Chapel Hill PO Box 2225 Chapel Hill NC 27515-2225

BERNER, ANDREW JAY, library director, writer; b. Bronx, NY, Apr. 5, 1952; s. Bernard and Phyllis (Stern) B. BA in History cum laude, Herbert H. Lehman Coll., 1974, MA in History, 1979; MS in Libr. and Info. Sci., Pratt Inst., 1982. Tchr. NYC Bd. Edn., NY, 1979-82; asst. libr. The Univ. Club Libr., NYC, 1982-84, assoc. libr., 1984-86, acting dir., 1986-87, dir., 1987-93, dir., curator of collections, 1993—. Co-founder, dir. OPL Resources, Ltd., 1984-99. Author: Time Management in the Small Library, 1987, (with Guy St. Clair) The Best of OPL, 1990, The Best of OPL II, 1997, Time Management in Libraries and Information Services, 1999, The University Club: An Architectural Celebration, 1999, Treasures of The University Club, 1999; author, editor The Illuminator, 1990—, The Univ. Club Libr. Quar., 1984-90; editor (newsletter) The One-Person Libr., 1984-98; contbr. articles to profl. jours. Fellow Spl. Librs. Assn. (chair, chair-elect mus., arts and humanities divsn. 1990-92, pres.-elect, pres. NY chpt. 1994-96, bylaws chair, pub. rels. chair, dir. awards); mem. Century Assn., Grolier Club. Office: The Univ Club Libr 1 W 54th St New York NY 10019-5404

BERNER, FREDERIC GEORGE, JR., lawyer; b. Washington, May 7, 1943; s. Frederic George and Florence Grace (Carlton) B.; m. Lorraine Anne Ouellette, Sept. 28, 1968; children: Frederic George, III, Christina Lorraine, Jennifer Jane. BA, Middlebury Coll., 1965; MBA, Am. U., 1970; JD, George Washington U., 1973. Bar: D.C. 1973, U.S. Dist. Ct. (D.C. dist.) 1973, U.S. Ct. Appeals (D.C. cir.) 1974, U.S. Ct. Appeals (4th cir.) 1977, U.S. Ct. Appeals (11th cir.) 1984, U.S. Ct. Appeals (10th cir.) 1994, U.S. Ct. Appeals (7th cir.) 2001, U.S. Supreme Ct. 1980. Econ. intelligence officer CIA, Washington, 1965-67, 70; assoc. Sidley & Austin LLP, Washington, 1973-80; ptnr. Sidley Austin LLP, Washington, 1980—. Contbr. articles to profl. jours.; bd. editl. advisors Pub. Utilities Fortnightly, 1992-2000. Gen. counsel, bd. dirs. Washington chpt. Nat. Hemophilia Found., 1976—80. 1st lt. US Army, 1967—70. Mem.: ABA (mem. house dels. 2007—), Charitable Found. of Energy Bar Assn. (bd. dirs. 2004—06), Found. of Energy Law Jour. (bd. dirs. 2004—06), Natural Gas Roundtable, D.C. Bar, Energy Bar Assn. (bd. dirs. 2004—, pres. 2005—06, bd. dirs. 1990—93), Order of Coif. Republican. Presbyterian. Home: 7605 Glenbrook Rd Bethesda MD 20814-1319 Office: Sidley Austin LLP 1501 K St NW Washington DC 20005 Office Phone: 202-736-8232. Business E-Mail: fberner@sidley.com.

BERNER, LEO DE WITTE, JR., retired oceanographer; b. Pasadena, Calif., Feb. 11, 1922; s. Leo De Witte and Maude Alena (Wright) B.; m. Arvetta Jo Hankins, June 28, 1947; children: Jo Anne Berner Thomas, Ernestine Elizabeth Berner Ice. BA, Pomona Coll., 1943; MS, UCLA-Scripps Instn. Oceanography, 1952, PhD, 1957. Fishery biologist U.S. Fish and Wildlife Svc., La Jolla, Calif., 1957-58; asst. rsch. biologist Scripps Instn. Oceanography, La Jolla, Calif., 1958-60, acting curator marine invertebrates, 1960-61; vis. asst. prof. U. Oreg., Oreg. Inst. Marine Sci., 1961; asso. program dir. NSF, Washington, 1961-65; adminstrv. scientist Tex. A&M U., College Station, 1965-66, asso. prof., 1966-72; asst. dean Tex. A&M U. (Grad. Coll.), 1967-71, assoc. dean, 1971-84, dean, 1984-87, prof. oceanography, 1972-87, prof. emeritus, dean emeritus, 1987—. Vol. George Bush Presdl. Libr. Archives, 1990-2002. Served with USNR, 1943-47. Fellow AAAS; mem. Am. Soc. Limnology and Oceanography, Oceanographic Soc., Assn. Tex. Grad. Schs. (1st v.p. 1981-82, pres. 1982-83), Sigma Xi. Home: 514 Helen Greathouse Cir Midland TX 79707-6116 Personal E-mail: bunsen@suddenlink.net.

BERNER, MARY G., publishing executive; married; 4 children. BA, Coll. Holy Cross, Worcester, Mass. Divisional mgr. Working Women Mag.; publisher Success Mag.; advertising dir. TV Guide, 1989—94, sr. v.p., publisher, 1994; publisher Glamour Mag., 1994—97; v.p. Conde Nast Publications, Inc., 1997—99; pres., CEO Fairchild Publications, Inc., NYC, 1999—2006; pres. Fairchild Divsn., Conde Nast Publications, Inc., NYC, 2006—07; officer Conde Nast Publications, Inc., 2006—07; pres., CEO The Reader's Digest Assn., Inc., Pleasantville, NY, 2007—. Bd. dir. Magazine Publishers Am. Started a fundraising and mentoring program St. Pius V High Sch., South Bronx; bd. dir. Partnership for a Drug-Free Am. Named Publishing Exec. Yr., Advertising Age, 2004. Office: The Reader's Digest Assn Inc Reader's Digest Rd Pleasantville NY 10570-7000*

BERNER, ROBERT FRANK, managerial statistics educator, administrator; b. Cleve., Nov. 30, 1917; s. Frank Otto and Marie (Gideon) B.; m. Ruth Harriet Levis, Nov. 6, 1943 (dec. Jan. 2005); children: Robert Frank, Mary Elizabeth, John David, Jean Harriet (dec.). BS, U. Buffalo, 1939, MBA, 1948; PhD, U. Chgo., 1961. Tchr. Palmyra (N.Y.) H.S., 1939-41; instr. stats. U. Buffalo, 1946-48, acting chmn. dept., 1948-49; asst. dean U. Buffalo (Evening Coll.), 1949-52, asst. prof. stats., 1952-63; assoc. prof. dept. mgmt. sci. SUNY, Buffalo, 1963-65, prof. mgmt. sci. and ops. analysis, 1965-81, prof. emeritus, 1981—; pres. emeritus Ctr. of SUNY, Buffalo, 1983-85; chmn. MBA program com., 1976-81. Adj. prof. internat. exec. program, 1982-90, acting dean divsn. continuing edn., 1952-55, dean, 1955-76; Fulbright prof. Robert Coll., Istanbul, Turkey, 1968-69, U. Nairobi, Kenya, 1975-76 Chmn. adult edn. com. Cmty. Welfare Coun. Buffalo and Erie County, 1962-64; bd. dirs. Creative Edn. Found., 1969-89, emeritus trustee, 1990; bd. dirs. Ch. Mission Help Western N.Y., 1990-96, sec., 1992, treas., 1993-96; mem. Rep. Coun. and Fund. Mgmt. Adv. Com., Canterbury Woods, western N.Y., 1999-2003. Capt. F.A., 10th Mountain divsn. AUS, 1941-45. Decorated Bronze Star, Silver Star; named to Creative Problem Solving Inst. Hall of Fame, 2005. Mem. AAUP, Assn. Univ. Evening Colls. (past pres.), Nat. Univ. Extension Assn., Am. Coun. Edn., Assn. Continuing Higher Edn., Am. Assn. Univ. Adminstrs., Am. Soc. Tng. Dirs. (chpt. sec. 1952-56), Equality Club (pres. 1986-87), Theta Chi, Beta Gamma Sigma, Alpha Sigma Lambda (past nat. pres.) Episcopalian (warden Calvary Ch. 1973-74, 76-77, 86-88, treas. 1996-2000, mem. commn. ministry Diocese Western N.Y. 1971, 95—, chmn. commn. on continuing edn. 1974-76, diocesan coun. 1988-91, diocese planning and vision com. 1989-92). Home: 715 Renaissance Dr Apt 113 Williamsville NY 14221-8033 Personal E-mail: berbob1@yahoo.com.

BERNER, ROBERT LEE, JR., lawyer; b. Chgo., Dec. 9, 1931; s. Robert Lee and Mary Louise (Kenney) B.; m. Sheila Marie Reynolds, Jan. 12, 1957; children: Mary, Louise, Robert, Sheila, John. AB, U. Notre Dame, 1953; LL.B., Harvard U., 1956. Bar: Ill. 1956, NY 1989. With Petit, Olin, Overmyer & Fazio, Chgo., 1957—63, Baker & McKenzie, Chgo., 1963—; ptnr., 1964—2000; sr. counsel, 2000—. Mem. vis. com. Northwestern U. Law Sch., 1981-85; mem. legal adv. com. N.Y. Stock Exch., 1995-98. Mem. vis. com. U. Chgo. Div. Sch., 1972—, chmn., 2001—05; mem. legal aid com. Met. Family Svcs., Chgo., 1972—, chmn., 1991—93; mem. adv. bd. Cath. Charities, Chgo., 1971—, Loyola U., 1972—; mem. coun. Coll. Arts and Letters, U. Notre Dame, 2001—; trustee Cath. Theol. Union, Chgo., 1999—; bd. dirs. Link Unltd., Chgo., 1972—, pres., 1990—92; bd. dir. World Trade Ctr. of Chgo., 1989—. Mem. ABA (chmn. bus. law sect. 1987-88), Ill. State Bar Assn., Chgo. Bar Assn., Legal Club Chgo. (pres. 1974-75), Law Club Chgo. (pres. 1991-92). Home: 932 Euclid Ave Winnetka IL 60093-1418 Office Phone: 312-861-2890. Business E-Mail: robert.l.berner@bakernet.com.

BERNER, THOMAS FRANKLYN, lawyer; b. Freeport, NY, July 20, 1954; s. Howard Everett and Elizabeth Ann (Phelan) B.; m. Ariel Holdsworth, May 8, 1982. BA, U. Wis., 1976; JD, Columbia U., 1979. Bar: NY 1980, Calif. 1989, U.S. Dist. Ct. (so. dist.) NY 1981, U.S. Dist. Ct. (ea. dist.) NY 2002. Assoc. Dewey, Ballantine, Bushby, Palmer & Wood, NYC, 1979-91; of counsel Katten, Muchin & Zavis, NYC, 1991-96; ptnr. Katten, Muchin Zavis Rosenman, NYC, 1996—2004, 2005—06; sr. legal adv. Afghanistan Reconstrn. Group, Kabul, 2004—05; gen. counsel First Capital, West Palm Beach, Fla., 2006—. Author: The Brooklyn Navy Yard, 1999. Bd. dirs. High Ridge House, Riverdale, NY, 1992-2001. Harlan Fiske Stone scholar, 1979. Mem. Assn. Bar City N.Y., Nat. Arts Club, Phi Beta Kappa. Republican. Office: FCC LLC 515 N Flagler Dr Ste 700 West Palm Beach FL 33401 Office Phone: 561-623-1923. E-mail: tberner@firstcapital.com.*

BERNER-HARRIS, CYNTHIA KAY, library director; b. Concordia, Kans., Aug. 31, 1958; d. William Clifford and Donna Darlene (Brown) B.; m. Dwight Harris, May 1, 1999. AA, Cottey Coll., 1978; BA, U. Kans., 1980; MALS, U. Denver, 1981. Sys. cons. Panhandle Libr. Network, Scottsbluff, Nebr., 1981-82; dir. Winfield Pub. Libr., Kans., 1982-84; Westlink br. mgr. coord. ext. svcs. Wichita Pub. Libr., Kans., 1984-95, coord. adminstrv. svcs., 1995—2000, dir. libr., 2000—. Editor: (mag.) Propeller mag., 1995-96, (newsletter) LWV, Wichita Met., 1993. Pres. PEO Sisterhood (chpt. IM), Wichita, 1989—90; active Jr. League Wichita; project chair STARBASE, 1997—98, dir. cmty. rels., 1998—99; trustee-at-large Bibliog. Ctr. Rsch., 2001—05, exec. com., 2002—04; tech. adv. bd. City of Wichita, 2000—; fin. chair Nat. Conf. for Cmty. and Justice Walk, 2003; chmn. affiliates bd. Kans. Ctr. for Book, 2005—; mem. exec. com. Kans. Book Festival, 2006—. Mem.: ALA, Kans. Libr. Assn. (chair pub. libr. sect. 1988—89, legis. com. 1997—2001, nominating com. 1998—99, legis. com. 2002—05, govt. affairs com. 2005—07, chair govt. affairs com. 2006—07), Mountain Plains Libr. Assn. (leadership inst. com. 2007—, chair profl. devel. grants com. 1983—84, 1986—87, chair pub. libr. sect. 1988—89, chair intellectual freedom com. 1988—90, sec. 1996—97, nominating com. 1998—2000), Pub. Libr. Assn. (dir. pub. libr. sys. sect. 1995—98, dir. pub. libr. sys. com. 1998—2001). Presbyterian. Office: Wichita Pub Libr 223 S Main St Wichita KS 67202 Office Phone: 316-261-8500. E-mail: ictbooks@yahoo.com.

BERNERS-LEE, SIR TIMOTHY JOHN, inventor of world wide web, research scientist, writer; b. London, June 8, 1955; BA with honors, Queens

Coll., Oxford U., Eng., 1976; DFA (hon.), Parsons Sch. Design, NYC, 1996; DU (hon.), Essex U., 1998, So. Cross. U., 1998, Open U., 2000; DLaw (hon.), Columbia U., 2001; DSc (hon.), Southampton U., 1996, Oxford U., 2001, U. Port Elizabeth, 2001. With Plessey Telecom. Ltd., Dorset, England, 1976—78, D.G. Nash Ltd., Dorset, England, 1978—80; ind. cons. software engr. CERN, Geneva, 1980, fellow, 1984; tech. design cons. Image Computer Systems Ltd., 1981—84; dir. World Wide Web Consortium, Lab. Computer Sci. MIT, Cambridge, Mass., 1994—, 3Com Founders chair & sr. rsch. scientist, Lab. Computer Sci. & Artificial Intel. Lab. (merged Computer Sci. & Artificial Intelligence Lab. (CSAIL)), 1999—. Spkr. in field. Author: Weaving the Web, 1999; contbr. articles to profl. publications. Co-recipient Assn. Computing Machinery Software Sys. award, 1995, Prize for Sci. and Tech. Rsch., Prince of Asturias Found., 2002; named one of 100 Greatest Minds of the Century, 1999; named to Order of the British Empire, 1997; recipient Young Innovator of Yr., Kilby Found., 1995, hon. Prix Ars Electronica, 1995, IEEE Koji Kobayashi Computers and Comm. award, 1997, Duddell Medal, Inst. Physics, 1997, Disting. Svc. award, Interactive Svcs. Assn., 1997, MCI Computerworld/Smithsonian award for Leadership in Innovation, 1997, Columbus prize, Internat. Comm. Inst., 1997, Charles Babbage award, 1998, Mountbatten medal, Elec. Coun., 1998, Lord Lloyd of Kilgerran prize, Found. for Sci. and Tech., 1998, Lifetime Achievement award in Tech. Excellence, PC Mag., 1998, The Eduard Rhein Tech. award, 1998, World Tech. award for Comm. Tech., 1999, Paul Evan Peters award of ARL, Educause and CNI, 2000, Pioneer award, Elec. Freedom Found., 2000, George R. Stibitz Computer Pioneer award, Am. Computer Mus., 2000, Spl. award for Outstanding Contbn., World TV Forum, 2000, Sir Frank Whittle medal, Royal Acad. Engring., 2001, Japan prize, Sci. and Tech. Found. Japan, 2002, Albert medal, Royal Soc. for the Encouragement of Art, Manufactures and Commerce, 2002, Fellow award, Computer Hist. Mus., 2003, Millennium Tech. Prize, Finnish Tech. Award Found., 2004, Spl. award, Am. Soc. Info. Sci. and Tech., 2004, Common Wealth award for Disting. Svc. for Mass Comm., 2005, Die Quadriga award, 2005, Inst. Physics President's medal, 2005, Fin. Times Lifetime Achievement award, 2005; fellow Guglielmo Marconi Found., 2002; MacArthur fellowship, 1998, Hon. Fellowship, Soc. Tech. Comm., 1999. Fellow: British Computer Soc., Royal Soc. (Royal medal 2000), Inst. Elec. Engrs. (hon.); mem.: NAE (fgn. assoc., Charles Stark Draper prize 2007), Am. Philos. Soc., Am. Acad. Arts & Scis. Achievements include writing the first World Wide Web server, "httpd", & the first client, "WorldWideWeb" a what-you-see-is-what-you-get hypertext browser/editor which ran in the NeXTStep environment in 1990; invention of the World Wide Web in 1991; knighted (KBE) by Queen Elizabeth II in 2004. Office: MIT Computer Sci and Artificial Intelligence Lab Stata Ctr Bldg 32 32 Vassar St Cambridge MA 02139 Office Phone: 617-253-5702. Office Fax: 617-258-5999. Business E-Mail: timbl@w3.org.*

BERNEY, BOB, film company executive; b. Okla., 1954; m. Jeanne Reinhart; children: Sean, Liam. BA in Film, U. Tex., 1976. Mgr. Greenway Theater, Houston, Showcase Theater, Dallas; owner Inwood Theater, Dallas; founder Inwood Films; sr. v.p. mktg. and distbn. IFC Films, NYC, 2000—02; ptnr. Newmarket Films, Beverly Hills, Calif., 2002—. Cons. Memento Newmarket Films. Recipient Trailblazer award, Deep Ellum Film Festival, 2003. Office: Picturehouse 597 Fifth Ave 7th Fl New York NY 10017

BERNEY, DAVID J., lawyer; BA magna cum laude, Lehigh U., 1989; JD, U. Pa., 1992; MA in Polit. Sci., New Sch. for Social Rsch., 2002. Bar: Pa., NY, US Ct. Appeals (3rd cir.), US Ct. Appeals (ea. dist.) Pa. Contract assoc. Pepper, Hamilton & Scheetz, Phila., 1992—93; law clk. to Hon. William J. Manfredi Civil Motions Ct., Ct. of Common Pleas, Phila., 1993—94; assoc. Sheller, Ludwig & Badey, Phila., 1994—96; mng. atty. Law Office of David J. Berney, Phila., 1996—. Contbr. articles to law jours. Office: 1528 Walnut St, 3rd Fl Philadelphia PA 19102 Office Phone: 214-545-5898. E-mail: djberney@berneylaw.com.

BERNHAGEN, LILLIAN FLICKINGER, retired school health consultant; b. Cleve., Oct. 1, 1916; d. Norman Henry and Bertha May (Rogers) Flickinger; m. Ralph John Bernhagen, Sept. 2, 1940; children: Ralph, Janet Elizabeth Darling, Penelope Anne Braat. Student, Ohio Wesleyan U., 1934—37; BSN, Ohio State U., 1940, MA, 1958; postgrad., LaVerne Coll., 1972—73. Cert. health edn. specialist; cert. holistic coach Journeys of Wisdom Inst. Asst. dir. Kiwanis Health Camp for Underprivileged Children, Steubenville, Ohio, summer 1940; asst. dir. nurses Jefferson Davis Hosp., Houston, 1940-41; ARC instr. Ohio State U., 1943, 63, elem. edn. lectr., 1970, health edn. instr., 1976-77; dir. health svcs. Worthington City Schs., Ohio, 1951-76; spl. cons. venereal disease and sex edn. Ohio Dept. Health, 1976-82; sch. health cons. Ohio Dept. Edn., 1976—82; vice chmn. medicine, edn. com. on sch. and coll. health AMA, 1976-78, chmn., 1978-80. Author: Sex Education: Understanding Growth and Social Development, 1968, What A Miracle You Are-Boys, 1968, 3d rev. edit., 1986, What A Miracle You Are-Girls, 1968, 3d rev. edit., 1986, Toward a Reverence for Life, 1971, Personality, Sexuality and Stereotyping, 1974, (with others) Growth Patterns and Sex Education: A Suggested Curriculum Guide K-12, 1967; mng. editor Holistic Discoveries, 2006—; contbr. articles to profl. jours., mags. Bd. dirs. Hearing and Speech Ctr. of Columbus and Franklin County, 1954-57, sec., 1957; mem. nat. adv. com. Nat. Ctr. for Health Edn., 1978-82; sec.-tres. Ohio Wesleyan U. Class of 38, 1968-78, 83-88; bd. dirs. V.D. Hotline Columbus and Franklin County, 1974-87, bd. expansion chmn., 1978-85, pres., 1985-86; mem. profl. adv. com. Ptnrs. Home Health Inc., 1991-97; mem. Worthington Hist. Soc., Doll Docent, 1982—; mem King Ave. United Meth. Ch., 1938—, mem. marriage counseling com., 1997-98, mem. choir, 1950—2004, pres., 1961-63, pastor/parish rels. com., 1985-88, bd. trustees, 1989-92, adminstrv. coun., 1992-98, homosexual study com., 1998-99, edn. commn., 1982-85, nominations and pers., 1992-94; treas. Franklin County Women's Golf Tournament, 1992. Recipient Outstanding Alumna award Ohio State U. Coll. Nursing, 1964, Centennial award Ohio State U., 1970, Disting. Svc. award Mich. Sch. Nurses Assn., 1972, Alumni Hon. award Ohio Wesleyan U., 1998; hon. mention La Sertoma Internat. Woman of Yr., 1972. Fellow Am. Sch. Health Assn. (v.p. 1974, pres. 1976, governing coun. 1973-88, chmn. health guidance in sex edn. com. 1963-67, 71-77, chmn. sr. adv. coun. 1983-89, Disting. Svc. award 1969, Howe award 1979, cert. of merit, 1985, mem. awards com. 1986-89, mem. hist. com. 1989-95, constn. and bylaws com. 1995-99), APHA (chmn. com. on urban health problems 1972); mem. NEA (life, ret.), Sex Edn. and Info. Coun. of U.S., Worthington Edn. Assn. (v.p. 1961-62, Tchr. of Yr. 1972-73), Ctrl. Ohio Tchrs. Assn. (chmn. sch. health svcs. sect. 1963), Ohio State U. Women's Golf Assn. (chmn. 1973, parliamentarian 1988—), Ohio Wesleyan U. Alumni Assn. (bd. dirs., chmn. alumni recognition com. 1994-95, chmn. bylaws revision com. 1991-96, mem. orgn. com. 1994-95), Columbus Women's Dist. Golf Assn. (treas. 1985, sec. 1987, v.p. 1989, pres. 1990, adv. bd. 1991-98, parliamentarian 1996-98), Chi Omega (pres. Columbus Alumnae chpt. 1947-49, fin. adv. Ohio Wesleyan U. 1964-76, Outstanding Alumna of Yr. State of Ohio 1986), Ohio State U. Nursing Alumni Soc. (Disting. Alumni award, 2004), Pi Lambda Theta (citation award 1971, mem. program com. 1986-89, chmn. by laws revision com. 1990-2000, parliamentarian), Journeys of Wisdom, Monnett Club, Worthington Women's Club, Sigma Theta Tau, Phi Delta Kappa. Home and Office: 5916 Linworth Rd Worthington OH 43085-3357 Personal E-mail: lfbern@aol.com.

BERNHARD, ALEXANDER ALFRED, lawyer; b. New Orleans, Sept. 28, 1936; s. John Helenus and Dora (Solosko) B.; m. Martha Ruggles, Nov. 21, 1959 (div.); children: John, Jason, Frederic; m. Joyce Harrington, Dec. 30, 1976 (div.); m. Myra Mayman, Nov. 2, 1986. BS, MIT, 1957; LLB, Harvard U., 1964. Bar: Calif. 1964, Oreg. 1965, Mass. 1966, N.H. 1991. Law clk. to judge U.S. Ct. Appeals (9th cir.), 1964-65; assoc. Johnson, Johnson & Harrang, Eugene, Oreg., 1965-66, Bingham, Dana & Gould, Boston, 1966-71, Hale and Dorr, Boston, 1971-73, jr. ptnr., 1973-75, sr. ptnr., 1975—2004, of counsel, 2005—. Trustee, bd. dirs. Mass. Eye and Ear Infirmary, chmn., 1992-96, chmn. emeritus, 1996—. Lt. (submarines) USNR, 1957-61. Mem.: Longwood Cricket Club, Union Boat Club. Office: Wilmer Cutler Pickering Hale and Dorr LLP 60 State St Boston MA 02109-1803 Office Phone: 617-526-6220. Business E-Mail: alexander.bernhard@wilmerhale.com.

BERNHARD, BERL, lawyer; b. NYC, Sept. 7, 1929; s. Morris and Celia B.; children— Peter Berl, Robin Churchill, Andrew Morris BA in Govt. magna cum laude (Rufus Choate scholar), Dartmouth Coll., 1951, A.M., 1974; JD, Yale U., 1954; LL.D., Central Ohio State Coll., 1963. Bars: D.C., 1954, U.S. Supreme Ct., 1957. Assoc. Davis, Polk, Wardwell, Sunderland & Kiendl, NYC, summer 1953; law clk. to U.S. dist. judge, 1954-56; assoc Turney & Turney, 1956-59; staff dir. U.S. Commn. on Civil Rights, 1961-63; ptnr. Hughes, Hubbard & Reed, Washington, 1972-75, Verner, Liipfert, Bernhard, McPherson and Hand and predecessor firms, 1959, 63—, chmn.; ptnr. Fed. Affairs & Legis., Govt. Affairs practices DLA Piper Rudnick Gray Cary, Washington, 2004—. Bd. dirs. UNC Inc.; gen. counsel, dir. Evening Star Newspaper Co., Washington, 1974-78, WJLA, Inc., Washington, 1976-80; staff dir. U.S. Commn. on Civil Rights, 1961-63, cons. under sec. polit. affairs Sec. State, 1963-65; adj. prof. law Georgetown U. Law Ctr., 1963-65; spl. counsel, dir. The White Ho. Conf. "To Fulfill These Rights," 1966; counsel Lawyers Com. for Civil Rights Under Law. Contbr. articles to profl. jours. Gen. counsel Dem. Senatorial Campaign Com., 1965-71; spl. counsel Dem. Nat. Com., 1965-71; staff dir. Senator Edmund S. Muskie, 1971, nat. campaign mgr., 1972; mem. D.C. Bd. Higher Edn., chmn. fin. com.; trustee Dartmouth Coll., 1974-84, Joe Davies Found., 1968-87; sr. advisor to Sec. of State, 1980-81; chmn., CEO Washington Federals, U.S. Football League; bd. dirs. Harriman Polit. Action Com., 1980-89; mem. bd. visitors Nelson A. Rockefeller Ctr. for Social Scis., 1983-90; mem. bd. overseers The Amos Tuck Sch. Bus. Adminstrn., Dartmouth Coll., 1985-90; bd. dirs. Aspen Inst., 1988—, chmn., 1991-96; trustee Fed. City Coun., 1988-92; bd. trustees Muskie Found., 1997. Recipient Arthur S. Flemming award D.C. Jr. C. of C., 1960, Ten Outstanding Young Men award U.S. Jr. C. of C., 1962 Mem. Am. Bar Assn., Bar Assn. D.C., Assn. Interstate Practitioners, Nat. Panel Arbitrators, Am. Arbitration Assn., Casque and Gauntlet, Phi Beta Kappa, Sigma Nu, Phi Delta Phi Clubs: Metropolitan (Washington); Yale (N.Y.C.). Home: 1693 Epping Farms Rd Annapolis MD 21401-6673 Office: DLA Piper Rudnick Gray Cary 1200 19th St NW Washington DC 20036-2412 Office Phone: 202-861-3839. Office Fax: 202-689-7494. Business E-Mail: berl.bernhard@dlapiper.com.

BERNHARD, HERBERT ASHLEY, lawyer; b. Jersey City, Sept. 24, 1927; s. Richard C. and Amalie (Lobl) B.; m. Nancy Ellen Hirschaut, Aug. 8. 1954; children: Linda, Alison, Jordan, Melissa. Student, Mexico City Coll., 1948; BEE, N.J. Inst. Tech., 1949; MA in Math., Columbia U., 1950; JD cum laude, U. Mich., 1957. Bar: Calif. 1958, U.S. Dist. Ct. (cen. dist.) Calif. 1958, U.S. Dist. Ct. (no., ea. and so. dists.) Calif. 1963, U.S. Ct. Claims 1966, U.S. Dist. Ct. (ea. dist.) Wis. 1982, U.S. Dist. Ct. (ea. and we. dists.) Ark. 1982, U.S. Dist. Ct. Nebr. 1982, U.S. Ct. Internat. Trade 1979, U.S. Tax Ct. 1969, U.S. Ct. Appeals (2d, 3d, 4th, 5th, 7th, 8th, 9th, 10th, 11th and D.C. cirs.) 1969, U.S. Supreme Ct. 1965. Research engr. Curtis-Wright Co., Caldwell, NJ, 1950-52, Boeing Aircraft Co., Cape Canaveral, Fla., 1952-55; assoc. O'Melveny & Myers, Los Angeles, 1957-62; ptnr. Greenberg, Bernhard, et al, Los Angeles, 1962-85, Jeffer, Mangels, Butler & Marmaro, Los Angeles, 1985—. Instr. math. U. Fla., Cape Canaveral, 1952-55; instr. elec. engring. U. Mich., Ann Arbor, 1955-57; referee L.A. Superior Ct., 1985—, arbitrator, 1988—, judge pro tem, 1988—; judge pro tem L.A. Mcpl. Ct., 1985—, Beverly Hills Mcpl. Ct., 1989—, Malibu Mcpl. Ct., 1994—. Contbr. articles to profl. jours. Chmn. adv. com. Skirball Mus., 1976-98; bd. overseers Hebrew Union Coll., 1976-98. With USAF, 1946-47. Recipient Disting. Achievement award N.J. Inst. Tech., 1998. Mem. Jewish Publ. Soc. (trustee 1986-96). Office: 78557 Alliance Way Palm Desert CA 92211-3069

BERNHARD, JAMES M., JR., engineering executive; m. Dana Bernhard. Grad., La. State U., 1976. Founder The Shaw Group, Inc., Baton Rouge, 1987—, CEO, 1987—, pres., 1987—2003, chmn., 1990—, La. State Dem. Party, 2005. Mem. Pipe Fabricators Inst. Mem. Com. of 100 for State of La.; chmn. Select Coun. for Revenues and Expenditures for La.'s Future; active La. State U. Alumni Assn., Tiger Athletic Found., La. Tech. U. Found., St. George Cath. Ch. and Sch., Ducks Unltd., Krewe of Endymion; supporter United Way, Baton Rouge Area Found., St. George Cath. Ch., St. George Cath. Sch., East La. Tech. U. Named Marketer of Yr., 1994, Entrepreneur of Yr. in La., 1995, Perpetual Founder of Cath. H.S.; named one of Top Ten CEOs, Greater Baton Rouge Bus. Report, 1993; recipient Prevent Child Abuse La.'s Corp. Champions for Children award, 1997, Ernst and Young Entrepreneru of Yr. award, 2001, Ace award, La. State U. Golf Program, Tiger Athletic Found. Augie Cross Meml. Mem. of Yr. award. Mem.: Associated Building Contractors, American Welding Society, Associated Gen. Contractors. Avocations: golf, duck hunting, horseback riding, bill fishing, coaching Little League sports. Office: Shaw Group Inc 4171 Essen Ln Baton Rouge LA 70809 Office Phone: 800-747-3322, 225-932-2500. Office Fax: 225-932-2661.*

BERNHARD, JEFFREY DAVID, dermatologist, educator, editor; b. Buffalo, Oct. 31, 1951; AB, Harvard Coll., 1973; MD, Harvard Med. Sch., 1978. Diplomate Am. Bd. Dermatology. Knox fellow St. John's Coll. Cambridge U., England, 1973—74; chief resident dermatology Harvard Med. Sch., Boston, 1982; fellow photomedicine Mass. Gen. Hosp., 1983; mem. faculty Med. Sch. U. Mass., Worcester, 1983—86, chief dermatology, assoc. prof. Sch. Medicine, 1986—2002, assoc. dean for admissions Med. Sch., 1989—95, prof. Med. Sch., 1992, prof. medicine and physiology, 2005, acad. chief dermatology, 2002—. Arthur Curtis vis. prof. U. Mich., 2007. Author: Itch: Mechanisms and Management of Pruritus, 1994; asst. editor Jour. Am. Acad. Dermatology, 1993-98, editor, 1998—; mem. editl. bd. Jour. European Acad. Dermatology and Venereology, Yearbook of Cancer, 1981-88, Yearbook of Dermatology, 1988-97, Internat. Jour. Dermatology, Jour. Geriat. Dermatology, 1993-97. Named J. Graham Smith, Jr., hon. lectr., 2000, Narins Meml. Lectr., 2001, Novy lectr., U. Calif., Davis, 2002, Lorincz lectr., Chgo. Derm. Soc., 2002, Luscombe lectr., Jefferson Med. Coll., 2003, Sydney Watson Smith lectr., Royal Coll. Physicians Edinburgh, 2004, Ervin Epstein lectr., Pacific Dermatol. Assn., 2004; named an hon. mem., Czech. Soc. Dermatol, 2002. Fellow: Royal Coll. Physicians (Edinburgh), Royal Soc. Medicine, Am. Dermatol. Assn.; mem.: French Soc. Dermatology and Venerology, Coun. Sci. Editors, European Soc. History of Dermatology, History Dermatology Soc., Quinsigamond Dermatol. Soc., Czech Soc. Dermatology (hon.), Austrian Soc. Dermatology nd Venerology (corr.), New Eng. Dermatol. Soc. (pres. 1990—91), Assn. Profs. Dermatology, Sir James Saunders Soc., European Acad. Dermatology and Venereology, Soc. for Investigative Dermatology (bd. dirs. 1981—83), Am. Acad. Dermatology (Presdl. citation 2000), James C. White Club, Aesculapian Club Boston, Sigma Xi, Alpha Omega Alpha, Phi Beta Kappa. Office: Jour Am Acad Dermatology 55 Lake Ave N Worcester MA 01655-0002

BERNHARD, NANCY LYNN, secondary school educator; d. Kenneth Lazell and Rosemary Bernhard; m. Jeffrey T. Heyer, July 19, 1999. BA, San Diego State U., 1975. Cert. secondary tchr. Calif. Clk. Golden State Fabrics, San Diego, 1974—76, Leather Bound, Ltd., San Diego, 1976—78, store mgr. Carmel, Calif., 1978—86; substitute tchr. San Diego County schs., 1976—78, Monterey County schs., 1987—89; tchr. English and theater Salinas Union HS Dist., Calif., 1989—. Mem. Calif. Thespian State Bd., Claremont, 2002—. Named Outstanding Tchr., Salinas Union HS Dist., 1997—98, 1999—2000, Salinas NW Rotary, 1999; named to Tchrs. for Tomorrow, Monterey Peninsula Coll., 2004. Mem.: Ednl. Theater Assn., Delta Kappa Gamma (Pub. Svc. award 2004—05). Episcopalian. Avocations: theater, reading, horseback riding, antique glass. Home: 977 Loyola Dr Salinas CA 93906

BERNHARD, PETER C., lawyer, state agency administrator; b. Apr. 24, 1949; BA cum laude, Harvard Coll., 1971; JD, George Washington U., 1975. Bar: Nev. Bar Assn. 1975, Clark County Bar Assn., US Ct. Appeals Ninth Circuit, US Dist. Ct., Dist. Nev., US Supreme Ct. Atty./ptnr. Bernhard & Leslie; pres., stockholder Bernhard, Bradley & Johnson; chartered counsel Bullivant, Houser & Bailey PC. Mem., chair Nev. Commn. Ethics, 1999; chair Nev. Gaming Commn., 2001, 2003—. Mem.: ABA, Harvard Club Nev., Assn. Trial Lawyers Am. Office: Nev Gaming Commn 555 E Washington St Ste 2600 Las Vegas NV 89101 Office Phone: 702-650-6565. Office Fax: 702-650-2995.*

BERNHARD, WILLIAM FRANCIS, thoracic and cardiovascular surgeon; b. Bklyn., Dec. 11, 1924; s. William and Helen (Conroy) B.; m. June Horne, Sept. 17, 1948; children: Susan, William Francis, Christine, Margaret, Catherine, John, Ann, James, Robert, Peter. BA, Williams Coll., 1946; MD, Syracuse U., 1950; MS (hon.), Harvard U., 1990. Intern Syracuse U. Hosp., 1950-51; asst. resident Children's Hosp. Med. Center, Boston, 1951-52; dir. surg. research lab. Children's Hosp., Boston, 1960—, assoc. surgeon, 1962-66; sr. assoc. in cardiovascular surgery Children's Hosp. Med. Center; asst. resident Peter Bent Brigham Hosp., Boston, 1952—57, attending staff cardiovascular surgery, 1973—, attending staff, 1974—; resident Bellevue Hosp., Columbia div., NYC, 1957-58; resident in surgery Columbia-Presbyn. Hosp., NYC, 1959; attending surgeon thoracic and cardiovascular surgery VA Hosp., West Roxbury, Mass., 1960—; Harvey Cushing fellow Harvard Med. Sch., 1954—55, clin. assoc. surgery, 1962-66, asst. clin. prof. surgery, 1966-68, assoc. clin. prof. surgery, 1968-71, prof. surgery, 1971—, prof. surgery emeritus, 1994; sr. surgeon Brigham and Woman's Hosp., Boston, 1987. Cons. in cardiothoracic surgery Beth Israel Hosp., Boston, 1986. Ensign USNR, 1944-46. Harvey Cushing fellow, Harvard Med. Sch., 1954—55. Mem. ACS., New Eng. Surg. Soc. (sr.), Am. Heart Assn., Mass. Med. Soc., Am. Assn. Thoracic and Cardiovasc. Surgery, Soc. Thoracic Surgery, Soc. Univ. Surgeons, Am. Acad. Pediatrics, New Eng. Cardiovasc. Soc., Internat. Soc. Heart Transplantation, Soc. Vascular Surgery, Am. Soc. Artificial Internal Organs, Am. Surg. Assn. Home: 58 Singletary Ln Framingham MA 01702-6161 Office: Children's Hosp 300 Longwood Ave Boston MA 02115-5737

BERNHARDT, ARTHUR DIETER, urban planner, consultant; b. Dresden, Germany; arrived in U.S., 1966; s. Rudolf B. and Charlotte (Apitz) B. Dipl. Ing., U. Tech., Munich, Fed. Republic Germany, 1965; postgrad., U. So. Calif., 1966-67; M. City Planning, MIT, 1969. Various positions constrn. cos., 1955-68; dir. Program in Industrialization of Housing Sector, MIT, Cambridge, Mass., 1969-76; pres. Program in Industrialization of Housing Sector, Cambridge, 1977-89; chief exec. officer, dir. Program in Industrialization of Housing Sector, Inc., Cambridge and NYC, 1989—2001; pres. DBG Berlin, Germany and N.Y.C., 2001—. Internat. building industry cons., Cambridge, Mass., and N.Y.C., 1973—; asst. prof. MIT, 1970-76 Author books; contbr. articles to profl. jours. Mem. exec. com. Mass. Gov.'s Adv. Com. on Manufactured Housing, 1974-75; NRC del. 8th Gen. Assembly Internat. Council Bldg. Research, 1974. Fed. Republic Germany fellow, 1965, 66, 67, 68; MIT fellow, 1968, 69; MIT grantee, 1970; Fed. Republic Germany grantee, 1965; Alfred P. Sloan Found. grantee, 1970; Dept. Commerce grantee, 1972; HUD grantee, 1972, 74. Mem. Internat. Coun. Bldg. Rsch., Am. Acad. Polit. and Social Sci., Am. Planning Assn., Am. Judicature Soc. (assoc.)

BERNHARDT, DAVID LONGLY, federal agency administrator; b. Rifle, Colo., Aug. 1969; m. Gena Rae Bernhardt; children: William, Katherine. BA in Polit. Sci., U. No. Colo., Greeley, 1990; JD, George Washington U. Nat. Law Ctr., 1994. Legis. dir. to Congressman Scott McInnis, assoc. to House Com. on rules & legal counsel US Congress, Washington, 1992—98; atty. Brownstein, Hyatt and Farber, P.C., Denver, 1998—2001; dir. congl. affairs, counselor to sec. US Dept. Interior, Washington, 2001—04, dep. chief of staff, counselor to sec., 2004—05, dep. solicitor Washington, DC, 2005—06, solicitor Washington, 2006—. Mem.: Colo. State Bar Assn. Office: US Dept Interior 1849 C St NW Washington DC 20240

BERNHARDT, MARCIA BRENDA, mental health counselor; b. Jersey, NJ, Aug. 22, 1938; d. Jerome and Mitzie (Cohen) B. BA, Fairleigh Dickinson U., 1960; MA, Columbia U., 1960-63, postgrad., 1968-70, Hunter Coll., 1973-74. Nat. cert. counselor. Rsch. asst. Tchrs. Coll., Columbia U., NYC, 1963-64; counselor JOIN, NYC, 1965-66; project assoc. Bd. Higher Edn. N.Y., NYC, 1966-68, Tchrs. Coll, Columbia U., NYC, 1968-70; counselor Nassau Community Coll., Garden City, N.Y., 1970-72; rsch. scientist Div. for Youth, NYC, 1972-73; rsch. assoc. Family Svc. Assn., NYC, 1974-76; counselor Div. Blind Svcs., West Palm Beach, Fla., 1984-96. Sec., chairperson adv. bd. com. Lighthouse for the Blind, West Palm Beach, 1984-90. Mem. AAUW, Am. Mental Health Counselors Assn., Am. Soc. for Handicapped Children in Israel, Hadassah. Democrat. Jewish. Avocations: theater, ballet, opera, art, swimming. Home: 40 Chatham B West Palm Beach FL 33417-1807 Personal E-mail: marciabrend@aol.com.

BERNHARDT, MARK, orthopedic surgeon, educator; b. Fayetteville, Ark., 1957; BA in Biology, U. Kans., Lawrence, 1979; MD, U. Kans., 1983. Lic. Kans., 1984, Mo., 1989, cert. Am. Bd. Orthop. Surgery, 1991. Intern orthop. surgery St. Francis/U. Kans., Wichita, 1983—84; resident spinal surgery U. Kans., Wichita, 1983—88; fellow Beth Israel Hosp./Harvard Med. Sch., Boston, 1988—89; instr. orthop. surgery Harvard Med. Sch., 1989; clin. asst. prof. U. Mo., Kans. City, 1990—94, clin. prof., 2000, 2002; staff mem. Dickson-Diveley Midwest Orthop. Clinic, 1990—, St. Luke's Hosp., Kans. City, Mo., 1993; staff mem. orthops. Children's Mercy Hosp., Kans. City, Mo., 2002. Contbr. articles to med. jours., chapters to books. Named one of Kans. City Super Doctors, 2007. Fellow: Scoliosis Rsch. Soc., Cervical Spine Rsch. Soc., Am. Acad. Orthop. Surgeons; mem.: AMA, North Am. Spine Soc., Kans. City Orthop. Soc., Mo. State Orthop. Assn., Mid-Ctrl. States Orthop. Soc., Met. Med. Soc. Greater Kans. City, Kans. Med. Soc., Mo. State Med. Assn., Phi Beta Kappa. Avocations: tennis, golf. Office: Dickson-Diveley Midwest Orthop Clinic Inc Medical Plz Bldg I Ste 610 4320 Wornall Rd Kansas City MO 64111 Office Phone: 816-531-5757. Office Fax: 816-531-5313.

BERNHEIM, DANIEL S., lawyer; b. Phila., Dec. 17, 1954; BA, U. Pa., 1976; JD, Villanova U., 1980; LLM in trial advocacy, Temple U., 1994. Bar: Pa. 1980, US Dist. Ct., Eastern Dist. Pa. 1980, US Tax Ct. 1985, US Ct. Appeals, Third Circuit 1985. Shareholder Silverman Bernheim & Vogel, P.C. Adj. faculty mem. Temple U. Sch. Law; lectr. in field Pa. Banker's Assn., Pa. Bar Inst., Nat. Bus. Inst. Named one of Pa. Super Lawyers, Phila. Mag., 2004. Mem.: Pa. Trial Lawyers Assn., Assn. Trial Lawyers Am., ABA (mem. section on bus. law and lit.), Phila. Bar Assn. (mem. state civil judicial com. 1984—, chmn. motion ct. subcommittee). Office: Silverman Bernheim & Vogel Two Penn Ctr Plz Ste 910 Philadelphia PA 19102 Office Phone: 215-569-0000. Business E-Mail: dbernheim@sbvlaw.com.

BERNHEIMER, G. MAX, art appraiser; MA in Classical Civilization, Harvard U.; attended, Intercollegiate Ctr. for Classical Studies, Rome, Am. Sch. of Classical Studies, Athens, London Inst. Archeology. With Christie's, NYC, 1992—, specialist in ancient Greek, Roman, Etruscan, Egyptian and Near Eastern Art, sr. v.p., internat. dept. head, antiquities. Author: Glories of Ancient Greece, 2001; co-author: Ancient Glass from the Collections of Dr. Elie Borowski. Office: Christie's/NY 20 Rockefeller Plz New York NY 10020 Office Phone: 212-636-2245. Office Fax: 212-636-4926. Business E-Mail: mbernheimer@christies.com.

BERNHEIMER, MARTIN, music critic; b. Munich, Sept. 28, 1936; came to U.S., 1940, naturalized, 1946; s. Paul Ernst and Louise (Nassauer) B.; m. Lucinda Pearson, Sept. 30, 1961 (div. Feb. 1989); children: Mark Richard, Nora Nicoll, Marina and Erika (twins); m. Linda Winer, Sept. 27, 1992. MusB with honors, Brown U., 1958; student, Munich Conservatory, 1958-59; MA in Musicology, NYU, 1961. Free-lance music critic, 1958—; contbg. critic N.Y. Herald Tribune, 1959-62; mem. music faculty NYU, 1959-62; contbg. editor Mus. Courier, 1961-64; temporary music critic N.Y. Post, 1961-65; N.Y. corr. Brit. Publ. Opera, 1962—65; L.A. corr., 1965—; corr. West Coast Brit. Opera Mag., 1965—; asst. to music editor Saturday Rev., 1962-65; mng. editor Philharmonic Hall Program, NYC, 1962-65; music editor, chief critic L.A. Times, 1965-96; N.Y. corr. Brit. Publ. Opera, 1997—. Mem. faculty U. So. Calif., 1966-71, music faculty UCLA, 1969-75, Calif. Inst. Arts, 1975-82, Calif. State U., Northridge, 1978-81, Rockefeller Program for Tng. of Music Critics; mem. Pulitzer Prize Music Jury, 1984, 86, 90; L.A. corr. for Swiss publ. Opernwelt, 1984—. Contbg. author New Groves Dictionary; contbr. liner notes for recordings; appearances on radio and TV, Met. Opera Broadcasts; contbr. articles to Vanity Fair, Music Quar., The Critic, Opera News, Mus. Am., Fin. Times, London, Sidewalk N.Y. (internet), others; N.Y. corr. Fin. Times and Opera mag.; lectr., moderator, essayist on Met. Opera Broadcast. Recipient Deems Taylor award ASCAP, 1974, 78, Headliners award, 1979, Pulitzer Prize for disting. criticism, 1982, Lifetime Achievement award Svc. to Music, Calif. Assn. Profl. Music Tchrs., 1990. Mem. Nat. Opera Inst. (ind. selection com. 1980), Pi Kappa Lambda (hon.). E-mail: mbern@earthlink.net.

BERNHOFT, FRANKLIN OTTO, psychotherapist, psychologist; b. Fargo, ND, Aug. 12, 1944; s. Otto and Irene Bernhoft; m. Dorothy Ann Larsen, Aug. 11, 1973; children: Kimberley, Brady, Heather. BA in English, N.D. State U., 1966; MA in Counseling Psychology, U. N.D., 1970; MA in English, Calif. State U., 1978; PhD in Counseling Psychology, Brigham Young U., 1985. Cert. therapist, hypnotherapist, counselor, secondary tchr.; lic. psychologist, marriage, family and child counselor, ednl. psychologist. Instr. Chapman Coll., Brigham Young U., U. N.D., U. S.I.U.; staff trainer Sacramento County Office Edn., 1977—82; therapist Lodi and Stockton, Calif., 1985—; devel. capable people trainer U. Pacific Behavioral Medicine Clinic, 1979—84, master trainer systematic helping skills, 1981—88, therapist, family fitness trainer, 1988—. Co-founder prevention/intervention project, Sacto County, 1977; presenter in field. Contbr. articles to profl. jours. Lt. U.S. Army, 1967-69. H.H. Kirk R. Askanase scholar, 1962-66; cert. achievement Ft. Carson, 1967; decorated Bronze star, combat med. badge Nat. Def. Svc. Vietnam, 1968-69; named Support Person of Yr. Phi Delta Kappa, 2000-2001. Mem. ACA, Children with Attention Deficit Disorders, Nat. Assn. Sch. Psychologists, Assn. Mormon Counselors and Psychotherapists, Calif. Assn. Marriage and Family Therapists, Calif. Psychol. Assn., Sacramento Area Sch. Psychologists Assn., Calif. Continuation Edn. Assn. (past treas.), Calif. Assn. Lic. Edn. Psychologists, Mensa, Eye Movement Desensitization and Reprocessing Internat. Assn., Calif. Assn. Psychologists, Am. Assn. Christian Counselors, Internat. Critical Incident Stress Found. Office: Creative Therapy 2000 W Kettleman Ln Ste 103 Lodi CA 95242-4334 Office Phone: 209-366-1516.

BERNHOLC, JERZY, physicist, educator; b. Szczecin, Poland, Feb. 12, 1952; arrived in U.S., 1978, naturalized, 1986; s. David and Irene Bernholc; m. Alissa Seligman, Aug. 1, 1982; children: Stuart, Judith. BS in Physics and Math., U. Lund, Sweden, 1973, PhD in Physics, 1977. Postdoctoral rschr. IBM Watson Rsch. Ctr., Yorktown Heights, NY, 1978-80; sr. physicist Exxon Corp. Rsch. Labs., Clinton, NJ, 1980-86; assoc. prof. physics NC State U., Raleigh, 1986-90, prof., 1990-2000, Drexel prof., 2000—; disting. vis. scientist Oak Ridge Nat. Lab., 2002—, dir. ctr. for high performance simulation, 2004—. Chmn. Electronic Structure Algorithms, Raleigh, 1992, organizing com. ann. workshops, 1992—; co-chmn. Grid, Wavelet and Multigrid Methods, Lyon, France, 1996; co-chmn. workshop multiscale methods in chemistry NATO, Eilat, Israel, 2000; mem. ONR Panel on Fgn. Field Offices, 1992; joint peer rev. bd. NSF Supercomputing Ctrs., 1988—91; adv. coun. NC Supercomputing Ctr., Research Triangle Park, 1990—92, Research Triangle Park, 1998—; chair NC Com. on Partnership for Advanced Computational Infrastructure, 1996—99; panel high performance computing NSF, Washington, 1992, com. visitors supercomputing ctrs. and computational infrastructure program, 99, Grand Challenges in Nanomaterials workshop, 2003; exec. com., leader nanomaterials/electronic structure team Nat. Computational Sci. Alliance, Urbana, Ill., 1998—2002; program com. Internat. Conf. on Computational Physics, San Diego, 2003; chair Prog. Com. Divsn. Computational Physics of APS, 2002; mem. southeastern sect. prog. com. of APS Prog. Com. Divsn. Computational Physics, 2003; sci. adv. com. Ctr. for Nanophase Materials Scis. Oak Ridge Nat. Lab., 2002—, adv. com. divsn. computer sci., 2003—; strategic planning workshop Dept. of Energy, 2003; rev. panel materials scis. divsn. Lawrence Berkeley Labs., 2003; NSF rev. panel, Ctr. Integrated Nanomechanical Sys. U. Calif., Berkeley, 2005; program com. Southeast Sec. APS, 2003; sci. com. 7th Internat. Conf. on Intermolecular and Magnetic Interactions in Matter, Poland, 2003, Workshop on Functional Materials, Athens, Greece, 2004—05; rev. com. Dir.'s Rsch. and Devel. Fund, 2004; organizing com. Workshop on Recent Devel. in Electronic Structure Algorithms, 2004—05, Fall Creek Falls Workshop on High-End Computing in Sci. and Engring., Tenn., 2004—05; panel mem. workshop Basic Rsch. Needs Effective Solar Energy Utilization Dept. Energy, Bethesda, 2005; panel mem. Crosscutting Areas: New Tools Dept. Energy, 2005; co-organizer Workshop on Enabling Petascale Sci. and Engring. Applications, Atlanta, 2005; chmn. sci. adv. com. Ctr. for Nanophase Sci.; chmn. Oak Ridge Nat. Lab., 2005—, chair users group Nat. Ctr. for Computational Scis., 2005—, mem. adv. com. Nat. Ctr. for Computational Scis., 2005—; co-organizer Workshop on Enabling Petascale Sci. and Engring. Applications, Atlanta, 2005; mem. Scientific Editl. Bd., Computational Sci. and Discovery Jour., Inst. of Physics, 2006—; rev. panel predictive sci. acad. alliance program Lawrence Livermore Nat. Lab., 2006; chmn. organizing com. Nineteenth Ann. Workship Recent Devel. Elec. Structure Algorithms, Raleigh, NC, 2007; mem. numerous rev. panels and organizing com. for confs. Specialist editor materials sci.: Computer Physics Comm., 1998—, mem. sci. editl. bd.: Computational Sci. and Discovery Jour., 2006—. Panel mem. AIChE, 2002. Recipient Outstanding Innovation award IBM Rsch. Divsn., Yorktown Heights, 1979, Alumni Oustanding rsch. award NC State U., Raleigh, 1992, Creativity Ext. award NSF, Washington, 1996 Fellow: Am. Phys. Soc. (vice-chair computational physics 2001, chmn.-elect 2002, chmn. fellowship com. 2002, chair computational physics 2002, chmn. ad hoc com. on condensed matter physics 2003, past chmn. program com. 2004, chmn. com. govt. rels. 2004, vice chmn. Rahman prize com. 2004, Jesse Beams award com. southeastern sect. 2004, chmn. Rahman prize com. 2005, chair comp. phys. 2002, Jesse Beams award for outstanding rsch. Southwestern sect. 2004); mem.: Materials Rsch. Soc., Sigma Xi. Home: 2309 Byrd St Raleigh NC 27608-1411 Office: Ctr High Performance Simulation PO Box 7518 Raleigh NC 27695-7518 Office Phone: 919-515-3126. Business E-Mail: bernholc@ncsu.edu.

BERNI, ROSEMARIAN RAUCH, rehabilitation and oncology nurse; b. Portland, Oreg., Sept. 30, 1925; d. George Laverne and Mabel (Rose) Rauch; m. Albert Hawthorne Berni, Oct. 25, 1947; children: George, Michael, William, Albert. Student, Oreg. State Coll., 1943-44; BS in Nursing, Univ. Oreg., 1947; M in Nursing, U. Wash., 1973. RN Wash., Oreg. Clin. nursing instr. Univ. Oreg. Sch. of Nursing, Portland; spl. duty nurse Doernbecher Hosp., Portland, Oreg., 1948; night supr. Halcyon Psychiat. Hosp., Seattle, Wash., 1962; staff nurse psychiat. nursing unit U. Wash. Hosp., Seattle, 1963, head nurse phys. medicine and rehab. nursing unit, 1964-66, asst. dir. nursing, 1966-67; dir. rehab. med. intermittent catheter team U. Hosp. and Harborview Med. Ctr., Seattle, 1973-82; rehab. clin. nurse specialist U. Wash. Med. Ctr., Seattle, 1973—. Clin. instr. U. Wash. Sch. Nursing, 1967-76, instr. dept. rehab. medicine, 1967-73; dir. nursing svc. Rehab. Nursing Unit, Dept. Rehab. Medicine, U. Wash., Seattle, 1967—; asst. prof. dept. rehab. medicine, U. Wash., 1973-78, assoc. prof. emeritus, 1981, mem. grad. sch. faculty, 1975—; dir. Rehab. Nursing Pathways in Depth, 1967—; chmn. rehab. nursing ctr., ARN 1981; presenter World Rehab. Fund, Cyprus; active on numerous hosp. and univ. coms., presenter many seminars and workshops in Wash. and nationwide. Author: (with Fordyce, Wilbert E.) Behavior Modification and the Nursing Process, 1973, 2nd edit., 1977; contbr. articles to profl. jours. and chpts. to books; producer films, audio and video presentations and course curricula. Vol. RN, Whidbey Island, Wash., 1981-2000; tutor pub. schs. Recipient Svc. award, Wash. State Health Facilities Assn., 1974, Wash. State Heart Assn., 1976, Leadership award, Rehab. Nursing Inst., 1981. Mem. ANA (coun. clin. nurse specialists), Nat. League of Nursing, Assn. of Rehab. Nurses (founding pres. Wash. chpt., nat. pres. 1980, Leadership award 1980), Assn. Women in Sci., N.Y. Acad. Sci., N.W. Neurological Rehab., Nat. Stroke Assn., Wash. State Head Injury Found., Univ. Wash. Alumni Assn., Sigma Theta Tau, Alpha Lambda Delta, Alpha Tau Delta. Home: PO Box 868 Freeland WA 98249-0868 Office: Stroke Support Group Whidbey Gen Hosp Dept Rehab Medicine Seattle WA 98195-0001

BERNICK, ALAN E., lawyer, accountant; b. St. Paul, June 20, 1958; s. Herbert Jay and Marcia Bernick; m. Elisa Kim Neff, Aug. 24, 1986; children: Joshua Norton, Daniel Noah, Matthew David. BA, U. Minn., 1980, JD, 1983. Bar: Minn. 1983, US Dist. Ct. Minn. 1983, US Tax Ct. 1985. Ptnr. Oppenheimer Wolff & Donnelly LLP, St. Paul, 1983-2000; sr. v.p., gen. counsel, corp. sec. Andersen Corp., Bayport, Minn., 2000—. Mem. exec. bd. Indianhead coun. Boy Scouts Am., 1993-2002, 2005—. Mem. AICPA, Minn. State Bar Assn. (chair tax sect. 1995-97), Minn. Soc. CPAs (chair tax sect. 1995-96). Avocations: outdoor activities, golf. Home: 621 Hampshire Dr Mendota Heights MN 55120-1935 Office: Andersen Corp 100 4th Ave N Bayport MN 55003-1096

BERNICK, CAROL LAVIN, consumer products company executive; 3 children. BA, Tulane U., 1974. Dir., v.p. Alberto-Culver Co., 1984, exec. v.p. worldwide mktg., 1990, chmn. bd., 2004—; pres. Alberto-Culver USA, 1994, Alberto-Culver N.Am., 1998, vice chmn., 1998; pres. Alberto Culver Consumer Products Worldwide, 2002. Founder Friends of Prentice; mem. women's bd. Boys and Girls Clubs, Chgo.; regent Lincoln Acad. Ill.; mem. exec. com. of adv. bd. Kellogg Sch., Northwestern U.; mem. Tulane U. Bd.; bd. dirs. Northwestern Meml. Healthcare. Recipient Leadership in Bus. award YWCA Met. Chgo., 1992, award for philanthropy Harvard Club of Chgo., Disting. Alumni award Tulane U., 2003. Mem. World Pres. Orgn., Econ. Club Chgo., Exec. Club Chgo., Com. 200 Chgo. Network. Office: Alberto-Culver Co 2525 Armitage Ave Melrose Park IL 60160-1163 Office Phone: 708-450-3000. Personal E-mail: cbernick@alberto.com.

BERNICK, DAVID M., lawyer; b. San Francisco, June 16, 1954; s. Herman Charles and Joan (Schutz) B.; m. Christine A. Clougherty, Aug. 13, 1983; 1 child, Evan Daniel. BA, U. Chgo., 1974, JD, 1978; MA, Yale U., 1975. Bar: Ill. 1978. Ptnr., mem. firm com. Kirkland & Ellis, Chgo., 1984—. Mem. Comml. Club, Mid-Am. Club, Phi Beta Kappa. Office: Kirkland & Ellis LLP 200 E Randolph Dr 54th Fl Chicago IL 60601-6636 Office Phone: 212-446-4806, 312-861-2248. Office Fax: 212-446-4900, 312-861-2200. E-mail: dbernick@kirkland.com.

BERNICK, HOWARD BARRY, manufacturing executive; b. Midland, Ont., Can., Apr. 10, 1952; came to U.S., 1974, naturalized, 1976; s. Henry and Esther (Starkman) B.; m. Carol Lavin, May 30, 1976; children: Craig, Peter, Elizabeth. BA, U. Toronto, Ont., 1973. Investment banker Wood Gundy Ltd., Toronto, 1973-74, First Boston Corp., Chgo., 1974-77; dir. of profit planning Alberto Culver Co., Melrose Park, Ill., 1977-79, v.p. corp. devel., 1979-81, group v.p., chief fin. officer, 1981-85, exec. v.p., 1985-88, pres., COO, 1988-94, also bd. dirs., pres., CEO, 1994—2006; pres. Bernick Holdings Inc., Chgo., 2006—. Bd. dirs. AAR Corp., Wm. Wrigley Jr. Co. Mem. Cosmetic, Toiletry & Fragrance Assn., Econ. Club Chgo. Office: Bernick Holdings Inc 401 N Michigan Ave Chicago IL 60611*

BERNIER, GEORGE MATTHEW, JR., oncologist, educator, dean; b. Portland, Maine, June 29, 1934; s. George Matthew and Lillián Theresa (Wallace) B.; m. Mary Jane Marron, June 29, 1963; children: George Matthew, III, Elizabeth Wallace. AB, Boston Coll., 1956; MD, Harvard U., 1960. Intern Univ. Hosps., Cleve., 1960-61, resident, 1961-62, 65-66, U. Fla. Hosps., Gainesville, 1964-65; fellow in biochemistry U. Fla., 1962-64; instr. Case Western Res. U., Cleve., 1966-67, asst. prof. medicine, 1967-72, assoc. prof., 1972-75, prof., 1975-78; dir. div. med. oncology Univ. Hosps., Cleve., 1974-78; prof., chmn. dept. medicine Dartmouth Med. Sch., Hanover, NH, 1978-86, Joseph M. Huber prof. medicine, 1982-86; dean, prof. medicine U. Pitts. Sch. Medicine, U. Pitts., 1987-95; dean medicine, v.p. acad. affairs U. Tex. Med. Br., Galveston, 1995-99, v.p. edn., 1999—2001, prof. emeritus, 2001—. Contbr. articles to profl. jours. Trustee Jackson Labs., Bar Harbor, Maine, 1973—; mem. White House Commn. on Complementary and Alternative Medicine. Served to lt. col. M.C. U.S. Army, 1967-70. Leukemia Soc. Am. scholar, 1970-75 Fellow A.C.P.; mem. Am. Soc. Hematology, Am. Soc. Clin. Oncology, Am. Soc. Clin. Investigation, Am. Assn. Immunologists., Assn. Am. Physicians, Am. Clin. and Climatological Assn., Nat Bd. Med. Examiners (mem.-at-large 2000—, mem. presdl. commn. policy for complementary and alter. medicine 2000-2002). Address: 287 Langley Rd Unit 11 Newton MA 02459 Personal E-mail: maberni3@aol.com.

BERNING, PAUL WILSON, lawyer; b. Marceline, Mo., Apr. 22, 1948; s. Harold John and Doris (Wilson) B. BJ, U. Mo., 1970; JD with honors, U. San Francisco, 1986. Bar: Calif. 1986, U.S. Dist. Ct. (no. dist., ea. dist., so. dist.) Calif. 1986, U. S. Dist. Ct. (cen. dist.) Calif. 1989, U.S. Ct. Appeals (9th cir.) 1986, U.S. Ct. Claims 1992, U.S. Supreme Ct. 1992, U.S. Ct. Appeals (D.C. cir.) 2005. Copy editor Chgo. Sun-Times, 1970-74, nat., fgn. editor, 1974-78; asst. news editor San Francisco Examiner, 1978-83; law clerk San Francisco dist. atty. Consumer Fraud Divsn., 1984; extern Calif. Supreme Ct., San Francisco, 1985, San Francisco Superior Ct., 1986; assoc. Thelen, Marrin, Johnson & Bridges, San Francisco, 1986-94, ptnr., 1995-98, Thelen Reid & Priest LLP, San Francisco, 1998—2006, Thelen, Reid, Brown, Raysman & Steiner, San Francisco, 2006—. Editor: Construction Web Links.com, 2000—; contbr. speeches and papers to profl. confs., chapters to books. Mem. ABA (forum on constrn. industry 1986—), Internat. Bar Assn., State Bar Calif., Bar Assn. San Francisco (coord. legal assistance for mil. pers. 1991-92, assoc. liaison to San Francisco lawyers com. urban affairs 1987-92). Avocations: horseback riding, sailing, reading. Office: Thelen Reid & Priest LLP 101 2nd St Ste 1800 San Francisco CA 94105-3401 Office Phone: 415-371-1200. Business E-Mail: pwberning@thelen.com.

BERNING, ROBERT WILLIAM, librarian; b. Carroll, Iowa, Dec. 2, 1949; s. Norbert John and Marjorie Lavine (Miller) B. BSE, N.W. Mo. State U., 1972; MLS, Emporia State U., 1974. Cert. pub. libr. Iowa. Sch. libr. Mount Ayr (Iowa) Cmty. Schs., 1974-76, Wall Lake (Iowa) Cmty. Schs., 1977-79, West Point (Nebr.) Pub. Schs., 1979-81; dir. Dubuque County Libr., Farley, Iowa, 1981-82; sch. libr. HLV Cmty. Schs., Victor, Iowa, 1982-84; dir. Carlisle (Iowa) Pub. Libr., 1985—. Mem. adv. bd. State Libr. Iowa, Des Moines, 1987, 89; mem. adv. com. Ctrl. Iowa Regional Libr., Clive, 1992-94, 98—. Libr. rep. Lanning Bequest com. City of Carlisle, 1995-97, Mng. Info. for Rural Am. (MIRA), 1998; mem. com., task force Iowans Can't Wait (Enrich Iowa), State Libr. Iowa, Des Moines, 1995-96; mem. Mayor's Select Com. on Property Taxes, Des. Moines, 1998-99. Mem. ALA, KC, Iowa Libr. Assn. (govtl. affairs com. 1988-91), Iowa Small Libr. Assn. (sec. 1985-87), Carlisle Lion's Club, Carlisle C. of C., Alpha Phi Omega (life). Roman Catholic. Avocations: collecting antiques, travel, gardening. Office: Carlisle Pub Libr 135 School St PO Box S Carlisle IA 50047 Office Phone: 515-989-0909. E-mail: carlpl1@mchsi.com.

BERNKNOPF, ALLISON CORI, pharmacist, educator; d. Judy Heyman. PharmD, U. Md., Balt., 2002. Registered pharmacist NJ, 2002, Mich., 2002. Resident drug info. Roche Pharms., Nutley, NJ, 2002—03; asst. prof. Ferris State U., Kalamazoo, 2003—. Mem.: Am. Pharm. Assn., Drug Info. Assn., Am. Soc. Health Sys. Pharmacists, Am. Coll. Clin. Pharmacy (chmn. elect drug info. practice and rsch. network 2006—), Creative Home Arts Club. Office: Ferris State Univ 1000 Oakland Dr Kalamazoo MI 49008 Office Phone: 269-599-5681. Office Fax: 269-337-4474. Business E-Mail: bernknopf@kcms.msu.edu.

BERNS, KENNETH IRA, physician; b. Cleve., June 14, 1938; s. Charles and Delnet (Cohn) Berns; m. Laura Louise Lawless, June 26, 1964; children: Jonathan Charles, Deborah Louise. Student, Harvard U., 1956—59; AB, Johns Hopkins U., 1960, PhD, 1964, MD, 1966. Intern Johns Hopkins Hosp., 1966—67; asst. prof. microbiology Johns Hopkins U. Sch. Medicine, 1970—74, asst. prof. pediat., 1970—76, asso. prof. microbiology, 1974—76; dir. Johns Hopkins U. Sch. Medicine (Yr. I program), 1973—76; prof., chmn. dept. immunology and med. microbiology, prof. pediat. U. Fla. Coll. Medicine, Gainesville, 1976—84, disting. prof., 2006—, dean, 1997—2002, v.p. health affairs, 2000—02; R.A. Rees Pritchett prof., chmn. dept. microbiology Cornell U. Med. Coll., 1984—97; pres., CEO Mt. Sinai Med. Ctr., NYC, 2002—03; dir. U. Fla. Genetics Inst., 2003—. Howard Hughes med. investigator, 1970—75; mem. microbiology test com. Nat. Bd. Med. Examiners, 1979—82, chmn., 1983—86, mem. exec. bd., 1986—95; mem. Recombinant DNA adv. com. NIH, 1980—83, chmn., 1982—83, mem. virology study sect., 1985—89; mem. genetic biology panel NSF, 1981—84; Fogarty sr. internat. fellow virology dept. Weizmann Inst. Sci., Rehovot, Israel, 1982—83; ad hoc mem. Bd. Sci. Counselors Nat. Inst. Allergy and Infectious Diseases, 1982, permanent mem., 1992—96; del. U.S.-Japan Coop. Program on Recombinant DNA, 1981; mem. Internat. Com. Taxonomy of Viruses, 1981—98; mem. virology and microbiology adv. com. Am. Cancer Soc., 1985—89, mem. liaison com. on med. edn., 1989—92; mem. composite com. U.S. Med. Licensing Exam., 1995—98; nat. adv. coun. Nat. Ctr. Rsch. Resources, 1999—2003. Bd. trustees Johns Hopkins U., 2000—06; bd. dir. Rosalind Franklin Soc., 2007—. With USPHS, 1967—70. Named Disting. Svc. Mem., Assn. Am. Med. Coll., 2003; recipient Faculty Rsch. award, Am. Cancer Soc., 1975—76, Disting. Svc. award, Nat. Bd. Med. Examiners, 1995; fellow Shell Oil, 1963—64; grantee Am. Cancer Soc., 1970—72, NIH, 1970—76, 1980—2005, NSF, 1973—75, 1979—80; Fogarty Sr. Internat. Fellowship, 1982—83. Fellow: AAAS; mem.: NAS, Inst. Medicine of NAS, Internat. Union Microbiol. Socs. (v.p. 1990—94), Soc. Pediatric Rsch., Soc. Gen. Microbiology, Am. Soc. Virology (pres. 1988—89), Assn. Med. Sch. Microbiology Chairmen (chmn. com. pub. policy 1979, counselor 1980—83, pres. 1985), Am. Soc. Microbiology (chair Public and Scientific Affairs Bd. 1990—96, pres. 1996—97), Am. Soc. Biol. Chemists, Am. Acad. Microbiology (bd. govs. 2003—), Alpha Omega Alpha, Sigma Xi, Phi Beta Kappa. Office: Univ Fla Coll of Medicine PO Box 103610 Gainesville FL 32610-3610 Office Phone: 352-273-8100. Business E-Mail: kberns@ufl.edu.

BERNS, PETER VERNON, lawyer; b. Newark, Sept. 22, 1956; s. Robert S. and Roslyn (Weinbaum) B.; m. Melissa Robin Zieve, Sept. 10, 1989; children: Eli L. Berns-Zieve, Rose W. Berns-Zieve, Jesse H. Berns-Zieve, Sarah R. Berns-Zieve. BA, U. Pa., 1978; JD, Harvard U., 1981; LLM, Georgetown U., 1983. Bar: Washington 1981, Md. 1983. Staff attorney, grad. fellow Inst. for Pub. Representation, Washington, 1981-83; asst. atty. gen. consumer protection div. Office of Atty. Gen., Balt., 1983-88, deputy chief consumer protection div., 1988-92; exec. dir. Md. Assn. Nonprofit Orgns., 1992—. Contbr. articles to profl. jours. V.p. Md. Food Com., Balt., 1989-94; sec. ACLU, Md., 1988; bd. dirs. Pub. Justice Ctr., 1994-96; bd. dirs. Balt. Jewish Coun., 1996—. Mem. Washington Bar. Assn. Office: Md Assn Nonprofit Orgns 190 W Ostend St Ste 201 Baltimore MD 21230-3797

BERNS, PHILIP ALLAN, lawyer; b. NYC, Mar. 18, 1933; s. Milton Benjamin and Rose (Aberman) Bernstein; m. Jane Klaw, June 7, 1959; children: David, Peter, Jay. BS in Marine Transp., N.Y. State Maritime Coll., 1955; LLB, Bklyn. Law Sch., 1960. Bar: N.Y. 1960, Calif. 1990, U.S. Ct. Appeals (2d cir.) 1962, U.S. Ct. Appeals (9th cir.) 1982. Admiralty atty. admiralty sect. U.S. Dept. Justice, NYC, 1960-71, asst. atty. in charge admiralty sect., 1971-77, atty. in charge torts br. San Francisco, 1977—2005, rep. to Supreme Ct. subcom. on admiralty rules, 1996—2005; pvt. practice cons. Henderson, Nev., 2005—. Adj. prof. McGeorge Law Sch., Sacramento, 1978-88; bd. dir. Pacific Admiralty Seminar, San Francisco. Assoc. editor Am. Maritime Cases, 1978-2005, cons. 2005-; mem. bd. editors Benedict's Maritime Bull., 2002—. Chmn. exec. com. S.I. (N.Y.) Community Bds., 1969-70, 1st vice chmn. no. 3 bd., 1975-77, treas. no. 3 bd., 1973-74; chmn. 122d Precinct, Community Counsel, S.I., 1968-71; pres. Walnut Creek (Calif.) Little League, 1984-85, v.p. 1978-83; pres. Chestnut Hill Civic Assn., S.I., 1968-74, Congregation B'nai Jeshurun, S.I., 1973-76, v.p., 1971-73; cub pack leader Boy Scouts Am., S.I., 1969-70; bd. dir. Mid-Island Little League, S.I., 1972-77, Jewish Community Ctr., S.I., 1976, Little League Dist. 4, Contra Costa (Calif.) County, 1984-90. Lt. USN, 1955-57 Named United Jewish Appeal Man of Yr., Congregation B'Nai Jeshurun, 1976. Mem. ABA (admiralty and maritime law com. 1991-94), Maritime Law Assn. U.S. (exec. com. 1991-94, vice chmn. practice and rules com. 1976-91, chmn. govt. liaison com. 1994—, mem. sec. 2002—, chmn. membership spl. subcom., no. dist. Calif. admiralty rules com. 1998-2005). Avocations: athletics, volunteer work. Home and Office: 2607 Savannah Springs Ave Henderson NV 89052-7160

BERNSEN, HAROLD JOHN, political scientist, educator, retired military officer; b. Boston, Nov. 25, 1936; s. Harold Arthur and Solveig Bachrud (Birkrem) B.; m. Doris Ann Champion, Mar. 5, 1960. BA, Dartmouth Coll., 1958. Commd. ensign USN, 1958, advanced through grades to rear adm., 1988, comdg. officer USS LaSalle, 1980-82, comdg. officer USS Lexington Pensacola, Fla., 1983-84, dir. plans and policy, staff comdr. in chief U.S. Cen. Command Tampa, Fla., 1985-86, comdr. Mideast Force, 1986-88, dir. plans and policy staff comdr. in chief Atlantic Fleet Norfolk, 1988-91; dep., chief of staff, comdr. in chief Atlantic Fleet, 1991; ret., 1991. Spkr. on Mid. East issues. Bd. dirs. Am. Bahraini Friendship Soc.; chmn. bd. dirs. Nat. Coun. on U.S.-Arab Rels.; trustee Physicians for Peace.; bd. dirs. Nat. US Arab C. of C. Decorated Disting. Svc. Medal, Def. Superior Svc. Medal, Legion of Merit; Royal Norwegian Order of Merit (Norway); Order 1st Class (Bahrain). Mem.: Assn. Naval Aviation, Sons of Norway, Army Navy Club, N.Y. Yacht Club. Avocations: sailing, cooking, gardening, skiing. Office Phone: 757-651-4811. E-mail: hbernsen@cox.net.

BERNSON, MARCELLA S., psychiatrist; b. NYC, Aug. 24, 1952; d. Maxwell Isaac and Priscilla Edith (Zuckerman) Bernson; m. Robert A. Foster, Aug. 7, 2001. BA in Biology summa cum laude, Hofstra U., 1973; MD, Albert Einstein Coll. Medicine, 1976. Diplomate Am. Bd. Psychiatry and Neurology. Resident in psychiatry Bronx (N.Y.) Mcpl. Hosp. Ctr., 1976—79; assoc. dir. med. student edn. in psychiatry U. Medicine and Dentistry N.J.-N.J. Med. Sch., Newark, 1979—81; pvt. practice psychiatry Westfield, NJ, 1981—86; cons. psychiatrist Healthwise EAP, Elizabeth, NJ, 1985—86; staff psychiatrist Elizabeth Gen. Med. Ctr., 1985—88, 1992—95, med. chief adult ambulatory svcs. dept. psychiatry, 1986—87, asst. dir. dept. psychiatry, 1987—88; dir. tng. psychiat. svc. VA Med. Ctr., East Orange, NJ, 1988—89; med. dir. partial care Occupl. Ctr. Union County, Roselle, NJ, 1989—92; cons. psychiatrist Union County Ednl. Svcs. Commn., Westfield, 1992—95; med. dir. Richard Hall CMHC, Bridgewater, NJ, 1995—99, staff psychiatrist, 2003—; with devel. disabilities ctr. Morristown (N.J.) Meml. Hosp., 1999—2003. Instr. U. Medicine and Dentistry N.J.-N.J. Med. Sch., Newark, 1979—81, asst. prof. clin. psychiatry, 1988—89; mem. human rights com. Divsn. Devel. Disabilities, State of N.J. Mem.: N.J. Psychiat. Assn. (Union County rep. 1989—90, Morris County rep. 2000—02), Am. Psychiat. Assn. Avocation: short fiction. Office: Richard Hall CMHC 500 N Bridge St Bridgewater NJ 08807

BERNSTEIN, ARTHUR HAROLD, venture capital executive; b. NYC, June 8, 1925; s. Charles and Eva (Aronson) B.; m. Barbara R. Ettinger, June 24, 1951; children: Jeffrey R., Diane. B of Chem. Engring., Cornell U., 1947, JD, 1950. Bar: N.Y. 1950, Fla. 1956, U.S. Supreme Ct. 1962, Calif. 1972. Staff atty. N.Y. Cen. R.R. Co., NYC, 1950-55; gen. counsel Ryder System, Inc., Miami, 1955-58, v.p., treas., dir., 1958-65; sr. assoc. Lazard Freres & Co., NYC, 1966-68; v.p. Norton Simon, Inc., Los Angeles, 1968-70; sr. v.p. Max Factor & Co., Los Angeles, 1970-77; mgr. gen. ptnr. Calif. Capital Investors, Ltd., LA, 1980-93; pres. Bancorp Capital Group Inc., Bancorp Venture Capital Inc., LA, 1988—, also bd. dirs. Trustee emeritus WM Group of Funds, Seattle. Chair emeritus bd. dir. Philips Grad. Inst., Encino, Calif.; trustee Idyllwild Arts Found., Calif. With USN, 1943—46, PTO. Mem. ABA, Fla. Bar Assn., State Bar Calif. Jewish. Office: 11661 San Vicente Blvd Ste 701 Los Angeles CA 90049-5115 Office Phone: 310-820-7222. E-mail: ahb10@cornell.edu.

BERNSTEIN, BARRY JOEL, lawyer; b. Charleston, SC, Feb. 11, 1961; s. Charles Stanley Bernstein and Sara Blum Baumwald; m. Charlene Wilkins, May 29, 1998; children: Brandi Nichole, Alexander Nicholas. BA, U. SC, 1983, JD, 1995; postgrad., US Army Command & Gen. Staff Coll., 2001. Bar: SC, US Dist. Ct. SC; cert. mediator SC Supreme Ct., 1998. Security mgr. Boeing, Wichita, Kans., 1986-88; pres. Security Cons., Inc., Charleston, SC, 1988-92; law clk. Bernstein and Bernstein, PA, Charleston, 1992-95; ptnr. Breland and Bernstein, Greenville, SC, 1995-97; owner, pres. Bernstein Law Firm, Greenville, 1998-2000; gen. counsel Adjutant Gen. of SC, 2000—. Dir. Homeless Animal Res. and Placement, Greenville, 1995-2000; active Kahol Kadosh Beth Elohim Synagogue. 1st lt. US Army, 1983-86, col. Operation Iraqi Freedom, 2006-07, col. JAG SC N.G., 1978—. SC Nat. Guard scholar U. SC, 1980, Helen Gullickson scholar U. SC Sch. of Law, 1994, Claude M. Sapp scholar; recipient Bronze Star Medal; named Officer of Yr. ROA, Kans. Mem. VFW (life, Bronze award), ABA, SC Trial Lawyers Assn., Comml. Law League Am., Scottish Rite, Masons (past master), Phi Delta Phi (magister 1994-95, province pres. 1996-98), Zeta Beta Tau. Jewish. Home: 304 Lost Creek Columbia SC 29212 Office: Adjutant General of SC 1 National Guard Rd Columbia SC 29201-4766 Business E-Mail: barry.bernstein@sc.ngb.army.mil.

BERNSTEIN, CARL, writer, journalist; b. Washington, Feb. 14, 1944; s. Alfred David and Sylvia (Walker) B.; m. Carol Ann Honsa, Apr. 28, 1968 (div.); m. Nora Ephron, Apr. 14, 1976 (div. 1980); children: Jacob Walker, Max Ephron; m. Christine Kuehbeck, July 4, 2003. Student, U. Md., 1961-64; LLD, Boston U., 1975. From copyboy to reporter Washington Star, 1960-65; reporter Elizabeth (N.J.) Jour., 1965-66, Washington Post, 1966-76; Washington bur. chief ABC, 1979-81; corr. ABC News, NYC, 1981-84; corr., contbr. Time mag., 1990-91; contbg. editor Vanity Fair, 1997—. Vis. prof. NYU, 1992; exec. editor voter.com Co-author: (with Bob Woodward) All The President's Men, 1974, The Final Days, 1976; (with Marco Politi) His Holiness: John Paul II and the History of Our Time, 1996; author: Loyalties: A Son's Memoir, 1989, A Woman in Charge: The Life of Hillary Rodham Clinton, 2007 Served with AUS, 1968. Recipient 1st prize feature writing, 1966, 1st prize gen. reporting N.J. Press Assn., 1966, 1st prize investigative reporting, 1966; Drew Pearson prize for investigative reporting of Watergate, 1972; George Polk Meml. award; Worth Bingham prize; Heywood Broun award Internat. Newspaper Guild; Sigma Delta Chi Disting. Service award; Sidney Hillman Found. award; gold medal U. Mo. Sch. Journalism, 1972; Pulitzer prize citation, 1972.*

BERNSTEIN, CAROL, molecular biologist; b. Paterson, NJ, Mar. 20, 1941; d. Benjamin and Mina (Regenbogen) Adelberg; m. Harris Bernstein, June 7, 1962; children: Beryl, Golda, Benjamin. BS in Physics, U. Chgo., 1961; MS in Biophysics, Yale U., 1964; PhD in Genetics, U. Calif.-Davis, 1967. NIH fellow zoology dept. U. Calif.-Davis, 1967—68; rsch. assoc. Dept. Microbiology to rsch. assoc. prof. U. Ariz., Tucson, 1968—2004, rsch. assoc. prof. cell biology and anatomy Coll. Medicine, 2004—. Proposal reviewer NSF, 1978—87, VA, 1983, Wellcome Trust, 2001—03, Michael Smith Found. for Health Rsch., Canada, 2003, Associazone Italiana Per La Ricerca Sul Cancro, 2003; exec. bd. Patient Quality Care Project; spkr. in field. Author (with Harris Bernstein): Aging, Sex and DNA Repair, 1991; mem. editl. bd.: Electronic Jour. Biotech.; contbr. articles to profl. jours. and encys. Panel mem. grad fellow rev. NSF, 1984—86, NAS, 1991—94, NSF, 1998, 1999, 2004. Grantee NSF, 1975—79, NIH, 1979—81, 1982—87, 1997—, Ariz. Disease Control, 1986—89, 1991—, Nat. Found., 1975—76, Vets. Affairs Merit Review, 2007—. Mem. AAUP (pres. Ariz. state conf. 1983-86, 90-2004, 2007-, Ariz. chpt. 1983, del. nat. coun. 1986-89, treas. nat. assembly state conf. 1990-92, designated lobbyist 1990—), Am. Assn. Cancer Rsch., Genetics Soc. Am., Whistleblower Week Wash. (treas. 2007-). Democrat. Jewish. Achievements include research in providing the molecular basis for the existence of sex and the cause of aging; led the passage of an Arizona faculty governance law for the American Association of University Professors. Home: 2639 E 4th St Tucson AZ 85716-4417 Office: U Ariz Coll Med Dept Cell Biology and Anatomy Tucson AZ 85724-5044 Home Phone: 520-324-0275; Office Phone: 520-626-6069. Personal E-mail: bernstein3@earthlink.net. Business E-Mail: bernstei@u.arizona.edu.

BERNSTEIN, CHARLES, poet, writer, educator; b. NYC, Apr. 4, 1950; s. Herman and Sherry (Kegel) B.; m. Susan Bee Laufer, Aug. 17, 1977; children: Emma Bee, Felix Laufer. AB, Harvard U., 1972. Vis. lectr., dept. lit. U. Calif. San Diego, 1987; vis. prof., dept. english Queens Coll., CUNY, 1988; vis. faculty/series coord. Wolfson Ctr. for Nat. Affairs, New Sch. for Social Rsch., 1988; lectr., creative writing program Princeton U., 1989, 1990; Butler Chair prof. (vis.), dept. english SUNY, Buffalo, 1989; vis. prof. CUNY, 1998, Columbia U., 2002; David Gray Prof. of Poetry and Letters, dept. english, dir. and co-founder poetics program, assoc. mem. program in comparative lit. SUNY, Buffalo, 1990—2003, SUNY Disting. Prof., 2002—03; Donald T. Regan Prof. English U. Pa., 2003—. Presenter of poetry readings, lectrs. worldwide; freelance writer, numerous med. publications and healthcare media prodrs., 1976-89; dir. rsch. Henny Youngman Ctr. for Stand-up Poetry and Avant-Garde Comedy; advisor, Transdisciplinary PhD program on Languages, Identities, and Globalization, Faculty of Arts & Sciences, U. Coimbra, 2005-; bd. mem. Ontological Hysteric Theatre, Ubuweb Found., Futurepoem Books, Ugly Duckling Presse; mem. adv. bd. New Works panel (lit. & criticism), Mass. Coun. Arts (1987) Greenwood Encyclopedia Am. Poetry, Gertrude Stein Awards (Los Angeles); Syntax Project for the Arts, Pengrove, Calif., Poems for the Millennium: The U. Calif. Book of Modern and Postmodern Poetry, ed. Jerome Rothenberg and Pierre Joris, NYC Poetry Calendar, Postwar Am. Poetry, ABES (Annotated Bibliography of English Studies), Macdowell Colony, 2003-04); Writing Workshop Leader, The Poetry Project, St. Mark's Church, 1980 81; vis. lectr., dept. English, U. Auckland, New Zealand,1986; writer in residence, grad. writing program, Brown U., 1988; vis. writer, grad. creative writing Program, Temple U., 1988; poet in residence, Kootenay Sch. of Writing, Vancouver,1989; vis. poet, Naropa Inst. Poetics Program, Boulder 1991, 2005, vis. instructor, Milton Avery Grad. Sch. Art, Bard Coll., 1992; vis. prof., Universidad de la Laguna, Tenerife, Spain, 1993. Author (full-length poetry) Asylums, 1975, Parsing, 1976, Shade, 1978, Poetic Justice, 1979, (with Bruce Andrews, Steve McCaffery, Ron Silliman, Ray DiPalma) Legend, 1980, Controlling Interests, 1980, Islets/Irritations, 1983, The Sophist, 1987, Rough Trades, 1991, Dark City, 1994, Republics of Reality: 1975-1995, 2000, With Strings, 2001, Shadowtime, 2005, Girly Man, 2006, (short collections, collaborations, and limited editions) Senses of Responsibility, 1979, Disfrutes, 1981, 2nd edit., 1999, The Occurance of Tune, 1981, Stigma, 1981, Resistance, 1983, Veil, 1987, Four Poems, 1988, The Nude Formalism, 1989, The Absent Father in Dumbo, 1990, (with Susan Bee) Fool's Gold, 1991, The Subject, 1995, (with Susan Bee) Little Orphan Anagram, 1997, (with Richard Tuttle) Reading Red, 1998, (with Susan Bee) Log Rhythms, 1998, Let's Just Say, 2003, World on Fire, 2004, Some of These Daze, 2005), (essays) Content's Dream: Essays, 1975-84, 1986, A Poetics, 1992, My Way: Speeches and Poems, 1999, A Conversation with David Antin, 2002, (libretti) Blind Witness News, A Psychiatric Opera, (with Ben Yarmolinsky) The Lenny Paschen Show, The Subject, 1995, Café Buffé, 2002, Shadowtime, 2005; dir. (with Al Filries) PennSound, 2003-; editor, co-founder (with Loss Pequeno Glazier) Electronic Poetry Ctr., 1995-, (with Hank Lazer), Modern Contemporary Poetics, 1998-; edited (with Bruce Andrews) L=A=N=G=U=A=G=E, 1984, (anthologies) Knock Knock, 1981, Language Sampler,1982, Realism: An Anthology of Language Writing, 1982, Translation: Experiments in Reading, 1983, In the American Tree, 1986, Annual Survey of American Poetry, 1987, American Poetry Since 1970: Up Late, 1987, Language Poetries: An Anthology, 1987, Broadway 2, 1989, Out of The World, 1991, The Best American Poetry 1992, Postmodern American Poetry: A Norton Anthology, 1994, Fifty: A Celebration of Sun & Moon Classics, 1994, From the Other Side of the Century: A New American Poetry 1960-1990, 1994, The Best Verse: Ten Years of Poetry, 1995, The Gertrude Stein Awards in Innovative North American Poetry: 1993, 1995, The Poetry Dictionary, 1996, American Poets Say Goodbye the Twentieth Century, 1996, The Gertrude Stein Awards in Innovative American Poetry: 1995-1996, 1998, Poems for the Millenium: The University of California Book of Modern and Postmodern Poetry, vol 2, 1998, Poetry Writing: Theme and Variations, 1999, Real Things: An Anthology of Popular Culture in American Poetry, 1999, Catalyst, 1999, The Norton Anthology of Jewish American Literature, 2000, The Body Electric: The Best Poetry from The American Poetry Review, 1972-1999, 2000, Jewish American Poetry: Poems, Commentary, and Reflections, 2000, The Norton Introduction to Literature, 7th edit., 1999, 2001, Best American Poetry 2002, Short Fuse: The Global Anthology of New Fusion Poetry, 2002, Great American Prose Poems: From Poe to the Present, 2003, The Norton Anthology of Modern and Contemporary Poetry, 3rd edit., 2003, 100 Poets Against the War, 2003, Enough, an anthology of poetry and writings against the war, 2003, The Norton Anthology of Poetry, 5th edit., 2004, Understanding Literature: An Introduction to Reading and Writing, 2004, Best American Poetry 2004, Understanding Poetry, 2005, 180 More: Extraordinary Poems for Everyday, 2005, The Gertrude Stein Awards in Innovative American Poetry: 2005, 2006, The Broadview Anthology of Poetry, 2nd edit., 2006, The Wadsworth Anthology of Poetry, 2006, The Longman Anthology of Poetry, 2006, The Oxford Book of American Poetry, 2006, and several others, (radio productions) poetry interviews, host/co-prodr. LINEbreak, 1995-96, Studio 111, 2004-, Close Listening, 2005-; listowner, founder, Poetics Listserve, 1993-; (Internet) Web Log, 2006-; editor 99 Poets, 1999; mem. editl. bd. boundary 2, Chain, Fgn. Lit. Studies, Sibila, Ariz. Quarterly Review, Boxkite, Revista Canaria de Estudios Ingleses; corr. Sulfur, 1985-2000; contbr. to several collaborations, compact discs, audio & video readings; curator and coord. of shows. Fellow William Lyon McKenzie King Simon Fraser U., 1973, Nat. Endowment for Arts Creative Writing, 1980, John Simon Guggenheim Meml., 1985, U. Auckland Found., 1986, N.Y. Found. for Arts, 1990, 1995; recipient Roy Harvey Pearce/Archive for New Poetry prize of the U. Calif. San Diego for Lifetime Contribution to Poetry and Scholarship, 1999; Adams House Coat-of-Arms, 1972. Fellow: Am. Acad. Arts & Sciences; mem.: Modern Language Assn. (mem. exec. com., Poetry Division 1998—2002, mem. exec. com. Discussion Group for Bibliography & Textual Studies 2004—), Poets and Writers Directory of Am. Writers, ASCAP (Standard award), Phi Beta Kappa (of Alpha). Office: Dept English U Pennsylvania 127 Fischer-Bennett Hall 3340 Walnut St Philadelphia PA 19104-6293 Business E-Mail: charles.bernstein@english.upenn.edu.

BERNSTEIN, CHARLES BERNARD, lawyer; b. Chgo., June 24, 1941; s. Norman and Adele (Shore) B.; m. Roberta Luba Lesner, Aug. 7, 1968; children: Edward Charles, Louis Charles, Henry Jacob. AB, U. Chgo., 1962; JD, DePaul U., 1965. Bar: Ill. 1965, U.S. Supreme Ct. 1972. Assoc. Axelrod, Goodman & Steiner, Chgo., 1966—67, Max & Herman Chill, Chgo., 1967—74, Bellows & Assocs., Chgo., 1974—81, Marvin Sacks Ltd., Chgo., 1981; sole practice Chgo., 1981—. Basketball press dir. U. Chgo., 1967-74. Author: (with Stuart L. Cohen) Torah and Technology: The History and Genealogy of the Anixter Family, 1986; (with Neil Rosenstein) From King David to Baron David: The Genealogical Connections Between Baron Guy de Rothschild and Baroness Alix de Rothschild, 1989; The Rothschilds of Nordstetten: Their History and Genealogy, 1989; contbr. articles to mags., profl. jours. Mem. nominating com. Hyde Park Coop. Soc., 1997—; officer Congregation Rodfei Zedek, 1979—83, 2002—04, bd. dirs., 1978—93, 2000—. Recipient Am. Jurisprudence award, 1963, My Brother's Keeper award Am. Jewish Congress, 1977, Kovod award Rodfei Zedek Men's Club, 1998; co-recipient 2d Century award Jewish Theol. Sem. Am., 1999. Mem. Chgo. Bar Assn., Ill. State Bar Assn., Decalogue Soc. of Lawyers, Chgo. Jewish Hist. Soc. (treas. 1977-79, v.p. 1979-82, dir. 1977—), Chgo. Pops Orch. Assn. (treas., exec. com. 1975-81), Am. Jewish Hist. Soc., Art Inst. of Chgo., Chgo. Hist. Soc., Jewish Geneal. Soc. (dir. 1977—), Nu Beta Epsilon, B'nai B'rith (citation meritorious svc. Dist. Grand Lodge 6 1969). Home: 5400 S Hyde Park Blvd Apt C10 Chicago IL 60615-5828 Office: 10 S LaSalle St Ste 1400 Chicago IL 60603-1080 Office Phone: 312-263-0005.

BERNSTEIN, DANIEL LEWIS, lawyer; b. Durham, NC, Aug. 19, 1937; s. Edward Morris and Edith (Lewis) B.; m. Ann Lust; children: Kenneth, Margaret. AB, Amherst Coll., 1959; LLB, Harvard U., 1962. Bar: N.Y. 1962, D.C. 1976. Assoc. Law Offices of A.L. Bienstock, NYC, 1962-66, Hale Russell & Gray, NYC, 1966-69, ptnr., 1970-84, Reid & Priest, NYC, 1984-91, mng. ptnr., 1990-91; ptnr. Mannheimer Swartling, Stockholm, Sweden, NYC, 1991-93, Law Office of Daniel L. Bernstein, NYC, 1994—2003; sr. v.p., gen. counsel Lantis Eyewear Corp., NYC, 1996—2003; ptnr. Sussman, Sollis, Tweedy & Wood LLP, NYC, 2001—06, Russin, Vecchi & Berg, LLP, NYC, 2007—. Trustee Georges Lurcy Charitable and Ednl. Trust, N.Y.C., 1982—. Dir. The Arts and Scis. Found. U. N.C., Chapel Hill, 1994-2000; trustee The Colleen Giblin Found. , Oradell, N.J., 1994—, Walnut Hill Sch., Natick, Mass., 1999—. Mem.: ABA, Bar Assn. of City of N.Y., Alumni Coun. Amherst Coll. (mem. exec. com. 2004—). Office: Russin Vecchi & Berg LLP 260 Madison Ave New York NY 10016

BERNSTEIN, DAVID, gastroenterologist; b. NYC; BA, Johns Hopkins U., 1984; MD, SUNY, Stony Brook, 1988. Attending hepatology U. Miami (Fla.) Sch. Medicine, 1994-96; chief clin. gastroenterology Winthrop Univ. Hosp., Mineola, N.Y., 1996-99; chief gastroenterology North Shore Univ. Hosp. and LI Jewish Med. Ctr., Manhasset, NY, 1999—. Mem. sci. adv. bd. Am. Liver Found., N.Y.C., 1996—. Fellow ACP, Am. Coll. Gastroenterology, Am. Assn. Study of Liver Disease, Am. Gastrointestinal Assn.; mem. Am. Soc. Gastrointestinal Endoscopy, NY Gastrointestinal Assn. Office: North Shore Univ Hosp 300 Community Dr Manhasset NY 11030-3801 Fax: 516-562-2683.

BERNSTEIN, DAVID WILLIAM, lawyer; b. Bklyn., Feb. 13, 1938; s. Sidney Abraham B. and Carol Elsa Silverman; m. Carol Ellen Lamberg, June 16, 1959 (div. 1977); m. Melissa Lewis, Mar. 7, 1980; children: Andrew, Donna, Lauren. BA magna cum laude, Harvard U., 1959, LLB magna cum laude, 1962. Bar: N.Y. 1962. Assoc. atty. Rogers & Wells, NYC, 1962-67; ptnr. Clifford Chance Rogers & Wells, NYC, 1967—, chmn. corp. dept., 1989-97. Contbr. numerous articles to Internat. Fin. Law Rev., 1996—. Bd. dirs. Internat. Preschs., 1966—. Mem. Inwood Country Club (sec. 1982-91). Republican. Jewish. Avocation: golf. Office: Clifford Chance US LLP 31 W 52d St New York NY 10019-0005 Office Phone: 212-878-8342. Fax: 212-878-8375. E-mail: david.bernstein@cliffordchance.com.

BERNSTEIN, DONALD SCOTT, lawyer; b. Bklyn., July 11, 1953; s. Emanuel and Shirley (Smithline) B.; m. Jo Ellen Finkel, May 31, 1987; children: Daniel Emanuel, Julia Clare. BA, Princeton U., 1975; JD, U. Chgo., 1978. Bar: NY 1979, US Dist. Ct. (ea. and so. dists.) NY 1979. Assoc. Davis Polk & Wardwell, NYC, 1978-86, ptnr., 1986—, head insolvency & restructuring practice group. Panelist Practicing Law Inst., NYC, 1983—, Am. Law Inst., ABA, 1991—, Am. Bankruptcy Inst., 1991—; mem. vis. com. U. Chgo. Law Sch., 1995-98, chmn., 1997-98; chmn. outside adv. com. Princeton U. program in law and pub. affairs, 2007; mem. ofcl. US del. Insolvency Working Group, UN Commn. on Internat. Trade Law. Contbg. author Collier on Bankruptcy, 1996—, bd. editors, 2000—. Bd. dirs. Altro Health and Rehab. Svcs., Bronx, NY, 1988-90, NY chpt. Am. Diabetes Assn., 1992-96, City Bar Justice Ctr., 2006-; mem. exec. com. bankruptcy lawyers div. United Jewish Appeal Fedn., 1985—. Fellow: Am. Bar Found; mem. ABA (bus. bankruptcy com., com. on legal opinions), Am. Coll. Bankruptcy (bd. dirs., 2001—), New York County Lawyers Assn. (bd. dirs. 1992-94), Nat. Bankruptcy Conf. (exec. com. 1996-99, chmn. 2004—), Am. Bankruptcy Inst., Assn. Bar City NY (audit com. chmn. 2000—, com. on bankruptcy and corp. reorgn. 1979-83, 85-88, chmn. 1993-96, mem. tribar opinion com. 1988—, chmn. 1998—), Internat. Insolvency Inst. (bd. dirs.). Office: Davis Polk & Wardwell 450 Lexington Ave Fl 21 New York NY 10017-3982 Office Phone: 212-450-4092. Office Fax: 212-450-3092. Business E-Mail: donald.bernstein@dpw.com.

BERNSTEIN, EDWARD CHARLES, rabbi; BA, Columbia U., NYC, 1989—93, Jewish Theol. Sem. Am., 1989—93; MA, JTSA William Davidson Grad. Sch. Jewish Edn., NYC, 1996—99. Lic. rabbi Jewish Theol. Sem. Am., 1999. Assoc. rabbi Beth El Synagogue Ctr., New Rochelle, NY, 1999—2003; rabbi Congregation Shaarey Tikvah, Beachwood, Ohio, 2003—. Mem. Mercaz USA, 2002—05. Grantee Crown fellowship, Jewish Theol. Sem. Am., 1994—96. Mem.: Profl. Edn. For Excellence Rabbis, Greater Cleve. Bd. Rabbis, Internat. Rabbinical Assembly. Jewish.

BERNSTEIN, EDWIN S., judge; b. Long Beach, NY, Aug. 15, 1930; s. Harry and Lena (Strizver) B.; children: Andrea, David. BA, U. Pa., 1952; LLB, Columbia U., 1955. Bar: NY 1955, U.S. Ct. Appeals (2d cir.) 1962, U.S. Dist. Ct. (ea. and so. dists.) NY 1962, U.S. Tax Ct. 1962, U.S. Supreme Ct. 1964, Md. 1981, DC 1982. Mem. bd. contract appeals Dept. Army, Heidelberg, Germany, 1968-72; regional counsel U.S. Navy, Quincy, Mass., 1972-73; adminstrv. law judge U.S. Dept. Labor, Washington, 1973-79, Fed. Mine Safety and Health Rev. Commn., Washington, 1979-81, U.S. Postal Svc., Washington, 1981-87, USDA, Washington, 1987-2000. Liaison rep. Administrv. Conf. of U.S., Washington, 1983-84; guest lectr. SUNY-Albany, 1978, U. Md., 1982, George Washington U., 1984. Author: U.S. Army Procurement Handbook, 1971; Establishing Federal Administrative Law Judges as an Independent Corps, 1984, also articles. Bd. dirs. Washington Hebrew Congregation, 1985-88. Recipient Meritorious Civilian Svc. award Dept. Army, 1972. Mem. ABA, Fed. Bar Assn., DC Bar Assn., Fed. Adminstr. Law Judges Conf. (pres. 1983-84), Papermill Assn. (pres. 1980-81), Masons. Avocations: golf, bridge, sailing, wines, opera. Home and Office: 5314 Angel Wing Dr Boynton Beach FL 33437 E-mail: edamber007@comcast.net.

BERNSTEIN, ELIZABETH ANN, retired executive secretary; b. London, Aug. 13, 1928; arrived in U.S., 1960; d. Eugene and Ethel (Housley) Horsfall-Ertz; m. Alvin Bernstein, Mar. 5, 1975. Sec. various firms, 1948—58, Icelandic Airlines, Reykjavik, Iceland, 1958—59; legal and med. sec. various firms, 1960—82, Wash., 1982—89; ret., 1990. Author: Tsunami, 1994, Pull of the Tides, 1998, Many Moons Rising, 2002, Walk Into The Wind, 2006, numerous pub. poetry. Mem.: Bay Area Poets Coalition, Calif. Fedn. Chaparral Poets (2nd prize poems 2004, first prize poem 2005, 2006). Democrat. Avocations: reading, writing, music, gardening, travel. Mailing: PO Box 94 Paradise CA 95967-0094

BERNSTEIN, ERIC MARTIN, lawyer; b. Passaic, NJ, May 5, 1957; s. Abbot Alan and Jean Hausman (Schwartz) B. BA, Drew U., Madison, NJ, 1979; JD, U. Okla., Norman, 1982; MS in Indsl. and Labor Rels., Cornell U., Ithaca, NY, 1985. Bar: NJ 1982, US Dist. Ct. NJ 1982, DC 1985, US Ct. Appeals (3d cir.) 1985, US Supreme Ct. 1986. Assoc. Mandelbaum Salsburg Gold & Lazaris, East Orange, NJ, 1982-83; pvt. practice Clifton, NJ, 1983-84; sr. assoc. Gerald L. Dorf, PA, Rahway, NJ, 1984-87; of counsel Vaida & Vaida, PC, Flemington, NJ, 1987-88; pvt. practice Bridgewater, Clifton and Three Bridges, NJ, 1988-92; ptnr. Weiner Lesniak, Parsippany, NJ, 1992-97, Mauro Savo Camerino & Grant, Somerville, NJ, 1998-00, Eric M. Bernstein & Assocs., LLC, Warren, NJ, 2000—. Co-adj. prof. Bur. Govt. Rsch. Rutgers U., 1984—; city atty. City of Passaic, N.J., 1990-92; mcpl. atty. Washington Twp.-Warren County, 1991-2004, Hardwick Twp.-Warren County, 1992-2001, West Windsor-Mercer County, 1993-97, North Plainfield-Somerset County, 1997—, Bethlehem Twp.-Hunterdon County, 1998-2000, Stillwater Twp.-Sussex County, 1998-2000, Paramus Borough-Bergen County, 1999-2001, Franklin Twp.-Hunterdon County, 1999-2004, Union City-Hudson County, 1999-2000, Lebanon Twp.-Hunterdon County, 2001—, High Bridge Borough, Hunterdon County, 2003-04, Fairfield Twp.-Cumberland County, 2005-07, Lavallette Borough-Ocean County, 2006—; bd. atty. Englewood Bd. Edn.-Bergen County, 1996-99, Lincoln Park Bd. Edn.-Morris County, 1997-2000; planning bd. atty. Bethlehem Twp.-Hunterdon County, 2000-02, Hillsborough Twp.-Somerset County, 2001—; city solicitor City Plainfield, 2001-05; gen. counsel Atlantic City Housing Authority, 2007-; lectr. in field. Asst. editor, co-author: Governing New Jersey Municipalities, 1984, co-editor, author, 6th edit., 1995; asst. editor NJ Mcpl. Attys. Mag., 1984-92; editor NJ State Bar Assn. Local Govt. Law Newsletter, 1995—; host "Legal Pad" YNOT Radio, 2006—. Vol. atty. Lawyers for the Arts, NJ, 1986—, First Amendment Lawters Assn., 2005-. Named Super Atty., NJ Monthly, 2006, 2007. Mem. ABA, Fed. Bar Assn., NJ Bar Assn. (1st vice chair local govt. law sect. 1995—), DC Bar Assn., Passaic County Bar Assn., Somerset County Bar Assn., Nat. Arbitration Forum (arbitrator). Republican. Jewish. Avocations: tennis, golf, stamp collecting/philately, classical and jazz music. Home: 10 Timberline Dr Bridgewater NJ 08807-1204 Office: 2 North Rd PO Box 4922 Warren NJ 07059-0922 Office Phone: 732-805-3360. Business E-Mail: embernstein@embalaw.com.

BERNSTEIN, GERALD WILLIAM, management consultant, researcher; b. Boston, Nov. 25, 1947; s. Alan Irwin and Anne B.; m. Kathleen Ann Chaikin, Jan. 12, 1985. BS in Aero. Engring., Rensselaer Poly. Inst., 1969; MS in Engring., Stanford U., 1978. Transp. engr., dept. transp. State of NY, Albany, 1969-70; transp. planner Kennebec Regional Planning Com., Winslow, Maine, 1974-77; dir. transp. dept. SRI Internat., Menlo Park, Calif., 1979-95; v.p. BACK Mgmt. Svcs., San Francisco, 1995-98; mng. dir. Stanford Transp. Group, San Francisco, 1998—2005; ptnr. Velocity Group, San Francisco, 2005—. Session chmn. aviation workshop NSF, 1985, 91, 99, 2002; profl. conf. chmn. Contbr. articles to profl. jours. Chmn. transp. com. Glenn Park Neighborhood Assn., San Francisco, 1982-85; dir. Balboa Terrace Neighborhood Assn., San Francisco, 1986-88; trustee Congregation Beth Israel-Judea, 1991-93. With U.S. Army, 1970-72. Recipient Cert. Appreciation City of Waterville, Maine, 1977. Mem. Am. Inst. Aeronautics and Astronautics (sr. mem.), Transp. Rsch. Bd. NRC (chmn. econs. and forecasting com.), Toastmasters Club (Menlo Park, pres. 1986). Democrat. Jewish. Avocations: flying, skiing. Office: Stanford Transp Group 236 W Portal Ave Ste 359 San Francisco CA 94127-1423 Business E-Mail: jerry@velocity-group.com.

BERNSTEIN, H. BRUCE, lawyer; b. Omaha, Dec. 9, 1943; s. David and Muriel (Krasne) B.; m. Janice Ostroff, Aug. 27, 1967; children: Daniel J., Jill M. AB, Cornell U., 1965; JD, Harvard U., 1968. Bar: Ill. 1968, Ill. Supreme Ct. 1968, US Dist. Ct. no. dist. Ill. 1969, ea. dist. Wis. 1997, US Ct. of Appeals 7th cir. 1981, 6th cir. 1995. Ptnr. secured transactions Sidley Austin LLP, Chgo., 1974—, mem. exec. com. Gen. counsel Comml. Fin. Assn. 1995-2001 Past bd. dirs. Jewish Family and Cmty. Svc. Agy. Mem. ABA, Ill. Bar Assn. (past chmn. Comml., Banking and Bankruptcy Law section), Chgo. Bar Assn. (past chmn. Uniform Comml. Code Com.), Am. Coll. Comml. Fin. Attorneys, Am. Coll. Bankruptcy, Nat. Bankruptcy Conf., Standard Club, Mid-Day Club, Northmoor Country Club, Harvard Club. Avocation: golf. Office: Sidley Austin LLP Ste 2500 One S Dearborn St Chicago IL 60603 Office Phone: 312-853-7635. Office Fax: 312-853-7036. Business E-Mail: bbernstein@sidley.com.

BERNSTEIN, I. MELVIN, dean, materials scientist; b. NYC, Oct. 14, 1938; s. Emanuel and Helen (Wolitzer) B.; m. Katherine Sarah Russo, June 7, 1964; 1 child, Elana BS, Columbia U., 1960, MS, 1962, PhD, 1965. Postdoctoral assoc. Central Electricity Generating Bd., Berkeley, Eng., 1966-67; scientist U.S. Steel Research Lab., Monroeville, Pa., 1967-72; from asst. prof. to prof. Carnegie-Mellon U., Pitts., 1972-87, assoc. dean engring., 1978-82, prof., head dept. metall. engring and materials sci., 1982-87; provost, acad. v.p. Ill. Inst. Tech., Chgo., 1987-90, chancellor, 1990-91; v.p. arts, scis. and engring., dean faculty Tufts U., Medford, Mass., 1991-2001; provost, sr. v.p. Brandeis U., 2001—03; dir. univ. programs Dept. of Homeland Security, Washington, 2003—06; v.p. rsch. U. Md., College Park, 2006—. Chief cons. MCL, Monroeville, 1972-82; liaison scientist Office Naval Research, London, 1977-78; mem. Nat. Materials adv. bd., 1990-96. Co-editor: Handbook of Stainless Steel, 1977, Hydrogen Effects in Metals, 1973, 76, 1981; assoc. editor Metall. Trans., 1977-82. Mem. Pitts. Dem. Com., 1971-75; bd. govs. Ben Gurion U., Israel, 1993—. Fellow: Am. Soc. Materials. Jewish. Office Phone: 307-405-4175. Personal E-mail: mel.berstein@att.net. Business E-Mail: mbern@umd.edu.

BERNSTEIN, JAY L., lawyer; b. NYC, Dec. 10, 1959; BA with highest honors, Lake Forest Coll., 1981; JD cum laude, Boston U., 1984. Bar: NY 1985. Ptnr. Clifford Chance, NYC, 1995—, co-head real estate funds and investment banking grp. Americas Region, co-head fin. instns. grp. Americas Region. Mem.: Phi Beta Kappa. Office: Clifford Chance 31 W 52nd St New York NY 10019-6131 Office Phone: 212-878-8527. Office Fax: 212-878-8375. E-mail: Jay.Bernstein@cliffordchance.com.*

BERNSTEIN, JOSEPH, lawyer; b. New Orleans, Feb. 12, 1930; s. Eugene Julian and Lola (Schlemoff) Bernstein; m. Phyllis Maxine Askanase, Sept. 4, 1955; children: Jill, Barbara, Elizabeth R., Jonathan Joseph. BS, U. Ala., 1952; LLB, Tulane U., 1957. Bar: La. 1957. Clerk to Justice E. Howard McCaleb of La. Supreme Ct., 1957; assoc. Jones, Walker, Waechter, Poitevent, Carrere & Denegre, 1957—60, ptnr., 1960—65; pvt. practice New Orleans, 1965—. Former gen. counsel Alliance for Affordable Energy. Past pres. New Orleans chpt. March of Dimes, New Orleans Jewish Cmty. Ctr.; past nat. exec. com. Am. Jewish Com.; trustee New Orleans Symphony Soc.; past mem. adv. council New Orleans Mus. Art. 2d lt. AUS, 1952—54. Mem.: ABA, La. Bar Assn., Zeta Beta Tau, Phi Delta Phi. Republican. Jewish. Home: 708 Explanade Ave Bay Saint Louis MS 39520 Office Phone: 228-466-4423. E-mail: Joelou1@bellsouth.net.

BERNSTEIN, JOSEPH, mathematician, researcher, educator; b. Moscow, Apr. 18, 1945; s. Naum and Sarah Bernstein; m. Elena Nekludova, Mar. 19, 1971 (div. 1989); children: Mira, Aaron; m. Tanya Khovanova, Feb. 21, 1990; 1 child, Sergei-Shlomo. MA, Moscow U., Russia, 1968, PhD, 1972. Jr. sci. Math. Biol. Lab. Moscow U., 1971-78; prof. Harvard U., Cambridge, Mass., 1983-93, Tel Aviv U., 1993—. Vis. prof. U. Md., 1981-82. Mem.: NAS. Office: Tel Aviv U Rm 225 Schreiber Bldg Dept Math Ramat Aviv Israel

BERNSTEIN, KENNETH J., secondary school educator; b. NYC, May 23, 1946; s. Louis Morton and Sylvia Livingston Bernstein; m. Jurretta Jordan Heckscher, Dec. 29, 1985. BA in Music, Haverford Coll., Pa., 1973; MA in Religious Studies, St. Charles Sem., Wynnewood, Pa., 1980; MA in Social Studies, Johns Hopkins U., Balt., 1996. Cert. data processor Inst. Cert. Computer Profls., Ill., 1984; National Board Certified Teacher - Social Studies - AYA Nat. Bd. for Profl. Tchg. Standards, 2005, cert. advanced profl. Md. State Dept. Edn., 2004. Supervisory sys. analyst Arlington County Govt. Office Tech. and Info. Svc., Va., 1985—94; social studies tchr. Kettering Mid. Sch., Upper Marlboro, Md., 1995—98, Eleanor Roosevelt H.S., Greenbelt, Md., 1998—2001, 2002—, Williamsburg Mid. Sch., Arlington, 2001—02. Bd. mem. William Penn House, 2006—; nat. co-coord. Educators for Dean, 2003—04; field dir. Hollings for Pres., 1983—84; mem. nat. dept. stewardship Orthodox Ch.Am., Syosset, NY, 1980—83; mem. audit com. Orthodox Ch. Am., Syossett, NY, 1980—86; choir dir. St Herman's Orthodox Ch., Wallingford, Pa., 1976—82; parish pres. St. Herman's Orthodox Ch., Wallingford, Pa., 1978, St Herman's Orthodox Ch., Wallingford, Pa., 1982; mem. alumni coun. Haverford Coll., Pa., 2000—06. With USMC, 1965—66. Mem.: NEA (bldg. rep. 2000—01), ASCD, Nat. Coun. Social Studies, Phi Lambda Theta. Mem. Soc. Of Friends. Avocations: music, coaching soccer, reading. Home: 4803 16th St N Arlington VA 22205-2624 Office: Eleanor Roosevelt HS 7601 Hanover Pkwy Greenbelt MD 20770 Home Phone: 703-525-9538. Personal E-mail: kber@earthlink.net.

BERNSTEIN, LARRY HOWARD, clinical pathologist; b. Highland Park, Mich., Dec. 28, 1941; s. David Mordecai and Lillian Cecilia (Schwartz) B.; m. Audrey Jean Mellen, Dec. 20, 1969; children: Rachel Laura, Naomi Beth. BS, Wayne State U., 1963, MS, 1966, MD, 1968. Intern pathology Kans. U. Med. Ctr., Kansas City, 1968-69; resident and fellow in pathology U. Calif.-San Diego, La Jolla, 1970-73; pathologist Armed Forces Inst. Pathology, Washington, 1973-75; asst. prof. pathology U. South Fla., Tampa, 1975-77; assoc. prof. pathology U. South Ala., Mobile, 1977-78; dir. chemistry Iowa Meth. Med. Ctr., Des Moines, 1979-80, United Health Svcs., Binghampton, N.Y., 1981-82; dir. chemistry and blood bank Bridgeport (Conn.) Hosp., 1983—. Cons. Beckman, Boehringer Mannheim, Eastman Kodak, Brea, Calif., Rochester, N.Y. and Indpls., 1985-95; Nat. Com. Clin. Lab. Scis. rev. com., Chgo., 1988-92. Contbr. articles to Nutrition, Clin. Chemistry, Cancer, Arch. Pathol. Lab. Medicine, Jour. Biol. Chemistry, Brit. Jour. Cancer, Jour. Molecular Cellular Cardiology. Bd. dir. Nat. Accrediting Agency for Clin. Laboratory Scis. Lt. cmdr. USNR. Fellow Am. Assn. Clin. Chemistry (lectr., program chmn. nat. mtgs. 1985—, Labbe-Garry award), Coll. Am. Pathologists, Am. Coll. Nutrition; mem. ASTM, Clin. Lab. Mgmt. Assn. (lectr., nat. mtgs. 1985), AHSR, others. Democrat. Jewish. Achievements include patents for lactate dehydrogenase method, malate dehydrogenase mthod; rsch. in effect of nutritional states; rsch. in determining decision values for laboratory tests using truth-table comprehension and quality management using data classification and analysis; rsch. in diagnosis of acute myocardial infarction (heart attack), and in cancer markers in serum and body fluids. Office: NY Meth Hosp Dept Pathology Brooklyn NY 11215 Home: 232 Fitch's Pass Trumbull CT 06611-5602 Home Phone: 203-261-3655; Office Phone: 718-780-5416.

BERNSTEIN, LAWRENCE R., inorganic chemist, pharmaceutical chemist; b. LA, Dec. 23, 1955; s. Emil O. and Eleanor R. (Mordell) B.; children: Hannah L., Aaron A. AB, Harvard U., Cambridge, Mass., 1977, AM, 1978; PhD, Stanford U., Calif., 1985. Tutor in geol. sci. Harvard U., Cambridge, Mass., 1977-78; exploration geologist Brit. Petroleum, San Francisco, 1979-81; geologist U.S. Geol. Survey, Menlo Park, Calif., 1982-86; sr. rsch. scientist Yaskawa Co., Mountain View, Calif., 1990-92; rsch. dir. Terrametrix, Menlo Park, Calif., 1992—. Founder, dir., cons. GeoMed, Inc., Menlo Park, 1995—. Author: Minerals of the Washington, D.C. Area, 1980; patentee in pharma. field. Fed. Jr. fellow US Govt., 1973-77; John Harvard hon. scholar, 1976, 77. Mem. Mineral Soc. Am., Am. Soc. for Bone and Mineral Rsch., Am. Chem. Soc., Internat. Ctr. for Diffraction Data (chmn. subcom. 1998—, minerals editor 1992—), Phi Beta Kappa, Sigma Xi. Achievements include discovery of compounds to administer gallium and other metals orally for the treatment of cancer; discovery of promising new treatments for neuropathic pain and psoriasis. Home: 285 Willow Rd Menlo Park CA 94025-2711 Office: Terrametrix 285 Willow Rd Menlo Park CA 94025-2711 Home Phone: 650-322-9244; Office Phone: 650-324-3344. Personal E-mail: larry.b@earthlink.net.

BERNSTEIN, LESLIE, academic administrator, biostatistician, epidemiologist; BA, U. Calif., 1965; MS, U. So. Calif., 1978, PhD, 1981. Rsch. assoc. dept. preventive medicine U. So. Calif., LA, 1981-82, asst. prof. biostats./epidemiology, 1982-88, assoc. prof. biostats./epidemiology, 1988-91, prof. biostats./epidemiology, 1991—, sr. assoc. dean faculty affairs, 1996—2003, AFLAC Inc. chair in cancer rsch., 1997—, vice provost med. affairs, 2003—05. Sci. dir. U. So. Calif. Cancer Surveillance program, 1988—; mem. bd. sci. counselors Nat. Cancer Inst., 2001-06; mem. sci. adv. panel Calif. Gov., 1989-92; mem. sci. com. Internat. Soc. Study Esophageal Diseases, 1994—; chair adv. com. L.I. Breast Cancer Cancer Study, Columbia U., 1994-2000; chair external adv. com. Nurse's Health Study Harvard U., 1995—; sci. adv. com. Registry for Rsch. on Transplacental Carcinogenesis, U. Chgo., 1997—; external adv. com. No. Calif. Cancer Ctr., Hawaii Cancer Ctr., 1997—. Contbr. over 350 articles to profl. jours. Office: U So Calif/Norris Cancer Ctr Keck Sch Medicine 1441 Eastlake Ave 4449 Los Angeles CA 90033-0804 Business E-Mail: lbern@usc.edu.

BERNSTEIN, LESTER, editorial consultant; b. NYC, July 18, 1920; s. Isidore and Rebecca (Axelrod) B.; m. Jacqueline Lipscomb, Feb. 6, 1946; children: Lynn, Nina, Paul, Daniel. AB, Columbia U., 1940. Reporter N.Y. Times, 1940-48; writer, fgn. corr., editor Time mag., 1948-58; dir. info. NBC, 1958-60, v.p. corp. affairs, 1960-62; nat. affairs editor Newsweek, 1963-65, exec. editor, 1965-69, mng. editor, 1969-72, editor, 1979-82; editorial cons., 1982-85; v.p. corporate communications RCA Corp., 1973-79. Cons. N.Y. Internat. Festival of the Arts, 1987-92. Recipient Nat. Mag. award for gen. excellence, 1981. Mem.: Century Assn. Home (Summer): PO Box 779 Castine ME 04421-0779

BERNSTEIN, MAUREEN ANN, theater educator, director; b. Modesto, Calif., Aug. 24, 1953; d. Francis Paul and Ann Bernice Abell; m. Lawrence A. Bernstein, Nov. 17, 1983; 1 child, Frankie Jonathan. BA in Theatre, U. Nev., 1976, MEd in Curriculum and Instrn., 1998, postgrad., 2005—. Cert. tchr. Nev., 1994. Student tchr. Eldorado HS, Las Vegas, 1994—94; theatre dir. Valley HS, 1994—97; grad. asst., urban tchg. partnership & instr. with nat. youth sports program as part of master's thesis project U. Nev., 1997—98; theatre dir. chair dept. performing and visual arts Desert Pines HS, 1999—, mem. school improvement com. Inst. for Integrated Studies. Mentor Student Theatrical Adjudicated Rev. Shows, Las Vegas, 2001—, bd. dirs.; mentor Student/Tchr. Mentorship Program, Desert Pines H.S., 2002—; mem. Nev. State Thespian Profl. Bd., 2003—; presenter, new tchr. training Clark County Sch. Dist., 2003—. Author: (plays) Hip Hop Goes the Shakespeare; dir.: (plays) Hip Hop Goes the Shakespeare (State Adjudicated Show: Nev. State Thespians, 2002), numerous plays, 1994—2007. Sponsor, dir. Thespian Troupe 6125, 2004—05; conf. dir., coach students Nev. State Thespians, bd. dirs., 2005—. Recipient Supporting Actress award, Am. Coll. Theatre Festival, 1974; Devos Talent scholar, U. Nev., Las Vegas Theatre Dept., 1972—76. Mem.: NEA, Actors Fund, Broadway Cares, Theatre Comm. Guild, Ednl. Theatre Assn. (profl. dir.), Nev. State Thespian Bd. Tchr. Profls., Clark Clounty Edn. Assn., Clark County Assn. Theatre Teachers (v.p. 2002). Liberal. Avocations: piano, musicals, antiques. Office: Desert Pines High School 3800 E Harris Ave Las Vegas NV 89110 Office Phone: 702-799-2196 ext 4051. Personal E-mail: bthespian@aol.com.

BERNSTEIN, MERTON CLAY, law educator, arbitrator; b. NYC, Mar. 26, 1923; s. Benjamin and Ruth (Frederica (Kleeblatt)) B.; m. Joan Barbara Brodshaug, Dec. 17, 1955; children: Johanna Karin, Inga Saterlie, Matthew Curtis, Rachel Libby. BA, Oberlin Coll., 1943; LL.B., Columbia U., 1948. Bar: N.Y. 1948, U.S. Supreme Ct. 1952. Assoc. Schlesinger & Schlesinger, 1948; atty. NLRB, 1949-50, 50-51, Office of Solicitor, U.S. Dept. Labor, 1950; counsel Nat. Enforcement Commn., 1951, U.S. Senate Subcom. on Labor, 1952; legis. asst. to U.S. Sen. Wayne L. Morse, 1953-56; counsel U.S. Senate Com. on R.R. Retirement, 1957-58; spl. counsel U.S. Senate Subcom. on Labor, 1958; assoc. prof. law U. Nebr., 1958-59; lectr., sr. fellow Yale U. Law Sch., 1960-65; prof. law Ohio State U., 1965-75; Walter D. Coles prof. law Washington U., St. Louis, 1975-96, Walter D. Coles prof. emeritus, 1997—; mem. adv. com. to Sec. of Treas. on Coordination of Social Security and pvt. pension plans, 1967-68. Prin. cons. Nat. Commn. on Social Security Reform, 1982-83; vis. prof. Columbia U. Law Sch., 1967-68, Leiden U., 1975-76; mem. adv. com. rsch. U.S. Social Security Adminstrn., 1967-68, chmn., 1969-70; cons. Adminstrv. Conf. of the U.S., 1989, Dept. Labor, 1966-67, Russell Sage Found., 1967-68, NSF, 1970-71, Ctr. for the Study of Contemporary Problems, 1968-71. Author: The Future of Private Pensions, 1964, Private Dispute Settlement, 1969, (with Joan B. Bernstein) Social Security: The System That Works, 1988; contbr. articles to profl. jours. Del White Ho. Conf. Aging, 1995; active Bethany (Conn.) Planning and Zoning Commn., 1962—65, Ohio Retirement Study Commn., 1967—68, City of St. Louis Bd. Health, 1993—2000, Brewster (Mass.) Bd. Health, 2001—05, chair, 2002—04; pres. bd. Met. Sch. Columbus, Ohio, 1974—75; co-chmn. transition team for St. Louis Mayor Freeman Bosley Jr., 1993; candidate for Dem. nom. US Senate, Mo., 1991—92; bd. dirs. St. Louis Theatre Project, 1981—84. With AUS, 1943—45. Fulbright fellow, 1975-76, Elizur Wright award, 1965. Mem. ABA (sec. sect. labor rels. law 1968-69), Internat. Assn. for Labor Law and Social Security (bd. dirs. U.S. chpt. 1973-83, 88-91), Indsl. Rels. Rsch. Assn., Nat. Acad. Social Ins. (founding mem., bd. dirs. 1986-91), Am. Arbitration Assn. (mem. adv. com. St. Louis region 1987-2000), Fulbright Alumni Assn. (bd. dirs. 1976-78). Democrat. Jewish. Office Phone: 508-896-8383. Business E-Mail: bernstein@wulaw.wustl.edu.

BERNSTEIN, MITCHELL HARRIS, lawyer; b. NYC, Sept. 19, 1949; s. Melvin and Gladys (Weissman) B.; m. Barbara Veitch, Oct. 8, 1978; children: Jonathan, Matthew, Emily. AB, U. Pa., 1970; JD, Yale U., 1973. Bar: N.Y. 1974, U.S. Ct. Appeals (2d cir.) 1974, U.S. Dist. Ct. (so. and ea. dists.) N.Y. 1974, U.S. Ct. Appeals (5th and D.C. cirs.) 1980, U.S. Supreme Ct. 1980, D.C. 1981, U.S. Ct. Appeals (4th cir.) 1981, U.S. Dist. Ct. D.C. 1982, U.S. Ct. Appeals (3d cir.) 1985. Assoc. Breed, Abbott & Morgan, NYC, 1974-77; sr. atty. U.S. EPA, Washington, 1977-81; assoc. Skadden, Arps, Slate, Meagher & Flom, Washington, 1981-83, ptnr., 1983-93; mem. Van Ness Feldman, Washington, 1994—. Bd. advisors Chem. Waste Litigation Reporter, Washington, 1985—. Mem. ABA, D.C. Bar. Assn. Office: Van Ness Feldman Ste 7 1050 Thomas Jefferson St NW Washington DC 20007-3837 Office Phone: 202-298-1820. E-mail: mhb@vnf.com.

BERNSTEIN, NADIA JACQUELINE, lawyer; b. Salford, Lançashire, Eng., Feb. 26, 1945; arrived in U.S., 1948; d. David Colin and Rose (Bolton) Cohen; m. David J. Adler, Mar. 1977 (div. 1992); m. Robert Bernstein, May 1997. BA, CCNY, 1966; JD, NYU, 1973. Bar: NY 1974, US Dist. Ct. (so. and ea. dists.) NY 1974, US Ct. Appeals (2d cir.) 1975, US Supreme Ct. 1983. Assoc. Rosenman Colin Freund Lewis & Cohen and predecessor firms, NYC, 1973-82; ptnr. Rosenman & Colin, NYC, 1983-87; v.p., gen. counsel Montefiore Med. Ctr., NYC, 1987-89, sr. v.p., gen. counsel, 1989-98; v.p., gen. counsel, corp. sec. C.R. Bard, Inc., Murray Hill, NJ, 1999—2004; prin. The NJ Bernstein Law Firm, 2004—. Mem. legal affairs com. Greater NY Hosp. Assn., NYC, 1987—99; mem. conf. bd. Coun. Chief Legal Officers, 1999—2004; mem. NJ Gen. Counsel's Group, 1999—2004; instl. rev. bd. Montefiore Med. Ctr., 2005—. Mem. bioethics task force, mem. commn. women's equality Am. Jewish Congress, NYC, 1989—94; mem. bd. ethics Village Briarcliff Manor, NY, 1997—2006; bd. dirs. Berkeley-in-Scarsdale Assn., NY, 1989—91. Mem.: ABA (forum on health care, law practice mgmt. com., corp. practices com. bus. law sect.), Am. Corp. Coun. Assn. (law mgmt. com. 2000—04), Advanced Med. Tech. Assn. (legal com. 2002—04), Women Bus. Leaders US Health Care Industry, Exec. Women NJ (honoree 2000), NY State Bar Assn. (exec. com. health law sect. 1996—99), Am. Health Lawyers Assn., Assn. Bar City of NY. Democrat. Office: 1 Sunnyside Ct Briarcliff Manor NY 10510 Business E-Mail: bernstelaw@optonline.net.

BERNSTEIN, PAUL, retired academic dean; b. Phila., Jan. 19, 1927; s. Abraham and Jennie (Geek) B.; m. Irma Shuster, Apr. 10, 1949; children: Jay Ira, Lisa Beth. BS, Temple U., 1949, MEd, 1950; PhD, U. Pa., 1955. Tchr. social scis. Phila. pub. schs., 1949-55; prof. European history, chmn. social scis. dept. Lock Haven (Pa.) State Coll., 1955-64, Plattsburg (N.Y.) State U. Coll., 1964-66; dean Coll. Gen. Studies, Rochester Inst. Tech., 1966-76, dean grad. studies, 1976-92, ret., 1993. Tchr. Elderhostel, Bradenton, Fla., 1998-99. Author: (with R. Green) History of Civilization, 2 vols., 1960, 62, Career Education and the Quality of Working Life, 1980, American Work Values, 1997, Letters to Eleanor: Voices of the Great Depression, 2004; mng. editor Lock Haven Bull., 1959-64; author articles on Swedish labor mgmt. issues capitalism and consumerism; manuscript reviewer Polity Press, 1998. Co-chmn. Citizens for Humphrey, Monroe County, N.Y., 1968. Served with AUS, 1944-47; mem. adv. bd. Rochester Bus. Hall of Fame Selection Group, 2002—05. Grantee Am. Philos. Soc., 1959; Grantee Swedish Bicentennial Com., 1980 Mem. Ind. Rel. Research Assn., Assn. Gen. and Liberal Studies (exec. bd., pres. 1978-79) Clubs: Elks. Republican. Jewish. Home: 1 Linden Cv Pittsford NY 14534-4614 Business E-Mail: pxbbbu@rit.edu.

BERNSTEIN, RICHARD, lawyer; b. 1974; B, U. Mich.; degree in Law, Northwestern U. Atty. Law Offices of Sam Bernstein, Farmington Hills, Mich. Adj. prof., Polit. Sci. U. Mich., Ann Arbor; bd. governors Wayne State U.; adv. bd. mem. Mich. Paralyzed Veterans; bd. mem. Tech Town; adv. com. mem. Mich. Anti-Defamation League, Am. Israel Pub. Affairs Com., Mich. Cmty. Scholars Prog., U. Mich., Max M. Fisher Found. Adv. bd. mem. United Jewish Fedn. of Metro. Detroit. Named one of 40 Under 40, Crain's Detroit Bus., 2006; named to Athletes with Disabilities Hall of Fame, 1999. Mem.: Mich. Assn. for Deaf & Hard of Hearing. Avocation: running. Office: Law Offices of Same Berstein 31100 Northwestern Highway Farmington Hills MI 48334 Office Phone: 248-737-8400.

BERNSTEIN, RICHARD, financial analyst, investment advisor; BA, Hamilton Coll.; MBA, NYU. Investment strategist Tucker Anthony, E.F. Hutton, Merrill Lynch, NYC, 1998—2001, chief U.S. investment strategist, 2001—. Author: Style Investing - Unique Insight into Equity Management, Navigate the Noise: Investing in the New Age of Media and Hype; commentator Wall Street Week and other TV shows, mem. editl bd. Jour. Portfolio Mgmt. Trustee Hamilton Coll.; mem. exec. com. Stern Sch. Bus. NYU. Named one of Power 30, SmartMoney Mag., All-Star Analysts, Fortune Mag.; named to All-Am. Rsch. Team, Institutional Investor. Office: Merrill Lynch 4 World Fin Ctr 250 Vesey St New York NY 10080*

BERNSTEIN, RICHARD ALLEN, food products executive; b. NYC, June 28, 1946; s. Sidney and Ethel Helen (Shankman) Bernstein; m. Amelia Fishman, Nov. 21, 1944; children: Bradley Ross, Jennifer Anne. BA in Econs., NYU, 1968. V.p. Pease & Ellman Inc., NYC, 1968-70; pres. P&E Properties Inc., NYC, 1970—; chmn. Western Pub. Co. Inc., NYC, 1984-96; chmn., pres., CEO Western Pub. Group Inc., NYC, 1984-96; chmn. Gen. Med. Corp., Richmond, Va., 1987-93, Harris Wholesale Co., Cleve., 1988-92; chmn., pres., CEO Rabco Health Svcs., Inc., NYC, 1991-93; chmn. Millbrook Distbn. Svcs., Inc., Leicester, Mass., 1997—; chmn., CEO, Rabco Luxury Holdings LLC, 1997—, Breguet LLC, 1997—, B. Manischewitz Co., 1998—. Chmn., pres., CEO Penn Corp., 1986—96; mem. adv. bd. Chase Manhattan Bank, 1985—; chmn., CEO R.A.B. Holdings, Inc., 1996—, Millbrook Distbn. Svcs., Inc., 1997—, Brequet LLC, NYC, 1997—2002, Rabco Luxury Holdings LLC, NYC, 1997—. Trustee Police Athletic Legaue, NYC, 1982—, NYU, 1988—; bd. dirs. Big Apple Circus, Inc., 1992—98, Hosp. for Joint Diseases, NYC, N.Y. State Employee Retirement Sys., NYC; mem. N.Y. State Commn. on Regulation of Lobbying, Albany, 1982—86; bd. overseers Stern Sch. Bus. NYU; candidate for comptr. City of N.Y., 1981. With US Army, 1969. Fellow, Yeshiva U., 1986. Mem.: Econ. Club N.Y. Republican. Jewish. Office: RAB Holdings 444 Madison Ave Ste 601 New York NY 10022-6903 Office Phone: 212-688-4500.

BERNSTEIN, ROBERT JAY, lawyer; b. Bklyn., July 1, 1948; s. Martin Emanuel and Vera (Muter) B.; m. Janet Rodolico, Oct. 28, 1978; 3 children. BA cum laude, cert. in pub. and internat. affairs, Princeton U., 1970; JD cum laude, U. Mich., 1975. Bar: Colo. 1976, N.Y. 1977. Law clk. to judge Richard P. Matsch U.S. Dist. Ct., Denver, 1975-76; assoc. Fried, Frank, Harris, Shriver & Jacobson, NYC, 1976-80, Cowan, Liebowitz & Latman, P.C., NYC, 1980-82, ptnr., 1982—2004; pvt. practice NYC, 2004—. Mem. faculty, lectr. on copyright devels. Practicing Law Inst. Program, 1986, 88, 91, New Music Sem., 1987; guest lectr. on entertainment law U. Mich., 1987, 90; lectr. copyright law and litig. Copyright Soc. USA, 1985, 87, 89, 93, 96, 99; lectr. in copyright law, Am. Intellectual Property Law Annual Mtgs., 1989, 93, 95, 98; guest lectr. copyright law, Fordham Law Sch., 1998. Co-author column on copyright law N.Y. Law Jour., 1987—; contbr. articles on copyright law to Billboard mag., Entertainment and Sports Lawyer mag., others. Mem. bd. trustees, Greenwich Reform Synagogue, Conn., 1986-92, co-pres., Men's Club, 1986, 90; vol. Internat. Assn. Jazz

Edn., 2007. Grantee Princeton U., 1969. Mem. ABA (sec. of patent, trademark and copyright lawyers, 1980—, forum com. on entertainment and sports law Music and Personal Appearances Div., 1980—, com. internat. copyright treaties and laws 1982-84, sub-com. on People's Republic of China., lectr. copyright law, forum com. on the entertainment and sports industries 1986, lectr. copyright law 1986, 1987, 1992, 1996), Am. Intellectual Property Law Assn. (sec., bd. dirs. 1990—93, chmn. copyright law com. 1988-90, moderator panel on negotiation recording contracts, 1990, lectr. current devel. copyright law ann. meeting 1989, 1993, 1995, 1998), Assn. Am. Pubs. (lawyers com. 1990-96, lectr. copyright and photography 2000), Assn. Bar City of N.Y. (com. copyright and literary property 2004—, lectr., copyright litigation 2005, 2007) lectr., current devel. copright law CLE program 2005, Copyright Soc. of the USA (v.p., pres.-elect 1998-2000, pres. 2000-02, hon. trustee 2002—, lectr. copyright law 1985, 1986, 1993, 1996, 1999), New York State Bar Association (Entertainment, Arts and Sports Law sect. 1988-, lectr., copyright and fair use, annual mtg. Entertainment and Sports Law sect., 1990). Avocations: tennis, jazz saxophone, piano, skiing, golf, romance languages. Office: The Law Office Robert J Bernstein 488 Madison Ave 9th Fl New York NY 10022 Home Phone: 203-328-7550; Office Phone: 212-705-4811. Business E-Mail: rjb@robert-bernsteinlaw.com.

BERNSTEIN, ROBERT M., dermatologic surgeon; b. NYC, July 13, 1952; BS in Psychology, Tulane U., New Orleans, 1973; MD, U. Medicine and Dentistry of N.J., 1978. Lic. N.Y., N.J., Calif., diplomate Nat. Bd. Med. Examiners, Am. Bd. Dermatology, Am. Bd. Hair Restoration Surgery. Resident in internal medicine U. Medicine and Dentistry of N.J., 1978—79; resident in dermatology Albert Einstein Coll. Medicine, NYC, 1979—81, chief resident in dermatology, 1981—82; pvt. practice dermatology, 1982—95; pvt. practice hair restoration surgery NYC, 1995—; founder Bernstein Med.-Ctr. Hair Restoration, 2005—. Asst. in clin. dermatology Coll. Physicians and Surgeons, Columbia U., NYC, 1982—85, instr. clin. dermatology, 1985—90, assoc. in clin. dermatology, 1990—95, asst. clin. prof. dermatology, 1995—2000, assoc. clin. prof. dermatology, 2000—; asst. attending dermatologist Manhattan Eye, Ear and Throat Hosp., NYC, 1982—2000; attending, dept. dermatology Englewood Hosp., NJ, 1982—, pharmacy and therapeutics com., NJ, 1982—88, chmn. quality assurance and compliance com., dept. dermatology, NJ, 1990—94; asst. dermatologist Presbyn. Hosp., NYC, 1982—90, assoc. dermatologist, 1990—96; asst. attending dermatology svc. N.Y. Presbyn. Hosp., 1996—2000, assoc. attending dermatology svc., 2000—; examiner Am. Bd. Hair Restoration Surgery, 2000—; mem. Almay Stress Info. coun. Almay Cosmetics, NYC, 1990—92, mem. Almay Health Watch Coun. adv. bd., 1992—96; evaluation com. World Hair Soc., Scientific Workshop, Orlando, Fla., 1999—2000; lectr. in field. Contbg. editor: Dermatologic Surgery, 1998—, Jour. Aesthetic Dermatology and Cosmetic Dermatologic Surgery, 1998—2000; contbr. articles, editorial reviews, book and textbook chapters; guest appearances ABC, CBS, and Fox 5 News, featured on Good Morning America, The Discovery Channel. Named Surgeon of the Month, Hair Transplant Forum Internat., The Best Doctors in NY, 2000, 2001, Top Doctors: NY Metro Area, 2001, America's Top Doctors 2001-Surgical Hair Restoration; recipient Continuing Med. Edn. award, Am. Acad. Dermatology, 1982—99, Platinum Follicle award for Outstanding Achievement in Scientific and Clin. Rsch. in Hair Restoration, Internat. Soc. of Hair Restoration Surgery, 2001; Tulane Scholar. Fellow: Am. Acad. Dermatology; mem.: Am. Hair Loss Coun., Am. Soc. for Dermatologic Surgery, Am. Acad. Aesthetic and Restorative Surgery, World Soc. of Hair Restoration Surgeons, North Jersey Dermatologic Soc., N.Am. Acad. Cosmetic and Restorative Surgery, Internat. Soc. Hair Restoration Surgery (mem. scientific and edn. com. 1999—2001, mem. certification com. 2002, ad hoc preceptorship com. 2001), Am.. Laser Medicine and Surgery, Am. Soc. Hair Restoration Surgery, Am. Acad. Cosmetic Surgery (mem. Am. hair loss coun.). Office: 125 E 63d St New York NY 10021 Address: 2150 Center Ave Fort Lee NJ 07024 Office Phone: 212-826-2400, 201-585-1115. Office Fax: 201-585-0464. Business E-Mail: contact@bernsteinmedical.com.

BERNSTEIN, SANFORD IRWIN, biology professor; b. Bklyn., June 10, 1953; s. Harold and Adele Dorothy B.; m. Laurel Spear, July 10, 1983. BS, SUNY, Stony Brook, 1974; PhD, Wesleyan U., 1979. Rsch. fellow U. Va., Charlottesville, 1979-82; asst. prof. biology San Diego State U., 1983-85, assoc. prof., 1985-88, prof., 1988—. Assoc. dir. Molecular Biology Inst., 1987-92, dir. 1992-95; co-dir. DNA cert. program, 1983—, chair biology dept., 1995-2000, coord. joint-doctoral program in cell and molecular biology with U. Calif. San Diego, 2000—; established investigatorship Am. Heart Assn., 1989-94; mem. grant rev. panels NIH, Am. Heart Assn. Mem. editl. bd. Devel. Biology, 1991-95, J. Muscle Rsch. and Cell Motility, 2006—; contbr. articles to profl. jours. Muscular Dystrophy Assn. fellow, 1979-82, grantee, 1984-2006; grantee NIH, 1983—, NSF, 1997-2000. Mem.: AAAS, Am. Physiol. Soc., Biophys. Soc., Am. Soc. Biochemistry and Molecular Biology, Am. Soc. Cell Biology, Genetics Soc. Am., Sigma Xi. Achievements include research in developmental regulation of muscle gene expression in Drosophila, muscle protein isoform function, alternative RNA splicing. Office: San Diego State U Biology Dept and Molec Bio Inst San Diego CA 92182-4614 Business E-Mail: sanford.bernstein@sdsu.edu.

BERNSTEIN, SOL, cardiologist, educator; b. West New York, NJ, Feb. 3, 1927; s. Morris Irving and Rose (Leibowitz) B.; m. Suzi Maris Sommer, Sept. 15, 1963; 1 son, Paul. AB in Bacteriology, U. So. Calif., 1952, MD, 1956. Diplomate Am. Bd. Internal Medicine. Intern Los Angeles County Hosp., 1956-57, resident, 1957-60; practice medicine specializing in cardiology LA, 1960—; physician dept. medicine Los Angeles County Hosp./U. So. Calif. Med. Ctr., LA, 1960—, chief cardiology clinics, 1964, asst. dir. dept. medicine, 1965-72, med. dir., 1974-94; med. dir. central region Los Angeles County, 1974-78; dir. Dept. Health Svcs., Los Angeles County, 1978; assoc. dean Sch. Medicine, U. So. Calif., LA, 1986-94, assoc. prof., 1968—; med. dir. Health Rsch. Assn., LA, 1995—2005. Cons. Crippled Childrens Svc. Calif., 1965—. Contbr. articles on cardiac surgery, cardiology, diabetes and health care planning to med. jours. Served with AUS, 1946-47, 52-53. Fellow ACP, Am. Coll. Cardiology; mem. Am. Acad. Phys. Execs., Am. Fedn. Clin. Research, NY Acad. Sci., Am. Heart Assn., LA Soc. Internal Medicine, LA Acad. Medicine, Sigma Xi, Phi Beta Phi, Phi Eta Sigma, Alpha Omega Alpha. Home: 4966 Ambrose Ave Los Angeles CA 90027-1756 Office: 1640 Marengo St Los Angeles CA 90033-1036 Home Phone: 323-666-8547. Business E-Mail: sol@hsc.usc.edu.

BERNSTEIN, STAN, federal bankruptcy judge; b. LA, 1941; m. Jane Ellen Hirschfield; 3 children. BA, Brandeis U., 1962; MA, U. Chgo., 1964; PhD, Harvard U., 1970; JD, Rutgers U., 1973. Bar: Mich. 1974, Ohio 1974, Calif. 1985, Ariz. 1989, Mass. 1991. Mem. faculty U. Calif., Davis, 1967-70, Rutgers U., 1970-73; assoc., ptnr. Honigman, Miller, Schwartz & Cohn, Detroit, 1974-82; bankruptcy judge for Ea. Dist. Mich., U.S. Bankruptcy Ct., Detroit, 1982-84; ptnr. Gendel, Raskoff, Shapiro & Quittner, LA, 1984-85, Dickinson, Wright, Detroit, 1985-89; shareholder Brown & Bain, Phoenix, 1989-90; ptnr. Foley, Hoag & Eliot, Boston, 1991-96; bankruptcy judge for Ea. Dist. N.Y., U.S. Bankruptcy Ct., Central Islip, 1996—. Mem.: Nat. Conf. Bankruptcy Judges. Office: US Bankruptcy Ct 290 Federal Plz Central Islip NY 11722-4437 Office Phone: 631-712-5742. Business E-Mail: stan_bernstein@nyeb.uscourts.gov.

BERNSTEIN, STANLEY JOSEPH, manufacturing executive; s. David William and Irene Mildred Bernstein; m. Cathy Ann Grey; children: Michael A., Geoffrey T. BA, Brown U., 1965; JD, U. Pa., 1968. Bar: Mass. 1968. Mgr. Am. Biltrite Inc., Chelsea, Mass., 1968-71, div. gen. mgr. Cambridge, Mass., 1971-78, v.p. corp. devel., 1978-82; exec. v.p. The Biltrite Corp., Waltham, Mass., 1983-85, chmn., chief exec. officer, 1986—, also bd. dirs. Bd. dirs. Shenzhen Biltrite-SPEC Soling Co., Ltd., Shenzhen, Atlanta, B. Hrite Corp., Waltham, Mass., Camera, Boston. Life trustee Roxbury Latin Sch., West Roxbury, Mass.; trustee Brown U.; bd. govs. Combined Jewish Philanthropies, Boston. Office: The Biltrite Corp PO Box 9045 51 Sawyer Rd Waltham MA 02454-9045 E-mail: stanley.bernstein@biltrite.com.

BERNSTEIN, STUART A., former ambassador; b. Washington, 1938; m. Wilma Bernstein; children: Brian, Adam, Alison. Leader in real estate devel., investment and mgmt. Mid-Atlantic region, Washington; U.S. amb. to Denmark US Dept. State, Copenhagen, 2001—05. Apptd. commr. Internat. Cultural and Trade Ctr., 1991; apptd. trustee John F. Kennedy Ctr. for Performing Arts, 1992—2001. Former bd. trustees Am. Univ.; former bd. dirs. Weizman Inst. of Sci. Personal E-mail: sbern11@aol.com.

BERNSTEIN, WARREN J., lawyer; AB cum laude, Rutgers U., 1977; JD, U. Pa., 1980. Bar: NY 1981. Ptnr., co-chair Real Estate Dept. Kaye Scholer LLP, NYC. Mem.: Assn. Bar. of City NY, NY State Bar Assn. Office: Kaye Scholer LLP 425 Park Ave New York NY 10022 Office Phone: 212-836-8073. E-mail: wbernstein@kayescholer.com.

BERNSTEIN, WILLIAM JOSEPH, glass artist, educator; b. Newark, Dec. 3, 1945; s. Jacob and Rosalind (Merliss) B.; m. Katherine Schachter, July 21, 1968; children: Joshua, Alex. BFA, Phila. U. of Arts, 1968. Artist in residence Penland (N.C.) Sch. of Crafts, 1968-70; instr. Summervail Workshop, Vail, Colo., U. So. Calif., LA, Pilchuck Glass Ctr., Stanwood, Wash., Naples (N.Y.) Mill Sch.; tchr. Bezalel Acad., Jerusalem, Israel, 1997—. One-man show Hodges Taylor Galley, Charlotte N.C., 1997; exhibited in group shows at Somerhill Gallery, Chapel Hill, N.C., Grohě Glass Gallery, Boston, Marx Gallery, Chgo., Am. Craft Mus., N.Y.C., John Michael Kohler Arts Ctr., Sheboygan, Wis., Spaso House, Moscow, U.S.S.R., The Denver Art Mus., Laguna Art Mus., Laguna Beach, Calif., Milwaukee Art Mus., J.B. Speed Art Mus., Louisville, Ky., Va. Mus. Fine Arts, Richmond, Ark. Arts Ctr. Decorative Arts Mus., Little Rock, Galerie Angela Hollings, Hameln, Germany, J&L Lobmeyr, Vienna, Austria, Galerie Rob van den Doel, The Hague, The Netherlands, Isetan Galleries, Japan; represented in permanent collections the Corning (N.Y.) Mus. of Glass, the Mint Mus. Art, Charlotte, N.C., Nat. Collection Fine Art, Washington, Greenville (S.C.) County Mus. Art, Austrialian Coun. for the Arts, Sidney, Morse Gallery Art, Winter Park, Fla., Ft. Lauderdale (Fla.) Mus. Arts, R.J. Reynolds Collection, Winston-Salem, N.C., Craft and Folk Mus., L.A., Glasmus., Frauenau, Germany, Ark. Art Ctr., Little Rock, Glasmus., Ebeltoft, Denmark, J&L Lobmeyr, Vienna, Austria, Asheville (N.C.) Mus. Art, Yamaha Corp., Japan, Chrysler Mus. Norfolk, Va., Newark (N.J.) Mus., Charles A. Wustan Mus. Arts, Racine, Wis. Louis Comfort Tiffany Found. grantee, 1975, NEA Master Craftsman Apprenticeship, 1976; NEA fellow, 1974, N.C. Arts Coun. fellow, 1983, masterworks fellow Creative Glass Ctr. Am., 1990. Office: 250 Chimney Ridge Rd Burnsville NC 28714 Personal E-mail: wberns1141@aol.com.

BERNSTEIN, WILLIAM ROBERT, banker; b. Newark, Apr. 14, 1947; s. Leonard H. and Gwen (Burstein) B.; m. Roberta Ann Sipkin, June 25, 1972; children: Carrie, Elizabeth, Michael. BS, Rensselaer Poly. Inst., 1969, BArch, 1970; M of Urban Planning, U. Wash., Seattle, 1972. Project planner Jersey City Redevel. Agy., 1972-74; v.p. Matthews & Wright Inc., NYC, 1974-79, Thompson Mckinnon Securities, NYC, 1979-81; mng. dir. Drexel Burnham Lambert, NYC, 1981-89; sr. v.p. The Tokai Bank, Ltd., NYC, 1990-99; mng. dir. Mesco Ltd., Ridgefield, Conn., 1999—; dir. Inceptor Ltd., Metro Mktg. Resources Inc., Hamden, Conn.; pres. Makris Berns Builders, 2005—. Pres. Nat. Leased Housing Assn., Washington, 1987-88, chmn., 1988-89, chmn. emeritus, 1989—; bd. dirs. Pixel Devices Internat., Inc Trustee Congregation B'nai Yisrael. Home: 29 Wampus Lake Dr Armonk NY 10504-1122 Office: Makris Bern Builders 120 County Rd Ste 209 Tenafly NJ 07670 Home Phone: 914-219-5061; Office Phone: 201-569-5909. E-mail: bill@makrisbros.com.

BERNSTINE, DANIEL O'NEAL, educational association administrator, law educator; b. Berkeley, Calif., Sept. 7, 1947; s. Annias and Emma (Jones) B.; m. Nancy Jean Tyler, July 27, 1971 (div. Mar. 1986); children: Quincy Tyler, Justin Tyler. BA, U. Calif., Berkeley, 1969; JD, Northwestern U., Chgo., 1972; LLM, U. Wis., 1975; LLD (hon.), Hanyang U., Seoul, Korea, 1999, Waseda U., Tokyo, 2003; PhD (hon.), Nizhny Novgorod Linguistics U., Russia, 2004. Bar: D.C. 1970, Wis. 1979. Prof. law Howard U. Law Sch., Washington, 1975-78, gen. counsel, interim dean, 1987-90; prof. law U. Wis. Law Sch., Madison, 1978-97, dean, 1990-97; pres. Portland State U., Oreg., 1997—2007, Law Sch. Admissions Coun., Newtown, Pa., 2007—. Author: Wisconsin and Federal Civil Procedure, 1986. Bd. dirs. Madison Cmty. Found., 1990-94, Portland Urban League, Legacy Health Sys., Willamette United Way, 2001—04; mem. Portland Multnomah Progress Bd., 1998—, Kellogg Commn. on the Future of State and Land-Grant Univs., 1997-2000. Mem. Am. Law Inst., Portland C. of C. (bd. dirs.). Office: Law Sch Admission Coun 661 Penn St Newtown PA 18940 Home Phone: 503-725-2376.

BERNT, BENNO ANTHONY, entrepreneur, investor; b. Bielitz, Austria, Mar. 14, 1931; came to U.S., 1953, naturalized, 1961; s. Victor and Grete Bernt; m. Constance Smigel, June 22, 1957; children: Karin, Eric, Steve. BS in Engring. cum laude, Fed. Inst. Tech., Vienna, Austria, 1952; DCS in Bus. and Econs. cum laude, U. Econs. & Bus. Adminstrn., Vienna, 1953; MBA, Carnegie Mellon U., 1954. Fin. and mfg. exec. Chrysler Corp., 1954-59; mfg. and bus. planning exec., subs. gen. mgr. Whirlpool Corp., 1959-68; pres. Cissell Mfg. Co., Louisville, 1968-70; gen. mgr. Simonds Abrasive Co., Phila., 1970-73; v.p. fin. ESB Ray-O-Vac Corp., Phila., 1973-76, exec. v.p., dir., 1977-78; pres., CEO RAYOVAC, Madison, Wis., 1979-82; sr. v.p. fin. and planning, CFO Nat. Intergroup Inc., Pitts., 1983-87; chmn. The Griffin Group, Pitts., 1988—, Univ. Ptnrs., Inc., 1997—. Dir. tech. transfer Carnegie Mellon U., 1992—97. Chmn. adv. bd. Sch. Computer Sci. and Sch. Music Carnegie Mellon U., 1993—; bd. dirs. Pitts. Symphony, Carnegie Sci. Ctr., Pitts., Pitts. Tissue Engring. Initiative. Mem. Duquesne Club, Pitts. Golf Club. Office: Griffin Group Ptnrs LP 308 Schenley Rd Pittsburgh PA 15217-1173 *I believe the measure of one's true success lies in how well we are using our own potential, and how well we are serving others.*

BERNTHAL, ERIC L., lawyer; b. Syracuse, NY, June 21, 1946; BA, Columbia U., 1967; JD with honors, George Washington U., 1970. Bar: DC 1970, U.S. Supreme Ct. 1975. Law clk. to Hon. Ruggero J. Aldisert U.S. Ct. Appeals (3rd cir.), 1970-72; ptnr. Arent, Fox, Kintner, Plotkin & Kahn, Washington, 1972—86; with Latham & Watkins LLP, 1986—, now mng. ptnr., Washington office. Mem. ABA, Fed. Comm. Bar Assn., Order of the Coif. Office: Latham & Watkins Ste 1000 555 11th St NW Washington DC 20004-1304

BERNTHAL, FREDERICK MICHAEL, research association executive; b. Sheridan, Wyo., Jan. 10, 1943; s. Erwin and Erna Bernthal; m. Heather A. Lancaster; 1 child, Justin. BS, Valparaiso U., 1964; PhD, U. Calif., Berkeley, 1969. Rsch. staff Yale U., New Haven, 1969-70; prof. Mich. State U., East Lansing, 1970-80; legis. asst. Senator Howard Baker, Washington, 1978-80, chief legis. asst., 1980-83; mem. U.S. Nuc. Regulatory Commn., Washington, 1983-88; asst. sec. oceans, environment, and sci. Dept. of State, Washington, 1988-90; dep. dir. NSF, Washington, 1990-94; pres. Univs. Rsch. Assn., Washington, 1994—. Bd. dir. PPL Corp., Sci. Svc, Inc., ISL, Inc. Contbr. 45 articles to sci. jours. NATO Sr. Scientist fellow U. Copenhagen, 1977; Congl. Sci. fellow Am. Phys. Soc., 1978-79. Fellow AAAS, Am. Phys Soc.; mem. Am. Chem. Soc., Cosmos Club. Republican. Lutheran. Office: Univs Rsch Assn 1111 19th St NW Ste 400 Washington DC 20036-3627 Office Phone: 202-293-1382. E-mail: bernthal@ura.nw.dc.us.

BERNTHAL, HAROLD GEORGE, health products executive, director; b. Frankenmuth, Mich., June 11, 1928; s. Wilfred Michael and Olga Bertha (Stern) B.; m. Margaret Hrebek, Jan. 25, 1958; children: Barbara Anne, Karen Elizabeth, James Willard. BS in Chemistry, Mich. State U., 1950. Pres. Am. Hosp. Supply Corp., Evanston, Ill., 1974-85; chmn. Cobern Inc., Lake Forest, Ill., 1986—. Life trustee Northwestern Meml. Hosp., Chgo.; hon. bd. dirs. Valparaiso (Ind.) U.; former chair Wheat Ridge Ministries; former governing mem. Chgo. Symphony Orch. Served with AUS, 1950-52. Recipient Lumen Christi medal Valparaiso U., 1988. Mem. Health Industries Assn. (past pres.), Health Industry Mfr.'s Assn. (past mem. exec. com.), Pharm. Mfrs. Assn. (past chmn. med. device com.), Knollwood Club, Old Elm Club, The Reserve, Bigfoot Country Club.

BERNTSON, GARY GLEN, psychiatry, psychology and pediatrics educator; b. Mpls., June 16, 1945; s. Edward Mathias and Meryle Berntson; m. Susan Berntson, July 11, 2002. BA, U. Minn., 1968, PhD, 1971. Postdoctoral fellow Rockefeller U., NYC, 1971-73; asst. prof. dept. psychology Ohio State U., Columbus, 1973-77, assoc. prof., 1977-81, prof., 1981—, prof. dept. pediatrics, 1983—, prof. of psychiatry, 1988—. Affiliate scientist Yerkes Regional Primate Rsch. Ctr., Emory U., Atlanta, 1984-95; mem. initial rev. group ADAMHA, Washington, 1989-91, NIMH, Washington, 1991-93, NIH, 2004—; mem. fellowship rev. panel NSF, Washington, 1991-95. Contbr. over 150 articles to profl. jours., 20 chpts. to books; co-editor: Handbook of Psychophysiology. Fellow NSF, 1969, USPHS, 1972. Mem. Soc. for Neurosci., Soc. for Psychophysiol. Rsch.; fellow AAAS. Achievements include novel concepts of control of the autonomic nervous system and psychosomatic relations. Office: Ohio State U Dept Psychology 1835 Neil Ave Columbus OH 43210-1222 Office Phone: 614-292-1749.

BEROFSKY, BERNARD, philosopher, educator; b. Jersey City, July 5, 1935; s. Charles and Etta Berofsky; m. Barbara Sailer; children: Adrienne Berofsky-Seyffert, Aaron. BA, NYU, NYC, 1956; MA, Columbia U., NYC, 1959, PhD, 1963. Instr. Vassar Coll., Poughkeepsie, NY, 1963—64; asst. prof. U. Mich., Ann Arbor, 1964—67; prof. Columbia U., NYC, 1967—. Editor: Freedom and Determinism, 1966; author: Freedom from Necessity, 1987, Liberation from Self, 1995; exec. editor: Jour. Philosophy, 1970—. Bd. acad. advisors Rothberg Sch. Hebrew U., NY, 1989—97. Grantee, Am. Philos. Soc., 1967; vis. scholar, Stanford U., 1972—73, Hebrew U., 1978—79, 1988; Fulbright Rsch. fellow, 1987—88, Rsch. fellow, Cambridge U., 1998—99. Avocation: magic. Home: 639 East St Lenox MA 01240

BEROLZHEIMER, KARL, lawyer; b. Chgo., Mar. 31, 1932; s. Leon J. and Rae Gloss (Lowenthal) B.; m. Diane Glick, July 10, 1954; children: Alan, Eric, Paul, Lisa. BA, U. Ill., 1953; JD, Harvard U., 1958. Bar: Ill. 1958, U.S. Ct. Appeals (7th cir.) 1964, U.S. Ct. Appeals (9th cir.) 1969, U.S. Supreme Ct. 1976. Assoc. Ross & Hardies, Chgo., 1958—66, ptnr., 1966—76; v.p. legal Centel Corp., Chgo., 1976-77, v.p., gen. counsel, 1977-82, sr. v.p., gen. counsel, 1982-88, sr. v.p., gen. counsel, sec., 1988-93; of counsel Ross & Hardies, Chgo., 1993—2003, McGuire Woods LLP, 2003—. Nat. adv. bd. Ctr. for Informatics Law, John Marshall Law Sch., Chgo., 1988-93; mem. Corp. Counsel Ctr., Northwestern U. Law Sch., 1987-93, mem. emeritus, 1993—; mem. adv. bd. Litigation Risk Mgmt. Inst., 1989-95; bd. dirs. Milton Industries, Chgo., 1973-2005, Devon Bank, Chgo., 1985—; cons. Mt. Pulaski Tel. and Elec. Co., Lincoln, Ill., 1981-86; sec., gen. counsel Consol. Water Co., Chgo., 1968-72; mem. human rels. task force Chgo. Cmty. Trust, 1988-90. Bd. dirs. The Nat. Conf. Commn. and Justice, Chgo., presiding co-chmn., 1987-90, mem. nat. exec. bd. dirs., 1988-98, chair investment com., 1991-94, nat. co-chair, 1992-95, pres., 1993-94, chair, 1995-98; exec. bd. Internat. Coun. Christians and Jews, 1996-2000, v.p., 1998-2000; bd. dirs. Evanston (Ill.) Mental Health, 1975-82, chair, 1978-80; dir. Evanston Cmty. Found., 1996-2003, vice chair, chair grants com., 1996-98, chair, 1999-2001, chair coun. advisors, 2003—; bd. dirs. Beth Emet Found., 1997; trustee Northlight Theatre, Evanston, 1992-2004, vice-chair, 1993-99; mem. coun. The Communitarian Network, 1993-96; trustee Beth Emet Synagogue, Evanston, 1985-87, 89, 2004-07, sec., 1985-89, exec. com. 2006-07; chair Capital Campaign Plan com., 1994-97; discrimination priority com. United Way, 1990-97, vice-chair, 1993; mem. assembly Parliament of the World's Religions, 1993; mem. Ill. atty. gen.'s ad hoc com. for creation of justice commn., 1994; adv. com. Ill. Justice Commn., 1995-96; adv. bd. Nat. Underground R.R. Freedom Ctr., 1997—. 1st lt. U.S. Army, 1953-55. Fellow Am. Bar Found.; mem. ABA (chair telcom. com. bus. law sect. 1982-86, dispute resolution com. 1986-90, office com. 1991-95, mem. Coalition for Justice 1993-97, bd. editors Bus. Law Today 1995-97, co-chair conflicts of interest com. 1997-2001, past chair 2001-03), Chgo. Bar Assn. (devel. of law com. 1963-77, chair 1971-73), Chgo. Coun. Lawyers. Democrat. Office: McGuire Woods LLP Ste 4100 77 W Wacker Dr Chicago IL 60601-1815 Home: 522 Church St Apt 6D Evanston IL 60201 Office Phone: 312-750-8642. Personal E-mail: dkberolz@comcast.net.

BERONA, DAVID A., library director, educator; b. Dayton, Ohio, Mar. 19, 1950; s. Daniel Anthony Berona and Dorothy Janet Voltz; m. Rose E. O'Brien, Aug. 11, 1981. BSc, Wright State U., Ohio, 1974; MSc, Simmons Coll., Boston, 1990; MA, U. NH, Durham, 2001. Libr. Westbrook Coll., Portland, Maine, 1990—96; sys. libr. U. New Eng., Biddeford, Maine, 1996—99; head, libr. computer sys. U. NH, 1999—2005; libr. dir. Lamson Libr., Plymouth State U., 2006—. Contbr. book of essays: language of comics Pictures Speak in Wordless Comics: An Examination of pictorial principles in the work of Milt Gross, Hendrik Dorgathen, Eric Drooker and Peter Kuper; reviewer Internat. Jour. of Comic Art, 1992—, The Comics Jour., 1998, INKS: Cartoon and Comic Art Studies, 1995—96, Print Quar., 2003—; contbr. articles to jours. on woodcut novels and wordless comics. Grantee Faculty Devel. grant, U. NH, 2002, Instrnl. Tech. grant, 2002, Parents Assn. grant, 2001, 2002, Bingham Foundaton Faculty Enrichment grant, Westbrook Coll., 1993—96. Mem.: AAUP, Comic Book Def. League, Popular Culture Assn., Soc. for the History of Authorship, Reading and Pub., New Eng. Libr. Assn., Libr. and Informational Tech. Assn., Assn. of Coll. and Rsch. Libraries, Am. Libr. Assn. Avocations: watercolors, swimming. Home: PO Box 448 Gilmanton NH 03237 Office: Plymouth State Univ Lamson Libr 17 High St Plymouth NH 03264 Office Phone: 603-535-2817. Business E-Mail: daberona@plymouth.edu.

BERRA, P. BRUCE, computer science educator; b. Smiths Creek, Mich., Apr. 14, 1935; s. Mike John and Dorothy (Nelson) B.; 1 son, Marshall R. BS, U. Mich., 1958, MS, 1962; PhD, Purdue U., 1968. Sr. engr. Hughes Aircraft Corp., Culver City, Calif., 1958-60; engr., tech. advisor Bendix Corp., Ann Arbor, Mich., 1960-63; instr. U. Mich.-Dearborn, 1964-65; asst. prof. info. engring. Boston U., 1965-66; assoc. prof. Syracuse U. (N.Y.), 1968-74, 74—, prof., chmn. indsl. engring. and ops. research, 1978-82, prof. elec. and computer engring., 1982-96; dir. N.Y. State Ctr. for Advanced Tech./Software Engring., 1991-96; dir. Info. Tech. Rsch. Inst., disting. prof. info. tech. Wright State U., Dayton, Ohio, 1997-2000. Cons. IBM Corp., Bell No. Rsch., IITRI, PAR Tech., SCEEE, Singer Link, TRW, KAMAN, Opticomp. Gen. chmn., organizer Workshop on Database Machines, 1980-89. USAF Office of Sci. Research univ. resident research fellow, 1982-83 Fellow IEEE; mem. IEEE Computer Soc. (editor-in-chief

CS Press 1981-83, vice chmn. publs. bd. 1984-85, governing bd. 1985-86, 89-91, disting. visitors program 1986-88, 89-91, gen. chmn. internat. conf. on data engring. 1986). Office Phone: 518-576-9109. E-mail: bberra@att.net.

BERRA, YOGI (LAWRENCE PETER BERRA), former professional baseball player, coach, manager; b. St. Louis, May 12, 1925; s. Peter and Pauline (Longsoni) B.; m. Carmen Short, Jan. 26, 1949; children—Lawrence A., Timothy Thomas, Dale Anthony. PhD (hon.), Montclair State U., 1996. Profl. baseball player with NY Yankees, 1946-63, mgr., 1964, coach, 1975-84, mgr., 1984-85; coach NY Mets, 1965-72, mgr., 1972-75; coach Houston Astros, 1986-89; former v.p. Yoo-Hoo Chocolate Beverage Co. Author: (with Ed Fitzgerald) Yogi Berra: The Autobiography of a Professional Baseball Player, 1961, (with Tom Horton): It Ain't Over., 1989, The Yogi Book: I Really Didn't Say Everything I Said, 1998, (with Dave Kaplan) When You Come to a Fork in the Road, Take It, 2001, 10 Rings-My Championship Seasons, 2003. Served with USNR, 1943-46. Recipient Am. League Most Valuable Player award, 1951, 54, 55, Golden Plate award, Acad. Achievement, 2005; elected to Baseball Hall of Fame, 1972; established Am. League record for most home runs by a catcher, lifetime: 313. Mem.: Lion, Elk, Moose. Achievements include being a mem. Am. League All-Star Team, 1949-62, mem. of record 10 World Series Championship teams, 1947, 49-53, 56, 58, 61-62; inducted into Baseball Hall of Fame, 1972. Office: Yogi Berra Mus and Learning Ctr Montclair State U 8 Quarry Rd Little Falls NJ 07424-2161*

BERRARD, STEVEN R., investment company and former automotive retail company executive; b. 1954; BS in Acctg., Fla. Atlantic U. Auditor Coopers & Lybrand; pres. Huizenga Holdings , Inc.; sr. v.p., treas., CFO Blockbuster Entertainment Corp., 1987—93, pres., COO, 1993—94, pres., CEO, 1994—96, vice chmn.; co-founder, co-CEO AutoNation, Inc. (formerly Republic Industries Inc.), 1996—99; co-founder, mng. ptnr. New River Capital Ptnrs., Ft. Lauderdale, 1997—; pres., CEO Spelling Entertainment Group, 1993—96. Bd. dirs. Blockbuster Entertainment Corp., 1989—94, Viacom, Inc., 1994—96, Boca Resorts, Inc., 1996—2004, HealthSouth Corp., 2004—. Office: New River Capital Ptnrs Ste 1140 401 E Las Olas Blvd Fort Lauderdale FL 33316

BERRESFORD, SUSAN VAIL, foundation administrator; b. NYC, Jan. 8, 1943; d. Richard Case and Katherine Vail (Marsters) Besserford Hurd; m. David F. Stein (div.); 1 child, Jeremy Vail Stein. Student, Vassar Coll., 1961-63; BA cum laude in Am. History, Radcliffe Coll., 1965. Vol. UN Vol. Services, NYC, summer 1962; sec. to Theodore H. White, summer 1964; program officer Neighborhood Youth Corps, NYC, 1965-67; program specialist Manpower Career Devel. Agy., NYC, 1967, human resources adminstrn. specialist, 1968; freelance cons., writer Europe & US, 1968-70; project asst. Nat. Affairs Div. Ford Found., NYC, 1970—72, program officer, 1972—80, officer in charge women's programs, 1980—81, v.p. US and Internat. Affairs programs, 1981-95, v.p. Worldwide Programming Div., 1989, exec. v.p., COO, 1995-96, pres., 1996—. Bd. mem. Coun. on Founds.; mem. Trilateral Commn., Coun. Fgn. Rels. Chair bd. dirs. United States Artists (USA) Bd.; adv. bd. mem. Trinidad Trust Fund, Calif.; mem. European Found. Centre's Governing Coun. Named one of 100 Most Powerful Women in World, Forbes mag., 2005—06. Mem.: Am. Acad. Arts and Scis. Office: Ford Foundation 320 East 43rd St New York NY 10017*

BERREY, ROBERT FORREST, lawyer; b. Oak Park, Ill., Dec. 7, 1939; s. Rhodes Clay and Regina (Kasprovich) B.; m. Rebecca L. Newell, Apr. 10, 1993; children from previous marriage: Adam Forrist, Ellen Catherine, Kevin Joseph. AB, Harvard U., 1962; JD, U. Chgo., 1968. Bar: Ill. 1969, Ohio 1986. Atty. Torshen, Fortes & Eiger, Chgo., 1970-75; atty. Jewel Cos., Inc., Chgo., 1975-76, sec., 1976-80, v.p., sec., gen. counsel, 1980-85; v.p., gen. counsel Tomkins (formerly Philips) Industries, Inc., 1986-91; ptnr. Chernesky, Heyman & Kress, Dayton, Ohio, 1991-98; formerly of counsel Bieser, Greer & Landis LLP, Dayton, Ohio; venture capital investments Chapel Hill, NC. With AUS, 1962-65. Mem. Governors Club, Old Chatham Golf Club. E-mail: robert@berrey.org.

BERRIDGE, GEORGE BRADFORD, retired lawyer; b. Detroit, June 9, 1928; s. William Lloyd and Marjorie (George) B.; m. Mary Lee Robinson, July 6, 1957; children: George Bradford, Elizabeth A., Mary L., Robert L. AB, U. Mich., 1950, MBA, 1953, JD, 1954. Bar: N.Y. 1954. Assoc. Chadbourne & Parke, NYC, 1954-61; gen. atty., v.p. law Am. Airlines, Inc., NYC, 1961-71; sr. v.p., gen. counsel Americana Hotels, Inc., NYC, 1971-74, Nat. Westminster Bank U.S.A., NYC, 1975-89, Nat. Westminster Bancorp, NYC, 1989-93; ret., 1993. Contbr. articles to U. Mich. Law Rev. Served to lt. (j.g.) USN, 1951-53. Recipient Howard P. Coblentz prize U. Mich. Law Sch., 1954. Episcopalian. Home: 2 Circle Ave Larchmont NY 10538-4219 Personal E-mail: gberr2@aol.com.

BERRIEN, JACQUELINE A., lawyer; b. 1961; BA in Govt. and English, Oberlin Coll.; JD, Harvard U. Bar: NY 1987. Atty. ACLU, NY, Voting Rights Project, Lawyers' Com. Civil Rights, Washington; asst. counsel NAACP Legal Def. Fund, 1994—2001, assoc. dir.-counsel, 2004—; prog. officer Peace & Social Justice Prog., Ford Found., 2001—04. Adj. prof. NY Law Sch. Contbr. articles to prof. legal jours. Office: NAACP Legal Def Fund Ste 1600 99 Hudson St New York NY 10013 Office Phone: 212-965-2200.*

BERRIGAN, HELEN GINGER, federal judge; b. New Rochelle, Apr. 15, 1948; m. Joseph E. Berrigan Jr. BA, U. Wis., 1969; MA, Am. U., 1971; JD, La. State U., 1977. Staff rschr. Senator Harold E. Hughes, 1971-72; legis. aide Senator Joseph E. Biden, 1972-73; asst. to mayor City of Fayette, Miss., 1973-74; law clk. La. Dept. Corrections, 1975-77; staff atty. Gov. Pardon, Parole and Rehab. Commn., 1977-78; prin. Gravel Brady & Berrigan, New Orleans, 1978-94, Berrigan, Litchfield, Schonekas, Mann & Clement, New Orleans, 1984-94; judge U.S. Dist. Ct. (ea. dist.) La., New Orleans, 1994—. Active La. Sentencing Commn., 1987. Active Com. of 21, 1989, pres., 1990-92, ACLU of La., 1989-94, Forum for Equality, 1990-94, Amistad Rsch. Ctr. Tulane U., 1990-95. Mem.: New Orleans Assn. Women Attys., La. Assn. Criminal Def. Lawyers, La. State Bar Assn. Office: US Dist Courthouse 500 Poydras St Rm C556 New Orleans LA 70130-3313

BERRING, ROBERT CHARLES, JR., law educator, librarian, association administrator; b. Canton, Ohio, Nov. 20, 1949; s. Robert Charles and Rita Pauline (Franta) B.; m. Leslie Applegarth, May 20, 1998; children: Simon Robert, Daniel Fredrick. BA cum laude, Harvard U., 1971; JD, MLS, U. Calif.-Berkeley, 1974. Asst. prof. and reference libr. U. Ill. Law Sch., Champaign, 1974—76; assoc. libr. U. Tex. Law Sch., Austin, 1976—78; dep. libr. Harvard Law Sch., Cambridge, Mass., 1978—81; prof. law, law libr. U. Wash. Law Sch., Seattle, 1981—82, U. Calif., Boalt Hall Law Sch., Berkeley, 1982—, dean sch. library and info. scis., 1986—89, Walter Perry Johnson Prof. Law, 1998—, dir. law libr., interim dean, 2003—04. Mem. Westlaw Adv. Bd., St. Paul, 1984-91; cons. various law firms; mem. on Legal Exch. with China, 1983—, chmn., 1991-93.; vis. prof. U. Cologne, 1993. Author: How to Find the Law, 8th edit., 1984, 9th edit., 1989, Great American Law Revs., 1985, Finding the Law, 1999; co-author: Authors Guide, 1981; editor Legal Reference Svc. Quar., 1981—; author videotape series Commando Legal Rsch., 1989. Chmn. Com. Legal Ednl. Exch. with China, 1991—93. Robinson Cox fellow U. Western Australia, 1988; named West Publishing Co. Acad. Libr. of Yr., 1994. Mem. Am. Assn. Law Libraries (pres. 1985-86), Calif. Bar Assn., ABA, ALA, Am. Law Inst. Office: U Calif Law Sch Boalt Hl Rm 345 Berkeley CA 94720-0001 Business E-Mail: berringr@law.berkeley.edu.

BERRINGTON, CRAIG ANTHONY, lawyer; b. Chgo., Aug. 9, 1943; s. Leo and Geraldine (Dale) Berrington; m. Susan Dale Olsen, Sept. 3, 1967; children: Jennifer, Emily, Lacy. BA, Am. U., 1965; JD, Northwestern U., 1968. Bar: D.C. 1969, U.S. Supreme Ct. 1989. Atty. U.S. Dept. Labor, Washington, 1968-75, assoc. solicitor, 1975-77, exec. asst. to under sec., 1977-79, dep. asst. sec. Employment Standards Adminstrn., 1979-86; sr. v.p., gen. counsel Am. Ins. Assn., Washington, 1986—2005; ptnr. Wily Rein LLP (formerly Wily, Rein & Fielding LLP), Washington, 2005—. Contbr. articles to profl. jours. Mem. ABA, U.S. Supreme Ct. Bar, D.C. Bar. Office: Wiley Rein LLP 1776 K St NW Washington DC 20006 Business E-Mail: cberrington@wileyrein.com.

BERRUGA-FILLOY, ENRIQUE, ambassador; b. Mexico City, Sept. 15, 1959; s. Arsenio Berruga and Eulalia Filloy; m. Delia Sanchez-Cervantes, Apr. 6, 1986; children: Mercedes, Bernardo. BA, El Colegio de Mexico, Mexico City, 1982; MA, Johns Hopkins U., 1984. Lic. in internat. rels. Advisor sec. Ministry Fgn. Affairs, Mexico City, 1984-87; sec. of info. Embassy of Mex. to U.S., Washington, 1987-89; sec. for polit. affairs Embassy of Mex. to U.K., London, 1989-90; chargé d'affaires Mexican Embassy in Ireland, Dublin, 1991-92; chief of cabinet of sec. Ministry of Fgn. Affairs, Mexico City, 1993; chief of advisors of sec. Ministry Fgn. Affairs, Mexico City, 1993; gen. dir. internat. rels. Ministry of Edn., Mexico City, 1993-94; chief of advisors to min. fgn. affairs Ministry Fgn. Affairs, 1993—97; rank of Amb. of Mex., 1996; amb. of Mexico to Costa Rica, 1997-2000; CEO Mexican Inst. for Internat. Cooperation, 1999—2000; dep. min. fgn. affairs Ministry Fgn. Affairs, 2000—03; perm. Mex. rep. UN, New York, 2004—. Sec.-gen. Mexican Commn. of UNESCO, Ministry of Edn., Mexico City, 1993. Author: Destino: Los Pinos, 1982, El Martes del Silencio, 1994, Propiedad Ajena, 2000; contbr. articles to newspapers. Fulbright scholar ITT, Washington, 1982-84. Mem. Asociacion del Servicio Exterior Mexicano. Avocations: fiction writing, reading, golf, running. Office: UN Two UN Plz 28th Fl New York NY 10017 Home: 178 E 72nd St New York NY 10021 E-mail: eberruga@sre.gob.mx, enriqueberruga@hotmail.com.

BERRY, ANDREW T., lawyer; b. 1940; BA cum laude, Princeton U., 1962; LLB, Harvard U., 1965. Bar: NJ 1965, NY 1981, U.S. Dist. Ct. (ea. dist. NY), U.S. Dist. Ct. (Tex.), U.S. Dist. Ct. (Colo.), U.S. Ct. Appeals (2d, 3rd, 5th, and 11th cir.), U.S. Supreme Ct. Ptnr. McCarter & English LLP, Newark, chmn., 1997—. Arbitrator U.S. Dist. Ct. (NJ Dist.), 1987—; spkr. in field. Contbr. articles to profl. jours. Bd. dirs. NJ Performing Arts Ctr., Newark Alliance. Fellow: Am. Acad. Appellate Lawyers, Am. Bar Found.; mem.: ABA, London Ct. Internat. Arbitration, Am. Arbitration Assn. (arbitrator, mem. comml. adv. coun. NJ), Am. Law Inst. (cons. various projects and coms.), Internat. Bar Assn., NJ State Bar Assn., Essex County Bar Assn., Assn. Bar City NY. Office: McCarter & English LLP Four Gateway Ctr 100 Mulberry St Newark NJ 07102 Office Phone: 973-628-4444. Office Fax: 973-624-7070. E-mail: aberry@mccarter.com.

BERRY, BARBARA COCHRAN, education educator, writer; b. Shreveport, La., Jan. 14, 1935; d. youree and Eartie Norris B.; m. Johnnie Cochran, Jr., July 10, 1960 (div. Apr. 1978); children: Melodie Trevania, Tiffany Krystal; m. David Berry, July 6, 1986 (dec. Dec. 1992). BS, UCLA, 1958, M. Educator L.A. Unified Sch., 1953-58, Miller-Unruh reading specialist, 1965-72, bilingual tchr., Spanish, 1972-79, mentor tchr., 1979-98; tng. tchr. Calif. State U., LA, 1980-98; master tchr., tng. tchr. Nat. U., LA, 1980—. Seminar leader L.A. Unified, 1979; workshop leader Occidental Coll., Pasadena, Calif., 1980; workshop participant UCLA, 1996. Author: (book) Life After Johnnie Cochran, 1995 (Excellence award 1997). Active Haven House Shelter for Battered Women, Pasadena, 1996; bd. dirs. WAVE Battered Women's Shelter, San Fernando Valley, 1998; co-chair Corina Alarcon for City Coun., L.A., 1998-99. Recipient Step Forward award Haven House, Inc., 1996. Mem. NEA, AAUW (nom. com. 1998), NAACP (life), Educare Ednl. Soc., United Tchrs. of L.A. Democrat. Baptist. Avocations: reading, speaking, travel, tennis, bridge. Home: 23020 Bretton Pl Woodland Hills CA 91364-4861

BERRY, BECKY, music educator; b. Ohio; m. Kim Berry; 1 child, Allison. BFA, Fla. Atlantic U., Boca Raton, 1976. Cert. tchr. Fla. Music/performing arts tchr. A.C.Perry Elem. Sch., Miramar, Fla., 1977—85, Nova Eisenhower Elem. Sch., Davie, Fla., 1985—91, Griffin Elem. Sch., Cooper City, Fla., 1991—98, Everglades Elem. Sch., Weston, Fla., 1998—. Music coord., youth choir dir. Pky. Christian Ch., Plantation, Fla., 1979—94. Dir.: (over 100 mus. prodns.). Finalist Arts Tchr. of Yr., Broward County Cultural Divsn., 2005; named Tchr. of Yr., Everglades Elem. Sch., 2005, Nova Eisenhower Elem. Sch.; recipient, A.C. Perry Elem. Sch. Mem.: Broward Music Educators Assn., Fla. Elem. Music Educator's Assn., Music Educator's Nat. Conf., Fla. Music Educators Assn. Avocations: singing, directing children's musicals. Office: Everglades Elem Sch 2900 Bonaventure Blvd Weston FL 33331 E-mail: becky.berry@browardschools.com.

BERRY, BRIAN JOE LOBLEY, geographer, educator, urban planner, political economist; b. Sedgley, Stafford, Eng., Feb. 16, 1934; arrived in U.S., 1955, naturalized, 1965; s. Joe and Gwendoline Alice (Lobley) B.; m. Janet Elizabeth Shapley, Sept. 6, 1958; children: Duncan Jeffrey, Carol Anne (dec.), Diane Leigh, Karen. BSc with honors, Univ. Coll., London, 1955; MA, U. Wash., 1956, PhD, 1958; AM (hon.), Harvard U., 1976. Instr. geography, civil engring. U. Wash., Seattle, 1957-58; asst. prof. geography U. Chgo., 1958-62, assoc. prof., 1962-65, prof., 1965-72, Irving B. Harris prof. urban geography, 1972-76, dir. Ctr. Urban Studies, chmn. dept. geography, 1974-76; Frank Backus Williams prof. urban and regional planning Harvard U., 1976-81, chmn. Ph.D. Program in Urban Planning, dir. Lab. for Computer Graphics and Spatial Analysis, fellow Inst. Internat. Devel., 1976-81, prof. sociology, 1978-81; dean H. John Heinz III Sch. of Pub. Mgmt. Carnegie-Mellon U., 1981-86, Univ. prof. urban studies and pub. policy, 1981-86; founders prof. U. Tex., Dallas, 1986-91, prof. polit. econ., 1986—, Lloyd Viel Berkner Regental prof., 1991—, chmn. Bruton Ctr. for Devel. Studies, 1988-95, dean Sch. Econ., Polit. and Policy Scis., 2005—. Author numerous books; contbr. articles to profl. jours. Named Lord of Hastingleigh, County Kent, 2000, Dist. Alumnus award in Social Scis., U. Wash., 2005, Vautrin Lud Laureate in Geography, 2005; recipient Victoria medal, Royal Geog. Soc., 1988, Rockefeller prize, Dartmouth U., 1992; fellow, Univ. Coll., U. London, 1983. Fellow AAAS, Am. Acad. Arts and Scis., Am. Inst. Cert. Planners, Urban Land Inst., Brit. Acad. (corr.), Weimer Inst. Real Estate and Land Econs., Royal Geog. Soc., So. Regional Sci. Assn.; mem. NAS (coun. 1999-2002), Assn. Am. Geographers (Hon. award 1968, pres. 1978-79, Anderson medal 1987), Acad. Medicine, Engring. and Sci. Tex., Regional Sci. Assn., Inst. Brit. Geographers, Sigma Xi. Office: U Tex Dallas Sch Econs Politics and Policy Scis Richardson TX 75083-0688 Home Phone: 972-562-1058; Office Phone: 972-883-4988. Business E-Mail: brian.berry@utdallas.edu.

BERRY, CHARLENE HELEN, librarian, musician; b. Highland Pk., Mich., Jan. 4, 1947; d. Harold Terry and Mattie Lou (Colvin) B. BSE, Wayne U., 1968, MA, 1970, MLS, 1974; diploma, Howard Sch. Broadcast Arts, 1992, Irene's Myomassology Inst., 1997; DMin (hon.), Univ. Sem. Ch., 1998; DD, Destiny Christian U., 07. Ordained music minister. Libr. asst. Wayne State U., Detroit, 1970-74; libr. serials cataloger SUNY, Stony Brook, 1975-79; cataloger Madonna U., Livonia, Mich., 1980—. Organist various area chs., Detroit, 1981—, 1st Ch. of Christ, Wyandotte, Mich., 1986—; music min. Gospel Light House Ministries, Detroit, 1991—; scholar, performer, tchr. hammer dulcimer, 1986—; libr. cons. Superior Twp. (Mich.) Libr. Bd., 1989-91; host Charlene Berry's Dulcimer World, Sta. WCAR, Garden City, Mich., WALE, Providence, R.I., WLLZ 560 AM, Southfield, Mich., 1997—, Sta. WPON AM 1460, Southfield, Mich., 1997—. Composer: Dulcimer Delights, 1991, Marches, Waltzes, Free Compositions, 1993, Dulcimer Praise, 1993, Fruits of the Spirit, 1993, Dulcimer Suits and Trreats, 2005, Dulcimer Inspirations, 2005, Old Village Dulcimer Collection, 2006, Little Collection of Music for all Occasion,s for Hammer Dulcimer and Other Instruments, 2006; solo recs.: Traditional Dulcimer, 1989, Christmas Dulcimer, 1989, Sacred Dulcimer, 1990, Dulcimer Fun, 1991, Dulcimer Praise, 1993, Fruits of the Spirit, 1993, Dulcimer Americana, 1994, Joy, Peace Healing, 1998, Hymns of Prayer and Praise, 1999, Appalachia, 2006, Nine Eleven, 2006; (video) Hammering the Hammer Dulcimer, 1994, Music of Light/Light and Life, 1995, Under der Linden, 1996, Joy, Peace, Healing, 1998, Hymms of Prayer and Praise, 1999; performed Carnegie Hall, 2006, Ellipse of the White House, 2006. Pres. Libr. Staff Assn., SUNY, 1978-79; ch. libr. Ch. Bds. Coms., Long Island, Detroit, 1975—; bd. dirs. Livonia Symphony Soc.; performing artist Mich. Touring Arts Agy., 1994—. Recipient Performance award Silver Springs Dulciner Soc., 1988, 89, 90, Interat. Order of Merit, ASCAP, Ronald Reagan award, 2004, Star of Stars Music award, 2006, Silver medal, Christian Music Connection, 2006; named Internat. Woman of Yr., 1992-93, Most Admired Woman of Decade, Businesswoman of Yr., 2003, 04. Fellow Internat. Biographical Assn. (life). Am. Biographical Inst. (Woman of Yr. 1993); mem. AAUW, ALA, NAFE, Am. Biographical Rsch. Assn. (hon. dep. gov.), Bus. and Profl. Women, Am. Soc. of Notaries, Am. Fedn. Musicians, Am. Guild Organists (bd. dirs. 1985-88), Plymouth C. of C., Luth. Ch. Musicians Guild, Order Ea. Star, Kappa Delta Pi. Office: Dulcimer Evente 49614 Oak Dr Lot 67 Plymouth MI 48170-2353 Office Phone: 800-550-0707. Business E-Mail: cberry@dulcimerworld.com.

BERRY, CHUCK (CHARLES EDWARD ANDERSON BERRY), musician, composer; b. St. Louis, Oct. 18, 1926; s. Henry William, Sr., and Martha Banks Berry; m. Themetta Suggs, Oct. 1948; 4 children: Darlen Ingrid, Melody Exes, Aloha Isa Lei, Charles Edward Anderson, Jr. Popular artist in rock and roll music, plays guitar, saxophone, piano; concert, TV appearances, 1955—; rec. artist Chess Records; appeared in film Go, Johnny Go, Rock, Rock, Rock, 1956, Jazz on a Summer's Day, 1960, Let the Good Times Roll, 1973; composer: Rock 'n' Roll Music; albums include: After School Sessions, 1958, One Dozen Berry's, 1958, Rockin' At The Hops, 1959-60, New Juke Box Hits, 1960, Chuck Berry, 1960, More Chuck Berry, 1960, On Stage, 1960, Twist, 1960, You Can Never Tell, 1964, Greatest Hits, 1964, 2 Great Guitars, 1964, Chuck Berry in London, 1965, Fresh Berrys, 1965, St. Louis to Liverpool, 1966, Golden Hits, 1967, At the Fillmore, 1967, Medley, 1967, In Memphis, 1967, Concerto in B Goods, 1969, Home Again, 1971, The London Sessions, 1972, Golden Decade, 1972, St. Louis to Frisco to Memphis, 1972, Let the Good Times Roll, 1973, Golden Decade, Vol. 2, 1973, Bio, 1973, Back in the U.S.A., 1973, Golden Decade, Vol. 5, 1974, I'm a Rocker, 1975, Chuck Berry 75, 1975, Motorvatin', 1976, Rockit, 1979, Chess Masters, 1983, The Chess Box, 1989, Missing Berries: Rarities, 1990, On the Blues Side, 1993, others; soundtrack Hail! Hail! Rock n' Roll, 1987; author: autobiography Chuck Berry, 1987. Recipient Grammy award for Lifetime Achievement, 1984; named to Rock and Rock Hall of Fame, 1986. Office: Berry Park 691 Buckner Rd Wentzville MO 63385-5442

BERRY, DAVID J., former financial services company executive; b. Columbus, Ohio, Apr. 14, 1944; s. Maurice Glenn Berry and Janice (Eshelman) Read; m. Janet Lynn Tewksbury, Mar. 24, 1977; children: Jeffrey James, Jennifer Jean, Jon Andrew, Amy Jo. Student, Miami U., Oxford, Ohio, 1963-64, Ohio State U., 1965-66. Registered prin. SEC. Ind. fin. svc. salesman, 1966-74; gen. agt. Sun Life Assurance Co. Can., Columbus, 1975-85; pres. Strategic Info. Svcs., Columbus, 1986-87; v.p. IDS Life Ins. Co., Mpls., 1990—; assoc. mgr. IDS Fin. Svcs. Inc., Columbus, 1988, region dir., 1989; v.p. IDS Life Ins. Co., Mpls., 1991-2000; ret., 2000. Chmn. Agy. Mgmt. Tng. Coun., Columbus, 1982-83. Bell ringer Salvation Army, Columbus, 1975-85; vol. instr. Learning Disabled Children, Columbus, 1980-83; pres. PTA, Worthington, Ohio, 1983. Fellow Life Underwriting Tng. Coun., Columbus, 1981. Mem. Nat. Assn. Securities Dealers, Gen. Agts. and Mgrs. Assn. (pres. 1979-82), Mpls. Life Underwriters Assn. Avocations: travel, sports, poetry. Office: IDS Life Ins Co IDS Tower # 10 Minneapolis MN 55402-2100

BERRY, DEAN C., lawyer; b. Lumberton, NC, July 17, 1957; AB magna cum laude, Harvard Univ., 1979, AM, 1979, JD cum laude, 1982; LLM, NYU, 1990. Bar: NY 1982. Ptnr., Trusts & Estates practice & chmn. recruiting com. Coudert Bros. LLP, NYC. Editor: Harvard Law Rev., 1981—82. Mem.: ABA, Soc. Trusts & Estates Practitioners, Assn. Bar City of NY, Phi Beta Kappa. Office: Coudert Bros LLP 1114 Ave of the Americas New York NY 10036 Office Phone: 212-626-4287. Office Fax: 212-626-4120. Business E-Mail: berryd@coudert.com.

BERRY, DEAN LESTER, lawyer; b. Chgo., Jan. 20, 1935; s. Ruben W. and Leonore C. (Nelson) B.; m. Donna J. Zack, Nov. 16, 1962 (dec.); children: Megan, Thomas. BA with distinction, DePauw U., 1955; JD with distinction, U. Mich., 1960. Bar: Ohio 1961, U.S. Dist. Ct. (no. dist.) Ohio 1962. Assoc. Squire, Sanders & Dempsey L.L.P., Cleve., 1960-70, ptnr., 1970—2002, counsel, 2002—03. Lectr. various programs, Order of Coif. Author: Local Government in Michigan, 1960; contbr. articles to profl. jours.; participant in Quiz Kids radio program, 1945-47. Mem. council City of Rocky River, Ohio, 1967-71; mem. cen. com. Cuyahoga County Rep. Orgn., Ohio, 1963-75, mem. exec. com., 1969-2001. Served to 1st lt. USAF, 1955-57. Mem. Ohio State Bar Assn., Portage County Bar Assn., Greater Cleve. Bar Assn. (com. chmn. 1978), Soc. Profl. Journalists. Avocations: travel, crossword puzzles. Home: 478 Ravine Dr Aurora OH 44202-8236 Personal E-mail: dlberry@adelphia.net.

BERRY, DENNIS (G. DENNIS BERRY), publishing executive; B in Advt. and Pub. Rels., U. Ga. Pub. Atlanta Jour.-Constn.; pres., CEO Manheim Auctions, 1995—2000; pres., COO Cox Enterprises, Inc., 2000—05, vice chmn., 2005—. Bd. dirs. Cox Comm., Inc., Cox Radio, Inc.; chmn. bd. AutoTrader.com. Mem. adv. bd. Grady Coll. Journalism and Mass Comm.; bd. dirs. Atlanta Area Coun., Boy Scouts Am., Ctrl. Atlanta Progress, Advt. Coun., United Way, Emory Bd. Visitors, Mission New Hope; mem. bd. advisors Ga. State U.; past chair bd. dirs. Better Bus. Bur. Met. Atlanta. Mailing: Cox Enterprises PO Box 105357 Atlanta GA 30348 Office: Cox Enterprises 6205 Peachtree Dunwoody Rd Atlanta GA 30328

BERRY, EDGAR ALLEN, music educator; b. Columbus, Ohio, Feb. 2, 1970; s. Richard A. and Janet L. Berry; m. Michelle W. Wickline, June 26, 1993; 1 child, Dawson J. MA, Ohio State U., 2002. Ohio Teaching Certificate Ohio Dept. of Edn., 1992. Music educator Huron City Schools, Huron, Ohio, 1992—2000; grad. asst. Ohio State U., Columbus, Ohio, 2000—02; music educator Bay Village City Schools, Ohio, 2002—. Grad. asst. Ohio State U. Marching, Athletic and Wind Bands, Columbus, Ohio, 2000—02. Musician (conductor): (performance) 2nd Annual Band Invitational at Severance Hall (Symphonic Band performance, 2005). Mem. Boy Scouts of Am., Huron, Ohio, 1983—2006. Named Ohio's Dir. Who Makes a Difference, Sch. Band and Orch., 2004; named one of Top 50 Most Effective Teachers across the U.S. representing Ohio, Sch., Band and Orch., 2004; recipient Nat. Music Honor Soc., Pi Kappa Gama, 2002, Superintendent's Best, Bay Village City Schools, 2003, 2004, Bay High Jazz Ensemble selected to perform at State Conv., Ohio Music Edn. Assn., 2005, Dedication and Achievement award, Huron Bd. of Edn., 1995, Spl. Appreciation award, Huron C. of C., 1994. Mem.: NEA, Ohio Edn. Assn., Ohio Arts Assn., Ohio Music Edn. (site coord. for large group adjudicated events 2004—05), Music Educators Nat. Conf., Rock 'n Roll Hall of Fame, Jazz at Lincoln Ctr., The Boy Scouts of Am. (Eagle Scout Recipient 1987), Nat. Order of the Arrow (lodge chief 1987—88, Vigil Honor 1988), Kappa Kappa Psi (chairperson 1990—2006). Avocations: golf, boating, basketball, travel. Home: 1233 Laguna Huron OH 44839 Office: Bay HS 29230 Wolf Rd Bay Village OH 44140 Home Phone: 419-433-6996; Office Phone: 440-617-7480. Office Fax: 440-617-7401; Home Fax: 440-617-7401. Personal E-mail: eberry@bex.net. E-mail: eberry@leeca.org.

BERRY, ESTER LORÉE, vocational nurse; b. St. Joseph, La., Sept. 19, 1945; d. Sim and Ruby Jordan; (div.); children: Roderick Bryant, Pamela Elaine. A in nursing and art, Calif. State U., 1996; diploma in poetry and writing, Internat. BIB Ctr. Lic. vocat. nurse. Ward clk. Santa Fe Hosp., Compton, Calif., 1969-72; supr. J.C. Penney's, Carson, Calif., 1973-80; asst. mgr. Std. Comm., Carson, 1981-84; lic. vocat. nurse, nurse King Drew Med., LA, 1984-94; medicine nurse Martin Luther Jr. Hosp., 1996-99; poet Nobles Theatre of the Mind, Paris, London, NYC, 2004—. Author numerous poems. Named hon. mem., Vets. Am., 1999—2001, Best Poet of Yr., 2001, Best Poet of Yr., Internat. Libr. Poetry, 2004, Poet of Yr., 2007; named to Comdrs. Club, DAV, 2002—03, Wall of Tolerance, Ala., 2004; recipient Editors Choice award, 1999—2001, Laureate award, Internat. Libr. Poetry, 2006, Editor's Choice award, 2006—, 2007, Bronze Merit Medallion award, 2007, Editor's Choice award, 2007, Christal Sataue Globe award, 2007, Bronze Leader award, Comdr. Club, DAV, 2001, Silver Internat. Poet of Merit, Bronze Commemorative medallion, Best Poet award, 2002—03, certificate, Profl. Women's Adv. Bd., Wall of Tolerance award, So. Poverty Law Ctr., 2004. Mem.: Am. Libr. Inst. (mem. profl. women's adv. bd. 2004). Avocations: fishing, sewing, photography, crocheting, camping. Home: Apt P230 27-700 Landau B Cathedral City CA 92234

BERRY, GAIL W., psychiatrist, educator; b. Kalamazoo, Mich., Nov. 7, 1939; BA, Kalamazoo Coll., 1960; MD, NYU, 1964; cert. in psychoanalysis, N.Y. Med. Coll., 1976. Lic. Am. Bd. Psychiatry and Neurology. Clin. instr. psychiatry Mt. Sinai Sch. Medicine, NYC, 1969—76, asst. clin. prof. psychiatry, 1976—; tng. and supervising psychoanalyst Psychoanalytic Inst. N.Y. Med. Coll., Valhalla, NY, 1980—; assoc. attending psychiatrist Mt. Sinai Hosp., NYC, 1981—. Adj. prof. psychiatry N.Y. Med. Coll., Valhalla, 1984—. Fellow: Am. Psychiat. Assn. (life; disting.); mem.: Am. Acad. Psychoanalysis (asst. editor jour. 1984—2002), Am. Acad. Psychoanalysis and Dynamic Psychiatry (consulting editor jour. 2002—).

BERRY, GUY CURTIS, polymer science educator, researcher; b. Greene County, Ill., May 11, 1935; s. Charles Curtis and Wilma Francis (Wickes) B.; m. Marilyn Jane Montooth, Jan. 26, 1957; children: Susan Jane, Sandra Jean, Scott Curtis. BSCh.E., U. Mich., 1957, MS in Polymer Sci., 1958, PhD, 1960. Fellow Mellon Inst., Pitts., 1960-65, sr. fellow, 1965—90; assoc. prof. chemistry Carnegie-Mellon U., Pitts., 1966-73, prof., 1973—2002, acting dean, 1981-82, acting head dept. chemistry, 1983-84, head dept. chemistry, 1990-95, Univ. prof., 2002—. Vis. prof. U. Tokyo, 1973, Colo. State U., Ft. Collins, 1979, U. Kyoto, Japan, 1983 Editor Jour. Polymer Sci., 1988-93, Progress in Polymer Sci., 2002--; mem. editl. bd. Jour. Rheology, 1990—, Chemtracts-Macromolecular Chemistry, 1990-94; contbr. over 200 articles to sci. jour. Recipient Bingham medal Soc. of Rheology, 1990; Polymeric Materials: Sci. and Engring. fellow. Fellow Am. Phys. Soc., Polymeric Materials: Sci. and Engring.; mem. AAAS, Am. Chem. Soc. (Pitts. Chemistry prize 1994), Soc. Rheology. Office: Carnegie Mellon U Dept Chem 4400 5th Ave Pittsburgh PA 15213-2617 Office Phone: 412-268-3131. Business E-Mail: gcberry@andrew.cmu.edu.

BERRY, HALLE MARIA, actress; b. Cleve., Aug. 14, 1966; d. Jerome and Judith (Hawkins) B.; m. David Christopher Justice, Dec. 31, 1992 (div. 1996); m. Eric Benet, Jan. 24, 2001 (div. Jan. 3, 2005). BA, Cuyahoga C.C., Cleveland, 1986. Spokeswoman, Revlon cosmetics, 1996-. Actress in films Jungle Fever, 1991, The Last Boy Scout, 1991, Strictly Business, 1991, Boomerang, 1992 (Image award nom. 1992), Father Hood, 1993, The Program, 1993, The Flintstones, 1994, Losing Isaiah, 1995, The Rich Man's Wife, 1996, Executive Decision, 1996, Race The Sun, 1996, Girl 6, 1996, B*A*P*S, 1997, Bulworth, 1998, Why Do Fools Fall in Love, 1998, Victims of Fashion, 1999, Ringside, 1999, X-Men, 2000, Swordfish, 2001, Monsters Ball, 2001 (Acad. award best actress 2002), Die Another Day, 2002, X2: X-Men United, 2003, Gothika, 2003, Catwoman, 2004, (voice) Robots, 2005, X-Men: The Last Stand, 2006, Perfect Stranger, 2007; (TV films) Solomon & Sheba, 1995, The Wedding, 1998, Oprah Winfrey Presents: Their Eyes Were Watching God, 2005; actress, exec. prodr., (TV films) Introducing Dorothy Dandridge, 1999 (Emmy award best actress 2000, Golden Globe award best actress 2000, Image award, SAG award and three NAACP Image awards 2000), exec. prodr. Lackawanna Blues, 2005; TV mini-series Queen, 1992; TV series include Living Dolls, 1989, Knots Landing, 1992; (TV appearances) Amen, 1991, A Different World, 1991 They Came From Outer Space, 1991, Martin, 1996, Frasier (voice only), 1998, The Bernie Mac Show, 2002. Named Miss Teen All-Am., 1985, Miss USA first-runner up, 1986, Miss U.S.A., 1987, Favorite Female Action Star, People's Choice awards, 2007. First African Am. actress to win Academy award for best actress for the film Monsters Ball, 2002. Mailing: Vincent Cirrincione Assoc Ltd Ste 205 8721 Sunset Blvd West Hollywood CA 90069*

BERRY, JACK K., lawyer; b. Colleton, SC, Aug. 30, 1930; s. Percy M. and Pearle A. (Garris) B.; m. Frances Marie Cassel, Apr. 24, 1954; children: J. Keith Jr., Karen B. Wharton, Christine B. Lloyd. BA in Polit. Sci., The Citadel, Charleston, SC, 1953; LLB, Emory U., 1958, JD, 1970. Bar: Ga. 1958, U.S. Dist. Ct. (so. dist.) Ga. 1990, U.S. Ct. Appeals (11th cir.), U.S. Supreme Ct. 2004. Assoc. Pierce, Ranitz & Lee, Savannah, Ga., 1958-63; ptnr. Pierce, Ranitz, Lee, Berry and Mahoney, Savannah, 1963-66, Pierce, Ranitz, Berry, Mahoney and Forbes, Savannah, 1968-76, Berry and McCallar, Savannah, 1976-87; asst. U.S. trustee Dept. of Justice, Savannah, 1987—2003. Chpt. 7 panel trustee U.S. Bankruptcy Ct., Savannah, 1965-74, chpt. 13 trustee, 1974-87. State legislator Ga. Ho. of Reps., 1968; bd. dirs. Jenkins Boys Club; pres. Coastal Empire Fair, 1992. Col. USAFR, 1953-83. Decorated Legion of Merit. Mem. Nat. Assn. Chpt. 13 Trustees (pres. 1980), Am. Bankruptcy Inst., Exch. Club Savannah (pres. 1968). Baptist. Office: Atty at Law PO Box 8516 302 Johnston St Savannah GA 31405 Office Phone: 912-355-8670.

BERRY, JACOB OBADIAH, not-for-profit developer, rancher; b. LA, Aug. 14, 1954; s. Francis Oscar and Harriet Leaf Beregi. BA, Denver U., 1976. Prin., owner 120 acre farm, Newell, SD, 1979—85; ranch hand various cattle ranches, SD, 1985—96; pres. Am. Cross Found., Amarillo, Tex., 1996—. Author: Horse Creek, 1999, (screenplays) Prince of Darkness, 2001. Achievements include patent for Cross design; utility patent for Cross structure. Avocations: country western dance, horseback riding. Office: American Cross Foundation PO Box 9492 Amarillo TX 79105 Office Phone: 806-374-6758. Business E-Mail: acf@americancross.org.

BERRY, JAMES F. (JIM BERRY), engineering executive; Dir. mfg. Command and Svc. Modules used in Skylab prog. and Apollo-Soyuz test project, 1971—75; positions up to divsn. dir. prodn. ops. Rockwell Space Divsn., 1975—86; v.p. tech., COO electronics sector Lockheed Martin Corp., 1994—97, pres. Vought Systems divsn. Dallas, 1997—99; pres. Lockheed Martin Missiles and Fire Control, 1999—. Recipient Disting. Pub. Svc. medal, NASA, 2000. Fellow: AIAA. Office: Lockheed Martin Missiles and Fire Control PO Box 650003 PT-42 Dallas TX 75265-0003*

BERRY, JOHN NICHOLS, III, publishing executive, editor; b. Montclair, NJ, June 12, 1933; s. John Nichols and Marian Petrea (Chase) B.; m. Louise Parker, June 5, 1982; children: Elizabeth Ann, John Nichols IV, Thomas Parker. AB in History, Boston U., 1958; MS in L.S, Simmons Coll., Boston, 1960. Youth-reference librarian Reading Pub. Library, Mass., 1959-60; reference librarian Simmons Coll., 1960-62, asst. dir. library, 1962-64; lectr. Sch. Library Sci., 1961-64; asst. editor Library Jour., R. R. Bowker Co. (div. Xerox), NYC, 1964-66; editor book editorial dept. R. R. Bowker Co. (div. Xerox), 1966-68, editor-in-chief Library Jour., 1969-89; journalist in residence Sch. of Libr. and Info. Sci. La. State U., 1989; v.p., editor-in-chief Libr. Jour. Reed Bus. Info., Inc., NYC, 1989—2006, editor-at-large Libr. Jour., 2006—. Vis. prof. Sch. Info. and Libr. Sci., Pratt Inst., Bklyn., 1994—, Dominican U., River Forest, Ill., 2000; adj. prof. Sch. Libr. Resources and Info. Studies, U. Ariz., Tucson, 2002—03; lectr. Sch. Libr. and Info. Sci., U. Pitts., 1972—73, Sch. Libr. and Info. Studies, U. Wash., Seattle, 1982; William Gillard lectr. dept. libr. and info. sci. St. John's U., 1986; Rudi Weiss lectr. N.Y. Libr. Assn., 1988. Contbg. author: Library Issues The Sixties, 1970; editor: Directory of Library Consultants, 1969, Bay State Libr., 1962-64 (ALA-H.W. Wilson Libr. periodical award 1962); contbr. articles to profl. jours. Active US Army, 1955—57. Recipient First Ann. Alumni Achievement award, Sch. Libr. Sci. Simmons Coll., 1970. Mem. ALA (Joseph W. Lippincott award, 1992), Am. Soc. for Info. Sci., Spl. Libr. Assn. (chmn. div. pub. 1969), Assn. Libr. & Info. Sci. Edn. (Spl. Svc. award, 1993), Archons of Colophon, Beta Phi Mu. Democrat. Office: Libr Jour 360 Park Ave S New York NY 10010 Home Phone: 203-359-2495; Office Phone: 646-746-6822. E-mail: jberry33@optonline.net, jberry@reedbusiness.com.*

BERRY, KAREN ANN, communications educator; d. Roy Hugh and Ann Fenwick Adair; m. Jan Raymond Berry, June 18, 1977; 1 child, James Berry. B in Edn., U. Mo., Columbia, 1976. Comm. arts and drama tchr. Marshall Pub. Sch., Mo., 1976—91, Bueker Mid. sch., Marshall, 1987—. Drama dir. Marshall H.S., 1976—80. Named Tchr. of Yr., Mid-Day Optimist, 2004—05. Office: Bueker Mid Sch 565 S Odell Marshall MO 65340 Home Phone: 660-837-3472. E-mail: kberry@marshallschools.com.

BERRY, KATHLEEN A., English language educator; b. LA, Calif., June 22, 1958; d. Raymond Albert and Robin Lee Berry. BA in Linguistics, U. Calif., Berkeley, 1981, MA in Edn., 1981, credential in single subject tchg./English, 1982. Instr. English U. Calif. Ext., Berkeley, 1992—2004, tchr. trainer, 1992—2004; instr. English U. Calif., Berkeley, 1994, Contra Costa C.C., San Pablo, Calif., 1996—, Laney C.C., Oakland, Calif., 2001—; instr. Las Positas C.C., Livermore, Calif., 2004—. Cons. grammar Am. Med. Writers Assn., San Francisco, 1999—. HS program coord. Albany Adult Sch., Calif., 1984. Mem.: Tchrs. of English to Spkrs. of Other Langs. Avocations: yoga, quilting. Office: Laney C C 900 Fallon St Oakland CA 94607 E-mail: katy622@yahoo.com.

BERRY, L. CLYEL, lawyer; b. Twin Falls, Idaho, July 17, 1949; s. Clyel J. and Nellie B.; m. Jill Brunzell, July 17, 1970; children: Jacob Clyel, Matthew Robert. BABA, Wash. State U., 1973; JD, U. Idaho, 1975. Bar: Idaho 1976, U.S. Dist. Ct. (dis. Idaho) 1976, U.S. Ct. Appeals (ninth cir.) 1982. Assoc. Emil F. Pike, Twin Falls, 1976-78; ptnr. Pike and Berry, Twin Falls, 1978-83; prin. Twin Falls, 1983—. Mem. Idaho State Bar Assn., Idaho Trial Lawyer Assn. (regional dir. 1981-82), Assn. Trial Lawyers of Am., Fifth Jud. Dist. Bar Assn. (sec.-treas. 1977-78). Avocations: white-water rafting, kayaking, skiing, fishing, travel. Office: PO Box 302 Twin Falls ID 83303-0302 Office Phone: 208-734-9962.

BERRY, LORRAINE LEDEE, state senator; b. St. Thomas, V.I., Nov. 15, 1949; d. Joseph and Emelda Ledee; m. Richard Berry; children: Roxanne, Kurt. Student, U. V.I. Mem. V.I. Legis., 1982—, pres., 1997-99, 2005—. Mem. econ. devel., agr., consumer protection, health, govt. and operation coms.; chair fin. com. Office: Capitol Bldg PO Box 1690 St Thomas VI 00804-1690 Home Phone: 340-774-4414; Office Phone: 340-693-3507. E-mail: LBerry19@hotmail.com, lberry@senate.gov.vi.

BERRY, MARION, congressman; b. Aug. 27, 1942; m. Carolyn Berry; 2 children. BS, U. Ark., 1965. Ptnr., gen. mgr. family farm, Gillett, Ark.; commr. Ark. Soil and Water Conservation Commn., 1986-94, chmn., 1992; spl. asst. to Pres. Agrl. Trade and Food Assistance, 1993; mem. US Congress from 1st Ark. dist., 1997—; mem. subcommittee on Energy and Water and Homeland Security US Ho. Appropriations Commn. Democrat. Avocations: hunting, fishing. Office: US Ho Reps 2305 Rayburn Ho Office Bldg Washington DC 20515-0401*

BERRY, MARK SEAN, music educator; s. Vernon Lyle and Judy Elaine Berry. B in Music Edn., Ohio State U., 1994; MusM in Percussion Performance, U. Mich., 1997, D of Musical Arts, 2004. State of Ohio Teaching Certificate Ohio, 1994. Percussion instr. Thomas Worthington (Ohio) H.S., Worthington, 1992—95, Marion Cadets Drum and Bugle Corps, Marion, Ohio, 1992—94, Whitehall (Ohio) H.S., Whitehall, 1991—94, Livonia (Mich.) Franklin H.S., Livonia, 1996—98; adj. prof. percussion U. Mich., Flint, 1996—97; vis. prof. percussion W.Va. U., Morgantown, 1998—99, Western Ky. U., Bowling Green, 2001—02, asst. prof. percussion, 2002—. Snare line mem. Ltd. Edit. Drum and Bugle Corps, Columbus, Ohio, 1988—89; percussionist Westerville (Ohio) Symphony Orch., 1992, Mich. Percussion Group, Ann Arbor, Mich., 1995—2001, Jackson (Mich.) Symphony Orch., 1995—97, Adrian (Mich.) Symphony Orch., 1996, Gt. Lakes Symphony Orch., Detroit, 1996, Ft. Wayne (Ind.) Philharm., Fort Wayne, Ind., 1997, W.Va. U. Faculty Laureate, Morgantown, 1998—99; timpanist Cleve. Baroque Ensemble, Novi, Mich., 1996; lead steel drummer and percussionist Panchita Steel Band, Ann Arbor, 1997—2001; drumset player Western Ky. U. Faculty Jazz Ensemble, Bowling Green, 2003—; timpanist and percussionist Bowling Green Western Symphony Orch., Ky., 2001—02; prin. timpanist Bowling Green Chamber Orch., 2001—; percussion faculty Mich. Summer Music Inst., Ann Arbor, 2001—02; mem. Ryu Sei Marimba Duo, Bowling Green, Ky., 2001—. Composer: (electro-acoustic composition) Haru No Bu-fu-u; contbr. percussion concerto; dir.: (steel band ensemble) Millenium Stage Concert, Kennedy Ctr.; musician: (recording) Coyote Dreams, Historic Works for Percussion, Soundscapes, Panchita!, Marimba Duo Playing, (marimba soloist) Westerville South Day of Percussion; contbr. Fellow, U. Mich. Sch. of Music, 1995—97, U. Mich., 1997—2001; grantee, Coun. of Postsecondary Edn., 2003, Coun. on Postsecondary Edn., 2003; scholar, Ohio State U., 1990—95. Mem.: Ky. Music Educator's Assn., Percussive Arts Soc. Office: Western Kentucky University - FAC Bldg 1 Big Red Way Bowling Green KY 42101 Business E-Mail: mark.berry@wku.edu.

BERRY, MARY FRANCES, history professor, former federal agency administrator; b. Nashville, Feb. 17, 1938; d. George Ford and Frances Southall (Wiggins) B. BA, Howard U., 1961, MA, 1962; PhD, U. Mich., 1966, JD, 1970; degree (hon.), Cen. Mich. U., Howard U., U. Akron, 1977, Benedict Coll., U. Md., Grambling State U., 1979, Bethune-Cookman Coll., Clark Coll., Del. State Coll., 1980, Oberlin Coll., Langston U., 1983, Marian Coll., Haverford Coll., 1984, Colby Coll., CUNY, 1986, DePaul U., 1987. Bar: D.C. 1972. Asst. prof. history Central Mich. U., Mt. Pleasant, 1966-68; asst. prof. Eastern Mich. U., Ypsilanti, 1968-69, assoc. prof., 1969-70, U. Md., College Park, 1969-76; acting dir. Afro-Am. studies, 1970-72, dir., 1972-74, acting chmn. div. behavioral and social scis., 1973-74, provost div. behavioral and social scis., 1973-76; prof. history, prof. law U Colo. at Boulder, 1976-80, chancellor, 1976-77; prof. history and law Howard U., Washington, 1980—87; Geraldine R. Segal prof. Am. Social Thought U. Pa., Philadelphia, 1987—; asst. sec. for edn. US Dept. Health Edn. & Welfare, Washington, 1977-80; vice chairperson U.S. Comm. on Civil Rights, Washington, 1980—82; chaiperson U.S. Commn. on Civil Rights, Washington, 1993—2004. Adj. assoc. prof. U. Mich., 1970-71; mem. com. visitors U. Mich. Law Sch., 1976-80; mem. nat. adv. panel on minority concerns Coll. Bd., 1980-84; mem. adv. bd. Feminist Press, 1980—; mem. research adv. com. Joint Ctr. for Polit. Studies, 1981—; mem. editorial adv. com. Marcus Garvey Papers, 1981—; mem. adv. bd. Inst. for Higher Edn. Law and Governance, U. Houston, 1983—. Author: Black Resistance/White Law, 1971 (rev. 1994), Military Necessity and Civil Rights Policy, 1977, Stability, Security and Continuity, Mr. Justice Burton and Decision-Making in the Supreme Court, 1945-58, 1978, (with John Blassingame) Long Memory: The Black Experience in America, 1982; Why ERA Failed, 1986, Politics of Parenthood: Child Care, Women's Rights, and the Myth of the Good Mother, 1993, The Pig Farmer's Daughter and Other Tales of American Justice, 1999, Health Care Challenge: Acknowledging Disparity, Confronting Discrimination, And Ensuring Equality, 1999, My Face Is Black Is True: Callie House and the Struggle for Ex-Slave Reparations, 2005; assoc. editor Jour. Negro History, 1974-78; contbr. articles, revs. to profl. jours. Bd. dirs. ARC, Washington, 1980—; trustee Tuskegee U., 1980—; mem. adv. bd. Project '87, 1978—; mem. council UN U., 1986— Recipient Athena (disting. alumni) award U. Mich., 1977, Roy Wilkins Civil Rights award NAACP, 1983, Image award, 1983, Allard Lowenstein award, 1984, President's award Congl. Black Caucus Found., 1985, Woman of Yr. award Nat. Capital Area YWCA, 1985, Hubert H. Humphrey Civil Rights award Leadership Conf. on Civil Rights, 1986, Rosa Parks award SCLC, Black Achievement award Ebony Mag., Woman of Yr. award Ms. Mag., 1986. Mem. ABA, Nat. Bar Assn., D.C. Bar Assn., Nat. Acad. Public Adminstrn., Orgn. Am. Historians (exec. bd. 1974-77), Assn. Study of Afro-Am. Life and History (exec. bd. 1973-76), Am. Hist. Assn. (v.p. for profession 1980-83), Am. Soc. Legal History, Coalition 100 Black Women (hon.), Delta Sigma Theta (hon.) Independent. Office: U Pa 208 College Hall Rm 216E Philadelphia PA 19104 E-mail: mfberry@sas.upenn.edu.

BERRY, MARYANN PARADISO, minister; d. Joseph and Mary Mainolfi Paradiso; m. Wayne Robert Berry, Jan. 4, 1975; children: Maria, John. BS in Bus. Adminstrn. cum laude, Marist Coll., 1975; cert. of studies, Faith Fellowship World, Sayreville, NJ, 1985, Sch. Bibl. Studies, Poughkeepsie, NY, 1996. Ordained min. Christian Faith Ctr., Bloomfield, NJ, 1990, Covenant Ministries, Sayreville, 1992. Co-owner Mid-Hudson Alarm Co., Poughkeepsie, 1975—80; children's music dir., elder, tchr. Bible Coll. Faith Fellowship Ministries, Sayreville, 1982—88; min. Christian Faith Ctr., Bloomfield, NJ, 1988—91; pastor, dean Sch. Bibl. Studies John 3:16 Christian Ctr., Unionvale, NY, 1991—. Co-host Christian radio broadcast Faith for Today, 2005—; host, spkr. Becoming A Woman of God Women's Conf., 2006—. Author: Answered Prayer, 1984. Vol. father's day parade Dutchess County Health Families, 2003—. Mem.: Covenant Ministries Internat., Assn. Faith Chs. and Ministries. Avocations: reading, hiking, piano, guitar. Office: John 3:16 Christian Ctr 3112 Rt 82 Verbank NY 12585 Office Phone: 845-677-0625. Personal E-mail: mab3331@verizon.net.

BERRY, MATTHEW M., aerospace engineer; s. Michael and Sue Berry; m. Megan Berry, Apr. 8, 2006. BS, Va. Tech, Blacksburg, 2000, MS, 2002, PhD, 2004. Intern Swales Aerospace, Beltsville, Md., 1997; student trainee US Naval Rsch. Lab., Washington, 1998—2004; grad. asst. Va. Tech Aerospace and Ocean Engring. Dept., Blacksburg, 2000—04; astrodynamics engr. Analytical Graphics, Inc., Exton, Pa., 2004—. Contbr. articles various profl. jours. Mem.: Am. Astronautical Soc. (John V. Breakwell Student Travel award 2002). Office: Analytical Graphics Inc 220 Valley Creek Blvd Exton PA 19341

BERRY, PATRICIA A., middle school educator; d. Robert E. and Mary Helen Trimpe; m. Michael L. Berry, June 12, 1971; children: David, Douglas. BS, Ind. State U., Terre Haute, 1972, MS, 1975. Cert. lang. arts tchr. Ind. U., 1990. Tchr. North White HS, Monon, Ind., 1974—77, Western Mid. Sch., Russiaville, Ind., 1990—. Coach social studies academic team Western Mid. Sch., Russiaville, Ind., 1991—, dir. drama club, 1994—, sponsor panther news network, 2004—06. Recipient Outstanding Grad. Asst., History Dept., Ind. State U., 1973, Golden Apple award, Kokomo Tribune, Ind., 2004. Avocations: travel, reading. Office: Western Mid Sch 600 W 250S Russiaville IN 46979 Office Phone: 765-883-5566. Business E-Mail: pberry@western.k12.in.us.

BERRY, PHIL HUNTER, JR., orthopedic surgeon; b. Jackson, Miss., June 18, 1937; married; 3 children. MD, U. Miss. Sch. Medicine, 1966. Intern Parkland Meml. Hosp., Dallas, 1966—67, resident, 1967—68, 1970, Baylor Med. Ctr., 1968, Tex. Scottish Rite Hosp., 1969; orthopedic surgeon pvt. practice, Dallas. Founder Southwest Transplant Found., 1994; mem. Health and Human Svc. Adv. Com. on Organ Transplantation. Recipient Max Cole Leadership award, 1996, Freedoms Found. award, Disting. Alumni award, U. Miss. Sch. Medicine, Champions of Hope award, Nat. Kidney Found., Pioneer Hero award, Internat. Organ Replacement. Mem.: AMA (precursor Live & Then Give Organ Donor Awareness Campaign, bd. trustees, AMA Foun., Benjamin Rush award for citizenship and cmty. svc. 2000), Tex. Orthopaedic Assn. (past pres.), Tex. Soc. Sports Medicine (past pres.), Dallas County Med. Soc. (past pres.), Tex. Med. Assn. (TMA) (founder Live & Then Give Organ Donor Awareness Campaign, pres. 1997—98, mem. TMA Found. (Tex. del. to AMA Ho. Del.)). Avocations: golf, skiing, tennis. Office Phone: 214-941-4243. Office Fax: 214-943-2671.

BERRY, PHILLIP SAMUEL, lawyer; b. Calif., 1937; s. Samuel Harper and Jean Mobley B.; children: David, Douglas, Dylan, Shane, Matthew; m. Carla Gilmer, Mar. 16, 2002. AB, Stanford U., 1958, LLB, 1961. Bar: Calif. 1962. Ptnr. Berry, Davis & McInerney, Oakland, Calif., 1968-76; owner Berry & Berry, Oakland, Calif., 1976—, pres., 1977—. Adv. com. Coll. Natural Resources, U. Calif., Berkeley; mem. Calif. State Bd. Forestry, 1974-86, vice-chmn., 1976-86. Trustee So. Calif. Ctr. for Law in Pub. Interest, 1970-87, Sierra Club Legal Def. Fund, 1975-90, Pub. Advs., 1971-86, chmn. bd., 1980-82; dir. Pacific Environment, 1997—. With AUS, 1961-67. Mem. ABA, Calif. State Bar Assn., Sierra Club (nat. pres. 1969-71, 91-92, v.p. conservation law 1971—, v.p. polit. affairs 1983-85, John Muir award), Am. Alpine Club. Office: 2930 Lakeshore Ave Oakland CA 94610-3614

BERRY, RICHARD LEWIS, information technology manager, writer, magazine editor, lecturer, programmer; b. Greenwich, Conn., Nov. 6, 1946; s. John William and Dorothy May (Buck) B.; m. Eleanor von Auw, June 7, 1968. BA, U. Va., 1968; MSc, York U., Can., 1972. Rsch. asst. MacMaster U., Hamilton, Ont., Canada, 1973-74; project engr. Intraspace Internat., Toronto, Ont., 1974-75; tech. editor Astronomy mag., Milw., 1976-78, editor, 1978-82, editor-in-chief, 1982-91; editor Telescope Making mag., Milw., 1978—91; editl. dir. Earth mag., 1990-91, cons., 1992; freelance writer, programmer, lectr., 1991—; editor Cookbook Camera Newsletter, 1994-99; founder, mng. ptnr. Digital Clarity Cons., 2003—. Mem. adv. bd. Global Network of Automatic Telescopes; com. chair Internat. Space Sta. Amateur Telescope Project, Astron. League, 2002—. Author: Build Your Own Telescope, 1985, Discover the Stars, 1987, (with others) The Star Book, 1984, Introduction to Astronomical Image Processing, 1991, AIP Image Processing Software, 1991, BatchPIX Image Processing Software, 1992, Choosing and Using a CCD Camera, 1992, The CCD Camera Cookbook, 1994, The Dobsonian Telescope: A Practical Manual for Building Large Aperture Telescopes, 1997, Handbook of Astronomical Image Processing, 2000; contbg. author: Robotic Observatories, 1989, ST6PIX Image Processing Software, 1992, CB245 Image Processing Software, 1994, Multi245 Image Compositing Software, 1995, QColor Color Synthesis Software, 1997, Astronomical Image Processing for Windows, 2000, 2d edit., 2004; editor: Telescope Optics, Design and Evaluation, 1988. Mem. adv. bd. Global Network of Automatic Telescopes; mem. Internat. Space Station Amateur Telescope com. Astron. League. Recipient Clifford-Holmes award Astronomy for Am., 1981, Dorothea

Klumpke-Roberts award Astron. Soc. Pacific, 1990, Omega Centauri award Tex. Star Party, Clyde W. Tombaugh award Riverside Telescope Makers Conf., 1995, G. Bruce Blair award Western Amateur Astronomers, 1998, Leslie C. Peltier award Astron. League, 2001, Astron. League award, 2002; Asteroid 3684 Berry named in his honor by Internat. Astron. Union, 1990. Mem. Internat. Amateur Profl. Photoelec. Photometry, Internat. Dark Sky Assn., Am. Astron. Soc. Avocation: photography. Office Phone: 503-859-3030. E-mail: rberry@wvi.com.

BERRY, RICHARD S., physician; s. David and Selma Berry; m. Beverly Berry; children: Ezra, Pamela, Ariella, Craig. MD, SUNY, Bklyn., 1974. Pvt. practice, Bklyn., 1978—. Clin. asst. prof. Downstate Med. Ctr., SUNY, Bklyn., 1978—. Fellow: Am. Acad. Dermatology. Office: 2820 Ocean Pky Brooklyn NY 11235

BERRY, ROBERT VAUGHAN, retired electrical manufacturing company executive; b. Newark, Mar. 24, 1933; s. Harold Silver and Elizabeth Lippincott (Vaughan) B.; m. Victoria Shaw, Mar. 8, 1958; children: Patricia E., Michael V. BA, Dartmouth Coll., 1954. With Thomas & Betts Corp., Memphis, 1957—95, dir., 1972—85, v.p. fin., 1975—83, sr. v.p., 1983—95; ret., 1995; pres. Thomas & Betts Internat., Inc., 1975. Bd. dirs. Ames Rubber Corp., Hamburg, N.J. Trustee Carrier Found. Psychiat. Hosp., Belle Mead, N.J., 1984-92. 1st lt. Airborne Corps U.S. Army, 1954-57. Mem. Baltusrol Golf Club (Springfield, N.J.), Harbour Ridge Golf Club (Stuart, Fla.), Summerlea Golf and Country Club (Montreal, Que., Can.), Mid Ocean Club (Bermuda), Royal and Ancient Golf Club of St. Andrews (Scotland), Hanover (N.H.) Country Club. Republican. *Have a little fun each day - if you wait until the end you might miss it.*

BERRY, ROBERT WORTH, lawyer, retired military officer, educator; b. Ryderwood, Wash., Mar. 2, 1926; s. John Franklin and Anita Louise (Worth) Berry. BA in Polit. Sci., Wash. State U., 1950; JD, Harvard U., 1955; MA, John Jay Coll. Criminal Justice, 1981. Bar: DC 1956, US Dist. Ct. (DC) 1956, US Ct. of Appeals (DC cir.) 1957, US Ct. Mil. Appeals 1957, Pa. 1961, US Dist. Ct. (ea. dist.) Pa. 1961, US Dist. Ct. (ctrl. dist.) Calif. 1967, US Supreme Ct. 1961, Calif. 1967, US Ct. Claims 1975, Colo. 1997, US Dist. Ct. Colo. 1997, US Ct. Appeals (10th cir.) 1997, US Tax Ct. 1959. Rsch. assoc. Harvard U., Cambridge, Mass., 1955—56; atty. Office Gen. Counsel US Dept. Def., Washington, 1956-60; staff counsel Philco Ford Co., Phila., 1960-63; dir. Washington office Litton Industries, 1967-71; gen. counsel US Dept. Army, Washington, 1971-74, civilian aide to sec. army, 1975-77; col. US Army, 1978-87; prof., head dept. law US Mil. Acad., West Point, NY, 1978-86; ret. as brig. gen. US Army, 1987; mil. asst. to asst. sec. of army, Manpower and Res. Affairs Dept. of Army, 1986-87; asst. gen. counsel pub. affairs Litton Industries, Beverly Hills, Calif., 1963-67; chair Coun. of Def. Space Industries Assns., 1968; resident ptnr. Quarles and Brady, Washington, 1971-74; dir., corp. sec., treas., gen. counsel G.A. Wright, Inc., Denver, 1987-92, dir., 1987-2000; pvt. practice law Fort Bragg, Calif., 1993-96; spl. counsel Messner & Reeves LLC, Denver, 1997—2004. Bd. dirs. G.A. Wright Mktg., Inc., v.p./gen. counsel, 2001-; bd. dirs. Denver Mgmt. Svcs. Inc., v.p., gen. counsel, 2001—; foreman Mendocino County Grand Jury, 1995-96. With US Army, 1944-46, 1951-53, 1978-87. Decorated Bronze Star, Legion of Merit, Disting. Service Medal; recipient Disting. Civilian Service medal U.S. Dept. Army, 1973, 74, Outstanding Civilian Service medal, 1977. Mem. Am. Corp. Counsel Assn. (ACCA), Calif. Bar Assn., Pa. Bar Assn., Colo. State Bar Assn., Denver Bar Assn., DC Bar Assn., Army-Navy Club, Army-Navy Country Club, Phi Beta Kappa, Phi Kappa Phi, Sigma Delta Chi, Lambda Chi Alpha. Protestant. Office: GA Wright Mktg Inc 10325 East 47th Ave Denver CO 80238 Office Phone: 303-333-4453. Business E-Mail: bobb@gawright.com.

BERRY, SHARON, medical/surgical nurse, legal nurse consultant; b. Manila, Philippines, Nov. 22, 1973; d. Reynaldo and Henrietta Dingcong; m. Jason Brad Berry, Apr. 10, 2000; children: Jake Ryan, Harley Lynn. ADN, No. Va. C.C., 1998. RN Commonwealth Va. Bd. Nursing, 1998. Nurse Sibley Meml. Hosp., Washington, 1998—99; travel nurse post-partum unit CrosscountryTravcorps, Boca Raton, Fla., 1999—2005; nurse post-partum, gynecology unit Meml. Med. Ctr., New Orleans, 1999—2001, nurse labor and delivery, 2001—03; nurse ICU Ochsner Clinic Found., 2003—05; nurse home health INOVA VNA Home Health, Springfield, Va., 2005—. Legal nurse cons. pvt. practice, Springfield, 2005—. Mem.: Am. Assn. Legal Nurse Cons., Am. Assn. Critical Nurses, Assn. Women's Health, Obs., and Neonatal Nurses. Avocations: violin, hiking, camping. Home Phone: 504-453-5384; Office Phone: 504-453-5384. Personal E-mail: sberry12002@yahoo.com.

BERRY, WENDELL, farmer, author; b. Henry County, Ky., Aug. 5, 1934; m. Tanya Amyx, May 29, 1957; children— Mary Dee, Pryor Clifford. AB, U. Ky., 1956, MA, 1957. Mem. faculty U. Ky., 1964-77, 87-93, Disting. prof. English, 1971-72. Author: (novels) Nathan Coulter, 1962, rev. edit., 1985, A Place on Earth, 1967, 2d. edit., 1985, The Memory of Old Jack, 1974, Remembering, 1988, A World Lost, 1996; (short stories) The Wild Birds, 1986, Fidelity, 1992, Watch With Me, 1994; (poetry) The Broken Ground, 1964, Openings, 1968, 2d edit., 1980, Findings, 1969, Farming: A Handbook, 1970, 2d edit., 1985, The Country of Marriage, 1973, 2 edit., 1985, Clearing, 1977, A Part, 1980, The Wheel, 1982, Collected Poems, 1985, Sabbaths, 1987, Entries, 1994, Hannah Coulter, 2004, Given, 2005; (essays) The Long-Legged House, 1969, The Hidden Wound, 1970, The Unforeseen Wilderness, 1971, A Continuous Harmony, 1972, The Unsettling of America, 1977, Recollected Essays, 1965-1980, 1981, The Gift of Good Land, 1981, Standing by Words, 1985, Sex, Economy, Freedom and Community, 1993; co-editor: (with Jackson and Colman) Meeting the Expectations of the Land, 1985, Home Economics, 1987, What Are People For, 1990, Harland Hubbard: Life and Work, 1990, Standing on Earth, 1991, Another Turn of the Crank.

BERRY, WILLIAM A., artist, educator; b. Jacksonville, Tex., Sept. 29, 1933; s. William Lafayette and Esther Cory Berry; m. Janet Rollins Berry, Dec. 12, 1970. BFA, U. Tex., Austin, 1955; MFA, U. So. Calif., 1957. Asst. prof. art U. Tex., Austin, 1968—74; assoc. prof. art Boston U., 1974—78; prof. art, dept. chair U. Mo., Columbia, 1978—99; freelance artist, 1999—. Illustrator periodicals including The Reporter, 1957—64, Opera News, TV Guide, Newsweek, Esquire, Holiday. Author: Paper Construction for Children, 1966, Drawing the Human Form, 1977, 2d edit., 1994; co-author: Paper Construction; Represented in permanent collections Boston Mus., Addison Gallery, Muscarelle Mus. Art, Hallmark Collection, Rutgers U., Hoyt Inst. Art, one-man shows include Charles Campbell Gallery, San Francisco, 1987, Mid-Am. Alliance-Nat. Endowment Arts; A Traveling Exhbn., 1990—93, exhibited in group shows at Smithsonian Instn. Traveling Exhbn., 1983—84, Faber-Birren Color Award Competitions, Bradley Nat. Print and Drawing Competitions, Fine Arts Inst. Nat. Exhbns., San Bernardino County Mus., Redlands, Calif. Fellow, MacDowell Colony, 1984, Carmago Found., France, 1989, Rockefeller Found., Italy, 1988. Mem.: Colored Pencil Soc. Am. Mailing: 908 Edgewood Ave Columbia MO 65203

BERRY, WILLIAM B., oil industry executive; b. Miss., Dec. 14, 1952; BA, Miss. State Univ., 1974; MA in Petroleum Engring., Miss. State. Univ., 1976. With Phillips Petroleum Co., Houston, 1976—77, El Dorado, Ark., 1977, London, 1977, Abidjan, South Africa, 1977, assoc. drilling enging. Stavanger, Norway, 1978, reservoir monitoring unit supr., engring. specialist Houston, 1981—84, planning dir. Bartlesville, Okla., 1984—86, ops. mgr. Odessa, Tex., 1987—89, mgr., corp. planning and budgeting Bartsville, 1991—92, mgr. internat. E & P China, 1992—96, v.p. internat. E & P Euroasia, 1998—2001; sr. v.p. Phillips Petroleum Co. (merger with Conoco Phillips), Euroasia-Middle East, 2001—02; pres. Conoco Phillips, Asia Pacific, 2002—03, exec. v.p., exploration & prodn. Houston, 2003—. Mem. bd. Tex. Alliance Minorties Engring., Beijing Internat. Sch., 1996—97. Named one of 31 Outstanding foreeign experts, Govt. of China, 1996. Office: Conoco Phillips 600 N Dairy Ashford Rd Houston TX 77079*

BERRY, WILLIAM LEE, business administration educator; b. Indpls., Dec. 24, 1935; s. George Lee and Anna Marie (Hansert) B.; m. Carol M. Berry; children: Ann Kathleen, Lee Michael, Lynn Colleen. BS, Purdue U., West Lafayette, Ind., 1957; MS, Va. Poly. Inst., Blacksburg, 1964; DBA, Harvard U., Cambridge, Mass., 1969. Mfg. trainee GE, various locations, 1957-60, supr. mfg. Salem, Va., 1960-64; from asst. prof. to assoc. prof. indsl. mgmt. Purdue U., West Lafayette, Ind., 1968-76; prof. prodn. mgmt. Ind. U., Bloomington, 1976-82; C. Maxwell Stanley prof. prodn. mgmt. U. Iowa, Iowa City, 1982-87, sr. assoc. dean Coll. Bus. Adminstrn., 1983-87, dir. Mfg. and Productivity Ctr., 1986-87; Belk prof. bus. adminstrn., chmn. ops. mgmt. area U. N.C., Chapel Hill, 1988-92; prof. bus. adminstrn. Ohio State U., Columbus, 1992—2007, Richard Ross chair in mgmt., dir. Ctr. Excellence in Mgmt., 1995—2006, prof. emeritus, 2007. Vis. prof. IMD, Lausanne, Switzerland, 1987-88; cons. in field. Co-author: Operations and Logistics Management, 1972, Production Planning, Scheduling and Inventory Control: Concepts, Techniques and Systems, 1974, Master Production Scheduling: Principles and Practice, 1979, Manufacturing Planning and Control for Supply Chain Management, 1984, 5th edit., 2005, ITEC: Manufacturing Planning and Control/Manufacturing Strategy Simulation, 1992, Production and Inventory Control Integrated, 1992; contbr. articles to profl. jours. 1st Enterprise fellow Kenan Inst., 1988-90. Fellow Decision Scis. Inst. (v.p. 1983-84, sec. 1985-86, pres.-elect 1987, pres. 1988); mem. Inst. Indsl. Engrs. (v.p. 1979-81, dir., Disting. Service award 1979), Ops. Mgmt. Assn. (v.p. 1981-85, pres.-elect 1985-86, pres. 1986-87, dir., Disting. Leadership award 1987), Am. Prodn. and Inventory Control Soc., Inst. Mgmt. Sci., Ops. Research Soc. Office: Fisher Coll of Bus Ohio State U Columbus OH 43210 Office Phone: 614-292-3173.

BERRY, WILLIAM WILLIS, retired utilities executive; b. Norfolk, Va., May 18, 1932; s. Joel Halbert and Julia Lee (Godwin) B.; m. Elizabeth Mangum, Aug. 23, 1958; children: Preston Blackburn, John Willis, William Godwin. BSEE, Va. Mil. Inst., 1954; MC in Commerce, U. Richmond, 1964. Registered profl. engr., Va. Engr. Gen. Electric Co., 1954-55; with Va. Power, Richmond, 1957-92, v.p. divsn. ops., then sr. v.p. comml. ops., 1976-78, exec. v.p., 1978-80, pres., COO, 1980-83, pres. CEO, 1983-85, chmn., CEO, 1985-86, Dominion Resources Inc., Richmond, 1986-90, chmn., 1990-92. Bd. dirs. New Market Corp., Richmond, 1983—2005. Chair ISO New Eng., Holyoke, Mass., 1997-2006. Mem. Commonwealth Club, Country Club Va. Republican. Home Phone: 804-285-2656. Personal E-mail: wwberry@earthlink.net.

BERRYHILL, HENRY LEE, JR., retired geologist; b. Charlotte, NC, Nov. 6, 1921; s. Henry Lee and Viola Estelle (Johnston) B.; m. Louise Randall Russell, Sept. 13, 1947; children: Stuart Randall, Keith Courtney. BS, U. N.C., 1947, MS in Geology, 1949. With U.S. Geol. Survey, 1948-86, chief publs. officer Denver, 1963-65, research marine geologist, 1965-66, chief marine geology Gulf of Mexico-Caribbean region office Corpus Christi, Tex., 1967-70; chief Office Marine Geology, Washington, 1970-73, sr. research marine geologist Corpus Christi, 1973-86; gen. cons., 1986-99; ret., 1999; Tech. adviser offshore prospecting com. ECAFE, 1972-73; Dept. Interior rep. Fed. Intragy. Com. on Marine Sci. and Engring., 1970-73; program mgr. integrated environ. assessment Outer Continental Shelf N.W. Gulf of Mexico, 1973-86; U.S. rep. marine geology panel U.S.-Japan Coop. Programs in Natural Resources, 1973-95; ret. Cons. Nat. Center for Geoscis., India, 1981-87. Author: Geology and Coal Resources of Belmont County, Ohio, 1963, Geology of the Ciales Area, Puerto Rico, 1965, Coal-Bearing Upper Pennsylvanian and Lower Permian Rocks, Washington Area, Pennsylvania, 1971, The Worldwide Search for Petroleum Offshore-A Status Report for the Quarter Century, 1947-72, 1974, Seismic Models of Late Qua ternary Facies and Structure, Northern Gulf of Mexico, 1986. Contbr. articles to sci. publs. Served with USAAF, 1942-45. Decorated DFC, Air medal with 3 oak leaf clusters; recipient Outstanding Performance award U.S. Geol. Survey, 1969, a seafloor feature of the Gulf of Mexico named Berryhill Basin in his honor, 1995. Fellow Geol. Soc. Am.; mem. Am. Assn. Petroleum Geologists (co-recipient Jules Braunstein meml. award 1987), Sierra Club (chmn. Coastal Bend group 1980-81, 86-89), Sigma Xi. Episcopalian. Home and Office: 922 Burnt Hickory Cir Marietta GA 30064 *Besides an innate enthusiasm for learning, the greatest single factor that has shaped my life has been the choice of a profession that I could pursue as if it were my hobby.True satisfaction comes from the heartfelt knowledge of work well done. No amount of praise can supplant that innermost feeling of achievement. Above all, never fear to try.*

BERRYMAN, CARL, veterinarian, retired epidemiologist; b. St. Louis, Nov. 6, 1942; s. Carl Jr. and Dora Mae Berryman; m. Barbara Ann Webb, Jan. 24, 1965; children: Craig, Nathan. BA, U. Mo., Columbia, 1965, DVM, 1969; MPH, U. Minn., Mpls., 1975. Diplomate Am. Coll. Vet. Preventive Medicine. Pvt. practice vet., Shelby, Mont., 1969—71; commd. 2d lt. US Army, 1971, advanced through grades to lt. col., 1989, with Vet. Corps, 1971—93, ret., 1993; epidemiologist Bur. Pub. Health, Charleston, W.Va., 1995—2000, Kanawha-Charleston Health Dept., 2001—03, ret., 2003. Author: 2013: World War III, 2004. Mem.: Am. Legion. Avocations: hunting, fishing, snowshoeing, skiing, reading. Home: 1652 Sesame St Worland WY 82401

BERRYMAN, GUY, musician; b. Fife, Scotland, Apr. 12, 1978; Student, U. Coll. London. Bassist Coldplay, 1998—. Musician: (albums) Parachutes, 2000 (Grammy award: Best Alternative Music Album, 2001), A Rush of Blood to the Head, 2002 (Grammy awards: Best Alternative Music Album, 2002, Best Rock Performance By A Duo Or Group With Vocal for song "In My Place", 2002, Grammy award: Record Of The Yr. for song "Clocks", 2003), Live 2003, 2003, X&Y, 2005, Love, Actually, 2006. Recipient Favorite Alternative Artist (Coldplay), Am. Music Awards, 2005. Office: Capital Records 1750 North Vine St 10th Floor Hollywood CA 90028

BERRYMAN, RICHARD BYRON, lawyer; b. Indpls., Aug. 16, 1932; s. Herbert Byron and Ruth Katherine (Mayerhoefer) B.; m. Virginia Marie Asti, June 9, 1957; children: Steven, Susan, Kenneth. BA, Carleton Coll., 1954; JD, U. Chgo., 1957. Bar: D.C. 1957. Atty. bur. of aeronautics U.S. Dept. Navy, Washington, 1957-59, atty. office gen. counsel, 1959-62; assoc. Cox, Langford & Brown, Washington, 1962-65, ptnr., 1965-68, Fried, Frank, Harris, Shriver & Jacobson, Washington, 1968-90; pvt. practice Washington, 1990—. Mem. vis. com. Law Sch. U. Chgo., 1978-82; trustee Carleton Coll., Northfield, Minn., 1982-86; dir. Pericles Inst., Washington, 1996-2000. Mem. ABA. Office: 6901 Old Gate Ln Rockville MD 20852 Office Phone: 301-881-7397. Personal E-mail: rbbesq@aol.com.

BERRYMAN, ROBERT GLEN, accounting educator, consultant; b. Freeport, Ill., Nov. 22, 1928; s. Loyd Vernon and Gladys Leone (Hicks) B.; m. Ruth Madelyn Bjorngjeld, Aug. 25, 1955; children: Peter, David, Kathryn. BSBA, Northwestern U., 1950, MBA, 1951; PhD, U. Ill., 1958. CPA, Ill., Minn. Staff auditor Deloitte & Touche, Chgo., 1951-54, mgr. Mpls., 1969-70; instr. U. Ill., Champaign, 1954-58; asst. prof. acctg. U. Minn., Mpls., 1958-61, assoc. prof., 1961-65, prof., 1965-95, dir. grad. studies in acctg., 1980-83, chmn. dept. acctg., 1963-65, 70-73, 1990-95; exec. dir. fin. Cedar Riverside Assocs., Mpls., 1974-75. Cons. in field.; PhD thesis adv. U. Minn., Mpls., Minn. Mem. editl. bd. Issues in Acctg. Edn., 1995-98; contbr. articles to profl. publs. Adviser to audit com. Minn. State Colls. and Univs., 1997-2001 Recipient Horace T. Morse-Amoco All Univ. Tchg. award U. Minn., 1976, Outstanding Tchr. award Carlson Sch. Mgmt., U. Minn., Green Eyeshade award Minn. Acctg. Assn., Tchg. award U. Minn. Alumni Assn., Mpls., 1978, Leon Radde Outstanding Educator award Inst. Internal Auditors, 1988. Mem. AICPA (chmn. acctg. theory subcom. 1979-83, continuing profl. edn. exec. com. 1979-82, bd. examiners 1980-83, Disting. Achievement in Acctg. Edn. award 1999), Inst. Internal Auditors (bd. regents 1979-83, bd. govs. Twin City chpt. 1981-91, cert. internal auditor), Minn. Soc. CPA (bd. dirs. 1965-69, 78-83, first recipient and honoree R. Glen Berryman award 1976), Accountability Minn. (pres. and bd. dirs.), Am. Acctg. Assn. (Outstanding Acctg. Educator 1994, Auditing Educator 1992). Home: 1462 Brenner Ave Saint Paul MN 55113-1671 Office: Univ MN Carlson Sch of Mgmt 321 19th Ave S Minneapolis MN 55455-0438

BERRYMAN, ROBERT MOGABGAB, systems engineer; s. William Joseph and Rose Berryman Mogabgab; m. Regina Stephans Berryman, June 5, 2004. Degree in Sys. Engring., U.S. Naval Acad., Annapolis, Md., 1993. Registered profl. engr., N.Y., 2004. Submarine officer USN, Groton, Conn., 1993—98; freelance pilot, flight instr. Groton, 1998—2000; aircraft sys. instr. pilot Commutair, Plattsburgh, NY, 2000—01; pilot Northwest Airlink, Memphis, 2001; sys. engr. CAE Marine Sys., Leesburg, Va., 2001—02; reactor insp. US Nuc. Regulatory Commn., King of Prussia, Pa., 2002—03, resident insp. Buchanan, NY, 2003—05, sr. reactor insp. Atlanta, 2005—. With USNR, 1998—. Decorated Achievement medal USN, Commendation medal, Meritorious Svc. medal; recipient Adm. McKee award, USN Submarine Sch., 1994. Mem.: ASME (assoc.), Nat. Assn. Flight Instrs. (master flight instr. 2002—04), Am. Soc. Naval Engrs. (assoc.), Soc. Naval Archs. and Marine Engrs. (assoc.). Roman Catholic. Avocations: running, aviation, shooting. Office: US Nuclear Regulatory Commn 61 Forsyth St NW Atlanta GA 30303 Home Phone: 770-565-9069; Office Phone: 404-562-4817. Personal E-mail: robberryman@earthlink.net. Business E-Mail: rmb1@nrc.gov.

BERS, ABRAHAM, electrical engineering and physics educator; b. Cernauti, Bukovina, Romania, May 28, 1930; came to U.S., 1949; s. Isaias and Berta (Lechter) B.; m. Anita Alden Burrage, June 17, 1966; children: Rachel, Joshua. BS with highest honors, U. Calif., Berkeley, 1953; SM, MIT, 1955, ScD, 1959. Rsch. asst. Rsch. Lab. Electronics MIT, Cambridge, Mass., 1953-58, instr. dept. elec. engring. and computer sci., 1958-59, asst. prof., 1959-63, assoc. prof., 1963-71, prof., 1971—. Dir. rsch. Ecole Polytechnique, Paris, 1979-80; vis. prof. U. Paris-Orsay, 1981-92; vis. scientist CEA-Euratom, Cadarache, France, 1995, Limeil-Valenton, France, 1995. Co-author: Waves in Anisotropic Plasmas, 1963, Physique des Plasmas, Vols. 1-2, 1994; contbr. chpts. to books, articles to profl. jours. Faculty Exch. fellow Ford Found., Tech. U. Berlin, 1966, fellow J.S. Guggenheim Meml. Found., U. Paris, 1968-69. Fellow: Am. Phys. Soc. (chmn. divsn. plasma physics 1991—92); mem.: AAAS, Univ. Fusion Assn. (pres. 1988—89), N.Y. Acad. Sci., St. Botolph Club Boston. Avocations: tennis, skiing.

BERSCHEID, ELLEN S., psychology professor, writer, researcher; b. Colfax, Wis., Oct. 11, 1936; d. Sylvan L. and Alvilde (Running) Saumer; m. Dewey Mathias Berscheid, Nov. 21, 1959. BA, U. Nev., 1959, MA, 1960; PhD, U. Minn., 1965. Market rsch. analyst Pillsbury Co., Mpls., 1960-62; asst. prof. psychology and mktg. U. Minn., Mpls., 1965-66, asst. prof. psychology, 1967-68, assoc. prof., 1969-71, prof., 1971-88, Regents' prof. psychology, 1988—. Mem. NRC Assembly Behavioral and Social Scis., 1973-77. Co-author: Interpersonal Attraction, 1969, 78, Equity: Theory and Research, 1978, Close Relationships, 1983, Psychology of Interpersonal Relationships, 2005, also numerous articles; mem. numerous editl. bds., past editorships. Recipient Disting. Scientist award Soc. Exptl. Social Psychology, 1993. Fellow APA (Donald T. Campbell award 1984, editor Contemporary Psychology Jour. 1985-91, Disting. Sci. Contbn. award 1997, Presdl. Citation 2003), Soc. Personality and Social Psychology (pres. 1985), Soc. for Psychol. Study Social Issues, Am. Acad. Arts and Scis.; mem. Internat. Soc. for the Study Personal Relationships (pres. 1990-92), Soc. Exptl. Social Psychology (exec. bd. 1971-74, 77-80, 85-89, Disting. Scientist award 1993). Lutheran. Avocation: interior design. Home: 329 Park Cir Menomonie WI 54751 Office: U Minn Dept Psychology N309 Elliott Hall Minneapolis MN 55455 Business E-Mail: bersc001@umn.edu.

BERSHAD, JACK R., retired lawyer; b. Phila., May 20, 1930; m. Helen Abby (Jay), Apr. 7, 1957; children: Thomas, Daniel, Robert. BS, Temple U., 1951; JD, Harvard U., 1954; LHD, Moore Coll. Art. Bar: D.C. 1954, Pa. 1955, U.S. Supreme Ct. 1985. Mem. firm Blank Rome LLP, Phila., 1958—2002, chmn., 1991—99, chmn. emeritus, 2000—, ret., 2002. Bd. dirs. Commerce Bancorp, Inc., Commerce Bank, N.A. Former chmn. bd. mgr. and trustees Moore Coll. Art, Phila.; trustee Phila. Mus. Art, 1989—; bd. trustees Jewish Fedn. Greater Phila.; bd. dirs. Opera Co., Phila., 1989—, Ben-Gurion U. Negev, Am. Assocs., 1998—, chair Mid. Atlantic Region; bd. govs. Mid. East Forum, 2000—; bd. dirs., pres. Phila. Chamber Music Soc., 2004-. With U.S. Army, 1954-56. Mem. ABA, Pa. Bar Assn., D.C. Bar Assn., Phila. Bar Assn. Office: Blank Rome LLP 1 Logan Sq Fl 3 Philadelphia PA 19103-6998 Office Phone: 215-569-5511. Business E-Mail: bershad@blankrome.com.

BERSHAD, NEIL JEREMY, electrical engineering educator; b. Bklyn., Oct. 20, 1937; BEE, Rensselaer Poly. Inst., 1958, PhD in Elec. Engring, 1962; MSEE, U. So. Calif., 1960. Mem. tech. staff Hughes Aircraft Co., Culver City, Calif., 1958—62, staff engr., 1964—69; prof. elec. engring. and computer sci. U. Calif., Irvine, 1966—94, prof. emeritus, 1994—. Contbr. more than 100 articles on communication theory, signal processing and adaptive filtering to profl. jours. 1st lt. USAF, 1962-65. Fellow IEEE (assoc. editor comm. jour., acoustics, speech and signal processing jour.). Office Phone: 949-824-6709. Business E-Mail: bershad@ece.uci.edu.

BERSI, ANN, lawyer; b. San Jose; BA, MA, San Diego State U.; JD, Calif. Western Sch. of Law; PhD in Higher Edn. Adminstrn., U. Conn. Bar: Calif. Past mem. law firms Morris, Brignone & Pickering, Lionel, Sawyer & Collins, Las Vegas; dir. employee rels. State of Nev., 1981-83; exec. dir. State Bar Nev., 1983-89; dep. dist. atty. civil divsn. Clark County Dist. Atty.'s Office, Las Vegas, 1995—2005. Past instr. pub. adminstrn. Pace U., N.Y.; legal counsel Clark County Sch. Dist. Bd. Trustees, Clark County Bd. Equalization, 1995-2005; mem. State Jud. Selection Commn., 2000—, Nev. Tax Commn., 2005— Mem. State Bar Nev. (pres. bd. govs. 1999-2000). Office: 5216 Painted Lakes Way Las Vegas NV 89149

BERSIA, JOHN CESAR, political science educator, editorial writer; b. Orlando, Fla., Nov. 23, 1956; s. Alfred and Rose-Marie (Idromasia) B. BA in Polit. Sci. and French, U. Ctrl. Fla., 1977, AA, 1977; MA in Govt., Georgetown U., 1979; MS in Pub. Info. Adminstrn., Am. U., 1980; MSc, London Sch. Econs., 1981. Distbr. Dexter Press Inc., Orlando, 1975-77; intern, analyst U.S. Dept. Labor, Washington, 1978-79; cons., staff assoc. Am. U., Washington, 1979-80; editor, cons. Global Perspectives, London, Washington, Orlando, 1981-83; pres. Global Perspectives Rsch. Group Inc., Casselberry, Fla., 1983-85; editorial bd. mem. The Orlando Sentinel, 1985—. Dir. Transnat. Studies Assn., Orlando, 1982-85; adj. prof. polit. sci. U. Ctrl. Fla., 1990—, Rollins Coll., Winter Park, Fla., 1993—; chmn. Shadows Know Regional sch. to work partnership, Orlando, 1996—; coordinator U.S. A.I.D. Seminar, Winter Park, Fla., 1984-85; speaker in field; del. editorial page editors and writers seminar Am. Press Inst., 1987; chmn. Global Connections for Ctrl. Fla., Orlando, 1999—. Editor-in-chief: Global Perspectives: An Interdisciplinary Jour. Internat. Rels., 1982-85.

Named to Outstanding Young Men Am., Jaycees, 1978, Outstanding Alumnus of Yr., U. Ctrl. Fla., 2000; fellow Knight Ctr. for Specialized Journalism, U. Md., 1991; recipient editl. award Florida Soc. Newspaper Mem. London Sch. Econs. Soc., Am. Friends London Sch. Econs., Citrus Club, Georgetown Club Metro Orlando (bd. dirs. 1996—), Phi Kappa Phi, Omicron Delta Kappa. Roman Catholic. Avocations: hiking, travel, cooking. Office: Orlando Sentinel Comm 633 N Orange Ave Orlando FL 32801-1349 E-mail: jbersia@orlandosentinel.com.

BERSIN, ALAN DOUGLAS, state agency administrator, lawyer; b. Bklyn., Oct. 15, 1946; s. Arthur and Mildred (Laikin) B.; m. Elisabeth Van Aggelen, Aug. 17, 1975 (div. Dec. 1983); 1 child, Alissa Ida; m. Lisa Foster, July 20, 1991; children, Madeleine Foster, Amalia Rose. AB magna cum laude, Harvard U., 1968; student, Oxford U., 1968-71; JD, Yale U., 1974; LLD (hon.), U. San Diego, 1994, Calif. Western Sch. Law, 1996, Thomas Jefferson Sch. Law, 2000. Bar: Calif. 1975, U.S. Dist. Ct. (ctrl. dist.) Calif. 1975, U.S. Ct. Appeals (9th cir.) 1977, Alaska 1983, U.S. Dist. Ct. Alaska 1983, U.S. Dist. Ct. Hawaii 1992, U.S. Dist. Ct. (so. dist.) Calif. 1992, U.S. Supreme Ct., 1996. Exec. asst. Bd. Police Commrs., LA, 1974-75; assoc. Munger, Tolles & Olson, LA, 1975-77, ptnr., 1978-92; spl. dep. dist. atty. Counties of Imperial and San Diego, Calif., 1993-98; supt. pub. edn. San Diego City Schs., 1998—2005; sec. edn. State of Calif., Sacramento, 2005—. Adj. prof. of law U. So. Calif. Law Ctr.; vis. prof. Sch. Law U. San Diego, 1992-93; named spl. rep. for U.S. s.w. border by U.S. Atty. Gen., 1995-98; mem. Atty Gen.'s adv. com. of U.S. Attys., 1995-98; tech. adv. panel Nat. Inst. of Justice Law Enforcement, adv. com. FCC/NTIA Pub. Safety Wireless; founder U.S./Mex. Binat. Lab. Program; chmn. bd. dirs. U.S. Border Rsch. Tech. Ctr., S.W. Border Coun.; chmn. Calif. Commn. on Tchr. Credentialing, 2000-02; mem. Nat. Bd. Profl. Tchg. Stds. Recognition, 2002; coun. visitors Calif. We. Sch. Law, 2002—; mem. bd. overseers Harvard U., 2004—. Named Rhodes scholar 1968; recipient Resolution of Merit award Mayor and City Coun. L.A., 1991, Spl. Achievement award Hispanic Urban Ctr., 1992, Peacemaker's award San Diego Mediation Assn., 1997, Morgan award San Diego LEAD, 1998, Learned Hand award, AJC, 2001, Courageous Leadership award, San Diego C. of C., 2003. Mem. Assn. Bus. Trial Lawyers (bd. govs. 1986-88), Inner City Law Ctr. (chmn. bd. dirs. 1987-90). Democrat. Jewish. Avocations: scuba diving, skiing, travel. Office: Gov's Office Office of Sec for Edn 1121 L St, Ste 600 Sacramento CA 95814 Office Phone: 916-323-0611. Office Fax: 916-323-3753.

BERSIN, RICHARD LEWIS, physicist; b. NYC, July 4, 1929; s. Maxwell Hilary and Virginia (Greenfield) B.; m. Lillian Freda Braudy, Mar. 21, 1954 (div.); children: Joshua Morris, Adam Samuel; m. Ruth Ann Hargrave, July 25, 1976; children: Jacob David Antonio, Rebekah Adeline Juana. BS in Physics, MIT, 1950; MS in Math. and Physics, Northeastern U., Boston, 1962. Physicist Tracerlab, Inc., Boston, 1950-58; divsn. mgr. Lab. for Electronics Corp., Waltham, Mass., 1958-69; pres., founder Internat. Plasma Corp., Berkeley, Calif., 1969-74; exec. v.p. Dionex Gas Plasma Sys., Hayward, Calif., 1974-79; dir. dry processing Perkin Elmer Corp., Wilton, Conn., 1979-83, dir. tech. mktg., 1983-84; pres., cons. Emergent Techs. Corp., 1985—; engring. specialist Ulvac Japan, Ltd., Chigasaki, Japan, 1989-92; sr. tech. staff mem. Ulvac Techs., Inc., Methuen, Mass., 1992—2002; dir. spl. projects Refugee Immigration Ministry, Malden, Mass., 2007—. Patentee in field. Mem. Am. Vacuum Soc. Democrat. Episcopalian. Personal E-mail: richard.bersin@verizon.net.

BERSOFF, DONALD NEIL, lawyer, psychologist, educator; b. NYC, Mar. 1, 1939; s. Irving and Mina (Cohen) B.; children by previous marriage: David, Judith; m. Deborah Leavy, Oct. 16, 1988; 1 child, Benjamin. BS, NYU, 1958, MA, 1960, PhD, 1965; student, U. Va. Law Sch., 1973-74; JD, Yale U., 1976. Bar: Md. 1976, D.C. 1984, Pa. 1990. Asst. prof. Ohio State U.; assoc. prof. U. Ga., U. Md. Sch. Law; ptnr. Ennis, Friedman & Bersoff, Washington, 1982-88, Jenner & Block, Washington, 1988-89; coord. joint JD and PhD program in law and psychology U. Md. Sch. Law and Johns Hopkins U. Dept. Psychology., 1976-82; dir. law and psychology program Med. Coll. Pa.-Hahnemann U., Phila., 1990-2001, Villanova (Pa.) U. Law Sch., 1990-2001, prof. emeritus, 2001—. Adj. prof. Drexel U., Phila., 2001—; psycholegal cons., 2001—. Author: Learning to Teach: A Decision-Making System, 1976, Ethical Conflicts in Psychology, 1995, 3d edit., 2003, Law and Mental Health-Pennsylvania, 1999. With USAF, 1965-68. N.Y. State Regents coll. teaching fellow. Mem. ABA, APA (mem. coun. of reps. 1991-94, bd. dirs. 1994-97, chair policy and planning bd. 1999, coun. of reps. 1999-2001), Am. Psychology-Law Soc. (pres. 1980-81. Lifetime Achievement award 2002). Home: 780 College Ave Haverford PA 19041-1205 Office: Villanova Law Sch Villanova PA 19085 Office Phone: 610-649-8448. E-mail: bersoffd@law.villanova.edu.

BERSON, ELIOT LAWRENCE, ophthalmologist, medical educator; b. Boston, Mass., 1937; MD, Harvard U., 1962. Intern Calif. Hosp., San Francisco, 1962-63; resident in ophthalmology Barnes and McMillan Hosps., St. Louis, 1963-66; clin. assoc. ophthalmologist Nat. Inst. Neurol. Diseases and Blindness, Bethesda, Md., 1966-68; asst. Mass. Eye and Ear Infirmary, Boston, 1968-73, asst. surgeon, 1974-78, dir. Berman-Gund Lab. for Study of Retinal Degenerations, Harvard Med. Sch., 1974—, assoc. surgeon in ophthalmology, 1979-84, surgeon in ophthalmology, 1984—. Instr. Harvard U. Sch. Medicine, Boston, 1968-70, asst. prof., 1971-76, assoc. prof. ophthalmology, 1976-82, Chatlos prof. ophthalmology, 1982—. Surgeon USPHS, 1966-68. Mem. AMA, Assn. for Rsch. in Vision and Ophthalmology, Am. Acad. Ophthalmology, Am. Ophthal. Soc. Office: Berman-Gund Lab Mass Eye and Ear Infirmary 243 Charles St Boston MA 02114-3002

BERSON, JEROME ABRAHAM, chemistry professor; b. Sanford, Fla., May 10, 1924; s. Joseph and Rebecca (Bernicker) B.; m. Bella Zevitovsky, June 30, 1946; children: Ruth, David, Jonathan. BS cum laude, CCNY, 1944; MA, Columbia U., 1947; PhD, 1949. NRC postdoctoral fellow Harvard U., 1949-50; asst. chemist Hoffmann-LaRoche, Inc., Nutley, NJ, 1944; asst. prof. U. So. Calif., 1950-53, asso. prof., 1953-58, prof., 1958-63, U. Wis., 1963-69, Yale U., 1969-79, Irénée du Pont prof., 1979-92, Sterling prof., 1992-94; Sterling prof. emeritus, 1994—; dir. div. phys. sci. and engring. Yale U., 1983-90. Vis. prof. U. Calif., U. Cologne, U. Western Ont., U. Karlsruhe, U. Lausanne; Fairchild Disting. scholar Calif. Inst. Tech.; cons. Riker Labs., Goodyear Tire & Rubber Co., am. Cyanamid Co., IBM, Cord Labs., SMC Corp., B.F. Goodrich Corp., Lubrizol Corp.; mem. medicinal chemistry study sect. NIH, 1969-73; mem. adv. panel chemistry NSF, 1964-70. Author: Chemical Creativity, 1999, Chemical Discovery and the Logicians' Program, 2003; mem. editorial adv. bd.: Jour. Organic Chemistry, 1961-65, Accounts of Chemical Rsch., 1971-77, 94-96, Nouveau Journal de Chimie, 1977-85, Chem. Revs., 1980-83, Jour. Am. Chem. Soc., 1988-93; contbr. articles to profl. jours. Served with AUS, 1944-46, CBI. Recipient Alexander von Humboldt award, 1980, Townsend Harris medal Alumni Assn. CCNY, 1984, Merit award NIH, 1989, Lit. award German Chem. Industry Assn., 2000; John Simon Guggenheim fellow, 1980 Fellow Am. Acad. Arts and Scis.; mem. NAS, Am. Chem. Soc. (Calif. sect. award 1963, James Flack Norris award 1978, Nichols medal 1985, Roger Adams award 1987, Arthur C. Cope scholar 1992, Oesper award 1998, chmn. div. organic chemistry 1971), Royal Soc. Chem., Chem. Soc. London, Phi Beta Kappa, Sigma Xi, Phi Lambda Upsilon. Office: Yale U Dept Chemistry PO Box 208107 New Haven CT 06520-8107 Home: 200 Leeder Hill Dr Apt 205 Hamden CT 06517 Business E-Mail: jerome.berson@yale.edu.

BERSTEIN, ROBERT L., investment company executive; b. Cambridge, Mass., July 12, 1975; s. Irving Aaron and Suzanne Berstein. BA magna cum laude in Classics, Cornell U., 1997. Investment banker Merrill Lynch, San Francisco, 1997—98, NYC, 1998—99; v.p. Advanta Ptnrs., NYC, 1999—2004, Needham & Co., LLC, Boston, 2005—; investment banker Jefferies Broadview, Waltham, Mass., 2004—05. Chmn. NY Pvt. Equity Network, NYC, 2001—04. Young alumni nat. chmn. ann. fund Cornell U., Ithaca, 2002—06, adv. coun. entrepreneurship enterprise program, 2002—07, mem. young alumni adv. coun. Coll. Arts and Scis., 2003—, mem. univ. coun., 2006—, mem. Student and Acad. Svcs. Com., 2006—. Mem.: Cornell U. Assn. Class Officers (v.p. bd. dirs. 2000—07), Univ. Club NYC, Harvard Club, Cornell Club, Epsilon Assn., Inc. (bd. dirs.), Sigma Phi (pres. 1996—97). Office: Needham & Co LLC 1 Post Office Sq Ste 1900 Boston MA 02109 Home: 110 Second St PH2 Cambridge MA 02141 Home Phone: 617-494-1812; Office Phone: 617-457-0942. Business E-Mail: rberstein@needhamco.com.

BERT, CHARLES WESLEY, mechanical and aerospace engineer, educator; b. Chambersburg, Pa., Nov. 11, 1929; s. Charles Wesley and Gladys Adelle (Raff) B.; m. Charlotte Elizabeth Davis (June 29, 1957); children: Charles Wesley IV, David Raff. BSME, Pa. State U., 1951, MS, 1956; PhD in Engring. Mechanics, Ohio State U., 1961. Registered profl. engr., Pa. Jr. design engr. Am. Flexible Coupling Co., State Coll., Pa., 1951-52; aero. design engr. Fairchild Aircraft div. Fairchild Engine and Airplane Corp., Hagerstown, Md., 1954—56; prin. M.E. Battelle Inst., Columbus, Ohio, 1956-61; sr. research engr., 1961-62; program dir., solid and structural mechanics research, 1962-63; cons., 1964-65; assoc. prof. U. Okla., 1963-66, prof., 1966—2004; Benjamin H. Perkinson Chair prof. engring. Sch. Aerospace and Mech. Engring., 1978—2004; George L. Cross rsch. prof. U. Okla., 1981—2004, prof. emeritus, 2004—. Instr. engring. mechanics Ohio State U., Columbus, 1959-61; dir.Sch. Aerospace and Mech. Engring. U. Okla., 1972-77, 90-95; vis. scholar U. Calif., San Diego, 1996; cons. in field; chmn. Midwestern Mechanics Conf., 1973-75; Honor lectr. Mid-Am. State Univs. Assn., 1983-84; seminar lectr. Midwest Mechanics, 1983-84; Plenary lectr. Internat. Conf. on Composite Structures, Paisley, Scotland, 1987. Mem. editl. bd. Composite Structures Jour., 1982—, Jour. Sound and Vibration, 1988—, Composites Engring., 1991-95, Mechanics of Composite Materials and Structures, 1993-2001, Applied Mechanics Revs., 1993—, Composites, 1996-98, Internat. Jour. Structural Stability and Dynamics, 2000—06, Jour. Sandwich Structures and Materials, 1997—, Mechanics of Advanced Materials and Structures, 2002-; assoc. editor: Exptl. Mechanics, 1982-87, Applied Mechanics Revs., 1984-87; contbr. chpts. to books, articles to profl. jours. 1st lt. USAF, 1952-54. Sr. Rsch. scholar U. Calif., San Diego, 1996; recipient Disting. Alumnus award Ohio State U. Coll. engring., 1985. Fellow AAAS, AIAA (nat. tech. com. structures 1969-72, chmn. Ctrl. Okla. sect. 1966-67), ASME (Cen. Okla. sect. exec. com. 1973-78, 90-95, 99-01, sec. 1990-91, region X mech. engring. dept. heads com. 1972-77, 90-95, chmn. 1975-77, 10-session symposium named in his honor 1999), Am. Soc. Composites (bd. dirs. 1996-98, Disting. Rsch. award 1999), Am. Acad. Mechs. (bd. dirs. 1978-82, pres.-elect 2001-02, pres. 2002-03), Soc. Exptl. Mechanics (monograph com. 1978-82, chmn. 1980-82, sec. Mid-Ohio sect. 1958-59, chmn. 1959-60, adv. bd. 1960-63), Soc. Engring. Sci. (bd. dirs. 1982-88); mem. NSPE, Okla. Acad. Sci., Okla. Soc. Profl. Engrs., Scabbard and Blade, Pa. State Alumni Assn. (Outstanding Engring. Alumnus award 1992), Sigma Xi, Sigma Tau, Pi Tau Sigma, Sigma Gamma Tau (Disting. Engr. award), Tau Beta Pi (Disting. Engr. award). Achievements include co-development of world's smallest pressure transducer capable of measuring both steady and fluctuating pressures; first general solution of cylindrically orthotropic plates of radially varying thickness under arbitrary body forces; origination of several minimum-weight optimal designs for multicell cylindrical pressure vessels, experimental techniques and associated data reduction equations for determining residual stresses in both flat-sheet and thick-walled cylindrical specimens of composite materials; first successful application of Kennedy-Pancu system identification method to shell structures, noninteger polynomial version of Rayleigh's method to heat conduction; first application of differential quadrature method to static structural problems, structural vibration problems and non-linear structural problems; first application of noninteger polynomial method to finite element analysis; first dynamic stability analysis of unicycles and monocycles; origination of concept of stress gages for composite materials; research on sandwich structures with bimodular facings, prediction of ply steer behavior of automobile tires, non-linear flutter of laminated composite panels; many others. Home and Office: 2516 Butler Dr Norman OK 73069-5059 Office: U Okla Sch Aerospace and Mech Engring 865 Asp Ave Norman OK 73019-1052 *Set high yet realistic goals, put forth the extra effort to achieve them, and practice the Golden Rule.*

BERT, CLARA VIRGINIA, retired secondary school educator, administrator; b. Quincy, Fla., Jan. 29, 1929; d. Harold C. and Ella J. (McDavid) Bert. BS, Fla. State U., 1950, MS, 1963, PhD, 1967. Cert. tchr. Fla., home economist, pub. mgr. Tchr. Union County HS, Lake Butler, Fla., 1950-53, Havana HS, Fla., 1953-65; cons. rsch. and devel. Fla. Dept. Edn., Tallahassee, 1967-75, sect. dir. rsch. and devel., 1975-85, program dir. home econs. edn., 1985-92, program specialist resource devel., 1992-96, program specialist, spl. projects, 1996-99, program dir. grants mgmt., 1999-2000; ret., 2000. Field reader US Dept. Edn., 1974—75; cons. Nat. Ctr. Rsch. Vocation Edn., Ohio State U., 1978. Author, editor: booklets. Mem. devel. bd., mem. adv. bd. Fla. State U. Coll. Human Scis. Family Inst., 1994—2004; mem. nat. com. for the capital campaign Fla. State U. Found., 2002—05. Named Disting. Alumna, Coll. Human Scis., Fla. State U., 1994; recipient Dean's award, 1995; US Office Edn. grantee, 1976, 1977, 1978. Mem.: Am. Edn. Rsch. Assn., Nat. Coun. Family Rels., Am. Vocat. Edn. Rsch. Assn. (nat. treas. 1970—71), Fla. Vocat. Home Econs. Assn., Fla. Vocat. Assn., Am. Vocat. Assn., Am. Home Econs. Assn. (state treas. 1969—71), Fla. State U. Alumni Assn. (bd. dirs. home econs. sect. 1976—81, pres.-elect 1978—79, 1979—80), Fla. State U. Ctr. Club, Havana Golf and Country Club, Phi Delta Kappa, Sigma Kappa (pres. corp. bd. 1985—91), Delta Kappa Gamma (pres. 1974—76), Kappa Omicron Nu (chpt. pres. 1965—66), Kappa Delta Pi.

BERTA, MELISSA ROSE, mathematics professor; b. Van Nuys, Calif., Apr. 29, 1966; d. Alexander Rocco and Patricia Ann Yguado; m. Brad Braden Berta, July 12, 1986; children: Joseph Brandon, Lisa Marie. AS in Math. and Sci., Coll. Canyons, 1989; BS in Math., Calif. State U., 1993; MS in Math., U. Nebr., 1996; EdD in Ednl. Leadership, Arogsu U., Calif., 2007. Marec fellow Calif. State U., Northridge, 1992—93; tchg. asst. Nat. Renewable Energy Lab., Golden, Colo., 1992—93, U. Nebr., Lincoln, 1994—96; exec. dir. Berta Engring., Laguna Hills, Calif., 1996—98; instr. math. Santiago Coll., Orange, Calif., 1998—2001, Orange Coast Coll., Costa Mesa, Calif., 1998—, Saddleback Coll., Mission Viejo, Calif., 1998—2005; dir. edn. in ednl. leadership Argo State U., 2006—. Leader Girl Scouts Am., Rancho Santa Margarita. With US Army, 1984—87. Larson Minority Grad. fellow, U. Nebr., 1994—95. Mem.: Math. Assn. Am., Am. Math. Assn. Two-Yr. Colls., Faculty Assn. Calif. CCs. Home: 17 Calle Espolon Rancho Santa Margarita CA 92688 Personal E-mail: mberta@occ.cccd.edu.

BERTE, NEAL RICHARD, academic administrator; b. May 7, 1940; s. Edward H. and Wenonah Maureen (Stevens) B.; m. Anne; children: Becky, Julie, Mark, Scott. BS in Polit. Sci, U. Cin., 1962, MS (Ford Found. scholar), 1963, EdD, 1966; Rockefeller Found. fellow, Union Theol. Sem., NYC, 1962-63; postgrad., Garrett Theol. Sem., Evanston, Ill., 1966-67, Harvard U., Cambridge, Mass., 1966; LHD (hon.), U. Cin., 1993. Asst. dir. Coll. Entrance Exam. Bd., Evanston, 1966-68; exec. asst. to pres., asst. prof. Ottawa U., Kans., 1968-70; dean New Coll.; assoc. prof. U. Ala., 1970-74; v.p. ednl. devel., dean New Coll., 1974-76; pres. Birmingham-So. Coll., Ala., 1976—, chancellor, 2004—, pres. emeritus, 2004—. Project dir. NSF grants, 1972; chmn. session Internat. Coun. on Edn. for Tchg. World Assembly, Nairobi, Kenya, 1973; faculty Danforth Found. sponsored CC Inst., Stephens Coll., 1973; steering com. Carnegie Found. funded project Coop. Assessment of Experiential Learning, 1974-77; mem. Commn. on Ednl. Credit, Am. Council Edn., 1975-81, Danforth Found. exec. com. for Danforth Fellows Program, 1974-75; nat. adv. council for career edn. HEW, Office Edn., 1976-79; sec.-treas. So. U. Conf., 1977-80, v.p., 1984-85, pres., 1985-86; vis. scholar Inst. for Ednl. Mgmt., Harvard Grad. Sch Edn., 1990-91; co-chmn. Region 2020, Ala., 1997—; bd. dirs. Ala. Ctr. for Law and Civic Edn. Contbr. articles to edn. jours. Mem. adminstrv. bd. Canterbury United Meth. Ch., Birmingham, 1977—, univ. senate United Meth. Ch., 1986-88; chmn. Univ. United Fund campaign, 1973; bd. dirs., mem. exec. com. United Fund, Tuscaloosa, Ala., 1974-75, chmn. edn. div., 1975; chmn. sect. for pvt. ednl. insts. Jefferson-Shelby-Walker Counties United Appeal, 1977; chmn. pub. employees div. United Way campaign, 1978; v.p. Coun. for Advancement Pvt. Colls. in Ala., 1977-82, pres., 1982-83; chmn. com. to select Man of Year in Birmingham, 1977; chmn. selection com. Rhodes Scholarships for Ala., 1976-81; bd. dirs. Jefferson-Shelby Counties Lung Assn., 1978-79, Ala. Partners for Progress with Guatemala Program, 1977—, Carraway Meth. Hosp., 1977-80, Brookwood Hosp., 1982-90, Neighborhood Housing Svc., Birmingham, 1977-78, Birmingham Symphony Assn., 1976-80, 82-87, Cmty. Affairs Com., 1976-87, Operation New Birmingham, 1976-89, 2006-09, Nature Conservancy of Ala., 2007; bd. govs. Relay House Club, Birmingham, 1983-87, Circle S Industries, Selma, Ala., 1983—, Parisian, Inc., Birmingham, 1983-88; bd. dirs. NCCJ, 1978—, Birmingham Summerfest, 1979—, March of Dimes, 1979-86, Am. Heart Assn., 1980-84, So. Rsch. Inst., 1982—, Leadership Birmingham, 1981—; bd. dirs., chmn. long range planning com., chmn. program for Scout Expn. Jefferson County coun. Boy Scouts Am., 1977—; exec. com. Men's Com., Birmingham Symphony Assn., 1977-84; bd. dirs. Jefferson Fed. Savs. and Loan Assn., Birmingham, 1978-91, Birmingham Festival Arts, 1982-89, bd. advisors, 1989, trustee, 1990, pres., 1981—; chmn. Birmingham Area United Way, 1983; trustee Advent Episc. Day Sch., 1977-87, Gorgas Scholarship Found., 1976-88, New Coll.-Sarasota, U. South Fla., 1977-79; founding mem., bd. dirs. Progressive Alliance, 1986—; bd. dirs. Met. Devel. Bd., 1987-88, Greater Birmingham Conv. and Visitors Bur., 1988; commn. pub. rels. Nat. Assn. Ind. Colls and Univs., 1992-94, bd. dirs., 1994; adv. bd. pub. Edn. Found. Jefferson County Bd. Edn., 1999—; bd. dirs. Civil Rights Inst., 2000; co-chair Campaign for Restoration of Birmingham's Hist 16th St. Bapt. Ch., mem. found. bd., 2004—; chmn. steering com. McWane Cmty. Adv. Panel, 2004—; bd. dirs. U. Ala. Health Svcs. Found., 2004—; v.p. Birmingham Civil Rights Inst., 2005, chmn. 2005-06; mem. adv. bd. Cmty. Grief Support Svc., 2005-; bd. dirs. Operation New Birmingham, 2006—, vice chmn. 2007; nat. adv. com. Robert Woods Johnson Found., 2007. Recipient Outstanding Citizens award Lawson State CC, 1977, Outstanding Citizen award in Birmingham Erskine Ramsay Award Com., 1978, Brotherhood award NCCJ, 1984, Outstanding Svc. award Black Student Union, 1986, Outstanding Cmty. Svc. award Mortar Bd., 1986, James M. Tingle award, 1986, Disting. Svc. award, Sigma Alpha Epsilon, 1991, Medal of Honor, DAR, 1995, Leadership award Birmingham Regional Planning Commn. promoting regional cooperation, 2000, award of distinction Nat. Interfrat. Coun., 2004, Outstanding Svc. award Martin Luther King, Jr. Unity Breakfast, 2005, James A. Head Lifetime Achievement award Nat. Conf. for Cmty. and Justice, 2007; elected to Ala. Acad. Honor, 1979; named one of 10 Outstanding Cmty. Leaders Birmingham Post-Herald, 1984, one of Top 10 Current Leaders in Birmingham, The Birmingham News, 1990, 99, one of 10 leaders Bus. First jour., 1990, Birmingham Citizen of Yr. award for outstanding civic and cmty. svc., 1986, Outstanding Ala. Civic Leader Nat. Soc. Fund-Raising Execs., 1991, Disting. Citizen City Coun. of Birmingham, 1992, one of top ten mems. of 1997 Class of Movers and Shakers, Birmingham Bus. Jour.; named to Sigma Alpha Epsilon Leadership Sch. Hall of Fame, 1994; named one of 2 recipients Ala. Humanities Found. award, 2005; honoree Ann. Benefit Am. Cancer Soc., 2005; King Beaux Arts Krewe Ball, Birmingham Mus. Art benefit, 2005. Mem. Am. Assn. Univ. Adminstrs. (pres. Alpha chpt. 1978-79), Greater Birmingham Area C. of C. (bd. dirs., exec. com. 1978-80, v.p. for govtl. rels., policy com. 1986, pres. 1988, chmn. exec. com. 1989), Am. Assn. Colls. (pres.'s adv. coun. 1977-78), Am. Assn. for Higher Edn. (chmn. Southeastern Regional Coun. 1973, chmn. panel on three-year degree programs 1973, program chmn. 1974, adv. bd. NEXUS Project 1974-75), Assn. for Innovation in Higher Edn. (adv. bd. 1973), Kiwanis Internat. (Disting. Pres. award 1992-93, George F. Hixon fellow 1995), Phi Beta Kappa (pres. 1975), Phi Delta Kappa. Clubs: The Redstone Club, The Jefferson Club, Downtown Birmingham Kiwanis (chmn. Ministers Day 1977, chmn. Youth-of-the-Year selection com. 1978, pres. 1992-93, Disting. Pres. award). Office: Pres Emeritus Birmingham So Coll 2100 First Ave N Ste 410 Birmingham AL 35203 E-mail: rberte@bsc.edu.

BERTELSMAN, WILLIAM ODIS, federal judge; b. Cin., Jan. 31, 1936; s. Odis William and Dorothy B.; m. Margaret Ann Martin, June 13, 1959; children: Kathy, Terri, Nancy. BA, Xavier U., 1958; JD, U. Cin., 1961. Bar: Ky. 1961, Ohio 1962. Law clk. firm Taft, Stettinius & Hollister, Cin., 1960-61; mem. firm Bertelsman & Bertelsman, Newport, Ky., 1962-79; judge U.S. Dist. Ct. (ea. dist.) Ky., Covington, 1979—, chief judge, 1991-98; instr. Coll. Law U. Cin., 1965-72; city atty., prosecutor Highland Heights, Ky., 1962-69. Adj. prof. Chase Coll. of Law, 1989—. Contbr. articles to profl. jours. Served to capt. AUS, 1963-64. Mem.: U.S. Jud. Conf. (standing com. on practice and procedure 1989—95, liaison mem. adv. com. on civil rules 1989—95, 6th cir. rep. 2004—06), Ky. Bar Assn. (bd. govs. 1978—79), ABA. Republican. Roman Catholic.

BERTENSHAW, WILLIAM HOWARD, III, radio and television producer; b. NYC, Nov. 28, 1930; s. William Howard Jr. and Grace Annette (Miller) B.; m. Betty J. Underriner, July 7, 1956 (dec. Nov. 1975); children: Jane Ann, Judith Ann, Jo Ann; m. Bobbi C. Slachofsky, Dec. 16, 1984 (div. Sept. 2002). BA in Communications, Ohio Wesleyan U., 1950. Asst. mktg. editor Bus. Week mag., NYC, 1953-55; radio-TV dir. Hardy Burt Assocs., NYC, 1955-57; radio-TV producer Empire Broadcasting Corp., NYC, 1957-60, Nat. Episcopal Ch., NYC, 1960-70; producer MBS, NYC, 1970-75; dir. communications Council of Chs. City of N.Y., 1975-84; exec. producer, chief exec. officer Radio & TV Roundup Prodns., NYC, 1984—; producer TKR Cable TV, NYC, 1987—. Guest lectr. Upsala U., East Orange, N.J., 1970-75, So. Meth. U., Dallas, 1972, Seton Hall U., South Orange, N.J., 1974, Pace U., N.Y.C., 1980, Syracuse (N.Y.) U., 1982; vice chmn. dept. communications N.J. Coun. Chs., 1986—; host People Working for People, Sta. WWOR-TV, N.Y.C., 1988-92; programmer Cable TV Network of N.J., 1985-2000; producer The Jersey Cape TV series, 1990-2002. Host Inner-Dimension Community Concerns, Union Eyes and Perspective on the News Sta. WOR Radio, WOR Special Report, N.Y., 1970—. Pres. Rep. Club, West Cape May, N.J., 1986-87; vice chmn. communications N.J. Coun. Chs., 1986-89; committeman Cape May County N.J. Rep. Orgn., 1987-90, Essex Coun. N.J. Rep. Orgn., 1960-85. Sgt. U.S. Army, 1951-53. Recipient Gabriel award Washington Conf., 1966-67, Radio Programming award Ohio State U., 1969, Columbus Film Festival award Ohio Coun. Chs., 1970, Radio-TV award N.J. Coun. Chs., 1983, Olive award, 1982-84, Cape award Cable TV Network NJ, 1987, Angel award Excellence in Media, Hollywood, Calif., 1999-. Mem. AFTRA, Delfon Recording Soc. (dir. comm. 2001—), Nat. Lima Bean Assn. (founder), Alpha Sigma Rho, South Jersey Bird Club. Clubs: Suburban Sports Car (N.J.) (v.p., co-founder 1956-61). Episcopalian. Home: 653 Sun Haven Dr Clayton NJ 08312-1955 Office Phone: 856-881-2570. Business E-Mail: delfon@att.net.

BERTENTHAL, BENNETT IRA, dean, psychologist, educator; b. NYC, Mar. 22, 1949; m. Meryl Bertenthal; 2 children. BA in Psychology, Brandeis U., 1971; MA in Devel. Psychology, U. Denver, 1976, PhD, 1978. Postdoctoral fellow Brain Rsch. Inst. and dept. pediats. UCLA Sch. Medicine, 1978-79; asst. prof. dept. psychology U. Va., 1979-85, assoc. prof., 1985, prof., 1991—, dir. devel. tng. program, 1989-96; asst. dir. NSF, Arlington, Va., 1997-99; prof. Dept. Psychology U. Chgo., 1999—2006; dean Coll. of Arts and Scis. Ind. U., Bloomington, 2007—. Mem. human devel. and aging study sect, Nat. Inst. Child Health and Human Devel., 1987, 91-96, chair, 1994-96; extramural reviewer NSF, Nat. Inst. Neurol. Diseases & Communicative Disorders, NIMH; cons. NINCDS; mem. performance and safety monitoring com. NINCDS, 1981-88; program com. Internat. Conf. Infant Studies, 1984, 88, 96, Southeastern Conf. Human Devel., 1988; mem. MacArthur Network on Transition From Infancy to Childhood, 1987-92; mem. MacArthur Network Task Force-Devel. of Computer Workstas. for Psychol. Rsch., 1988-92. Assoc. editor Devel. Psychology, 1988-90, mem. editl. bd., 1988-90; mem. editl. bd. Jour. Exptl. Child Psychology, 1985-88, Child Devel., 1980-83; reviewer Psychophysiology, infant Behavior and Devel., Perception and Psychophysics, Devel. Psychology, Child Devel., SRCD Monographs, Internat. Jour. Behavioural Devel., Jour. Exptl. Psychology, Human Perception and Performance. Recipient Boyd R. McCandless Young Scientist award, 1985, rsch. career devel. awarrd NIH, 1985-90, Cattell Sabbatical award, 1990, MHTP postdoctoral fellowship, 1978-79; grantee U. Va. Rsch. Policy Coun., 1979-80, 87-90, 89—, NIMH, 1979-80, 85-90, 91—, NINCDS, 1980-81, NIH, 1982-84, 85-88, 89—, John D. and Catherine T. MacArthur Found., 1984-85, 89—, Va. Ctr. Innovative Tech., 1985-86, NATO, 1989—, United Cerebral Palsey Rsch. and Edn. Found., 1989-90, McDonnell-Pew Program Cognitive Neuroscis., 1991-93 Fellow APA (program com. 1987, 88, nominations com. divsn. 7 1988, mem.-at-large divsn. 7 exec. com. 1995-98, mem. com. on sci. awards, 1991-94, chair, 1994), Am. Psychol. Soc.; mem. AAAS, Soc. Rsch. in Child Devel. (co-chair program com. 1995-97), Assn. Rsch. in Vision and Ophthalmology, Internat. Soc. Infant Studies, Internat. Soc. Study Behavioural Devel., Internat. Soc. Study of Posture and Gait, Psychonomic Soc. Office: Dean's Office Kirkwood Hall 104 130 S Woodlawn Ave Bloomington IN 47405-7104*

BERTHELSEN, RICHARD A., lawyer; b. Racine, Wis., Sept. 14, 1944; BS, U. Wis., 1966, JD, 1969. Bar: Wis. 1969, U.S. Dist. Ct. Wis., 1969. Assoc. Murphy, Huiskamp, Stolper, Brewster & Desmond, Madison, Wis., 1969-72; gen. counsel Nat. Football League Players Assn., Washington, 1984—. Gen. counsel U.S. Football League Players Assn., Washington, 1983-86, N.Am. Soccer League Players Assn., Washington, 1982-86, Major Indoor Soccer League Players Assn., Washington, 1983-91; lectr. various legal/sports seminars. Mem. Nat. Sports Law Inst. (bd. advisors), Sports Lawyers Assn. (bd. dirs.), Wis. Bar Assn. Office: NFL Players' Assn 2021 L St NW Washington DC 20036

BERTHOT, JAKE, artist, educator; b. Niagara Falls, NY, Mar. 30, 1939; Student, New Sch. Social Rsch., 1960-61, Pratt Inst., 1960-62. Mem. faculty Cooper Union, 1960-62, Yale U., New Haven, 1982-90, Sch. Visual Arts, NYC, 1992—. Artist in residence Dartmouth U., 1995. One-man shows include O. K. Harris Gallery, N.Y.C., 1970, 1972, 1975, Portland (Oreg.) Ctr. Visual Arts, 1973, Galerie de Gestlo, Hamburg, Germany, 1973, 1977, David McKee Gallery, N.Y.C., 1976, 1978, 1982, 1983, 1986, 1988, 1989, 1991, 1995—2004, Nina Nielsen Gallery, Boston, 1979, 1984, 1992, 1995, 1996, 2000—02, Nigel Greenwood Gallery, London, 1979, 1991, U. Calif. Berkeley, 1984, Galleri Olsson, Stockholm, 1987, 1990, 1996, Nat. Art Gallery, Washington, 1989, Cork Gallery Lincoln Ctr., N.Y.C., 1991, Jaffe-Friede and Strauss Gallery, Hanover, N.H., 1995, The Phillips Collection, Washington, 1996, Cooper Union, N.Y.C., 1999, Marist Coll., 2005, Betty Cunningham Gallery, 2005, Kleiner/James Art Ctr., Woodstock, NY, 2006, exhibited in group shows at Whitney Mus. Art, N.Y.C., 1969, McKee Gallery, 2000, 2003, Randolph-Macon Woman's Coll., 2003, Whitney Mus. Art, N.Y.C., 1972, 1974, 1978, Art Inst. Chgo., 1971, Mus. Modern Art, N.Y.C., 1977, 1981, 1983—85, Meadows Art Gallery, Dallas, 1985, others, Represented in permanent collections Australian Nat. Gallery, Balt. Mus. Art, U. Calif. Berkeley Mus., Dallas Mus. Fine Arts, Fogg Mus. Harvard U., Guggenheim Mus., Mus. Modern Art, Whitney Mus. Art, others. Named academician, Nat. Acad. Design; recipient Acad. Inst. award, Am. Acad. Arts & Letters, 1994; grantee, The Elizabeth Found., 1995—96; Guggenheim fellow, 1981. Address: Betty Cuningham Gallery 541 W 25th St New York NY

BERTIN, JOHN JOSEPH, aeronautical engineer, educator, researcher; b. Milw., Oct. 13, 1938; m. Ruth Easterbrook; children: Thomas Alexander, Randolph Scott, Elizabeth Anne, Michael Robert. BA, Rice Inst., Houston, 1960; MS, Rice U., 1962, PhD, 1966. Aerospace technologist NASA Johnson Space Ctr., Houston, 1962-66; prof. U. Tex., Austin, 1966-89; program mgr. for space initiative MTS, Sandia Nat. Labs., Albuquerque, 1989-94; vis. prof. USAF Acad., Colorado Springs, Colo., 1988-89, prof. aero. engring., 1994—2004, prof. emeritus, 2004—. Cons. McGinnis, Lochridge & Kilgore, Austin, 1978-83, Sandia Nat. Labs., Albuquerque, 1980-89, BPD Difesa e Spazio, Rome, 1980-82, NASA, 1994-96, Sci. Applications Internat. Corp., 1996, Return to Flight, 2004-2005; detailed to Office of Space, U.S. Dept. Energy Hdqs., 1991-92; dir. Ctr. Excellence for Hypersonic Tng. and Rsch., 1985-89; mem. sci. adv. bd. USAF, 1989-93, mem. adv. group Flight Dynamics Labs., 1989-93; tech. chmn. Space 2000 Conf., 1998-99; aerothermodynamics cons. Columbia Accident Investigation Bd., 2003; adj. prof. Rice U., 2003-. Author: Engineering Fluid Mechanics, 1987, Hypersonic Aerothermodynamics, 1994, Aerodynamics for Engineers, 2002; contbg. author Letterwinner, 1999—; editor: Hypersonics, 1989, Advances in Hypersonics, 1992; assoc. editor Jour. Spacecraft and Rockets, 2000-01. Pres. Western Hills Little League, Austin, 1975; mem. arts subcom. NASA, 1987—91; mem. Aerospace Engring. Bd. Panel NRC, 1996—97, mem. USAF hypersonics program rev. com., 1997—98; mem. attendance com. Rice Athletic Dept., 2002—; mem. adv. bd. Rice Owl Club, 2002—05; mem. athletic coun. Rice U., 2007—. Recipient Gen. Dynamics Tchg. award U. Tex. Coll. Engring., 1978, Tex. Exec. Tchg. award Ex-Students Assn. U. Tex., 1982, Faculty award Tau Beta Pi, 1986, award for meritorious civilian svc. Dept. Air Force, 1993, Gen. Daley award USAFA, 1996, Exemplary Civilian Svc. Award medal, 1996, F.J. Seiler Rsch. award, USAFA, 1997, Disting. Alumni award, Rice U., 2005. Fellow: AIAA (dir. region IV 1983—86, publs. bd. 1998—2000, disting. lectr., Thermophysics award 1997); mem.: Columbia Accident Investigation Bd. (aerothermodynamic cons. 2003, Outstanding Civilian Career Svc. award 2004), Assn. Rice Alumni (bd. dirs. 2006—). Office Phone: 713-784-4092. Personal E-mail: wiseoldowl60@pcisys.net.

BERTIN, MARGARET A.H, museum administrator; b. Quito, Equador, June 2, 1948; d. Francis W. and Ellen D. Herron; m. Michael Bertin Heinlein, June 23, 1970; children: Madeleine E., M. Richard O. BA in Art History and Theory, George Washington U., Washington, DC, 1970. Pub. info. officer The Metro. Mus. of Art, NYC, 1971—77; asst. to dir. Yale Ctr. for British Art, New Haven, 1977—79; pub. rels. cons. Am. Fedn. of Arts, NYC, 1979—80; dir. pub. affairs Nat. Mus. African Art, Washington, 1983—88; exec. asst. to provost Smithsonian Inst., Washington, 1988—95; asst. dir. external affairs Nat. Mus. Am. Indian Smithsonian Inst., Washington, 1996—2007; assoc. dir. mus. resources Nat. Mus. Am. Indian Smithsonian, Washington, 2007—. Author: (course book) Willful Neglect: The Smithsonian Institution and U.S. Latinos, 1994. Chair pub. rels. com. Am. Assn. Mus., Washington, 1984; advisor Latino task force Smithsonian Inst., 1993—94. Recipient Silver Anvil award, Pub. Rels. Soc. Am., 2005, Golden World award, Internat. Pub. Rels. Assn., 2005. Mem.: Am. Assn. Mus. Avocations: reading, travel, cooking. Home: 2645 Ft Scott Dr Arlington VA 22202 Office: Nat Mus Am Indian MRC 590 Box 37012 4th St and Independence Ave SW Washington DC 20013-7012 Office Phone: 202-633-6928. Business E-Mail: bertinm@si.edu.

BERTINE, DOROTHY WILMUTH, artist, educator, accountant, genealogist, poet, writer; b. Madill, Okla., Sept. 28, 1916; d. Oliver Olen Wilkerson and Nina Keortinka Bennett; m. George Franklin Bertine II (dec. 1995). BS, Okla. State U., 1942; MA, Tex. Woman's U., Denton, 1975; advanced studies with many famous art tchrs. in painting workshops worldwide as, Dong Kingman, Mildred Sheets, Milford Zornes, Frances Skinner, Clara Ely, Edgar Whitney. CPA Tex., 1944. Acct., CPA, Dallas, 1943—45, Houston, 1945—68, Brownsville, Tex., 1963—68; instr., life mem. Brownsville Art League, 1959—70; student to Frances Skinner Houston Museum Art Sch., Houston, 1956—63; tchr. Tex. Women's U., Denton, Tex., 1973—75; tchr., head art dept. Denton Parks and Recreation, 1976—85; instr. in continuing edn. U. North Tex., 1982—83; lectr. workshops local painting groups Okla., Tex., Colo., 1976—96; acct., CPA Austin, Tex., 1944—. Bd. mem. Southwestern Watercolor Soc., Dallas, 1983—84; bd. mem., founding mem. Denton Hist. Landmark Commn., 1983—85; bd. mem., genealogist Denton Hist. Commn., 1976—85; regent, geneologist Daughers of Am. Revolution, 1999—2001. Author, illustrator Design Elements Used in High Victorian Houses, 1975, Principles and Elements of Design:, 1989, Pierre Bertine 1686 and Allied Families, 1994, Ancestors and Descendants of Lucy Ann and George E.C. Bennett, 1989, DeHaven Ancestry Book, 1994; over 20 solo art exhibits and over 40 group exhibits; contbr. artistic works to profl publs.; Represented in permanent collections Brownsville Art League, Laredo Art Ctr, Tex., Heard Mus. Sci., McKinny, Tex., State Mus. NJ, Trenton, Citizens Nat. Bank, Tex., Charles B. Goddard Ctr. for Visual and Performing Arts, Ardmore, Okla., over 40 more permanent collections throughout the US; contbg. artist (book) The Collected Best of Watercolor America, 2002, International Dictionary Encyclopedia of Modern and Contemporary Art, 2004 (cert. merit and medal, 2004), 2005 (cert. merit and medal, 2005), La Mer. Regards de Pientres et d'ecrivains, 2005, International Dictionary Encyclopedia of Modern and Contemporary Art, 2006 (cert. merit and medal, 2006), Art, Peintres et Sculpteurs du XV au XXI Siecle, 2006, Portraits D'Artists Regards, Pau France, 2007. Asst. precinct chmn. Rep. Party, Houston, 1953—63; artist in residence Tex. and Denton Hist. Commn., Denton, 1980—83; tchr. adult bible classes Ch. of Christ, Houston, 1960—, Brownsville, 1960—, Denton, 1975—; pres. co-founder Nat. Registry for DeHaven Family 1698. Named Best of Watercolor painting light and shadow, 1997; recipient Grumbacher Art award, Southwestern Watercolor Soc., Dallas, Tex. 1982, Best of Show Pres. award, Soc. Watercolor Artists, Ft. Worth, Tex., 1986, Tex. Fine Arts Regional citation, Tex., 1967, 1st Place Graphics, Nacogdoches Ann., 1973, Dist. Svc. award, Tex. Hist. Commn., 1980—81, Acad. Knight of Verbano, 2004—05; Ann. Scholarship award, Delta Psi Delta Nat. Hon. Art Orgn., Denton, Tex., 1974—75. Mem.: Soc. Watercolor Artists (signature mem. 1986), So. Watercolor Soc. (exhibiting mem. 1982), Associated Creative Artists (signature mem. 1984—), Southwestern Watercolor Soc. (signature mem., bd. mem. 1982—), Laredo Art Ctr. (life), La. Watercolor Soc. (life; academical mem. 1980—2007), Brownsville Art League (life; instr., bd. mem. 1959—). Republican. Ch. Of Christ. Avocations: poetry, genealogy. Office: studio d'Bertine PO Box 2965 Denton TX 76202 Office Phone: 940-387-9993. Personal E-mail: dwbertine@netzero.net.

BERTINO, JOSEPH ROCCO, oncologist, educator; b. Port Chester, NY, Aug. 16, 1930; s. Joseph and Madaleine (Posillipo) B.; m. Mary Patricia Hagemeyer, Sept. 29, 1956; children: Frederick, Amy Marie, Thomas Allen, Paul Phillip. Student, Cornell U., 1947-50; MD, SUNY Downstate Med. Ctr., 1954. Resident, internal medicine Veteran's Adminstrn. Hosp., Phila., 1955—56; fellow, hematology U. Washington, Seattle, 1958—61; US Pub. Health Svc. Rsch. fellow, hematology U. Wash. Sch. Medicine, Seattle, 1958-61; dir. Yale Comprehensive Cancer Ctr., including dir. & assoc. dir. for clin. rsch., 1973—86; mem. faculty Yale U. Sch. Medicine, 1961-87, assoc. prof. pharmacology and medicine, 1964-67, prof., 1967-87, Am. Cancer Soc. prof., 1975—; chmn. molecular pharmacology and therapeutics prog., mem., co-head prog. in develop. therapy and clin. investigation Meml. Sloan Kettering Inst. for Cancer Rsch., 1987—; prof. medicine and pharmacology Cornell U. Sch. Medicine, NYC, 1987—; joined Cancer Inst. NJ, New Brunswick, NJ, 2002, assoc. dir., chief scientific officer, 2004, acting chair, interim dir., 2007—; disting. prof. medicine and pharmacology UMDNJ-Robert Wood Johnson Med. Sch., 2002—. State scholar for medicine, 1950—54; prof. Am. Cancer Soc. Contbr. articles to profl. jours. Recipient Honor medal Am. Cancer Soc., 1992. Mem. Am. Soc. for Clin. Investigation, Am. Soc. Hematology, Biol. Chemists, Pharmacology and Therapeutics. Home: 117 Sunset Hill Rd Branford CT 06405-6419 Office: Cancer Inst NJ 195 Little Albany St New Brunswick NJ 08903 Office Phone: 732-235-8510, 732-235-2465. Office Fax: 732-235-7355. Business E-Mail: bertinoj@umdnj.edu.

BERTLES, JOHN FRANCIS, physician, educator; b. Spokane, Wash., June 8, 1925; s. John Francis and Henrita Swart (Brown) B.; m. Jeannette Winans, 1948 (div. 1978); children: Mark Dwight, Jacquelyn Eve, John Francis; m. Lila Rodriguez, 1981. BS, Yale U., 1945; MD, Harvard U., 1952. Diplomate Am. Bd. Internal Medicine. Intern Presbyterian Hosp., NYC, 1952-53, asst. resident in medicine, 1953-55; research fellow in hematology U. Rochester and Strong Meml. Hosp., 1955-56; research fellow in immunohematology Harvard U. Med. Sch. and Mass. Gen. Hosp., Boston, 1956-58, research fellow in hematology, 1958-59; instr. in medicine Harvard U. Med. Sch. at Mass. Gen. Hosp., 1959-61; dir. hematology-oncology div. St. Luke's Hosp. Center, NYC, 1962-95, asst. attending physician, 1962-64, assoc. attending physician, 1964-71, attending physician, 1971-95; dir. transfusion services St. Luke's Roosevelt Hosp. Ctr., 1981-95; sr. research assoc. dept. biol. scis. Columbia U., 1970-71, asst. clin. prof. medicine, 1962-67, assoc. clin. prof., 1967-71, assoc. prof., 1971-74, prof., 1974-95, prof. emeritus of medicine, 1995—; attending physician Montefiore Med. Ctr., NYC, 1995-97; clin. prof. medicine Albert Einstein Coll. Medicine, NYC, 1995-97. Vis. prof. medicine Nuffield dept. clin. medicine Radcliffe Infirmary, U. Oxford, Eng., 1977-78; cons. to various govt. agys., including hematology study sect. NIH, 1972-76, 82-84, blood rsch. rev. group, 1978-82; mem. dirs. coun. N.Y. Heart Assn., 1974-90; mem. basic rsch. adv. com. Nat. Found. March of Dimes, 1977-80. Contbr. articles to profl. publs. Ensign USNR, 1945-46. Fellow ACP; mem. Am. Soc. Clin. Investigation, Am. Physiol. Soc., Am. Soc. Hematology, Am. Fedn. Clin. Rsch., Am. Chem. Soc., Alpha Omega Alpha. Office: 72 Pondfield Rd W Apt 3K Bronxville NY 10708

BERTOLAMI, CHARLES NICHOLAS, dean, dental educator, oral surgeon; b. Lorain, Ohio, Dec. 31, 1949; s. Salvatore Charles and Michela (Orlando) B.; m. Linda Silva, June 27, 1977; children: Michela, Joseph. AA, Lorain CC, 1969; DDS summa cum laude, Ohio State U., 1974; DMS, Harvard U., 1979. Diplomate Am. Bd. Oral and Maxillofacial Surgery. Chief resident Mass. Gen. Hosp., Boston, 1979-80, asst. oral surgeon, 1983; asst. prof. U. Conn., 1980-83, Harvard Sch. Dental Medicine, Boston, 1983-89; assoc. prof. UCLA Sch. Dentistry, 1989-90, prof., 1990—95, chmn. sect. oral & maxillofacial surgery, 1989—95, assoc. dean faculty affairs; chief dental svcs. UCLA Med. Ctr., 1990—95; dean, prof. oral and maxillofacial surgery Sch. Dentistry U. Calif., San Francisco, 1995—2007; dean NYU Coll. Dentistry, 2007—. Mem. editl. bd. Jour. of Oral and Maxillofacial Surgery; contbr. articles to profl. jours. Recipient Callahan Meml. award Ohio Dental Assn., 1974; named Disting. Alumnus, Ohio State U. Coll. Dentistry, 1996, Harvard Sch. Dental Medicine, 2000; grantee USPHS, 1983-. Fellow Am. Assn. Oral and Maxillofacial Surgeons (exec. com. 1983-84), Am. Coll. Dentists, Internat. Coll. Dentists; mem. ADA , Internat. Assn. Dental Rsch. (program chmn. 1984-85), Am. Assn. Dental Rsch. (v.p. 2000-01, pres.-elect, 2001-02, pres. 2002-03). Achievements include Contribution to understanding the origin of abnormal wound healing in conditions of excessive scar formation. Office: NYU Coll Dentistry Office of Dean 345 E 24th St New York NY 10010 Office Phone: 212-998-9898.*

BERTOLET, CAROLINE LYNNE GEORGEANNE, special education educator, labor union administrator; b. Phila., Oct. 16, 1948; d. George Clayton and Caroline E. Werner; m. William B. Bertolet, II, June 6, 1980; 1 child, Leslie Lynne Hollingsworth. BS, Indiana U. Pa., 1970; MA in Psychology, West Chester U., Pa., 1974; cert. in spl. edn. supervisory, Pa. State U., 1983, cert. elem. and secondary prin., 1996. Tchr. Marple Newtown Sch. Dist., Newtown Square, Pa., 1970—, chairperson student assistance program, 1998—2004, mem. negotiating team, 2005—06. Chairperson registration SPCA Walk for Paws, Chester County, Pa.; treas. SPCA Aux., Chester County, Pa. Mem.: Pa. State Edn. Assn. (profl. rights and responsibilities commr. 2002—), Marple Newtown Edn. Assn. (pres. 2002—, grievance chair 1988—), Pi Lambda Theta. Avocations: gardening, reading, knitting, swimming, aerobics. Home: 1181 Fielding Dr West Chester PA 19382 Office: Marple Newtown Sch Dist 120 Media Line Rd Newtown Square PA 19073

BERTOLET, RODNEY JAY, philosophy educator; b. Allentown, Pa., Mar. 22, 1949; s. Frank and Helen (Johnson) B. BA, Franklin & Marshall Coll., 1971; PhD, U. Wis., 1977. Asst. prof. philosophy Purdue U., West Lafayette, Ind., 1977-82, assoc. prof. philosophy, 1982-90, prof. philosophy, 1990—, dept. head, 1991—. Author: What Is Said, 1990. Mem. Am. Philos. Assn., Ind. Philos. Assn. (pres. 1983-84). Office: Purdue Univ Dept Philosophy 100 N University St West Lafayette IN 47907-2098 Office Phone: 765-494-4275. E-mail: bertolet@purdue.edu.

BERTOLINI, MARK T., insurance company executive; BSc in bus. adminstrn., Wayne State U.; MBA in fin., Cornell U. CEO, previously COO SelectCare, 1992—95; exec. v.p. NYLCare Health Plans; sr. v.p., nat. sales & delivery Cigna Corp., 2000—02, sr. v.p., regional & middle market, 2002—03; sr. v.p., splty. products Aetna Inc., Hartford, Conn., 2003—05, sr. v.p. specialty group, 2005, sr. v.p. regional bus., 2005—06, exec. v.p. regional bus., 2006—07, exec. v.p. bus. ops., 2007—. Office: Aetna Inc 151 Farmington Ave Hartford CT 06156*

BERTOLINI, ROBERT J., pharmaceutical executive; BA in Econs., Rutgers U. CPA. With Coopers & Lybrand, 1983; ptnr. Pricewaterhouse-Coopers, 1993—2003; exec. v.p., CFO Schering-Plough Corp., 2003—. Mem.: Am. Coll. Emergency Physicians. Office: Schering-Plough Corp 2000 Galloping Hill Rd Kenilworth NJ 07033-0530*

BERTOLINO, DEAN A., lawyer; b. Nyack, NY, Nov. 7, 1968; BA, U. Ariz., 1990; JD, Harvard U., 1994. Bar: Mass. 1994, NY 1995. Assoc. Brown & Wood LLP, NYC, 1994—99; asst. gen. counsel BOC Group, Murray Hill, NJ, 1999—2001; v.p., gen. counsel Airgas, Inc., Radnor, Pa., 2001—. Mem.: ABA, Assn. of Bar City of NY. Office: Airgas Inc 259 N Radnor Chester Rd Ste 100 PO Box 6675 Radnor PA 19087-8675 Office Phone: 610-230-3070. Office Fax: 610-687-1052.*

BERTOLUCCI, BERNARDO, film director; b. Parma, Italy, Mar. 16, 1941; s. Attilio and Ninetta Bertolucci; m. Clare Peploe, 1978. Attended, Rome U., Italy. Dir.(films): The Grim Reaper, 1962, Before the Revolution, 1964 (Young Critics award Cannes Film Festival), La Via del Petrolio, 1965, His Partner, 1968, The Conformist, 1970 (Nat. Film Critics Best Dir. award), The Spider's Strategem, 1970, Last Tango in Paris, 1972, 1900, 1976, Luna, 1979, Tragedy of a Ridiculous Man, 1981, The Last Emperor (Golden Globe award for Best Dramatic Picture, 1987, Best Dir., Best Screenplay, Best Original Score, Best Editor, Best Cinematography, Best Sound, Best Prodn. Design, Art Dir., Best Costume Design, Acad. award fo, Acad. award for Best Picture of Yr., Best Dir., Best Screenplay Adaptation, Best Film honor Brit. Acad. Film and TV Arts, The Sheltering Sky, 1990, Little Buddha, 1994, Stealing Beauty, 1996, Besieged, 1998 (Globo D'Oro award for Best Film 1999; actor: (of poems). Office: care Recorded Picture Co 24 Hanway St London W1T 1UH England also: care Jeff Berg ICM 8942 Wilshire Blvd Beverly Hills CA 90211-1934

BERTONE, THOMAS LEE, management consultant; b. Pittsburg, Kans., Nov. 15, 1938; s. Anthony and Gaye Kittle Bertone; m. Ellen Reville Kniffin, Sept. 6, 1969; children: Elizabeth Reville, Katherine Logan. AB cum laude, Harvard U., 1960; MA, Stanford U., 1963; D Pub. Adminstrn., George Washington U., 1971. Budget examiner on det. U.S. Bur. Budget, Washington, 1964-67; cons., assoc. Booz Allen & Hamilton, Washington, 1967-69, 78-80; dir. budget rev. Office Fiscal Affairs, N.J. Legislature, Trenton, 1973-75, exec. dir. Office Fiscal Affairs, 1975-78; regional dir. state and local govt. cons. Coopers & Lybrand, Phila., 1980-82; dir. internat. cons. Grant Thornton, Chgo., 1986-90; pres. Thomas L. Bertone & Assocs., Pennington, N.J., 1982-86, 90—. World Bank decentralization adviser to permanent sec. Sri Lanka Ministry Local Govt., 1985-89; ADB advisor to budget dir. Budget Office, Federated States Micronesia, 1993-95; IMF budget advisor to min. fin. Palestine Authority, Gaza and West Bank, 1995; U.S. AID intergovtl. fiscal rels. advisor to prime min. and min. fin. Fedn. Bosnia Herzegovina, 1997; evaluator for U.S. Agy. Internat. Develop. fiscal reform program in Kosovo, 2003. Sr. advisor on state fin. and mgmt. to gov. candidate State of W.Va., Charleston, 1970-72; pro bono cons. NJ Office Mgmt. and Budget, Trenton, 1999; dir. Dummerston Sch. Bd., Vt., 2006-. 2d lt. US Army, 1964, Korea. Mem. ASPA, Inst. Mgmt. Cons. (cert.), Assn. Govt. Accts. (cert. govt. fin. mgr.). Democrat. Avocations: scuba diving, skiing, horseback riding, shooting and gun collecting, dogs. Home and Office: 337 Waterman Rd East Dummerston VT 05346 Home Phone: 802-387-4567; Office Phone: 802-387-4567. Business E-Mail: tom_bertone_ab60@post.harvard.edu.

BERTOZZI, CAROLYN R., chemistry professor; b. Boston, 1966; AB in Chemistry summa cum laude, Harvard U.; PhD, U. Calif., Berkeley, 1993. Summer intern Bell Labs, 1987; predoc. fellow Office of Naval Rsch., 1988—91; postdoc. fellow U. Calif., San Francisco, prof. chemistry Berkeley, 1996—, Joel H. Hildebrand chair in chemistry, 1998—2000, T. Z. and Irmgard Chu disting. prof. Contbr. articles to profl. jours. including J. Org. Chem., Chem. and Biol., Biochem. Recipient MacArthur Found. award, 1999, Presdl. Early Career award in Sci. and Engring., 2000, Donald Sterling Noyce prize for excellence in undergrad. tchg., 2001, Irving Sigal Young Investigator award, Protein Soc., 2002. Fellow: Am. Acad. Arts and Sciences; mem.: NAS, Am. Chem. Soc. (Arthur C. Cope Scholar award 1999, Award in Pure Chemistry 2001). Office: U Calif Berkeley Chemistry Dept 820 Latimer Hall Berkeley CA 94720-0001 Office Phone: 510-643-1682. Office Fax: 510-643-2628. E-mail: bertozzi@cchem.berkeley.edu.

BERTRAM, JEAN DESALES, writer; b. Burlington, Iowa, Sept. 28; d. Val Randall and Ruth Cecilia Bertram; 1 child, Larkin Bertram-Cox Montgomery. BA, U. N.C., Greensboro, 1942; MA, U. Minn., 1951; PhD, Stanford U., 1963. Reporter Greensboro News Record, 1942-43; founder dept. pub. rels. Burlington Industries, Greensboro, 1943-49; asst. to dean edn. U. N.C., Greensboro, 1949-50; instr. U. Minn., Mpls., 1950-51; dir. radio performance Mpls. Vocat. High Sch., 1951-52; dir. Children's Theatre Touring Co., Jr. League Mpls., 1951-52; prof. theatre arts San Francisco State U., 1952-88. Cons. Wadsworth Pub. Co., Belmont, Calif., 1966; dir. Readers' Repertory, San Francisco State U., 1967-72; dir. Jean De Sales Bertram Players, San Francisco, 1971-74; founder, developer storytelling program San Francisco State U., 1971-88; cons. Scott-

Foresman, Chgo., 1983; senator acad. senate San Francisco State U., 1983-84, dir. com. for lectures, arts and spl. programs, 1985-87; tax preparer, 1994; founder, dir. The O'Connor Woods Drama Soc., 2004—. Author: (textbooks) The Oral Experience of Literature, 1967, The Actor Speaks, 4 edits., 1981-87, Tell Me a Story!, 5 edits., 1982-88; author, dir. Girl Scout Nat. Conv. pageant Finding Your Own Adventure, 1955; prodr., dir., adapter, editor: (religious plays) A Symphonetic Easter Drama, 1954, The Awakening, 1954, The Vision of Isaiah, 1970, The Cherry Tree, 1971; author, dir.: (plays) American Cameos, 1976, Jeremiah The Prophet, 1999; author: (poem) Cosmorama, 1971; actress one-woman show numerous women from Shakespeare's plays, 1971-88; author: (short story) The Giraffe and the Canary, 1999; contbr. articles to profl. jours. Stanford-Wilson fellow Stanford U., 1962-63. Mem. Acad. Am. Poets, O'Connor Woods Drama Soc. (founder, dir. 2004—), Phi Beta Kappa (sec. Omicron of Calif. chpt. 1977-79, 83-88, pres. 1979-81, v.p. 1981-83, ofcl. del. Triennial coun. 1979, 82). Avocations: sculpturing in clay, poetry writing, photography. Office Phone: 209-477-1355.

BERTRAM, MANYA M., retired lawyer; b. Denver; d. Samuel and Ruby (Feiner) Boran; m. Barry Bertram, June 19, 1938; children: H. Neal, Carel. JD magna cum laude, Southwestern U., 1962. Ptnr. Most and Bertram, LA; ret. Former trustee Southwestern U. Sch. Law, former pres. Southwestern U. Sch. Law Alumni Assn.; former bd. advisor Whittier Coll. of Law and LA Beverly Coll. Law; commr. Calif. Commn. on Aging, Sacramento, 1977-82; bd. dirs. Jewish Family Svc., LA, 1963-2001. Mem.: ABA, Calif. State Bar Assn., Federacion Internac. de Abagados, B'nai B'rith (life), Hadassah (life), Iota Tau Tau. Avocation: genealogy. Personal E-mail: manyamin@california.com.

BERTRAND, BETTY HARLEEN, nurse; b. Little Rock, Ark., July 17, 1960; d. Harley Walter and Joyce Elaine (Bryant) Baker; m. Robert K. Bertrand, June 13, 1980; children: Mary, Jessie, Alyssa, Jared. AA, Cerro Coso C.C., 1981; ADN, Texarkana Coll., 1989; BSN, U. Ark. Med. Sch., 1994. RN, Tex.; lic. vocat. nurse; cert. low risk neonatal care. Nurse asst. Ridgecrest (Calif.) Cmty. Hosp., 1982-85; lic. vocat. nurse Wadley Regional Med. Ctr., Texarkana, Tex., 1986-89, RN, 1989-92; field supervising nurse HealthCor Home Health, Texarkana, 1992-93; nurse Blankenship Dialysis Ctr., Texarkana, 1993-95; clin. instr. Texarkana Coll., 1995-97, instr. vocat. nursing program, 1997—; nurse St. Michael Health Care Ctr., 1995—. Baptist. Avocations: reading, cross stitching, crochet, parenting, piano. Home: 461 Knottingham Texarkana TX 75501-1316 Office Phone: 903-838-4541 ext. 3410. E-mail: dadmomb@msn.com, bbertran@texarkanacollege.edu.

BERTRAND, FREDERIC HOWARD, retired insurance company executive; b. Montpelier, Vt., Aug. 5, 1936; s. George Joseph and Dolores Gertrude (Mallory) B.; m. Elinor Maude Pierce, June 11, 1960; children: Kimberly Sue, Michael Scott, John Frederic (dec.). BSCE magna cum laude, Norwich U., 1958; postgrad., Georgetown U. Law Sch., 1961-63, Carnegie-Mellon U. Sch. Indsl. Adminstrn., 1967-68; JD, Coll. William and Mary, 1967; D in Bus. Mgmt. (hon.), Norwich U., 1991. Bar: Va. 1967, Vt. 1970; registered profl. engr., Vt. Engr.-adminstr. CIA, Washington, 1960-70; asst. counsel, assoc. counsel, v.p., sr. v.p., bd. dirs. Nat. Life Ins. Co., Montpelier, 1970-83, exec. v.p., chief oper. officer, 1983-85, pres., chief oper. officer, 1985-87, chmn., chief exec. officer, 1987-97, also bd. dirs. Bd. dirs., chair Chittenden Bank, Burlington, 2004-07; bd. dirs. Union Mut. Fire Ins. Co., New Eng. Guaranty Ins. Co., Montpelier; bd. dirs. Cen. Vt. Pub. Svcs. Co., Rutland, 1985-2007, chair, 1997-2006; bd. dirs. Vt. Elec. Transmission Co., 1998-2007; bd. dirs. Catamount Energy Corp., 1995—2004, chair, 1997-2002; bd. dirs. The Home Svc. Store, Rutland, 2000-07; civilian aide to Sec. of Army, Washington, 1981-93. Alderman City of Montpelier, 1974-76, pres. city coun., 1975-76, mayor, 1976-78; bd. dirs. Ctrl. Vt. Econ. Devel. Corp., 1985-98; chmn. Vt. Bus. Roundtable, 1995-97, bd. dirs., 1987-98; trustee Norwich U., Northfield, Vt., 1979-85. Recipient Outstanding Alumnus award Norwich U., 1980, Citizen of Yr. award Vt. C. of C., 1992, U.S. Army Disting. Civilian Svc. award, 1993. Mem. Am. Coun. Life Ins. (bd. dirs. 1989-94, chmn. 1993), Vt. Bar Assn., Washington County Bar Assn., Theta Chi, Epsilon Tau Sigma. Republican. Roman Catholic.

BERTRAND, LUC, stock exchange executive; b. Feb. 14, 1951; BA in philosophy, Univ. Ottawa, Can. Co-founder Pollit, Bertrand brokerage firm, Canada, 1985; v.p. and mng. dir. Instl. Sales Group Nat. Bank Fin., Canada; bd. dir. Montreal Stock Exch., Canada, 1992—94, mem. exec. com., 1994—96, vice chmn., 1996—97, chmn., 1998—2000, pres. and CEO, 2000—; ptnr., exec v.p., & resident dir. Deacon Capital Corp., Canada, 1993—98. Former gov. Canadian Securities Inst.; gov. Canadian Investor Protection Fund, 1996—2002; vice chmn. bd. Boston Options Exch. Group LLC; mem. bd. Internat. Fin. Ctr. Montreal, Regulatory Svc. Inc., Securities Industry Adv. Coun., Canadian Derivatives Clearing Corp. Office: Bourse de Montreal Inc PO Box 61 800 Victoria Square Montreal H4Z1A9 Canada Office Phone: 514-871-2424.

BERTSCH, FREDERICK CHARLES, III, appraiser, finance company executive; b. Bklyn., Mar. 17, 1942; s. Frederick Charles and Norma Elizabeth (Hodgkins) B.; m. Ana Maria Carmen Natteri, Aug. 20, 1971; children— Frederick C., Ana Cecilia BA, Wesleyan U., Middletown, Conn., 1965; MBA, U. Pa., 1967. Accredited sr. appraiser. Supr. Ford Motor Co., Dearborn, Mich., 1967-69; cons. Cresap, McCormick & Paget Inc., NYC, 1969-73; dir. corp. devel. IU Internat., Phila., 1973-76; v.p. corp. devel. Enterra Corp., Radnor, Pa., 1976-84, v.p. fin., chief fin. officer, 1985-86; founder F.C. Bertsch & Co., Inc., St. Davids, Pa., 1988—; v.p., CFO Gladwin Corp., Coraopolis, Pa., 1995; accredited sr. appraiser Am. Soc. Appraisers, 2006—. Pres. Radnor ABC (A Better Chance), Wayne, Pa., 1984-85, now bd. dirs Avocations: golf, fishing, gardening. Home and Office: 416 Round Hill Rd Saint Davids PA 19087-4728 Personal E-mail: fcb@fcbertsch.com.

BERTSCH, GARY KENNETH, political science professor; b. Vallejo, Calif., June 8, 1944; s. Gideon and Freda (Hepper) B.; m. Joan Elizabeth Brubacher, Feb. 29, 1964; children: Dawn, Todd, Jason. BA, Idaho State U., 1966; MA, U. Oreg., 1968, PhD, 1970. Vis. prof. U. Zagreb, Yugoslavia, 1969-70; prof. polit. sci. U. Ga., Athens, 1970—. Vis. prof. nat. security affairs Air U., Dept. Def., Maxwell AFB, Ala., 1981-82; Fulbright prof. politics U. Lancaster, Eng., 1984-85; dir. Ctr. Internat. Trade and Security, 1987—. Author: East-West Strategic Trade and the Atlantic Alliance, 1983, Reform and Revolution in Communist Systems, 1991, others; editor: Engaging India, 1999, Dangerous Weapons, Desperate States, 1999, Crossroads and Conflict, 2000; contbr. articles to profl. jours. Recipient Tchg. award U. Ga., 1970-2005, profl. chair for disting. tchg., 1982—, numerous rsch. grants, 1970—. Mem. Am. Polit. Sci. Assn., Internat. Studies Assn. Home: 228 Henderson Ave Athens GA 30605-1037 Office: Univ Ga Ctr for Internat Trade and Security Athens GA 30602 Home Phone: 706-549-5198; Office Phone: 706-542-2985. Business E-Mail: gbertsch@uga.edu.

BERTSCH, PATRICIA ANN, nature center director; b. Orange, NJ, Jan. 14, 1969; d. Margaret Mary and John Patrick Murray; m. Leon James Bertsch, Oct. 19, 1997. BS in Marine Biology, Richard Stockton Coll., 1991. Instr. Marine Sci. Consortium, Wallops Island, Va., 1992—93, Barrier Island Environ. Edn. Ctr., John's Island, SC, 1993—94; ednl. coord. Jenkinson's Aquarium, Point Pleasant, NJ, 1995—95; pk. naturalist Trailside Nature & Sci. Ctr., Mountainside, NJ, 1995—98, asst. dir., 1998—2002, dir., 2002—. Intern Kewalo Basin Marine Mammal Lab., Honolulu, 1995—96; vol. Earthwatch, Mass., 1999; exec. dir. Trailside Mus. Assn., Mountainside, 2002—; mem. Cranford Environ. Commn., 2004—. Mem.: Alliance N.J. Environ. Edn. (assoc.). Avocations: bird-watching, camping, hiking, kayaking, travel. Home: 110 Kenilworth Blvd Cranford NJ 07016 Office: Trailside Nature & Sci Ctr 452 New Providence Rd Mountainside NJ 07092 Home Phone: 908-497-0379. Office Fax: 908-789-3270. E-mail: pbertsch@ucnj.org.

BERTSCH, PAUL M., ecologist, director; b. Oct. 28, 1956; BS in Plant Sci., U. Conn., 1978; MS in Soil Chemistry, Va. Poly. Inst., 1980; PhD in Soil Phys. Chemistry-Mineralogy, U. Ky., 1983. Rsch. specialist dept. agronomy U. Ky., Lexington, 1983, asst. prof. dept. agronomy, 1984; asst. rsch. prof. divsn. biogeochemistry Savannah River Ecology Lab., Aiken, SC, 1984—89; vis. scientist applied and atomic physics Nat. Synchrotron Light Source, Brookhaven Nat. Lab., Upton, NY, 1992—93; assoc. rsch. prof. divsn. bigeochemistry Savannah River Ecology Lab., Aiken, SC, 1989—95; prof., dir. Advanced Analytical Ctr. for Environ. Scis., U. Ga., Savannah River Ecology Lab., Aiken, SC, 1995—, dir., 1999—; faculty mem. Med. U. S.C., Charleston, 2001—; affiliate facutly mem. engring. U. Ga., 2002—. Presenter in field. Contbr. articles to profl. jours. Fellow: Soil Sci. Soc. Am. (assoc. editor 1994—2001, selection com. 1999—, evaluation com., chmn. divisn. soil chemistry 2003—04, Career Achievement award 2004, Jackson award 1996), Am. Soc. Agronomy; mem.: AAAs, Internat. Soil Sci. Soc., Internat. Clay Minerals Soc., Clay Minerals Soc. (coun. 1997, awards com. 2001, v.p. 2001, program devel. com. 2004—), Am. Geophysical Union, Am. Chem. Soc., Sigma Xi, Phi Sigma, Phi Kappa Phi, Gamma Sigma Delta. Achievements include patents for in-situ groundwater remediation by selective colloid mobilization, 1998. Office: Savannah River Ecology Lab Univ Ga Drawer E Aiken SC 29808 Business E-Mail: bertsch@srel.edu.

BERTSCHY, TIMOTHY L., lawyer; b. Pekin, Ill., Nov. 12, 1952; AB magna cum laude, U. Ill., 1974; JD, George Washington U., 1977. Bar: Ill. 1977, U.S. Dist. Ct. (cen. dist.) Ill., U.S. Ct. Appeals (7th cir.) 1982, U.S. Supreme Ct. Atty. Heyl, Royster, Voelker & Allen, Peoria, Ill., 1977—84, ptnr., 1984—. Author articles in law jours. Pres. Ill. Lawyers Assistance Prog., Ill. Equal Justice Found.; past pres. Ill. Coalition Equal Justice; co-chmn. Ill. Needs Study II. Fellow Ill. State Bar Found., Am. Bar Found.; mem. ABA (ho. dels. 1995—, co-chair sect. litigation bus. torts com. 2003-, bd. gov. 2004-), Ill. State Bar Assn. (bd. gov. 1984-90, pres. 1998-99, Lincoln Legal Writing Award), Peoria County Bar Assn (chmn. Diversity Comm.,bd. mem.); Am. Judicature Soc.; Bar Assn. Cent. & So. Dist. (co-chmn. Rules & Practices); Ill. Township Attys. Assn. (pres. 1989-93, bd. dir. 1985-92 & 2002-). Office: Heyl Royster Voelker & Allen PC 124 SW Adams St Ste 600 Peoria IL 61602-1352 E-mail: tbertschy@hrva.com.*

BERTSIMAS, DIMITRIS J., mathematician, researcher, educator; MS in Ops. Rsch., MIT, 1987, PhD in Ops. Rsch. and Applied Math., 1988. Asst. prof. mgmt. science Sloan Sch. Mgmt., MIT, 1988—92, assoc. prof. ops. rsch., 1992—93, E. Pennell Brooks prof. ops. rsch., 1993—94, prof. ops. rsch., 1995—97, Boeing prof. ops. rsch., 1997—. Vis. prof. Stanford U., 1996; Miller vis. prof. U. Calif., Berkeley, 2002. Mem.: NAE, Inst. Ops. Rsch. and Mgmt. Scis., Am. Math. Soc., Soc. Industrial and Applied Math., Math. Programming Soc., Econometrics Soc., Am. Fin. Soc., Inst. Math. Statistics. Office: MIT Sloan Sch Mgmt E53-363 Cambridge MA 02139 Office Phone: 617-253-4223. Office Fax: 617-258-7579. E-mail: dbertsim@mit.edu.

BERTUCELLI, ROBERT EDWARD, accountant, educator; b. Bklyn., Mar. 23, 1948; s. Leo and Gertrude Augusta (Roggenkamp) B.; children: Nikole, Gina; m. Loretta Strand, Jan. 7, 2005. AAS, Suffolk C.C., 1968; BS, C.W. Post Coll., 1970; MS, L.I. U., 1974. CPA, N.Y.; cert. fin. planner; chartered life underwriter. Acct. Arthur Young & Co., Westbury, N.Y., 1970-72; sr. tax. mgr. Peat Marwick Mitchell & Co., Jericho, N.Y., 1972-77; prof. acctg. and taxation C.W. Post Coll., 1977—; pvt. practice Smithtown, N.Y., 1977-83, Hauppauge, N.Y., 1989-94; ptnr. Bertucelli Barragato & Co., Smithtown, 1983-89, Bertucelli & Malaga L.L.P., Ronkonkoma, NY, 1994—. Lectr. Person Wolinsky Assocs., 1977—. Mem. St. Patrick's Sch. Bd., Smithtown, N.Y., 1982-92, pres., 1985-88, 90-92; bd. trustees, St. Charles Hosp. and Rehab. Ctr., Port Jefferson, NY, 2003—. Mem.: AICPA, Estate Planning Coun. (pres. 1996—97), Nat. Assn. Accts., N.Y. Soc. CPAs (author, lectr. 1989—, Haskins Silver medal 1972), Smithtown C. of C. (treas. 1988—90). Roman Catholic. Office Phone: 631-738-0200. Business E-Mail: reb@taxprofs.com.

BERTUZZI, TODD, professional hockey player; b. Sudbury, Ont., Can., Feb. 2, 1975; m. Julie Bertuzzi; children: Tag, Jaden. Right wing NY Islanders, 1995—98, Vancouver Canucks, 1998—2006, Fla. Panthers, 2006—07, Detroit Red Wings, 2007, Anaheim Ducks, 2007—. Mem. Team Can., Olympic Games, Torino, Italy, 2006. Named to NHL All-Star Game, 2003, 2004, First All-Star Team, NHL, 2003. Office: Anaheim Ducks 2695 E Katella Ave Anaheim CA 92806*

BERUBE, BRIAN A., lawyer, chemicals executive; b. 1962; BA, Coll. Holy Cross; JD, Boston Coll. Bar: 1988. Law clk. New Hampshire Supreme Ct.; mem. corp. dept. Choate, Hall & Stewart, Boston; of counsel Cabot Corp., Boston, 1994—2003, v.p., gen. counsel, 2003—. Bd. dirs. New Eng. Legal Found. Mem.: ABA, Boston Bar Assn., Am. Corp. Counsel Assn. Office: Cabot Corp Two Seaport Ln Ste 1300 Boston MA 02210-2019 Office Phone: 617-342-6175. Office Fax: 617-342-6103.*

BERVEN, NORMAN LEE, counselor, psychologist, educator; b. Des Moines, May 14, 1945; s. Arthur N. and Ruth N. (Sharp) B.; m. Estella Stone, Oct. 11, 1969; 1 child, Jennifer. BS, U. Iowa, 1967, MA, 1969; PhD, U. Wis., 1973. Lic. psychologist; cert. rehab. counselor, lic. profl. counselor. Rehab. counselor San Mateo County Mental Health Svc., San Mateo, Calif., 1969-71; rsch. assoc. Internat. Ctr. for Disabled, NYC, 1973-75; asst. prof. counseling and spl. svcs. Seton Hall U., South Orange, N.J., 1975-76; asst. prof. to prof. rehab. psychology, program chair U. Wis., Madison, 1976—. Cons. to univ., govt. and pvt. non-profit programs. Editor: Rehab. Counseling Bull., 1985-92, assoc. editor, 1982-85, editorial bd., 1980-82, 92—; mem. editl. bd. Rehab. Psychology, 1981-99, Vocat. Evaluation and Career Profl. Jour., 1980—, Assessment in Rehab. and Exceptionality, 1992-96, Jour. Counseling and Devel., 2006—; co-editor: Counseling Theories and Techniques for Rehabilitation Health Professionals, 2004; contbr. articles to profl. jours., chpts. to books. Mem. bd. visitors U. Wis. Sch. Edn., Madison, 2007—. Recipient Varsity Disting. Alumni award rehab. psychology program U. Wis., 1994, Disting. Alumni award grad. programs in rehab. U. Iowa, 1997; grantee U.S. Dept. Edn., 1986—, Spencer Found., 1981-82, Wis. Alumni Rsch. Found., 1979-80. Fellow APA (rehab., counseling and evaluation, measurement and stats. divsn.); mem. ACA (rsch. award 1986), Am. Rehab. Counseling Assn. (disting. profl. award 1990, rsch. award 1981, 84, 86, 92, 93, 95, 2000, 04, Disting. Career Rsch. award 1998), Nat. Rehab. Counselors and Educators Assn. (bd. dirs. N.J. chpt. 1975-76, bd. dirs. Wis. chpt. 1981-83, bd. dirs. Calif. chpt. 1971, Meritorious Svc. award Wis. chpt. 1992), Nat. Rehab. Assn. (Grad. Lit. award 1968, bd. dirs. S.W. Wis. chpt. 1980-2003, San Mateo chpt. 1969-71, Disting. Svc. award Wis. chpt. 1997), Assn. for Counselor Edn. and Supervision, Assn. for Assessment in Counseling and Edn., Assn. for Specialists in Group Work, Vocat. Evaluation and Work Adjustment Assn., Nat. Coun. on Rehab. Edn., Nat. Coun. Measurement Edn., NAMI (Nat. Alliance for the Mentally Ill) Wis. Home: 417 Samuel Dr Madison WI 53717-2144 Office: U Wis Madison Rehab Psychology 432 N Murray St Madison WI 53706-1407 Home Phone: 608-833-3055; Office Phone: 608-263-7917. Business E-Mail: nlberven@wisc.edu.

BERWICK, DONALD MARK, medical institute administrator; b. NYC, Sept. 9, 1946; m. Ann Greenberg; children: Ben, Dan, Jessica, Rebecca. MPA summa cum laude, Harvard U., MD cum laude, 1972. Assoc. pediatrics Children's Hosp., Boston; cons. pediatrics Mass. Gen. Hosp.; co-founder, co-principal investigator Nat. Demonstration Project on Quality Improvement in Healthcare, 1987—91; pres., CEO Inst. Healthcare Improvement, Boston. Clinical prof. pediatrics and health care policy Harvard Med. Sch.; vice-chmn. US Preventive Services Task Force, 1990—96; mem. adv. commn. Consumer Protection & Quality in Health-care Industry, 1997, 98. Co-author: Curing Health Care, New Rules: Regulation, Markets and the Quality of American Health Care; editl. bd. The British Med. Jour.; contbr. articles to profl. jour. Ind. mem., bd. trustees Am. Hosp. Assn., 1996—99; mem. judges panel Malcolm Baldrige Nat. Quality Award Program, 1989—91. Mem.: Inst. Med. (coun. mem.), Nat. Acad. Sci. (mem., Inst. Medicine), Internat. Soc. Med. Decision-Making (pres.), Agency Healthcare Rsch. and Quality (chmn., nat. adv. coun.), Agency Healthcare Policy and Rsch. (chmn., Health Services Rsch. Rev. Study Sect. 1995—99). Office: Inst Healthcare Improvement 20 University Rd, 7th Fl Cambridge MA 02138 also: 375 Longwood Ave 4th Floor Boston MA 02215 Office Phone: 617-754-4852. Office Fax: 617-754-4865. E-mail: dberwick@ihi.org.*

BERWICK, FRANCES, broadcast executive; b. U.K. Former dir., internat. distbn. Channel 4, England; sr. v.p., programming, production Bravo, 1996—2006, exec. v.p., programming, production, 2007—. Prodr.: (TV films) Cirque du Soleil: Alegria, 2001, Straight Talk, 2006; (TV series) Inside the Actors Studio, The Art of Influence, 1998, Queer Eye for the Straight Guy, 2003— (Emmy award for outstanding reality program, 2004), Boy Meets Boy, 2003, Celebrity Poker Showdown, 2004, Kathy Griffin: My Life on the D-List, 2005, Project Runway, 2004—06, 30 Even Scarier Movie Moments, 2006. Office: Bravo 3000 W Alameda Ave Ste 250 Burbank CA 91523*

BERWICK, PHILIP, law librarian, director, dean; BA, U. Pa., 1973; JD, U. Toledo, 1978; AMLS, U. Mich., 1979. Mem. libr. staff U. Toledo Coll. Law, Law Libr. Congress; dir. law libr. George Mason U. Sch. Law; assoc. dean info. resources Law Libr., lectr. law Wash. U. Sch. Law, St. Louis. Mem.: ABA, Mid-Am. Assn. Law Librs., Am. Assn. Law Librs. Office: Wash U Sch Law Anheuser-Busch Hall One Brookings Dr Saint Louis MO 63130 Office Phone: 314-935-6440. E-mail: berwick@wulaw.wustl.edu.*

BERZ, DAVID RICHARD, lawyer; b. Chgo., May 21, 1948; m. Sherry Kirschner, Sept. 5, 1970; children: Douglas, Alexander. BA, George Washington U., 1970, JD with honors, 1973. Bar: DC 1973, US Supreme Ct. 1977, NY 1985. Mng. ptnr. Weil, Gotshal & Manges, LLP, Washington, 1985—, head environmental practice. Lectr. in field. Co-author (environmental treatise): Environmental Law in Real Estate and Business Transactions, 3 vols., 1992; contbr. articles to profl. jours.; mem. editl. bd. Chemical Waste Litigation Reporter 1986-; environmental editor Inside Litigation 1991- Bd. dirs., pres. Washington Hebrew Congregation; mem. exec. bd. Am. Jewish Com.; mem. bd. overseers Hebrew Union Coll., 2004—; mem. adv. bd. George Washington Univ. Nat. Law Ctr. Fellow Am. Bar Found.; mem. US C. of C. (mem. environ. com. 1993-), DC Bar, Fed. and ABA (Fellow (ABA), mem. environmental controls com., corp., banking and bus. law sect., vice-chmn. environmental quality control com. sect. administrv. law 1978-81). Office: Weilgotshallmanges 1300 I St NW Frnt 1 Washington DC 20005-3343 Office Phone: 202-682-7190. Office Fax: 202-857-0940. Business E-Mail: david.berz@weil.com.

BERZOFSKY, JAY A., medical researcher; b. Balt., Apr. 13, 1946; AB summa cum laude, in chemistry, Harvard U., 1967; PhD in biochemistry/biophysics, Albert Einstein Coll. Medicine, 1971, MD, 1973. Rsch. asst. rediat. rsch. unit Sinai Hosp., Balt., 1962—65; rsch. asst. dept. pharmacology, organic synthesis lab. Johns Hopkins Sch. Medicine, Balt., 1966; vis. scientist Ctr. Nat. de la Recherche Sci., Lab. d'Enzymologie, Gif-sur-Yvette, France, 1967; med. intern Mass. Gen. Hosp., Boston, 1973—74; rsch. assoc. Nat. Inst. Arthritis, Metabolism, and Digestive Diseases, NIH, Lab. Chem. Biology, Bethesda, Md., 1974—76; investigator metabolism br. Nat. Cancer Inst., NIH, Bethesda, 1976—79, sr. investigator, 1979—87, named head molecular immunogenetics and vaccine rsch. sect., metabolism br., 1987; chief Vaccine Br. Ctr. Cancer Rsch., Nat. Cancer Inst., NIH, Bethesda, 2003—. Hollister-Stier's Disting. lectr. Washington State U., 1986; McLaughlin vis. prof. U. Tex. Med. Sch., Galveston, 1992. Assoc. editor: Jour. Immunology, 1980—84, adv. editor: Molecular Immunology, 1985—88, mem. editl. bd.: Jour. Human Virology, 1997—, consulting editor: Jour. Clin. Investigation, 1998—. Named Disting. Alumnus of Yr., Albert Einstein Sch. Medicine, 2007; recipient Superior Svc. Award, USPHS. Fellow: AAAS (chair med. scis. sect. 2007—); mem.: Assn. Am. Physicians, Am. Soc. for Clin. Investigation (sec.-treas. 1989—92, pres.-elect 1992—93, pres. 1993—94), Am. Soc. Biol. Chemists (coun. mem. 1989—94), Am. Fedn. for Clin. Rsch., Am. Assn. Immunologists, N.Y. Acad. Scis., Assn. Harvard Chemists, Phi Beta Kappa. Achievements include research in T-lymphocyte recognition of antigens and applications; regulation of tumor immunosurveillance. Office: Ctr Cancer Rsch Vaccine Br Bldg 10 Rm 6B-04 10 Center Dr Bethesda MD 20892-1578 Office Phone: 301-496-6874. Office Fax: 301-480-0681. Business E-Mail: berzofsk@helix.nih.gov.

BERZON, FAYE CLARK, retired nursing educator; b. New Britain, Conn., Sept. 26, 1926; d. Bernard Francis and Elizabeth Tillie (Gross) Clark; m. Harry Berzon, June 18, 1961. Diploma, Beth Israel Hosp., 1947; BSN, Boston U., 1957, MSN, 1959; cert. advanced grad. studies, U. Mass., 1987, cert. in gerontology, 1993, adv. cert. in gerontology, 1994. Staff, head nurse, instr. Beth Israel Hosp., Boston, 1948-58; instr. nursing Simmons Coll., Boston, 1958-62, Cath. Labore Sch. Nursing, Dorchester, Mass., 1962-67; asst. prof. nursing Boston U. Sch. Nursing, 1967-70; div. chmn. human svcs. Massasoit C.C., Brockton, Mass., 1973-79, prof. nursing, 1970-92, chair nursing dept., 1988-91. Mem. acad. adv. com. to Mass. Bd. Higher Edn., 1975-76; ombudsman in nursing home South Shore Elder Svcs., 1993—. Author: (with Govoni, Berzon, Fall) Drugs and Nursing Implications, 1965, Nursing Outlook, 1970. Vol. Milton Meals on Wheels, Mass., 1978—90; scholarship com. New Eng. Sinai Hosp., 1992—, bd. advisors, 1996—; bd. dirs. Temple Israel-Saaron, 2000—, coun. aging, 2004—; adv. com. Respiratory Therapy Dept. Massasua C.C., 1976—. Mem. ANA, Nat. League Nursing (scholar 1963-79, accreditation visitor 1976-86), Nursing Archives, Mass. Assn. Older Ams., Mass. Gerontology Assn., Beth Israel Hosp. Nurses Alumnae Assn. (co-pres.), Hadassah-Landy-Kaplan Nurses Coun. (life), Sigma Theta Tau. Jewish. Home: 52 Harold St Sharon MA 02067-2544

BERZON, MARSHA S., federal judge; b. Cin., Apr. 17, 1945; BA, Radcliffe Coll., 1966; JD, Boalt Hall Sch. Law, 1973. Bar: Calif. 1973, DC 1975. Clerk Judge James Browning, 9th Cir., 1973—74, Justice William Brennan, 1974—75; atty. Woll & Mayer, Washington, 1975—77, Altshuler, Berzon, Nussbaum, Berzon & Rubin, San Francisco, 1978—2000; judge US Ct. Appeals (9th cir.), 2000—; assoc. gen. counsel AFL-CIO, 1987—99. Lectr. U. Calif. Sch. Social Welfare, Berkeley, Calif., 1992, La. State U. Sch. of Law, 2003; practitioner-in-residence Cornell Sch. of Law, NY, 1994, Ind. U. Law Sch., 1998. Mem.: Fed. Bar Assn., State Bar of Calif., DC Bar Assn., Am. Law Inst., Am. Bar Found. Office: US Ct Appeals 9th Cir 95 7th St San Francisco CA 94103-1526 Office Phone: 415-556-7800. Office Fax: 415-556-9491.*

BERZOW, HAROLD STEVEN, lawyer; b. Bklyn., Oct. 22, 1946; s. Julius and Lillian (Hershkowitz) Brzozowsky; m. Lynore Kushner, Aug. 22, 1970; children: Alan, Jason, Rachel. BA, Bklyn. Coll., 1968; JD,

Bklyn. Law Sch., 1971. Bar: N.Y. 1972, U.S. Dist. Ct. (so. and ea. dists.) 1973, U.S. Dist. Ct. (no. dist.) N.Y. 1998, U.S. Ct. Appeals (2d cir.) 1975, U.S. Supreme Ct. 1978. Assoc. Finkel, Nadler & Goldstein, NYC, 1971-77; ptnr. Finkel, Goldstein, Berzow, Rosenbloom & Nash, LLP, NYC, 1977—2004; ptnr., chmn. bus. reorganization practice group Ruskin Moscou Faltischek P.C., Uniondale, NY, 2004—. Mem. ABA, N.Y. County Bar Assn., N.Y. State Bar Assn., Am. Bankruptcy Inst. Jewish. Office: Ruskin Moscou Faltischek PC E Tower 15th Fl 1425 Reckson Plz Uniondale NY 11556 Office Phone: 516-663-6600. Business E-Mail: hberzow@rmfpc.com.

BESANT, LARRY XON, retired librarian, administrator, consultant; b. Centralia, Ill., Mar. 13, 1935; s. Ben Vern and Marjorie Loyce (Jarboe) B.; m. A. Jean Hofstetter, Dec. 31, 1953; children: Vicki, Lizabeth, Paul, Peter, Mary. AA, Centralia Jr. Coll., Ill., 1959; BS in Chemistry, U. Ill., Urbana, 1961, MSL.S., 1962. Asst. librarian Chem. Abstract Assn., Columbus, Ohio, 1962-68; asst. dir. U. Houston Library, 1968-71, Ohio State U. Library, Columbus, 1972-82; dir. libraries Linda Hall Library, Kansas City, Mo., 1982-85; dir. libraries Camden-Carroll Library Morehead (Ky.) State U., Ky., 1985—2004. Library cons. in field; speaker in field Contbr. numerous articles, revs. to Library Mgmt. Bull., Am. Libraries, other profl. publs. Served with USAF, 1954-57. Mem. ALA, Spl. Libre. Assn. (pres. Ky. chpt. 1996-97, 2002-2003), Ky. Libr. Assn. Democrat. Baptist. Avocations: fishing, book collecting (jack london). Home: 428 N Wilson Ave Morehead KY 40351-1172 Office: Morehead State U Camden-Carroll Libr Morehead KY 40351 Home Phone: 606-784-3933. Personal E-mail: l.besant@adelphia.net.

BESCH, EMERSON LOUIS, physiologist, educator, retired dean; b. Hammond, Ind., June 9, 1928; s. Ernest Henry and Carolyn (Dieckmann) B.; m. H. Jean Whitstine, May 28, 1955; children: Karen J., Kevin D., Kathleen L., Kristine A. BS in Biology/Chemistry, S.W. Tex. State U., 1952, MA in Biology/Chemistry, 1955; PhD in Physiology, U. Calif., Davis, 1964. Grad. instr. biology dept. S.W. Tex. State U., San Marcos, 1954-55; research asst., NIH trainee U. Calif., Davis, 1960-64, research physiologist, lectr., 1964-67; research assoc. Pacific Missile Range, USN, Point Mugu, Calif., 1960-64; from assoc. to full prof., head dept. physiology Kans. State U., Manhattan, 1967-74, from assoc. to full prof. mech. engring., 1967-74; prof. mech. engring. U. Fla., Gainesville, 1974-93; prof. physiology U. Fla. Coll. Vet. Medicine, Gainesville, 1974-93, assoc. dean, 1974-87, acting dean, 1980-81, exec. assoc. dean, 1987-88, prof. emeritus, 1993—. Served to capt. USNR. Fellow Aerospace Med. Assn. (exec. council 1985-88, profl. excellence award 1987); mem. Am. Physiology Soc., Soc. for Exptl. Biology & Medicine, Aerospace Physiologist Soc. (pres. 1984-86), Am. Soc. Heating, Refrigerating & Air Conditioning Engring. Achievements include research in environmental physiology and acceleration biology. Home: 15207 Rompel Trail Dr San Antonio TX 78232-4255 Office: U Fla Coll Vet Medicine PO Box 100144 Gainesville FL 32610-0144 E-mail: ebesch@satx.rr.com.

BESCH, EVERETT DICKMAN, veterinarian, dean emeritus, educator; b. Hammond, Ind., May 4, 1924; s. Ernst Henry and Carolyn (Dieckmann) B.; m. Mellie Darnell Brockman, Apr. 3, 1946; children: Carolyn Darnell, Ceryl Lynn, Cynthia Lee, Charlotte Ann, Everett Dickman. D.V.M., Tex. A&M Coll., 1954; M.P.H., U. Minn., 1956; PhD, Okla. State U., 1963. Instr. U. Minn., 1954-56; asst. prof. Okla. State U., 1956-64, prof., head dept. vet. parasitology and pub. health, 1964-68; dean Sch. Vet. Medicine, La. State U., 1968-88, prof., 1988-89. Sec.-treas. Assn. Am. Vet. Med. Colls., 1973-78, sec. coun. deans, 1976-80, chmn. coun. deans, 1980-81; mem. Nat. Adv. Coun. Health Professions Edn., 1982-86; treas. Am. Vet. Med. Found., 1991-93, v.p., 1993-94, pres., 1994-95, mem., 1995-97; bd. dirs. Coun. Agrl. Sci. and Tech., 1991-95; bd. dirs., divsn. agr., Nat. Assn. State Univs. and Land Grant Colls., 1980-82, mem. commn. on vet. medicine, 1972-82; cons. U.S. Army Surgeon Gen. in Vet. Med. Edn., 1973-85; cons. in pub. health and vet. edn. NIH, WHO, Pan Am. Health Orgn., NAS, others. Contbr. articles to profl. jours., chapters to books. Served with USN, 1942-48. Mem. AVMA (ho. of dels. 1988-91, exec. bd. 1991-97, award 1999), Assn. Tchrs. Vet. Pub. Health and Preventive Medicine (pres. 1968-69), La. Vet. Med. Assn. (named Vet. of Yr. 1976), Tex. Vet. Med. Assn., Conf. Pub. Health Veterinarians (pres. 1971-72), Am. Assn. Food Hygiene Veterinarians (pres. 1976-77), Am. Assn. Vet. Parasitologists (pres. 1964-65). Achievements include research in arthropod vectors of disease, internal parasites of ruminants. Home: 1453 Ashland Dr Baton Rouge LA 70806-7838

BESCHLOSS, MICHAEL, historian, writer, lecturer, commentator; b. Chgo., Nov. 30, 1955; s. Morris and Ruth Beschloss; m. Afsaneh Mashayekhi, Oct. 20, 1991; children: Alexander, Cyrus. BA, Williams Coll., 1977; MBA, Harvard U., 1980; LHD (hon.), St. Mary's Coll., 2001; LDH (hon.), Williams Coll., 2003, Lafayette Coll., 2007. Historian Smithsonian Instn., Washington, 1982—85; sr. assoc. mem. St. Anthony's Coll., U. Oxford, England, 1985—86; vis. fellow Russian Rsch. Ctr. Harvard U., Cambridge, Mass., 1986—87; fellow Annenberg Found., Washington, 1988—96. Commentator The News Hour with Jim Lehrer, PBS, Arlington, Va., 1994—; contbr. ABC News, NYC, 1998—2005. Author: Kennedy and Roosevelt: The Uneasy Alliance, 1980, Mayday: Eisenhower, Khrushchev and the U-2 Affair, 1986, The Crisis Years: Kennedy and Khrushchev, 1991, Taking Charge: The Johnson White House Tapes, 1963-1964, 1997, Reaching for Glory: Lyndon Johnson's Secret White House Tapes, 1964-1965, 2001, The Conquerors: Roosevelt, Truman and the Destruction of Hitler's Germany, 2002, Decisions That Shook the World, Discovery Channel, 2005 (Emmy award, 2005), Presidential Courage: Brave Leaders and How They Changed America, 1789-1989, 2007; co-author (with Strobe Talbott): At the Highest Levels: The Inside Story of the End of the Cold War, 1993; editor: American Heritage: The Presidents, 2003; contbr. NBC News, N.Y.C., 2005-. Trustee White House Hist. Assn., Washington, 1998—, Thomas Jefferson Found., Charlottesville, Va., 1999—2006, Urban Inst., Washington, 1999—2004, Nat. Archives Found., Washington, 2000—; commr. Pres.' Commn. on White House Fellowships, Washington, 1993—96. Recipient Ambassador Book prize, English-Speaking Union of U.S., N.Y.C., 1991, Harry S. Truman Pub. Svc. award, Truman Pub. Svc. Award Commn., Independence, Mo., 2004, Order of Lincoln, Lincoln Acad. Ill., Chgo., 2004. Fellow: Soc. Am. Historians; mem.: Am. Hist. Assn., Century Assn., Cosmos Club.

BESDINE, RICHARD WILLIAM, medical educator, researcher; b. NYC, Apr. 12, 1940; s. Alan Xerus and Betty (Bronstein) Besdine; m. Judith Anne Bailey, June 22, 1963 (div. May 1980); m. Fox Wetle, July 1, 1981; children: Molly Bailey Besdine, Sarah Besdine Freedman. BS cum laude, Haverford Coll., 1961; MD, U. Pa. Sch. Medicine, 1965. Diplomate in internal medicine and in infectious diseases and geriatrics Am. Bd. Internal Medicine; diplomate Nat. Bd. Med. Examiners. Intern Beth Israel Hosp. Medicine, Boston, 1965-66, asst. resident in internal medicine, 1966-67, fellow in immunology and infectious diseases, 1969-72; rsch. fellow in medicine Harvard Med. Sch., Boston, 1969-72, instr. in medicine, 1972-75, asst. prof. medicine, 1975-86, lectr. in medicine, 1986-89, co-founder, divsn. aging, developer, academics geriatrics fellowship training program; assoc. prof. medicine, cmty. medicine and healthcare U. Conn. Health Ctr. Sch. Medicine, 1986-89, dir. Travelers Ctr. on Aging, assoc. prof. family medicine, 1988-2000; prof. medicine, cmty. medicine and healthcare U. Conn. Sch. Medicine, 1990-2000, chief divsn. geriatrics, dept. medicine; dir. U. Conn. Geriatric Edu. Ctr.; from asst. to assoc. in medicine Beth Israel Hosp., 1972-75, asst. physician in medicine, 1975-82; assoc. physician in medicine Brigham and Women's Hosp. and Beth Israel Hosps., 1982-88; prof. medicine, Greer prof. geriatric medicine, dir. Ctr. Gerontology and Health Care Rsch., dir. divsn. geriat. Brown Med. Sch., 2000—; interim dean medicine and biol. scis. Brown U., 2002—05. Staff internist Hebrew Rehab. Ctr. for Aged, Roslindale, Mass., 1972-86, dir. geriatric med. edn., 1981-86; attending med. staff John Dempsey Hosp., 1986—, Hebrew Home and Hosp., 1987—, McLean Home and Village, 1987—; mem. cons. med. staff Inst. Living, Newington VA Med. Ctr.; cons., presenter in field; Noble Wiley Jones lectr. U. Oreg. Health Scis. Ctr., Portland, 1980; mem. Harvard-Hastings Project on Ethical Issues in Care of Elderly, 1982-86; vis. prof. U. Toronto Sch. Medicine, 1983, Montreal (Can.) Neurol. Inst., 1984, U. Geneva, 1990, U. Mich., 1991, U. Wis., 1991, Baylor U., 1991, U. Kans. Med. Ctr., 1992, Fallon Clinic and Health Plan, 1992; chair fed. task force on geriatric edn. NIH, 1986; mem. adv. bd. John A. Hartford Found. grant Johns Hopkins U. Sch. Medicine, 1994; chmn. western delegation Seminar on Aging, Singapore, Hong Kong, Taipei and Kuala Lumpur, 1987; mem. spl. adv. group White House Conf. on Aging and Mental Health, 1980-81; mem. task force on reversible dementia in the elderly Nat. Inst. on Aging, 1978-80, cons. geriatric medicine, prin. investigator, Claude Pepper Older Americans Independence Ctr.; dir. health stds. and quality bur., chief med. officer Healthcare Fin. Adminstrn., 1995-97; sr. adv. healthy aging project, Healthcare Financing Adminstrn. Co-author: Handbook of Geriatric Care, 1982; editor: Health and Disease in Old Age, 1982, 2d edit., 1988; mem. editl. bd. Geriat. Rev. Syllabus, 1989, 93, 96, assoc. editor, 1991, 93, 96; contbr. chpts. to books and articles to profl. jours. Surgeon USPHS Nat. Ctrs. for Disease Control, 1967—69; bd. dirs. Inst. for Cmty. Rsch., Hartford, 1987—2000, New Britain Meml. Hosp., 1993, Am. Fedn. for Aging Rsch., 1993—, Am. Geriat. Soc., 1994—, pres.; bd. dirs. Alzheimers Assn., 1998; bd. trustee Am. Soc. of Cons. Pharmacists, 2000—. Royal Soc. Medicine Found. travelling fellow U. Glasgow, 1972; grantee Geriatric Edn. Ctr., 1983-91, John A. Hartford Found., 1988-94, Charles A. Dana Found., 1988-90, Conn. State Dept. on Aging, 1989-91, Travelers Rsch. Inst. on Health Promotion and Aging, 1990, Howard and Bush Found. , 1990, Robert Wood Johnson Found., 1991-93, Travelers Found., 1991, 92, 94, NIH Pepper Ctr., 1996. Fellow ACP, Am. Geriat. Soc. (pres.-elect 2002, pres., 2003-04, chmn., 2004-05, Milo D. Leavitt award 1991), Gerontol. Soc. Am. (Joseph T. Freeman award 1995), Am. Soc. Aging (Pres. award 1997). Office: Brown Med Sch Box G-B Providence RI 02912 E-mail: richard_besdine@brown.edu.

BESEN, STANLEY MARTIN, economist; b. Bklyn., Dec. 17, 1937; s. Moe and Sylvia (Forgang) B.; m. Marlene Dublirer, June 10, 1961; children: Roberta Ann, Elizabeth Rebecca. BBA, CCNY, 1958; MA, Yale U., 1960, PhD, 1964. Acting asst. prof. econs. U. Calif.-Santa Barbara, 1962-63; economist Inst. Def. Analyses, 1963-65; mem. faculty Rice U., Houston, 1965-80, prof. econs., 1974-79, Cline prof. econs. and fin., 1979-80; co-dir. network inquiry spl. staff FCC, 1978-80; sr. economist Rand Corp., Washington, 1980-92; v.p. CRA Internat., Washington, 1992—. Vis. Henley prof. law and bus. Columbia U., 1988—89; vis. prof. law and econs. Georgetown U. Law Ctr., 1990—91; mem. task force nat telecomms. policy making Aspen Inst. Program Comms. and Society, 1977; mem. adv. panel on intellectual property rights in an age of electronics and info. Office of Tech. Assessment, 1984—85, mem. adv. panel on comms. sys. for an info. age, 1986—88; mem. com. on internet searching and the domain name sys. The Nat. Acads. Computer Sci. and Telecomm. Bd., 2001—04; mem. bd. on earth scis. and resources, com. on licensing geographic data and svcs. NRC, 2003—04. Author: Misregulating Television: Network Dominance and the FCC, 1984, also articles; co-editor Rand Jour. Econs., 1985-88; mem. editorial bds. profl. jours. Fellow Brookings Instn., 1971-72, NSF, 1973-75 Office: CRA Internat 1201 F St NW Ste 700 Washington DC 20004-1204 Home: 5610 Wisconsin Ave #306 Chevy Chase MD 20815-4429 Personal E-mail: sbesen@crai.com.

BESHAR, CHRISTINE, lawyer; b. Paetzig, Germany, Nov. 6, 1929; came to US, 1952, naturalized, 1957; d. Hans and Ruth (vonKleist-Retzow) von Wedemeyer; m. Robert P. Beshar, Dec. 20, 1953; children: Cornelia, Jacqueline, Frederica, Peter. Student, U. Hamburg, 1950-51, U. Tuebingen, 1951-52; BA, Smith Coll., 1953. Bar: NY 1960, US Supreme Ct. 1971. Assoc. Cravath, Swaine & Moore, NYC, 1964-70, ptnr., 1971—. Bd. dirs. Catalyst for Women Inc., 1977-94; trustee Colgate U., 1978-84, Smith Coll., 1987-97; mem. state bd. Nature Conservancy, NY, 1993-96. Inst. Internat. Edn. fellow, 1952-53; recipient Disting. Alumnae medal Smith Coll., 1974. Fellow: Am. Coll. Probate Counsel; mem.: Fgn. Policy Assn. (bd. dirs. 1978—87), UN Assn. (bd. dirs. 1975—89), NY Bar Found. (bd. dirs. 1977—2001), NY State Bar Assn. (ho. of dels. 1971—80, v.p. 1979—80), Assn. Bar City NY (exec. com. 1973—75, v.p. 1985—86), Am. Bar Found., Gipsy Trail Club, Cosmopolitan Club. Office: Cravath Swaine & Moore 825 8th Ave 43d Fl New York NY 10019-7475 also: Stone House Farm PO Box 533 Somers NY 10589-0533 Office Phone: 212-474-1698. Business E-Mail: cbeshar@cravath.com.

BESHAR, PETER JUSTUS, lawyer, insurance company executive; b. NYC, Nov. 20, 1961; s. Robert Peter and Christine (Wedemeyer) Beshar; m. Sarah Elizabeth Eggleston Jones, Jan. 5, 1991; children: Isabel Emma, Henry Frederick, Sophie Charlotte. BA, Yale U., 1984; JD, Harvard U., 1989. Bar: NY 1989. Law clk. to the Hon. Vincent L. Broderick, NYC, 1989-90; assoc. Simpson, Thacher & Bartlett, NYC, 1990—92; spl. asst. to the Hon. Cyrus Vance Internat. Conf. on the Former Yugoslavia, 1992-93; asst. atty. gen. Office of Atty. Gen., NYC, 1994; assoc. Gibson, Dunn & Crutcher, NYC, 1995—99, ptnr., 1999—2004; exec. v.p., gen. counsel Marsh & McLennan Cos. Inc., NYC, 2004—. Mem. gen. counsel com. Nat. Ctr. State Courts, Williamsburg, Va., 2004—; spkr. Gen. Counsel Leadership Series, 2007. Trustee Rye Country Day Sch. Mem. Coun. Fgn. Rels. Office: Marsh & McLennan Cos Inc 1166 Ave of the Americas New York NY 10036-2774

BESHAR, ROBERT PETER, lawyer; b. NYC, Mar. 3, 1928; m. Christine von Wedemeyer, Dec. 20, 1953; children: Cornelia, Jacqueline, Frederica, Peter. AB honors with exceptional distinction, Yale U., 1950, LLB, 1953. Bar: N.Y. 1954. Asst. gen. counsel Waterfront Commn. N.Y. Harbor, 1954-55; law sec. Hon. Charles D. Breitel, Appellate div. 1st dept. N.Y. Supreme Ct., NYC, 1956-58; spl. hearing officer Justice Dept., 1967-68; dep. asst. sec. Commerce; dir. Bur. Internat. Commerce; nat. export expansion coordinator Commerce Dept., Washington, 1971-72; pvt. practice, NYC, 1972—2004; pres. various family enterprises, 1993—. Bd. dirs. Nat. Semicondr. Corp. (audit and dir's. affairs coms., counsel to bd. dirs. 1972-98); mem. bus. adv. panel Nat. Commn. for Rev. of Antitrust Laws, 1978-79; mem. Mcpl. Securities Rulemaking Bd., 1982-85; bd. govs. Fgn. Policy Assn., 1991-1998. Author: Current Legal Aspects of Doing Business With Sino-Soviet Nations, 1973; editor: Manhattan Auto Study, 1973. Trustee Westchester Coll. Found., 1992—; mem. Planning Bd. of Somers, 1984-97. Scholar of the House, Yale U., 1950. Mem. ABA (chmn. corp. and antitrust law com. 1982-85), N.Y. State Bar Assn., Elizabethan and Gypsy Trail Clubs, Phi Beta Kappa. Home: 120 E End Ave New York NY 10028-7552 also: PO Box 533 Somers NY 10589-0533 Office Phone: 914-276-2425. E-mail: rpbeshar@netscape.net.

BESHEAR, STEVEN LYNN, lawyer; b. Dawson Springs, Ky., Sept. 21, 1944; AB, U. Ky., Lexington, 1966, JD, 1968. Bar: N.Y. 1969, Ky. 1971. Assoc. White and Case, NYC, 1968-70; later ptnr. Beshear, Meng and Green, Lexington; mem. Ky. Ho. of Reps., 1974-79; atty. gen. State of Ky., Frankfort, 1979-83, lt. gov., 1983-87; ptnr. Stites & Harbison, Lexington, 1987—2006; Dem. candidate gov. Commonwealth of Ky., 2007—. Bd. editors, Ky. Law Jour., (1967-68.). Mem. Fayette County Bar Assn., Ky. Bar Assn., ABA, Order of Coif, Phi Beta Kappa, Phi Delta Phi, Omicron Delta Kappa. Office: Stites & Harbison Ste 2300 250 W Main St Lexington KY 40507-1758 Office Phone: 859-226-2300. E-mail: sbeshear@stites.com.

BESHERS, DANIEL NEWSON, retired materials scientist; s. Hugh Monahan and Caroline Newson Beshers; m. Barbara Renata Algin, Aug. 22, 2004; m. Maxine McArthur Beshers, Sept. 5, 1953 (dec.); children: George McArthur, Samuel Newson, Robert Neil, Clifford Monahan. PhD in Physics, U. Ill., Urbana-Champaign, 1956. Physicist US Naval Rsch. Lab., Washington, 1955—57; from asst. prof. to prof. metallurgy Columbia U., NYC, 1957—69, prof. metallurgy, 1969—2000, spl. lectr. applied physics and prof. emeritus, 2000—. Vis. prof. U. Poitiers, France, 1979—80, U. Ballearic Isles, Palma de Mallorca, Spain, 2006; cons. in field. Contbr. numerous articles to profl. jours. Mem.: ASM (life; mem. exec. com. NY chpt.), The Minerals, Metals and Materials Soc., Am. Phys. Soc., Sigma Xi. Unitarian-Universalist. Office: Columbia University MC4701 Dept Applied Physics 500 W 120th St New York NY 10027 Home Phone: 646-414-2202; Office Phone: 212-854-2918.

BESHUR, JACQUELINE E., retired animal trainer, farmer, writer; b. Portland, Oreg., May 8, 1948; d. Charles Daniel and Mildred (Domreis) Beshears. BA, UCLA, 1970; MBA, Claremont U., 1980; postgrad., City U., Seattle, 1989-90. Dir. and founder L.A. Ctr. for Photog. Studies, 1972-76; precious gem distbr. Douglas Group Holdings, Australia, 1976-78; small bus. owner BeSure Cleaning, 1981-90; animal trainer, exotic livestock farmer, writer, 1990-2000. Dir. County Citizens Against Incineration, 1987—90, Ames Lake Protection Com., 1989—2004. Mem. Bridges for Peace, Nature Conservancy, Wash. Wilderness Coalition, Humane Farming Assn., Issaquah Alps Club. Republican. Office: BeSure Tng PO Box 225 Carnation WA 98014-0225

BESIER, JAMES LOUIS, pharmacist, educator; b. Waukegan, Ill., Feb. 23, 1954; s. Louis Clark and Jessie Olive Besier; m. Janice Lynn Halloran, Nov. 2, 1979; children: Matthew, Christopher, Robert. BS, U. Cin., 1977, MS, 1990; PhD, Union Inst. & U., 2004. Lic. pharmacist Ohio, Ky. Staff pharmacist Children's Hosp. Med. Ctr., Cin., 1977—89; svc. chief pediat. Strong Meml. Hosp., Rochester, NY, 1989—90; staff pharmacist U. Cin. Hosp., 1990—91; pharmacy mgr. U. Hosp., Cin., 1991—97; asst. dir. pharmacy St. Luke Hosps., Ft. Thomas, Ky., 1997—2004, adminstr. bar code medication adminstrn., 2005—, dir. health alliance pharmacy residency program, 2005—. Adj. asst. prof. Coll. Pharmacy U. Cin., 1991—2004, adj. assoc. prof. Coll. Nursing, 2004—; spkr. Glaxo Pharm. Rsch., Triangle Park, NC, 1994—97; lectr. Coll. Nursing, U. Cin., 1998—; adv. coun. Gateway Cmty. & Tech. Coll., Edgewood, Ky., 2002—04. Contbr. articles to profl. jours. Bus. edn. cons. Jr. Achievement, Cin., 1995—99. Mem.: Am. Assn. Coll. Pharmacy, Am. Soc. Health Sys. Pharmacists. Home: 914 Cedarpark Dr Cincinnati OH 45233 Office: Dept Pharmacy Services Alliance Business Ctr 3 South Cincinnati OH 45229 Office Phone: 859-572-3345, 513-585-7223.

BESING, RAY GILBERT, lawyer, educator; b. Roswell, N.Mex., Sept. 14, 1934; s. Ray David and Maxine Mable (Jordan) B.; children: Christopher, Gilbert, Andrew, Paul. Student, Rice U., 1952—54; BA, Ripon Coll., 1957; postgrad., Georgetown U., 1957; JD, So. Meth. U., 1960. Bar: Tex. 1960. Ptnr. Geary, Brice, Barron, & Stahl, Dallas, 1960-74; sr. ptnr. Besing, Baker & Glast, Dallas, 1974-77; prin. Law Offices of Ray G. Besing, P.C., Dallas, 1977—96. Sr. rsch. fellow Faculty Laws U. Coll. London, 2002-03; lectr. in field, 1998—. Author: Who Broke Up AT&T?: From Ma Bell to the Internet, 2000, The Intersection of Sherman Section 2 and the Telecommunications Act of 1996: What Should Congress Do?, 2005; mng. editor So. Meth. U. Law Jour., 1959-60. Pres. Dallas Cerebral Palsy Found., 1970; trustee Ripon Coll., 1969—76; mem. Tex. Gov.'s Transition Team on Telecom., 1982; mem. exec. coun. Episc. diocese Dallas, 1969—72; bd. dirs. Dallas Symphony, 1972, Dallas Theatre Ctr., 1971, Found. for Santa Fe C.C., 2001—03, Found. for Santa Fe Concert Assn., 1998—2001. Tex. Moot Ct. champion, 1958. Mem. Tex. Bar Assn., Dallas Bar Assn., Dallas Jr. C. of C. (v.p. 1964), Sigma Chi. Democrat. Episcopalian. Office Phone: 505-988-1553. E-mail: raybesing@nets.com.

BESLEY, MORRISH ALEXANDER (TIM BESLEY), civil engineer; b. New Plymouth, New Zealand, Mar. 14, 1927; arrived in Australia, 1950; s. Hugh Morrish and Isobel (Alexander) B.; m. Nancy Marguerite Cave, Feb. 15, 1952 (dissolved 2001); children: Trevor J., Grant A., Rodney G.; m. Sarah Harrington, Aug. 11, 2001; children: Hugh I., Hannah Alice. BE in Civil Engring., U. New Zealand, 1950; B Legal Studies, Macquarrie U., Sydney, Australia, 1984, DSc (hon.), 2002, FIE (hon.), 2005. Chartered profl. engr., Australia. Engr. Ministry of Works, New Zealand, 1950; with Snowy Mountains Hydro-Electric Authority, 1950-67; 1st asst. sec. Dept. External Territories, 1967-72; exec. mem. Fgn. Investment Review Bd., 1975-76; 1st asst. sec. Dept. of Treasury, 1973-76; sec. Commonwealth Dept. Bus. and Consumer Affairs, ACT, Australia, 1976-81; comptroller gen. Customs, 1976-81; mng. dir. Monier Ltd., Sydney, 1982-87, chmn., CEO, 1987; chmn. Monier Redland Ltd., 1988, Redland Australia, 1988-95; exec. chmn. Commonwealth Indsl. Gases Ltd., Sydney, 1988-90; chmn. The CIG Group, 1988-93, Commonwealth Banking Corp., 1988-91, Commonwealth Bank Australia, Sydney, 1991-99. Pres. Metal Trades Industry Assn., Sydney, 1989—91, nat. pres., 1990—92; chmn. Leighton Holdings Ltd., Sydney, 1990—2001. Chmn. Royal Bot. Gardens, Sydney, 1989—92; dir. O'Connell St. Assocs. Pty. Ltd., 1990—; active Red Shield Appeal Com., Sydney, 1987—99; Sydney adv. bd. Salvation Army, 1994—99; active Legacy Appeal Com., Sydney, 1988—2003; mgmt. bd. Australian Grad. Sch. Mgmt., 1983—92, Chancellor Macquarie U., 1994—2001; chmn. Co-op Rsch. Ctr. for Greenhouse Gases, 2003—, Wheat Export Authority, 2005—, Australian Rsch. Coun., 2002—05. Decorated mem., officer and companion Order of Australia. Fellow: Australian Acad. Tech. Sci. and Engring. (pres. 1998—2002); mem.: Australian Club Sydney, Elanora Country Club, Union Club, Nat. Press Club, Royal Sydney Yacht Sqadron. Home: Pvt Box 304 Cammeray NSW 2062 Australia Personal E-mail: baroona@ozemail.com.au.

BESLOW, WILLIAM S., lawyer; b. Paterson, NJ, June 7, 1948; s. Harry George and Marion Gertrude (Doan) B.; m. Evelyn Z. Beslow, Dec. 20, 1970; children: Lauren Allegra, Jonathan Doan. BA, Yale U., 1969; JD, Columbia U., 1972; LLM in Taxation, NYU, 1977. Bar: N.Y. 1973, U.S. Dist. CT. (so. dist.) N.Y. 1979. Assoc. Davis, Polk & Wardwell, NYC, 1972-79; sole practice NYC, 1980—. Fellow: Am. Acad. Matrimonial Lawyers; mem. ABA, Assn. Bar City N.Y., N.Y. State Bar Assn. Office: Law Office of William S Beslow Rockefeller Ctr 620 Fifth Ave New York NY 10020*

BESOSA, FRANCISCO AUGUSTO, federal judge; b. San Juan, 1949; AB, Brown U., 1971; JD, Georgetown U. Law Ctr., 1979. Ptnr., chmn. litig. dept. Adsuar Muniz Goyco & Besosa, PSC, San Juan, 1979—83, 1986—2006; asst. US atty. US Dept. Justice, 1983—86; judge US Dist. Ct. PR, 2006—. US Army, 1971—77. Office: Clemente Ruiz-Nazario US Courthouse CH-119 150 Carlos Chardon St San Juan PR 00918 Office Phone: 787-772-3241.*

BESOZZI, PAUL CHARLES, lawyer; b. NYC, Aug. 22, 1947; s. Alfio Joseph and Lucy Agnes (Ducibella) B.; m. Caroline Lisa Hesterberg, Oct. 7, 1978; 1 child, Christina Claire. BS cum laude in Intl. Affairs, Georgetown U., 1969, JD, 1972; MBA in Bus./Govt. Rels., George Washington U., 1977. Bar: Va. 1972, D.C. 1973, U.S. Ct. Mil. Appeals 1972, U.S. Ct. Appeals (4th cir.) 1978, U.S. Ct Appeals (3d cir.) 1996, U.S. Supreme Ct.

1977. Assoc. Arnold & Porter, Washington, 1977-80; gen. counsel, minority counsel U.S. Senate Com. on Armed Svcs., Washington, 1980-84; ptnr. Hennesey, Stambler & Siebert, P.C., Washington, 1984-86, Besozzi & Gavin, Washington, 1987-93, Besozzi, Gavin & Craven, Washington, 1993-95, Besozzi, Gavin, Craven & Schmitz, Washington, 1995-96, Patton Boggs LLP, Washington, 1996—. Editor Georgetown Law Jour., 1971-72; contbr. articles to profl. jours. Alumni interviewer Georgetown U. Alumni Assn., Washington, 1981—, dir. Procurement Roundtable, 1991—; mem. bd. visitors Georgetown U. Sch. Fgn. Svc. Capt. JAGC, U.S. Army, 1972-76. Mem. Fed. Comms. Bar Assn., Georgetown U. Alumni Assn. (bd. govs. 1993—), Phi Beta Kappa, Phi Alpha Theta, Pi Sigma Alpha. Office: Patton Boggs LLP 2550 M St NW Ste 400 Washington DC 20037-1301 Home Phone: 301-949-0361; Office Phone: 202-457-5292. Business E-Mail: pbesozzi@pattonboggs.com.

BESS, CHARLES WAYNE, lawyer; b. Denver, Mar. 23, 1958; s. Howard Heber and Helen Faye (Esau) B.; m. Jennifer Anne Murray, Feb. 28, 1981; children: Caroline Tempel, Madelaine Kate. BS, Colo. State U., 1980; JD, U. Denver, 1984. Bar: Colo. 1984, U.S. Dist. Ct. Colo. 1985, U.S. Ct. Appeals (10th cir.) 1986. Assoc. Roath & Brega P.C., Denver, 1984-86, La Salle Ptnrs., Denver, 1986-87, sr. assoc., 1987-89, gen. mgr., 1989-90, mktg. mgr., 1990-91; dir. office brokerage EquiVentures, Inc., Denver, 1991-92; assoc. Jensen, Byrne, Parsons, Ruh & Tilton P.C., Denver, 1992-94; dir. shareholder Byrne, Ruh & McDermott, P.C., Denver, 1994-95; ptnr. Davis & Ceriani, P.C., Denver, 1995-2000; shareholder, dir. Ducker, Montgomery Aronstein & Bess, P.C., Denver, 2000—. Mem. ABA (mem. adv. panel), Colo. Bar Assn., Denver Bar Assn., Denver Country Club, Wigwam Club (sec. 2006—), Riverside Club Co. (pres. 2000-02), Arapahoe Tennis Club (pres. 1998-99), Rotary (bd. dirs. Denver club 1990-93, chmn. word cmty. svc. com. 1996-97). Republican. Congregationalist. Avocations: martial arts, hunting, bicycling, tennis. Office: Ducker Montgomery Aronstein & Bess PC Ste 1400 1560 Broadway Denver CO 80202-5151 Home Phone: 303-741-1516; Office Phone: 303-861-2828. Business E-Mail: cbess@denverlaw.com.

BESS, RONALD W., advertising executive; b. Bloomington, Ill., July 9, 1946; s. Bloice Monroe and Mary (Trussel) B.; m. Teresa N. Shute, July 22, 1970; children: Daniel, Laura. BS in Mktg., U. Ill., Champaign, 1968, M, 1972. Account exec. Foote, Cone and Belding, Chgo., 1972-75; v.p. account dir. Needham, Harper and Steers, Chgo., 1975-81; sr. v.p. group account dir. DDB Needham, Chgo., 1981-87; pres. Bayer Bess Vanderwarker, Chgo., Foote, Cone & Belding, Chgo.; chmn., CEO diversified group Young Rubicam Inc., NYC, 2001—03, vice chmn, Integration and Bus. Dev., 2003; CEO Euro RSCG-Chgo, Canada, 2004—. Office: Euro RSCG 36 E Grand Ave Chicago IL 60611

BESSANT, CATHY (CATHERINE POMBIER), bank executive, marketing professional; b. Jackson, Mich. m. John E. Clay; 2 children. BBA in Fin., Mktg. and Eng. Lit., U. Mich. Joined NationsBank, 1982; pres., cmty. devel. bank Bank Am. Corp. (formerly NationsBank), 1998—2000; pres., mortgage lending ops. Bank Am. Corp., pres., consumer real estate banking, 1999—2000, pres., Fla. ops., 2000—01, chief mktg. exec., 2001—06, pres. global treasury services, 2006—. Trustee Enterprise Found. Bd. dirs. Children's Theatre Charlotte, Blue Cross Blue Shield Fla., Inc. Named one of Most Powerful Women in Banking, US Banker Mag., 2003. Office: Bank Am Corp 100 N Tryon St Charlotte NC 28255*

BESSER, GRETCHEN ROUS, writer, educator; b. Bklyn., Dec. 1, 1928; d. Ben and Sidonya (Menkes) Rous; m. Albert Gordon Besser, Dec. 28, 1952; children: James, Neal, Brian. BA in French with honors, Wellesley Coll., 1949; MA, Middlebury Coll., 1950; PhD, Columbia U., 1967. Instr. Fairleigh Dickinson U., Rutherford, NJ, 1955-57, Columbia U., NYC, 1957-59, 63-67; asst. prof. Lehman Coll., CUNY, Bronx, 1967-70, Rutgers U., Newark, 1972-73; PhD examiner Monash U., Victoria, Australia, 1979; instr. in lit. N.J. Com. for The Humanities, New Brunswick, 1985-90; faculty mem. New Sch. U., NYC, 1989—2005, instr. Distance Instrn. for Adult Learners program, 1994—2000; ski columnist Recorder Pub. Co., Stirling, NJ, 1993—; instr. New Sch. Online U., 2000—05. Author: Balzac's Concept of Genius, 1969, Nathalie Sarraute, 1979, The National Ski Patrol, 1983, Germaine de Staël, Revisited, 1994; contbr. World Lit. Today, 1978—, French Rev., 1973—, Ski Patrol Mag., 1978—, Skiing Heritage, 2000—, Snow East, 2006—. Instr. first aid ARC, 1971-82; internat. liaison Nat. Ski Patrol, 1980-85, nat. historian, 1980—; mem. selection com. U.S. Nat. Ski Hall of Fame, 1982—, bd. dirs., 1997—; bd. dirs. Internat. Skiing History Assn., 1997-2004; bd. dirs. Vt. Humanities Coun., 2001—, sec., 2005—; pres. Wellesley Class of 1949, 2004—. Fulbright Commn. grantee, 1949-50; Wellesley scholar, 1949; recipient Ullr award Internat. Skiing History Assn., 1997. Mem. Am. Assn. Tchrs. French, Ea. Ski Writers Assn., N.Am. Snowsports Journalists Assn. Avocations: opera, skiing, hiking. Home and Office: 3679 Stagecoach Rd Morrisville VT 05661 Personal E-mail: grbesser@comcast.net.

BESSEY, PALMER QUINTARD, surgeon; BA, Williams Coll., 1967; MA in Chemistry, U. Oregon, 1970; MD, U. Vt., 1975; MS in Epidemiology and Public Health, Columbia U., 2006. Diplomate Am. Bd. Surgeons, Am. Bd. Critical Care Surgery. Intern U. Ala. Hosp., Birmingham, 1975-76, resident in surgery, 1976-81; fellow metabolism and nutrition Brigham and Women's Hosp., Boston, 1981-83; assoc. dir. Burn Ctr. N.Y. Presbyterian Hosp., 2000—; prof. surgery Weill Med. Coll. Cornell U., 2000—. Mem. ACS (region chief), Assn. Acad. Surgery, Soc Univ. Surgeons, Am. Assn. Surgery Trauma, ASPEN, Soc. Critical Care Medicine, Ctrl. Surg. Assn., Am. Surg. Assn., Am. Bd. Surgery (bd. dirs.), Am. Burn Assn. (com. on trauma). Office: Dept Surgery Box 137 P-703 525 E 68th St New York NY 10021

BESSIE, SIMON MICHAEL, publisher; b. NYC, Jan. 23, 1916; s. Abraham and Ella (Brainin) B.; m. Constance Ernst, Sept. 12, 1945; children: Nicholas, Katherine; m. Cornelia Schaeffer, Dec. 21, 1968. BA magna cum laude, Harvard U., 1936. Reporter Newark Star Eagle, 1936; with rsch. dept. RKO-Radio Pictures, 1936-38; editor Market Rsch. Monthly, 1938; free-lance writer Europe, Africa, 1938-39; assoc. editor, war editor, war corr. Look mag., 1940-42; editor Harper & Bros., 1946-52, gen. editor, 1952-59; co-founder Atheneum Pubs., 1959, pres., 1963-75; sr. v.p. Harper & Row, NYC, 1975-81, v.p., 1988-91, also bd. dirs., 1975-87; pres. Joshuatown Pub. Assocs., Lyme, Conn., 1981—; co-pub. Cornelia and Michael Bessie Books, 1981—. Cons. editor Counterpoint Press, 1995-2002, Perseus Books Group, 1999-2002; lectr. English, Columbia U., 1953-59; dir. novel workshop New Sch., 1959-63, dir. Franklin book programs, 1963-72; chmn. vis. com. Harvard U. Press, 1972-78, bd. dirs., 1980-91; bd. dirs. Am. Book Pubs. Coun., 1964-69, Ctr. for Comm., 1981—; chmn. trade book div. Assn. Am. Pubs., 1970-72, bd. dirs., 1972-76, chmn., 1974-75, chmn. freedom to read com., 1975-78, internat. freedom to pub. com., 1975—; mem. exec. com. Ctr. for the Book, Libr. of Congress, 1979—, chmn., 1983—. Author: Jazz Journalism, 1938; contbr. numerous articles to mags. Bd. overseers vis. com. dept. history Harvard U., 1964-77; chmn. lit. panel Nat. Arts Council, 1971-74, chmn. spl. projects panel, 1974-81; chmn. bd. advisors Sta. WNET, 1979-83, trustee, 1983-96, life trustee, 1997—; chmn. book com. Alfred P. Sloan Found., 1986-91, mem. tech. book com., 1992-2001. Served as chief news bur. psychol. warfare br., 1943-44, Algiers, Sicily, Italy; chief psychol. warfare combat team 1944, So. France; dep. dir. USIS, 1944-46, France. Recipient Presdl. Medal of Freedom, 1946, Curtis Benjamin award Assn. Am. Pubs., 1986. Mem. Council Fgn. Relations, Assn. Harvard Alumni (dir. 1974-77), Phi Beta Kappa. Clubs: Century Assn. (N.Y.C.), Harvard (N.Y.C.); Federal City (Washington). Home and Office: 296 Joshuatown Rd Lyme CT 06371-3035 Office Phone: 860-526-2486. Personal E-mail: mbessie@snet.net.

BESSLER, MARC, surgeon, educator; b. NYC, Oct. 21, 1964; BA cum laude, Yeshiva U., NYC, 1985; MD, NYU Sch. Medicine, 1989; Advanced Operative Laparoscopy for Gen. Surgery, Advanced Laparoscopy Tng. Ctr., Marietta, Ga., 1991; Course in Laparoscopic Suturing, Anastomosis and Intracorporeal Knot Tying, Microsurgery and Operative Endoscopy Tng. Inst., San Francisco, Calif., 1992; Basic Microsurgery Course, Columbia U. Coll. Physicians and Surgeons, NYC, 1992; Endosurgical Techniques of the Foregut and Hindgut, U. So. Calif., LA, 1993; Vertical Banded Gastroplasty and Mgmt. of Morbid Obesity, U. Iowa, Iowa City, 1996; Gastric Bypass and Mgmt. of Morbid Obesity, Med. Coll. Va., Richmond, Va., 1996. Cert. Am. Bd. Surgery. Resident, gen. surgery NY-Presbyn. Hosp./Columbia U. Med. Ctr., NYC, 1989—96, fellow, surgical endoscopy, 1993—94, asst. attending surgeon, 1997—, dir., NY Presbyn. Ctr. for Obesity Surgery, 1997—, dir., laparoscopic surgery, 1997—, dir., network relationships, divsn. gen. surgery, 2005—; instr. clin. surgery Columbia U. Coll. Physicians and Surgeons, NYC, 1996—97, asst. prof. surgery, 1997—. Presenter in field. Contbr. articles to profl. jours. Recipient Blackmore award for Surgical Rsch., 1992, 1993, 1996, Soc. Laparoendoscopic Surgeons Resident Achievement award, Best Resident Presentation, SAGES, 1995. Fellow: ACS (assoc.); mem.: Soc. for Surgery Alimentary Tract, Am. Soc. for Bariatric Surgery, Assn. Academic Surgery, Soc. Am. Gastrointestinal Endoscopic Surgeons. Achievements include patents for Gastrointestinal Staplescope, 1993; Gastrointestinal Tissue Approximating and Attaching Device, 1995; Device and Method for Performing Laproscopic Vertical Banded Gastroplasty; Device and Method for Percutaneous Removal and Replacement of Cardiac Valves; Bessler Treat Laparoscopic Suturing Assistant Forreps. Office: NY Presbyn Hosp Columbia U Med Ctr Irving Pavilion Rm 6-620 161 Fort Washington Ave New York NY 10032 Office Phone: 212-305-9506. Office Fax: 212-305-5992.*

BESSMAN, SAMUEL PAUL, pediatrician, educator, biochemist; b. Newark, Feb. 3, 1921; m. Alice Neuman, July 3, 1945; children: Joel David, Ellen. Student, Coll. William and Mary, 1938-41; MD, Washington U., St. Louis, 1944. Intern, asst. resident St. Louis Children's Hosp., 1944-45; asst. prof. pediatrics George Washington U., 1947-54; dir. research Children's Hosp., Washington, 1947-54; asso. prof. pediatrics U. Md., 1954-59, prof. pediatric research, 1959-68, prof. biochemistry, 1962-68; prof., chmn. dept. pharmacology and nutrition U. So. Calif., 1968-91, prof. pediatrics, 1969-91, prof. emeritus, 1991—. Dir. research Rosewood State Hosp., Md., 1962-68, Jewish Home for Retarded Children, Washington, 1962-68 Founding editor Biochem. Medicine; mem. editorial bd. Analytical Biochemistry. Pres. First Dist. Cmty. Coun., Balt., 1965; trustee Robert Lindner Found.; pres. Molly Towell Found., Alsam Found. Served with USPHS, 1945-47. Recipient Crawford Long award U. Ga., 1963, Creative Scholar award U. So. Calif., 1978, Maimonides award Technion, 1979, Disting. Sci. Achievement award Am. Heart Assn., 1984, Inst. for Advanced Studies award Louis Pasteur Libr. and Sci. Found., 1986, Alumni Achievement award Washington U. Med. Sch., 1994. Fellow AAAS, Am. Acad. Pediat.; mem. Am. Soc. Biol. Chemists, Soc. Pediat. Rsch., Am. Inst. Nutrition, Am. Soc. Pharmacology and Exptl. Therapeutics, Sigma Xi, Alpha Omega Alpha. Achievements include introduction of EDTA treatment of lead poisoning, theoretical basis of hepatic coma, mechanism of insulin action chemistry mental retardation, genetic basis of malnutrition, artificial implantable pancreas, creatine phosphate energy shuttle. Home: 7404 Woodrow Wilson Dr Los Angeles CA 90046-1323 E-mail: bessman@usc.edu.

BEST, EVE (EMILY BEST), actress; b. London, Eng., 1971; BA in English Lit. with hons., Oxford U.; attended, Royal Acad. Dramatic Art. Actress (plays) 'Tis Pity She's a Whore, 1999 (London Critics Cir. award most promising newcomer, 1999, London Evening Standard Theatre award best newcomer, 1999), The Three Sisters, The Cherry Orchard, The Heiress, Macbeth, Prime Suspect, 2006, The Coast of Utopia, Mourning Becomes Electra (London Critics Cir. award best actress, 2003), Hedda Gabler (Laurence Olivier award best actress, 2006, London Critics Cir. award best actress), A Moon for the Misbegotten, 2007 (Outer Critics Cir. award outstanding actress in a play, 2007, Drama Desk award outstanding actress in a play, 2007), (films) The Lodge, 2004, (TV films) Shackleton, 2002, Lie with Me, 2004, The Inspector Lynley Mysteries: In Divine Proportion, 2005, (TV series) The Infinite Worlds of H.G. Wells, 2001, Vital Signs, 2006. Avocations: singing, painting, travel, sailing.*

BEST, FRANKLIN LUTHER, JR., lawyer; b. Lock Haven, Pa., Dec. 14, 1945; s. Franklin L. and Hazel M. (Yearick) B.; m. Kimberly R., May 1, 1982 BA, Yale U., 1967; JD, U. Pa., 1970; postgrad., Columbia U., 1994. Bar: Pa. 1970. Assoc. MacCoy, Evans & Lewis, Phila., 1970—74; asst. counsel Penn Mut. Life Ins. Co., Phila., 1974—77, asst. gen. counsel, 1978—84, assoc. gen. counsel, 1985—99, mng. corp. counsel, 1999—2004, mng. corp. counsel, sec., 2004—; counsel, asst. sec. Penn Ins. and Annuity Co., Phila., 1983—96, counsel, sec., 1996—. Lectr. Pa. Bar Inst., 1976-84. Author: Pennsylvania Insurance Law, 1991, 3d edit., 2005; contbr. articles to profl. jours. Bd. dirs. Ctr. City South Neighborhood Assn., 1979-80, pres., 1978-79; mem. Com. of Seventy, 1978-84; sec. Washington Sq. Assn., 1977-87; mem. 30th Ward Rep. Exec. Com., 1972-84, West Pikeland Twp. Open Spaces Com., 1987-99, chair, 1995-99, planning commn., 1994—, chair, 1996—. Mem.: ABA, Phila. Bar Assn., Internat. Claim Assn. (exec. com. 1979—81, 1985—88, sec. 1995—2000, exec. com. 1995—, pres. 2002—03, treas. 2005—), Yale Club Phila. Baptist. Office: Penn Mut Life Ins Co 600 Dresher Rd Horsham PA 19044-2204 Office Phone: 215-956-7754. Business E-Mail: best.frank@pennmutual.com.

BEST, JACOB HILMER, JR., retired hotel chain executive; b. Evanston, Ill., July 21, 1937; s. Jacob Hilmer and Clara (Cornell) B.; m. Janet Patricia Donnelly, June 20, 1959; children: Jacob Hilmer III, Peter B., Julie Donnelly Best. BS in Hotel Adminstrn., Mich. State U., 1959; postgrad, Stanford U., 1979. From sales rep. to dir. of sales Sheraton Hotels, Chgo., Wash., 1960-62; asst. to owner Camelback Inn, Scottsdale, Ariz., 1963-64; from sales mgr. to exec. v.p. Marriott Hotels, 1964-84; pres. Ramada Inns, Phoenix, 1984-85; pres., CEO, Wyndham Hotels, Dallas, 1985-87, Red Lion Hotels & Inns, Vancouver, Wash., 1987-91, Omni Hotels, Hampton, NH, 1992-96; ind. cons., 1996-98; COO Tauck Tours, Westport, Conn., 1998-99. Named charter mem. Mich. State U. Sch. of Hospitality Hall of Fame, 1995. Mem. Am. Hotel and Motel Assn. Republican. Roman Catholic. Avocations: golf, reading, fishing. Home: PO Box 56 Rancho Santa Fe CA 92067-0056 Personal E-mail: pops7217@aol.com.

BEST, JUDAH, lawyer; b. NYC, Sept. 4, 1932; s. Sol and Ruth (Landau) B.; 1 child, Stephen Andrew. AB, Cornell U., 1954; LLB, Columbia U., 1959. Bar: NY 1959, DC 1961, U.S. Supreme Ct. 1963. Trial atty. Solicitor's Office, U.S. Dept. Labor, Washington, 1960-61; asst. U.S. atty. for D.C., 1961-64; assoc. to ptnr. Chapman, DiSalle & Friedman, Washington, 1964-70; ptnr. Dickstein, Shapiro & Morin, Washington, 1970-80, Steptoe & Johnson, Washington, 1980-87, Debevoise & Plimpton, Washington, 1987—2002, of counsel, 2003—04, LeBoeuf Lamb Greene MacRae LLP, Washington, 2004—. Participant trial advocacy program U. Va. Sch. Law, 1981—. Contbr. articles to profl. publs. Served with U.S. Army, 1954-56 Fellow Am. Coll. Trial Lawyers; mem. ABA (coun., litigation sect. 1977-81, chmn. subcom. on litigation 1982-84, mem. fed. regulation securities com., corp. bank and bus. law sect., pub. contracts sect., vice chmn. ABA Task Force Report on RICO 1983-85, chmn. litigation sect. 1988-89, sect. del. 1989-95, mem. standing com. on fed. judiciary 1990-93, chmn. 1996-97, mem. spl. com. on governance 1993-95), Fed. Bar Assn. (commr.), DC Bar Assn., Am. Bar Found., Am. Law Inst., Cosmos Club, Washington Golf and Country Club, Smithsonian Am. Art Mus. (commr.): 125 W 55 St New York NY 10019-5389 Office: LeBoeuf Lamb Greene MacRae LLP 1101 New York Ave NW Washington DC 20005 Office Phone: 202-986-8004. Business E-Mail: jbest@LLGM.com.

BEST, LAURENCE EDWARD, lawyer; b. New Orleans, June 14, 1949; s. Kermit Roosevelt and Frances Elizabeth (Hicks) Best; m. Julie B. Guten (div.); children: Erin Lynn, Mark Edward, Kevin John; life ptnr. Kory Chatelain, Oct. 13, 2001. BS in Acctg., U. New Orleans, 1971; JD, Tulane U. Sch. Law, 1974. Bar: La. 1974, U.S. Dist. Ct., ea. dist., La. 1974, U.S. Dist. Ct., western dist., La., U.S. Dist. Ct., middle dist., La. 1974, U.S. Supreme Ct. 1979, U.S. Dist. Ct., so. dist., Tex. 1991, U.S. Dist. Ct., so. dist., Miss. 1991. Atty. Waitz & Downer, Houma, La., 1974—78, Waitz, Downer & Best, Houma, 1978—83, Hebert & Abbott, New Orleans, 1983—84; ptnr. Abbott, Webb, Best & Meeks, New Orleans, 1984—88, Abbott, Best & Meeks, New Orleans, 1985—91, Best Koeppel, New Orleans, 1991—. Invited guest U.S. Ct. Appeal (5th cir.) Jud. Conf., San Antonio, 2000. Presenter, panelist numerous radio shows, meetings, TV shows. Treas. Forum for Equality, 1992-93, chair-elect and chair, 1993-95; mem. Forum for Equality/Equality Club; cmty. dir. Forum for Equality, 2001; founder, bd. mem. New Orleans Lesbian and Gay Cmty. Ctr., 1994-95; mem. adv. com. City of New Orleans Human Rels. Commn., 1994-96; mem. La. Log Cabin Reps. 2003, Human Rights Campaign Fed. Club, Svc. Members Legal Def. Network, Parents and Friends of Lesbians and Gays, donor to annual scholarship fund, 1996-; mem. Lambda Legal Def. Fund. Recipient Legal Eagle award, La. Electorate of Gays and Lesbians, 1996, award for outstanding leadership and svc. to the Lesbian and Gay Counsel, New Orleans Human Rights Campaign, 2001, Annual Acclaim award for lesbian and gay polit. activism, New Orleans Forum for Equality, 2003. Mem.: Nat. Lesbian and Gay Bar Assn., Fed. Bar Assn. New Orleans, La. Trial Lawyer Assn., La. Assn. Def.Counsel, Def. Rsch. Inst., Tex. Bar Assn., La. Bar Assn., Maritime Law Assn., U. New Orleans Alumni Assn., Tulane U. Alumni Assn. and Assoc. Club. Democrat. Avocations: reading, cooking, wine. Office Phone: 504-598-1000. Office Fax: 504-524-1024. Business E-Mail: lebest@bestkoeppel.com.

BEST, LAWRENCE C., retired medical products executive; BBA, Kent State U. From acct. to ptnr. Ernst & Young, Akron, Ohio, 1971—81, ptnr., 1981—92; fellow Securities and Exchange Commn., Washington, 1979—80; exec. presdl. exchange The White House, Washington, 1981; sr. v.p., CFO Boston Scientific Corp., Natick, Mass., 1992—2007. Bd. dirs. Biogen, Inc., 2003, Biogen Idec. Inc., 2003—, Haemonetics Corp., Archemix.*

BEST, MELVYN EDWARD, geophysicist; b. Victoria, BC, Can., Mar. 8, 1941; s. Herbert Best and Irene Jessie (Kelly) MacKenzie; m. Virginia Marie Pignato, July 19, 1970; children: Lisette Anne, Aaron Michael. BSc in Math. and Physics with honors, U. B.C., Vancouver, 1965, MSc in Physics, 1966; PhD in Theoretical Physics, MIT, 1970. Geophysicist mineral exploration Shell Can. Resources Ltd., Calgary, Alta., Canada, 1972-77, divsn. geophysicist minerals, 1980-82, mgr. petroleum engring. rsch., 1982-85; head non-seismic rsch. Royal Dutch Shell Exploration and Prodn. Labs., The Hague, Netherlands, 1978-80; geophys. advisor Teknica Resource Devel. Ltd., Calgary, 1985-86; head basin analysis subdivision Atlantic Geoscience Ctr. Geol. Survey Can., Dartmouth, N.S., 1986-90, dir. Pacific Geosci. Ctr. Sidney, B.C., 1990-94, sr. rsch. scientist, 1994-97; geophys. cons. Bemex Consulting Internat., Victoria, B.C., 1997—; environ. geophys. Lockheed-Martin Corp., Edison, NJ, 2001—. Vis. lectr., rsch. assoc. dept. physics McGill U., Montreal, Que., 1970—72; mem. panel Jeanne d'Arc hydrocarbon resource assessment Can. Govt., 1987—90; mem. petroleum geology working group Office Energy R&D, 1987—92; mem. oil and gas com. Can. Nfld. Offshore Petroleum Bd., 1990—94, official Can. rep. coom. coordination joint prospecting for mineral resources in Asian offshore waters, 1992—94; sessional lectr. Sch. Earth and Ocean Scis. U. Victoria, 1995—, adj. prof. earth and ocean scis., 1998—; adj. prof. geology and geophysics U. Calgary, 1998—2004; part-time sr. geophysicist Lockheed Martin Corp., Edison, NJ, 2001—. Author: Resistivity Mapping and Electromagnetic Imaging, 1992; editor: (with J.B. Boniwell) A Geophysical Handbook for Geologists, 1989, (with T.P. Ng) Development and Exploitation Scale Geophysics, 1995; assoc. editor Bull. of the Can. Soc. Petroleum Engrs., 2004—. Vol. lectr. Can. Coll. Chinese Studies, Victoria, B.C., 1995-99; vol. Victoria chpt. Habitat for Humanity, 1996-97. Recipient meritorious svc. award Can. Soc. Exploration Geophysicists, Calgary, 1996. Mem. Can. Soc. Exploration Geophysicists (chmn. continuing edn. com. 1982-85, mem. tech. com. 1985 conv., assoc. editor jour. 1986-93, 95-2003, editor jour. 1993-95), Soc. Exploration Geophysicists (prodn. and devel. geophysics com. 1985-88, geophys. rsch. com. 1988—, organizer workshop 1989, instr. continuing edn. 1985-2000, global affairs com. 2005—), Soc. Environ. and Engring. Geophysics (assoc. editor jour. 1995-97, 2000-02, editor 1997-2000, v.p. coms. 2003-05, gen. chmn. symposium on application geophysics to environ. and engring. problems meeting 2006, grant selection com., natural sci. and engring. rsch. coun. solid earth scis. 2006—), Assn. Profl. Engrs., Geologists and Geophysicists Alta. (cert.), Assn. Profl. Engrs. and Geoscientists B.C. (cert.). Avocations: competitive badminton, squash, tennis, hiking, sailing. Home and Office: Bemex Cons Internat 3701 Wild Berry Bend Victoria BC Canada V9C 4M7 Office Phone: 250-658-4225. Personal E-mail: best@islandnet.com.

BEST, ROBERT MULVANE, insurance company executive; b. Newcomerstown, Ohio, May 9, 1922; s. Chester R. and Beatrice (Mulvane) Best; m. Shirley Marie Smith, Nov. 25, 1994; children: Eric, Linda, Grant. BS, Ohio State U., 1947. Agt. Bus. Men's Assurance Co. Am., Columbus, Ohio, 1946-48; mgr. group sales Security Mut. Life Ins. Co., Binghamton, NY, 1948-49, asst. supt. agys., 1949-51, dir. sales, 1951-53; mgr. Bus. Men's Assurance Co., Columbus, 1952-61; v.p. in charge agys. Security Mut. Life Ins. Co. N.Y., Binghamton, 1961-66, exec. v.p., 1966-69, pres., 1969—, chief exec. officer, 1972-87, chmn. bd., 1977-90; chmn., chief exec. officer Home Mut. Ins. Co., 1986-89. Mem. exec. com. Life Inst. Guaranty Corp., NYC, 1980—89; mem. N.Y. Nat. bd; chmn. bd. trustees bus. coun. Inst. Trust. Trustee Bus. Coun. N.Y. State, Inc.; former dir. Valley Devel. Found., Binghamtom; mem. coun. SUNY; bd. govs. Internat. Ins. Seminars; bd. dirs. Twin Tier Home Health Care, Inc., Binghamton; former mem. N.Y. State Bd. Regents, Am. Coun. Life Ins.; chmn. Med. Index Bur., Inc., Boston, 1989; dir. Greater Broome Cmty. Found., Inc. Lt. (j.g.) USNR, 1942-46. Mem. Am. Soc. CLUs (regional v.p. 1967-70), Am. Council Life Ins. (bd. dir.), Life Ins. Council N.Y. (bd. dir.), Broome County C. of C. (bd. dir. 1970-75, pres. 1974), Empire State C. of C. (former pres., bd. dirs.). Clubs: Binghamton City (bd. dirs. 1969-73); Oteyokwa Lake (Hallstead, Pa.) (pres. 1970-71); Econ. (N.Y.C.). Home: 41A Crestmont Rd Binghamton NY 13905-4117 Office Phone: 570-874-2764. Personal E-mail: sbest12@aol.com.

BEST, ROBERT WAYNE, gas transmission company executive, lawyer; b. Nappanee, Ind., Oct. 8, 1946; s. Wayne and Helen F. (Kendall) B.; m. Mary Beth Hoffman, Apr. 7, 1967; children— Stephanie, Sean, Ashley BS, Ind. State U., 1968; JD, Ind. U., 1974. Bar: Ky., Ind. Atty. Tex. Gas Transmission Corp., Owensboro, Ky., 1974-79, sr. atty., 1979-81, gen. counsel, 1981-82, v.p., gen. counsel, 1982-85, pres., chief exec. officer, 1985-89, pres., chief operating officer, 1989-1995; chmn., pres. & CEO Atmos Energy Corp., Dallas, 1997—. Dir. Cardinal Fed. Savs. Bank. Bd. dirs. Leadership Owensboro, Brescia Coll., Mercy Hosp., Ky. Ind. Coll. Fund., United Way Owensboro-Daviess County; mem. exec. com. Stategies for Tomorrow; mem. Ky. Econ. Devel. Corp. Mem. ABA, Ky. Bar Assn., Ind. Bar Assn., Fed. Energy Bar Assn. Democrat. Roman Catholic. Avocations: golf, reading. Office: Atmos Energy Corp PO Box 650205 Dallas TX 75265-0205 Home: 440 Flint Point Dr Houston TX 77024-6749*

BEST, WANDA, career planning consultant; d. Herbert and Coretta Best; 1 child, Sharona Joy Anderson. BA in Sociology, LI U., Bklyn., 1999; M in Human Svcs., Lincoln U., Pa., 2006. Lic. nurse technician, Bklyn.; cert. tchr. NYC Bd. Edn. Nurse technician NY Meth. Hosp., Bklyn., 1993—2000; cons. Adolescent Career Devel. Ctr., Bronx, NY, 2000—; CEO Vocat. Career Planning, Cons., NYC, 2003—. Cons. Adolescent Career Devel. Ctr., Bronx; vocat. cons. Bronx Children's Psychiat. Ctr. Author, editor: Volunteer Training Program for At-Risk Adolescents, 2006, My Soul Awakes. Vol. Harlem C. of C., NYC, 2002—, Women in Need, NYC, 1998; mentor HS Transitions Intensive English Lang. Program, NYC; mem. Feed the Children Partnership, Oklahoma City, 2003—, Effective Tchg. Program for Exceptional Students, NYC, 2000—; outreach counselor Greater Refuge Temple Ch. of Our Lord Jesus Christ, NYC, 1995—. Named to Wall of Tolerance, Rosa Parks So. Poverty Law Ctr., Montgomery, Ala., 2004; recipient You Never Fail Until You Stop Trying award, LI U., 1997, Appreciation for Dedication and Commitment award, Adolescent Career Devel. Ctr., 2002, cert. achievement, State Senator, 4th Dist., 2006. Mem.: Nat. Alliance for Mentally Ill. Democrat. Mem. Apostolic Faith Ch. Avocations: creative writing, reading, art, travel. Home: 1875 3d Ave New York NY 10029-5407

BEST, WILLIAM ROBERT, internist, educator, dean; b. Chgo., July 14, 1922; s. Gordon and Marian Burton (Shapland) B.; m. Ruth Johanna Stuchlik, Sept. 2, 1944; children: Barbara Ann Best Mulch, Patricia Marian Best Williams. BS, U. Ill., 1945; MD, U. Ill., Chgo., 1947, MS, 1951; postgrad. math. biology, U. Chgo., 1964-65. Diplomate Am. Bd. Internal Medicine, Am. Bd. Hematology. From intern to fellow in hematology then to resident U. Ill. Hosp., 1947-51; asst. prof., assoc. prof. medicine U. Ill. Coll. Medicine, Chgo., 1953-67, prof., assoc. dean, 1972-81; chief Midwest Rsch. Support Ctr., VA Hosp., Hines, Ill., 1967-72, chief staff, 1981-92, sr. health svcs. rschr., 1992—; prof. medicine, assoc. dean for VA affairs Loyola U. Stritch Sch. Medicine, Maywood, Ill., 1981-92; chief staff U. Ill. Hosp., Chgo., 1976-81. Contbr. numerous articles to sci. jours. 1st lt. US Army, 1951—53. Named Alumnus of Yr., U. Ill. Med. Alumni Assn., 1980. Fellow ACP; mem. AMA (br. pres. 1985), Am. Statis. Assn., AAAS. Episcopalian. Avocations: sailing, computing, radio-controlled model airplanes. Home: 1712 Waverly Cir Saint Charles IL 60174-5869 Office: Ctr for Mgmt Complex Chronic Care Edward Hines Jr VA Hosp Hines IL 60141 Personal E-mail: w.and.r.best@sbcglobal.net. Business E-Mail: william.best@va.gov.

BESTERMAN, DOUGLAS, composer, orchestrator; BA in Music History and Theater, U. of Rochester, 1985. Orchestrator Broadway shows: Damn Yankees, 1994—95; Big, 1996; King David, 1997; Fosse, 1999—2001 (Tony award Best Orchestrations, 1999); The Music Man, 2000—01; The Producers, 2001— (Tony award Best Orchestrations, 2001); Seussical, 2000—01; Thoroughly Modern Millie, 2002—04 (Tony award Best Orchestrations, 2002); Dracula, The Musical, 2004—05; A Christmas Carol; Radio City Music Hall Christmas Spectacular; orchestrator off-Broadway shows: Weird Romance; Jack's Holiday; Johnny Pye and the Foolkiller; The Gifts of the Magi; Godspell; orchestrated ballet: But Not for Me; orchestrated for film/TV: Pocahontas, 1995; Cinderella, 1997; Anastasia, 1997; orchestrated for film/TV Mulan, 1998, Gepetto, 2000, South Pacific, 2001, Fosse, 2001, Chicago, 2002; arranger for vocalist: Toni Braxton; Kathy Lee Gifford; Jerry Hadley; Patti LuPone; Mandy Patinkin; Chita Rivera. Office: Local 802 AFM 320 W 48th St New York NY 10036-1302

BESTLER, J. MICHAEL, columnist, retired surgeon; b. Hinsdale, Ill., Sept. 21, 1930; s. Edward Thomas and Margaret Marie Bestler; m. Brenda B. Barber, Oct. 12, 1993; m. Jean Wade, June 10, 1954 (div. 1984); children: Susan Marie Gordon, Emily Eileen, Michael Wade. BSc in Naval Sci., Coll. of Holy Cross, 1952; MD, U. Rochester, NY, 1960. Lic. NY State Bd. Medicine, 1960, Va. State Bd. Medicine, 1966. Midshipman, naval aviation, instr. naval acad. USN, Annapolis, Md., 1948—56; intern gen. surgery U. Rochester, 1960—62, resident, chief resident head and neck surgery, 1962—66; surgeon Martinsville Meml. Hosp., Martinsville, Va., 1966—80; pres. Beaver Creek Surg. Clinic, Martinsville, Va., 1980—97. Fellow ACS, Chgo., 1968—97; founder Am. Bd. Cosmetic Surgery, Chgo., 1983—97. Contbr. articles to profl. jours. Candidate ho. rep. NY State, Rochester, 1965—65; co-founder Carlisle Sch., Martinsville, Va., 1976—78. Lt. 5th and 6th fleet USN, 1950—54. Decorated Svc. medals Navy. Mem.: Am. Assn. Cosmetic Surgeons, Chatmoss Country Club. Conservative. Roman Catholic. Avocations: cooking, writing, music. Home: 650 Axton Rd Axton VA 24054 Home Phone: 276-650-2305.

BESWICK, ELLEN J., research scientist; d. Edward L. and Ellen J. Gramme; m. Kurt F. Beswick, Oct. 20, 2001. BS, Fla. So. Coll., Lakeland, Fla., 1996; PhD, So. Ill. U., Springfield, Ill., 2002. Lab. asst. Fla. So. Coll., Lakeland, 1994—96; tchg. asst. So. Ill. U., Carbondale, 1998—99, rsch. asst. Springfield, 1999—2002; postdoctoral fellow U. Tex. Med. Br., Galveston, Tex. Mentor, med. student and undergrad. student rsch. projects U. Tex. Med. Br., Galveston, 2002—. Contbr. articles to profl. jours., chapters to books. Recipient McLaughlin award, U. Tex. Med. Br., 2005, 2006; grantee Infectious Diseases Tng. grant, 2003—06; Presdl. scholar, Fla. So. Coll., 1993—96. Mem.: Am. Gastroent. Soc. (assoc.), Am. Assn. Cancer Rsch. (assoc.), Amercian Assn. Immunologists (assoc.). Achievements include discovery of a novel receptor for Helicobacter pylori.

BESWICK, KURT F., artist, graphic designer; s. James F. and Barbara A. Beswick; m. Ellen J. Gramme, Oct. 20, 2001. BFA, Fla. Atlantic U., Boca Raton, 1995—99. Asst. studio artist Miami Med. Art, Inc., Fla., 1993—96; graphic designer Internet Solutions Worldwide, Coral Springs, Fla., 1996—98; sr. designer Ideas Design, Inc., Ft. Lauderdale, Fla., 1998—2000; visual comm. specialist Levi, Ray & Shoup, Springfield, Ill., 2000—02; art dir. Quest Displays & Prodn., LLC., Stafford, Tex., 2002—07. Cons. DaKeegan Design, Katy, Tex.; visual design cons. LGI Devel., Ltd., The Woodlands, Tex. Exhibition, Houston Heights Gallery Tour, T3 Featured Artist, televised exhibition, Fox 26 News Featured Artist, exhibition, One Allen Center Exhibition; dir.: (display graphic design) Taylor Woodrow Homes Sales Center Design (Nat. Assn. Home Builders Gold Award, 2006), Marriot Hotels Sales Center Design (Am. Resort Devel. Assn. Award for Excellence, 2004), Hilton Hotels Sales Center Design (Am. Resort Devel. Assn. Award for Excellence, 2004), Engle Homes Sales Center (Nat. Assn. Home Builders Regional Award, 2006), Goodman Family of Builders Sales Center (Nat. Associations Homebuilders Silver Award, 2006), Old Kinderhook Sales Center (Nat. Associations Homebuilders Regional Award, 2007), The Woodlands Welcome Center (Nat. Associations Homebuilders Regional Award, 2007); contbr. exhibition, journal illustration, text book illustration; author: (journal article) Design Graphics. Recipient Grand Prize, Natural Sci. and Engring. Found., 1994, Gold Award, ULead Animation Challenge, 1999, Gold Award in Advt. for the Arts Electronic Media, Greater Ft. Lauderdale Advt. Assn., 1999, Silver Award in Advt. for the Arts Electronic Media, 1999, Self Promotional award, Am. Graphic Design Awards, 2000, Judges Choice Award, Ctrl. Ill. Advt. Assn., 2001, Gold Award in Illustration, 2001, Excellence in Logo and Trademark Design, 2001, Silver Award in Advt. for the Arts Electronic Media, 2002. Achievements include invention of novel undersea based resource extraction platform.

BETANCOURT, JOSE A., dean, public health service officer; s. Carlos M. and Concepcion G. Betancourt; m. Mary S. Cahill, Feb. 4, 1989; children: Carlos M., Mateo J., Philip J., John (Jack) T., Mariela F., Therese G. MS, Def. Intelligence Coll., DC, 2002; DPH, George Wash. U., DC, 2003; MS, U.S. Army War Coll., Carlisle, Pa., 2006. Dir. internat. med. programs Office of the Army Surgeon Gen., Falls Church, Va., 2001—03; program dir. med. ops. and planning Office of Mil. Cooperation-Afghanistan, Kabul, 2004—05; assoc. dean Acad. of Health Scis., Army Med. Dept. Ctr. and Sch., Ft. Sam Houston, Tex., 2005—. Author: articles in profl. jours. Lt. col. Med. Svc. Corps US Army, 1985—, San Antonio, Tex. Decorated Bronze Star Combined Forces Command - Afghanistan. Achievements include served as principal advisor to the Afghanistan National Army Surgeon General in all sectors of health systems support to the Afghanistan National Army. Office: US Army Med Dept Ctr & Sch 2250 Stanley Rd Fort Sam Houston TX 78234 Home Phone: 210-479-2417; Office Phone: 210-221-7399. Business E-Mail: jose.betancourt@us.army.mil.

BETANCOURT, PHILIP P., art historian, archaeologist, educator; Faculty Temple Univ., Phila., 1970—, Laura H. Carnell Prof. of Art History and Archaeology; and adj. prof., history of art Univ. Pa. Fellow: Soc. Antiquaries of London, European Acad Sciences, Am. Acad. Arts & Scis.; mem.: Archaeol. Inst. Am. (Gold Medal for Disting Archaeol. Achievement). Office: Art History Temple Univ 1801 N Broad St Philadelphia PA 19122 Office Phone: 215-782-2899. Business E-Mail: philip.betancourt@temple.edu, betancou@temple.edu.

BETANCOURT LOPEZ, ANTONIO L., association executive; b. Belen de Umbria, Colombia, Jan. 9, 1944; came to U.S., 1967; s. Angel Maria and Pastora (Lopez) B.; m. Kyoko Funayama-Kagawa, July 1, 1982; children: Kiantar, Annika, Kyboter, Isaac. Sec. gen. CAUSA Internat., NYC, 1979-89; asst. to pres. New World Comms., NYC, 1980-83; exec. v.p. Internat. Security Coun., Washington, 1984-90; exec. dir. Assn. for the Unity of Latin Am., Washington, 1983—, Summit Coun. for World Peace, Washington, 1981—; dep. sec. gen. Fedn. for World Peace, Washington, 1991—; pres. Young Gruppe, Inc., Washington, 1992—, News & Communication, Inc., 1993—. Pres. Group Internat. Arte, Washington, 1996—, World Inst. for Devel. and Peace, 1996—; sec.-gen. Interreligious and Internat. Fedn. for World Peace-N.Am., 2002-06; chmn. exec. bd. Internat. Assn. Educators for World Peace, 2002—; exec. dir. internat. office govt. rels. Universal Peace Fedn., 2006—. Exec. editor jour. Global Affairs, 1984-90; exec. dir. conf. procs. Mem. Family Fedn. for World Peace and Unification, NYC, 1996—; bd. dirs., bd. mem. Universal Ballet Acad. and Universal Ballet Found., 2004-06, Martin Luther King Jr. Family Life Inst., 2005, Tiempos del Mundo Found., 2005-07, Kirov Ballet Acad., 2006—; pres. Universal Cultural Found., 2006—. Recipient commendation Cath. U., La Plata, Argentina, 1984, Acad. award Mexican Acad. Internat. Law, 1985, Grand Medal of Peace, Dem. People's Republic of Korea, 1996, Academician of honor U. San Andres, Chile, 2003; named hon. citizen Santo Domingo City, 1987. Mem. N.Y. Acad. Sci., Oxford Club, Korea Soc., Wilson Ctr. for Scholars. Avocations: gardening, antiques, hiking, fishing. Home: 6305 Queens Chapel Rd University Park MD 20782-2131 Office: Summit Coun for World Peace 3600 New York Ave NE Washington DC 20002-1947 Business E-Mail: abetancourt@peacefederation.org.

BETENSON, GAYE BRINTON, secondary school educator; b. Salt Lake City, Utah, Aug. 4, 1953; d. Brinton Phil and Helen Rae Reese Brinton; m. Donald Blaine Betenson, June 7, 1974; children: Bryan Donald, Brandon Blaine, Amber Betenson Mann, Ashley, Michelle, Michael Phil. BA in Bus. and Edn., So. Utah State Coll., 1984. Cert. tchr. Utah, 1973. Tchr. Bingham HS, South Jordan, Utah, 1973—79, Indian Hills Mid. Sch., Sandy, Utah, 1980—81; asst. coord., competency-based testing Utah State Office Edn., Salt Lake City, 1985—89, coord., competency-based testing, 1989—94; tchr. West Jordan HS, Utah, 1997—; tchr., adult HS South Pointe HS, Sandy, 2004—. Tchr. teen mother program Valley HS, Sandy, 1976—, tchr., home and hosp., 1997. Mem.: Utah Bus. Educators Assn., Utah Assn. Career and Tech. Educators. Lds Ch. Avocations: sewing, quilting, embroidery. Home: 11275 Rick Cir South Jordan UT 84095-4065 Office: West Jordan HS 8136 S 2700 W West Jordan UT 84088 Home Phone: 801-619-6285; Office Phone: 908-256-5600. Office Fax: 801-256-5670. Personal E-mail: gayebetenson@msn.com. Business E-Mail: gaye.betenson@jordan.k12.ut.us.

BETHANCOURT, JOHN E., oil industry executive; b. Dallas, Nov. 12, 1951; BS in Petroleum U., Tex. A&M U., 1974. Field engr., then various engring. and mgmt. positions Getty Oil, Kilgore, Tex., 1974—84; area mgr. South Tex. Texaco U.S.A., Midland, Tex., 1984—89, asst. divsn. mgr. Midland producing divsn., 1989—91, asst. to mgmt. office of pres. and CEO White Plains, NY, 1991—93, mng. dir. bus. devel Mid. East/Far East divsn., 1993—96, v.p. bus. devel. internat. mfg. and mktg. divsn., 1996—97, v.p. corp. devel. upstream devel. orgn. Houston, 1997—2000, pres. prodn. ops., 2000—01, v.p., 2000—01; v.p. human resources ChevronTexaco Corp., San Ramon, Calif., 2001—03, exec. v.p. tech. services, 2003—. Office: ChevronTexaco 6001 Bollinger Canyon Rd San Ramon CA 94583-2324*

BETHEA, ELIZABETH, social sciences educator, psychologist, minister; b. Hattiesburg, Miss., May 10, 1950; d. David Ball Jr. and Molly Mayo Bethea. BA, Univ. Tex., Austin; MSW, Univ. Denver, 1982; PhD, Union Inst. and Univ., Cin., 1999; ThD, Univ. Wales, Lampter, 2004—. Social worker, faculty trainer Boulder Valley Pub. Sch., 1983—94; med. social worker Adventist Health Sys., Denver, 1983—95; social work adj. faculty Univ. Denver, Denver, 1991—93; social sci. adj. faculty Front Range Cmty. Coll., Boulder, 2000—03; psychology adj. faculty Naropa U., Boulder, Colo., 2003; social work adj. faculty Colo. State Univ., Ft. Collins, Colo., 2003—04. Dir. Bether Inst. for Rsch. on the Transformation of Humanity Inc., Colo., 1994—; pyschotherapist Elizabeth Bethea, PhD, Boulder, Colo., 1983—. Author: A Critical Mass: A Primer for Personal, Social & Global Transformation, 1999; contbr. chapters to books, articles pub. to profl. jour. Chair of peace, world friendship Womens Internat. League, Boulder, Colo., 1980—85; cmty. organizer Eco Cycle, Boulder Pks. and Open Space, Doris Day Annual League, Am. Humane Soc., Boulder, Colo., 1978—. Mem.: AARP, Colo. Chautquague Assn., Doris Day Animal League, Am. Humane Soc., Sierra Club. Avocations: studying Sanskirt and Hinduism, walking, spiritual ministry.

BETHEA, LOUISE HUFFMAN, allergist; b. Jackson, Miss., Mar. 27, 1947; d. Theodore G. and Frances (Allen) Huffman; m. Henry L. Bethea, Sept. 15, 1946; children: Mary, Samuel, Sarah. BS, Miss. Coll., Clinton, 1968; MD, U. Miss., 1974. Diplomate Am. Bd. Allergy and Immunology, Am. Bd. Pediatrics. Resident pediatrics U. Miss., Jackson, 1973-75; fellow allergy and immunology U. Fla., 1977-79; pvt. practice Houston, 1983—. Instr. pediatrics U. Miss., 1975-77, U. Fla., 1979-80; active staff Houston Northwest Med. Ctr., 1983—, Meml. Hermann Hosp. The Woodlands, St. Luke's Hosp. The Woodlands; cons. in field. Fellow Am. Acad. Allergy, Asthma and Immunology, Am. Coll. Allergy, Am. Acad. Pediatrics. Republican. Episcopalian. Avocations: photography, travel, arts and crafts. Home: 92 Hollymead Dr The Woodlands TX 77381-5121 Office: 17070 Red Oak Dr Ste 107 Houston TX 77090-2615 Office Phone: 281-580-6494. Business E-Mail: bethea@dbmed.net.

BETHEL, DENISE, art appraiser; MA, Courtauld Inst. Art, U. London. Dir., photography Swann Galleries, NYC, 1980—90; with Sotheby's, NYC, 1990—, sr. v.p., dir., photographs. Lectr. in field. Contbr. articles to photography jours. Office: Sotheby's 1334 York Ave New York NY 10021 Office Phone: 212-894-1149. Office Fax: 212-894-1150. Business E-Mail: denise.bethel@sothebys.com.

BETHEL, KATHLEEN EVONNE, librarian; b. Washington, Aug. 4, 1953; d. Frederick Errington and Helen Evonne (Roy) B. BA, Elmhurst Coll., Ill., 1975; MALS, Rosary Coll., River Forest, Ill., 1977, MA Northwestern U., Evanston, Ill., 1989. Receptionist Newberry Library, Chgo., 1975-77; br. and reference librarian Maywood Pub. Library, Ill., 1977-78; asst. librarian Johnson Pub. Co., Chgo., 1978-81; librarian African-Am. studies Northwestern U., Evanston, Ill., 1982—. Trustee DuSable Mus. African Am. History, Chgo. Mem. ALA, NAACP, Black Caucus of ALA, Assn. for the Study of African Am. Life and History, Inc., Caribbean Studies Assn., Toni Morrison Soc., Alpha Gamma Phi. Office: Northwestern Univ Library 1970 Campus Dr Evanston IL 60208 Office Phone: 847-491-2173. Business E-Mail: kbethel@northwestern.edu.

BETHKE, FREDERICK RANDALL, microbiologist, researcher; b. Balt., Apr. 27, 1963; s. Frederick Carroll Bethke and Sue Bethke Carole; m. Candace Ann Snyder; children: Brooks Randall, Kara Sue, Blair Micah. BS, W.Va. U., Morgantown, 1985; MS, Hood Coll., Frederick, Md., 1991. Biol. sciences asst. US Army Med. Rsch. Inst. Infectious Diseases, Frederick, Md., 1986—90; sr. rsch. assoc. Henry M. Jackson Found., Rockville, Md., 1990—94; rsch. assoc. Sci. Applications Internat. Corp., Md., 1994—98; rsch. scientist Intervet, Inc., Millsboro, Del., 1998—. Musician (prodr.): (album) Christmas Guitars: Sounds of the Season, 2006. Praise & worship musician Frederick Christian Fellowship, Frederick, 1993—98, Bayshore Cmty. Ch., Gumboro, Del., 1998—2007, class instr., 2005, leader missions trip to Albania, 2007. With US Army, 1986—90. Decorated Achievement medal US Army, Good Conduct medal, Commendation medal, Achievement medal for Civilian Svc.; recipient Shining Star award, Mentoring Del., 2004, User Analyst of Yr., Intervet, Inc., 2007. Mem.: Am. Soc. Rickettsiology (assoc.), Am. Soc. Microbiology (assoc.), R-Consevative. Achievements include patents pending for vaccines for protection from Bartonella and related methods; scale-up and Fermentation of Bartonella henselae for vaccine antigen; novel Bartonella antigen lysate extracts for use in ELISA diagnostic; infection and propagation of Ehrloichia species in feline embryonic cell lines. Avocation: little league baseball. Home: 5 Mill Landing Millsboro DE 19966 Office Phone: 302-934-4301. Personal E-mail: randy.bethke@mchsi.com.

BETHKE, LOUISE VIRGINIA, music educator, writer; b. Neenah, Wis., Mar. 22, 1932; d. Herbert August and Sigrid Natalie Bethke. Diploma in Theology and Music, Patten U., 1957; student, U. Calif., Berkeley, 1958—60, Holy Names U., Oakland, Calif., 1978—81. Performer (piano/organ) Christian Cathedral, Oakland, 1954—82; music instr. Patten U., Oakland, 1955—81, Music Studio in Home, Oakland, 1982—. Composer: (complete Easter cantata words and music) Behold, The Lamb of God, author numerous poems. Named Honoree For Exceptional Achievement, Leadership & Svc., Patten U. Alumni Walk of Honor, 1997; recipient Talent award for organ, Patten Conservatory Music, 1957, Achievement award trophy, 1960. Mem.: Internat. Soc. Poets (life), Music Tchrs.' Assn. Calif. (life), Alumni Assn. Patten U. (life). Avocations: reading, writing, piano, organ, harp. Personal E-mail: lbethke@msn.com.

BETHOUX, FRANÇOIS ANDRE, physiatrist, researcher; b. Paris, May 31, 1964; arrived in U.S., 1997; s. Pierre Andre and Janine Gabrielle (Monin) Bethoux; m. Sandrine Christine Delclaud, Apr. 9, 1988; children: Nicolas, Ambre. MD, A. Carrel Med. Sch., Lyon, France, 1990; Bd. Phys. Med. and Rehab., J. Monnet U., St. Etienne, France, 1994; DEA Handicap and Rehab., Bourgogne U., Dijon, France, 1994. Diplomate specializing in physical med and rehab. Resident U. Hosps., St. Etienne, France, 1991-94, acad. physiatrist, 1995-97; rsch. fellow Case We. Res. U., Cleve., 1994-95; fellow in neuroimmunology Mellen Ctr. Multiple Sclerosis, Cleve., 1997-2000, clin. assoc., 2001—02, staff physician, dir. rehab. svcs., 2003—. Rschr. Jean Monnet U., St. Etienne, 1992—97, tchr., 1995—97, Sch. Phys. Therapy, St. Etienne, 1992—97, Inst. Social Scis., St. Etienne, 1996—97; assoc rschr. Page Ctr Outcomes Rsch. Cleve. Clin, 2000—. Contbr. chapters to books, articles to profl jours; co-editor: Guide of Evaluation and Measurement Tools in Physical Medicine and Rehabilitation, 2003. Grantee, French Assn. Paralyzed People, 1994, Nat. Multiple Sclerosis Soc., 2002. Mem.: Am Acad Neurology, Int Soc Quality Life, French Soc Physical Med and Rehab. Avocations: music, reading, bicycling. Office: Cleve Clin Found 9500 Euclid Ave Cleveland OH 44195-0001 Business E-Mail: bethouf@ccf.org.

BETON, JOHN ALLEN, communications company executive; b. Chgo., Aug. 25, 1950; s. John Henry and Anne Marilyn (Joseph) Beton. BS, U. Ill., 1972; MBA, DePaul U., 1975. Market analyst ITT Telecomm., Des Plaines, Ill., 1972—73, mgr. mktg. svcs., 1973—75, mgr. market planning Hartford, Conn., 1975—77, area mgr. Detroit, 1977—80, mgr. mktg. ops. Des Plaines, 1980—81; v.p. mktg. NEC Tele., Inc., Melville, NY, 1981—82, Summa Four, Inc., Manchester, NH, 1982—85; pres. Alston divsn. Conrac Corp., Niles, Ill., 1985—. Pres. Daniel Radiator Corp., 1989—; sr. v.p. Go/Dan Industries, New Haven, 1990—; prin. Beton Assocs., Chgo., 1992—. Mem.: Am. Mktg. Assn., Pitcairn Islands Study Group, Am. Philatelic Soc., Beta Gamma Sigma, Phi Kappa Phi, Phi Eta Sigma. Presbyterian. Office: 7850 N Harlem Ave Niles IL 60714-3202

BETSKY, AARON, art museum director; b. Missoula, Mont., 1958; BA, Yale U., 1979, MArch, 1983. Tchr. U. Cin., 1983—85; designer office of Frank Gehry, 1985—87, Hodgetts & Fung Design, 1987, pvt. practice, LA, 1987; instr., coord. Special Projects Southern Calif. Inst. Architecture; curator, Architecture and Design San Francisco Mus. Modern Art, 1995—2001; dir. Netherlands Architecture Inst., Rotterdam, 2001—06, Cin. Art Mus., 2006—. Co-founder San Francisco Prize, 1995; founder first biannual San Francisco Forum, Architecture of Imagination, 1997; adj. prof. Calif. Coll. Arts and Crafts; dir. First Internat. Architecture Biennale Rotterdam, 2002. Author: Violated Perfection: Architecture and the Fragmentation of the Modern, 1990, James Gamble Rogers and the Architecture of Pragmatism, 1994, Building Sex: Men, Women, Architecture and the Construction of Sexuality, Queer Space: The Spaces of Same Sex Desire, 1997, Architecture Must Burn, 2000; exhibitions include Magnets of Meaning, 1997. Office: Cincinnati Art Museum 953 Eden Park Ave Cincinnati OH 45202

BETT, ROBERT SCOTT, music educator; b. Kingman, Kans., Aug. 31, 1953; s. Robert Lawrence and Juanita Maxine Bett; m. Wendy Diane Wheaton, June 1, 1979; children: Jessica Lynn, Diana Rebecca. B in music edn., U. North Colo., 1975, M in music edn., 1981. Music educator Thornton Elem., Colo., 1975—79, Baseline Jr. High, Boulder, 1979—81, West Jefferson Jr High, 1983—84, West Arvlda H S, 1984—86, Mandalay Mid. Sch., Westminister, Colo., 1986—88, Moore Mid. Sch., Arvada, Colo., 1988—2005. Mid. level rep. Music Assn. of Jefferson County, 1984—86. Mem.: Am. Sch. Band Dir. Assn., Colo. Bandmasters Assn., Music Educators Nat. Conf., Phi Beta Mu. Avocations: golf, skiing, bicycling. Home: 8800 W 81st Dr Arvada CO 80005

BETTAC, ROBERT EDWARD, lawyer; b. Ashland, Ohio, Aug. 13, 1949; s. Donald Albert and Ruth Lavina (Foos) B.; m. Suzanne Lee Shepherd, June 30, 1979; children: Jacqueline Lee, Robert Mitchell. BA in Polit. Sci., Ashland U., 1972; JD, U. Cin., 1979. Bar: U.S. Dist. Ct. (we.

and so. dists.) Tex. 1983, U.S. Dist. Ct. (no. dist.) Tex. 1989, U.S. Ct. Appeals (5th and 11th cirs.) 1981, U.S. Dist. Ct. (ea. dist.) Tex. 2001. Assoc. Foster & Assocs., Inc., San Antonio, 1979-84; ptnr. Foster, Bettac & Heller, P.C., San Antonio, 1984-89, Akin Gump Strauss Hauer & Feld, San Antonio, 1989—2003. Author: (with others) Texas Practice Guide, 2d ed., 1983. Mem. Witte Mus. Coun., San Antonio, 1984—, San Antonio Public Library Found. Bd., 2003—. Home: 126 Rosemary Ave San Antonio TX 78209-3841 Office: Ogletree Deakins Nash Smoak & Stewart 112 E Pecan St Ste 2600 San Antonio TX 78205 Office Phone: 210-354-1300. E-mail: bob.bettac@odnss.com.

BETTERIDGE, FRANCES CARPENTER, small business owner, retired lawyer, mediator; b. Aug. 25, 1921; d. James Dunton and Emily (Atkinson) Carpenter; m. Albert Edwin Betteridge, Feb. 5, 1949 (div. 1975); children: Anne, Albert Edwin, James, Peter. AB, Mt. Holyoke Coll., South Hadley, Mass., 1942; JD, NY Law Sch., 1978. Bar: Conn. 1979, Ariz. 1982. Tech. in charge blood banks Roosevelt Hosp. and Mountainside Hosp., NYC, Montclair, NJ, 1943-49; sub. tchr. Greenwich H.S., Conn., 1978-79; intern and asst. to labor contracts office Town of Greenwich, 1979-80; vol. referee Pima County Juvenile Ct., Tucson, 1981-85; pvt. practice Tucson, 1982—87; judge Pro Tempore Pima County Justice Cts., 1988-91; owner, tour leader Betteridge Imports and Tours, LLC, Tucson, 2004—. Commr. Juvenile Ct., Pima County Superior Ct., Tucson, 1985-87; hearing officer Small Claims Ct., Pima County Justice Cts., Tucson, 1982; mediator Family Crisis Svc., Tucson, 1982-85. vol. referee Pima County Superior Ct., 1981-85; lectr. Tucson Mus. Art, 1994—. Pres. H.S. PTA, Greenwich, 1970, PTA Coun., 1971; mem. Greenwich Bd. Edn., 1971-76, sec. 1973-76; com. chmn. LWV Tucson, 1981, bd. dirs., 1984-85; bd. dirs., sec. Let The Sun Shine Inc., Tucson, 1981—; bd. dirs. Ariz. Sr. Acad., 2003-05; medicare vol. Pima Coun. on Aging, 2003—; chair adv. bd. Acad. Village Homeowners Assn., 2005-07. Mem. ABA, Ariz. Bar Assn., Pima County Bar Assn., Tucson Sr. Acad., Point o'Woods Club. Republican. Avocations: travel, folk art. Home and Office: Betteridge Imports & Tours LLC 7659 S Vivaldi Ct Tucson AZ 85747 Office Phone: 520-577-7795. E-mail: fmotz@aol.com.

BETTI, JOHN ANSO, federal official, retired automotive executive; b. Ottawa, Ill., Jan. 6, 1931; s. Louis and Ida (Dallari) B.; m. Joan Doyle, Aug. 22, 1953; children: Diane , Denise, Donna (dec.), Joan. BSMechE, Ill. Inst. Tech., 1952; MS in Engring., Chrysler Inst. Engring., 1954. Registered profl. engr., Mich. Student engr. to asst. chief engr. Chrysler Corp., 1952-62; with Ford Motor Co., 1962-89, from exec. engr. body engring. to v.p., gen. mgr. truck ops., 1962-76; v.p. product devel. Ford of Europe, Inc., Warley, England, 1976-79, also dir.; with N.Am. Automotive Ops., Dearborn, Mich., 1979-84, v.p. powertrain and chassis ops., 1979-83, v.p. mfg. and bus. devel., 1983-84; exec. v.p. tech. affairs and operating staffs Ford Motor Co., Mich., 1985—88, bd. dirs. fin. and exec. coms., 1985—89, exec. v.p. diversified products ops. Dearborn, Mich., 1988-89; undersecretary of def., acquisition and nat. armaments dir. Dept. Def., Washington, 1989-91. Instr. Lawrence Inst. Engring., Wayne State U., Detroit, 1953-59; chmn. bd. Ford Motor Co., Caribbean Inc., 1979-84, Ensite Ltd. Can., 1979-84, Ford Aerospace corp., 1988-89, Ford Electronics and Refrigeration Corp., 1988-89; dir. collins & Aikman Corp., 1991-94; mem. dir. compensation com. Breed Tech., 1992-94, Kaysor-Roth Corp., 1993-94. Bd. dirs. Mich. Opera Theatre, 1984-87; trustee Detroit Inst. for Children, 1985-89; mem. nat. adv. com. U. Mich. Engring. Sch., 1985-89; chmn. bd. trustees GMI Engring. and Mgmt. Inst., 1985-89. Recipient Alumni Profl. Achievement award Ill. Inst. Tech., 1980; John Morse Meml. scholar. Mem. Lost Tree Club (North Palm Beach, Fla.), Jupiter Hills Club (Tequesta, Fla.), Bloomfield Hills C.C., Tau Beta Pi, Pi Tau Sigma, Alpha Sigma Phi, Beta Omega Nu. Personal E-mail: jbetti@bellsouth.net.

BETTINGER, WALTER W., II, investment company executive; b. Nov. 29, 1960; m. Laura G. Bettinger (div.); 3 children; m. Teri Farnsworth. BBA summa cum laude in Finance and Investments, Ohio U., 1983; completed Gen. Mgmt. program, Harvard Bus. Sch. Joined pension dept. Westfield Cos., Medina County, Ohio, 1981; founder The Hampton Co. (acquired by The Charles Schwab Corp.), Bath Township, Ohio, 1983—95; gen. mgr. SchwabPlan, COO and then pres. Retirement Plan Services Enterprise The Charles Schwab Corp., 1995—2001, pres. corp. services divsn., 2001—04, exec. v.p., 2004—05, COO individual investor enterprise, 2004—05, pres. individual investor enterprise, 2005—07, pres., COO, 2007—. Exec. advisory bd. Ohio U. Coll. Bus.; chmn. Walter W. Bettinger II Charitable Found. Mem.: Am. Soc. Pension Actuaries, Nat. Defined Contribution Coun. (bd. dirs., exec. com.). Office: Charles Schwab Corp 101 Montgomery St San Francisco CA 94104*

BETTINGHAUS, ERWIN PAUL, research scientist; b. Peoria, Ill., Oct. 28, 1930; s. Erwin Paul and Paula (Bretscher) B.; m. Carole Irma Overmier, Apr. 5, 1952; children: Karen Lee, Joyce Anne, Bruce Alan. BA, U. Ill., 1952, PhD, 1959; MA, Bradley U., 1953. Instr. Mich. State U., East Lansing, 1958-60, asst. prof., 1960-64, assoc. prof., 1964-69, prof., 1969-97, prof. emeritus, 1997—, chmn. dept. comm., 1972-76, dean Coll. Comm. Arts and Scis., 1976-96, dean emeritus, 1997—; dep. dir. AMC Cancer Rsch. Ctr., Denver, 1997—2002; sr. scientist Cooper Inst., 2002—05, assoc. v.p., 2003—05; sr. scientist Klein Buendel, Inc., 2005—. Vis. prof. U. Okla., 1970-71 Author: The Nature of Proof, 1971, Persuasive Communication, 1994. Mem. Nat. Cancer Adv. Bd., 1988-94. With U.S. Army, 1953-56. Mem. AAAS, APA, Internat. Comm. Assn. (pres. 1982), Am. Comm. Assn., Assn. for Edn. in Journalism, Assn. Comm. Adminstrn. (pres. 1991). Home: 2170 S Parfet Dr Lakewood CO 80227-1900 Office: 1667 Cole Blvd Ste 225 Golden CO 80401 Office Phone: 303-565-4341. Business E-Mail: ebettinghaus@kleinbuendel.com.

BETTIS, JEROME ABRAM, sports commentator, retired professional football player; b. Detroit, Feb. 16, 1972; s. Johnnie and Gladys Bettis. Student, U. Notre Dame. Running back L.A. Rams, 1993—94, St. Louis Rams (formerly L.A. Rams), 1995, Pitts. Steelers, 1996—2006; studio analyst NFL Sunday Night Football NBC, 2006—. Co-author (with Teresa Varley): Driving Home: My Unforgettable Super Bowl Run, 2006. Founder The Bus Stops Here Foundation, 1997—. Named NFL Rookie of Yr., Sporting News, 1993; named to Pro Bowl, 1993, 1994, 1996, 1997, 2001, 2004; recipient Walter Payton Man of the Yr. Award, 2002. Mem.: Super Bowl XL Champions, Pittsburgh Steelers, 2006. Avocation: bowling. Office: NBC 30 Rockefeller Plz New York NY 10112*

BETTISON, CYNTHIA ANN, museum director, archaeologist; b. St. Louis, Sept. 8, 1958; d. William Leslie and Barbara Ann (Yunker) B. BA in Anthropology and Biology, Pitzer Coll., 1980; MA in Anthropology, Eastern N.Mex. U., 1983; ABD in Anthropology, U. Calif., Santa Barbara, 1986, PhD in Anthropology, 1998. Cert. profl. archaeologist Archaeol. Stds. Bd., 2004. Asst. curator dept. anthropology U. Calif., Santa Barbara, 1988-89, curator dept. anthropology, 1990-91; dir. Western N.Mex. U. Mus., Silver City, 1991—. Co-dir. Western N.Mex. U. Archaeol. Field Sch., 1992, 94, 95; lectr. Western N.Mex. U., 1992, 93, adj. asst. prof. dept. social scis., 1994—; various archaeol. positions, 1981—. Contbr. articles to profl. jours. Recipient Conservation Assessment Program grant, 1994-95, NEH, 1994; Gila Nat. Forest grantee, 1992, 94, 95, Silver City Lodgers Tax Bd. grantee, 1992, Andrew Isabell Meml. Fund grantee U. Calif., 1990, SIMSE grantee, 1994-95, 95-96. Mem. AAUW, Am. Assn. Mus., Am. Anthrop. Assn., Am. Soc. Conservation Archaeology, N.Mex. Mus. Assn. (pres. 2002-04), Soc. for Am. Archaeology, Archaeol. Soc. N.Mex., N.Mex. Archaeol. Coun. (sec. 1993-94), Coun. Mus. Anthropology (sec. 1992-94), Assn. of Coll. and Univ. Mus. and Galleries (bd. dirs. 2004—, sml. mus. adminstrn. com. bd. mem.)), Mountain Plains Mus. Assn., Univ. Women's Club, Univ. Club, Optimist Club (sec. Silver City chpt. 1992), Silver City Rotary Club (v.p. 1999-2000, pres. elect 2000-2001, pres. 2001-2002, dist. 5520 asst. gov. 2002-04), Silver City Grant County C. of C., Chpt. BR PEO, Phi Kappa Phi. Office: Western NM Univ Mus 1000 W College Ave Silver City NM 88061-4158 E-mail: bettisonc@wnmu.edu.

BETTMAN, GARY BRUCE, national hockey league commissioner; b. NYC, June 2, 1952; s. Howard G. and Gretel J. (Pollack) B.; m. Michelle Weiner, Aug. 24, 1975; children: Lauren, Jordan, Brittany. BS, Cornell U., 1974; JD, NYU, 1977. Bar: N.Y. 1978, N.J. 1978, U.S. Dist. Ct. (so. and ea. dists.) N.Y. 1979. Assoc. Proskauer Rose, NYC, 1977-80, Gutkin, Miller et al, Milburn, NJ, 1980-81; asst. gen. counsel NBA, NYC, 1981-84, v.p., gen. counsel, 1984-89, sr. v.p., gen. counsel, 1989-93; commr. NHL, NYC, 1993—. Mem. N.Y. State Bar Assn., Assn. of Bar of City of N.Y. (chmn. com. on sports law), N.J. Bar Assn., Sports Lawyers Assn. (bd. dirs. 1985-93, entertainment and sports law com. 1990-93), Phi Kappa Phi. Avocations: skiing, sailing, tennis. Office: NHL 47th Flr 1251 Ave of the Americas New York NY 10020*

BETTMAN, JAMES ROSS, management educator; b. Laurinburg, NC, Sept. 15, 1943; s. Roland David and Virginia Gertrude (Hare) B.; m. Joan Carol Scribner, Dec. 16, 1967; 1 child, David James. BA, Yale U., 1965, MPhil, PhD, Yale U., 1969. Prof. mgmt. Grad. Sch. Mgmt., UCLA, 1969-82; IBM rsch. prof. Fuqua Sch. Bus., Duke U., Durham, NC, 1982-83, Burlington Industries prof., 1983—. Author: An Information Processing Theory of Consumer Choice, 1979, The Adaptive Decision Maker, 1993, Emotional Decisions: Tradeoff Difficulty and Coping in Consumer Choice, 2001; co-editor Jour. of Consumer Rsch., 1981-87, editor monographs, 2002--; contbr. chpts. to books, articles to profl. jours. Named ISI Highly Cited Rschr., Econs./Bus., 2003; recipient Melamed prize bus. rsch., 2000, Disting. Sci. Achievement award Soc. for Consumer Psychology, 2006. Fellow APA, Am. Psychol. Soc.; mem. Assn. Consumer Rsch. (bd. dir. 1976-79, pres. 1987, fellow in consumer behavior 1992), Inst. Ops. Rsch. and Mgmt. Sci., Am. Mktg. Assn. (Harold M. Maynard award 1979, Paul D. Converse award 1992, Irwin/McGraw-Hill Disting. Mktg. Educator award 2000). Democrat. Episcopalian. Home: 213 Huntington Dr Chapel Hill NC 27514-2419 Office: Duke U Fuqua Sch of Bus Durham NC 27708-0120 Office Phone: 919-660-7851. Business E-Mail: jrb12@mail.duke.edu.

BETTMAN, SUZANNE (SUE BETTMAN), lawyer; b. June 1964; BA, Northwestern U.; JD, U. Ill. Sr. v.p., gen. counsel R.R. Donnelley & Sons Co., Chgo., 2004—. Spkr. in field. Office: RR Donnelley & Sons Co 111 S Wacker Dr Chicago IL 60606 Home: 521 W Stratford Pl Apt 2 Chicago IL 60657 Office Phone: 312-326-8000. Office Fax: 312-326-8594.

BETTS, BARBARA STOKE, artist, educator; b. Arlington, Mass., Apr. 19, 1924; d. Stuart and Barbara Lillian (Johnstone) Stoke; m. James William Betts, July 28, 1951; 1 child, Barbara Susan (dec.). BA, Mt. Holyoke Coll., South Hadley, Mass., 1946; MA, Columbia U., NYC, 1948. Cert. tchr. NY, Calif., Hawaii. Art tchr. Walton Union Schs., NY, 1947-48, Presidio Hill Sch., San Francisco, 1949-51; freelance artist San Francisco, 1951; art tchr. Honolulu Acad. Arts, summer 1952, 59, 63, 85, spring 61, 64; libr. aide art rm. Libr. of Hawaii, Honolulu, 1959; art tchr. Hanahauoli Sch., Honolulu, 1961-62, Hawaii State Dept. Edn., Honolulu, 1958-59, 64-84; owner Ho'olaule'a Designs, Honolulu, 1973—; art editor Scrapbook Press, 2002—, Portfolio Cons. of Hawaii, 1990—. Cons.: Strategy of The Baltimore & Ohio Railroad 1930-1932; staff artist: The Arcadian newsletter, 2000—, James W. Betts & Co.; illustrator: Cathedral Cooks, 1964, In Due Season, 1986, From Nowhere To Somewhere On A Round Trip Ticket, 2003; exhibited in Hawaii Pavilion Expo '90, Osaka, Japan, State Found. Culture and Arts; exhibited in group shows since 1964; one-woman shows include 1991, 96, 99; represented in Arts of Paradise Gallery, Waikiki, 1990-2001, Hale Ku'ai, a Hawaiian Coop., 1998-2001, Art Exch., Hot Springs, Ark., artexchange.com, Hot Springs, Ark., 2005—, NEOCON 2006, Chgo., 2006; traveling exhbns. include Pacific Prints, 1991, Printmaking East/West, 1993-95, Hawaii/Wis. Watercolor Show, 1993-94. Mem. Hawaii Watercolor Soc. (newsletter editor 1986-90), Nat. League Am. Pen Women (art chmn. 1990-92, sec. 1992-94, 2000-02, nat. miniature art shows 1991, 92, 93, 95), Honolulu Printmakers (dir. 1986, 87), Assn. Hawaii Artists, scholarship aid programs, Mount Holyoke Coll., Mary Lyon Soc., Rutgers Univ., Col. Henry Rutgers Soc. Republican. Episcopalian. Avocations: art, travel, writing, photography. Home and Office: 1434 Punahou St Apt 1028 Honolulu HI 96822-4740 Office Phone: 808-955-7817. Personal E-mail: kimorail@aol.com.

BETTS, BERT A., retired treasurer, accountant; b. San Diego, Aug. 16, 1923; s. Bert A. and Alma (Jorgenson) B.; m. Barbara Lang; children: Terry Lou, Linda Sue, Sara Ellen, Bert Alan, Randy Wayne, LeAnn, John Chauncey, Frederick P., Roby F., Bruce H. BBA, Calif. Western U., 1950. CPA, Calif. Accountant John R. Gillette, 1946-48; ptnr. Gillette & Betts, 1949-50; pvt. accounting practice, 1951-54; ptnr. Betts & Munden, Lemon Grove, Calif., 1954-57; sr. ptnr. Bert A. Betts & Co., 1958-59; treas. State of Calif., 1959-67; prin. Bert A. Betts & Assos., 1967-77; ret., 1977. CEO Internat. Prodn. Assocs., 1970-87; dir. Lifetime Cmtys. Inc.; gen. ptnr. Sacramento Met. Airport Properties 4, Ltd., 1970-02. Author (with Barbara Lang Betts): A Citizen Answers. Mem. Lemon Grove Sch. Bd., 1954-57; Calif. chmn. Max Baer Heart Fund; state employees chmn. Am. Cancer Sco., 1962-64, bd. dirs. county br., 1963-69, Sacramento County campaign chmn., mem. exec. com., 1965, pres. Sacramento chpt., 1967-68; sponsor All Am. B-24 Liberator Collings Found. Served as 1st lt. USAAF, 1942-45. Decorated D.F.C., Air medal with four clusters; recipient Louisville award Municipal Finance Officers Assn. U.S. and Can., 1963; honored by Calif. Mcpl. Treas.'s Assn., 1964; inductee Hoover H.S. Hall of Fame, San Diego, 1998, Grossmont Health Dist. Gallery of Honor, 2002. Mem. Nat. Assn. State Auditors, Comptrs. and Treas's Mcpl. Forum N.Y., Calif. Soc. CPAs, San Diego Squadron Air Force Assn. (past vice comdr.), Am. Legion, 2d Air Div. Assn., 8th Air Force Hist. Soc., VFW, Commemorative Air Force (col.), Native Sons. Golden West, Internat. B-24 Liberator Club, Foresters, Masons, Calif. Scholarship Fedn. (life), DFC Soc., Sigma Phi Epsilon, Beta Alpha Psi (hon.), Alpha Kappa Psi (hon.). Clubs: Eagles; Men's (Lemon Grove) (pres.), Lions (Lemon Grove) (treas.); Commonwealth. Presbyterian. Home: 441 Sandburg Dr Sacramento CA 95819-2559 also: 1830 Avenida Del Mundo Apt 1608/9 Coronado CA 92118-3018 Personal E-mail: blbbabbetts@sbcglobal.net.

BETTS, DIANNE CONNALLY, economist, educator; b. Tyler, Tex., Sept. 23, 1948; d. William Isaac and Martine (Underwood) Connally; m. Floyd Galloway Betts Jr., Feb. 14, 1973. BA in History, So. Meth. U., 1976, MA in History, 1980; MA in Econ., U. Chgo., 1986; PhD in Econ., U. Tex., 1991. Affiliated scholar Inst. for Rsch. on Women and Gender/Stanford U., 1993—; economist, tech. analyst, fin. cons. Smith Barney, Dallas, 1994—2000; economist, fin. cons. Morgan Keegan, Dallas, 2000—. Mem. women studies coun. So. Meth. U., 1993-94, Fulbright campus interviewing com. mem. 1992-93, pub. rels. and devel. liaison dept. econ., 1990-92, faculty mentor U. honors first year mentoring program, adj. asst. prof. dept. econ. and history, 1992—, vis. asst. prof. 1990-92; faculty, Oxford, summer 1991-93, adj. instr. dept. history, 1989-90, adj. instr. dept. econ., 1985-89, tchg. asst. dept. history, spring 1980; lectr. dept. polit. economy U. Tex., Dallas, summer 1988. Author: Crisis on the Rio Grande: Poverty, Unemployment, and Economic Development on the Texas-Mexico Border, 1994, Historical Perspectives on the American Economy: Selected Reading, 1995; contbr. articles to profl. jours. Rsch. Planning grant NSF, 1992; recipient Marguereta Deschner Teaching award, 1991; Humanities and Scis. Merit scholar, 1978. Mem. Am. Econ. Assn., Am. History Assn., Econ. History Assn., Cliometric Soc., Social Sci. History Assn., N.Am. Conf. on British Studies, Nat. Coun. for Rsch. on Women (affiliate), Omicron Delta Epsilon, Phi Alpha Theta. Home: 7802 Bryn Mawr Dallas TX 75225 Office: Morgan Keegan 5956 Sherry Ln # 1900 Dallas TX 75225-6531 Office Phone: 214-365-5525. E-mail: dcbetts@airmail.net.

BETTS, EDWARD, artist; b. Yonkers, NY, Aug. 4, 1920; s. Harrison and Mildred (Waterbury) B.; m. Jane Burke, June 2, 1949 (dec. 1984); children: Peter, John, Wendy; m. Edis Hatch, 1986. BA, Yale U., 1942; MFA, U. Ill., 1952. From instr. to prof. art U. Ill., 1949-84, prof. emeritus, 1984—; assoc. Ctr. for Advanced Study, 1968-69. Watercolor and acrylic painter, 1937—; one-man shows include Contemporary Arts Gallery, N.Y.C., 1953, 55, John Heller Gallery, 1956, 59, Charles Feingarten Gallery, Chgo., 1954, 56-57, Midtown Galleries, N.Y.C., 1961, 65, 68, 72, 76, 89, Krannert Art Mus., U. Ill., 1970; group shows include Corcoran biennial exhbns. Contemporary Am. Painting, 1947, 51, 55, 57, 59, Met. Mus. Am. Painting Today, 1950, Bklyn. Internat. Watercolor Exhbn., 1953, 55, 61, NAD, 1953—, Audubon Artists, Am. Water Color Soc., Calif. Water Color Soc., Bklyn. Mus., 1961, Pa. Acad., 1953-54, 59, 61, Nat. Inst. Arts and Letters, 1962, Water Color USA, Springfield (Mo.) Art Mus., 1963-64, 20th Am. Drawing Ann., Norfolk Mus. Arts and Scis., 1963, Hassam Purchase Fund Exhibit, 1961, 63, Maine 100 Artists of the 20th Century, Colby Coll., 1964; represented in permanent collections Fogg Art Mus., Upjohn Pharm. Co., La Jolla Art Ctr., Indpls. Mus. Art, Stephens Coll. (Mo.), Sandoz Pharm. Co., Atlanta U., St. Lawrence U., Irving Trust Co., N.Y.C., USIA Art in Embassies Program, New Britain Mus. Am. Art, Kans. State U., Rochester (N.Y.) Meml. Art Gallery, Springfield (Mo.) Art Mus., Davenport (Iowa) Mcpl. Gallery, Ball State U., Va. Mus. Fine Arts, Butler Inst. Am. Art, Calif. Watercolor Soc., Tupperware Internat., Orlando, Fla., 1st Nat. Bank Boston, Prudential Life Ins. Co., Newark, also pvt. collections; author: Master Class in Watercolor, 1975, Creative Landscape Painting, 1978, Creative Seascape Painting, 1981, Master Class in Watermedia, 1993. "Creative Lives: Four Maine Artists", Ogunquit Museum of American Art, 1996—; retrospective one man show Irvine Gallery of Art, River Tree Ctr. for the Arts, Kennebunk, 2002. Recipient 1st prize oil painting Brick Store Mus. Exhbn., Kennebunk, Maine, 1949, Arts and Artists Miss. Exhbn., Davenport, Iowa, 1950; Grumbacher award Allied Artists, 1950, Bronze medal of honor, 1956; Audubon Artists award, 1951, 72, Gold medal of honor, 1952; Pennell medal Phila. Water Color Club, 1953, award Portland Mus. Summer Art Festival, 1957, Purchase award Hassam Fund Exhbn., 1966, Winsor and Newton award Ga. Water Color Soc., 1979. Mem. NAD (2d Altman prize 1954, Benjamin Altman prize 1957, 59, 66), Am. Water Color Soc. (Silver medal of honor 1953, 59, Remmey award 1966, Cooper award 1977), Art Students League, Ogunquit Art Assn. (past pres.), Nat. Acad. Design, Am. Watercolor Soc., Century Assn. N.Y.C. Home: 2 Wonderbrook Dr Kennebunk ME 04043-6738

BETTS, GENE M., telecommunications industry executive; BBA, MBA, U. Kans. CPA. Various positions in audit and tax depts. Arthur Young, 1975; ptnr. Arthur Young & Co.; asst. v.p. tax dept. Sprint Corp., Overland, Kans., 1987-88, v.p., 1988-90, sr. v.p. fin. svcs. and taxes, 1990-98, sr. v.p., treas., 1998—. Office: Sprint World Hdqrs 6200 Sprint Pkwy Overland Park KS 66251

BETTS, JAMES EDWARD, lawyer; b. Holyoke, Mass., Oct. 9, 1940; s. James Archibel and Ruth Owen Betts; m. Carol Sue Hanser, June 19, 1962; children: James Hanser, Laurie Jane Betts Hemler. AB, Colgate U., Hamilton, NY, 1962; JD, U. Richmond, Va., 1965; LLM, Harvard Law Sch., Cambridge, Mass., 1966. Bar: Va. 1965. Assoc. Christian & Barton, LLP, Richmond, Va., 1966—72, ptnr., 1972—, mng. ptnr., 1990—. Adj. assoc. prof. antitrust law U. Richmond Law Sch., Richmond, Va., 1973—83, 2005—; chmn. antitrust sect. Va. State Bar, 1977, mem. lawyer disciplinary bd., 1990—93, chmn. com. on lawyer discipline, 1999—2000. Sec. Richmond First Club, 1972; pres. Friends of Richmond Libr., Va., 1974; chmn. Profls. Divsn. United Way Svcs. Greater Richmond, 1996; mem., moderator diaconate First Presbyn. Ch., Richmond, 1989—95, elder, clk. of session, 1996—2002; sec. and mem. Mary Baldwin Coll. Bd. Trustees, Staunton, Va., 1976—89, 1991—96; v.p. and mem. bd. dir. The Steward Sch., Richmond, 1977—79; chmn. U. Richmond Nat. Alumni Coun., 1979—80. Fellow: Am. Bar Found. (Va. state chair); mem.: John Marshall Found. (pres. 2006—), U. Richmond Law Sch. Assn. (pres. 1979—80), Va. Bar Assn. (pres. 2002), Farmington Country Club (Charlottesville, Va.), US Supreme Ct. Hist. Soc. (Va. state chmn. 2004), Phi Delta Phi, Omicron Delta Kappa. Presbyterian. Avocations: reading, exercise, sports. Office: Christian and Barton LLP 909 E Main St Richmond VA 23219 Office Phone: 804-697-4156. Business E-Mail: jbetts@cblaw.com.

BETTS, JAMES WILLIAM, JR., financial analyst, consultant; b. Oct. 11, 1923; s. James William and Cora Anna (Banta) B.; m. Barbara Stoke, July 28, 1951; 1 child, Barbara Susan (dec.). BA, Rutgers U., 1946; postgrad., New Sch. for Social Rsch., 1948—49; MA, U. Hawaii, 1957. With Dun & Bradstreet, Inc., 1946-86, svc. cons., 1963-64, reporting and svc. mgr., 1964-65, sr. fin. analyst Honolulu, 1965-86; owner Portfolio Cons. of Hawaii, 1979—. Cons. Saybrook Point Investments, Old Saybrook, Conn., 1979—; owner James W. Betts & Co., 1996—, Scrapbook Press, 2002—. Author: From Nowhere to Somewhere on a Round Trip Ticket, 2003, Strategy of the Baltimore & Ohio Railroad, 1930-1932, 2006; contbr. articles to mags. With AUS, 1943. Mem. Am. Econ. Assn., Nat. Assn. Bus. Economists, Col. Henry Rutgers Soc., Internat. Inst. Forecasters. Republican. Episcopalian. Home and Office: 1434 Punahou St #1028 Honolulu HI 96822-4740 Office Phone: 808-955-7817. Personal E-mail: kimorail@aol.com.

BETTS, JOE DELTON, retired religious studies educator; b. Fairy, Tex., July 24, 1922; s. Thomas Lester and Beulah Ardenia Betts; m. Wilma Ruth Majors, Dec. 24, 1950; children: Donna Jean Hanson, Rebecca Louise Tribble, Robert Joseph, Thomas Walter. BA in Bible and Social Sci., Harding Coll., Seary, Ark., 1952, MA, 1953. Prof. Ibaraki Christian Coll., Hitachi, Ibaraki, Japan, 1956—96, ret., 1996. Supt. Nazare-en Old Peoples' Home, Urizura, Ibaraki, 1962—65; missionary Ch. of Christ, Hitachi, 1956—. Author: Biblical Exegesis, Charis in Romans, 1958. Chief petty officer USN, 1942—48, Pacifc Theater. Recipient Outstanding Alumnus award, Harding U. Sch. of Religion, 1987. Republican. Achievements include patents for eternal calendar. Home: 668 EN 23d St Abilene TX 79601 Home Phone: 325-232-7319. Personal E-mail: joeandruthbetts@suddenlink.net.

BETTS, NICOLE LAVETTE, elementary school educator, consultant; b. Houston, Tex., Apr. 7, 1979; d. Thomas Holloway and JoAnn Kelly-James; 1 child, Nakita Morgan. BS in Criminal Justice, U. Houston, Tex., 2002; MEd, Tex. So. U., Houston, Tex., 2004. Cert. tchr. Tex. Edn. Agy., 2003. Ednl. asst. N.Q. Henderson Houston (Tex.) Ind. Sch. Dist., 1999—2002, tchr. N.Q. Henderson, 2002—, coord. after sch. program N.Q. Henderson, 2005—. Mem. tchr. adv. bd. McGovern Mus. Health and Med. Scis., Houston, 2004—05, Children's Mus., Houston, 2006—; tchr. liaison Nat. Space Found., 2006. Contbr. curriculum units. Named Tchr. of Yr., N.Q. Henderson Elem., 2006; recipient Jordan Fundamentals award, Nike and Michael Jordan, 2005; fellow, Baylor Coll. Medicine, 2004—06. Fellow: Houston (Tex.) Tchrs. Inst. (tchr. rep. 2004—, mentor 2004—); mem.: Houston Area Alliance Black Sch. Educators (named Tchr. of Yr.), Nat. Sci. Tchrs. Assn. Home: 3907 Portman Glen Houston TX 77047 Office: NQ Henderson HISD 701 Solo Houston TX 77020 Office Phone: 713-671-4195. Business E-Mail: nbetts@houstonisd.org.

BETTS, REBECCA A., lawyer; b. Memphis, Nov. 25, 1951; BA, Dickinson Coll., 1972; JD, W.Va. U., 1976. Bar: W.Va., U.S. Dist. Ct. (so.

dist.) W.Va. 1976, U.S. Ct. Appeals (4th cir.) 1978, U.S. Supreme Ct. 1984. Assoc. Spilman, Thomas, Battle & Klostermeyer, Charleston, W.Va., 1976—77; asst. U.S. atty. U.S. Atty.'s Office, 1977—81, chief civil divsn., 1979—81; founding ptnr. King, Betts & Allen, Charleston, W.Va.; U.S. atty. U.S. Dist. Ct. So. Dist., W.Va., 1994—2001; ptnr. Allen Guthrie McHugh & Thomas PLLC, 2001—. Adv. com. on rules & procedures 4th Cir., 1995—2001; civil justice reform act adv. com. So. Dist. W.Va., 1991, com. for local rules and subcom. on criminal rules, 92. Mem. editl. bd.: W.Va. Law Rev. Mem.: The Legal Aid Soc. of Charleston (bd. dirs.), W.Va. State Bar (past mem. com. on legal ethics), Order of Coif. Office: Allen Guthrie McHugh & Thomas PO Box 3394 Charleston WV 25333 Office Phone: 304-345-7250. Business E-Mail: rabetts@agmtlaw.com.

BETTS, RICHARD KEVIN, political science professor; b. Easton, Pa., Aug. 15, 1947; s. John Rickards and Cecelia Agnes (Fitzpatrick) B.; m. Adela Maria Bolet, July 25, 1987; children: Elena, Michael, Diego. BA, Harvard U., Cambridge, Mass., 1969, MA, 1971, PhD, 1975. Lectr. in government Harvard U., Cambridge, Mass., 1975-76, vis. prof., 1985-88; rsch. assoc. Brookings Instn., Washington, 1976-81, sr. fellow, 1981-90; dir. Saltzman Inst. War and Peace Studies, Columbia U., NYC, 1997—, Shifrin prof. polit. sci., 1998—2002, Saltzman prof., 2002—; dir. nat. securities studies Coun. on Fgn. Rels., 1996-2000. Mem. staff Senate Select Com. on Intelligence, Washington, 1975-76, NSC, Washington, 1977; adj. prof. Johns Hopkins U., Washington, 1978-85, 88-90; cons. CIA, 1980-91, 93-99, 2003—; dir. ctrl. intelligence Nat. Security Adv. Panel, 1993-99; mem. Nat. Commn. on Terrorism, 1999-2000; occasion lectr. Nat. War Coll., Fgn. Svcs. Inst., U.S. Mil. Acad. Author: Soldiers, Statesmen and Cold War Crises, 1977 (2d edit. 1991, Lasswell award 1979), Surprise Attack, 1982, Nuclear Blackmail and Nuclear Balance, 1987, Military Readiness, 1995, Enemies of Intelligence, 2007; co-author: The Irony of Vietnam, 1979 (Woodrow Wilson award 1980), Nonproliferation and U.S. Foreign Policy, 1980; editor: Cruise Missiles, 1981, Conflict After the Cold War, 1994, 2d edit., 2001, Paradoxes of Strategic Intelligence, 2003. Mem. foreign policy staff Mondale Presdl. Campaign, Washington, 1984; mem. Assn. for Retarded Citizens, Bergen County, NJ, 1990—. Recipient Sumner prize Harvard U., 1976, Article award Nat. Intelligence Study Ctr., Washington, 1979, 81, Disting. Scholar award Internat. Studies Assn., 2005. Mem. Internat. Inst. for Strategic Studies, Am. Polit. Sci. Assn., Internat. Studies Assn. (Disting Scholar award 2005), Soc. for Historians Am. Fgn. Rels., Consortium for Study Intelligence. Democrat. Avocation: cinema history. Home: 1199 The Strand Teaneck NJ 07666-2020 Office: Columbia U Saltzman Inst War & Peace Studies 420 W 118th St New York NY 10027-7213

BETZ, A. LORRIS, pediatrician, educator; b. LaCrosse, Wis., Feb. 9, 1947; s. Alert L. and Charlotte M. (Kopp) B.; m. Ann C. Doyle, Aug. 30, 1968; children: Jennifer A., Bryan L. BS, U. Wis., 1969, MD., PhD, 1975. Intern pediatrics U. Calif., San Francisco, 1975, resident in pediatrics, 1975-79; asst. prof. pediatrics and neurology U. Mich., Ann Arbor, 1979-83, assoc. prof. pediatrics and neurology, 1983-87, prof. pediatrics, surgery, neurology, 1987—99, dir. neurosurg. rsch., surgery, 1987—99, assoc. dean for faculty affairs, 1993-97, interim dean Med. Sch., 1997—99; dean, sr. v.p. health sci. U. Utah Med. Sch., Salt Lake City, 1999—, sr. v.p. Cons. NIH, Bethesda, Md., 1985—. Editorial bd.: Jour. Neurochemistry, 1986-94; contbr. articles to Sci., Brain Rsch., Sci. Am., Stroke, Am. Jour. Physiology. Grantee, NIH, Univ. Mich., 1980—; named Established Investigator, Am. Heart Assn., Univ. Mich., 1981. Mem. Internat. Soc. Cerebral Blood Flow and Metabolism (bd. dirs. 1991—, sec. 1995—), Internat. Soc. Neurochemistry, Am. Physiol. Soc., Soc. for Pediatric Rsch., Am. Pediatric Soc., Phi Beta Kappa, Sigma Xi, Alpha Omega Alpha. Achievements include research in basic mechanisms that are responsible for moving nutrients and electrolytes between the blood and the brain of mammals, processes that produce brain injury following a stroke. Office: Health Sci Ctr Moran Eye Ctrs Fl 5 50 N Med Dr Salt Lake City UT 84132-0001

BETZ, HANS DIETER, theology studies educator; b. Lemgo, Lippe, Germany, May 21, 1931; came to U.S., 1963, naturalized, 1973; s. Ludwig and Gertrude Betz; m. Christel Hella Wagner, Nov. 10, 1958; children: Martin, Ludwig, Arnold. Student, Kirchliche Hochschule, Bethel, Fed. Republic Germany, 1951—52, U. Mainz, Fed. Republic Germany, 1952—55, U. Mainz, 1956—58, Westminster Coll, Cambridge, Eng., 1955—56; Doctor Theologiae, U. Mainz, Fed. Republic Germany, 1957; Habilitation, U. Mainz, 1966. Pastor Evangelical Ch., Rhineland, Fed. Republic Germany, 1961-63; from asst. prof. to prof. Sch. Theology, Claremont Grad. Sch., Calif., 1963-78; prof. N.T. and early Christian lit. U. Chgo., 1978-2000, Shailer Mathews prof., 1989—; prof. emeritus; chmn. dept. N.T. and early Christian lit. U. Chgo., 1985-94. Rsch. fellow Inst. Advanced Study, Hebrew U., Jerusalem, 1999. Author, editor numerous books and articles in German and English, 1959— Recipient Humboldt Rsch. prize, 1986; Lady Davis fellow Hebrew U., Jerusalem, Israel, 1990, Sackler scholar Tel Aviv U., 1995, McCarthy scholar Pontifical Biblical Inst., Rome, 2004; NEH rsch. grantee, 1970-83, Am. Assn. Theol. Schs. grantee, 1977, 84. Mem. Soc. Bibl. Lit. (pres. 1997), Studiorum Novi Testamenti Societas (pres. 1999-2000), Chgo. Soc. Bibl. Rsch. (pres. 1983-84). Office: U Chgo 1025 E 58th St Chicago IL 60637-1509

BETZER, SUSAN ELIZABETH BEERS, physician, geriatrician; b. Evanston, Ill., Aug. 24, 1943; d. Thomas Moulding and Mary Ella (Waidner) Beers; m. Peter Robin Betzer, June 18, 1965; children: Sarah Elizabeth, Katherine Hannah. AB in Biol. Scis. magna cum, Mount Holyoke Coll., 1965; PhD in Oceanography, U. R.I., 1972; MD, U. Miami, 1978. Diplomate Am. Bd. Family Practice, Am. Bd. Geriat. Rsch. assoc. dept. marine sci. U. South Fla., St. Petersburg, 1973-74, rsch. scholar, scientist, 1975-76; resident in family practice Bayfront Med. Ctr., St. Petersburg, 1978-81; clin. asst. prof. dept. family medicine U. South Fla., Tampa, 1982—2007; pvt. practice St. Petersburg, 1982—. Cons. physician Fed. Employee Health Clinic, Honolulu, 1981-82. Contbr. articles to profl. jours. Adv. com. St. Petersburg H.S., 1996-2002; bd. dir. Fla. Orch., Tampa, 1983-86, 88-, pres., 1985-86, mem. exec. com., 1988-, vice-chair bd. trustees 1996-2002, sec., 2002-, founder, chair audience devel. com., St. Petersburg, 1990-94; bd. dirs. Suncoast Ctr. Cmty. Mental Health, St. Petersburg, 1992-93; trustee Bayfront Health Found., 1996-2004, chmn., 2001-03; trustee Bayfront Health Svcs., 1992-96, vice-chair, 1993-96; vol. physician St. Petersburg Free Clinic, 1979-. Named Woman of Distinction, Suncoast coun. Girl Scouts U.S., 1994; named one of Best Doctors in Am., 1996—; recipient Golden Baton award, St. Petersburg Fla. Orch. Guild, 1994, Chmns. award, Fla. Orch., 1997, Svc. award, Pinellas County Med. Soc., 1999, Philanthropy Vol. of Yr., Tampa Bay chpt. Assn. Fundraising Profls., 2003, Humanitarian Physician of Yr., Tampa Bay Area, Fla. Med. Bus., 2004. Mem.: Mt. Holyoke Coll. Campaign Steering Com., Fla. Acad. Family Physicians (Dr. of the Day, Fla. Legislature 1995, 1996), Am. Med. Women's Assn., Am. Acad. Family Physicians (Mead Johnson award 1980), Mount Holyoke Alumnae Assn. (alumnae honor rsch. com. 1988—91, alumnae devel. com. 1996—2003, pres. 2003—06, Alumnae medal of honor 2000), Phi Beta Kappa. Avocations: symphony, birding, cooking, reading. Home: 1830 7th St N Saint Petersburg FL 33704-3322 Office: 461 7th Ave S Saint Petersburg FL 33701-4818 Office Phone: 727-823-0402.

BETZJITOMIR, SUSAN MARIE, lawyer, educator, policy analysis researcher; b. Bangor, Maine, Apr. 7, 1961; d. Andrew Kurchey and Trudy Louise (Box) Runyan; m. Howard Steven Jitomir; children: Roxanne Jitomir, Jennifer Stergion, Jean Jitomir, Susan Jitomir II, Ebony Jitomir. AS with honors and distinction, Corning C.C., 1994; BS, Cornell U., 1997, JD, 2000. Model Vogue Agy., NYC, 1980-81; elder deacon Campbell (N.Y.) Presbyn. Ch., 1982-86; farmer Thurston, NY, 1985-93, Beaver Dams, NY, 1995—; supplemental instrn. leader Corning (N.Y.) C.C., 1991-94; fin. svcs. rep. 1st Investors, Elmira, NY, 1997. Chmn. faculty senate Alfred State Coll., 2001—02. Contbr. articles to profl. jours. Lectr. Merchantville Grange, Thurston, 1986—91; councilman Twp. of Thurston, 1987—93, coord. CD, 1989—93. Fellow, Equal Justice Am., 1999. Mem. AAAS, N.Y. State Bar Assn. (exec. com. criminal justice section, co-chair sentencing alternatives com.), Schuyler County Bar Assn. (v.p. 2001-), NY State Magistrates Assn. Avocations: farming, photography, writing, politics, research. Office: 8 Buell St Bath NY 14810 Office Phone: 607-776-4200, 212-736-3200. Business E-Mail: lawyer@betzjitomir.com.

BEUCHERT, EDWARD WILLIAM, lawyer; b. NYC, Feb. 13, 1937; s. August Vincent and Anna Beuchert; m. Elizabeth Sadowsky, Aug. 5, 1961; children: Edward, Jon, Philip, Suzanne, Alexandra. BA cum laude, Fordham U., 1958; JD cum laude, Harvard U., 1961. Bar: N.Y. 1962. Assoc., then ptnr. and counsel Seward & Kissel, NYC, 1963-99. Bd. dirs. Cotswold Assn., Inc., 1977-85, 1996-2002, v.p. 1979-80, 98-99, pres., 1980-82. Contbr. articles to profl. jours. Bd. dirs. Edgemont Cmty. Coun., Inc., 1984-90, sec., 1984-86, v.p., 1987-90. 1st lt. U.S. Army, 1961-63. Recipient Silver Box award, Edgemont Cmty. Coun., 1998. Republican. Roman Catholic. Home: 53 Inverness Rd Scarsdale NY 10583-3525

BEUGEN, JOAN BETH, communications executive; b. Mar. 9, 1943; d. Leslie and Janet (Glick) Caplan; m. Sheldon Howard Beugen, July 16, 1967. BS in Speech, Northwestern U., 1965. Founder, prin., pres. The Creative Establishment, Inc., Chgo., NYC, San Francisco and L.A., 1969—87; founder, pres. Cresta Comm. Inc., Chgo., 1988—. Spkr. on entrepreneurship for women. Contbr. articles to profl. jours. Trustee Mt. Sinai Hosp. Med. Ctr.; del. White House Conf. on Small Bus., 1979; bd. dirs. Chgo. Network, Chgoland Enterprise Ctr., Girl Scouts Chgo. Named Entrepreneur of Yr., Women in Bus.; recipient YWCA Leadership award, 1985. Mem.: Overseas Edn. Fund Women in Bus. Com., Nat. Women's Forum, Com. of 200, Women in Film, Chgo. Film Coun., Chgo. Audio-Visual Prodrs. Assn., Midwest Soc. Profl. Cons., Chgo. Assn. Commerce and Industry, Ill. Women's Agenda, Nat. Assn. Women Bus. Owners (pres. Chgo. bhpt. 1979), Econ. Club Chgo. Office: The Cresta Group 1050 N State St Chicago IL 60610-7829

BEUGNOT, BERNARD ANDRE HENRI, literature educator; b. Paris, July 3, 1932; s. Raoul P.H. Beugnot; m. Brigitte L'Hermite, June 11, 1960; children: Marie-Christine, Nicolas, Sophie. Student, Ecole Normale Superieure, Paris, 1954; licence, U. Sorbonne, Paris, 1955, MA, 1956, PhD, 1969; agregation, U. France, Paris, 1958. Prof. Coll. Chartres, France, 1960-62; assoc. prof. French U. Montreal, Que., Canada, 1962-69, prof. French lit. Que., 1970—, chmn. French dept. Que., 1965-69, 85-91, prof. emeritus French dept., 1997—. Mem. editing com. Can. Coun. Humanities, Ottawa, 1970-75, 78-81; editor: J.L.G. Balzac, Entretiens, 1972, F. Ponge, Oeuvres Completes, 2 vols., 1999-2002, 20 other books and over 150 articles on 17th-century and contemporary lit.; co-author (monograph) Boileau, 1973, Manuel Bibliographie, 1982. Lt. inf. French Army, 1958-60. Recipient Prix Halphen Acad. Française, 1974, Prize 2000 for Humanities, ACFAS, Ordre Nat. du Merite, Govt. France, 1977, Palmes Academiques, 1988, Ordre Nat. du Québec, 2003. Fellow Royal Soc. Can. Home: 4720 Grosvenor Montreal PQ Canada H3W 2L8 E-mail: beugnotmontreal@videotron.ca.

BEUKEMA, JOHN FREDERICK, lawyer; b. Alpena, Mich., Jan. 30, 1947; s. Christian F. and Margaret Elizabeth (Robertson) B.; m. Cynthia Ann Parke, May 25, 1974; children: Frederick Parke, David Christian. BA, Carleton Coll., 1968; JD, U. Minn., 1971. Bar: Minn. 1971, US Ct. Mil. Appeals 1974, US Dist. Ct. Minn. 1975, US Ct. Appeals (8th cir.) 1981, US Ct. Appeals (fed. cir.) 1984, US Supreme Ct. 1988, US Dist. Ct. (we. dist.) Wis. 1997, US Ct. Appeals (9th cir.) 1999. Assoc. Faegre & Benson, Mpls., 1971, 75-79, ptnr., 1980—. Vestryman Cathedral Ch. St. Mark, Mpls., 1983-86, 2002-05, junior warden, 2006-07, senior warden, 2007-; bd. dirs. Neighborhood Involvement Program, Mpls., 1986-90, pres., 1989-90; bd. dirs. Ronald McDonald House of Twin Cities, 1991-97, sec., 1995-97. Lt. JAGC, USNR, 1972-75. Mem. ABA, Minn. State Bar Assn., Hennepin County Bar Assn. Republican. Episcopalian. Business E-Mail: jbeukema@faegre.com.

BEUMER, RICHARD EUGENE, retired engineering executive; b. St. Louis, Feb. 26, 1938; s. Eugene Henry and C. Florence (Braun) Beumer; m. Judith Louise Rockett, June 25, 1960; children: Kathryn, Karen, Mark. BSEE, Valparaiso U., Ind., 1959. Registered profl. engr., Mo., Ill., Ariz., Md., Okla., Ohio, Ga., Va., Mich., D.C., Mass., N.Y., N.C. With Sverdrup Corp. Cos., 1959—; v.p. Sverdrup & Parcel and Assocs., St. Louis, 1974—78; sr. v.p., exec. v.p., dir. Sverdrup & Parcel Assocs., St. Louis, 1979—81; pres. Sverdrup & Parcel Assos., St. Louis, 1982—85; sr. v.p. Sverdrup Corp., 1986—88, exec. v.p., 1989—92, pres., 1993; pres., CEO Sverdrup Corp., 1994—95; chmn., CEO Sverdrup Corp., 1996—99; vice chmn. Jacobs Engring. Group, Inc., 1999—2003; ret., 2003. Ret. vice-chmn. Thrivent Fin. for Luths.; bd. dirs. Valparaiso U. Chmn. St. Louis Regional Chamber and Growth Assn., 1998—99; divsn. chmn. United Way St. Louis, 1980; bd. dirs. Downtown St. Louis, Inc., 1982—91, Jr. Achievement, St. Louis Sci. Ctr.; past chmn. Luth. Med. Ctr., St. Louis; trustee, chmn. St. Louis Luth. High Schs. Recipient Disting. Alumni award, Valparaiso U., 1983. Mem.: NSPE, Mo. Soc. Profl. Engrs., Constrn. Industry Round Table (past chmn.), Design Profls. Coalition (past chmn.), Cons. Engrs. Coun. Mo. (pres. 1980), Am. Cons. Engrs. Coun. (nat. bd. dirs. 1979—82), St. Louis Elec. Bd. (pres. 1983), The Bogey Club, Old Warson Club, The Moles. Lutheran. Personal E-mail: rebeumer@att.net.

BEUSCH, JOHN ULRICH, engineer, researcher; b. Erie, Pa., Apr. 22, 1938; s. Andrew and Ruth B. Beusch; m. Donna Marie Williams, Dec. 23, 1961; children: Cheryl Susan, Laura Kristine. BS, Rochester Inst. Tech., NY, 1961; MBA, Boston U., 1971; PhD, MIT, Cambridge, 1965. Sr. staff MIT Lincoln Lab., Lexington, 1965—, group leader, 1965—, divsn. head, 1965—, sr. staff, 2006—. Chair Stow (Mass.) Conservation Commn., 1974—80; trustee Randell Libr. Fund, Stow, 1980—86; pres., dir. Stow Conservation Trust, 1986—. Achievements include patents in field. Avocations: aerobics, exercise, carpentry. Home: 416 Taylor Rd Stow MA 01775 Office: MIT Lincoln Lab 244 Wood St Lexington MA 02420 Office Phone: 781-981-7908. Business E-Mail: beusch@ll.mit.edu.

BEUTHIEN, GAYLE DAWN, special education educator, swim coach; d. Milo and Jessie Dawn Beuthien. BS, Siler Lake Coll., Wis., 1991; MS, U. Wis., Oshkosh, 2006. Cert. DVI U. Wis., Oshkosh, 1996, ednl. leadership in social justice U. Wis., Oshkosh, 2005. Spl. edn. instr., volleyball, basketball, track and swim coach Manitowoc Pub. Schs., Wis., 1991—95; spl. edn. instr., swim coach Appleton Area Sch. Dist., Wis., 1995—. Vocational specialist for sch. dist. Tech-Prep, Manitowoc, Wis., 1991—95, C. of C., Manitowoc, Wis., 1991—95. Mem.: Council for Exceptional Children. Achievements include development of apartment program to teach students with disabilites functional life skills; school-tech. work program. Avocations: water-skiing, swimming, bicycling, reading. Business E-Mail: BEUTHIENGAYLE@AASD.K12.WI.US.

BEUTLER, ARTHUR JULIUS, manufacturing executive; b. LaCrosse, Wis., Sept. 2, 1924; s. Arthur Julius and Augusta Henrietta (Dobe) B.; m. Carolee Yvonne Crawford, Dec. 28, 1952; 1 child, Karen Elizabeth. BSEE, U. Wis., 1948, Grad. in EE, 1968. Registered profl. engr., Wis. Trainee inventor program Gen. Electric Co., Schenectady, NY, 1948-51, devel. engr. Milw., 1951-59, project engr., 1959-61, sr. engr., 1961-64; chief engr. Dings Magnetic Separator Co., Milw., 1964-67; pres., owner Creative Engring. Assocs., Inc., Greendale, Wis., 1967-72, 88—; v.p. mfg. Gettys Mfg. Co., Racine, Wis., 1972-79, v.p. internat., 1979-81; v.p. tech. planning div. motion control div. Gould, Inc. (formerly Gettys Mfg. Co.), Racine, 1981-88. Cons. in field. Patentee elec. controls. Served with U.S. Army, 1943-46, PTO. Mem. IEEE (sr., chpt. chmn. 1969-72), NSPE, Soc. Mfg. Engrs. (cert.), Tau Beta Pi, Eta Kappa Nu.

BEUTLER, ERNEST, physician, research scientist; b. Berlin, Sept. 30, 1928; arrived in U.S., 1936, naturalized, 1943; s. Alfred David and Kaethe (Italiener) Beutler; m. Brondelle Fleisher, June 15, 1950; children: Steven Merrill, Earl Bryan, Bruce Alan, Deborah Ann. PhB, U. Chgo., 1946, BS, 1948, MD, 1950; PhD (hon.), Tel Aviv U., Israel, 1993. Cert. Am. Bd. Internal Medicine, 1958, in Hematology 1976. Intern U. Chgo. Clinics, 1950—51, resident in medicine, 1951—53; asst. prof. U. Chgo., 1956—59; chmn. divsn. medicine City of Hope Med. Ctr., LA, 1959—78; chmn. dept. clin. rsch. The Scripps Rsch. Inst., La Jolla, 1978—82, chmn. dept. basic and clin. rsch., 1982—89, chmn. dept. molecular and exptl. medicine, 1989—2007. Clin. prof. medicine U. So. Calif., 1964—79, U. Calif., San Diego, 1979—; mem. hematology study sect. NIH, 1970—74, 1989—91, nat. heart, lung, and blood adv. coun. mem., 1994—97; Spinoza chair U. Amsterdam, 1991; mem. med. adv. com. Red Cross Blood Program, 1972—78; mem. adv. com. Blood Products FDA, 1984—88; chmn. sci. adv. com. Puget Sound Blood Ctr., Seattle, 1975—81; mem. sci. adv. coun. Cystic Fibrosis Found., 1976—78; mem. sci. bd. vis. Okla. Rsch. Found., 1980—84; chmn. sickle cell disease task force Nat. Heart, Lung and Blood Inst., NIH, 1990; mem. sci. adv. bd. Burnham Inst., La Jolla, Calif., 1996—, chmn., 1998—. Author: 8 books; contbr. numerous articles in med. jours.; mem. editl. bds. profl. jours.:. Dem. nom. for Gov. State of Ky. 1st lt. US Army, 1953—55. Recipient Gairdner award, 1975, Blundell prize, 1985, Nat. Heart, Lung, and Blood Inst. Merit award, NIH, 1987, Nat. Acad. Clin. Biochemistry Lectureship award, Kodak Instruments, 1990, Mayo Soley award, Western Soc. Clin. Investigation, 1992, 5th ann. Excellence award, Gen. Clin. Rsch. Program, 1993, City of Medicine award, 1994, Outstanding Rsch. award, Am. Soc. Clin. Pathologists, 2000, Profl. Achievement citation, U. Chgo., 2003. Mem.: NAS, Inst. Medicine, Am. Soc. Human Genetics (mem. exec. com. 1968—72), Am. Soc. Hematology (mem. exec. com. 1968—72, v.p. 1977, pres. 1979, Stratton Medal 1974, E. Donnall Thomas Lecture and Prize 2003), Western Assn. Physicians (pres. 1989), Am. Soc. Clin. Investigation, Assn. Am. Physicians, Am. Acad. Arts and Scis. Jewish. Achievements include invention of screening tests for galactosemia and other genetic disorders; co-discovery of glucose-6-phosphate dehydrogenase deficiency; origination of X inactivation hypothesis; research in glycolipid disorders; hemochromatosis. Avocation: music. Personal E-mail: beshear@peodigy.net.

BEUTLER, FREDERICK JOSEPH, information scientist; b. Berlin, Oct. 3, 1926; came to U.S., 1936, naturalized, 1943; s. Alfred David and Kaethe (Italiener) B.; m. Suzanne Armstrong, Jan. 5, 1969; children—Arthur David, Kathryn Ruth, Michael Ernest. SB, MIT, 1949, SM, 1951; PhD, Calif. Inst. Tech., 1957. Faculty U. Mich., Ann Arbor, 1957—, prof. info. and control engring., 1963-90, prof. emeritus, 1990—, chmn. computer info. and control engring., 1970-71, 77-90, chmn. grad. elect. engring. systems program, 1985-90. Vis. prof. Calif. Inst. Tech., 1967-68; vis. scholar U. Calif. at Berkeley, 1964-65 Editorial cons. Math. Rev., 1965-67, 75-88; contbr. articles to profl. jours. and books. Bd. dirs. Ann Arbor Civic Theatre, 1976-78, 91-94. With AUS, 1945-46. Rsch. grantee NSF, 1971-81, 92-94, Air Force Office Sci., 1970-80, NASA grantee, 1959-69. Fellow IEEE (life); mem. Soc. Indsl. and Applied Math. (coun. 1969-74, mng. editor Jour. Applied Math. 1970-75, editor 1984-90, editor Rev. 1967-70), Am. Math. Soc., U. Mich. Retirees Assn. (bd. dirs., sec.-treas. 1994—), Barton Boat Club, Racquet Club of Ann Arbor, Rotary Club of Ann Arbor. Office: Elec Engr and Comp Sci Bldg Univ Michigan Ann Arbor MI 48109-2122 Business E-Mail: fjb@umich.edu.

BEUTLER, LARRY EDWARD, psychologist, educator; b. Logan, Utah, Feb. 14, 1941; s. Edward and Beulah (Andrus) B.; children: Jana, Kelly, Ian David, Gail. BS, Utah State U., 1965, MS, 1966; PhD, U. Nebr., 1970. Diplomate Am. Bd. Clin. Psychology. Asst. prof. psychology Duke U., Ashville, NC, 1970-71; asst. prof. Stephen F. Austin State U., Nacogdoches, Tex., 1971-73; assoc. prof. Baylor Coll. Medicine, Houston, 1973-79; prof. U. Ariz., Tucson, 1979-90, U. Calif., Santa Barbara, 1990—, Pacific Grad. Sch. Psychology, Stanford U., Palo Alto, Calif., 2002—. Co-author: Systematic Treatment Selection, 1990, Guidelines for the Systematic Treatment of the Depressed Patient, 2000, Integrative Assessment of Adult Personality, 2003, Principles of Therapeutic Change That Work, 2006, others; editor Jour. Cons. Clin. Psychology, 1990-96, Psychology of Terrorism, 2007; editor Jour. Clin. Psychology, 1997—2004. Fellow APA (pres. divsn. psychotherapy, 1997, pres. divsn. clin. psychology, 2002), Am. Psychol. Soc.; mem. Soc. Psychotherapy Rsch. (pres. 1986-88). Home: 2620 Piedra Verde Ct Placerville CA 95667 Office: Pacific Grad Sch Psychology 935 E Meadow Palo Alto CA 94303 Home Phone: 530-642-1353. Business E-Mail: lbeutler@pgsp.edu.

BEUTLER, SUZANNE A., retired secondary school educator, artist; b. Cin., Oct. 23, 1930; d. Robert and Marguerite (Pierson) Armstrong; m. Frederick J. Beutler, Jan. 5, 1969; children: Richard and Mark Ireland. BA, U. Wis., 1954; MA, U. Mich., 1966, PhD, 1974, BFA, 2000. Cert. tchr. Middle sch. tchr. Ann Arbor (Mich.) Pub. Schs. Vis. lectr. U. Mich., Ann Arbor; adj. lectr. Eastern Mich. U., Ypsilanti. Author 3 manuals with Lang. Art Projects; contbr. articles to profl. jours.; developed writing program using personal classroom experiences. Recipient Tchr. Recognition award, 1986; grantee in field. Mem. Ann Arbor Rotary Club, Phi Delta Kappa (Svc. Key award 1992). Home: 1717 Shadford Rd Ann Arbor MI 48104-4543 Office Phone: 734-663-4870. E-mail: sbeutler@umich.edu.

BEUTNER, ERNST HERMAN, microbiology educator; b. Berlin, Aug. 27, 1923; came to U.S., 1923; s. Reinhard and Hermine (Aye) B.; children: Eric, Karen, Jean. BA, Pa. State U., 1947; PhD, U. Pa., 1951. Cert. Am. Bd. Med. Microbiology, Am. Bd. Med. Lab. Immunology, Am. Bd. Bioanalysis. Rsch. supr. Sias Labs. at Brook Hosp., Brookline, Mass., 1951-55; rsch. assoc. Harvard Sch. of Dental Medicine, Boston, 1955-56; prof. microbiology and dermatology SUNY at Buffalo, 1956—. Mem. editorial bd. Internat. Jour. of Dermatology Autoimmunity. Fellow Phila. Coll. of Physicians; mem. AAAS, Am. Soc. Microbiologists, Soc. Investigative Dermatology, Am. Acad. Dermatology, Soc. for History of Dermatology, Am. Assn. Immunologists, N.Y. Acad. Scis., Acad. Microbiology of ASM, Am. Acad. Dermatology, Japanese Soc. for Investigative Dermatology. Office: Univ at Buffalo SUNY Dept Of Microbiology Buffalo NY 14214

BEUTTENMULLER, RUDOLF WILLIAM, lawyer; b. St. Louis, Dec. 20, 1953; s. Paul A. and Doris R. (Henle) B.; m. Ragina Lee Winters, July 14, 1984. AB cum laude, Princeton U., 1976; JD with distinction, Duke U., 1980. Bar: Tex. 1980, U.S. Dist. Ct. (no. dist.) Tex. 1980. Assoc. Jenkens & Gilchrist, Dallas, 1980-83; ptnr. Gregory, Self & Beuttenmuller, Dallas, 1983-88, Bradley, Bradley & Beuttenmuller, Irving, Tex., 1988-93; dir. Thomas Cinclair & Beuttenmullen, Dallas, 1994—. Articles editor Duke Law Jour., Durham, 1979-80. Mem. Rep. Nat. Com., Washington, 1984. Mem. ABA, Dallas Bar Assn., Duke Law Alumni Assn., Princeton Alumni Assn. Home: 4428 Irvin Simmons Dr Dallas TX 75229-4247 Office: 5335 Spring Valley Rd Dallas TX 75254-3009 Office Phone: 972-991-2121. Business E-Mail: rudybeutt@tcblawfirm.com.

BEVAN, ROBERT LEWIS, lawyer; b. Springfield, Mo., Mar. 23, 1928; s. Gene Walter and Blanche Omega (Woods) B.; m. Ronice Diane Gartin, Jan 25, 1977; children: Matthew Gene, Lisa Ann. AB, U. Mo., 1950; LLB,

U. Kansas City, 1957. Bar: Mo. 1957, D.C. 1969. Adminstrv. asst. U.S. Senator T. Hennings Jr., Washington, 1957-60; legis. asst. U.S. Senator E.V. Long, Washington, 1960-69; sr. govt. relations counsel Am. Bankers Assn., Washington, 1970-84; ptnr. Hopkins & Sutter, Washington, 1984-95; of counsel Stinson, Mag and Fizzell, Kansas City, Mo., 1995-2001. Ghost author: The Intruders, 1967; contbg. editor U.S. Banker, 1985-88. Fieldman Dem. Nat. Com., 1968. Served with U.S. Army, 1946-47, 1951-53. Mem. ABA (bus. law sect., chmn. banking law com. 1988-92, commn. on IOLTA 1997-2000, co-chmn. joint banking com. 1999-2000), Echequer Club. Avocation: art and antiques. Office: Ste 301 4545 Wornall Rd Kansas City MO 64111

BEVAN, TIM, film producer; b. Queenstown, New Zealand, 1958; m. Joely Richardson, January 1992 (div. July 12, 1997); 3 children. Co-founder Working Title Prodns. Formed Working Title Films (with Eric Fellner) 1982-; Prodr. films (with Sarah Radclyffe) My Beautiful Laundrette, 1986, Sammy and Rosie Get Laid, 1987, Paperhouse, 1989; Personal Svcs., 1987, For Queen and Country, 1989, Dark Obsession, 1990, The Tall Guy, 1990, Chicago Joe and the Showgirl, 1990, London Kills Me, 1992, Rubin and Ed, 1992; (with Graham Bradstreet) A World Apart, 1988, Fools of Fortune, 1990; (with Carlos Davis and Anthony Fingleton) Drop Dead Fred, 1991, (with Paul Webster and Ronna B. Wallace) Bob Roberts, 1992; (with Eric fellner) French Kiss, 1995, Moonlight & Valentino, 1995, Bean, 1997, The Matchmaker, 1997, The Borrowers, 1997,The Hi-Lo Country, 1997, Elizabeth, 1998 (BAFTA Best British Film, ALFS awd., 1999), What Rats Won't Do, 1998, Plunkett & MaCleane, 1999; For TV Tales of the City, 1993, The Borrowers, 1993, More Tales of the City, 1998, High Fidelity, 2000, Bridget Jones Diary, 2001, Captain Corelli's Mandolin, 2001, 40 Days and 40 Nights, 2002, Ali G Indahouse, 2002, About A Boy, 2002, The Guru, 2002, Johnny English, 2003, Love Actually, 2003, The Calcium Kid, 2004, Thunderbirds, 2004, Wimbledon, 2004, Bridget Jones: The Edge of Reason, 2004, The Interpreter, 2005, Pride & Prejudice, 2005, Nanny McPhee, 2005, United 93, 2006, Sixty Six, 2006, Smokin' Aces, 2006; exec. prodr.: The Rachel Papers, 1989, Year of the Gun, 1991, A Kiss Before Dying, 1991, Posse, 1993, Romeo is Bleeding, 1993, The Hawk, 1993, Four Weddings and a Funeral, 1994, The Hudsucker Proxy, 1994, Panther, 1995, Dead Man Walking, 1995, Loch Ness, 1995, Fargo, 1996, The Big Lebowski, 1998, Notting Hill, 1999, O Brother, Where Art Thou?, 2000, The Man Who Cried, 2000, The Man Who Wasn't There, 2001, Long Time Dead, 2002, My Little Eye, 2002, Thirteen, 2003, The Shape of Things, 2003, Ned Kelly, 2003, The Italian Job, 2003, Gettin' Square, 2003, Shaun of the Dead, 2004, Mickybo and Me, 2004, Inside I'm Dancing, 2004, No. 2, 2006; prodr. TV: Frankie's House, 1992, Underbelly (exec.), 1992. Recipient ShowEast's Kodak award for excellence in filmmaking (with Eric Fellner), 2003.*

BEVAN, WILLIAM ARNOLD, JR., emergency physician; b. Sault St. Marie, Mich., June 23, 1943; s. William Arnold and Syneva Lois (Martin) B.; m. Martha Lynn Peterson, Dec. 29, 1973; children: Terry Eugene, Brian William, Patrick Jon. BS, U. Minn., 1966, MD, 1970. Diplomate Am. Bd. Family Practice, Am. Bd. Emergency Medicine. Intern U. Utah, 1970—71; family practitioner Vail Mountain Med. Profl. Corp., Vail, Colo., 1972—83; emergency physician Vail Valley Emergency Physicians, 1983—; dir. Vail Valley Med. Ctr., 1990—. Dir. Vail Valley Emergency Dept., 1992—, pres. med. staff, 1977; adviser Western Eagle County Ambulance Dist., 1983—. Trustee Shattuck St. Mary's Sch., Faribault, Minn., 1977—; football coach Battle Mountain H.S., Vail, 1978—; trustee, bd. dirs. Vail Christian H.S., 1998—, football coach; Eagle Scout. Named Man of Yr. Boy Scouts Am., 1966, 77. Fellow Am. Coll. Emergency Physicians; mem. AMA, Rocky Mountain Med. Soc., Colo. Med. Soc., U. Minn. Alumni Assn. (life). Republican. Lutheran. Home: 25 Cottonwood Rd Eagle CO 81631 Office: Vail Valley Emergency Dept 181 W Meadow Dr Vail CO 81657-5058 Mailing: Box 1143 Avon CO 81620 Home Phone: 970-949-7093; Office Phone: 970-476-8065.

BEVELACQUA, JOSEPH JOHN, physicist, researcher; b. Waynesburg, Pa., Mar. 17, 1949; s. Frank and Lucy Ann Bevelacqua; m. Terry Sanders, Sept. 4, 1971; children: Anthony, Jeffrey, Megan, Peter, Michael, Karen. BS in Physics, Calif. State Coll., Pa., 1970; postgrad., U. Maine, Orono, 1970—72; MS in Physics, Fla. State U., Tallahassee, 1974, PhD, 1976. Diplomate Am. Bd. Health Physics; cert. radiol. shield survey engr.; cert. health physicist (comprehensive and power reactors), sr. reactor operator cert. Teaching/rsch. asst. U. Maine, 1970-72; tchg. and rsch. asst. Fla. State U., 1973-76; rsch. asst. NSF, 1975-76, rsch. assoc., 1976; nuc. engr. Bettis Atomic Power Lab., West Mifflin, Pa., 1973, sr. nuc. engr., 1976-78; ops. rsch. analyst US Dept. Energy, Oak Ridge, 1978-80, chief physicist advanced laser isotope separation program, 1980-83; sr. radiol. engr. Three Mile Island Sta.-Unit 2 GPU Nuc. Corp., Middletown, Pa., 1983-84, Three Mile Island emergency preparedness mgr., 1984-86, mgr. TMI-2 safety rev. group, 1986-89, dir. radiol. controls TMI-2, 1989; supt. health physics Point Beach Nuc. Power Plant Wis. Electric Co., Two Rivers, 1989-95; prodn. planning mgr. Point Beach Nuc. Plant, 1995—96; pres., CEO Bevelacqua Resources, Richland, Wash., 1993—; sr. radiol. controls tech. advisor USDOE-Office River Protection, Hanford, 1996—2005, acting dir. environ. divsn., 2000; assoc. AJC & Assocs. Inc., 2005—. Cons. US Dept. Energy Process Evaluation Bd. of Isotope Separation, Washington, 1981-82; acting asst. mgr. environ., safety, health, and quality USDOE- Office River Protection, Hanford, 2000. Author: Contemporary Health Physics: Problems and Solutions, 1995, Basic Health Physics: Problems and Solutions, 1999, 20 health physics tng. manuals pub. by Bevelacqua Resources, 3 CD-ROMS for health physics tng.; contbr. articles to profl. jours. including Physical Rev. Letters and Physics Letters. Mem. Rep. Presdl. Task Force, Nat. Rep. Senatorial Com. Recipient Outstanding Performance award, Dept. of Energy, 1982, 1996—2004, Profl. Excellence award, California U. of Pa., 2000; grantee, USAF, NSF, Von Humboldt fellow, U. Hamburg. Mem. Am. Nuc. Soc. (Ea. Wash. chpt., Silver Cert. award 2007), Am. Phys. Soc., Am. Math. Soc., The Math. Assn. Am., Am. Acad. Health Physics (profl. devel. com. 1992-94, chmn. 1994, nom. com. 1994-96), Health Physics Soc., Susquehanna Valley Health Physics Soc. (mem. exec. com.), NY Acad. Scis., Soc. Nuc. Medicine, Nuc. Utility Coordinating Group on Emergency Preparedness Implementation, Babcock and Wilcox Owners Group on Emergency Preparedness, Profl. Reactor Operators Soc., Health Physics Soc. (Columbia chpt., placement com. 1989-92, nominating com. 1994-97), Am. Bd. Health Physics (vice chmn. comprehensive panel of examiners 1990, chmn. 1991, nat. office mem.), Nat. Rifle Assn. Am., US Golf Assn., Tri Cities Ams. Ice Hockey Booster Club, Oak Ridge Sportsman's Club, Sigma Pi Sigma, Soc. Physics Students. Independent. Lutheran. Achievements include research in theoretical studies of light nuclei, few nucleon transfer reactions, radiation shielding, laser isotope separation, uranium enrichment, free electron lasers, neutron nuclei; symmetry violations in nuclei, grand unification theories, quark models of nuclear forces, neutrino interactions; nuclear fuel cycle, generation III and IV fission reactors, laser fusion, gravitational collapse of stars, beta dosimetry, internal dosimetry, health effects of ionizing radiation; nuclear reactor safety, accident analysis, fusion reactor safety, muon catalyzed fusion, health physics at fusion reactors, radon health effects and mitigation, radioactive and mixed waste management; applied health physics, internal and external dosimetry, dark matter, strange matter, symmetry violations in nuclei, cosmology, radiation effects during low earth orbit, lunar missions; planetary missions, quantum field theory, astrophysics, supersymmetry, quantum gravity, string theory, twister theory, muon colliders, neutrino dose equivalents, genetic approaches for cancer research; heavy ion cancer therapy, therapy applications using microbeams and nanotechnology; quantum chromodynamics, differential geometry, general relativity, gravitation, neutrino dosimetry; special relativity, standard model of particle physics and radiation induced immune system activation; heavy ion therapy, radiotherapy using microbeams and nanotechnology. Avocations: golf, hockey, lacrosse, running, rock climbing. Home and Office: Bevelacqua Resources 343 Adair Dr Richland WA 99352-8563 Office Phone: 509-628-2240. Personal E-mail: bevelresou@aol.com.

BEVELHYMER, DARLENE PEARL, lawyer, retired secondary school educator; b. Napoleon, Ohio, Oct. 31, 1950; d. Herbert S. and N. Lorene (Skelton) B. BS in Edn., Ohio U., 1972, MS in Environ. Studies, 1977; JD, U. Toledo, 1987. Bar: Ohio 1987; permanent cert. comprehensive sci. tchr., Ohio. Tchr. sci. Napoleon City Schs., 1972—2007; pvt. practice Bowling Green, Ohio, 1987—. Mem. Napoleon Community Band, 1986—, Cantare, choral ensemble, Wauseon, Ohio, 1987-93; treas. Choral and Performing Arts Assn. N.W. Ohio, Wauseon, 1987-93; mem. Sing Out Toledo Chorus, 1996-2005. Recipient local svc. award NW Ohio Edn. Assn., 1989. Mem. NEA, Ohio Bar Assn., Ohio Edn. Assn. (legis. commn. 1991-93), Napoleon Faculty Assn. (pres., negotiator 1987-89). Democrat. Presbyterian. Avocations: choral singing, stained glass. Home Phone: 419-352-8095.

BEVELS, ESTHER MARIE, medical technician, director; b. Aberdeen, Miss., June 1, 1956; d. Robert Williams and Janie Mae Brandon; children: Connelia Capote, Nyshea Simpson. Grad., Perdue U., 1992. Surgical asst. Star Inst. Tech., Stratford, NY, 2001—03; dir. sterile processing Our Lady of Lourdes Hosp., Willingboro, NJ, 1990—. Adv. bd. Harrison Career Inst., Phila., 1999—. Recipient Wall of Tolerance, So. Proverty Law Ctr., Ala., 2004. Mem.: So. Proverty Law Ctr. (leadership coun. mem. 2004), Order Eas. Star. Baptist. Avocation: reading. Office: Lourdes Med Ctr Burlington 218A Sunset Rd Willingboro NJ 08046

BEVERIDGE, ANDREW ALAN, sociologist, educator, consultant; b. Madison, Wis., Apr. 27, 1945; s. Jacob Melvin and Bonnie Belle Beveridge; m. Fredrica Rudell, Apr. 17, 1970; 1 child, Sydney Jocelyn. BA, Yale U., 1967, MPhil, PhD, Yale U., 1973. From asst. to assoc. prof. sociology Columbia U., NYC, 1973—81; from assoc. prof. to prof. sociology Queens Coll. and Grad Ctr. CUNY, NYC, 1981—. Demographic and census cons. N.Y. Times, Newspaper Divsn., NYC, 1993—; demographic litig. cons. in redistricting, housing and jury composition cases, 1993—; monthly demographic topic columnist Gotham Gazette, NYC, 2001—. Author: African Businessmen and Development in Zambia, 1979; contbg. author: New York and Los Angeles: Politics, Society and Culture, A Comparative View, 2003; contbr. articles to profl. jours. Trustee, pres. Yonkers (N.Y.) Sch. Bd., 1986—90; founding mem., v.p. Citizens and Neighbors Organized to Protect Yonkers, 1987—92; 2d v.p. Yonkers Dem. Party, 1991. Grantee, NSF, 1976—78, 2002—05, NEH, 1984—85, Robert Wood Johnson Found., 1994—2001, Ford Found., 2000—01; ACLS fellow, 1978—79, Regional Econ. History Rsch. Ctr. fellow, Hagley Found., 1978—79. Mem.: Am. Assn. Pub. Opinion Rsch., Ea. Sociol. Soc. (v.p. 1997—98), Social Sci. History Assn., Population Assn. Am., Am. Sociol. Assn. (Pub. Understanding of Sociology award 2007). Democrat. Achievements include social explorer mapping and visual display system; patents pending for. Avocation: bicycling. Home: 50 Merriam Ave Bronxville NY 10708 Office: Queens Coll Sociology- 233 PH 65-30 Kissena Blvd Flushing NY 11367-1597 Home Phone: 914-337-6237; Office Phone: 718-997-2837. Personal E-mail: andy@socialexplorer.com. Business E-Mail: andrew.beveridge@qc.cuny.edu.

BEVERIDGE, CRAWFORD W., information technology executive; BSc in Social Scis., U. Edinburgh; MSc in Indsl. Adminstrn., U. Bradford, Eng.; D (hon.), U. Edinburgh, Napier U., Edinburgh, Robert Gordons U., Aberdeen, Scotland. Human resources mgmt. positions Hewlett-Packard Co., Digital Equipment Corp., Analog Devices; v.p. corp. resources Sun Microsystems, Inc., 1985—91, exec. v.p. people and places, chief human resources officer Santa Clara, Calif., 2000, exec. v.p., chmn. Europe, Mid. East and Africa, Asia Pacific and the Ams.; CEO Scottish Enterprise, Scotland, 1991—2000. Bd. dirs. Autodesk, Memec, Scottish Equity Ptnrs., Ltd. Recipient Comdr. of Order of Brit. Empire, 1995. Office: Sun Microsystems Inc 4150 Network Cir Santa Clara CA 95054 Office Phone: 800-555-9786. Office Fax: 650-960-1300, 408-276-3804.*

BEVERIDGE, TERRANCE JAMES, microbiology professor, researcher; b. Toronto, Ont., Can., Apr. 29, 1945; s. Fredrick Charles and Doris Elizabeth (Hooks) B.; m. Janice Elizabeth Barnett, Sept. 9, 1970; children: Braden Charles, Jennifer Bree. BS, U. Toronto, 1968, Diploma in Bacteriology, 1969, MS, 1970; PhD, U. Western Ont., 1974. Rsch. assoc. U. Western Ont., London, 1975-78; from asst. prof. to assoc. prof. U. Guelph, Ont., 1978-86, prof. Ont., 1986—, Killam prof. Ont., 1995-97, Can. rsch. chair Ont., 2002—. Vis. prof. Zentrum für Ultrastrucktturforschung, Vienna, Austria, 1984, Biozentrum, Universtät der Basel, Switzerland, 1987; dir. Nat. Scis. and Engring. Rsch. Coun. of Can. (NSERC) Gueiph Regional STEM Facility, 1980—. Editor: Metal Ions and Bacteria, 1989, Advances in Bacterial Paracrystalline Surface Layers, 1993; editor Can. Jour. Microbiology, 1982-88, Jour. Bacteriology, 1988-97, Biorecovery, 1987—, Internat. Jour. of Resource and Environ. Biotech., 1994—, Microbiology, 1997—, Arch. Microbiology, 1998—. Recipient Steacie prize, Nat. Sci. and Engring. Rsch. Coun. of Can., 1984, Can. Soc. Microbiology award, 1994, Sigma Xi award, 1994, Culling medal, 2001. Fellow Royal Soc. Can. (dir. life scis. 1992-95), Am. Acad. Microbiology, Austrian Acad. Sci.; mem. Can. Soc. Microbiologists, Microscopical Soc. Can., Am. Soc. Microbiology (divsnl. award 1984), Electron Microscopic Soc. Am., Nat. Centre Excellence, Can. Bacterial Disease Network, Can. Inst. Advanced Rsch. (assoc. 1988—). Avocations: hiking, cross country skiing. Office: U Guelph Coll Biol Scis Dept Molecular and Cellular Biology Guelph ON Canada N1G 2W1 Office Phone: 519-824-4120 x 53366. E-mail: tjb@uoguelph.ca.

BEVERLAND, JACK EDWIN, retired retail executive, folk artist; b. Idaho Falls, Idaho, May 15, 1939; s. John Banks and Vern Louise (Stouct) B.; m. Linda Wilson (dec.); children: Dusti Dawn Lynn, Traci Diana Collins, Durk Edwin. Degree in bus. mgmt., La Salle Ext. U., Chgo., 1966; police officer tng., Aux. Officer Sch., Fla., 1975; degree in personal mgmt., Cornell U., 1970. Dist. mgr. Winn-Dixie, Tampa, Fla., 1958—90; folk artist Mr. B's Folk Art, San Antonio, 1995—. Resident artist for Fla. VSA Arts, Tampa, 1996—. Author: 25 Stories for 25 Years, 1999, Extraordinary in Interpretations, 2005, Just Above the Water, 2006; one-man shows include Office of Gov. Jeb Bush, Tallahassee, 2002, exhibitions include African Am. Mus., Dallas, 1996—98, Mekee Botanical Gardens, Vero Beach, Fla., 1996—2002, Capitol Complex, Tallahassee, 1997—98, Riverfest, Columbus, Ga., 1998—2006, Hillsborough County Ctr. Bldg., 1998—2007, Mennello Mus., Orlando, 1999—2007, Safety Harbor Mus., 1999—2007, Folk Art Soc. Am., 1999—2007, Oldsmar Art Gallery, Fla., 2000—07, Jimmie B. Keel Libr., Tampa, Fla., 2003—07, Tampa Mus. Fine Art, 2007, St. Petersburg Mus. Fine Art, 2007, Cotton Club Mus., Gainesville, Fla., 2007, Freedom Park, Tampa, Fla., 2007. Capt. Sheriff's Dept., Hillsborough County, Fla., 1974—87. Recipient Emerging Artist award, Hillsborough County, 1997, Best in Show, Princeton Med. Ctr., 2005, 2006. Republican. Mem. Church Of Christ. Avocation: art. Home: 10422 Moshie Ln San Antonio FL 33576 Studio: Mr Bs Folk Art San Antonio FL 33576 Office Phone: 352-668-3047. Personal E-mail: jbeverland@tampabay.rr.com.

BEVERLEY, CORDIA LUVONNE, gastroenterologist; b. Jamaica, W.I., Oct. 19, 1950; d. Hurdley Aston and Joyce Ruby (Baker) Beverley. BA, Hunter Coll., 1971; MD, NYU, 1975. Diplomate Am. Bd. Gastroenterology, Am. Bd. Internal Medicine. Intern Columbia U., Harlem Hosp. Ctr., 1975—76, resident in medicine, 1976—78; clin. fellow divsn. gastroenterology NY Hosp./Cornell U. Med. Coll., 1979—82; asst. physician Rockefeller U. Hosp., 1978—81; pvt. practice gastroenterology, 1981—; assoc. med. staff mem. Lenox Hill Hosp., 1985—. Fellow Postdoctoral fellow, Nat. Inst. Alcohol Abuse and Alcoholism, 1980—82. Mem.: Women's Med. Assn. N.Y.C. Office: 1085 Park Ave New York NY 10128-1168 Office Phone: 212-876-1886.

BEVERS, THERESE BARTHOLOMEW, physician, educator; b. Amarillo, Tex., Apr. 5, 1960; d. James Oliver Bartholomew and Ruth Ann Berg. BS, Tex. Woman's U., 1981; MD, U. Tex. Health Scis. Ctr., San Antonio, 1987. Intern, then resident U. Tex. Health Sci. Ctr., San Antonio/Bexar County Hosp., 1987-90; physician pvt. practice, Wichita Falls, Tex., 1990-91, Dallas, 1991-94; chief med. dir. Medi Clinic, Houston, 1994-96; asst. prof. clin. cancer prevention U. Tex. M.D. Anderson Cancer Ctr., Houston, 1996—2003, med. dir. cancer prevention ctr., 1996—, assoc. prof. clin. cancer prevention, 2003—. Chmn. expert panel Nat. Comprehensive Cancer Network Breast Screening and Diagnosis Com., Nat. Comprehensive Cancer Network Breast Cancer Prevention Com. Mem. editl. bd. Oncolog, Breast Diseases: A Year Book Quarterly. Mem. bd. regents Tex. Woman's U., 2001—07, chair bd. regents, 2005—07. Mem.: Anderson Physician Network (bd. dirs. 2001—06), Am. Cancer Soc. Tex. (breast cancer detection com., colorectal cancer detection com., health sci. adv. bd., bd. dirs.). Avocations: skiing, hiking, antiques, decorating, reading. Office: U Tex MD Anderson Cancer Ctr 1515 Holcombe Blvd Unit 1322 Houston TX 77030-4009

BEVERSDORF, DAVID QUENTIN, neurologist, researcher; b. Bloomington, Ind., May 28, 1965; s. Samuel Thomas and Norma (Beeson) B.; m. Suzanne E. Lentz, Aug. 6, 2005. BS, Ind. U., 1987; MD, Ind. U., Indpls., 1992. Med. resident Meth. Hosp. Ind., Indpls., 1992-93; neurology resident Dartmouth-Hitchcock Med. Ctr., Lebanon, N.H., 1993-96; behavioral neurology fellow U. Fla. Coll. Medicine, Gainesville, 1996-98; asst. prof. neurology Ohio State U. Med. Ctr., Columbus, 1998—. Contbr. articles to profl. jours. including Procs. Nat. Acad. Scis., Lancet, Neurology, Psychiatry Rsch.-Neuroimaging, Jour. Neurology, Jour. Cognitive Neurosci., Neurosurgery and Psychiatry, and Physiology and Behavior. Rsch. grant Stallone Fund, L.A., 1994, grantee Nat. Inst. on Drug Abuse, 2002, Nat. Inst. Neurol. Diseases and Stroke, 2002, Nat. Alliance for Autism Rsch., 2005. Mem. Internat. Neuropsychol. Soc., Am. Acad. Neurology, Soc. for Neurosci., Cognitive Neurosci. Soc., Phi Beta Kappa. Office: Ohio State U Med Ctr Dept Neurology 1654 Upham Dr Columbus OH 43210-1250 Office Phone: 614-293-8531. Business E-Mail: david.beversdorf@osumc.edu.

BE VIER, WILLIAM A., retired religious studies educator; b. Springfield, Mo., July 31, 1927; s. Charles and Erma G. (Ritter) Be V.; m Jo Ann King, Aug. 11, 1949; children: Cynthia, Shirley. BA, Drury Coll., 1950; ThM, Dallas Theol. Sem., 1955, ThD, 1958; MA, So. Meth. U., 1960; EdD, ABD, Wayne State U., 1968. With Frisco Rlwy., 1943-45, 46-51, John E. Mitchell Co., Dallas, 1952-60; instr. Dallas Theol. Sem., 1958-59; prof. Detroit Bible Coll., 1960-74, registrar, 1962-66, dean, 1964-73, exec. v.p., 1967-74, acting pres., 1967-68; prof., dean edn., v.p. for acad. affairs Northwestern Coll., Roseville, Minn., 1974-81, prof., 1981-95, prof. emeritus, 1995—. Editor The Discerner. Bd. dirs. Religion Analysis Svc., Mpls., 1979-2004, pres., 1989-2004. With USMC, 1945-46, 50-51; ret. col. Army Res. Mem. Res. Officers Assn., Ind. Fund Chs. of Am. (nat. exec. com. 1991-94, v.p. 1993-94), Huguenot Hist. Soc., Bevier-Elting Family Assn., Phi Alpha Theta.

BEVILACQUA, LOUIS J., lawyer; b. Boston, Dec. 21, 1948; BA, Coll. Holy Cross, 1970; MBA, NYU, 1977; JD, Fordham U., 1977. Bar: N.Y. 1977. Assoc. to ptnr. Sage Gray Todd & Sims, NYC; ptnr. Cadwalader, Wickersham & Taft, NYC, 1987—, chmn. Corp. Mergers & Acquisitions Dept. & mem. mgmt. com. Mem. ABA, N.Y. County Lawyers Assn. Office: Cadwalader Wickersham & Taft LLP 1 World Fin Ctr New York NY 10281 Office Phone: 212-504-6057. Office Fax: 212-504-6666. Business E-Mail: louis.bevilacqua@cwt.com.

BEVILACQUA, MAURIZIO, member of Canadian parliament; b. Sulmona, Italy, June 1, 1960; m. Elena Cesaroni; 2 children. BA, York U., Toronto. Exec. asst. Members of Provincial and Federal Parliaments, Toronto, Ottawa, Can., 1982-88; mem. parliament Ho. of Commons, Ottawa, 1988—, chmn. standing com. on fin., 1997—2002, parliamentary sec. to the min. of labour (human resources develop.), 1993—95, parliamentary sec. to the min. of employment & immigration (human resources develop.), 1993—96, sec. of state sci., rsch. and develop., 2002, sec. state internat. fin. instns., 2002—03. Opposition critic for employment: youth and disabled, assoc. opposition critic for energy, mines and resources, 1988-90; mem. standing coms. on Energy, Mines and Resources; Labour, Employment and Immigration and Human Rights and Status of Disabled Persons, 1988-90; chair of standing com. on Human Resources Devel., 1995-97; chair standing com. on fin., 1997-2002. Co-founder Vaughn Comty. of Assns. to Restore Environ. Safety; past pres. Coun. York Student Fedn.; active on many local bds. and in local assns. Office: Can Ho of Commons Rm 540 N Ctr Block Ottawa ON Canada KIA0A6

BEVILAQUA, PAUL M., aeronautical engineer; BS, U. Notre Dame; MS, Purdue U., PhD in Aeronautics and Astronautics. Dep. dir. Energy Conversion Lab., Wright Patterson AFB; mng. advanced programs Rockwell Intern. Navy Aircraft Plant; chief aeronautical scientist Lockheed Advanced Aeronautics Co. Lockheed Martin Aeronautics Co., Palmdale, Calif., chief engr. Advanced Development Projects. Capt. USAF. Recipient Engr. of Yr. award, Design News mag., 2004. Mem.: NAE. Office: Lockheed Martin Aeronautics Co 1011 Lockheed Way Palmdale CA 93599

BEVINGTON, DAVID MARTIN, English literature educator; b. NYC, May 13, 1931; s. Merle Mowbray and Helen (Smith) B.; m. Margaret Bronson Brown, June 4, 1953; children: Stephen, Philip, Katharine, Sarah. BA, Harvard U., 1952, MA, 1957, PhD, 1959. Instr. English Harvard U., 1959-61; asst. prof. U. Va., 1961-65, asso. prof., 1965-66, prof., 1966-67; vis. prof. U. Chgo., 1967-68, prof., 1968—, Phyllis Fay Horton disting. svc. prof. in the humanities, 1985—. Vis. prof. NYU Summer Sch., 1963, Harvard U. Summer Sch., 1967, U. Hawaii Summer Sch., 1970, Northwestern U., 1974 Author: From Mankind to Marlowe, 1962, Tudor Drama and Politics, 1968, Action is Eloquence, Shakespeare's Language of Gesture, 1984, Shakespeare, 2002 2d edit., 2005, This Wide and Universal Theater: Shakespeare in Performance Then and Now, 2007; editor: Medieval Drama, 1975, The Complete Works of Shakespeare, 5th edit., 2003, The Bantam Shakespeare, 1988, English Renaissance Drama: A Norton Anthology, 2002. Served with USN, 1952-55. Guggenheim fellow, 1964-65, 81-82; sr. fellow Southeastern Inst. Medieval and Renaissance Studies, summer 1975; sr. cons. and seminar leader Folger Inst. Renaissance and Eighteenth-Century Studies, 1976-77 Mem. MLA, AAUP, Renaissance Soc. Am., Shakespeare Assn. Am. (pres. 1976-77, 95-96), Am. Acad. Arts and Scis., Am. Philos. Soc., Brit. Acad. Office: U Chgo English Dept 1115 E 58th St Chicago IL 60637-5418 Office Phone: 773-702-9899. Business E-Mail: bevi@uchicago.edu.

BEVINGTON, EDMUND MILTON, electrical machinery manufacturing company executive; b. Nashville, Oct. 31, 1928; s. John Laurence and Mary (Halloran) B.; m. Elizabeth Anne Rickey, Sept. 8, 1951 (dec. June 1962); children: Milton, Rickey, Peter (dec.); m. Paula Maureen Lawton, Apr. 24, 1965; children: George, Mary-Laurence, Christian, Charles, Justin. Grad., Canterbury Sch., 1945; S.B. in Chem. Engring, Mass. Inst. Tech., 1949; MBA, Harvard, 1951. Plant supr. Dewey & Almy Chem. Co.

(name changed to W.R. Grace Co., 1954), Cambridge, Mass., 1951-54, marketing research mgr., 1954-56; merchandising mgr. Westinghouse Electric Co., Staunton, Va., 1956-58, So. zone sales mgr. Atlanta, 1958-59; with The Trane Co., Atlanta and LaCrosse, Wis., 1959—, v.p., gen. mgr. consumer products div., 1969-70, exec. v.p., 1970-73; chmn., pres. Servidyne Systems, Inc., Atlanta, 1974—2002, Bevington & Co., Atlanta, 2002—. Bd. dirs. AAA South. Mem. corp. devel. com. MIT, 1978—, bd. dirs. MIT Corp., 1985-91; chmn. Ga. Conservancy, 1989-92, bd. dirs.; bd. dirs. Atlanta coun. Boy Scouts Am., also v.p., 1989-90, pres., 1990-92; bd. dirs. So. region Boy Scouts Am.; pres. Metro Group, 1992-97; bd. dirs. Ga. Dept. Cmty. Affairs, 1988-92; bd. dirs. Flannery O'Connor-Andalusia Found, 2002. Mem. Pres.' Cir. of NAS, MIT Alumni Assn. (v.p. 1983-85, pres. 1985-86), Harvard Club, (NYC), Piedmont Driving Club (Atlanta), Tau Beta Pi, Sigma Alpha Epsilon.

BEWKES, EUGENE GARRETT, JR., investment company executive, consultant; b. Norwood, Mass., Sept. 28, 1926; s. Eugene Garrett and Helen (Van Vlaanderen) B.; m. Marjorie Louise Klenk, Aug. 20, 1949; children: Eugene Garrett III, Jeffrey Lawrence, Robert David. BA, Colgate U., 1948; JD, Yale U., 1951; LLD, Colgate U., 1991. Bar: N.Y. 1952. With firm Chapman, Bryson, Walsh & O'Connell, NYC, 1951-55; atty.-adviser also asst. Office Sec. USAF, 1955-57; with Am. Mgmt. Assn., 1957-61, gen. mgmt. div., mgr., 1959-61; gen. counsel, sec., asst. v.p. Reuben H. Donnelley Corp, 1961-67; v.p. law and adminstrn., sec. Canada Dry Corp., 1967-68; v.p. Norton Simon, Inc., NYC, 1968-72, sr. v.p., 1972-73, exec. v.p., 1973-77, vice chmn. bd., 1977-81; chmn., pres., chief exec. officer Am. Bakeries Co., 1982-88; cons. Paine Webber Group, Inc., NYC, 1988—2003. Chmn. emeritus bd. trustees Colgate U., Hamilton, N.Y. With USNR, 1945-46. Mem. Yale Club (N.Y.C.), Johns Island Club, Redstick Golf Club, Sankaty Club Nantucket, Phi Beta Kappa, Delta Kappa Epsilon, Phi Delta Phi. Home: 51 Marker Way Vero Beach FL 32963

BEWKES, JEFFREY L., television broadcasting company executive; b. Paterson, NJ, May 25, 1952; s. Eugene Garrett Bewkes Jr.; m. Margaret Brim; 1 child. BA in Philos., Yale U., 1974; MBA, Stanford U., 1977. Ops. dir. Sonoma Vineyards, Inc., Healdsburg, Calif.; acct. officer Citibank, NA, NYC; exec. v.p., CFO HBO, NYC, 1987—91, pres., COO, 1991—95, chmn., CEO, 1995—2002; chmn. entertainment. & networks grp. Time Warner Inc., NYC, 2002—, pres., COO, 2005—. Bd. dirs. Time Warner Inc., 2007—. Mem. adv. coun. Yale U., Stanford U. Grad. Sch. Bus., Am. Mus. Nat. Hist. Office: Time Warner Inc 75 Rockefeller Plz New York NY 10019*

BEWLEY, JEFFREY MICHAEL, lawyer; BA, Princeton U., NJ, 1967; JD, U. Ariz., Tucson, 1972. Bar: Calif. 1972, Ariz. 1972. Prin. Law Office J. Michael Bewley, San Jose, Calif., 1976—. Named one of Best Employment Lawyers in Silicon Valley, San Jose Mag., 1999—2006, Top Employment Lawyers in Bay Area, Employment Law Mag./Recorder, 2004; recipient Disting. Advocacy, Internat. Trial Lawyers, 1972. Mem.: Nat. Employment Lawyers Assn., Calif. Employment Lawyers Assn. Office: 160 W Santa Clara St Ste 625 San Jose CA 95113

BEWLEY, JOHN DEREK, botany researcher, educator; b. Preston, Lancashire, Eng., Dec. 11, 1943; s. Clifford and Marion (Garner) B.; m. Christine E. Nee Kite, Sept. 3, 1966 (dec. Mar. 2006); children: Alexander, Janette Louise. BSc, U. London, 1965, PhD, 1968, DSc, 1983. Asst. prof. U. Calgary, Alta., 1970-73, assoc. prof. Alta., 1973-77, prof. biology Alta., 1977-85; prof., chmn. dept. botany U. Guelph, Ont., 1985-90, prof. botany, 1990—2005, Univ. prof. emeritus, 2005—, dir. plant biol. program, 1993-94. E.W.R. Steacie Meml. fellow in natural scis. and engring. Rsch. Coun. Can., 1979-81; recipient Career Rsch. Excellence award Sigma Xi, 1993, Disting. Biologist award Can. Coun. Univ. Chairs, 1994; named Highly Cited Author, ISI, 2002. Fellow Royal Soc. Can. (rapporteur plant biology div. 1984-85, convenor 1985-87); mem. Am. Soc. Plant Physiology (corr.), Can. Soc. Plant Physiologists (C.D. Nelson award 1978, Gold medal 1992, sec. 1983-85, v.p. 1987-88, pres. 1988-90), Natural Scis. and Engring. Rsch. Coun. Can. (chmn. plant biology grant selection com. 1988-90), Internat. Soc. Seed Sci. (pres. 2005—). Home: 26 Waverley Dr Guelph ON Canada N1E 6C8 Office: U Guelph Dept Molecular andCellular Biology Guelph ON Canada N1G 2W1 Business E-Mail: dbewley@uoguelph.ca.

BEWLEY, PETER DAVID, lawyer; b. Atlantic City, Aug. 4, 1946; s. Philip Bessor and Gladys Elizabeth Bewley; m. Barbara L. Sell, June 1, 1968 (dec. June 25, 1971); 1 child, Peter David Jr.; m. Lee D. Catanese, Aug. 12, 1972; 1 child, Stephen Philip. BA in politics cum laude, Princeton U., 1968; JD, Stanford U., 1971. Bar: Calif. 1971, DC 1972, US Ct. Appeals DC cir. 1972, US Supreme Ct. 1976. Law clk. O'Melveny and Myers, LA; assoc. Wilmer, Cutler & Pickering, Washington, 1972-76; atty. Johnson & Johnson, New Brunswick, NJ, 1977—85, asst. gen. counsel, 1985—90, assoc. gen. counsel, 1990—94; sr. v.p., gen. counsel, sec. NovaCare, Inc., King of Prussia, Pa., 1994-98, The Clorox Co., Oakland, Calif., 1998—2005. Bd. dirs. Non Prescription Drug Mfrs. Assn., Washington, 1991-94, Access Worldwide Comm Inc., Boca Raton, Fla., 1998-2001. Mem. editl. bd. Food and Drug Law Jour., 1992-94. City councilman, Gladstone, NJ, 1993—94; vice chair bd. dirs. Children Now, chair fin. com.; exec. campaign adv. com. United Negro Coll. Fund of the Bay Area; exec. com. bd. visitors Stanford Law Sch. Capt. USAF, 1971—72. Mem. ABA, Am. Corp. Counsel Assn., Am. Soc. Corp. Secretaries, Order of Coif. Avocations: travel, skiing, reading.

BEXTERMILLER, THERESA MARIE, architect, computer engineer; b. St. Charles, Mo., Feb. 9, 1960; d. Charles Frederick and Loretta Joan (Unterreiner) Bextermiller; m. Paul James Metzger III, Nov. 29, 2000. BArch, Kans. State U., 1983; MFA in Computer Graphics, Pratt Inst., 1990. Registered arch., NY, Mo., cert. Nat. Coun. Architectural Registration Bds., 1996; lic. real estate broker Mo., 2000. Grad. arch. Mackey/Mitchell Assocs., St. Louis, 1983-84, Fleming Corp., St. Louis, 1984-85; grad. project arch., prototype mgr. Casco Corp., St. Louis, 1985-87; grad. arch. H.B.E Corp., St. Louis, 1987-88; with telecomm. Western Union, 1992-93; with telecomm. spl. projects Lucent Techs. (formerly AT&T Network Sys.), 1993—94; contract arch. indsl. projects Washington Group Internat. (formerly M.K-Ferguson Group), 1994-95; contract arch. Fru-Con Engring. Inc. and other firms, various locations, 1995-98; pvt. practice St. Louis, 1997—; arch. Le Pique and Orne Archs.-Inc., 1998—, Hellmuth, Obata & Kassabaum, Inc., St. Louis, 1998—, Infante Assocs., LLC, 1999—. Cons. with 3D modeling and animation software, NY, LA, St. Louis, 1990—; with Maya Video Products Inc., NY, 1990, Barlow Prodns., St. Louis, 1991, Tad Tech. Svcs., Lake Forest, Calif., 1992, So. Ill. U., Edwardsville, 1992, Washington U., St. Louis, 1996; substitute tchr. St. Louis Pub. Schs., 2001—02; mem. US Green Bldg. Coun., LA, 2005—. Mem.: AIA (environ. com. St. Louis chpt. 1998—2005), Assn. Computing Machinery-Spl. Interest Group Graphics, Nat. Fire Protection Assn. Roman Cath. Avocations: bicycling, camping. Home and Office: 1120 Blendon Pl Saint Louis MO 63117-1911 Personal E-mail: illege666@aol.com.

BEYELER, JULIA, retired academic administrator; b. Orrville, Ohio, Nov. 13, 1938; d. Milton D. and Ella Amstutz Rohrer; m. Robert V. Beyeler, Aug. 19, 1961; children: Michael, Steven, Suzanne. BS in Edn., Goshen Coll., Ind., 1960; MS in Edn., Kent State U., Ohio, 1965; PhD in Elem. Edn., U. Akron, 1995. Tchr. grade 4 Wooster City Schs., Ohio, 1960—61, tchr. grades 3, 1964—65, spl. reading tchr. grades 1-9, 1965—75; tchr. grades 3 and 4 Goshen City Schs., Goshen, Ind., 1961—64; spl. reading tchr. grades 11 and 12 Wayne County Career Ctr., Smithville, Ohio, 1975—77; reading tchr. U. Akron-Wayne, Orrville, Ohio, 1977—78, dir. learning support svcs., 1978—2006, dir. emeritus, 2006—. Author: Instructor's Resources Manual, 2004. Mem. literacy com. Wayne County Career Ctr., 2004—; trustee Ctrl. Christian Schs., Kidron, Ohio, 1987—93, 2004—07. Recipient Grant award, Ohio Bd. Regents, 2005. Mem.: Internat. Reading Assn., Am. Ednl. Rsch. Assn., Ohio Assn. for Developmental Edn. (pres. 2004—05, Outstanding Developmental Educator 2006), Delta Kappa Gamma. Business E-Mail: juliabeyeler@uakron.edu.

BEYENE, NAHOM MINASSIE, aerospace engineer; b. Dallas, Jan. 4, 1980; s. Minassie and Rebecca (Tesfaye) Beyene. BSMechE, U. Tex., Austin, 2002; MS in Biomechanical Engring., Stanford U., Calif., 2004; postgrad., U. Pitts., 2007—. Aerospace engr. NASA Johnson Space Ctr., Houston, 2000—07. Adv. Ethiopian Students Assn. Internat., Washington, 2000—; lead facilitator Ethiopian Students Assn. Tex.; task force Ethiopian Orthodox Tewahido Ch. Internat. Parishoners Orgn., Dallas, 2006—07; Sunday sch. tchr. Medhanealem Ethiopian Orthodox Ch., Houston. Mem.: Nat. Soc. Black Engrs. (Alumni Leadership award 2006). Ethiopian Orthodox Tewahido. Home Phone: 281-280-0824. Personal E-mail: nahom.beyene@gmail.com.

BEYER, AARON JAY, lawyer; b. Plainfield, NJ, Mar. 26, 1946; s. Solomon and Pearl (Lieberman) B.; m. Francine Simmons, Apr. 21, 1974; 1 child, Jared Solomon. BA, Rutgers U., 1968; JD, Temple U., 1971. Bar: N.J. 1971, D.C. 1974, Pa. 1977, U.S. Supreme Ct. 1976. Assoc. Smith, Stratton, Wise & Heher, Princeton, N.J., 1971-74, Howrey & Simon, Washington, 1974-77, Ballard, Spahr, Andrews & Ingersoll, Phila., 1977-79; ptnr. Meltzer & Schiffrin, Phila., 1979-87, Fox, Rothschild, O'Brien & Frankel, Phila., 1987—. Bd. dirs. Jewish Nat. Fund, Phila., 1987-88, chmn. lawyers' divsn.; pres. Soc. Hill Civic Assn., Phila. 1987-89. Lefferts scholar, Rutgers U., 1966-68. Mem.: Nassau Club. Republican. Home: 632 Spruce St Philadelphia PA 19106-4114 Office: Fox Rothschild O'Brien & Frankel 2000 Market St Ste 10 Philadelphia PA 19103-3231

BEYER, BARBARA LYNN, transportation executive, consultant; b. Miami, Fla., Feb. 16, 1947; d. Morten Sternoff and Jane (Hartman) Beyer. BA, George Washington U., 1978. Supr. printing office Saudi Arabian Airlines, 1966-67; ops. coord. Modern Air Transport, Miami, 1968-70, acct. Berlin, 1970-72; rep. Johnson Internat. Airlines, Washington, 1974-75; v.p., bd. dirs. Avmark, Inc., Washington, 1975—, pres., 1989—; chmn., bd. dirs. Avmark Internat., London, 1985—; mng. dir. Avmark Asia Ltd., Singapore, 1988-89, also bd. dirs., chmn. bd. dirs. Hong Kong, 1989—; pub. Avmark Aviation Economist, London, 1986—. Mem. adv. bd. aviation bus. dept. Embry-Riddle Aero. U. Mem.: Nat. Bus. Aircraft Assn., Aviation Space Writers (internat. bd. dirs. 1986—88, award 1978), Am. C. of C., Nat. Press Club, Internat. Aviation Club, Aero Club, Fgn. Corr. Club. Avocations: reading, horseback riding, home improvement. Office: Avmark Inc 415 Church St NE Ste 203 Vienna VA 22180 Office Phone: 703-528-5610. Personal E-mail: bbeyer@avmarkinc.com.

BEYER, GERRY WAYNE, lawyer, educator; b. Sept. 12, 1956; s. O. Frank and Lorraine Hazel (Kopper) B.; m. Margaret Mary Brewer, June 17, 1983. BA summa cum laude, Ea. Mich. U., Ypsilanti, 1976; JD summa cum laude, Ohio State U., 1979; LLM, U. Ill., 1983, JSD, 1990. Bar: Ohio 1980, Ill. 1980, Tex. 1984, US Ct. Mil. Appeals 1990, US Supreme Ct. 1991. Assoc. Knisley, Carpenter, Wilhelm & Nein, Columbus, Ohio, 1980; instr. law U. Ill., Champaign, 1980-81; asst. prof., assoc. prof. law St. Mary's U., San Antonio, 1981-87, prof., 1987—2005; Gov. Preston E. Smith regents prof. Tex. Tech. U., Sch. Law, Lubbock, 2005—. Vis. prof. Boston Coll. Law Sch., 1992-93, U. N.Mex., 1995, So. Meth. U. Sch. Law, 1997, Santa Clara U. Sch. Law, 1999-2000; lectr. Inst. Tex. Bar Rev., Austin, 1984-88, BAR/BRI Bar Rev., Houston, 1984-90, 99—, SMH Bar Rev., Boston, 1990-95, West Bar Rev., 1996-97; adv. bd. paralegal divsn. S.W. Sch. Ct. Reporting, 1990-92. Author quar. jour. articles in Estate Planning Devels. for Tex. Profls., 1981—, Texas Wills and Estates: Cases and Materials, 1987, 3d rev. edit., 2006, Tex. Estate Planning Statutes Student Edit., 2006, Teaching Materials on Estate Planning, 1995, 2005, Wills, Trusts, and Estates: Examples and Explanations, 1999, 4th rev. edit., 2007, West's Legal Forms- Real Estate Transactions - Residential (vols. 19 & 19A), 2002, Texas Law of Wills, 3d ed., 2002; co-author: West's Legal Forms - Real Estate Transactions (vols. 19-23), 1986, West's Texas Forms - Probate and Administration of Estates (vols. 12, 12A, 12B), 1996, Texas Law of Wills, 2d edit., 1992, ann. supplement to Tex. Will Manual, 1986-2004, Modern Dictionary for the Legal Profession, 1993, 3d edit., 2001, Wills, Trusts and Estates for Legal Assistants, 2002, 06. Mem. ABA (vice chair significant current lit. com., probate and trust divsn. of real property, probate and trust law sect. 1990-95, vice-chair non-tax issues in drafting wills and revocable trusts 1996-99), ACTEC, ATLA, Tex. Bar Assn., Ill. State Bar Assn., Order Coif, Order Barristers, Southwest Found. for Biomed. Rsch. (animal rsch. com. 1986-91). Home: Ste 212 4414 82nd St Lubbock TX 79424 Office: Tex Tech Univ Sch Law 1802 Hartford St Lubbock TX 79409-0004 Office Phone: 806-742-3990 ext. 302. Business E-Mail: gwb@ProfessorBeyer.com.

BEYER, KAREN HAYNES, social worker; b. Cleve., Jan. 30, 1942; BA, Ohio State U., Columbia, 1965; MSW, Loyola U., Chgo., 1969; postgrad. Family Inst., Northwestern U., Evanston, Ill., 1979; MPA, Roosevelt U., Chgo., 1992; CBA, U. Ill., Chgo., 1995; MBA, Keller Grad. Sch. Mgmt., Elgin, Ill., 2004. Lic. clin. social worker, Ill. With Cuyahoga County Divsn. Child Welfare, Cleve., 1965, Dallas County Child Welfare Unit, Dallas, 1966, Luth. Social Svsc. Ill., Chgo., 1967-73; pvt. practice psychotherapy, family mediation Schaumburg, Ill., 1975-93; therapist Family Svcs. Assn. Greater Elgin (Ill.), 1973-77, dir. prof. svcs., 1977-83; dir. HHS Village of Hoffman Estates, Ill., 1983-93; exec. dir. Larkin Ctr., Elgin, Ill., 1993-2000, Ecker Ctr., Elgin, 2000—. Mem.: NASW, Cosmopolitan Club, Rotary. Unitarian Universalist. Office: Ecker Ctr for Mental Health 1845 Grandstand Pl Elgin IL 60123 Office Phone: 847-695-0484.

BEYER, LISA, journalist; b. Lafayette, La., 1961; BJ, U. Tex., 1983. Staff Austin American-Statesman; editor Daily Texan; sr. correspondent Asiaweek, Singapore, 1984-88; staff writer Time Internat., NYC, 1988—90, assoc. editor, World Sect., 1990—91; Jerusalem bur. chief Time Mag., 1991—2000, sr. editor, Soc. Sect. editor NYC, 2000—01, sr. editor, World Sect. editor, 2001—04, asst. mng. editor, Nation Sect. editor, 2004—07. Interviewed leaders such as Yassar Arafat, Yitzhak Rabin, Benjamin Neanyahu and Ehud Barak. Office Fax: 212-522-0023.*

BEYER, MARCUS PAUL, lawyer; b. 1975; BA cum laude, St. Olaf Coll., 1997; JD, William Mitchell Coll. Law, 2000. Bar: Minn. 2000, US Dist. Ct. (dist. Minn.). Law clk. to Hon. Michael J. Roith Anoka County Dist. Ct., Minn.; atty. Steffens & Rasmussen; ptnr. Gadtke & Beyer, L.L.C., Edina, Minn. Named a Rising Star, Minn. Super Lawyers mag., 2006. Mem.: Minn. State Bar Assn., Hennepin County Bar Assn. Office Phone: 952-345-8004. E-mail: marcus.beyer@gadtkelaw.com.*

BEYER, MOLLY M., museum program director; m. Michael K. Beyer, Aug. 22, 1970; children: Claire E., Elsa M. BA, U. Calif., Berkeley, 1974. Mgr. mus. amb. program Fine Arts Mus., San Francisco, 1995—. Recipient Coming Up Taller award, President's Com. Arts and Humanities, 2004. Office: Fine Arts Museums of San Francisco 50 Hagiwara Tea Garden Dr San Francisco CA 94118 Home Phone: 415-563-3698; Office Phone: 415-750-3521. Office Fax: 415-750-3540. E-mail: mbeyer@famsf.org.

BEYER, ROBERT D., corporate financial executive; BS, Univ. So. Calif.; MBA, UCLA. Investment banker Bear Stearns & Co., 1983—91; co-founder, co-CEO Crescent Capital Corp., 1991—95; CEO TCW Group Inc., 1995—. Bd. dir. Kroger Co., Societe Generale Asset Mgmt., Allstate Corp. Chmn. bd. trustees Harvard-Westlake Sch.; mem. bd. vis. Anderson Sch. Mgmt. UCLA; mem. bd. councilors Coll. Letters Arts & Sci. Univ. So. Calif.; past. commr. LA City Employees Retirement Sys. Office: TCW Group Inc 865 S Figueroa St Los Angeles CA 90017

BEYER, ROBERTA BONNIE, dean, education professor, writer, researcher; d. Raymond B. and Florentine R. Beyer; children: Leonard, Elizabeth Ann, James. BA, Elmhurst Coll., Ill., 1978; MS in Edn., No. Ill. U., 1979; EdD, Vanderbilt U., 1988. Cert. tchr. 9-12 Ill., adminstr. K-12 Ill., supt. Ill., adminstr. K-12 NY. Adminstr., tchr. K-12, Chgo. area, 1969—92; asst. prof. Sch. Edn., Bemidji State U., 1992—93, West Tex. A&M U., Canyon, 1993—95; asst. prof. U. Mich., Dearborn, 1995—99, assoc. prof., 2000—07, assoc. dean, 2000—06, prof., 2007—. Mem. ednl. adv. bd. Henry Ford C.C., Dearborn, 2000—. Author: Special and Compensatory Programs, 1997, Special Programs and Services in Schools, 2005. Mem. Dearborn Cmty. Coun. for Edn., 2004—05; mem. editl. review bd. Scholar Practitioner Quarterly, Ednl. Leadership Review; domain editor NCPEA Connexions. Mem.: Mich. Assn. Coll. of Tchr. Edn., Mich. Coun. Profs. of Ednl. Adminstrn., Nat. Coun. Profs. of Ednl. Adminstrn., Assn. Supervision and Curriculum Devel., Am. Edn. Rsch. Assn., Am. Assn. Colls. for Tchr. Edn., Ill. State Deans' Assn. (hon. life, past pres.), Phi Delta Kappa, Phi Beta Delta (pres. Alpha Psi chpt. 1994—95). Avocations: art, sports, reading, cooking, dance. Office: U Mich-Dearborn Sch Edn 19000 Hubbard Dr Dearborn MI 48126

BEYER, SUZANNE, advertising agency executive; b. NYC; d. Harry and Jennie Hillman; m. Isadore Beyer; children: Pamela Claire, Hillary Jay. Grad., Conservatory of Mus. Art, NYC, 1947; student, Nassau C. C., NYC, 1963-65. Singer, tchr. piano, NYC, 1947-66; asst. to v.p. media dir. Robert E. Wilson, Advt., NYC, 1967-72; media planner, media buyer frank J. Corbett div. BBDO Internat., NYC, 1972-77, Lavey/Wolff/Swift divsn. BBDO Advt., NYC, 1977-80; sr. media planner Lavey/Wolff/Swift (divn. BBDO Advt.), NYC, 1980-83, media supr., 1983-94, Lyons, Lavey, Nichel, Swift, NYC, 1995-96; pharm. advt. med. media cons., 1996—. Soprano Opera Assn., Nassau, N.Y., 1976-99; soprano United Choral Soc., Woodmere, L.I., 1970-99, soprano Armand Sodero Chorale, Baldwin, Long Is., 1980-86, soprano Rockville Ctr. Choral Soc., 1986—. Mem. Pharm. Advt. Coun., L.I. Advt. Club, Healthcare Bus. Women's Assn. Home and Office: 66 Fonda Rd Rockville Centre NY 11570-2751 Personal E-mail: pianoredhead@yahoo.com.

BEYER-MEARS, ANNETTE, physiologist; b. Madison, Wis., May 26, 1941; d. Karl and Annette (Weiss) Beyer. BA, Vassar Coll., 1963; MS, Fairleigh Dickinson U., 1973; PhD, Coll. Medicine and Dentistry NJ, 1977. NIH fellow Cornell U. Med. Sch., 1963-65; instr. physiology Springside Sch., Phila., 1967-71; teaching asst. dept. physiology Coll. Medicine & Dentistry NJ, NJ Med. Sch., 1974-77, NIH fellow dept. ophthalmology, 1978-80; asst. prof. dept. ophthalmology U. Medicine and Dentistry NJ., NJ Med. Sch., Newark, 1979-85, asst. prof. dept. physiology, 1980-85, assoc. prof. dept. physiology, 1986—, assoc. prof. dept. ophthalmology, 1986—. Vis. assoc. prof. dept. ophthalmology and vision sci. U. Wis., Madison, 1995—; cons. Alcon Labs. Contbr. articles in field of diabetic lens and kidney therapy to profl. jours. Chmn. admissions No. NJ, Vassar Coll., 1974-79; mem. minister search com. St. Bartholomew Episcopal Ch., NJ, 1978, fund-raising chmn., 1978, 79; del. Episc. Diocesian Conv., 1977, 78; long range planning com. Christ Ch., Ridgewood, NJ, 1985-87, vestry, 1994-95. Recipient NIH Nat. Rsch. Svc. award, 1978-80, Found. CMDNJ Rsch. award, 1980; grantee Juvenile Diabetes Found., 1985-87, NIH, NEI grantee, 1980-95, Pfizer, Inc. grantee, 1985-89, 93—. Mem. Am. Physiol. Soc., NY Acad. Scis., Soc. for Neurosci., Am. Soc. Pharmacology and Exptl. Therapeutics, Assn. for Rsch. Vision & Ophthalmology, Internat. Soc. for Eye Research, AAAS, The Royal Soc. Medicine, Internat. Diabetes Found., Am. Diabetes Assn., European Assn. Study of Diabetes, Aircraft Owners and Pilots Assn., Sigma Xi. Home: 120 Ely Pl Madison WI 53726-4015

BEYERS, WILLIAM BJORN, geography educator; b. Seattle, Mar. 24, 1940; s. William Abraham and Esther Jakobia (Svendsen) B.; m. Margaret Lyn Rice, July 28, 1968. BA, U. Wash., 1962, PhD, 1967. Asst. prof. geography U. Wash., Seattle, 1968-74, assoc. prof., 1974-82, prof., 1982—, chmn. dept. geography, 1991-95, 2005—08. Mem.: Western Regional Sci. Assn., Regional Sci. Assn., Assn. Am. Geographers. Home: 7159 Beach Dr SW Seattle WA 98136-2077 Office: U Wash Dept Geography PO Box 353550 Seattle WA 98195-3550 Home Phone: 206-935-6282; Office Phone: 206-543-5871. Fax: 206-543-3313. E-mail: beyers@u.washington.edu.

BEYLKIN, GREGORY, mathematician; b. St. Petersburg, Mar. 16, 1953; came to U.S., 1980; naturalized citizen, 1985; s. Jacob and Raya (Pripshtein) B.; m. Helen Simontov, 1974; children: Michael, Daniel. Diploma in Math., U. St. Petersburg, Leningrad, 1975; PhD in Math., NYU, 1982. Assoc. rsch. sci. NYU, 1982-83; mem. profl. staff Schlumberger-Doll Research, Ridgefield, Conn., 1983-91; prof. dept. applied math. U. Colo., Boulder, 1991—. Contbr. articles to profl. jours. Mem. Am. Math. Soc., Soc. for Indsl. and Applied Math., Soc. Exptl. Geophysicists. Office: U Colo Dept Applied Math 526 UCB Boulder CO 80309-0526 Business E-Mail: beylkin@boulder.colorado.edu.

BEYMAN, JONATHAN ERIC, investment company executive; b. Newark, Dec. 31, 1955; s. Bernard B. and Miriam (Simon) Beyman; m. Susan Elizabeth Bleckman, Aug. 23, 1981; children: Michael, Daniel, Max. BS, U. Ct., 1976; MBA, Cornell U., 1981. CPA Conn. Sr. acct. Arthur Young and Co., NYC, 1976-79; asst. v.p. Chem. Bank, 1981-84; sr. cons. Am. Mgmt. Systems, 1985; v.p. Citibank North Am. Investment Bank, 1985-86, Lehman Bros., 1986-88, sr. v.p., 1988-91, mng. dir., 1991-94, 99-00, mng. dir., chief info. officer, 2000—02, global head ops., tech. divsn., 2002—; exec. v.p., chief ops. and tech. Lehman Bros. Holdings Inc., NYC, 2002—; chief info. officer, sr. v.p. CUC Internat., Stamford, Conn., 1994-97; co-chief info. officer, exec. v.p. Cendant Corp., 1997-98; pres. Cendant Interactive, 1998-99. Bd. dirs. Depository Trust and Clearing Corp., Dice, Inc.; N.Y. adv. bd. Donors Choose Org. Mem.: AICPA. Democrat. Jewish. Avocations: bicycling, reading, carpentry. Business E-Mail: jbeyman@yahoo.com.

BEYONCÉ, (BEYONCÉ GISELLE KNOWLES), singer; b. Houston, Sept. 4, 1981; d. Matthew and Tina Knowles. Mem. group Destiny's Child, Houston, 1990—. Spokesperson L'Oreal, Tommy Hilfiger for fragrance "True Star"; launched House of Dereon fashion line (with Tina Knowles), 2005. Singer: (albums) Destiny's Child, 1998, The Writing's on the Wall, 1999 (Platinum album 7 times, Grammy awards: Best R&B Song for Say My Name, 2000, Best R&B Performance By A Duo Or Group With Vocal, 2000), Survivor, 2001 (debuted at #1 Billboard Album Chart, Platinum 3 times, Grammy award: Best R&B Performance By A Duo Or Group With Vocal, 2001), 8 Days of Christmas, 2001, Destiny Fulfilled, 2004 (Am. Music Awards Favorite R&B Album, 2005), #1's, 2005, (solo albums) Dangerously in Love, 2003 (Grammy awards: Best Female R&B Vocal Performance, 2003, Best R&B Performance By A Duo Or Group With Vocals for song The Closer I Get To You, 2003, Best R&B Song for Crazy In Love, 2003, Best Contemporary R&B Album, 2003, Best Rap/Sung Collaboration for song Crazy in Love, 2003, MTV Video Music award Best Female Video for the song Naughty Girl, 2004), Live at Wembley, 2004, B'day, 2006 (Grammy award for Best Contemporary R&B Album, 2007); actor: (films) Austin Powers in Goldmember, 2002, I Know, 2003, The Fighting Temptations, 2003, The Pink Panther, 2006, Dreamgirls, 2006 (Best Song, Listen, 2006 Critics Choice award, Broadcast Film Critics

Assn., 2007); composer: (films) Romeo Must Die, Charlie's Angels, Austin Powers in Goldmember, Bad Boys II, Fighting Temptations, Bridget Jones: The Edge of Reason, Soul Plane; actor: (TV Guest Appearances) Oprah Winfrey Show, 2003, 2004, The View, 2004, 20 / 20, 2004, Top of the Pops, 2004, Saturday Night Live, 2004, 106th & Park Top 10 Live, 2005; On front cover Sports Illustrated Swimsuit Issue: The Music Issue, 2007. Co-recipient Best R&B Video award for Check on It, MTV Video Music Awards, 2006; named Pop Songwriter of Yr., ASCAP, 2001, Best Female R&B artist, Black Entertainment TV (BET) Awards, 2004, 2007; named one of 50 Most Influential African-Americans, Ebony Mag., 2004; recipient 4 Billboard Music awards, 2000, 2 Billboard Music awards, 2001, Am. Music award, 2000, 2 Am. Music awards, 2001, Favorite R&B Group, Am. Music Awards, 2005, MTV Music Video award, 2001, Video of Yr. for the song Irreplaceable, Black Entertainment TV (BET) Awards, 2007, 4 World Music awards, 2001, Image award, NAACP, 2000, 2001, 2006, Sammy Davis, Jr. award, 2000, Soul Train award, 2000, Soul Train award for Best R&B Single, 2007, World's Best-Selling Pop Group, World Music Awards, 2006, World's Best-Selling R&B Group, 2006, Best-Selling Female Group of All Time, 2006, World's Best R&B Artist, 2007, 3 Music of Black Origin (MOBO) awards, 2006. Office: 1505 Hadley Houston TX 77002 Office Phone: 713-772-5175.*

BEYRLE, JOHN R., ambassador; BA, Grand Valley State; MS, Nat. War Coll. Polit. officer US Embassy-Moscow, Russia, US Embassy-Sofia, Bulgaria, 1985—87; mem. US Delegation to the CFE Negotiations, Vienna; staff officer to Sec. State George Shultz, Sec. State James Baker; fgn. policy advisor to Senator Paul Simon; dir. for Russian, Ukrainian and Eurasian Affairs NSC, Washington, 1993—95; counselor for polit. and econ. affairs US Embassy-Prague, Czech Republic, 1997—99; dep. spl. advisor to sec. for the New Independent States US Dept. State, Washington; dep. chief of mission US Embassy-Moscow, Russia, 2002—05; US amb. to Bulgaria US Dept. State, Sofia, 2005—. Address: American Embassy Sofia Bulgaria 16 Kozyak St 1407 Sofia Bulgaria Office: American Embassy Sofia Bulgaria Dept of State 5740 Sofia Pl Washington DC 20521-5740 Office Phone: 359-2-937-5100. Office Fax: 359-2-937-5320. Business E-Mail: irc@usembassy.bg.

BEYSTEHNER, JOHN J., transportation executive; m. Anne Beystehner; 3 children. BS in Fin., Boston Coll., 1973; JD, Suffolk U., 1977. Part-time audit clk. to various mgmt. positions UPS, Inc., Atlanta, 1971-83, mktg. profl., 1983-86, head legal and regulatory aspects Louisville, 1986-92, air dist. mgr., 1992-94, v.p. airline opers., 1994-97, v.p., dir. sales Atlanta, 1997-99, sr. v.p., worldwide sales and mktg., 1999—2003, mem. mgmt. com., 1999—, COO, sr. v.p., dir., 2004—; pres. UPS Airlines, 2004—. Office: UPS Inc 55 Glenlake Pkwy NE Atlanta GA 30328-3474

BEYTAGH, FRANCIS X., law educator; b. Savannah, Ga., July 11, 1935; BA magna cum laude, U. Notre Dame, Ind., 1956; JD, U. Mich., 1963. Bar: Ohio 1964, US Supreme Ct 1967, Ind. 1972. Clk. Fuller, Seney, Henry, and Hodge, Toledo, 1961; sr. law clk. to Chief Justice Earl Warren US Supreme Ct., Washington, 1963-64; assoc. Jones, Day, Cockley, and Reavis, Cleve., 1964-66; asst. to solicitor gen. US Dept. Justice, Washington, 1966-70; prof. law U. Notre Dame, 1970-74, 75-76; prof., dean U. Toledo, 1976-83; Cullen prof. law U. Houston, 1984-85; prof., dean Ohio State U. Coll. Law, 1985-93, prof., 1993-97; spl. counsel Jones, Day, Reavis, and Pogue, Columbus, Ohio, 1993-96; pres., prof. Fla. Coastal Sch. Law, Jacksonville, 1997-98, prof., 1998—, founders' chair, 2000—. Vis. prof. law U. Va., Charlottesville, 1974—75, U. Mich., 1983—84, So. Meth. U., Dallas, 1997. Editor in chief: Mich. Law Rev., 1962—63; author: Supplement to Kauper's Constitutional Law: Cases and Materials, 1977, Constitutional Law: Cases and Materials, 5th edit., 1980, supplements, 1981, 1984, Constitutionalism in Contemporary Ireland, 1997; contbr. articles to profl. jours. Ret. capt. USNR. Fulbright fellow, 1994. Fellow: Am. Bar Found. (life); mem.: ABA, Jacksonville Bar Assn., Fla. Bar, Am. Jud. Soc. (assoc.), Order of Coif. Home: 49 Marsh Creek Rd Amelia Island FL 32034-6414 Office: Fla Coastal Sch Law 8787 Baypine Rd Jacksonville FL 32256-8528 Business E-Mail: fbeytagh@fcsl.edu.

BEZANILLA, FRANCISCO, biomedical researcher; BS in Biology, Cath. U., Santiago, Chili, 1964; MS in Biophysics, Cath. U., 1967, PhD in Biophysics, 1968. Instr. physics Cath. U. Sch. Medicine, 1964—68; instr. neurophysiology lab. Cath. U., 1965—69; postdoctoral fellow lab. biophysics NIH Nat. Inst. Neurol. and Communication Disorders and Stroke, Bethesda, Md., 1969; postdoctoral fellow dept. physiology U. Rochester, NY, 1969—71, rsch. assoc. dept. biology sch. medicine, 1974; asst. prof. dept. biology faculty of scis., U. Chile, Santiago, 1972—74, prof. dept. biology faculty of scis., 1974—77; prof. neuroscience dept. physiology UCLA, 1977—95, Susumu Hagiwara prof. neuroscience, 1995—; prof. dept. pediat. U. Chgo. Inst. Molecular Pediatric Scis. Chilean coun. sci. rsch., 1968—69; fellow Rockefeller Found., 1969—71; vis. asst. prof. dept. physiology U. Pa. Sch. Medicine, Philadelphia, 1975—76; mem. coun. Soc. Gen. Physiologists, 1985—87; sec. Soc. Latin Am. Biophysicists, 1986—87. Contbr. articles to sci. jours. Recipient Kenneth S. Cole award, 1990. Fellow: Biophysical Soc. (mem. exec. com. 1984—86); mem.: Latin Am. Acad. Scis., NAS. Office: Inst for Molecular Pediatric Scis U Chgo 5721 S Maryland Ave MC 8000 Chicago IL 60637 also: Box 951778 Bh-550 CHS Los Angeles CA 90095-1778

BEZANSON, THOMAS EDWARD, lawyer; b. Hartford, Conn., Aug. 1, 1945; s. Philip Thomas and Lillian (Carlson) Bezanson; m. Janie H. Bezanson, Aug. 10, 1969; children: Philip, Jeffrey. BA, Grinnell Coll., 1967; MA, Rutgers U., 1971; JD, 1974. Bar: NY 1975, US Dist. Ct. (Ea. and So. Dists.) 1975, US Ct. Appeals (2nd Cir.) 1975, US Ct. Appeals (6th Cir.) 1980, US Supreme Ct. 1991, US Dist. Ct. (Dist. Ariz.) 1992, US Ct. Appeals (5t Cir.) 1995. Assoc. Chadbourne & Parke LLP, NYC, 1974—81, ptnr., 1981—, chmn., Products Liability Practice Group. Author: 42 poems, 1993; mgn. editor Rutgers Law Rev., 1973—74. Bd. dirs. Westchester Philharm., 1992—98, NY Lawyers Pub. Interest Inc., 1997—, Legal Aid Soc., 1999—2002, Duke U. Sch. Law, 2003—. With US Army, 1967—69. Mem.: ABA, Fed. Bar Coun. (program com.), NY State Commn. on the Jury, Assn. Bar City NY. Office: Chadbourne & Parke 30 Rockefeller Plz Fl 31 New York NY 10112-0129 Office Fax: 212-541-5369. Business E-Mail: tbezanson@chadbourne.com.

BEZKOROVAINY, ANATOLY, medical educator, retired biochemist; b. Riga, Latvia, Feb. 11, 1935; s. Ignatius and Olga (Solovey) Bezkorovainy; m. Marilyn Grib, June 14, 1964; children: Gregory, Alexander. BS, U. Chgo., 1956; PhD, U. Ill., 1960; JD, Ill. Inst. Tech., 1977. Bar: Ill. 1977. Rsch. assoc. Oak Ridge Nat. Lab., Tenn., 1960—61; chemist USDA, Ames, Iowa, 1961—62; mem. faculty Rush-Presbyn. St. Luke's Med. Ctr., Chgo., 1962—, asst. prof., 1962—67, assoc. prof., 1967—73, prof. biochemistry, 1973—2004, emeritus prof., 2004, assoc. chmn., dir. ednl. programs biochemistry dept., 1980—2000. Adj. prof. Dr. Scholl Coll. Podiatric Medicine, North Chicago, Ill., 2000—. Author: Basic Protein Chemistry, 1970, Biochemistry of Nonheme Iron, 1980; co-author (with Rafelson and Hayashi): Basic Biochemistry, 1980; co-author: (with Miller-Catchpole) Biochemistry and Physiology of BifidoBacteria, 1989; co-author: (with Rafelson) Concise Biochemistry, 1995; contbr. articles to profl. jours. Numerous grants, NSF, NIH, Am. Heart Assn., indsl. instns., 1962—90. Mem.: Inst. Food Technologists, Am. Chem. Soc., Am. Soc. Biol. Chemists, Am. Dairy Sci. Assn. Eastern Orthodox. Home: 4 Northbend Ln Galena IL 61036 Personal E-mail: marilynb38@hotmail.com.

BEZOLD, CLEMENT, futurist; b. Coral Gables, Fla., 1948; BS, Georgetown U., 1970; PhD, U. Fla., 1976. Asst. dir. Ctr. Govtl. Responsibility, Fla.; vis. scholar The Brookings Inst., 1974-77; pres. Inst. for Alternative Futures, Alexandria, Va., 1977—. Pres. Alternative Futures Assocs., 1982—; cons. to local, state, fed. govts. in U.S. and internat., WHO, major corps. including Disney, AT&T, pharm. and health care cos.; tchr. Am. U., U. Fla., Antioch U.; spkr. in field. Editor: Anticipatory Democracy (introduction by Alvin Toffler), 1978; co-author: (with R. Carlson and J. Peck) The Future of Work and Health, 1985 (Am. Health Mag. book award); co-editor: (with Erica Mayer) Future Care: Responding to the Demand for Change, 1996, The Future of Complementary and Alternative Approaches (CAAs) in US Healthcare, 1998, (with J. Frenk & S. McCarthy) 21st Century Health Care in Latin American and the Caribbean, 1998, Genomics and Society Project for UK-ESRC, 2002. Bd. dirs. World Future Soc. Office: Inst Alternative Futures 100 N Pitt St Ste 235 Alexandria VA 22314-3134 Office Phone: 703-684-5880. Business E-Mail: cbezold@altfutures.com.

BEZOS, JEFFREY PRESTON, multimedia company executive; b. Albuquerque, Jan. 12, 1964; s. Miguel and Jacklyn Bezos; m. Mackenzie Tuttle, 1993; 3 children. Degree in Elec. Engring. and Computer Sci. (summa cum laude), Princeton U., 1986. With FITEL, NY, 1986—88, Bankers Trust Co., NY, 1988-90, v.p. NY, 1990, D.E. Shaw & Co., NY, 1990-94, sr. v.p. NY, 1992-94; founder Amazon.com Inc., Seattle, 1994—, chmn., 1994—, pres., 1994—99, 2000—, CEO, 1996—, treas., sec., 1996—97; founder Blue Origin, Seattle, 2000—. Mem. staff FITEL, NY, 1986-88; bd. dirs., Drugstore.com, 1998- Named Person of Yr., TIME mag., 1999; named one of 40 Under 40 Richest, Fortune, 2003, 50 Who Matter Now, CNNMoney.com Bus. 2.0, 2006, 2007, Forbes' Richest Ams., 2005—, World's Richest People, Forbes mag., 2006—. Mem. Phi Beta Kappa. Live on the Internet July 16, 1995, first book sold: "Fluid Concepts & Creative Analogies: Computer Models of the Fundamental Mechanisms of Thought"; Funding Blue Origin, builders of low cost vehicles that would send passengers into space on short flights; On November 13, 2006, launched and landed Goddard, a first development vehicle in the New Shepard program at Blue Origin. Office: Amazon com Inc 1200 12th Ave S Ste 1200 Seattle WA 98144*

BEZOZO, KENNETH K., lawyer; b. Bklyn., Sept. 14, 1955; BA cum laude, Syracuse U., 1977; JD cum laude, Yeshiva U., Benjamin N. Cardozo Law Sch., 1980; LLM in Taxation, cum laude, NYU, 1981. Bar: NY 1981, Tex. 1981. Ptnr., tax, bus. and estate planning Haynes and Boone LLP, NYC. Spkr. in field. Mem.: NY State Bar Assn., ABA (Taxation Sect., corp. tax com.). Office: Haynes And Boone Attorneys 153 E 53rd St Rm 4900 New York NY 10022-4636 Office Phone: 212-659-4999. Office Fax: 212-884-8222. Business E-Mail: kenneth.bezozo@haynesboone.com.

BHABHA, HOMI K., humanities educator, writer; b. Mumbai, India, 1949; BA, U. Bombay, 1970; M.Phil, U. Oxford, 1974, MA, 1977, D.Phil, 1990. Chester D. Tripp prof. in humanities U. Chgo.; Anne F. Rothenberg prof. English and Am. lit. Harvard U., Cambridge, 2001—; dir. Harvard Humanities Ctr., 2005—. Sr. fellow Old Dominion U.; vis. prof. Princeton U., U. Pa.; faculty fellow Sch. of Criticism and Theory Dartmouth Coll.; lectr. Richard Wright lecture series, Ctr. Black Lit. and Culture, U. Pa., 1991, Annual Interdisciplinary Lecture, Sch. Oriental and African Studies, U. London, 1995, W.E.B. Du Bois Lectures, Harvard U., 1999, Presdl. Lectr., Stanford U., 2000, Clarendon Lectures, U. London, 2001—02. Editor: Nation and Narration, 1990; author: The Location of Culture, 1993; editl. bd. mem. Critical Inquiry, October, contbr. Artforum. Fellow Radcliffe Inst., 2004—05. Office: Harvard U Humanities Ctr Barker Ctr 136 Cambridge MA 02138 Office Phone: 617-495-0739, 617-495-0730. E-mail: hbhabha@fas.harvard.edu.

BHADA, ROHINTON KHURSHED, chemical engineering educator; b. Bombay, Mar. 23, 1935; s. Khurshed A. and Goola K. (Press) B.; m. Patricia Ann Bergman, Jan. 18, 1959; children: John, James, Sarah, Naomi, Jenny, Nikki, Cyndie. BS, U. Mich., 1955, MS, 1957, PhD, 1968; MBA, U. Akron, 1964. Registered profl. engr., Tex. Rsch. asst. U. Mich., Ann Arbor, 1955-59; rsch. engr. Babcock & Wilcox, Alliance, Ohio, 1959-64, group leader, 1964-72, sect. mgr., 1972-77, dept. mgr., 1977-88; assoc. dean, prof. N.Mex. State U., Las Cruces, 1988-92, prof., assoc. dean of engring., 1992—99, assoc. dean emeritus, dir., 1999—. Adj. prof. Youngstown (Ohio) State U., 1978-85; dir. Wast Edn. & Rsch. Consortium, Las Cruces, 1989—. Contbr. articles to profl. jours.; patentee in field. Local pres. Alliance Jaycees, 1964-65; state v.p. Ohio Jaycees, Marion, 1965-66; nat. dir. US Jaycees, Tulsa, 1966-67; vice-chair City Environment Com., Las Cruces, 1989—. Named Outstanding Pres. U.S. Jaycees, 1965, Outstanding Nat. Dir., 1967. Mem. AIChE (chmn. 1967-68), NSPE (Outstanding Engring. Achievement award 1991), Am. Acad. Environ. Engrs. (diplomate, Grand Prize award 1998), Am. Soc. Engring. Edn., N.Mex. Soc. Profl. Engrs., Phi Lambda Upsilon, Beta Gamma Sigma, Tau Beta Pi. Jehovah'S Witness. Avocations: racquetball, religious study, gardening. Office Phone: 678-313-0938. Personal E-mail: ronbhada@aol.com.

BHADRA, JAYANTA, computer scientist, electrical engineer; B Computer Sci. and Engring., Jadavpur U., Calcutta, 1993; M Computer Sci. and Engring., Indian Inst. Tech., Kharagpur, India, 1994; PhD Elec. and Computer Engring., U. Tex., 2001. Software engr. Motorola India Electronics Ltd., Bangalore, Karnataka, 1995—96; rsch. asst. Ga. Inst. Tech., Atlanta, 1997, U. Tex., Austin, 1997—2001; tech. lead, R&D custom tools front-end semiconductor products sect. Motorola Inc., Austin, 2001—04; tech. lead, R&D custom tools front-end Freescale Semiconductor Inc., Austin, 2004—. Recipient Silver medal, Indian Inst. Tech., 1994, Motorola Sci. and Tech. Soc., 2003; fellow, Grad. Aptitude Test Engring., 1993—94; scholar, Tex. Advanced Tech. Program Devel., 1999—2000. Mem.: IEEE. Achievements include research in modeling design constraints to avoid false results in dynamic circuit verification; elimination of gate/switch level simulations; model checking security protocols using pre-configuration; automatic validation of chip-level assertions in verifying high performance circuits; methodology for validating manufacturing test vector suites for custom designed scan-based circuits; design constraints in verifying high performance embedded dynamic circuits; program slicing for hierarchical test generation; language formalism for verification of powerPC(TM) custom memories using compostions of abstract specifications; full chip false timing path identification; automatic formal verification of interacting finite state machines; method to identify false critical paths using ATPG techniques; automatic validation test generation using extracted control models; solidarity of functional verification and manufacturing test generation using enhanced equivalence checking; hierarchical test generation approach using program slicing techniques on hardware description languages; automatic generation of high performance embedded memory models for powerPC microprocessors; genCRAM: Testview Generation for Memories; verification of a system-on-chip using computation slicing; theory and practice of automatic design constraint generation; patents for analysis tool for path extraction and false path identification and method thereof; patents pending for. Home Phone: 512-426-4859.

BHADRA, NARENDRA, biomedical engineer, researcher; s. Narayan Bhadra. MBBS, Calcutta U., India, 1977; MS in Biomed. Engring., Case We. Res. U., Cleve., 1993; PhD, Case We. Res. U., 2001. Rsch. scientist Jadavpur U., Calcutta, 1985—87; asst. prof. Nat. Inst. Orthop. Handicapped, Calcutta, 1988—90; staff scientist Axon Engring., Inc., Cleve., 1995—2001; rsch. fellow Case We. Resesrve U., 2004—. Translator (poetry book) Instructions for the Mind, by Shri Annada Thakur, 2003. Organizer Annada Found., Cleve., 2005—07. Mem.: Am. Assn. Sci., Indian Soc. Med. Stats. (life), Indian Soc. Biomaterials and Artificial Organs (life). Achievements include patents for nerve cuff electrode carrier; combined stimulation of ventral and dorsal sacral roots for control of bladder function. Office: Case We Reserve Univ 10900 Euclid Ave Cleveland OH 44106

BHADRIRAJU, SUBRAMANYAM VENKATA, entomologist, consultant; b. Visakhapatnam, India, Nov. 5, 1958; s. Krishnamurti and Syamala Bhadriraju; m. Kameswari Chandrapati, Apr. 27, 1992; 1 child, Vamsi Krishna. MS, U. Minn., St. Paul, 1988. Assoc. prof. Kans. State U., 1999—2003, prof., 2003—. Cons. Alternative Pest Mgmt. Technologies, Manhattan, Kans., 1989—. Author: (text book) Fundamentals of Stored-Product Entomology (EPA's Stratospheric Ozone Protection award, 2004); editor: (book) Integrated Management of Stored Product Insects, Alternatives to Pesticides in Stored Product IPM (Coll. of Agr. Outstanding Tchg. Award, 2002). Mem.: Entomol. Soc. of Am., Food Protection Com. of the Internat. Assn. of Operative Millers (hon.). Office: Kans State Univ 201 Shellenberger Hall Manhattan KS 66506 Office Phone: 785-532-4092. Office Fax: 785-532-7010. E-mail: sbhadrir@ksu.edu.

BHAGAT, PHIROZ MANECK, mechanical engineer; b. Oct. 28, 1948; came to U.S., 1970; s. Maneck Phirozshaw and Khorshed Eduljee (Batliwala) B.; m. Patricia Jane Steckler, Oct. 13, 1979; children: Kay, Sarah. BTech, Indian Inst. Tech.-Bombay, 1970; MS in Engring., U. Mich., 1971, PhD, 1975. Rsch. fellow in applied mechanics Harvard U., Cambridge, Mass., 1975-77; asst. prof. engring. Columbia U., NYC, 1977-81; staff engr. Exxon Mobil Rsch. & Engring. Co., Florham Park, N.J., 1981-83, sr. staff engr., 1983-2001; sr. engring. assoc. Exxon Mobil Rsch. and Engring. Co., Annandale, NJ, 2001—03; founder, prin. Internat. Strategy Engines, LLC, Westfield, NJ, 2004—. Adj. asst. prof. Columbia U., N.Y.C., 1981-84; head sci. computing group Exxon/Mobil Rsch. & Engring. Co., Florham Park, 1988-90; mng. dir. Janus Enterprise Internat., 1992-94. Author: Pattern Recognition in Industry, 2005; contbr. articles to profl. jours. K.C., Mahindra scholar, 1970, J.N. Tata scholar, 1970; Horace Rackham predoctoral fellow, 1973-74, 74-75. Mem. AIChE, ASME, N.Y. Acad. Scis., Tau Beta Pi, Sigma Xi. Achievements include research and development of neural nets and pattern recognition technology in technical and business applications, providing cutting edge data driven modeling solutions for improved operations and profitability in the financial and process industries; first to develop the application of pattern recognition technology for technical and business operations in the petroleum and chemical industry. Office: 519 Alden St Westfield NJ 07090-3040 Home Phone: 908-233-3690;, Office Phone: 908-232-1190. Business E-Mail: pmbhagat@strategyengines.com.

BHAGAT, SHAUM P., speech educator; b. Pullman, Wash., June 20, 1968; s. Surinder Kumar and Louise S Bhagat; m. Geeta S. Srinivasan, June 24, 2001; children: Rajinder Kumar, Ravi Chandran. PhD, U. Tex., Austin, 2003. Cert. audiologist Am. Speech and Hearing Assn., 1996. Asst. prof. La. State U., Baton Rouge, 2003—05, U. Memphis, 2005—. Vol. Peace Corps, Guatemala City, Guatemala, 1991—92. Fellow: Am. Acad. Audiology; mem.: Phi Kappa Phi. Liberal. Hindu. Avocations: travel, reading, jogging, theatre, music. Office: Univ Memphis 807 Jefferson Ave Memphis TN 38105 Home Phone: 901-522-6678; Office Phone: 901-678-5800.

BHALLA, SANJEEV, radiologist; b. Chgo., July 15, 1968; s. Brahm and Rama Bhalla. BS, Yale U., New Haven, Conn., 1990; MD, Columbia Coll. Physicians and Surgeons, NY, 1994. Lic. physician Mo., 1995, diplomate Am. Bd. Radiology, 1999. Asst. dir. residency Mallinckrodt Inst. Radiology, St Louis, 2002—, dir. chest radiology, 2007—. Cons. radiologist Barnes-Jewish Hosp., St Louis. Home: 4545 Forest Pk Pkwy 5B Saint Louis MO 63108 Office: Mallinckrodt Inst Radiology 510 South Kingshighway Saint Louis MO 63110 Home Phone: 314-361-6950; Office Phone: 314-362-2927. Office Fax: 314-362-2976. Personal E-mail: bhallaster@gmail.com. Business E-Mail: bhallas@mir.wustl.edu.

BHALOO, SALIM, otolaryngologist; DO, U. North Tex., Ft. Worth, 1998. Physician, Granbury, Tex., 2004—. Named Student DO of Yr., Coun. Student Coun. Presidents, 1998. Mem.: AMA (assoc.), Am. Osteo. Assn., Am. Acad. Otolaryngology/Health and Neck Surgery, Am. Osteo. Coll. Otolaryngology and Opthamology (assoc.).

BHANDARI, AKSHAY, urologist; b. Jaipur, Rajasthan, India, May 14, 1976; s. Mahendra and Sushma Bhandari; m. Smita Goyal, Feb. 4, 2001. MBBS, GSVM Med. Coll., Kanpur, India, 1998. Sr. rsch. asst. Henry Ford Health Sys., Detroit, 2000—03, fellow robotic surgery, 2003—05; resident Vattikuti Urology Inst., Henry Ford Health Sys., Detroit, 2006—. Contbr. articles to profl. jours. Recipient Gold Merit cert. in Biology, Indian Sch. Cert. Edn., 1993, Cert. of merit in Internal Medicine, Kanpur U., 1998. Mem.: Am. Urol. Assn. Office: Henry Ford Health Sys 2799 W Grand Blvd Detroit MI 48202 Home Phone: 248-588-1320. Business E-Mail: abhanda1@hfhs.org.

BHANGALE, TUSHAR, biomedical engineer, researcher; b. India; MB, BChir, U. Mumbai, India, 1998; PhD in Bioengring., U. Wash., Seattle, 2006. Sr. fellow genome scis. U. Wash., Seattle, 2006—. Achievements include invention of new algorithm to automate detection of insertion-deletions from DNA resequencing data. E-mail: tbhangale@gmail.com.

BHARADWAJ, PREM DATTA, physics professor; b. Gorakhpur, India, May 20, 1931; arrived in U.S., 1960; s. Ganga Dhar and Bhagwati Devi (Sharma) B.; m. Vidya Wati Sharma, Feb. 14, 1949; children: Rakesh Kumar, Rajnesh Kumar, Vidhu Rani Eranki, Sudha Kar. BS 1st class with merit, NREC Coll. Khurja, 1950; MS 1st class, IST, Agra U., 1952; PhD, SUNY, Buffalo, 1964. Asst. prof. physics B.R. Coll. Agra, India, 1952—54, 1959—60; lectr. physics GPIC Tehri, Tehri Garhwal, India, 1954—56, Govt. Coll. Meerut, India, 1956—59; grad. asst. physics SUNY, Buffalo, 1960—62; from asst. prof. physics to assoc. prof. physics Niagara U., Niagara Falls, NY, 1962—66, prof. physics, 1966—, chmn. dept. physics, 1976—86. Cons. NSF, 1966-71; reviewer NY State Regents Exams. in Medicine and Dentistry, 1976; co-founder India Assn. Buffalo, 1961, Hindi Samaj Greater Buffalo, 1986; summer rsch. participant NSF, La. State U., Baton Rouge, 1965; vis. prof. dept. crystallography Rosewell Park Cancer Inst., Buffalo, 1970-71 Co-author: Intermediate Agriculture Physics and Climatology, 1954; contbr. articles to profl. jours. Pres. Sathya Sai Ctr. Buffalo, Amherst, NY, 1990-93, Hindi Samaj Greater Buffalo, Amherst, 1996-97; trust com. Hindu Cultural Soc. Western NY, 1999-2001 Recipient Rajiv Gandhi Nat. Unity award for excellence Govt. India, 1995, Hind Rattan (Jewel of India) award Govt. of India, 1995; named Internat. Man of Yr. Internat. Biog. Ctr., Cambridge, Eng., 1999. Mem. India Assn. of Buffalo (award for outstanding work in edn. and cmty. 1997), Hindi Samaj of Greater Buffalo, Am. Phys. Soc. Democrat. Hindu. Home: 100 N Parrish Dr Amherst NY 14228-1477 Office: Niagara U Physics Dept Lewiston Rd Niagara Falls NY 14109 Personal E-mail: bharadwaj14228@netzero.com.

BHARGAVA, ASHOK, retired economics professor; b. Agra, India, July 1, 1943; came to U.S., 1966; s. Mahabir Prasad and Chandra Kanti Bhargava; m. Deviyani J. Bhatt, June 11, 1970 (dec. Oct. 1999); children: Amit, Kamini. BA with honors, Delhi U., India, 1963, MA, 1965; MS, U. Wis., 1969, PhD, 1975. Lectr. Siri Ram Coll. Commerce, Delhi, 1965-66; asst. U. Wis., Madison, 1967-70, instr. Whitewater, 1970-75, asst. prof., 1975-77, assoc. prof., 1977-80, prof., 1980—2003, chmn. dept. econs., 1981-87, 1999—2003, asst. dir. global bus. resource ctr., 1998—2003; prof. emeritus, 2003—; comptroller Feingold Senate Com., 2003—04, vol. cons., 2005—. Cons. Wis. Exports Coop., Madison, 1988-92; dir. Ctr. for

Bus. and Mgmt. Svcs., U. Wis. Whitewater, 1989-91, coord. rsch., 1989-92, dir. Ctr. for Econ. Edn. 1995-99; pres. Bhargava Assocs., Bus. and Econ. Cons. Editor: Indian Economics Studies, 1984, Studies of the Indian Economy, 1985; mem. editl. bd. Bull. Concerned Asian Scholars, 1978-2003, Issues in Internat. Bus., 1986-92; mng. editor Devel. Update, 1988—; contbr. articles to profl. publs. Bd. dirs. Indian Devel. Svc., Chgo., 1975-95, v.p., 2007; bd. dirs. Madison Area Tech. Coll. Found., 2000-03, 05-, Shama, Inc.; treas. Combat Blindness Found., Madison, 1985-2000; mem. Gov.'s Coun. on Asian Affairs, 1985-96, sec., 1988-96; bd. dirs. minority bus. devel. fund State of Wis., 1989-2003; co-chair Wis. Orgn. of Asian Ams., 1995-2000; founder Village Libr. Fund, 1995—. Mem. Assn. Indian Econ. Studies (sec.-treas. 1981-89, chmn. 1989-91), Assn. Managerial Econs. (sec. 1984-2003), Assn. Internat. Bus. Studies, Eastern Econ. Assn. (area rep. 1988-96), Courtyard Village Homes Assn. (pres.). Avocations: squash, volunteer work. Home: 5631 Longford Ter Apt 102 Fitchburg WI 53711-6909 E-mail: ashokbhargava1@hotmail.com.

BHARGAVA, MANJUL, mathematics professor, researcher; b. Can., 1975; AB summa cum laude in Math., Harvard U., Cambridge, Mass., 1996; PhD in Math., Princeton U., NJ, 2001. Tchg. fellow Harvard U., Cambridge, Mass., 1993—95; vis. lectr. US/Can. Mathcamps, 1997—98; rschr. Ctr. Comm. Rsch., Princeton, NJ, 1996, Inst. Advanced Study; vis. lectr. Princeton U., prof. math., 2003—. Fellow Clay Math. Inst., Cambridge, 2000—. Contbr. articles to profl. jours. Named one of Brilliant 10, Popular Sci. mag., 2002; recipient First prize, NY State Sci. Talent Search, 1992, Morgan prize for Outstanding Rsch., Am. Math. Soc., 1997, Merten M. Hasse prize for Exposition, Math. Assn. Am., 2003, Leonard M. and Eleanor B. Blumenthal award for Advancement of Rsch. in Pure Math., 2005; grantee Fellowship in Mathematics, Hertz Found., 1996—2000, Packard Found. fellowship in Sci. and Engring., 2004. Office: Princeton U Math Dept Fine Hall Washington Rd Princeton NJ 08544 Office Phone: 609-258-4192. Office Fax: 609-258-1367. E-mail: bhargava@math.princeton.edu.*

BHARGAVA, RAMESHWAR NATH, physicist; b. Allahabad, UP, India, Dec. 25, 1939; came to U.S., 1960; s. Gajadhar Prasad and Rupkanti Bhargava; m. Veena Bhargava, Aug. 15, 1965; children: Sidharth, Amitabh. BS, U. Allahabad, 1957, MS, 1959; PhD, Columbia U., 1966. Fellow IBM Watson Lab., Columbia U., NYC, 1965-66; cons. IBM Watson Rsch. Ctr., Yorktown Heights, NY, 1966-67; mem. tech. staff Bell Labs, Murray Hill, NJ, 1967-70, Philips Labs, Briarcliff Manor, NY, 1970-78, dept. head, 1978-89, assoc. dir., 1989-93; pres. Nanocrystals Tech., Briarcliff Manor, NY, 1993—. Organizer symposia and internat. profl. confs.; chmn. Gordon Conf., N.H., 1977. Patentee inventor 3-D TV, Harmonics in High Temperature Superconductors, Doped nanocrystals, digital x-ray imaging. Recipient Chancellor's Gold medal U. Allahabad, 1959. Fellow IEEE, Am. Phys. Soc. Home: 5 Morningside Ct Ossining NY 10562-3003 Office: Nanocrystals Tech PO Box 820 Briarcliff Manor NY 10510-0307

BHARGAVE, ASHISH A., research scientist; s. Arvind Vasant and Mangala Bhargave; m. Supriya Shirolkar, Dec. 24, 2004. BS in Tech., Nat. Inst. Tech., 1996; MSEE in Computer Sci., U. Calif., Irvine, 2001, PhD in Elec. Engring. and Computer Sci., 2006. Software engr. IT Solutions, Bangalore, India, 1997—99; systems engr. Broadcom Corp., Irvine, Calif., 2003; rsch. engr. U. Calif., Irvine, 2002—. Recipient Painting Recognition award, 1991, Computer Aided Design Software First prize, Indian Inst. Technolgy, Delhi, 1995; fellow, U. Calif., Irvine, 2002, 2004. Mem.: IEEE (treas. student chpt. 1995—96), Computer Soc. India, Sigma Xi, Phi Beta Kappa. Achievements include patents pending for wireless LAN receiver; multi stage receiver for wireless MIMO systems. Home: 20560 Anza Ave #27 Torrance CA 90503 Home Phone: 949-331-2509. Personal E-mail: ashish.bhargave@gmail.com.

BHARTIA, PRAKASH, defense research management executive, educator; b. Calcutta, West Bengal, India, Jan. 6, 1944; arrived in Can., 1967, arrived in US, 2003, permanent resident, 2004; s. Benarshi Prasad and Bhagwati Devi (Chirimar) B.; m. Savitri Kanhai, Apr. 27, 1971; children: Sanjay Manish, Anil Manoj. B in Tech. with honors, Indian Inst. Tech., Bombay, 1966; MSc, U. Man., Winnipeg, Can., 1968, PhD, 1971. Assoc. prof. U. Regina, Sask., Canada, 1976, asst. dean Sask., 1975-77; def. scientist, chief R&D br. Nat. Defence, Ottawa, Ont., Canada, 1977—; head navigation sect. Defence Rsch. Establishment Ottawa, 1981-85; dir. R&D air Defence Hdqrs., Govt. of Can., Ottawa, 1985-86; dir. R&D commnications and space Nat. Defence, Govt. of Can., 1986-89; dir. sonar div. Defence Rsch. Establishment Atlantic, Halifax, 1989-91; dir. radar div. Defence Rsch. Establishment Ottawa, 1991—; chief Defence Rsch. Establishment Atlantic, 1992-97; dir.-gen. Def. Rsch. Establishment, Ottawa, 1997—2003; exec. v.p. Natel Engring. Co. Inc., Chatsworth, Calif., 2004—. Adj. prof. U. Ottawa, 1977-96, Daltech, 1997—; dir. Can. Microelectronics Centre, Kingston, 1986-88; mem. elec. engring. grant selection com. Natural Scis. and Engring. Rsch. Coun., Ottawa, 1990—, chmn. ind. chair evaluation com., Victoria, 1991; bd. dirs. Tradex Investment Funds, Ottawa, Canadian Ctr. Marine Communication. Author: Microstrip Antennas, 1980, Millimeter Wave Engineering and Applications, 1984, E Plane Integrated Circuits, 1987, Millimeter Wave Microstrip and Printed Circuit Antennas, 1990; author, editor: Microwave Solid State Circuit Design, 1988, Microstrip Lines and Slotlines, 1996, RF and Microwave Coupled Line Circuits, 1999, Microstrip Antenna Design Handbook, 2000; patentee in field. Mem. engring. adv. com. Queen's U., Kingston, 1989-92, chmn. bd., 1992. Decorated Order of Canada; recipient Queen's Golden Jubilee Medal. Fellow: IEEE, Can. Acad. Engrs., Royal Soc. of Can., Instn. Elec. and Telecomm. Engrs.; mem.: India Soc. Engrs., Eng. Inst. Can. Hindu. Home: 21026 Schoenborn St Canoga Park CA 91304 Office: Natel Engring Co Inc 9340 Owensmouth Ave Chatsworth CA 91311 Home Phone: 818-349-9617; Office Phone: 818-734-6511. Personal E-mail: bhartiaprakash@hotmail.com. Business E-Mail: pbhartia@natelengr.com.

BHARUCHA, JAMSHED, academic administrator; b. July 24, 1956; BA, Vassar Coll.; MA in Philosophy, Yale U.; PhD in Psychology, Harvard U. Asst. prof. Dartmouth Coll., 1983—89, assoc. prof., 1989—95, prof., 1995—97, John Wentworth chair in psychol. and brain scis., 1997—2002, assoc. dean faculty for social scis., 1997—2000, dep. provost, 2000—01, dean faculty, 2001—02; provost, sr. v.p. Tufts U., Medford, Mass., 2002—, prof. psychology, 2002—. Mem. Linguistics and Cognitive Sci. program Dartmouth Coll., mem. Electro-Acoustic Music program; commentator various segments NPR; mem. adv. panel NSF; fellow Ctr. for Advanced Study in the Behavioral Scis. Stanford U. Contbr. articles to profl. jours. Fellow: Am. Inst. Indian Studies. Avocation: violin. Office: Provosts Office Tufts Univ Medford MA 02155

BHASIN, MADAN MOHAN, research scientist; b. Lahore, India, June 23, 1938; came to U.S., 1959; s. Late L. Mela Ram and Bahain Devi (Sahni) B.; m. Anand Kumari Chugha, Aug. 5, 1961; children: Madhu Lata, Anoop Kumar. BS with hon., Delhi U., New Delhi, India, 1958; postgrad., Indiana U., 1959-60; PhD, U. Notre Dame, 1964. Chemist Union Carbide Corp., South Charleston, W.Va., 1963-69, project scientist, 1969-77, research scientist, 1977-81, group supr., 1981-82, sr. research scientist, group supr., 1982-88, corp. fellow., group supr., sr. scientist, 1988—. Spkr., lectr. in field. Patentee in field; contbr. articles to profl. jours. Chmn. India Ctr., Charleston, W.V., 1986-96, co-chair, India Heritage Fair, 1996—; bd. dirs. United Way, 2000. Recipient Eugene J. Houdry Award in Applied Catalysis, Catalysis Soc. N. Amer., 1995, Scientific Achievement Awd., Kanawka Valley Section of ACS (Am. Chem. Soc.), 1995, Amer. Chem. Soc. Awd. in Indsl. Chem., 1999, AZKO Nobel. Mem. AIChE, NAE, Am. Chem. Soc. (chmn. summer symposium Indsl. and Engring. Chem. div. 1986-88, exec. com. mem. 1983-87, chmn. I & EC div. 1990), Catalysis Secretariat (chair 1997), India Assn. (pres. 1979-80). Avocations: photography, tennis, badmington, gardening. Office: Union Carbide Corp 437 Maccorkle Ave SW South Charleston WV 25303 E-mail: bhasin2m@excelonline.com.

BHASKAR, K.S., information technology executive; Studied at, Indian Inst. Tech., Kanpur; grad., U. Nebr., Lincoln; MBA, U. Wash. Bus. Sch., Seattle. V.p. Bancware; pres. Greystone Software Tech.; v.p., Greystone group Sanchez Computer Associates, Inc. (acquired by Fidelity Nat. Fin. Inc. in 2004); v.p., product mgr. GT.M Fidelity Nat. Info. Svcs., Inc., Malvern, Pa.; COO WorldVistA, dir., 2003—04, 2005—. Presenter in field. Contbr. of Technical Articles. Co-recipient Rave award-Medicine, WIRED Mag., 2007; recipient GNU/Linux Med. News Achievement award, 2002. Achievements include patents in field; part of team responsible for a medical-records program called, VistA at US Department Veterans Affairs. Office: Fidelity Nat Info Svcs 2 W Liberty Ste 300 Malvern PA 19355

BHAT, RAJIV, physicist, researcher; b. Mulki, Karnataka, India, Aug. 10, 1978; s. K. N. and Anusuya Bhat. MS, Indian Inst. Tech., Kanpur, 2001. Bus. analyst McKinsey & Co., Inc., Mumbai, Maharastra, India, 2001—03; rsch. assoc. JILA, U. Colo., Boulder, 2004—. Mem.: Am. Physics Soc. Achievements include research in theoretical physics. Office: JILA Univ Calif 440 Ucb Boulder CO 80309-0440 Personal E-mail: rajiv.bhat@gmail.com. Business E-Mail: rajiv.bhat@colorado.edu.

BHATIA, KARAN K., ambassador; m. Sara Levine; 2 children. AB, Princeton U., 1989; MSc, London Sch. Econs., 1990; JD, Columbia U., 1993. Law clk. to Hon. Milton Pollack US Dist. Ct. (so. dist.) NY, 1993—94; ptnr. Wilmer, Cutler & Pickering LLP, Washington, 1994—2001; chief counsel for export adminstrn. Office Gen. Counsel US Dept. Commerce, Washington, 2001—02, dep. under sec., Bur. Industry & Security, 2002—03; asst. sec. for aviation & internat. affairs US Dept. Transp., Washington, 2003—05; dep. US Trade Rep. Exec. Office of the Pres., Washington, 2005—. Adj. prof. Georgetown U. Law Ctr., Washington, 2000—03. Mem.: Coun. on Fgn. Rels. Office: US Trade Rep 600 17th St NW Washington DC 20508

BHATIA, PETER K., editor, journalist; b. Pullman, Wash., May 22, 1953; s. Vishnu N. and Ursula Jean (Dawson) B.; m. Elizabeth M. Dahl, Sept. 27, 1981; children: Megan Jean, Jay Peter. BA, Stanford U., 1975. Polit. reporter, asst. news editor Spokesman Rev., Spokane, Wash., 1975-77; news editor Dallas Times Herald, 1980-81; asst. news editor San Francisco Examiner, 1977-80, news editor, 1981-85, dep. mng. editor/news, 1985-87; mng. editor Dallas Times Herald, 1987-88; editor York Dispatch, York, Pa., 1988-89; mng. editor The Sacramento Bee, 1989-93; exec. editor The Fresno Bee, 1993; mng. editor The Oregonian, Portland, 1993-97, exec. editor, 1997—. Pulitzer Prize juror, 1992-93, 98-99; pres. Accrediting Coun. on Edn. in Journalism and Mass Comm., 2007—; bd. dirs. Am. Press Inst. Mem. adv. bd. Knight Ctr. Specialized Journalism U. Md.; mem. adv. bd. Murrow Sch. Communication Wash. State U.; mem. new media adv. bd. Oreg. State U.; bd. chmn. Albertina Kerr Ctrs. for Children, 2001—02, found. chair, 2004—05; chmn. bd. St. John Fisher Sch., 2000—04; bd. trustees Jesuit HS, Portland, 2007—, St. Andrew Nativity Sch., Portland, 2007—. Mem.: Investigative Reporters and Editors, South Asian Journalists Assn., Nat. Assn. Minority Media Execs., Asian Am. Journalists Assn., AP Mng. Editors (bd. dirs. 1991—97), Am. Soc. Newspaper Editors (bd. dirs. 1997—, treas. 2000—01, sec. 2001—02, v.p. 2002—03, pres. 2003—04, chair awards bd. 2006), Stanford U. Alumni Assn. (bd. dirs. 1998—2001), Theta Delta Chi, Sigma Delta Chi. Office: The Oregonian 1320 SW Broadway Portland OR 97201-3499 Home Phone: 503-293-1006; Office Phone: 503-221-8393. Business E-Mail: pbhatia@news.oregonian.com.

BHATIA, RAJAN, engineer, physicist, researcher; arrived in U.S., 1985, permanent resident; s. Prem S. and Shakun Bhatia. Student, U. Mont., Butte, 1985—88; BS in Engring. Physics, U. Maine, Orono, 1991. Laser systems rsch. engr. Amoco Laser Co., Naperville, Ill., 1990—90, Amoco Corp. - Amoco Tech. Co., Naperville, 1990—92; laser systems tech. engr., non-linear acoustics physicist Johnson & Johnson, Claremont, Calif., 1992—95, sr. laser systems engr. Palo Alto, Calif., 1996—97; laser systems rsch. engr. Cygnus, Monroe, Wash., 1995—96; sr. rsch. scientist IRIS/IRIDEX, Sunnyvale, Calif., 1997—99, Qculight Inc., Bothell, Wash., 1999—2000; sr. mem. tech. staff Tyco Internat., Eatontown, NJ, 2001—01; prin. photonics staff engr. NIS, San Jose, Calif., 2001—. Electro-optical sys. engr. NASA, Greenbelt, Md., 1990; presenter in field. Contbr. articles to profl. jours. Scholar, U. Maine, 1988—91. Mem.: ASM Internat., Japanese Soc. Applied Physics, Internat. Soc. Optical Engring., Optical Soc. Am. Achievements include research in in various diverse areas of Laser Engineering, Photonics, Electro-Optics, Biomedical Lasers, High Power Lasers, Non-Linear Optics, Fiber-Optics, Biomedical Acoustics & Ultrasound; design of various in Biomedical Lasers, High Power Lasers, Non-Linear Optics, Fiber-Optics, Biomedical Acoustics & Ultrasound. Personal E-mail: gumalaser24@mail.com.

BHATIA, SANGEETA N., biomedical engineer, educator; b. Boston, June 24, 1968; d. Narain D. and Vidya N. (Hingorany) Bhatia; m. Jagesh Vijaykumar Shah, Aug. 9, 1997; 1 child. BS in Biomedical Engring., Brown U., 1990; MS in Mech. Engring., MIT, 1993, PhD in Med. Engring., 1997; MD, Harvard Med. Sch., 1999. Process engr. ICI Pharms., Wilmington, Del., 1990-91; rsch. asst. Harvard Med. Sch., Boston, 1991-97; design engr. med. products divsn. Pfizer, NYC, 1993; postdoctoral fellow Mass. Gen. Hosp., Boston, 1997-98; asst. prof. bioengineering U. Calif. San Diego, La Jolla, 1998—2005; assoc. prof. dept. elec. engring. and computer sci. and Harvard-MIT Divsn. of Health Scis. and Tech. MIT, Cambridge, 2005—, dir. Lab. Multiscale Regenerative Technologies, 2005—. Asst. adj. prof. medicine Divsn. Gastroenterology, U. Calif. San Diego, 1999. Author: (book) Microfabrication in Bioartificial Organs, 1999; co-inventor in field; contbr. articles to profl. jours., chpts. to books; patentee in field. Co-founder, bd. dirs. Keys to Empowering Youth, MIT, Cambridge, 1993-94; mem. subcommittee, chmn. ASTM, 1998-99. Mem. ASME, AMA, Soc. Women Engrs., Biomedical Engring. Soc., Am. Liver Found. Democrat. Hindu. Avocations: running, reading, travel. Office: Lab Multiscale Regenerative Technologies MIT 77 Mass Ave Bldg E19-502d Cambridge MA 02139 Office Phone: 617-324-0610. E-mail: sbhatia@mit.edu.*

BHATNAGAR, ABHA, school system administrator, department chairman; arrived in US, 2003; s. Jagat Narayain and Laxmi Bhatnagar. MSc, U. Rajasthan, 1981; degree in Computer Edn., U. Ulster, 1985; PhD, Rajasthan U., 1988; diploma in Computer Mgmt., Indian Inst. Mgmt., 1994; MEd, Annamalai U., 1995; MBA, India Gandhi Nat. Open U., 1997. Web page design Auckland U. Tech., New Zealand, 2000; classroom mgmt. NC Dept. Pub. Instrn., 2002. Chemistry lectr. Nat. Coun. Ednl. Rsch. & Tng., India, 1981—91; sci. lectr. State Coun. Ednl. Rsch. & Tng., Delhi, India, 1991—99; sub. tchr. Auckland Colls., New Zealand, 1999—2000; sci. tchr. Blue Mountain Coll., West Otago, New Zealand, 2000; head sci., math. & ICT Te Waha O Rerekohu Area Sch., Te Araroa, New Zealand, 2001—02; sci. tchr. Northampton County HS, Conway, NC, 2002—03; curriculum coord. Garinger HS, Charlotte Mecklenburg Schs., Charlotte, NC, 2003—. Author: (book) Computer An Introduction.; contbr. articles to profl. publs. Coord. Soka Gakki Internat., Young Women's Divsn. Leader, Charlotte, 2003—05. Recipient scholarship, Nat. Coun. Edn., Rsch. & Tng., India, 1976—79, rsch. grant, NCERT, India, 1981—88; scholar, Brit. Govt., 1985. Mem.: Nat. Sci. Tchr. Assn. (assoc.), Youth Hostal Assn. (life). Avocations: camping, track, sports, culture. Personal E-mail: bhatnagar_abha@yahoo.com. Business E-Mail: abha.bhatnagar@cms.k12.nc.us.org.

BHATT, MANISHA HEMENDRA, lawyer; BA in History and Spanish, Boston Coll., 1995; JD, Suffolk U. Law Sch., 1999. Intern Boston Med. Ctr.; pvt. practice civil litig.; staff atty. Family Law Unit Greater Boston Legal Services, 2001—. Office: Greater Boston Legal Services 197 Friend St Boston MA 02114 Office Phone: 617-371-1234. Office Fax: 617-371-1222.

BHATTACHARYA, DEBASHISH, environmental scientist, educator; s. Bonaj Bhushan and Sujata Bhattacharya; m. Susanne Elisabeth Ruemmele, Sept. 23, 1995; children: Lydia Sanjana, Ashim Alexander. BS with honors, Dalhousie U., Halifax, NS, Can., 1981, M in Environ. Sci., 1983; PhD, Simon Fraser U., Burnaby, B.C., Can., 1989. Asst. prof. U. Iowa, Iowa City, 1997—2003, assoc. prof., 2003—, dir. genetics program, 2004—. Assoc. editor: Jour. Molecular Evolution, 2003—; contbr. articles to profl. jours. Grantee, NASA, 1994—97, NSF, 1994—99, 2001—04, 2001—05, 2002—05, 2004—05; Postdoctoral fellow, Alfred P. Sloan Found., 1989—91, Humboldt scholar, Alexander von Humboldt Found., Germany, 1991—93. Achievements include playing critical role in elucidating how photosynthesis originated in plants and algae through endosymbiosis; clarifying the evolutionary history of catalytic RNAs (ribozymes). Office: U Iowa 446 Biology Bldg Iowa City IA 52242 Home Phone: 319-341-8159; Office Phone: 319-335-1977. Office Fax: 319-335-1069. Business E-Mail: debashi-bhattacharya@uiowa.edu.

BHATTACHARYA, SATYAJIT, research scientist; came to U.S., 1993; s. Amal and Rekha B. BS, U. Poona, Pune, Maharashtra, India, 1985, MS, 1987; diploma in Computer Sci., Indian Inst. Computer Studies, Pune, 1988; MS, U. Toronto, 1993; PhD, Calcutta U., India, 2001. Rsch. assoc. Mt. Sinai Sch. Medicine Vets. Affairs Med. Ctr., NYC, 1993-94, asst. rsch. scientist, 1994-95, NYU Med. Ctr., NYC, 1994-95; rsch. assoc. Amgen Inc., Thousand Oaks, Calif., 1995-96; rsch. scientist Meml. Sloan-Kettering Cancer Ctr., NYC, 1996—. Inventor in field; contbr. articles to profl. jours. Coun. Sci. and Indsl. Rsch. fellow, 1991. Fellow Royal Microscopic Soc.; mem. AAAS, Am. Chem. Soc., N.Y. Acad. Scis., Histochem. Soc. (Outstanding Young Investigator award 1999), Metastasis Rsch. Sic., European Soc. Analytical and Cell Pathology (Best Oral Presentation award 2002), Internat. Soc. Quality and Diagnostic Pathology, Am. Molecular Pathology Soc., Harlem Children Soc. (founder, CEO, pres. 2000—), Sigma Xi (pres. Rockefeller U. chpt. 2003). Avocations: reading, writing, swimming, sports, music. Office: Meml Sloan-Kettering Cancer Ctr Dept Pathology Box 105 1275 York Ave New York NY 10021 E-mail: bhattacs@mskcc.org.

BHATTACHARYA, SYAMAL KANTI, biomedical scientist, educator; b. Calcutta, West Bengal, India, Feb. 13, 1949; arrived in U.S., 1974, naturalized, 1983; s. Sudhir Chandra Bhattacharya and Prabhabati Battacharya; m. Keka Karabi Ghoshal; children: Sumoulindra Titu, Julie Keka, Syamal Dave. BS in Chemistry, with honors, U. Calcutta, India, 1968, BA in English, 1969; MS, Murray State U., Ky., 1976; AM, Washington U., St. Louis, 1978; PhD in Chemistry, Memphis State U., 1979. Diplomate Am. Bd. Bioanalysis; cert. profl. chemist Nat. Cert. Commn. Chemistry and Chem. Engring., lic. med. lab. dir. Tenn. Dept. Pub. Health. R&D chemist Swastik Household and Indsl. Products Pvt. Ltd., Bombay, 1970—74; sr. rsch. tech. Washington U. Med. Sch., St. Louis, 1976—77; rsch. assoc. U. Tenn. Med. Ctr., Memphis, 1979—80, instr. medicine, 1980—82, mem. surgery faculty, 1983—, dir. surg. rsch. labs., 1982—, founding dir. chemistry and nutrient data output lab., 1982—, instr. surgery, 1983—84, asst. prof. surgery, 1984—88, assoc. prof. surgery, 1988—98, asst. prof. medicinal chemistry, 1985—91, assoc. prof. medicinal chemistry, 1991—99, assoc. prof. anatomy and neurobiology, 1988—95, prof. surgery, 1998—, prof. pharm. scis., 1999—, prof. neurology, 1999—, prof. medicine, 2006—; prof. biomed. engring. U. Memphis, 2006—. Adj. prof. surgery NY Med. Coll., 1988—97; vis. prof. surgery Yale U. Sch. Med., 1985; vis. prof. pediats. U. Cin. Med. Ctr. and Cin. Children's Hosp., 1985; vis. prof. pediatric surgery Johns Hopkins U. Sch. Med., 1987; vis. prof. surgery Rush-Presbyn.-St. Luke's Med. Ctr., Chgo., 1987, NY Med. Coll., 1987—88; vis. prof. biochemistry George Washington U. Sch. Medicine, Washington, 1988, Howard U., 1989; vis. prof. surgery East Tenn. State U., 1989; vis. prof. microbiology Bose Inst., Calcutta, 1999, Calcutta, 2001; external examiner doctoral dissertation faculty engring. U. Memphis, 1999—; external examiner doctoral dissertation faculty scis. Jadavpur U., Calcutta, 2002—; commr. Nat. Cert. Comm. Chemistry & Chem. Engrg., Washington, 1987—; v.p. Nat. Registry in Clin. Chemistry, Washington, 1999—2000, pres., 2000—01; grant reviewer, mem. pathology-A study sect. NIH, 1993—95; clin. chemistry and surgical pathology cons. various hosps., 1982—2003. Contbr. numerous publs. to biomed. and sci. jours., to nat. and internat. sci. confs.; ad hoc reviewer: for numerous sci. and profl. jours. Grantee Muscular Dystrophy Assn. Am., 1983—84; recipient Presdl. rsch. fellowship, Memphis State U., 1978—79, Indian Nat. scholarship, Govt. India, New Delhi, 1965—69, Govt. India scholarship, Bank of India, 1974—75, rsch. grant, U. Physician's Found., 1985—86, Am. Heart Assn., 1986—87, Varian Instrument Group of Am., 1986—99, U. Tenn. Med. Group, 1997—99, Nat. Rsch. Svc. award in medicine, NIH, 1979—81, 1988—95, 1990—97, 2004—. Fellow: Am. Coll. Nutrition, Indian Chem. Soc., Am. Instn. Chemists (cert. profl. chemist 1980); mem.: ACS, AAAS, Am. Oil Chemists' Soc., Internat. Soc. Brain Rsch., Soc. Neurosci., NY Acad. Scis., Am. Soc. Molecular Biology and Biochemistry, Coll. Am. Pathologists, Am. Fedn. Clin. Rsch., Royal Soc. Chemistry (chartered chemist 1981), U. Tenn. Health Sci. Ctr. Faculty Senate (Memphis), Phi Kappa Phi, Sigma Xi. Office: U Tenn Health Sci Ctr Dept Surgery and Medicine 956 Court Ave Ste B220 Memphis TN 38163-2814 Business E-Mail: sbhattachary@utmem.edu.

BHATTACHARYYA, DEV, information technology executive, consultant; s. Santosh and Bela Bhattacharyya; m. Sheena Mukhopadhyay, Oct. 9, 1984; children: Rupsha, Reeshav. BS/MS, Birla Inst. Tech. and Sci., 1982. Cert. JBuilder 5 Enterprise Borland Software Corp., 1990, Visibroker C+ Borland Software Corp., 1990, Visibroker Java Borland Software Corp., 1990, C+ Builder Borland Software Corp., 1990, Java Programming Brainbench, 1997, Delphi Programming Brainbench, 1999. Prin. cons. Borland Software Corp., Princeton, NJ, 1998—2002; dir. distributed technologies Starwood Hotels and Resorts Worldwide Inc., White Plains, NY, 2002—05; v.p. tech. solutions ITC Infotech USA, Princeton, 2005—. Pres. Emryn Internat. LLC, Sparta, NJ, 2000—05. Author: (book) BPB Publications - From Delphi 2 You, 1997; contbr. technical articles in field. Mem.: IEEE, IEEE Computer Soc., Assn. Computing Machinery, Planetary Gemologists Assn., Coun. of Vedic Astrology. Achievements include development of value ERP open source; GrafxShop - graphics editor and publisher; Mystic Prediction Engine - astrology; FTP-Shop - FTP Client. Home: 678 Glen Rd Sparta NJ 07871 Home Phone: 973-726-8085. Personal E-mail: devb@ieee.org.

BHAUMIK, MANI LAL, physicist; b. Calcutta, India, Jan. 5, 1932; came to U.S., 1959, naturalized, 1968; s. Gunadhar and Lolita (Pramanik) B. BS, U. Calcutta, 1951, MS, 1953; PhD, Indian Inst. Tech., 1958, DSc (hon.), 1995. Fellow UCLA, 1959—63; with Xerox Electro-Optical Sys., Pasadena, Calif., 1961—67, Northrop Corp. Labs., Hawthorne, Calif., 1968—71, dir. rsch., 1971—75; mgr. Laser Tech. Lab., Northrop Rsch. and Tech. Ctr., 1976—84, sr. staff scientist, 1984—86. Lectr. physics Calif. State U., Long Beach, 1967-69. Author: Code Name GOD, 2005; contbr. articles to profl. jours. Fellow Am. Phys. Soc., IEEE. Achievements include patents in field. Office: Laser Tech Lab PO Box 24050 Los Angeles CA 90024-0050 *A strong and innate belief in basic human goodness has often pulled me out of hostile circumstances where one is likely to lose faith in humanity.*

BHAVSAR, DHAVAL, medical researcher; s. Rameshchandra and Virbala Bhavsar; m. Noopur Pathak; 1 child, Ishya. MD, Nathiba Hargovandas Lalubhai Med. Coll., Ahmedabad, India, 1996. Cert. in surgery Gujarat State Med. Bd., 2000, in plastic surgery Gujarat State Med. Bd., 2003. Vis. scholar U. Calif. San Diego Med. Ctr., 2003—05, sr. clin. fellow, 2005—. Contbr. chapters to books. Recipient David Bessinger award, North Am. Burn Soc., 2005. Mem.: Plastic Surgery Rsch. Coun. Achievements include research in the use of biomechanical barrier to reduce post-opertaive adhesions. Office Phone: 619-543-3908.

BHIDE, MANOHAR GOPAL, nuclear scientist, educator; b. Pune, Maharashtra, India, Nov. 9, 1935; arrived in U.S., 1994, naturalized, 2001; s. Gopal Ramchandra and Manorama Gopal Bhide; m. Meena Mohiniraj Joshi, Jan. 7, 1981; children: Unmesh, Amit, Sonia. BSc in Math., U. Mumbai, India, 1954; MSc in Physics, U. Mumbai, 1956; PhD, U. Mumbai, India, 1971. Registered profl. engr., Argonne Nat. Lab., IL., USA, 1958, cert. Atomic Energy Rsch. Establishment, Harwell, U.K., 1960; Yoga tchr. Kaivalyadham, Lonavala, Maharashtra, India, 1984. Fellow Ramnarain Ruia Coll., Mumbai, Maharashtra, 1954—56; sci. officer Bhabha Atomic Rsch. Ctr., Trombay, Mumbai, 1956—94; adj. faculty physics No. Va. CC, Annandale, 1997; substitute tchr. Fairfax County Pub. Schs., Va., 1998—. Exch. scientist Atomic Energy Rsch. Establishment, Harwell, Didcot, Berkshire, United Kingdom, 1958—60; affiliate Internat. Inst. Nuc. Sci. & Engring., Argonne, Ill., 1960—62; sec. disarmament study group Govt. of India, Dept. Atomic Energy, Mumbai, 1962—67; sci. sec. XII Pugwash Conf. on Sci. & World Affairs, Udaipur, Rajasthan, India, 1964; Indian del. IAEA Seminar on Physics of Fast & Intermediate Reactors, Vienna, 1961, Second UN Conf. on Peaceful Uses of Atomic Energy, Geneva, 1958; adj. prof. Southeastern U., Ct. for Allied Health Edn., Washington, 1999—. Editor: Vidnyan Kutuhal, Marathi Mahasangh-Vidnyan; contbr. articles to profl. jours. Co-founder, treas. Marathi Vidnyan Mahasangh, Mumbai, 1980—82; founder, treas., sec. Madhyamumbai Marathi Vidnyan Sangh, Mumbai, 1971—93; co-founder, treas. Mumbai Shubham Karoti Parivar, 1979—88; camp leader Student Voluntary Work Camps, Turbhe, Gorkamat & Kadav, Maharashtra, 1953—54; active Bhabha Atomic Rsch. Ctr. Maharashtra Mandal, Mumbai, 1970—94, Kokannagar Yuvak Mandal (Youth Club), Mumbai, 1965—75; vis. lectr. Shramik Vidyapeeth Ministry Non-formal Edn. Govt. India, 1973—82. Recipient V. K. Bhagawat prize, Ramnarain Ruia Coll., Mumbai, India, 1954, Homi J. Bhabha Commemorative Medallion, Bhabha Atomic Rsch. Ctr., Trombay, Mumbai, 1982. Fellow: Soc. for Advancement Electrochem. Sci. and Tech. (life; internal auditor Mumbai chpt. 1988—93); mem.: ACLU, AAUP, Am. Nuc. Soc., Indian Nuc. Soc. (life), Nat. Assn. for Applications Radiation and Radioactive Isotopes (life), Assn. Med. Physicists India (life), Indian Assn. for Radiation Protection (life; organizing com. ann. conf. 1990), Indian Physics Assn. (life), Vienna Photographic Soc., Sierra Club. Avocations: photography, nature walks, music, museums, yoga. Home: 8156 Larkin Lane Vienna VA 22182-5232 Personal E-mail: mhbhide@hotmail.com.

BHIDE, PRADEEP G., neuroscientist, researcher; s. Gopal Narayan and Kamala Bhide. B of Vet. Sci., Vet. Coll., Bangalore, India, 1979; PhD, U. Aberdeen, Scotland, 1983. Rsch. asst. U. Aberdeen, Scotland, 1980—84; postdoctoral rsch. fellow Indian Inst. of Sci., Bangalore, Karnataka, India, 1984—85, U. Coll. London, 1985—88, Yale U. Sch. of Medicine, New Haven, 1988; rsch. fellow in neurology Mass. Gen. Hosp., Boston, 1988—90, asst. in devel. neuroscience, 1990—2005; instr. in neurology Harvard Med. Sch., Boston, 1990—96, asst. prof. of neurology, 1996—2005, assoc. prof. of neurology, 2005—; assoc. neuroscientist Mass. Gen. Hosp., Boston, 2005. Mem. Fin. Com., Boxford, Mass., 2005—, Capital Budgeting Com., Boxford, Mass., 2005—. Mem.: Soc. for Neuroscience. Office: Mass Gen Hosp 149 Thirteenth St Charlestown MA 02129

BHOLA, RAHUL, ophthalmologist; b. New Delhi, Delhi, India, Aug. 25, 1974; arrived in US, 2003; s. Ved and Veena Bhola; m. Richa Singh. MD, U. Coll. Med. Scis., Delhi, India, 1996. Diplomate Med. Coun. India, 1997. Clin. instr. pediatric ophthalmology U. Iowa, Iowa City, 2004—06; ophthalmologist U. Louisville, 2006—. Vis. asst. prof. dept. ophthalmology UCLA, 2003—04. Contbr. articles to profl. jours. Recipient Clin. Rsch. award, Jules Stein Eye Inst., UCLA, 2004, Above and Beyond the Call of Duty award, U. Iowa Hosps. and Clinics, 2005; scholar, Internat. Strabismological Assn., 2003—04. Mem.: Ky. Med. Assn., Am. Assn. Pediatric Ophthalmology and Strabismus (assoc.), Am. Acad. Ophthalmology (assoc.). Achievements include research in new surgical technique on recession of inferior oblique muscle of eye. Home: 3116 Running Deer Cir Louisville KY 40241 Office: U Louisville Dept Ophthalmology Louisville KY 40202 Home Phone: 310-980-7166. Personal E-mail: drrahulbhola@gmail.com.

BHUIYAN, SHAFIQUR RAHMAN, materials scientist; b. Chandpur, Bangladesh, Oct. 30, 1974; MSc in Mech. Engring., U. Houston, PhD (hon.) in Materials Engring., 2004. Rsch. asst. U. Houston, 2000—04; rsch. assoc. Oak Ridge Nat. Lab., Tenn., 2005—. Lectr. Bangladesh U. Eng. & Tech., Dhaka, 1998—2000. Contbr. articles to profl. jours. Recipient Warner Von Siemens Excellence award, 1998. Mem.: AAAS (assoc.). Achievements include first to New oxide materials. Home: 105 Inn Ln Apt 205 Oak Ridge TN 37830 Office: Oak Ridge National Laboratory 1 Bethel Valley Rd Oak Ridge TN 37831 Home Phone: 865-384-6395; Office Phone: 865-574-4943. Personal E-mail: bhuiyant@yahoo.com. E-mail: s9r@ornl.gov.

BHUSHAN, BHARAT, mechanical engineer; b. Jhinjhana, India, Sept. 30, 1949; came to U.S., 1970, naturalized, 1977; s. Narain Dass and Devi (Vati) B.; m. Sudha Bhushan, June 14, 1975; children: Ankur, Noopur. BE Mech. Engring. with honors, Birla Inst. Tech. and Sci., 1970; MSME, MIT, 1971; MS in Mechanics, U. Colo., 1973, PhD in Mech. Engring., 1976; MBA, Rensselaer Poly. Inst., 1980; DSc, U. Trondheim, Norway, 1990; D of Tech. Scis., Warsaw U. Tech., Poland, 1996; D honoris causa, Metal Polymer Rsch. Inst., Nat. Acad. Scis. at Gomel, Belarus, 2000. Mem. rsch. staff dept. mech. engring. MIT, Cambridge, 1971-72; rsch. asst., instr. dept. mech. engring. U. Colo., Boulder, 1973-76; phys. tribology program mgr. R&D divsn. Mech. Tech. Inc., Latham, NY, 1976-80; rsch. scientist, tech. svcs. divsn. SKF Industries, Inc., King of Prussia, Pa., 1980-81; devel. engr., mgr., gen. products divsn. lab. IBM Corp., Tucson, 1981—86; rsch. staff mem., mgr. head-disk interface Almaden Rsch. Ctr., IBM Rsch. Divsn., San Jose, Calif., 1986-91; Ohio eminent scholar, Howard D. Winbigler prof. mech. engring. Ohio State U., Columbus, 1991—, dir. Nanotribology lab. info. storage, 1991—. Expert investigator Automotive Specialists, Denver, 1973-76; vis. sr. scientist dept. machine design and materials tech., Royal Norwegian Coun. for Sci. and Indsl. Rsch., U. Trondheim, 1987, USSR Acad. Sci., Moscow, Gomel, Vilnuis, Leningrad, 1989; vis. scholar dept. mech. engring., chemistry and materials sci. and mineral engring. U. Calif., Berkeley, 1989; Sony sabbatical chair prof. Sony Corp. Rsch. Ctr., Fujitsuka, Japan, 1997; guest prof. dept. physics and engring. U. Cambridge, 1999; Inst. Fine Tech., Tech. U. Vienna, 1999; sr. academic visitor, Ecole Polytechnique Federale de Lausanne, Inst. de Physique de la Matiere Complexe, Switzerland, 2003; gust prof. Eidgennoessische Tech. Hochschule, Switzerland, 2005; invited prof. Lab. Physicque des Solides, U. Paris, France, 2006; rsch. student supr.; spkr. over 250 invited presentations, 60 keynote and plenary addresses, and internat. confs. worldwide. Author: Tribology and Mechanics of Magnetic Storage Devices, 1990, 2d edit. 1996, Mechanics and Reliability of Flexible Magnetic Media, 1992, 2d edit. 2000, Principles and Applications of Tribology, 1999, Introduction to Tribology, 2002; co-author (with B.K. Gupta) Handbook of Tribology: Materials, Coatings and Surface Treatments, 1991; mem. editl. bd. Jour. Friction and Wear of Belarus, Tribology Letters and Storage; assoc. editor Jour. Tribology, 1986-90; co-editor Proceedings on Tribology and Mechanics of Magnetic Storage Systems Symposia, 1984-90; editor Handbook of Micro/Natrotribiology, 1995, 2d edit., 1999, Modern Tribology Handbook, Vol. 1 Principles of Tribology, 2001, Vol. 2 Materials, Coatings and Industrial Applications, 2001, Springer Handbook of Nanotechnology, 2004; editor 25 books; co-editor-in-chief Microsystem Technologies: Micro-& Nanosystems and Information Storage and Processing Systems, 2002; editor-in-chief, founding editor ASME series Advances in Info. Storage Sys., 1991-93, World Scientific, 1994-99; editor-in-chief CRC Mechanics and Materials Sci. series, Jour. Info. Storage and Processing Sys., 1999-2001; contbr. over 70 handbook chpts., 600 tech. papers, 60 tech. reports, 4005 articles to profl. jours. in field. Recipient Alfred Noble prize ASCE, IEEE, ASME, AIME, Western Soc. Engrs., 1981, George Norlan award, U. Colo., 1983, Regents Disting. Svc. award, 1985, GPD Achievement award IBM Corp., 1983, Invention Achievement award, 1985, Rsch. Divsn. award for Outstanding Achievement, 1987, Outstanding Tech. Achievement award, 1990, Tech. Excellence award Am. Soc. Engrs. India, 1989, Cert. Appreciation award NASA, 1987, Lumley Rsch. award, Ohio State U., 1997, 2001, Alexander von Humboldt Rsch. prize for Sr. Scientists U. Ulm, 1998-99, U. Karlsruhe, 1998-99, Fulbright Sr. Scholar award Tech. U. Vienna, 1999, UN Sr. TOKTEN Expert award, Dehli, Bangalore, India, 1999, Max Planck Found. Rsch. award for Outstanding Fgn. Scientists Max Planck Inst. for Metals Rsch., Düsseldorf, Germany, 2002; Ford Found. fellow MIT, 1971; grantee USN, NASA, Dept. Energy, USAF, Franco-Am. Commn. for Ednl. Exch. Interfound. grantee Ecole Ctrl. Lyon, 1999. Fellow STLE, IEEE, ASME (cert. of recognition Design Engring. Conf., Henry Hess award 1980, Burt L. Newkirk award 1983, Gustus L. Larson Meml. award 1986, Tribology Divsn. Best Paper award 1989, Melville medal for Best Current Original Paper 1992, Bd. Govs. award for Valued Svcs. as Founding Chair of ISPS Divsn. 1997, Bd. Govs. award for Valued Svcs. as Chair of ISPS Divsn. 1998, Charles Russ Richards Meml. award 2000, Robert Henry Thurston Lect. award, 2004), NY Acad. Scis.; mem. NSPE, IEEE (sr.), ASEE, Soc. Tribologists and Lubrication Engrs., Am. Soc. Lubrication Engrs., Am. Acad. Mechanics, Internat. Humanists Soc., Tri-City India Assn., Internat. Acad. Engring. Russia (fgn.), Byelorussian Acad. of Engring. and Tech. (fgn.), Acad. of Triboengring. of Ukraine (fgn.), Soc. of Tribologists of Belarus (hon.), Soc. Tribologists and Lubnicetim Engr., Rotary, Sigma Xi, Tau Beta Pi, Pi Tau Sigma. Hindu. Achievements include 16 US and fgn. patents in field; pioneer in tribology and mechanics of magnetic storage devices; leading researcher in field of micro/nanotribology using single probe microscopy. Home: 10235 Widdington Close Powell OH 43065-9059 Office: Ohio State University 650 Ackerman Rd Columbus OH 43202-4500 Office Phone: 614-292-0651. Business E-Mail: bhushan.2@osu.edu.

BHUTTA, ADEEL ASLAM, computer engineer, educator; arrived in US, 2003; s. M. Aslam Bhutta and Naheed Pervaiz; m. Gul Hina, July 28, 2002; 1 child, Afaaf Adeel. M in Computer Sci., U. Ctrl. Fla., Orlando, 2006, postgrad. in Computer Engring., 2005—. Design engr. Enabling Technologies, Islamabad, Pakistan, 2000—02; grad. tchg. asst. Sch. Elec. Engring. and Computer Sci. U. Ctrl. Fla., 2003—. Recipient Grad. Tchg. Asst. award, Sch. Elec. Engring. and Computer Sci., 2007, award of achievement, Nat. Scholars Honor Soc., 2006; scholar, Student Govt. Assn., U. Ctrl. Fla., 2006; Grad. Merit fellow, U. Ctrl. Fla., 2003, 2005, Grad. Rsch. fellow, 2006. Mem.: IEEE, Assn. Computing Machinery, Inst. Elec. Engrs., Pakistan Engring. Coun. (life). Achievements include research in blind blur estimation using low rank approximation of cepstrum. Office: U Ctrl Fla Sch Elec Engring and Computer Sci 4000 Central FL Blvd Orlando FL 32816 Office Phone: 407-823-0016. Personal E-mail: abhutta@gmail.com.

BIAGIOTTI, GUY A., urologist, medical association administrator, director; b. Cleve., May 20, 1927; s. Eliseo Biagiotti and Rose Coreno; m. Gloria J. Buccieri, June 1, 1963; children: Victoria, Guy Rocco. BS in Chemistry, Adelbert Coll., Cleve., 1949; MA in Physiology, Oberlin Coll., Ohio, 1950; MD, Ohio State U., Columbus, 1955. Cert. Am. Bd. Urology, 1965. Intern Orange County Hosp., Calif., 1955—56; resident gen. surgery Crile VA Hosp, UN Hosp. Cleve., 1956—57; resident urology UN Hosp., Western Res. and Crile Hosp., Cleve., 1957—60; pvt. practice urology Orange County, 1960—; med. dir. Orange County Litho Ctr., Garden Grove, Calif., 1986—; ass. clin. prof. urology U. Calif. Med. Ctr. Orange County, Irvine, 1969—2006; med. dir. Orange County Kidney Stone and Oclitho Ctr., Garden Grove, 1986—. Chmn. urology Children's Hosp., Orange, 1969, 75, 78; staff St. Joseph Hosp., Orange, 1967, 75, 78; chief urology, mem. exec. com. Drs. Hosp., Santa Ana, Calif.; head urology Canyon Gen. Hosp., Anaheim, Calif., 1974—78; staff AMI Garden Grove Hosp.; past. med. dir. Mobile Lithotripters, Inc., 1990—93; design cons. Calumet Coach Co., Chgo., 1991. Contbr. articles to profl. jours. Charter mem. Orange County Kidney Stone Ctr., 1986; vol. tchg. staff U. Calif., Irvine, 1969—2006. Cpl. med. corp US Army, 1945—46, Colo. Mem.: AMA, Am. Lithotripter Soc., Am. Urol. Assn., Orange County Med. Assn., Calif. Med. Assn., Orange County Urol. Soc. Achievements include development of techniques in treating lower ureteral stones in 1986 and presacral Ureteral stone in 1988 on the dornier HM3 lithotripter.

BIALASIEWICZ, JAN TADEUSZ, electrical engineering educator; b. Pruszkow, Poland, June 1, 1939; came to U.S., 1985; s. Piotr Pawel and Wanda Henryka Bialasiewicz; m. Ewa Teresa Wanasz, Sept. 30, 1967; children: Luiza, Seweryn. MS in Elec. Engring., Warsaw U. Tech., Poland, 1962; PhD in Elec. Engring., Silesian Tech. U., Gliwice, Poland, 1966; DSc in Elec. Engring., Silesian Tech. U., 1972. Registered profl. engr., Colo. Head, computer control software dept. Indsl. Inst. Automation and Measurements, Warsaw, 1969-78; assoc. prof. elec. engring. Higher Inst. Electronics, Malta, 1979-80; head, computer control software dept. Nuc. Rsch. Inst., Warsaw, 1980-85; assoc. prof. elec. engring. U. Colo., Denver, 1985—. Vis. rsch. assoc., NASA Langley Rsch. Ctr., Hampton, Va., summers, 1990, 91, NASA/ASEE fellow, 1993; cons. Nat. Renewable Energy Lab., Golden, Colo., 1994—; vis. prof., Warsaw Tech. U., 1997; prof. comp. engring. Polish-Japenese Inst. Comp. Tech., Warsaw, 2004—. Author: Wavelets and Approximations, 2000; editor (assoc.): IEEE Trans. Ind. Electronics; contbr. articles to profl. jours. Pres. Rocky Mountain chpt. Kosciuszko Found., Denver, 1993—. Named Prof. Tech. Scis., Pres. Republic of Poland, 2001. Mem. IEEE, AAUP, Polish Inst. Arts and Scis. in Am. Roman Catholic. Avocations: travel, skiing, classical music. Office: U Colo at Denver CB110 PO Box 173364 Denver CO 80217 Business E-Mail: jan.bialasiewicz@cudenver.edu.

BIALEK, PAUL RICHARD, mathematics professor; b. Chgo., Dec. 1965; s. Richard Paul and Leona Katherine Bialek; m. Nancy Ann Nagle, 1998. BS, U. Ill., 1986, MS, 1988, PhD, 1994. Instr. math. Coll. Wooster, Ohio, 1993—94; asst. prof. math. Westmont Coll., Santa Barbara, Calif., 1994—95; assoc. prof. math. Trinity Internat. U., Deerfield, Ill., 1995—. Reader advanced placement calculus exam Ednl. Testing Svc., Princeton, NJ, 2001—07. Deacon North Suburban Evang. Free Ch., Deerfield, 1997—2002. Mem.: Associated Colls. Chgo. (Ill.) Area (chmn. math. divsn. 2001—02), Math. Assn. Am., Assn. Christians in Math. Scis. Avocations: cooking, reading, languages. Office: Trinity International University 2065 Half Day Road Deerfield IL 60015 Home Phone: 847-945-9268. Business E-Mail: pbialek@trin.edu.

BIALKIN, KENNETH JULES, lawyer, director; b. NYC, Sept. 9, 1929; s. Samuel and Lillian (Kastner) B.; m. Ann Eskind, Aug. 19, 1956; children: Lisa Beth, Johanna. AB, U. Mich., 1950; cert. of attendance, London Sch. Econ., 1952; JD, Harvard U., 1953. Bar: N.Y. 1953, U.S. Dist. Ct. (ea. dist.) N.Y. 1955, U.S. Supreme Ct. 1964, U.S. Dist. Ct. (so. dist.) N.Y. 1972, U.S. Ct. Appeals (2d cir.) 1976. Assoc. Willkie Farr & Gallagher, NYC, 1953-60, ptnr., 1960-88, Skadden, Arps, Slate, Meagher & Flom, NYC, 1988—. Adj. prof. law NYU, 1967-87; lectr., commentator legal and fin. symposia; mem. N.Y. Stock Exch. Legal Adv. Commn., 1983-92, 98—, chmn. internat. securities subcom., 1989-98; bd. dirs. Mcpl. Assistance Corp. City of NY, 1977-, chmn. audit com.; bd. dirs. Citigroup, Inc., 1986-02, St. Paul Travelers Property and Casualty Co. 1986-05; mem. Adminstrv. Conf. of U.S., 1987-92; chmn. Com. on Fin. Svcs.; bd. govs. grad. faculty New Sch. U., 1992-. Editor: The Business Lawyer, 1980; bd. editors Corp. Governance Jour., 1992—; contbr. articles on corp., fin. investment law to profl. jours. Chmn. Conf. Pres. Major Am. Jewish Orgns., 1984-86; chmn. Am.-Israel Friendship League, 1995—; nat. chmn. Anti-Defamation League B'nai Brith, 1982-86; pres. Jewish Cmty. Rels. Coun. N.Y., 1989-92; vice-chmn., dir. Jerusalem Found., Inc., 1975—; sec., trustee Carnegie Hall, 1980-. Mem. ABA (chmn. fed. regulation securities com. 1974-79, chmn. com. to study fgn. investment in U.S. 1978-80, chmn. ad hoc com. on insider trading regulation 1988—, chmn. sect. corp. banking and bus. law 1981-82, 88), Am. Jewish Hist. Soc. (pres. 1997—03, chmn. 2003—), N.Y. State Com. on Edn reform, 2003-04, N.Y. County Lawyers Assn. (pres. 1986-88), Am. Bar Retirement Assn. (dir. 1981-84), Coun. Fgn. Rels., Harvard Club. Home: 211 Central Park W New York NY 10024-6020 Office: Skadden Arps Slate Meagher & Flom Fl 44 4 Times Sq New York NY 10036-6595 Office Phone: 212-735-2130. Business E-Mail: kbialkin@skadden.com.

BIALLER, NANCY, art appraiser; AB, Vassar Coll.; MA, MPhil, PhD in 16th & 17th Century Dutch Art, Yale U. With Sotheby's, London, 1976, head, Old Master Drawings NYC. Fullbright Fellow, Vienna, 1972. Office: Sotheby's 1334 York Ave New York NY 10021 Office Phone: 212-606-7230. Office Fax: 212-606-7107. Business E-Mail: nancy.bialler@sothebys.com.

BIALO, KENNETH MARC, lawyer; b. NYC, Nov. 21, 1946; s. Walter and Mildred (Miller) B.; m. Katherine Ann Burghard; children: Darren Andrew, Caralyn Alyssa, Jacquelyn Anne, Matthew Joseph Geronimo, Kelsey Elizabeth Ariel. BS, U. Rochester, 1968; JD cum laude (Univ. scholar), NYU, 1971; LLM, London Sch. Econs., 1973. Bar: N.Y. 1972, U.S. Ct. Appeals (2d cir.) 1974, U.S. Ct. Appeals (fed. cir.) 1988, U.S. Supreme Ct. 1975. Law clk. Hon. L.W. Pierce U.S. Dist. Ct. (so. dist.) N.Y., 1971—72; assoc. Sullivan & Cromwell, NYC, 1973—80; counsel, sr. counsel Exxon Corp., NYC, 1980—90; sr. counsel, chief litigation atty. Exxon Chem. Co., Darien, Conn., 1990—91; ptnr. Baker Botts, LLP, NYC, 1992—2003, Emmett, Marvin & Martin, LLP, NYC, 2003—, leader litigation group, 2005. Lectr. Practicing Law Inst., NYC, 1982, 88, N.Y. State Bar Assn., 1997; vice chmn. bd. State of N.Y. Mcpl. Bond Bank Agy., NYC, 2000—, State of N.Y. Tobacco Settlement Fin. Corp., 2003—. Contbg. editor: Family Legal Guide, 1974; contbr. articles to profl. jours.; note and comment editor: NYU Law Rev.; host The Larchmont Report, WVOX, Whitney Radio Group, New Rochelle, N.Y., 1995—, co-host Larchmont Today, LMC-TV, Mamaroneck, N.Y., 1995—; co-founder, prin. contbr.: Plugged In, Rep. Party Pub. Svc. Newsletter, 1996—. Trustee Village of Larchmont, NY, 1991-2002, mayor, 2002-06; mem. PLI Adv. Com. on Litig., 1994—; bd. govs., Univ. Club Larchmont, 1995-1999, pres., 1998-1999; v.p., bd. dirs. Little League, Larchmont, 1985-94, recreation com., 1987-89; treas., exec. com. L.I. Sound Watershed Intermcpl. Coun., Westchester County, NY, 2000-2002; mem. Westchester County Legis. Stormwater Adv. Com., 2001-. Mem. ABA (litig. sect. task force on client concerns 1994-95, subcom. class action, litig. sect.), N.Y. State Bar (antitrust com., fed. and comml. litig. sect., former chmn. corp. counsel com. 1989-91), Assn. of Bar of City of N.Y. (arbitration com. 1983-85), Fed. Bar Coun. (com. 2d cir. cts. 1985-87), Am. Arbitration Assn. (mem. arbitrators panel), Order of Coif. Avocations: tennis, baseball, opera, symphony. Office: Emmett Marvin & Martin LLP 120 Broadway New York NY 10271 Office Phone: 212-238-3058.

BIALOSKY, DAVID L., lawyer, automotive executive; b. 1958; AB in Engring. Scis., Dartmouth Coll.; JD, Northwestern U. Bar: Calif., Mich., Ohio. Mech. engr. Std. Oil Co. Ohio; assoc. Thompson, Hine & Flory, Cleve.; joined TRW, 1989, counsel automotive sector, sr. counsel occupant restraints and controls group, 1989; sr. counsel TRW Info. Sys. and Svcs., Orange County, Calif., 1996—97; v.p., asst. gen. counsel TRW Automotive, v.p., gen. counsel Livonia, Mich., 2002—04, exec. v.p., gen. counsel, 2004—. Office: TRW Automotive 12025 Tech Center Dr Livonia MI 48150 Office Phone: 734-266-2600. Office Fax: 734-266-4594.*

BIAN, ZHIXI, research scientist; PhD, U. Calif., Santa Cruz, 2004. Lectr. Beijing U., 1996—99; rsch. scientist U. Calif., 2004—. Contbr. articles to profl. jours. Mem.: IEEE, APS, MRS. Office: Univ Calif Sch Engring Santa Cruz CA 95064 Business E-Mail: zxbian@soe.ucsc.edu.

BIANCHI, HOLLIS DOLCE, writer, poet, artist; b. Orange, NJ, June 25, 1952; d. Ovid Carlo Bianchi and Matilda Florence Dolce. Student in studio drawing, Corcoran Sch. Art, Washington, 1975—76; AAS, Marymount U., Arlington, Va., 1978. Freelance writer Atlantic Highlands Herald Newspaper, 2004—. Author: Poems for the Holidays, 1998 (Writer's Digest Cert. of Merit awards), Collage: A Collection of Poems, 1999, Images of America: Leonardo, 2002 (Cert. of Appreciation award), Earth's Spirits, 2004; contbr. short stories and poems to newspapers and mags.; lyricist: songs Redrock and Hilltop Records, 1998—2000; Former Am. Chamber Orch., Washington, NJ Coast Guard Aux. Monmouth Country. Mem.: The Arts for Aging, Atlantic Highlands Hist. Soc., Nat. Trust Hist. Preservation, Met. Opera Guild, Summer Opera Theatre Guild (artist newsletter), Washington Ballet (mem. women's com.), Corcoran Gallery Art, Nat. Mus. Women in Arts. Avocations: playing the harmonica, embroidery, reading. Home: 49 Florence Ave Leonardo NJ 07737 Personal E-mail: dmapelli@aol.com.

BIANCHI, MARIA, critical care specialist, acute care nurse practitioner; b. Springfield, Mass. B in Nursing, Catherine Laboure Sch. Nursing, Boston, 1979; BSN, Fitchburg State Coll./U. Mass., Amherst, 1985; MS in Critical Care and Nursing Adminstrn., Russell Sage Grad. Coll., Troy, NY, 1993. Cert. post-anesthesia care nurse; critical care clin. specialist; expert witness, Mass., Conn. Recovery as mgmt. educator; mktg. and recruitment cons.; cons. in critical care nursing; clin. faculty Am. Internat. Coll., Springfield; adminstr. dept. spl. svcs., mgr. critical care Baystate Med. Ctr., Springfield, Mass., 1980-89; recruitment adminstrn. and sr. faculty St. Francis Med. Ctr. Sch. of Nursing, Hartford, Conn., 1989-92; grad. faculty U. Mass. Med. Ctr., Worcester, 1995-97; asst. prof. Grad. Sch. U. Mass., Amherst, 1998-99; faculty U. Mass. Sch. of Nursing, Amherst, per diem nurse practitioner dept. surgery Worcester, 1995—97, 1999—; CS/NP Mass Gen. Hosp., Boston; nurse dept. emergency medicine St. Francis Hosp. and Med. Ctr., Hartford, Conn., 2006—; critical care specialist adminstrn. program Sage, Troy, NY. Pres. ProLase Medi-Spa & Clinic, Worcester and Springfield, Mass., TI Healthcare; nat. cons. critical care/post anesthesia issues; medicolegal cons.; laser med. provider; lectr. critical care and post anesthesia issues, empowerment, acute pain, holistic techniques, medicological documentation, trauma; lectr. cardiac and non-cardiac chest pain issues. Invited amb. del. People's for People's, Fed. Govt. Mem. AACN, Am. Soc. Post-Anesthesia Nursing (Boston chpt. editl. cons.), Soc. Critical Medicine, Mass. Gen. Hosp. Alumni Assn., Catherine Laboure Alumni Assn., Sigma Theta Tau. Achievements include research in pain, burn trauma, stress reduction, holistic methods for high risk individuals in maximum security penitentiary and critical care patients. Office: PO Box 614 Suffield CT 06078-0614 Office Phone: 888-750-5273. Personal E-mail: mariatih@comcast.net.

BIANCHI, MATT, neurologist, researcher; s. Richard and Elizabeth Bianchi. BA in Neuroscience, Brandeis U., Waltham, Mass.; MD, PhD, U. Mich., Ann Arbor, 2004. Postdoctoral fellow Vanderbilt U., Nashville, 2003—04; resident neurology Mass. Gen. Hosp. and Brigham and Women's Hosp., Boston, 2005—. Contbr. chapters to books, articles to profl. jours. Recipient Publ. award, U. Mich. Neuroscience Program, 2001, Rsch. Publ. award, Blue Cross Blue Shield of Mich., 2003, 2004; grantee, NIH, 1999, 2000. Mem.: Soc. Neuroscience (Rsch. award Mich. chpt. 2000, 2001), Am. Acad. Neurology (Extended Neuroscience award 2004, Neuroscience Rsch. award 2004). Independent. Achievements include research in kinetic mechanisms of GABA-A receptor function using patch clamp electrophysiology; mechanisms of pharmacological modulation of GABA-A receptors by endogenous neurosteroids. Avocations: philosophy, hiking, bicycling, writing, travel. Personal E-mail: thebianchi74@hotmail.com.

BIANCHINI, GINA, Internet company executive; BA, MBA, Stanford Univ. With CKS Group, Goldman Sachs & Co.; co-founder, pres. Harmonic Comm. (sold to Dentsu); co-founder Ning, Palo Alto, Calif., 2004—. Named one of 50 Who Matter Now, Business 2.0, 2007. Office: Ning Ste 300 167 Hamilton Ave Palo Alto CA 94301*

BIANCO, ANTHONY JOSEPH, III, newswriter; b. Oceanside, Calif., May 17, 1953; s. Anthony Joseph Jr. and JoAnn (Reavill) B.; 1 child, Marissa. BA, U. Minn., 1976. Reporter Mpls. Tribune, 1977; bus. editor Willamette Week newspaper, Portland, Oreg., 1978-80; corr. Bus. Week mag., San Francisco, 1980-82, dept. editor NYC, 1982-84, assoc. editor, 1984-85, sr. writer, 1985-92, 1996—2005, nat. corr., 2005—. Author: Rainmaker, 1991, The Reichmanns, 1997, Ghosts of 42nd Street, 2004, The Bully of Bentonville, 2006. Recipient media award for econ. understanding Amos Tuck Sch., Dartmouth Coll., 1979, award for feature writing Oreg. Newspaper Pubs., 1979, award for excellence in fin. writing N.Y. State Soc. CPA's, 1987, Disting. Editorial Achievement award McGraw-Hill, 1986, Nat. Bus. Book award, Can., 1997. Mem. Soc. Profl. Journalists. Home: 17 1st St Brooklyn NY 11231-5001 Office Phone: 212-512-3201.

BIANCO, JAMES A., research and development executive; b. Bronx, NY, July 26, 1956; married; 3 children. BS cum laude with honors, NYU, 1979; MD, Mt. Sinai Sch. of Medicine, 1983. Intern, then resident Mt. Sinai Med. Ctr., NYC, 1983-87; fellow in oncology U. Wash., Seattle, 1987-91, asst. prof. medicine, 1991-92; dir. bone marrow transplant program VA Med. Ctr., Seattle, 1990-92; asst. mem. Fred Hutchinson Cancer Rsch. Ctr., Seattle, 1991-92; pres., CEO Cell Therapeutics, Inc., Seattle, 1992—. Spkr. in field. Recipient Corp. Visionary award, Gilda's Club, Seattle, 2006. Mem. Alpha Omega Alpha. Achievements include profile in Bus. Week Mag., 2006. Avocations: cooking, guitar. Office: Cell Therapeutics Inc 201 Elliott Ave W Ste 400 Seattle WA 98119-4237*

BIARD, JAMES ROBERT, retired electrical engineer, consultant; b. Paris, Tex., May 20, 1931; s. James Christopher and Mary Ruth (Bills) B.; m. Amelia Ruth Clark, May 23, 1952; children: James Clark, Jan Elaine; 1 adopted child, Becky Dell. AS, Paris Jr. Coll., 1951; BSEE, Tex. A&M U., 1954, MSEE, 1956, PhD in Elec. Engring., 1957. Sr. engr. Tex. Instruments, Inc., Dallas, 1957-69; v.p. R & D Spectronics, Inc., Richardson, Tex., 1969-78; chief scientist Honeywell Optoelectronics, Richardson, 1978-88, Honeywell Micro Switch, Richardson, 1988-98; ret., 1998. Prof. elec. engring. dept. Tex. A&M U., College Station, 1980—; presenter at nat. and internat. symposia, 1957—; cons. in field. Contbr. over 23 articles to profl. jours. Entertainer for various svc. clubs, radio, TV, bus. and chs., 1957—. Recipient Disting. Alumnus award Tex. A&M U., 1986, Paris Jr. Coll., 1993. Fellow IEEE; mem. Am. PHys. Soc., Nat. Acad. Engring., Sigma Xi, Tau Beta Pi, Eta Kappa Nu, Phi Kappa Phi. Republican. Mem. Ch. of Christ. Achievements include 41 U.S. and 17 foreign patents for gallium arsenide light emitting diode, schottky clamped silicon integrated logic circuits, metal-oxide-semiconductor read only memory, others. Office: Advanced Optical Products 6000 Millennium Dr Allen TX 75013 Office Phone: 214-509-2731. Business E-Mail: bob.biard@finisar.com.

BIAS, DANA G., lawyer; b. Lexington, Ky., Mar. 12, 1959; d. Cyrus Dana and Betty Jo (Haddox) B. BA with highest honors, U. Louisville, 1981; JD magna cum laude, Boston U., 1984. Bar: Mass. 1985, N.Y. 1985, Ky. 1995, Tex. 2000, U.S. Dist. Ct. (so. and ea. dists.) N.Y. 1986, U.S. Dist. Ct. (ea. dist.) Tex. 2000. Counselor Mass. Half-Way Houses, Inc., Boston, 1982-83; sr. trial atty. Criminal Def. div. Legal Aid Soc., NYC, 1984-89, mng. atty., 1989-94; sole practitioner Hauppauge, N.Y., 1995; sr. trial atty. Louisville-Jefferson County Pub. Defender Corp., 1995-97; asst. public advocate, capital trial atty. Dept. of Public Advocacy, 1997-2000; mng. atty. Lone Star Legal Aid, Nacogdoches, 2000—03, Beaumont, Tex., 2002—04; project dir. East Tex. Fair Housing Svc. Ctr., Nacogdoches, Tex., 2004—06; mng. atty., pvt. atty. involvement coord. Lone Star Legal Aid, Nacogdoches, 2006—. Lectr. N.Y.C. Pub. Schs., 1989. Contbr. articles to profl. jours. Mem. Nacogdoches Mayor's Com. on People with Disabilities. Mem. ABA, ACLU, N.Y. State Bar Assn., Nat. Assn. Criminal Def. Lawyers, Mass. Bar Assn., Ky. Bar Assn., Tex. Bar Assn., Smith County Bar Assn. (lectr. 2005), NLADA, N.Y. Civil Liberties Union, Woodcock Soc., Mortar Bd., Phi Kappa Phi, Phi Eta Sigma. Democrat. Office: Lone Star Legal Aid PO Box 631070 Nacogdoches TX 75963-1070 Office Phone: 936-560-1455. Business E-Mail: dbias@lonestarlegal.org.

BIASOTTI, ROBERT E., lawyer; BA, LI U., 1993; JD cum laude, Stetson U., 1996. Cert.: Fla. Bar (specialist in appellate practice), bar: NY, Fla., admitted to practice: US Supreme Ct., US Dist. Ct. (No. Dist.) Fla., US Dist. Ct. (Mid. Dist.) Fla., US Dist. Ct. (So. Dist.) Fla., US Ct. Appeals (11th Cir.). Computer programmer, systems analyst Gilman Paper Co., NY; treas., v.p. fin., CFO Columbia Artists Mgmt., Inc., NY, 1983—94, adminstr. pension, profit sharing, employee stock ownership and VEBA plans NY, trustee NY; clk. to Hon. John Robert Blue Fla. 2nd Dist. Ct. Appeal, 1997—98; assoc., appellate practice Carlton Fields, St. Petersburg, Fla., 1998, shareholder, 2003—. Adj. prof. appellate practice, legal practice, Coll. Law Stetson U. Recipient E. Harris Drew award for excellence in written and oral advocacy, 1996. Mem.: Fed. Bar Assn., US Supreme Ct. Bar, St. Petersburg Bar Assn. (chair, appellate practice com. 2002—03), ABA, The Fla. Bar (appellate ct. rules com. 2001—, chair, record subcom. 2004—05, vice chair, gen. subcom. 2004—05). Office: Carlton Fields One Progress Plz 200 Central Ave Ste 2300 Saint Petersburg FL 33701-4352 Office Phone: 727-824-0003. Office Fax: 727-822-3768. E-mail: rbiasotti@carltonfields.com.

BIBB, DANIEL ROLAND, art restorer; b. Gadsden, Ala., June 10, 1951; s. Cassius Roland and Louise Selma B. Student, Jefferson State, 1969-70, DeKalb Coll., 1971-72. Sales cons. Macy's Antique Gallery, Atlanta, 1973; dir. Collector's Gallery, Atlanta, 1974-76, Connoisseur's Gallery, New Orleans, 1977-79; painting conservator Daniel R. Bibb Fine Painting Conservation & Restoration, Atlanta, 1980—; chief fund raiser Atlanta Rabbit Rescue. Researcher for pvt. collectors and museums, Atlanta, 1977-89; listed conservator, New Orleans Museum List of Restorers, New Orleans, 1988. Discovered a lost major painting of Philip IV of Spain; exhibited lost painting Atlanta High Mus. Art, 1980; publ. of discovered painting, High Mus. Monthly, 1980; conservator Anglo-Am. Art Mus., Baton Rouge, New Orleans Mus. Art.; owner Fabergè collection on loan to New Orleans Mus. Art, 1996; icon collection touring mus., La., Miss. and Ala., 1998—; contbr. articles to popular mags. Fund raiser Am. Heart Assn., Atlanta, 1987-88, March of Dimes, 1987-88, Atlanta Rabbit Rescue, 1984—; active High Mus. Art, Atlanta; vol. ARC Disaster Relief Team, Atlanta, 1992, Art Care Art Auction for fight against AIDS, 1992-93, chmn. Live Auction, 1993; vol. relief work Hurricane Katrina, Atlanta, New Orleans, 2005. Recipient Design award, Most Authentic Design, Patio Planters of the Vieux Carre, New Orleans, 1977. Mem. Nat. Trust for Historic Preservation. Republican. Baptist. Achievements include raising funds and pub. awareness of animal cruelty. Home and Office: Bibb Painting Restoration 807 Summit North Dr NE Atlanta GA 30324-5641

BIBB, PAUL E. (BUCK BIBB), bank executive; B in Mktg., Fla. State U., Tallahassee. With Commonwealth Corp., Tallahassee, 1973, Commonwealth Mortgage Corp., Houston; positions up to exec. v.p. Bank United Mortgage/Commonwealth United Mortgage, 1990—97; with Nat. City Corp., 1997—, CEO Nat. City Mortgage, sr. v.p. Mem.: Mortgage Bankers Assn. Am. (mem. residential lending com.). Office: Nat City Corp Nat City Ctr 1900 E Ninth St Cleveland OH 44114-3484 Office Phone: 216-222-2000.*

BIBBO, MARLUCE, physician, educator; b. Sao Paulo, Brazil, July 14, 1939; d. Domingos and Yolanda (Ranciaro) Bibbo. MD, U. Sao Paulo, 1963, ScD, 1968. Intern Hosps. das Clinicas, U. Sao Paulo, 1963, resident in morphology, 1964-66; instr. dept. morphology and ob-gyn. U. Sao Paulo, 1966-68, asst. prof., 1968-69; fellow in cytology U. Chgo., 1969-70, asst. prof. sect. cytology dept. ob-gyn., 1971-73, assoc. prof., 1973-77, assoc. prof. pathology, 1974-77, prof. ob-gyn. and pathology, 1978-92; assoc. dir. Cytology Lab., Approved Sch. Cytotech and Cytocybernetics, AMA-Am. Soc. Clin. Pathologists, 1970-91; dir. Cytology Lab., Phila., 1992—; prof. pathology and cell biology Thomas Jefferson U., Phila., 1992—, Warren R. Lane prof. pathology & cell biology, 1993—. Mem. rsch. com. Ill. divsn. Am. Cancer Soc., 1976-91. Contbr. numerous articles to profl. jours.; editor: Comprehensive Cytopathology, 1991, 1997, 2008. Fellow Internat. Acad. Cytology (pres.-elect, v.p. 1987, pres. 1992, dep. editor Acta Cytologica, editor 1995—), Am. Soc. Clin. Pathologists (coun. on cytopathology); mem. Am. Soc. Cytology (exec. com., pres. 1982-83), U.S. Acad. Pathology, Can. Acad. Pathology, Soc. Analytical Cytology, Coun. Cytopathology. Home: 250 S 9th St Philadelphia PA 19107-5734 Office: Cytology Lab Rm 260 Main Bldg 132 S 10th St Philadelphia PA 19107-5244 Office Phone: 215-955-1197. Business E-Mail: bibbo@cytology-iac.org.

BIBBY, DOUGLAS MARTIN, mortgage association executive; b. Endicott, NY, Aug. 24, 1946; s. Dause Leveridge and Virginia (Martin) B.; m. Lorraine C. Creer, Sept. 6, 1969; children: Mariah, Ian. BA in Econs., Denison U., 1968; MBA, U. Tex, 1970. Sr. v.p. J. Walter Thompson Co., NYC, Washington, San Juan, P.R., and Toronto, Can., 1971-82; v.p. Russell Reynolds Assocs., Inc., Washington, 1982-83; sr. v.p. adminstrn. Fed. Nat. Mortgage Assn., Washington, 1983-98; ptnr. The Fin. Group, Potomac, Md., 1999—. Bd. dirs. Martha's Table, 1985—, Arena Stage, 1992—, The Summit Fund of Washington, 1992—. Avocations: tennis, community affairs.

BIBBY, MIKE, professional basketball player; b. May 13, 1978; Attended, Univ. Ariz. Basketball player Vancouver Grizzlies, 1998—2001, Sacramento Kings, 2001—. Named Pac-10 Player Yr., 1998; named to NBA All-Rookie First Team, 1999, Men's National Team, USA Basketball, 2003. Office: Sacramento Kings One Sports Pkwy Sacramento CA 95834

BIBEAULT, DONALD BERTRAND, corporate executive, investor; b. Woonsocket, RI, Nov. 14, 1941; s. George Bertrand and Renee (Herbert) B.; m. Gigi Loving, June 18, 1994 (div. June 2002); children: Zachary James, Jessica Renee, Dorothy Leigh; m. Lynne S. Barr, April 17, 2006. BSEE, U. RI, 1963; MBA, Columbia U., 1965; PhD, Golden Gate U., 1979, JD (hon.), 2000. COO Pacific States Steel, Union City, Calif., 1975-78, PLM Internat., San Francisco, 1979-81; turnaround advisor Varity Corp., 1981-82; pres., CEO Best Pipe and Steel Co., San Francisco, 1983-86; workout advisor Bank of Am., 1987-89; chmn. Am. Nat. Petrol, Houston, 1990-91; chmn., CEO Tyler Dawson Supply Co., Tulsa, 1990-91, Iron Oak Supply Co., Sacramento, 1990-93; pres. Bibeault and Assocs., Inc., San Rafael, Calif., 1976—; chmn. Bsquare Corp., Bellevue, Wash., 2003—. Trustee Golden Gate U., San Francisco, 1986-97; bd. advisors U. R.I. Bus., Kinsgton, 1993—; bd. overseers Columbia Grad. Sch. Bus., N.Y.C., 1994—2001; bd. visitors Golden Gate U. Law Sch., San Francisco, 2000—; CEO adviser underperforming cos., 1993—; chmn. bd. dirs. Bsquare Corp., Seattle, 2003—. Author: Corporate Turnaround, 1982 (Fortune award 1982); contbr. articles to profl. jours. Adv. bd. on trade Dept. Commerce, Washington, 1988-92. Lt. U.S. Army Combat Engrs., 1963-65. Recipient Lifetime Achievement award, Assn. Cert. Turnaround Practitioners, 2005. Mem. Turnaround Mgmt. Assn. (founding dir. 1987-91), Bankers Club San Francisco. Home and Office: Bibeault Assocs 1 Dooley Ct Novato CA 94945 Home Phone: 415-892-5250; Office Phone: 415-781-7200. Personal E-mail: bibeault@aol.com.

BIBER, PATRICK D., oceanographer; b. Sydney, NSW, Australia, 1971; PhD, U. Miami, 2002. Postdoctoral rsch. assoc. U. N.C., Morehead City, 2002—04; asst. prof. Gulf Coast Rsch. Lab., Ocean Springs, Miss., 2005—. Rsch. asst. Rosenstiel Sch. of Marine and Atmospheric Sci., Miami, Fla., 1994—2002. Contbr. chpt. to books and articles to profl. jours. Grantee, EPA- Star, 2003-2004, NOAA, Miss. Dept. Marine Resources, 2005—07, Miss. Dept. Marine Resources, 2006—07, Miss.-Ala. Sea Grant Consortium, 2006—08, NSF, 2006—07; scholar Rsch. assistantship, U. Miami, 1994—2002. Mem.: World Seagrass Assn., Am. Soc. of Limnologists and Oceanographers, Estuarine Rsch. Fedn., U. Miami Dive Orgn. (life; v.p. 1996—97). Achievements include research in Software for determining seagrass survival - Seagrass CriteriaBase v1. Office: Gulf Coast Rsch Lab 703 E Beach Dr Ocean Springs MS 37564 E-mail: patrick.biber@usm.edu.

BIBERMAN, LUCIEN MORTON, retired physicist; b. Phila., May 31, 1919; s. Lewis and Eva (Kerns) Biberman; m. Anne H. Wilner, Mar. 8, 1941 (dec. 1997); children: Leslie Biberman Gordon, Judith Biberman Robinson, Candace Biberman Evans; m. Virgina L. Hewitt, May 25, 2002. BS, Rensselaer Poly. Inst., 1940; postgrad., Harvard U., Cambridge, Mass., 1940-41, Stevens Inst., Hoboken, NJ, 1941-42. Phys. chemist Nairn Rsch. Labs., 1942-43; physicist in charge Mayport Magnetic Survey Area, Navy Dept., 1943-44; various positions from physicist in charge phys. measurements group to cons. Aviation Ordnance Dept. and Weapons Devel. Dept. Naval Ordnance Test Sta., 1944-57; assoc. dir. Labs. for Applied Scis. U. Chgo., 1957-63; rsch. staff rsch. and engring. support div. Inst. for Def. Analysis, Alexandria, Va., 1963-71, rsch. staff sci. and tech. div., 1972-96; emeritus, 1996—; ret., 1996. Vis. prof. dept. elec. engring. U. R.I., 1971-72; fellow Mil. Sensing Symposium, 1999. Decorated citation U.S. Army Ctr. for Night Vision and Electro Optics; recipient Andrew J. Goodpaster award, 1989. Fellow: Washington Acad. of Sci. (Disting. Career in Sci. award), Soc. Photo-optical Instrumentation Engrs. (emeritus), Soc. Info. Display (emeritus), Optical Soc. Am. (emeritus), IEEE (life), Military Sensors Symposium, Infrared Info. Symposia. Home and Office: 3731 Glen Eagles Dr Silver Spring MD 20906 Home Phone: 301-460-1673; Office Phone: 301-460-2692. Personal E-mail: lucienmb@verizon.net.

BIBICOFF, HILLARY SUE, lawyer; b. Ft. Riley, Kans., June 26, 1966; d. Harvey and Jacqueline Ruth (Marks) Bibicoff. BA, UCLA, 1988; JD, Loyola U., LA, 1991. Bar: Calif. 1991, DC 1993, Colo. 1994. Assoc. Cooper, Epstein & Hurewitz, Beverly Hills, Calif., 1991-93; dir. legal and bus. affairs Live Entertainment, Inc., Van Nuys, Calif., 1993-96; dir. theatrical bus. and legal affairs Rysher Entertainment Inc., Santa Monica, Calif., 1996, v.p. theatrical bus. and legal affairs, 1997; assoc. Greenberg Glusker Fields Claman Machtinger & Kinsella LLP, LA, 1997-2000, ptnr., 2001—. Exec. bd. mem. Women in Film, 2006—; active Hollywood Women's Polit. Com., LA, 1993—97; bd. govs. Loyola Law Sch., 1997—. Named Woman of Achievement, Century City Women's Bus. Coun., 2002, So. Calif. Super Lawyer, Law & Politics and LA Mag., 2004, 2006, 2007; named one of Top 20 Hollywood New Generation Dealmakers, LA Bus. Jour., 2001; recipient award, Nat. Assn. Women Lawyers, 1991; Burns scholar, Loyola Law Sch., 1988—91. Mem.: Women in Film (bd. dirs. 2006—), Calif. Bar Assn., Beverly Hills Bar Assn., Los Angeles County Bar Assn. (bd. dirs. intellectual property sect. 1995—98), Saxophone Club (mem. steering com. 1995—2000). Avocations: bicycling, tennis, skiing, horseback riding. Office: Greenberg Glusker Fields Claman & Machtinger LLP 1900 Avenue Of The Stars Fl 20 Los Angeles CA 90067-4301 Home Phone: 310-827-5667; Office Phone: 310-785-6823. Business E-Mail: hbibicoff@ggfirm.com.

BIBLIOWICZ, JESSICA M., financial analyst; b. 1959; d. Sanford and Joan Weill; 2 children. Grad., Cornell U. Formerly with assesment mgmt. divsn. Shearson Lehman Bros.; dir. sales and mktg. Prudential Mutual Funds, 1992—94; exec. v.p., oversees mutual funds and insured investor group Smith Barney, NYC, 1994—97; pres., COO John A. Levin & Co., 1997—99; pres., CEO Nat. Financial Partners, NYC, 1999—. Dir. Eaton Vance Mutual Funds, Gov. Com. Scholastic Achievement, Securities Industry Assn.; mem., hedge funds adv. group, investment com. Cornell U. Gov. Boys & Girls Club of Am.; regional chair, N.E. Region. Office: NFP 787 7th Ave, 49th Fl New York NY 10019

BICCHIERI, CRISTINA, science educator; b. Milano, Italy, Oct. 26, 1950; d. Ettore and Vanna (Bianco) B.; m. Michael Woodford, Sept. 14, 1984 (div. May 1, 1992); m. Massimo Bigliardo, June 6, 1992. Degree (hon.) in Philosophy, U. Milano, Italy, 1976; MA in Philosophy of Sci., Cambridge U., Eng., 1979, PhD in Philosophy of Sci., 1984. Asst. prof. Columbia U. Barnard Coll., NYC, 1984-86, U. Notre Dame, Ind., 1986-89; assoc. prof. Carnegie Mellon, Pitts., 1989-95; prof., 1996—. Bd. editors Econ. and Philisophy, 1990-95. Author: Rationality and Coordination, 1993; editor: Knowledge, Belief, and Strategic Interaction; contbr. articles to profl. jours. Grantee ONR, 1995—, Nat. Rsch. Coun., 1987, 91, NSF Scholars award in History and Philosophy of Sci., 1987-88, Faculty Devel. Fund, 1990, 94, NSF Grant for US/Italy Workshop on Knowledge, Belief, and Strategic Interaction, 1992. Democrat. Roman Catholic. Avocations: sailing, skiing, opera, movies, travel. Office: Carnegie Mellon University 5000 Forbes Ave Pittsburgh PA 15213-3890 Home: 649 N Chester Rd Swarthmore PA 19081-1014

BICE, EDNA JEWEL, artist, educator; b. Bridge Port, Ala., Dec. 27, 1927; d. Edward Jack and Suzanne Reeves; m. Ronald H. Bice, June 27, 1954; children: Ronald H. Jr., Randy Reeves. Grad., Bridge Port Schs., 1945. Mothers patrol officer Charra Police Dept., Tenn., 1963—70; merchandiser Chattanooga, 1973—78; ceramics tchr. Soddy Daisy, Tenn., 1978—2004. Recipient Leadership award, Chattanooga Schs., 1965, award for commitment and svc. to elderly, City of Chattanooga, 1980. Mem.: NAACP, Nat. Hist. Soc. (life). Democrat. Presbyterian. Avocations: ceramics, arts and crafts, knitting, gardening, cross stitch. Home: 12209 Posey Hollow Rd Soddy Daisy TN 37379

BICE, SCOTT HAAS, dean, law educator; b. LA, Mar. 19, 1943; s. Fred Haas and Virginia M. (Scott) B.; m. Barbara Franks, Dec. 21, 1968. BS, U. So. Calif., 1965, JD, 1968. Bar: Calif. 1971. Law clk. to Chief Justice Earl Warren, 1968-69; asst. prof., assoc. prof., prof. law U. So. Calif., Los Angeles, 1969—, assoc. dean, 1971-74, dean Law Sch., 1980-2000, Carl Mason Franklin prof., 1983-2000, Robert C. Packard prof. law, 2000—; CEO Five B Investment Co., 1995—. Vis. prof. polit. sci. Calif. Inst. Tech., 1977; vis. prof. U. Va., 1978-79; bd.dirs. Western Mut. Ins. Co., Residence Mut. Ins. Co., Imagine Films Entertainment Co., Jenny Craig, Inc., Arena Pharms., Inc. Mem. editl. adv. bd. Calif. Lawyer, 1989-93; contbr. articles to law jours. Bd. dirs. LA Family Housing Corp., 1989-93, Stone Soup Child Care Programs, 1988—, LA Child Guidance Clinic, 2003; trustee Bice Passavant Found., 2000-, trustee Sigma Phi Epsilon Ednl. Foun., 2006-. Affiliated scholar Am. Bar Found., 1972-74. Fellow Am. Bar Found. (life); mem. Am. Law Inst. (life), Calif. Bar, Los Angeles County Bar Assn., Am. Law Deans Assn. (pres. 1997-99), Calif. Club, Chancery Club (treas. 2001-02, sec. 2002-03, v.p. 2003-04, pres. 2004-05), Econ. Roundtable, Catalina Island Yacht Club (judge adv. 2002—). Home: 787 S San Rafael Ave Pasadena CA 91105-2326 Office: Univ So Calif Sch Law Los Angeles CA 90089-0071 Home Phone: 626-441-2432; Office Phone: 213-740-4549. Business E-Mail: sbice@law.usc.edu.

BICHSEL, HANS, physicist, consultant, researcher; b. Basel, Switzerland, Sept. 2, 1924; came to U.S., 1951; s. Paul and Anna Maria Bichsel; m. Sue O. Greenwalt, Sept. 12, 1959; children: Elizabeth Christine, Joseph Oliver. MA, PhD, U. Basel, 1951. Rsch. asst. Princeton (N.J.) U., 1951-55; rsch. assoc. Rice U., Houston, 1955-57; asst. prof. physics U. Wash., Seattle, 1957-59; affiliate prof. physics U. Wash., Seattle, 1992—; assoc. prof., prof. radiology U. Wash., Seattle, 1969-80; asst. prof., assoc. prof. physics U. So. Calif., LA, 1959-68; assoc. prof. U. Calif., Berkeley, 1968-69. Cons. Internat. Commn. on Radiation Units, Bethesda, Md., 1970—, Los Alamos (N.Mex.) Nat. Lab., 1978-83, IAEA, Vienna, Austria, 1990—; vis. scientist Nat. Inst. Radiol., Scis., Chiba, Japan, 1991-96, U. Sherbrooke Med. Sch., Que., Can.; rschr. Relativistic Heavy Ion Collider, Brookhaven Nat. Lab., 1999—; referee Phys. Rev., Nuclear Instruments and Methods, Physics in Medicine and Biology, also others. Contbr. articles to profl. jours. Fellow Am. Phys. Soc.; mem. Swiss Phys. Soc. Achievements include research in heavy ion radiation therapy. Home and Office: 1211 22nd Ave E Seattle WA 98112-3534 Office Phone: 206-329-2792. Personal E-mail: hbichsel@scientist.com.

BICHSEL, RUTH J., psychologist, educator; d. Edwin John Bichsel and Doris May Dickinson. BS in Psychology, U. Oreg., Eugene, 1980, MS in Counseling, 1990, PhD, 1997. Lic. psychologist Oreg., 1998. Faculty U. Oreg., 1995—97; instr. Lane CC, Eugene, 1995—. Vol. Animal Rescue and Rehab., Eugene, 1998—2007. Named Instr. of Yr., Lane CC, 1995-1996, Outstanding Instr., 2005; recipient Social Interest award, Oreg. Soc. Individual Psychologists, 2003. Fellow: Am. Coll. Forensic Examiners; mem.: Am. Hort. Therapists Assn., Am. Fedn. Police and Concerned Citizens (Citizenship award 1993). Avocation: animal training. Office: Lane CC 4000 E 30th Ave Eugene OR 97405 Office Phone: 541-463-5819.

BICK, KATHERINE LIVINGSTONE, neuroscientist, educator, researcher; b. Charlottetown, Can., May 3, 1932; came to U.S., 1954; d. Spurgeon Arthur and Flora Hazel (Murray) Livingstone; m. James Harry Bick, Aug. 20, 1955 (div.); children: James A., Charles L. (dec.); m. Ernst Freese, 1986 (dec. 1990). BS with honors, Acadia U., Can., 1951, MS, 1952; PhD, Brown U., 1957; DSc (hon.), Acadia U., 1990. Rsch. pathologist UCLA Med. Sch., 1959-61; asst. prof. Calif. State U., Northridge, 1961-66; lab. instr. Georgetown U., Washington, 1970-72, asst. prof., 1972-76; dep. dir. neurol. disorder program Nat. Inst. Neurol. and Communicative Disorders and Stroke, NIH, Bethesda, Md., 1976-81, acting dep. dir., 1981-83, dep. dir., 1983-87; dep. dir. extramural rsch. Office of Dir. NIH, 1987-90; sci. liaison Centro Studio Multicentrico

Internazionale Sulla Demenza, Washington, 1990-95. Cons. Nat. Rsch. Coun., Italy, 1991-97, The Charles A. Dana Found., N.Y.C., 1993-98, Edn. Commn. of the States, 1996-99. Editor: Alzheimer's Disease: Senile Dementia and Related Disorders, 1978, Neurosecretion and Brain Peptides, Implications for Brain Functions and Neurol. Disease, 1981, The Early Story of Alzheimer's Disease, 1987, Alzheimer Disease, 1994, 2d edit., 1999, Alzheimer Disease: The Changing View, 2000; contbr. articles to profl. jours. Pres. Woman's Club, McLean, Va., 1968-69; bd. dirs. Fairfax County (Va.) YWCA, 1969-70; pres. Avenel Homeowner's Assn., 1998; pres. Emerson Unitarian Ch., 1964-66; mem. Bethesda Pl. Cmty. Coun., 1992-95, pres., 1993-94; mem. Dana Alliance for Brain Initiatives, 1993—; bd. dirs. Wilmington NC Child Advocacy Commn., 1998-2002; mem. vol. guild St. John's Mus. Art, Wilmington; chair Vol. Guild Cameron Art Mus., Wilmington, 2002-03, Cameron Art Mus. Bd., 2003-06; vestry St. Andrew's on the Sound, Wilmington, 2004-06. Recipient Can. NRC award Acadia U., 1951-52, NIH Dir.'s award, 1978, Spl. Achievement award NIH, 1981, 83, Superior Svc. award USPHS, 1986, Presdl. Rank award meritorious sr. exec., 1989, Genesis award Alzheimer's Assn., 2005; Universal Match Found. fellow Brown U., 1956-57, Fed. Exec. Inst. Leadership fellow, 1980 Fellow AAAS; mem. Am. Neurol. Assn., Internat. Brain Rsch. Orgn., World Fedn. Neurology Rsch. Group on Dementias (exec. sec. Am. region 1984-86, chmn. 1986-93), Alzheimer's Disease Internat., Soc. for Neurosci. (emeritus), Acad. of Medicine Washington, Dana Alliance for Brain Initiatives.

BICK, RODGER LEE, hematologist, researcher, oncologist, educator; b. San Francisco, May 21, 1942; s. Jack Arthur and Pauline (Jensen) B.; m. Marcella Bick, Mar. 3, 1980 (dec. Feb. 1995); children: Shauna Nicole, Michelle Leanne. MD, U. Calif., Irvine, 1970; PhD, Acad. Medicine, Bialystok, Poland, 1995. Diplomate Am. Bd. Quality Assessment, Am. Bd. Forensic Medicine in Oncology, Hematology, Thrombosis, Hemostasis and Product Liability, Internat. Bd. Thrombosis, Hemostasis & Vascular Medicine, Am. Bd. Pain Mgmt. Med. intern Kern County Gen. Hosp., UCLA, Bakersfield, Calif., 1970-71, internal medicine resident, 1971-72; fellow in hematology-med. oncology UCLA/Bay Area Hematology Oncology Med. Group, West Los Angeles, Calif., 1974-76; med. staff various hosps., Calif., 1974-77, med. staff, extensive adminstrv. and com. work Bakersfield, Calif., 1977-92; med. dir. oncology hematology Presbyn. Comprehensive Cancer Ctr., Presbyn. Hosp., Dallas, 1992-95. Staff hematologist/oncologist Bay Area Hematology Oncology Med. Group, Santa Monica, Calif., 1976-77, med. dir. Calif. Coagulation Labs., Inc., Bakersfield, 1977-92, San Joaquin Hematology Oncology Med. Group, 1977-92, Regional Cancer and Blood Disease Ctr. Kern, Bakersfield, 1986-92; asst. clin. prof. to clin. prof. medicine UCLA Ctr. Health Scis., 1976-94, assoc. prof. to prof. allied health profns. Calif. State U., Bakersfield, 1980-92, clin. prof. nursing and health scis., 1982-92; adj. assoc. prof. medicine/physiology, Wayne State U., Detroit; adj. clin. faculty Wesley Med. Ctr. and U. Kans. Med. Sch., Wichita, 1984-86; clin. prof. medicine U. Tex. Southwestern Med. Ctr., 1993—, clin. prof. pathology, 1993—; prof. hematology U. Tasmania Sch. Medicine, 1996; hematology cons. NASA; med. dir. UCLA/Kern Cancer Program, 1991-92, Ctrl. Calif. Heart Inst., 1990-92; invited spkr. and presenter in field, numerous internat. symposia and confs.; dir. numerous workshops in field. Author: Disseminated Intravascular Coagulation and Related Syndromes, 1983, Disorders of Hemostasis and Thrombosis: Principles of Clinical Practice, 1985, 2d. edit., 1992, 3d edit., 1997, Disorders of Thrombosis and Hemostasis, 2002; guest editor, contbr.: Thrombohemorrhagic Disorders Perplexing to the Hematologist Oncologist, 1992; guest editor: Laboratory Diagnosis of Hemostasis Problems, I, 1994, II, 1995, (monograph) Seminars in Thrombosis and Hemostasis, 1994, Common Bleeding and Clotting Problems for the Internist, 1994; editor-in-chief: Hematology: Principles of Clinical and Laboratory Practice, 2 vols., 1993, Paraneoplastic Syndromes, Hematology Oncology Clinics of North America, 1996, Hematological Complications of Obstetrics, Pregnancy and Gynecology, 2006; editor: Current Concepts of Thrombosis, 1998; contbr. numerous chpts. to books; author monographs and lab. manuals; contbr. over 250 articles and papers and numerous revs. to profl. jours. and conf. procs.; patentee in field; editor-in-chief Jour. Clin. and Applied Thrombosis/Hemostasis & Vascular Medicine, Thrombosis and Thrombophilia, 2003; mem. editl. bd. Am. Jour. Clin. Pathology, Internat. Jour. Haematology. Bd. dirs., exec. com. Bakersfield Symphony Orch., 1988-92. Fellow ACP, Am. Soc. Clin. Pathologists, Assn. Clin. Scientists, Am. Soc. Coagulationists, Internat. Soc. Hematology, Am. Coll. Angiology, Internat. Coll. Angiology, Nat. Acad. Clin. Biochemistry, Am. Heart Assn. (coun. on thrombosis, circulation and atherosclerosis; rsch. and grant peer rev. com. 1980-86), Am. Geriat. Soc. (founding fellow, Am. Stroke Assn., Am. Soc. Angiology; mem. AMA, AAAS, Am. Assn. Blood Banks, Am. Soc. Internal Medicine, Am. Soc. Hematology, Internat. Soc. Thrombosis and Haemostasis, Am. Assn. Study of Neoplastic Disease, Am. Assn. Clin. Rsch., Am. Cancer Soc., Internat. Assn. Study of Lung Cancer (founding mem.), Fedn. Am. Scientists, N.Y. Acad. Scis., Calif. Soc. Internal Medicine, Calif. Med. Assn., Calif. Thoracic Soc., Haematology Soc. Australia, Internat. Consensus Com. on Autithrombotic Therapy, numerous others. Lutheran. Avocations: ocean sailing, classical piano, brass musical instruments, photography, target archery, astronomy and astrophotography. Office: 10455 N Central Expy Ste 109 Dallas TX 75231-2215 Office Phone: 214-668-2425. Business E-Mail: rbick@thrombosis.com.

BICKART, THEODORE ALBERT, university president emeritus; b. NYC, Aug. 25, 1935; s. Theodore Roosevelt and Edna Catherine (Pink) B.; m. Carol Florence Nichols, June 14, 1958 (div. Dec. 1973); children: Karl Jeffrey, Lauren Spencer; m. Frani W. Rudolph, Aug. 14, 1982; 1 stepchild, Jennifer Anne Cumming. B Engring. Sci., Johns Hopkins U., 1957, MS, 1958, DEng, 1960; D Univ. (hon.), Dneprodzerzhinst State Tech. U., Ukraine, 1996. Asst. prof. elec. and computer engring. Syracuse (N.Y.) U., 1963-65, assoc. prof., 1965-70, prof., 1970-89, assoc. to vice chancellor for acad. affairs for computer resources devel., 1983-85, dean L.C. Smith Coll. Engring., 1984-89; prof. elec. engring., dean engring. Mich. State U., East Lansing, 1989-98; pres. Colo. Sch. Mines, Golden, 1998-2000. Vis. scholar U. Calif., Berkeley, 1977; Fulbright lectr. Kiev Poly Inst., USSR, 1981; vis. lectr. Nanjing Inst. Tech., China, 1981; hon. disting. prof. Taganrog Radio Engring. Inst., Russia, 1992—; fellow Accreditation Bd. for Engring. and Tch., Engring. Accreditation Commn., exec. com., 1998-2000; chmn. Engring. Workforce Commn., 1996-98; elected-mem. Johns Hopkins U. Soc. Scholars, 2001. Co-author: Electrical Network Theory, 1969, Linear Network Theory, 1981; contbr. numerous articles to profl. jours. Served to 1st lt. U.S. Army, 1961-63 Recipient numerous rsch. grants. Fellow IEEE (best paper awards Syracuse sect. 1969, 70, 73, 74, 77, chmn. com. on engring. accreditation activities 1996-98, bd. ednl. activities 1999, chmn. accreditation policy coun. 2001-2003, Meritorious Achievement award 2006, Meritorious Svc. citation 2006), Am. Soc. Engring. Edn. (v.p. 1997-99); mem. Am. Math. Soc., Assn. for Computing Machinery, Soc. for Indsl. and Applied Math., N.Y. Acad. Scis., Ukrainian Acad. Engring. Scis.), Internat. Higher Edn. Acad. Scis. (Russia), Internat. Acad. Informatics (Russia), Johns Hopkins U. Soc. Scholars., Johns Hopkins U. Alumni Assn. (Disting. Alumnus award), ABET Avocations: bicycling, hiking, gardening. Home: 541 Wyoming Cir Golden CO 80403-0900 Home Phone: 303-277-0125. Personal E-mail: tabickart@comcast.net. Business E-Mail: tbickart@mines.edu.

BICKEL, FLOYD GILBERT, III, investment counselor; b. St. Louis, Jan. 10, 1944; s. Floyd Gilbert and Mary Mildred (Welch) B.; m. Martha Wohler, June 11, 1966; children: Christine Carleton, Susan Marie, Katherine Anne, Jennifer Anne, Laura Elizabeth, Andrew Barrett (dec.) BS in Bus. Adminstrn., Washington U., St. Louis, 1966; MS in Commerce, St. Louis U., 1968. Rschr. Yates, Woods & Co., St. Louis, 1966-67; asst. br. mgr. E.F. Hutton & Co., Inc., St. Louis, 1967-70, v.p. dir. consulting svcs., 1980-88; asst. v.p., resident mgr. Bache & Co., Inc., St. Louis, 1970-72; pres. Donelan-Phelps Investment Advisors, Inc., St. Louis, 1972—80; v.p. Merrill Lynch & Co., St. Louis, 1988—2003; sr. v.p. Morgan Stanley, St. Louis, 2003—. Bd. dirs. Summit Mktg. Group, Eagle River LLC, Washington U., St. Louis Regional Commerce and Growth Assn., Innovate St. Louis. Mem. City of Des Peres (Mo.), Planning and Zoning Commn., 1975-76; chm. St. Louis County Bd. Equalization, 1976-79; pub. safety commr. City of Des Peres, 1977-80, mem. audit and fin. com., 1980-86; mem. State of Mo. Gov.'s Crime Commn., 1981-92; bd. dirs. Villa Duchesne Sch., 1986-92; alderman City of Huntleigh, 1998-2002, mayor, 2002—; chmn. St Louis Arch Angels; trustee Washington U., 2005-07. Recipient Disting. Alumni award, Washington U., 2002, Washington U. Olin Sch. Bus., 2005. Mem.: St. Louis Acad. Sci. (bd. dirs. 2007—), John M. Olin Bus. Sch. Washington U. Alumni Assn. (pres. 1995—96, nat. coun. 2001—), St. Louis Soc. Fin. Analysts, Internat. Soc. Cert. Employee Benefit Specialists, St. Louis Club, John's Island Club, Eagle Springs Golf Club, Cordillera Golf Club, Beaver Creek Club, Bellerive Country Club. Republican. Roman Catholic. Home: 30 Huntleigh Woods Saint Louis MO 63131-4813 Office: Morgan Stanley 700 Corp Park Dr Saint Louis MO 63105 Home Phone: 314-965-1030; Office Phone: 314-889-9836. Business E-Mail: gil.bickel@morganstanley.com.

BICKEL, JOHN W., II, lawyer; b. Champaign, Ill., Sept. 9, 1948; s. John William and Virginia Bickel; children: Hannah, Molly, Sarah. BS, U.S. Mil. Acad., 1970; JD, So. Meth. U., 1976. Bar: N.Y. 1988, Tex. 1976, U.S. Ct. Appeals (5th and 11th cirs.) 1980, U.S. Supreme Ct. 1983. Assoc. Thompson & Knight, Dallas, 1980-83; ptnr. Brown, Thomas, Karger & Bickel, Dallas, 1983-84; co-mng., co-founder, ptnr. Bickel & Brewer, Dallas, 1984—; co-founding ptnr. Bickel & Brewer Storefront, PLLC, Dallas; founder Bickel & Brewer Foundation. Adv. mem. Tex. Supreme Ct. Jury Charge Task Force, 1992; mem. com. for qualified judiciary. Co-author: "Exhibits and other Evidence," Chpt. 13, Lawyers Cooperative Fed. Practice Guide. Mem. exec. bd. So. Meth. U. Sch. Law.; mem. Hiram A. Boaz Soc. So. Meth. U.; mem. Tex. Com.: A Time to Lead--The Campaign for So. Meth. U.; mem. adv. com. Southwestern Ball, 1997-2000, co-founder Future Leaders Program, Bickel & Brewer Nat. Pub. Policy Forum. Named a Tex. Super Lawyer, Tex. Monthly Mag., 2003, 2004, 2005, Best Lawyer in Dallas, D Mag. Fellow Tex. Bar Found., Dallas Bar Found. (sustaining life); mem. ABA, State Bar Tex. (past chmn. litigation com. of environ. and natural resource law sect.), N.Y. Bar Assn., Dallas Bar Assn., Markey/Wigmore Inns of Ct. (Chgo. chpt.), West Point Assn. Grads. (trustee 1997-2000, strategic planning com. 1997-2005, adv. com. to bd. trustee, 2006-), West Point Soc. North Tex. (bd. dirs. 1992-2002). Office: Bickel & Brewer 4800 Bank One Ctr 1717 Main St Ste 4800 Dallas TX 75201-4651 E-mail: jwb@bickelbrewer.com.

BICKEL, PETER JOHN, statistician, educator; b. Bucharest, Romania, Sept. 21, 1940; arrived in U.S., 1957, naturalized, 1964; s. Eliezer and P. Madeleine (Moscovici) B.; m. Nancy Kramer, Mar. 2, 1964; children: Amanda, Stephen. AB, U. Calif., Berkeley, 1960, MA, 1961, PhD, 1963; PhD (hon.), Hebrew U. Jerusalem, 1988. Asst. prof. stats. U. Calif., Berkeley, 1964-67, assoc. prof., 1967-70, prof., 1970—, chmn. dept. stats., 1976-79, dean phys. scis., 1980-86, chmn. dept. stats., 1993-97. Vis. lectr. math. Imperial Coll., London, 1965-66; fellow J.S. Guggenheim Meml. Found., 1970-71, J.D. and Catherine T. MacArthur Found., 1984-89; NATO sr. sci. fellow, 1974; chmn. com. on applied and theoretical stats. NRC, 1998-2000, mem. bd. on math. scis., 2000—, chmn., 2000-03; chmn. sci. adv. coun. Stats. and Applied Math. Inst., NSF. Author: (with K. Doksum) Mathematical Statistics, 1976, 2d edit., 2000, (with C. Klaassen, Y. Ritov and J. Wellner) Efficient and Adaptive Estimation in Semiparametric Models, 1993; assoc. editor Annals of Math. Stats., 1968-76, 86-93, PNAS, 1996—2000, Bernouilli, 1996—, Statistica Sinica, 1996—2003; contbr. articles to profl. jours. Decorated comdr. Order Orange Nassau (Netherlands);J.D. and Catherine T. MacArthur Found. fellow, 1984-89. Fellow AAAS (chair sect. U 1996-97), Inst. Math. Stats. (pres. 1980), Am. Statis. Assn.; mem. NAS, Royal Statis. Soc., Internat. Statis. Inst., Am. Acad. Arts and Scis., Royal Netherlands Acad. Arts and Scis., Bernoulli Soc. (pres. 1990). Office: U Calif Dept Stats Evans Hall Berkeley CA 94720 Home Phone: 510-526-4055; Office Phone: 510-642-1381. Business E-Mail: bickel@stat.berkeley.edu.

BICKERS, DAVID RINSEY, dermatologist, educator, department chairman, health facility administrator; b. Richmond, Va., Sept. 23, 1941; s. William McKenzie and Helen Virginia (Fitzpatrick) B.; m. Melinda Lee Jarger, May 30, 1970 (div. 2003); 1 child, McKenzie Winchester; m. Sara Hurcburt Patterson, Nov. 13, 2004. AB, Georgetown U., 1963; MD, U. Va., 1967. Intern in medicine U. Iowa Hosps., Iowa City, 1967-68; resident in dermatology skin and cancer unit N.Y.U. Med. Center, 1970-73; NIH tng. fellow, guest investigator Rockefeller U., 1971-73, R.J. Reynolds scholar in clin. medicine, asst. prof., asso. physician, 1976-77; asst. prof. dermatology Columbia U. Coll. Physicians and Surgeons, 1973-76; asst. attending dermatologist Presbyn. Hosp., NYC, 1973-76, med. dir., 1997—; prof. dermatology, chmn. dept. Case Western Res. U. Med. Sch., 1977-93, assoc. dean, 1990-93; med. dir. N.Y. Hosp., NYC, 1997—. Dir. dermatology svc. U. Hosps., 1977-93, sr. v.p. med. program planning, 1977-89, chief staff, sr. v.p. med. affairs, 1990-93; dir. dermatology svc. Cleve. VA Hosp., 1977-89; mem. gen. medicine A study sect., NIH, 1980-84, chmn., 1982-84; adv. coun. Nat. Inst. Arthritis, Musculoskeletal and Skin Diseases, NIH, 1988-92; Carl Truman Nelson prof. dermatology, chmn. Dept. Coll. Physicians and Surgeons, Columbia U., 1994—; dir. dermatology svc. NY Presbyn. Hosp., 1994—. Author: (with L.C. Harber) Photosensitivity Diseases: Principles of Diagnosis and Treatment, 1981, 2d. edit., 1989, (with Hazen and Lynch) Clinical Pharmacology of Skin Disease, 1984; mem. editorial bd. Jour. Am. Acad. Dermatology, 1979-85, Physicians Drug Alert, 1982—, Today's Therapeutic Trends, 1983-2004, Photodermatology, 1983-88; assoc. editor Jour. Investigative Dermatol., 1987-97. Served as officer M.C. USAF, 1968-70. Decorated Air Force Commendation medal. Mem. Assn. Am. Physicians, Am. Soc. Clin. Investigation, Am. Soc. Pharmacology and Exptl. Therapeutics, Am. Fedn. Clin. Rsch., Am. Soc. Photobiology, Am. Acad. Dermatology (hon.), Am. Dermatol. Assn., Soc. Investigative Dermatology (bd. dirs. 1985-89, sec.-treas. 1989—, pres. 2003), Pasteur Club (Cleve.), Med. Strollers, Skin Pharmacology Soc. (sec. 1985-87, pres. 1987-89), Dermatology Found. (sec.-treas. 1984, chmn. bd. 1987-88), Bicontinental Assn. Edn. and Rsch. in Dermatology (founding mem.), German Dermatol. Soc. (hon.), Am. Univ. Beirut (bd. trustees, 1996-, chair health sci. com., 2005-), Austrian Dermatol. Soc. (hon.), Commanderie De Bordeaux, Confrérie des Chevaliers du Tastevin, Expert Panel Rsch. Inst. for Fragrance Materials (chair, 2002-2005), Am. Bd. Dermatology (bd. dirs. 1997-2005, pres. 2005) Office: Columbia Univ Med Ctr IP-1214 161 Fort Washington Ave New York NY 10032-3713 Office Phone: 212-305-5565. Business E-Mail: drb25@columbia.edu.

BICKERSTAFF, BERNIE (BERNARD TYRONE BICKERSTAFF SR.), professional sports team executive, former professional basketball coach; b. Benham, Ky., Nov. 2, 1944; m. Eugenia King; children: Tim, Robin, Cydni, Bernard, John. Grad., U. San Diego. Asst. coach U. San Diego, 1968—69, head coach, 1969—73; asst. coach Washington Bullets, 1973—85; head coach Seattle SuperSonics, 1985—90, v.p. ops., 1990; pres., gen. mgr. Denver Nuggets, 1990-97, head coach, 1994—96, Washington Wizards, 1997-98; part owner, gen. mgr., head coach Internat. Basketball League St. Louis Swarm, 1999; gen. mgr. Charlotte Bobcats, 2004—07, head coach, 2004—07, exec. v.p., 2007—. Named Coach of Yr., NBA, 1987; named to U. San Diego Hall of Fame, 1995. Office: Charlotte Bobcats 333 E Trade St Charlotte NC 28202*

BICKETT, BRENT B., insurance company executive; BSBA, U. So. Calif., LA, 1986; MBA, UCLA, 1990. Mng. dir. real estate, gaming, lodging and leisure group Bear, Stearns & Co. Inc., 1997—99, mem. investment banking divsn., 1990—99; with Fidelity Nat. Fin., Inc., Jacksonville, Fla., 1999—, exec. v.p. fin., co-pres. Office: Fidelity Nat Fin Inc 601 Riverside Ave Jacksonville FL 32204 Office Phone: 888-934-3354.*

BICKFORD, MARGARET WYATT, minister; b. Cleve., Nov. 3, 1936; d. Ralph Moore and Virginia Hixon Wyatt; m. William Edwin Bickford, Oct. 12, 1963; children: Virginia Musumeci, William Ralph. BA, Wellesley Coll., 1958; BArch, Boston Arch. Ctr., 1965; MDiv, Episc. Divinity Sch., 1978; DMin, Boston U. Sch. Theology, 1996. Ordained elder N.H. Conf. United Meth. Ch.; cert. grief counselor Assn. Death Edn. and Counseling. Sec. Bourne & Nichols, Archs., Boston, 1958—62, Todesco & Assocs., Boston, 1962—63, Polaroid Corp., Cambridge, Mass., 1963—64; intern Bon Secours Hosp., Methuen, Mass., 1976—77, Mass. Rehab. Hosp., Boston, 1977—78; educator Mental Health Ctr. So. N.H., 1978—81; pastor, counselor First United Meth. Ch., Methuen, Mass., 1981—89; coord. bereavement, chaplain Rockingham Hospice, Salem-Derry, NH, 1983—89; chaplain Lawrence Gen. Hosp., Mass., 1981—85; pastor Ayers Village United Meth. Ch., Haverhill, Mass., 1983—89; intern Tewksbury State Hosp., Mass., 1985—86, Elliott Hosp., Manchester, NH, 1986—87; pastoral counselor, bereavement coord. Lourdes Hospice, Paducah, Ky., 1989—93; pastor Grace United Meth. Ch., Canaan, Vt., 1993—98, Farnham United Meth. Ch., Pitts., NH, 1993—98, Plymouth (N.H.) United Meth. Ch., 1998—2004, Thornton (N.H.) United Meth. Ch., 1998—2004, Ashland (N.H.) United Meth. Ch., 2000—04, Milan (N.H.) Cmty. Ch., 2004—. Co-founder, pres. Rockingham Hospice, Derry, NH, 1983—89; chaplain Lawrence Gen. Hosp., NH, 1981—85, Pemi-Baker Home Health and Hospice, Plymouth, NH, 2001—, chmn. hospice com., pastoral counselor, 2001—. Author: Headwaters Harvest, 1997, Getting A Grip on Grief, 2006, United in Service, 2006. Fellow: Assn. Profl. Chaplains; mem.: Am. Acad. Bereavement, Nat. Hospice and Palliative Care Orgn. Coun. Hospice Profls., Assn. Death Edn. and Counseling (grief counselor 1991—). Avocations: music, travel, history, reading. Office Phone: 603-786-2475. Personal E-mail: webmbkfd@emailmv.com.

BICKFORD, MERIS J., lawyer, bank executive; JD, Univ. Maine, 1986. Asst. v.p. Merrill Merchants Bank, Bangor, Maine. Mem.: Maine State Bar Found. (bd. of gov.), Maine State Bar Assn. (pres.-elect 2004, past dist. 5 gov., pres. 2005). Office: Merrill Merchants Bank 201 Main St PO Box 925 Bangor ME 04402-0925 Business E-Mail: mbickford@merrillmerchants.com.

BICKS, PETER ANDREWS, lawyer; b. Washington, Dec. 5, 1959; s. Robert Alan and Patricia (Hughes) B.; m. Linda Danovitch, Nov. 16, 1997; children, Avery Andrews, Isabella Sara Celia, Phoebe Hannah. BA, Pomona Coll., 1982; JD, Georgetown U., 1986. Bar: N.Y. 1987, U.S. Dist. Ct. (so. dist.) N.Y. 1990, U.S. Dist. Ct. (ea. dist.) N.Y. 1993, U.S. Dist. Ct. Ariz. 1994, U.S. Ct. Appeals (2nd cir.) 1998. Asst. press sec. John Anderson Presdl. Campaign, Washington, 1980; lead advance person Mayor Ed Koch, NYC, 1981-82; mgmt. analyst N.Y.C. (N.Y.) Dept. Sanitation, 1982-83; ptnr. Donovan Leisure Newton Irvine, NYC, 1995-98; ptnr., litigation dept. Orrick, Herrington & Sutcliffe, LLP, NYC, 1998—. Pres. 175 E. 73d St. Corp., N.Y.C., 1987-97. Mem. ABA, N.Y. State Bar Assn., Seawanhaka Corinthian Yacht Club, Castine Golf Club, The Creek Club. Republican. Avocations: sailing, tennis, golf. Home: 1150 5th Ave Apt 6C New York NY 10128-0724 Office: Orrick Herrington & Sutcliffe LLP 666 5th Ave New York NY 10103-1798 Office Phone: 212-506-3742. Business E-Mail: pbicks@orrick.com.

BIDART, FRANK, English educator, poet; b. Bakersfield, Calif., 1939; Attended, U. Calif., Riverside, Harvard U. Faculty mem. Wellesley Coll., Mass., 1972—, Andrew W. Mellon prof. English Mass. Poet Golden State, 1973, The Book of the Body, 1977, The Sacrifice, 1983, In the Western Night: Collected Poems 1965-90, 1990, Desire, 1997, Music Like Dirt, 2002; co-editor (with David Gewanter): Collected Poems of Robert Lowell, 2003. Recipient Bernard R. Conners prize, The Paris Review, 1981, Lila Wallace Reader's Digest Found. Writer's award, 1993, Shelley award, Poetry Soc. Am., Rebekka Bobbitt award for Poetry, 1998, Lannan Writer's award, 1998, Bollingen Prize in Am. Poetry, Yale U. Libr., 2007. Mem.: Am. Acad. Poets (chancellor 2003—, Wallace Stevens award), AAAL (Morton Dauwen Zabel award 1995). Office: Wellesley Coll Founders Hall Rm 124B 106 Central St Wellesley MA 02481-8268 Office Phone: 781-283-2710.*

BIDDLE, BRUCE JESSE, social psychologist, educator; b. Ossining, NY, Dec. 30, 1928; s. William Wishart and Loureide Jeanette (Cobb) B.; m. Ellen Catherine Horgan; children: David Charles, William Jesse, Jennifer Loureide; m. Barbara Julianne Bank, June 19, 1976. AB in Math., Antioch Coll., Yellow Springs, Ohio, 1950; postgrad., U. N.C., 1950-51; PhD in Social Psychology, U. Mich., 1957. Asst. prof. sociology U. Ky., 1957-58; assoc. prof. edn. U. Kansas City, 1958-60; assoc. prof. psychology and sociology U. Mo., Columbia, 1960-66, prof., 1966-2000, prof. emeritus, 2000—, dir. Ctr. Rsch. in Social Behavior, 1966-96. Vis. assoc. prof. U. Queensland, Australia, 1965; vis. prof. Monash U., Australia, 1969, vis. fellow Australian Nat. U., 1977, 85, 93. Author: (with R.S. Adams) Realities of Teaching: Explorations with Videotape, 1970, (with M.J. Dunkin) The Study of Teaching, 1974, (with T.L. Good and J. Brophy) Teachers Make a Difference, 1975, Role Theory: Expectations, Identities and Behaviors, 1979, (with D.C. Berliner) The Manufactured Crisis: Myths, Fraud, and the Attack on America's Public Schools, 1995, (with L.J. Saha) The Untested Accusation: Principals, Research Knowledge, and Policy Making in Schools, 2002; editor: (with W.J. Ellena) contemporary Research on Teacher Effectiveness, 1964, (with E.J. Thomas) Role Theory: Concepts and Research, 1966, (with P.H. Rossi) The New Media: Their Impact on Education, 1966, (with D.S. Anderson) Knowledge for Policy: Improving Education Through Research, 1991, (with T.L. Good and I.F. Goodson) International Handbook of Teachers and Teaching, 1997, Social Class, Poverty, and Education, 2001. Served with U.S. Army, 1954-56. Fellow APA, Am. Psychol. Soc., Australian Psychol. Soc.; mem. Am. Ednl. Research Assn., Australian Assn. Rsch. Edn., Am. Sociol. Assn., Midwest Sociol. Soc. Home: 924 Yale Columbia MO 65203-1874 Office: U Mo Dept Psychology McAlester Hall Rm 210 Columbia MO 65211-0001 Business E-Mail: BiddleB@missouri.edu.

BIDDLE, DONALD RAY, aerospace transportation executive; b. Alton, Mo., June 30, 1936; s. Ernest Everet and Dortha Marie (McGuire) B.; m. Nancy Ann Dunham, Mar. 13, 1955; children: Jeanne Kay Northington, Mitchell Lee, Charles Alan. Student, El Dorado Jr. Coll., Kans., 1953-55, Pratt Jr. Coll., 1955-56; BSME, Washington U., St. Louis, 1961; postgrad. computer sci., Pa. State U. Ext., 1963; cert. bus. mgmt., Alexander Hamilton Inst., 1958. Design group engr. Emerson Elec. Mfg., St. Louis, 1957-61; design specialist Boeing Vertol, Springfield, Pa., 1962; cons. engr. Ewing Tech. Design, Phila., 1962-66; chief engr. rotary wing Gates Learjet, Wichita, Kans., 1967-70; dir. engring., R&D, BP Chems., Inc. Advanced Material Divsn., Stockton, Calif., 1971-93; prin. Biddle & Assocs., Consulting Engrs., Stockton, 1993—; pres., CEO, Big Valley Aviation, Inc., Stockton, 1997-98; CEO, Propulsion Technologies, Inc., Stockton, 1999—, United Propeller Technologies, Inc., Stockton, 1999—. Guest lectr. on manrated structures, devel. proprietary designs, small bus. devel. to various univs. and tech. socs. Patentee landing gear designs, inflatable rescue sys., glass retention sys., adjustable jack sys., cold weather start flourescent lamp, paper honeycomb core post-process sys. Scoutmaster, counselor, instl. rep. Boy Scouts Am., St. Ann, Mo., 1956-61; mem.

Springfield Sch. Bd., 1964. Mem. ASME, ASTM, AIAA, Am. Helicopter Soc. (sec.-treas. Wichita chpt. 1969), Am. Mgmt. Assn., Exptl. Pilots Assn., Soc. for Advancement of Metals and Process Engring. Republican. Methodist. Home: 6449 Embarcadero Dr Stockton CA 95219-3800 Office: United Propeller Inc 2478 Wilcox Rd Stockton CA 95215-2319

BIDDLE, FLORA MILLER, art patron, museum administrator; Granddaughter of Gertrude Vanderbilt Whitney; m. Sydney; 4 children BA, Manhattanville Coll., 1978. V.p. Whitney Mus. Am. Art, NYC, 1958—77, pres., 1978-85, chair, 1985—95, hon. trustee. Author: The Whitney Women and the Museum They Made, 1999. Mem.: NYC Art Commn. (mem. 1980—90). Home: 17 E 97th St Apt 6A New York NY 10029 Personal E-mail: florabiddle@gmail.com.

BIDDLE, JUDITH ANN, retired writer; b. Knoxville, Tenn., Feb. 11, 1940; d. Charles Eugene Sexton and Molly Katherine Sise; m. Clarence Edward Biddle, Apr. 20, 1957; children: Clarence Edward, Robert Allen, Mandy Aleesa, David Eugene. Columnist Tri-County News, Seymour, Tenn., 1980—83; supr. Ho. Lloyd/Christmas Around the World, Kansas City, Mo., 1991—2000; feature writer Strawberry Plains Chronicle, Tenn., 1998—99. Guest editl. writer The Knoxville Jour., Tenn., 1987; guest spkr. Aglow Internat., Sevierville, Tenn., 2003. Author: (book) On the Outside of life, Looking in; contbr. articles to mags. Recipient First Pl. Book prize, Rutledge Hill Press, Nashville, 1986. Republican. Personal E-mail: cbiddle070@comcast.net.

BIDDLE, MICHAEL, plastics company executive; BS in Chemical Engring., U. Louisville; MS in mgmt. sci., Stanford U. Graduate Sch. of Bus.; PhD in Polymer Sci. and Engring., Case Western Reserve U. With Gen. Electric, Cummins Engine Co., Dow Chemical; founder, CEO MBA Polymers Inc., 1994—. Contbr. scientific papers about recycling plastics; spkr. in field (recycling plastics). Fellow Sloan Fellow (Exec. MBA Program), Dow Chemical at Stanford U. Graduate Sch. of Bus. Office: MBA Polymers Inc 500 West Ohio Ave Richmond CA 94804 Office Phone: 510-231-9031. Office Fax: 510-231-0302. E-mail: mbiddle@mbapolymers.com.

BIDELMAN, WILLIAM PENDRY, astronomer, educator; b. LA, Sept. 25, 1918; s. William Pendry and Dolores (De Remer) B.; m. Verna Pearl Shirk, June 19, 1940; children: Lana Louise Stone (dec. Mar. 2000), Linda Elizabeth McKinley, Billie Jean Little, Barbara Jo Talley. Student, U. N.D., 1936-37; SB, Harvard, 1940; PhD, U. Chgo., 1943. Physicist, Aberdeen Proving Ground, Md., 1943-45; instr., then asst. prof. astronomy Yerkes Obs., U. Chgo., 1945-53; asst. astronomer, then. assoc. astronomer Lick Obs., U. Calif., 1953-62; prof. U. Mich., 1962-69, U. Tex. at Austin, 1969-70, Case Western Res. U., Cleve., 1970-86, prof. emeritus, 1986—. Chmn. dept., dir. Warner and Swasey Obs., 1970-75; mem. adv. panel on astronomy NSF, 1959-62; mem. NRC adv. com. on astronomy Office Naval Rsch., 1964-67. Contbr. articles to profl. jours. Mem. Am. Astron. Soc. (councilor 1959-62, participant vis. prof. program 1961-65), Astron. Soc. Pacific (editor Publs. 1956-61), Internat. Astron. Union (commns. 29, 45, pres. 1964-67), Phi Beta Kappa. Presbyterian. Achievements include discovery of lines of mercury, krypton and xenon in stellar spectra; discovery of phosphorus stars; co-discovery of barium stars; research in spectral classification, astronomical data and observational astrophysics. Home: 3171 Chelsea Dr Cleveland Heights OH 44118-1256 Office: Case Western Res U Dept Astronomy 10900 Euclid Ave Cleveland OH 44106-7215 Office Phone: 216-368-4003. Business E-Mail: wsobs@grendel.astr.cwru.edu.

BIDEN, BEAU (JOSEPH ROBINETTE BIDEN III), state attorney general, lawyer; b. Del., Feb. 3, 1969; s. Joseph Robinette and Jill Tracy (Jacobs) Biden; m. Hallie Biden; 2 children. BA in European Hist., U. Pa., 1991; JD, Syracuse U. Coll. Law, 1994. Bar: Del., Md., US Dist. Ct. Del. Law clk. to Hon. Steven J. McAuliffe US Dist. Ct. NH, 1994—95; counsel, Office of Policy Devel. US Dept. Justice, Washington, 1995, fed. prosecutor, 1995—2002, legal adv. Kosovo, 2001, fed. prosecutor (ea. dist.) Pa. Phila., 1997—2002; atty., civil litig. Monzack and Monaco, Wilmington, Del., 2002—04; ptnr. Bifferato, Gentilotti, Biden & Balick LLC (formerly Bifferato Gentilotti & Biden LLC), Washington, 2004—; atty. gen. State of Del., Dover, 2007—. Mem., Bd. Dirs. Met. Wilmington Urban League, Wilmington Housing Partnership, World Affairs Coun. Wilmington. Capt., Del. Army Nat. Guard, mem. 261st Signal Brigade JAGC, Smyrna, Del. Mem.: Richard Rodney Inn of Ct. Office: Off of Atty Gen Carvel State Office Bldg 820 N French St Wilmington DE 19801 Office Phone: 302-425-5200, 302-577-8338.*

BIDEN, JOSEPH ROBINETTE, JR., senator; b. Scranton, Pa., Nov. 20, 1942; s. Joseph Robinette Sr.and Jean Finnegan Biden.; m. Jill Tracy Jacobs, June 17, 1977; children: Ashley Blazer, Joseph Robinette III, Robert Hunter. BA in History and Polit. Sci., U. Del., 1965; JD, Syracuse U., 1968. Bar: Del. 1968. Practiced law, Wilmington, 1968-72; US Senator from Del., 1973—; US Rep. to Gen. Assembly UN, 2000. Mem. New Castle County Coun., Del., 1970-72; adj. prof. Widener U. Sch. Law, 1991-; mem. com. fgn. relations US Senate, chmn., 2001-03, mem. com. judiciary, chmn., 1987-95. Recipient Friend of Zion Tribute award, Jerusalem Fund, 1998, Spirit of Enterprise award, US C. of C., 1998, Silver medal of Appreciation, Czech Republic, 1999, Senator of the Year, Nat. Assn. Police Organizations, 2000, Charles Dick medal of Merit, DE chapter, Nat. Guard Assn. of the US, 2002, Balkan Peace award, Albanian Amer. Civic League, 2002, Rail Spike award, Delmarva Rail Passenger Assn., 2003, Nat. Leadership award, Coalition for Juvenile Justice, 2004, Harry S. Truman award, Democratic Leadership Coun., 2005. Democrat. Roman Catholic. Office: US Senate 201 Russell Senate Bldg Washington DC 20510-0001 also: District Office Ste 2000 1105 North Market St Wilmington DE 19801-1233 Office Phone: 202-224-5042, 302-573-6345. Office Fax: 202-224-0139, 302-573-6351.*

BIDERMAN, CHARLES ISRAEL, diversified financial services company executive; b. NYC, Oct. 24, 1946; m. Brenda Carol Nicholson (div.); 1 child, John Patrick; m. Cheryl Marie Johnson, Sept. 8, 1985 (div.); 1 child, Christopher Isaac. BA, Bklyn. Coll., 1967; MBA, Harvard U., Cambridge, Mass., 1971. Assoc. editor Barron's Fin. Weekly, 1971-73; pres. Charles Biderman & Co., NYC and Nashville, 1980-89, Market St. Devel. Corp. (formerly Nashville Mgmt. Corp.), 1976-80; pres., CEO, Trimtabs Fin. Svcs., Inc., Santa Rosa, Calif., 1990—. Fin. editor Wall St. Final, NYC; editor Market Trim Tabs. (constructed over 200 home including) Gaslite Condominiums and Lafayette Townhouses, Seaside Park, N.J., Three Pence Brooke Townhomes, Jackson, N.J., N.J. Quail Farms, Jackson; author: (book) Trim Tabs Investing, 2005. Bd. dris. Tenn. Dance Theater, 1977—80, Children & Family Ctr., 1989. With USAF, 1966—67. Office: Trim Tabs Fin Svcs Inc 520 Mendocino Ave Ste 350 Santa Rosa CA 95401-5258 Office Phone: 707-525-1001.

BIDERMAN, PAUL LEONARD, lawyer, educator; b. Bklyn., Apr. 29, 1947; s. Samuel and Edith (Sherwin) B.; m. Ellen Naomi Geffner, Aug. 25, 1968; children: Eric Justin, Seth Jeremy. BA, CCNY, 1967; JD, NYU, 1970. Bar: N.Mex. 1971, U.S. Dist. Ct. N.Mex. 1971, U.S. Ct. Appeals (10th cir.) 1975, U.S. Supreme Ct. 1991. Staff atty., office dir. D.N.A. Legal Svcs., Inc., Crown Point & Window Rock, Navajo Nation, 1970-73; atty. pvt. practice, Albuquerque, 1973-75; staff atty., divsn. dir. Atty. Gen.'s Consumer Divsn., Santa Fe, 1975-78, 79-82; litigation dir. No. N.Mex. Legal Svcs., Santa Fe, 1978-79; sec. energy & minerals Energy & Minerals Dept., Santa Fe, 1983-86; atty. pvt. practice, Santa Fe, 1987-91; dir. Jud. Edn. Ctr. U. N.Mex. Sch. Law, Albuquerque, 1991—2005, dir. Inst. of Pub. Law, 2005—. Bd. dirs. Ghost Ranch/Plaza Resolana Conf. Ctrs., pres. 1996—. Co-author: Consumer Law in New Mexico, 1980. Bd. dirs. N.Mex. Cmty. Devel. Loan Fund, Albuquerque, 1992-97, past pres. Grantee State Justice Inst., Alexandria, Va., 1992-98, McCune Found., Santa Fe, 1993-98; recipient Jud. Edn. award ABA, 1997. Mem. Nat. Assn. State Jud. Educators (western regional dir. 1992-94, nat. sec. 1994-96). Democrat. Jewish. Avocations: jogging, hiking, weightlifting, reading. Office: U NMex Sch Law 1117 Stanford NE Albuquerque NM 87106-3700 Office Phone: 505-277-8789. E-mail: biderman@unm.edu.

BIDLACK, JEAN MARIE, pharmacologist, educator, researcher; b. Rochester, NY, Dec. 4, 1953; d. William Henry and Mary Louise (Naughton) Bidlack; m. Carl T. Helmers, Jr., Nov. 1, 2003. BA in Biology and Chemistry, Skidmore Coll., 1975; PhD in Biophysics, U. Rochester, 1979. Postdoctoral fellow U. Rochester, 1979-80, sr. instr. Ctr. Brain Rsch., 1980-81, asst. prof. brain rsch., 1981-87, assoc. prof. pharmacology, 1987-97, prof. pharmacology and physiology, 1997—. Cons. NSF, Washington, 1983—89, VA, Washington, 1986—88, Nat. Inst. Drug Abuse, Rockville, Md., 1987—, AIDS Study Sect., 1996—2002; mem. secretariat Internat. Narcotics Rsch. Conf., 1999, treas., 2004—. Contbr. articles to profl. jours. Recipient Sr. Sci. award, KO5 NIH, 1998—; fellow U. Rochester, 1975—79. Mem.: Internat. Narcotics Rsch. Conf. (v.p. and treas. 2004—), Soc. NeuroImmune Pharmacology (pres. 2004—05), Soc. Neurosci., Am. Soc. Pharmacology and Exptl. Therapeutics, Coll. on Problems of Drug Dependence Inc. Achievements include patents in field. Office: U Rochester/Sch Med and Dentistry Dept Pharm and Physiology 601 Elmwood Ave Rochester NY 14642-8711

BIDLACK, JERALD DEAN, manufacturing executive; b. Oakwood, Ohio, Nov. 18, 1935; s. Ansel Carol and Vivian Irene (Huff) B.; m. Ruth Heidenescher, Dec. 24, 1953; children: Jeffrey, Cynthia, Timothy, Bethann, Deborah. BSM.E., Tri-State U., 1956; postgrad., Wayne State U., 1959. Registered profl. engr., N.Y. Sr. engr. Cadillac Gage Co., Warren, Mich., 1956-63; engring. mgr. indsl. Moog Inc., East Aurora, NY, 1963-67, mng. dir. Boeblingen, Republic of Germany, 1967-69, pres. internat. ops. East Aurora, 1969—92; pres. Griffin Automation, Inc., West Seneca, NY, 1992—. Bd. dir. Graham Corp., Bush Industries, Inc.; trustee Keuka Coll. Patentee in field. Mem. com. Boy Scouts Am., East Aurora, 1973-76. Mem. Young Pres.'s Orgn. (chpt. chmn. 1981-82), Fluid Power Soc., Nat. Soc. Profl. Engrs., Buffalo and Erie County C. of C. Clubs: Country of Buffalo. Home: 323 Windsor Ln East Aurora NY 14052-1321 Office: Griffin Automation Inc 240 West Munster Rd West Seneca NY 14224 Home Phone: 716-652-9025; Office Phone: 716-674-2300. Business E-Mail: jbidla@griffinautomation.com.

BIDLACK, WAYNE ROSS, nutritional biochemist, toxicologist, food scientist; b. Waverly, NY, Aug. 12, 1944; s. Andrew L. Bidlack and Vivian Pearl Cowles Williams; m. Wei Wang. BS, Pa. State U., 1966; MS, Iowa State U., 1968; PhD, U. Calif., Davis, 1972. Postdoctoral fellow dept. pharmacology U. So. Calif., LA, 1972-74, asst prof. sch. medicine, 1974-80, assoc. prof., 1980-92, prof., 1992—, asst. dean student affairs, 1988-91, chmn. dept. pharmacology and nutrition, 1991-92; chmn. dept. food sci. and human nutrition Iowa State U., Ames, 1992-95; dean Coll. Agr. Calif. State Poly. U., Pomona, 1995—2007, prof. dept. human nutrition and food sci., 2007—. Assoc. editor Biochem. Medicine and Metabolic Biology, 1986-87; mem. editl. bd. Jour. Am. Coll. Nutrition, 1995—, Environ. Nutritional Interactions, 1996-2000, Toxicology, 2000-04. Chmn. Greater L.A. Nutrition Coun., 1982-83, So. Calif. Inst. Food Technologists, 1988-89, Toxicology and Safety Evaluation divsn. Inst. Food Technologists, 1989-90, food sci. communicator, 1986-90; chmn. Nat. Coun. Against Health Fraud, 1983-85; expert panel on foods and nurtrition, 1989-93. Recipient Outstanding Tchr. Award, U. So. Calif. Sch. Medicine, 1987-88, Meritorious Svc. award Calif. Dietetic Assn., 1990, Disting. Achievement award So. Calif. Inst. Food Technologists, 1990, Bautzer Faculty award Calif. State U., 1998; fellow Inst. Food Technologists, 1998, Wang Family award Calif. State U., 2002. Mem. Soc. Toxicology (chair awards com. food safety sect. 1993-94, chair 1994-95), Calif. State Bd. Food and Agr., Nat. Golden Key Soc. (hon.), Gamma Sigma Delta. Republican. Avocations: golf, book collecting. Office: Calif State Polytech U Coll of Agrl 3801 W Temple Ave Pomona CA 91768-2557 Business E-Mail: wrbidlack@csupomona.edu.

BIDWELL, CHARLES EDWARD, sociologist, educator; b. Chgo., Jan. 24, 1932; s. Charles Leslie and Eugenia (Campbell) B.; m. Helen Claxton Lewis, Jan. 24, 1959; 1 son, Charles Lewis. AB, U. Chgo., 1950, AM, 1953, PhD, 1956. Lectr. on sociology Harvard U., 1959-61; asst. prof. edn. U. Chgo., 1961-65, assoc. prof., 1965-70, prof. edn. and sociology, 1970-85, Reavis prof. edn. and sociology, 1985-2001, Reavis prof. emeritus edn. and sociology, 2001—, chmn. dept. edn., 1978-88, chmn. dept. sociology, 1988-94, dir. Ogburn-Stouffer Ctr., 1988-94. Author books in field; contbr. numerous articles to profl. jours.; editor Sociology of Edn., 1969-72, Am. Jour. Sociology, 1973-78, Am. Jour. Edn., 1983-88. With U.S. Army, 1957-59. Guggenheim fellow, 1971-72 Fellow AAAS; mem. Sociol. Rsch. Assn., Nat. Acad. Edn. (sec.), Phi Beta Kappa. Office: Dept Sociology 1126 East 59th St Chicago IL 60637 Office Phone: 773-702-0388. E-mail: c-bidwell@uchicago.edu.

BIDWELL, DUANE R., religious studies educator; b. Champaign, Ill., June 22, 1966; s. Jack L. and Phyllis A. Bidwell; m. Karee J. Galloway, Nov. 4, 1989; 1 child, Ben Thu Ngoc. BS, Tex. Christian U., Ft. Worth, 1988, MDiv, 1997, PhD, 2003. Cert. pastoral counselor Am. Assn. Pastoral Counselors (v.p.), 2000, lic. spiritual theology and direction U. Dallas Anglican Sch. Theology, 1997. Exec. dir. Tarrant County AIDS Interfaith Network, Ft. Worth, 1991—94; dir. Pastoral Care and Tng. Ctr., Tex. Christian U. Brite Div. Sch., Ft. Worth, 2002—07; asst. prof. pastoral theology, care, and counseling, dir. Presbyn. Formation, Phillips Theol. Sem., Tulsa, 2007—. Author: (profl. text) Short-Term Spiritual Guidance, 2004; editor: The Formation of Pastoral Counselors: Challenges and Opportunities, 2007. Chair profl. adv. group. clin. pastoral edn. program Harris Meth. Hosp., Ft. Worth. Mem.: Tarrant County Med. Soc. (mem. ethics consortium 2005—), Soc. Study Christian Spirituality, Soc. Buddhist-Christian Studies, Spiritual Dirs. Internat., Soc. Pastoral Theology. Liberal. Presbyterian. Office: Phillips Theol Sem 901 N Mingo Rd Tulsa OK 74116 Home Phone: 817-320-7042; Office Phone: 918-610-8303. Business E-Mail: duane.bidwell@ptstulsa.edu.

BIDWELL, JAMES TRUMAN, JR., lawyer; b. NYC, Jan. 2, 1934; s. James Truman and Mary (Kane) B.; m. Gail S. Bidwell, Mar. 6, 1965 (div.); children: Hillary Day Bidwell Mackay, Kimberley Wade, Cortney E.; m. Katherine T. O'Neil, July 15, 1988 (dec. Nov. 2003). BA, Yale U., 1956; LLB, Harvard U., 1959. Bar: NY 1959. Atty. USAF, Austin, Tex., 1959-62; assoc. Donovan, Leisure, Newton & Irvine, NYC, 1962-68, ptnr., 1968-84, White & Case, NYC, 1984-98; sr. counsel Linklaters, NYC, 1998—2003; ptnr. Thelen, Reid, Priest LLP, 2003—04, sr. counsel, 2005—06; ptnr. Sullivan & Worcester, LLP, 2006—. Pres. Youth Consultation Svc., 1973-78; trustee Berkeley Divinity Sch. Mem. ABA, Fed. Bar Assn., NY State Bar Assn., NY County Lawyers Assn., Ch. Club NY (trustee). Episcopalian. Office Phone: 212-660-3032. Business E-Mail: jtbidwell@sandw.com.

BIDWELL, ROGER GRAFTON SHELFORD, biologist, educator; b. Halifax, NS, Can., June 8, 1927; came to U.S., 1965; s. Roger Edward Shelford and Mary B.; m. Shirley Mae Rachael Mason, July 1, 1950; children— Barbara, Alison, Roger, Gillian. B.Sc., Dalhousie U., 1947; BA, Queen's U., 1950, MA, 1951, PhD, 1954. Tech. officer Canadian Def. Research Bd., Kingston, Ont., 1951-56; asst. research officer Nat. Research Council, Halifax, 1956-59; assoc. prof. biology U. Toronto, Ont., 1959-65; prof. biology Case Western Res. U., Cleve., 1965-69, chmn. dept., 1966-68; prof. biology Queen's U., Kingston, Ont., Canada, 1969-79, prof. emeritus, 1979—; I.W. Killam research prof. Dalhousie U., Halifax, 1980-85; sr. ptnr. Atlantic Research Assocs. Ltd., Wallace, N.S., 1980-91; exec. dir. Atlantic Inst. Biotech., Halifax, 1985-88. Vis. prof. Cornell U., 1961-63; vis. scientist Atlantic Regional Lab., NRC, Halifax, 1966, 76; cons. Faculty Edn., Simon Fraser U., 1966; Can. Sci. Exch. visitor to People's Republic of China, 1975, 77; participant Dark Skies Symposium; co-founder scotobiology program Ecology of Night Symposium, Muskoka, Ont., 2005. Author: Plant Physiology, 1974, 79; co-editor: Plant Physiology: A Treatise, 1978-90; contbr. over 160 articles to profl. jours., chpts. books. Active Crime Stoppers, Cumberland region, 1993-97, chmn., 1994-97; com. mem. Anglican Diocese N.S.; pres., chmn. bd. Pugwash Coop. Ltd., 1995-2000; warden Parish of Pugwash/River John, 1998-2002, parish treas., 2004-05; mem. diocesan coun. Diocese of N.S. and P.E.I., 1999-2001; active Pugwash and Area Cmty. Health Bd., 2001-2005 Recipient Queen Elizabeth II Silver Jubilee medal, 1977. Fellow AAAS, Royal Soc. Can.; mem. Canadian Soc. Plant Physiologists (founder, past sec.-treas., pres. 1972-73, Gold medal 1979), Biol. Council Can. (sec. 1973-76), Am. Soc. Plant Biology. Achievements include research in biochem. mechanisms in plants, protein metabolism, CO2 metabolism in leaves, photosynthesis and metabolism in marine algae; global climate change and the discovery and development of the science of scotobiology, the biology of darkness. Avocations: bicycling, walking, skiing, bird watching.

BIDWILL, WILLIAM V., professional sports team executive; s. Charles W. and Violet Bidwill; m. Nancy Bidwill; children: William Jr., Michael, Patrick, Timothy, Nicole. Grad., Georgetown U. V.p. Ariz. Cardinals (formerly St. Louis Cardinals Football Team), co-owner, 1962-72, owner, 1972—, also chmn., 1972—, pres. Mem. NFL Broadcasting Com., NFL Bus. Ventures Com. Bd. trustees Bert Bell/Pete Rozelle Player Benefit Plan. Office: Ariz Cardinals PO Box 888 Phoenix AZ 85001-0888*

BIEBEL, PAUL PHILIP, JR., lawyer; b. Chgo., Mar. 24, 1942; s. Paul Philip Sr. and Eleanor Mary (Sweeney) B.; divorced; children: Christine M., Brian E., Jennifer A., Susan E. AB, Marquette U., 1964; JD, Georgetown U., 1967. Bar: Ill. 1967, U.S. Dist. Ct. (no. dist.) Ill. 1967, U.S. Ct. Appeals (6th cir.) 1985, U.S. Supreme Ct. 1972. Asst. dean of men Loyola U., Chgo., 1967-69; asst. state's atty. Cook County State's Atty., Chgo., 1969-75, dep. state's atty., 1975-81; 1st asst. atty. gen. Ill. Atty. Gen., Chgo., 1981-85; pub. defender Cook County Pub. Defender, Chgo., 1986-88; ptnr. Winston & Strawn, Chgo., 1985-86, 88-94, Altheimer & Gray, Chgo., 1994-96; judge Cir. Ct. Cook County, Ill., 1996—. Contbr. articles to profl. publs. Mem. Fed. Bar Assn. (bd. dirs., pres. 1994-95), Cath. Lawyers Guild (bd. dirs., Cath. Lawyer of Yr. 1988), Ill. Judges Assn., Ill. Appellate Lawyers, 7th Cir. Bar Assn., Chgo. Bar Assn. (chmn. com. 1991-93), Georgetown Law Alumni Assn. (bd. dirs. 1991-96). Roman Catholic. Avocations: reading, golf. Home: 5415 N Forest Glen Ave Chicago IL 60630-1523 Office: Presiding Judge Criminal Divsn RM 101 2600 S California Ave Chicago IL 60608 Home Phone: 773-725-9211; Office Phone: 773-869-3160. Personal E-mail: jorich73@cs.com.

BIEBER, FREDERICK ROBERT, medical geneticist; b. Regina, Sask., Can., Feb. 9, 1950; s. Frederick John and Marjorie (Davidson) B.; m. Jane Marie McNamara, June 23, 1973. BA, SUNY, Oswego, 1972; MS, U. Rochester, 1976; PhD, Med. Coll. Va., 1981. Diplomate Am. Bd. Med. Genetics. Asst. prof. Harvard Med. Sch., Boston, 1985-91; assoc. prof. pathology Brigham Womens Hosp., Boston, 1992—. Mem. DNA adv. bd. FBI, Royal Can. Mounted Police, U.S. Dept. Def. Author: The Malformed Fetus and Stillbirth, 1988; mem. editl. bd. Clin. Genetics; contbr. articles to profl. jours. Bd. dirs. Greyhound Friends, Hopkinton, Mass., 1992. Capt. US Army Res., 2001—. Office: Brigham & Women's Hosp Dept Pathology 75 Francis St Boston MA 02115-6106

BIEBER, SANDER M., lawyer; b. LA, 1950; AB, Princeton U., 1972; JD, Case Western Reserve U., 1976. Bar: D.C. 1976. Intern to Chief Justice U.S. Supreme Ct., 1974; atty. office of chief counsel fed. railroad adminstrn. Dept. Transp., 1976-78; assoc. Wolfe, Block Schoor & Solis-Cohen, 1978—81, Dechert LLP (formerly Dechert Price & Rhoads), Washington, 1981—86, ptnr., 1986—. Assoc. editor Case Western Reserve Law Review. Mem. ABA (corp. banking and bus. law sect., Mex. law com., internat. law and practice sect.), D.C. Bar Assn. Office: Dechert LLP 1775 I St NW # 9 Washington DC 20006-2402 Office Phone: 202-261-3308. E-mail: sander.bieber@dechert.com.

BIEBER-ROBERTS, PEGGY EILENE, communications educator, editor, journalist, researcher; b. Mobridge, SD, Jan. 8, 1943; d. John J. and Lenora (Schlepp) Bieber; m. Phil Roberts. BS, No. State U., Aberdeen, SD, 1966; MA, U. Wyo., Laramie, 1984; PhD, U. Wash., Seattle, 1990; LLM in Human Rights and Internat. Law, U. Edinburgh, Scotland, 2005. Vol. Peace Corps, Turkey, 1966-68; tchr. secondary pub. schs., Idaho, 1968-69, Pine Ridge (S.D.) Reservation, 1969-71; co-founder Medicine Bow Post weekly newspaper, 1977; legis. reporter various weekly newspapers, Wyo., 1980-82; owner, pub. Capitol Times mag., Cheyenne, Wyo., 1982-84; pub. Skyline West Press, 1983—; lectr. pub. rels. and advt. U. Wash., Seattle, 1986-88; rsch. analyst Elway Rsch./Jay Rockey Co., Seattle, 1989-90; asst. prof. mass media U. Wyo., Laramie, 1990-96; journalism faculty comm. tech. Higher Colls. of Tech., Dubai, United Arab Emirates, 1996-98; polit. campaign mgr. Phil Roberts gubernatorial campaign, Wyo., 1998; assoc. prof. journalism and mass comms. Am. U. in Cairo, 1999—2003, chair dept. journalism and mass comm., 2000—02; office mgr. Albany County Dem. Party, 2004. Indexer McGraw/Hill, Bedford Books, also others, 1988—94. Author, editor: hist. almanacs for various states, 1984—87; contbr. articles to profl. jours., chapters to books. Publicity chmn. Laramie County Dem. Com., Cheyenne, 1982; publicity chmn., precinct committeewoman Albany County Dems., 1999—2000, 2004—06. Named Stout fellow, U. Wash., 1990; recipient 1st Place award for feature writing, co-1st Place award for editorials, Wyo. Press Assn., 1982, Alumni Assn. Faculty Growth award, U. Wyo., 1994. Mem.: Internat. Assn. Media and Comm. Rsch., Assn. Ednl. Journalism and Mass Comm. Office Phone: 307-745-8205. Personal E-mail: bieberroberts@yahoo.com.

BIEBUYCK, JULIEN FRANCOIS, anesthesiologist, medical administrator, educator; b. South Africa, Feb. 2, 1935; came to U.S., 1971, naturalized, 1985; s. Lucien Jean and Drix J. B.; m. Jeanette A. Sumner, May 10, 1961; children: Gavin L., Richard M., Clare E. MB, U. Capetown, 1959; DPhil, Oxford U., Eng., 1971. Diplomat Am. Bd. Anesthesiology. Nuffield scholar Oxford U., Eng., 1969-71; asst. prof. anesthesiology Harvard Med. Sch., Mass. Gen. Hosp., Boston, 1971-76; Eric A. Walker prof., chmn. dept. anesthesia Pa. State U. Coll. Medicine, Hershey, 1977-97, assoc. dean, 1991-97, sr. assoc. dean for acad. affairs, 1997—2000; Robert G. Petersdorf scholar-in-residence Assn. Am. Med. Coll., Washington, 2001—02, sr. cons. acad. mgmt. programs, 2002—. Mem. anesthetic and life support drugs adv. com. FDA, 1995-97. Mem. editorial bd. Anesthesiology, 1985-93; co-editor Current Opinion in Anaesthesiology; contbr. chpts. to books, articles to med. jours. Med. Found. Boston fellow, 1972-76. Fellow Royal Coll. Anaesthetists (hon.), Australian and New Zealand Coll. Anaesthetists (hon.); mem. AMA, Am. Med. Coll., Assn. Univ. Anesthesiologists, Am. Soc. Anesthesiologists (chair com. on rsch. 1994-97), Am. Physiol. Soc., Soc. Acad. Anesthesia Chmn. (past pres.), Coun. Acad. Socs., Assn. Am. Med. Colls., Biochem. Soc., Soc. Parenteral Nutrition, Soc. Neurosci., Soc. Neurosurg. Anesthesia, Pa.

Med. Soc., Trinity Coll. Soc., Cosmos Club, Alpha Omega Alpha. Office: 2105 Carey Way Hummelstown PA 17036-6800 Office Phone: 717-583-2679. E-mail: jbiebuyck@comcast.net.

BIECK, ROBERT BARTON, JR., lawyer; b. Wiesbaden, Germany, Apr. 13, 1952; arrived in US, 1954; s. Robert Barton and Mary-Jean (Boeck) B.; m. Julia A. Dietz, Apr. 20, 1991. BA in Polit. Sci., U. Nebr., 1974; JD with high honors, Tex. Tech. U., 1977. Bar: Tex. 1977, La. 1977, US Dist. Ct. (ea. dist.) La. 1977, US Dist. Ct. (mid. dist.) La. 1978, US Dist. Ct. (we. dist.) La. 1979, US Supreme Ct. 1980, US Ct. Appeals (5th and 11th cirs.) 1981, US Dist. Ct. (no. and so. dists.) Tex. 1991, DC 1992, US Ct. Appeals (DC cir.) 1992, US Dist. Ct. DC 1994, US Dist. Ct. (ea. dist.) Tex. 2006. Assoc. firm Jones, Walker, Waechter, Poitevent, Carrere & Denegre, New Orleans, 1977-82, ptnr., 1982—. Chmn. profl. liability practice group Jones, Walker, et al. Recipient West Horn Book award West Pub. Co., 1976; Fulbright and Jaworski scholar, 1976. Mem. ABA (litigation sect., bus. law sect., federal regulation of securities com.), Securities Industry Assn., Nat. Soc. Compliance Profls., New Orleans Bar Assn., La. Bankers Assn., 5th Cir. Bar Assn., Order of Coif, Phi Kappa Phi, Phi Delta Phi. Home: 5708 Annunciation St New Orleans LA 70115 Office: Jones Walker Waechter Poitevent Carrere & Denegre 201 Saint Charles Ave Ste 5200 New Orleans LA 70170-5100 Home Phone: 504-891-3901; Office Phone: 504-582-8202.

BIEDERMAN, BARRON ZACHARY (BARRY), advertising agency executive; b. NYC; s. William and Sophye (Groll) B.; m. Susan Howard, Apr. 1, 1967; children: Rachel, David. BA with distinction, Cornell U., 1952; MS in Journalism, Columbia U, 1953; postgrad., U. London, 1954. Copy group head Mogul, Williams & Saylor, NYC, 1955-59; sr. writer Lennen & Newell, NYC, 1960-62; v.p., assoc. creative svcs. dir. Cunningham & Walsh, NYC, 1962-64; sr. v.p. Needham, Harper & Steers, NYC, 1964-84, exec. creative dir., 1964-74, mgmt. rep., 1974-79, dir., 1981-84; mng. dir. NH&S Corp. Futures, 1979-80; chmn., chief exec. officer NH&S/Issues & Images, 1981-84; chmn. Biederman & Co., Inc. (name changed to Biederman, Kelly & Shaffer, Inc. 1989), 1984—; chmn. emeritus Biederman, Kelly, Krimstein Ptnrs., 1998—2001; ret., 2001. Lectr. in field. Bd. dirs. Liberty Club, N.Y., 1983-87, Alvin Ailey Dance Theatre, N.Y., 1974. Recipient various advt. awards; Ford Found. fellow Eng., India, 1953-55 Mem. Fin. Comms. Soc. (bd. dirs. 1982-89, pres. 1986-87), Internat. Advt. Assn., Bank Mktg. Assn., Copywriters Club N.Y. (bd. dirs. 1960-64). Avocations: history, literature, music, gardening, travel. Home: 425 E 58th St Apt 17G New York NY 10022-2300

BIEDERMAN, EDWIN WILLIAMS, JR., retired geologist; b. Stamford, Conn., June 30, 1930; s. Edwin Williams and Thelma Frances (Morrow) B.; m. Margaret-Jane Bell White, Aug. 23, 1958; children: Robert, Mary, Jane, James. BA, Cornell U., 1952; PhD, Pa. State U., 1958. Cert. petroleum geologist. Project leader Cities Svc. Co., Tulsa, 1958-68, pres. staff Cranbury, N.J., 1968-72; asst. dir. Pa. Tech. Assistance Program, University Park, 1972-77; sr. tech. specialist Pa. Tech. Assistance program, 1980—2001; field ctr. dir. NSF Chautauqua Courses, University Park, 1977-80; ret. Author: Atlas of Oil and Gas Reservoir Rocks From North America, 1986; contbr. articles to profl. jours.; holder 5 patents for geochem. exploration, in situ acidulation of phosphate rock, grate for vertical oil shale kiln, fire retardant foam, lightweight cement for oil wells. Petroleum officer USAF, 1952-54. Pa. State U. scholar 1956-58; am. Assn. Petroleum Geologists grantee 1957; recipient First Place award Project of Yr. Nat. Assn. Mgmt. and Tech. Assistance Ctrs., 1985. Mem. AAAS, Am. Assn. Petroleum Geologists, Soc. Econ. Paleontologists and Mineralogists, Geochem. Soc., Assn. Profl. Geol. Scientists.

BIEDRON, THEODORE JOHN, publishing and advertising executive; b. Evergreen Park, Ill., Nov. 30, 1946; s. Theodore John and Ione Margaret B.; m. Gloria Anne DeAngelo, Nov. 7, 1970; children: Jessica Ann, Lauren. BA in Polit. Sci., U. Ill., 1968. Recruitment advt. mgr. Chgo. Sun-Times, 1968-74; classified advt. mgr. Pioneer press, Wilmette, Ill., 1974-76, v.p. advt. and promotion, 1993-94, sr. v.p. sales and mktg., 1994-97, exec. v.p., 1997-2000. Pub. North Shore mag., 1997-2000; classified mgr., v.p. Lerner Newspapers, Chgo., 1976-79, assoc. pub., 1980-82, advt. dir., 1982-87; v.p., classified advt. mgr. Chgo. Sun-Times, 1987-92; pres. Chicagoland Pub. Co. divsn. Chgo. Tribune, 2000—. Pres. Northeastern Ill. U. Found., 1998-2002; trustee Northlight Theater, 1993-98. Home: 404 Jackson Ave Glencoe IL 60022- Office: Chicagoland Pub Co 2000 S York Rd Oak Brook IL 60523 Personal E-mail: tbiedron@gmail.com.

BIEGEL, DAVID ELI, social worker, educator; b. NYC, July 3, 1946; s. Jack and Estelle (Lentin) B.; m. Margaret S. Smoot, Jan. 31, 1976 (div.); 1 child, Geoffrey S.; m. Ronna Kaplan, Oct. 26, 2003. BA, CCNY, 1967; MSW, U. Md., 1970, PhD, 1982. Field coord. United Farm Workers, AFL-CIO, Balt., 1971; exec. dir. Junction, Inc., Westminster, Md., 1971—72; dir. office planning and program devel. Cath. Charities, Balt., 1973—76; ctr. assoc., dir. neighborhood and family svcs. project U. So. Calif., Washington Pub. Affairs Ctr., 1976—80; asst. prof. social work U. Pitts., 1980—85, assoc. prof., 1985—86; Henry L. Zucker prof. social work practice Mandel Sch. Applied Social Scis., Case Western Res. U., 1987—, prof. psychiatry and sociology, 1987—, co-dir. Ctr. for Practice Innovations, 1991—97, chair doctoral program, 1998—2001, 2005. Co-dir. Cuyahoga County Cmty. Mental Health Rsch. Inst., 1994—2002; pres. Inst. for the Advancement of Social Work Rsch., 1999—2002; dir. rsch. and evaluation Ohio Substance Abuse and Mental Illness Coord. Ctr. Excellence, 2000—05; co-dir. Ctr. Substance Abuse and Mental Illness, 2002—. Co-editor: Evidence-Based Practices Serves, Innovations in Practice and Service Delivery with Vulnerable Populations Series, Family Caregiving Applications Series, Evidence-Based Practices Series; editor Practice Concepts sect., The Gerontologist, 2002-04; co-author: Neighborhood Networks for Humane Mental Health Care, 1982, Community Support Systems and Mental Health: Practice, Policy and Research, 1982, Building Support Networks for the Elderly: Theory and Applications, 1984, Social Networks and Mental Health: An Annotated Bibliography, 1985, Social Support Networks: A Bibliography 1983-1987, 1989, Aging and Caregiving: Theory, Research and Policy, 1990, Family Preservation Programs: Research and Evaluation, 1991, Family Caregiving in Chronic Illness: Alzheimer's Dsiease, Cancer, Heart Disease, Mental Illness, and Stroke, 1991, Family Caregiving: A Lifespan Perspective, 1994, The Jewish Aged in the U.S. and Israel: Diversity, Programs and Services, 1994, Innovations in Practice and Service Delivery with Vulnerable Populations Across the Lifespan, 1999; contbr. articles to profl. jours., chpts. to books. Cons. Vol. VISTA, Raton, N.Mex., and Balt., 1967-70; active Big Bros. Am., Balt., 1974-77' pres. bd. trustees Bridgeway, Inc., 2004-07; sec. bd. trustees Cmty. Care Network, Inc., 2006-07—. N.Y. State Incentive scholar, 1963-64; VISTA Fellows Program fellow, 1968-70. Fellow Gerontol. Soc. Am.; mem. NASW, Acad. Cert. Social Workers, Soc. Social Work Rsch. Democrat. Jewish. Home Phone: 216-371-3108; Office Phone: 216-368-2308. Business E-Mail: david.biegel@case.edu.

BIEGEL, DEBRA JEANNE, music educator; b. Billings, Mont., July 29, 1955; d. Oscar Herman and Doris Jeanne Biegel. MusB, U. Mont., 1977; M in Curriculum and Instr., Mont. State U., 1991. Music tchr. Bozeman Pub. Schools, Mont., 1980—, Ennis Pub. Schools, Mont., 1977—80. Choir dir. Hawthorne After Sch., Bozeman, Mont., 2003—; dir. piano studio Hawthorne Sch., 2000—. Recipient Mont. Tchr. of Yr., 2006, Gov. Arts award, Hawthorne Sch., 2005, Boyer Ctr. award, 2004. Mem.: Mont. Gen. Musta Tchrs. Assn., Bana Masters Assn., Music Edn. Nat. Conf., NEA. Avocations: travel, sports, movies, reading. Home: 406 Meagher Ave Bozeman MT 59718 Office: Bozeman Pub Sch 114 North Rouse Bozeman MT 59715*

BIEGLER, DAVID W., energy executive; b. 1946; married. BS, St. Mary's U., 1968; postgrad., Harvard U., 1979. With Enserch Exploration Inc., 1966—79, petroleum engr., 1968—70, dist. petroleum engr., 1970—72, staff petroleum engr., then mgr. revenue control, 1972—74, chief engr., 1974—75, dir. engring. mktg. planning, then v.p. processing engring. mktg., 1975—77, v.p. land and mktg., 1977—78; exec. v.p. Pool Arabia, 1978—79; exec. v.p. ea. hemisphere Pool Intairdril, 1979—80; pres. Pool Well Servicing Co., 1980—84; pres. U.S. ops. Pool Co., 1984—85; pres., COO, CEO, chmn. Enserch Corp., Dallas, 1985—97; pres., COO, vice-chmn. TXU Corp. (formerly Tex. Utilities), Dallas, 1997—2001; CEO Estrella Energy, LP, Dallas, 2003—. Office: Estrella Energy LP 1700 Pacific Ste 2350 Dallas TX 75201 Office Phone: 214-393-7501. Business E-Mail: d.biegler@estrellaenergy.com.

BIEGLER, LORENZ THEODOR, chemical engineering educator; b. Chgo., Sept. 10, 1956; s. Lorenz and Cecilie (Hoegele) B.; m. Lynne Morgan Webber, May 23, 1987; 1 child, Matthew. BS, Ill. Inst. Tech., 1977; PhD, U. Wis., 1981. Asst. prof. in chem. engring. Carnegie Mellon U., Pitts., 1981-86, assoc. prof., 1986-90, prof., 1990—, bayer prof., 1996—; scientist in residence Argonne (Ill.) Nat. Lab., 1990-91. Trustee Cache Corp., Austin, Tex., 1990—; cons. to various chem. and software cos. Contbr. more than 200 papers to profl. jours. and books. Recipient Presdl. Young Investigator award NSF, 1985, Best Paper award of 1988, 95, Computers and Chem. Engring. Jour., 1989, Alumni award Ill. Inst. Tech., 1977, ASEE McGraw award 1996; Disting. faculty visitor U. Alta., Can., 1990; Gambrinus fellow 1995. Fellow AIChE (dir. CAST 1989-92, sec./treas. 1993, Pitts. sect. chmn. 1993, chair 1999), Am. Chem. Soc., Ops. Soc. Am., Soc. Indsl. and Applied Math. Office: Carnegie Mellon U Chem Engring Dept Pittsburgh PA 15213

BIEHL, MICHAEL MELVIN, lawyer, writer; b. Milw., Feb. 24, 1951; s. Michael Melvin Biehl and Frieda Margaret (Krieg) Davis. AB, Harvard U., 1973, JD, 1976. Bar: Wis. 1976, U.S. Dist. Ct. (ea. dist.) Wis. 1976. Assoc. Foley & Lardner, Milw., 1976-84, ptnr., 1984—. Adj. prof. law Marquette U. Law Sch., 2001—. Author: Medical Staff Legal Issues, 1990, Doctored Evidence, 2002, Lawyered to Death, 2003; editor: Physician Organizations and Medical Staff, 1996. Mem. Mt. Sinai Med. Ctr. Clin. Investigations Com., Hastings Ctr.; election monitor first multi-party elections in Rep. Ga., 1990; dir. Colorlines Found. for Arts and Culture, Inc., chmn., bd. dirs. Milw. Psychiat. Hosp. and Aurora Behavioral Health Svcs. Mem. ABA, Am. Health Lawyers Assn., Am. Coll. of Med. Quality, Am. Soc. Law and Medicine, Sarasota Conservation Found. Mem. Unitarian Ch. Achievements include having the Michael Biehl Park in Venice, Florida named in his honor. Office: Foley & Lardner 777 E Wisconsin Ave Ste 3800 Milwaukee WI 53202-5367 Home: 908 Scherer Way Osprey FL 34229-6867 Office Phone: 414-297-5648.

BIEL, JESSICA, actress, model; b. Ely, Minn., Mar. 3, 1982; d. John and Kim Biel. Attended, Tufts U., 2000. Spokesmodel L'Oreal. Actor: (plays) Annie, Beauty and the Beast, Anything Goes, The Sound of Music; (TV series) 7th Heaven, 1996—2002; (films) Ulee's Gold, 1997, I'll Be Home for Christmas, 1998, Summer Catch, 2001, The Rules of Attraction, 2002, The Texas Chainsaw Massacre, 2003, Cellular, 2004, Blade: Trinity, 2004, Stealth, 2005, Elizabethtown, 2005, The Illusionist, 2006, Home of the Brave, 2006, Next, 2007, I Now Pronounce You Chuck and Larry, 2007, (voice) It's a Digital World, 2004. Named Sexiest Woman Alive, Esquire mag., 2005; recipient Rising Star award, Palm Springs Internat. Film Soc., Palm Springs Internat. Film Festival, 2007. Mailing: Creative Artists Agy 9830 Wilshire Blvd Beverly Hills CA 90212-1825*

BIEL, LEONARD, JR., urologist; b. NYC, Jan. 17, 1922; s. Leonard and Eleanor Roberta (Abrahams) B.; m. Lynn Arnstein, June 27, 1958; children: Pamela, Alix. AB, Yale U., New Haven, 1943; MD, NY Med. Coll., 1946. Diplomate Am. Bd. Urology. Intern Paterson Gen. Hosp., NJ, 1946-47; resident in surgery Flower and Fifth Ave. Hosps., NYC, 1950-51, Bellevue Hosp., NYC, 1951-52; resident in urology Mt. Sinai Hosp., NYC, 1952-54; pvt. practice NYC, 1954—. Asst. attending physician Mt. Sinai Hosp. Capt. U.S. Army, 1947-49; ETO. Fellow ACS; mem. AMA, NY Acad. Medicine, NY Med. Soc., NY County Med. Soc., Am. Urol. Assn. Avocation: photography. Home and Office: 114 E 90th St New York NY 10128-1550 Office Phone: 212-369-7070. Personal E-mail: lbieljr@mindspring.com.

BIELE, HUGH IRVING, retired lawyer; b. Bridgeport, Conn., July 28, 1942; s. Ray James and Blanche (McClellan) B.; m. Pamela Althea Johnson, Aug. 21, 1965 (div.); children: Jonathan Christopher, Melissa Lynne. BA, St. Lawrence U., Canton, NY, 1965; JD, U. Utah, 1968. Bar: Utah 1968, U.S. Dist. Ct. Utah 1968, Calif. 1972, U.S. Dist. Ct. Calif. 1972, U.S. Ct. Appeals (9th and 10th cirs.). Instr. San Francisco Law Sch., 1971-73; atty. United Calif. Bank, San Francisco, 1974—81; v.p., sr. counsel First Interstate Bank, LA, 1974-81; ptnr. Biele & Stuehrmann, LA, 1981-83; sr. ptnr. Biele, Stuehrmann & Lapinski, LA, 1983-84; founding ptnr. Biele & Lapinski, LA, 1985-89; ptnr. Barton, Klugman & Detting, LA, 1989-91; ptnr., dir. comml. law and litigation Grace, Skocypec, Cosgrove & Schirm, LA, 1992-95; ret., 1995. Bd. govs. Fin. Lawyer Conf., L.A., 1976-2000, pres. 1984-85, original developer, ptnr. Engine Co. No. 28 rehabilitation, 1978-88, ptnr. Engine Co. No. 28 Restaurant, 1988—, owner Biele Enterprises. Author screenplay: Corporate Cancer, 1989, Hedge of Thorns, 1990. Chmn. Vols. in Parole, LA, 1979—80, 1989—90, Lawyers for Human Rights, 1988—2000, co-pres. elect, 1998, co-pres., 1999; commr. Episc. Diocese AIDS Ministry, LA, 1988—93; bd. dirs. Cmty. Counseling Svc., LA, 1989—99, pres., 1993—95, chmn. bd. dirs., 1995—99; bd. dirs. Casa de Rosa and the Sunshine Mission, 1997—2001, treas., 2001; bd. dirs., v.p., sec. Project New Hope, Inc., LA, 1990—92. Decorated Army Commendation medal, Bronze Star with oak leaf cluster. Mem.: FBA, ABA, Internat. Bankers Assn. Calif., Calif. State Bar (fin. inst. com.), L.A. County Bar Assn. (internat. sect. exec. com. 1978—97, chmn. 1981—82, exec. com. comml. law and bankruptcy sect. 1986—2000, chair 1992—93), Fin. Lawyers Conf. (pres. 1986—87), Internat. Bar Assn., Hollywood Knolls Cmty. Club (bd. dirs. 2002—), St. Lawrence U. Alumni Assn. (pres. 1979—91). Republican. Episcopalian. Avocations: skiing, jogging, aerobics, travel. Home: 3478 Wonder View Dr Los Angeles CA 90068-1536 Office: 3478 Wonder View Dr Los Angeles CA 90068-1536 E-mail: hughbiele@aol.com.

BIELEMA, BRET, university football coach; b. Prophetstown, Ill., Jan. 13, 1970; BA in Mktg., Iowa Univ., 1992. Asst. coach Univ. Iowa, 1993—2001; co-defensive coord. Kansas St., 2002—03; defensive coord. Univ. Wis., 2004—05, head coach, 2006—. Achievements include being youngest head football coach in Div. I, NCAA, 2006. Office: Univ Wisconsin Dept Athletics Kellner Hall 1440 Monroe St Madison WI 53711

BIELIAUSKAS, VYTAUTAS JOSEPH, psychologist, educator; b. Plackojai, Lithuania, Nov. 1, 1920; came to U.S., 1949, naturalized, 1955; s. Antanas and Anele (Kasparaite) B.; m. Danute G. Sirvydaite, Mar. 12, 1947; children— Linas A., Diana B., Aldona O., Cornelius V. PhD in Psychology, U. Tuebingen, 1943; PsyD, Xavier U., 2005. Diplomate Clin. Psychology, Marital Family Therapy, Am. Bd. Profl. Psychology. Asst. prof. U. Munich, Germany, 1944-48; instr. King's Coll., Wilkes-Barre, Pa., 1949-50; mem. faculty Sch. Clin. and Applied Psychology, Coll. William and Mary, 1950-58, prof. psychology, 1953-58, head dept. psychology, 1951-57; assoc. prof. Xavier U., Cin., 1958-60, chmn. dept. psychology, 1959-78, prof., 1960-78, Riley prof. psychology, 1978-88, disting. prof. psychology emeritus, 1988—. Author: A Psychologist Looks at the Dealth Penalty, Social Justice Review, 1993 (7-8), 2002, Community Relations Training for Police Supervisors, 1969; CSSS for the H-T-P Drawings, 1981, Politics, Ethics and Morality, Social Justice Review, 1994 (3-4), 2003; contbr. articles to profl. jours. Pres., exec. officer Lithuanian World Cmty., 1988-92; exec. v.p. Lithuanian-Am. Cmty., Inc., 1994-2000; adviser on spl. programs Pres. of Republic of Lithuania, 1995-96. Lt. col. M.S.C., USAR, 1958-65. Recipient Ellis Island medal of honor, 1990. Fellow APA (pres. divsn. 13, 1986, Dist. Svc. award divsn. 36 1998); mem. Ohio Psychol. Assn. (pres. 1978-79, Disting. Svc. award 1980), Soc. Personality Assessment, Internat. Assn. for Study Med. Psychology and Religion (pres. 1972-75), Cin. Acad. Profl. Psychology, Psychologists Interested in Religious Issues (pres. 1971, exec. sec. 1973-75), Cath. Acad. Scis. in the U.S.A. (academician 1987—). Office: Xavier U Dept Psychology Cincinnati OH 45207 Office Phone: 513-745-3710. Personal E-mail: vbieliaus@aol.com. Business E-Mail: bieliaus@xavier.edu.

BIELORY, LEONARD, allergist, immunologist, medical school administrator; b. Neptune, NJ, Nov. 17, 1954; s. Max and Bessie (Spielberg) B.; m. Marilyn Miriam Gilan, July 5, 1981; children: Brett Phillip, Barry Mark, Amy Beth BS, MS, Lehigh U., 1976; MD, NJ Med. Sch., 1980. Intern, resident U. Md. Hosp., Balt., 1980-82; clin. assoc. NIH, Bethesda, Md., 1982-85; dir. divsn. allergy, immunology & rheumatology NJ Med. Sch., Newark, 1985—, co-dir. immuno-ophthalmology svcs., prof. medicine, pediats. and ophthalmology, 1992—2002, dir. devel. & clin. rsch. dept. medicine; pres. med. staff U. Medicine and Dentistry NJ-U. Hosp., 1993-95; pres., chmn. U. Physician Assocs., 1996-2000. Pres. med. staff ex-oficio mem. NIH Safety and Data Mgmt. Bd., 1993-98; bd. dirs. Univ. Health Care Corp., acting med. dir., 1995-97; dir. Asthma and Allergy Rsch. Ctr., 1992—; prof. medicine, pediat. and ophthalmology, 2002—; chmn. clin. treatment study sect. NIH, 1993; prin. investigator Nat. Ctr. for Complementary and Alternative Medicine, NIH, 2002-04. Assoc. editor: Annals of Allergy, Asthma & Immunology, 1996-; contbr. rsch. papers to profl. jours., chpt. to books. Bd. dirs. Congregation Israel, Springfield, NJ, 1988, pres., 1999-01; v.p. Kushner Yeshiva, pres. 2005-; bd. dirs. St. John's Cmty. Svc., 2002-. Recipient Young Investigator award Am. Acad. Allergy and Immunology, 1985; Schering Corp. Travel grantee, 1985. Fellow ACP, Am. Acad. Allergy and Immunology; mem. Med. Soc. NJ. Jewish. Avocations: skiing, camping, rafting, bicycling. Office: NJ Med Sch Divsn Allergy Immunology & Rheumatology 90 Bergen St Ste 4700 Newark NJ 07103-2425 Office Phone: 973-972-2768. E-mail: bielory@umdnj.edu.

BIELUCH, WILLIAM CHARLES, judge; b. Nov. 12, 1918; AB magna cum laude, Brown U., 1939; JD, Yale U., 1942. Bar: Conn. 1942. Assoc. Covington, Burling, Rublee, Acheson & Shorb, Washington, 1942-43; ptnr. Bieluch, Barry & Ramenda and predecessors, Hartford, 1946-68; judge Cir. Ct. Conn., 1968-73, Ct. Common Pleas Conn., 1973-76, Superior Ct. Conn., 1976-85, Appellate Session, 1979-83, Appellate Ct. Conn., 1985-88; ret., 1988; judge trial referee, 1988—. Trustee emeritus S. S. Cyril and Methodius Roman Cath. Ch., Hartford; corporator St. Francis Hosp. and Med. Ctr., Hartford. Lt. (j.g.) USCG, WWII. Decorated Knight St. Gregory, Pope Paul VI, 1972; recipient Merit award Polish Legion Am. Vets., 1952, Man of Yr. award United Polish Socs., 1968, Archdiocesan medal of appreciation Archbishop John F. Whealon, 1970, Disting. Grad. award Nat. Cath. Elem. Sch., 1995. Mem. Conn. Bar Assn. (chmn. Jr. Bar Sect. 1948-49), Hartford County Bar Assn., KC, Phi Beta Kappa. Republican. Office: 95 Washington St Hartford CT 06106-4431 Office Phone: 860-548-2850.

BIEN, JOSEPH JULIUS, philosophy educator; b. Cin., May 22, 1936; s. Joseph Julius and Mary Elizabeth (Adams) B.; m. Françoise Neve, Apr. 8, 1965. BS, Xavier U., MA, 1958; DTC, U. Paris, 1968; postgrad., Laval Univ., 1958, Emory U., 1961-62, U. Edinburgh, 1962; D (hon.), Lucian Blaga U., 1999. Asst. prof. philosophy Univ. Tex., Austin, 1968-73; asso. prof. philosophy Univ. Mo., Columbia, 1973-79, prof. philosophy, 1979—, chmn. dept. philosophy, 1976-80, 81-83, 1993—99; vis. prof. Tex. A&M U., 1980, Dubrovnik Inst. Postgrad. Studies, Yugoslavia, 1983, 84, 85, 89, co-dir. Croatia, 1990—; Mid-Am. States Univs. Assn. hon. lectr. in philosophy, 1985-86. Rsch. assoc. Russian and Slavic Rsch. Ctr., 1989-91; vis. prof. Lucian Blaga U., 1996, Hubei U., 1997, Wichita State U., 1998, U. Western Cape, 2000, Lille 3 U, 2002. Author: History, Revolution and Human Natue: Marx's Philosophical Anthropology, 1984; transl.: (M. Merleau-Ponty) Adventures of the Dialectic, 1973; editor: Phenomenology and the Social Sciences, A Dialogue, 1978, Political and Social Essays by Paul Ricoeur, 1974, Leviathan, 1986, Contemporary Social Thought, 1989, Ethics and Politics, 1992, Philosophical Issues and Problems, 1998. Am. Council Learned Socs. grantee, 1973; Dubrovnik Inst. Postgrad. Studies grantee, 1984; recipient U. Mo. faculty alumni award, 1998. Mem. Soc. Social and Polit. Philosophy (pres. 1979-80, 86-87, 93-94, 97-98), Ctrl. States Philos. Assn. (pres. 1978-79), Ctrl. Slavic Conf. (sec.-tres. 1977, 84), Southwestern Philosophy Soc. (pres. 1997-98). Democrat. Home: 100 W Brandon Rd Columbia MO 65203-3508 Office: Univ Mo Dept Philosophy Columbia MO 65211-0001

BIEN, PETER ADOLPH, language educator, writer; b. NYC, May 28, 1930; s. Adolph F. and Harriet (Honigsberg) B.; m. Chrysanthi Yiannakou, July 17, 1955; children: Leander, Alec, Daphne. Student, Harvard U., 1948-50; BA, Haverford Coll., 1952; MA, Columbia U., 1957, PhD, 1961; postgrad., Bristol U., Eng., 1958-59, Woodbrooke Coll., 1970-71; PhD (hon.), U. Thessaloniki, 2007. Lectr. Columbia U., NYC, 1957-58, 59-61; instr. dept. English Dartmouth Coll., Hanover, NH, 1961-62, asst. prof., 1963-65, assoc. prof., 1965-68, prof., 1969-97, Geisel prof., 1974-79, Frederick Sessions Beebe '35 prof. in art of writing, 1989-97, prof. emeritus, 1997—. Vis. prof. Harvard U., 1983, U. Melbourne, Australia, 1983, Woodbooke Coll., 1995, U. Thessaloniki, Greece, 1996, 2000, Princeton (N.J.) U., 2001, Columbia U., 2004, Brown U., 2005, San Francisco State U., 2005, U. Crete, 2007. Author: L.P. Hartley, 1963, Constantine Cavafy, 1964, Kazantzakis and the Linguistic Revolution in Greek Literature, 1972, Nikos Kazantzakis, 1972, Antithesis and Synthesis in the Poetry of Yannis Ritsos, 1980, Three Generations of Greek Writers, 1983, Tempted by Happiness: Kazantzakis' Post-Christian Christ, 1984, Kazantzakis: Politics of the Spirit, vol. 1, 1989, vol. 2, 2007, Nikos Kazantzakis-Novelist, 1989, Words, Wordlessness, and the Word: Quaker Silence Reconsidered, 1992, (with Darren J.N. Middleton) God's Struggler: Religion in the Works of Nikos Kazantzakis, 1996, (with Chuck Fager) In Stillness There Is Fullness: A Peacemaker's Harvest, 2000, On Retiring to Kendal (and Beyond), 2003, A Literary Excursion, 2003, The Mystery of Quaker Light, 2006, Eight Lectures by Peter Bien, 2007; co-author: Demotic Greek I, 1972, Demotic Greek II, 1982, Greek Today, 2004, A Century of Greek Poetry 1900-2000, 2004; translator: The Last Temptation of Christ, 1960, Saint Francis, 1962, Report to Greco, 1965 (all by Nikos Kazantzakis), Life in the Tomb (Stratis Myrivilis), 1977, 87, 2004; co-editor: Modern Greek Writers, 1972; assoc. editor Byzantine and Modern Greek Studies, 1975-82; assoc. editor Jour. Modern Greek Studies, 1983-89, editor, 1990-99. Trustee Kinhaven Music Sch., Weston, Vt., 1972-78, 81-84, 86-92, pres., 1988-90; trustee Pendle Hill, Wallingford, Pa., 1977-92, 94-2005, presiding clk., 1983-84, 86, Quaker in Residence, 1998; mem. corp. Haverford Coll., 1974-2001; pres. bd. trustees Hanover Monthly Meeting, Soc. of Friends, 1977-84; chair bd. overseers Kendal at Hanover, 1989-95, chair bd. dirs., 1995-96, pres. residents coun., 2006—07; trustee Am. Farm Sch., 1998—. Recipient E. Harris Harbison award for disting. teaching, Danforth Found., 1968, Golden Cross, St. Andrew Greek Orthodox Archdiocese Australia, 2000; Fulbright fellow, 1958, 1983, 1987. Mem. Modern Greek Studies Assn. (pres. 1982-84, 99-2002, mem. exec. com. 1968-75, 99-2005), Yale Club (N.Y.C.). Democrat. Home: 80 Lyme Rd # 171 Hanover NH 03755 Home (Summer): Terpni 207 Waddell Rd Riparius NY 12862 Home Phone: 603-643-5524; Office Phone: 603-643-5524. E-mail: peter.bien@dartmouth.edu.

BIENEK, DIANE ROSE, research scientist; d. Gerhard K. and Rosemarie E. Bienek. BA, Weber State U., Ogden, Utah, 1991; MS, Utah State U., Logan, 1994; PhD, U. Alta., Edmonton, Can., 2001. Sr. scientist in cell physiology/immunology Henry M. Jackson Found., Rockville, Md., 2003—06, Gen. Dynamics Info. Tech., Frederick, Md., 2006—, Naval Inst for Dental and Biomed., Great Lakes, Ill. Youth advisor LDS Ch., Lake Villa, Ill., 2004. Recipient Am. Soc. Parasitologists prize, Can. Soc. Zoologists, 1997—98. Republican. Mem. Lds Ch. Office: Naval Inst Dental and Biomed 310A B-St Bldg 1-H Great Lakes IL 60088-5259 Home Phone: 847-265-0917; Office Phone: 847-688-5647. Office Fax: 847-688-4279. Business E-Mail: diane.bienek@med.navy.mil.

BIENEN, HENRY SAMUEL, academic administrator, political scientist, educator; b. NYC, May 5, 1939; s. Mitchell Richard and Pearl (Witty) Bienen; m. Leigh Buchanan, Apr. 28, 1961; children: Laura, Claire, Leslie. BA with honors, Cornell U., 1960; MA, U. Chgo., 1961, PhD, 1966. Ssst. prof. politics U. Chgo., 1965—66; asst. prof. politics & internat. affairs Princeton U., NJ, 1966—69, assoc. prof., 1969—72, prof., 1972—95, William Stewart Tod prof. politics and internat. affairs, 1981—85, James S. McDonnell Disting. Univ. prof., 1985, dir. Ctr. Internat. Studies, 1985—92, chair dept. politics, 1973—76, dir. African studies progrm, 1977—78, 1983—84, dir. rsch. Woodrow Wilson Sch. Pub. & Internat. Affairs, 1979—82, dean, 1992—94; pres. Northwestern U., Evanston, Ill., 1995—. Mem. exec. com. Inter-Univ. Seminar on Armed Forces and Soc., 1968—78, Chgo. Coun. Global Affairs; mem. sr. review panel CIA, 1982—88; nat. co. dir. Movement for A New Congress, 1970—71; mem. Inst. Advanced Study, 1984—85, Ctr. Advanced Study in the Behavioral Scis., 1976—77; vis. prof. Makerere Coll., Kampala, Uganda, 1963—65, U. Coll., Nairobi, Kenya, 1968—69, U. Ibadan, 1972—73, Columbia U.; mem. Coun. on Fgn. Rels., Matthews Internat. Capital Mgmt., LLC, Consortium on Financing Higher Edn., John G. Shedd Aquarium, Steppenwolf Theatre, Alain Locke Charter Sch., Com. on Roles of Acad. Health Ctrs. in the 21st Century at Nat. Acad.'s Inst. of Medicine; Acad. fellow Carnegie Corp. on Internat. Devel. Program; cons. in field. Editor: World Politics, 1970—74, 1978—, Voices of Power: World Leaders Speak, 1995—; author: Tanzania: Party Transformation and Economic Development, 1967, The Military Intervenes: Case Studies in Political Change, 1968, Violence and Social Change, 1968, The Military and Modernization, 1970, Kenya: The Politics of Participation and Control, 1974, Armies and Parties in Africa, 1978, The Politcal Economy of Income Distribution in Nigeria, 1981, Political Conflict and Economic Change in Nigeria, 1985, Arms and the African Military Influence in Africa's International Relations, 1985, Of Time and Power: Leadership Duration in the Modern World, 1991, Power, Economics, and Security: The U.S.-Japanese Relationship, 1992. Bd. dirs. The Bear Stearns Co., Inc., Rasmussen Coll.; bd. govs., chair nominating & governance com., mem. exec. com. Coun. Fgn. Rels.; bd. dirs., mem. exec. com. Chgo. Coun. Global Affairs; bd. trustees John G. Shedd Aquarium, Steppenwolf Theatre, Alain Locke Charter Sch.; bd. govs. exec. & nominating com. Argonne Nat. Lab.; bd. trustees The Scholarly Jour. Archives. Recipient Profl. Achievement award, U. Chgo., 2000, Acad. Leadership award, Carnegie Corp., 2005; grantee, Rockefeller Found., 1968—69, 1972—73; Seeger fellow, 1989. Mem.: Assn. Am. Univs. (mem. big tea network branding com., chmn.), Am. Acad., Am. Polit. Sci. Assn., Civil Com. Comm. Club. Office: Northwestern U Z-130 Crown 633 Clark St Evanston IL 60208-0001 Business E-Mail: nu-president@northwestern.edu.

BIENENSTOCK, ARTHUR IRWIN, physicist, educator, federal official; b. NYC, Mar. 20, 1935; s. Leo and Lena (Senator) Bienenstock; m. Roslyn Doris Goldberg, Apr. 14, 1957; children: Eric Lawrence, Amy Elizabeth-(dec.) , Adam Paul. BS, Poly. Inst. Bklyn., 1955, MS, 1957; PhD, Harvard U., 1962; PhD (hon.), Poly. U., 1998, Lund U., 2006. Asst. prof. Harvard U., Cambridge, Mass., 1963—67; mem. faculty Stanford (Calif.) U., 1967—, prof. applied physics, 1972—, vice provost faculty affairs, 1972—77, dir. synchrotron radiation lab., 1978—97, dir. Lab. for Advanced Materials, 2002—03, vice provost, dean rsch. and grad. policy, 2003—06, spl. asst. to the pres., 2006—; assoc. dir. sci. Office of Sci. and Tech. Policy, Washington, 1997—2001. Mem. U.S. Nat. Com. Crystallography, 1983—88; mem. sci. adv. com. European Synchrotron Radiation Facility, 1988—90, 1993—96; mem. com. condensed matter and materials physics NRC, 1996—97, mem. bd. chem. scis. and techs., 2001—03. Contbr. scientific papers to profl. jours. Bd. dirs. Calif. chpt. Cystic Fibrosis Rsch. Found., 1970—73, mem. pres.'s adv. coun., 1980—82; trustee Cystic Fibrosis Found., 1982—88. Recipient Sidhu award, Pitts. Diffraction Soc., 1968, Disting. Alumnus award, Poly. Inst. N.Y., 1977; NSF fellow, 1962—63. Fellow: AAAS, Am. Phys. Soc. (gen. councilor 1993—96, v.p. 2006, pres. elect 2007—); mem.: Materials Rsch. Soc., Am. Crystallographic Assn. Jewish. Home: 967 Mears Ct Stanford CA 94305 Office: Bldg 160 Rm 223 Stanford CA 94305-2205 Office Phone: 650-723-8845. Business E-Mail: arthurb@stanford.edu.

BIENENSTOCK, JOHN, pathologist, educator, health facility administrator; b. Budapest, Hungary, Oct. 6, 1936; s. Maurice and Anne (Horn) Bienenstock; m. Dody Sanders, Nov. 24, 1961; children: Jimson Andrew, Adam Sebastian, Robin Anne. MB, BChir, Westminster Med. Sch., London, 1960; postgrad., Harvard Med. Sch., 1964—66, SUNY, Buffalo, 1966—68; MD (hon.), U. Göteborg, Sweden, 1998; CM, Order of Canada, 2002. Fellow Harvard U. Med. Sch., Boston, 1964; Buswell fellow SUNY, Buffalo, 1966—68, asst. rsch. prof. medicine, 1967—68; asst. prof. medicine McMaster U., Hamilton, Ont., Canada, 1968—74, assoc. dean rsch., 1972—78, prof. medicine and pathology, 1974—, chmn. dept. pathology, 1978—89, v.p. health scis., 1989—97, dean health scis., 1992—97, univ. prof., 1997—; dir. Brain-Body Inst. St. Joseph's Healthcare, Hamilton, 2001—. Founder AB Biol. Supply, Inc., 1977, Agritech Rsch. Inc., 1980; D. W. Harrington lectr. SUNY, Buffalo, 1986; Rayne vis. prof. U. Western Australia, Perth, 1987; cons. WHO, Geneva, 1970—; chief sci. officer Oratol Inc., 1997—99; chmn. sci. adv. bd. Internat. Med. Innovations, 1999; bd. dirs. Prometic Life Sci. Inc.; cons. various pharm. cos.; dir. Brain-Body Inst. St. Joseph's Healthcare, Hamilton. Editor: (book) Immunology of Lung, 1984, Mast Cell Differentiation, 1986, Recent Advances in Mucosal Immunology, 1987, Handbook of Mucosal Immunology, 1994, Mucosal Immunology, 1998, 3d edit., 2004; contbr. over 400 articles to profl. jours. Chmn., bd. dirs. Can. Red Cross Soc.; chmn. bd. Dundas Valley Sch. Art., Ont., 1984—86; chmn. adv. com. nat. blood svcs., 1985—90. Recipient Prukynje medal, Assn. Czechoslovak Socs., Prague, 1989, Ross A. McIntyre Gold medal, U. Nebr., Omaha, 1989, Finkelstein prize, Crohn's and Colitis Found., Can., 1996. Fellow: RCP (London), RCP (Can.), Royal Soc. Can.; mem.: Coll. Internat. Allergologicum (pres. 1998—2002), Soc. Mucosal Immunology (pres. 1990—92), Internat. Union Immunological Socs. (mem. coun.), Am. Thoracic Soc., Swiss Soc. Allergy and Immunology (hon.), Am. Soc. Clin. Investigation, Assn. Am. Physicians, Can. Soc. Immunology (pres. 1985—87). Jewish. Avocation: painting. Office: Brain-Body Inst St Josephs Healthcare 50 Charlton Ave E Tower 3304 Hamilton ON Canada L8N 4A6 Home: 801-19 Brant St Toronto ON Canada M5V 2L2 Office Phone: 905-522-1155 35203. Office Fax: 905-540-6593. Business E-Mail: bienens@mcmaster.ca.

BIENENSTOCK, MARTIN J., lawyer; b. NYC, Nov. 14, 1952; s. Arthur H. and Elaine (Schulman) B. BS in Econs., U. Pa., 1974; JD cum laude, U. Mich. Law Sch., 1977. Bar: NY 1978, US Dist. Ct. (So. and Ea. Districts) NY 1978, US Dist. Ct. So. Dist. Ala. 1983, US Ct. Appeals (2nd Cir.) 1986, US Supreme Ct. 1987, US Dist. Ct., No. Dist. Tex., 1988, US Ct. Appeals (5th Cir.) 1989. Assoc. Weil, Gotshal & Manges LLP, NYC, 1977-85, ptnr., co-chair bus. fin. and restructuring dept., 1985—. Tchr. of Advanced Reorganization Harvard Law Sch. Writer (treatise) Bankruptcy Reorganization. Named one of 100 Most Influential Lawyers, Nat. Law Jour., 2006; named to The Best Lawyers in America, 2007. Mem. ABA, Am. Coll. Bankrupty Lawyers, S.W. Legal Found.; fellow Am. Coll. Commercial Fin. Lawyers Jewish. Office: Weil Gotshal & Manges LLP 767 5th Ave New York NY 10153-0119 Office Phone: 212-310-8530. Office Fax: 212-310-8007. Business E-Mail: martin.bienenstock@weil.com.*

BIENIAWSKI, ZDZISLAW TADEUSZ RICHARD, engineering educator, writer, consultant; b. Cracow, Poland, Oct. 1, 1936; came to U.S., 1978, naturalized; m. Elizabeth Hyslop, 1964; 3 children. Student, Gdansk Poly. Inst., Poland, 1954—58; BS in Mech. Engring., U. Witwatersrand, Johannesburg, South Africa, 1961, MS in Engring. Mechanics, 1963; PhD in Rock Engring., U. Pretoria, South Africa, 1968; DEng (hon.), U. Madrid, 2001. Prof. mineral engring. Pa. State U., Univ. Park, 1977—96, prof. sci., tech. & society, 1994-96, prof. emeritus, 1996—; pres. Bieniawski Design Enterprises, Prescott, Ariz., 1996—; Disting. prof. geol. engring. U. Madrid, Spain, 2001—. Vis. prof. U. Karlsruhe, Germany, 1972, Stanford U., 1985, Harvard U., 1990, Cambridge (Eng.) U., 1997; chmn. U.S. Nat. Com. on Tunneling Tech., 1984-85; U.S. rep. to Internat. Tunnel Assn., 1984-85. Author: Rock Mechanics Design in Mining and Tunneling, 1984, Strata Control in Mineral Engineering, 1987, Aiming High-A Collection of Essays, 1988, Engineering Rock Mass Classifications, 1989, A Tale of Three Continents, 1991, Design Methodology in Rock Engineering, 1992, Gaudeamus Igitur Poems, 1997, Alec's Journey, 1999, Beasts in the Onion Leaves and Renaissance Dialogues, 2006; editor: Tunneling in Rock, 1974, Exploration for Rock Engineering, 1976, Milestones in Rock Engring., 1996; contbr. over 170 articles to profl. jours. Recipient Mayor's Proclamation of City of State Coll. Bieniawski Day, 1983, Rock Mechanics Rsch. award, 1984, Disting. Toastmaster Internat. award, 1974; Bieniawski Auditorium at U. Madrid Sch. Mines named in his honor, 2003. Avocations: genealogy, cosmology, foreign policy, financial planning. Home: The Ranch 3023 Sunnybrae Cir Prescott AZ 86303-5770

BIENVENU, JOHN CHARLES, lawyer; b. Modesto, Calif., Sept. 11, 1957; s. Robert Charles and Martha Louise (Beard) B.; m. Sarah Luciene Brick, May 10, 1983; children: Reed Charles, Loren John. Student, U. Calif., Berkeley, 1975-78; BA summa cum laude, U. N.Mex., 1985; JD with distinction, Stanford U., 1988. Bar: Calif., 1988, N.Mex., 1990; U.S. Ct. Appeals (9th cir.) 1988, U.S. Ct. Appeals (10th cir.) 1990; U.S. Ct. Fed. Claims, 1991. Assoc. Brobeck, Phleger & Harrison, San Francisco, 1988-90, Rothstein, Walther, Donatelli, Hughes, Dahlstrom & Cron, Santa Fe, N.Mex., 1990-93; prin. Santa Fe, 1993—. Mem. ACLU (cooperating atty. N.Mex.), N.Mex. State Bar. Democrat. Home: 1580 Cerro Gordo Rd Santa Fe NM 87501-6143 Office: PO Box 2455 1217 Paseo de Peralta Santa Fe NM 87501-1883 Office Phone: 505-988-8004. Business E-Mail: jbienvenu@rothsteinlaw.com.

BIER, KARLA, manufacturing engineer, chemical engineer, educator; d. Mary and Charles Stiefermann; m. Gregory Bier, Dec. 20, 1986; children: Kirstin, Bridget, Brandon. BS in Chem. Engring., U. Mo.- Rolla, 1988, MS in Chem. Engring., 1994, PhD in Chem. Engring., 1998. Asst. prof. Stephens Coll., Columbia, Mo., 1999—2006; rsch. asst. U. Mo.-Rolla, 1983—89; semivolatile gc dept. chemist and mgr. Savannah Labs. and Environ. Svcs., Savannah, Ga., 1990—93; mfg. engr. 3M, Columbia, 2006—. Tchr. sci. using inquiry. Advisor Students in Free Enterprise, Columbia, 2000—04, Sigma Sigma Sigma Sorority, Columbia, 2000—06; vol. sci. workshops Stephens Natural Sci. Dept., Columbia, 2000—06; canstruction participant Ctrl. Mo. Food Bank, Columbia, 2002—06; catechist St. Thomas More Newman Ctr., Columbia, 2001—06. Mem.: Soc. Women Engrs. (treas. middle Mo. sect. 2006), Tau Beta Pi, Alpha Chi Sigma. Avocation: scuba diving. Office Phone: 573-886-1865.

BIER, LOUIS HENRY GUSTAV, minister; b. Chgo., Jan. 12, 1933; s. Louis Wilfred and Ethel Lea (Laue) Bier; m. Helene Mueller, July 29, 1962; children: Richard Allen, Karen Elizabeth, Lisa Anne. BE, Chgo. Tchrs. Coll., 1954; B in Theology, Concordia Sem., 1959, MDiv in Theology, 1959; MEd, Boston State Coll., 1962; DRE, Smith Bapt. U., 1987, DD, 1986. Ordained ministry Luth. Ch., 1959; lic. social worker. Vicar Redeemer Luth. Ch., Phila., 1957, 1st Luth. Ch., Holyoke, Mass., 1957—58; pastor St. Paul's Luth. Ch., West Frankfort, Ill., 1959—61, Trinity Luth. Ch., Boston, 1961—98, emeritus, 1999—; chaplain VA New Eng. Health Care Sys., Boston, 1965—; instr. psychology Boston State Coll., 1967—81; mem. adj. faculty Holy Cross Greek Orthodox Sem., Brookline, Mass., 1998. Chaplain German Home Elderly, Boston, 1962, also trustee, clk. corp., 1971—; chaplain Arbour, Boston, 1969, West Roxbury VA Hosp., 1978—86; circuit counselor Luth. Ch. Mo. Synod; trustee Chapel Four Chaplains, Valley Forge, Pa., 2000; cons. Slavik Rsch. Inst.; mem. animal studies com. Beth Israel-Deaconess Hosp., Havard Med. Sch., 2000; bd. dirs. Interfaith Bible Readings, Inc. Active Boy Scouts Am., Boston, 1970—; mem. USO Coun. New Eng.; bd. mgrs. Sophia Snow Ho.; br. pres. A.A.L., 1982. Seved to lt. col. CAP, 1975—2005, col. chaplain Mass. State Def. Fort. Co-recipient 40 Yr. award, Friends of Old Sturbridge Village, 2005; recipient Honored Citizen award, Kennedy VFW, 1973, Cmty. Svc. award, Greater Boston Assn. Retarded Citizens, 1974, Lamb award, Luth. Coun., 1975, George Meany Youth Svc. award, AFL-CIO, 1983, Dist. Eagle Scout award, Boy Scouts Am., 1993, Recognition award, Slovik Rsch. Inst., 1999, Svc. award, Concordia Seminary, Ft. Wayne, Ind., 1999, 30 Yr. citation, CAP, 2005; West fellow, Boy Scouts Am., 1999, Emerson fellow, Mil. Chaplains Assn. USA, 1999. Mem.: Am. Assn. Mental Retardation (20 Year Citation 2002, Humanitarian award Northeast region 2002), Concordia Sem. (Servus Ecclesia Christi award), Mass. Chaplains Assn., German Aid Soc. Boston (trustee), Assn. Profl. Chaplains (life; cert., 25th Anniversary citation 2000), Mil. Chaplains Assn. (life; treas., v.p., pres.), Luth. Edn. Assn. (life), Friends of Jackson Lab. of Bar Harbor, Slovik Assn. (life), Westwood Hist. Soc., Franklin County Hist. Soc. (life), Bar Harbor Hist. Soc. (life), Nat. Eagle Scout Assn. (life), New Eng. Luth. Hist. Soc. (life), Vanderbilt Club. Avocations: swimming, golf, reading. Home: 169 Nahatan St Westwood MA 02090-3607 Office Phone: 617-232-9500 ext. 45065.

BIERBAUM, J. ARMIN, petroleum company executive, consultant; b. Oak Park, Ill., June 29, 1924; s. Armin Walter and Harriett Cornelia (Backmann) B.; m. Janith Turnbull, Apr. 17, 1948; children: Steve, Todd, Charles, Peter, Mark. BS, Northwestern U., 1945, MS, 1948. Project engr. Am. Oil Co., Ind., 1948-53; sales engr. Universal Oil Products Co., Des Plaines, Ill., 1953-56; tech. dir. Nat. Coop. Refinery Assn., McPherson, Kans., 1956-58; asst. plant mgr., treas., v.p., dir. Gen. Carbon & Chem. Corp., Robinson, Ill., 1958-61; cons. Williston, ND, 1962-64; v.p. ops. Midland Coops., Inc., Mpls., 1964-72; sr. v.p. ops. Tosco Corp., Los Angeles, 1972-77; pres., chief exec. officer Gary Energy Co., Englewood, Colo., 1977-79, U.S. Ethanol Corp., Englewood, 1979-82; cons., 1983—. Served with USNR, 1942-45. Mem. Am. Inst. Chem. Engrs., Sigma Xi, Phi Epsilon Pi. Office: 1609 Ridgecrest Dr Loveland CO 80537-9073

BIERBAUM, JANITH MARIE, artist; b. Evanston, Ill., Jan. 14, 1927; d. Gerald Percy and Lillian (Sullivan) Turnbull; m. J. Armin Bierbaum, Apr. 17, 1948; children: Steve, Todd, Chad, Peter, Mark. BA, Northwestern U., 1948; student, Mpls. Art Inst., 1964; postgrad., St. Paul Art Inst., 1969-70. Rsch. asst. AMA, Chgo., 1948-49; tchr. Chgo. high schs., 1949-51; freelance artist Larkspur, Colo., 1951—. Exhibited in group shows at Foot Hills Art Ctr., 1985, 86, 87, Palmer Lake (Colo.) Art Assn., 1986-87, 88-89, Gov.'s Mansion, Bismarck, N.D., 1960; oil painting appeared in 1989 Women in Art Nat. calendar pub. by AAUW. Recipient 1st Place Purchase award, U. Minn., Mpls., 1966, Coors Classic award, Coors Beer, Golden, Colo., 1987. Mem.: Colo. Artist Assn. Republican. Avocations: cross country skiing, swimming, hiking. Home and Office: 1609 Ridgecrest Dr Loveland CO 80537-9073

BIERBAUM, ROSINA M., federal agency administrator; BS in Biology, Boston Coll., 1974, BA in English, 1974; PhD in Ecology and Evolution, SUNY, Stony Brook, 1985. Congressional fellow, 1980; sr. assoc. environ. program Office of Tech. Assessment U.S. Congress, Washington, 1991-93, sr. policy analyst Sci. Tech. Policy Office, 1993-96, asst. dir. environ. Sci. Tech. Policy Office, 1996, acting assoc. dir. Sci. Tech. Policy Office, 1996-97, apptd. assoc. dir. environ. Office Sci. Tech. Policy for the Pres., 1998—2001; dean, prof, environ. and natural resource policy and mgmt. Sch. of Natural Resources & Environment, U. Mich., 2001—. U.S. scientific expert, Permanent Ct. of Arbitration of Disputes Relating to Natural Resources and/or the Environ., in Hague, on the Bd. on Atmospheric Scis. and Climate of the Nat. Rsch. Coun. of the Nat. Academies; mem. exec. com., Inst. for Social Rsch., U. Mich.; mem. oversite com., Environ. and Energy Study Inst.; mem. design com., "The State of Nation's Ecosystems", H. John Heinz III Ctr.; lectr. in field. Mem. adv. bd. Frontiers in Ecology & the Environment, Ecological Soc. Am., mem. editl. bd. Consequences, reviewer International Panel on Climate Change; contbr. articles to profl. jours. Co-chair Def. Strategic Environ. R&D Program. Mem. Nat. Sci. & Tech. Coun. (mem. com. on environ. and natural resources), Nat. Ocean Rsch. Leadership Coun., Am. Geophysical Union (Waldo E. Smith medal, 2000), Energy Found., NAS (bd. dir. Atmospheric Chemistry and Climate); bd. dir. Fedn. Am. Scientists; fellow AAAS, Am. Acad. Arts & Scis. Office: U Mich Sch of Natural Resources and Environment 440 Church St 2046a Dana Ann Arbor MI 48109-1041 Office Phone: 734-764-6453, 734-764-2550. Business E-Mail: rbierbau@umich.edu.*

BIERIG, JACK R., lawyer, educator; b. Chgo., Apr. 10, 1947; s. Henry J. and Helga (Rothschild) B.; m. Barbara A. Winokur; children: Robert, Sarah. BA, Brandeis U., 1968; JD, Harvard U., 1972. Bar: Ill. 1972, US Dist. Ct. (no. dist.) Ill. 1972, US Ct. Appeals (1st-3d, 5th-11th and DC cirs.) 1974, US Supreme Ct. 1980. Ptnr. Sidley Austin, LLP, Chgo., 1972—; prof. Ill. Inst. Tech.-Chgo. Kent Coll. Law, 1974-95; lectr. law. U. Chgo. Law Sch. and Harris Sch. Pub. Policy, 2000—. Chmn. legal sect. Am. Soc. Assn. Execs., 1994-95. Contbr. articles to profl. jours. Pres. Neighborhood Justice Chgo., 1983-87; pres. Jewish Vocat. Svc., 1997-99. Mem. Ill. Assn. of Hosp. Attys. (pres. 1991), Chgo. Bar Assn. (bd. govs., 1982-84). Clubs: Standard (Chgo.). Jewish. Office Phone: 312-853-7614. Business E-Mail: jbierig@sidley.com.

BIERLY, EUGENE WENDELL, meteorologist, science foundation director; b. Sept. 11, 1931; m., 1953; 3 children AB, U. Pa., 1953; cert., U.S. Naval Postgrad. Sch., 1954; MS, U. Mich., 1957, PhD, 1968. Asst. dept. civil engring. meteorol. labs. U. Mich., Ann Arbor, 1956-60, asst. research meteorologist dept. engring. mechanics, 1960-63, lectr., 1961-63; meteorologist U.S. AEC, 1963-66; dir. meteorology NSF, Washington, 1966-71, coordinator global atmospheric research program, 1971-74, head office climate dynamics, 1974-75, head climate dynamics research sect., 1975-79, dir. div. atmospheric scis., 1979-92; dir. edn. and rsch. Am. Geophys. Union, 1992-98, sr. scientist, 1998—2006, acting dir. outreach and rsch. support, 2006—. Mem. biol. and environ. rsch. adv. com. Dept. Energy, 1992—; chmn. adv. cons. bd. Geophys. Inst., U. Alaska, 1993—; chmn. adv. bd. U. Okla. Sch. Meteorology, 1994—; cons. Fla. State U., U. Okla., U. Ariz., Univs. Space Rsch. Assn., Soundprint Media Ctr. Cons. editor: Meteorology & Climatology, Encyclopedia Sci. and Tech., 9th edit., Yearbook Scis. and Tech., 2000, 2002. Congl. fellow, 1970-71 Fellow AAAS, Am. Meteorol. Soc. (pres. 1984, Charles Franklin Brooks award 1990, Cleveland Abbe award 2000); mem. Chinese Meteorol. Soc., Am. Geophys. Union, Sigma Xi (presdl. rank merit excellence sr. exec. svc. 1982). Office: AGU Directorate Outreach and Rsch Support 2000 Florida Ave NW Washington DC 20009-1277 Home: 300 King Farm Blvd #204 Rockville MD 20850 Office Phone: 202-777-7506. Business E-Mail: ebierly@agu.org.

BIERLY, SHIRLEY ADELAIDE, communications executive; b. Waterbury, Conn., Jan. 19, 1924; d. Samuel and Frances Ada (Bogorad) Brown; m. Leroy Elwood Bierly, Jan. 19, 1946 (div. 1951); children: Lee Jr., Dennis Ray, David Lincoln. Student, Orange Coast Coll., 1963—66, L.A. City Coll., 1967—69. Mgr. Pacific Telephone, San Francisco, Calif., 1953-82; exec. dir. Sr. Power Office, San Francisco, 1982—. Cmty. activist, 1982—. Editor: Sr. Power newsletter, 1990—. Treas. Calif. Legis. Coun. for Older Am., San Francisco, 1984—; pres. Calif. Assn. Older Am., 1984—, bd. dirs. Sr. Action Network, San Francisco, 1991—, Congress of Calif. Sr., Sacramento, 1994—; trustee Agape Found., 1994-2001; policy bd. Nat. Coun. Sr. Citizens, 1995-2001; commr. San Francisco Residential Arbitration and Stabilization Bd., 1997-2000, Calif. Commn. on Aging, 2000-03; bd. Planning for Elders in Central City, 2000-02; v.p. Yerba Buena Consortium, San Francisco, 1992—; mem. San Francisco Bd. Suprs. Pedestrian Safety Adv. Com., 2003—; exec. bd. Calif. Alliance for Ret. Ams., 2003-06, v.p., 2006—; mem. Kaiser Sr. Adv. Bd., San Francisco, 2004—; adv. bd. Sr. Survival Sch., 2005—, planning com., 2004—. Mem. Am. Civil Liberties Union, Older Women's League, Gray Panthers, Alliance Ret. Ams. (charter, exec. bd., cmty. rep. 2003—). Avocations: photography, theater, reading, philately. Office: Calif Assn for Older Ams (aka Sr Power) 325 Clementina St San Francisco CA 94103-4104 Office Fax: 415-541-9630.

BIERMACHER, KENNETH WAYNE, lawyer; b. Hartford, Conn., Oct. 15, 1953; s. Donald David and Ethel Pearl (Biermacher) Lawton; m. Joan; children; Carl Joseph II (dec.), Matthew Robert, Michelle Renee; 1 step child Brent Cohen. BS summa cum laude, U. New Haven, 1976; JD with honors, Drake U., 1979. Bar: Iowa 1980, Tex. 1985, U.S. Dist. Ct. (so. dist.) Iowa 1980, U.S. Dist. Ct. (no. dist.) Iowa, 1981, U.S. Ct. Appeals (8th cir.) 1981, U.S. Supreme Ct. 1983, U.S. Dist. Ct. (no. dist.) Tex. 1984, U.S. Dist. Ct. (so. and we. dists.) Tex. 1985, U.S. Dist. Ct. (ea. dist.) Tex. 1993, U.S. Ct. Appeals (5th cir.) 1985; cert. scuba diver NAUI, 1999; advanced scuba diving cert. PADI, 2001. Assoc. Whitfield, Musgrave, Selvy, Kelly, Eddy, Des Moines, 1980-84; shareholder Geary, Stahl & Spencer, P.C., Dallas, 1984-89, Leonard Marsh Hurt Terry & Blinn, Dallas, 1989-90; ptnr.-in-charge Dallas office Small, Craig & Werkenthin, P.C., Dallas, 1990-93; v.p., ptnr., dir., gen. counsel Kane, Russell, Coleman & Logan, P.C., Dallas, 1993—. Lectr. Iowa Defense Counsel Assn. Annual Meeting, 1982, Des Moines Area Community Coll. Legal Asst. Program, 1981-82, Human Resources Forum, Am. Electronics Assn., Dallas, 1986; legal research asst. Iowa State Bar Assn. Com. on Study Fed. Rules Evidence, 1982; chmn. spl. com. on Friends of Moot Ct. Drake Law Sch. Bd. Counsellors, 1983-84; founder shareholder, dir. Recruit TV, Inc., 2001—, Xlantic Records, Inc., Dallas, 2001—, Xlantic Music Pub., Inc., Dallas, 2001—, founder, pres., dir. Frontrunner Capital Corp., 1999—, CDRK, Inc., 2001—, Geyser Petroleum, Inc., 2004—, others; bd. dirs. Retractable Techs., Inc., compensation com., nominating com.; bd. dirs., sec. MT Auctions.com, Inc., Dallas. Contbg. author: Understanding Iowa Law, 1984; editor: Energy and Nat. Resources Guide for Iowa, 1979; contbr. articles to law jours. Advisor U. New Haven Law Enforcement Explorers Post Boy Scouts Am., 1975; coach Johnston Sr. HS Mock Trial Teams, Iowa, 1984; chmn. scholarship and fin. aid com. Canyon Creek Christian Acad., 1985—87; v.p., dir. Boys and Girls Clubs of Greater Dallas, Inc., 1997—2004, chmn. circus com., 1998—2000, chmn. resource devel. com., 1999—2001, mem. exec. com., 1999—2001, strategic planning com., 2000—01; bd. govs. U. New Haven, 2007—; del. Polk County Rep. Conv., Des Moines, 1980, Iowa Rep. State Conv., 1980; deacon Canyon Creek

Bapt. Ch., 1986—87; bd. dirs. Henry C. Lee Inst. Forensic Sci., 1997, 2003—. Recipient Acad. Scholarship U. New Haven, 1973-76, Disting. Svc. Recognition award Boys and Girls Clubs Greater Dallas, Inc., 1999-2001, Nat. Svc. To Youth award Boys and Girls Club Am., 2003, Points Inspiration Alumni Svc. award, U. New Haven, 2006. Mem. ABA (subcom. on fraudulent and deceptive trade practices, sect. tort and ins. practice 1985-86, vol. atty. post-conviction death penalty representation project 1988-89), ATLA, FBA, Iowa State Bar Assn. (mem. Young Lawyer Sect. ethics com. 1981, law schs. panel com. 1982, law-related edn. com. 1983-84), Def. Rsch. Inst., Iowa Assn. Trial Lawyers (founding dir., chmn. Drake U. Law Sch. student bd. dirs. 1978-79, ex-officio mem. bd. dirs. 1978-79), Dallas Bar Assn. (mock trial com., law in changing soc. com. 1985, speech com. 1985-86, bus. litigation sect. ethic and courtesy com. 1988, qualified mediator 1989—, mem. cts. com. 1995, mem. fee dispute com. 1995), State Bar Tex. (legal assts. com. 1988-91), Dallas Assn. Young Lawyers (liaison with other profls., fed. opinions com. 1986), Order of Barristers, Atty.-Mediator Assn., Drake U. Law Sch. bd. counselors (regional v.p. for Tex. and Okla. 1986-89), Dallas Tower Club (trustee 1999-2003), Alpha Chi (vice chmn. Conn. chpt. 1975-76). Avocations: scuba diving, hunting, furniture making, off-roading. Home: 4324 Hollow Oak Dr Dallas TX 75287-6847 Office: Kane Russell Coleman & Logan PC 1601 Elm St Ste 3700 Dallas TX 75201-7207 Home Phone: 972-380-1302; Office Phone: 214-777-4250. Business E-Mail: kbiermacher@krcl.com.

BIERMAN, ARNOLD, optometrist; b. NYC, May 6, 1943; s. William Leonard and Dora Bierman; m. Carol F. Bierman, Dec. 26, 1965; 1 child, Julie Elise. BS, OD, Pa. Coll., 1968. Pvt. practice, Lansdale, Pa., 1968—. Clin. instr. Pa. Coll. Optometry, Phila., 1968—72, asst. prof., 1972—79; visual cons. Montgomery County Intermediate Unit, Norristown, Pa., 1976—87; mem. eyecare quality assurance com. U.S. Healthcare, Blue Bell, Pa., 1992—99. Editor: Jour. Pa. Optometrist, 1979—81. Chmn. Jaycees Amblyopia Clinic, Lansdale, Pa., 1969—70. Mem.: Am. Optometric Assn., Pa. Optometric Assn., Am. Acad. Optometry (pres. ea. Pa. chpt. 1980—82), Beta Sigma Kappa. Achievements include expertise in remediating reading and/or learning problems in children and adults. Avocations: art, music, bowling, photography. Office: 2302 N Broad St PO Box 1369 Lansdale PA 19446-0749 Office Phone: 215-822-1365. Personal E-mail: arnoldbierman@comcast.net.

BIERMAN, GEORGE WILLIAM, retired food scientist; b. Cleve., Mar. 2, 1925; s. George Henry and Esther Josephine (Johnson) B.; m. Nyo Jeanne Iserloth; children: Cynthia, Barbara, Marsha, Jill, Wendy, Mindy, G. Steven, Chris. BS, Rutgers U., 1951; PhD, MIT, 1956. Technician R&D Am. Can Co., Maywood, Ill., 1943-45, Schering Corp., Bloomfield, NJ, 1947-48; tech. dir. Friend Bros., Inc., Malden, Mass., 1951-58; v.p. Herbert V. Shuster, Inc., Boston, 1958-75, pres. Quincy, Mass., 1975-89, vice chmn. bd., 1989-95, sr. scientist, 1995-96; tech. cons. Shuster Labs. Inc., 1996—98; ret., 1998. Sgt. U.S. Army, 1945-47. Mem.: Nat. Fisheries Inst. (smoked fish com. 1968—98), Inst. Food Technologists, Assn. Smoked Fish Processors (tech. dir. 1968—98). Presbyterian. Avocations: gardening, motorcycling. Home: 19 Curwen Rd Peabody MA 01960-1205

BIERMAN, JAMES L., health products executive; BA, Dickinson Coll., 1974; MBA, Cornell U., 1976. Ptnr. Arthur Andersen LLP, 1976—98; sr. v.p. corp. devel. Quintiles Transnational, Research Triangle Park, NC, 1998—2000, exec. v.p., CFO, 2000—07; CFO Owens & Minor Inc., Mechanicsville, Va., 2007—. Spkr. in field. Contbr. articles to profl. jours. Mem.: N.C. Assn. CPAs. Office: Owens & Minor Inc 9120 Lockwood Blvd Mechanicsville VA 23116*

BIERMAN, JAMES NORMAN, lawyer; b. St. Louis, Nov. 23, 1945; s. Norman and Margaret (Loeb) B.; m. Catherine Best, Apr. 10, 1983; 1 child, James Norman. AB magna cum laude, Washington U., 1967; JD, Harvard Law Sch., 1970. Bar: D.C. 1970, U.S. Supreme Ct. 1973. Assoc. Hogan & Hartson, Washington, 1970-72; asst. dean Harvard Law Sch., Cambridge, Mass., 1973-75; assoc. Foley & Lardner LLP, Washington, 1975-79, ptnr., 1979—, ptnr. in charge, 1985-2001, mgmt. com., 1989—98. Mem. nat. coun. Washington U. Coll. Arts and Scis., 1999—. Mng. editor Harvard Jour. Legis., 1969-70. Mem. Civil Rights Reviewing Authority HEW, Washington, 1979-80. Mem. ABA, Fed. Bar Assn., Supreme Ct. Bar, Washington Lawyers Com. for Civil Rights and Urban Affairs (bd. dirs. 2000—, co-chmn. 2005-06), Phi Beta Kappa, Omicron Delta Kappa, Pi Sigma Alpha, Phi Eta Sigma. Home: 906 Peacock Station Rd Mc Lean VA 22102-1021 Office: Foley & Lardner LLP 3000 K St NW Fl 5 Washington DC 20007-5143 Office Phone: 202-672-5358. Business E-Mail: jbierman@foley.com.

BIERMAN, SANDRA, artist; b. Bklyn., 1938; d. John Charles Riesberg and Martha Lee Blair; m. Arthur Bierman, Oct. 1, 1983; children: Cheryl, Steven, James. Represented by Contemporary S.W. Gallery, Santa Fe, 1994—, David Haslam, Boulder, Colo., 1992—, Gallery East, Loveland, Colo., 1996—, Augustine Arts, Lake Tahoe, Nev., 1997—, Bakersfield (Calif.) Mus., 2001; instr. workshop Am. Acad. Women Artists, Wickenburg, Ariz., 1997, Oil Painting with Sandra Bierman, Kauai, Hawaii, 2000. One-person shows include Contemporary S.W. Galleries, 1996, Lincoln Ctr. for the Arts, Ft. Collins, Colo., 1998, Bakersfield (Calif.) Mus. Art, 2001; group shows include C.S. Lewis Summer Inst. Show on Tour, 1994, Queens Coll. Art Gallery, Cambridge, Eng., 1994, 99th Nat. Exhbn. Nat. Arts Club, N.Y.C., 1995, 67th Grand Nat. Show, Salmagundi Club, N.Y.C., 1995, Artistes Americaines, Maison du Terroir, Genouilly, France, 1996, Colo. History Mus., 1996, Clymer Mus., Ellensburg, Wash., 1996, Desert Caballeros Mus., Wickenburg, Ariz., 1997, Colo. Gov.'s Invitational Show, Loveland (Colo.) Mus., 1997-2002, Art Expo, N.Y.C., 1998-99; works in permanent collections at City of Loveland, CSI Ltd., Cambridge, Eng., El Pomar Found., Colorado Springs, Colo., Gilford, Inc., N.Y.C., Herzog & Adams, N.Y.C., Loveland Mus., Storage Tek, Louisville, Colo., Boulder Cmty. Hosp., Colo., Telluride Gallery of Fine Art, Colo., Kaiser Permanente, Denver, Kohn Family Trust, Balt., Mfrs.-Hanover trust, N.Y.C., Mayo Women's Clinic, Scottsdale, Penrose Conf., Ctr., Colorado Springs, Philip Chamberlan Inc., Madison, Conn.; featured in Southwest Art Mag., Art Trends Mag., Mountain Living mag., Woman's Mag., Radiance mag., Sun Storm Fine Art Mag., US Art, Art World News, Art Bus. News, others. Recipient Colo. Gov.'s Purchase award, Loveland, 1988, Best of Show award Western Images, Boulder, 1993, medal of honor award Am. Artists Profl. League, N.Y.C., 1995. Mem. Am. Artists Profl. League, Bus. Coun. for the Arts N.Y.C., Nat. Mus. of Women in the Arts, Oil Painters Am., Am. Acad. Women Artists (nominating juror, exec. bd. dirs. 1997—). Office Phone: 303-447-8871. E-mail: art@sandrabierman.com.

BIERS, MARTIN HENRY, physician; b. Bklyn., Oct. 10, 1931; s. Louis and Sarah (Naidich) Bierfass; m. Elizabeth Jaros Biers, Feb. 11, 1962; children: Eric, Carl, John. BA, NYU, 1951; MD, SUNY, Bklyn., 1955. Cert. in internal medicine and hematology. Intern Kings County Hosp., Bklyn., 1955—56; med. resident Bklyn. Vets. Hosp., 1956—57, Montefiore Hosp., Bronx, NY, 1957—58; hematology resident Mt. Sinai Hosp., NYC, 1958—59; pvt. practice White Plains, NY, 1961—. Attending medicine and chief emeritus hematology dept. White Plains Hosp. Capt. USAF, 1959-61. Mem. Am. , N.Y. Med. Soc., Westchester Med. Soc. Office: 170 Maple Ave White Plains NY 10601-5115 Office Phone: 914-328-0932. Business E-Mail: edbiers@aol.com.

BIERSTEDT, PETER RICHARD, entertainment industry consultant, lawyer; b. Rhinebeck, NY, Jan. 2, 1943; s. Robert Henry and Betty Bierstedt; m. Carol Lynn Akiyama, Aug. 23, 1980 (div. Oct. 1995); m. Lieschen van Straaten, Aug. 11, 2000. AB, Columbia U., 1965, JD cum laude, 1969; cert., U. Sorbonne, Paris, 1966. Bar: N.Y. 1969, Calif. 1977, U.S. Supreme Ct. 1973. Atty. with firms in, NYC, 1969-74; pvt. practice cons. legal and entertainment industry, 1971, 75-76, 88—; with Avco Embassy Pictures Corp., LA, 1977-83, v.p., gen. counsel, 1978-80, sr. v.p., 1980-83, dir., 1981-83; gen. counsel New World Entertainment (formerly New World Pictures), LA, 1984-87, exec. v.p., 1985-87, sr. exec. v.p. Office of Chmn., 1987-88, also bd. dirs.; pres. subs. New World Prodns. and New World Advt. New World Pictures, 1985-88. Guest lectr. U. Calif., Riverside, 1976-77, U. So. Calif., 1986, 91, UCLA, 1987, 95-96; bd. dirs. New World Pictures (Australia) Ltd., FilmDallas Pictures, Inc., Cinedco, Inc. Exec. prodr. (home video series) The Comic Book Greats. Mem. Motion Picture Assn. Am. (dir. 1980-83), Acad. Motion Picture Arts and Scis. (exec. br.), LA Copyright Soc., ACLU. Democrat. Avocations: astronomy, literature, tennis, scuba diving. Office Phone: 323-667-2698. Business E-Mail: peter@bierstedt.com.

BIERY, EVELYN HUDSON, lawyer; b. Lawton, Okla., Oct. 12, 1946; d. William Ray and Nellie Iris (Nunley) Hudson. BA in English and Latin summa cum laude, Abilene Christian U., Tex., 1968; JD, So. Meth. U., 1973. Bar: Tex. 1973, US Dist. Ct. (we. dist.) Tex. 1975, US Dist. Ct. (so. dist.) Tex. 1977, US Dist. Ct. (no. dist.) Tex. 1979, US Ct. Appeals (5th cir.) 1979, US Ct. Appeals (11th cir.) 1981, US Supreme Ct. 1981. Atty. Law Offices of Bruce Waitz, San Antonio, 1973-76; mem. LeLaurin & Adams, PC, San Antonio, 1976-81; ptnr. Fulbright & Jaworski, San Antonio, 1982—2003, head bankruptcy, reorgn. and creditors' rights sect. Houston, 1990—. Policy com. Fulbright & Jaworski, 1996-98; spkr. on creditors' rights, bankruptcy and reorganization law; lectr. Southwestern Grad. Sch. Banking, Dallas, 1980, La. State U. Sch. Banking, 1994; presiding officer, U. Tex. Sch. of Law Bankruptcy Conf., 1976, 94, State Bar Tex. Creditors' Rights Inst., 1985, 88, State Bar Tex. Advanced Bus. Bankruptcy Law Inst., 1985, State Bar Tex. Inst. on Advising Officers, Dirs. and Ptnrs. in Troubled Bus., 1987, U. Tex. Sch. Law Bankruptcy Conf. 2006; mem. bankruptcy adv. com. 5th cir. jud. coun., 1979-80; vice-chmn. bankruptcy com. Comml. Law League Am., 1981-83; mem. exec. bd. So. Meth. U. Sch. Law, 1983-91; founding dir., com. chair, Internat. Insolvency Inst., 1998-. Editor: Texas Collections Manual, 1978, Creditor's Rights in Texas, 2d edit., 1981; author: (with others) Collier Bankruptcy Practice Guide, 1993. Del. to US/Republic of China joint session on trade, investment and econ. law, Beijing, 1987; designated mem. Bankruptcy Judge Merit Screening Com. State of Tex. by Tex. State Bar Pres., 1979-82; patron McNay Mus., San Antonio; rsch. ptnr. Mind Sci. Found., San Antonio; diplomat World Affairs Coun., San Antonio. Fellow: Soc. Internat. Bus. Fellows (chair bd. dirs.), San Antonio Bar Found. (life), Tex. Bar Found. (life); mem.: San Antonio Young Lawyers Assn. (pres. 1979—80, Outstanding Young Lawyer award 1979), Tex. Assn. Bank Counsel (bd. dirs. 1988—90, 2001—04), Tex. Bar Assn. (chair bankruptcy com. 1982—83, chair corp., banking and bus. law sect. 1989—90), Am. Coll. Bankruptcy Attys. (chair bd. dirs. 2006—07, pres. 2003—05), Zonta (Chair Z club com. 1989—90), Plaza Club San Antonio (bd. dirs. 1982—), Order of Coif. Office: Fulbright & Jaworski LLP 1301 McKinney St Ste 5100 Houston TX 77010-3031 Office Phone: 713-651-5544. Office Fax: 713-651-5246. Business E-Mail: ebiery@fulbright.com.

BIES, SUSAN SCHMIDT, former federal official; b. Buffalo, May 5, 1947; d. Louis Howard and Gladys May (Metke) Schmidt; m. John David Bies, Aug. 29, 1970; children: John Matthew, Scott Louis. BS, State U. Coll.-Buffalo, 1967; MA, Northwestern U., 1968, PhD, 1972. Banking structure economist Fed. Res. Sys., St. Louis, 1970-72; asst. prof. econs. Wayne State U., Detroit, 1972-77; assoc. prof. Rhodes Coll., Memphis, 1977-80; tactical planning mgr. First Tenn. Nat. Corp., Memphis, 1980-81, dir. corp. devel., 1982-83, treas., 1983-84, sr. v.p., CFO, 1984-85, exec. v.p., CFO, 1985—95, exec. v.p. for risk mgmt., auditor, 1995—2001; mem. bd. govs. Fed. Res. Sys., Washington, 2001—07. Mem. fin. adv. com. City of Germantown, Tenn., 1978—; mem. investment adv. com. Tenn. Consol. Retirement System, Nashville, 1981-86; instr. MidSouth Sch. Banking, 1985-86; mem. Com. on Corp. Reporting, Fin. Exec. Inst.; mem. Bank Adminstrn. Inst. Pres., bd. dirs. North Germantown Homeowners Assn., 1978-83; treas. Germantown Area Soccer Assn., 1985-86; treas. Fury Soccer Club, 1988—; vice chmn. task force Com. on 21st Century, Rhodes Coll., Memphis, 1986-87; mem. exec. adv. bd. Sch. Accountancy Memphis State U.; bd. dirs. Memphis Youth Initiative, 1988, Memphis Ptnrs.; mem. BAI Acctg. and Fin. Commn., 1988—, Internat. Women's Forum Fellow Ctr. for Urban Affairs, 1968-69, Fed. Res. Bank Chgo., 1970. Mem. Am. Bankers Assn. (exec. com. 1986-88), Nat. Assn. Bus. Economists, Am. Econ. Assn., End Users of Derivatives Assn., Planning Execs. Inst., Fin. Execs. Inst., (bd. dirs. Memphis chpt. 1988—), Planning Forum (Managerial Excellence award Memphis chpt. 1986), Memphis Area C. of C. (bd. dirs. 1988—, tax com. 1988—, chair 1989—), Econ. Club Memphis (bd. dirs. 1986—, vice chmn. 1987-88, chmn. 1988-89), Omicron Delta Epsilon, Lambda Alpha. Episcopalian. Avocations: gardening, golf, soccer.

BIESELE, JOHN JULIUS, biologist, educator; b. Waco, Tex., Mar. 24, 1918; s. Rudolph Leopold and Anna Emma (Jahn) B.; m. Marguerite Calfee McAfee, July 29, 1943 (dec. 1991); children: Marguerite Anne, Diana Terry, Elizabeth Jane; m. Esther Aline Eakin, Mar. 9, 1992 (dec., 2007). BA with highest honors, U. Tex., 1939, PhD, 1942. Fellow Internat. Cancer Rsch. Found., U. Tex., 1942—43, Barnard Skin and Cancer Hosp., St. Louis, U. Pa., Phila., 1943—44, instr. zoology, 1943—44; temporary rsch. assoc. dept. genetics Carnegie Instn. of Washington, Cold Spring Harbor, 1944—46; rsch. assoc. biology dept. MIT, Cambridge, 1946—47; asst. Sloan-Kettering Inst. Cancer Rsch., 1946—47, rsch. fellow, 1947, assoc., 1947—55, head cell growth sect., divsn. exptl. chemotherapy, 1947—58, mem., 1955—58, assoc. scientist divsn., 1959—78; asst. prof. anatomy Cornell U. Med. Sch., 1950—52; assoc. prof. biology Sloan-Kettering divsn. Cornell U. Grad. Sch. Med. Scis., 1952—55, prof. biology, 1955—58; prof. zoology, mem. grad. faculty U. Tex., Austin, 1958—78, also mem. faculty Coll. Pharmacy, 1969—71, prof. edn., 1973—78, prof. emeritus zoology, 1978—99; prof. emeritus sect. molecular cell and developmental biol. U. Tex. Sch. Biol. Scis., Austin, 1999—. Cons. cell biology M.D. Anderson Hosp. and Tumor Inst., U. Tex., Houston, 1958-72; dir. Genetics Found., 1959-78; mem. cell biology study sect. NIH, 1958-63; Sigma Xi lectr. NYU Grad. Sch. Arts and Scis., 1957; Mendel lectr. St. Peter's Coll., Jersey City, 1958; featured spkr. on first Earth Day, Old Westbury Campus of N.Y. Inst. Tech., 1970; Mendel Club lectr. Canisius Coll., Buffalo, 1971; adv. com. rsch. etiology of cancer Am. Cancer Soc., 1961-64, pres. Travis County unit, 1966, adv. com. on pers. for rsch., 1969-73; counsellor Cancer Internat. Rsch. Coop., Inc., 1962-90; cancer rsch. tng. com. Nat. Cancer Inst., 1969-72; gen. chmn. Conf. Advancement Sci. and Math. Tchg., 1966. Author: Mitotic Poisons and the Cancer Problem, 1958; mem. editorial bd. Year Book Cancer, 1959-72; mem. editorial adv. bd. Cancer Rsch., 1960-64, assoc. editor, 1969-72; cons. editor: Am. Jour. Mental Deficiency, 1963-68; mem. editorial bd. The Jour. of Applied Nutrition, 1987-91; contbr. articles to profl. jours. Rsch. Career award NIH, 1962, 67, 72, 77 Fellow AAAS, N.Y. Acad. Scis., Tex. Acad. Scis.; mem. Am. Assn. Cancer Rsch. (dir. 1960-63), Am. Soc. Cell Biology, Am. Inst. Biol. Scis., Phi Beta Kappa, Sigma Xi (pres. Tex. chpt. 1963-64), Phi Eta Sigma, Phi Kappa Phi. Achievements include rsch. in provision of early evidence for abnormal chromosome numbers in cancer cells, for occasional excessively multiple-stranded state of cancer chromosomes; demonstration of a direct relation of chromosomal size in mammalian tissues and organs to the local metabolic activity, as evidenced by the local content of B vitamins, of differential toxicity in certain antimetabolites to cancer cells in culture. Home: 2500 Great Oaks Pky Austin TX 78756-2908

BIESENBACH-LUCAS, SIGRUN, language educator, consultant; b. Remscheid, Germany, Mar. 28, 1960; arrived in US, 1984; d. Heinz Wilhelm and Ingrid Biesenbach; m. Randolph Joel Pitcher Lucas, 1984; children: Benjamin Noah Lucas, Cameron Raymond Lucas. BA, U. Bonn, 1983; MA in Tchg., Georgetown U., Washington, 1986, PhD, 1994. Asst. professorial lectr. ESL/English fgn. lang. George Washington U., Washington, 1988—98; asst. professorial lectr. applied linguistics Georgetown U., Washington, 1992—98, instr. Ctr. for Lang. Edn. and Devel., 2006—; asst. prof. TESOL Am. U., Washington, 1998—2006. Site reviewer Commn. on English Lang. Program Accreditation; cons. Svc. English, Ashburn, Va., 2006—; presenter in field. Revs. editor Lang. Learning and Tech., 2005—, mem. editl. bd., 2006—; contbr. articles to profl. jours. Guest panelist AAUW, Washington, 2003—04. Mem.: TESOL (World Tchr. honoree 2005—06), Washington Area TESOL, Internat. Soc. Lang. Studies, Linguistic Soc. Can. and US, Am. Assn. Applied Linguistics. Achievements include research in email requests in higher education. Office: Georgetown Univ Box 571054 ICC 481 Washington DC 20057 Home Phone: 703-729-3347; Office Phone: 202-687-5869. Business E-Mail: biesenbs@georgetown.edu.

BIESTY, JENNIFER, chef; Grad., Culinary Inst. Am. Chef de partie Aquavit, NYC; sous chef Charlotte, NYC; chef Bizou, San Francisco, 1994—97, chef de cuisine; exec. chef Coco500 (formerly Bizou), San Francisco; chef de partie The River Café, London, 1997—98; chef Jardiniere, San Francisco, 1998; exec. chef Universal Cafe. Named one of San Francisco's Rising Stars, StarChefs.com, 2007. Office: Coco500 500 Brannan St San Francisco CA 94107 Business E-Mail: jb@coco500.com.*

BIFFLE, TONY, editor; Copy editor Sun Herald, Biloxi, Miss., 1993—94, assoc. editor, 1994—, mem. editorial bd., 1994—. Recipient Walker Stone award for editorial writing, Scripps Howard Found., 2006. Office: The Sun Herald 205 DeBuys Rd Gulfport MS 39507 Mailing: The Sun Herald PO Box 4567 Biloxi MS 39535-4567 Office Phone: 228-896-2387. Office Fax: 228-896-2104. E-mail: tdbiffle@sunherald.com.

BIG BOI, See PATTON, ANTWAN

BIG BOY, (KURT ALEXANDER), radio personality, actor; b. Chgo., 1969; s. Ida Alexander. Bodyguard for rap group Pharcyde; with KPWR/Power 106 FM, LA, 1994—. Host (radio show) Big Boy's Neighborhood, announcer (TV series) Vibe, 1998; actor: (films) The Players Club, 1998, Deuce Bigalow: Male Gigolo, 1999, 3 Strikes, 2000, Malibu's Most Wanted, 2003, Charlie's Angels: Full Throttle, 2003, Soul Plane, 2004; (TV series) Fastlane, 2002—03; voice actor: (video games) Grand Theft Auto: San Andreas, 2004; (TV films) The Proud Family Movie, 2005. Named Personality of Yr., Radio Music Awards (4 time winner), Radio & Records mag. (3 time winner); recipient Marconi Radio award for Major Market Personality of Yr., Nat. Assn. Broadcasters, 2002, 2004. Office: Power 106 8th Fl 2600 W Olive Ave Burbank CA 91505 E-mail: bigboy@power106.emmis.com.

BIGBY, JUDYANN, medical educator; b. Jamaica, NY, 1951; children: Kenan, Naima. BA, Wellesley Coll., 1973; MD, Harvard U., 1978. Henry J. Kaiser fellow in gen. internal medicine Harvard Med. Sch. and Brigham and Women's Hosp., Boston; primary care internal medicine resident U. Wash. Affiliated Hosps., Seattle; assoc. prof. medicine Harvard Med. Sch., Boston, dir. Ctr. of Excellence in Women's Health, mem. faculty, 1983—; med. dir. Cmty. Health Programs Brigham and Women's Hosp., Boston, attending physician, 1983—. Mem. com. Assuring the Health of the Pub. in 21st Century, Inst. Medicine; mem. minority women's health panel of experts Office on Women's Health, Dept. HHS. Mem. bd. dirs. Boston Pub. Health Commn. Recipient Edna W. Smith Pioneer in Cmty. Health Care award, 2000.

BIGELEISEN, JACOB, chemist, educator; b. Paterson, NJ, May 2, 1919; s. Harry and Ida (Slomowitz) Bigeleisen; m. Grace Alice Simon, Oct. 21, 1945; children: David M., Ira S., Paul E. AB, NYU, 1939; MS, Wash. State U., 1941; PhD, U. Calif., Berkeley, 1943. Rsch. scientist Manhattan Dist., Columbia, 1943-45; rsch. assoc. Ohio State U., Columbus, 1945-46; fellow Enrico Fermi Inst., U. Chgo., 1946-48; sr. chemist Brookhaven Nat. Lab., Upton, NY, 1948-68; prof. chemistry U. Rochester, NY, 1968-78, chmn. dept., 1970-75; Tracy H. Harris prof. U. Rochester (Coll. Arts and Scis.), 1973-78; v.p. research, dean grad. studies SUNY, Stony Brook, 1978-80, Leading prof. chemistry, 1978-89, Disting. prof., 1989, Disting. prof. emeritus, 1989—. Vis. prof. Cornell U., 1953; NSF sr. fellow, vis. prof. Eidgen Techn. Hochschule, Switzerland, 1962—63; chmn. Assembly Math. and Phys. Scis. NRC-Nat. Acad. Scis., 1976—80. Mem. editl. bd.: Jour. Phys. Chemistry, Jour. Chem. Physics. Trustee Sayville Jewish Ctr., 1954—68. Recipient Gilbert N. Lewis lectr., 1963, E. O. Lawrence award, 1964, Disting. Alumnus award, Wash. State U., 1983, Meliora award, Univ. Rochester, 1978; fellow John Simon Guggenheim, 1974—75. Fellow: AAAS, Am. Acad. Arts and Sci., Am. Chem. Soc., Am. Phys. Soc. (Nuc. award 1958); mem.: Nat. Acad. Scis. (councilor 1982—85), Phi Lambda Upsilon, Sigma Xi, Phi Beta Kappa. Achievements include research in photochemistry in rigid media; isotopes; isotope separation; quantum statistics of gases; liquids and solids. Office: 900 N Taylor St Apt 1809 Arlington VA 22203 E-mail: jacob_bigeleisen@comcast.net. *As a youth I became interested in a career in science because it offered the opportunity to test ideas and hypotheses objectively by experiment. This unique aspect of science, which differentiates it from all other branches of learning and knowledge, has been a guiding principle both in my professional and my personal life. My career has included research, teaching, administration and public service.*

BIGELOW, DANIEL JAMES, aerospace executive; b. Harrisville, Pa., Mar. 26, 1935; s. Raymond James and Hilda Irene (Graham) Bigelow; m. Elizabeth Jane Allison, Sept. 10, 1955; 1 child, Allison Jane. BFA in Art Advt., Kent State U., Ohio, 1957; MA in Edn., La. Tech. U., 1974; MS in Polit. Sci., Auburn U., 1986; MS, Air U., 1987; postgrad., Ohio State U., 1989—, Kent State U. Commd. 2d lt. USAF, 1957, advanced through grades to col., 1979, ret., 1987; command pilot 167 combat missions Vietnam; air attaché to Soviet Union, 1983—85; dir. Soviet program Air War Coll. Air U., Ala., 1985—87; gen. mgr. aerospace divsn. Modern Techs. Corp., Dayton, Ohio, 1988—98, dir. programs corp. hdqrs., 1998—2001, dir. bus. svcs. corp. hdqrs., 2002—03; dir. investor rels. and corp. comm. MTC Tech., Inc., Dayton, 2003—. Designer artwork, writer text MTC Annual Reports, 2002—06; designer MTC Website, 2003—07. Author, editor: Soviet Studies, 1968—88; contbr. articles to profl. jours. Comdr. Army and Air Force ROTC Corps of Cadets, 1957, Kent State U. Decorated Legion of Merit with one oak leaf cluster, DFC, 14 Air medals, Def. Superior medal; named Disting. Mil. Grad., Air Force ROTC, 1957, Disting. alumni, East Liverpool (Ohio) HS Alumni Assn., 2004; recipient U.S. Am. Nat. award, CIA Dir. William J. Casey, 1985. Mem.: AIAA, Intelligence and Nat. Security Alliance, Am. Electronics Assn., Nat. Mus. US Army (founding sponsor), Wright "B" Flyer Assn., Strategic Air Command Assn., 3rd Mil. Airlift Squadron Assn., Kent State U. Alumni Assn., Nat. Investor Rels. Inst., Nat. Mil. Intelligence Assn., Nat. Def. Indsl. Assn., Electronic Engring. and Mfg. Group (bd. dirs. 2006—), Internat. Test and Evaluation Assn., Inst. Navigation, Miami Valley Mil. Affairs Assn., Def. Planning and Analysis Soc., Dayton Area Def. Contractors Assn. (pres. 1999—2000, bd. dirs.), Internat. Platform Assn., Am. Def. Preparedness Assn., Acad. Polit. Sci., Intelligence & Nat. Security Alliance, Waco Hist. Soc., Nat. Aviation Hall of Fame, DFC Soc., Air Force Assn. Cmty. Ptnrs., Assn. Former Intelligence Officers, Air Rescue Assn. (historian 1998—, chmn. reunion and symposium 2003, nat. bd. dirs.), Air Force Assn. (v.p. state legis. affairs 2001—02), F-86 Sabre

Pilots' Assn., B-52 Stratofortress Assn., Ret. Officers' Assn., Airlift/Tanker Assn., Armed Forces Comm. and Electronics Assn., Pararescue Assn., Pedro Helicopter Assn., Air Force Mus. Found., Mil. Officer Assn. Am., Dayton Art Inst., Dayton Area C. of C. (vice-chmn. mil. and fed. affairs com. 2003—04, chmn. 2004—), Mil. Officers Assn. Am., Assn. U.S. Army, Royal Air Force Club, Discussion Club Dayton (v.p. 1999—2000), Am. Legion, Assn. Old Crows, Order Daedalians (flight capt., pres. 2001—02), Order Quiet Birdmen, Anciente Order Quiet Birdmen, Shriners, Scottish Rite, Masons, Blue Key. Presbyterian. Avocations: art, photography, jogging. Home: 2537 Indian Wells Trl Xenia OH 45385-9373 Office Phone: 937-610-0275. Business E-Mail: daniel.bigelow@mtctechnologies.com.

BIGELOW, GEORGE E., psychology and pharmacology scientist; b. Washington, Aug. 31, 1943; BS in Psychology, with honors, U. Md., College Park, 1965; PhD in Psychology, U. Minn., 1969. Dir. behavioral pharmacology unit Johns Hopkins U., Balt.; asst. prof., Dept. Psychiatry & Behavior Sci. Johns Hopkins U. Med. Sch., Balt., 1971—76, assoc. prof., 1976—89, prof., 1990—. Mem., Drug Abuse Adv. Com. FDA, 1987—93, cons., 1993—2002. Recipient Nyswander/Dole (Marie) award, Am. Methadone Treatment Assn., 1997. Fellow: APA (pres., div. psychopharmacology 1987—88, div. psycholpharmacology & substance abuse, div. experimental analysis behavior, div. health psychology), Soc. Behavioral Medicine, Am. Psychol. Soc., Coll. of Problems of Drug Dependence (pres. 1993—94, bd. dir. 1989—98, treas. 1995—98); mem.: Am. Pub. Health Assn., Rsch. Soc. Alcoholism, Assn. for Advancement Behavior Therapy, Behavioral Pharmacology Soc. Office: Johns Hopkins U Behavioral Pharma Unit 5510 Nathan Shock Dr Baltimore MD 21224-6823

BIGELOW, MARGARET ELIZABETH BARR (M.E. BARR), retired botany educator; b. Elkhorn, Man., Can., Apr. 16, 1923; d. David Hunter and Mary Irene (Parr) Barr; m. Howard Elson Bigelow, June 9, 1956 (dec.). BA with honors, U. B.C., Vancouver, Can., 1950, MA, 1952; PhD, U. Mich., 1956. Rsch. attaché U. Montreal, Que., Can., 1956-57; instr. U. Mass., Amherst, 1957-65, asst. prof., 1965-71, assoc. prof., 1971-76, prof., 1976-89, prof. emeritus, 1989—. Author: Diaporthales in N.A., 1978, Prodromus to Loculoascomycetes, 1987, Prodromus to Nonlichenized Members of Class Hymenoascomycetes, 1990; contbr. articles to profl. jours. With Can. Women's Army Corps, 1942—46. Mem. Mycol. Soc. Am. (v.p. to pres. 1980-82, editor 1975-80, Disting. Mycologist Award, 1993), Brit. Mycol. Soc., Am. Inst. Biol. Sci. (gen. chmn. ann. meeting 1986). Avocations: gardening, reading. Home and Office: 9475 Inverness Rd Sidney BC Canada V8L 5G8

BIGELOW, MARTHA MITCHELL, retired historian; b. Talladega Springs, Ala., Sept. 19, 1921; children: Martha Frances, Carolyn Letitia. BA, Montevallo U., 1943; MA, U. Chgo., 1944, PhD, 1946. Assoc. prof. history Miss. Coll., Clinton, 1946-48, Memphis State U., 1948-49; Assoc. prof. history U. Miss., 1949-50; assoc. curator manuscripts Mich. Hist. Collections, U. Mich., Ann Arbor, 1954-57; prof. history Miss. Coll., 1957-71, chmn. dept. history and polit. sci., 1964-71. Dir. Bur. of History, Mich. Dept. State, 1971-90; sec. Mich. Hist. Commn., Mich. Dept. State, state historic preservation officer, 1971-90; coord. for Mich., Nat. Hist. Publs. and Recs. Commn., 1974-90. Contbr. articles to profl. publs. Fellow, Ency. Britannica, 1944—45; scholar Julius Rosenwald scholarship, 1943—44, Cleo Hearson scholarship, 1944. Mem. Am. Assn. State and Local History (v.p. 1979-80, pres. 1980-81, fellow summers 1958, 59), Orgn. Am. Historians, Nat. Assn. State Archives and Recs. Assn., So. Hist. Assn., Mich. Hist. Soc., Miss. Hist. Soc. Home: 201 Jefferson St Clinton MS 39056-4237 Office Phone: 601-924-2822. Personal E-mail: mbigelow@bellsouth.net.

BIGELOW, NICHOLAS PIERRE, physicist, researcher; b. Princeton, NJ, Dec. 26, 1958; s. Julian Himley and Mary Agnes (Milward) B.; m. Judith Anderson, July 26, 1981; children: Ian, Eric. BS in Elec. Engring. with high honors, Lehigh U., 1980, BS in Physics with high honors, 1981; MS, Cornell U., 1984, PhD, 1989. Lic. pilot. Mem. tech. staff AT&T Bell Labs., Holmdel, NJ, 1989-91; sr. rsch. assoc. dept. physics and astronomy U. Rochester, NY, 1991-92, asst. prof. physics NY, 1992-97, assoc. prof. NY, 1997—, sr. staff scientist Lab. for Laser Energetics NY, 1992—, prof., 2000, Lee A. DuBridge prof. physics, prof. optics, 2001—. Rsch. assoc. Ecole Normale Supèrieure, Paris, 1991-92, vis. prof., 1992-95. Mem. editl. bd. Laser Physics, Optics Letters; contbr. chpts. to books, numerous articles to profl. jours. and encys. Alfred P. Sloan Found. fellow, 1993-95; NSF grantee, 1994—; David and Lucile Packard Found. fellow, 1994—. Fellow Am. Phys. Soc., Optical Soc. Am., Tau Beta Pi Achievements include theoretical and experimental investigations the fields of quantum optics and atomic physics. Office: U Rochester Dept Physics and Astronomy Rochester NY 14627

BIGELOW, PETER, electronics executive; b. Mineola, NY, Sept. 28, 1953; s. Benjamin and Anne (Lehr) B.; m. Margaret (Baldwin) B.; children: Emily Anne, Catherine Clare, David Ellis. BA in Bus., Ohio No. U., 1976. Supr. costing & pricing Burndy Corp., York, Pa., 1977-81; mgr. product mktg. & planning Champion Internat., Inc., Stamford, Conn., 1981-85; dir. mktg. Catty divsn. Rostra Holdings, Fairfield, Conn., 1985-86; dir. sales & mktg. M.H. Rhodes, Inc., Avon, Conn., 1986-90; ind. cons. Darien, Conn., 1990-92; v.p. sales & mktg. Beaver Brook Circuits, Inc., Bethel, Conn., 1992-94, pres., CEO, 1994—2001; prin. Conn. Coining, Inc., Bethel, 2001—02; pres., CEO IMI Inc., Haverhill, Mass., 2002—. Dir. Record-Jour. Pub. Co., Meriden, Conn., IPC, Northbrook, Ill., 1999-; dir., pres. Houston Edn. for Advanced Tech., 1999-2001. Contbr. columns in mags.; monthly columnist: Printed Circuit Design and Manufacture Mag., 2003—. Chmn., pres. Darien Nature Ctr., Inc., 1996-99, dir., 1991-99; commr. Planning & Zoning Commn., Darien, 1999. Episcopalian. Home: 9 Clock Ave Darien CT 06820-5323 Office: IMI Inc 140 Hilldale Ave Haverhill MA 01832 E-mail: pbigelow@IMIPCB.com.

BIGELOW, REBA SEETIN, artist; b. Lawrence, Kans., Apr. 16, 1928; d. George Jackman and Irene (Harrison) Seetin; m. Dwight Ernest Bigelow, Apr. 16, 1954; children: David Dwight, Brad Seetin. Assoc. Degree, Tacoma C.C., 1971; BA, U. Wash., 1974, 5th Yr. Degree for Tchg., 1983. Bus. dir. Capitol Truck Co., Topeka, 1946-49; ins. sec. Iowa Home Mutual Ins., Topeka, 1949-52; psycho record typist Topeka State Hosp., 1952-53; tchr. left/right brain art spl. edn. Seguin Sch., Seattle, 1980-83, Seattle Acad. Greater Achievement Sch., Seattle, 1983-85; sec., dir. Art/Not Terminal Gallery, Seattle, 1988—. Vol. art tchr. Pacific Arts Ctr., Seattle, 1986-88, Sch. for the Homeless, Seattle, 1987-89. Works exhibited at Crystal Star Gallery, 1991, Art/Not Terminal Gallery, 1991, Adirmal Pub, 1995. Vol. Rep. Party, Seattle, 1983. Mem. Art/Not Terminal Gallery (fundraiser 1992-93), New Horizons for Learning (vol., student 1980-88). Avocations: line dancing, volunteering. Home: 7520 12th Ave NE Seattle WA 98115-4318

BIGELOW, ROBERT P., lawyer, arbitrator, mediator, journalist; b. NYC, Jan. 17, 1927; s. Robert R.L. and Doris W.S. (Bissell) B.; m. Katharine W. MacKenty Apr. 14, 1951; children: Katharine R., Robert S., Sanford W., Edward G. AB cum laude, Harvard U., 1950, JD, 1953. Bar: Mass. 1953. Law clk. Supreme Ct. Mass., 1953-54; assoc. Bingham Dana & Gould, Boston, 1954-56; atty., asst. counsel John Hancock Mut. Life Ins. Co., Boston, 1956-66; pvt. practice Woburn and Boston, Mass., 1966-86; of counsel Hennessy Kilburn Killgoar & Ronan, Boston, 1973-84; ptnr. Bigelow & Saltzberg, Woburn, 1980-86; counsel Warner & Stockpole, Boston, 1986-87; pvt. practice, 1987-91, 95-97, 2003—; counsel Bird & Bird, London, 1995-97; arbitrator, mediator, 1966—; hearing officer Mass. Bd. of Bar Overseers, 2003—06. Adj. prof. Dartmouth Coll., 1982-84, Suffolk Law Sch., 1986-92; acting dir. New Eng. Law Inst., 1974-75. Author: (with Susan Nycum) Your Computer and the Law, 1975, Contracting for Computer Hardware, Software and Services, 1984-95, Computer Contracts, 1987-92; editor Law Office Econs. and Mgmt., 1969-78, Computer Law Svc., 1973-81, Computer Law and Tax Report, 1974-84, Computer Law Newsletter, 1979-87, cons. editor, 1988-91; cons. editor Bull. Computer Law Assn., 1971-97, editor, 1997-98; contbg. editor Cyberspace Lawyer, 1998-2007, Lawyers Competitive Edge, 1999-2007; mem. adv. bd. Guide to Computer Law, 1998-2001; contbr. articles to profl. jours. With U.S. Army, 1945-46, 51-64. Fellow AAAS, Brit. Computer Soc. (life, qualified arbitrator), New Zealand Computer Soc., I.S.P. Can. Info. Processing Soc., Am. Bar Found. (life), Mass. Bar Found. (life), Coll. Law Practice Mgmt. (hon.), Australian Computer Soc. (sr. life); mem. ABA (life, editor Computers and the Law 1966, 69, 81, Jurimetrics Jour. 1971-74, Bull. Law, Sci. and Tech. 1977-80, chmn. com. law relating to computers 1979-80, briefs editor Law Practice Mgmt. 1979-91, 93-96), Mass. Bar Assn. (life, chmn. econs. com. 1969-73, mem. com profl. ethics 1973-79, mem. coun. law practice 1981-84, chmn. bus. law sect. 1984-85), Computer Law Assn. (now Internat. Tech. Law Assn.) (pres. 1977-79, dir. 1973-84, adv. bd. 1984—), Boston Bar Assn. (chmn. com. on automation 1963-68). Office Phone: 781-729-2334.

BIGELOW, SHARON LEE, elementary school educator; b. Chgo., Ill., Oct. 13, 1942; d. Clarence Ellsworth and Frances Lorraine Bigelow. BA in Edn., SUNY, 1964; MA in Ednl. Psychology, N.Y.U., 1965. Tchr. Union Free Sch. Dist., Pleasantville, NY, 1966—. Art dir. Chappaqua Recreation, Chappaqua, NY, 1961—64. Named a Sharon Lee Bigelow Day, Town Bd. & Mayor, 2001. Mem.: N.Y. State Tchrs. Assn., Pleasantville Tchrs. Assn. (pres., deleg.). Avocations: reading, calligraphy, travel.

BIGELOW, VIVIAN LOU, elementary school educator, secondary school educator; b. Redding, Calif., Apr. 24, 1943; d. Lloyd Vivian and Minnie Marie Keefer; m. Robert Buckland Bigelow, Aug. 14, 1965; 1 child, Christine Ann; m. Thomas Bateman, July 24, 1992. AA, Shasta Jr. Coll., Calif., 1963; BA, Chico State U., Calif., 1966. Cert. tchr. 6-12 Calif., 1966, advanced tchg. cert. Idaho, 1972. Tchr. Fortuna Union HS, Calif., 1967—68, Parsons Jr. High, Redding, Calif., 1968—73, Lowell Scott Jr. High, Meridian, Idaho, 1973—75, Cascade HS, Idaho, 1975—77, Payette Lakes Mid. Sch., McCall, Idaho, 1977—. Developing sci. curriculum com. McCall Donnelly Sch. Dist. #421, McCall, Idaho. Avocations: hunting, hiking.

BIGGART, NICOLE WOOLSEY, dean; m. James Biggart; 1 child, Scott. BA, Simmons Coll., 1969; MA, U. Calif., Davis, 1977; PhD, U. Calif., Berkeley, 1981. Asst. prof. adminstrn. and sociology U. Calif., Davis, 1981—87, assoc. prof. mgmt. and sociology, 1987—90, prof., 1991—2002; Jerome J. and Elsie Suran chair in tech. mgmt. Grad. Sch. Mgmt., U. Calif., Davis, 2002—, dean, 2003—. Adv. bd. Sloan Found. social sci. rsch. coun. program on corp. as social instn., 1999—; mem. editl. bd. Orgn.: The Interdisciplinary Jour. of Orgn., Theory, and Soc., 1993—, Calif. Mgmt. Rev., 1993—. Co-author: (books) Governor Reagan, Governor Brown: Sociology of Executive Power, 1984, Enhancing Organizational Performance, 1997, The Changing Nature of Work, 1999; author: Charismatic Capitalism: Direct Selling Organizations in America, 1989; editor: Economic Sociology: A Reader, 2001. Mem.: Macro-Orgnl. Behavior Soc. Office: Grad Sch Mgmt Univ Calif Davis 115 AOB IV One Shields Ave Davis CA 95616-8609 Office Phone: 530-752-7366. Office Fax: 530-754-5824. Business E-Mail: nwbiggart@ucdavis.edu.*

BIGGERT, JUDITH BORG, congresswoman, lawyer; b. Chgo., Aug. 15, 1937; d. Alvin Andrew and Marjorie Virginia (Mailler) Borg; m. Rody Patterson Biggert, Sept. 21, 1963; children: Courtney Ray, Alison Mailler, Rody Patterson, Adrienne Taylor. BA, Stanford U., 1959; JD, Northwestern U., 1963. Bar: Ill. 1963. Law clk. to presiding justice US Ct. Appeals (7th cir.), Chgo., 1963-64; sole practice Hinsdale, Ill., 1964—99; mem. Ill. Gen. Assembly, 1993—98, asst. Rep. leader, 1995—98; mem. US Congress from 13th Ill. dist., 1999—, mem. fin. svcs. com., edn. and workforce com. stds. ofcl. conduct, chmn. sci. com. subcom. on energy, mem. bipartisan working group on youth violence. Mem. bd. editors Law Rev., Northwestern U. Sch. Law, 1961-63. Pres. Hinsdale Twp. HS Dist. 86 Bd. Edn., 1983-85; pres. Jr. League Chgo., 1976-78, treas., bd. mgrs., 1966—; chmn. Hinsdale Antiques Show, 1980; pres. Oak Sch. PTA, Hinsdale, 1976-78; pres.-treas. Chgo. jr. bd. Travelers Aid Soc., 1965-70; Sunday sch. tchr. Grace Episcopal Ch., Hinsdale, 1978-80, 82-85; chair, treas., 2d v.p. bd. dirs. Vis. Nurses Assn. Chgo., 1978; bd. dirs. Salt Creek Ballet, 1990-98. Recipient Servan award Jr. aux. U. Chgo. Cancer Rsch. Foun., Woman Yr. in Govt., Politics, and Civic Affairs DuPage YWCA, 1995, Hero of the Taxpayer, Am. for Tax Reform. 2000, 02, award for pub. svc., Am. Chem. Soc., 2003, Excellence in Edn., Nat. Assn. Coll. Admission Counseling, 2002, Friend of Edn., Ill. & Nat. Edn. Assn., 2002, Outstanding Leadership to Homeless and Victims of Domestic Violence, Chgo., Pub. Sch., 2002, Disting. Achievement for Protecting and Expanding Opportunities for Children and Youth Who Are Homeless, Chgo. Coalition for the Homeless, 2002, Spirit of Enterprise award US C. of C.; named one of 100 Women Making a Difference; inductee to Hinsdale Ctrl. HS Hall Fame, 1997. Mem. ABA, Ill. Bar Assn., DuPage Bar Assn., Coalition Women Legislatures. Republican. Office: US Ho Reps 1317 Longworth Ho Off Bldg Washington DC 20515-1313 also: Dist Off Ste 305 6262 S Rte 83 Willowbrook IL 60527 Office Phone: 202-225-3515.*

BIGGINS, J. VERONICA, bank executive; m. Franklin Biggins; children: Dawn, Kenzie. B, Spelman Coll.; M, Ga. State U.; postgrad., U. Md. Asst. br. mgr. Citizens and So. Nat. Bank, Atllanta, affirmative action officer, compliance mgr., employee relations mgr., mgr. Atlanta personnel, exec. v.p., dir. human resources; exec. NationsBank (now Bank of Am.); asst. to Pres. The White House, Washington, dir. presdl. personnel; mng. ptnr. Heidrick& Struggles, Atlanta. Vice chair US Delegation UN's Fourth World Conf. on Women, Beijing; lectr. in field; chair Czech Slovak Am. Enterprise Fund. Bd. dirs., co-chmn. freedom fund dinner NAACP; bd. dirs. Atlanta chpt. Urban League, AirTran Airways, Avnet, NDC Health; chmn. personnel com., bd. dirs. United Way; bd. dirs., chmn. student affairs com., vice chmn. fundraising Spelman Coll.; mem. governing bd., vice chmn. Zoo Atlanta Capital Campaign; mem. exec. com. Leadership Atlanta, 1983; mem. bd. visitors Grady Hosp.; mem. bd. trustees YWCA, Exodus, Inroads Inc., Ga. Rsch. Alliance, Woodruff Arts Ctr., Down Atlanta Rotary, Intenat. AIDS Fund; chmn. nominating com. NW Girl Scout Council; mem. Atlanta women's fund adv. com. Recipient Outstanding Performance award Inroads, Atlanta, 1986, Urban Bankers, 1987, trail blazer award Nat. Assn. Negro Bus. and Profl. Women's Clubs, Inc. Mem.: Internat. Bus. Fellows, Chautaugua Cir., Dogwood City Links, Am. Bankers Assn. (chmn. human resource divsn.). Episcopalian. Office: Heidrick & Struggles 303 Peachtree St NE Ste 4300 Sun Trust Plz Atlanta GA 30308

BIGGIO, CRAIG, professional baseball player; b. Smithtown, NY, Dec. 14, 1965; m. Patty Biggio; children: Conor Joseph, Cavan Thomas, Quinn Patricia. Second baseman Houston Astros, 1988—. Named to The Sporting News Coll. All-Am. Team, 1987, Nat. League All-Star Team, 1991-92, 94-98, Tex. Baseball Hall of Fame, 2004, Tex Sports Hall of Fame, 2004; named Houston Astros Player of Yr., 1998 recipient: Nat. League Silver Slugger award, 1989, 94-97, Nat. League Gold Glove award, 1994-97, Branch Rickey award for Exceptional Community Svc., 1997, Hutch award, 2005, Heart & Hustle award, 2006 Achievements include becoming the 27th player in major league history to reach 3,000 hits, June 28, 2007. Office: Houston Astros PO Box 288 Houston TX 77001-0288*

BIGGS, ALAN RICHARD, plant pathologist, educator; b. Lewisburg, Pa., June 22, 1953; s. Edgar Harold and Yvonne S. Biggs; m. Lise N. Sade, Oct. 3, 1981 (div) 2005; children: Benjamin Jesse Biggs Sade, Skylar Rose Biggs Sade. BS, Pa. State U., 1976, MS, 1978, PhD, 1982. Rsch. scientist Can. Dept. Agr., Vineland, Ont., 1983-89; assoc. prof. W.Va. U., Kearneysville, 1989-95, prof., 1995—. Editor: Defense Mechanisms of Woody Plants Against Fungi, 1992, Cytology, Histology and Histochemistry of Fruit Tree Diseases, 1992; assoc. editor Phytopathology, 1986-88, Plant Disease, 1994-96; sr. editor Plant Disease, 1998-2000, editor-in-chief, 2001-2003. Recipient Lee M. Hutchins award, 1993, USDA Sec. Honor award, 2001, 2002. Mem. Am. Phytopath. Soc. (Lee M. Hutchins award 1993). Avocations: photography, bicycling, jazz guitar. Office: WVa U Tree Fruit Rsch and Edn Ctr PO Box 609 Kearneysville WV 25430-0609

BIGGS, ARTHUR EDWARD, retired chemicals executive, social services administrator; b. NYC, Jan. 3, 1930; s. Arthur Edward and Pauline (Maier) B.; m. Charlotte Marion Elliott, Sept. 10, 1955; children— Arthur Edward III, William Elliott, Nancy Catherine, Andrew David BS in Acctg. and Fin. Magna cum laude, U. Md., 1951; MBA in Fin. and Prodn. with distinction, Harvard U., 1957. Mgmt. cons. McKinsey & Co., Inc., NYC, 1957-62; asst. controller Mobil Oil Co., NYC, 1963-66, controller, 1966-68; v.p., gen. mgr. plastics div. Mobil Chem. Co., Rochester, NY, 1969-73, exec. v.p. NYC, 1974-82, pres., 1982-86. Chmn. bd. dir. The Century Group, 1987-91. Vice pres. bd. dir. Vis. Nurse Svc. N.Y., 1975-88; bd. advisers Pace U., N.Y.C., 1976-88; trustee Quinnipiac Coll., Hamden, Conn., 1982-92, chmn., 1986-90; bd. dirs. Ptnrs. in Care, N.Y.C., 1983-88, chmn., 1983-88; trustee Conn. Conf. Ind. Colls., chmn., 1987-89; trustee Harvard Sch. Bus. 1st lt., pilot USAF, 1951-55. Baker scholar, Harvard U., 1957. Mem. Monarch Country Club, Woodfield Country Club (Boca Raton). Avocation: tennis.

BIGGS, DOUGLAS LEE, historian, educator; b. Ames, Iowa, June 1, 1960; s. Donald Lee and Carolyn Nina Biggs; m. Gloria Jean Betcher, 1993. BA, Iowa State U., 1982, MA, 1985; PhD, U. Minn., 1996. Assoc. prof. history Waldorf Coll., Forest City, Iowa, 1997—. Academic cons. for history Ednl. Testing Svc., Princeton, NJ, 2002—; vis. prof. U. York, England, 2000. Editor: (collection of essays) Traditions and Transformations in Fifteenth Century England, 2003, Henry IV: The Establishment of the Regime, 1399-1406, 2004; author: Reputation and Representation: Essays in Late Medieval History, Three Armies in Britain: The Irish Campaign of Richard II and the Usurpation of Henry IV, 1397-1399, 2006; contbr. articles to profl. publs. Named Alpha Chi Prof. Yr., Waldorf Coll., 2005—06; recipient Profl. Excellence award, 2003. Fellow: Royal Hist. Soc.; mem.: Am. Hist. Soc., White Hart Soc. (pres.). Progressive. Roman Catholic. Avocations: running, travel. Office: Waldorf Coll 214 Salveson Hall 106 South Sixth St Forest City IA 50436 Home Phone: 515-292-5177; Office Phone: 641-585-8217. Business E-Mail: biggsd@waldorf.edu.

BIGGS, JASON, actor; b. Pompton Plains, NJ, May 12, 1978; s. Gary and Angela Biggs. Student, NYU, Montclair State U. Actor: (films) Conversations With My Fahter, 1991, The Boy Who Cried Bitch, 1991, American Pie, 1999, Boys and Girls, 2000, Loser, 2000, Saving Silverman, 2001, American Pie 2, 2001, Prozac Nation, 2001, American Wedding, 2003, Jersey Girl, 2004, Guy X, 2005, Eight Below, 2006; (TV series) Drexell's Class, 1991, As the World Turns, 1994—95; (Broadway plays) The Graduate, 2002. Office: c/o SFM 1122 S Robertson # 15 Los Angeles CA 90035

BIGGS, JEFFREY ROBERT, political scientist; b. New Castle, Pa., May 2, 1941; s. Wallace R. and Janice E. Biggs; m. Janet Allen Mathews, May 24, 1969; children: Jennifer M., Jessica E. BA, Harvard U., 1963; MA, Victoria U., Wellington, New Zealand, 1965; PhD, George Washington U., 1975. With U.S. Consulate Gen., Rio de Janeiro, 1974-78; attache U.S. Embassy, Lisbon, Portugal, 1978-81; dir., pres. bur. inter-Am. affairs Dept of State, Washington, 1981-84; deputy chief of mission Am. Embassy, La Paz, Bolivia, 1985-87; press sec. spkr. of house U.S. Ho. Reps., Washington, 1987-94; sr. advisor Office Nat. Drug Control Policy, Washington, 1995; dir. congl. fellowship program Am. Polit. Sci. Assn., Washington, 1997—. Mem. adv. bd. sr. Fulbright enhancement program, Pub. Diplomacy Coun. Co-author: Honor in the House: Speaker Tom Foley, 1999, A Congress of Fellows: Fifty Years of the American Political Science Association Congressional Fellowships Program 1953-2003, 2003; contbr. articles to profl. jours. Fulbright fellow, Wellington, New Zealand, 1964-65, Congl. fellow Am. Polit. Sci. Assn., 1984-85. Mem. Am. Polit. Sci. Assn., Diplomatic-Consular Officers Ret. Assn., Pub. Diplomacy Coun., Nat. Capitol Hist. Soc. (alumni steering com.), Wash. Inst. Fgn. Affairs, Phi Beta Delta. Avocations: fly fishing, hiking, writing. Home: 6406 Kenhowe Dr Bethesda MD 20817-5446 Office: Am Polit Sci Assn 1527 New Hampshire Ave NW Washington DC 20036-1203 Business E-Mail: jbiggs@apsanet.org.

BIGGS, JOHN HERRON, retired insurance company executive; b. St. Louis, July 19, 1936; s. Peter Willis and Lillian (Herron) B.; m. Penelope Frances Parkman, June 13, 1959; 1 child, Henry. AB magna cum laude, Harvard U., 1958; PhD in Econ., Washington U., St. Louis, 1983. V.p., contr. Gen. Am. Ins. Co., 1970-77; vice chancellor for adminstrn. and fin. Washington U., St. Louis, 1977-85; chmn., pres., chief exec. officer Centerre Trust Co., 1985-89; pres., COO Tchrs. Ins. and Annuity Assn./Coll. Retirement Equities Fund, 1989-93, chmn., pres., CEO, 1993—2002; exec. in residence Stern Sch., NYU, 2004—. Bd. dirs. Boeing Co., JPMorganChase Co.; emeritus trustee, past pres. Mo. Bot. Garden. Dir., past chmn. Nat. Bur. Econ. Affairs; trustee Washington U.; chmn. Emeriti Health Svcs., S. Paul Getty Trust; trustee Danforth Found.; past chmn. United Way N.Y.C., J. Paul Getty Trust. Fellow: Soc. of Actuaries; mem.: Am. Acad. Arts and Scis., Coun. Fgn. Rels., St. Louis Club, Harvard Club N.Y., Westchester Country Club. Home: 240 E 47th St Apt 23D New York NY 10017-2137 Office: 780 3d Ave 18th Fl New York NY 10017 Office Phone: 212-838-8071. E-mail: jbiggs@nyu.stern.edu.

BIGGS, ROBERT DALE, Near Eastern studies educator; b. Pasco, Wash., June 13, 1934; s. Robert Lee and Eleonora Christina (Jensen) B. BA in Edn, Eastern Wash. Coll. Edn., 1956; PhD, Johns Hopkins U., 1962. Rsch. assoc. Oriental Inst. U. Chgo., 1963—64, asst. prof. Assyriology, 1964-67, assoc. prof. Assyriology, 1967-72, prof. Assyriology, 1972—2004, prof. emeritus, 2004—. Author: ŠA.ZI.GA: Ancient Mesopotamian Potency Incantations, 1967, Inscriptions from Tell Abu Salabikh, 1974, Inscriptions from al-Hiba-Lagash: The First and Second Seasons, 1976; co-author: Cuneiform Texts from Nippur, 1969, Nippur II: The North Temple and Sounding E, 1978; editor: Discoveries from Kurdish Looms, 1983; assoc. editor: Assyrian Dictionary, 1964-87; editor Jour. Near Ea. Studies, 1971-2007; mem. editl. bd. Assyrian Dictionary, 1995—. Fulbright scholar Univ. Toulouse, France, 1956-57; fellow Baghdad Sch., Am. Schs. Oriental Rsch., 1962-63, Am. Rsch. Inst. in Turkey, 1972, Danforth fellow, 1956-62. Mem. Am. Oriental Soc. (pres. Mid. Western br. 1978-79), Archaeol. Inst. Am. (pres. Chgo. soc. 1985-92), Brit. Sch. Archaeology Iraq. Office: U Chgo 1155 E 58th St Chicago IL 60637-1540 Office Phone: 773-702-9540. Business E-Mail: r-biggs@uchicago.edu.

BIGHAM, ROBERT ERIC, engineer; b. Lampasas, Tex., Feb. 10, 1940; s. George Thomas and Mildred Lee (Abney) B.; m. Opal Miller, May 30, 1970 (div. 2000); 1 child, Watt Raburn. BS, Tex. A&M U., 1963, MS, 1969. Registered profl. engr., pub. surveyor, Tex. Engr. Buchanan Soil Mechanics, Inc., Bryan, Tex., 1968—2001; sole practice Robert E. Bigham, P.E. Consulting Engr., 2001—. Mem. drainage system adv. bd. City of Bryan, 1985-92, chmn., 1989-92, mem. bd. adjustments and appeals, 1992-98. Served in Corps of Engrs. US Army, 1964—67. Mem. ASCE, Geo-Inst.

ASCE, Tex. Soc. Profl. Surveyors (cert.). Home and Office: 211 Tee Dr Bryan TX 77801-3046 Office Phone: 979-822-0719. Personal E-mail: rebighampe@earthlink.net.

BIGHAM, WANDA DURRETT, religious organization administrator; b. Barlow, Ky., June 19, 1935; d. Herbert Martin and Ada Florene (Baker) Durrett; m. William M. Bigham, Jr., June 7, 1958; children: William M. III, Janet Kaye, Julia Lynn. BME, Murray State U., 1956; MM, Morehead State U., 1971, MHE, 1973; EdD, U. Ky., 1978; cert., Inst. For Ednl. Mgmt. -Harvard U., 1982; LittD (hon.), Loras Coll., 1989. Dir. TRIO programs Morehead (Ky.) State U., 1972-85, assoc. dean acad. affairs, dir. instructional sys., 1982-85, acting dean grad. and spl. acad. programs, 1984-85; exec. asst. to pres. Emerson Coll., Boston, 1985, v.p. for devel., 1986; pres. Marycrest Coll., Davenport, Iowa, 1986-92, Huntingdon Coll., Montgomery, Ala., 1993—2003; asst. gen. sec. for schs., colls. and univs. The United Meth. Ch., Nashville, 2003—. Bd. dirs. Nat. Assn. Ind. Coll. U., 2002-03, Secretariat, 2007-; bd. dirs., pres. Asia-Pacific Fedn. Christian Schs.; bd. dirs. Internat. Assn. Meth.-Related Schs., Colls. and Univs., Montgomery Symphony Orch., 1993-2003, Ala. Shakespeare Festival, 1996-2003, NASCUMC, 1996-2003; exec. com., pres. Univ. Senate United Meth. Ch., Ctrl. Ala. chpt. ARC, Montgomery, 1995-2003, pres, 2001-2002; mem. Leadership Ala., 1994—; co-chair Quad Cities Vision for the Future, Davenport, 1987-92. Recipient Pres.'s award Davenport C. of C., 1988, Women of Spirit and Note award Cmty. Com. of Davenport, 1991, Hope for Humanity award Jewish Fedn. of QC, Rock Island, Ill., 1993, Women's Acad. of Honor award Ala. Bus. and Profl. Women's Found., 2004; named to Alumni Hall of Fame, Morehead State U., 1988, Disting. Alumna, Murray State Coll., 1988, Woman of Distinction award Girl Scouts South Ctrl. Ala., 2001. Mem. Am. Coun. on Edn. (mem. coun. of fellows, bd. dirs. 1994-97, fellow in higher edn. adminstrn. 1983-84), Internat. Assn. Univ. Pres., Montgomery C. of C., Com. of 100, Sigma Alpha Iota (Sword of Honor 1956), Phi Kappa Phi, Kappa Delta Pi. Office: United Meth Ch Gen Bd Higher Edn and Ministry 1001 19th Ave S PO Box 340007 Nashville TN 37203-0007 Mailing: PO Box 340007 Nashville TN 37203-0007 Office Phone: 615-340-7406. Business E-Mail: wbigham@gbhem.org.

BIGHAM, WILLIAM J., lawyer; b. Bryn Mawr, Pa., July 4, 1949; s. Robert H. and Regina B.; m. Cindy K. Elkins, Aug. 12, 1972; children: Justin K., Joel M., Meredith E. BBA with honors, Siena Coll., 1971; JD with honors, Rutgers U., 1974. Bar: N.J. 1974, D.C. 1977, U.S. Ct. Appeals (3d cir.) 1983, U.S. Supreme Ct. 1985. Jud. law clk. to Hon. Samuel D. Lenox, Jr. Chancery Divisn. Superior Ct. of N.J., Trenton, NJ, 1974-75; mng. dir., shareholder Sterns & Weinroth, Trenton, 1975—. Mem.: ABA, N.J. Bar, D.C. Bar, Mercer County Bar Assn. Roman Catholic. Office: 50 W State St Ste 1400 Trenton NJ 08607-1220 Office Phone: 609-392-2100.

BIGLARI, HAMID, investment banker; s. Manouchehr and Parvin Biglari; m. Laya Khadjavi, Apr. 1, 1994; children: Roxana Sahar, Mandana Yasmine. BA, BS, Cornell U., 1978—81; MS, Princeton U., 1981—84, PhD, 1984—87. Ptnr. McKinsey & Co., NYC, 1991—2000; head of corp. strategy Citigroup, NYC, 2000—. Bd. mem. Graham Windham, NYC, 2000—02. Home: 447 East 57th St Apt 11 New York NY 10022 Office: Citigroup 388 Greenwich St 35th Flr New York NY 10013 E-mail: biglarih@citigroup.com.

BIGLER, HAROLD EDWIN, JR., retired investment company executive; b. NYC, Apr. 27, 1931; s. Harold Edwin and Elizabeth Augusta (Cutler) B.; m. Lorinda Jennings Bailey, June 21, 1980; children by previous marriage: John Stephen, Diane Elizabeth Bigler Whatley, William Campbell. AB, Brown U., 1953; MBA, Babson Inst., 1957; postgrad., Harvard U. Bus. Sch., 1975. Investment analyst Conn. Gen. Life Ins. Co., 1957-64, asst. sec., 1964, sec., 1964, 2d v.p., 1966-68; v.p. Securities Group, Hartford, 1968-81; chmn. C.G. Investment Mgmt. Co., Inc., 1975-81; pres., dir. Conn. Gen. Fund, Income Fund, Mcpl. Bond Fund, Money Market Fund, Companion Fund, Companion Income Fund, 1975-81. Chmn. Bigler Investment Mgmt. Co.; chmn. bd. Bigler Ptnrs., Inc.; gen. ptnr. Crossroads Fund, Crossroads Capital Fund; dir. Conn. Water Service, Inc., Vantage Computer Systems, Inc., various CIGNA mutual funds; chmn. investment adv. com., State of Conn., 1972-78; mem. investment com. Brown U., Providence, R.I., 1968-80; former chmn. Conn. Higher Edn. Student Loan Authority; bd. dirs. New Eng. Asset Mgmt. Co. Inc.; bd. dirs. New Eng. Monthly, Inc. Served as lt. (j.g.) USN, 1953-55. Mem. Am. Council Life Ins. (chmn. securities investment com. 1972-76), Fin. Analysts Fedn. (dir. 1974-76), N.Y. Soc. Security Analysts, Hartford Soc. Fin. Analysts (pres. 1966-67), The Hartford Club, Hartford Golf Club, The Moorings Club (Vero Beach, Fla.). Republican. Home: 180 Springline Dr Vero Beach FL 32963

BIGUM, RANDALL K., retired military officer; b. Lubbock, Tex., Dec. 11, 1949; BS in Bus., Ohio State U., 1973; student pilot tng., Williams AFB, Ariz., 1973-74; student F-4 pilot tng., 71st Tactical Fighter Squadron, MacDill AFB, Fla., 1974; student, USAF Fighter Weapons Sch., Nellis AFB, Nev., 1977; student F-15 pilot tng., 58th Tactical Tng. Wing, Luke AFB, Ariz., 1979; student, Squadron Officer Sch., 1980; M in Mil. Art and Sci., Army Command and Gen. Staff Coll., 1985; student, Nat. War Coll., 1993, Syracuse U., 1996. Commd. 2d lt. USAF, 1973, advanced through grades to brig. gen., 1998, various pilot assignments, 1974-77; weapons officer 59th Tactical Fighter Squadron, Eglin AFB, Fla., 1977-79, F-15 instr. pilot, 1979-80; various positions Nellis AFB, 1980-84; air ops. staff officer advanced program office Hdqs. Tactical Air Command, Langley AFB, Va., 1985-88, dep. chief. staff for requirements, 1985-88; ops. officer then comdr. 53rd Tactical Fighter Squadron, Bitburg Air Base, Germany, 1988-91; chief fighter devel. br. Office Undersec. Air Force Acquisition, Pentagon, Washington, 1991-92; comdr. 18th Ops. Group, Kadena Air Base, Japan, 1993-95; exec. officer to dep. comdr. in chief U.S. European Command, Stuttgart-Vaihingen City, Germany, 1995-97; comdr. 4th Fighter Wing, Seymour Johnson AFB, N.C., 1997-99; dep. dir. combat weapon sys. Hdqrs. Air Combat Command, Langley AFB, Va., 1999-2000, dir. combat weapon sys., 2000; dir., strategic initiatives Lockheed Martin Missiles and Fire Control, 2001—02, v.p., strike weapons bus. Orlando, Fla., 2002—. Dir. requirements, Hdqrs. Air Combat Command, Langley AFB, Va., 2000-01. Decorated D.F.C., Legion of Merit, Air medal with three oak leaf clusters, Small Arms Expert Marksmanship Ribbon. Office: Lockheed Martin Missiles and Fire Control 5600 Sand Lake Rd MP 455 Orlando FL 32819-8907

BIGWOOD, DAVID P., librarian, writer; b. 1953; Sr. libr. Ctr. Info. and Rsch. Svcs. Lunar and Planetary Inst., Houston. Office: Lunar and Planetary Inst 3600 Bay Area Blvd Houston TX 77058 Office Phone: 281-486-2134. E-mail: bigwood@lpi.usra.edu.

BIHLDORFF, JOHN PEARSON, hospital director; b. Boston, Aug. 3, 1945; s. Carl Birger and Martha Bowling (McCandless) B.; m. Jane Sargent Lyman, Mar. 30, 1968; children: Jennifer, Nathan, David. AB, Harvard U., 1969; MPH, Yale U., 1971. With McMaster U. Med. Ctr., Hamilton, Ont., Canada, 1971-77, assoc. exec. dir., 1975-77; dir. program planning, asst. prof. divsn. med. adminstrn. Vanderbilt U. Med. Ctr. & Sch. Medicine, 1977-78; assoc. hosp. dir., COO U. Conn. Health Ctr.-John Dempsey Hosp., Farmington, 1978-81; asst. exec. dir. U. Conn. Health Ctr., 1981-82, hosp. dir., 1982-86; pres., CEO St. Luke's Health Found. and Hosp., New Bedford, Mass., 1986-91, Newton-Wellesey Hosp., Newton, Mass., 1991-2001. Chmn. bd. dirs. VHA of Mass., Inc., 1995-97; chmn. bd. dirs. VHA Healthfront, 1995-97; bd. dirs. Tufts Assocs. Health Plan, 1994-96; adj. faculty Mt. Olive Coll., 2006—. Home: 107 Elm St Canton MA 02021-1255

BIJOL, VANESA, nephrologist, educator, pathologist, researcher; b. Banja Luka, Bosnia-Herzegovina, Aug. 22, 1971; arrived in US, 1997; d. Emira and Ivan Bijol. MD, U. Zagreb, Croatia, 1996. Diplomate Am. Bd. Pathology, 2005. Resident U. Rochester, 2000—04; asst. prof. Emory U. Sch. Medicine, Atlanta, 2005—; attending nephropathologist Emory Healthcare, Atlanta, 2005—. Contbr. articles to profl. jours. Fellow, Bigham and Women's Hosp., Harvard Med. Sch., 2004—05. Mem.: Am. Soc. Clin. Pathology, Coll. Am. Pathologists, US Coll. Am. Pathologists, Internat. Soc. Nephrology. Office: Emory Univ Sch Medicine EUH-H188 1364 Clifton Rd NE Atlanta GA 30322 Office Phone: 404-712-8843. Office Fax: 404-727-3133. Business E-Mail: vbijol@emory.edu.

BIJUR, PETER I., retired petroleum company executive; b. NYC; m. Kjestine Anderson; children from previous marriage: Kristin Anne, Matthew Montgomery, David Barrett. BA in Polit. Sci., U. Pitts., 1964; MBA, Columbia U., 1966. Various dist. and regional sales positions Texaco, Inc., 1966—71, mgr. Buffalo sales dist., 1971—73, asst. to sr. v.p. for pub. affairs, 1973—75, staff coord. dept. strategic planning, 1975—77, asst. to exec. v.p. Buffalo sales dist., 1977—80; mgr. Rocky Mountain Refining & Mktg., 1980—81, asst. to chmn. bd., 1981—84; pres. Texaco Oil Trading and Supply Co., 1984, v.p. spl. projects, 1984—86; pres., chief exec. officer Texaco Can. Inc., Don Mills, Canada, 1987—89; chmn. Texaco Ltd., London, 1989—91; pres. Texaco Europe, 1990—92; sr. v.p. Texaco, Inc., White Plains, NY, 1992—96, vice chmn. bd., 1996, chmn. bd. dirs., CEO, 1996—2001. Strategic adv. coun. Gas Tech. Inst.; bd. dirs. AB Volvo, Gulf Mark Offshore, Inc.

BIKALES, NORBERT M., chemist, science administrator; b. Berlin, Jan. 7, 1929; arrived in U.S., 1946; s. Salomon and Bertha (Bander) Bikales; m. Gerda V. Bierzonski, Apr. 28, 1951; children: Marguerite Sarlin, Edward A. BS in Chemistry, CCNY, 1951; MS in Chemistry, Polytech. U., 1956, PhD in Chemistry, 1961. Rsch. chemist Am. Cyanamid Co., Stamford, Conn., 1951-62; tech. dir. Gaylord Assocs., Newark, 1962-65; pres. N.M. Bikales & Co., Cons., Livingston, NJ, 1965-76; prof. chemistry, dir. continuing edn. in scis. Rutgers U., New Brunswick and Newark, NJ, 1973-79; dir. polymers program NSF, Washington, 1976-95, head Europe office Paris, 1995-98. Trustee Gordon Rsch. Conf., 1990—97, Fedn. Materials Soc., 1998—2002. Editor: Ency. Polymer Sci. and Tech., 1962—77; mem. editl. bd. Ency. Polymer Sci. and Engring., 1982—90; contbr. chpts. in books, articles to profl. jours. Pres. Friends of Livingston Libr., NJ, 1968—72, Livingston Symphony Orch., 1970—76; judge internat. Tech. Film '89 Festival, Pardubice, Czech Republic, 1989; v.p., sec. OSE-USA, 2000—05, pres., 2006—; hon. bd. mem. Oeuvre de Secours aux Enfants, Paris, 2007—. Recipient Twp. of Livingston award, 1976, Great Medal, City of Paris, 1985, Disting. Alumnus award, Poly. U., Bklyn., 1986, Disting. lectr. award, Soc. Polymer Sci., Tokyo, 1986, Chevalier des Palmes Académiques award, French Govt., 1993, Krakow award, Polish Acad. Scis., 1997, Disting. Svc. award, NSF, 1999, Lifetime Achievement award, Queens Coll., 2001. Fellow: AAAS, Am. Phys. Soc., Internat. Union Pure and Applied Chemistry (titular, sec. 1979—87, 1993—97, chmn. commn. on recycling of polymers 1993—98), N.Y. Acad. Sci. (life); mem.: Groupe Français des Polymères (sci. counselor 1994—99), Soc. Plastics Engrs. (sr.; bd. dirs. 1979—82), Polish Chem. Soc. (hon.), Am. Chem. Soc. (councilor 1987—89, chmn. polymer divsn. 1983, emeritus 2000—). Achievements include patents for materials, chemicals and chemical processes. Personal E-mail: nbikales@msn.com.

BIKEL, THEODORE, actor, singer; b. Vienna, May 2, 1924; came to U.S., 1954, naturalized, 1961; s. Josef and Miriam (Riegler) B.; m. Rita Weinberg, 1967. Student, U. London; grad., Royal Acad. Dramatic Art, London, 1948; DFA (hon.), U. Hartford, 1992; LHD, Seton Hall U., 2003; DFH, Hebrew Union Coll., 2005. Apprentice with Habimah Theatre, Tel Aviv, 1942-44, a founder, Israel Cameri, 1944-46; theatrical prodns. include A Streetcar Named Desire, London, 1950, The Love of Four Colonels, London, 1950-52, Tonight in Samarkand, N.Y.C., 1954, The Lark, N.Y.C., 1955-56, Rope Dancers, N.Y.C., 1957-58, Sound of Music, N.Y.C., 1959-61, Fiddler on the Roof, various cities, 1968-72, 74, 77, 79, 80, 82-83, 85, 87-96, 98, 00, 01, 02, The Rothschilds (nat. co.), 1972, Jacques Brel is Alive and Well and Living in Paris, various cities, 1974-75, The Good Doctor, various cities, 1975, Zorba, various cities, 1976, 78, Inspector Gen., N.Y.C., 1978, Threepenny Opera, Mpls., 1983, My Fair Lady, Phoenix, 1988-89, She Loves Me, various cities, 1989-90, Sholom Aleichem Lives, 1997, The Disputation, Miami, 1999, Washington, 2005, The Gathering, N.Y.C., Miami, 1999, The Chosen, Miami and N.J., 2004; opera prodns. include La Gazza Ladra, Phila., 1990, Abduction from the Seraglio, Cleve., 1992, Ariadne auf Naxos, L.A. Opera, 1992; motion pictures include African Queen, 1951; The Little Kidnappers, 1951, The Enemy Below, 1957, I Want to Live, 1958, The Defiant Ones, 1958 (Academy award nomination), Blue Angel, 1959, My Fair Lady, 1964, Sands of the Kalahari, 1965, The Russians are Coming, 1966, Sweet November, 1967, My Side of the Mountain, 1969, Darker Than Amber, 1970, The Little Ark, 1971, See You in the Morning, 1989, Shattered, 1991, My Family Treasure, 1993, Crime and Punishment, 1993, Shadow Conspiracy, 1995, Second Chances, 1997; also numerous TV appearances, 1954—; star: TV prodns. The Eternal Light, 1958, Look Up and Live, 1958-60; host-editor: TV prodn. Directions 61, 1961; weekly radio program At Home with Theodore Bikel, 1958-63; concert folk singer, 1955-, rec. artist for, Elektra and Reprise; reader books on tape including The Hope (Herman Wouk), The Glory (Herman Wouk), The Name of the Rose (Umberto Eco); Author: Folksongs and Footnotes, 1960, (autobiography) Theo, 1994, rev. edit., 2002. Mem. Nat. Coun. for Arts, 1977-82; founder arts chpt. Am. Jewish Congress, 1961-63, nat. v.p., 1963-70, chmn. governing coun., 1970-80, sr. v.p., 1980-2002; del. Democratic Nat. Conv., 1968. Recipient Emmy award, 1988, Lifetime Achievement award Nat. Found. for Jewish Culture, 1997. Mem. AFTRA, SAG, AGMA, Acad. TV Arts and Scis. (gov. 1961-65), AEA (councillor 1961-64, 1st v.p. 1964-73, pres. 1973-82, pres. emeritus 1982—), Am. Coun. Arts (bd. dirs. 1970-80), Internat. Fedn. Actors (v.p. 1981-91), Associated Actors and Artists of Am. (pres. 1989—), Acad. Motion Picture Arts and Scis., Am. Fedn. Musicians. Address: Associated Actors & Artists of Am Fl 16 165 W 46th St New York NY 10036-2501 E-mail: theoLXX@aol.com. *If I am a universalist-and I believe myself to be one-I derive my general standard of humanity from a particularist experience. For, above all and before all else, I am a Jew. That, to me, means a heightened awareness of the human condition and the sad-sweet knowledge that where we stand someone has stood before. It means a mode of living and a method of survival. Spiritually and culturally to be a Jew is to be a man on the road from Jerusalem to Jerusalem. I am an American; this is my home and my daily solace. Jerusalem, however, is my hope and my inspiration.*

BIKLE, DANIEL DAVID, research physician; b. Harrisburg, Pa., Apr. 25, 1944; s. Charles Augustus and Sarah Elizabeth (Yaukey) B.; m. Mary Elizabeth Wanner, June 20, 1965; children: Christine, Hilary. BA, Harvard U., 1965; MD, U. Pa., 1969, PhD, 1974. Diplomate Am. Bd. Internal Medicine; cert. Nat. Bd. Med. Examiners. Intern, resident Peter Bent Brigham Hosp., 1969—71; asst. prof. medicine U. Calif., San Francisco, 1979-86, assoc. prof. medicine, 1986-91, prof. medicine, 1991—, prof. dermatology, 1993—; co-dir. spl. diagnostic treament unit VA Med. Ctr., San Francisco, 1979—. Chmn. academic Senate U. Calif., San Francisco, 2001—03, chmn. sch. medicine faculty coun., 2005—. Editor: Assay of Calcium Regulating Hormones, 1982, Hormonal Regulation of Bone Mineral Homeostasis, 1995; contbr. articles to profl. jours., chpts. to books. Served to col. USAR, 1974-97. Research grantee NIH, 1979—, NASA, 1979—, VA, 1979—. Fellow ACP; mem. Endocrine Soc. (mem. editl. bd. 1984—), Am. Soc. Clin. Investigation, Am. Soc. for Bone and Mineral Rsch., Advances in Mineral Metabolism, Assn. Am. Physicians, Commonwealth Club Calif., Harvard Club (San Francisco). Republican. Mem. Christian Ch. Avocations: bicycling, skiing, tennis, sailing. Office: VA Med Ctr 4150 Clement St San Francisco CA 94121-1598 Office Phone: 415-221-4810. E-mail: daniel.bikle@ucsf.edu.

BIKLEN, STEPHEN CLINTON, retired diversified financial services company executive; b. Phila., Jan. 27, 1943; s. Paul Frederick and Anne (Chenoweth) Biklen; m. Britta Jorgensen Anderson, Oct. 21, 1989; children: Robert, Theodore. BA, Brown U., 1964; MBA, U. Pa., 1966. Auditor, acct. Coopers & Lybrand, NYC, 1970-73; fin. analyst, contr. Citibank, NYC, 1973-78; v.p. fin. Citibank N.Y. State, Rochester, 1978-80, bus. mgr. student loans, 1980-92, also bd. dirs.; pres., CEO, Student Loan Corp., Rochester, 1993-97, also bd. dirs.; ret., 1997. Mem. Nat. Adv. Com. Student Fin. Assistance, Washington, 1988—96; bd. dirs. Am. Student Assistance, Postsecondary Electronic Standards Coun., treas. Mem.: Consumer Bankers Assn. (chmn. edn. funding com. 1988—90, 1994—97). Avocation: golf. Office Phone: 585-393-0997. Personal E-mail: sbiklen@aol.com.

BIKOFF, J. DARIUS, beverage company executive; b. NYC; s. William and Suzie Bikoff; m. Nanne Puritz, May 28, 1994 (div.); m. Jill Bikoff, Nov. 2003; 1 child. BA in Humanities and Literature, Colgate U., 1983. Pres. William Bikoff Associates, Whitestone, NY, 1986; founder, CEO Energy Brands Inc., Whitestone, NY, 1996—, launched Go-Go beverage products, launched Glaceau line vitaminwater, smartwater and fruitwater. Recipient Marketers of the Next Generation, Brandweek, 2000. Jewish. Avocations: water-skiing, sailing, yoga, windsurfing. Office: Glaceau 17-20 Whitestone Expwy Whitestone NY 11357

BIKRAM, MALAVOSKLISH, medical educator; BS with honors, U. Denver, 1996; PhD, U. Utah, Salt Lake City, 2004. Analytical chemist West-Ward Pharm. Corp., Eatontown, NJ, 1996—97; assoc. analytical chemist Osteotech Inc., Eatontown, NJ, 1998—99. Student rep., biol. scis. dept. Grad. Steering Com., U. Utah, 1999—2000; chair grad. student adv. com., dept. pharm. chemistry U. Utah, 2002—03, grad. student recruiter, 2003; mem. and student chair, det. pharmaceutical chemistry Am. Assn. Pharm. Scientists, U. Utah, 2002—04; sci. judge Calvin Smith Elem. Sci. Fair, Taylorsville, Utah, 2004; sci. judge, summer undergrad. internship program Rice U., Houston, 2005; faculty rep. Houston-Louis Stokes Alliance for Minority Participation Nat. Conf., 2006; com. mem., dept. pharmacological & pharm. scis. U. Houston, 2006—, com. mem., grad. edn. com., dept. pharmacological & pharm. scis., 2006—. Contbr. articles to profl. jours. Vol. Sq. Meal, Jersey City, 1992—93. Mem.: Am. Assn. Pharm. Scientists (chair 2002—04). Office: Univ Houston 1441 Moursund St Rm 516 Houston TX 77030 Office Fax: 713-795-8305. Business E-Mail: mbikram@uh.edu.

BILANCIA-VITTUM, DENISE, secondary school educator; m. John S. Vittum, Oct. 6, 1974; children: Alexis Vittum, Eric Vittum. BA, Ohio Wesleyan U., Delaware, 1973; MBA, U. Akron, Ohio, 1986. HS tchr. Akron Pub. Schs., 1977—. Named Tchr. of Yr., Harfield HS, Akron, 2003; Disseminator grantee, State of Ohio. Mem.: Jr. Women's Civic Club (pres. 2004—05).

BILAND, ALAN THOMAS, computer integrated manufacturing executive; b. Pontiac, Mich., Sept. 13, 1958; s. Alfred T. and Janice J. (Bortreger) B.; m. Martha R. Wegner, Sept. 15, 1979; children: Benjamin A., Elizabeth L. BA in Biology and Psychology, Kalamazoo Coll., 1980; MBA, U. Wis., 1990. Computer aided design/computer aided mfg. Ronningen Rsch., Vicksburg, Mich., 1980-83; sr. industry cons. Computervision, Bedford, Mass., 1981-83; mgr. CAD/CAM N.Am. J.I. Case Co., Racine, Wis., 1985-91; mgr. U.K. Info. Svcs. J.I. Case, Doncaster, England, 1991—98; v.p. & CIO Snap-On Inc., Kenosha, Wis., 1998—2001, v.p. & CIO and pres. diagnostics and info group, 2001—. Mem. Computer and Automated Systems Assn., Soc. Mfg. Engrs. Republican. Lutheran. Avocations: fishing, travel, studying german. Office: Snap-On Inc 10801 Corporate Dr Pleasant Prairie WI 53158-1603

BILANIUK, LARISSA TETIANA, neuroradiologist, educator; b. Ukraine, July 15, 1941; arrived in U.S., 1951; d. Yaroslav and Myroslava Zubal; m. Oleksa-Myron Bilaniuk, Nov. 14, 1964; children: Larissa Indira, Laada Myroslava. BA, Wayne State U., 1961, MD, 1965. Diplomate Am. Bd. Radiology, Am. Bd. Neuroradiology. Resident in radiology Hosp. of U. Pa., Phila., 1966-70; fellow Fondation Ophtalmologique, Paris, 1972; assoc. in radiology U. Pa. Sch. Medicine, Phila., 1973-74, asst. prof., 1974-79, assoc. prof., 1979-82, prof., 1982—; with Children's Hosp. of Phila., 1992—. Reviewer grants rsch. NIH, Washington, 1983—86; vis. prof. Grosshadern Clinics U. Munich, 1988; vis. prof. Inst. Med. Radiology, Kharkiv, Ukraine, 1996; lectr. in field. Co-editor: 3 radiology books; contbr. articles to profl. jours., chapters to books. Rsch. fellow, Cancer Rsch. Ctr., Heidelberg, Fed. Republic Germany, 1967—68. Fellow: Am. Coll. Radiology; mem.: Acad. Med. Sci. Ukraine (elected), Ukranian Med. Assn. N.Am., Soc. Pediatric Radiology, European Soc. Neuroradiology, Am. Soc. Neuroradiology, Radiol. Soc. N.Am., Sigma Xi. Avocations: downhill skiing, alpine hiking, glider flying, photography. Office: Childrens Hosp of Phila 324 S 34th St Philadelphia PA 19104-4345

BILANIUK, OLEKSA MYRON, physicist, researcher; b. Ukraine, Dec. 15, 1926; arrived in U.S., 1951, naturalized, 1957; s. Petro and Maria B.; m. Larissa T. Zubal, Nov. 14, 1964; children: Larissa, Laada. Student, U. Louvain, 1947—51; MS, U. Mich., 1953, MA, 1954, PhD, 1957; Dr. honoris causa (hon.), Nat. Univ. Lviv, Ukraine, 2002. Postdoctoral fellow U. Mich., 1957-58; rsch. assoc., asst. prof. U. Rochester, 1958-64; assoc. prof. physics Swarthmore (Pa.) Coll., 1964-70, prof., 1970-82, Swarthmore Centennial prof., 1982—. Vis. scientist Argentine Atomic Energy Commn., Buenos Aires, 1961-62, Institut de Physique Nucléaire, Orsay, France, spring 1980, Laboratori Nazionali di Frascati, Italy, spring 1984, U. Munich, fall 1988; vis. prof., cons. Delhi U., summer 1966, Shivaji U., Kolhapur, India, summer 1969, Faculté des Scis., Rabat, Morocco, spring 1978, Kiev U. Ukraine, spring 1994, Inst. Med. Radiology, Kharkiv, Ukraine, summer 1996; Fulbright prof. Lima, Peru, summer 1971, Kinshasa, Zaïre, fall 1975. NSF fellow Max Planck Inst., Heidelberg, Germany, 1967-68, Inst. Physique Nucléaire, Orsay, 1972; NAS exch. scientist Kiev, Ukrainian SSR, 1976. Mem. Am. Phys. Soc., Nat. Acad. Scis. Ukraine, Ukrainian Acad. Arts and Scis. in U.S. (pres. 1998-2006), Schevchenko Sci. Soc. in U.S., European Phys. Soc., Société Française de Physique, Phi Beta Kappa, Sigma Xi. Achievements include research on nuclear structure; with Deshpande and Sudarshan challenged the view that Einstein's relativity precludes the possibility of existence of particles that travel faster than light, 1962. Office: Swarthmore Coll Dept Physics Swarthmore PA 19081 E-mail: obilani1@swarthmore.edu. *The most cherished possession of humanity is its spiritual and intellectual heritage. Contributing to the enrichment of this heritage I consider to be a human's loftiest goal.*

BILAS, RICHARD A., economist; b. Passaic, NJ, Feb. 3, 1935; s. Nestor Joseph and Helen Evelyn (Smith) B.; m. Janet Lianne Harris, June 23, 1956; children: Cathy, David, Ami. AB in Math., Duke U., 1956; PhD in Econs., U. Va., 1963. Asst., then assoc. prof. U. So. Calif., LA, 1962-67; from assoc. prof. to prof. Ga. State U., Atlanta, 1967—70; E.C. Reid prof. econs. Calif. State U., Bakersfield, 1970-87, prof. emeritus Calif., 2002—; commr. Calif. Energy Commn., Sacramento, 1987-95; Brock chair in energy econs. and policy Sarkeys Energy Ctr., Norman, Okla., 1995—96; commr. Calif. Pub. Utilities Commn., San Francisco, 1997—2002. Program on workable energy regulation bd. U. Calif., 1990—95; pres. Calif.

Pub. Utilities Commn., 1998—99; adj. prof. bus. adminstrn. The Citadel, Charleston, 2006—. Author: Microeconomics, 1967, 71, Problems in Microeconomics, 1972, Macroeconomics, 1974; mem. editl. bd. Western Econ. Assn.'s Contemporary Econ. Policy, 1990—, Contemporary Economic Policy, 1997-. Active Rep. Ctrl. Com., Kern County, Calif., 1978-82; pres. bd. dirs. Mendocino Art Ctr., 2000-05; treas. Cmty. Found. Mendocino County, 2003-05. Nat. Def. fellow U. Va., 1959-62, Fulbright fellow to the Philippines, 1966-67; recipient Honor cert. Freedoms Found., 1977, 79. Mem. Mont Pelerin Soc., Masons, Phi Beta Kappa. Republican. Episcopalian. Avocation: model trains. Home: 1513 Oakhurst Dr Mount Pleasant SC 29466 Office Phone: 943-216-7973. Business E-Mail: richardbilas@comcast.net.

BILBO, THOMAS EARL, biology professor; b. Moss Point, Miss., Feb. 12, 1944; s. Prentiss Lanier Bilbo and Doris Elizabeth Adams; m. Jerre Lynne Kannon; children: Jonathan Dayton, Erika Leeann. BS in Edn., Miss. Coll., Clinton, 1966; M in Combined Scis., U. Miss., University, 1970; EdM, Auburn U., Ala., 1971; PhD, U. So. Miss., Hattiesburg, 1976. Sci. tchr. Pascagoula Jr. H.S., Miss., 1966—68; sci. tchr., dept. chair William M. Colmer Jr. High, 1968—69; itenerate tchr. Elem. Secondary Edn. Act Title III Mobile Sci. Lab., Gulfport, Miss., 1970—72; sci. tchr. Pass Christian H.S., Miss., 1972—73; NSF project dir., instr. Prentiss Inst. Jr. Coll., Miss., 1974—75; sci. supr. Middle Ga. Coop. Ednl. Svc. Agy., Ft. Valley, Ga., 1976; biology prof. U. Mobile, Ala., 1976—, chair dept. phys. scis., 1994—96. Mem. SACS vis. com. Mobile County Pub. Schs., 1978, 1980, sci. fair judge, 1980—2006, sci. workshop presenter, 1987—88; pres. Saraland Elem. Sch. PTA, Ala., 1992—93. Recipient Uncommon Fox award, Mobile Coll. Student Govt. Assn., 1984, William A. Megginson Tchg. award, Megginson Found., 1996—97. Mem.: Ala. Sci. Tchrs. Assn., Ala. Acad. Sci. (chmn. sci. edn. sec. 1995—96, chmn. date and place of meeting com. 1998—2006), Alpha Sigma Lambda. Baptist.

BILBRAY, BRIAN PATRICK, congressman; b. Coronado, Calif., Jan. 28, 1951; m. Karen Walker; 5 children. Grad., Southwestern Coll. Mem., city coun. City of Imperial Beach, Calif., 1976—78, mayor Calif., 1978—85; mem. San Diego County Bd. Supervisors, 1985—95, US Congress from 49th Calif. dist., Washington, 1995-2001; mem US Congress from 50th Calif. dist., Washington, 2006—. Co-chair Nat. Bd. Advisors Fedn. Am. Immigration Reform. Avocations: sailing, surfing, horseback riding. Office: US Ho Reps 2350 Rayburn Ho Office Bldg Washington DC 20515-0550*

BILBRAY, JAMES HUBERT, retired congressman, lawyer, consultant; b. Las Vegas, Nev., May 19, 1938; s. James A. and Ann E. (Miller) B.; m. Michaelene Mercer, Jan. 1960; children: Bridget, Kevin, Erin, Shannon Student, Brigham Young U., 1957—58, U. Nev., Las Vegas, 1958—60; BA, Am. U., 1962; JD, Washington Coll. Law, 1964; D of Laws (hon.), U Nev. Las Vegas, 2001. Bar: Nev. 1965. Staff mem. Senator Howard Cannon U.S. Senate, 1960-64; dep. dist. atty. Clark County, Nev., 1965-68; mem. Lovell, Bilbray & Potter, Las Vegas, 1969-87, Nev. Senate, 1980-86, chmn. taxation com., 1983-86, chmn. interim com. on pub. broadcasting, 1983; mem. 100th-103rd Congresses from 1st Nev. dist., 1987-95; mem. fgn. affairs com., 1987-88; mem. house armed svs. com., mem. small bus. com., chmn. procurement, taxation and tourism subcom., 1989-95; ptnr. Alcalde & Fay, Arlington, Va., 1995; of counsel Kummer Kaempfer Bonner Renshaw & Ferrario, Las Vegas. Mem. subcoms. Africa, trade exports and tourism, select com. on intelligence, 1993-95; alt. mcpl. judge City of Las Vegas, 1987-89; del. North Atlantic Alliance, 1989-95; bd. visitors U.S. Mil. Acad., West Point, 1995-99, vice chmn., 1996-97; mem. adv. bd. Ex-Import Bank U.S., 1996-97; mem. adv. com. U.S. Nat. Security Policy, 2000-01; mem. Calif. Nev. High Speed Train Commn., 2005 Base Closing and Realignment Commn. Mem. bd. regents U. Nev. Sys., 1968—72; mem. Nat. Coun. State Govts. Commn. on Arts and Historic Preservation; mem. bd. visitors USAF Acad., 1991—93; mem. U.S. Nat. Security Policy Bd. Adv. Com., 2000—01, Calif. Nev. High Speed Train Commn., Base Closing and Rearmament Commn., Dem. Nat. Com., 1996—; Nev. chmn. Kerry for Pres., 2004; mem. Calif.-Nev. High Speed Train Commn., 2005—, US Base Closing Commn., 2005; mem. bd. govs. US Postal Svc. Named Outstanding Alumnus U. Nev., Las Vegas, 1979, Man of Yr. Am. Diabetes Assn., 1989, Man of Yr. Haddassah (Nev.), 1990 Mem. Nev. State Bar Assn., Clark County Bar Assn., U. Nev.-Las Vegas Alumni Assn. (pres. 1964-69, Humanitarian of Yr. 1984), Rotary, Phi Alpha Delta, Sigma Chi, KC. Democrat. Roman Catholic. Office Phone: 702-792-7000.

BILDERSEE, ROBERT ALAN, lawyer; b. Albany, NY, Jan. 22, 1942; s. Max U. and Hannah (Marks) B.; m. Ellen Bernstein, June 9, 1963; 1 child, Jennifer M. BA, Columbia Coll., 1962, MA, 1964; LLB, Yale U., 1967. Assoc. Wolf Block Schorr & Solis Cohen, Phila., 1967-72; sole practice Phila., 1972-73; assoc., then ptnr. Fox Rothschild, O'Brien & Frankel, Phila., 1973-80; ptnr. Morgan Lewis & Bockius LLP, Phila., 1980-97; founding ptnr. Bildersee & Silbert, LLP, Jenkintown, Pa., 1997—. Lectr. Temple U. Sch. Law, Phila., 1978-91; asst. in instrn. Yale U. Law Sch., New Haven, 1966; bd. dirs. ASPA Benefits Coun. Delaware Valley; mem. Northeast region and Mid-Atlantic region pension liaison coms. IRS. Author: Pension Regulation Manual, Pension Administrator's Forms and Checklists, 1987; contbg. author: Employee Benefits Handbook, 1982-98; editor: Beyond the Fringes; contbr. articles to profl. jours. Woodrow Wilson fellow, 1962. Mem. ABA, Pa. Bar Assn., Phila. Bar Assn. Avocation: wildlife photography. Office: Bildersee and Silbert LLP PO Box 599 Abington PA 19001-0599 Home Phone: 215-947-5131; Office Phone: 215-914-0414. Business E-Mail: erisaplus@aol.com.

BILECKI, RONALD ALLAN, financial planner; b. Cin., July 15, 1942; s. Allan Frederick and Ruth H.; m. Judy A. Newberry, Jan. 25, 1964; children: Sherry D. Pavan, Sean P. BA in Chemistry, Calif. State U., 1968. Cert. fin. planner; investment adv. rep. Ins. agt. N.Y. Life Ins., Covina, Calif., 1973-75, asst. mgr. Los Angeles, 1975-79; pvt. practice Rosemead, Calif., 1979-81; pres. Fin. Designs Corp., San Gabriel, Calif., 1981—. Fin. planning cons. So. Calif. Edison, Rosemead, 1986—, So. Calif. Gas Co., 1991—, Disney/ABC, 1991—. Mem. Gideons, Covina, 1987. Mem. Internat. Assn. Fin. Planning. Republican. Avocations: chess, jogging, hiking, western dancing. Home Phone: 909-626-9244; Office Phone: 909-626-1642. E-mail: fdc@earthlink.net.

BILELLO, JOHN CHARLES, engineering educator, director; b. Bklyn., Oct. 15, 1938; s. Charles and Catherine (Buonadonna) B.; m. Mary Josephine Gloria, Aug. 1, 1959; children: Andrew Charles, Peter Angelo, Matthew Jonathan. B.E., NYU, 1960, MS, 1962; PhD, U. Ill., 1965. Sr. rsch. engr. Gen. Telephone & Electronics Lab., Bayside, NY, 1965-67; mem. faculty SUNY, Stony Brook, 1967-87, asst. prof., 1967-71, assoc. prof., 1971-75, prof. engring., 1975-87, dean, 1977-81; dean Sch. Engring and Computer Sci., prof. mech. engring. Calif. State U., Fullerton, 1986-89; prof. materials sci. and engring., prof. applied physics U. Mich., Ann Arbor, 1989—2004, dir. Ctr. Nanomaterials Scis., 1995—, emeritus, 2005—; v.p. R&D Metaglass Coatings, LLC, Ann Arbor, 2005—. Vis. rsch. assoc., Calif. Inst. Tech., Pasadena, 2003, vis. prof. Poly. of Milan, 1973-74; vis. scholar King's Coll., London U., 1983; vis. fellow NATO exchange scholar Oxford U., 1986; project dir. synchrotron topography project Univ. Consortium, 1981-86; NATO vis. fellow Oxford (Eng.) U., 1998—. NATO sr. faculty fellow Enrico Fermi Center, Milan, Italy, 1973 Fellow Am. Soc. for Metals; mem. AIME, Am. Phys. Soc., Materials Rsch. Soc. Office: U Mich Dept Material Sci Engring Ann Arbor MI 48109

BILES, CHARLES LEE, plant pathologist, physiologist, educator; b. Ft. Worth, Nov. 24, 1957; s. Betty LaRue Biles; m. Merrianne Densie Daughtery, May 24, 1986; children: Robert Josiah, Caleb Lincoln, Peter Battle. BS, Stephen F. Austin State U., Nacogdoches, Tex., 1980; MS, Colo. State U., Ft. Collins, 1984; PhD, Tex. A&M U., College Station, 1988. Asst. prof. N.Mex. State U., Las Cruces, 1990—93; prof. biology East Ctrl. U., Ada, Okla., 1993—. Cons. Ada Biolab Cons., LLC, 2002—. Author: Human Physiology Laboratory Workbook. Recipient Tchg. Excellence award, East Ctrl. U., 1997, 2004; Summer Acad. Forensic Biology grantee, Okla. State Regents for Higher Edn., 1998—2005, Grantee for preformed and induced disease def. mechanisms of cantaloupe, USDA Agr. Rsch. Svc., 1996—2000, Rsch. and Engring. Apprenticeship Program grantee, Acad. Applied Sci., 2006, 2007. Mem.: Okla. Acad. Scis. (vice-chair microbiology 2006—07), Brit. Mycol. Soc., Beta Beta Beta (sponsor East Ctrl. U. Campus Soc., Psi Delta 1994—2007). Conservative. Avocations: bicycling, hiking. Office: East Central Univ 1100 East 14th St Ada OK 74820 Home Phone: 580-436-3023; Office Phone: 580-559-5498. Business E-Mail: cbiles@ecok.edu.

BILES, GLORIA C., historian, educator; d. George Graham and Lillian Oriol Crevenstene; m. Wiley Biles, June 21, 1949. BBA, U. Houston, 1947, MEd, 1957, MA, 1972; PhD, Rice U., 1979. Cert. tchr. Tex. Tchr. mid. and high sch. Houston Ind. Sch. Dist., 1957—67; lectr. U. Houston, Clear Lake, 1979—81, U. Houston, West Houston, 1979—81; adj. prof. Houston Bapt. Univ., 1984—86, asst. prof., 1986—93, assoc. prof., 1993—2002; ret., 2002. Mem. Houston Grand Opera, 1952—, Gilbert and Sullivan Soc., 1952—, Heritage Soc., 1979—, PBS, 1988—, Am. Carousel Soc., 1989—, Houston Symphony Soc., 1989—, Bush Presdl. Libr., Coll. Station, Tex., 1999—, Nat. Trust for Hist. Preservation, Mus. of Printing History, 1999—. Mem.: NEA, AAUP, Am. Hist. Assn., Phi Kappa Phi, Delta Kappa Gamma (chair coms.), Phi Alpha Theta, Phi Gamma Nu, Alpha Mu Gamma (hon.). Avocation: collecting antique carousel horses, Steuben glass and miniature animals.

BILEYDI, SUMER, advertising agency executive; b. Antalya, Turkey, Feb. 7, 1936; came to U.S., 1957; s. Abdurrahman M. and Neriman (Akman) B.; m. Lois E. Goode, Dec. 30, 1961; children: Can M., Sera N. BA, Mich. State U., 1961, MA, 1962. Mktg. cons. Export Promotion Ctr., Ankara, 1962; planner Gardner Advt. Agy., St. Louis, 1963-65; planning supr. Batten, Barton, Durstine & Osborn, NYC, 1965-69; assoc. dir. Ketchum, Macleod & Grove, Pitts., 1969-73; sr. ptnr., dir. Carmichael Lynch, Inc., Mpls., 1974-91, sr. ptnr., 1992-98; CEO, pres. Manajans Thompson AS, Istanbul, Turkey, 1999-2001, ret., 2001. Cons. Carmichael-Lynch, Mpls., 1999-2004; cons. Leading Ind. Advt. Agy. Network, 1987-89, chmn., pres., 1989-91; CEO, pres. Global Mktg. Comm. Cons., Naples, Fla. Contbr. articles to profl. jours. Mem. Am. Mktg. Assn., Advt. Rsch. Found. Home: 4718 Navassa Ln Naples FL 34119-9554 Office Phone: 239-594-5056. E-mail: lbileydi@aol.com.

BILGER, BRUCE R., lawyer; b. Balt., Feb. 27, 1952; BA, Dartmouth Coll., 1973; MBA, JD, U. Va., 1977. Bar: Tex. 1977. Mem. Vinson & Elkins LLP, Houston, chair Energy Practice Group, co-head Bus. & Internat. Law Sect. Mem. Phi Beta Kappa. Office: Vinson & Elkins LLP 2500 First City Tower 1001 Fannin St Houston TX 77002-6760 Business E-Mail: bbilger@velaw.com.

BILGINSOY, CIHAN, economics professor; arrived in U.S., 1977; s. Sadi and Raika Bilginsoy; m. Gunseli Berik; children: Alev, Mehmet. BS, Mid. East Tech. U., Ankara, 1976; MS, U. Minn., 1979; PhD, U. Mass., 1986. Prof. econ. U. Utah, Salt Lake City, 1993—. Contbr. articles to profl. jours. Office: U Utah Dept Econ 1645 Central Campus Dr Room 308 Salt Lake City UT 84112 Office Fax: 801-585-5649. Business E-Mail: bilginsoy@economics.utah.edu.

BILGUTAY, NIHAT MUSTAFA, engineering educator, associate dean; b. Ankara, Turkey, Mar. 31, 1952; s. Sabahattin and Utarit Bilgutay; m. Kathleen Ann Evans, Sept. 10, 1977; children: Canan Ayse, Aylin Nur, Deniz Oya. BSEE, Bradley U., 1973; MSEE, Purdue U., 1975, PhD, 1981. Assoc. dean engring. for grad. programs and rsch. Drexel U., Phila., 1990—95, head elec. and computer engring. dept., 1995—2006, Vernon L. Newhouse prof. elec. engring., 2004—, assoc. dean engring dept., 2006—. Contbr. articles to profl. jours. Fellow: IEEE (Third Millennium award 2000, Second Pl. award in the Transactions on Sonics and Ultrasonics Best Paper Competition 1976); mem.: Am. Soc. for Non-Destructive Testing, Eta Kappa Nu, Tau Beta Pi. Achievements include development of split-spectrum processing (SSP) technique, which provides a unique and effective means of suppressing coherent noise; research in Evaluation of a Random Signal Correlation System for Ultrasonic Flaw Detection. Office: Drexel Univ 3141 Chestnut St Philadelphia PA 19104 Home Phone: 610-565-1969; Office Phone: 215-895-6806. Business E-Mail: bilgutay@ece.drexel.edu.

BILINSKY, YAROSLAV, political scientist; b. Lutsk, Ukraine, Feb. 26, 1932; s. Peter Bilinsky and Natalia (Balabaj) Bilinska; m. Wira Rusaniwskyj, Feb. 18, 1962; children: Peter Yaroslav, Sophia Vera Yaroslava, Nadia Yaroslava, Mark Paul Yaroslav. AB magna cum laude, Harvard U., 1954, postgrad. in Soviet affairs, 1956-57; PhD, Princeton U., 1958. Asso. Harvard U. Russian Research Center, 1956-58; instr. polit. sci. Douglass Coll., Rutgers U., New Brunswick, NJ, 1958-61; asst. prof. U. Del., Newark, 1961-65, assoc. prof., 1965-69, prof., 1969—2002, prof. emeritus, 2002—. Vis. instr. U. Pa., 1961; vis. prof. Columbia U., 1976 Author: The Second Soviet Republic: The Ukraine after World War II, 1964, Endgame in NATO's Enlargement: The Baltic States and Ukraine, 1999. Corr. sec. Peter and Paul Ukrainian Orthodox Ch., Wilmington, Del., 1965-66, trustee, 1967-71. Mem. Am. Assn. Advancement Slavic Studies (pres. Mid-Atlantic Slavic Conf. 1992-93), Ukrainian Acad. Arts and Scis. in U.S. (pres. 1987-90). Home: 2 Mimosa Dr Newark DE 19711-7523 Office Phone: 302-831-2355. E-mail: yby@udel.edu. *My favorite quotation is from Shakespeare: The readiness is all. I have tried to be always prepared to serve my country, my students, and my family. I am ready to live and, if it be God's will, ready to die.*

BILIONIS, LOUIS D., dean, law educator; b. Fitchburg, Mass., July 19, 1957; s. Charles L. and Angela (Despotopulos) B.; m. Sara Bullard, Aug. 20, 1983 (div. 1986), Ann Hubbard; 1 child: Graciela. AB in econs. and english, U. NC, 1979; JD magna cum laude, Harvard U., 1982. Bar: Mass 1983, U.S. Dist. Ct. Mass. 1984, N.C. 1985, U.S. Supreme Ct. 1987. Law clk. to hon. Francis D. Murnaghan Jr. U.S. Ct. Appeals (4th cir.), Balt., 1982-83; assoc. Ropes & Gray, Boston, 1983-84; asst. appellate defender State of N.C., Raleigh, 1984-88; asst. prof. law. Sch. of Law U. NC, Chapel Hill, 1988—93, assoc. prof., 1993—97, prof., 1997—99; Samuel Ashe Disting. Prof. of Constitutional Law, U. Cin. Coll. Law, Cin., 1999—2005, dean and nippert prof. law, 2005—. Vis. prof. Nat. Law Ctr., George Washington U., 1994. Contbr. articles to profl. journs. Mem.: Order of the Grail, Order of the Old Well, Order of the Golden Fleece, Phi Beta Kappa. Office: U Cin Coll Law Clifton Ave Calhoun St Cincinnati OH 45221 Office Phone: 513-556-0121. Office Fax: 513-556-2391. Business E-Mail: louis.bilionis@uc.edu.

BILIRAKIS, GUS MICHAEL, congressman, former state representative; b. Gainesville, Fla., Feb. 8, 1963; s. Michael Bilirakis; m. Eva Bilirakis; 4 children. BA, U. Fla., 1986; JD, Stetson U., 1989. Atty. Bilirakis Law Group, Holiday, Fla.; mem. Fla. Ho. of Reps from Dist. 48, 1998—2006, vice chmn. Real Property & Probate Com., mem. Fin. & Taxation, Elder Affairs & Long-Term Care and Utilities & Comm. Coms., 1998—2006; mem. US Congress from 9th Fla. Dist., 2007—. Adj. prof. St. Petersburg Jr. Coll., 1997. Mem.: Clearwater Bar Assn., Am. Hellenic Edn. Progressive Assn., Elks Club. Republican. Office: 1630 Longworth House Office Bldg Washington DC 20515 also: 35111 United States Highway 19 N Palm Harbor Profl Ctr, Ste 3 Palm Harbor FL 34684*

BILIRAKIS, MICHAEL, former congressman, lawyer, corporate financial executive; b. Tarpon Springs, Fla., July 16, 1930; s. Emmanuel and Irene (Pikramenos) B.; m. Evelyn Miaoulis, Dec. 27, 1959; children: Emmanuel, Gus. BS in Engring., U. Pittsburgh, 1959; student, George Washington U., 1959-60; JD, U. Fla., 1963; JD (hon.), Stetson U.; degree (hon.), U. Tampa. Bar: Fla. 1964; cert. coll. tchr., Fla. Atty., small businessman, Pinellas and Pasco Counties, Fla., 1968—; mem. US Congress from 9th Dist. Fla., 1983—2007, mem. energy & commerce com., vice chair vets. affairs com., chair health subcom. Mem. Rep. Task Force on Social Security; co-chmn. Task Force on Infant Mortality; founder, charter pres. Tarpon Springs Vol. Ambulance Service; dir. Greek Studies program U. Fla.; dir. emeritus Juvenile Diabetes and Hospice; mem. Pres.' Coun. U. Fla. Sgt. USAF, 1951-55. Named Citizen of Yr. Greater Tarpon Springs, 1972-73, Man of Yr. United Way, 1989-90. Mem. Am. Legion (comdr. 1977-79), VFW, Amvets, USAF Sgts., NCOA, Air Force Assn., Greater Tarpon Springs C. of C. (past pres., dir.), Pinellas C. of C. (gov.), West Pasco Bar Assn., Am. Judicature Soc., Fla. Bar Assn., Gator Boosters, Fla. Blue Key (hon.), Mason (33 degree), Shriner, Jester, Moose, Elks, Rotary, Eastern Star, Phi Alpha Delta, Sigma Pi. Lodges: Masons; Shriners; Moose; Tarpon Springs Rotary; Elks; Eastern Star; White Shrine of Jerusalem; Am. Bar Assn. Republican. Greek Orthodox.*

BILKA, PAUL JOSEPH, retired physician; b. NYC, Oct. 12, 1919; s. John and Josephine (Hlavaty) B.; m. Madge Ayres Mussey, Dec. 26, 1943. BS, Trinity Coll., Hartford, Conn., 1940; MD, Columbia U., 1943; MS in Medicine, U. Minn., 1950. Intern Hartford Hosp., 1944-45; fellow in internal medicine Mayo Found, Rochester, Minn., 1947-50; asst. in rheumatology Mayo Clinic, 1949-50; practice medicine specializing in rheumatology Mpls., 1950-91; med. staff Mpls. VA Hosp., 1991—; clin. prof. medicine U. Minn. Med. Sch. Clin. prof. medicine U. Minn. Med. Sch., 1960-2007; cons. Mpls. VA Hosp., 1955-2007, mem. med. staff, 1991-. Author numerous papers in field; also producer films on rheumatology. Served to capt. M.C. AUS, 1945-47. Mem. Am. Coll. Rheumatology (master designation 1992), Nat. Soc. Clin. Rheumatology (pres. 1985-87). Clubs: Lafayette (Minnetonka, Minn.). Home: 4384 Manitou Rd Excelsior MN 55331-9445

BILL, TONY, producer, director; b. San Diego, Aug. 23, 1940; Student, Notre Dame U. Founder Bill/Phillips Prodns. (with Julia and Michael Phillips), 1971-73; ind. producer, 1973—. Bd. govs. Acad. Motion Picture Arts and Scis. Prodr.: Deadhead Miles, Steelyard Blues, 1973, The Sting, 1974, Going in Style, 1979, Hearts of the West, 1975, Harry and Walter Go to New York, 1976, Boulevard Nights, 1979; exec. producer: The Little Dragons, 1978; dir.: The Ransom of Red Chief, 1977, My Bodyguard, 1980, Six Weeks, 1982, Love Thy Neighbor, 1984, Five Corners, 1987, Crazy People, 1990, Untamed Heart, 1993, A Home of Our Own, 1993, Next Door, 1995, Beyond the Call, 1996, Oliver Twist, 1997, A Chance of Snow, 1998, Harlan County War, 2000, In the Time of the Butterflies, 2001, Whitewash the Clarence Brandley Story, 2002, Last Call, 2002; dir. Flyboys, 2006. Office: Barnstorm Films 73 Market St Venice CA 90291-3603

BILLAUD, LOUISE ANN, musician, educator; b. Hamilton, Ohio, Sept. 24, 1959; d. Albert and Donna Franzmann; m. Jean-Paul Billaud; 1 child, Kéran John. MusB in Performance, U. Alaska, Anchorage, 1985; MA, Radford U., Va., 1997. Pvt. piano instr., Anchorage, 1992-95; grad. asst. Radford U., 1995-97, instr. music, 1997—99, New River C.C., Dublin, Va., 2001—07, asst. prof., 2007—. Musician (pianist): concerts and lecture-recitals, 1986—; musician: (recording) Louise Billaud, 1999, From Bartók to the Popol Vuh, 2000, Passion, 2004, (DVD) Mazeppa - An Inspirational Living Legend, 2006. Named semifinalist, Web Concert Hall Internat. Competition, 2004; recipient First prize, Internat. Bartok-Kabalevsky Piano Competition, 1987, award for Exemplary Performance, Radford U., 1997. Mem.: Coll. Music Soc., Music Educators Nat. Conf., Music Tchrs. Nat. Assn., Phi Kappa Phi. Office: PO Box 1127 Dublin VA 24084 Office Phone: 540-674-3600 4351. Business E-Mail: nrbilll@nr.edu.

BILLAUER, BARBARA PFEFFER, lawyer, educator; b. Aug. 9, 1951; d. Harry George and Evelyn (Newman) Pfeffer. BS with honors, Cornell U., 1972; JD, Hofstra U., 1975; MA, NYU, 1982; cert. in risk scis. and pub. policy, Johns Hopkins U., 1999. Bar: N.Y. 1976, Fed. Dist. Ct. N.Y. 1977, U.S. Ct. Appeals (2d cir.) 1978, U.S. Supreme Ct. 1984. Assoc. Bower & Gardner, NYC, 1974-78; sr. trial atty. Joseph W. Conklin, NYC, 1978-80; assoc. dept. head Curtis, Mallet-Prevost, Colt & Mosle, NYC, 1980-82; ptnr. Anderson, Russell, Kill & Olick, NYC, 1982-86, Stroock & Stroock & Lavan, NYC, 1986-90; ptnr., chair environ. and toxic tort practice Keck, Mahin, Cate & Koether, 1990-93; prin. Barbara P. Billauer & Assocs., Lido Beach, N.Y., 1993—. Vis. scholar Johns Hopkins U. Sch. Pub. Health, 1998-99; faculty SUNY Stony Brook Med. Sch.; adj. assoc. prof. NYU Grad. Sch., 1982-88; lectr. Rutger's U. Med. Sch.; jud. screening com. Coordinated Bar Assn., 1983-86; mem. spl panel Citywide Ct. Adminstrn. 1982-85; bd. dirs. Weizmann Inst., Am. Com. Co-author: The Lender's Guide to Environmental Law: Risk and Liability, 1993. Fellow Am. Bar Found.; mem. ABA (indoor air polution 1990-93), Met. Womens Bar Assn. (v.p. 1981-83, pres. 1983-85, chmn. bd. 1985-87), Nat. Conf. Womens Bar Assn. (bd. dirs., v.p. 1989-95), Internat. Coun. Shopping Ctrs. (environ. com.), Brit. Occupl. Hygiene Soc., Environment Toxic Torts. Home: 2867 Tilden St NW Washington DC 20008-3837 E-mail: omniscience@starpower.net.

BILLER, JOEL WILSON, lawyer, retired diplomat; b. Milw., Jan. 17, 1929; s. Saul Earl and Mildred (Wilson) B.; m. Geraldine Pollack, May 1, 1955; children— Sydney, Andrew, Charles. BA, U. Wis., 1950; JD, U. Mich., 1953; MA, Northwestern U., 1959. Bar: Wis. 1953. Atty., Milw., 1953-55; vice consul Am. consulate, Le Havre, France, 1956-58; econ. officer Am. Embassy, The Hague, Netherlands, 1959-62; internat. relations officer State Dept., Washington, 1962-66; econ. officer, asst. dir. AID mission, Quito, Ecuador, 1966-69; econ. counselor Am. embassy, Buenos Aires, 1969-71; dir. AID mission, Santiago, Chile, 1971-73; spl. asst. to undersec. state for econ. affairs Washington, 1973-74; spl. asst. to dep. sec. state, 1974; dep. asst. sec. state for comml. and spl. bilateral affairs, 1974-76; dep. asst. sec. state for transp., telecommunications and comml. affairs, after, 1976; sr. v.p. Manpower Inc., Milw., 1979-97, sr. v.p., gen. counsel, 1997-98, sr. v.p. internat. corp. affairs, 1999—; pres. Internat. Confedn. of Pvt. Employment Agys., 2004—. Mem. Am. Fgn. Service Assn. Office: Manpower Inc 5301 N Ironwood Rd PO Box 2053 Milwaukee WI 53201-2053

BILLER, JOSE, neurologist, educator; b. Montevideo, Uruguay, Jan. 18, 1948; B in Medicine, A.V. Acevedo Inst., Montevideo, Uruguay, 1965; MD, U. de la Republica, Montevideo, Uruguay, 1974. Diplomate Am. Bd. Neurology and Vascular Neurology. Intern Maciel Hosp., Montevideo, Uruguay, 1974—76, Columbus Hosp., Chgo., 1976-77; resident in neurology Henry Ford Hosp., Detroit, 1977-78, Loyola U. Hosp., Hines VA Hosp., Ill., 1978-80, chief resident neurology Ill., 1979—80; fellow cerebral vascular diseases Bowman Gray Sch. Med., Winston Salem, NC, 1980-81, instr. neurology, 1981; asst. prof. neurology Loyola U., Chgo., 1982-84, prof., assoc. chmn. dept. neurology Stritch Sch. Med., 2003—, dir. neurology residency training program, 2003—05, acting chmn. dept. neurology, 2004—05, prof., chmn. dept. neurology, 2005—; asst. prof. neurology U. Iowa Coll. Medicine, Iowa City, 1984-87, assoc. prof. neurology, 1987-90, prof. neurology, 1990-91; prof. Northwestern Sch.

Medicine, Chgo., 1991-94; dir. stroke program, dir. acute stroke care unit Northwestern Meml. Hosp., Chgo., 1991-94; prof., chmn. dept. neurology Ind. U., 1994—2003. Prof. ad-hororem U. of the Republic Sch. Medicine, Uruguay, 1997—; cons. physician neurology svc. VA Hosp., Iowa City, 1984—91; staff physician Northwestern Meml. Hosp., Chgo., 1991—94; neurology cons. Rehab. Inst. Chgo., 1991—94; active med. staff Ind. U. Hosps., 1994—2003, Loyola U. Hosp., 2003—; cons. Roudebush VA Med. Ctr., 1994—2003. Mem. editl. bd. Stroke, Stroke-Clin. Update, Neurol. Rsch., internat. bd. editors CNS Drugs; editor: Seminars in Cerebrovascular Diseases and Stroke, Jour. Stroke and Cerebrovascular Diseases; contbr. articles to profl. jours., chapters to books. Fellow: ACP, Am. Heart Assn., Am. Acad. Neurology; mem.: AMA, Am. Neurol. Assn., Inter-Am. Coll. Physicians and Surgeons, Uruguayan Internal Medicine Soc. (hon.), Argentinian Neurol. Assn. (hon.), Uruguayan Neurol. Soc. (hon.), Internat. Stroke Soc., Am. Soc. Neurology Investigation, N.Y. Acad. Sci. Office: Maguire Bldg 105/2700 2160 S First Ave Maywood IL 60153 Office Phone: 708-216-2438. Business E-Mail: jbiller@lumc.edu.

BILLERA, LOUIS J(OSEPH), mathematics professor; b. NYC, Apr. 12, 1943; s. Joseph James and Florence Ann B.; m. Jeanne Marie Kebba, June 20, 1964; children: John L., Mark A. BS, Rensselaer Poly. Inst., 1964; postgrad., Princeton U., 1964-65; MA, CUNY, 1967, PhD, 1968. Asst. prof. Cornell U., Ithaca, N.Y., 1968-73; postdoctoral fellow Hebrew Univ., Jerusalem, Israel, 1969; assoc. prof. Cornell U., Ithaca, N.Y., 1973-80, prof. math., 1980—, Rutgers U., New Brunswick, N.J., 1985-89, assoc. dir. DIMACS Ctr. Discrete Math./Theoretical Computer, 1988-89; acting dir. Ctr. for Applied Math., Cornell U., Ithaca, N.Y., 1995-96; rsch. prof. Math. Sci. Rsch. Inst., Berkeley, 1996-97. Vis. rsch. assoc. Brandeis U., Waltham, Mass., 1974-75; prof. invité CORE, U. Catholique de Louvain, Belgium, 1980; vis. prof. Mittag-Leffler Inst., Sweden, 1992, 2005. Contbr. over 65 articles to profl. jours. Fellow Ednl. Testing Svc., 1964-65, NDEA, 1965-68, NSF, 1969; recipient D.R. Fulkerson prize Am. Math. Soc. and Math. Programming Soc., 1994. Mem.: Math. Assn. Am., Am. Math. Soc. Office: Cornell U Dept Math Malott Hall Ithaca NY 14853-4201

BILLETER, ROBERT JAMES, newspaper publisher; b. Clarksburg, W.Va., Aug. 16, 1926; s. Arch and Mabel Edith (Westfall) B.; m. Eileen Billie Horvath, Apr. 14, 1972; 1 child, William Fletcher. BS, W.Va. U., Morgantown, 1951. Editor Pendleton Times, Franklin, W.Va., 1951-53; copy editor Herald-Dispatch, Huntington, 1953-54; reporter The Post, Morgantown, 1954-56; copy editor Sun-Telegraph, Pitts., 1956-60, Post-Gazette, Pitts., 1960-81, night city editor, 1981-85, makeup editor, 1985-91; pub. The Weston (W.Va.) Democrat, 1992—. With U.S. Army, 1945-47. Episcopalian. Avocations: wine tasting, sailing, hiking, skiing. Home: One E 4th St Weston WV 26452 Office: The Weston Democrat 306 Main Ave Weston WV 26452-2046 Office Phone: 304-269-1600. Business E-Mail: news@westondemocrat.com.

BILLIAS, GEORGE ATHAN, historian, educator; b. Lynn, Mass., June 26, 1919; s. Athan O. and Grace (Papadakis) B.; m. Joyce Baldwin, Dec. 28, 1948 (dec.); children: Stephen, Athan, Nancy; m. Margaret Neussendorfer, Aug. 17, 1986. BA magna cum laude, Bates Coll., Lewiston, Maine, 1948; MA, Columbia U., NYC, 1949, PhD, 1958. Nat. def. historian USAF, 1951-54; instr. U. Maine, 1954-57, asst. prof., 1957-59, assoc. prof., 1959-62, Clark U., Worcester, Mass., 1962-66, prof. Am. history, 1966—, Jacob and Frances Hiatt prof. history, 1983-89, Jacob and Frances Hiatt prof. emeritus, 1989—. Author: Massachusetts Land Bankers of 1740, 1959, General John Glover and His Marblehead Mariners, 1960, Elbridge Gerry: Founding Father and Republican Statesman, 1976; editor, contbr.: George Washington's Generals, 1964, Law and Authority in Colonial America: Selected Essays, 1965, The American Revolution: How Revolutionary Was It?, 1965, 4th edit., 1989, Interpretations of American History: Patterns and Perspectives, 2 vols., 1967, 7th edit., 2000, George Washington's Opponents, 1969, The Federalists: Realists or Ideologues?, 1970, American History: Retrospect and Prospect, 1971, Perspectives on Early American History, 1973, American Constitutionalism Abroad, 1990, The Republican Synthesis Revisited: Essays in Honor of George Athan Billias, 1992, George Washington's Generals and George Washington's Opponents, 1993, George Bancroft, Master Historian, 2004; contbr. articles to profl. jours. With M.C., U.S. Army, 1941-46, ETO. Decorated Bronze Star; Am. Philos. Soc. grantee, 1965; Guggenheim fellow, 1961-62, Am. Coun. Learned Socs. fellow, 1968-69, NEH fellow, 1970-71, 79, 86, Huntington Libr. fellow, 1989-90. Mem.: Orgn. Am. Historians, Am. Antiquarian Soc. (honoree symposium The Republican Synthesis Revisited 1989), Mass. Hist. Soc., Inst. Early Am. History and Culture (coun. 1969—72), Columbia Seminar in Early Am. History, Phi Beta Kappa. Office: Clark U Dept History Worcester MA 01610

BILLICK, BRIAN, professional football coach; b. Fairborne, Ohio, Feb. 28, 1954; m. Kim Billick; children: Aubree, Keegan. Student, Brigham Young U. Mem. Dallas Cowboys, 1977; asst. coach U. Redlands, 1977-78; grad. asst. Brigham Young U., Provo, Utah, 1978; asst. dir. pub. rels. San Francisco 49ers, 1979-80; coach receivers, tight ends, quarterbacks San Diego State U., 1981-85; offensive coord. Utah State U., 1986-88; asst. coach Stanford (Calif.) U., 1989-91; offensive coord. Minn. Vikings, 1992-98; head coach Balt. Ravens, 1999—. Earned All Western Athletic Conf. honors and honorable mention All-America in 1976 as a tight end, Brigham Young U. Achievements include being the architect of Minnesota Vikings offense that scored 556 points to break NFL record of 541 points. Office: Baltimore Ravens 1 Winning Dr Owings Mills MD 21117-4776

BILLIG, DONAL MICHAEL, surgeon; b. NYC, Feb. 19, 1931; s. Richard Leon and Sylvia Irma Billig; m. Bonny Brown Billig, Jan. 19, 1985; 1 child, Samuel Richard; 1 child from previous marriage, Andrea Lynn. BA cum laude, U. Louisville, 1952, MD cum laude, 1956. Diplomate Am. Bd. Surgery, Am. Bd. Thoracic Surgery, Am. Bd. Urgent Care Medicine, lic. physician NY, DC, Md., Va. Intern Bellevue Hosp., NYC, 1956—57, resident in internal medicine, 1957—58; fellow in cardiopulmonary lab. Columbia Presbyn. Med. Ctr., NYC, 1958—59; surg. officer Naval Hosp., Portsmouth, NH, 1959—61; resident in gen. surgery Baylor Affiliated Hosps., Houston, 1961—65, resident in thoracic surgery, 1965—66; chief thoracic and cardiovasc. surgery VA Hosp., Houston, 1966—68; chief thoracic and cardiac surgery Boston Floating Hosp., 1968—72; surgeon New Eng. Med. Ctr. Hosps., Boston, 1968—72; staff cardiothoracic surgeon Naval Hosp., Bethesda, Md., 1983—85; asst. in surgery Baylor U. Coll. Medicine, Houston, 1961—66, instr. in surgery, 1966—68, dir. and lectr. sr. med. student surg. anatomy course, 1967—68; asst. prof. surgery Tufts U. Sch. Medicine, Boston, 1968—72; assoc. prof. surgery Hahnemann Med. Coll. & Hosp. of Phila., 1972—73, prof. surgery, 1973—81, Uniformed Svcs. Univ. of Health Sci., Bethesda, 1983—85; pvt. practice Prompt Care Med. Ctr., Washington, 1990—93, Beauregard Med. Ctr., Ltd., Alexandria, Va., 1992—96; assoc. med. dir., staff physician Briggs Chaney Med. Ctr., Silver Spring, Md., 1996—2004; staff physician Concentra Med. Ctrs., Linthicum, Md., 2004—07; med. dir. Concentra-Rosedale Med. Ctr., Balt., 2007—, 2007—. Chmn. dept. cardiothoracic surgery, dir. thoracic surgery residency program Naval Hosp., Bethesda, 1983—85; thoracic surg. advisor Naval Med. Command, Washington, 1984—85, med. officer physical qualifications and rev. divsn., 1985—86; prof. surgery Uniformed Svcs. Univ. of Health Scis., 1983—85; dir. divsn. cardiothoracic surgery Hahneman Med. Ctr. & Hosp. of Phila., 1972—76; assoc. attending thoracic and cardiovasc. surgeon Monmouth Med. Ctr., Long Branch, NJ, 1976—81, dir. vascular lab., 1979—81; attending thoracic and cardiovasc. surgeon Freehold Area Hosp-Centra State Med. Ctr., NJ, 1978—81; staff thoracic and cardiovasc. surgeon Montefiore Hosp., Pitts., Braddock Gen. Hosp., Pa., 1981—83; staff physician No. Va. Doctors Hosp., 1991—99, Nat. Hosp. Med. Ctr., 1990—98; mem. adv. bd. cardiovasc. surgery Pa. Blue Shield, 1972—76; mem. exec. com. Monmouth County Med. Soc., 1978—81, sec.-treas., 1980—81; del. NJ State Med. Soc., 1978—80; mem. constn. and by-laws com. Med. Soc. DC, Washington, 1990—94; mem. credentials com. Fairfax County Med. Soc., 1994—96. Author: (textbook) Management of Neonates and Infants with Congenital Heart Disease, 1973; sr. editor CHEST, 1974—79. Comdr. USN, 1984—88. Recipient award for outstanding prof. and tchr., Baylor U., 1968, Phi Chi award for tchg., 1968; Student Rsch. scholar, Ky. Heart Assn., 1953—56. Fellow: ACS (coun. on cardiovasc. surgery), Am. Heart Assn.; mem.: Am. Assn. Ambulatory Care, Md. Acad. Family Physicians, Am. Acad. Family Physicians, Soc. Vascular Surgery (sr. disting. fellow), Va. Acad. Family Physicians, Michael E. DeBakey Internat. Cardiovasc. Soc., Alpha Epsilon Delta. Jewish. Home: 10945 Rocky Mount Way Silver Spring MD 20902 Office: Concentra-Rosedale Med Ctr B101 Pulaski Hwy Baltimore MD 21237

BILLIG, ETEL JEWEL, theater director, actress; b. NYC, Dec. 16, 1932; d. Anthony and Martha Rebecca (Klebansky) Papa; m. Steven S. Billig, Dec. 23, 1956 (dec. Aug. 1996); children: Curt Adam, Jonathan Roark. BS, NYU, 1953, MA, 1955; student, Herbert Berghof Studio, NYC, 1955-56. Cert. elem. and high sch. tchr. Actress Washington Square Players, NYC, 1950-55, Dukes Oak Theatre, Cooperstown, NY, 1955, Triple Cities Playhouse, Binghampton, NY, 1956, Candlelight Dinner Playhouse, Summit, Ill., 1970, 73, 77, 79, 90; mng. dir. Theatre 31, Park Forest, Ill., 1971-73; asst. mgr. Westroads Dinner Theatre, Omaha, 1973-76; mng. dir., actress Forum Theatre, 1973, 94; mng. dir., actress, producing dir. Ill. Theatre Ctr., Park Forest, 1976—; mng. dir., actress Goodman Theatre, Chgo., 1987, 95, Ct. Theatre, 1990, Wisdom Bridge Theatre, 1991; dir. drama Rich Ctrl. H.S., Olympia Fields, Ill., 1978-86. Del. League of Chgo. Theatres Russian Exchange to Soviet Union, 1989; actress Drury Lane, Oak Brook, Ill., 1989; mem. adj. faculty theatre program Prairie State Coll., 2004—; cons. and lectr. in field. Appeared in films including the Dollmaker, Running Scared, Straight Talk, Stolen Summer; (TV series) Hawaiian Heat, Missing Persons, Untouchables. V.p. Nat. Coun. Jewish Women, Park Forest, 1968-70; sec. Community Arts Coun., Park Forest, 1984-86; pres. Southland Regional Arts Coun., 1986-92. Recipient Risk Taking award NOW, 1982, Athena award Matteson Area C. of C., 1997, Abby Found. award, 1997; grantee Nebr. Arts Coun., 1975, Ill. Arts Coun., 1995, 96, 2000; named Best of Chgo. drama muse for children Chgo. Mag., 2004, Entertainer of Yr. Star Pub. Newspaper, 2006; named to Park Forest Hall of Fame, 2000. Mem. AFTRA, SAG, Actors' Equity Assn., League Chgo. Theatres, Ill. Arts Coun. Theatre Panel, Prodrs. Assn. Chgo. Area Theatre (sec. 1988-89), Bus. in the Arts Coun. of C. of C. (charter), Rotary (bd. dirs. Park Forest chpt. 1988-97, sec. 2000, hall of fame 2000). Avocations: travel, antiques. Office: Ill Theatre Ctr PO Box 397 Park Forest IL 60466-0397 Office Phone: 708-481-3510. E-mail: ilthctr@sbcglobal.net.

BILLINGS, CHARLES EDGAR, physician; b. Boston, June 15, 1929; s. Charles Edgar and Elizabeth (Sanborn) B.; m. Lillian Elizabeth Wilson, Apr. 16, 1955; 1 dau., Lee Ellen Billings Kreinbihl. Student, Wesleyan U., 1947-49; MD, N.Y. U., 1953; M.Sc. (Link Found. fellow), Ohio State U., 1960. Diplomate: Am. Bd. Preventive Medicine. Instr. to prof. depts. preventive medicine and aviation Sch. Medicine Ohio State U., 1960-73, dir. div. environ. health Sch. Medicine, 1970-73, clin. prof. Sch. Medicine, 1973-83, prof. emeritus, 1983—; rsch. scientist indsl. and systems engring., 1992—. Med. officer NASA Ames Rsch. Ctr., Moffett Field, Calif., 1973-76; chief Aviation Safety Rsch. Office, 1976-80, asst. chief for rsch. Man-Vehicle Systems rsch. divsn., 1980-83, sr. scientist, 1983-91; chief scientist Ames Rsch. Ctr., 1991-92; cons. Beckett Aviation Corp., 1962-73; surgeon gen. U.S. Army, 1965-77, FAA, 1967-70, 75, 83; mem. NATO-AGARD Aerospace Med. Panel, 1980-86; assoc. advisor USAF Sci. Adv. Bd., 1978-90; mem. human factors adv. panel U.K. Civil Aviation Authority, 1999-2001; mem. aviation adv. bd. Ohio U., 2000-01. Contbr. chpts. to books, numerous articles in field to med. jours. Served to maj. USAF, 1955-57. Recipient Air Traffic Svc. award FAA, 1969, Walter M. Boothby rsch. award, 1972, PATCO Air Safety award, 1979, Disting. Svc. award Flight Safety Found., 1979, John A. Tamisea award, 1980, Laura Taber Barbour Air Safety medal, 1981, Outstanding Leadership medal NASA, 1981, 90, Jeffries Aerospace Med. Rsch. medal AIAA, 1986, Lovelace award NASA Soc. Flight Surgeons, 1996, Forrest and Pamela Bird award Civil Aviation Med. Assn., 2001, Henry L. Taylor Founders award Aerospace Human Factors Assn, 2002; Ames Rsch. Ctr. fellow, 1989. Fellow AIAA (assoc.), Royal Aero. Soc., Aerospace Med. Assn. (pres. 1979-80); mem. AMA, Internat. Acad. Aviation and Space Medicine. Office: 210 Baker ISE Bldg 1971 Neil Ave Columbus OH 43210-1210 Home: 1897 Fontenay Ct Columbus OH 43235-7317 Personal E-mail: chasbill@ix.netcom.com.

BILLINGS, FRANKLIN SWIFT, JR., federal judge; b. Woodstock, Vt., June 5, 1922; s. Franklin S. and Gertrude (Curtis) B.; m. Pauline Gillingham, Oct. 13, 1951; children: Franklin, III, Jireh Swift, Elizabeth, Ann. S.B., Harvard U., 1943; postgrad., Yale U. Law Sch., 1945; JD, U. Va., 1947; DL (hon.), Vt. Law Sch., 1997. Bar: Vt. 1948, U.S. Supreme Ct., 1958. With dept. electronics Gen. Electric Co., Schenectady, NY, 1943; bldg. dept. Vt. Marble Co., Proctor, 1945-46; pvt. practice law Woodstock, 1948-52; mem. firm Billings & Sherburne, Woodstock, 1952-66; asst. sec. Vt. Senate, 1949-55, sec., 1957-59; sec. civil and mil. affairs State of Vt., 1959-61; exec. clk. to gov., 1955-57; judge Hartford Mcpl. Ct., 1955-63; mem. Vt. Ho. of Reps., 1961-66, chmn. jud. com., 1961, speaker of ho., 1963-66; judge Vt. Superior Ct., 1966-75, assoc. justice, 1975-83, chief justice, 1983-84; judge U.S. Dist. Ct. Vt., 1984-94, chief judge, 1988-92, sr. ct. judge, 1994—. Active, Town of Woodstock, 1948—. Served as warrant officer 1st class attached Brit. Army, 1944-45. Decorated Purple Heart; Brit. Empire medal. Mem. Vt. Bar Assn., Delta Theta Phi. Office: US Dist Ct PO Box 598 Woodstock VT 05091-0598

BILLINGS, HAROLD WAYNE, retired library director, editor, writer; b. Cain City, Tex., Nov. 12, 1931; s. Harold Ross and Katie Mae (Price) B.; m. Bernice Schneider, Sept. 10, 1954; children: Brenda, Geoffrey, Carol. BA, Pan Am. Coll., 1953; MLS, U. Tex., 1957. Tchr. Pharr-San Juan-Alamo (Tex.) H.S., 1953-54; catalog libr. U. Tex., Austin, 1954-57, asst. chief catalog libr., 1957-65, chief acquisitions libr., 1965-67, asst. univ. libr., 1967-72, assoc. dir. gen. librs., 1972-77, acting dir. gen. librs., 1977-78, dir. gen. librs., 1978—2003. Sec. Tex. Bd. Libr. Examiners; mem. adv. com. Tex. Higher Edn. Coordinating Bd. Libr. Formula, 1987-92, acad. support formula adv. com., 1993-94; mem. steering com. Tex-Share Project, 1993-94; trustee Amigos Bibliographic Coun., 1980-83; chmn. Coun. Acad. Rsch. Librs., 1979-81; chmn. rsch. librs. adv. com. Online Computer Libr. Ctr. (OCLC), 1980-82, 87-88, mem. OCLC Users Coun.; bd. dirs. Ctr. Rsch. Librs., Chgo., 1989-96, Assn. Rsch. Librs., 1989-92; mem. Tex. Coun. State Univ. Librs., Assn. Rsch. Librs. Preservation Com., Collection Devel. Com., Coun. on Libr. Resources Preservation and Access Com., Coun. on Libr. Resources/Assn. Am. Pubs. Joint Working Group on Electronic Info., 1993-94; mem. adv. bd. Project Muse-Johns Hopkins U. Press, Balt., 1995-98; mem. N.Am. adv. bd. Lit. Online, 1997—; assoc. Tex. Telecomm. Policy Inst., 1996-2003; mem. coun. on libr. and info. studies area studies materials task force ACLS, 1998-99; mem. adv. coun. for Stanford U. Librs., 1998-2003; mem. steering com. Digital Libr. Fedn., 1999-2003; vis. coms. U. Tenn., U. Wyo.; project dir. numerous fed. grants. Author: Education of Librarians in Texas, 1956, Edward Dahlberg: American Ishmael of Letters, 1968, A Bibliography of Edward Dahlberg, 1972, The Leafless American, 2d edit., 1986, Magic and Hypersystems: Constructing the Information-Sharing Library, 2002, Texas Beast Fables, 2006, M.P. Shiel: A Biography of His Early Years, 2005; editor books in field; contbr. The Texas Book, 2007, to profl. jours.; mem. editl. bd. Libr. Chronicle, 1970-97. Sec., trustee Littlefield Fund for So. History, 1977-2003. Recipient Morley-Montgomery Meml. award, Baker St. Irregulars, 2006. Mem. ALA (Hugh C. Atkinson Meml. award 2002), Tex. Libr. Assn., Assn. Coll. Rsch. Librs. (chmn. tech. svcs. group, 1979-80). Democrat. Protestant. Avocations: book collecting, pottery, literature. Office: U Tex Librs PO Box P Austin TX 78713-8916 Office Phone: 512-442-8597. Personal E-mail: hbillings@mac.com. Business E-Mail: billings@mail.utexas.edu.

BILLINGS, JOSHUA, literature scholar; b. Cambridge, Mass. BA in German and Classics, Harvard Univ., 2007, MA in Comparative Lit., 2007; master's student in European Lit., Oxford Univ., 2007—. Editor: (pub.) Harvard Book Rev. Rhodes Scholar. Achievements include being a HS debate coach and tutor, and curriculum developer for an after-sch. enrichment prog; and studying in Berlin, Vienna, and St. Petersburg. Home: 115 Hilliard St Cambridge MA 02138*

BILLINGS, RICK, chef; Grad. from Advanced Placement Prog., New England Culinary Inst., Montpelier, Vt. Internship L'Espalier, Boston; chef Metropolitan, Utah; pastry chef No. 9 Park, Boston, Clio, Boston. Named one of Boston's Rising Stars, StarChefs.com, 2006, 7 Best New Chefs, Boston Mag., 2006. Office: Clio 370 Commonwealth Ave Boston MA 02215 Home Phone: 617-913-2288; Office Phone: 617-913-2288. Personal E-mail: rick_billings_2000@yahoo.com.

BILLINGS, THOMAS NEAL, computer and publishing executive, management consultant, entrepreneur, journalist, writer; b. Milw., Mar. 2, 1931; s. Neal and Gladys Victoria (Lockard) B.; m. Barta Hope Chipman, June 12, 1954 (div. 1967); children: Bridget Ann, Bruce Neal; m. Marie Louise Farrell, Mar. 27, 1982 (dec. Jan. 2003). AB with honors, Harvard U., 1952, MBA, 1954. V.p. fin. and adminstrn. and technol. innovation Copley Newspapers Inc., LaJolla, Calif., 1957-70; group v.p., dir. tech. Harte-Hanks Comm. Inc., San Antonio, 1970-73; exec. v.p. United Media Inc., Phoenix, 1973-75; asst. to pres., dir. corp. mgmt. systems Ramada Inns, Inc., Phoenix, 1975-76; exec. dir. NRA, Washington, 1976-77; pres. Strategic Ideation Inc., NYC, 1977—; chmn. Bergen-Billings Inc., NYC, 1977-80; pres. The Assn. Svc. Corp., San Francisco, 1978—, Recorder Printing and Pub. Co. Inc., San Francisco, 1980-82; v.p. adminstrn. Victor Techs. Inc., Scotts Valley, Calif., 1982-84; mng. dir. Saga-Wilcox Computers Ltd., Wrexham, Wales, 1984-85; chmn. Thomas Billings & Assocs., Inc., Reno, 1978—, Intercontinental Travel Svc. Inc., Reno, 1983-88, Oberon Optical Character Recognition Ltd., Hemel-Hemstead, Eng., 1985-86. Bd. dirs. 5M Corp., San Francisco, Intercontinental Rsch. Coun., London, Corp. Comm. Coun., Alameda, Digital Broadcasting Corp., Mountain View, Calif., Lenny's Restaurants, Inc., Wichita, Kans., Tymyndr Corp., Dover, Del., Zzyzzyx Corp., Reno, Harrod's Hotel & Casino Corp., Las Vegas, Pandemonium Pictures, Inc., San Moteo, Calif., Bonanza Enterprises, Inc., Virginia City, Nev., Quillmill Ltd., London, Better Betting Systems, Inc., Alameda, Calif., Video Stream, Inc., Cupertino, Calif., ResuMaster Corp., Walnut Creek, Calif., ProcessMaster Corp., Pleasanton, Calif., Enterprise House, Alameda, Chut! Cheri's Chic Chit Choppe, S.A., Laguna Beach, Calif., Waters Equipment Co., Inc., San Francisco, Goldstein Miller and Assocs. Inc., San Bruno, Calif., Silicon World Search Group, Inc., Alameda, Calif., Knicker's Ltd., Reno; dir., CEO Insignia Software Solution Group, High Wycombe, Eng., Cupertino, Calif., 1986-89; chmn. Intercontinental News Svc. Inc., London and Alameda, Calif., 1989—; v.p. Cromer Equipment Co., Oakland, Calif., 1991-94; chmn. Newton Group of Cos., Las Vegas, 1993—, Info. Integrity Internat., Inc., Las Vegas, London, 1994—, WordMaster Corp., Reno, 1995—, GolfDoctor!Inc., Las Vegas, 1998—, First Impact Inc., Alameda, Calif., 2000—, Alameda Industries Inc., 2006—; CEO Assurant Software, Inc., Palo Alto, Calif., 2002—; editor, pub., CEO The-View-Less-Seen.com, Alameda, Calif., 2001—; adj. prof. U. Phoenix, San Jose, Calif., 1999—, Coll. San Mateo, Calif., 2000—, Monterey (Calif.) Inst. Internat. Studies, 2001—, Deep Springs Calif. Coll., 2002—; spkr. and seminar leader; co-inventor StrokSavr Software, 1994. Author: Creative Controllership, 1978, Our Credibility Crisis, 1983, Non-Euclidean Theology, 1987, Ruminations on Meta Mentality, 1990, Fixing our Broken System, 1992, Our Dissembling Society, 1997, Our Co-Dependent World, 1998, A Christmas Carol-The Musical!, 1999, All Roads Lead to Ausfardt, 2000, The View Less Seen, 2002; (series) The Ethnic Epicure, 1995—, The View Less Seen, 2000—; editor: The Vice President's Letter, 1978-92; pub. The Microcomputer Letter, 1982-94, Synthetic Hardware Update, 1987-93, Windows on Tomorrow Magazine, 1994-99; editor: Intercontinental News Svc. London and Alamedia, Calif., 1985—; theatre critic, editl. columnist The Alameda Jour., 1998—. Bd. dirs. Nat. Allergy Found., 1973—, The Wilderness Fund, 1978—, San Diego Civic Light Opera Assn., 1965-69; chief exec. San Diego 200th Anniversary Expn., 1969; founder, exec. dir. Am. Majority Party, 1993—, The Millenium Three Found., 1996—, The Remembrance Soc., 1996—, People Finders' Inc., 1996—, Corp. Comm. Counsel Inc., 1996—, Alameda County Theatre Alliance, 1998—, Alameda Repretory Theatre, 1999—; founder, exec. dir. Heathen Haven, 2005—; sr. assoc. Rand Global, Inc., San Francisco, 2006—; voice talent Voice Wizardry, Alameda, Calif., 1999-; bass cantor and lector St. Joseph Basilica, Alameda, Calif., 1994-; soloist with Kol Truah, Temple Israel, Almeda, 2004-; sr. assoc. Rand Global Inc., San Francisco, 2006-. With U.S. Army, 1955-57. Recipient Walter F. Carley Meml. award, 1966, 69. Fellow U.K. Inst. Dirs.; mem. Am. Newspaper Pubs. Assn., Inst. Execs. Inc. (dir.), Inst. Newspaper Fin. Officers, West Side Tennis Club, LaJolla Country Club, Washington Athletic Club, San Francisco Press Club, Am. Contract Bridge League, Harvard Club (N.Y.C.), Elks, ACBL, Sigma Delta Chi. Office: PO Drawer I Alameda CA 94501-0262 Home Phone: 510-814-9000; Office Phone: 510-769-2000. E-mail: himself@tnbillings.com.

BILLINGSLEY, ROBERT THAINE, lawyer; b. Wichita, Jan. 9, 1954; s. Thaine Edward and Anita (Moore) B.; m. Anna Barron, Dec. 31, 1983; children: Carol Carothers, Leslie Hope. AB, Coll. William and Mary, 1976; JD, U. Richmond, 1980. Bar: Va. 1980. Law clk. to presiding justice U.S. Dist. Ct., Roanoke, Va., 1980—81; assoc. McGuire, Woods & Battle, Richmond, Va., 1981—87, Hirschler, Fleischer, Weinberg, Cox & Allen, Richmond, 1987—96; fin. advisr Kramnick & Assocs., Fredericksburg, Va., 1996—2001; rep. Northwestern Mut. Fin. Network, Fredericksburg, 2001—. Bd. dirs. Make A Wish Found., Ctrl. and Western Va. Bd. editors The Virginia Lawyer, 1984-86; mem. adv. bd. U. Richmond Law Rev., 1986-97; contbr. articles to profl. publs. Bd. dirs. Bethlehem Ctr., Richmond, 1985-89, United Meth. Found. of Va. Conf., Inc., sec., 2000-02; bd. dirs. Hanover Indsl. Air Pk. Bus. Assn., 1994-96; mem. adminstrv. bd. Trinity United Meth. Ch., Richmond, 1986-89, trustee, 1988-96, chmn. bd. trustees, 1992-95, chmn. commitment campaign, 1995; team capt. United Way Greater Richmond, 1989, sect. chmn., 1991, divsn. chmn., 1993; team capt. Rappahannock Area United Way, 1998, divsn. chair, 1999; mem. Leadership Metro Richmond Class, 1992-93; bd. dirs. Arts Coun. of Richmond, Inc., 1994-96, exec. com., 1996; chmn. fin. com. Fredericksburg United Meth. Ch., 1999-2001; co-chair Capital Funds Campaign, 2005; bd. dirs. College Heights Swimming Pool Assn Mem.: ABA (litig. sect., state membership chmn., young lawyers divsn. 1985—89, state membership chmn. 1989—96), Fredericksburg Bar Assn., Richmond Bar Assn. (program com., vice chmn. 1990—91, chmn. 1991—92, adminstrn. of justice com. 1992—96), Va. State Bar Assn. (bd. govs. young lawyers conf. 1985—89, spl. com. on professionalism, legal edn., admission to bar), Va. Bar Assn. (com. on alternative dispute resolution), William and Mary Alumni Assn. (bd. dirs. Richmond chpt. 1993—95), Rotary (Rappahannock chpt. bd. dirs., pres. 2003—05), Richmond Jaycees (bd. dirs. 1984—86). Avocations: sports, travel, theater. Office: Northwestern Mutual

Fin Network 725 Jackson St Ste 211 Fredericksburg VA 22401 Home: 661 Lancaster St Fredericksburg VA 22405 Office Phone: 540-370-1886. Business E-Mail: robert.billingsley@nmfn.com.

BILLINGTON, BARRY E., lawyer; b. Bruceton, Tenn., June 24, 1940; s. Charles Raymond and Edith Virginia (Bowles) Billington; m. Bonnie Leslie Johnson, Oct. 16, 1971 (div. Mar. 23, 1990); children: Erin Alexis, Barry E. Jr. AB in Econs., Davidson Coll., 1964; JD, Emory U., 1968. Bar: Calif. 1969, U.S. Dist. Ct. (ctrl. dist.) Calif. 1969, Ga. 1971, U.S. Dist. Ct. (no. dist.) Ga. 1971. Assoc. Surr & Hellyer, San Bernardino, Calif., 1968-70; with Mfrs. Life Ins. Co., Atlanta, 1970-71; assoc. Carter, Ansley, Smith & McClendon, Atlanta, 1971-72; of counsel Raiford & Hills, Decatur, Ga., 1972-75; ptnr. Raiford, Hills, Billington & McKeithen, Atlanta, 1975-77; mem. Rich, Bass, Kidd, Witcher & Billington, Decatur, 1977-82; ptnr. Billington & Beasley, Decatur, 1982-83, Billington & Turner, Atlanta, 1983-85; owner Barry E. Billington & Assocs., Atlanta, 1985—. Editor: Ga. Rep. Party Newsletter, 1968. Candidate 4th dist. U.S. Ho. Reps., 1980; publicity dir. San Bernardino County Reps., 1969—70; alt. del. Rep. Ctrl. Com. Calif., 1969—70; publicity dir. San Bernardino County Ronald Reagan Com., 1970; chmn. 4th dist. Conservative Caucus, 1977—79; candidate 52d dist. Ga. Ho. Reps., 1978. With Police Corps US Army, 1958—60. Mem.: ATLA, ABA (mem. litig. sect. 1969—89), Diplomat Nat. Coll. Advocacy Trial Advocacy Course, Nat. Assn. Criminal Def. Lawyers, Ga. Assn. Criminal Def. Lawyers, Ga. Trial Lawyers Assn., Decatur-DeKalb Bar Assn. (chmn. spkr.'s com. 1977—78), Atlanta Bar Assn. (mem. spkr.s com., litig., family law, criminal law sects. 1974—77). Home: 7208 Peachford Circle Atlanta GA 30338 Office: 3 Dunwoody Park Ste 103 Atlanta GA 30338-6709 Office Phone: 770-396-7286. Business E-Mail: barry@billingtonandassociates.com.

BILLINGTON, DAVID PERKINS, civil engineering educator; b. Bryn Mawr, Pa., June 1, 1927; s. Nelson and Jane Newkirk (Coolbaugh) B.; m. Phyllis Bergquist, Aug. 26, 1951; children: David Jr., Elizabeth Billington Fox, Jane Billington Flucker, Philip, Stephen, Sarah BS in Engring., Princeton U., 1950; postgrad. (Fulbright fellow), U. Louvain, Belgium, 1950-51, U. Ghent, 1951-52; DHL (hon.), Union Coll., 1990; DSc (hon.), Grinnell Coll., 1991; DEng (hon.), Notre Dame U., 1997. Registered profl. engr., N.J. Structural engr. Roberts & Schaefer Co., NYC, 1952-60; assoc. prof. civil engring. Princeton U., NJ, 1960-64, prof. civil engring., 1964—, Gordon Y.S. Wu prof. engring., 1996—. A.D. White prof.-at-large Cornell U., 1987-93; Robert Noyes vis. prof. Grinnell Coll., 2006; guest curator Princeton U. Art Mus., 2003; cons. in field. Author: Robert Maillart's Bridges, 1979 (Dexter award 1979), Thin Shell Concrete Structures, 1982, The Tower and the Bridge, 1983, Robert Maillart and the Art of Reinforced Concrete, 1990, The Innovators: The Engineering Pioneers Who Made America Modern, 1996, Robert Maillart: Builder, Designer, Artist, 1997, The Art of Structural Design: A Swiss Legacy, 2003, (with Donald C. Jackson) Big Dams of the New Deal Era: A Confluence of Engineering and Politics, 2006, (with David P. Billington Jr.) Power, Speed and Form: Engineers and the Making of the Twentieth Century, 2006. With USN, 1945-46. Recipient Dana award, Charles A. Dana Found., 1990, N.J. Prof. of Yr. award, Carnegie Found., 1995, Sarton medal, U. Ghent, Belgium, 1999, Sarton chair award, 1999—2000, Dir.'s award, NSF, 2003, John P. McGovern Lecture award in sci., Cosmos Club Found., 2004, Charles Zollman award, Pre-stressed & Pre-cast Concrete Inst., 2004; grantee NEH, 1969—89, NSF, 1963—83, NEA, 1977—79, NSF, 1991—94, 2001—06, Walter L. Robb Sr. Engring. Edn. fellow, Nat. Acad. Engring., 2005—06; vis. scholar, Phi Beta Kappa, 1984—85. Fellow Am. Acad. Arts and Scis., Am. Concrete Inst. (hon.); mem. NAE, ASCE (hon., 3 awards 1956-57, History and Heritage award 1986, George Winter award 1992), Internat. Assn. for Bridge and Structural Engring., Internat. Assn. Shell Structures (hon.), Soc. for History Tech. (Usher prize with J. Doig 1995). Republican. Episcopalian. Home: 45 Hodge Rd Princeton NJ 08540-3011 Office: Princeton U Dept Civil and Environ Enging Princeton NJ 08544-0001 Home Phone: 609-497-9069; Office Phone: 609-258-4606. Business E-Mail: billington@princeton.edu.

BILLINGTON, JAMES HADLEY, librarian, historian; b. Bryn Mawr, Pa., June 1, 1929; s. Nelson and Jane (Coolbaugh) B.; m. Marjorie Anne Brennan, June 22, 1957; children: Susan Billington Harper, Anne Billington Fischer, James Hadley, Jr., Thomas Keator. BA with highest honors, Princeton U., 1950; PhD, Oxford U., 1953, LittD (hon.), 2002, Lafayette Coll., 1981; DLitt (hon.), U. Pitts., 1988, Duke U., 1995, William & Mary, 2005; LHD (hon.), LeMoyne Coll., 1982, RI Coll., 1982, Cath. U. Am., 1983, NYU, 1987, Va. Theol. Sem., 1990, Williams Coll., 1991, Hood Coll., 1992, U. Scranton, 1992, U. Albany, 1993, Georgetown U., 1993, Bates Coll., 1993, Am. U., 1995, Mt. Holyoke Coll., 1995, U. San Diego, 1998, Lawrence U., 1999, Washington Coll., 1999, U. South, 1999, Quinnipiac U., 2000, Carthage Coll., 2002, St. Norbert Coll., 2003, Jewish Theol. Sem., 2005, St. Mary's Coll., 2005; HHD (hon.), Furman U., 1986, Ball State U., 1988, Russian State U. Humanities, 2001; D in Pub. Svc. (hon.), George Washington U., 1990; LLD (hon.), Dartmouth Coll., 1990, U. Notre Dame, 1995; D in Humane Scis. (hon.), U. Tblisi, Georgia, 1999; EdD (hon.), Montreat Coll., 2000; D (hon.), Russian State U. for Humanities, Moscow, 2001; MBA (hon.), Jones Internat. U., 2005. Instr. history Harvard U., Cambridge, Mass., 1957-58, fellow Russian Rsch. Ctr., 1958-59, asst. prof. history, 1958-61; assoc. prof. history Princeton U., NJ, 1962-64, prof., 1964-73; dir. Woodrow Wilson Internat. Ctr. for Scholars, Washington, 1973-87; Libr. of Congress Washington, 1987—. Chmn. Bd. Fgn. Scholarships (Fulbright program), 1971-73, mem. 1973-76; vice-chmn. Atlantic Coun.'s Working Group on the Successor Generation, 1982-86; trustee St. Alban's Sch., 1979-82; dir. Am. Assn. for Advancement of Slavic Studies, 1968-71; spl. cons. to Chase Manhattan Bank on East-West Matters, 1971-73; vis. rsch. prof. to Inst. History of Acad. Scis. of USSR in Moscow, 1966-67, U. Helsinki, 1960-61, École des Hautes Études en Sciences Sociales, Paris, 1985, 88; vis. lectr. to various univs. in Europe and Asia; founder Woodrow Wilson Quarterly, 1976. Author: Mikhailovsky and Russian Populism, 1958, The Icon and the Axe: An Interpretive History of Russian Culture, 1966, (Serbian transl., 1988, Japanese transl., 2000, Russian transl., 2001), The Arts of Russia, 1970, Fire in the Minds of Men: Origins of the Revolutionary Faith, 1980, (Italian transl., 1986), Russia Transformed: Breakthrough to Hope, Moscow, August 1991, 1992, The Face of Russia, 1998 (Russian transl., 2001); writer, host: (3-part TV series) The Face of Russia, 1998; mem. adv. bd. Fgn. Affairs, 1974-92, Theology Today, 1974-84; script writer and host of Humanities Film Forum, 1973; contbr. chpts. to books, numerous articles to profl. jours. Trustee John F. Kennedy Ctr. for Performing Arts, Ctr. Theol. Inquiry, Nat. Bldg. Mus., Woodrow Wilson Internat. Ctr. for Scholars, Am. Folklife Ctr.; bd. regents Nat. Libr. Medicine. 1st lt. US Army, 1953—56. McCosh faculty fellow Princeton U., Guggenheim fellow, 1960-61; Rhodes scholar, 1950-53; Fulbright rsch. prof. U. Helsinki, 1960-61; decorated Chevalier, Order of Arts and Letters of France, 1985, Comdr., 1991; recipient Gwanghwa medal Republic of Korea, 1991, Woodrow Wilson award Princeton U., 1992, Russian Orthodox medal, 1994, Knight Comdr.'s Cross of Order of Merit Fed. Republic of Germany, 1995, Vologda Universal Sci. Lib. award, 1999, Pushkin medal Internat. Assn. Teachers of Russian Language and Culture, 1999, UCLA medal, 2000. Mem. Am. Philos. Soc., Am. Acad. Arts and Scis., Russian Acad. Scis., Cosmos Club, Phi Beta Kappa. Office: The Library of Congress 101 Independence Ave SE Washington DC 20540-0002*

BILLION, JOHN JOSEPH, surgeon, retired state representative; b. Sioux Falls, SD, Mar. 4, 1939; s. Henry Alphonse and Evelyn Margaret (Heinz) B.; div.; children: Matthew, Suzanne, John, James, Jane; m. Deborah Wagner, Mar. 22, 1980; children: Timothy, Allyson. BA, Loras Coll., 1960; MD, Stritch-Loyola U., 1964. Diplomate Am. Bd. Orthopedic Surgery. Resident orthopedics St. Francis Hosp., Peoria, Ill., 1964-69; orthopedic surgeon Sioux Falls, 1971-96; state rep. State of S.D., 1992-96. Vice-chair SD Dem. Party, 1997-98, Chair, 2006—; chair Minnehaha Dem. Party, 2005-06; Dem. candidate for Gov. of S.D., 2006. Maj. USAF, 1969-71. Fellow Am. Acad. Orthopedic Surgeons. Democrat.

BILLMAN, IRWIN EDWARD, publishing executive; s. Herman Frank and Ruth (Dutchen) B. BS in Econs, Wharton Sch., U. Pa., 1962. Asst. controller Whelan Drug Co., 1965-66; v.p., treas. Curtis Circulation Co., Phila., 1966-71; exec. v.p., COO Penthouse Internat. Ltd. & Gen. Media Internat. Ltd., 1971—81; pres., publisher Oui Mag., NYC, 1981-82; pres. Billman Media Group; ptnr. Mag. Communications Cons. Pres. Global Distribution Svcs., Inc. Mem. Periodical and Book Assn. Am. (pres. 1977-81, bd. dirs. 2004—), Am. Circulation Execs. Soc. (pres. 1998-2000), Assn. Circulation Execs. (UK), Distripress Coun. Home: PO Box 350 Westhampton NY 11977-0350 Office: PO Box 850 Remsenburg NY 11960-0850

BILLS, JENNIFER LEAH, lawyer; b. Wichita, Kans., Feb. 10, 1969; BA, Haverford Coll., 1991; JD, Northeastern U. Sch. Law, 2001. Bar: Mass. 2002, US Ct. Appeals (1st Cir.) 2002, US Dist. Ct. (Dist. Mass.) 2002, NY 2003. Law clk. to Hon. Gene Carter US Dist. Ct. (Dist. Maine), 2001—02; atty. Law Offices of Howard Friedman PC, Boston. Mem.: Nat. Lawyers Guild, Assn. Trial Lawyers Am., Mass. Gay and Lesbian Bar Assn., Women's Bar Assn. Office: Law Offices of Howard Friedman PC 5th Floor 90 Canal St Boston MA 02114 Office Phone: 617-742-4100. Office Fax: 617-742-5858.

BILLS, PEGGY NANNETTE, parochial school educator; b. Mt. Calm, Tex., May 9, 1932; d. Dudley Whiteside Castellaw and Willie Mae Kelley; children: Sherry Denise, Randy Dean, Vicki Darcel, Sarah Diane. BA, Baylor U., Waco, Tex., 1968, M in Sci. Edn., 1978, postgrad., 1980—81, Tarleton State U., Stephenville, Tex., 1979. Cert. tchr., sch. prin., tchr. ESL Tex. Edn. Agy. Classroom tchr. Waco Ind. Sch. Dist., 1968—77, elem. sch. prin., 1977—90, ombudsman, 1990—93; rsch. libr. Waco-McLennan County Libr., 1973—79; classroom tchr. St. Mary's Cath. Sch., West, Tex., 1993—. Mentor prin. Waco Ind. Sch. Dist., Baylor U., 1980; curriculum developer Waco Ind. Sch. Dist., 1970—2000, tchr. in-svc. dir., 1980—. Recipient Golden Apple award, 2006. Mem.: Mensa, Delta Kappa Gamma. Methodist. Avocations: interior decorating, gardening, reading, writing, environmental concerns. Home: 207 N 6th W Hubbard TX 76648 Office: St Mary's Cath Sch 207 Spruce St West TX 76691

BILLS, ROBERT HOWARD, political party executive; b. North Conway, NH, Jan. 13, 1944; s. Howard William and Mary Catherine (Jackson) B.; m. Donna Gail Florian; children: Emily Ida, Katherine Mary. Staff writer Weekly People Newspaper, Bklyn., 1970-74, Palo Alto, Calif., 1974-76; nat. sec. Socialist Labor Party, Sunnyvale, 1980—, mem. nat. exec. subcom., 1976-79. Office: Socialist Labor Party of Am PO Box 218 Mountain View CA 94042-0218 Home Phone: 650-969-4838. Business E-Mail: socialists@slp.org.

BILLUPS, CHAUNCEY, professional basketball player; b. Sept. 25, 1976; m. Piper Riley; 2 children. Student, U. Colo., 1997. Guard Boston Celtics, 1996-97, Toronto Raptors, 1997-98, Denver Nuggets, 1998-00, Minn. Timberwolves, Mpls., 2000—02, Detroit Pistons, 2002—07. Named NBA Finals MVP, 2004; named to Ea. Conf. All-Star Team, NBA, 2007. Achievements include being a member of NBA Championship Team, 2004. Avocation: music. Office: c/o Detroit PIstons Palace of Auburn Hills 2 Championship Dr Auburn Hills MI 48326*

BILSKY, MARK HARVEY, neurosurgeon; b. Atlantic City, June 13, 1962; BS in Biology with highest Distinction, U. Mich., Ann Arbor, 1983; MD magna cum laude, Emory U., Atlanta, 1988. Lic. physician N.Y., 1990, diplomate Am. Bd. Neurologic Surgeons. Intern in neurosurgery N.Y. Hosp./Cornell Med. Ctr., 1988—89, resident in neurosurgery, 1988—94, clin. assoc. in surgery, asst. neurosurgeon, 1988—93, sr. clin. assoc. in surgery, chief resident, 1993; rsch. fellow dept. neurology Meml. Sloan Kettering Cancer Ctr., 1991—92, mem., 2001—; acting chief neurosurgery svc. Meml. Hosp. for Cancer and Allied Diseases, NYC, 1995—96, clin. asst. surgeon, 1995—2001, asst. attending surgeon, 2001—04, assoc. attending surgeon, 2004—. Asst. prof. N.Y. Presbyn. Hosp., NYC, 2000—05, assoc. prof., 2005—; cons. Hosp. for Spl. Surgery, 2000—. Contbr. numerous articles, monographs to profl. jours., chapters to books. Recipient Lange Med. Pubs. award, 1985, Harrison's Prins. of Internal Medicine Book award, 1986, Sandoz Pharm. award, 1988; scholar, Barnstrom scholar, 1981, James B. Angel scholar, 1982. Mem.: AMA, Am. Assn. Neurol. Surgeons, Congress of Neurol. Surgeons, Am. Soc. Clin. Oncology, N.Y. State Neurosurg. Soc., N.Am. Skull Base Soc., N.Am. Spine Soc., Alpha Omega Alpha. Home: 404 E 76th St Apt 21A New York NY 10021 Office: Memorial Sloan Kettering Cancer Ctr Neurosurgery Svc 1275 York Ave New York NY 10021 Office Phone: 212-639-8526. Business E-Mail: bilskym@mskcc.org.

BILSTROM, JON WAYNE, lawyer; b. Chgo., Mar. 1946; m. Kathy Bilstrom. BS, U. Iowa, 1968, JD, 1974. Bar: Iowa 1974, Ill. 1974, Mo. 1991. Gen. counsel Exchange Nat. Bank, Chgo.; v.p., gen. counsel First Wis. Corp., Milw.; ptnr. Katten Muchin & Zavis, Chgo.; gen. counsel, sec. Merc. Bancorp Inc., St. Louis, 1990—99; pres., CEO The Bar Plan Mut. Ins. Co., St. Louis, 2001—02; exec. v.p. governance, regulatory rels., and legal affairs, sec. Comerica Inc., Detroit, 2003—. Served US Army. Office: Comerica Inc Comerica Tower at Detroit Ctr 500 Woodward Ave MC 3391 Detroit MI 48226*

BILTONEN, RODNEY LINCOLN, biochemistry and pharmacology educator; b. Ont., Can., Aug. 24, 1937; came to U.S., 1941; s. Frank Emil and Frances Cecilia (Castren) B.; m. Margaret Jane Kobel, Aug. 6, 1960; children— Michael Andrew, Eric Franklin AB, Harvard Coll., 1959; PhD, U. Minn., 1965. Asst. prof. Johns Hopkins U., Balt., 1966-72; assoc. prof. biochemistry and pharmacology U. Va., Charlottesville, 1972-77, prof., 1977—2003, prof. emeritus, 2003—, assoc. dean, 1979-81, assoc. provost, 1981-84. Vis. prof. Gulbenkian Inst., Portugal, 1970-71, U. Lund, Sweden, 1971, Cayetano, Lima, Peru, 1976, U. N.C., Chapel Hill, 1980, CNR, Genoa, Italy, 1993, The Technical U. Denmark, 1995; James Disting. prof. physics St. Francis Xavier U., Antigonish, N.S., 1984; cons. in field. Assoc. editor Biophys. Jour., 1991-95; mem. editl. bd. Chemistry and Physics of Lipids, 1995—; contbr. numerous articles to profl. jours. Recipient G.T. Walker award, Sigma Xi, 1965, Huffman Meml. award, Calorimetry Conf., 1989; fellow, NIH, 1965—66; grantee, NSF, 1968—99, NIH, 1970—. Fellow: Biophys. Soc. (councilor 1984—86); mem.: Am. Calorimetry Conf. (chmn. 1976—77). Office: Univ Va Dept Pharmacology 1300 Jefferson Park Ave Charlottesville VA 22908-0735 E-mail: rlb1t@virginia.edu.

BIN, JOO WON, physician; b. Seoul, Republic of Korea, July 17, 1937; arrived in US, 1963; s. Bong Sup and Jung Yae Bin; m. Angelita M. Bin, May 24, 1967; children: Steven, Joanne. BS, MD, Yonsei U., Seoul, 1962; PhD, Cath. U., 1974. Diplomate Am. Soc. Plastic Surgery, 1969. Home Phone: 305-275-2536; Office Phone: 305-378-0006. Personal E-mail: jwbin@hotmail.com.

BINDENAGEL, JAMES DALE, university executive; b. Huron, SD, June 30, 1949; s. Gordon Dean and Patricia Jean (Williams) B.; m. Jean Kathleen Lundfelt, Dec. 26, 1971; children: Annamarie, Carl Jakob. BA, U. Ill, 1971, MPA, 1977. Officer U.S. Embassy U.S. Dept. State, Seoul, Republic of Korea, 1975—77; U.S. consul U.S. Consulate, Bremen, Germany, 1977-79; econ. officer Office Ctrl. European Affairs U.S. Dept. State, Washington, 1980-83; polit. officer Am. Embassy, Bonn, Germany, 1983-86; acting dir. Can. affairs U.S. Dept. State, 1988-89; dep. chief mission Am. Embassy, Berlin, 1989-90; divsn. chief developing countries and trade orgns. U.S. Dept. State Econ. and Bus. Affairs Bur., 1991; dir. Rockwell Internat., 1991-92; dir. Office Ctrl. European Affairs U.S. Dept. State, Washington, 1992-94; dep. chief mission Am. Embassy, Bonn, Germany, 1994-96, chargé d'affaires, acting amb., 1996—97; sr. coord. New Transatlantic Agenda German Marshall Fund, 1997-98; dir. Washington Conf. on Holocaust-era Assets; amb. spl. envoy for Holocaust issues, 1999—2002; spl. negotiator Conflict Diamonds, 2002—03; v.p. Chgo. Coun. on Fgn. Rels., 2003—05, De Paul U., 2005—. Trustee Remembrance, Responsibility and Future Fund, 1999-02, Arthur F. Burns Fellowship, German-Am. C. of C. Midwest, Catholic Theol. Union, Am. Jewish Comm., Berlin, Am. Inst. Contemporary German Studies, Humanitarian Aid Found., Internat. Human Rights Law Inst., Internat. Aviation Law Inst., Grant Park Conservancy. Capt. USAR, 1971-74. Decorated comdrs. cross Order of Merit Germany; recipient V.P. Nat. Performance award, 1998, Disting. Honor award, U.S. State Dept., 2000, Presdl. Meritorious Svc. award, 2002. Mem.: Coun. Fgn. Rels., Am. Coun. on Germany, Am. Polit. Sci. Assn. (Congl. fellow 1987—88), Pi Sigma Alpha. Roman Catholic. Avocations: tennis, hiking. Home: 3740 N Lake Shore Dr Apt 4B Chicago IL 60613-4201 Office Phone: 312-362-8100. Personal E-mail: jbindenagel@earthlink.net. Business E-Mail: jbindena@depaul.edu.

BINDER, AMY FINN, public relations company executive; b. NYC, June 13, 1955; d. David and Laura (Zeisler) Finn; children: Ethan Max, Adam Finn, Rebecca Eve. BA with honors, Brown U., 1977; MBA, Columbia U. Freelance photographer, NYC, 1977-78; account exec. Newton & Nicolazza, Boston, 1978-79, Agnew, Carter, McCarthy, Boston, 1979-80; dir. pub. relations City of New Rochelle, N.Y., 1980-82; dir. urban communications Ruder-Finn, NYC, 1982-85, v.p., 1985-86, exec. v.p., 1986-87; pres. Ruder-Finn America, NYC, 1987; CEO, exec. mng. dir. RFBinder Partners, Inc. Ruder Finn Group, 2001—. Photographer: Museum without Walls, 1975, The Spirit of Man: Sculpture of Kaare Nygaard, 1975, Knife Life and Bronzes, 1977, St. Louis: Sculpture City, 1988, The Triumph of the American Spirit: Johnstown, Pennsylvania, 1989. Mem. Internat. Ctr. of Photography (mem. pres. coun.), Pres. Assn. of Am. Mgmt. Assn. Democrat. Jewish.

BINDER, DAVID FRANKLIN, lawyer, writer; b. Beaver Falls, Pa., Aug. 1, 1935; s. Walter Carl and Jessie Maivis (Bliss) Binder; m. Deana Jacqueline Pines, Dec. 25, 1971; children: April, Bret. BA, Geneva Coll., Beaver Falls, Pa., 1956; JD, Harvard U., Cambridge, Mass., 1959. Bar: Pa. 1960, US Ct. Appeals (3d cir.) 1963, US Supreme Ct. 1967. Law clk. to chief justice Pa. Supreme Ct., 1959—61; counsel Fidelity Mut. Life Ins. Co., Phila., 1964—66; ptnr. Bennett, Bricklin & Saltzburg, Phila., 1967—68; mem. Richter, Syken, Ross, and Binder, Phila., 1969—72, Raynes, McCarty, Binder, Ross and Mundy, Phila., 1972—2006, Gold, Silverman, Goldenberg & Binder, Phila., 2007—. Mem. faculty Pa. Coll. Judiciary; judge pro tempore Phila. Common Pleas Ct., 1991—97; lectr., course planner Pa. Bar Inst.; mem. civil procedural rules com., ad hoc com., mem permanent com. evidence Supreme Ct. Pa. Author: Hearsay Handbook, 1975, ann. supplements, 4th edit., 2001, Binder on Pennsylvania Evidence, 1999, 4th edit., 2005. Recipient Disting. Alumnus award, Geneva Coll., 1981. Mem.: ATLA (lectr.), ABA, Am. Coll. Trial Lawyers, Am. Bd. Trial Advs., Pa. Trial Lawyers Assn., Phila. Bar Assn., Pa. Bar Assn., Harvard Law Sch. Assn., Union League. Home: 331 Trillium Ln Wayne PA 19087 Office: The Meadows 485 Devon Pk Dr Ste 115 Wayne PA 19087 Office Phone: 215-563-6067. Business E-Mail: dave@gsgattorneys.com.

BINDER, ELAINE KOTELL, associations consultant; b. Boston, Oct. 12, 1938; d. Maxwell and Florence (Blumsack) Kotell; m. Richard A. Binder, Aug. 28, 1960; children: Mark Stephen, Jonathan Stuart. AB, Radcliffe Coll., 1960; MA, U. Md., 1975. Tchr. City of Medford, Mass., 1960-62; project dir. Wider Opportunities for Women, Washington, 1971-75, Women's Equity Action League Fund, Washington, 1976-78; mng. ptnr. Binder, Elster, Mendelson, Wheeler, Bethesda, Md., 1978-80; adminstrn. dir. AAUW, Washington, 1980-85; exec. dir. B'nai B'rith Women, Washington, 1985-94. Pres. Binder Assocs., Bethesda, 1994—; prin. ptnr. Tecker Consultants, Trenton, N.J., 1994—; cons. Bethesda, 1975-76. Co-author: Careers for Peers, 1973; contbr. articles to profl. jours. Trustee Temple Shalom, Silver Spring, Md., 1974-76; pres., v.p. Montgomery County Commn. for Women, Rockville, Md., 1978-80; commr. Anti-Defamation League, N.Y., 1985—; bd. dirs. Jewish Coun. for the Aging, 1996—. Fellow Am. Soc. Assn. Execs. (bd. dirs. 1990-93, vice chmn. 1994), Greater Washington Soc. Assn. Execs. (com. chair 1989—). Democrat. Jewish. Avocations: music, art, collecting native american art and artifacts, reading. Office: Tecker Consultants 427 River View Exec Park Trenton NJ 08611 also: Binder Assocs 6704 Bradley Blvd Bethesda MD 20817-3045

BINDER, GORDON M., venture capitalist; b. St. Louis, 1935; m. Adele Binder, 1964. BS in elec. engring., Purdue U., 1957; MBA, Harvard U., 1962. Asst. to v.p. Litton Industries, 1962-64; fin. mgmt. Ford Motor Co., 1964-69; CFO Sys. Devel. Corp., 1971-81; v.p., CFO Amgen, Thousand Oaks, Calif., 1982-88, CEO, 1988-2000, chmn. bd., 1990-2000; mng. dir. Coastview Capital LLC, LA, 2001—. Former chmn. Pharm. Rsch. and Mfrs. of Am. (PhRMA), Biotechnology Industry Assn. (BIO), MIT. Am. Cancer Soc. Found. Baker scholar Harvard U. Office: Coastview Capital LLC Ste 1850 11111 Santa Monica Blvd Los Angeles CA 90025

BINDER, JEFFREY R., medical products executive; BA, Yale Univ.; MPP, Woodrow Wilson Sch., Princeton Univ. Cons. Boston Consulting Group; sr. mgmt. positions Howmedica Orthopedics; pres. DePuy Orthopedics, 1998—2000; pres., CEO Spinal Concepts, 2000—03; pres. Spinal Concepts unit Abbott Laboratories, 2003—05, v.p., 2004—05, v.p., pres. Abbott Spine, 2005—06, sr. v.p. diagnostic ops., 2006—07; pres., CEO Biomet Inc., Warsaw, Ind., 2007—. Office: Biomet Inc 56 E Bell Dr Warsaw IN 46582 Mailing: Biomet Inc PO Box 587 Warsaw IN 46581-0587*

BINDER, L. JAMES, retired magazine editor, journalist; b. Jackson, Mich., June 21, 1926; s. Leonard George and Ethel Cecile (Lilly) B.; m. Margery Elizabeth Rose, Sept. 6, 1950; children: Timothy James, Michael Paul, Douglas Harold. BS, Central Mich. U., 1952. Editor Wingfoot Clan, Goodyear Tire & Rubber Co., 1952-54, Wayne (Mich.) Eagle, 1954-55; news editor Pontiac (Mich.) Press, 1955-57; editor, newsman AP, 1957-60; state editor Detroit News, 1960-67; editor-in-chief Army mag., Washington, 1967-93; corr., book reviewer Nat. Observer, 1962-67; v.p publs. Assn. U.S. Army, 1992-94; ret., 1993. Author: Lemnitzer: A Soldier for His Time, 1997; editor: Front and Ctr., 1991; contbr. articles to various publs. Served with USN, 1944-46; with USAR, 1950-54. Recipient George Washington Honor medal Freedoms Found., 1975, George Washington award editorial, 1974, 76 Mem. VFW, Am. Soc. Mag. Editors, Soc. Profl. Journalists, Cosmos Club, Nat. Press Club, Detroit Press Club, Ends of Earth Club, Soc. of Midland Authors, Am. Legion, Tin Can Sailors. Methodist. Home: 12728 Inverness Way Woodbridge VA 22192-5036 Personal E-mail: ptsable@aol.com.

BINDER, PHILIPPE-MICHEL, physicist, educator; b. Medellin, Colombia, Mar. 28, 1961; arrived in U.S., 1977; s. Paul Binder and Claire de Bourmont; m. Penelope Rodriguez, Dec. 7, 2000; 1 stepchild, Shalila Baena. BS with high distinction, U. Va., Charlottesville, 1982; MA, St.

John's Coll., 1988; PhD, Yale U., 1989. Jr. fellow Wolfson Coll. U. Oxford, 1990—93; cons. Los Alamos (N.Mex.) Nat. Lab., 1994; assoc. prof. U. de Los Andes, Bogota, Colombia, 1995—2001; asst. prof. U. Hawaii, Hilo, 2001—04, assoc. prof., 2004—. Project reviewer NSF, Washington, 2002; peer reviewer Colombian U. Accreditation Bd., Bogota, 2000. Mem. editl. bd.: Complexity, 1995—96; contbr. papers to profl. jours. Grantee, Colombian Sci. Found., 1996—98, 2000—02, Rsch. Corp., Tucson, Ariz., 2003—; scholar, Kavli Inst. Theoretical Physics, U. Calif., 2006—. Achievements include research in kinetic theory; polymer phase transitions and theory of chaos and complex systems. Office: U Hawaii Natural Scis Divsn Hilo HI 96720-4091 Home Phone: 808-935-1237. E-mail: pbinder@hawaii.edu.

BINDLEY, WILLIAM EDWARD, pharmaceutical executive; b. Terre Haute, Ind., Oct. 6, 1940; s. William F. and Gertrude (Lynch) B.; children: William Franklin, Blair Scott, Sally Ann. BS, Purdue U., 1961; grad. wholesale mgmt. program, Stanford U., 1966. Asst. treas. Controls Co. Am., Melrose Park, Ill., 1962-65; vice-chmn. E.H. Bindley & Co., Terre Haute, 1965-68; pres., chmn. bd., CEO Bindley Western Industries, Inc., Indpls., 1968—2001; CEO Priority Healthcare, Lake Mary, Fla., 1994—97, pres., 1996, now chmn. Scholl scholarship guest lectr. Loyola U., Chgo., 1982; guest lectr. Young Pres. Orgn., Palm Springs, Calif. and Dallas, 1981, 82, 84, Ctr. for Entrepreneurs, Indpls., 1983, Purdue U., West Lafayette, Inc., De Pauw U., Greencastle, Ind., disting. lectr. Georgetown U., Washington, 1989—, mem. adv. bd.; bd. dirs. Key Bank NA, Cleve., Shoe Carnival, Inc.; former owner basketball team Ind. Pacers. State dir. Bus. for Reagan-Bush, Washington and Indpls., 1980; trustee Marian Coll., Indpls., Indpls. United Way, St. Vincent Hosp., Indpls.; bd. dirs. Indpls. Entrepreneurship Acad., Nat. Enterpreneurship Found., U.S. Ski Team, chmn. fin., exec. com. mem.; mem. adv. bd. Rose Hulman Inst. Tech.; mem. pres.'s coun. Purdue U., dean's adv. bd. Named Hon. Ky. Col., 1980, Sagamore of the Wabash, Gov. Orr, State of Ind., 1989, Entrepreneur of Yr., State of Ind., 1992. Mem. Young Pres. Orgn. (area dir., chmn. 1982, award 1983), Nat. Wholesale Druggists Assn. (dir. 1981-84, Svc. award 1984), Purdue U. Alumni Assn. (life), Woodstock Club, Meridian Hills Countryn Club. Republican. Roman Catholic. Avocations: skiing, golf, tennis, boating. Office: Priority Healthcare 250 Technology Pk Lake Mary FL 32746

BINEGAR, BIRNE, mathematics professor; b. Seattle, Mar. 6, 1954; m. Yumi Binegar, 1990; children: Cosmo, Skye. Student, Temple Univ.; PhD in physics, UCLA, 1982. Joined math dept. Okla. State Univ., Stillwater, 1988, now assoc. prof. math. Achievements include being one of 18 top mathematicians and computer scientists (Atlas of Lie Groups Project) from the US to successfully map E8, one of the largest and most complicated structures in mathematics. Avocation: guitar. Office: 430 Math Sci Bldg Okla State Univ Stillwater OK 74078 Office Phone: 405-744-5793. Business E-Mail: binegar@math.okstate.edu.

BINES, HARVEY ERNEST, lawyer, educator, writer; b. Winthrop, Mass., Nov. 25, 1941; s. Carl and Lillian (Cooper) B.; m. Joan Carol Paller, Dec. 27, 1964; children: Jonathan W., Joel T., Susanne R., Benjamin E. BS, MIT, 1963; JD, U. Va., 1970. Bar: Mass 1971, Va. 1971, U.S. Dist. Ct. Mass., U.S. Dist. Ct. (ea. dist.) Va., U.S. Ct. Appeals (1st, 3d, 4th, 7th and D.C. cirs.), U.S. Supreme Ct. Law clk. to hon. John D. Butzner Jr. U.S. Ct. Appeals (4th cir.), Richmond, Va., 1970-71; asst. prof. Law Sch. U. Va., Charlottesville, 1971-74, assoc. prof. Law Sch., 1974-76; assoc. Sullivan & Worcester, Boston, 1976-79, ptnr., 1980—. Adj. prof. Boston Coll. Law Sch., Chestnut Hill, Mass., 1981-88, bd. dirs., treas., sec. Schweitzer Fellowship, Boston. Author: Investment Management Law and Regulation, 1978, 2d edit., 2004, supplement, 2007. Lt. USNR, 1963-67. Mem.: Va. Bar Assn., Boston Bar Assn., Am. Law Inst. Home: 36 Clarke St Lexington MA 02421-4916 Office: Sullivan & Worcester 1 Post Office Sq Ste 2300 Boston MA 02109-2129 Home Phone: 781-861-6218; Office Phone: 617-338-2828. Business E-Mail: hbines@sandw.com.

BINFORD, GREGORY GLENN, lawyer; b. Canton, Ohio, Oct. 8, 1948; s. Edwin and Helen Marie B. BA, Case Western Res. U., 1970, JD, 1973. Bar: Ohio 1973. Ptnr. Guren, Merritt, Cleve., 1973-84, Benesch, Friedlander, Cleve., 1984—. Councilman, Bratenahl, Ohio. Mem. ABA, Nat. Health Lawyers Assn., Cleve. Bar Assn. (former chair health law sect.). Office: BP America Bldg 200 Public Sq Ste 2300 Cleveland OH 44114-2378 Office Phone: 216-363-4617. Business E-Mail: gbinford@bfca.com.

BING, RICHARD MCPHAIL, lawyer; b. Lewes, Del., Aug. 23, 1950; s. Arden E. and Ellen Louise (Judd) B.; m. Valerie Lynn Wasson, Dec. 18, 1971; children: Jennifer Lynn, Kristin Tyler. BA, U. Richmond, 1972, JD, 1978. Bar: Va. 1979, U.S. Dist. Ct. (ea. and we. dists.) Va. 1979, U.S. Dist. Ct. (we. dist.) Pa. 1990, U.S. Dist. Ct. (no. dist.) N.Y. 1990, U.S. Dist. Ct. (ctrl. dist.) Ill. 1996, U.S. Ct. Appeals (4th cir.) 1979, U.S. Ct. appeals (2d cir.) 1990, U.S. Supreme Ct. 1994, U.S. Dist. Ct. (ctrl. dist.) Ill. 1996. Dir. ins. Bur. of Ins., Richmond, Va., 1978-79; resident gen counsel Va. Gasoline Retailers Assn., Richmond, 1979-83; ptnr. Pearce & Bing, Richmond, 1983-93, Bing & Assocs., P.C., Richmond, 1993—. Adj. prof. law J. Sargent Reynolds Community Coll., Richmond, 1984-85. Mem. Henrico County Rep. Com; bd. dirs. Three Chopt PTA, Richmond, 1984-85. Mem. ABA, Va. Bar Assn., Va. Bar, Richmond Bar Assn., Fed. bar Assn., Assn. Trial Lawyers Am., Va. Trial Lawyers Assn., Nat. Lawyers Club, Tuckahoe Jaycees (pres. 1981-82), Bull and Bear Club, Hermitage Country Club, Tobacco Co. Club, The Spider Club (bd. dirs.), Am. Assn. of Franchisees and Dealers, Svc. Sta. Dealers of Am., Inc., Affiliate Attys. Group. Avocations: golf, bicycling, photography. Home: 1701 Habwood Ln Richmond VA 23233-4451 Office: Bing & Assocs PC 7400 Beaufont Springs Dr Ste 300 Richmond VA 23225 Home Phone: 804-346-0069; Office Phone: 804-272-7900. Personal E-mail: rmcpbng@juno.com.

BING, STANLEY See SCHWARTZ, GIL

BING, STEVE, film producer; b. Mar. 31, 1965; s. Peter S. and Helen Bing; 1 child, Damien. Writer (films) Missing in Action, 1984, Missing in Action 2: The Beginning, 1985, Kangaroo Jack, 2003, (TV series) Married.With Children, 1987—97; prodr.: (films) Without Charlie, 2001, Night at the Golden Eagle, 2002, The Big Bounce, 2004; exec. prodr.: Get Carter, 2000; actor: The Dark Backward, 1991. Named one of 50 Most Powerful People in Hollywood, Premiere mag., 2005. Address: 1801 Avenue of the Stars #150 Los Angeles CA 90067

BING, XU, artist; b. Chongqing, China, 1955; arrived in US, 1990; Grad., Central Acad. of Fine Arts, Beijing, 1981, MFA, 1987. Instr. Central Acad. of Arts, Beijing, 1988; lectr. Sch. Design La. State U., Princeton U., McGill U., Montreal, Quebec, Canada. Former dir. Chinese Artists Assn.; honorary fellow U. Wisconsin, 1990; art residency Am. Acad., Berlin, 2003—04. Exhbns. include: Modern Chinese Prints, British Mus., London, 1986, Xu Bing: A Book from the Sky, Nat. Fine Arts Mus., Beijing, 1989, Looking for Tree of Life: A Journey to Asian Contemporary Art, Mus. Modern Art, Saitama, Japan, 1992, Maos Goes Pop: China Post-1989, Mus. Contemporary Art, Sydney, 1993, Transversions, 2nd Johannesburg Biennale, Johannesburg, South Africa, 1997, Beyond the Form: The Transformation and Symbolic of Chinese Character in Arts, NY Lincoln Ctr. Cork Gallery, NYC, 1998, Crossings, Nat. Gallery of Can., Ottawa, 1998, Banner Project, MOMA, NYC, 1999, Half A Century of Chinese Woodblock Prints, Mus. Art Ein Harod, Israel, 1999, 1st Fukuoka Asian Art Triennale, Fukuoka Asian Art Mus., Japan, 1999, Concerning Truth, Gallery 400, Sch. of Art Inst. Chgo., 1999, Tobacco Project, Duke U., NC, 2000, Word Play: Contemporary Art by Xu Bing, Arthur M. Sackler Gallery, Smithsonian Instn., Wash., DC, 2001, Where Does the Dust Collect Itself?, Wales, 2001 (Artes Mundi prize), Commons Gallery, U. Hawaii, Honolulu, 2002, Living Word 2, Herbert F. Johnson Mus. Art, Cornell U., Ithaca, NY, 2002, Biennale of Sydney, Mus. Contemporary Art, Australia, 2002, Asia Pacific Triennial, Queensland Art Gallery, Brisbane, Australia, 2002, ES 2002 Tijuana: Bienal Internacional de Estandartes, Centro Cultural Tijuana, Mexico, 2002, The First Guangzhou Triennial - Reinterpretation: A Decade of Exptl. Chinese Art 1990-2000, Guang Dong Mus. Art, China, 2002, 4th Shanghai Biennale, Shanghai Art Mus., China, 2002, Book from Sky, Princeton U. Art Mus., NJ, 2003, Fukuoka Asian Art Mus., Japan, 2003, Drawing the Line: Contemporary Artists Reassess Traditional East Asian Calligraphy, Pacific Asia Mus., Pasadena, Calif., 2003, Drawing the World: Masters to Hipsters, Vancouver Art Gallery, Can., 2003, Love and/or Terror: Contemporary Book Art, U. Ariz. Mus. Art, Tucson, 2003, First Beijing Internat. Art Biennale, China Nat. Mus. Fine Arts, Beijing, 2003, Happiness, Mori Art Mus., Tokyo, 2003, Chinese Printmaking Today, Brit. Libr., London, 2003, Artes Mundi Prize Exhbn., Nat. Gallery Mus. Wales, Cardiff, 2004. Named to Art in Am. Ann. Guide, 2004—05; recipient Youth Friends award, NYC Dept. Edn., Sch. Art League, 2005, Artes Mundi prize, 2004; Coca-Cola fellow, Am. Acad. Berlin, 2004. Mailing: Art Beatus Gallery 3rd Floor 138 Queen's Road Central Central Hong Kong Office Phone: 718-388-4228. Business E-Mail: xubing@xubing.com.

BINGAMAN, JEFF, JR., (JESSE FRANCIS BINGAMAN), senator; b. El Paso, Tex., Oct. 3, 1943; s. Jesse and Beth (Ball) B.; m. Anne Kovacovich, Sept. 13, 1968, 1 child BA in Govt., Harvard U., 1965; JD, Stanford U., 1968. Bar: N.Mex. 1968. Atty. Stephenson, Campbell & Olmsted, 1971-72; ptnr. Campbell, Bingaman & Black, Santa Fe, 1972-78; asst. atty. gen. State of N.Mex., 1969, atty. gen., 1979—82; US Senator from N.Mex., 1983—. Mem. com. energy and natural resources US Senate, com. fin., com. health, edn., labor and pensions, joint econ. com. Served with USAR, 1968—74. Recipient Disting. Svc. award, Am. Dietetic Assn., 1997, Public Servant Outstanding award excellence, 3Com Corp. and Consortium for Sch. Networking, 2000, Public Svc. award, Am. Chem. Soc., 2001, Congressional award, Small Bus. Coun. Am., 2001, Public Svc. award, Am. Assn. Public Health Dentistry, 2002, Capitol Dome award, Am. Cancer Soc., 2003, Outstanding Lifetime Achievement award, Friends of Nat. Inst. Dental and Craniofacial Rsch., 2003, Excellence in Public Svc. award, Am. Acad. Pediatrics, 2004, Joseph F. Boyle award disting. pub. svc., Am. Coll. Physicians, 2004, Disting. Cmty. Health Champion award, Nat. Assn. Cmty. Health Centers, 2005. Democrat. Meth. Office: US Senate 703 Hart Senate Bldg Washington DC 20510-0001 also: District OFfice Ste 101 119 East Marcy Santa Fe NM 87501 Office Phone: 202-224-5521, 505-988-6647. Office Fax: 202-224-2852.*

BINGER, ERIKA L., foundation administrator; BA, Pepperdine U.; MA in Orgnl. Leadership, Bethel Coll., Arden Hills. Athletic dir. Jack Cornelius Boys and Girls Club, Minneapolis, 1994—2000. Adv. bd. mem. Bolder Options; bd. mem. Minn. Coalition for Adolescent Females; mem. Minneapolis Junior League; bd. dirs. McKnight Found., 1994—, chair, bd. dirs., 2004—. Named Nat. Duathlon Champion, Nat. Triathlon Champion, 2-Time World Triathlon Champion, Athena category; recipient Heroes in the Making award, Minn. Lynx and Timberwolves. Office: McKnight Found 710 S Second St Ste 400 Minneapolis MN 55401 Business E-Mail: ebinger@mcknight.org.

BINGHAM, CHRISTOPHER, statistics educator; b. NYC, Apr. 16, 1937; s. Alfred Mitchell and Sylvia (Knox) B.; m. Carolyn Higinbotham, Sept. 23, 1967 AB, Yale U., 1958, MA, 1960, PhD, 1964. Research fellow Conn. Agrl. Expt. Sta., New Haven, 1958-64; research assoc. in math. and biology Princeton U., NJ, 1964-66; asst. prof. stats. U. Chgo., 1967-72; assoc. prof. applied stats. U. Minn., Mpls., 1972-79, prof., 1979—. Contbr. articles to profl. jours. Fellow Am. Statis. Assn., Inst. Math. Stats.; mem. Royal Statis. Soc., Biometric Soc., Soc. Indsl. and Applied Math Home: 605 Winston Ct Mendota Heights MN 55118-1039 Office: U Minn Sch Stats 313 Ford Hall 224 Church St SE Minneapolis MN 55455-0493 E-mail: kb@umn.edu.

BINGHAM, GEORGE WALTER CHANDLER, retired sales executive; b. Cambridge, Mass., Jan. 1, 1925; s. George Hutchins Bingham Jr. and Audrey Wellington (Wack) Bingham Suter; m. Carolyn Susan Webb, Nov. 25, 1967; 1 child, Susan Cordelia. Student, Dartmouth Coll., 1943—44, student, 1946—48; BA, Gettysburg Coll., 1950; postgrad., Columbia U., 1950—51. With CBS TV, NYC, 1951—55; account exec. Gill-Perna Sta. Reps., NYC, 1955—56, Walker Representation Co., NYC, 1956—57; v.p., mgr. New Eng. sales Walker-Rawalt, Inc., Boston, 1957—61; pres. New Eng. Spot Sales, Inc., Boston, 1961—95; mgr. New Eng. sales Stone Reps., 1960—70; mgr. New Eng. sales Jack Masla & Co., Boston, 1970—80, Weiss & Powell, Boston, 1983—86, Katz & Powell, Boston, 1987—95, New Eng. Spot Sales Inc., Belmont, Mass., 1995—2000; ret., 2000. Treas., co-owner So. Maine Broadcasting Corp., Sanford/York County, 1975-83, Essex Broadcasting Corp., Newburyport, Mass., 1977-83. Exec. com. Dartmouth Coll. Class of 1947; dir. Camp Allen, Bedford, NH, 1983—. With USNR, 1943-46. Mem. New Eng. Assn. Radio and TV Sta. Reps. (pres. 1963-64), Broadcasters Found., Mass. Soc. SAR, Mass. Soc. Mayflower Descs. (officer, dep. gov. 1976-87), Am. Legion (comdr. post 281 1974-76, 85-92), Boston's Advt. Post, Harvard Faculty Club, Boston Athenaeum, Kiwanis, Phi Alpha Theta, Kappa Kappa Kappa (hon.). Democrat. Episcopalian. Avocations: history, theater. Home: 208 Lewis Rd Belmont MA 02478-3833

BINGHAM, J. PETER, electronics research executive; married; 2 children. BS in Physics cum laude, Polytechnic Inst., NYC; MS in Exptl. Physics, U. Md., PhD in Elec. Engring. With RCA Consumer Electronics, David Sarnoff Rsch. Ctr.; exec. v.p., tech. Thomson Consumer Electronics; v.p. engring. Philips Consumer Electronics Co., 1982-91; with Philips Rsch. Philips Electronics N.Am. Corp., 1991; pres. Philips Rsch., 1991—. Bd. dirs. Indsl. Rsch. Inst. Recipient David Sarnoff award, RCA Lab. Achievements award; Named in his honor Bingham Peak in Antarctica, Arctic Inst. of North Am. Office: 23 Brookwood Dr Briarcliff Manor NY 10510-2040

BINGHAM, JINSIE SCOTT, broadcast company executive; b. Greencastle, Ind., Dec. 28, 1935; d. Roscoe Gibson and Alpha Edith (Robinson) Scott; m. Frank William Wokoun, Jr. (dec.); children: Douglas Scott, Richard Frank; m. Richard Innes Bingham, June 24, 1964. Student, DePauw U., Greencastle, 1952-53, Northwestern U., Evanston, Ill., 1953, Coe Coll., Cedar Rapids, Iowa, 1953-54. Exec. sec. Ind. Young Dems., 1958-60; receptionist Ind. Ho. of Reps., Indpls., 1959; saleslady Avon Products, Greencastle, 1961-64; sales mgr. Sta. WJNZ (formerly WXTA), Greencastle, 1969-77, owner, pres., gen. mgr., 1977-94; owner Radio Greencastle, 1977—. Owner, pres. gen. mgr. Sta WJNZ, 1977-94; past ptnr. Sta. WVTL, Monticello, Ill., Sta. KBIB, Monette, Ark.; speaker DePauw U. Comm. Seminar, 1981-85; vis. lectr., 1986—. Co-author: Putnam County Indiana Land Patents, 2004. Com. chair Legis. Awareness Seminar, 1978—86; co-chair Greencastle Gaelic Festival, 1983—84; charter mem. Greencastle 2001, 1985—, Greencastle Civic League, 1984—, Greencastle Merchant's Assn., 1983—97, Cmty. Resources Com., 1982—87; charter mem., corp. sec. Main St. Greencastle, 1983—87, v.p., 1987—88, pres., 1989—90, chmn., 1990—91; v.p. United Way, 1996—97, bd. dirs., 1989—97, campaign chair, 1996—97, campaign advisor, 1998—99; announcer Putnam County Fair Parade, 1977—; co-chmn. centennial com. Putnam County Courthouse, 2001—05; v.p. Putnam County Mus., 2002, 2005—06, sec., 2006—, pres., 2003—04; tour guide Putnam County Conv. and Visitors Bur., 1998—; active Putnam County Coun. on Aging and Aged, 1999—; pres. Putnam County Hist. Soc., 1996—97, sec., 1998—; bd. dirs., v.p., sec., pres., hon. dir. Putnam County Found.; co-founder Greencastle H.S. Alumni Assn., 1995, founding chmn. scholarship fund, 1995—; active Govs. Commn. for a Drug Free Ind., 1991—; v.p. West Ctrl. Ind. Econ. Devel. Coun., 2003—; mem. Lilly Scholar Selection Com., 1998—; vice chmn. Putnam County Dem. Ctrl. Com., 2001—; bd. dirs. Putnam County Comprehensive Ctr., 1994—2000, Opportunity Housing, 1995—2002, Greencastle Devel. Ctr., 1988—89; charter mem., bd. dirs. Greencastle Cmty. Child Care Ctr., 1983—87; v.p. Greencastle Zoning Bd. Appeals, 1985—, pres., 1988—; charter mem., bd. dirs. Greencastle Vol. Fire Dept., 1986. Sagamore of the Wabash, Ind. Gov. Evan Bayh, 1995; Limestone State Seal, 1996, Seal of City, Greencastle, 1996; named Hoosier Know It All Champion, Sta. WTTV, Indpls., 1998; named to Ind. Broadcasters Hall of Fame, 1999; named Outstanding Citizen Greencastle Jaycees, 1981; named one of Ind.'s Trail-Blazing Women, 2000; named to Putnam County Agr. Hall of Fame Putnam County Farm Bur., 2002; recipent Disting. Hoosier Award, conferred by Gov. Joseph Kernan, 2004 Mem. AARP (Capital City task force 2000), Nat. Soc. DAR (Centennial chmn. Washburn chpt. 2002, sec. 1994-2003, chaplain 1988-2004, chpt. regent 2003—), Broadcast Pioneers (life), Putnam County Bd. Realtors, Am. Women in Radio and TV (pres. Ind. chpt. 1979-82, Lifetime Achievement award 1996), Indpls. Network Women in Bus. (charter), Women in Comm., Inc. (bd. dirs. 1983-84, MATRIX co-chair 1984, Frances Wright award 1993), Am. Legion Aux., Nat. Assn. Broadcasters, Soc. Profl. Journalists, Ind. Broadcasters Assn. (v.p. FM 1982), Putnam County Extension Adv. Coun. (4H), Natural Resources Svc. Land Use Study Group, Greencastle Bus. and Profl. Women's Club (pres. 1975-76, 78-79, Woman of Yr. 1994), Indpls. Ad Club, Women's Press Club Ind., Indpls. Press Club, Nat. Fedn. Press Women, Ind. Dem. Editl. Assn. (sec. 1987, v.p. 1988, pres. 1990), Ind. C. of C., Greencastle C. of C. (bd. dirs. 1979-83, pres. 1982, amb. 2001—, Citizen of Yr. 1997), VFW (pres. ladies aux. 1966-68), NSDAR (good citizen chair 1992-, Ind. Geneal. Soc. (bd. dirs. West Ctrl. divsn. 2005—), Packard Club Ind., Ind. Soc. Pioneers, Daus of 1812 (pres. Tippecanoe chpt. 1981, state v.p. 1982), Daus. of the Union, Internat. Order Job's Daus., Ind. DAR Chmn.'s Club (sec. regent 2004—), Soc. Descs. of Valley Forge, Rotary (bd. dirs., pres. 1994-95, bull. editor 1995—, dist. conf. planner 1997, Paul Harris fellow 1998, del. world conf. 1998), Order Ea. Star, Women of Moose, Milestone Car Soc., Geneal. Soc. (bd. dirs., 2005-), Delta Theta Tau, Sigma Delta Chi. Mem. Christian Ch. (Disciples Of Christ). Office Phone: 765-653-3565. Business E-Mail: jinsie@ccrtc.com.

BINGHAM, JUNE, playwright; b. White Plains, NY, June 20, 1919; d. Max J.H. and Mabel (Limburg) Rossbach; m. Jonathan B. Bingham, Sept. 20, 1939 (dec. July 1986); children: Sherry B. Downes, Micki B. Esselstyn (dec. 1999), Timothy, Claudia B. Meyers; m. Robert B. Birge, Mar. 28, 1987; 1 stepchild, Robert R. Student, Vassar Coll., 1936-38; BA, Barnard Coll., 1940; LittD (hon.), Lehman Coll., 2002. Writer, editor U.S. Treasury, Washington, 1943-45; editorial asst. Washington Post, 1945-46; writer Tarrytown (N.Y.) Daily News, 1946. Author: Do Cows Have Neuroses?, Do Babies Have Worries?, Do Teenagers Have Wisdom?, Courage to Change: An Introduction to Life and Thought of Reinhold Niebuhr, 1961, Courage to Change: An Introduction to Life and Thought of Reinhold Niebuhr, paperback edit., 1992, U Thant: The Search for Peace, 1970, (plays) Triangles, 1986, Eleanor and Alice, 1996, You and the I.C.U., 1990; author: (with others) The Inside Story: Psychiatry and Everyday Life, 1953, The Pursuit of Health, 1985; author: (mus.) Squanto and Love, 1992, Young Roosevelts, 1993, The Other Lincoln, 1995, The Strange Case of Mary Lincoln, 2001; contbr. articles to nat. mags., newspapers and profl. jours. Bd. dirs. Riverdale Mental Health Assn., 1983-2005, Woodrow Wilson Found., Princeton, NJ, 1959-64, 83-89, Lehman Coll. Found., 1983-90, Ittleson Ctr. for Childhood Rsch., 1958-90, Franklin and Eleanor Roosevelt Inst., 1992-2002; founder T.L.C.; trained liaison comforter Vol. Program of Presbyn. Hosp., NYC, hosp. ethics com., 2003-06. Named Alumna of the Yr., Rosemary Hall, 1976. Mem. Authors Guild (nominating com. 1987-90), Dramatists Guild, PEN, Cosmopolitan Club. Democrat. Avocations: theater, movies, reading. Home: 5000 Independence Ave Bronx NY 10471-2804

BINGHAM, MARIAN, artist, printmaker; b. Oakland, Calif., July 5, 1940; d. Woodbridge and Ursula Wolcott (Griswold) Bingham; m. William Bradford Hubbell, Jr. (div. 1990); children: Drika B. Hubbell, Jonathan Bradford Hubbell; m. Kenneth George McAdams, Feb. 28, 1998. BS (magna cum laude), Conn. Coll., New London, 1991; M.Liberal Arts, Wesleyan U., Middletown, Conn., 1995. Exhibitions include Garde Arts Ctr. and Vangard Gallery, New London, Conn., 1994, Mill Gallery, 1994, Paul Mellon Arts Ctr., Wallingford, Conn., 1994, Slater Mus., Norwich, 1994, Gallery B.A.I., N.Y.C., 1995, 1997—99, Nat. Mus. Women in the Arts, Washington, 1995, New Haven Coun. Small Gallery, New Haven, Conn., 1996, Fernbank Mus. Natural History, Atlanta, 1996, New Britain Mus. Art, Conn., 1997—99, Silvermine Guild Arts Ctr., 1997—99, So Hyun Gallery, N.Y.C., 2000, 2002, Greene Art Gallery, Guilford, Conn., 1998—2001, Alexey von Schlippe Gallery of Art, Groton, Conn., 1998—2001, 2002, 2004, Conn. Graphics Art Ctr., Norwalk, 2001—06, Hotel Abbye-Ecole, Soreze, France, 2003, 4 Star Gallery, Indpls., 2004, Albany Mus. Art, Ga., 2004, Moon Gallery, Berry Coll., Mt. Berry, Ga., 2005, Bendheim Gallery, Greenwich, Conn., 2005, Opelousas (La.) Mus. Art, 2005, numerous others. Avocations: hiking, skiing, travel, poetry.

BINGMAN, CHARLES FRANKLIN, government executive, educator; b. West Allis, Wis., Sept. 11, 1929; s. Clyde James and Bernice (Hengstler) B. BBA, U. Wis., 1952, MBA, 1956. Mgr. planning and control Nasa-Johnson Space Ctr., Houston, 1962-66; dep. dir. mgmt. programs Office Manned Space Flight Nat. Aero. and Space Adminstrn., Washington, 1967-71; dep. assoc. dir. orgn. mgmt. U.S. Office Mgmt. and Budget, Washington, 1971-76; dep. adminstr. Urban Mass Transp. Adminstrn. U.S. Dept. Transp., Washington, 1976-79, spl. asst. to dep. sec., 1982-83; exec. dir. Pres.'s mgmt. improvement coun. Exec. Office of The Pres., Washington, 1979-80, mgmt. advisor White House Office of Policy Devel., 1980-81; vis. prof. pub. adminstrn. dept. George Washington U., Washington, 1984-97; cons. U.S. and internat. govts., 1985—; fellow Ctr. for Study of Am. Govt., Johns Hopkins U., Washington, 1997—. Author: Revitalizing Federal Management, 1983, Japanese Government Leadership and Management, 1989, Serving Two Presidents: A History of the Bureau of the Budget, 1992, Why Governments Go Wrong, 2006; contbr. articles to profl. jours. Pres. Woodlake Towers Condo Assn., 1996—2002. Capt. US Army, 1951—65. U.S. Info. Agy. grantee, 1992. Fellow Nat. Acad. Pub. Adminstrn.; mem. Sr. Execs. Assn. (pres. 1968-69, bd. dirs. 1982-85), Fed. Exec. Inst. Alumni Assn. (bd. dirs. 1983-86), William A. Jump Found. (bd. dirs. 1987-2006), Cosmos Club Republican. Avocations: writing, jogging, hiking, reading. Home: 3100 S Manchester St Apt 815 Falls Church VA 22044-2716 E-mail: user7352@aol.com.

BINIENDA, JOHN J., state legislator; b. Worcester, Mass., June 22, 1947; s. Thaddeus Andrew and Mary Gertrude (O'Coin) B.; children: Julie Ann, John Joseph Jr., Jamie Thaddeus. BA, Worcester State Coll., 1970, postgrad., 1970-74. State rep. Dist. 17 Mass. Ho. of Reps., 1987—, chmn. Com. on Revenue. Mem. Ward 7 Dem. Com., 1987—; mem. South Worcester Neighbor Ctr. Mem. Worcester State Coll. Alumni Assn., Am. Legion (Main St. chpt.), Polish Naturalization Ind. Club, Polish Am. Vet. Club, K.C. (3d degree), Loyal Order Moose. Office Phone: 617-722-2320. Business E-Mail: Rep.JohnBinenda@hou.state.ma.us.

BINION, CELIOUS, retired parochial school educator; b. Carthage, Jan. 31, 1940; d. George Lewis and Ellene Steel; children from previous marriage: Vicki Pearson, Yolanda Davis. BS, Jackson State U., 1961; MA, Chgo. State U., 1981, Olivet Nazarene U., Kankakee, Ill., 2001. Tchr. Bd.

Edn., Chgo., 1964—69, libr., 1970—2001; tchr. Dist. 143, Posen, Ill., 1969—70, St. Clotilde Cath. Sch., Chgo., 2001—03; ret., 2003. Counselor Ill. Young Authors, Bloomington, 1986—; sec. Connexion, Inc., Chgo., 1998—. Author: (children's book) Buffy Goes Skating, 1987, (poems) Poetry for the Soul, 2004. Drama helper vol. Washington Pk. Field House, Chgo., 1986—97; vol. Sherman Pk. Libr., Chgo., 1999—2003, Connexions, Chgo., 1999—; sec. Chgo. State's Libr. Club, 1999—2001; Sunday sch. tchr. God's House of All Nations, 1989—. Named Tchr. of the Yr., Leary Corp., 2003; grantee, Kate Maremont Assn., 1987, Kizzy Found., 2001. Mem.: Phi Beta Kappa. Avocations: reading, writing, music, tennis. Home: 7747 S King Dr Chicago IL 60691-2928

BINKLEY, DAVID A., human resources specialist; BS, Mich. State U. Regional mgr. human resources Whirlpool Corp., Benton Harbor, Mich., 1984—86, mgr. employee rels. parts distbn. ctr. LaPorte, Ind., 1986—89, dir. exec. devel. corp. human resources, 1989—92; dir. human resources Whirlpool Corp. Europe, Comerio, Italy, 1992—94; dir., human resources Whirlpool Corp. Asia, Singapore, 1994—95, v.p. human resources Greater China, 1995—96; corp. dir. mgmt. resources Whirlpool Corp., Benton Harbor, Mich., 1996—98, v.p. human resources N.Am. divsn., 1998—2001, corp. v.p. global human resources, 2001—04, sr. v.p. global human resources, 2004—. Office: Whirlpool Corp 2000 N M-63 Benton Harbor MI 49022-2692 Office Phone: 269-923-5000. Office Fax: 269-923-5443.*

BINKLEY, DAVID MARTIN, electrical engineer, educator, musician; b. Knoxville, Tenn., July 19, 1955; s. Jerry White and Carol Dexter Binkley; m. Jacqueline Lee Wimsatt, Apr. 23, 1988; children: Anna Marie, Christopher Michael Dexter. PhD in Elec. Engring., U. Tenn., 1992, MS in Elec. Engring., 1984, BS in Elec. Engring., 1978. Registered profl. engr., Tenn., 1983. Devel. engr. Tech. for Energy Corp., Knoxville, Tenn., 1978—85; sr. scientist CTI PET Systems, Knoxville, 1985—98; v.p. integrated circuit devel. Concorde Microsystems, Knoxville, 1998—2000; assoc. prof., elec. and computer engring. U. NC, Charlotte, 2000—. Bd. dirs. Concorde Microsystems, Knoxville, 1992—2007, cons., 2000—04. Contbr. articles to profl. jours.; musician: Dave Binkley and Friends, 1972—. Pres. West Forest Neighborhood Assn., Knoxville, 1988—2000. Recipient Most Influential Engring. Prof., Tau Beta Pi, U. NC at Charlotte, 2000; Rsch. grant, Dept. of Def., DARPA, 2001—04, NIH, Nat. Cancer Inst., 1991—93. Mem.: IEEE (sr.; chmn., East Tenn. sect. 1995—96, Outstanding Sect. award 1996), Research! Am. Achievements include patents in field. Avocations: photography, amateur radio, jazz. Home Phone: 704-598-0056.

BINKLEY, LUTHER JOHN, philosophy educator; b. Wernersville, Pa., Oct. 7, 1925; s. Harry Garfield and Jennie Theresa (Yoder) B.; m. Betty Jane Bowman, June 5, 1964. AB, Franklin and Marshall Coll., 1945; BD, Lancaster Sem., Pa., 1947; PhD, Harvard U., 1950. Ordained to ministry United Ch. of Christ, 1949. Instr. philosophy Franklin and Marshall Coll., Lancaster, 1949-51, asst. prof., 1951-56, assoc. prof., 1956-62, prof., 1962-91, prof. emeritus, 1991—, chmn. dept., 1962-74, dir. humanities program, 1972-74. Vis. fellow Cambridge (Eng.) U., 1959-60, Princeton (N.J.) U., 1967, 69; adj. prof. Temple U., Phila., 1965-83, Pa. State U., Harrisburg, 1975-88. Author: The Mercersburg Theology, 1953, Contemporary Ethical Theories, 1961, Conflict of Ideals: Changing Values in Western Society, 1969. Mem. Pub. Coun. for Humanities in Pa., Phila., 1975-79; mem. instnl. ethics com. Lancaster Regional Med. Ctr., 1985—; mem. instnl. rev. bd. Lancaster Gen. Hosp., 1988—, mem. cmty adv. bd. Penn State Ambulatory Rsch. Network. Recipient Disting. Coll. Tchg. award Lindback Found., 1962. Mem. AAUP (pres. Franklin and Marshall chpt. 1962-63, 50 Yr. Svc. award 2000), Am. Philos. Assn., Philos. Soc. for Study Sport (pres. 1977-78), Hershey Country Club, Lancaster Torch Club (pres. 1956-57, Silver award 1999), Phi Beta Kappa (pres. Theta chpt. Pa. 1970-71). Avocations: travel, golf, tennis, attending opera and symphony concerts, reading. Home: PO Box 473 Hershey PA 17033-0473 Office: Franklin and Marshall Coll PO Box 3003 Lancaster PA 17604-3003 Personal E-mail: ljbinkley@aol.com.

BINKLEY, TIMOTHY, computer graphics designer, educator; b. Balt., Sept. 14, 1943; s. Enos G. and Grace (Joy) Binkley; m. Sonya Shannon, 1993. BA in Math. with honors, U. Colo., 1965, MA in Math., 1966; PhD in Philosophy, U. Tex., 1970; postgrad. in computer sci., Courant Inst., NYU, 1979-82. Asst. prof. Notre Dame U., Ind., 1970-73; postdoctoral fellow Temple U., Phila., 1973-75; mem. faculty New Sch. for Social Rsch., NYC, 1975-77; chair dept. humanities and scis. Sch. Visual Arts, NYC, 1976-88, dir. computer edn., 1982—98, dir. Inst. for Computers in the Arts, 1986—98, chair MFA program in computer art, 1988—98; pres. Artware, 1996—. Co-dir. telecom. event Heinrich Hertz Centennial Celebration, Bronx, Bklyn., 1987. Author: Wittgenstein's Language, 1973; author: (with others) Reason and Violence, 1974, Culture and Art, 1976, Philosophical Perspectives on Metaphor, 1981, Philosophy Looks at the Arts, 1987; author: (software) Paint Brush, 1983, Starmaker, 1988, Symmetry Studio, 1990, GAIN Engine, 1999, Agent Wrangler, 2000; contbr. articles to profl. jours.; exhibitions include computer installations Face to Face and Drawn to the Light in Computer and Art Exhbn., IBM Gallery Sci. and Art, N.Y.C., 1988, Ctr. Fine Arts, Miami, Fla., 1988, Represented in permanent collections Franklin Inst., Phila., Autoform in Gretta Sarfaty's retrospective exhbn. Musea Da Imagem E Do Som, Sao Paulo, Brazil, collaborative paintings with G. Sarfaty, Symmetrical Reincarnations I and II; computer art dir.: (videos) A Price for Every Progress, 1987; Pink Slip Out of Nowhere, 1988; dir.: (films) Portrait of Sean, 1972, The Seasons, One Minute of Pure Chance, 1973, Existence, Synchrony, 1974; mem. editl. adv. bd. Philosphy and Lit., 1976—85, Art & Academe, 1988—. NEH Younger Humanist fellow, 1973—74, Ford Found. fellow, 1974—75, Oldright fellow, NDEA fellow, O'Brien Rsch. grantee, 1971, NEH Grantee, 1977. Mem.: Am. Soc. Aesthetics (trustee 1981—84), Assn. Computing Machinery (bd. dirs. N.Y.C. 1987—, chair spl. interest group computer graphics 1988—), Phi Beta Kappa. Personal E-mail: tbinkley@artware.com.

BINN, JASON, publishing executive; b. 1967; m. Haley Lieberman. B. in mktg., Boston U., 1989. Co-founder, pub. Ocean Drive, Miami, 1993—; founder & CEO Niche Media LLC, NYC, 1998—; pub. Hamptons, NY, 1998—, Gotham, 2001—, Los Angeles Confidential, 2002—, Aspen Peak, 2004—, Boston Common, 2005—, Capitol File, 2005—. Named one of 40 Under 40, Crain's NY Bus., 2007; named to Advt. Hall of Achievement, Am. Advt. Fedn., 2006. Office: Niche Media 5th Fl 257 Park Ave S New York NY 10010 Office Phone: 646-835-5205. E-mail: jasonbinn@gotham-magazine.com.*

BINNEY, JAN JARRELL, publishing executive, marketing professional; b. Frankfort, Ind., Aug. 16, 1941; d. Robert and Susie (Meek) Jarrell; m. Joseph M. Binney, June 23, 1962; 1 child, Robert J. BS, Purdue U., 1962; MA, Coll. N.J., 1972. Speech-lang. pathologist pub. schs., various locations, 1962-84; pvt. practice speech pathology East Brunswick, NJ, 1982-85; pres. The Speech Bin, Inc. Pub., Vero Beach, Fla., 1984—. Editor profl. publs. Deacon Presbyn. Ch., 1985-87, elder, 1987-90; bd. dirs., chpt. chmn. ARC, Indian River County, Fla. Fellow Am. Speech, Lang. Hearing Assn. (legis. councilor 1981-89, bd. dirs. pub. info. exch. 1987-89, com. on equality 1988-90, bd. dirs. polit. action com.), N.J. Speech, Lang. Hearing Assn. (pres. 1981-82, hon. 1984), Exch. Club Indian River (sec. 1998-99, bd. dirs. 2001-2002), Exch. Club Indian River Found. (charter, sec. 2002—), Pi Beta Phi Alumnae Club (treas.). Office: The Speech Bin Inc 1965 25th Ave Vero Beach FL 32960-3000 Office Phone: 772-770-0007. Business E-Mail: jan@speechbin.com.

BINNEY, ROBERT HARRY, bank executive; b. London, Oct. 21, 1945; s. Roy and Barbara (Poole) B.; m. Valerie Kay Greene, May 4, 1979; children: Alexandra, Christopher, Nicholas, Paul. MA in Mech. Scis., Cambridge U., Eng., 1967; MBA, Manchester Bus. Sch., Eng., 1971. Mktg. exec. Rank Xerox, Birmingham, Eng., 1967-69; with Chase Manhattan Bank, various locations, 1971-96; exec. Orion Bank, London, 1971-72; various positions including mng. dir. Asia merchant banking, Hong Kong and country mgr. Japan Chase Manhattan Bank, 1972—91, bus. exec. Europe and Mid. East for global securities svc., 1991—96; mng. dir. Europe, Mid. East, Africa worldwide securities svcs. Citibank, N.A., London, 1996—2005; with Citigroup, 1998—2005, mng. dir. global transaction svcs. in Europe, Mid. East, Africa London, 2003—04, mng. dir. global client devel., 2004—05; vice chmn. Fortent Inc., London, 2005—. Mem. Surrey County Cricket Club. Anglican. Avocations: travel, tennis, bridge. Office: Fortent Ltd Prospect House 80-110 New Oxford St London WC1A 1HB England Office Phone: +44 20 7255 1065. Business E-Mail: r.binney@fortent.com.

BINNIE, BRIAN, pilot, transportation executive; BS in Aerospace Engring., Brown U., MS in Fluid Mechanics; MS in Aeronautical Engring., Princeton U.; grad., US Navy Test Pilot Sch., Patuxent River, Md., Naval Aviation Safety Sch., Monterey, Calif. Lic. Airline Transport Pilot. Program bus. mgr., test pilot Scaled Composites, Mojave, Calif. Flight test experience includes: Scaled's Model 318 White Knight, Scaled's Model 316 SpaceShipOne, Roton Flight Test, F/A-18 Electronic Warfare Suite Testing and Integration, F/A-18 TSSAM Weapon Launch Envelope Expansion, A-6E TSSAM Weapon Launch Envelope Expansion, F/A-18 SLAM-ER Weapon Launch Envelope Expansion, A-6E SLAM-ER Weapon Launch Envelope Expansion, F/A-18 LEX Fence Performance Map, F/A-18 ATARS Transonic Handling Evaluation, A-7E Structural Flight Test Qualification Program, F/A-18 KC-10 Wing Tip Refueling Pod Evaluation, A-7E KC-10 Wing Tip Refueling Pod Evaluation, F/A-18 F404 2nd Source (Pratt & Whitney vs GE) Engine Envelope Expansion, F/A-18 Hi-Energy Nose Strut -T/Off and Landing Eval, F/A-18 First LGB Weapon Delivery Using Self-Lasing FLIR. Mem.: Am. Inst. Aeronautics and Astronautics (pub. mem.), Soc. Exptl. Test Pilots. Achievements include completing the ROTON: Hazard Analysis / Aircrew Checklists / Normal & Emergency Procedures; conducting Flight Test / Developed Operational Flight Procedures (Tactics)/ providing Fleet Training (1 to 5 day course) for F/A-18 and AV-8B EW Suites; expanding curriculum to include Foreign Military Customers and provided in-country training to Finland, Malaysia and Italy; writing all the operational checklists and providing the Fleet Tactics Manual for the TSSAM Weapon System; planning and executing the first (and only) radar chase of the Tomahawk cruise missile to demonstrate more effective surface fleet training; preparing and briefing the Australian Air Force on new Operational Flight Software for their F/A-18 aircraft; pilot for the second record flight of Space ShipOne on October 4, 2004, which won the Ansari X prize; second person in history to earn his commerical astronaut wings as a result of historic flight on Space ShipOne. Office: Scaled Composites Inc Mojave Airport 1624 Flight Line Mojave CA 93501 Office Phone: 661-824-4541. Office Fax: 661-824-4174.

BINNING, BETTE FINESE (MRS. GENE HEDGCOCK BINNING), athletic association official; b. Brandon, Manitoba, Canada, Sept. 20, 1927; father is an Am. citizen. d. Henry Josiah and Beatrice Victoria (Harrop) Ames; m. Gene Hedgcock Binning, May 3, 1952; children: Gene Barton, Barbara Jo, Bradford Jay. Grad., Brandon Coll., 1944; student, Brandon U., 1944—46. Exec. sec. to mgr. Gardner Denver Co., Denver, 1950—52; mem. age. group swimming com. Amateur Athletic Union U.S., 1966—68, women's swimming com., 1968—69, age group swimming objectives subcom., 1970—71, mem. age. group swimming com., 1970—72, del. Conv., 1971—77, women's swimming com., 1972—76, del. Conv., 1979—80. Okla. state chmn. age group swimming Amateur Athletic Union, 1966-68, 70-72, chmn. women's swimming com., 1968-69, 72-79, mem. Okla. exec. bd. for all amateur sports, also registration com., 1971-79; mem. U.S. Olympic com., 1972-80; nat. dir. swimming records, 1972-81; U.S. rep. to records com. Amateur Swimming Assn. Am., 1975-83, dir. records com., 1975-83; dir., sec. records com. Union Amateur de Natacion de las Americas, 1979-83; tech. ofcl. Pan Am. Games, Mex. City, 1975, San Juan, P.R., 1979; ofcl. XXI Olympiad, Montreal, PQ, Can., 1976; mem. interim organizing com. U.S. Olympic Festival, 1986; athletic adv. dir. U.S. Olympic Festival 1989, 1987-88. Team capt. YMCA fund drives, 1966-78; mem. adv. com. Internat. Gymnastics Hall of Fame, 1996-99. Mem. Kerr Mcgee Swim Club (dir. 1968-75), Quail Creek Golf and Country Club(sports dir. women's golf assn. 2003, pres. 2005, rep. to Oklahoma City Golf Assn. 2006, 07), Gaillardia Country Club, Ski Club, Vail Athletic Club Colo. Presbyterian. Home: 3101 Rolling Stone Rd Oklahoma City OK 73120-1841 also: Vail Internat 205 300 E Lionshead Cir Vail CO 81657-5204 Home Fax: 405-751-6906. E-mail: Bettebinning@yahoo.com.

BINNING, GENE BARTON, real estate company executive; b. Denver, Feb. 7, 1953; s. Gene Hedgcock and Bette Finice (Ames) B. BA in Econs. and Bus. Adminstrn., Vanderbilt U., 1975; MBA, U. Okla., 1977; EdD, Okla. State U., 1996. Br. controller Trane Air Conditioning Dist. Office, Okla. City, 1977-86; cons. pvt. practice, Okla. City, 1986-99; instr. U. Cen. Okla., Edmond, Okla., 1988-99; v.p. bus. devel. Aetenitas Inc., Oklahoma City, 1999—2002; commercial broker assoc. Prudential Alliance Realty, 2002—. Tech. editor On the Horizons, 1996-99. Vol. coord. Sooner State Games, Okla. City, 1985-87; state regents faculty adv. com., 1992-93; pres. edn. com. Okla. Assn. of Realtors, 2003—. Mem. AAUP, Assn. Info. Tech. Profl., Assn. Info. Sys., Okla. Higher Edn. Faculty Assn. of U. Ctrl. Okla. (pres. 1992-93), Faculty Assn. (pres. 1991-92), Quail Creek Golf and Country Club. Republican. Home: 2933 Rolling Stone Rd Oklahoma City OK 73120-1921 Office: 4101 NW122 Oklahoma City OK 73120

BINNING, WILLIAM CHARLES, political science professor; b. Mar. 8, 1944; m. Maureen G. Fannon, Nov. 26, 1966; children: Patrick, Catherine. BA in Politics, St. Anselm's Coll., 1966; PhD in Govt. and Internat. Rels., U. Notre Dame, 1970. Asst. prof. polit. sci. Youngstown (Ohio) State U., 1970—77, assoc. prof., chmn. polit. sci., 1977—84, prof., 1984—. Project dir. NSF, 1978—79, grant evaluator, 1979; part-time staff mem. Office of Gov. G. Voinovich, Ohio, 1991—2000; arbitrator Am. Arbitration Assn., 2000—. Fellow, NDEA. Mem.: AAU, ASPA, Midwest Polit. Sci. Assn., Am. Polit. Sci. Assn. Office: Dept Polit Sci Youngstown State U 410 Wick Ave Youngstown OH 44555-0001 Business E-Mail: wcbinning@ysu.edu.

BINNS, JAMES EDWARD, retired banker; b. Alameda, Calif., Oct. 5, 1931; s. Guy Vivian and Beatrice (Jury) B.; m. Marjean Friesen, Feb. 21, 1951; children: Cheryl Jean Binns Smith, Jana Lee Binns Gualco, Lori LeAnn Binns Mauer. Student, U. Nev., 1950-51; grad., Sch. Bank Audit and Control, U. Wis., 1963, Am. Inst. Banking, 1964. With Sierra Pacific Power Co., Reno, 1948-50; with First Interstate Bank of Nev., Reno, 1951-91, asst. cashier, 1957-63, asst. to cashier, 1963-65, auditor, 1965-84, asst. v.p., 1968-75, v.p., 1975-91; Cameo Jewelry and Loan, Reno, 1992-93; instr. Am. Inst. Banking. Past chmn. internal audit com. City of Reno. Mem. Sierra Nevada Cmty. Access TV, Reno Hot August Nights. Mem. AARP (past pres. Western Nev. chpt., treas., bd. dirs., dir. weekly TV prodn. N. Nev. chpt.), Am. Inst. Banking (past pres. Sierra-Nev. chpt., past nat. assoc. coun.), Bank Adminstrn. Inst. (cert. bank auditor, charter pres. chpt., past state dir.), Data Processing Mgmt. Assn. (charter mem. Sierra-Nev. chpt., past pres.), Inst. Internal Auditors (cert. internal auditor, past charter pres. chpt.), Western Indsl. Nev., Masons, Shriners, Elks, Lakeridge Tennis Club, Reno Toastmasters (past pres.), Reno H.S. Alumni Assn. (life, 1st treas.), E. Clampus Vitus (Las Plumas Del Oro chpt.), Graeagle Tennis Club, Reno C. of C. (mem. spl. events coun. diplomates, Vol. of Yr. award 2001, Outstanding Svce. award 2003), Good Old Days Club. Home: 1720 Allen St Reno NV 89509-1252 *A true leader must accept all reasonable challenges being fully cognizant that his and the group's success can only be achieved through the combined efforts of all participants.*

BINNS, JAMES HAZLETT, JR., entrepreneur; b. Lancaster, Pa., June 5, 1945; s. James Hazlett and Ruamie (Hill) B.; m. Connie Hoffman, Nov. 26, 1981; children: Corissa, Marian, Alexandra. BA with great distinction, Stanford U., 1967; JD magna cum laude, Harvard U., 1973. Bar: Ariz. 1974. Assoc. Meyer, Hendricks, Victor, Osborn & Maledon, Phoenix, 1973-74; v.p. Advanced Diagnostic Rsch. Corp., Tempe, Ariz., 1974-76, pres., 1976-82, Marcor Inc., Phoenix, 1982-88; prin. dep. asst. sec. def. for internat. security policy US Dept. Def., Wash., 1988—; former chmn. Parallel Design Inc., Phoenix, 1991—. Bd. dirs. Ind. Newspapers Inc., Dover, Del., Sundance Broadcasting Wis., Milw. Editor: Harvard Law Review, 1972. Asst. to mayor City of Phoenix, 1984-85; chmn. Phoenix Meml. Hosp. Found., 1985-86; participant Anglo-Am. Conf. for Successful Generation, Sch. Advanced Internat. Studies, Johns Hopkins U., Oxford, Eng., 1985. Recipient Prometheus award, 1985. Mem. Ariz. Bar Assn., Young Pres. Orgn. (chmn. Ariz. chpt. 1982-83), Skanaetales Country Club. Republican. Avocations: writing, golf. Office: Parallel Design Inc 4313 E Cotton Center Blvd Ste 100 Phoenix AZ 85040 Office Phone: 480-222-7000. Office Fax: 208-474-3374.

BINNS, JANE CAMILLE, humanities educator; b. Ann Arbor, Mich., Aug. 4, 1967; d. Robert Caryl and Lenore Eloise Binns; m. Michael James Monkman, Aug. 11, 1990 (div. Apr. 4, 2002); 1 child, Cale August Monkman. BS, Ea. Mich. U., Ypsilanti, 1989; MEd, Syracuse U., NYC, 1995; MFA, Naropa U., Boulder, Colo., 1999. Survey analyst, tech. writer Syracuse U., NY, 1993—97; instr. English Met. State Coll. of Denver, 2000—. Author: (short stories) Pocket Change, 2004, (manual and audio tape) Talking to the Media: A How-to for New Readers; contbr. articles to profl. jours. Process and procedures manual editor Women's Polit. Caucus, Ann Arbor, Mich., 1991—93; newsletter editor NOW, Ann Arbor, 1991—93. Finalist Fiction/Prose Contest, The Litchfield Rev., 2006, Summer Literary Seminars Fiction Contest, 2006, Progenitor Fiction Contest, 2007. Avocations: swimming, playing piano, writing.

BINNS, TOM, jewelry designer; b. Belfast, Ireland; BA, Middlesex Polytechnic, 1981. Head designer Tom Binns Accessories. Recipient Accessory Designer of Yr. award, Coun. of Fashion Designers of Am., 2006. Office: c/o Cristina Viera-Newton 1405 Pacific Ave Venice CA 90291 Office Phone: 310-395-8078. Office Fax: 310-399-7452.

BINOCHE, JULIETTE, actress; b. Paris, Mar. 9, 1964; children: Raphael, Hannah. Student, Nat. Conservatory of Drama. Appearances in films include Les Nanas, La Vie de Famille, Rouge Baiser, 1985, Rendez-Vous, 1985, Mon beau-Frère a tué ma soeur, Mauvais Sang, 1986, Un tour de Manège, The Unbearable Lightness of Being, 1988, Les amants du Pont-Neuf, 1991, Wuthering Heights, 1992, Damage, 1992, Trois Couteurs: Bleu, 1993, The Horseman on the Roof, 1995, A Couch in New York, 1995, Le Hussard Sur Le Toit, 1995, The English Patient, 1996 (Academy award, 1996), Alice et Martin, 1998, Les Enfants du Siecle, 1999, La Veuve de Saint-Pierre, 2000, Chocolat, 2000, Decalage Horaire, 2002, Country of My Skull, 2004, Cache, 2005, Bee Season, 2005, Mary, 2005, Paris, je t'aime, 2006. Avocation: painting.*

BINSFELD, CONNIE BERUBE, former state official; b. Munising, Mich., Apr. 18, 1924; d. Omer J. and Elsie (Constance) Berube; m. John E. Binsfeld, July 19, 1947; children: John T., Gregory, Susan, Paul, Michael. BS, Siena Heights Coll., 1945, DHL (hon.), 1977; LLD (hon.), No. Mich. U., 1998; DHL (hon.), Mich. State U., 1998, Thomas Cooley Sch. of Law, 1999; LLD (hon.), Saginaw Valley State U., 2000, Lake Superior State U., 2000; DHL (hon.), U. Notre Dame, 2000, Grand Valley State U., 2000, DHL (hon.). County commr. Leelanau County, Mich., 1970-74; mem. Mich. Ho. of Reps., 1974-82, asst. rep. leader, 1979-81; del. Nav. Conv., 1980, 88, 92; mem. Mich. Senate, 1982-90, asst. rep. leader, 1979, 81; lt. gov. State of Mich., 1990-98. Mem. adv. bd. Nat. Park Sys. Named Mich. Mother of Yr., Mich. Mothers Com., 1977; Northwestern Mich. Coll. fellow; named to Mich. Women's Hall of Fame, 1998. Mem. Nat. Coun. State Legislators, LWV, Siena Heights Coll. Alumnae Assn. Republican. Roman Catholic. E-mail: Connieltgov@mailstation.com.

BINSTOCK, ROBERT HENRY, public policy educator, writer; b. New Orleans, Dec. 6, 1935; s. Louis and Ruth (Atlas) B.; m. Martha Burns, July 27, 1979; 1 dau., Jennifer. AB, Harvard U., 1956, PhD, 1965. Lectr. Brandeis U., Waltham, Mass., 1963-65, asst. prof., 1965-69, assoc. prof., 1969-72, Stulberg Prof. law and politics, 1972-84, dir. Policy Ctr. Aging, 1979-84; prof. aging, health and soc. Case Western Res. U., Cleve., 1985—. Mem. com. on an Aging Soc. Nat. Acad. Scis., Washington, 1982-86. Author: America's Political System, 1972, 5th edit., 1991, America's Political System: Urban, State and Local, 1972, 3d edit., 1979, Feasible Planning for Social Change, 1966; editor: The Politics of the Powerless, 1971, Too Old for Health Care?, 1991, Dementia and Aging, 1992, International Perspectives on Aging: Population and Policy Changes, 1982, Handbook of Aging and the Social Sciences, 1976, 5th edit., 2001, 6th edit., 2006, The Future of Long Term Care, 1996, Home Care Advances: Essential Research and Policy Issues, 2000, The Lost Art of Caring: A Challenge to Health Professionals, Families, Communities and Society, 2001, The Fountain of Youth: Cultural, Scientific, and Ethical Perspectives on a Biomedical Goal, 2004, Aging Nation: The Economics and Politics of Growing Older in America, 2006. Bd. dirs. White House Task Force on Older Ams., 1967-68; chmn. adv. panel Office Tech. Assessment, U.S. Congress, 1982-84; tech. adviser, del. White House Conf. on Aging, 1971, 81; trustee Boston Biomed. Research Inst., 1971-84; mem. gov.'s adv. com. Dept. of Elder Affairs Mass., 1974-84; chair, adv. bd. Nat. Acad. on Aging, 1991-95. Recipient Haak-Lilliefors award Mich. State U., 1979, Arthur S. Flemming award Nat. Assn. State Units on Aging, 1988, Key award APHA, 1992, Am. Soc. Aging award, 1994, Hall of Fame award, Am. Soc. Aging, 2006; fellow Ford Found., 1959-69; Rsch. grant NIH, 1968-73. Fellow Gerontol. Soc. Am. (pres. 1976, Donald P. Kent award 1981, Brookdale Prize award 1983), Assn. Gerontol. in Higher Edn. (Tibbitts award, 2007); mem. APHA (chair gerontol. health sect. 1996-97, Lifetime Achievement award 2005). Office: Case Western Res Univ 2040 Adelbert Rd Cleveland OH 44106-4901

BINTLIFF, BARBARA ANN, library director, law educator; b. Houston, Jan. 14, 1953; d. Donald Richard and Frances Arlene (Appling) Hay; m. Byron A. Boville, Aug. 20, 1977 (dec. 2006); children: Bradley, Bruce. BA in Political Sci. with hon., Cen. Wash. U., Ellensburg, 1975; JD, U. Wash., Seattle, 1978, MLL, 1979. Bar: Wash. 1979, U.S. Dist. Ct. (ea. dist.) Wash. 1980, Colo. 1983, U.S. Dist. Ct. Colo. 1983. Atty., libr. Gaddis and Fox, Seattle, 1978-79; reference libr. U. Denver Law Sch., 1979-84; assoc. libr., sr. instr. Sch. Law U. Colo., Boulder, 1984-88, assoc. prof., libr. dir., 1989—2001, prof., dir. Law Libr., 2001—, Nicholas Rosenbaum prof. law, 2002—. Legal cons. Nat. Ctr. Atmospheric Rsch., Environ. and Societal Impacts Group, Boulder, 1980; vis. prof. U. Wash., Seattle, 1996, chair U. Colo. Boulder, Faculty Assembly, 2003-05. Co-author: Colorado Legal Resources: An Annotated Bibliography, 2004; co-editor, Public Services in Law Libraries: Evolution and Innovation in the 21st Century, 2007; editor: A Representative Sample of Tenure Documents for Law Librarians, 1988, 2nd edit., 1994, Chapter Presidents' Handbook, 1989, Representatives Handbook, 1990, Marketing Toolkit for Academic Law Libraries, 2004; assoc. editor: Legal Reference Svcs. Quarterly, Perspectives: Teaching Legal Research and Writing; co-editor: Public Services in the 21st Century

Evolution and Innovation, 2007; contbr. articles to profl. jours. Named Disting. Alumnus, Ctrl. Wash. U., 2000; recipient Boulder Faculty Assembly Excellence Svc. award, 2001, Calhoun Svc. award, U. Colo., 2002. Mem. Am. Assn. Law Librs. (v.p./pres.-elect 2000-01, pres. 2001-02; Frederick Charles Hicks award 2005, Presdl. citation 2006, Spectrum article of Yr. 2007), Am. Law Inst. (elected), Colo. Assn. Law Librs. (pres. 1982), Southwestern Assn. Law Librs. (pres. 1987-88, 91-92). Episcopalian. Office: U Colo Law Sch 2450 Kittredge Loop Dr Rm 424 Boulder CO 80309-0402 Business E-Mail: barbara.bintliff@colorado.edu.

BINTZ, EDWARD E., lawyer; b. Sept. 29, 1958; BS, Fordham Univ., 1980; JD, George Washington Univ., 1984; LLM, Georgetown Univ., 1992. Bar: N.Y. 1985, D.C. 1988. Ptnr., Benefits & Employment Law Practice Group Arnold & Porter, Washington. Contbr. articles to profl. jours. Office: Arnold & Porter 555 Twelfth St NW Washington DC 20004-1206 Office Phone: 202-942-5045. Office Fax: 202-942-5999. Business E-Mail: edward.bintz@aporter.com.

BINZEL, RICHARD P., astrophysicist, educator; B in Physics, Macalester Coll., St. Paul; PhD in Astronomy, U. Tex., 1986. Prof. dept. earth, atmospheric and planetary scis. MIT, Cambridge. Margaret MacVicar faculty fellow MIT, 1994—, chair prog. in planetary sci. Contbr. articles to profl. jours., chapters to books; co-editor: Asteroids II, 1990, Asteroids III, 2002. Recipient Presdl. Young Investigator award, 1990, Harold C. Urey prize, Am. Astron. Union, 1991. Fellow: AAAS. Achievements include development of the Torino Impact Hazard Scale, which assigns a number to the likelihood that an asteroid will strike Earth; made the first definitive observations showing the onset of the Pluto-Charon mutual events in 1985. Office: Dept Earth Atmospheric and Planetary Scis MIT 77 Mass Ave 54-426 Cambridge MA 02139-4307 E-mail: rpb@mit.edu.

BINZEN, PETER HUSTED, journalist; b. Montclair, NJ, Sept. 24, 1922; s. Frederick William and Lucy Beckwith (Husted) B.; m. Elisabeth Virginia Flower, June 12, 1951; children: Lucy Binzen Wildrick, Jennifer Binzen Cardoso, Jonathan Peter, Katherine. BA in Polit. Sci, Yale U., 1947; postgrad. (Nieman fellow), Harvard U., 1962. Reporter UP, NYC, 1947, Passaic (N.J.) Herald-News, 1947-50; reporter, editor Phila. Bull., 1951-82; reporter Phila. Inquirer, 1982-87; columnist Inquirer, 1987—2005. Author: Whitetown U.S.A, 1970, (with Joseph R. Daughen) The Wreck of the Penn Central, 1971, The Cop Who Would Be King, 1977; editor: Nearly Everybody Read It, 1998. Served with U.S. Army, 1943-45. Decorated Bronze Star.

BIOLCHINI, ROBERT FREDRICK, lawyer; b. Detroit, Sept. 22, 1939; s. Alfred and Erma (Barbetti) Biolchini; m. Frances Lauinger, June 5, 1965; children: Robert F., Douglas C., Frances E., Tobin M., Thomas A., Christine M. BA, U. Notre Dame, 1962; LLB, George Washington U., 1965. Bar: Okla., Mich., 1965. Assoc. Doerner, Stuart, Saunders, Daniel, Anderson & Biolchini, Tulsa, Okla., 1968-71, ptnr., 1971-94, Stuart, Biolchini & Turner, Tulsa, 1994—. Pres., CEO Pennwell Corp.; chmn. bd. dirs., CEO, PennEnergy, Inc., Valley Nat. Bank, Ameritrust Holding Co., Bank of Jackson Hole, Old Faithful Underwriting Ltd.; dir. Am. Bus. Media; mem. Lloyds of London, 1979—; bd. dirs. Bank of The Lakes. Bd. dirs. Thomas Gilcrease Mus., past pres., chmn. bd., 1977-80, dir. emeritus, 1980—; bd. dirs., sec., legal clk. Tulsa Ballet Theatre, Inc., 1976-84; trustee Monte Cassino Endowment, 1978—; pres. Monte Cassino Sch. Bd., 1970-77; chmn. Christ the King Parish Coun., 1974-75; mem. adv. coun. U. Notre Dame Law Sch., 1982-2000, trustee U. Notre Dame, 2001—; chmn. Cath. Diocese Tulsa Fund for Future, 1998—; bd. dirs. legal counsel Tulsa Area United Way, 1986—; mem. pres.'s coun. Regis Coll., 1986—; Okla. chmn. Lawyers for Bush, 2000. Capt. U.S. Army, 1965-67. Mem. Okla. Bar Assn., Mich. Bar Assn., Met. Tulsa C. of C. (bd. dirs. 1992—), Summit Club, Southern Hills Country Club, Club Ltd., Knights of Malta, Knights of the Holy Sepulchre. Roman Catholic. Home: 1744 E 29th St Tulsa OK 74114-5402 Office: First Place Tower 15 E 5th St Ste 3300 Tulsa OK 74103-4340

BIONDI, LAWRENCE, academic administrator, priest; b. Chgo., Dec. 15, 1938; s. Hugo and Albertina (Marchetti) B. BA, Loyola U., Chgo., 1962, Ph.L., 1964, M.Div., S.T.L., Loyola U., Chgo., 1971; MS, Georgetown U., 1966, PhD in Socioloinguistics, 1975. Ordained priest Roman Cath. Ch., 1970. Joined Soc. Jesus; asst. prof. sociolinguistics Loyola U., Chgo., 1974-79, assoc. prof., 1979-81, prof., 1982-87, dean Coll. Arts and Scis., 1980-87; pres. St. Louis U., 1987—. Mem. Joint Commn. on Accreditation of Health Care Orgs., 1998—. Author: The Italian-American Child: His Sociolinguistic Acculturation, 1975, Poland's Solidarity Movement, 1984; editor: Poland's Church-State Relations in the 1980s, 1980, Spain's Church-State Relations, 1982. Trustee Xavier U., 1981-87, Loyola Coll., Balt., 1988-94, Santa Clara U., 1988-98, Kenrick-Glennon Sem., 1988-94, St. Louis U., 1982—, Loyola U., Chgo., 1988-97; bd. dirs. Epilepsy Found. Am., 1985-95, Civic Progress, St. Louis, 1987—, Regional Commerce and Growth Assn., 1987—, Mo. Bot. Gardens, 1987—, St. Louis Zoo, 1994, St. Louis Symphony, 1994, Harry S. Truman Inst. for Nat. and Internat. Affairs, 1987—, Tenet Health Care Sys., 1998—, St. Louis Sci. Ctr., 2000—, Boys Hope Girls Hope, 1996—, St. Louis Art Mus., 1997—, Grand Ctr., St. Louis, 1987—. Mellon grantee, 1974, 75, 76, 82; Humanitarian of Yr., Arthritis Found., 1999; Leon R. Strauss Urban Pioneer award, 2001. Mem. Linguistic Soc. Am., MLA, Am. Anthrop. Assn.; Knight of Italian Order of Merit. Office: St Louis U 221 N Grand Blvd Saint Louis MO 63103-2006 Office Phone: 314-977-7777.*

BIONDI, MANFRED ANTHONY, physicist; b. Carlstadt, NJ, Mar. 5, 1924; s. Manfred Anthony and Helen Biondi; m. Elaine Theresa Leitkam, May 12, 1952; children: David Mark, George Philip BS in Physics, MIT, 1944, PhD, 1949. Research assoc. MIT, Cambridge, 1948-49; with Westinghouse Research Labs, Pitts., 1949-60, adv. physicist, 1952-57, mgr. physics dept., 1957-60; prof. physics U. Pitts., 1960-86, prof. emeritus, 1987—; also dir. Atomic Scis. Inst., 1968-79; exchange prof. U. Paris, 1976-86. Trustee Upper Atmosphere Rsch. Corp.; mem. adv. com. Army Rsch. Office, Durham, N.C., NAS, 1962-64; mem. exec. coun. Fedn. Am. Scientists, 1966-68; mem. adv. panel physics NSF, 1970-72; mem. Army basic rsch. steering com. NRC, 1985-88, chmn., 1987-88. Mem. editl. bd. Jour. Applied Physics, 1966-68. Served with USNR, 1943-46. Fellow AAAS, Am. Phys. Soc. (chmn. div. electron and atomic physics 1957, chmn. gaseous electronics conf. 1962-64, Davisson-Germer prize 1984); mem. Am. Geophys. Union, Earth and Sky (adv. bd. 1992-94). Office: U Pitts Dept Physics And Astro Pittsburgh PA 15260 Home: 4953 Cline Hollow Rd Apt 233 Murrysville PA 15668-1591 Office Phone: 412-624-9287. Business E-Mail: biondi@pitt.edu.

BIPPUS, DAVID PAUL, manufacturing executive; b. Evansville, Ind., Nov. 29, 1949; s. James Paul and Mary Louise (Elder) B.; m. Kohnne Susann Heikens, Aug. 28, 1971; 1 child, Laura. BS, Iowa State U., 1971; MBA with honors, Boston U., 1975. Cert. CPCU. Tech. mgr. Ill. Dept. Transp., Springfield, 1976; asst. dir. planning Horace Mann Ins. Co., Springfield, 1976-79; mgr. fin. planning Hydro-Transmission div. Sundstrand Corp., Ames, Iowa, 1979-82; controller Hydraulics div. Sundstrand Corp., Rockford, Ill., 1982-84; v.p. fin., sec., treas. Suntec Industries, Inc., Rockford, 1984-89, v.p. ops., sec., treas., 1989-94; corp. controller Reliant Industries, Inc., Rock Falls, Ill., 1994, CFO, 1995-99; v.p. fin. and info. tech. Haldex Hydraulics, Co., 1999—. Instr. Lincoln Land Community Coll., Springfield, 1976-78. Bd. dirs. New Am. Theater, Rockford, 1991-97, pres., 1993-95; bd. dirs. Parents for Gifted Edn., Rockford, 1989-91; bd. dirs. Rockford Civic New Comers, 1982-85; mem. Story County Planning and Zoning Commn.; mem. ch. coun. Zion Luth. Ch., 1998-2001, pres., 2000-2001. 1st lt. U.S. Army, 1972-76. Mem. Fin. Exec. Inst. (bd. dirs. local chpt. 1989—, pres. 1993-94), Soc. of CPCU's, Nat. Assn. Accts., Am. Legion, Forest Hills Country Club. Republican. Avocations: photography, woodworking. Home: 113 Rivers Edge Dr Cherry Valley IL 61016-8802 Office: Haldex Hydraulics Co 2222 15th St Rockford IL 61104-7313

BIRBAHADUR, DINDIAL, secondary school educator; b. Albion Estate, Guyana, Oct. 28, 1944; came to the U.S., 1980; s. Pandit and Mangree Birbahadur; m. Rabby Devi Jaikaran, Feb. 23, 1969; 1 child, Devendra. BA, U. Guyana, 1971, diploma in edn., 1972; advanced diploma in ednl. studies, U. Leeds., 1976; MEd, U. V.I., 1984. Elem. tchr. Dept. Edn., Guyana, 1963-71, secondary tchr., 1971-74; math. lectr. Lilian Dewar Coll. Edn., Guyana, 1974-80; secondary math. tchr. V.I. Dept. Edn., 1980-89, master tchr., 1989—, chmn. math. dept., 1986—99, registrar/sys. analyst, 1999—. Math. lectr. U. Guyana, 1975-80; instr. U. V.I., 1981-89; math. examiner Caribbean Examination Coun., Barbados, 1978-80; statis. advisor U. V.I., 1982—; mem. Territorial Tech. Com., V.I., 1994—; state coord. for Presdl. award in elem. and secondary math. Author: Use of Objective Testing in Mathematics, 1976. Fellow Govt. of U.K., 1975; recipient Presdl. award for excellence in math. teaching Pres. of U.S., 1995. Mem. Nat. Coun. Tchrs. Math., Math. Assn. Am., V.I. Math. Tchrs. Assn., St. Croix Fedn. Tchrs., Coun. Presdl. Awardees in Math., Lions. Avocations: reading, playing chess, swimming, fishing, touring. Home: PO Box 2811 Frederiksted VI 00841-2811 Office: Arthur A Richards Jr High 20 & 21 Stoney Ground Frederiksted VI 00840 Personal E-mail: dbirbah@yahoo.com.

BIRCH, ADOLPHO A., JR., retired state supreme court justice; b. Washington, Sept. 22, 1932; 3 children. Attended, Lincoln U., Pa., 1950—52; BA, JD, Howard U., 1956. Bar: Tenn. 1957. Pvt. practice, Nashville, 1958—66; asst. pub. defender Davidson County, 1963—66, asst. dist. atty., 1966—69; judge Davidson County Gen. Sessions Ct., 1969—78, Tenn. Criminal Ct. (20th Jud. Dist.), 1978—87; presiding judge Trial Cts. of Davidson County, 1981—82; mem. Ct. of the Judiciary, 1983—86; former judge Tenn. Ct. Criminal Appeals; chief justice Tenn. Supreme Ct., Nashville, 1996—97, assoc. justice, 1994—2006. Former assoc. prof. legal medicine Meharry Medical Coll.; former law lecturer Fisk U., Tenn. State U.; assoc. prof. Nashville Sch. of Law, 1991—; disting. jurist-in-residence U. Memphis. Mem. Harvard Law Review, 1954—56. With USNR, 1956—58. Mem.: ABA, Nat. Bar Assn. Jud. Coun., Napier Lobby Bar Assn. (past pres.), Nashville Bar Assn., Tenn. Bar Assn., Nat. Bar Assn.*

BIRCH, IAN, editor-in-chief; With EMAP, London, 1984—90, 1994—2004; editor-in-chief Us, Wenner Media, 1990—94; editl. dir. Heat, EMAP, London, Closer, EMAP, London; editor-in-chief TV Guide Mag. Gemstar - TV Guide Internat. Inc., NYC, 2004—, exec. v.p., chief content editor, 2006—. Mem.: British Soc. Mag. Editors (chair). Office: Gemstar TV Guide Internat Inc 4th Floor 1211 Avenue of the Americas 28th Fl New York NY 10036 Office Phone: 212-852-7500. Office Fax: 212-852-7323.*

BIRCH, LORNA MAY, geriatrician; b. Grand Bahamas, May 18, 1970; d. Lloyd Moore and Laurel Maude McFarlane; m. Canute Robert Birch; children: Alexa, Dorian. BA in Biology, Wesleyan U., Middletown, Conn., 1992; MD, SUNY, Stony Brook, 1997. Diplomate Am. Bd. Internal Medicine, cert. added qualifications in geriatric medicine Am. Bd. Internal Medicine. Staff physician Sarah Neuman Ctr. for Health Care and Rehab., Mamaroneck, NY, 2001—05; clin. instr. medicine Albert Einstein Coll. Medicine, Bronx, NY, 2001—05; staff physician Alexian Brothers Cmty. Svcs., Chattanooga, 2005—; clin. instr. medicine U. Tenn. Health Sci. Ctr., Memphis, 2006—. Asst. edn. sec. Duramis Seventh-Day Adventist Ch., Bklyn., 2003—05. Named Resident of Yr. Ambulatory Care, Montefiore Med. Ctr., Bronx, 2000. Mem.: ACP, Am. Geriatric Soc. Adventist. Avocations: gardening, reading. Home: 7720 Tranquility Dr Ooltewah TN 37363

BIRCH, STANLEY FRANCIS, JR., federal judge; b. Langley Field, Va., Aug. 29, 1945; BA, U. Va., 1967; JD, Emory U., Atlanta, 1970, LLM in Taxation, 1976. Law clk. to Hon. Judge Sidney O. Smith Jr. US Dist. Ct. (no. dist.) Ga., 1972—74; mem. firm Greer, Sartain & Carey, Gainesville, Ga., 1974—76, Deal, Birch, Jarrard & Link, Gainesville, 1976—83, Birch, Hartness & Link, Gainesville, 1983—85, Vaughan, Davis, Birch & Murphy, Atlanta, 1984—90; judge US Ct. Appeals (11th cir.), Atlanta, 1990—. Lt. US Army, 1970—72. Mem.: Lawyers Club Atlanta, 11th Cir. Hist. Soc., Gainesville Northeastern Bar Assn., Atlanta Bar Assn., Ga. Bar Found., State Bar Ga., Calvert Hall Alumni Assn., Emory U. Sch. Law Alumni Assn. (past pres.), U. Va. Alumni Assn., Ga. Legal History Found., Old Warhorse Lawyers Club, Theta Delta Chi. Office: US Ct Appeals 11th Cir 56 Forsyth St NW Atlanta GA 30303*

BIRCHER, ANDREA URSULA, retired psychiatric mental health clinical nurse specialist; b. Bern, Switzerland, Mar. 6, 1928; arrived in US, 1947; d. Franklin E. Bircher and Hedy E. Bircher-Rey. Diploma, Knapp Coll. Nursing, Santa Barbara, Calif., 1957; BS, U. Calif., San Francisco, 1961, MS, 1962; PhD, U. Calif., Berkeley, 1966. RN. Staff nurse, head nurse Cottage Hosp., Santa Barbara, 1957—58; psychiat. nurse, jr., sr. Langley-Porter Neuropsychiatric Inst., San Francisco, 1958—66; asst. prof. U. Ill. Coll. Nursing, Chgo., 1966-72; prof. U. Okla. Coll. Nursing, Oklahoma City, 1972-93, prof. emeritus, 1993—. Contbr. articles to profl. jours. Mem.: ANA, AAUP, N.Am. Nursing Diagnosis Assn., Internat. Soc. Psychiat.-Mental Health Nursing, Am. Psychotherapy Assn. (diplomate), Ventura County Writers Club, Phi Kappa Phi, Sigma Theta Tau. Republican. Avocations: indoor gardening, reading, writing. Home: 1161 Cypress Point Ln Apt 201 Ventura CA 93003-6074

BIRCHFIELD, JOHN KERMIT, JR., lawyer; b. Roanoke, Va., Jan. 8, 1940; s. John Kermit and Christine (Luke) B.; m. Glenys Garnell, Nov. 14, 1964; 1 child, Guthrie Kathryn BS in Econs., Roanoke Coll., 1968; JD, U. Va., 1971. Bar: N.Y., 1972, U.S. Dist Ct. (so. dist.) N.Y., 1972, U.S. Ct. Appeals (2d cir.), 1972. Assoc. Shearman & Sterling, NYC, 1971-81; ptnr. Holtzmann, Wise & Shepard, NYC, 1981-83; sr. v.p. legal and govtl. affairs, gen. counsel Ga. Pacific Corp., Atlanta, 1983-88; mng. dir. Century Ptnrs., Atlanta, Darien, Conn., 1988—; sr. v.p., gen. counsel, corp. sec. M/A-COM, Boston, 1990-95. Chmn. and lead ind. dir. Mass. Fin. Compass Group Mutual Funds, 1998—; bd. dirs. Intermountain Industries, Inc., Mass. Fin. Offshore Funds, Displaytech, Inc., chmn., 1996—2001; bd. dirs. Dessin Fourir Co.; former chmn. bd. dirs. Chas. P. Young Co.; chmn. bd. dirs. Dairy Mart Convenience Stores, Inc., 1999—2003. Author: How to Borrow on the Eurodollar Market, 1981, The Multinational Joint Venture, 1981. Chmn. adv. bd. Park Pride, 1986-90; bd. dirs., exec. com. Atlanta Ballet, 1984-88, chmn., 1987-88, vice chmn., 1986-87; bd. dirs. Atlanta Music Festival Assn., 1984-90, Friends Piedmont Hosp., 1985-90; bd. dirs., exec. com., treas. Assn. Am.-Indian Affairs, 1983-86; bd. dirs. High Mus. Art, 1986-91, exec. com., 1988-89; bd. visitors Emory U., 1985-88, bd. dirs. Emory U. Mus. Art and Archaeology, 1988-92; bd. dirs., chmn. collections com. Cape Ann Hist. Assn., 1993—; trustee Roanoke Coll., 1988—, Chatham Hall, 1988-94. Mem. ABA, Atlanta Bar Assn., Assn. Bar City N.Y., N.Y. State Bar Assn., Am. Law Inst., Am. Arbitration Assn., Racquet and Tennis Club, India House Club, Piedmont Driving Club, Farmington Country Club, Shendoah Club, Annisquam Yacht Club, Union Boat Club, Somerset Club. Home: Cranberry Hill 33 Way Rd Gloucester MA 01930-4315 Business E-Mail: kermitb@displaytech.com.

BIRD, ANDY, film company executive; BA with honors, U. Newcastle Upon Tyne, Eng., 1985. Breakfast show prodr. Piccadilly Radio, Manchester, England; with Music Box Virgin Broadcasting Co., London, head programming Radio Radio; various radio and TV positions, 1989—94; head Unique TV Unique Broadcasting, 1992; sr. v.p., gen. mgr. Turner Entertainment Networks Ltd. Time Warner, 1994—2000, pres. TBS Internat., 2000—04; pres. Walt Disney Internat., Burbank, Calif., 2004—. Office: Walt Disney Co 500 S Buena Vista St Burbank CA 91521-0001*

BIRD, CAROLINE, author; b. NYC, Apr. 15, 1915; d. Hobart Stanley and Ida (Brattrud) B.; m. Edward A. Menuez, June 8, 1934 (div. Dec. 1945); 1 dau., Carol (Mrs. John Paul Barach); m. John Thomas Mahoney, Jan. 5, 1957 (dec. 1981); 1 son, John Thomas. Student, Vassar Coll., 1931-34; BA, U. Toledo, 1938; MA, U. Wis., 1939; LHD (hon.), Keene State U., 1988. Desk editor N.Y. Jour. Commerce, 1943-44; editl. rschr. Newsweek mag., NYC, 1942-43, Fortune mag., NYC, 1944-46; with Dudley-Anderson-Yutzy, pub. relations, NYC, 1947-68; Froman Disting. prof. Russell Sage Coll., 1972-73; Mather prof. Case Western Res. U., Cleve., 1977. Author: The Invisible Scar, 1966, Born Female, 1968, rev. edit., 1970, The Crowding Syndrome, 1972, Everything a Woman Needs to Know to Get Paid What She's Worth, 1973, rev., 1982, The Case Against College, 1975, Enterprising Women, 1976, What Women Want, 1979, The Two-Paycheck Marriage, 1979, The Good Years, 1983, Second Careers, 1992, Lives of Our Own, 1995; chief writer: The Spirit of Houston, 1978; also articles in nat. mags. Mem. review bd. Dept. State, 1974. Mem. Am. Soc. Journalists and Authors, Am. Sociol. Assn. Address: The Meadows 2088 Coley Davis Rd 30 Nashville TN 37221

BIRD, DAVID R., lawyer; b. June 7, 1949; BS, Brigham Young U., 1973, JD, 1977. Bar: Utah 1977, U.S. Ct. Appeals (10th Cir.) 1978, U.S. Dist. Ct. (Dist. Utah) 1977, U.S. Supreme Ct. 1987. Atty., shareholder environ., energy and natural resources dept. Parsons, Behle & Latimer, Salt Lake City. Spkr. in field. Co-author: Utah Environmental and Land Use Permits and Approval Manual, 1980, Brownfields Law and Practice, 2003, others. Bd. dirs. Utah Found.; trustee Barrick Mercer Gold Mine Found.; mem. workers compensation adv. coun. Labor Commn.; mem. environ. adv. coun. Salt Lake Valley Health Dept.; past chair legis. affairs com. Salt Lake Area C. of C. Mem.: ABA, Utah State Bar (mem. legis. affairs com. 1979—2001, chmn. water com. 1981—83, environ. law com. 1983—85, energy and natural resources sect. 1988—89, pres.-elect 2004, jud. coun., pres. 2005), Utah Mfrs. Assn. (mem. legis. com., environ. com.), Utah Mining Assn. (exec. com., tax com., environment com.), Boy Scouts Am., Phi Kappa Phi. Office: Parsons Behle & Latimer One Utah Ctr 201 S Main St Ste 1800 PO Box 45898 Salt Lake City UT 84145-0898 Office Phone: 801-532-1234. Office Fax: 801-536-6111. E-mail: dbird@pblutah.com.*

BIRD, HECTOR RAMÓN, child psychiatrist, psychoanalyst, educator; b. San Juan, P.R., Feb. 5, 1939; s. Hector F. and Yvette (Baker) B.; m. Sandra Lopez, May 23, 1970; 1 child, Alejandra Y. BA, U. Mich., 1960; MD, Yale U., 1965; cert. in psychiatry and child psychiatry, Columbia U., 1972; cert. in psychoanalysis, W.A. White Inst., NYC. Diplomate Am. Bd. Psychiatry and Neurology. Asst. dir. child psychiatry St. Luke's Hosp., NYC, 1972-78; dir. tng. in child psychiatry Columbia U., NYC, 1978-80, prof. clin. psychiatry, 1984—; dir. child psychiatry U. P.R. Med. Sch., San Juan, 1980-86; dep. dir. child psychiatry N.Y. State Psychiat. Inst., NYC, 1986—2006. Contbr. articles to profl. jours. Founding dir., pres. bd. dirs. Teatro de la Opera, San Juan, 1982-86; dir. Pro-Arte Musical, San Juan, 1982-86. Lt. USN, 1966-68. Recipient Profl. Achievement award Boricua Coll., N.Y.C., 1987, Wilfred C. Hulse Meml. award N.Y. Coun. on Child and Adolescent Psychiatry, 2001. Fellow Am. Acad. Child and Adolescent Psychiatry, Am. Acad. Psychoanalysis (trustee); mem. Am. Psychopathological Assn., Soc. Rsch. in Child and Adolescent Psychopathology, William A. White Psychoanalytic Soc. Roman Catholic. Office: 424 West End Ave 20E New York NY 10024 Office Phone: 212-874-5311. Personal E-mail: hecbird@aol.com.

BIRD, KAI, journalist, historian; b. Eugene, Oreg., Sept. 2, 1951; s. Eugene Hall and Jerine Newhouse Bird; m. Susan Gloria Goldmark, June 7, 1975; 1 child, Joshua Kodai Goldmark. BA in History, Carleton Coll., 1973; MS in Journalism, Northwestern U., 1975. Assoc. editor Newsweek Internat., NYC, 1977, The Nation, NYC, 1978-82, columnist, 1983-86, contbg. editor, 1987—. Author: The Chairman: John J. McCloy, The Making of the American Establishment, 1992, The Color of Truth: McGeorge Bundy & William Bundy, Brothers in Arms, 1998; co-author (with Martin J. Sherwin): American Prometheus: The Triumph and Tragedy of J. Robert Oppenheimer 2005 (Nat. Book Critics Circle award for biography 2005, Pulitzer Prize for biography, 2006); co-editor: (anthology) Hiroshima's Shadow: Writings on the Denial of History and the Smithsonian Controversy, 1998. Fellow Thomas J. Watson Found., Providence, 1973-74, John Simon Guggenheim Found., N.Y.C., 1984, Alicia Patterson Journalism Found., Washington, 1984-85, German Marshall Fund, Washington, 1986-87, John D. and Catherine T. Macarthur Found., 1993-95; residency fellow Rockefeller Found. Study Ctr., Bellagio, Italy, 1997, Woodrow Wilson Internat. Ctr. for Scholars, 2001-02. Home: 1914 Biltmore St NW Washington DC 20009-1510 E-mail: Kai@igc.org.

BIRD, LARRY JOE, professional sports team executive, retired professional basketball player; b. West Baden, Ind., Dec. 7, 1956; s. Joe and Georgia B; m. Dinah Mattingly Oct. 1, 1989; children: Corrie, Connor. Student, Ind. U., 1974, Northwood Inst., West Baden, Ind., 1974; BS, Ind. State U., 1979. Player Boston Celtics, 1979—92, spl. asst. to exec. v.p., 1992—97; head coach Ind. Pacers, Indpls., 1997—2000, pres. basketball ops., 2003—. Mem. US Men's Basketball Team World Univ. Games (gold medal), Sophia, Bulgaria, 1977, Barcelona Olympic Games (gold medal), Spain, 1992. Author: (with Bob Ryan) Drive, 1989; actor (film) Blue Chips, 1994. Named Collegiate Player of Yr., AP, UPI and Nat. Assn. Coaches, 1979, NBA Rookie of Yr., 1980, NBA All-Star Game MVP, 1982, NBA Finals MVP, 1984, 86, NBA MVP, 1984, 85, 86; named to NBA All-Rookie team, 1980, NBA All-Star Team, 1980-88, 90-92, All-NBA 1st team, 1980-88, NBA All-Def. 2nd team, 1982-84, NBA All-NBA 2nd team, 1990, Basketball Hall of Fame, 1998; named one of 50 Greatest Players in NBA hist., 1996. Achievements include winning NBA Championships as a member of the Celtics, 1981, 84, 86. Office: Ind Pacers 125 S Pennsylvania St Indianapolis IN 46204*

BIRD, LEWIS L., III, apparel executive; Fin. mgmt. position BayBanks, Inc., Ford Motor Co., AlliedSignal Inc., dir. bus. analysis and planning, 1998—99; v.p. fin. and ops. Gateway, Inc., 1999—2001; CFO Old Navy divsn. Gap Inc., 2001—03, COO North Am. divsn., 2003—05, exec. v.p. new bus. devel., 2005—06; pres. subsidiaries Nike, Inc., Beaverton, Oreg., 2006—. Office: Nike Inc One Bowerman Dr Beaverton OR 97005-6453 Office Phone: 503-671-6453.*

BIRD, MARY LYNNE MILLER, professional society administrator; b. Buffalo, Feb. 25, 1934; d. Joseph William and Mildred Dorothy (Wallette) Miller; m. Thomas Edward Bird, Aug. 23, 1958; children: Matthew David, Lisa Bronwen. AB magna cum laude, Syracuse U., 1956; postgrad., Columbia U., 1956-58. Mem. rsch. staff Ctr. for Rsch. in Personality, Harvard U., Cambridge, Mass., 1959-62, Ctr. Internat. Studies, Princeton (N.J.) U., 1962-66, Inst. Internat. Social Rsch., Princeton, 1965, Sch. Internat. Affairs, Columbia U., NYC, 1966-67, Coun. Fgn. Rels., NYC, 1967-69, Twentieth Century Fund, NYC, 1969-72; asst. to pres. World Policy Inst., NYC, 1972-74; dir. devel. Fund for Peace, NYC, 1974-78; dir. fellows program Exec. Council Fgn. Diplomats, NYC, 1978-79; dir. devel. Engender Health, NYC, 1979—83; exec. dir. Am. Geog. Soc., NYC, 1983—. Cons. Fedn. Am. Scientists, Washington, 1974-75. Trustee Bel

Canto Opera Co., NYC, 1975—90. Maxwell Citizenship scholar Syracuse U., 1952-56. Fellow AAAS; mem. NAS (com. on geography, liaison mem. 1984-2000), Assn. Am. Geographers, Soc. Woman Geographers, Inst. for Current World Affairs (trustee), Nat. Coun. Geog. Edn., 100-Yr. Assn. N.Y., Conf. Latin Americanist Geographers, Planning Com. for Nat. Assessment on Ednl. Progress in Geography, Nat. Music Theatre Network (bd. dirs.), St. David's Soc. (past pres.), Colonial Dames Am., Daus. of Colonial Wars, Daus. of 1812, Pilgrims of U.S., Mid-Atlantic Club N.Y.C. (bd. dirs.), Princeton Club, Welsh Women's Club NY, Am. Soc. Assn. Execs., The Bohemians, Phi Beta Kappa, Phi Kappa Phi, Eta Pi Upsilon, Pi Beta Phi. Avocations: singing, sailing. Office Phone: 212-422-5456. Business E-Mail: MLBird@amergeog.org.

BIRD, PAUL S., lawyer; b. Nov. 21, 1960; BA, Yale U., 1983, JD, 1987. Bar: NY 1989, Conn. 1989, Paris 1992. Law clerk to Hon. Robert W. Sweet US Dist. Ct., So. Dist. NY, 1987—88; assoc. Debevoise & Plimpton LLP, NYC, Paris, 1988—95, ptnr. NYC, 1995—, co-head Mergers & Acquisitions Group. Mem.: ABA, Assn. Bar of City NY, Internat. Bar Assn. Office: Debevoise & Plimpton LLP 919 Third Ave New York NY 10022 Office Phone: 212-909-6435. E-mail: psbird@debevoise.com.

BIRD, ROBERT BYRON, chemical engineering educator, author; b. Bryan, Tex., Feb. 5, 1924; s. Byron and Ethel (Antrim) Bird. Student, U. Md., 1941—43; BS, U. Ill., 1947; PhD, U. Wis., 1950; postdoctoral fellow, U. Amsterdam, 1950—51; DEng (hon.), Lehigh U., 1972, Washington U., 1973, Tech. U. Delft, Holland, 1977, Colo. Sch. Mines, 1986; ScD (hon.), Clarkson U., 1980, The Technion, Israel, 1993, Tex. A&M U., 1999; D in engring. sci. (hon.), Eidgenössische Tech. Hochschule, Zürich, Switzerland, 1994; DrEngring (hon.), Kyoto U., Japan, 1996; DSc (hon.), Iowa State U., 2007. Asst. prof. chemistry Cornell U., 1952—53, Debye lectr., 1973, Julian C. Smith lectr., 1988; rsch. chemist DuPont Exptl. Sta., 1953; mem. faculty U. Wis., 1951—52, 1953—57, prof. chem. engring., 1957—92, C.F. Burgess distinguished prof. chem. engring., 1968—72, John D. MacArthur prof., 1982—92, Vilas research prof., 1972—92, chmn. dept., 1964—68, emeritus prof., 1992—; Burgers prof. Technische Univ. Delft, The Netherlands, 1994. Vis. prof. U. Calif., Berkeley, 1977, Univ. Catholique de Louvain, Belgium, 1994; D. L. Katz lectr. U. Mich., 1971; W. N. Lacey lectr. Calif. Inst. Tech., 1974; K. Wohl Meml. lectr. U. Del., 1977; W. K. Lewis lectr. MIT, 1982; R. H. Wilhelm lectr. Princeton U., 1991; G. N. Lewis lectr. U. Calif., Berkeley, 1993; Ascher Shapiro lectr. MIT, 1997; lectr. Lectures in Sci. Humble Oil Co., 1959, 61, 64, 66; lecture tour Am. Chem. Soc., 1958, 75, Canadian Inst. Chemistry, 1961, 65; cons. to industry, 1965—90; mem. adv. panel engring. sci. divsn. NSF, 1961—64. Author (with others): Molecular Theory of Gases and Liquids, 2d printing, 1964; author: Transport Phenomena, 64th printing, 2002, Spanish edit., 1965, Czech edit., 1966, Italian edit., 1970, Russian edit., 1974, Chinese edit., 1990, revised 2d English edit., 2007, Chinese translation, 2004, Portuguese edit., 2004, Spanish edit., 2006, Een Goed Begin: A Contemporary Dutch Reader, 1963, 2d edit., 1971, Comprehending Technical Japanese, 1975, Chinese edit., 1985, Dynamics of Polymeric Liquids, Vol. 1, Fluid Mechanics, Vol. 2, Kinetic Theory, 1977, 2d edit., 1987, Japanese transl. Vol. 1, 1999, Vol. 2, 2004, Reading Dutch: Fifteen Annotated Stories from the Low Countries, 1985, Basic Technical Japanese, 1990, Technical Japanese Supplements: Polymer Science and Engineering, 1995, 100 Years of Chemical Engineering at the University of Wisconsin, 2005, also numerous rsch. publs.; Am. editor (with others) Applied Sci. Rsch., 1969—86, 1989—98; mem. adv. bd.: Indsl. and Engring. Chemistry, 1970—72, mem. editl. bd.: Jour. Non-Newtonian Fluid Mechanics, 1975—; contbr. Served to 1st lt. AUS, 1943—46. Decorated Bronze Star, knight Order Orange Nassau Netherlands; recipient Curtis McGraw award, Am. Assn. Engring. Edn., 1959, Westinghouse award, 1960, Corcoran award, 1987, Centennial Medallion, 1993, Nat. Medal Sci., 1987; Fulbright fellow, Holland, 1950, Guggenheim fellow, 1958, Fulbright lectr., 1958, Japan, 1962—63, Sarajevo, Yugoslavia, 1972. Fellow: AIChE (William H. Walker award 1962, Profl. Progress award 1965, Warren K. Lewis award 1974, Founders award 1989, Inst. Lect. award 1992 1992), Am. Acad. Arts and Scis., Am. Phys. Soc.; mem.: NAE, NAS, Royal Flemish Acad. Belgium for Scis and Arts (fgn.), Royal Dutch Acad. Scis. (fgn.), Soc. Rheology, Soc. Chem. Engrs. Japan (hon.), Am. Chem. Soc. (chmn. Wis. sect. 1966, unrestricted rsch. grant Petroleum Rsch. Fund 1963), Am. Assn. Netherlandic Studies, Wis. Acad. Scis., Arts and Letters, Am. Acad. Mechanics, Arts and Letters, Sigma Tau, Omicron Delta Kappa, Phi Kappa Phi, Alpha Chi Sigma, Tau Beta Pi, Sigma Xi (v.p. Wis. sect. 1959—60), Phi Beta Kappa. Office: U Wis Dept Chem and Biol Engring 3004 Engring Hall 1415 Engineering Dr Madison WI 53706-1607 Business E-Mail: bird@engr.wisc.edu.

BIRD, SAMUEL N., judge; b. El Dorado, Ark., Jan. 19, 1940; m. LeAnne McElveen; 2 children. BS, Fla. State U., 1962; JD, U. Ark., 1970. Commd. 2d lt. USAF, 1962, advanced through ranks to capt., 1966, with Air Force Security Svc. Turkey, resigned, 1967; ptnr. Williamson, Ball & Bird, Monticello, Ark., 1970-91; cir. chancery judge 10th Jud. Cir., 1991—97; assoc. judge Ark. Ct. of Appeals, Little Rock, 1997—. Pres. S.E. Ark. Legal Inst., 1974. Pres. Monticello Rotary, 1976-77. Home: 10119 Garrison Rd Little Rock AR 72223 Office Phone: 501-682-7477. Business E-Mail: sam.bird@arkansas.gov.

BIRD, SHELLEY, communications executive; MA in Communication Mgmt., U. South Australia. Cert. bus. communicator Internat. Assn. Bus. Communicators. With J. Walter Thompson, Toronto, Canada; mgmt. positions mktg. and comm. Asia Pacific region Motorola Electronics; with Hill and Knowlton, Hong Kong, dep. gen. mgr. Singapore office; v.p. mktg. comm. and pub. rels. Philips Consumer Comm.; chief comm. officer NCR Corp.; exec. v.p. comm. Cardinal Health. Tchr. retail mgmt. Named Corp. PR Profl. of Yr., PR News, 2004. Office: Cardinal Health 7000 Cardinal Pl Dublin OH 43017

BIRD, SUE (SUZANNE BRIGIT BIRD), professional basketball player; b. Syosset, NY, Oct. 16, 1980; d. Herschel and Nancy Bird. Grad. in Comm. Sci., U. Conn., 2002. Guard Seattle Storm, 2002—. Member USA Basketball Women's Sr. Nat. Team, 2002, 04. Named Naismith Player of Yr., 2002, AP Player of Yr., 2002, Best Female Coll. Athlete, ESPY Awards, 2002; named to All-WNBA First Team, 2002, 2003, 2005, WNBA Western Conf. All-Star Team, 2002, 2003, 2007; recipient Wade Trophy, 2002, Honda Award for Women's Coll. Basketball Player of Yr., 2002. Achievements include being a member of the NCAA Divsn. 1 Nat. Championship Team, U. Conn., 2000, 02; member, US Women's Basketball FIBA World Championship Gold Medal Team, 2002; selected as the number 1 overall pick in the 2002 WNBA Draft; member, US Women's Basketball Team, Athens Olympics, 2004. Office: Seattle Storm 351 Elliott Ave W Ste 500 Seattle WA 98119*

BIRD, TERRY W., lawyer; b. LA, Feb. 11, 1946; BA, Stanford U., Calif., 1967; JD, UCLA, 1970. Bar: Calif. 1970. Law clk. Calif. Ct. Appeals (2nd dist.), 1970—72; asst. US atty., 1972—77; prin. atty. Bird, Marella, Boxer, Wolpert, Nessim, Drooks & Lincenberg, LA. Mem. 9th Cir. Jud. Conf. Magistrates Adv. Com., 1988—91, 9th Cir. Exec. Com., 1989—93, 9th Cir. Gender Bias Task Force, 1991—94, 9th Cir. Adv. Bd., 2002—05. Mem.: Am. Coll. Trial Lawyers, Inns of Ct. (pres. complex litig. 1993—94), Assn. Bus. Trial Lawyers (bd. dirs. 1991—93), LA County Bar Assn. (chmn. fed. cts. com. 1991—95), ABA (mem. white collar crime com.). Office: Bird Marella Boxer Wolpert Nessim Drooks & Lincenberg PC 23rd Fl 1875 Century Pk E Los Angeles CA 90067-2561 Office Phone: 310-201-2100. Office Fax: 310-201-2110.

BIRD, THOMAS EDWARD, foreign language and literature educator; s. Harry J. and Paula W. (Boyce) B.; m. Mary Lynne Miller, Aug. 23, 1958; children: Matthew David, Lisa Bronwen. AB magna cum laude, Syracuse U., 1956; postgrad., Harvard U., 1958-59; MA, Middlebury Coll., 1960; AM, Princeton U., 1965; postgrad., Warsaw U., 1990—. Lectr., assoc. prof. Slavic langs. and lit. Queens Coll., CUNY, Flushing, 1965—; dir., co-dir. Ctr. Jewish Studies, 1996-98. Bd. dirs. Pax Romana, Benyumin Shekhter Found., Cymdeithas Madoc, St. David's Soc., St. Nicholas Soc., Soc. of Colonial Wars, chmn. Flag Svc. Com., 1997—. Gen. Soc. of the War of 1812 (pres. New York State Soc.), Soc. of Mayflower Descendants, Nat. Gavel Soc., Vet. Corps Art. NY State. Author: Patriarch Maximos IV, 1964; editor: Aspects of Religion in the Soviet Union, 1971, The Hard Life of Jura Odcesty, 1980, The 1863 Uprising in Byelorussia, 1980, Skovoroda: An Anthology, 1994, Zapisy; mem. editl. bd. Diakonia, Nationalities Papers, Polish Rev. Served with US Army (Military Intelligence) 1957-62. Recipient George Arents Library award, Isaiah award for interreligious dialogue, Amer. Jewish Com., 1996, Maxwell Citizenship Scholar, 1952-56, NDFL fellow, 1962-65, Woodrow Wilson Fell., 1965, Presdl. Tchg. Awd., 1991. Fellow Soc. for Values in Higher Edn., Phi Beta Kappa Soc.; mem. AAUP, MLA, SAR, Amer. Assn. for Advancement Slavic Studies, Am. Assn. Tchrs. Slavic and East European Langs., Amer Coun.Tchrs. Russian, Columbia U. Faculty Seminars, Belarusan Inst. Arts and Scis., Internat. Assn. Belarusan Studies (v.p.), Polish Inst. Arts and Scis., Russian-American Scholars Assn., Shevchenko Scientific Soc., Ukrainian Acad. Arts and Scis., Hon. Soc. Cymmrodorion, Dobro Slovo, Princeton Club N.Y., Nassau Club Princeton, Sons Am. Colonists (gov. gen. 2007—), Colonial Order of the Acorn, Phi Beta Kappa, Phi Kappa Alpha. Office: Queens Coll CUNY Rufus King Hall 65-30 Kissena Blvd Flushing NY 11367-1597 Office Phone: 718-997-5982.

BIRD, VINCENT G., urologist, researcher, educator; b. Boston, Jan. 24, 1968; s. Patrick J. and Mary T. Bird; m. Victoria Y. Lu-Contreras, Sept. 9, 2003; children: Victoria B., Veronica I. BA in Biology, Boston U., 1991, BA in Classical Civilization, 1991; MD, SUNY, Stony Brook, 1995. Asst. prof. urology and transplant surgery U. Miami Sch. Medicine, Fla., 2002—. Tchr. Miami Dade Coll., 2006. Fellow, Endourologic Soc., 2002. Mem.: Am. Urol. Assn. (assoc.). Achievements include research in urologic disease. Office: U Miami Sch Medicine 1400 NW 10th Ave Ste 509 Miami FL 33136 Office Phone: 305-243-9935. Office Fax: 305-243-3381. Business E-Mail: vbird@med.miami.edu.

BIRD, WENDELL RALEIGH, lawyer; s. Raleigh Milton and R. Jean Bird. BA summa cum laude, Vanderbilt U., 1975; JD, Yale U., 1978. Bar: Ga. 1978, Ala. 1980, Calif. 1981, Fla. 1982, U.S. Ct. Appeals (2d, 3d, 4th, 5th, 6th, 7th, 8th, 9th, 10th and 11th cirs.) 1979-83, U.S. Supreme Ct. 1983. Law clk. to judge U.S. Ct. Appeals (4th cir.), Durham, NC, 1978-79, U.S. Ct. Appeals (5th cir.), Birmingham, Ala., 1979-80; pvt. practice San Diego, 1980-82; atty. Parker, Johnson, Cook & Dunlevie, Atlanta, 1982-86; sr. ptnr. Bird & Loechl, LLC, Atlanta, 1986—. Adj. prof. Emory U. Law Sch., Atlanta, 1985—90; lectr. Washington Non-Profit Tax Conf., 1982—. Author: The Origin of Species Revisited, 2 vols., 1987; contbg. author: Federal and State Taxation of Exempt Organizations, 1994, CCH Federal Tax Service, 1988—; mem. bd. editors Yale U. Law Jour., 1977-78, others; contbr. articles to profl. jours. Recipient Egger prize Yale U., 1978, Vanderbilt U. award, 1972. Mem.: ABA (litigation sect., taxation sect., com. on exempt orgns., past chmn. subcom. on religious orgns., past chmn. subcom. on state and local taxes, chmn. subcom. on charitable contbns., sect. on real property probate and trust, com. charitable gifts), Am. Law Inst., Ga. Bar Assn., Fla. Bar Assn., Calif. Bar Assn., Ala. Bar Assn., Phi Beta Kappa. Republican. Avocations: piano, skiing, photography, genealogy, architecture, science. Home: 92 Blackland Rd NW Atlanta GA 30342-4420 Office: Bird & Loechl LLC 1150 Monarch Plz 3414 Peachtree Rd NE Atlanta GA 30326-1153 Office Phone: 404-264-9400.

BIRDSALL, CHARLES KENNEDY, electrical engineer; b. NYC, Nov. 19, 1925; s. Charles and Irene Birdsall; m. Betty Jean Hansen, 1949 (dec.); children: Elizabeth(dec.) , Anne(dec.) , Barbara, Thomas, John; m. Virginia Pletcher, Aug. 21, 1981. BS, U. Mich., Ann Arbor, 1946, MS, 1948; PhD, Stanford U., Calif., 1951. Various microwave amplifier projects Hughes Aircraft Co., Culver City, Calif., 1951—55; leader GE Microwave Lab., Electron Physics Group, Palo Alto, Calif., 1955-59; prof. elec. engring. U. Calif., Berkeley, 1959-91; prof. U. Calif., Grad. Sch., Berkeley, 1994—. Founder Plasma Theory and Simulation Group, 1967—; founder, chmn. Energy and Resources Group, 1972—74; cons. on fusion simulations Lawrence Livermore Lab. of U. Calif., 1960—86; prof. Miller Inst. Basic Rsch. in Sci., 1963—64; sr. vis. fellow U. Reading, England, 1976; rsch. assoc. Inst. Plasma Physics Nagoya (Japan) U., 1981; co-founder Nagoya (Japan) U., Undergrad. Program Computational Engring. Sci, 2000; Chevron vis. prof. energy Calif. Inst. Tech., 1982; area coord. phys. electronics/bioelectronics, 1984—86; lectr. Plasma Sch. Internat. Ctr. for Theoretical Physics, Trieste, Italy, 1985—99; vis. prof. Inst. Plasma Physics, Nagoya U., Fusion Theory joint U.S.-Japan, 2002, Gunma U., Kiryu, Japan, 2003; Intergovtl. Personnel Act AirForce Rsch. Lab., Albuquerque, 2002—. Author: (with W.B. Bridges) Electron Dynamics of Diode Regions, 1966, (with A.B. Langdon) Plasma Physics via Computer Simulation, 1985, 91, 93, 2002, 2005, (with S. Kuhn) Bounded Plasmas, 4 vols., 1994. With USNR, 1944—46. U.S.-Japan Coop. Sci. Program grantee, 1966-67; Fulbright grantee U. Innsbruck, 1991; recipient Berkeley Citation, 1991; first recipient (with A.B. Langdon) of Dawson award for pioneering plasma simulation, 2003. Fellow IEEE (1st recipient Plasma Sci. and Applications award June 1988), AAAS, Am. Phys. Soc.; mem. Plasma Theory and Simulation Group, Energy and Resourses Group, Internat. Ctr. for Theoretical Physics, Inst. Plasma Physics, Sigma Xi, Tau Beta Pi, Eta Kappa Nu. Achievements include being the co-originator many-particle plasma simulations in two and three dimensions using cloud-in-cell/particle-in-cell methods, 1966; holder 24 patents. Office: U Calif EECS Dept Cory Hall Berkeley CA 94720-1770 Office Phone: 510-643-6631. Business E-Mail: birdsall@eecs.berkeley.edu.

BIRDSALL, MELINDA R., gynecologist; d. Charles Matthew and Nancy Virginia Ropar; m. Christopher Pennock Birdsall, Sept. 19, 1987; children: Ryan, Andrew. BS, Youngstown State U.; MD, Med. U. Ohio, Toledo. Intern in gen. surgery Med. U. Ohio; resident in ob-gyn. Loyola U./St. Francis Hosp., Chgo.; physician Hale Hosp., Haverhill, Mass., Beverly Hosp., Mass., Lahey Clinic, Burlington, Mass. Asst. prof. ob-gyn. Boston U. Med. Ctr.; mem. consulting and adv. bds. contraceptive mgmt. and menopausal health. Named one of Best Drs., Boston Mag. Fellow: ACOG; mem.: AMA, Am. Assn. Gynecol. Laparoscopists, Ipswich Country Club (bd. govs., chmn.). Achievements include research in cryoblation of the uterine cavity. Avocations: golf, skiing, running. Office: Lahey Clinic Found 1 Essex Center Dr Peabody MA 01960 Office Phone: 978-538-4620. Office Fax: 978-538-4708. E-mail: melinda_r_birdsall@lahey.org.

BIRDSALL, WILLIAM FOREST, retired librarian; b. Farmington, Minn., Oct. 30, 1937; s. Herman Elden and Mae Elizabeth (Daugherty) B.; m. Ann Elizabeth Page, Dec. 20, 1965; children— Sarah, Stephanie, Thomas BA, U. Minn., 1955, MA, 1964; PhD, U. Wis., 1973. Reference libr. Iowa State U., Ames, 1961-63; head pub. svcs. Wis. State U., La Crosse, 1965-70; asst. dir. for pub. svcs. U. Man., Winnipeg, Canada, 1973-77, assoc. dir. for pub. svcs.ervices, 1977-81; univ. libr. Dalhousie U., Halifax, N.S., Canada, 1981-97; exec. dir. Novanet, Inc., Halifax, 1998—2002; ret., 2002. Author: Myth of the Electronic Library, 1994, Understanding Telecommunications and Public Policy, 1998; contbr. articles to profl. jours. Mem. Atlantic Provinces Library Assn. (pres. 1984), Man. Library Assn. (pres. 1981), Can. Library Assn. (council 1981, 84) Home: 54 Village Crescent Bedford NS Canada B4A 1J2 Personal E-mail: billbirdsall@accesswave.ca.

BIRDSONG, ALTA MARIE, volunteer; m. Kenneth Layne Birdsong; children: Suzanne Denise Huff, Jeffrey Layne Birdsong. BBA in Acctg. magna cum laude, U. North Tex., 1955. Cost engr. Tex. Instruments, Inc., Dallas, 1955-62; part-time acct. Atlanta, 1972—. Mem. DeKalb County Cmty. Rels. Com., 1981-93, chair, 1984-87; mem. Atlanta Regional Com. Adv. Group, 1981-88, Met. Atlanta United Way, 1985-98, resource investment vol. sch. age children; chair Sch. Age Child Care Coun., 1987-90; mem. Dekalb County Task Force on Personal Care Homes, Dekalb County Task Force on Domestic Violence; mem. steering com. for bond referendum Dekalb B. Edn.; mem. Vision 2020 Governance Stakeholders ARC, 1994-95; mem. Camp Fire Boys and Girls. Recipient John H. Collier award for Camp Fire, 1991, Luther Halsey Gulick award for Camp Fire, 1993, Frederic E. Ruccius award for Camp Fire, 1993, Mortar Bd. Alumni Achievement award, 1991, Woman of Yr. award Atlanta Alumnae Panhellenic, 1983, Women Who Have Made a Difference award DeKalb YWCA, 1985, Ember award Camp Fire, 1998, Tom Murphy State Service Good Heart Vol. award, 2002. Mem.: AAUW (rec. sec. 1982—84, mem. v.p. 1984—86, pres. elect 1986—87, divsn. pres. 1987—89, assn. nominating com. 1993—97, chair 1995—97, Atlanta chpt. pres. 2001—03, co-chair Sister-to-Sister Summit 2002, chair Woman to Woman Summit 2002, Achievement award 1999), Freedoms Found. at Valley Force (sec. 1983—85, treas. 1985—87, v.p. publicity 1988—89, v.p. 1990—91, Atlanta chpt. pres. 1991—92, ea.-so. region adv. 1994—97, treas. 1999—2000, Atlanta chpt. pres. 2000—01), Atlanta Alumnae Panhellenic (v.p. 1977—78, pres. 1978—79), Atlanta Coun. Camp Fire (region fin. officer 1989—90, v.p. 1990—92, pres. 1992—94), Delta Gamma Alumnae (treas. 1972—74, Atlanta chpt. 1st v.p. 1985—87, Oxford award 1992).

BIRDSONG, GEORGE YANCY, manufacturing executive; b. Suffolk, Va., Nov. 8, 1939; s. William McLemore and Yancey (Brooking) B.; m. Sue Benton, June 10, 1961; children: Anne Cabell, David Jefferson, Charles Randolph. BA, Washington and Lee U., Lexington, Va., 1961; LLB, U. Va., 1964, diploma in basic advanced mgmt., 1968. Bar: Va. 1964. Mem. Godwin & Godwin, Suffolk, 1964-66; sec.-treas. Birdsong Peanuts divsn. Birdsong Corp., Suffolk, 1965—, exec. v.p., 1981-97, pres., 1997—99, CEO, 1999—. Bd. dirs. SunTrust Bank. Dir. Suffolk Redevel. and Housing Authority, 1966—85, chmn., 1966—83; pres. Louise Obici Meml. Hosp. Found., Suffolk, 1980—; chpt. pres. Tri-County Area Planned Parenthood, 1969—; mem. pres.'s adv. coun. Va. Wesleyan Coll., 1971—89, trustee, 1989—; mem. exec. com. Future of Hampton Roads, 1983—96; founding dir. Suffolk YMCA, 1987—91; mem adv. bd. Young Leaders Soc. of Hampton Roads, 2001—; bd. dirs. Hampton Roads United Way , 1980—84; sec., bd. dirs. Suffolk Cmty. Health Ctr., 1992—99; bd. dirs. Va. Found. Ind. Colls., 1994—. Recipient Disting. Svc. award Suffolk Jaycees, 1971, Order of the Red Triangle YMCA of South Hampton Rd., 1993, Humanitarian award Tidewater chpt. NCCJ, 1997; named 1st Citizen, Suffolk, 1997. Mem. Va. Bar Assn., Suffolk Bar Assn., Va. Mfrs. Assn. (bd. dirs. 1977-79, 87-89), Suffolk C. of C., Suffolk Sports Club, Suffolk Tennis Assn., Elks, Rotary. Methodist. Home: 608 Riverview Dr Suffolk VA 23434 Office: Birdsong Corp 612 Madison Ave Suffolk VA 23434

BIRDWELL, JAMIE, music educator, department chairman; b. Honolulu, Mar. 5, 1973; s. Sarah Jane Birdwell; m. Michelle Marie Burdett, Apr. 1997. MusB in Edn., Troy U., Ala., 1995, MS in Music Edn., 1996. Cert. instrumental music edn. Fla., 2006. Music tchr. East Gate Sch., Ozark, Ala., 1996—98; band, choir, french tchr. Dale County HS, Midland City, Ala., 1998—2001; dir. bands A. Crawford Mosley HS, Lynn Haven, Fla., 2001—. Dir.: US Pres. Bush Performance, Disney Honors performance. Mem.: Music Educators Nat. Conf., Nat. Bandmasters Assn., Fla. Bandmasters Assn. (chmn. dist. 2, exec. bd. dirs. 2003—), Phi Kappa Phi. Democrat. Roman Catholic. Avocations: reading, gardening, music, travel. Office: A Crawford Mosley HS 501 Mosley Dr Lynn Haven FL 32444 Home Phone: 850-271-5032; Office Phone: 850-872-4400 3834. Office Fax: 850-784-6311. Personal E-mail: jamiebirdwell@aol.com. Business E-Mail: birdwj@bay.k12.fl.us.

BIRDWELL, MICHELLE MARIE, music educator; b. Panama City, Fla., Nov. 22, 1974; d. Bennie Gene and Darlene Carroll Burdett; m. Jamie Birdwell, Apr. 5, 1997. MusB Edn., Troy State U., 1997, MS in Edn., 1998. Professional Teacher Certification State of Fla., 2001, State of Ala., 1998. Adminstrv. grad. asst. to dir. bands Troy (Ala.) State U. Sch. Music, 1997—98; elem. music tchr. Enterprise (Ala.) City Schs., 1999—2001; choir dir. Surfside Mid. Sch., Panama City Beach, Fla., 2001—02, dir. bands, 2002—. Musician: Southeast Alabama Community Band. Com. mem. quality stds.-basedDesign SERVE R&D Project, Panama City, Fla., 2002—; host John Philip Sousa Nat. Jr. Honors Band. Chancellor's fellow, Troy State U., 1996—97. Mem.: Nat. Band Assn., So. Assn. Colls. and Schs. (mem. sch. leadership team surfside mid. sch.), NEA, Fla. Bandmasters Assn. (sec. dist. 2), Music Educators Nat. Conf., Women Band Dirs. Internat., Phi Kappa Phi. Avocations: performing, gardening, travel, reading, walking. Office: Surfside Middle Sch Band 300 Nautilus St Panama City Beach FL 32413 Business E-Mail: birdwmm@mail.bay.k12.fl.us.

BIRELY, WILLIAM CRAMER, investment banker; b. Thurmont, Md., Nov. 13, 1919; s. Victor Morris and Dorothy Grace (Rouzer) B.; m. Luelle Avis Langness, July 21, 1943. Student, Strayer U., 1937-38, USDA Graduate Sch., Washington, 1940, Babson Inst., 1940, Am. U., 1941-42. With Nat. Wildlife Assn., U.S. Govt., 1938—47, Folger, Nolan, Inc., Washington, 1947-52, v.p., 1950-52; gen. partner Rouse, Brewer & Becker (now Morgan Stanley), Washington, 1952-55; exec. v.p., treas. Birely & Co., Washington, 1955-62, pres., 1962-67; also dir.; v.p. Mason & Co. (now Legg, Mason, Wood, Walker, Inc.), 1967-70; investment banker Lang & Co., Washington, 1970-85, Chapin, Davis & Co., Balt., 1985-89, Lang Div. Moors & Cabot, Inc., Alexandria, Va., 1989—. V.p., dir. Thurmont Bank (now Bank of Am.), Md., 1962-73;; elected share funding mem. US Capitol Hist. Soc., 1963, chmn. fin. com.; adv. bd. Farmers & Mechanics Nat. Bank, Thurmont (now P.N.O. Fin.), 1975-76; mem. adv. council SBA, 1962-66; mem. adv. commn. Nat. Defense Office of Production Mgmt., War Prodn. Bd., War Assets Adminstrn., Indsl. Analyst. Mem. gen. inaugural coms. Eisenhower and Nixon, 1953, 1957, Nixon and Agnew, 1968, 1972, Reagan and Bush, 1980, 1984, Bush and Quayle, 1988; bd. appeals Montgomery County, 1965; mem. Montgomery County Coun., 1965—66; treas. Young Rep. Club of Montgomery County, 1947, pres., 1948; elected del. Md. Rep. Conv., 1952, 1956, 1980; apptd. on Nat. Alcohol Beverage Control Assn. Constn., Laws Com., Fed. Affairs and Legis. Com., 1966. Served with FA AUS, 1943—44. Recipient Gov.'s citation for outstanding service to Md. Mem. NRA (life), Am. Legion (life), Huguenot Soc. Washington (life, former v.p.), S.A.R. (life, former nat. trustee), Soc. Mayflower Descs., Soc. Colonial Wars (life), Soc. War 1812, St. Andrews Soc., Frederick County Hist. Soc. (life), Carroll County Hist. Soc. (life), Washington Hist. Socs. (life), Montgomery County Hist. Soc. (life; mem. bd. mgmt.), Nat. Geneol. Soc. (former v.p.), Md. Geneol. Soc. (life), Bond Club, Nat. Press Club, Army and Navy Club, Izaak Walton League Am. (nat. life), Assn. Childhood Edn. Internat. (chmn. fin. com.), N.Am. Blue Bird Soc. Home: PO Box 590 Olney MD 20830 Office: Lang Div Moors & Cabot Inc 1600 Prince St Ste 113 Alexandria VA 22314-2836 Office Phone: 301-924-2521.

BIRENBAUM, LEO, retired engineering educator; b. N.Y.C., Dec. 1, 1927; s. Morris and Esther (Ditman) B.; m. Mary Giurato, Feb. 17, 1961; children: Eric, Nellie, Maija. BSEE, Cooper Union, 1946; MSEE, Poly. Inst. N.Y., 1958, MS in Physics, 1974. Electronics engr. N.Y. Naval Shipyard, Bklyn., 1948-51; from rsch. asst. to assoc. prof. U. N.Y., Bklyn., 1951-93, prof. emeritus, 1993—. Sec. C95.4 com. Am. Nat. Standards Inst., N.Y.C., 1969-79. Patentee microwave devices. Served with USN, 1946-47. Mem. IEEE (sr.), Bioelectromagnetics Soc., N.Y. Acad. Scis., Sigma Xi, Tau Beta Pi. Home: 44 Mohawk Rd Yonkers NY 10710-5010 Office: Poly Univ ECE Dept 6 Metrotech Ctr Brooklyn NY 11201 Home Phone: 914-771-8342; Office Phone: 718-260-3319. Business E-Mail: lbirenba@duke.poly.edu.

BIRENBAUM, WILLIAM M., former university president; b. Macomb, Ill., July 18, 1923; s. Joseph and Rose (Whiteman) B.; m. Helen Bloch, Mar. 8, 1951; children: Susan, Lauren Amy, Charles. Dr. Law, U. Chgo., 1949; L.H.D., Columbia Coll., Chgo., 1970. Dean students Univ. Coll., 1955-57. Dir. research, conf. bd. Asso. Research Councils, Ford Found. project study post-doctoral internat. ednl. exchanges, 1954-55; asst. v.p. Wayne State U., 1957-61; dean New Sch. Social Research, N.Y.C., 1961-64; v.p., provost Bklyn. Center, L.I. U., 1964-67; pres. Edn. Affiliate, Bedford-Stuyvesant Devel. & Services Corp., Bklyn, 1967-68, S.I. Community Coll., 1968-76; pres. Antioch U., 1976-85. Author: Overlive: Power, Poverty and the University, 1968, Something for Everybody is Not Enough: An Educator's Search for His Education, 1971; Contbg. author: Student Personnel Work in Urban Colleges. Cons. Austrian Ministry Edn., Vienna, 1969; higher edn. adviser Republic of Zambia, 1972; cons. U. Zambia, 1972; faculty Salzburg Seminar in Am. Studies, 1976; founder Nat. Student Assn., 1946-48; chmn. Mich. Cultural Commn., 1960-61; founder, original dir. Detroit Adventure, vol. assn. cultural instns., 1958-61; bd. adv. Bklyn. Acad. Music, 1965—, Bklyn Inst. Arts and Scis; trustee Friends World Coll., Westbury, NY, Hasbro Childrens Found., 1985-99, Lit. Vols. NYC, 1986-98, Met. Coll. NY, 1994-. Mem. Chgo. Bar Assn., Delta Sigma. Home: 108 Willow St Brooklyn NY 11201-2202

BIRGENEAU, ROBERT JOSEPH, academic administrator, physicist, researcher; b. Toronto, Ont., Can., Mar. 25, 1942; arrived in US, 1963; s. Peter Duffus and Isobel Theresa (Meehan) B.; m. Mary Catherine Ware, June 20, 1964; children: Michael, Catherine, Patricia, Michelle. BSc, U. Toronto, 1963; PhD in physics, Yale U., 1966. Vis. tchr. Benedict Coll., Columbia, SC, summer 1965; instr. dept. engring. and applied sci. Yale U., New Haven, 1966-67; Nat. Research Council Can. postdoctoral fellow Oxford U., England, 1967-68; mem. tech. staff Bell Labs, Murray Hill, NJ, 1968-74, research head scattering and low energy, physics dept., 1975; guest sr. physicist Brookhaven Nat. Lab., Upton, NY, 1968—; vis. scientist RisNational Lab., Roskilde, Denmark, 1971, 79; prof. physics MIT, Cambridge, 1975—2000, Cecil and Ida Green prof. physics, 1982—2000, assoc. dir. Rsch. Lab. of Electronics, 1983-86, head solid state, atomic and plasma physics, 1987-88, head dept. physics, 1988-91, dean Sch. Sci., 1991-2000; pres., prof. physics U. Toronto, 2000—04; chancellor U. Calif., Berkeley, 2004—. Cons. Bell Labs., 1977-80, IBM Rsch. Labs., Yorktown Heights, NY, 1980-83, Sandia Nat. Labs., Albuquerque, 1985-92; mem. steering com. Panel on Neutron Scattering, NAS, 1977, mem. exec. com. Major Materials Facilities Com., 1984; co-chmn. Gordon Conf. on Quantum Solids and Fluids, 1979, Gordon Conf. on Condensed Matter Physics, 1986; mem. external adv. com. physics divsn. Los Alamos Nat. Lab, 1982-86; mem. policy and adv. bd. Cornell High Energy Synchrotron Source, 1980-84, chmn., 1983-84; mem. rev. panel on neutron scattering Dept. Energy, 1980, 82, mem. Basic Energy Sciences Adv. Com., 1991-94, chair Panel on Rsch. Reactors, 1996, Panel on Synchrotron Radiation Sources & Sci., 1997; mem. materials rsch. adv. com. NSF, 1989-90; mem. adv. coun. NEC Rsch. Inst., 1995-2000; mem. sci. policy com. Lawrence Berkeley Nat. Lab., 1997-2000; co-chair Polaroid Sci. and Tech. Bd., 1998-2001; mem. external adv. com. physics dept., Oxford U., 2000-; chair. vis. com. ETH Domain, Switzerland, 2002; mem. DOE Task Force on the Future of Sci. Programs, 2003. Contbr. articles to profl. jours.; assoc. editor for condensed matter physics, Physical Review Letters, 1980-83; mem. editorial bd. Physical Review B, 1987-89. Trustee Associated Univs., Inc., 1990-97, Boston Mus. Sci., 1992-2001, Brookhaven Sci. Assocs., 1997-2000, Univ. Health Network, 2000-, Royal Ont. Mus., 2000-, United Way Greater Toronto Campaign Cabinet, 2000-, Univs. Rsch. Assn., Inc., 2000-; bd. govs. Argonne Nat. Lab., 1992-2001; mem. physics fellow selection com. Sloan Found., 1995-2001; bd. dirs. St. Michael's Hosp., 2000-04. Recipient Yale Sci. and Engring. Alumni Achievement Award, 1981, Wilbur Lucius Cross Medal, Yale U., 1986, Bertram Eugene Warren Award, Am. Crystal Assn., 1988, Magnetism Award, Internat. Union Pure and Applied Physics, 1997; 48th Richtmyer Meml. lectr. Am. Assn. Physics Tchrs., 1989, A.W. Scott lectr. Cambridge U., 2000. Fellow AAAS (exec. coun. 1992-94), Am. Phys. Soc. (Oliver E. Buckley prize com. 1981, 90-2001, Oliver E. Buckley Prize for Condensed Matter Physics 1987, Julius E. Lilienfeld award 2000), Am. Acad. Arts Sci. (membership com. 1989-92, Founders award 2006), Royal Soc. London, Royal Soc. Can, Inst. Physics; mem. NAS (fgn. assoc., 2004), Am. Philos. Soc. Roman Catholic. Avocations: landscaping, squash, basketball. Office: U Calif Office Chancellor 200 Calif Hall Berkeley CA 94720 Office Phone: 510-642-7464. E-mail: chancellor@berkeley.edu.

BIRI, TONI ROPPOLO, elementary school educator; b. New Orleans, Sept. 21, 1957; d. Anthony Rocco and Helen Ellis (Ferguson) Roppolo; m. Gerard Michael Biri, Aug. 8, 1992; children: Michael A. Greenfield, Stephen R. Buford Jr., Kaitlyn Marie. BS, Our Lady of Holy Cross Coll., New Orleans, 1981. Cert. elem. edn. La., 1981. Tchr. 3rd grade Catherine Strehle Elem. Sch., Avondale, La., 1983—89; tchr. 6th grade Wilkerson Intermediate Sch., The Woodlands, Tex., 1989—90; tchr. 4th grade Galvez Primary Sch., Prairieville, La., 1990—. Bldg./area rep. Jefferson Fedn. Tchrs., Avondale, 1984—86; co-leader 4-H, Prairieville, La., 1995—2002. Grantee, Ascension Fund, 2000—01. Home: 40461 Myrtle St Prairieville LA 70769 Office: Galvez Primary Sch 16093 Henderson Bayou Rd Prairieville LA 70769 Home Phone: 225-622-5070.

BIRIBAUER, RICHARD FRANK, lawyer; b. May 30, 1950; s. Frank Anton and Mary M. (Valle) Biribauer; m. Linda Carey, Aug. 26, 1972; children: James Richard, David Tyler, Tia Renee. AB, Rutgers U., 1972; JD, Washington and Lee U., 1975. Bar: Va. 1975, DC 1976. Assoc. Law Offices of Fulton Brylawski, Washington, 1975—77; trademark counsel Johnson & Johnson, New Brunswick, NJ, 1977—83, internat. trademark counsel, 1984—91, chief trademark counsel, 1991—. Contbr. articles to Washington and Lee U. Law Rev., to Mng. Intellectual Property. Mem.: ABA, Va. State Bar Assn., DC Bar Assn., Pharm. Trademarks Group, Inter Am. Assn. Indsl. Property, Internat. Trademark Assn. Office: Johnson & Johnson One Johnson & Johnson Plz New Brunswick NJ 08933 Home Phone: 908-735-2166; Office Phone: 732-524-2845. Business E-Mail: rbiriba@corus.jnj.com.

BIRINYI, LASZLO, financial analyst, investment advisor; b. Hungary; B, Univ. NC; MBA, NYU. Dir., investment analyst Salomon Brothers, NYC, 1976—89; founder, pres. Birinyi Associates, Westport, Conn., 1989—. Contbr. articles to Forbes Mag., Bloomberg Personal Fin.; commentator CNBC, Wall Street Week (named to WSW Hall of Fame, 1999). Named to Power 30, SmartMoney Mag. Office: Birinyi Associates 61 Wilton Rd Westport CT 06880*

BIRK, DAVID R., lawyer, electronics executive; BA, U. Fla., Gainesville, 1969; JD, Cornell U., Ithaca, NY, 1972. Bar: NY 1973. Assoc. Jacobs, Persinger & Parker, NYC, 1974-77; ptnr. Burstein & Marcus, White Plains, NY, 1977-80; sr. atty. Avnet, Inc., Great Neck, NY, 1980-89, gen. counsel, 1989—, sr. v.p., 1992—, corp. sec., 1997—. Bd. dirs. UAP Holding Corp., Greeley, Colo., 2007—. 1st lt. US Army, 1972—74. Mem. NY State Bar (mem. corr. law com.), Assn. of Bar of City of NY (mem. profl. discipline com.). Office: Avnet Inc 2211 S 47th St Phoenix AZ 85034-6403 Office Phone: 480-643-2000.*

BIRK, IAN, lawyer; b. Seattle, Sept. 22, 1978; BA summa cum laude, Univ. Wash., 1997, JD, 2001. Bar: Wash. 2001. Assoc. atty. Keller Rohrback LLP, Seattle, Wash., 2001—. Contbr. articles to numerous profl. jours. Named Seattle Rising Star, SuperLawyer Mag., 2006. Mem.: ABA, Wash. Bar Assn. Office: Keller Rohrback LLP Ste 3200 1201 Third Ave Seattle WA 98101-3052

BIRK, JOHN RICHARD, management consultant; b. Boston, Aug. 11, 1951; s. Harold F. and Jane Birk; m. Susan Arnold, Feb. 9, 1980; children: John R. Jr., Andrew A. BA in Econs. and English, Colgate U., 1974; Advanced Mgmt. Program, Harvard Bus. Sch., 1991. Sales rep. Procter & Gamble, NYC, 1975-76, dist. field rep. White Plains, NY, 1976, unit mgr. Dallas, 1976-78; sales devel. mgr. Pepsi Cola Co., Purchase, NY, 1978-80, regional sales mgr. San Francisco, 1980-83; dir. sales and mktg. MCI Comm. Inc., Atlanta, 1983-84, v.p. sales and mktg., 1984-85; pres., bd. dirs. U.S. Telecomm Svcs. Co., Kansas City, 1985; pres. N.E. divsn. US Sprint, Purchase, 1986-87, pres. we. group San Francisco, 1987-88; exec. v.p., COO, dir. ADVO, Inc., 1988—89; pres., COO, dir. ADVO Inc., Windsor, 1989-92; pres., CEO, dir. Wright Express Corp., South Portland, Maine, 1992-94, chmn., 1994-95; pres. Ideon Group Inc. (formerly Safe Card Svcs., Inc.), Jacksonville, Fla., 1995; mgmt. cons. John R. Birk & Assocs., Ponte Vedra Beach, Fla., 1995—; oper. exec. Evercore Ptnrs., 1996—2006, adv. bd., 2006—. Bd. dirs. Nat. Sys., Inc., Splty. Products Insulation Inc., chmn.; fin. commr. Ctrl. Beach Fire Dist., Charlestown, RI, bd. govs. Bd. dirs. Prevent Blindness, Atlanta, 1984-85, United Way, White Plains, 1986-87, Westchester County Assn., 1986-87, Bay Area Coun., 1987-88, United Way Greater Portland, 1993-95, Found. for Blood Rsch., Inc., 1993-95, Colgate U. Alumni Corp., 1995-99; chmn. Colgate U. Pres. Club, 1996-99. Republican. Roman Catholic. Avocations: tennis, golf, skiing. Office Phone: 904-273-7819. Personal E-mail: jrbirk@aol.com.

BIRK, ROBERT EUGENE, retired internist; b. Buffalo, Jan. 7, 1926; s. Reginald H. and Florence (Diebolt) B.; m. Janet L. Davidson, June 24, 1950; children— David Eugene, James Michael, Patricia Jean, Thomas Spencer, Susan Margaret AB, Colgate U., Hamilton, NY, 1948; MD, U. Rochester, NY, 1952. Diplomate Am. Bd. Internal Medicine. Intern, resident Henry Ford Hosp., Detroit, 1952-57, chief 2d med. div., 1961-66, asst. to chmn. dept. medicine, 1965-66; practice medicine specializing in internal medicine Grosse Pointe, Mich., 1966-89; sr. active staff St. John Hosp., 1966-89, chief dept. medicine, 1967-70, dir. health edn., dir. grad. med. edn., 1975-86, exec. dir. continuing med. edn., 1975-86; dir. med. affairs St John Ambulatory Care Corp., St. John Home Care Svcs., 1980-89; v.p. clin. affairs St. John Health Corp., 1985-89. Assoc. prof. medicine Wayne State U., 1969-89 Contbr. articles to profl. jours. Mem. trustee's coun. U. Rochester, 1973-75, Med. Ctr. alumni coun., 1974-75; bd. trustees St. John Hosp., Macomb Ctr., 1986-89; corp. mem. bd. Boys Clubs Met. Detroit, 1973-89; trustee Mich. Cancer Found., 1980-89, bd. dirs., 1982-85. With US Army, 1943-46. Fellow ACP, Detroit Acad. Medicine; mem. AMA, Assn. Hosp. Med. Edn. (trustee region IV 1986-87), Mich. Assn. Med. Edn. (trustee 1985-86), Am. Soc. Internal Medicine, Am. Acad. Med. Dirs., Alpha Tau Omega. Republican. Episcopalian. Home: 8 Eagle Claw Dr Hilton Head Island SC 29926-1853

BIRKELAND, BRYAN COLLIER, lawyer; b. Hibbing, Minn., May 29, 1951; s. Lionel Owen and Peggy Jean Birkeland; m. D.J. Loras, Jan. 5, 1974; children: Brett Holton, Blair Leigh, Blake Owen. Student, Washington and Jefferson Coll., 1969-70; BA with high honors, U. Tex., 1973, JD with honors, 1975. Bar: Tex. 1976. Ptnr. Jackson Walker, LLP, Dallas, 1982—. Pres., dir. Globalaw, Ltd.; dir. Real Estate Coun. Grantee, Moody Found., 1971. Mem. ABA, State Bar Tex., Dallas Bar Assn., Order of Coif, Phi Beta Kappa, Phi Kappa Phi, Delta Sigma Rho, Tau Kappa Alpha. Presbyterian. Office: Jackson Walker LLP 901 Main St Ste 6000 Dallas TX 75202-3797 Office Phone: 214-953-5934. E-mail: bbirkeland@jw.com.

BIRKELBACH, ALBERT OTTMAR, retired oil industry executive; b. Oak Park, Ill., Feb. 22, 1927; s. August and Ann B.; m. Shirley M. Spandet, Aug. 21, 1948; children: J.A., Lisa M., Grace L. Birkelbach Boland, Ann C. Birkelbach. BSCh.E., U. Ill., 1949. Various engring., supervisory and mgmt. positions Globe Oil & Refining Co., Lemont, Ill., 1949-53, Anderson Prichard Oil Corp., Cyril, Okla., 1953-58, Signal Oil & Gas Co., Los Angeles, 1958-64; mng. dir. Raffinerie Belge de Petroles, Antwerp, Belgium, 1964-74; v.p. Occidental Petroleum Corp., London, Eng., 1972-74; cons. in field, 1974-75; pres. ATC Petroleum Inc., NYC, 1975-81, also dir.; pres. Amorient Petroleum Corp., Laguna Niguel, Calif., 1981-84; mgmt. cons., 1984-87. Served with USCG, 1945-47. Decorated knight Order Leopold Belgium). Home: 33957 N 66th Way Scottsdale AZ 85262 Address: 33957 N 66th Way Scottsdale AZ 85262-7231

BIRKELUND, JOHN PETER, investment company executive; b. Chgo., June 23, 1930; s. George R. and Ruth (Olsen) B.; m. Constance I. Smiles, Oct. 25, 1958; children: Gwynne Tibbetts, Elizabeth Oberbeck, Constance Olivia, Diana. AB, Princeton U., 1952; doctorate (hon.), Brown U., 2002. Cons. Booz Allen & Hamilton, Chgo., 1956; v.p. Amsterdam Overseas Corp., NYC, 1956-67; co-founder, chmn. New Court Securities Corp., NYC, 1967-81; pres. Dillon, Read & Co., Inc., NYC, 1981-86, CEO, 1986-93, chmn., 1994-97; sr. advisor UBS Warburg LLC, NYC, 1998—2002; gen. ptnr. Saratoga Ptnrs., NYC, Darby Overseas Ptnrs., Washington. Chmn. Polish-Am. Enterprise Fund, Polish.-Am. Freedom Found., Nat. Humanities Ctr., N.C. Chair Thomas J. Watson Inst. for Internat. Studies, Providence; trustee N.Y. Pub. Libr., NYC, 1990—, Frick Collection, 2004. Lt. USNR, 1953—55. Mem. Coun. Fgn. Rels., Phi Beta Kappa (senate, 2004-), The Links Club, Univ. Club, The Blind Brook Club, Clove Valley Rod and Gun Club. Home: 510 Weed St New Canaan CT 06840-6127 Office: Saratoga Ptnrs 535 Madison Ave 4th Fl New York NY 10022

BIRKENHEAD, THOMAS BRUCE, theater producer, educator; b. NYC, Dec. 19, 1931; s. Thomas A. and Florence (Morison) B.; m. Susan Leslie Arkin, Dec. 3, 1954 (div. 1983); m. Maria Martins, May 26, 1999; children: Peter Lawrence, David Andrew, Richard James, Alison Jane, Leila Alessandra. BA, Bklyn. Coll. CUNY, 1954, MA, 1958; PhD, New Sch. Social Rsch., 1963. From lectr. to prof. econs. Bklyn. Coll. CUNY, 1957-72, prof., 1972-75; dean Sch. Social Scis., 1972-75; prof. emeritus Bklyn. Coll. CUNY, 1975—. Bus. mgr. Theatre II, Glen Cove, NY, 1970—74; mgmt. cons. Keystone Ctr. Performing Arts, 1999—. Co-mgr. Do Black Patent Leather Shoes Really Reflect Up?, Present Laughter, Master Harold and the Boys, Children of a Lesser God, Ain't Misbehavin, Brighton Beach Memoirs, Biloxi Blues, Broadway Bound, Barbara Cook in Concert, Run For Your Wife, Rumors, Lost in Yonkers, Jake's Women, Goodbye Girl; gen. mgr.: Cape Cod Melody Tent, 1969—71, Twyla Tharp on Broadway, 1980—81; gen. mgr. Joe Egg, 1985, Social Security, 1986, Long Days Journey Into Night, London and Tel Aviv, 1986, Ain't Misbehavin, N.Y.C., 1988—89, Japan, 1990, Fresh Air Taxi, 1993, Honky Tonk Highway, 1994—96, Dream a Little Dream, 1994—95, Duke and the Dutchess, 2001—; co-prodr.: 1995 Tony Award Broadcast, N.H.K. Japan, —; prodr.: High Mountain Ghost, 1996—98; sec.-treas.: Highly Ent., 1995—2001. Founding mem., sponsor U.S. Shooting Team, U.S. Holocaust Meml. Mus., Am. Air Mus., Eng., U.S. Naval Meml. Found., WWII Meml., U.S. Olympic Com.; mem. negotiating team ATPAM, 2005-06, bd. trustees, 2007; mem. negotiating com., ATPAM Broadway Contract, 2006—. Named T. Bruce Birkenhead scholarship in his honor, Performing Arts Mgmt. Program Bklyn. Coll. Mem. NRA, US Naval Inst., Habitat for Humanity, Amnesty Internat., Women in Mil. Svc. for Am., Groucho Club (Eng.), World Jewish Congress, Carter Ctr., Victorian Soc., Friends of Israel Def. Force. Home and Office: 353 W 44th St Apt 1A New York NY 10036-5416 E-mail: brucebirkenhead@yahoo.com.

BIRKERTS, GUNNAR, architect; b. Riga, Latvia, Jan. 17, 1925; came to U.S., 1949, naturalized, 1954; s. Peter and Meria (Shop) B.; m. Sylvia Zvirbulis, July 29, 1950; children— Sven Peter, Andra Sylvia, Erik Gunnar. Diplomingeneur Architekt, Technische Hochschule, Stuttgart, Germany, 1949; D (hon.), Riga Tech. Univ., Latvia, 1990. Designer Perkins & Will, Chgo., 1950-51, Eero Saarinen & Assos., Bloomfield Hills, Mich., 1951-55; prin. chief designer Minoru Yamasaki & Assos., Birmingham, Mich., 1955-59; pres. Gunnar Birkerts & Assos., Inc., Birmingham, 1959; asst. prof. architecture U. Mich., 1961, asso. prof., 1963-69, prof., 1969-90; Graham fellow, 1970; architect in residence Am. Acad. in Rome, 1976; 1st Lawrence J. Plym. disting. prof. architecture U. Ill., 1982; Thomas S. Monaghan architect-in-residence prof. U. Mich., Ann Arbor, 1984; Bruce Alonzo Goff prof. of creative architecture U. Okla., 1990. Prin. works include Schwartz House, Northville, Mich. (First Honor award AIA 1962, Merit award Detroit chpt. AIA 1963, Archtl. Record award 1961), Univ. Reformed Ch., Ann Arbor Mich. (award Ch. Archtl. Guild Am. 1962), Peoples Fed. Savs. & Loan Bank, Royal Oak, Mich., 1963 (Merit award Detroit chpt. AIA 1963), Fisher Adminstrv. Ctr., Detroit (award of merit Mich. Soc. Architects 1967, Merit award Detroit chpt. AIA 1967), Detroit Inst. Arts addition (25 Yr. award AIA 2002), 1300 Lafayette Apts., Detroit, Tougaloo (Miss.) Coll. (award of honor Mich. Soc. Architects 1974), Vocat.-Tech. Campus, So. Ill. U., Glen Oaks Community Coll. Campus, Centreville, Mich., Lincoln Sch., Columbus, Ind. (AIA Detroit chpt. and nat. Honor awards 1968, 70, 25 yr. award Mich. AIA), Fed. Res. Bank, Mpls. (award excellence Am. Inst. Steel Constrn. 1974, design award Am. Iron and Steel Inst. 1975), IBM Corp. Computer Center, Sterling Forest, N.Y. (honor award Detroit chpt. AIA 1973), Contemporary Arts Mus., Houston (honor award Detroit chpt. AIA 1975), Dance Instructional Facility at Purchase (award honor Mich. Soc. Architects 1977, Honor award Detroit chpt. AIA 1978), Calvary Baptist Ch., Detroit (Honor award Mich. Soc. Architects 1979, award of excellence Am. Inst. Steel Constrn. 1979), IBM Office Bldg., Southfield, Mich. (Honor award Mich. Soc. Architects 1980, energy conservation award Owens Corning Fiberglas Corp. 1977), Duluth Public Libr. (Honor award Mich. Soc. Architects 1981), Fire Sta., Corning, N.Y. (honor award Mich. Soc. Architects 1977), Corning Mus. of Glass, Law Libr. Addition, U. Mich. (award of excellence AIA and ALA 1985), U.S. Embassy bldg., Helsinki, Finland, Coll. of Law bldg., U. Iowa (Award of Honor-Mich. Soc. Architects 1987), Uris Library addition, Cornell U. (honor award Mich. Soc. Architects 1984), Dist. Office Bldg., Green Bay, Wis., Ferguson Residence, Kalamazoo, Mich. (award of honor Mich. Soc. Architects 1986), Chapel & Ednl. Facility, Camp Wildflecken, Fed. Republic Germany (Silver Castle award U.S. Army Corps. Engrs., European div. 1986), St. Peter's Luth. Ch., Columbus, Ind. (award of honor Detroit chpt. AIA 1986, 90), Domino's world hdqrs., Ann Arbor, Mich. (bldg. recognition award Engring. Soc. Detroit 1987, M award for Excellence in Masonry Design Masonry Inst. Mich., 1989), Libr. Addition Conservatory Music Oberlin Coll., Ohio, Prototype Franchise Bldg. Domino's Pizza, Inc. (award of honor Mich. Soc. Architects 1989), Jackson, Mich., Cen. Libr. addition U. Calif., San Diego, Sports Svcs. Bldg. U. Mich., U.S. Embassy, Caracas, Venezuela , Libr. U. Mich., Flint (Design and Constrn. showcase '94 award), Coll. Law Ohio State U., (award of honor AIA Mich., 1995), Kemper Mus. Contemporary Art and Design, Kans. City Mo. (Lighting award, 1995), Ch. Servant, Kentwood, Mich.; exhbns. include Akron Inst. Art, 1954, Sao Paulo (Brazil) Bienniale, 1962, 40 under 40, USA-NY, Architects League, 1965, Mus. Modern Art, N.Y.C., 1971, Notre Dame U., 1973, N.Y. Mus. Modern Art, 1979, Neuberger Mus., Purchase, N.Y., 1981, Am. Acad. and Inst. Arts and Letters, N.Y.C., 1981, U. Ill., 1983, U. Md., College Park, 1985, Saginaw Art Mus., Mich., 1985, Notre Dame U., 1985, Pratt Inst., Bklyn., 1986, NYU, 1986, The Triennale, Milan, Italy, 1986, Judah L. Magnes Mus., Berkeley, Calif., 1986, Nat. Ctr. for Study of Frank Lloyd Wright, Ann Arbor, 1988, St. Peter's Cathedral, Riga, Latvia, 1989, Torino '90, Turin, Italy, 1990, The 3d Belgrade Triennial of World Architects, 1991, The Athenaeum Music and Art Libr., LaJolla, Calif., 1991, Kansas City Art Inst., 1992, Lawrence Tech. U., Southfield, Mich., 1993, Latvian Nat. Libr., 2000 (Am. Archtl. award Chgo. Atheanum), Venezia and Archtl. Bieniale, 2002. Named Young Designer of Year Akron Inst. Art, 1954, Mich. Artist of Yr. Mich. Artrain, 1993; recipient 1st prize Internat. Furniture competition, Cantu, Italy, 1955; 3d prize Internat. competition for Cultural Centre, Belgian Congo; Design award Progressive Architecture mag., 1957, 59, 61, 71; award of excellence Archtl. Record, 1968; Nat. Gold medal Tau Sigma Delta, 1971; Gold medal Detroit chpt. AIA, 1975; Gold medal Mich. Soc. Architects, 1980; Brunner Meml. prize Am. Acad. and Inst. Arts and Letters, 1981; Mich. Art award Arts Found. Mich., 1988, Disting. Prof. Assn. Collegiate Schs. Architecture, 1990; Order of Three Stars, Republic of Latvia. Fellow AIA, Graham Found., Latvian Architects Assn.; mem. Mich. Soc. Architects (Award of Honor 1989), Ch. Archtl. Guild, Hon. Order Ky. Cols. Office: PO Box 812115 Wellesley MA 02482-0013 Office Fax: 781-235-4167. Personal E-mail: gunnarbirk@aol.com.

BIRKESTOL, ANNABELLE MOLLIE ELSIE, retired elementary school educator; b. Stanwood, Wash., May 29, 1923; d. Ole and Ingeborg Birkestol. BA in Edn., Pacific Luth. U., Tacoma, Wash., 1945; grad. studies (hon.), U. Wash., Seattle, 1969. Elem. tchr. Woodinville Sch., Woodinville, Wash., 1945—47, Wilson Sch., Mukilteo, Wash., 1948—54, Conway Sch., Conway, Wash., 1954—76; ret., 1976. Mem. Wash. State Edn. Assn., Olympia, Wash., 1945—76, NEA, 1945—76. Mem.: Wash. State Sch. Retirees' Assn., Am. Assn. U. Women, Nat. Women's Hist. Mus., Stanwood Area Hist. Soc. (life; pres. 1978—79), Norwegian Am. Mus. Vesterheim (life), Pacific Lutheran U. Q Club, Fritjov Lodge No. 17 Sons of Norway Stanwood. Republican. Lutheran. Avocations: opera, museums, historic preservation. Home: 4515 Norman Rd Stanwood WA 98292

BIRKETT, NORMAN MYLES, private school educator, writer; s. Ronald M. and Grace G. Birkett; m. Katharine Givotovsky, May 3, 1986. AB, Princeton U., 1984. Sr. programmer/analyst Key Fin. Sys., Parsippany, NJ, 1984—86, Advanced Data Mgmt., Kingston, NJ, 1986—87, Prudential-Bache Securities, NYC, 1987—89; v.p. Bankers Trust Co., NYC, 1989—93, Goldman, Sachs & Co, NYC, 1993—99; tchr. Trinity Christian Sch., Montville, NJ, 1999—. Writer, pub., propr. Classical Legacy Press, Montville, 2002—. Author: (textbook) Logic I: Tools for Thinking, 2003. Mem., sec., pres. Princeton Evang. Fellowship, 1980—84. Mem.: Assn. Christians in Math. Scis. Republican. Baptist. Avocations: carpentry, military history, kayaking, photography. Office: Trinity Christian Sch 160 Changebridge Rd Montville NJ 07045

BIRKETVEDT, GRETHE STØA, medical scientist, writer, musician; b. Sarpsborg, Norway, Sept. 17, 1942; d. Arne and Aase (Oscarsdatter) Støa; 1 child, Camilla Støa. Student, Tchrs. Tng. Coll., Stord, Norway, 1964; MMus, U. Oslo, 1969; M of Phys. Edn., U. of Sport, Oslo, 1972; MD, Oslo U., 1983; MD, PhD, U. Tromsø, Norway, 1995. Diplomate, lic. med. NY; cert. tchr. phys. edn., music diplomate. Tchr. Norwegian Tchg. Assn., Sarpsborg, 1964-67; Fulbright scholar U.S., 1968-69; musician, composer Norwegian Composers Assn., Oslo, 1969-83; gen. practitioner Med. Assn. Oslo, 1983-92; med. scientist Gen. Practice Orgn., Oslo, 1992-93; asst. prof. Tromsö Hosp., 1993-95; vis. scientist U. Pa., Phila., 1995-99. Rschr. U. Tromaö, Norway; asst. rsch. prof. Mt. Sinai Sch. Medicine, NYC, 2000—; hon. prof. Albert Schweitzer Internat. U. Geneva, Geneva, 2000—. Author: (poems) At a Distance, 1976, 2d edit., 1977, These are the

Days, 1978, Hildelin, A Symphonic Poem, 1980, In the Light of the Planet, 1994, textbook for medical student and geneeral practioners; composer: (plays) Musikklek, 1980, Laughting Street No. 2, 1986, Circus in Town, 1994, Vriompeisen, 1997, Treatment of Overweight and Obesity in General Practice, 2000; contbr. articles to profl. jours., chapters to books. Recipient Writer's award, U. Altertumskunde, Munich, 1980, Golden Acad. award, Lifelong Achievement, Am. Biog. Inst., 1999, Peace and Sci. Commemorative medal, Albert Schweitzer Internat. U., 2002; Norwegian Coun. Med. Rsch. grantee, 1996. Mem.: AAAS, NY Acad. Scis., Norwegian Assn. Music Composition, Norwegian Assn. Gen. Practitioners, Norwegian Assn. Gastroenterology, TONO Assn. Protection Musical Original Work, Soc. Study Ingestive Behavior, Norwegian Writers Ctr., Fulbright Alumni Assn. Avocations: music, writing, riding, painting, reading. Home: 74 Oak Knoll Dr Berwyn PA 19312 Office: Aker Univ Hosp Oslo Norway Personal E-mail: gsb42nor@aol.com.

BIRKHEAD, GUTHRIE SWEENEY, JR., political scientist, dean; b. Holden, Mo., Oct. 28, 1920; s. Guthrie Sweeney and Yula Donna (Glass) B.; m. Louise Gartner, Aug. 16, 1952; children— Guthrie Sweeney III, Richard Gartner, Evan Clark. AA, Jefferson City Jr. Coll., 1940; AB, U. Mo., 1942, A.M., 1947; MA, Princeton, 1949, PhD in Politics, 1951. Mem. faculty Syracuse U., 1950—, prof. polit. sci., 1960—, chmn. dept., 1959-62, 66-67, dir. met. studies program, 1968-73; asso. dean Maxwell Sch., 1973-77, dean, 1977-88. Also dir. pub. adminstrn. programs, 1959-62; dir. research UN Inst. Pub. Adminstrn. for Turkey and Middle East, 1955-56; cons. Pakistan Adminstrv. Staff Coll., Lahore, 1962-64, Ford Found., Pakistan, 1967-68 Co-author: River Basin Administration and the Delaware, 1960, Science and State Government in New York, 1960, Decisions in Syracuse, 1962; Editor: Administrative Problems in Pakistan, 1966, A Look to the North: Canadian Regional Experience, 1974, Education for Public Service, 1980; Contbr. articles to profl. jours. Chmn. pub. finance com. Community Renewal Plan, Syracuse, N.Y., 1970-72; exec. dir. com. local govt. and home rule N.Y. State Constl. Conv., 1967, Syracuse Charter Commn., 1972-74; mem. Nat. Com. Water Quality Policy Nat. Acad. Scis.-NRC, 1974-76; com. to review the metropolitan Washington area water supply study Nat. Acad. Engring/Nat. Research Council, 1977-84. Served with inf. AUS, 1942-46. Fellow Nat. Mcpl. League, 1952-53. Fellow Nat. Acad. Pub. Adminstrn.; mem. AAAS, Am. Soc. Pub. Adminstrn., Phi Beta Kappa, Sigma Xi. Home: 220 Lockwood Rd Syracuse NY 13214-2035 Personal E-mail: guthrietwo@msn.com.

BIRKINBINE, JOHN, II, philatelist; b. Chestnut Hill, Pa., Mar. 29, 1930; s. Olaf Weimer and Gertrude Marie (Tyson) B.; m. Ausencia Barrera Elen, Dec. 19, 1969; children: John III, Bayani Royd. Degree, Haverford Sch., 1948. Chmn., CEO Am. Philatelic Brokerages, Tucson, 1946—. Chmn. bd. dirs. Ariz. Philatelic Rangers, Tucson, 1987—; bd. dirs. Postal History Found. Chmn. bd. 1869 Pictorial Rsch. Assn., 1969, bd. dirs., 1970-76, chmn. Baha'i Faith Adminstrv. Body, Pima County, Ariz., 1977-81, 83-91; sheriff, chmn. Santa Catalina Corral of Westerners Internat., Tucson, 1986; bd. dirs. Tucson chpt. Nordmanns-Forburdet (Norse Fedn.), 2002-05, Future of Philately Commn., 2005-06; participant Arago rsch. project Smithsonian Inst., 2005—. Recipient Large Gold and Spl. award Spanish Soc. Internat., San Juan, P.R., 1982, New Zealand Soc. Internat., Auckland, 1990, Large Internat. Gold award Australian Soc. Internat., Melbourne, 1984, Swedish Soc. Internat., Stockholm, 1986, Singapore Soc. Internat., 1995, U.S. Soc. Internat., San Francisco, 1997, Internat. Gold award U.S. Soc. Internat., Chgo., 1986, Bulgarian Soc. Internat., Sofia, 1989. Mem. Am. Philatelic Soc. (U.S. Champion of Champions award 1985), U.S. Philatelic Classics Soc. (disting. philatelist award 1995), Am. Philatelic Congress (McCoy award 1969, 97), Scandinavian Collectors Club, Collectors Club N.Y., Western Cover Soc. Avocations: swimming, travel, music, West U.S. historical research, Japanese antiques. Office: Am Philatelic Brokerages PO Box 36657 Tucson AZ 85740-6657 Office Phone: 520-297-1544. Personal E-mail: jb2nd@earthlink.net. *To look for and appreciate the good qualities in each individual, to have sympathy and empathy for their problems, and to provide exceptional service in an attempt to satisfy their needs and desires.*

BIRKY, JOHN EDWARD, banker, financial consultant; b. Minier, Ill., July 16, 1934; s. John G. and Gertrude K. (Nafziger) B.; m. Susan Becker, Dec. 13, 1937; children: John Brian, Kathleen Debera. BS in Indsl. Adminstrn., U. Ill., 1957; postgrad., Ohio State U., 1957; MBA, Case Western Res. U., 1975. Cert. data processor. Asst. to mgr. Caterpillar Tractor Co., Peoria, Ill., 1957-61; cons. Sutherland Co., Peoria, 1961-63; mgr. United Research Services, San Mateo, Calif., 1963-69; dir. Case Western Res. U., Cleve., 1969-72; v.p. Fed. Res. Bank, Cleve., 1972-79; exec. v.p. Banc Systems Assn., West Lake, Ohio, 1979-83, Citizens Banking Corp., Flint, Mich., 1983-92, also chmn. auto com., mem. corp. exec. com., 1986-92; fin. planner Bonita Springs, Fla., 1992-98; fin. adviser Amex Fin. Advisors, Inc.; ind. fin. cons. Hopedale, Ill. Bd. dirs. Citizens Bank, Flint, Comml. Nat. Bank, Berwyn, Ill., Citizens Leasing Corp., Grand Rapids, Mich., Flin Inst. Music; chmn. Magicline Inc., 1989-91; speaker various profl. confs. Contbr. articles to banking jours. Mem. Rep. precinct com., Sierra Vista, Ariz., 1964-65; life mem. Pres.'s Task Force, Washington, 1980; advisor automation commn. ARC, Flint, 1987; mem. exec. bd., treas. Flint Inst. Music, 1986-88, vice chmn.; mem. Am. Bank Adminstrn. Ins.; bd. dirs. Flint Inst. Music; elder, lay pastor 1st Presbyn. Ch., Flint, 1988-91; past mem. adv. com. U. Mich., Flint, Boys Club Cleve., Cuyahoga C.C., Ashland Coll.; bd. dirs. Catalina coun. Golden Eagle Club Boy Scouts; pres. Friends of Catalina Resource Svcs. Capt. USAF, 1957-60. Mem.: Data Processing Mgmt. Assn., Am. Bankers Assn., Acacia, U. Ill. Alumni Assn. (life; pres. coun.), Am. Legion, Tucson Alumni Club (v.p.), Saddlebrooke Country Club, Scottish Rite, Shriners, Masons. Republican. Avocations: golf, tennis, barbershop singing.

BIRLE, JAMES ROBB, investor; b. Phila., Jan. 25, 1936; s. John George and Mildred C. (Donnelly) B.; m. Mary Margaret McDaniels, Jan. 28, 1961; children— James Robb, Jr., Anne Margaret, Alexandra Lea, John George II BSM.E., Villanova U., 1958. With Gen. Electric Co., San Jose, Calif., 1958, gen. mgr. nuclear energy bus., 1969-77, v.p., gen mgr. far east business div. NYC, 1977-81, v.p., gen mgr. air condition div. Louisville, 1981-82, sr. v.p., group exec. constrn. and engring. svcs. group Westport, Conn, 1982-85, sr. v.p. corp. trading ops. NYC, 1985-88; ptnr. The Blackstone Group, NYC, 1988-94; co-chmn., CEO Collins & Aikman Group, NYC, 1988-94; chmn. Resolute Ptnrs., LLC, Village of Golf, Fla., 1994—; non-exec. chmn. Mass. Mut. Fin. Svcs. Co., 2005—. Bd. dirs. Mass. Mut. Fin. Svcs. Co. 1992-, chmn. bd. Mass Mutual Fin. Group; former mem. Transparency Internat. Former trustee Villanova U., 2005-. Republican. Avocations: tennis, golf, reading, sailing. Office: Resolute Ptnrs LLC 2 Pine Ln East Village Of Golf FL 33436 Home: 2 Pine Ln E Village Of Golf FL 33436

BIRMAN, JOSEPH LEON, physics professor; b. NYC, May 21, 1927; m. Joan Sylvia Lyttle, Feb. 22, 1950; children: Kenneth, Deborah, Carl-David. BS, CCNY, 1947; MA, Columbia U., 1950, PhD, 1952; DSc honoris causa, U. Rènnes, France, 1974. From sr. physicist to head luminescence sect. GTE Research Labs., NY, 1952-62; Mary Amanda Wood vis. prof. U. Pa., 1960; assoc. prof. physics NYU, 1962-64, prof., 1964-74; Henry Semat prof. physics CCNY, 1974-88; Disting. prof. physics CCNY and Grad. Sch. CUNY, 1987—. Cons. rsch. labs.; vis. prof. U. Paris VI, Ecole Normale Superieure, 1969-70, Japan Soc. Promotion of Sci., Rsch. Inst. Fundamental Physics, U. Kyoto, Japan, 1978, 1980, Inst. Hautes Etudes Scientifiques, Bures/Yvette, France, 1976, 1978, 1980, 1982, 1986, 1987-88, 1991, U. Regensburg, 1983, 1984, 1985, Oxford U., Eng.,1981, 1984, 1985, 1986, Technion, Israel, 1981, 1995-2007, Peking, Fudan, Nanking, Xian Univs., 1980, 1982, 1985, U. Stuttgart, 1986, U. Paris VI, 1987-88, 1991, Weitzmann Inst., Rehovoth, 1988, Nankai U., 2004, 07; founder, chmn. Am. coordinating com. Chinese Scholars Program, joint program Am. Phys. Soc. and Chinese Acad. Sci./Chinese State Com. Edn., 1983-86. Author: Theoretical Physics, 1952, Handbuch der Physik, Vol. 25/2b, 1974, reprinted 1984 (Russian transl. 1978); editor: Light Scattering in Solids, 1976, 79; co-editor: Laser Optics of Condensed Matter, 1988; mem. editl. bd., consulting editor: Springer Verlag, Plenum Press, Nova Pubs., World Sci. Press; US Physics Del., Oxford U. Press; contbr. more than 300 articles to profl. jours. Served with USNR, 1945-46. Rsch. grantee NSF, NRC-U.S., Army Rsch. Office, Aerospace Rsch. Labs., Dept. Def.; J.S. Guggenheim Meml. Found. fellow, 1980-81. Fellow Am. Phys. Soc. (com. Internat. Freedom of Scientists 1991-93, chmn. Forum Internat. Physics, 1993, 1999), AAAS (com. sci. freedom and responsibility 1991-93), NY Acad. Scis. (human rights com. 1980—, chair 1993-05, gov.-at-large 1989-90, v.p. 1991-92, Heinz Pagels Human Rights award 2006), Com. Concerned Scientists (vice chair), Human Rights in China (hon. bd. mem. 2005-, bd. mem. 1988-05). Office: CCNY Physics Dept Rm MR424 138th St And Convent Ave New York NY 10031

BIRMELIN, ROBERT, artist; b. Newark, 1933; BFA, Yale U., 1956, MFA, 1960. Tchr. Queens Coll., NYC. One-man shows include Galerie Claude Bernard, Paris, 1981, Montclair Art Mus., Montclair, NJ, 1984, Schaefer Gallery Custavus Adolphus Coll., St. Peter, Minn., 1986, Galeria Mara, Buenos Aires, 1990, Rider U. Art Gallery, Lawrenceville, NJ, 1991, Morris Mus., Morristown, NJ, 1991, Jaffe Baker Gallery, Boca Raton, Fla., 1992, Contemporary Realist Gallery, San Francisco, 1993, 1995, Ralph Greene Galllery, Albuquerque, 1994, Godwin-Ternbach Mus. Queens Coll., Flushing, NY, 1996, Jersey City Mus., Jersey City, NJ, 1997—98, Hackett-Freedman Gallery, San Francisco, 2001, others. Recipient Carnegie Prize, NAD Annual, Altman Prize, Purchase award, Am. Inst Arts and Letters, San Francisco Mus., H.G. Scheidt Meml. Prize, Pa. Acad. Art; grantee, Am. Acad. Rome, 1961—64, Nat. Inst. Arts and Letters, 1968, Louis Comfort Tiffany Found., 1973, NJ Coun. for Arts, 1980, 1988, Nat. Endowment of Arts, 1976, 1982, 1989. Address: Peter Findlay Gallery 41 E 57th St New York NY 10022

BIRMINGHAM, RICHARD GREGORY, lawyer; b. Buffalo, Aug. 14, 1929; s. William Anthony and Laura Louise (Reimann) B.; m. Suzanne M. Cannon, May 20, 1961; children: Barbara A. McCarty, Maureen E., Gregory S. BA, U. Notre Dame, 1951; JD, SUNY, Buffalo, 1957. Bar: N.Y. 1957, Del. 1984, Pa. 1993. Law clk. to justices appellate div. N.Y. Supreme Ct. (4th dept.), Rochester, 1957-60; ptnr. Phillips, Lytle, Hitchcock, Blaine & Huber, Buffalo, 1960-84, 90-94, ret., 1994, ptnr. Wilmington, Del., 1984-90. Lt. comdr. USN, 1951-54, Korea. Mem. ABA, N.Y. State Bar Assn., Del. Bar Assn., Erie County Bar Assn., Rivermont Country Club. Republican. Roman Catholic. Office: 510 Shelli Ln Roswell GA 30075-2988 Personal E-mail: rgsb510@hotmail.com.

BIRMINGHAM, RICHARD JOSEPH, lawyer; b. Seattle, Feb. 26, 1953; s. Joseph E. and Anita (Loomis) B. BA cum laude, Wash. State U., 1975; JD, Seattle U., 1978; LLM in Taxation, Boston U., 1980. Bar: Wash. 1978, Oreg. 1981, U.S. Dist. Ct. (we. dist.) Wash. 1978, U.S. Tax Ct. 1981. Ptnr. Davis Wright Tremaine, Seattle, 1982-93; shareholder Birmingham Thorson & Barnett, P.C., Seattle, 1993—. Mem. King County Bar Employee Benefit Com., Seattle, 1986, U.S. Treasury ad hoc com. employee benefits, 1988—. Contbg. editor: Compensation and Benefits Mgmt., 1985—; contbr. articles to profl. jours. Mem. ABA (employee benefits and exec. compensation com. 1982—), Wash. State Bar Assn. (speaker 1984-86, tax sect. 1982—), Oreg. State Bar Assn. (tax sect. 1982—), Western Pension Conf. (speaker 1986), Seattle Pension Round table. Democrat. Avocations: jogging, bicycling, photography. Home: 3820 49th Ave NE Seattle WA 98105-5234 Office: Birmingham Thorson & Barnett PC 3315 Two Union Square 601 Union St Seattle WA 98101-2341 Business E-Mail: RBirmingham@BTBPC.com.

BIRMINGHAM, STEPHEN, writer; b. Hartford, Conn., May 28, 1931; s. Thomas J. and Editha (Gardner) B.; m. Janet Tillson, Jan. 5, 1951 (div.); children: Mark, Harriet, Carey. BA cum laude, Williams Coll., 1950; postgrad., Univ. Coll., Oxford U., Eng., 1951. Advt. copywriter Needham, Harper & Steers, Inc., 1953-67. Author: Young Mr. Keefe, 1958, Barbara Greer, 1959, The Towers of Love, 1961, Those Harper Women, 1963, Fast Start, Fast Finish, 1966, Our Crowd: The Great Jewish Families of New York, 1967, The Right People, 1968, Heart Toubles, 1968, The Grandees, 1971, The Late John Marquand, 1972, The Right Places, 1973, Real Lace, 1973, Certain People: America's Black Elite, 1977, The Golden Dream: Suburbia in the 1970's, 1978, Jacqueline Bouvier Kennedy Onassis, 1978, Life at the Dakota, 1979, California Rich, 1980, Duchess, 1981, The Grandes Dames, 1982, The Auerbach Will, 1983; The Rest of Us, 1984, The LeBaron Secret, 1986, Americas Secret Aristocracy, 1987, Shades of Fortune, 1989, The Rothman Scandal, 1991, Carriage Trade, 1993, The Wrong Kind of Money, 1997; contbr. numerous articles to numerous periodicals. Served with AUS, 1951-53. Mem. New Eng. Soc. of City of N.Y., Phi Beta Kappa. Democrat. Episcopalian. Address: 1247 Ida St Cincinnati OH 45202-1525 Office Phone: 513-241-8919.

BIRMINGHAM, THOMAS F., lawyer, former state legislator; b. Aug. 4, 1949; married; two daughters. AB in Social Studies cum laude, Harvard Coll., 1972; Rhodes Scholar, Oxford Univ., 1972—75; JD cum laude, Harvard Coll., 1978. Bar: Mass., US Dist. Ct. Mass., US Ct. Appeals (1st cir.), US State Supreme Ct. Asst. gen. counsel Internat. Union Electrical Workers, 1978-80; assoc. atty. Flamm, Kaplan, Paven & Feinberg, 1980-83; ptnr. Flamm & Birmingham, 1984-93; mem. Mass. Senate, Boston, 1991—2002, pres., 1996—2002; ptnr. Feinberg, Charnas & Birmingham, 1994—; sr. counsel Edwards Angell Palmer & Dodge, Boston. Faculty mem. Boston Labor Guild Sch. Indsl. Rels., 1980-85; senate chair Edn. Arts and Humanities Com., 1991-92, Ways and Means Com. State Mass., 1993-2002; mem. Steering and Policy Com. State Mass., 1993-2002. Commr. Chelsea Redevelopment Authority, 1985-88; bd. dirs. New England Higher Edn., 1991—, Boston Plan for Excellence (bd. trustees), Boys & Girls Clubs Boston Inc., PreservatiON MASS (bd. dirs.), Am. Cancer Soc., Bay Windows, Children Trust Fund, Mass. Coalition of Police, Project Bread, Meals on Wheels, Mass. Alliance for Arts and Edu. Harvard Coll. Academic scholar, 1969-72, U. Coll. Galway scholar, 1970, Rhodes scholar, 1972-75; Teaching fellow Harvard Coll., 1971. Mem. Mass. Bar Assn. (labor law sec. coun. mem.), Mass. Mcpl. Assn., Women's Bar Assn., Unified Veterans Assn. Office: Edwards Angell Palmer & Dodge 101 Federal St Boston MA 02110 Office Phone: 617-239-0228. Office Fax: 617-439-4170. Business E-Mail: tbirmingham@eapdlaw.com. E-mail: Tbirming@sen.state.ma.us.*

BIRMINGHAM, WILLIAM JOSEPH, retired lawyer; b. Lynbrook, NY, Aug. 7, 1923; s. Daniel Joseph and Mary Elizabeth (Tighe) B.; m. Helen Elizabeth Roche, July 23, 1955; children: Deirdre, Patrick, Maureen, Kathleen, Brian. ME, Stevens Inst. Tech., Hoboken, NJ, 1944; MBA, Harvard U., Cambridge, Mass., 1948; JD, DePaul U., Chgo., 1953. Bar: Ill. 1953, U.S. Patent and Trademark Office, 1955, U.S. Dist. Ct. (no. dist.) Ill. 1960, U.S. Supreme Ct. 1961, U.S. Ct. Appeals (7th cir.) 1962, U.S. Ct. Appeals (3rd cir.) 1968, U.S. Ct. Mil. Appeals 1973, U.S. Ct. Appeals (Fed. cir.) 1982, U.S. Ct. Claims 1986; registered profl. engr., Ill., Ind. Chem. engr. Standard Oil Co. Ind., Chgo., 1948-53; patent atty., 1953-59; assoc. Neuman, Williams, Anderson & Olson, Chgo., 1959-60, ptnr., 1961—91, Leydig, Voit & Mayer, Ltd., Chgo., 1991-93, of counsel, 1994—96; ret., 1997. Served to capt. USNR, 1942-75, ret. Mem. ABA, ASME, Fed. Cir. Bar Assn., Am. Intellectual Property Law Assn., Intellectual Property Law Assn. Chgo. Home: 233 Pine St Deerfield IL 60015-4853

BIRN, STUART R., lawyer; b. Bklyn., Jan. 30, 1947; BA, U. Cin., 1968, JD, 1971. Bar: Ohio 1973, Mich. 1982. Atty. Auto-Owners Ins. Co., Lansing, Mich., 1974—91, sr. v.p., sec., gen. counsel. Mem.: State Bar Mich., Ohio State Bar Assn. Office: Auto-Owners Insurance Co 6101 Anacapri Blvd Lansing MI 48917 Office Phone: 517-323-1200. Office Fax: 517-323-8796. E-mail: birn.stuart@aoins.com.*

BIRNBAUM, BARRY WILLIAM, special education educator; b. Chgo., Oct. 9, 1952; s. Irving and Beatrice (Factoroff) B. BS, So. Ill. U., 1974; MA, Northeastern Ill. U., 1980; EdD, Nova U., 1991. Cert. secondary spl. edn. tchr., elem. tchr., middle sch. tchr. Tchr. Wood Dale (Ill.) Sch. Dist., 1982-86, Palm Beach (Fla.) Cmty. Schs., Palm Beach County, 1985-93; program prof. Nova U., Ft. Lauderdale, Fla., 1993-95; inclusion specialist Sch. Dist. # 59, Arlington Heights, Ill., 1996-97; prin. Neumann Sch., Chgo.; ednl. svcs. adminstr. South Ctrl. Comm. Svcs., Chgo., 1997-98; prof. spl. edn. Chgo. State U., 1997-2000, Northeastern Ill. U., Chgo., 2000—. Named Fla. Tchr. of Yr., Fla. Assn. for Gifted, 1991, IBM/Tech. and Learning Tchr. of Yr., 1992, Prof. Recognized Spl. Educator in Teaching and Adminstrn., Coun. for Exceptional Children. Mem. Phi Delta Kappa. Democrat. Jewish. Avocations: theater, reading, technology. Home: 5225 W Eddy St Chicago IL 60641-3309 Office: Northeastern Ill U Classroom 4052 Spl Edn 5500 N St Louis Ave Chicago IL 60625 Office Phone: 773-442-5593. E-mail: b-birnbaum@neiu.edu.

BIRNBAUM, CHARLES A., landscape architect; Pvt. practice; coord. landscape initiative Nat. Pk. Svc., 1992—. Loeb fellow Grad. Sch. Design Harvard U., 1998, instr. profl. devel. program Grad. Sch. Design; instr. Nat. Preservation Inst.; founder Cultural Landscape Found. Editor: Preserving Modern Landscape Architecture I and II, Pioneers of American Landscape Design, Design with Culture: Claiming America's Landscape Heritage. Recipient Samuel H. Kress fellow, Am. Acad. in Rome. Fellow: Am. Soc. Landscape Archs. Office: Nat Park Svc 1201 Eye St Washington DC 20005

BIRNBAUM, EDWARD LESTER, lawyer; b. Bklyn., Aug. 2, 1939; s. Isaac and Rita Birnbaum; m. Madeleine Birnbaum, Apr. 10, 1965; children: Amanda, Jordan. BA, CUNY, 1961; LLB, NYU, 1964. Bar: NY 64, US Dist. Ct. (so. and ea. dists.) NY 67, US Ct. Appeals (2d cir.) 70, US Supreme Ct. 71, US Dist. Ct. (we. dist.) NY 83. Assoc. Korkus & Korkus, NYC, 1964—66, Herzfeld & Rubin, P.C., NYC, 1967—. Lectr. field; mem. faculty NYU Sch. Continuing Edn., Law Taxation, 1987—; arbitrator small claims night ct. Contbr. articles to profl. jours.; co-author: NY Trial Notebook, 2005. Coach Little League Baseball, Little League Basketball; pres., v.p. Village Saddle Rock Civic Assn., chmn. bd. appeals; town counsel North Hempstead, NY; del. jud. conv. Liberal Party County Com.; chair Village of Saddle Rock Bd. Appeals. Mem.: ATLA, ABA, NY Bar Found., NY State Trial Lawyers Assn., Am. Arbitration Assn. (arbitrator), Nassau County Bar Assn., Queens County Bar Assn., NY County Bar Assn., NY State Bar Assn. (chmn. com. Supreme Ct., chmn. action unit #6). Home: 70 Shelly Ln Great Neck NY 11023-1822 Office: Herzfeld & Rubin PC 40 Wall St New York NY 10005-2349 Office Phone: 212-471-8540. E-mail: ebirnbaum@herzfeld-rubin.com. *Life is to be lived with understanding and consideration for others and with understanding and consideration from others.*

BIRNBAUM, IRWIN MORTON, educational consultant, lawyer; b. Bklyn., July 15, 1935; s. Sol N. and Rose (Cohen) B.; m. Arlene R. Burrows, June 8, 1957; children: Bruce J., Leslie R. Birnbaum Ventura, Amy G. Birnbaum Heath. BS in Acctg., Bklyn. Coll., 1956; JD, NYU, 1961. Bar: N.Y. 1962. Budget officer Montefiore Med. Ctr., Bronx, NY, 1962-70, v.p., chief fin. officer, 1970-86; counsel Proskauer & Rose LLP, NYC, 1986-89, ptnr., 1989-97; COO Yale Univ. Sch. Medicine, New Haven, 1997—2004, sr. advisor to the dean, 2004—05, sr. advisor Robert Wood Johnson Clin. Scholars Program, 2005—. Chmn. bd. dirs. FFH/North East Ins. Com., 1998-2004, Fedn. Jewish Philanthropies Svcs. Corp., 2006; mem. exec. com. and chair fin. com. Med. Ctr. Ins. Co. Vt., Inc., 1997-2005; adj. prof. Yale U. Sch. Medicine; lectr. pub. health, health policy, adminstrn. Sch. Medicine Yale U.; trustee South County Hosp., South Kingstown, RI, 2007. Editor: Health Care Law Treatise, 1990. Trustee, treas., exec. com. Malmonides Med. Ctr., Bklyn., 1988—; sec./treas., exec. com. Hosp. Trustees N.Y. State, 1990-97; bd. dirs. Jewish Home for the Aged, New Haven Fellow N.Y. Acad. Medicine; mem. Assn. of Bar of City of N.Y. (sec. com. on medicine and law 1989-90, sec. health law com. 1995-96), Am. Acad. Hosp. Attys. (spl. com. in health care systems). Avocations: sailing, tennis, reading, travel. Home: 383 Temple St New Haven CT 06511-6801 Office Phone: 203-785-3782. Business E-Mail: irwin.birnbaum@yale.edu.

BIRNBAUM, NORMAN, writer, humanities educator; b. NYC, July 21, 1926; s. Silas Jacob and Jean (Bermen) B.; children: Anna, Antonia. BA, Williams Coll., 1947; MA, Harvard U., 1951, PhD, 1958. Editor OWI, 1943-45; tchg. fellow Harvard U., 1948-52; tutor Adams House, 1949- 52; asst. lectr. London Sch. Econs. and Polit. Sci., U. London, 1953-55, lectr., 1955-59; fellow Nuffield (Eng.) Coll., Oxford (Eng.) U., 1959-66; vis. prof. faculty letters and human scis. U. Strasbourg, France, 1964-66; prof. grad. faculty New Sch. Social Rsch., 1966-68; prof. Amherst Coll., 1968—. Mem. Inst. Advanced Study, 1975-76; guest fellow Wissenschaftskolleg, Berlin, 1986; Mellon vis. prof. humanities Georgetown U. Law Ctr., 1979-81; prof. Georgetown U., 1981-2001, prof. emeritus, 2001— sr. scholar Inst. for Policy Studies, 2002-; cons. NSC, Exec. Office Pres., 1978; vis. prof. Ecole des Hautes Etudes en Scis. Sociales, Paris, 1991; chair scholarly adv. bd. Internat. Inst. Peace, Vienna, 1991—. Author: Sociological Study of Ideology (1940-60), 1962; (with others) Sociology and Religion, 1968, Crisis of Industrial Society, 1969, Towards a Critical Sociology, 1971, Beyond the Crisis, 1977, Social Structure and the German Reformation, 1980, The Radical Renewal, 1988, Searching for the Light, 1993, After Progress, 2001; contbg. editor Change mag. of Higher Edn., 1970-74; mem. editl. bd. Praxis, 1986-92, The Nation, 1978—; editl. cons. Patisan Rev., 1971-83. Cons. Giovanni Agnelli Found., 1972-75; mem. Wellfleet Psychohistory Conf., 1970-; adviser UAW, Congrl. Progressive Caucus, 1996-; mem. exec. com. New Dem. Coalition, 1978-, chmn. policy adv. coun., 1980-82; mem. nat. exec. com. Dem. Socialist Organizing Com., 1973-77, nat. adv. bd., 1980-82; mem. founding editl. bd. New Left Rev., London, 1959; sec. com. sociology religion Internat. Sociol. Assn., 1959-, chmn., 1970-74; adviser Dem. Nat. Campaign, 1976, Edward M. Kennedy campaign, 1979, Cranston campaign, 1980, Jackson campaigns, 1980, 1988; adviser European Socialist Parties, 1979—; founding com. Campaign for Am. Future, 1996; Fulbright chair Univ. Bologna, 1998; visitor London Sch. of Econs., 1998, Nuffield Coll., 2001. Guggenheim fellow, 1971. Fellow: Inst. Policy Studies (sr.); mem.: Am. Sociol. Assn. (coun. 1979—82, columnist El Pais 1993—, exec. com. for rep. 2006—). Office: Georgetown U Law Ctr 600 New Jersey Ave NW Washington DC 20001-2075 Home Phone: 202-342-0241; Office Phone: 202-662-9062. Business E-Mail: birnbaum@law.georgetown.edu. *I have always thought that one of the strongest ethical and biological forces propelling us is a concern for our children— for our own children and for the continuation of humanity. This elementary sense of care seems increasingly challenged, by doctrines of callousness and selfishness, poorly disguised as recognition of the sovereignty of the market. It is that sovereignty which threatens us as citizens, and which accounts for the outbursts of hatred and rage we know as the new ethnicity, the new fundamentalism, the new nationalism--all of them, alas,very old.*

BIRNBAUM, ROBBY H., lawyer; b. Milw., May 8, 1974; BA, U. Wis., Madison, 1996, JD, 1999. Law clk. to Hon. Jeffrey Wagner, Milw., 1994; intern to Hon. William Bablitch Wis. Supreme Ct., Madison, 1997; atty. Greenpea Marder, PA, Ft. Lauderdale, Fla., 1998—. Mem.: Assn. Settlement Cos., State Bar Wis., State Bar Fla., Broward County C. of C.

BIRNBAUM, SHEILA L., lawyer, educator; b. Mar. 5, 1940; BA, Hunter Coll., 1960, MA, 1962; LLB, NYU Sch. Law, 1965. Bar: NY 1965. Legal asst. Superior Ct., NYC, 1965; assoc. Berman & Frost, NYC, 1965-70, ptnr., 1970-72; prof. Fordham U., NYC, 1972-78; prof. law NYU, NYC, 1978—84, assoc. dean, graduate divsn., 1982-84; ptnr. mass tort and insurance litigation Skadden, Arps, Slate, Meagher & Flom, LLP, NYC, 1984—. Chair NY State Adv. Com. on Civil Practice, 1981—86; adj. prof. law NYU Sch. Law, 1984—; mem. 2nd Cir. Com. on the Improvement of Civil Litigation, 1986—88, NY State Jud. Commn. on Minorities, 1988—91; exec. dir. Second Cir. Task Force for Racial, Ethnic and Gender Fairness, 1994—97; mem. jud. conf. adv. com. on rules and civil procedure US Supreme Ct., 1997—2004; chair, Commn. Fiduciary Appointments NY State Court System, 2000—; lectr. in field; mem. adv. com. to the Restatement of the Law of Product Liability and Complex Litigation Project. Author: (with Rheingold) Products Liability, Law, Practice Science, 1974; co-author: Practitioner's Guide to Litigating Insurance Coverage Actions; columnist NY Law Jour., Nat. Law Jour.; contbr. articles to profl. jours. First pres. and founding mem. Judges and Lawyers Breast Cancer Alert. Named one of 50 Most Powerful Women in Am. Bus., Fortune Mag., 75 Most Influential Women in Bus., Crain's NY Bus., 100 Most Outstanding Members of the Legal Profession, Nat. Law Jour., 100 Most Influential Lawyers, 2006, The 50 Most Influential Women Lawyers in Am., 2007; named to, Hunter Coll. Hall of Fame; recipient John J. McCloy Meml. award, Fund for Modern Courts, 2003, Florence E. Allen award, NYU Sch. Law and NY Women's Bar Assn., Louis D. Brandeis award, Am. Jewish Congress, Law and Society award, NY Lawyers for the Public Interest, NYU Law Alumni award for Outstanding Achievement in the Legal Profession, George A. Katz Torch of Learning award, Milton S. Gould award for Outstanding Appellate Advocacy, Award for Achieving the Highest Standards of Professional Excellence, Touro Law Sch. Mem. NYC Bar Assn. (mem. exec. com. 1978—, jud. com. 1977), NY Women's Bar Assn. (pres. 1974-75), ABA (coun. of the sect. of torts and insurance practice 1982-86, spl. com. on the future of the legal profession 1996-97, House of Delegates 1997-98, chmn. product gen. liability, consumer land coms., Margaret Brent Women Lawyers of Achievement award), Am. Law Inst. (mem. coun. 1989-), Assn. of Bar of City of NY (exec. com. 1978—, 2nd century com. 1984-86, v.p. 1987), Phi Beta Kappa, Phi Alpha Theta, Alpha Chi Alpha. Office: Skadden Arps Slate Meagher & Flom LLP 4 Times Sq New York NY 10036 Office Phone: 212-735-2450. Office Fax: 917-777-2450. E-mail: sbirnbau@skadden.com.*

BIRNBERG, JACK, financial executive; b. June 15, 1937; s. Max and Yetta (Halpern) B.; m. Louise Rothstein, June 7, 1959; children: Michael, Steven, John, Jeffrey. BS, Fairleigh Dickinson U., 1959. Acct. firm Scholtz, Simon & Miller, 1960-61; contr., officer Scott, Harvey Co., Inc., 1962-63; pres. M.A. Allan & Co., Inc., Clifton, NJ, 1963-71, dir., 1963-71; chmn. bd. Edios, Inc., 1969-77, Jack Birnberg & Assocs., Inc.; pres. NE Regional Assn. Small Bus. Investment Corp., NY, 1970—71, Internat. Equities, Ltd., Clifton, 1970-71. Chmn. bd., dir. Tappan-Zee Capital Corp., 1973-2005, exec. com. NE Region; chmn. bd. BB Energy Corp., Waldorf Auto Leasing Corp., Waldorf Group, Inc.; dir., chmn. exec. com. Ferdon Equipment Corp.; chmn. bd. dirs. Met. Fin. Corp., 1968—, AIP Risk Group, 1968—, Ascot Solutions, Inc., 1980; mem. Midwest Stock Exch., 1968-76, Phila.-Balt.-Washington Stock Exch., 1968-76; guest lectr. Fla. Atlantic U., 2000-01. Co-host radio program Off The Record, Sta. WPBR, 2001-01; radio talk show host Jack Birnberg Speaks Out, NYC, 2001-, Sta. WVNJ, 2001-. Pres. Passaic County Children's Shelter, 1967-68; bd. dirs. Birnberg Found., 1969—, Boys Club, Paterson, NJ, 1970-75, Barnert Hosp., 1971-91, Employee Retirement Benefit Assn., 1975-1985, Barnert Temple, 1976-1995; chmn. met. divsn. United Jewish Appeal, 1970; dir. greater Paterson YW-YMHA, 1970-75; pres. Daus. Miriam Home for Aged, 1995-1997, bd. mem., 1971—, bd. dirs., 1995-97; chmn. Expo 200 Barnert Temple, 1976—; trustee various corps., U.S. Bankruptcy Ct. Mem. N.E. Regional Assn. Small Bus. Investment Corps. (pres. 1985-86), Nat. Assn. Small Bus. Investment Corps. (bd. govs. 1985-93), B'nai B'rith (trustee Greater Clifton chpt. 1962-64), Preakness Hills Country Club (bd. govs. 1992-96, treas. 1994-95), Polo Club Boca Raton. Office: 25 Whitney Rd Mahwah NJ 07430 Office Phone: 201-560-1180. Personal E-mail: jackbirnberg@aol.com.

BIRNE, KENNETH ANDREW, lawyer; b. Englewood, NJ, Apr. 2, 1956; s. Alvin Aaron and Rita May (Gorsky) B.; m. Pamela Beth Ross; children: Jennafer Sara, Allison Francie, Jonathan Ross. BA in Polit. Sci., Ohio State U., 1978; JD, Case Western Res. U., 1981. Bar: Ohio 1981, U.S. Dist. Ct. (no. dist.) Ohio 1981. Sole practice, Cleve., 1981-85; ptnr. Peltz & Birne, Cleve., 1985—. Instr. Am. Inst. Paralegal Studies, Cleve., 1982-93, pers. dir. Cleve. area, 1984-93; cons. in field. Mem. Ohio Bar Assn., Cleve. Bar Assn. (chmn. practice and procedure clinic 1984-86, vol. Call for Action 1986, meritorious service award 1986), Cuyahoga County Bar Assn., Phi Eta Sigma, Zeta Beta Tau, Phi Delta Phi. Lodges: Masons. Office Phone: 216-292-4900.

BIRNEY, WALTER LEROY, religious administrator; b. Garden City, Kans., Apr. 25, 1934; s. Claude David and Mildred Elizabeth (Ferris) B.; m. Iva Lou Mosher, June 18, 1954; children: Mickey, Scotty, Gary, Lorrie, Lindie. BA, Dallas Christian Coll., 1956. Min. First Christian Ch., Benjamin, Tex., 1954-57, Bellaire Christian Ch., San Antonio, 1957-58, Copeland (Kans.) Christian Ch., 1958-84; coord. Nat. Missionary Conv., Copeland, 1966—. Dean, promoter Ashland (Kans.) Christian Camp, 1961-84; promoter S.W. Sch. Missions, Copeland, 1973-84. Named Outstanding Alumnus Dallas Christian Coll., 1988, Named to Dallas Christian Coll. Basketball Hall of Fame, 2004. Mem. Christian Ch. Avocation: running. Office: Nat Missionary Conv PO Box 11 Copeland KS 67837-0011 Office Phone: 620-668-5259. E-mail: wbirne11@aol.com.

BIRNKRANT, HENRY JOSEPH, lawyer; b. Phila., Jan. 24, 1955; s. Harry Philip and Myra Arlene (Hendler) B.; m. Lynn Rachel Goldin, Oct. 23, 1983; children: Aviva Michelle, Beth Elana. BA magna cum laude, U. Rochester, 1976; JD, Columbia U., 1979; LLM, NYU, 1983. Bar: D.C. 1979, U.S. Dist. Ct. D.C. 1980; U.S. Ct. Appeals (D.C. cir.) 1980, U.S. Tax Ct. 1984. Assoc. Bergson, Borkland, Margolis & Adler, Washington, 1979-82, Covington & Burling, Washington, 1983-88, Cole, Corette & Abrutyn, Washington, 1988-90, ptnr., 1991-96; ptnr., co-chair, tax sect. Alston & Bird LLP, Washington, 1997—. Author: (with others) Butterworth's International Taxation of Financial Instruments and Transactions, 1989; editor: Columbia Jour. Law and Social Problems, 1979; contbr. articles to profl. jours.; bd. advisors Jour. Internat. Taxation. Fellow Am. Coll. Tax Counsel; mem. ABA (tax section), Internat. Bar Assn., Thomson West Tax Adv. Bd., Tax Treaty Subcommittee of U.S. Council for Internat. Bus. (chair). Home: 5506 Durbin Rd Bethesda MD 20814-1012 Office: Alston & Bird LLP Atlantic Bldg 950 F St NW Washington DC 20004-1404 Office Fax: 202-756-3333. Business E-Mail: hbirnkrant@alston.com.

BIRNS, IRA MICHAEL, corporate financial executive; b. Long Beach, NY, Sept. 12, 1962; s. Alfred and Edith (Moskovich) B.; m. Francine Silver, Mar. 19, 1988. BBA in Pub. Acctg., Hofstra U., 1983. CPA, Cert. Treas. Profl. Internal auditor Culbro Corp., NYC, 1983-85, fin. analyst, 1985-86, asst. treas., 1986-89, Arrow Electronics, Inc., Melville, NY, 1989—96, treas., 1996—2003, v.p., treas., 2003—04, v.p. investor rels. & treas., 2004—07; exec. v.p., CFO World Fuel Services Corp., Miami, Fla., 2007—. Mem., past vice-chmn., Assn. Fin. Professionals; mem. AICPAs, N.Y. State Soc. CPAs, Nat. Corp. Cash Mgmt. Assn., Treasury Mgmt. Assn. L.I. (co-founder 1991). Republican. Jewish. Avocation: rare coin collecting. Office: World Fuel Services Ste 400 9800 NW 41st St Miami FL 33178*

BIRNS, MARK THEODORE, physician; b. Bklyn., Sept. 24, 1949; s. Leon and Naomi B.; m. Ann Krieger, Aug. 15, 1976; children: Samantha Lynn, Michael Eric, Kevin Douglas. BA, Case Western Res. U., 1971; MD, Albert Einstein Coll. Medicine, 1974. Diplomate: Am. Bd. Internal Medicine, Am. Bd. Gastroenterology. Intern Bronx Mcpl. Hosp. Ctr. Albert Einstein Hosps., 1974-75, resident in medicine, 1975-77; fellow in gastroenterology U. Oreg. Health Scis. Ctr., 1977-79; asst. chief gastroenterology Walter Reed Army Med. Ctr., 1979-83; asst. prof. medicine U. Health Scis., 1980-83; emergency physician Shady Grove Adventist Hosp., part time, 1980-83, Frederick Meml. Hosp., Washington, 1980-83; practice medicine specializing in gastroenterology and endoscopic biliary surgery Rockville, Md., 1983—; active staff Shady Grove Adventist Hosp.; sec. med. staff, 1986-87, chief gastroenterology sect., vice chmn. dept. medicine, 1988, 89, mem. exec. com., 1990-92, mem. laser com., 1992, 93, 94, 95, mem. OR com., 1996-97; assoc. clin. prof. medicine dept. gastroenterology Georgetown U., Washington, 1988—; active staff Suburban Hosp.; courtesy staff Montgomery Gen. Hosp. Vice chmn. Health Delivery Orgn., Mid Atlantic Med. Svcs. Health Plan, 1997-2004, peer review com., 2005-; treas., contract coord. Gastrointestinal Endoscopy Assocs., LLC, 1995—, Gastrointestinal Rsch. Assocs., LLC, 1999—. Major contbg. author: Radiology of the Liver, Biliary Tract, Pancreas and Spleen, 1987. Synagogue chair Israel Bonds Congregation B'nai Tzedek, 1994—, synagogue divsn. chair Washington, 2003—; alumni rep., mem. admissions com. Case Western Res. U., 1998—; healthcare adv. com. Eagle Bank, Md., 2000—. Served to maj. USAR. Named one of Top Doctors, Wash. Mag., 1993, 1994, 1995, 1999, 2004, 2005. Fellow ACP, Am. Coll. Gastroenterology, Am. Gastroent. Assn.; mem. AMA (Physician Recognition award 1978, 81, 84, 87, 90, 93), Am. Gastroent. Assn., Am. Soc. Gastrointestinal Endoscopy (postgrad. edn. com. 1991-92), Md. Soc. Gastrointestinal Endoscopy (exec. bd.), Montgomery County Med. Soc. Home: 11413 Twining Ln Rockville MD 20854-1860 Office: 9711 Medical Center Dr Ste 308 Rockville MD 20850-3388 Home Phone: 301-279-9256; Office Phone: 301-251-1244.

BIRNS, NICHOLAS BOE, literature educator, editor; b. NYC, May 30, 1965; s. Laurence Richard Birns and Margaret Ann Boe. AB, Columbia U., 1988; MA, NYU, 1990, PhD, 1992. Mem. faculty New Sch. U., NYC, 1995—, Coll. New Rochelle, Bronx, 1996—2002. Vis. asst. prof. Western Conn. State U., Danbury, 1992-93; invited lectr. U. Stockholm, 1997-98; vis. rsch. fellow U. Newcastle, Australia, 2001. Editor: Powys Notes, 1998-2002; book rev. editor: Antipodes, 1994-2001, editor, 2001—; author: Understanding Anthony Powell, 2004; contbr. articles to profl. jours. Sec., treas. Coun. Editors Learned Jours., 2007—. Devel. fellow NYU, 1988-89. Mem.: Guild of Scholars of Episcopal Ch. (pres. 2007—). Episcopalian. Avocations: baseball, music, following current events. Home: 205 E 10th St New York NY 10003-7634 Office: New Sch U 66 W 12th St New York NY 10011-8603 Office Phone: 646-469-3124. Business E-Mail: birnsn@newschool.edu.

BIRNSTIEL, CHARLES, consulting engineer; b. NYC; s. Charles Conrad and Margarete (Heckel) B. BCE, NYU, 1954, MCE, 1957, EngScD, 1962. Mem. faculty NYU, Bronx, 1954-73, prof. civil engring., 1968-73, Poly Inst. N.Y., Bklyn., 1973-74; cons. structural and mech. engring. NYC; head engring. firm, 1974—; prin. assoc. Hardesty & Hanover LLP, NYC. Adj. prof. civil engring. Columbia U., N.Y.C., 1989-2000. Patentee elevated rail transit guideway with noise attenuators; contbr. chpt. to book and articles to profl. jours. Fellow ASCE (State-of-the-Art paper award, Roebling award Met. sect. 2003), Instn. Civil Engrs. (U.K.); mem. Am. Railway Engring. and Maintenance of Way Assn., Internat. Assn. Bridge and Structural Engring., Structural Stability Rsch. Coun. Lutheran. Home and Office: 68-19 Fleet St Flushing NY 11375 Home Phone: 718-268-9188; Office Phone: 718-268-9188. Personal E-mail: cbirnstiel29@msn.com. Business E-Mail: cbirnstiel@compuserve.com.

BIRO, FRANK M., pediatrics educator; b. Allentown, Pa., Apr. 25, 1952; s. Francis M. and Irene C. Biro; m. Nancy Bloemer, Dec. 1, 2001; 1 child, F. Noah. MD, Harvard Med. Sch., Boston, 1979. Lic. internal medicine Am. Bd. Internal Medicine, pediats. Am. Bd. Pediats., adolescent medicine Am. Bd. Pediats. Prof. pediats. Cin. Children's Hosp., 1984—. Assoc. dir. divsn. adolescent medicine Cin. Children's Hosp., 1990—2007, dir. divsn. adolescent medicine, 2007—. Named Adele Hofmann vis. professorship in adolescent medicine, 2005; recipient Puberty and Cancer Initiation grant, NIH, 2003—. Fellow: Am. Bd. Pediats. (chair certifying com. 2005—); mem.: Soc. Adolescent Medicine (Adele Hofmann vis. prof. 2005), N.Am. Soc. for Pediat. and Adolescent Gynecology (pres. 2006—07, Evelyn Green Laufer award 2004). Roman Catholic. Home: 7895 Stonehouse Rd Melbourne KY 41059 Office: Cini Children's Hosp Med Ctr 3333 Burnet Ave Cincinnati OH 45229 Office Phone: 513-636-8580.

BIRO, LASZLO, dermatologist; b. Czechoslovakia, May 31, 1929; came to U.S., 1956; s. Sandor and Margaret (Klein) B.; m. Dolores Macchiaroli, July 9, 1961; children: David, Lisa, Deborah, Michele. MD, Univ. Med. Sch., Debrecen, Hungary, 1953. Diplomate Am. Bd. Dermatology. Intern Kings County Hosp., Bklyn., 1957-58; resident Bellevue Hosp., NYC, 1958-60; pvt. practice medicine specializing in dermatology NYC, 1960-61, Bklyn., 1960—; emeritus dept. dermatology Bklyn. Hosp., Luth. Med. Ctr.; clin. prof. dermatology SUNY, Downstate Med. Ctr., 1971—. Contbr. articles on skin tumors to profl. jours. Fellow ACP, Am. Acad. Dermatology, N.Y. Acad. Medicine; mem. AMA, Kings County Med. Assn., Bay Ridge Med. Soc. (pres. 1987-88), N.Y. State Dermatol. Soc., Bklyn Dermatol. Soc., Internat. Soc. Tropical Dermatology, N.Y. Acad. Scis., Am. Coll. Cryosurgery (v.p. 1996), Semmelweis Sci. Soc. (pres. 1985). Office: 9921 4th Ave Brooklyn NY 11209-8347 Office Phone: 718-833-7616. Personal E-mail: laszlobiro@aol.com.

BIRÓ, MARCEL, chef; b. Germany, 1973; m. Shannon Kring Biró. Chef Au Crocodile; personal chef German Chancellor Helmut Kohl; owner, chef Biró Restaurant and Wine Bar, Sheboygan, Wis., Ó, Sheboygan, Wis., 2005—, Macel Biró Culinary Sch.; CEO, chef Biró Internationale LLC, Sheboygan, Wis. Amb. German Cuisine German Fed. Gov., 2006—. Co-author: Biró: European-Inspired Cuisine, 2005; featured in (newspaper) Wall St. Jour., (magazines) SmartMoney Mag., TV Guide, featured on Nat. Pub. Radio, host (TV series) The Kitchens of Biró, PBS. Achievements include becoming one of youngest European chefs to aquire Master Chef de Cuisine title. Office: Biro Internationale PO Box 1012 Sheboygan WI 53082-1012 Office Phone: 920-457-6940.

BIRON, CHRISTINE ANNE, medical science educator, researcher; b. Woonsocket, RI, Aug. 8, 1951; d. R. Bernard and Theresa Priscilla (Sauvageau) B. BS, U. Mass., 1973; PhD, U. N.C., 1980. Rsch. technician U. Mass., Amherst, 1973—75; grad. rschr. U. N.C., Chapel Hill, 1975—80; postdoctoral fellow Scripps Clinic and Rsch., La Jolla, Calif., 1980; fellow U. Mass. Med. Sch., Worcester, 1981—82, instr., 1983, asst. prof., 1984—87; vis. scientist Karolinska Inst., Stockholm, 1984; asst. prof. Sch. Medicine Brown U., Providence, 1988—90, assoc. prof., 1990—96, prof., 1996—, Esther Elizabeth Brintzenhoff prof., 1996—, chair Dept. Molecular Microbiology & Immunology, 1999—, dir. grad. program in pathobiology, 1995—99; sci. adv. bd. Trudeau Inst., 2004—. Mem. AIDS and related rsch. study sect. 3 NIH, 1991-93; mem. exptl. immunology study sect. NIH, 1993-97, immunology working group sci. rev.; co-organizer Keystone Symposium on Innate Immunity to Pathogens, 2005; bd. sci. counselors subcom. basic scis. Nat. Cancer Inst., 2005—. Assoc. editor: Jour. Immunology, 1990—94, 2000, bd. editors: Procs. of Soc. for Exptl. Biology and Medicine, 1993—99, sect. editor: Jour. Immunology, 1995—99; editor: Jour. Nat. Immunity, 1994—98, Jour. Leukocyte Biology, 1999—2000; mem. editl. bd.: Virology, 2001—03; contbr. articles, revs. to sci. jours.; mem. adv. bd. editors: Jour. Exptl. Medicine, 2002—, mem. editl. bd.: Immunity, 2005—. Leukemia Soc. Am. fellow, 1981, Spl. fellow, 1983, scholar, 1987; grantee NIH, 1985—; rsch. grantee MacArthur Found., 1991-96. Fellow AAAS (scholar 2002—); mem. Am. Assn. Immunologists (co-chmn. symposium 1990, 94, 95, 96, 98, 99), Am. Soc. Virology, Am. Assn. Immunology (block co-chair nat. meetings 1996-99, program com. 1998-2000), Soc. Natural Immunity (co-chair program for 2001 meeting), Sigma Xi. Office: Brown U PO Box G-B618 Providence RI 02912-0001

BIRON, MARTIN, professional hockey player; b. Lac-St-Charles, Que., Can., Aug. 15, 1977; m. Ann Marie Biron; children: Jacob Mathieu, Grace. Goalie Buffalo Sabres, 1995—2007, Phila. Flyers, 2007—. Recipient Harry Holmes Meml. Trophy, Am. Hockey League, 1999, Baz Bastien Meml. Trophy, 1999. Office: Phila Flyers 3601 S Broad St Philadelphia PA 19148*

BIRREN, JAMES EMMETT, research and development company executive; b. Chgo., Apr. 4, 1918; m. Elizabeth S., 1942; children: Barbara Ann, Jeffrey Emmett, Bruce William. Student, Wright Jr. Coll., 1938; BEd, Chgo. State U., 1941; MA, Northwestern U., 1942, PhD, 1947, ScD (hon.), 1985; postgrad., U. Chgo., 1950—51; PhD (hon.), U. Gothenberg, Sweden, 1983; LLD (hon.), St. Thomas U., Can., 1990. Tutorial fellow Northwestern U., 1941—42; rsch. asst. project for study of fatigue Office Sci. Rsch. and Devel., 1942; rsch. fellow NIH, USPHS, 1946—47; rsch. psychologist gerontology unit NIH, 1947—51; rsch. psychologist NIMH, 1951—53, chief sect. on aging, 1953—64; dir. aging program Nat. Inst. Child Health and Human Devel., Bethesda, Md., 1964—65; dir. Gerontology Ctr.; prof. psychology U. So. Calif., 1965—89, Disting. prof. emeritus, 1992—, dean Davis Sch. Gerontology, 1975—86, Brookdale Disting. scholar, 1986—90, dir. Inst. Advanced Study in Gerontology and Geriat., 1981—89; dir. Borun Ctr. Gerontol. Rsch. UCLA, 1989—93, assoc. dir. Ctr. on Aging, 1990—. Fellow Ctr. for Advanced Study in Behavioral Scis., Stanford, Calif., 1978-79; Green vis. prof. U. B.C., 1979; vis. scientist Cambridge (Eng.) U., 1960-61; Harold E. Jones meml. lectr. U. Calif., Berkeley, 1965; mem. LA County Bd. Suprs.' Com. on Aging, 1967-69; sr. fellow U. So. Calif. Urban Ecology Inst., 1968-70; mem. Dean's Coun., U. So. Calif., 1970-86; chmn. aging rev. com. Nat. Inst. Aging, 1974-75; program dir. Integration of Info. on Aging: Handbook Project, 1973-76; mem. steering com. Care of Elderly, Inst. of Medicine, 1976-77; bd. dirs. Sears Roebuck Found., 1977-80; chmn. life course prevention rsch. rev. com. NIMH, 1985-87; cons. Roche Seminars on Aging Series, 1980-82. Author: Psychology of Aging, 1964; editor: Handbook of Aging and the Individual, 1959, (with K.W. Schaie) Handbook of the Psychology of Aging, 1996, Encyclopedia of Gerontology, 1996, (with R.B. Sloane) Handbook of Mental Health and Aging, 1992; contbr. articles to books, profl. publs.; bd. collaborators: Gerontologia, 1956-89; asst. editor: Jour. Gerontology, 1956-61, assoc. editor 1961-63, editor-in-chief 1968-74, chmn. publs. com., 1975-78, adv. editl. bd., 1956-69; bd. adv. editors: Devel. Psychobiology, 1967-69; adv. editor: Jour. Human Devel., 1957-58. Mem. adv. com. and del. White House Conf. on Aging, 1995. With USNR, 1943-46; to scientist dir. USPHS Scientist Corps, 1947-65. Recipient award for rsch. on problems of aging CIBA Found., 1956, Stratton award Am. Psychopath. Assn., 1960, Sr. 65er award Dist. 65 Retail Workers and Dept. Store Union, Sr. 65er award AFL-CIO, 1962, medal for meritorious svc. USPHS, 1965, citation Am. Assn. Ret. Persons, 1970, Am. Pioneers in Aging award U. Mich., 1972, commendation for disting. contbns. to field of gerontology Mayor of LA, 1968, 74, Merit award Northwestern U. Alumni Assn., 1976, Creative Scholarship and Rsch. award U. So. Calif., 1979, Disting. Educator award Assn. Gerontology in Higher Edn., 1983, Eminent Svc. award Stovall Found., 1984, award of Distinction Am. Fedn. for Aging Rsch., 1986, Sandoz prize for rsch. on aging, 1989, Can. Assn. Gerontology award, 1990, Disting. Emeritus award U. So. Calif., 1992, Pres.'s award Am. Soc. on Aging, 1996, Disting. Career Contbn. to Gerontology award Gerontol. Soc. Am., 2002, Ollie Randall award Nat. Coun. on Aging, 2004, Hall of Fame award Am. Soc. on Aging, 2004; USPHS rsch. fellow, 1946-47. Fellow AAAS, Am. Geriat. Soc. (founding fellow Western divsn.), Am. Psychol. Assn. (Disting. Sci. Contbn. award 1968, chmn. membership com. 1969, Disting. Contbn. award Divsn. Adult Devel. and Aging 1978, pres. divsn. 1955-56, editor newsletter 1951-55), Gerontol. Soc. (pres. 1961-62, chmn. publs. com. 1974-77, award for meritorious rsch. 1966, Brookdale award 1980); mem. Am. Physiol. Soc., Internat. Assn. Gerontology (chmn. exec. com. 1966-69, chmn. program com. 1968-69), Psychonomic Soc., Western Gerontol. Soc. (dir. 1965-, pres. 1968-69), Golden Key Club, Skull and Dagger Club, Sigma Xi, Phi Kappa Phi. Office: UCLA Ctr on Aging 10945 Le Conte Ave Los Angeles CA 90024-2828

BIRSTEIN, ANN, writer, educator; b. NYC, May 27, 1927; d. Bernard and Clara (Gordon) B.; m. Alfred Kazin, June 26, 1952 (div. 1982); 1 child, Cathrael. BA, Queens Coll., 1948. Lectr. The New Sch. Queens Coll., NYC, 1953-54; writer-in-residence CCNY, 1960; lectr. The Writers Workshop, Iowa City, 1966, 72; lectr. Sch. Gen. Studies Columbia U., NYC, 1985-87; dir., founder Writers on Writing Barnard Coll., NYC, 1988—. Adj. prof. English Hofstra U., L.I., 1980, Barnard Coll., N.Y.C., 1981-93; film critic Vogue mag. Author: Star of Glass, 1950, The Troublemaker, 1955, The Sweet Birds of Gorham, 1966, Summer Situations, 1972, Dickie's List, 1973, American Children, 1980, The Rabbi on Forty-Seventh Street, 1982, The Last of the True Believers, 1988, What I Saw at the Fair, 2003; co-editor: The Works of Anne Frank; contbr. articles to numerous mags. Nat. Endowment of Arts grantee, 1983; Fulbright fellow, 1951-52. Mem. PEN (former mem. exec. bd., former chair admissions com.), Authors Guild (former mem. coun.), Phi Beta Kappa (hon.). Democrat. Jewish. Home: 1623 3rd Ave # 27jw New York NY 10128-3638 Personal E-mail: abirstein@aol.com.

BISANZO, MARK THOMAS, retired sales executive; b. Port Chester, NY, Sept. 28, 1941; s. Dominic Daniel and Pauline Ann (Zak) B.; m. Mary Jane Ann Baldino, July 2, 1966; 1 child, Mark Christopher. AAS, Westchester C.C., 1963; BSME, N.Y. Inst. Tech., 1966; MBA, Fordham U., 1972. Instrument engr. Bechtel, NYC, 1966-68, M.W. Kellogg, NYC, 1968-70; sr. controls engr. Power Gas Corp., NYC, 1970-71, Am. Electric Power, NYC, 1971; sr. v.p. Control Assocs., Allendale, NJ, 1971—2000—. Mem. adv. bd. Fisher Controls Co., Marshalltown, Iowa, 1997—; bd. dirs. Control Assocs. Pres. Bergen Cath. H.S. Fathers' Club, Oradell, N.J., 1991-94; coach Park Ridge (N.J.) Athletic Assn., 1980-90; mem. Our Lady of Mercy Roman Cath. Ch. Noctornal Adoration Soc., Park Ridge; v.p. Middlebury Collegiate Alumni Coll. Parents Alumni Assn., 2005—. Mem. Soc. Gas Operators (pres. 2006-07), Instrument Soc. Am. (v.p. N.Y. chpt. 1984-85, v.p. 2005). Avocations: skiing, photography, travel, golf. Home: 67 Degroff Pl Park Ridge NJ 07656-1406 Office: Control Assocs 20 Commerce Dr Allendale NJ 07401-1600 Office Phone: 201-825-7700. Business E-Mail: mark.bisanzo@coldwellbankermoves.com.

BISBEE, GERALD ELFTMAN, JR., investment company executive; b. Waterloo, Iowa, July 12, 1942; s. Gerald Elftman and Maxine Cole (Prather) Bisbee; m. Linda Elaine Ude, Aug. 22, 1970; children: Gerald Elftmann III, Katherine Elizabeth. BA, North Cen. Coll., Naperville, Ill., 1967; MBA, U. Pa., 1972, PhD, Yale U., 1975. Adminstr. Med. Ctr. Northwestern U., Chgo., 1968-70; asst. prof. Yale U., New Haven,

1974-78, assoc. dir. health svcs., 1975-78; pres. Hosp. Rsch. and Ednl. Trust, Chgo., 1978-84; v.p., shareholder Kidder, Peabody & Co., NYC, 1984-88; chmn., chief exec. officer Sequel Corp., New Canaan, Conn., 1988-89, Apache Med. Systems, Inc., Washington, 1989-97; chmn., CEO Health Mgmt. Acad., Alexandria, Va., 1998—; chmn., pres., CEO ReGen Biologics, Inc., Franklin Lakes, NJ, 1998—. Adj. prof. Northwestern U. Kellogg Sch. Mgmt., Evanston, Ill., 1979—83; mem. exec. adv. com. Weatherhead Sch. Mgmt. Health Sys. Program, Case Western Res. U., Cleve., 1984—86; mem. vis. com. Harvard U. Health Svcs., Boston, 1986—92; bd. dirs. Cerner Corp., ReGen Biologics Inc., Health Mgmt. Acad. Co-author: Musculo-Skeletal Disorders: Their Frequency of Occurrence and Their Impact on the Population of the United States, 1978, Financing of Health Care, 1979, Managing the Finances of Health Institutions, 1980; author: Multihospital Systems: Policy Issues for the Future, 1981. Mem. adv. com. Waveney Care Ctr., New Canaan, 1987. Grantee, USPHS, 1972—75. Mem.: Yale Club (NYC). Home and Office: The Bisbee Group 110 Wellesley Dr New Canaan CT 06840-3530 Personal E-mail: gbisbee@aol.com.

BISBEE, JOYCE EVELYN, retired utility company executive; b. Portage, Wis., May 15, 1941; d. Orris Dean and Helen Paulina (Golz) B. BS, U. Wis., Stout, 1963; MEd, U. N.C., 1971. Cert. family and consumer sci. Ext. home economist U. Wis., Racine, 1964-68; tchr., dept. chair Oshkosh (Wis.) Pub. Schs., 1963-64, 68-74; mgr. ednl. rels. J.C. Penney, NYC, 1974-78; v.p. Creamer Dickson Basford, PR, 1978-81; consumer affairs rep. Bklyn. Union, 1983-85, consumer advocate, 1986-92, mgr. consumer outreach and edn., 1992-98; dir. consumer comm. and advocacy KeySpan Corp., 1998—2003; ret., 2004. Mem. consumer affairs com. Bar Assn. City N.Y., 1993-98. Mem. adv. com. N.Y.C. 4-H Youth Program, 1985-96; active East 60s Neighborhood Assn., N.Y.C., 1993-2003. Recipient Alumni Disting. Svc. award, U. Wis., Stout, 1978. Lutheran. Avocations: craft shows, cultural performances, cats, travel. Home: 5815 American Pkwy # 101 Madison WI 53718

BISCARDI, CHESTER, composer, educator; b. Kenosha, Wis., Oct. 19, 1948; s. Chester Frank and Anne Rose (Rizzo) B. Student, Università di Bologna and Conservatorio di Musica G. B. Martini, Italy, 1969-70; BA in English Lit. with honors, U. Wis., 1970, MA in Italian Lit. (Ford Found. fellow), 1972, MM in Composition, 1974; MMA, Yale U., 1976, DMA, 1980. Tchg. asst. Italian U. Wis., Madison, 1970—73, tchg. asst. theory, 1973—74, ad hoc instr. Italian for reading knowledge, 1973—74; tchg. fellow Italian for singers Yale U., New Haven, 1975—76; seminar instr. Fed. Correctional Instn. Oxford U., 1978; faculty mem. music dept. Sarah Lawrence Coll., 1977—; seminar and program faculty Acad. Yr. in N.Y.C., 1984; dir. music program Sarah Lawrence Coll., 1987—, William Schuman chair music, 1995—2007, Margaret C. Bogart Disting. Svc. chair, 2007—. Vis. prof. summer program in Florence at Villa Corsi-Salviati in Sesto Fiorentino with U. Mich., 1987, 94; composer-in-residence U. Wis., 1985, The Chamber Music Conf. and Composers' Forum of the East, Bennington, Vt., 1990. Composer: Tartini, 1972, Turning, 1973, Chartres, 1973, Indovinello, 1974, orpha, 1974, Heabakès: Five Sapphic Lyrics, 1974, they had ceased to talk, 1975, Trusting Lightness, 1975, Tenzone, 1975, Music for the Duchess of Malfi, 1975, Trio, 1976, At the Still Point, 1977, Eurydice, 1978, Mestiere, 1979, Trasumanar, 1980, Di Vivere, 1981, Good-bye, My Fancy!, 1982, Music for Witch Dance, 1983, Chêz Vous, 1983, Piano Concerto, 1983, Incitation to Desire (tango), 1984, 1993, Tight-Rope, 1985, Piano Sonata, 1986, rev., 1987, Traverso, 1987, No Feeling is the Same as Before, 1988, Companion Piece (for Morton Feldman), 1989, 1991, Netori, 1990, Music for an Occasion, 1992, rev., 2003, The Gift of Life, 1990—93, Baby Song of the Four Winds, 1994, Guru, 1995, Resisting Stillness, 1996, What a Coincidence, 1997, I Wouldn't Know About That, 1997, Modern Love Songs, 1997—2002, Prayers of Steel, 1998, Now You See It, Now You Don't, 1998, The Child Comes Every Winter, 1999, Someone New, 1999, Music for NASDAQ Market Site TV, 1999, Recovering, 2000, In Time's Unfolding, 2000, At Any Given Moment, 2002, Piano Quintet, 2004, The Viola Had Suddenly Become a Voice, 2005, Recognition, 2007. Recipient Prix de Rome, Am. Acad. in Rome, 1976-77, Aaron Copland award, 2001; Composer/Librettist grantee Nat. Endowment for Arts, 1977-78, 80-81; Composers' Conf. fellow, Johnson, Vt., 1974-75; Wis. Arts Bd. grantee, 1976; Nat. Acad. and Inst. Arts and Letters Charles E. Ives scholar, 1975-76; Guggenheim fellow, 1979-80; Mellon Found. grantee, 1979; Am. Music Ctr. grantee, 1980; McDowell Colony fellow, 1981, 84, 92, 94-95, 98, 2000, 04; Martha Baird Rockefeller Fund grant, 1982; Creative Artists Pub. Svc. Program fellow in music, 1983; Japan Found. fellow, 1989-90; N.Y. Found. for Arts Artists fellow in music composition, 1990, 98; Rockefeller Found. Bellagio Study and Conf. Ctr. residency, Lago di Como, Villa Serbelloni, Italy, 1993; Humanities residency Bogliasco Found., Villa Orbiana, Italy, 1999, 2005, Fromm Music Found. at Harvard Commn., 1999-2002, Acad. award Am. Acad. Arts and Letters, 2007. Mem. Am. Composers Alliance, Am. Acad. in Rome, Am. Music Ctr., Broadcast Music, MacDowell Colony, Century Assn., also others. Office: Sarah Lawrence Coll Music Dept Bronxville NY 10708 Home: 380 Riverside Dr 4C New York NY 10025-1819 Office Phone: 914-395-2334. Business E-Mail: biscardi@slc.edu.

BISCHEL, MARGARET DEMERITT, physician, consultant; b. Moorhead, Minn., Nov. 8, 1933; d. Connie Magnus Nystrom and Harriett Grace (Petersen) Zorner; m. Raymon DeMeritt, 1953 (div. 1958); 1 child, Gregory Raymon; m. John Bischel, 1961 (div. 1964); m. Kenneth Dean Serkes, June 7, 1974. BS, U. Oreg., Eugene, 1962; MD, U. Oreg., Portland, 1965. Diplomate Am. Bd. Internal Medicine, Nat. Bd. Med. Examiners. Resident, straight med. intern Los Angeles County/U. So. Calif. Med. Ctr., 1965-68, NIH fellow nephrology, 1968-70, asst. prof. renal medicine, 1970-74; asst. prof., instr. medicine U. So. Calif., 1968-74; instr. nephrology East L.A. City Coll., 1971-74; dir. med. edn. Luth. Gen. Hosp., Park Ridge, Ill., 1974-78, dir. nephrology sect., 1977-80, pres. med. staff, 1974-88; founding mem., med. dir., dir. med. svcs. Luth. Health Plan, Park Ridge, 1983-87; clin. assoc. prof. medicine Abraham Lincoln Sch. Medicine U. Ill., 1975-80; sr. cons. Parkside Assocs., Inc., Park Ridge, 1986-88; pvt. practice Chgo., 1974-88; physician Buenaventura Med. Clinic, Ventura, Calif., 1989-94, med. dir., 1992-94; prin. Apollo Managed Care Cons., Santa Barbara, Calif., 1988—. Trustee Luth. Health Care System, Park Ridge, 1986-90, Unified Med. Group Assn., Seal Beach, Calif., 1993-94; hon. lifetime staff mem. Luth. Gen. Hosp., Park Ridge; mem. formulary com. HealthNet, 1992-94, med. adv. com. TakeCare, 1993-94, quality assurance com. PacifiCare, 1993-94; mem. doctor's adv. network AMA, 1994-96; JCAHO advisor for behavioral health care providers, 2000—2006. Author: Managing Behavioral Healthcare, 2d edit., 2006, 3rd edit., 2007, The Credentialing and Privileges Manual, 2d edit., 2005, 3d edit., 2007, Medical Review Criteria Guidelines for Managed Care, 5th edit., 2006, 6th edit., 2007; editor: Med. Mgmt. Manual, Managed Care Bull.; mem. editl. bd. Capitation Mgmt. Report, 1998-2006; contbr. chpts. to books and articles to profl. jours. Fellow: ACP (Calif. Gov.'s advisor 1993—95); mem.: Am. Coll. Physician Execs. Avocations: real estate, gardening. Office: Apollo Managed Care Cons 860 Ladera Ln Santa Barbara CA 93108-1626 Office Phone: 805-969-2606. Personal E-mail: mbischel@cox.net. Business E-Mail: mbischel@apollomanagedcare.com.

BISCHOFF, DAVID CANBY, retired university administrator; b. Bellefonte, Pa., May 27, 1930; s. Eugen Carl and Jean Stuart (Canby) B.; m. Patricia A. Halfacre, Aug. 15, 1954; children: Cynthia, Steven, Ingrid. BS, Pa. State U., 1952, PhD, 1958; MS, U. N.C., 1953. Asst. prof. dept. phys. edn. U. Mass., Amherst, 1957-60, asso. prof., 1960-63, prof., 1963—, asso. provost for profl. schs., 1972-79, dep. provost, 1982-84; assoc. chancellor, 1983-92; dean U. Mass. Sch. Phys. Edn., 1973-92. Vis. prof. Wesleyan U., 1968-69; bd. dirs. Bay State Games. Past pres. Amherst Community Chest, Amherst Am. Field Service; mem. Amherst Planning Bd., 1958-62; trustee The Hotchkiss Sch., 1990-96; trustee Portland (Maine) Mus. Art. Capt. USAF, ret., 1953-55. Mem. AAHPER, Nat. Coll. Phys. Edn. Assn. (past pres.) Clubs: Algonquin, Hillsboro, Anglers (N.Y.C.). Home: 46 Burbank Farm PO Box 462 Yarmouth ME 04096-0462

BISCHOFF, MARILYN BRETT, clinical social worker, personal life coach, psychotherapist; b. Mt. Vernon, NY, Apr. 16, 1930; d. Arthur Cushman and Mary Kathryn (Clark) Brett; m. Walter A. Bischoff, Mar. 25, 1961; children: Holly, Robert. BA magna cum laude, CCNY, 1959; MSSW, Columbia U., 1961; PhD in Social Work, Boston Coll., 1985; cert. in gerontology, U. Mass., Dartmouth, 2000. Diplomate clin. social work Am. Bd. Examiners Social Work, bd. cert. diplomate clin. social work NASW. Clin. social worker Providence Child Guidance Clinic, 1961-65, 69-73; pvt. practice clin. social worker Attleboro, Mass., 1994—, Providence, 1965-94; instr. Providence Coll., 1988-89. Personal life coach; spkr. field. Active Attleboro (Mass.) Area Mental Health Assn., 1975—94. Fellow, Columbia U., 1959—60; grantee, NIMH, 1960—61. Mem.: NASW (sec.-treas. (S.E. Mass. chpt.) 1967—68, mem. speaker's bur. (RI chpt.) 1987), RI Group Psychotherapy Soc. (chair membership com. 1985—96), Acad. Cert. Social Workers, Attleboro Ski Club, Columbia U. Alumni Assn., Phi Beta Kappa. Avocations: travel, photography, sewing, gardening. Home and Office: 10 Norfolk Row Attleboro MA 02703-1629 Home Phone: 508-222-2531; Office Phone: 508-222-7085. E-mail: drmarilynb@aol.com.

BISCHOFF, RICK, admissions director; BA in Math., Macalester Coll.; MBA in Info. Sys., U. Minn. Assoc. dir. admissions Macalester Coll., U. Chgo.; dir. admissions Calif. Inst. Tech., Pasadena, 2004—. Office: Calif Inst Tech Office of Undergrad Admissions Mail Code 1-94 Pasadena CA 91125 Office Phone: 626-395-8375. E-mail: rbisch@caltech.edu.*

BISCHOFF, SUSAN ANN, newspaper editor; b. Indpls., July 31, 1951; d. Thomas Anthony and Betty Jean (Coons) Bischoff; m. Jim B. Barlow, June 20, 1975; 1 child, Samantha Lynn Barlow Martinez. BA, Ind. U., 1973. Rschr., reporter Congl. Quar., Washington, 1973-74; city desk reporter Houston Chronicle, 1974-75, bus. reporter, 1975-79, asst. bus. editor, 1979-84, bus. editor, 1984-86, asst. mng. editor, 1986-2000, dep. mng. editor, 2000—03, assoc. editor, 2003—06; pres. Houston Pub. Libr. Found., 2007—. Houston corr. Kiplinger, Tex. Letter, Washington, 1980-85; juror Pulitzer Prizes in Journalism, 2004, 05. Mem. class policy Leadership Houston, 1992—94; mem. exec. com. Gulf Coast affiliate United Way, 1994—2002; pres. Friends of Houston Girl Scouts, 2002—; bd. dirs. Houston Chronicle Employees Fed. Credit Union, 1980—87, San Jacinto Coun. Girl Scouts US, 1997—2003, Child Adv., 1999—2005, US Olympic Festival VII, Houston, 1985—86, Gulf Coast Mar. of Dimes Birth Defects Found., 1989—2001, YES Coll. Prep. Sch., 1999—2002, AIDS Found., Houston, 2002—, Psychology Works, 2006—, Houston A+ Challenge, 2007—; founding bd. dir. Greater Houston Women's Found.; mem. bd. visitors Anderson Cancer Ctr. U. Tex. Named Outstanding Woman in Houston Journalism, YWCA, 1989, Fabulous Femme, Greater Houston Women's Found., 1994, Woman of Distinction, Crohn's & Colitis Found., 1996; recipient Outstanding Vol. Achievement award, Gulf Coast United Way, 1995, Outstanding Media award, Nat. Soc. Fund Raising Execs., 1997, Nat. Thanks award, San Jacinto Girl Scouts, 2001, Mayborn award, Cmty. Leadership Tex. Daily Newspaper Assn., 2001, honoree, Jewish Cmty. Ctr. of Houston Children's Scholarship Ball, 2002, Strong, Smart and Bold award, Houston Girls, Inc., 2003. Mem.: Am. Assn. Sunday and Feature Editors (named to Features Hall of Fame 2003), Am. Soc. Newspaper Editors (bd. dirs.). Home: 2929 Buffalo Speedway # 112 Houston TX 77098 Office: Houston Pub Libr Found 500 McKinney St Houston TX 77002

BISCHOFF, THERESA ANN, not-for-profit association executive; b. Rockville Ctr., NY, Nov. 16, 1953; d. Robert and Colette (Burke) Peters. BS in Acctg. cum laude, U. Conn., 1975; MBA, NYU, 1991. Cert. CPA, 1977. Sr. dir. acctg. svcs. NYU Med. Ctr., NYC, 1984-87, v.p. fin., 1987-93, dep. provost, exec. v.p., 1993—98, pres., 1998—2003; clin. prof. health care mgmt. NYU Sch. Medicine, NYC, 1993—2003; CEO ARC in Greater NY, NYC, 2004—. Bd. dirs. Combined Coord. Coun., 1984-03, chair, 1998-02; mem. adv. com. United Hosp. Fund, 1994-03; mem. adminstrv. bd. Coun. Tchg. Hosp., 1995-03. Mem. AAMC (chair 2002-03), Greater NY Hosp. Assn. (mem. bd. dirs. 1994-03, mem. health care exec. forum 1987—, sec. 1990-92), Assn. Am. Recital Colls., Healthcare Assn. NY State (trustee 1994-02), Soc. Health Svc. Adminstrs., Mut. Am. (trustee 2001-), Dov Pharm. (trustee 2003-), U. Conn. Found. Bd. Office: ARC 520 W 49th St New York NY 10019

BISCIOTTI, STEPHEN J., staffing company executive, professional sports team executive; b. Phila., Apr. 10, 1960; s. Bernard and Patricia; m. Renee Foote; children: Jason, Jack. BA, Salisbury State U., 1982. Cofounder (with Jim Davis) Allegis Group, Inc. (formerly Aerotek), chmn. Minority owner Baltimore Ravens, 2000—04, owner, 2004—. Bd. dirs. Catholics Charities, Mother Seton Acad., Balt. Named one of Forbes' Richest Americans, 2006. Catholic. Avocations: golf, boating, cigar enthusiast. Office: Allegis Group Inc 7301 Parkway Dr Hanover MD 21076

BISCOE, BELINDA P., academic administrator, psychologist; d. Walter Marks and Luetta Marks-Perry; children: Brandi, Ashley. BA in Sociology cum laude, Fisk U., 1971, MA in Sociology, 1973; PhD in Psychology, U. Okla., 1982. Cert. drug and alcohol dir. Okla. Drug and Alcohol Profl. Counselors Assn., prevention specialist Okla. Drug and Alcohol Profl. Counselors Assn. Evaluator, adminstr., instr. MeHarry Med. Coll., Nashville, 1975—78; pres., founder Higher Horizons, Inc., Oklahoma City, 1991—; dir. Region VII Comprehensive Ctr. U. Okla., Coll. Continuing Edn., Norman, 1997—2006, dir. rsch. and evaluation, 2001—, asst. v.p., 2001—. Co-founder, cons. Eagle Ridge Inst., Oklahoma City, 1989, dir. Mid-Continent Comprehensive Ctr.; cons., trainer, rschr. U.S. Dept. Ctr. for Substance Abuse Treatment, Washington, 1996—; adj. prof. depts. advanced programs and human rels. U. Okla., 1999—; evaluation cons. Child Devel., Inc., Russellville, Ark., 1999—2001. Author/developer: psychol. assessment tool Adult Resiliency Attitudes Scale, 1994, Children's and Adolescent's Resiliency Tool, 1994; author: (tng. manual) Funding: To Be or Not To Be, 1995. Founding bd. mem. Regional Civic League, Oklahoma City, 1995—97; bd. dirs. YWCA, Oklahoma City, 1980—85. Named Woman of Yr. in Edn., Redland Chpt. of the Girl Scouts, 1992—93, Outstanding Woman of Yr., Am. Fedn. Colored Women; recipient Leadership award in edn., Women in Comm., 1995, E. Neal Stone Superior Performance award, Adminstrv. Staff Coun.-U. Okla., 2004, Making a Difference in Okla. award, Journal Record Newspaper, 2005, Continuing Edn. Profl. award, Regional U. Continuing Edn. Assn., 2006, Continuing Edn. award, Nat. U., 2006; Join Together fellow, Nat. Substance ABuse Coalition. Mem.: APA, Oklahoma County Mental Health Assn. (bd. dirs. 1984—86, 2002), U. Continuing Edn. Assn., Am. Evaluation Assn., Links (Oklahoma City chpt.). Democrat. Methodist. Avocations: hydroponic gardening, reading, crocheting, bicycling, water-skiing, snow skiing. Office: Univ Okla 555 Constitution Norman OK 73072 Office Phone: 405-325-1711. Business E-Mail: BpBiscoe@ou.edu.

BISCONTI, ANN STOUFFER, public opinion research company executive; b. Chgo., Nov. 22, 1940; d. Samuel Andrew Stouffer and Ruth Rachel McBurney; m. Raffaele Ludovico Bisconti (dec. Oct. 19, 1999); children: Alessandra Ilus Wilkes, Giulia Rachel; m. Charles William Dyke, Oct. 13, 2002. Student, Harvard U., 1958—60; BA with honors, McGill U., 1962; PhD, The Union Inst., Cin., 1978. Assoc. study dir. Nat. Commn. on Allied Health Edn., Washington, 1977—79; dir. Washington office Higher Edn. Rsch. Inst., 1979—80; ptnr. Human Resources Policy Corp., Washington, 1980; dir. Nat. Ctr. for Allied Health Leadership, Washington, 1981—83; v.p. rsch. Nuc. Energy Inst., Washington, 1983—96; pres. Bisconti Rsch., Inc., Washington, 1996—. Mem. adv. com., risk comm. program EPA, Washington, 1988; advisor tech. cooperation program in Malaysia IAEA, Vienna, 1990; mem. adv. com., risk comm. Orgn. for Econ. Cooperation and Devel., Paris, 1991. Author: College and Other Stepping Stones, 1980; co-author: Higher Education and the Disadvantaged Student, 1972, The Power of Protest, 1975, College as a Training Ground for Jobs, 1977. Pres. Congl. Award Coun., 8th Congl. Dist., Md., 1990—93; advisor long-range planning com. Town of Somerset, Chevy Chase, Md., 2002; career advisor Harvard U., Cambridge, 1996; rsch. advisor NASA Alumni League, Washington, 1998. Recipient Disting. Svc. Award, Am. Soc. Allied Health Professions (now Assn. Schs. Allied Health Profls.), 1983. Mem.: World Assn. Pub. Opinion Rsch., Am. Nuc. Soc. (bd. dirs. 1993—96, 2004—07, Best Paper award 1989, Outstanding Session award 1990, 1992), Am. Assn. Pub. Opinion Rsch. Avocations: geography/travel, languages, gardening. Office: Bisconti Rsch Inc 5530 Greystone St Chevy Chase MD 20815

BISHAR, JOHN JOSEPH, JR., utilities executive, lawyer; b. NYC, Jan. 22, 1950; s. John Joseph Sr. and Mildred (Marron) B.; m. Noreen Ellen Leddy, Aug. 5, 1972; children: Kimberly, Kelly, Lauren. BA, Georgetown U., 1971; JD, Fordham U., 1974. Bar: NY 1975, U.S. Dist. Ct. (so., ea. dist. NY) 1975. Assoc. Cullen & Dykman, Garden City, NY, 1974-80; sr. v.p., gen. counsel, corp. sec. LITCO Bancorporation, 1980-87; ptnr. Cullen & Dykman, Garden City, NY, 1987—2002, mng. ptnr., 1993—2002; sr. v.p., gen. counsel Keyspan Corp., Bklyn., 2002—05, corp. sec., 2003—05, exec. v.p., gen. counsel, corp. sec., chief governance officer, 2005—. Bd. dirs. YMCA of Long Island, Huntington, N.Y., 1981—; bd. of trustees Family Life Ctr., Garden City, 1985—; gov. Cath. Sch. of St. Mary, Garden City, 1985—. Named Man of Yr. YMCA of Long Island, 1986. Mem. ABA, N.Y. State Bar Assn., Nassau County Bar Assn., N.Y. State Bankers Assn. (lawyers adv. com.), Assn. Bank Holding Cos. (lawyers com.). Clubs: Cherry Valley (Garden City), Atlantic Beach (N.Y.). Republican. Roman Catholic. Avocations: sports, golf, basketball, tennis, coaching kids. Office: Keyspan Energy 21st Fl One Metro Tech Ctr Brooklyn NY 11201*

BISHARA, AMIN TAWADROS, management and consulting firm executive; b. Cairo, Oct. 22, 1944; came to U.S., 1973; s. Tawadros and Fakha (Boules) B.; m. Suzi Guirguis, Aug. 27, 1977; children: James A., Robert A. BSME, Ain Shams U., Cairo, 1968; MSME, Poly. U. N.Y., 1976. Registered profl. engr., N.Y., Tex., Ill., Ariz., Pa., Fla. Field engr. Gen. Engring. Co., Cairo, 1968-71; mech. engr. Engring. Co. for Indsl. Enterprises, Cairo, 1971-73; project engr. Cosentini Assocs., NYC, 1973-76; sr. engr. Ebasco Svcs., Inc., NYC, 1976-79, lead engr., 1979-84; chmn., chief exec. officer PTS Tech. Svcs., Inc., Hurst, Tex., 1985-96; v.p. Metzler & Assocs., 1997-98; sr. mgr. Ernst & Young LLP, 1999—. Mem. adv. bd. Entrepreuneurship Inst., Ft. Worth, 1990—. Lectr. in nuclear industry; strategic and bus. cons. Contbr. articles to profl. publs. Mem. NSPE, ASME Nuc. Air Treatment Sys. (main com.), Masons, Moslah Temple of Ft. Worth. Roman Catholic. Home: 2625 Brookridge Dr Hurst TX 76054-2761 Office Phone: 972-556-7189. Personal E-mail: amin.bishara@capgemini.com.

BISHARA, SAMIR EDWARD, orthodontist; b. Cairo, Oct. 31, 1935; children: Dina Marie, Dorine Gabrielle, Cherine Noelle. B. Dental Surgery, Alexandria U., Egypt, 1957; diploma in orthodontics, 1967; MS, U. Iowa, 1970, cert. in orthodontics, 1970, D.D.S., 1972. Diplomate Am. Bd. Orthodontics (pres. Coll. Diplomates 1992). Practice gen. dentistry, Alexandria, 1957-68; specializing in orthodontics Iowa City, 1970—; fellow in clin. pedontics Guggenheim Dental Clinic, NYC, 1959-60; resident in oral surgery Moassat Hosp., Alexandria, 1960-61, mem. staff, 1961-68; asst. prof. dentistry U. Iowa, 1970-73, assoc. prof., 1973-76, prof., 1976—. Vis. prof. Alexandria U., 1974. Contbr. articles profl. jours., chpts. in books. Fellow Am. Coll. Dentists, Internat. Coll. Dentists; mem. ADA, AAAS, World Fedn. Orthodontists (hon.), Am. Assn. Orthodontics, Internat. Dental Fedn., Internat. Assn. Dental Research, Am. Cleft Palate Assn., Assn. Egyptian Am. Scholars, Egyptian Orthodontic Soc. (hon.), Columbian Orthodontic Soc. (hon.), Greek Orthodontic Soc. (hon.), Mexican Bd. Orthodontists (hon.), Brit. Orthodontic Conf. (hon.), Omicron Kappa Upsilon, Sigma Xi Home: 1014 Penkridge Dr Iowa City IA 52246-4930 Office: U Iowa Coll Dentistry Orthodontic Dept Iowa City IA 52242

BISHER, JAMES FURMAN, journalist, writer; b. Denton, NC, Nov. 4, 1918; s. Chisholm and Mamie (Morris) B.; m. Lynda Landon; children: Roger, James Furman Jr., Monte. Student, Furman U., Greenville, SC, 1934—36; AB in Journalism, U. NC, Chapel Hill, 1938; D in Arts and Letters (hon.), Furman U., Greenville, SC, 1999. Editor Lumberton (N.C.) Voice, 1938-39; reporter High Point (N.C.) Enterprise, 1939-40; reporter, state editor Charlotte (N.C.) News, 1940-42, sports editor, 1946-50, Atlanta Constn., 1950-57, Atlanta Jour., 1957—; columnist The Sporting News, St. Louis; moderator weekly TV show, Football Rev., 1950-68. V.p. Bisher Hosiery Mill, Denton, N.C. Author: With A Southern Exposure, 1962, Miracle in Atlanta, 1966, Strange But True Baseball Stories, 1966, Arnold Palmer— The Golden Year, 1971, Aaron, 1974, The College Game, 1974, The Masters, 1976, The Furman Bisher Collection, 1989, Thankful, 1997, Atlanta Half-Century, 1997, Peachtree Golf Club, 2004, Face to Face, 2005, also numerous articles; contbr. to: anthologies including Best Sports Stories of Year, 23 times. Chmn. Ga. Christmas Seal campaign, 1961; charter mem. Atlanta-Fulton County Stadium Authority.; mem. selection com. Pro Football Hall of Fame, Coll. Football Hall of Fame, Ga.; bd. dirs. Salvation Army Boys Club, mem. adv. bd. Sarazen World Open Golf Tournament; mem. Atlanta Sports Coun. Served to lt. USNR Air Corps, 1943-46. Named Ky. col., 1958, Sportswriter of Yr. Ga. (19 times); hon. Tar Heel, 1961; Disting. Alumnus of Yr. Furman U., 1978, Disting. Alumnus 20th Century, 2006; named to U. NC Journalism Hall of Fame, 1985; Nat. Sportscasters and Sportswriters Hall of Fame, 1989, Internat. Golf Writers Hall of Fame, 1989, Ga. Sports Hall of Fame, 1990, N.C. Sports Hall of Fame, 1995, Ga. Soccer Hall of Fame, 1997, Ga. Golf Hall of Fame, 2004; recipient Ga. A.P. Sports Writing award, 18 times; UPI Sports Writing award, 4 times; Turf Writing award Fla. Throughbred Breeders Assn., 1972, 75; Jake Wade award Coll. Sports Info. Dirs. Am., 1979; Sigma Delta Chi awards best sports commentary, 1982, 93, 90; Bert McGrane award disting. svc. to coll. football, 1982; N.C. Gov.'s award, 1986; Red Smith award disting. and meritorious contbn. to art of sportswriting, 1988, Bobby Jones Sportsman of Yr. award, 1994, Lifetime Achievement in Journalism award PGA in Am., 1996, Meml. Golf Journalism award, 1997, Marvin Francis Svc. award, 2001, Nat. Conf. Cmty. and Justice award, 2001, Lincoln Werden Meml. award, N.Y. Golf Assn., 2001; sponsor Furman Bisher Acad.-Athletic scholarship Furman U., Roger C. Bisher Scholarship Ga. Tech. Mem. Nat. Sportscasters and Sportswriters Assn. (pres. 1974-76), Football Writers Assn. Am. (pres. 1959-60), Golf Writers Assn. Am. (pres. 1992-94), Assn. Golf Writers (Europe) (life), Canongate Golf Club, Legends at Chateau Elan, Capital City Club, The European Club, Sea Island Golf Club, Gridiron Club, Chi Psi. Presbyterian. Home: 431 Lester Rd Fayetteville GA 30215-4930 Office: 72 Marietta St NW PO Box 4689 Atlanta GA 30302-4689: 21 Dunbar Creek Pte Saint Simons Island GA 31522 Office Phone: 404-526-5335. E-mail: furman@ajc.com. *My good fortune in life is not to be confused with success, whose definition yet remains vague to me. Success is some mythical goal clamored and struggled for, and whose pursuit is never-ending. One level leads to a requirement to seek another. Success, in my mind, must be related to the status of that person who achieves happiness, and yet may never have been outside his county.*

BISHOP, ALFRED CHILTON, JR., lawyer; b. Alexandria, Va., Oct. 3, 1942; s. Alfred Chilton and Margaret (Marshall) Bishop; 1 child, Alfred Chilton III. BA with distinction, U. Va., 1965, LLB, 1969; LLM in Taxation, Georgetown U., 1974. Bar: N.Y. 1970, U.S. Ct. Appeals (2d cir.) 1970, U.S. Tax Ct. 1971, U.S. Ct. Claims 1971, D.C. 1977. Assoc. Shearman and Sterling, NYC, 1969—70; assoc. trial atty. Office of Chief Counsel, IRS, Washington, 1970—74, sr. trial atty., 1974—80, sr. tech. reviewer, 1980—81, br. chief, 1981—. Recipient Am. Jurisprudence award, 1968. Mem.: Sr. Exec. Assn., Sr. Exec. Svc. Candidate Network (v.p. 1980—81, pres. 1981—82, dir. 1983), D.C. Bar Assn., Phi Delta Phi. Episcopalian. Home: 9891 Burke Pond Ct Burke VA 22015 Home Phone: 703-408-1140; Office Phone: 202-622-8483. Business E-Mail: alfred.c.bishop@irscounsel.treas.gov.

BISHOP, BRUCE TAYLOR, lawyer; b. Hartford, Conn., Sept. 13, 1951; s. Robert Wright Sr. and Barbara (Taylor) B.; m. Sarah M. Bishop, Aug. 31, 1974; children: Elizabeth, Margaret. BA in Polit. Sci., Old Dominion U., 1973; JD, U. Va., Charlottesville, 1976. Bar: Va. 1977, U.S. Supreme Ct., Va. 1976, U.S. Dist. Ct. (ea. dist.) Va., U.S. Dist. Ct. (we. dist.) Va., U.S. Ct. Appeals (4th cir.); diplomate Am. Bd. Trial Advocates. Law clk. to chief judge U.S. Dist. Ct. (ea. dist.) Va., 1976-77; assoc. Willcox & Savage, P.C., Norfolk, Va., 1977-82, ptnr., 1983—. Bd. dirs. Nautical Adventures, Inc., Norfolk FestEvents, Ltd., 1981—, pres., 1982-85; pres. Va. OpSail 2000 Found.; bd. visitors Old Dominion U., 1972-83, sec., 1979-81, chmn., com. mem.; speaker in field. Treas. Norfolk Reps., 1978-82, com. mem.; bd. dirs., chmn. regional Key Club campaign United Way South Hampton Roads; chmn., co-chmn. United Negro Coll. Fund, 1981, Four Cities United Way Campaign; trustee Va. Stage Co., 1982; pres. Cmty. Promotion Corp.; commr. Norfolk Redevel. and Housing Authority, chmn., 2000-02; pres. Old Dominion U. Ednl. Found., 2003-2005. Named Outstanding Young Man in Norfolk, Norfolk Jaycees, 1982; recipient Disting. Alumni award Old Dominion U., Dominion Vol. of Yr. award, 1993. Mem. ABA, Fed. Bar Assn. (pres. Tidewater chpt. 1980-81), Am. Bd. Trial Advocates, Va. Assn. Def. Lawyers, Va. Bar Assn., Norfolk-Portsmouth Bar Assn., Def. Rsch. Inst., Internat. Assn. Def. Counsel (nat. trial acad. faculty 1997), Assn. Def. Attys., Def. Rsch. Inst., Old Dominion U. Alumni Assn. (bd. dirs. 1978-83), Old Dominion U. Ednl. Found. (bd. dirs. 1987—, sec. 2000-02, pres. 2003-05), Norfolk C. of C. (chmn. downtown devel. com. 1980-81), James Kent Am. Inn of Ct. (master). Avocations: basketball, tennis, gardening. Office: Willcox & Savage PC One Commercial Place Norfolk VA 23510 Office Phone: 757-628-5573. Business E-Mail: bbishop@wilsav.com.

BISHOP, BUDD HARRIS, retired museum director; b. Canton, Ga., Nov. 1, 1936; s. James M. and Mary E. (Ponder) B.; m. Julia Crowder, Nov. 30, 1968. AB, Shorter Coll., Rome, Ga., 1958; M.F.A., U. Ga., 1960; student, Arts Adminstrn. Inst. Harvard, 1970. Instr. art Ensworth Sch., Nashville, 1961-63; dir. creative services Transit Advt. Assn., NYC, 1964-66; dir. Hunter Mus. of Art, Chattanooga, 1966-76, Columbus (Ohio) Mus. Art, 1976-87, Samuel P. Harn Mus. Art, U. Fla., Gainesville, 1987-98, dir. emeritus. Vis. lectr. Vanderbilt U., 1962; past pres. bd. Intermuseum Conservation Lab., Oberlin, Ohio Past trustee Fla. Arts Celebration, Gainesville; mem. Gainesville Art in Pub. Places Trust; mem. faculty Ctr. for Arts and Pub. Policy, Tenn. Arts Commn., 2007—; bd. dirs. Fla. Assn. Mus. Found., Inc.; mem. nat. adv. bd. Philharm. Ctr. for Arts, Naples, Fla.; trustee Hist. Rugby, Inc., Tenn.; bd. dirs. Cordell Hull Mus. and Bhplace, Upper Cumberland Arts Alliance; pres. Livingston-Overton County C. of C.; appointee Tenn. Arts Commn., 2007—. Recipient gov.'s award Tenn. Art Commn., 1971, 73, Alumni Arts achievement award Shorter Coll., 1979, arts leadership award Columbus Day, 1986, Person of Yr. award in arts Gainesville Sun, 1995, Lifetime Achievement Mus. Svc. award Fla. Assn. Mus., 1997. Mem. Am. Assn. Museums, Assn. Art Mus. Dirs. (past trustee), Southeastern Museums Conf. (James R. Short award 1998), Fla. Art Mus. Dirs. Assn. (Lifetime Achievement award 1998). Home Phone: 931-823-7114; Office Phone: 931-823-1106.

BISHOP, C. DIANE, state agency administrator, educator; b. Elmhurst, Ill., Nov. 23, 1943; d. Louis William and Constance Oleta (Mears) B. BS in Maths., U. Ariz., 1965, MS in Maths., MEd in Secondary Edn., 1972. Lic. secondary educator. Tchr. math. Tucson Unified Sch. Dist., 1966-86, mem. curriculum council, 1985-86, mem. maths. curriculum task teams, 1983-86; state supt. of pub. instrn. State of Ariz., 1987-95, gov.'s policy advisor for edn., 1995-97, dir. gov.'s office workforce devel. policy, 1996-2000; asst. dep. dir. Ariz. Dept. Commerce, 1997-2000; exec. dir. Gov.'s Strategic Partnership for Econ. Devel., 1997—2000; pres. The Vandegrift Inst., 2000—06; exec. dir. Maricopa Health Found., 2002—. Mem. assoc. faculty Pima C.C., Tucson, 1974-84; adj. lectr. U. Ariz., 1983, 85; mem. math. scis. edn. bd. NRC, 1987-90, mem. new standards project governing bd., 1991; dir. adv. bd. sci. and engring. ednl. panel, NSF; mem. adv. bd. for arts edn. Nat. Endowment for Arts. Active Ariz. State Bd. Edn., 1984-95, chmn. quality edn. commn., 1986-87, chmn. tchr. crt. subcom., 1984-95, mem. outcomes based edn. adv. com., 1986-87, liaison bd. dirs. essential skills subcom., 1985-87, gifted edn. com. liaison, 1985-87; mem. Ariz. State Bd. Regents, 1987-95, com. on preparing for U. Ariz., 1983, HS task force, 1984-85, bd. Ariz. State Community Coll., 1987-95, Ariz. Joint Legis. Com. on Revenues and Expenditures, 1989, Ariz. Joint Legis. Com. on Goals for Ednl. Excellence, 1987-89, Gov.'s Task Force on Ednl. Reform, 1991, Ariz. Bd. Regents Commn. on Higher Edn., 1992; mem. governing bd. Phoenix Union HS Dist. 2005—; mem. bd. dirs. Great Heart Prep. Acad., 2005-. Woodrow Wilson fellow Princeton U., summer 1984; recipient Presdl. Award for Excellence in Teaching of Maths., 1983, Ariz. Citation of Merit, 1984, Maths. Teaching award Nat. Sci. Research Soc., 1984, Distinction in Edn. award Flinn Found., 1986; named Maths. Tchr. of Yr. Ariz. Council of Engring. and Sci. Assns., 1984, named One of Top Ten Most Influential Persons in Ariz. in Field of Tech., 1998. Mem. AAUW, NEA, Nat. Coun. Tchrs. Math., Coun. Chief State Sch. Officers, Women Execs. in State Govt. (bd. dirs. 1993), Ariz. Assn. Tchrs. Math., Women Maths. Edn., Math. Assn. Am., Ednl. Commn. of the States (steering com.), Nat. Endowment Arts (adv. bd. for arts edn.), Nat. Forum Excellence Edn., Nat. Honors Workshop, Ariz. Bioindustry Assn. (bd. dirs. 1997—, sec. 2000—), Phi Delta Kappa. Republican.

BISHOP, CHARLES EDWIN, academic administrator, economist, educator; b. Campobello, SC, June 8, 1921; s. Fred and Hattie Bess (Wall) B.; m. Lee N., June 1, 2002; children from a previous marriage: Susan Ann, Mary Catherine, Charles Edwin. BS, Berea Coll., 1946; MS, U. Ky., 1948; PhD (Farm Found. fellow 1948-49), U. Chgo., 1952. Research asst. agrl. econs. U. Ky., 1947-48; research assoc. econs. U. Chgo., 1949-50; mem. faculty N.C. State U., 1950-70, prof. agrl. econs., 1956-70, head dept. agrl. econs., 1957-65, head dept. econs., 1965-66, William N. Reynolds Disting. prof., 1957-70; v.p. U. N.C., Chapel Hill, 1966-70; exec. dir. Agrl. Policy Inst., 1960-66; chancellor U. Md., College Park, 1970-74; pres. U. Ark., Fayetteville, 1974-80, U. Houston System, 1980-86. Vis. prof. Grad. Sch. Bus., U. Va., 1961-63; cons. Universidad Agraria, Lima, Peru, 1961-65; mem. Nat. Com. Agrl. Policy, Nat. Planning Assn., 1958-70; agrl. bd. Nat. Acad. Scis., 1963-68; sci. adv. com. to sec. agr., 1962-68; mem. Nat. Manpower Adv. Com., 1962-68; exec. dir. Pres. Johnson's Nat. Adv. Com. on Rural Poverty, 1966-67; mem. food adv. com. Pres. Nixon's Cost of Living Council, 1972; mem. Pres. Carter's adv. com. White House Conf. on Balanced Nat. Growth and Econ. Devel., 1978 Co-author: Introduction to Agricultural Economic Analysis, 1958. Mem. com. on vet. med. edn. So. Regional Edn. Bd., 1974; trustee Farm Found., 1968-78; bd. dirs. Winthrop Rockefeller Found., 1975-78, Resources for the Future, 1976-90, chmn., 1987-90; co-chmn. bd. Nat. Rural Ctr., 1975-79; mem. N.C. Rural Econ. Devel. Ctr., 1986-96, chmn., 1991-96; mem. Pres. Carter's Commn. on Agenda for Eighties, 1980; bd. dirs. Houston Industries, 1984-92. Sr. fellow M.D.C., 1991-2000. Fellow Am. Agrl. Econ. Assn. (pres. 1967-68); mem. Internat. Assn. Agrl. Econs., Commn. on Cen. European Econ. Devel., Alpha Zeta, Phi Kappa Phi, Gamma Sigma Delta.

BISHOP, CHARLES JOSEPH, retired manufacturing executive; b. Gary, Ind., June 22, 1941; s. Charles K. and Angela (Marich) Yelusich; m. Yvonne M. Stazinski, June 8, 1963; children: Stephen, Scott. BS, Purdue U., 1963; PhD, U. Wash., 1969. Mgr. advanced energy systems Boeing Co., Seattle, 1969-77; mgr. sys. devel. Solar Energy Rsch. Inst., Denver, 1977-81; sr. v.p. tech. A.O. Smith Corp., Milw., 1981—2006; ret. Mem. adv. bd. S.W. Wis. Rsch. Ctr., Milw., 1987; bd. dirs. Indsl. Rsch. Inst., 1989—92, v.p., 1993, pres., 1995—96. Contbr. articles to profl. jours. Treas. Cedarburg Cmty. Scholarship Com., Wis., 1985—91; mem. Gov.'s Coun. Sci. and Tech., 1992—94; mem. nat. coun. Alverno Coll.; mem. indsl. liaison coun. U. Wis., Milw., 1985—, U. Wis. Coll. Engring., Madison, 1990—95. Recipient Cert. of Recognition award, NASA, 1975. Mem.: Milw. Athletic Club. Republican. Roman Catholic. Avocations: fishing, travel, golf.

BISHOP, CHRISTY B., lawyer, researcher; b. Akron, Ohio, Mar. 10, 1960; m. Dennis R. Thompson; 1 stepchild, Jeffrey Thompson. BA in Rhetoric, U. Akron, Ohio, 1985, MA in Rhetoric, 1991, JD cum laude, 2002. Bar: Ohio 2003, Ohio (US Dist. Ct. (no. dist.)) 2003, Ohio (US Dist. Ct. (so. dist.)) 2006, (US Supreme Ct.) 2006. Journalist Village Views, Akron, 1982—85; mng. editor Great Lakes Sailor Mag., Akron, 1986—89; prof. U. Akron, 1991—94; law clk. Thompson Law Office, Akron, 1992—2002; ptnr. Thompson & Bishop, Akron, 2002—. Mem. Southern Poverty Law Ctr., 2003—, mem. Tchg. Tolerance Campaign, 2003—; mem. Democratic Nat. Campaign Com., 1992—. Recipient Westlaw Excellence award, 1998, Anderson Book award, 2001, Hon. Arthur Goldberg prize Constitutional Law, 2002. Mem.: Nat. Employment Lawyers Assn. (mem. comms. com. 2003—), Ohio Employment Lawyers Assn. (mem. amicus brief com. 2002—, mem. judiciary com. 2004—, chmn. Akron chpt. 2002—). Democrat. Episcopalian. Avocations: writing, music, boating, hiking. Office: Thompson & Bishop 2719 Manchester Rd Akron OH 44319

BISHOP, CLAIRE DEARMENT, small business owner, retired librarian; b. Youngstown, Ohio, Oct. 12, 1937; d. Eugene Howard and Ruth (Bright) DeArment; m. Carl R. Meinstereifel, 1956 (div. 1964); children: Paul, Dawn; m. Olin Jerry Dewberry, Jr., 1974 (div. 1979); m. J. Bruce Bishop, May 6, 1992 (dec. Oct. 2005). BS, Clarion State U., 1967; MLS, Ga. State U., 1977. Cert. libr. media specialist, Ga. Libr. Henry County, Stockbridge, Ga., 1967-69; head libr. Russell H.S., East Point, Ga., 1969-84; engring. libr. Rockwell Internat., Duluth, Ga., 1984-88; rep. Govt. Industry Data Exch. Program, Corona, Calif., 1984-88; libr. Raytheon Co., 1990, Missile Sys. Divsn., Bristol, Tenn., 1988-90; owner, mgr. Claire's Collectibles, rubber stamp store, St. Augustine, Fla. Author newsletter Grin and Stamp It. Sec. San Marco Avenue Mchts. Assn. Mem. St. Augustine IBM Users Group (sec.), Six-Ninety-Six Investment Club (fin. officer), Mensa. Democrat. Avocations: computers, writing, information broker. Home: 78A San Marco Ave Saint Augustine FL 32084-3258 Office Phone: 904-825-1122.

BISHOP, ELIZABETH SHREVE, psychologist; b. Ann Arbor, Mich., Nov. 18, 1951; d. William Warner Jr. and Mary Fairfax (Shreve) B. AB, U. Mich., 1972; MA, Ohio State U., 1973, PhD, 1976. Lic. psychologist Mich. Psychologist Franklin County Program for the Mentally Retarded, Columbus, Ohio, 1974, WC Mental Health, Willmar, Minn., 1977-83; chief psychologist Battle Creek Child Guidance Ctr., Mich., 1981; dir. psychometrics Meridian Profl. Psychol. Cons., East Lansing, Mich., 1983-92; pres. Arbor Psychol. Cons., Ann Arbor, 1991—. Trainer Girl Scouts USA, 1993—, troop leader, 1968—69, 1971—72, 1973—74, 1980—82, 1984—86; deacon 1st Congl. Ch., 1996—2000, 2002—. Assoc. Univ. London Inst. Edn., 1976. Mem. APA, AAUW, LWV (Willmar v.p. 1979-81), Mich. Psychol. Assn., Mich. Women Psychologists (treas. 2002-06, pres.-elect 2005-06, pres. 2006-07), Coun. Exceptional Children (local pres. 1977-78), Internat. Coun. Psychologists (bd. dir. 1999-2002). Avocations: reading, travel, birdwatching, photography, music. Home: 1612 Morton Ave Ann Arbor MI 48104-4441 Office: Arbor Psychol Cons 1565 Eastover Pl Ann Arbor MI 48104-6316 Office Phone: 734-741-8844. Personal E-mail: arborpsych@sbcglobal.net.

BISHOP, GENE HERBERT, corporate financial executive; b. Forest, Miss., May 3, 1930; s. Herbert Eugene and Lavonne (Little) B.; m. Kathy S. Bishop, May 27, 1983. BBA, U. Miss., Oxford, 1952. With First Nat. Bank, Dallas, 1954-69, sr. v.p., chmn. sr. loan com., 1963-68, exec. v.p., 1968-69; pres., dir. SBIC subs. First Dallas Capital Corp.; pres. Lomas & Nettleton Fin. Corp., Dallas, 1969-75, Lomas & Nettleton Mortgage Investors, Dallas, 1969-75; chmn., CEO Merc. Nat. Bank, Dallas, 1975-81, MCorp., Dallas, 1975-90; vice-chmn., CFO Lomas Fin. Corp., 1990-91; pres., COO Lomas Mortgage USA, Dallas, 1990-91; chmn., CEO Life Ptnrs. Group, Inc., Dallas, 1991-94, also bd. dirs. Adv. dir. Tolleson Wealth Mgmt. Bd. dirs. State Fair Tex., Dallas; trustee Children's Med. Ctr., Dallas Meth. Hosps. Found.; mem. Dallas Citizens Coun. 1st lt. USAF, 1952-54. Mem. Terpsichorean Club, Idlewild Club, Brook Hollow Golf Club, Eldorado Country Club, Vintage Club, Dallas Country Club. Methodist. Office: 5500 Preston Rd Ste 250 Dallas TX 75205-2699

BISHOP, GEORGE FRANKLIN, political scientist, educator; b. New Haven, July 26, 1942; s. George Elwood and Mary Bridget (Trant) B.; m. Pama Mitchell, July 15, 1995; 1 child, Kristina. BS in Psychology, Mich. State U., 1966; MS in Psychology, Mich. State U., East Lansing, 1969; PhD, Mich. State U., 1973. Instr. multidisciplinary social sci. program Mich. State U., East Lansing, 1972-73; asst. prof. dept. sociology and anthropology U. Notre Dame, Ind., 1973-75; dir. Greater Cin. Survey, 1981-95; rsch. assoc. behavioral sci. lab U. Cin., 1975-77, sr. rsch. assoc. Inst. for Policy Rsch., 1981-93, dir. behavioral scis. lab., 1994-95, assoc. prof. polit. sci., 1982-87, prof., 1987—, dir. grad. cert. program in pub. opinion and survey rsch., 1999—; dir. Internet Pub. Opinion Lab. Univ. Cin., 2000—. Assoc. dir. Ohio Poll, 1981-95; guest prof. Zentrum für Umfragen, Methoden und Analysen, Mannheim, Germany, 1985, 90, 92, 2007; fellow Ctr. Study of Dem. Citizenship, Dept. Polit. Sci., U. Cin., 1992-99, fellow Inst. Data Scis., 1996-98; summer inst. faculty Survey Rsch. Ctr., Inst. Social Rsch., U. Mich., summer 1993; sr. cons. Burke Mktg. Rsch., Inc., Cin., 1996-98. Author: The Illusion of Public Opinion, 2005 (Outstanding Academic Title Choice Mag., 2005); sr. editor: Presdl. Debates: Media, Electoral and Policy Perspectives, 1978; sr. author various articles in profl. jours.; mem. editl. bd. Pub. Opinion Quar., 1987-90, Free Inquiry, 1999-2005; mem. editl. adv. bd. Pub. Perspective, 2000—03. Bd. trustees Clifton Town Meetings, Cin., 2004—, chair pub. safety com., 2004—. With N.G. US Army, 1960—63. NSF grantee, 1977-84. Mem. AAUP (Maita Levine Svc. award 2002), Midwest Assn. Pub. Opinion Rsch. (pres. 1977-78, Mapor fellow Disting. Scholarship in pub. opinion rsch. 1994), Am. Assn. Pub. Opinion Rsch., Am. Polit. Sci. Assn., World Assn. Pub. Opinion Rsch. (treas. 1983-85). Avocation: genealogy. Home: 825 Dunore Rd Cincinnati OH 45220-1416 Office: U Cin Cincinnati OH 45221-0001

BISHOP, GORDON BRUCE, journalist; b. Paterson, NJ, Jan. 1, 1938; s. Charles E. and Freda Mary (Romyns) B.; m. Jeanne Ann Reed, June 30, 1962; children: Jennifer, Elizabeth. Student, Am. Acad. Dramatic Arts, 1957; BA, Rutgers U., NJ, 1967. Reporter, columnist Herald-News, Passaic, NJ, 1959—68; pres., TV prodr. Bishop Pub. Programs, Inc., Ocean, NJ, 1969—. Spl. writer Star-Ledger, Newark, 1969-96; lectr. Rutgers U., Princeton U. Author: (with Frank Papps) The Purple Canary, 1963, Holding Onto Nothing, 1969, Gems of New Jersey, 1985, Greater Newark: A Microcosm of America, 1989, Gateway to America, 1994, The Greatest Century: 1901-2001 Upper Montclair Country Club, 2002, Quest for Survival, 2002, Three Little Girls, 2005, The Hacky, 2007; prodr. 12 documentaries including It's My Home for PBS, 1980, Every Day Is Earth Day, 1990, The Baykeeper, 1993, Global War on Pollution, 1994, Gateway to America, 1995; prodr.-collaborator (mus.) Crispus, 1986; columnist NJ Mayors mag., The Patriot NJ, The Courier; syndicated columnist AH-Hearld.com, AmericanDaily.com, Etherzone.com, Newsbull.com; host. NJ Issues TV Program, 1988-96. Environ. commr. Eatontown, NJ, 1973-76; chmn. NJ Lit. Hall of Fame, 1988-96; dir. Battleship NJ Found., 1998-2001; pres. US Mil. Mus., Ft. Hancock, NJ, 2002—. Recipient Disting. Pub. Service award NJ Profl. Soc. Engrs., Nat. Environ. awards Scripps-Howard Found., 1971-75; Nat. Conservation awards Washington Journalism Ctr., 1971-72, Conservation award NJ Audubon Soc., 1973, NJ Press Assn. awards, 1971-88, NJ Pub. Health Assn. award, 1987, Mid-Atlantic States Air Pollution Control Assn. Disting. Service award, 1987, Pub. Svc. award NJ Profl. Journalism Soc., 1972, 73, 74, 76, 78, NJ, Nat. Recycling award Nat. Recycling Assn., 1973, Conf. Mayors award, 1994,; Gold medal NJ Garden Club, 1980, award Ballew/McFarland Found., 1981, NJ Agrl. Soc., 1981, Nat. Wildlife Fedn.'s Nat. Conservation Achievement award, 1987, Good Journalism award Nat. Assn. Water Cos., 1992, Monmouth County Planning Award, 1989, Inst. Internat. Edn. scholar, U. Manchester, Eng., 1972, Environ. Edn. award NJ Edn. Assn., 1990, Environ. award Am. Soc. Landscape Architects, 1993, 94, Broadcaster award Radio Club of Am., 2005; named NJ Journalist of Yr., 1986 (1st in NJ), Man of Yr. AABC Congregation, Irvington, NJ; inductee Literary Hall of Fame, 1990, chmn., 1988-96. Mem. Rutgers U. Alumni Assn. *The will to live, to learn, and to inspire others flows from a genuine desire to want to work at your best and to share your love with those who seek it. This is our destiny: Work and Love. Without either, you can never realize your full potential as an individual.*

BISHOP, INA SUE MARQUIS (INA SUE MARQUIS BISHOP), retired dean; b. Charleston, W.Va., Sept. 30, 1939; d. Harold Edwin and Ina Mabel (Walkup) Marquis; m. Randal Young Bishop, Feb. 27, 1960; children: Jon Marquis, Heather Suzanne. RN, Norton Infirmary Sch. Nursing, 1960; BSN, Murray State U., 1963; MSN, Ind. U., 1967, PhD, 1983. RN, Ky., Ind., Fla., N.C. Ind. staff nurse psychiatry Norton Infirmary, Louisville, 1960-61; head nurse obstetrics, nursing supr. Murray (Ky.) Gen. Hosp., 1961-62; primary care nurse, crisis counselor infirmary Murray State U., 1962-63; staff nurse, clin. instr. Madison (Ind.) State Hosp., 1963-65; instr. through assoc. prof. Ind. U. Sch. Nursing, Indpls., 1967-89, developer child/adolescent psychiat., mental health nursing program, 1982-83, chairperson grad. dept., 1983-89; prof., asst. dean Coll. of Nursing U. South Fla., Tampa, 1989-91; dean Coll. Nursing U. N.C., Charlotte, 1992-95, dean Coll. of Nursing and Health Professions, 1995—2004, dean Coll. Health and Human Svcs., 2002—04, dean emerita, 2004—; ret., 2004. Pvt. practice marital and family therapy, 1975-89; cons. in field. Founding editor-in-chief Jour. of Child and Adolescent Psychiatric and Mental Health Nursing, 1987-91; contbr. articles to profl. jours. Bd. dirs. Carolinas blood svcs. region ARC, 1997-2002, chmn. bd. dirs., 2000—. NIMH trainee Ind. U., 1965-67, USPHS profl. nurse trainee Ind. U., 1977-78; recipient Youth Advocacy award Ind. Advs. for Child Psychiat. Nursing, 1987, Disting. Svc. award Ind. U. Sch. Nursing Alumni Assn., 1989, Nat. Youth Advocacy award Advs. for Child Psychiat. Nursing, 1990, Disting. Alumni award Ind. U. sch. Edn., 2000. Fellow Am. Acad. Nursing; mem. ANA, Psychiat. Mental Health Nursing Coun., Soc. for Edn. and Rsch. in Psychiat. Mental Health Nursing (pres. 1988-90), Am. Assn. Marital and Family Therapy, So. Nursing Rsch. Soc., So. Piedmont Alzheimer's Assn. (bd. dirs. 1999-2000), New South Hospice of Charlotte and Lincoln County (bd. dirs. 1995—2004, chair 2002-04), Sigma Theta Tau.

BISHOP, JAMES DODSON, lawyer, mediator; b. Washington, Sept. 28, 1957; s. James William and Jane Lillian (Dodson) B. BA magna cum laude in Polit. Sci., Lincln U., Pa., 1979; JD, Howard U., Washington, 1982. Bar: Pa. 1985, DC 1986. Dir. Atty./Client Arbitration Bd. DC Bar, Washington, 1987-93; dir. Archdiocesan Legal Network of Cath. Cmty. Svcs., Washington, 1993—. Mediator, DC Superior Ct., Washington, 1987—; lay reader St. Georges Episcopal Ch., Washington, 1984—; chair Catholic Cmty. Svcs. Diversity Com., 1997-2002; bd. dirs. Coun. for Ct. Excellence and Episcopal Sr. Ministries. Recipient award, Griffith Found., 2002, Order of Merit award, Archdiocese Wash., 2003, Benemerenti medal, 2006. Democrat. Episcopalian. Avocation: church activities. Home: 5157 33rd St NW Washington DC 20008-2011 Office: Catholic Community Svcs 924 G St NW Washington DC 20001-4532 Home Phone: 202-669-5781; Office Phone: 202-772-4325. Personal E-mail: bishopjim@verizon.net. Business E-Mail: james.bishop@ccs-dc.org.

BISHOP, JAMES FRANCIS, personnel director, consultant; b. Chgo., Mar. 14, 1937; s. Francis Joseph and Margaret Rose (Nagle) B.; m. Shirley Ann McNulty, Oct. 13, 1962; children: Michael Francis, Noreen Maura, James Francis Jr. BA, Marquette U., 1961, MA, 1965. Spl. agt. Office of Naval Intelligence, Chgo., 1962-65; sr. assoc. Burke & O'Brien Assoc., Inc., NYC, 1965-67, v.p., 1967-74, sr. v.p., 1974-78, pres., 1978-83, CEO, 1983—2005; ret., 2005. Trustee George St. Playhouse, 1988-93, NJ Hosp. Assn., 1996-2002, St. Francis Med. Ctr., Trenton, NJ, 1989—, chmn. bd., 1991-96; chmn., bd. trustees St. Francis Med. Ctr. Found., 1998—; councilman Piscataway, 1968-71. With USMC, 1954—57. Mem.: NJ Hosp. Assn., Marquette U. Alumni Assn. (v.p. 1985—87, pres. 1987—88), Marquette Club (NY), Springdale Golf Club (Princeton). Republican. Roman Catholic. Home: 2 Allura Ct Lawrenceville NJ 08648 Personal E-mail: jmsbishop@aol.com.

BISHOP, JEROME C., lawyer; BA, Georgetown U., 1994, JD, 2001. Bar: Ohio 2002, US Dist. Ct. Southern Dist. Ohio. Assoc. Katz, Teller, Brant & Hild, Cin. Named one of Ohio's Rising Stars, Super Lawyers, 2006. Avocations: running, golf. Office: Katz Teller Brant & Hild 255 E 5th St Ste 2400 Cincinnati OH 45202-4724 Office Phone: 513-721-4532. Office Fax: 513-762-0061.

BISHOP, KIM IRENE, pharmaceutical consultant, psychopharmacologist; b. Williamsport, Pa., Nov. 12, 1960; arrived in Switzerland, 1996; d. Harold Dane and Irene (Pelletier) B. BA, Franklin and Marshall Coll., Lancaster, Pa., 1982; MS, Villanova U., Pa., 1986; PhD, U. London, 1995; DipPM, U. Basel, 2001. Coord. clin. rsch. Scheie Eye Inst. U. Pa., Phila., 1984-88; sr. clin. rsch. assoc. Allergan Pharms., Irvine, Calif., 1988-90; cons. Clin. Trials Rsch. Ltd., Maidenhead, Eng., 1994; sr. drug safety scientist Ciba Geigy, Basel, Switzerland, 1996-97; global projects liaison mgr. Novartis, Basel, Switzerland, 1997-99; founder, prin. cons. Global Pharma Cons., Basel, 1999—, cons. clin. devel. and psychopharm. svcs. Contbr. articles to profl. jours. Alumni regional amb. Villanova U. Overseas rsch. scholar Brit. com. for Vice Chancellors and Prins., London, 1991-94; European Behavioral Pharmacology Soc. scholar, 1994; scholar Brit. Assn. Psychopharmacology Bursary, Eng., 1993, 94. Mem. APA, INS, ECNP, Am. Acad. Neurology, Drug Info. Assn., Royal Soc. Medicine. Avocations: skiing, scuba diving, dance, horseback riding, bicycling. Office Phone: 570-546-7833. Business E-Mail: kib@globalpharmaconsultancy.com.

BISHOP, LEAH MARGARET, lawyer; b. NYC, Nov. 2, 1954; d. Franklin Gerald and Evelyn (Fremed) B.; m. Gary M. Yale, Aug. 10, 1975; children: Elizabeth Yale, Rebecca Yale. BA summa cum laude, Brandeis U., 1975; JD, Columbia U., 1979. Bar: NY 1980, US Dist. Ct. (ea. and so. dists. NY) 1980, Calif. 1981, US Dist. Ct. (ctrl. dist. Calif.) 1981; cert. State Bar Calif. Bd. Legal Specialization (estate planning, trust and probate law). Law clk. to Hon. Edmund Palmieri US Dist. Ct. (so. dist. NY),

1979-80; assoc. O'Melveny & Myers, LA, 1980-87, ptnr., 1987—2006, Loeb & Loeb, LLP, LA, 2006. Named one of Top 100 Attys., Worth mag., 2006. Fellow Am. Coll. Trust and Estate Counsel; mem. LA County Bar Assn. (mem. exempt orgn. com.), Phi Beta Kappa. Democrat. Jewish. Office: Loeb & Loeb LLP Ste 2200 10100 Santa Monica Blvd Los Angeles CA 90067-4120 Office Phone: 310-282-2353. Office Fax: 310-919-3963. E-mail: lbishop@loeb.com.

BISHOP, LEO KENNETH, clergyman, educator; b. Britton, Okla., Oct. 11, 1911; s. Luther and Edith (Scovill) B.; m. Pauline T. Shamburg, Sept. 15, 1935; 1 dau., Linda Paulette. AB, Phillips U., 1932, LHD, 1958; MA, Columbia U., 1944; MBA, U. Chgo., 1957; LittD, Kansas City Coll. Osteopathy and Surgery, 1964. Assoc. min. Univ. Place Ch., Oklahoma City, 1932-35; min. First Ch., Paducah, Ky., 1935-41, Ctrl. Ch., Des Moines, 1941-45; dir. St. Louis office NCCJ, 1945-48, v.p., dir. ctrl. divsn. Chgo., 1949-63; dir. pub. affairs People-to-People, Kansas City, Mo., 1963-66; v.p. Chgo. Coll. Osteopathy, 1966-72; pres. Bishop Enterprises, Colorado Springs, Colo., 1972—, also lectr. Contbr. religious and ednl. jours.; Developed: radio series Storm Warning; TV series The Other Guy, 1954. Cons. Cmty. Social Planning Coun., Mayor's Race Rels. Com., YMCA, St. Louis; Am. del. Conf. World Brotherhood, Paris, 1950; bd. dirs. Am. Heritage Found. Recipient Most Useful Citizen award Paducah Jr. C. of C., 1937, Disting. Svc. award Dore Miller Found., 1958, Freedom Found. of Valley Forge award, 1961; named Chicagoan of Year, 1960. Mem.: Rotary, Union League, Winter Night. Home and Office: Montara Meadows A342 3150 E Tropicana Ave Las Vegas NV 89121

BISHOP, MARK D., finance company executive, director; b. Roanoke, Va., Oct. 25, 1959; s. John W. Bishop, Jr. and Chris R. Bishop-Bohon; life ptnr. Brandon Y. Kim, Mar. 10, 1978; 1 child, Daniel. BA, Fla. Atlantic U., Boca Raton, 1983. V.p., legal dept. Sun Trust Bank, N.A., Ft. Lauderdale, Fla., 1980—85; fin. dir. Williamsburg Ford, Va., 1985—90, First Team Hampton Chevrolet, Va., 1990—95, Tidewater Nissan, Newport News, Va., 1995—99, Toyota, N. Hollywood, Calif., 1999—2003, Northridge Toyota/Hitchcock Automotive, Calif., 2003—. Author: How to Re-Establish Your Credit After Bankruptcy. Vol. capt. Roanoke County Fire Dept., Cave Spring, Va., 1975—78; emergency med. tech Clearwater Rescue Squad, Va., 1975—78; dealer bd. mem. Rt. One, Farmington Hills, Mich., 2006—07. Recipient Finance Mgr. of Yr. award, GMAC, 1996. Master: Am. Fin. & Ins. Profls. (assoc.); mem.: Am. Assn. Finance Profls. Business E-Mail: mbishop@northridgetoyota.com.

BISHOP, MICHAEL, writer; Writer-in-residence LaGrange Coll., 1997—. Author: A Funeral for the Eyes of Fire, 1975, And Strange at Ecbatan the Trees, 1976, A Little Knowledge, 1977, Stolen Faces, 1977, Catacomb Years, 1979, Transfigurations, 1979, Eyes of Fire, 1980, No Enemy But Time, 1982 (Nebula award), Blooded on Arachne, 1982, Who Made Stevie Crye?, 1984, One Winter in Eden, 1984, Ancient of Days, 1985, Close Encounters with the Deity, 1986, Philip K. Dick is Dead, Alas, 1987, Unicorn Mountain, 1988 (Mythopoeic Fantasy awrd for best novel, 1988), Emphatically Not SF, Almost, 1990, Count Geiger's Blues, 1992, Brittle Innings, 1994 (Locus award for best fantasy novel, 1994), At The City Limits of Fate, 1996, Blue Kansas Sky, 2000, Brighten to Incandescence: 17 Short Stories, 2003; author: (with Ian Watson) (novels) Under Heaven's Bridge, 1981; author: (collection of poems) Time Pieces, 2000, (nonfiction collection) A Reverie for Mister Ray, 2005; co-author (with Paul Di Filippo under penname Philip Lawson): Would It Kill You to Smile?, 1998, Muskrat Courage, 2000; editor: 3 Nebula award anthologies (Nebula awards 23, 1988, Nebula awards 24, 1990, Nebula awards 25, 1991), (anthology) Light Years and Dark, 1984 (Locus award Best Anthology, 1984); co-editor (with Ian Watson): Changes, 1983. Home and Office: PO Box 646 Pine Mountain GA 31822-0646 E-mail: mlbishop@juno.com.

BISHOP, MICHAEL, lawyer, state senator; b. 1967; Studied, Universidad de Sevilla, 1988, Cambridge U., U. Paris Sorbonne, 1992; BA, U. Mich., 1989; JD, Detroit Coll. Law, 1993. Admitted to Bar: Mich. 1993, Washington DC. Atty Booth Patterson P.C.; clerk Oakland County Cir. Ct., 1989—92; real estate broker, pres., owner Freedom Realty Inc, Rochester, Mich., Pro Management Inc., Rochester, Mich.; sr. atty. Simon, Galasso & Frantz PLC, Troy, Mich.; mem. Mich. Legis., 1998—; asst. majority leader Mich. Senate, Lansing, 2002—. Mem. Mich. State Com., 1995—97; chmn. Senate Banking and Fin. Inst. Com. Named one of 40 Under 40, Crain's Detroit Bus., 2006. Mem.: State Bar of Mich., Mich. Assn. Realtors, Sports Lawyer Assn., ABA, Michigamua Honorary Soc. Office: Simon, Galasso & Frantz PLC 363 W Big Beaver Rd Ste 300 Troy MI 48084 Office Phone: 248-720-0290. Office Fax: 248-720-0291.

BISHOP, MICHAEL D., emergency physician; b. Anna, Ill., Feb. 10, 1945; m. Mary Susan Wilkens, Dec. 28, 1965; children: Amy Elizabeth, Amanda Marie. AB, GreenvilleColl., 1967; MD, U. Ill., 1971. Diplomate Am. Bd. Emergency Medicine (oral examiner 1980—, dir. 1988-96, mem. exec. com. 1990-95, mem. several bd. coms., sec.-treas. 1991-92, pres.-elect 1992-93, pres. 1993-94). Intern Meth. Hosp. Dallas, 1971-72; emergency physician Bloomington (Ind.) Hosp., 1972—, Morgan County Meml. Hosp., Martinsville, Ind., 1978—, Fayette Meml. Hosp., Connersville, Ind., 1989—, Jackson County Meml. Hosp., Seymour, Ind., 1989—; gen. dir. Immediate Care Ctrs. in Ind., various cities, 1981—; clin. assoc. prof. med. scis. Ind. U., Bloomington, 1980—; pres., CEO Unity Physician Group P.C., Bloomington, Ind., 1971—. Bd. trustee, Sunday sch. tchr. Ellettsville (Ind.) Christian Ch.; bd. dirs. Peoples State Bank, Ellettsville; bd. dirs., sec. Ellettsville Bancshares, Ellettsville Elem. Sch. Bldg. Corp. Fellow Am. Coll. Emergency Physicians (charter, pres. Ind. chpt. 1979-80, nat. councillor 1976-81, 83, mem. nat. multi-hosp./multi-state blue ribbon task force 1981, mem. nat. ins. com. 1976-77, mem. coun. long-range planning com. 1981-82, mem. coun. steering com. 1983-85, chmn. medicare task force 1984-86, chmn. task force on physician payment reform 1986-88, mem. govt. affairs com. 1983-88, 89-93, chmn. 1984-87, 89-93, mem. nat. emergency medicine polit. action com. bd. trustees 1984-88, 89-93, chmn. 1987, 89-93, mem. fin. com. 1987-93, James D. Mills Outstanding Contbn. to Emergency Medicine award 1990, mem. awards com. 1991-93, mem. reimbursement com. 1992—, dir. 1995—, lectr. in field), AHA (mem. Ind. affil. faculty, ACLS), Am. Coll. Physician Execs., Soc. Acad. Emergency Medicine, Christian Med. Dental Soc., Ind. State Med. Assn., Med. Group Mgmt. Assn., Owen Monroe County Med. Soc. Office: Unity Physician Group PC 1155 W 3rd St Bloomington IN 47404-5016

BISHOP, OLIVER RICHARD, retired state official; b. El Dorado, Kans., Dec. 5, 1928; s. Oliver Harrison and Hazel May (Garabrandt) B.; m. Fuyo Oyake, Aug. 14, 1959; children: Lisa Naomi, Rachel Eri. BS in Pub. Adminstrn. magna cum laude, U. So. Calif., 1963; MS in Econs cum laude, U. S.D., 1971. Cert. planner, office automation profl., assisted housing mgr. Commd. 2d lt. USAF, 1956, advanced through grades to maj., 1966, ret., 1971; city mgr. City of Slater, Mo., 1971-73, City of Highland, Ill., 1973-76, City of Napoleon, Ohio, 1976-77; village mgr. Village of Westmont, Ill., 1977-85; revenue and fiscal advisor State of Ill., Chgo., 1985-99. Planning cons. Bishop's Cons. Services, Westmont, Ill., 1985—. Precinct committeeman Rep. Ctrl. com., Dupage County, Ill., 1987-88; candidate for County Bd. Dupage County Dist. 3, 1988; com. chmn. Westmont Planning Commn., 1986-95, 97-2004; bd. dirs. T.E.A.C.H., Inc., I-Care, Inc. Mem.: Inst. Cert Planners, Am. Planning Assn., Intertel, Mensa, Shriners, Masons, Elks, Omicron Delta Epsilon (pres. Lambda chpt.), Pi Sigma Alpha. Avocations: stamp collecting/philately, photography. Personal E-mail: obishop@aol.com.

BISHOP, ROB, congressman; b. Kaysville, Utah, July 13, 1951; m. Jeralynn Hansen; 5 children. BA magna cum laude in Polit. Sci., U. Utah. Tchr. Box Elder HS, Brigham City, Utah, 1974, tchr. govt. and US hist., 1985—2002; mem. Utah State Ho. Reps., 1979—84, speaker, 1992—94; tchr. German Ben Lomond HS, Ogden, Utah, 1980—85; chmn. Utah State Rep. Party, 1997—2002; mem. US Congress from 1st Utah dist., 2003—, mem. rules com. Co-founder Western States Coalition. Republican. Mem. Lds Ch. Office: US Ho Reps 124 Cannon Ho Office Bldg Washington DC 20515-4401 Office Phone: 202-225-0453.*

BISHOP, ROBERT CALVIN, pharmaceutical company executive; b. LA, Jan. 13, 1943; s. Harold Eames and Mary Frances (Allen) B.; m. Susan Elizabeth Ogden, Nov. 18, 1966; children: John Ogden, James Allen, Bryan Hutchings. AB in Psychology, U. So. Calif., 1966, PhD in Biochemistry, 1976; MBA, U. Miami, 1981. Rsch. assoc. Hyland Labs., Glendale, Calif., 1966-69; cons. LA, 1970-75; program mgr. Am. Hosp. Supply Corp., Glendale, 1976-78, rsch. dir. Dade div. Miami, Fla., 1978-81, v.p. Evanston, Ill., 1981-85; pres. Allergan Med. Optics, Irvine, Calif., 1986-88; sr. v.p. Allergan Inc., Irvine, 1989; pres. Allergan Pharmaceuticals, Irvine, 1989-91, Allergan Therapeutics Group, 1991-92; pres., CEO, dir. AutoImmune, Inc., Pasadena, Calif., 1992—. Bd. dirs. MFS/Sun Life Series Trust & Compass Accts., Caliper Life Scis. Inc., Millipore Corp. Contbr. articles to profl. jours.; patentee in field. Bd. dirs. Eye Bank Assn. Am., Washington, 1988-90, Amyotropic Lateral Sclerosis Assn., LA, 1984-87, Quintiles Transitional Corp., 1994-2003, Optobionics Corp., 2003-07. With USAR, 1963—69. Mem. Annandale Golf Club (Pasadena, Calif.). Republican. Presbyterian. Avocation: golf. Home: 1199 Madia St Pasadena CA 91103-1961 Office: AutoImmune Inc 1199 Madia St Pasadena CA 91103

BISHOP, ROBERT HAROLD, aerospace engineering educator; b. Vicenza, Italy, June 8, 1957; s. William Robert and Anna Maria (DiPietro) Bishop; m. Lynda R. Ferrera, July 27, 1985; children: Robert Emerson, Joseph Taylor. BS, MS, Tex. A&M U., 1980; PhD in Elec. and Computer Engring., Rice U., 1990. Registered profl. engr., Tex. Tech. staff mem. Charles Stark Draper Lab., Cambridge, Mass., 1980-90; assoc. prof. aerospace engring. and engring. mechanics to Joe J. King prof. engring., chair U. Tex., Austin, 1990—. Author: Modern Control Systems Analysis and Design Using Matlab and Simulink, 1997, (with R. Dorf) Modern Control Systems, 1998, Learning with LabVIEW, 1999; contbr. articles to sci. jours. Recipient Excellence in Engring. Tchg. award, Lockheed Martin Tactical Aircraft Systems, 1997, John Leland Atwood award, 1999. Fellow AIAA; mem. IEEE, Am. Astronautical Soc., Am. Soc. Engring. Educators. Office: Dept Aerospace Engring and Engring Mechanics U Tex Austin 1 Univ Sta C0600 Austin TX 78712 Office Phone: 512-471-4596. E-mail: rhbishop@mail.utexas.edu.*

BISHOP, ROBERT LYLE, retired economist, educator; b. St. Louis, June 4, 1916; s. Lyle Austin and Helen (Craden) B.; m. Joan Frances Fiss, Sept. 12, 1942 (dec.). AB, Harvard, 1937, MA, 1942, PhD, 1949; postgrad., Princeton, 1938-39. Instr. econs. Harvard, 1939-42; mem. faculty Mass. Inst. Tech., 1942—, successively instr., asst. prof., asso. prof., 1942-57, prof. econs., 1957-86, prof. econs. emeritus, 1986—, head dept. econs. and social sci., 1958-65; dean Sch. Humanities and Social Scis., 1964-73. Vis. lectr. Harvard; vis. prof. Brandeis U. Mem. Am. Econ. Assn., Econometric Soc., Am. Acad. Arts and Scis., Phi Beta Kappa. Home: 650 Concord Ave Apt 103 Cambridge MA 02138

BISHOP, ROBERT R., computer company executive; BS in Math. Physics with honors, U. Adelaide; MS, NYU. Sr. exec. Digital Equip. Corp., 1968—82, Apollo Computer, Inc., 1982—86; pres. world trade corp. Silicon Graphics, Inc., 1986—95, non-executive chmn. bd., world trade corp., 1996—99, chmn., COO, 1995—, chmn. bd. dir., CEO, 1999—. Internat. adv. panel Multimedia Super Corridor, Malaysia; invited prof. Swiss Fed. Inst. Tech., Lausanne; adj. prof. Stockholm Sch. Econs.; lectr. U. St. Gallen, Wirtschafts Tech.; spkr. in field. Mem.: Govs. World Econ. Forum Info.Techs., World Intellectual Property Orgn., Industry Adv. Commn., Swiss Acad. Engring. Scis. Office: Silicon Graphics Inc 1500 Crittenden Ln Mountain View CA 94043-2776 Office Phone: 650-960-1980. Office Fax: 650-961-0595.

BISHOP, SANFORD DIXON, JR., congressman, lawyer; b. Mobile, Ala., Feb. 4, 1947; s. Sanford and Minnie Bishop; m. Vivian Creighton; 1 child, Aayesha J. Reese. BA in Polit. Sci., Morehouse Coll., 1968; JD, Emory U., 1971. Ptnr. Bishop & Buckner, P.C., Columbus, Ga., 1972—92; mem. Ga. Ho. Reps. from 94th dist., 1977—90, Ga. State Senate, 1991—92, US Congress from 2nd Ga. dist., 1993—, mem. appropriations com. Del. Dem. Nat. Conv. 1980, 84, 88. Named Man of the Yr. Men's Progressive Club Columbus, Ga., 1977, Black Georgian of the Yr., 1983, Most Influential Black Men in Ga.; recipient Outstanding Legis. award Ga. NOW, 1983-84, Legis. Svc. award, Ga. Mcpl. Assn., 1984, 86, Friend of the Children award Child Adv. Coalition, Disting. Eagle Scout award; Earl Warren fellow, 1971-72; named one of Most Influential Black Americans, Ebony mag., 2006. Mem. ABA, Nat. Bar Assn., Ga. Bar Assn., Ala. Bar Assn., Am. Judicature Soc., Shriners, Masons (32 degree), Phi Delta Phi, Pi Sigma Alpha, Kappa Alpha Psi, Sigma Pi Phi. Democrat. Baptist. Office: US Ho Reps 2429 Rayburn Ho Office Bldg Washington DC 20515-1002 also: Albany Towers Ste 114 235 Roosevelt Ave Albany GA 31701 Office Phone: 202-225-3631. Fax: 202-225-2203. Business E-Mail: bishop.email@mail.house.gov.*

BISHOP, SID GLENWOOD, union official; b. Gladehill, Va., Nov. 11, 1923; s. Clarence Glenwood and Lillian Helen (Onks) B.; m. Patrice Frances Collier, Nov. 14, 2004. Grad., US Naval Trade Sch., 1942; cert. in labor rels., Concord Coll., Athens, W.Va., 1961. Telegraph operator Virginian R.R., 1946-47, C & O R.R., 1947-62; local chmn. Order R.R. Telegraphers, 1960-62; gen. chmn. C & O-Virginian R.R.'s, 1962-68; 2d v.p. Transp-Communication Employees Union, St. Louis, 1968-69; v.p. transp. com. divsn. Brotherhood Ry. and Airline Clks., Rockville, Md., 1969-73, asst. internat. v.p., 1973—. Mem. subcom. Labor Rsch. Adv. Coun., Dept. Labor, 1975, mem. com. on productivity, tech., growth Bur. Labor Statistics, 1975-77. With USN, 1941-46. Mem. AFL-CIO, Can. Labor Congress, Hunting Hills Homeowners Assn., VFW, Chantilly Nat. Golf and Country Club, Elks, Masons, K.T., Shriners. Home and Office: 676 NE 28th Ave Okeechobee FL 34972-3323 Personal E-mail: bishlite@adelphia.net.

BISHOP, SUSAN KATHARINE, executive search company executive; b. Palm Beach, Fla., Apr. 3, 1946; d. Warner Bader Bishop and Katharine Sue (White) McLennan; m. Robert Uchitel, Dec. 27, 1973 (div. 1979); 1 child, Rachel. BA, Briarcliff Coll., 1968; MBA, Fordham U., 1985. Actress, NYC, 1968-72; producer, hostess Sta. KIMO-TV, Anchorage, 1972-74; dir. programming Visions Pay TV, 1974-79; recruiter Joe Sullivan & Assocs., NYC, 1980-82; prin. Johnson, Smith & Knisely, 1982-88; ptnr. Schmitt Bishop Tolette, NYC, 1989-91; pres. Bishop Ptnrs., Ltd., NYC, 1991—. Mem. Cable TV Adminstrn. and Mktg. Soc., Women in Cable, Assn. Exec. Search Cons. (bd. dirs.). Office: Bishop Ptnrs 708 3rd Ave New York NY 10017-4201

BISHOP, TILMAN MALCOLM, retired state legislator; b. Colorado Springs, Jan. 1, 1933; m. Pat Bishop, 1952; 1 son, Barry Alan. BA, MA, U. No. Colo., Greeley. Adminstr., dir. student svcs. Mesa State Coll., Grand Junction, Colo., 1962-94; mem., pres. pro tem Colo. Senate, 1971-99, ret., 1999. Bd. dirs. Rocky Mountain Pub. Broadcasting TV, Colo. Duck Stamp Commn. Mem. World Series com. Nat. Jr. Coll. Baseball; elected commr. Mesa County, 2003-07; trustee El Pomar Found.; mem selection com. Colo. Sports Hall of Fame; elected bd. regents U. Colo., 2007—. With US Army. Mem. Elks, Lions. Republican. Methodist. Avocations: fishing, small game hunting. Home: 2255 Piazza Way Grand Junction CO 81506 Personal E-mail: tilmanmb@bresnan.net.

BISHOP, TIMOTHY H., congressman; b. Southampton, NY, June 1, 1950; m. Kathryn Bishop; children: Molly, Meghan. AB in Hist., Coll. Holy Cross, Worcester, Mass., 1972; MPA, LI U., 1981. Admissions counselor to provost Southampton Coll., NY, 1973—2002; mem. US Congress from 1st NY dist., 2003—. Mem. transp. and infrastructure com. US Congress, mem. edn. and labor com., mem. budget com. Mem. Southampton Town Bd. Ethics; bd. dirs., treas. Bridgehampton Childcare and Recreation Ctr; bd. mem. Ea. LI Coastal Conservation Alliance. Democrat. Roman Catholic. Office: US House Reps 225 Cannon House Office Bldg Washington DC 20515 Office Phone: 202-225-3826. Office Fax: 202-225-3143.*

BISHOP, VIRGINIA WAKEMAN, retired librarian, humanities educator; b. Portland, Oreg., Dec. 28, 1927; d. Andrew Virgil and Letha Evangeline (Ward) Wakeman; m. Clarence Edmund Bishop, Aug. 23, 1953; children: Jean Marie Bishop Johnson, Marilyn Joyce. BA, Bapt. Missionary Tng. Sch., Chgo., 1949, Linfield Coll., 1952; MEd, Linfield Coll., McMinnville, Oreg., 1953; MA in Librarianship, U. Wash., 1968. Ch. worker U. Bapt. Ch., Seattle, 1954—56, 1959—61, tchr. parent coop presch., 1965—66; libr. N.W. Coll., Kirkland, Wash., 1968—69; undergrad. libr. U. Wash., Seattle, 1970; libr., instr. Seattle Ctrl. CC, 1970—91; co-owner small bus. Seaside, Oreg., 1972—2004. Leader Totem coun. Girl Scouts U.S., 1962-65; pres. Wedgwood Sch. PTA, Seattle, 1964-65; chair 46th Dist. Dem. Orgn., Seattle, 1972-73; precinct com. officer Dem. Party, 1968-88, 96-2000; candidate Wash. State Legislature, Seattle, 1974, 80; bd. dirs. U. Bapt. Children's Ctr., 1989-95, chair, 1990-95; vol. Ptnrs. in Pub. Edn., 1992-96. Recipient Golden Acorn award Wedgwood Elem. Sch., 1966. Mem. AAUW Seaside, LWV Seattle (2d v.p. 1994-96), U. Wash. Grad. Sch. Libr. and Info. Sci. Alumni Assn. (1st v.p. 1986-87, pres. 1987-88). Baptist. Avocations: swimming, walking, reading. Home: 3032 NE 87th St Seattle WA 98115-3529

BISHOP, WILLIAM PETER, management consultant, rancher, musician; b. Lakewood, Ohio, Jan. 18, 1940; s. William Hall and Ethel Laverle (Evans) B.; m. Sarah Gilbert, Sept. 1, 1963. BA in Chemistry with honors (Nat. Merit scholar), Coll. Wooster, Ohio, 1962; PhD (NDEA fellow), Ohio State U., 1967. Resident research assoc. Ohio State U., 1967-69; mem. staff Sandia Labs., Albuquerque, 1969-75; head nuclear waste program NRC, Washington, 1975-78; dep. dir. environ. observation div. NASA, 1978-81, dep. dir. life scis. div., 1981-83; dep. asst. adminstr. satellites NOAA, 1983-85, acting asst. adminstr. satellites and info. services, 1985-87; v.p. SAIC, Washington, 1987-89; v.p. for rsch. Desert Rsch. Inst., Las Vegas, Nev., 1989-94; assigned to U.S. Dept. of Energy, 1995-99; pres. B-plus, Inc., Paonia, Colo., 1999—. Mem. Nat. Acad. Com. Earth Studies, 1989-91, Task Group on Priorities in Space Rsch., 1990-94; chair Adv. Commn. on Geoscis. NSF, 1994-97. Author articles in field. Trustee Keystone (Colo.) Ctr., 1986-95, Nev. Devel. Authority, 1989-95, Univ. Corp. for Atmospheric Rsch., 1991-97; bd. dirs. Opportunities Industrialization Ctrs., Albuquerque, 1974-75, Cave Rsch. Found., 1967-74; dir. Western Slope Environ. Resources Coun., 200-04. Recipient Meritorious Service award NRC, 1977; Spaceship Earth award NASA, 1981; Meritorious Service award U.S. Dept. Commerce, 1985, Spl. Act or Svc. awrad, U.S. Dept. Energy, 1999. Fellow Nat. Speleological Soc. (conservation editor bull. 1974-78), Am. Astron. Soc. (v.p. tech. 1987-88); mem. AAAS, Am. Meteorol. Soc., Rotary, Sigma Xi, Phi Lambda Upsilon. Personal E-mail: bplusine@tds.net.

BISHOP, WILLIAM WADE, advertising executive; b. Mt. Vernon, NY, Apr. 17, 1939; s. Kenneth Farrington and Dorothea (Renz) B.; m. Jacqueline Kenton, May 21, 1966; children: William Jr., Christopher. BA, Ohio Wesleyan U., 1961. Account exec. Ogilvy & Mather, Grey, BBDO, NYC, 1964-72; v.p. Ted Bates, NYC, 1972-74; category mgr. Gen. Foods Corp., White Plains, NY, 1974-79; mng. dir. Mktg. Corp. Am., Westport, Conn., 1979-80; exec. v.p. MCA Advt., NYC, 1980-84, pres., CEO, 1984-86, MCA Comm. Group, 1986-89; pres. Ally & Gargano, NYC, 1986-89; chmn., CEO CHC Advt., 1989-92; CEO CHC Advt. and M.E.D. Comm., 1992—; pres., CEO Ryan Direct, Westport, 1992-94; dir. South Beach Beverages, 1995—; chmn., CEO Sierra Comm. Group, 1995-2001; COO South Beach Beverage Co., 1999-2001; CEO Blue Buffalo Co. Owner LI Lizards, Lacrosse; ptnr. Blue Buffalo Co., 2002, B Group, 2001—. Served with USMC, 1962-68. Mem. Salem Golf Club. Republican. Congregationalist. Avocations: lacrosse, golf. Office: B Group 43 Danbury Rd Wilton CT 06897-4065 Home Phone: 203-762-9332. Business E-Mail: wbishop@bluebuffalocompany.com.

BISHOPRIC, KARL, insurance company executive, retired investment banker, real estate company executive, retired advertising executive; b. Greensboro, NC, Jan. 5, 1925; s. James Robert Karl and Frances (Farrell) B.; m. Rose Anne Straub, Mar. 4, 1944 (div. Jan. 1972); children: Robert Lewis, James Nelson (dec.), Bruce Graham; m. Carmen Deruth Dunlop, May 26, 1973; stepchildren: Jannette Marie Eyles, Kathryn Ruth Engelhardt. BA, U. N.C., 1945. With Houck & Co., Roanoke, Miami, Va., Fla., 1946-54, pres. Miami, Fla., 1948-54, Bishopric-Green-Fielden, Inc., Miami, NYC, 1954-68, chmn. bd., 1968-73, Lando-Bishopric, Inc., 1973-74; chmn., dir. Advt. & Marketing Internat. Network, Inc., 1972-74; pres. Miami Nat. Bank, 1974-75; assoc. Oscar E. Dooly Assos., Inc., 1974-76; prin. 1st Equity Corp. of Fla., 1976-2000; pres. 1st Equity Properties, Inc., 1976-2000; v.p., dir. Fundamental Mgmt. Corp., 1986-89; pres. Swiss Atlantic Corp., 1999-2000; prin. William R. Hough & Co., Miami, 2001—04; fin. cons. RBC Dain Rauscher, 2004, Adcock Fin. Group, Tampa, Fla., 2005—. Pres. United Fund Dade County, 1967-68, trustee, 1963-; chmn. Port Action Com., 1969-71; bd. dirs. Community TV Found. S. Fla., 1965-67, v.p., 1969-72; mem. citizens bd. U. Miami, 1968-, pres. citizens bd., 1982-83, trustee, 1983-85; bd. dirs. Econ. Soc. S. Fla., 1969-73, Urban Coalition Greater Miami, 1968-72, Fla. Philharmonic Orchestra Found., 1992-98, Miami Lighthouse for the Blind, 1993-2004, chmn. fin. com., 1994-98; bd. dirs. Urban League Greater Miami, 1956-65, pres., 1956-60; chmn. budget leaders conf. United Funds and Community Councils Am., 1968; trustee Lowe Art Mus., 1973-86. Served to lt. (j.g.) USNR, 1944-46. Recipient Printer's Ink Silver medal. Mem. Greater Miami C. of C. (dir. 1971-74, trustee 1976—2003), Alpha Delta Sigma, Beta Theta Pi. Home: 600 Biltmore Way Coral Gables FL 33134-7541 Office: Adcock Fin Group 311 W Fletcher Ave Tampa FL 33612 Home Phone: 305-448-8036; Office Phone: 305-448-8036. Business E-Mail: karlbishopric@bellsouth.net.

BISI, ARNAB, management educator; m. Somdutta Bisi; 1 child, Sayan. BSc with honors, U. Calcutta, India, 1990; M in Stats., Indian Statis. Inst., 1992; PhD, Hong Kong U. Sci. and Tech., 1997. Asst. prof. mgmt. Purdue U., West Lafayette, Ind., 2002—. Contbr. articles to profl. publs. COE-MITACS postdoctoral fellow, U. BC, 1999—2001. Mem.: MSOM, INFORMS. Office: Purdue U 403 W State St West Lafayette IN 47907-2056 Office Phone: 765-494-4416.

BISIGNANO, FRANK, diversified financial services company executive; Sr. v.p. Shearson Lehman Bros., 1986—90; exec. v.p., chief consumer lending officer First Fidelity Bancorporation, 1990—94; with Smith Barney, 1994—2000; sr. exec. v.p., chief administrv. officer, Global Corp. and Investment Banking Group Citgroup, Inc., NYC, 2000—. Bd. dirs. Depository Trust & Clearning Corp., The Options Clearing Corp., Euroclear.

BISKIN, BRUCE HOWARD, psychometrician; b. Bronx, NY, Nov. 21, 1950; s. George and Theresa (Bolinsky) B.; m. Barbara R. Gronsky, Feb. 14, 1982; children: Lee Jordan, Eric Daniel. BBA cum laude, Baruch Coll., 1972; MA, U. Minn., 1975; PhD, U. Md., 1982. Cons. psychol. and behavioral assessment Univ. Md., Univ. Coll., College Park, 1979-88; rsch. assoc. Am. Psychol. Assn., Washington, 1979-81; cons. psychol. svcs. rev., 1981-82; rschr. Johnson O'Connor Rsch. Found., Chgo., 1983; test and measurement specialist NYC Bd. Edn., 1984; psychometrician AICPA, NYC, 1985-88, sr. psychometrician, 1988—2005; dir. learning assessment Thomas Edison State Coll., Trenton, NJ, 2006—. Project mgr. Practice Analysis of CPAs in Pub. Acctg., AICPA, NYC, 1988-91, 1998-2001, Ednl. & Psychol. Measurement, 1998-2001; organizer Nat. Inst. on the Assessment of Experiential Learning, 2007-. Editorial bd. mem.: Advances in Accounting, 1986—, Measurement & Evaluation in Counseling and Development, 1986—; mem. adv. bd.: Professional Education Research Quarterly, 1991-93; contbr. articles to profl. jours. Mem. AACD, APA, Am. Ednl. Rsch. Assn., Nat. Coun. on Measurement in Edn., Assn. Psychol. Sci., Nature Conservancy, Psi Chi (pres. Baruch Coll. chpt. 1971-72). Avocations: gardening, sci. fiction, puzzles. Office: Thomas Edison State Coll 101 W State St Trenton NJ 08608-1146

BISKUPIC, STEVEN M., prosecutor, lawyer; b. Mar. 1961; BA, JD, Marquette U. Asst. US atty. (ea. dist.) Wis. US Dept. Justice, 1989—2002, US atty. (ea. dist.) Wis., 2002—. Office: 530 Fed Bldg 517 E Wisconsin Ave Milwaukee WI 53202*

BISKUPSKI, MIECZYSLAW BOLESLAW, historian, writer; b. Chgo., Sept. 24, 1948; s. J.F. and Virginia H. Biskupski; children: Aleksandra, Jadwiga, Mieczyslaw. BA with honors, UCLA, 1972, MA, 1972; MPhil, PhD, Yale U., New Haven, 1981. Prof. history St. John Fisher Coll., Rochester, NY, 1984—2002; S. A. Blejwas endowed chair Polish history Ctrl. Conn. State U., New Britain, 2002—. Author: Pastor of the Poles, 1982, Polish Democratic Thought, 1990, Poland and Europe: Historical Dimensions, 1993; mng. editor East Cen. Europe, 1982—. Bd. dirs. Inst. for Polish Studies, Rochester, 1984—, Polish Inst. Arts and Scis., N.Y.C., 1990—, Rochester-Krakow Sister Cities Com., 1984—. Fulbright fellow, 1976, Woodrow Wilson Ctr. rsch. fellow, 1989, Internat. Studies Assn. fellow, 1976, Yale U. grad. fellow, 1972-76. Mem. Polish Am. Hist. Assn. (pres. 1989-90), Am. Hist. Assn., Am. Assn. for Advancement of Slavic Studies, Joseph Pilsudski Inst. Conservative. Roman Catholic. Avocation: opera. Office: CCSU History Dept 1615 Stanley St New Britain CT 06050 Home Phone: 860-666-2587; Office Phone: 860-832-3010. Office Fax: 860-832-3010. Business E-Mail: biskupskim@mail.ccsu.edu.

BISMUTH, PIERRE, artist; b. Paris, 1963; Writer (screenplays) Eternal Sunshine of the Spotless Mind, 2004 (Acad. Award for best original screenplay, 2005); exhibitions include (solo), FRAC Languedoc Roussillion, Montpellier, 1995, Lisson Gallery, London, 1996, Palais de Beaux Arts, Brussels, 1997, Kunsthalle, Vienna, 1997, Witte de With Mus., Rotterdam, 1997, Galerie Yvon Lambert, Paris, 1998, The Showroom, London, 1998, Galerie Jan Mot, Brussels, 2000, 2003, Kunsthalle Basel, 2001, Dvir Gallery, Tel Aviv, 2001, Centre d'art Contemporain de Bretigny, 2001, Sprengel Mus., Hannover, 2002, Christine Konig Galerie, Vienna, 2004, Art Basel, 2004, Galeria Sonia Rosso, Milan, 2004, Erna Hecey Gallery, Luxembourg, Cosmic Gallery, Paris, exhibitions include (group), 49th Venice Biennale, 2001, Manifesta 4, Frankfurt, 2002, Stedelijk Mus., Amsterdam, Casino, Luxembourg, MAMCO, Geneva, Musee d'Art Moderne de la Ville de Paris. Office: c/o Focus Features 100 Universal City Plz Universal City CA 91608

BISPING, BRUCE HENRY, photojournalist; b. St. Louis, Apr. 27, 1953; s. Harry and Marian B.; m. Joan M. Berg, Sept. 29, 1984; children: Erin Elizabeth Giovanna, Trevor Thomas. B.J., U. Mo., Columbia, 1975. Freelance Tribune, Columbia, Mo., 1968—71; Summer intern Cleve. Press, 1974, The Virginian/Pilot-Ledger Star, Norfolk, 1975; staff photojournalist Mpls. Tribune, 1975-82, Mpls. Star and Tribune, 1982—. Freelance photographer Black Star Pub. Co., N.Y.C., 1975—, Sporting News, St. Louis, Business Week, Time, U.S. News World Report, Newsweek, Am. Illustrated, N.Y. Times, Los Angeles Times, other nat. and local publs.; past mem. faculty Mo. Photojournalism Workshop. Mem. Nat. Press Photographers Assn. (assoc. dir. Region 5 1981-82, dir. Region 5 1983-86, rep. to exec. com. 1984, Nat. Newspaper Photographer of Year award 1976, Regional Newspaper Photographer of Year award 1977, citation for dedication to profession 1985), Twin Cities News Photographers Assn. (pres. 1979-80), Profl. Assn. Diving Instrs. (open water instr. rating), Oldsmobile Club of Am. (bd. dirs. Minn. Club, news editor), Minn. Oldsmobile Club. Avocations: photography, reading, movies, walking, travel. Office: Mpls Tribune 6020 View Ln Edina MN 55436-1827 Home Phone: 952-927-5753; Office Phone: 612-673-7205. E-mail: bruceb65@citilink.com.

BISSADA, NABIL KADDIS, urologist, educator, researcher, author; b. Cairo, Sept. 2, 1938; s. Kaddis B. and Negma Bissada; m. Samia; children: Sally, Nancy, Mary, Amy, Andrew. MD, Cairo U., 1963. Diplomate Am. Bd. Urology. Intern Cairo Univ. Hosp., 1964-65; resident in surgery Babelsharia Gen. Hosp., 1965-69; resident in urology U. N.C. Hosp., 1970-72, chief resident, 1972-73; asst. prof. urology U. Ark. for Med. Scis., 1973-77, assoc. prof., 1977-79; cons. urologist King Faisal Specialist Hosp. and Rsch. Ctr., Riyadh, Saudi Arabia, 1979-87; prof., chief urologic oncology Med. U. S.C., 1987—2003; chief urologic surgery Ralph H. Johnson Med. Ctr., 1987—2003; vice-chmn. dept. urology Med. U. S.C., 1999—2003; prof. urology U. Ark. for Med. Scis., Little Rock, 2003—, exec. vice chmn. dept. urology, 2003—06, interim chmn., 2006—; chief urology Ark. Children's Hosp., 2003—. Spkr. in field. Author: Lower Urinary Tract Function and Dysfunction: Diagnosis and Management, 1978; Pharmacology of the Urinary Tract and the Male Reproductive System, 1982; cons., guest editor several med. jours. and periodicals; mem. editl. bd. Archives of Andrology, Arab J. Urol., Jour. Urology Nephrology; contbr. articles to profl. jours.; chpts. to books; pioneered several significant surgical and med. urologic treatment methods, developed the Charleston Pouch Technique for continent urinary diversion; rsch. in urologic reconstructive techniques. Fellow ACS, Internat. Coll. Surgeons (co-chmn. divsn. urology U.S. sect. 1989-91, chmn. 1991-93), Soc. Pediat. Urology; mem. Am. Urol. Assn., , Egyptian-Am. Urol. Assn. (pres. 1990-92), Arab-Am. Urol. Assn. (pres. 1993-96), Carolina Urol. Assn. (pres. 1997-99), Soc. Internat. D'Urologie, Soc. Urologic Oncology, Urodynamic Soc., Soc. Urology and Engring., Sigma Xi. Office: U Ark Med Ctr Dept Urology 430 W Markham # 540 Little Rock AR 72205-7199 Office Phone: 501-364-3632. Business E-Mail: bissadanabilk@uams.edu.

BISSELL, GEORGE ARTHUR, architect; b. LA, Jan. 31, 1927; s. George Arthur and Ruby Zoe (Moore) B.; m. Laurene Conlon, Nov. 21, 1947; children: Teresa Ann, Thomas Conlon, William George, Robert Anthony, Mary Catherine. BArch, U. So. Calif., 1953. Registered architect, Calif. Ptnr. Bissell Co., Covina, Calif., 1953-57, Bissell & Durquette, A.I.A., Pasadena, Calif., 1957-61; owner George Bissell, A.I.A., Laguna Beach, Calif., 1961-65; ptnr. Riley & Bissell, A.I.A., Newport Beach, Calif., 1965-72; pres. Bissell/August, Inc., Newport Beach, 1972-83, Bissell Architects, Inc., Newport Beach, 1983—. Bd. dirs. Newport Ctr. Assn., 1973-78, Lido Isle Community Assn., Newport Beach, 1985-87, Hamilton Cove Assn., 1991-92. With U.S. Mcht. Marine, 1944-46. Fellow AIA (pres. Orange County chpt. 1975, Calif. coun. 1978, nat. bd. dirs. 1980-83, Progressive Arch. award 1974, Nat. AIA Honor award 1978, 98, Merit award Calif. Coun. 1988, AIA Calif. Coun. Lifetime Achievement award 2000); mem. Newport Harbor Yacht Club, Lido Isle Yacht Club. Avocations: sailing, skiing, travel. Home: 108 Via Havre Newport Beach CA 92663-4905 also: Yacht Banshee Newport Beach CA 92663 Office: Bissell Architects 3422 Via Lido Newport Beach CA 92663 Office Phone: 949-675-9901. E-mail: Bisarch@aol.com.

BISSELL, JAMES DOUGAL, III, motion picture production designer; b. Charleston, SC, Aug. 6, 1951; s. James Dougal Sr. and Elizabeth McPherson (Jones) B.; m. Teresa Ann Atkinson, June 1, 1974 (div. Sept. 1987); m. Martha Wynne Snetsinger, Oct. 22, 1995; children: James Dougal, Alexander Wynne, Elizabeth Wynne. BFA in Theatre, U. N.C., 1973. Art dir. various TV movies, LA, 1976-81; prodn. designer E.T. The Extra-Terrestrial, LA, 1981, Twilight Zone-The Movie, LA, 1982, The Falcon and The Snowman, Mexico City, 1983-84; prodn. designer, 2d unit dir. The Boy Who Could Fly, Vancouver, B.C., Canada, 1985, Harry and the Hendersons, LA, 1986; prodn. designer Someone to Watch Over Me, LA and NYC, 1986-87, Twins, LA and Santa Fe, 1988—. Visual cons. St. Elmo's Fire, Hollywood, 1984; title co-designer Amazing Stories, Hollywood, 1985; art dir. The Last Starfighter, Hollywood, 1983; prodn. designer, 2nd unit dir. Always, LA, Libby Mt., Epharata, Wash., 1989; prodn. designer Arachnophobia, Venezuela, Cambria, Calif., LA Prodn. designer Rocketeer, 1990, The Pickle, NYC and LA, Dennis the Menace, Chgo., 1992, Blue Chips, LA, Chgo., New Orleans, 1993, Jumanji, Vancouver, New Eng., 1994-95, Tin Cup, Tucson, Houston, 1995, My Fellow Americans, LA, Asheville, NC, The Sixth Day, 1999, Cats and Dogs, 2000, Confessions of a Dangerous Mind, 2002, Hollywood Homicide, LA, 2002; visual cons., 2d unit dir. 50 First Dates, LA, 2003, Ring II, LA, 2004, Good Night and Good Luck, LA, 2005 (Oscar nomination 2005, Satellite award 2005, 300 award Montréal, 2005), Spiderwick Chronicles, Montréal, 2006, Leatherheads, NC, SC. Mem.: Acad. Motion Picture Arts and Scis., Dir.'s Guild Am., Art Dir.'s Guild (past v.p.).

BISSELL, MINA J., lab administrator, biochemist; b. Tehran, Iran, May 14, 1940; Student, Bryn Mawr Coll., 1959-61; AB in Chemistry cum laude, Radcliff Coll., Cambridge, Mass., 1963; MA in Bacteriology and Biochemistry, Harvard U., Cambridge, Mass., 1965, PhD in Microbiology-Molecular Genetics, 1969. Milton rsch. fellow, 1969-70; Am. Cancer Soc. rsch. fellow, 1970-72; staff biochemist Lawrence Berkeley Nat. Lab. U. Calif., Berkeley, 1972-76, mem. sr. staff, 1976—, co-dir. div. biology and medicine Lab. Cell Biology, 1980—, dir. divsn., 1988-92, coord. life scis., 1989-91, assoc. lab. dir. bioscience, 1989, dir. life scis. divsn. Lawrence Berkeley Nat. Lab., 1992—. mem. faculty dept. comparative biochemistry, 1979—. Vis. prof. Kettering Inst., U. Cin. Med. Schs., 1986-88; disting. vis. scientist Queensland Inst. Med. Rsch., Brisbane, Australia, 1982; mem. coun. Gordon Rsch. Conf., 1991-94; George P. Peacock lectr. pathology U. Tex., Dallas, 1992; Dean's lectr. Mt. Sinai Med. Sch., N.Y.C., 1993; presenter numerous lectures, condr. symposia; keynote spkr. Gordon Conf. on Proteoglycans, 1994, others. Mem. editl. bd. and sect. editor In Vitro Cell and Devel. Biology Rapid Comm., 1986—; mem. editl. bd. Jour. Cellular Biochemistry, 1990-92; assoc. editor In Vitro Cellular and Devel. Biology, 1990—, Molecular and Cellular Differentiation, 1992—, Molecular Carcinogensis, 1993-97, Devel. Biology, 1993—, Cancer Rsch., 1994—, Breast Jour., 1994—; contbr. numerous articles to sci. jours. Recipient 1st Joseph Sadusk award for breast cancer rsch., 1985, Ernest Orlando Lawrence award Dept. Energy, 1996, Krakower award in Pathology, 2003, Discovery Health Channel Med. Honors, 2004; Fogarty sr. fellow NIH, Imperial Can. Rsch. Fund Labs., London, 1983-84, Guggenheim fellow, 1992-93,; honored by Susan G. Komen Breast Cancer Found. Fellow AAAS; mem. Am. Soc. for Cell Biology (mem. coun. 1989-91, Women in Cell Biology Career Recognition award 1993, pres. 1997), Internat. Soc. Differentiation (bd. dirs. 1990-96). The pioneer in postulating, and then proving that the extracellular matrix (ECM), the mass of fibrous and globular proteins that surrounds cells performs a critical role in dictating a tissue's organization and function. In 1981, Dr. Bissell formulated the concept of a "dynamic reciprocity." This communication scheme between the nucleus, the cells and their microenvironment suggests that signals are sent into the cell through ECM receptors which attach to the cell's outer skeleton and convey important information to the nucleus and the chromosomes. Office: Lawrence Berkeley Nat Lab Div Life Scis 1 Cyclotron Rd Ms 83 101 Berkeley CA 94720-8260 Business E-Mail: mjbissell@lbl.gov.

BISSELL, PHIL (CHARLES P. BISSELL), cartoonist; b. Worcester, Mass., Feb. 1, 1926; s. Ralph Kenneth and Dorothy Earle (Pennell) B.; m. Beverly Barrows, Sept. 17, 1948; children: Steven Barrows, Christopher William. Student, Sch. Practical Art, Boston, 1946-48; degree (hon.), Art Instrn. Sch., Mpls., 1971; BFA (hon.), Lesley U., Cambridge, Mass., 2007. Theatrical and editl. sports cartoonist Christian Sci. Monitor, 1949-53; sports cartoonist Boston Globe, 1953-65; sports and editl. cartoonist Worcester Telegram and Evening Gazette, 1967-75; sports cartoonist Boston Herald, 1975-77; editl. cartoonist Lowell (Mass.) Sun, 1980-87; illustrator, cartoonist Cartoon Corner Syndicate, Rockport, Mass., 2004. Cons. D.C. Graphics, Lexington, Mass., 1987—; originator football helmet logo New England Patriots, 1960; portrait artist City of Lowell Bridge Placque, 1982. Represented in permanent collections Basketball Hall Fame, Springfield, Mass., Football Hall of Fame, Canton, Ohio, Baseball Hall of Fame, Cooperstown, N.Y., Internat. Swimming Hall of Fame, Ft. Lauderdale, Fla., Dwight D. Eisenhower Meml. Libr., Abilene, Kans., New Eng. Patriots Hist. Mus.; cartoonist: (book) Sportspot, 1978, World Ency. of Cartooning, 1980, Tall Tales from Tall Ships, 1992. Recipient N.Am. Racing Assn. award, 1958, Scarlet Quill award Boston U., 1976, Hockey award Mass. Bay Chiefs, 1981. Mem. Baseball Writers Assn. Am. (hon. life.), Rockport Art Assn. Home and Office: 19 Landmark Ln Rockport MA 01966-1262 *Humor and laughter can hold mankind together, and if you can share it with your fellow-man, I feel it's a successful day's work!.*

BISSET, JACQUELINE, actress; b. Weybridge, Eng., Sept. 13, 1946; Student, French Lycée, London. Made film debut in: The Knack, 1965; other motion pictures include Cul de Sac, 1965, Two for the Road, 1965, Casino Royale, 1966, The Sweet Ride, 1967, The Detective, 1967, Bullitt, 1968, The First Time, 1968, Airport, 1969, The Grasshopper, 1968, The Mephisto Waltz, 1969, Believe in Me, 1971, The Life and Times of Judge Roy Bean, 1972, Stand Up and Be Counted, 1972, The Thief Who Came to Dinner, 1972, Day for Night, 1972, Murder on the Orient Express, 1974, The Spiral Staircase, 1974, End of the Game, 1974, St. Ives, 1975, The Deep, 1975, Le Magnifique, 1973, Sunday Woman, 1974, The Greek Tycoon, 1976, Secrets, 1969, Who is Killing the Great Chefs of Europe?, 1976, Amo Non Amo, 1979, When Time Ran Out, 1979, Rich and Famous, 1980, Inchon, 1979, Class, 1983, Under the Volcano, 1984, High Season, 1986, Hoffman's Honger, 1993, Les Marmottes, 1993, East & West: Paradise Lost, 1993, Crimebroker, 1993, La Cérémonie, 1995, Once You Meet a Stranger, 1996, The Honest Courtesan, 1996, Let the Devil Wear Black, 1999, New Year's Day, 2001, Latter Days, 2003, Swing, 2003, Fascination, 2004, Domino, 2005; appeared in TV films Anna Karenina, 1984, Forbidden (Home Box Office), 1985, Choices, 1985, Summer Solstice, 2005; appeared in miniseries Napoleon and Josephine, 1987; La Maison de Jade, 1988, Wild Orchid, 1989, Scenes From The Class Struggle in Beverly Hills, 1989, The Maid, 1990, Rossini Rossini, 1990, Leave of Absence, 1994, September, 1996, End of Summer, 1996, Steve McQueen: The King of Cool, 1998, Witch Hunt, 1998, Brittanic, 2000, In the Beginning, 2000, Dancing at the Harvest Moon, 2002, America's Prince: The John F. Kennedy Jr. Story, 2003, The Survivors Club, 2004. Address: care William Morris Agency 151 S El Camino Dr Beverly Hills CA 90212-2704 also: care VMA 10th Ave George V 75008 Paris France

BISSETTE, WINSTON LOUIS, JR., lawyer, mayor; b. Statesville, NC, Sept. 18, 1943; s. Winston Louis and Rubye (Goode) B.; m. Sara Oliver, Aug. 21, 1965; children: W. Louis III, Thomas Anderson. BA, Wake Forest U., 1965; JD, U. N.C., Chapel Hill, 1968; MBA, U. Va., 1970. Bar: N.C. 1968. Asst. v.p. Wachovia Bank & Trust Co., Winston-Salem, N.C., 1970-74; v.p., treas. Western Carolina Bank, Asheville, N.C., 1974-76; ptnr. McGuire, Wood & Bissette, P.A., Asheville, 1976—. Chmn. Forest Comml. Bank. Co-chmn. I-26 corridor Assn., 1987—; chmn. West NC Devel. Assn., 1995—98; regional adv. coun. HUD, 1986—90; mem. Gov.'s Task Force on Urban Transp., 1986, Yr. of the Mtns. Commn., 1995—97; chmn. Asheville Sports Com., 1991—97, Buncombe County Econ. Devel. Commn., 1997—2003, NC Arboretum Soc., 2003—, Grove Arcade Pub. Market Found., 2002—, Asheville Cmty. Betterment Found., 1992—; mayor City of Asheville, 1985—89, city coun., 1983—89; bd. trustees Wake Forest U., 1996—, Western Carolina U., 1995—2003; chmn. Advantage Asheville, 1996—, Grove Arcade Pub. Mkt. Found., 1992—; bd. dirs. Mission-St. Joseph's Health Sys., Inc., 1996—99; vice chmn. Sisters of Mercy Svcs. Corp.; bd. dirs. AB Tech. Coll. Found., Asheville Merchants Corp., 2002—, Inst. at Biltmore, 2001—07, Blue Ridge Pkwy. Found.; vice-chmn. Inst. Biltmore, 2002—07, Met. Sewerage Dist. Buncombe County; bd. dirs. Western Carolina Industries, 2002—, chmn., 2005. Mem. ABA, N.C. Bar Assn., Asheville Area C. of C. (pres. 1991-92), Wake Forest U. Alumni Assn. (pres. 1992-93), Bald Head Island Club, Biltmore Forest Country Club, Cliffs at Walnut Cove. Republican. Presbyterian. Avocations: golf, running. Home: 321 Old Toll Rd Asheville NC 28804-3716 Office: McGuire Wood & Bissette PA 48 Patton Ave PO Box 3180 Asheville NC 28802-3180 Office Phone: 828-254-8800. Business E-Mail: lbissette@mwbavl.com.

BISSINGER, FREDERICK LEWIS, retired manufacturing executive; b. NYC, Jan. 11, 1911; s. Jacob Frederick and Rosel (Ensslin) B.; m. Julia E. Stork, Aug. 4, 1935 (dec. Dec. 1989); children: Frederick Louis, Elizabeth Julia; m. Barbara S. Simmonds, Dec. 4, 1993. ME, Stevens Inst. Tech., 1933, MS in Chemistry, 1936, DEng (hon.), 1973; JD, Fordham U., 1938. Bar: D.C. 1937, N.Y. 1939, Ohio 1943, U.S. Supreme Ct. 1943. Instr. chemistry Stevens Inst. Tech., Hoboken, NJ, 1933-36; assoc. Pennie, Davis, Marvin & Edmonds, NYC, 1936-42; counsel, bus. cons. Pennie, Davis, Marvin & Edmonds (name now Pennie & Edmonds), NYC, 1976—; with Indsl. Rayon Corp., Cleve., 1942-61, v.p. charge rsch., 1948-57, group v.p. mktg. and rsch., 1957-59, v.p., gen. mgr., 1959-60, pres., chief exec. officer, 1960-61; group v.p. Midland-Ross Corp., Cleve., 1961-62; v.p., dir., mem. exec. com. Stauffer Chem. Co., NYC, 1962-65; v.p. Allied Chem. Corp., NYC, 1965-66, exec. v.p., 1966-69, pres., chief oper. officer, 1969-74, vice chmn., 1974-76. Chmn. emeritus bd. trustees Steven Inst. Tech.; trustee emeritus Fordham U.; mem. N.Y. State Econ. Devel. Bd., 1975. Mem. AAAS, Am. Chem. Soc., Soc. of Chem. Industry (Am. sect.), Societe de Chimie Industrielle, Chemists Club, Sky Club, Sakonnet Golf Club, Met. Club. Home: 9 W Irving St Chevy Chase MD 20815-4218

BISSINGER, MARK CHRISTIAN, lawyer; b. Steubenville, Ohio, June 4, 1957; s. Emerson Melvin and Nancy (Osbun) B.; m. Julie Furber, Sept. 28, 1985; children: Lucas Christian, Nathan Kenneth. BS in Civil Engring., Purdue U., 1979; JD, U. Cin., 1983. Bar: Ohio 1983, U.S. Dist. Ct. (so. dist.) Ohio 1983, U.S. Ct. Appeals (6th cir.), Ky. 1993. Assoc. Dinsmore & Shohl, Cin., 1983-90, ptnr., 1990—. Spkr. Ohio Continuing Legal Edn., Cin., 1990—; lectr. Nat. Bus. Inst., 1990—; commn. cert. attys. as splsts. Supreme Ct. Ohio; mem. Supreme Ct. Ohio's Bd. Bar Examiners; lectr. Lorman Edn. Svcs. Pres. Ctr. for Comprehensive Alcoholism Treatment, Cin., 1989-92; mem. pk. commn. Anderson Township, 2004—. Named Order of Coif, Cin., 1983; inducted class of 1999 Cin. Acad. of Leadership for Lawyers. Mem. ABA, Cin. Bar Assn., Ohio Bar Assn., No. Ky. Bar Assn., Ky. Bar Assn, Anderson Twp. Park Commn. Avocations: travel, sports. Office: Dinsmore & Shohl 255 E 5th St Cincinnati OH 45202-4700

BISSLER, JOHN JOSEPH, nephrologist, educator; b. Ravenna, Ohio, Nov. 12, 1960; m. Gloria M. Beuck. MD, Northeastern Ohio U., Rootstown, 1985. Assoc. prof. U. Cin., Coll. Medicine, Cin., 1988—. Office: Cin Children's Hosp Med Ctr 3333 Burnet Ave Cincinnati OH 45229-3039 Home Phone: 513-984-5450; Office Phone: 513-636-4531.

BISSLER, RICHARD THOMAS, mortician; b. Ravenna, Ohio, Nov. 23, 1953; s. Richard Samuel and Ruth Marion (Cowan) B.; m. Jane H. Vair, Aug. 23, 1975; children: Stephanie Ann (Shawn) Arden, Carlie Jane. BS in Mortuary Sci., U. Minn., 1976; grad., Nat. Found. Funeral Svc. Mgmt., 1983. Lic. funeral dir. and embalmer Ohio; cert. crematory operator Cremation Assn. N.Am. Funeral svc. asst. Bissler & Sons Funeral Home, Kent, Ohio, 1970-74, mortician, 1976—, corp. sec., 1983-86, corp. sec.-treas., 1986-88, pres., 1988—. Bd. dirs. Home Savs. Bank, Kent; bd. dirs., treas. NSM Ins. Co. Ltd., 1997—2001. Trustee Kent Free Libr., 1986—, trustee St. Patrick's Sch. Endowment Fund, 1994—, Nat. Selected Morticians Ins. Trust, 1995-2001; bd. dirs. Selected Ind. Funeral Homes, 2003-06, sec.-treas, 2005-06; past bd. dirs., pres. Portage County A.C.S., Kent; past treas. NEO-SIDS Found., Akron, Ohio; past mem. adult edn. adv. com. Kent City Schs.; past steering com. Portage County Hospice; past devel. com. United Christian Ministries, 1996-98; mem. Vision 2000 com. City of Kent; past mem. Kent Bus. and Edn. adv. com.; bd. dirs. Portage Area Regional Transit Authority, 2002—. Recipient Disting. Svc. award Kent Jaycees, 1986. Mem. Nat. Funeral Dirs. Assn., Ohio Embalmers Assn., Ohio Funeral Dirs. Assn., Selected Ind. Funeral Homes (meeting chair 1989), Funeral Ethics Assn., Kent Area C. of C. (dir. 1985-89, Outstanding Bus. Person award 1992), Order of the Golden Rule, Kent Rotary (dir. 1991-93, pres. 1995-96), KC. Republican. Roman Catholic. Avocations: golf, photography, travel. Office: Bissler & Sons Funeral Home 628 W Main St Kent OH 44240-2212 E-mail: rbissler@bisslerandson.com.

BISSON, CASEY, library and information scientist; Info. arch. Lamson Libr., Plymouth State U. Named one of the Movers & Shakers, Libr. Jour., 2007; recipient Mellon award for Tech. Collaboration, Andrew W. Mellon Found., 2006. Achievements include design of Scriblio (formerly WPopac). Office: Plymouth State U Lamson 220c 17 High St Plymouth NH 03264-1595 Office Phone: 603-535-2458.

BISSON, ROGER, middle school educator; b. Biddeford, Maine, Oct. 16, 1944; s. Napoleon and Simonne (Desrochers) B.; m. Janet Elizabeth Gerace, Aug. 9, 1969. BA in Biology, St. Michael's Coll., Winooski, Vt., 1969; MEd in Adminstrn. and Planning, U. Vt., 1991; tech. edn. cert., Lyndon State Coll., 1991. Cert. sci. tchr. grades 7-12, tech. edn. tchr. grades 7-12, prin. grades K-12, sci. and tech. edn. middle grades 5-8, mid. level endorsement Vt. Dept. Edn., 2001. 5th and 7th grade tchr. Sacred Heart Sch., Sharon, Mass., 1964-66; algebra I, French I and II and Latin I tchr. Notre Dame H.S., Fitchburg, Mass., 1966-68; 7th and 9th grade sci. tchr. Meml. Jr. and Sr. H.S., Bellingham, Mass., 1968-79; sci. and tech. edn. instr. grades 6, 7, 8 Folsom Sch., South Hero, Vt., 1979—2002, 8th grade sch.-to-work instr., 1992—2002; 8th grade sci. tchr. Albert D. Lawton Sch., Essex Junction, Vt., 2002—. Mem. info. tech. com. Grand Isle Supervisory Dist., North Hero, Vt., 1985-2002; tech. edn. cons. Alburg (Vt.) Elem. Sch., 1992-2002; sch.-to-work lead tchr. New Am. Sch.-Folsom, South Hero, 1992-2002, sci. lead tchr., 1994-2002; mem. tchr./bus. internship program Vt. Math. Coalition, Montpelier, summer 1994; initiator Electronic Portfolio Project 6, 7, 8, 1994-2002, Student/Bus. Internship Program, 1994—2002; tech. cons. Burlington Sch. Sys., 1996; presenter Nat. Ednl. Computing Conf., Boston, spring 1994, Vt. Fest '94, Fairlee, Vt., fall 1994, Sch.-to-Work Initiative Conf., Burlington, summer 1996, Regional Edn. Television Network Conf., Burlington, fall 1997, Vt. Fest '98 Info. Tech. Conf.; presenter in field. Contbr. articles to profl. jours. Initiator Grand Isle County Networking Initiative, Grand Isle County, Vt., 1991, Grand Isle County Peer Coaching Program, Grand Isle County, 1991. Recipient Sch.-to-Work Initiative Gov.'s Office, 1995, award Lake Champlain

Regional C. of C., 1996, Vocat. Edn. award Grand Isle Rotary Club, 1998; co-recipient IBM Test Flight 1991 award, Essex Junction, Vt., 1992. Mem. ASCD, NEA, NSTA, Vt. Edn. Assn., Vt. Sci. Tchrs. Assn., Vt. Tech. Edn. Assn., Grand Isle Supervisory Union (bldg rep., negotiator, grievance com., past pres.), Vt. State Tech. Coun., Vt. Inst. Sci., Math. and Tech., Vt. Info. Tech. Assn. for Avancement of Learning. Roman Catholic. Avocations: woodworking, furniture refinishing, carpentry, computer technology, fine dining. Office: Albert D Lawton Intermediate Sch 104 Maple St Essex Junction VT 05452 Business E-Mail: rbisson@ejhs.k12.vt.us.

BISSOON, CATHY, lawyer; b. NYC; married; 2 children. BA in polit. sci. summa cum laude, Alfred U., NY, 1990; JD, Harvard U., 1993; exec. leadership program, The Wharton Sch., U. Pa., 2004. Bar: Pa. 1993, US Dist. Ct. We. Dist. Pa. 1993, Supreme Ct. Pa. 1994, US Ct. Appeals 4th Cir. 1995, US Ct. Appeals 3rd Cir. 1997, US Ct. Appeals 6th Cir. 2001. Law clk. to Hon. Gary L. Lancaster US Dist. Ct. We. Dist. Pa., 1994; joined Reed Smith LLP, Pitts., 1993, ptnr., 2001—, dir. diversity, 2001—, former head employment group. Bd. mem. Girl Scouts Trillium Coun., Pitts. Zoo & PPG Aquarium. Named a Nat. Hispanic Scholar, Alfred U., Harvard U. Mem.: Pitts. Met. Area Hisp. C. of C., Hispanic Nat. Bar Assn., Phipps Conservatory and Botanical Gardens. Office: Reed Smith LLP 435 Sixth Ave Pittsburgh PA 15219 Office Phone: 412-288-3268. Office Fax: 412-288-3063. Business E-Mail: cbissoon@reedsmith.com.

BISTRIAN, BRUCE RYAN, internist, educator; b. Southampton, NY, Oct. 22, 1939; s. Peter and Mary Laura (Ryan) B.; m. Eleanor Alice Dix, Sept. 3, 1964; children: Tennille Ryan, Jordan Brooke, Britton Perry. BA, NYU, 1961; MD, Cornell U., 1965; MPH, Johns Hopkins U., 1971; PhD, MIT, 1975; AM (hon.), Harvard U., 1990. Diplomate in internal medicine and critical care medicine Am. Bd. Internal Medicine. Intern Cornell U., NYC, 1965-66; metabolism fellow U. Vt., Burlington, 1968-69, resident in medicine, 1969-70; from asst. clin. prof. to assoc. prof. Harvard U. Sch. Medicine, Boston, 1975-90, prof. medicine, 1990—. Clin. assoc. physician rsch. resources divsn. NIH, 1975-78; lectr. MIT, 1981-84. Mem. editl. bd. Jour. Parenteral and Enteral Nutrition, Harvard Health Letter, Women's Health Watch, Critical Care Medicine, European Jour. Clin. Nutrition; contbr. more than 400 sci. articles to profl. publs. Capt. U.S. Army, 1966-68. Recipient Goldberger award in clin. nutrition AMA, 2004; grantee Nat. Inst. Gen. Med. Scis., 1977-80, Nat. Inst. Arthritis, Metabolism and Digestive Disease, 1979-83, Nat. Inst. Arthritis, Diabetes, Digestive and Kidney Diseases, 1985-95, Nat. Cancer Inst., 1984-87. Fellow: ACP, Am. Soc. Nutritional Scis.; mem.: Inst. Medicine (com. on military nutrition rsch. 2001—), Mass. Med. Soc., Soc. Critical Care Medicine, Am. Soc. Parenteral and Enteral Nutrition (pres. 1989—90), Am. Soc. Clin. Nutrition (sec. 1993—96, v.p.-elect 1998, v.p. 1999, pres. 2000), Fedn. Am. Soc. Exptl. Biologists (bd. dirs. 2001—07, pres. 2005—06), Mass. Soc Mayflower Descs. (bd. assts. 2007—). Presbyterian. Achievements include more than 40 patents in field. Subspecialties: Nutrition (medicine); Biochemistry (medicine). Current work: protein calorie malnutrition; total parenteral nutrition; nutrition and infection. Home: Argilla Rd Ipswich MA 01938 Office: Beth Israel Deaconness Med Ctr 1 Deaconess Rd Boston MA 02215-5321 Business E-Mail: bbistria@bidmc.harvard.edu.

BITNER, BETTY L., education educator; b. Antrim Township, Pa., Feb. 7, 1945; d. Arthur Robert and Anna Elizabeth (Foreman) B. BA in Classical Langs., Thiel Coll., Greenville, Pa., 1967; MEd in Mental Retardation, Edinboro U. of Pa., 1973; EdD in Sci. Edn., U. Maine, 1983. Cert. tchr., NY, Maine, Mo. Tchr. Jamestown Pub. Schs., NY, 1967-69, 71-78, S.A.D. # 5, Rockland, Maine, 1978-81; grad. asst., instr. U. Maine, Orono, 1981-83; asst. prof. Ark. Tech. U., 1983-86; asst. prof. edn. S.W. Mo. State U., Springfield, 1986-89, assoc. prof., 1989-94, prof., 1994—2002, prof. emeritus, 2002—; prof. edn., chmn. Thiel Coll., Greenville, Pa., 2002—05; prof. edn., dir. MA in Tchg. Wilson Coll., Chambersburg, Pa., 2006—. Contbr. numerous articles to profl. jours. Founding sponsor Martin Luther King Jr. Nat. Meml. Recipient numerous grants in field. Mem. ASCD, Internat. Assn. Tech. Edn., Pa. Assn. Coll. Tchr. Educators, Nat. Assn. for Rsch. in Sci. Tchg., Nat. Audubon Soc., Nat. Sci. Tchrs. Assn. (com. on rsch. and sci. tchg. 1987-89), Southern Poverty Law Ctr., Phi Delta Kappa, Phi Kappa Phi. Avocations: the arts, hiking, reading. Office: Wilson Coll 1428 Alexander Ave Chambersburg PA 17201 Office Phone: 717-264-4141. Business E-Mail: bbitner@wilson.edu.

BITNER, JOHN HOWARD, lawyer; b. Indpls., Feb. 27, 1940; s. Harry M. Jr. and Jeanne B. (Eshelman) B.; m. Vicki Ann D'Ianni, 1961; children: Kerry, Holly, Robin. AB in English and History, Northwestern U., 1961; JD cum laude, Columbia U., 1964. Bar: Ill. 1964. Assoc. Bell, Boyd & Lloyd LLC, Chgo., 1964-71, mem., 1972—, chair corp. and secs. dept., 1988-99, vice chmn., 1992—99. Contbr. articles to profl. jours.; editor Columbia Law Rev. Active St. Gregory Episcopal Sch. Bd.; bd. visitors Columbia Law Sch, tutor, GED students at Jobs for Youth Fellow Am. Bar Found.; mem. ABA, Ill. Bar Assn., Union League, Mid-Day Club, Glen View Club, Lawyers Club, Delta Upsilon, Phi Delta Phi Episcopalian. Avocations: tennis, reading, chess, golf. Home: 2329 Lincolnwood Dr Evanston IL 60201-2048 Office: Bell Boyd & Lloyd LLC 70 W Madison St Chicago IL 60602 Fax: (312) 827-8048. E-mail: jbitner@bellboyd.com.

BITNER, JOHN WILLIAM, banker; b. Jersey Shore, Pa., July 6, 1948; s. John W. and Gertrude Elizabeth Bitner; m. Joy Lin. BS in Econs., Lebanon Valley Coll., Annville, Pa., 1970; MBA, Boston Coll., Chestnut Hill, Mass., 1983. V.p. Commonwealth Bank, Williamsport, Pa., 1970-78, Neworld Bank, Boston, 1978-81; fixed income mgr. Digital Equipment Co., Maynard, Mass., 1981-84; sr. v.p. Ea. Bank, Boston, 1984—. Author: Successful Bank Asset/Liability Management, 1992; contbr. articles to profl. jours.; guest Wake Up Call, CNBC TV, NBC Nightly News, NECN News, WBZ Radio. Mem.: Boston Com. on Fgn. Rels., Boston Econ. Club.

BITNER, TEDDY DWIGHT, history professor, military officer; b. Butler, Mo., July 27, 1950; s. Dwight Dixon and Ella Loraine Bitner; m. Nancy Lorena Stephens, Aug. 6, 1971; children: Rebekah Sue, Hannah Colleen, Miriam Kristin. BS, U. Ctrl. Mo., Warrensburg, 1972; MA, Wheaton Coll., Ill., 1982; M of Mil. Art and Sci., US Army Command & Gen. Staff Coll., Fort Leavenworth, Kans., 1983; D of Ministry, Trinity Theol. Sem., Newburgh, Ind., 1983. Cert. mil. historian US Army, 1983, mil. parchutist US Army, 1975, inspector gen. US Army, 1990. Comdr. 2nd Bn., 52nd Air Def. Arty., Fort Bragg, NC, 1990—92; chief, contingency initiative brand and sr. nato planner Allied Forces So. Europe, Naples, Italy, 1994—96; comdr. Army Theater Missile Def. Element, Colorado Springs, 1996—97; dep. dir. Space and Missile Def. Battle Lab., Colorado Springs, 1997—98; sr. mil. analyst SY Coleman, Colorado Springs, 1998—; assoc. prof. history Calvary Bible Coll., Kansas City, Mo., 2000—. Dir. Nat. Vietnam and Gulf War Vets. Coalition, Washington, 2005—, Vets. Modern Warfare, Kansas City, 2006—; chmn. bd. Hwy. Mission, Raymore, Mo., 2007—. Author: (history book) Unreconstructed: Vietnam to Iraq, 2005, Kesselring at Anzio, 2005. Mem. Freedom Fest, Inc., Skidmore, Mo., 2004—07. Decorated Def. Superior Svc. medal Dept. Def., Legion of Merit awards Dept. of Army, Bronze Star medal, Valorous Unit award; recipient Rescuer award, Assn. of Gospel Rescue Missions, 2006. Mem.: IFCA Internat., Assn. US Army, Vietnam Veterans Am., Rolling Thunder, Cycle Disciples Motorcycle Club (pres. 2000—07), 82nd Airborne Divsn. Assn. (life). Baptist. Avocation: motorcycling. Office: Calvary Bible Coll 15800 Calvary Rd Kansas City MO 64147 Home Phone: 816-914-5119; Office Phone: 816-322-0110. Personal E-mail: teddybitner@aol.com. Business E-Mail: assessment@calvary.edu.

BITRAN, JACOB DAVID, internist; b. Thessaloniki, Greece, Sept. 23, 1947; arrived in U.S., 1952; s. David Jacob and Martha (Faratzl) Bitran; m. Linda Sue Androw, Dec. 26, 1970; children: Lauren, Dina. BS, U. Ill., Chgo., 1968, MD, 1971. Diplomate Am. Bd. Internal Medicine, Am. Bd. Med. Oncology, Am. Bd. Hematology. Intern in medicine Michael Reese Med. Ctr., Chgo., 1971-72, resident in internal medicine, 1973-75, clin. asst. prof. medicine, 1977-81, clin. assoc. prof., 1981-84; resident in pathology Rush Presbyn. St. Luke's Med. Ctr., Chgo., 1972-73; fellow in hematology/oncology U. Chgo., 1975-77, assoc. prof., 1984-88, prof., 1988-91; dir. divsn. hematology/oncology Luth. Gen. Hosp., Park Ridge, Ill., 1991—; prof. medicine U. Ill., Chgo., 1996-98. Mem. sci. adv. bd. Lederle Labs., Wayne, NJ, 1986—89. Editor: Lung Cancer, 1988. Fellow: ACP, Am. Coll. Chest Physicians; mem.: Am. Soc. Clin. Oncology (program chmn. 1990—91), Am. Assn. Cancer Rsch. (program chmn. 1988—89). Democrat. Achievements include development of usable chemotherapy regimen for non small cell lung cancer that has been in clinical use since 1976; research in dose intensive chemotherapy in breast cancer. Avocations: tennis, rowing. Office: Luth Gen Hosp 1700 Luther Ln Park Ridge IL 60068-1270 Office Phone: 847-268-8200. Business E-Mail: jbitran@oncmed.net.

BITSBERGER, TIMOTHY S., finance company executive, former federal agency administrator; BA, Yale U., 1981; MBA, Harvard U., 1985. Trader Drexel Burnahm Lambert, NYC, 1985—89; sr. trading mgr., v.p. NationsBanc Capital Markets, NYC, 1989—98; sr. v.p. investments Solomon Smith Barney, NYC, 1999—2001; dep. asst. sec. fed. fin. US Dept Treasury, Washington, 2001—04, asst. sec. for fin. markets, 2004—05; sr. v.p. Freddie Mac, McLean, Va., 2005—. Cons. J.F. Lehman & Co., NYC, 1999. Office: Freddie Mac 8200 Jones Branch Dr Mc Lean VA 22102

BITTENBENDER, BRAD JAMES, safety engineer; b. Kalamazoo, Mich., Dec. 4, 1948; s. Don J. and Thelma Lu (Bacon) B.; m. Patricia Stahl Hubbell, June, 1992. BS, Western Mich. U., 1972; Cert. Hazardous Material Mgmt., U. Calif., Irvine, 1987; Cert. Environ. Auditing, Calif. State U., Long Beach, 1992. Cert. safety profl. of the Ams.; cert. hazardous materials mgr. Supr. mfg. Am. Cyanamid, Kalamazoo, 1973-77, Productol Chem. div. Ferro Corp., Santa Fe Springs, Calif., 1977-79, environ. adminstr., 1979-80; sr. environ. engr. Ferro Corp., Los Angeles, 1980-87; mgr. environ. safety and indsl. hygiene dept. Composites divsn. Ferro Corp., Los Angeles, 1988-91, Structural Polymer Systems, Inc., Montedison, Calif., 1991-95; dir. environ. safety and health dept. Culver City (Calif.) Composites Corp., 1996-98; mgr. safety, health and environ. dept. Cytec Fiberite-Calif. Divsn., LA, 1998-99; sr. safety specialist CH2M Hill Gen. Electric Aviation, Lynn, Mass., 2000—. Bd. dirs., mem. adv. bd. safety and health extension program U. Calif. Irvine, 1985-91. Bd. dirs. adv. com. hazardous materials Community Right to Know, Culver City, Calif., 1987-91; mem. Calif. Mus. Found., L.A., 1985-90, Mus. Contemporary Art, L.A., 1985-2000; founding sponsor Challenger Ctr.; mem. R.I. Driving Club, 1999—. Mem. DAR, Am. Inst. Chem. Engrs., Nat. Assn. Environ. Mgmt., Acad. Cert. Hazardous Materials Mgrs., Suppliers of Advanced Composites Materials Assn. (mem. environ. health and safety com. 1989-92), Am. Indsl. Hygiene Assn., Am. Soc. Safety Engrs., Nat. Fire Protection Assn., Beta Beta Beta. Republican. Presbyterian. Avocations: breeding morgan horses, skiing, distance running, reading, equestrian carriage driving. Home: 215 Everett St Wrentham MA 02093-1105 E-mail: bradbittenbender@yahoo.com.

BITTENBENDER, CHARLES A., lawyer; b. Plainfield, NJ, 1949; married, 2 children. BA, Claremont McKenna Coll., Claremont, Calif., 1971; JD, Cleveland State U., 1979. Bar: Ohio 1980. Various positions Ohio Bell Telephone Co., Cleveland, Ohio; atty. Jones, Day, Reavis & Pogue, Cleveland, Ohio; dep. gen. counsel G. D. Searle & Co., Chicago, Ill.; v.p., sec., gen. counsel Nacco Industries, Inc., Mayfield Heights, Ohio, 1990—. Mem.: ABA. Office: Nacco Industries Inc 5875 Landerbrook Dr Mayfield Heights OH 44124

BITTERMAN, MARY GAYLE FOLEY, foundation executive; b. San Jose, Calif., May 29, 1944; d. John Dennis and Zoe (Hames) Foley; m. Morton Edward Bitterman, June 26, 1967; 1 child Sarah Fleming. BA, Santa Clara U., 1966; MA, Bryn Mawr Coll., 1969, PhD, 1971. Exec. dir. Hawaii Pub. Broadcasting, Honolulu, 1974-79; dir. Voice Am., Washington, 1980-81, Dept. Commerce, Honolulu, 1981-83, E.-W. Ctr. Inst. Culture, Comm., 1984-88; cons. pvt. practice, 1989-93; pres., CEO KQED, Inc., San Francisco, 1993—2002, The James Irvine Found., 2002—03; Dir. Osher Lifelong Learning Inst., 2003; pres. The Bernard Osher Found., 2004—. Vice chmn. TIDE 2000, Tokyo, 1984—93; adv. coun. mem. Stanford Inst. Econ. Policy Rsch. Prodr.: (film) China Visit, 1978; contbr. numerous articles on internat. telecomms. to various pubs. Bd. dir. Bank of Hawaii, Honolulu, Honolulu, 1984—, United Way, Honolulu, 1986—1993, World Affairs Coun., 1994-2002, McKesson Corp., San Francisco, 1995—1999, Bernard Osher Found., Barclays Global Investors, Bay Area Econ. Forum, Bay Area Coun., exec. com., 1994-2002; bd. dirs. Assn. Pub. TV Sta., 1994-2002, chmn. 2001-2002; trustee Am.'s Pub. TV Stas., 1997—2002, Santa Clara U., 2004-07; chmn. Kuakini Health System, 1991—1994; bd. dir. PBS, chmn. Recipient Candle of Understanding award Bonneville (Utah) Internat. Corp., 1985; named hon. mem. Nat. Fedn. Press Women, 1986; Doctor of Humane Letters (honoris causa), Dominican Coll. of San Rafael, 1999; Doctor of Public Svc. (honoris causa), Santa Clara U., 2003; Ralph Lowell award, 2007. Mem.: Pacific Forum, CSIS (bd. gov.), Commonwealth Club Calif. (bd. dir.), Nat. Acad. Pub. Admin. (fellow). Office: One Ferry Bldg Ste 255 San Francisco CA 94111 Address: 229 Kaalawai Pl Honolulu HI 96816-4435 Office Phone: 415-677-5946. Business E-Mail: mbitterman@osherfoundation.org.

BITTERMAN, MORTON EDWARD, psychologist, educator; b. NYC, Jan. 19, 1921; s. Harry Michael and Stella (Weiss) B.; m. Mary Gayle Foley, June 26, 1967; children— Sarah Fleming, Joan, Ann BA, NYU, 1941; MA, Columbia U., 1942; PhD, Cornell U., 1945. Asst. prof. Cornell U., Ithaca, N.Y., 1945-50; assoc. prof. U. Tex., Austin, 1950-55; mem. Inst. for Advanced Study, Princeton, N.J., 1955-57; prof. Bryn Mawr Coll., Pa., 1957-70, U. Hawaii, Honolulu, 1970—; dir. Békésy Lab. Neurobiology, Honolulu, 1991—2000. Author: (with others) Animal Learning, 1979; editor: Evolution of Brain and Behavior in Vertebrates, 1976; co-editor: Am. Jour. Psychology, 1955-73; cons. editor Jour. Animal Learning and Behavior, 1973-76, 85-88, Jour. Comparative Psychology, 1988-92. Recipient Humboldt prize Alexander von Humboldt Found., Bonn, W.Ger., 1981; Fulbright grantee; grantee NSF, Office Naval Research, NIMH, Air Force Office Sci. Research, Deutsche Forschungsgemeinschaft. Fellow Soc. Exptl. Psychologists (Warren medal 1997, E.R. Hilgard award 2004), Am. Psychol. Assn. (D. O. Hebb award 2001), AAAS; mem. Psychonomic Soc. Home: 229 Kaalawai Pl Honolulu HI 96816-4435 Office: Univ Hawaii Bekesy Lab of Neurobiology 1993 E West Rd Honolulu HI 96822-2321 Office Phone: 808-956-6987. Business E-Mail: jeffb@pbrc.hawaii.edu.

BITTING, WILLIAM M., lawyer; b. Santa Monica, Calif., Apr. 17, 1939; AB, UCLA, 1962, JD, 1965. Exec. v.p., gen counsel Pabst Brewing Co., San Antonio, chmn., CEO, 1998—2000; former CEO, co-chmn., gen. counsel S&P Co., Mill Valley, Calif.; sr. ptnr Hill Farrer & Burrill LLP, Los Angeles, Calif. Office: Hill Farrer & Burrill LLP 300 S Grand Ave 37th Fl Los Angeles CA 90071 Business E-Mail: wbitting@hillfarrer.com.

BITTNER, VERA, cardiologist; b. Mainz, Germany, July 31, 1957; d. Friedrich and Lieselotte Bittner. MD, U. South Ala., Mobile, 1981; MSPH, U. Ala., 1995. Asst. prof. medicine U. Ala., Birmingham, 1987—93, assoc. prof. medicine, 1993—2000, dir. cardiovasc. disease residency program, 1998—, prof. medicine, 2000—, sect. head preventive cardiology, 2005—. Contbr. articles to profl. jours. Fellow, CDC and Am. Heart Assn., 1995. Fellow: ACP, Soc. Geriatric Cardiology, Am. Heart Assn. (clin. exercise com. 2005—, fellow 1991), Am. Coll. Cardiology (cardiovasc. disease prevention com. 2004—); mem.: Birmingham Cardiovasc. Soc. (pres. 2004—05), SE Lipid Assn. (pres. 2003—04), Nat. Lipid Assn. (bd. dirs. 2005—), Am. Assn. Cardiovasc. and Pulmonary Rehab. (bd. dirs. 2001—03), Delta Omega, Alpha Omega Alpha. Office: U Ala 701 19th St S - LHRB 310 Birmingham AL 35294 Office Phone: 205-934-7336.

BITZER, DONALD LESTER, electrical engineer, educator, retired lab administrator; b. East St. Louis, Ill., Jan. 1, 1934; s. Jess L. and Marjorie (Look) B.; m. Maryann Drost, July 2, 1955; 1 son, David. BS, U. Ill., 1955, MS, 1956, PhD, 1960; PhD (hon.), MacMurray Coll., Jacksonville, Ill. Mem. faculty U. Ill.-Urbana, 1955—, asst. prof., 1960-63, assoc. prof., 1963-67, prof. elec. engring., 1967—, dir. Computer-Based Edn. Research Lab., 1967-89; disting. prof. rsch. N.C. State U., 1989—. Cons. in field. Contbr. articles to profl. jours.; pioneer PLATO-large computer-based edn. system; co-inventor plasma display panel. Recipient Indsl. Rsch. 100 award, 1966, Bobby Connelly Meml. award Miami Valley Computer Assn., 1973, Recognition award Soc. for Info. Display, 1979, Edn. award Am. Fedn. Info. Processing Socs., 1989, Elec. Engring. Disting. Alumni award U. Ill., 1992, Emmy award NATAS, 2002; named to Consumer Electronics Hall of Fame, 2006; named laureate Lincoln Acad of Ill., 1982; Internat. Engring. Consortium fellow, 1994. Fellow AAAS, IEEE, Assn. Devel. Computer-Based Instrnl. Sys., Internat. Engring. Consortium; mem. NAE (Vladimir K. Zworykin award), Data Processing Mgmt. Assn. (Computer Sci. Man of Yr. award), Am. Soc. Engring. Edn. (Chester Carlson award), Nat. Acad. Engring. Home: 104 Christofle Ln Cary NC 27511-6473 Office: NC State U Dept Computer Sci PO Box 8206 Raleigh NC 27695-0001

BIVENS, CAROLYN VESPER, sports association administrator, former advertising executive; m. Bill Bivens. Various sales and mktg. positions Xerox Corp., Dallas, Washington; with USA Today, 1982—2000, dir. nat. sales, v.p. nat. circulation sales Arlington, Va., 1985—91, sr. v.p., assoc. pub., 1991—2000; mng. dir. Western Region Initiative Media, 2000—01; pres., COO Initiative Media N.Am., LA, 2001—05; commr. LPGA, Daytona Beach, Fla., 2005—. Chmn. bd. govs. Children's Miracle Network; bd. dirs. Ad Coun., Nat. Steppenwolf Theatre. Named one of Most Powerful Women in TV, Electronics Media mag., 2002. Mem.: Am. Assn. Advt. Agencies (mem. Media Policy Com.), Congl. Country Club. Achievements include becoming the first female commissioner in the 55 year history of the Ladies Professional Golf Association. Avocation: golf. Office: LPGA 100 International Golf Drive Daytona Beach FL 32124-1092 Office Phone: 386-274-6200. Office Fax: 386-274-1099.*

BIVENS, MITCHEL LEE, school system administrator, minister; s. Willie Fred and Elvira Bivens; m. Etta Faye Collier, Apr. 15, 1979; children: Devara Anita Richardson, Donovan Bernard, Charles Frederick, Anthony James, Ann Marie. AA, U. Md., 1990, B in Mgmt., 1994; M in Adminstrv. Supr. and Leadership, State U. West Ga., 2004. Police identification tech. Fulton County Police Dept., Atlanta, 1995—97; paraprofessional Birney Elem. Sch., Marietta, Ga., 1997—2000, tchr., 2000—04, adminstr. asst., 2004—. Bd. mem. Young Adult Guidance Ctr., Atlanta, 1997—2003. Rev. Crown of Life Bapt. Ch., Powder Springs, Ga., 2004. Served in US Army, 1972—77, adminstrv. supr. 3d Infantry Divsn. US Army, 1977—79, adminstrv. supr. 7th Adjutant Gen. Co. US Army, 1979—80, adminstrv. supr. 7th Eng. Brigade US Army, 1980—83, Germany, instr./adminstrv. supr. Tulane U. US Army, 1983—87, drill sgt. 277th Quartermaster Battalion US Army, 1987—89, detachment sgt. Hdqrs. and Hdqrs. Co. US Army, 1989—92, Germany, first sgt. 369th Adjutant Co. US Army, 1992—93. Mem.: ASCD, Profl. Assn. Ga. Educators (bldg. coord. 2000—05), Pi Lambda Theta. Baptist. Avocations: reading, gardening, travel, cooking, baking. Home: 2551 Hencley Cir Marietta GA 30008-5682 Home Phone: 770-428-0792. Business E-Mail: mike.bivens@cobbk12.org.

BIVINS, SUSAN STEINBACH, systems engineer; b. Chgo., June 5, 1941; d. Joseph Benard and Eleanor Celeste (Mathes) S.; m. James Herbert Bivins, June 7, 1980. BS, Northwestern U., 1963; postgrad., U. Colo., 1964, U. Ill., 1965, UCLA, 1971. With IBM, 1967-94, support mgr. East White Plains, NY, 1977-78, sys. support mgr., western region LA, 1978-81, br. market support mgr., 1981-84, mgr. IBM ops. and support L.A. Summer Olympics, 1984, mgr. IBM office supporting devel. FAA air traffic control sys. for 1990's, 1984-88, mgr. complex sys. mktg., 1988-89, acct. devel. mgr. aerospace engring. and mfg., 1989-91, mgr. cons. and outsourcing indsl. sector trading area, 1991-92, cons. orgn. task forces, 1992-93; project exec. IBM Integrated Sys. Solutions Corp., 1993-94; exec. dir. BDM Internat. Inc., 1995-98; sr. dir. Hitachi, 1998—2002; dir. project mgmt. Habitat for Humanity Internat., 2003—07, pres., 2007; prin. cons. Tier Technologies, Inc., 2007—. Pres. Jastech, 1986—. Developed program to retrieve data via terminal and direct it to any appropriate hardcopy device, 1973. Vol. tchr. computer sci. Calif. Mentally Gifted Minor Programs; vol. L.A. Youth Motivation Task Force; dir. pub. rels. Lake of the Ozarks Jazz Festival, 1993-95; bd. dirs. Greater Lake Area Arts Coun., 1993-95. Mem.: Project Mgmt. Inst. (mem. sys. engring. symposium, mem. OPM3 and PPM Stds. Teams, cert. PMP 2003, mem. MS project orange Bslt 2004), Pi Lambda Theata. Achievements include developed program to retrieve data via terminal and direct it to any appropriate hardcopy device, 1973, PMI cert. PMP, 2003; vol., PMI orgnl. project mgmt. maturity model, program/portfolio mgmt. std. Home: 18 Suji Point Four Seasons MO 65049-9024 Business E-Mail: sue.bivins@onemain.com.

BIX, HERBERT PHILIP, historian, educator; b. Boston, Sept. 21, 1938; s. James and Francis Bix; m. Toshie Watanabe, 1961 (dec.); children: Mark, Deborah, Meriam. BA, U. Mass., Amherst, 1960; MA, Harvard U., 1968, PhD, 1972. With U. Mass., Boston, 1970-77, Hosei U., Tokyo, 1978-88; prof., grad. sch. social sci. Hitotsubashi U., Japan, 1997—2001; prof., history, sociology SUNY, Binghamton, 1988—; assoc. in rsch. E.O. Reischauer Inst. for Japanese Studies, Harvard U., Cambridge, Mass., 1992—. Author: Peasant Protest in Japan 1590-1884, 1986, Hirohito and the Making of Modern Japan, 2000 (Pulitzer Prize in gen. nonfiction, 2001, Nat. Book Critics Circle award, 2001); translator: The Japanese Monarchy; contbr. articles to profl. jours., books and newspapers. Lt. (j.g.) USNR, 1962-64, Japan. Nat. Def. Fgn. Langs. fellow U.S. Govt., 1965-69, Fulbright-Hayes Postdoctoral fellow, 1977-78; recipient Rsch. Grant award U.S.-Japan Edn. Commn., 1992-93. Mem.: Am. Soc. Internat. Law, Am. Hist. Assn., Soc. for Historians Am. Fgn. Policy, Hist. Sci. Soc. (Japan). Office: Binghamton U Dept History PO Box 6000 Binghamton NY 13902 Business E-Mail: hbix@binghamton.edu.

BIXBY, FRANK LYMAN, retired lawyer; b. New Richmond, Wis., May 25, 1928; s. Frank H. and Esther (Otteson) B.; m. Katharine Spence, July 7, 1951; children— Paul, Thomas, Edward, Janet. AB, Harvard U., 1950; LLB, U. Wis., 1953. Bar: Ill. 1953, Wis. 1953, Fla. 1974. Ptnr. firm Sidley Austin Brown & Wood LLP, Chgo., 1963—97, sr. counsel, 1998—2005; ret., 2005. Editor-in-chief Wis. Law Rev, 1952-53; mem. editorial bd. Chgo. Reporter, 1973-89. Trustee MacMurray Coll., Jacksonville, Ill., 1973-85; bd. dirs. Chgo. Urban League, 1962-2006, v.p., 1972-86, gen. counsel, 1972—, chmn. 1986-89; bd. dirs. Community Renewal Soc., 1973-86, Voices for Ill. Children, 1987-90; chmn. trustees Unitarian Ch., Evanston, Ill., 1962-63; bd. dirs. Spencer Found., 1967-2001, chmn. 1975-90; mem. dist. 202 bd. edn. Evanston Twp. High Sch., 1975-81, pres., 1977-79. Recipient Man of Year award Chgo. Urban League, 1974 Mem. ABA, Ill. Bar Assn., Chgo. Bar Assn., Chgo. Coun. Lawyers, Chgo. Coun. Fgn. Rels., Order of Coif, Harvard Club (pres. 1964-65), Mid-Day Club.,

Phi Beta Kappa. Home: 505 N Lake Shore Dr Apt 4607 Chicago IL 60611-3409 Office: Sidley Austin LLP 1 S Dearborn St Chicago IL 60603-2000 Office Phone: 312-853-7429. Business E-Mail: fbixby@sidley.com.

BIXLER, R. JEFFREY, lawyer; b. 1945; BS, U. Dayton; JD, U. Toledo, 1972. V.p., gen. counsel, sec. Manor Care Inc., Toledo, 1991—. Mem.: ABA. Office: HCR Manor Care 333 N Summit St Toledo OH 43604 Office Phone: 419-252-5500.

BIZIOU, PETER, cinematographer; Cinematographer: (films) Bugsy Malone, 1978, Monty Python's Life of Brian, 1979, Time Bandits, 1981, Pink Floyd-The Wall, 1982, Another Country, 1984 (Cannes award best artistic contbn.), 9 1/2 Weeks, 1986, A World Apart, 1988, Mississippi Burning, 1988 (Academy award best cinematography 1988, British Acad. award 1989, award British Soc. Cinematographers 1989), Rosencrantz and Guildenstern Are Dead, 1991, City of Joy, 1992, Damage, 1992, In the Name of the Father, 1993, Road to Wellville, 1994, Richard III, 1995, The Truman Show, 1998, Unfaithful, 2001, Ladies in Lavender, 2003, Festival Express, 2004, Derailed, 2005.

BIZUB, JOHANNA CATHERINE, law librarian; b. Denville, NJ, Apr. 13, 1957; d. Stephen Bernard and Elizabeth Mary B.; m. Scott Jeffrey Smith, 1992. BS in Criminal Justice, U. Dayton, 1979; MLS, Rutgers U., 1984. Law libr. Morris County (NJ) Law Libr., 1981-83, Clapp & Eisenberg, Newark, 1984-86; dir. libr. Sills Cummis, 1986-94; libr. dir. Montville (NJ) Twp. Pub. Libr., 1994-97; libr. dir. law dept. Prudential Ins. Co. Am., Newark, 1997—. Mem. ALA, NJ Law Librs. Assn. (treas. 1987-89, v.p./pres.-elect 1989-90, 99-2000, pres. 1990-91, 2000-01, past pres. 1991-92, 2001-02), Am. Assn. Law Librs. (pvt. law librs. SIS, vice chair 1992-93, chair 1993-94, chair awards com. 1992-93, 2005—, mem. bylaws com. 2006—), NJ Libr. Assn., Assoc. Libr. of Morris County (v.p. 1995, pres. 1996, treas. 1997-2001), Spl. Libr. Assn. NJ (treas. 1990-92), Am. Legion Aux. (treas. Rockden unit 175 1983-93). Democrat. Roman Catholic. Home: 11 Elm St Rockaway NJ 07866-3108 Office: Prudential Ins Co Am 4 Plz 751 Broad St Newark NJ 07102-3714 Business E-Mail: jbizub@prudential.com.

BIZZI, EMILIO, neurophysiologist, educator; b. Rome, Feb. 22, 1933; arrived in U.S., 1963, naturalized, 1982; s. Vittorio and Anna (Galeazzi) Bizzi. MD summa cum laude with highest honors, U. Rome, 1958. Postdoctoral trainee Inst. Med. Pathology, U. Siena, Italy, 1958-60; postdoctoral trainee Inst. Physiology, U. Pisa, Italy, 1960-63; rsch. assoc. neurophysiol. lab., dept. zoology Washington U., St. Louis, 1963-64; vis. assoc. sect. physiology, lab. clin. sci. NIMH, Bethesda, Md., 1964-66; rsch. assoc. dept. psychology MIT, Cambridge, 1966-67, lectr. dept. psychology, 1967-68, assoc. prof. neurophysiology, 1969-72, prof., 1972-80, Eugene McDermott prof. brain scis. and human behavior, 1980—2002, inst. prof., 2002—, dir. Whitaker Coll., 1983-88, chmn. dept. Brain and Cognitive Scis., 1986-97. Mem. editl. bd.: Brain Theory Newsletter, 1980—, Jour. Motor Behavior, 1981—, Jour. Neurobiology, 1981—; contbr. articles to profl. jours., chapters to books. Recipient Alden Spencer award, Columbia U. Coll. Physicians and Surgeons, 1978, Hermann von Hlmholtz award, 1992; fellow Found. Rsch. Psychiatry, 1978—. Mem.: NAS, Inst. Medicine, Am. Acad. Clin. Neurophysiol., Acad. dei Lincei, Am. Acad. Arts and Scis. (pres. 2006—), Internat. Brain Rsch. Orgn. Office: MIT Dept Brain & Cognitive Scis Cambridge MA 02139-4307 Office Phone: 617-253-5769. Office Fax: 617-258-5342. Business E-Mail: ebizzi@mit.edu.

BJERKAAS, ALLAN WAYNE, associate dean, physicist; b. Alexandria, Minn., Nov. 25, 1944; s. Jay Oscar and Marie Anna Bjerkaas; m. Judith Louise Egstad, Sept. 4, 1965; children: Douglas Wayne, Robert Allan, James Kevin, Stephen Matthew Bjekaas. BS in Physics & Math., U. ND, Grand Forks, 1962—66; PhD in Physics, U. Ill., Urbana-Champaign, 1966—71. Postdoctoral rsch. assoc. U. Pitts., 1971—73; prin. staff physicist Johns Hopkins Applied Physics Lab., Laurel, Md., 1973—2004; assoc. dean Johns Hopkins Whiting Sch. Engring., Balt., 2004—. Home: 4922 Snowy Reach Columbia MD 21044 Office: Johns Hopkins Univ 3400 N Charles St Baltimore MD 21218 Home Phone: 410-997-3609. Personal E-mail: abjerkaas@comcast.net. Business E-Mail: bjerkaas@jhu.edu.

BJERKAAS, CARLTON LEE, information technology executive; b. Fergus Falls, Minn., Apr. 17, 1948; s. Jay Oscar and Anna Marie (Bangert) Bjerkaas; children: Kristopher Scott, Eric Stefan, Todd Philip. BS, U. N.D., 1970; MS, MIT, 1977; MPA, Auburn U., Montgomery, Ala., 1983. Commd. 2d lt. USAF, 1970, advanced through grades to col., 1992; forecaster Weather Detachment, Homestead AFB, Fla., 1971-73; flight examiner Weather Reconnaissance Squadron, Andersen AFB, Guam, 1973—75; radar rsch. meteorologist A.F. Geophysics Lab., Hanscom AFB, Mass., 1976-82; chief support br. operational requirements & testing Hdqrs. Mil. Airlift Command, Scott AFB, Ill., 1983-85; chief aerospace environ. requirements Hdqrs. A.F. Systems Command, Andrews AFB, Md., 1985-87; comdr. Weather Detachment, Lajes Field, Azores, Portugal, 1987-89; asst. chief of staff Hdqrs. Air Weather Svc., Scott AFB, 1989-91, dir. resource mgmt., 1991-92, dir. program mgmt., integration, 1992-94; dir. sys. and comm., 1994-95; dir. tech., plans and programs, 1995—; sr. scientist Hdqrs. Air Weather Svc., Scott AFB, Ill., 1995-96; divsn. mgr. Sci. Applications Internat. Corp., O'Fallon, Ill., 1996—2001, ops. mgr., 2001—05, v.p. ops., 2005—07, v.p. program mgmt. Sioux Falls, SD, 2007—. Contbr. articles to profl. jours. Mem. Sch. Dist. Com., Lajes Field Azores, 1987; chmn. Sch. Bd., Lajes Field Azores, 1988—89; coach, referee youth sports, O'Fallon, 1989—; com. chmn. Boy Scouts Am., O'Fallon, 1991—92. Fellow: Am. Meteorol. Soc.; mem.: ASPA, AAAW, Air Lift and Tanker Assn., Air Weather Assn., Acad. Polit. Sci., N.Y. Acad. Scis., Rotary, Sigma Xi, Phi Beta Kappa, Pi Alpha Alpha, Phi Eta Sigma. Methodist. Avocations: computers, soccer coaching, boy scouts. Office: Sci Applications Internat Corp 47914 252d St Sioux Falls SD 57198

BJERKE, DANA, librarian; MLS, U. Wis., Madison. Outreach libr. St. Croix County Libr., Minn.; reference libr. East Ctrl. Regional Libr., Cambridge, Minn.; reference & children's svcs. libr. Anoka County Libr., Minn.; youth svcs. libr. Ridgedale Libr., Minnetonka, Minn., 1999—. Recipient NY Times Libr. award, 2006. Office: Hennepin County Libr 12601 Ridgedale Dr Minnetonka MN 55305 Office Phone: 952-847-8800.

BJERREGAARD, PREBEN, cardiologist, educator; b. Hansted, Denmark, Feb. 6, 1942; arrived in U.S., 1989; s. Emil Robin and Karen Bjerregaard; m. Ria Skovholm Knudsen, June 4, 1965; children: Torsten, Dorte, Jens. MD, U. Aarhus, 1969, DMSc, 1983. Diplomate in Cardiology Denmark, 1978. Cardiology fellow U. Okla., Oklahoma City, 1972—74; rsch. fellow U. Aarhus, Denmark, 1977—81, lectr., 1981—83, Aarhus Amtssygehus, 1983—84; asst. prof. medicine Aarhus Kommune Hosp., 1984—88; cons. cardiologist Ibn Al Bitar Hosp., Baghdad, Iraq, 1988—89; prof. medicine St. Louis U. Hosp., 1989—2006, St. Louis VA Med. Ctr., 2006—. Bd. mem. IRB, St. Louis U., 1990—2003. Author: Electrocardiographic Atlas, 1981; co-editor: Cardiac Repolarization, 2003. 2d lt. Denmark Navy, 1970—71, Frederikshavn, Denmark. Achievements include discovery of a new disease called Short QT-Syndrome in 1999. Avocations: jazz, boating, Iraq history. Office: VA Med Ctr 915 N Grand Saint Louis MO 63106 Home: 8 Portland Ct Saint Louis MO 63108 Office Phone: 314-289-6329. Business E-Mail: preben.bjerregaard@va.gov.

BJONTEGARD, ARTHUR MARTIN, JR., foundation executive; b. Lynn, Mass., Mar. 23, 1938; s. Arthur M. and Irma W. (Cook) B.; m. Wilma Joy Golding, Oct. 15, 1966; children— Arthur M., Karla Kristin BA, Duke U., 1959; JD, U. Va., 1962; postgrad., Rutgers U., 1966; grad. advanced mgmt. program, Harvard U. Sch. Bus., 1974. Bar: N.J. 1962, S.C. 1967. Bank examiner U.S. Treasury Dept., Richmond, Va., 1962-66; trust officer S.C. Nat. Bank, Columbia, 1966-74, sr. v.p., 1974-81; pres. S.C. Nat. Corp., Columbia, 1981-84, vice-chmn., 1984-92; pres. Ind. Colls. and Univs. of S.C. Inc., 1992—. Commr. Columbia Housing Authority, 1995—. Pres. United Way of the Midlands, Columbia, 1984-85, S.C., 1986-87, Univ. Assocs., Columbia, 1984-85, Friday Luncheon Club, Columbia, 1984, Spring Valley Ednl. Found., 1986—, Ctrl. Carolina Community Found., 1990-96; chmn. Columbia Community Resl. Coun., 1984, Fedn. of the Blind, 1992—. Named Vol. of Yr., Urban League, Columbia, 1984; recipient Order of Palmetto award, S.C. Gov., 1992. Mem. S.C. Bar Assn., Palmetto Soc., Thomas Jefferson Soc., S.C. C. of C., Forest Lake County Club, Palmetto Club, Spring Valley Country Club. Episcopalian. Avocations: tennis, swimming, sports. Office: Ind Colls and Univs of SC PO Box 12007 Columbia SC 29211-2007

BJÖRK, (BJÖRK GUÐMUNDSDÓTTIR), singer, composer; b. Reykjavik, Iceland, Nov. 21, 1965; d. Gudmundur and Hildur Runa; m. Thor Eldon, 1986 (div. 1988); 1 child, Sindri Eldon; m. Matthew Barney, 2000; 1 child, Isadora Rec. artist solo album at age 11; performer with several bands; formed theatrical/rock ensemble KUKL, 1980s; rec. artist with The Sugarcubes: (albums) Life's Too Good, 1986, Here Today, Tomorrow, Next Week, 1989; solo artist: (albums) Debut, 1993, Post, 1995, Telegram, 1997, Homogenic, 1997, Vespertine, 2001, Family Tree, 2002, Greatest Hits, 2002, Medulla, 2004, Volta, 2007; (soundtracks) Selmasongs: Dancer in the Dark, 2000, Drawing Restraint 9, 2005; actor: (films) Juniper Tree, 1990,Prêt-à-Porter , 1994, Dancer in the Dark, 2000 (Best Actress, Cannes Film Festival), Drawing Restraint 9, 2005, (voice only) Anna and the Moods, 2007. Recipient Brit Award for Internat. Female, 1994, Q Inspiration award, 2005. Office: Electra Records 75 Rockefeller Plz New York NY 10019-6908*

BJORKLUND, NANCY BASLER, history professor; b. Santa Ana, Calif., Dec. 20, 1940; d. Herman Henry and Virginia Eleanor Basler; m. Lawrence Paul Bjorklund (div. Aug. 27, 1987); children: Julie, Kristen, David. BA, UCLA, 1962, MA, 1964; PhD, U. Calif., Irvine, 1987. Instr. Leeward Coll., Pearl City, Hawaii, 1971—72, Saddlebrook Coll., Mission Viejo, Calif., 1973—76, Rancho Santiago Coll, Santa Ana, 1974—84; tchg. assoc. and asst. U. Calif., Irvine, 1978—84; prof. history Fullerton Coll., Calif., 1984—. Contbr. articles to profl. jours. Chair bd. higher edn. and campus ministeries Meth. Ch., Calif.-Pacific Conf., 1999—2003. Grantee, U. Calif., Irvine, 1982, 1984. Mem.: Pacific Coast Conf. Brit. Studies, Nat. Endowment Humanities, Phi Beta Kappa. Methodist. Office: Fullerton Coll 321 E Chapman Ave Fullerton CA 92832 Business E-Mail: nbjorklund@fullcoll.edu.

BJORKLUND, VICTORIA B., lawyer; b. Glen Cove, NY, Feb. 20, 1952; BA magna cum laude & phi beta kappa, Princeton U., 1973; PhD, Yale U., 1977; JD, Columbia U., 1983. Bar: N.Y. 1984. Ptnr. Simpson, Thacher & Bartlett LLP, NYC, head firm exempt orgn. group, co-chmn. pro bono com. Dir., sec., pro bono legal counsel Doctors Without Borders, 1989—2001; dir., pro bono legal counsel Robin Hood Found. Co-author: N.Y. Nonprofit Law & Practice, 1997. Recipient Commr.'s Award, Commr. IRS, 2003. Mem.: Assn. Bar City N.Y.- com. nonprofit orgn. (mem. 1991—97), ABA-sub com. international philanthropy (co-chmn.), ABA-tax sect. com. exempt orgn. (co-chmn., sub-com. private found. 1997—99, vice chmn. 1999—2001, chmn. 2001—03, co-chmn., sub-com. private found. 2003—, co-chmn., sub-com. precedential guidance 1995—97, Pro Bono Lawyer Year 2002). Office: Simpson Thacher & Bartlett LLP 425 Lexington Ave New York NY 10017-3954 Office Phone: 212-455-2875. Office Fax: 212-455-2502. Business E-Mail: vbjorklund@stblaw.com.

BJORNSON, EDITH CAMERON, foundation administrator, communications consultant; b. Orlando, Fla., Sept. 12, 1937; d. Hilliard Francis and Edith Muriel (McBride) Cameron; m. Carroll N. Bjornson, Jan. 11, 1963; children: Lisa Carol, Karl Cameron (dec.). BA, U. Fla., Gainesville, 1953. MA, 1956; profl. cert., Ecole de Cuisine LaVerenne, Paris, 1983. Copywriter Sta. WGGG, Gainesville, Fla., 1953—54; exec. asst. Actors' Studio, NYC, 1956—58; prodn. asst. Omnibus, NYC, 1958—59; assoc. prodr. Robert Saudek Assocs., NYC, 1958—60, ABC News Adlai Stevenson Reports, NYC, 1960; asst. gen. mgr. Sta. WNDT-TV, NYC, 1960—63; co-prodr. The Open Mind, NYC, 1963—69; dir. local programming Teleprompter, Inc., NYC, 1979—80; corp. v.p. programming Westinghouse Broadcasting and Cable, NYC, 1980—83; cons. Sta. WNYC-TV, NYC, 1984—86; v.p., sr. program officer The Markle Found., NYC, 1986—98. Working group Carter Commn. on Radio and TV, Atlanta, 1992—96; chmn. NY New Media Assn., NYC, 2002; bd. dirs. Conn. Pub. TV and Radio, 1999—, co-chair strategic planning com., 2006, v.p., bd. advisor to Culture Connect, 2003—; exec. dir. Fulfilling the Promise project on digital comm. Century Found. and Carnegie Corp., 1999—2001; sr. advisor, Morningside Ventures Columbia U., 1999—2001; project dir., website designer Fulfilling the Promise The Century Found. Carnegie Corp., 1999—2001; website editor Digital Promise Project, 2002—03; project dir., website designer The Open Mind Digital Archive Project, Columbia Tchrs. Coll., 2002—; sr. advisor Fathom.com Columbia U., 1999—2001; sr. advisor video oral history project Healthcare Chaplaincy, 2002—05; dir. oral history project The Healthcare Chaplaincy, 2003—05; prin. Recorded Oral Histories, LLC; sr. cons. Liberty Concepts LLC; bd. dirs. MOUSE, 2007—; cons. in field. Project advisor: (computer software) Voyager Co., 1993, SimHealth, 1994, (Internet software, multi-player online games) ReInventing America, 1995, President '96; contbr. articles to profl. jours. Vice chmn. bd. dirs. HealthCare Chaplaincy, N.Y.C., 1989-96; bd. dirs. Pro-Natura USA, N.Y.C., 1995-99; life trustee Health Care Chaplaincy, N.Y.C., 1997. Recipient Emmy award Acad. TV. Arts and Scis., 1960. Mem. Internat. Assn. Culinary Profls., Night Kitchen (computer software developers bd. dirs. 1996-98), Mortar Board, Delta Gamma. Republican. Avocation: cooking. Home: 34 E Lyon Farm Dr Greenwich CT 06831-4349 Office Phone: 212-481-3949.

BLACHLY, JACK LEE, lawyer; b. Dallas, Mar. 8, 1942; s. Emery Lee and Thelma Jo (Budd) B.; m. Lucy Largent Rain, Jan. 15, 1972; 1 son, Michael Talbot. BBA, So. Meth. U., 1965, JD, 1968. Bar: Tex. 1968, U.S. Ct. Appeals (5th cir.) 1969, U.S. Supreme Ct. 1975, U.S. Tax Ct. 1977. Trust officer First Nat. Bank in Dallas, 1968-70; ptnr. firm Reese & Blachly, Dallas, 1970-71; assoc. firm Rain Harrell Emery Young & Doke, Dallas, 1971-76; staff atty. Sabine Corp., Dallas, 1976-77, mgr. legal dept., 1977-80, v.p., gen. counsel, 1980-89; asst. gen. counsel Pacific Enterprises Oil Co. USA (merger Sabine Corp. and Pacific Enterprise Oil Co. USA), Dallas, 1989-90; pvt. practice Dallas, 1990—2005; v.p. legal Tex. Credit Union League, Farmers Br., Tex., 2005—. Mem.: Dallas Bar Assn., Tex. Bar Assn., Dallas Gun Club. Baptist. Office: Tex Credit Union League 4455 LBJ Freeway Farmers Branch TX 75244 Office Phone: 469-385-6411.

BLACHMAN, MICHAEL JOEL, lawyer; b. Portsmouth, Va., Aug. 16, 1944; s. Zalmon I. and Rachel G. (Grossman) B.; m. Paula D. Levine, Nov. 23, 1969; children: Dara R., Erica Dale. BS, Am. U., 1966; JD, U. Tenn., 1969. Bar: Va. 1969, U.S. Dist. Ct. (ea. dist.) Va. 1971, U.S. Supreme Ct. 1974, U.S. Ct. Appeals (4th cir.) 1977. Asst. commonwealth's atty. Commonwealth of Va., Portsmouth, 1970-72; assoc. Bangel, Bangel & Bangel, Portsmouth, 1972-77, ptnr., 1977—. Chmn. Portsmouth Juvenile Adv. Com., 1975-78. Mem. Va. Dem. Steering Com. 1980-85; vice chmn. Indsl. Devel. Authority and Port and Indsl. Commn., Portsmouth, 1987-89, chmn. 1989-93; bd. dirs. United Jewish Fedn. Tidewater, 1980—, v.p. 1989—. With USCGR, 1966-72. Recipient Young Leadership award United Jewish Fedn. Tidewater, 1983. Mem. ABA, Assn. Trial Lawyers Am., Va. Bar Assn., Va. Trial Lawyers Assn. (v.p. 1985-88, pres. 1989-90), So. Trial Lawyers Assn. (bd. dirs. 1991—), Portsmouth Bar Assn., Portsmouth C. of C., Kiwanis (bd. dirs. Portsmouth club 1973-75), B'nai B'rith. Jewish. Avocations: tennis, travel, reading.

BLACK, ALLEN DECATUR, lawyer; b. Pitts., July 27, 1942; s. Gerald Richard and Amy Elizabeth (Haymaker) B. AB, Princeton U., 1963; LLB magna cum laude, U. Pa., 1966. Bar: D.C. 1967, Pa. 1971, U.S. Supreme Ct. 1975. Law clk. to Hon. John Minor Wisdom, New Orleans, 1966-67; trial atty. Dept. Justice, 1967-68; asst. prof. law U. N.D., Grand Forks, 1971; practice comml. and antitrust litigation law Fine, Kaplan & Black, Phila., 1975—. Lectr. in law Rutgers U., 1972-77, Temple U., 1978, U. Pa., 1985. Chmn. Bucks County Airport Authority, 1999—. Served with JAGC USN, 1968-71. Fellow Am. Coll. Trial Lawyers; mem. Am. Law Inst. (2d v.p. 2004—), Pa. Bar Assn., Phila. Bar Assn. Republican. Episcopalian. Office: 1835 Market St Philadelphia PA 19103

BLACK, BARBARA ANN, publisher; b. Eureka, Calif., Dec. 11, 1928; d. William Marion and Letitia (Brunia) Black; m. Vinson Brown, June 18, 1950 (dec Dec. 1991); children: Tamara Pinn, Roxana Hodges, Keven Brown. BA, Western State Coll., Gunnison, Colo., 1950. Cert. tchr., Colo. Editor/proofreader Naturegraph Pubs., Los Altos, Calif., 1950-53, co-owner, mgr. San Martin, Calif., 1953-60, Healdsburg, Calif., 1960-76, owner/mgr. Happy Camp, Calif., 1976—. Author: Barns of Yesteryear, 1993; co-author: Sierra Nevada Wildlife, 1996, The Californian Wildlife Region, 1999; pub. over 100 titles on natural history and Native American subjects. Mem. Am. Booksellers Assn. Baha'i Faith. Avocations: gardening, backpacking. Home: PO Box 1045 3633 Indian Creek Rd Happy Camp CA 96039-9706 Office: Naturegraph Publishers Inc 3543 Indian Creek Rd Happy Camp CA 96039-9706 Home Phone: 530-493-2845; Office Phone: 800-390-5353, 530-493-5353.

BLACK, BARBARA ARONSTEIN, legal history educator; b. Bklyn., May 6, 1933; d. Robert and Minnie (Polenberg) A.; m. Charles L. Black, Jr., Apr. 11, 1954; children— Gavin B., David A., Robin E. BA, Bklyn. Coll., 1953; LLB, Columbia U., 1955; MPhil, Yale U., 1970, PhD, 1975; LLD (hon.), N.Y. Law Sch., 1986, Marymount Manhattan Coll., 1986, Vt. Law Sch., 1987, Coll. of New Rochelle, 1987, Smith Coll., 1988, Bklyn. Coll., 1988, York U., Toronto, Can., 1990, Georgetown U., 1991. Assoc. in law Columbia U. Law Sch., NYC, 1955-56; lectr. history Yale U., New Haven, 1974-76, asst. prof. history, 1976-79, assoc. prof. law, 1979-84; George Welwood Murray prof. legal history Columbia U. Law Sch., NYC, 1984—, dean faculty of law, 1986-91. Editor Columbia Law Rev., 1953-55. Active N.Y. State Ethics Commn., 1992-95. Recipient Fed. Bar Assn. prize Columbia Law Sch., 1955 Mem. Am. Soc. Legal History (pres. 1986-90), Am. Acad. Arts and Scis., Am. Philos. Soc., Mass. Hist. Soc., Supreme Ct. Hist. Soc., Selden Soc., Century Assn. Office: Columbia U Sch Law 435 W 116th St New York NY 10027-7201 Office Phone: 212-854-5735. Business E-Mail: BAB@law.columbia.edu.

BLACK, BOYD CARSON, small business owner; b. Spencer, Nebr., Mar. 31, 1926; s. Royal Mitchel and Gladys Emma (Carlson) B.; m. Margaret Ann Prchal, June 26, 1948; children: Barton, Cheryl, Brian, Roger, Eric. Student, Wayne State Coll. Boiler maker various firms, 1947-56; owner, operator Blacco Splicing and Rigging Loft, Columbus, Ohio, 1956—. Seminar instr. Am. Recreational Equipment, Greenville, N.C., 1979-88; tng. insp. Ohio State Agrl. Insps., Columbus, 1980-82; instr. safety seminars on lift equipment, Ohio, 1980—. Patentee in field. Mem. Heath City (Ohio) Charter Commn., 1963-64; chmn. Heath Zoning Bd. Appeals, 1963-68; del. Ohio Leadership Initiative, Yugoslavia, USSR, Poland, Hungary, 1990. With USN, 1943-46, PTO. Named Small Bus. Person of Yr., 1985. Mem. Am. Subcontractors Assn., Newark C. of C., Moundbuilders Babe Ruth Assn. (bd. dirs.), Am. Legion, Masons, USN Armed Guard Vets, SAR. Methodist. Avocations: fishing, camping, antique collecting, history. Home: 140 Claren Dr Newark OH 43056-1276

BLACK, BRUCE D., judge; b. Detroit, July 27, 1947; BA, Albion Coll., 1969; JD, U. Mich., 1971. Pvt. law practice, N.Mex., 1972—91; judge N.Mex. Ct. Appeals, 1991-96, US Dist. Ct. N.Mex., 1996—. Office: US Dist Ct NMex 106 Federal Pl Santa Fe NM 87501 Office Phone: 505-955-8830. Office Fax: 505-955-8835.

BLACK, BUD (HARRY RALSTON BLACK), professional baseball manager; b. San Mateo, Calif., June 30, 1957; s. Harry Black. BS in Fin., San Diego State U., 1979. Pitcher Seattle Mariners, 1981, Kans. City Royals, 1982—88, Cleve. Indians, 1988—90, 1995, Toronto Blue Jays, 1990, San Francisco Giants, 1991—94; pitching coach LA Angels of Anaheim, 1999—2006; mgr. San Diego Padres, 2006—.*

BLACK, CANDACE REGAN, language educator; d. Elizabeth Anne and John Joseph Black. BA, SUNY, Potsdam, 1992; MBA, U. Rochester, N.Y., 1994, MA in Tchg., 1997. Cert. French, bus., social studies tchr. N.Y., 2000, world langs. other than English Nat. Bd. for Profl. Tchg. Stds., 2005. Tchr. French, Rush-Henrietta Sr. H.S., Henrietta, NY, 2000—06; french tchr. Eastridge H.S., Rochester, NY, 2006—. V.p., chair edn. com. Linkages of Rochester, Inc., NY, 2005—06; bd. mem., newsletter editor Rennes Rochester Sister Cities Orgn., NY, 2005—06. Office: Eastridge HS 2350 Ridge Rd E Rochester NY 14622 Home Phone: 585-872-0294.

BLACK, CAROLE, broadcast executive; b. Cin. BA in English Lit., Ohio State U. With Procter & Gamble, Cin.; account supr., sr. v.p., mgmt. rep. DDB Needham, Chgo., 1983—86; v.p. worldwide mktg. home video Walt Disney Co., 1986—88, sr. v.p. mktg., TV, 1988—94; pres., gen. mgr. NBC 4, LA, 1994—99; pres., CEO Lifetime Entertainment Svcs., 1999—2005. Named one of 100 Most Powerful Women in Entertainment, Hollywood Reporter, 2004; recipient CTAM Hall of Fame Award, 2000, Nat. Breast Cancer Coalition Leadership Award, 2000, Muse Award, NY Women in Film & Television, 2000, Impact Award, Nat. Hispanic Media Coalition, 2001, Women Who Change the World Award, NY Women in Communications, 2002, Matrix Award, 2002. Office: Lifetime Entertainment Svcs 309 W 49th St New York NY 10019-7404

BLACK, CAROLINE KAPUSTA, lawyer; b. Derby, Conn. BS, Cornell U., 1982; JD, Stetson Coll. Law, 1984. Asst. state atty. Hillsborough County State Atty.'s Office, Tampa, Fla., 1985-89; ptnr. Sessums, Mason Black & Caballero, Tampa, 1989—. Pres. Ctr. for Women, Tampa, 1995-97; chair Fla. Bar Grievance Com. 13A, Tampa, 1995. Mem. Fla. Bar (mem. exec. coun. family law sect. 1995-2002, chair 2002-03), Hillsborough County Bar Assn. (bd. dirs. family law sect. 2003—, pres.-elect 2006—). Office: Sessums Mason Black and Caballero 307 S Magnolia Ave Tampa FL 33606-2237 Office Phone: 813-251-9200.

BLACK, CAROLYN REBECCA, music educator; b. Fayetteville, NY, May 6, 1945; d. Henry Andrew Black Sr. and Madeline Jackson Black; m. Arthur Jerome Hightower Sr., Dec. 28, 2002; m. Thomas Benjamin Berrien (div.); children: Dawn Berrien, Jenelle Berrien, Todd Berrien. MusB, U. N.C., 1968; MA, Columbia U., 1976. Music tchr. Mt. Vernon (N.Y.) Pub. Sch., 1968—75; choral music tchr. Ossining (N.Y.) H.S., 1975—2002. Choral dir., organist St. Matthews United Meth. Ch., Ossining, 1977—85, St. Paul's on the Hill Episcopal Ch., Ossining, 1989—, NY Acad. of Tchg. and Learning, 1997. Bd. dirs. Ossining Children's Ctr., 2004—, sec. bd. dirs., 2004. Named Tchr. of Yr., Ossining Parents, Tchrs. and Students, 1991, Nat. Honor Soc., Astra chpt., 1996. Mem.: N.Y. State Sch. Music

Assn. (h.s. music chair 2002—), N.Y. State Tchrs. Theatre Edn. Assn. (nomination chair), Music Educators Nat. Conf. Episcopalian. Avocations: gardening, reading. Home: 639 Kissam Rd Peekskill NY 10566

BLACK, CATHLEEN PRUNTY, publishing executive; b. Chgo., Apr. 26, 1944; d. James Hamilton and Margaret (Harrington) Black; m. Thomas E. Harvey, May 20, 1982; children: Alison, Duffy. BA, Trinity Coll., 1966. Advt. sales rep. Holiday mag., NYC, 1966-69, Travel & Leisure mag., NYC, 1969-70, New York mag., 1970-72; advt. dir. Ms. mag., 1972-75, assoc. pub., 1975-77, New York mag., 1977-79, pub., 1979-83; pres. USA Today, 1983, pub., 1984-91; exec. v.p. mktg. Gannett Co., Inc., 1985—91, also bd. dirs.; pres., CEO Newspaper Assn. Am., Reston, Va., 1991—95; pres. Hearst Mags., NYC, 1996—. Bd. dirs. iVillage, Coca-Cola Co., 1990—91, 1993—, IBM, 1995—. Trustee U. Notre Dame. Named Pub. Exec. of Yr., Advt. Age, 2000, Corp. Pub. of Yr., Delaney Report, 2006; named one of Most Powerful Women in Am. Bus., Fortune mag., 100 Most Influential Bus. Leaders, Crain's N.Y. Bus., 2002, 100 Most Powerful Women in World, Forbes mag., 2005—06, 50 Most Powerful Women in Bus., Fortune mag., 2005, 2006, Next 20 Female CEOs, Pink Mag. & Forté Found., 2006; recipient Muriel Fox Award for Comm. Leadership Toward a Just Soc., NOW, 2000, Stephen P. Duggan Award, Inst. Internat. Edn., 2002, Henry Johnson Fisher award for lifetime achievements, Mag. Pub. Am., 2006. Mem.: Coun. on Fgn. Rels., Advt. Coun. (bd. mem.). Office: Hearst 250 W 55th St New York NY 10019-5201*

BLACK, CLANTON CANDLER, JR., biochemistry professor, researcher; b. Tampa, Fla., Nov. 27, 1931; s. Clanton Candler Black and Cora (Winfred) Eady B.; m. Betty Louise Dantzler, Apr. 10, 1952; children—Marjorie Kay, Clanton Candler III, Julia Renee BSA., U. Fla., 1953, MSA., 1957, PhD, 1960. NIH postdoctoral fellow Cornell U., Ithaca, NY, 1960-62; C. F. Kettering Found. fellow Kettering Research Lab., Antioch Coll., Yellow Springs, Ohio, 1962-63, staff scientist, asst. prof., 1963-67; prof. biochemistry U. Ga., Athens, 1967—, disting. rsch. prof. biochemistry/molecular biology, 1982—. Cons. plant biochemistry, physiology Internat. Atomic Energy Agy. Nat. Agr. U., Lima, Peru, 1981—Editor: CO2 Metabolism and Plant Productivity, 1976, Net Carbon Dioxide Assimilation in Higher Plants, 1972, Handbook of Biosolar Resources, Vol. IA, IB, 1982. Served to cpl. U.S. Army, 1953-55 Recipient Merit award Bot. Soc. Am., 1981, Alex Laurie award Am. Soc. Hort. Sci., 1984, Gold medal Bulgarian Acad. Scis., 2004; Fulbright scholar, 1976, 98-99. Fellow AAAS; mem. Am. Soc. Plant Physiology (sec.-treas., v.p., pres. 1975-79), Am. Soc. Biol. Chemists, Russian Soc. Plant Physiology (hon.), Sigma Xi, Phi Kappa Phi, Phi Sigma, Gamma Sigma Delta. Baptist. Office: U Ga Dept Biochem and Molecular Bio Life Scis Bldg Athens GA 30602 Office Phone: 706-542-1778. Business E-Mail: ccblack@bmb.uga.edu.

BLACK, CLIFFORD MERWYN, academic administrator, sociologist, educator; b. Lafayette, Ohio, Mar. 6, 1942; s. Richard Allen and Ivaloo Mae (Mosher) B.; m. Angelica Hernandez; children: Jonathan Andrew, Marisela, Jose Angel, Carlos Alberto. BA, Adrian Coll., 1963; MDiv, Meth. Theol. Sch., 1966; PhD, Northwestern U., 1972. Cert. clin. sociologist; lic. profl. counselor. Asst. prof. Wilberforce (Ohio) U., 1973-74, The Ohio State U., Mansfield, 1974-78; instr. U. North Tex., Denton, 1978-79, asst. prof., 1979-83, sociology program dir., 1982-83, assoc. prof., 1983-89, chair Ctr. for Pub. Svc., 1984-86, chair dept. sociology, 1986-87, assoc. dean Sch. Cmty. Svc., 1986-88, 91-92, acting dean Sch. Cmty. Svc., 1988-90, prof., 1989-92, Tex. A&M Internat. U., Laredo, 1989-92, dean Sch. Edn. and Arts and Scis., 1992-94, dean Coll. of Arts and Humanities, 1994-96, 96-2001, Webb Co. Tex. Planning Coun., 1996-2001, Webb Co. Tex. Drug Planning Com., 1996-2001, Webb Co. Tex. Jail Case Mgmt. Supervision, 1998-2001, Webb Co. Drug Ct. Supervising Com., 1998-2001; prin. investigator US Dept. Justice/Webb Co. Tex., Laredo, Tex., 1996—2001, 3d Party Payment Com.; adminstrv. cons. Webb County Sheriff's Dept., 2005—; dir. Internat. Justice Ctr., 1996—2002; pres. CJUS Rsch. and Program Cons. Internat. Inc., 2002—; adminstrv. coord. Webb County Sheriff's Dept., 2005—. Cons. Denton County Sheriff's Dept., Denton, 1984-89; mem. state coordinating bd. com. on Two Yr. Coll. Curriculum, 1986-89. Author: (book) Alternative Sentencing: Electronically Monitored Correction Supervision, 1992; contbg. editor for Clin. Sociology Newsletter, 1983-84; mem. editorial bd. Sociol. Practice, 1984-89; contbr. numerous articles to profl. jours. Pres. Sam Houston Elem. PTA, Denton, 1985-86; trustee Denton Ind. Sch. Dist., 1986-89; mem. United Way Bd., Laredo, 1994-95; active St. Martin de Porres Cath. Ch. Recipient U.S. Dept. Justice award for Rsch. Prgms. for Elimination of Illegal Drugs. Mem. Nat. Clin. Sociology Assn. (v.p. 1984-86, certification bd. mem. 1984-90, nat. certifier 1985-92, nat. program chair for ann. meeting 1984-85), Clin. Sociology Assn. Tex. (pres. 1982-84), Nat. Sociol. Practice Assn. (exec. bd. 1990-91), Nat. Sociol. Practice Assn. (certification bd. 1990-91), Am. Sociol. Assn. (sect bd. 1981-84, sociol. practice sect. sec./treas. 1981-84), Southwestern Sociol. Assn. (chair com. on professions 1983-86), Am. Criminology Soc., Acad. Criminal Justice Scis. Avocations: field archaeology, walking, reading, writing, drawing. Home and Office: 8506 Callow Ct Laredo TX 78045-1983

BLACK, CORA JEAN, evangelist, wedding consultant; b. Mt. Pleasant, Pa., July 30, 1941; d. Alfred John and Ruby Isabel (Waugaman) B.; m. Arthur Byron Everett, Mar. 27, 1974. Student, Greensburg Bus. Coll., 1962, Moody Bible Inst., 1966; DD, Internat. Bible Inst., 1972; postgrad., Seton Hill Coll., 1986. Ordained evangelist, 1962; notary pub.; diplomate Clin. Forensic Counseling, 2000. Advt. display silk-screen artist West Penn Power Co., Greensburg, Pa., 1962—63; missionary to W.I. Gospel Light Ministry, New Stanton, Pa., 1964; dir. pub. rels. Assn. Internat. Gospel Assemblies of DeSota, Mo., 1982—; founder, pres. America for Christ Ministry, New Stanton, 1974—; owner, founder Sea-Jay's All Faith Wedding Chapel, New Stanton; chaplain Westmoreland County Prison, 1999—2001; cert. signing agt., full agt. Harrisburg for Notary Svc., Pa., 2000—. Coord. Holy Land Tours, 1971—83; owner Sea-Jay All Pet Hotel, New Stanton; ordained mem. Internat. Pentecostal Holiness Ch. Pa. Conf. Author Christian literature; composer: (pub. and recorded Gospel music including) Christ is Coming! Are You Ready?, America for Christ, and the Joy of Life; host weekly radio programs. Mem. disaster action ARC, 2002—, vol. DAT- mass care response family svc.; mem. Internat. Critical Incident Stress Found., Inc., 2002—; historian Aux. AM. Legion unit 446, 2004—; pres. C.S.W. Regents Club, 2004—; queen Sea-Jay's Red Hatter's Soc., 2005—. Recipient award, Nat. Notary Assn., 2001. Mem.: DAR (regent chpt. Pa. 76 chpt. 2001—, pres. Ctrl. SW Pa. Regent Club 2004—, 1st v.p. Ctrl. NW Regents Club 2007—), Assn. Civil War Women (pres. tent 156 2002—03), Women in Christ, God and Country Nat. Heritage Soc. (pres. 2000—), Women's Relief Corp., Tri-State Gospel Music Assn. (treas. 1998—2000), Assn. Internat. Gospel Assemblies, Internat. Platform Assn., Pa. Assn. Notaries, Am. Assn. Christian Counselors (charter, counselor), Ctrl. Westmoreland C. of C., Am. Acad. Bereavement Assn. (cert. bereavement facilitator), Am. Psychotherapy Assn. (cert.), Assn. Internat. Gospel Assemblies (internat. pub. rels. dir.), Am. Acad. Cert. Forensic Counselors, BMI, New Stanton Hist. Soc. (sec.-treas. 1995—), Westmoreland Hist. Soc. (nat. chaplain 2001—02), Ladies Grand Army Rep. (nat. chaplain 2001—), Aux. Sons. Union Vets. Civil War, Daus. Union Vets. Civil War 1861-1865 (chaplain 2002—03). Republican. Achievements include having married over 3,500 couples since 1962. Avocations: travel, photography, decorating and designing, painting, animals. Home: 440 N Center Ave PO 192 New Stanton PA 15672-0192 Home Phone: 724-516-7797; Office Phone: 724-925-2366. E-mail: seajay77@juno.com.

BLACK, CREED C., JR., lawyer; BA magna cum laude, Yale U., 1973; JD cum laude, U. Pa., 1976. Bar: Pa. 1976, US Supreme Ct. 1989. Law clk. to Hon. Herbert A. Fogel US Dist. Ct. (ea. dist.) Pa., 1976-77; trial atty. criminal divsn. US Dept. Justice, Washington, 1977-78; spl. asst. to U.S. atty. US Dist. Ct. (ea. dist.) Va., 1978; mem. organized crime and racketeering sect. Cleve. Strike Force, 1978-80, Phila. Strike Force, 1980-82; atty. Ballard Spahr Andrews & Ingersoll, Phila., 1982-96; pvt. practice Phila., 1996—. Mem.: ABA, Pa. Assn. Criminal Def. Lawyers, Nat. Assn. Criminal Def. Lawyers, Phila. Bar Assn., Fed. Bar Assn., Order of Coif. Office: 1700 Market St Ste 3025 Philadelphia PA 19103-3913 Office Phone: 215-564-4060. Business E-Mail: ccb@creedblack.com.

BLACK, CREED CARTER, newspaper executive; b. Harlan, Ky., July 15, 1925; s. Creed Carter and Mary (Cole) B.; m. Mary C. Davis, Dec. 28, 1947 (div. 1976); children: Creed Carter, Steven D., Douglas S.; m. Elsa Goss, Dec. 9, 1977; 1 child, Michelle. BS with highest distinction and honors in Polit. Sci., Northwestern U., 1949; MA, U. Chgo., 1952; LLD (hon.), Davidson Coll., 1991; LHD (hon.), Ctr. Coll., 1996. Reporter Paducah (Ky.) Sun-Democrat, 1942-43, 46; editor Daily Northwestern, 1947; copy editor Chgo. Sun-Times, 1949, Chgo. Herald-Am., 1950; editl. writer Nashville Tennessean, 1950-57, exec. editor, 1957-59; v.p., exec. editor Savannah (Ga.) Morning News and Savannah Evening Press, 1959-60, Wilmington (Del.) Morning News and Evening Jour., 1960-64; mng. editor Chgo. Daily News, 1964-68, exec. editor, 1968-69; asst. sec. for legislation HEW, 1969-70; editor Phila. Inquirer, 1970-77; chmn., pub. Lexington (Ky.) Herald-Leader, 1977-88; pres., trustee Knight Found., Miami, Fla., 1988-98. With 100th Inf. divsn. AUS, WWII, ETO. Decorated Bronze Star; recipient Northwestern U. Alumni medal, 1973 Mem. Newspaper Assn. of Am., So. Newspaper Pubs. Assn. (pres. 1987—), Am. Soc. Newspaper Editors (pres. 1983), Nat. Conf. Editl. Writers (pres. 1962), Riviera Country Club, Kappa Tau Alpha, Lambda Chi Alpha. Methodist. Home: 11044 SW 77th Court Cir Miami FL 33156-3766

BLACK, DANIEL HUGH, retired social studies educator; b. Arab, Ala., July 4, 1947; s. Lehmon Ray and Lillian Geneve (Divine) B. BS, U. Ala., Tuscaloosa, 1970; MEd, Ala. A&M U., 1976; PhD, Vanderbilt U., 1981; MA, St. John's Coll., Annapolis, Md., 1988. Social studies tchr., advanced placement govt. tchr. Grissom High Sch., Huntsville, Ala., 1970-98. Adj. instr. history Calhoun C.C., 1982—99, Ala. A&M U., 1989—94, Great Books in the Western World, U. Ala., Huntsville; essay reader advanced placement Am. govt. and politics exam. Ednl. Testing Svc., 1991—96; internet store mgr. Blacks Furniture City. Mem. NEA, Ala. Edn. Assn., Huntsville Edn. Assn., Nat. Trust for Hist. Preservation (master class James Madison and Federalist Papers 1989), Phi Delta Kappa. Home: 1019 Old Monrovia Rd NW Apt 232 Huntsville AL 35806-3505 Office: Black's Furniture City 124 N Brindlee Mountain Pkwy Arab AL 35016-1316 Office Phone: 256-931-2529. Personal E-mail: bfc@hiwaay.net.

BLACK, DAVID, writer, educator; b. Boston, Apr. 21, 1945; s. Henry Arnold and Zelda Edith (Hodosh) B.; m. Deborah Hughes Keehn, June 22, 1968 (div. 1994); children: Susannah Haden, Tobiah Samuel McKee; m. Barbara Weisberg, June 20, 1996. BA cum laude, Amherst Coll., 1967; MFA, Columbia U., 1971. Free-lance writer, 1971—; writer-in-residence Mt. Holyoke Coll., South Hadley, Mass., 1982-86. Scholar-in-residence Kirkland House Mt. Holyoke Coll., Harvard U.; guest lectr. Tisch Sch. of the Arts, Harvard Coll., 2002—. Author: Like Father, 1978 (Notable Book of Yr. NY Times, 1978, One of 7 Best Novels of Yr. Washington Post), Minds, 1982, Peep Show, 1986, An Impossible Life, 1998; (non-fiction) Ekstasy, 1975, The King of Fifth Avenue (Notable Book of Yr. NY Times AP, NY Mag. 1981), Murder at the Met, 1984, Medicine Man, 1985, The Plague Years, 1986 (Nat. Mag. award reporting, Nat. Assn. Sci. Writers award); (play) An Impossible Life, 1998; (screenplay) The Confession, 1999 (Winner Writers Guild Best TV Movie of Yr., Adaptation 1999), (teleplay) Final Jeopardy; contbr. articles and stories to Harper's, The Atlantic, NY Times Mag., others; story editor Hill Street Blues; prodr. Miami Vice; supervising prodr. H.E.L.P., Gidgon Oliver, Law and Order (Golden Globe nominee 1992, Edgar nominee 1992, 99, Emmy nominee 1992, 98, ABA Certificate of Merit 1998); co-creator, supervising prodr.: The Nasty Boys; co-creator, exec. prodr.: Under Fire, The Good Policeman, The Cosby Mysteries, co-exec. prodr.: Sidney Lumet's 100 Centre Street, 1999-2002; exec. prodr.: CSI-Miami, 2003; creator, exec. prodr. Copshop, 2004, Kojak, 2005, Law and Order Trial by Jury, 2005; cons. prodr. Richard Dreyfuss, The Education of Max Bickford, 2002, Monk, 2002; contbg. editor Rolling Stone, 1986-89; prodr.: Cardgnio, Willamstown Theater Festival, 2006; mng. editor: Perfect 10, 2005-07. Recipient Atlantic Firsts award Atlantic Monthly, 1973, Playboy's Best Article of Yr. award Playboy Mag., 1979, Nat. Assn. Sci. Writers award, 1985, hon. mention for Best Essay of Yr., 1986, Giorgi award, Cert. Merit for excellence in writing, 1998; grantee Nat. Endowment Arts, 1979. Mem. SAG, Mystery Writers Am. (former bd. dirs.), PEN, Internat. Assn. Mystery Writers, Authors Guild, Writers Guild East, Williams Club, Century Assn., Players, Explorer's Club, Columbia Club. Jewish/Unitarian.

BLACK, DONNA LORD, psychologist; d. Clarence Gaither and Edith Wade Lord; m. Ronald Gregory Black, Oct. 6, 1949; children: Jason Andrew, Allison Pauline Handler. AA, San Jacinto Coll., Pasadena, Tex., 1972; BS, U. Houston, Clear Lake, 1988, MA, 1992. Lic. Specialist in Sch. Psychology Tex. State Bd. Examiners of Psychologists, 1996, Psychol. Assoc. Tex. State Bd. Examiners of Psychologists, 1994, cert. instr. Nonviolent Crisis Intervention Internat. Assn. Nonviolent Crisis Intervention Cert., 2000. Caseworker, investigator Galveston County Children's Protective Svcs., Tex., 1988—90; intern Tex. Children's Hosp., Houston, 1992; lic. specialist sch. psychology Dickinson Ind. Sch. Dist., Tex., 1992—99; coord. student support svcs. Santa Fe Ind. Sch. Dist., Tex., 1999—2001; specialist sch. psychology Pasadena Ind. Sch. Dist., Tex., 2001—02; cons. Houston, 2002—04; coord. psychol. and diagnostic svcs. East Wharton County Co-Op, Tex., 2004—. Adj. faculty U. Houston Clear Lake, 2002—04; commentator radio talk show Attack on America: A Nation Recovers; apptd. lic. bd. mem. Tex. State Bd. Examiners of Psychologists, 2007. Vol. Wharton County Spl. Olympics; chairperson Clear Brook H.S. Project Graduation, Friendswood, Tex., 1994—95; youth coord. Cokesbury United Meth. Ch., Houston, 1991—93; chairperson Tex. Air N.G., 147th Fighter Wing Family Readiness Group, Houston, 2001—04. Named to, Nat. Dean's List, 1988—89; recipient Outstanding Coll. Students Am. award, 1989; scholar, Ch. Women United, 1986; Scholarship, Assn. Bus. and Profl. Women, Bay Area chpt., 1986, 1987. Mem.: NASP, Tex. Assn. Sch. Psychologists (newsletter editor, sec., area rep. 2000—06, Outstanding Sch. Psychologist of Yr. 2005), Tex. Coun. of Administrators of Spl. Edn. Methodist. Avocations: baseball, music, digital slideshow productions. Office: Region 4 Edn Svc Ctr 7145 W Tidwell Houston TX 77092 Home Phone: 281-346-0034. E-mail: dblack@esc4.net.

BLACK, EDWARD G., lawyer; BA with honors, Brown Univ., 1986; JD, Univ. Calif., Berkeley, 1989. Bar: Calif. 1989, Mass. 1997. Law clk. Judge D. Lowell Jensen, US Dist. Ct. (no. Calif.); ptnr. corp. dept. & co-head Fish & Neave IP group Ropes & Gray, Boston. Mem.: Boston Bar Assn. (past co-chmn. Intellectual Property com.). Office: Ropes & Gray 1 International Pl Boston MA 02110-2624 Office Phone: 617-951-7984. Office Fax: 617-951-7050. Business E-Mail: edward.black@ropesgray.com.

BLACK, GARY D., investment company executive; Grad., U. Pa.; MBA, Harvard U., 1988. Analyst Sanford C. Bernstein & Co., Alliance Bernstein, exec. v.p., head Instl. Asset Mgmt., 1999—2001; mng. dir. US Internat. And Third Party Bus. Goldman Sachs & Co., 2001—02; chief investment officer Global Equities Goldman Sachs Asset Mgmt., 2002—04; pres. Janus Capital Group Inc., Denver, 2004—05, chief investment officer, 2004—, CEO, 2006—. Office: Janus Capital Group Inc 151 Detroit St Denver CO 80206-4923 Office Phone: 303-333-3863. Office Fax: 212-642-8442. E-mail: gary.black@janus.com.

BLACK, GINGER ELIZABETH, elementary school educator; d. Richard Temple and Mary Helen Crouch; 1 child, Caitlin Emily. BA in Edn., Lynchburg Coll., 1970; MA, U. Va., Charlottesville, 1974. Advanced profl. ednl. cert. Md. Reading specialist Montgomery County Schs., Rockville, Md., 1973—. Ednl. cons., tutor, McLean, Va., 1995—. Author: Making the Grade, 1989. Mem. Friends of the Nat. Zoo, Washington, 1993—98. Mem.: Montgomery County Edn. Assn. (Broome award for outstanding pub. 1992), Md. State Tchrs. Assn. (assoc.), Internat. Reading Assn. (assoc.), U. Va. Alumni Assn. Episcopalian. Avocations: travel, gardening, reading. Home: 7208 Evans Mill Rd Mc Lean VA 22101 Home Phone: 703-556-0856; Office Phone: 301-320-6555. Personal E-mail: gblack4720@aol.com.

BLACK, HENRY RICHARD, physician; b. NYC, June 1, 1942; s. David Robert and Beatrice (Morris) Black; m. Benita L. Daniels, Apr. 19, 2002; children: Matthew, Dana. AB, Columbia U., NYC, 1963; MD, NYU, 1967. Diplomate Am. Bd. Internal Medicine, cert. hypertension specialist Am. Soc. Hypertension, 2001. Intern Johns Hopkins Hosp., Balt., 1967—68, resident in internal medicine, 1970—71; resident Yale-New Haven Hosp., 1971—72, chief resident internal medicine, 1974—75; fellow Yale U., New Haven, 1972—74, practice medicine specializing in preventive cardiology and hypertension, 1975—92; asst. prof. Yale U. Med. Sch., New Haven, 1975—79, assoc. prof., 1979—88, prof., 1988—92, dir. hypertension svcs., 1975—92; Charles J. and Margaret Roberts prof. preventive medicine Rush U. Med. Ctr., Chgo., 1992—2006, chmn. dept. preventive medicine, 1992—2005; assoc. v.p. rsch., assoc. dean rsch. NYU Sch. Medicine, 2000—05, clin. prof. internal medicine, 2007—. Bd. dirs. Am. Heart Assn., Conn., 1985—87; fellow Coun. on Hypertension. Contbr. articles to profl. jours. With USPHS, 1968—70. Fellow: ACP, Am. Soc. Hypertension (exec. com. 1991—96, exec. coun. 2002—, pres. elect 2006—), Am. Heart Assn. (coun. epidemiology & prevention, fellow coun. on nutrition), Internat. Soc. Hypertension; mem.: Am. Soc. Preventive Cardiology (pres. 1994—95), Columbia Coll. Alumni Assn. (bd. dirs. 1983—87, v.p., acad. affairs 1986—87), Am. Fedn. Clin. Rsch. Jewish. Home: 60 E 9th St Apt 526 New York NY 10003 Office: NYU Sch Medicine 530 First Ave Stairwell 9V New York NY 10016 Office Phone: 212-263-7751. Personal E-mail: hrbmd63@gmail.com.

BLACK, HILLEL MOSES, publisher; b. NYC, Apr. 8, 1929; s. Isidore and Ida (Feldstein) B. BA, U. Chgo., 1949, M.English and Fgn. Langs., 1952. Copy boy N.Y. Times, NYC, 1952-53; reporter AP, Pitts., Newark and Phila., 1954-58; freelance writer NYC, 1959-65; editor Saturday Evening Post, NYC, 1966-67; sr. editor William Morrow & Co., NYC, 1967-77, editor-in-chief, 1977-82; pub. gen. books div. Macmillan Pub. Co., NYC, 1983-87; pub. Richardson, Steirman & Black, NYC, 1987-88; pres. Birch Lane Press, 1989-99; editorial dir. Carol Pub. Group, NYC, 1989-99; exec. editor Sourcebooks, Naperville, Ill., 2000—. Author: The Watch Dogs of Wall Street, Buy Now, Pay Later, The American Schoolbook. Mem. Century Assn., Pubs. Club. E-mail: hillwen@aol.com.

BLACK, JACK (THOMAS BLACK), actor; b. Santa Monica, Calif., Aug. 28, 1969; s. Thomas Black and Judith Cohen; m. Tanya Haden, Mar. 14, 2006; 1 child. Student, UCLA. Mem. The Actors Gang, LA. Actor: (films) Bob Roberts, 1992, Airborne, 1993, Demolition Man, 1993, The Never Ending Story III, 1994, Blind Justice, 1994, Dead Man Walking, 1995, Bye Bye Love, 1995, Waterworld, 1995, Crossworlds, 1996, Bio-Dome, 1996, The Cable Guy, 1996, The Fan, 1996, Mars Attacks!, 1996, The Jackal, 1997, Johnny Skidmarks, 1998, I Still Know What You Did Last Summer, 1998, Bongwater, 1998, Enemy of the State, 1998, Cradle Will Rock, 1999, The Love Letter, 1999, Jesus' Son, 1999, High Fidelity, 2000, Frank's Book, 2001, Saving Silverman, 2001, Shallow Hal, 2001, Ron Ronnie Run, 2002, Orange County, 2002, (voice only) Ice Age, 2002, Tenacious D: The Complete Masterworks, 2003, Melvin Goes to Dinner, 2003, The School of Rock, 2003 (nominated Golden Globe for Best Performance by an Actor in a Motion Picture-Musical or Comedy, 2003), Envy, 2004, Anchorman: The Legend of Ron Burgundy, 2004, (voice only) Shark Tale, 2004, King Kong, 2005, Danny Roane: First Time Director, 2006, Nacho Libre, 2006, The Holiday, 2006; actor, writer: Tenacious D: The Pick of Destiny, 2006; actor: (TV films) Our Shining Moment, 1991, Marked for Murder, 1993, The Innocent, 1994, Heat Vision and Jack, 1999, Lord of the Piercing, 2002, Jack Black: Spider-Man, 2002; (TV series) Tenacious D, 1999, Computerman, 2003, (voice) Crank Yankers, 2002,: (TV appearances) The Golden Palace, 1991, Life Goes On, 1993, Northern Exposure, 1993, All-American Girl, 1995, Pride & Joy, 1995, The X Files, 1995, Touched By an Angel, 1995, The Single Guy, 1995, Picket Fences, 1995, Mr. Show with Bob and David, 1996, Clone High, 2002, Will & Grace, 2003, Player$, 2003, Cracking Up, 2004; singer, songwriter with Tenacious D: albums Tenacious D, 2001. Recipient Best Performance by a Human-Male (Peter Jackson's King Kong: The Official Game of the Movie), Spike TV Video Game Awards, 2005. Office: United Talent Agy 9560 Wilshire Blvd Ste 500 Beverly Hills CA 90212*

BLACK, JAMES ISAAC (JIB), III, lawyer; b. Lakeland, Fla., Oct. 26, 1951; s. James Isaac Jr. and Juanita (Feemster) B.; m. Vikki Harrison, June 15, 1973; children: Jennifer Leigh, Katharine Ann, Stephanie Marie. BA, U. Fla., 1973; JD, Harvard U., 1976. Bar: Fla. 1976, NY 1977, US Tax Ct. 1984. Assoc. Sullivan & Cromwell, NYC, 1976-84, ptnr., 1984—, and mng. ptnr. estates and personal practice group, 1995—. Mem. ABA, NY State Bar Assn. (persons under disability com. trusts and estates law sect. 1984-90), Leader Shape, Inc. (bd. dirs.), Assn. of Bar of City of NY (sec. 1980-81, trusts estates and surrogates ct. com. 1980-83), Scarsdale Golf Club (past pres.), Alpha Tau Omega Found., Flagler Found., Sheridan Arts Found. Office: Sullivan & Cromwell LLP 125 Broad St Fl 28 New York NY 10004-2489 Office Phone: 212-558-3948. Office Fax: 212-558-3588. Business E-Mail: blackj@sullcrom.com.

BLACK, JAMES JENS, plastic surgeon; b. Torrance, Calif., May 14, 1959; s. J. Ralph and Gladys Olava Black; m. Karen Seitzer Black, Apr. 27, 1991; children: KAty, James, Sherry, Joey, Jonny. MD, Chgo. Med. Sch., 1988. Bd. cert. AM. Bd. Plastic Surgery, 1997. Intern UCLA, Torrance, Calif., 1988—92; resident Baylor Coll. Medicine, Houston, 1992—94; clin. assoc. prof. plastic surgery UCLA, LA, 1996—2002; chief plastic surgery Little Company Mary Hosp., Torrance, 2002—05. Mayor City Rolling Hills, Calif. Fellow, U. Tex., Houston, 1994—95. Fellow: Am. Coll. Surgeons; mem.: Calif. Soc. Plastic Surgeons, Am. Soc. Plastic Surgeons. Office: 22930 Crenshaw Blvd Torrance CA 90505 Office Phone: 310-530-4200.

BLACK, JAMES ROBERT, industrial engineer; b. Davenport, Iowa, Feb. 17, 1948; s. Robert James and Anne Louise (Johnson) Black; m. Mary Ann O'Malley, June 5, 1971; 1 child, Robert Joseph. BS in Indsl. Engring., Iowa State U., Ames, 1970, MS, 1971; MBA, U. Chgo., 1976. Indsl. engr. Inland Steel Co., East Chicago, Ind., 1971-76, sr. indsl. engr., 1976-77; indsl. engring. supr. Clark Equipment Co., Jackson, Mich., 1977-78; indsl. engring. mgr. Harrison plant Graphic Sys. divsn. Rockwell Internat., Rockford, Ill., 1978-83; corp.supr. adminstrv. work mgmt. Kohler Co., Wis., 1983-87; mgr. mgf. svcs. Frigidaire Co.-Wet Products, Jefferson, Iowa, 1987—89, assembly ops. mgr., 1989—91, Kaizen facilitator Webster City, Iowa, 1991—93, paint process mgr., 1993, plant engring. mgr., 1993-95; sr. project mgr. Ctr. for Indsl. Rsch. and Svc., Iowa State U., 1995—; pres. James R. Black & Assocs., 1997—. Co-leader, guest lectr. Am. Mgmt. Assn., 1979-80; mem. adv. coun. Iowa State U. Ctr. Indsl.

Rsch. and Svc., 1992-94, pres. adv. coun., 1994; mem. planing com. Iowa conf. Mfg., 1991-93, chmn., 1993. Contbr. articles to profl. jours. Cons. project bus. divsn. Jr. Achievement, 1980; pack com. chmn. Boy Scouts Am., 1980—83, den leader, 1982—83, asst. scoutmaster, 1983—84, scoutmaster, 1984—88, dist. vice-chmn., 1984—86, dist. boy scouting chmn., 1986—88, unit commr., 2000—05, dist. mem.-at-large, 2000—01, 2006—07, asst. dist. commr., 2001, dist. vice-chmn., 2000—01, dist. commr., 2002—04, asst. coun. commr., 2004—05, woodbadge tng. staff, 2005; asst. soccer coach, 1981—83; coach, 1984—85; mem. bd. dirs. Habitat for Humanity, exec. com., 2003—, chair ptnr. family rels. com., 2003, pres., 2004—, co chair faith rels. com., 2006—; bd. dirs. Youth and Shelter Svcs., 2007—, mem. fin. com., 2007—, sec.-treas., 2007—, exec. com., 2007—, chair strategic planning com., 2007—. Fisher Governor scholar, 1968-69, Maytag scholar, 1969-70; recipient Woodbadge Boy Scouts Am., 1986, Dist. award of Merit, 2003, Silver Beaver, 2005, Woodbadge Tng. Staff, 2005, named Disting. Commr., 2006. Mem.: Soc. Mfg. Engrs., Kohler Engring. and Tech. Orgn. (program chmn. 1986, chmn. 1987), Assn. Mfg. Excellence, Am. Soc. Quality, Inst. Indsl. Engrs. (sr.; treas. 1979—80, pres. 1980—81, bd. dirs. 1989—91, v.p. 1991—92), Mainstream Living and Story County Devel. Ctr. (phonathon co-chmn. 1993—95, bd. dirs. 1994—2001, treas. 1995—97, v.p. 1997—99, pres. 1999—2001), Rotary Internat. (web page chmn. 2001—05, bd. dirs. 2005—07), Epsilon Sigma Phi, Alpha Phi Omega (univ. advisor 2000—02), Beta Gamma Sigma, Psi Chi, Gamma Epsilon Sigma, Tau Beta Pi, Phi Kappa Phi. Home: 3416 Valley View Rd Ames IA 50014-4613 Office: CIRAS/Iowa State U Coll Engring 2272 Howe Hl Ste 2620 Ames IA 50011-0001 Office Phone: 515-294-1507. Business E-Mail: jimblack@iastate.edu.

BLACK, JEFFREY P., manufacturing executive; s. Lennox K. Black. B in Criminal Justice, Old Dominion U., 1983. Head automotive and indsl. groups Teleflex Inc., Limerick, Pa., pres., 2000—, CEO, 2002—, chmn. bd., 2006—. Recipient Disting. Alumni award, Old Dominion U., 2001. Office: Teleflex 155 S Limerick Rd Royersford PA 19468*

BLACK, JERRY BERNARD, lawyer; b. Bklyn., Sept. 16, 1940; s. Paul A. and Esther (Rosenberg) B.; m. Joyce Fenmore, Nov. 29, 1975; children: Abigail B., Andrew S. AB, Harvard U., 1962, LLB, 1965. Bar: N.Y. 1966, U.S. Supreme Ct. 1976. Assoc. Cravath, Swaine & Moore, NYC, 1966-77; asst. sec., sr. counsel Revlon, Inc., NYC, 1978-83; v.p., dep. gen. counsel Hertz Corp., NYC, 1984-86; ptnr. Hill, Betts & Nash, NYC, 1987-90, Wilson, Elser, Moskowitz, Edelman & Dicker, LLP, NYC, 1990—. Mem. ABA (loan documentation subcom. of comml. fin. svcs. com. 1995), Assn. of Bar of City of N.Y. (com. inter-Am. affairs 1973-75), N.Y. State Bar Assn. Home: 149 E 73rd St New York NY 10021-3592 Office: Wilson Elser Moskowitz Edelman & Dicker LLP 150 E 42nd St New York NY 10017-5612 E-mail: jerry.black@wilsonelser.com.

BLACK, KEITH LANIER, neurosurgeon, educator; b. Tuskegee, Ala., Sept. 13, 1957; m. Carol J. Bennett; children: Teal Etoile, Keith Quinten. BS in Biomed. Sci. with distinction, U. Mich., 1978, MD with distinction, 1981. Lic. MD, Mich., Calif.; diplomate Am. Bd. Med. Examiners, Am. Bd. Neurol. Surgery. Intern, gen. surgery U. Mich. Med. Ctr., Ann Arbor, Mich., 1981—82, resident, neurol. surgery, 1982—87; head neuro-oncology UCLA Med. Ctr., 1988—97, asst. prof., divsn. neurosurgery, 1987—91, assoc. prof., divsn. neurosurgery, 1991—94, head, UCLA Comprehensive Brain Tumor Program, 1991—97, prof. surgery, divsn. neurosurgery, 1994—97, Ruth and Raymond Stotter chair dept. surgery, 1992—97, prof. neurosurgery, dept. neurology, 1995—97; Ruth and Lawrence Harvey chair in neuroscience Cedars-Sinai Med. Ctr., 1997—, dir., Comprehensive Brain Tumor Program, Dept. Surgery, 1997—, dir., divsn. neurosurgery, dept. surgery, 1997—2006, dir., Maxine Dunitz Neurosurgical Inst., Dept. Surgery, 1997—, chmn., dept. neurosurgery, 2006—; prof., chmn., dept. neurol. surgery U. Calif., Irvine Med. Ctr., LA, 1998—2000, prof., neurol. surgery, dept. neurol. surgery, 2000—03. Mem. Internat. Congress of the Skull Base Study Group, 1988; mem. scientific adv. bd., Found. for Neurosurgical Rsch., Valhalla, NY, 1990; founder, Microsurgeon, Inc., 1997, Imagine Pharm., 2003; bd. sci. counselors Nat. Inst. Neurol. Disorder and Stroke, NIH, 1994-; vis. prof. Howard U., Washington, 1986, Taiwan U., 1993, U. Mich., Ann Arbor, 1995; various univ. and hosp. com. positions, UCLA and Cedars-Sinai Med. Ctr.; bd. dir. LA World Affairs Coun., 1997-2001; med. adv. bd. mem., Nat. Brain Tumor Assn., 1997-, U. Mich. Life Sci. Inst., 2003; U. Mich. Med. Ctr. Alumni Soc. bd., 2000-2002; mem. Musella Found. for Brain Tumor Rsch. and Info., 2001-; com. mem. Calif. Inst. for Regenerative Medicine Independent Citizens Oversight Com. created under Proposition 71, 2004-2006; lect., presenter in field. Mem. editl. bd. UCLA Cancer Trials Newsletter, 1989-97, Critical Reviews in Neurosurgery, 1990-99, Perspectives in Neurological Surgery, 1992-97, Journal of Neuro-Oncology, 1994-98, Neurological Research, 1995-, Journal Radiosurgery, 1997-2001, Gene Therapy and Molecular Biology, 1998-, Neurosurgery Quarterly, 2001-, Frontiers in Bioscience, 2003-; Net editor, Neuroscience Medicine and Technology, 2001-; profiled along with patients undergoing the first clinical trials of the drug RMP-7, PBS program, The New Explorers, Outsmarting the Brain, 1996; Editor, reviewer and contbr. to profl. jours.; contbr. chpts to books. Recipient Richard F. and Eleanor W. Dwyer award for excellence in cancer rsch., 1990, LEVI Human Rights award in medicine, 1994, Medal Honor, Charles R. Drew U. Medicine and Sci., Medal Honor, 1995, Humanitarian award honoree, Calif. Hosp. Med. Found., 1996, Pres. Medal Honor, Charles M. Drew Med. Soc., 1998, Don Newcombe Humanitarian award, San Fernando Valley Chpt. Links, Inc, Top Hat award Benefit, 1998, Golden Plate award, Am. Acad. Achievement, 1999, Nat. Med. Fellowships Disting. Svc. award, 1999, Spl. Recognition, NAS, 2000, Thomas Bradley Disting. Citizen award, Kappa Alpha PSI Fraternity, Inc., 2000, Jacob Javits award, Nat. Inst. Neurol. Disorder and Stroke, NIH, 2000, Essence award, 2001, Annual Martin Luther King, Jr. Day Nat. Holiday Honored Recipient, 2002, Candle award in Sci. and Tech., Morehouse Coll., 2003, "From Whence We Came" Honored recipient, All State Ins., 2004, Highlight award, Women Pasadena, 2004, Innovator award, Nat. Role Models, Minority Access, Inc., 2004, Minorities In Bus., Corp. Angel award, 2004, Southeast Symphony Humanitarian award, Walt Disney Hall, 2005, March of Dimes Honoree, 2005, Trumpet Found. award in medicine, Turner Broadcasting, 2006; grantee Nat. Cancer Inst., 1993-96, NIH, 1994-99, Robert Wood Johnson Found., 1990, Alkermes Inc., 1994-96; named one of the Heros of Medicine, Time Mag.-Cover, 1997, Key Players in the 21st Century, Newsweek Japan-Cover, 1999, The 21 Most Important People of the 21st Century, Esquire Mag., 1999, 1000 Most Creative Individuals in the U.S.A., 2002, 40 Mist Insiring African Americans, Essence Mag., 2002; Shering scholar ACS, 1985. Mem. AMA, AAAS, Am. Assn. Neurol. Surgeons (young neurosurgeons com., 1991, scientific program com.-young neurosurgeons rep., 1993, registration com., 1994), Am. Acad. Neurol. Surgery, Brain Rsch. Inst. UCLA (adv. com.), Jonsson Comprehensive Cancer Ctr., Calif. Assn. Neurol. Surgeons, Congress of Neurol. Surgeons (sergeant-at-arms com., 1988, host com., 1989, chmn., pub. relations com., 1990, scientific program com., co-chmn., luncheon discussions, 1991, scientific program com., chmn., practical courses, 1992, scientific program com. chmn. gen. scientific session II, 1993, scientific program com., chmn. spl. courses, 1994, exec. com., 1995-96 and in conjunction with Joint Am. Assn. Neurol. Surgeons-Tumor Sect. program com., 1995-96, chmn. program com.-tumor sect., 1997), Neurosurgical Soc. Am., N. Am. Skull Base Soc. (founding mem., rsch. com. mem., 1989, membership and credintials com., 1992-95, nominating com., 1992), Soc. Neuroscience, So. Calif. Neurosurgical Soc., S.W. Oncology Group (brain com., 1994-95), Western Neurosurgical Soc., Soc. for Neuro-oncology, Pituitary Soc., Am. Assn. for Cancer Rsch. (minorities in cancer rsch. minority scholar in cancer rsch. awards com., 2006-07, Alpha Omega Alpha Hon. Med. Soc. Achievements include patents in field: method for selective opening of abnormal brain tissue capillaries, 1994, enhanced opening of abnormal brain tissue capillaries, 1998, gene associated with neoplastic disease or malignancy associated gene, 1998, A herpes simplex virus type-1 (HSV-1)-derived vector for selectively inhibiting malignant cells and methods for its use to treat cancers and to express desired traits in malignant and non-malignant mammalian cells, 1999, method for using potassium channel agonists for delivering a medicant to an abnormal brain region and/or malignant tumor, 2006. Address: 8631 W Third St Ste 800 E Los Angeles CA 90048 Office Phone: 310-423-7900. Office Fax: 310-423-0777.*

BLACK, KENNETH, JR., retired insurance company executive; b. Norfolk, Va., Jan. 30, 1925; s. Kenneth and Margaret Virginia (Wolf) B.; m. Mabel Llewellyn Folger, Sept. 20, 1948; children— Kenneth III, Kathryn Anne Shoji. AB, U. N.C., 1948, MS, 1951; PhD, U. Pa., 1953. Ptnr. Colonial Ins. Agy., Chapel Hill, N.C., 1948-50; instr. U. Pa., 1952-53; chmn. ins. dept. Ga. State U., 1953-69, Regents' prof. ins., 1959-92, C.V. Starr prof. internat. ins., 1984-92, Regent's prof. emeritus, 1992—, dean Coll. Bus. Adminstrn., 1969-84, dean emeritus Coll. Bus. Adminstrn., 1992—; pres., CEO Internat. Ins. Soc., Inc., 1988-92, vice chmn., bd. dirs., 1992—2001. Author (with Huebner): Property Insurance, 1957, Life Insurance, 1958, 1964, 1969, 1972, 1979, 1982; author: (with Russell) (books) Human Behavior and Life Insurance, 1963, 1993; author: Human Behavior and Property and Liability Insurance, 1964; author: (with Keir and Surrey) Cases in Life Insurance, 1965; author: (with Huebner and Webb) Property and Liability Insurance, 1968, 1996; author: (with Huebner and Cline), 1968, 1976, 1982; author: (with Skipper) Life Insurance, 1987, 1994; author: (with Russell) (books) Human Behavior in Business, 1972, Understanding and Influencing Human Behavior, 1981; author: (with Skipper) Life and Health Insurance, 2000; editor: (jour.) Jour. Soc. Fin. Svc. Profls., 1959—2001, (ins. series) Prentice Hall, Inc., 1959—. Vice chmn. Pres.'s Commn. R.R. Retirement, 1971-73; trustee Village of St. Joseph, 1969-80; exec. dir., trustee Ednl. Found., Inc., 1969-96. Served with USN, 1944-46. Recipient Solomon S. Huebner gold medal, Am. Coll., 1985, Laureate Ins. Hall Fame, 1993, Order of the Golden Fleece, UNC, 1948, John Newton Russell Meml. award, 1999, Round Table of N.Y. Lifetime Achievement award, 2001. Mem. Am. Risk and Ins. Assn. (pres. 1964), Phi Beta Kappa, Beta Gamma Sigma, Omicron Delta Kappa, Alpha Kappa Psi. Roman Catholic. Home: 1762 Nancy Creek Blf NW Atlanta GA 30327-1912 Office Phone: 404-651-4200.

BLACK, KENNETH W., JR., retail executive; b. Aug. 13, 1959; m. Shandra Black; 2 children. BBA, Appalachian State U., MS in Acctg. CPA. Sr. mgr., fin. instns. and retail cos. Deloitte & Touche, LLP, 1983—86; v.p., corp. controller Lowe's Cos., Inc., Wilkesboro, NC, 1997—99, sr. v.p., chief acctg. officer, 1999—. Office: Lowes Cos Inc 1000 Lowes Blvd Mooresville NC 28117

BLACK, KRIS SUSAN LYNN, marketing company executive, speaker, author, poet; b. Ladysmith, Wis., Sept. 19, 1950; d. Bruce Roger and Christine Mae (Sweet) B. AA with honors, Bakersfield Coll.; student, Phoenix Coll. Asst. mgr. jewelry dept. K Mart, Rapid City, SD, 1965-68; beauty titilist, actress, model, tchr. Patricia Stevens, Phoenix, 1968-72; Country Musics' 1st lady internat. promotional dir. for TV series Hee Haw (Buck Owens), Bakersfield, Calif., 1972-76; dir. K.B. Properties, Dallas, 1976-78; v.p. Wynn Investments, Dallas, 1978—; pres. Sunflower Mktg., Dallas, 1982—. Cons. CBI Labs., Aloe Labs. of Tex., 1979—, Richard Simmons, 1983, March of Dimes, 1976; dir. mktg. Colibri Skin Care Coming Home, healing retreat ctr.; internat. spkr. on mktg. and bus., relationships, mental health and illness, bi-polar rsch., healing from rape to internat. prosecution; Reiki master. Mem. DAR, NAMI, MHA, DBSA, M.K. Gandhi Inst. for Non-Violence. Avocations: horseback riding, water sports, singing, human and animal rights, environment protection.

BLACK, LAWRENCE, librarian; b. Bronx, NY, May 28, 1940; s. Reuben and Florence (Kuhnberg) B.; m. Linda Perlis, Dec. 8, 1968; 1 child, David. BA, Long Island U., 1963; MLS, Pratt Inst., 1965; MA in Edn., NYU, 1973; cert. in Advanced Librarianship, Columbia U., 1981. Libr. U.S. VA Hosp., Northport, NY, 1965-66; libr. assoc. NYU Librs. Gen. U. Libr., NYC, 1967-68; libr. N.Y. State Inst. for Basic Rsch. in Devel. Disabilities, Staten Island, 1968—. Mem. adv. com. of librs. Med. Libr. Ctr. of N.Y., N.Y.C., 1969—2003; compiler of bibliographies, 1975-. Trustee Temple Emanu-El, Staten Island, N.Y., 1989—, founder, coord. book club 1999—. Scholarship N.Y. Libr. Club, N.Y.C., 1965; recipient Small award NYU Dept Hebrew Culture, 1969. Mem. Govt. Agy. Librs. N.Y. State, Med. Libr. Assn. N.Y., N.J. chpt., N.Y. Libr. Club., Spl. Librs. Assn., Medical Libr. Assn. (institutional rep.), Met. NY Libr. Council (institutional rep.) Democrat. Jewish. Avocation: history. Office: NY St Inst Basic Rsch Devel Disabilities 1050 Forest Hill Rd Staten Island NY 10314-6356 Business E-Mail: lawrence.black@omr.state.ny.us.

BLACK, LEON DAVID, private investment company executive; s. Eli Black; m. Debra Ressler; 4 children. AB summa cum laude in Philos., Dartmouth Coll., 1973; MBA, Harvard U., 1975. With Drexel Burnham Lambert Inc., NYC, 1977—90, joined as assoc. fin. dept., 1977, head mergers and acquisitions, 1985—90, co-head corp. fin. dept.; co-founder The Apollo Orgn. (includes Apollo Mgmt. LP, Apollo Advisors LP, Apollo Real Estate Advisors LP), 1990—. Bd. dirs. Vail Resorts Inc., Sequa Corp., United Rentals Inc., Allied Waste Industries Inc., 2000—, AMC Entertainment Inc., 2001—, Sirius Satellite Radio Inc., 2001—, Wyndham Internat. Inc. Trustee Mus. Modern Art, Mt. Sinai Hosp., Lincoln Ctr. for Performing Arts, Met. Mus. Art, Prep for Prep, The Jewish Mus., Cardozo Sch. of Law, The Asia Soc., Spence Sch., The Vail Valley Found., Dartmouth Coll. Named one of Top 200 Collectors, ARTnews Mag., 2004, 2005, 2006, 400 Richest Ams., Forbes mag., 2006. Avocation: Collecting Old Masters, Impressionist, Modern and Contemporary Art, and Chinese Sculpture. Office: Apollo Advisors 2 Manhattanville Rd Purchase NY 10577*

BLACK, LEWIS, comedian, actor; b. Silver Spring, Md., Aug. 30, 1948; s. Sam and Jeannette. Grad., U. NC, Chapel Hill, 1970; MFA in drama, Yale U., 1977. Head of repertory co., Colo.; ran and performed at West Bank Cafownstairs Theatre Bar, NYC. Actor: (films) Hannah and Her Sisters, 1986, Jacob's Ladder, 1990, The Hard Way, 1991, Joey Breaker, 1993, The Night We Never Met, 1993, Sidesplitters: The Burt & Dick Story, 2000, American Dummy, 2002, The Gynecologists, 2003, Accepted, 2006, Man of the Year, 2006, Unaccompanied Minors, 2006; writer, prodr. (films) The Deal, 1998, Contbr. (TV series) The Daily Show, 1996—, comedian, writer (TV specials) Comedy Central Presents: Lewis Black, 2000, 2002, comedian, writer, prodr. Lewis Black: Taxed Beyond Belief, 2002, Lewis Black: Black on Broadway, 2004, Lewis Black: Red, White and Screwed, 2006; author: (autobiography) Nothing's Sacred, 2005. Recipient Grammy award for Best Comedy Album: The Carnegie Hall Peformance, 2007. Office: c/o Jackie Miller-Knobbe Agy for Performing Arts 9200 Sunset Blvd Ste 900 Los Angeles CA 90069*

BLACK, LOUIS ENGLEMAN, lawyer; b. Washington, Aug. 5, 1943; s. Fischer Sheffey and Elizabeth (Zemp) B.; m. Cecelia Whidden, Sept. 5, 1966; 1 child, Kerrison Todd. BA, NYU, 1968, JD, 1971, LLM in Taxation, 1978. Bar: N.Y. 1972. Assoc. Carter, Ledyard & Milburn, NYC, 1972-79; ptnr. Van Ginkel & Benjamin, NYC, 1979-83; of counsel Zimet, Haines, Moss & Friedman, NYC, 1983-84, DeForest & Duer, NYC, 1984-86, ptnr., 1986—2001, Black & Assocs., 2002—; mng. dir. Aleutian Capital Ptnrs., LLC, NYC, 2004—. Vice-chmn. bd. dirs. MacMillan Ring-Free Oil Co., Inc., 1986-87; chmn. bd. Lee's Gourmet Farms, Inc., 1993-97, United Compressor, LLC, 2002—, Kingdom Techs., LLC, 2002—. Editor: NYU Jour. Internat. Law and Politics, 1970-71; author: Partnership Buy/Sell Agreements, 1977. Mem. ABA, N.Y. State Bar Assn. Home: 220 E 65th St Apt 24M New York NY 10021-6629 Office: Black & Associates Ste 6710 350 5th Ave New York NY 10118-6710 Office Phone: 917-656-6263. Business E-Mail: lblack@blackesq.com.

BLACK, LYNANNE, psychologist, educator; b. Johnstown, Pa., Sept. 2, 1970; d. Ronald Linn and Deborah Ann Black. BA, Cath. U. Am., 1992; EdM, Temple U., 1994, PhD, 2001. Cert. sch. psychology Del., Pa. Sch. psychologist Colonial Sch. Dist., New Castle, Del., 1996—2003; asst. prof. Indiana (Pa.) U. Pa., 2003—. Adj. prof. U. Del., Newark, 2000—03, Wilmington Coll., New Castle, 2001—03; mental health cons. Indiana County Head Start, 2005—. Mem.: Coun. for Exceptional Children, Internat. Dyslexia Assn., Nat. Assn. Sch. Psychologists. Office: IUP 250 Stouffer Hall 1175 Maple St Indiana PA 15705

BLACK, PAGE MORTON, civic worker, vocalist, musician; b. Chgo. d. Alexander and Rose Morton; m. William Black, Mar. 27, 1962. Student, Chgo. Mus. Coll. Singer, pianist Pierre Hotel, NYC, Warwick Hotel, One Fifth Ave. Sherry Netherland Hotel; singer radio show and comml. Chock Full O'Nuts Corp.; rec. artist Atlantic Records, Den Records. Co-founder Page and William Black Post-Grad. Sch. Medicine, Mt. Sinai Med. Sch., 1965—; chmn. mem. exec. bd. Parkinsons' Disease Found., Columbia U. Med. Ctr.; mem. nat. vis. coun. Columbia U. Health Scis. Faculties; hon. chmn. Chock Full O' Nuts Corp., 1983—90; active Columbia Presbyn. Health Scis. Adv. Coun.; founding mem. ASPCA; mem. neurosci. com. Neurol. Inst. of NY at Columbia Presbyn. Med. Ctr., Columbia Presbyn. Med. Ctr. Mem. neuroscience com. Columbia Presbyn. Health Sci. Adv. Coun. Recipient Ann. award, Parkinsons' Disease Found., 1987, Police Athletic League, 1992, Manhattan Mag. award, 1992, Lifetime Achievement award, Parkinson's Disease Found., 1997, Disting. Svc. award, 2005, Humanitarian award, 2005, Dean's award for Disting. Svc., Columbia U. Coll. Physicians & Surgeons, 1998. Achievements include being honored with a laboratory and the Page & William Black Chair at Columbia U. Home: Premium Pt New Rochelle NY 10801

BLACK, PAUL HENRY, medical educator, researcher; b. Boston, Mar. 11, 1930; s. Samuel Louis and May (Goldberg) B.; m. Sandra Merkin, June 2, 1962; children: Scott, Marc, Jeffrey. AB, Dartmouth Coll., 1952; MD, Columbia U., 1956. Diplomate Am. Bd. Internal Medicine. Intern Mass. Gen. Hosp., Boston, 1956-57, asst. resident in medicine, 1957-58, clin. and rsch. fellow, 1958-60, resident in medicine, 1960-61; sr. asst. surgeon Lab. Infectious Diseases USPHS Nat. Inst. Allergy and Infectious Diseases, NIH, Bethesda, Md., 1961-63; sr. surgeon Lab. Infectious Diseases USPHS Nat. Inst. Allergy and Infectious Diseases, U. Glasgow Inst. Virology, Scotland, 1963-64; sr. surgeon, comdr. Lab. Infectious Diseases USPHS Nat. Inst. Allergy and Infectious Diseases, NIH, Bethesda, Md., 1964-67; asst. prof. medicine Harvard U. Med. Sch., Boston, 1967-70, assoc. prof. medicine, 1970-80; asst. physician Mass. Gen. Hosp., Boston, 1967-70, assoc. physician, 1970-80, hon. physician, 1980—; dir. Hubert H. Humphrey Cancer Rsch. Ctr. Boston U., 1979-83; chmn., prof. microbiology, research prof. surgery, prof. medicine Boston U. Sch. Medicine, 1979-96, prof. emeritus, 1996—. Cons. Roswell Park Meml. Inst., Buffalo, 1976-80, Monsanto Chem. Corp., St. Louis, 1976-82, Collaborative Rsch., Inc. (Oscient Pharm.), Waltham, Mass., 1984-90; mem. subcom. on evaluation cancer ctrs. Nat. Cancer Adv. Bd., Bethesda, 1975-80; sci. cons. U.S.-Israel Binat. Sci. Found., Jerusalem, Israel, 1974—; mem. NIH Study Sect. Virology, 1968-72, Tumor Virus Detection Segment, Spl. Virus Cancer Program, Bethesda, 1972-76; mem. subcom. on environ. carcinogens, Am. Cancer Soc. Task Force on Cancer Prevention, 1975-82 , sci. adv. bd. Worcester Found. for Exptl. Biology, Mass., 1976-78, sci. adv. bd. Dartmouth-Hitchcock Med. Ctr., Hanover, N.H., 1976-80, Gov.'s Task Force on AIDS, Commonwealth of Mass., Boston, 1983-94; chmn. spl. virus cancer program contract rev. com., Nat. Cancer Inst., 1977-79 Author monograph; contbr. 226 articles to profl. jours., chpts. to books Nat. Cancer Inst. grantee, 1967-87. Fellow AAAS; mem. Am. Soc. Clin. Investigation, Infectious Diseases Soc., Am. Soc. Microbiology, Am. Soc. Virology, Am. Assn. Med. Sch. Microbiology Chmn., Soc. Gen. Microbiology, Sigma Xi. Democrat. Jewish. Office: Boston U Sch Medicine 715 Albany St Boston MA 02118-2307 Home: 9 Commonwealth Ave Apt 6 Boston MA 02116-2111 Home Phone: 617-247-8795; Office Phone: 617-414-5881. Business E-Mail: pblack@bu.edu.

BLACK, PETE, retired state legislator, educator; b. Ansbach, Germany, Sept. 16, 1946; came to U.S., 1948; s. Howard and Kadi (Fietz) B.; m. Ronda Williams, July 12, 1970; 1 child, Darin. BS, Idaho State U., 1975, MEd, 1998. Cert. elem. tchr. Tchr. Pocatello (Idaho) Sch. Dist., 1975—; mem. Idaho Ho. Reps., Boise, 1983-96, asst. minority leader, 1987-96; tech. tng. specialist Sch. Dist. 25, 1996—, info. officer, 2003—. Mem. edn. tech. coun.; mem. adv. coun. chpt. II ESEA. Bd. dirs. Arts for Idaho; mem. State Libr. Bd.; mem. Idaho Pers. Commn., Pocatello Civil Svc. Commn., Pocatello Parks and Recreation Bd. With USNR, 1964. Mem. NEA, Idaho Edn. Assn. (bd. dirs.), Idaho Libr. Assn., Idaho State U. Alumni Bd. Democrat. Home: 2249 Cassia St Pocatello ID 83201-2059 Office: Idaho House of Reps Statehouse Mail Boise ID 83720-0001 Home Phone: 208-237-1779; Office Phone: 208-235-3251. E-mail: blackcat1@cableone.net.

BLACK, PETER, neurosurgeon, educator; b. Calgary, Alta., Can., Apr. 3, 1944; s. Thomas Herbert and Harriet Elizabeth (Peterson) B.; m. Katharine C. Black, June 15, 1967; children: Winifred, Libby, Katy, Peter Thomas, Christopher. AB, Harvard U., 1966; MD, CM, McGill U., 1970; PhD, Georgetown U., 1978. Diplomate Am. Bd. Neurosurgery. Staff neurosurgeon Mass. Gen. Hosp., Boston, 1980—87; neurosurgeon-in-chief Brigham and Women's Hosp., Boston, 1987—2007, chmn. dept. neurosurgery, 2000—07; neurosurgeon-in-chief Children's Hosp., Boston, 1987—2004, chmn. dept. neurosurgery, 1987—2005; chief neuro-surg. oncology Dana Farber Cancer Inst., Boston, 1987—; Franc D. Ingraham prof. neurosurgery Harvard Med. Sch., Boston, 1987—. Author Self-Assessment Test in Neurological Surgery, 4th edit., 1990, The Surgical Art of Harvey Cushing, 1992, Harvey Cushing at the Brigham, 1993, Astrocytomas: Diagnosis, Management and Biology, 1993, Surgical Treatment of Epilepsy in Children, Neurosurgery Clinics of North America, 1995, Cancer of the Nervous System, 1997, 2d edit., 2004, Operative Neurosurgery, 1999, Brain Tumors in Adults. Neurological Clinics, Angiogenesis in Brain Tumors, 2004, Minimally Invasive Neurosurgery, 2005, Living with a Brain Tumor, 2006; contbr. more than 500 articles. Office: Brigham and Women's Hosp 75 Francis St Boston MA 02115-6106 Office Phone: 617-525-7796. Business E-Mail: pblack@partners.org.

BLACK, RICHARD BRUCE, corporate executive, consultant; b. Dallas, July 25, 1933; s. James Ernest and Minerva (Braden) B.; m. Heather Bilandic; children: Kathryn Braden, Paula Anne (dec.), Erica Lynn. BS in Engring., Tex. A&M U., 1954; MBA, Harvard U., 1958; PhD (hon.), Beloit Coll., 1997. With Vulcan Materials Co., Birmingham, Ala., 1958—62; v.p. fin. Warner Electric Brake & Clutch Co., Beloit, Wis., 1962—67, dir., 1973-85; pres. automotive group, exec. v.p. corp. Maremont Corp., Chgo., 1967-72, pres. corp., COO, 1972-76, pres., chmn., CEO, 1976-79; pres., CEO, dir. Alusuisse of Am., Inc., NYC, 1979-81; chmn., CEO, dir. AM Internat., Inc., Chgo., 1981-82; owner R. Black & Assocs., 1983—; chmn. ECRM, Boston, 1983—2002, pres., CEO, 2002—; gen. ptnr. KBA Ptnrs., LP, 1988-98, OpNet Ptnrs., LP, 2000—; pres. Oak Tech., Inc., Sunnyvale, Calif., 1998—99, vice chmn., 1999—2003, dir., 1988—2003. Bd. dirs. GSI Group, Inc., chmn. 2005-; bd. dirs. ECRM, Inc., Applied Optoelectronics, Inc., Alliance Fiber Optics Products, Inc., Trex Enterprises, Inc.; lectr.

econs. Beloit (Wis.) Coll., 1964-67. Author: (with Jack Pierson) Linear Polyethylene-Propylene: Problems and Opportunities, 1958. Trustee Beloit Coll., Am. Indian Coll. Fund., Teton Sci. Sch., Inst. Advanced Study, vice chmn., Princeton, NJ, Snake River Conservancy Found.; trustee, nat. chmn. Inroads, Inc., 1973-77. 1st lt. USAF, 1954-56. Recipient Flame of Hope Lifetime Achievement award, Am. Indian Coll. Fund, 1998, Inroads Lifetime Achievement award, 1979. Mem. Am. Alpine Club, Harvard Club (N.Y.C.). Office: ECRM Inc 554 Clark Rd Tewksbury MA 01876 Home Phone: 917-626-7476; Office Phone: 978-851-0207. Business E-Mail: r_black@ecrm.com.

BLACK, ROBERT ALLEN, lawyer; b. Ocala, Fla., Aug. 15, 1954; s. Allen Harrison and Rose Marie (Dupree) B. BA, U. Tex., El Paso, 1977; JD summa cum laude, Tex. Tech U., 1980. Bar: Tex. 1980, U.S. Ct. Appeals (5th and 11th cirs.) 1980, U.S. Supreme Ct. 1985. Ptnr. Mehaffy & Weber, Beaumont, Tex., 1980—, mng. ptnr., 1998—. Case note editor Tex. Tech Law Rev., 1979-80. Pres. Humane Soc. S.E. Tex., Beaumont, 1983-89; bd. dirs. YMCA, Beaumont, 1985-87, Beaumont Cmty. Players, 1989-91; host TV show Pets on Parade, Beaumont, 1986-87; mem. Beaumont City Planning and Zoning Commn., 1987-90; mem. Beaumont Hist. Landmark Commn., 1989-90. Named Super Lawyer, Tex. Monthly, 2004, 05, 06, 07. Fellow: ABA, Tex. Bar Found. (bd. trustees 2007—); mem.: Am. Bar Assn. Found., Am. Contract Bridge League (pres. unit 201 1991—93, bd. govs. 1992—96, pres. 1994—96), State Bar Tex. (chmn. bd. dirs. 2006—07), Jefferson County Bar Assn. (treas. 1994—95, pres.-elect 1996—97, pres. 1997—98). Democrat. Avocations: book collecting, tennis, history. Home: 601 22nd St Beaumont TX 77706-4915 Office: Mehaffy & Weber 2615 Calder St Ste 800 Beaumont TX 77702-1993 Office Phone: 409-835-5011. Business E-Mail: BobBlack@mehaffyweber.com.

BLACK, ROBERT COLEMAN, judge, lawyer; b. Greenville, Ala., July 3, 1934; s. James Monroe and Mabel (Coleman) B.; m. Carolyn Musselwhite, Dec. 20, 1960; children: Elizabeth Anne, Robert C., Carolyn Jane. BS in Commerce and Bus. Adminstrn, U. Ala., 1960, LL.B., 1961. Bar: Ala. 1961. Law clk. to justice Ala. Supreme Ct., 1961-62; partner firm Hill, Hill, Carter, Flanco, Cole & Black, Montgomery, Ala., 1968—, spl. asst. atty. gen. Ala., 1969—; judge Circuit Ct., 1979—. Prof. law Jones Law Sch., Montgomery; instr. bus. law U. Ala. at Montgomery, Auburn U.; lectr. continuing legal edn. Ala. Bar Assn.; faculty Ala. Jud. Coll. City chmn. March of Dimes, 1966; bd. dirs. Montgomery YMCA, St. James Parrish Sch.; trustee Ala. Indsl. Sch. Served with USMCR, 1954-57. Mem. Ala. Bar Assn., Montgomery County Bar Assn. (chmn. exec. com. 1969-70, pres. 1971), Phi Delta Phi, Beta Gamma Sigma. Office: 425 S Perry St Montgomery AL 36104-4235

BLACK, ROBERT FREDERICK, retired gas industry executive; b. Mansfield, Ohio, Jan. 9, 1920; s. Judson Ammi and Pauline (Remy) B.; m. Conita Fay McCoslin, June 25, 1944; children: Ronald Gregory, Peggy Lynn. Student, Miami U., Oxford, Ohio, 1946-47. Asst. mgr. Warner Bros. Theatres, Mansfield, 1935-42; asst. treas. Red Arrow Freight Lines, Inc., Houston, 1947-56; contr., sec. Cactus Petroleum Inc., Houston, 1956-62; project contr. Del E. Webb Corp., Clear Lake City, Tex., 1962-65; treas. Mitchell Energy & Devel. Corp., The Woodlands, Tex., 1965-82. Choir dir. New Song United Meth. Ch., 2005. With USAAC, 1942-46, CBI, with USAF Inactive Reserve, 1946-1952. Named to Honorable Order of Ky. Colonels. Mem. Fin. Execs. Inst. (life, past bd. dirs. Houston chpt.), CBI Vets Assn., DeMolay Alumni Assn., Burma Star Assn., Masons (life, grand organist Grand Lodge of Ariz. 1997-98). Republican. Home: 10800 N 115th Ave Apt 19 Youngtown AZ 85363-1429 E-mail: cfbrfb@msn.com.

BLACK, ROBERT LINCOLN, pediatrician, educator; b. LA, Aug. 25, 1930; s. Harold Alfred and Kathryn (Stone) Black; m. Jean Wilmott McGuire, June 27, 1953; children: Donald J., Douglas L., Margaret S. AB, Stanford U., Calif., 1952, MD, 1955. Diplomate Am. Bd. Pediat. Intern Kings County Hosp., Bklyn., 1955—56; resident and fellow Stanford U. Hosp., 1958—62; practice medicine specializing in pediat. Monterey, Calif., 1962—. Clin. prof. Stanford U., 1962—; cons. Calif. Dept. Health, Sacramento, 1962—; mem. Calif. State Maternal, Child, Adolescent Health Bd., 1984—93. Author (with others): California Health Plan for Children, 1979. Mem. Monterey Peninsula Unified Sch. Bd., 1965—73, pres., 1968—70; mem. Mid-Coast Health Sys. Agy., Salinas, Calif., 1975—80, pres., 1979—80; bd. dirs. Lucile Packard Found. for Child Health, 2000—, Lyceum of Monterey Peninsula, 1963—, Carmel Bach Festival, Calif., 1972—81. With USAF, 1956—58. Fellow: Am. Acad. Pediat. (Child Advocacy award sr. sect. 2002); mem.: Physicians for Social Responsibility, Monterey County Med. Soc., Calif. Med. Assn., Inst. Medicine of NAS. Democrat. Home: 976 Mesa Rd Monterey CA 93940-4612 Office: 920 Cass St Monterey CA 93940-4507 Office Phone: 831-372-5841.

BLACK, ROBERT PERRY, bank executive; b. Hickman, Ky., Dec. 21, 1927; s. Burwell Perry and Veola (Moore) B.; m. Mary Rives Ogilvie, Oct. 27, 1951; children: Patty Rives, Robert Perry. BA, U. Va., 1950, MA, 1951, PhD, 1955. Research assoc. Fed. Res. Bank, Richmond, Va., 1954-55, assoc. economist, 1956-58, economist, 1958-60, asst. v.p., 1960-62, v.p., 1962-68, 1st v.p., 1968-73, pres., 1973-92. Instr. U. Va., 1953—54, lectr., 1956—57; asst. prof. U. Tenn., 1955—56; J. Boone Aiken vis. prof. banking Francis Marion Coll., Florence, SC, 1991; mem. Gov.'s Adv. Bd. Revenue Estimates, 1976—92, Va. Econ. Recovery Commn., 1991—92; adv. bd. Health Corp. Va., 1981—93; bd. govs. Capital Area Assy., 1989—93, exec. com., 1989—93; bd. dirs. Winchester Evening Star, Inc., Rockingham Publ. Co. Contbr. articles to profl. jours. Past dir. Ctrl. Richmond Assn.; former trustee Collegiate Schs., past chmn.; chmn. Main to the James Devel. Com., 1971-73; adv. coun. Robert E. Lee coun. Boy Scouts Am., 1977-78; bd. dirs. Retreat Hosp., 1988-98; past pres. United Way Greater Richmond; bd. dirs., mem. exec. com., treas., chmn. fin. com. Downtown Devel. Unltd., 1975-86; chmn. adv. com. Ctr. Banking Edn., Va. Union U., 1977-79; trustee E. Angus Powell Endowment for Am. Enterprise, 1980-88, Acad. for Econ. Edn., 1990-94; mem. adv. bd. Ctr. for Advanced Studies, U. Va., 1986-94; mem. Forum Club, 1987—; bd. dirs. Va. United Meth. Homes, Inc., 1990-94, v.p., 1991-92, chmn., 1992-94; mem. Gov.'s Com. on Def. Conv. and Econ. Adjustment, 1992-94; dir. Va. Biotech. Rsch. Park, 1992-94. With AUS, 1946-47. Recipient George Washington Honor medal award Freedoms Found., Valley Forge, 1978, Brotherhood citation NCCJ, 1991, J. Curtis Hall award Va. Coun. Econ. Edn., Outstanding Svc. award Ctrl. Richmond Assn., 1991, Silver Hope award Ctr. Va. chpt. Nat. Multiple Sclerosis Soc., 1992, Disting. Citizen award Robert E. Lee coun. Boy Scouts Am., 1993, Robert P. Black Rsch. Professorship in Econs. U. Va. established by friends, 1993. Mem. Va. Inter-Govt. Inst. (bd. dirs. 1986-93), Country Club Va. (bd. dirs. 1980-85, 88, v.p. 1981-83, pres. 1983-85), The Commonwealth Club, Kinloch Golf Club, Raven Soc., Phi Beta Kappa (past pres. Richmond chpt.), Beta Gamma Sigma, Alpha Kappa Psi, Kappa Alpha. Methodist. Home: 2133 Cedarfield Ln Richmond VA 23233-1937

BLACK, ROBERT W., health products executive; BS, SUNY, Buffalo, 1982; MBA, Harvard U., 1984. Sr. positions in planning, devel. and gen. mgmt. Baxter Healthcare; with McKinsey & Co.; various sr. leadership positions in mktg., strategy, corp. devel. and internat. mgmt. Steelcase, Inc., 1994—2004, pres. Steelcase Internat. Strasbourg, France, 2000—04; COO Sammons Enterprises, 2004—05; sr. v.p., chief strategy officer Kimberly-Clark Corp., 2006—. Office: Kimberly-Clark Corp PO Box 619100 Dallas TX 75261-9100 Office Phone: 972-281-1200.*

BLACK, RONNIE DELANE, religious organization administrator, mayor; b. Poplar Bluff, Mo., Oct. 26, 1947; s. Clyde Olen and Leona Christine Black; m. Sandra Elaine Hulett, Aug. 27, 1966; 1 child, Stephanie. BA, Oakland City Coll., Ind., 1969; M Div, So. Bapt. Theol. Sem., 1972. Ordained to ministry Gen. Assn. of Gen. Bapts., 1967. Pastor Gen. Bapt. Ch., Fort Branch, Ind., 1972-78; stewardship dir. Gen. Bapt. Hdqrs., Poplar Bluff, Mo., 1978-97, exec. dir., 1997—; councilman City of Poplar Bluff, 1985-97, mayor, 1990-92, 95-96. Mem. Gen. Bapt. Ch. Office: Gen Bapts 100 Stinson Dr Poplar Bluff MO 63901-8736

BLACK, ROY, lawyer; b. NYC, Feb. 17, 1945; s. Richard and Minna (Benett) B. BA, U. Miami, Fla., 1967, JD, 1970. Bar: Fla. 1970. Sr. asst. pub. defender Miami-Dade County, 1971-76; ptnr. Roy E. Black, PA, Miami, 1976-79, Black and Furci, PA, 1979-93, Black & Seiden, Miami, 1993-96, Black, Srebnick & Kornspan, Miami, 1996—2002, Black Srebnick Kornspan & Stumpf, Miami, 2002—. Legal analyst NBC, 2003—; legal commentator several nat. TV networks. Author: Black's Law: A Criminal Lawyer Reveals his Strategies in Four Cliffhanger Cases, 1999. Fundraising events sponsor Bay Point Sch., Miami, 1998—. Recipient Nelson Potyner award ACLU, 1982, Criminal Justice award Dade County Bar Assn., 1991, U. Miami William R. Butler Cmty. Svc. award, 2005. Fellow: Am. Coll. Trial Lawyers; mem.: ABA, NACDL (life), Eugene Spellman Inns of Ct., Dade County Bar Assn., Internat. Acad. Trial Lawyers, Fla. Assn. Criminal Def. Lawyers, Fla. Bar Assn. Office: Black Srebnick Kornspan & Stumpf PA 201 S Biscayne Blvd Ste 1300 Miami FL 33131-4311 Office Phone: 305-371-6421. Business E-Mail: rblack@royblack.com.

BLACK, SCOTT C., career military officer, lawyer; married; 4 children. BA in Polit. Sci., Calif. Poly. State U.; degree, Calif. Western Sch. Law, San Diego; MS in Nat. Resource Strategy, Nat. Def. U.; postgraduate student, Judge Adv. Basic and Grad. Courses, Army Command and Gen. Staff Coll., Indsl. Coll. Armed Forces. Advanced through ranks to maj. gen. US Army; judge adv., chief legal assistance br., trial counsel, chief criminal law br., contract atty. Ft. Bliss, Tex.; gen. law atty. Office of JAG Army, Washington; asst. counsel to Pres. The White House, Washington; dep. staff judge adv. 7th Inf. Divsn. (light) Fort Ord, Calif., 1990; chief mil. and civil law divsn. US Army Europe and 7th Army, Germany, staff judge adv. 3rd Inf. Divsn.; legis. counsel Office of Sec. of Army, Washington, 1996, chief investigations and legis. divsn.; chief pers., plans and tng. office US Army Europe and 7th Army, staff judge adv. V Corps; asst. JAG mil. law and ops. US Army, 2001—03; commdg. gen., comdt. JAG Legal Ctr. and Sch., 2003—05; JAG US Army, 2005—. Decorated Legion of Merit with oak leaf cluster, Meritorious Svc. medal with four oak leaf clusters, Army Commendation medal with oak leaf cluster, Army Achievement medal with oak leaf cluster. Office: JAG 2700 Army Pentagon Washington DC 20310-2700 Office Phone: 703-697-5151.*

BLACK, SCOTT M., diversified financial services company executive; b. Portland, Maine; BS in Applied Math., Econ., Johns Hopkins Univ., 1968; MBA in Finance, Harvard Univ., 1971. Worked in finance Joseph E. Seagram then Xerox, 1972—75; various positions to head, corp. develop. Merrill Lynch, 1975—77; portfolio mgr. William O'Neil Co., Calif., 1977; mgr. Delphi Value Fund; founder, pres. Delphi Mgmt. Inc., Boston, 1980—. Adv. bd. Portland Mus. Art, Mus. Fine Arts, Boston, John F. Kennedy Sch. Govt, Harvard Univ., Boston, Johns Hopkins Univ., Northeastern Univ. With US Army. Named one of Top 200 Collectors, ARTnews Mag., 2004, 2005, 2006. Achievements include personally endowing Scott M. Black Professorship, Harvard Univ. Kennedy Sch. Avocation: Collecting impressionist and modern art. Office: Delphi Mgmt Inc 50 Rowes Wharf Boston MA 02110 Office Phone: 617-330-1025.

BLACK, SHIRLEY TEMPLE (MRS. CHARLES A. BLACK), retired ambassador, retired actress; b. Santa Monica, Calif., Apr. 23, 1928; d. George Francis and Gertrude Temple; m. John Agar, Jr., Sept. 19, 1945 (div. 1950); 1 dau., Linda Susan Falaschi; m. Charles A. Black, Dec. 16, 1950 (dec. Aug. 4, 2005); children: Charles Alden Jr., Lori Alden. Grad., Westlake Sch. Girls, 1945; D (hon.), Santa Clara Univ., Lehigh Univ. Rep. to 24th Gen. Assembly UN, NYC, 1969-70; amb. to Ghana Accra, 1974-76; chief of protocol White House, Washington, 1976-77; amb. to Czechoslovakia Prague, 1989-92. Mem. U.S. Delegation on African Refugee Problems, Geneva, 1981; mem. public adv. com. UN Conf. on Law of the Sea; dep. chmn. U.S. del. UN Conf. on Human Environment, Stockholm, 1970-72; spl. asst. to chmn. Pres.'s Coun. on Environ. Quality, 1972-74; del. treaty on environment USSR-USA Joint Commn., Moscow, 1972; mem. U.S. Commn. for UNESCO, 1973; hon. U.S. Fgn. Svc. officer. Began film career at age 3 1/2; first full-length film was Stand Up and Cheer; other films included Little Miss Marker, Baby Take a Bow, Bright Eyes, Our Little Girl, The Little Colonel, Curly Top, The Littlest Rebel, Captain January, Poor Little Rich Girl, Dimples, Stowaway, Wee Willie Winkie, Heidi, Rebecca of Sunnybrook Farm, Little Miss Broadway, Just Around the Corner, The Little Princess, Susannah of the Mounties, The Blue Bird, Kathleen, Miss Annie Rooney, Since You Went Away, Kiss and Tell, 1945, That Hagen Girl, War Party, The Bachelor and the Bobby-Soxer, Honeymoon, 1947; narrator, actress: TV series Shirley Temple Storybook, NBC, 1958, Shirley Temple Show, NBC, 1960; author: Child Star: An Autobiography, 1988. Dir. Bank of Calif.; dir. Fireman's Fund Ins. Co., BANCAL Tri-State Corp., Walt Disney, Del Monte Corp.; Mem. Calif. Adv. Hosp. Council, 1969, San Francisco Health Facilities Planning Assn., 1965-69; Republican candidate for U.S. Ho. of Reps. from Calif., 1967; bd. dirs. Nat. Wildlife Fedn., Nat. Multiple Sclerosis Soc., UN Assn. U.S.A.; bd. dirs. exec. com. Internat. Fedn. Multiple Sclerosis Socs. Appointed col. on staff of Gov. Ross of Idaho, 1935; commd. col. Hawaiian N.G.; hon. col. 108th Rgt. N.G. Ill.; dame Order Knights Malta, Paris, 1968; recipient Ceres medal FAO, Rome, 1975, numerous other state decorations; Kennedy Center Honoree, 1998; recipient Chubb Fellowship Yale Univ., Screen Actors Guild Life Achievement award for career achievement and humanitarian accomplishment, 2005. Mem. World Affairs Coun. No. Calif. (dir.), Coun. Fgn. Rels., Nat. Com. for U.S./China Rels. Clubs: Commonwealth of Calif.

BLACK, STEPHEN FRANKLIN, lawyer, writer; b. NYC, Nov. 28, 1944; s. Theodore Russell Black and Zelma Carmel Bernstein; m. Laurie N. Bromberg, June 25, 1967 (div. Oct. 1988); children: Hilary F., Jane S., Katharine L.; m. Anne M. Richmond, Oct. 14, 1989. AB magna cum laude, Harvard U., 1965; JD magna cum laude, U. Mich., 1968; MLitt, Oxford U., Eng., 1970. Bar: DC 1969. Ptnr. Wilmer, Cutler & Pickering, Washington, 1970—2001. Author: Internal Corporate Investigations, 1985, Der Zivilprozess in Den Vereinigten Staaten, 1986, Complying with Foreign Corrupt Practices Act, 1997, (plays) Candlefire, 2003, Kennedy, 2005; contbr. articles to profl. jours. Trustee Shakespeare Theatre Co., Washington, 2001—07; bd. dirs. Am. Soc. Legal History, 1979—82, English Speaking Union, Washington, 2004—. Marshall scholar, 1970. Mem.: Cosmos Club (Washington). Home: 1605 22nd St NW Washington DC 20008-1921 Home Phone: 202-232-6895.

BLACK, STEPHEN L., lawyer; b. Cin., Dec. 3, 1948; AB magna cum laude, in economics, Harvard U., 1971, JD, 1974. Bar: Ohio 1974, U.S. Ct. Appeals (6th cir.). Law clerk to Hon. George Edwards U.S. Ct. Appeals (6th cir.), 1974-75; mayor City of Indian Hill, Ohio, 1995-99; ptnr. Graydon, Head & Ritchey, Cin., 1980—. Bd. trustee, pres. Children's Home Cin. Inc., Cin. Law Libr. Assn., Harvard Club Cin., 1988-89, Harvard Alumni Assn., 1989-92, Seven Hills Sch., 1992-2001, Village of Indian Hill (councilman, 1989-99, mayor 1995-99), Am. Lung Assn. SW Ohio, Summerbridge Cin. Inc., Cin. Nature Ctr., 1989-95. Recipient Goodall Disting. Alumni award, Seven Hills Sch., 2003. Mem. Ohio State Bar Assn., Cin. Bar Assn. Avocation: small aircrafts. Office: Graydon Head & Ritchey 511 Walnut St 1900 5th 3rd Ctr Cincinnati OH 45202-3157 Office Phone: 513-629-2723. Office Fax: 513-651-3836. Business E-Mail: sblack@graydon.com.

BLACK, STEVEN D., bank executive; Vice chmn. Salomon Smith Barney; head instl. equities bus. J.P. Morgan Chase & Co., NYC, 2000—01, dep. head investment bank, 2001—04, co-CEO investment bank, 2004—. Office: JP Morgan Chase and Co 270 Park Ave New York NY 10017-2070

BLACK, SUSAN HARRELL, federal judge; b. Valdosta, Ga., Oct. 20, 1943; d. William H. and Ruth Elizabeth (Phillips) Harrell; m. Louis Eckert Black, Dec. 28, 1966. BA, Fla. State U., 1965; JD, U. Fla., 1967; LLM, U. Va., 1984. Bar: Fla. 1967. Atty. US Army Corps of Engrs., Jacksonville, Fla., 1968—69; asst. state atty. Gen. Counsel's Office, Jacksonville, 1969—72; judge County Ct. of Duval County, Fla., 1973—75; judge 4th Jud. Cir. Ct. of Fla., 1975—79; judge US Dist. Ct. (mid. dist.) Fla., Jacksonville, 1979—90, chief judge, 1990—92; judge US Ct. Appeals (11th cir.) Fla., Jacksonville, 1992—. Faculty Fed. Jud. Ctr.; mem. U.S. Jud. Conf. Com. onInns of Ct., 1984—87; trustee Am. Inns Ct. Found., 1985—91; pres. US Dist. Judge's Assn (11th Cir.), 1987—88; mem. Jud. Improvements Com., 1987—90, Com. on Court Admin. and Case Mgmt., 1990—92, Jud. Conference Com. on Fed.-State Jurisdiction, 1998—2004. Trustee emeritus Law Sch. U. Fla.; past pres. Chester Bedell Inn of Ct. Mem.: Chester Bedell Inn of Ct. (founding mem.), Jacksonville Bar Assn., Fla. Bar Assn. Presbyterian.*

BLACK, THOMAS See BLACK, JACK

BLACK, THOMAS DONALD, retired religious organization administrator; b. Mercer, Pa., Feb. 7, 1920; s. Harry Alexander and Bessie (Gilkey) B.; m. Frances Anna Greenan, Mar. 1, 1923; children: David Alan, Donald Francis, Joseph Harry, Timothy John (dec.). BA, Grove City Coll., 1942, DD, 1955; MDiv, Pitts.-Xenia Theol. Sch., 1945; MST, Temple U., 1954. Ordained to ministry United Presbyn. Ch. N.Am., 1945. Founding pastor Creston Hills United Presbyn. Ch., Oklahoma City, 1945-50; pastor Blvd. United Presbyn. Ch., Phila., 1950-54, Am. Ch. in London, 1973-76; exec. sec. United Presbyn. Bd. Fgn. Mission, Phila., 1954-58; assoc. gen. sec. Commn. on Ecumenical Mission and Relations United Presbyn. Ch.-U.S.A., NYC, 1958-70, gen. sec. Commn. on Ecumenical Mission and Relations, 1970-72, assoc. gen. dir. Program Agy., 1977-84; exec. dir. Gen. Assembly Council Presbyn. Ch. (USA), NYC and Atlanta, 1985-87; acting assoc. gen. sec. Nat. Coun. Chs. in U.S.A., 1989-90; interim dir. U.S. Office World Coun. Chs., NYC, 1991-92. Chmn. bd. dirs. Christian Lit. Fund, Geneva, 1964-69, Ravemcco, Lit-Lit, N.Y.C., 1962-66. Author: Merging Mission and Unity, 1986; contbr. articles and pamphlets to mission and ch. publs. Interim assoc. Riverside Ch., 1992-93; pastoral assoc. Abington Presbyn. Ch., 1994-98. Presbyterian. Home: 1515 The Fairway Apt 617 Jenkintown PA 19046 *We want to be appreciated for what we are, but uncertain of being accepted, we try to justify our lives by what we have accomplished. God accepts us for what we are.*

BLACK, TODD RONALD, music educator; b. Effingham, Ill., Feb. 1, 1962; s. Ted Ronald and Eula Jean Black; m. Angelique Susann Katz, Oct. 10, 1992; children: Matt, Suzanne, Gabe. BS in Music Edn., Ea. Ill. U., Charleston, 1985; MS in Music Performance, So. Ill. U., Carbondale, 1993. Cert. tchr. spl. edn. K-12 Ill. Dir. bands Franklin Park Mid. Sch., Salem, Ill., 1986—88, Trinity Christian Jr./Sr. H.S., Cedar Hill, Tex., 1988—90, St. Joseph Mid. Sch., Olney, Ill., 1990—91, Mattoon Jr. H.S., Ill., 1991—94, Mattoon H.S., 1994—. Band chmn. Ill. Music Educators Assn., Dist. V, 1993—, Mid-Ill. Hon. Wind Symphony, Mattoon, 1996—, Big 12 Conf., 1994—95; co-founder, trumpet player Sounds of Swing Big Band, Ill., 1990—. Mem.: Internat. Trumpet Guild, Internat. Assn. Jazz Edn., Nat. Band Assn., Sigma Chi, Kappa Kappa Psi, Mortar Bd. (pres. 1984—85), Phi Kappa Phi. Assemblies Of God. Avocations: tennis, golf, basketball. Home: 705 S 5th Pl Mattoon IL 61938 Office: Mattoon HS 2521 Walnut Ave Mattoon IL 61938 E-mail: mrb@mattoon.k12.il.us.

BLACK, WILFORD REX, JR., retired state legislator; b. Salt Lake City, Jan. 31, 1920; s. Wilford Rex and Elsie Isabell (King) B.; m. Helen Shirley Frazer; children: Susan, Janet, Cindy, Joy, Peggy, Vanna, Gayle, Rex. Locomotive engr. Rio Grande R.R., 1941-81; mem. Utah Senate, Salt Lake City, 1972-96, spkr. 3d House, 1975-76, majority whip, 1977-78, minority leader, 1981-90. Sec. Utah State Legis. Bd., United Transp.; chmn. bd. Rail Operators Credit Union , 1958—87. Mission pres. Rose Park Stake Mormon Ch. Rose Park Stake Mormon Ch.; high priest group leader Rose Park 9th Ward, 1980—83, 10th Ward, 1996—99; mem. Rose Park Stake High Coun., 1957—63. With USAR, 1942—45. Recipient various awards r.r. and legis. activities. Democrat. Office: 826 N 1300 W Salt Lake City UT 84116-3877

BLACK, WILLIAM B., JR., federal agency administrator; b. N.Mex. m. Iris Black; 3 children. BA in Polit. Sci., U. Md., 1971; postgrad., George Washington U., 1978—79, Nat. War Coll., Ft. McNair, Wash., 1979. Operational linguist/analyst Nat. Security Agy., Ft. George, Md., 1959—75, chief office of customer rels. and support to mil. ops., 1975—78, chief ops. maj. field installation, 1979—82, dep. chief, 1982—84, chief, 1984—86, chief office of collection mgmt., 1986—87, assoc. dep. dir. ops./mil. support, 1987—89, chief NSA/CSS rep. Europe office, 1989—92, chief of ops. analysis Group A, 1992—96, spl. asst. to dir. info. warfare, 1996—97, dep. dir., 2000—, acting dir., 2005; asst. v.p., dir. info. ops. Sci. Applications Internat. Corp./Info. Ops. Advanced Technologies and Solutions Group, 1997—2000. With US Army, 1956—59. Recipient Meritorious Civilian Svc. award, US Dept. Def., 1974, Sr. Exec. Svc. Presdl. Rank award, 1984, Exceptional Civilian Svc. award, 1986, 1997, Meritorious Civilian Svc. award, US Dept. Def., 1992, Nat. Intelligence Disting. Svc. medal, 1996, Disting. Civilian Svc. award, US Dept. Def., 2005. Office: Nat Security Agy Central Security Svc 9800 Savage Rd Fort George G Meade MD 20755-6000

BLACK, WILLIAM CORMACK, IV, insect geneticist, statistician; b. Denver, Jan. 6, 1957; s. William Cormack III and Katherine (Marshall) B.; m. Nancy Marie DuTeau, Aug. 15, 1981; children: Christine, Emma. BA, Grinnell Coll., 1979; MS, Duke U., 1981; PhD, Iowa State U., 1985. Psotdoctoral rsch. fellow U. Notre Dame, South Bend, Ind., 1985-88; asst. prof. Kans. State U., Manhattan, 1988-91; asst. prof. dept. microbiology Colo. State U., Ft. Collins, 1991—. Contbr. articles to Theoretical/Applied Genetics, Genetical Rsch., Heredity, Genetics, Bull. Entomol. Rsch. Democrat. Unitarian Universalist. Achievements include, in ecological genetics, use of allozymes and molecular genetic markers to monitor patterns of breeding in insect populations; molecular systematics of Deltocephaline leafhoppers, ticks and aedine mosquitoes. Office: Colo State U Dept Microbiology Immunology & Pathology B416 Microbiology Building Fort Collins CO 80523 Office Phone: 303-491-1081. Office Fax: 303-491-1815. Business E-Mail: William.Black@colostate.edu.

BLACK, WILLIAM REA, lawyer; b. NYC, Nov. 4, 1952; s. Thomas Howard and Dorothy Chambers (Dailey) B.; m. Kathleen Jane Owen, June 24, 1978; children: William Ryan, Jonathan Wesley. BSBA, U. Denver, 1978, MBA, 1981; JD, Western State U., Fullerton, Calif., 1987. Bar: Calif., US Ct. Appeals (fed. cir.), US Dist. Ct., US Supreme Ct.; lic. real estate broker, pvt. investigator. Bus. mgr. Deere & Co., Moline, Ill., 1979-85; dir. Mgmt. Resource Svc. Co., Chgo., 1985-86; sr. v.p. Geneva Corp., Irvine, Calif., 1986-91; pvt. practice Newport Beach, Calif.,

1991-92; gen. counsel Sunclipse, Inc., 1992—97; spl. counsel Amcor, Ltd., 1992—97; dir. gen. Amcor de Mex., S.A. de C.V., 1993—97; secretario KHL de Mex. S.A. de C.V., 1995—97; v.p., gen. counsel LL Knickerbocker Co., 1997-99; CEO Kuroi Kiku Corp., Kuroi Ryu Corp., First Reconnaissance Co., 1997—; v.p., gen. counsel Thales N.Am., 1999—2005; gen. counsel Ground Systems divsn. BAE Systems, Inc., 2006—. Mng. editor Western State U. Law Rev., Fullerton, 1984-87. Instr. Pai Lum Kung Fu Karate, Hartford, Conn., 1970-75, US Judo Assn., Denver, 1975-80, United Studios Kenpo, L.A., 1995—. Recipient Am. Jurisprudence award Bancroft-Whitney Co., 1984, 85, 86; Pres.'s scholar full acad. merit scholarship, 1983. Mem. ABA, Am. Soc. Appraisers, Am. Employment Law Coun., Orange County Bar Assn., Orgn. Fgn. Investment, Internat. Gov. Contractors (adv. bd. Washington 2004—), Mu Kappa Tau. Avocations: Karate (third degree black belt), Judo (black belt), skiing, scuba diving, golf. Business E-Mail: william.black@baesystems.com. E-mail: wrblack0001@cs.com.

BLACKADAR, ALFRED KIMBALL, meteorologist, educator; b. Newburyport, Mass., July 6, 1920; s. Walter Lloyd and Harriett (White) B.; m. Beatrice J. Fenner, Mar. 23, 1946; children: Bruce Evan, Russell Lloyd, Thomas Alan. AB, Princeton U., 1942; PhD, NYU, 1950. From instr. to asso. prof. NYU, 1946-56; lectr. climatology Columbia U., 1953-55; mem. faculty Pa. State U., 1956—, prof. meteorology, 1961—, prof. emeritus, 1985—, head dept., 1967-81. Mem. exec. com. Univ. Corp. Atmospheric Rsch., 1965-68; mem. exec. com. divsn. earth scis. NRC, 1966-69; mem. Internat. Commn. on Dynamical Meteorology, 1978-94, chair working group A, 1978-85; vis. prof. Christian-Albrechts U., Kiel, Germany, 1985-95. Editor: Meteorological Research Revs., 1957; exec. editor: Weatherwise, 1981-95. Sec. Univ. Christian Assn., 1964-68. Served to maj. USAAF, 1942-46. Recipient Sr. Scientist award Alexander von Humboldt Found., 1973 Fellow AAAS, Am. Meteorol. Soc. (sec. 1965-69, pres. 1971-72, editor monographs, Charles F. Brooks award 1969, Cleveland Abbe award 1986, award for outstanding contbns. to the advance of applied meteorology 2002, chmn. publs. commn. 1978-84, chair com. on awards 1989-90), Am. Geophys. Union, Deutsche Meteorologische Gesellschaft (fgn. mem.), North Plainfield (N.J.) Hall of Fame. Baptist. Office: Pa State U 503 Walker Bldg University Park PA 16802-5013 Home: 330 Lions Hill Rd #w221 State College PA 16803 Business E-Mail: akb1@psu.edu.

BLACK BEAR, TRISTAN See MACAVERY, TRISTAN

BLACKBOURN, DAVID GORDON, history professor; b. Spilsby, Eng., Nov. 1, 1949; s. Harry and Pamela Jean (Youngman) B.; m. Deborah Frances Langton; 2 children. BA with honors, Cambridge U., England, 1970, PhD, 1976. Lectr. Queen Mary Coll., U. London, 1976-79, Birkbeck Coll., U. London, 1985-89, prof. history, 1989-92, Harvard U., Cambridge, Mass., 1992-97, Archibald Carey Coolidge prof., 1997—. Vis. Kratter prof. history Stanford (Calif.) U., 1989-90; guest lectr. U.S., England, Italy, Yugoslavia, Germany, 1976—; George C. Windell lectr. New Orleans U., 2006; Crayenborgh lectr. Leiden U., 2007; ann. lectr. German Hist. Inst., London, 1998; Malcolm Wynn lectr. Stetson U., Fla., 2002; hist. cons. Channel 4 TV (UK), History Channel (US); mem. adv. com. Edmund Spevack Meml. Trust, 2002—; dir. Ctr. European Studies Harvard U., Cambridge, 2007-. Author: Class, Religion and Local Politics in Wilhelmine Germany, 1980, (with G. Eley) The Peculiarities of German history, 1984, Populists and Patricians: Essays in Modern German History, 1987; co-editor: (with R.J. Evans) The German Bourgeoisie, 1991, Marpingen: Apparitions of the Virgin Mary in Bismarckian Germany, 1993 (Am. Hist. Assn. prize best book), The Long Nineteenth Century: A History of Germany, 1780-1918, 1998, 2d edit., 2003, The Conquest of Nature: Water, Landscape and the Making of Modern Germany, 2006; mem. editl. bd. Past and Present, 1988—; numerous appearances on Brit. Broadcasting Sys., 1977—; contbr. articles to profl. jours. Gov. Goodrich Sch., London, 1983—86. Rsch. fellow Jesus Coll., Cambridge, 1973-76, Inst. European History, Mainz, Germany, 1974-75, Alexander von Humboldt Found. fellow, 1984-85, John Simon Guggenheim Meml. Found. fellow, 1994-95, Walter Channing Cabot fellow Harvard, 2004; German Acad. Exch. grantee, 1977. Fellow: Am. Acad. Arts & Scis., Royal Hist. Soc.; mem.: Friends of the German Hist. Inst. Washington (bd. dirs.), Am. Hist. Assn. (com. on honorary foreign membership 2001—03, pres. conf. group on ctrl. European history 2003), German History Soc. (sec. 1979—81, com. 1981—86), Inst. European History Mainz (adv. bd. 1995—2005), German Hist. Inst. London (acad. adv. bd. 1983—92). Avocations: writing, reading, jazz, politics, classical music. Office Phone: 617-495-4303 x228. Business E-Mail: dgblackb@fas.harvard.edu.

BLACKBURN, AUDREY PEYTON, lawyer; b. Camden, NJ, July 10, 1938; d. Robert Leon and Catherine (Collins) Peyton; m. Lemuel H. Blackburn, May 1, 1959; children: Hope Renee, Lisa Dawn. BA, Douglass Coll., 1960; JD, Rutgers U., 1974. Bar: NJ 1974, US Dist. Ct. NJ 1974. Tchr. English, Moorestown Jr. HS, NJ, 1961-64, Ewing HS, NJ, 1964-67; ptnr. Blackburn and Blackburn, Trenton, 1974—; dean of students Sch. Law Rutgers U., Camden, NJ, 1987-90; presiding judge Trenton Mcpl. Ct., 1990-99; judge Superior Ct. NJ State, 1999-. Mem. NJ Supreme Ct. Ethics Com., 1985—89, Mayor's Overall Devel. Com., Trenton, 1978—90, Judiciary Alternate Dispute Resolution Com., 2000-02; commr. Trenton Housing Authority, 1980—90; trustee Mercer County Cmty. Coll., Trenton, 1979-82, Mercer council Girl Scouts USA, 1985—90, Children's Home Soc., 1987-89; chair Mercer County NJ State Judiciary Minority Concerns Com., 1999-. Recipient Outstanding Service award Carver Ctr. YMCA, 1981, Outstanding Service award Las Chaperones Sorority, 1982, cert. recognition for excellence in law Mt. Zion Women's Club, 1985. Mem. ABA, NJ Bar Assn., Mercer County Bar Assn., Nat. Assn. Women Lawyers, Nat. Assn. Female Execs., Jack and Jill Am., AAUW. Democrat. Methodist. Club: Links. Avocations: piano, violin, singing, writing, reading. Home: 11 Kensington Ave Trenton NJ 08618-3327 Office: Civil Courts Bldg 175 S Broad St Trenton NJ 08650 Business E-Mail: audrey.blackburn@judiciary.nj.us.

BLACKBURN, JAMES B., III, lawyer; b. Pitts., Nov. 16, 1946; s. James B. Jr. and Ethel Louise (Herrod) B.; m. Cynthia Jan Coote, Aug. 10, 1974; children: Sarah Louise, James B. IV, Natalie Alice. BA, Princeton U., 1969; MPA, N.C. State U., 1974; JD, Duke U., 1980. Bar: N.C. 1980. Staff atty. Gen. Rsch. Divsn, N.C. Gen. Assembly, Raleigh, 1980-84; gen. counsel N.C. Assn. County Commrs., Raleigh, 1984—. Sgt. U.S. Army, 1970-72. Mem. Internat. Mcpl. Lawyers Assn., N.C. Bar Assn. Home: 801 Kings Mill Rd Chapel Hill NC 27517 Office: NC Assn County Commrs PO Box 1488 Raleigh NC 27602-1488 Office Phone: 919-715-2893. Business E-Mail: jim.blackburn@ncacc.org.

BLACKBURN, JOHN D. (JOHN DAVID BLACKBURN), lawyer, educator; b. Connersville, Ind., Dec. 19, 1949; s. James Edwin and Julia Jane (Hubbard) Blackburn; m. Vitalia Berezina, Oct. 29, 1999; children: Jennifer Anne, Melissa Christine, Iris Mae. BS, Ind. State U., Terre Haute, 1971; JD, U. Cin., 1974. Bar: Ohio 1974. Instr. bus. adminstrn. Ohio State U., Columbus, 1975—80, assoc. prof., 1981—. Vis. asst. prof. Ind. U., Bloomington, 1980, U. Pa., Phila., 1980—81; vis. assoc. prof. U. Fla., Gainesville, 2002. Author (with Julius Getman): Labor Relations: Law, Practice and Policy, 1983; author: (with Jack Steiber) Protecting Unorganized Employees Against Unjust Discharge, 1984; author: (with others) Law and Business, 1987, Modern Business Law 3d edit., 1990; author: (with Eliot I. Klayman) Legal Environment of Business 8th edit., 2006; editor-in-chief: Am. Bus. Law Jour., 1986—89, Jour. Legal Studies Edn., 1990—92. Mem.: Am. Bus. Law Assn. (Best Article award 1980). Home: 220 Winthrop Rd Columbus OH 43214 Office: Ohio State Univ 2100 Neil Ave Columbus OH 43210 Office Phone: 614-292-5204. Business E-Mail: blackburn_3@cob.osu.edu.

BLACKBURN, JOHN D., insurance company executive; BA, W Ill. Univ.; MA, Univ. Ill., Springfield, 1979. CLU. Agent through sr. v.p. mktg. Country Ins. & Fin. Services, Bloomington, Ill., 1982—2001, CEO, 2001—. Chmn. Cotton States Ins., Holyoke Mutual Ins. Co., Middlesex Mutual Assurance Co., MSI Preferred Ins. Co. Office: Country Insurance 1701 N Towanda Ave Bloomington IL 61702*

BLACKBURN, JOHN LESLIE, small business owner; b. Malta Bend, Mo., Dec. 21, 1924; s. Clarence Oliver and Vivian (Mitchener) B.; m. Gloria Bullington, June 10, 1950; 1 child, Holly. BS, Mo. Valley Coll., 1950; MEd, U. Colo., 1952; PhD, Fla. State U., 1969. Counselor to men Fla. State U., Tallahassee, 1952-56; from asst. dean of men to dean student devel. U. Ala., Tuscaloosa, 1956-69, v.p. devel., 1978-90; vice chancellor student affairs U. Denver, 1969-74, vice chancellor univ. resources, 1974-78; pres. Blackburn Ednl. Techs., Tuscaloosa, 1990—; gen. sec. Am. Assn. of U. Administrators, Tuscaloosa, Ala., 1993-97; interim dir. Challenge 21, Tuscaloosa, 1998-99. Mem. Model City Mayor's Adv., Denver, 1970-73, Nat. Adv. Coun. on Extension and Continuing Edn., Washington, 1976-78; cons. to sec. HEW, Washington, 1976; mem. Ala. Commn. on Aging, 2000—; mem. Gov.'s Task Force on Devel. of Economically Distressed Counties, 2000-01. Contbr.: Pieces of Eight, 1978. Sgt. AUS, 1943-46, CBI. The Blackburn Inst. was created in his honor by U. Ala., 1995, John L. Blackburn Exemplary award in his honor by AAUA, 1991. Mem. AAUA (pres. 1977-79), Am. Coun. on Edn. (acad. affairs commn. 1970-73), Nat. Assn. Student Pers. Adminstrn. (pres. 1973-74), Nat. Inst. Rsch. and Devel. (founder 1974). Home: 1601 St Andrews Dr Tuscaloosa AL 35406-2058 Office: Blackburn Ednl Techs PO Box 2615 Tuscaloosa AL 35403-2615 E-mail: johnblackburn1@hotmail.com.

BLACKBURN, JOHN OLIVER, economist, consultant; b. Miami, Fla., Sept. 13, 1929; s. Elmer E. and Proxie (Hughes) B.; m. Jeanne Elise Miles, Nov. 29, 1957; children: Katherine Elise, John Parkinson, David Laurence. AB, Duke U., 1951; postgrad., U. Miami, 1951-52; PhD, U. Fla., 1959. CPA, Fla. From asst. prof. econs. to prof. Duke U., 1959-81, provost, 1970-71, chancellor, 1971-76; asst. prof. bus. adminstrn. Am. U., Beirut, 1961-62. Vis. prof. Davidson Coll., 1983. Author: The Renewable Energy Alternative, 1987, Solar Florida: A Sustainable Energy Future, 1993. Bd. dirs. U.S. Found. of Univ. of the Valley of Guatemala, Orlando Philharm. Orch., Fla. With USNR, 1952—55. Mem. Phi Beta Kappa. Democrat. Mem. United Ch. of Christ. Home: 47 Forest at Duke Dr Durham NC 27705 Home Phone: 919-489-5511.

BLACKBURN, JOY MARTIN, retired librarian; b. Marietta, Ohio, Oct. 28, 1925; d. Jonathan George and Helen Joy (Smith) Martin; m. Paul Edward Blackburn, Dec. 18, 1948 (dec. Dec. 1996); children: Paul Conrow, Amy Joy. BA, Ohio Wesleyan U., 1947; MA, U. Minn, 1948. Student counselor Ohio State U., Columbus, 1948—54; editor/libr. Jones & Laughlin Steel Co., Pitts., 1955—57; rsch. libr. Tech. Mktg. Assn., Concord, Mass., 1964—66; mgr. corp. libr. Washington Nat. Ins., Evanston, Ill., 1966—85; systems libr. Luth. Gen. Hosp., Park Ridge, Ill., 1986—88; info. specialist C. Berger & Co., Carol Stream, Ill., 1989—93; ret., 1993. Rschr./editor U. Pitts. Med. Sch., 1959. Author: J&L Rsch. Bull., 1955—57. Vol. Chgo. Bot. Garden Libr., Glencoe, Ill., 1997—99, U. Va. Health Sys. Mktg. and Cmty. Outreach, 2002—, U. Va. Alderman Libr., 2002—, Va. Found. Humanities, 2004—. Mem.: U. Va. Libr. Assocs. (bd. dirs. 2001—, 2004—), Cook County Hort. Soc. (hon.), Phi Beta Kappa. Avocations: history, photography, Arctic travel, art.

BLACKBURN, LARRY H., builder; b. Houston, Tex., Nov. 13, 1948; s. Ephraim S. and Hollie B. Blackburn; m. Judith L. McCubbin, May 28, 1977; children: Wendy L. Blackburn Owens, Ashley G., Courtney L., Kelly L. BBA in Acctg., U. Houston, Tex., 1973; MBA, Calif. Coast U., Santa Ana, Calif., 2004, PhD in Strategic Mgmt., 2007. Classified FBI, Houston, 1970—73; profl. builder E. G. Lowry, Houston, 1974—88, LeBlanc, Houston, 1989—93, Linbeck, Houston, 1994—2002, E. E. Reed, Houston, 2003—. Prin., owner Blackburn Investment Properties, Houston, 1980—2000. Cub master Boy Scouts Am., Houston, 1984—88; coach YMCA, Houston, 1984—94; mem. parish coun. St. Ambrose Cath. Ch., Houston, 2000—04; pastoral adv. St. Edwards Cath. Ch., Houston, 2004—06; chmn. com. St. Pius X Cath. HS, Houston, 2000—03, mem. sch. bd., 2000—03. Sgt. USMC, 1968—74. Recipient Outstanding Carpenter Apprentice award, US Dept. Labor, 1967, Nat. Def. medal, USMC, 1968, Svc. medal, 1970, Cold War Victory medal, 1970, Hon. Svc. medal, 1970. Mem.: Calif. Coast U. Alumni Assn. (assoc.), U. Houston Alumni Assn. (assoc.), Delta Epsilon Tau (assoc.). Independent. Roman Catholic. Avocation: golf. Home Phone: 281-320-8437.

BLACKBURN, MARSHA, congresswoman; b. Laurel, Miss., June 6, 1952; m. Chuck Blackburn; 2 children. BS, Miss. State U., 1973. Retail mktg.; mem. Tenn. State Senate, Nashville, 1998—2002, US Congress from 7th Tenn. dist., 2003—, mem. energy and commerce com., founder Songwriters Caucus, 2003. Del. Am. Coun. Young Polit. Leaders, S.E. Asia, 1993; appointed by Gov. Don Sundquist exec. dir. Tenn. Film, Entertainment and Music Commn., 1995; chmn. Gov.'s Prayer Breakfast, 1996; bd. dirs. Benton Hall Sch., Nashville Symphony Guild, Arthritis Found., Nashville Zoo Friends; appointed Econ. Coun. on Women, 1999. Named a Small Bus. Adv., Small Bus. Survival Com., 2003; recipient Spirit of Enterprise award, US C. of C., 2004. Mem. Nat. Acad. Rec. Arts and Scis., Country Music Assn., Rotary, C. of C. Republican. Office: US Ho Reps 509 Cannon Ho Office Bldg Washington DC 20515-4305 Office Phone: 202-225-2811.*

BLACKBURN, MICHAEL DALE, lawyer, educator; b. Mt. Pleasant, Utah, June 28, 1951; m. Celia W. Blackburn, Aug. 21, 1973; children: Lauren, Alison, Erin, Andrew, Megan. BS in Acctg., U. Utah, 1973; JD, Stanford U., 1978. Bar: Utah 1978, U.S. Tax Ct. 1980; CPA, Utah. Acct. John F. Forbes & Co., San Francisco, 1973-76; pvt. practice acctg. San Jose, Calif., 1976-78; ptnr. Snow, Christensen & Martineau, Salt Lake City, 1978-93, Blackburn & Stoll, LC, Salt Lake City, 1993—. Prof. taxation U. Utah, Salt Lake City, 2001—; trustee Hansen Planetarium Found., Salt Lake City, 1980—; presenter in field. Contbr. articles to profl. jours. Planned giving com. Primary Children's Hosp., Salt Lake City, 1987-89. Fellow Am. Coll. Trust and Estate Coun.; mem. AICPA (Outstanding Instr. 1988, 98), ABA, Utah State Bar Assn. (chmn. estate planning sect. 1988-89, chmn. task force multidisciplinary practice 2001-2003), Utah Assn. CPAs (pres. 2001, CPA of Yr. 1997). Office: Blackburn & Stoll LC 257 E 200 S Ste 800 Salt Lake City UT 84111

BLACKBURN, ROBERT PARKER, lawyer; b. Tacoma, Sept. 24, 1956; s. John Griffin and Dorothy Joan (Parker) B. BS with honors, Case Western Res. U., 1978; JD, Am. U., 1981. Bar: D.C. 1982, Calif. 1987, US Patent and Trademark Office 1981. Atty. Banner, Birch, McKie and Beckett, Washington, 1981-84; asst. patent counsel Agrigenetics Research Corp., Boulder, Colo., 1984-86; atty. Ciotti and Murashige, Menlo Park, Calif., 1986-87; ptnr. Irell & Manella, Menlo Park, 1987-89; dir. intellectual property Chiron Corp., Emeryville, Calif., 1989-91, v.p., chief patent counsel, 1991—2005; pvt. practice Berkeley, Calif., 2005—. Disting. scholar Berkeley Ctr. for Law and Tech., U. Calif. Berkeley Sch. Law, 2001—. Mem. AAAS, ABA, Am. Chemical Soc., Am. Intellectual Property Law Assn. (biotech. task force mem., chem. practice com., biotechnology subcom. mem.). Office: 2930 Domingo Ave #209 Berkeley CA 94705 Office Phone: 510-898-5000.

BLACKBURN, SADIE GWIN ALLEN, conservation executive; b. San Angelo, Tex., Oct. 14, 1924; d. Harvey Hicks Allen and Helen (Harris) Weaver; m. Edward Albert Blackburn Jr., Feb. 25, 1946; children: Edward III, Catherine Ledyard, Robert Allen. BA, Rice U., 1945, MA, 1975. Bookkeeper, trust dept. State Nat. Bank, Houston; tchr. elem. sch. Galveston, Tex.; mng. ptnr. Storey Creek Partnership, Houston, 1969—; dir. spl. projects San Jacinto State Park; dir. master plan State Hist. Park. Lectr. in landscape design history; spkr. in field. Co-author: Houston's Forgotten Heritage, 1822-1914, 1991; contbr. articles to gardening publs. Newsheet chmn. Jr. League, Galveston, 1950-53, art chmn., Houston Jr. League, 1957-58, chmn. garden/design com., 1991-93, mental health study com., 1959-61, 2d v.p., 1962-63, provisional chmn., 1962-63, interview chmn., 1963-64; adv. bd. Bayou Bend Gardens chmn. Mus. Fine Arts, 1973-74, Bayou Bend adv. com., 1987-89; v.p. Mental Health Assn., 1957-62, Botanic Garden Houston, 2005—; asst. treas. Child Guidance Assn., 1962-65; mem. Rice U. Hist. Commn., 1974-75; pres. River Oaks Garden Club, Houston, 1975-76; mem. adv. com. Bayou Bend Gardens, 1991—; active Buffalo Bayou Partnership, Houston Nature Conservancy, 1993, Friends of Herman Park, 1994, Meml. Park Adv., 1995, Scenic Houston Bd., 1999. Named Scenic Visionary, Scenic Houston, 2003; recipient Sweet Briar Disting. Alumna award, 1991, award, Friends of Herman Park, 2003, Stewardship Excellence award, Cultural Landscape Found., 2005, honor, San Jacinto Mus. History, 2006. Mem. Garden Club Am. (zone chmn. 1977-79, founders fund vice chmn. 1979-80, dir. 1980-82, rec. sec. 1982-84, v.p. 1984-86, archive co-chmn. 1986-87, 1st v.p. 1987-89, pres. 1989-91, Achievement medal 2002), Nat. Wildflower Rsch. Ctr. (bd. dirs.), Nat. Parks and Conservation Assn. Bd. (v.p. 1995-97, sec. 1997-99), San Jacinto Mus. History (pres. bd. 1975-77, bd. dirs.), Pi Beta Phi (Carolyn Herman Lichtenberg Crest award for disting. alumnae achievement 1998). Republican. Episcopalian. Avocations: gardening, fishing, hunting, bridge, golf. Home: 1030 Potomac Houston TX 77057-1916

BLACKBURN, TERRY L., systems administrator; b. Garden Grove, Calif., May 11, 1957; s. James W Blackburn and Blackburn R Ramona; m. Launa Rae Mathews, Nov. 16, 1997; children: Chantel C, Chelsea M Cafferky, Michael A, Lindsey R Cafferky. BA, Walla Walla Coll., Coll. Place, 1996. Sys. svcs. mgr. Tuality Healthcare, Hillsboro, Oreg., 1989—. Composer: (piano solo) Four Short Detours (1st Pl., Oreg. Music Teacher's Assn. Composition Contest, 1975), (musical) The Great Lewis & Clark Extravaganza of 1905 -or- Paddle Your Own Canoe, (duo for soprano and flute) Summoned by the Tides. Pres. Rotary Club, Hillsboro, Oreg., 2006—07. Mem.: Am. Mensa. Achievements include development of first automated report distribution system for IBM AS/400 - still in use world wide; Recognized as a leader in the field of 3D photography and color anaglyph production. Office: Tuality Healthcare 335 SE 8th Av Hillsboro OR 97123 Home Phone: 503-531-9158; Office Phone: 503-681-1774. Personal E-mail: whoswho@terryblackburn.us.

BLACKBURN, WILLIAM STANLEY, lawyer; b. Nashville, Nov. 7, 1951; s. William Hodge and Margaret Virginia (Ware) B.; m. Laura Ross Wilson, July 23, 1983; children: William, Margaret. BS in Economics, Auburn U., 1973; JD, U.Va., 1976. Assoc. Kilpatrick & Cody (now Kilpatrick Stockton, LLP), Atlanta, 1976—82, ptnr., 1982—. Co-chair Bus. Transactions Group, 1996—2001; mem. bus. law sect. State Bar Ga., sect. sec., 1998, sect. vice chair, 99, sect. chair, 2000, mem. legal opinions com., 1991—, chair, 1992—98, younger lawyers sect. long range planning com., 1979—80, pub. com., 1979—80, credit union com., 1980—81. Notes Editor Va. Law Review, 1975-76, mem. editorial bd., 1974-75. Sec. Boys and Girls Clubs of Metro Atlanta, Inc., 1984—, mng. bd. dirs., 1982—, mem. exec. com., 1984—; chmn. legal divsn. Fulton County, Am. Heart Assn., 1981; mem. Leadership Atlanta, 1983-84; sec. Young Men's Round Table, High Mus. Art, 1984-85, pres., 1985-86, mem., 1983-86; group chmn. United Way Atlanta, 1984, account exec.; bd. dirs. Japan-Am. Soc. Ga., 1986-90. Fellow: Am. Coll. Investment Counsel; mem.: ABA (young lawyers sect. banking law subcom. 1980—81, com. legal opinions 1992—, sect. bus. law), Cobb County C. of C. (internat. bus. coun. 1984—89), Can. Am. Soc. Atlanta (bd. dirs. 1998—2001), Atlanta Bar Assn. (cts. com. 1982—83, co-chmn. joint task force mcpl. ct. City of Atlanta 1982—83, law day com. 1984), Piedmont Diving Club, Lawyers Club Atlanta, Omicron Delta Epsilon, Phi Eta Sigma, Omicron Delta Kappa, Phi Kappa Phi, Order of Coif. Avocation: golf. Home: 2595 Habersham Rd NW Atlanta GA 30305-3557 Office: Kilpatrick Stockton LLP 1100 Peachtree St NE Ste 2800 Atlanta GA 30309-4530 Office Phone: 404-815-6400. Business E-Mail: sblackburn@kilpatrickstockton.com.

BLACKBURN, WYATT DOUGLAS, insurance executive; b. July 6, 1954; s. Wyatt W. and Marjorie C. (Wyre) B.; m. Deborah L. Garland, Feb. 28, 1987; children: Wyatt Woodrow, Taylor Lynne. BBA, West Tex. State U., 1976. Staff acct. Harvey, Messenger & Co. CPAs, Amarillo, 1974-77; audit mgr. Martin W. Cohen & Co. CPAs, Dallas, 1977-78, sr. v.p. adminstrv. ops., 1978-88, sr. v.p., CFO, 1988-94, sr. v.p., COO, 1995-97; exec. v.p., COO State Nat. Cos., Ft. Worth, 1997—. Bd. dirs. State & County Mut. Fire Ins. Co., State Nat. Ins. Co., Nat. Specialty Ins. Co., United Specialty Ins. Co. Tex., United Splty. Ins. Co. Mem. AICPA, Tex. Soc. CPAs, Omicron Delta Epsilon. Home: 1028 Diamond Blvd Southlake TX 76092-6208 Office: State Nat Cos 8200 Anderson Blvd Fort Worth TX 76120-3620 Office Phone: 817-265-2000. Business E-Mail: wblackburn@statenational.com.

BLACKBURNE-RIGSBY, ANNA, state supreme court justice; b. Washington; BA in Polit. Sci., Duke U.; JD, Howard U. Sch. of Law, 1987. Assoc. atty. Hogan and Hartson, 1987—92; special counsel DC Office of Corp. Counsel, 1992—94, dep. corp. counsel of family services div., 1994—96; hearing commsr. DC Superior Ct., 1996—2000, assoc. judge, 2000—06, DC Ct. Appeals, 2006—. Mem. judicial ed. com. DC Superior Ct.; lecturer Harvard Law Sch.; adjunct prof. U. DC David A. Clarke Sch. of Law. Recipient Women Meritorious Svc. award, Nat. Assn. of Professional Women. Mem.: Internat. Assn. of Women Judges (bd. managerial trustees), Nat. Assn. of Women Judges (v.p. dist. 4, chair nominating com.), Wash. Bar Assn. (former chair judicial council). Office: DC Ct of Appeals Moultrie Courthouse 500 Indiana Ave NW Washington DC 20001*

BLACKER, DEBORAH, epidemiologist, educator, psychiatrist; b. Glendale, Calif., 1956; MD, Harvard U., Boston, 1984, DSc, 1992. Diplomate Am. Bd. Psychiatry and Neurology, Am. Bd. Psychiatry and Neurology. Assoc. prof. epidemiology sch. pub. health Harvard U., Boston, 2002—, assoc. prof. psychiatry med. sch., 2002—; dir. gerontology rsch. unit dept. psychiatry Mass. Gen. Hosp., Boston, 2003—, asst. vice chmn. rsch. dept. psychiatry, 2006—. Office Phone: 617-726-5571.

BLACKETOR, PAUL GARBER, minister; b. Birmingham, Ala., Feb. 10, 1927; s. Everly B. and Marie (Scokel) B.; m. Sandra Blacketor; children: A. Wade, Paula. Christopher, Racheal. BS, Samford U., Birmingham, Ala., 1953; MS, Auburn U., 1954, MA, 1955, EdD, 1956. Ordained to ministry, Bapt. Ch., 1952. Pastor Heidrick (Ky.) Bapt. Ch., 1962-63, Clarks Summit (Pa.) Bapt. Ch., 1963-64, Dalton (Pa.) Bapt. Ch., 1963-65, Wilmington (Vt.) Bapt. Ch., 1969-88, Fitzwilliam (N.H.) Bapt. Ch., 1990—. Prof. Keene State Coll., N.H., 1966-97. Mem. N.H. Gen. Ct., 1984-90. Capt.

U.S. Army, 1987, ret. Mem.: Internat. Conf. Police Chaplains, Assn. U.S. Army, Ret. Officers Orgn., Assn. Mil. Surgeons U.S., Am. Legion, VFW. Democrat. Home: 104 Chimney Hill Dr Colchester VT 05446-7364

BLACKFORD, BARBARA L., lawyer, manufacturing executive; Ptnr. Kutak Rock, Long Aldridge & Norman LLP; assoc. gen. counsel Monsanto Co., 1997—2000, head corp. securities and mergers and acquisitions law groups, gen. counsel Cereon Genomics; v.p., gen. counsel, sec. AirGate PCS, 2000—04; exec. v.p., gen. counsel, sec. Superior Essex, Inc., Atlanta, 2004—. Mem.: Soc. Corp. Secretaries and Governance Profls. (bd. dirs.). Office: Superior Essex Inc 150 Interstate N Parkway Atlanta GA 30339*

BLACKFORD, ROBERT NEWTON, lawyer, director; b. Cin., Feb. 5, 1937; s. Robert Criley and Virginia Pendleton (Yowell) B.; m. Margaret Ann Williams, July 22, 1961; children: William Pendleton, John Whitner. BSBA, U. Fla., Gainesville, 1960; JD, Emory U., Atlanta, 1968. Bar: Fla. 1968, Ga. 1968. Mem., dir. Maguire, Voorhis & Wells, P.A., Orlando, Fla., 1972-98, sec., treas., 1972-95; ptnr. Holland & Knight LLP, Orlando, 1998—2001. Sec. Hughes Supply, Inc., Orlando, 1972-96, asst. sec., 1996-98; sec. Princeton Fin. Corp., 1987-94. Mem. Orlando Mcpl. Planning Bd., 1969-75, Orlando Downtown Devel. Bd., 1972-77, chmn., 1975-77, bd. dirs. Crime Commn., Inc., 1985-88; mem. Orange County's Refuse Disposal Citizens Coordination Com., 1988-90, Orange County Solid Waste Adv. Bd., 1992-96; mem. neighborhood concerns com. Orlando Naval Tng. Ctr. Base Closing Commn., 1994-96; trustee Chelsey G. Magruder Found., Inc., 1981—, pres., 1982-85, 92-94, 2000-02, sec./treas., 1998-2000; trustee Orlando Mus. Art, 1980-82, 85-91, pres. 1985-86, chmn. bd., 1986-87, v.p. 1989-91; ruling elder First Presbyn. Ch., Orlando, 1989-2003, tchr., 1970-2000; bd. dirs. Univ. Club Orlando, 1994-97, sec., 1994-96; active The Cathedral Ch. of St. Luke, 2004—. Mem. Fla. Bar Assn., State Bar Ga. (emeritas), Orlando Area C. of C. (pres. 1980, chmn. bd. dirs. 1981), Orange County Hist. Soc. (bd. dirs. 1980-83), Country Club Orlando, Rotary Club Orlando (pres. 1991-92). Democrat. Personal E-mail: rblackf398@aol.com.

BLACKHAM, ANN ROSEMARY, realtor; b. NYC, June 16, 1927; d. Frederick Alfred and Letitia L. (Stolfe) DeCain; m. James W. Blackham Jr., Aug. 18, 1951; children: Ann C., James W. III. AB, St. Mary of the Springs Coll. (now Ohio Dominican U.), 1949; postgrad., Ohio State U., 1950. Mgr. br. store Filene & Sons, Winchester, Mass., 1950—52; broker Porter Co. Real Estate, Winchester, 1961—66; sales mgr. James T. Trefrey, Inc., Winchester, 1966—68; pres., founder Ann Blackham & Co. Inc. Realtors, Winchester, 1968—2001; v.p. Coldwell Banker, Winchester, 2001—. Bd. econ. advisors to Gov., 1969-74; participant White House Conf. on Internat. Cooperation, 1965; mem. Presdl. Task Force on Women's Rights and Responsibilities, 1969; exec. coun. Mass. Civil Def., 1965-69; chmn. Gov.'s Commn. on Status of Women, 1971-75; regional dir. Interstate Assn. Commn. on Status of Women, 1971-74; mem. Gov. Task Force on Mass. Economy, 1972; mem. Gov.'s Jud. Selection Com., 1972, Mass. Emergency Fin. Bd., 1974-75; bd. registration Real Estate Brokers and Salesman Commonwealth of Mass., 1991—, chmn. 1994—, Mass. Housing Authority, 2005—. Bd. visitors Ohio Dominican U., 1995—, nat. fund raising chair, 1998-99; corporator, trustee Charlestown Savs. Bank, 1974-84; corporator Winchester Hosp., 1983—, chair fund raising emergency room; bd. dirs. Winchester Hosp. Found., 1996—; mem. Winchester 350th Anniversary Commn.; design rev. commn. Town of Winchester, 1981-2003, Mass. Housing Authority, 2006—; bd. dirs. Phoenix Found., 1980-90, Bay State Health Care, Mass. Taxpayers Found., Speech and Hearing Found., Baystate Health Mgmt., Realty Guild Inc., v.p. 1995-96, bd. dirs. 1996-99, pres. 1997-98; regional selection panel White House Fellows, 1973-74; com. on women in svc. U.S. Dept. Def., 1977-80; 2d v.p. Doric Dames, 1971-74, founding mem., 1969; dep. chmn. Mass. Rep. State Com., 1965-66; sec. Mass. Rep. State Conv., 1970, del., 1960, 62, 64, 66, 70, 72, 74, 78, 90, 98, 2002, 06; state vice-chmn. Mass. Rep. Fin. Com., 1970; alt. del.-at-large Rep. Nat. Conv., 1968, 72, del., 1980, 84, 88, 92, 96; Rep. State Committeewoman, 1996—; pres. Mass. Fedn. Rep. Women, 1964-69; v.p. Nat. Fedn. Rep. Women, 1965-79; pres. Scholarship Found., 1976-78, Mass. Fedn. Women's Clubs; alumnae liaison The Beaumont Sch. for Girls; mem. Women for Romney, 2002; mem. Gov. Romney Inaugural Com.; mem. com. Bush Reelection, 2004; Gov.'s appointee to Housing Authority, 2006—, treas. Recipient Pub. Svc. award Commonwealth of Mass., 1978, Merit award Rep. Party, 1969, Pub. Affairs award Mass. Fedn. Women's Clubs, 1975; named Civic Leader of Yr. Mass. Broadcasters, 1962, Banker and Tradesman Leader Making a Difference, 1999; recipient Bus. Owner of Yr. award New England Women Bus. Owners, 1995, Disting. Alumnae award Ohio Dominican Coll., 1999, Disting. Service Citation Town of Winchester, 2003 Mem. Greater Boston Real Estate Bd. (hon., bd. dirs.), Eastern Middlesex Bd. Realtors (life mem. multi-million dollar club), Mass. Assn. Realtors (bd. dirs.), Nat. Assn. Realtors (women's coun.), Brokers Inst. (cert.), Coun. Realtors (cert., pres. 1983-84), Winchester C. of C. (bd. dirs.), Greater Boston C. of C., Nat. Assn. Women Bus. Owners, ENKA Soc. (treas. 2001—04), Rotary Internat., Tequesta Fla. Country Club, Capitol Hill Club, Ponte Vedra Club, Winchester Boat Club, Winchester Country Club, Wychmere Harbor Club, Womens City Club, Winton Club (sec., bd. dirs.), Hyannis Yacht Club. Office: Coldwell Banker 3 Church St Winchester MA 01890-2903 Home Phone: 781-729-3459. Business E-Mail: ann.blackham@nemoves.com.

BLACKLEDGE, BRETT J., reporter; b. Baton Rouge; married; 1 child. Grad., La. State U., 1986. Reporter AP, New Orleans, Jackson, Miss., Tulsa, Okla., Jour. Newspapers, Washington, Edn. Daily, Washington; local govt. reporter, edn. & state govt. reporter Mobile (Ala.) Register, 1993—98; gen. assignment & spl. projects reporter Birmingham (Ala.) News, 1998—. Recipient Pulitzer Prize for Investigative Reporting, 2007. Office: Birmingham News PO Box 2553 Birmingham AL 35202 Office Phone: 205-325-3123. E-mail: bblackledge@bhamnews.com.*

BLACKLEDGE, DAVID WILLIAM, retired academic administrator; b. Cin., Mar. 10, 1930; s. William Clinton and Helen Louise (Van Curen) B.; m. Diana Marjorie Wiley, June 5, 1953; children: David Noel, William Dean, Alan Keith, Naomi Karen. BS, Purdue U., W. Lafayette, Ind., 1953; MA, Rutgers U., New Brunswick, NJ, 1965; grad., Nat. War Coll., Wash., 1975. Commd. 2d lt. US Army, 1953, advanced through grades to col., 1974; asst. prof. mil. sci. Rutgers U., New Brunswick, NJ, 1961-64; instr. Am. history U. Md.-Far East Divsn., Bangkok, 1967-68; dir. nat. security studies US Army War Coll., Carlisle, Pa., 1978-83; dir. fin. aid Pa. State U. Dickinson Sch. Law, Carlisle, 1983—84, dir. admissions and fin. aid, 1984-94, exec. asst. to the dean, 1994-2000; ret., 2000. Co-compiler: Blackledges in America: A Genealogy of Blackledge/Blackledge Descendants with Roots in the USA, 2002. Bd. dirs. Carlisle area United Way, 1983-86, Sarah Todd Retirement Home, Carlisle, 1989-95. Decorated Legion of Merit with oak leaf cluster.

BLACKLEY, CHERYL ANN, musician, freelance/self-employed educator; b. Woods Cross, Utah, June 8, 1960; d. LeGrande and Patricia Green Blackley. MusB in Secondary Edn., BS in Secondary Edn., Utah State U., 1988. Sole propr./owner and dir. S & D Music Studio, Woods Cross, 1988—; freelance musician on clarinets, saxophones, oboe/english horn & bassoon No. Utah area, 1988—. Prin. clarinet Utah State U. Alumni Band, Logan, 1984—; orch. mgr. Westminster Chamber Orch., Salt Lake City, 1992—94; founding exec. bd. mem., orch. mgr. Intermountain Chamber Orch., Salt Lake City, 1994—96; orch. mem.-reeds Former Utah Musical Theatre, Ogden, 1994—2006; orch. mgr. Utah Musical Theatre, 1999—2006, asst. music dir., 2004, assoc. music dir., condr., 2005—06. Composer: (orchestral works) The Mist, 1993—94, (clarinet solo) 2257 (Utah Best of Category Instrumental Composer's Guild Composition Contest, 1999), (songs) Trio No. 1 for Flute, Oboe & Clarinet (1st pl. Tchr. Composition Competition Utah Music Tchrs. Assn., 1997, 3rd pl. music for children category Composer's Guild Composition Contest, 1995), Gently Raise the Sacred Strain, arr. for Mixed Woodwind Trio (award of merit instrumental divsn. LDS Ch. Music Competition, 1996). Mem.: Utah Music Tchrs. Assn., Music Tchrs. Nat. Assn., Utah Music Educators Assn., Music Educators Nat. Conf., Golden Key, Phi Kappa Phi. Mem. Lds Ch. Avocations: reading, gardening, off-road desert racing, cooking, baking. Home: 1985 S 800 W Woods Cross UT 84087 Office: S & D Music Studio 796 W 2000 S Woods Cross UT 84087 Office Phone: 801-292-8707. Business E-Mail: sdmusic@netzero.net.

BLACKLOW, ROBERT STANLEY, internist, educator; b. Cambridge, Mass., June 24, 1934; s. Leo Alfred and Clara Edna (Cumenes) Blacklow; m. Winifred Young, Dec. 7, 1958; children: Stephen Charles, Kenneth Lawrence, David Alan. AB summa cum laude, Harvard U., 1955, MD cum laude, 1959; DSc (hon.), Kent State U., 1998; DMed. (hon.), U. Pecs, Hungary, 2001. Intern Peter Bent Brigham Hosp., Boston, 1959-60, resident, 1960-61, 63-64, 67-68; instr. Harvard U., 1967-70, asst. prof. medicine, 1970-76, assoc. prof., 1976-78, asst. to dean faculty of medicine, 1969-73, assoc. dean, 1973-78; prof. internal medicine Rush Med. Coll., 1978-85, dean, 1978-81; v.p. for med. affairs Rush-Presbyn.-St. Luke's Med. Center, Chgo., 1978-81; prof. medicine Jefferson Med. Coll., Phila., 1985-92, sr. assoc. dean, 1985-92; pres., dean Northeastern Ohio Univs. Coll. Medicine, Rootstown, 1992—2002, prof. cmty. medicine, prof. medicine, 1992—2002, prof. emeritus cmty. medicine, 2002—, 2002—; sr. scholar health policy Assn. Acad. Health Ctrs., Washington, 2002—05; vis. prof. social medicine Harvard Med. Sch., Boston, 2005—07, sr. lectr. social medicine, 2007—. Mem. sci. adv. com. Nat. Fund Med. Edn., 1981—84, Nat. Cancer Inst., 1986—95; bd. dir. Nat. Resident Matching Program, 1993—2003, pres.-elect, 1994—95, pres., 1995—96, treas., 1998—99, 2001—03, pres.-elect, 1999—2000, pres., 2000—01; spl. cons. to dir. Nat. Inst. Alcohol Abuse and Alcoholism, 2003—06. Editor: (book) Signs and Symptoms, 1971, Signs and Symptoms, 6th edit., 1983; mem. editl. bd. Jour. Med. Humanities, 1997—. Trustee Chestnut Hill Sch., Newton, Mass., 1970—79, Belmont (Mass.) Hill Sch., 1973—79, Chgo. chpt. ARC, 1979, Greater Akron (Ohio) Musical Assn., 1993—2002, mem. exec. com., 1998—2002; dir. Akron Regional Devel. Bd., 1998—2003; mem. Ill. health svc. corps task force Ill. Dept. Pub. Health, 1980; corporator Belmont Hill Sch., 1978—. With USPHS, 1961—63. Sr. scholar, Assn. Acad. Health Ctrs., 2002—05. Fellow: ACP, Chgo. Soc. Internal Medicine, Inst. Medicine Chgo.; mem.: AAAS, Assn. Acad. Health Ctrs., Assn. Am. Med. Colls., N.Y. Acad. Sci., St. Rotolph Club (Boston), Literary Club (Chgo.), Badminton & Tennis Club (Boston), Harvard Musical Assn., Longwood Cricket Club (Boston), Cliff Dwellers Club (Chgo.), Franklin Inn (Phila.), Rowfant Club, Alpha Omega Alpha, Sigma Xi, Phi Beta Kappa. Home: 16 Birchwood Ln Lincoln MA 01773 Office: Dept Social Medicine 641 Huntington Ave Boston MA 02115 Business E-Mail: blacklow@neoucom.edu.

BLACKMAN, DOROTHY J., library director; b. Lynn, Mass., Sept. 11, 1935; d. Harvey William and Marion Marie (Hooper) Loyte; m. John A. Blackman, June 11, 1955; children: David John, Deborah DeForest, Karen, Kathy Felker. Student, Gordon Coll., Mass., 1952—54. Data processing Gilman Brothers Wholesale Druggists, Boston, 1944—55; data processor CBS Hytron, Danvers, Mass., 1955—56, Bomac Labs, Beverly, Mass., 1956—58; dir., mgr. Edmeston Free Libr., NY, 1982—. Substitute tchr. Edmeston Ctrl. Sch., 1964—94. Author: The Long Sleep, 1992, Zeke, 1992; contbr. articles to profl. jours. and mags. Spkr., rep. Alcohol Edn. for Youth, NY, 1966—76. Recipient Cmty Svc. award, Wharton Valley Grange, Edmeston, N.Y. Baptist. Avocations: gardening, reading, cooking. Home: 60 High St Edmeston NY 13335 Office: Edmeston Free libr 6 West St Edmeston NY 13335 Home Phone: 607-965-8597; Office Phone: 607-965-8208.

BLACKMAN, ERIC GLEN, physics and astronomy professor; b. Rochester, NY, Sept. 21, 1968; s. Jerome Robert Blackman and Esther Ruth Miller. SB in Physics, MIT, Cambridge, 1990; CASM with honors, Cambridge U., Eng., 1991; AM, Harvard U., Cambridge, 1993, PhD, 1995. Rsch. fellow Cambridge U. Inst. Astronomy, 1995—98; postdoctoral scholar Calif. Inst. Tech., Pasadena, 1998—99; asst. prof. physics and astronomy U. Rochester, Rochester, 2000—03, assoc. prof. physics and astronomy, 2003—04, prof. physics and astronomy, 2004—, sr. scientist, lab. laser energetics, 2004—. Def. sci. study group Inst. Def. Analyses, Alexandria, Va., 2006—; vis. prof. in field to numerous univs. throughout US and internat.; chair to various dept. unvi. coms.; spkr. and lectr. in field to numerous unvis. and orgns. Contbr. over 100 articles and conf. proceedings to profl. jours. Bd. trustees Harley Sch., Rochester, 2002—03. Recipient Faculty Devel. award, Dept. Energy, 2000—04; fellow, Am. Nuc. Soc., 1989—90; grantee, Dept. Energy, 2000—04, Telescope Sci. Inst., 2004—05, NASA, 2005—; scholar, Harley Sch., Rochester, 1985—86; Travel grant, AAS, 2001, grants, NSF, 2004—. Fellow: Am. Astron. Soc., Am. Phys. Soc. (exec. com. mem. plasma astrophysics 2003—06). Avocations: exercise, music, ornithology. Office: Univ Rochester Dept Physics and Astronomy Rochester NY 14627

BLACKMAN, EVERETT ALLAN, writer; b. Chgo., Feb. 25, 1927; s. Charles and Margaret Hertha Blackman. BA, New Sch., NYC, 1950. Film prodr., dir. Everett Blackman Prodns., Chgo., 1966—84; author Chgo., 1985—. Dir. Chgo. Pk. Dist., Chgo. Stage Guild, 1964—68. Author: So You Want to be President, 1973; author: (with Mark Bell, illustrator) (book) Pyramids & Puns: the 1st Book of Egyptian Humor, 1988 (archived by the Brit. Mus. Ctrl. Libr. Humanities Divsn., 1994); author: (short stories) Wolf Creek Tales, 2005, (plays) In Praise of Walnuts, 2006, From the Tales of Burdock Mountain, 1991 (winner of Salinas River New Works Play Festival, 1993), Old-Fashioned Girl, 2001, The General's Pants, 2002, Salable Livestock Receipts (America, You're Beautiful!), 2002, (book, non fiction) Crisis Studies in Human Affairs, 1999, (poetry, essays) Meanderings of a Soul in Transit, 2003. Sponsor Paralyzed Vets. Am., Wilton, NH, 1988—2007. Sgt. US Army, 1945—47, Ft. Dix, NJ, Pine Camp, NY. Scholar Graphic Design award, Mpls. Art Instrn. Co., 1944—45. Avocations: photography, travel. Office: Norcor Enterprises 6147 N Sheridan Rd Chicago IL 60660-2803 Office Phone: 773-743-6792. Personal E-mail: norcorent@juno.com.

BLACKMAN, JEFFREY WILLIAM, lawyer; b. LA, Oct. 24, 1948; s. Ralph Leonard and Judith Esther (Glantz) B. BA, U. Ariz., 1970, JD, 1976. Bar: Ariz. 1976, U.S. Dist. Ct. Ariz. 1977, U.S. Ct. Appeals (9th cir.) 1980, U.S. Supreme Ct. 1980, U.S. Dist. Ct. (no. dist.) Calif. 1988. Pvt. practice, Oracle, Ariz., 1977-85; assoc. various law firms, Phoenix, Tucson, 1986-87; pvt. practice Tucson, 1988—. Participant March for the Animals, Washington, 1990, 96. 2d lt. ROTC, U.S. Army. Recipient Cert. of Appreciation, Ctr. Environ. Edn. Whale Protection Fund, 1984, UNICEF, Defenders of Wildlife, Nat. Humane Edn. Soc., ASPCA, Humane Soc. US, Tiger Haven, Wine Diploma, San Francisco Wine Inst. Wine Adv. Bd., 1964, Cert. of Appreciation for Service in Israel during the Gulf War, Nation of Israel; named Ptnr. for Life, Cal Farley's Boy Ranch, Amarillo, Tex., 1982. Mem. State Bar Ariz., Mensa, Alliance Francaise, Animal Legal Def. Fund. Avocations: rock drummer, tennis, hiking, gardening. Office: PO Box 41624 Tucson AZ 85717-1624 Office Phone: 520-795-3321.

BLACKMAN, JOHN CALHOUN, IV, lawyer; b. Monroe, La., Dec. 13, 1944; s. John Calhoun Blackman III and Marie (Collens) Bernstein; m. Judy Swayze, Apr. 19, 1986; children: Carrie Marie, Caroline Frances, Mary Winston. BA, La. State U., 1966, JD, 1969. Bar: La. 1969, U.S. Ct. Appeals (5th cir.) 1969, U.S. Tax Ct. 1972, U.S. Supreme Ct. 1976. Ptnr. Hudson, Potts & Bernstein, Monroe, 1969-79, Blackman, Arnold & Pettway, Monroe, 1979-88, Jones, Walker, Waechter, Poitevent, Carrere & Denegre, Baton Rouge, 1988—. Adj. prof. law La. State U., Baton Rouge, 1990-93; mem. com. of 100 econ. devel., 1993—; mem. trust code com. La. State Law Inst., 1982—. Mem. La. State U. Found.; mem. adv. commn. Estate Planning and Adminstrn. Cert., 1994—99, chmn., 1998—99. Fellow Am. Coll. Trusts and Estates Counsel (bus. planning com.), Am. Coll. Tax Counsel; mem. ABA (litigation task force, employee benefits com., taxation sect.), La. Bar Assn. (cert. tax specialist, cert. estate planning and adminstrn. specialist, chmn. taxation sect. 1976-77, chmn. liaison com. with dist. dir. IRS 1981-82, liaison com. with regional commrs. office), Estate Planning Coun. N.E. La. (pres. 1975-76), NASD (arbitrator), Estate and Bus. Planning Coun. Baton Rouge. Republican. Episcopalian. Office: Jones Walker et al 8555 United Plaza Blvd Ste 500 Baton Rouge LA 70809 Home Phone: 225-383-6342; Office Phone: 225-248-2070. Business E-Mail: jblackman@joneswalker.com. E-mail: jcbandjsb@bellsouth.net.

BLACKMAN, KENNETH ROBERT, lawyer; b. Providence, May 19, 1941; s. Edward and Beatrice (Wolf) B.; m. Meryl June Rosenthal, June 7, 1964; children: Michael, Susan, Kevin. AB, Brown U., 1962; LLB, MBA, Columbia U., 1965. Bar: N.Y. 1966. Law clk. to U.S. Dist. Judge, 1965—66; ptnr. Fried, Frank, Harris, Shriver & Jacobson, LLP, NYC, 1966—. Mem.: ABA, N.Y. Bar Assn., Assn. Bar City of N.Y., Phi Beta Kappa, Beta Gamma Sigma. Office: Fried Frank Harris Shriver & Jacobson LLP 1 New York Plz Fl 22 New York NY 10004-1980 Office Phone: 212-859-8000. Business E-Mail: blackke@friedfrank.com.

BLACKMAN, LANI MODICA, copy editor; d. Salvatore Modica; m. Ronald Lewis Blackman, Sept. 17, 1969; 1 child, Lezlie Bianca Hepburn. Student, Ind. U., 1952—53; BS in Bus. Adminstrn., Bryant Coll., 1957; postgrad., SUNY, New Paltz, 1965—67; MFA in Theatre Arts, Brandeis U., 1972. Columnist Onterora Record, Woodstock, NY, 1962—64; dir. acting workshops Nashua (N.H.) and Manchester (N.H.) Inst. Arts and Scis., 1970—72; instr. acting and directing Berkshire C.C., Pittsfield, Mass., 1976—77; copy editor SUNY Press, Albany, NY, 1984—; editl. dir., copy editor, owner Renaissance Style, Ontario, NY, 1986—; editor Greenhaven Press, Mpls., 1986—87; copy editor Macmillan Pub., NYC, 1988—91. Lectr. on Shakers Old Chatham (N.Y.) Mus., 1973—75; writer, editor Connections Episcopal Diocese Rochester, 1991—93; artist-in-residence Dorset (Vt.) Colony House, 2002. Author poetry, plays. Pres. Friends of the Walworth-Sealy Libr., Walworth, NY, 2005—; vestry mem. St. Luke's Episcopal, Catskill, NY, 1987, conv. del. Fairport, NY, 1989—91. Democrat. Avocations: English riding and jumping, reading, gardening. Office: Renaissance Style 641 Haley Rd Ontario NY 14519 Office Phone: 315-524-4718.

BLACKMAN, LEE L., lawyer; b. Phila., Aug. 28, 1950; s. Harold H. and Mary Elizabeth Blackman; m. Kathryn M. Forte, Oct. 5, 1979; 1 child, Shane Forte. BA, U. So. Calif., 1973, JD, 1975. Bar: Calif. 1975, U.S. Dist. Ct. (ctrl. dist.) Calif. 1975, U.S. Ct. Appeals (9th cir.) 1977, U.S. Supreme Ct. 1980, U.S. Dist. Ct. (ea. dist.) Calif. 1984, U.S. Dist. Ct. (no. dist.) Calif. 1988, Hawaii 2005, U.S. Dist. Ct. Hawaii 2005. Atty. Kadison, Pfaelzer, Woodard, Quinn & Rossi, LA, 1975-81, assoc., ptnr., 1981-87; ptnr. McDermott, Will & Emery, LA, 1987-2000; atty. pvt. practice, 2000—. Arbitrator LA Superior Ct., 1986—90; judge pro tem Superior Ct. State of Calif., 1986—92; spkr. in field. Mem. editl. adv. bd. Airport Noise Report, 1989—99; article editor: ABA Health Litig. Reporter, 1996—97. Mem.: State Bar Hawaii, Legion Lex Inn of Ct. (master bencher 1989—2000), State Bar Calif. Office: 1562 Granvia Altamira Palos Verdes Estates CA 90274 E-mail: llblackman@aol.com.

BLACKMAN, SUE ANNE BATEY, economics research specialist; b. Hamilton AFB, Calif., June 21, 1948; d. Wayman C. and Lela M. (Fasgold) Batey; m. Martin R. Blackman, Apr. 7, 1977; 1 child, Emily Batey Blackman. BA in Polit. Sci., U. Colo., 1970. Econs. rsch. aide dept. econs. Princeton U., NJ, 1972-79, econs. rsch. asst. dept. econs., 1979-86, sr. rsch. asst. dept. econs., 1987—2004, sr. rsch. specialist, 2005—. Author: (with W.J. Baumol and E.N. Wolff) Productivity and American Leadership: The Long View, 1989, (with Baumol) Perfect Markets and Easy Virtue, 1991; contbr. articles to profl. jours. Office: Princeton U Dept Econs 101 Fisher Hall Princeton NJ 08544-1021 Business E-Mail: sabb@princeton.edu.

BLACKMER, DONALD LAURENCE MORTON, political scientist; b. Boston, July 6, 1929; s. Alan Rogers and Josephine (Bedford) B.; m. Joan Dexter, Aug. 25, 1951; children: Stephen, Alexander, Katherine. AB magna cum laude, Harvard U., 1952, AM, 1956, PhD, 1967. Sheldon traveling fellow Harvard U., 1952-53; exec. asst. to dir. Ctr. for Internat. Studies, MIT, Cambridge, 1956-61, asst. dir., 1961-68, lectr., 1960-61, asst. prof. polit. sci., 1961-67, assoc. prof., 1967-73, prof., 1973-95; prof. emeritus, 1995—; assoc. dean Sch. Humanities and Social Sci., 1973-81; dir. Program in Sci., Tech. and Soc., 1977-81, head dept. polit. sci., 1981-88. Research asso. West European studies Harvard U., 1973— Author: Unity in Diversity: Italian Communism and the Communist World, 1967, (with Annie Kriegel) The International Role of the Communist Parties of Italy and France, 1975; co-author, editor: (with Max F. Millikan) The Emerging Nations: Their Growth and United States Policy, 1961, (with Sidney Tarrow) Communism in Italy and France, 1975; The MIT Center for International Studies: The Founding Years 1951-1969, 2002. With U.S. Army, 1953-55. Home: 266 Main St Concord MA 01742-4942 Office: MIT E53-373 Cambridge MA 02139

BLACKMON, WILLIE EDWARD BONEY, judge, military officer; b. Houston, Apr. 16, 1951; s. A. L. and Florence (Joseph) Blackmon. BBA in Mktg., Tex. A&M U., 1973; JD, Tex. Southern U., 1982. Bar: Nebr. 1984, U.S. Dist. Ct. (ea. dist.) Mich. 1984, U.S. Ct. Mil. Appeals 1984, Mich. 1985, U.S. Supreme Ct. 1987, Tex. 1989, U.S. Dist. Ct. (no. dist.) Tex. 1990, U.S. Dist. Ct. (so. dist.) Tex. 1993. Terr. sales mgr. Gillette Co., 1977-79; sales and mktg. coord. Drilco divsn. Smith Internat., 1973-77; legal intern Gulf Coast Legal Found., Houston, 1982; intern, ind. counsel City of Detroit, 1982-84; judge advocate USAF, Ellsworth AFB, Offutt AFB, S.D., 1984-89, USAFR, Reese AFB, Randolph AFB, Bergstrom AFB, Tex., 1989-94, asst. staff judge advocate lt. col. Randolph AFB, 2004—; staff judge advocate lt. col. Tex. Air N.G., Ellington Field, 1994—2004. Asst. criminal dist. atty. Lubbock County, Tex., 1990—91, Harris County, Tex., 1991—92; admissions liaison officer USAF Acad., 1990—; pvt. practice, Houston, 1992—97, 2005—; assoc. mcpl. judge City of Houston, 1995—97, mcpl. judge, 1997—2004; adj. instr. Judge Adv. Gen.'s Sch. Air U., Maxwell AFB, Ala., 1996—2000; staff judge adv. 101st Air Refueling Wing, Pisa, Italy, 1996; internat. election supr. Orgn. Security and Coop. in Europe, Bosnia-Herzegovina, 1997; exec. dir. Assn. Minority Mil. Officers, 2000—01; mediator State of Tex. and Nat. Guard Bur., 2005—; lectr. in field. Bd. adv. Mickey Leland Libr. and Mus., 2003—. Decorated numerous mil. decorations; co-recipient Gerald R. Ford medal disting. pub. svc., 2006; named Disting. Alumni, Tex. A&M U., 2005; named to Tex. A&M U. Athletic Hall of Fame, 1994, Wheatley High Disting. Grad. Hall of Fame, 2002, Hall of Honor; recipient numerous awards. Mem.: SAR, NAACP (Alex award 1999), ABA, Aggie Officers Assn., Houston Bar Assn., Mex.-Am. Bar Assn., Tex. Mcpl. Cts. Assn., Am. Judges Assn., Houston Lawyers Assn., Tex. Assn. African Am. Lawyers, Nat. Bar Assn. (Living Legend award 1990), Nebr. Bar Assn., Soc. War of 1812, Masons. Baptist. Avocations: scuba diving, skiing, hiking, bicycling, dance. Office: 143 Nelson Pl Meadowlakes TX 78654-6442 Office Phone: 830-693-0044. Personal E-mail: weblackmon@yahoo.com.

BLACKMUN, BARBARA WINSTON, art historian, educator, academic administrator; b. Merced, Calif., June 29, 1928; d. Walter Lafayette and Marian Lewelyn (Warner) Winston; m. Rupert Beall Blackmun, Apr. 16, 1951; children: Monica Blackmun Visona, William Winston, Karl Warner. BA in Fine Art, UCLA, 1949, PhD in Art History, 1984; MA in Art History, Ariz. State U., 1971. Life credentials in gen. elem. and secondary art tchg. Calif. Tchr. elem., secondary schs., Calif., 1949—64; instr. humanities Malawi Poly. Coll., Blantyre, 1965—66; lectr., chairperson arts and crafts bd. U. Malawi, Limbe, 1967—69; instr. art history San Diego Mesa Coll., 1971—76, prof. chmn. dept. art, 1976—79, 1983—85, prof. emeritus, 2000—; curator African art collection Mesa Coll., 1986—; adj. lectr. visual arts dept. U. Calif., San Diego, 1987, adj. faculty art history, 2004; adj. assoc. prof. art history dept. UCLA, 1987, vis. assoc. prof. art history, 2000. Nat. program dir. African Am. Inst., Malawi, 1968—69; mem. Nat. Craft Devel. Com., Malawi, 1968—69, Nat. Com. for Devel. O Level Syllabus in Art, Malawi, 1968—69; mem. edn. coun., contemporary arts com. San Diego Mus. Art, 1975—78, founding mem. African arts coun., 1976—, guest curator, 2003; bd. mem. San Diego Mesa Coll. Found., 1983—; curatorial cons. Chgo. Field Mus., 1990—93, Chgo. Art Inst., 1994, 2006—, Detroit Inst. Art, 2002—, Mus. fuer Voelkerkunde, Vienna, 2003—, Ethnologisches Mus. Berlin, 2003—; curator Glass Gallery exhbns. Mesa Coll., 2003—; bd. mem. African and African-Am. Studies Rsch. Program U. Calif., San Diego, 2004—. Contbr. articles, chpts. to profl. pubs. Founding chmn. San Diego County Pub. Arts Adv. Coun., 1976—78. Recipient NEH Summer Rsch. Stipend, Lisbon, 1987; fellow Fulbright-Hays doctoral dissertation rsch. abroad, Benin City, Nigeria, 1981—82; grantee Calif. Cmty. Coll. Faculty rsch., Internat. Coll., Glasgow, Scotland, 1978, UCLA dept. art Dickson history of art travel, Europe, Russia, 1980; NEH fellow for coll. tchrs., 1992, Advanced Area Rsch. grantee, Social Sci. Rsch. Coun./Am. Coun. Learned Socs., 1993, Interpretive Rsch. grantee, Nat. Endowment for the Arts, 1993—99. Mem.: Arts Coun. African Studies Assn., UCLA Fowler Mus. Cultural Art, Mingei Mus. Internat. Art, San Diego Mus. Art, Archaeol. Inst. Am., African Studies Assn., Coll. Art Assn., Art Historian So. Calif., Delta Kappa Gamma (Beta Gamma chpt.). Methodist. Personal E-mail: bwblackmun@earthlink.net.

BLACKSHEAR, A. T., JR., lawyer; b. Dallas, July 5, 1942; s. A. T. and Janie Louise (Florey) Blackshear; m. Stuart Davis Blackshear. BBA cum laude, Baylor U., 1964, JD cum laude, 1968. CPA Tex.; bar: Tex. 1968, U.S. Ct. Appeals (5th cir.) 1970, U.S. Tax Ct. 1970. Acct. Arthur Andersen & Co., Dallas, 1964-66; assoc. Fulbright & Jaworski, Houston, 1969-75, ptnr., 1975—2004, chmn. exec. com., 1992—2002, of counsel, 2005—. Bd. dirs. Tex. Med. Ctr., Inc. Bd. dirs. Sam Houston Area coun. Boy Scouts Am.; bd. dirs. chmn. Spiritual Leadership Inst. Mem.: Houston Bar Assn., State Bar Tex., Houston Country Club, Coronado Club. Baptist. Office: Fulbright & Jaworski 1301 Mckinney St Fl 51 Houston TX 77010-3031

BLACKSTOCK, JAMES FIELDING, lawyer; b. LA, Sept. 19, 1947; s. James Carne and Justine Fielding (Gibson) B.; m. Kathleen Ann Weigand, Dec. 12, 1969; children: Kristin Marie, James Fielding. AB, U. So. Calif., 1969, JD, 1976. Bar: Calif. 1976, Tenn. 1994, U.S. Dist. Ct. (ctrl. dist.) Calif. 1977, U.S. Supreme Ct. 1980. Assoc. Hill Farrer Burrill, LA, 1976-80, Zobrist, Garner, Garrett, LA, 1980-83; ptnr. Zobrist & Vienna, LA, 1983; v.p., gen. counsel Tatum Petroleum, La Habra, Calif., 1983; atty. Thorpe, Sullivan, Workman & Thorpe, LA, 1984; ptnr. Sullivan, Workman & Dee, LA, 1985-91; prin. James F. Blackstock, PLC, LA, 1992-93; v.p., gen. counsel Nat. Auto/Truckstops, Inc., Nashville, 1993-97, Cracker Barrel Old Country Store, Inc., Lebanon, Tenn., 1997-98; sr. v.p., gen. counsel CBRL Group, Inc., Lebanon, 1998—2005; exec. v.p., gen. counsel Shoney's USA, Inc., Nashville, 2007—. Pres. Commerce Assocs., U. So. Calif., 1990-93. Mem. Town Hall, L.A., 1980-90; bd. dirs. Tenn. Valley region ARC, 2002-04, Nashville chpt. ARC, 2004—; interim CEO, Nashville area chpt. ARC, 2006. Served to lt. USN, 1969-73; capt. USNR ret. Mem. ABA, Tenn. Bar Assn., Nashville Bar Assn., U. So. Calif. Alumni Assn. (bd. govs. 1990-92), Pasadena Tournament of Roses Assn., Saddle and Sirloin Club, Rancheros Visitadores. Republican. Roman Catholic. Home: 533 Turtle Creek Dr Brentwood TN 37027-5632 Office: 1717 Elm Hill Pike Ste B-1 Nashville TN 37210 Home Phone: 615-371-5183; Office Phone: 615-231-2348. Personal E-mail: jim.blackstock@comcast.net. Business E-Mail: jim_blackstock@shoneys.com.

BLACKSTOCK, JERRY B., lawyer; b. Monticello, Ga., Mar. 9, 1945; s. J.B. and Eugenia (Jones) B.; m. Margaret Owen, June 10, 1967; children: Towner Anson, Michael Owen, Kendrick. BA, Davidson Coll., 1966; JD, U. Ga., 1969. Bar: Ga. 1969, U.S. Ct. Appeals (5th cir.) 1970, U.S. Supreme Ct. 1978, U.S. Ct. Appeals (11th cir.) 1981, U.S. Ct. Appeals (fed. cir.) 1984. With Powell, Goldstein, Frazer & Murphy, Atlanta, 1969—2002; chair Atlanta litigation team Hunton & Williams, LLP, 2002—. Adj. prof. law Emory U., Atlanta, 1975-81; mem. adv. bd. Jour. Intellectual Property Law, U. Ga. Sch. Law, 1992-2005; chair Ga. Jud. Qualifications Commn., 1994-2002. Author: Georgia Appellate Practice Handbook, 1977, Preparation of a Lawsuit for Trial, Pre-Trial Practice, Appellate Practice, 1980; (with others) Georgia Lawyers Basic Practice Handbook, 2d edit. Pres. parents coun. Trinity Sch. Inc., 1981-82; pres. parents club Woodward Acad. Lower Sch., 1986-88, bd. dirs., treas., Woodward Acad. Upper Sch., 1988-91, v.p., 1991-92, pres., 1992-94; chmn. Ga. Athlete Agt. Regulatory Commn., 1989-2000; chmn. bd. dirs. Pastoral Counseling Svc. Atlanta; chmn. bd. visitors U. Ga. Sch. Law, 2001-04; bd. trustees Ga. Legal History Found., 1990-93; mem. Leadership Ga., 1980; mem. Leadership Atlanta, 1990, exec. com., 1991-92; chair bd. trustees Riverside Mil. Acad., 1996—. Recipient Tradition of Excellence award for Def. Lawyer of Yr., State Bar Ga., 2002. Fellow Am. Bar Found., Am. Coll. Trial Lawyers, Internat. Acad. Trial Lawyers, Ga. Bar Assn. (editor-in-chief jour. 1984-85, bd. govs. 1982-98, exec. com. 1990-95, intellectual property law, tech. law and gen. practice and trial sects.), Ga. Bar Found.; mem. ATLA (intellectual property litig. com.), ABA (intellectual property, sci. and tech., tort and ins. practice and litig. sects.), So. Trial Lawyers Assn., Ga. Trial Lawyers Assn., Atlanta Bar Assn. (editor-in-chief Atlanta Lawyer 1972-73), Am. Law Inst., Atlanta Legal Aid Soc. (adv. bd. 1979-86), Atlanta Lawyers Club, Ga. Def. Lawyers Assn. (bd. dirs. 1989-91, dir. Trial Acad. 1987), Am. Bd. Trial Advs. (diplomate, bd. dirs. 1990—, state exec. com. 1985—), Am. Arbitration Assn. (arbitrator, comml. and constrn. panels, Ga.-Ala. adv. com. for large complex cases), Licensing Execs. Soc., Internat., Am. Intellectual Property Law Assn., Computer Law Assn., Davidson Coll. Atlanta Alumni Assn. (pres. 1982-83), Bleckley Am. Inn of Ct. (master of the bench), Commerce Club, Old War Horse Lawyers Club, Cherokee Town and Country Club, 191 Club. Methodist. Avocation: running. Home: 3364 Chatham Rd NW Atlanta GA 30305-1140 Home Phone: 404-231-1632; Office Phone: 404-888-4298. Business E-Mail: jblackstock@hunton.com.

BLACKSTONE, DARA, music educator, conductor; b. Conn. d. Dan and Barbara; m. Hayashi, 1995. BS, U. Conn., 1977, MusM, 1980, DPhil, 1996. Grad. asst. U. Conn., Storrs, 1978-80, 84-85; choir dir. Mansfield Bapt. Ch., Conn., 1979-87, OBesa Cantavit, 2002—, Griswold Cmty., 1997—, United Ch. Stonington, 2004—; tchr., choral dir., drama dir. Tolland HS, 1979-96; lectr., conductor U. Conn., 1985-87; cons., vocal coach, conductor pvt. practice, 1978—. Vol. instr. YMCA; bd. dirs. North Stonington Citizens Land Alliance. Mem. Am. Choral Dirs. Assn. (life), Music Edn. Nat. Conf., Internat. Fedn. Choral Musicians. Avocations: hiking, canoeing, skiing, skydiving, travel.

BLACKWELDER, BRENT FRANCIS, environmentalist; b. Buffalo, Jan. 4, 1943; s. Francis Winfield and Evelyn Hellen B.; m. Teresa Ann Stotzer, Apr. 5, 1975; children: Matthew, Laura. AB summa cum laude, Duke U., 1964; MA in Math., Yale U., 1966; PhD in Philosophy, U. Md., 1975. Chmn. math. dept. Philander Smith Coll., Little Rock, 1966-68; founder Environ. Policy Ctr., Washington, 1972; chmn., founder Am. Rivers, Washington, 1973-85; founder, staff mem. Environ. Policy Inst., Washington, 1974—; v.p. Friends of the Earth, Washington, 1989-94, pres., 1994—. Bd. mem. 20/20 Vision, Washington, 1990—, Am. Rivers, Washington, 1973-93. Author: Water Conservation, 1982, Bankrolling Successes I, 1988, II, 1995. Pres. Plan Takoma, Takoma Park, Washington, 1977-83; bd. mem. League Conservation Voters, 1980-97, chmn., 1981-91. Grad. fellow NSF, 1964, Woodrow Wilson fellow, 1964; recipient Disting. Alumni award U. Md., 2001, one of Best Stewards of Environment, Vanity Fair Mag., 2005 Episcopalian. Avocations: canoeing, golf, piano, magic, squash. Home: 3517 Rodman St NW Washington DC 20008-3118 Office: Friends of the Earth 1717 Massachusetts Ave NW Washington DC 20036 Office Phone: 202-783-7400.

BLACKWELL, ANNA NELLE, medical educator, medical technician; b. Sylva, NC, Jan. 8, 1945; d. Felix William and Nell Dodson Potts; m. Eugene Baxter Blackwell, Oct. 29, 1978; children: Denise Blackwell Nielsen, Ross Andrew Dillingham. BS in Biology, Lenoir Rhyne Coll., Hickory, NC, 1967. Lic. med. technologist ASCP, 1970. Anatomy/physiology tchr. C.D.Owen H.S., Black Mountain, NC, 1984—; clin. chemist Mission/St. Josephs Hosp., Asheville, NC, 1988—; med. technologist Sisters of Mercy Urgent Care, Asheville, NC, 1996—2005. Prom chair person C.D.Owen H.S., Black Mountain, NC, 1984—2005. Ch. coun. St. Marks Luth. Ch., Asheville, NC, 1980—82. Named Tchr. of Yr., Owen HS, 2007. Mem.: NCAE, Nat. Soc. H.S. Scholars. D-Liberal. Luthern. Avocations: cooking, gardening, reading. Home: 210 Blue Ridge Rd Black Mountain NC 28711 Office: CDOwen High School 99 Lake Eden Rd Black Mountain NC 28711 Home Phone: 828-669-8897; Office Phone: 828-686-3852. Personal E-mail: apblackwell210@bellsouth.net. E-mail: anna.blackwell@bcsemail.org.

BLACKWELL, BRUCE BEUFORD, lawyer; b. Gainesville, Fla., July 23, 1946; s. Benjamin B. and Doris Juanita (Heagy) B.; m. Julie McMillan, July 12, 1969; children: Blair Allison, Brooke McMillan. BA, Fla. State U., 1968, JD with honors, 1974. Bar: Fla. 1975, Ga. 1977, NY 1980, U.S. Supreme Ct. 1979. Atty. So. Bell Tel. & Telegraph Co., Charlotte, NC, 1975-76, Atlanta, 1976-78; antitrust atty. AT&T, Orlando and NYC, 1978-80; atty. Sun Banks of Fla. Inc., Orlando, 1980; assoc. Peed & King PA, Orlando, 1981-84; shareholder King & Blackwell PA, Orlando, 1984-97, King, Blackwell, Downs & Zehnder PA, Orlando, 1997—. Counselor, master to First Ctrl. Fla. Inn of Ct., 1999—. Bd. dir. Legal Aid Soc., Orlando, 1986-88; chmn. Winter Park (Fla.) Civil Svc. Bd., 1992-94; trustee Fla. State U. Found., 1985-86; trustee SC Hist. Commn., 2007—. Capt. USAF, 1968-72. Recipient award of excellence Orange County Bar Assn. Legal Aid Soc., 1993, Judge J.C. Stone Pro Bono Disting. Svc. award, 1996, Annual Friend of FAWL award Fla. Assn. Women Lawyers, 1998; named Legal Elite Fla. Trend Mag., 2004-07; named to Best Lawyers in Am., 2006, 07. Mem. Fla. Bar (chmn. 9th cir. grievance com. 1985-87, chmn. mid-yr. meeting 1986, chmn. 9th cir. fee arbitration com. 1992-94, bd. govs. 1994-98, vice chair statewide disciplinary rev. com. 1995-96, co-chair 1997-98, vice-chmn. access to cts. com. 1995-97, chmn. annual meeting com. 1997, mem. supreme ct. spl. com. on pro bono svcs. 1996-97, mem. edn. work force 1996-97, chair spl. com. on solo/small firm practice 1997-98, mem. rules com. 1997-98, mem. com. to determine need for a new DCA 1998, Chief Justice's adv. counsel 2006, Fla. Bar Presidents' Pro Bono Svc. award 1997), Fla. Bar Found. (pres. 2007—), Orange County Bar Assn. (exec. coun. 1983-86, pres. 1987-88, co-chair fair campaign practices com. 1998-2001, William E. Trickel, Jr. Professionalism award 2003), Fla. State U. Coll. Law Alumni Assn. (pres. 2006-07), Fla. State U. Alumni Assn. (nat. pres. 1985-86), Orlando Touchdown Club (pres. 1996-97), Gold Key, Order of Omega, Omicron Delta Kappa. Democrat. Presbyterian. Avocation: study of China. Home: 1624 Roundelay Ln Winter Park FL 32789-4042 Office: PO Box 1631 Orlando FL 32802-1631 Office Phone: 407-422-2472. Business E-Mail: bblackwell@kbdzlaw.com.

BLACKWELL, F. ORIS, environmental scientist, educator; b. Feb. 27, 1925; s. Floyd Weaver and Mary Olive Blackwell; m. Eleanor Louise Edwards, May 5, 1951; children: Susan, Betsy, Mary Ruth, Stephen. BS in Bacteriology and Pub. Health, Wash. State U., Pullman, 1950; MS in Bacteriology and Pub. Health, U. Mass., 1954; MPH in Environ. Health Adminstrn., U. Calif., Berkeley, 1965, DPh in Health Adminstrn., 1967. Rsch. scientist Calif. Gen. sanitarian Benton-Franklin Dist. Health Dept., Pasco, Wash., 1950—53; health and sanitation advisor USAID Program, Peshawar, Pakistan, 1954—56, sr. sanitation advisor Dacca, East Pakistan, 1957—59; asst. prof., acting chair dept. environ. health S.P.H. Am. U. Beirut, 1967—71; assoc. prof. environ. health Rutgers U., New Brunswick, NJ, 1967—71; assoc. prof. environ. health Sch. Medicine U. Vt., 1971—74; prof. environ. health East Carolina U., Greenville, NC, 1974—82; prof., chair dept. environ. health sci. Ea. Ky. U., Richmond, 1982—90; ret., 1990. Mem. gov. coun. USPHA, Washington, 1984—88; mem. various site visits accreditation Nat. Coun. Environ. Curriculum, Ind. State U., Ferris State U., others, 1977—78; curriculum cons. dept. bacteriology Wash. State U., Pullman, 1977; cons. water supply devel. USAID-MetaMetrics Inc., Sri Lanka, 1980; leader pub. health del. People to People Program to People's Republic of China, 1987. Editor: (book revision) Health and Safety in the School Environment, 1978. Apptd. Citizen's Task Force on Chem. Weapons Disposal, Ky., 1984—90. With USNR, 1943—46. Named a Ky. Col., Gov. W. Wilkerson, 1988; recipient Walter Mangold award, Nat. Environ. Assn., 1989. Mem.: Am. Acad. Sanitarians (bd. dirs. 1972—77, bd. cert. diplomate, Laureate diplomate 1977), Nat. Enivron. Health Assn. (life; pres. 1975—77). Democrat. Mem. Soc. Of Friends. Avocations: gardening, nature studies, conservation.

BLACKWELL, HELEN E., chemistry professor; b. 1972; BA, Oberlin Coll., 1994; PhD in Organic Chemistry, Calif. Inst. Tech., 1999. Postdoctoral rschr. Schreiber Lab. Harvard U., 1999—2002; asst. prof. dept. chemistry U. Wis., Madison, 2002—. Contbr. articles to profl. jours. Named one of Top 35 Innovators Under the Age of 35, MIT Tech. Rev., 2005; recipient Early Career award, NSF, 2004, PROGRESS/Dreyfus award, Am. Chem. Soc., 2004, Shaw Scientist award, Greater Milw. Found., 2004, Cottrell Scholar award, Rsch. Corp., 2005. Office: Dept Chemistry Rm 5211a U Wis Madison 1101 University Ave Madison WI 53706-1396 Office Phone: 608-262-1503. E-mail: blackwell@chem.wisc.edu.*

BLACKWELL, JAMES E., retired science educator; b. Anniston, Ala., Mar. 4, 1926; s. Edward Lee and Celia Hayes Blackwell; m. Myrtle Dapremont. BS in biology and sociology, Western Reserve U., 1948, MA in sociology, 1949; PhD in sociology, Wash. State U., 1959. Instr. biology Benedict Coll., Columbia, SC, 1949—51, Shorter Coll., Little Rock, 1951—52; asst. prof. sociology and biology sci. Grambling Coll., Grambling, La., 1952—55; asst. to assoc. prof. sociology San Jose State U., San Jose, Calif., 1959—63; acting dir. US Peace Corps, Dar Es Salaam, Tanzania, 1963—64, dir. Blantyre, Malawi, 1964—65; prof., chair sociology U. Mass., Boston, 1970—89; ret., 1990. Dir. US Peace Corps Tng. Ctr., U. Wis., Milw., 1965—66; dir. Panchayat devel. US Agency for Internat. Devel., Kathmandu, Nepal, 1966—69; assoc. prof. sociology Case Western Reserve U., Cleve., 1969—70. Author: Black Sociologists: Historical and Contemporary Perspectives, 1972, The Black Community: Diversity and Unity, 1975, 1980, 1991, Mainstraming Outsiders: The Production of Black Professionals, 1981, 1987, Cities, Suburbs and Blacks, 1983, Networking and Metoring: A Cross-Generational Study of Blacks in Graduate and Professional Schools, 1983. Pres. NAACP, Local Chpt., San Jose, Calif., 1962—63; nat. adv. panel on minority affairs The Coll. Bd., NYC, 1980—85; rsch. adv. panel Ednl. Testing Svc., Princeton, NJ, 1981—86; chair desegregation rsch. task force Southern Edn. Found., Atlanta, 1976—86; expert witness various higher edn. desegregation cases, 1984—94. Recipient Regents Dist. Alumni award, Wash. State U., 2002, Dist. Alumni award, Case Western Reserve U., 1998, James E. Blackwell Founders' award, Assn. of Black Sociologists, 2002, DuBois-Johnson-Frazier award, Am. Sociological Assn., 1986, Lee-Founders' award, Soc. for the Study of Social Problems, 1988, Merit award, Eastern Sociological Soc., 1988, Spivak award, Am. Sociological Assn., 1979. Mem.: NAACP, Nat. Urban League, New Orleans Mus. of Art, Amistad Rsch. Ctr. Tulane U., Foreign Relations Assn. of New Orleans, Am. Sociological Assn. (coun. 1970—71, 1989—92), Soc. for the Study of Social Problems (pres. 1980—81), Eastern Sociological Soc. (pres. 1981—82), Assn. of Black Sociologists (founding pres. 1970—72). Avocations: tennis, reading, theater, travel. Home: 5990 Eastover Dr New Orleans LA 70128

BLACKWELL, JEAN STUART, manufacturing executive; b. Dublin, Ga., Sept. 13, 1954; d. Price Barron and Jean Stuart (Babb) B. BA in Econs., Coll. William and Mary, 1976; JD cum laude, U. Mich., 1979. Bar: Ind. 1979, U.S. Dist. Ct. (so. dist.) Ind. 1979, U.S. Ct. Appeals (7th cir.) 1983, U.S. Supreme Ct. 1983. Assoc. Bose, McKinney & Evans, Indpls., 1979-85, ptnr., 1985-91, 1995—97; exec. dir. Ind. State Lottery Commn., Indpls., 1991-93; Ind. state budget dir., 1993—95; v.p., gen. counsel Cummins Inc., Columbus, Ind., 1997, v.p. HR, 1997—2001, v.p. bus. services, 2001—03, v.p., CFO, chief of staff, 2003—05, exec. v.p., CFO, 2005—. Commr. Supreme Ct. Commn. on Legal Edn., Ind., 1989-92; chairperson State Ethics Commn., Ind., 1991-92; adj. prof. Butler U., Indpls., 1989-91. Bd. mem. Ind. Leadership Celebration, 1986-92, Heritage Pl., Bd., 1991-92; govs. audit team Health and Human Svcs., Ind., 1991; mem. Regional Ctr. Planning Task Force, Indpls., 1991-92. Named Sagamore of the Wabash, Ind. Gov., 1991. Mem. ABA (vice chair 1985-91), Nat. Assn. Women Lawyers (bd. mem. 1990-92), Am. Coll. Mortgage Attys., Ind. Bar Assn. (bd. govs. 1988-92), Stanley K. Lacy Alumni, Mortar Bd., Omicron Delta Kappa, Omicron Delta Epsilon. Democrat. Methodist. Avocations: soccer, biking, camping, golf. Mailing: Cummins Inc PO Box 3005 Columbus IN 47202-3005 Office: Cummins Inc 500 Jackson St Columbus IN 47201*

BLACKWELL, JOHN, science educator; b. Oughtibridge, Sheffield, Eng., Jan. 15, 1942; came to U.S., 1967; s. Leonard and Vera (Brook) B.; m. Susan Margaret Crawshaw, Aug. 5, 1965; children: Martin Jonathan, Helen Elizabeth. BSc in Chemistry, U. Leeds, Eng., 1963, PhD in Biophysics, 1967. Postdoctoral fellow SUNY-Syracuse Coll. Forestry, 1967-69; vis. asst. prof. Case Western Res. U., Cleve., 1969-70, asst. prof., 1970-74, assoc. prof., 1974-77, prof. macromolecular sci., 1977—, chmn. dept., 1985-95, F. Alex Nason prof., 1991-2000, Leonard Case Jr. prof., 2001—, assoc. dean rsch. and grad. studies Case Sch. Engring., 2005—07. Vis. prof. Kennedy Inst. Rheumatology, London, 1975, Centre National de Recherche Scientifique, Grenoble, France, 1977, U. Frieburg, Fed. Republic Germany, 1982; chmn. Gordon Conf. on Liquid Crystalline Polymers, 1992; cons. in field. Author: (with A.G. Walton) Biopolymers, 1973; mem. editorial bd. Macromolecules, 1989-92; adv. bd. Jour. Macromolecular Sci.-Physics, 1986—; internat. adv. bd. Acta Polymerica, 1992—; contbr. articles to profl. jours. Recipient award for disting. achievement Fiber Soc., 1981, Sr. Scientist award Alexander von Humboldt Found., Max Planck Inst. for Polymer Rsch., Mainz, Fed. Republic Germany, 1991, Rsch. Career Devel. award, 1973-77. Fellow Am. Phys. Soc. (exec. com. divsn. high polymer physics 1986-90, vice chmn. 1987-88, chmn. 1988-89); mem. Am. Chem. Soc. (chmn. cellulose divsn. 1999, Anselm Payen award 1999, divsn. councillor 2000-03), Am. Crystallography Soc. (chmn. fiber diffraction spl. interest group 1993-94), Biophys. Soc. (chmn. biopolymer subgroup 1975-76), Fiber Soc. Episcopalian. Home: 12614 Cedar Rd Cleveland Heights OH 44106-3220 Office: Case Western Res U Case Sch Engring Cleveland OH 44106-7220 Office Phone: 216-368-6370. Business E-Mail: john.blackwell@case.edu.

BLACKWELL, JOHN ADRIAN, JR., computer company executive; b. Tulsa, Okla., Aug. 1, 1940; s. John Adrian and Daisy Edith (Webb) Blackwell; m. Carol Ann Blackwell. MusB, Westminster Choir Coll., 1962, MusM, 1963. Minister of music 1st Presbyn. Ch., Warren, Ohio, 1963-68, Oklahoma City, 1968-79; artistic dir. Okla. Choral Assn., Oklahoma City, 1980-82; pres. Okla. Digital Technologies Inc., Oklahoma City, 1987-92; ptnr. JJ Enterprises (now Megabyn Assocs., Inc.), pres., owner Oklahoma City, 1992—; program mgr. S. Systems Corp., Oklahoma City, 1995-98. Cons. Union Oil Co. Calif., Oklahoma City, 1989-98; conductor Warren (Ohio) Symphony Orch., 1965-68; choral dir. NBC-TV Stars and Stripes Shows, Oklahoma City, 1975-76. Commd. ch. worker Presbyn. Ch. in the U.S.A., 1965. Recipient Paul Harris award Rotary Found., 1993. Mem. Rotary Internat. (pres. NW Oklahoma City chpt. 2001-02). Office: Megabyn Assocs 2413 NW 112th Ter Oklahoma City OK 73120-7202 Home Phone: 405-751-1392; Office Phone: 405-751-1392. Personal E-mail: jbmegabyn@aol.com. Business E-Mail: jblackwell@megabyn.com.

BLACKWELL, KEN (JOHN KENNETH BLACKWELL), former state official, former mayor; b. Feb. 28, 1948; m. Rosa Blackwell; children: Kimberly, Rahshann, Kristin. BS, Xavier U., Cin., 1970, MEd, 1971. Cert. govt. fin. mgr. Mem. city coun., City of Cin., 1977-89, vice mayor, 1977-78, 85-86, mayor, 1979-80; vice-chmn. Cin. Employees Retirement Sys. Fund., 1988; dep. undersec. U.S. Dept. HUD, 1989-90; mem. Nat. Commn. Econ. Growth and Tax Reform, 1995; participant Nat. Summit on Retirement Income Savings, 1998; ptnr. Bituminex Co., 1978-82; coord. urban affairs, Xavier U., 1971-74, asst. prof. edn., 1974-77, assoc. prof., 1977-91, dir. cmty. rels., 1975-79, assoc. v.p., 1979-91; assoc. prof. U. cin., 1993; chmn. bd. adv. trustees Govt. Investment Found., Inc., 1999; ambassador U.N. Human Rights Commn., 1992-93; adv. bd. John M. Ashbrook Ctr. Pub. Affairs Ashland U., 1997; Children's Ednl. Opportunity Am. Found., 1999; bd. dirs. Black Alliance for Edn. Options; pres. Nat. Electronic Commerce Coord. Coun., 2002; bd.dir. Nat. Coun. UN, Internat. League Human Rights, nat. coun. Lawyer's Com. for Human Rights, Pub. Tech., Inc., Internat. City Mgmt. Assn./Ret. Corp., Internat. Rep. Inst.; mem. Fed. Election Commn. adv. panel, 1999; bd. trustees Am. Coun. Young Polit. Leaders, 1995' treas. State of Ohio, 1994-99; sec. State of Ohio, 1999-2006; mem. Coun. Fgn. Rels. Contbr. articles to profl. jours. Mem. The Jerusalem com., 1981, Harvard Policy Group on Network-Enabled Svcs. and Givt.; co-chmn. Hamilton County Reagan-Bush campaign, Ohi, 1984; mem. exec. com. Nat. Conf. Rep. Mayors; co-chmn. Blacks for Bush campaign, Ohio, 1988; mem. adv. coun. Ohio victims of Crime, 1989; bd. dirs. Internat. Rep. Inst., 1993, Campaign Finance Inst., Physicians for Human Rights, Congressional Human Rights Found.; nat. chmn. Steve Forbes for Pres. campaign, 1999; bd. dirs. Wilberforce U., 1989; chmn. Cin. Riverfront Classic and Jamboree, 2000-01; mem. exec. bd. Youth Voter Corps, 2001; mem. nat. bd. visitors Mazza Collection, U. Findlay, 1999; hon. co-chair Meml. to Our Lost Children, 1995; trustee Grant/Riverside Hosps., 1996, Wilmington Coll., 1996; v.p. Nat. Electronic Commerce Coordinating Coun., 2001, 02; mem. bd. advisors John M. Ashbrook Ctr. Pub. Affairs, Ashland U., 1997; exec. bd. Youth Voter Corps., 2001; fellow Nat. Acad. of Pub. Adminstrn.; mem. nat. adv. bd. Princeton Review, Youth for Christ, Jewish Inst. for NAt. Security Affairs; adv. coun. Employee Welfare and Pension Plan U.S. Dept. of Labor. Fellow Harvard U., 1987, The Aspen Inst., 1984, Salzburg Seminar, Austria, 1988, Heritage Found., 1992, The Ditchley Found., 1993; scholar Urban Morgan Inst. Human Rights, 1993; recipient Disting. Alumnus award Xavier U., 1992, Superior Honor award U.S. Dept. State, 1993, Peace of City award Cin. Jewish Cmty. Rels. Coun., 1994, Family of Yr. award Nat. Coun. Negro Women, 1994, Advocacy award U.S. Small Bus. Adminstrn., 1995, Martin Luther King Dream Keeper award, 1996, Veritas award Albertus

Magnus Coll., 1998, Thomas A. Van Meter scholar award Ashbrook Ctr., 1997, Pub. Svc. award NAACP, 1996, John M. Ashbrook award American Conservative Union and Ashbrook Ctr. Pub. Affairs, 2004; named one of Top 25 Pub. Sector Leaders, Govt. Tech. Mag., 2002. Mem. Nat. Govt. Fin. Officers Assn. (excellence award 1999), Nat. Assn. State Treasurers, Nat. Assn. State Auditors, Comptrs. and Treasurers (exec. com. 1995-99, Pres. award, 1996), Nat. Taxpayers Union, Nat. Assn. of Secs. of State (v.p. midwest region 2001), Nat. Assn. Securities Profls., Internat. City Mgmt. Assn. (bd. dirs. 1999), Federalist Soc., Econ. club of Columbus, Sigma Pi Phi. Republican. Office Phone: 614-466-2655. Office Fax: 614-644-0649. Business E-Mail: blackwell@sos.state.oh.us.*

BLACKWELL, LOIS MOORE, fashion designer, educator, visual artist; d. Lawrence Wilbert and Ruth Jenkins Moore; m. Paul Marvin Blackwell, July 27, 1957 (dec. May 9, 1999); children: Daphne Paula, Ursula Paulette. BSc, Howard U., 1963, MSc, 1967; EdD, George Washington U., 1980. Cert. tchr. D.C. Tchr. DC Pub. Schs., Washington, 1967—74; asst. prof. Morgan State U., Balt., 1974—76, Univ. DC, Washington, 1975—77; fashion cons. Woodward & Lothrop Corp., Columbia, Md., 1978—85; cons. Westinghouse Electrical, Columbia, 1985—89; cmty. coord. Duke Ellington Sch. Arts, Washington, 1989—92; asst. prof. George Washington U., Washington, 1990—92; tchr. DC Schs., Washington, 1989—2001. Mem. English Inst. Harvard U., 1990—; mem. The Actors' Ctr., 2006—. Exhibitions include A Proud Continuum: Eight Decades of Art, Howard U., 2005; actor: HBO Cable TV series "The Wire", 2005—06; actor, actor: Twenty Questions, 2006. Recipient Merit award, All-Island Juried Art Show, 2003; fellow, Nat. Fellowships Fund, 1978. Mem.: Nat. Mus. Women in Arts. Achievements include created uniform concept designs for Oprah Winfrey's Leadership Academy for Girls, South Africa; designed sportswear for Gospel recording artist, Joii Foxx. Avocations: designing, painting, music, dramatic arts. Office Phone: 240-374-4266. Personal E-mail: lois.moore1@verizon.net.

BLACKWELL, PAUL EUGENE, SR., military officer; b. York, SC, Aug. 19, 1941; s. Paul Webb and Ruby Mae (Hartness) B.; m. Janet Gail Glenn, June 23, 1963; 1 child, Paul Eugene Jr. BS, Clemson U., SC, 1963, MS, 1965, postgrad., 1970-72, LLD, 1992. Commd. 1st lt. U.S. Army, 1963, advanced through grades to lt. gen., 1994, comdr. 1st Bn., 4th inf., 3d inf. divsn. Aschaffenburg, W. Ger., 1980-82, ops. officer 9th Inf. Div. Ft. Lewis, Wash., 1983-85, chief staff 9th Inf. Div., 1985-86, comdr. 1st Brigade, 9th Inf. Div., 1986-88, dep. dir. ops. Nat. Mil. Command Ctr., Joint Staff Washington, 1988-89; asst. div. comdr. 3d Armored Div., Germany, 1989-91; comdg. gen. 2d Armored Div., Garlstedt, Germany, 1991-92; comdr. 24th Inf. Div., Ft. Stewart, Ga., 1992-94; dep. chief staff ops. Dept. Army, Washington, 1994-96; v.p. integrated command ctrl. and comm. Raytheon Co., 2000—. Def. cons., 1996—. Ruling elder Presbyn. Ch., Puyallup, Wash., 1985—88, Beth Shiloh Presbyn. Ch., 1998—2001, clerk of session, 1999—2001, supt., 1997—99. Decorated DSM with oak leaf cluster, Silver Star with oak leaf cluster, Legion of Merit with oak leaf cluster, Bronze Star with V device with eight oak leaf clusters, Purple Heart, Air medal, Army Commendation medal with V device and three oak leaf clusters, others. Mem. 82d Airborne Div. Assn., 9th Inf. Div. Assn. (pres. 1986-88), Marine Corps Assn., Assn. of U.S. Army, Tiger Brotherhood (hon.), Am. Ordnance Assn., Octofoil Assn., 3d Armored Div. Assn., 2d Armored Div. Assn., 24th Inf. Div. Assn., Assn. U.S. Army, DAV, Masons, Shriners, Ft. Stewart Skeet Club, Phi Kappa Phi, Gamma Sigma Delta, Alpha Zeta, Alpha Tau Alpha. Avocations: hunting, skeet shooting, running. Home: 650 N Shiloh Rd York SC 29745-8378 Office Phone: 321-427-3943. Personal E-mail: peblackwell@raytheon.com.

BLACKWELL, TODD V., human resources specialist; BA in Edn., NC State U. Various positions including team leader, ops. team leader, store team leader, dist. human resources mgr., dist. team leader, regional v.p., sr. v.p. Mervyn's (a former subsidiary of Target Corp.), 1986—2000; sr. v.p. human resources Target Corp., Mpls., 2000—03, exec. v.p. human resources, assets protection, COO AMC world-wide sourcing co., 2003—. Chmn. Associated. Merchandising Corp. Bd. dirs. Kids Fitness for Life. Mem.: Omega Psi Phi. Office: Target Corp 1000 Nicoillet Mall Minneapolis MN 55403 Office Phone: 612-304-6073. Office Fax: 612-696-3731.

BLACKWELL, WILLIAM ERNEST, broadcast executive; b. Rocky Mount, NC, Apr. 1, 1932; s. Rosser I. and Ellen W. (Wilkinson) Blackwell; m. Elizabeth Levitan Blackwell, Mar. 22, 1973. BS, Davidson Coll., 1954; MBA, U. N.C., 1958. Security analyst Jefferson Standard Life Ins. Co., Greensboro, NC, 1958—66, asst. treas., 1966—69, 2d v.p., 1969—81; v.p. corp. devel. Jefferson-Pilot Corp., Greensboro, 1981—83, sr. v.p. corp. devel., 1983—85, exec. v.p., 1986; pres. Jefferson-Pilot Comm. Co., 1991—97, OmniVest Svcs., 1998—. Served in US Army, 1954—56. Mem.: Nat. Assn. Life Underwriters, N.C. Soc. Fin. Analysts, Inst. Chartered Fin. Analysts. Office: OmniVest Svcs PO Box 3384 Greensboro NC 27402-3384

BLACKWELL, WILLIAM J., geophysicist; b. San Antonio, Tex., July 16, 1971; s. Joseph E. and Lucy A. Blackwell; m. Megan L. Hepler. DSc, MIT, Cambridge, Mass., 2002. Mem. tech. staff Lincoln lab. MIT, Lexington, Mass., 2002—. Fellow, NSF, 1995—98. Mem.: IEEE (chmn. chpt. 2004—). Home: 1010 Massachusetts Ave 44 Cambridge MA 02138 Office: MIT Lincoln Lab 244 Wood St S3-237 Lexington MA 02420 Home Phone: 617-547-0894; Office Phone: 781-981-5324.

BLACKWILL, ROBERT D., former federal agency administrator; b. Kellogg, ID, Aug. 8, 1939; m. Wera Hildebrand; 5 children. BA, Witchita St. U., 1962. Volunteer Peace Corps, Malawi, 1964—66; polit. counselor Am. Embassy US Dept. State, Tel Aviv, 1978—79; dir. West European affairs Nat. Security Coun. Nat. Security Coun., 1979—81; prin. dep. asst. sec. of state for polit.-mil. affairs US Dept. State, 1981—82, dep. asst. sec. of state for European affairs, 1982—83; assoc. dean Harvard U. John F. Kennedy Sch. Govt., 1983—85; spl. asst. for Nat. Security Affairs to President George Bush Exec. Office of the Pres., 1989—90; Belfer lectr. internat. security Harvard U. John F. Kennedy Sch. Govt.; U.S. amb. to India US Dept. State, 2001—03; dep. asst. to the Pres. & coord. for strategic planning Nat. Security Coun., 2003—04; pres. Barbour Griffith & Rogers Internat., Washington, 2004—. Editor: Arms Control and the US-Russian Relationship, 1996; co-editor: Conventional Arms Control and East-West Security, 1989, A Primer for the Nuclear Age, 1990; co-editor: (with Albert Carnesale) New Nuclear Nations, 1993; co-editor: (with Sergei Karaganov) Damage Limitation or Crisis? Russia and the Outside World, 1994; co-editor: (with Rodric Braithwaite and Akihiko Tananka) Engaging Russia, 1995; co-editor: (with Michael Sturmer) Allies Divided: Transatlantic Policies for the Greater Middle East, 1997; co-editor: (with Paul Dibb) America's Asian Alliances, 2000; contbr. articles to profl. jours. Recipient Comdrs. Cross of the Order of Merit, Fed. Republic of Germany. Office: Barbour Griffith & Rogers LLC 10th Fl 1275 Pennsylavania Ave NW Washington DC 20004

BLACKWOOD, (R.) DUKE, library director; Asst to fin. chmn. Rep. Gov. George Deukmejian's campaign, Calif.; exec. dir. U. So. Calif. Assocs.; dir. Ronald Reagan Presdl. Libr., Simi Valley, Calif., 2000—; polit. cons. in field. Office: Ronald Reagen Libr 40 Presidential Drive Simi Valley CA 93065-0600 Office Phone: 800-410-8354.*

BLADEN, EDWIN MARK, judge, lawyer; b. Detroit, Feb. 2, 1939; s. Philip and Ruth Sara (Millstein) B.; m. Paula Dee Maskin, Sept. 2, 1962; children: Philip, Sara, Jeffrey. BA, Wayne State U., 1962, JD, 1965. Asst. atty. gen. State of Mich., Lansing, 1965-86; mng. atty. Moran & Bladen, Lansing, 1987-93; pvt. practice, East Lansing, Mich., 1994-97; adminstrv. law judge USCG, 1997—2003, Dept. Homeland Security, 2003—. Author: Consumer Law of Michigan, 1978. Mem. Dem. Polit. Reform Comm., Mich., 1968. With U.S. Army Security, 1957-60, Korea. Recipient Alexander Freeman scholarship Wayne State U., Detroit, 1962-65. Mem. State Bar Mich. (chmn. anti-trust sect., treas./sec. 1990-94), Nat. Assn. Fraud Units (pres. 1985-86). Office: 3448 Jackson Fed Bldg 915 2nd Ave Seattle WA 98174-1009

BLADES, G(ENE) GRANVILLE, accountant; b. Easton, Md., Nov. 17, 1967; s. Gene William and Jean (Wise) B. BA, Washington Coll., Chestertown, Md., 1986; PhD, Catholic U., Washington, 1990; JD, U. Md., 1994; student in theology studies, St. Mary's Seminary & U., Balt., 1999—2005. CPA. Instr. Chesapeake Coll., Wye Mills, Md., 1990-93; ptnr. Kent & Blades, Denton, Md., 1994-95; pvt. practice Easton, 1995-98; pvt. practice, CPA Trappe, Md., 1998—. Cons. Blades Design, LLC, Trappe, 1994-98; v.p. Wise-Blades Farm Group, 1999—; pres. Trappe Acctg. Svcs., 2000-; dep. to Gen. Conv. of Episc. Ch., 2000-06. Author: Politics of Sectional Avoidance, 1990, Brief History of White Marsh Parish, 1997, The Kings of France, 2004; editor: The Epistle, 1995, 2006-07. Treas. Habitat for Humanity Talbot Co., Easton, 1997-99; dir. Talbot Co. Humane Soc., Easton, 1996-99, Cmty. of the Ascension, 2001; sec. Old White Marsh Cemetery Corp., Trappe, 1997—; dep. Gen. Conv. Episc. Ch., 2000-06. Mem. AICPA, Am. Hist. Assn., Md. Assn. CPA's, Md. Soc. Accts., Md. Hist. Soc., New Eng. Geneal. Soc., Nat. Cathedral Assn. Republican. Episcopal. Avocations: photography, travel. Home: 2814 Ocean Gtwy Trappe MD 21673-1764

BLAGA, OTILIA M., psychologist, researcher; d. Gavril and Florica Blaga; m. F. Anthony Romero, July 2, 2005. PhD, U. Kans., Lawrence, 2007. Grad. rsch. asst. U. Kans., Lawrence, 2000—. Contbr. articles to profl. jours. Office: U Kans Psychology Dept 1415 Jayhawk Blvd Rm 426 Lawrence KS 66045

BLAGOEV, KRASTAN BLAGOEV, physicist, biophysicist; b. Sofia, Bulgaria, July 18, 1964; s. Blagoi Krastev Blagoev and Snezhanka Dimitrova Blagoeva; m. Elizabeth Juliana Pare, Aug. 10, 1996; children: Kiril Krastan, Tavian Krastan. PhD, Boston Coll., Chestnut Hill, Mass., 1998. Rsch. fellow Cambridge U., Cambridgeshire, England, 1998—99, Harvard U., Boston, 1999—2000; rsch. asst. prof. Boston Coll., Chestnut Hill, 2000—02; asst. in physics Mass. Gen. Hosp., Boston, 2001—03; tech. staff mem. Los Alamos Nat. Lab., N.Mex., 2002—; rsch. scientist Mental Illness and Neurodiscovery (MIND) Inst., Albuquerque, 2006—. Contbr. articles to profl. jours. Recipient Disting. Career award, Boston Coll., 2004. Mem.: Internat. Soc. for Magnetic Resonance in Medicine, Am. Physics Soc. Achievements include research in Proof of Luttinger's theorem for one dimensional metals; prediction of the coexistence of superconductivity and weak ferromagnetism; prediction of a new recognition mechanism of DNA damage caused by ultra-violet light; large scale computations of the magnetic field in cortical tissue. Home: 9652 Merion Cir Albuquerque NM 87111 Office: Los Alamos National Laboratory Ms K710 Los Alamos NM 87545 Home Phone: 505 822n 6362; Office Phone: 505-667-3397. E-mail: krastan@lanl.gov.

BLAGOJEVIC, GORAN, electrical engineer, consultant; b. Belgrade, Serbia and Montenegro, Oct. 11, 1963; s. Gradimir and Menka Blagojevic; m. Stanislava Sasic, Apr. 24, 1993; children: Viktor Alexander, Alexander Marko. BS in Elec. Engring., Belgrade U. Faculty of Elec. Engring., Serbia and Montenegro, 1989. Lic. profl. engr., C. of C. Serbia-Montenegro, 1991. Sr. project mgr. Clifford Dias P.E., P.C., NYC, NC, 1998—2001, chief elec. engr., 2001—. Mem.: IEEE, Nat. Fire Protection Assn. Achievements include design of elec.sys; mission critical sys; emergency power sys. Personal E-mail: goranb@diaseng.com.

BLAGOJEVICH, ROD R., governor, former congressman; b. Chgo., Dec. 10, 1956; s. Rade and Millie (Govedarica) Blagojevich; m. Patti Mell; children: Amy, Annie. BA in History, Northwestern U., 1979; JD, Pepperdine U., 1983. Pvt. practice law, Chgo., 1983—86; asst. state atty. Cook County, Ill., 1986—88; mem. Ill. Ho. of Reps., 1992—96, US Congress from 5th Ill. dist., 1997—2003, mem. govt. reform and armed svcs. coms.; gov. State of Ill., Springfield, 2003—. Democrat. Office: Office of the Governor 207 State House Springfield IL 62706 also: 100 W Randolph Ste 16-100 Chicago IL 60601 Office Fax: 217-524-4049.*

BLAHA, MICHAEL DOUGLAS, research biologist; b. Bronx, NY, Nov. 14, 1950; s. George Joseph Blaha and Marie Clare; m. Agerica S. Blaha, Oct. 26, 1996. BS in Biology, CW Post Coll., Greenvale, LI, 1972; MS in Food/Nutrition, Framingham State Coll., Mass., 1989. Med. tech. U.S. Dept. of the Army, 1986. Phys. sci. technician USDA, Ft. Collins, Colo., 1975—77; med. technologist V.A. Outpatient Clinic, Boston, 1977—83; rsch. biologist U.S. Army Rsch. Inst. of Environ. Medicine, Natick, Mass., 1983—. Contbr. articles and abstracts to profl. jours. With US Army, 1973—75. Named to Primary Leadership Devel. Course Commandant's List, U.S. Army, 1991. Mem.: New Eng. Soc. Microscopy, Sigma Xi (chmn. admissions com. Natick chpt. 2000—). Independent. Roman Catholic. Avocations: racquetball, international travel. Home: 4 Walden Dr Natick MA 01760-3858 Office: US Army Rsch Inst Environ Medicine Kansas St Natick MA 01760-5007 Office Phone: 508-233-4264. Office Fax: 508-233-5298. E-mail: michael.blaha@us.army.mil.

BLAHA, VERLE DENNIS, consumer products company executive, electrical engineer; b. Detroit, Nov. 21, 1929; s. Maurice Lee and Clarice Annette Blaha; m. LuVeral Alma Blaha, Aug. 11, 1956; children: Bryan Jay, Lynn Renee Blaha Melchior. BS in Bus., U. Minn., Mpls., 1966, MBA, 1969. Field supr. Aero. Radio Inc., Washington, 1952-56; mgr. quality assurance Gen. Mills Electronics, Mpls., 1956-63; sr. v.p. Litton Microwave Cooking, Mpls., 1963-82; v.p., gen. mgr. Holaday Industries Inc., Eden Prairie, Minn., 1982-86; pres. Celsion Corp., Columbia, Md., 1986-91, New Opportunities Ltd., North Oaks, Minn., 1984—, Thumper Pond Golf Course, Thumper Pond, Inc., Ottertail, Minn., 1998—; pres. Thumper Pond Clinic, LLC Thumper Pond Svcs., Inc., 2004—. Lectr. on investments, U. St. Thomas, 1982-86. With USN, 1947-50, PTO. Fellow Internat. Microwave Power (chmn. bd. dirs. 1976-82). Republican. Lutheran. Avocations: hunting, fishing, building wildlife habitat. Office: New Opportunities Ltd 43207 Topaz Tr Ottertail MN 56571 Office Phone: 218-367-2431. E-mail: verle77@aol.com.

BLAHD, WILLIAM HENRY, nuclear medicine physician, director; b. Cleve., May 11, 1921; s. Moses and Rae (Lichtenstader) B.; m. Miriam Weiss, Jan. 29, 1971; children— Andrea Margery, William Henry, Karen Ruth. Student, Western Res. U., 1939-40, U. Ariz., 1940-42; MD, Tulane U., 1945. Diplomate Am. Bd. Nuclear Medicine (chmn. 1982, v.p. 1986-97, exec. dir. 1998-2003), Am. Bd. Internal Medicine (bd. govs. 1981). Resident in pathology and internal medicine VA Wadsworth Med. Ctr., 1948-52, ward officer metabolic rsch. ward, 1951-52, asst. chief radioisotope svc., 1952-56, chief nuclear medicine dept. LA, 1956-97, dir. nuclear medicine tng. program, 1997—; nuc. medicine residency program dir. Am. Bd. Nuc. Medicine, LA. Prof. dept. medicine U. Calif., Los Angeles; mem. ACGME residency rev. com. for nuclear medicine, 1979-97, chmn., 1991-97; mem. Joint Rev. Com. on Edn1. Programs in Nuclear Medicine Tech., 1986-93; mem. subcom. on naturally occurring and accelerator produced radioactive materials Com. on Interagency Radiation Rsch. and Policy Coordination, 1988-92; cons. nuclear medicine; mem. adv. com. on human uses radioisotopes Calif. Dept. Health Svcs.; mem. HEW Interagy. Task Force on Ionizing Radiation, 1978; dir. nuclear medicine Mt. Sinai Hosp., L.A., 1955-76, Valley Presbyn. Med. Ctr., Van Nuys, Calif., 1959-85, St. Joseph Hosp. Med. Ctr., Burbank, Calif., 1958-83. Author 3 textbooks on nuclear medicine. Contbr. numerous articles to med. jours. Served with U.S. Army, 1946-48. Grantee Muscular Dystrophy Assn. Am., 1965-69, Nat. Cancer Inst., 1973-76; recipient Lifetime Achievement award Wadsworth Physicians and Surgeons Alumni Assn., 2000, William H. Oldendorl Lifetime Achievement award West L.A. Med. Ctr., 2000. Fellow ACP, Am. Coll. Nuclear Physicians (bd. regents 1974-80); mem. AMA, Soc. Nuc. Medicine (trustee 1966-74, pres. 1977-78, Disting. Scientist award No./So. Calif. chpts. 1975, Disting. Sci. award We. Regional chpts. 1995, Disting. Pub. Svc. Career award Fed. Exec. Bd. L.A. 1998, Presdl. Disting. Svc. award 2000, 02), Health Physics Soc. (pres. So. Calif. chpt. 1964-66), Calif. Med. Assn. (sci. bd. 1975-81, chmn. adv. bd. nuclear medicine 1976-84), Am. Bd. Med. Spltys., COCERT, Soc. Exptl. Biology and Medicine, Los Angeles County, Calif. Med. Assns., We. Assn. Physicians, Am. Fedn. Clin. Rsch., Nat. Assn. VA Chiefs Nuclear Medicine (pres. 1985-87), We. Soc. Clin. Rsch., Alpha Omega Alpha. Office: Nuclear Med Dept VA Greater LA Healthcare 691/W115 11301 Wilshire Blvd Los Angeles CA 90073

BLAHER, NEAL JONATHAN, lawyer; b. Lowell, Mass., Nov. 6, 1960; BA in Psychology, U. Pa., 1981; JD, Villanova U., 1986. Bar: Pa. 1986, N.J. 1986, U.S. Dist. Ct. N.J. 1986, Fla. 1987, U.S. Dist. Ct. (ea. dist.) Pa. 1987, U.S. Ct. Appeals (3rd cir.) 1987, U.S. Ct. Appeals (11th cir.) 1988, U.S. Dist. Ct. (mid. dist.) Fla. 1988, U.S. Supreme Ct. 1997. Intern law clk. to presiding justice Cir. Ct., Phila., 1984-85; paralegal Fineman & Bach, Phila., 1982-83, assoc., 1986-88, Allen, Dyer, Doppelt, Milbrath & Gilchrist, P.A., Orlando, Fla., 1988-93; pvt. practice Orlando, 1993—. Mem.: Fla. Bar, Pub. Investors Arbitration Bar Assn. Avocation: music. Home and Office: PO Box 804 Orlando FL 32802-0804 Office Phone: 407-895-5050.

BLAHOUS, CHARLES P., federal official; B in Chemistry, Princeton U., 1985; PhD, U. Calif. Berkeley, 1989. Legis. dir. for Sen. Alan K. Simpson US Senate, policy dir. for Sen. Judd Gregg, 1996—2000; exec. dir. Alliance for Worker Retirement Security, 2000—01; spl. asst. to Pres. for econ. policy The White House, Washington, 2001—; mem. Nat. Econ. Coun., Washington, 2001—. Author: (book) Reforming Social Security for Ourselves and Our Posterity, 2000; contbr. articles to profl. jours. Mem.: Soc. Am. Baseball Rsch. Office: Nat Econ Coun 1600 Pennsylvania Ave Washington DC 20500

BLAHUT, RICHARD EDWARD, electrical and computer engineering educator; b. Orange, NJ, June 9, 1937; s. Edward John and Julia Anna (Chamer) B.; m. Barbara Ann Krachenfels, Aug. 30, 1958; children: Gregory, Kenneth, Janice, Jeffrey. BS in Elec. Engring., MIT, 1960; MS in Physics, Stevens Inst. Tech., Hoboken, NJ, 1964; PhD in Elec. Engring., Cornell U., 1972. Engr. Kearfott (GPI), Little Falls, NJ, 1960-64, IBM, Owego, NY, 1964-94; courtesy prof. elec. engring. Cornell U., 1974-94; Henry Magnuski prof. and dept. head elec. and computer engring. U. Ill., Urbana, 1994—, adj. prof. elec. engring., 1986-94. Sys. cons. Ioptics Corp., Bellevue, Wash., 1994-99. Author: Theory and Practice of Error Control Codes, 1983, Fast Algorithms for Digital Signal Processing, 1985, Principles and Practice of Information Theory, 1987, Digital Transmission of Information, 1990, Algebraic Codes for Data Transmission, 2003, Theory of Remote Image Formation, 2005. IBM fellow, 1980. Fellow IEEE (pres. info. theory group 1982, editor Transactions on Info. theory, Alexander Graham Bell award 1998, Claude E. Shannon award 2005), NAE. Republican. Roman Catholic. Home: 1502 BridgePoint Ln Champaign IL 61822-9272 Office: U Ill Dept of Elect and Computer Engring Urbana IL 61801 E-mail: blahut@uiuc.edu.

BLAIN, CHARLOTTE MARIE, internist, educator; b. Meadeville, Pa., July 18, 1941; d. Frank Andrew and Valerie Marie (Serafin) Blain; m. John G. Hamby, June 12, 1971 (dec. May 1976); 1 child, Charles J. Hamby. Student, Coll. of St. Francis, 1958—60, DePaul U., 1960—61; MD, U. Ill., Chgo., 1965. CLU; diplomate Am. Bd. Family Practice, Am. Bd. Internal Medicine. Intern, resident U. Ill. Hosps., 1967—70; fellow in infectious diseases U. Ill., 1968—69; pvt. practice specializing in internal medicine and family practice Elmhurst, Ill., 1969—. Instr. U. Ill. Hosp., 1969—70; asst. prof. Loyola U., 1970—71; mem. staff Elmhurst Meml. Hosp., 1970—; clin. asst. prof. Chgo. Med. Sch., 1978—95, U. Ill. Med. Sch., 1995—, Rush Med. Coll., 1997—. Contbr. articles to profl. jours., chapters to books. Bd. dirs., v.p. Elmhurst Art Mus. Fellow: ACP, Am. Acad. Family Practice; mem.: AMA, DuPage Med. Soc., Am. Profl. Practice Assn., Am. Soc. Internal Medicine, Univ. Club (Chgo.). Roman Catholic. Avocations: Hapki Do (Black Belt), Tae-Kwan-Do (Black Belt), skiing. Home: 320 Cottage Hill Ave Elmhurst IL 60126-3302 Office: 135 Cottage Hill Ave Elmhurst IL 60126-3330 Office Phone: 630-832-6633. Business E-Mail: cblain@mybclinic.com.

BLAIN, PETER CHARLES, lawyer; b. Milw., Nov. 15, 1949; s. Emile Octave and Mary Catherine (Usalis) B.; m. Katherine Stauber, June 12, 1971; children: Thomas Peter, Timothy Charles, Katherine Elizabeth, Peter James. BS, Wis. State U., Stevens Point, 1971; JD, Georgetown U., 1978. Bar: Wis. 1978. Budget analyst VA, Washington, D.C., 1974-78; atty. Reinhart, Boerner, Van Deuren S.C. and predecessor firms, Milw., 1978—. Chmn. Wis. State Bar Insolvency Sect., 1995-97; lectr. U. Wis., Milw., 1984—. Contbr. articles to profl. jours. Active Open Space Com. Mequon, Wis. 2d Lt. U.S. Army, 1972-74 Mem. Am. Coll. Bankruptcy, Milw. Bar Bankruptcy Sect. (prog. chmn. 1984-85, sect. chmn. 1986-87, co-chair bankruptcy sect. bench/bar com. 1998—), EDWI (bankruptcy local rules com. 2002—, bd. dirs. 2002—). Democrat. Avocation: reading. Office: Reinhart Boerner Van Deuren 1000 N Water St Ste 1800 Milwaukee WI 53202-6650 Home Phone: 262-242-9270; Office Phone: 414-298-8129. Business E-Mail: pblain@reinhartlaw.com.

BLAINE, DAVID, magician; b. Brooklyn, NY, Apr. 4, 1973; Performed in TV spl. (also exec. prodr.) David Blaine: Street Magic, 1996, David Blaine: Magic Man, 1998, David Blaine: Premature Burial, 1999, David Blaine: Frozen in Time, 2000, David Blaine: Fearless, 2002, David Blaine: Vertigo, 2002, David Blaine: Above the Below, 2003, David Blaine: Drowned Alive, 2006, David Blaine: Shackled, 2006; guest performances include TV programs Rosie O'Donnel Show, Late Night with Conan O'Brien; author (book) Mysterious Stranger, 2002. Office: Creative Artists Agy 9830 Wilshire Blvd Beverly Hills CA 90212

BLAINE, DAVIS ROBERT, valuation consultant, investment banker; b. Gary, Ind., Oct. 30, 1943; s. Jack Davis and Virginia Sue (Mintzer) B.; m. Karen Ellen Levenson, Dec. 28, 1981; children: Davis Justin, Tristan D., Brittara K., Whitney K. BA, Dartmouth Coll., 1965; MBA, U. Mich., 1969. Founder, sr. v.p. Am. Valuation Cons., Chgo., 1971-78, chmn. bd., 1978; exec. v.p. Valuation Rsch., Chgo., 1978-80, pres. LA, 1980-83; sr. v.p. Arthur D. Little Valuation, Inc., Woodland Hills, Calif., 1983-87; owner, chmn. bd. Olesen, 1989-92; founder, mng. ptnr. Profls. Network Group, 1988—. Founder, chmn. bd. The Mentor Group Inc., L.A., 1981-; founder, pres. ICS Corp., Chgo., 1976-82, v.p. bd., 1982-87. Served to lt. (j.g.) USNR, 1966-68. Mem.: Beta Theta Pi. Office Phone: 818-597-3559. Business E-Mail: dblaine@thementorgrp.com.

BLAIR, ANDREW LANE, JR., lawyer, educator; b. Oct. 10, 1946; s. Andrew Lane and Catherine (Shaffer) B.; m. Catherine Lynn Kessler, June 21, 1969; children: Christopher Lane, Robert Brook. BA, Washington & Lee U., 1968; JD, U. Denver, 1972. Bar: Colo. 1972, U.S. Dist. Ct. Colo. 1972, U.S. Ct. Appeals (10th cir.) 1972. Assoc. Dawson, Nagel, Sherman

& Howard, Denver, 1972-78; mem. Sherman & Howard LLC, Denver, 1978. Lectr. U. Denver Law Sch., 1980-83, U. Colo., Colorado Springs, 1984, U. Colo. Law Sch., Boulder, 1991. Author: Uniform Commercial Code sects. for Colorado Methods of Practice, 1982; contbr. articles to profl. jours. Mem. ABA, Colo. Bar Assn. Democrat. Methodist. Home: 1111 Humboldt St Denver CO 80218-3123 Office: Sherman & Howard 633 17th St Ste 2900 Denver CO 80202-3665 E-mail: ablair@sah.com.

BLAIR, ANN, historian; BA, Harvard U., 1984; MPhil, U. Cambridge, 1985; MA, Princeton U., 1987, PhD, 1990. Instr. U. Calif., Irvine, 1992—96; prof. history Harvard U., 1996—. Contbr. articles numerous publ. Fellow Postdoc. fellow, NSF-NATO, 1990—91, NEH, 1996, MacArthur Found. fellow, 2002. Office: Harvard U Robinson 216 Cambridge MA 02138

BLAIR, BONNIE KATHLEEN, former professional speedskater, former Olympic athlete; b. Cornwall, NY, Mar. 18, 1964; d. Charlie and Eleanor Blair; m. David Cruikshank; 1 child, Grant B. Cruikshank Student, Mont. Tech. Univ. Mem. U.S. Olympic Team, Sarajevo, Yugoslavia, 1984; Gold medalist, 500m Speedskating, Bronze medalist 1,000m Calgary Olympic Games, 1988; Gold medalist, 500m Speedskating Albertville Olympic Games, 1992, Gold medalist, 1000m Speedskating, 1992; Gold medalist, 500m Speedskating Lillehammer Olympic Games, 1994, Gold medalist, 1000m Speedskating, 1994; pro tour speedskater, 1994-95; ret. from competitive speedskating, 1995; motivational speaker, 1995—. ABC sports commentator; motivational spkr.; founder Bonnie Blair Charitable Fund; active fundraiser Am. Brain Tumor Assn. Author: Bonnie Blair: A Winning Edge. Recipient James E. Sullivan award for Outstanding U.S. amateur athlete, 1993, Sportswoman of the Year, Sports Illustrated, 1994; named Female Athlete of Yr., AP, 1994; inducted into Nat. Speedskating Hall of Fame, Internat. Women's Sports Hall of Fame, US Olympic Hall of Fame. Achievements include 1st American woman in any sport to win gold medals in consecutive Winter Olympics; 1st American speedskater to win a gold medal in more than one Olympics. Most decorated female Olympian of all time -- five gold medals, six total. Office: Octagon Mgmt Ste 300 2 Union St Portland ME 04101

BLAIR, BRUCE G., think-tank executive; b. Creston, Iowa, Nov. 16, 1947; s. Donald Gentry and Betty Ann Blair; m. Sally Onesti. BS, U. Ill., 1970; PhD, Yale U., 1984. Project dir. Congl. Office Tech. Assessment, 1982-85; project leader Cornell U., Am. Acad. Arts and Scis., 1985-87; sr. fellow Brookings Instn., Washington, 1987—2000; pres. Ctr. Def. Info., Washington, 2000—04, World Security Inst., Washington, 2004—. Vis. prof. Yale U.; vis. lectr. Princeton U. Exec. prodr.: Azimuth Media, Foreign Exchange with Fareed Zakaria, 2001-; pub.: Washington ProFile, Washington Observer, Washington Prism, Taqrir Washington, 2001-; author: Strategic Command and Control: Redefining the Nuclear Threat, 1985, The Logic of Accidental Nuclear War, 1993, Global Zero Alert for Nuclear Forces, 1995; contbg. author: The Nuclear Turning Point: A Blueprint for Deep Cuts and De-Alerting of Nuclear Weapons, 1999; co-editor: (with K. Gottfried) Crisis Stability and Nuclear War, 1988; contbr. chpts. to books and articles to profl. jours. With Strategic Air Command USAF, 1970—74. MacArthur Found. Prize fellow, 1999. Office: World Security Inst 1779 Massachusetts Ave NW Washington DC 20046-2109 Office Phone: 202-797-5116.

BLAIR, DAVID CLARK, information scientist, educator; b. Salem, Oreg., May 23, 1947; s. Jay William and Jessica Blakney Blair; m. Barbara Kerekes, Oct. 3, 1978; children: Alain Kerekes, Christopher Kerekes. BA, Whitman Coll., 1968; PhD, U. Calif., 1976. Info. scientist Sch. Info. Systems, U. Calif., Berkeley, 1976—79; asst. prof. computer and info. systems U. Mich., 1979—85, prof. computer and info. systems, 1985—98. Author: Language and Representation in Information Retrieval (named Best Info. Sci. Book of the Yr., 1991), Wittgenstein, Language and Information: Back to the Rough Ground!, 2006. Recipient Worldtech Technology award, Control Data Corp., 1984, Annual Quest for Tech. award, Inst. Sci. and Tech., 1983. Mem.: Am. Soc. Info. Sci. and Tech. (mem. editl. bd. 1989—, named Outstanding Internat. Rschr. of Yr. 1999, Best Refereed Paper of Yr. 1980). Home Phone: 734-971-4869. Home Fax: 734-936-0279. E-mail: dcblair@umich.edu.

BLAIR, DAVID F., biochemist, educator; b. Martinsville, Va., Jan. 19, 1957; s. Robert Jerome and Elizabeth Blair; m. Patricia Renfranz; children: Caroline, Camille. AB, Princeton U., NJ, 1979; PhD, Calif. Inst. Tech., Pasadena, 1985. Postdoctoral fellow Calif. Inst. Tech., Pasadena, 1985—87, Harvard U., Cambridge, Mass., 1987—91; asst., assoc. prof. U. Utah, Salt Lake City, 1991—2002, prof. biology, 2002—. Contbr. articles to profl. jours. Rev. panel mem. NSF, Arlington, Va., 1998—99, NIH, Bethesda, Md., 2006—. Fellow, NIH, 1980—85, 1987, Del Webb Found., 1986, Life Sci. Rsch. Found., 1988—90; Rsch. grants, NIH, 1991—, NSF, 1992—99. Mem.: Am. Soc. Microbiology (editl. bd. mem. 2005—). Achievements include research in elucidation of molecular mechanisms of bacterial movement. Office: Univ Utah Dept Biology 257 S 1400 East Salt Lake City UT 84112 Home Phone: 801-582-2293; Office Phone: 801-585-3709.

BLAIR, DENNIS CUTLER, career officer; m. Diane Blair; children: Duncan, Pamela. BA, U.S. Naval Acad.; postgrad., Oxford U., Eng. Commd. ensign USN, advanced through grades to vice adm.; comdr. USS Cochrane, Yokosuka, Japan, 1984-86, Naval Sta. Pearl Harbor, 1989-90, Kitty Hawk Battlegroup, 1993-95; assoc. dir. Ctrl. Intelligence Mil. Support, 1995-96; mem. staff NSC; dir. Joint Staff, 1996-99; comdr. in chief U.S. Pacific Command, Camp H.M. Smith, Hawaii, 1999. Bd. dirs. Tyco Internat. Ltd., 2003—. Decorated Legion of Merit with 3 gold stars, Def. Disting. Svc. medal with 2 oak leaf clusters; Rhodes scholar Oxford U.; White Ho. fellow; Naval Ops. fellow. Office: 711 Timber Branch Pkwy Alexandria VA 22307

BLAIR, DIKE, sculptor, painter; b. New Castle, Pa., 1952; Attended, Skowhegan Sch. Painting & Sculpture, Maine, 1974; B, U. Colo., 1975; attended, Whitney Mus. Ind. Study Program, NY, 1976; MFA, Sch. Art Inst. Chgo., 1977. One-man shows include Nancy Lurie Gallery, Chgo., 1980, Stefanotti Gallery, NYC, 1981, Christminster Gallery, 1986, Baskerville + Watson, 1986, Cash/Newhouse, 1987, Galerie Hubert Winter, Vienna, 1987, Carl Solway Gallery, Cin., 1988, 121 Gallery, Antwerp, Belgium, 1988, Koury Wingate Gallery, NYC, 1989, Ealan Wingate Gallery, 1991, Daniel Newburg Gallery, 1994, Galerie Hubert Winter, Vienna, 1995, Feature, Inc., 1998, 2001, Mary Goldman Gallery, LA, 2005, exhibited in group shows at Ctr. Georges Pompidou, Paris, 2000, NY Works on Paper, LA, 2001, Whitney Biennial Am. Art, 2004, Wexner Ctr. Arts Ohio State U., Columbus, 2005. Mailing: 235 E 11th St New York NY 10003 E-mail: dblair2@nyc.rr.com.

BLAIR, DONALD W., apparel executive; b. West Chester, Pa., Apr. 4, 1958; BS in Econs., U. Pa., Phila., 1980, MBA, 1981. CPA NY, 1982. Sr. acct. Deloitte, Haskins & Sells, 1981-84; sr. fin. analyst PepsiCo, Inc., 1984-85, v.p., planning Pizza Hut divsn., 1996-97; mgr. fin. planning Pepsi-Cola USA, 1985-86, group mgr. bus. planning, 1986-88; fin. dir. Pepsi-Cola New Eng., 1988-90, Pepsi-Cola Japan, Tokyo, 1990-92; v.p. fin. Pepsi-Cola Asia, Hong Kong, 1992-96; sr. v.p., fin. The Pepsi Bottling Group Inc., 1997-99; v.p., CFO Nike, Inc., Beaverton, Oreg., 1999—. Office: Nike Inc One Bowerman Dr Beaverton OR 97005-6453 Office Phone: 503-671-6453.*

BLAIR, FRED EDWARD, social services administrator; b. Huntington, W.Va., Oct. 6, 1933; s. Fred E. and Pearl Amy (King) B.; m. Lois Ann Thomas, Aug. 16, 1958; children: Lesli Winifred, Annlyn Paige, Carter Thomas. BBA, Marshall U., 1955; MA, U. Iowa, 1965. Cert. healthcare exec. Adminstrv. asst. Jefferson Med. Coll. Hosp., Phila., 1964-66; asst. adminstr. Barberton (Ohio) Citizen Hosp., 1966-67; sr. asst. adminstrn. U. Ala. Hosp. and Clinics, 1967-68; exec. dir. Ohio Valley Med. Ctr., Wheeling, W.Va., 1969-83; pres. Ohio Valley Health Svcs. and Edn. Corp., 1983-86; pres., chief exec. officer United Care Inc. (formerly Peoples Community Hosp. Authority), Wayne, Mich., 1986-90; pres. Blair Ltd., Inc., 1991—. Instr. health services mgmt. U. Ala., Birmingham; dir. W.Va. Hosp. Service, Inc. (Blue Cross); preceptor health adminstrn. George Washington U., Med. Coll. Va. Bd. dirs. W.Va. Health Systems Agy., treas., 1978; bd. dirs. W.Va. Heart Assn., Wheeling Country Day Sch.; mem. exec. com. W.Va. Regional Med. Program; elder Vance Meml. Presbyn. Ch.; elder Mt. Pleasant (S.C.) Presbyn. Ch. Fellow Am. Coll. Healthcare Adminstrs.; mem. Am. Coll. Healthcare Execs., Am. Hosp. Assn., W.Va. Hosp. Assn., Nat. League Nursing, Am. Assn. Mental Health Adminstrs., Am. Pub. Health Assn., Mich. Hosp. Assn. (legis. and pub. policy com., svc. corp. com., HAPAC team, com. on govt. relations), S.E. Mich. Health Council (vice chair com. on health facilities planning, trustee), SAR, Rotary.

BLAIR, GARY WESLEY, pharmacist; BS in Pharmacy, Southwestern Okla. State U., Weatherford, 1978; MPA, U. Okla., Norman, 1988. Registered pharmacist practitioner DHHS/Indian Health Svc., 1981, pharmacist Tex., 2004. Chief pharmacist Indian Health Svc. Hosp., Eagle Butte, SD, 1978—80, Carnegie Indian Health Ctr., Okla., 1982—88, Kincheloe Indian Health Ctr., Mich., 1980—82; chief statistician Nashville Area Indian Health Svc., 1990; pharmacist cons. Ctrs. Medicare and Medicaid Svcs., Dallas, 1997—2005, chief pharmacist, 2005—; survey and certification specialist Health Care Financing Adminstrn., Dallas, 1990—92, med. rev. program cons., 1992—97. Capt. USPHS, 1978—. Various. Decorated Surgeon Gen.'s Exemplary Svc. award USPHS, Commendation medal, Outstanding Unit Commendation medal, Achievement medal. Mem.: CAP (assoc.), Commd. Officers Assn. (assoc.), Mil. Officers Assn. (assoc.), Assn. Mil. Surgeons US (life; com. chmn. 1997—98). Office: Ctrs Medicare and Medicaid 1301 Young St Rm 833 Dallas TX 75088 Office Phone: 211-767-4438.

BLAIR, JAMES PEASE, freelance photographer; b. Phila., Apr. 14, 1931; s. Jacob Jackson and Dorothy Flagg (Pease) B.; m. Patricia Carol Wohlgemuth, Aug. 13, 1964 (dec. Nov. 2000); children: Matthew Ward, David Alexander; m. Elise de Vries-Ostroff, May 4, 2002. BS, Ill. Inst. Tech., 1954. Reporter, film photographer Sta. WIIC-TV, Pitts., 1958-59; freelance photojournalist, 1959—62; staff photographer Nat. Geog. Soc., Washington, 1962-94; ret., 1994. Instr. Rochester Inst. Tech., 1978, Internat. Ctr. of Photography, N.Y.C., 1992, Maine Photog. Workshops, 1988-2004, disting. vis. prof. U. Mo., 1992. Photographer: Listen With The Eye, 1964, As We Live And Breathe, 1971, Our Threatened Inheritance, 1984, Wooden Fences, 1997, Geography of Religion, 2004; one-man shows in Pitts., 1962, New Haven, 1977, Teheran, 1975, St. Louis, 1990, Washington Cosmos Club, 2000. Lt. (j.g.) USN, 1954-56. Poynter fellow Yale U., 1977; recipient Overseas Press Club Best Photog. Reporting from Abroad award, 1977 Mem. White House News Photographers Assn., Am. Soc. Picture Profls., Nat. Press Photographers Assn., Cosmos Club. Home: 5116 Lowell Ln NW Washington DC 20016-2608 also: 27 Washington St Middlebury VT 05753

BLAIR, M. WAYNE, lawyer; b. Spokane, Wash., Oct. 17, 1942; BS in Elec. Engr., U. Washington, 1965, JD, 1968. Bar: Wash. 1968. Mem. Wash. State Bd. for Jud. Adminstrn., 1995-2000. With USAF, 1968-72. Recipient Helen M. Geisness award, 1987, President's award, 1990. Mem. ABA (Ho. of Dels. 1988-91), Am. Judicature Soc., Washington State Bar Assn. (bd. govs. 1991-94, pres. 1998-99, Lifetime Service award, 2004), Seattle-King County Bar Assn. (trustee 1981-83, pres. 1987-88). Office: 5500 Bank of America Twr 701 5th Ave Seattle WA 98105-7097

BLAIR, MARGARET MENDENHALL, economist, consultant, law educator; b. Bartlesville, Okla., Nov. 8, 1950; d. Harold Leroy and Mary Winifred (Simmons) Mendenhall; m. Forrest Randall Blair, May 29, 1971 (div. Sept. 1979); m. Roger Lisle Conner, June 22, 1991; 1 child, Elizabeth LeeAnn Conner. BA, U. Okla., 1973; postgrad., Harvard U., 1982-83; MA, MPhil, PhD, Yale U., 1989. Reporter Houston Chronicle, 1973-75; reporter, bur. mgr. Fairchild Publ., Houston, 1975-77; corr. Bus. Week, Houston, 1977-79, bur. chief, 1979-82; economist Fed. Res. Bank N.Y., NYC, 1985; rsch. asst. Yale U., New Haven, 1985-86, lectr., 1986-87; rsch. assoc. Brookings Instn., Washington, 1987-94, sr. fellow, 1995-99; dir. Brookings Project on Corps. and Human Capital, 1996-99; co-dir. Brookings Project on Intangible Sources of Value, 1998-2001; rsch. dir., vis. prof. Sloan-GULC project bus. inst. Georgetown U. Law Ctr., 2000—04; prof. law Vanderbilt U., Nashville, 2004—. Adj. faculty U. Md. Coll. Bus. and Mgmt., 1993—94; vis. prof. Georgetown U. Law Ctr., 1996—2004; steering com., rapporteur Woodstock Seminar Series on Bus. Ethics, Washington, 1989—90; subcoun. on capital allocation Competitiveness Policy Coun., 1993—96; rapporteur Salzburg (Austria) Seminar on Internat. Fin. Markets, 1989; steering com. time horizons project Coun. on Competitiveness, Washington, 1990; mem. Task Force on Restructuring America's Labor Market Instns., MIT/Sloan Sch. Mgmt., 1997—2001, World Econ. Forum Corp. Performance Coun., 1999—2003; non-resident sr. fellow Brookings Instn., 2000—04; bd. advisors George Washington U. Sloan Program on Bus. and Soc., 1998—2002; trustee Woodstock Theol. Ctr., 2001—04; bd. dir. Worldwide Responsible Apparel Prodn. Author: The Deal Decade Handbook, 1993, Ownership and Control: Rethinking Corporate Governance for the Twenty-first Century, 1995; co-author: Unseen Wealth: Report of the Brookings Task Force on Intangibles, 2001; editor: The Deal Decade: What Takeovers and Leveraged Buyouts Mean for Corporate Governance, 1993, Wealth Creation and Wealth Sharing: A Colloquium on Corporate Governance and Investments in Human Capital, 1996, Employees and Corporate Governance, 1999, The New Relationship Human Capital in the American Corporation, 2000; contbr. articles to profl. jours. Vol. Big Sisters Washington Met. Area, 1989-92; organizer neighborhood watch group, Washington, 1990; mem. bd. advisors Ctr. for Cmty. Interest, 1993-98; mem. bd. dir. Christ Edn. Rock Spring United Ch. Christ, 2000-03; mem. Arlington County Adv. Coun. Instrn., 1999-2003. Univ. fellow Yale U., 1983-86, Leo Model fellow Brookings Instn., 1987-88; rsch. grantee Boston U. Mfrs. Roundtable, 1990, Columbia U. Instnl. Investor Project, 1994, Alfred P. Sloan Found., 1995, 96, 98, 99. Mem.: ABA (assoc.), Am. Law Econs. Assn., Am. Econ. Assn. Avocations: ballet, religious studies, cooking. Office: Vanderbilt Univ Law Sch 131 21st St S Nashville TN 37203-1181

BLAIR, MAUDINE, psychotherapist, communications executive, management consultant; d. Eugene Goode and Della Wright Blair. MA, U. Ga., Athens, 1964; PhD, Fla. State U., Tallahassee, 1969. Cert. group psychotherapist Nat. registry of Cert. Group Psychotherapists, transactional analyst, lic. psychotherapist Fla., cert. relationship specialist. Assoc. dir. of counseling and pers. svcs. Fla. State U., Tallahassee, 1964—67; dir. and founder Blair's Counseling Svc., Tallahassee, 1970—, Blair's Counseling Satellite Ctr., Tifton, Ga., 1971—92, Tenn. Comm. & Mgmt. Inst., Townsend, Tenn., 1980—89, Blair's Lodge, Townsend, Tenn., 1981—89; founder, pres. Fla. Comm. & Mgmt. Inst., Tallahassee, 1972—; co-founder, co-dir. CE Studies LLC, Tallahassee, 2005—. Co-editor: Transactional Analysis Rsch. Index vol. I, 1976, Transactional Analysis Rsch. Index vol. II, 1979; contbr. articles to profl. jours. Fellow: Am. Psychotherapy Assn., Am. Orthopsychiatric Assn.; mem.: APA, Fla. Assn. Marriage and Family Therapy (clin. mem.), Am. Assn. Marriage and Family Therapy (life; clin. mem.), Internat. Transactional Analysis (clin. mem.), Am. Group Psychotherapy Assn. (clin. mem.). Avocations: reading, travel, writing. Office: Blair's Counseling Svc PO Box 12697 Tallahassee FL 32317 also: CE Studies LLC PO Box 12337 Tallahassee FL 32317 Office Phone: 850-297-2190, 850-580-2600. Business E-Mail: BlairCare@att.net, CEStudies@att.net.

BLAIR, MICHAEL WALTER, lawyer; b. Balt., July 22, 1955; s. Joseph E. and Mary Christine (Hathaway) B.; m. Edith Baily Moore, Sept. 9, 1978; children: Edith Baily, Katherine Hathaway, Michael Walter Jr. BA, Yale U., 1977; JD, U. Chgo., 1981. Bar: N.Y. 1982. Assoc. Debevoise & Plimpton LLP, NYC, 1981-89, ptnr., 1989—, chair Corp. Dept. Bd. dirs. N.Y. Legal Aid Soc., 1992—. Mem. Country Club of Fairfield. Office: Debevoise & Plimpton LLP 919 Third Ave New York NY 10022 Office Phone: 212-909-6775. E-mail: mwblair@debevoise.com.

BLAIR, PAUL ALEX, otolaryngologist, plastic surgeon; b. Huntington, W.Va., June 4, 1951; s. Alex and Patricia Maureen (Cowgill) B.; m. Jane Anne Kurucz; children: Kathryn Jane, Elizabeth Anne, Suzanne Patrice, Robert Alex. BS in Chemistry, W.Va. U., 1973, MD, 1977. Diplomate Am. Bd. Otolaryngology, Head and Neck Surgery, Am. Bd. Plastic Surgery. Intern. Geneva Surgery Charleston Area Med. Ctr., W.Va., 1977-78; residency W.Va. U., Morgortown, 1978-81; asst. prof. Tulane Med. Ctr., New Orleans, 1983-88; pvt. practice Huntington, 1988—2003, Hurricane, W.Va., 2003—. Contbr. articles to med. jours., chpt. to book. Maj. USAF, 1981-83. Fellow ACS, Am. Acad. Facial Plastic and Reconstructive Surgery, Am. Acad. Otolaryngology/Head and Neck Surgery; mem. AMA, Am. Med. Soc., W.Va. Med. Soc., Cable County Med. Soc., Am. Acad. Cosmetic Surgery. Republican. Roman Catholic. Avocations: skiing, reading. Office: 3667 Teays Valley Rd Hurricane WV 25526-9656 Office Phone: 304-201-3223. Office Fax: 304-201-6555.*

BLAIR, PHILIPPA MARY, artist, educator; d. Ian Douglas Blair and Grace Evelyn Mackenzie; m. James Drummond Hutchison (div.); children: Alice Hutchison, Taisha Hutchison; m. John Rolf Porter, Mar. 7, 1991. Student in English and Art History, Massey U., 1968; BA in English and Art History, Auckland U., 1968; diploma in Fine Arts, Canterbury U., 1968; diploma in tchg., Secondary Tchrs. Coll., Auckland, New Zealand, 1976. Instr. art Wairoa Coll., Hawkes Bay, New Zealand, 1968; graphic artist ABC TV2, Brisbane, Australia, 1969; art tchr. Henderson HS, Auckland, 1970—84; lectr. painting Canterbury U., Christchurch, 1985; tutor Auckland U., 1987—93; vis. artist Art Ctr. Coll. Design, Pasadena, Calif., 1995—2001; tutor Santa Reparata Internat. Sch. Art, Florence, Italy, 2002—. Artist in residence Canberra Sch. Art, Australia, 1984, Griffis Art Ctr., New London, Conn., 2002; workshop tutor, 1987—2003; vis. painting tutor Canterbury U., Christchurch, 1991; pvt. art tutor, 2000—07; instr. painting emeritus Santa Monica Coll., Calif., 2004; tutor painting Otis Coll. Art and Design, 2000—01. One-woman shows include Double Vision Gallery, LA, 2001, 2004, Janne Land Gallery, Wellington, New Zealand, 2002, Washington, 2007, Pfizer Internat., New London, Conn., 2003, Warwick Henderson Gallery, Auckland, New Zealand, 2004, 2005, Lawrence Asher Gallery, LA, 2007, Janne Land Gallery, Wellington, 2007, exhibited in group shows at W. LA Coll., 2002, Walter Wickerson Gallery, NYC, 2002, Cartelle Gallery, Marina del Rey, Calif., 2004, Cypress Coll., 2005, Coca, Christchurch, New Zealand, 2005, Riverside Art Mus., Calif., 2005, New Zealand Embassy, Washington, 2006, Crossroads Sch., Santa Monica, Calif., 2006, Chan Liu Mus., Taiwan, 2006, Torrance Art Mus., Calif., 2007, Art Taipei Artfair, 2007, Torrance Art Mus., Calif., 2007, Auckland Art Fair, 2007. Recipient Queen Elizabeth II Arts Travel award, 1987; Queen Elizabeth II Arts Coun. grantee, 1980, 1984. Avocations: music, hiking, reading, theater, travel.

BLAIR, PHYLLIS E., artist; b. NYC, Oct. 5, 1922; d. Franz Joseph and Marian Jane (Burke) Emmerich; m. Thomas Slingluff Blair, Sept., 17, 1946 (dec. May, 2003); children: Joan Dix, George Dike, Hadden Slingluff. Student, Skidmore Coll., 1940—42, Art Students League, 1945, Westminster Coll., 1970—72, Bennington Coll., 1989. Student asst. art dept. Skidmore Coll., Saratoga Springs, NY, 1940—42; art illustrator & engring. draftsman GE, Schenectady, NY, 1942—44, Bell Labs., NYC, 1944—46; tchr. elem. Clinton, Tenn., 1946—47. One-woman shows include Hoyt Inst. Fine Arts, New Castle, Pa., 1971, 93, Butler Inst. Am. Art, Youngstown, Ohio, 1982, Westminster Coll., New Wilmington, Pa., 1983, Butler Inst. Am. Art, Salem, Ohio, 1994, Cornell Mus., Delray Beach, Fla., 2004-05, Ann Norton Sculpture Gardens, West Palm Beach, Fla., 2006. Art curator Human Svcs. Ctr., New Castle, 1968-89, Jameson Health Sys., 1978-99, Jameson Care Ctr., Jameson Retirement Pl., 1978-99, Jameson Rehab Ctr., 1978-99, Almira Home, New Castle, 1990-99, Lawrence County Children and Youth Svcs., 2000, The Soup Kitchen, Boynton Beach, Fla., 2000; founding mem. Nat. Mus. of Women in the Arts, Washington, D.C. Recipient Benjamin Rush award Pa. Med. Soc., 1991. Mem. Hoyt Inst. Fine Arts (chair art com. & permanent collection 1967-99, trustee, 1967-99, Blair Sculpture Walkway named in her honor 1996), Am. Heart Assn. (Disting. Svc. award Lawrence County chpt. 1978). Avocations: golf, painting, sculpting. Home (Summer): 1611 Cold Spring Rd Williamstown MA 01267-2771

BLAIR, ROBERT ALLEN, lawyer; b. Suffolk, Va., June 25, 1946; s. Thomas Francis and Ossie Blair; m. Linda Britt, Dec. 27, 1970; children: Robert Allen II, Thomas Edward. BA in Math., Coll. William and Mary, 1968; JD, U. Va., 1973. Bar: Mass. 1974, US Dist. Ct. Mass. 1974, US Ct. Appeals (DC cir.) 1976, US Dist. Ct. DC 1980. Assoc. Goodwin, Procter & Hoar, Boston, 1973-74, Surrey & Morse, Washington, 1974-78, ptnr., 1979-81; mng. ptnr. Anderson, Hibey & Blair, Washington, 1981-95; ptnr., chair govt. practice group Manatt, Phelps & Phillips, 1995-99, co-chmn.; pres. The Blair Law Firm P.C., Washington, 1999—. Chmn. nat. adv. bd. IPG Photonics Corp., 1999—2004, vice chmn. bd. dirs., 2000—04, chmn. compensation com., 2006—; trustee Winkler Family Trust, 1996—. Mem. editorial bd. Law Rev. U. Va., 1971-73. Chmn. bd. Inst. on Terrorism and Subnat. Conflict, Washington, 1982-95; co-counsel Citizens for Dem. Alternatives in 1980, Washington, 1979-81; mem. adv. panel on fgn. policy, def. and arms control Dem. Nat. Com., Washington, 1982-85; mem. drafting team for fgn. policy, def. and arms control issue workshop Dem. Nat. Conf., Phila., 1982, mem. bus. coun., 1988-90, 94—, mng. trustee, 1994-95; mem. Senate Dem. Roundtable, Washington, 1983-2000; mem. Senate Dem. Leadership Circle, Washington, 1983-2000; vice chmn. Potomac Group, Washington, 1983-84, chmn., 1984-85; mem. adv. council Dem. Platform Com., Washington, 1984; spl. counsel 1984 Dem. Nat. Conv., San Francisco, 1984; spl. counsel to nat. fin. chmn. Dem. Nat. Com., Washington, 1984-85, mem. fin. bd. dirs., 1983-85, 88; mem. Nat. Dem. Club, Senate Dem. Majority Trust, 1992-99; vice chmn. Washington Fgn. Affairs Soc., 1984-87; mem. Gov.'s Econ. Adv. Council, Va., 1986-94; commr. Va. Port Authority, Commonwealth Va., 1991-96, vice chmn. finance/planning com., 1992-94, chmn., 1994-96; chmn. S Corp. Assn., Washington 1996-2000, chmn. emeritus, 2000—, chmn. reform project, 1993-96; advisory bd. Thomas Jefferson Program Pub. Policy, 1996—, chmn. devel. com., 1999-2004; bd. dirs. Everybody Wins, 1997-2000; mem. bd. of vis. William and Mary, 2004—, chmn. bldg. a grounds com., 2006-, chmn. design review bd., 2006-. Named to Outstanding Young Men Am., U.S. Jaycees, 1976; recipient Alumni Medallion award William and Mary Coll., 2005 Mem.: ABA. Home: 4936 Rodman St NW Washington DC 20016-3239

BLAIR, ROSEMARY MILES, retired art educator, environmentalist; d. George Bernard and Kathryn Gannon Miles; m. David William Blair, Jan. 30, 1954; children: Karen, Barbara, Mira, Amanda, David Belmont,

Rachel. BA, Coll. New Rochelle, 1951; MA, Columbia U. Tchrs. Coll., 1969; post grad., Princeton U., 1975. Cert. adminstrn. N.J., 1973, N.Y., 1973, art instr. K-12 N.J., N.Y., prin. NJ, 1973. Art tchr., coord. and supr. Princeton Regional Schs., NJ, 1965—96; spl. cons. tchr. preparation program Princeton U.; ret., 1996. Chair 12th dist. U.S. Congressional Art Competition. One woman and group shows, US and Can., work in corp. and pvt. collections. Founding parent, vol. Stuart County Day Sch., Princeton, 1963—; cmty. activist Princeton Cmty. Dem. Org., 1979—; lector Aquinas Found. Princeton U.; bd. trustees St. Saviour Sch., Bklyn., 1990—95; founding pres. and chmn. bd. Friends Princeton Open Space, 1979—89; mem. alumni coun. Coll. New Rochelle, NY, 1983—87; pres. Del. & Raritan Canal Coalition, 1985—; founder, trustee Del. Raritan Greenway Land Trust, Princeton, 1989—; mem. Princeton Environ. Commn., 1998—2006. Mem.: Montgomery Ctr. Arts, Consortium Arts Edn. (exec. dir. 1983—93), Art Educators NJ (conf. chmn. 1981, pres. 1982), Nova Scotia Nature Trust. Democrat. Avocations: painting, environment and land preservation. Home (Summer): 1371 Summerside Rd Bayfield NS Canada B0H 1A0 Personal E-mail: rosemaryblair@cs.com.

BLAIR, RUTH REBA, retired government official, notary public; b. New Orleans, Aug. 21, 1934; d. Joseph Aloysius and Ruth (Labostrie) Porter; m. William Jennings Blair, Sept. 22, 1961 (dec.); children: Joseph Vernon, Constance Eileen. AS in Bus. Adminstrn., Loyola U., New Orleans, 1980; BA in English, U. New Orleans, 1984; masters cert. in govt. contracting, George Washington U., 1992. Cert. assoc. contracts mgr. (life); cert. mem. fed. acquisition corps. Profl. intern and various positions NASA Michoud Assembly Facility, New Orleans, 1964-84; contract specialist NASA, Marshall Space Flight Ctr, Ala., 1985-86; contracting officer USCG, New Orleans, 1986-87; contract adminstr. (supercomputers) Naval Rsch. Lab., Stennis Space Ctr., Miss., 1987-96; dir. adminstrn. Tech. Ventures, Inc., New Orleans. Author numerous poems, short stories. Adminstr. Primary Oceanographic Prediction System Recipient Special Act award Naval Rsch. Lab., 1994. Mem. Nat. Assn. Ret. Fed. Employees (past chpt. pres.). Home: 19 Osprey Ct La Place LA 70068 E-mail: rblairtv1@aol.com.

BLAIR, SYLVIA H., aerospace engineer; BS in Physics, Lamar U., 1976. Computer resources project engr. on F-16 and F-22 fighter aircraft Ft. Worth divsn. Gen. Dynamics, 1979—89; avionics project engr. Sikorsky Aircraft Co., Stratford, Conn., 2005—. Session chmn., tutorials chmn. AIAA/IEEE Digital Avionic Systems Conf., 1983—86; conf. chmn., tech. program chmn. AIAA Aerospace Engring. Conf. and Show, LA, 1983—85; chmn. AIAA Digital Avionic Tech. Com., 1987—89. Recipient Navy Superior Pub. Svc. medal, U.S. Sec. of the Navy, 1988. Mem.: Am. Inst. Aeronautics and Astronautics (sr.). Avocations: writing, reading, fishing, travel. Office: Sikorsky Aircraft MS S328A 6900 Main St PO Box 9729 Stratford CT 06615-9129 Business E-Mail: sblair@sikorsky.com.

BLAIR, VIRGINIA DEVOTO, music educator; b. Santa Rosa, Calif., Sept. 26, 1950; d. Albert and Thelma Helen (Devoto) Gugliamo; m. Ted Leroy Blair, June 15, 1974; children: Eric Tobias, Rebecca Kristine. AA, Santa Rosa Jr. Coll., 1970; BA, Calif. State U., 1973. Music tchr. San Juan Unified Sch. Dist., Sacramento, 1976; tchr. asst. Sacramento (Calif.) Montessori, 1976—79; music tchr. Concordia Montessori Sch., Concord, Calif., 1990—2004, self-employed, Concord, 1990—2006. Violinist Santa Rosa Symphony, Santa Rosa, Calif., 1967—70, Sacramento Symphony, Sacramento, 1971—74. Finalist 2d pl., Press Democrat Etude Contest, 1967; recipient 1st pl., 1968; scholar, Calif. State U., 1970. Mem.: Nat. Piano Guild. Avocations: gardening, scrapbooks, jogging, reading, informal piano and violin performing. Home: 4129 Cheshire Dr Concord CA 94521 Office Phone: 925-408-6115. Office Fax: 925-459-0995. E-mail: gdb564@yahoo.com.

BLAIR, WILLIAM GRANGER, retired reporter; b. Chgo., Nov. 17, 1925; s. William Mitchell and Martha (Granger) B.; m. Sue Cunningham, Apr. 19, 1952 (div.); children: Robert, Bruce (dec.), Laura; m. Ellen Lopin, Sept. 29, 1970. AB in English cum laude, Princeton U., 1950. Reporter Kansas City (Mo.) Star, 1950-52; mem. staff N.Y. Times, 1953-90. Fgn. corr., Paris, 1956-62, London, 1965-67, bur. chief, Jerusalem, 1962-65, mgr. employee communications, 1968, mgr. pub. relations, 1969-70, dir. pub. relations, 1970-73, broadcast corr., 1973-79, met. reporter, 1980-90. Served with USMCR, 1943-46, PTO. Mem. reporting team whose news coverage of regional flood helped to earn Pulitzer award for The Kansas City Star, 1952; corr. in France and Algeria when N.Y. Times won 1st Pulitzer prize awarded specifically to a fgn. news staff for internat. reporting, 1958. Mem. Ivy Club. Home: 425 E 58th St New York NY 10022 Personal E-mail: wblair@nyc.rr.com.

BLAIR, WILLIAM MCCORMICK, JR., lawyer; b. Chgo., Oct. 24, 1916; s. William McCormick and Helen (Bowen) B.; m. Catherine Gerlach, Sept. 9, 1961; 1 son, William McCormick III (dec.). AB, Stanford U., 1940; LL.B., U. Va., 1947. Bar: Ill. 1947, D.C. 1972. Assoc. firm Wilson & McIlvaine, Chgo., 1947-50; adminstrv. asst. to Gov. Adlai E. Stevenson of Ill., 1950-52; ptnr. firm Stevenson, Rifkind & Wirtz, Chgo., 1955-61, Paul, Weiss, Rifkind, Wharton & Garrison, NYC, 1957-61; U.S. ambassador to Denmark, 1961-64, to Philippines, 1964-67; gen. dir. John F. Kennedy Ctr., 1968-72; ptnr. firm Surrey & Morse, Washington, 1978-84, of counsel, 1984-86. Bd. dirs. Am.-Scandinavian Found., N.Y.C.; v.p. bd. dirs. Albert and Mary Lasker Found., N.Y.C., 1968-98. Capt. USAAF, 1942-46. Decorated Bronze Star U.S.; officer Order of Crown, Belgium; Order of Sikatuna, Philippines; comdr. cross Order of Dannebrog 1st class, Denmark). Mem. Am. Coun. Ambs. (vice chmn., pres. 1985-89), River Club (N.Y.C.), Phi Delta Phi. Address: 435 E 52nd St New York NY 10022

BLAIS, ROGER NATHANIEL, physics professor, academic administrator; b. Duluth, Minn., Oct. 3, 1944; s. Eusebe Joseph and Edith Seldina (Anderson) Blais; m. Mary Louise Leclerc, Aug. 2, 1971; children: Christopher Edward, Laura Louise. BA in Physics and French Lit., U. Minn., 1966; PhD in Physics, U. Okla., Norman, 1971; cert. in computer programming, Tulsa Jr. Coll., 1981; cert. in bus., UCLA, 1986. Registered profl. engr., Okla. Instr. physics Westark C.C., Ft. Smith, Ark., 1971-72; asst. prof. physics and geophys. scis Old Dominion U., Norfolk, Va., 1972-77; asst. prof. engring. physics U. Tulsa, 1977-81, assoc. prof., 1981-98, prof., 1998—; assoc. dir. Tulsa U. Artificial Lift Projects, 1983—98, chmn. physics, 1986-88, vice-provost, 1989-92, provost, v.p. acad. affairs, 1998—. Contbr. articles to profl. jours. Active Leadership Okla. XVI, 2003; bd. dirs. Light Opera Okla., 2003—, Hillcrest Splty. Hosps., 2003—, Okla. Acad. Fellow Instrumentation Sys. and Automation Soc. (dir. test measurement divsn. 1995-97, v.p. automation and tech. dept. 2003-04); mem. AAAS, AAUP, NSPE, Am. Phys. Soc., Am. Geophys. Union, Soc. Petroleum Engrs., Am. Assn. Physics Tchrs., Am. Soc. Engring. Edn., NY Acad. Scis., Iron Wedge Soc., Phi Beta Kappa, Sigma Xi, Sigma Pi Sigma, Tau Beta Pi, Phi Kappa Phi. Home: 5348 E 30th Pl Tulsa OK 74114-6314 Office: U Tulsa Office of Provost 600 S College Ave Tulsa OK 74104-3189 Office Phone: 918-631-2554. Personal E-mail: rblais71@cox.net. Business E-Mail: roger.blais@utulsa.edu.

BLAISE, CLARK LEE, writer, educator; b. Fargo, ND, Apr. 10, 1940; s. Léo Roméo Blais and Anne Marion Vanstone; m. Bharati Mukherjee, Sept. 19, 1963; children: Bart Anand, Bernard Sudhir. BA, Denison U., 1961, D (hon.), 1979; MFA, U. Iowa, 1964; Doctorate (hon.), McGill U., 2004. Prof. Concordia U., Montreal, Que., Can., 1966-78, York U., Toronto, Ont., Can., 1978-80, Skidmore Coll., Saratoga Springs, N.Y., 1980-84; vis. prof. Emory U., Atlanta, 1984-85, U. Calif., Berkeley, 1998-2000; adj. prof. Columbia U., NYC, 1986-89, NYU, NYC, 1986-89; prof., dir. internat. writing U. Iowa, Iowa City, 1990-98, Southampton Coll., L.I. U., 2002—05. Book reviewer, lectr., presenter workshops in field. Author: A North American Education, 1973, Tribal Justice, 1974, Days and Nights in Calcutta, 1977, Lunar Attractions, 1979, Lusts, 1982, Resident Alien, 1985, The Sorrow the the Terror, 1987, Man and His World, 1992, I Had a Father: a post-modern autobiography, 1993, Here, There and Everywhere: Modern Canadian, Australian, American and Post Modernist Theory, 1994, If I Were Me, 1997, New and Selected Stories (4 vols.), 2000-2004, Time-Lord, 2001; contbr. stories, essays to over 90 anthologies. Recipient award NEA, Guggenheim Found., Can. Coun., St. Lawrence award, Great Lakes Colls. award, Books in Can. First Novel award, Book of Yr. award Can. Booksellers, 1995, Pearson prize, 2002. Avocation: languages. Home: 130 Rivoli St San Francisco CA 94117

BLAJCHMAN, MORRIS AARON, science educator, physician; b. Montreal, Jan. 3, 1940; s. Joseph and Dora (Najman) B.; m. Isabel Janet Selick, June 13, 1965; children: Aviva Rhona, Joel Philip. BSc, McGill U., 1960, MD, 1964. Fellow in hematology and internal medicine Royal Coll. Physicians (Can.). Hematologist Hamilton (Ont.)Civic Hosp., 1970-75, McMaster Univ. Med. Ctr., Hamilton, 1975-98, chief of svc. hematology, head transfusion medicine svc., 1985-98; asst. prof. McMaster U., Hamilton, 1970-76, assoc. prof., 1976-82, prof., 1982—; med. dir. Can. Red Cross Soc., Hamilton Ctr., 1975-98, Can. Blood Svcs., Hamilton Ctr., 1998—. Head transfusion med. svcs. health scis. McMaster U., 1998—2007; chair steering com. NIH Clin. Trials Network Transfusion Medicine and Hemostasis, 2007—. Founding editor, editor-in-chief: Transfusion Medicine Reviews, 1987—; co-author: Blood Transfusion: A Conceptual Approach, 1984, Immunomodulatory Effects of Blood Transfusion, 1999, Global Perspectives in Transfusion Medicine, 2006; sect. editor: Transfusion, BloodMed.com, 2002—; contbr. more than 360 articles to profl. jours. and books. Recipient Commemorative medal 125th Gov. Gen. of Can., 1994, medal in medicine Royal Coll. Physicians and Surgeons Can., 1979, Lifetime Achievement award Can. Blood Svcs., 2003; named Found. lectr. Royal Coll. Pathologists, U.K., 2004. Mem. AAAS, Am. Assn. Blood Banks (Cooley award 2004), Am. Soc. Hematology, Can. Soc. for Transfusion Medicine (pres. 1990-92, Ortho award 2004), N.Y. Acad. Sci., Internat. Soc. for Thrombosis and Hemostasis (investigator recognition award, 1993), Internat. Soc. Hematology, Internat. Soc. Blood Transfusion. Avocations: judaica, stamp collecting/philately, tennis, antiquarian books. Home: 118 Cline Ave S Hamilton ON Canada L8N 1X1 Office: McMaster U Med Ctr 1200 Main St W Hamilton ON Canada L8N 3Z5 Business E-Mail: blajchma@mcmaster.ca.

BLAKE, AILEEN B., finance company executive; b. 1968; Fin. analyst Quaker Oats, Co. (now PepsiCo Inc.), 1993, PepsiCo Inc., 2001, v.p. fin. planning and analysis, 2003; exec. v.p., controller-designate Northern Trust Corp., Chgo., 2004—05, exec. v.p., controller of registrant and bank, 2005—. Named one of 40 Under Forty, Crain's Bus. Chgo., 2005. Office: Northern Trust Corp 50 S LaSalle Chicago IL 60675 Office Phone: 312-630-6000. Office Fax: 312-444-7843.*

BLAKE, ALLEN H., bank executive; b. Chgo., 1942; Student, Washington U., 1964, student, 1965. Joined First Bank, Inc., St. Louis, 1984—, sr. v.p., CFO, 1984—99, COO, 1998—2003, pres., 1999—, CFO, 2001—05; CEO St. Louis, 2003—. Office: First Banks Inc 135 N Meramec Ave Saint Louis MO 63105 Office Phone: 314-854-4600.

BLAKE, BUD (JULIAN WATSON), cartoonist; b. Nutley, NJ, Feb. 13, 1918; s. George Wilbur and Hazel (Metcalfe) B.; m. Doris Gaskill, Jan. 4, 1941; children: Julian G., Mariana. Student, Nat. Acad. Design, 1935-36. Sketch artist, art dir., exec. art dir. Kudner Agy., NYC, 1937-43, 46-54. Cartoonist: Ever Happen To You, syndicated by King Features; also free lance cartooning for various mags. and ads, 1954-65; cartoonist: syndicated comic strip Tiger, 1965—; Paperback cartoon books include Tiger, Tiger Turns On; others. Served with inf. AUS, 1943-46. Mem. Nat. Cartoonists Soc. (Best Humor Strip award 1971, 78, 2000), Newspaper Features Coun. Home and Office: PO Box 146 Damariscotta ME 04543-0146

BLAKE, CATHERINE C., judge; b. Boston, July 27, 1950; d. John Ballard and Jean Place (Adams) B. BA magna cum laude, Radcliffe Coll., 1972; JD cum laude, Harvard Law Sch., 1975. Bar: Mass. 1975, Md. Ct. Appeals 1977, U.S. Ct. Appeals (4th cir.) 1977, U.S. Dist. Ct. Md. 1977, D.C. 1979. Assoc. Palmer & Dodge, Boston, 1975-77; asst. U.S. atty. Dist. of Md., Balt., 1977-83, first asst. U.S. atty., 1983-85, 86-87, U.S. atty. (court-appointed), 1985-86; U.S. magistrate judge U.S. Dist. Ct. Md., Balt., 1987-95, U.S. dist. ct. judge, 1995—. Mem.: FBA, Fed. Judges' Assn., Nat. Assn. of Women Judges, Md. Bar Assn., Bar Assn. Baltimore City. Office: US Courthouse 101 W Lombard St Ste 7310 Baltimore MD 21201-2639

BLAKE, D. STEVEN, lawyer; b. Saginaw, Mich., June 2, 1940; BA, Mich. State U., 1963; JD, U. Calif., Davis, 1971. Bar: Calif. 1972. Of counsel Downey Brand LLP, Sacramento, 1971—; arbitrator, mediator. Adj. prof. law U. Pacific, 1998-2000. Co-author: California Real Estate Finance and Construction Law, 1995. Mem. ABA (bus. law sect.), Am. Arbitration Assn. (arbitrator), State Bar Calif. (co-chair corp. com., sect., fin. instns. com., bus. law sect., panelist, presenter numerous seminars Calif. State Bar Continuing Edn. Bar 1981-91, co-chair corps. com. bus. law sect. 1997), Yolo County Bar Assn. Office: Downey Brand LLP 555 Capitol Mall Ste 1050 Sacramento CA 95814-4601 Office Phone: 916-444-1000.

BLAKE, ELIZABETH K., lawyer; b. June 1951; m. Frank Blake; 3 children. BA with honors, Smith Coll., 1973; JD, Columbia U., 1977; degree (hon.), Cin. State Tech. CC, Coll. Mt. St. Joseph. Bar: NY, Ohio. Assoc. Davis Polk & Wardell, NYC; assoc., ptnr. Frost & Jacobs (now Frost Brown Todd LLC), Cin.; gen. counsel S.W. Ohio Regional Transit Authority; dir. Star Gas Corp.; v.p., chief of staff Cinergy Corp., 1996—98; v.p., gen. counsel GE Power Sys., 1998—2002; sr. v.p., gen. counsel Trizec Properties, 2002; exec. v.p., corp. affairs and gen. counsel US Airways Group, Inc., US Airways, Inc., Arlington, Va., 2003, corp. sec., 2004; sr. v.p. advocacy and corp. affairs, gen. counsel Habitat for Humanity Internat., Inc., Atlanta, 2006—. Bd. dirs. Patina Oil & Gas Corp. Chmn. Aronoff Ctr.; vice chmn. Cin. Arts Assn.; mem. adv. bd. Civic Forum; bd. dirs. Ohio Bd. Regents, 1990, sec. of the bd., 1994, 1995, chmn., 1996; bd. dirs. Cin. Parks Found., Greater Cin. Conv. and Visitors Bur., Lighthouse Youth Svcs., World Affairs Coun., Children's Svcs. Levy Com. Harlan Fiske Stone scholar, Columbia U. Sch. Law. Office Phone: 404-962-3403. Business E-Mail: eblake@habitat.org.

BLAKE, FRANK (FRANCIS STANTON), consumer products company executive, lawyer; b. Boston, July 30, 1949; s. George Baty and Rosemary (Shaw) Blake; m. Anne McChristian, Jan. 1, 1977; children: Francis S., Margaret D. BA, Harvard U., 1971; JD, Columbia U. Sch. Law, 1976. Bar: DC 1978. Legis. aide to Joint Com. on Social Welfare Mass. Legis., Boston, 1971—73; law clk. to Hon. Wilfred Feinberg US Ct. Appeals (2nd Cir.), NYC, 1976—77; law clk. to Justice John Paul Stevens US Supreme Ct., Washington, 1976—78; assoc. Leva, Hawes, Symington, Martin & Oppenheimer, Washington, 1978-81; dep. counsel to v.p. The White House, Washington, 1981-83; ptnr. Swidler Berlin & Strelw, Washington, 1983-85; gen. counsel EPA, Washington, 1985—88; v.p., gen. counsel GE Power Systems, Schenectady, NY, 1991—95, v.p. bus. devel. & alliances, 1995—98, v.p. bus. devel., 1998—2000; sr. v.p. corp. bus. devel. GE, 2000—01; dep. sec. US Dept. Energy, Washington, 2001—02; exec. v.p. bus. devel. & corp. ops. The Home Depot, Inc., Atlanta, 2002—07, vice-chmn., 2006—07, chmn., CEO, 2007—. Bd. dirs. So. Co., Atlanta, 2004—. Republican. Episcopalian. Office: Home Depot Inc 2455 Paces Ferry Rd Atlanta GA 30339-4024*

BLAKE, GEORGE ROWLAND, soil scientist, educator, environmental scientist, researcher; b. Provo, Utah, Mar. 14, 1918; s. Samuel Henry and Annie Matilda (Bevan) B.; m. Kathryn M. Sumsion, Feb. 26, 1941; children: Carla Paul (dec.), Rowland, Lorraine Blake Phillips, Henry; m. Helen M. Patten, May 25, 1985. BA, Brigham Young U., 1943; PhD, Ohio State U., 1949. Missionary LDS Ch., Germany, 1937-39; with FBI, Washington, 1941-42; research fellow, teaching asst. Ohio State U., Columbus, 1946-49; asst. prof., asst. research specialist Rutgers U., New Brunswick, NJ, 1949-55; assoc. prof. dept. soil sci. U. Minn., St. Paul, 1955-60, prof., 1960-84, prof. emeritus, 1984—, dir. Water Resources Research Ctr., 1979-84. NSF sr. postdoctoral fellow, Braunschweig, Fed. Republic of Germany, 1962-63; Fulbright guest prof. U. Hohenheim, Fed. Republic of Germany, 1970-71; Ford Found. cons., Chile, 1967; guest prof. U. Kesthely, Hungary, 1974, U. Warsaw, Poland, 1981; USAID cons., Morocco, 1979-88; adj. prof. Institut Agronomique et Veterinaire Hassan II Rabat Morocco, 1982-88; guest prof. Humboldt U., Berlin, German Dem. Republic, 1986; Benson Inst. cons., Guatemala, 1990, 94. Contbr. articles to profl. jours. Pub. affairs vol. LDS Ch., Frankfurt, Germany, 1996-97. Recipient Georgicon award U. Kesthely, 1974, Müncheberg Plaque Acad. of Sci., German Dem. Republic., Spl. Emeritus Recognition award Brigham Young U. Emeritus Assn., 1996. Fellow Am. Soc. Agronomy, Soil Sci. Soc. Am.; mem. Internat. Soc. Soil Sci., Soil Sci. Soc. Am., Soil Conservation Soc. Am., Sigma Xi, Gamma Sigma Delta, Omicron Delta Kappa Home: 2215 N 1400 E Provo UT 84604-2103 Personal E-mail: grblake@iveracity.com.

BLAKE, GERALD RUTHERFORD, retired banker; b. Knoxville, Tenn., Apr. 2, 1939; s. Roy Carl and Katherine Marie (Rutherford) B.; m. Jeanne Avonne Jones, May 11, 1962; children: Robert Alan, Douglas Mark. Student, U. Tenn., 1957-58, Sch. Bank Adminstrn., U. Wis., 1971-73. With Miller's. Inc., Knoxville, 1959—62, First Tenn. Bank, Knoxville, 1963—, eastern regional bldg. mgr., 1973—. Vice-chmn. planning com. Knoxville United Way, 1973—; pres. Ramsey Cmty. Club, 1966-67, Ramsey Elem. Sch. PTO, 1976-80; bd. dirs. Planned Parenthood Assn., 1976-77. Mem. Am. Inst. Banking, Bank Adminstrn. Inst. (pres., dir. Smoky Mountain chpt. 1976-77, state dir. 1977-79, 2d vice-chmn. Tenn. Title XX com.) Baptist. Home: 5233 Straw Plains Pike Knoxville TN 37914-6340 Office: 800 S Gay St Knoxville TN 37929-9729 *I always seem to be caught between the old and the new-in the middle of change from one accepted method or life-style to the new method or life-style, which has yet to be fully accepted. Perhaps everyone in every age is at the same situation. The time is upon us and the need is clear for a return to individualism and self-reliance, and a return to basic moral and religious principles. In doing so, one may just find the answers to most of life's problems.*

BLAKE, JAMES RILEY, professional tennis player; b. Yonkers, NY, Dec. 28, 1979; s. Thomas and Betty Blake. Student, Harvard U., 1998—99. Pro tennis player ATP Tour, 1999—; model IMG Models, 2002—. Mem. U.S. Davis Cup Team, 2001—03. Achievements include 6 career singles titles, 5 doubles titles; winner Sydney Internat., 2006, 2007, Tennis Channel Open, 2006, RCA Championships, 2006, Thailand Open, 2006, Countrywide Classic, 2007, Pilot Pen Tennis, 2007; attained No. 1 ranking in the United States, 2006. Office: c/o ATP Tour 201 ATP Boulevard Ponte Vedra Beach FL 32082*

BLAKE, JEFF, film company executive, lawyer; m. Barbara Blake; 4 children. B. in Economics, Northwestern U.; JD, Whittier Coll. Law. Sales booker Chgo. territory Paramount, 1974, sales mgr. Detroit territory, 1976, branch mgr. Detroit territory, 1976, branch mgr. Milwaukee/Indpls. territory, 1977, branch mgr. Chgo. territory, 1978; asst. gen. sales mgr. Buena Vista Distribution Walt Disney Co., 1980; mgr. Western div. Paramount, 1981, v.p. theatrical distribution, 1984; exec. v.p., gen. sales mgr. domestic distbn. Columbia Pictures, 1987—92, pres. domestic distbn., 1992—94; pres. Sony Pictures Releasing Sony Corp. Am., 1994, pres. worldwide mktg. distbn. Columbia TriStar Motion Picture Group, 2000—05, vice chmn. Sony Pictures Entertainment, 2002—, chmn. worldwide mktg. distbn. Columbia TriStar Motion Picture Group, 2005—. Office: Sony Pictures Entertainment 10202 W Washington Blvd Culver City CA 90232

BLAKE, JONATHAN DEWEY, lawyer; b. Long Branch, NJ, June 14, 1938; s. Edgar Bond and Haven (Johnstone) B.; m. Prudence Anne Rowsell, Dec. 22, 1964 (div. June 1977); children: Juliet Haven, Deborah Anne, Susanna Rowsell; m. Elizabeth L. Shriver, Dec. 9, 1977; children: Jonathan Shriver-Blake, Molly Shriver-Blake. BA magna cum laude, Yale U., 1960, LLB cum laude, 1964; BA, MA, Oxford U., Eng., 1962. Bar: D.C. 1965, U.S. Supreme Ct. 1973, U.S. Dist. Ct. D.C. 1965, U.S. Dist. Ct. Md. 1985, U.S. Ct. Appeals (D.C. cir.) 1965, U.S. Ct. Appeals (2d cir.) 1973. Assoc. Covington & Burling, Washington, 1964-72, ptnr., 1972—; chmn. mgmt. com., 1996—2002. Tchr. Howard U., Washington, 1965-70, U. Va., Charlottesville, 1965-70. Contbr. articles to profl. jours. Exec. com., bd. dir. Deerfield Acad., Mass., 1980—85. Rhodes scholar, 1960; recipient Gordon Brown prize, 1959. Mem. ABA (chair internat. telecomm. com. 1993-2000), Fed. Comm. Bar Assn. (pres. 1980-85). Office: Covington & Burling 1201 Pennsylvania Ave NW Washington DC 20004-7566 Home: 3020 Cambridge Pl NW Washington DC 20007 Home Phone: 202-362-7696; Office Phone: 202-662-5506. E-mail: jblake@cov.com.

BLAKE, KIMBERLY BOSWORTH, pharmacist; b. Birmingham, Ala., Apr. 23, 1975; d. Johnny R. and Gwen Bosworth; m. Paul M. Blake, III, Aug. 2, 2003. BS, Auburn U., Ala., 1998, PharmD, 1999; MBA, W.Va. U., Morgantown, 2006. Registered pharmacist W.Va., Ala. Pharmacy practice resident Erlanger Health Care Sys., Chattanooga, 1999—2000; clin. pharmacist Carraway Meth. Med. Ctr., Birmingham, 2000—01; clin. pharmacy specialist Bapt. Montclair, Birmingham, 2001; clin. and staff pharmacist Meml. Healthcare Sys., Chattanooga, 2001—02; pharmacist, leader IV room project St. Mary's Med. Ctr., Huntington, W.Va., 2002—04; dir. pharmacy Option Care, Huntington, 2004—05, Cornerstone Hosp., Huntington, 2005—. Mem.: Cabell County Med. Soc. Alliance, Am. Soc. Health-Sys. Pharmacists, Am. Mensa, Beta Gamma Sigma, Phi Kappa Phi. Avocations: reading, hiking, playing violin. E-mail: KDBOZAU@hotmail.com.

BLAKE, KING CHARLES, humanities educator, writer; life ptnr. David Gordon. AA, St. Paul's Coll., 1975; BA, Concordia U., 1978; MDiv, Luth. Theol. Sem., 1993; MA, Loyola Coll., 2004. Advisor to pastors Faith Ch., Balt., 1996—2004; individual support counselor Athelas Inst., Inc., Columbia, 2000—04; outreach coord. Luth. U. Ministry, 2003—. Contbr. short stories, poems. Comm. specialist Thrivent Fin., Appleton, Wis., 2002. Mem.: Dr. Cleo Johnson's Fellowship Love Concert Choir (assoc.; chaplain, advisor, songster, comm. specialist 2003). Lutheran. Avocations: music, art, planning and organizing community events, assisting the unfortunate, reading.

BLAKE, LORETTA L., music educator; b. Bonham, Tex., Feb. 2, 1967; d. David F. and M. Cynthia Redding; m. Paul D. Blake, May 5, 2006; children: Hannah McGaughy, Alyssa, Audrey McGaughy, Preston, Benjamin. BS, Arlington Bapt. Coll., Tex., 1989; MA in Tchg., U. Ark., Monticello, 2003. Cert. tchr. vocal music, instrumental music, P-12, ESL P-12 Ark. Dept. Edn., 2002. Libr. asst. Arlington Bapt. Coll., 1986—88; instrumental ensemble instr. Northside Bapt. Ch., Carrollton, Tex.,

1986—91; recruiter Flying Nurses, Inc., Dallas, 1989—91; pvt. voice instr. Tuscola, Tex., 1991—96; preschool tchr. Dallas Ave. Christian Acad., Mena, Ark., 2002; music tchr. K-12 Wickes Sch. Dist., Ark., 2002—06, Springfield Public Sch., Mo., 2006—. Mem.: Ark. Edn. Assn., Ark. Choral Dirs. Assn., Ark. Sch. Band and Orch. Assn. Office: Springfield Public Sch Weller Elementary 1630 Weller Ave Springfield MO 65803 Personal E-mail: loretta.blaka@mchsi.com.

BLAKE, MARGARET MARY, director; d. Joseph Edward and Elizabeth Lynch; m. Laurence Stephen Blake, June 28, 1957; children: Steven Joseph, Anita Marie Furrow, Michelle Denise Michaud, Jennifer Ann. BS in Edn., Salem Coll., 1956; MA in Edn., Tufts U., 1978. Cert. tchr. Mass., 1956. Classroom tchr. Everett Pub. Schs., Mass., 1956—57, North Reading Pub. Schs., Mass., 1958—70; reading specialist Melrose Pub. Schs., Mass., 1971—73; tchr. Baldwin Cartier Sch. Commn., Montreal, Que., Canada, 1974—76; reading clinician Everett Pub. Schs., Mass., 1977—84, dir. Title 1, 1985—, sch. prin., 1993—94. Presenter in field. Bd. dirs. Coun. of Advisors to Compensatory Edn., Title 1, Mass., 1980—82; organizer activities/programs State Title 1 Dissemination Bd., Mass. Recipient Great Seal of United States for excellence in edn., 1985, 1987, 1989. Mem.: Coun. of Advisors to Compensatory Edn. (assoc.; presenter), Oxford (Eng.) Roundtable Alumna (hon.), Pi Lambda Theta. Achievements include presentor Massachusetts Title 1 Conf.-10 successive years; completing 50 years in education, 2007. Avocations: writing, travel, water aerobics. Office: Everett Pub Schs 121 Vine St Everett MA 02149 Home Phone: 978-535-8826; Office Phone: 617-389-7950 ext. 151. Office Fax: 617-387-2951. Business E-Mail: mblake@everett.k12.ma.us.

BLAKE, NORMA E., library director; BA, Montclair State Coll., NJ; MLS, Rutgers U., New Brunswick. Asst. dir. South River Pub. Libr., NJ; dir. West Deptford Pub. Libr., NJ, Gloucester County Libr. System, NJ, Burlington County Libr. System, NJ; state libr. NJ State Libr., Trenton, 2001—. Bd. dirs. NJ Reads, NJ Network Citizens Adv. Bd., So. NJ Devel. Coun., Com. Distance Edn., State Coun. Adult Literacy Edn. Services. Recipient Disting. Svc. award, NJLA-CUS-ARCL NJ, 2005. Mem.: NJ Libr. Assn. (pres. 1993—94, Libr. of Yr. 1999). Office: Office of the State Librarian NY State Library PO Box 520 Trenton NJ 08625-0520 Office Phone: 609-292-6200.*

BLAKE, PETER A., state agency administrator; BA, MS, Va. Commonwealth U. Assoc. dir. State Coun. of Higher Edn. for Va.; staff House Appropriations Com., Va. Gen. Assembly; dep. sec. edn. State of Va., Richmond, 2002—05, sec. edn., 2005; vice chancellor Va. Cmty. Coll. Sys., Richmond, 2006—. Adj. faculty mem. Va. Commonwealth U. Office: VCCS Workforce Develop Services James Monroe Bldg 101 N 14th St 15th Fl Richmond VA 23219 Home Phone: 804-272-5959; Office Phone: 804-786-1151. Office Fax: 804-371-0154, 804-752-4772. E-mail: SOE-CS@governor.virginia.gov.*

BLAKE, RANDOLPH, psychology professor; b. Dallas, Tex., Dec. 22, 1945; BA with highest honors, U. Tex., Arlington, 1967; MA, Vanderbilt U., 1969, PhD, 1972. Nat. Inst. Mental Health postdoctoral fellow Baylor Coll. Medicine & U. Tex. Sensory Sciences Ctr., 1972—74; dir. undergrad. studies Dept. Psychology Northwestern U., 1976—77, asst. prof. psychology, 1974—77, assoc. prof. psychology, 1977—81, prof. psychology and neurobiology/physiology, 1981—88; investigator Vanderbilt Vision Ctr. Vanderbilt U., 1989—, Kennedy Ctr. investigator, 1988—, chmn. Dept. Psychology, 1988—96, 2002, 2004—, prof. psychology, 1988—2000, Centennial prof. psychology, 2000—. Fellow Kennedy Ctr. for Human Develop. Recipient Early Career award, APA, 1977, Career Devel. award, NIH, 1978—83. Fellow: Am. Acad. Arts and Sciences, Japan Soc. Promotion Sci., Am. Assn. Advancement Sci., Am. Psychological Soc.; mem.: Visual Sciences Soc., Psychonomic Soc., Assn. Rsch. Vision and Ophthalmology (program com. 1983—85, chmn. program com. 1985), Sigma Xi. Office: Dept Psychology Vanderbilt Univ 512 Wilson Hall Nashville TN 37203 Office Phone: 615-343-7010. Office Fax: 615-343-8449. E-mail: randolph.blake@vanderbilt.edu.

BLAKE, ROB, professional hockey player; b. Simcoe, Ont., Can., Dec. 10, 1969; m. Brandy Blake; 1 child, Jack. Defenseman LA Kings, 1989—2001, 2006—, Colo. Avalanche, 2001—06. Player NHL All-Star Game, 1994, 1999—2004; mem. Team Can., Olympic Games, Salt Lake City, 2003. Named to First All-Star Team, NHL, 1998, Second All-Star Team, 2000—02; recipient James Norris Trophy, 1998. Achievements include being a member of Stanley Cup Champion Colo. Avalanche, 2001; being a member of gold medal Canadian Hockey team, Salt Lake City Olympic Games, 2002. Office: LA Kings Ste 3100 1111 S Figueroa St Los Angeles CA 90015

BLAKE, ROBERT WILLIAM, retired literature and language professor, writer; b. Springfield, Vt., Jan. 25, 1930; s. Kenneth Davidson Blake and Erma Rhoda Curtis; m. Carol Ann Clark; children: David Whittier, Brett Elizabeth, Robert William Jr. BA in English, Am. Internat., Springfield, Mass., 1952; MA in English, Boston U., 1954; EdD in Curriculum, U. Rochester, 1964. Cert. tchr. Mass., secondary English NY, secondary sch. prin. NY, supt. NY. English tchr. Amherst (Mass.) Jr. HS, 1957, West Springfield (Mass.) HS, 1954—58, Canandaigua (NY) Acad., 1958—60, supervising vice prin., 1960—62; assoc. prof. SUNY, Brockport, 1963—64, prof., 1964—95, prof. emeritus, 1995—. Lit. cons. Internat. Reading Assn., Bismarck, ND, 2004, NY State Reading Assn., Saratoga, 2004, NY State English Coun., Albany, 2004, pres., 1971. Co-author: Literacy and Learning, 2002, Literacy, A Primer, 2005; editor: Literature as a Way of Knowing, 1991. Regional v.p. Day Sailor Assn., Eugene, Oreg., 1970—95; lay reader, vestryman St. Luke's Episcopal, Brockport, 1964—65; treas., bd. dirs. Brockport Yacht Club, 1964—70. Served to sgt. US Army, 1955—56. Mem.: Nat. Coun. Tchrs. English, UK Lit. Assn. Home: 66 Lynnwood Dr Brockport NY 14420 Personal E-mail: bobbillydumpling@aol.com.

BLAKE, SIMONE ELAISE, retired school librarian; b. Fitchburg, Mass., Nov. 24, 1939; d. Pierre and Elaise Trottier; children: Scott Michael, Bethany Ann. BA, Fitchburg State Coll., Mass., 1987; MS, Simmons Coll., Boston, 1990. Pre-profl. libr. Fitchburg Pub. Libr., 1958—60; libr. St. Bernard Ctrl. Cath. H.S., Fitchburg, 1961—85; tech. svcs. libr. Fitchburg State Coll./Gallucci-Cirio Libr., 1986—2007; ret., 2007. Rsch. asst., 1989—97. Editor: Guide to the Montachusett Heritage Trail (Nat. Trust for Hist. Preservation award, 1973). Camp dir., troop leader, neighborhood chairperson Girl Scouts U.S.A., Fitchburg, 1961—79. Mem.: Assn. Coll. and Rsch. Librs. (New Eng. chpt.), Fitchburg Hist. Soc. (life; pres., bd. dirs.), Beta Phi Mu.

BLAKE, STEWART PRESTLEY, retired ice cream company executive; b. Jersey City, Nov. 26, 1914; s. Herbert P. and Ethel (Stewart) B.; m. Helen Davis, Nov. 16, 1982; children by previous marriage: Nancy Blake Yanakakis, Benson Prestley. Student, Trinity Coll., 1934-35, LLD, 1976; PhD, Western New Eng. Coll., 1980, Springfield Coll., 1982; PhD (hon.), Path Bay Coll., 1993; PhD (hon.), Quinnipiac Coll., 1993; PhD (hon.), Elms Coll. Co-founder Friendly Ice Cream Corp., 1935, chmn., to 1979. Past chmn. bd. trustees Bay Path Coll., Longmeadow, Mass. Mem.: Colony (Springfield), Longmeadow Country, Sailfish Point Yacht (Stuart). Home: 700 Hall Hill Rd Somers CT 06071-1058 E-mail: helenblake@aol.com.

BLAKE-INADA, LOUIS MICHAEL, cardiologist, researcher; b. Osaka, Japan, June 4, 1956; came to U.S., 1959; s. Edward Kneeland, Sr. and Setsuko (Inada) Blake. BA in Biochemistry and Molecular Biology, U. Calif., Santa Barbara, 1979; MD, Case Western Res. U., 1983. Diplomate in internal medicine and cardiovasc. diseases Am. Bd. Internal Medicine; diplomate Am. Bd. Nuc. Medicine, Am. Bd. Nuc. Cardiology. Intern in gen. surgery Letterman Army Med. Ctr., San Francisco, 1983-84; resident in internal medicine Sch. Medicine Stanford U., Calif., 1988-90, resident in nuc. medicine, 1990-92, chief resident in nuc. medicine, 1991-92; fellow in cardiology Calif. Pacific Med. Ctr., San Francisco, 1992-93; fellow in cardiology, cardiac imaging U. Calif., San Francisco, 1993-95; fellow in invasive cardiology U. N.Mex. Health Sci. Ctr., 1997-98; asst. prof. medicine (cardiology), asst. prof. radiology U. Nev. Sch. of Medicine, Reno, 1998-2000; dir. echocardiography lab. Sierra Nevada VA Med. Ctr., Reno, 1999-2000; dir. nuclear cardiology Sierra Nevada Med. Ctr., Reno, 1999-2000; staff cardiologist Swedish Heart Inst., Seattle, 2000—, med. dir. Jiang Nuc. Medicine Lab. Med. dir. Swedish Cardiology Lab., Swedish Heart Inst., Seattle, 2005—. Contbr. articles to med. jours. including Am. Jour. Radiology, Jour. Nuc. Medicine, others; contbr. editor Jour. Am. Coll. Cardiology, 1993-95. Capt. U.S. Army, 1979-88. Recipient Evelyn Neizer srch. fellow, Stanford U., 1992. Fellow ACP, Am. Coll. Angiology, Am. Coll. Cardiology; mem. Am. Coll. Nuc. Physicians, Am. Heart Assn. (coun. on cardiovascular radiology), Am. Heart Assn. (coun. on vascular biology, coun. on cardiovascular and critical care medicine 1999—. coun. on vascular and molecular biology 1999—), Soc. Nuc. Medicine, Assn. Military Surgeons of the U.S., Stanford U. Alumni (life). Home: PO Box 1805 Edmonds WA 98020 Office: Swedish Med Ctr Seattle WA 98122

BLAKELY, ALLISON, history professor; b. Clinton, Ala., Mar. 31, 1940; s. Ed Walton and Alice Blakely; m. Shirley Ann Reynolds, July 5, 1968; children: Shantel, Andrei. Student, Oreg. State Coll., Corvallis, 1958-60; BA, U. Oreg., 1962; MA, U. Calif., Berkeley, 1964, PhD, 1971. Instr. history Stanford (Calif.) U., 1970-71; asst. prof. history Howard U., Washington, 1971-77, assoc. prof. history, 1977-87, assoc. dean Coll. Liberal Arts, 1989-90, dir. honors program, Coll. Liberal Arts, 1990-93, prof. history, 1987-2001, Boston U., 2001—. Reader and test devel. cons., Ednl. Testing Svc., Princeton, NJ, 1974-2001; fellowship selection panelist, Am. Coun. Learned Socs., 2001, NEH, 1979-80, chair fellowship selection panel, Ford Found., NYC, 1992-94; world history nat. stds. rev. panelist, Coun. Basic Edn., Washington, 1995-96. Author: Russia and the Negro: Blacks in Russian History and Thought, 1986 (Am. Book award, 1988), Blacks in the Dutch World: The Evolution of Racial Imagery in a Modern Society, 1994; contbr. articles to profl. jours., chpts. to books. Mem. Dem. Nat. Com., Washington, 1982—; pub. mem. Fgn. Svc. Selection Bd., US State Dept., 1995. Mem. Am. Hist. Assn. (nom. com. 1999—, chmn. com. on minority historians 1993-97), World History Assn., Am. Assn. Advancement of Slavic Studies, US Fgn. Svc. Pub. Mems. Assn. (bd. dirs.), Phi Beta Kappa Soc. (sen. at large 1993—, pres. 2006-). Democrat. Unitarian Universalist. Avocations: music, swimming, tai chi. Home: 1 Sunnyside Rd Silver Spring MD 20910 Office: Boston U 226 Bay State Rd Boston MA 02215 E-mail: ablakely@bu.edu.

BLAKELY, CAROLINE MILLER, retired editor; b. Legrande, Ky., Apr. 12, 1924; d. John Brison and Mary Brown (Eilliott) Miller; m. Charles William Lynch, II (div. 1947); children: Carol Lynn Lynch Berry, Charles William Lynch III; m. Durward Earl Blakely, Aug. 25, 1947 (dec. 1952); children: Donna Blakely Pohl, John Durward, David Elliott. BA summa cum laude, Bethel Coll., McKenzie, Tenn., 1958; MA in Journalism, Syracuse U., 1960. Homebound tchr. McKenzie Sch. Bd., 1956—58; tchr. English to fgn. adults Syracuse Dept. Edn., 1959—60; editor News for You Laubach Literary Internat., Syracuse, 1960—67; editl. dir. New Readers Press, Syracuse, 1967—83; bd. assessment rev. Syracuse Common Coun., 1985—95; ret. Author: (memoirs) I Am One of These, 2004; co-author (with Robert Laubach): (book) Literacy Journalism at Syracuse University: A 30-Year History, 1996. Del. 12th ward com. Dem. Party of Syracuse, 1998—2002. Recipient Valedictorian award, McKenzie H.S., 1942, Literacy award, Cumberland Presbyn. Home Mission, 1960. Mem.: Peace Action of Cen. N.Y. (bd. dirs., Peace award 2001). Democrat. Avocations: pinochle, reading. Home: 403 Onondaga Ave Syracuse NY 13207 Home Phone: 315-474-3530.

BLAKELY, DELORES PHINELLA, financial consultant, business advisor, evangelist; b. Manning, SC, May 4, 1960; d. Aaron Jr. and Daisy (Kennedy) McF.; m. Lenard Jerome Blakely, Nov. 7, 1989 (div.); children: Seneca Duwayne McFadden, Crystal, Lynnette, Faith, Joshua. BA in Bus. Mgmt., U. S.C., 1985; MBA in Fin. Mgmt., Morgan State U., 1988. Cert. fin. coord.; lic. mortgage broker. Learning mgr. Sumter (S.C.) Area Tech., 1981-85; sales assoc. Fed. Machine Corp., Des Moines, 1985-87; pres. McFadden and Assocs., Sumter, 1987-90; CEO Blakely and Assocs., Sumter, 1990—, bus. advisor, 1993—. Min. at confs. and chs. Vol. Mental Health Assn., Sumter, 1994-95; mentor Salvation Army Boys and Girls Club, 1993. Mem. NAFE, NOW, Acad. Polit. Sci., Nat. Assn. Fin. Cons., Internat. Alliance of Fin. Cons., S.C. Sheriff Assn. Republican. Full Gospel Ch. Avocations: knitting, gourmet cooking, aerobics, nature walks. Office: Blakely and Assocs Fin Svcs PO Box 2910 Sumter SC 29151-2910 Home Phone: 803-469-6419; Office Phone: 803-469-6348. E-mail: blakelyfinance@aol.com.

BLAKELY, EDWARD JAMES, city manager, economics professor; b. San Bernardino, Calif., Apr. 21, 1938; s. Edward Blakely and Josephine Elizabeth (Carter) Proctor; m. Maaike C. Vander Sleesen, July 1, 1971; children: Pieta C., Brette D. BA, U. Calif., Riverside, 1960; MA, U. Calif., Berkeley, 1964; MBA, Pasadena Nazerene Coll., 1967; EdD in Edn. and Mgmt., UCLA, 1971. Mgr. Pacific Telephone Co., Pasadena, Calif., 1960-65; exec. dir. Western Community Action Tng., Los Angeles, 1965-69; spl. asst. US Dept. State, Washington, 1969-71; asst. chancellor, assoc. prof. U. Pitts., 1971-74; assoc. dean and prof. applied econs. and behavioral scis. U. Calif., Davis, 1974-77, asst. v.p. Berkeley, 1977-85, prof., chmn. dept. city and regional planning, 1985—2004; dean Milano Sch. Mgmt. and Urban Policy New Sch. U., NYC, 2004—; chair urban & regional planning U. Sydney, 2004—; exec. dir. for recovery mgmt. City of New Orleans, 2006—. Expert advisor Orgn. Econ. Cooperation and Devel., asst. to Mayor Elihu Harris, City of Oakland. Author: Rural Communities in Advanced Industrial Society, Community Development Research, Taking Local Development Initiative, Planning Local Economic Development SAGE, 1988, Separate Societies: Poverty and Inequality in U.S. Cities (Paul Davidoff award 1993), 1992, Fortress America: Gated Communities in the U.S., 1998. Chmn. fin. com. Pvt. Industry Council of Oakland (Calif.), 1978-85; vice chmn. Ecole Bilingue Sch., Berkeley, 1982-85, chmn., 1988—; chmn. bd. Royce Sch., Oakland, Calif., 1988—; sec., treas. Econ. Devel. Corp., Oakland, 1983; expert advisor Orgn. Econ. Corp. and Devel., Paris, 1986; apptd. to pres. trust Pres. Bill Clinton, 1997—; mayoral candidate City of Oakland, Calif., 1998. Served to 1st lt. USAF, 1961-63. Named 125th Anniversary Prof., U. Calif. at Riverside Berkeley Campus, 1992; named to, Athlete Hall of Fame, U. Calif. Riverside Alumni Press, 1992, Pres. Trust by Pres. Bill Clinton, 1997; recipient San Francisco Found. award, 1991, Paul Davidoff award, 1993, Rsch. award, Cmty. Devel. Soc., 2002; fellow, German Acad. Exch., 1984, Urban Studies Australian Inst. Urban St., 1985, John Simon Guggenheim fellow, 1995—96; scholar Fulbright St. scholar, Internat. Exch. Scholars, 1986. Fellow Nat. Acad. Pub. Adminstrn.; mem. Cmty. Devel. Soc. (bd. dirs. 1980-84, svc. award 1983, disting. svc. award 1990), Calif. Local Econ. Devel. (standing com. 1980-81), Am. Planning Assn. (accreditation com.), Am. Assn. Collegiate Schs. of Planning, Nat. Assn. State and Land Grant Colls. (exec. com. 1987), Phi Delta Kappa, Lambda Alpha. Clubs: Rueful Order. Office: City Hall 1300 Perdido St New Orleans LA 70112 Office Phone: 504-658-8400. Personal E-mail: ejbakely@cityofu.com.

BLAKELY, JESSE ALAN, military officer; b. Heidelberg, Germany, Jan. 17, 1976; s. Jerrel Dean and Catherine Ann Blakely; m. Sara Rose Mauer, Aug. 1, 2003; children: Truitt Alan, Isabella Rose Blakeley. AA in Liberal Arts, St. Leo U., 2004, BA in Bus. Adminstrn., 2007. Cert. six sigma green belt USN, 2005, six sigma champion USN, 2006. Aviation electrician mate USN, 2002—03, shop supr., 2004—05, divsn. electronics supr. Virginia Beach, 2005—. Decorated Achievement medal USN, Good Conduct medal, Flag Letter Commendation medal. Avocation: basketball.

BLAKELY, KEVIN M., management association executive; b. 1952; BS Fin., So. Ill.; MBA, Case W. Res. U. Dep. comptr. for spl. supervision, Office Comptr. of the Currency US Dept Treasury; chief risk officer KeyCorp, 1994—2005; chmn. The Risk Mgmt. Assn., 1999—2000, regulatory rels. chmn., ex officio dir., pres., CEO, 2007—; grp. exec. v.p., risk mgmt. KeyCorp. Office: The Risk Mgmt Assn 10 Penn Ctr 1801 Market St Ste 300 Philadelphia PA 19103 Office Phone: 215-446-4000. Office Fax: 215-446-4101.*

BLAKELY, ROBERT T., financial executive; b. Dec. 16, 1941; B in Mech. Engring., Cornell U., 1964, MBA, 1965; Doctorate, MIT, 1970; postgrad., Dartmouth U., 1976. Mng. dir. Morgan Stanley & Co., 1970-81; v.p., CFO U.S. Synthetic Fuels Corp., Washington, 1981; exec. v.p., CFO Tenneco, 1981—99, exec. v.p., 1996—99; exec. v.p., CFO Lyondell Chemical Co, 1999—2002; pres. Performance Enhancement Group, Inc., 2002—03; exec. v.p., CFO MCI, Inc., 2003—05; CFO Fannie Mae, 2006—. Bd. dirs. Solutia, Inc., Vlasic Foods Internat., Inc. Trustee, mem. audit and fin. coms. Cornell U.; bd. dirs. N.Y.C. Ballet, Manhattan and Bronx Coun. Boy Scouts Am., United Way Greenwich. Office: Fannie Mae 3900 Wisconsin Ave NW Washington DC 20016

BLAKELY, WILLIAM D., lawyer; b. Darien, Wis., Oct. 15, 1945; BA, Univ. Wis., Madison, 1968; JD, Univ. Detroit, 1977. Bar: Mich. 1977, DC 1980, Va. 1984, US Dist. Ct. (DC, Va. dist.), US Ct. Appeals (4th cir.). Atty. civil div. torts branch, US Dept. of Justice, 1977—82; ptnr., co-chmn. Aviation Litigation practice group, head No. Va. Litigation group DLA Piper Rudnick Gray Cary, Reston, Va. Editor (in chief): Univ. Detroit Law Rev. Served to Lt. Col. pilot, naval aviation, & JAG Corps USMC. Recipient Spurgeon award, Boy Scouts of Am. Mem.: ABA, Million Dollar Advocates Forum, Am. Inst. Aeronautics & Astronautics, USMC Ret. Officers Assn.

BLAKEMORE, AMY, photographer; b. Tulsa, Okla., 1958; MFA, 1985. Profl. photog., 1986—. Prin. works include Jill in Woods, 2005, Exhibited in group shows at Inman Gallery, Houston, Tex., Grace Mus. Achievements include appearing in the Whitney Biennial, Whitney Mus. Art, NYC, 2006. Office: c/o Inman Gallery 3901 Main St Houston TX 77002

BLAKENEY, ALLAN EMRYS, Canadian government official, lawyer, educator; b. Bridgewater, NS, Can., Sept. 7, 1925; s. John Cline and Bertha (Davies) B.; m. Mary Elizabeth Schwartz, 1950 (dec. 1957); m. Anne Louise Gorham, May 1959; children: Barbara, Hugh, David, Margaret. BA, Dalhousie U., 1945, LLB, 1947, LLD (hon.); BA, Oxford U., 1949, MA, 1955; DCL (hon.), Mount Allison U.; LLD (hon.), York U., Toronto, U. Western Ont., London, 1991, U. Regina, 1993, U. Sask., 1995. Bar: N.S. 1950, Sask. 1951. Queen's counsel, 1961; sec. to govt. fin. office Govt. Sask., Canada, 1950-55; chmn. Sask. Securities Commn., 1955-58; ptnr. Davidson, Davidson & Blakeney, Regina, Sask., 1958-60, Griffin, Blakeney, Beke, Koskie & Lueck, Regina, 1964-70; premier of Sask., 1971-82; mem. Sask. Legislature, 1960-88; prof. Osgoode Hall Law Sch. York U., 1988—90; prof. U. Sask., 1990—. Leader of the opposition Sask. Legislature, 1970-71, 82-87; min. of edn., Sask., 1960-61, provincial treas., 1961-62, min. pub. health, 1962-64; mem. Royal Commn. on Aborginal Peoples, 1991-93. Decorated Officer Order of Can., Sask. Order of Merit; Rhodes scholar, Oxford U., 1948—49. Fellow Royal Soc. Can. Home: 1752 Prince of Wales Ave Saskatoon SK 3E5 Office: U Sask Coll Law 15 Campus Dr Saskatoon SK Canada S7N 5A6 Office Phone: 306-966-5881.

BLAKENEY, BARBARA A., public health service officer; BS, MS, U. Mass.; diploma, Worcester City Hosp. Sch. of Nursing. Primary care nurse practitioner Amherst Med. Assoc., Amherst, Mass., Boston City Hosp., Boston; prin. pub. health nurse for homeless svcs., addiction svcs. Dept. Health and Hosp., Divsn. Pub. Health, Boston; currently dir. health svcs. for homeless Boston Pub. Health Comm.; leave of absence. Named one of 100 Most Powerful People in Healthcare, Modern Healthcare mag., 2002, 2003, 2004, 2006; recipient Pearl McIver Pub. Health Nurse award, Am. Nurses Assn., Theta Alpha chpt. Ann Kibirck Nursing Leadership award, Sigma Theta Tau. Mem.: ANA (pres. 2002—06). Office: Am Nurses Assn Ste 400 8515 Georgia Ave Silver Spring MD 20910

BLAKE RAMOS, DEBRA BARBARA, writer; b. Bklyn., June 17, 1959; d. Rebecca Simmons and Jack Blake; m. Manuel Joseph Ramos, Apr. 2, 1957; children: Michael Young, Shameeka Shontele Ramos, Sarah Barbara Ramos, Abraham Joseph Ramos. Bus. degree, N.Y. Bus. Sch., 1981. Telephone technician, 1983; sec. Queensboro Correctional Facility, Queens, NY, 1984; writer, 1980—2003, 2003. Author (artist): (book) A New Birth Of Poetry (Editor's Choice award, 2001), Let Them Cry (Editor's Choice award, 2002), (CD) Serenity and Passion, 2000, Let Them Cry, 2002; songwriter Hill Top Record, 2001—03; contbr. articles to profl. jours. Mem.: Internat. Soc. Of Poets (hon. Internat. Poet of Merit award 2001). E-mail: dedebpoet@earthlink.net.

BLAKESLEE, DIANE PUSEY, financial planner; b. West Chester, Pa., Apr. 12, 1933; d. Norman S. and Leona (Ruth) Pusey; m. Earle B. Blakeslee, June 11, 1954 (dec. July 1999); children: Samuel N., Barbara Blakeslee Porteous, David E., Ruth D. Blakeslee Overton; m. Joseph E. Brocato, Mar. 3, 2007. BA, Hood Coll., 1988. CLU; cert. fin. planner. Dist. mgr. Tchrs. Mgmt. and Investment Corp., Newport Beach, Calif., 1972-78, Walt Becker, Inc., Fresno, Calif., 1978-80; pres. Blakeslee & Blakeslee, San Luis Obispo, Calif., 1980—. Small firm adv. bd. NASD; statutory disqualification bd. Author: (column for Sr. Mag. and syndicated for radio) Dollars and Sense; co-editor: How to Survive on $50,000 to $150,000 a Year, 1984; host monthly TV program Welcome to The World of Financial Planning, 1984-87. Bd. dirs., treas. Pvt. Industry Coun., 1979-84, treas. Child Devel. Ctr., 1980-83; bd. dirs. Cuesta Coll. Found., 1985—; bd. dirs., 1st v.p. San Luis Obispo Art Assn.; 1st v.p. San Luis Obispo Estate Planning Coun.; bd. dirs. Cert. Fin. Planners Bd. of Standards, Ethics and Profl. Rev., 1993-97; regent Coll. Fin. Planning, 1980-85; chmn. planned giving com. Cuesta Coll., 1984-86, pres. found. Named Bd. Mem. of Yr., Econ. Opportunity Coun., San Luis Obispo County, 1983, Woman of Achievement of Yr., Ctrl. Calif. region Bus. and Profl. Women, 1985-86, Nat. Cert. Fin. Planner of Yr., 1986; recipient Disting. Alumni award George Sch., 1991. Mem.: NASD (dist. 2 com. 1999—2002, statutory disqualification com. 1999—, small firm adv. com. 2000—), Bur. Nat. Affairs Tax Mgmt. (bd. advisors 1986—), Nat. Life Underwriters Assn., Inst. Cert. Fin. Planners (bd. dirs. 1978—82, chmn. pub. rels.), Internat. Assn. Fin. Planners, San Luis Obispo Rotary Club (bd. dirs., treas. 2005—), Womens' Network (San Luis Obispo). Republican. Mem. Soc. Of Friends. Avocations: hiking, gardening, sketching. Home: 88 Country Club Dr San Luis Obispo CA 93401-8908 Office: Blakeslee & Blakeslee 299 Madonna Rd San Luis Obispo CA 93405-5430

BLAKESLEE, EDWARD EATON, lawyer, insurance company executive; b. NYC, July 23, 1921; s. Edward Eaton and Ada Rainbow (Harris) B.; m. Janice Callaghan, Mar. 19, 1944; children— Edward, David. LLB cum laude, NYU, 1947, LLM in Taxation, 1957; grad. exec. program in bus. adminstrn., Columbia U., 1966. Bar: N.Y. 1947. Atty. Mut. Life Ins. Co. N.Y., 1947-69, 2d v.p., gen. solicitor, 1969-73, v.p., gen. solicitor, 1973, gen. counsel, 1974-85; gen. counsel, bd. dirs. Am. Life Ins. Co. of N.Y., 1986-88; mng. dir., chief exec. officer Sargasso Mut. Ins. Co., Ltd., Hamilton, Bermuda, 1986-93, also bd. dirs. Pres. Securities Investors Indemnification Co., Ltd., Hamilton, Bermuda, 1989-90; spl. counsel Rosenman & Colin, 1990-92; of counsel Shea & Gould, 1992-94, Werner & Kennedy, 1994-99; assessor Ins. Marketplace Stds. Assn., 1997—; cons. Nat. Exec. Svc. Corps, 2001—. With AC US Army, 1942—46. Mem. ABA, Assn. Bar City of N.Y., Assn. Life Ins. Counsel, NYU Alumni Fedn. (pres. 1981-83, dir. emeritus), Fellows Am. Bar Found. (life mem.), NYU Law Alumni Assn., Univ. Club. Home: 495 Birchtree Rd Oradell NJ 07649-1303 Personal E-mail: edwardb743@aol.com.

BLAKESLEE, WESLEY DANIEL, lawyer, consultant, director; s. Daniel Leo and Ann Blakeslee; m. Georgia Carroll Croft, July 28, 1973; children: Jaime Kiersten, Christopher Justin, Shaun Michael. BS, Pa. State U., 1969; JD, U. Md.-Balt., 1976. Bar: Md. 1976, U.S. Dist. Ct. Md. 1977, U.S. Tax Ct. 1984. Sys. analyst NASA, Greenbelt, Md., 1969-76; assoc. Semmes, Bowen & Semmes, Balt., 1976-78; with Dulany & Davis, Westminster, Md., 1978-83; pvt. practice Westminster, 1984—2000; of counsel Blakeslee & Wallace PC, Westminster, 2000—. Lectr. Md. Inst. Profl. Edn. of Lawyers, 1980-, Md. State Jud. Inst., 1990-; bd. govs. Md. Law Sch. Fund, 1982-94, chair, 1991; assoc. gen. counsel Johns Hopkins U., 1999-, lectr., 2002-, exec. dir. tech. transfer, 2006—; dir. computer devel. U. Md. Law Sch., Balt., 1984-89, lectr., 1985-87; dir. Union Nat. Bank, 1988-00; bd. govs. Md. Law Sch. Alumni Assn., 1999-03; mem. Md. Bus. and Tech. Ct. Task Force, 2000-, Md. Bus. and Tech. Coalition, 2004-; presenter in field. Author: (manual) Understanding Computers: A Primer for the Technically Challenged, 1995, rev. edit., 2003. County bd. mgrs. YMCA, 1986—92, 1993—98, chair bldg. com., 1990; mem. county bd. Am. Cancer Soc., 1989—95, pres., 1992—94. Mem. ABA, Fed. Bar Assn. (bd. govs. 1981-99, treas. Balt. chpt. 1984-90), Md. Bar Assn. (litig. sect. coun. 1982-01, chair litig. sect. 1995-96), Carroll County Bar Assn. (treas. 1984), Nat. Assn. Coll. and Univ. Attys. (co-chmn. intellectual property sect. 2000-02, mem. CLE com., First Decade award (inaugural recipient) 2006), Assn. Univ. Tech. Masters, Order of Coif, Delta Theta Phi. Roman Catholic. Home: 980 Hook Rd Westminster MD 21157-7335 Office: Johns Hopkins U Tech Transfer 5th Fl 100 N Charles St Baltimore MD 21201 Office Phone: 410-516-8300. Business E-Mail: starman@jhu.edu.

BLAKESLEY, DAVID EDWARD, language educator, small business owner; b. Hemet, Calif., Feb. 15, 1960; s. Merrill Kimble and Pearl Beatrice Blakesley; m. Julie Lynn Reiske, Dec. 30, 1992; children: Meagan Belle, Matthew Michael. BA, San Diego State U., 1978—83, MA, 1983—86; PhD, U. So. Calif., LA, 1986—90. Asst. prof. English So. Ill. U., Carbondale, 1989—90, assoc. prof. English, 1997—2000, Purdue U., W.Lafayette, Ind., 2000—06, prof. English, 2006—; founder, pres. Parlor Press, LLC, W.Lafayette, 2002—. Dir. profl. writing dept. English Purdue U., 2000—. Author: (textbooks) The Thomson Handbook, The Thomson Handbook, Brief Edition, (book) The Elements of Dramatism; editor: (books) Late Poems, 1968-1993, The Terministic Screen. Commr. Tippecanoe County Human Rels. Commn., Lafayette, 2004—. Mem.: NCTE, Coun. Writing Program Adminstrs., Kenneth Burke Soc. (web developer, conf. planner 2002—, Disting. Svc. award 2005). Home: 816 Robinson St West Lafayette IN 47906 Office: Purdue Univ Dept English 500 Oval Dr West Lafayette IN 47907 Home Phone: 765-746-0175. Office Fax: 765-494-3780; Home Fax: 206-600-5076. Business E-Mail: blakesle@purdue.edu.

BLAKESLEY, KIMBERLY KAY, art educator, consultant; b. Hampton, Iowa, Aug. 17, 1959; d. Jay Francis and Sharon Kay (Pieters) Kurth; m. Jay Kevin Hoodjer, July 22, 1977 (div. Sept. 1990); children: Joshua, Tylor, Kathryn; m. Bruce Carl Blakesley, Oct. 22, 1999. AA, Ellsworth C.C., Iowa Falls, Iowa, 1990; BA, U. No. Iowa, Cedar Falls, 1993, MA in Ednl. Leadership, 2002, postgrad. Cert. tchg. U. No. Iowa, 1997. Owner, mgr. Skay's Variety Store, Ackley, Iowa, 1983-88; mgr. Pronto Market, Ackley, 1989-90; state coord. Iowa region Nacel Cultural Exchs., St. Paul, 1994—98; art bus. instr. Waterloo, Iowa, 1998—2002; art instr., yearbook adv., coach Wapsie-Valley, Fairbanks, 2002—06; owner Turning Page Cons., 2006—. Artist, creator electroplated container, Container I (hon. mention 1993); exhibited in group shows at Denver Art Show (1st pl. 2002-06). Mem. NEA, ASCD, Sch. Adminstrs. Iowa, Nat. Art Educators Assn., Iowa Art Educators Assn., Phi Theta Kappa, Beta Sigma Phi. Avocations: fine arts, golf, cross country skiing. Home: 2512 Cedar Heights Dr Cedar Falls IA 50613 Office Phone: 319-939-4356. E-mail: kbangels@cfu.net.

BLAKESLEY, WAYNE LAVERE, JR., retired production engineer; b. Goshen, Ind., Mar. 26, 1926; s. Wayne L. Blakesley Sr. and Thelma (Brown) Cobb. Test engr. Bendix Missile Div., Mishawaka, Ind., 1952-53, engring. tech., 1955-59; field engr. RCA Service Co., Camden, NJ, 1953-55; design engr. Crown Internat., Elkhart, Ind., 1959-72, prodn. engr., 1978—95; pres. Blakesley Electronics, Syracuse, Ind., 1972-78; ret. Inventor, designer automated system for radio stas., printed circuit bd. prototyping system, printed circuit bd. multilayer overlay; designer multi-unit electronic learning lab. Mem. So. Mfg. Engrs. (sr. mem. Robotics Internat. div.), Mensa, Intertel. E-mail: wayne@npcc.net.

BLAKEY, G(EORGE) ROBERT, law educator; b. Burlington, NC, Jan. 7, 1936; BA, U. Notre Dame, 1957, JD, 1960. Bar: NC 1960, DC 1960, Colo. 1986, admitted to practice: U.S. Supreme Ct. 1963. Participated in Atty. General's Honor Program US Dept. Justice, 1960, spl atty. Organized Crime and racketeering sect., 1960—64; asst. prof. U. Notre Dame Law Sch., Ind., 1964—67, prof. law, 1967—74, 1980—85, William J. and Dorothy O'Neill prof. law, 1985—; spl. cons. Pres. Commn. for Law Enforcement and Adminstrn. of Justice, 1966—67, U.S. Senate Judiciary Com., Title III on wiretapping and electronic surveillance, 1967—68, Nat. Commn. on Reform of the Fed. Penal Law, 1968; chief counsel U.S. Senate Judiciary Com., Subcommittee on Criminal Laws and Procedures, 1969—73; prof. law, Cornell U., Ithaca, NY, 1973—80; dir. Cornell Inst. on Organized Crime, Cornell Law Sch., 1973—80; presdl. mem. Nat. Commn. on the Review of Fed. and State Law Relating to Wiretapping and Electronic Surveillance, 1974—75; chief counsel Nat. Comn. on the Review of Policy Toward Gambling, 1974—76; chief counsel, staff dir. U.S. House Select Com. on Assassinations, 1977—78; spl. cons. U.S. Judiciary Com. White Collar Crime, 1985—86, U.S. House Judiciary Com., White Collar Crime and RICO reform, 1988. Assoc. editor Law Review; author: (novels) Develop. of Law of Gambling, 1978; contbr. articles to profl. jours. Recipient Legal award, Assn. Fed. Investigators, 1969, Award of Merit, Nat. Acad. Forensic Sciences, 1979, Appreciation award, FBI, 1985, Pub. Justice Achievement award, Trial Lawyers for Pub. Justice, 1995, Charles Crutchfield Profl. Excellence award, NDLS Black Law Students Assn., 1996. Mem.: Am. Law Inst., Order of the Coif, Nat. Commn. for Rev. of Fed. and State Law Relating to Wiretapping and Electronic Surveillance (mem. 1974—76), Nat. Commn. on Rev. of Policy toward Gambling (mem. 1974—76), Nat. Commn. on Reform of Fed. Penal Law (mem. 1968), Phi Beta Kappa. Office Phone: 574-631-5717. Office Fax: 574-631-4197. Business E-Mail: G.R.Blakey.1@nd.edu.

BLAKEY, MARION CLIFTON, federal agency administrator; b. Gadsden, Ala., Mar. 26, 1948; B Internatl Studies, Mary Washington Coll., U. Va.; postgrad., Johns Hopkins U. Dir. pub. affairs NEH, 1982—84; dir. pub. affairs & spl. asst. to the sec. US Dept. Edn., Washington, 1985—87; adminstr. Nat. Hwy. Traffic Safety Adminstrn., 1992—93; prin. Blakey & Assocs., Washington, 1993—2001; chmn. Nat. Transp. Safety Bd., 2001—02; adminstr. FAA, 2002—. Office: FAA 800 Independence Ave SW Washington DC 20591-0004*

BLAKLEY, BENJAMIN SPENCER, III, lawyer; b. DuBois, Pa., Sept. 1, 1952; s. Benjamin Spencer Jr. and Mary Jane (Campney) B.; m. Kathleen M. Ellermeyer, Oct. 20, 1989; children: Benjamin Spencer IV, Kevin Charles, Kyra Jane. BA, Grove City Coll., 1974; JD, Duquesne U., 1977. Bar: Pa. 1977. With Blakley & Jones, DuBois, 1977—. Pub. defender Clearfield (Pa.) County, 1977-84; instr. Pa. State U., DuBois, 1979-85; solicitor City of DuBois, 2000. Mem. adv. bd. Salvation Army Pa. Corp., DuBois, 1978-98, 00-06, chmn., 1988-91; mem. DuBois Area Youth Aid Panel, 1984-87; mem. Citizens for Effective Govt., DuBois, 1985-97; trustee DuBois Vol. Fire Dept., 1986-87, treas., 1987-90, mem., instr., 1972-; mem. DuBois Ednl. Found., 1990—, Cath. Counseling and Adoption Svcs., 1996—; bd. dirs. DuBois Sr. and Cmty. Ctr., 1992-97; mem. Jaffa Shrine Temple, Altoona, Pa., 2006—. Mem. Pa. Bar Assn., Clearfield County Bar Assn., DuBois Vol. Fire Dept. Relief Assn. (pres. 1998-00), Garfield Lodge, Free and Accepted Masons. Democrat. Methodist. Office: Blakley & Jones 90 Beaver Dr Box 6 Du Bois PA 15801-2440 Office Phone: 814-371-2730. Business E-Mail: bjlaw@choiceonemail.com.

BLAKNEY, JUANITA MOSLEY, psychotherapist; d. George Spellman Mosley and Clarissa Lee Whitlock; children: Denise, Donna Blakney-Williams. BS in Edn., Cheyney U., Pa., 1959; MEd, Antioch U., Yellow Springs, Ohio, 1977; EdD, Nova Southeastern U., Ft. Lauderdale, Fla., 1991. Cert. counselor Pa., lic. profl.counselor NJ. Tchr. Sch. Dist. Phila., 1959—92, Girard Coll., Phila., 1992—97; in home therapist Delaware Valley Psychol. Svcs., Moorestown, NJ, 1999—; provider Magellan Behavioral Health, 2003—. Part-time therapist CEC Counselors and Cons., Haddon Heights, NJ, 1993—96; clin. coord. Youth Advocate Programs, Camden, NJ, 2004—05; provider divsn. Youth and Family Svc., NJ, 2005—. Bd. dirs. Faces of Survivors, Arlington, Tex., Boys and Girls Club, Burlington, NJ. Recipient cert. of merit, Women in Edn., 1992. Mem.: APA, Nat. Assn. Parliamentarians, Continental Socs., Inc (Ea. regional dir. 2003—, past pres. South Jersey chpt., past v.p. South Jersey chpt., past sec. South Jersey chpt.), Order Ea. Star, Grand Chpt. (sec., PM), Alpha Kappa Alpha. Avocations: walking, dance, travel, theater, reading. Home: 322 Society Hill Cherry Hill NJ 08003 Office Phone: 609-744-2758. Business E-Mail: nitablak@comcast.net.

BLALACK, K. LEE, lawyer; b. 1964; BA, U. Memphis, 1990, JD, 1994, MA, 1996. Bar: Washington, DC. Law clerk US Ct. of Appeals, Sixth Cir.; counsel US Senate Com. on Govtl. Affairs; chief counsel, staff dir. US Senate Permanent Subcommittee on Investigation; ptnr. O'Melveny & Myers LLP, Washington. Polit. commentator CNN, CNBC, MSNBC, FOX News, C-Span. Served with Second Marine Divsn. USMC, Persian Gulf. Decorated Combat Action Ribbon, Kuwait Liberation Medal; named one of Washington DC's Top Lawyers, Washingtonian, Litigation's Rising Stars, The Am. Lawyer, 2007. Mem.: Tenn. Bar Assn., Md. Bar Assn., DC Bar Assn., ABA. Office: OMelveny & Myers LLP 1625 Eye St NW Washington DC 20006 Office Phone: 202-383-5374. Office Fax: 202-383-5414. Business E-Mail: lblalack@omm.com.*

BLALOCK, ANN BONAR, evaluation researcher; b. Parkersburg, W.Va., Apr. 16, 1928; d. Harry and Fay (Conley) Bonar; m. Hubert Blalock, Jr., 1951 (dec. 1991); children: Susan Blalock Lyon, Kathleen Blalock McCarrell, James W.; m. Gerhard E. Lenski, 1996. AB, Oberlin Coll., 1950; MA, U. N.C., 1954; MSW, U. Wash., 1978. Pvt. cons. Admiralty Inlet Consulting, Hansville, Wash. Cons. OECD, Paris, 1990, European Commn., Brussels, 1995. Author: Introduction to Social Research, 2d edit., 1982; contbg. author: Quicker, Better, Cheaper: Managing Performance in American Government, 2001; editor, reviewer: Evaluation Forum, 1986-97; editor: Evaluating Social Programs, 1990; co-editor: Methodology in Social Research, 1968; contbr. articles to profl. jours. Past pres. bd. dirs. Cmty. Mental Health Clin.; mem. Gov.'s Task Force on Accountability in Govt. Recipient Rsch. award, Partnership for Employment and Tng. Careers, 1988, Gov.'s Golden Apple award. Mem. NASW (past pres. Wash. state chpt.), Am. Eval. Assn. (past com. chair). Home: PO Box 409 Hansville WA 98340-0409 Personal E-mail: aglenski@earthlink.net.

BLALOCK, LOUISE, librarian, public administrator; b. Neptune, NJ, Jan. 25, 1934; BS, TCNJ, 1955; MLS, SUNY, Albany, 1971; M in Pub. Adminstrn., NYU, 1987. Acting dir. Empire State Coll., NY, 1972; instr. sch. library sci. SUNY, Albany, 1973—74; coordinator children's services East Providence (R.I.) Pub. Library, 1974—77; regional coordinator Island Interrelated Library System, RI, 1977—79; dir. Barrington Pub. Library, RI, 1979—81, New Canaan (Conn.) Library, 1981—92; chief libr. Hartford (Conn.) Pub. Libr., 1994—. Chairperson State Library Standards Task Force, 1984; active Notable Books Council, 1988-90, Conn. Inter-Agy. Library Planning Com., 1982-86, White House Conf. Libraries and Info. Services. 1979, Recipient Outstanding Libr. award, Conn. Libr. Assn., 1999, Libr. of Yr., Libr. Jour., 2001, Nat. Award Libr. Svc., IMLS, 2002. Mem. ALA, Am. Soc. Pub. Adminstrn., Conn. Library Assn., Fairfield Adminstrs. Group (pres. 1987), New Eng. Library Assn. (exec. bd. 1975-77), R.I. Library Assn. (pres. 1979-80). Home Phone: 860-247-6062; Office Phone: 860-695-6280. E-mail: lblalock@hplct.org.

BLALOCK, REBECCA A., information technology specialist; BS in Mktg., State U. West Ga.; M in Fin., Mercer U., Ga. Sr. v.p., chief info. officer Southern Co. Svc. Inc. Chair Bd. Leadership Atlanta. Named Ga. CIO of Yr., Ga. CIO Leadership Assn., 2003, Power Woman of the Yr., Atlanta Woman Mag., 2006; named one of Premier 100 IT Leaders, Computerworld, 2006; named to Acad. of Woman Achievers, YWCA Atlanta, 2005. Office: Southern Co Svc Inc 241 Ralph McGill Blvd Atlanta GA 30308

BLALOCK, SHERRILL, investment advisor; b. Newport News, Va., June 9, 1945; d. David Graham and Martha Lee (Bennett) B.; m. Jonathan L. Smith, Oct. 27, 1985; 1 child, Graham C.G. BA, Smith Coll., 1967. Chartered fin. analyst. Investment broker Legg Mason & Co., Washington, 1968-77, Blyth Eastman Dillon, Washington, 1977-80; portfolio mgr., mng. dir. Mitchell Hutchins, NYC, 1980-88; gen. ptnr., portfolio mgr. Weiss Peck & Greer, NYC, 1988-95; gen. ptnr. Delphi Asset Mgmt., NYC, 1995-98; founder, mng. mem. Chesapeake Asset Mgmt., NYC, 1998—. Chair investment com., trustee Diocese of NY of Episcopal Ch., 2001—; trustee, vice chmn. bd. trustees, chair investment com. Estate and Property of Diocese Conv. of N.Y., 1996—2002; trustee Cathedral of St. John the Divine, 1998—, chair investment com., 1999—. Mem. Washington Soc. Investment Analysts, Inst. Chartered Fin. Analysts. Office: Chesapeake Asset Mgmt 1 Rockefeller Plz Rm 1210 New York NY 10020-2002 Office Phone: 212-218-4040, 212-218-4041.

BLALOCK, THOMAS SULLIVAN, JR., military officer; b. Winston-Salem, NC, Nov. 5, 1963; s. Thomas Sullivan and Elizabeth Weir Blalock; m. Lisa Gardner Blalock, Aug. 4, 1964. BA, Wake Forest U., 1986. Dir., squadron weapons, tactics and tng. 43rd Electronic Combat Squadron, Davis-Monthan AFB, Ariz., 1998—99; dir., wing C-130 weapons and tactics 355th Ops. Support Squadron, Davis-Monthan AFB, Ariz., 1999—2001; asst. ops. officer 41st Electronic Combat Squadron, Davis-Monthan AFB, Ariz., 2001—02, 755 Ops. Support Squadron, Davis-Monthan AFB, Ariz., 2002—03; dep. chief, spl. tech. ops. Air Combat Command, Langley AFB, Va., 2003—, chief, non-lethal SEAD (suppression enemy air def.), 2003—. Chief, electronic warfare plans Combined Air Ops. Ctr., Prince Sultan AB, Saudi Arabia, 2002—03. Maj. USAF, 1988—2005. Decorated Aerial Achievement medal US Ctrl. Command, Air Force Commendation medal 355th Wing, Commendation medal USN, Air Medal US Air Forces Europe, Air Force Commendation medal 355th Wing, Def. Meritorious Svc. Medal US Ctrl. Command; named Directorate of Ops. Action Officer of Yr., Dir. of Air and Space Ops., Air Combat Command, 2005; recipient Outstanding Grad. award, USAF Weapons Sch., 1998. Mem.: Assn. Old Crows (Joint Svc. award 2004), Alpha Phi Omega (life). Independent. Avocations: golf, sports. Home: 112 Cattail Br Hudgins VA 23076 Office: Hdqs Air Combat Command 205 Dodd Blvd Ste 101 Langley Afb VA 23665 Home Phone: 804-725-1034. Personal E-mail: thomas.blalock@langley.af.mil.

BLAMER, STEVEN W., former advertising executive; b. Whittier, Calif., Apr. 19, 1956; m. Linda Blamer; 2 children. Grad., Ariz. State U., 1979. With FCB, Chgo., 1979—81, LA, 1984—87, DDV Needham, 1981—84; dir. new bus, exec. v.p., dir. client svcs. Grey L.A., 1989—97; mng. dir., exec. v.p. Grey LA, Grey Worldwide, 1997—98; CEO Grey London, Grey Worldwide, 1998—2000; pres., CEO Grey Worldwide NY, Grey Worldwide, 2000—03, Grey Worldwide North Am., NYC, 2003—05, FCB Worldwide, 2005—06. Poast bd. dirs. Jr. Achievement. Mem.: Am. Assn. Advt. Agys. (bd. dirs.).

BLAN, OLLIE LIONEL, JR., retired lawyer; b. Ft. Smith, Ark., May 22, 1931; s. Ollie Lionel and Eva Ocie (Cross) B.; m. Allen Conner Gillon, Aug. 19, 1960; children: Bradford Lionel, Elizabeth Ann, Cynthia Gillon. AA, Ft. Smith Jr. Coll., Ark., 1951; LLB, U. Ark. Law Sch., 1954. Bar: Ark. 1954, Ala. 1959, US Dist. Ct. (no. dist.) Ala. 1959, US Dist.Ct. (mid. and so. dist.) Ala. 1960, US Ct. Appeals (5th cir.) 1960, US Ct. Appeals (11th cir.) 1982, US Supreme Ct. 1991. Rsch. analyst Ark. Legis. Coun., 1954-55; law clk. to judge US Dist. Ct. (no. dist.) Ala., Birmingham, 1959-60; assoc. Spain, Gillon & Young, Birmingham, Ala., 1960-64; ptnr. Spain & Gillon and predecessor firms, Birmingham, Ala., 1965-2001; tchr. Am. Inst. Banking, 1965-68; ret., 2001. Spkr. Ala. Inst. Continuing Edn., 1978—2001. Contbr. articles to profl. jours. Treas. Jefferson County Hist. Assn., 1972-81, vice chmn., 1981-86, chmn., 1986-93; mem. Jefferson County Rep. Exec. Com., 1973-76; mem. Briarwood Sch. Bd., Birmingham, 1982-86; chmn. Here's Life Birmingham, 1986-88. Capt. USMCR, 1955-58, ret. Mem. ABA, Am. Bd. Trial Advocates, Ark. Bar Assn., Ala. Bar Assn. (com. on admissions and legal edn. 1971-74, com. jud. office 1972-76, com. ins. programs, bd. bar commrs. 1987-92, chmn. task force om. on disciplinary rules and enforcement 2001-03), Birmingham Bar Assn. (exec. com. 1986-89), Ala. Def. Lawyers Assn. (v.p. 1983-84, 91-93, bd. dirs. 1988-91, sec.-treas. 1993-94, pres. elect. 1994-95, pres. 1995-96), Am. Coun. Life Ins., Internat. Assn. Def. Counsel (chmn. accident, health and life ins. com. 1987-90), Def. Rsch. Inst. (Ala. state rep. 1996-99, Louis B. Potter profl. svc. award 2000). Baptist. Home: 2100 English Village Ln Birmingham AL 35223-1729 Personal E-mail: olblan@bellsouth.net. *My desire has been to achieve the highest standard in whatever area of life I am thrust, guided by principles of ethics and Christianity.*

BLANC, MAUREEN, public relations executive; Founder (with Simone Otus) Blanc & Otus Pub. Rels., Inc., San Francisco, 1985. Office: Blanc and Otus 303 2nd St Ste 800 San Francisco CA 94107-1327

BLANC, ROGER DAVID, lawyer; b. NYC, Dec. 26, 1945; s. Robert Smith and Ara Jeanne (Ponchelet) B.; m. June Chunchin Ku, Sept. 17, 1972; children: David Jung-Wei, Gregory Jung-Lee, Cynthia Jung-Lin. BA, Yale U., 1967; JD, Columbia U., 1970. Bar: N.Y. 1971. Ptnr. Willkie Farr & Gallagher, NYC. Lectr. various profl. orgns. Contbr. articles to profl. jours. Dir. Yale Alumni Schs. Com. Westchester, 1994—. Mem.: Assn. Bar City NY, Univ. Club (NYC). Office: Willkie Farr & Gallagher 787 Seventh Ave New York NY 10019-6099 Office Phone: 212-728-8206. E-mail: rblanc@willkie.com.

BLANCH, HARVEY WARREN, chemical engineering educator; BS in Chem. Engring., U. Sydney, Australia, 1968; PhD, U. NSW, 1971. Lectr. Sch. of Biol. Technology U. NSW, 1971; asst. prof. dept. chem. engring. U. Del., 1974-77, assoc. prof., 1977-78; assoc. prof. dept. chem. engring. U. Calif., Berkeley, 1978-82, prof. dept. chem. engring., 1982—, chair dept. chem. engring., 1997—2001; sr. faculty scientist Lawrence Berkeley Nat. Lab., 1984—; assoc. dir. Marine Bioproducts Engring. Ctr., 1998—2004. Mem. numerous adv. bds. and panels in field, including NIH Cell Culture Ctr., 1991—, rsch. program com. Dept. Energy, Basic Energy Scis., 1993; numerous univ. coms.; cons. and lectr. in field. Author: (book) Biochemical Engineering, 1995; editor: Jour. Bioprocess Engring., 1986—, The Chem. Engring. Jour./Biochem. Engring. Jour., 1985—, (books) Applied Biocatalysis, 1991, Comprehensive Biotechnology, 1980-84, others; mem. editl. bd.: Biotechnology and Bioengring., 1990—, Advances in Biochem. Engring., 1992—; author more than 250 publs. in field; patentee in field. Fellow Internat. Inst. Biotechnology, Am. Inst. for Med. and Biol. Engring. (founder); mem. NAE, Am. Inst. Chem. Engrs. (recipient Food, Pharm. and Bioengring. Divsn. award 1996), Am. Chem. Soc. (Johnson award 1995, Enzyme Engring award 1997), Am. Soc. Engring. Edn. Office: U Calif/Berkeley Chem Engrg 420 Latimer Hall Berkeley CA 94720 Office Phone: 510-642-1387. E-mail: blanch@socrates.berkeley.edu.

BLANCH, PAUL BRADFORD, biomedical engineer, researcher; b. Boston, Mar. 25, 1949; s. Euan True and Ethel Elizabeth Blanch; m. Laurel Ann McNamara, Aug. 18, 1980; children: David Paul, Kathryn Rogers Hazzard, Kimberly Bradford; m. Lorrie Rogers Wilkes, July 21, 1971 (div. Nov. 1, 1977). AA, U. Chgo., 1976; BA, Colby Coll., Waterville, Maine, 1972. Registered respiratory therapist Nat. Bd. Respiratory Care, 1977, lic. Fla. Dept. Health Divsn. Med. Quality Assurance, 1990. Technologist Carney Hosp., Dorchester, Mass., 1972—73; staff therapist Seton Hosp., Waterville, Maine, 1973—74; staff therapist Shands Hosp U. Fla., Gainesville, 1974—75, supr. blood gas and stat chemistry lab. Shands Hosp., 1975—80, respiratory equipment specialist Shands Hosp., 1980—, courtesy asst. anesthesiology Dept. of Anesthesiology Coll. Medicine, 1995—. Mem. Fla. Soc. for Respiratory Care, St. Petersburg, 1990—, Nat. Bd. Respiratory Care, Dallas, 1977—; cons. VersaMed Inc, Trenton, NJ, 1999—2001, Allied Med., St. Louis, 1992—97; instr. Santa Fe C.C., Gainesville, 1974—90; v.p. engring. and R&D Airon Corp., Melbourne, Fla., 1997—. Co-author: Mechanical Ventilators, in Clinical Applications of Ventilatory Support, 1990, Respiratory Care in Atlas of Anesthesia: Critical Care, vol. 1, 2000, Tracheal Pressure Ventilator Control in Innovations in Mechanical Ventilation, 2000, Mechanical Ventilators in Respiratory Care - A Guide to Clinical Practice, 1991, Mechanical Ventilation in Critical Care, 2d edit., 1992, Mechanical Ventilators in Neonatal and Pediatric Respiratory Care, 2d edit., 1993, Mechanical Ventilation in Critical Care, 3d edit., 1996; mem. editl. bd.: Respiratory Care Jour., 1993—; contbr. articles to profl. jours. Coach Babe Ruth Baseball Program, Alachua, Fla., 1993—97. Recipient Lit. award, Am. Respiratory Care Found., 1992, 1994, 1997, 1999; grantee, Am. Coll. Chest Physicians, 1994. Independent. Episcopalian. Achievements include design of mechanical ventilator for use during transportation of patients; pNeuton ventilator for use in a magnetic resonance imaging environment or during transportation of patients; patents in field; patents pending for. Home: 15214 NW 94th Ave Alachua FL 32615 Office: Shands Hospital at the Univ of Florida 1600 SW Archer Road Gainesville FL 32610 Home Phone: 386-462-5547; Office Phone: 352-265-0078. Office Fax: 352-338-9891. Business E-Mail: blancpb@shands.ufl.edu.

BLANCHARD, BRUCE, civil engineer, consultant; b. Ft. Stotsenburg, Philippines, Dec. 26, 1932; s. Wendell and Marcella (Palmer) B.; m. Mary Josie Cain, July 31, 1992; children: Wendell, Laura, Renee. SB in Civil

Engring., MIT, 1957, SM in Civil Engring., 1964; diploma (hon.), Commd. Gen. Staff Course, Ft. Leavenworth, Kans., 1980. Tchg. and rsch. asst. MIT, 1957-59, asst. lacrosse coach, 1958-59, 64; hydraulic engr. Bur. Reclamation, Dept. Interior, Denver, 1959-60, 60-61; water resources planning engr. Phoenix, 1961-66; sr. staff specialist Water Resources Coun., Washington, 1966-69; environ. specialist Office of Sec. Dept. Interior, Washington, 1970-71; dir. Office Environ. Project Rev., Washington, 1971-89; dep. dir. US Fish and Wildlife Svc., Dept. Interior, Washington, 1989-97; spl. asst. for tribal self-governance Office of Sec. of Interior, 1997—2004; asst. to dep. asst. sec. mgmt. office Indian Affairs Dept. Interior, Washington, 2004—05, dir. planning and policy analysis, 2005—06; cons. natural resources mgmt. Editor: The Nation's Water Resources, 1968. With US Army, 1951-53, 60; col. Md. N.G., 1967-85; lt. Ariz. N.G., 1961-66. Decorated Army Commendation medal, Army Meritorious Svc. medal, Army Achievement medal; recipient Commendation medal State of Md., 1976, 78, 79, Meritorious Svc. medal State of Md., 1983, Meritorious Svc. medal Dept. Interior, 1985, Disting. Svc. medal, 1999. Fellow: AAAS; mem.: ASCE, Sr. Execs. Assn., Am. Soc. Pub. Adminstrn., US Armor Assn., N.G. Assn. US, Am. Water Resources Assn., Am. Geophys. Union, MIT Alumni Assn. (bd. dirs. 2001—03), Explorers Club (Washington group treas. 1997—), MIT Club of Washington (bd. dirs. 1997—, v.p. 1998—99, pres. 1999—2000), Phi Gamma Delta (Disting. Fiji award). Home and Office: 80 Observatory Cir NW Washington DC 20008-3611 Personal E-mail: bruce_blanchard@alum.mit.edu.

BLANCHARD, CHARLES ALAN, lawyer, retired state senator; b. San Diego, Apr. 14, 1959; s. David Dean and Janet (Laxson) B.; m. Allison Major, 2001. BS, Lewis & Clark Coll., 1981; M of Pub. Policy, Harvard U., 1985, JD, 1985. Bar: Ariz. 1987, U.S. Dist. Ct. Ariz. 1988, U.S. Ct. Appeals (D.C. cir.) 1988, U.S. Ct. Appeals (9th cir.) 1988, U.S. Supreme Ct. 1994. Law clk. to hon. Harry T. Edwards, Washington, 1985-86; law clk. to hon. Sandra Day O'Connor U.S. Supreme Ct., Washington, 1986-87; assoc. ind. counsel Ind. Counsel James McKay, Washington, 1987-88; atty. Brown & Bain, P.A., Phoenix, 1988-97; state senator State of Ariz., Phoenix, 1991-95; dir. Office of Legal Counsel Office of Nat. Drug Control Policy, Washington, 1997-99; gen. counsel U.S. Army, 1999-2001; ptnr. Brown & Bain PA, Phoenix, 2001—04, Perkins Coie Brown & Bain PA, Phoenix, 2004—. Adj. prof. Ariz. State U. Coll. Law, 1996, 2003—; chmn. Senate Judiciary Com., Phoenix, 1991-93; Dem. candidate U.S. Congress, 1994; dir. homeland security State of Ariz., 2003; mem. regulatory rev. coun., Gov., 2004—. Contbr. articles to profl. jours. Bd. dirs. Luth. Vol. Corps., Washington, 1986-88, Florence (Ariz.) Immigrant and Refugee Rights Project, 1990-97, 2001-, Homeless Legal Assistance Project, Phoenix, 1992-97, Tempe Comty. Action Agy., 1994-97, ABA Com. on Immigration Law, 1996-98, ABA Com. on Substance Abuse, 1998-02, Childrens Action Alliance, Phoenix, 2005—, Ariz. Found. for Legal Svc. and Edn., 2005—; state committeeman Ariz. Dem. Party, Phoenix, 1991-97, 2005—07; chmn. Ariz. Dem. Leadership Coun., Inc., 1992-97. Recipient Disting. Svc. award Ariz. Atty. Gen., 1992, Disting. Civilian Svc. award U.S. Army, 2001; Toll fellowship Coun. of State Govts., 1991; named Disting. Young Alumni Lewis and Clark Coll., 1987. Mem. ABA. Home: 1814 Palmcroft Dr NE Phoenix AZ 85007 Office: PO Box 400 Phoenix AZ 85001-0400 Home Phone: 602-254-5851; Office Phone: 602-351-8000. E-mail: cblanchard@perkinscoie.com.

BLANCHARD, DANIEL G., cardiologist; b. Mnpls., Mar. 13, 1959; s. Robert and Jeannine Blanchard; m. Jennifer Neely, Apr. 20, 2002; children: Rachel, Rebecca, Daniel. MD, U. Calif. San Diego Sch. of Medicine, 1985; BS, Calif. State U., 1980. Cert. Am. Bd. of Internal Medicine, 1988, Subspecialty in Cardiology Am. Bd. of Internal Medicine, 1991, Am. Bd. of Internal Medicine, 2002. Dir. cardiac noninvasive labs. U. Calif. San Diego Med. Ctr., 1994—2004; prof. of medicine U. Calif. San Diego Sch. of Medicine, 2003—; chief clin. cardiology Thornton Hosp, U. Calif. San Diego Med. Ctr., 2002—. Author: (sci. articles, book chpts.) Cardiologic Medical Literature. Fellowship, Am. Coll. of Cardiology, 1994, Am. Heart Assn., 2000. Achievements include research in noninvasive cardiac imaging, transesophageal echocardiography. Office: Univ Calif San Diego Cardiology Ste 1D 9350 Campus Point Dr La Jolla CA 92037 Office Phone: 858-657-8530.

BLANCHARD, DONALD PIERRE, JR., engineer; b. Napoleonville, La., Oct. 12, 1962; s. Donald Pierre and Billie Ann Eris Blanchard; m. Alisa Marie Landry; children: Jennifer Marie, Donald Pierre III. Sheriff's dep. Assumption Parish Sheriff's Dept., Napoleonville, La., 1981—89; sr. process technician Rubicon, L.L.C., Geismar, La., 1989—; owner, comml. pilot pipeline and powerline patrol Bayou Air, Napoleonville, La., 1999—. Fire chief Napoleonville Vol. Fire Dept., La., 1975—; third degree mem. K. of C., Napoleonville, 1988—. Recipient Achievment award, Napoleonville Vol. Fire Dept., 2000, Fireman of Yr., 2003. R-Consevative. Roman Cath. Avocations: flying, skiing, golf. Office: Napoleonville Vol Fire Dept PO Box 911 Napoleonville LA 70390 Home Phone: 985-369-2851; Office Phone: 985-369-2558. Office Fax: 985-369-2558. Business E-Mail: bayouair1@aol.com.

BLANCHARD, DOROTHY HARDT, academic administrator, volunteer; b. Chgo., Apr. 12, 1930; d. Carl Frederick and Meta Jandt Hardt; m. Benjamin Seaver Blanchard, Aug. 4, 1956; children: Rebecca, Benjamin III, Lisa. BS in Edn., Concordia Tchrs. Coll., 1953; MS in Adult and Continuing Edn., Va. Tech. U., 1984. Tchr. St. Paul Luth. Sch., Patterson, NJ, 1950—51, Concordia Luth. Sch., Seattle, 1953—56; v.p., developer programs Ctr. Vol. Devel. Va. Tech. U., Blacksburg, Va., 1981—86. Adv. bd. Med. Clinic New River Valley, Christiansburg, Va., 1984—87; mem. adv. bd., trainer Ctr. Vol. Devel., Blacksburg, Va., 1981—86. Contbr. articles to profl. jours. Vol. ops. Girl Scouts U.S.A., NYC, 1992—97; leader Genessee Valley Girl Scout Coun., Penfield, NY, 1963—71, Va. Skyline Girl Scout Coun., Roanoke, Va., 1971—75, chmn. program com., 1974—75, pres., 1975—80, past pres. adv. group, 1980—; dir. vol. programs Luther Meml. Ch., Blacksburg, Va., 1999—; founder, organizer Christ the King Luth. Ch., Nashua, NH, 1960—62; v.p., bd. dirs. Luth Campus Ministry Va. Tech. U. and Radford U., Va., 1977—80. Recipient Thanks Badge award, Va. Skyline Girl Scouts Coun., 1978, Citizen Recognition award, Rotary Internat., 1993, Cmty. Women Distinction award, 1998. Lutheran. Avocations: walking, reading, travel. Home: 160 Slate Creek Dr Christiansburg VA 24073-6189 Home Phone: 540-394-3311. Personal E-mail: dotblanchard@verizon.net.

BLANCHARD, ERIC ALAN, lawyer; b. 1956; BBA, U. Mich., 1978; JD, Harvard U., 1981. Bar: Ill. 1981. Atty. Schiff, Hardin & Waite, 1981-86; corp. atty. Dean Foods Co., Franklin Park, Ill., 1986-88, gen. coun., sec., v.p., pres. dairy divsn., 1988—; pres. Dean foods, 1999—2002; sr. v.p., sec., gen. counsel Tennant Co., Mpls., 2002, United Stationers Inc., Deerfeild, 2006—. Office: United Stationers Inc 1 N Parkway Blvd Ste 100 Deerfield IL 60015-2559 Office Phone: 847-627-7000. Office Fax: 847-627-7001.

BLANCHARD, JAMES HUBERT, finance company executive; b. Augusta, Ga., July 22, 1941; BBA, U. Ga., 1963, LLB, 1965. With Page Scranon Harris McGlanney and Chapman, 1964-70; with Columbus Bank and Trust Co., 1970—; with Synovus Fin. Corp., Columbus, Ga., 1972—, CEO, 1971—2005, chmn., 2005—. Chmn.-elect Fin. Service Roundtable, 2005—; chmn. exec. com., bd. dirs. TSYS; bd. dirs. Columbus Bank and Trust Co., BellSouth Corp., W.C. Bradley Co., Sea Island Co. Trustee Columbus State U. Found.; Emory Com. Robert T. Jones, Jr. Scholarship; Carter Center Board of Councilors mem.; bd. visitors Morehouse Sch. Med.; mem. Trust for Public Land Chattahoochee River Land Protection Campaign Com.; bd. councilors Carter Ctr.; bd. visitors, mem. Advisory Com. Ga. Partnership Excellence in Education; bd. curators Ga. Historical Society. 1st Lt. and Finance Officer US Army, 1965—67. Mem.: Ga. C. of C. (dir.), Ga. Rsch. Alliance (dir., past chmn.), Ga. Dept. Econ. Develop. (past chmn.), Banker Information Technol. Secretariat (dir., former chmn.), Financial Services Roundtable (dir.), Am. Bankers Assn. (dir.). Office: Synovus Fin Corp 901 Front Ave Columbus GA 31901-2722

BLANCHARD, JAMES JOHNSTON, ambassador, retired governor; b. Detroit, Aug. 8, 1942; m. Janet Eifert; 1 son, Jay. BA, Mich. State U., Lansing, 1964; MBA, Mich. State U., 1965; JD, U. Minn., 1967; JD (hon.), Mich. State U., U. Mich., 1985, Wayne State U., 1985, Oakland U., 1984, Alma Coll., 1987, Grand Valley State U., 1988. Bar: Mich. 1968, DC 2000, US Dist. Ct. (ea. & we. dist. Mich.), US Ct Appeals (6th cir.), US Supreme Ct. Legal aid elections bur. Office Sec. State, State of Mich., 1968-69; asst. atty. gen. State of Mich., 1969-74, adminstrv. asst. to atty. gen., 1970-71, asst. dep. atty. gen., 1971-72; mem. Congress from 18th Mich. Dist., 1974-82; gov. State of Mich., 1983-91; ptnr. Verner, Liipfert, Bernhard, McPherson & Hand, Washington, 1991—93; U.S. amb. to Canada, 1993-96; ptnr. Verner, Liipfert, Bernhard, McPherson & Hand, Washington, 1996—2002; ptnr. Energy, Fed. Affairs & legis., Govt. Affairs practices DLA Piper Rudnick Gray Cary, Washington, 2002—. Former mem. Pres.'s Commn. on Holocaust, Nat. Govs. Assn. Exec. Com.; former chmn. Dem. Nat. Platform Com., Dem. Govs. Assn.; bd. drs. Ctr. for the Great Lakes; founding mem. Dem. Leadership Coun. Mem. Oakland County exec. club Mich. State U.; bd. advisors Ctr. for Policy Research. Recipient Outstanding Achievement award U. Minn., 1983-84, Tree of Life award Jewish Nat. Fund., 1984, supporter of entrepreneurship award Inc. mag., 1991, Disting. alumni award Mich. State U., 1991, Fgn. Affairs award for pub. svc., 1996; named one of Outstanding Young Men Am., U.S. Jaycees, 1978, a Michiganian of Yr. Detroit News mag., 1980. Mem. Assn. Asst. Attys. Gen., Ferndale Jaycees, State Bar Mich., Am. Bar Assn., LWV, Nat. Gov's. Assn. (chmn. legal affairs com. 1987, mem. finance com., human resources com.), Dem. Gov's. Assn. (chmn., 1988), U. Minn. Law Sch. Alumni Club, Mich. State Alumni Assn., Delta Tau Alumni Assn., U. Detroit Titan Club. Democrat. Office: DLA Piper Rudnick Gray Cary 1200 19th St NW Washington DC 20036-2412 Office Phone: 202-861-6415. Office Fax: 202-689-8565. Business E-Mail: james.blanchard@dlapiper.com.

BLANCHARD, KIMBERLY STAGGERS, lawyer; b. Ann Arbor, Mich., May 17, 1954; d. Theodore R. and Bette Lee (Clark) Staggers; m. John Sears Blanchard, May 31, 1980; children: Charles Stuart, Virginia Greene. BA, Dartmouth Coll., 1976; MS, U. Wis., 1978; JD, NYU, 1981. Bar: N.Y. 1982. Assoc. Paul, Weiss, Rifkind, Wharton & Garrison, NYC, 1981-83, Haythe & Curley, NYC, 1983—99, ptnr., Weil, Gotshal & Manges LLP, 2000—. Mem. ABA, N.Y. State Bar Assn. (exec. com., former chair tax sect.), Pelham Country Club (Pelham Manor, N.Y.). Democrat. Avocation: golf. Office: Weil, Gotshal & Manges LLP 767 Fifth Avenue New York NY 10153 E-mail: kim.blanchard@weil.com.

BLANCHARD, LEONARD ALBERT, writer, consultant, educator; b. New Britain, Conn., July 30, 1947; s. Albert Edward and Sophie Marian (Lemanski) B.; children: Sarah Maddin Henniger, Henry Wyche Hunter. BA in English cum laude, Washington & Lee U., 1969; MA, Emory U., 1974, PhD, 1975. Instr. English, coach Oak Ridge (N.C.) Mil. Inst., 1969-71, St. Mark's Sch., Dallas, 1974-75; instr. English El Centro Coll., Dallas, 1975-79; writer, developer, liaison Southland Corp., Dallas, 1979-87; dir. devel. Franchise Group Internat., Little Rock, 1987-88; cons. Len Blanchard, Bradenton, Fla., 1988—. V.p. human resources Harken Internat., Bedford, Tex., 1989—90; mgmt. cons. Tropical Breeze Inn, Sarasota, 1996—99; instr. English Manatee C.C., Bradenton, Fla., 1999—. Author: An American Passion, 2001, Provocations of the Birds and the Beach, 2005, numerous poems. Mem.: Acad. Am. Poets, Musical Heritage Soc., Amnesty Internat., Smithsonian Assn. Democrat. Avocations: swimming, hiking, classical music. Office: Manatee CC Dept English 5840 26th St W Bradenton FL 34207-3522 Business E-Mail: blanchl@mccfl.edu.

BLANCHARD, MARYANN N., state legislator; b. NJ, Oct. 12, 1942; d. Joseph Charles and Mary (Longo) Navatta; m. Raymond P. Blanchard, 1967; children: Mary Beth, Catherine Anne, Daniel, Frances Elizabeth. BA, St. Joseph's Coll., 1966. Mem. Rockingham County Dist. 26 N.H. Ho. of Reps., Concord, 1982-90, mem. dist. 33, 1996-2000, ranking minority mem., mem. resources, recreation and devel. com., mem. fin. com., 2000—05. Trustee Strawberry Banke, 1993-96, Portsmouth Pub. Libr., 1981-83; commr. Portsmouth Police Commn., 1991-96; mem. adv. coun. Coop-Ext., Rockingham, 1992-93; mem. Portsmouth Hosp. Guild; leader Swiftwater coun. Girl Scouts USA, 1978-82; mem. Portsmouth PTA; mem. Atlantic States Marine Fisheries Commn., 2001—. Mem. LWV (past pres., bd. dirs. 1967-71), Soc. Protection N.H. Forests, Audubon Soc., Parents Music Club. Roman Catholic. Office Phone: 603-271-2136.

BLANCHARD, RICHARD EMILE, SR., retired management services executive, consultant; b. Thompson, Conn., July 13, 1928; s. Lionel A. and Bernadette L. (Jolicoeur) B.; m. Lorraine Patricia Lachapelle, July 3, 1954; children: Michele Welling, Richard E., Danielle Wornstaff, Marie Blanchard Oser, Robert Allen, Janine Lippert. BS in Biology, Providence Coll., 1952; postgrad., U. Conn. Sch. Law, West Hartford, 1952-53. Cert. mgmt. cons. Chemist Charles Pfizer Co., Inc., NYC, 1953-56, med. salesman, 1956-60, coll. rels. mgr., 1960-63, pers. mgr., 1963-67; dir. manpower and orgn. devel. Sky Chef divsn. Am. Airlines, NYC, 1967-70; dir. manpower ARA Svcs., Inc., Phila., 1970-72, v.p., 1972-76; v.p. pers. Jerrico, Inc., Lexington, Ky., 1976-78; chmn., CEO Career Mgmt., Inc., C.M. Temporary Svcs., C.M. Mgmt. Svcs., Lexington, 1978-99; ret., 1999. Cons. pers. svcs. Bd. dirs. Ky. Higher Edn. Coun., Bluegrass United Way, 1979-99, Jr. Achievement, 1979—, Better Bus. Bur., 1985—, United Way of the Bluegrass, 1998-2000, U. Ky. Small Bus. Devel. Ctr., Ky. Econ. Devel. Coun.; v.p. Bluegrass Ednl. Work Coun., 1980—, Bluegrass Better Bus. Bur., 1990-98, bd. dirs., past pres.; chmn. adv. bd. U. Ky. C.C., 1987—; divsn. chmn. United Way, 1990, 92—; Bd. dirs., vice-chmn. Human Rights Commn., 1991-94; co-chmn. bd. dirs. Bluegrass MS Soc., 1996; mem. adv. bd. C.C. divsn. U. Ky., Muscular Dystrophy Bluegrass Coun. With USN, 1946-48. Mem. Inst. Mgmt. Cons., Am. Mgmt. Assn., Am. Soc. Pers. Assocs. (past pres. N.Y. chpt.), Nat. Assn. Temporary Svcs., Ind. Temporary Svcs. Assn., Ky. Assocs. Temporary Svcs. (past pres.), Ky. State C. of C. (bd. dirs.), Lexington C. of C. (bd. dirs. 1996-99), Lexington Country Club, Exec. Fitness and Sports Ctr., Lexington Tennis Club, Rotary (bd. dirs. 1996-99, Bluegrass Bus. Hall of Fame, 2003). Republican. Roman Catholic. Home: 16279 Edgemont Dr Fort Myers FL 33908-3658 Personal E-mail: chezmemere@aol.com.

BLANCHARD, RICHARD FREDERICK, construction executive; b. Orange, NJ, Feb. 8, 1933; s. William F. and Dorothy Dew (Wright) B.; m. Jill Isles, Nov. 23, 1985 BA, Dartmouth Coll., 1955; MBA, Harvard U., 1957. Apprentice Wm. Blanchard Co., Newark, 1958—62, estimator, 1962—65, project mgr. Springfield, NJ, 1965—72, pres., 1972—2004, vice chmn., 2004—. V.p. Newark Mus., 1986—. With U.S. Army, 1957-58 Mem. Bldg. Contractors Assn. N.J. (trustee 1986-2003), N.J. State C. of C. (bd. dirs. 1980-88) Presbyterian. Avocations: mountain climbing, skiing. Office Phone: 973-376-9100.

BLANCHARD, SUSAN MANNING, academic administrator, director, engineering educator; b. Knoxville, Tenn., Sept. 15, 1946; d. Frederick Claude and Florence Chapin Manning; m. Donald Gray Blanchard, Oct. 11, 1980; 1 child, Whitney Blanchard O'Brian; m. James Wilson Henderson, Jan. 30, 1968 (div. Jan. 0, 1980); children: Paul Manning Henderson, Sara Tiers Henderson. AB, Oberlin Coll., Ohio, 1968; MS, Duke U., Durham, NC, 1980, PhD, 1982. Mem. tech. staff Rockwell Internat., Chapel Hill, 1982—83; rsch. assoc. med. ctr. Duke U., 1983—88, asst. med. rsch. prof. dept. surgery med. ctr., 1988—90, rsch. asst. prof. dept. biomedical engring., 1990—93; from assoc. prof. to prof. dept. biol. and agrl. engring. NC State U., Raleigh, NC, 1993—2003, dir. biomedical engring. grad. programs joint dept. biomedical engring. U. NC, 2003—05; founding dir. U.A. Whitaker sch. engring. Fla. Gulf Coast U., Fort Myers, Fla., 2005—. Program evaluator Accreditation Bd. Engring. and Tech., Inc., NY, 2003—. Author: (book) Introduction to Biomedical Engineering, 2d edit.; contbr. over 50 articles to profl. jours. Recipient Outstanding Tchg. award, NC State U., 2001. Fellow: IEEE (exec. dir. 1990—93, v.p. mem. and student activities engring. in medicine and biology soc. 1994—95, pres. engring. medicine and biology soc. 1996, Svc. award Medicine and Biology Soc. 1998, Third Millennium award 2000), Am. Inst. Med. and Biol. Engring. (v.p. at large 1998—99, chmn. coun. socs. 1999—2000, v.p. at large 2007—), Biomedical Engring. Soc.; mem.: Computers in Cardiology, Inc. (bd. dirs. 1994—99), Am. Soc. Engring. Edn. (mem. bd. biomedical engring. divsn. 2002—05, Theo C. Pilkington Outstanding Educator award 2004), Tau Beta Pi, Sigma Xi. Unitarian. Office: Florida Gulf Coast Univ 10501 FGCU Blvd South Fort Myers FL 33965-6565 Office Phone: 239-590-7399.

BLANCHARD, TOWNSEND EUGENE, retired service companies executive; b. Du Quoin, Ill., Jan. 30, 1931; s. Townsend and Anna Belle Blanchard; m. Norma Louise Barr, Dec. 18, 1960; children: John Barr, Susan Melody, Jayne Ann Blanchard Reishus, Stephen Eugene. BS, U. Ill., 1952; MBA, Harvard U., 1957. Cons. Ill. Sch. Bond Svc., Monticello, 1958-62; co-founder, treas., chief fin. officer Americana Nursing Ctrs., Monticello, 1962-75; v.p. fin., treas., CFO, chief of staff Cenco, Inc., Chgo., 1975-79; sr. v.p., CFO DynCorp., Reston, Va., 1979-97. Chmn. Employee Stock Ownership Plan DynCorp, 1997—2003. Elder, deacon Presbyn. Ch.; bd. dirs. Combined Health Appeal, 1986-96; bd. advisors Cameron Glen Care Facility, 1989-92. Lt. USNR, 1952-55. Decorated Spl. Commendation letter. Mem. Fin. Execs. Inst. (chpt. pres. 1988-89, nat. v.p. and bd. dirs. 1991-94), U. Ill. Alumni Club, Harvard U. Bus. Sch. Club, Harvard Club, Am. Legion, Delta Sigma Phi (trustee nat. found. 1982-89, pres. nat. found. 1988-89, Harvey W. Herbert award 1975, Mr. Delta Sig award 1988).

BLANCHET, BERTRAND, archbishop; b. Montmagny, Que., Can., Sept. 19, 1932; s. Louis and Alberta (Nicole) B. BA, Coll. Ste-Anne-de-la Pocatiere, 1952; LTh, Laval U., 1956, DSc, 1975. Ordained priest Roman Cath. Ch., 1956, consecrated bishop 1973. Tchr. biology Coll. and Coll. d'Enseignement Gen. et Profl., La Pocatiere, 1963-73; bishop of Gaspe, Que., Canada, 1973-92; archbishop of Rimouski, Canada, 1992—. Mem. Chevaliers de Colomb, Rimouski. Roman Catholic. Address: CP 730 34 Eveche Ouest Rimouski PQ Canada G5L 4H5 Office Phone: 418-723-3320. E-mail: bblanchet@globetrotter.net.

BLANCHET, JEANNE ELLENE MAXANT, artist, educator, performer; b. Chgo., Sept. 25, 1944; d. William H. and L. Barbara (Martin) Maxant; m. Yasuo Shimizu, Apr. 28, 1969 (div. 1973); m. William B. Blanchet, Aug. 21, 1981 (dec. May 1993). BA summa cum laude, Northwestern U., 1966; MFA, Tokyo U., 1971; MA, Ariz. State U., 1978; postgrad., Ill. State U., 1979-80; PhD, Greenwich U., 1991. Instr. Tsuda U., Kodaira, Japan, 1970-71; free-lance visual, performing artist various cities, U.S., 1973—; artist in residence YMCA of the Rockies, Estes Park, Colo., 1976-81 summers; prof. fine arts Rio Salado Coll., Surprise, Ariz., 1976-91. Lectr. Ariz. State U. West, Sun City, 1985-93; evaluator several arts couns. including Ariz. Humanities Coun., 1993, Ariz. Humanities Coun. Scholar's SPkrs. Bur., 1998—; Prescott Melodrama ragtime pianist, 1993, 94; artist with Performing Arts for Youth, 1994—. Selected for regional, state, nat. juried art shows, 1975—, mus. and gallery one-woman shows of computer art, 1988—; author: Original Songs and Verse of the Old (And New) West, 1987, A Song in My Heart, 1988, Reflections, 1989, The Mummy Story, 1990; contbr. articles to newspapers, profl. jours. Founding mem. Del Webb Hosp. Woodrow Wilson fellow, 1966; ADA B.C. Welsh scholar, 1980; recipient numerous art, music awards, 1970—, major computer art awards in regional, nat., and internat. shows, 1990—. Mem. Nat. League Am. Pen Women (sec. chpt. 1987, v.p. 1988, pres. 1990-92, pres. Colo. chpt. 1996-97), Ariz. Press Women (numerous awards in original graphics and writing 1980s, 90s), Nat. Fedn. Press Women, Northwestern U.'s John Evans Club, Henry W. Rogers Soc., P.E.O. (rec. sec. chpt. BV 1998—), Phi Beta Kappa. Avocations: computers, ragtime piano, hiking, parapsychology, duplicate bridge (silver life master). Home and Office: 10330 W Thunderbird Blvd # C-311 Sun City AZ 85351 *To live is to think, to create.*

BLANCHET, JOSE H., statistics educator, researcher; m. Citlalli Salinas. PhD in Mgmt. Sci., Stanford U., Calif., 2004. Asst. prof. stats. Harvard U., Cambridge, Mass., 2004—. Achievements include research in applied probability, simulation. Office: Harvard U Holyoke St Cambridge MA 02138 Home Phone: 617-496-8318; Office Phone: 617-496-8318.

BLANCHETT, CATE (CATHERINE ELISE BLANCHETT), actress; b. Melbourne, Victoria, Australia, May 14, 1969; d. Robert and June Blanchett; m. Andrew Upton, Dec. 29, 1997; children: Dashiell John, Roman Robert. Grad., Nat. Inst. Dramatic Art, Australia, 1992. Performed with Sydney Theatre Co., Belvoir St. Theatre Co.; joint artistic dir. Australia's Sydney Theatre Co., 2006—. Appeared in theatre prodns. including Top Girls, Kafka Dances (Newcomer Sydney Theatre Critics Circle award 1993), Oleanna (Rosemont and Sydney Theater Critics Cir. Best Actress Award 1993), Hamlet (nominated Green Rm. award), 1995, Sweet Phoebe, The Tempest, The Seagull, The Blind Giant is Dancing, Plenty, 1999, Hedda Gabler (Prestigious Helpmann award best female actor in a play 2006), 2006; actress: (films) Police Rescue, 1994, Parklands, 1996, Paradise Road, 1997, Thank God He Met Lizzie, 1997 (Australian Film Inst. award 1997, Sydney Film Critics awards best supporting actress 1997), Oscar and Lucinda (Am. Film Inst. nomination best actress 1997), 1997, Elizabeth (Golden Globe for best actress in a drama, 1999, Brit. Acad. Film and TV Arts award best actress in leading role 1999, Chgo. Film Critics Assn. award best actress 1999, London Film Critics Assn. award 1999, Toronto Film Critics Assn. award 1999, On-line Film Critics award 1999, Variety Critics and Eng. Empire award 1999), 1998, The Talented Mr. Ripley (Brit. Acad. Film and TV Arts nomination best supporting actress 1999), 1999, An Ideal Husband, 1999, Pushing Tin 1999, The Man Who Cried (Best Supporting Actress award 2000), 2000, The Gift, 2000, Bandits (Golden Globe award nomination 2001, SAG nomination outstanding supporting actress 2001), 2001, Charlotte Gray, 2001, The Shipping News (Best Supporting Acress award 2001), 2001, Galadriel, 2001, The Lord of the Rings: The Fellowship of the Ring, 2001, Heaven, 2002, The Lord of the Rings: The Two Towers, 2002, Veronica Guerin (Golden Globe nomination best performace actress in a motion picture-drama 2003, Film Critics Assn. best actress 2003), 2003, Coffee and Cigarettes (nomination best supporting female 2005 Ind. Spirit awards), 2003, The Missing, 2003, The Lord of the Rings: The Return of the King, 2003 (SAG award outstanding performance by a cast in a motion picture 2004), The Life Aquatic with Steve Zissou, 2004, The Aviator (Acad. award best supporting acress 2004, Brit. Acad. Film and TV Assn. award 2004, SAG award 2004, Hollywood Fgn. Press Assn. nomination 2004), 2004 (Acad. Award for best actress in a supporting role, 2005, SAG award for best actress in a supporting role 2005), Little Fish, 2004, Babel, 2006, Notes on a Scandal, 2006 (Best Supporting Actress Fla. Film Critics Cir., 2006), The Good German, 2006; (TV miniseries) Heartland, 1994, Bordertown, 1995; actor, prodr. (films) Bangers, 1999. Nominee Best Actress, SAG, Acad. Motion Picture, Arts and Scis.; named one of The World's Most Influential People, TIME mag., 2007, 100 Most Powerful

Celebrities, Forbes.com, 2007; recipient Career Achievement award, Palm Springs Internat. Film Soc., Palm Springs Internat. Film Festival, 2007. Office: Creative Artists Agy c/o Hylda Queally 9830 Wilshire Blvd Beverly Hills CA 90212*

BLANCHETTE, OLIVA, philosophy educator; b. Berlin, NH, May 6, 1929; s. Delphis and Odelia (Morneau) B.; m. Dorothy M. Kennedy, May 25, 1975; children: Nicole Elizabeth, Frances Kathleen. AB in Philosophy, Boston Coll., 1953, MA, 1958; Licentiate in Philosophy, Coll. St. Albert de Louvain, Belgium, 1954; Licentiate in Sacred Theology, Weston Coll., 1961; PhD in Philosophy, U. Laval, Que., Can., 1966. Prof. Latin, Greek and English Boston Coll. High Sch., 1954-57; instr. philosophy Boston Coll., 1964-65, asst. prof., 1965-67, asso. prof., 1967-74, prof., 1974—; dean Sch. of Philosophy, 1968-73. Dir. Inst. for Social Thought. Author: Initiative in History: A Christian-Marxist Exchange, 1967, For a Fundamental Social Ethic: A Philosophy of Social Change, 1973, The Perfection of the Universe According to Aquinas: A Teleological Cosmology, 1992, Philosophy of Being: A Reconstructive Essay in Metaphysics, 2003; contbr. articles on philosophy of history, metaphysics, philosophy of religion, and social ethics to scholarly jours. Mem. Hegel Soc. Am., Metaphys. Soc. Am., Internat. Soc. Metaphys. Home: 28 Florence St Natick MA 01760-2121 Office: Dept Philosophy Boston Coll Chestnut Hill MA 02467

BLANCHFIELD, FRANCIS J., JR., lawyer; b. Chgo., Sept. 19, 1945; BA, Coll. of Holy Cross, 1967; JD, NYU, 1970, LLM in Tax., 1974. Bar: NJ 1970, NY 1974, Ga. 1976, NC 1981, US Supreme Ct., US Tax Ct., US Ct. of Fed. Claims, 5th and 11th Courts of Appeal, ea. dist. NC. Law clk. Judge Samuel Allcorn Jr., Superior Ct. (Chancery Divsn.), Newark, 1970—71; ptnr. Hull, Towill, Norman, Barrett & Johnson, Augusta, Ga., 1973—76; spl. asst. to asst. atty. gen., tax divsn. Dept. of Justice, Washington, 1977—79, dep. asst. atty. gen., appeals, settlements and legis., tax divsn., 1979—80; shareholder Johnson and Blanchfield, Charlotte, NC, 1981—88, Blanchfield & Moore PA, Charlotte, NC, 1988—89; ptnr., practice area leader for tax Smith Helms Mulliss & Moore, Charlotte, Greensboro, Raleigh and Washington, 1989—92; shareholder Blanchfield Cordle & Moore PA, Charlotte, NC, 1992—98; ptnr. Mayer, Brown, Rowe & Maw LLP, Charlotte, 1998—, ptnr.-in-charge, Charlotte office, 1998—2004. 1st lt., instr., criminal and military law mil. police sch. US Army, 1971—73, Fort Gordon, Ga. Recipient US Atty. Gen. Medal, 1980. Fellow: Am. Coll. of Tax Counsel; mem.: ABA, Fed. Bar Assn., NC Bar Assn., Charlotte Tax Roundtable. Office: Mayer Brown Rowe & Maw LLP Ste 3800 214 N Tryon St Charlotte NC 28202 Office Phone: 704-444-3510. Office Fax: 704-377-2033. Business E-Mail: fblanchfield@mayerbrownrowe.com.

BLANCK, RONALD RAY, academic administrator, internist, military officer; b. Lancaster, Pa., Oct. 8, 1941; s. Harvey Ray and Mildred Katherine (Smith) B.; m. Donna Rae Ault, Sept. 17, 1971; children: Jennifer, Susan. BS, Juniata Coll., 1963; DO, Phila. Coll. Osteo. Medicine, 1967; DSc in Osteopathy (hon.), New Eng. Coll. Osteo. Medicine, 1982; LLD (hon.), Phila. Coll. Osteo. Medicine, 1991. Diplomate Am. Bd. Internal Medicine. Intern Lancaster Osteo. Hosp., 1967-68; resident in internal medicine Walter Reed Army Gen. Med. Ctr., 1970-73; commd. capt. U.S. Army, 1968, advanced through grades to lt. gen., 1996, ret., 2000, gen. med. officer Vietnam, 1968-69, Ft. Myer, Va., 1969-70; asst. chief gen. med. svc. Walter Reed Army Med. Ctr., Washington, 1973-74, asst. chief dept. medicine, 1974-76; asst. dean student affairs Sch. Medicine Uniformed Svcs. U., Bethesda, Md., 1976-79; chief dept. medicine Brooke Army Med. Ctr., San Antonio, Tex., 1979-82; chief med. corps career activities office Army Med. Dept. Pers. Support Act, Washington, 1982-85; comdr. U.S. Army Hosp., Berlin, 1986-88, Army Regional Med. Ctr., Frankfurt, Germany, 1988-90; dir. prof. svcs., chief med. corps affairs Office of Surgeon Gen., Fall Church, Va., 1990-92; comdr. Walter Reed Army Med. Ctr., Washington, 1992-96; surgeon gen., comdr. MECOM U.S. Army, Falls Church, Va., 1996-2000; pres. U. North Tex. Health Sci. Ctr., Ft. Worth, 2000—. Asst. prof. clin. medicine Georgetown U., Washington, 1972—78; clin. instr. medicine Howard U., Washington, 1975—77; assoc. prof. medicine USUHS, Bethesda, 1976—; clin. prof. medicine U. Tex., San Antonio, 1979—80, San Antonio, 1980—82; disting. prof. mil. medicine USUHS, Bethesda, Md., 1998—. Guest editor Osteopathic Annals, 1981; mem. editorial adv. bd. History of Medicine in Vietnam, 1981. Advisor bd. regents Uniformed Svcs. U. Health Scis., Bethesda, 1992; bd. dirs. Nat. Med. Vets. Soc., Chgo., 1993; bd. regents Potomac Inst. for Policy Studies, 2000; bd. dirs. Annapolis Ctr., 2002. Decorated DSM, Bronze Star, Legion of Merit, Def. Superior Svc. medal; recipient Founder's award Tex. Coll. Osteo. Medicine, 1991. Master ACP (gov.); mem. AMA (alt. del.), Am. Osteo. Assn., Assn. Mil. Surgeons U.S. (John Shaw Billings award 1976), Berlin Internat. Med. Soc., Assn. Mil. Osteo. Physicians and Surgeons, Soc. Med. Cons. Armed Forces (assoc.), Nat. Bd. Med. Examiners. Episcopalian. Avocations: reading, jogging. Office: U North Tex Health Sci Ctr 3500 Camp Bowie Blvd Fort Worth TX 76107-2699

BLANCK, SUSAN, insurance company executive; BS in Edn., U. Mo., Columbia. With actuarial dept. in US pricing area AFLAC Inc., 1993, second v.p., asst. actuary, 1998—2000, v.p., 2000, sr. v.p., dep. corp. actuary, 2004—06, sr. v.p., corp. actuary, 2006—. Bd. mem. Fla. Health Reinsurance Program. Bd. mem. Chattahoochee Riverkeeper. Fellow: Soc. Actuaries (chair cancer experience studies com.); mem.: Am. Acad. Actuaries. Office: AFLAC Inc 1932 Wynnton Rd Columbus GA 31999 Office Phone: 706-323-3431.*

BLANCO, HUMBERTO, soil scientist, researcher; arrived in US, 2000; m. Vilma A. Vasquez; children: Luis A, Pablo A. BSc in Agrl. Engring., Tech. U., Oruro, Bolivia, 1990; PhD in Soil Sci., U. Mo., Columbia, 2003. Assoc. prof. Tech. U., Oruro, Bolivia, 1996—99; rsch. scientist soil sci. Ohio State Univ., Columbus, Ohio, 1999—. Contbr. articles to profl. jours.; assoc. editor: Soil Sci. Soc. Am. Jour. Scholar, Fulbright Found., 1993. Mem.: Soil Sci. Soc. Am. (assoc. editor Soil Sci. Am. Jour. 2007—). Achievements include research in crop residue management for biofuel production. Home: 686 Riverview Dr Apt 57 Columbus OH 43202 Office: The Ohio State Univeristy 2021 Coffey Road 412C Kottman Hall Columbus OH 43210 Office Phone: 614-292-2299.

BLANCO, KATHLEEN BABINEAUX, governor; b. New Iberia, La., Dec. 15, 1942; m. Raymond S. Blanco, Aug. 8, 1964; 6 children. BS in Bus. Edn., U. La.at Lafayette, 1964. Tchr. Breaux Bridge High Sch.; with La. State Legis. Dist. 45, 1984-88, mem. house edn. com., mem. house transp., hwys., and pub. works com., Pub. Svc. Commn., La., 1988-94, chair La., 1993-95; lt. gov. State of La., 1995—2003, gov., 2004—. Democrat. Catholic. Achievements include being first woman gov. of La. Office: Office of Gov PO Box 94004 Baton Rouge LA 70804-9004 Office Phone: 225-342-7015. Office Fax: 225-342-7099.*

BLANCO, LAURA, interior designer; b. Havana, Cuba, July 3, 1956; came to U.S., 1960; d. Lauro and Marina (Mardones) B.; m. Robert F. Shainheit, 1988. Studied landscape design, NY Botanical Gardens, 2000—03; studied interior design, NY Sch. Interior Design, 2002—04. Asst. box office treas., press agt. Zev Bufman Entertainment, Inc., Orlando, St. Petersburg, Fla., 1978-83; press agt. Kool Jazz Festival and Heritage Fair, Orlando, 1982; producer La. World Exposition Inc., New Orleans, 1983-84, Festival Ventures, Inc., Miami, Fla., 1985-86; producer/dir. hispanic events Festival Prodns., Inc., NYC, 1986-87; pres. Blanco Shainheit Prodns., Blanco Shainheit Music, NYC, 1988—99; ptnr. unanimo, 1992—99; pres. Laura Blanco Interiors, NYC, 2004—. Prodr. (short film) The Summer of My Dreams, 1994, La Ciudad, 1995, (feature film, award winner Havana Film Festival, 1998), Perdida, 1998. Bd. dirs. Artists Community Fed. Credit Union, 1988-90; bd. mem. Off World Theatre, 2003-05. Mem. ASCAP, Am. Latin Music Assn. Office Phone: 212-876-0053. E-mail: info@laurablanco.com.

BLAND, CALVIN, foundation administrator; BS in economics, U. Pa.; MS in adminstrv. medicine, Columbia U., 1974. Program officer The Robert Wood Johnson Found., Princeton, NJ, 1974—77; pres., CEO St. Christopher's Hosp. for Children, Phila., 1977—99; adminstr. South Phila. Med. Ctr.; adminstrv. resident Pa. Hosp., Phila.; rejoined The Robert Wood Johnson Found., 2000, sr. program adv. and interim dir. Health Care Group, now chief of staff and spl. adv. to pres./CEO. Office: The Robert Wood Johnson Found PO Box 2316 College Road E and Rt 1 Princeton NJ 08543 Office Phone: 888-631-9989.

BLAND, FREDERICK AVES, architect; b. Galveston, Tex., Dec. 21, 1945; s. David and Florence (Aves) B.; m. Morley Anne Thomson, Dec. 21, 1968; 1 child, Chloe Thomson. BA, Yale U., 1968, MArch, 1972. Registered architect, N.Y., Conn., Fla., Va., NJ, Md., Ky. Assoc. Beyer Blinder Belle, Architects & Planners, NYC, 1974-77, dir. design, 1977-79, ptnr., 1979—2004, mng. ptnr., 2004—. Chief architect Yale Archeol. project Royal Abbey St. Denis, Paris, 1970-80; adj. prof. NYU Sch. Fine Arts, 1990—. V.p. Bklyn. Heights Assn., 1981-86, pres., 1992-94; panel mem. N.Y. State Coun. Arts, 1985-86; exec. com. Friends of Edn., Mus. Modern Art, 1992-00; trustee Bklyn. Bot. Garden, 1993—, chmn. horticulture com., 1996-03, exec. com., 1996—, vice-chmn., 1999-2007, chmn. 2007—; trustee Bklyn. Hist. Soc., 1998, 04, The Evergreens Cemetery, 1998—; v.p. N.Y. Found. Architecture, 1998, pres., 1999; mem. vestry Trinity Ch. Wall St., 2004—, chair ch. properties and bus. enterprises com.; bd. mem. James Marston Fitch Charitable Found., 2006—. Mem. AIA (nat. com. on design, coll. of fellows, jury of fellows 1995-97), Am. Inst. Cert. Planners, Mcpl. Art Soc. NY, Yale Arch. Sch. Dean's Coun., Heights Casino Club (bd. govs. 1981-87, pres. 1987-90), Rembrandt Club (pres. 2001-03), Century Assn. (NYC). Democrat. Episcopalian. Home: 26 Pierrepont St Brooklyn NY 11201-7209 also: Wallace Rd Branford CT 06405 Office: Beyer Blinder Belle Architects 41 E 11th St New York NY 10003-4673 Office Phone: 212-777-7800.

BLAND, JAMES THEODORE, JR., lawyer; b. Memphis, June 16, 1950; s. James Theodore and Martha Frances (Downen) B.; m. Pattie L. Martin, Apr. 12, 1974. BBA magna cum laude, Memphis State U., 1972, JD, 1974. Bar: Tenn. 1975, U.S. Dist. Ct. (we. dist.) Tenn. 1976, U.S. Tax Ct. 1976, U.S. Supreme Ct. 1983, U.S. Ct. Claims 1987; cert. Estate Planning specialist. Estate tax atty. IRS, Memphis, 1974—76; atty. Armstrong, Allen, Braden, Goodman, McBride & Prewitt, Memphis, 1976—91; prin. James T. Bland, Jr. and Assocs., Memphis, 1991—. Instr. in taxation, bus. law State Tchr.'s Inst., Memphis, 1975-83; bd. dirs. Thomas W. Briggs Found., Memphis. Fellow Am. Coll. Trust and Estate Counsel, Tenn. Bar Found., Memphis Bar Found., Shelby County Bar Found. (pres. 1991-93); mem. ABA (legis. initiatives com., taxation sect., specialization in estate planning real property, probate and trust sect., Achievement award 1983, 85), Fed. Bar Assn. (pres. 1987-88, nat. coun. 1979—, bd. dirs. young lawyers divsn. 1979-84, pres. Memphis mid south chpt. 1979-80), Tenn. Bar Assn. (chmn. tax sect. 1984-85, bd. govs. 1984-85, 89-90, 90-91), Tenn. Young Lawyers Conf. (pres. 1985), Memphis Bar Assn. (bd. dirs. 1990-91), Tenn. Soc. CPA Republican. Methodist. Office: PO Box 25345 Christiansted VI 00824 Business E-Mail: blandjr@viaccess.net. E-mail: blandjr@vipowernet.net.

BLAND, JOHN LLOYD, lawyer; b. Wichita Falls, Tex., Sept. 20, 1944; Student, Vanderbilt U.; BA, U. Tex., 1967, JD with honors, 1969. Bar: Tex. 1969. Mem. Bracewell & Giuliani, LLP, Houston, 1969—. Mem. State Bar Tex., Houston Bar Assn., Phi Delta Phi. Office: Bracewell & Giuliani LLP 2300 S Tower Pennzoil Pl 711 Louisiana St Houston TX 77002-2781 Home Phone: 713-522-0787; Office Phone: 713-221-1310. E-mail: john.bland@bracewellgiuliani.com.

BLAND, J(OHN) RICHARD, lawyer; b. Denver, Oct. 30, 1946; s. Harry Edward and Julia Lenora (Bjelland) B.; m. Carole Jeanne Martin, Aug. 25, 1968. BS, Augustana Coll., 1968; JD, Drake U., 1971. Bar: Iowa 1971, Minn. 1971, U.S. Supreme Ct. 1976. Assoc. Meagher & Geer PLLP, Mpls., 1971-75, ptnr., 1975—. Lectr. Minn. Inst. of Legal Edn., Mpls., 1985—. Fellow Am. Coll. Trial Lawyers; mem. Minn. Bar Assn., Minn. Def. Lawyers Assn. (bd. dirs. 1986-88). Home: 17225 5th Ave N Plymouth MN 55447-3593 Office: Meagher & Geer PLLP 33 S 6th St Ste 4400 Minneapolis MN 55402-3722 Office Phone: 612-338-0661. Business E-Mail: DBland@Meagher.com.

BLAND, LEONARD A., auditor, consultant; b. SI, NY, Apr. 23, 1941; s. Leonard H. and Helen A. Bland; m. Ruth Ellen Bland, June 2004; m. Mary Susan Fogarty (div.); children: Heather, Leonard, Rachel, Craig. BS in Econs., U. Pa., Phila., 1963; MBA, NYU, NYC, 1965. Acctg. mgr. Alpine Electronics, Greenwood, Ind., 1995—96; CFO Hickory Furniture, Shelbyville, Ind., 1997—98; controller Onkyo Am., Columbus, Ind., 1998—2000; fin. mentor Myers Spring, Logansport, Ind., 2000—02; cons. pvt. practice, Logansport, 2003; fin. cons. Nelson Acquisition, Logansport, 2005—06; auditor Resources Connection/Robert Half, Indpls., 2004—07. 1st lt. US Army, 1965—67. Avocation: stamp collecting/philately. Home: 2424 Stadium Dr Logansport IN 46947

BLAND, PAMELA JUNE, special education educator; b. Chgo., Ill., Oct. 12, 1947; d. Arnold Richard Johnsen and June Florence Meisenhelder Johnsen; m. William Lawrence Bland, Jan. 24, 1970; children: Eric, Todd. BS, No. Ill. U., 1969; MEd, Nat. Louis U., 1996. Lead tchr. Keeler Sch. Multiply Handicapped, Aurora, Ill., 1975—78, substitute tchr., 1979—83; case mgr. Kennedy Rehab. Ctr., 1983—86; lead tchr. DeKalb County Spl. Edn. Assn., Cortland, 1986—88, Batavia Pub. Schs. Dist. 101, 1989—94, Maywood Pub. Schs. Dist. 89, Maywood, 1994—; partime faculty early childhood spl. edn. Morton C.C., Cicero, 2003—. Mem. St. Mark's Child Care Adv. Bd., Aurora, 1990—93; presenter in field. Actor: (of poems). Mem. Fox Valley Festival Chorus, Aurora, 1970—90, Naperville Chorus, 1990—; mem., Highland dancer Tunes of Glory Pipe Band, Batavia, 1980—84; high sch. youth leader St. Mark;s Luth. Ch., Aurora, 1990—98. Recipient Editors Choice award, Nat. Libr. Poetry, 1995. Mem.: ASCD, NEA, Nat. Assn. Edn. Young Children, Maywood Edn. Assn. Lutheran. Avocations: travel, camping, boating, genealogy, history. Office: Dist 89 Roosevelt Sch Maywood Pub Schs 1925 S 15th Broadview IL 60155

BLANDA-HOLTZBERG, MARIANNE LOURDES, education educator, consultant; b. Rochester, NY, Aug. 8, 1956; d. Andrew Joseph and Rosemary Reynolds Blanda; m. Richard Harry Holtzberg, Nov. 11, 1979; children: Rachael Molly Holtzberg, Vanessa Elizabeth Holtzberg, Alexandra Blanda Holtzberg. AAS, Monroe C.C., NY, 1976; BSc in Social Sci., Nazareth Coll. Rochester, 1980; MSc in Edn., SUNY, Brockport, 1990; PhD, Union Inst. & U., Cin., 2003. Cert. Tchr. NYU, 1990, in Spl. Edn. NYU, 1992, in Sch. Adminstrn., Supervision NYU, 2002. Spl. edn. tchr. Hillside Children's Ctr., Rochester, NY, 1980—82, Rochester City Sch. Dist., 1992—2002; asst. prin. Webster Ctrl. Sch. Dist., Webster, 2002—04; adj. faculty Roberts Wesleyan Coll., Rochester, 2005—, asst. prof. divsn. tchr. edn., 2006—; asst. prof. spl. edn. St. John Fisher Coll., Rochester, 2005—06. Ednl. cons. Holtzberg Ednl. Cons., Rochester, 2003—; lectr. in field; biennial conf. presenter Internat. Assn. Spl. Edn., 2005. Chair inclusion com. Rochester City Sch. Dist., 1994—2002. Mem.: ASCD, Coun. Exceptional Children, Learning Disabilities Assn. Am., Sch. Adminstrs. NY State. Catholic. Achievements include research in the effects of academic placements on self-esteem. Avocations: golf, tennis, photography, travel. Office: Holtzberg Ednl Cons 2586 Browncroft Blvd Rochester NY 14625 Home Phone: 585-385-5891; Office Phone: 585-594-6248. Home Fax: 585-385-4199. E-mail: mholtzberg4@aol.com.

BLANDFORD, COLLEEN M., lawyer; b. Cin., Apr. 15, 1969; BA in Polit. Sci., U. Cin., 1990, BA in Journalism, 1990; JD, U. Cin. Coll. Law, 1993. Bar: Ohio 1993, US Dist. Ct. Southern Dist. Ohio 1994, Commonwealth of Ky. 1999, US Ct. of Appeals Sixth Cir. 1999, US Dist. Ct. Eastern Dist. Ky. 2000. Arbitrator Hamilton County Ct. of Common Pleas; atty. Kohnen & Patton LLP, Cin. Named one of Ohio's Rising Stars, Super Lawyers, 2006. Mem.: Phi Beta Kappa. Office: Kohnen & Patton LLP PNC Ctr Ste 800 201 E 5th St Cincinnati OH 45202 Office Phone: 513-381-0656. Office Fax: 513-381-5823.

BLANDFORD, JIM, JR., social studies educator; b. Paducah, Ky., May 17, 1961; s. James Robert and Mary Frances (Campisano) Blandford. BS, U. Louisville, 1984, MA in Tchg., 1986. Cert. tchr., Ky. K-8 phys. edn. tchr. St. Anthony Elem. Sch., Clarksville, Ind., 1986—88, Sacred Heart Elem. Sch., Jefferson, Ind., 1986—88; tchr. jr. high sch. social studies St. Albert the Great Sch., Louisville, 1988—93; tchr., coach St. Xavier HS, Louisville, 1993—. Class agt. St. Xavier High Sch., Louisville, 1988—. Youth minister Tri-Parish Youth Group, Louisville, 1989—; coach Lyndon Recreation, Louisville, 1982—. Named Asst. Coach of Yr., St. Xavier HS, 2004—05; named to, Hon. Order Ky. Cols. Mem. AAHPERD, Nat. Coun. for Social Studies, Nat. Geog. Soc., Ky. Coun. for Social Studies, Nat. Cath. Edn. Assn. Democrat. Roman Catholic. Avocations: golf, fantasy baseball, movies, music, television. Office: ST Xavier HS 1609 Poplar Level Rd Louisville KY 40217 Office Phone: 502-637-4712. Business E-Mail: blandfordj@saintxfac.com.

BLANDFORD, ROGER DAVID, science educator; b. Grantham, Eng., Aug. 28, 1949; s. Jack George and Janet Margaret (Evans) B.; m. Elizabeth Kellett, Aug. 5, 1972; children: Jonathan, Edward. BA, Magdalene Coll., Cambridge U., 1970; MA, PhD, Cambridge U., 1974. Rsch. fellow St. John's Coll., Cambridge U., 1973-76; asst. prof. astronomy Calif. Inst. Tech., Pasadena, 1976-79, prof., 1979-89, Richard Chace Tolman prof. theoretical astrophysics, 1989—; mem. Inst. Advanced Study, Princeton, 1974-75; Luke Blossom prof. particle astrophysics and cosmology Stanford U., 2003—, Pehong and Adele Chen dir. Kvali Inst. for Particle Astrophysics and Cosmology, 2003—. Contbr. articles to profl. publs. W.B.R. King scholar, 1967-70; Charles Kingsley Bye fellow, 1972-73; Alfred P. Sloan research fellow, 1980, Guggenheim fellow, 1988—. Fellow Royal Soc., Royal Astron. Soc. (Eddington medal 1999), Cambridge Philos. Soc.; mem. NAS, Am. Astron. Soc. (Warner prize 1982, Heineman prize 1998), Am. Acad. Arts and Scis. Office: PO Box 20450 MS29 Stanford CA 94309 Home: 820 Monte Rosa Dr Menlo Park CA 94025-6723 Office Phone: 650-926-2600. Business E-Mail: rdb3@stanford.edu.

BLANE, HOWARD THOMAS, alcohol/drug abuse services professional, researcher; b. De Land, Fla., May 10, 1926; s. Chesley Thomas and Olive Henrietta (Van Heest) B.; children: Benjamin, Eva. BA cum laude, Harvard U., 1950; MA, Clark U., 1951, PhD, 1957. Instr. Harvard Med. Sch., Cambridge, Mass., 1957-66, asst. clin. prof., 1966-70; assoc. prof. U. Pitts., 1970-72, prof., 1972-86; rsch. prof. SUNY, Buffalo, 1986—96, prof. emeritus, 1996—; dir. Rsch. Inst. Addictions, Buffalo, 1986-96. Cons. Nat. Inst. on Alcohol Abuse and Alcoholism, Washington, 1970-98; v.p. Health Edn. Found., Washington, 1975-2006; bd. dirs. Rsch. Found. for Mental Hygiene, Albany, NY, 1986-96; principal investigator numerous grants. Author: The Personality of the Alcoholic, 1968; editor: Frontiers of Alcoholism, 1970, Youth, Alcoholism and Social Policy, 1979, Psychological Theories of Drinking and Alcoholism, 1987, 2nd edit., 1999. Bd. dirs. Jellinek Meml. Fund, Toronto, 1995-2005. Clark U. scholar, 1950-51. Fellow APA, Am. Psychol. Soc.; mem. APHA, AAAS, Rsch. Soc. on Alcoholism. Home and Office: Rsch Inst on Addictions 600 Main St # 904 Buffalo NY 14202-1972 Office Phone: 716-852-0858. E-mail: blaneonfmb@gmail.com.

BLANK, A(NDREW) RUSSELL, lawyer; b. Bklyn., June 13, 1945; s. Lawrence and Joan B.; children: Adam, Marisa. Student, U. N.C., 1963-64; BA, U. Fla., 1966; postgrad., Law Sch., 1966-68; JD, U. Miami, 1970. Bar: Ga. 1971, Fla. 1970; cert. civil trial advocate Nat. Bd. Trial Advocacy. Law asst. Dist. Ct. Judge, Atlanta, 1970-72; ptnr. A. Russell Blank & Assocs., PC, Atlanta, 1985—. Contbr. articles to profl. jours. Pub. adv. com. Atlanta Regional Commn., 1972-74. Recipient Merit award Ga. Bar Assn., 1981. Mem. ABA, ATLA, Atlanta Bar Assn., Ga. Bar Assn. (Merit award 1981), Ga. Trial Lawyers Assn. (officer), Lawyers Club Atlanta, Fla. Bar Assn., Am. Bd. Trial Advocates (advocate, bd. dirs. 2000—, pres. Ga. chpt., southeastern design v.p., 2004-05, pres. Southeastern regional divsn. 2006—), Xenix Soc. (bd. dirs.). Office: 3166 Mathieson Dr Ste 280 Atlanta GA 30305 Office Phone: 404-523-7400. Business E-Mail: rblank@arussellblank.com.

BLANK, ARTHUR M., professional sports team and retired lumber company executive; b. Queens, NY, 1942; BS, Babson Coll., LLD (hon.), 1998. Acct. Arthur Young & Co., NYC, 1963-67; with Daylin Inc., Los Angeles, 1967-74; v.p., treas. Handy Dan Home Improvement Ctrs. Inc., Los Angeles, 1974-78; co-founder Home Depot Inc., Atlanta, 1978, pres., COO, 1978—97, pres., CEO, 1997—2000, co-chmn., 2000—01; chmn. Arthur M. Blank Family Found., 1995—; chmn., pres., CEO AMB Group LLC, 2001—; owner, CEO Atlanta Falcons Football Club, 2002—. Bd. dir. Cox Enterprises, Staples Inc.; disting. exec. in residence Goizueta Bus. Sch., Emory Univ., 2001. Trustee Carter Ctr., Emory Univ., Cooper Inst.; bd. mem. NC Outward Bound Sch. Co-recipient Ga. Philanthropist of the Year, Nat. Soc. Fundraising Exec., 2000, Abe Goldstein Human Rels. award, Anti-Defamation League, 2001; named Ga. Most Respected CEO, Ga. Trend mag., 2001, 2003; named one of 50 Most Generous Philanthropists, BusinessWeek, 2005, Forbes' Richest Americans, 2006; named to Acad. Disting. Entrepreneurs, Babson Coll., 1995, Bus. Hall of Fame, Junior Achievement Atlanta, 2001, Ga. State Univ., 2002; recipient Brotherhood / Sisterhood award, Nat. Conf. of Christians & Jews, 1994. Mem.: Commerce Club. Office: Atlanta Falcons 4400 Falcon Pkwy Flowery Branch GA 30542

BLANK, EUGENE, pediatrician, radiologist, educator; b. Balt., May 8, 1924; s. Maurice Blank and Fannie Edith Jacob; m. Esther Honikberg, June 22, 1958; children: Lisa, Anne, Linda. BA, Johns Hopkins U., 1948, MD, 1954. Diplomate Am. Bd. Pediat., Am. Bd. Radiology. Prof. emeritus in pediats. and radiology Oreg. Health Scis. U., Portland, 1991—. Author: Pediatric Images Casebook of Differential Diagnosis, 1997, USMC 457703, 2006. 2d lt. USMC, 1942—45, South Pacific. Democrat. Avocation: writing. Home: 4940 SW Humphrey Park Rd Portland OR 97221

BLANK, LENORE KIM, literature and language professor, consultant; b. Seoul, Republic of Korea, Apr. 17, 1930; d. Yong-Bae Kim and Dae-Ran Park; children: Kimberly, Melanie, Jonathan. BA in English Lit., Seoul Nat. U. Tchrs. Coll., 1953; MA in English Edn., N.J. State Tchrs. Coll., 1957; MA in Tchg. English to Spkrs. of other Langs., Columbia U., 1958; EdD in Curriculum and Instrn., U. San Francisco, 1981. Lifetime cert. secondary educator, std. tchg. credential State of Calif. Bd. Edn. Tchr. English Coll. H.S., 1954—55; instr. English Yun-sei U., Tong-Guk U., 1958—60; ESL tchr., resource specialist San Francisco Unified Sch. Dist., 1970—87; bilingual resource specialist U. San Francisco, 1981—98, coord. Korean lang. programs, 1995—98; ret., 1998. Korean lang. instr. U. Calif., Berkeley, 1994. Fellow, N.J. Fedn. Women, 1957—58; grantee, Nat.

Fng. Lang. Ctr., Washington, 1994; scholar, Korean-Am. Found., 1955—57. Mem.: NEA, Am. Assn. Tchrs. Korean, Calif. Tchrs. Assn., Calif. Ret. Tchrs. Assn. Democrat. Achievements include development of curiculum guides for the school district as well as national academic standard tests of SAT-Korean (for students) and SSAT-Korean (for teachers). Home: 6301 Galaxy Ln Rocklin CA 95677 E-mail: lenorekblank@yahoo.com.

BLANK, MARION SUE, psychologist, educator; b. NYC, Dec. 20, 1933; d. Morris David and Tillie Jean (Sherman) Hersch; m. Martin Blank, July 3, 1955; children: Donna, Jonathan, Ari. BA, CCNY, 1955, MS in Edn, 1956; PhD, Cambridge U., Eng., 1961. Asst. prof. Albert Einstein Coll. Medicine, 1965-70, assoc. prof., 1970-73; prof. dept. psychiatry Rutgers Med. Sch., Piscataway, NJ, 1973-83; mem. adj. faculty dept. psychiatry Columbia Coll. Physicians and Surgeons, NYC, 1980—83; pres. Darj on Learning, Inc., 2001—; co-dir. Devel. Neuropsychiatry Program, Columbia U., NYC, 2004—; dir. A Light on Literacy, 2005—. Dir. reading disabilities rsch. inst., pvt. practice, cons., 1983—; Nat. Tour lectr. Speech Pathology Assn. Australia, 1996. Author: Teaching Learning in the Preschool - A Dialogue Approach, Preschool Language Assessment Instrument, 1978, (with Rose and Berlin) The Language of Learning, 1978, Sentence Master, 1990-96, (with Berlin) A Parent's Guide to Educational Software, 1991, (with Marquis and Klimovitch) Directing School Discourse, 1994, Directing Early Discourse with Marquis and Klimovitch, 1995, The Reading Remedy, 2006. Pinsent-Darwin fellow, 1960; recipient award of commendation N.J. Speech and Hearing Assn., 1979, Spl. Edn. award Software Pubs. Am., 1990, N.J., USPHS Career Devel. award, 1965-73; named N.J. nominee Kleffner Lifetime Svc. award Am. Speech Lang. Hearing Assn., 1994, 95. Fellow APA; mem. Assn. for Children with Learning Disabilities (profl. adv. bd., instr., adv. N.J. chpt.) Home: 157 Columbus Dr Tenafly NJ 07670-1635 Office Phone: 212-305-4663. Personal E-mail: msblank@optonline.net. Business E-Mail: msb5@columbia.edu. *It is heartening, albeit at times difficult, to live in a period of revolutionary change for women.*

BLANK, MATTHEW C., broadcast company executive; m. Susan McGuirk; children: Meredith, Gordon. Degree, U. Pa.; MBA, Baruch Coll. Past sr. v.p. consumer mktg. Home Box Office; exec. v.p. mktg. Showtime Networks, Inc. (Showtime, The Movie Channel, Fliz, Showtime Extreme, Showtime en Español, Showtime Event TV), NYC, 1981-91, pres., COO, 1991—, past CEO, also chmn. bd. dirs., bd. dirs., mem. exec. com. Sundance Ch. Bd. dirs. Comedy Central, Phoenix Pictures; chmn., CEO Showtime Network, Inc. Trustee Rheedlen Ctrs. Children and Families; bd. dirs. Walter Kaitz Found.; mem. exec. com. Cable Positive, active Nat. Minorities in Cable. Recipient Vanguard award for mktg., 1991, Chmn.'s award Cable TV and Mktg., 1991, Friends of Children award Rheedlen Ctrs. Children and Families, 1996, 1991, Chmn.'s award Cable TV and Mktg., 1991, Friends of Children award, Rheedlen Ctrs. Children and Families, 1996, Fairness award, Gay and Lesbian Alliance Against Defamation, 1997. Mem.: Pub. Edn. Needs Civic Involvement in Lng., Nat. Cable TV Assn. (bd. dirs.), Nat. Acad. Cable Programming (bd. govs.), NCCJ (mem. exec. bd. dirs). Office: care Showtime Networks 1633 Broadway New York NY 10019-6708

BLANK, REBECCA MARGARET, economist; b. Columbia, Mo., Sept. 19, 1955; d. Oscar Uel and Vernie (Backhaus) B.; m. Johannes Kuttner, 1994; 1 child, Emily. BS, U. Minn., 1976; PhD, MIT, 1983. Cons. Data Resources, Inc., Chgo., 1976-79; asst. prof. econs. Princeton U., 1983-89; assoc. prof. econs. Northwestern U., Chgo., 1989-94, prof. econs., 1994-99; sr. staff economist Coun. of Econ. Advisors, Washington, 1989-90, mem., 1998-99; dean, Henry Carter Adams prof. Gerald R. Ford Sch. Pub. Policy, U. Mich., Ann Arbor, 1999—; co-dir. Nat. Poverty Rsch. Ctr., U. Mich., 2002—. Author: It Takes A Nation: A New Agenda for Fighting Poverty, 1997, Is the Market Moral?, 2004, other books; contbr. articles to profl. jours. Vis. Professorships for Women grantee, 1988-89; Sloan Found. fellow, 1982-83; recipient Jr. Faculty Teaching award Princeton U., 1985, David Kershaw award Assn. Pub. Policy Analysis and Mgmt., 1993, Richard Lester award for best book on labor econs., 1997. Mem. Am. Acad. Arts and Scis., Nat. Bur. Econ. Rsch., Am. Econs. Assn., Assn. of Pub. Policy Analysis and Mgmt., Indsl. Rels. Rsch. Assn. United Ch. of Christ.

BLANK, STEVEN A., energy executive; B in History, SUNY; M in Internat. Bus., Columbia U. V.p. fin., treas. Ultramar Diamond Shamrock Corp., 1996—2002; chief acctg. officer, CFO Valero GP, LLC, San Antonio, 1999—2002, sr. v.p., CFO, 2002—. Office: Valero PO Box 696000 San Antonio TX 78269-6000 Office Phone: 210-370-2000.

BLANKE, CHARLES D., medical educator; BS in Medicine, Northwestern U., 1986, MD, 1988. Diplomate Nat. Bd. Med. Examiners, Am. Bd. Internal Medicine. Intern, resident Gundersen Med. Found., La Crosse, Wis., 1988-91; with Vanderbilt U. Hosp., Nashville Vets. Adminstrn. Med. Ctr., 1994-98; asst. prof. divsn. hematology/med. oncology Oreg. Health Scis. U., Portland Vets. Adminstrn. Med. Ctr., 1998, assoc. prof. Media cons., ABC News, Today Show, WebMD; lectr., cons., presenter in field. Contbr. articles to profl. jours. Am. Cancer Soc. fellow, 1997-98. Fellow, Am. Coll. Physicians; mem. Am. Gastroenterological Assn., Am. Soc. Clin. Oncology, Alpha Omega Alpha. Office: Oreg Health Scis U Physicians Pavilion 3181 SW Sam Jackson Park Rd Portland OR 97201-3011 also: Cancer Care Ctr Ctr Health & Healing 7th floor 3303 SW Bond Ave Portland OR 97239 Office Phone: 503-494-6594. Business E-Mail: blankec@ohsu.edu.*

BLANKE, HENRY H., JR., retired theater educator; b. Geneva, Nebr., May 15, 1931; s. Henry H. Blanke, Sr. and Fern L. Cruse; m. Phyllis Anne Chard, June 30, 1957; children: Gregory W., Annette LaRae Blanke Hinrichs. BA, Doane Coll., 1953; postgrad., Kans. State U., 1954; MA, U. Nebr., 1958; postgrad., Ind. U., 1961—63. Tchr. English and speech Superior H.S., Nebr., 1953—57; assoc. prof. Tarkio Coll., Mo., 1959—61; instr. speech and theatre Ind. U., Bloomington, 1961—63; assoc. prof. theatre arts Nebr. Wesleyan U., Lincoln, 1958—59, 1963—99, dir. theatre arts, 1963—93; ret., 1999. Founder, artistic dir. Brownville (Nebr.) Village Theatre, 1967—97; designer Nebr. Wesleyan Elder Speech-Theatre Art Ctr., 1981. Actor: (various plays), 1949—2007; dir.: (various plays, musicals, operas), 1953—2002. Chmn. Nebr. Centennial Playwriting Com., Brownville Repertory Theatre Found.; chmn. adv. bd. Tada Theatre Prodns. Named Outstanding Alumni, Hixon-Lied Coll. Fine Arts, 2000; recipient Eyes on Nebr. award, Nebr. Optometric Assn., 1972, Nebr. Govs. Arts award, Nebr. Gov. J. J. Exon, 1979, Kersenbrock Humanitarian award, Doane Coll., 1993, Lincoln Mayor's Arts award, Lincoln Nebr. Arts Coun., 2001, Play Directing award, Kennedy Ctr./Am. Coll. Theatre Festival, 1986—87, Kennedy Ctr./Am. Coll. theatre Festival, 1987, Kennedy Ctr./Am. Coll. Theatre Festival, 1994, 1998, Medallion of Excellence award, 1999. Mem.: Nat. Collegiate Players, Theta Alpha Phi, Alpha Psi Omega, Phi Kappa Phi. Democrat. Presbyterian. Home: 2221 N 61st St Lincoln NE 68505

BLANKE, RICHARD BRIAN, lawyer; b. St. Louis, Oct. 28, 1954; s. Robert H. and Phyllis I. (Kessler) Schaffler. BA, U. Pa., 1977; JD, U. Mo., 1980. Bar: Mo. 1980, U.S. Dist. Ct. (ea. and we. dists.) Mo. 1980. Ptnr. Blanke & Assocs., St. Louis County, Mo., 1980-90, Uthoff, Graeber, Bobinette & Blanke, St. Louis, 1991—. Mem. ABA, ATLA, Mo. Bar Assn., Mo. Assn. Trial Attys., St. Louis Met. Bar Assn. Office: Uthoff Graeber Bobinette & Blanke 906 Olive St Ste 300 Saint Louis MO 63101-1426 Office Phone: 314-621-9550. Business E-Mail: rblanke@ugbblaw.com.

BLANKENSHIP, BILLY JIM, surgeon; b. Longview, Tex., Feb. 13, 1928; s. John O. Blankenship and Jimmie S. Baggett; m. Carolyn Elizabeth Keeling, Jan. 26, 1952; children: Roberta Jean, Jimmie Lynn, Jean Ann. BS, Stephen F. Austin State, Nacogdoches, Tex., 1953, BA, MEd, 1954; DDS, U. Tex., 1958, MD, 1963. Lic. dentist Tex., physician Tex., diplomate Am. Bd. Oral and Maxillofacial Surgery, Am. Bd. Family Practice, Am. Bd. Hyperbaric Medicine. Able seaman US Mcht. Marine, 1945—46, boatswain, 1948—51; sonarman USN, 1946—48; chief, div. oral & maxiofacial surgery UTMB, Galveston, Tex., 1966—69; with div. sur 3rd mardiv, Force Sur Third Mar Amphb Force, 1980—81; commanding officer combat support hosp. USN, 1983—85, diving officer spl. boat unit, 1985—87; capt. med. corps USN, USMC, 1958—83; exec. officer US Naval Hosp., Corpus Christi, Tex., 1981—83; sr. Navy med. officer NATO, 1987—88; med. dir. Hyperbaric Med. Assoc., Corpus Christi and Houston, 1983—. Asst. prof. surgery U. Tex. Med. Br., Galveston, 1967—69; prof. surgery and pharmacology U. Tex. Health Sci. Ctr., San Antonio, 1971—75; prof. dental sci. Del Mar Coll., Corpus Christi, 1989—92. Contbr. articles to profl. jours. Mem.: AMA, ADA, Tex. Med. Assn., 3d Marine Divsn. Assn., Submarine Vets. of US, Omicron Kappa Upsilon, Alpha Omega Alpha, Sigma Xi. Baptist. Avocations: flying, fishing. Home: 13810 Suntan Ave Corpus Christi TX 78418 Fax: 361-949-8020. E-mail: bjblanks@aol.com.

BLANKENSHIP, COLLEEN MARIE-KRICK, secondary school educator, writer; b. Myrtle Beach, SC, Feb. 19, 1962; d. Roger Lenwood and Barbara Holbrook Krick; children: Allen Reeves, Emily Catherine, Rebecca Lynne. BA, Berry Coll., Mt. Berry, Ga., 1984; MEd, U. Ga., Athens, 1997. Tchr. Shiloh H.S., Gwinnett County Schs., Snellville, Ga., 1988—2000, Brookwood H.S., Gwinnett County Schs., Snellville, 2000—. Writer Prentice Hall, Boston, 2005—; curriculum writer Ga. Online Sch., Atlanta, 2005—. Chmn. election campaign Com. to Elect Phyllis Miller to State Legislature, Snellvillle, 2004; chmn. election com. Campaign to Elect Warren Auld to State Legislature, Snellville, 2005. Nominee Disney Hand Tchr., Disney Co., 2006; named Tchr. of Yr., Shiloh H.S., 2000, Gwinnett County Law Tchr. of Yr., Gwinnett Bar Assn., 2000. Office: Brookwood High School 1255 Dogwood Rd Snellville GA 30078 Home Phone: 770-845-0470; Office Phone: 770-972-7642.

BLANKENSHIP, DON L., energy executive; b. W. Va., 1950; B in Acctg., Marshall Univ. With Keebler and Flowers Industries, 1972—82; joined A.T. Massey Coal (now Massey Energy), 1982—, chmn., pres., CEO, 1992—2000, Massey Energy Co., 2000—. Bd. dir. Bluesprings Coal Co., Maxann Coal Co., Pikco Mining Co., Tall Timber Coal Co., Blackberry Creek Coal Co., Big Bottom Coal Co., Allburn Coal Co., Rawl Sales & Processing Co.; bd. dir., pres. Snowball Ptnrs., Ziebold Sapphire Ptnrs. Bd. dir. US C. of C. Named Disting. Alumni, Marshall Univ., 1999; named to Tug Valley Mining Inst. Hall of Fame, 1999, Am. Inst. CPA Bus. & Industry Hall of Fame, 2002. Office: Massey Energy 4 N Fourth St PO Box 26765 Richmond VA 23261 Office Phone: 804-788-1800. Office Fax: 804-788-1870.*

BLANKENSHIP, EDWARD G., architect; b. Martin, Tenn., June 22, 1943; BArch, Columbia U., 1966, MSc in Arch., 1967; MLitt in Arch., Cambridge U., Eng., 1971. Sr. v.p. Landrum & Brown, Inc., Chgo. Office: 218 Park Crest Dr Newport Beach CA 92657 Office Phone: 949-252-5214.

BLANKENSHIP, J. RICHARD, former ambassador; b. Troy, Ala. married. Diploma, Fla. State U. Former ptnr., dir. Capital South Group, Jacksonville, Fla.; former pres., CFO St. John's Capital; former mcpl. and govt. financing officer Raymond James and Assocs., St. Petersburg, Fla.; former acct. Peat, Marwick, and Mitchell, Jacksonville; former ptnr. J. Richard Blankenship & co.; U.S. amb. to The Bahamas US Dept. State, 2001—03; former acct. Price Waterhouse & Co., Tampa, Fla. Apptd. mem. State of Fla. Transp. Outreach Program; mem. Fla. Joint Task Force Evaluation Team.

BLANKENSHIP, JAMES COLEGROVE, cardiologist; s. John Harnly and Marian (Colegrove) Blankenship; m. Mary Stark, June 9, 1984; children: Leah Shikany, Bart James, Peter Stark. MD, Cornell U., 1980. Diplomate in internal medicine and interventional cardiology Am. Bd. Internal Medicine. With Marshfield (Wis.) Clinic, 1987—89; dir. Catheterization Lab., Geisinger Med. Ctr., Danville, Pa., 1997—; prof. medicine Jefferson Med. Coll., Phila., 1989—. Office: Geisinger Med Ctr 100 N Academy Dr Danville PA 17822 Office Phone: 570-271-8067.

BLANKENSHIP, LAWRENCE L., retired minister; b. Pensacola, Fla., July 9, 1950; s. Erskin D. and Willie L. Blankenship; m. Zelmer J. Blankenship, Jan. 25, 1986; children: Lucille J. French, La'Rhonda B. Smith. Student, U. W. Fla. Ordained 88; cert. occupl. proficiency Pensacola Jr. Coll., 71. Minister Mt. Moriah Missionary Bapt. Ch.; ret. Author: The Divine Law: Women in a Changing World, The Divine Law: The Law of God, The Divine Law: The Law of The States. Avocations: reading, writing. Home: PO Box 2971 Pensacola FL 32503

BLANKENSHIP, ROBERT EUGENE, biochemistry educator; b. Auburn, Nebr., Aug. 25, 1948; s. George Robert and Jane (Kehoe) Leech; m. Elizabeth Marie Dorland, June 26, 1971; children: Larissa Dorland, Samuel Robert. BS, Wesleyan U., Nebr., 1970; PhD, U. Calif., Berkeley, 1975. Postdoctoral fellow Lawrence Berkeley Lab., Berkeley, 1975-76, U. Washington, Seattle, 1976-79; asst. prof. Amherst Coll., Mass., 1979-85; assoc. prof. Ariz. State U., Tempe, 1985-88, prof., 1988—2006, dir. Ctr. Study of Early Events in Photosynthesis, 1988-91, chair, dept. chem. and biochem., 2002—06; Lucille P. Markey Disting. Prof. Arts and Scis. in biology and chemistry Washington U., St. Louis, 2006—. Author: Molecular Mechanisms of Photosynthesis, 2002; editor Anoxygenic Photosynthetic Bacteria, 1995; editor-in-chief Photosynthesis Rsch., 1988-99; cons. editor Advances in Photosynthesis, 1991-98; mem. editl. bd. Biophys. Jour., 2000-03, Biochemistry, 2001—, Internat. Jour. Astrobiology, 2001—, Chem. Biology, 2006—; contbr. 235 articles to sci. jours. Recipient Alumni award Nebr. Wesleyan U., 1991, Disting. Rsch. award Ariz. State U., 1992, Mentoring award Ariz. State U., 1998. Fellow AAAS, Ariz. Arts, Scis. & Tech. Acad.; mem. Am. Chem. Soc., Am. Soc. Microbiology, Biophys. Soc., Union Concerned Scientists, Internat. Soc. Photosynthesis Rsch. (pres. 2001-04), Internat. Soc. for Study of Origin of Life. Democrat. Avocations: hiking, cooking, travel, fossil collecting. Home: 6924 Columbia Ave Saint Louis MO 63130 Office: Washington Univ Depts Biology and Chemistry Campus Box 1137 Saint Louis MO 63130 Business E-Mail: blankenship@wustl.edu.

BLANKENSHIP, ROY, conservator, artist, writer; b. Phila., Nov. 26, 1943; m. Lynn Ann Wilkers, Apr. 6, 1968 (div. May 1993); children: Troy Insley, Beth Lynn; m. Lois Showalter, Apr. 1, 2000. BAAS Arts and Sci., U Del., 1973. Art restoration apprentice/asst. Salter Studio, Arden, Del., 1966—72; art conservation student apprentice Winterthur (Del.) Mus., 1968—72; painting conservation asst. Ted Segal Studio Phila. Mus. Art, 1969—70; painting restoration asst./apprentice Twistback Conservation Ctr., Oxford, Pa., 1970—72; gen. mgr., layout design artist The Little Giant Shopper, Newark, Del., 1970—72; art tchr. Marbrook Elem., Wilmington, Del., 1971—72; part-time art tchr. Ursuline Acad., Wilmington, 1971—72; art history and studio art tchr. Brandywine H.S., Wilmington, 1972—73; curator, exhbn. coord. Morris Libr., U. Del., Newark, 1972—73; painting conservator-in-residence Carspecken-Scott Gallery, Wilmington, 1972—78; founder Blankenship Painting and Conservation Studio, Wilmington, 1975—81; dir., owner Blankenship Conservation Ctr., Wilmington, 1981—; founder Blankenship's mail order bus., 1985—. Profl. fine art painting conservationist IIC, 1972; instr. art history U. Del., Newark, 1972; lectr., cons. in field, 1973—; curator, lectr. Albert Babb Insley retrospective exhbn. (traveling), 1984—85, Nardin Fine Arts, Ltd., Cross River, NY, 1988; organizer, guest curator, lectr. The McKissick Mus., U. S.C., Columbia, 1995; collections and chief painting conservator Boggs Fed. Bldg., Wilmington, Del., 1973—; curator Hastings Gallery, New Canaan, Conn., 1987; painting collections cons., restorer Del. Art Mus., Wilmington, Del., 1972—83; personal collections cons. to Ernest Dodge, dir. Peabody-Essex Mus., Salem, Mass., 1973—85; fellow, rsch. scientist AIC, Wash., DC, 1973—; conservators in pvt. practice Am. Inst. Cons., 1975—; chief painting conservator NEHGS, Boston, 1996—. Columnist Collecting (Gannett Papers), 1975—85; author, compiler, designer, pub.: The Delicate Palette of Albert Insley, 1982; editor: The Life and Times of Frank G. Speck (1881-1950), 1992; one-man shows include Atlas Chem. Emporium (photography), Wilmington, 1970, Swarthmore Coll., Pa., 1960, Bicentennial Retrospective exhbn., Wilmington Libr., Lou Polack Gallery, Rockport, Mass., 1978, 1983, Nancy Richardson Art and Antique Gallery, Essex, Conn., 1981, R.M. Worth Antiques and Fine Art, Chadds Ford, Pa., 2000, 2000, exhibited in group shows at Grand Opera Ho. and Del. Art Mus., Wilmington, Del., 1968, Del. Art Mus. Ceramics Retro., 1970, 1973, Chester County (Pa.) Art Assn., 2002, Hagley Mus., Wilmington, 2000, Rockport Contbg. Members Show, 2001, Main Hall, Kendal at Longwood, Pa., 2001, North Shore Ann. Exhbn., 1972—, Oil Painters of Am., 2002, one-man shows include R.M. Worth Antiques and Fine Art, Pa., 2000, exhbn. with wife, Main Hall, Kendal at Longwood, 2001, Wilmington Libr., Del., 2002, Sawyer Free Libr., Gloucester, Mass., 2002, Crosslands, Kennett Sq., Pa., 2003. Founder, organizer, head chairperson 1st Ann. Arden Ctr. Antiques Show and Sale, 1977; founder Blankenship Conservation Ctr., Wilmington, 1973—; organizer, co-chair 1st F.G. Speck Seminar, U. Pa., Phila., 1986. With USN, 1962—66, with USN, 1962—66. Mem.: NSAA, Am Artists Prof. League (Salmagundi Club), Am. Soc. Marine Artists, Soc. Del. Artists, Chester County Artist Assn. Address: PO Box 7221 Wilmington DE 19803

BLANKENSHIP, TRENT, school system administrator, educator; married; 3 children. BS in sci. Edn., U. Wyo., 1986, MA in Ednl. Adminstrn., 1991, PhD in Leadership and Human Devel., 1995. Chemistry tchr. Riverton H.S., Wyo.; chemistry and physics tchr. Heidelburg H.S. Dept. of Defense, Germany; asst. prin. Sheridan Jr. H.S., Sheridan County, Wyo.; prin. DuBois H.S. and Middle Sch., Wyo.; supt. Fremont Sch. District, DuBois, Wyo., Carbon County Sch. Dist., Rawlins; state supt. pub. instrn. State of Wyo., Cheyenne, 2003—05; dist. supt. North Slope Borough, Alaska, 2005—. Mem. Wyo. CAS Policy Com. Mem. adv. bd. U. Wyo. Coll. Edn.; mem. Gov.'s Substance Abuse Com. Office: North Slope Borough Sch Dist PO Box 169 829 Aivik St Barrow AK 99723-0169 E-mail: champion4children@yahoo.com.

BLANKENSTEIN, ELIZABETH M., director, educator; b. Dorchester, Mass., Feb. 16, 1958; d. Frederick F. and Elizabeth A. MacQueen; m. Ronald G. Blankenstein, May 3, 1998; 1 child, Heather L. BA, Westfield State Coll., 1980; MS, U. Bridgeport, 1983. Cert. career and tech. edn. adminstr. N.H., 2004, faculty instr. Intel, 2003. Learner services coord. Coll. Lifelong Learning, North Country Region, NH, 1985—97; dir. of the office of grad. and evening admissions and asst. dean Rivier Coll., Nashua, NH, 1997—98; dir. office grad. admissions and continuing edn. Notre Dame Coll., Manchester, NH, 1998—99; implementation specialist Jenzabar, Inc., Harrisonburg, Va., 1999—2002; dir. vocat. planning and accountability N.H. Cmty. Tech. Coll. Sys., Concord, 2002—05; assoc. v.p. acad. affairs N.H. Tech. Inst., Concord, 2005—. Faculty Granite State Coll., Manchester, NH, 1985—; cons. Office Grad. Studies Plymouth (N.H.) State U., 1989—97. Mem. adv. bd. Kennett H.S. Mktg. Program, Conway, NH, 1992—93; elected mem. Town of Madison Planning Bd., NH, 1992—97, chair, 1993—95; mem. Rte. 16 corridor study team NH Dept. Transp., Concord, 1996—97; mem. supr. adminstrv. unit 9 and 13 Sch. to Work Com., Conway, NH, 1996—97; eucharistic min. St. Elizabeth Seton Parish, Bedford, NH, 2002—; mem. Vis. Nurse Svcs. No. Carroll County, NH, 1986—88, Mt. Wash. Valley Econ. Coun., Conway, NH, 1995—97; mem. cmty. adv. bd. Internat. Paper Corp., Madison and Freedom Operations, NH, 1996—97. Fellow, Rotary Internat., 1992. Mem.: Assn. Continuing Higher Edn. (region I exceptional program com. chair 1997—), Nat. Tech Prep Network, Nat. Assn. State Dirs. Career and Tech. Edn. Consortium (assoc.). Independent. Roman Catholic. Avocations: painting, ballroom dancing. Home: 101 Crestview Rd Manchester NH 03104 Office: NH Tech Inst 31 College Dr Concord NH 03301 Home Phone: 603-624-1831; Office Phone: 603-271-1754.

BLANKFEIN, LLOYD C., diversified financial services company executive; b. Bronx, NY, Sept. 20, 1954; m. Laura Susan Jacobs; 3 children. BA, Harvard U., 1975, JD, 1978. Corp. tax lawyer Donovan, Leisure, Newton & Irvine; joined J. Aron & Co. Currency and Commodities Divsn. Goldman Sachs Co., NYC, 1982, co-head, J. Aron currency and commodities divsn., 1994—97; co-head fixed income, currency and commodities divsn. Goldman Sachs Group, Inc., NYC, 1997—2004, vice chmn., 2002—04, pres., COO, 2004—06, chmn., CEO, 2006—. Bd. dirs. Goldman Sachs Group, Inc., 2003—; former mem. fgn. exch. com. Fed. Res. Bank, NY. Co-chair fin. aid task force Harvard U., mem. exec. com. com. on univ. resources; bd. trustees NY Hist. Soc.; bd. overseers Cornell U. Weill Med. Coll.; bd. dirs. Partnership NYC, Robin Hood Found. Office: The Goldman Sachs Group 85 Broad St New York NY 10004*

BLANKFEIN, ROBERT JEROME, retired neurologist; b. Nov. 5, 1931; s. Jules and Freda S. Blankfein; m. Leslie Wald Blankfein, June 27, 1998; 1 child, David. Grad., Hotchkiss Sch., 1950; BA, Yale U., New Haven, Conn., 1954; MD, NY Med. Coll., 1958. Diplomate in neurology Am. Bd. of Neurology and Psychiatry, 1971. Intern San Francisco Gen. Hosp. (Stanford U. Svc.), 1958—59; resident in internal medicine Bx VA Hosp., 1959—60, resident in neurology, 1960—63; vis. fellow neurology and myasthenia Clinic Columbia Presbyn. Hosp., 1962—63; neurophysiology fellow EEG Hosp. U. Penn., 1963—65; clin. asst. prof. neurology NY Med. Coll., 1971-74, clin. assoc. prof. neurology, 1975—2002; attending neurologist Met. Hosp. NY, NYC, 1986—2002, NY Hosp. Med. Ctr. Queens, 1979-95; fed. examiner neurology US Dept. Labor, 1992—2002; ret., 2002. Dir. neurology, Physicians Hosp., 1967-90, pres. med. bd., 1971-81; coord. Jour. Club Neurology Residents, NY Med. Coll., 1971-89; disting. lectr. dementia and aging, Sandoz-Dorsey Pharms., 1973-74; lectr. delirium, McNeil Pharms., 1984; presenter in field. Mem. editl. bd., consulting editor in neurology, Jour. Hosp. Physician, 1977-95; contbr. articles to profl. jours. Class agt. Hotchkiss Sch. 55th Reunion; vice-chmn. Hotchkiss Fund, 2005—06. Fellow ACP, Am. Acad. Neurology, NY Acad. Medicine, Royal Soc. Medicine, Stroke Coun. of Am. Heart Assn., Yale Sci. and Engring. Soc.; mem. Assn. Rsch. Nervous and Mental Disease, NY Neurol. Soc., Am. Epilepsy Soc., Am. EEG Soc., Assoc. Alumni Neurol. Inst. NY Columbia Presbyn. Med. Ctr., Queens Acad. Medicine (mem. continuing edn. com. 1980-85), Yale Crew Assn., Yale Club NYC. Personal E-mail: robertblankfein@verizon.net.

BLANKFEIN-TABACHNICK, DAVID H., philosophy educator; b. New Haven, Aug. 6, 1971; s. Robert J. Blankfein and Leslie J. Wald. BA, Ithaca Coll., NY, 1993; MA, U. Rochester, NY, 1995; PhD, U. Va., 2007. Instr. U. Va., 2007—. Fellow law, philosophy and ethical thought Inst. Practical Ethics, U. Va., 2001—03. Mem.: Am. Philos. Assn. Democrat. Jewish. Home: 107 1st Street South Charlottesville VA 22902 Office: Corcoran Department of Philosophy 121 Cocke Hall University of Virginia Charlottesville VA 22903 Home Phone: 434-293-0684; Office Phone: 434-924-7701. Business E-Mail: dht3b@virginia.edu.

BLANKFIELD, BRYAN J., lawyer, automotive executive, accountant; BS, Drake U.; JD, Northwestern U. CPA. In-house legal counsel and cons. Waste Management, Inc., 1990—2002, assoc. gen. counsel, asst. sec., 1995—2002, v.p., 1998—2002; exec. v.p., gen. counsel, sec. Oshkosh Truck Corp., Wis., 2002—. Also advisor to CEO, bd. dir., sr. mgmt. OshKosh Truck Co. Office: Oshkosh Truck Corp 2307 Oregon St PO Box 2566 Oshkosh WI 54903 Office Phone: 920-235-9151.*

BLANKFORT, LOWELL ARNOLD, newspaper publisher; b. NYC, Apr. 29, 1926; s. Herbert and Gertrude (Butler) B.; m. April Pemberton; 1 child, Jonathan. BA in History and Polit. Sci., Rutgers U., 1946. Reporter, copy editor LI Star-Jour., NY, 1947—49; columnist London Daily Mail, Paris, 1949—50; copy editor The Stars & Stripes, Darmstadt, Germany, 1950—51, Wall St. Jour., NYC, 1951; bus., labor editor Cowles Mags., NYC, 1951—53; pub. Pacifica Tribune, Calif., 1954—59; freelance writer Europe, Asia, 1959—61; co-pub., editor Chula Vista Star-News, Calif., 1961—78; co-owner Paradise Post, Calif., 1977—2003. Co-owner Monte Vista Jour., Colo., Ctr. Post-Dispatch, Colo., Del Norte Prospector, Colo., 1978—93, Plainview News, Minn., St. Charles Press, Minn., Lewiston Jour., Minn., 1980—98, Summit Sentinel, Colo., New Richmond News, Wis., 1981—87, Yuba City Valley Herald, 1982—85, TV Views, Monterey, Calif., 1982—87, Summit County Jour., 1982—87, Alpine Sun, Calif., 1987—93, Bassics Mag., 1998—, Fingerstyle Guitar Mag., 1999. *Mr. Blankfort has received many awards including Best Editorials in California, non-dailies; 1st or 2nd place seven consecutive years, California Newspaper Publishers Association; Best Editorial in the United States, National Newspapers Association; Best Editorial U. S. suburban newspapers. Suburban Publishers Newspapers of America; Headliner of the Year, San Diego Press Club; John Swett Award, California Education Association; and Citizen of the Year, Sweetwater Education Association. Special Media Award, National Conference of Christians and Jews. Mr. Blankfort is a widely traveled writer. He has interviewed many heads of state including Fidel Castro in Cuba, Li Peng and Li Xiannin in China, and Benezir Bhutto in Pakistan.* Columnist, contbr. articles on fgn. affairs to newspapers. Active Calif. Dem. Ctrl. Com., 1963; bd. dirs. Mus. Photographic Arts, San Diego, 2003—04. Named Citizen of Yr., Sweetwater Edn. Assn., Outstanding Layman of Yr., 1966, Citizen of Yr., City of Chula Vista, 1976, Headliner of Yr., San Diego Press Club, 1980; recipient Best Editl. in Calif., non-dailies, 1st or 2d place seven consecutive yrs., Calif. Newspaper Pub. Assn., Best Editl. in US, Nat. Newspaper Assn., Best Editl. US Suburban Newspapers, Suburban Pubs. Newspapers Am., John Swett award, Calif. Edn. Assn., Spl. Media award for articles on S.Am., Nat. Conference Christians and Jews. Mem.: ACLU (pres. San Diego chpt. 1970—71), Soc. Profl. Journalists, Calif. Newspaper Pubs. Assn., East Meets West Found. (nat. v.p. 1992—98), World Federalist Assn. (pres. San Diego chpt. 1984—86, nat. bd. 1992—2000), UN Assn. (pres. San Diego chpt. 1991—93, nat. coun. 1992—97, nat. bd. 1997—2001, chpt. bd. 1999—), Internat. Ctr. Devel. Policy (nat. bd. 1985—90), Ctr. Internat. Policy (bd. dirs. 1991—), World Affairs Coun. San Diego (pres. 1996—99, v.p. 2005—06), Inst. of the Ams. (assoc.; internat. coun. 1994—). Achievements include interviewing many heads of state including Fidel Castro in Cuba, Li Peng and Li Ziannin in China, Benazir Bhutto in Pakistan, Kim Dae Jung in Korea, Paul Kagame in Rwanda. Home: 4008 Old Orchard Ln Bonita CA 91902-2337 Office: Ste C25 310 3rd Ave Chula Vista CA 91910-3970

BLANKLEY, TONY, editor; b. London, 1948; m. Davis C. Lynda; 3 children. BA Polit. Sci., UCLA; JD, Loyola Law Sch., LA. Prosecutor Calif. Atty. General's office, 1972—88; policy analyst and speechwriter Pres. Reagan Adminstrn., 1982—88; staff writer Congresswoman Bobbi Fiedler, 1988—90; press. sec. Ho. Spkr. Newt Gingrich US Congress, 1990—97; contbg. editor George Mag., 1997—99; weekly polit. columnist The Washington Times, 1999—2002, editl. page editor, 2002—. Co-host Left, Right & Ctr. Radio Talk Show, The McLaughlin Grp., The Diane Rehm Show. Actor: (films) The Harder They Fall, 1955; author: (novels) The West's Last Chance: Will We Win the Clash of Civilizations?, 2005, Am. Grit: What It Will Take to Survive and Win in the 21st Century, 2007; contbg. editor and monthly columnist (articles) George Mag. Office: The Washington Times 3600 NY Ave NE Washington DC 20002-1947 Office Phone: 202-636-2869.*

BLANTON, EDWARD LEE, JR., lawyer; b. nr. Hope Mills, NC, Oct. 31, 1931; s. Edward Lee and Margaret M. (Bullard) B.; m. Cathleen Estelle Edwards, Aug. 13, 1960; children: Edward Lee III, Cathleen Estelle, Margaret Ellyn. BS, Davidson Coll., 1953; MA, Vanderbilt U., 1954; LLB, U. Md., 1960. Bar: Md. 1960. Tchr. math. Balt. City schs., 1956-59; law clk. to judge Washington, 1960-62; assoc. Cross & Shriver, Balt., 1962—65; ptnr. Manger, Maxwell Hughes & Blanton, 1965—68, Adelberg, Rudow & Blanton, 1969-72, Blanton & McCleary, 1973-93; asst. atty. gen. State Md., Balt., 1965-68. Chmn. subcom. drafting revision Md. election laws Md. Legis. Coun., 1966-67; chmn. subcom. drafting revision Md. income tax laws Hughes Commn., 1966-67. Bd. dirs. United Christian Citizens, 1971-92, pres., 1974-75; pres. Ctrl. Balt. Ecumenical Sch. Christian Edn., 1971-74, Hist. Long Green Valley, Inc., 1980-86, Long Green Valley Assn., 1979-89; dir. Ctr. for Prevention of Child Abuse, 1991-96; mem. State Rep. Ctrl. Com., 1982-86; mem. citizens adv. com. Charles H. Hickey Sch., 1983-91, chmn., 1987-91; mem. Ctrl. Towson Com. Christian Businessmen, Balt. Coun. Fgn. Affairs; v.p., dir. Long Green Valley Conservancy, Inc., 1995-98; trustee com. Presbyn. Ch., Balt., St. James Acad., Monkton, Md., 1989-95, Egenton Home, Balt.; Rep. nominee for Atty. Gen. of Md., 1990. 1st lt. AUS, 1954-56; capt. Md. N.G., 1957-62. Mem. Nat. Lawyers Assn., Bar Assn. Balt. County, Newcomen Soc. N.Am., Christian Legal Soc., Richard III Soc., Center Club, Masons, Delta Theta Phi. Presbyterian (elder). Home: Avondell Glen Arm MD 21057 Office: 305 W Chesapeake Ave Baltimore MD 21204-4255 E-mail: eblantonjr@msn.com.

BLANTON, ELIZABETH ANNE, secondary school educator; b. Saint Louis, Nov. 30, 1975; d. Christopher Michael and Pamela Greer Blanton. BA, Washington U., 1997; MS, St. Louis U., 2001, Miss. State U., 2006. Educator Villa Duchesne/Oak Hill Sch., St. Louis, 1998—. Home: 128 Hollywood Ln Saint Louis MO 63122 Office: Villa Duchesne/Oak Hill Sch 801 South Spoede Rd Saint Louis MO 63131 Home Phone: 314-821-3137; Office Phone: 314-810-3412. Personal E-mail: blantonea@aol.com. Business E-Mail: eblanton@vdoh.org.

BLANTON, FAYE WESTER, legislative official; b. Tallahassee, Nov. 9, 1946; m. Edwin F. "Ed" Blanton; children: Wade, Doug, Laurel McDaniel. Staff asst. govtl. efficiency com. Fla. Senate, Tallahassee, asst. to dir. mgmt. staff, asst. sec., sec., 1996—. Advisor, counselor Girls State, Boys State, YMCA Youth Legislature, Silver-Haired Legislature; pres. PTO Leon County Sch. Dist., mem. adv. bd. Mem. Am. Soc. Legis. Clks. and Secs. (exec. com., past assoc. v.p., mem. exec. and nominating com., chair, vice-chair, mem. various coms.) Baptist. Avocations: gardening, walking, reading. Home: 610 Summerbrooke Dr Tallahassee FL 32312 Office: Fla Senate 404 S Monroe St Tallahassee FL 32399-1100 Fax: 850-487-5174. E-mail: blanton.faye@flsenate.gov.

BLANTON, HOOVER CLARENCE, lawyer; b. Green Sea, SC, Oct. 13, 1925; s. Clarence Leo and Margaret (Hoover) B.; m. Cecilia Lopez, July 31, 1949; children: Lawson Hoover, Michael Lopez. JD, U. S.C., 1953. Bar: S.C. 1953. Ordained deacon, Bapt. Ch. Assoc. Whaley & McCutchen, Columbia, SC, 1953—66; ptnr. McCutchen, Blanton, Johnson and Barnette LLP, Columbia, 1967—. Dir. Legal Aid Service Agy., Columbia, chmn. bd., 1972-73. Gen. counsel S.C. Rep. Conv., 1962; del. Rep. State Conv., 1962, 64, 66, 68, 70, 74; bd. dirs. Midlands Cmty. Action Agy., Columbia, vice chmn., 1972-73; bd. dirs. Wildewood Sch., 1976-78; mem. Gov.'s Legal Svcs. Adv. Coun., 1976-77, Commn. on Continuing Legal Edn. for Judiciary, 1977-84, Commn. on Continuing Lawyer Competence, 1988-92, Commn. on Continuing Legal Edn. and Specialization, 1992-2000, sec. 1995, chmn., 1996-99. Mem. ABA. SC Bar (ho. of dels. 1975-76, chmn. fee disputes bd. 1977-81), Richland County Bar Assn. (pres. 1980), Def. Trial Attys. (state chmn. 1971-77, 80-95, exec. coun. 1977-80), Am. Bd. Trial Advs. (pres. SC chpts. 1989, Trial Lawyer of Yr. 2001), Toastmasters Club (pres. 1959), Palmetto Club, Phi Delta Phi. Home: 3655 Deerfield Dr Columbia SC 29204-3730 Office: 1414 Lady St Columbia SC 29201-3304

BLANTON, JACK SAWTELLE, oil industry executive; b. Shreveport, La., Dec. 7, 1927; s. William Neal and Louise (Wynn) B.; m. Laura Lee Scurlock, Aug. 20, 1949; children: Elizabeth Louise Blanton Wareing, Jack Sawtelle Jr., Eddy Scurlock. BA, U. Tex., 1947, LLB, 1950. Bar: Tex. 1950. With Scurlock Oil Co., Houston, 1950-88, v.p., 1956-58, pres., 1958-83, chmn. bd., 1983-88; pres. Eddy Refining Co., Houston, 1988—. Chmn. bd. trustees Houston Endowment, Inc.; pres. Eddy Refining Co.; bd. dirs. Pogo Producing Co., Burlington No. Santa Fe, Inc. Past chmn. bd. trustees St. Luke's United Meth. Ch., Houston; past chmn. bd. regents U. Tex. System, 1985-89; past vice chmn., bd. dirs. Meth. Hosp., Houston. Mem. Nat. Petroleum Coun., Mid-Continent Oil and Gas Assn. (past pres.) Houston C. of C. (life), Sons Republic of Tex. (past pres. San Jacinto chpt.), Sam Houston Meml. Assn., Nat. Tennis Assn., U.S. Lawn Tennis Assn., Tex. Ind. Oil Producers and Refiners, Ex-Students Assn. U. Tex. (past pres.), Greater Houston Partnership (chmn. 1985-86), Delta Kappa Epsilon, Phi Delta Phi, Phi Alpha Delta. Clubs: Houston (Houston) (past pres.), River Oaks Country (Houston); El Dorado Country (Palm Springs, Calif.). also: Houston Endowment Inc 600 Travis St Ste 6400 Houston TX 77002-3000

BLANTON, JOHN ARTHUR, architect, writer; b. Houston, Jan. 1, 1928; s. Arthur Alva and Caroline (Jeter) Blanton; m. Marietta Louise Newton, Apr. 10, 1954 (dec. 1976); children: Jill Blanton Milne, Lynette Blanton Rowe(dec.) , Elena Diane. BA, Rice U., 1948, BS in Architecture, 1949. With Richard J. Neutra, LA, 1950-64; pvt. practice Manhattan Beach, Calif., 1964—. Lectr. UCLA Ext., 1967—76, 1985. Columnist: Easy Reader newspaper, 1994—96; contbr. articles to profl. jours. City commr. Bd. Bldg. Code Appeals, Manhattan Beach; chmn. Zoning Adjustment Bd., 1990, Planning Commn., 1993—99. With Signal Corps US Army, 1951—53. Recipient local and nat. awards (published internationally). Mem.: AIA (contbr. book revs. to jour. 1972—76). Office: John Blanton AIA Architect 1456 12th St # 4 Manhattan Beach CA 90266-6187 Office Phone: 310-546-1200.

BLANTON, LEWIS M., federal judge; b. Cape Girardeau, Mo., Mar. 5, 1934; AB, St. Louis U., 1958, MA, 1962; JD, U. Mo., 1965. Bar: Mo. Atty. Thompson, Walther & Shewmaker, St. Louis, 1965-69, Blanton, Rice & Sickal, Sikeston, Mo., 1969-71, Robison & Blanton, Sikeston, 1971-78; assoc. judge Cir. Ct. of Scott County, Mo., 1979-91; magistrate judge U.S. Dist. Ct. (ea. dist.) Mo., Cape Girardeau, 1991—. Contbr. articles to profl. jours. Mem. ABA, Mo. Bar, Scott County Bar Assn., Cape Girardeau County Bar Assn., Bar Assn. Met. St. Louis, Fed. Magistrate Judges Assn. Office: 111 US Courthouse 339 Broadway St Cape Girardeau MO 63701-7330

BLANTON, THOMAS N., chemist, researcher; PhD in Chemistry, Emory U., Atlanta, Ga., 1981; MS in Materials Sci. and Engring., Rochester Inst. Tech., NYC, 1986. Rsch. scientist Eastman Kodak Co., Rochester, NY, 1982—95, sr. scientist, 1996—2000, rsch. assoc., 2001—. Lectr. in field. Co-editor: Rigaku Jour.; contbr. over 115 articles to profl. jours. Fellow: Internat. Ctr. Diffraction Data (bd. dirs. 2004—, cons. editor 2001); mem.: Am. Crystallographic Assn. Achievements include 33 patents in field; 13 patents pending. Office: Eastman Kodak Company Research Laboratories B82 Rochester NY 14650-2106 Office Phone: 585-722-3323. Business E-Mail: thomas.blanton@kodak.com.

BLANTON, VALLYE J., elementary school educator; b. Valdosta, Ga., Sept. 4, 1953; d. Louie Sloan and Tomie Jean (Roberts) B. BS in edn., U. Ga., 1975; MEd, Valdosta State Coll., 1977, cert., 1977-79. Tchr. Lowndes County Sch. System, Valdosta, Ga., 1975-89; assessment specialist Coastal Plains Regional Assessment Ctr., Valdosta, Ga., 1989-90; tchr. Lowndes County Sch. System, Lake Park, Ga., 1990—. Bd. dirs. Ga. Partnership for Excellence in Edn., Atlanta, 1994—; tchr. adv. com. Southeastern Regional Vision for Edn., Greensboro, N.C., 1994—; editorial bd. Tchr. Learning Resource Ctr., Dayton, Ohio, 1994—; scholarship selection com. U.S. Space & Rocket Ctr., Huntsville, Ala., 1994—. Bd. dirs. Valdosta Jr. Svc. League, 1985—, Valdosta State U. Alumni Bd., 1993—, U. Ga. Booster Club, 1982—. Named Ga. Tchr. of Yr. Ga. Dept. Edn., 1994; recipient Milken Nat. Educator award Milken Family Found., 1994. Mem. Ga Assn. Educators (profl. devel. chmn. 1975-94), Profl. Assn. Ga. Educators, Ga. Coun. Tchrs. Math., Nat. State Tchrs. of Yr. Orgn., Kappa Delta Pi, Phi Delta Kappa. Baptist. Avocations: reading, walking, volunteer work. Home: 2832 Fawnwood Cir Valdosta GA 31602-4105 Office: Lake Park Elementary School 604 W Marion Ave Lake Park GA 31636-5068

BLANTON, W. C., lawyer; b. LaRue County, Ky., Apr. 13, 1946; s. Crawford and Lillian (Phelps) B. BS in Math., Mich. State U., 1968, BA in Social Sci., 1968; MEd, U. Vt., 1970; JD, U. Mich., 1975. Bar: Ind. 1975, Minn. 1998, Mo. 2002, Kans. 2006, U.S. Dist. Ct. (no. and so. dists.) Ind. 1975, U.S. Dist. Ct. Minn. 1996, U.S. Dist. Ct. (we. dist.) Wis. 1996, U.S. Dist. Ct. (we. and ea. dists.) Mo. 2002, U.S. Ct. Appeals (7th cir.) 1977, U.S. Ct. Appeals (8th cir.) 1996, U.S. Ct. Appeals (6th cir.) 1998, U.S. Ct. Appeals (10th cir.) 2005. Residence hall dir. U. Wis., Madison, 1970-72; assoc. Ice Miller Donadio & Ryan, Indpls., 1975-81, ptnr., 1982-94, Popham, Haik, Schnobrich & Kaufman, Ltd., 1995-97, Oppenheimer Wolff & Donnelly LLP, Mpls., 1997—2002, Blackwell Sanders, LLP, Kansas City, Mo., 2002—, head of environ. practice group. Mem. ABA. Democrat. Avocations: skiing, travel, bridge. Office: Blackwell Sanders Peper Martin LLP Ste 1000 4801 Main St Kansas City MO 64112 E-mail: wblanton@blackwellsanders.com.

BLANTZ, ROLAND C., nephrologist, educator; b. Portland, Oreg. BA in Humanities and Chem. Engring., Johns Hopkins U., Balt., 1961, MD, 1965. Diplomate Am. Bd. Internal Medicine, Am. Bd. Nephrology. Intern U. Colo. Med. Ctr., 1965—66, resident medicine, 1968—69; fellow U. Tex. Southwestern Med. Sch., 1969—72; resident Parkland Meml. Hosp., Dallas, 1971—72; attending physician VA Med. Ctr., San Diego; chief nephrology VA San Diego Healthcare Sys.; prof. nephrology U. Calif., San Diego. Contbr. articles to profl. jours. Recipient William S. Middleton award, Dept. Vets. Affairs, 2006. Mem.: AAP, AFCR, ASCI, Am. Soc. Nephrology (pres. 2001—02). Office: Dept Medicine U Calif San Diego 9500 Gilman Dr #9111H La Jolla CA 92093 Office Phone: 858-552-8585 ext. 7528. E-mail: rblantz@ucsd.edu.*

BLAS, BRYAN ALLYN, postal maintenance worker, artist; b. Astoria, NY, Dec. 10, 1948; s. Seymour Edmund and Milred Posner Blas. AA, Ulster County CC, Stone Ridge, NY; BS in Art Edn., SUNY, Buffalo. Cert. art tchr. NY. Art tchr. Poughkeepsie Mid. Sch., NY, 1977—79; graphic artist Channel Master, Ellenville, NY, 1980—84; clerk US Postal Svc., Hurley, NY, 1984—93, maintanence worker NY, 1993—; self-employed graphic fine artist Creative Person, Kingston, NY, 1980—. Artist, illustrator (book) Question of Balance "Tryptic", 1974, Payla The Dog, 1979, (book cover design) Nici Records "Ash", 1985. Specialist 4 US Army, 1972—75, Pentagon. Mem.: Buick Club Am. Independent. Jewish. Avocation: photography. Office: US Postal Service 99 Enterprise Dr Newburgh NY 12550

BLAS, MARLENE JAMBARO, academic administrator, educator; d. Jose Garcia and Mindanita Jambaro Blas; life ptnr. Thomas Duran. AA in Fashion Merchandising, San Diego Mesa CC, 1993; BA in Journalism and Mktg., Calif. State U., Long Beach, Calif., 1996; degree in Event Mgmt., U. San Diego, 2002; MA in Tourism Adminstrn., George Wash. U., 2007. Coord. conf. Kushi Inst., Becket, Mass., 1999; meeting planner Duran and Assocs., San Diego, 1999—2000; sales adminstr. Peregrine Sys., San Diego, 2001—02; assoc. dir. mtgs. and events Calif. We. Sch. of Law, San Diego, 2002—. Instr. Calif. State U., San Marcos, 2005—; spkr. in field, 2004—. Vol. Helen Woodward Animal Ctr., Rancho Santa Fe, Calif., 2003—. Mem.: Internat. Spl. Events Soc. (assoc.; mktg. com. 2002—04), Meeting Profls. Internat. (assoc. Wyndham International-United Airlines scholarship 2005), Long Beach (Calif.) Jr. C. of C. (bd. dirs. 1997—98), Toastmasters Internat. (assoc.). Avocations: yoga, travel, running, cooking, massage therapy. Office: California Western School of Law 225 Cedar Street San Diego CA 92101

BLASBAND, DAVID, lawyer; b. Phila., Feb. 21, 1934; s. Alfred and Gertrude Blasband; m. Francie Alexander, May 28, 1994; children: Katherine, Jane Feldman. BA, Cornell U., Ithaca, NY, 1955; LLB, U. Pa., Phila., 1958. Bar: NY 1962, US Supreme Ct. 1990. Ptnr. Deutsch Klagsbrun & Blasband, NYC, 1963—2001, McLaughlin & Stern LLP, NYC, 2001—. Vis. lectr. copyright law Cardoza Law Sch., NYC, 2000—06. Trustee Trisha Brown Dance Co., NYC; gen. counsel Hebrew Hosp. Home, New York, Pa., 1976—2006. Recipient Client Svc. All Star award, BTI Consulting Group, 2006. Mem.: NYC Bar Assn., Am. Bar Assn. Office: McLaughlin & Stern LLP 260 Madison Ave New York NY 10016 Office Phone: 212-448-1100. Business E-Mail: dblasband@mclaughlinstern.com.

BLASCHKE, LAWRENCE RAYMOND, electronic security services professional; b. Elgin, Ill., Feb. 24, 1950; s. Raymond Otto and Margaret Irma (Palm) B.; m. Diane Charlotte Hartwell, Apr. 12, 1974 (dec. 1986); children: Matthew Robert, Bryan Raymond; m. Karen Juliann Larson, Feb. 14, 1987 (dec. Aug. 1993); m. Terry Leigh, July 29, 1995. AS, William Rainey Harper Coll., Palatine, Ill., 1973; student, Valparaiso U., Ind., 1974—. Cert. power engr., Ind.; registered elec. maintenance Am. Coun. on Edn. Audio visual technician multi-media systems William Rainey Harper Coll., Palatine, Ill., 1970-71; jr. engr., then assoc. engr. No. Ind. Pub. Svc. Co., Hobart, 1974-79, dist. engr., 1979-84, project engr., 1984-87, Gary, 1987-92, project engr. level III Merrillville, 1992-93, spl. projects engr. level III, 1994, project leader product strategic planning, 1994-96; dispatcher power sys. and utility svcs. dept. mgmt. supr. Bethlehem Steel Corp., Burns Harbor Divsn., Chesterton, Ind., 1996—2003; customer svc. rep. Cedar Lake br. Grand Rapids Sash & Door, Ind., 2003—04, small bus. sales rep. Ind., 2006; core comml. sales rep. Valparaiso br. ADT Security Svcs. Inc. divsn. Tyco Internat., Valparaiso, 2004—06; ptnr., v.p., CFO, treas., regional sales mgr., dir. human resources Independence Sound & Security Inc., Valparaiso, Ind., 2005—. Co-owner, pres. TL Spectrum, Valparaiso, 2001—. Chmn. bd. social ministry Immanuel Luth. Ch., Valparaiso, 1983-84, sec. bd. evangelism, 1981-83, asst. Sunday sch. supt., 1984-85; cubmaster Boy Scouts Am., Valparaiso area, 1984-88, merit badge counselor, 1992—, asst. scoutmaster, 1992-95, com. mem., 1992-95, co-chmn. Dunes Moraine dist. advancement com., 1996-97, chmn. advancement com., 1996-97, mem. bd. rev., 1995-97; supervisory com. No. Ind. Fed. Credit Union, 1996-99, chmn., 1987-88, 90-96; treas. Montessori Sch. Porter County, 1981-83; bldgs. and grounds co-supt., 1983-84; sec.-treas. Quality Devel., Inc., 1990-93; active Nat. Arbor Day Found., 1992-99; jr. varsity adult leader Awana Club, Christ Cmty. Ch., Hobart, Ind., welcome team, usher, 1992-98; pres. Hobart Pub. Svc. Club, 1979-81; active Project Teach, 1992-96; loaned exec. Lake Area United Way, 2003-04; mem. coun. Nat. Assn. Home Builders Remodelers; edn. com. and county coun. North Porter, 2007-. Recipient Edward A. Filene award Ind. Credit Union League and Credit Union Nat. Assn., Inc., 1991. Mem.: IEEE-Stds. Assn., IEEE (sr.; power soc. chmn. Calumet sect. 2002—), Nat. Assn. Home Builders (remodelers coun. 2007—), Greater Portage Area C. of C., Merrillville C. of C. (econ. devel. com., edn. com., amb. 2005—07), Porter County Builders Assn. (edn. com., remodelers coun.), Assn. Energy Engrs., Nat. Trust Hist. Preservation, Smithsonian Instn., Nat. Pks. and Conservation Assn., Ind. Sheriffs Assn. (assoc.), Consumers Union (life), Wilderness Soc., Handyman Club Am. (life; adv. coun. 2005, 2006, 2007). Republican. Avocations: computers, stereo audio equipment and recording, woodworking, electronics. Home: 396 W Southfield Ln Valparaiso IN 46385-9633 Office: Independence Sound & Security Inc 786 N McCool Rd Ste 5 Valparaiso IN 46385 Office Phone: 219-759-4200. Office Fax: 219-759-4300. Personal E-mail: lrbtlb@yahoo.com.

BLASE, ANTHONY IDOMENEUS, retired electronics executive, writer, poet; b. Chgo., July 30, 1929; s. Nicholas George and Tousa Marie Blase; m. Aspacia Mary Manos, Aug. 31, 1952; children: Mary Kadie Burgner, Nicolette Stephane Young. BSBA, Loyola U., Chgo., 1955. Lic. gen. ins. broker Ill.; real estate broker Ill. Contr. Universal Wire and Cable Co., Chgo., 1958—64; v.p., contr. Rockola Mfg. Corp., Chgo., 1964—78; exec. v.p., treas., CFO, Wells-Gardner Electronics, Chgo., 1978—88, also bd. dirs. Author: In Search of Alexander, 1990, Contemplating Forms, 1989, Thus the Gods Taught Man, 1991, On Moral Purpose, 1992, Byzantium, 1992, Religious Paradigm?, 1993, Vessels Without Dimension, 1994, The Ultimate Comprehension, 1995, The History of Western Philosophy, 1996, The Universal Will, 1997, Historical Essays, 1998, Embracing the Universe, 1998, But Grain of Sand, 1999, The Etaireia, 1999, Uncompromising Nature, 2000, As I Understand Aristotle, 2000, Hellenism in the Post Classical World, 2001, Idomenian Ethics, 2002, From Acorn to Oak--Princip to Ground Zero, 2003, The Unlosable Wager, 2003, Unscripted Shadows, 2004, The Ideal Concept, 2004, Eternal Recurrence, 2004, Of Cardinal Virtues, 2004, Criterion of Truth, 2005, Analogous to Man, 2005, The Glow of Words in all their Prism, 2005, Philosophic Edicts, 2005, Of Laurels Bright, 2005;: Of Wreaths and Thorns, 2005, A Nation Keens, 2005, Unjeweled Crown, 2005, Twilight's Smold'ring Embers, 2005, A Lightning's Bolt, 2005, A Leapt Relief, 2005, A Depth Unknown, 2005, A Harvest's Glean, 2005, Ontology's Demand, 2005, Time in Space, 2005, Orphaned World, 2005, Affectation's Deceypt, 2005, Credulity in Crept, 2005, Surgical Precision, 2005, A Mind Distilled, 2005, A Heart Fulfilled, 2005, To Fate's Unknow, 2005, A Meadow Lark, 2005, A Sonrous Hark, 2006, A Book to Mark, 2006, Climactic Clime, 2006, Sieving Mind, 2006, Pandemics Rise, 2006, Charting the Theogonies, 2006;: The Whirlwind Creeps, 2006, Kinder, Gentler Thoughts, 2006, Realities Apprise, 2006, A Promise Bid, 2006, In Darkness Hid, 2006, A Horror's Rid, 2006, A Future's Hid, 2006, Of Ages Tolled, 2006, Beauty Compromised, 2006, Silver Lining Blurred, 2006, Confounded World, 2007, A Martyr's Crown, 2007, A Mount to Climb, 2007, A Sights Behold, 2007, Collective Consciousness, 2007, Warfare's Scourge, 2007, Avoiding the Apocalypse, 2007, Our Daily Bread, 2007, Historical Behold, 2007, Universal Greet, 2007. Cpl. US Army, 1948—50. Avocation: world travel. Home: 3011 Applegate Ln Glenview IL 60025 Personal E-mail: tekanis5@aol.com.

BLASER, BROCK CAMERON, agronomist; s. Greg Ernest and Kira Archer Blaser; m. Jessica Williams Blaser, June 22, 2002; children: Davis Kiralyn, Duke Gregory. BS, Brigham Young U., Provo, Utah, 2002; MS, Iowa State U., Ames, 2003. Grad. tchg. asst. Iowa State U., Ames, 2003—. Leader various orgns. Ch. Jesus Christ of Latter-day Saints, Ames, Iowa. Mem.: Gamma Sigma Delta, N.Am. Colls. and Tchrs. Agr., Am. Soc.

Agronomy, Crop Sci. Soc. Am., ISU Agronomy Club. Office: Iowa State Univ Agronomy Hall Ames IA 50010-1010 Office Phone: 515-294-2230. Business E-Mail: blaserb@iastate.edu.

BLASER, MARTIN JACK, medical educator, researcher; b. NYC, Dec. 18, 1948; s. Frederick S. and Irene J. Blaser; m. Ronna W. Blaser, Sept. 3, 1979; children: Daniel, Genia, Simone. BA, U. Pa., 1969; MD, NYU, 1973. Cert. Nat. Bd. Med. Examiners. Intern in medicine U. Colo., Denver, 1973-74, resident in medicine, 1974-77, fellow in infectious diseases, 1977-79, from asst. prof. medicine to assoc. prof. medicine, 1981-89; Epidemic Intelligence Svc. officer Ctrs. for Disease Control, Atlanta, 1979-81; Scoville prof. Vanderbilt U., Nashville, 1989-2000; Frederick H. King prof. and chmn. dept. medicine NYU, NYC, 2000—, prof. dept. microbiology, 2000—. Chair bacteriology study sect. NIH, Bethesda, 1994; guest investigator Rockefeller U., N.Y.C., 1987-88; invited prof. Inst. Pasteur, Paris, 1991, 92, 94, 96; v.p. Enteric Rsch. Lab., Inc., NY, 1988—; bd. sci. counselors, Nat. Cancer Inst., 2005-; spkr. in field. Editor: (book) Infections of the GI Tract, 1995, 2003; holder 22 U.S. patents for bacterial products. Recipient Young Investigator award West Soc. Clin. Investigation, 1989, Am. Assn. Cancer Rsch. ACS award cancer epidemiology, 2003. Master ACP, APHA (Wade Hampton Frost award 2001); fellow Infectious Disease Soc. Am. (councillor 1993-96, v.p. 2003, pres.-elect 2004, pres. 2005, Squibb award 1992), Am. Epidemiol. Soc., Am. Acad. Microbiology; mem. Am. Bd. Internal Medicine (mem. subsplty. bd. infectious disease 1996-02), Assn. Am. Physicians, Am. Soc. Clin. Investigation, Am. Clin. Climat Assn., Interurban Club. Avocations: hiking, Go. Office: Bellevue A606 Adminstrn NYU Sch Medicine 550 1st Ave New York NY 10016 Business E-Mail: martin.blaser@med.nyu.edu.

BLASI, ALBERTO, Romance languages educator, writer; b. Buenos Aires, Jan. 21, 1931; s. Alberto B. and Emma (Raffo) B. Diploma en Letras, U. Buenos Aires, 1957, Licenciado en Letras, 1965; D. Letras, U. La Plata, 1976; postgrad. (fellow), U. Iowa, 1975. Sr. lectr. U. Buenos Aires, 1965-69; prof. U. Rosario, Argentina, 1969-73; vis. writer U. Iowa, 1974-75; assoc. prof. Spanish Bklyn. Coll., CUNY, 1975-79, prof. modern langs, 1979—; prof. Spanish CUNY Grad. Sch., 1979—. Author: Los Fundadores, 1962, Introducción a Lucio López, 1965, La tarea del cuento en Fin de Siglo, 1968, Güiraldes y Larbaud: Una amistad creadora, 1970, Manuel Podestá, 1982, La luna del cazador, 2002; editor: La gran aldea, 1965, Fin de Siglo, 1968, Essays on Lucio Victorio Mansilla, 1981, Movimientos literarios del siglo XX en Iberoamérica: Teoría y práctica, 1982, Don Segundo Sombra, 1983, 2d edit., 1996; contbr. articles to profl. jours. Recipient French Govt. award, Bourse de Marque, 1972, Argentine Writers Soc. Book award, 1960, CUNY rsch. award, 1980—83, 1999—2000, Argentine Found. for the Arts award, 1966, 1969, Municipality of Buenos Aires Book award, 1967. Mem. PEN Club Internat., Internat. Assn. Hispanists, Internat. Comparative Lit. Assn. Office: CUNY Bklyn Coll Dept Modern Langs Brooklyn NY 11210

BLASIER, COLE, political scientist; s. Stewart Parnell and Helen (Cole) B.; m. Martha Hiett; children: Peter Cole, Holly. AB, U. Ill.; postgrad., U. Mex.; AM, Columbia U., cert. Russian Inst., PhD in Polit. Sci., 1955. Career fgn. svc. officer U.S. Dept. State, Belgrade, Yugoslavia, 1951-54, Bonn, Federal Republic of Germany, 1954-57, Washington, 1957-60, Moscow, 1958; exec. asst. to pres., sec. bd. trustees Colgate U., Hamilton, NY, 1960—63; prof. polit. sci. U. Pitts., 1964-88; chief hispanic div. Libr. Congress, Washington, 1988-93; sr. rsch. assoc. North-South Ctr. U. Miami, Coral Gables, Fla., 1993-95. Dir. ctr. Latin Am. studies U. Pitts., 1964-74; adv. bd. Handbook Latin Am. Studies, 1972-88; exchange scholar Polish Inst. Internat. Affairs, Warsaw, Poland, 1978, Inst. Latin Am., Moscow, 1979; U.S. chmn. U.S./USSR Exch. in Latin Am. Studies, 1980-86; mgmt. cons. project to revive ancient libr., Alexandria, Egypt, 1993; Far Ea. State U., Vladivostok, Russia, 1999; adj. prof. Georgetown U., 1993-94; field work in Russia and Germany, 1996-2000; cons. in field. Author: The Hovering Giant, U.S. Responses to Revolutionary Change in Latin America, 1976, rev., 1985, The Giant's Rival, The USSR and Latin America, 1983, rev., 1987, Cuba in the World, 1979, The End of the Soviet-Cuban Partnership, Cuba After the Cold War, 1993, Russia's Institute of Europe, 1996, Electing Putin Po-Tartarski, 2000, Soviet Impact on Latin America, 2002; editor U. Pitts. Press Latin Am. series, 1968-91. Pres. UN Assn. Pitts., 1985. Lt. (j.g.) USNR, PTO, 1943-46. Fellow Rotary Santiago Chile 1947-48, Kennan Inst. Woodrow Wilson Ctr., 1978, Fulbright, Buenos Aires, Argentina, 1986, Heinz Endowment, 1988; Rockefeller Found. grantee, Cali, Colombia, 1963-64; decorated Knighthood of Isabel la Catolica (Spain), 1993. Mem. Lat. Am. Studies Assn. (pres. 1986-87), Am. Polit. Sci. Assn., Am. Fgn. Svc. Assn., Diplomatic and Consular Officers Ret., Washington Inst. for Fgn. Affairs, Cosmos Club. Home: 10450 Lottsford Rd #5009 Mitchellville MD 20721

BLASIER, ROBERT DALTON, JR., lawyer; b. Pitts., Feb. 27, 1945; s. Robert D. Blasier Sr.; m. Charlotte M. Blasier, Aug. 17, 1990; children: Matthew, Elizabeth. BS, Carnegie Inst. Tech., Pitts., 1967; JD, Harvard U., 1970. Bar: Calif 1971. Dep. dist. atty. Contra Costa County Office, Martinez, Calif., 1970-78; dir. enforcement Calif. Fair Polit. Practices Commn., Sacramento, 1978-84; prv. practice El Dorado Hills, Calif. State Bar Calif. Avocations: golf, sailing. Office: 3600 Peidra Montana Rd El Dorado Hills CA 95762-9405 Office Phone: 916-933-7289. Office Fax: 916-933-7452. E-mail: bobblasier@aol.com.*

BLASING, MUTLU KONUK, English language educator; b. Istanbul, Turkey, June 27, 1944; arrived in U.S., 1963; d. Mustafa Celal Konuk and Muzeyyen (Uzun) Dursunoglu; m. Randolph Charles Blasing, Aug. 21, 1965; 1 child, John Konuk. Student, Carleton Coll., 1963-65; BA, Coll. William and Mary, 1969; PhD, Brown U., 1974. Lectr. English U. Mass., 1974-76; asst. prof. Pomona Coll., Claremont, Calif., 1977-79, Brown U., Providence, 1979-83, assoc. prof., 1983-88, prof. English dept., 1988—. Dir. Copper Beech Press, Providence. Author: The Art of Life, 1977, American Poetry: The Rhetoric of Its Forms, 1987, Politics and Form in Postmodern Poetry, 1995, Lyric Poetry: The Pain and the Pleasure of Words, 2007; translator: Epic of Sheik Bedreddin (Nazim Hikmet), 1975, Things I Didn't Know I Loved (Nazim Hikmet), 1975, Human Landscapes (Nazim Hikmet), 1982, Rubaiyat (Nazim Hikmet), 1985, Selected Poetry (Nazim Hikmet), 1986, Poems of Nazim Hikmet, 1994, 02, Human Landscapes from My Country (Nazim Hikmet), 2002. Fellow, U. Mass., 1974—76. Office: Brown U English Dept PO Box 1852 Providence RI 02912-1852 Home Phone: 401-351-1253; Office Phone: 401-863-3744. Business E-Mail: mutlu_blasing@brown.edu.

BLASIOTTI, ROBERT VINCENT, accountant, consultant; b. Phila., Nov. 15, 1949; s. Vincent Mario Blasiotti and Hilda (Romani) Greer; m. Katheryn Phyllis Ombres, Dec. 15, 1973 (div. Apr. 1982); m. Gilda Maria Cipriani, June 17, 1988; children: Gabriella, Robert Jr. BS, Pa. State U., 1971, MBA, 1973. CPA, Pa. Jr. acct. Goldenberg, Rosenthal & Co., Phila., 1971-73, sr. acct., 1973-75; mgr. acctg. Gross & Co., Jenkintown, Pa., 1975-77; owner Blasiotti & Co. CPAs, West Chester, Pa., 1977—. CPA, advisor Big Bros. Chester County, West Chester, 1985—; cons. Presdl. Adv. Coun., 1984; fin. advisor Exton Sq. Mall Merchants Assn., 1978-89; bd. advisors Med-Trans, Inc., 1982-84. Mem. Big Bros.-Big Sisters Chester County, 1978—, PSPA (SE chpt.), 2006—; trustee Rep. Presdl. Task Force, 1982—; mem. coun. St. Maximilian Kolby Ch., 1994-97; bd. advisors Our Lady's Missionaries of Eucharist, 1999—; treas. Boy Scouts Am. Pack 153, 1999-2002; Pa. chmn. Congressional Bus. Adv. Coun., 2003—. Served from 2d lt. to capt. U.S. Army, 1971-79. Mem. C. of C., PSU Alumni Assn. (life), Jaycees (chmn. 1980-84), Italian Social Club (fin. sec. 1992-96), KC (treas. 1994, dep. grand knight 1995, grand knight 1996, trustee 1997-99), Lions (treas. 1980-81), Men of Malvern. Roman Catholic. Avocations: stamp collecting/philately, numismatology, golf, horticulture, fishing. Office: Blasiotti & Co CPAs Ste 108 882 S Matlack St West Chester PA 19382 Office Phone: 610-436-8686. E-mail: bblasiotti@earthlink.net.

BLASKE, NATHAN H., lawyer; b. Louisville, July 1, 1978; BBA, U. Ky., 2000; JD, Salmon P. Chase Coll. of Law, 2003. Bar: Ohio 2003, US Dist. Ct. Southern Dist. Ohio 2003, Ky. 2004, Ind. 2004, US Dist. Ct. Northern Dist. Ind. 2004, US Dist. Ct. Southern Dist. Ind. 2004, US Dist. of Appeals Sixth Cir. 2004. Assoc. Wood & Lamping, L.L.P., Cin. Named one of Ohio's Rising Stars, Super Lawyers, 2006. Mem.: Ky. Bar Assn., Ind. State Bar Assn., Ohio State Bar Assn., Cin. Bar Assn., ABA. Office: Wood & Lamping LLC 600 Vine St Ste 2500 Cincinnati OH 45202-2491 Office Phone: 513-852-6000. Office Fax: 513-852-6087.

BLASKO, BARBARA ANN, secondary school educator; b. Pitts., Nov. 17, 1957; d. Roy Edward and Shirley Marie Newbould; m. Robert Stephen Blasko, Jr., Aug. 4, 1990. BS in Secondary Edn. Biology, Calif. U., Pa., 1979, BS in Earth Sci., 1985, EdM in Guidance Counseling, 1995. 8th grade sci. tchr. Bethel Park Schs., Pitts., 1979—80; HS tchr. Bentworth Schs., Bentleyville, Pa., 1980—. Jr. class sponsor, advisor Bentworth Sch. Dist., Bentleyville, Pa., 1982—, advisor, sponsor student coun., 1985—89, counselor student assistance team, 1993—, co-dir. HS musicals, 2002—. Worthy advisor, grand officer Order of Rainbow, Pitts., 1970—88, grand officer; coord. blood drive ARC, Mon Valley, Pa., 1982—94; coord., vol. Am. Cancer Soc., Washington County, Pa., 1984—; treas. Sunday sch., mem. adult choir Concord Presbyn. Ch., 1977—79; deacon First Presbyn. Ch., California, 1988—, moderator, 1992—95. Recipient Grand Cross award for svc., Internat. Order of Rainbow, 1974—77, Second Pl. Donors award, ARC, 1985—93; grantee, Sci. in Medieval Times Consortium, 1997—99. Mem.: Bentworth Edn. Assn. (treas., rep.), Pa. State Tchrs. Assn., Nat. Tchrs. Assn., Friends Nat. Park, Nat. Air Disaster Support League (life), Order of Eastern Star, Alpha Xi Delta (pres., treas. 1976—79). Avocations: walking, forensics, swimming, crafts, singing. Home: 1961 Rostraver Rd Belle Vernon PA 15012 Office: Bentworth Sch Dist 75 Bearcat Dr Bentleyville PA 15314 Business E-Mail: bblasko@bentworth.k12.pa.us.

BLASS, JOHN PAUL, physician, biochemist; b. Vienna, Feb. 21, 1937; arrived in U.S., 1938; s. Gustaf and Jolan (Wirth) B.; m. Birgit Annelise Knudsen, Dec. 20, 1960; children: Charles, Lisa. AB summa cum laude, Harvard U., 1958; PhD, U. London, 1960; MD, Columbia U., 1965. Postdoctoral fellow Am. Cancer Soc., Columbia U., 1962-63; intern Mass. Gen. Hosp., Boston, 1965-66, resident in medicine, 1966-67; research assoc. Nat. Heart and Lung Inst., Bethesda, Md., 1967-70; asst. prof. psychiatry and biol. chemistry UCLA, 1970-76, assoc. prof., 1976-78; mem. staff UCLA Hosps. Clinics, 1970-78; Winifred Masterson Burke prof. neurology, prof. medicine Cornell U. Med. Center, 1978—2005, prof. emeritus, 2005—. Attending neurologist N.Y. Hosp.; mem. NBS-1 rev. com. NIH, 1981-84; councilor Nat. Inst. Aging, 1986-89; chmn. Nat. Adv. Panel on Alzheimers's Disease U.S. Congress, 1987-91, mem., 1993-96. Jour. Neurochemistry, 1981—86, Neurochem. Rsch., 1984—86, Neurochem. Pathology, Neurobiol. Aging, Jour. Neurol. Sci., 1990—2000, Jour. Molecular Neurosci., 1999—, assoc. editor Jour. Am. Geriatric Soc., 1982—87, Age, 1993—95, Yearbook of Neurology and Neurosurgery, 1992—; co-editor: Caring for Alzheimer's Patients, 1990—, Familial Alzheimer's Disease, 1989—, Treatment of Alzheimer's Disease, 1989—, Principles of Geriatrics and Gerontology, 2d edit., 1990—, Principles of Geriatrics and Gerontology, 3d edit., 1994—, Principles of Geriatrics and Gerontology, 4th edit., 1998—, Concise Clinical Pharmacology: LNS Therapeautics, 2006; contbr. articles to profl. jours. Mem. sci. adv. bd. Will Rogers Inst., 1981-97, Allied Signal Aging Award Com., 1993-95. Served as asst. surgeon USPHS, 1967-70. Marshall scholar, 1958-60. Mem. Soc. Neurosci. (chmn. social issues com.), Biochem. Soc., Am. Soc. Biol. Chemists, Am. Soc. Neurochemistry (council, chmn. public policy com.), Internat. Soc. Neurochemistry (council, chmn. clin. com.), Am. Soc. Clin. Investigation, Am. Geriatrics Soc., Am. Fedn. Aging Rsch. (v.p., chmn. research com. 1982-87, pres. 1994-96), Assn. Alzheimers and Related Disease (sci. adv. bd. 1982-86), Am. Chem. Soc., Phi Beta Kappa, Sigma Xi, Alpha Omega Alpha. Jewish. Office: Burke Med Rsch Inst 785 Mamaroneck Ave White Plains NY 10605-2523 Home: 93 Mercer St Apt 3E New York NY 10012 Office Phone: 914-597-2351. Personal E-mail: jpblass@yahoo.com. Business E-Mail: jpblass@mail.med.cornell.edu.

BLASS, WALTER PAUL, management consultant, educator; b. Dinslaken, Germany, Mar. 31, 1930; s. Richard B. and Malvi (Rosenblatt) B.; m. Janice L. Minott, Apr. 2, 1954; children: Kathryn, Christopher, Gregory. BA, Swarthmore Coll., 1951; postgrad., Princeton U., 1951-52; MA, Columbia U., 1953. Asst. Laos and Cambodia desk officer ICA, Wash., 1957—58; gen. mgr. R.B. Blass Co., Deal, NJ, 1958—61; economist AT&T, NYC, 1961—65; country dir. Peace Corps, Afghanistan, 1966—68; asst. v.p. revenue requirement studies NY Telephone Co., NYC, 1968—70; dir. corp. planning AT&T, 1970—82, dir. strategic planning, 1982—85; ret., 1985—. Pres., Strategic Plans, Unltd., Warren, N.J., 1985—. Exec. Fellow-in-Residence Martino Grad. Sch. Bus. Adminstrn., Fordham U., N.Y.C., 1986-90; cons. McKinsey & Co., Telecom. Authority Ireland, McDonnell Douglas, Heller Fin., Inc.; lectr. in field; vis. prof. U. Grenoble, France, 1988, Ecole Superieure de Commerce, Chambery and Grenoble, France, 1989-2005; trustee Guilford Coll., 1975—, chmn. planning com., 1992-99, vice chmn. acad. affairs com., 1999—. Co-author: The Strategic Planning Handbook, 1982, Handbook of Strategic Planning, 1986. Lt., j.g., USNR, 1953-56, Woodrow Wilson Found., sr. fell., 1974-85. Mem., NY Acad. Scis., Soc. Values in Higher Edn. (dir. 1983-86, 2005—), Am. Econ. Assn., Nat. Assn. Bus. Economists, The Planning Forum (bd. dirs. 1972), Royal Econ. Soc. Home and Office: 6 Casale Dr Warren NJ 07059-6703 Office Phone: 908-647-5769.

BLASSBERG, FRANCI J., lawyer; b. Sept. 28, 1953; m. Joseph Rice III, 1991. BA, Cornell U., 1975, JD magna cum laude, 1977. Bar: NY 1978. Ptnr., co-head Private Equity Group, mem. Mgmt. Com. Debevoise & Plimpton LLP, NYC. Editor-in-chief Debevoise & Plimpton Private Equity Report; co-editor: The Debevoise & Plimpton European Private Equity Handbook, 2004. Bd. trustees Cornell U., NY City Ballet, New Sch. U. Named a Dealmaker of the Yr., Am. Lawyer mag., 2006; named one of 100 Most Influential Lawyers, Nat. Law Jour., 2006, The 50 Most Influential Women Lawyers in Am., 2007, 30 most influential lawyers in global private equity, Private Equity Internat. Mem.: NY County Lawyers Assn., Assn. Bar of City of NY (mem., com. on corp. law 1985—89). Office: Debevoise & Plimpton LLP 919 Third Ave New York NY 10022 Office Phone: 212-909-6531. Business E-Mail: fjblassberg@debevoise.com.*

BLASZKIEWICZ, DAVID, investment company executive; b. 1968; Dir. fin. Detroit Renaissance, 1994, sec., treasurer; pres. Detroit Investment Fund. Mgmt. and loan com. Lower Woodland Housing Fund; works with Real Estate Assistance Fund, Woodward Corridor Devel. Fund; bd. mem. Detroit Cmty. Loan Fund, Wayne State U. Rsch. and Tech. Park, Mich. Magnet Loan Fund, Detroit Downtown Devel. Authority. Named one of 40 Under 40, Crain's Detroit Bus., 2006. Office: Detroit Investment Fund 600 Renaissance Ctr Ste 1710 Detroit MI 48243 Office Phone: 313-259-6368. Office Fax: 313-259-6393.

BLATT, GREGORY R., lawyer; BA, Colgate U.; JD, Columbia U. Assoc. Wachtell, Lipton, Rosen & Katz, Grubman, Indursky & Schindler; exec. v.p. bus. affairs, gen. counsel, sec. Martha Stewart Living Omnimedia Inc.; sr. v.p., gen. counsel, sec. IAC/InterActiveCorp., 2003—05, exec. v.p., gen. counsel, sec., 2005—.

BLATT, MORTON BERNARD, medical illustrator; b. Chgo., Jan. 9, 1923; s. Arthur E. and Hazel B. Blatt. Attended, Ctrl. YMCA Coll., 1940—42, U. Ill., 1943—46. Tchr. Ray-Vogue Art Schs., Chgo., 1946—51; med. illustrator VA Ctr., Wood, Wis., 1951—57, Swedish Covenant Hosp., Chgo., 1957—76. Med. illustrator Laidlaw Bros., River Forest, Ill., 1956—59, cons., artist health textbooks, 1956—59; illustrator Standard Edn. Soc., Chgo., 1960; art editor Covenant Companion, 1958—82, Covenant Home Altar, 1972—83. Atlas and Demonstration Technique of the Central Nervous System, numerous med. jours., Covenant Hymnal, books, record jackets. With USAAF, 1943—44. Mem.: Art Inst. Chgo., Chgo. Press Club. Address: 373 Eliseo Dr Greenbrae CA 94904-1326

BLATT, SIDNEY JULES, psychology professor, psychoanalyst, investigator; b. Phila., Oct. 15, 1928; s. Harry and Fannie (Feld) Blatt; m. Ethel Shames, Feb. 1, 1951; children: Susan, Judith, David. BS, Pa. State U., 1950, MS, 1952; PhD, U. Chgo., 1957; postgrad., Western New Eng. Inst. for Psychoanalysis, 1972. Postdoctoral fellow Neuropsychiat. Inst. of U. Ill. Med. Ctr., Psychiat. and Psychosomatic Inst. of Michael Reese Hosp., 1957—59; instr. Univ. Coll. U. Chgo., 1959-60; mem. faculty Yale U., New Haven, 1960—, prof. psychology and psychiatry, 1974—; mem. faculty Western New Eng. Inst. for Psychoanalysis, 1975—, Sigmund Freud prof. psychoanalysis, 1988—89. Ayala and Sam Zacks prof. art history Hebrew U., 1988—89; Fulbright sr. rsch. fellow, 1988—89; mem. Rsch. Fellowship Rev. Panel NIMH, 1966—69, mem. Psychology Tng. Rev. Panel, 1969—74; vis. prof. Ben Guron U., 1992, 96, Univ. Coll., London, 1999—2003, Cath. U. Leuven, 2003, George Washington U., 2006, Bar Ilan U.; Fulbright sr. specialist, 2006—. Author: Experiences of Depression: Theoretical, Research and Clinical Perspectives, 2004; co-author (with J. Allison and C. Zimet): Interpretation of Psychological Tests, 1968, Interpretation of Psychological Tests, 2d edit., 1988; co-author: (with C.M. Wild) Schizophrenia: A Developmental Analysis, 1976; co-author: (with E.S. Blatt) Continuity and Change in Art: The Development of Modes of Representation, 1984; co-author: (with R.Q. Ford) Therapeutic Change: An Object Relations Perspective, 1994; editor (with D. Diamond): Attachment Research and Psychoanalysis, vols. I-III, 1999—2003; co-editor (with Z.V. Segal): The Self in Emotional Distress, 1993; co-editor: (with J. Corveleyn, P. Luyten) The Theory and Treatment of Depression: Towards a Dynamic Interaction Model.; co-editor: (with D. Diamond & J. Lichtenberg) Attachment and Sexuality. Named Disting. Practitioner of Psychology, Nat. Acad. Practice, 1983; recipient Disting. Contbns. to Rsch. award, Assn. Med. Sch. Profs. Psychology and APA Divsn. Psychoanalysis, 2000, Founders' Disting. Tchg. prize, We. New Eng. Psychoanalytic Soc., 2001, Hans H. Strupp Disting. Contbns. to Psychoanalysis award, 2000, Bruno Klopfer and Marguerite R. Hertz awards for dist. contbns. to psychol. assessment, Soc. for Personality Assessment, 1989, 1994, Disting. Sci. Contbns. award, APA Divsn. Clin. Psychology, 2004, Otto Weininger award, Can. Psychol. Assn., 2006; fellow Found. Fund Rsch. in Psychiatry, 1961—64. Mem.: AAUP, AAAS, APA, Soc. Personality Assessment (pres. 1984—86), Am. Psychoanalytic Assn. (Outstanding Sci. Paper prize 2005, Mary S. Sigourney award 2006). Office: Yale Univ 300 George St Ste 901 New Haven CT 06511 Home Phone: 203-397-0167; Office Phone: 203-785-2090. Business E-Mail: sidney.blatt@yale.edu.

BLATTER, FRANK EDWARD, travel company executive; b. Denver, Jan. 9, 1939; s. Anthony John and Irene Marie (Tobin) B.; m. Barbara E. Drieth, Sept. 6, 1959; children: Dean Robert, Lisa Kay Faircloth, Paul Kelly. BS, Regis U., Denver, 1961; grad., Colo. Sch. Banking, 1966, Sch. Bank Adminstrn., 1973. CPA, Colo. Acct. McMahon, Maddox & Rodriguez CPAs, Denver, 1960-63, United Bank Denver, 1963-65; with United Banks Colo., Inc., Denver, 1965-86; pres. Cath. Cmty. Svcs., Denver, 1987, Premiere Travel and Cruises, Denver, 1988—. Mem. nat. adv. coun. and devel. com., chmn. ann. funds coun. Regis U.; chmn. adv. coun. Camp Santa Maria; crusade chmn. Am. Cancer Soc., Denver. Mem. AICPA, Tax Execs. Inst. (past pres. Denver), Colo. Soc. CPAs, Fin. Execs. Inst. (dir.), Bank Adminstrn. Inst. (dir.), Arrowhead Golf Club. Roman Catholic. Office: 3900 S Wadsworth Blvd Ste 475 Denver CO 80235-2207

BLATTNER, WILLIAM ALBERT, physician, epidemiology researcher; b. St. Louis, Oct. 16, 1943; s. Russell John and Marian Edith (Koeneke) B.; m. Diane Mach, Dec. 27, 1974; chidlren: Michael and Mary (twins), John, Matthew, Timothy. AB, Wash. U., 1966, MD, 1970. Diplomate Am. Bd. Internal Medicine, Am. Bd. Med. Oncology. Intern Strong Meml. Hosp., NYC, 1970-71, asst. resident internal medicine, 1971-72; assoc. resident, asst. chief resident Sloan-Kettering Meml. Hosp., NYC, 1972-73; staff assoc. Nat. Cancer Inst., Bethesda, Md., 1973-75, clin. investigator, 1975-76, sr. clin. investigator, 1976-81, chief family studies sect., 1981-87, chief viral epidemiology sect., 1987-91, founding chief viral epidemiology br., 1991—95; co-founder, assoc. dir. Inst. Human Virology, U. Md., Balt., 1996—, dir. Epidemiology and Prevention Divsn. Chmn. Balt. City Commn. on HIV/AIDS Prevention and Treatment; elected mem. adv. bd. Internat. AIDS Soc., Washington, 1989; participant 5th annual Russell J. Blattner lecture Tex. Children's Hosp., 1984. Editor: Human Retrovirology HTLV, 1990; co-editor-in-chief: Jour. AIDS, 1987—. Recipient Commendation medal USPHS, 1982, Meritorious Svc. medal, 1988, John Snow Award, Am. Health Assn., 2002. Mem. AAAS, Am. Assn. for Cancer Rsch., Am. Fedn. for Clin. Rsch., Am. Soc. Clin. Oncology, Am. Coll. Epidemiology, Internat. AIDS Soc., Phi Beta Kappa, Alpha Omega Alpha. Office: U Md Inst Human Virology 725 W Lombard St Baltimore MD 21201

BLATZ, KATHLEEN ANNE, former state supreme court justice; BA summa cum laude, U. Notre Dame, 1976; MSW, U. Minn., 1978, JD cum laude, 1984; LHD (hon.), Hamline U., 1999. Psychiat. social worker, 1979—81; mem. Minn. Ho. of Reps., St. Paul, 1979—93, chmn. crime and family law, fin. instns. and ins. coms., 1985—86; judge Dist. Ct., Henne Pin County, 1993—96; justice Minn. Supreme Ct., 1996—98, chief justice, 1998—2005. Asst. minority leader Minn. House of Reps., 1987—90, 1993; dir. employee assistance prog. Fairview Community Hospital, 1979—81; assoc. atty. Popham, Haik, Schnobrich & Kaufman, 1984—88; asst. county atty. Hennepin County Attorney's Office, 1992—93; mem. Health and Human Services Com., Rules and Legislative Administration Com., Judiciary, Gen. Legislation Veterans Affairs and Elections Com., Taxes Com.; chair Nat. Ctr. for State Cts. Rsch. Advisory Council; mem. Conference of Chief Justices; bd. dirs. Riversource Funds, 2006—. Trustee Fairview Southdale Hospital; former mem. Children's Defense Fund Advisory Council, Governor's Task Force on Fetal Alcohol Syndrome; former vice-chair Minn. Supreme Ct. Foster Care and Permanency Task Force; former bd. mem. Big Brothers Big Sisters of Greater Minneapolis. Recipient Women in State Govt. "A Minn. Treasure" award, 27th Annual Women & Bus. Conference Career Achiev. award, 1999, Minn. Women Lawyers Myra Bradwell award, 2002, Minn. Council of Child Caring Agencies Disting. Service award, 2004. Mem.: Minn. State Bar Assn.

BLATZ, LINDA JEANNE, sales manager; d. William Edmund and Jeanne Grace (Hyman) B. BS, U. Md., 1972. Mgr. sales Milliken & Co., NYC, 1972-81; retail market mgr. Greenwood Mills Mktg. Co., NYC, 1981-89; dist. mgr. Steelcase Inc., NYC, 1989-94, tng. cons., 1994-95, tng. mgr., 1995-2000, tng. dir., 2000—03, sales tng. cons., 2003; regional sales mgr. Nat. Bus. Furniture, NYC, 2003—. Contbr. articles to profl. jours. Mem. N.Y.C. Ballet Guild; corr. sec., v.p., pres. PEO; mem. jr. com. N.Y.C. Ballet; v.p. membership, bd. mgrs. exec. com. N.Y. Jr. League (Outstanding Vol. award 1991-92); nominating dir. Assn. Jr. Leagues Internat., 1997, centennial adv. bd., 1999—. Recipient Outstanding Vol. of the Yr. award N.Y. Jr. League, 1992. Mem.: ASTD, AAUW, Am. Woman's Econ. Devel. Corp., N.Y. Women's Agenda, U. Md. Alumni Assn., Cosmopolitan Club,

Nat. Arts Club, East River Rowing Club, Women's City Club N.Y., Alpha Gamma Delta. Congregationalist. Avocations: ballet, aerobic dancing, swimming, reading. Personal E-mail: ljbeje@aol.com.

BLAU, BARRY, marketing professional, financial consultant; b. NYC, Oct. 4, 1927; s. Emanuel B. and Henrietta Marsha (Moses) B.; m. Eileen Diane Lefkowitz, Aug. 28, 1948; children: Shawn, Peter, Emily, Juliet. With Huber Hoge & Sons, NYC, 1952-57, Sullivan, Stauffer, Caldwell & Bayles, 1958-67, O&M Direct Response, 1968-77; founder Blau Mktg. Techs. Group, 1978-98. Mem. Birchwood Country Club. Jewish. Office: Bayberry Assocs No 4 LLC 9 Bayberry Ridge Rd Westport CT 06880-1713 Personal E-mail: barryblau@aol.com.

BLAU, HARVEY RONALD, lawyer, manufacturing executive; b. NYC, Nov. 14, 1935; s. David and Rose (Kuchinsky) B.; m. Arlene Joan Garrett, Mar. 21, 1964; children: Stephanie Elizabeth Kramer, Melissa Karen, Victoria Gayle. AB, NYU, 1957, LLM, 1965; JD, Columbia U., 1961. Bar: N.Y. 1961. Practiced in, NY, 1961—2002; law sec. to U.S. Dist. Judge Cooper So. Dist. N.Y., 1962—63; asst. U.S. atty. So. Dist. N.Y., 1963—66; vice-chmn. Aeroflex Inc., Plainview, NY, 1983—91, chmn., CEO, 1991—; CEO Griffon Corp., Jericho, NY, 1982—. Chmn. Griffon Corp., Aeroflex Corp.; trustee Mt. Sinai Hosp., N.Y. Mayor Village of Old Westbury. Served to capt. JAGC, AUS, 1958-66. Mem. Assn. Bar City of N.Y., Bar Assn. of Nassau County. Home: 125 Wheatley Rd Old Westbury NY 11568-1210 Office: Griffon Corp 100 Jericho Quadrangle Jericho NY 11753-2708

BLAU, HELEN MARGARET, pharmacology educator; b. London, May 8, 1948; (parents Am. citizens); d. George E. and Gertrude Blau; m. David Spiegel, July 25, 1976; children: Daniel Spiegel, Julia Spiegel. BA in Biology, York U., Eng., 1969; MA in Biology, Harvard U., 1970, PhD in Biology, 1975; Doctorate (hon.), U. Nijmegen, Netherlands, 2003. Predoctoral fellow dept. biology Harvard U., Cambridge, Mass., 1969-75; postdoctoral fellow div. med. genetics, dept. biochemistry and biophysics U. Calif., San Francisco, 1975-78; asst. prof. dept. pharmacology Stanford (Calif.) U., 1978-86, assoc. prof. dept. pharmacology, 1986-91, prof. dept. molecular pharmacology, 1991—99, prof. dept. microbiology and immunology, 2002—, chair dept. molecular pharmacology, 1997—2001, dir. gene therapy tech., 1997—, Donald E. and Delia B. Baxter prof., 1999—, dir. Baxter Lab. in Genetic Pharmacology, 2002—. Rolf-Sammet-Fonds vis. prof., U. Frankfurt, 2003; plenary talk on stem cells, Academic des Sci. della France at Pontifical Acad., the Vatican, Modern Biotech. Symposium, 2003; co-chmn. various profl. meetings; spkr. in field. Mem. editorial bd. 14 jours. including Jour. Cell Biology, Somatic Cell Molecular Genetics and Exptl. Cell Rsch., Molecular and Cellular Biology, Genes to Cells, Molecular Therapy; contbr. articles to profl. jours. Mem. ad hoc molecular cytology study sect. NIH, 1987-88; mem. five-yr. planning com genetics and teratology br. NICHHD/NIH, 1989. Recipient Rsch. Career Devel. award NIH, 1984-89, SmithKline & Beecham award, 1989-91, Women in Cell Biology Career Recognition award, 1992, Excellence in Sci. award FASEB, 1999, McKnight Endowment Fund for Neurosci. award, 2001; Mellon Found. faculty fellow, 1979-80, William H. Hume faculty scholar, 1981-84; grantee NIH, NSF, Ellison Med. Found., Muscular Dystrophy Assn., March of Dimes, 1978—; Yvette Mayent-Rothschild fellow for vis. profs. Inst. Curie, Paris, 1995. Fellow AAAS, Havard Overseers; mem. NAS (del. to China 1991), Internat. Soc. Differentiation (pres. 2002-04), Am. Soc. for Cell Biology (nominating com. 1985-86, program com. 1990), Soc. for Devel. Biology (pres. 1994-95), Inst. Medicine (coun. mem.) Nat. Acad. Scis. , Am. Soc. Gene Therapy (bd. dirs. 1999-2002). Avocations: skiing, swimming, hiking, music, theater. Office: Stanford U Sch Medicine 269 Campus Dr CCSR 4215 Stanford CA 94305-5175 Fax: (650) 736-0080. E-mail: hblau@stanford.edu.*

BLAU, MONTE, retired radiology educator; b. NYC, June 17, 1926; s. Samuel and Rose (Cohen) B.; m. Guitta Drimer, June 30, 1946; children: Saul, Hannah. BS in Chemistry, Poly. Inst. Bklyn., 1948; PhD in Phys. Chemistry, U. Wis., 1952. Rsch. chemist Geochronometric Lab., Yale U., 1952-53; with div. neoplastic diseases Montefiore Hosp., NYC, 1953-54; cancer rsch. scientist Roswell Park Meml. Inst., Buffalo, 1954-75; prof., chmn. dept. nuclear medicine SUNY, Buffalo, 1975-83; vis. prof. radiology Harvard Med. Sch., Boston, 1983-90. Mem. USP adv. panel on radiopharms.; chmn. med. adv. com. N.Y. State bur. Radiol. Health; chmn. med. isotopes adv. com. Los Alamos Nat. Lab. Mem. editorial bd. Jour. Nuclear Medicine. With USN, 1944-46. Mem. Soc. Nuclear Medicine (v.p. 1964, pres. 1972), Am. Chem. Soc., Am. Assn. Physicists in Medicine. Home: PO Box 605 South Wellfleet MA 02663-0605

BLAU, ROBERT, editor; BA, SUNY Albany; MA, Columbia U. Assoc. mng. editor Chgo. Tribune, 1998—2004; v.p. & mng. editor Balt. Sun, 2004—. Author: The Cop Shop. Finalist Pulitzer prize, 1997; fellow Nieman fellow, Harvard U., 1997. Office: Baltimore Sun Co 501 N Calvert St PO Box 1377 Baltimore MD 21278 Office Phone: 410-332-6000.*

BLAUFOX, MORTON DONALD, hypertension specialist, nuclear medicine physician, educator; b. NYC, July 19, 1934; s. Emanuel and Elizabeth (Rosenblum) B.; m. Paulette Goldberg, Dec. 20, 1958; children: Laurie Beth, Ellen Ruth, Andrew David. Student, Harvard U., 1952-55; MD, SUNY, 1959; PhD, U. Minn., 1964. Diplomate Am. Bd. Internal Medicine, Am. Bd. Nuc. Medicine (bd. dirs. 1985-91). Intern Jewish Hosp. of Bklyn., NYC, 1959-60; fellow in medicine Mayo Found. Med. Edn. and Rsch., Rochester, Minn., 1960-64; advanced rsch. fellow Am. Heart Assn., 1964-66; rsch. fellow in medicine Harvard Med. Sch., Boston, 1964-66; asst. in medicine and radiology Peter Bent Brigham Hosp., Boston, 1964-66; asst. prof. radiology, also assoc. in medicine Albert Einstein Coll. Medicine, Bronx, NY, 1966-71, dir. sect. nuc. medicine, 1966-76, dir. unified dept., 1976-82, chmn. unified dept., 1982—, assoc. dir. clin. rsch. ctr., 1968-72, assoc. prof. radiology, 1971-76, prof. radiology, 1976—, assoc. prof. medicine, 1972-78, prof. medicine, 1978—; asst. attending physician Bronx Mcpl. Hosp. Ctr., 1966-71, assoc. attending, 1972, attending physician, 1972—; dir. divsn. nuc. medicine Montefiore Med. Ctr., 1976-82, chmn. dept. nuc. medicine, 1982—. Cons. kidney disease control program USPHS, 1967-72; mem. adminstrv. coun. nuc. medicine VA, 1972-73; mem. panel on radiopharms. U.S. Pharmacopeia, 1970-76; mem. hypertension adv. com. N.Y.C. Dept. Health, 1975-76; mem. Am. Bd. Nuc. Medicine, 1984-90; treas. exec. com., 1987-89, chmn., 1990; mem. clin. trials rev. com. Nat. Heart, Lung and Blood Inst., 1988-92, reviewer ready rsch., 1992—; mem. subcom. on non-pharmacologic therapy of Joint Nat. Com. on Detection Evaluation and Treatment of High Blood Pressure, 1991-92; mem. Brookhaven Linac Isotope Producer Users' adv. com. Brookhaven Nat. Lab., 1992-96; mem. internat. liaison com. World Fedn. Nuc. Medicine and Biology, 1992-94; active Coun. Cardiovasc. Radiology, hon. lifetime prof. medicine Shanxi U. Med. Sch., China, 1997; mem. adv. bd. Mobile Med. Mus. Author: An Ear to the Chest: An Illustrated History of the Evaluation of the Stethoscope, 2002; co-author: Blood Pressure Measurement: An Illustrated History, 1998; editor (with others): Seminars in Nuclear Medicine, 1970—; editor: Evaluation of Renal Function and Disease with Radionuclides, 1972—, 2d edit., 1989—, Procs. Internat. Symposium, 1972—, 1975—, 1980—, 1987—, 1990—, PDR for Nuclear Medicine and Radiology, 1971—80, Unilateral Renal Function Studies, 1978; editor: (with others) Secondary Hypertension: Current Diagnosis and Management, 1981; editor: Non-Pharmacologic Therapy of Hypertension, 1987, Newer Diagnostic Methods in Nephrology and Urology, 1986; editl. bd.: Radionuclides in Nephrology, 1980, Jour. Nuclear Medicine, 1973—81, Nephron, Uroradiology, 1978—, Nuclear Medicine Comm., 1979—, Jour. Nuclear Medicine and Allied Sci., 1982, Renal Failure, 1985—89, Am. Jour. Hypertension, 1987—, Current Hypertension Reviews, 2004—; editl. bd. Current Med. Imaging Reviews, 2004, editor-in-chief, 2005; assoc. editor: Garnet's Pediatrics, 1972—, sect. editor for diagnostics and techniques: Current Opinions in Nephrology and Hypertension, 1992—96, contbr.: The Merck Manual, 14th, 15th and 16th edits., 1982—91, Merck Manual Medical Information Home Edit., 1997; contbr. articles to profl. jours. Recipient Edward Nobel Found. award, 1963, Albert Lasker pub. health svc. award, 1980, Lifetime Achievement award Internat. Soc. Radionuclides in Nephro Urology, 2001. Fellow ACP, Am. Nephrology Soc., Am. Coll. Nuc. Physicians, Coun. on High Blood Pressure Rsch., Coun. Cardiovasc. Radiology, N.Y. Acad. Medicine (libr. com. 1985—, chmn. sect. on nuc. medicine 1993-95, chmn. ad hoc com. artifact collection, chmn. history of medicine adv. com. 1995—); mem. AMA, Am. Heart Assn., Am. Physiol. Soc., Am. Fedn. Clin. Rsch., Am. Soc. Hypertension (membership com.), Soc. Nuc. Medicine (pres. Greater N.Y. chpt. 1975-76, chmn. acad. coun. 1976-77, exec. and sci. coms., chmn. publ. com. 1979-82, trustee, Berson-Yalow award 1989), Ind. Soc. Nuc. Medicine, Internat. Soc. Nephrology, Internat. Hypertension Soc., Coun. on High Blood Pressure Rsch. (med. adv. bd.), N.Y. Med. Soc., Am. Nephrology Soc., Med. Collectors Assn. (pres. 1983-2004), Swiss Soc. Nuc. Medicine (hon., corr.), Nat. Atomic Mus. (life), Sigma Xi. Achievements include research in hypertension, renal function and evaluation of renal function with radioisotopes, renal blood flow and renin secretion. Home: 101 Drake Smith Woods Ln Rye NY 10580-4316 Office: Montefiore Med Park 1695A Eastchester Rd Bronx NY 10461-2374 Office Phone: 718-405-8454. Business E-Mail: blaufox@aecom.yu.edu. *My life has been directed toward the acquisition, clarification and dissemination of knowledge in the health sciences. The use of such goals to help train young people embarking on a career, with honesty and integrity, has been a particularly rewarding experience.*

BLAVAT, JERRY (GERALD JOSEPH BLAVAT), television personality, actor; b. Phila., July 3, 1940; s. Louis Blavat and Lucille Capuano; children: Kathi, Geraldine, Stacy, Deserie. Grad. high sch., Phila. Dancer Bandstand TV show, Phila., 1953-55; record promoter Cameo/Parkway Records, Phila., 1956-59; road mgr., mgr. various rock and roll groups including Danny and the Juniors, also Don Rickles, 1957-59; night club performer, live radio show host various clubs, radio stas., Phila., 1959-62; disc jockey radio stations including WCAU, WFIL, WCAM, WPGR, WSSJ, WTKU, WVLT, WPEN, WPAZ, WPEN, WXPN, Phila. and Delaware Valley, 1962—; program dir. Geator Gold Radio Network, Pa. Del., Md., N.J., 1989—. Owner night club Memories, Margate, N.J., 1972—; mem. nominating com. Rock & Roll Hall of Fame, Phila., 1988—; host live radio show on geatorgold.net, 1999—. TV appearances include The Monkees, Mod Squad, Joey Bishop Show, Tonight Show, Mike Douglas Show, Pat Boone Show, Merv Griffin Show; movie appearances include Baby, It's You, 1983, Desperately Seeking Susan, 1985, Cookie, 1989; producer, host TV shows Discophonic Scene, 1965-66, Jerry Blavat Show, 1966-70, On the Air with the Geator, 1991—, Backstage with Blavat, 1992—; co-prodr. Rock Rhythm and Doo Wop series PBS, 1999—; prodr. Legends of Rock, Legends of Soul, Legends of Harmony at Kimmel Regional Performing Arts Ctr., Phila.; prodr. over 30 record albums of collections/anthologies; rec. artist 5 pop singles; contbr. articles, biographies, liner notes to profl. jours., programs and record albums. Bd. dirs., performer Hero Scholarship Fund, Phila., 1963-70; bd. dirs. Police Athletic League, Phila., 1966-70; fundraiser numerous schs., chs., founds., and pub. TV. Recipient U.S. Congl. Horizon award, 2002; inductee Phila. Rock & Roll Hall of Fame, 1986, installed in permanent exhibit Rock and Roll Hall of Fame, Mus. of Radio and Records, 1998, Phila. Music Alliance Walk of Fame, 1993, Broadcast Pioneers of Phila., 2002. Mem. AFTRA, SAG, Am. Guild Variety Artists, Nat. Music Found. (adv. bd. 1989—). Avocations: horseback riding, bicycling, native american history, fitness. Office: Celebrity Showcase PO Box 25010 Philadelphia PA 19147-0210 Office Phone: 215-923-0550. E-mail: geatorgold@yahoo.com.

BLAVATNIK, LEONARD, investment company executive; b. Russia, 1958; married. Grad., Moscow Inst. transport Engring.; MBA, Harvard Univ.; PhD computer sci., Columbia Univ. Mgmt. positions Arthur Anderson & Co., Macy's Dept. Stores, Gen. Atlantic Partners; founder, chmn. Access Industries, NYC, 1986—. Bd. dir. TNK-BP, OAO SUAL, Access Industries (Eurasia), Svenska Bredbandsbolaget AB. Mem. global adv. bd. Ctr. for Internat. Bus. & Mgmt., Cambridge Univ.; mem. bd. Dean's advisors Harvard Bus. Sch.; bd. dir. Eurasia Group, NYC; vice-chmn. Kennan Council Woodrow Wilson Ctr., Washington. Named one of Forbes Richest Americans, 2004—, World's Richest People, Forbes Mag., 2004—. Office: Access Industries 730 Fifth Ave New York NY 10019*

BLAYDES, SOPHIA BOYATZIES, English language educator; b. Rochester, NY, Oct. 16, 1933; d. James George and Helene (Bougdanos) Boyatzies; m. David Fairchild Blaydes, June 4, 1961; children: Stephanie Anne, Jeffrey Glenn. BA, U. Rochester, 1955; MA, Ind. U., 1958, PhD, 1962. Teaching asst. English Ind. U., 1955-62; instr. to asst. prof. Am. Thought and Lang. dept. Mich. State U., 1962-65; instr. to prof. English W.Va. U., Morgantown, 1966-99, chair faculty senate, 1990-91, coord. program for sr. and retired faculty, 1994—; pres. Carolinas Symposium for British Studies, 1990-91. Co-dir. Lit. Discussion Group for Sr. Citizens, 1978—; mem. faculty Elderhostel, 1985, 87, 88, 90, 94; mem. ctrl. exec. com. Folger Inst., 1992-99; chair faculty senate, bd. advisors W.Va. U., 1990-91, rep. to adv. coun. to bd. trustees, 1993-99; state del. to the 1995 White House Conf. on Aging; bd. trustees Univ. Sys., 1998-99, Women in Sci. and Health, Robert C. Byrd Health Scis. Ctr., 2004-. Author: Christopher Smart as a Poet of His Time: A Re-Appraisal, 1966, (with others) Sir William Davenant, 1981, Sir William Davenant: An Annotated Bibliography, 1986; editor: (with others) Selected Papers from the W.Va. Shakespeare and Renaissance Association, 1976, The Literary Discussion Group, 1982, 85; contbr. chpts. to books, articles to profl. jours., encys., dictionaries, bibliographies. Mem. cen. exec. com. Folger Inst., 1992-99. Recipient Disting. Manuscript award Mich. State U., 1965, Gerontology Ctr. award, 1983; named Disting. West Virginian, W.Va. Gov., 1995; grantee W.Va. Found., 1973, W.Va. Humanities, 1980; W.Va. U. Senate rsch. grantee, 1984, 89; Folger fellow, 1981, Folger grantee, 1988, 91; recipient Sigma Tau Delta Outstanding Tchg. award, 1996. Mem. Am. Soc. 18th Century Studies, MLA, W.Va. Assn. Coll. English Tchrs. (pres. 1977), Shakespeare and Renaissance Soc. W.Va. (chmn. 1978, 84), Carolinas Symposium on Brit. Studies (chair program 1989, pres. 1990, conf. chair 1993), Women in Sci. and Health (WISH), W. Va. U. Health Scis. Ctr., Order of Vandalia. Home: 652 Bellaire Dr Morgantown WV 26505-2421 Office: W Va U PO Box 6296 Morgantown WV 26506-6296

BLAYLOCK, JAMES CARL, clergyman, librarian; b. Guntown, Miss., Jan. 27, 1938; s. Carl Houston and Katie Lee (Pugh) Blaylock; m. Jo Ann Enlow, May 3, 1962; children: Jacquelin Ann, John Thomas. AA, Southeastern Bapt. Coll., 1962; BTh, N.Am. Theol. Sem., 1964; BA, U. Tex., Tyler, 1976; MRE, Bapt. Missionary Sem., 1977; MSLS, Tex A&M U., 1980. Ordained to ministry Bapt. Ch., 1962. Pastor Mt. Pleasant Ch., Bedias, Tex., 1962—64, Buena Vista Ch., Timpson, Tex., 1964—70, 1st Bapt. Ch., Maydelle, Tex., 1970—86, Corinth Ch., Jacksonville, Tex., 1986—; asst. dir. Bapt. News Svc., Jacksonville, 1969—88, dir., 1988—99; asst. editor Directory and Handbook of Bapt. Missionary Assn., Jacksonville, 1969—88, editor, 1988—99; libr. Bapt. Missionary Assn. Theol. Sem., Jacksonville, 1972—. Editor: Mt. Olive Evangel, 1965—70; author: History of 1st Baptist Church Maydelle, Texas, 1966, Buena Vista Baptist Church, 1986, Glimpses from the Past, 2003. Mem.: ALA, Tex. Libr. Assn., Am. Theol. Libr. Assn. Office: Bapt Missionary Assn Theol Sem 1530 E Pine St Jacksonville TX 75766-5407 Home: 1105 Robs Rd Jacksonville TX 75766-3527 Home Phone: 903-586-4594; Office Phone: 903-586-2501.

BLAZAR, ANDREW S., reproductive endocrinologist; b. Providence, Jan. 19, 1934; s. Milton and Evelyn Kortick Blazar; m. Beverly Ann Resnik, June 17, 1956; children: Judith Westrick, Philip, Faye. AB, Brown U., Providence, 1955; MD, Tufts U., Boston, 1959. Cert. bd. cert. Am. Bd. Ob-Gyn. Physician Ob-Gyn. Assocs., Inc., Providence, 1969—93; attending physician Women and Infants' Hosp. of R.I., Providence, 1993—; assoc. clin. prof. Brown U., Providence, 1984—. Contbr. scientific papers to profl. jours.; ad hoc editor: Obstetrics and Gynecology, Fertility and Sterility. Recipient Disting. Svc. award, med. staff Women and Infants' Hosp. of R.I., 2001, Man of Yr. award, Planned Parenthood of R.I., 1993. Mem.: ACOG, AMA, Am. Soc. Reproductive Medicine. Office: Women and Infants' Hosp of RI 101 Dudley St Providence RI 02905

BLAZE, MATTHEW, computer science educator, researcher; BS, CUNY (Hunter Coll.), 1986; MS in Computer Sci., Columbia U., 1988; MA in Computer Sci., Princeton U., 1989, PhD in Computer Sci., 1993. Rsch. scientist AT&T Labs-Rsch./AT&T Bell Labs, NJ; assoc. prof. computer and info. sci. U. Pa., Phila., 2004—, acting dir., Distributed Systems Lab. Testified before various committee's of the US Congress and European Parliament; chair USENIX Security, 2004. Achievements include co-publishing a paper presenting a protocol swIPe in 1993; co-designing of swIPE, a predecessor of the current standard IPSEC protocol for protecting Internet traffic; coining the term and one of the inventors of Trust Management, this provides the abstract layer in which a system decides whether to allow a potentially dangerous action to take place; discovering a serious flaw in the US Government's Clipper encryption system in 1994; applying cryptologic techniques to analyse physical security systems, this resulted in powerful and practical attacks against virtually all commonly used master-keyed mechanical locks; active in the analysis of the FBI's Carnivore Internet wiretap system. Office: Dept Computer and Info Sci 506 Levine Hall 3330 Walnut St Philadelphia PA 19104-6389 Office Phone: 215-573-2696. Business E-Mail: blaze@cis.upenn.edu.

BLAZEK-WHITE, DORIS, lawyer; b. Easton, Md., Nov. 17, 1943; d. George W. and Nola M. (Buterbaugh) Defibaugh; m. Thacher W. White; children: Christine T., Judson M. BA, Goucher Coll., 1965; JD, Georgetown U., 1968. Bar: DC 1969, VI 1969, Md. 1978, registered: US Ct. Appeals (3rd cir.) 1969, US Ct. Appeals (DC cir.) 1971. Gen. practice with Judge Warren H. Young, St. Croix, VI, 1968-70; assoc. Covington & Burling, Washington, 1970-76, ptnr., 1976—, chmn. Estates & Trust Practice Group. Mem.: ABA (tax sect.), DC Superior Ct. (adv. com., probate and fiduciary rules), Washington DC Estate Planning Coun., Am. Coll. Trust & Estate Counsel. Office: Covington & Burling 1201 Pennsylvania Ave NW Washington DC 20004 Office Phone: 202-662-5490. Office Fax: 202-778-5490. Business E-Mail: dblazek-white@cov.com.

BLAZER, DAN GERMAN, II, psychiatrist, epidemiologist; b. Nashville, Feb. 23, 1944; s. Dan German and Mary Elizabeth (Owsley) Blazer; m. Sherrill Walls, Aug. 19, 1966; children: Dan German III, Natasha Leigh. BA, Vanderbilt U., 1965; MD, U. Tenn., 1969; MPH, U. N.C., 1979, PhD, 1980. Diplomate Am. Bd. Psychiatry and Neurology, cert. geriatric psychiatry. Fellow Montefiore Hosp. and Med. Ctr., NYC, 1975—76; asst. prof., assoc. prof., then prof. psychiatry Duke U. Med. Ctr., Durham, NC, 1976—, J.P. Gibbons prof. psychiatry, 1990—, interim chair of psychiatry, 1990—93, prof. cmty. and family medicine, 1986—; dean of med. edn. Duke U., 1992—99. Chair, bd. dirs. Am. Geriat. Soc., NY, 1983; bd. dirs. ret. persons svcs. Am. Assn. Ret. Persons, Alexandria, Va., 1987—92; pres. Psychiat. Rsch. Soc., Salt Lake City, 1988; chmn. epidemiology and disease control study sect. NIH, Bethesda, Md., 1988—. Author: Life is Worth Living, 1987, Depression in Late Life, 1993, Freud vs. God, 1998, Introduction to Clinical Research in Psychiatry, 1998, The Age of Melancholy, 2005. Named Outstanding Alumnus, U. Tenn. Coll. Medicine, 2003; recipient Rsch. Career Devel. award, NIMH, 1977, Alex Haley award, East Tenn. Bapt. Hosp., Knoxville, 1986, Disting. Svc. award, U. N.C. Sch. Pub. Health, Chapel Hill, 1989, Milo Leavitt award, Am. Geriat. Soc., 1997, Rema LaPouse award, APHA, 2001, Disting. Faculty award, Duke U. Med. Ctr., 2005. Fellow: Am. Assn. Geriatric Psychiatry (disting. life) (pres. 2005—06), Am. Psychopathol. Assn., Gerontol. Soc. Am. (Klecmeier award 2005), Am. Psychiat. Assn., Am. Coll. Psychiatrists (Geriatric Psychiatry Rsch. award 2003); mem.: Inst. Medicine NAS, 1995. Democrat. Avocations: hiking, reading. Office: Duke U Med Ctr PO Box 3003 Durham NC 27715-3003 Business E-Mail: blaze001@mc.duke.edu.

BLAZINA, JANICE FAY, pathologist; d. Joseph and Cordelia Evelyn B. BS, Youngstown State U., 1975; MD, Ohio State U., 1978. Diplomate Am. Bd. Pathology. Resident in anat. and clin. pathology U. Ala. Med. Ctr., Birmingham, 1978-82; assoc. pathologist various hosps., Bryan, Tex., 1982-83, High Plains Bapt. Hosp., Amarillo, Tex., 1983-84; fellow in blood banking Baylor U. Med. Ctr., Dallas, 1984-85; asst. prof. dept. pathology Ohio State U., Columbus, 1985-93, asst. prof. Sch. Allied Med. Professions, 1987-93. Asst. dir. transfusion svc. Ohio State U. Hosp., 1985-89, assoc. dir., 1989-90, dir., 1990-93, med. dir. histocompatibility, paternity, apheresis and phlebotomy svcs., 1987-93, divsn. med. tech., 1987-93; asst. med. dir. Carter Blood Ctr., Ft. Worth, 1993-95, med. dir., 1995-96. Contbr. articles to profl. publs. Bremer Found. grantee, 1987. Mem. AMA, Am. Soc. Apheresis, Am. Soc. Histocompatibility and Immunogenetics, Am. Assn. Blood Banks (insp. 1987—), Ohio Assn. Blood Banks (trustee 1990-93, sec. 1992-93), Assn. Women Sci. Cen. Ohio (v.p. 1989-90, pres. 1990-91), Nat. Alliance Mentally Ill Tarrant County (sec. 2003). Mem. Church of Christ. Avocation: gardening. Personal E-mail: bbpathd1@yahoo.com.

BLAZING, MICHAEL AUGUST, internist; b. 1961; MD, U. Calif., San Francisco, 1987. Postdoctoral fellow Duke U. Med. Ctr., now asst. prof. medicine, 1991—. Recipient Clinician-Scientist award Am. Heart Assn., 1995-96. Home: 2113 Carriage Way Chapel Hill NC 27517-9466 Office: Duke U Med Ctr Dept Cardiology Rm 7403 PO Box 3126 Durham NC 27710-0001

BLAZY, LOUIS JOSEPH, III, federal agency administrator; b. Ft. Beloir, Va., Apr. 2, 1952; s. Louis Joseph Blazy Jr. and Dorothy Virginia Blazy; m. Suzan Mary Rike-Blazy, June 1, 1975; children: Damian Louis, Christopher Michael. BA, George Mason U., 1979, MA, 1981; PhD, U. Md., 1985; MBA, George Washington U., 2002. Engr. Army Rsch. Inst., Alexandria, Va., 1980—83; computer scientist CIA, McLean, 1983—93; dir., U.S. Dept. Agrl., Washington, 1993—98; dir. IVEV NASA, AMES, Fairmont, W.Va., 1998—2003; dep. asst. sec. U.S. Dept. Housing & Urban Devel., Washington, 2003—05; astl dir. FBI, 2005—. Prof. U. Md., College Park, 1985—; pres. Intelligent Sys. Applications, Fairfax, Va., 1993—96. With USN, 1970—71. Mem.: AAAS, Internat. Soc. Sys. Engring., Psi Chi, Sigma Chi, Beta Gamma Sigma. Avocation: collecting Japanese wood block prints. Office: FBI 935 Pennsylvania Ave NW Washington DC 20535

BLAZY, PIERRE FRANÇOIS, science educator; b. Foix, France, May 18, 1931; s. Martial and Suzanne (Rouan) B.; m. Andrée Baptiste, July 25, 1955. Ingenieur geologue degree, Ecole Nationale Superieure Geologie, Nancy, France, 1954; PhD, U. Nancy, 1958. Prof. U. Nancy, 1964-71, Inst. Nat. Poly., Nancy, 1971-99; adminstr. Tech. Transfer Cons., 1993-96. Cons. Panamerican Union, Washington, 1967-68; adminstr. Soc. Nouvelle Acieries Pompey (Steel), Paris, 1984, Ascometal (Steel), Paris, 1984 geology operation systems, Paris, 1986, Guyanor Gold and Diamond Resources, Cayenne, 1998-2001, Golden Star Resources, Denver, 1998; expert European Commns., Brussels, 1985—; pres. Ecole Nat. Superieure Geologie, Nancy, 1971-79 Author: Valorisation des Minerais, 1970, El Beneficio de los Minerales, 1976, La Métallurgie Extractive des Métaux Non Ferreux,

1979, Energétique Industrielle II, 1981; contbr. 250 articles to profl. jours. With French Mil., 1958-60. Mem. Russian Acad. Scis. Achievements include 17 patents in the fields of flotation reagents, ionic flottation, phosphate roasting and removal of metals contained in phosphoric acid, environmental engineering. Office: Ecol Nationale euperieure de Geologie BP 40 54501 Vandoeuvre-les-Nancy France Office Phone: (33)383596111. Personal E-mail: pf.b@wanadoo.fr.

BLEAKLEY, PETER KIMBERLEY, lawyer; b. Franklin, Pa., Aug. 19, 1936; s. Rollin R and Marion (St James) Bleakley; m. Mary B DeRosa; children: Jennifer A, Sarah A, Nicholas D. BA, U. Va., 1958, LL.B., 1962. Bar: Va 1962, DC 1966, US Ct Appeals (2d cir), US Ct Appeals (3d cir), US Ct Appeals (5th cir), US Ct Appeals (6th cir), US Ct Appeals (7th cir), US Ct Appeals (8th cir), US Ct Appeals (9th cir), US Ct Appeals (DC cir), US Supreme Ct, US Ct Appeals (fed cir). Trial atty. Fed. Trade Commn., Washington, 1962-66; trial atty. Dept. Justice, Washington, 1966; assoc. Arnold & Porter, Washington, 1966-70, ptnr., 1971—. Fellow: Am Col Trial Lawyers; mem.: ABA. Democrat. Avocations: tennis, skiing, bicycling, golf. Home: 3103 Hawthorne St NW Washington DC 20008-3540 Office: Arnold & Porter 555 12th St NW Washington DC 20004-1206 E-mail: peter_bleakley@aporter.com.

BLEAM, NANCY KAY, physical education educator; b. Adrian, Mich., May 17, 1957; d. Donald Fay and Evelyn Ruth Bleam. BA in Elem. Edn., Adrian Coll., Mich., 1980; MEd in Athletic Adminstrn., Austin Peay State U., Clarksville, Tenn., 1984. Cert. athletic trainer Nat. Athletic Trainer's Assn., 1987. Tchr., athletic trainer Unified Sch. Dist. 495., Larned, Kans., 1980—81; rehab. aide Herrick Meml. Hosp., Tecumseh, Mich., 1982—83; tchr., athletic trainer Greenville (Mich.) Pub. Schs., 1985—90; athletic trainer, instr. Culver-Stockton Coll., Canton, Mo., 1990—94; athletic trainer Hannibal (Mo.) Regional Hosp., 1994—96; athletic trainer, instr. Keene (N.H.) State Coll., 1996—. Avocations: travel, photography, reading. Home: 20 Gates Road 15 Marlborough NH 03455 Office: Keene State College 229 Main Street Keene NH 03435 Home Phone: 603-876-4632; Office Phone: 603-358-2825. Personal E-mail: nbleam@hotmail.com. Business E-Mail: nbleam@keene.edu.

BLECH, ILAN ASRIEL, retired technology company executive; b. Nov. 1936; Pres. Flexus Corp., Los Altos & Mountian View, Calif.; ret. Mem.: NAE.

BLECHMAN, R. O., artist, filmmaker; b. Bklyn., Oct. 1, 1930; s. Samuel and Mae Blechman; m. Moisha Kubinyi, Mar. 3, 1960; children: Nicholas, Max. BA, Oberlin Coll., 1952. Freelance illustrator, NYC, 1953—; freelance producer, designer animated films, 1975—; pres. R.O. Blechman, Inc., NYC, 1978—, The Ink Tank, NYC, 1979—. Author, illustrator: The Juggler of Our Lady, 1952, Onion Soup, 1963, Behind the Lines, an autobiography and anthology, 1980, The Life of Saint Nicholas, 1996, The Book of Jonah, 1997; exhibited one-man shows, Gallery Delpire, Paris, 1968, Graham Gallery, N.Y.C., 1978, ITC Gallery, 1981, Galerie Bartsch & Chariau, Munich, 1982, 92, 2000, Mark Borghi Gallery, 2007; represented in permanent collections, Mus. Modern Art, N.Y.C., Chase Manhattan Bank; executed murals, Mus. Natural History, U.S. Pavilion Expo '67, Folger Shakespeare Library.; films include The Juggler of Our Lady, 1958, Abraham and Isaac, 1971, Exercise, 1974, Simple Gifts, 1978, No Room at the Inn, 1978 (Clio award 1968, 69, 73), L'Histoire du Soldat, 1984 (Emmy award 1984); retrospective Mus. Modern Art, N.Y.C., N.Y., 2003. Trustee Swann found. Mem. Alliance Graphique Internat., Am. Inst. Graphic Arts, Graphic Artists Guild. Home and Office: 205 Tompkins RD Ancram NY 12502-5351 Home Phone: 518-329-0531; Office Phone: 518-329-0531. Business E-Mail: ro@roblechman.com.

BLECHMAN, WILBUR JORDAN, medical educator; b. Washington, May 7, 1932; s. Charles and Florence (Goodman) B.; m. Sidell Ray Cohen, June 26, 1955 (dec. Mar. 1983); children: Michele, Michael, Ivy; m. Rachel Simonhoff Rudin, May 26, 1985. BS, Yale U., 1954; MD, Med. Coll. of Va., 1957. Diplomate Am. Bd. Internal Medicine and Rheumatology. Pvt. practice, North Miami Beach, Fla., 1961-94; clin. prof. of medicine U. Miami Sch. Medicine, 1980-95; dir. Resources for Children, Inc., Miami, 1994-95; state health officer Fla., 1995-96; courtesy prof. pub. health U. South Fla., 1996—2000; sr. cons. Fla. Dept. Health, Dept. Children and Families, 1996-98; program officer Lawton & Rhea Chiles Ctr. for Healthy Mothers & Babies, 1997-98, cons., 1998. Co-dir. Miami Arthritis Ctr., 1985-93; cons. Bertha Abess Children's Ctr., Miami, 1999-2007; co-chair child health and well-being task force Miami-Dade County Early Childhood Initiative, 1999—; sec. Youth Ethics Initiative, Inc., 2005-; cons. in field. Contbr. articles to profl. jours. Chmn. Fla. Kids Count Adv. Coun., 1992-94; mem. U.S. Kids Count Adv. Group, 1991-94; vice-chmn. Children's Trust, Miami-Dade County, 2003—; bd. dirs. Fla. Children's Forum, 1991—, sec. Youth Ethics Initiative, Inc., 2003—. Recipient Disting. Svc. award The Arthritis Found., 1971, Physician's award for Outstanding Cmty. Svc. Fla. Med. Assn., Wyeth-Ayerst Labs., 1990, Hannah G. Solomon award Nat. Coun. Jewish Women, 1992, State Health Office Cmty. Friend award, 1993, Help and Hope award for Excellence in Rheumatology Arthritis Found. S.E. Fla., 1994, Recognition letter Sec. U.S. Dept. Health and Human Svcs., 1995, 5th Annual Lawton Chiles Advocacy award Fla. Chpt. March Dimes, 2005; named 1993 Champion for Children Miami-Dade C.C., Friend of Coop. Extension, 1993. Mem. ACP, Am. Coll. Rheumatology, Fla. Soc. of Rheumatology (pres. 1970-71), Internat. Coun. for Control of Iodine Deficiency Disorders (bd. dirs. 1994-96), Kiwanis (pres. Internat. 1990-91, Citizen of Yr. Biscayne club 1992), Fla. Assn. Infant Mental Health (charter pres. 2001-03, pres. 2006-). Home and Office: 5250 SW 84th St Miami FL 33143-8434 Office Phone: 305-904-7912. Personal E-mail: wilblechman@aol.com.

BLECHNER, MARK JACOB, psychologist, educator; b. NYC, Nov. 6, 1950; BA, U. Chgo., 1972; MS, Yale U., 1975, PhD, 1977; cert. in psychoanalysis, William Alanson White Inst., 1983. Trainee in clin. psychology NIMH, 1973-76; rsch. assoc. Haskins Lab., New Haven, 1974-77; pvt. practice clin. psychology, NYC, 1977—. Asst. clin. prof. psychology dept. psychiatry Columbia Coll. Physicians and Surgeons, 1981-94; dir., HIV-Clini. Svcs., tng. analyst, supr., dir. curriculum William Alanson White Inst., 1984—, Manhattan Inst. for Psychoanalysis, 1985-90; asst. clin. prof. psychology postdoctoral program in psychoanalysis NYU, 1995—. Author: The Dream Frontier; editor Hope and Mortality; editor-in-chief: Contemporary Psychoanalysis, 2007—; contbr. articles to profl. jours. Mem. AAAS, APA, N.Y. Acad. Scis., Sigma Xi. Address: 145 Central Park W New York NY 10023-2004 Office Phone: 212-595-4648. E-mail: mblechner@psychoanalysis.net.

BLECKLEY, JEANETTE A., lawyer; b. Columbia, SC, Feb. 2, 1943; d. Thomas Marcus and Amanda Elizabeth (Cobb) B.; m. Nathan G. Pearce, Dec. 3, 1967 (div. 1979); 1 child, Angelique Nicole Pearce. AA, Young Harris Coll., Ga., 1963; student, American River Coll., Sacramento, 1966—67; JD, Lincoln U., Sacramento, 1974; JD (hon.), U. No. Calif., 2002. Bar: Calif., U.S. Dist. Ct. (3d dist.) Calif.; cert. tchr., Calif. Gen. office staff Procter & Gamble, Atlanta, 1962-64; contract negotiator, adminstr., purchasing agt., pub. rels. Am. Cable Elec. Supply, Inc., Sacramento, 1965-74; engring. asst. R&D,s. Ban Electronics, Sacramento, 1970; owner Sunshine Carpet, 2003—, Going Postal 4 U, 2004—, Absolute Glass Protection, 2005—; pvt. practice Sacramento, 1974—; prof. U. No. Calif., 2000—. Contbr. articles to Reflections; author, writer, composer album Willows, Wisps and Wishes, 1994. Mem. Calif. Bar Assn., Sacramento Bar Assn., Calif. Women Lawyers, Sacramento Valley Legal Svcs., Weave, Sigma Beta Sigma. Avocations: music, antique cars, writing, dance, football. Home and Office: 1808 Del Paso Blvd Sacramento CA 95815-3041 Office Phone: 916-567-4060. Personal E-mail: bleckleylaw@aol.com.

BLEDEL, ALEXIS (KIMBERLY ALEXIS BLEDEL), actress; b. Houston, Sept. 16, 1981; d. Martin and Nanette Bledel. Attended, Page Parkes Ctr. of Modeling and Acting; studied Film, NYU Tisch Sch., NYC, 1999—2000. Actor: (TV series) Gilmore Girls, 2000—07; (films) Rushmore, 1998, Tuck Everlasting, 2002, DysEnchanted, 2004, Bride & Prejudice, 2004, The Orphan King, 2005, Sin City, 2005, The Sisterhood of the Traveling Pants, 2005; guest appearances The Late Late Show with Craig Kilborn, 2003, Late Show with David Letterman, 2005, The View, 2005. Named one of 25 Hottest Stars under 25, Teen People mag., 2002; recipient Family Friendly Forum Award, best actress in a drama, 2002. First language Spanish. Office: 17 Little West 12th St #333 New York NY 10014-1311

BLEDSOE, DREW, retired professional football player; b. Ellensburg, Wash., Feb. 14, 1972; s. Mac and Barbara Bledsoe; m. Maura Bledsoe; children: Stuart, John, Henry, Healy. BA in Edn., Wash. State U., 1993. Quarterback New Eng. Patriots, 1993—2002, Buffalo Bills, 2002—04, Dallas Cowboys, 2005—07. Internat. chmn. Children's Miracle Network; co-founder Drew Bledsoe Found., 1999—; sponsor Parenting with Dignity, 1996—; established Albert"Stu" Bledsoe Endowed Football Scholarship. Named to Am. Football Conf. Pro Bowl Team, 1994, 1996—97, 2000. Achievements include holding NFL single season record for most passes attempted (691), 1994; single game record for most pass completions (45); led NFL in total passing yards (4,555), 1994; led NFL in completions 1994, 1996. Office: Drew Bledsoe Found 730 Capistrano Kalispell MT 59901

BLEIBERG, LEON WILLIAM, surgeon, podiatrist; b. Bklyn., June 9, 1932; s. Paul Pincus and Helen (Epstein) B.; m. Beth Daigle, June 7, 1970; children: Kristina Noel, Kelley Lynn, Kimberly Ann, Paul Joseph. Student, L.A. City Coll., 1950-51, U. So. Calif., 1951, Case Western Res. U., 1951-53; DSc with honors, Temple U., 1955; D in Podiatric Medicine, Pa. Sch. Podiatric Medicine, 1965; PhD, U. Beverly Hills, 1970. Intern various hosps., Phila., 1954—55; resident Bella Vista Hosp., Montebello, Calif., 1956—58; surg. podiatrist So. Calif. Podiatry Group, Westchester, Calif., 1956—75; health care economist, rschr. Drs. Home Health Care Svcs., 1976—; chmn. bd. Unltd. Healthcare, Metro Manila, Philippines; v.p. pub. rels. Bilbao Wellness Found., Upland, Calif.; CEO Med. Trianon, Newbury Park, Calif.; dir. biomechanics dept. Anti-Aging and Rejuvenation Clinic, Torrance, Calif.; CFO mktg. and devel. Immigration Ctr. for Law and Justice. Podiatric cons. U. So. Calif. Athletic Dept., Morningside and Inglewood (Calif.) High Schs., Royal Naval Assn., Long Beach (Calif.) Naval Sta.; exec. cons. Thomas Med. Group, Pomona, Calif., 1995, Cardiotel, Van Nuys, Calif., 1995; lectr. in field; healthcare affiliate Internat. divsn. CARE/ASIA, 1987; pres. Medica, Totalcare, Cine-Medics Corp., Strategic World-Wide Health Care Svcs.; exec. dir. Internat. Health Trust; developer Health Banking Program; adminstr. Orthotic Concepts, 1993; prof. health care econs. and med. rehab. Global U., Ontario, Calif., chmn. dept. health care econs., chmn. dept. biomechanics and phys. rehab.; CEO Integrated Wellness Ctrs., The Med. Trianon Found.; exec. dir. Med. Trianon; exec. dir. wellness divsn. Crown Golden Eagles; mem. nat. leadership Temple U., Phila.; CEO Global Health Share 2000. Prodr. (films) The Gun Hawk, 1963, Terrified, Day of the Nightmare; contbr. articles to profl. jours. Hon. Sheriff Westchester 1962-64; commd. mem. Rep. Senatorial Inner Circle, 1984-86; lt. comdr. med. svcs. corps Brit.-Am. Sea Cadet Corps, 1984—; co-chmn. health reform com. United We Stand Am., Thousand Oaks, Calif., exec. coun. State of Calif.; active 1st Security and Safety, Westlake Village, Calif., 1993—; track coach Westlake HS, Westlake Village; exec. sec. Nat. Coalition Parents Anti-Drug/Violence Corp., Inc. LA World Affairs Coun.; active Agoura C. of C., Oak Park C. of C., Las Virgenes C. of C.; exec. dir. healthcare dept. H. Martin Found.; county inspector U.S. Election Com., Calif.; bd. dirs. Power Search Unltd. Ministries, Philippines and U.S.; U.S. coord. Luntiang Pilipinas (Philippine Ecology Program); chmn., bd. dirs. Philippine Vets. Found.; leader healthcare dept. H. Martin Found. With USN, 1955-56 Recipient Medal of Merit, U.S. Presdl. Task Force, Grand award Top Personalities mag., 1999. Mem. Filipino Vets. Found. (chmn., bd. dirs.), Philippine Pvt. Hosp. Assn. (Cert. of Appreciation 1979, Outstanding Svc. trophy 1979), Calif. Podiatric Med. Assn. (hon.), Am. Podiatric Med. Assn. (hon.), Acad. TV Arts and Scis., Royal Soc. Health (Eng.), We. Foot Surgery Assn., Am. Coll. Foot Surgeons, Am. Coll. Podiatric Sports Medicine, Internat. Coll. Preventive Medicine, Hollywood Comedy Club, Sts. and Sinners Club, Westchester C. of C. (hon. sheriff), Las Vegas C. of C., Hals Und Beinbruch Ski Club, Beach Cities Ski Club, Orange County Stamp Club, Las Virgenes Track Club, Am. Legion, Masons, Shriners, Scottish Rite. Home and Office: 55 N Wendy Dr Newbury Park CA 91320-4351 Office Phone: 805-499-6900. Personal E-mail: medicaltrianon@verizon.net.

BLEICH, JEFFREY LAURENCE, lawyer, educator; b. Neubreuke, Germany, May 17, 1961; came to U.S., 1964; s. Charles Allen Bleich and Linda Sue Caplan; m. Rebecca Lee Pratt, Aug. 12, 1984; children: Jacob, Matthew, Abigail. BA in Polit. Sci., Amherst Coll., 1983; MA in Pub. Policy, Harvard U., 1986; JD, U. Calif., Berkeley, 1989. Bar: Calif. 1989, D.C. 1990, U.S. Ct. Appeals (D.C. cir.) 1990, U.S. Dist. Ct. (no. dist.) Calif. 1992, U.S. Ct. Appeals (4th cir.) 1993, U.S. Supreme Ct. 1993, U.S. Ct. Appeals (9th cir.) 1994. Law clk. US Ct. Appeals, Washington, 1989-90, US Supreme Ct., Washington, 1990-91; legal asst. Iran-U.S. Claims Tribunal, The Hague, 1991-92; ptnr. Munger, Tolles & Olson LLP, San Francisco, 1992—. Adj. prof. U. Calif., Berkeley, 1993—. Editor-in-chief Calif. Law Rev., Nat. Debt; columnist San Francisco Atty. Dir. White Ho. Youth Violence Initiative, 1999-2000, vice chair, Calif. State U., 2006; v.p. State Bar. Calif., 2006. Recipient James Madison award Soc. Profl. Journalists, 1998, Learned Hand award, 2007; named Atty. of Yr., Calif. Lawyer, 2007. Mem. ABA (amicus curiae com., top 100 lawyers in Calif., 2006, Pro Bono Publico award 1996), State Bar Calif. (pres. 2007-), Bar Assn. San Francisco (pres.), Lawyers' Com. Civil Rights of San Francisco Bay Area (co-chair), Lawyers Com. Human Rights (bd. dirs. 1998—), Legal Aid Soc. (bd. dirs. 1998—), Barristers Club San Francisco (pres.), Am. Law Inst. Democrat. Avocations: short story writer, tennis, camping. Office: Munger Tolles & Olson 560 Mission St Fl 27 San Francisco CA 94105 Home Phone: 510-655-2192; Office Phone: 415-512-4000. Business E-Mail: jeff.bleich@mto.com.

BLEICHER, MICHAEL NATHANIEL, mathematics professor; b. Cleve., Oct. 2, 1935; s. David B. and Rachel (Faigin) B.; m. Betty Isack, June 4, 1957; children: Helene, Laurence, Benjamin; m. E. Jeanne Smith, Dec. 31, 1980; stepchildren: Kathryn, Robert, Zaka. BS, Calif. Inst. Tech., 1957; MS, Tulane U., 1959, PhD, 1961; doctorate degree, U. Warsaw, 1961. Teaching and research asst. Tulane U., 1957-60; fellow U. Warsaw, Poland, 1960-61; NSF fellow U. Calif., Berkeley, 1961-62; mem. faculty U. Wis., Madison, 1962—93, dept. chmn., 1972-74, prof. dept. math., 1968—93, prof. emeritus, 1993—; chief adv. and liaison U.S. Dept. Energy, 1979-81. Assigned to coll. preparatory studies Inst. of Tech. Mara, Shah Alam, Selangor, Malaysia, 1987-90; founder Wis. Emerging Scholars program; chair Dept. Math. Sci. Clark Atlanta U., 1998-05.; prof. Kennesaw State U., 2005—. Author: (with A. Beck, D. Crowe) Excursions into Mathematics, 1968; co-translator: A. Mathematical Guidebook for Technologists and Engineers, 1962. Mem. Dem. Nat. Com., 1972-79; chmn. Dem. Party Wis., 1977-79. Recipient Regents award of distinction, U. Wis., 1973. Mem. Am. Math. Soc., Math. Assn. Am., Polish Math. Soc. Democrat. Jewish. Achievements include research on length and size of denominators of Egyptian fractions, least length subdivision of a region into cells of a given area. Home: 540 Celevaras Dr Atlanta GA 30350-4002 Home Phone: 770-393-9957; Office Phone: 770-423-6103. Office Fax: 770-423-6629. Business E-Mail: bleicher@math.wisc.edu.

BLEICHER, PAUL ALAN, information technology executive, physician; b. Bklyn., Dec. 31, 1954; s. Henry William and Annette Bleicher; m. Julia Lea Greenstein, June 19, 1977. BS cum laude, Rensselaer Poly. Inst., Troy, NY, 1976; PhD in Microbiology and Immunology, U. Rochester Medicine and Dentistry, NY, 1983. Med. diplomate Mass., 1984, cert. Am. Bd. Dermatology, 1988. Resident in medicine Beth Israel Hosp., Boston, 1983—85; resident in dermatology Harvard Med. Sch., Boston, 1985—87; rsch. fellow in molecular immunology Dana Farber Cancer Inst., Boston, 1987—88; asst. prof., instr. Mass. Gen. Hosp., Harvard Med. Sch., Boston, 1988—92; dir. PAREXEL Internat., Waltham, Mass., 1992—94; v.p. clin. affairs Alpha-Beta Tech., Worcester, Mass., 1994—97; founder, chmn. Phase Forward Inc., Waltham, Mass., 1997—, CEO, pres., 1997—98, 2002—03, chief strategy officer, 2004—. Profl. adv. com. Rabb Sch., Brandeis U., 2006; mem. life sci. adv. bd. Mass. Tech. Leadership Coun., 2007—; mem. organizing com. Mass. Life Sci. Collaborative, 2007—. Bd. mem. Drug Info. Assn. Found., 2003—06; bd. overseers Mus. Sci., Boston, 2006—. Named Entrepreneur of Yr., New Eng., Ernst and Young, 2002; named one of PharmaVoice 100 Most Inspiring Leaders in Life Scis., 2005; recipient Robert Kates award, U. Rochester, 1983, Innovators award, Smaller Bus. Assn. of New Eng., 2002, Rensselaer Alumni Assn. Fellows award, 2003, Champions in Healthcare award, Boston Bus. Jour., 2006; Burroughs-Wellcome fellowship, Dermatology Found., 1989. Mem.: Drug Info. Assn. (chmn. steering com. N.Am. 2001—03, bd. dirs. 2003—, Outstanding Svc. award 2004). Achievements include first to comercialize web-based clinical trials; United States Patent clinical trial data management system and method; United States Patent discovery of Role of CD1 as target for T cells. Avocations: technical rock climbing, tennis, bridge, skiing, sailing. Office: Phase Forward 880 Winter St Ste 100 Waltham MA 02451-1465 Office Phone: 781-890-7878. Office Fax: 781-902-4668. Business E-Mail: paul.bleicher@phaseforward.com.

BLEICHER, SAMUEL ABRAM, law educator, consultant; b. Omaha, June 21, 1942; s. David Bernard and Rachael Bleicher; m. Beatrice Koretsky, June 16, 1965 (dec. Nov. 12, 1995); children: Leo, Zena; m. Emily Blair Chewning, May 17, 1997 (div. 2002). BA, Northwestern U., 1963; JD, Harvard U., 1966. Bar: Nebr. 1966, Ohio 1972, D.C. 1979, Va. 1989, Md. 1991. Prof. law U. Toledo Coll. Law, 1966-76; dep. dir. for regulation and enforcement Ohio EPA, 1972-75; issues generalist Carter-Mondale Presdl. Campaign, Atlanta, 1976; policy analyst Carter-Mondale Transition Planning Group, Washington, 1976-77; spl. asst. to adminstr. NOAA Dept. Commerce, Washington, 1977, dir. Office Ocean Mgmt., 1977-78, dep. asst. adminstr., 1978-80, dep. gen. counsel, 1980-81; of counsel Blank, Rome, Comisky & McCauley, Washington, 1981-85; ptnr. Frank, Bernstein, Conaway & Goldman, Tysons Corner, Va., 1985-90; prin. Miles & Stockbridge P.C., Washington, 1990—2001; legis. affairs asst. Overseas Bldg. Ops. Bur., U.S. Dept. State, 2001—03, New Initiatives Divsn. dir., 2003—06, chief strategist new initiatives, 2006—. Vis. prof. law, Moscow, 2007, Beijing, 07. Democrat. Jewish. Personal E-mail: sambleicher@comcast.net.

BLEICHER, SHELDON JOSEPH, endocrinologist, medical educator; b. NYC, Apr. 9, 1931; s. Max and Fannie (Klieger) B.; m. Diane D. Cole, Aug., 1990; children from previous marriages: Erick Max, Phillip Thaddeus Samuel, Deborah Ann Cote, Sandra Lynn Gable, Jodie Lisa Cole. AB, NYU, 1951; MS, Western Ill. U., 1952; MD, SUNY Downstate Med. Center, Bklyn., 1956. Intern L.I. Jewish Hosp. Ctr., New Hyde Park, N.Y., 1956-57; resident Boston City Hosp., 1959-60; chief rsch. fellow in medicine Harvard-Thorndike Meml. Lab., Boston, 1962-63; chief metabolic research unit Jewish Hosp. Med. Center, Bklyn., 1963-67, chief div. endocrinology and metabolism, 1967-77; pvt. practice specializing in endocrinology and diabetes Woodbury, 1990—2004; prof. medicine SUNY Downstate Med. Center, 1975—2004; chmn. dept. internal medicine The Bklyn. Hosp. Ctr., 1978—90. Cons. IAEA, Vienna, 1966—90; mem. attending staff North Shore Univ. Hosp. at Syosset, North Shore Univ. Hosp. at Plainview, North Shore Univ. Hosp. at Manhasset. Mem. editl. bd. Diabetes in News, Practical Diabetes; contbr. articles to profl. jours. Vice pres. Locust Valley Central Sch. Bd., 1981-82, pres., 1982-85. Served to capt. M.C., USNR, 1957-92, ret. NIH fellow, 1960-63; NIH research career devel. award, 1970-75; recipient Torch of Liberty award Anti-Defamation League of B'nai Brith, 1982. Fellow: ACP, Am. Coll. Endocrinology; mem.: AMA, Mass. Med. Soc., Juvenile Diabetes Found. Internat., Internat. Diabetes Fedn., Am. Coll. Endocrinologists, Am. Assn. Clin. Endocrinologists, Endocrine Soc., Bklyn. Soc. Internal Medicine (treas. 1983—85, sec. 1985—87, pres. 1987—89), N.Y. State Soc. Internal Medicine (state bd. dirs., treas. Bklyn. chpt., chmn. continuing edn. com.), L.I. Diabetes Assn. (pres. 1978—81), N.Y. Diabetes Assn. (bd. dirs. 1965—93, pres. 1976—78), Am. Diabetes Assn. (bd. dirs. 1979—85, nat. com. quality care Achievement award 1986, 1990, Provider Recognition award), Am. Soc. Internal Medicine, Nassau County Med. Soc., N.Y. State Soc. Medicine, Sagamore Yacht Club (fleet surgeon 1983—86). Jewish. Personal E-mail: SJBleich@comcast.net.

BLEIDT, BARRY ANTHONY, pharmacy educator; b. South Charleston, W.Va., Mar. 29, 1951; s. Robert Anthony and Mary Frances (Gash) B.; 1 child, Brittany Alice. B in Gen. Studies, BS in Pharmacy, U. Ky., 1974; PhD, U. Fla., 1982; PharmD, Xavier U., 1994. Registered pharmacist, Fla., Calif., Ga., W.Va., Tex. Pres. Health Resources Cons., 1979—; asst. prof. pharmacy Northeastern U., Boston, 1983—86, U. Houston, 1986—89; assoc. prof. pharmacy adminstrn. Xavier U., 1989—94; med. info. scientist Astra/Merck Group, 1994—95; clin. coord., dir. postgrad. profl. edn. sch. pharmacy Hampton U., 1995—2002; prof., chair social and adminstrv. scis. dept. Loma Linda U. Sch. Pharmacy, 2002—05; assoc. dean acad. affairs Coll. Pharmacy Tex. A&M Health Sci. Ctr., Kingsville, 2005—. Faculty dir. Practicing Pharmacists Inst., Boston, 1983-86. Author, editor: Clinical Research in Pharmaceutical Development, 2000-2005; contbr. articles to profl. jours.; guest editor Jour. Pharm. Mktg. and Mgmt., 1988; mem. editl. bd. Clin. Rsch. Reg. Affairs, 1983—, editor, 1999. Recipient Local Assn. Pres. of Yr., Va. Pharm. Assn., 2001. Mem.: APHA (leadership award 1999), Nat. Pharm. Assn. (James Tyson award 2001), Am. Soc. Health-Sys. Pharmacists, Am. Assn. Colls. Pharmacy (parliamentarian 1983—2006), Fla. Blue Key, Nat. Eagle Scout Assn., U. Fla. Hall of Fame, Phi Lambda Sigma, Omicron Delta Kappa, Rho Chi, Sigma Xi. Avocations: music, travel, ethnic restaurants, films. Home and Office: PO Box 3037 Kingsville TX 78363-8330 Office Phone: 757-593-7245, 361-593-4533. E-mail: bbleidt@aol.com, bbleidt@pharmacy.tamhsc.edu.

BLEIER, MICHAEL E., lawyer, director; b. NYC, Mar. 23, 1942; BA, U. Tulsa, 1962; JD, Georgetown U., 1965. Bar: Pa., DC. Atty. Office Gen. Counsel, Bd. Govs. Fed. Res. Sys., 1971-78, sr. counsel, 1979-81, asst. gen. counsel, 1981-82; mng. counsel Mellon Bank Corp., Pitts., 1982-88; asst. gen. counsel Mellon Fin. Corp., 1989-91, dep. gen. counsel, 1991-92, gen. counsel, exec. v.p., 1992—2006, sr. mgmt. com., spl. counsel to chmn., 2006—. Contbr. articles to profl. jours. Mem. Am. Bankers Assn. (vice chmn. bank counsel com. 1996-98), Lawyers Coun. Fin. Svcs. Roundtable (chmn. 1993-98). Office: Mellon Fin Corp 1 Mellon Ctr 28th Fl Pittsburgh PA 15258-0001 Office Phone: 412-234-1537. Business E-Mail: bleier.me@mellon.com.*

BLEIFELD, STANLEY, sculptor; b. Bklyn., Aug. 28, 1924; s. Benjamin and Rose (Molshatsky) B.; m. Naomi Kaplan Ruby, Sept. 5, 1949; children: Becky Paula, Emily Harriet. BFA, BSEd, Temple U., 1949, MFA, 1950; D of Fine Arts (hon.), Lyme Acad. Fine Arts, Conn., 1997. Asst. prof. art

Western Conn. State Coll., New Haven, 1953-55; instr. Silvermine Guild Art, New Canaan, Conn., 1963-66; dir. Bleifeld Sculpture Group, New Canaan, Conn., 1966—; fellow Tyler Sch. Fine Arts, Temple U., 1967—; commd. Civil Rights Meml., Richmond, Va., 2005-. One-person shows Peridot Gallery, N.Y.C., 1963, 65, 68, Fairfield U., Conn., 1967, FAR Gallery, N.Y.C., 1971, 73, 77, New Britain Mus. Art, Conn., 1974, Kenmore Gallery, Phila., 1967, Franz Bader Gallery, Washington, 1987, 91; exhibited in group shows Internat. Art Festival, Newport, RI, 1964, Am. Fedn. Arts, 1966, 67, Conn. Commn. on Arts, 1972, Parrish Art Mus., Southampton, N.Y., 1968, Century Assn., 2003; represented in permanent collections Mus. of City of N.Y., Fairfield U., Conn., New Britain Mus. Art, Tampa Bay Art Ctr., Fla., Temple U., Phila., Westmoreland Mus., Pa., Pa. State Mus., U. Edinburg, Scotland, L.B. Johnson Libr., Tex.; executed relief sculptures The Prophets, Vatican Pavilion, NY Worlds Fair, 1964-65, Stazzema, Italy, 2003, Magic Carpet, Kokomo Pub. Libr., 1970, Family of Acrobats, Civic Ctr., Orlando, Fla., 1973, Alberta Family, Century Gardens, Calgary, Can., 1981, Father McGivney Meml. KC Internat. Hdqrs., New Haven, 1982, Christopher Columbus, 8'n KC Mus. of States, New Haven, 2000; sculptor U.S. Navy Meml., Washington, 1982—, Jacksonville, Fla., 1988, Great Lakes, Ill., 1997, San Diego, Calif., 1998, Fort Lauderdale, Fla., 2006, Henry C. Singleton, Sr. Monument, Key West, Fla., 1994, Marine Relief, Brookgreen Gardens, SC, 1996, Life Size Pitcher and Catcher Baseball Hall of Fame, Cooperstown, N.Y., 2000, Lone Sailor, Vista Point Golden Gate Bridge, San Francisco, 2000, Homecoming, Norfolk, Va., 2000, Woman at Bat, 2005, Satchel Paige, 2006; designer Medal of Liberty ACLU, 1984. Served with USNR, 1944-46. Recipient Shikler award, Nat. Acad. Design, 1977, Agopoff prize for Classical Sculpture, 2001, Meiselman prize, 1997, 1998, Internat prize for sculpture, Pietrasanta Versilia in the World, XI edit., 2001; fellow Tiffany, 1967. Fellow: Nat. Sculpture Soc. (pres. 1991—93, chmn. editl. bd. Sculpture Rev., treas. 1994, John Gregory award 1964, Bronze medal 1970, Proskauer award 1977, Hexter award 1990, Henry Hering award 1990, Silver medal 1991, Bronze medal 1994, Chilmark award 1994, Hexter award 1998, Henry Hering award 2000); mem.: NAD (accademician coun. 2001—, corr. sec. 2001—), N.Am. Sculpture Soc., Century Assn., Fedn. Internationale de la Medialle, Portrait Soc. Am. (adv. bd. 2000—, Agopoff prize 2001). Jewish. Avocation: tennis. Home: 27 Spring Valley Rd Weston CT 06883-1546

BLEILER, CHARLES ARTHUR, lawyer; b. Boston, Mar. 16, 1945; s. Charles Edward and Grace Rita Bleiler; m. Joyce Ann Kohlmyer, Oct. 6, 1972; children: Charles Edward. BS, Tufts U., 1967; JD, U. San Diego, 1973. BAr: Calif. 1973, U.S. Dist. Ct. (so. dist.) Calif. 1973. Commd. ensign U.S. Navy, 1967, advanced through grades to lt. comdr., resigned, 1978; ptnr. Williams, Clodig & Bleiler, San Diego, 1974-85, Bleiler & Reiter, San Diego, 1985-91, Malowney, Chialtas & Bleiler, San Diego, 1991-93; pres. Charles A. Bleiler A.P.C., San Diego, 1987—. Lectr. San Diego Trial Lawyers Assn., 1982. Bd. dirs. Rancho Santa Fe Cmty. Ctr., Calif., 1990-94, 2001-06, pres., 1993-94, bd. govs., 2006—; mem. San Dieguito Soccer Bd., Encinitas, Calif., 1991-92; bd. dirs. Torrey Pines HS Found., Del Mar, Calif., 1996-98, pres., 1997-98; founding mem., lector Nativity Ch., Rancho Santa Fe; bd. dirs. Rancho Santa Fe Little League, 1989-92; fundraiser for charitable orgns. Named to, So. Calif. Super Lawyer Mag., 2007. Mem. Calif. State Bar, Consumer Attys. San Diego, Calif. Employment Lawyers Assn., Optimist Club (charter pres. Kearny Mesa club 1987-89). Republican. Roman Catholic. Avocations: sailing, horseback riding, skiing, coaching youth baseball and soccer. Home: PO Box 1653 Rancho Santa Fe CA 92067-1653 Office: 12555 High Bluff Dr Ste 150 San Diego CA 92130-2060 Office Phone: 858-350-9833. E-mail: bleiler@worldnet.att.net.

BLEILER, EVERETT FRANKLIN, writer, publishing company executive; b. Boston, Apr. 30, 1920; s. Joseph Eugene and Rose Caroline (Mayor) B.; m. Ellen Haas, May 12, 1956; children: Richard, John, Constance, Dorothy. AB cum laude, Harvard U., 1942; MA, U. Chgo., 1951; Diploma, U. Leiden, The Netherlands, 1952. Freelance writer, 1952-55; advt. mgr. Dover Publs., NYC, 1955-60, mng. dir., 1960-65, exec. v.p., 1965-78; editorial cons. Charles Scribners Sons, NYC, 1978-83. Author more than 60 books including The Checklist of Fantastic Literature, 1948, Essential Japanese Grammar, 1963, Best Tales of Hoffmann, 1967, Mother Goose's Melodies, 1970, Eight Dime Novels of the Victorian Period, 1974, Wagner, The Wehrwolf by G. W. M. Reynolds, 1975, Seventeenth Century Floral Engravings of Emanuel Sweerts, 1976, Richmond, Exploits of a Bow Street Runner, 1976, (under name Liberte E. LeVert) Prophecies and Enigmas of Nostradamus, 1979; A Treasury of Victorian Detective Stories, 1979, A Treasury of Victorian Ghost Stories, 1981, Science Fiction Writers, 1982, The Guide to Supernatural Fiction, 1983, Supernatural Fiction Writers, 1985, Science-Fiction: The Early Years, 1991, Science-Fiction: The Gernsback Years, 1998, Alice and the Snark, 2002, Magistrate Mai and the Invisible Murderer, 2006, Firegang, 2006, others; co-author: (with Wendell C. Bennett) Northwest Argentine Archeology, 1948, (with Guy Stern) Essential German Grammar, 1961. Sgt. U.S. Army, 1942-46. Recipient World Fantasy award World Fantasy Com., Providence, 1978, World Fantasy award (lifetime), London, 1988, Pilgrim award Sci. Fiction Rsch. Assn., 1984, Pres.'s award World Sci. Fiction Assn., 1986, Locus award for best non-fiction book, 1992, Living Legend award Internat. Horror Guild, 2004; named to N.J. Literary Hall of Fame, 1979; knight comdr. Order of Star, Realm of Redonda; Fulbright fellow, 1952. Democrat. Home: 4076 Interlaken Beach Rd Interlaken NY 14847-9632

BLEIWEISS, SHELL J., lawyer; b. Chgo., Mar. 7, 1950; s. Ben and Berte (Melin) B.; m. Patricia Lynn Heck, Dec. 19, 1970 (div. 1976); m. Jo Ellen Rosencrans, May 21, 1985; children: Michael Lawrence, Lowell Rosencrans. BA, So. Ill. U., 1971, MS, 1974; JD, Northwestern U., 1982. Bar: Ill. 1982, U.S. Dist. Ct. (no. dist.) Ill. 1982. Wildlife ecologist Jack McCormick & Assoc., Devon, Pa., 1973-76; project mgr. Betz Converse Murdoch, Plymouth Meeting, Pa., 1976-78; cons. McGraw Hill Publ., NYC, 1978-79; assoc. Sidley & Austin, Chgo., 1981-85, Coffield, Ungaretti, Harris & Slavin, Chgo., 1985-88; ptnr. McDermott, Will & Emery, Chgo., 1988-97; atty. pvt. practice, 1998—. Environ. advisor Roland Burris for Atty. Gen. Campaign, Ill., 1986. NSF fellow, 1970. Mem. ABA (former chair environ. ADR com.), Chgo. Bar Assn. Office: 321 S Plymouth Ct Ste 1200 Chicago IL 60604-3996 Office Phone: 312-360-8782. E-mail: sbleiweiss@shellbleiweiss.com.

BLEKE, DIANE K., music educator, director; b. Springfield, Mo., Jan. 10, 1951; d. Karl William Engeking and Mary Ida Cotler; m. Earl Howard Bieke, Mar. 20, 1982; children: Christine, John, Angela; 1 child, Tanya. MusB, S.W. Mo. State U., 1972; MusM, U. Austin, 1979; degree in Organ, Concordia U., 1995. Pvt. music tchr., Oconomowoc, Wis., 1965—90; social worker Dept. Human Resources, Austin, Tex., 1975—83; dir. choir H.S. St. Paul's Evang. Luth. Ch., Austin, 1982—90; min. music Hope Luth. Ch., Milw., 1990—91; tchr. music Lake Bluff and Atwater Elem. Schs., 1990—91; dir. music St. Paul's Evang. Luth. Ch., Oconomowoc, 1990—. Dir. children's choir King of Kings United Meth. Ch., Sprinfield, Mo., 1970—72; dir. choir Crest View United Meth. Ch., Austin, 1975—82; coach, accompanist U. Tex., Austin, 1972—73; dir. choir, accompanist Austin (Tex.) Children's Choir Concordia Coll., 1987—90. Mem.: Choral Dirs. Assn., Nat. Assn. Tchrs. Singing, Oconomowoc Music Club. Luth. Avocations: harp, guitar, drums, gardening. Home: W358 N5971 Misty Ct Oconomowoc WI 53066-2436 Office: St Pauls Church and School 210 E Pleasant Oconomowoc WI 53066-3050 Office Phone: 262-567-5001 x242. Business E-Mail: ebleke@wi.rr.com.

BLENCOWE, PAUL SHERWOOD, lawyer, private investor; b. Amityville, NY, Feb. 10, 1953; s. Frederick Arthur and Dorothy Jeanne (Ballenger) Blencowe; m. Mary Frances Faulk, Apr. 11, 1992; children: Kristin Amanda, Alison Michelle, Caitlin Emily. BA with honors, U. Wis., 1975; MBA, U. Pa., 1976; JD, Stanford U., 1979. Bar: Tex. 1979, Calif. 1989. Assoc. Fulbright & Jaworski, Houston, 1979-86, London, 1986-87, ptnr., 1988-89, Fulbright & Jaworski L.L.P., LA, 1989-2000, of counsel, 2000—. Editor: China's Quest for Independence: Policy Evolution in the 1970s, 1980; editor-in-chief Stanford Jour. of Internat. Law, 1978-79; contbr. articles on U.S. securities and corp. law to profl. jours. Mem. The Calif. Club, Phi Beta Kappa, Phi Kappa Phi, Beta Theta Pi. Office: Fulbright & Jaworski LLP 555 S Flower St Fl41 Los Angeles CA 90071 Office Phone: 213-892-9332. Business E-Mail: pblencowe@fulbright.com.

BLENDON, ROBERT JAY, health policy educator; b. Dec. 19, 1942; s. Edward and Theresa Blendon; m. Marie C. McCormick, Dec. 31, 1977. BA, Marietta Coll., Ohio, 1964; MBA, U. Chgo., 1966; MPH, Johns Hopkins U., 1967, DSc, 1969. Fellow Ind. U. Med. Ctr., Indpls., 1965—66; instr. dept. med. care and hosps. Johns Hopkins U. Sch. Hygiene and Pub. Health, Balt., 1969—70, asst. to assoc. dean for health care programs Sch. Medicine, 1969—70, asst. prof. dept. med. care and hosps., 1970—71; asst. dir. planning and devel. Office of Health Care Programs, Johns Hopkins Med. Instns., Balt., 1970—71; spl. asst. for health affairs to dep. undersec. for policy coordination HEW, Washington, 1971—72, spl. asst. for policy devel. to asst. sec. to health and sci. affairs, 1971—72; sr. v.p. Robert Wood Johnson Found., Princeton, NJ, 1987; prof. health policy and polit. analysis Harvard U. Sch. Pub. Health and Kennedy Sch. of Govt., Boston, 1987—; dep. dir. health policy Harvard U. Vis. lectr. Princeton U., 1972—87; sr. policy analyst com. on health svcs. industry Cost of Living Coun., Washington, 1971. Mem. editl. bd.: Jour. of Am. Med. Assn., 1992—. Mem.: Inst. Medicine NAS, Council Fgn. Rels. Home: 478 Quinobequin Rd Newton MA 02468-2127 Office: Harvard U Sch Pub Health 677 Huntington Ave Boston MA 02115-6028 Office Phone: 617-432-4502. Business E-Mail: rblendon@hdph.harvard.edu.

BLENKO, WALTER JOHN, JR., lawyer; b. Pitts., June 15, 1926; s. Walter J. and Ardis Leah (Jones) B.; m. Joy Kinneman, Apr. 9, 1949; children: John W., Andrew W. BS, Carnegie-Mellon U., 1950; JD, U. Pitts., 1953. Bar: Pa. 1954. Pvt. practice law, Pitts., 1954—; ptnr. Eckert, Seamans, Cherin & Mellott, Pitts., 1984-93, of counsel, 1993—. Mem. adv. bd. dept. mech. engring. Carnegie-Mellon U., 1992—2000; arbitrator NASD, Coun. of Better Bus. Burs. Active Churchill Vol. Fire Co., 1970-82; charter and hon. mem. Wilkinsburg Emergency Med. Svc.; sec. Hampton Twp. Zoning Hearing Bd., 1991-92, vice-chmn., 1993; mem. Hampton Twp. Sch. Bd., 1993-97, pres. 1996; mem. Allegheny County Parks adv. bd., 2000-02; trustee, v.p. Classic Car Club Am. Mus., 2005-; bd. dirs. Pitts. Civic Light Opera, Gateway to the Arts. With U.S. Army, 1944-46, ETO Decorated Bronze Star, Combat Inf. badge; recipient Disting. Svc. award Carnegie-Mellon U. Alumni Assn., 1993, Recognition award Carnegie Mellon U. Andrew Carnegie Soc., 2002. Fellow Am. Coll. Trial Lawyers, Allegheny County Bar Found.; mem. ASME, Pa. Bar Assn., Allegheny County Bar Assn., Assn. Bar of City of N.Y., Pitts. Intellectual Property Law Assn. (pres. 1977-78), Engrs. Soc. Western Pa., Carnegie-Mellon U. Alumni Assn. (exec. bd. 1996-2001, exec. com. 1997-2001), Duquesne Club, Princeton Club (N.Y.), Rolls-Royce Owners Club (bd. dirs. 1982-84, v.p. publs. 1984-87, treas. 1987-89), Pitts. Athletic Assn. Avocation: classic cars. Home: 4073 Middle Rd Allison Park PA 15101-1207 Office: Eckert Seamans Cherin & Mellott 600 Grant St Pittsburgh PA 15219-2702 Office Phone: 412-566-6000.

BLESER, PHILIP F., diversified financial services company executive; AAS, Pace U. Lubin Sch. Bus., 1981, BBA, 1984, MBA, 1994; grad., Am. Inst. Banking. Banker Mfrs. Hanover Trust Co.; sr. v.p., divsn. exec. J.P. Morgan Chase & Co. Mem. adv. bd. Pace U. Lubin Sch. Bus. Office: JP Morgan Chase and Co 270 Park Ave New York NY 10017-2070

BLESSEN, KAREN ALYCE, freelance/self-employed journalist, artist; b. Columbus, Nebr. BFA, U. Nebr., 1973. Freelance illustrator, 1973-86; designer Dallas Morning News, 1986-89, freelance illustrator, designer, 1989—; owner, illustrator Karen Blessen Illustration, Dallas, 1989—; artist Times Square Bus. Improvement Dist., NYC, 1994—. Illustrator Be An Angel, 1994; Peace One Day, 2005; contbr. (art and articles) Dallas Morning News; commd. by Absolut to represent Tex. in Absolute Statehood series; co-founder (non-profit arts orgn.) Today Marks the Beginning. Recipient Pulitzer Prize for explanatory journalism, 1989, awards, N.Y. Art Dirs. Club, Soc. Newspaper Design, Dallas Press Club. Home and Office: Karen Blessen Illustration 6327 Vickery Blvd Dallas TX 75214-3348 E-mail: kblessen@aol.com, kblessen@sbcglobal.net.

BLESSING, EDWARD WARFIELD, petroleum company executive; m. Kalita Hardin Beck, June 11, 2005; 1 child, Megan Louise. BA, San Diego State U., 1960; MBA, Harvard U., 1965. Rep. Shearson, Hammill & Co, La Jolla, Calif., 1961-63; cons. McKinsey & Co. Inc., San Francisco and L.A., 1965-68; assoc. mng. dir. Canadawide Investments, Vancouver, BC and Calgary, 1968-69; misc. investor energy and fin. related activities, 1969-75; mng. ptnr. Dexer Assocs., LA and Sharjah, United Arab Emirates, 1975-78; exec. v.p. Okla. Oil & Gas Co., Oklahoma City, 1978-80; pres. Blessing Petroleum Co., Blessing Oil Co., Oklahoma City, 1980-87; dir., pres., CEO Strategic Petroleum, Inc., Dallas, 1987-89; mng. ptnr. The Blessing Group, Dallas, 1989—2000; mng. dir. Blessing Petroleum Group, LLC, Dallas, 2000—. Ind. dir.; chair Governance Com., Nominating Com.; mem. audit com. Natural Gas Ptnrs. Capital Resource Co.; vis. instr., adj. prof. U. Okla. Grad. Sch. Bus. Adminstrn., Okla. City, 1983-84; spkr. in field. Res. dep. sheriff Okla. County Sheriff's Dept., Okla. City, 1986-87, Dallas County Sheriff's Dept., 1987-89; mem. Mayor's Adv. Com. on Crime, Dallas, 1988-91; Rep. candidate Calif. 79th Assembly Dist., 1960; hon. dir., chmn. bd. dirs. Calif. Pediatric Ctr., LA, 1973—; mem. energy subcom. Okla. Dept. Commerce, Okla. City, 1987; mem. planning com. Okla. Gov.'s 1987 Energy Conf., Oklahoma City; chmn. stewardship com., lay eucharist min., vestryman Trinity Episcopal Ch.; lay eucharist min., stewardship com., lector St. Michael's & All Angels Episcopal Ch., Dallas; mentor, judge So. Meth. U. Cary M. Maguire Ctr. Ethics and Responsibility. With USMC, 1960-61. Mem. Ind. Petroleum Assn. Am. (regional gov., exec. com., trustee North Ctrl. Tex. region, fin. com., v.p., dir., Roustabout, mem. econs. policy com., crude oil policy com., econ. task force 1980—), Tex. Ind. Prodrs. and Royalty Owners Assn., Dallas C. of C. (energy subcom. 1987-90), Tex. Alliance Energy Prodrs. (chmn.'s coun.), Harvard Bus. Sch. Alumni Assn. (sponsor), Tex. Energy Edn. Partnership (dir. mem. exec. com.), Bus. and Industry Action Com. (dir.), Oklahoma City C. of C. (chmn. energy coun. 1982-87), Hard Hatters, Dallas Wildcat Com., Dallas Petroleum Club (bd. dirs. 1992-94), Calgary Petroleum Club, Houston Petroleum Club, Harvard Club (NY), Dubai Offshore Sailing Club, Royal Vancouver Yacht Club. Office: Blessing Petroleum Group LLC 8235 Douglas Ave Ste 1325 Dallas TX 75225 Office Phone: 972-490-0200.

BLESSING, LEONARD C., secondary school educator; b. Newark, Oct. 16, 1920; s. David L. and Mildred Blessing; m. Frances Meeker Blessing, Apr. 8, 1944; children: Lynn C. Blessing Hogan, Leslee C. Blessing Mabee. BA, Montclair U., Montclair, NJ, 1950; MA, Montclair U., 1951; postgrad., U. Sussex, Eng., 1973. Cert. tchr. N.J. Home office calculator Prudential Ins. Co., N ewark, 1938—47; sci. tchr. Wayne H.S., Wayne, NJ, 1950—52; biology, chemistry tchr. Millburn H.S., 1952—58, sci. dept. head., 1958—80; sci. supr. Millburn Sch. Dist., 1980—88; ret., 1988; track coach Millburn H.S., 1952—60. Author: Crossing Your Bidding Bridges, 1957, Unified Science, 1967. Pianist New Providence United Meth. Ch., 1994—. Named Outstanding Biology Tchr., Theobold Smith Microbiology Soc., 1967, Outstanding Adminstr., N.J. Sci. Suprs. Assn., 1983, 1987, Outstanding Educator, N.J. Senate, 1970; named one of Six Outstanding Biology Tchrs. in U.S., Nat. Assn. Biology Tchrs., 1966; recipient Bob Ryder Outstanding Sportsmanship award, N.J. Contract Bridge Assn., 2004, Plaque of Appreciation, N.J. Sci. League, 2002, Spl. Citation Scroll, N.J. Sci. Tchrs. Assn., 1977;, Fulbright Found. fellow, 1960—61. Fellow: AAAS (internat. com. 1998—, officer internat. divsn.), N.J. Sci. Tchrs. Assn. (pres. 1967); mem.: Nat. Assn. Biology Tchrs. (dist. rep. 1969—72, chmn. internat. com. 1991—2001, Outstanding Biology Tchr. 1967). Achievements include being a national championship bridge player. Avocation: travel. Home: 103 Primrose Dr New Providence NJ 07974

BLESSING, MAXINE LINDSEY, secondary school educator; b. Skirum, Ala., Mar. 27, 1920; d. John Amos and Lizzy Maude (Croft) Lindsey; m. Alvin Reed Blessing, June 24, 1939; 1 child, Deanna Dawn Blessing Gilbert. BS in Secondary English Edn., Jacksonville State U., Ala., 1956; postgrad., Auburn U., 1974-75. Tchr. DeKalb County (Ala.) Schs., 1943-97; ret., 1997. Beta Club sponsor Crossville (Ala.) H.S., 1960—, drama dir. jr. and sr. plays, 1960—, interim counselor. Sunday sch. tchr., pianist, organist Skirum Bapt. Ch., Crossville. Mem. AAUW, NEA, Nat. Coun. Tchrs. English, Ala. Coun. Tchrs. English, Ala. Edn. Assn., DeKalb County Edn. Assn. (mem. English textbook com. 1988-89), Ea. Star (worthy matron 1944-45), Skirum Cmty. Club (various coms.). Democrat. Baptist. Avocations: music, church and community activities, bridge, reading, attending plays. Home: 2314 County Road 46 Dawson AL 35963-3400 Office: Crossville HS PO Box 38 Crossville AL 35962-0038

BLESSING-MOORE, JOANN CATHERINE, allergist, pulmonologist; b. Tacoma, Sept. 21, 1946; d. Harold R. and Mildred (Benson) Blessing; m. Robert Chester Moore; 1 child, Ahna. BA in Chemistry, Syracuse U., 1968; MD, SUNY, Syracuse, 1972. Diplomate Am. Bd. Pediatrics, Am. Bd. Allergy Immunology, Am. Bd. Pediatric Pulmonology. Pediatric intern, then resident Stanford U. Sch. Medicine, Palo Alto, Calif., 1972-75, allergy pulmonology fellow, 1975-77; co-dir. pediatric allergy pulmonology dept. Stanford U. Children's Hosp., Palo Alto, Calif., 1977-84; clin. asst. prof. dept. Allergy Immunology Respiratory Disease (AIR) Stanford U. Sch. Medicine, Palo Alto, Calif., 1977-84, co-dir. pediatric pulmonology lab., 1977-84; clin. asst. prof. dept. immunology Stanford U. Hosp., 1984—; allergist Palo Alto Med. Clinic, 1984-90; pvt. practice allergy immunology-pediatric-pulmonary Palo Alto, San Mateo, Calif., 1990—. Dir. ednl. program for children with asthma Camp Wheeze, Palo Alto, 1975-90; cons. FDA, Allergy Pulmonary Adv. Bd., 1992-97; cons. in field. Author handbooks, camp program manuals; co-editor jour. supplements; mem. edit. bd. Allergy jours.; contbr. articles to sci. publs. Fellow Am. Acad. Allery, Asthma, Immunology (various offices 1980—, joint task force parameters of care asthma and allergy 1989—, Outstanding fellow 1998, Women in Allergy award 2000), Am. Coll. Chest Physicians (com. mem. 1980—), Am. Coll. Asthma, Allergy and Immunology (mem. regent com. 1995-98); mem. Am. Thoracic Soc., Am. Lung Assn., No. Calif. Allergy Found. (bd. dirs., pres.), Peninsula Women's Assn., Santa Clara and San Mateo County Med. Soc. (bd. dirs. 1999-2004), Chi Omega. Republican. Presbyterian. Avocations: music, sailing, skiing, horseback riding, scuba diving. Office: 780 Welch Rd Ste 204 Palo Alto CA 94304-1518 also: Stanford Univ Hosp Dept Immunology Palo Alto CA 94304 Office Phone: 650-696-8236. Business E-Mail: j_blessingmoore@hotmail.com.

BLESZINSKI, CLIFF (CLIFFORD MICHAEL BLESZINSKI), game designer; b. North Adover, Mass., Feb. 12, 1975; Working on video games since, 1994—; lead designer Epic Games, Inc., Raleigh, NC. Spkr. in field. Featured in NY Times, LA Times, Entertainment Weekly and other mainstream publications, creator games Unreal, Jazz Jackrabbit, The Palace of Deceit: Dragon's Plight, Dare to Dream, Unreal Tournament series, lead designer Gears of War, 2006, co-host G-Phoria. Co-recipient Rave award-Games, WIRED Mag., 2007.

BLETHEN, FRANK A., newspaper publisher; b. Seattle, Apr. 20, 1945; BS in Bus., Ariz. State U. Pub. Walla Walla Union-Bulletin, Wash., 1975-79; exec. in circulation, advt., mktg. & labor Seattle Times Co., 1980—85, pub. & CEO circulation mgr., 1985—. Chmn. Walla Walla Union-Bull., Yakima (Wash.) Herald Republic, Blethen Maine Newspapers, Portland, Augusta, Waterville; pres. Blethen Corp. Mem. pres.' adv. bd. Wash. State U. and U. Wash.; campaign chair United Way King County, 1996, 97, bd. dirs., 1996; bd. dirs. Maynard Inst. for Minority Journalism Edn., 1994—. Recipient Pulitzer prize (3) for best newspaper reporting and investigative reporting, 1997, Nat. Reports, 1991, Ida B. Wells award for lifetime achievement in advancement of minority employment, 1997, Leadership Conf. on Civil Rights Chairperson's award for spl. merit, 1999, Edward R. Murrow award Wash. State U., 1998, Weldon B. Gibson Disting. Vol. award Wash. State U., 1998; named to Wash. State Hall of Journalistic Achievement, 1998. Mem. Nat. Assn. of Minority Media Execs., Am. Newspaper Pubs. Assn. (bd. dirs., chmn. telecomm. com.), Sigma Delta Chi. Office: Seattle Times PO Box 70 Seattle WA 98111 also: Seattle Times 1120 John St Seattle WA 98109*

BLETHEN, SANDRA LEE, pediatric endocrinologist; b. San Mateo, Calif., May 16, 1942; d. Howard Albion and Laura Katherine (Wolf) B.; m. Fred I. Chasalow, Nov. 26, 1966. BS in Biochemistry, U. Chgo., 1961; PhD in Biochemistry, U. Calif., Berkeley, 1965; MD, Yeshiva U., 1975. Diplomate Am. Bd. Pediat. Fellow biochemistry Brandeis U., Waltham, Mass., 1965-68; instr. biochemistry U. Calif., San Diego, 1968-69; asst. prof. San Francisco State U., 1969-71; resident in pediat. Columbia Presbyn. Med. Ctr., NYC, 1975-77; fellow pediatric endocrinology U. N.C., Chapel Hill, 1977-79; asst. prof. pediatrics Washington U., St. Louis, 1979-84; assoc. prof. pediat. SUNY, Stony Brook, 1985-96; assoc. attending pediatrician L.I. Jewish Med. Ctr., New Hyde Park, NY, 1984-90; attending pediatrician Univ. Hosp., Stony Brook, 1991-96; cons. Genentech, Inc., South San Francisco, Calif., 1985-96, sr. endocrinologist, 1996—99, assoc. dir. product experience, 1997-2000, sr. clin. scientist, 1999—2002; v.p. med. affairs metabolic endocrinology Serono, Inc., Rockland, Md., 2002—. Cons. Diagnostic Systems Labs., Webster, Tex., 1989-96. Mem. editl. bd. Steroids, 1990—, Jour. of Endocrinology and Metabolism, 1995-98; contbr. more than 90 articles to profl. jours. Predoctoral fellow NSF, 1961-63, Postdoctoral fellow USPHS, 1965-67. Mem. Am. Pediatric Soc. (program com. 1994), Endocrine Soc., Lawson Wilkens Pediatric Endocrine Soc. (membership chair 1994-95), Soc. for Pediatric Rsch., Phi Beta Kappa, Alpha Omega Alpha. Avocation: sailing. Office: Serono Inc 1 Tech Pl Rockland MA 02370 Office Phone: 781-681-2433. Personal E-mail: sandra.blethen@serono.com.

BLEUSTEIN, JEFFREY L., motorcycle company executive; b. 1939; BS in Mech. Engring., Cornell U.; MS in Engring. Mechanics, PhD in Engring. Mechanics, Columbia U. Assoc. prof. engring. & applied sciences. Yale U., 1966—71; mem., ctrl tech. staff AMF, Inc., 1971; with Harley-Davidson Inc., Milw., 1975—, pres., Trihawk, Inc., 1984—85, v.p. parts and accessories divsn., 1985—88, exec. v.p., 1990—93, pres., COO, 1993—97, pres., CEO, 1997—98, chmn., CEO, 1998—2005, chmn., 2005—. Mem. bd. dirs. Harley Davidson Inc., 1996—, Brunswick Corp., 1997—, The Kohler Corp., 2003—; mem. Pres. Coun. on 21st Century Workplace US Dept. Labor, 2002—03. Mem. bd. dirs. Greater Milw. Com., Milw. Jewish Fedn., Milw. Florentine Opera, Med. Coll Wis.; regent emeritus Milw. Sch. Engring. Office: Harley Davidson Inc 3700 W Juneau Ave Milwaukee WI 53208*

BLEVEANS, JOHN, lawyer; b. Danville, Ill., Mar. 29, 1938; s. Edward Harold and Angelita (Robinson) B.; m. Luanna Harrison Burdick, Aug. 17, 1962; children: Lincoln Edward, Melanie Catherine. BA, Trinity U., 1960;

LLB, U. Tex., 1965. Bar: Tex. 1965, D.C. 1967, U.S. Supreme Ct. 1969, Ill. 1971. Mem. gen. counsel's office Acacia Mut. Life Ins. Co., Washington, 1967-68; trial and appellate atty., civil rights div. U.S. Dept. Justice, Washington, 1966-67, 69-70; exec. dir. Washington Lawyers' Com., Civil Rights Under Law, 1970-71; chief counsel Lawyers' Com., Civil Rights Under Law, Cairo, Ill., 1971-72; assoc. Mayer, Brown & Platt, Chgo., 1972-74, ptnr., 1974-83, 91-92; sr. v.p., assoc., gen. counsel Continental Ill. Nat. Bank and Trust Co. of Chgo., 1983-89; dep. gen. counsel Continental Bank N.A., Chgo., 1989-91; ptnr. Mayer, Brown & Platt, Chgo., 1991-92; of counsel Arthur Andersen & Co., Chgo., 1992-95, Hong Kong, 1996-97, Sydney, Australia, 1995-96. Tour guide Tri State Travel, Galena, Ill., 2002—, bus driver; pres. Hanover Ambulance, Inc., 2000, treas. 2006-07. Alderman City of Evanston, Ill., 1981-89; chmn. Evanston Zoning Bd. Appeals, 1991-92; vol. Hanover Ambulance, 1999—. Capt. USNR ret. Mem. Tex. Bar Assn., D.C. Bar Assn., Nat. Ski Patrol, Law Club Chgo. Home: 8634 Fisher Rd Hanover IL 61041-9561 E-mail: jakeb@netexpress.net.

BLEVINS, CHARLES RUSSELL, publishing executive; b. Kittaning, Pa., Apr. 6, 1942; s. Clarence Ray and Elizabeth Sarah (Warren) B.; m. Gale Watkins Crittenden, Dec. 16, 1967; children: Charles Jr., Rush. BS, Ind. U., 1964. Asst. prodn. exec. Wall St. Jour., Cleve., D.C. and Princeton, 1964-71, Gannett Co. Inc., El Paso Agy., El Paso, Tex., 1971-76; prodn. exec. Rockford Newspapers, Rockland, Ill., 1976-77; corp. prodn. dir. Gannett Corp. Hdqrs., Rochester, N.Y., 1977-79, v.p., prodn. Arlington, Va., 1979-89; CEO Blevins Harding Group, Vienna, Va., 1989-98; pres., CEO Chuck Blevins & Assocs., Vienna, 1998—. Speaker European Printing Conf., Newspaper Quality Meeting Conf.; chmn. Conf. Quality-Newspaper Assn., Conf. Research & Engring. Council, Chgo., Rsch. and Engring. Coun. Com. Graphic Arts Techs. Standards Unit Loading. Creator quality standards, operating procedures USA Today, 1981-86. Judge RIT/USA Today Quality Cup for Individuals and Teams, 1992-2000; chmn. long range planning com. Vanderbilt Country Club. Mem. Am. Newspaper Pub. Assn. (tech. com. 1985-89, officer internat. newspaper group 1989—), Rsch. and Engring. Coun. of Graphic Arts (v.p. 1985-94), Rochester Inst. Tech. Coun., W.Va. Inst. Tech. Adv. Coun., Inca Fiej Rsch. Assn. (press com. 1984-89), Vanderbilt Country Club (chmn. long range planning com.). Office: Chuck Blevins & Assocs 8396 Northhampton Naples FL 34120 Business E-Mail: chuckblevins@chuckblevins.com.

BLEVINS, DALE GLENN, agronomy educator; b. Ozark, Mo., Aug. 29, 1943; s. Vernon Henry and Edna Gertrude Blevins; 1 child, Jeremy. BS in Chemistry, S.W. Mo. State U., 1965; MS in Soils, U. Mo., 1967; PhD in Plant Physiology, U. Ky., 1972. Postdoctoral fellow botany dept. Oreg. State U., Corvallis, Oreg., 1972-74; asst. prof. botany U. Md., College Park, 1974-78; assoc. prof. agronomy dept. U. Mo., Columbia, 1978-86, prof., 1986—. Mem. Am. Soc. Plant Physiology, Am. Soc. Agronomy, Crop Sci. Soc. Am. Office: Univ Mo Divsn Plant Scis 1-31 Agriculture Building Columbia MO 65211-7140

BLEVINS, ERNEST EVERETT, genealogist, researcher, historian; b. Spartanburg, SC, Nov. 16, 1968; s. Maurice Everett Blevins and Anne Soule Lapham; m. Lisa Ann Schlosser, Dec. 30, 1975; children: Everett(dec.) , Ana Grace, Cameren Everett. BA in Studio Art, Coll. Charleston, SC, 1987—92, BS in Anthropology, 1987—92; MFA in Hist. Preservation, Savannah Coll. Art and Design, Ga., 2001; postgrad. in History, Ga. State U., Atlanta, 2004—06; postgrad. in Public History, History, State U. West Ga., Carrollton, 2003—. Asst. prodn. manger, stagehand Charleston Symphony Orch., SC, 1989—99, prodn. mgr., 1996; stagehand Savannah Symphony Orch., Ga., 1995—99; archtl. conservator Liollio Architecture, Charleston, SC, 1997—98; owner Blevins Hist. Rsch., Villa Rica, Ga., 1997—; guest lectr., hist. preservation Coll. Charleston, SC, 1998; hist. preservation planner, housing specialist, E. Tenn. Devel. Dist., Knoxville, 1999—2000; historian, assoc. transp. planner Ga. Dept. Transp., Atlanta, 2000—01; prof. history Ga. Highlands Coll., 2005—. Bd. dirs. Warehouse Teen Ctr., Spartanburg, SC, 1986—87; chmn. Villa Rica Hist. Preservation Com., Ga., 2003—07, chair, 2005—06; cmdr. Kennesan Mountain SU-VCW Camp, 2006. Actor: (films) Gods and Generals, The Hunley, An American Tempest, Close to Danger; tech. mgr.: (webpage) The Real Story of the American Revolution; contbr. articles to profl. jours., columns in newspapers, articles to newspapers. Vol. Bill Workman for Congress, Spartanburg, SC, 1986. 2nd lt. S.C. State Guard, 1998—99, Charleston. Recipient Ray A. Croc Citizenship Award, McDonald's Corp., Spartanburg H.S., 1987. Mem.: Assn. Ga. State U. Historians (sec. 2004—05), S.C. Hist. Soc., Am. Planning Assn., Am. Hist. Assn., New Eng. Hist. & Geneal. Soc., Nat. Coun. on Pub. History, Ga. Trust for Hist. Preservation, Assn. for State and Local History, Assn. Profl. Genealogists (scribe, Ga. chpt. 2004—05), Nat. Trust for Hist. Preservation, E. Tenn. Hist. Soc., Ga. Hist. Soc., Huguenot Soc., Order Founders and Patriots Am. (registrar 2005—07), 10th SC Vol. Infantry Reenactors (sec. 1997—98), Sons of Union Veterans of the Civil War (patriotic instr. 2005—, cmdr. 2006—), Alden Kindred Am. (assoc. Genealogist's Award for Complete Documentation 2004), SAR (assoc.; historian 2005—06, webmaster 2005—06, genealogist 2007—, Best Chapt. Webpage 2005—06), Sons of Confederate Vetrans (life), Soc. of Mayflower Descendants (life; asst. dep. gov., S.C. historian 1995—96), Alpha Phi Omega (life; v.p., adminstrn., alumni sec., historian 1988—98). Conservative. Avocations: genealogy, travel, writing, music, history. Home: 110 Evergreen Way Villa Rica GA 30180 Office: Blevins Hist Rsch 110 Evergreen Way Villa Rica GA 30180 Home Phone: 770-456-1876; Office Phone: 770-456-1876. Personal E-mail: blevins@alumni.cofc.edu.

BLEVINS, JAMES RAY, lawyer, insurance company claims executive; b. Jefferson, NC, Mar. 20, 1949; s. Oscar Ray and Helen Marie (Clark) B.; m. Patricia Fay Faltermann, Dec. 27, 1970; children: Jennifer Renee, James Ray Jr. BA, Wake Forest U., 1971, JD, 1978; MS in Edn., U. So. Calif., 1975. Bar: N.C. 1978, S.C. 1993; registered profl. adjuster. Claims atty. Integon Ins. Co., Winston-Salem, N.C., 1979-80, field claims mgr., asst. v.p., 1980-85; Mid-Atlantic regional claims mgr. Amerisure Ins. Co., Charlotte, 1985-90; v.p., claims mgr. Sedgwick James of the Carolinas, Columbia, S.C., 1990-92; pvt. practice claims cons. and lawyer Columbia, 1992-94; litigation mgr. Seibels Bruce Ins. Co., Columbia, S.C., 1994-98; dir. spl. claims Burlington (N.C.) Ins. Co., 1998—. Del. N.C. Dem. Conv., Raleigh, 1976, S.C. Dem. Conv., Columbia, 1996. 1st lt. U.S. Army, 1971-75, capt. N.C. Army Nat. Guard, 1975-87, lt. col. judge adv. USAR, 1987-97. Mem. ABA, N.C. Bar Assn., S.C. Bar Assn. Democrat. Presbyterian. Avocation: reading.

BLEVINS, JEFFREY ALEXANDER, lawyer; b. Forest Hills, NY, June 18, 1955; s. William E. and Mary J. Blevins; m. Pamela A. Manos, Nov. 26, 1983 (div. Mar. 1995); 1 child, Mary Alexandria; m. Diane L. Bannon, June 12, 1999; stepchildren: Meagan Elizabeth, Laura Leigh, Jeffrey Daniel. BA, Denison U., 1977; JD, DePaul U., 1981. Bar: Ill. 1981, U.S. Dist Ct. (no. dist.) Ill. 1981, U.S. Dist. Ct. (we. dist. Wis. 1984, U.S. Ct. Appeals (7th cir.) 1984, U.S. Supreme Ct. 1990. Personnel specialist Comerica Bank, Detroit, 1979-80; assoc. Bell, Boyd & Lloyd, Chgo., 1981-88, ptnr., mem., 1988—2001; mng. atty. The Law Office of Jeffrey A. Blevins LLC, Naperville, Ill., 2001—02; employment counsel Prairie State Legal Svcs., 2002—. Lectr., author Ill. Inst. Continuing Legal Edn., others; chair employment sect. Ctr. for Disability and Elder Law, 1999—. Editor in chief DePaul Law Rev., 1980. Mem. Ill. State Bar Assn. (labor and employment coun. 1992-95), Chgo. Bar Assn., Omicron Delta Epsilon. Republican. Lutheran.

BLEVINS, STANLEY NANCE, minister, educator; b. Comanche, Tex., Oct. 2, 1938; s. A.J. and Ruby Blevins; m. Betty Jo Westfall, Apr. 17, 1960; children: Ronald, Kristi Dean. BA, Hardin-Simmons U., 1961; MDiv, Southwestern Bapt. Theol. Sem., 1964, D of Ministry, 1982. Sr. pastor First Bapt. Ch., Lueders, Tex., 1964—66, Jackson Ave. Bapt. Ch., Lovington, N.Mex., 1966—69, Oakwood Bapt. Ch., Lubbock, Tex., 1969—79, Ctrl. Bapt. Ch., Bryan, Tex., 1979—86, Highland Bapt. Ch., Lubbock, 1986—. Adj. prof. Wayland Bapt. U. , Lubbock, 2000—; trustee Hardin-Simmons U., Abilene, Tex., 1988—97, bd. of devel., 1998—; exec. bd. Bapt. Gen. Conv. of Tex., Dallas, 1972—79, 1981—86. Contbr. articles to profl. jours. Recipient Disting. Alumnus award, Logsdon Sch. of Theology Hardin-Simmons U., 1999. Mem.: Aircraft Owners & Pilots Assn., Colo. R.R. Hist. Found., Rocky Mountain R.R. Club. Avocations: narrow gauge railroad history, photography, writing. Home: PO Box 93777 Lubbock TX 79493-3777 Office: Highland Baptist Ch 4316 34th St Lubbock TX 79410 Office Phone: 806-795-6453.

BLEVINS, WILLIAM EDWARD, management consultant; b. Boissevan, Va., Oct. 18, 1927; s. Howard Muncey and Elsie Jane (Wire) B.; m. Mary Hester Jenkins, Aug. 25, 1951; children— Jeffrey Alexander, Jennifer Lynn, Bradley Edward. AB, Marshall Coll., 1951; MPA, CCNY, 1960. Personnel mgr. Equitable Life, NYC, 1951-66; asst. v.p., dir. mgmt. devel. Nat. Bank Detroit, 1966-69, v.p., dir. personnel, 1969-74, sr. v.p., dir. personnel, 1974-91; exec. v.p., dir. human resources NBD Bancorp, Inc., Detroit, 1980-92; pres. WEB Communications Co., Detroit, 1993—2004. Trustee Bon Secour Hosp., Grosse Pointe, Mich., 1975-84; chmn. St. John Sr. Cmty., 1995-2004, St. John Health Sr. Svcs., 2000-04; bd. dirs. Oxford Inst., 1987-89, Holy Cross Hosp., 1996-98, Mich. Diabetes Assn., 1982-86, Mich. Soc. for Mental Health, 1984-87, Lancaster Heart and Stroke Found., Susquehanna Assn. Blind and Visually Impared, 2005-07; corp. adv. bd. Am. Heart Assn., 1995-98; trustee Frances Rhodes, M.D. Meml. Found., 1999-2004; personnel com. Lancaster County Coun. Chs. Recipient Outstanding Alumnus award Marshall U., 1976, Hall of Fame award Lambda Chi Alpha, 1996. Mem. Am. Bankers Assn. (bd. dirs. 1974-75), Am. Inst. Banking (bd. dirs., bd. regents, chmn. 1983-90), Am. Soc. Employers (bd. dirs. 1970-94, treas. 1970-90, vice chmn. 1991-92, chmn. 1992-94), Alpha Bank Pers Group (founder, chmn. 1972-74, 86), Mich. Pers. Indsl. Rels. Group (chmn. 1980-92), Bank Adminstr. Inst. (human resources commn. 1983-88), Detroit Athletic Club, Country Club Detroit, Conastoga Country Club. Republican. Office: 611 Willow Valley Lakes Dr Willow Street PA 17584-9647 Office Phone: 717-464-2875. Personal E-mail: webmjb@comcast.net. *How lucky I am to live in the USA. It offers a fine education to those who want it; meaningful jobs to those who prepare and strive, a wonderful place for romance, an ideal place to raise a family. I have been truly blessed with lots of help along the way.*

BLEWETT, DAVID LAMBERT, English literature educator; b. Calgary, Alta., Can., Dec. 18, 1940; s. John and Sydney Catherine (Cole) B. BA with honors, U. Man., Winnipeg, 1962, MA, 1963; PhD, U. Toronto, Ont., Can., 1971. Lectr. McMaster U., Hamilton, Ont., Canada, 1969-71, asst. prof., 1971-77, assoc. prof., 1977-84, prof., 1984—2003, prof. emeritus, 2003—. Author: DeFoe's Art of Fiction, 1979, The Illustration of Robinson Crusoe: 1719-1920, 1995, Japanese trans., 1998; editor: Roxana, 1982, Amelia, 1987, Moll Flanders, 1989, Roderick Random, 1995, Passion and Virtue; Essays on the Novels of Samuel Richardson, 2001, Satire, Fantasy, and Writings on the Supernatural by Daniel Defoe, Vol. 5, 2005; editor Eighteenth-Century Fiction, 1988—2003; contbr. chpts. to books. Grantee Social Scis. and Humanities Rsch. Coun. Can., 1989-90, 96-99. Mem. Am. Soc. for Eighteenth-Century Studies, Can. Assn. for Eighteenth-Century Studies, Reform Club, McMaster U. Faculty Assn. (pres. 1992-93). Avocations: travel, music. Home: 390 Wellesley St E # 16 Toronto ON Canada M4X 1H6 E-mail: blewett@mcmaster.ca.

BLEWITT, THOMAS MICHAEL, chief US magistrate judge; b. Pittston, Pa., Nov. 20, 1949; m. Evelyn Bubser; three children. BA, U. Scranton, 1972; MPA, Marywood Coll., 1979; JD, Temple U., 1983. Bar: Pa. 1983. Spl. investigator Pa. Bur. Consumer Protection, Harrisburg, 1972-80; assoc. Law Office Marshall E. Anders, Stroudsburg, Pa., 1983-84; asst. dist. atty. Lackawanna County, Scranton, Pa., 1984-86; asst. fed. pub. defender for mid. dist. Pa. Office Fed. Pub. Defender, Scranton, 1986-92; assoc. Lenahan & Dempsey, Scranton, 1988-89; magistrate judge for mid. dist. Pa., U.S. Magistrate Ct., Scranton, 1992—; chief magistrate judge Mid. Dist. Ct. Pa., 2002—. Office: US Magistrate Ct 217 Fed Bldg PO Box 443 235 N Washington Ave Scranton PA 18501-0443

BLEY, CARLA BORG, composer; b. Oakland, Calif., May 11, 1938; d. Emil Carl and Arlene (Anderson) Borg; m. Paul Bley, Jan. 27, 1959 (div. Sept. 1967); m. Michael Mantler, Sept. 29, 1967 (div. 1992); 1 dau., Karen. Student public schs., Oakland. Mem. adv. bd. Jazz Composers Orch. Assn. Freelance jazz composer, 1956—, pianist, Jazz Composers Orch., N.Y.C., 1964—, European concert tours, Jazz Realities, 1965-66; founder, WATT, 1973—, toured Europe with Jack Bruce Band, 1975; leader, Carla Bley Band, touring, U.S. and Europe, 1977—; composed, recorded: A Genuine Tong Funeral, 1967, (with Charlie Haden) Liberation Music Orch., 1969; opera Escalator Over the Hill, 1970-71 (Oscar du Disque de Jazz 1973), Tropic Appetites, 1973; composed: chamber orch. 3/4, 1974-75; film score Mortelle Randonnèe, 1983; recorded: Dinner Music, 1976, The Carla Bley Band: European Tour, 1977, Musique Macanique, 1979, (with Nick Mason) Fictitious Sports, 1980, Social Studies, 1980, Carla Bley Live!, 1981, Heavy Heart, 1984, I Hate to Sing, 1985, Night Glo, 1985, Sexted, 1987, Duets, 1988, Fleur Carnivor, 1989, The Very Big Carla Bley Band, 1991, Go Together, 1993, Big Band Theory, 1993, Songs with Legs, 1995, Goes to Church, 1996, Fancy Chamber Music, 1998, Are We There Yet?, 1999, 4x4, 2000, Looking for America, 2003, The Lost Chords, 2004. Named winner internat. jazz critics poll Down Beat mag., 1966, 71, 72, 78, 79, 80, 83, 84; Best Composer of Yr., Down Beat Readers' Poll, 1984, composer/arranger of yr., 1985-92; Guggenheim fellow, 1972; Cultural Coun. Found. grantee, 1971, 79; Nat. Endowment for the Arts grantee, 1973, Oscar du Disque de Jazz (for Escalator Over the Hill) 1973; named Best in Field Jazz Times critics poll, 1990, Best Arranger, Downbeat Critics Poll, 1993, 94, Best Arranger, Downbeat Readers' Poll, 1994; recipient Prix Jazz Moderne from Academie du Jazz for The very Big Carla Bley Band album, 1992. Office: Watt Works PO Box 67 Willow NY 12495-0067 E-mail: watt@ulster.net.

BLEY, JOHN L., financial executive; BA in Econs. and Polit. Sci., Pacific Lutheran U., 1980; JD, MBA Willamette U., 1985. Atty. Graham & Dunn, 1985—88; dep. supr. banking Wash. State Div. Banking, 1988—91, supr. banking, 1991—93; dir. Wash. State Dept. Fin. Instns., Olympia, 1993—2002; CEO Integra Advisors, Seattle, 2002—. Office: Integra Advisors LLC 2801 Alaskan Way Ste 300 Seattle WA 98121-1128

BLEZNICK, DONALD WILLIAM, Romance languages educator; b. NYC, Dec. 24, 1924; s. Louis and Gertrude (Kleinman) B.; m. Rozlyn Burakoff, June 15, 1952; children— Jordan, Susan. BA, CCNY, 1946; MA, U. Nacional de Mex., 1948; PhD, Columbia U., 1954. Instr. romance langs. Ohio State U., 1949-55; prof. Pa. State U., 1955-67, U. Cin., 1967—, head dept., 1967-72. Vis. prof. Hebrew U., Jerusalem, 1974. Bibliographer, MLA Internat. Bibliography, 1966-81; rev. editor Hispania, 1965-73, editor-in-chief, 1974-83, editor's adv. coun., 1984—. El Ensayo Espanol del Siglo Veinte, 1964, Historia del Ensayo Espanol, 1962, Duelo en el Paraiso (Goytisolo), 1967, Madrugada (Buero Vallejo), 1969, (with W.T. Pattison) Representative Spanish Authors, 1971, Quevedo, 1972, Variaciones interpretativas en torno a la nueva narrativa hispanoamericana, 1972, Directions of Literary Criticism in the Seventies, 1972, Sourcebook for Hispanic Literature and Language, 1974, 3d expanded edit., 1995, Homenaje a Luis Leal, 1978, Studies on Don Quixote and other Cervantine Works, 1984, Critical Edition of La Diana (Jorge de Montemayor), 1990, The Thought of Contemporary Spanish Essayists, 1993, Studies in Honor of Donald W. Bleznick, 1995; translator (from Spanish and Portuguese) Identity in Dispersion: Selected Memoirs from Latin American Jews, 2000, History of the University of Cincinnati Faculty Council on Jewish Affairs, 2004; founder, exec. editor Cin. Romance Rev., 1982-88; field editor: Twayne Spanish Literature Series, 1981—; contbr. articles to profl. jours., Ency. Americana. With US Army CIC, 1946-47. Decorated Knight's Cross Order Civil Merit (Spain); Am. Philos. Soc. rsch. grantee, 1964; Downer fellow CCNY, 1947-48; U. Cin. Taft rsch. and publ. grantee, 1972, 75, 78, 83, 88, 89, 92; named 1 of 15 outstanding scholars in Spanish lit. in Cuadernos Salmantinos de Filosofia, Salamanca, Spain, 1977; recipient Rieveschl award for excellence in rsch. U. Cin., 1980, award Hispania, U. So. Calif., 1983; fellow U. Cin. Grad. Sch., 1984. Mem. AAUP, Am. Assn. Tchrs. Spanish and Portuguese (exec. com. 1975—, award 1984, v.p. 1992, pres. 1993, Honored for Outstanding Career 1995, disting. svc. award 1997), MLA, Los Ensayistas (adv. bd. 1976—), Comediantes, Midwest Modern Lang. Assn., Conf. Editors of Learned Jours. (exec. com. 1978-79), Celestinesca, Cervantes Soc. Am., Phi Beta Kappa (pres. Delta chpt. of Ohio 1971-72, 86-87), Sigma Delta Pi (state dir. Ohio 1968-74, Order of Don Quijote 1970, v.p. Midwest 1975-83, Jose Martel award 1980, hon. pres. 1998-), Phi Sigma Iota, Kappa Delta Pi. Home: 2444 Madison Rd Apt 1806 Cincinnati OH 45208-1255 Office: U Cin Dept Romance Langs Cincinnati OH 45221-0001 E-mail: donald.bleznick@uc.edu.

BLICKENSDERFER, MATTHEW C., lawyer; b. Tuscola, Ill., July 16, 1970; BA, Northwestern U., 1992; JD, Harvard U., 1995. Bar: Ill. 1995, US Dist. Ct. Northern Dist. Ill. 1995, US Ct. of Appeals Sixth Cir. 1996, US Ct. of Appeals Seventh Cir. 1999, US Dist. Ct. Southern Dist. Ohio 2001, US Dist. Ct. Eastern Dist. Mich. 2002, US Supreme Ct. 2003. Law clerk US Ct. of Appeals Sixth Cir., 1996—97; adj. prof. U. Cin. Coll. Law, 2002—06; editor-in-chief Sixth Cir. Practice Manual, Third Edition, 2006; atty. Frost Brown Todd LLC, Cin. Named Cin. Leading Lawyer, Cincy Bus. mag., 2006; named one of Ohio's Rising Stars, Super Lawyers, 2005, 2006. Office: Frost Brown Todd LLC 2200 PNC Ctr 201 E 5th St Cincinnati OH 45202-4182 Office Phone: 513-651-6162. Office Fax: 513-651-6981.

BLICKWEDE, DONALD JOHNSON, retired metal products executive; b. Detroit, July 20, 1920; s. Frederic H. and Laura L. (Johnson) B.; m. Meredith Lloyd, Aug. 23, 1943; children: Karen (Mrs. Kimball J. Knowlton), Jon Frederic. BS, Wayne U., 1943; postgrad., Stevens Inst. Tech., 1943-45; ScD, Mass. Inst. Tech., 1948; postgrad., Harvard, 1969. Metallurgist Curtiss Wright Corp., 1943-45; head high temperature alloys br. Naval Research Lab., 1948-50; rsch. engr. Bethlehem Steel Corp., Pa., 1950-52, div. head, 1952-63, v.p., 1964-82. Campbell Meml. lectr. Am. Metal Congress, 1968, William Park Woodside Meml. lectr., 1969, Zay Zeffries Meml. lectr., 1970; Andrews Meml. lectr. Porcelain Enamel Inst., 1972. Pres. Ea. Shore Art Ctr., Ala., 1990; leader Hazardous Abandoned Mine Finders, Green Valley, Ariz. Fellow Am. Soc. Metals (hon., pres. 1983); mem. AIME, Am. Acad. Engring., Am. Iron and Steel Inst. (chmn. gen. rsch. com. 1971-73), Indsl. Rsch. Inst. (pres. 1975), Iron and Steel Inst. Japan (hon., Yukawa Meml. lectr. 1984). Home: Apt 2415 8580 Woodway Houston TX 77063 E-mail: blickwede@sbcglobal.com.

BLIESNER, JAMES DOUGLAS, municipal/county official, consultant; b. Milw., Mar. 19, 1945; s. Milton Carl and Dorothy (St. George) B.; m. Phyllis Jean Byrd, June 15, 1966 (div. 1985); children: Tris, Cara. BA in Philosophy, Ea. Nazarene Coll., 1968; MA in Social Ethics, Andover, Newton Theol. Sch., 1973; postgrad., Boston U., 1969-70; student, N.Y. Studio Sch./Decordoua, Mus. Sch., Milw. Tech. Art Sch. Exec. dir. San Diego Youth and Community Svcs., 1974-78; cons., analyst San Diego Housing Commn., 1979-84; dir. San Diego City-County Reinvestment Task Force, 1984—. Bd. dir. Calif. Cmty. Reinvestment Corp.; vice chmn. Calif. Reinvestment Com., 1989-91; founder, chmn. City Heights Cmty. Devel. Corp., San Diego, 1980-89; fin. com. chair Mid-City Revitalization Com., San Diego, 1988; founder San Diego Capital Collaborative; founding bd. dirs. Neighborhood Nat. Bank; instr. San Diego State U. Author monographs, 1979; visual arts exhbns. include San Diego Arts Inst., Soc. Western Artists, Santa Barbara Contemporary Arts Forum, Calif. Coun. for Humanities; films exhibited in Centro Cultural, Tijuana, Mex.; exhibited in group shows in Venice, Paris, Jerusalem, Mex., Eng., China; internat. invitee Habana Bienale. Coun. appointee City of San Diego Com. on Reapportionment, 1990, Com. on Growth and Devel., San Diego, 1989; gov. appointee Gov.'s Office of Neighborhoods, Calif., 1987; mem. City Heights Redevel. Project Com., San Diego, 1992; pres. San Diego Housing Consortium; bd. dirs. Advocates for Social Justice; com. appointee S.D. Cmty. Found. and United Way; internat. juror Shanghai Pub. Sculpture Competition. Named Citizen of Yr. Mid-City C. of C., 1986; recipient Award of Honor, Am. Planning Assn., 1987, Spl. Project award, 1987, Merit award, 1989, Lifetime Achievement award Non-Profit Fedn. San Diego, Outstanding Achievement award Calif. Reinvestment Commn., 1999, award Calif. Coun. Humanities, Nat. Leadership award Nat. Cmty. Reinvestment Com., 2000, Visionary award Urban Land Inst., 2006; U.S.-Mex. Fund for Culture grantee, 2000, 02. Mem.: S.D. Artists Guild. Methodist. Avocation: visual arts. Home: 4106 Manzanita Dr San Diego CA 92105-4508 Office: City County Reinvestment Task Force 3989 Ruffiu Rd San Diego CA 92123 E-mail: jdbarte@sbcglobal.net, jim.bliesner@sdcounty.ca.gov.

BLIGE, MARY JANE, singer; b. Yonkers, NY, Jan. 11, 1971; d. Cora Blige; m. Kendu Isaacs, Dec. 7, 2003; 3 stepchildren. Singer: (albums) What's the 411?, 1992, (NY Music award for Best R&B Album, 1993), My Life, 1994 (Billboard Music award for R&B Album of Yr., 1995), Mary Jane, 1995, Share My World, 1997 (Am. Music award for Favorite R&B Album, 1998, Soul Train Lady of Soul award for R&B Soul Album of Yr., 1998), Mary, 1999 (Soul Train Music award for Best R&B Album & Lady of Soul award for Album of Yr., 2000), The Tour, 1999, No More Drama, 2001, Dance For Me, 2002, Love & Life, 2003, The Breakthrough, 2005 (Favorite Album, Am. Music Awards, 2006, Billboard R&B Album of Yr., 2006, Best R&B Album, Grammy Awards, 2007, Best Album, Soul Train awards, 2007), Reflections: A Retrospective, 2006, Mary J. Blige and Friends, 2006;(songs) I'll Do For You, 1991, Real Love, 1991 (Soul Train Music award for Best Female Single, 1993), I'll Be There for You/You're All I Need (with Method Man), 1995 (Grammy award for Best Rap Duo Performance, 1996, named one of 100 Greatest Videos Ever Made, MTV, 1999), Not Gon' Cry, 1996, No More Drama, 2001 (Best R&B Video, MTV Video Music awards, 2002), He Think I Don't Know, 2001 (Grammy award for Best Female R&B Vocal Performance, 2003), Whenever I Say Your Name (with Sting), 2003 (Grammy award for Best Pop Collaboration With Vocals 2004), Be Without You, 2005 (BET Video of Yr. award, 2006, Billboard R&B Song of Yr., Hot 100 Airplay Song of Yr., R&B Song Airplay of Yr., & Videoclip of Yr., 2006, Best Female R&B Vocal Performance & Best R&B Song, Grammy Awards, 2007, NAACP Image award for Music Video, 2007); actress: (films) Angel, 2001, Prison Song, 2001. Recipient Soul Train Music award for Best New Artist 1993, Best Debut R&B Artist & Rising Star award, NY Music Awards, 1993, Source award for R&B Artist of Yr., 1994, 1995, Heroes award, RIAA, 1999, Patrick Lippert award, Rock the Vote, 2001, Best Female R&B award, Black Entertainment TV (BET), 2001, 2006, Favorite R&B Female Artist, Am. Music Awards, 2003, 2006, Legend award, Vibe mag., 2005, 9 Billboard Music awards, including R&B Artist of Yr., Female R&B Artist of Yr., R&B Songs Artist & Album Artist of Yr., 2006, Female Artist award, NAACP Image Awards, 2007, Voice of Music award, ACAP Rhythm & Soul Music Awards, 2007; co-recipient Best Collaboration for Runaway Love (with Ludacris), Black Entertainment TV (BET) Awards, 2007.

BLILEY, THOMAS JEROME, JR., former congressman; b. Chesterfield County, Va., Jan. 28, 1932; s. Thomas J. and Carolyn F. Bliley; m. Mary Virginia Kelley, June 22, 1957; children: Mary Vaughan, Thomas Jerome III. BA, Georgetown U., 1952. Pres. Joseph W. Bliley Funeral Home, 1972-80; mem. U.S. Congress from 7th Va. dist., Washington, 1981-2001; former ranking minority mem. D.C. com.; former chmn. House Commerce Com.; sr. adv. govt. rels. and pub. policy Collier Shannon & Scott, Washington, 2001—. Vice-mayor Richmond City Council, 1968-70, mayor, 1970-77; past bd. dirs. Nat. League Cities; past pres. Va. Mcpl. League Past bd. dirs. Crippled Children's Hosp.; past bd. dirs. St. Mary's Hosp.; bd. visitors Va. Commonwealth U.; bd. govs. Va. Home for Boys. Served with USN. Republican. Roman Catholic. Office: Collier Shannon & Scott Washington harbour, Ste 400 3050 K St NW Ste 400 Washington DC 20007-5108

BLIM, RICHARD DON, retired pediatrician, health facility administrator; b. Kansas City, Mo., Nov. 8, 1927; s. Miles G. and Latha Mae (Daniels) Blim; m. Myrle Rae Blim, Apr. 12, 1952; children: Richard David, Carol Rae, John Miles. BA, U. Kans., 1949, MD, 1953. Diplomate Am. Bd. Pediat. Intern U. Kans., 1953—54, resident in pediat., 1954—56; practice medicine specializing in pediat.; pres. Pediatric Assocs., Kansas City, Mo., 1956—89; dir. med. affairs St. Lukes Hosp., Kansas City, 1989—99. Peter T. Bohan lectr. U. Kans., Kansas City, 1978; Max Seham lectr. U. Minn., Mpls., 1982; mem. editl. bd. Mo. Medicine, 1978—92, Pediatric Annals, 1982—92, Pediatric News, 1983—92, Health Care Mgmt. Rev.; mem. VHA Phys. Leadership Coun. Bd. dirs. Marillac Spl. Sch. for Children, 1976—79, Cmty. Blood Ctr., Crittenton Children's Hosp.; mem. advancement bd. Kans. U. Med. Ctr. Served to sgt. US Army, 1946—48, PTO. Named Outstanding Med. Alumnus, U. Kans. Sch. Medicine, 1978; recipient Clifford G. Grulee award, 1984, Katherine Berry Richard MD award, Children Mercy Hosp., 1997. Fellow: Am. Acad. Pediat. (chmn. Mo. chpt. 1964—67, exec. bd. 1973—80, pres. 1980—81); mem.: AMA, Coun. Med. Spltys. Soc. (rep., exec. bd. 1974—80), Met. Med. Soc. (merit award 1996), Mo. Med. Assn., S.W. Pediatric Assn. (pres. Kansas City 1963), Jackson County Med. Soc. (pres. 1973), Inst. Medicine NAS, Kans. U. Med. Alumni (pres. 1973), Loch Lloyd Club, Alpha Omega Alpha. Republican. Presbyterian. Home: 100 W 172d St Belton MO 64012 Personal E-mail: rdonblimmd@earthlink.net.

BLINDER, ALAN STUART, economist, educator; b. Bklyn., Oct. 14, 1945; s. Morris and Shirley (Rothberg) Blinder; m. Madeline D. Schwartz, July 9, 1967; children: Scott, William. AB, Princeton U., 1967; MSc, London Sch. Econs., 1968; PhD, MIT, 1971. Instr. fin. Rider Coll., Trenton, NJ, 1968—69; instr. econs. Boston State Coll., 1969; asst. prof. econs. Princeton U., 1971—76, assoc. prof., 1976—79, prof., 1979—82, Gordon S. Rentschler Meml. prof. econs., 1982—, chmn. dept. econs., 1988—90, mem. pres.'s coun. econ. advisers, 1993—94; vice chmn. bd. governors Fed. Res. Bd., Washington, 1994—96. Author: Hard Heads, Soft Hearts: Tough Minded Economics for a Just Society, 1987, Central Banking in Theory and Practice, 1998, The Quiet Revolution: Central Banking Goes Modern, 2004; co-author (with C. Goodhart, P. Hildebrand, D. Lipton, and C. Wyplosz): How Do Central Banks Talk?, 2001; co-author: (with W. Baumol and E. Wolff) Downsizing in America: Reality, Causes, and Consequences, 2003; contbr. articles to profl. jours. such as Jour. Pub. Econs. Recipient W.S. Woytinsky award, 1981. Office: Dept of Econ Princeton Univ 105 Fisher Hall Princeton NJ 08544

BLINDER, ALBERT ALLAN, judge; b. NYC, Nov. 27, 1925; s. William and Sarah (Gold) B.; m. Meredith Zaretzki, Nov. 16, 1961 (dec.); 1 child, Adam Z.; m. Joan Goodman, Jan. 20, 1985 (dec.) AB, NYU, 1944, postgrad., 1944—45; JD, Harvard U., 1948. Bar: N.Y. 1949, U.S. Dist. Ct. (so. dist.) N.Y. 1953, U.S. Ct. Appeals (2d cir.) 1953, U.S. Supreme Ct. 1967. Asst. U.S. atty. (so. dist.) N.Y., 1950—53; asst. counsel N.Y.C. Bd. High Edn., 1953—54; asst. dist. atty. County of Bronx, NY, 1954—60; ptnr. Saxe, Bacon & O'Shea, NYC, 1960—64, Blinder, Steinhaus & Hochhauser, NYC, 1965—73; judge N.Y. State Ct. Claims, 1973—96; jud. hearing officer N.Y. State Supreme Ct., 1996—. Rsch. counsel N.Y. Commn. on Law of Estates, 1965; assoc. counsel N.Y. Commn. Revision of Penal Law, 1966-70; asst. counsel N.Y. Commn. on Eminent Domain, 1970-73; rsch. asst. N.Y. Commn. State Ct. Sys., 1971-73 Assoc. editor Am. Criminal Law Quar., 1968-70, mem. adv. bd., 1969-70 Mem.: ABA, Am. Judges Assn., N.Y. County Lawyers Assn., Assn. Bar City N.Y., N.Y. State Bar Assn. Office: 115 Broadway Fl 15 New York NY 10006-1604 Home Phone: 212-795-5555; Office Phone: 212-577-2800. Personal E-mail: ABLINDER@aol.com.

BLINDER, MARTIN S., management consultant, art dealer; b. Bklyn., Nov. 18, 1946; s. Meyer and Lillian (Stein) Blinder; m. Janet Weiss, Dec. 10, 1983. BBA, Adelphi U., 1968. Acct. exec. Bruns, Nordeman & Co., NYC, 1968-69; v.p. Blinder, Robinson & Co., Westbury, NY, 1969-73; treas. BHB Prodns., LA, 1973-76; pres. Martin Lawrence Ltd. Edits., Van Nuys, Calif., 1976-94, chmn., 1986-94, bd. dirs., 1994—; dir. AZ/NY Gallery, Scottsdale, Ariz., 2000—. Pres., dir. Corp. Art Inc., Visual Artists Mgmt. Corp., Art Consultants Inc.; pres., owner, founder MSB Fine Art, Phoenix, 1994—; lectr. bus. symposia. Contbr. articles to mags. and newspapers; appeared on TV and radio. Mem. Dem. Nat. Com., benefit com. AIDS project, L.A., 1988; bd. dirs. Very Spl. Arts, 1989—; chmn. visual arts Internat. Very Spl. Arts Festival, 1989; patron Guggenheim Mus., N.Y.C., Mus. Modern Art, N.Y.C., L.A. County Mus. Art, L.A. Mus. Contemporary Art (hon. founder), Whitney Mus. Am. Art, Palm Springs Mus. Art, Hirschorn Mus., Washington, Skirball Mus., L.A., Diabetes Found. of City of Hope, B'nai B'rith Anti-Defamation League, 1999, Very Spl. Arts, Scottsdale (Ariz.) Ctr. for the Arts, Scottsdale Mus. Contemporary Art (lectr. on Keith Haring); mem. Citizens for Common Sense; bd. dirs., pres. Rsch. Found. for Crohns Disease; mem. benefit com. Art Against AIDS, 1989; co-chair artists com. for Don't Bungle the Jungle Companions of Arts and Nature, 1989; prin. sponsor, ann. fundraiser AIDS Project, L.A., 1990; patron Ariz. Stat U. Art Mus., Sylvia Plotkin Mus. Recipient resolution of commendation L.A. City Coun., 1983, State of Calif. resolution for contbn. to arts in Calif., 1983, Merit award Republic Haiti for contbn. to arts, 1985, U.S. Senate commendations, 1983, County of L.A. Bd. Suprs. resolution for contbn. to arts in So. Calif., 1983, Gov. of R.I. resolution for contbns. to arts, 1985, commendation County of L.A.-Supr. Ed Edelman, 1991, commendation for contbns. to the arts and the healing arts City of L.A., 1991, commendation for contbns. to arts and philanthropy Mayor David Dinkins, N.Y.C., 1992; Nov. 18, 1985 declared Martin S. Blinder Day in L.A. in his honor by Mayor Tom Bradley, spl. award San Diego Youth and Cmty. Svcs., Bruin Bear award for establishing Blinder Rsch. Found., UCLA Sch. Medicine, 1994. Mem. Fine Art Pub.'s Assn. (bd. dirs. 1990-94), Med. Art Assn. at UCLA. Office: MSB Fine Art PO Box H82013 Scottsdale AZ 85251

BLINDER, SEYMOUR MICHAEL, chemistry and physics professor, researcher; b. NYC, Mar. 11, 1932; s. Morris and Ida (Styszynskaya) B.; m. Frances Ellen Bryant, July 8, 1978; children: Michael Ian, Stephen Earl, Matthew Bryant, Amy Rebecca, Sarah Jane. AB, Cornell U., 1953; MA, Harvard U., 1955, PhD, 1958. Sr. physicist Applied Physics Lab., Johns Hopkins U., 1958-61; asst. prof. chemistry Carnegie Inst. Tech., 1961-62; vis. prof. Harvard U., 1962-63; prof. chemistry and physics U. Mich., 1963—95, prof. emeritus, 1995—. Author: Advanced Physical Chemistry, 1969, Foundations of Quantum Dynamics, 1974, Introduction to Quantum Mechanics in Chemistry, Materials Science and Biology, 2004; Mem. bd. editors: Jour. Am. Chem. Soc., 1978-80; contbr. rsch. articles to profl. jours. Guggenheim fellow, 1965-66; NSF sr. postdoctoral fellow, 1970-71 Mem. AAAS, Am. Phys. Soc., Philos. Soc. Washington, Phi Beta Kappa. Home: 1240 Ferdon Rd Ann Arbor MI 48104-3635 Office: U Mich Dept Chemistry Ann Arbor MI 48109-1055 Business E-Mail: sblinder@umich.edu.

BLINKEN, DONALD, ambassador, investment banker; b. NYC, Nov. 11, 1925; s. Maurice Henry and Ethel (Horowitz) B.; m. Vera Evans, Oct. 15, 1975; 1 child, Antony John. BA magna cum laude, Harvard U., 1947. Cons. Marks & Spencer, Ltd., London, 1950-51; pres. Exchange Trading Corp., NYC, 1952-53; v.p. Stein's Stores, Inc., NYC, 1953-58, E.M. Warburg & Co., Inc., 1961-72; sr. v.p., chmn. exec. com. E.M. Warburg, Pincus & Co., Inc., NYC, 1970-81, mng. dir., 1981-86, dir., 1987-94; U.S. amb. Budapest, Hungary, 1994-97; dir. Ion Track Instruments, Inc., 2000—02. Author: Wool Tariffs and American Policy, 1948; chmn. publ. com. Commentary, 1984-87. Pres. Bklyn. Acad. Music, 1971—76, Mark Rothko Found., 1976—88; mem. trustees' coun. Nat. Gallery Art, 1984—94; trustee SUNY, 1976—2000, chmn. bd., 1978—90; bd. dirs. NY Philharm. Soc., 1986—94, vice chmn., 1989—94, hon. bd. dirs., 1999—; mem. US 2d Cir. Nominating Panel, 1979; trustee Manville Personal Injury Settlement Trust, 1986—91, NY Pub. Libr., 1990—94, hon. trustee, 1998—; dir. Inst. Internat. Edn., 1990—94; trustee Isamu Noguchi Found., 1987—94; bd. overseers Nelson Rockefeller Inst. Govt., 1985—94; chancellor Internat. Coun. Ctrl. European U., 1998—2001; trustee Ctrl. European U., 2001—; mem. adv. bd. Sch. Internat. and Pub. Affairs, Columbia U., 1998—; mem. exec. com. Citizens Devel. Corps, 1999—; sec.-gen. World Fedn. UN Assns., 2000—04; trustee Nat. Com. Am. Fgn. Policy, 2006—. With USAAF, 1944—45. Mem.: Coun. Am. Ambs., Coun. Fgn. Rels., Century Assn., River Club. Home: 435 E 52nd St New York NY 10022-6445 Office: 466 Lexington Ave New York NY 10017-3140 Office Phone: 212-878-0835.

BLISS, DONALD TIFFANY, JR., ambassador; b. Norwalk, Conn., Nov. 24, 1941; s. Donald Tiffany and Marina (Popova) B.; m. Nancy Arnold, Sept. 14, 1974; children: Evan Hale, Bion Northam. JD, Harvard U., 1966. Bar: N.Y. 1969, D.C. 1971, U.S. Dist. Ct. D.C. 1975, U.S. Ct. Appeals (D.C. cir.) 1971, 84, U.S. Supreme Ct. 1975. Atty. Peace Corps, Micronesia, 1966-67; legis. counsel Congress of Micronesia, 1968; cons. judiciary, American Samoa, 1968; assoc. firm LeBoeuf, Lamb, Leiby & McCrae, NYC, 1969; asst. to sec. HEW, 1969-72; spl. asst. to adminstr. EPA, 1972-73; exec. sec. AID, 1973-74; dep. gen. counsel U.S. Dept. Transp., 1975-77, acting. gen. counsel, 1976-77; chair, transp. practice group firm O'Melveny & Myers LLP, Washington, 1979—2006; U.S. amb. to Internat. Civil Aviation Orgn., Montreal, 2006—. Mem. Maritime Adv. Com., 1984-85; pres. Harvard Law Sch. Assn. D.C., 1985-86; chmn. transp. sect. FBA, 1987-90; mem. interior task force Grace Commn.; nat. pres. The Ripon Soc. Author: The Law of Airline Customer Relations: Stability, Security, Safety and Service, 2002, Drug Testing and Federal Employees: Lessons from the Transportation Experience, 1988, Economic Deregulation and Safety: Are The Compatible, 1989, A Challenge to the U.S. Aviation Leadership: Launching the New Era of Global Aviation, 1991, Supreme Court Preemption Analysis: Differentiating the Hamiltonians and Jeffersonians, 1993; play The Return of Halley's Comet, 2002. Trustee Studio Theatre, Arts for the Aging, Inc., pres. exec. com., 2003-. Recipient spl. citation HEW, 1972, 73, Pres.'s Cert. Exec. Mgmt., 1973, Superior Achievement award Dept. Transp., 1976. Mem. ABA (chmn. air and space law forum 1997-99), DC Bar Assn. (co-chmn. sect. adminstrv. law and agy. practice 1988-90), Chevy Chase Club. Office Phone: 514-954-8304. E-mail: dbliss@icao.int.

BLISS, ROBERT HARMS, lawyer; b. Paris, Tex., Nov. 20, 1940; s. Jack Edward and Ruth Eugenia (Harms) B.; m. Juliee Dixie Fuselier, Dec. 29, 1964; 1 child, Katherine Elaine. BA, U. Colo., 1964; JD, U. Tex., 1967. Bar: Tex. 1967; cert. civil trial specialist, mediator-arbitrator, spl. master. Since practiced in, Dallas; assoc. Johnson, Bromberg, Leeds & Riggs, 1967-72; ptrn. Bliss, Danner & Bishop, 1972-74; individual practice, 1974; pres. Bliss & Hughes, P.C., Dallas, 1978-88; pvt. practice Robert Harms Bliss P.C., 1988-98; ptnr. Glast, Phillips & Murray, PC, 1998—2002; pvt. practice, 2002—. Mem. faculty advanced real estate law State Bar Tex., 1985, 92-93, 95, 97, 99, 2000, 02; mem. faculty CLE series So. Meth. U. Sch. Law, Dallas, 1989, 92, 94, 97, 98, 99, 2000, mem. faculty The Leasing Inst., 2004-05, course dir., 2007; mem. faculty Mortgage Lending Inst., U. Tex. Sch. Law, 1994, 97, 98, 99, 2000, mem. faculty advanced real estate drafting course, 1995, 2000-04, course dir., 2002. Contbr. articles to profl. jours. Bd. dirs. Dallas Symphony Orch., Dallas Symphony Orch. Guild, Dallas Classic Guitar Soc.; mem. Gov.'s Task Force on Immigration, 1983-84, Tex. Real Estate Commn., 1983-87; adv. bd. Tex. Real Estate Rsch. Ctr., Tex. A&M U., 1985-87; ch. atty. Episcopal Diocese Dallas. Fellow Tex. Bar Found. (sustaining life); mem. Am. Coll. Real Estate Lawyers, State Bar Tex. (past chair real estate, probate and trust sect.), Dallas Bar Assn. (past chmn. real property sect.), Tex. Coll. Real Estate Attys., Assn. Atty.-Mediators (pres. North Tex. chpt.), U. Tex. Tchg. Quiz-Masters Assn., Phi Delta Phi. Home: 29 Ashton Ct Dallas TX 75230-1977 Office: PO Box 12825 Dallas TX 75225 Home Phone: 972-726-0605; Office Phone: 214-521-0190.

BLISSETT, WILLIAM FRANK, English literature educator; b. East End, Sask., Can., Oct. 11, 1921; s. Ralph Richardson and Gladys (Jones) B. BA, U. B.C., 1943; MA, U. Toronto, 1946, PhD, 1950. Lectr dept. English U. Toronto, 1946-50, prof. English, 1965-87, prof. emeritus, 1987; assoc. prof. dept. English U. Sask., 1950-57, prof., 1957-60; prof., head dept. English Huron Coll., London, Ont., 1960-65. Author: The Long Conversation, 1981; editor: Editing Illustrated Books, 1980; editor U. Toronto Quar., 1965-76; adv. bd.: Ency. of Shakespeare and Music, 1991, Chesterton Rev., 1984—; co-editor: Spenser Ency., 1982-90; joint editor: A Celebration of Ben Jonson, 1974; subject of book: Craft and Tradition: Essays in Honour of William Blissett, 1990. Huron Coll. hon. fellow, 1966; Royal Soc. Can. fellow, 1979 Mem. Internat. Assn. Univ. Profs. English, David Jones Soc. Anglican.

BLISSMER, BRYAN, medical researcher, educator; b. Aurora, Ill., Aug. 1, 1972; s. Fred and Charmaine Blissmer; m. Anne Pinneo, Aug. 9, 1997; children: Evan, Nathan. BS, U. Ill., Urbana-Champaign, 1996, PhD, 2000; MS, Miami U., Oxford, Ohio, 1997. Rsch. assoc. Cancer Prevention Rsch. Ctr., Kingston, RI, 2000—; assoc. prof. U. RI, Kingston, 2000—. Faculty sponsor Colls.Against Cancer. Mem.: Am. Coll. Sports Medicine, Soc. Behavioral Medicine. Office: Univ RI Rm 108 210 Flagg Rd Kingston RI 02881 Home Phone: 401-828-5910; Office Phone: 401-874-5435. Business E-Mail: blissmer@uri.edu.

BLITMAN, HOWARD NORTON, construction executive; b. NYC, Dec. 9, 1926; s. Charles H. and Anna (Palestine) B.; m. Maureen Lefcort-Winter, 1975. CE, Rensselaer Poly. Inst., 1950; MA, New Sch. Social Research, 1973. Registered profl. engr., N.Y., N.J., Conn., Mass., S.C. Field engr. Drier Structural Steel Co., NY, 1950-51; design engr. Blitman & Tischler, NYC, 1952-60; project engr. Blitman Constrn. Corp., NYC, 1960-61, coordinator, 1961-62, exec. v.p., 1962-69, pres., 1969-81; pres., dir. Blitman Bldg. Corp., 1981—. Mem. housing com. State Constnl. Conv., 1968; mem. N.Y.C. Commn. Investigation Water Main Breaks; chmn. adv. bd. to dept. civil engring. Rensselaer Poly. Inst., 1999—, adj. trustee, 2005; trustee Deconstructionist Rabbinical Coll. Mem. sch. bd. Mt. Pleasant Cottage Sch., Union Free Sch. Dist., Pleasantville, N.Y.; pres., bd. dirs. Jewish Child Care Assn. N.Y.; v.p. bd. dirs. Beth Israel Med. Ctr.; mem. coun. Rensselaer Poly. Inst., adj. trustee 2004-05; chmn. archtl. rev. bd. Town of Scarsdale, N.Y., trustee 1989-93; trustee Village of Scarsdale, 1989, dep. mayor, 1992—; mem. Planning Bd. Scarsdale, 1994—, chmn., 1998—; trustee Rensselaer Poly. Inst., 2004. 2d lt. Chem. Corps AUS, 1944-47; 1st lt., 1951-53. Recipient Norman Tishman Human Rels. award, 1967, Albert DeMers medal, Rensselaer Poly. Inst., Outstanding Alumni Achievement award, 2006. Fellow: ASCE, NSPE (chmn. profl. engrs. in constrn., pres. 1997, chmn. 1996—97, nat. treas. 1999—2001, pres.-elect 2001—02, pres. 2002—03); mem.: ASME, N.Y. State Soc. Profl. Engrs. (pres. 1978, pres. N.Y. chpt. 1974—75), Harmonie Club (N.Y.C.), Masons (N.Y.C.). Home: 3 Elmdorf Dr Scarsdale NY 10583-4203 Office Phone: 914-244-8600.

BLITT, RITA LEA, artist; b. Kansas City, Mo., Sept. 7, 1931; d. Herman Stanley and Dorothy Edith (Sofnas) Copaken; m. Irwin Joseph Blitt, Apr. 18, 1951; 1 child, Chela ne Connie. Student, U. Ill., 1948-50; BA, Kans. City U., 1952; postgrad., Kans. City Art Inst., 1951-55. Painter/sculptor, Aspen, Colo., Emeryville, Calif., Leawood, Kans. Author: Nessie the Sculpture, 1978; author: (video), 1993; author: (7-minute video) Flag: 1976, 1976; subject (audio interview) Goodnewsbroadcast, collaborations with dancers and musicians St. Joseph Ballet, Santa Ana, Calif., 1995, dancer/choreographer David Parsons, 1996, cellist Yehuda Hanani, 1986, creator words and paintings for internat. distributed poster "Kindness is Contagious, Catch It!", led to the founding of the Kindness Program sponsored by the Stop Violence Coalition, creator, presenter (multi-discipline program) CLAL Gala, 2005—; one-woman shows include Unitarian Gallery, Kansas City, Mo., 1965, Hall's, 1967, Spectrum Gallery, N.Y.C., 1969, Johnson County C.C., Overland Park, Kans., 1974, 1979, Angerer Gallery, Kansas City, Mo., 1974, Battle Creek (Mich.) Civic Art Ctr., 1975, Harkness Gallery, N.Y.C., 1977, Martin Schweig Gallery, St. Louis, 1977, Gargoyle Gallery, Aspen, Colo., 1978, Tumbling Waters Mus., Montgomery, Ala., 1978, St. Louis U., 1980, Rockhurst Coll., Kansas City, Mo., 1984, Jewish Cmty. Ctr., Omaha, Nebr., 1984, 2001, Ctrl. Exch., Kansas City, Mo., 1985, 1991, 1995, Leedy-Voulkos Gallery, 1987, Joy Horwich Gallery, Chgo., 1987, Goldman Gallery, Haifi, Israel, 1989, Bet Shmuel, Jerusalem, 1989, Mark Twain Bank, Kansas City, Mo., 1989, 1990, Goldman Kraft Gallery, Chgo., 1990, Singapore Nat. Mus., 1991, Albrecht-Kemper Mus., St. Joseph, Mo., 1991, Aspen (Colo.) Inst., 1992, Foothills Art Ctr., Golden, Colo., 1992, Mackey Gallery, Denver, 1992, Jewish Cmty. Campus, Overland Park, Kans., 1992, U. Ill., Urbana, 1994, Kennedy Mus., U. Ohio, Athens, 1994, Krasl Art Ctr., St. Joseph, Mich., 1994, La Quinta Sculpture Park, La Quinta, Calif., 1994, Baker U., Baldwin, Kans., 1995, Aatchison (Kans.) Muchnik Gallery, 1996, Marines Meml. Theater, San Francisco, 1997, Resourceful Women, 1997, City Ctr., N.Y., 1998, Brandeis U., Waltham, Mass., 2000, Leedy Voulkos Art Ctr., Kansas City, Mo., 2001, Aspen Dance Theater, Colo., 2001, Nev. Mus. Art, Reno, 2003, Penn Valley CC, Kansas City, 2003, Michelson Mus., Marshall, Tex., 2003, Tex. A&M, College Station, 2003, College Station, Tex., 2004, 4 Star Gallery, Indpls., 2005, Marion Meyer Contemporary Art, Laguna Beach, Calif., 2005, Hallar Gallery, Kansas City, Mo., 2005, Walton, Fayetteville, Ark., 2006, Ezair Gallery, Southampton, NY, 2006, Marion Meyer Contemporary Art, 2006, Hudgens Ctr., Deluth, Ga., 2006, Wayne Ctr., Wooster, Ohio, 2006, Thornhill Gallery, Kansas City, Mo., 2007, many group shows including most recently, exhibited in group shows at Marion Meyer Contemporary Art, Laguna Beach, Calif., 2005, Florence (Italy) Biennale, 2005, Hallar Gallery, Kansas City, Mo., 2005, Ezair Gallery, N.Y.C., 2005, Thomas Ctr., Gainesville, Fla., 2005, Represented in permanent collections Albrecht Kemper Mus., St. Joseph, Mo., also exhibits, Represented in permanent collections Am. Embassy, Barbados, Ga. Inst. Tech., JFK Libr., Cambridge, Mass., Kennedy Mus. Ohio U., Athens, Nat. Mus. Singapore, Kemper Mus. of Contemporary Art, Kansas City, Mo., Skirball Mus., L.A., Spencer Mus. Art. U. Kans., Lawrence, Spertus Mus., Chgo., Kansas City (Mo.) Children's Mus., Ga. Tech. Ctr. for the Arts, I-Lan Taiwan City Hall, other numerous pub. and pvt. collections, Conservatory of Music and Sci. Bldgs., U. Mo., Kansas City; sculptures in numerous pub. places including Australia, Calif., Ill., Kans., Mo., Md., N.Y., N.J., Japan, Singapore, Israel, print sent to every country in the UN and Palestinian Liberation Orgn. in honor of Norway helping Israel and the Palestinian Liberation Orgn.'s first steps toward peace, 1993; choreographer, Aspen, Colo., Williamstown, Mass., Ojai Calif., Berkeley Film Festivals (award). Mem. Soc. Fellow The Nelson Gallery Found., The Aspen Inst.; bd. dirs. Trio Found.; mem. The Stop Violence Coalition; rsch. assoc. The Internat. Rsch. on Jewish Women. Co-honoree Parsons Dance Co., 2000. Mem. Internat. Sculpture Ctr., Kansas City Artists Coalition. Avocations: music, dance, travel, walking. Office Phone: 800-627-7689. Personal E-mail: ritablitt@aol.com.

BLITZ, NELSON, JR., entrepreneur; m. Catherine Woodard; children: Perri, Allison. Pres. Nelson Air Device Corp., Maspeth, NY, Nelson Acquisition Corp., Rye, NY. Named one of Top 200 Collectors, ARTnews Mag., 2004, 2005, 2006. Avocation: Collecting Viennese furniture, prints and works on paper, especially Munch, Picasso, Kirchner and Johns. Office: Nelson Air Device Corp 46-28 54th Ave Maspeth NY 11378 also: Nelson Acquisition Corp 10 Pine Island Rd Rye NY 10580

BLITZ, STEPHEN M., lawyer; b. NYC, July 29, 1941; s. Leo and Dorothy B.; m. Ellen Sue Mintzer, Sept. 23, 1962; children: Catherine Denise, Thomas Joseph. BA, Columbia U., 1962, BS, 1963; LLB, Stanford U., 1966; MS in Acctg., U. Colo., 2001. Bar: Calif. 1967, U.S. Dist. Ct. (ctrl. dist.) Calif. 1967, Colo. 1996, Wis. 2004. Law clk. to judge U.S. Dist. Ct. (ctrl. dist.) Calif., 1966-67; ptnr. Gibson, Dunn & Crutcher, LA, 1967-96, Denver, 1996-2001; of counsel Fleishman & Shapiro, Denver, 2001—. Adj. prof. law U. West L.A. Sch. Law, 1978-80, dir. Pub. Counsel, 1981-83, 94-96. Bd. dirs. Colo. Preservation, Inc., 1999-2005. Mem. ABA, L.A. County Bar Assn. (exec. com. 1986-96, chmn. 1994-95, real property sect.), Colo. Bar Assn., Denver Bar Assn., Order of Coif, Beta Gamma Sigma. Office: Fleishman & Shapiro PC 1600 Broadway Ste 2600 Denver CO 80202-4926 Office Phone: 303-861-1000.

BLITZER, ANDREW, otolaryngologist, educator, research scientist, writer; b. Apr. 25, 1946; s. Martin Hollander and Lyrene Iris (Lave) Blitzer; children: Peter Morgen, Polly Volk. BA, Adelphi U., 1967; DDS, Columbia U. Sch. of Dental and Oral Surgery, 1970; MD, Mt. Sinai Sch. Medicine, 1973. Diplomate Am. Bd. Otolaryngology. Resident in gen. surgery Beth Israel Hosp., NYC, 1973—74; resident in otolaryngology Mt. Sinai Hosp., NYC, 1974—77; asst. prof. otolaryngology Coll. Phys. & Surg. Columbia U., NYC, 1977—82, assoc. prof. otolaryngology and oral surgery, 1982—84, prof. clin. otolaryngology and oral surgery, 1984—, prof. clin. otolaryngology in neurology, 1993—95; prof. clin. otolaryngology Coll. Physicians and Surgeons, Columbia U., acting chmn. dept. otolaryngology NYC, 1991—94; vice chmn. dept. otolaryngology Columbia U., NYC, 1983—91; dir. divsn. head and neck surgery Columbia-Presbyn. Med. Ctr., NYC, 1980—94, dir. multidiscipline head and neck tumor bd., dir. residency edn., 1978—94; acting dir. Otolaryngology Svc. Presbyterian Hosp.; lectr. dept. otolaryngology Mt. Sinai Sch. Medicine, NYC, 1977—; sr. attending otolaryngologist and dir. NY Ctr. for Voice and Swallowing Disorders St. Luke's/Roosevelt Med. Ctr., 1994—. Dir. NY Ctr. for Clin. Rsch.; cons., mem. spl. senses and lang. study sect. NIH. Co-author several books, author several textbooks; mem. editl. bd.: Otolaryngology-Head and Neck Surgery, The Laryngoscope, Jour. Otolaryngology, Jour. Rhinology; contbr. chapters to books, articles to profl. jours. Recipient award for excellence, Am. Assn. Orthodontists, 1970, Tchr.-Investigator award, Nat. Inst. Neurol. Communicative Disorders and Strokes, 1978—83, Maxwell Abramson Meml. award, Excellence in Resident Teaching, 1993, James A. Newcomb award, Am. Laryngological Assn. Fellow: ACS, Am. Bronchoesophagological Assn. (Chevalier Jackson award), Am. Acad. Otolaryngology-Head and Neck Surgery (bd. dirs. 2002—, Disting. Svc.

award 1996, Honor award), Am. Laryngol., Rhinol., and Otol. Soc., Am. Laryngol. Assn. (James Newcomb award 1998), Am. Acad. Facial Plastic and Reconstructive Surgery, Am. Soc. Head and Neck Surgery, NY Acad. Medicine. Achievements include being a pioneer and leading authority in the use of Botox for conditions with excessive muscle function, muscle pain, tremor & muscle spasm, including spasmodic dysphonia and facial lines & wrinkles; a pioneer in the field of neurolaryngology and has one of the ten fellowship programs in the country; developed new surgical techniques for the rehabilitation the paralyzed vocal cord; world leader in the management of voice and swallowing disorders, nasal and sinus surgery, laser surgery, management of facial lines and wrinkles and head and neck surgery. Avocations: running, skiing, photography, fly fishing. Office: 425 W 59th St 10th Fl New York NY 10019-1104 Office Phone: 212-262-9500. Office Fax: 212-523-6364.

BLITZER, WOLF, news correspondent; b. Buffalo, Mar. 22, 1948; m. Lynn Greenfield; 1 child, Elana. BA in History, SUNY, Buffalo; MA in Internat. Rels., Johns Hopkins U. of Advanced Internat. Studies, Washington, DC; doctorate (hon.), King's Coll., Wilkes-Barre, Pa., Gannon Univ., Erie, Pa., Quinnipiac Coll., New Haven, Conn., SUNY, Buffalo. With Reuters New Agy., Tel Aviv, 1971—73; Washington corr. Jerusalem Post, 1973—89; mil. affairs corr. at the Pentagon CNN, Washington, 1990-92, sr. White House corr., 1992-99, host Late Edition, 1998—, sr. anchor, The World Today, 1999—, anchor, Wolf Blitzer Report, 2000—, anchor, America Votes 2004. Author: Between Washington & Jerusalem: A Reporter's Notebook, 1985, Territory of Lies, 1989 (most notable book of 1989, NY Times); contbr. articles to profl. publs. Recipient Emmy for Coverage of Oklahoma City bombing, 1996, Best in the Bus. award Am. Journalism Rev., 1994, Disting. Alumnus award Johns Hopkins U. Alumni Assn., 1999, Lowell Thomas Broadcast Journalism award for outstanding contbns. to broadcast journalism, Internat. Platform Assn., 1999, Hubert H. Humphrey First Amendment Freedoms prize, Anti-Defamation League, 2002, Ernie Pyle Journalism award for excellence in military reporting, Am. Veteran awards, 2002, Daniel Pearl award, Chgo. Press Veterans Assn., 2003; co-recipient Golden CableACE for coverage of the Persian Gulf War, Nat. Acad. of Cable Programming. Jewish. Achievements include coverage of many key events that have shaped the international political landscape and has interviewed some of recent history's most notable figures. Office: Cable Network News 820 1st St NE Washington DC 20002-4243 E-mail: wolf@cnn.com.

BLIVAISS, DAVID HARVEY, lawyer, accountant; b. Chgo., May 4, 1949; s. Dr. Ben B. and Helen F. (Friedman); m. Karen N. Rosenberg, Aug. 20, 1972; children: Jeffrey E., Amanda R. BSBA, Roosevelt U., 1971; JD, Loyola U., 1974. Bar: Ill. 1974, N.J. 1991; CPA: Ill. 1975, N.Y. 1984, N.J. 1990. Various positions Arthur Andersen & Co., Chgo., 1974-83, ptnr. NYC, 1983-91, Eisner LLP, NYC, 1991—. Mem. AICPA, NYSSCPA, ABA, Wall Street Tax Assn. Office: Eisner LLP 750 3rd Ave New York NY 10017 Office Phone: 212-891-4038. Business E-Mail: dblivaiss@eisnerllp.com.

BLIWISE, LESTER MARTIN, lawyer; b. Phila., Dec. 22, 1945; s. Sanford and Mollie (Cohen) B.; m. Ilene Estelle Hisiger, June 23, 1968; children: Matthew Scott, Howard Michael. BA, Rutgers U., 1967; JD, Bklyn. Law Sch., 1970. Bar: N.Y. 1971, U.S. Dist. Ct. (no. dist.) N.Y. 1971, U.S. Dist. Ct. (so. dist.) N.Y. 1975. Law asst. appellate div. 3d dept. N.Y. State Supreme Ct., Albany, 1970-71, law sec. appellate div. 3d dept., 1971-72; assoc. Burstein and Marcus, White Plains, N.Y., 1972-73, Trubin Sillcocks Edelman & Knapp, NYC, 1973-78, ptnr., 1978-84, Milgrim Thomajan Jacobs & Lee, NYC, 1984-85, Curtis, Mallet-Prevost, Colt & Mosie, NYC, 1985-87, Schulte Roth & Zabel, LLP, NYC, 1987-97, LeBoeuf, Lamb, Greene & MacRae LLP, NYC, 1997—. Mem. coun. advisors Ticor Title Ins. Co., N.Y.C., 1990—. Contbr. chpts. in books Real Estate Titles, 1984, rev., 1988, 2d edit., 1994, rev. edit., 1998, Foreign Investment in the U.S., 1989, rev. 1990, 92; notes editor Bklyn. Law Rev., 1969-70. Mem. planning bd. Town of Mamaroneck, 1984-88. Mem. N.Y. Sate Bar Assn. (del. to Ho. of dels., 1992-94, chair real estate financing and liens com., real property law sect. 1980-88, 98—, chair real property law sect. 1991-92, sec. 1988-89, 2d vice chair 1989-90, 1st vice chair 1990-91), Am. Coll. Real Estate Lawyers. Home: 155 Franklin St New York NY 10013-2936 Office: LeBoeuf Lamb Greene & MacRae LLP 125 W 55th St New York NY 10019-5369

BLIX, HANS MARTIN, retired international organization official; b. Uppsala, Sweden, June 28, 1928; s. Gunnar and Hertha (Wiberg) B.; m. Eva Kettis, Mar. 17, 1962; children: Marten, Goran. LL.B., U. Uppsala, 1951; PhD, Cambridge U., 1959; LL.D., Stockholm U., 1960. Assoc. prof. U. Stockholm, 1960; legal adviser Ministry Fgn. Affairs, Stockholm, 1963-76, under sec. of state in charge of internat. devel. coop., 1976-78, 79-81; minister fgn. affairs Sweden, 1978-79; dir. gen. Internat. Atomic Energy Agy., Vienna, 1981-97; exec. chmn. UN Monitoring, Verification and Inspection Commn., 2000—03. Mem. Swedish Del. UN Gen. Assembly, N.Y., 1961-81, Swedish Del. Conf. Disarmament, Geneva, 1962-78; chair Assembly States Mems. Chernobyl Shelter Fund, 1998—, Weapons of Mass Destruction Commn., 2004-06. Author: Treaty Making Power, 1959, Statsmyndigheternas Internationella Forbindelser, 1964, Sovereignty, Aggression and Neutrality, 1970, The Treaty Maker's Handbook, 1974, Disarming Iraq, 2004, Weapons of Terror--Freeing the World of Nuclear, Biological and Chemical Arms, 2006. Mem. Inst. de Droit Internat.

BLIXSETH, TIMOTHY, real estate developer; b. Roseburg, Oreg., 1951; m. Edra Blixseth; 4 children. Founding ptnr. Crown Pacific Ltd., 1988—90; owner Big Sky Lumber Co., 1992; CEO The Blixseth Grp.; developer, owner Yellowstone Club, Big Sky, Mont. Composer: (songs) Pray For Peace, 2001 (Proceeds went to victims of the 9/11 attacks.), Heart of America, 2005 (Proceeds went to Habitat for Humanity for Hurricane Katrina victims.). Named one of Forbes' Richest Americans, 2006. Office: c/o The Blixseth Group Inc 71534 Sahara Rd Rancho Mirage CA 92270 Office Phone: 760-776-6622. Office Fax: 760-776-6626.

BLIXT, CHARLES A., lawyer; b. Rockford, Ill., Aug. 18, 1951; m. Leslie Blixt; children: Allison, Katherine. BS, U. Ill., 1974, JD, 1977. Litigation atty. Foster, Swift, Collins and Coey, P.C., Lansing, Mich., Overholser, Ray, Flannery and Glick Ltd., Libertyville; atty. Fiat-Allis Constrn. Machinery Inc., 1979-81, Caterpillar Tractor Co., 1981-85; assoc. counsel R. J. Reynolds Tobacco Co., Winston-Salem, NC, 1985-87, counsel-litigation, 1987-89, staff v.p., asst. gen. counsel, 1994-95, v.p., asst. gen. counsel, 1995, sr. v.p., gen. counsel, 1995—99, exec. v.p., gen. counsel, 1999—2006; interim gen. counsel Krispy Kreme Doughnuts, Inc., 2006—07. Bd. dirs Salem Coll. & Acad., Wake Forest U. Sch. Law, Targacept Inc., NC Tech. Concepts & Design Inc., Krispy Kreme Doughnuts Corp.*

BLIZNAKOV, MILKA TCHERNEVA, architect, educator; b. Varna, Bulgaria, Sept. 20, 1927; came to U.S., 1961, naturalized, 1966; d. Ivan Dimitrov and Maria Kesarova (Khorozova) Tchernev; m. Emile G. Bliznakov, Oct. 23, 1954 (div. Apr., 1974). Architect-engr. diploma, State Tech. U., Sofia, 1951; PhD, Engring.-Structural Inst., Sofia, 1959; PhD in Architecture, Columbia U., 1971. Sr. researcher Ministry Heavy Industry, Sofia, 1950-53; pvt. practice architecture Sofia, 1954-59; assoc. architect Noel Combrisson, Paris, 1959-61; designer Perkins & Will Partnership, White Plains, NY, 1963-67; project architect Lathrop Douglass, NYC, 1967-71; assoc. prof. architecture and planning Sch. Architecture, U. Tex., Austin, 1972-74; prof. Coll. Architecture, Va. Poly. Inst. and State U., Blacksburg, 1974-98, prof. emerita, 1998—; prin. Blacksburg, 1975—. Bd. dirs. founder Internat. Archives Women in Architecture, Va. Poly. Inst. and State U., The Parthena award, 1994. Prin. works include Speedwell Ave. Urban Renewal, Morristown, N.J., 1967—69, Wilmington (Del.) Urban Renewal, 1968—70, Springfield (Ill.) Ctrl. Area Devel., 1969—71, Arlington County (Va.) Redevel., 1975—77; author (with others): Utopia e Modernitá, 1989, Reshaping Russian Archtecture, 1990, Russian Housing in the Modern Age, 1993, Nietzsche and Soviet Culture, 1994, New Perspectives on Russian and Soviet Artistic Culture, 1994, The Eastern Dada Orbit: Russia, Georgia, Ukraine, Central Europe, 1996, Signs of Times, Culture and the Emblems of Apocalypse, 1998, Women Architects in Eastern Europe: The Contributions of the Bulgarians, 1997, International Archive of Women in Architecture, 1997; author: (with others) 5th edit., 2003; author: (with others) Encyclopedia of Eastern Europe, 2000, Centropa, 2001; author: (with others) 2d edit., 2003; author: (with others) Women Architects in Japan, 2002, Housing in Russia: 20th Century, 2002; author: (with others) Encyclopedia of Twentieth Century Architecture, 2003. Recipient Parthena award, 1994, CAUS Diversity award, 2007; William Kinne scholar, 1970, vis. scholar Inst. Advanced Russian Studies, The Wilson Ctr. of Smithsonian Instn., 1988; NEA grantee, 1973-74, Am. Beautiful Found. grantee, 1973, Internat. Rsch. and Exch. Bd. grantee, 1984, 93; Fulbright Hays rsch. fellow, 1983-84, 91. Mem. Internat. Archive Women in Architecture (founder, chair bd. dirs.), Am. Assn. Tchrs. Slavic and East European Langs., Soc. Archtl. Historians, Nat. Trust Hist. Preservation, Am. Assn. Advancement of Slavic Studies, Assn. Collegiate Schs. of Planning, Inst. Modern Russian Culture (chairperson architecture, co-founder, dir.), Bulgarian Studies Assn., Assn. Collegiate Schs. of Architecture. Home: 2813 Tall Oaks Dr Blacksburg VA 24060-8109 Office: Va Poly Inst and State U Coll Architecture Blacksburg VA 24061 Office Phone: 540-231-5480. Business E-Mail: mbliznak@vt.edu.

BLIZZARD, ALAN, artist; b. Boston, Mar. 25, 1939; s. Thomas and Elizabeth B. BFA, Mass. Coll. Art; MA, U. Ariz.; MFA, U. Iowa, 1963. Instr. in art U. Iowa; vis. asst. prof. art Albion Coll., U. Okla.; asso. prof. UCLA; now prof. painting Scripps Coll. and; Claremont Grad. Sch. Represented in permanent collections Bklyn. Mus., Met. Mus. Art, N.Y.C., Art Inst. Chgo., Denver Art Mus., La Jolla (Calif.) Mus. Art, Ashland U., Columbia U., McGeorge Sch. Law, Pomona Coll., Sacramento State U., Pitzer Coll., Fluor Corp., Kouri Capital Corp., N.Y.C., Crocker Mus. Art, Sacramento, Office: Scripps Coll Art Dept Claremont CA 91711

BLOBEL, GÜNTER, cell biologist, educator; b. Waltersdorf, Silesia, Germany, May 21, 1936; MD, U. Tübingen, Germany, 1960; PhD in Oncology, U. Wis., 1967. Intern, Germany, 1960-62; fellow lab. cellular biology Rockefeller U., 1967-69, asst. prof. cell biology NYC, 1969-73, assoc. prof., 1973-76, prof., 1976—; investigator Howard Hughes Med. Inst., 1986—. Founder, pres. Friends of Dresden, Inc. Contbr. articles to profl. jours. and chpts. to books. Recipient Gairdner Found. award, 1982, Warburg medal German Biochem. Soc., 1983, Wilson medal Am. Soc. Cell Biology, 1986, U.D. Mattia award Roche Inst. Molecular Biology, 1986, Louisa Gross Horwitz prize Columbia U., 1987, Waterford Biomedical Sci. award, 1989, Albert Lasker Basic Med. Rsch. award, 1993, King Faisal internat. prize for sci., 1996, Mayor's award for Excellence in Sci. and Tech., 1997, Massry Prize, 1999, Nobel Prize for Medicine, 1999, Ellis Island Medal of Honor, 2000. Mem. Nat. Acad. Scis. (U.S. Steel award in molecular biology 1978, Richard Lounsbery award 1983), Am. Acad. Arts and Scis., Japan Biochem. Soc. (hon.), Am. Soc. Cell Biology (pres. 1990), German Soc. Cell Biology (hon.), Am. Philos. Soc., European Molecular Biol. ORgn. (assoc.). Office: Rockefeller U Cell Biology Lab 66th and York Ave New York NY 10021-6339

BLOCH, ANTHONY MICHAEL, mathematician, educator; b. Johannesburg, Republic South Africa, Feb. 28, 1955; s. Harry and Mary Elizabeth (Gotlop) B.; m. Sheila Janet Hurwitz, Dec. 30, 1984; 1 child, Mitchell Keith. BS with honors, U. Witwatersrand, Johannesburg, 1978; MS, Calif. Inst. Tech., 1979; M of Philosophy, Cambridge U., England, 1981; PhD, Harvard U., 1985. Teaching fellow Harvard U., Cambridge, Mass., 1982-84; T.H. Hildebrandt research asst. prof. math. U. Mich., Ann Arbor, 1985-88; research fellow Math Sci. Inst. Cornell U., Ithaca, N.Y., 1988-89; asst. prof. math. Ohio State U., Columbus, 1988-92, assoc. prof. math., 1992-95, U. Mich., Ann Arbor, 1994-97, prof. math., 1997—, Alexander Ziwet Collegiate prof., 2005—, chair math. dept., 2005—. Contbr. articles to scholarly jours. Recipient Presdl. Young Investigator award, 1991; NSF grantee, 1987—; Guggenheim fellow, 1996-97. Fellow IEEE; mem. Am. Math. Soc., Soc. Indsl. and Applied Math.

BLOCH, CLIFFORD ALAN, pediatric endocrinologist; b. Johannesburg, Republic of South Africa, May 13, 1953; came to U.S., 1984; s. Leonard E. and Audrey (Silver) B.; m. Natalie Cohen, Dec. 5, 1976; children: Tracy L., Jennifer K. B Medicine and Surgery, Witwatersrand U., 1976. Diplomate Am. Bd. Pediatrics (subbd. pediatic endocrinology). Med. and surg. intern U. Witwatersrand, Johannesburg, Republic of South Africa, 1977; med. officer S.A. Med. Corps, Johannesburg, 1978-79; pediatric resident U. Witwatersrand, 1980-83, cons. pediatrician, 1984; pediatric endocrine fellow U. Cin., 1984-87; asst. prof. Childrens Hosp. of Denver, 1987—; pediatric endocrinology, pediatrician Pediatric Endocrine Associates, Englewood, Colo. Contbr. articles to profl. jours. Served to capt. SAMC, 1983. Grantee U. Colo. (BRS), 1988, Childrens Hosp. Denver (kempe research ctr.), 1987. Fellow Am. Acad. Pediatrics; mem. Am. Diabetes Assn., Endocrine Soc., Pediatric Endocrine Soc., Western Soc. for Pediatric Research, Colo. Soc. for Endocrinology and Metabolism. Jewish. Discovered the link in 2007 between lavender oil and tea tree oils found in shampoos, soaps, and lotions can temporarily leave boys with large breasts. Home: 5791 S Havana Ct Englewood CO 80111-3927 Office: Pediatric Endocrine Associates 499 E Hampden Ave Suite 290 Englewood CO 80113-2792*

BLOCH, DONALD MARTIN, lawyer; b. Lynn, Mass., May 16, 1939; s. Meyer James and Bertha (Berman) B.; m. Ellen Ann Green, June 18, 1961; children: Andrew Louis, Linda Phyllis, David Michael. BA, Bowdoin Coll., Brunswick, Maine, 1960; LLB, Harvard U., Cambridge, Mass., 1963. Bar: Mass. 1963, U.S. Dist. Ct. Mass. 1974. Assoc. Lane, Altman & Owens LLP , Boston, 1966-71; ptnr. Lane, Altman & Owens LLP, Boston, 1972-2001; of counsel Posternak, Blankstein & Lund, LLP, Boston, 2001—. Mem. Framingham Town Meeting, Mass., 1970-95, Town Charter Commn., Framingham, 1978-79, Mass. Adv. Com. to US Civil Rights Commn., 1991-93, Town Finance Com., 2002-06; bd. dirs. South Middlesex Assn. for Retarded, Framingham, 1980-86, Metrowest Mental Health Assn., Framingham, 1983-95, Mary Morse Healthcare Inc., 1997—, vice chair, 2000-01, chair, 2001—; bd. dirs. Jewish Cmty. Housing for Elderly, Inc., 2005—; dir., sec. Metrowest Jewish Day Sch., 2006-07, pres., 2007—. Capt. US Army, 1963—65. Named one of Outstanding Citizens, Greater Framingham Jewish Fedn., 1983. Mem. Bowdoin Club Boston (officer, bd. dirs.), Phi Beta Kappa. Republican. Office: Posternak Blankstein & Lund LLP 800 Boylston St Boston MA 02199 Home Phone: 508-879-1672; Office Phone: 617-973-6169. Personal E-mail: donmbloch@aol.com. Business E-Mail: dbloch@pbl.com.

BLOCH, ERICH, retired electrical engineer, science foundation director; b. Sulzburg, Germany, Jan. 9, 1925; arrived in U.S., 1948, naturalized, 1952; s. Joseph and Tony Bloch; m. Renee Stern, Mar. 4, 1948; 1 child, Rebecca Bloch Rosen. Student, Fed. Poly. Inst., Zurich, Switzerland, 1945—48; BSEE, U. Buffalo, 1952; degrees (hon.), U. Mass., George Washington U., Colo. Sch. Mines, SUNY Buffalo, U. Rochester, Oberlin Coll., U. Notre Dame, Ohio State U.; degree (hon.), Rensselaer Poly. Inst., 1989, Washington Coll., 1989, CUNY, NYC, 1991, Poly. U., Bklyn., 1993, St. Thomas Aquinas Coll. With IBM, 1952—75, v.p. gen. mgr. East Fishkill, NY, 1975—80, v.p. tech. personnel devel. Armonk, NY, 1980—84; mem. com. computers in automated mfg. NRC, 1980—84; dir. NSF, Washington, 1984—90; fellow Coun. on Competitiveness, 1990—; prin. Washington Adv. Group, 1998—; mem. Pres.'s Coun. of Advisors for Sci. and Tech., 2001—. Past vis. disting. prof. George Mason U. Patentee in field. Recipient U.S. medal of tech., 1985, Computer World/Smithsonian award for innovation, 1991, Swedish Royal Order of the Polar Star, Robert Noyce award, Semiconductor Industry Assn., 1999, Eugene Merchant Mfg. medal, ASME and Soc. Mfg. Engrs., Vanevar Bush award, Nat. Sci. Bd., 2002, Fellow award, Computer History Mus., 2004. Fellow: AAAS, IEEE (Founder's award 1990, Computer Pioneer award 1993, 1994), Am. Acad. Arts & Sciences; mem.: NAE (Arthur M. Bueche award 1997), Japan Acad. Engring., Royal Swedish Acad. Engring. Scis., Am. Soc. Mfg. Engrs. (hon.), Am. Soc. Engring. Edn. Office Phone: 202-682-0164. Business E-Mail: ebloch@theadvisorygroup.com.

BLOCH, HENRY WOLLMAN, diversified financial services company executive; b. Kansas City, Mo., July 30, 1922; s. Leon Edwin and Hortense Bienenstok; m. Marion Ruth Helzberg, June 16, 1951; children: Robert, Thomas M., Mary Jo, Elizabeth Ann. BS, U. Mich., 1944; D of Bus. Adminstrn. (hon.), Avila Coll., Kansas City, Mo., 1977, U. Mo., Kansas City, 1989; LLD (hon.), N.H. Coll., 1983, William Jewell Coll., Liberty, Mo., 1990, Kansas City Art Inst., 1999. Ptnr. United Bus. Co., 1946-55; hon. chmn., past CEO H & R Block, Inc., Kansas City, 1955—, also dir. Bd. dirs. Commerce Bancshares, Inc., Kansas City, CompuServe, Inc., Valentine Radford Advt.; past chmn. Midwest Rsch. Inst. Past bd. dirs. Menorah Med. Ctr.; bd. dirs., past pres. Menorah Med. Ctr. Found.; former mem. pres.'s adv. coun. Kansas City Philharmonic Assn.; chmn., dir. H & R Block Found.; past pres. of trustees U. Kansas City, Nelson-Atkins Mus. Art, trustee, dir., past chmn. bus. coun.; past bd. dirs. Jewish Fedn. and Coun. Greater Kansas City; dir., past pres. Civic Coun. Greater Kansas City; gen. chmn. United Negro Colls. Fund, 1986; bd. dirs. St. Luke's Hosp. Found., Internat. Rels. Coun., Kansas City Cmty. Found.; former mem. bd. dirs. Coun. of Fellows of Nelson Gallery Found., Am. Jewish Com.; former mem. bd. govs. Kansas City Mus. History and Sci.; bd. dirs. Midwest Rsch. Inst., vice chmn.; bd. dirs. Kansas City Symphony, past dir.; bd. dirs. Greater Kansas City Community Found.; gen. chmn. Heart of Am. United Way Exec. Com., 1978; past met. chmn. Nat. Alliance Businessmen; former mem. bd. regents Rockhurst Coll.; former mem. bd. chancellor's assocs. U. Kans. at Lawrence; former mem. bd. dirs. Harry S. Truman Good Neighbor Award Found.; bd. dirs. Internat. Rels. Coun.; bd. dirs., v.p. Kansas City Area Health Planning Coun.; past pres. Found. for a Greater Kansas City; dir. Mid-Am. Coalition on Health Care, St; Luke's Found.; trustee Jr. Achievement of Mid-Am.; vice chmn. corp. fund Kennedy Ctr. 1st lt. USAAF, 1943-45. Decorated Air medal with 3 oak leaf clusters; named Mktg. Man of Yr. Sales and Mktg. Execs. Club, 1971, Chief Exec. Officer of Yr. for svc. industry Fin. World, 1976, Mainstreeter of Decade, 1988, Entrepreneur of Yr., 1986; recipient Disting. Exec. award Boy Scouts Am., 1977, Salesman of Yr. Kansas City Advt. Club, 1978, Civic Svc. award Hyman Brand Hebrew Acad., 1980, Golden Plate award Am. Acad. Achievement, 1980, Chancellor's medal U. Mo.-Kansas City, 1980, Pres.'s trophy Kansas City Jaycees, 1980, W.F. Yates medal for disting. svc. in civic affairs William Jewell Coll., 1981, bronze award for svc. industry Wall Street Transcript, 1981, Disting. Missourian award NCCJ, 1982, Lester A. Milgram Humanitarian award, 1983, Hall of Fame award Internat. Franchise Assn., 1983; named to Bus. Leader Hall of Fame Jr. Achievement, 1980; honoree Sales and Mktg. Execs. Internat. Acad. of Achievement, 1991. Mem. Greater Kansas City C. of C. (past pres.), C. of C. Greater Kansas City (Mr. Kansas City award 1978), Acad. Squires, Golden Key Nat. Honor Soc. (hon.), Oakwood Country Club, River Club, Carriage Club, Kansas City Country Club. Jewish. Office: H&R Block Inc 4400 Main St Kansas City MO 64111-1812

BLOCH, JOSHUA J., software designer; b. Southampton, NY, Aug. 28, 1961; s. Fritz W. and Renée (Spear) B.; m. Cynthia L. Fink, Apr. 1, 1993; children: Timothy David, Matthew Jeremy. BS in Computer Sci., Columbia U., 1982; PhD in Computer Sci., Carnegie-Mellon U., 1990. Rsch. assoc. IBM Rsch., Yorktown Heights, N.Y., 1982, 83, San Jose, Calif., 1985; mem. tech. staff Bell Labs., Holmdel, N.J., 1984; sr. systems designer Transarc, Pitts., 1989; sr. staff engr. Sun Microsystems, Inc., disting. engr., 2004; prin. engr. Google, Inc., Mountain View, Calif., 2004—. Co-author: Camelot and Avalon: A Distributed Transaction Facility, 1991, Java Puzzlers: Traps, Pitfalls, and Corners Cases, 2005, Java Concurrency in Practice, 2006; author Effective Java Programming Language Guide, 2001. Achievements include helping architect Java's core platform. Home: 1199 Cordelia Ave San Jose CA 95129-4211 Office: Google Inc 1600 Amphitheatre Pkwy Mountain View CA 94043 E-mail: joshua@bloch.us.

BLOCH, JULIA CHANG, not-for-profit developer; b. Mar. 2, 1942; came to U.S., 1951, naturalized, 1962; d. Fu-yun and Eva (Yeh) Chang; m. Stuart Marshall Bloch, Dec. 21, 1968. BA, U. Calif., Berkley, 1964; MA, Harvard U., 1967, postgrad. in Mgmt., 1987; DHL (hon.), Northeastern U., Boston, 1986. Vol. Peace Corps, Sabah, Malaysia, 1964-66; tng. officer East Asia and Pacific region, Washington, 1967-68, evaluation officer, 1968-70; mem. minority staff U.S. Senate Select Com. on Nutrition and Human Needs, Washington, 1971-76, chief minority counsel, 1976-77; dep. dir. Office of African Affairs U.S. Internat. Comm. Agy., Washington, 1977-80; fellow Inst. Politics Harvard U., Cambridge, Mass., 1980; asst. adminstr. Bur. for Food For Peace and Voluntary Assistance AID, Washington, 1981-87; asst. administr. Bur. for Asia and Near East, 1987-88; assoc. U.S.-Japan Rels. Program, Ctr. for Internat. Affairs Harvard U., Cambridge, Mass., 1988-89; amb. Kingdom of Nepal, 1989-93; group exec., v.p. Bank Am., San Francisco, 1993-96; pres. The U.S.-Japan Found., 1996-98; dir. Am. West Airlines, 1994-98, Penn Mut. Life Ins., 1997; prof. Am. studies Beida U., Beijing, 1998; amb. in residence U. Md., 2000—; pres. US-China Edn. Trust, Washington, 2004—. Trustee Eisenhower Exch. Fellowship, 1995-97, Nat. Com. U.S. China Rels., 1998—; U.S. Senate rep. World Conf. on Internat. Women's Yr., Mex., 1975; advisor U.S. Del. to Food and Agr. orgn. Conf., Rome, 1975; rep. Am. Coun. Young Polit. Leaders, Peoples Republic China, 1977; charter mem. Sr. Exec. Svc., 1979; head U.S. del. Biennial Session World Food Programme, Rome, 1981-86, Devel. Assistance Com. Meeting on Non-Govtl. Orgns., Paris, 1985, Intergovtl. Group on Indonesia, The Hague, Netherlands, 1987, World Bank Consultative Group Meeting, Paris, 1987, mem. exec. women in govt., 1988-93, mem. coun. fgn. rels., 1991—; vis. prof. internat. rels. Peking U., 1998—; Starr sr. fellow U.S. China Rels. Fudan U., Shanghai, adj. prof. Author: A U.S.-Japan Aid Alliance, 1991; co-author: Chinese Home Cooking, 1986. Exec. bd. mem. Internat. Ctr. for Rsch. on Women, 1974-81; mem. adv. bd. Women's Campaign Fund, 1976-78; mem. nat. adv. coun. Experiment in Internat. Living, 1981-83; mem. U.S. Nat. Com. for Pacific Econ. Cooperation, 1984—, Nat. Presdl. Debate Forum, 1987-92; bd. trustees Atlantic counsel, 2004-; mem. presdl. adv. couns. Peace Corps, 1988-89; mem. com. to visit art mus. Harvard U., 1989; founder Women Fgn. Policy Group; mem. Am. Refugee Com. Bd., 1993; mem. Am. Himalayna Found. Bd., 1994; commr. Asian Art Mus., San Francisco, 1994; trustee, bus. leadership cir., 1994—; bd. trustees Coun. Am. Ambs., 2003-; chmn. bd. dirs. F.Y. Chang Found. Hon Fulbright fellow, 1996, Woodrow Wilson fellow, 2000-; recipient Hubert Humphrey award for internat. svc., 1979, Humanitarian Svc. award AID, 1987, Leader for Peace award Peace Corps, 1987, Asian Am. Leadership award, 1989, Brotherhood/Sisterhood award NCCJ, 1996; named Outstanding Woman of Color, Nat. Inst. for Women of Color, 1982, Woman of Distinction, Nat. Conf. for Coll. Women Student Leaders and Women of Achievement, 1987, Disting. Pub. Svc. award Nat. Assn. Profl. Asian Pacific Am. Women, 1989; Ford Found. Study fellow for internat. devel. Harvard U., 1966, Paul Harris award Rotary, 1992, Award of Honor Narcotic Enforcement Assn., 1992.

Fellow Nat. Acad. Pub. Adminstrn.; mem. Orgn. Chinese Am. Women (founder, chair 1977—, bd. dirs., Woman of Yr. 1987), Asia Soc. (pres. coun. 1989, trustee, 1994), Am. Studies Ctr. (vice-chair), Prytannean Honor Soc., Coun. Fgn. Rels., Mortar Bd., Cosmos Club. Republican. Avocations: ceramics, gourmet cooking, collecting art. Office Phone: 202-884-8533. E-mail: jcbloch@aol.com.

BLOCH, KURT JULIUS, physician; b. Germany, Oct. 17, 1929; s. Max and Mathilde B.; m. Margot Bendit, June 25, 1953; children: Kenneth D., Donald B. BS, CCNY, 1951; MD, NYU, 1955. Diplomate Am. Bd. Internal Medicine, Am. Bd. Allergy and Immunology, subspecialties Rheumatology, Diagnostic Lab. Immunology. Intern, asst. resident Bellevue Hosp., NYC, 1955-57; resident in medicine Mass. Gen. Hosp., Boston, 1960-61, physician, 1974—2003, sr. physician, 2003—, chief clin. immunology and allergy units, 1976—2000, chief clin. immunology unit, dir. clin. immunology lab., 2000—02; instr. medicine Harvard Med. Sch., Boston, 1965-68, asst. prof., 1968-70, assoc. prof., 1970-74, prof., 1974—2003, prof. emeritus, 2003—. Sr. investigator Arthritis Found., 1964-69 Contbr. articles to profl. jours. With USPHS, 1957-60. Mem. Am. Soc. Clin. Investigation, Am. Assn. Physicians. Achievements include research on the biologic functions of antibodies, mechanisms of inflammation of the intestine, the immunobiology of sensorineural hearing loss, and the clinical significance of antibodies to heat shock proteins. Office: Mass Gen Hosp Cardiovascular Rsch Ctr Boston MA 02114 Business E-Mail: kbloch@partners.org.

BLOCH, PAUL, public relations executive; b. Bklyn., July 17, 1939; s. Edwin Lionel and Antoinette (Greenberg) B. B.B. Polit. Sci., UCLA, 1962. Publicist Rogers & Cowan, Beverly Hills, Calif., 1962-70, v.p., 1970-75, sr. v.p., ptnr., 1975-83, exec. v.p., sr. ptnr., 1983—, also vice chmn., co-chmn. Asst. Am. Cancer Soc., United Way, Am. Diabetes Assn., UNICEF, 1975—; adv. council Orange County Sheriff's Dept., 1980—. Served with U.S. Army, 1957. Recipient Les Mason award Publicity Guild Am., 1991. Mem. Publicists Guild of Am. (award for publicity campaign for Brian's Song 1972), Country Music Assn. Office: Rogers & Cowan 8687 Melrose Ave Ste G700 Los Angeles CA 90069-5721 *I wouldn't trade my life for the world.*

BLOCH, SCOTT J., lawyer; m. Catherine Bloch; 7 children. B, JD, U. Kans. Ptnr. Stevens & Brand, LLP, Lawrence, Kans.; assoc. dir. then dep. dir. and counsel, task force for faith-based and cmty. initiatives US Dept. Justice, 2001—03; nominated for position of spl. counsel US Office of Special Counsel, 2003, spl. counsel Washington, 2004—. Served on state bd. of discipline, Kans.; adj. prof. U. Kans. Sch. Law. Bd. editors Kans. Law Review, Kans. Criminal Procedure Review. Chair of his county Bar Ethics and Grievance Com. Office: US Office Spl Counsel 1730 M St NW Ste 218 Washington DC 20036-4505

BLOCH, STUART MARSHALL, lawyer, banker; b. Detroit, Nov. 5, 1942; s. A. Howard and Pauline Betty (Rappaport) B.; m. Julia Chang, Dec. 21, 1968. AB, U. Miami, 1964; LLB, Harvard U., 1967. Bar: Mich. 1968, DC 1968. Ptnr. Ingersoll and Bloch, Washington, 1972—; chmn. Real Estate Reporter, Ltd., Washington, 1978—; chmn. bd. Congl. Bank; bd. dirs. ULLILO. Author: A Periodical Guide to FIRREA, 1989, The Workout Game, 1987, 90, The Liability Game, 1988; editor State Digest of Land Sales, 1977—, DC Real Estate Reporter, 1979—; fellow Salzburg Seminar, 1988. Chmn. Land Devel. Inst., Washington, 1974—; trustee Arena Stage, 1983, Black Student Fund, Washington, 1983; major gifts chmn. Harvard U. Law Sch., 1983; 25th reunion chmn. U. Miami, 1989; pres. Internat. Found. for Timesharing, 1983; mem. corp. Northeastern U., Boston, 1983; bd. individual vol. svc. Jewish Nat. Fund, 1994. Recipient Spl. Citation Am. Land Devel. Assn., 1980; citation DC City Coun., 1982, Jewish Nat. Fund Tree of Life award, 1991. Mem. ABA, D.C. Bar Assn., Mich. Bar Assn., Univ. Club (Washington). Home Phone: 202-812-1814; Office Phone: 202-744-6947.

BLOCH, SUSAN LOW, law educator; b. NYC; d. Ernest and Ruth Low; m. Richard I. Bloch; children: Rebecca, Michael. BA in Math., Smith Coll., 1966; MA in Math., U. Mich., MA in Computer Sci., PhC, 1972, JD, 1975. Bar: D.C. 1975. Law clk. to chief judge U.S. Ct. Appeals, Washington, 1975-76; law clk. to assoc. justice Marshall U.S. Supreme Ct., Washington, 1976-77; assoc. Wilmer, Cutler & Pickering, Washington, 1978-82; prof. Georgetown U. Law Ctr., Washington, 1983—. Legal analyst for impeachment procs. CBS, 1998; impeachment expert U.S. Ho. of Reps. Jud. Com., 1998. Author: Supreme Court Politics: The Institution and Its Procedures, 1994, Inside the Supreme Court: The Institution and Its Procedures, 2007; contbr. articles to profl. jours. including Constl. Commentary, Duke Law Jour., Mich. Law Rev., Am. U. Law Rev., Wis. Law Rev., Law and Contemporary Problems, Georgetown Law Rev., St. Louis U. Law Jour., ABA Jour., Supreme Ct. Preview, Voice of Am., chapters to books. Active Common Cause, Women's Legal Def. Fund. Recipient Smith Coll. medal, 2005. Mem. ABA, Am. Bar Found., Am. Law Inst., D.C. Bar (Bicentennial of Constn., mem. ethics com., jud. evaluation com.), D.C. Cir. Judicial Conf. (prog. chair 1993, 96), U. Mich. Com. Visitors, 1982—, Inst. Pub. Representation (bd. dirs.), Order of Coif, Phi Beta Kappa, Sigma Xi. Home: 4335 Cathedral Ave NW Washington DC 20016-3560 Office: Georgetown U Law Ctr 600 New Jersey Ave NW Washington DC 20001-2075 Office Phone: 202-662-9063. Business E-Mail: bloch@law.georgetown.edu.

BLOCK, ALLAN JAMES, communications executive; b. Oct. 1, 1954; s. Paul Jr. and Marjorie (McNab) B. BA, U. Pa., 1977. Coord. electronic tech. planning Toledo Blade Co., 1981-83, dir. electronic planning, 1984-85; dir. mktg. Buckeye Cablevision Inc., Toledo, 1985-87; v.p. cablevision and TV Blade Communications, Inc., Toledo, 1987-88, exec. v.p., 1989; co-CEO Blade Comm., Inc., Toledo, 1989—; vice-chmn. bd. Block Comm., Inc. (formerly known as Blade Comm., Inc.), Toledo, 1990—2001, mng. dir., prin. exec. officer, 2002—04, chmn. bd., prin. exec. officer, 2005—. Bd. dirs. Toledo Blade Co., P.G. Pub. Co., Buckeye Cablevision Inc. Bd. dirs. C-SPAN, Med. Coll. Ohio, 1991-2000, Nat. Cable TV Coop., Inc., 2000-03, Am. Cable Assn., 2002—. Mem. Toledo Club, Met. Club (N.Y.C.), Penn Club (N.Y.C.), Downtown Assn. (N.Y.C.), Duquesne Club (Pitts.), Inverness Club. Home: 235 14th St Toledo OH 43624-1401 Office: 6450 Monroe St Sylvania OH 43560 Home Phone: 419-242-6739; Office Phone: 419-724-6035. Business E-Mail: ABlock@blockcommunications.com.

BLOCK, ALVIN GILBERT, academic director; b. Moline, Ill., Sept. 15, 1946; s. Sylvan Emory Block and Pauline (Kutten) Salzman; m. Sarah Cannon Michael, June 17, 1977 (div. 1984); m. Ellen Marie Chapman, Jan. 19, 1992; children: Will Chapman Block, Thomas Chapman Block BA, Bradley U., 1968. Editl. asst. Playboy mag., Chgo., 1970; exec. Salzman & Co., Davenport, Iowa, 1971-74; editor Ketchum (Idaho) Tomorrow, 1975-77; reporter Idaho Statesman, Ketchum, 1978-80; freelance writer, Sacramento, 1980-82; mng. editor Calif. Jour., Sacramento, 1983-94, editor, columnist, 1995-2000, 2004—05, editor-in-chief news and publs., 2000—03, pub., 2003. Commentator Sta. KXPR-FM, Sacramento, 1985—88; co-editor Calif. Polit. Almanac; editor Calif. Govt. and Politics Annual, 1995—2005; v.p., editor-in-chief State Net, 1996—2003; vis. scholar Inst. Govt. Studies, U. Calif., Berkeley, 2004—05; dir. public affairs journalism program U. Calif., Sacramento, 2005—. Councilman City of Ketchum, 1979; bd. dirs. Calif. Common Cause, 2006—. With U.S. Army, 1969-74. Recipient award for column Idaho Newspaper Assn., 1975, Soc. Profl. Journalists, 1995. Avocations: baseball, military history, railroading, writing. Home: 1133 Marian Way Sacramento CA 95818-3718 Home Phone: 916-446-4785; Office Phone: 916-445-7300. Personal E-mail: ag.block@sbcglobal.net. Business E-Mail: ag.block@ucop.edu.

BLOCK, ANDREW, lawyer; b. Washington, July 12, 1972; BA in Polit. Sci., Univ. Md., 1994; JD, Emory Univ., Atlanta. Ga., 1998. Bar: Ala. 1998, Ga. 2001. Ptnr. Nelson Mullins Riley & Scarborough LLP, Atlanta. Bd. mem. CURE childhood cancer org., 2006—. Mem.: ABA, Am. Health Lawyers Assn. Office: Nelson Mullins Ste 1400 999 Peachtree St NE Atlanta GA 30309-3964 Fax: 404-817-6091.

BLOCK, ARTHUR R., communications executive, lawyer; BS in Econs., U. Pa., 1975, BA, 1975; JD, U. Mich., 1978. Ptnr. Corp. Dept. Wolf, Block, Schorr and Solis-Cohen, 1978—89; atty. Comcast Corp., Phila., 1989—, v.p., sr. dep. gen. counsel, 1994—2000, gen. counsel, 2000—, sr. v.p., 2002—, sec., 2002—. Bd. mgrs. Moore Coll. of Art & Design, Phila.; site bd. City Yr. Greater Phila. Office: Comcast Corp 1500 Market St Philadelphia PA 19102 Office Phone: 215-981-7564. E-mail: ablock@comcast.net.*

BLOCK, BARTLEY CAVANOUGH, biologist, educator; b. Chgo., Apr. 12, 1933; s. David and Anne (Been) B.; m. Janet Jacobs, May 26, 1963; children: Kenneth, Deborah, Steven. BS, Northwestern U., 1954, MS, 1955; student, Pa. State U., 1955-58. Entomologist USDA, Beltsville, Md., 1959; asst. prof. Lycoming Coll., Williamsport, Pa., 1959-63, Drexel Inst. Tech., Phila., 1964-65, So. Conn. State Coll., New Haven, 1965-67, U. Bridgeport, Conn., 1967-74, assoc. prof. biology, 1974-92; chief med. writer Pharmedica Comm., New Haven, 1992-96; sr. sci. editor Pharos Healthcare Comm., Inc., Greenwich, Conn., 1996-97. Freelance med. writer, 1998—; cons. in field. Author: Man, Microbes and Matter, 1974; inventor in field. Chmn. Milford Conservation Commn., 1982-86; mem. Inland Wetland Agy., 1988-90. Grantee U.S. AEC, 1960, USDA, 1960-62, NSF, 1962-63, Mellon Found., 1980; vis. fellow Yale U., 1988-89. Mem. AAAS, Am. Med. Writers Assn., Am. Inst. Biol. Sci., Am. Soc. Zool., Entomol. Soc. Am., Ecol. Soc. Am., Animal Behavior Soc. Democrat. Jewish. Avocation: photography. Home: 355 Blackstone Blvd Apt 349 Providence RI 02906-4951 Personal E-mail: jbblock2@cox.net.

BLOCK, DENNIS JEFFREY, lawyer; b. Bronx, NY, Sept. 1, 1942; s. Martin and Betty (Berger) B.; m. Lauren Elizabeth Troupin, Nov. 27, 1967; children: Robert, Tracy, Meredith. BA, U. Buffalo, 1964; LLB, Bklyn. Law Sch., 1967. Bar: N.Y. 1968, U.S. Dist. Ct. (ea. dist.) N.Y., U.S. Dist. Ct. (so. dist.) N.Y., U.S. Ct. Appeals (2d, 3d, 5th, 6th, 7th, 8th, 9th, 10th and 11th cirs.), U.S. Supreme Ct. Br. chief SEC, NYC, 1967-72; assoc. Weil, Gotshal & Manges, L.L.P., NYC, 1972-74, ptnr., 1974-98, Cadwalader, Wickersham & Taft, LLP, NYC, 1998—. Co-author: The Business Judgment Rule: Fiduciary Duties of Corporate Directors and Officers, Law & Business, Inc., 1987, 5th edit., 1998; co-editor: The Corporate Counselor's Desk Book, 1982, 5th edit., 1999; contbr. articles to profl. jours. Chmn. major gifts lawyers div., United Jewish Appeal Fedn., 1987-89, chmn. lawyers div., 1989-91. Named one of 100 Most Influential Lawyers, Nat. Law Jour., 2006. Mem.: ABA (coun. litigation sect., com. on corp. laws sect. bus. law), Assn. Bar City NY, Am. Law Inst. Office: Cadwalader Wickersham & Taft LLP Ste 32-106 One World Finl Ctr New York NY 10281 Office Phone: 212-504-5555. Business E-Mail: dennis.block@cwt.com.

BLOCK, EMIL NATHANIEL, JR., retired air force officer; b. Newark, Ohio, Oct. 3, 1930; s. Emil Nathaniel and Louise Jeanette (Palmer) B.; m. Marian Lou Davis, June 9, 1956; children: Eric, Emil Darin. BS, U.S. Naval Acad., 1956; MSE in Instrumentation, U. Mich., 1961, MSE in Aero. and Astronautical Engring, 1961; MS in Bus. Adminstrn, George Washington U., 1966. Commd. 2d lt. U.S. Air Force, 1956, advanced through grades to maj. gen., 1979; spl. asst. for B-1 matters, dep. chief staff for research and devel. Hdqrs. USAF, Washington, 1976-78; chief of staff mil. airlift command, dir. Air Force C-X task force, Scott AFB, Ill., 1978-80; dir. plans Hdqrs. USAF, Pentagon, Washington, 1980-81; ret., 1981; pres. Blime, Inc., 1981—2005. Decorated D.S.M. (2), Legion of Merit (3), D.F.C., Bronze Star, Meritorious Service medal (2), Air medal (5); Jimmy Doolittle fellow, 1978 Mem. Air Force Assn. Home Phone: 703-866-7897. Personal E-mail: blime@cox.net.

BLOCK, FRANCESCA LIA, writer; b. Hollywood, Calif., Dec. 3, 1962; d. Irving Alexander and Gilda Rona (Klein) B.; children: Jasmine Angelina Schuette, Samuel Alexander Schuette. BA in English Lit., U. Calif., Berkeley, 1986. Author: Weetzie Bat, 1989 (ALA Best Book award, 1989), Witch Baby, 1991 (Sch. Libr. Jour. Best Book award), Cherokee Bat and the Goat Guys, 1992 (ALA Best Book award, N.Y. Times Book Rev. Notable Book), Ecstasia, 1993, Missing Angel Juan, 1993 (ALA Best Book award, 1993), Primavera, 1994, The Hanged Man, 1994, Baby Be Bop, 1995 (Pub.'s Weekly Best Book award, 1995, ALA Best Book award, 1995), Girl Goddess # 9, 1996, Dangerous Angels, 1998 (L.A. Times Rev. Best Seller), I Was a Teenage Fairy, 1998; author: (with Hillary Carlip) Zine Scene, 1998, Violet and Claire, 1999 (L.A. Times Rev. Best Seller), The Rose and the Beast, 2000 (L.A. Times Rev. Best Seller, Pub.'s Weekly Best Book award, 2000), Nymph, 2000, Echo, 2002; author: Guarding the Moon, 2003 (L.A. Times Rev. Best Seller, 2003), Wasteland, 2003, Goat Girls, 2004, Beautiful Boys, 2004;: Necklace of Kisses, 2005, Psyche in a Dress, 2006; author: (with Carmen Staton) Ruby, 2006; author: various translations into French, Italian, German, Japanese, Czech, Danish, Finnish and Norwegian. Recipient Margaret A. Edwards Lifetime Achievement award, ALA, 2005. Mem. Phi Beta Kappa. Democrat. Jewish. Office: c/o Lydia Wills Paradigm Agy New York NY 10019-5206

BLOCK, GENE DAVID, academic administrator, biologist, educator; b. NYC, Aug. 17, 1948; s. Philip and Roslyn (Klein) B.; m. Carol Sue Kullback, June 28, 1970. AB, Stanford U., 1970; MS, U. Oreg., 1972, PhD, 1975. NIH postdoctoral fellow Stanford U., 1975-78; asst. prof. U. Va., Charlottesville, 1978-83, assoc. prof., 1983-88, prof. biology, 1988—2007, prof. medicine, 1991—2007, dir. Biodynamics Inst., 1989-91; dir. NSF Biol. Timing Ctr. NSF Biol. Timing Ctr., Charlottesville, 1991—2002; Alumni Coun. Thomas Jefferson Prof. of Biology U. Va., Charlottesville, 1993—2007, v.p. rsch., 1993—2001, v.p., provost, 2001—07; chancellor UCLA, 2007—. Disting. prof. psychiatry and behavioral sci. UCLA, 2007—. Contbr. articles on biol. timing to profl. jours.; patentee in field. Home Phone: 310-825-9980; Office Phone: 310-825-2151.

BLOCK, HOLLY, museum director; Programs coord. Washington Project for the Arts (WPA); curator The Brox Mus., Bronx, NY, 1985—88; exec. dir. Art in General, NYC, 1988—2006, The Bronx Mus., 2006—. Co-commr. Cairo Biennial U.S. Dept. of State, 2003; advisor Nat. Assn. of Aritsts Orgns.; bd. dirs. ArtTable; co-studio theme chair Coll. Art Assn. Nat. Conf., NYC, 1997; mem. steering com. NYC Arts Coalition. Author: Art Cuba: The New Generation, 2001. Office: The Bronx Mus of the Arts 1040 Grand Concourse at 165th St Bronx NY 10456-3999

BLOCK, ISAAC EDWARD, professional society administrator; b. Phila., Aug. 8, 1924; s. Louis Emanuel and Stella Florence (Goodman) B.; m. Marline Beryl Lewin, June 16, 1957; children: Nancy Anne, Kathie Sue, Stephen Edward BS in Physics, Haverford Coll., Pa., 1944; MA in Math., Harvard U., Cambridge, Mass., 1947, PhD in Math., 1952. Math. cons. Philco Corp., Phila., 1951-54; mgr. computer ctr. Burroughs Corp., Phila., 1954-59; mgr. engring. computer ctr. Univac div. Sperry Rand Corp., Phila., 1959-61, mgr. applied math. systems Blue Bell, Pa., 1961-64; tech. advisor Auerbach Corp., Phila., 1964-65; mgr. Auerbach Info. Inc., Phila., 1965-67, v.p., gen. mgr., 1967-72; v.p., dir. product planning and devel. Auerbach Pub. Inc., Phila., 1972-76; mng. dir. Soc. for Indsl. and Applied Math., Phila., 1976-94, cons., 1994—. Sec./founder, 1951-53, chmn. pubs. com., 1954-63, v.p., 1964-74, council, 1957-65, trustee, 1971-75, chmn. bd. trustees, 1974-75; lectr. Computation Lab, Wayne State U., summers 1954-55 With USNR, 1944—45. Fellow: AAAS; mem.: Am. Math. Soc., Soc. Indsl. and Applied Mech., Sigma Xi, Phi Beta Kappa. Avocations: photography, music. Home: 7904 Cobden Rd Glenside PA 19038-7255 Personal E-mail: ieblock@hotmail.com.

BLOCK, JANICE L., lawyer; BA magna cum laude, Princeton U.; MS in Journalism, Northwestern U.; JD, Columbia U. Ctrl. regional counsel Microsoft Corp., 1998—2002, cons., 2002—04; ptnr. Tech., Telecommunications and Media Group Greenberg Traurig, LLP, Chgo., 2004—05; sr. v.p., gen. counsel, sec. Career Edn. Corp., Hoffman Estates, Ill., 2005—. Office: Career Edn Corp Ste 600 2895 Greenspoint Parkway Hoffman Estates IL 60169*

BLOCK, JOHN ROBINSON, newspaper publisher, editor-in-chief; b. Toledo, Oct. 1, 1954; s. Paul Jr. and Marjorie Jane (McNab) B.; m. Susan Lynn Jones, July 20, 2002; 1 child Caroline McNab Jones Block. BA, Yale U., 1977. Reporter AP, Miami, Fla., 1977-78, NYC, 1978-80; Washington corr. The Toledo Blade, 1980-82, European corr. London, 1982-83, Sunday editor, 1983-85, asst. mng. editor, 1985-87, exec. editor, 1987-89; co-pub., editor-in-chief The Blade, Toledo, 1989—2001; co-pub. Pitts. Post-Gazette, 1989—2001, editor-in-chief, 1993—, pub., 2001—, The Blade and Pitts Post-Gazette, 2001; v.p., bd. dirs. P.G. Pub. Co., Pitts. Vice chmn., bd. dirs. Block comms., Inc., Toledo. Chmn. City Mgr.'s Hist. Preservation Com., Toledo, 1983-85; chmn. airport com. Toledo-Lucas County Port Authority, 1994-97. Mem. Am. Soc. Newspaper Editors, Soc. Profl. Journalists, Internat. Press Inst., Nat. Press Club (Washington), Yale Club (NYC), Belmont Country Club (Perrysburg, Ohio), Grolier Club (NYC), Duquesne Club (Pitts.), Athletic Club (Columbus, Ohio), Rockwell Springs Trout Club (Castalia, Ohio), Golf Club (Pitts.). Avocations: flying, book collecting. Home: 725 Devonshire St Pittsburgh PA 15213-2905 Office: The Blade 541 N Superior St Toledo OH 43697-0921 also: Pitts Post-Gazette 34 Blvd Of The Allies Pittsburgh PA 15222-1204

BLOCK, JOSEPH G., lawyer; b. Johnstown, Pa. BA with high honors, U. Mich., 1969; JD, Harvard U., 1972. Bar: Pa. 1972, DC 1977, Calif. 1981. Trial atty. Defender Assn. of Phila., 1972—76; gen. counsel to minority Permanent Sub-com. on Investigations, Govtl. Affairs Com., US Senate, 1977—79, chief counsel to minority, 1979—81; atty. Law Offices of Barry Tarlow, LA, 1981—84; trial atty. Environ. Crimes Sect., Environment and Natural Resources Div., Dept. Justice, 1985—91, asst. chief, 1987—88, chief, 1988—91; atty. EPA, 1991; spl. asst. criminal enforcement Office of Enforcement, 1991; ptnr. Environ. and Corp. Defense Depts. Venable LLP, Washington, DC. Mem. Prin., Trade and Environ. Policy Adv. Com. US Trade Rep. and EPA, 1994—. Contbr. articles to profl. jours. Master: Edward Bennett Williams Inn of Ct.; mem.: ABA (vice chair Environ. Crimes Com. 1988—), Am. Law Inst. (co-chair Annual Conf. on Environ. Crimes). Office: Venable LLP 575 7th St NW Washington DC 20004 Office Phone: 202-344-4878. Office Fax: 202-344-8300. E-mail: jgblock@venable.com.

BLOCK, KEITH, computer software company executive; BS in Info. Systems, Carnegie-Mellon U., Pitts., MS in Mgmt. Sr. cons. Booz, Allen and Hamilton, 1984—86; with Oracle Corp., Redwood City, Calif., 1986—, v.p. Ams. Consumer Packaged Goods consulting, group v.p. East Consulting, sr. v.p. N.Am. Comml. Consulting, exec. v.p. N.Am. Consulting, mem. exec. mgmt. com., 2001—, exec. v.p. N.Am., 2002—. Bd. trustees Concord Mus.; bd. visitors Carnegie-Mellon U. Office: Oracle Corp 500 Oracle Pky Redwood City CA 94065 Office Phone: 650-506-0024.*

BLOCK, LAWRENCE, writer; b. Buffalo, June 24, 1938; s. Arthur Jerome and Lenore Harriet (Nathan) B.; m. Loretta Kallett, Mar. 10, 1960 (div. 1973); children: Amy Jo Block Reichel, Jill Diana, Alison Elspeth; m. Lynne Wood, Oct. 2, 1983. Student, Antioch Coll., 1955-59. Editor Scott Meredith Lit. Agy., NYC, 1957-58; editor Whitman Pub. Co., Racine, Wis., 1964-66; free lance writer, 1957—. Pres., seminar leader Write for Your Life, NYC and Ft. Myers Beach, Fla., 1983-88; instr. Hofstra U., Hempstead, N.Y., 1981 Author: (novels) Mona, 1961, Death Pulls a Doublecross, 1962, The Girl With the Long Green Heart, 1965, The Thief Who Couldn't Sleep, 1966, The Cancelled Czech, 1966, Deadly Honeymoon, 1967, Tanner's Twelve Swingers, 1967, Two for Tanner, 1968, Tanner's Tiger, 1968, Here Comes A Hero, 1968, After the First Death, 1969, The Specialists, 1969, Such Men are Dangerous, 1969, Me Tanner, You Jane, 1970, No Score, 1970, Ronald Rabbit Is A Dirty Old Man, 1971, Chip Harrison Scores Again, 1971, Five Little Rich Girls, 1976, The Topless Tulip Caper, 1975, The Sins of the Fathers, 1976, In the Midst of Death, 1976, Time to Murder and Create, 1977, Burglars Can't be Choosers, 1977, The Burglar in the Closet, 1978, The Burglar Who Liked to Quote Kipling (Nero Wolfe award), 1979, Ariel, 1980, The Burglar Who Studied Spinoza, 1980, A Stab in the Dark, 1981, Eight Million Ways to Die, 1982, The Burglar Who Painted Like Mondrian, 1983, When the Sacred Ginmill Closes (Japanese Maltese Falcon award), 1986, Random Walk, 1988, Out on the Cutting Edge, 1989, A Ticket to the Boneyard, 1990, A Dance at the Slaughterhouse, 1991, A Walk Among the Tombstones, 1992, The Devil Knows You're Dead, 1993, The Burglar Who Traded Ted Williams, 1994 (German Marlowe award), A Long Line of Dead Men, 1994, The Burglar Who Thought He Was Bogart, 1995, Even the Wicket, 1997, The Burglar in the Library, 1997, Hit Man, 1998, Tanner on Ice, 1998, Everybody Dies, 1998, The Burglar in the Rye, 1999, Hit List, 2000, Hope to Die, 2001, Small Town, 2003, The Burglar on the Prowl, 2004, All the Flowers Are Dying, 2005, Hit Parade, 2006, Lucky at Cards, 2007; (nonfiction) Writing the Novel From Plot to Print, 1979, Telling Lies for Fun and Profit, 1981, Write for Your Life, 1985, Spider, Spin Me a Web, 1988; (with Delbert Ray Krause) Swiss Shooting Talers and Medals, 1965; (with Cheryl Morrison) Real Food Places, 1981; (with Harold King) Code of Arms, 1981, (with Ernie Bulow) After Hours, 1994; (short story collections) Sometimes They Bite (trophy 813 Societe of France), 1983, Like A Lamb to Slaughter, 1984, Some Days You Get The Bear, 1993, Ehrengraf for the Defense, 1994, One Night Stands, 1999, The Lost Cases of Ed London, 2001, Enough Rope, 2002, (anthologies) Death Cruise, 1999, Master's Choice, 1999, Opening Shots, 2000, Master's Choice 2, 2000, Speaking of Lust, 2000, Speaking of Greed, 2001, Opening Shots 2, 2002, Blood on Their Hands, 2003, Manhattan Noir, 2006; contbg. editor Writer's Digest, 1976-90; contbr. stories to various mags. including Cosmopolitan, Playboy, GQ, Am. Heritage, mystery mags; exec. story cons. ESPN series, Tilt!, 2005-. Named Suspense Writer of Yr., Romantic Times, 1984, Grand Maitre du Roman Noir, Calibre 38, 1996, Gumshoe award, 2005. Fellow Flat Earth Soc. of Can. (U.S. plenipotentiary 1971—), Va. Ctr. for the Creative Arts; mem. Mystery Writers Am. (pres. 2000, Edgar Allan Poe award 1985, 92, 94, 98, Grand Master award 1994), Pvt. Eye Writers Am. (pres. 1984, Shamus award 1983, 85, 96, Life Achievement award 2002), Internat. Assn. Crime Writers, Internat. Narcotics Enforcement Officers Assn., Internat. Assn. for Study of Organized Crime, Crime Writers Can., Crime Writers Assn. (U.K., Cartier Diamond Dagger Life Achievement award 2004), Crime Writers of Norway. E-mail: LB@lawrenceblock.com.

BLOCK, LAWRENCE J., federal judge; b. NYC, Mar. 15, 1951; BA magna cum laude, NYU, 1973; JD, John Marshall Law Sch., Chgo., 1981. Law clk. to Hon. Roger J. Miner US Dist. Ct. (no. dist. NY), 1981—82; assoc. Skadden Arps Slate Meagher & Flom, NYC, 1983—86; atty. comml.

litig. br. US Dept. Justice, 1986, sr. atty. adv. Office Legal Policy & Policy Devel., 1987—90; dep. asst. gen. counsel legal policy US Dept. Energy, 1990—94; sr. counsel Senate Judiciary Com., Washington, 1994—2002; judge US Ct. Fed. Claims, Washington, 2002—. Adj. prof. George Mason U. Sch. Law, 1990—91. Contbr. articles to profl. jours. Office: US Ct Fed Claims Suite 708 717 Madison Pl NW Washington DC 20005 Office Phone: 202-357-6508.

BLOCK, MARTIN, lawyer; b. NYC, July 14, 1937; s. Leonard and Rose (Tenzer) B.; m. Linda Zuckerman, Dec. 25, 1965 (div. 1979); children: Sarin, Bryson; m. Ann Block, July 15, 1990. Student, Bklyn. Coll., 1959-61, NYU, 1962-63; LLB, Bklyn. Law Sch., 1965. Bar: N.Y. 1965, U.S. Dist. Ct. (so. and ea. dists.) N.Y.C. 1966, U.S. Ct. Appeals (2d cir. 1979). Assoc. Seymour L. Colin, NYC, 1965-70; assoc. then. ptnr. Queller, Fisher, Block & Wisotsky, NYC, 1970-85; ptnr. Sanders, Sanders, Block & Woycik, P.C., 1985—. Instr. Hofstra U. Trial Adv. Program, 1994—; guest lectr. Lawline-Cable TV, N.Y.C., 1984. Staff sgt. USNG, 1959-64. Recipient Cert. in Civil Trial Adv. Nat. Bd. Trial Adv., 1993. Mem. ATLA, Nassau County Bar Assn. (chair Plaintiffs Roundtable com.), Assn. Trial Lawyers City of N.Y., N.Y. State Trial Lawyers Assn. (lectr. 1984), Nassau-Suffolk Trial Lawyers Assn. (treas. 1998 sect., bd. dirs. 1994-97, vice chmn. 1999-2001), Am. Arbitration Assn. Democrat. Jewish. Office: Sanders Sanders Block & Woycik PC 100 Herricks Rd Mineola NY 11501-3652

BLOCK, MICHAEL KENT, economics and law professor, former government official; b. NYC, Apr. 2, 1942; s. Philip and Roslyn (Klein) B.; m. Carole Arline Polansky, Aug. 30, 1964 (div.); children: Robert Justin, Tamara Nicole; m. Olga Vyborna, Dec. 1, 1996. AB, Stanford U., 1964, A.M., 1969, PhD, 1972. Research analyst Bank of Am., San Francisco, 1965-66; research assoc. Planning Assocs., San Francisco, 1966-67; asst. prof. econs. U. Santa Clara, 1969-72; asst. prof. econs. dept. ops. research and adminstrv. sci. Naval Postgrad. Sch., Monterey, Calif., 1972-74, assoc. prof., 1974-76; research fellow Hoover Instn., Stanford U., 1975-76, sr. research fellow, 1976-87; dir. Center for Econometric Studies of Justice System, 1977-81; ptnr. Block & Nold, Cons., Palo Alto, Calif., 1980-81; assoc. prof. mgmt., econs. and law U. Ariz., Tucson, 1982-85, prof. econs. and law, 1989—; mem. U.S. Sentencing Commn., Washington, 1985-89; exec. v.p. Cybernomics, Tucson, 1991—2002; pres. Goldwater Inst. for Pub. Policy, Phoenix, 1992—2002; sr. policy adviser State of Ariz. Gov. Symington, 1996-97. Chair Basis Sch. Bd., 1998—; mem. Ariz. Residential Utility Consumer Bd., 1995-96, chmn. Ariz. Constl. Def. Coun., 1994-97, Ariz. Juvenile Justice Adv. Coun., 1996-97; seminar dir. Econ. Devel. Inst./World Bank, 1992-95; cons. in field. Author: (with H.G. Demmert) Workbook and Programmed Guide to Economics, 1974, 77, 80, (with James M. Clabault) A Legal and Economic Analysis of Criminal Antitrust Indictments:, 1955-80; contbr. articles to profl. publs. Fellow NSF, 1965, Stanford U. Fellow Progress and Freedom Found.; mem. Am. Econ. Assn., Phi Beta Kappa. Office: U Ariz Econ Dept McClelland Hl Rm 401 Tucson AZ 85721-0001

BLOCK, NEAL JAY, lawyer; b. Chgo., Oct. 4, 1942; s. William Emmanual and Dorothy (Harrison) Block; m. Frances Keer, Apr. 19, 1970; children: Jessica, Andrew. BS, U. Ill., 1964; JD, U. Chgo., 1967. Bar: Ill. 1967, U.S. Dist. Ct. (no. dist.) Ill. 1967, U.S. Ct. Appeals (3d and 6th cirs.) 1968, U.S. Claims Ct. 1990, U.S. Ct. Appeals (fed. cir.) 1991. Atty., advisor U.S. Tax Ct., Washington, 1967-69; assoc. Baker & McKenzie, Chgo., 1969-74, ptnr., 1974—, client credit dir., 1989—2002. Adj. prof. law Kent Law Sch., Ill. Inst. Tech., Chgo., 1986—90. Mem.: AICPA (honorable mention award 1964), ABA, Ill. Soc. CPAs (silver medal 1964, Leading Ill. Atty. 1997), Ill. State Bar Assn., Chgo. Bar Assn. (chmn. fed. tax com. 1983—84). Office: Baker & McKenzie 1 Prudential Pla 130 E Randolph St Ste 3500 Chicago IL 60601-6342 E-mail: neal.j.block@bakernet.com.

BLOCK, NED, philosopher, educator; b. Chgo., Aug. 22, 1942; s. Eli William and Blanche (Rabinowitz) Block; m. Susan Carey, May 17, 1970; 1 child, Eliza. SB in Physics and Philosophy, MIT, 1964; postgrad., Oxford U., Eng., 1964-66; PhD, Harvard U., 1971. Asst. prof. philosophy MIT, Cambridge, Mass., 1971-77, assoc. prof., 1977-83, prof., 1983-96, chair dept. philosophy, 1989-95, chair press cognitive rev. bd., 1992—95; prof. NYU, NYC, 1996—2004, Silver prof., 2004—. Mem. faculty NEH Inst., 1981, 93; grant reviewer NSF, Can. Coun.; vis. rschr. Ecole Poly., Paris, 1995—96; vis. prof. Harvard U., 2002—03, Edole Normal, Paris, 2007. Adv. editor: Contemporary Psychology; mem. editl. bd. Cognition, Cognition and Brain Theory, Cognitive Sci., mem. adv. editl. bd. Lang. and Cognitive Processes, Mind and Lang. Philos. Studies, mem. bd. editl. advisors Behavioral and Brain Scis.; contbr. articles to profl. jours. Recipient Robert A. Muh award, MIT, 2005; fellow, Old Dominion Found., 1973—74, Sloan Found., 1980—81, Am. Acad. Arts Scis., 2004—, NEH, 2006—07; grantee, U.S. Nat. Com. Internat. Union History and Philosophy Sci., 1979, 1983, NEH, 1979—82, NSF, 1985—86, 1988—90, Am. Coun. Learned Socs., 1988—89; Postdoctoral fellow, NIH, 1970—71, Sr. fellow, Ctr. Study Lang. and Info., Stanford U., 1984—85. Mem.: Assn. Sci. Study Consciousness (pres. 2003). Home: 37 Washington Sq W New York NY 10011-9181 Office: NYU Dept Philosphy 5 Washington Pl New York NY 10003 Office Phone: 212-998-8322. Business E-Mail: ned.block@nyu.edu.

BLOCK, NORMAN LOUIS, oncologist, educator; b. NYC, Aug. 31, 1938; s. Abraham Harold and Rose (Bodatsky) B.; m. Carolyn Lee Peck, May 12, 1967; children: Joseph, David, Adam, Nathaniel, Jessica. BA, NYU, 1959, MD, 1963. Diplomate Am. Bd. Urology. Intern Baylor U. Med. Ctr., Dallas, 1963-64, resident in surgery, 1966—67; resident in urology NYU Med. Ctr., NYC, 1967—71; fellow in urologic oncology Meml. Sloan Kettering Cancer Ctr., NYC, 1971-72; attending physician Miami VA Med. Ctr., 1972-96, Jackson Meml. Hosp., Fla., 1972—; chief urology VA Med. Ctr., 1975—85; assoc. prof. urology U. Miami, 1976-82, prof. urology, 1982—, prof. biomed. engring., 1982—, L. Austin Weeks prof., 1982—, prof. oncology, 1985—. Editl. reviewer 6 jours. Contbr. numerous articles to profl. jours., including Cancer Jour. Urology, Jour. Urology, Jour. Surg. Oncology. Capt. U.S. Army, 1964-66. Recipient numerous awards, fellowships, lectureships. Mem. AMA, ACS, AAAS, Internat. Urology Soc., Internat. Soc. for Artificial Organs, Am. Fertility Soc., Am. Urol. Assn. (Southeastern sect.), Am. Soc. for Artificial Internal Organs, Am. Assn. Lab. Animal Sci. (Fla. divsn.), Southeastern Cancer Rsch. Assn., Soc. Surg. Oncology, Soc. Univ. Urologists, Southeastern Coop. Oncology Group, Soc. Govt. Svc. Urologists, So. Med. Assn., Confedn. Am. Urologists, Soc. Urologic Oncology, Colombian Urol. Soc., Fla. Med. Assn., Fla. Urologic Assn., Greater Miami Urologic Soc., Dade County Med. Soc., Bellevue Urologic Alumni Assn. Republican. Jewish. Achievements include holder six patents; research in new treatment for prostate cancer; development of new diagnostic test for bladder cancer; applied a new model for prostate cancer in animals; development of an artificial bladder, ureter, urethra sphincter. Avocation: wildlife photography. Office: U Miami Sch Medicine Dept Urology M 814 PO Box 16960 Miami FL 33101-6960 Office Phone: 305-243-6518. Business E-Mail: nblock@med.miami.edu.

BLOCK, PHILIP DEE, III, retired investment company executive; b. Chgo., Feb. 14, 1937; married; 2 children. BS in Indsl. Adminstrn. with high honors, Yale U., 1958. Trainee and engr. Inland Steel Co., Chgo., 1958-60, raw materials coordinator, 1961-65, gen. mgr. purchases, 1966-72, gen. mgr. corp. planning, 1973-76, v.p. materials and services, 1977-79, v.p. purchases, 1980-85; sr. v.p. Capital Guardian Trust Co., Chgo., 1986—2004; ret., 2004. Trustee Chgo. Hist. Mus., Shedd Aquarium Soc.; alumni trustee Latin Sch. of Chgo., 2005—; bd. dirs. Children's Meml. Hosp. With USAFR, 1959—64. Home: 1430 N Lake Shore Dr Chicago IL 60610-6682

BLOCK, ROBERT CHARLES, nuclear engineering educator; b. Newark, Feb. 11, 1929; s. George and Sue (Ehrenkranz) B.; m. Rita Adler, June 28, 1952; children: Keith, Robin. BSEE, Newark Coll. Engring., 1950; MA in Physics, Columbia U., 1953; PhD in Nuc. Physics, Duke U., 1956. Elec. engr. Nat. Union Radio Corp., West Orange, NJ, 1950-51, Bendix Aviation Co., Teterboro, NJ, 1951; physicist Oak Ridge Nat. Lab., 1955-66; prof. nuc. engring. and sci. Rensselaer Poly. Inst., 1966-96, head dept. nuc. engring. and engring. physics, 1987-93, assoc. dean engring. for acad. and student affairs, 1993-96, prof. emeritus, 1997—; founder, v.p., treas. Becker, Block & Harris Inc., 1981-92. Vis. scientist Atomic Energy Rsch. Establishment, Harwell, Eng., 1962-63, Am. Inst. Physics, 1961-67; vis. prof. Kyoto (Japan) U., 1973-74; vis. physicist Brookhaven Nat. Lab., 1975, mem. vis. com. nuc. energy dept., 1982-86; cons. GE, 1968-79; cons., mem. nuc. cross sect. adv. com. AEC, 1969-72; mem. U.S. Nuc. Data Com., 1974—; mem. Cross Sect. Evaluation and Working Group, exec. com. 2003—; mem. NRC panel on low and medium energy neutrons, 1977; dir. Gaerttner Linac Lab., 1976—; vis. faculty Sandia Nat. Lab., 1986; mem. adv. com. West Point Mil. Acad., 2004—; mem. nuc. program adv. com. Los Alamos Nat. Lab., 2004—; mem. faculty senate Rensselaer Polytech. Inst., 2003-2005. Co-author chpts. in books. Recipient Glenn Murphy award Am. Soc. Engring. Edn., 1991, William H. Wiley Disting. Faculty award Rensselaer Poly. Inst., 1995; Japanese Ministry Edn. rsch. grantee, 1973-74. Fellow Am. Nuc. Soc. (Seaborg medal 2005); mem. AAAS, AAUP, IEEE, Am. Phys. Soc., Sigma Xi, Sigma Pi Sigma, Phi Beta Tau, Tau Beta Pi. Achievements include research on neutron physics, radiation effects in electronics, and radiation applications. Home: 114 3rd St Troy NY 12180 Office: Rensselaer Poly Inst Gaerttner LINAC Lab 110 8th St Troy NY 12180-3590 Office Phone: 518-276-6404. Business E-Mail: blockr@rpi.edu.

BLOCK, STANLEY HOYT, pediatrician, allergist; b. NYC, Oct. 28, 1943; s. Julius and Zilla Augustus (Freidman) B. BA, U. Chgo., 1963; MD, Yale U., 1966. Diplomate Am. Bd. Pediatrics, Am. Bd. Allergy and Immunology. Intern Children's Hosp. of Phila., 1966-67; resident Babies Hosp., Columbia Presbyn. Med. Ctr., NYC, 1967-69; pediatrician, allergist pvt. practice Lynn and Lowell, 1971-77; med. dir. Providence (R.I.) Cmty. Health Ctrs., Inc., 1977—. Major U.S. Army, 1969-71. Recipient Tchg. award in pediatrics R.I. Hosp. House Officers Assn., 1982, Dr. Charles L. Hill award for Pub. Svc., R.I. Med. Soc., 1995, Cmty. Partnership award Brown U. Howard R. Swearer Ctr., 1999, Disting. Tchr. award Brown U., 2000, Bert Jaffe award, R.I. Pub. Health Assn., 2002. Fellow Am. Acad. Pediatrics, Am. Acad. Allergy, Asthma and Immunology, R.I. Soc. of Allergy (former pres., sec.); mem. R.I. Med. Soc. Avocations: hiking, cross country skiing. Office: Providence Cmty Health Ctrs Inc 375 Allens Ave Providence RI 02905-5010 Business E-Mail: sblockmd@providencechc.org.

BLOCK, STEVEN MICHAEL, biophysicist, educator; b. Durham, NC, Oct. 4, 1952; s. Martin M. and Beate S. (Sondhelm) B.; m. Kathleen Ann Beasley, Aug. 15, 1985. BA with honors, Oxford U., 1974, MA in Physics, 1978; MA in Biology, U. Colo., 1982; PhD, Calif. Inst. Tech., 1985. Postdoctoral rschr. Stanford U., 1985—87, prof. applied physics and biol. scis. Calif., 1999—, sr. fellow Freeman Spogli Inst. Internat. Studies; lectr. Harvard U., Cambridge, Mass., 1987-91, assoc., 1991-93; fellow Rowland Inst., Cambridge, 1987-93; assoc. prof. Princeton U., NJ, 1994-98, prof., 1998—99. Contbr. articles to sci. jours.; mem. editl. bd.: The Scientist, 1986—97, Biophysical Jour., 1995. Fellow Am. Acad. Arts & Scis., AAAS; mem. Biophysical Soc. (mem. exec. bd. 1995-97, coun. mem. 1995-98, pres. 2005-06, Young Investigator award 1994), NAS, Sigma Xi. Jewish. Avocations: bluegrass banjo, alpine skiing. Office: Dept Biol Scis Stanford U Gilbert Hall 371 Serra Mall M/C5020 Stanford CA 94305-5020 Office Phone: 650-724-4046. E-mail: sblock@stanford.edu.*

BLOCK, WILLIAM K., JR., media executive; b. New Haven, Nov. 28, 1944; s. William and Maxine (Horton) B.; m. Carol Pauline Zurheide, Aug. 1, 1970; children: Diana, Nancy, Katherine. BA, Trinity Coll., Hartford, Conn., 1967; JD, Washington and Lee U., 1972. Staff mem. Red Bank (N.J.) Register and Toledo Blade, 1972-77; advtg. mgr. Red Bank (N.J.) Register, Shrewsbury, NJ, 1977-79, sales mgr., 1979-80, pub., 1980-82; dir. ops. Toledo Blade Co., 1983-84, v.p. ops., 1984-86, v.p., gen. mgr., 1986-87, pres., 1987—, co-pub., 1990—, Pitts. Post Gazette, 1990—; v.p. Block Com., Inc., Toledo, 1987-88, pres., 1989—2001, chmn., 2002—. V.p. Toledo Sesquicentennial Commn., 1986-87; pres. Inland Press Assn., 1998-99; bd. dirs. Toledo Symphony, St. Luke's Hosp., Ohio Hist. Soc.; pres. Read for Literacy, Inc., 1989-2001; campaign chmn. United Way of Greater Toledo, 2003. With U.S. Army, Vietnam, 1968-70. Mem. Toledo Country Club, Toledo Club. Avocations: reading, travel, fishing. Office: Block Communications Inc 541 N Superior St Toledo OH 43660-0001

BLOCK, ZENAS, retired management consultant, educator; b. NYC, Dec. 7, 1916; s. Joshua and Celia (Kaplow) B.; m. Lillian Bialek, June 12, 1938 (dec. 1985); children: Richard, Karen Block Chase Graubard, Margaret Block Walker; m. Janet Andre, Aug. 13, 1988. BS, CCNY, 1938; postgrad., Bklyn. Poly. Inst., 1939-41. Chemist Clairol Inc., NYC, 1938-39; chief chemist Am. Dietaids Co., Yonkers, N.Y., 1938-48; dir. labs. DCA Food Industries, NYC, 1948-55, v.p. rsch., 1955-60, pres. bakery divsn., 1960-64, group v.p., 1964-71, exec. v.p., 1971-77, vice chmn. bd., 1977-79, also bd. dirs. Chmn. bd. dirs. Nisshin DCA Foods Inc., Tokyo, 1975-79, DCA Industries Ltd., Eng., 1976-79; founder, pres. Haystack Cable Vision Inc., Lakeville, Conn., 1978-80, v.p. and treas., 1980-82; adj. prof. Grad. Sch. Bus. Adminstrn., U. Conn., 1979-81; clin. prof. NYU, 1984-94, adj. prof. entrepreneurship grad. divsn. Stern Schs. Bus., NYU, 1995-2001, entrepreneur-in-residence Stern Sch. Bus., 1999-2000, founder, assoc. dir. Ctr. for Entrepreneurial Studies, 1984-89; adj. prof. mgmt. Lally Sch. Mgmt., Rensselaer Poly. Inst., 1991-92, 97-98, vis. prof., 1996-97, curriculum cons., 1997-99; founder Salisbury Sch. Ednl. Enrichment Fund, 2001— Author: It's All on the Label, 1981; (with I.C. MacMillan) Corporate Venturing: Creating New Businesses Within the Firm, 1993; mem. editl. bd. Jour. Bus. Venturing; contbr. articles to acad. and profl. jours.; patentee food processing field. Bd. dirs. N.Y.C. Mission Soc., 1983-87, Salisbury Family Svcs., 1983-87; trustee Salisbury Assoc., 1992-95; mem. bd. fin. Town of Salisbury, 1996—; mem. bd. govs. Sharon Hosp., 2002—. Home and Office: PO Box 530 Salisbury CT 06068-0530

BLODGETT, ELSIE GRACE, small business owner, property manager; b. Eldorado Springs, Mo., Aug. 2, 1921; d. Charles Ishmal and Naoma Florence (Worthington) Robison; m. Charles Davis Blodgett, Nov. 8, 1940; children: Carolyn Doyel, Charleen Bier, Lyndon, Daryl(dec.). Student, Warrensburg State Tchrs. Coll., Mo., 1939—40; BA, Fresno State Coll., Calif., 1953. Tchr. schs., Mo., 1940—42, Calif., 1947—72; owner, mgr. rental units, 1965—; exec. dir. San Joaquin County Rental Property Assn., Stockton, Calif., 1970—81; prin. Delta Rental Property Owners and Assoc., 1981—82; propr. Crystal Springs Health World, Inc., Stockton, 1980—86. Active PTA, Girl Scouts U.S., Boy Scouts Am., Vols. in Police Svc., 1993—2004; capt. Delaware Alpine Neighborhood Watch, 1994—2003; past bd. dirs. Stockton Better Bus. Bur.; bd. dirs. Stockton Goodwill Industries, 1994—2003. Named (with husband) Mr. and Mrs. Apt. Owner of San Joaquin County, 1977. Mem.: Nat. Apt. Assn. (state treas. women's divsn. 1977—79), Calif. Ret. Tchrs. Assn., Mil. Wives, DAV Aux., Stockton Zonta Lodge. Republican. Methodist. Home: 4350 St Andrews Dr Stockton CA 95219

BLODGETT, FRANK CALEB, retired food company executive; b. Janesville, Wis., Apr. 22, 1927; s. Frank Caleb Pickard and Dorothy (Korst) B.; m. Jean Ellen Fountain, June 23, 1951; children: Caleb J., Barbara F., David K. Grad., Beloit Coll., 1950; postgrad., Advanced Mgmt. Program, Harvard U., 1969. 1st v.p., dir. Frank H. Blodgett Inc., Janesville, 1947-61, pres., dir., 1961-62; with Gen. Mills Inc., Mpls., 1961-92, v.p., dir. mktg., 1967-69, gen. mgr., v.p., 1969-73, group v.p., 1973-76, exec. v.p., 1976-80, vice chmn., 1981-92, chief fin. and adminstrv. officer, 1985-92, dir., 1980-92; ret., 1992. Bd. dirs. Medtronic, Inc., Reliastar Fin. Corp. and subs., Northwestern Nat. Life Ins. Co., HealthSpan Health Sys. Corp.; dir. Waldorf Corp., 1993—. Trustee Gen. Mills Found., 1980-92, Washburn Child Guidance Ctr., 1972-75, Beloit Coll., 1976—, Nutrition Found., 1980-84; bd. dirs. Cereal Inst., 1970-76, chmn., 1973-74; bd. dirs. Abbott Northwestern Hosp. With USN, 1944-46, PTO. Recipient Disting. Svc. citation Beloit Coll., 1990. Mem. Millers Nat. Fedn., Young Millers Orgn. (past pres.), U.S. C. of C. (bd. dirs. 1982-88), Greater Mpls. C. of C. (bd. dirs. 1975-76), Phi Kappa Psi (trustee alumni bd. Beloit 1961-62), Phi Eta Sigma. Home: 688 Hillside Dr Wayzata MN 55391-9643

BLODGETT, J. KEVIN, lawyer; BA, Tex. A&M U.; JD, U. Houston Law Ctr. Assoc. corp. dept. Baker Botts, LLP; with legal grp. Dynegy Inc., Houston, 2000, grp. gen. counsel corp. fin. & securities, corp. sec., 2003—04, sr. v.p. human resources, 2004—05, gen. counsel, exec. v.p. adminstrn., 2005—. Mem.: Houston Young Lawyers Assn., Houston Bar Assn., Tex. Bar Assn. Office: Dynegy Inc 1000 Louisiana St Ste 5800 Houston TX 77002 Office Phone: 713-507-6400. Office Fax: 713-507-6808.*

BLODGETT, LYNN R., information technology company executive; Grad., Brigham Young U., Utah Tech. Coll. Co-founder Unibase Technologies, Inc., 1985; pres. ACS Bus. Process Solutions, Inc., 1990—99; exec. v.p., group pres. comml. solutions Affiliated Computer Svcs., Inc. (ACS), Dallas, 1999—2005, v.p., COO, 2005—06, bd. dirs., 2005—, pres., CEO, 2006—. Office: ACS 2828 N Haskell Dallas TX 75204*

BLODGETT, WARREN TERRELL, public affairs educator; b. Ranger, Tex., Sept. 15, 1923; s. William Serle Sr. and Alice Louise (Furman) B.; m. Dorothy Jean Chapin, Mar. 7, 1946; children: Robert Harold, William Arthur, Katherine Ann. BA, Baylor U., 1943; MS Pub. Adminstrn., Syracuse U., 1947. Research assoc. U. Tex., Austin, 1947-50, assoc. dir. policy rsch inst., 1982-90, Mike Hogg prof. urban mgmt., 1982-95, Mike Hogg prof. emeritus in urban mgmt., 1995—; personnel dir. City of Austin, 1950-52, adminstrv. asst. to city mgr., 1952-55, asst. city mgr., 1955-60; city mgr. City of Waco, Tex., 1960-63, City of Garland, Tex., 1963-64; adminstrv. asst. to gov. State of Tex., Austin, 1964-69; prin. in charge govt. cons. Peat, Marwick and Mitchell, Austin, 1969-82. Cons. Tex. Dept. Water Resources, Austin, 1984-86, Legis. Audit Com., Austin, 1984-85; Tex. Com. Economy and Efficiency in Govt., Austin, 1985-87, Tex. Office of Speaker, Austin, 1985-87. Chmn. bd. Tex. Mcpl. Retirement System, 1961-62. Served to 1st lt. U.S. Army, 1943-46. Mem. Nat. Acad. Pub. Adminstrn., Internat. City Mgmt. Assn. (fund for profession 1986-89, chmn. Found. 1980-84), Internat. City-County Mgmt. Assn. ((Disting. Svc. award 1993), Nat. Civic League (hon. life dir. 1989, chmn. 1986-87, vice chmn. 1987-88), Austin Area Urban League (treas. 1985-87). Democrat. Mem. Christian Ch. Avocation: tennis. Home and Office: 1801 Lavaca St Austin TX 78701-1341 Personal E-mail: blodgett@mail.utexas.edu.

BLODIG, ALLISON MARIE, environmental services administrator; b. Atchison, Kans., Nov. 12, 1967; d. Donald Lloyd Jones and Marlene Marie Walker, Richard Walker (Stepfather); m. Jeffrey George Blodig, May 17, 1997; 1 child, Alex James Crough. BA in Biology, Benedictine Coll., Atchison, KS, 1992. Registered environ. health specialist Nat. Environ. Health Assn., 1996. Food, drug, lodging surveyor Kans. Dept. Health and Environ., Topeka, 1992—95; environ. health specialist Johnson County Environ., Lenexa, Kans., 1996—2001; regulatory affairs mgr. Bio-Microbics, Inc., Shawnee, Kans., 2000—; owner Apple Valley Farm Resort, Ozawkie, Kans., 2002—. Chair Kans. Small Flows Assn., Conf. Com., Mullinville, Kans., 2004—, pres., 2005—06. Author: (paper) Bottled Water Survey in Kansas (Kans. Assn. of Sanitarians Achievement, 1995). Liturgical min. St. Theresa Cath. Ch., Perry, Kans., 1998—2007. Mem.: Nat. Onsite Wastewater and Recycling Assn. R-Conservative. Catholic. Avocations: travel, billiards, motorcycling. Home: 9259 Apple Valley Ln Ozawkie KS 66070 Personal E-mail: alimarie86@yahoo.com.

BLOEDE, VICTOR CARL, lawyer, consultant, director; b. Woodwardville, Md., July 17, 1917; s. Carl Schon and Eleanor (Eck) B.; m. Ellen Louise Miller, May 9, 1947; children: Karl Abbott, Pamela Elena. AB, Dartmouth Coll., 1940; JD cum laude, U. Md., Balt., 1950; LLM in Pub. Law, Georgetown U., 1967. Bar: Md. 1950, Fed. Hawaii 1958, U.S. Supreme Ct. 1971. Pvt. practice, Balt., 1950-64; mem. Goldman & Bloede, Balt., 1959-64; counsel Seven-Up Bottling Co., Balt., 1958-64; dep. atty. gen. Pacific Trust Ter., Honolulu, 1952-53; asst. solicitor for ters. Office of Solicitor, U.S. Dept. Interior, Washington, 1953-54; atty. U.S. Justice, Honolulu, 1955-58; assoc. gen. counsel Dept. Navy, Washington, 1960-61, 63-64; spl. legal cons. Md. Legislature, Legis. Coun., 1963-64, 66-67; assoc. prof. U. Hawaii, 1961-63, dir. property mgmt., 1964-67; house counsel, dir. contracts and grants U. Hawaii Sys., 1967-82; house counsel U. Hawaii Rsch. Corp., 1970-82; legal counsel Law of Sea Inst., 1978-82; legal cons. Rsch. Corp. and grad. rsch. divsn. U. Hawaii, 1982—92; spl. legal cons. 1st Unitarian Ch. Honolulu, 1992—. Spl. counsel to Holifield Congl. Commn. on Govt. Procurement, 1970—73. Author: Hawaii Legislative Manual, 1962, Maori Affairs, New Zealand, 1964, Oceanographic Research Vessel Operations, and Liabilities, 1972, Hawaiian Archipelago, Legal Effects of a 200 Mile Territorial Sea, 1973, Copyright-Guidelines to the 1976 Act, 1977, Forms Manual, Inventions: Policy, Law and Procedure, 1982; writer, contbr. Coll. Law Digest and other publs. on legis. and pub. law. Mem. Gov.'s Task Force Hawaii and The Sea, 1969, Citizens Housing Com. Balt., 1952-64; bd. govs. Balt. Cmty. YMCA, 1954-64; bd. dirs. U. Hawaii Press, 1964-66, Coll. Housing Found., 1968-80; apptd. to internat. rev. commn. Can.-France Hawaii Telescope Corp., 1973-82, chmn., 1973, 82; co-founder, incorporator First Unitarian Ch. Honolulu. Served to lt. comdr. USNR, 1942-45, PTO. Grantee ocean law studies, NSF and NOAA, 1970—80. Mem.: ABA, Fed. Bar Assn., Am. Soc. Internat. Law, Nat. Assn. Univ. Attys. (founder & 1st chmn. patents & copyrights sect. 1974—76), Balt. Bar Assn. Home: 635 Onaha St Honolulu HI 96816-4918

BLOEM, JAMES H., managed health care executive; BA, Calvin Coll.; MBA, Harvard Univ.; JD, Vanderbilt U. Sch. Law. cert. CPA. CFO Herman Miller, Inc.; pres. personal care divsn. Perrigo Co., 1998—99; pvt. fin. and bus. cons., 1999—2001; sr. v.p., CFO Humana, Inc., Louisville, 2001—. Bd. dir. Rotech Healthcare Inc., NeighborCare Inc. Office: Humana Inc 500 W Main St Louisville KY 40202*

BLOEMBERGEN, NICOLAAS, physicist, researcher; b. Dordrecht, Netherlands, Mar. 11, 1920; arrived in U.S., 1952, naturalized, 1958; s. Auke and Sophia M. (Quint) Bloembergen; m. Huberta D. Brink, June 26, 1950; children: Antonia, Brink, Juliana. BA, Utrecht U., 1941, MA, 1943; PhD, Leiden U., 1948; MA (hon.), Harvard U., 1951, LHD (hon.), 2000; DSc (hon.), Laval U., 1987, U. Conn., 1988, U. Hartford, 1991, Moscow State U., 1997; LHD (hon.), U. Mass., Lowell, 1994, U. Ctrl. Fla., 1996, N.C. State U., 1998. Tchg. asst. Utrecht U., 1942—45; rsch. fellow Leiden U., 1948; mem. Soc. Fellows Harvard U., 1949—51, assoc. prof., 1951—57, Gordon McKay prof. applied physics, 1957—, Rumford prof. physics, 1974, Gerhard Gade univ. prof., 1980, prof. emeritus, 1990; prof. optics U. Ariz., 2001—. Vis. prof. U. Paris, 1957, U. Calif., 1965, Coll. de France, Paris, 1980, U. Ariz., 2001—; Lorentz guest prof. U. Leiden, 1973; Raman vis. prof., Bangalore, India, 79; Fairchild Disting. scholar Calif. Inst. Tech., 1984; hon. prof. Fudan U., Shanghai; Disting. vis. prof. CREOL U. Ctrl. Fla., 1995. Author: Nuclear Magnetic Relaxation, 1948, Nonlinear Optics, 1965, Enconters in Magnetic Resonance, 1996, Encounters in Nonlinear Optics, 1996; contbr. articles to profl. jours. Recipient Stuart Ballantine medal, Franklin Inst., 1961, Half Moon trophy, Netherlands Club N.Y., 1972, Nat. Medal of Sci., 1975, Lorentz medal, Royal Dutch Acad., 1978, Frederic Ives medal, Optical Soc. Am., 1979, von Humboldt sr. scientist award, Munich, 1980, Nobel prize in Physics, 1981, Dirac medal, U. New South Wales, Australia, 1983, Medal of Honor, Inst. Elec. and Electronic Engrs., 1983, Von Humboldt Sr. Scientist award, 1987, von Humboldt medal, Munich, 1989, Byvoet medal, U. Utrecht, 2001, Russell Varian prize, Euromar, 2005; fellow Guggenheim, 1957. Fellow: IEEE (Morris Liebmann award 1959), Am. Acad. Arts and Scis., Am. Phys. Soc. (Buckley prize for solid state physics 1958); mem.: NAE, Norwegian Soc. Scis. and Letters (fgn.), Paris Acad. Scis. (fgn. assoc.), Koninklyke Nederlandse Akademie von Wetenschappen (corr.), Indian Acad. Scis. (hon.), Optical Soc. Am. (hon.), Deutsche Akademie der Naturforscher Leopoldina, Am. Philos. Soc., Nat. Royal Dutch Acads. Scis. Office: Optical Scis Ctr Univ Ariz 1630 E Univ Blvd Tucson AZ 85721 Business E-Mail: nbloembergen@optics.arizona.edu.

BLOEMEN, CRYSTAL LYNN, secondary school educator; b. Ft. Collins, Colo., July 10, 1958; d. M.L. Pat and Mildred L. Chaffin; m. Michael W. Bloemen, Dec. 17, 1988; children: Elizabeth, Patrick, Christina. BA in Elem. Edn., U. No. Colo., 1980, MS in Biology and Earth Scis., 1989. Lic. principal Colo., 2001, cert. tchr. mid. sch. sci. and elem. edn. Colo., 1980. Tchr. Newcastle Sch. Dist., Colo., 1980—82; tchr. sci. Littleton Pub. Sch., Colo., 1982—2002, Poudre Sch. Dist., Ft. Collins, Colo., 2002—. Cons. in field. Bd. advisors Space Coalition. Recipient Colo. Tchr. of Yr. award, Colo. Dept. Edn., 1999. Mem.: Assn. Supr. Curriculum Develop., Colo. Assn. Sci. Tchrs., Nat. Sci. Tchrs., Civil Air Patrol (A. Scott Crossfield Nat. Tchr. of Yr. award 2002, Crown Cir. Aerospace Educator award 2002). Avocations: reading, flying, camping, water-skiing. Home: 9935 N County Rd 19 Fort Collins CO 80524-9741

BLOEMSMA, MARCO PAUL, investor; b. Heemstede, The Netherlands, July 20, 1924; s. Philippus and Wilhelmina Geertruida (Bonebakker) Bloemsma; m. Mieke Harten, Sept. 23, 1955; children: Marco Reinier, Barbara Patricia, Michiel Alexander. LLM, Leyden U., 1948. Lawyer firm van der Feltz, Voûte & Riechelmann, 1948—49; assoc., then ptnr. Blackstone, Rueb & van Boeschoten, 1951—72; pres. C. Harten Holding B.V., The Hague, 1972—85; positions formerly held include chmn. KTI-Group; chmn. ten Doesschate-group; chmn. Euroma Holding; dir., pres., chmn. Patino-group; chmn. Lips United-group, ICL Nederland B.V., Auto-Palace group, Bloemsma Holding B.V., Nebim Handelmaatschappy B.V. With Dutch Naval Reserve, 1949—51. Hon. Ky. col. since 1962. Mem.: Cercle Litteraire (Lausanne), Cercle Interalliée (Paris). Home: 5 Ave de Crousaz 1010 Lausanne Switzerland Personal E-mail: mpbloemsma@bluewin.ch.

BLOES, RICHARD K., audio-visual specialist, artist; b. Waterloo, Iowa, Sept. 1951; m. Caitilin Driscoll-Bloes; children: Ryan, Eric. BFA, U. Iowa, Iowa City, 1973, MFA, 1977. Audio visual technician Whitney Mus. Am. Art, NY, 1979—. Exhibited in group shows at Feature Inc., 2000, NY, 2005, CAC, Cin., Ohio, 2006, Ball State U. Art Mus., Ind., 2006—07. Fellow, Guggenheim Found., 1994; grantee, Jerome Found., 1984, NY Found. for Arts, 1985, NEA, 1987, NY State Coun. for Arts, 1988, NYSCA, 1990. Home Phone: 845-228-5752.

BLOHM, KENNETH E., lawyer; b. Green Bay, Wis., Sept. 10, 1956; s. Melvin A. and Ruth M. (Schwalen) B.; m. Helen M. Marinak, Sept. 24, 1983. BA, U. Wis., 1977; JD, Harvard U., 1981. Bar: Calif. 1982, DC, NY, US Ct. Appeals (9th cir.) 1982. Law clk. to presiding justice U.S. Ct. Appeals (9th cir.), San Francisco, 1981-82; assoc. Morrison & Foerster, San Francisco, 1982; ptnr. Latham & Watkins, San Francisco. Mem. ABA, Calif. Bar Assn., Phi Beta Kappa, Phi Kappa Phi. Clubs: Asian Bus. League. Office: Latham & Watkins 505 Montgomery St Ste 2000 San Francisco CA 94111 Office Phone: 415-395-8079. Office Fax: 415-395-8095. Business E-Mail: ken.blohm@lw.com.

BLOKZYL, MATTHEW AUGUSTUS, respiratory therapist; b. Lawrence, Kans., Apr. 20, 1972; s. Glenn Bernard Blokzyl and Dianne Carol Laughter; m. Anna Marie Miller, Dec. 17, 2004; m. Melanie Bonebreak, June 22, 1993 (div. Sept. 1, 2000); children: Zoe Madia, Ema Nenet. B in Psychology, U. Tex., San Antonio, 2002. Cert. respiratory therapist Nat. Bd. Respiratory Care, 2003. Staff respiratory therapist U. Hosp., San Antonio, 2003—05, Wilford Hall Med. Ctr., San Antonio, 2005—. With USAF, 1994—97, Landstuhl, Germany. Decorated Nat. Def. Svc. medal USAF, Air Force Outstanding Unit award, Air Force Good Conduct medal. Mem.: Mensa. Buddhist. Avocation: running. Home: 5523 Red Canyon San Antonio TX 78252 Office: Wilford Hall Medical Center Lackland Air Force Base San Antonio TX 78228 Home Phone: 210-643-7715; Office Phone: 210-292-5825. Personal E-mail: mblokzyl1@satx.rr.com.

BLOM, DANIEL CHARLES, lawyer, investor, retired insurance company executive; b. Portland, Oreg., Dec. 13, 1919; s. Charles D. and Anna (Reiner) B.; m. Ellen Lavon Stewart, June 28, 1952; children: Daniel Stewart (dec.), Nicole Jan Heath. BA magna cum laude, U. Wash., 1941, postgrad., 1941-42; JD, Harvard U., 1948; postgrad., U. Paris, 1954-55. Bar: Wash. 1949, U.S. Supreme Ct. 1970. Tchg. fellow speech U. Wash., 1941—42; law clk. to justice Supreme Ct. Wash., 1948—49; since practiced in Seattle; assoc. Graves, Kizer & Graves, 1949—51; gen. counsel Northwestern Life Ins. Co., 1952—54; ptnr. Case & Blom, 1952—54; assoc., ptnr., of counsel Ryan, Swanson & Cleveland, 1956—; exec. v.p., gen. counsel Family Life Ins. Co., 1964—85, spl. counsel, 1985—91. Vice chmn. Wash. Bd. Bar Examiners, 1970-72, chmn., 1972-75; mem. industry adv. com. Nat. Assn. Ins. Commrs., 1966-68; pres. Wash. Ins. Coun, 1971-73, gen. counsel, 1975-78; mediator Arbitration Forums, Inc. Editor Wash. State Bar Jour., 1951-52; assoc. editor The Brief, 1975-76; author: Life Insurance Law of the State of Washington, 1980, Banking and Insurance, Deregulatory Cross-Currents, 1985, Hostile Insurance Company Takeovers: New Frontier of the Law, 1990, Administrative Finality Under the Washington Insurance Code, 1991, Business and Professionalism, 1994, The Civility Problem, 1995, Technics and the Civilization of Law Practice, 1997, Varieties of Regulatory Experience, 1998, Legislative Review of Administrative Rules in the State of Washington; A Light that Failed?, 2003. Chmn. jury selection Wash. Gov.'s Writer's Day Awards, 1976; bd. dirs. Crisis Clinic; trustee Bush Sch., 1971-79, v.p., 1976-77; trustee, v.p. Frye Mus., Seattle, 1976-82, World Affairs Coun. Seattle, 1972-94, Friends of Seattle Pub. Libr., 1982-87; bd. visitors U. Wash. Libr., 1988-92, Friends of U. Wash. Librs., bd. dirs., 1991-95, pres., 1991-92. 2d lt. AUS, 1942-45, PTO. Decorated Bronze Star; Rhodes scholarship finalist, 1949. Fellow: Am. Bar Found.; mem.: ABA (vice chmn. com. on life ins. law. sect. tort and ins. pratice 1971—76, chmn. 1976—78, sect. program chmn. 1978—79, mem. coun. 1979—83, chmn. pub. rels. com. 1981—83, chmn. com. on profl. independence of the lawyer 1984—85, chmn. com. on scope and correlation 1985—86, policy coord. tort and ins. practice sect. 1986—90, del. ABA to Union Internat. des Avocats 1986—91, chmn. com. on handbook and bylaws 1987—88, chmn. hist. com. 1991—94), Fedn. Regulatory Counsel (dir. 1995—97, 2002—04), Found. UIA (coun. 1990—97), Am. Arbitration Assn., Am. Coun. Life Ins. (legis. com. 1982—85), Assn. Life Ins. Counsel, Am. Judicature Soc., N.Am. Found. for Internat. Legal Practice (pres. 1987—89, dir. 1987—95, chmn. 1990—95), Union Internat. des Avocats (v.p. 1987—92), Seattle Bar Assn., Wash. Bar Assn. (chmn. legal edn. liaison com. 1977—78, award of merit 1975), Harvard Assn. Seattle and Western Wash. (trustee 1976—77), Harvard Law Sch. Assn., Rainier Club, Tau Kappa Alpha, Phi Beta Kappa. Home: 100 Ward St # 602-3 Seattle WA 98109-5613 Office: Ryan Swanson & Cleveland 1201 3rd Ave Ste 3400 Seattle WA 98101-3034 Home Phone: 206-283-6258; Office Phone: 206-654-2280. Personal E-mail: blomdc@msn.com.

BLOMQUIST, ALAN CHARLES, film producer; b. Arlington, Mass., July 21, 1953; s. Robert C. and Marjorie H. B.; children: Samuel Ellis, William Hamilton, Annika Carpenter. B in Gen. Studies in Film, U. Mich., 1976. First asst. dir. (feature film) Iron Eagle, (TV and film) The Lone Star Kid; unit prodn. mgr. (features) La Bamba, 1987, Uncle Buck, 1989, The Check is in the Mail, Breach of Contract, (Movie of the Week) A Different Affair, The Summer My Father Grew Up, 1991; co-prodr. (feature film) Guilty By Suspicion, Everybody's All American, The Cider House Rules, 1999, Bounce, 2000, (TV series) Sledge Hammer; prodr. (TV pilot) The Time of Their Lives, (schoolbreak spl.) The War Between Classes (Emmy award); exec. prodr. (features) Beautiful Girls, Of Mice and Men, 1992, What's Eating Gilbert Grape, 1993, A Little Princess, 1995, Spawn, 1997, (short film) Detached, 1998, Chocolat, 2000, View from the Top, Duplex, 2003, Taking Lives, 2004, Walk the Line, 2005, (TV movies) Vanishing Point, 1997, Blue Collar Comedy Tour: The Movie, Blue Collar Comedy Tour Rides Again, Blue Collar Comedy Tour - One For The Road, (films) Larry the Cable Guy: Health Inspector, Delta Farce. Mem. Dirs. Guild Am.

BLOMQUIST, DAVID WELS, journalist; b. Detroit, June 16, 1956; s. August Wels and Sally Lou (Ball) B. AB, U. Mich., 1976; AM, Harvard U., 1978. Tchg. fellow Harvard U., Cambridge, 1978-82, asst. sr. tutor, 1981-82; supervising sect. editor CBS Inc., NYC, 1982-84; staff writer The Record of Hackensack, N.J., 1984-86, state polit. corr. N.J., 1986-89, chief polit. writer N.J., 1990-92, chief Trenton bur. N.J., 1992-94; dir. The Record Poll, Hackensack, 1992-99, dir. online devel., 1998-99; dir. new media Detroit Free Press, 1999—2001, sr. editor tech. and rsch., 2002—. Author: Elections and the Mass Media, 1982; contbr. articles to profl. jours. Mem. Am. Polit. Sci. Assn. (edn. com. 1984-86), N.J. Legis. Corrs. Club (pres. 1992), Harvard Club of N.Y., Nat. Press Club Washington. Avocations: music, ballet. Office: Detroit Free Press 600 W Fort St Detroit MI 48226-2706 E-mail: blomquist@freepress.com.

BLOMSTEDT, ERIK RAGNAR, library administrator; b. Lulea, Sweden, May 10, 1947; came to US, 1956, naturalized, 1965; s. Ragnar Johan and Anna Viktoria (Sundkvist) B.; m. Lily Anna Yakich, May 18, 1974; children: James, Jennifer. BA, Northeastern Ill. U., 1969; MS, U. Ill., 1973; MPA, Roosevelt U., 1976; student Universidad de las Americas, 1967. Reference librarian Chgo. Pub. Library, 1973-75; dir. Cook County Corrections Library Program, Chgo., 1975-77; dir. Three Rivers Pub. Libr. Dist., Channahon, Ill., 1977—. Contbr. articles on folk music to profl. jours. Mem. exec. bd. Sunny Ridge Family Ctr., Wheaton, Ill., 1982—, Midwest Baptist Conf., Park Ridge, Ill., 1981—. Served with US Army, 1969-72; Vietnam. Decorated Bronze Star. Ill. State Libr. scholar, 1972. Mem. Am. Libr. Assn., Ill. Libr. Assn. (treas. DLRT 1978-79), Beta Phi Mu, Psi Chi. Home: 915 Surrey Ct Joliet IL 60431-9313 Office: Three Rivers Pub Library Dist 210 Channon Dr Channahon IL 60410-9637

BLOMSTRAND, DOREEN KATHRYN, retired physician assistant; b. Superior, Wis., Sept. 25, 1929; d. Wesley Lawrence and Ann Kattrine (Okerstrom) Wright; m. Fritz Joseph Blomstrand, 1948 (dec. Dec. 26, 1982); children: Cynthia Dawn Reynolds, Heidi Jo Thomas, Jace Wright-(dec.). Physician Asst. Program, U. of Wash., Seattle; Cmty. Health Adv. Program, Yakima Valley C.C., Wash. Physician Assistant MEDEX NW, U. of WA, 1985, Pa. Bd. Cert. Nat. Commn. on Cert. of Physician Assistants Bd., 1986, cert. EMT Ctrl. Wash. U., 1978; Tng. the trainer-qualified to teach others Ministry Tng. Ctrs., Oreg., 1997; Community Health Advocate Yakima Valley C.C., Wash., 1983, Cambodian Lang. study SE Asian Summer Study Intst. of Lang., U. of Hawaii, 1988. Full-time faculty MEDEX NW, U. of Wash., Seattle, 1990—2000; ret., 2000. Physician asst., health edn. coord. CAMA Svcs., United Nations Border Relief Ops., Thailand, 1986—90. Contbr. articles (Awarded second pl. in nonfiction articles, 2002). Ministry team, small group leader, mentor Eastside Foursquare Ch., Bothell, Wash., 1992—2003; vol. supplies and time with orphans Chang Mai, Thailand, 1998; vol. at distbn. ctr. for Russian immigrants Christian Friend's of Israel, Jerusalem, 1999; short-term vol. work with the poor IMPACT, Ensenada, Mexico, 1999; short term med. mission Project Mercy, Yetebon, Ethiopia, 2000; vol. Northshore Sr. Ctr., Bothell, Wash., 2000—03, Kirkland Sr. Ctr., Wash., 2001—03; short term vol. team Eastside Foursquare Ch., Metro Manila, Philippines, 2002—. Recipient Humanitarian Svc. award, MEDEX NW Alumni Assn., 2003. Mem.: Fellowship of Christian Physician Assts., U. of Wash. Retirement Assn., Wash. Acad. of Physician Assts. (past bd. mem., student affairs chair 1995—2000), MEDEX NW Alumni Assn. (life; bd. mem. 1996—), Toastmasters, Writer's Info. Network, NW Christian Writers Assn. Avocations: short-term international missions, writing, teaching, reading, dance. Personal E-mail: dblomstrand@earthlink.net.

BLOND, STUART RICHARD, magazine editor; b. LA, Sept. 1, 1953; s. Elmer George and Anne G. Blond; m. Stella Pyrtek, July 28, 1986. BA in Art, Calif. State U., 1977. V.p. advt. Packard Automobile Classics, Fords, NJ, 1988-97; sales Packard Industries, Boonton, NJ, 1989—. Editor newsletter The Cormorant News Bull., 1988-2004; edit mag. The Packard Cormorant, 2004—. Home and Office: 84 Hoy Ave Fords NJ 08863-1938 E-mail: stuartrblond@earthlink.net.

BLONDIN, C. J., trade association administrator, lawyer; b. Paterson, NJ, May 13, 1930; s. Joseph and Margaret (DeMarco) Blondin; m. Barbara Helen Barker, May 28, 1955; children: Jacqueline, Chris, Elizabeth, Barbara, David, Jennifer. BS in Engring., U.S. Coast Guard Acad., 1955; JD, George Washington U., 1962. Bar: DC 1962, U.S. Supreme Ct. 1966, appointed mil.judge: 1971. Dir. internat. affairs Nat. Marine Fisheries Svc./Nat. Oceanic & Atmospheric Adminstrn. Dept. Commerce, Washington, 1972—79, dep. asst. adminstr., 1979—86; commr. Internat. Atlantic Ocean Commn. and Internat. North Pacific Commn. Dept. Commerce, Washington, 1980—90; judge U.S.-USSR Maritime Claims Ct., Washington, Moscow, 1982—91; sr. trade assoc. U.S. Dept. Commerce, Washington, 1986—88, dep. asst. sec. internat., 1988—94; pres. Internat. Trade Assocs., Northern Neck, Va., 1994—2004. US rep. Internat. Pension Commn., Wahington, Ottawa, Can., 1984—93; vice chmn. Monitor Internat. Bd., Washington, 1989—2000; cons. internat. and maritime affairs US and Europe, 1994—. Editor (bus. editor): George Washington U. Law Rev., 1961—62; contbr. articles on internat. and maritime law to profl. jours. Dist. chmn. Boy Scouts Am., Nat. Capitol Area and Va., 1988—92; parliamentarian 1st Rep. Congl. Dist. Va., 1995—2000; chmn. Northumberland County Rep. Com., Va., 2001—04. With USN, 1948, Korea, comdr. USCG, 1955—74. Recipient Meritorious Svc. medal, U.S. President, 1973, Silver medal, Sec. of Commerce, 1984, Sec. of State, 1989. Mem.: Christian Men's Assn., Am. Legion (vice commander 2000—03), Mil. Officers Assn. Am. (chpt. pres. 1995—98). Republican. Roman Catholic. Avocations: boating, camping, golf, hiking, sailing.

BLONZ, EDWARD ROBERT, nutritionist, biochemist; b. Chgo., Nov. 17, 1949; s. Robert Blonz and Ruth Stella Eisner; m. Karen Leslie Fisher, June 27, 1982; 1 child, Joshua Aaron. BA, U. of Wis., 1971; MS, U. of Calif., Davis, 1977, PhD, 1984. Sea grant rsch. fellow U. of Calif., Davis, 1975—77, rsch. asst., vis. lectr., 1977—84; asst. prof. U. of Minn., St. Paul, 1984—87; adminstrv. project mgr. USDA Western Human Nutrition Rsch. Ctr., San Francisco, 1987—90; sci. dir. / dir. of nutrition More.com, San Francisco, 1998—2000; prin. Edward R. Blonz Cons., Kensington, Calif., 1990—; syndicated columnist United Media, NYC, 1993—. Instr. U. Calif. Extension, Berkeley, 2005—. Author: (scientific text) Controversies in Nutrition: Obesity and Fad Diets, (book) The Really Simple No Nonsense Nutrition Guide, Your Personal Nutritionist: Fiber and Fat, Your Personal Nutritionist: Antioxidants, Your Personal Nutritionist: Food Additives, Your Personal Nutritionist: Calcium and other Minerals, Power Nutrition, The Nutrition Doctors A to Z Food Counter. Food adv. com. dietary supplements U.S. FDA, Washington, 2003—. Recipient Sci. Writing award, James Beard Found., 1995; grantee Rsch. grantee, Sigma Xi, 1975. Fellow: N.Am. Assn. for Study of Obesity, Am. Coll. Nutrition (cert.); mem.: APHA, Assn. Health Care Journalists, N.Y. Acad. Scis., Inst. Food Technologists, Am. Soc. Journalists and Authors, Nat. Assn. Sci. Writers, Assn. Food Journalists, Soc. for Nutrition Edn., Sigma Xi. Personal E-mail: ed@blonz.com, er@blonz.com.

BLOODWORTH, ALBERT WILLIAM FRANKLIN, lawyer; b. Atlanta, Sept. 23, 1935; s. James Morgan Bartow and Elizabeth Westfield (Dimmock) B.; m. Elizabeth Howell, Nov. 24, 1967; 1 child, Elizabeth Howell. AB in History and French, Davidson Coll., 1957; JD magna cum laude with 1st honors, U. Ga., Athens, 1963. Bar: Ga. 1962, US Supreme Ct. 1971. Asst. dir. alumni and pub. relations Davidson Coll., NC, 1959-60; assoc. Hansell & Post, Atlanta, 1963-68, ptnr., 1969-84, Bloodworth & Nix, Atlanta, 1984-95, Bloodworth & McSwain, Atlanta, 1996—2003; pvt. practice Atlanta, 2003—. Counsel organized crime com. Met. Atlanta Commn. on Crime, 1965-67; asst. sec., counsel Met. Found. Atlanta, 1968-76. Bd. dirs. Atlanta Presbytery, 1974-78; trustee Synod of S.E., Presbyn. Ch. in U.S.A., Augusta, Ga., 1982-87; trustee Big Canoe Chapel, Ga., 1983-86, 88-91, chmn. bd. trustees, 1985-86, 90-91; mem. pres.'s adv. coun. Presbyn. Homes, 1989—; mem. president's adv. coun. Thornwell Home and Sch. for Children, 1998—. elder North Ave Presbyn. Ch., Atlanta. 1st lt. Intelligence Corps, USAR, 1957-59. Recipient Jessie Dan MacDougal Scholarship award U. Ga. Found., 1963, Outstanding Student Leadership award Student Bar Assn., U. Ga., 1963. Fellow: Am. Coll. Trust and Estate Counsel; mem.: ABA, Atlanta Estate Planning Coun., Atlanta Bar Assn., State Bar Ga., Gridiron Club, Sphinx Club, Lawyers Club, Capital City Club, Phi Delta Phi (pres. chpt. 1963, Grad. of Yr. 1963), Alpha Tau Omega (pres. chpt. 1957), Omicron Delta Kappa, Phi Kappa Phi, Phi Beta Kappa. Republican. Presbyterian. Home: 3784 Club Dr NE Atlanta GA 30319-1108 Office: 706 Monarch Plz 3414 Peachtree Rd NE Atlanta GA 30326-1153 Home Phone: 404-233-5510; Office Phone: 404-231-9331. Office Fax: 404-231-9330. Personal E-mail: awfb@bellsouth.net.

BLOODWORTH, GLADYS LEON, elementary school educator; b. Natchitoches, La., July 9, 1946; d. Rudolph and Mary (LeRoy) Leon; m. John Edward Bloodworth, Aug. 14, 1971; children: John, Jeremy. BA, Southern U., Baton Rouge, 1968; MA, Calif. State U., Dominguez Hills, 1989. Nat. bd. cert. tchr. mid. childhood generalist NBCT/MC, 2001. Lang. arts tchr. grades 6-10 Natchitoches Parish Schs.; categorical program adviser LA Unified Schs., mentor tchr., 1999—, coord. gifted coord., 1988. Named Outstanding Math Tchr., 1987-88. Mem. NEA, United Tchrs. LA, Calif. Tchrs. Assn., Women in Ednl. Leadership, Kappa Kappa Iota. Methodist.

BLOODWORTH, RICK KEITH, minister; b. Boulder, Colo., June 14, 1960; s. Ed Ray and Linda Earle Bloodworth; m. Carolyn King Moudy, June 5, 1982; children: A.J., Cherise Marie, Rebecca Elyse. BS in Bus. Adminstrn., Lubbock Christian Coll., Tex., 1982; MS in Fin. magna cum laude, West Tex. State A & M U., Canyon, 2006. Cert. residential appraiser Wyo., 2000. Owner, valuation svcs. residential Appraisal firm, Casper, Wyo., 1982—95; gospel preacher Ch. of Christ, Happy, Tex., 1995—. Adv. Disaster Relief - Tornado Recovery, Happy, 2002; co-creator The Happy Champions basketball team; coach Little League; adv. Crime Stoppers, Tulia, Tex., 1998—2005. Mem.: Mensa. Avocations: coin collecting/numismatics, basketball. Office: Church of Christ 300 W Main St Happy TX 79042

BLOODWORTH, VELDA JEAN, librarian, educator; b. Campobello, SC, June 28, 1929; d. Lloyd Ernest and Nora Frances (McNeal) Burke; m. Clifford Burton Bloodworth, Aug. 14, 1949; children: Jill Henderson, Jackie Herschberger. BA, So. Coll., Collegedale, Tenn., 1967; MS, Fla. State U., 1968; MAT, Rollins Coll., 1979. Libr. Forest Lake Acad., Apopka, Fla., 1968-74, Rollins Coll., Winter Park, Fla., 1974—99, assoc. prof. emerita; ret., 1999. Cons. libr. Forest Lake Acad., Apopka, 1987-88. Editor, curator: (catalog for art mus. exhibit) Jessie B. Rittenhouse Poetry Collection, 1984. Mem. Beta Phi Mu. Home: 3162 Holliday Ave Apopka FL 32703-6634 Office: Rollins Coll Olin Libr 1000 Holt Ave Winter Park FL 32789-4499 Business E-Mail: jbloodworth@msn.com.

BLOOM, ALFRED HOWARD, academic administrator, educator; b. NYC, Feb. 27, 1946; s. Alfred H, and Martha (Berrol) Bloom; m. Margaret Hennigan, Aug. 22, 1971. BA, Princeton U., 1967; PhD, Harvard U., 1974. Asst., assoc. prof. Swarthmore Coll., Pa., 1974—86, assoc. provost, 1985—86, pres., 1991—; dean of faculty, v.p. acad. affairs Pitzer Coll., Claremont, Calif., 1986—90, exec. v.p., 1990—91. Author: The Linguistic Shaping of Thought, 1981; contbr. articles to profl. jours. Fellow, Fulbright-Hays, 1968; grantee, SSRC, 1978, 1981, NEH, 1975, 1986. Mem.: Assn. Asian Studies. Avocations: study of languages and cultures, intercultural gastronomy. Office: Swarthmore Coll Office of Pres 500 College Ave Swarthmore PA 19081-1306 Office Phone: 610-328-8314. E-mail: abloom1@swarthmore.edu.*

BLOOM, BARRY MALCOLM, research and development company executive, consultant; b. Roxbury, Mass., Aug. 12, 1928; s. Morris and Ann (Levine) B.; m. Joan Martha Ensign, June 27, 1956; children: Catherine, Brian, Joanna. SB, MIT, 1948, PhD, 1951, postgrad., 1967; LHD (hon.), Conn. Coll., 1992. Rsch. chemist Pfizer, Inc., Groton, Conn., 1952-63, dir. medicinal chems. and rsch., 1963-71, pres. ctrl. rsch. divsn., 1971-90, v.p. rsch., 1971-90, bd. dirs., 1973—93, corp. mgmt. com., 1984-93, sr. v.p. R & D, 1990-92, exec. v.p. R & D, 1992-93; cons. pvt. practice, 1993—2004. Bd. dirs. Congl. Commn. on Fed. Drug Approval Process, PMA Commn. on Drugs for Rare Diseases; cons. U.S. Congress Office Tech. Assessment, 1976-77; mem. Conn. Tech. Adv. Bd., 1985-90. Mem. editl. bd. Ann. Reports in Medicinal Chemistry, 1968-70; patentee in field. NRC postdoctoral fellow U. Wis., 1952; Poly. Inst. Tech. fellow N.Y.C., 1980; recipient Spl. Achievement award CT Innovations, Inc., 1997. Mem. Am. Chem. Soc. (chmn. divsn. medicinal chemistry 1967), Conn. Acad. Sci. and Engring., Pharm. Mfrs. Assn. (chmn. R & D sect. 1976). Home and Office: Mackintosh Rd Lyme CT 06371

BLOOM, BARRY R., dean, medical educator; BS in Biology, Amherst Coll., DSc (hon.), 1990; MA, Harvard U.; PhD in Immunology, Rockefeller U., 1963. Joined faculty Albert Einstein Coll. Medicine, 1964, named prof., 1973, chmn. dept. microbiology and immunology, 1978—90, Weinstock Prof. of Microbiology and Immunology; dean faculty Harvard Sch. of Pub. Health, Cambridge, Mass., 1998—, Joan L. and Julius H. Jacobson Prof. of Pub. Health. Cons. White House, 1977—78; investigator Howard Hughes Inst., 1990—98; mem. Global Adv. Com. on Health Rsch. WHO; chair emeritus Internat. Vaccine Inst.; mem. sci. adv. bd. Ellison Med. Found., Wellcome Trust Ctr. for Human Genetics; mem. external adv. bd. Earth Inst., Columbia U.; mem. UN Devel. Programme: Millennium Devel. Goals Working Group on Tuberculosis. Contbr. articles to profl. jours. Co-recipient Award in Immunology, Novartis, 1998; recipient Award for Disting. Rsch. in Infectious Diseases, Bristol-Myers Squibb, 1991, John Enders Award, Infectious Diseases Soc. Am., 1994, Robert Koch Gold medal for lifetime rsch. in infectious diseases, Robert Koch Found., Bonn, Germany, 1999. Fellow Am. Acad. Arts and Scis.; mem. NAS, Inst. Medicine, Am. Assn. Immunologists (pres., 1984) Office: Sch Pub Health Harvard U Kresge Bldg Rm 1005 677 Huntington Ave Boston MA 02115

BLOOM, CLAIRE, actress; b. London, Feb. 15, 1931; d. Edward Max and Elizabeth (Grew) B.; m. Rod Steiger, Sept. 19, 1959 (div. Jan. 1969); 1 child, Anna Justine; m. Philip Roth, Apr. 29, 1990 (div. Mar. 1995). Student, Badminton Sch., Bristol, Eng., Fern Hill Manor, New Milton, Eng., Guildhall Sch. Music and Drama, London. Disting. vis. prof. Hunter Coll., N.Y.C., 1989-90. Appeared as Ophelia, Stratford-Upon-Avon, 1948; plays include Ring Around the Moon, London, 1949-51, Romeo and Juliet, also as Juliet in Old Vic tour of U.S., Six Lessons in Six Weeks, 2006; film roles in Limelight, Richard III, 1956, Alexander the Great, 1956, The Brothers Karamazov, 1958, Look Back in Anger, 1958, The Brothers Grimm, 1962, The Chapman Report, 1962, The Haunting, 1963, 80,000 Suspects, 1963, Alta Infidelita, 1963, Il Maestro di Vigeevano, 1963, The Outrage, 1964, The Spy Who Came in from the Cold, 1965, The Illustrated Man, 1969, Three into Two Won't Go, 1969, A Severed Head, 1971, A Doll's House, 1973, Islands in the Stream, 1976, Clash of the Titans, 1981, Always, 1984, Sammy and Rosie, 1987, Crimes and Misdemeanors, 1989, Daylight, 1995, The Book Eve, 2002, Imagining Argentina, 2002, Daniel and the Superdogs, 2003; Broadway prodns. include Rashomon, 1959; other theatre appearances include Duel of Angels, London, 1958, Altona, Royal Court Theatre, London, 1960, Ivanov, London, 1964, A Doll's House, Hedda Gabler, 1971, Vivat! Vivat Regina!, 1972; N.Y. appearance The Innocents, 1976; London appearances A Doll's House, 1973, A Streetcar Named Desire, 1974, Rosmersholm, 1977, The Cherry Orchard, 1981, These are Women, 1982-83, When We Dead Awaken, 1990, Daughters, Wives and Mothers, 1991, Silenced Voices, 1992, Women in Love, 1993, The Cherry Orchard, 1994, Long Days Journey into Night, 1996, Electra, 1998, Conversations After a Burial, 2000, A Little Night Music, 2001, A Little Night Music NYCO, 2003, Whistling Psyche, 2004, Six Dance Lessons in Six Weeks, 2006-; many roles Brit. and U.S. TV including In Praise of Love, 1975, A Legacy, 1975, Henry VIII, 1979, Hamlet, 1979, The Ghost Writer, 1983, Cymbeline, 1983, King John, 1983, Brideshead Revisited, 1981, Shadowlands, 1984, Time and the Conways, 1985, miniseries Queenie, 1987, Anastasia, 1987, Shadow in the Sun, 1988, The Camomile Lawn, 1991, The Mirror Crack'd, 1992, Remember, 1993, Village Affairs, 1994, Family Money, 1996, When the Dead Man Heard, 1997, The Lady in Question, 1999, Law and Order, 2003, Ten Commandments, 2005, Trial and Retribution, 2005, Miss Marple, 2005, Doc Martin, 2005, Lady Chatterley, 2006; author: Limelight and After, 1982, Leaving A Doll's House, 1996. Recipient Evening Standard award, London, 1974, Brit. Film and TV award, London, 1984; nominee Tony award, 1998, 99, Ibsen award, Oslo, 2006. Office: Marion Rosenberg Agy 1345 N Hayworth Ave Ste 104 Los Angeles CA 90046 Home: 14 Rosaville Rd London SW6 7BL England

BLOOM, DAVID ANDREW, communications operations director; s. Joel Barnet and Mavis June Bloom. BSCS, Strayer U., 1993—95. Dir. of telecom. Internat. Data Products Corp., Gaithersburg, Md., 1995—99; v.p. and chief tech. officer F-Square Comm., Damascus, Md., 1999—2000; v.p. telecom. Facilities PLUS, Inc., Gaithersburg, Md., 2000—04; dir. of ops., telephony MTM Techs., Inc., Wilmington, Del., 2004—. Dir. Harp and Shamrock Soc., Gaithersburg, Md., 1999—2005. Mem.: Internat. Alliance of Avaya Users (assoc.), Building Industry Cons. Svc. Internat. (assoc.). Non-Partisan. Avocation: ballroom dancing. Office: MTM Techs Inc 590 Century Blvd Wilmington DE 19808 Home Phone: 240-344-3524.

BLOOM, DAVID I., lawyer; b. Washington, Mar. 27, 1954; AB magna cum laude, Brown U., 1975; JD, Yale U., 1978. Bar: D.C. 1978, U.S. Dist. Ct. (D.C. dist.) 1978, U.S. Ct. Appeals (D.C. cir.) 1979, U.S. Ct. Appeals (5th cir.) 1983, U.S. Ct. Appeals (7th cir.) 1984. With Mayer, Brown, Rowe & Maw LLP (formerly Mayer, Brown & Platt), Washington, 1978—; ptnr. Mayer, Brown, Rowe & Maw LLP, Washington, 1985—. And chmn., tech. com. Asst. and articles editor: Energy Law Jour., 1984-99. Mem. ABA, Am. Gas Assn. (mem. legal sect. mng. com. 1990-92), Fed. Energy Bar Assn., D.C. Bar. Office: Mayer Brown Rowe & Maw LLP 1909 K St NW Washington DC 20006-1101

BLOOM, FLOYD ELLIOTT, internist, neuroscientist; b. Mpls., Oct. 8, 1936; s. Jack Aaron and Frieda (Shochman) B.; m. D'Nell Bingham, Aug. 30, 1956 (dec. May 1973); children: Fl'Nell, Evan Russell; m. Jody Patricia Corey, Aug. 9, 1980. AB cum laude, So. Meth. U., Dallas, 1956; MD cum laude, Washington U., St. Louis, 1960; DSc (hon.), So. Meth. U., 1983, Hahnemann U., 1985, U. Rochester, 1985, Mt. Sinai U. Med. Sch., 1996, Thomas Jefferson U., 1997, Washington U., 1998, The Scripps Rsch. Inst., 2005. Intern Barnes Hosp., St. Louis, 1960—61, resident internal medicine, 1961—62; rsch. assoc. NIMH, Washington, 1962—64; fellow depts. pharmacology, psychiatry and anatomy Yale Sch. Medicine, 1964—66, asst. prof., 1966—67, assoc. prof., 1968; chief lab. neuropharmacology NIMH, Washington, 1968—75, acting dir. divsn. spl. mental health, 1973—75; commd. officer USPHS, 1974—75; dir. Arthur Vining Davis Ctr. for Behavorial Neurobiology; prof. Salk Inst., La Jolla, Calif., 1975—83; dir. divsn. preclin. neurosci. and endocrinology Scripps Rsch. Inst., La Jolla, 1983—89, chmn. dept. neuropharmacology, 1989—2005, prof. emeritus, 2005—; editor in chief Sci. Mag., 1995—2000; founding CEO Neurome, Inc., LaJolla, Calif., 2000—06, chmn. bd., 2000—06, chief scientific officer, 2000—06. Mem. Pres. Commn. on Alcoholism, 1980—81, Nat. Adv. Mental Health Coun., 1976—80; chmn. sci. adv. bd. Pharmavene, Inc., 1994—98, Advancis Corp., 2000—07, Middlebrook Pharms., 2007—; mem. Rsch. Adv. Com. Gulf War Vets. Illnesses, 2005—, President's Coun. Bioethics, 2006—; bd. dirs. Alkermes, Inc., Elan Pharmaceuticals. Author: (with others) Biochemical Basis of Neuropharmacology, 1971, 8th edit., 2002, (with Lazerson and Hofstadter) Brain, Mind and Behavior, 1984, (with Lazerson) 2d edit., 1988, (with C.A. Nelson) 3d edit., 2000, (with W. Young and Y. Kim) Brain browser, 1989; editor: Peptides: Integrators of Cell and Tissue Function, 1980, Progress in Brain Research, vol. 199, 1994, vol. 100, 1997, (with D.J. Kupfer) Neuro-Psychopharmacology: The Fourth Generation of Progress, 1994, Handbook of Chemical Neruoanatomy, 1997, The Primate Nervous System, 1997, vol. II, 1998, vol. III, 1999, (with Beal and Kupfer) The Dana Guide to Brain Health, 2003; co-editor: Regulatory Peptides, 1979-90, (with M. Randolph) Funding Health Sciences Research, 1990, The Best of the Brain from Scientific American, 2007; assoc. editor: Biological Psychiatry, 1993-95; editor-in-chief Science, 1995-2000, Brain Rsch., 2000-. Trustee Washington U., St. Louis, 1998—, chmn. nat. med. coun., 2000—. Recipient A. Cressy Morrison award NY Acad. Scis., 1971, A.E. Bennett award for basic rsch. Soc. Biol. Psychiatry, 1971, Arthur A. Fleming award Science mag., 1973, Mathilde Solowey award, 1973, Biol. Sci. award Washington Acad. Scis., 1975, Alumni Achievement citation Washington U., 1980, McAlpin Rsch. Achievement award Mental Health Assn., 1980, Lectr.'s medal College de France, 1979, Steven Beering medal, 1985, Janssen award World Psychiat. Assn., 1989, Passerow Found. award, 1990, Herman von Helmholtz award, 1991, Pythagora award, 1994, Presdl. award Soc. for Neurosci., 1995, Golgi prize U. Brescia, 1996, Meritorious Achievement award Coun. Biology Editors, 1999, Gold medal Soc. Biol. Psychiatry, 1997, Disting. Svc. award Am. Psychiat. Assn., 2000, Thomas William Salmon medal, NY Acad. Medicine for Psychiatry and Mental Hygiene, 2004, Dedmar Coll. Disting. Grad. award, So. Meth. U., 2005, Rhoda and Bernard Sarnat Internat. prize in Mental Health, Inst. of Medicine of the Nat. Academies, 2005; Disting. Fellow Am. Psychiat. Assn., 1986; named Sci. of Yr. Achievement Rewards for Coll. Scientists, 1996. Fellow AAAS (bd. dirs. 1986-90, pres.-elect 2001, pres. 2002, chmn. bd. dirs. 2003), Am. Coll. Neuropsychopharmacology (coun. 1976-78, chmn. program com. 1987, pres. 1988-89, Hoch award 1998); mem. NAS (chmn. sect. neurobiology 1979-83, co-chair reports rev. com. 2004—, chair com. publs. 2007—), Inst. Medicine (coun. 1986-89, 93-95, Walsh McDermott medal 2004, Rhoda and Bernard Garnet award in Mental Health 2005), Am. Philos. Soc. (chmn. Lashley award com. 2001—), Am. Acad. Arts and Scis., Soc. Neurosci. (sec. 1973-74, pres. 1976, chmn. publs. com. 1999-2002), Am. Soc. Pharmacology and Exptl. Therapeutics, Am. Soc. Cell Biology, Am. Physiol. Soc., Am. Assn. Anatomists, Am. Neurol. Assn., Rsch. Soc. Alcoholism (chmn. program com. 1985-87, pres.-elect 1989-91, pres. 1991-93), Swedish Acad. Sci. (fgn. assoc. 1989). Home: 628 Pacific View Dr San Diego CA 92109-1768 Business E-Mail: fbloom@scripps.edu. E-mail: fbloom@bloomsciassocs.net.

BLOOM, GARY L., data processing executive; b. Sept. 1960; m. Judy Bloom. BS in Computer Sci., Calif. Poly. State U., San Luis Obispo. Various tech. positions IBM Corp., Chevron Corp.; various positions Oracle Corp., Redwood Shores, Calif., 1986—2000, v.p. mainframe and integration tech. divsn., 1992—96, v.p. massively parallel computing divsn., 1992—96, sr. v.p. product and platform techs. divsn., 1996—97, sr. v.p. woldwide alliances and techs. divsn., 1997, sr. v.p. sys. products divsn., 1997—98, exec. v.p. systems product, 1998—99, exec. v.p., 1999—2000; mem. bd. dir., pres., CEO Veritas Software Corp., Mountain View, Calif., 2000—, chmn. bd. dis., 2002—, also mem. exec. mgmt. com., mgmt. com., product devel. mgmt. com.; pres., vice chmn. Symantec (merged with Veritas), 2005—06. Serves on President's Cabinet Calif. Polytechnic State U., San Luis Obispo. Office Phone: 650-527-8000.

BLOOM, HAROLD, humanities educator, writer; b. NYC, July 11, 1930; s. William and Paula (Lev) B.; m. Jeanne Gould, May 8, 1958; children: Daniel Jacob, David Frank. BA, Cornell U., 1951; PhD, Yale U., 1955; LHD, Boston Coll., 1973, Yeshiva U., 1976, U. Bologna, 1997, St. Michael's Coll., 1998, U. Rome, 1999, U. Coimbra, 2001, U. Mass at Dartmouth, 2002. Mem. faculty Yale U., 1955—, prof. English, 1965-77, DeVane prof. humanities, 1974-77, prof. humanities, 1977—, Sterling prof. humanities, 1983—. Vis. prof. Hebrew U., Jerusalem, 1959, Breadloaf Summer Sch., 1965-66, Soc. for Humanities, Cornell U., 1968-69; vis. Univ. prof. New Sch. Social Rsch., NYC, 1982-84; Charles Eliot Norton prof. of poetry Harvard U., 1987-88; Berg prof. Eng., NYU, 1988—2004. Author: Shelley's Mythmaking, 1959, The Visionary Company, 1961, Blake's Apocalypse, 1963, Commentary on Blake, 1965, Yeats, 1970, The Ringers in the Tower, 1971, The Anxiety of Influence, 1973, Wallace Stevens: The Poems of Our Climate, 1977, A Map of Misreading, 1975, Kabbalah and Criticism, 1975, Poetry and Repression, 1976, Figures of Capable Imagination, 1976, The Flight to Lucifer: A Gnostic Fantasy, 1979, Agon: Towards a Theory of Revisionism, 1981, The Breaking of the Vessels, 1981, The Strong Light of the Canonical, 1987, Freud: Transference and Authority, 1988, Poetics of Influence: New and Selected Criticism, 1988, Ruin the Sacred Truths, 1988, The Book of J, 1990, The Am. Religion, 1992, The Western Canon, 1994, Omens of Millennium, 1996, Shakespeare: The Invention of the Human, 1998, How to Read and Why, 1999, Stories and Poems for Extremely Intelligent Children of all Ages, 2000, Genius, 2002, Hamlet: Poem Unlimited, 2003, Best Poems of the English Language: Chaucer to Hart Crane, 2004, Where Shall Wisdom Be Found?, 2004, The Names Divine: Jesus and Yahweh, 2005, Fallen Angels, 2007; editor Chelsea House Modern Critical Views and Interpretations, 1984—. Recipient John Addison Porter prize Yale U., 1955; Newton Arvin award, 1967; Melville Cane award Poetry Soc. Am., 1970; Zabel prize Am. Inst. Arts and Letters, 1982, Christian Gauss prize Phi Beta Kappa, 1989, Internat. prize Catalonia, 2002; Reyes Internat. Prize, Mexico, 2003, Hans Christian Andersen prize of Denmark, 2005; Guggenheim fellow, 1962; Fulbright fellow, 1955; MacArthur prize fellow, 1985. Mem. Am. Acad. Arts and Letters (Gold medal 1999), Am. Philos. Soc. Home: 179 Linden St New Haven CT 06511-2407 Office Phone: 203-432-0029. Business E-Mail: haroldbloom@yale.edu. *Most instances of religion are mere manifestations of religiosity, which is endemic in our nation, where nine of ten say that God loves them. Spinoza observed that we should love God without expecting that God would love us in return.*

BLOOM, HYMAN (CHAIM MELAMED), artist; b. Brunoviski, Latvia, Mar. 29, 1913; came to U.S., 1920; parents Joseph Melamed and Anna Soloman; m. Nina Bohlen, 1954 (div. 1961); m. Stella Caralis, 1978. Student, West End Community Center, Boston; studied under, Harold K. Zimmerman, Danman Waldo Ross. Instr. Wellesley (Mass.) Coll., 1949-51, Harvard U., Cambridge, Mass., 1951-53. One-man shows, Stuart Gallery, Boston, 1945, Inst. Contemporary Art, Boston, Whitney Mus. Art, N.Y.C., 1945, 54, 68, Albright Knox Art Gallery, Buffalo, 1954, Wadsworth Atheneum, 1957, U. Conn. Mus. Art, 1969, Terry Dintenfass Gallery, 1972, 75, retrospective, Paul Mus., U. N.H., 1992, U. N.H. Mus., 1992, Bateo Coll. Mus., 2001, Nat. Acad. Design, 2002, others; exhbns. include Butler Inst. Am. Art, 1972, Esther Robles Gallery, Brentwood Park, 1976, Ind. U. Mus., Bloomington, 1977, Ind. Mus. Art, 1977-78, Inst. Contemporary Art, Boston, 1979, others; represented in permanent collections, Hirshorn Mus., Washington, Mus. Modern Art, N.Y.C., Whitney Mus. Art, Harvard U., Kalamazoo Inst. Arts, Mich., Minn. Mus. Art, St. Paul, Mus. Fine Arts, Boston, Jewish Mus., N.Y.C., Bloom Found., The Pan Orient Arts Mus. Fellow, Ford Found.; Guggenheim fellow. Mem.: Nat. Acad. Design, Am. Acad. Arts and Letters. Office Phone: 603-886-1710.

BLOOM, JAMES EDWARD, commodity trading and financial executive; b. Milw., Aug. 24, 1941; s. Edward Harry and Clarina Louise (Hoppe) B. Cert. in radiology tech., Columbia Hosp., 1963; AA in Edn. with honors, Milw. Area Tech. Coll., 1964; BBA in Sales Mktg. with honors, Concordia U., 1968, BBA in Bus. Mgmt. with honors, 1968; postgrad., Marquette U., 1969-72. Radiologic technologist Columbia Hosp., Milw., 1963-69; asst. adminstr. Bel Air Convalescent Ctr., Inc., Milw., 1969-70; asst. mktg. mgr. Champion Internat. Inc., Milw., 1970-72, human resources mgr., safety and tng. dir., 1972-75; corp. dir. indsl. rels. Weyenburg Shoe Mfg. Co., Milw., 1975; gen. mgr. Aqua Spray, Inc., Milw., 1976; mgmt. cons. Bloom & Assocs., Milw., 1976—; pres. M.F.C., Milw., 1985—; internat. agt. Superior Coffee and Foods divsn. Sara Lee Corp., Milw., 1991—; internat. and U.S. rep. Al-Sabah Internat., Safat, Kuwait, 1992—; internat. and US rep. shipping and trading and contracting svc. W.L.L., Kuwait, Switzerland, US, 1992—; internat. agt. Moti Enterprises Internat., 1992—, Protea Diamond Corp. (site holders: DeBeers Cons. Mines), 1992—. Guest lectr. mgmt. Milw. Area Tech. Coll., 1974-75, Marquette U., Milw., 1975, U. Milw., 1975; advisor bus. devel. State Wis., 1978—; internat. disting. agt. Al-Ewan Med. Establishment, 1993—, Kingdom Saudi Arabia, 1993—, Hovercraft Am., 1993—, Mico Farms, Malaysia, 1993—, Steenberg Homes, 1994—, Lemke Seed Farms, Inc., 1994—, Xiangtan Fgn. Econ. Rels. and Trade Corp., China, 1994—, Greg Orchards and Produce, Inc., 1994—, Miller Brewing Co., 1994—, Holsum Foods, 1994—, Manipal Printers and Pubs. Ltd., India, 1994—; Protea site holder DeBeers Mines Ltd., Alpha Remarketing Corp.; internat. distbn. agt. Polfa Tarchomin, S.A., Poland, B.B.M. Internat. S.A., De C.V., Mex., 1995—, Valezzi, S.A., De C.V., Mex., 1996, DIMSA, Mex., Intercon Internat., Bulk Connection, Inc., 1997; brand mgmt. and mktg. ptnr. Wis. gold Harvest, 1998; mktg. ptnr. Cuming County Cattle Co., Sioux-Preme Packing Co., Intermountain Pork; Harker's Distbn. Inc., 1999, Right Time Foods, Inc., 1999, Great Plains Pork, 1999, Farm Connect, U. Minn., 2001, Roode Packing Co./Roode Feedlots, 2001, North Platte Feeders, 2001; commodity agt. Archer Daniels Midland Co., 1998; mktg. agt. DuQuoin Processing Co., Inc., DuQuoin Specialty Meats, 2000, E.H. Wolf & Sons, Inc., 2001, Parker Products, Inc., 2007—, Am. Pasteurization Co., 2007-, High Pressure Solutions, 2007; ptnr. in R&D mktg. consortium with U. Wis.: Dairy Foods/Reproductive Physiology/Meat Sci., 2003—, with Milw. Pub. Mus./U. Wis.:Confectionary/Dairy Sci., 2003—. Mem. ASTD, Am. Mgmt. Assn., Indsl. Rels. Rsch. Assn., Am. Soc. Human Resource Mgmt., Am. Soc. Safety Engrs., Assn. Corp. Growth, Am. Soc. Radiologic Technologists, Nat. Assn. Purchasing Mgmt., Mfr.'s Agts. Nat. Assn., Wis. Agri-Svc. Assn., Inc. Home: 8060 N Navajo Rd Fox Point WI 53217-2726 Office: 1009 W Glen Oaks Ln Ste 204 Mequon WI 53092-3383 Office Phone: 262-241-2800.

BLOOM, JANE MAGINNIS, emergency physician; b. Ithaca, NY, June 22, 1924; d. Ernest Victor and Miriam Rebecca (Mansfield) M.; m. William Lee Bloom, Mar. 31, 1944; children: David Lee, Jan Christopher, Carolyn Wells, Eric Paul, Joseph William, Robert Carl, Mary Catherine, Thomas Mark, Patrick Martin (dec.), Arthur Emerson. BS, U. Mich., 1968, MD, 1974. Diplomate Am. Bd. Internal Medicine. Rotating intern Wayne County Gen. Hosp., Eloise, Mich., 1974—75; resident in internal medicine St. Mary's Hosp., Rochester, NY, 1975-77; emergency physician Emergency Physicians Med. Group, Ann Arbor, 1986—2003. Fellow: Am. Coll. Emergency Physicians (life); mem.: AMA, Mich. State Med. Soc., Am. Coll. Physicians, Am. Med. Womens Assn., Am. Assn. Women Emergency Physicians, Washtenaw County Med. Soc. Avocations: bird watching, planting trees, classical music, walking. Home and Office: 537 Elm St Ann Arbor MI 48104-2515 Office Phone: 734-761-2435. Personal E-mail: jbmdfacep@aol.com.

BLOOM, JOEL N., science museum director; b. NYC, Aug. 5, 1925; s. Philip M. and Minnie (Shainmark) B.; m. Paula Yakira, Mar. 21, 1948; children: Margo, Ron, Dan. BSChemE, Poly. Inst. Bklyn., 1949; MS in Ops. Rsch., Columbia U., 1954. Research engr. Ministry Def. Israel, Tel Aviv, 1949-52; engr. Inland Machinery Co., NYC, 1953-54; sr. engr. US Army Ordnance, NYC, 1954-55; chief engr. Aywon Wire & Metal Co., NYC, 1955-58; sr. staff engr. to dir. system sci. dept. Research Labs., Franklin Inst., Phila., 1958-69; v.p., dir. Sci. Mus. and Planetarium, 1969-85, pres., dir., 1985—. Mem. adv. council Nat. Mus. Act, 1979-81; mem. adv. com. on sci. edn. NSF, 1978-81; mem. Pa. Gov.'s Transp. Com., 1968-69, Phila. Mayor's Cultural Adv. Coun., 1984; mem. adv. council Parkway Program, 1968-72; cons., mem. mus. adv. panel Nat. Endowment for Arts, 1973-79; cons. Exec. Office of Pres., 1965-68, NEH, 1977; mem. hwy. research bd. Nat. Acad. Sci., NRC, 1965-69; mem. joint com. on museums Indo-US Subcommn. on Edn. and Culture, 1975-79; mem. US Nat. Commn. for UNESCO, 1981; co-chmn. Commn. on Mus. for a New Century, 1981-84 Bd. dirs. Lower Delaware County United Jewish Appeal; mem. govt.-univ.-industry roundtable working group on talent Nat. Acad. Sci., 1984; pres. Greater Phila. Cultural Alliance, 1983; mem. edn. adv. com. US Nat. Holocaust Meml. Commn., 1985. Served with AUS, 1943-46, ETO. Recipient Distinguished Svc. Awd., Am. Assn. Museums, 1993. Mem. Assn. Sci. and Tech. Centers (pres., dir.), Assn. Sci. Mus. Dirs. (pres., council mem.), N.E. Conf. Mus. (bd. govs.), Internat. Com. Sci. and Tech. Mus., Internat. Council Mus. (US com., dir., v.p., nat. com. sci. and technol. museums), Am. Assn. Museums (accreditation commn. 1975-79, legis. com. 1979, v.p. 1982-84; named to Centennial Honor Roll, 2006), Franklin Inst., Sigma Xi. Jewish (dir. synagogue). Home: 2401 Pennsylvania Ave Apt 17c51 Philadelphia PA 19130-7709 Office: Franklin Inst Sci Mus 20th St B Franklin Pky Philadelphia PA 19103*

BLOOM, JOEL S., academic administrator; BA, CUNY; MA, PhD, Columbia U. Tchr., sch. adminstr. NYC Pub. Schs.; dir. rsch., instr. Columbia U. Tchrs. Coll., NY; mgr. N.E. Ednl. Improvement Ctr. US Dept. Edn.; asst. commr. divsn. gen. acad. edn. NJ Dept. Edn., 1984—90; v.p. acad. affairs NJ Inst. Tech., Newark, 1990—, dean Albert Doman Honors Coll., 1997—. Chair NJ Coll. Bound Adv. Bd., Greater Newark Consortium Bd. for Pre-Coll. Edn.; mem. NJ Bd. for Cmtys. and Schs., NJ Pres. Coun. Task Force on Transfer and Mission Differentiation; bd. mem. Phila. Alliance for Minority Participation, NJ Assn. Ptnrs. in Edn. Office: Office of the VP NJ Inst Tech Newark NJ 07102*

BLOOM, JOSEPH D., psychiatrist, medical educator; MD, Albert Einstein Coll. Medicine. Diplomate in psychiatry and in forensic psychiatry Am. Bd. Psychiatry and Neurology. Intern Mt. Zion Hosp. and Med. Ctr., San Francisco; resident in psychiatry Harvard U.; chief psychiat. resident Southard Clinic Mass. Mental Health Ctr.; chief mental health unit Alaska Native Health Svc. USPHS; pvt. practice Anchorage; dir. cmty. psychiatry tng. program Oreg. Health Sci. U., Portland, 1977, chmn. dept. psychiatry, 1986-94, interim dean Sch. Medicine, 1993-94, dean Sch. Medicine, 1994-2001. Office: Oreg Health Sci U Sch Medicine 3181 SW Sam Jackson Park Rd Portland OR 97201-3011 Home Phone: 503-978-5156; Office Phone: 503-494-6689. E-mail: bloomj@ohsu.edu.

BLOOM, KATHRYN RUTH, public relations executive; d. Morris and Frances Sondra (Siegel) B. BA, Douglass Coll.; MA, U. Toronto, Can. Dir. spl. projects United Jewish Appeal, NYC, 1973-78; mgr. pub. affairs Bristol-Myers-Squibb Co., NYC, 1978-86; mgr. pub. rels. pharm. and nutritional Bristol-Myers Squibb Co., 1986-90, dir. pharm. and rsch. comms., 1990-91; dir. comms. Biogen Idec, Inc., 1992—2001, sr. dir. pub. affairs Cambridge, Mass., 2001—05; dir. Biogen Idec Found., 2005—. Bd. overseers Beth Israel Deaconess Med. Ctr., 2000—, Hebrew Coll., 2004—. Mem.: Am. Friends of the Magen David Adom (bd. dirs.), Boston Club, Phi Beta Kappa. Office: Biogen Idec 14 Cambridge Ctr Cambridge MA 02142-1481

BLOOM, LAWRENCE STEPHEN, retired clothing company executive; b. New Rochelle, NY, Apr. 30, 1930; s. Hyman and Eleanor (Bursch) B.; m. Mary Ann Hendricks, Aug. 15, 1959; children: Mark, Julie. BS in Commerce and Fin, Bucknell U., Lewisburg, Pa., 1952. Trainee Gimbels, NYC, to 1954; with Warnaco Inc., 1954-90; former chmn. Warnaco Men's Knitwear (Puritan, Thane and Hathaway Knitwear), Altoona, Pa. Bd. dirs. Woolknit Assocs., Nat. Sportwear and Outerwear Assocs.; chpt. chair Svc. Corps Ret. Execs. Mem. Logan Twp. (Pa.) Planning Commn. Served with AUS, 1952-54. Home: 340 Deer Run Rd Hollidaysburg PA 16648-3110 E-mail: blooml@msn.com.

BLOOM, LEE HURLEY, lawyer, consultant, retired consumer products company executive; b. NYC, June 21, 1919; s. Harry and Harriet (Bresel) B.; m. Mary Louise Tolan, Dec. 15, 1945; children: Daniel, Louise, Douglas. BS, MIT, 1940; LL.B., Harvard U., 1943. Bar: Mass. 1947, N.Y. 1951. Atty. legal div. Lever Bros. Co., NYC, 1947-67, v.p., sec., gen. counsel, 1968-70, adminstrv. v.p., dir., 1970-82; pres. Unilever U.S., Inc., 1978-82, vice chmn., 1982-83. Donald L. Wilson prof., Grinnell Coll., Iowa, 1986. Chmn. bd. Larchmont (N.Y.) chpt. ARC, 1961—63; mem. Mamaroneck Planning Bd., 1959—69, Mamaroneck Town Bd., 1969—85, dep. supr., 1982—83; coord. N.Y. State Sch. and Bus. Alliance for Yonkers Pub. Schs., 1987—93; chmn. Ctr. for Performing Arts Lehman Coll., 1987—93, Sheldrake Environ. Ctr., 1995—2003; mem. Town of Mamaroneck (N.Y.) Rep. Com., 1957—69. Served to lt. comdr. USNR, 1941—46. Mem. Soap and Detergent Assn. (dir. 1971-83, vice chmn. 1978-79, chmn. 1980-82), Assn. Pvt. Enterprise Edn. (exec. com. 1985-93), Internat. C. of C. (trustee U.S. coun. 1978-86, exec. com. 1980-86, vice chmn. 1982-85, sr. trustee 1987—), UN Assn. U.S.A. (pres. so. N.Y. state divsn. 1989-93). Home and Office: 22 Myrtle Blvd Larchmont NY 10538-1823 E-mail: leehbloom@aol.com.

BLOOM, LISA READ, lawyer; b. Phila., Sept. 20, 1961; d. Peyton Huddleston Bray and Gloria Allred; children: Sarah Wong Bloom, Samuel Bloom Wong. BA, UCLA, 1983; JD, Yale U., 1986. Bar: N.Y., 1987, Calif., 1992; U.S. Dist. Ct. (so. and ea. dists.) N.Y., 1987, U.S. Dist. Ct. (cen. dist.) Calif. 1992. Assoc. Meister, Leventhal & Slade, NYC, 1986-87, Robinson, Silverman, Pearce, Aronsohn & Berman, NYC, 1987-91, Allred, Maroko & Goldberg, LA, 1992—2001; co-host Closing Arguments Court TV,

2001—03, co-anchor Trial Heat, 2003—. Spkr. in field. Numerous TV and radio appearances. Recipient Cert. of Merit, Courage to Tell Found., Calif., 1993. Office: Court TV Network LLC 600 Third Ave New York NY 10016

BLOOM, MARK DAVID, lawyer; b. Phila., Sept. 25, 1953; s. Sheperd and Muriel Esther (Wallner) B.; m. Annette Rodriguez, July 17, 1982; children: Sara Michelle, Stefan Jacob. BA in Polit. Sci., Yale U., 1975; JD, U. Md., 1979. Bar: Md. 1979, D.C. 1980, Fla. 1980, U.S. Dist. Ct. Md. 1980, U.S. Ct. Appeals (4th cir.) 1980, U.S. Dist. Ct. (so. dist.) Fla. 1981, U.S. Ct. Appeals (5th and 11th cirs.) 1981, U.S. Dist. Ct. (mid. dist.) Fla. 1986. Law clk. U.S. Dist. Ct. Md., Balt., 1979-80; assoc. Greenberg, Traurig, Askew, Hoffman, Lipoff, Rosen & Quentel, Miami, Fla., 1980-86; shareholder, nat. co-chair reorganization, bankruptcy, restructuring dept. Greenberg, Traurig LLP (formerly Greenberg Traurig Hoffman, Lipoff, Rosen & Quentel, P.A.), Miami, 1986—. Lectr., author on bankruptcy and reorgn. for ALI-ABA, Norton Bankruptcy Law Inst., Exec. Enterprises, Fla. Bar Assn. Mem. Bankruptcy Bar Assn. (bd. dirs. So. Dist. Fla. 1986-87, officer 1987-90). Democrat. Jewish. Avocations: swimming, travel, wine. Office: Greenberg Traurig LLP 1221 Brickell Ave Miami FL 33131-3224 Office Phone: 305-579-0537. Office Fax: 305-579-0717. Business E-Mail: bloomm@gtlaw.com.

BLOOM, ORLANDO, actor; b. Canterbury, England, Jan. 13, 1977; s. Harry Bloom and Sonia Copeland-Bloom. Attended, Nat. Youth Theatre London, British Am. Drama Acad.; grad., Guildhall Sch. Music and Drama, 1996—99. Actor: (films) Wilde, 1997, The Lord of the Rings: The Fellowship of the Rings, 2001 (Empire award for best debut, 2001, Best Breakthrough Star award MTV Movie Awards, 2002), Black Hawk Down, 2001, The Lord of the Rings: The Two Towers, 2002, Ned Kelly, 2003, Pirates of the Caribbean: The Curse of the Black Pearl, 2003, The Lord of the Rings: The Return of the King, 2003, Troy, 2004, Kingdom of Heaven, 2005, Elizabethtown, 2005, Love and Other Disasters, 2006, Pirates of the Caribbean: Dead Man's Chest, 2006, Pirates of the Caribbean: At World's End, 2007; actor, co-prodr. (films) Haven, 2004; actor: (TV series) Midsomer Murders; (plays) Casualty, London's Burning, Twelfth Night, Uncle Vanya, Little Me, Peer Gynt. Recipient Choice Hottie-Male, Teen Choice Awards, 2006. Mailing: c/o ICM Oxford House 76 Oxford St London W1D 1BS England*

BLOOM, SHERMAN, retired pathology educator, photographer; b. Bklyn., Jan. 26, 1934; s. Philip and Sadie (Kaplan) B.; m. Miriam Fishman, Feb. 11, 1960; children: Naomi, Stephanie. BA, NYU, 1955, MD, 1960. Diplomate Am. Bd. Anat. Pathology. Intern in medicine Kings County Hosp., Bklyn., 1960-61; fellow in exptl. pathology, resident in anatomic and clin. pathology NYU Med. Ctr. and Bellevue Hosp., NYC, 1961-65; instr. pathology NYU Sch. Medicine, 1965-66; asst. prof. U. Utah Coll. Medicine, Salt Lake City, 1966-70, assoc. prof., 1970-72, U. South Fla. Coll. Medicine, Tampa, 1973-76, prof. pathology, 1976-77, George Washington U. Coll. Medicine, Washington, 1977-88; prof., chmn. dept. pathology U. Miss. Med. Ctr., Jackson, 1988-2000, prof. emeritus, 2000—, ret., 1999; pres. PhotoTov Fine Arts, 2004. Cons. Sci. Rev., NIH; mem. cardiovascular study sect. NSF, FDA; dir. coun. on cardiovascular and geriatric health Amer Coll. Nutrition, 1998-01; bd. dirs. Scientists Ctr. Animal Welfare, pres. elect, 1987, pres., 1988. Mem. editl. bd. Jour. Am. Coll. Nutrition, 1982, Am. Jour. Cardiovascular Pathology, 1985; assoc. editor Cardiovascular Pathology, 1990; fine art photo pub. Jour. Miss. State Med. Assn.; contbr. numerous articles to profl. publs. Del. Utah State Dem. Party, 1968. NIH fellow, 1962; Dilthey Found. fellow, 1982. Fellow Am. Coll. Nutrition; mem. Internat. Acad. Pathologists, Am. Physiol. Soc., Am. Assn. Pathologists, Internat. Soc. Heart Research, Soc. Cardiovascular Pathology (pres. 1986-87), Photograph Soc. Am.(pres.). Jewish. Home: 4433 Wedgewood St Jackson MS 39211-6219 Office Phone: 601-982-1800. Personal E-mail: shermanbloom@mac.com.

BLOOM, TERRY RAYMOND, chemical engineer; b. Dayton, Ohio, Apr. 11, 1950; s. Chester Raymond and Velma Ilene Bloom; m. Geraldine Marie Miller; children: Heather Marie Kaiser, Travis Raymond, Trevor Ryan, Tyler Russell. BS in Chem. Engring., TriState U., Angola, Ind., 1972. With R&D CTS Corp., Elkhart, Ind., 1972—92, mgr. materials and processing tech., 1992—2004, mem. tech. staff, 2004—. Founder Little River Steam RR, Coldwater, Mich., 1974—2007. With USNG, 1972—78. Mem.: Internat. Microelectronics and Packaging Soc. (John A. Wagnon, Jr. Tech. Achievement award 1995). Republican. Achievements include patents for 24 patents in materials, processes, and equipment for thick film electronics. Avocations: ride trains, water sports, mountains, snowmobiling. Office: CTS Corp 1142 W Beardsley Ave Elkhart IN 46514 Home Phone: 574-825-9182; Office Phone: 574-389-2736.

BLOOM, WILLIAM MILLARD, furnace design engineer; b. New Kensington, Pa., Aug. 10, 1925; s. William Lewis and Nellie Tillbrook (McMillan) B.; m. Judith Ann Callen, May 23, 1953; children: Kimberly Ann, Stacey Ellen. BA, Geneva Coll., 1951; BSME, Carnegie Inst. Tech., 1951. Registered profl. engr., Pa. Fuel engr. maintenance dept. Brackenridge (Pa.) Plant, Allegheny Ludlum Steel, 1951-56; fuel engr. gen. engring. divsn. Allegheny Ludlum Steel Corp., Brackenridge, 1956-59, sr. engr. furnaces and fuels, gen. engring. divsn., 1959-61; chief engr. furnaces and fuels gen. engring. divsn. Allegheny Ludlum Industries, Pitts., 1961-71; asst. to v.p. engring. spl. assignments Allegheny Ludlum Steel Corp., Brackenridge, 1971-81, mgr. furnace design engring., mfg. engring. Pitts., 1981-92; pvt. practice cons. indsl. furnaces Pitts., 1992—. Cons. Alloy Rods Corp., Hanover, Pa., 1989, Timet Corp., Henderson, Nev., Toronto, Ohio, IPM Corp., Ridgeway, Pa., Columbus, Ohio, Tube Turn Corp., Louisville, True Temper, Geneva, Ohio, Arnold Engring., Chgo., Altech, Dunkirk, N.Y., Posco, Korea, Kuhlman Electric, Lexington, Ky., 1961-92. With US Army, 1944—46, ETO. Mem. NSPE, Assn. Iron and Steel Engrs. (life, bd. dirs., chmn. combustion com., AISE-KELLY award 1st pl. 1979), 70th Divsn. Assn. (life), Theta Xi (life). Republican. Methodist. Achievements include patents for Bar Furnace Seals, Annealing Apparatus, Coil Quench, Conveyor Roll, Tunnel Furnace, Annealing Furnace, Steel Scrap Preheater, Apparatus Scrap Preheater, Roll Turner/Remover, Jet Heat Reucperator, Replaceable Ladle Heater Seals, High Temp Fan Plug, Hot Strip Mill Cover Heat Retention; developed high temperature hydrogen anneal tunnel furnace for grain oriented silicon steels that significantly lowered watt losses/pound to develop class of steel, jet heat recuperators that reduce continous anneal furnaces fuel input by 50% and increases production 50%. Home: 1522 King John Dr Pittsburgh PA 15237-1590

BLOOMBERG, COE ARTHUR, lawyer; b. Laurel, Md., Oct. 6, 1943; s. Arthur Eugene and Elaine (Howell) B.; m. Kathleen Marshall; children: Christopher Arthur, Laura Anne. BME, Ga. Inst. Tech., 1966; JD, Loyola Marymount U., Los Angeles, 1972. Bar: Calif. 1972, NY 1974, registered: US Patent and Trademark Office. Patent counsel Mobil Oil, NYC, 1972-74; ptnr. Lyon & Lyon, LA, 1974, Jones Day, LA. Mem. ABA, N.Y. Patent Law Assn., Los Angeles Patent Law Assn., Ga. Inst. Tech. Alumni Assn. So. Calif. (pres. 1984-86). Office: Jones Day 50th Floor 555 S Flower St Los Angeles CA 90071 Office Phone: 213-489-3939. Office Fax: 213-489-2539. E-mail: cabloomberg@jonesday.com.

BLOOMBERG, MIKE (MICHAEL RUBENS), mayor; b. Medford, Mass., Feb. 14, 1942; s. William and Charlotte Bloomberg; m. Susan Brown, 1975 (div. 1993); children: Emma, Georgina. BEE, Johns Hopkins U., 1964; MBA, Harvard U., 1966. Processing clerk Salomon Brothers, 1966—72, gen. ptnr. NYC, 1972—81; pres. founder Bloomberg L.P., NYC, 1981—, pres., CEO; pub. Bloomberg Business News, NYC; gen. mgr. Bloomberg Television, Bloomberg Radio, Sta. WBBR-AM 1130, NYC; pub. Bloomberg Mag./Bloomberg Personal Mag., Princeton, NJ, Bloomberg Personal, Skillman, NJ; mayor NYC, 2002—. Chmn. World Trade Ctr. Meml. Found., 2006—. Co-author (with Matthew Winkler): Bloomberg by Bloomberg, 1997. Chmn. bd. trustees Johns Hopkins U., 1996-2002; trustee Big Apple Circus, Ctrl. Park Conservancy, Met. Mus. Art, H.S. Econs. And Fin., Inst. Advanced Study, Lincoln Ctr. Performing Arts, Jewish Mus., N.Y. Police and Fire Widows' and Childrens' Fund, Spence Sch., Prep for Prep, S.L.E. Found., U.S. Ski Team Ednl. Found., Serpentine Gallery, London. Named New Yorker of the Yr., Daily News, 2006; named one of Forbes Richest Americans, 1999—, World's Richest People, Forbes Mag., 2001—, 50 Most Generous Philanthropists, Fortune Mag., 2005, The World's Most Influential People, TIME mag., 2007; recipient Golden Plate award, Acad. Achievement, 2004. Fellow Am. Acad. Arts & Scis.; mem. U.S. C. of C. (trustee). Jewish. Office: City Hall 52 Chambers St New York NY 10007-1222*

BLOOMER, HAROLD FRANKLIN, JR., retired lawyer; b. NYC, Nov. 4, 1933; s. Harold Franklin and Ailene (Cress) Bloomer; m. Mary Jane Lloyd, July 16, 1955 (div. June 1976); children: Sara Ailene, Margaret Gail, Leslie Lloyd; m. Freya Donald, Nov. 30, 1985; children: Katharine Roma, Alice Donald. AB, Amherst Coll., 1956; LLB, Columbia U., 1967. Bar: Conn. 1967, N.Y. 1968, U.S. Dist. Ct. Conn. 1968, U.S. Dist. Ct. (so. and ea. dists.) N.Y. 1974, U.S. Ct. Appeals (2d cir.) 1974. Assoc. Debevoise, Plimpton, Lyons & Gates, NYC, 1967-77; counsel Burlington, Underwood & Lord, Jeddah, Saudi Arabia, 1977-78; chief internat. counsel Saudi Rsch. & Devel. Corp., London, 1978-80; counsel Morgan, Lewis & Bockius LLP, London, NYC, 1980-81, ptnr., 1981-2000; ret., 2000. Adj. prof. Pepperdine U. Sch. Law, London, 1985. Trustee San. Products Trust, Riverside, Conn., 1965—74; trip leader Adventure Cycling Assn., Missoula, Mont., 2000; mem. Conn. Com. East Coast Greenway, 2001—; co-chmn. bd. Coastal Corridor Transp. Investment Area, State of Conn., 2001—07; chmn. Greenwich (Conn.) Safe Cycling, 1999—; pres. Calf Island Conservancy, Inc., Greenwich, 2004—05, sec., 2005—; mem. Rep. Town Meeting, Greenwich, Conn., 1964—74, 1992—, chmn. pub. works com., 1971—74, chmn. land use com., 1998—; mem. Rep. Town Com., Greenwich, Conn., 1973—74. Lt. (j.g.) USNR, 1957—60. Kent scholar, Columbia U., 1965—66, Stone scholar, 1966—67. Mem.: Am. Arbitration Assn. (panel arbitrators 1990—), Riverside Yacht Club. Republican. Episcopalian. Avocations: sailing, canoeing, skiing, bicycling, running.

BLOOMER, JOSEPH ROBERT, physician, educator; b. Indpls., Ind., Sept. 29, 1940; s. Betty Glore Bloomer; m. Anne Vaughn Macintyre, June 26, 1965; children: Jennifer Anne Jeans, Jeffrey Neil. BS, MIT, Cambridge, 1962; MD, Western Res. Med. Sch., Cleve., 1966. Diplomate Am. Bd. Internal Medicine. Assoc. prof. medicine Yale U Sch. Medicine, New Haven, 1976—79; prof. medicine U. Minn., Mpls., 1979—95, dir. gastroenterology, 1983—95; prof. medicine and genetics, dir. liver ctr. U. Ala., Birmingham, 1995—. Investigator Howard Hughes Med. Inst., 1974—79; bd. govs. Am Bd. Internal Medicine; lectr. in field. Pres. Am. Assn. for Study of Liver Diseases, 1998—99. Lt. comdr. USPHS, 1968—71. Recipient Merit award, NIH, 1994—2002. Mem.: Am. Clin. Climatol. Assn. (Theodore Woodward award 1999), Assn. Am. Physicians. Office: Univ Ala 1918 University Blvd MCLM 281 Birmingham AL 35294-0005 Office Phone: 205-975-9699.

BLOOMER, KENT CRESS, architecture educator; b. Mt. Vernon, NY, May 31, 1935; s. Harold Franklin Bloomer and Vera Allene Cress; m. Leonor Golay Bloomer, June 13, 1959; children: Mark Clifford, May Bloomer Bartels. MFA, Yale U., New Haven, Conn., 1960. Asst. prof. Carnegie Inst. Tech., Pitts., 1961—66; prof. Yale Sch. Architecture, New Haven, 1966—. Prin. Bloomer Studio, New Haven, 1964—; spkr. in field. Co-author (Charles Moore): Body, Memory, and Architecture, 1977; author: The Nature of Ornament, 2000; one-man shows include Mus. Art, Pitts., 1962, exhibitions include Mus. Modern Art, 1959, Yale Art Gallery, 2001, exhibitions include sculpture and architectural ornament Central Park Lights, NYC, 1982, Treedomes, New Orleans Worlds Fair, 1984, Harold Washington Libr. Ctr., Chgo., 1993, Reagan National Airport, Washington, 1997, Gt. Platte River Rd. Monument, Kearny, Nebr., 2000, Entrance Gate, Class of 1954 Chem. Rsch. Bldg., Yale U., 2005. Exec. com. Yale-New Haven Tchrs. Inst., 1993—2007. Fellow: Whitney Ctr. for Humanities. Home: 988 Leetes Island Rd Guilford CT 06437 Office: Yale Univ Sch Arch 180 York Str New Haven CT 06520 Home Phone: 203-453-4073; Office Phone: 203-432-7039, 203-562-7559. Office Fax: 203-432-7175. Business E-Mail: kent.bloomer@yale.edu. E-mail: kent@bloomerstudio.com.

BLOOMER, WILLIAM DAVID, radiologist, oncologist, educator; b. Aug. 19, 1944; s. Ward LaVern and Vera Catherine (Rochefort) B.; m. Lauren S. Taslitz, Aug. 10, 1986; children: Whitney Dana, Brian Andrew, Gregory Stewart. AB, U. Pa., 1966; MD, Jefferson Med. Coll., Phila., 1970. Diplomate Am. Bd. Radiology, Am. Bd. Nuclear Medicine. Intern Univ. Hosps., Cleve., 1970-71; clin. fellow in radiation therapy Harvard U. Med. Sch., Boston, 1971-74, instr., 1974-76, asst. prof., 1976-80, assoc. prof., 1980-83; rsch. mem. Harvard MIT Divsn. Health Scis. and Tech., Boston, 1978-83; mem. sr. common room Lowell House Harvard Coll., Boston, 1983-87; dir. radiotherapy, radiotherapist-in-chief Mt. Sinai Hosp., NYC, 1983-87; prof., chmn. dept. radiation oncology U. Pitts. Sch. Medicine, 1987-92; dir. Joint Radiation Oncology Ctr., 1987-92; dir. radiation oncology Presbyn. U. Hosp., Magee-Women's Hosp., Shadyside Hosp., 1987-92; assoc. dir. Pitts. Cancer Inst., 1987-92; pres. U. Radiotherapy Assocs., Inc., 1989-92; sr. lectr. engring. in medicine Carnegie Mellon U., 1989-92; chmn. radiation medicine Evanston Northwestern Healthcare, 1992—. Prof. radiology Northwestern U. Med. Sch., 1992—, pres. Radiation Medicine Inst., 1992—; dir. radiation oncology svcs. Condell Med. Ctr., 2004—. Contbr. articles to profl. jours. Mem. AAAS, Am. Coll. Radiology, Am. Soc. Therapeutic Radiologists, Soc. Nuclear Medicine, Am. Assn. Cancer Rsch., Am. Soc. Clin. Oncology, Am. Coll. Radiation Oncology (Gold medal 1998). Office: Evanston Northwestern Healthcare 2650 Ridge Ave Evanston IL 60201-1718

BLOOMFIELD, APRIL, chef; b. Birmingham, England, 1974; Grad., Birmingham Coll. of Food, Tourism and Creative Studies. Chef Kensington Place, London, Bibendum, London, River Cafe, London, Roscoff, Belfast, Ireland, Chez Panisse, Berkeley, Calif.; co-owner, exec. chef The Spotted Pig, NYC, 2004—. Featured in O Mag., 2005. Named one of Best New Chefs, Food and Wine Mag., 2007. Office: The Spotted Pig 314 W 11th St at Greenwich St New York NY 10014 Office Phone: 212-620-0393.*

BLOOMFIELD, CLARA DERBER, oncologist, educator, medical institute administrator; b. Flushing, L.I., NY, May 15, 1942; d. Milton and Zelda (Trenner) Derber; m. Victor A. Bloomfield, June 11, 1962 (div. 1983); m. Albert de la Chapelle, Jan. 1, 1984. Student, U. Wis., 1959-62; BA, San Diego State U., 1963; MD, U. Chgo., 1968. Diplomate Am. Bd. Internal Medicine, Nat. Bd. Med. Examiners. Intern in medicine U. Chgo. Hosps. and Clinics, 1968-69, resident internal medicine, 1969-70, U. Minn., Mpls., 1970-71, med. oncology fellow, 1971-73, chief resident in medicine, Jan.-June, 1972, instr., 1972-73, asst. prof. medicine, 1973-76, assoc. prof., 1976-80, prof. medicine div. oncology, 1980-89, dir. fellowship program med. concology, 1987—89, mem. univ. senate, 1986-89, mem. all univ. Commn. on Women, 1988-89; prof. medicine, chief div. oncology SUNY, Buffalo, 1989—97; head dept. medicine Roswell Pk. Cancer Inst., Buffalo, 1989—97; William G. Pace III prof. cancer research Ohio State U. Coll. Med. & Pub. Health, 1997—, dir., div. hematology & oncology, dept. Internal Medicine, 1997—. Mem. Kettering selection com. GM Cancer Rsch. Found., 1986-87; cons. Office Tech. Assessment, U.S. Congress, 1988; participant, chair various coms. Internat. Human Gene Mapping Workshops, Helsinki, Finland, 1985, France, 1987, Internat. Workshops Chromosomes in Leukemia, Lund, Sweden, 1980, Chgo., 1982, Tokyo, 1984, London, 1987, Buffalo, 1991; mem. nat. and sci. adv. bds. NIH, 1977—, mem. bd. sci. counselors divsn. cancer treatment, 1991—, organizer Internat. Hodgkins Disease Symposium, 1981; bd. dirs. cancer and leukemia group B, 1982—, mem. other coms., 1973— sponsored clin. trial groups, Nat. Cancer Inst., cons. S.W. oncology group; mem. nat. and sci. adv. bd. Don and Sybil Harrington Cancer Ctr., Amarillo, Tex., 1979—, Med. Coll. Pa., 1988—; bd. trustees Berlex Oncology Found., 1992—; vis. prof. dept. medicine W.Va. U., 1973, U. Ariz., Tucson, 1979, U. Fla., Gainesville, 1979, Emory U., Atlanta, 1980, U. Chgo., 1982, George Washington U., Washington, 1982, U. Tex., San Antonio, 1982, Brown U., Providence, 1982, Mayo Clinic, Rochester, Minn., 1982, U. Zurich, Switzerland, 1983, U. P.R., 1984, U. Witwatersand, S. Africa, 1984, Nihon U., Tokyo, 1984, Leukemia Soc. Mass., 1991; frequent invited speaker, guest lectr. symposia, workshops, continuing edn. courses, seminars, med. congresses, univs. in U.S., Europe, S. Am., Scandinavia, Eng., Japan, Republic of South Africa, New Zealand. Author: (with others) Recent Advances in Bone Marrow Transplantation, Vol. VII, 1983, New Prospectives in Human Lymphoma, 1984, Neoplastic Diseases of the Blood, 1985, Current Therapy in Hematology/Oncology 1984-85, 1985, Medical Genetics: Past, Present, Future, 1985, Directions in Oncology, Vol. 1, 1985, Medical Oncology, Basic Principles and Clinical Management of Cancer, 1985, Tumor Aneuploidy, 1985, Malignant Lymphomas and Hodgkins Disease: Experimental and Therapeutic Advances, 1985, Current Therapy in Internal Medicine, 1987, Genetic Maps, Vol. 4, 1987; contbr. over 250 articles, abstracts to profl. jours.; editor ann. Adult Leukemia series in Cancer Treatment and Rsch., 1979-85; cons. editor Leukemia and Lymphoma Yearbook of Cancer, 1980—; assoc. editor Cancer Rsch., 1981-88, editor, 91, Leukemia Rsch., 1984-87, Leukemia, 1987-89; mem. editorial bd. Jour. Clin. Oncology, 1983-88, Cancer Genetics and Cytogenetics, 1983-87, Directions in Oncology, 1984-86, Cancer Rsch. Bull., 1984-85, Med. and Pediatric Oncology, 1987—, Blood, 1988—, Annals of Medicine, 1989—, Seminars in Oncology, 1989—; editorial bd. Am. Jour. Hematology, 1985, assoc. editor, 1988—; reviewer 23 med. jours. Recipient Nat. Bd. award Med. Coll. Pa., 1981, Past State Pres.' Bus. and Profl. Women award U. Tex. System Cancer Ctr., M.D. Anderson Hosp. and Tumor Clinic, Houston, 1987, Joseph H. Burchenal Clinical Rsch. award, Am. Assn. Cancer Rsch., 2004; prin. or co-prin. investigator 8 grants, NIH, 1975—, also ACS, 1980-84, Minn. State Spl. Coleman Leukemia Rsch. Fund, 1981-89, Coleman Leukemia Rsch. Fund Endowment, 1981—, Baltzar W.A. von Platen Found., 1984-85, Genentech/Hoffman -LaRoche, 1988—. Mem. ACP, AAAS, Am. Assn. Cancer Rsch., Am. Soc. Hematology, Am. Soc. Clin. Oncology (bd. dirs. 1991—), Am. Fedn. Clin. Rsch., Cen. Soc. Clin. Rsch., N.Y. Acad. Scis., Inst. Medicine, Internat. Assn. Comparative Rsch. Leukemia and Related Diseases, Med. Soc. Finland (external mem.), Phi Beta Kappa, Alpha Omega Alpha, Sigma Delta Epsilon. Office: Comprehensive Cancer Ctr 320 W 10th Ave Columbus OH 43210

BLOOMFIELD, DAVID CHARLES, lawyer, educator, not-for-profit public executive; b. NYC, Feb. 19, 1952; BA, Brandeis U., Waltham, Mass., 1975; JD, Columbia U., NYC, 1984; MPA, Princeton U., NJ, 1984. Bar: N.Y. 1984, D.C. 1985; cert. primary and elem. tchr., Mass.; cert. prin./supr., N.J.; cert. supt. N.Y. Tchr. New Lincoln Sch., NYC, 1975-79; analyst Advocates for Children of N.Y., Queens, N.Y., 1979-80; law clk. to Judge Robert L. Carter U.S. Dist. Ct. (so. dist. N.Y.), NYC, 1984-85; assoc. Hogan & Hartson, Washington, 1985-86; atty. N.Y.C. Law Dept., 1986-89; adminstr. N.Y.C. Bd. Edn., Bklyn., 1989-90, gen. counsel, 1990-91; gen. counsel, sr. edn. advisor Manhattan Borough Pres., NYC, 1991-94; exec. dir. Partnership for Effective Edn. Mgmt., NYC, 1994-96; adj. asst. prof. Tchrs. Coll. Columbia U., NYC, 1996—98; assoc. prof. Bklyn. Coll., CUNY, 1999—. Head edn. leadership program Bklyn. Coll., 2001; pres. N.Y. Citywide Coun. on High Schs., 2004—. Author: African Ethnicity, 1976, Attendance Improvement Programs in N.Y.C. Schools, 1979, Children First: NYC School Governance Legislation, 1993, Strategic Management of NYC Schools, 1997, 2d edit., 2003, Technology Based Peer Education, 1999, Technology-Based Peer Education, 1999, Church/State Separation, 2001, No Child Left Behind Act, 2003, No Child Left Behind, 2003, High School Reform, 2005, Legal Issues in the Classroom, 2005, American Public Education Law: A Primer, 2007; contbg. author: Praeger Handbook of Special Education; appeared on Colo. Pub. Radio, N.Y. Pub. Radio, N.Y.C. Pub. TV (Ch. 13, WNET), RNN-TV Metro News, N.Y.C. and Hudson Valley, Come Clean on Small Schools, 2006; contbr. chpts. to books and articles to profl. jours. Recipient Paul Robeson prize Columbia U., N.Y.C., 1982, Harlan Fiske Stone scholar, 1982, Princeton (N.J.) U. fellow, 1982, African-Am. Inst. fellow, N.Y.C., 1976; Disting. Educator NY State Edn. Dept., 2006. Office: Bklyn Coll CUNY Rm 2205 James Hall 2900 Bedford Ave Brooklyn NY 11210 Office Phone: 718-951-5608. Personal E-mail: david11201@nyct.net. Business E-Mail: davidb@brooklyn.cuny.edu.

BLOOMFIELD, LINCOLN PALMER, political scientist; b. Boston, July 7, 1920; m. Irirangi Pamela Coates, 1948; children: Pamela, Lincoln Jr., Diana. SB, Harvard U., 1941, MPA, 1952, PhD, 1956. With US Dept. State, Washington, 1946-57, spl. asst. to asst. sec., 1952-57; sr. staff ctr. for internat. studies MIT, Cambridge, 1957—99, prof. polit. sci., 1963-91, prof. emeritus, 1991—; dir. global issues NSC, Washington, 1979-80. Mem. Presdl. Commn. 25th Anniversary UN, 1970—71; vis. prof. Grad. Inst. Advanced Internat. Studies, Geneva, 1965, Geneva, 72, Geneva, 77, Geneva, 79, Salzburg Seminar faculty, 1982, 86, 92, 95; moderator State Dept. seminar fgn. policy and global issues, 1992—99. Host (TV series) Christian Sci. Monitor Fifty Years Ago Today, 1989—92; author: Evolution or Revolution?, 1957, The UN and U.S. Foreign Policy, rev. edit., 1967, In Search of American Foreign Policy, 1974, The Foreign Policy Process: A Modern Primer, 1982, Accidental Encounters With History, 2005, co-author; editor: International Military Forces, 1964, Kruschchev and the Arms Race, 1966, Outer Space: Prospects for Man and Society, rev. edit., 1968, Controlling Small Wars, 1969, The Management of Global Disorder, 1987, Prospects for Peacemaking, 1987, Managing International Conflict, 1997. Moderator First Parish Ch., Cohasset, Mass.; bd. dirs. Unitarian-Universalist Assn., 1958—64, World Affairs Coun. Boston, 1975—2002, World Peace Found., Nat. Def. U., 1984—89, Can. Inst. Internat. Peace and Security, 1989—92. Lt. USNR, 1942—46. Recipient Chase prize, Harvard U., 1956, EDUCOM prize, Disting. Software, 1988, New Eng. Emmy award, 1992, Disting. Vis. Lectr. award, State Dept. Fgn. Svc. Inst., 1995, Leadership award, UN Assn. Greater Boston, 1997; Littauer fellow, 1952, Rockefeller fellow, 1954, 1975, Internat. Leadership Forum fellow, 2006—. Fellow: World Acad. Art and Sci.; mem.: Coun. Fgn. Rels., Harvard Club NY, Cohasset Golf Club.

BLOOMFIELD, LOUIS AUB, physicist, researcher; b. Boston, Oct. 11, 1956; s. Daniel Kermit and Frances (Aub) B.; m. Karen Shatkin, Aug. 28, 1983; children: Elana, Aaron. BA in Physics, Amherst Coll., 1979; PhD in Physics, Stanford U., 1983. Postdoctoral physicist AT&T Bell Labs., Murray Hill, NJ, 1983-85; asst. prof. U. Va., Charlottesville, Va., 1985-91, assoc. prof., 1991-96, prof, 1996—. Author: (Book) How Things Work: The Physics of Everyday Life, How Everything Works: Making Physics Out of the Ordinary. Recipient Alumni Tchr. award U. Va., 1992, Pres.'s Rsch. prize, 1994; named Presdl. Young Investigator NSF, 1986, Young Investigator Office of Naval Rsch., 1988, Va. Outstanding Faculty award, 1998; Alfred P. Sloan fellow, 1989. Fellow Am. Phys. Soc. (Apker award 1980, Pegram medal 2001). Jewish. Office: Univ of Va Dept Physics PO Box 400714 Charlottesville VA 22904-4714 Office Phone: 434-924-6595. E-mail: bloomfield@virginia.edu.

BLOOMFIELD, MAXWELL HERRON, III, retired history and law professor; b. Galveston, Tex., Aug. 17, 1931; s. Maxwell Herron and Violet Clemons (Turner) B.; m. Helen Lorraine Anderson, Sept. 11, 1965. BA, Rice U., 1952; LLB, Harvard U., 1957; PhD in History, Tulane U., 1962. Bar: Tex. 1957. Lectr. Tulane U., 1961-62; instr. Ohio State U., 1962-66; asst. prof. history Cath. U. Am., Washington, 1966-68, assoc. prof., 1968-74, prof., 1974—98, chmn. dept. history, 1977-80, prof. law, 1985-98, prof. emeritus, 1998—. Vis. prof. U. Va., 1973. Author: Alarms and Diversions: The American Mind Through American Magazines, 1967, American Lawyers in a Changing Society, 1776-1876, 1976, (with John McWilliams and Carl Smith) Law and American Literature, 1983, Peaceful Revolution: Constitutional Change and American Culture from Progressivism to the New Deal, 2000; mem. editl. bd. Md. Hist. Mag., 1974-75, Capitol Studies, 1979-80, Legal Studies Forum, 1985-96. With U.S. Army, 1952-54. Am. Bar Found. fellow, 1968-69, Project '87 fellow, 1981; ABA grantee, 1979-80. Mem. State Bar Tex., Am. Soc. Legal History, Am. Hist. Assn., Am. Cath. Hist. Assn., Orgn. Am. Historians, Tex. Supreme Ct. Hist. Soc. (trustee 2006-), Phi Beta Kappa. Democrat. Roman Catholic. Home: 4 Legas Dr Galveston TX 77551-1568

BLOOMFIELD, NEIL JON, lawyer, real estate broker, educator; b. NYC, July 25, 1945; s. Elmer Joel and Charlotte (Orlov) B.; children: Jennifer, Violet. BA cum laude, Princeton U., 1966, BA cum laude Woodrow Wilson Sch. Pub. and Internat. Affairs, 1966; JD cum laude, Harvard U., 1969. Bar: NY 1969, Calif. 1972; cert. proficiency in pub. and internat. affairs, expert in real estate law and trusts related to real estate Calif. Superior Ct.; Assoc. Willkie, Farr & Gallagher, NYC, 1969-73; ptnr. Bloomfield & Greene, 1974-80; pres. Bloomfield White & Whitney, Inc., Sausalito, Calif., 1974-77, pvt. practice, 1980—. Bd. dirs. Vol. Lawyers for Arts, NYC, 1970-72; adj. prof. law U. San Francisco, 1982-83; judge pro-tem Marin Mcpl. Ct., 1983, 84; spl. master, discovery referee Marin County Superior Ct., other various appts., 1987-91, 2003-. Mem. Marin County Bar Assn., San Francisco Bar Assn., Clolsrer Inn, Lincolns Inn Soc. (Cambridge). Editor: Community and Racial Crises, 1966; contbr. articles to profl. jours. including U. Southern Calif. Law Rev., 1970. Office: 901 E St Ste 100 San Rafael CA 94901-2928 E-mail: njb@earthlink.net.

BLOOMFIELD, SARA J., museum director; BA in English Lit., Northwestern Univ.; MA in Education. V.p. Cleveland Financial Group; dep. dir. for ops. U.S. Holocaust Meml. Coun., Washington, 1986—88, exec. dir., 1988—94; assoc. dir. for mus. programs U.S. Holocaust Memorial Museum, Washington, 1994—98, acting dir., 1998—99, dir., 1999—. Established the first Learning Disability Program for the Shaker Heights City School System. Recipient of the Young Leadership award from the American Jewish Com., 1986, Jan Karski award from the Anti-Defamation League, Washington Chap. Bd. mem, Women's Political Caucus, the Cleveland City Club and the American Jewish Com. Office: US Holocaust Meml Mus 100 Raoul Wallenberg Pl SW Washington DC 20024-2126

BLOOMGARDEN, GARY MICHAEL, neurosurgeon; b. NYC, Apr. 12, 1954; s. Leonard J. and Annette B.; m. Jennifer Anne Frenzilli, Mar. 16, 1957; children: Jessica Ellen, Kara Elizabeth. BA summa cum laude, SUNY, Buffalo, 1976; MD, NYU, 1980; MBA, U. NH, 1997. Diplomate Am. Bd. Neurosurgery, 1988. Surg. intern Parkland Meml. Hosp., Dallas, 1980-81; resident in neurosurgery Yale-New Haven Hosp., 1981-86, courtesy neurosurgeon, 1986—, Hosp. of St. Raphael, New Haven, 1986—, Milford (Conn.) Hosp., 1986—, St. Mary's Hosp., Waterbury, Conn., 1995—. Clin. asst. prof. in surgery Yale U. Sch. of Medicine, 1987—. Fellow ACS, Internat. Coll. Surgeons; mem. AMA, Am. Assn. Neurologic Surgeons, Congress of Neurologic Surgeons, Conn. State Med. Soc., Conn. State Neurol. Soc., New Eng. Neurolosurgical Soc. Republican. Jewish. Avocation: skeet shooting. Office: Ste 316 330 Orchard St New Haven CT 06511-4430 Office Phone: 203-781-3400. E-mail: gmbloom@aol.com.

BLOOMGARDEN, KARENNE JO, elementary school educator, small business owner; b. NYC, July 5, 1951; d. Kermitt and Carol (Lane) B. BS, Bradley U., 1973; M Secondary Edn., Mercy Coll., 2000. Health and phys. edn. tchr. N.J. Bd. Edn., Plainfield, 1973-76, phys. edn. tchr. Orange, 1976-79; camp dir. Orange YWCA, 1977-85; health and phys. edn. tchr. Newark Bd. Edn., 1980-83; exec. dir. Am. Camping Assn., NYC, 1984-87; tchr., trainer N.Y.C. Bd. Edn., 1988-90, adaptive phys. edn. tchr., 1990—; pres. KB Camp Svc., Inc., 1985—. Camp dir. Balt. Cancer Soc., 1977-85, 86-91; dir. The Summer Camp, N.Y.C., 1985-92; stds. accreditation vis. Am. Camping Assn., N.Y.C., 1980—; spokesperson Children and Adults with Attention Deficit Disorder, N.Y.C., 1993—; pres. KB Camp Svc., Inc., 1985—. Contbr. articles to mags. Vol. Starlight Found., N.Y.C., 1989—, Ronald McDonald House, N.Y.C., 1990-92, Coalition for the Homeless, N.Y.C., 1990—, Yorkville Pantry Shelter, N.Y.C., 1993—, Kwazulu Natal-Mduku Cmty., South Africa, 2000—; founder Girl Club of Am., Peoria, Ill., 1973. Named Tchr. of Yr., P.U.S.H., N.J., 1975; featured in Time Mag., 1986, N.Y. Times,1994, LA Times, 2001. Mem. Am. Camping Assn. (cert. camp dir.). Home and Office: 351 E 84th St New York NY 10028-4423 Office Phone: 212-772-6633. Personal E-mail: kbcamp@rcn.com.

BLOOMGARDEN, KATHY FINN, public relations executive; b. NYC, June 9, 1949; d. David and Laura (Zeisler) Finn; m. Zachary Bloomgarden; children: Rachel, Keith, Matthew. BA, Brown U., 1970; MA, PhD, Columbia U.; cert., East Asian Inst. Pres. Rsch. & Forecasts, NYC; pres., dir. Ruder-Finn, Inc., NYC, 1988—98, pres., 1998—, co-CEO, 2001—. Mem. comm. com. Brown U. Mem. comms. com. Brown U., Providence. Recipient PR Industry's All-Star award. Mem.: Women's Forum, Fgn. Policy Assn., Coun. Fgn. Rels., Am. Mgmt. Assn. (bd. dirs.), Pub. Rels. Soc. Am. Jewish. Office: Ruder Finn 301 E 57th St New York NY 10022-2900

BLOOMINGDALE, LEWIS MORGAN, retired psychiatrist; s. Lewis Morgan Bloomingdale; m. Eileen Grace Crutchlow, July 25, 1947; 1 child, Kerry Lewis. BS with honors, Yale U., New Haven, Conn., 1940; B in Chem. Engring. with highest honors, Yale U., New Haven, 1941; MD magna cum laude, Harvard U., Cambridge, Mass., 1950. Diplomate Am. Bd. Psychiatry and Neurology, lic. physician NY, Conn., Mass.; qualified examiner NY. Chem. engr. Am. Cyanamide, Wallingford, Conn., 1941—42, Manhattan Project, NYC, 1942—43; clin. assoc. prof. N.Y. Med. Coll., Valhalla, 1972—98; faculty assoc. Coll. Med. Spltys., Fla. North Gulf U., Ft. Myers, 2001—02; pvt. practice child and forensic psychiatry, 1955—97. Psychiat. cons. Yonkers Family Svc., NY, 1957—65; spl. psychiat. cons. Child Protective Svcs. of Westchester County, NY, 1989—97; founder, pres. Profl. Group for Rsch. in Attention and Related Disorders; mem. adv. bd. Mental Health Dept., Westchester County, NY, 1957, 60; advisor on mental health US Congressman Ottinger, Westchester County, 1965; mem., chair several coms. Westchester Med. Soc., 1955—97; pres. Westchester Psychiat. Soc., 1968—69; founder, 1st pres. Westchester Soc. Sex Edn.; cofounder Assn. Adolescent Psychiatry (merged with Assn. Child Psychiat.). Editor: Attention Deficit Disorder, 4 vols., 1983—88; co-editor: Attention Deficit Disorder, 2 vols., 1988; contbr. articles to profl. jours. With AUS, 1943—45. Fellow: Am. Psychiat. Assn. (disting. life); mem.: Coll. Forensic Psychiatry, Coll. Forensic Psychology, Am. Assn. Law and Psychiatry, World Psychiat. Assn., NY Acad. Scis., Nat. Acad. Neuropsychology, Mt. Vernon Bar Assn. (hon.), Internat. Neuropsychology Soc., NY Med. and Psychiat. Socs., Mental Health Soc. Westchester, Mass. Med. and Psychiat. Socs., Am. Acad. Child and Adolescent Psychiatry, Alpha Omega Alpha, Sigma Xi, Phi Beta Kappa. Avocations: tennis, travel photography, neurosciences. Home: 20 Longwood Dr Apt 378 Westwood MA 02090 Home Fax: 781-329-2444. Personal E-mail: bloompgard@yahoo.com.

BLOOMQUIST, KENNETH GENE, music educator, director; b. Boone, Iowa, Dec. 29, 1931; s. Carl Arvid and Alma Florence (Lindahl) B.; m. Carole Ann Murphy, Feb. 14, 1954; children: Leslie Ann, Laurie Kathleen, Daniel John. BS in Music Edn., U. Ill., 1953, MusM, 1957. Band dir. Urbana (Ill.) Pub. Schs., 1956-57; band dir., supr. music Taylorville (Ill.) Pub. Schs., 1957-58; asst. band dir., trumpet tchr. U. Kans., Lawrence, 1958-68, dir. bands, 1968-70, Mich. State U., East Lansing, 1970-78, 88-93, dir. Sch. Music, 1978-88; dir. bands, 1988-93; dir. bands emeritus Mich. State U., East Lansing, 1993. Guest band condr., U.S., Europe, Asia, 1968—; condr. fgn. tours, 1964, 75, 76, 78, 85, 92, 95, 98, 2001, 04; vis. prof. Musashino Acadamia Musicae, Tokyo, 1998, 2000, 02, 05; cons. adjudicator of music, U.S., Europe, Mex., Taiwan, Indonesia, Japan, Thailand, Korea, Czech Republic. Contbr. articles to profl. jours., others. Pres. Music Boosters Okemos (Mich.) Pub. Schs., 1970—72, Northport (Mich.) Cmty. Arts Ctr., 2001—03; bd. dirs. Lansing Symphony Orch., 1978—84, Okemos Cmty. Ch., 1984—87, Traverse Symphony Orch., 2003—. Sgt. US Army, 1953—55. Recipient Alumni award U. Ill., 1966. Mem. Nat. Band Assn. (nat. pres. 1980-82), Am. Band Masters Assn. (nat. pres. 1995-96), Coll. Band Dirs. Assn., Music Educators Nat. Conf., Nat. Bd. Assn. Acad. Winds and Percussion Arts (Hall of Fame for Disting. Band Condrs., NBA Hall of Fame, Midwest Clinic medal of honor), Phi Mu Alpha. Avocations: golf, bridge, tennis, travel, reading. E-mail: kennannbloomquist@yahoo.com.

BLOOMQUIST, MICHAEL, lawyer; BA, Hamilton Coll., 1991; JD, Washington Univ., St. Louis, 1995; LLM, George Washington Univ., 1997. Mem. honors program Office of US Solicitor Gen., Washington; assoc. Patton Boggs LLP, Washington, 1999—2003; assoc. gen. counsel, Com. on Sci. US Ho. of Reps, Washington, 2003, gen. counsel, Com. on Sci., 2003—05, dep. gen. counsel, Com. Energy and Commerce, 2005—. Office: Committee on Energy and Commerce 2125 Rayburn HOB Washington DC 20515

BLOOMQUIST, PAUL FREDERICK, music educator, director, secondary school educator, musician; b. Clarion, Iowa, Oct. 18, 1977; s. Marlan Paul and Margaret Ann Bloomquist; m. Kelli Patricia Linn, Sept. 10, 2005; 1 child, Grace Margaret. MusB, Simpson Coll., Indianola, Iowa, 2000. Dir. band mid. sch. Meservey-Thornton Ctrl. Sch. Dist., Iowa, 2000—01, Lake Mills Ctrl. Sch. Dist., 2001—03; dir. band Manson N.W. Webster HS, 2003—06; dir. bands Iowa Ctrl. CC, Fort Dodge, 2006—. Mem. Karl L. King Mcpl. Band, Fort Dodge, Iowa, 1997—; dir. jazz band Celebration Iowa Luther Coll., 2002—05; mem. Jive for Five Brass Quintet, Fort Dodge, 2003—. Recipient Cmty. Leader award, Lake Mills (Iowa) Chamber Devel. Corp., 2002, Golden Apple Tchg. award, KIMT Channel 3, Mason City, Iowa, 2003. Mem.: Iowa Bandmaster Assn., Iowa Ctrl. Edn. Assn., North Ctrl. Iowa Bandmasters (sec. 2005—06, treas. 2005—06, v.p. 2006—07), Manson Meridian Singers (Iowa) (v.p. 2004—05). Avocations: golf, gardening, baseball. Business E-Mail: bloomquist@iowacentral.com.

BLOOMQUIST, RODNEY GORDON, geologist; b. Aberdeen, Wash., Feb. 3, 1943; s. Verner A. and Margaret E. (Olson) B.; m. Linda L. Lee, Dec. 19, 1964 (div. July 1968); m. Bente Brisson Jørgensen, Aug. 4, 1977; 1 child, Kira Brisson. BS in Geology, Portland State U., 1966; MS in Geology, U. Stockholm, 1970, PhD in Geochemistry, 1977. Rschr. U. Stockholm, 1974-77; asst. prof. Oreg. Inst. Tech., Klamath Falls, 1978-80; geologist Wash. State Energy Office, Olympia, 1980-96; chief scientist Wash. State U., Olympia, 1996—2007, dir. CHP Application Ctr., 2003—, dir. Ctr. Distributed Generation and Thermal Distbn., 2004—. Author: Regulatory Guide to Geothermics, 1991; mem. editl. bd. Geothermics, 1985-88; contbr. articles to profl. jours. Smitts fellow, Sweden, 1974, Royal Rsch. fellow, Sweden, 1975-77; Rsch. grant U. Stockholm, 1975-77. Mem.: N.Am. Dist. Heating and Cooling Inst. (bd. dirs. 1988—92), Internat. Geothermal Assn. (chmn. edn. com. 1988—2004, bd. dirs. 1990—2001, 2004—, chmn. fin. com. 2004—, chair 2010 world congress steering com.), Internat. Dist. Energy Assn. (western sect. bd. dirs. 1990—2000, bd. dirs. 1994—97, chmn. com. govt. rels. 1997—2002, bd. dirs. 2001—04), Geothermal Resources Coun. (pres. Pacific N.W. sect. 1982—85, bd. dirs. 1985—92, pres. 1989, bd. dirs. 2001—04), Am. Blade Smith Soc. (bd. dirs. 1989—2002). Democrat. Lutheran. Avocations: skiing, backpacking, fishing, hunting. Office: Wash State Univ 925 Plum St SE Olympia WA 98501-1529 Office Phone: 360-956-2016. Business E-Mail: bloomquistr@energy.wsu.edu.

BLOOSTON, ROSELEE, cultural organization administrator, writer; b. Washington, Sept. 29, 1952; d. Arthur and Leone Isaacs Blooston; m. Jerry Michael Mosier, Sept. 9, 1983; 1 child, Oliver Blooston Mosier. BA in Drama, Vassar Coll., Poughkeepsie, NY, 1973; MFA in Theater, Trinity U., San Antonio, Tex., 1975. Drama instr. Smithsonian Instn., Washington, 1976; acting instr. U. Tex., Austin, 1976—79; faculty New Sch. for Social Rsch., NYC, 1982—83; master tchr., dir. Paper Mill Playhouse, Millburn, NJ, 1991—96; dir., tchg. artist NJ Performing Arts Ctr., Newark, 1997; adj. faculty Montclair State U., 1992—2000; founder, dir. Tunnel Vision Writers' Project, Inc., Montclair, 1998—2005. Cons. Job Performance Seminars, Bklyn., 1984—89; dir., playwriting coord. The Gathering/Whole Theater, Montclair, 1988—89; head speech dept. Action Theater Conservatory, Clifton, NJ, 1995—97; adult edn. workshop leader Montclair Art Mus., 2005. Author short stories; prodr.: 5 plays. Mem. edn. com. Montclair Editors and Writers, 2001—; mem. pub. programs com. Montclair Art Mus., 2001—04; mem. steering com. Montclair Arts Coun., 2004, trustee, 2006—. Recipient Greer Garson Theater Arts award, Dallas Theater Ctr., 1974. Mem.: Internat. Womens Writers Guild, Dramatists Guild, Actors Equity Assn., Phi Beta Kappa. Office Phone: 973-783-2372. E-mail: rblooston@mac.com.

BLOS, JOAN WINDSOR, writer, critic, educator; b. NYC, Dec. 9, 1928; m. Peter Blos, Jr., 1953; 2 children, 1 deceased. BA, Vassar Coll., 1950; MA, CCNY, 1956; DHL (hon.), Bank St. Coll. Edn., 2001. Asso. publs. div., mem. tchr. edn. faculty Bank St. Coll. Edn., NYC, 1958-70; lectr. Sch. Edn., U. Mich., Ann Arbor, 1972-80; U.S. editor Children's Literature in Education, 1976-81. Author: "It's Spring!" She Said, 1968, (with Betty Miles) Just Think!, 1971, A Gathering of Days: A New England Girl's Journal, 1830-32, 1979 (ALA Newbery medal 1980, ALA Notable Children's Books, 1980, Am. Book award 1980, Nat. Book award 1980, IRA Tchrs. Choices, 1980, Best Books of Yr., Sch. Libr. Jour., 1980), Martin's Hats, 1984, Brothers of the Heart: A Story of the Old Northwest, 1837-38, 1985, (dramatized 2000), Old Henry, 1987 (Honor book Boston Globe/Horn Book award, 1987), Trans. Ce sacré vieil Henri, 1987, Oh Dieser Heinrich, 1987, Vreemde Vogels, 1987, El Viejo Henry, 1987, Lottie's Circus, 1989, The Grandpa Days, 1989, One Very Best Valentine's Day, 1990, The Heroine of the Titanic,1991 (Juvenile Non-Fiction award, Soc. of Midland Authors, 1991, Annie award For Excellence in Lit. Arts-Fiction, Washtenaw Council for the Arts, 1992), A Seed, A Flower, A Minute, An Hour, 1992, Brooklyn Doesn't Rhyme, 1994, The Days Before Now, 1994, Hungry Little Boy, 1995, Hello, Shoes (Best Book award Bank St. Coll. Edn. 1999). Letters from the Corrugated Castle: A Novel of Gold Rush California, 2007. Office Phone: 212-473-5400.

BLOSKAS, JOHN D., retired finance company executive; b. Waco, Tex., July 13, 1928; s. George and Alvina (Schrader) B.; m. Anna Louise Nelson, Feb. 7, 1955; children: Suzzanne (dec.), John D., Kenneth Douglas. Exec. sec. Waco Jr. C. of C., 1953—55; assoc. editor Mexia Daily News, Tex., 1955—56; dir. publicity Valley C. of C., Weslaco, Tex., 1956—57; religion editor Houston Chronicle, 1957—58; v.p. pub. rels. annuity bd. So. Bapt. Conv., Dallas, 1984—90, v.p., endowment officer annuity bd., 1984—90; v.p. Lady Love Cosmetics, Dallas, 1981—83; ret., 1990. Chmn. Greenville (Tex.) Airport adv. bd.; cons., spkr. in field. Author: Staying in the Black, Financially, Living Within Your Means; editor: THe Years Ahead. Chmn. adv. bd. Greenville (Tex.) Airport. Served with USNR, 1945-49, 50-51. Mem. Southern Bapt. (past pres.), Tex. Bapt. Assn. (past pres.), Pub. Rels. Assn., Pub. Rels. Soc. Am. (accredited), Religious Pub. Rels. Coun., Sales and Mktg. Execs., Bapt. Devel. Officer's Assn., Assn. Bapt. Found. Execs., Dallas Estate Planning Coun., Fellowship Christians in Arts, Media and Entertainment. Home: 7508 Blossom Ln Frisco TX 75034-5470 Office Phone: 214-450-6805. Personal E-mail: jbloskas@sbcglobal.net, anjoblossom@hotmail.com.

BLOSSER, HENRY GABRIEL, physicist; b. Harrisonburg, Va., Mar. 16, 1928; s. Emanuel and Leona (Branum) B.; m. Priscilla May Beard, June 30, 1951 (div. Oct. 1972); children: William Henry, Stephan Emanuel, Gabe Fawley, Mary Margaret; m. Mary Margaret Gray, Mar. 16, 1973 (dec. Jan. 1995); m. Amy June Conley, May 11, 1995 (div. Feb. 1997); m. Lois Pearlena Lynch, Oct. 17, 1998. BS, U. Va., 1951, MS, 1952, PhD, 1954. Physicist Oak Ridge (Tenn.) Nat. Lab., 1954-56, group leader, 1956-68; assoc. prof. physics Mich. State U., East Lansing, 1958-61, prof., 1961-90, Univ. Disting. prof., 1990—, dir. Cyclotron Lab., 1961-89. Cons. Harper Hosp., Detroit, 1983—, Ion Beam Applications, Belgium, 1996—, others; adj. prof. radiation oncology Wayne State U., Detroit, 1996—. Bd. dirs. Midwest Univs. Rsch. Assocs., 1960-63. With USNR, 1946-48. Predoctoral fellow NSF, 1953-54, sr. postdoctoral fellow, 1966-67; Guggenheim fellow, 1973-74. Fellow Am. Phys. Soc. (Bonner prize 1992); mem. Sigma Xi, Phi Beta Kappa, Kappa Alpha. Home: 2350 Emerald Forest Cir East Lansing MI 48823-7200 Office: Mich State U Nat Cyclotron East Lansing MI 48824-1321 Business E-Mail: blosser@nscl.msu.edu.

BLOSSEY, ERICH CARL, chemistry professor; b. Toledo, June 10, 1935; s. Erich Fredrich and Marguerite F. (Steinmiller) B.; m. Shirley Ann Stanford, Sept. 6, 1954 (div. Nov. 1978); m. Elizabeth Diane Frye, Aug. 11, 1979 (div. Aug. 1995); children: Christina E., Elizabeth N., Erich G.; m. Sandra C. Blossey, Jan. 22, 2000 BS, Ohio State U., 1957; MS, Iowa State U., 1959; PhD, Carnegie Mellon U., 1963. Prof. chemistry Rollins Coll., Winter Park, Fla., 1965—, AG Bush prof., 1981-87, prof. and D.J. and J.M. Cram chair chemistry, 2002—. Cons. White Labs, Orlando, Fla., 1978-84; vis. prof. Okla. State U., Stillwater, 1985-86; vis. scholar Harvard U., 1991-92. Author: (with others) Preparative Chemistry Using Supported Reagents, 1987, Comprehensive Polymer Science, Vol. 6, 1988. Bd. dirs. div. accreditation Am. Coll. Nurses-Midwives, Washington, 1986-97. Rsch. Corp. grantee Rollins Coll., 1972-75, NSF Instrumentation and Lab. Improvement, 1986—; Arthur Vining Davis Found. fellow, 1978-79, NIH sr. fellow U. N.Mex., 1974-75. Mem. AAAS, ACLU, Am. Chem. Soc. (sect. chmn. 1970-71, 1981-82), Royal Soc. Chemistry (London), Sierra Club. Achievements include U.S. and Canadian patents in field. Office: Rollins Coll Dept Chemistry Box 2743 1000 Holt Ave Winter Park FL 32789-4499 Office Phone: 407-646-2140. E-mail: eblossey@rollins.edu.

BLOSSMAN, ALFRED RHODY, JR., banker; b. Madisonville, La., Oct. 21, 1931; s. Alfred Rhody and Mabel (Perrin) Blossman; m. Royanne Elaire Hurd, Dec. 28, 1957; children: Alfred Rhody III, Roy Edward, Gary Bennett, Christopher Hurd, David Quintin, John Eric. AB in Gen. Bus., La. State U., 1955. Pres. Blossman Hydratane Gas, Inc., Covington, La., 1963—67; chmn. First Nat. Corp., First Nat. Bank, Covington, 1968—84; pres., CEO First Nat. Bank, 1980—84, Parish Nat. Bank, Covington, 1986—, also chmn. bd. dirs. Capt. USAF, 1956—58. Mem.: Phi Delta Theta. Republican. Roman Catholic. Home: 10 Blossman Ln Covington LA 70433-4707 also: 503 Norriego Dr Destin FL 32541 Business E-Mail: fredb@parishnational.com. *My formula for life is shaped by the moral and ethical guidelines of my religious faith and my own personal code of ethics. Thank God, strong self discipline has made that possible, as well as channelling my enthusiasm for whatever role I have played; being it business, or hobby; educational, military service, parent or grandparent, in a positive direction.*

BLOSSOM, BEVERLY, choreographer, educator; b. Chgo., Aug. 28, 1926; d. Theodore and Florence (Pfeiffer) Schmidt; m. Roberts Blossom, 1966 (div.); 1 child, Michael. BA, Roosevelt U., 1950; MA, Sarah Lawrence, 1953. Dancer Alwin Nikolais Co., NYC, 1952-62; instr. Adelphi U., LI, NY, 1964-66; prof. dance dept. U. Ill., Urbana, 1967-90. Choreographer Festival Theatre, Krannert Ctr., Black Traveler, 1961, Poem for the Theater #6, 1963, Brides, 1981, Urbana, Radio Show, 1985, Quick-Step, 1985, Heartbeat, 1985, Interlude from Veranda, 1985; choreographer: Rehearsal for a Class Act, 1983, You Are Still With Me, Fred, 1983, Dad's Ties, 1983, Ordinary Heartbreak, 1984, Egg, 1984, Weatherwatch, 1986, Potpourri, 1986, Eye of the Beholder, 1986, Russian Tea Room, 1986, Entitled, 1987, Grass Widow, 1987, Inch, 1987, Castles in Spain, 1988, Swansong, 1989,.Exit, 1990, The Cloak, 1990, Onward, 1991, Shards, 1993, Dead Monkey, 1996, Cynicism, 1996, Cello Lessons, 2003, The Incomplete Lament of an Old Dancer, 2005, others. Choreography grantee Nat. Endowment for the Arts, 1986-90, 92-95, Ill. Arts Coun. Choreography grantee, 1980-82; recipient Bessie award, 1993. Mem.: Am. Guild of Musical Artists (cert.), Screen Actors Guild (cert.), Union of Profl. Employees (cert.). Office Phone: 312-347-0981. E-mail: bblossom@jps.net.

BLOUCH, TIMOTHY CRAIG, food company executive; b. Lebanon, Pa., June 26, 1954; s. Charles and Elaine (Krick) B.; m. Donna Joyce Walmer, June 18, 1977. AA, Harrisburg Area Community Coll., 1974; BBA, Pa. State U., 1977, MBA, 1991. Prodn. supr. Kraft, Inc., Allentown, Pa., 1977-78, Hershey (Pa.) Chocolate USA, 1978-82, mgr. inbound and fleet ops., 1982-83, mgr. inbound ops., 1983-84, mgr. transp. rates, 1984-86, mgr. traffic services, 1986-90, transp. planning mgr., 1990-93, mgr. transp. planning and rates, 1993—2001, mgr. tranps. financials and analysis, 2002—05; dir. transp. Maines Paper and Food Svc., Inc., Conklin, NY, 2006—07; mgr. inbound transp. Rite Aid Corp., Camp Hill, Pa., 2007—. Republican. Avocation: fine arts. Office: Rite Aid Corp 30 Hunter Ln Camp Hill PA 17011 Office Phone: 717-730-8342. Office Fax: 717-975-5943. Business E-Mail: tblouch@riteaid.com.

BLOUIN, FRANCIS XAVIER, JR., history professor; b. Belmont, Mass., July 29, 1946; s. Francis X. and Margaret (Cronin) B.; m. Joy Alexander; children: Benjamin, Tiffany. AB, U. Notre Dame, 1967; MA, U. Minn., 1969, PhD, 1978. Asst. dir. Bentley Library U. Mich., Ann Arbor, 1974-75, assoc. archivist Bentley Library, 1975-81, dir. Bentley Library, 1981—, asst. prof. history and library sci., 1979-83, assoc. prof., 1983-89, prof., 1989—. Author: The Boston Region., 1980, Vatican Archives: An Inventory and Guide to Historical Documentation of the Holy See, 1998; editor: Archival Implications Machine., 1980, Intellectual Life on Michigan Frontier, 1985, Archives Documentation and Institutions of Social Memory, 2006. Trustee Much. Student Found., 1986-91; dir. Am. Friends of Vatican Libr., 1981—, Coun. on Libr. and Info. Resources, 2001—. Fellow Soc. Am. Archivist (mem. governing council 1985-88); mem. Am. Hist. Assn., Hist. Soc. Mich. (trustee 1982-88, pres. 1987-88), Assn. Records Mgrs. and Adminstrs., Internat. Council on Archives. Office: U Mich Bentley Hist Libr 1150 Beal Ave Ann Arbor MI 48109-2113 E-mail: fblouin@umich.edu.

BLOUNT, BENROE WAYNE, physician, department chairman; b. Augusta, Ga., Feb. 8, 1950; s. Benroe and Loreen Moellering B.; m. Merry Teresa Van Dam, Feb. 14, 1974 Dec. May 8, 1974); m. Young Hui Cho, Nov. 23, 1976; children: Teresa Jana, Daniel Paul. BS, US Mil. Acad.,

1972; MA, U. Calif., Berkeley, 1975; MD, U. Miami, 1983; MPH, U. Wash., Seattle, 1990. Commd. 2d lt. U.S. Army, 1972, advanced through grades to lt. col., 1990, ret., 1994; intern, resident DeWitt Army Hosp., Alexandria, Va., 1983-86; divsn. chief, dept. vice-chair Emory Sch. Medicine, Atlanta, 1994-99, 2004—; chair dept. family medicine U. Tenn., Memphis, 1999—2002; prof. Emory U., 2002—; chief family practice Kaiser, S.E., 2002—04. Contbr. articles to profl. jours., chpts. to books. Named one of Outstanding Young Men of Am., Nat. Jaycees, Top Family Physicians in US, 2007; recipient Chmn. of Joint Chief of Staff award for Excellence in Mil. Medicine, 1993, Best Dr. in Am., 2000, 2001, 2002. Independent. Avocation: church. Office Phone: 404-778-6920. Business E-Mail: bwbloun@emory.edu.

BLOUNT, CHARLES WILLIAM, III, lawyer; b. Independence, Mo., Nov. 14, 1946; s. Charles William and Mary Marguarette (Van Trump) B.; children: Charles William IV, Chaille Elizabeth; m. Bonnie M. Harp., Jan. 1, 1991. BS in Journalism, U. Kans., 1968; JD cum laude, U. Toledo, 1981. Bar: Mo. 1981, U.S. Dist. Ct. (we. dist.) Mo. 1981, Tex. 1985, U.S. Dist. Ct. (no. dist.) Tex. 1988, U.S. Ct. Appeals (5th cir.) 1995, U.S. Supreme Ct. 1997; cert. in civil appellate law Tex. Bd. Legal Specialization. Litigation assoc. Shugart, Thomson & Kilroy, Kansas City, Mo., 1981-84, Hughes & Luce, Dallas, 1984-87, Simpson & Dowd L.L.P., Dallas, 1987-91, ptnr., 1991-94; mem. Dowd & Blount, Dallas, 1994-99; ptnr. Perry-Miller & Blount, L.L.P., Dallas, 1999—2002; sr. counsel Underwood, Perkins & Ralston, PC, Dallas, 2002—. Mem. West Group Tex. Editl. Bd., 1999. Bd. govs. U. Toledo Coll. Law, 1980-81; trustee Episcopal Diocese We. Mo., Kansas City, 1983-84; mem., chmn. com. Boy Scouts of Am., Kansas City, 1983-84, Richardson, Tex., 1984-92. 1st lt. U.S. Army, 1968-72. Mem. Phi Kappa Phi, Phi Kappa Tau (pledge pres., social chmn., activities chmn., 1965—). Avocations: music, reading. Office: Underwood Perkins & Ralston PC 5420 LBJ Frwy Ste 1900 Dallas TX 75240 Home Phone: 214-373-7760; Office Phone: 972-661-5114. Business E-Mail: cblount@suplaw.com.

BLOUNT, CINDY KAREN, web site designer, web programmer; b. Concord, NC, May 16, 1970; d. Calvin Randall Barringer and Emma Jean Martain; m. Andrew Franklin Blount, Jan. 28, 1950; children: Tiffany Renee' Pino, Cheyenne Autumn. AA in Internet Tech., Blue Ridge Cmty. Coll., Flat Rock, NC, 2006. Asst. to distance learning specialist/webmaster Blue Ridge Cmty. Coll., 2003—; owner KC webVisions, Hendersonville, NC, 2005—; dir. mktg. & visual comm. Quality Recycling, Hendersonville, 2007. Recipient USAA Nat. Collegiate Computer Sci. award, US Achievement Acad., 2005, Gold Metal award, Web Masters of World Internat. Web Design Competition, 2005. Mem.: Guardiam ad Litem, Assn. Info. Tech. Profls. (pres. 2003—06, Outstanding Leadership 2004, 2005), Nat. Tech. Honor Soc. (life), Phi Theta Kappa (life; webmaster 2005—06, pres., v.p., treas. 2003—06, 4th Pl. NC State Java Programming award 2005, 2d Pl. NC State Web Devel. award 2005, 1st Pl. Nat. Web Devel. award 2005). Baptist. Office: KC webVisions 330 Pressley Rd Hendersonville NC 28792 Personal E-mail: afbckb@mchsi.com. Business E-Mail: cindy@kcwebvisions.com.

BLOUNT, DANIEL J., lumber company executive; BS, U. Ill., Urbana; MBA, St. Ambrose U. Sr. v.p. fin. Montgomery Elevator Co., 1989-97; joined Riverwood Internat. Corp., Atlanta, 1998, v.p., CFO, 1999—2003; sr. v.p. integration Graphic Packaging Corp., Atlanta, 2003—. Office: Graphic Packaging Corp 814 Livingston Court Marietta GA 30067

BLOUNT, MICHAEL EUGENE, lawyer; b. Camden, NJ, July 9, 1949; s. Floyd Eugene and Dorothy Alice (Geyer) Durham; m. Janice Lynn Brown, Aug. 22, 1969; children: Kirsten Marie, Gretchen Elizabeth. BA, U. Tex., 1971; JD, U. Houston, 1974. Bar: Tex. 1974, Ill. 1980, D.C. 1981, U.S. Ct. Appeals (D.C. cir.) 1978, U.S. Ct. Mil. Appeals 1975, U.S. Supreme Ct. 1977. Atty. advisor Office of Gen. Counsel SEC, Washington, 1977-78, legal asst. to chmn., 1978-79; assoc. Gardner, Carton & Douglas, Chgo., 1980-84; ptnr. Arnstein, Gluck, Lehr, Barron & Milligan, Chgo., 1984-86, Seyfarth Shaw LLP, Chgo., 1987—. Lt. JAGC USN, 1974—77. Mem.: ABA (fed. regulation of securities com.), Internat. Bar Assn., Chgo. Bar Assn., Order of Barons, Assn. SEC Alumni, Univ. Club (Chgo.), Phi Alpha Delta (chpt. treas. 1973). Home: 1711 Galloway Dr Inverness IL 60010-5737 Office: Seyfarth Shaw LLP 131 S Dearborn St Ste 2400 Chicago IL 60603-5577 Home Phone: 847-991-9830; Office Phone: 312-460-5962. E-mail: mblount@seyfarth.com.

BLOUNT, ROBERT HADDOCK, management consultant, retired military officer; b. Miami, Fla., Dec. 8, 1922; s. Uriel and Aleve Sadie (Haddock) B.; m. Jeannette Mae Barclay, May 13, 1951 (dec. 1998); children: Barbara Mae, Jennifer. B.E.E., MIT, 1947; MS in Systems Engring, George Washington U., 1970; student, Naval War Coll., 1958-59. Commd. ensign USNR, 1946; transferred to U.S. Navy, 1947, advanced through grades to rear adm., 1973; comdr. submarines, service in MTO, PTO, Scotland, Panama; chief staff, aide to comdr. Submarine Flotilla 6, 1970-72; comdr. Naval Sta., Naval Base Charleston, SC, 1972-73; comdr. U.S. Naval Forces, So. Command; also comdt. 15th Naval Dist. Ft. Amador, C.Z., 1973-75; dir. undersea and strategic warfare div. Office Chief Naval Ops. Washington, 1975-77; dep. dir. research, devel., test and evaluation OPNAV, 1977-78; comdr. Operational Test and Evaluation Force, 1978-82, ret., 1982; pvt. industry cons., 1986-90; ret. Va. Ops. div. EDO Corp., 1990. Pres. C.Z. coun. Boy Scouts Am., 1974. Decorated D.S.M., Meritorious Service medal with star, Navy Expeditionary medal; recipient Scroll of Honor Navy League, 1974 Mem. Naval Submarine League, U.S. Naval Inst., Norfolk Yacht and Country Club, Rotary. Address: 1516 Blanford Cir Norfolk VA 23505-1706 Personal E-mail: rhblount@aol.com.

BLOUNT, STANLEY FREEMAN, marketing educator; b. Detroit, June 12, 1929; s. Harry Alfred and Thelma (Freeman) B.; m. Constance Parker, Aug. 30, 1957; children— Jeffrey Parker, Lori Maria. BA, Wayne State U., 1952, MA, 1959; PhD, Northwestern U., 1962. Account exec. Jam Handy Corp., Detroit, 1952-54; marketing mgr. Chrysler Corp., Detroit, 1954-58; instr. Northwestern U., 1961-62; asst. prof. U. Ill., 1962-63; assoc. prof. Kent State U., 1963-67; prof., dept. chmn. State U. N.Y. at Albany, 1967—, chmn. ednl. policies council, 1970—. Disting. vis. prof. U. of Americas, Mexico, 1966; dir. Femtec Inc.; exec. dir. U. Albany Found. Chmn. sub-com. legis. affairs N.Y. State affiliate Am. Heart Assn., 1974-99. Served with AUS, 1946-48. Named Outstanding Faculty Mem. Kent State U., 1964 Mem. Sigma Xi, Gamma Theta Upsilon. Clubs: Essayons, Audubon, Phalanx. Achievements include research on environment analysis and preception, digitized land use mapping, land use and resource mgmt. Home: 11 Pheasant Ln Delmar NY 12054-4109 Office: SUNY at Albany Sch Business Albany NY 12222-0001

BLOUNT, SUSAN L., insurance company executive, lawyer; b. Pitts., July 8, 1957; d. Eugene Irving and Mary Jane Thomas (Langeluttig) B.; m. Richard A. Bard, Aug. 20, 1977; children: Sean, Abigail, Nathaniel. Student, U. Chgo., 1974-76; BA, U. Tex., 1978, JD, 1981. Assoc. Kirkland & Ellis, Chgo., 1981-85; asst. gen. counsel Prudential Residential Svcs. Co., Newark, 1989-95; staff legal positions Prudential, Newark, 1985-89, v.p., corp. sec., 1995—2004, v.p., chief investment counsel, 2004—05, sr. v.p., gen. counsel, 2005—. Mem. NJ Commn. on Higher Edn., 2005—; bd. trustees Montclair State U., 1996—. Office: Prudential Ins Co Am 751 Broad St 21st Fl Newark NJ 07102-3714 Office Phone: 973-802-7001. E-mail: susan.blount@prudential.com.*

BLOUNT, WINTON MALCOLM, III, investment executive; b. Albany, Ga., Dec. 14, 1943; s. Winton Malcolm Jr. and Mary Katherine (Archibald) B.; m. Riley Sikes; children: Sikes, McLeod, Winton Malcolm IV, K. Stuart, William, Judkins. Student, U. Ala., 1962-63; BA, U. South, 1966; MBA, U. Pa., 1968. With Blount Bros. Corp., Montgomery, Ala., 1968-73, project mgr., 1972-73; with Mercury Constrn. Corp., Montgomery, 1973-77, pres., 1975-77; chief exec. officer, chmn. bd. Benjamin F. Shaw Co., Wilmington, Del., 1977-80; pres., chief operating officer Blount Internat., Ltd., Montgomery, 1980-83, pres., chief exec. officer, 1983-85, chmn., chief exec. officer, 1985-87; sr. v.p. Blount Inc., 1985-87, vice chmn., 1987-89; chmn., chief exec. officer Winton Blount III & Assocs., 1989—. Chmn., CEO Wright Plastics Co., 1989-2001, Cobb Pontiac-Cadillac & Royal Motor Co., 1990-2000, Blount-Strange Ford, Lincoln, Mercury, 1991-2000, Blount-Pittman and Assoc., 2004—. Fin. com. Ala. Rep. Com., 1980-82, chmn., 1999-01; bd. dirs. So. Rsch. Inst., 1995-99, Montgomery YMCA, Episcopal High Sch., 1988-89, 95-2001, Ala. Pub. Affairs Rsch. Coun., 1979-83, Bus. Coun. Ala.; active Tukabatchee Area coun. Boy Scouts Am., 1980-83; bd. visitors U. Ala. Coll. Commerce and Bus. Adminstrn., 1983-88; mem. bd. control Com. of 100; bd. dirs. Leadership Ala., 1989-93, 95-98, chmn. bd., 1997-98, Ala. Coun. Econ. Edn. Mem. Chief Execs. Orgn., World Pres.'s Orgn.), Montgomery C. of C. (dir. 1981-88), Del. C. of C. (dir. 1979-80), NAM (dir. 1982-85). Episcopalian. Office: Winston Blount III & Assoc 2821 Eastern Blvd Montgomery AL 36116

BLOUNT, YOLANDA DENISE, social services administrator, psychologist; m. Osborn Blount, Oct. 21, 1989; 1 child, Osborn LaVonte. BA, Columbia Coll., Mo., 1996; MA Clin. Psychology, Ctr. Humanistics Studies, Detroit. Lic. psychologist Mich. Therapist N.W. Behavioral Health Svcs., Jacksonville, Fla., 1998—99, Child Guidance Ctr., Jacksonville, 1999, Renaissance Behavioral Health Sys., Jacksonville, 2000; social svc. specialist Cmty. Hospice N.E. Fla., Jacksonville, 2001—; psychol. specialist Fla. State Prison, Raiford, 2002—03. Psychologist Disaster Med. Assistance Team, Jacksonville, 2004—. With USNR. Decorated various mil. awards. Office: Comty Hospice NE Fla 4266 Senbeam Rd Jacksonville FL 32257 Home Phone: 904-220-1954.

BLOW, GEORGE, lawyer; b. Chgo., Oct. 4, 1928; s. George Waller and Katharine Rowland (Cooke) B.; m. Sarah Wendel Kuhn, Nov. 4, 1957; children: Mary Allmand Blow Prevost, George Rowland, Wendel Matthiessen. AB cum laude, Harvard U., 1950; JD, U. Va., 1953. Bar: Va. 1953, D.C. 1954, U.S. Ct. Appeals (D.C. cir.) 1954, U.S. Ct. Mil. Appeals, 1955, U.S. Supreme Ct. 1956, U.S. Ct. Appeals (4th cir.) 1961, U.S. Ct. Appeals (fed. cir.) 1982. Assoc. Covington & Burling, Washington, 1953-63; ptnr. Patton, Boggs & Blow, Washington, 1963-93. Mem. adv. coun. Internat. Human Rights Law Group, Washington, 1988-98. Mem. Com. of 100 on Fed. City, Washington, 1984—2004, trustee, 1985-87; mem. Washington Inst. Fgn. Affairs, 1976—, bd. dirs., 1976-98; bd. dirs. Sheridan-Kalorama Hist. Assn., Washington, 1987-89. Mem. D.C. Bar, Va. State Bar, Soc. of Cincinnati in State of Va., Soc. Colonial Wars, Met. Club Washington, Order of Coif, Phi Delta Phi.

BLOWERS, HELENE, library and information scientist; m. David Blowers; children: Kathryn, Jessica. BS, U. Wis., Stevens Pt., 1986. Cert. project mgmt. trainer. Staff trainer Pub. Libr. Charlotte & Mecklenburg County, NC, 1996—98, web dir. NC, 1998—, pub. svcs. tech. dir. NC. Co-author: Weaving a Library Web: A Guide to Developing Children's Websites, 2004; developer Learning 2.0 online discovery program, co-developer (websites) Readersclub.org, 1998 (Nat. Assn. Counties Achievement award, 2001), BookHive.org, 1999 (Assn. Libr. Svc. to Children Notable award, 2000, Nat. Assn. Counties Achievement award, 2000, Learning Mag. Teacher's Choice award, 2001, StudyWeb Academic Excellence award for Literature), StoryPlace.org, 2000 (USA Today Edn. Best Bet Web Site, Lightspan StudyWeb Academic Excellence award, Bonus.com Editor's Choice award), Brarydog.net. Named one of the Movers & Shakers, Libr. Jour., 2007. Office: Pub Libr Charlotte & Mecklenburg County 310 N Tryon St Charlotte NC 28202 Office Phone: 704-336-2725. E-mail: hblowers@plcmc.org, helene.blowers@gmail.com.

BLOXHAM, JEREMY, geophysicist, educator; BA in Math., U. Cambridge, Eng., 1982, MA in Math., 1986, PhD in Geophysics, 1986; AM (hon.), Harvard U., Cambridge, Mass., 1993. Postdoctoral rsch. fellow dept. geol. scis. Harvard U., 1985—87, asst. prof. geophysics dept. earth & planetary scis., 1987—90, John L. Loeb assoc. prof. natural scis., 1990—93, prof. geophysics, 1993—2004, chair dept. earth & planetary scis., 2000—06, Harvard Coll. prof., 2002—07, Mallinckrodt prof. geophysics, 2004—, prof. computational sci. divsn. engring. & applied scis., 2006—, divisional dean phys. scis., 2006—. Assoc. editor: Jour. Geophys. Rsch., 1992—94; editor: Geophys. Jour. Internat., 1993—95; North Am. coordinating editor:, 1995—2005. Recipient Presdl. Young Investigator award, 1991; grantee Packard Found. fellowship, 1990. Fellow: Royal Astron. Soc. (Chapman medal 2001), Am. Geophys. Union (James B. Macelwane Young Investigator medal 1994), Royal Soc. Office: Dept of Earth and Planetary Scis Harvard U 20 Oxford St Cambridge MA 02138-2902 Office Phone: 617-495-9517. E-mail: jeremy_bloxham@harvard.edu.*

BLUE, CATHERINE ANNE, lawyer; b. Boston, Feb. 17, 1957; d. James Daniel and Angela Devina (Savini) Mahoney; m. Donald Sherwood Blue, 1980 (dec. 2001); children: Mairead Catherine, Edward Pierce. BA, Stonehill Coll., 1977; JD, Coll. William and Mary, 1980. Bar: Pa. 1980, N.Y. 1999, Mass. 2000, DC 2006. Atty. Aluminum Co. Am., Pitts., 1980-83, Pa. Dept. Revenue, Harrisburg, 1983-85, State Workmen's Ins. Fund, Pitts., 1985-87, Met. Pitts. Pub. Broadcasting (now QED Comm. Inc.), 1987-91, gen. counsel, 1991-95; regional gen. counsel ctrl. region AT&T Wireless Svcs., Paramus, NJ, 1995-97, dir. N.E. region, 1997-98, chief counsel land use, 1998-2000, v.p. land and comml. trans., 2000—05; chief counsel land use Cingular Wireless, Paramus, 2004—05; sr. counsel Holland & Knight, Washington, 2005—06; ptnr. Donohue & Blue, Alexandria, Va., 2006—. Mem. Pa. Bar Assn., Mass. Bar Assn. Democrat. Home: 1200 1st St Apt 1123 Alexandria VA 22314 Office: 801 N Fairfax St Ste 209 Alexandria VA 22314 Office Phone: 703-549-5382. Business E-Mail: catherine.blue@donohueblue.com.

BLUE, FREDERICK JUDD, retired history professor, writer; b. S.I., NY, Apr. 18, 1937; s. Leonard Anderson and Helan Judd Blue; m. Judith Ann Hertwig, June 9, 1962; children: Karen Evenson, Eric. BA, Yale U., New Haven, 1958; MA, U. Wis., Madison, 1962, PhD, 1966. Prof. dept. history Youngstown State U., Ohio, 1964—2004. Adj. prof. history U. Oreg., Bend, 2005—. Author: The Free Soilers: Third Party Politics, 1848-54, 1973, Salmon P. Chase: A Life in Politics, 1987 (Midland Authors Non-Fiction award, 1988), No Taint of Compromise: Crusaders in Anti-slavery Politics, 2005. With US Army, 1958—60, Germany. Mem.: So. Hist. Assn., Soc. Historians of the Early Republic, Orgn. Am. Historians. Democrat. Presbyterian. Avocations: hiking, singing. Home: 900 Victoria Falls Dr Redmond OR 97756-7359 Personal E-mail: bluefj@bendbroadband.com.

BLUE, JOHN RONALD (J. RONALD BLUE), evangelical mission executive; b. Milw., Sept. 4, 1935; s. Earl R. and Wretha J. (Teater) B.; m. Elizabeth F. Wood, Sept. 7, 1962; children: Elisa, Laurie, David. BA, U. Nebr., 1957; cert. contact lens fitter, Ohio State U., 1960; ThM, Dallas Theol. Sem., 1965; PhD, U. Tex., Arlington, 1983. Contact lens fitter Ohio State U., Columbus, 1960-61; field dir. Ctrl. Am. Mission, 1965—75; dept. chmn. Dallas Theol. Sem., 1975-92; pres. CAM Internat., Dallas, 1992-2000; coord. Spanish-lang. Doctor Minsitries program Dallas Theol. Seminary, 2001—. Mem. adv. bd. Proclamation, Inc., Dallas, 1998—, Christar, Reading, Pa., 1999—; mem. edit. bd. Evang. Missions Quar. Contbg. author: Walvoord: A Tribute, 1982, Bible Knowledge Commentary, 1983, 85, Essays in Honor of J.D. Pentecost, 1986, Devotions for Kindred Spirits, 1995, Basic Theology Applied, 1996; author: Evangelism and Missions, 2001. Lt. USN, 1957-59. Mem. Pi Epsilon Pi, Theta Xi. Republican. Avocation: travel. Home: 3504 Halifax Dr Arlington TX 76013-1909 Office: Dallas Theol Seminary 3909 Swiss Ave Dallas TX 75204 Business E-Mail: rblue@dts.edu.

BLUE, MONTE LYNN, college president; b. Ft. Worth, Feb. 25, 1945; s. Bert Leonard and Mary Lee (Cooper) B.; m. Sheryl Doris O'Connor, July 1, 1966; children: Michelle Denea, Laura Lynn. BA, North Tex. State U., 1967, MA, 1972; EdD, U. Houston, 1979. Illustrator Gen. Dynamics, Ft. Worth, 1967-71; instr. advt. art, Cen. Campus San Jacinto Jr. Coll., Pasadena, Tex., 1971-74, dist. dir., instr. media, 1975-79, dean student services, South Campus, 1979-81, dean student services, Cen. Campus, 1981-83, pres., 1983—. Bd. dirs. Deer Park Ednl. Found., 1996—; bd. dirs. Southeast Econ. Devel. Coun., 1995—, chmn. bd., 1997-98; moderator Bd. of Southmore Med. Ctr.; consumer credit counselor svc. bd. dirs., 1999-2000; spkr. numerous presentations to various comty., civic and profl. groups. Contbr. articles to profl. jours.; speaker numerous presentations to various community, civic and profl. groups. Vice chmn. bd. dirs. San Jacinto YMCA, Pasadena, 1986-87, chmn., 1987-88. Named Outstanding Alumni, Ft. Worth Ind. Sch. Dist., 1984. Mem.: Tex. Pub. Cmty. Jr. Coll. Assn., Assn. Tex. Colls. and Univs., Nat. Orgn. on Legal Problems in Edn., Am. Assn. Higher Edn., Am. Assn. Cmty. Jr. Colls., LaPorte/Bayshore C. of C. (bd. dirs. 1987—89, pres. 1989), Rotary (local pres. 1986—87), Phi Theta Kappa (hon. mem. Mu Omicron Chpt., Hall of Honor 1985). Republican. Baptist. Avocation: painting. Office: San Jacinto Coll Cen 8060 Spencer Hwy Pasadena TX 77505 Office Phone: 281-542-2000.

BLUE, VIOLET (ADA MAE JOHNSON), blogger; b. Aberdeen, Wash., Mar. 27, 1977; 2 children. Host (blog) TinyNibbles.com (Named one of Top 25 Web Celebs, Forbes mag., 2007), columnist San Francisco Chronicle, writer (news tech. blog) Techyum, corr. Geek Entertainment TV; actor: adult videos (Adult Video News Best New Starlet award, 2002). Office: care of ICM 10250 Constellation Blvd Los Angeles CA 90067*

BLUEDORN, TODD M., manufacturing executive; BS with distinction, U.S. Mil. Acad., West Point, 1985; MBA with distinction, Harvard Univ., 1992. Engagement mgr. McKinsey & Co.; dir. strategic planning United Technologies, 1995—96, v.p. N.Am. truck & trailer, Carrier Transicold, 1996—98, v.p. SE Asia, Carrier Corp., pres. Hamilton Sundstrand Indsl., pres. N.Am. HVAC, Carrier Corp., 2002—04, pres. Otis Elevator, 2004—07; CEO Lennox Internat., Richardson, Tex., 2007—. Ranger, combat engr. US Army, 1985—90. Office: Lennox Internat 2140 Lake Park Blvd Richardson TX 75080*

BLUEITT, ODIS R., financial analyst, military officer; s. Ada J. and Nathaniel Phillips (Stepfather); m. Pauletta D. Brown, 1982; children: Brittany C., Brawnlyn C., Briana C. Student, US Mil. Acad., West Point, NY, 1978—80; BS, Tex. A&M U., College Station, 1982; MBA, So. Ill. U., Edwardsville, 1989; MA, Midwestern State U., Wichita Falls, Tex., 1997. Cert. Level I acquisition ofcl. HHS, 2003. Comdr., col. USAR, Ft. Sam Houston, Tex., 1982—; asst. regional bus. dir. Tex. Dept. Human Svcs., San Antonio, 1992—96; chief fin. and bus. ops. Rolling Plains Cmty. Mental Health Mental Retardation Ctrs., Graham, Tex., 1996—99; productivity mgr. Peoples First Cmty. Bank, Panama City, Fla., 1999—2001; dir. fin. mgmt. and analysis Helen Farabee Regional Mental Health Mental Retardation Ctrs., Wichita Falls, Tex., 1998—99; adminstrv. officer NIH, Bethesda, Md., 2002—04; supevisory fin. adminstrn. and program analyst Navy Expeditionary Med. Support Command, Williamsburg, Va., 2004—06; fin. analyst US Army Med. Command, Ft. Sam Houston, 2006—. Mem. funds allocation team United Way, San Antonio, 1991—96; mentor David Robinson Found., San Antonio, 1992—96; pres. Black Profl. Leadership Network, San Antonio, 1992—94; trustee St. John Bapt. Ch., Wichita Falls, 1996—99, Mt. Calvary Bapt. Ch., Rockville, Md., 2001—03; bd. dirs. Leadership San Antonio Alumn Assn., 1994—96; agt., mem. leadership coun. Tex. A&M U. Assn. Former Students, College Station, 2002—. Col. US Army, 1982. Decorated Army Commendation medals (8) US Army, Army Res. Components Achievement medals, Army Achievement medal, Meritorious Unit commendation, SW Asia Svc. medal with 3 bronze svc. stars, Nat. Def. Svc. medal, Kuwait Liberation medal, Armed Forces Res. medal, Meritorious Svc. medal, Global War on Terrorism Svc. medal; finalist Wichita Falls Family of Yr., 1997; named Quality of Life Champion, SW Empowerment Network, 1996; named to HS All-Am. All-Academic Football Team, 1978, Leadership San Antonio, Greater San Antonio C. of C., 1993; recipient Congl. Appointment to US Mil. Acad., 1978, Cmty. Svc. Pacesetters award, Saphronia Holmes Found., 1994, awards for exemplary performance, Fed. Govt. Fellow: Am. Coll. Healthcare Execs. (cert.); mem.: Assn. Mil. Surgeons US, Res. Officer Assn. (life), Am. Soc. Mil. Comptrs. (cert. def. fin. mgr. 2006), Alpha Phi Alpha (life). Home: 24923 Birdie Ridge San Antonio TX 78258-4843 Office: US Army Med Command 2050 Worth Rd Ste 09 Fort Sam Houston TX 78234 Home Phone: 210-483-8971; Office Phone: 210-295-2881.

BLUEMER, BEVAN, acrobatics company executive; b. 1970; married. Owner, ind. cons. Arbonne Internat.; owner, dir. Ariz. Acrobatics. Prog. facilitator GEARUP, Amphitheater High Sch.; dir. campus campaign, The Vagina Monologues. Mem. Beowolf Alley Theatre. Named one of 40 Under 40, Tucson Bus. Edge, 2006. Office: The Honors College Slonaker House 1027 E 2nd St Tucson AZ 85721

BLUESTEIN, HOWARD BRUCE, meteorology educator; b. Chelsea, Mass., Oct. 8, 1948; BSEE, MIT, 1971, MSEE, 1972, MS in Meteorology, 1972, PhD in Meteorology, 1976. Asst. prof. meteorology U. Okla., Norman, 1979-83, assoc. prof., 1983-90, prof., 1990—, George Lynn Cross rsch. prof., 2004—. Vis. asst. prof. meteorology U. Okla., Norman, 1976-79. Author: Synoptic-Dynamic Meteorology in Midlatitudes, Vol. I, 1992, Vol. II, 1993, Tornado Alley, 1999. Named Okla. Prof. of Yr., Coun. Advancement and Support of Edn., 1989. Fellow Am. Meteorol. Soc. (chair severe local storms com. 1993-95, recipient Louis J. Battan Author's award, 2001, Tchg. Excellence award, 2004). Avocations: photography, folkdancing. Office: U Okla Sch Meteorology Ste 5900 120 David L Boren Blvd Norman OK 73072 Business E-Mail: hblue@ou.edu.

BLUESTEIN, VENUS WELLER, retired psychologist, educator; b. Milw., July 16, 1933; d. Richard T. and Hazel (Beard) Weller; m. Marvin Bluestein, Mar. 7, 1954. BS, U. Cin., 1956, MEd, 1959, EdD, 1966. Diplomate Am. Bd. Profl. Psychology. Psychologist-in-tng. Longview State Hosp., Cin., 1956-58; sch. psychologist Cin. Pub. Schs., 1958-65; asst. prof. psychology U. Cin., 1965-70, assoc. prof., 1970-79, prof., 1979-93, prof. emerita, 1993—, dir. sch. psychology program, 1965-70, co-dir. sch. psychology program, 1970-75, dir. undergrad. studies, 1976-91, dir. undergrad. advising, 1991-93. Cons. child psychologist. Sec., U.S. exec. com. rsch. Children's Internat. Summer Villages, 1964—68; chmn. Ohio Interuniv. Coun. Sch. Psychology, 1967. Editor Ohio Psychologist, 1961-68, co-editor, 1972-79; contbr. articles to profl. publs. Vol. Hamilton County Parks, 1982—, vol. naturalist, 1995—; vol. educator Cin. Zoo, 1982— Recipient George B. Barbour award, 1985, 20 Yrs. of Svc. award Cin. Zoo, 2002, Hamilton County Parks Dist., 2002. Mem. AAUP, APA, Nat. Assn. School Psychologists, Ohio Psychol. Assn. (citation 1972, Disting. Svc. award 1968), Southwestern Ohio Sch. Psychol. Assn., Cin. Psychol. Assn. (sec. 1961-62), Sch. Psychologists Ohio, Forum for Death Edn. and Counseling, Kappa Delta Pi, Sigma Delta Pi, Psi Chi (award for outstanding mentor 1985, award for outstanding contbns. to undergrad. psychology students 1994). Avocations: horseback riding, photography. Office: U Cin Dept Psychology Ml 376 Cincinnati OH 45221-0001

BLUESTONE, ELLEN HOPE, literature, writing, and women's studies professor, writer; b. Miami, Fla, Oct. 8, 1950; d. Alexander Herbert and Shirley Anne (Kalin) Bluestone; m. Christopher Albert Wilmot (div.); children: Jessica Dawn Wilmot, Richard Alexander Wilmot, Andrew S. H. Wilmot. BA in Art History, Wellesley Coll., Mass., 1971; MA in English, Villanova U., Pa., 1986; grad. Philosophy and Appreciation of Art, The Barnes Found., Merion, Pa.; doctoral cand. in English, Rutgers U., New Brunswick, NJ. Instr. English Harcum Coll., Bryn Mawr, Pa., 1981—82, União Cultural Brasil- U.S., Sao Paulo, Brazil, 1982—84, Harcum Coll., Bryn Mawr, Pa., 1984—86; tchg. asst. and English instr. Rutgers U., New Brunswick, NJ, 1987—92, Douglas Coll., 1991; instr. English West Chester U., Pa., 1997—99, Pa. State U., Media, 1999—2001, West Chester U., 2000—02, 2003—05, Immaculata U., 2003—04, Widener U., 2004—05; instr. English and women's studies Pa. State U., Media, 2004—06; instr. bus. and rsch. writing Strayer U., 2006—. Conf. organizer Edn. in New Communities, Washington, 1972; corp. English instr. Banco Crefisul, Sao Paulo, Brazil, 1982—84; dir. Main Line Arts Ctr., 1986; instr. tech. writing Rohm and Haas, Ft. Washington, Pa., 1999; instr. writing Am. Inst. Chartered Property Casualty Underwriters, Malvern, Pa., 2000; tchr. art history Acad. Learning in Retirement Widener U., Exton, Pa., 2004—05; tech. writer InGrid, Inc., 2006; instr. ESL Corp. Lang. Workshops, 2006—; fellow Pa. Writing and Lit. Project, 2005, Nat. Writing Project, 2005; freelance writer, 1975—; resume cons., Gladwyne, Pa., 1979—81. Juried Art Exhibition, Delaware County C.C., 2000. Jr. Great Books tchr. The Gladwyne Sch., Pa., 1983, 1987; inner city vol. Phila., 1996. Named Outstanding Faculty Mem., Interfraternity and Panhellenic Council, West Chester U., 2005; recipient Margaret Esmonde award, Grad. Sch. Arts and Scis. Villanova U., 1986. Mem.: Sisters in Crime (Del. Valley chpt.). Avocations: painting, writing, gardening, swimming, pets. Home: A 508 750 Old Lancaster Rd Berwyn PA 19312 Office Phone: 484-913-1490.

BLUFORD, GUION STEWART, JR., engineering company executive; b. Phila., Nov. 22, 1942; s. Guion Stewart and Harriet Lolita (Brice) B.; m. Linda M. Tull, Apr. 7, 1964; children: Guion Stewart, James Trevor. BS in Aerospace Engring., Pa. State U., 1964; grad., Squadron Officers Sch., 1971; MS in Aerospace Engring., Air Force Inst. Tech., 1974, PhD in Aerospace Engring., 1978; MBA, U. Houston, 1987; DSc (hon.), Fla. A&M U., Tallahassee, 1983, Tex. So. U, Houston, Va. State U., Petersburg, Morgan State U., Balt., Stevens Inst. Tech., Hoboken, NJ, Tuskegee U., Ala., Bowie State Coll., Md., Thomas Jefferson U., Phila., Chgo. State U., Georgian Ct. Coll., Drexel U., Phila., Kent State U., Ohio, Ctrl. State U., Wilberforce, Ohio. Commd. 2d lt. U.S. Air Force, 1965, advanced through grades to col., 1993, F-4C fighter pilot 12 Tactical Fighter Wing Cam Ranh Bay, Vietnam, 1966-67, T-38 instr. pilot 3630 Flying Tng. Wing Sheppard AFB, Wichita Falls, Tex., 1967-72; chief aerodynamics and airframe br. Air Force Flight Dynamics Lab., Wright-Patterson AFB, Dayton, Ohio, 1975-78; NASA astronaut Johnson Space Ctr., Houston, 1978-93; ret., 1993; v.p., gen. mgr. div. engring. svcs. NYMA Inc., Greenbelt, Md., 1993-97; v.p., gen. mgr. aerospace sector Fed. Data Corp., Bethesda, Md., 1997—2000; v.p. microgravity R&D ops. Northrup Grumman Info. Tech., Herndon, Va., 2000—02; pres. The Aerospace Tech. Group, 2002—. Decorated Air medal with 9 oak leaf clusters, Def. Superior Svc. medal, Legion of Merit, Air Force Commendation medal, Air Force Meritorious Svc. medal; named Black Engr. of Yr., 1991; named to Internat. Space Hall of Fame, 1997; recipient Mervin E. Gross award Air Force Inst. Tech., 1974, Disting. Nat. Scientist award Nat. Soc. Black Engrs., 1979, Group Achievement award, NASA, 1980, 1981, 1989, 2003, Nat. Intelligence medal of achievement, 1993, Space Flight medal, 1983, 1985, 1991, 1992, Def. Meritorious Svc. medal, 1989, 1992, 1993, NASA Disting. Svc. medal, 1994, NASA Exceptional Svc. medal, 1992, Disting. Alumni award, Pa. State U. Alumni Assn., 1983, Pa. Disting. Svc. medal, 1984, Disting. Alumni award, Air Force Inst. Tech., 2002, Univ. Houston, 2003. Fellow: AIAA (bd. dirs.); mem.: ENSCO (bd. dirs.), US Space Found. (bd. dirs.), Aerospace Corp. (trustee), Nat. Rsch. Coun. Aeronautics and Space Engring. Bd., Omicron Delta Kappa, Tau Beta Pi. Christian Scientist. Office: The Aerospace Tech Group PO Box 549 North Olmsted OH 44070-0549 Personal E-mail: gsbluford@adelphia.net.

BLUH, BONNIE, scriptwriter, actress, novelist, playwright; b. NYC, Mar. 29; d. Morris and Mary (Steinberg) Bluh; children: Craig, Kenn, Brian. Cons. Lincoln Repertory Theater, N.Y.C., 1962; dir. improvisational theater East Brunswick (N.J.) Jr. H.S., 1965; creative drama tchr., Phila., 1968-71; Emmy judge, 1989—; mentor Young Writers Inst., West Hartford, Conn., 1995—; lectr. in field. Author: Woman to Woman, 1974, Banana, 1976, The Old Speak Out, 1979, The Eleanor Roosevelt Girls, 1999, (plays) N, My Name is Nicki, 1962, Light a Candle for Charlie, 1964, Lifetime Policy, 1975, The Day God Died, 1992; co-editor: Broadway's Fabulous Fifties, 2002; actor: Many Wonder, 1989, Jesus Christ is Alive, 1990, One Woman Show, 1991, and assorted TV roles. Recipient Best Actor award, Festival Short Films, N.Y., 1990. Mem. AFTRA, Authors Guild, New Dramatists (alumna exec. com.), Dramatists Guild. Jewish.

BLUH, PAMELA M., library director, library association executive; BA, Vanderbilt U.; MA, Northwestern U.; MLS, George Peabody Coll. With Milton S. Eisenhower Libr., Johns Hopkins U.; asst. dir. tech. services U. Md. Sch. Law Libr., Balt., 1980—94, assoc. dir. tech. services and adminstrn., 1994—. Mem.: Assn. Libr. Collections and Tech. Services (pres.-elect 2006—07, pres. 2007—). Office: U Md Sch of Law 500 W Baltimore St Baltimore MD 21201-1786 Office Phone: 410-706-2736. Business E-Mail: PBluh@law.umaryland.edu.*

BLUHER, GREGORY, computer scientist, mathematician; b. Odessa, Ukraine, May 9, 1960; arrived in U.S., 1979; s. Froim and Alla (Shvetz) Blyukher; m. Antonia Rose Wilson, May 25, 1986; children: Andrew Emmanuel, Julia Elizabeth, Sarah Elena. MA in Math. with honors, Johns Hopkins U., 1983; PhD in Math., Princeton U., 1988; MS in Computer Sci., UCLA, 1992. Asst. prof. The Coll. of N.J., Trenton, 1987-88, Whittier (Calif.) Coll., 1988-89; programmer The Software Toolworks, LA, 1989-90; rschr. computer sci. dept. UCLA, 1990-92; staff programmer IBM, San Jose, 1992-93; project leader ORACLE, Redwood City, Calif., 1993-95; computer specialist Social Security Adminstrn., Balt., 1995-96; sr. computer scientist Dept. of Def., Washington, 1996-2001; IT Apps. team leader EPA, Washington, 2001—. Translator: Introduction to the Classical Theory of Abelian Functions, 1990. Interviewer alumni coun. Johns Hopkins U., Balt., 1985-89. IBM scholar, 1983. Mem. IEEE-Computer Soc. (cert. software devel. profl. 2003), Assn. Computing Machinery, Project Mgmt. Inst. (project mgmt. profl. 2004), Phi Beta Kappa. Home: PO Box 252 Simpsonville MD 21150-0252 Personal E-mail: gbluher@access4less.net.

BLUHER, JOHN H., lawyer, diversified financial services company executive; BS, JD, U. Wyo. Sr. counsel SEC, Disnv. Enforcement, 1987—92; exec. v.p. & gen. counsel AIG Sun America, 1997—2001; sr. v.p. & global chief compliance officer Prudential Securities, 2001—02; gen. counsel, corp. sec. & dir. risk mgmt. Knight Trading Group, 2002—04; sr. v.p., gen. counsel & chief pub. affairs officer Janus Capital Group, Denver, 2004—, exec. v.p., mem. exec. com. & operating com., 2005—. Office: Janus Capital Group 151 Detroit St Denver CO 80206-4923 Office Phone: 303-333-3863. Office Fax: 303-639-6662.

BLUHM, BARBARA JEAN, communications agency executive; b. Chgo., Mar. 5, 1925; d. Maurice L. and Clara (Miller) B. Student Coll. William and Mary, 1943-45; BS, U. Wis., 1947. Exec. tng. program Carson Pirie Scott & Co., Chgo., 1947-52; home economist Lever Bros. Co., Chgo., 1952-57; field rep. The Merchandising Group, Chgo., 1957-62, v.p. NYC, 1962-82, pres., 1982-87, chmn., 1987-90. Publicity chmn. James Lenox House Assn., NYC, 1980—90; vol. Venice Little Theatre; active Coll. Club of Venice, Venice Art Ctr., Venice Symphony, Friends of the Venice Libr. Mem. Venice Yacht Club, Venice Area Hist. Soc. Republican. Presbyterian. Home: 1470 Colony Pl Venice FL 34292-1550 Personal E-mail: bbluhm@iopener.net.

BLUHM, NEIL GARY, real estate company executive; b. 1938; married. BS, U. Ill.; JD, Northwestern U. CPA Ill.; bar: Ill. Ptnr. firm Mayer, Brown & Platt, Chgo., 1962-70; pres. JMB Realty Corp., Chgo., from 1970; pres., trustee JMB Realty Trust, Chgo., 1972—. Bd. dir. Chgo. Cares Inc., Urban Shopping Ctrs. Inc., 1993—2000, Northwestern U., Alzheimer's Disease & Related Disorders Assn., Whitney Mus. Am. Art; bd. trustees Art Inst. Chgo. Named one of Forbes' Richest Americans, 2006. Mem.: Bar State Ill., Real Estate Roundtable, Standard Club, Chgo. Club. Office: Urban Shopping Ctrs Inc 132 E Delaware Ste Ste 6501 Chicago IL 60611 also: JMB Realty Corporation 900 N Michigan Ave Fl 19 Chicago IL 60611-1542*

BLUHM, WILLIAM THEODORE, political scientist, educator; b. Newark, Oct. 13, 1923; s. Frederick Theodore and Charlotte Catherine (Walz) B.; m. Eleanor Elizabeth Kearns, Apr. 22, 1950; children: Catherine Elizabeth, Susanna Marie, Andrew Edward Frederick. BA, Brown U., Providence, RI, 1948; MA, Tufts U., Medford, Mass., 1949; PhD, U. Chgo., 1957. Instr. polit. sci. U. Rochester, 1952-53, asst. prof., 1957-63, assoc. prof., 1963-67, prof., 1967-92, prof. emeritus, 1993—; instr. polit. sci. Brown U., 1953-57. Cons. C.H. Beck Verlag, Munich, 1966-70. Author: Theories of the Political System, 1965, Building an Austrian Nation: The Political Integration of a Western State, 1973, Ideologies and Attitudes, 1974, Force or Freedom?: The Paradox in Modern Political Thought, 1984; co-author: The World of the Policy Analyst, 1990, 3d edit. 2002, Ethics and Public Policy, 2006; editor: The Paradigm Problem in Political Science, 1982; contbr. articles profl. jours. Served with Signal Corps AUS, 1943-46. Decorated Bronze Star Medal; U. Rochester rsch. grantee, 1963-64, 68-69; Fulbright rsch. fellow Austria, 1965-66; NSF summer grantee, 1967, 68; U. Rochester Bridging fellow, 1980-81; Nat. Endowment Humanities grantee, 1976. Mem. Am. Polit. Sci. Assn., Sigma Nu. Democrat. Roman Catholic. Office: U Rochester Dept Polit Sci Rochester NY 14627 Business E-Mail: bluh@mail.rochester.edu.

BLUM, ARTHUR, social worker, educator; b. Cleve., May 25, 1926; s. Rebecca (Pivowar) Blum; m. Lenore Sharrie Secord, Dec. 26, 1954; children: Alex, Joel. AB, Western Res. U., 1950, MS in Social Adminstrn., 1952, DSW, 1960. Group worker Cleve. Jewish Community Ctr., 1952, Cleve. Child Guidance Ctr., 1954-58; project dir. Case Western Res. U., Cleve., 1958-60, prof. social work, 1960—, Grace Longwell Coyle chair, 1987—; prof. Smith Coll., Northampton, Mass., 1961-63. Cons. Bellefaire Regional Treatment Ctr., Cleve., 1962-85, City of East Cleve., 1967-70, Jewish Welfare Fedn., Cleve., 1968-72, Fedn. Cmty. Plannning, Cleve., 1976-78, others; vis. prof. Tel Aviv U., 1971-72, 79-80. Editor: Healing Through Living, 1971, Aging and Care Giving, 1990, Innovations in Practice and Service Delivery, 1999; contbr. numerous articles to profl. jours. Sgt. U.S. Army, 1945-46, with Med. Svcs. Corp, 1952-54. Recipient Outstanding Alumnus award Case Western Res. U., 1968. Mem. AAUP, Nat. Assn. Social Workers, Coun. Social Work Edn., Assn. Group Workers. Democrat. Jewish. Avocations: camping, sailing, racquetball, gardening. Office: Case Western Res U Sch Applied Social Scis Univ Circle Cleveland OH 44106

BLUM, BARBARA DAVIS, investor; b. Hutchinson, Kans. d. Roy C. and Jo (McKinnon) Davis; children: Devin, Hunter, Ragan, Davis. BA, Fla. State U., 1960, MSW, 1961. Founder, ptnr. Mid-Suffolk Ctr. for Psychotherapy, Hauppage, L.I., NY, 1965-67; v.p. Restaurant Assocs. Ga., Inc., Atlanta, 1967-75; dep. adminstr. U.S. EPA, Washington, 1977-81; mem. Pres.'s Interagy. Coordinating Coun.; chair, pres., CEO Abigail Adams Nat. Bancorp and Adams Nat. Bank, Washington, 1983-98; CEO BDB Investment Partnership, 1998—; chair MainSt. Bank, 2003—. Chair U.S./Japan Environ. Agreement, 1977—81; head 1st U.S. Environ. Del. to China, 1978; chmn. Environ. Policy Inst., 1981—84; sr. advisor UN Environ. Program, 1981—84; pres. UN Univ. Peace, 1986—89; chair emeritus Ctr. for Policy Alternatives; trustee Fed. City Coun., 1988—99; nat. adv. bd. U.S. SBA, 1993—2001; chmn. D.C. Econ. Devel. Fin. Corp., 1986—2002. Del. UN Mid Decade Conf. on Women, 1980; Presdl. appointee trustee and treas. Inst. Am. Indian Art, 1992—; founder, chmn. Leadership Washington, 1989—; trustee, treas. Southeastern U., 1998—2007; trustee, chmn. investment com. DC Retirement Bd.; bd. chmn. Main St. Bank; dep. dir., trustee, treas. Carter-Mondale U.S. Presdl. campaign, 1976; dir. Carter-Mondale Transition Team, Washington, 1976—77; panelist Clinton-Gore Econ. Conf., Little Rock and Atlanta; bd. dirs., chmn. performance com. Kaiser Found. Health Plan Mid Atlantic, 1989—2004; bd. dirs., chair compensation com. Kaiser Found. Health Plan, Inc., 2001—05; bd. dirs., chair exec. com. Kaiser Found. Hosp., 2002—04; bd. dirs., treas. Stimpson Ctr., 2002—; bd. dirs. Smart Growth Am., 2006—. Decorated comdr.'s cross Order of Merit W. Ger.; recipient Disting. Svc. award Federally Employed Women, Spl. Conservation award Nat. Wildlife Fedn., Orgn. of Yr. award Ga. Wildlife Fedn., 1974, Disting. Svc. award Americans for Indian Opportunity; named Bus. Woman of Yr. Nat. Assn. Bus. Women, Leukemia Soc., Assn. Women Contractors, Vol. of Yr., Leadership Greater Washington, 2006. Mem. Washington Women's Forum, Internat. Women's Forum, Cosmos Club. Democrat. Home Phone: 202-251-2020; Office Phone: 202-332-0601. Personal E-mail: bdavisblum@verizon.net.

BLUM, BRADLEY D., former food service executive; BA, Denison U., Ohio, 1976; MA, Northweatern U., 1978. Mktg. asst. Betty Crocker General Mills, 1978, v.p. mktg. Cereal Ptnrs. Worldwide, 1990—94; sr. v.p. mktg. then pres. Olive Garden N.Am., 1994—96; exec. v.p., mem. bd. of dirs., vice chmn. Darden Restaurants Inc., 1997—2002; CEO Burger King, Corp., 2003—04. Chmn. Economic Devel. Bd., City of Winter Park, Fla. Bd. trustees Atlantic Ctr. for Arts, Fla.; adv. bd. Sun Trust Bank. Recipient Operator of the Year, Multi-Unit Foodservice, 2000. Avocations: skiing, tennis, race car driving.

BLUM, DAVID J., former editor-in-chief; b. Queens, NY, Dec. 25, 1955; m. Terri Minsky; children: Sam, Annie. BA, U. Chgo., 1977. Staff reporter Wall St. Jour., NYC, 1979—83; assoc. editor Esquire, NYC, 1983—85; contbg. editor New York, 1985—92; contbr. NY Times Mag., 1995—2000; TV critic NY Sun, 2002—; editor-in-chief Village Voice, NYC, 2006—07; editor-in-chief, editorial dir. cmty. newspaper group NY Press, NYC, 2007—. Adj. prof. Columbia U. Grad. Sch. Journalism, NYC, 2002—. Author: Flash in the Pan: The Life and Death of an American Restaurant, 1992, Tick.Tick.Tick.: The Long Life & Turbulent Times of 60 Minutes, 2002. Office: Manhattan Media NY Press 79 Madison Ave 16th Floor New York NY 10016 E-mail: dblum@villagevoice.com.*

BLUM, ELIZABETH DIAN, history professor; b. Pensacola, Fla., Jan. 26, 1970; d. Kenneth Dale Oden and Mildred Larraine Crayton; m. Sean Patrick Blum, June 4, 1994; 1 child, Aidan Gabriel. BA, U. Tex., Austin, 1991; MA, U. Houston, 1997, PhD, 2000. Asst. prof. Troy U., Ala., 2000—06, assoc. prof., 2006—. Acting archivist Troy U., Troy, Ala., 2001—. Author: Instructor's Manual for The African-American Odyssey; contbg. author: To Love the Wind and the Rain, 2006, Energy Intensive Metropolis, 2007, The Influence of Star Trek on Television, Film & Culture, 2007, Pollution A to Z. Cons. SE Ala. Regional In-service Ctr., 2000—06; bd. advisors Ala. Hist. Commn., 2004; vol. leader Montgomery County 4-H, Ala., 2004—05; vol. Elmore County 4-H, Ala., 2005—06, Pinchona Pony Club, Ala., 2006—. Grantee Chancellor's Symposium on So. History, Ala. Humanities Found., 2003. Mem.: Am. Soc. Environ. History, Am. Hist. Assn. (Rachel Carson prize com. 2003). Avocations: horseback riding, quilting. Home: 2344 Wentworth Dr Montgomery AL 36106 Office: Troy Univ Dept of History Troy AL 36082 Home Phone: 334-396-8751; Office Phone: 334-670-5663. Office Fax: 334-670-3515. Business E-Mail: sblum@troy.edu.

BLUM, EVA TANSKY, lawyer; b. Pitts., July 29, 1949; d. Harry and Jeanette N. Tansky; 1 child. BA, U. Pitts., 1970, JD, 1973. Bar: Pa. 1973. Atty. U.S. Dept. Commerce, Washington, 1973-76, U.S. Air, Washington, 1976-77; sr. v.p., dir. cmty. devel. PNC Fin. Group, Pitts., 1990—, chair PNC Found., 2002—, dir. PNC Grow Up Great, 2003—. Mem. com. Pitts. Health and Welfare Planning Assn., 1985-89; bd. dirs. Family Health Coun., Pitts., 1987-94, Forbes Health Found., 1992-96, WQED, Pitts., 1994—, U. Pitts. Alumni Assn., 1992-98, 2000—, The Ellis Sch., 1996-2002; bd. dirs., sec. ARC Western Pa. chpt. 1992-94; trustee Am. Jewish Com., Pitts., 1977—. Mem. ABA, Pa. Bar Assn., Allegheny County Bar Assn. Office: PNC Fin Svcs Group One PNC Plaza 249 5th Ave Pittsburgh PA 15222-2709 Office Phone: 412-762-2748. Business E-Mail: eva.blum@pnc.com.

BLUM, GARY BERNARD, lawyer; b. Brighton, Eng., Feb. 1, 1946; came to U.S., 1947; s. Peter and Alice (Fenchel) B.; m. Marsha Weinberg, Sept. 9, 1973; children: Annette, Jesse, Alyce. BA, U. Colo., 1968, JD, 1971. Bar: Colo. 1971, U.S. Dist. Ct. Colo. 1971, U.S. Ct. Appeals (10th cir.) 1971, U.S. Supreme Ct. 1985. Dep. pub. defender State of Colo., Denver, 1971-74, asst. atty. gen., 1975-78; shareholder Long & Jaudon P.C., Denver, 1978—2001; dir. Silver & DeBoskey P.C., 2001—. Lectr. law U. Colo.; mem. grievance com. Colo. Supreme Ct., 1988-93, 99—, mem. civil justice com.; mem. com. on lawyer conduct Fed. Ctr., 1995—, chair, 2000—; mem. Faculty Fed. of Advocates, bd. dirs. 2001—. Named Super Lawyer in health care, Colo., 2006; named one of Best Lawyers in Am. in alternative dispute resolution and health care law, 2005—07; recipient Super Lawyer in health care, Colo., 2007. Mem. ATLA, Colo. Bar Assn. (past chmn. ethics com., bd. govs. alt. dispute resolution sect., litigation sect. health law sect.), Denver Bar Assn., Colo. Def. Lawyers Assn., Am. Bd. Trial Advocates (pres. 2006—07), Am. Health Lawyers Assn., Am. Arbitration Assn. Democrat. Jewish. Avocations: jogging, reading, skiing, tennis. Office: Silver and DeBoskey 1801 York St Denver CO 80206 Office Phone: 303-399-3000. Business E-Mail: blumg@s-d.com.

BLUM, GERALD HENRY, retired retail executive; b. San Francisco, 1926; s. Abe and Mildred B.; children: Shelly, Todd, Ryan, Derek. AB, Stanford U., Calif., 1950. Mdse. trainee Emporium, San Francisco, 1950—51; with Gottschalks Inc. (formerly E. Gottschalk & Co., Inc.), Fresno, Calif., 1951—98; v.p. Gottschalks Inc., Fresno, 1954—63, exec. v.p., 1963—82, pres. and vice chmn., 1982—94, ret., 1995, bd. dirs. Bd. dirs. Fresno Conv. Bur., 1954—, pres., 1985-87; bd. dirs. BBB, Fresno, 1954-77, Blue Cross, Calif. 1972-85; chmn. C.A.R.E., Fresno County, 1957—, Eagle Scout Awards Banquet, 1993, Calif. State U. Bus. Coun., Fresno, 1997-98; adv. com. Fresno County Arts Ctr., 1982-85, bd. dirs., 1958-66, v.p. 1961, 88-94; mem. Area VII Calif. Vocat. Edn. Com., 1972-75, Mayor's Bi-Racial Com., 1968-69; founding v.p. Jr. Achievement, Fresno County, 1957-63; bd. dirs. Fresno Boys Club, 1958-62, Ctrl. Calif. Employers Coun., 1956-62, treas. 1958; bd. dirs. Fresno Philharm. Orch., 1954-58, Salvation Army, Fresno, 1956-67, Youth Edn. Svc., 1956-57, Fresno County Taxpayers Assn., 1954, San Joaquin Valley Econ. Edn. Project, 1953; bd. dirs., bus. adv. coun. Fresno City Coll., 1955-57; trustee Valley Children's Hosp., 1955-57, United Crusade, Fresno, 1952-62; adv. bd. Liberty Mut. Ins. Co., 1990-2001. Recipient Disting. Svc. award Fresno Jaycees, 1959; winner World's Championship Domino Tournament, 1969, 86, 88. Mem. Nat. Retail Fedn. (dir. 1978-94), Calif. Retailers Assn. (dir. 1964-94), Fresno C. of C. (dir. county, city 1955-57, Boss of Yr., Jr. C. of C. 1980), Retail Mmgt. Inst., U. Santa Clara (dir. 1986-98), Nat. Secs. Assn. (Boss of Yr. 1978), Fresno County Stanford U. Alumni Assn. (pres. 1952), Pres. Club of Calif. State U., Rotary (v.p. Fresno club 1962), Univ. Sequoia Sunnyside Club, Downtown Club (Fresno, pres. 1978). Personal E-mail: gblum2020@aol.com.

BLUM, JACOB JOSEPH, physiologist, educator; b. Bklyn., Oct. 3, 1926; s. Paul and Anna (Brown) B.; m. Ruth Marsey, June 3, 1960; children: Mark, Douglas, Lisa, Laura. BA, NYU, 1947; MS, U. Chgo., 1950, PhD, 1952. Mem. staff Naval Med. Rsch. Inst., Bethesda, Md., 1953-56; chief biophysics sect. gerontology br. NIH, Balt., 1958-62; prof. physiology Duke U., Durham, NC, 1962—, James B. Duke prof., 1980-97, James B. Duke prof. emeritus, 1997—. With AUS, 1945-46. Merck postdoctoral fellow, 1952, Guggenheim fellow, 1969, Fogarty sr. internat. fellow, 1992. Mem. Am. Physiol. Soc., Soc. Protozoologists (pres. 1991). Home: 16 Stoneridge Cir Durham NC 27705 Office Phone: 919-684-6937. Business E-Mail: j.blum@cellbio.duke.edu.

BLUM, JOAN KURLEY, not-for-profit fundraiser, marketing executive, consultant; b. Palm Beach, Fla., July 27, 1926; d. Nenad Daniel and Eva (Milos) Kurley; m. Robert C. Blum, Apr. 15, 1967 (dec. Apr. 2001); children: Christopher Alexander, Martha Jane, Louisa Joan. BA, U. Wash., 1948. Cert. fund raising exec. U.S. dir. Inst. Mediterranean Studies, Berkeley, Calif., 1962-65; devel. officer U. Calif., Berkeley, 1965-67; pres. Blum Assocs., Fund-Raising Cons., San Anselmo, Calif., 1967-92; ptnr. Philmark Australia, 1980—2001; pres. The Blums of San Francisco, 1992-2001, ret., 2001. Mem. faculty U. Calif. Extension, Inst. Fund Raising, S.W. Inst. Fund-Raising U. Tex., U. San Francisco, U.K. Vol. Movement Group, London, Australasian Inst. Fund Raising. Contbr. numerous articles to profl. jours. Mem. Marin County Civil Grand Jury, 2004—05. Recipient Golden Addy award Am. Advt. Fedn., Silver Mailbox award Direct Mail Mktg. Assn., Best Ann. Giving Time-Life award, others; decorated commdr. Sovereign Order St. Stanislas. Mem. Nat. Soc. Fund-Raising Execs. (dir.), Nat. Assn. of Hosp. Devel., Women Emerging, Rotary (pres., 2007—), Fund Raising Inst. (Australia), Tahoe Yacht Club. Office: 202 Evergreen Dr Kentfield CA 94904-2708 Business E-Mail: sugarblum@aol.com.

BLUM, JOHN CURTIS, agricultural economist; b. Terryville, Conn., July 5, 1915; s. John A. and Marion D. (Curtis) B.; m. Mable L. Brooks, Oct. 21, 1939; children— Joanne M. Blum Kraft, John Curtis, Nancy J. BS, U. Conn., Storrs, 1937, MS, 1939; postgrad., U. Wis., Madison, 1941, US Dept. Agr. Grad. Sch., Washington, 1946, Indsl. Coll. Armed Forces, 1965—66. With Dept. Agr., 1939-75; asst. dir. dairy div. Agrl. Marketing Service, 1960-61, dir. div., 1961-63; economist Office of Adminstr., 1963-64, asst. dept. adminstr., 1964-67, dep. adminstr., 1967-74, asso. adminstr., 1974-75; economist E.A. Jaenke & Assos., Inc., Washington, 1975-83. Violinist Fairfax Symphony Orch., Va., 1957-95, bd. dir., 1957-70, pres., 1959-61, treas., 1965-67; violinist McLean Symphony, Va., 1995—, Reston Cmty. Orch., Va., 1998—; dist. dir. North Va. dist. PTA, 1961-63; treas. Va. Congress Parents and Tchrs., 1963-65, regional v.p., 1965-67, chmn. extension com. 1967-69, budget chmn., 1969-71, bd. mgrs., 1961-71. Lt. (j.g.) USNR, 1944-46, PTO. Mem. Am. Agr. Econ. Assn., Grange. Home: Apt 1310 20510 Falcons Landing Cir Sterling VA 20165-7596

BLUM, JOHN MORTON, historian, educator; b. NYC, Apr. 29, 1921; s. Morton Gustave and Edna (LeVino) B.; m. Pamela Louise Zink, June 28, 1944; children: Pamela, Ann, Thomas Tyler. AB, Harvard U., 1943, MA, 1947, PhD, 1950, LLD (hon.), 1980; MA, Cambridge U., Eng., 1963; DHL (hon.), Trinity Coll., 1970; LLD (hon.), Colgate U., 1978. Research assoc., then asst. prof. history, assoc. prof. M.I.T., 1948-57; prof. history Yale U., 1957-91, ret., 1991; Pitt prof. Cambridge U., 1963-64; Harmsworth prof. Oxford U., 1976-77. Author: Joe Tumulty and the Wilson Era, 1951, The Republican Roosevelt, 1954, Woodrow Wilson and the Politics of Morality, 1956, From the Morgenthau Diaries, Vol. I, 1959, Vol. II, 1965, Vol. III, 1967, Yesterday's Children, 1959, The Promise of America, 1966, Roosevelt and Morgenthau, 1970, V Was for Victory, 1976, The Progressive Presidents, 1980, Years of Discord, 1991, Liberty Justice Order, 1993, A Life with History, 2004, An Old Blue Corpse, 2005; assoc. editor: (with Elting E. Morison) Letters of Theodore Roosevelt (8 vols.), 1951-54; editor: The National Experience, 1963, The Price of Vision, 1973; Public Philosopher, 1985. Trustee Buckingham Sch., 1954-56, Hotchkiss Sch., 1964-70; mem. Andover Alumni Council, 1957-60. Served from ensign to lt. USNR, 1943-46. Harvard U. fellow, 1970-79. Mem. Am. Acad. Arts and Scis., Mass. Hist. Soc., Century Assn., Phi Beta Kappa. Home: 313 St Ronan St New Haven CT 06511-2327

BLUM, LENORE, mathematician, computer scientist, educator; m. Manuel Blum; 1 child, Avrim. B in Math., Simmons Coll., 1963; PhD, MIT, 1968; LLD Mills Coll. (hon.), 1999. Postdoctoral fellow, lectr. U. Calif., Berkeley, 1968—73; vis. asst. prof. Mills Coll., Oakland, Calif., 1973—74, founder, head and co-head, math. and computer sci. dept., 1974—87, Lettis-Villard Rsch. prof., 1979—96; vis. prof. CUNY, 1984—85; vis. scientist IBM TJ Watson Rsch. Ctr., NY, 1987; rsch. scientist, theory group Internat. Computer Sci. Inst., Berkeley, 1988—99; dep. dir. Math. Sciences Rsch. Inst., Berkeley, 1992—96; vis. prof. City Univ. Hong Kong, 1996—98; disting. career prof. computer sci. Carnegie Mellon U., Pitts., 1999—. Co-dir. NSF-ITRx ALADDIN Ctr. (ALgorithm ADaptation Dissemination and INtegration); co-PI Mills Summer Math. Inst.; faculty advisor Women@SCS (Sch. Computer Sci.), Carnegie Mellon Univ.; mem. President's Diversity Adv. Coun.; spkr. in field. Author (with F. Cucker, M. Shub, S. Smale): Complexity and Real Computation, 1997; contbr. articles to profl. jours. Founder Math/Sci. Network and its Expanding Your Horizons Confs., co-dir., 1975—81. Recipient Career Advancement award, NSF, 1983. Fellow: AAAS (chair math. sect. 1998—99); mem.: Am. Math. Soc. (v.p., coun. 1990—92), Math/Sci. Network, Assn. for Women in Math. (pres. 1975—78, founding mem.), Math. Scis. Rsch. Inst. (co-dir. 1975—81), Internat. Computer Sci. Inst. Achievements include being well-known for work in increasing the participation of girls and women in mathematics and scientific fields. Office: Dept Computer Sci Wean 4105 Carnegie Mellon Univ Pittsburgh PA 15213-3891 Office Phone: 412-268-8139. Office Fax: 412-268-5576. E-mail: lblum@cs.cmu.edu.*

BLUM, LISA CARRIE, social worker, researcher; b. NY, Nov. 11, 1961; BA magna cum laude, Douglass Coll., 1983; MSW, Rutgers U., 1985, PhD, 1996. LCSW Bd. of Social Work Examiners, N.J., 1994. Clin. program coord. Women Aware, Inc. Abused Women's Svcs., New Brunswick, NJ, 1986—94; planning rsch. cons. Atlanta (Ga.) Jewish Fedn., 1994—98; grants evaluator Friedman Supporting Found., Atlanta, 1996—98; coord. outpatient geriatric svcs. Jewish Family and Vocat. Svc., Edison, NJ, 2000—03; trainer Women Aware, Inc. Abused Women's Svcs, 2001—; sr. program coord. Highland Park Sr./Youth Ctr., NJ, 2004—. Adj. faculty Sch. Social Work Rutgers U., New Brunswick, 1985—91; cons. in field. Adv. bd. Project SPAN, Edison, 1989—; commr. Middlesex County Commn. on Missing and Exploited Children, New Brunswick, 1990—92; mem. Middlesex County Child/Adult Protection Coalition, New Brunswick, 1986—94. Grantee, Fahs-Beck Found., 1992; scholar, Rutgers U., 1986—89. Mem.: NASW, N.J. Coalition Battered Women, Nat. Coun. Family Rels., Phi Beta Kappa. Achievements include development of National Model for Domestic Violence Response Teams now mandated under New Jersey Law. Office: Highland Park Sr Youth Ctr 220 S Sixth Ave Highland Park NJ 08904

BLUM, MANUEL, computer science educator; b. Caracas, Venezuela, Apr. 26, 1938; s. Bernardo and Ernestine (Horowitz) B.; m. Lenore Epstein, July 30, 1961; 1 child, Avrim. BS in Elec. Engring, MIT, 1959, MS, 1961, PhD in Math., 1964. Research asst. to research assoc. Research Lab. Electronics, MIT, 1960-65; asst. prof. dept. math. MIT, 1966-68; vis. asst. prof. to prof. dept. elec. engring. and computer scis. U. Calif.-Berkeley, 1968—, chmn. for computer sci., 1977-80, faculty rsch. lectr., 1995—; Bruce Nelson prof. computer sci., Univ. prof. Carnegie Mellon U., Pitts. Contbr. articles to profl. jours. Sloan Found. fellow, 1972-73.A.M. Turing awd, Assn. Computing Machinery. 1995. Fellow AAAS, IEEE, NAE, Nat. Acad. Scis., Am. Acad. Arts and Scis.; mem. Assn. for Computing Machinery (A.M. Turing award 1995), Sigma Xi (Monie A. Ferst award 1991). Home: 4770 Bayard St Pittsburgh PA 15213-1766 Office: Computer Sci Dept Carnegie Mellon U 5000 Forbes Ave Pittsburgh PA 15213-3890 Home Phone: 412-687-8730; Office Phone: 412-268-3742. E-mail: mblum@cs.cmu.edu.

BLUM, MELVIN, chemical company executive, researcher; b. NYC, Jan. 8, 1936; s. Paul Henry and Dora (Schneiderman) B.; m. Paula Linda Weiss, July 11, 1969; 1 child, Lara Joyce. BS, Columbia U., 1957, MA, 1959; PhD, Duke U., 1964, Burlington Inst., 1970. Pres. Atomergic Chemetals Corp., Farmingdale, NY, 1963—2004, Burlington Sci. Corp., Farmingdale, 1974—2004; v.p. Am. Roland Chem. Co., Farmingdale, NY, 1984—2004; mng. dir. Viachem LLC, East Farmingdale, NY, 2004—. Author: Handbook of Rare Elements, Encyclopedia of Chemical Technology, Strategic Metal Investments, (mag.) DMSO Reporter. Capt. USAFR, 1959-65. Mem. Am. Chem. Soc., Am. Soc. Metals, N.Y. Acad. Scis., Chemists Club. Home: 1385 Lyon Pl Wantagh NY 11793-2919 Office Phone: 631-752-8700. E-mail: mblum@optonline.net, melblum@gmail.com.

BLUM, PAUL, retail executive; b. 1960; V.p., prin. The Blum Cos., 1982—90; with Kenneth Cole Prodns., Inc., 1990—2006, sr. v.p., 1992—96, exec. v.p., 1996—98, CEO, 1998—2002, pres., 2002—06; CEO David Yurman, Inc., NYC, 2006—. Office: Yurman Design Inc 24 Vestry St New York NY 10013 Office Phone: 877-226-1400, 212-896-1550.

BLUM, RICHARD HOSMER ADAMS, foundation administrator, educator; b. Ft. Wayne, Ind., Oct. 7, 1927; s. Hosmer and Imogene (Heino) B. AB with honors magna cum laude, San Jose State Coll., 1948; PhD, Stanford U., 1951. Rsch. dir. Calif. Med. Assn., San Francisco, 1956-58, San Mateo County (Calif.) Mental Health Service, San Mateo, 1958-60; lectr. Sch. Criminology, U. Calif., Berkeley, 1960-62; mem. faculty Stanford (Calif.) U., 1962-78, prof. dept. psychology, 1970-75, prof. dept. gynecology and obstetrics, 1982-97; mem. faculty Stanford (Calif.) U. Law Sch., 1975-78; chmn. bd. Am. Lives Endowment, Portola Valley, Calif., 1979—. Chmn. Internat. Rsch. Group on Drug Legis. and Programs, Geneva, 1969—78; pres. Bio-Behavioral Rsch. Group, Inc., Palo Alto, 1964—87; owner, operator Shingle Mill Ranch, 1964—; vis. fellow Wolfson Coll. U. Cambridge, 1984; vis. prof. social and polit. sci. U. Cambridge, 1997—98; dir. ethics program World Jurist Assn./World Peace Through Law Ctr., Washington, 2000—; dep. chmn. Commn. for the World Equity Ct.; prof. St. Josephs of Arimanthea Theol. Sem., Berkeley, Calif., China U. Polit. Sci. and Law, Beijing; officer Superior Ctr. Conservator for Health Care; guest prof. Northeastern U., Changchun; disting. vis. prof. Dalian U., China; pres. Knightsbridge Castle Found. Author: 29 books. Trustee Palace Mus. of the Last Emperor Puye, Manchuria, China. With U.S. Army, 1951-53, Korea. Decorated Bronze Star; recipient APA Presdl. citation. Fellow APHA (coun. sr. advisors), AAAS, Am. Psychol. Soc., Soc. Advanced Legal Studies (hon., life); mem. Archaeol. Inst. Am., Sigma Xi, Cosmos Club, Athenaeum Club, San Francisco Univ. Club. Unitarian. Home: PO Box 620482 Woodside CA 94062-0482 Office Phone: 650-529-1282.

BLUM, ROBERT M., lawyer; b. NYC, July 12, 1954; BS cum laude, Northwestern U., 1975; JD, Duke U., 1978. Bar: Calif. 1978, US Dist. Ct. (No. Dist.) Calif., US Dist. Ct. (Ea. Dist.) Calif., US Dist. Ct. (So. Dist.) Calif. Ptnr. Thelen, Marrin, Johnson & Bridges, San Francisco; gen. counsel Thelen Reid & Priest LLP, San Francisco. Article & notes editor Adminstrv. Law Issue, Duke Law Jour., 1977—78; contbr. articles to profl. jours., chapters to books. Office: Thelen Reid & Priest LLP 101 Second St Ste 1800 San Francisco CA 94105-3601 Office Phone: 415-369-7277. Office Fax: 415-371-1211. Business E-Mail: rblum@thelenreid.com.

BLUM, ROBIN N., elementary school educator; b. Reading, Pa., Dec. 23, 1953; d. Richard E. and Ruth N. Latch; m. Robert C. Latch, Oct. 9, 1976; children: Geoffrey R., Pamela N. BS, Kutztown U., Pa., 1975. Cert. tchr. secondary edn. Pa., 1975. Tchr. Gov. Mifflin Sch. Dist., Shillington, Pa., 1999—. Advisor Gay-Straight Student Alliance Club. Mem.: Internat. Reading Assn., Nat. Coun. Tchrs. English. Independent. Avocation: travel. Home: 25 Matthew Dr Sinking Spring PA 19608 Office: Governor Mifflin Sch Dist 10 S Waverly St Shillington PA 19607 Home Phone: 610-777-4102; Office Phone: 610-775-5089. Business E-Mail: rblum@gmsd.k12.pa.us.

BLUM, SAMUEL, retired research scientist; b. Aug. 1920; BS Chemistry, Rutgers U., 1942, PhD Phys. Chemistry, 1950; cert. meterology, weather forecasting, UCLA. Ret. rsch. scientist IBM Watson Rsch. Ctr., 1990. Active alumni work Rutgers U. Mem. U.S. Navy. Recipient Nat. Inventors Hall of Fame, 2002. Achievements include invention of Far Ultraviolet Surgical and Dental Procedures. Avocations: travel, gardening.

BLUM, SCOTT ALLEN, Internet company executive; b. San Jose, Calif., Jan. 3, 1964; m. Audrey Blum; 2 children. Student, Saddleback CC. Founder MicroBanks, 1985, Pinnacle Micro, 1987, Buy.com, Inc., Aliso Viejo, Calif., 1997, chmn., CEO, 1997—99; mng. ptnr. Think Tank Holdings, LLC, Jackson, Wyo., 1999—. Bd. dirs. TechSpace. Office: Buy dot com Inc 85 Enterprise Ste 100 Aliso Viejo CA 92656 also: ThinkTank Holdings LLC PO Box 8378 Jackson WY 83002 Office Phone: 949-389-2000. Office Fax: 949-389-2800.

BLUM, STEVEN (H. STEVEN BLUM), career military officer; b. 1946; BA in History, U. Balt., 1968; MS in Social Sci., Morgan State Coll., 1973; grad., Army War Coll., 1989. Joined Army Nat. Guard, 1971, advanced through grades to lt. gen., 2003; S-3, detachment B-3, Company B, 19th Spl. Forces Group (Airborne) 1st Spl. Forces Md. Army Nat. Guard, 1971—72, air ops. officer, hdqrs. detachment, 5th Spl. Forces Bn. 20th Spl. Forces Group, 1972—74, Bn. S-2, hdqrs. detachment, 1974—76, recruiting & retention officer, 1976—77, 1978, comdr. spl. forces ops. detachment-A, Company B, 5th Spl. Forces Bn., 20th Spl. Forces, 1977—78, spl. forces ops. officer command & control, 1978—81, marksmanship program adminstr. hdqrs., 1981, tng. adminstr. hdqrs. detachment, 1981—82, dir. plans, ops. & tng. hdqrs., 1982—84, mobilization ops. officer hdqrs. state area command, 1984—85, bn. comdr. hdqrs. 1st Bn., 115th Inf., 29th Inf. Divsn., 1985—87, exec. officer hdqrs. 3rd Brigade, 29th Inf. Divsn., 1987—88, ops. and tng. officer hdqrs. State Area Command, 1988—89, dir. plans, ops. and tng. hdqrs., 1989—92, comdr. 3rd Brigade, 29th Inf. Divsn., 1992—95, asst. divsn. comdr. 29th Inf. Divsn., 1996—99; commdg. gen. 29th Inf. Divsn. Va. Army Nat. Guard, 1999—2001, 2002; commdg. gen. Multi Nat. Divsn. SFOR-10, Operation Joint Force Bosnia-Herzegovina, 2001—02; chief of staff US No. Command, Peterson AFB, Colo., 2002—03; chief Nat. Guard Bur., Arlington, Va., 2003—. Decorated Def. Superior Svc. medal, Legion of Merit with 2 bronze Oak Leaf Clusters, Army Meritorious Svc. medal with 2 bronze Oak Leaf Clusters, Army Commendation medal with 1 bronze Oak Leaf cluster, Army Achievement medal with 1 bronze Oak Leaf Cluster, Army Res. Component Achievement medal with 1 silver Oak Leaf Cluster, Nat. Def. Svc. medal with bronze star device, Army Forces Expeditionary medal, Armed Forces Res. medal, NATO medal. Office: Nat Guard Bur 1411 Jefferson Davis Hwy Arlington VA 22202-3231*

BLUM, TERRY CHRISTINE, dean; b. Bklyn., Dec. 25, 1953; m. Paul M. Roman; children: Luke, Faith Elisabeth. BA in Sociology with honors, Bklyn. Coll., 1976; MA, Columbia U., 1978, MPhil, 1980, PhD, 1982. Asst. prof. Dept. Sociology, adj. prof. biostatistics and edpidemology Sch. Pub. Health and Tropical Medicine, Tulane U., 1982—86; asst. prof. orgnl. behavior and human resource mgmt. Ga. Inst. Tech. Coll. Mgmt., 1986—88, assoc. prof., 1988—92, prof., 1992—99, dir. Ctr. Entrepreneurship and New Venture Devel., 1996—2000, Tedd Munchak chair in entrepreneurship, 1999—, dean, 1999—2006, dir. Inst. Leadership and Entrepreneurship, 2006—. Mem. Prevention and Epidemiology Initial Review Group Nat. Inst. Alcohol Abuse and Alcoholism, 1988—92; mem. cmty. prevention and control study section NIH, 1997—2000. Grantee, Nat. Inst. Alcohol Abuse and Alcoholism, 1982, 1983, 1987, 1988, Nat. Inst. Drug Abuse, 1991, 1999, NIH, 1993, 1994, Coleman Found., 1999; special opportunities grant, Whitaker Found., 1998. Office: Inst Leadership and Entrepreneurship Ga Inst Tech 800 W Peachtree St NW Atlanta GA 30332-0520 Office Phone: 404-894-4924. Office Fax: 404-894-1517. Business E-Mail: terry.blum@ile.gatech.edu.*

BLUM, WILLIAM GEORGE, hematologist, clinical researcher educator; b. Lynn, Mass., Dec. 16, 1970; m. Kristie Ann Uber, May 21, 2001. BS, U. Notre Dame, 1993; MD, Med. Coll. Ga., Augusta, 1997. Cert. in hematology and med. oncology Nat. Bd. Med. Examiners, in internal medicine Nat. Bd. Med. Examiners. Asst. prof. medicine Ohio State U., Columbus, 2003—. Office: Ohio State Univ B310 Starling Loving 320 W 10th Ave Columbus OH 43210 Office Phone: 614-293-9808.

BLUMBERG, BARUCH SAMUEL, research scientist, educator; b. NYC, July 28, 1925; s. Meyer and Ida (Simonoff) B.; m. Jean Liebesman, Apr. 4, 1954; children: Anne, George, Jane, Noah. BS, Union Coll., Schenectady, NY, 1946; MD, Columbia U., 1951; PhD, Oxford U., Eng., 1957; 22 hon. doctoral degrees. Intern, then resident Columbia divsn. Bellevue Hosp., NYC, 1951—53; fellow in medicine Columbia-Presbyn. Med. Ctr., NYC, 1953—55; chief geog. medicine and genetics sect. NIH, Bethesda, Md., 1957—64; assoc. dir. clin. rsch. Fox Chase Cancer Ctr., Phila., 1964—86, v.p. population oncology, 1986—89, Fox Chase disting. scientist, 1989—, sr. advisor to pres., 1989—; univ. prof. medicine and anthropology U. Pa., 1977—; master Balliol Coll., Oxford, England, 1989—94; dir. NASA Astrobiology Inst., Moffett Field, Calif., 1999—2002; sr. adv. to the adminstr. NASA Hdqs., Washington, 2000—01; disting. scientist NASA Fundamental Space Biology, 2003—04. George Eastman vis. prof. Oxford U., 1983—84; Raman vis. prof. Indian Inst. Scis., Bangalore, India, 1986; Ashland vis. prof. U. Ky., Lexington, 1986—87; Lee Kuan Yew disting. vis. prof. Nat. U. Singapore, 1992; vis. prof. U. Otago, Dunedin, New Zealand, 1994; James W. McLaughlin vis. prof. U. Tex.; vis. prof. Med. Ctr. Stanford U.; sr. advisor to pres. Fox Chase Cancer Ctr., 1989—; fellow Ctr. Advanced Study Behavioral Scis. Stanford U., Larry Lokey disting. vis. prof. human biology. Contbr. articles to profl. jours. Lt. USNR, 1943—46. Recipient Albion O. Berstein, M.D. award Med. Soc. State of N.Y., 1969, Grand Sci. award Phi Lambda Kappa, 1972, Ann. award Eastern Pa. br. Am. Soc. Microbiology, 1972, Passano award Williams & Wilkens Co., 1974, Modern Medicine Disting. Achievement award, 1975, Internat. award Gairdner Found., 1975, Karl Landsteiner Meml. award Am. Assn. Blood Banks, 1975, Nobel prize in physiology or medicine, 1976, Scopus award Am. Friends of Hebrew U., 1977, Strittmatter award Philadelphia County Med. Soc., 1980, Disting. Svc. award Pa. Med. Soc., 1982, Zubrow award Pa. Hosp., 1986, Achievement award Sammy Davis Jr. Nat. Liver Inst., 1987, John P. McGovern award Am. Med. Writers Assn., 1988, Gov.'s Award in the Scis. Commonwealth of Pa., 1989, John Blundell award Brit. Blood Transfusion Soc., 1989, Gold Medal award Can. Liver Found. and Can. Assn. Study of Liver, 1990, Showa Emperor Meml. award Japan, 1994, Outstanding Leadership medal NASA, 2002, Lifetime Achievement award Am. Liver Found., 2005; named to Nat. Inventor Hall of Fame, 1993. Fellow ACP, Royal Coll. Physicians; mem. NAS, AAAS, Inst. Medicine NAS, Am. Acad. Arts and Scis., Assn. Am. Physicians, Am. Soc. Human Genetics, Am. Philos. Soc. (pres. 2005), Explorers Club NY, Athenaeum (London). Office: Fox Chase Cancer Ctr 333 Cottman Ave Philadelphia PA 19111 Business E-Mail: baruch.blumberg@fccc.edu.

BLUMBERG, EDWARD ROBERT, lawyer; b. Phila., Feb. 15, 1951; BA in Psychology, U. Ga., 1972; JD, Coll. William and Mary, 1975. Bar: Fla., 1975, U.S. Dist. Ct. Fla. 1975, U.S. Ct. Appeals, 1975, U.S. Supreme Ct. 1979. Assoc. Knight, Peters, Hoeveler & Pickle, Miami, Fla., 1976-77; ptnr. Deutsch & Blumberg, P.A., Miami, 1978—. Adj. prof. U. Miami Sch. Paralegal Studies; mem. adv. coun. legal studies Fla. Internat. U., 2004—. Author: Proof of Negligence, Mathew Bender Florida Torts, 1988. Mem. ABA (ho. of dels. 1996-2002), ATLA, Dade County Bar Assn., Fla. State Bar (bd. govs., pres.-elect 1996-97, pres. 1997-98), Acad. Fla. Trial Lawyers, Nat. Bd. Trial Advocacy (cert. civil trial adv.), Fla. Bar Found. (bd. dirs. 1996-99, bd. govs. 1996-99), Bankers Club (chmn. bd. govs. 2003-05). Office: Deutsch & Blumberg PA 100 Biscayne Blvd Fl 28 Miami FL 33132-2304 Home Phone: 305-667-4884; Office Phone: 305-358-6329.

BLUMBERG, GRACE GANZ, lawyer, educator; b. NYC, Feb. 16, 1940; d. Samuel and Beatrice (Finkelstein) Ganz; m. Donald R. Blumberg, Sept. 9, 1959; 1 child, Rachel. BA cum laude, U. Colo., 1960; JD summa cum laude, SUNY, 1971; LLM, Harvard U., 1974. Bar: N.Y. 1971, Calif. 1989. Confidential law clk. Appellate Divsn., Supreme Ct., 4th Dept., Rochester, NY, 1971-72; tchg. fellow Harvard Law Sch., Cambridge, Mass., 1972-74; prof. law SUNY, Buffalo, 1974-81, UCLA, 1981—. Reporter Am. Law Inst., Prins. of the Law of Family Dissolution, 2002. Author: Community Property in California, 1987, Community Property in California, rev. edit., 1999, 2003, Blumberg's California Family Code Annotated; contbr. articles to profl. jours. Office: UCLA Sch Law Box 951476 Los Angeles CA 90095-1476

BLUMBERG, JOEL MYRON, cardiologist; b. NYC, Oct. 17, 1940; s. Howard Godfrey and Lily Ruth (Goldberg) B.; BA, DePauw U., 1962; MD, NYU, 1966; m. Judith Ellen Green, Aug. 23, 1964; children: Amy, Hillary, Michelle. Intern, NYU-Bellevue Med. Center, NYC, 1966-67, resident in internal medicine, 1969-71; fellow in cardiology Cornell U.-NY Hosp., 1971-73; pvt. practice internal medicine and cardiology, Greenwich, Conn., 1973—; attending staff Greenwich Hosp., 1973—, coronary care cons., 1973—; physician to out-patients NY Hosp., 1973-77; clin. instr. Cornell U. Med. Coll., 1971-77; clin. asst. prof. Yale Sch. Medicine, 1975—; lectr. in preventive cardiology to civic groups; bd. visitors DePauw U., bd. incorporators Greenwich Hosp. Diplomate Am. Bd. Internal Medicine. Fellow A.C.P., Am. Coll. Cardiology, Am. Heart Assn. (council on clin. cardiology). Named to Best Doctors in Am., 2005, Best Doctors in NY, 2005, Best Doctors in Conn., 2006; recipient Excellence in teaching award, 2002; mem. Am. Soc. Internal Medicine, NY Heart Assn., Greenwich, Fairfield County, Conn. State med. socs. Club: B'nai B'rith (Stamford, Conn.). Contbr. articles to profl. jours. Home: 59 Old Stone Bridge Rd Cos Cob CT 06807-1511 Office: 55 Holly Hill Ln Ste #210 Greenwich CT 06830 Home Phone: 203-869-9055; Office Phone: 203-661-4242.

BLUMBERG, MARK STUART, health service researcher, scientist, director; b. NYC, Nov. 16, 1924; s. Sydney N. and Mollie (Leshrowitz) B.; m. Luba Monasevitch, 1952; children: Bart David, Eve Luise; m. 2d Elizabeth R. Conner, 1974. Student, Johns Hopkins U., 1942-43, Harvard U., 1943-44, student Sch. Pub. Health, 1955, DMD, 1948, MD, 1950. Intern, children's med. service Bellevue Hosp., NYC, 1950-51; ops. analyst Johns Hopkins U. Ops. Research Office, Chevy Chase, Md., 1951-54; exchange analyst Army Ops. Research Group (U.K.), West Byfleet, Eng., 1953-54; staff Occupational Health Program, USPHS, Washington, 1954-56; assoc. ops. analyst to dir. health econs. program Stanford (Calif.) Research Inst., 1956-66; asst. to v.p. adminstrn. to dir. health planning, office of the pres. U. Calif., Berkeley, 1966-70; corp. planning advisor to dir. spl. studies Kaiser Found. Health Plan, Inc., Oakland, Calif., 1970-94; dir. Kaiser Found. Health Plan of Conn., Hartford, 1982-94, Kaiser Found. Health Plan Mass., 1987-94; cons. risk adjusted measures Oakland, 1994—; co-founder, sr. scientist TruRisk LLC, 1998—. Various times cons. Pan Am. Health Orgn., Calif. State Dept. Mental Hygiene, Carnegie Commn. on Higher Edn., various agys. HHS. Contbr. writings to profl. publs. Vol. Grenfell Med. Mission, Harrington Harbour, Que., Can., summer 1948; mem. tech. adv. com. AB 524 State of Calif., 1992—. Served with USNR, 1943-45; with USPHS, 1954-56. Mem. Ops. Research Soc. Am. (past mem. council, Health Applications sect.), Hosp. Mgmt. Systems Soc. (charter), Inst. of Medicine of Nat. Acad. Scis. Office Phone: 510-601-9536.

BLUMBERG, MICHAEL ZANGWILL, allergist; b. Phila., July 29, 1945; s. Jerome Blumberg and Vivian Rose (Liebman) Steiger; m. Barbara Sue Gurman, June 9, 1973; children: Jessica Lynn, Jason Mark. AB, Brandeis U., 1967; MD, Jefferson Med. Coll., 1971; MSHA., Va. Commonwealty U., 1998. Diplomate Am Bd Pediatrics, Am Bd Allergy and Immunology. Intern, resident N.Y. Hosp., Cornell U. Med. Ctr., 1971-73; fellow in allergy and immunology Nat. Jewish Hosp.-U. Colo. Med. Ctr., 1973-75; chief allergy sect. major Scott Air Force Base, Ill., 1975-77; physician-ptnr. Va. Adult and Pediat. Allergy and Asthma, Richmond, 1977—, mng. ptnr., 1998—; assoc. clin. prof. pediatrics Med. Coll. Va., Richmond, 1977—2002, 2000—; chief of allergy Children's Hosp. of Richmond, 1987-2000; ptnr. Clin. Rsch., Richmond, 1998—. Med advisor Sanofi-Adventec, Astra Zeneca, Glaxo SmithKline, Merck. Contbr. articles and abstracts to profl jours; contbg. editor: Review in Allergy, 1978; mem ed bd: Jour Asthma, 1996—. Mem exec comt, pres, bd dirs, chmn Beth Shalom Home Va, Richmond, 1987—95; bd dirs Jewish Community Ctr, Richmond, 1984—87; bd dirs endowment fund, mem budget comt Jewish Fedn; pres. Richmond Jewish Found., 2002. Recipient Maimonides award, Jewish Fedn. Richmond, 2006. Fellow: Am Acad Pediatrics, Col Chest Physicians, Am Col Allergy, Asthma and Immunology (pub. rels.com.); mem.: Allergy and Asthma Soc. Va. (pres. 2002—04), Am Thoracic Soc, Am Acad Allergy, Asthma and Immunology (managed care com.), Am Col Allergy Sports Med (practice standards com. 1994—95), Friends of Brandeis Athletics, Masons, Phi Kappa Phi. Jewish. Avocations: American history, exercise. Office: Va Adult & Pediat Allergy and Asthma 7605 Forest Ave Ste 103 Richmond VA 23229-4936 Home: 149 W Square Court Richmond VA 23238 Office Phone: 804-288-0055. Personal E-mail: mshadoc@comcast.net. Business E-Mail: mblumberg@vaallergy.com.

BLUMBERG, NEIL, hematologist, educator; b. NYC, June 14, 1948; s. Abraham Samuel and Mildred Blumberg; m. Joanna Mary Heal, May 2, 1981; children: David Anthony Heal, Eric Lawrence Heal. BS, Yale U., 1970, MD, 1975. Cert. Am. Bd. Pathology. Dir. clin. labs. and transfusion medicine, prof. pathology and lab. medicine U. Rochester Med. Ctr., NY, 1980—. Fellow: Am. Coll. Pathologists. Achievements include in collaboration with Dr. Joanna Heal and other colleagues, redefining the boundaries and clinical importance of transfusion immunology and the role of the ABO blood group system in transfusion. Office: Univ Rochester Med Ctr 601 Elmwood Ave Box 608 Rochester NY 14642 Home Phone: 585-586-9778; Office Phone: 585-275-3189. Business E-Mail: neil_blumberg@urmc.rochester.edu.

BLUMBERG, PHILLIP IRVIN, law educator; b. Balt., Sept. 6, 1919; s. Hyman and Bess (Simons) B.; m. Janet Helen Mitchell, Nov. 17, 1945 (dec. 1976); children: William A.M., Peter M., Elizabeth B., Bruce M.; m. Ellen Ash Peters, Sept. 16, 1979. AB, Harvard U., 1939, JD, 1942; LLD (hon.), U. Conn., 1994. Bar: N.Y. 1942, Mass. 1970. Assoc. Willkie, Owen, Otis, Farr & Gallagher, NYC, 1942—43, Szold, Brandwen, Meyers and Blumberg, NYC, 1946—66; pres., CEO United Ventures Inc., 1962—67; pres., CEO, trustee Federated Devel. Co., NYC, 1966—68, chmn. fin. com., 1968—73; prof. law Boston U., 1966—74; dean U. Conn. Sch. Law, Hartford, 1974—84, prof. law, 1984—89, dean, prof. law emeritus, 1989—. Bd. dirs. Verde Exploration Ltd.; legal adv. com. to bd. dirs. N.Y. Stock Exch., 1989-93; adv. com. on transnat. corps. U.S. Dept. State, 1976-79; advisor corp. governance project, restatement of suretyship and restatement of agy. Am. Law Inst.; vis. lectr. U. Brabant, Tilburg, Netherlands, 1985, U. Internat. Bus. and Econs., Beijing, 1989, U. Sydney, 1992, Jagiellonian U., Cracow, Poland, 1992. Author: Corporate Responsibility in a Changing Society, 1972, The Megacorporation in American Society, 1975, The Law of Corporate Groups: Procedure, 1983, The Law of Corporate Groups: Bankruptcy, 1985, The Law of Corporate Groups: Substantive Common Law, 1987, The Law of Corporate Groups: General Statutory Law, 1989, The Law of Corporate Groups: Specific Statutory Law, 1992, The Multinational Challenge to Corporation Law, 1993, The Law of Corporate Groups: State Statutory Law, 1995, The Law of Corporate Groups: Enterprise Liability, 1998, Blumberg on Corporate Groups, 2d edit., 2005, The Law of Corporate Groups - Jurisdiction, Practice, and Procedure, 2007; mem. editl. bd. Harvard Law Rev., 1940-42, treas., 1941-42; contbr. articles to profl. jours. Trustee Black Rock Forest Preserve, Inc.; trustee emeritus Conn. Bar Found. Capt. USAAF, 1943-46, ETO, maj. USAF JAGD Res. 1946-55. Decorated Bronze Star. Mem. ABA, Conn. Bar Assn., Am. Law Inst., Hartford Club, Harvard Club (Boston), Army & Navy Club (Washington), Phi Beta Kappa, Delta Upsilon. Home: 791 Prospect Ave Apt B-5 Hartford CT 06105-4224 Office: U Conn Sch Law 65 Elizabeth St Hartford CT 06105-2290 Office Phone: 860-570-5192. Business E-Mail: phillip.blumberg@law.uconn.edu.

BLUME, FRED, lawyer; b. Phila., Mar. 14, 1941; married; three children. BS, Temple U., 1963; LLB, U. Penn. Law Sch., 1966. Bar: Pa. 1966, Fla. 1975, NY 1994. Law clerk to Judge D. Donald Jamieson Ct. of Common Pleas; assoc. Blank Rome LLP, Phila., 1967—72, ptnr., 1972—, adminstrv. ptnr., 1996—2002, co-chmn., 2000—02, COO, 2001—02, ptnr., privately held and emerging cos. group, mng. ptnr., CEO, 2003—06, chmn. emeritus, mem. exec. com., 2006—. Chmn. bd. dirs. law sch. U. Pa. Corp. exec. bd. Phila. Mus. Art; mem. Inst. of Law & Econ. U. Penn. Law Sch.; bd. dirs. Nati. Museum Am. Jewish History, Greater Phila. Film Office; bd. visitors Temple U. Fox Sch. of Bus. & Mgmt. Mem.: ABA (bus. section), NY Bar Assn., Fla. Bar Assn., Pa. Bar Assn., Phila. Bar Assn. Office: Blank Rome LLP One Logan Sq Philadelphia PA 19103-6998 Home Phone: 610-667-5358; Office Phone: 215-569-5512. Office Fax: 215-832-5512. Business E-Mail: blume@blankrome.com.

BLUME, JAMES BERYL, investment advisor; b. NYC, Apr. 9, 1941; s. Philip Franklin Blume and Mary Kirschman Asch; m. Kathryn Weil Frank, Jan. 20, 1984; 1 child, Zachary Thomas Philip. BA, Williams Coll., Williamstown, Mass., 1963; MBA, Harvard U., Boston, 1966; M. Psychology, The Wright Inst., Berkeley, Calif., 1983, PhD in Psychology, 1986. Security analyst Faulkner, Dawkins & Sullivan, NYC, 1966-68; sr. v.p. Faulkner, Dawkins & Sullivan Securities, Inc., NYC, 1968-73; ptnr. Omega Properties, NYC, 1973-74; exec.v.p. Arthur M. Fischer, Inc., NYC, 1974-77; pvt. practice psychotherapist Berkeley, Calif., 1985—91; fin. cons., 1987—93; pres. Blume Capital Mgmt., Inc., Berkeley, 1987—. Bd. dirs. Ploughshares Fund. Bd. dirs. ACLU No. Calif., San Francisco, 1988—94, 2004—, treas., 1993—94; bd. dirs. East Bay Clinic Pyschotherapy, Oakland, Calif., 1981—85, Marin Psychotherapy Inst., Mill Valley, Calif., 1986—87; trustee Wright Inst., 1981—85. Mem.: Williams Club (bd. govs. 1968—72), Berkeley Tennis Club. Democrat. Jewish. Avocations: tennis, politics. Office: 1708 Shattuck Ave Berkeley CA 94709-1700 Office Phone: 510-549-3534. Business E-Mail: jbb@blumecapital.com.

BLUME, JUDY, author; b. Elizabeth, NJ, Feb. 12, 1938; d. Rudolph and Esther (Rosenfeld) Sussman; m. John M. Blume, Aug. 15, 1959 (div. Jan. 1975); children: Randy Lee, Lawrence Andrew; m. George Cooper, June 6, 1987; 1 stepchild, Amanda. BA in Edn., NYU, 1960; LHD (hon.), Kean Coll., 1987, Endicott Coll., 1995. Author: (fiction) including The One in the Middle is the Green Kangaroo, 1969, Iggie's House, 1970, Are You There God? It's Me, Margaret (selected as outstanding children's book 1970), Freckle Juice, 1971, Then Again, Maybe I Won't, 1971, It's Not the End of the World, 1972, Tales of a 4th Grade Nothing, 1972, Otherwise Known as Sheila the Great, 1972, Deenie, 1973, Blubber, 1974, Forever, 1975, Starring Sally J. Freedman as Herself, 1977, Superfudge, 1980, Tiger Eyes, 1981, The Pain and the Great One, 1984, Just As Long As We're Together, 1987, Fudge-A-Mania, 1990, Here's to You, Rachel Robinson, 1993, Double Fudge, 2002 others; (adult novels) Wifey, 1977, Smart Women, 1984, Summer Sisters, 1998; (other writings) Letters to Judy: What Kids Wish They Could Tell You, 1986; exec. producer (25 min. film) Otherwise Known As Sheila The Great, Barr Films, 1988. Founder, trustee The Kids Fund, 1981. Recipient Carl Sandburg Freedom to Read award Chgo. Pub. Libr., 1984, The Civil Liberties award ACLU, 1986, John Rock award Ctr. for Population Options, 1986, Margaret A. Edwards for lifetime achievement ALA, 1996, medal for disting. contbn. to Am. letters, Nat. Book Found., 2004; numerous Children's Choice award, U.S.A., Europe, Australia. Mem. Authors Guild (bd. dirs.), Nat. Coalition Against Censorship (adv. bd.), Soc. Children's Book Writers (bd. dirs.). Jewish. Office: c/o William Morris Agy 1325 Ave of Ams New York NY 10019

BLUME, MARSHALL EDWARD, finance educator; b. Chgo., Mar. 31, 1941; s. Marshall Edward Blume and Helen Corliss (Frank) Gilbert; m. Loretta Ryan, June 25, 1966; children: Christopher, Caroline, Catherine. SB, Trinity Coll., Hartford, Conn., 1963; MBA, U. Chgo., 1965, PhD, 1968; MA (hon.), U. Pa., 1970. Lectr. applied math. Grad. Sch. Bus., U. Chgo., 1966, instr. bus. fin. and applied math., 1967; lectr. fin. U. Pa., Phila., 1967, asst. prof., 1968-70, assoc. prof., 1970-74, prof., 1974-78, Howard Butcher prof., 1978—, chmn. dept., 1982-86, assoc. dir. Rodney White Ctr., 1978-86; prin. Prudent Mgmt. Assocs., 1982—; dir. Rodney White Ctr., 1986—. Mem. U.S. Compt. Gen. adv. bd. on Oct. 1987 stock market crash, 1987-88; prof. fin. European Inst., Brussels, 1975-76, New U. Lisbon, Portugal, 1982; vis. prof. Stockholm Sch., spring 1976, U. Brussels, 1975. Author: Mutual Funds and Other Institutional Investors, 1970, The Changing Role of the Individual Investor, 1978, The Structure and Reform of the U.S. Tax System, 1985, Revolution on Wall Street: The Rise and Fall of the New York Stock Exchange, 1993; editor: Encyclopedia of Investments, 1982, The Complete Guide to Investment Opportunities, 1984; assoc. editor Jour. Fin. and Quantitative Analysis, 1967-76, Jour. Fin. Econs., 1976-81, Jour. of Portfolio Mgmt., 1985—; mng. editor Jour. Fin., 1977-80, assoc. editor, 1985-88, Jour. of Fin. Income, 1990—. Contbr. articles to profl. publs. Trustee Trinity Coll., Hartford, Conn., 1980-86, Rosemont (Pa.) Sch., 1991—; commr. Bi-Partisan Commn. on Pa. Pension Fund Investments, 1989-93. Mem. Am. Fin. Assn. (officer 1977-80), Am. Econs. Assn., Fin. Economist Roundtable, Corinthian Yacht Club Phila., New Castle (Del.) Sailing Club, NASD (chmn. econ. adv. bd. 1998), NASDAQ Ednl. Found. (dir. 2000-2001), Measey Found. (mgr. 1997—, acad. adv. coun. 2004-), Shadow Regulatory Commn. Home: 204 Woodstock Rd Villanova PA 19085-1419 Office: U Penn Rodney L White Ctr Fin Rsch 3250 Steinberg Hall Philadelphia PA 19104

BLUME, MARTIN, physicist; b. Bklyn., Jan. 13, 1932; s. Julius and Frances (Cohen) B.; m. Sheila Bierman, June 12, 1955; children— Frederick, Janet. AB, Princeton U., 1954; A.M., Harvard U., 1956, PhD, 1960. Fulbright rsch. fellow Tokyo U., 1959-60; rsch. assoc. Atomic Energy Rsch. Establishment, Harwell, England, 1960-62; with Brookhaven Nat. Lab., Upton, NY, 1962—, sr. physicist, 1970—, head solid state physics, dep. chmn. physics dept., 1975-79, assoc. dir., 1981-84, dep. dir., 1984-96; editor-in-chief Am. Phys. Soc., Ridge, NY, 1997—. NSF grantee, 1973-78; recipient E.O. Lawrence award Dept. of Energy, 1981, A.H. Compton award, 2003, Meritorious Achievement award Coun. Sci. Editors, 2005. Fellow Am. Acad. Arts and Scis., Am. Phys. Soc., AAAS, N.Y. Acad. Scis.; mem. Phi Beta Kappa, Sigma Xi. Home: 284 Greene Ave Sayville NY 11782-3003 Office: Am Phys Soc 1 Rsch Rd Ridge NY 11961 also: Brookhaven Nat Lab Physics Dept Bldg 510 Upton NY 11973 Business E-Mail: blume@aps.org.

BLUME, PETER FREDERICK, museum director; b. Syracuse, NY, June 5, 1946; s. Edward Frederick and Charlotte (Murray) B.; m. Karolyn Waller Vreeland, Oct. 4, 1980 (div. 1998); 1 child, Susanna. BFA, Syracuse U., 1967, postgrad., 1972-73, Attingham Summer Sch., Eng., 1976, Mus. Mgmt. Inst., Berkeley, Calif., 1986. Curator Allentown (Pa.) Art Mus., 1974-84, dir., 1984—2002, Ball State U. Mus. Art, Ind., 2003—. Mem. museums panel Pa. Council on Arts, Harrisburg, 1983-87. Author exhbn. catalogs. Mem. Hist. Archtl. Rev. Bd., Allentown, 1978-83; mem. Old Allentown Preservation Assn., 1977—. Served with U.S. Army, 1967-73. Rockefeller Found. fellow Met. Mus. Art, N.Y.C., 1973-74. Mem. Rotary. Home: 2600 Fern Brook Way Muncie IN 47304 Office Phone: 765-285-3373. Business E-Mail: pfblume@bsu.edu.

BLUMENAUER, EARL, congressman; b. Portland, Oreg., Aug. 16, 1948; m. Margaret Kirkpatrick; 2 children. BA, Lewis and Clark Coll., Portland, Oreg., 1970, JD, 1976. Asst. to pres. Portland State U., Oreg., 1971-73; mem. Oreg. State Ho. Reps., 1973-79, Multnomah County Bd. Commrs., Portland, Oreg., 1979-87; commr. pub. works City Coun., Portland, 1987-96; mem. US Congress from 3rd Oreg. dist., 1996—, mem. ways and means com., mem. budget com., mem. select com. on energy independence and climate change. Mem. Gov.'s Commn. Higher Edn., Oreg., 1990—91. Named Legislator of Yr., Am. Planning Assn., 1999; recipient Apgar award, Nat. Bldg. Mus., 2000, Nat. Bicycle Advocacy award, League of Am. Bicyclists, 2001; fellow German Marshall, 1995. Democrat. Avocations: bicycling, running. Office: 729 NE Oregon St Ste 115 Portland OR 97232 Office Phone: 202-225-4811. Office Fax: 503-230-5413.*

BLUMENCRANZ, PETER WILLIAM, surgeon; b. NYC, Mar. 8, 1946; s. Bernard and Evelyn (Guttman) B.; m. Ann Frances Garfes, June 6, 1970; children: Brett, Lisa, Jennifer, Deborah, Todd. BA, U. Pa., 1966; MD, Cornell U., 1970. Diplomate Am. Bd. Surgery. Resident in surgery N.Y. Hosp.-Cornell U. Med. Ctr., NYC, 1970-76; fellow in surg. oncology Meml. Hosp.-Sloan Kettering Cancer Ctr., NYC, 1976-77; surgeon Diagnostic Clinic, Largo, Fla., 1977-79, Fla. Surg. Assocs., Clearwater, Fla., 1980-95; pres. Surg. Assocs. West Fla., Clearwater, 1995—. Bd. dirs. Morton Plant Mease Health Care; trustee Morton Plant Hosp., Clearwater, Fla., 1992—98, 2005—; med. dir. Moffitt Morton Plant Cancer Care, Tampa, Fla., 2001—. Trustee Shorecrest Prep. Sch., St. Petersburg, Fla., 1982-88; bd. dirs. Pinellas unit Am. Cancer Soc., 2006—. Lt. comdr. USN, 1972-74. Fellow Soc. Surg. Oncology, Am. Coll. Surgeons, Southeastern Surg. Congress; mem. Am. Soc. Breast Diseases, Fla. Soc. Clinical Oncology, Fla. Med. Assn., Am. Soc. Breast Surgeons, State Fla. Cancer Coun., Fla. Soc. Gen. Surgeons. (bd. dirs. 1998—). Avocations: tennis, running. Office: Surg Assocs West Fla 303 Pinellas St Clearwater FL 33756-3354 Office Phone: 727-462-2131.

BLUMENFELD, CHARLES RABAN, lawyer; b. Seattle, May 24, 1944; s. Irwin S. and Freda I. (Raban) B.; m. Karla Axell; children: David, Lisa. BA, U. Wash., JD, 1969. Bar: Wash. 1969, U.S. Dist. Ct. (we. dist.) Wash. 1969, U.S. Ct. Appeals (9th cir.) 1975, U.S. Supreme Ct. 1979, U.S. Dist. Ct. D.C. 1981, U.S. Ct. Appeals (D.C. cir.) 1981. Legis. counsel U.S. Senator Henry M. Jackson, Washington, 1969-72; ptnr. Bogle & Gates, Seattle, 1973-99, PerkinsCoie, Seattle, 1999—2007; assoc. v.p. alumni rels. U. Washington, Seattle, 2007—. Office: U Washington Alumni Assn 1415 NE 45th St Seattle WA 98105 Home Phone: 206-323-4868; Office Phone: 206-685-6929. Business E-Mail: cblumenfeld@u.washington.edu.

BLUMENFELD, JEFFREY, lawyer, educator; b. NYC, May 13, 1948; s. Martin and Helen Kay (Smith) B.; m. Laura Madeline Ross, June 11, 1970; children: Jennifer B. Schwarz, Joshua Ross Blumenfeld. AB in Religious Thought cum laude, Brown U., Providence, RI, 1969; JD, U. Pa., Phila., 1973. Bar: DC 1973. Asst. US atty. US Atty. for DC, Washington, 1975-79; trial atty. Antitrust div. US Dept. of Justice, Washington, 1973-75, sr. trial atty. US versus AT&T staff, 1979-82, asst. chief spl. regulated industries, 1982-84, chief US versus AT&T staff, 1984, spl. counsel, 1995-97; ptnr. Blumenfeld & Cohen, Washington, 1984—2002; sr. trial counsel, antitrust divsn. US Dept. Justice, 1996-97; gen. counsel, chief legal officer Rhythms Net Connections, 1997-2001; ptnr. Gray, Cary, Ware & Freidenrich, LLP, Washington, 2002—04, Crowell & Moring, 2004—. Adj. prof. Georgetown U. Law Ctr., Washington, 1983—; spl. counsel antitrust divsn. US Dept. Justice, 1995-97. Bd. dirs. Charles E. Smith Jewish Day Sch., Washington, 1991-93. Democrat. Jewish. Office: Crowell & Moring LLP 1001 Pennsylvania Ave NW Washington DC 20004 Home Phone: 202-966-6614; Office Phone: 202-624-2919. Business E-Mail: jblumenfeld@crowell.com.

BLUMENGARTEN, JERRY, educational consultant; b. Bklyn., Feb. 14, 1948; s. Nathan and Jeanne G Blumengarten; m. Gail Rachel Weiner, Aug. 7, 1977; children: Neil J, Shira F. BA, U. Pitts., 1968; MA, Hunter Coll., CUNY, 1974. Lead tchr. NYC Bd. Edn., Bklyn., 1969—2001; writer, ednl. cons. Culver Co., Inc., Larkspur, Calif., 1979—. Chairperson Nat. Coun. Social Studies, Washington, 1977—78. Author: (educational booklet) The Safest You Can Be, Planning for Your Work Future. Libr. trustee Bellmore Meml. Libr., Bellmore, NY, 1992—96; cmty. curriculum advisor Mashpee (Mass.) Pub. Schools, 2002—05; charter commr. Mashpee Charter Commn., 2003—04; publicity chairperson Mashpee Civic Assn., 2004—05. With USAR, 1969—75, Ft. Tilden, NY. Recipient Outstanding Young Men of Am. award, U.S. Jaycees, 1979. Jewish. Home: 9240 SE La Creek Ct Hobe Sound FL 33455 Home Phone: 772-545-2127. Personal E-mail: lib218@yahoo.com.

BLUMENGOLD, JEFFREY GENE, health facility administrator; b. Dec. 25, 1950; s. Irving and Marjorie (Freeman) B.; m. Vivienne Colletti, Oct. 15, 1972; children: Stacey, Craig. BBA, Bernard M. Baruch Coll., 1973, CUNY, 1973, MBA, 1976. CPA NY, NJ. Asst. mgr. royalty acctg. MacMillan Pub. Corp., NYC, 1973-74; tchr. acctg. Port Richmond H.S., SI, 1974-75; dir.-provider audit dept. Empire Blue Cross and Blue Shield, NYC, 1976-77, 78-88; acct. Pannell, Kerr, Foster & Co., NYC, 1977-78; dir. fin. Cath. Med. Ctr. Bklyn. and Queens, 1988-91; ptnr. in charge health care svcs. Weiser LLP, NYC, 1990—; ptnr. and leader health care forensic and dispute svcs. Deloitte Fin. Adv. Svcs. LLP, 2006. Former vice chmn. bd. Ctr. for Home Health Devel., 1995—97; bd. dirs. HomeHealth Assembly of N.J.; adj. prof. acctg. Coll. S.I., CUNY, N.Y. Inst. Tech. With USAR, 1972—. Mem. AICPA, NJ Soc. CPAs (healthcare com. 2000—), Healthcare Fin. Mgmt. Assn. (nat. prin. and practices bd. 1999-2002), Nat. Assn. Home Care-Fin. Mgrs. Forum, NY State Soc. CPAs (past chmn. health care instns. com.). Office: Weiser LLP 399 Thornall St Edison NJ 08837-2246 E-mail: jblumengold@weiserllp.com.

BLUMENKRANZ, DAVID BENJAMIN, chemical engineer, consultant; b. Palo Alto, Calif., June 1, 1967; s. Jerald M. Blumenkranz and Anthony Cancilla (Stepfather), Karen L. Cancilla, Judy Blumenkranz (Stepmother); m. Julie E. White, Sept. 16, 1995; 1 child, Zoe V. BS, Calif. Poly. State U., 1990. Registered profl. engr., Wash., 1995. Engr. Westinghouse Hanford Co., Richland, Wash., 1990—94, CH2M Hill Hanford, Richland, 1994—2000; sr. engr. Sci. Applications Internat. Corp., Richland, 2000—03; waste chemistry engr. Wash. Group Internat., Richland, 2003—. Mem.: Am. Ceramics Soc. Avocations: Karate, beer judge. Office: Washington Group International 2435 Stevens Center Place Richland WA 99354 Home Phone: 509-967-5484; Office Phone: 509-371-3525. Office Fax: 509-371-3508.

BLUMENTHAL, DAVID, health policy expert; b. NYC, Aug. 31, 1948; s. Martin and Jane (Rosenstock) B.; m. ellen G. Blumenthal, Aug. 9, 1970; children: Daniel, Karen. BA, Harvard U., 1970, MD, 1975; MPP, Kennedy Sch. Govt., Boston, 1975. Mem. profl. staff subcom. on health U.S. Senate, Washington, 1977-79; exec. dir. ctr. for health policy Kennedy Sch. Govt., Cambridge, Mass., 1980-87; sr. v.p. Brigham & Women's Hosp., Boston, 1987-91; chief health policy rsch. unit Mass. Gen. Hosp., Boston, 1991—; assoc. prof. Harvard Med. Sch., Boston. Mem. editorial bd. New Eng. Jour. Medicine, Boston, 1995—. Contbr. over 100 articles to profl. jours. Chmn. Mass. Peer Rev. Orgn., Waltham, 1997—. Office: Health Policy R&D Unit Med Practices Eval Ctr 50 Staniford St Boston MA 02114-2517

BLUMENTHAL, GEORGE, academic administrator, astronomy and astrophysics professor; BS, U. Wis.-Milw.; PhD in Physics, U. Calif., San Diego. Faculty mem. U. Calif., Santa Cruz, 1972—, chair Astronomy and Astrophysics Dept., chair Academic Senate, 2001—03, acting chancellor, 2006—; chair U. Calif. Academic Senate, 2004—05. Office: U Calif Santa Cruz 1156 High St Santa Cruz CA 95064-1077 E-mail: chancellor@ucsc.edu.*

BLUMENTHAL, JANE LEONARDI, library director; d. William F. and Gwenlyn M. Banks; m. Don Michael Blumenthal. MSLS, Cath. U. Am.; BA, Coll. William and Mary. Asst. libr. Georgetown U. Med. Ctr., Wash., 1990—95, assoc. libr., 1995—96, med. ctr. libr., 1996—2000; asst. dean knowledge mgmt. Georgetown U. Sch. Medicine, Wash., 2000—06; cataloger Sci. Libr., NCI-Frederick Cancer Rsch. Facility, 1980—82, tech. svcs. libr., 1982—84, asst. mgr., 1984—85; libr. dir. AMA Wash. Office, 1985—90; dir. Health Scis. Librs. U. Mich., Ann Arbor, 2006—. Chpt. assembly dir. Am. Soc. Info. Sci., 1990—92; regional adv. com. S.E. Atlantic Region Nat. Network Librs. Medicine, Balt., 2001—06. Mem.: Acad. Health Info. Profls. (disting.), Assn. Acad. Health Scis. Librs. (bd. dirs. 2002—05), Med. Libr. Assn. (sr. assoc. editor bulletin 1994—96, mem. editl. bd. bulletin 1996—99, chair leadership & mgmt. sect. 2004—05, co-chair nat. program com. 2006—). Office: U Mich Taubman Med Libr 1135 Catherine St 0726 Ann Arbor MI 48109

BLUMENTHAL, RICHARD, state attorney general; b. NYC, Feb. 13, 1946; m. Cynthia Blumenthal; 4 children. BA, Harvard Coll., 1967; JD, Yale U., 1973. Law clk. to Hon. Jon O Newman US Dist Court Conn, 1973—74; law clk. to Justice Harry A. Blackmun US Supreme Ct., 1974—75; adminstr. asst. to Senator Abraham Ribicoff US Senate, 1975—76; U.S. atty. Dist. Conn. US Dept. Justice, 1977—81; ptnr. Cummings & Lockwood, 1981—84, Silver Golub & Teitell, 1984—90; mem. from Dist. 27 Conn. Gen. Assembly, 1984—87; mem. Conn. State Senate, 1987—90; state atty. gen. State of Conn., 1990—. Volunteer counsel NAACP Legal Def. Fund, 1981—86. Sgt. USMC, Res. Recipient Raymond E. Baldwin award for Pub. Svc., Quinnipiac U. Sch. Law, 2002. Democrat. Office: Office of Attorney General 55 Elm St Hartford CT 06141 Office Phone: 860-808-5318.*

BLUMENTHAL, ROGER SCOTT, cardiologist; b. Washington, Jan. 17, 1960; s. Stanley and Anita B.; m. Wendy Post, Apr. 12, 1997. MD, Cornell U., 1985. Diplomate Am. Bd. Internal Med. Intern Johns Hopkins Hosp., Balt., 1985-86, resident in Internal Medicine, 1986-88, fellow in Cardiology, 1988-92, mem. staff, 1992—; asst. prof. Johns Hopkins U., dir. Ciccarone Preventive Cardiology Ctr. Editl. bd. Cardiology Rev., Today in Cardiology, Jour. Cardiovascular Nursing, Jour. Women's Health. Mem. AMA, Am. Col. Physicians, Am. Col. Cardiologists, Md. chpt. Am. Heart Assn. (past v.p.), Balt. divsn. Am. Heart Assn. (bd. dir.), SE Lipid Assn. (pres. 2004), Nat. Lipid Edn. Coun. Avocation: golf. Office: Johns Hopkins Hosp Divsn Cardiology--Blalock 524C 600 N Wolfe St Baltimore MD 21287 Business E-Mail: rblument@jhmi.edu.*

BLUMENTHAL, RONNIE, lawyer; b. Passaic, NJ, Nov. 27, 1944; d. Paul and Marga (Stern) B. BA, George Washington U., 1966, JD, 1969. Bar: D.C. 1969. Gen. atty. EEOC, Washington, 1969-71, spl. asst. to commr., acting chmn., 1971-78, sr. atty., 1978-82, dir. spl. svcs. staff, 1982-85, dir. compliance programs, 1985-91, acting dir. Office of Communications-Legis. Affairs, 1991-92; spl. asst. U.S. atty. Dept. Justice, Washington, 1992, dir. Office Fed. Ops., 1992-99, mediator, 1999—. Legis. fellow U.S. Senate, 1982; chmn. Performance Review Bd., Exec. Resources Bd; lectr., cons. in field. Mem. ABA, D.C. Bar Assn., Fed. Bar Assn., Exec. Women in Govt., Womens Bar Assn., Soc. Profls. in Dispute Resolution. Home: 853 Vanderbilt Beach Rd # 327 Naples FL 34108-8746 Office Phone: 202-297-1191. Personal E-mail: ronnieblum@aol.com.

BLUMENTHAL, SUSAN JANE, physician, psychiatrist, educator; m. Edward John Markey. BA, Reed Coll., Portland, Oreg., 1971; MD, U. Tenn., 1976; MPA, Harvard U., Cambridge, Mass., 1982; PhD (hon.), Trinity Coll., Washington, 1996, Ben Gurion U., Israel, 2005, Pine Manor Coll., Chestnut Hill, Mass. Diplomate Am. Bd. Psychiatry and Neurology. Intern. Stanford U. Sch. Medicine, 1976-77, residency and fellowship, 1977-80; fellow NIMH, 1980-81, assoc. dir. Psychiatry Tng. Rev., head suicide rsch. unit and coord. of project depression, 1982-85, chief behavioral medicine program, 1985-93, chief behavioral and basic prevention rsch. br., 1991-93; clin. asst. prof. Tufts Med. Ctr., 1981-82; clin. asst. prof. psychiatry George Washington Sch. Medicine, 1982-86; clin. assoc. prof. psychiatry Georgetown Sch. Medicine, 1986-91, clin. prof. psychiatry Washington, 1991—; first dep. asst. sec. women's health HHS, Washington, 1993—97, asst. surgeon gen., 1996—2005, sr. med. and e-health advisor, 2002—05, sr. sci. advisor, 2002—05, sr. global health advisor, 2003—05; clin. prof. psychiatry Tufts Sch. Medicine, 1995—; assoc. v.p. for health affairs George Washington U. Med. Ctr., 1998; pres. Global Health Inst. LLC, Washington, 2006—; disting. advisor for sci., health and medicine Ctr. Study of the Presidency, Washington, 2006—. Vis. prof. ob-gyn. George Washington U. Med. Ctr., 1998-99; disting. vis. prof. women's studies Brandeis U., 1999—; vis. prof. Stanford U., 2004-05, Mayo Clinic, 2005; hon. prof. Ben Gurion U. Sch. Medicine, 2004-, med. dir. Discovery Channel/AFI global health series, 2006; chief med. advisor PBS Health Instn., 2006—; chair NIH Coord. Com. on Health and Behavior, 1991-94; co-chair NIH Reunion Task Force, 1992-94; chair Fed. Coord. Com. Breast Cancer, fed. coord. com. women's health and the environ., co-chair nat. breast cancer action plan; coord. Com. Women's Health Issues and Domestic Violence, 1994-98; mem. Pres.'s Interagy. Coun. on Women; sr. advisor pub. health White House Coun. on Youth Violence, 2000-02, sr. med. advisor on pub. health and sci. to the sec., USDA, 2000-02; vis. fellow Harvard U. Sch. Govt., 2004-05; chair Save the Children, Nat. Adv. Coun. on Obesity Prevention, 2007—. Editor: Suicide Over the Life Cycle, 1989, Premenstrual Syndrome, 1985; mem. editl. bds.: Jour. Women's Health, Depression, health columnist: Elle Mag., Ladies Home Jour., U.S. News and World Report; med. dir.: Discovery/AFI global health film series; chief med. advisor: PBS Health Initiative; contbr. articles to sci. jours. Mem. Nat. Commn. on Sleep Disorders Rsch., workgroup on mental health Pres. Task Force on Health Care Reform; U.S. rep. global commn. on Women's Health WHO; trustee Meridian Internat. Ctr., 2005—, Save the Children, Acad. Achievement, Hadassah HMO. Capt. USPHS, 1992-94, rear adm., 1994—. Recipient Outstanding Svc. medal, 1989, Commendation medal, 1990, Meritorious Svc. medal, USPHS, 1992, Sec.'s Honor award for Domestic Violence, 1996, Asst. Sec. for Health's award for Breast Cancer, 1996, Am. Med. Writers award, 1996, Gretchen Poston award, The Nat. Race for the Cure, 1996, Founder's award, 1996, Pub. Svc. award, Nat. Alliance for the Mentally Ill, 1996, Surgeon Gen.'s Exemplary Svc. medal, 1997, Gracie award, Assn. Women Radio and TV Profls., 1997, Inspiration Leader award, Pa. Diabetes Assn., 1997, Spl. Assignment Svc. medal, 1998, 2002, Women of Distinction award, Nat. Assn. Women in Higher Edn., 1998, Woman of Valor award, United Jewish Fedn., 1999, Mosaic award, Komen Found., 2000, Founder's award, 2000, Feminist First award for Health, Feminist Majority, 2000, Congl. award, 2001, Congl. citation, 2002, Achievement medal, 2002, Women's Ctr. Leadership award, 2003, Leadership award, Save the Children, 2004, Nat. Breast Cancer Awareness Pub. Svcs. Leadership award, 2004, Disting. Svc. award, Spirit of Life Found., 2004, Presdl. Sacher Medallion, Brandeis U., 2005, DSM, USPHS, 2006; fellow, Harvard U. Sch. Govt., 2004. Fellow AMA (disting.); mem. Am. Psychiat. Assn. (cons. Joint Coun. on Pub. Affairs, Francis Braceland award for pub. svc. 1998), Am. Coll. Psychiatrists, Am. Med. Women's Assn. (past chair com. on publicity and pub. rels., Pres.'s citation, 1996), Congl. Club, Nat. Assn. Bus. and Profl. Women (Magnificent Seven award 1996), Internat. Club, Internat. Women's Forum, Am. Suicide Found. (past bd. dirs. Washington divsn., pres.), Starlight Found. (past chmn. sci. adv. bd.). Office: Ctr Study Presidency 1020 19th St NW Ste 250 Washington DC 20036 Office Phone: 202-872-9800. Personal E-mail: healthinstitutes@aol.com.

BLUMENTHAL, W. MICHAEL (WERNER MICHAEL BLUMENTHAL), retired manufacturing company executive, former secretary of the treasury; b. Oranienburg, Germany, Jan. 3, 1926; s. Ewald and Rose Valerie (Mark) Blumenthal; m. Margaret Polley, 1951; children: Jane, Anne, Jill; m. Barbara Bennett; 1 child, Michael. BS, U. Calif., Berkeley, 1951; MA, MPA, Princeton U., 1953, PhD, 1956. Rsch. assoc. Princeton U., 1954-57; v.p., bd. dirs. Crown Cork Internat. Corp., 1957-61; dep. asst. sec. for econ. affairs US Dept. State, 1961; dep. spl. rep. for trade negotiations The White House, 1963-67; pres. Bendix Internat., 1967-70; vice-chmn. Bendix Corp., 1970-71, pres., COO, 1971-72, chmn., pres., CEO, 1972-77; sec. US Dept. Treasury, Washington, 1977-79; vice-chmn., CEO Unisys Corp. (formerly Burroughs Corp.), Detroit, 1980-81, chmn., CEO, 1981-1990; sr. adv. Lazard Frères & Co., LLC, 1990—96; dir. Jewish Mus. Berlin, 1997—. Bd. Bendix Corp., 1967-77, Tenneco, Inc., DaimlerChrysler Services AG; mem. internat. adv. bd. Chem. Bank. Author: Invisible Wall: 300 Years of a German-Jewish Family, 1998. Recipient Bundesverdienstkreuz, Fed. Rep. Germany, 1999, Leo Baeck medal, 1999, Goethe medal, 2002, Culture Prize of Berlin, 2002, Great Cross of Merit with Star, Fed. Rep. Germany, 2006. Mem. Bus. Coun., U.S.-Japan Bus. Coun. (steering com.).

BLUMENTHAL, WILLIAM, lawyer; b. White Plains, NY, Nov. 4, 1955; s. Louis and Mary (Meyer) B.; m. Marjory Susan Spodick, Dec. 30, 1979; 1 child, Deborah Louise. AB, MA, Brown U., 1977; JD, Harvard U., 1980. Bar: D.C. 1980, U.S. Dist. Ct. D.C. 1986. Cons. Policy & Mgmt. Assocs., Inc., Boston, 1977-80; teaching fellow Harvard U., Cambridge, Mass., 1978-80; assoc. Jones, Day, Reavis & Pogue, Washington, 1980-83, Sutherland, Asbill & Brennan, Washington, 1983-87, ptnr., 1988-93, Kelley Drye & Warren, Washington, 1993-95, King & Spalding LLP, Washington, 1995—2005; gen. counsel Fed. Trade Commn., Washington, 2005—. Editor Horizontal Mergers: Law and Policy, 1986; contbr. to book: The Merger Review Process, 1995, Mergers & Acquisitions Handbook, 1986. Harvey A. Baker fellow Brown U., 1977. Mem. ABA (chmn. Clayton Act com. 1992-94, chmn. monograph com. 1989-92, vice chmn. antitrust sect. 1997-98, internat. officer antitrust sect. 2003-2005). Office: Office of General Counsel Federal Trade Commission 600 Pennsylvania Ave NW Washington DC 20580 Business E-Mail: wblumenthal@ftc.gov.

BLUMER, FREDERICK ELWIN, retired philosophy educator; b. Glencoe, Okla., Sept. 16, 1933; s. Edward H. and Eva Marie (Forbes) B.; m. Ann Louise Anderson, June 9, 1956; children: Frederick Edward, William Robert. BA, Millsaps Coll., 1955; BD, Emory U., 1958, PhD, 1962; postgrad., Georg August U., Goettingen, Germany, 1960-61. Ordained to ministry United Meth. Ch., 1962; chaplain, instr. philosophy and religion Nebr. Wesleyan U., Lincoln, 1962-63, asst. prof., 1963-65, assoc. prof., 1965-67, prof., 1967-76, v.p. acad. affairs, 1967-70, provost, v.p. acad. affairs, 1970-76; pres. Lycoming Coll., Williamsport, Pa., 1976-89; Moll prof. faith and life Baldwin-Wallace Coll., Berea, Ohio, 1989-99, prof. emeritus, 1999—. Dean, dir. Graz Ctr., Austria, 1972-73; mem. univ. senate United Meth. Ch., 1980-88, 93-97, pres., 1980-88, chmn. Commn. on Theol. Edn.; exec. com. Commn. Ind. Colls. and Univs. Pa., 1978-81, treas., 1988-89. Editor: Nebr. Wesleyan Univ. Press, 1967-76; Contbr. articles to profl. jours. Dir. edn. Lincoln United Way, 1971; bd. dirs. NE Lincoln YMCA, 1968-71, Lincoln Symphony Orch., 1971-76, Williamsport/Lycoming United Way, 1976-83; bd. mgrs. Williamsport Hosp., 1982-89; chmn. Found. Ind. Colls. Pa., 1987-88; bd. dirs. Pine Street Found., 1982-86, Lycoming Found., 1985-89. Recipient Pres.'s award Nebr. Wesleyan U., 1966; Cokesbury fellow, Dempster fellow, Rockefeller doctoral fellow Emory U. Mem. Nat. Assn. Schs., Colls., Univs. of United Meth. Ch. (pres. 1987-89), Williamsport-Lycoming C. of C. (dir., exec. com. 1976-85), Phi Kappa Phi, Pi Gamma Mu, Theta Phi, Omicron Delta Kappa. Republican. Home: 20798 Burgandy Dr Strongsville OH 44149-5602

BLUMIN, STUART M., history professor; b. Miami, Fla., Mar. 29, 1940; s. Harry and Faye Blumin; m. Deborah A. Adelman, June 12, 1965; children: Jennifer A., Daniel A. BS in Econ., U. Pa., 1962, MA, 1963, PhD, 1968. Asst. prof. am. studies Skidmore Coll., Saratoga Springs, NY, 1967—69; asst. prof. hist. MIT, Cambridge, Mass., 1969—73; faculty mem. Cornell U., Ithaca, NY, 1974—82, prof. am. hist., 1982—, dir., 1998—. Author: The Urban Threshold: Growth and Change in a Nineteenth-Century Community, The Short Season of Sharon Springs: Portrait of Another New York, The Emergence of the Middle Class: Social Experience in the American City, 1760-1900; editor: New-York by Gaslight and Other Urban Sketches by George G. Foster; co-author Rude Republic: Americans and their Politics in the Nineteenth Century; author: The Encompassing City: Streetscapes in Early Modern Art and Culture. Mem. NY State Hist. Assn., Cooperstown, NY, 2000—06. Recipient Kerr History prize, NY State Hist. Assn., 1975, Best Book in North Am. Urban Hist. award, Urban Hist. Assn., 1990, Binkley-Stephenson prize, Orgn. of Am. Historians, 2000; fellowship, Charles Warren Ctr. for Studies in Am. Hist., Harvard U., 1971-72, NEH, 1987-88, 1997-98. Mem.: Urban Hist. Assn., Orgn. of Am. Historians, Am. Hist. Assn. Home Phone: 607-257-6130; Office Phone: 607-255-3359.

BLUMKIN, LINDA RUTH, lawyer; b. Aug. 25, 1944; d. Louis and Edith (Fortus) Blumkin. AB cum laude, Barnard Coll., 1964; LLB cum laude, Harvard U., 1967, LLM, 1973. Bar: NY 1968, US Dist. Ct. (so. dist.) NY 1969, US Ct. Appeals (2nd cir.) 1969, US Supreme Ct. 1982. Assoc. Fried, Frank, Harris, Shriver & Jacobson, NYC, 1967—71, ptnr., 1979—2005, of counsel, 2005—. Lectr. Boston U., 1971, asst. prof. mgmt., 1972—73; assoc. Breed, Abbott & Morgan, NYC, 1973—77; asst. dir. Bur. Competition, Fed. Trade Commn., 1977—79. Mem.: ABA, NYC Bar Assn. Office: Fried Frank Harris Shriver & Jacobson 1 New York Plz Fl 24 New York NY 10004-1901 Office Phone: 212-859-8085. Business E-Mail: linda.blumkin@friedfrank.com.

BLUMROSEN, ALFRED WILLIAM, law educator; b. Detroit, Dec. 14, 1928; s. Sol and Frances (Netzorg) B.; m. Ruth L. Gerber, July 3, 1952; children: Steven Marshall, Alexander Bernet. BA, U. Mich., Ann Arbor, 1950, JD, 1953. Bar: Mich. 1953, N.J. 1961, N.Y. 1981. Solo practice, Detroit, 1953-55; mem. faculty Rutgers Law Sch., Newark, 1955—, prof., 1961—, acting dean, 1974-75, Herbert J. Hannoch scholar, 1984, Thomas A. Cowan prof., 1986—. Dir. fed.-state rels., chief conciliations U.S. EOOC, 1965-67, cons. to chmn., 1977-79; advisor U.S. Dept. Justice, HUD, 1968-72, U.S. Dept. Labor, 1995-96; of counsel Kaye, Scholer, Fierman, Hays & Handler, N.Y.C., 1979-82; dir. Ford Found. intentional discrimination project Rutgers U., Law Sch., 1998—. Author: Black Employment and the Law, 1971, Modern Law: The Law Transmission System and Equal Employment Opportunity, 1993; author: (with Ruth Blumrosen) The Realities of Intentional Job Discrimination in Metropolitan America, 1999, Slave Nation: How Slavery United the Colonies and Sparked the American Revolution, 2005; contbr. articles to profl. jours. Fulbright scholar, South Africa, 1993, Rockefeller Inst. Resident scholar Bellagio Conf. Ctr., 1995. Mem. ABA (Ross essay prize 1983), Internat. Soc. for Labor Law and Social Security, Indsl. Relations Rsch. Assn., Order of Coif. Office: Rutgers U Sch Law 123 Washington St Newark NJ 07102-3026 Office Phone: 917-670-8878. E-mail: theblumrosen@aol.com.

BLUMSTEIN, ALFRED, urban and public affairs educator; b. NYC, June 3, 1930; m. Dolores Reguera, Jan. 26, 1958; children: Lisa, Ellen, Diane. BS in Engring. Physics, Cornell U., 1951, PhD in Ops. Rsch., 1960; MS in Stats., U. Buffalo, 1954; JD (hon.), John Jay Coll., 1996. Prin. ops. analyst Cornell Aero. Lab., Buffalo, 1951-61; rsch. staff Inst. Def. Analyses, Arlington, Va., 1961-69; dir. sci. and tech. task force Pres.'s Commn. Law Enforcement and Adminstrn. Justice, Washington, 1966-67; J. Erik Jonsson Univ. prof. urban sys. and ops. rsch. H. John Heinz III Sch. Pub. Policy and Mgmt. Carnegie-Mellon U., Pitts., 1969—, dean, 1986-93, dir. Nat. Consortium on Violence Rsch., 1996—. Overseas fellow Churchill Coll. Cambridge U., 1983—; chmn. various panels NRC Com. Rsch. Law Enforcement and Adminstrn. Justice, 1982-86, chmn. com., 1980-83; mem. NRC Commn. Behavioral and Social Scis. and Edn., 1994-2000. Mem. editl. bd. Ops. Rsch. Letters, Jour. Rsch. in Crime and Delinquency, Evaluation Rev., Jour. Criminal Justice, Sci. Commn. of Internat. Soc. of Criminology, 1985-91, others; co-editor Cambridge Criminology Series; contbr. articles to profl. jours. Chmn. Pa. Commn. Crime and Delinquency, Harrisburg, 1979-90; mem. Pa. Commn. on Sentencing, 1986-96; bd. dirs. Police Found., 1990-96; nat. adv. com. Inst. Rsch. on Poverty at U. Wis., 1989-94; trustee Jewish Healthcare Found., 2001-2006. Recipient Stockholm prize in Criminology, 2007. Fellow AAAS, Am. Soc. Criminology (pres. 1991-92, Sutherland award 1987); mem. NAE, Ops. Rsch. Soc. Am. (pres. 1977-78, Kimball medal 1985, Pres.'s award 1993), Am. Statis. Assn., Inst. Ops. Rsch. and Mgmt. Scis. (pres. 1996, Morse lectr. 2004-05), Law and Soc. Assn., Inst. Mgmt. Scis. (pres. 1987-88), Internat. Fedn. Operational Rsch. Socs. (v.p. N.Am. 1992-94), Consortium of Social Sci. Assn. (pres. 1999-2002), Cosmos Club, Omega Rho. Home: 5025 5th Ave # 2D Pittsburgh PA 15232 Office: Carnegie-Mellon U H John Heinz III Sch Pub Policy Mgmt Pittsburgh PA 15213 Office Phone: 412-268-8269. Business E-Mail: ab0q@andrew.cmu.edu.

BLUMSTEIN, EDWARD, lawyer; b. Phila., Aug. 24, 1933; s. Isaac and Mollye (Rodofsky) B.; m. Susan Perloff, Aug. 13, 1983; 1 child, Daniel Blumstein. BS in Econs., U. Pa., 1955; JD, Temple U., 1958. Bar: U.S. Dist. Ct. (ea. dist.) Pa. 1959, U.S. Ct. Appeals (3rd cir.) 1959. Pvt. practice, Phila., 1959-85; ptnr. Blumstein, Block & Pease, Phila., 1985—2002, Edward Blumstein, PC, Phila., 2002—. Adj. prof. Sch. Law Temple U., 1994-2006. Gen. Counsel to North American Ski Journalists Assn. With U.S. Army, 1958-64. Mem. ABA, Pa. Bar Assn., Phila. Bar Assn. (bd. govs. 1984-85, past chmn. family law sect. 1984), Assn. Conflict Resolution (pres. delaware valley chpt. 2007), Family Mediation Assn. Del. Valley (pres. 1990-91), B'nai B'rith. Jewish. Avocations: skiing, reading, photography. Office: Ste 1100 1528 Walnut St Philadelphia PA 19102 Office Phone: 215-790-9666. Personal E-mail: edmediates@hotmail.com.

BLUMSTEIN, JAMES FRANKLIN, lawyer, educator, consultant; b. Bklyn., Apr. 24, 1945; s. David and Rita (Sondheim) B.; m. Andree Kahn, June 25, 1971 BA in Econs., Yale U., 1966, MA in Econs., LLB, 1970. Bar: Tenn. 1970, U.S. Ct. Appeals (6th cir.) 1970, U.S. Dist. Ct. (mid. dist.) Tenn. 1971, U.S. Supreme Ct. 1974, N.Y. 1985. Instr. econs. New Haven Coll., 1967-68; pre-law adviser office of dean Yale U., New Haven, 1968-69, sr. pre-law adviser office of dean, 1969-70, asst. in instrn. law shc., 1969-70; asst. prof. law Vanderbilt U., Nashville, 1970-73, assoc. prof., 1973-76, prof., 1976-99, spl. advisor to chancellor for acad. affairs, 1984-85, Centennial prof., 1999—2003, Univ. prof. constl. law and health law and policy, 2003—, chair faculty senate, 2001—02, univ. prof., 2003—. Assoc. dir. Vanderbilt Urban and Regional Devel. Ctr., 1970-72, dir. ctr., 1972-74; sr. rsch. assoc. Vanderbilt Inst. for Pub. Policy Studies, 1976-85, sr. fellow, 1985—, dir. health policy ctr., 1995—; Commonwealth Fund fellow, vis. assoc. prof. law and policy scis. law sch. Duke U. and Inst. of Policy Scis. and Pub. Affairs, 1974-75; adj. prof. health law med. sch. Dartmouth U., scholar-in-residence intermittently, 1976-78; John M. Olin vis. prof. Sch. Law, U. Pa., 1989; elected mem. Inst. Medicine NAS, 1990—; bd. dirs. St. Thomas Health Scis. Found., Alive Hospice, Nashville; cons. law, health policy, civil and voting rights, land use, state taxation, torts; lectr. in field. Editor: (with Eddie J. Martin) The Urban Scene in the Seventies, 1974, (with Benjamin Walter) Growing Metropolis: Aspects of Development in Nashville, 1975, (with Lester Salamon) Growth Policy in the Eighties (Law and Contemporary Problems Symposium), 1979; (with Frank A. Sloan and James M. Perrin) Uncompensated Hospital Care: Rights and Responsibilities, 1986, (with Frank A. Sloan and James M. Perrin) Cost, Quality, and Access in Health Care: New Roles for Health Planning in a Competitive Environment, 1988; (with Frank A. Sloan) Organ Transplantation Policy: Issues and Prospects, 1989, (with Frank A. Sloan) Antitrust and Health Care Policy (Law and Contemporary Problems Symposium), 1989, (with Clark C. Havighurst and Troyen A. Brennan) Health Care Law and Policy, 1998, supplement, 2007, bd. Jour. Health Politics, Policy and Law, 1981-01; mem. adv. bd. Nat. Fedn. Ind. Bus. Legal Found., 2003-; mem. pub.'s adv. bd. Nashville Banner, 1982-98; contbr. articles to profl. jours., op-ed articles to newspapers. Mem. Health Econs. Task Force, Middle Tenn. Health Sys. Agy., 1979; mem. Nashville Mayor's Commn. on Crime, 1981; chmn. Yale Alumni Schs. Com. Middle Tenn., 1983—; sec. Martin Luther King Jr. Holiday Com., State of Tenn., 1985—87; mem. Tenn. Gov.'s Task Force Medicaid, 1992—94; active Inst. Medicine Com. on Adequacy of Nursing Staffing, 1994—96; chmn. Tenn. adv. com. U.S. Commn. on Civil Rights, 1985—91, mem., 1991—97; bd. dirs. Alive Hosp., 2005—, St. Thomas Health Svcs. Found.; mem. adv. bd. LWV, 1979—80; bd. dirs. Jewish Fedn. Nashville and Middle Tenn., 1981—90, mem. exec. com., 1988—90, chmn. cmty. rels. com., 1980—82, chmn. campus com., 1987—89; chmn. task force cost containment and med. malpractice Rand Corp., 1991—92; mem. adv. panel Office Tech. Assessment study of defensive medicine and use of med. tech., 1991—94; mem. adv. com. on The Records of Congress, 1997—99; cons. Leadership Nashville, 1977—, Tenn. Motor Vehicle Commn., 1986—87, Leadership Music, 1989—2002, Tenncare Reform Project, Office Gov. Phil Bredesen, 2004—, Acad. Country Music, 2005; panelist Am. Arbitration Assn., 1977—2002. Bates Jr. fellow, 1968-69; grantee Ford Found./Rockefeller Found. Population Program, 1970-73, Health Policy grantee HCA Found., 1986-90; grantee State Justice Inst., 1991—2000, Robert Wood Johnson Found., 1994—2000; named One of Outstanding Young Men in Am., 1971; recipient award Univ. Rsch. Coun., 1971-72, 73-74, 79-80, 94-95, Earl Sutherland prize achievement in rsch. Vanderbilt U., 1992, Paul J. Hartman award Outstanding Prof., 1982. Mem. ABA (sec. sect. legal edn. and admissions to bar 1982-83 , chmn. subcom. on state and local taxation com. on corp. law and taxation sect. on corp., banking and bus. law 1983—, mem. accreditation com. sect. legal edn. and admissions to bar 1983-89, mem. com. on state and local taxation sect. on taxation 1983—), NAS (inst. of medicine), Assn. Am. Law Schs. (chmn. law, medicine and health care sect. 1987-88, mem. exec. com. 1988-92, 2d vice chmn. sect. local govt. law 1976-78, mem. sect. coun. 1980-86), Tenn. Bar Assn. (Pres.'s award 2004), N.Y. State Bar Assn., Nashville Bar Assn. (Liberty Bell award 1987), Assn. Yale Alumni (del.), Yale U. Law Sch. Alumni Assn. (exec. com. 1985-88), Univ. Club (Nashville). Home: 2113 Hampton Ave Nashville TN 37215-1401 Office: Vanderbilt U Sch Law 21st Ave S Nashville TN 37240-0001 Office Phone: 615-322-2615.

BLUNCK, TEDDE, lawyer, engineer, engineering company executive; b. Milw., Aug. 19, 1946; s. George C. Blunck and Pauline L. Hillebran Murphy; m. Quita R. Lininger, June 27, 1965 (div. June 1984); children: Kelle M. Blunck Gliem, Kenneth M. Blunck (dec.); m. Cathy A. Terrell, May 26, 1988; 1 child, Richard T. Antoine. BSCE, Iowa State U., 1970; JD magna cum laude, Tex. Wesleyan U., 1995. Bar: Tex. 1995, D.C. 1998, U.S. Dist. Ct. (no. dist.) Tex. 1996, U.S. Supreme Ct. 2002; lic. profl. engr., lic. profl. land surveyor. Project engr. Shive Hattery & Assocs., Iowa City, 1976-77; county engr. Madison County, Winterset, Iowa, 1977-83; head dept. transp. Veenstra & Kimm Inc., West Des Moines, Iowa, 1983-84; v.p. Huitt-Zollars, Inc., Dallas, 1984-89; project leader Parsons Brinckerhoff Quade & Douglas, Inc., Tempe, Ariz., 1989-90; asst. to project dir. PB/MK Team, waxahachie, Tex., 1990-95; legal asst. Ford Yungblut White & Salazar, P.C., Dallas, 1995-96; sr. constrn. mgr. Parsons Brinckerhoff Constrn. Svcs., Inc., Ft. Worth, 1996-97, v.p., asst. sec., mgr. legal svcs. Herndon, Va., 1997—2002; sr. assoc. counsel Parsons Brinckerhoff Quade & Douglas, Inc, Austin, Tex., 2002—06, PB Americas, Inc., Austin, 2006—. County engr. Taylor County, Bedford, Iowa, 1973-76; dir. pub. works City of Charles City, Iowa, 1970-73. Bd. dirs. Cmty. and Econ. Devel. Corp., Duncanville, Tex., 1996-97; mem. City Coun., City of Sharpsburg, Iowa, 1976. Republican. Roman Catholic. Home: 10809 Olympia Fields Loop Austin TX 78747 Office: PB Americas Inc Barton Oaks Plz Two 901 MoPac Expy South Bldg 2 Ste 595 Austin TX 78746-5148 Office Phone: 512-347-3515. Business E-Mail: blunckt@pbworld.com.

BLUNDELL, WILLIAM RICHARD CHARLES, retired electric company executive; b. Montreal, Apr. 13, 1927; s. Richard C. and Did Aileen (Payne) B.; m. Monique Audet, Mar. 20, 1959; children: Richard, Emily, Michelle, Louise. BSc, U. Toronto, 1949. Registered profl. engr., Ont. Sales engr. Can. Gen. Electric Co., Toronto, 1949-51, travelling auditor, 1951, various fin. positions, 1951-66, treas., 1966-68, v.p.-fin., 1968-70, v.p., exec. consumer div., 1970-72, v.p., exec. apparatus div. Lachine, Que., 1972-79; pres., CEO, Camco Inc., Weston, Ont., 1979-83; pres., COO, Can. Gen. Electric Co. Ltd., Toronto, 1983-84; chmn., CEO Gen. Electric Can. Inc., Toronto, 1985-90; ret., 1991. Chmn. Mfrs. Life Ins. Co., 1994—98, chmn. pub. sector pension investment bd., 2000—03; vice chair Can. Inst. for Advanced Rsch., 1998—2006; bd. dirs. Metallic Ventures Gold Inc. Decorated officer Order of Can.; recipient Engring. Alumni medal U. Toronto, 1990; honoree Public Policy forum, 1995. Home: 29 Rothmere Dr North York ON Canada M4N IV3 Personal E-mail: bill_blundell@rogers.com.

BLUNT, EMILY OLIVIA L., actress; b. London, Feb. 23, 1983; Actor: (plays) The Royal Family, 2001 (Evening Standard Brit. Film award for Most Promising Newcomer), Romeo & Juliet, 2002; (films) Boudica, 2003, My Summer of Love, 2004 (Evening Standard Brit. Film award for Most Promising Newcomer, 2005), Irresistible, 2006, The Devil Wears Prada, 2006; (TV films) Henry VIII, 2003, The Strange Case of Sherlock Holmes & Arthur Conan Doyle, 2005, Gideon's Daughter, 2005 (Golden Globe award for Supporting Actress, 2007); (TV miniseries) Empire, 2005. Office: ICM London 4-6 Soho Sq London W1D 3PZ England*

BLUNT, JAMES HILLIER, singer; b. Tidworth, Wiltshire, England, Feb. 22, 1974; Grad., Royal Mil. Acad., Sandhurst. Signed to Custard Records, Calif., 2003—. Singer: (albums) Back to Bedlam, 2005, Chasing Time: The Bedlam Sessions, 2006, All the Lost Souls, 2007, (songs) High, 2004, Wisemen, 2005, You're Beautiful, 2005 (MTV Australia Video Music award for Song of Yr., 2006, 2 Ivor Novello awards: Most Performed Work, and Internat. Hit of Yr., 2006, 2 MTV Video Music awards: Best Male Video, Best Cinematography, 2006). Capt. Life Guards Rgt. Brit. Army, 1998—2002, Kosovo. Recipient Best New Act award, MTV Europe Music Awards, 2005, Q Awards, 2005, Best Pop Act award, Brit. Awards, 2006, Best Male, 2006, Best Internat. Newcomer award, NRJ Music Awards, France, 2006, ECHO Awards, Germany, 2006, Choice Music: Male Artist, Teen Choice Awards, 2006, Best New Artist award, World Music Awards, 2007, Best-Selling British Artist, 2007. Office: Twenty-First Artists Ltd 1 Blythe Rd London W14 OHG England also: Custard Records 8939 1/2 Santa Monica Blvd West Hollywood CA 90069 Office Phone: 44-207-348-4800. Personal E-mail: info@wabbie.com. Business E-Mail: info@custardrecords.com.*

BLUNT, JOYCE OMEGA, special education educator; d. Herbert and Rosemary Blunt. BA, So. U. New Orleans, 1978; MA, Xavier U., 1982; postgrad., Southeastern U., 1986. Chair, black history, grade, student coun. advisor Harahan, La., 1998—2004; mem. spl. edn. adv. coun. Jefferson Parish, Harvey, 1995—2005; spl. edn. tchr. Granville T. Woods Elem. Sch., Kenner, La., 2005—. Parent tchr. rep. Harahan, 1998—2003, dollars for scholars, 1998—2004. Named Outstanding Young Educator, Metairie Jaycees, 1994, Walmart Tchr. Yr., 2002, Reading Tchr. Yr., La. Reading Coun., Jefferson, 2002. Mem.: Nat. Assn. Univ. Women (edn. chair), Jefferson Fed. Tchrs. Union (mem.-at-large 1996—). Baptist. Avocations: travel, shopping. Home: 7924 Macon St Metairie LA 70003

BLUNT, MATT (MATTHEW ROY BLUNT), governor, former state official; b. Strafford, Missouri, Nov. 20, 1970; s. Roy Blunt; m. Melanie Blunt, Mar. 1997; 1 child, William Branch. BA in History, US Naval Acad., Annapolis, Md., 1993. Mem. Mo. Gen. Assembly, 1999—2001; sec. state State of Mo., Jefferson City, 2001—05, gov., 2005—. USN, 1993—98, lt. comdr. USNR, 1998—, engring. officer, USS JACK WILLIAMS, navigator, adminstrv. officer, USS PETERSON. Decorated achievement award USN, US Marine Corps, Humanitarian Svc. Medal. Mem.: Mo. Farm Bureau, Am. Legion, State Historical Soc. Mo. Republican. Baptist. Achievements include serving in Operation Support Democracy in Haiti and in southern England in support of Operation Enduring Freedom while in the USN. Office: Office of Gov Mo Capitol Bldg Rm 216 Jefferson City MO 65101 also: PO Box 720 Jefferson City MO 65102 Office Phone: 573-751-3222. Office Fax: 573-526-3291. Business E-Mail: mogov@mail.state.mo.us.

BLUNT, ROY D., congressman; b. Niangua, Mo., Jan. 10, 1950; s. Leroy and Neva (Letterman) B.; m. Roseann Blunt (div. 2003), children: Matthew Roy, Amy Roseann, Andrew Benjamin.; m. Abigail Perlman, 2003. BA in Hist., S.W. Bapt. U., 1970; MA in Hist. & Govt., S.W. Mo. State U., 1972. Tchr. Marshfield HS, Mo., 1970-73; instr. Drury Coll., Springfield, Mo., 1973-82; clk. Greene County, Mo., 1973-85; sec. of state State of Mo., 1985-93; pres. S.W. Bapt. U., 1993-96; mem. US Congress from 7th Mo. dist., 1997—, chief dep. majority whip, 1999—2002, majority whip, 2002—07, interim majority leader, 2005—06, minority whip, 2007—.

Mem. Fed. Election Commn. Adv. Panel; del. Atlantic Treaty Assn. Conf., 1987; mem. Congl. Com. on Commerce, 1999—2004, Internat. Rels., 1997-98, 2004-, Ho. Reps. Steering Com., 1997-; del. Nat. Hist. Publs. and Records Commn., 1997—; mem. ho. appropriations com., 1999. Co-author: Mo. Election Procedures: A Layman's Guide, 1977, Jobs Without People: The Coming Crisis for Missouri's Workforce, 1989; Voting Rights Guide for the Handicapped Bd. dirs. Ctr. Democracy; mem. Mo. Mental Health Advocacy Coun., 1998-99; mem. exec. bd. Am. Coun. of Young Polit. Leaders, 1998-99; chmn. Mo. Housing Devel. Commn., Kans. City, 1981, Rep. State Conv., Springfield, 1980; chmn. Gov.'s Adv. Coun. on Literacy; co-chmn. Mo. Opportunity 2000 Commn., 1985-87; Rep. candidate for lt. gov. of Mo., 1980; active local ARC, Muscular Dystrophy Assn., others. Named One of 10 Outstanding Young Americans US Jaycees, 1986, Springfield's Outstanding Young Man Jaycees, 1980, Mo.'s Outstanding Young Civic Leader, 1981, Mo. Republican of Yr. 2002; Recipient Disting. Mem. of Congress award, Am. Wire Producers Assn., 2002, Health Leadership award Am. Assn. of Nurse Anesthetists, 2003, Arthur T. Marix Congl. Leadership award Mil. Officers Assn. Am., 2004, Cmty. Health Defender award Nat. Assn. Cmty. Health Ctrs. Inc., 2005. Mem. Nat. Assn. Secs. of State (chmn. voter registration and edn. com., sec., v.p. 1990), Am. Coun. Young Polit. Leaders, Kiwanis, Masons. Republican. Baptist. Office: US House Reps 217 Cannon Ho Office Bldg Washington DC 20515-2507 Office Phone: 202-225-6536, 202-225-5604. E-mail: blunt@mail.house.gov.*

BLUST, LARRY D., lawyer; b. Bushnell, Ill., Feb. 16, 1943; BS with high honors, U. Ill., 1965, JD with high honors, 1968. Bar: Ill. 1968; CPA, Ill. Former mem. Jenner & Block, Chgo.; ptnr., bus. practice Barnes and Thornburg LLP, Chgo., 2001—. Mem. Ill. Bd. CPA Examiners, 1978-81. Contbr. articles to profl. jours. Mem. ABA (tax sect., partnerships com. 1975-80, 1982-85), Order of the Coif. Office: Barnes and Thonrburg Ste 4400 One No Wacker Dr Chicago IL 60606-2833 Office Phone: 312-214-8320. Business E-Mail: larry.blust@letlaw.com.

BLUTH, B. J. (ELIZABETH JEAN CATHERINE BLUTH), sociologist, aerospace technologist; b. Phila., Dec. 5, 1934; d. Robert Thomas and Catherine Cecelia (Boxman) Gowland; m. Thomas Del Bluth, Aug. 20, 1960 (dec. Aug. 6, 1980); children: Robert Thomas, Richard Del. BA in Sociology (Washington semster fellow), Bucknell U., 1953; MA, Fordham U., 1960; PhD, UCLA, 1970. Teaching fellow in methods of social research Fordham U., 1957-58; reading instr. St. Margaret's High Sch., Tappahannock, Va., 1958-59; instr. history, civics and English, Rosary High Sch., San Diego, 1959-60; successively instr., asst. prof. sociology Immaculate Heart Coll., Los Angeles, 1960-65; prof. sociology Calif. State U., Northridge, 1965-87; grantee NASA Ames Research Ctr., Moffett Field, Calif., 1982-83; grantee space sta. program NASA, Washington, 1983-87, aerospace technologist system engrng. div. space sta. program office Reston, Va., 1987-90, spl. asst. to dep. program dir. space sta. freedom program and ops., 1990-94, spl. tech. asst. to dir. edn. divsn., mgr. edn. evaluation Washington, 1994—2006, program mgr. on-line edn. evaluation program, 1994—2006. Cons. Immaculate Heart Cmty., L.A., 1967-69; engrng. rsch. NASA Space Sta. design Boeing Aerospace Co., 1982-83; mem. Presdl. Citizens Adv. com. on Space, Coun. Nat. Space Policy, Nat. Tech. Com. on Soc. and Tech., UN team on relevance of space activities to econ. and social devel.; professor emeritus Calif. State U., 1987—; computational scis. and informatics inst. dir.'s search com. George Mason U., 1992-93. Editor: (with others) Search for Identity Reader, vol. I and II, 1973, (with S.R. McNeal) Update on Space, vol. I, 1961, Parson's General Theory of Action, 1982, Space Station Habitability Report, 1983, Soviet Space Station Analog, 1983, Space Station Human Productivity Study NASA, 1986, Russian Mir Space Station Analog, 1993, Marching with Sharpe, 2001; contbr. articles to profl. jours. Recipient Alpha Omega faculty awards, 1966, 1974. Fellow Am. Astronautical Soc.; mem. AIAA (chpt. award for outstanding program 1980), Am. Sociol. Assn., L5 Soc., Brit. Interplanetary Soc., Inst. Social Sci. Study of Space (acad. adv. bd.), Space Studies Inst., Internat. Acad. Astronautics (com. on space econs. and benefits), Phi Beta Kappa. Republican. E-mail: bjb@patriot.net. *To seed the universe with intelligence you must: never give up, no matter how little progress you see day-to-day for it's the "big picture" where the changes show up; always concentrate on the practical, no matter how enticing theories appear; never forget that ideas and systems and institutions are nothing more than ideas, and ideas can change— that is the true vehicle to freedom. Always reach beyond the horizon, knowing that horizons have no limit save that of our imagination.*

BLY, CAROL MCLEAN, writer, educator; b. Duluth, Minn., Apr. 16, 1930; d. Charles Russell and Mildred Barr (Washburn) McLean; divorced; children: Mary, Bridget, Noah, Micah. BA in English, Wellesley Coll., 1951; DHL, Northland Coll., 1985. Instr. writing U. Minn., Mpls., 1981—. Vis. disting. Benedict prof. Carleton Coll., U. Minn., 1990; co-founder Collaborative Tchrs. & Sch. Social Workers, St. Paul, 1993; Edelstein-Keller disting. author Carleton Coll., U. Minn., 1998—99; bd. dirs. The Loft, Mpls.; founder Bly & Loveland Press, Mpls., 2003. Author: (book) Letters from the Country, 1981, 1999, My Lord Bag of Rice, 2000, Beyond the Writers' Workshop, 2001, Three Readings for Republicans and Democrats, 2003, Stopping the Gallop to Empire, 2004; author: (with Cynthia Loveland) A Shout to American Clergy, 2005, Against Workshopping Manuscripts, 2006; author: (book) others. Bd. dirs. Episc. Cmty. Svcs., Mpls., 1980. Democrat. Avocation: tree planting. Home: 1668 Juno Ave Saint Paul MN 55116-1415 Office Phone: 952-925-2684. E-mail: carolbly@visi.com, loveland@m1ecmn.net.

BLY, JAMES CHARLES, JR., finance company executive; b. Kane, Pa., Jan. 24, 1952; s. James Charles Bly Sr. and Dorothy Hau Bly Smith; m. Laurie Ann Ramadon, June 6, 1987; children: Alana W., Bridget R., James C. III, Chase N. BA, St. Bonaventure U., 1973. CLU, cert. mergers and acquisitions. Mgmt. trainee Conn. Gen. Life, Washington, 1974-76; rep. CIGNA Fin. Svcs., McLean, Va., 1976-79; mng. exec. Integrated Resources Equity Corp., NYC, 1980-82; pres. Source Capital, Ltd., Pitts., 1982—; chmn., CEO Source Cos., LLC, 1998—; co-chmn. Bus. Growth Alliance LLC, 2005—; mng. dir. de Visscher & Co., 2006—; prin. Park Ave. Equity Ptnrs. Mem. adv. bd. John J. Kirlin, Inc., Rockville, Md., 1980—2004, Energy Alloys, LLC, 2005—; mem. bus. adv. bd. TCIM, Inc., 2005—, C.H. Brigg's Hardware, Inc., 2006—, Path North, LLC, 2006—, Legacy Bus. Governance , LLC, 2006—; prin. Arrow Capital Advisors, LLC, 2006—. Mem.: Alliance of Merger and Acquisition Advisors, Assn. Corp. Growth, Soc. Fin. Svcs. Profls., Allegheny Country Club, Edgeworth Club, The Stonedale Guns, Duquesne Club. Republican. Avocations: music, automobiles, history, travel, golf. Home: 730 Chestnut Rd Sewickley PA 15143 Office: Source Cos LLC Ste 300 1606 Carmody Ct Sewickley PA 15143 Personal E-mail: info@sourcecos.com.

BLYNN, GUY MARC, lawyer; b. Bklyn., May 26, 1945; s. S. Jerry and Viola T. Vogel Blynn; children: Daniel Scott, Harlan Sterling, Aaron Seth. BS in Econs. cum laude, U. Pa., Wharton Sch. of Fin. Commerce, 1967; JD cum laude, Harvard U., 1970. Bar: N.C., N.Y., U.S. Ct. of Appeals for Fed. Cir., U.S. Ct. of Appeals for the 2d Cir., U.S. Dist. Cts. for the Middle Dist. of N.C., Southern and Eastern Dist. N.Y. Assoc. Kaye, Scholer, Fierman, Hays & Handler, NYC, 1970-78; assoc. counsel R.J. Reynolds Industries Inc., Winston Salem, N.C., 1978-79; sr. counsel RJR Nabisco Inc., Winston Salem, N.C., 1979-86; dep. gen. counsel R.J. Reynolds Tobacco Co., Winston Salem, N.C., 1986-1989, v.p., 1989—; dep. gen. counsel R.J. Reynolds Global Products, Inc., 1989—2006, gen. counsel, 2006—. Lectr. Wake Forest U. Sch. of Law, 1980-93; cons. Dept. Commerce, 1987-90. Contbr. articles to profl. jours. Chmn. Brand Names Edn. Found., 1988-94; bd. dirs. N.C. Vol. Lawyers for the Arts, 1985-91, pres., 1987-91; bd. dirs. Urban League Winston-Salem. Mem. ABA, Am. Arbitration Assn. (panel of arbitrators 1975-95), Carolina Patent Trademark & Copyright Law Assn. (v.p. 1979-80, pres. 1980-81), Am. Intellectul Property Law Assn. (chmn. taxation and fin. matters com. 1991-92), Am. Bar Assn. Forum Com. on Entertainment And Sports Industries, Assn. of Bar of City Of N.Y. (chmn. com. on trademarks and unfair competition 1975-78, subcommittee on patent and trademark office practice 1976-77), Anti-Defamation League (N.C. regional adv. bd. 1987—, chmn. elect 1991-93, chmn. 1993—, vice chmn. 1990-91), U.S. Trademark Assn. (bd. dirs. 1982-90, v.p. 1984-85, exec. v.p. 1985-86, pres., chmn. 1986-87). Home: PO Box 20383 Winston Salem NC 27120-0383 Office: R J Reynolds Global Products Inc 401 N Main St Winston Salem NC 27101-3804

BLYSTONE, ROBERT VERNON, cell biologist, educator; b. El Paso, Tex., July 4, 1943; s. Edward Vernon and Cecilia (Mueller) Blystone; m. Donna Joan Moore, Mar. 26, 1964; 1 child, Daniel Vernon. BS in Biol. Sci., U. Tex., El Paso, 1965; MA in Zoology, U. Tex., Austin, 1968, PhD in Zoology, 1971. Instr. U. Tex., El Paso, 1965, tchg. asst. Austin, 1965-68, NIH predoctoral fellow, 1968-70; from asst. prof. to assoc. prof. biology Trinity U., San Antonio, 1971—84, prof., 1984—, chmn. dept., 1984-86. Cons. Ednl. Testing Svc., Princeton, NJ, others; text and trade book cons. McGraw-Hill, 1987, Harper-Collins, 1991—93, Oxford U. Press, 1988, Addison-Wesley, 1987—91, others. Contbr. articles to profl. jours., chapters to books. Asst. dir., dir., sec., v.p., historian Alamo Regional Sci. Fair, 1973—85; bd. dirs. Sci. Collaborative, San Antonio, 1987—95. Named Piper Prof., Tex. Piper Found., 1986; Scott fellow for tchg., 1991, Rsch. grantee, USAF Office Sci. Rsch., 1990—91, 2000—, NSF, 1991, 1995. Fellow: AAAS (film/book reviewer 1982—95), Tex. Acad. Sci. (life; exec. bd. 1976—79); mem.: Tex. Soc. Electron Microscopy (program chmn., assoc. jour. editor 1982—83), Nat. Assn. Biology Tchrs., Am. Soc. Cell Biology (mem. edn. com. 1985—89, 1991—), Microscopy Soc. Am., Am. Inst. Biol. Scis. (assoc. editor BioScience 1995—2002), Sigma Xi (pres. chpt. 1990—91). Avocation: computer graphics. Office: Trinity U Dept Biology One Trinity Pl San Antonio TX 78212-3104 Office Phone: 210-999-7243. E-mail: rblyston@trinity.edu.

BLYTH, JOHN E., lawyer, educator; b. Rochester, NY, Oct. 19, 1931; s. Ray G. and Ruby Luella (Spaulding) B.; m. Joanna E. Jennings, Aug. 24, 1963; children: Geoffrey E., Jennifer E. Blyth-Schmandt, Jane Blyth Warren, James E. AB, Colgate U., Hamilton, NY, 1953; LLB, NYU, 1960; Dr.jur., Goethe U., 1962. Bar: NY 1961. Ptnr. Harter, Secrest & Emery, Rochester, 1961-93, Hiscock & Barclay, Rochester, 1994-95, Blyth & Lamb, Rochester, 1995-2000, Fix Spindelman Brovitz & Goldman, Rochester, NY, 2000—02; lawyer Blyth Law Offices, 2002—. Speaker in field; adj. prof. Cornell U. Law Sch., Ithaca, NY, 1990—; past trustee Keuka Coll., Keuka Pk., NY, 1986—. Mem. editl. bd. Warren's Weed; contbr. articles to profl. jours. Pres. Palmyra (NY) Macedon Sch. Bd., 1969-72, Citizen's Tax League, Rochester, 1984-86. Sgt. US Army, 1954-57, ETO. Named Internat. Exec. of Yr., Rochester C. of C., 1994. Mem. NY State Bar Assn. (chair real property law sect. 1990-91, Professionalism award 2004), Am. Coll. Real Estate Lawyers Avocation: organist. Home: 1428 Hidden Pond Ln Walworth NY 14568-9538 Office: 141 Sully's Trail Ste 12 Pittsford NY 14534 Home Phone: 315-986-4226; Office Phone: 585-586-0590. E-mail: blyth.john@gmail.com.

BLYTH, MYRNA GREENSTEIN, publishing executive; b. NYC, Mar. 22, 1939; d. Benjamin and Betty (Austin) Greenstein; m. Jeffrey Blyth, Nov. 25, 1962; children: Jonathan, Graham. BA, Bennington Coll., Vt., 1960. Sr. editor Datebook mag., NYC, 1960-62, Ingenue mag., NYC, 1963-68; book editor Family Health mag., 1968-71; book and fiction editor, then assoc. editor Family Circle mag., NYC, 1972-78, exec. editor, 1978-81; editor-in-chief Ladies' Home Jour., 1981—2002, pub. dir., sr. v.p., 1987—2002, former editor-in-chief, pub. dir.; editor-in-chief, pub. dir. More Mag., 1998—2002, v.p. , editl. dir., 2002—03; with new product devel. Meredith Corp., 2002—03; freelance writer. Chmn. Pres.' commn. White House Fellows, 2002—; mem. adv. com. for ORIWH, NIH. Author: Cousin Suzanne, 1975, For Better and For Worse, 1978, Spin Sisters, 2004, How to Raise an American, 2007; columnist: Nat. Rev. Online, NY Sun; contbr. articles to New Yorker mag., New York mag., Redbook mag., Cosmopolitan mag., Readers Digest. Del. White House Conf. on Aging; mem. nat. adv. bd. Susan G. Komen Breast Cancer Found.; mem. adv. com. ORWH at NIH; mem. Pres.'s Commn. on White House Fellows, chmn. Recipient Headliner award Women in Comms., Inc., 1992, Human Rels. award, Am. Jewish Com.'s Pub. Divsn., 1992, Henry Johnson Fisher award, 1999. Mem.: Women's Forum, Women's Media Group, N.Y. Women in Comm., Inc. (past pres., Amb. of Excellence, Matrix award 1988), Am. Soc. Mag. Editors, Overseas Press Club (bd. govs.), Authors League. Personal E-mail: myrnablyth@aol.com.

BLYTHE, JAMES DAVID, II, lawyer; s. James David and Marjorie M. B.; m. Sara S. Frantz, Nov. 21, 1974; 1 child; Amanda Renee. BS, Butler U., 1962; JD, Ind. U., 1966. Bar: Ind. 1966, U.S. Supreme Ct. (so. dist.) Ind., 1966, U. S. Supreme Ct. 1980, U.S. Ct. Appeals (7th cir.), 1993. Diplomate, U.S. congl. staff asst. Ct. Practice Inst., 1965-69; majority atty. Ind. Ho. of Reps., 1967, 69; dep. prosecutor Marion County Prosecutor's Office, 1966, 68; pvt. practice Indpls., 1966—; sr. ptnr. Blythe & Ost, 1994—. Mem. com. on character and fitness Ind. Supreme Ct., 1974-94; host TV show Ask a Lawyer, 1977-79. Bd. dirs. Marion County chpt. Am. Cancer Soc., 1971-76 (pres. 1975-76), Cen. Ind. coun. Boy Scouts Am., 1969-72, exec. com., 1969-71, Crossroads of Am. coun., 1972-87, exec. com. 1976-84, pres., 1979-81, life mem 1987, Salvation Army, 1975—, vice chmn., 1986, chmn., 1987, 88, life mem., 2003; Ind. chmn. W.I. Amb. Exch., Jaycees, 1972-73; pres. North Ctrl. H.S. Alumni Assn., 1996-98, life mem., 2002; lawyers fund raising com. Indpls. Mus. Art., 1973-74; co-membership chmn, Friends of Channel 20, 1975; hon. chmn. ann. dinner Muscular Dystrophy Family Found., 2001. Named Man of Yr., Am. Cancer Soc., 1974, Sagamore of the Wabash, Gov. of Ind., 1981; named to North Ctrl. H.S. Hall of Fame, 1999; recipient cert. of merit, Am. Cancer Soc., 1971, 1974—75, Outstanding Svc. award, Indpls. by Am. Cancer Soc., 1972—73, Richard E. Rowland award, Jaycees, 1971—72, Stanley K. Lacy Meml. award, 1974, Dist. Svc. award, Ind. Jaycees, 1974, Silver Beaver award, Boy Scouts Am., 1981, commendation, Gov. State of Ind., 1973, Day named in his honor, Mayor of Indpls., 1976. Mem. Ind. Bar Assn. (legal ethics com. 1995—), Indpls. Bar Assn. (bd. mgrs. 1978-81, 89-90, chmn. grievance com. 1980-88), Nat. Eagle Scout Assn. (life), Kiwanis (v.p. Indpls 1986-87, pres. 1987-88, found pres. 1988-89, Indpls. found. 1989-99, pres. Ind. Dist. Found. 1995-98, civic award, 1991, Abe Lincoln Fellow, 1993, Man of Yr., 1997), Gyro Club Indpls. (bd. dirs. 2000-01, 03-04), Kappa Sigma, Phi Delta Phi. Republican. Office: 10585 N Meridian St Ste 200 Indianapolis IN 46290-1067 Business E-Mail: jdb-2@sbcglobal.net.

BLYWISE, BARBARA, mental health services professional; b. Cleve., Nov. 17, 1947; d. Robert Taussig Blywise and Ruth Eleanor Schimberg; m. Richard Erwin Porter (div.); 1 child, Michael Blywise Porter. BA, U. Wash., Bothell, 1996; MA, Seattle U., Wash., 2000. Lic. mental health counselor Wash. Mgr. Martin of London, LA, 1974—81; office mgr. Kings Cabinet, LA, 1981—83; adminstrv. asst. Bear Stearns, LA, 1983—88, Shearson Lehman, Seattle, 1989—90; adminstrv. asst., human resources Oppenheimer Co., Seattle, 1990—93; adminstrv. asst. Merrill Lynch, Belleuve, Wash., 1993—96; clinician III Federal Way Youth and Family, Wash., 1999—2004; pvt. practice, 2004—. Mem.: Am. Mental Health Counselor Assn., Am. Psychol. Assn. Democrat. Jewish. Avocation: jewelry making. Home: 31849 48th Cir SW Federal Way WA 98023 Office: Agy Ctr 402 S 333d St Ste 129 Federal Way WA 98003 Office Phone: 253-929-1529. Office Fax: 253-874-4382. Business E-Mail: b.blywise@comcast.net.

BOAC, THELMA BLANTUCAS, principal; b. Bohol, Philippines, Feb. 13, 1950; d. Diego Campos and Crispina Blantucas de Vera; m. Danilo Sales Boac, July 7, 1973; children: Roland Culajara, Maria Rosalie Culajara. BA, San Francisco State U., 1972; MA in Edn., San Jose State U., 2001. Professional Clear Adminstrv. Credential Calif., 2002. Resource specialist Independence H.S., San Jose, Calif., 1981—90, h.s. villa prin., 2001—05; prin. Silver Creek H.S., San Jose, Calif., 2005—. Edn. cons. Northside Cmty. Ctr., San Jose, 1999—. Bd. mem. Benevolent Assn. Eastside Employees, San Jose, 2005, Human Develop. Internat., 2005. Recipient Dr. Martin Luther King, Jr. Good Neighbor award, Martin Luther King Assn. of Santa Clara County, 2005. Mem.: Nat. Assn. of Secondary Sch. Prins. (assoc. Dr. Jose Rizal Heroes Award 2001). Roman Catholic. Avocations: playing the piano, singing, dancing, travel, kickboxing. Home: 839 Clearview Dr San Jose CA 95133 Office: Silver Creek High Sch 3434 Silver Creek Rd San Jose CA 95121 Home Phone: 408-258-6276; Office Phone: 408-347-5610. Home Fax: 408-937-0358. Personal E-mail: dboac@comcast.net. Business E-Mail: boact@esuhsd.org.

BOACHIE-ADJEI, OHENEBA, orthopedic surgeon; b. Kumasi, Ghana, Dec. 16, 1950; MD, Columbia P & S, NYC, 1980. Diplomate Am. Bd. Orthopaedic Surgery. Intern Saint Vincents Hosp., NYC, 1980-81, res. genl. surg., 1981-82; fellowship orthopaedic pathology Hosp. of Special Surgery, NYC, 1982-83, res. orthopaedic surgery, 1983-86; fellowship spinal surgery Twin Cities Scoliosis Ctr. U. Minn., Mpls., 1986-87, Mpls. Spine Ctr., 1986-87; assoc. staff Abbott-Northwestern Hosp., Minn., 1987-90; med. dir. U. Minn.-Low Back Ctr., 1988-90; assoc. med. dir. Southern Calif. Complex Spine Scoliosis Ctr., 1990-94; ortho. cons. Spine Deformity Svc.,Rancho Los Amigos Hosp., 1990-94; ortho. surg. U. Calif.-Irvine Med. Ctr., 1993-94; staff Long Beach Meml. Med. Ctr., 1993-94; chief scoliosis physician Hosp. Special Surgery, NYC, 1994—, assoc. orthop. surgeon, 1994—; attending orthop. surgeon NY Hosp., 1994—; assoc. attending ortho. surg. Meml. Sloan Kettering Cancer Ctr., 1994—. Instr. orthop. surgery Cornell U. Med. Coll., 1983-86, asst. prof. U. Minn., Twin City Scoliosis Ctr., 1987-90, clin. asst. prof. U. Southern Calif., 1990-94, assoc. clin. prof. orthop. Cornell U. Med. Coll., 1994—. Named one of Best Doctors in NY, NY Mag., 2001, Best Doctors, 2005. Mem. Am. Acad. Ortho. Surg., AMA, N. Am. Spine Soc., Scol. Assn. Chapt. Manhat., Scol. Assn. Long Isl., Scoliosis Rsch. Soc. Office: Hosp Special Surgery 535 E 70th St New York NY 10021-4872 Office Phone: 212-606-1948. E-mail: boachie@hss.edu.

BOADLE-BIBER, MARGARET CLARE, physiologist, educator; b. Melbourne, Australia, Jan. 18, 1943; arrived in U.S., 1967; d. Campbell Dean and Constance Ellen (Browne) Boadle; m. Thomas Ulrich Leonard Biber, Oct. 8, 1969; 1 child, Eric Gustav Nicholas Biber. BS, U. Coll. London, 1964; DPhil, Oxford U., Eng., 1967. Rsch. assoc. pharm. dept. Yale U. Sch. Medicine, New Haven, 1968-69, instr. pharm. dept., 1969-71, asst. prof. pharm. dept., 1971-75; assoc. prof. physiology dept. Va. Commonwealth U., Richmond, 1975-87, prof., 1987—, interim chair, 1991-93, chair, 1993—. Contbr. articles to profl. jours. Mem.: Soc. Neuroscience, Am. Soc. Pharm. and Exptl. Therapeutics, Am. Soc. Neurochemistry. Office: Va Commonwealth U 1101 E Marshall St Richmond VA 23298-0551 Office Phone: 804-828-9756. Business E-Mail: mbiber@vcu.edu.

BOAHEN, KWABENA, bioengineering educator; BS in Elec. and Computer Engrng., MS in Elec. and Computer Engrng., Johns Hopkins U., Balt., 1989; PhD in Computation and Neural Systems, Calif. Inst. Tech., 1997. Asst. prof. depts. bioengineering and elec. engrng. U. Pa., Phila.; assoc. prof. bioengineering Stanford U., Calif., 2006—. Contbr. articles to sci. jours. Recipient Faculty Early Career award, NSF, 2001, Young Investigator award, Office of Naval Rsch., 2002, NIH Dir.'s Pioneer award, 2006; grantee Packard Found. fellowship in Sci. and Engrng., 1999—2004. Achievements include development of a silicon retina able to process images in the same manner as a living retina. Office: Brains in Silicon Stanford U Clark Ctr W3 1 318 Campus Dr W Stanford CA 94305-5441 Office Phone: 650-724-5633. Office Fax: 650-724-5791. E-mail: boahen@stanford.edu.*

BOAL, BERNARD HARVEY, cardiologist, educator, author; b. Winnipeg, Man., Can., May 14, 1937; arrived in US, 1964. s. Charles and Bessie (Carr) B.; m. Pamela Sures Brownstone, Oct. 28, 1962; children: Steven, Jeremy, Hilary. BS in Medicine, U. Man., 1962, MD, 1962. Licentiate Med. Coun. Can.; diplomate Nat. Bd. Med. Examiners, Am. Bd. Internal Medicine in medicine and cardiology. Intern Winnipeg Gen. Hosp., 1962-63, resident in medicine, 1963-64, U. Utah Hosps., Salt Lake City, 1964-66; USPHS trainee in cardiology NYU Med. Ctr., NYC, 1966-68; chief sect. cardiology Booth Meml. Med. Ctr., 1969-87; chief cardiology Cath. Med. Ctr. Bklyn. and Queens, 1987—2002; cons. L.I. Jewish Hosp.; mem. staff NYU Hosp., Bellevue Hosp., 1968-81; clin. assoc. prof. medicine N.Y. Med. Coll., 1981-89, Cornell U. Med. Coll., 1989-95; assoc. prof. medicine Albert Einstein Coll. Medicine, 1995-2000, N.Y. Med. Coll., 2000—03; chief cardiology Bklyn.-Queens region St. Vincents Cath. Med. Ctrs. N.Y., Jamaica, 2000—02; physician, electrophysiology sect. North Shore Univ. Hosp., Manhasset, NY, 2003—. Lectr. in field. Guest editor several major cardiology jours.; asst. editor: HeartNet; contbr. chpts. to books, articles to med. jours. Co-inventor Kolker-Boal Cardiac Pacemaker Electrode. Chmn. physicians divsn. Queens County Cabinet United Jewish Appeals of Greater N.Y., 1978-80; charter mem., founding treas. B'nai B'rith UN unit, 1984—; U.S. physician rep. pacemaker working group of the Internat. Standards Orgn., Geneva, 1988-2004, chmn., 1990-2004. With US Army, 1966—68. Master Am. Coll. Cardiology (chmn. med. devices com., Heart House campaign 1976-78, chmn. bequests and endowments com. 1980-85, pacemaker com. 1987-95, trustee 1985-90, electrocardiology com. 1995-2001, budget/fin./investment com. 1996-2002, devel. com. 1997-2003); fellow ACP (treas. Queens chpt. 1976-78, sec. 1978-79, v.p. 1979-81, pres. 1981-85; govs. adv. coun. NY State 1982-85); fellow NY Cardiol. Soc., Am. Heart Assn., Heart Rhythm Soc. (founding mem., nat. adv. coun. 1984-85, exec. com. 1985-88, chmn. fin. com. 1985-88, trustee 1987-91); mem. AMA, Assn. Advancement Med. Instrumentation (pacemaker com. 1976-2004, chmn. pacemaker com. 1988-2004, bd. dirs. 1983-86, co-chmn. strategic planning com. 1983-85), Am. Heart Assn. (fellow coun. clin. cardiology), NY Heart Assn., Am. Soc. Internal Medicine, Queens Soc. Internal Medicine, US divsn. Israeli Med. Assn. (founding mem.). Office: North Shore Univ Hosp Manhasset NY Office Phone: 516-562-2300. Business E-Mail: bboal@nshs.edu.

BOAL, DEAN, retired arts center administrator, educator; b. Longmont, Colo., Oct. 20, 1931; s. Elmer C. and L. Mildred (Snodgrass) B.; m. Ellen Christine TeSelle, Aug. 23, 1957; children: Brett, Jed. B.Music, B.Music Edn., U. Colo., 1953; M.Music, Ind. U., 1956; D. Musical Arts, U. Colo., 1959. Mem. faculty Hastings (Nebr.) Coll., 1958-60; head piano dept. Bradley U., Peoria, Ill., 1960-66; dean, pianist Peabody Conservatory, Balt., 1966-70; prof. piano, chair music SUNY, Fredonia, 1970-73; pres. St. Louis Conservatory, 1973-76; dir. radio sta. KWMU, St. Louis, 1976-78; v.p., gen. mgr. Sta. WETA-FM, Washington, 1978-83; dir. arts and performance programs Nat. Pub. Radio, Washington, 1982-89; pres. Interlochen (Mich.) Ctr. for the Arts, 1989-95; pres. emeritus, 1995—. Author: Concepts and Skills for the Piano, Book I, 1969, Book II, 1970, Interlochen: A Home for The Arts, 1998; contbr. articles to profl. jours.

Mem. adv. bd U. Colo. Coll. Music, 1987-2000; trustee Alma Coll., 1992-95; bd. dirs., chmn. Peak Assn. of the Arts, 1998-2000. Served with U.S. Army, 1953-55. Woodrow Wilson teaching fellow, 1983-89; recipient Disting. Alumnus award in Profl. Music Univ. Colo., 1987. Mem. Eastern Public Radio Network (chmn. 1979-82), Coll. Music Soc., Pi Kappa Lambda, Mu Phi Epsilon, Phi Mu Alpha. Presbyterian.

BOAL, ELLIS, lawyer; b. Evanston, Ill., Sept. 27, 1944; s. Stewart and Susan (Ballard) Boal; AB, Bowdoin Coll., 1966; JD, Wayne State U., 1972. Bar: Mich. 1973, U.S. Dist. Ct. (ea. dist.) Mich. 1973, U.S. Ct. Appeals (D.C. and 6th cirs.) 1978, U.S. Ct. Appeals (1st cir.) 1981, U.S. Ct. Appeals (7th cir.) 1993. Sole practice, Detroit, 1974—. Author: Teamster Rank and File Legal Rights Handbook, rev. edit., 1984. Mem.: Nat. Lawyers Guild. Green Party. Office Phone: 231-547-2626. E-mail: ellisboal@voyager.net.

BOAL, LYNDALL ELIZABETH, social worker; b. London, Feb. 19, 1936; came to U.S., 1953; d. George Woodall and Mary Barbara (Pearce) Cadbury; m. R. Bradlee Boal Aug. 29, 1959 (div. Sept. 1983); children: Jennifer, Peter. BA with honors, Swathmore Coll., Pa., 1957; MS, Simmons Coll., Boston, 1959. Cert. sch. social worker, N.Y.; lic. social worker, Mass., NY. Social worker Beth Israel Hosp., Boston, 1959-60, Mt. Sinai Hosp., NYC, 1960-61, Meml. Sloan-Kettering Hosp, NYC, 1961-63; cons. Dist. Nursing Svc., Mt. Kisco, N.Y., 1964-65; exec. dir. Planned Parenthood, Mt. Kisco, N.Y., 1965-68; dir. social worker No. Westchester Hosp., Mt. Kisco, N.Y., 1968-78; social worker Fox lane High Sch., Bedford Schs, 1978-81; chmn. com. on handicapped Bedford (N.Y.) Schs., 1981-86; social worker Chappaqua (N.Y.) Sch., 1988—; instr. Fordham U. Sch. Social Svcs., 1994—2003. Bd. dirs. No. Westchester Guidance Ctr., Mt. Kisco, 2003-05; pres. Soc. Hosp. Social Work Dirs., Westchester, N.Y., 1976-78; mem. adv. bd. Mercy Coll. Social Work Program, 1997—, Concordia Coll. Social Work Program, 2001—; v.p. Westchester Children's Assn., 1999-2004, adv. coun., 2007—; mem. N.Y. State Bd. for Social Work, 2004—. Chmn. Narcotics Guidance Coun., Bedford, 1972-75; No. Westchester Coun. Equality pres., Bedford, 1984-86; bd. dirs. Sherrill House, Boston, 1986-88; Dem. committeeman, Bedford, 1983-86. Mem. NASW (sec. N.Y. state chpt. 1993-95, pres. N.Y. State chpt. 1996-98, chair state pers. com. 1993-94, pres. Westchester divsn. 1969-71, 91-92, Merit Svc. award Westchester divsn. 1993, sch. social work sect. steering com. 1994-96), N.Y. State Sch. Social Workers Assn., Kappa Delta Pi. Democrat. Mem. Soc. Of Friends. Avocations: skiing, travel, spending time with family. Home: 508 Millwood Rd Mount Kisco NY 10549-3700 Office: Chappaqua Schs Off of Sch Social Worker Chappaqua NY 10514 Office Phone: 914-238-6170 X 237.

BOAL, PETER CADBURY, performing company executive; b. Bedford, NY, Oct. 18, 1965; s. Richard Bradlee and Lyndall Elizabeth (Cadbury) B.; m. Kelly Cass, Aug. 15, 1992; 3 children: Sebastian Bradlee, Oliver, Sarah. Student, Sch. Am. Ballet, NYC, 1975-83, N.Y. State Summer Sch. Arts, 1981-82. With corps de ballet NYC Ballet, 1983-87, soloist, 1987-89, prin., 1989—2005, Ballet Du Nord, Roubaix, France, 1988; artistic dir. Pacific NW Ballet, Seattle, 2005—. Performed in NYC Ballet's Balanchine Celebration, 1993, also Apollo, Divertimento from Le Baiser de la Fée, Harlequinade. Trustee Profl. Children's Sch. Recipient Award Dance Mag., 1996. Mem. Am. Guild Mus. Artists. Democrat. Avocation: skiing. Office: Pacific NW Ballet 301 Mercer St Seattle WA 98109*

BOALER, JO, education educator; BSc in Psychology, U. Liverpool, Eng., 1985; MA in Math. Edn., London U., 1991, PhD in Math. Edn., 1996. Tchr. secondary sch. math., Camden, London, 1986—89; dep. dir. math. assessment project King's Coll., London U., 1989—93, lectr., rschr. on math. edn., 1993—98; assoc. prof. Stanford (Calif.) U., 2000—. Mem. Math. Edn. Study Panel; bd. dirs. Gender and Edn. jour. Mem.: Internat. Orgn. for Women in Math. Edn. Office: Stanford U Sch Edn 485 Lasuen Mall Stanford CA 94305-3096

BOAMAH-WIAFE, DANIEL, geographer, researcher; arrived in U.S., 1970, naturalized, 1980; s. Daniel Kwabena Boamah and Elizabeth Akosua Adutwumwah; m. Lydia Ampomah, Sept. 11, 1949; children: Michael Yaw, Daniel Kwabena Jr. BA in Geography with honors, U. Ghana, Legon, 1967; MS, U. Wis., 1973, PhD, 1978. Cert. tchr. Ghana Edn. Svc. Assoc. prof. U. Nebr., Omaha, 1977—; prof. geography and Black studies Calif. State U., Chico, 1991—92. Dir. Black studies Calif. State U., Chico, 1991—92. Contbr. Encyclopedia of the Great Plains. Independent. Methodist. Avocations: travel, writing, photography. Office: U Nebr 60th and Dodge Omaha NE 68182-0041 Home Phone: 402-933-5307; Office Phone: 402-554-2412.

BOARD, JOSEPH BRECKINRIDGE, JR., political scientist, educator; b. Princeton, Ind., Mar. 5, 1931; s. Joseph Breckinridge and Rachel Eleanor (Unthank) B.; children from previous marriage: Ian Robert, Annika Caroline, Amanda Anne; m. Mary Squire, Jan. 1, 1998. AB with highest honors, Ind. U., 1953, JD, 1958, PhD, 1962; BA (Rhodes scholar 1953-55), Oxford U., Eng., 1955, MA, 1961; PhD (hon.), Umea U., Sweden, 1973. Tchg. fellow govt. Ind. U., 1955-58, lectr. govt., 1958; asst. prof. polit. sci. Elmira Coll., 1959-61; assoc. prof. polit. sci., chmn. dept. Cornell Coll., 1961-64; prof. polit. sci., chmn. dept. Union Coll., Schenectady, 1964—, Robert Porter Patterson prof. govt., 1973—, chmn. faculty, 1983-85; pres. Paralegals-Plus Assocs., Inc., 1986—. Acad. visitor London Sch. Econs. and Polit. Sci., 1972-73; adj. prof. Albany Law Sch., 1974—; lectr. Green Mountain Acd. Lifelong Learning; scholar-in-residence Sch. Law Ind. U., 1999—; acting prof., chmn. dept. polit. sci. U. Umea, 1979; vis. prof. U. Paris (Sorbonne), 1987; mem. Rhodes Scholarship Selection Com. Nebr., 1961-62, Iowa, 1963-64, N.Y., 1991, 92; mem. regional selection com. for Woodrow Wilson Fellowships, 1966—; mem. exec. coun. Iowa Conf. Polit. Scientists, 1963-65; spl. adv. coll. and univ. affairs Young Citizens for Johnson, 1964; cons. Nat. Endowment Humanities, 1968, N.Y. State Dept. Edn., 1968; mem. polit. sci. adv. com. Fulbright-Hays Program, 1969-73; assoc., adv. com. for Western Europe Coun. for Internat. Exchange of Scholars; chmn. Scandinavian peer rev. com. Linkages Project; mem. U.S. Com. on NATO Fellowships; cons., co-host Nobel Prize broadcast Nat. Pub. Radio, 1976; vis. fellow Oriel Coll., Oxford, 1994—; acad. assoc. The Atlantic Coun.; chair bd. advisors Transnat. Rsch. Project on Effects of European Unification; bd. dirs. Fulbright Assn., Vt. Author: The Government and Politics of Sweden, 1970. Mem. bd. advisors Schenectady Salvation Army; trustee, treas. Schnectady County C.C.; trustee, patron Oriel Coll. (Oxford U.), Devel. Trust, 1991—; pres. bd. trustees Martha Canfield Libr., Arlington, Vt.; vestry mem. Zion Episcopal Ch., Manchester, Vt.; bd. dirs. Vt. Coun. on World Affairs; mem. diocesan coun. Episc. Ch. Vt. Fulbright lectr. Sweden, 1968-69; Ctrl. Am. fellow Assoc. Colls. Midwest, 1962, NDEA fellow, Portuguese, 1963, Acad. Law Sch. Alumni fellow Ind. U.; recipient Disting. Svc. award SUNY Bd. Trustees Cmty. Colls., 1997. Mem. AAUP, Am. Assn. Rhodes Scholars, Am. Polit. Sci. Assn., Ind. Bar, Am. Arbitration Assn., Am-Scandinavian Found. (com. on fellowships 1981-), Northeastern Polit. Sci. Assn. (exec. Coun. 1972), Soc. for Advancement Scandinavian Studies (exec. coun. 1972), United Oxford and Cambridge U. Club (London), The Anglers' Club of NY, Trout Unlimited, Soc. Letters (Lund U.), Acacia, Phi Beta Kappa. Democrat. Episcopalian. Home: 3740 Rt 313 W Arlington VT 05250-8998 Office: Union Coll Political Sci Dept Schenectady NY 12308 Fax: 802-375-8314. Personal E-mail: boardj@sover.net.

BOARDMAN, DAVID, editor-in-chief; m. Barbara Winslow; children: Emily, Madeline. BS in Journalism, Northwestern U., 1979; M in Comm., U. Wash., 1983. Copy editor Football Weekly, Chgo., 1977-79; reporter Anacortes (Wash.) American, 1979-80, Skagit Valley Herald, Mt. Vernon, Wash., 1980-81; reporter, copy editor The News Tribune, Tacoma, 1981-83; copy editor The Seattle Times, 1983, editor, reporter, 1984, nat. editor, 1984-86, local news editor, 1986-87, asst. city editor, 1987-90, regional editor, 1990-96, metro. editor, 1997—, asst. mng. editor, 1997—2003, mgn. editor, 2003—. Vis. faculty Poynter Inst. Media Studies, St. Petersburg, Fla. Recipient Goldsmith Prize in Investigative Reporting JFK Sch. Govt. Harvard U., 1993, Worth Bingham prize, 1993, Investigative Reporters and Editors award, 1993, AP Mng. Editors Pub. Svc. award, 1992, 1st place nat. reporting Pulitzer Prize, 1990, lead editor Pulitzer Prize in investigative reporting, 1997; finalist Pulitzer Prize, 1993, 98, 99, 2002, 03; juror Pulitzer Prizes, 1999-2000; fellow Japan-IBCC fellowship Ctr. Fgn. Journalists, 1995. Office: Seattle Times 1120 John St Seattle WA 98109 also: Seattle Times PO Box 70 Seattle WA 98111 E-mail: dboardman@seattletimes.com.*

BOARDMAN, D(ENNIE) DIXON, investment banker; b. Nov. 7, 1945; s. T. Dennie Boardman and Vivian Dixon; m. Pauline Munn Baker (div. 1999); children: Serena Pauline, Samantha Vivian; m. Princess Arriana Hohenlohe, June 30, 2001. Student, McGill U. Sr. v.p. Kidder, Peabody; mem. chairman's coun. UBS PaineWebber; founder Optima Group, 1988—; mng. gen. ptnr. Optima Fund Mgmt., LLC, NYC; chmn. Optima Mgmt. Partners, LP, Optima Fund Mgmt., LP, Hamilton, Bermuda. Dir. Fla. Crystals Corp.; adv. bd. J.C. Bamford Excavators, England; frequent lectr. in field. Trustee The Game Conservancy Trust; past chmn. Special Projects Com. Meml. Sloan Kettering Cancer Ctr., mem. Pres.'s Coun. Mem.: Deepdale Golf Club (pres.). Office: Optima Fund Mgmt 10 E 53rd St 29th fl New York NY 10022 also: Optima Fund Mgmt 73 Front St Hamilton HM12 Bermuda Office Phone: 212-484-3000. Office Fax: 212-484-3001.

BOARDMAN, ELIZABETH DRAKE, computer security professional; b. Columbus, Ohio, Oct. 14, 1955; d. Jack Martin and Marilyn Hawk Boardman; children: Melissa Grimsley, Stephanie Grimsley. BS Bus. Adminstrn., Ohio State U., 1977; BS in Computer sci., We. Ill. U., 2003; MS in Computer Engring. and Info. Assurance, Iowa State U., 2007. Officer (lt., unrestricted line) U.S. Navy, Various, 1977—85; sr. computer software analyst Analysis & Tech., North Stonington, Conn., 1985—88; database adminstr. We. Ill. U., Macomb, Ill., 2000—02; tchg. asst. computer sci. Iowa State U., Ames, 2003; info. security specialist Boeing, 2005—. Mem., bd. of dirs. Girl Scouts Shining Trail Coun., Burlington, Iowa, 1995—99; fin. com. Trinity United Meth. Ch., Keokuk, Iowa, 2000—02; blue & gold officer U.S. Naval Acad., Annapolis, Md., 1992—94; vol. Girl Scouts of U.S.A., various, 1990—99; life mem. Girl Scouts. Comdr. USNR, 1985—2006. Named Iowa Cmty. Hero Olympic Torch Bearer, Iowa Com. for Olympic Torch Run, 1996. Mem.: Western Ill. Alumni Assn., Mil. Officers Assn. Am., The Ohio State U. Alumni Assn., Naval Res. Assn., Phi Kappa Phi, Upsilon Pi Epsilon, Chi Omega. Avocations: volunteer work, computers, travel.

BOARDMAN, EUNICE, retired music educator; b. Cordova, Ill., Jan. 27, 1926; d. George Hollister and Anna Bryson (Feaster) Boardman. B. Mus. Edn., Cornell Coll., 1947; M. Mus. Edn., Columbia U., 1951; Ed.D., U. Ill., 1963; DFA (hon.), Cornell Coll., 1995. Tchr. music pub. schs., Iowa, 1947-55; prof. music edn. Wichita State U., Kans., 1955-72; vis. prof. mus. edn. Normal State U., Ill., 1972-74, Roosevelt U., Chgo., 1974-75; prof. mus. edn. U. Wis., Madison, 1975-89, dir. Sch. Music, 1980-89; prof. music, dir. grad. program in music edn. U. Ill., Urbana, 1989-98; ret. Author: Musical Growth in Elementary School, 1963, 6th rev. edit., 1996, Exploring Music, 1966, 3d rev. edit., 1975, The Music Book, 1980, 2d rev. edit., 1984, Holt Music, 1987; editor: Dimensions of Musical Thinking, 1989, Dimensions of Musical Thinking: A Different Kind of Music, 2002, Up the Mississippi: A Journey of the Blues, 2002. Named to MENC Hall of Fame, 2004. Mem. Soc. Music Tchr. Edn. (chmn. 1984-86), Music Educators Nat. Conf. Avocations: reading, antiques.

BOARDMAN, HAROLD FREDERICK, JR., lawyer, retired corporate financial executive; b. Darby, Pa., Nov. 23, 1939; s. Harold Frederick and Juanita (Sorzano) B.; m. Martha Eltie, May 23, 1987; children: Kimberly, Leslie, Ashley, Kyle BS, Trinity Coll., Hartford, Conn., 1961; JD with honors, George Washington U., 1964; grad. advanced mgmt. program, Duke U., 1988. Bar: D.C. 1964, Hawaii 1971, N.J. 1974, U.S. Dist. Ct. D.C. 1965, U.S. Ct. Appeals (D.C. cir.) 1965, U.S. Ct. Mil. Appeals 1965, U.S. Supreme Ct. 1969. Gen. atty. Fed. Home Loan Bank Bd., Washington, 1964-66; atty. Hoffmann-LaRoche, Inc., Nutley, NJ, 1966, with, 1973-94, sec., 1979-94, assoc. gen. counsel, 1981-88, v.p., gen. counsel, bd. dirs., exec. com., 1989—94; of counsel Crummy, Del Deo, Dolan, Griffinger & Vecchione, Newark, 1995-96; exec. v.p., gen. counsel, bd. dirs. Rhone-Poulenc Inc., Princeton, NJ, 1996—97; sr. v.p., gen. counsel, bd. dirs., exec. com Rhone Poulenc Rorer, Collegeville, Pa., 1998-99; sr. v.p.-legal Aventis Pharms., 1999-2000, retired, 2000; of counsel Gibbons, Del Deo, Dolan, Griffinger & Vecchione, Newark, 2001—05. Bd. suprs. Hideaway Beach Tax Dist., 2004—06; bd. dirs.m sec. Hideaway Beach Assn., 2004—06. Capt. JAGC USAF, 1966—73. Mem.: Pharm. Mfrs. Assn. (exec. com. law sect. 1991—94), D.C. Bar Assn., Hawaii Bar Assn., N.J. Bar Assn. Episcopalian. Avocations: golf, skiing. Home: PO Box 2296 Middleburg VA 20118 Personal E-mail: rickboardman@earthlink.net.

BOARDMAN, JOHN MICHAEL, mathematician, educator; b. Manchester, Eng., Feb. 13, 1938; arrived in U.S., 1969, naturalized, 1973; s. William Edgar and Carrie (Brown) B.; m. Jacqueline O'Brien Schulman, 1967 (div. 1977); children: Susan, Andrew. BA, Trinity Coll., Cambridge U., 1961, PhD, 1965. Vis. lectr. U. Chgo., 1966-67; asst. lectr. U. Warwick, England, 1967-68; assoc. prof. Johns Hopkins U., Balt., 1969-72, prof., 1972—. Author: Singularities of Differentiable Maps, 1967, (with R.M. Vogt) Homotopy Invariant Algebraic Structures on Topological Spaces, 1973, Modular Representations on the Homology of Powers of Real Projective Space, 1993; (with D.C. Johnson and W.S. Wilson) Unstable Operations on Generalized Cohomology, 1995, Conditionally Convergent Spectral Sequences, 1999. Served with RAF, 1956-58. Sci. Rsch. Coun. fellow, 1964-66; NSF grantee, 1970-88. Mem. Am. Math. Soc. Mem. Soc. Of Friends. Home: 6217 Northwood Dr Baltimore MD 21212-2802 Office: Johns Hopkins U Dept Math 3400 N Charles St Baltimore MD 21218-2686

BOARDMAN, JOSEPH H., federal agency administrator; b. Dec. 1948; m. Joanne Boardman; children: Joe Jr., Emily, Philip. BS, Cornell U.; MS in Mgmt. Sci., SUNY, Binghamton. Mgr. Rome Transp., Rome Parking Authority; commr. pub. transp. Broome County, NY, 1981—88; CEO Progressive Transp. Svcs., Inc., Elmira, NY; dep. commr. NY State Dept. Transp., 1995, asst. commr. Office Pub. Transp., acting commr., 1997, commr., 1997—2005; adminstr. Fed. R.R. Adminstrn., Washington, DC, 2005—. With USAF, 1966—69. Mem.: Am. Pub. Transit Assn., NY Pub. Transit Assn. (pres. 1987—89). Office: Fed Railroad Adminstrn 1120 Vermont Ave NW, 7th Fl Washington DC 20590 Office Phone: 202-493-6014. Office Fax: 202-493-6009.

BOARDMAN, MARK SEYMOUR, lawyer; b. Birmingham, Ala., Mar. 16, 1958; s. Frank Seymour and Flora (Sarinopoulos) B.; m. Cathryn Dunkin, 1983; children:Wilson Paul, Joanna Christina. BA cum laude, U. Ala., University, 1979, JD, 1982. Bar: Ala. 1982, US Dist. Ct. (no., so. and mid. dists.) Ala. 1982, US Ct. Appeals (11th cir.) 1983, US Supreme Ct. 1987. Assoc. Spain, Gillon, Riley, Tate & Etheredge, Birmingham, 1982-84; ptnr. Porterfield, Scholl, Bainbridge, Mims and Harper, P.A., Birmingham, 1984-93, Boardman Carr & Hutcheson PC, Birmingham, 1993—. Pres. Holy Trinity Holy Cross Greek Orthodox Cathedral, 1991, 1992, 2006, sec., 1987, asst. treas., 1986, treas., 1988, 1989, v.p., 1990, 1996—2005, bd. auditors, 1994; mem. coun. Greek Orthodox Diocese of Atlanta, 1992—95; sec. Shelby County Work Release Commn., Ala., 1996; mem. ednl. adv. com. Homewood Bd. Edn., 1999—2002, 2006—07, strategic planning com., 2000—02; pres. Beta Theta Pi House Corp. U. Ala., 2004—07; bd. dirs. Ala. Coun. Sch. Sch. Bd. Attys., 2001—06, Homewood HS PTO, 2004—07; pres. Shades Cahaba PTO, 1999—2000. Mem.: ABA, Ala. Assn. Mcpl. Attys., Ala. Claims Assn., Def. Rsch. Inst., Ala. Def. Lawyers Assn., Birmingham Bar Assn. (co-chmn. econs. of law com. 1997, local bar liaison com. 1997), Shelby County Bar Assn. (treas. 1992—93, sec. 1994, v.p. 1995, pres. 1996, treas. 2007—), Ala. Workers Compensation Claims Assn., Ala. State Bar, Order of Barristers, Pi Sigma Alpha, Delta Sigma Rho-Tau Kappa Alpha, Phi Beta Kappa. Greek Orthodox. Home: 1915 Wellington Rd Birmingham AL 35209-4026 Office: Boardman Carr & Hutcheson PC PO Box 382886 Birmingham AL 35238-2886 also: 400 Boardman Dr Chelsea AL 35043-8211

BOARDMAN, ROBERT A., retired lawyer; b. 1947; BA, Muskingum Coll., 1969; JD, Case Western Reserve U., 1972. Bar: Ohio 1972, Colo. 1976. Assoc. atty. Roetzel & Andress, 1972-75, atty., 1975-83; asst. gen. coun., sec. Manville Corp., Denver, 1983-87, v.p., sec., 1988-90; sr. v.p., gen. coun. Navistar Internat. Corp., Chgo., 1990—2004, ret., 2004. Office: Navistar Internat Corp 4201 Winfield Rd Warrenville IL 60555 Business E-Mail: robert.boardman@nav-international.com.

BOARTFIELD, ERNEST WILLIAM, music educator; b. Montgomery, Ala., Jan. 17, 1973; s. Ernest G. and Rebecca Blakey Boartfield. MusB in edn., Troy State U., 1997, MusM in edn., 1999. Cert. Instrumental Music k-12 Ala. State Dept. of Edn., 1997. Band dir. McIntyre Jr. H.S., Montgomery, Ala., 1997—98, Kendrick H.S., Columbus, Ga., 1998—99; asst. band dir. Prattville Jr. H.S., Prattville, Ala., 2000—01; band dir. Isabella H.S., Maplesville, Ala., 2001—04; band dir., asst. band dir. Millbrook Jr H.S., Stanhope Elmore H.S., Millbrook, Ala. Sec. Nat. H.S. Band Dirs. Assn., Columbus, Ga., 2005—; cons. Nat. H.S. Band Dir. Hall of Fame, Columbus, Ga., 2005—. Paul Yoder scholarship for outstanding svc., Troy State U. Music Dept., 1997. Mem.: Ala. Band Masters Assn., Music Educators Nat. Conf., Phi Mu Alpha, Kappa Kappa Psi. Achievements include tour manager for the Muscogee Troupers, Columbus, Ga. at the 1997 Presidential Inaugural Parade, Washington, D.C. Home: 817 Cottage Ln Prattville AL 36067 Office: Stanhope Elmore HS 4300 Main St Millbrook AL 36054 Home Phone: 334-358-0734; Office Phone: 334-285-7342.

BOAS, FRANK, retired lawyer; b. Amsterdam, North Holland, The Netherlands, July 22, 1930; arrived in U.S., 1940; s. Maurits and Sophie Boas; m. Edith Louise Bruce, June 30, 1981 (dec. July 1992); m. Jean Scripps, Aug. 6, 1993 (div. Dec. 2000). *Father, Maurits Boas, was a pioneer for the International Business Machines Corporation in Europe. He brought the Hollerith Punched Card System, first used in the United States for the 1890 census, to Holland and Belgium after World War I and he founded the IBM organizations in those countries.* AB cum laude, Harvard U., 1951, JD, 1954. Bar: US Dist. Ct. DC 1955, US Ct. Appeals (DC cir.) 1955, US Supreme Ct. 1958. Atty. Office of the Legal Adviser US State Dept., Washington, 1957-59; pvt. practice Brussels and London, 1959-79; of counsel Patton, Boggs & Blow, Washington, 1975-80; pres. Frank Boas Found., Inc., Cambridge, Mass., 1980—2005. Mem. U.S. delegation UN Conf. Law of Sea, Geneva, 1958, 1960; hon. sec. Am. C. of C., Belgium, 1966—78; bd. dirs. Found. European Orgn. Rsch. and Treatment Cancer, Brussels, 1978—87, Paul-Henri Spaak Found., Brussels, 1981—, East-West Ctr. Found., Honolulu, 1990—2001, Law of Sea Inst., Honolulu, 1992—97, Pacific Forum CSIS, Honolulu, 1996—, Honolulu Acad. Arts, 1997—, U. Hawaii Found., 2000—; vice chmn. Commn. Ednl. Exch., Brussels, 1980—87; mem. vis. com. Harvard Law Sch., 1987—91, Ctr. Internat. Affairs, 1988—2005. With US Army, 1955—57. Decorated officer Order of Leopold II Belgium, comdr. Order of Merit Luxembourg, comdr. Order of Crown, comdr. Order of Leopold Belgium; recipient Tribute of Appreciation award, US State Dept., 1981, Harvard Alumni Assn. award, 1996, Resolution of Appreciation, Hawaii Ho. Reps., 2002, Nat. Jefferson award for Outstanding Pub. Svc., 2004, Hawaii award, Am. Bd. Trial Advs., 2005, Bachman Meml. award, Pacific and Asian Affairs Coun., 2006; fellow, Hawaii Pacific U., 2004. Mem.: ABA, Honlulu Social Sci. Assn., Honolulu Com. Fgn. Rels., Pacific and Asian Affairs Coun. (pres. 1998—2004), Fed. DC Bar Assn., Am. and Common Market Club (Brussels pres. 1981—85), Travellers Club (London), Pacific, Outrigger Canoe Clubs (Honolulu). Home: 4463 Aukai Ave Honolulu HI 96816-4858

BOAST, MOLLY SHRYER, lawyer; b. Cin., Apr. 10, 1948; d. Davis Maxwell Shryer and Mary Stratton (Bowlby) Baird; m. Thomas Hansen Boast, Sept. 4, 1971; 1 child, Emma Alice. BA with gen. honors, Coll. William & Mary, 1970; MS in Journalism, Columbia U., 1971, JD, 1979. Bar: N.Y. 1980, U.S. Dist. Ct. (so. dist.) N.Y., U.S. Dist. Ct. (ea. dist.) N.Y., U.S. Ct. Appeals (1st cir.), U.S. Ct. Appeals (2d cir.), U.S. Ct. Appeals (3d cir.), U.S. Supreme Ct. Teaching asst. Columbia U. Grad. Sch. Journalism, NYC, 1971-72; writer, pub. rels. George Jr. Republic, Dryden, NY, 1973-76; assoc. Le Boeuf, Lamb, Leiby & MacRae, NYC, 1979-87, ptnr., mem. exec. com., chmn. litigation dept., 1988; sr. dep. dir. and dir. Bur. of Competition, FTC, 1999—2001; ptnr., mem. litig. dept. Debevoise & Plimpton LLP, NYC, 2001—. Sec., bd. dirs. N.Y. Lawyers for the Pub. Interest, N.Y.C., 1989-99; bd. dirs. Vols. Legal Svc., Inc., N.Y.C. Named Harlan Fiske Stone scholar Columbia U. Sch. Law, N.Y.C., 1979; recipient Jane Marks Murphy prize Columbia U. Sch. Law, N.Y.C., 1979. Mem. ABA (chair ins. industry com. antitrust sect. 1992-95, coun. 1995-98, editl. vice-chmn. Antitrust Law Jour. 1990-92), Fed. Bar Coun. (chair com. on second cir. cts. 1990-93, v.p. 1991-94, trustee 1995-99), City Bar Assn. (chair fed. ctr. com. 2004—), Mortar Bd. Avocations: bicycling, swimming, gardening, reading, music. Office: Debevoise & Plimpton LLP 919 Third Ave New York NY 10022 Office Phone: 212-909-1069. Fax: 212-909-6836. E-mail: msboast@debevoise.com.

BOAT, THOMAS FREDERICK, pediatrician, pulmonologist, researcher, educator; b. Pella, Iowa, Sept. 7, 1939; s. Bert Reuben and Anne Marie (Schoenbohm) B.; m. Barbara Mary Walling, June. 9, 1962; children: Sarah Elizabeth, Mary Barbara, Anne Christine. BA, Cen. Coll., Pella, 1961; MS, U. Iowa, 1965, MD, 1966. Diplomate Am. Bd. Pediat., Am. Bd. Pediat. Pulmonology. Resident in pediat. U. Minn., Mpls., 1966-68; clin. assoc. NIH, Bethesda, Md., 1968-70; fellow in pediat. pulmonology Case Western Res. U., Cleve., 1970-72, instr. pediat., 1972-73, asst. prof., 1973-76, assoc. prof., 1976-81, prof., 1981-82; prof., chmn. dept. pediat. U. N.C., Chapel Hill, 1982-93; chmn. dept. pediat. U. Cin. Sch. Medicine, 1993—; dir. Cin. Children's Hosp. Rsch. Found., 1993—. Prin. investigator Pediat. Pulmonary Specialized Ctr. Rsch., NIH, 1991-93; chmn. Am. Bd. Pediat., 1994. Mem. editl. bd. Lung Rsch. Jour. Bd. dirs. Ronald McDonald House, Chapel Hill, 1985-88, Cystic Fibrosis Found., chmn. rsch. devel. program, 1983—. Lt. comdr. USPHS, 1968-70. Fellow: Am. Acad. Pediat.; mem.: Assn. Accreditation Human Rsch. Programs (v.p. 2007—), Inst. of Medicine, Assn. Med. Sch. Dept. Chairs (pres.-elect 1994—97, pres. 1997—99), Am. Thoracic Soc. (chmn. pediat. assembly 1983—84), Am. Pediat. Soc. (pres. 2000—01). Office: Children's Hosp Med Ctr 3333 Burnet Ave SEC D6 Cincinnati OH 45229-3039 Office Phone: 513-636-4588. Business E-Mail: thomas.boat@cchmc.org.

BOATNER, LYNN ALLEN, research physicist; b. Clarksville, Tex., Aug. 3, 1938; s. Fred Leroi and Nila Allen Boatner; m. Martha Alice Goodwin, Sept. 6, 1961; children: Mark Jesse, Ivan Aaron, Philip Gordon. BS, Tex. Tech U., 1960, MS, 1961; PhD, Vanderbilt U., 1966. With LTV Rsch. Ctr., Dallas, 1966-74, Ecole Poly. Fed. de Lausanne (Switzerland), 1975-77; group leader solid state divsn. Oak Ridge (Tenn.) Nat. Lab., 1977-87, sect. head solid state divsn., 1987—, corp. fellow, 1993—. Gen. chmn. editor procs. workshop Alt. Nuclear Waste Forms and Interactions in Geologic

Media, Gatlinburg, Tenn., 1980; co-chmn. program com. Eighth Am. Conf. on Crystal Growth, Vail, Colo. Assoc. editor: Jour. of Optical Materials, 1991—; contbr. articles to profl. jours. Past. v.p., bd. dirs. Assn. for Retarded Citizens, Anderson County, Tenn.; past. treas., mem. Oak Ridge Sertoma Club; past. chmn. com. on comm. and events parents coun. U. of the South, Sewanee, Tenn. Named for one of 100 Most Significant Tech. Achievements in 1985, Sci. Digest mag.; recipient IR-100 award R&D Mag., 1982, 85, Significant Implications for Energy Tech. in Solid State Physics award U.S. Dept. Energy, 1984. Fellow AAAS, Am. Phys. Soc., ASM Internat. (Francis F. Lucas award 1988), Am. Ceramic Soc., Mineral. Soc. Am., Inst. Materials Mineralogy and Mining (U.K.); mem. Am. Assn. for Crystal Growth (mem. exec. com. 1987, chmn. workshop on crystal growth of high Tc superconducting materials at conf. 1987, Frank Spedding award 2002, Jesse W. Beams prize 2001, Crystal Growth award 2003), Materials Rsch. Soc. (sec. 1992-93, chair membership com. 1989, gen. chmn. meeting 1982), Internat. Metallographic Soc. (Pierre Jacquet Gold Medal award 1988). Achievements include 14 patents in field. Home: 112 Greystone Dr Oak Ridge TN 37830-5607 Office: Oak Ridge Nat Lab MS 6056 PO Box 2008 Oak Ridge TN 37831-2008

BOATWRIGHT, CHARLOTTE JEANNE, marketing professional, public relations executive; b. Chattanooga, Dec. 12, 1937; d. Clifton Jentry and Veltina Novella (Braden) Blevins; m. Robert W. Boatwright; children: Lynn Kay, Janis Ann, Karen Jean, Mary Ruth, Melody Susan, April Celeste. Diploma, Erlanger Sch. Nursing, Chattanooga, 1963; BS in Psychology, U. Tenn., Chattanooga, 1976, MEd, 1981; student in Ministry, U. of the South, Sewanee, Tenn., 1984; PhD in Health Svc. Adminstrn., Columbia Pacific U., San Rafael, Calif., 1987. Diplomate Nat. Assn. Forensic Counselors, Nat. Bd. Addiction Examiners; RN Erlanger Med. Ctr., Tenn., 1963; cert. domestic violence counselor IV Nat. Assn. Forensic Counselors; lic. profl. counselor Tenn., 1976, cert. mediator Mediation Assn., family mediator Tenn. Supreme Ct., 2000. Surgeon's asst. William Robert Fowler, M.D., Chattanooga, 1963—64; instr. med.-surg. nursing Baroness Erlanger Hosp. Sch. Nursing, Chattanooga, 1964—67, instr. fundamentals nursing, 1971—74, chmn. dept. mental health-psychiat. nursing, 1977—81; staff nurse Meml. Hosp., Chattanooga, 1967—68, supr. nursing, 1968—70; dir. inservice edn. Hutcheson Med. Ctr., Ft. Oglethorpe, Ga., 1970—71; youth work cons. Sewanee Dist. Episcopal Chs., Chattanooga, 1975—76; dir. spl. projects N. Park Hosp., Chattanooga, 1984—87, dir. mktg. and pub. rels., 1987—. Pres. CBB Comm.; freelance writer, 1991—; expert witness in field; sr. med. writer Chattanooga HealthScope Mag. Mem. editl. bd.: Rsch. Mag. Founder, pres. Domestic Violence Coalition Greater Chattanooga, 1994; mem. Cmty. Ptnrs. Neighborhood Change-Crime and Neighborhood Safety; crisis intervention homes prevention com. Partnership Families, Children and Adults, residential adv. com.; mem. coalition eliminate homelessness Faith Cmty. Svc. Network, Chatanooga; founding mem. Family Justice Alliance of Chattanooga, 2004; mem. Chattanooga Area Law Enforcement Commn., Chattanooga Fair Housing Roundtable, Chattanooga Endeavors Re-entry Roundtable; mem. Safe in My Wjorld and Leadership Camp Project, Girls, Inc.; mem. Regional Interagy. Coun. on Homelessness; mem. com. on legis. SE Tenn. Coun. on Children & Youth; mem. Tenn. Coalition Against Domestic Violence and Sexual Abuse; mem. gender-specific project Tenn. Dept. Probation & Parole; mem. SE Devel. Adv. Coun. Tenn. Econ. Coun. on Women; mem. campus violence prevention project U. Tenn. Chattanooga Transformation Project; leadership faculty fellow doctoral leadership and learning program U. Tenn. Chattanooga, instr. Tenn. State Victims Assistance Acad.; founding mem., pres. Coalition Against Domestic and Cmty. Violence of Greater Chattanooga, Inc.; founding mem., coord., adv. com. Chattanooga/Hamilton County Family Justice Alliance, 2004; founding mem. Hamilton County Domestic Violence Fatality Rev. Team, 2006; mem. residential programs adv. com. Partnership Families, Children and Adults; mem. oversight bd. Hamilton County Domestic Violence Task Force Law Enforcement Prosecution Unit, 1997—2001; mem. Hamilton County adv. bd. Tenn. Dept. Children's Svcs.; mem. steering com. Tenn. Conf. Social Welfare; mem. Blue Monarch/Blue Chair Program for abused/addicted women and their children, Grundy County, Tenn.; mem. steering com. M.L. King Weed and Seed Project; mem. planning and devel. team Legal Aid of East Tenn.; mem. dept. youth work Episcopal Diocese Tenn., 1975—77, mem. violence in soc. resource team, pres. diaconate formation com., 2002, mem. crisis response team; bd. dirs. Family Violence Shelter Com., Sexual Abuse Resource Ctr., Child Abuse Prevention Coun., Opportunity Home, Chattanooga; mem. oversight bd. Hamilton County Domestic Violence Task Force; bd. dirs. Crisis/Homelessness Prevention Svcs.; bd. dirs., chair homelessness prevention/crisis intervention subcom., chair family violence shelter/svcs. and sexual assault resource ctr. subcom. Partnership Families, Children and Adults; vice chmn. Brynewood Park Cmty. Assn., 1985, 1986; coord. Chattanooga Family Justice Alliance, 2004. Recipient Liberty Bell award, Chattanooga Bar Assn., 1997, Outstanding Advocacy for Children, Families and Cmty. award, SE Tenn. Coun. Children and Youth, 2000, Mayor's Best Practices award, 2000, Cmty. Svc. award, United Way Tapestry of Vols., 2005, Shirley Chisholm Unbought and Unbossed award to women who have changed Chattanooga, Girls, Inc., 2006. Mem.: Nat. Assn. Forensic Counselors, Chattanooga C. of C., Chattanooga Press Assn., Tenn. Soc. Hosp. Mktg. and Pub. Rels., Tenn. Hosp. Assn., Am. Coll. Healthcare Execs. (nominee), U. Tenn. Alumnae Assn. Republican. Avocations: music, reading, gardening, travel.

BOAZ, DAVID DOUGLAS, foundation executive; b. Mayfield, Ky., Aug. 29, 1953; s. Seth Thomas Jr. and Martha Elizabeth (Pruitt) B. BA, Vanderbilt U., 1975. Exec. dir. Young Am.'s Found., Sterling, Va., 1975-76; editor New Guard Mag., Sterling, Va., 1976-78; exec. dir. Coun. for a Competitive Economy, Washington, 1978-80; rsch. dir. Clark for Pres. Com., Washington, 1980; v.p. Cato Inst., Washington, 1981-89, exec. v.p., 1989—. Bd. dirs. Ctr. for Ind. Thought, NYC, Women's Freedom Network; bd. regents Congl. Schs. Va., 1991-2003. Author: Libertarianism: A Primer, 1997; co-editor: Beyond the Status Quo, 1985, An American Vision, 1989, Market Liberalism: A Paradigm for the 21st Century, 1993, Cato Handbook for Congress, 2001; editor: Left, Right and Babyboom, 1986, Assessing the Reagan Years, 1988, The Crisis in Drug Prohibition, 1990, Liberating Schools: Education in the Inner City, 1991, The Libertarian Reader, 1997, Toward Liberty, 2002; contbr. Encyclopedia Brittanica, also books and newspapers. Office: Cato Inst 1000 Massachusetts Ave NW Washington DC 20001-5400

BOBAK, MARK T., lawyer; b. 1959; JD cum laude, St. Louis U. Sch. Law, 1984. With Anheuser-Busch Cos., St. Louis, 1992—96, assoc. gen. counsel, 1996—2000, v.p., corp. human resources, 2000—04, group v.p., chief legal officer, 2004—. Office: Anheuser-Busch Cos One Busch Pl Saint Louis MO 63118 Office Phone: 314-577-2000.

BOBANGO, JOHN ALLEN, lawyer; b. Bremerton, Wash., July 11, 1955; s. Charles John and Myrtie Bonita Bobango; m. Lisa Walker, July 31, 1982; children: Allen, Mary Lauren. BA, Ark. State U., 1978; JD, U. Memphis, 1983; LLM in Taxation, U. Fla., 1984. Bar: Tenn. 1983, Ark. 1984, Fla. 1986. With Black Bobango & Morgan, Memphis, 1994—99, Farris Matthews Branan Bobango Hellen & Dunlap, PLC, Memphis, 2000—. Bd. dirs. Street Ministries, Memphis, 2003—; city councilman Memphis City Coun., 1996—2000; chmn. City of Memphis, Shelby County, 2000—, Cmty. Redevelopment Agy.; mem. Meth. Healthcare Found., 2005—; bd. dirs. Riverfront Devel. Corp., Memphis, 2004—. Mem.: Econ. Club Memphis (bd. mem.), Pi Kappa Alpha Internat. (legal counsel to Supreme Coun. 2004—). Republican. Meth. Office: Farris Matthews Branan BobangoHellen & Dunlap 1100 Ridgeway Loop Ste 400 Memphis TN 38120 Office Phone: 901-259-7120. Office Fax: 901-259-7180.

BOBBITT, JUANITA CRAWFORD, international organization executive; b. NYC, Sept. 4, 1938; d. Philip Theodore and Lillian Beatrice (Nelson) Crawford; 1 child, Edmund Michael. BA in Romance Lang., CUNY, Bklyn., 1959; MA in Econ., NYU, 1982; MPA, Harvard U., 1984. Pub. adminstrn. officer UN, NYC, 1974-84, econ. affairs officer, 1984-92, sr. pub. adminstrn. officer, 1992-97, head gender adv. svcs. unit, 1998, internat. devel. cons., 1999—. Contbr. articles to profl. jours. Exec. com. St. George's Cmty. Devel. Corp., Bklyn., 1994-99; rep. provincial coun. Episcopal Ch., 1993-96. Mem.: ASPA (exec. com., sect. internat. comparative adminstrn.), Tri-State J.F. Kennedy Alumni Assn. (exec. com. 1987—), Harvard Club (admissions com. 2001—03, program com. 2002—04, 2005—07), Delta Sigma Theta (pres. Bklyn. chpt. 1966—68, nat. projects com. 1973—74, chair internat. com. 1993—99, nat. social action commn. 2002—). Episcopalian. Avocations: reading, walking, dance, arts.

BOBBITT, LEROY, lawyer; b. Jackson, Miss., Nov. 1, 1943; s. Leroy and Susie (Catchings) B.; m. Andrea Marie James, Sept. 18, 1965; children: Dawn, Antoinette. BA, Mich. State U., 1966; JD, Stanford U., 1969. Bar: Calif. 1969, N.Y. 1970. Atty. East Palo Alto (Calif.) Legal Aid, 1969-70; assoc. Paul, Weiss, Rifkind, Wharton & Garrison, NYC, 1970-74, Loeb and Loeb, LA, 1974—96, ptnr. dept. entertainment; ptnr. Bobbitt & Roberts, Santa Monica, Calif. Mem. Friends of NAACP Legal Def. Fund, L.A., 1991—; bd. advisors Operation Hope, L.A., 1992—. Named one of Am.'s Top Black Attys., Black Enterprise mag., 2003. Mem. ABA, Nat. Bar Assn., Langston Bar Assn., Black Entertainment and Sports Lawyers Assn. (pres., bd. dirs. 1991-94). Democrat. Avocation: golf. Office: Bobbitt & Roberts 6100 Ctr Dr Ste 910 Los Angeles CA 90045 Office Phone: 310-645-4100. Business E-Mail: lbobbitt@bobroblaw.com.

BOBBITT, PHILIP CHASE, law educator, writer; b. Temple, Tex., July 22, 1948; s. Oscar Price and Rebekah Luruth (Johnson) B.; m. Selden Anne Wallace (div. 1990). AB, Princeton U., 1971; JD, Yale U., 1975; PhD, Oxford U., 1983, MA, 1984. Bar: Tex. 1977, U.S. Supreme Ct. 1989. Law clk. to Judge Henry Friendly U.S. Ct. Appeals (2d cir.), 1975-76; asst. prof. law U. Tex., Austin, 1976-79, prof., 1979—, A.W. Walker chair in law, 1996—. Assoc. counsel to Pres. U.S. for intelligence and internat. security, 1980-81; legal counsel U.S. Senate Select Com. on Secret Mil. Assistance to Iran and Nicaraguan Opposition, 1987-88; counselor on internat. law U.S. Dept. of State, 1990-93; dir. for intelligence NSC, 1997-98, sr. dir. critical infrastructure, 1998-99, sr. dir. strategic planning, 1999; mem. faculty Salzburg Seminar, 1987; vis. fellow Internat. Inst. Strategic Studies, 1981-82; jr. rsch. fellow Nuffield Coll., Oxford U., 1982-84, rsch. fellow, 1984-85, Anderson sr. rsch. fellow, 1985-91, mem. modern history faculty, 1984-91; guest scholar Woodrow Wilson Ctr. for Internat. Scholars, 1994; sr. rsch. fellow war studies King's Coll./U. London, 1994-97. Author: Democracy and Deterrence, 1988; (with Guido Calabresi) Tragic Choices, 1979, Constitutional Fate, 1982; (with Lawrence Freedman and Gregory Treverton) Nuclear Strategy, 1988, Constitutional Interpretation., 1991, The Shield of Achilles: War, Peace and the Course of History, 2002. Trustee Princeton U. Mem. Am. Law Inst., Internat. Inst. Strategic Studies (London), Austin Coun. Fgn. Affairs (pres. 1983—), Coun. Fgn. Rels. (N.Y.C.), Adminstrv. Conf. U.S. (spl. com. on ethics in govt.), Pacific Coun. on Internat. Policy, Nat. Infrastructure Assurance Coun., Tex. Philos. Soc., Am. Acad. Art & Scis. (fellow 2004-). Democrat. Baptist. Office: U Tex Law Sch 727 E 26th St Austin TX 78705-3224

BOBBY, THEODORE N., lawyer, food products executive; m. Mary Kathryn Bobby; 2 children. BS, Univ. Pitts., 1973, JD, 1977. Atty. H.J. Heinz Co., Pitts., 1980—97, assoc. gen. counsel, 1997—99, v.p. legal affairs, 1999—2005, sr. v.p., gen. counsel, 2005—. Office: HJ Heinz Co 800 Grant St Pittsburgh PA 15219*

BOBCO, WILLIAM DAVID, JR., consulting engineering company executive; s. William David and Eleanor Josephine (Dvojack) B.; m. Donna Domenica DiFrancesca, Sept. 13, 1969; 1 child, Christina Marie. BS in Engring., U. Ill., Chgo., 1969; MBA in Prodn. Mgmt., U. Chgo., 1983. Prodn. mgr. Am. Can Co., Maywood, Ill., 1972-73; with Footlik & Assocs., Evanston, Ill., 1973—, exec. v.p., 1986—2006, pres., 2006—. Mem. indsl. adv. bd. U. Ill. Coll. Engring., Chgo., 1992-2004, chmn. alumni devel. com., 1991-95, mem. dean selection com., 1994, com. mem. 40th Anniversary Chgo. Campus, 2004. Vol. Art Inst. Chgo., 1983—84, Animal Care League, Oak Park, Ill., 2000—02; vol. warehousing cons. Am. Red Cross, Chgo., 2007—; facilities and grounds com. St. Giles Parish, 1995—97, co-chair, 1997—2001, lions leap com., 1998—2001, chmn. golf scholarship com., 1999—, treas. golf com., 2000—, chmn., 2001—, chmn. golf com., 2002—, steering com. capitol campaign, 2002, mem. fin. com., 2003—; Eucharistic Minister St. Giles Ch., 2000—, bus. mgr. selection com., 2004; sec. St. Giles Men's Soc., 2007. Capt. Ordnance Corp. US Army, 1969—72, W. Germany, Vietnam. Mem. ASME (bd. dirs. Chgo. sect. 1984-2001, newsletter editor 1987-98, vice chmn. 1991, chmn. Chgo. sect. 1992-94, 2007—, region VI rep. to A World in Motion K-12 tng. program), SAE(co-sponsor 1993), Engring. Alumni Assn. U. Ill. Chgo. (pres. 1984-88, bd. dirs. 1975-99), U. Ill. Alumni Assn. (bd. dirs. 1985-91, nominating com. 1991, mem. pres.' coun. 1988—, Loyalty award 1988, Constituent Leadership award 1991, Disting. Svc. award 1994). Independent. Roman Catholic. Avocations: travel, art, music. Office: Footlik & Assocs 2521 Gross Point Rd Evanston IL 60201-4993 Office Phone: 847-328-5644. Personal E-mail: wocbobjr@comcast.net.

BOBEK, NICOLE, professional figure skater; b. Chgo., Aug. 23, 1977; Competitive history includes: mem. of 1st place team Hershey's Kisses Challenge, 1997, placed 13th in World Championships, 1997, 3rd in Nat. Sr., 1997, 2nd (team) U.S. Postal Svc. Challenge, 1996, 3rd (team) Hershey's Kisses Challenge, 1996, 10th place Centennial on Ice, 1996, 1st place Starlight Challenge, 1995, 3rd in World Championships, 1995, 1st in Nat. Sr., 1995, 2d place, World Pro Championship, 2000, 3d place, Canadian Open, 2001, numerous others. Champions on Ice Tour, 2000-. Avocations: dance, drawing, poetry, modeling, designing clothes. Office: USFSA 20 1st St Colorado Springs CO 80906-3624

BOBER, JOANNE L., lawyer, retail executive; b. NYC, Dec. 14, 1952; BA, Wash. U., 1974; JD, Georgetown U., 1980. Bar: Tex. 1980. Assoc. Moore & Peterson, 1980—82, Jones, Day, Reavis & Pogue, NYC, 1983—88, ptnr., 1989—96; sr. v.p., gen. counsel, sec. Gen. Signal Corp., Stamford, Conn., 1997—99; sr. v.p., gen. counsel Chubb Corp., Warren, NJ, 1999—2005; exec. v.p., gen. counsel, sec. J.C. Penney Corp. Inc., Plano, Tex., 2005—. Mem.: ABA, Tex. Bar Assn., Phi Beta Kappa. Office: JC Penney Corp Inc 6501 Legacy Dr Plano TX 75024*

BOBER, LAWRENCE HAROLD, retired banker; b. NYC, Mar. 29, 1924; s. Michael N. and Julia (Verschleiser) B.; m. Natalie S. Birnbaum, Aug. 27, 1950; children: Stephen, Marc, Elizabeth. BS, NYU, 1949; postgrad., Grad. Sch. Bus. Adminstrn., 1949-50. With Hanover Bank (now J.P. Morgan-Chase), 1941-87, asst. sec., 1950-52, asst. treas., 1953-55, asst. v.p., 1955-60, v.p., 1960-71, sr. v.p. (North Am. div.-II), 1971-87; ret., 1987. Dir., past chm. The Renesselaerville Inst.; past vice chmn., bd. fellows Brandeis U.; past pres. Congregation Emanuel of Westchester; past pres. Cobblefield Homeowners Assn. White Plains, NY. 1st lt. USAAF, 1942-45. Decorated D.F.C. with two oak leaf clusters, Air medal with three oak leaf clusters; recipient Human Relations award Am. Jewish Com., 1968, Community Service award Nat. Jewish Hosp. and Research Center, 1980, Community Service award Am. Jewish Congress, 1988. Home: 7 Westfield Ln White Plains NY 10605-5459

BOBERG, DOROTHY KURTH, author; b. Lincoln, Nebr., Mar. 17, 1930; d. Herman R. and Regina E. Kurth; m. John Elliott Boberg, Sept. 17, 1951; 1 child, Mark. BA, U. Nebr., 1951; postgrad., Calif. State U., Northridge, 1959-62, U. So. Calif., 1981. Libr. Nebr. Legis. Coun., Lincoln, 1952; child welfare worker L.A. County, 1953-57, 67-68; rsch. assoc. Nuclear Facilities/Radiation Monitoring in Calif. Another Mother for Peace, Beverly Hills, Calif., 1975; exec. v.p. So. Calif. divsn. UN Assn., LA, 1977-78. Author: Evolution and Reason Beyond Darwin, 1993; editor Nebraska Blue Book. Resolutions chair LA County Dem. Cen. Com.; chair UN Internat. Solar Exhibition, LA, 1978, Mayor's Lifeline Com., Earthquake Prediction Task Force; pres. Northridge Civic Assn., 1971-73; founding bd. mem. Northridge East Neighborhood Coun., 2004; bd. dirs. Nat. Alliance for Democracy, 2004-05. Recipient Achievement award Nebr. Sec. State, 1993, Admiral, Nebr. Navy/Gov. State Nebr., 1993. Mem. AAAS, Soc. Study Evolution, AAUW (pres. San Fernando Valley Br. 1966-67), Phi Beta Kappa, Psi Chi, Alpha Kappa Delta. Home: 10912 Nestle Ave Northridge CA 91326-2849

BOBINS, NORMAN R., banker; m. Virginia Bobins. BS, U. Wis., 1964; MBA, U. Chgo., 1967. Sr. v.p. Am. Nat. Bank & Trust Co., 1967—81; sr. exec. v.p., chief lending officer Exch. Nat. Bank Chgo., 1981—90; sr. exec. v.p. ABN AMRO Bank N.V., Netherlands; chmn., pres. & CEO LaSalle Nat. Bank, Chgo., 1990—; pres. & CEO LaSalle Bank Corp., Chgo. Vice chmn. Standard Fed. Bank, N.A., bd. dirs.; mem. bd. Ill. Bus. Roundtable; mem. bd. trustees CenterPoint Properties Trust. Treas., bd. dirs. Fin. Svcs. Roundtable, Washington; former chmn. bd. Chicagoland C. of C.; mem. Bd. Edn., Chgo., 1994—; bd. trustees Chgo. Cmty. Trust; exec. bd. Auditorium Theatre Coun., Chgo.; bd. dirs. Terra Found. Arts; bd. trustees Field Mus., Art Inst. Chgo., U. Chgo. Hospitals. Recipient Human Rights medallion, Am. Jewish Com., 1992, Keshet Rainbow award, 1997, Reach for Excellence award, Midtown Ednl. Found., 1998, Bus. Leadership award, DePaul U., 1999, Jane Addams Hull House medal, 2000, Chmn.'s award, Boys & Girls Clubs, 2002, Lifetime Achievement award, Assn. Corp. Growth, 2003, Richard J. Daley medal, 2005. Mem.: Comml. Club Chgo. (civic. com.), Banker's Club of Chgo. (pres.), Anti-Defamation League of B'nai B'rith (bd. dirs., Disting. Svc. award 1982). Office: LaSalle Bank NA 135 S La Salle St Fl 3 Chicago IL 60603-4404*

BOBINSKI, GEORGE SYLVAN, librarian, educator; b. Cleve., Oct. 24, 1929; s. Sylvan and Eugenia (Sarbiewski) B.; m. Mary Lillian Form, Feb. 20, 1953; children-George Sylvan, Mary Anne. BA, Case Western Res. U., 1951, MS in Libr. Sci., 1952; MA, U. Mich., 1961, PhD, 1966. Rsch. asst. Bus Info. Bur., Cleve. Pub. Libr., 1954-55; asst. dir. Royal Oak (Mich.) Pub. Libr., 1955-59; dir. librs. State U. Coll. at Cortland, NY, 1960-67; prof., asst. dean Sch. Libr. Sci. U. Ky., 1967-70; prof. SUNY, Buffalo, 1970—2001, dean Sch. Info. and Libr. Studies, 1970-99, prof. emeritus, 2002—. Fulbright-Hays lectr. in libr. sci. U. Warsaw, Poland, 1977; trustee Western N.Y. Libr. Rsch. Coun., 1971-87, pres., 1972, 82; vis. scholar Jagiellonian U., Krakow, Poland, 1992, 97. Author: A Brief History of the Libraries of Western Reserve University, 1826-1952, 1955, Carnegie Libraries, Their History and Impact on American Public Library Development, 1969, Dictionary of American Library Biography, 1978, Libraries and Librarianship: Sixty Years of Challenge and Change, 1945-2005, 2007; contr. articles to profl. jours. Mem. N.Y. Gov.'s Commn. on Librs., 1990—95. With AUS, 1952-54. Recipient Meritorious Svc. medal Jagellonian U., Krakow, Poland, 1997. Mem. ALA (mem. pub. com., mem. coun.), N.Y. Libr. Assn., Assn. Am. Libr. Schs. (chmn. coun. of deans 1985-86) Home: 69 Little Robin Rd Buffalo NY 14228-1125 Office: SUNY Buffalo Dept Libr and Info Studies Baldy Hall Buffalo NY 14260 Office Phone: 716-645-2412. Personal E-mail: gsbobinski@aol.com. Business E-Mail: bobinski@buffalo.edu.

BOBIS, DANIEL HAROLD, lawyer; b. NYC, May 1, 1918; s. Morris N. and Sarah C. Bobis; m. Selma Linder, May 15, 1960 (dec. Mar. 26, 2003); children: Jodee E. Bobis Verbow, Stacee M. Bobis Miccio. LLB, St. Lawrence U., 1939; BS, Columbia U., 1947. Bar: N.Y. 1949, U.S. Patent and Trademark Office 1950, U.S. Supreme Ct. 1961, U.S. Ct. Appeals (3d cir.) 1963, N.J. 1964, U.S. Dist. Ct. N.J. 1964, U.S. Ct. Appeals (fed. cir.) 1982. Patent atty. Worthington Corp. (name now Studebaker-Worthington Corp.), Harrison, NJ, 1946-1952, patent counsel, until 1969; mem. firm Popper, Bain, Bobis, Gilfillan & Rhoades, Newark, 1969-74, Popper & Bobis, Newark, 1974-79, Popper, Bobis & Jackson, Newark, 1979-88; of counsel Lerner, David, Littenberg, Krumholz & Mentlik, Westfield, NJ, 1988—. Founder Ann. Outstanding Patent Award N.J. Coun. R & D, 1966; former instr. intellectual property matters and causes Horizon Sch. Paralegal Tng., Linden, NJ. Capt. pilot AC US Army, ETO. Decorated Air medal with one silver and 2 bronze oak leaf clusters, Purple Heart. Mem.: ABA (chmn., mem. intellectual property coms.), N.J. Patent Law Assn. (pres. 1966, chmn., mem. intellectual property coms.), N.J. Bar Assn. (chmn., mem. intellectual property coms.). Home: 30 Burnham Ct Scotch Plains NJ 07076-3129 Office: Lerner David Littenberg Krumholz & Mentlik 600 South Ave W Ste 300 Westfield NJ 07090-1497 Home Phone: 732-388-3665; Office Phone: 908-654-5000. Business E-Mail: dbobis@ldlkm.com.

BOBISUD, LARRY EUGENE, mathematics professor; b. Midvale, Idaho, Mar. 16, 1940; s. Walter and Ida V. (Bitner) B.; m. Helen M. Meyer, June 15, 1963. BS, Coll. of Ida., 1961; MA, U. N.M., 1963, PhD, 1966. Vis. mem. Courant Inst. Math. Scis. NYU, NYC, 1966-67; prof. math. U. Idaho, Moscow, 1967—2002, prof. emeritus, 2002—. Contbr. articles to profl. jours. Mem. Am. Math. Soc. Home: 860 N Eisenhower St Moscow ID 83843-9581 Office: Univ Idaho Dept Math Moscow ID 83844-1103 Business E-Mail: bobisud@uidaho.edu.

BOBO, LAWRENCE D., sociologist; b. Nashville, Feb. 18, 1958; married. BA in sociology, Loyola Marymount U., 1979, DHL (hon.), 2001; MA in sociology, U. Mich., 1981, PhD in sociology, 1984; MA (hon.), Harvard U., 1997. With sociology dept. U. Wis., Madison, 1984—90, UCLA, 1990—97; with Harvard U., 1997—, Norman Tishman and Charles M. Diker prof. sociology and African Am. studies, 2001—05; Martin Luther King Jr. Centennial prof. sociology Stanford U., 2005—, dir. Ctr. Comparative Study of Race and Ethnicity, 2005—, chair Program in African and African Am. Studies, 2005—. Bd. mem. Am. Inst. Rsch., Roper Ctr., Ctr. Comparative Study Race and Ethnicity, Stanford U., Inst. Govt. and Pub. Affairs, U. Ill. Founding co-editor Dubois Review: Social Sci. Rsch. Race; co-author: Racial Attitudes in America: Trends and Interpretations, 1997; sr. editor Prismatic Metropolis: Inequality in LA, 2000; co-editor: Racialized Politics: The Debate on Racism in America, 2000, Urban Inequality: Evidence from Four Cites, 2001. Fellow: Am. Acad. Arts and Sciences; mem.: NAS. Office: Dept Sociology Stanford Unive 450 Serra Mall Bldg 120 Stanford CA 94305 Office Phone: 650-723-3956. Office Fax: 650-725-6471. Business E-Mail: bobo@wjh.harvard.edu. E-mail: lbobo@stanford.edu.

BOBOC, MARIUS, education educator; b. Constanta, Romania, Aug. 31, 1967; s. Nicolae and Marcela Boboc. MA in Edn., Roosevelt U., 1997; EdD, U. No. Iowa, 2002. Progam asst. U. No. Iowa, Cedar Falls, 2001—02; asst. prof. Cleve. State U., 2002—. Asst. prof. Ovidius U., Constanta, Romania, 1997—99. Grantee, Roosevelt U., 1995—96; scholar, 1996—97; John J. Kamerick fellow, U. No. Iowa, 2001—02, C.A. & Katherine Bemler Edn. scholar, 2000—01, 2001—02, John S. Latta Endowed Doctoral scholar, 2001—02. Mem.: ASCD, Am. Assn. Colleges Tchr. Edn., Am. Assn. Higher Edn., Am. Edl. Rsch. Assn. Office: Cleveland State University 2121 Euclid Ave Cleveland OH 44115 Office Phone: 216-687-4581.

BOBRINSKOY, CHARLES KELLOGG, investment banker; b. Chgo., Aug. 7, 1959; s. George V. and Elizabeth (Shaw) B.; m. Mary Anne Kane, May 11, 1985; children: Gregory, Amy, Nicholas, Michael, Alexander. AB, Duke U., 1981; MBA, Univ. Chgo., 1983. Assoc. Salomon Bros. Inc., NYC, 1983-86, v.p. Chgo., 1986-89, dir. fin., 1989-94; mng. dir. Citigroup Global Mkts. (formerly Salomon Bros. Inc.), 1994—2004; vice-chmn., dir. rsch. Ariel Capital Mgmt., Chgo., 2004—. Bd. dirs., Envirolyne Industries, Oak Brook, Ill., 1989—. Bd. dirs. Juvenile Protection assn., Chgo., LaRabida Children's Found., Mus. Sci. & Industry, Chgo. Urban League, Big Shoulders Fund, Duke Univ. Libr. Bd. Mem. North Shore Country Club, Chgo. Club. Republican. Office: Ariel Capital Mgmt Ste 2900 200 E Randolph Dr Chicago IL 60601*

BOBROW, RICHARD S., lawyer, former diversified financial services executive; BSBA, MSBA, Kans. Univ. With Ernst & Young LLP, NYC, 1976—2004, ptnr., 1984—2004, tech. specialist nat. tax on real estate and partnership matters, 1985—88, dir. West Region, real estate adv. svcs. LA, 1988—91, dir. tax Indpls., 1991—93, nat. dir. tax, 1993—96, vice chair tax practice initiatives NYC, 1996—98, sr. vice chair assurance and adv. bus. svcs., 1998—2000, CEO Americas, 2002—02, global CEO, 2002—03; COO Chadbourne & Parke LLP, NYC, 2006—. Office: Chadbourne & Parke LLP 30 Rockefeller Plz New York NY 10112 E-mail: rbobrow@chadbourne.com.

BOBROW, SUSAN LUKIN, retired lawyer; b. Cleve., Jan. 18, 1941; d. Adolph and Yetta (Babkow) Lukin; m. Martin J. Bolhower, Nov. 28, 1986 (div. Dec. 1988); children from previous marriage: Elizabeth Bobrow Pressler, Erica, David. Student, Antioch Coll., Yellow Springs, Ohio, 1958-61; BA, Antioch Coll., LA, 1975; JD, Southwestern U., LA, 1979. Bar: Calif. 1980. Pvt. practice, Beverly Hills, Calif., 1983-88; assoc. Schulman & Miller, Beverly Hills, 1988-89; staff counsel Fair Polit. Practices Commn., Sacramento, 1990-96; sr. counsel Calif. State Lottery, Sacramento, 1996-98; asst. gen. counsel Employment Tng. Panel, Sacramento, 1998—2003, acting. gen. counsel, 2004—06; ret., 2006. Panel for paternity defense L.A. Superior Ct., 1984. Exhibited paintings at Death and Trasnfiguration Show, Phantom Galleries, Sacramento, 1994; exhibited photography Phantom Galleries, Sacramento, 1997, Camera Arts, Sacramento, 1998, Viewpoint Gallery Exhibit, Sacramento, 1998-2006, Nimbus Winery, 2005, Woodbridge Winery, 2006 (award), Appel Gallery, Sacramento, The Univ. of Pacific, 2006, Old Sugar Mill, Clarksburg, Calif., 2007. Broadcast vol. Access News, Assn. Blind, Sacramento, 2004-2005; reader Calif. Access News Sys., Sacramento Assn. Blind; bd. dir. San Fernando Valley Friends Homeless Women and Children, North Hollywood, Calif., 1985-88, Jewish Family Svcs., 1997, Sacramento Jewish Family Svcs., 1997-98, Viewpoint Photographic Arts Ctr., 2006; mem. adv. bd. Project Home, Sacramento Interfaith Svc. Coun., 1990-91; v.p. cmty. affairs B'nai Israel Sisterhood, Sacramento, 1991-93. Recipient commendation Bd. Govs. State Bar of Calif., 1984. Mem. Inst. Noetic Scis., Sacramento Inst. Noetic Scis. (steering coun. 1994), Los Angeles County Bar Assn. (Barristers com. on adminstrn. of justice 1985), Sacramento County Bar Assn. (com. on profl. responsibility 1993-94, alt. del. to state bar conv. 1991), Viewpoint Photog. Arts Ctr. Democrat.

BOBZIEN, DAVID P., lawyer; b. 1946; BA in Polit. Sci., Coll. Holy Cross, 1968; JD, U. Va., 1971; LLM, George Washington U. Former judge advocate gen. U.S. Army; pvt. practice; with office profl. responsibility Justice Dept.; county atty. Fairfax, Va., 1993—. Chmn. goals commn. Fairfax County, mem. planning commn.; bd. dirs. Va. Law Found.; bd. dirs., past pres. Fairfax Law Found. Mem.: Local Govt. Attys. Va. (past pres.), Va. State Bar (pres. 2004—05, past chmn. local govt. sect., mem. budget and fin. com.). Office: 12000 Government Ctr Pkwy Fairfax VA 22035-0065 Home Phone: 703-758-9609; Office Phone: 703-324-2603. E-mail: david.bobzien@fairfaxcounty.gov.

BOBZIN, STEVE, chemist, researcher; s. Clyde (Pat) Frederick and Dolores Benish Bobzin; m. Karie Kristine Hahn; children: Seabastian Daniel, Elizabeth Lea Estella. BS in Chemistry, Calif. State U., Fullerton, 1985; PhD in Oceanography, U. Calif., San Diego, 1990. Rsch. assoc. dept. chemistry U. Hawaii, Honolulu, 1990—92; scientist GD Searle, St. Louis, 1992—98; group leader Monsanto, St. Louis, 1998—2000; dir. natural products chemistry Galileo Labs., Santa Clara, Calif., 2000—03, Ceres, Inc., Malibu, Calif., 2003—06, dir. tech. planning, protection, and acquisition Thousand Oaks, Calif., 2007—. Adj. prof. U. Miss., Oxford, 1995—. Grantee, USDA, 2007—. Mem.: Am. Chem. Soc. Office: Ceres Inc 1535 Rancho Conejo Blvd Thousand Oaks CA 91320 Home Phone: 310-456-2756; Office Phone: 805-376-6515. Business E-Mail: sbobzin@ceres-inc.com.

BOCANEGRA, CARLOS, professional soccer player; b. Upland, Calif., May 25, 1979; Attended, UCLA. Defender Chgo. Fire, 2000—03, Fulham FC, England, 2003—. 40 caps, 6 goals U.S. Nat. Soccer team, 2001—; mem. U.S. World Cup team, 2006. Named Major League Soccer Defender of the Yr., 2002—03; named to Major League Soccer All-Star team, 2002—03. Mailing: US Soccer Fedn 1801 S Prairie Ave Chicago IL 60616

BOCH, DAVID PAUL, engineering technical specialist; b. Pitts., Mar. 21, 1964; s. Edward Francis and Dorothy Jean Boch; m. Paula Jean Bridgman, May 20, 1989; children: Chelsea, Olivia. BME, Duke U., 1986; MS, Rensselaer Poly. Inst., 1999. Registered profl. engr., Ohio. Assoc. mfg. engr. Inland divsn. GM, Vandalia, Ohio, 1986—89, reliability engr. IFG divsn., 1989—91, product mgr., 1991—93, sr. product mgr. Delphi Interior, 1993—97, sr. project mgr., 1997—98; supr. product engring. Delphi Interior, Vandalia, 1998—2001, supr. materials engring., 2001—05, sr. tech. specialist, 2006—. Office coord. Thunder-Rd. Bike-a-thon, Dayton, Ohio, 1989—90; demonstrator Bring Children to work day, Vandalia, Ohio, 2003, office coord., 2004; H.S. sci. fair judge, 2006. Recipient Most Innovative Use of Plastics award, Automotive divsn. Soc. Plastics Engrs., 2003. Mem.: ASME, K. C. (sir knight 1998—, recorder 2000—03). Republican. Roman Catholic. Avocations: Lionel trains, fishing, bicycling, running, hiking. Office Phone: 937-356-2470. Business E-Mail: david.p.boch@delphi.com.

BOCHERT, LINDA H., lawyer; b. East Orange, NJ, May 13, 1949; BA, U. Wis., 1971, MS, 1973, JD, 1974. Bar: Wis. 1974. Dir. environ. protection unit Wis. Atty. Gen. Office, 1978-80; exec. asst. to the secy. Wis. Dept. Natural Resources, 1980-91; ptnr. Michael, Best & Friedrich, Madison, Wis., 1991—. Mem. ABA, Wis. State Bar Assn. Office: Michael Best & Friedrich PO Box 1806 Firstar Plaza 1 S Pinckney St Madison WI 53701-1806 Office Phone: 608-283-2271. Business E-Mail: lhbochert@michaelbest.com.

BOCHETTO, GEORGE ALEXANDER, lawyer; b. Bklyn., Oct. 7, 1952; m. Paula Agins, Aug. 6, 1987; children: David, Evan. BA, SUNY, Albany, 1975; JD cum laude, Temple U., 1978. Bar: Pa. 1978, N.Y. 1995, U.S. Dist. Ct. (ea. dist.) Pa. 1979, U.S. Supreme Ct. 1992, U.S. Tax Ct. 1986. Pvt. practice, 1979-90; assoc. Pelino & Lentz, P.C., Phila., 1978-79, Monteverde & Hemphill, P.C., Phila., 1990-93, Bochetto & Lentz, P.C., Phila., 1993—. Contbr. articles to profl. jours. Bd. dirs. Pa. Spl. Olympics, 1986—; mem. Rep. State Com., Pa., 1992—; appt. Pa. State Athletic Commr. Gov. Ridge, 1995—. Mem. ABA, Pa. Bar Assn., Phila. Bar Assn. (subcom. chairperson profl. responsibility com. 1978—). Avocations: amateur boxing, boating, sports. Office: Bochetto & Lentz PC 1524 Locust St Philadelphia PA 19102-4401

BOCHICCHIO, VITO SALVATORE, lawyer; b. Pitts. s. Richard John and Francesca (Romano) B.; m. Giovanna Febbraro, Nov. 21, 1992; children: Richard, Giosue, Francesco, Paolo. BA, MA, Duquesne U., 1984, JD, 1987. Bar: Pa. 1987, U.S. Dist. Ct. (we. dist.) Pa. 1987. Asst. dist. atty. Office Allegheny County Dist. Atty., Pitts., 1988-90; assoc. Rothman Gordon, Pitts., 1990-94; ptnr. O'Brien, Rulis & Bochicchio, Pitts., 1994—. Sec. Big Jim's Inc., Pitts., 1992—. Committeeman Allegheny County Dem. Com., Pitts., 1981—. Mem. Allegheny County Bar Assn., Small Mfrs. Coun., Calabria Club. Roman Catholic. Avocation: Karate. Office: O'Brien Rulis & Bochicchio 555 Grant St Ste 120 Pittsburgh PA 15219 Business E-Mail: vbochicchio@orbslaw.com.

BOCHNER, BERNARD H., urologic surgical oncologist; s. Solomon and Harriet Bochner; m. Robin Bochner. MD, UCLA, 1990. Diplomate Am. Bd. of Urology. Asst. prof. of urology U. So. Calif., LA, 1999—2000; asst. attending surgeon Meml. Sloan-Kettering Cancer Ctr., NYC, 2000—05, assoc. attending surgeon, 2005—; asst. prof. urology Weill Med. Coll. Cornell U., NYC, 2000—05. Fellow: Am. Coll. Surgeons; mem.: Am. Urol. Assn. Office: Meml Sloan-Kettering Cancer Ctr 1275 York Ave New York NY 10021 Office Phone: 646-422-4387. Office Fax: 212-988-0759.

BOCHNER, BRUCE SCOTT, immunologist, educator; BA in Natural Scis. with honors, Johns Hopkins U., 1978; MD with honors, U. Ill., Chgo., 1982. Diplomate Am. Bd. Internal Medicine, Am. Bd. Allergy and Immunology. Intern, then resident in internal medicine U. Ill. Hosps., Chgo., 1982-85; fellow in clin. immunology Johns Hopkins U., Balt., 1985-88, instr. in medicine, 1988-89, asst. prof., 1989-94, assoc. prof., 1994—98, prof., 1999—, dir., Divsn. of Allergy and Clin. Immunology, 2003. Assoc. editor, mem. editl. bd. Jour. Allergy and Clin. Immunology, 1993—; reviewer various jours.; contbr. more than 165 articles to profl. jours. NIH grantee, 1989-; recipient Developing Investigator award Burroughs Wellcome Fund, 1992. Mem. Am. Assn. Immunology, Am. Acad. Asthma Allergy and Immunology (Charles Reed lectureship 1993, 2004), Am. Soc. Clin. Investigation, Alpha Omega Alpha. Office: Johns Hopkins Asthma and Allegy Ctr 5501 Hopkins Bayview Cir Baltimore MD 21224-6821

BOCHNER, MEL, artist; b. Pitts., 1940; B.F.A., Carnegie Inst. Tech., 1962. Former instr. Sch. Visual Arts, NYC. One-man shows Galerie Heiner Friedrich, Munich, Galerie Konrad Fischer, Dusseldorf, Germany, Ace Gallery, Los Angeles, 1969, Galleria Sperone, Torino, Italy, 1970, Galleria Toselli, Milan, Italy, 1970, Mus. Modern Art, N.Y.C., 1971, Galerie Sonnabend, Paris, 1972, 73, 74, 78, Sonnabend Gallery, N.Y.C., 1972, 73, 76, 80, 82, 83, Lisson Gallery, London, 1972, Univ. Art Mus., Berkeley, Calif., 1974, Balt. Mus. Art, 1976, Bernier Gallery, Athens, 1977, Gallerie Schema, Milan and Florence, Italy, 1978, Galerie Art in Progress, Dusseldorf, Germany, 1979, Daniel Weinberg Gallery, San Francisco, 1981, Centre Internat. de Creation Artistique, 1982, Abbaye de Senanque, Gordes, France, 1982, Yarlow Salzman Gallery, Toronto, 1983, Daniel Weinberg Gallery, San Francisco, 1983, Pace Editions, N.Y.C., 1983, Santa Barbara Contemporary Arts Forum, 2003, Walker Art Ctr., Mpls., 2003, Galerie Grimm/Rosenfeld, Munich, 2003, Hammer Mus., L.A., 2004; group shows include Finch Coll. Mus. Art, 1967, Paula Cooper Gallery, N.Y.C., 1968, Seattle Art Mus., 1969, Mus. Modern Art, N.Y.C., 1970, Museo Civico D'Arte Moderna, Turin, Italy, 1970, Gallery Nachet St. Stephen, Innsbruck, 1971, Spoleto Festival, Itlay, 1972, Documenta V. Kassel, Germany, 1972, Sonnabend Gallery, N.Y.C., 1972, 77, 81, Kunstmuseum, Basel, Switzerland, 1972, Fogg Mus., Harvard U., Cambridge, Mass., 1973, Seattle Art Mus., Seattle, 1973, Whitney Mus. Am. Art, N.Y.C., 1973, Princeton Art Mus., 1974, Art Inst. Chgo., 1974, Mus. Modern Art, N.Y.C., 1975, Am. Drawings' Mus., Leverkusen, 1975, Art Gallery Ont., 1975, Mus. Modern Art, N.Y.C., 1976, Chgo. Art Inst., 1976, Fort Worth Mus., 1976, Detroit Inst. Art, 1976, Whitney Mus. Am. Art, N.Y.C., 1977, 83, Mus. Contemporary Art, Chgo., 1977, Phila. Mus. Art, 1978, Leo Castelli Gallery, 1978, Whitney Mus. Am. Art, N.Y.C., 1979, Palazzo Reale, Milan, Italy, 1979, W Centre Georges Pomipdou, Beauborg, Paris, 1979, MIT, 1980, Beaubourg Centre Nationale d'Art et de Culture, 1981-82, Centre Georges Pompidou, 1981-82, Chgo. Art Inst., 1982, Yale U. Art Gallery, 1982, Janet Steinberg Gallery, Sonnabend Gallery; invited exhibitor 2004 Biennial Exhbn., Whitneys Mus. Am. Art, N.Y., 2004; represented in permanent collections Los Angles County Mus., Mus. Nat. d'Art Moderne, Paris, Whitney Mus. Am. Art; film Walking a Straight Line Through Grand Central Station, 1965, N.Y.C. Windows, 1965, Dorothea in Fifteen Positions Stasis, 1970; contbr. articles to profl. jours. Recipient Acad.-Inst. award for art, 1990. Office: care Sonnabend Gallery 420 W Broadway New York NY 10012-3764

BOCHTLER, STANLEY EDWIN, education educator; s. Edwin Chris and Ruth Emma (Von Behren) Bochtler; children: Edwin, Christina Rice, Elizabeth, Eric. MS, So. Ill. U., Carbondale, 1964, MS, 1967, PhD in Curriculum & Instrn., 1971. 4th grade tchr. Frankfort Elem. Sch., 1966—67, 5th grade tchr., 1967—68, 5th grade tchr., asst. to supr., 1967—68; asst. prof. edn. St. Mary's Coll., Notre Dame, Ind., 1971—74; assoc. prof. edn. McKendvee Coll., Lebanon, Ill., 1974—80; prof. edn. Buena Vista U., Storm Lake, Iowa, 1980—. Mem. promotion & tenure com. Buena Vista U., 2004—07, advisor student senate, 2005—06. Advisor Students Concerned About Environ., 2006—07; trip advisor Alternative Week Learning, Seattle, 2007; participant Project Analysis Fund Drive, Storm Lake, 2005, McCorkle Fellows Trip, Argentina, 2006, Peru, 2006. Recipient Wythe Tchg. award, Buena Vista U., 2001, McCorkle Fellows award, 2006. Mem.: Nat. Coucils Tchrs. Math., Nat. Sci. Tchrs. Assn., Internat. Reading Assn. Democrat. Luth. Office: Buena Vista Univ 610 W Fourth Storm Lake IA 50588

BOCHY, BRUCE, professional baseball team manager and retired player; b. Landes de Boussac, France, Apr. 16, 1955; m. Kim B.; children: Greg, Brett. Catcher Houston Astros, 1978—80, NY Mets, 1982, San Diego Padres, 1983—87, third base coach, 1993-94, mgr., 1994—2005, San Francisco Giants, 2006—. Named Nat. League Mgr. of Yr., MLB, 1996, The Sporting News, 1996, 1998. Office: San Francisco Giants Pac Bell Park 24 Willie Mays Plz San Francisco CA 94107*

BOCIAN, PETER, corporate financial executive; BA, Mich. State U., M in Acctg., 1982. Various mgmt. positions NCR Corp., Dayton, Ohio, 1983—2002, CFO, v.p. retail solutions divsn., 1999—2002, CFO retail and fin. group, 2002—03, v.p., fin., CFO, 2003—07; exec. v.p., CFO Starbucks Corp., Seattle, 2007—. Office: Starbucks Corp 2401 Utah Ave S Seattle WA 98134*

BOCK, BROOKS FREDERICK, emergency physician; b. Orange, NJ, Sept. 19, 1943; MD, Wayne State U., 1969. Intern Detroit Gen. Hosp., 1969-70; resident in surgery Wayne State U., 1970-71, resident in urology, 1971-73, prof., chmn. Dept. Emergency Medicine, 1985—2005; pvt. practice; specialist-in-chief emergency medicine Detroit (Mich.) Med. Ctr., 1985—2005, pres. Harper-Huntzel Hosp., 2005—. Mem. Am. Bd. Emergency Medicine, 1995—2004, pres., 2002—03. Mem. AMA, Am. Coll. Emergency Physicians, Mich. State Med. Soc., Wayne County Med. Soc. Home: 5764 Bloomfield Glens West Bloomfield MI 48322-2501 Office: 3990 John R Detroit MI 48201-2445 Home Phone: 248-626-6603; Office Phone: 313-745-6211.

BOCK, JANINE SCHMELZER, music educator; b. Nelsonville, Ohio, June 14, 1963; d. Maurice David Schmelzer and Jeanne Marie Flemming; m. James David Bock, Sept. 6, 1953; children: Christopher David McCabe, LeeAnn Marie McCabe. MusB in Edn., Ohio State U., 1985, MA, 2004. Cert. tchg. Ohio, 1985. Band dir. Franklin Local Sch. Dist., Duncan Falls, Ohio; dir. of bands Licking Valley Local Sch., Newark, Ohio, 1991—2001, music tchr., 2001—. Guest condr. , clinician Zanesville Meml. Concert Band, Zanesville, Ohio, 2001—; tuba soloist Women in Music, Columbus, Ohio; tuba player, guest conductor Muskingum Valley Winds, 2004—; area clinician, guest condr. wind bands. Musician tuba performance, (concerto soloist) Tubby in Tubby the Tuba, Wind Band Music, 2005. Sec. Zanesville Meml. Concert Band, Ohio, 1996—2003; pres. St. Benedict Cath. Sch. Home & Sch. Assn., Cambridge, Ohio, 2002—04; mem. Rep. Club of Guernsey County, Cambridge, Ohio, 1997—. Mem.: Music Educators Nat. Conf., Licking Valley Edn. Assn., Ohio Music Edn. Assn., Ohio State U. Marching Band TBDBITL Alumni Club. R-Consevative. Roman Cath. Achievements include i dotter-first female to dot the i in the Script Ohio Marching manuever in a single script in front of a home football crowd while a member of The Ohio State Univ Marching Band, Fall 1984. Avocations: travel, sewing, sports. Personal E-mail: jbock@muskingum.edu.

BOCK, WALTER JOSEPH, zoology educator; b. NYC, Nov. 20, 1933; s. Paul and Anne (Kalsch) B.; m. Katharine Lippitt, June 29, 1957; children: Katharine Rose, Susan Ruth, Walter David. BS, Cornell U., 1955; MA, Harvard U., 1957, PhD, 1959. NSF postdoctoral fellow Universität Frankfurt Main, 1959-61; asst. prof. dept. zoology U. Ill., 1961-64, assoc. prof., 1964-65; asst. prof. dept. biol. scis. Columbia U., 1965-66, assoc. prof., 1966-73, prof., 1973—. Rsch. assoc. Am. Mus Natural History, 1965—. Author: (with J.J. Morony and J. Farrand) Reference List of the Birds of the World, 1975; Contbr. articles to profl. jours. Pres. Tenafly (N.J.) Nature Ctr., 1977-80; permanent sec. Internat. Ornithol. Com., 1986-98; pres. 23d Internat. Ornithol. Congress, 2002; v.p. Internat. Congress Zoology, 2004. NSF grantee, 1962-79 Mem. Am. Ornithologists Union (Coues award 1975), Am. Soc. Zoologists, Am. Soc. Naturalists (treas. 1978-80), Soc. Study Evolution, Soc. Systematic Biology, AAAS, Brit. Ornithologists Union (corres. mem.), Deutschen Ornithologen-Gesellschaft (hon.) Home: 114 Hudson Ave Tenafly NJ 07670-1004 Office: Columbia U Dept Biological Scis New York NY 10027 Office Phone: 212-854-4487. Business E-Mail: wb4@columbia.edu. *Humans are not independent of the earth's environment in which they live and of their evolutionary history. As a scholar, I hope to learn about evolutionary and ecological mechanisms; as a teacher I hope to pass this knowledge on to others; and as a person I hope to preserve and enjoy the beauty of nature that exists about us.*

BOCKER, HANS JURGEN, editor-in-chief, consultant, finance educator; b. Thuringia, Germany, July 13, 1939; s. Hans Alfred and Liselotte (Böttcher) B.; m. Megan Elizabeth Sutton, Jan. 4, 1960; children: Adrian Alexander, Chloe April. MS in Engring., Tech. Univ., Darmstadt, 1964; MBA, Tech. Univ., Munich, 1968; Dr. Commerce, Univ. S. Africa, Pretoria, 1978. Cert. mech. engr., mgmt. prof., editor. Lectr. Univ. S. Africa, Pretoria, 1968-72, sr. lectr., 1972-78; pvt. practice indsl. and economic cons. various internat. companies and govts., 4 continents, 1969-86; assoc. prof. Wilfrid Laurier U., Waterloo, Ont., Can., 1978-84, Western Ill. U., 1984-86; editor-in-chief Finanz und Wirtschaft (Finance and Economy), London, 1986-91, Zollikerberg, B.C., Switzerland, 1992—; prof. EBS, London, 1986-91, Internat. Sch. Mgmt., 1993—. Front-page columnist for Finanz und Wirtschaft; permanent vis. prof. bus. schs.; work with Treuhand Anstalt, Berlin; presenter in field; pres. Internat. Sch. Mgmt., Dortmund, 1993—; cons. to Internet Initial Pub. Offerings; chmn. bd. numerous cos.; pres. SwissAm, Inst. Corp. Orgn. and Comm. Author: books, study guides, case studies, interviews with famous personalities. Sometime TV and radio performer. Grantee Volkswagen Found. W. Germany 1964-66, many rsch. grants. Mem. Inst. Mgmt. Sci, Am. Inst. Decision Scis., Acad. Mgmt., Canadian Purchasing Assn., Swiss Fedn. Journalists, Inst. Corp. Orgn. and Comm. Switzerland (pres.), British Assn. Fgn. Journalists, Swiss Am. Ltd., Surrey Country and Tennis Club, Rotary Internat. Avocation: classical pianist. Office: Bruenigstr 12 CH-6055 Alpnach Switzerland

BOCKHORST, BARBARA ALICE, retired secondary school educator; b. St. Louis, Feb. 2, 1939; d. Harold Calvert and Lillian Amelia (Smith) Cox; m. William Dreon Bockhorst (div.); children: William Dreon Jr., Walter Richard. BEd, U. Mo., 1961; MEd, Washington U., 1972. Tchr. sci., phys. edn. RIII Sch. Dist., Troy, Mo., 1961—64; tchr. Ft. Zumwalt Sch. Dist., O'Falllon, Mo., 1965—2006; ret., 2006. Mem. Ft. Zumwalt Edn. Assn., O'Fallon, Mo., 1965—97, pres., 1994; coach track and field Ft. Zumwalt Sch. Dist., 1983—95; mem. state standards com., Mo., 1994; mem. textbook review com. Rosalia Tilles Non-Sectarian Fund scholar, Mo. U., 1957—61. Mem.: NEA (del. 1994—97), Mo. Edn. Assn. (del. 1982—97, women's com.), Lions, Mensa. Independent. Avocations: reading, embroidery, paper cutting. Home: 401 W Collier Troy MO 63379-1212

BOCKIUS, RUTH BEAR, nursing educator; b. Groffdale, Pa., Dec. 19, 1925; d. Weidler Romaine and Ruth Mary (Jacoby) Bear; m. Thomas B. Bockius Jr., Dec. 15 1945; children: Donna Ruth, Dawn Eileen. AA, Phoenix Coll., 1970; BSN, Ariz. State U., 1973, MEd, 1978. Instr. nursing Glendale (Ariz.) Community Coll.; coord. health edn. Samaritan Health Svcs., Phoenix; dir. patient/community edn. Maryvale Samaritan Hosp., Phoenix, edn. dir., ret., 1994. Grantee Fed. Nursing; AMA scholar, 1st Nat. Bank scholar. Mem. Am. Soc. Hosp. Edn. and Tng., Am. Hosp. Assn., Phi Theta Kappa, Phi Kappa Phi.

BOCKSERMAN, ROBERT JULIAN, chemist; b. St. Louis, Dec. 20, 1929; s. Max Louis and Bertha Anna (Kremen) B.; m. Clarice K. Kreisman, June 9, 1957; children: Michael Jay, Joyce Ellen, Carol Beth. BSc, U. Mo., 1952, MSc, 1955; postgrad., Far East Intelligence Sch, Tokyo, 1954. Chemist Sealtest Corp., Peoria, Ill., 1955-56; prodn. mgr. Allan Drug Co., St. Louis, 1957-59; rsch. chemist Monsanto Co., St. Louis, 1960-65, purchasing agt. Sauget, Ill., 1966-67; founder, pres. Pharma-Tech Industries, Inc., Union, Mo., 1967-84; tech. dir. Overlock-Howe Consulting Group, St. Louis, 1984-85; founder, pres. Conatech Consulting Group, Creve Coeur, Mo., 1985—. Sec., mem. industry packaging adv. com. Sch. of Engring. U. Mo., Rolla, 1979—, adj. prof. dept. food sci./nutrition, Columbia, adj. prof. dept. engring. mgmt., Rolla, vis. lectr., Clayton, Northwestern U., Evanston, Ill.; vol. tutor Ladue Sch. Dist.; tutor Parkway Sch. Dist., St. Louis, Clayton (Mo.) Sch. Dist.; tech. cons. Creve Coeur Fire Protection Dist.; cons. HAZMAT Team St. Louis County; mentor U. Mo. Dept. Food Sci. and Nutrition; tech. cons. hazardous products EPA, CPSC; mem. safety panel Info. Resources, Inc. Tech. reviewer Jour. Inst. of Packaging Profls., Jour. Packaging Tech., Mo. Waste Control Scholarship Grants and Research, Medical Device and Diagnostic Industry Jour., Medical Plastics and Biomaterials Publication.; mem. editl. adv. bd. The Forensic Examiner, Processing Mag.; panelist (Help Desk column) Medical Device and Diagnostic Industry mag., The Forensic Examiner; contbg. author: Packaging Forensics - Package Failure in the Courts. Mem. Mo. Waste Control Coalition; mem. stormwater engring. com. City of Creve Coeur, Mo., also mem. recycling and environ. com.; tech. cons. Hazmat Team, St. Louis County, Mo.; mem. St. Louis Emergency Response Team; nat. mem. Libr. Congress, Mo. Hist. Soc. With U.S. Army, 1952-54, Korea. Grantee Small Bus. Innovation, Clear Seas Rsch. Found. Mem. ASTM, Am. Coll. Forensic Examiners, Cons. Packaging Engring. Coun., Inst. Packaging Profls. (cert. packaging profl.), Am. Technion Soc., Inst. Food Technologists Arrangements (St. Louis), Nat. Forensic Ctr., Teltech Resource Network, Am. Chem. Soc., Am. Plastics Coun., Mo. Acad. Scis., N.Y. Acad. Sci., Acad. Sci. St. Louis, Assn. Cons. Chemists and Chem. Engrs., Am. Nutraceutical Assn., Nat. Dir. Expert Witnesses, Rotary Internat., Wash. U. Century Club, Juvenile Diabetes Rsch. Found., Sigma Xi. Achievements include research on toxicological effects of additives from packaging materials upon foodstuffs, on biological and photo degradation of polymers, on technology of form/fill/seal packaging engineering, new sterilization technologies for medical devices and pharmaceuticals, barrier properties of polymer films, toxicology of chemical dusts and fumes, and food irradiation effects on humans, neurotoxicity of organic solvents. Home: 54 Morwood Ln Creve Coeur MO 63141-7621 Office: Conatech Cons Group 501 N Lindbergh Blvd Ste 105 Creve Coeur MO 63141-7844 Office Phone: 314-995-9767. Business E-Mail: rjbockserman@conatech.com.

BOCKSTEIN, HERBERT, lawyer; b. NYC, Jan. 27, 1943; s. Stanley Joseph and Sylvia (Tannenbaum) B.; m. Bonnie Sue Ritt, Sept. 2, 1967 (div.); children: Andrew, Jana; m. Nadine Bernstein, June 27, 1988. BA, NYU, 1963, JD cum laude, 1971; MBA, Cornell U., Ithaca, NY, 1966. Bar: NY 1972, Mo. 1979. Assoc. Stroock & Stroock & Lavan, NYC, 1971-78, Stolar, Heitzmann & Eder, St. Louis, 1978-80, Finley, Kumble, Wagner, Heine, Underberg, Manley & Casey, NYC, 1980-83; ptnr. Finley, Kumble, NYC, 1983-87, Myerson & Kuhn, NYC, 1988-89, Ashinoff, Ross & Korff, NYC, 1989-90, Newman Tannenbaum, NYC, 1990—96, Blank Rome LLP, NYC, 1996—. Mem.: N.Y. State Bar Assn., Estate Planning Coun. N.Y.C., Order of Coif. Avocations: tennis, golf. Home: 70 Garth Rd Apt 3C Scarsdale NY 10583 Office: Blank Rome LLP 405 Lexington Ave New York NY 10174-0002 Home Phone: 914-725-0651; Office Phone: 212-885-5312. Business E-Mail: hbockstein@blankrome.com.

BOCKSTRUCK, LLOYD DEWITT, librarian; b. Vandalia, Ill., May 26, 1945; s. Harry Earl and Olive Elsie (Blankenship) B. AB cum laude, Greenville Coll., Ill., 1967; MA, So. Ill. U., 1969; MS, U. Ill., 1973; student, Samford U., 1973. Teaching asst. So. Ill. U., Carbondale, 1967—69; tchr. Mombasa (Kenya) Bapt. High Sch., 1969—71; teaching asst. U. Ill., Urbana, 1972—73; libr. Dallas Pub. Libr., 1973—. Instr. Inst. Genealogy and Hist. Rsch., Samford U., Birmingham, Ala., 1973—; instr. Sch. Continuing Edn., So. Meth. U., Dallas, 1974-91; instr. Geneal. Inst. of Mid-Am., U. Ill., Springfield, 1994-2005; columnist Dallas Morning News, 1991—. Author: Virginia's Colonial Soldiers, 1988, Genealogical Research in Texas, 1992, Revolutionary War Bounty Land Grants Awarded by State Governments, 1996, Family Tree Weekly Newspaper Columns from the Dallas Morning News, 1001-1996, 1999, Naval Pensioners of the United States, 1800-1851, 2002, Denizations and Naturalizations in the British Colonies in America, 1607-1775, 2005, Bounty and Donation Land Grants in British Colonial America, 2007; contbr. articles to profl. jours. Recipient Scholarship Key award Phi Alpha Theta, 1967, History award DAR, 1989, Profl. award for hist. preservation Dallas County Hist. Commn., 1992, Filby prize for Genealogical Librarianship, 1999, Lifetime Achievement award N.E. Tex. Libr. Sys., 2003; Nat. Geneal. Soc. fellow, 1992; Gold Good Citizenship award, SAR, 2005. Mem. ALA (life), SAR (libr. gen. 1981-83), SCW (dep. gov. gen. 2000), Soc. of the Cincinnati, Jamestowne Soc., Order of Ams. of Armorial Ancestry (genealogist gen. 1993-99), Order of Founders and Patriots of Am. (genealogist gen. 1986-2000), Dallas Geneal. Soc. (dir. 1979—). Republican. Avocation: genealogy. Office: Dallas Pub Libr 1515 Young St Dallas TX 75201-5499 Office Phone: 214-670-1406.

BOCKWOLDT, TODD SHANE, nuclear engineer; b. Spirit Lake, Iowa, July 31, 1967; s. Larry Ray and Gale Glee (Bobzien) B. BS in Nuclear Engring., Ga. Tech, 1989, MS in Nuclear Engring., 1990. Lic. profl. engr., 1999. Grad. rsch. asst. Ga. Inst. Technology, Atlanta, 1989-90; S5W (submarines) and A1G (carriers) fleet reactor engr. DOE/USN Naval Reactors Hdqrs., Arlington, Va., 1990-95; asst. naval reactors rep. DOE/USN Norfolk Naval Shipyard, Portsmouth, Va., 1995-98; control drive mechanism design/mfg. engr. naval reactors hdqs. DOE/USN, Arlington, Va., 1998—2004, naval reactors rep. Norfolk, 2004—. Tech. program chmn. Am. Nuclear Soc. Student Conf., Atlanta, 1988; nuclear engring. rep. Mech. Engring. Student Adv. Com., Ga. Tech, 1988-89. Comdr. USN, 1990—. Scholar NROTC, 1985-89, MCDAC, 1985-89, Am. Soc. Naval Engrs. scholar, 1987-89; recipient Gold medal Soc. Am. Mil. Engrs., 1988, Ga. Tech Honor award Soc. Am. Mil. Engrs., 1989, Outstanding Coll. Students of Am. award, 1989. Mem. Am. Nuclear Soc. (grad. scholar 1989-90), Tau Beta Pi, Mensa, Alpha Nu Sigma. Lutheran. Home: 1604 Tapgallant Quay Chesapeake VA 23321-6613 Personal E-mail: bockwoldt@cox.net.

BOCOBO-BALUNSAT, DALISAY, librarian, journalist; b. Metro Manila, Philippines, Jan. 22, 1926; d. Jorge Bocobo; m. Anthony Anton Balunsat. PhB, U. Philippines, 1950. Faculty mem. Adamson U., Manila, 1950—53; corr., columnist Philippine-Am. press, 1953—; ref. libr. San Francisco Pub. Libr., 1958—84. Founder, dir. Philippine-Am. Cultural Celebration, San Francisco, 1973—. Named Outstanding Filipino-Am. of No. Calif. award in field of culture and art, 1984, Outstanding Filipino-Am. Journalist award, 1986, June 8, 1991 Dalisay Bocobo-Balunsat Day, San Francisco Mayor Art Agnos, 1991, Top Fgn. Contbr., Philippines Free Press; named to KGO-TV's Salute to Prominent Asian-Pacific-Am. San Francisco Bay Area list, 2002; recipient Recognition award, Philippine-Am. Press and Media, 1973—2005, Calif. State Senators George Moscone and Milton Marks, 1975, Calif. State Assembly, 2005, Honor award, Mayor and Bd. Suprs. San Francisco and Calif. Legislatures, 1973—2005, Salutes to Asian-Am. award, 2002, Outstanding Achievement award, 2004—05, Cert. of Appreciation, Philippine Consulate-Gen., 1975, Asian-Am. Role Model award, US Navy Filipino Employees, 1975, US Bicentennial award, Filipino Arts Fiesta, 1976, Outstanding Pub. Svc. award, Mayor Dianne Feinstein of San Francisco, 1984, Fiesta Islands Recognition award, Philippine Tourism, 1989, Commendation award, San Francisco Pub. Libr. Commn. and City Librarian, 1998, Bd. Supr. City and County of San Francisco, 2006, Outstanding Cmty. Svc. award, San Francisco Bd. of Supr. and Legis., 2004, Hon. cert., City and County of San Francisco, 2004, Commendation cert., Mayor and City Coun. Daly City, Calif., 2004—05, Literary and Cmty. Svc. Calatagan award, Philippine-Am. Writers and Artists, 2004—05, Commendation award, Calif. Governor Jerry Brown, Woman Warrior award, Pacific Asian Am. Women, Outstanding Sch. Vol. award, San Francisco Pub. Sch., certificate of honor, Mayor Gavin Newsom, San Francisco, 2006, San Francisco Bd. Suprs., 2006, Calif. State Sen. Tom Leland, 2006, Assemblyman Mark Leno, 2006. Mem.: ALA (Dana Nat. Libr. award 1975), Phillipine-Am. Press Corr., Filipino Artists, Writers, and Performers (founder 1973—, dir. 1973—, various Recognition awards 1973—2006). Avocations: travel, writing, reading, movies. Office: Filipino Artists Writers and Performers 1437 19th Ave San Francisco CA 94122

BOCOCK, SCOTT GREGORY, historian; b. Hammond, Ind., Sept. 26, 1967; s. Carman Robert and Mary Ann Bocock. B in Gen. Studies, Ind. U. N.W., Gary, 1993. Hist. interpreter, groundskeeper Buckley Homestead Lake County Pk., Lowell, Ind., 1990; pres. Cedar Lake (Ind.) Hist. Assn., 1993—95; historian Town of Cedar Lake, 1994—2001, City of Westminster, Colo., 2001—; Ind. rm. page Gary (Ind.) Pub. Libr., 1999—2000. Vol. Cedar Lake Hist. Assn., 1989—2001, Adams County Hist. Soc., Brighton, Colo., 2002; vol. site dig/rschr. Kankakee Valley Hist. Soc., 2005. Recipient cert. for contbn., Cedar Lake Hist. Assn., Lake of Red Cedars Mus., Ind., 1992, plaque, Cedar Lake Town Coun., 2001; scholar Cornelius O'Brien Confs. on Historic Preservation, Ind U., 1990—91. Mem.: Archaeological Conservancy, Ind. Hist. Soc., Kankakee Valley Hist. Soc., Cedarlake Hist. Assn., Nat. Trust for Historic Preservation, Orgn. Am. Historians, Am. Assn. State and Local History. Achievements include helping in development of Lake of Red Cedars Museum; listing Old Monon Park Dancing Pavilion in Cedar Lake on the National Register of Historic Places. Avocations: reading, writing, antiques, preserving artifacts, genealogy. Home: 13206 Parrish Ave Cedar Lake IN 46303-2608

BODAGER, DEAN W., epidemiologist; b. Goshen, Ind., Aug. 29, 1958; s. Donald E. and Doris J. Bodager; m. Anita M. Sallas, July 25, 1984; children: Aaron S., Adam D. BS, Ind. State U., Terre Haute, 1981; MPA, U. Ctrl. Fla., Orlando, 1996. Diplomate Am. Acad. Sanitarians, 1998. Environ. health specialist Fla. Dept. Health and Rehabilitative Svcs., Marathon, 1982—87, environ. health supr., 1987—88, environ. health cons. Orlando, 1988—91, dist. supr. office of restaurant programs; mgmt. rev. specialist Fla. Dept. Bus. and Profl. Regulation, Orlando; regional environ. epidemiologist Fla. Dept. Health, Orlando. Contbr. articles to profl. jours. Mem.: Nat. Environ. Health Assn. (tech. editl. adv. bd. Jour. Environ. Health 1998—, registered sanitarian 1988), Fla. Environ. Health Assn. (v.p. 1990—91, dir. 1992—95, pres. 1996—97, dir. 2004—, tech. editor Jour. Environ. Health, registered sanitarian 1988, Billy G. Tennant award 2005), Phi Kappa Phi. Home: 513 Wilmington Cir Oviedo FL 32765 Office: Florida Dept Health 400 W Robinson St S Tower S529 Orlando FL 32801 Home Phone: 407-366-8328; Office Phone: 407-245-0468. Office Fax: 407-317-7319. Personal E-mail: dbodager@cfl.rr.com. Business E-Mail: dean_bodager@doh.state.fl.us.

BODANSKY, DAVID, physicist, researcher; b. NYC, Mar. 10, 1924; s. Aaron and Marie (Syrkin) B.; m. Beverly Ferne Bronstein, Sept. 7, 1952; children: Joel N., Daniel M. BS, Harvard U., 1943, MA, 1948, PhD, 1950. Instr. physics Columbia U., NYC, 1950-52, assoc., 1952-54; mem. faculty U. Wash., Seattle, 1954—, assoc. prof. physics, 1958-63, prof., 1963-93, prof. emeritus, 1993—, chmn. dept., 1976-84. Co-author: (with Fred H. Schmidt) The Energy Controversy: The Fight over Nuclear Power, 1976, (with others) Indoor Radon and Its Hazards, 1987, Nuclear Energy: Principles, Practices, and Prospects, 1996, 2d edit., 2004; editl. bd.: Rev. Sci. Instruments, 1967-69. With Signal Corps AUS, 1943-46. Sloan Rsch. fellow, 1959-63, Guggenheim fellow, 1966-67, 74-75. Fellow Am. Phys. Soc. (chair Panel on Pub. Affairs 1995), AAAS; mem. Am. Assn. Physics Tchrs., Am. Nuc. Soc., Health Physics Soc., Phi Beta Kappa. Achievements include research in nuclear physics, nuclear astrophysics and energy policy. Office: U Wash Dept Physics Seattle WA 98195-1560 Business E-Mail: bodansky@phys.washington.edu.

BODANSKY, ROBERT LEE, lawyer; b. NYC; BA cum laude, Syracuse U., 1974; JD with honors, George Washington U., 1977; cert. postgrad. studies, Ctr. Internat. Legal Studies, Salzburg, Austria, 1978. Bar: Md. 1978, DC 1978, U.S. Dist. Ct. Md. 1978, U.S. Ct. Appeals (DC cir.) 1980, U.S. Dist. Ct. DC 1980, U.S. Ct. Appeals (4th cir.) 1981, U.S. Supreme Ct. 1982, Va. 2000, U.S. Dist. Ct. (ea. dist.) Va. 2001. First assoc., then ptnr. Feldman, Krieger, Goldman & Tish, Washington, 1978-83; ptnr. Feldman, Bodansky & Rubin, Washington, 1984-95; prin. Freer, McGarry, Bodansky & Rubin, P.C., Washington, 1995-97; ptnr. Nixon, Hargrave, Devans & Doyle, LLP (now Nixon Peabody LLP), Washington, 1997—2004, Seyfarth Shaw LLP, Washington, 2004—. Advisor internat. bus. law and taxation programs McGeorge Sch. Law, Sacramento, 1985—. Author: Special Problems of Subcontractors and Suppliers, 1987. Legal advisor Parkwood Resident's Assn., Kensington, Md., 1984; bd. dirs. Ridgeleigh Residents' Assn., 1987-2001, Congregation Har Shalom, 1989-91, pres. 2003-04; tchr. Adas Israel Congregation, Washington, 1975-91. Mem. ABA (chmn. subcom. internat. and fgn. bus. law young lawyers divsn. 1978-80), Md. State Bar Assn., DC Bar Assn., Va. Bar Assn. Office: Seyfarth Shaw LLP 815 Connecticut Ave NW Ste 500 Washington DC 20006-4004 Business E-Mail: rbodansky@seyfarth.com.

BODANSZKY, MIKLOS, chemist, educator; b. Budapest, Hungary, May 21, 1915; came to U.S., 1957, naturalized, 1964; s. Lajos and Maria (Friedner) B.; m. Agnes A. Vadasz, Apr. 21, 1950; 1 child, Eva. Diploma in chem. engring, Tech. U. Budapest, 1939, DSc, 1949. Sr. lectr. Tech. U. Budapest, 1950-56; research assoc. Cornell U. Med. Coll., 1957-59; sr. research assoc. Squibb Inst. Med. Research, New Brunswick, N.J., 1959-66; prof. chemistry and biochemistry Case Western Res. U., Cleve., 1966-83, Charles Frederic Mabery prof. research in chemistry, 1978-83, prof. emeritus, 1983—. Author: Peptide Synthesis, 1966, 2d edit., 1976, Principles of Peptide Syntheses, 1984, 2d edit, 1993, The Practice of Peptide Synthesis, 1984, 2d edit., 1994, Greek transl., 1984, Indonesian transl., 1998, Peptide Chemistry, 1988, 2d edit., 1993, The World of Peptides, 1991; mem. editl. bd. Jour. Antibiotics, 1971-87, Internat. Jour. Peptide Protein Rsch., 1978-89. Recipient Pierce award, 1977; Morley medal, 1978; A. von Humboldt award, 1979 Mem. Am. Chem. Soc., Am. Soc. Biol. Chemistry, Hungarian Acad. Scis. (fgn.). Achievements include research in Nitrophenyl ester method of peptide synthesis, 1954; first synthesis gastrointestinal hormone secretin, 1966; synthesis vasoactive intestinal peptide, 1973.

BODDIE, ARTHUR WALKER, JR., surgeon, cancer researcher; b. Detroit, Dec. 21, 1941; s. Arthur Walker Sr. and Ellena Louise B.; m. Joy Marie Marchbanks, Aug. 20, 1966; children: Elise Catherine, Ellena Lois. BA, Yale U., 1963, MD, 1967. Diplomate Am. Bd. Surgery. Commd. capt. USAF, 1968, advanced through grades to lt. col., 1976; assoc. prof. surgery M.D. Anderson Hosp., Houston, 1980-90, U. Ill., Chgo., 1990-93, prof. surgery, 1993—, vice-chair dept. surg. oncology, 1997—. Patentee in field; contbr. articles to profl. jours. Recipient Med. Instrumentation award Am. Assn. for Advancement Med. Instrumentation, 1984. Fellow Internat. Coll. Surgery (mem. Japanese sect., hon.); mem. Am. Mensa Soc., Chgo. Surg. Soc. (pres. 1997-98), Sixteen Prof. Socs., VA (mem. oncology subcom. merit rev. bd. 1996—), Sigma Pi Phi. Avocations: golf, sailing. E-mail: awboddiejr@aol.com, midway@webmail.uic.edu.

BODDIE, DON O'MAR, recording industry executive; b. St. Louis, Mo., Nov. 22, 1944; s. George Palmer and Lucille (Owens) Johnson-Boddie; m. Martha Lee Brown, Oct. 11, 1970 (div. Dec. 1979); children: Don O'Mar, Anthony, Shawn, Shellie; m. Paula R. Smith, 1991; children: Courtney, George, Kyle. BS in Bus. Mgmt., Tarkio Coll., 1988, BS in Mgmt., 1988, St. Louis Music Inst., 1968; MA in Tchg., Webster U., 2002. Cert. cross categorical K-12, Mo. Rec. artist Bamboo Records, St. Louis, 1966-70; producer, writer Puzzletown Prodns., St. Louis, 1970-77, James Earl World Prodns., East St. Louis, Ill. and, Memphis, 1975-79, Hi Records, Memphis, 1975-79, Motown Records, Los Angeles, 1976-78; owner, prodr., writer, artist Chrome Records, St. Louis, 1978—. Cons. Archway Studios, St. Louis, 1970-85, Music Assocs. in Mo. Corp, Jefferson City, Mo., 1978—, JD Mgmt., St. Louis, 1978—; v.p. Scorpio Prodns., Pine Lawn, Mo., 1980-82, music prodr., 1980-84. Producer: Lets Be Lovers, 1985 (Heritage award), The Legend, 1986 (Heritage award); rec. artist Can't Stop the Fire, 1987 (Heritage award), New Thing Between Us (charted Top 5 on Midwest Survey 1990, 91), True Love (charted Top 5 on Midwest Survey, 1990, 91); host, presenter Gateway Music Awards Ceremony, 1991; headliner for Cigarettes/Salem Spirit Festival, 1985; featured performer Shock Wave Music TV Show, Friends of the Black Music Soc. Gateway Awards Lacledes Landing, 1991. Mem. entertainment com. to elect Irene Smith, St. Louis, 1982, Music Assocs. Mo. (pres. 1986—), St. Louis Bd. Edn. State Mo., 1991, Chpt. 1 reading tchr. (basic skills), 1995, secondary edn. gen. edn. devel. (ABE), sr. master tchr., Adult Basic Edn., 1997, 98, music dir., Clay Cmty. Edn. Ctr.; chpt. 1 reading tchr. St. Louis Pub. Sch. Dist., 1991—, vocal music tchr., 1996—, instrumental music tchr., 1996—, spl. edn. cross categorical tchr., 1998—. Recipient Named New R&B Rec. Artist of Yr. Gateway Music award, 1990, 91, citation for exceptional performance in edn. of children with spl. needs St. Louis Pub. Sch. Dist., 2002 Democrat. Roman Catholic. Avocations: basketball, martial arts. Office: Pierre Toussaint L'Ouverture Accelerated Mid Sch 3021 Hickory St Saint Louis MO 63118 E-mail: player112244@yahoo.com.

BODDIE, REGINALD ALONZO, lawyer; b. New Haven, June 14, 1959; s. Gladys Geraldine (Harrell) B. BA, Brown U., 1981; JD, Northeastern U., 1984. Bar: N.Y., U.S. Dist. Ct. (ea. and so. dists.) N.Y. 1986, D.C. 1987, U.S. Ct. Appeals (2d cir.) 1989, U.S. Supreme Ct. 1990. Staff atty. Legal Aid Soc., NYC, 1984-86, Harlem Legal Svcs., NYC, 1986-88; asst. counsel Ctr. for Law and Social Justice Medgar Evers Coll. CUNY, 1988-95; pvt. practice NYC, 1995—. Arbitrator Lemon Law, N.Y. Atty. Gen. and Am. Arbitration Assn., N.Y.C., 1986-94. Founder, pres., exec. dir. United Youth Enterprises, Inc., New Haven, 1976—; founder, dir. Coll. Prep. program Ctrl. HS, Providence, 1980-81; bd.dirs. Claremont Neighborhood Ctrs., Inc., Bronx, NY, 1994-96; vol. instr. ARC, New Haven, 1975-90; bd. dirs. Boys and Girls' Clubs of Union County, NJ, 1996-97; vol. law edn. instr. NYC Pub. Schs., 1992—; mem. judicial screening com. Kings & Richmond Counties, 2004-. Recipient Good Citizenship award Civitan Internat. Club, New Haven, 1977, 2 commendations Brown U., 1981, Outstanding Cmty. Svc. award New Haven Police Dept., 1984, Cmty. Svc. award Pub. Sch. 21, Bklyn., 1993, Trailblazer award for Cmty. Svc. Nat. Coun. of Negro Women, 2000, Cmty. Svc. award for Law Related Edn., Sch. Dist. 16, N.Y.C., 2000, others; named Vol. Lawyer of the Yr., N.Y.C. Civil Ct., 2000. Mem. Bklyn. Bar Assn., Optimist Internat. Club (v.p. 2003—, Optimist of Yr. 2003-04) Office: 19 Fulton St Ste 408 New York NY 10038-2100 Office Phone: 212-406-8032.

BODE, JOYCE SCRUGGS, lawyer; b. Waco, Tex., Nov. 18, 1953; d. James Harry and Jane Reese (Rich) Scruggs; m. Clive Denis Bode, Sept. 5, 1987. BA Criminology with highest honors, U. Calif., Berkeley, 1975; JD cum laude, Harvard U., 1979. Bar: Tex. 1979, U.S. Dist. ct. (no. dist.) Tex. 1986, U.S. Tax Ct. 1979, U.S. Ct. Appeals (5th cir.) 1985. Jud. clk. to Judge Richard C. Wilber US Tax Ct., Wash., 1979-81; assoc. Vinson & Elkins, Houston, 1981-87, Fulbright & Jaworski, Dallas, 1987-89, ptnr. Austin, 1989—. Spkr. in feilds. Contbr. Recipient Best Lawyers in Am. Tax, Tex. Super Lawyer, Tex. Monthly mag., Best of Bus. Attys. & Corp. Counsel, Austin Bus. Jour. Mem. ABA (taxation sect.), Nat Assn. Bd. Lawyers, State Bar Tex. (taxation sect., tax exempt fin. com., vice chmn. fed. ct. procedure). Republican. Methodist. Avocations: travel, snorkeling, tennis, hiking. Office: Fulbright & Jaworski 600 Congress Ave Ste 2400 Austin TX 78701-2978 Office Phone: 512-474-5201, 512-536-4511. Office Fax: 512-536-4598. Business E-Mail: jbode@fulbright.com.

BODEN, GUENTHER, endocrinologist; b. Ludwigshafen, Germany, Jan. 8, 1935; came to U.S., 1965; s. Alwin and Irma (Godelman) B.; m. Irene Ulrike Dingeldein, Dec. 12, 1970; children: Karin, Stephanie, Eric, Dirk. MS, Heidelberg U., Germany, 1956; MD, Munich U., 1959. Intern City Hosp. Hamburg, Germany, 1960-62; rsch. fellow in biochemistry U. Tübingen, Germany, 1963-65; rsch. fellow in medicine P.B. Brigham Hosp., Boston, 1965-67; resident physician Rochester (N.Y.) Gen. Hosp., 1967-70; rsch. prof. biochemistry Temple U. Sch. Medicine, Phila., 1986—, prof. medicine, 1977—2000, Laura H. Carnell prof. of medicine, 2000—. Chief div. endocrinology/metab. Temple U. Sch. Medicine, Phila., 1987—, dir. gen. clin. rsch. ctr., 1989—. Mem. editl. bd. Jour. Clin. Endocrine Metabolism, 1985-88, Clin. Diabetes, 1995—, Am. Jour. Physiology, 1998—; assoc. editor, Diabetes, 2001—; contbr. articles to profl. jours. Rsch. grantee NIH, 1973—, Am. Diabetes Assn., 1985—; recipient Rochester N.Y. Diabetes award Rochester Acad. Medicine, 1970, Novartis Long Standing Achievement award in Diabetes, 2005. Fellow ACP; mem. Am. Diabetes Assn., Am. Soc. Clin. Investigation, Am. Endocrin Soc. Office: Temple Univ Hosp 3401 N Broad St Philadelphia PA 19140-5189 E-mail: bodengh@tuhs.temple.edu.

BODEN, SCOTT DAVID, orthopedic surgeon, spine surgeon, educator; b. Bklyn., Sept. 15, 1960; MD, U. Pa. Sch. Medicine, 1986. Cert. Am. Bd. Orthopedic Surgery. Intern George Washington U. Hosp., 1986—87, resident, 1987—91; spine fellowship Case Western Reserve U. Hosp., Cleve., 1991—92; clin. dir. Whitesides Orthop. Rsch. Lab.; assoc. prof. orthop. Emory U. Sch. Medicine, 1995, prof. orthop.; dir. Emory Spine Ctr., Atlanta, 1994—2004, Emory Orthop., Spine Ctr. & Sports Medicine Ctr., Atlanta, 2004—; staff mem. Emory U. Hosp., Crawford Long Hosp., Atlanta. Founder, chmn. Nat. Spine Network, Marietta, 1994—. Articles published on Spine-health.com When is back pain a fracture?, Bone graft substitutes for lumbar spine fusion surgery, 4 proven steps to prevent osteoporosis fractures. Fellow: Am. Acad. Orthop. Surgeons; mem.: Orthop. Rsch. Soc., Internat. Soc. for the Study of the Lumbar Spine, N.Am. Spine Soc. Achievements include being founder of the National Spine Network, a group of physicians, hospitals and institutions who specialize in the diagnosis and treatment of all problems of the spine. Office: Emory Orthop, Spine Ctr & Sports Medicine Ctr 59 Executive Park S Ste 3000 Atlanta GA 30329 Address: Nat Spine Network 3020 Roswell Rd NE Marietta GA 30062 Office Phone: 404-778-7143. Office Fax: 404-778-7117.*

BODEN, WILLIAM EDWARD, cardiologist, educator; b. June 21, 1948; BS, LeMoyne Coll., Syracuse, 1970; MD, SUNY Upstate Med. Ctr., 1974. Cert. Internal Medicine, Cardiovascular Disease. Resident Boston Univ. Med. Ctr., 1977; chief resident, tchg. assoc. Univ. Hosp., Boston, 1977; clin. fellow cardiology Tufts-New England Med. Ctr., Boston, 1977—79; asst. prof. medicine Brown Univ. Sch. Medicine, 1979—86; assoc. prof. medicine Wayne State Univ., 1986—89; prof. medicine Boston Univ. Sch. Medicine, 1989—96; prof. medicine, assoc. chair dept. medicine SUNY Health Sci. Ctr., Syracuse, 1996—2000; prof. medicine Univ. Conn. Sch. Medicine, 2000—06; chief cardiology Henry Low Heart Ctr., Hartford Hosp., Conn., 2000—06; med. dir. cardiovascular services Kaleida Health, 2006—; chief of cardiology Buffalo Gen. and Millard Fillmore Hospitals, 2006—; prof. medicine and pub. health Univ. at Buffalo Sch. of Medicine and Biomedical Sciences, 2006—, prof. medicine. Chair COURAGE Trial; co-chair AIM-HIGH Trial. Contbr. several articles to profl. jours. Named Top Cardiology Physician in Conn., Conn. Mag. and Hartford Mag. Office: Univ Buffalo Sch Medicine and Biomedical Sciences 100 High St Buffalo NY 14203 Business E-Mail: wboden@kaleidahealth.org.*

BODENHAMER, DAVID JACKSON, historian, educator; b. Macon, Ga., May 4, 1947; s. David Jackson and Mary Elizabeth (Cox) B.; m. Penny Jo McClelland, Dec. 27, 1988. BA, Carson-Newman Coll., 1969; MA, U. Ala., 1970; PhD, Ind. U., 1976. Asst. prof., then assoc. prof. U. So. Miss., Hattiesburg, 1976-84, prof., asst. v.p. acad. affairs, 1985-88; dir. Polis Ctr. Ind. U., Indpls., 1989—. Head N.Am. team, exec. com. Electronic Cultural Atlas Initiative, 1997—. Author: Pursuit of Justice, 1986, Fair Trial, 1991; author, editor: Encyclopedia of Indianapolis, 1994; co-editor: Ambivalent Legacy, 1984, Bill of Rights in Modern America, 1992, History of Indiana Law, 2006, Our Rights, 2006; editor-in-chief Indiana Online: An Electronic Encyclopedia. Chmn. bd. dirs. South Miss. Community Action Agy., Hattiesburg, 1978-82; bd. dirs. Pine Belt Family YMCA, Hattiesburg, 1982-86; steering com. Regional Ctr. Plan, Indpls, 1989-92; mem. steering com. New Ind. State Mus. Task Force, 1998—, regional ctr. plan, 2002. With U.S. Army, 1970-72. Mem. Am. Soc. Legal History, Orgn. Am. Historians. Office: Polis Ctr Ste 100 1200 Waterway Blvd Indianapolis IN 46202-5140 Office Phone: 317-274-2455. E-mail: intu100@iupui.edu.

BODENHEIMER, GEORGE, broadcast executive; b. Meriden, Conn., May 6, 1958; m. Ann Bodenheimer, Aug. 4, 1984; 3 children. BA in economics, Denison U., 1980. With adminstrv. dept. ESPN Inc., Bristol, Conn., 1981—82, mktg. rep. south ctrl. region Tex., 1982—85, mktg. rep. ctrl. region, 1985, nat. accounts mgr. Rocky Mountain region, 1985—88, dir. affiliate sales and mktg. ea. divsn., 1988—89, v.p. affiliate sales and mktg. ea. divsn. Bristol, Conn., 1989—91, v.p. nat. affiliate sales, 1991—92, v.p. affiliate sales and mktg., 1992—93, sr. v.p. affiliate sales and mktg., 1993—95, sr. v.p. sales and mktg., 1995—96, exec. v.p. sales and mktg., 1996—98, pres. domestic ops., 1998—99, pres., 1999—, ABC Sports, 2003—; co-chair Media Networks divsn. Walt Disney Co., 2004—. Bd. mem. Cable & Telecom. Assoc. for Mktg., Cable TV Advt. Bur., Cable in the Classroom. Office: ESPN Inc Espn Plz Bristol CT 06010-1099 also: ABC Sports 47 W 66th St New York NY 10023

BODENSTEIN, IRA, lawyer; b. Atlantic City, Nov. 9, 1954; s. William and Beverly (Grossman) B.; m. Julia Elizabeth Smith, Mar. 9, 1991; children: Sarah Rose, George William, Jennie Kathryn. Student, Tel Aviv U., 1974-75; BA in Govt., Franklin & Marshall Coll., 1977; JD in Econs., U. Miami, 1980. Bar: Ill. 1980, U.S. Dist Ct. (no. dist.) Ill. 1980, U.S. Ct. Appeals (7th cir.) 1982, Fla. 1983. Assoc. James S. Gordon Ltd., Chgo., 1980-85, mem., 1985-89, Portes, Sharp, Herbst & Fox, Ltd., Chgo., 1990-91; shareholder Towbin & Zazove, Ltd., Chgo., 1991-93; ptnr. D'Ancona & Pflaum, Chgo., 1993-98; U.S. Trustee Region 11, Chgo., 1998—2006, Region 9, Cleve., 2001—02; mem. Shaw, Gussis, Fishman, Glantz, Wolfson & Towbin, LLC, Chgo., 2006—. Pres., bd. dirs., benefit chmn. Gus Giordano Jazz Dance, Chgo., 1990—; treas. Chgo. Pub. Art Group, 1995-99. Mem. ABA (bus. law sect., rep. young lawyers divsn. dist. 15, 1986-87, ann. meeting adv. com. 1990, spkr. spring meeting 1996, 97), Chgo. Bar Assn. (bd. dirs. young lawyers sect. 1985-87, chmn.-elect 1987-88, chmn. 1988-89, antitrust com., chmn. athletics com. 1984-85, bd. mgrs. 1990-92, chmn. pub. affairs and media rels. com., chmn. assn. meetings com., memberships com. 1996, cert. of appreciation 1984-93, 96-97). Democrat. Jewish. Home: 2848 W Wilson Ave Chicago IL 60625-3743 Office: Shaw Gussis Fishman et al 321 N Clark St Ste 800 Chicago IL 60610 Office Phone: 312-666-2861. Office Fax: 312-275-0556. E-mail: ibodenstein@shawgussis.com.

BODENSTEINER, LISA M., former utilities executive, lawyer; BS in Bus. Adminstrn. and Acctg., U. Nev., 1985; JD, Santa Clara U., 1989. Assoc. Thelen, Reid & Priest, 1994—96; assoc. counsel Calpine Corp., 1996—99, v.p., gen. counsel, 1999—2001, sr. v.p., gen. counsel, 2001—02, asst. sec., exec. v.p., gen. counsel, 2002—06.

BODEY, BELA, immunologist, pathologist, oncologist; b. Sofia, Bulgaria, Jan. 18, 1949; arrived in US, 1985, naturalized, 1994; s. Joseph and Rossitza (Derebeeva) B.; m. Victoria Psenko, Aug. 29, 1979; children: Bela Jr., Vivian. MD, Med. Acad., Sofia, 1973; PhD in Immuno-Biology, Inst. Morphology, Bulgarian Acad. Sci., Sofia, 1977. Lic. physician, exptl. pathologist, embryologist, immuno-morphologist, thymologist, exptl. oncologist. Asst. prof. Semmelweis Med. U., Budapest, 1977-80; prof. Inst. Hematology, Budapest, 1980-83; rsch. assoc. Tufts U., Boston, 1985; rsch. fellow immuno-pathology Mass. Gen. Hosp./Harvard U., Boston, 1986; rsch. fellow Childrens Hosp. L.A., 1987-90, rsch. scientist, 1991-92; asst. prof. rsch. pathology, Sch. of Medicine Univ. Southern Calif., 1992—, prof. pathology Sch. Medicine, 1995—. Vis. prof. Alexander von Humboldt Found., Ulm, Fed. Republic Germany, 1984. Mem. Am. Assn. Cancer Rsch., Am. and Can. Acad. Pathology, French Soc. Cell Biology, French Soc. Electronmicroscopy, Internat. Soc. Exptl. Hematology, Internat. Soc. Comparative Oncology, N.Y. Acad. Scis., Free Masons. Roman Catholic. Avocations: travel, swimming, dance. Office: Childrens Hosp Los Angeles 4650 W Sunset Blvd Los Angeles CA 90027-6062 Home: 6820 Remmet Ave Unit 201 Canoga Park CA 91303 Office Phone: 818-886-1082. Personal E-mail: bodey18@aol.com.

BODEY, GERALD PAUL, retired medical educator; b. Hazelton, Pa., May 22, 1934; s. Allen Zartman and Marie Frances (Smith) B.; m. Nancy Louise Wiegner, Aug. 25, 1956; children: Robin Gayle Sparwasser, Gerald Paul Jr., Sharon Dawn Brantley. AB magna cum laude, Lafayette Coll., 1956; MD, Johns Hopkins U., 1960. Diplomate Nat. Bd. Med. Examiners, Am. Bd. Internal Medicine, Am. Bd. Infectious Diseases, Am. Bd. Oncology. Intern Johns Hopkins U., Balt., 1960-61, resident, 1961-62; clin. assoc. Nat. Cancer Inst., Bethesda, Md., 1962-65; resident U. Wash., Seattle, 1965-66; internist to prof. medicine U. Tex./M.D. Anderson Cancer Ctr., Houston, 1975—95, emeritus prof. medicine, 1995—, ret., 2004. Mem. Am.-Soviet Meetings on Cancer Chemotherapy, 1974—78; adj. prof. microbiology, immunology and medicine Baylor Coll. of Medicine, Houston, 1975—99; active collaborative cancer treatment rsch. program Pan Am. Health Orgn., 1976—84; prof. internal medicine and pharmacology Med. Sch. U. Tex. Health Sci. Ctr., 1976—2004, clin. prof. Dental Sch., 1977—95; mem. orphan products devel. initial rev. group FDA, 1984—95; mem. lunar quartine ops. team Apollo 11-14, Manned Spacecraft Ctr., NASA, joint commn. accreditation healthcare orgns. Hospital-wide Indicators Task Force, 1987—89; hon. prof. U. Peruana Cayetano Heradia, 2007—. Mem. editl. bd.: European Jour. Clin. Microbiol. Infectious Diseases; former mem. editl. bd.: Cancer Rsch., Antimicrobial Agts. and Chemotherapy, Brazilian Jour. Infectious Disease; contbr. over 1000 articles to profl. jours. Past trustee Med. Benevolence Found. Nat. AIDS Prevention Inst.; past bd. dir. Christian Coalition Reconciliation. Recipient Am. Chem. Soc. prize, 1956, Merck award, 1956, Robert B. Youngman Greek prize Lafayette Coll., 1956, Eugene Yourassowsky award U. Libre de Bruxelles, Belgium, 1995, Gran Ofcl. de Orden, Hipolito Unanue, Peru, 2007; scholar Leukemia Soc. Am., 1969-74; Henry Strong Denison fellow Johns Hopkins Sch. Medicine, Balt., 1958-60. Fellow ACP, Am. Coll. Chest Physicians, Am. Coll. Clin. Pharmacology, Royal Coll. Medicine, Royal Soc. Promotion Health; mem. AMA, Nat. Acad. Medicine Peru (hon.), Am. Soc. Clin. Oncology, Infectious Diseases Soc. Am., Am. Soc. Clin. Pharmacology and Therapeutics, Am. Soc. Hematology, Am. Soc. Microbiol., Am. Sci. Affiliation, Internat. Soc. Complexity, Info. and Design, Christian Med. Soc., Tex. Med. Assn., Academia Peruana de Cirugia (hon.), Academia Nacional Medicina (hon.), Mediterranean Med. Soc. (hon.), Le Soc. Peruana Cancerologia (hon.), La Costarricensa Oncologie (hon.), Soc. Brasileira Cancerologia (hon.), Phi Beta Kappa, Sigma Xi. Methodist. Office: U Tex MDACC Box 402 1515 Holcombe Blvd Houston TX 77030-4009 Business E-Mail: gbodey@mdanderson.org.

BODEY, RICHARD ALLEN, minister, educator; b. Hazelton, Pa., Nov. 27, 1930; s. Allen Zartman and Marie (Smith) B.; m. Ruth Lois Price, 1955; children: Bronlynn Beth Spindler, Richard Allen Jr. Student, Muhlenberg Coll., 1948—49; AB, Lafayette Coll., 1952; postgrad., Moravian Theol. Sem., 1952; MDiv, Princeton Theol. Sem., 1955; postgrad., Wycliffe Coll., 1961, Knox Coll., 1961, Emmanuel Coll., 1961, Gannon Coll., 1963-64, Winona Lake Sch. Theology, 1963; ThM, Westminster Theol Sem., 1972; DMin, Trinity Evang. Div. Sch., 1984, Seabury-We. Theol. Sem., 1985. student licentiate Evang. Congl. Ch, 1948-52; ordained to ministry Presbyn. Ch. Am., 1955. Student pastor Zion Welsh Presbyn. Ch., Wind Gap, Pa., 1951; student supply pastor Italian Presbyn. Ch., Roseto, Pa., 1951; student pastor Westminster Presbyn. Ch., Allentown, Pa., 1952—55; supply pastor Presbyn. Ch., Brackney, Pa., 1955; pastor Marshall Meml. Presby. Ch., Lebanon, Ill., 1955—56; instr. Bible McKendree Coll., Lebanon, 1956; pastor 3d Presbyn. Ch., North Tonawanda, NY, 1956—62; instr. Buffalo Bible Inst., 1961; pastor 1st Presbyn. Ch., Corry, Pa., 1962—64, Dales Meml. United Presbyn. Ch., Phila., 1964—66; asst. pastor Westminster Presbyn. Ch., Jackson, Miss., 1966; founding prof. preaching, chmn. Practical Theol. Dept. Reformed Theol. Sem., Jackson, Miss., 1966—73; interim pastor 1st Presbyn. Ch., Hazlehurst, Miss., 1967—68; stated supply pastor Presbyn. Ch., Union Church, Miss., 1970—73, supply pastor Fayette, Miss., 1970—73; head of staff 1st Assoc. Reformed Presby. Ch., Gastonia, NC, 1973—79; chaplain Civitan, 1975; founder, dir. Gastonia Sch. Bibl. Studies, 1978—79; founding bd. chmn. Gastonia Christian Sch., 1978—79; assoc. prof. practical theol. Trinity Evang. Div. Sch., Deerfield, Ill., 1979—87, prof., 1987—95. Dir. continuing edn. Trinity Evang. Div. Sch., 1982-87, DMin coord. and examiner, 1989-95; examiner Moody Bible Inst. Corr. Sch., Chgo., 1982-86; vis. instr. Westminster Theol. Sem., Phila., 1987, 88; lectr., 1990; cons. in continuing edn., 1990-91; seminar leader Nat. Conf. on Preaching, 1990-94; DMin examiner, 1994-96, 2002-03, 2007; instr. North Chgo. Theol. Inst., 1991-94, Seabury Western Theol. Sem., Chgo., 1993; vis. instr. Our Lady of the Lake Coll., Chgo., 1993; vis. faculty Columbia (SC) Internat. U. and Sem., 1991; asst. to rector Aquia Episcopal Ch., Stafford, Va., 2007—; spkr. in field. Author: You Can Live Without Fear of Death, 1980; editor, contbr. Good News for All Seasons: 26 Sermons for Special Days, 1987, (Korean edit., 1990), Inside the Sermon: Thirteen Preachers Discuss Their Methods of Preparing Sermons, 1990, The Voice from the Cross: Seven Sermons on the Last Words of Our Lord, 1990, 2d edit., 2000, If I Had Only One Sermon to Preach, 1994; editor: Voices Trinity Evang. Div. Sch., 1980-88, Trinity Book Bull., 1989-94, The Lamb of God (Sermons by Clarence Edward Macartney), 1994; co-editor: Come to the Banquet, 1998; contbr. Ministers Manual, 1974, 82, Zondervan Pictorial Ency. of the Bible, 1975, Handbook of Contemporary Preaching, 1993, The Complete Library of Christian Worship, 1996, Ministry to the Aging, 2005; contbr.: Serving and Challenging Seniors, 2005; contbr. articles and revs. to profl. jours. Chmn. Here's Life Metrolina, Gastonia Area, 1976; founding bd. chmn. Gaston Evang. Assn., 1978-79; bd. dirs. Gaston Christian Sch., 1978-79; chmn. planning com. Evang. Affirmations, 1989; chaplain Civitan, 1974. Recipient Porter Bible prize Lafayette Coll., 1950, David Fowler Atkins Jr. prize, 1952, Gastonia Evang. Assn. award, 1979. Mem. Am. Acad. Ministry (charter, adv. bd. mem.). Avocations: travel, collecting miniature cathedral and church models, collecting Christian art and artifacts, books and records, music. *To me life's highest meaning and deepest satisfaction lie in a personal relationship with Jesus Christ my Saviour and Lord. My supreme aim and motive are to honor Him in everything I do. I can think of no worthier pursuit, no more challenging goal, for anyone in any age.*

BODIN, KATE, dean; BFA, Boston U.; MEd in Creative Arts and Learning, Endicott Coll. Dean of faculty Montserrat Coll. Art, Beverly, Mass., 1992; acad. dean Coll. Art and Craft, Portland, Oreg., 2005—. Office: Oreg Coll Art and Craft 8245 SW Barnes Rd Portland OR 97225 Office Phone: 502-397-5544 x 125. E-mail: kbodin@ocac.edu.

BODINE, CHRIS W., retail executive; V.p. bus. devel. CVS Pharmacy, Inc., 1997—98, sr. v.p. health care svcs., 1998—2000, v.p. merchandising, 2000—02; exec. v.p. merchandising and mktg. CVS Pharmacy, Inc. and CVS Corp., 2002—07; exec. v.p. CVS Corp., 2007—; pres. CVS Health Services, 2007—. Office: CVS Caremark Corp Corp Hdqrs 1 CVS Dr Woonsocket RI 02895*

BODINE, GEOFF, race car driver; b. Chemung, NY, Apr. 18, 1949; children: Matthew, Barry. Profl. race car driver NASCAR, 1979—; owner, driver, 1993—. Named Rookie of Yr., NASCAR, 1982, winner, Daytona 500, 1986, Internat. Race of Champions, 1987, Holly Farms 400, 1989, Hanes 500, 1990, AC Spark Plug 500, 1990, Goody's 500, 1990, 1992, Mello Yello 500, 1991, Tyson/Holly Farms 400, 1992, Save art 300, 1993, Miller 500, 1994, Goodwrench 400, 1994, Tyson 400, 1994, Winston Select, 1994, The Bud at the Glen, 1996; named one of 50 Greatest Drivers, NASCAR; recipient Busch Pole award, 1996. Office: c/o NASCAR PO Box 2875 Daytona Beach FL 32120-2875

BODINE, SUSAN P., federal agency administrator; AB, Princeton U., 1983; JD, U. Penn., 1988. Atty. Covington & Burling, Washington, 1988—95; counsel Subcommittee on Water Resources & the Environment, Com. on Transportation & Infrastructure, US Ho. Reps., Washington, 1995—2002, staff dir., sr. counsel, 2002—05; asst. admin. for solid waste & emergency response EPA, Washington, 2005—. Office: EPA Rm 3146 1200 Pennsylvania Ave NW Washington DC 20460 Office Phone: 202-566-0200. Office Fax: 202-566-0207.

BODINE, WILLIAM BEEKMAN, JR., museum director; b. New Brunswick, NJ, Sept. 30, 1948; s. Alice Flanders Jeffries and William Beekman Bodine. BA, U. Va., 1970. Program adminstr. Nat. Endowment for Arts, Washington, 1974—80; devel. office mgr. Mus. Fine Arts, 1980—83; asst. dir. Corcoran Gallery of Art, Washington, 1983—92; assoc. dir. High Mus. of Art, Atlanta, 1992—94; chief curator Columbia (SC) Mus. of Art, 1994—2002; dir. Frick Art and Hist. Ctr., Pitts., 2002—. Bd. dirs. Greater Pitts. Arts Coun., 2004, Greater Pitts. Conv. and Visitors Bur., 2005. Mem.: Am. Assn. Museums, Assn. Art Mus. Directors, Pitts. Golf Club. Episcopalian. Avocation: travel. Office: Frick Art and Hist Ctr 7227 Reynolds Street Pittsburgh PA 15208 Home Phone: 412-781-1411. Office Fax: 412-371-6104.

BODIS, STEPHAN B., radiologist, oncologist, educator; b. Basel, Switzerland, Feb. 16, 1958; s. Istvan and Ruth (Kipfer) B.; m. Mirjam Christeler, Sept. 30, 1989; 4 children. BS, U. Baden, Switzerland, 1978; MD, U. Basel, 1985. Lic. cert. profl. physician, Switzerland; diplomate Am. Bd. Radiation Oncology, Swiss Bd. Radiation Oncology. Resident physician Dist. Hosp., Baden, 1985—87, U. Hosp., Zurich, 1987—89; clin. fellow, rsch. fellow Inst. Gustave Roussy, Villejuif/Paris, 1989—91; resident, rsch. fellow Joint Ctr. Radiation Therapy Harvard Med. Sch., Boston, 1991—95; attending physician Joint Ctr. for Radiation Therapy, Boston, 1995; head rsch. lab., dept. radiation oncology U. Zurich, 1995—99, assoc. physician, 2000—, asst. prof., 1999—2001, assoc. prof., 2001—03, prof., 2004—; chmn. Inst. for Radiation Oncology, Aargau State Hosp, Switzerland, 2004—. Contbr. articles to profl. jours. including Jour. Clin. Oncology, Blood, Cancer, Cancer Rsch. Grantee, Swiss NIH, 1997, Swiss Cancer League, 1995, 1999, 2001, 2006. Mem.: Swiss Cancer League (pres. radiation oncology sect. 2000—), European Soc. Med. Oncology, European Soc. Therapeutic Radiation Oncology (radiobiology com. 1999—2005, bd. dirs. 2001—04, pres. sci. com.), Am. Soc. Therapeutic Radiation Oncology, Swiss Soc. Radiation Oncology (exec. com. 1997—2002). Avocations: classical music, travel. Office: Institut für Radio-Onkolgie Kantonsspital AG 5001 Aargau Switzerland Office Phone: 01141-62-838-5371. E-mail: stephan.bodis@ksa.ch.

BODKIN, HENRY GRATTAN, JR., lawyer; b. LA, Dec. 8, 1921; s. Henry Grattan and Ruth May (Wallis) B.; m. Mary Louise Davis, June 28, 1943; children: Maureen L. Dixon, Sheila L. McCarthy, Timothy Grattan. BS cum laude, Loyola Marymount U., Los Angeles, 1943, JD, 1948. Bar: Calif. 1948. Pvt. practice, Los Angeles, 1948-51, 53-95; ptnr. Bodkin, McCarthy, Sargent & Smith (predecessor firms), LA; of counsel Sullivan, Workman & Dee, LA, 1995—. Mem. L.A. Bd. Water and Power Commrs., 1972-74, pres., 1973-74; regent Marymount Coll., 1962-67; trustee Loyola-Marymount U., 1973-91, vice chmn., 1985-86. With USNR, 1943-45, 51-53. Fellow Am. Coll. Trial Lawyers; mem. Calif. State Bar (mem. exec. com. conf. of dels. 1968-70, vice chmn. 1969-70), California Club, Chancery Club (pres. 1990-91), Riviera Tennis Club, Tuna Club, Phi Delta Phi. Republican. Roman Catholic. Home: 956 Linda Flora Dr Los Angeles CA 90049-1631 Office: Sullivan Workman & Dee 800 S Figueroa St Fl 12 Los Angeles CA 90017-2521 Home Phone: 310-472-3441; Office Phone: 213-624-5544. E-mail: bodkin01@cs.com.

BODKIN, LAWRENCE EDWARD, inventor, essayist, research and development company executive, consultant; b. Sapulpa, Okla., May 17, 1927; s. Clarence Elsworth and Lillie (Moore) B.; m. Ruby Emma Pate, Jan. 15, 1949; children: Karen Bodkin Snead, Cinda, Lawrence Jr. Student, Fla. State U., 1947-50; grad., Gemological Inst., 1969. Chief announcer, program dir., mgr. various radio stations, Winter Haven, Fla., Tallahassee and Jacksonville, Fla., 1947-60; ind. jewelry salesman and appraiser Underwood Jewelers, 1961-87; pres. Bodkin Jewelers and Appraisers, Jacksonville, 1984—, Telanon, Jacksonville, 1981—, Bodkin Co., Jacksonville, 1974—; chmn., chief exec. officer Bodkin Corp., Jacksonville, 1975—; dir. elec. safety R&D in U.S. and Orient Innovative Designer Products Div. Brooke Shields Beauty Care, Kendall Park, NJ, 1989-92. Cons. gem and mineral groups, Jacksonville, 1960—, numerous corps. and industries (on inventions); lectr. in field. Author: Dual Imagery of Ultra Speed Bodies, 1971, Miniatures, 1976, Bodkin's Revised Law of Buoyancy, 2000; contbr. articles to sci. publs.; inventor Universal-Fault Circuit-Interrupter (Bodkin Circuit), TIP (tested immersion protection), Auto Test and Reset GFCI (ground fault cir. interrupter), Bodkin Jewelry Clasp, Height Measure, others. Mem. Jacksonville Mus. Sci. and Hist., 1981—, Jacksonville Symphony Assn., 1985—, Cummer Gallery Art, Jacksonville, 1985—, Ye Mystic Revellers, 1997—. Served with U.S. Army, 1945-47, ETO. Mem. Fla. State U. Alumni Assn., Mensa Internat., San Jose Country Club. Achievements include inventor in field. Avocations: fossil collecting, beach combing, philosophy, writing, theoretical physics. Home: 1149 Molokai Rd Jacksonville FL 32216-3273 Office: 1043 Park St Jacksonville FL 32204 Office Phone: 904-350-9600. Personal E-mail: larubodkin@aol.com.

BODKIN, RUBY PATE, retired real estate broker, educator; b. Frostproof, Fla., Mar. 11, 1926; d. James Henry and Lucy Beatrice (Latham) P.; m. Lawrence Edward Bodkin Sr., Jan. 15, 1949; children: Karen Bodkin Snead, Cinda, Lawrence Jr. BA, Fla. State U., 1948; MA, U. Fla., 1972. Lic. real estate broker Fla. Banker Barnett Bank, Avon Park, Fla., 1943-44, Lewis State Bank, Tallahassee, 1944-49; ins. underwriter Hunt Ins. Agy., Tallahassee, 1949-51; tchr. Duval County Sch. Bd., Jacksonville, Fla., 1952-77; pvt. practice realty Jacksonville, 1976—2007; ret., 2007. Tchr. Nassau County Sch. Bd., Jacksonville, 1978—83; sec., treas., v.p. Bodkin Corp., R&D/Inventions, Jacksonville, 1983—2007. Author: 100 Teacher Chosen Recipes, 1976, Bodkin Bridge Course for Beginners, 1996, (autobiography) Grandma Bodkin, 2000, Essay on Death, 2003; author numerous poems. Mem. Jacksonville Symphony Guild, 1985—, Southside Bapt. Ch. Recipient 25 Yr. Svc. award Duval County Sch. Bd., 1976, Tchr. of Yr. award Bryceville Sch., 1981, 30 Yr. Svc. award State of Fla. Dept. Edn. Mem. Am. Contract Bridge League, Nat. Realtors Assn., Southside Jr. Woman's Club, Garden Club Sweetbriar (bd. dirs.), Oak St. Woman's Club Jacksonville (fin. dir. 1991-92, 3rd v.p. social dir. WCOJ, 1992-99), UDC (Martha Reid chpt. #19), Fla. Edn. Assn. (pers. problems com. 1958), Duval County Classrooms Tchrs. (v.p. membership 1957), Woman's Club Jacksonville Bridge Group, Fla. Ret. Tchrs. Assn., Fla. Realtors Assn., N.E. Fla. Realtors Assn., Jacksonville Geneal. Soc. (practicing genealogist, family historian 1986—), Friday Musicale of Jacksonville, San Jose Golf Country Club, Jacksonville Sch. Bridge. Baptist. Avocations: reading, writing, genealogy, photography, bridge. Home: 1149 Molokai Rd Jacksonville FL 32216-3273 Office: Bodkin Jewelers & Appraisers c/o G Exchange 1043 Park St Jacksonville FL 32204 Personal E-mail: larubodkin@aol.com. *Ruby Pate Bodkin, geneaologist and honored teacher (1955-83) has traced her Pate and Bodkin ancestors back to England and Ireland. Son Lawrence (Larry) Bodkin, Jr., 40, MEd, Fla. State U., Tallahasse, is currently a prosperous owner and CEO of his own founded company, Bodkin Management and Consulting (New Directions for Associations). Daughter Karen, 53, wed C.T. Snead III in 1976, grandson (by adoption) of U.S. congressman, congressman Carl Vinson of Milledgeville, Ga. Ruby's husband of 56 years, Larry Bodkin, Sr. has more than 25 US patents on his own inventions. Also, he has written many timely essays on varied subjects which he has for sale on website. He works daily at his job appraising fine jewelry for the public for their insurance purposes since he was duly certified by The American Gem Soc. years ago and enjoys the work still at age 78.*

BODLEY, HARLEY RYAN, JR., sportswriter, announcer, editor; b. Dover, Del., Nov. 24, 1936; s. Harley Ryan and Mildred Olivia (Carver) Bodley; m. Patricia Jean Hall, Dec. 4, 1981. BA, U. Del., 1959; postgrad., Am. U., 1960. Sports editor Del. State News, Dover, 1959-60; sports dir. Radio WDOV, Dover, 1958-62; sports writer News-Jour. Papers, Wilmington, Del., 1960-63, night sports editor, 1963-67, asst. sports editor, 1967-71, sports editor, 1971-82; baseball editor USA Today, McLean, Va., 1982—. Discussion leader Am. Press Inst., Reston, Va., 1967—76; TV host Sta. WHYY-TV, Wilmington, 1967—74; columnist The Sporting News, St. Louis, 1978—83; commentator NBC-TV Baseball: An Inside Look, 1987, USA Today Radio Report, 1987—89, USA Today: The TV Show, 1988—89; commentator and host Baseball Sunday United Syndications Radio Network, 1988—90; baseball analyst CNN, 1989—91; commentator CBS Radio Network baseball pre-game, 1990—97, Comcast Sports Net, 2000—05. Author: I Learned To Fly, So Can You, 1967, The Team That Wouldn't Die, 1981, Countdown to Cobb, 1985; writer Best Sports Stories, 1967-71, 1977-79, 1982, 1985 Flight safety counselor FAA, Phila., 1968-72. Served as sgt. U.S. Army N.G. 1956-64. Named Sportswriter of Yr., Nat. Sportscasters and Sportswriters Assn., 1961, 63, 65, 67-70, 73-75, 78-79; recipient Best of Gannett award Gannett Co., Inc., 1981, Mark Twain award AP, 1980, 25th Year award Baseball Commr., 1983, USA Today All-Star award, 2000, 01; inducted Del. Baseball Hall of Fame, 2002, Del. Sports Hall of Fame, 2004. Mem. AP Sports Editors (pres. 1981-82, Best Sports Story award 1981, 1st place award 1982), Baseball Writers Assn. Am. (Phila. chpt. chmn. 1977-78), Wilmington Sportswriters and Broadcasters (pres. 1963 sec-treas. 1965-83), Sigma Delta Chi (Top Sports award 1982) Clubs: Wilmington Country; Northeast Yacht. Episcopalian. Avocations: golf, pilot, boating. Address: care Athletes & Artists 421 7th Ave New York NY 10001-2002 Business E-Mail: hbodley@usatoday.com.

BODMAN, SAMUEL WRIGHT, III, secretary of energy, former specialty chemicals and materials company executive; b. Chgo., Nov. 26, 1938; s. Samuel W. Jr. and Lina (Lindsay) B.; m. M. Diane Barber, July 31, 1997; children: Elizabeth L., Andrew M., Sarah H. BS in Chemical Engring., Cornell U., 1961; ScD, MIT, 1964. Tech. dir. Am. R & D, Boston, 1964-70; prof. MIT, Cambridge, Mass., 1964-70; v.p. Fidelity Venture Assn., Boston, 1970-74; pres. Fidelity Venture Assocs., 1974-77; chmn. Fidelity Venture Assn., 1977; pres. Fidelity Mgmt. & Rsch. Co., Boston, 1976-86; pres., COO FMR Corp., 1982-86; exec. v.p., dir. Fidelity Group Mut. Funds, 1980-86; pres., COO Cabot Corp., Boston, 1987-88, chmn., CEO, also bd. dirs., 1988—2001; dep. sec. US Dept. Commerce, Washington, 2001—04, US Dept. Treasury, 2004—05; sec. US Dept. Energy, Washington, 2005—. Bd. dirs. Westvaco, Inc., N.Y.C., John Hancock Fin. Svcs., Thermo Electron Corp., Houston, Security Capital Group Inc. Trustee, mem. exec. com. MIT, Cambridge; trustee Isabella Stewart Gardner Mus., Boston, New England Aquarium, Boston. Mem.: NAE. Episcopalian. Office: US Dept Energy Forrestal Bldg 1000 Independence Ave SW Washington DC 20585

BODNAR, LISA M., medical educator; b. Pitts., May 9, 1976; d. Robert and Patricia Bodnar; m. Steve Potter, Sept. 1, 2001; 1 child, Cole. BS of Pub. Health, U. NC, Chapen Hill, 1998; MPH, U. NC, Chapel Hill, 1999, PhD, 2002. Registered dietitian Commn. Dietetic Registration, 2000. Asst. prof. U. Pitts.; Pitts., 2004—. Office: Univ Pitts 130 DeSoto St Pittsburgh PA 15261

BODNAR, PETER O., lawyer; b. Queens, NY, Mar. 19, 1945; s. John and Edith (Schultz) B. BA in Govt., NYU, 1966; JD, Fordham U., 1970. Bar: N.Y. 1971, U.S. Dist. Ct. (so. dist.) N.Y. 1973. Confidential law sec. to Hon. Evans V. Brewster Family Ct. and County Ct. Westchester County, NY, 1970-73; pvt. practice White Plains, NY, 1973-77; ptnr. Bodnar & Greene, P.C., White Plains, NY, 1977-80, Bender & Bodnar, White Plains, NY, 1980-98; prin. Law Offices of Peter O. Bodnar, White Plains, NY, 1998-99, Bodnar & Milone LLP, White Plains, NY, 1999—; mng. mem.

Organica USA II LLC, 2004—07. Pres., CEO P.A.J. Am. Ltd./The Olo Corp., 1990—97; CEO Organica, USA, Inc., 1998—2007; lectr. Pace U. Sch. Law Women's Justice Ctr., 2001—, Appellate Divsn. 2d Dept. Law Guardian Program, 2003—; supervisory bd. Organica RT, Budapest, Hungary, 2001—07, Vertis Environ. Fin., KFT, Budapest, Hungary, 2002—. Trustee Village of Ossining, N.Y., 1975-77. Fellow: Am. Acad. Matrimonial Lawyers (parliamentarian 2007—); mem.: ABA (family law sect.), Westchester County Bar Assn. (family law sect., exec. com. 1992—, chair 2000—02), N.Y. State Bar Assn. (family law sect., exec. com. 2000—, lectr. custody and visitation 2003—). Office: 140 Grand St White Plains NY 10601-4831 Home Phone: 516-627-0774; Office Phone: 914-997-2500. Personal E-mail: usorganica@aol.com.

BODNER, BRUCE IRA, ophthalmologist; b. Norfolk, Va., Nov. 5, 1945; s. Herman Bodner and Freda Glazier; m. Joanne Berson. BA in Biology, Va. Mil. Inst., 1967; MD, U. Va., 1971. Diplomate Am. Bd. Ophthalmology. Intern U. Mich. Hosp., Ann Arbor, 1971-72; resident in ophthalmology Emory U. Sch. of Medicine, Grady Meml. Hosp., others, Atlanta, 1975-78; chief resident in ophthalmology Emory U. Sch. of Medicine, Grady Meml. Hosp., Atlanta, 1977-78; various ednl. and staff positions to dir. Cornea and Contact Lens Clinic Sentara Hosps., 1980-97; asst. to assoc. prof. dept. ophthalmology Ea. Va. Med. Sch., 1980—; founder, med. dir. Lions Med. Eye Bank and Rsch. Ctr. of Ea. Va., 1979—. Founder, med. dir. Lions Med. Eye Bank & Rsch. Ctr. Ea. Va., Inc., 1979—; commr. Joint Commn. Allied Health Pers. Ophthalmology, 1990—97; adv. bd. Contact Lens Coun., Washington, 1992—98; bd. councillors Am. Acad. Ophthalmology, 1993—95; med. dir. Laser Optic Ctr. Norfolk, Va., 1996—2002; presenter in field. Named in Best Doctors in Am., S.E. region, 1996—97, nat. listing, 1998—2003; fellow Cornea & External Disease, Emory U. Sch. Medicine, Atlanta, 1978—79, Melvin Jones, Lions Internat., 1989; scholar Norfolk Found., U. Va., 1967—71; Florence Smith scholar. Fellow: Am. Acad. Ophthalmology; mem.: AMA (Physicians Recognition awards 1978, 1990, 1991, 1993), Castroviejo Soc., Va. Ophthalmology and Otolaryngology Soc., Norfolk Acad. Medicine, Va. Soc. Medicine, Tidewater Ophthalmology and Otolaryngology Soc., Am. Soc. Cataract and Refractive Surgery, Occular Immunology and Microbiology Study Group, Internat. Soc. Keratorefractive Surgery, Eye Bank Assn. Am. (mem. accreditation bd. 2003—), Contact Lens Assn. Ophthalmologists (dir. 1992—97), Am. Assn. Ophthalmology, Alpha Omega Alpha. Avocations: computer, astronomy. Office Phone: 757-622-2200. Personal E-mail: vaeye@aol.com. Business E-Mail: bbodner@vec2020.com.

BODNER, DONALD ROGER, urologist, medical educator; b. Indpls., Aug. 31, 1953; s. Robert Stewart and Elizabeth (Wolf) B.; m. Linda Joy Abrams, Oct. 5, 1985; children: Robert, Daniel, Richard. BS, Trinity Coll., Hartford, Conn., 1975; MD, Ind. U., Indpls., 1979. Resident in urology Case Western Res. U., Cleve., 1979-84, instr. urology, 1984-85, asst. prof., 1985-92, assoc. prof., 1992—99, prof., 1999—. Editor Jour. Spinal Cord Medicine, 2006—; guest editor: Urologic Clinical Procedures - Spinal Cord Injury, 1993. Mem. Am. Urologic Soc., Internat. Spinal Cord Soc., Am. Paraplegia Soc. (pres. 1993-95). Office: Case Western Res Univ Dept Urology 11100 Euclid Ave Cleveland OH 44106-1736 Office Phone: 216-844-3009. E-mail: donald.bodner@uhhospitals.org.

BODNER, JOHN, JR., lawyer; b. Dover, NJ, May 4, 1927; s. John and Anna (Kushman) B.; m. Anne Potter; children: John Edward, Brit-Marie, Anne Kristin, Peter Andrew. Student, Cornell U., 1946-50; JD, Northwestern U., 1953; MLA, Johns Hopkins U., 1969. Bar: D.C. 1954. Bigelow teaching fellow U. Chgo. Law Sch., 1953-54; atty. Dept. Justice, Washington, 1954-56; assoc. Howrey & Simon, Washington, 1956-64; ptnr. Howrey, LLP and predecessors, Washington, 1964—. Law lectr. various univs. With U.S. Army, 1945-46. Mem. ABA, FBA, D.C. Bar Assn., Met. Club. Roman Catholic. Home: 4707 Reservoir Rd NW Washington DC 20007-1906 Office: Howrey LLP 1299 Pennsylvania Ave NW Washington DC 20004-2420 Home Phone: 202-333-0292; Office Phone: 202-383-6899. Business E-Mail: bodnerj@howrey.com.

BODNER, RANDALL WAYNE, lawyer; b. Danville, Ky., May 24, 1959; s. Jack Kenneth Elsie Marie (Elmore) B.; m. Elizabeth Hendrik Evans, May 31, 1986. AB summa cum laude, Dartmouth Coll., 1981; JD magna cum laude, Harvard U., 1985. Bar: Mass. 1987, U.S. Dist. Ct. Mass. 1987, U.S. Ct. Appeals (1st crct.) 1987, U.S. Ct. Appeals (2d crct.) 1991. Law clk. to Hon. Ellsworth A. Van Graafeiland U.S. Ct. Appeals (2d cir.), NYC and Rochester, N.Y., 1985-86; assoc. Ropes & Gray, Boston, 1986-90; asst. U.S. atty. criminal div. so. dist. N.Y. U.S. Dept. Justice, NYC, 1990—95; ptnr. litigation dept. Ropes & Gray, Boston, 1995, head securities and corp. litigation practice group. Mem. ABA, Mass. Bar Assn., Phi Beta Kappa. Avocations: sailing, squash, golf. Office: Ropes & Gray 1 International Pl Boston MA 02110-2624 Home Phone: 781-383-7062; Office Phone: 617-951-7776. Office Fax: 617-951-7050. Business E-Mail: randall.bodner@ropesgray.com.

BODOFF, JOSEPH SAMUEL UBERMAN, lawyer; b. Bryn Mawr, Nov. 2, 1952; s. Bernard David and Ruth Irma (Uberman) B. BS, Pa. State U., 1974; JD, Villanova U., 1977. Bar: Pa. 1977, U.S. Dist. Ct. (ea. dist.) Pa. 1979, U.S. Ct. Appeals (3d cir.) 1980, U.S. Supreme Ct. 1988, Mass. 1987, U.S. Dist. Ct. Mass. 1988, U.S. Ct. Appeals (1st cir.) 1988, R.I. 1998, U.S. Dist. Ct. R.I. 1999. Jud. law clk. Phila. County Ct. of Common Pleas, 1977—79; assoc. Pincus, Verlin, Hahn & Reich, Phila., 1979—86; ptnr. Kaye, Fialkow, Richmond & Rothstein, Boston, 1986—91, Gaston & Snow, Boston, 1991, Warner & Stackpole, Boston, 1991—94, Hinckley, Allen & Snyder, Boston, 1994—98, Shechtman & Halperin, Boston, 1998—2000, Bodoff & Slavitt LLP, Boston, 2003—06, Bodoff & Assocs., Boston, 2000—03, 2006—. Co-chair Am. Bankruptcy Inst. Unsecured Trade Creditor Com., Alexandria, 1993—98, Am. Bankruptcy Inst. Creditors' Com. Manual Task Force, 1993—94; chair Am. Bankruptcy Inst. Task Force on Preferences, 1995—97; dir. Am. Bankruptcy Inst., Alexandria, Va., 1995—2003, mem. exec. com., 2000—03, co-chmn. task force bankruptcy rules, 2006—; chair NACM Bankruptcy and Insolvency Group, Portland, 1998—; dir. Am. Bd. Certification, Alexandria; exec. editor ABI World, 2002—. Author: Cramdown: The Ultimate Chapter 11 Threat, 1992, (with others) Bankruptcy Business Acquisitions, 1998; exec. editor: ABI World, 2002-07; contbr. articles to profl. publs. Mem. Mus. Coun. of Mus. of Fine Arts, Boston, 1997—99. Mem. ABA, Am. Bankruptcy Inst. (dir. 1995-2003, exec. com. 2000-03, co-chair task force on bankruptcy rules), Am. Bd. Certification (dir. 1996-2000), Boston Bar Assn., Nat. Assn Credit Mgmt. Avocations: skiing, tennis, wine collecting, piano. Home: 64 Forest St Chestnut Hill MA 02467-2930 Office: Bodoff & Assocs 225 Friend St Boston MA 02114 Home Phone: 617-734-8611; Office Phone: 617-742-7300. Business E-Mail: jbodoff@bodofflaw.com.

BODOVITZ, JAMES PHILIP, lawyer; b. Evanston, Ill., Aug. 20, 1958; s. Philip Edward and Dosha (Laurman) B. BS, U. So. Calif., 1980, JD, 1984. Bar: N.Y. 1985, D.C. 1989, Calif. 1990. Assoc. Shearman & Sterling, NYC, 1984-89, San Francisco, 1989-92; br. chief divsn. broker-dealer enforcement U.S. Securities Exch. Commn., NYC, 1992-96; v.p., assoc. gen. counsel law dept. The Equitable Life Assurance Soc. of U.S., NYC, 1996—2004; sr. v.p., gen. counsel AXA Advisors, LLC, 1999—2004; chief compliance officer Pk. Ave. Securities Guardian Life Ins. of Am., NYC, 2004—07; chief compliance officer Royal Alliance Assocs., Inc., NYC, 2007—. Mem. ABA, Assn. Bar City N.Y. (Thurgood Marshall award 1998). Democrat. Office: Royal Alliance Assocs Inc 1 World Financial Ctr 15th Fl New York NY 10281 Business E-Mail: jbodovitz@aigroyalalliance.com.

BODSWORTH, FRED, writer, ecologist; b. Port Burwell, Ont., Can., Oct. 11, 1918; s. Arthur John and Viola B.; m. Margaret Neville Banner, July 8, 1944; children: Barbara (Mrs. Edward Welch), Nancy (Mrs. Richard Hannah), Neville. Student pub. schs., Port Burwell. Reporter St. Thomas (Ont.) Times-Jour., 1940-43; reporter, editor Toronto (Ont.) Daily Star, 1943-46; staff writer, editor Maclean's Mag., Toronto, 1947-56; novelist, 1956—. Organizer, leader numerous natural history tours Author: Last of the Curlews, 1954, 2d edit., 1995, The Strange One, 1960, The Mating Call, 1961, The Atonement of Ashley Morden, 1964, The Sparrow's Fall, 1967 (also pub. in Eng., fgn. translations), The Pacific Coast, Illustrated Natural History of Canada series, 1970; (with others) Wilderness Canada, 1970; editor: Illustrated Natural History of Canada series, 1980-81. Bd. dirs. Natural Sci. of Can., 1980-88; hon. bd. dirs. Long Point Bird Obs., 1970—; chmn. bd. trustees James L. Baillie Meml. Fund for ornithol. field research, 1975-88. Mem. Fedn. Ont. Naturalists (hon. life, pres. 1964-66), Internat. PEN, Writers Union of Can. Clubs: Ornithological, Field Naturalists (past pres.), Brodie (Toronto), Writer's Tust of Can. (Lifetime Achiev. award, 2003). E-mail: fbodsworth@sympatico.ca.

BODWELL, LORI, lawyer; b. Oct. 1966; AB, Bowdoin Coll., 1988; JD, Boston Coll., 1991. Bar: Alaska 1992, Maine 1993, Mass. 1992, Dist. of Alaska (US Dist. Ct.) 1994, 9th Air 1995. Mem.: Tananeu Valley Bar Assoc., Nat. Assoc. of Criminal Def. Lawyers, Alaska Bar Assn. (pres. 2002—03).

BOE, DAVID STEPHEN, musician, educator, dean; b. Duluth, Minn., Mar. 11, 1936; s. Egbert Thomas and Beatrice Ella (Steen) Boe; m. Sigrid North, July 23, 1961; children: Stephen, Eric. BA, St. Olaf Coll., Northfield, Minn., 1958; M.Mus., Syracuse U., 1960. Asst. prof. music U. Ga., 1961-62; mem. faculty Oberlin Coll. Conservatory Music, Ohio, 1962—, prof. organ and harpsichord, 1976—, dean, 1976-90; organ recitalist U.S. and Europe, 1962—. Mem. advanced placement music com. Coll. Entrance Exam. Bd., 1980—83; vis. prof. Fla. State U., 1991, U. Notre Dame, 1991—92. Trustee Westfield Ctr., 2000—; chmn. scholarship com. Presser Found., 2002—; dir. music, organist First Luth. Ch., Lorain, Ohio, 1962—2002. Scholar Fulbright, Germany, 1960—61. Mem.: Nat. Assn. Schs. Music (trustee, sec. 1981—87), Phi Beta Kappa, Pi Kappa Lambda (nat. pres. 1986—90). Business E-Mail: david.boe@oberlin.edu.

BOECKMAN, ROBERT KENNETH, JR., chemistry professor, organic chemistry researcher; b. Pasadena, Calif., Aug. 26, 1944; s. Robert Kenneth Sr. and Orletta Christine (Brinck) B.; m. Mary Helen Delton, June 19, 1976 BS, Carnegie Inst. Tech., 1966; PhD, Brandeis U., 1971. NIH fellow Columbia U., NYC, 1970-72; from asst. prof. to prof. chemistry Wayne State U., Detroit, 1972-79; prof. chemistry U. Rochester, NY, 1980—, chmn. dept. chemistry, 2003—. Cons. Eastman Kodak, 1986—, Ricerca Inc., Painesville, Ohio, 1983-01, Novartis Pharma AG, Basel, Switzerland, 1981—, Procter & Gamble Pharm., Cin., 1988—, Sanofi-Aventis, SA, 1992-99, 2001—, Emisphere Technologies, Hawthorne, N.Y., 1999-02; bd. dirs. Organic Syntheses, Pet Pride of N.Y., Inc.; v.p. Organic Syntheses, Inc., 2002—. Mem. editl. bd. Organic Syntheses, 1988-96; mem. editl. adv. bd. Can. Jour. Chemistry, 2000—03; assoc. editor Jour. Organic Chemistry, 1997—; contbr. articles to profl. jours. Recipient Career Devel. award NIH, 1976-81, award for acad. achievement Probus Club, 1979, Von Humboldt Rsch. prize for sr. scientists, 1992-93; fellow A.P. Sloan Found., 1976-80; Marshal Gates scholar, 1996-2001; Marshall Gates Jr. Prof., 2002-. Fellow Japanese Soc. for Promotion Sci.; mem. Am. Chem. Soc. (chmn. organic chemistry divsn. 2001, past chair 2002, Arthur C. Cope Scholar award 2006), Royal Soc. Chemistry, Deutscher Chemiker Gesellschaft, Oakhill Country Club Rochester, Sigma Xi. Republican. Roman Catholic. Avocations: golf, basketball, ping pong/table tennis. Office: U Rochester Hutchinson Hall Dept of Chemistry Rochester NY 14627 Home Phone: 585-624-2023; Office Phone: 585-275-4229. Business E-Mail: rkb@rkbmac.chem.rochester.edu.

BOECKMANN, ALAN L., engineering and construction management company executive; BSEE, U. Ariz., Tucson. Engr. Fluor Corp., 1974; pres., CEO Fluor Daniel; pres. Fluor Daniel's Energy & Chem. group; pres., COO Fluor Corp., 2001—02, chmn. bd., CEO, 2002—. Dir. Burlington No. Santa Fe, Am. Petroleum Inst., Bus. Coun. Internat. Understanding, Nat. Petroleum Coun., Archer Daniels Midland Co. Dir. Orange County Performing Arts Ctr., Hearing & Speech Found.; mem. Bus. Roundtable; chmn. engring. & constrn. gov. World Econ. Forum; mem. adv. coun. U. Ariz. Coll. Engring. & Mines; dir. So. Meth. U. Cox Sch. Bus. Office: Fluor Corp 6700 Las Colinas Blvd Irving TX 75039 Office Phone: 469-398-7000. Office Fax: 469-398-7255.*

BOED, ROMAN A., legal administrator; arrived in U.S., 1979; s. Viktor and Eva Boed; m. Molly Bradshaw, May 29, 1995; children: Julian, Owen, Charles. BA, Lawrence U., 1987; JD, DePaul U., Chgo., 1994; LLM, Cambridge U., Eng., 1998, Columbia U., 1999. Assoc. legal protection officer UN High Commr. for Refugees, Moscow, 1995—97; judgment coord. UN Internat. Criminal Tribunal for Rwanda, Arusha, Tanzania, 1999—2004; legal officer UN ICTR Appeals Chamber, The Hague, Netherlands, 2004—. Author (with Michael Bohlander and Richard J. Wilson): Defense in International Criminal Proceedings, 2006; bd. editors: Internat. Criminal Law Rev., 2002—; contbr. articles to profl. jours. Office: UN Internat Criminal Tribunal for Rwanda Churchillplein 1 2517 JW The Hague Netherlands Home Phone: 630-665-8512; Office Phone: 31-70-5128804. E-mail: boed@un.org.

BOEDER, THOMAS L., lawyer; b. St. Cloud, Minn., Jan. 10, 1944; s. Oscar Morris and Eleanor (Gile) B.; m. Carol-Leigh Coombs, Apr. 6, 1968. BA magna cum laude, Yale U., 1965, LLB, 1968. Bar: Wash. 1970, U.S. Dist. Ct. (We. Dist.) Wash. 1970, U.S. Dist. Ct. (Ea. Dist.) Wash. 1972, U.S. Ct. Appeals (9th Cir.) 1970, U.S. Supreme Ct. 1974, U.S. Ct. Appeals (D.C. Cir.) 1975, U.S. Ct. Appeals (10th Cir.) 1993. Litigation atty. Wash. State Atty. Gen., Seattle, 1970-72, antitrust div. head, 1972-76, chief, consumer protection and antitrust, 1976-78, also sr. asst. atty. gen. and criminal enforcement, 1979-81; ptnr., Litig. Practice Area Perkins Coie LLP, Seattle, 1981—. With US Army, 1968—70, Vietnam. Mem. ABA (antitrust sect.), Wash. State Bar Assn. (antitrust sect.), Phi Beta Kappa. Lutheran. Office: Perkins Coie LLP 1201 3rd Ave Fl 40 Seattle WA 98101-3029 Home Phone: 206-523-2795; Office Phone: 206-359-8416. Office Fax: 206-359-9416. Business E-Mail: tboeder@perkinscoie.com.

BOEHEIM, JIM, college basketball coach; b. Lyons, NY, Y, Nov. 17, 1944; BA in Social Sci., Syracuse U., 1966, M in Social Sci. Full-time asst. basketball coach Syracuse (N.Y.) U., 1972-76, head basketball coach, 1976—. Mem. coaching staff U.S. basketball team Goodwill Games, Seattle, 1991 (silver medal), World Championships, Argentina (bronze medal), World Univ. Games, 1989. Hon. chmn. Kidney Found.; active orgns. Multiple Sclerosis, Cystic Fibrosis, Children's Miracle Network, Make-A-Wish, Pioneer Ctr. for Blind and Disabled, Lighthouse, People in Wheelchairs, Easter Seals, Spl. Olympics. Named Dist. II Coach of Yr., Nat. Assn. Basketball Coaches nine times, U.S. Basketball Writers Assn., 1979, 80, 91; named Big East Conf. Coach of Yr., 1984, 91 and 2000; Basketball court at the Carrier Dome named "Jim Boeheim Court" 2002. Achievements include coaching NCAA Championship team, Syracuse, 2003; coaching Syracuse to 12 "Sweet 16" appearances and to three NCAA championship games. Office: Syracuse Univ Basketball Dept Manley Field House Syracuse NY 13244-0001

BOEHLERT, CARL JOSEPH, materials scientist, educator; b. Vestal, NY, Feb. 10, 1969; s. James Thomas and Rose Marie Boehlert; m. Paula Maria Somohano, Feb. 5, 1995; children: Victoria Rose, Nicolas Joseph, Lucas Samuel. BS in Agr. and Biol. Engring., Cornell U., 1991; MS in Materials Sci. and Enring., U. Dayton, 1993, PhD in Materials Sci. and Engring., 1997. Rsch. assoc. U. Dayton, Ohio, 1991-93; materials scientist UES Inc., Dayton, 1993-97; postdoctoral fellow Johns Hopkins U., Balt., 1998-99; postdoctoral rsch. assoc. Los Alamos Nat. Lab., 2000-01; asst. prof. Alfred U., NY, 2001—04, Mich. State U., 2005—. Contbr. numerous articles to profl. jours. Recipient Career award, NSF, 2002, Presdl. Early Career award, 2002. Mem.: Am Soc. Engring. Edn., Am. Soc. Mech. Engrs., Materials Rsch. Soc., The Materials Soc. (young leader 1999), Am. Soc. Materials Internat. (award 2002). Roman Catholic. Office: Mich State U 2527 Engring Bldg East Lansing MI 48824 Home Phone: 517-347-3791; Office Phone: 517-353-3703. Business E-Mail: boehlert@egr.msu.edu.

BOEHLERT, SHERWOOD LOUIS, former congressman; b. Utica, NY, Sept. 28, 1936; s. Sherwood John and Elizabeth Monica (Champoux) Boehlert; div.; children: Mark C. Brooks, Tracy Boehlert Suk, Leslie; m. Marianne Willey Phillips, July 10, 1976; 1 stepchild, Laura Brooke Drahzal. BS in Pub. Rels., Utica Coll., 1961. Staff asst. Wyandotte Chems. Corp., Mich., 1961—63, mgr. pub. rels., 1963—65; chief of staff to Rep. Alexander Pirnie US Congress, Washington, 1964—72, chief of staff to S Rep. Donald J. Mitchell, 1973-79; exec. Oneida County, NY, 1979—82; mem. US Congress from 24th (formerly 23rd) NY dist., 1983—2007, mem. sci. com., 1983—2006, chmn. sci. com., 2001—06, mem. transp. and infrastructure com.; vis. scholar Woodrow Wilson Pub. Policy Ctr., 2007—. Del. NATO parliamentary assembly; mem. N.E.-Midwest Congl. Coalition; co-chmn. N.E. Agr.; chmn. Fire Svcs. Caucus, Minor League Baseball Caucus. Author: Telling the Congressman's Story: The Voice of Government, 1968. Bd. dirs. Utica Coll. Found. Served in US Army, 1956—58. Named one of the 50 Most Effective Lawmakers in Washington DC, Congl. Quarterly, 1999; recipient Environmental Leadership award, Interfaith Impact Found., Friend of the Farmer award, NY Farm Bur., 2002, Pub. Svc. award, Am. Astron. Union, 2003, Edgar Wayburn award, Sierra Club. Mem.: Rotary. Republican. Roman Catholic. Office Phone: 202-225-3665.

BOEHM, BARRY WILLIAM, computer science educator; b. Santa Monica, Calif., May 16, 1935; s. Edward G. and Kathryn G. (Kane) B.; m. Sharla Perrine, July 1, 1961; children: Romney Ann, Tenley Lynn. BA, Harvard U., 1957; PhD, UCLA, 1964; ScD (hon.), U. Mass., 2000. Programmer, analyst Gen. Dynamics, San Diego, 1955-59; head infosci. dept. Rand Corp., Santa Monica, 1959-73; chief scientist TRW Def. Sys. Group, Redondo Beach, Calif., 1973-89; dir. infosci. and tech. office Def. Advanced Rsch. Agy. Dept. Def., Arlington, Va., 1989-92, dir. software and computer tech. office, dir. def. rsch. and engring., 1992; TRW prof. software engring., dir. Ctr. for Software Engring. U. So. Calif., LA, 1992—. Co-chmn. Fed. Coordinating Coun. Sci., Engring. and Tech. High Performance Computing WG, Washington, 1989-91; chmn. DOD Software Tech. Plan WG, Arlington, 1990-92, NASA G & C/Infosystems Adv. Com., Washington, 1973-76; guest lectr. USSR Acad. Sci., 1970; chmn. bd. visitors Carnegie Mellon U. Software Engring. Inst., 1997—; chmn. USAF-Sci. Adv. Bd. Info. Tech. Panel, 1994-97, Army/DARPA Future Combat Systems Software Steering Com., 2001—, vis. prof. Chinese Acad. Sci., 2005. Author: ROCKET, 1964, Software Engineering Economics, 1981; co-author: Characteristics of Software Quality, 1978, Software Risk Management, 1989, Software Cost Estimation with COCOMO II, 2000, Balancing Agility and Discipline, 2004, Software Engineering: Barry W. Boehm's Contributions, 2007; co-editor: Planning Community Information Utilities, 1972, Foundations of Empirical Software Engineering, 2005, Value-Based Software Engineering, 2005, Unifying The Software Process Spectrum, 2005. Recipient Warnier prize Soc. Software Analysts, 1984, Freiman award Internat. Soc. Parametric Analysts, 1988, Award for Excellence Office of Sec. of Def., 1992. Fellow Internat. Coun. on Sys. Engring., Assn. for Computing Machinery (Disting. Rsch. award in Software Engring. 1997), NAE, AIAA (chair TC computers 1968-70, Info. Sys. award 1979), IEEE (gov. bd. computer sci. 1981-82, 86-87, H.D. Mills award 2000). Office: U So Calif Computer Sci Dept Los Angeles CA 90089-0781 Business E-Mail: boehm@sunset.usc.edu.

BOEHM, EDWARD GORDON, JR., college administrator, educator; b. Washington, Jan. 30, 1942; s. Edward and Catherine (Murray) B.; m. Regina Ellen Evans, June 25, 1966; children: Evan Arnold, Andrew Edward. BS in Edn., Frostburg State U., 1964; MEd, The Am. U., 1970, D of Higher Edn., 1977. Dir. univ. devel., dean for student devel., assoc. dean/dir. admissions, instr. Coll. Arts & Scis. The Am. U., Washington, 1968-79; assoc. vice chancellor acad. affairs, asst. prof. edn., dean admissions Tex. Christian U., Ft. Worth, 1979-89; sr. v.p., asst. prof. Coll. Edn., exec. dir. Found. Marshall U., Huntington, W.Va., 1989-95; pres. Keystone Coll., La Plume, Pa., 1995—. Mem. adv. coun. Tandy Tech. Scholars, Ft. Worth, 1989-99; trustee, mem. com. The Coll. Bd., N.Y.C., 1987-91. Contbr. book chpt.: Student Services and the Law, 1988; contbr. articles to profl. jours. Bd. dirs., v.p. Boys & Girls Club, Huntington, 1989-95, Tri-State coun. Boy Scouts Am., Huntington, 1989-95; bd. dirs., pres. United Way River Cities, Huntington, 1989-95; bd. dirs. Leadership W. Va., Charleston, 1992-95, Leadership Tri-State, Ironton, Ohio, 1991-95; mem. scholastic evaluation panel Am.'s Jr. Miss, 1995-2005; bd. dirs. Tyler Hosp., 1995-2001, Waverly Cmty. House, 1996-2000; mem. Leadership Wilkes-Barre Exec. Program, Class of '96, Leadership Lackawanna Exec. Program, Class of '96, N.E. Regional Cancer Inst. Adv. Bd.; pres. bd. dirs. Pa. Assn. of Nonprofit Orgns., 1998; mem. nonprofit adv. bd. Nonprofit Resource Ctr., U. Scranton, 1998—; mem. Pa. Soc., 1997—, Team Pa. Amb., 1999—; life mem. Lackawanna Indsl. Fund Enterprises, 1999—; mem. task force Healthy N.E. Pa. Intiative, 1999-2001; bd. govs. Scranton Area Found., 2002—; bd. dir. PACU, 2003—, Pa. Campus Compact, 2003—; commr. Middle States Commn. on Higher Edn., 2005—. Named W.Va. Outstanding Fundraising Exec., Nat. Soc. Fundraising Execs., 1993, Citizen of Yr., Herald Dispatch, 1993, Disting. West Virginian, 1995; recipient Cir. of Excellence in Fundraising award Coun. for Advancement and Support of Edn., 1993, Nat. Tchr.'s award Radio Shack Adv. Coun., 2000; John Deaver Drinko Acad. fellow Marshall U. Mem. Huntington C. of C., Lawrence County C. of C., Greenup County C. of C., Engrs. Club Huntington, Huntington Rotary Club (bd. dirs. 1989-95). Avocations: tennis, soccer, history, golf, hiking. Home: 29 College Ave La Plume PA 18440 Office: Keystone Coll One College Green La Plume PA 18440-0200 Office Phone: 570-945-8500. Business E-Mail: Edward.Boehm@keystone.edu.

BOEHM, ERIC HARTZELL, information technology executive; b. Hof, Germany, July 15, 1918; came to U.S., 1934, naturalized, 1940; s. Karl and Bertha (Oppenheimer) Boehm; m. Inge Pauli, June 5, 1948 (dec.); children: Beatrice(dec.) , Ronald James, Evelyn(dec.) , Steven David. BA, Wooster Coll., Ohio, 1940, Litt.D. (hon.), 1973; MA, Fletcher Sch. Law and Diplomacy, 1942; PhD, Yale U., 1951. With Dept. Air Force, 1951-58; chmn., CEO BoehmGroup.com; bd. dirs. ABC-CLIO, Santa Barbara, Calif., 1960—; pres. Internat. Sch. of Info. Mgmt., 1987-94. Chmn. bd. dirs. Internat. Acad. at Santa Barbara, 1970—2003; pub. Environ. Studies Inst., 1971—2003, Info. Inst., 1980—2003; cons. on bibliography, info. sys. Author: We Survived, 1949, 83, 2004; microfilm Policy-making of the Nazi Government, 1969; editor Historical Abstracts, 1955-83, cons., 1983; editor America: History and Life, 1964-83, cons., 1983; editor Bibliographies on International Relations and World Affairs, an Annotated Directory, 1965, Blueprint for Bibliography, a System for Social Sciences and Humanities, 1965, Clio Bibliography Series, 1973; co-editor Historical Periodicals, 1961, 2d edit., 1983-85; pub. Advanced Bibliography of Contents: Political Science, 1969, ART Bibliographies: Modern, 1972,

Environ. Periodicals Bibliography, 1972; bd. advisors Info. Strategy, The Exec.'s Jour., 1984; contbr. articles to profl. jours. Bd. dirs. UN Assn., Santa Barbara, 1973-77, Santa Barbara's Adv. Bd. Internat. Relationships (Sister Cities), 1974, Friends of Public Library, Friends of U. Calif. at Santa Barbara Library; mem. affiliates bd. U. Calif.-Santa Barbara; vice chmn. New Directions Found., 1984-88; adv. bd. Nuclear Age Peace Found., 1985; chmn. BoehmGroup.com, 2003—. With USAAF, 1942-46. Recipient Disting. Alumnus award Wooster Coll., 1990. Mem. AAAS, Am. Soc. Info. Sci., Assn. Bibliography in History (v.p. 1986, pres. 1987), Calif. Library Soc., Nat. Trust Historic Preservation, Santa Barbara Com. Fgn. Rels., Santa Barbara C. of C. (dir. 1980-84), Univ. Club, Rotary, Phi Beta Kappa. Home and Office: 800 E Micheltorena St Santa Barbara CA 93103-2220 Office Phone: 805-965-6266. Personal E-mail: eboehm1918@aol.com.

BOEHM, FELIX HANS, physicist, researcher; b. Basel, Switzerland, June 9, 1924; came to U.S., 1952, naturalized, 1964; s. Hans G. and Marquerite (Philippi) B.; m. Ruth Sommerhalder, Nov. 26, 1956; children: Marcus F., Claude N. MS, Inst. Tech., Zurich, 1948, PhD, 1951. Research assoc. Inst. Tech., Zurich, Switzerland, 1949-52; Boese fellow Columbia U., 1952-53; faculty Calif. Inst. Tech., Pasadena, 1953—, prof. physics, 1961—, William L. Valentine prof., 1985-94, William L. Valentine prof. emeritus, 1995—; Sloan fellow, 1962-64; NSF sr. fellow Niels Bohr Inst., Copenhagen, 1965-66, CERN, Geneva, 1971-72, Laue-Langevin Inst., 1980. Recipient Humboldt award, 1980, 84. Fellow Am. Phys. Soc. (Tom W. Bonner prize 1995); mem. Nat. Acad. Scis. Achievements include research on nuclear physics, nuclear beta decay, neutrino physics, atomic physics, muonic and pionic atoms, parity and time-reversal. Home: 2510 N Altadena Dr Altadena CA 91001-2836 Office: Calif Inst Tech Mail Code 161 33 Pasadena CA 91125-0001 E-mail: boehm@caltech.edu.

BOEHM, KENNETH, legal association administrator; 1 child, Christine. Talk show host Sta. WWDB-AM-FM, Phila.; prosecutor; adminstrv. asst. to Congressman Christopher Smith; legis. dir. Howard Jarvis' Am. Tax Reduction Movement; co-founder, chmn. Nat. Legal Policy and Ctr., Falls Church, Va., 1991—. Counsel to bd. dirs. Legal Svcs. Corp. Office: Nat Legal and Policy Ctr 107 Park Washington Ct Falls Church VA 22046 Office Phone: 703-237-1970.

BOEHM, STEVEN BRUCE, lawyer; b. NYC, May 22, 1954; s. Henry and Irene (Jonas) B. BA, Rutgers U., New Brunswick, NJ, 1975; JD, Rutgers U., Newark, 1978. Bar: N.J., 1978, D.C., 1982, U.S. Dist. Ct. N.J., U.S. Dist. Ct., D.C. Enforcement atty. SEC, Washington, 1978-81, atty. office gen. counsel, 1982, counsel to the commr., 1982-83; assoc. Sutherland Asbill & Brennan, LLP, Washington, 1983-87, ptnr., 1988—. Philip J. Levin scholar Rutgers U., 1975-78. Mem. ABA (corp., banking and bus. law com.), D.C. Bar Assn., Phi Beta Kappa, Pi Sigma Alpha. Office: Sutherland Asbill & Brennan LLP 1275 Pennsylvania Ave NW Washington DC 20004-2415 Business E-Mail: steven.boehm@sablaw.com.

BOEHM, THEODORE REED, state supreme court justice; b. Evanston, Ill., Sept. 12, 1938; s. Hans George and Frances (Reed) B.; children from previous marriage: Elisabeth, Jennifer, Sarah, Macy; m. Margaret Stitt Harris, Jan. 27, 1985. AB summa cum laude, Brown U., 1960; JD magna cum laude, Harvard U., 1963. Bar: D.C. 1964, Ind. 1964, U.S. Supreme Ct. 1975. Law clk. to Chief Justice Warren, Justices Reed and Burton, U.S. Supreme Ct., Washington, 1963-64; assoc. Baker & Daniels, Indpls., 1965-70, ptnr., 1970-88, 95-96, mng. ptnr., 1980-87; gen. counsel major appliances GE, Louisville, 1988-89; v.p., gen. counsel GE Aircraft Engines, Cin., 1989-91; dep. gen. counsel Eli Lilly & Co., 1991-95; justice Ind. Supreme Ct., Indpls., 1996—. Pres. Ind. Sports Corp., 1980-88; chmn. organizing com. 1987 Pan Am. Games, Indpls.; chmn. Indpls. Cultural Devel. Commn., 2001—. Mem. ABA, Am. Law Inst., Ind. Bar Assn., Indpls. Bar Assn. Office: Ind Supreme Ct State House Rm 324 Indianapolis IN 46204-2728 Office Phone: 317-232-2547. E-mail: tboehm@courts.state.in.us.

BOEHMER, ANN, mathematics professor; d. Donald and Nancee McCarthy; 1 child, Max. BA in Math., U. Mo., St. Louis, 1997, MA in Math., 2000. Asst. prof. math. East Ctrl. Coll., Union, Mo., 2000—. Faculty devel. co-chair East Ctrl. Coll., Union, 2005—06, faculty welfare co-chair, 2006—, faculty devel. chair, 2006—, faculty assn. v.p., 2006—07, faculty assn. pres., 2007—. Mem.: Am. Math. Assn. Two Yr. Colls., Nat. Assn. Devel. Edn. Office: East Central College 1964 Prairie Dell Rd Union MO 63084 Home Phone: 636-239-7122; Office Phone: 636-583-5193. Business E-Mail: boehmera@eastcentral.edu.

BOEHNE, EDWARD GEORGE, banker; b. Evansville, Ind., May 15, 1940; s. Edward John and Lucy Naomi (Strieter) Boehne; m. Patricia Graffis, Jan. 24, 1960; 1 child, Lisa Elena. BS, Ind. U., 1962, MBA, 1963, MA, 1967, PhD in Econs, 1968; LLD (hon.), Widener U., 1989, U. Del., 2001, U. So. Ind., 2002, Holy Family U., 2004. Economist Fed. Res. Bank, Phila., 1968—70, rsch. officer, economist, 1970—71, v.p., dir. rsch., 1971—73, sr. v.p., 1973—81, pres., 1981—2000. Tchr. Bradley U., 1963—65, Ind. U., 1965—67, Temple U., 1969—70; bd. dirs. Haverford Trust, 2000—, AAA Mid-Atlantic Co., 2000—, Beneficial Savs. Bank, 2000—, Toll Bros., 2000—, PennMut. Life Ins. Co., 2001—. Chmn. Pa. Hosp., 1993-97; chmn. University City Sci. Ctr., 1998-99. Recipient Lieber award Ind. U., 1967, Gov.'s citation for outstanding svc. to Pa., 1978, Whitney Young Leadership award 1986, Stephen Girard award, 1987. Office: 313 Devon State Rd Devon PA 19333-1411 Fax: 610-687-4748. E-mail: egboehne@msn.com.

BOEHNEN, DANIEL A., lawyer; b. Mitchell, SD, Aug. 5, 1950; s. Lloyd and Mary Elizabeth (Buche) B.; m. Joan Bensing, May 22, 197 (dec. 2006); children: Christopher, Lindsey. BS in Chem. Engring. cum laude, Notre Dame U., 1973; JD, Cornell U., 1976. Bar: Ill, U.S. Dist. Ct. (no. dist.) Ill., U.S. Ct. Appeals (7th and fed. cirs.), U.S. Supreme Ct. Atty. Allegretti, Newitt, Witcoff & McAndrews Ltd., Chgo., 1976—, assoc., 1982—; ptnr. Allegretti & Witcoff, Ltd., Chgo., 1986—, bd. dirs., 1993—95; founder McDonnell Boehnen Hulbert & Berghoff, LLP, Chgo., 1996—. Named one of Top IP Lawyers in Ill., Crain's Chgo. Bus., Super Lawyers for IP Litigation, Chgo. Mag., The Best Lawyer's in Am., Best Lawyers Pubs., Best Patent Trial Lawyers in Am., Chambers USA. Fellow Am. Bar Found.; mem. ABA, AIPLA, Cornell Law Assn. Chg. (past chmn.), Fed. Cir. Bar Assn. (past bd. dirs.), Assn. Patent Law Firms (past pres., bd. dirs.), Leading Lawyers Network (Ill., founding mem.). Office: McDonnell Boehnen Hulbert & Berghoff LLP 300 S Wacker Dr Chicago IL 60606-6709 Home Phone: 847-498-0486. Business E-Mail: boehnen@mbhb.com.

BOEHNEN, DAVID LEO, food service executive, lawyer; b. Mitchell, SD, Dec. 3, 1946; s. Lloyd L. Boehnen and Mary Elizabeth (Buche) Roby; m. Shari A. Bauhs, Aug. 9, 1969; children: Lesley, Michelle, Heather. AB, U. Notre Dame, 1968; JD with honors, Cornell U., 1971. Bar: Minn. 1971. Assoc. Dorsey & Whitney, Mpls., 1971—76, ptnr., 1977—89; sr. v.p. law and external rels. Supervalu Inc., Mpls., 1991—97, exec. v.p., 1997—. Vis. prof. law Cornell U. Law Sch., Ithaca, NY, 1982. Bd. govs. U. St. Thomas Law Sch.; mem. adv. coun. on arts and letters U. Notre Dame, 1993—; mem. adv. coun. Cornell U. Law Sch., 1983—92, chmn. coun., 1986—90; bd. dirs. Guthrie Theatre. Mem.: Spring Hill Golf Club, Minikahda Club (Mpls.). Roman Cath. Office Phone: 612-828-4151. E-mail: david.boehnen@supervalu.com.

BOEHNER, JOHN ANDREW, congressman; b. Cin., Nov. 17, 1949; s. Earl Henry and Mary Ann (Hall) Boehner; m. Deborah Lane Gunlack, 1973; children: Lindsay Maria, Tricia Ann BS in Bus., Xavier U., Cin., 1977. Mgr. Merrell-Dow Pharms., Inc., 1972—76; staff to pres. Nucite Sales, Inc., 1976—90; mem. Ohio State Ho. Reps., 1984-90, US Congress from 8th Ohio dist., 1991—, majority leader, 2006—07, minority leader, 2007—, chmn. edn. and the workforce com., 2001—06. Trustee Union Twp., 1982-84 Active Ohio Farm Bur. Named Friend of the Farm Bur., Friend of the Farm Bur. Assn., 2002; recipient Watchdog of the Treasury award, 1992, Jefferson award, Citizens for a Sound Economy, 1998, Golden Bulldog award, Watchdogs of the Treasury, 1998, Guardian of Seniors Rights, 60-Plus Coalition, 1998, Adam Smith Fed. Official award, Bus. Industry Polit. Action Com., 2001, Ground Water Protector award, Nat. Ground Water Assn., 2003, Bryce Harlow award, Bryce Harlow Found., 2005. Mem. Am. Heart Assn., Am. Legion, Butler County Farm Bur., Ohio Farm Bur., KC, Lakota Hills Homeowners Assn., Cin. C. of C., Dayton C. of C., Middletown C. of C. Republican. Roman Catholic. Office: US House Reps 1011 Longworth House Office Bldg Washington DC 20515-3508 Office Phone: 202-225-6205. Office Fax: 202-225-0704.*

BOEHNER, LEONARD BRUCE, lawyer; b. Council Bluffs, Iowa, Apr. 19, 1930; s. Bruce and Flora (Kruse) B. AB, Harvard U., 1952, JD, 1955. Bar: N.Y. 1956, U.S. Dist. Ct. (so. dist.) N.Y. 1963, U.S. Ct. Appeals (2d cir.) 1963, U.S. Supreme Ct. 1964. Assoc. Dewey, Ballantine, Bushby, Palmer & Wood, N.Y.C., 1959-66; ptnr. Clare & Whitehead, N.Y.C., 1966-73, Morris & McVeigh LLP, N.Y.C. 1973—. Served to lt. USN, 1955-59. Mem. Assn. Bar City N.Y. Club: Union (N.Y.C.). Home: 210 E 73rd St New York NY 10021 Office: Morris & McVeigh 767 3rd Ave New York NY 10017-2023 Office Phone: 212-418-0540.

BOEHNKE, MICHAEL, biostatistics educator; b. Eugene, Oreg., May 16, 1956; m. Betsy Foxman; children: David, Kevin, Richard. BA Honors Coll. in Math. with Distinction, U. Oreg., 1977; PhD in Biomathematics, UCLA, 1983. Rsch. assoc. Cedars-Sinai Med. Ctr., 1979—80; tchg. asst., dept. biology UCLA, 1979—81, rsch. asst., dept. biomathematics, 1980—83; asst. prof., dept. biostatistics U. Mich., 1984—89, assoc. prof., dept. biostatistics, 1989—93, prof., dept. biostatistics, 1993—, Richard G. Cornell Collegiate Prof. Biostatistics, 2005—; dir. U. Mich. Genome Sci. Tng. Program, 1995—, U. Mich. Ctr. for Statistical Genetics, 1999—. Lectr. in field; co-organizer with Nancy Cox, chair steering com., mem. analysis and mapping com. Internat. Type 2 Diabetes Linkage Analysis Consortium, 1997—; mem., genetics steering com. NIMH, 2003—; mem. external adv. bd., Internat. Type 1 Diabetes Genetics Consortium Nat. Inst. of Diabetes and Digestive and Kidney, 2003—; mem., external adv. bd. European Acad. Bolzano Inst. for Genetic Medicine, Italy, 2004—; mem. ext. adv. bd., program for genomic applications Seattle SNP, 2004—. Contbr. articles to profl. jours.; assoc. editor American Journal of Human Genetics, 1989—91, Journal of the American Statistical Association, 1993—2003, Human Hereditary, 1992—, mem. editl. adv. bd. Genome Rsch., 1995—99, Genetic Epidemiology, 1997—, referee for several profl. publications. Named a Myrto Lefkopoulou Disting. Lectr., Harvard U. Sch. Pub. Health, 1994, Pharmacia Rsch. Prof. Biostatistics, 1999—2005, Bernard Greenberg Lectr., Dept. Biostatistics, U. NC Sch. Pub. Health, 2002; named NIH Pre-Doctoral Trainee, 1978—83; recipient DeCou prize winner as outstanding math. undergraduate, U. Oreg., 1977; Fulbright Scholar, Freiburg, West Germany, 1977—78. Fellow: Am. Statistical Assn. (co-recipient with Kenneth Lange, Snedecor award for Outstanding Statistical Applications Paper 1993); mem.: AAAS, Internat. Genetic Epidemiology Soc., Biometric Soc., Am. Soc. for Human Genetics (mem. awards com. 2005—07, bd. dir. 2006—), Phi Beta Kappa. Office: Dept Biostatistics Sch Pub Health U Mich M4108 SPH II 1420 Washington Heights Ann Arbor MI 48109-2029 Office Phone: 734-936-1001. Office Fax: 734-615-8322. Business E-Mail: boehnke@umich.edu.*

BOELHOWER, PATRICIA LEE, history educator; d. Louis Frank and Mary Frances (Thelen) Wahoske; children: Rebecca Lynn Boelhower-Santi, Joel Francis, Matthew Jacob. BA in History, Marian Coll., Fond du Lac, Wis., 1973, MA in Edn., 1995. Tchr. St. Mary and Joseph Sch., Fond du Lac, 1976—92, Marian Coll., Fond du Lac, 1993—; dir. Christian formation Holy Family Cath. Cmty., Fond du Lac, 2000—. Bd. dirs. Mt. Tabor Retreat Ctr., Menasha, Wis., 2006—07. Named Adj. Tchr. of Yr., Marian Coll., 2004—05. Mem.: Nat. Cath. Ednl. Assn. Roman Catholic. Avocations: reading, travel, quilting, knitting, aerobics. Home: 111 East 11th St Fond Du Lac WI 54935 Office: Holy Family Cath Cmty 678 Western Ave Fond Du Lac WI 54935 Office Phone: 920-921-0580.

BOELTER, PHILIP FLOYD, real estate company officer, construction executive; b. Independence, Iowa, Mar. 25, 1943; s. Floyd Joseph and Eileen R. (Wilson) B.; m. Linda Lee Franck, June 7, 1964; children: Carrie Lynn, John Philip. BS in Indsl. Engring., Iowa State U., 1965; JD, U. Iowa, 1968. Ptnr. Dorsey & Whitney, Mpls., 1968—2002; exec. v.p., chief oper. officer Kraus-Anderson Cos., Inc., Mpls., 2002—. Trustee Gustavus Adolphus Coll., 1996-2005; bd. dir. Jr. Achievement of the Upper Midwest, 2003-04. Mem. Mpls. Athletic Club (treas. 1992, sec. 1993, v.p. 1994, pres. 1995). Lutheran. Avocations: landscape gardening, skiing, golf, reading, volleyball. Office: Kraus-Anderson 525 S 8th St Minneapolis MN 55404 Home Phone: 952-941-5438; Office Phone: 612-335-2704. E-mail: phil.boelter@k-a-c.com.

BOENNING, HENRY DORR, JR., investment banker; b. Phila., Oct. 16, 1914; s. Henry Dorr and Clara Virginia (Smith) B.; m. Clare Huston Miller, Feb. 18, 1946; m. Sara Ann Perkins, Aug. 19, 1964. BS, U. Pa., 1935; postgrad., Harvard Bus. Sch., 1935-37. Partner Boenning & Co., Phila., 1946-70; v.p. Boenning & Scattergood, Inc., 1970—. Served from 2d lt. to maj. AUS, 1939-46. Mem. Phi Gamma Delta. Office: 4 Tower Bridge 200 Barr Harbor Dr Fl 3D West Conshohocken PA 19428-2977 Home: 51 Pature Ln Bryn Mawr PA 19010

BOER, F. PETER, chemical company executive; b. 1940; AB, Princeton U., 1961; PhD, Harvard U., 1965. With Tex Div. Lab. Dow Chem. Co., 1965-78, dir; v.p., mgr. R & D Am. Can Co., 1978-83; v.p., pres. rsch. div., corp. tech. group W.R. Grace & Co., from 1983, sr. v.p., until 1989, exec. v.p., until 1995; pres., CEO, Tiger Scientific Inc., 1995—. Bd. dirs. Nova Corp., ENSCO, Inc., Rhodes Techs. Inc.; former adj. prof. Sch. Mgmt. and chem. engring. Yale U.; mem. evaluation com. for nat. medals of tech. Dept. Commerce, 1990-97. Author: Valuation of Technology, 1999, The Real Options Solution, 2002, Technology Valuation Solutions, 2004. Mem. Nat. Acad. Engring. Office: Tiger Scientific Inc 47 Country Rd S Village Of Golf FL 33436-5615 Business E-Mail: fpboer@boer.org.

BOER, RALF REINHARD, lawyer; b. Berlin, Oct. 31, 1948; came to U.S., 1965; s. Karl Wolfgang Boer and Ingeborg (Krause) Serafin; m. Kathleen Marie Steinmetz, Jan. 5, 1974; children: Jessica, Charles, Alexander. BA cum laude, U. Wis., Milw., 1971; JD magna cum laude, U. Wis., Madison, 1974. Bar: Wis. 1974, U.S. Dist. Ct. (ea. dist.) Wis. 1974. Ptnr. Foley & Lardner, Milw., 1974—, ptnr.-Berlin office, 1975—76, mng. ptnr., 1992—, chmn. of firm, CEO, chmn. mgmt. com. Bd. dirs. Fiskars, Helsinki, Finland, Dynea, Hayward, Wis., Plexus Corp., Neenah, Wis. Author: German Labor-Management Relations Act, 1976. Bd. dirs. Internat. Inst. Wis., Milw., 1985-89; bd. dirs., adv. coun. U. Wis.-Milw. Internat. Bus. Ctr., 1987—. Mem. ABA, Wis. Bar Assn., Milw. Bar Assn. Fluent in german. Office: Foley & Lardner LLP 777 E Wisconsin Ave Ste 3800 Milwaukee WI 53202-5367 Office Phone: 414-297-5609. Business E-Mail: rboer@foley.com.

BOERSMA, JUNE ELAINE (JALMA BARRETT), retired writer, photographer; b. NYC, Apr. 27, 1926; d. Arthur Oscar and Gertrude Ann (Connolly) Schiefer; m. Kenneth Thomas McKim, June 8, 1946 (div. 1957); children: Kenneth Thomas McKim Jr., Mark Rennie McKim, Juliana Jaye, Dirk John; m. Lawrence Allan Boersma, Nov. 22, 1962. Student, Edgewood Park Jr. Coll., 1944—46. Writer non-fiction; co-owner, photographer Allan/The Animal Photographers, San Diego, 1980—2005; co-owner Animal Art, San Diego, 1999—2005. Author: (series) Wildcats of North America-Bobcat, Cougar, Feral Cat, Lynx, 1998, The Dove Family Tale, A True Story, 1998, Wild Canines of North America--Coyote, Foxes, Wolf, 2000, El Lince, 2002, El Lince Rojo, 2002, El Puma, 2002, El Coyote, 2002, El Lobo, 2002, Los Zorros, 2002; co-author: One Day in the Life of a Little Couger, 2001, One Day in the Life of a Coyote Pup, 2001; contbr. articles to Ladies' Home Jour., Horse Illus., Cat Fancy, Dog Fancy, Popular Photography, Studio Photography, Petersen's Photographic, Dog World, others. Mem.: Doris Day Animal League, Humane Soc. U.S., Preserve Our Wildlife Orgn., Natural Resources Def. Coun., Defenders of Wildlife, Wilderness Soc. Home: 4238 65th Terr East Sarasota FL 34243

BOERSMA, LAWRENCE ALLAN (LARRY ALLAN), animal welfare administrator, photographer; b. London, Ont., Can., Apr. 24, 1932; s. Harry Albert and Valerie Kathryn (DeCordova) B.; m. Nancy Noble Jones, Aug. 16, 1952 (div. 1962) children: Juliana Jaye, Dirk John; m. June Elaine Schiefer McKim, Nov. 22, 1962; children: Kenneth Thomas McKim, Mark Rennie McKim. BA, U. Nebr., Omaha, 1953, MS, 1955; PhD, Sussex U., 1972; postgrad., Oxford U., Eng., 1996; ScD (hon.), U. Calif., Berkeley, 2005. Journalism tchr. Tech. H.S., Omaha, 1953-55; dir. pub. rels., chair journalism dept. Adams State Coll., Alamosa, Colo., 1955-59; advt. sales analyst, advt. salesman Better Homes and Gardens, Des Moines, NYC, 1959-63; advt. account exec. This Week Mag., NYC, 1963-66; eastern sales dir., mktg. dir. Ladies' Home Jour., NYC, 1966-75; v.p. assoc. pub., v.p. pub. Saturday Evening Post and The Country Gentleman, NYC, 1975; v.p., dir. mktg. and advt. sales Photo World Mag., NYC, 1975-77; advt. mgr. LaJolla (Calif.) Light, 1977-80; owner, photographer Allan/The Animal Photographers, San Diego, Sarasota, 1980—; pres., CEO The Photographic Inst. Internat., 1982-86; dir. cmty. rels. San Diego Humane Soc./Soc. for Prevention Cruelty to Animals, 1985-94; assoc. exec. dir. The Ctr. for Humane Edn. for So. Calif., 1994-98; owner Animal Art, San Diego, 1999—, Sarasota, Fla., 1999—. Adj. asst. prof. Grad. Sch. Bus., Pace U., NYC, 1964-65; adj. instr. NY Inst. Advt., 1974-77, others; adj. prof. Sch. Bus. Mesa Coll., San Diego, 1981-84, City Coll., San Diego, 1982-86, Winona Internat. Sch. Profl. Photography, Des Plaines, Ill., 1984-87, U. Calif., San Diego, 1985; adj. prof. Coll. Bus. Adminstrn. U. LaVerne, San Diego, 1985; tchr. Winona Internat. Sch. Profl. Photography, Photog. Inst. Internat., San Diego Natural History Mus., U. Calif. San Diego, Adams State Coll. of Colo.; pres., CEO United Animal Welfare Found., San Diego, 1992-94; chmn., CEO Internat. Dolphin Project, 1995; spkr. in field. Author: Strange Events at the House on Park Avenue: A Jack and Jimmy Mystery, 1996; (as Larry Allan) Creative Canine Photography, 2004, Keep Wild Animals in Our Lives!, 2005; co-author: One Day in the Life of a Little Cougar, 2001, One Day in the Life of a Coyote Pup, 2001; photographer: (as Larry Allan) Wildcats of North Am. book series, 1998, Wild Canines of North America book series, 2000, Show Biz Tricks for Birds, 2001, El Lince, El Lince Rojo, El Puma El Coyote, El Lobo, Los Zorros, 2002; wildlife/environ. columnist Venice Gondolier Sun, Fla., 2005—; contbr. photography and articles to mags. and newspapers; photographer calendars, books, and greeting cards; photographer: (motion picture) The Truth About Cats and Dogs; exhbns.: Sierra Club, Art Photo Expo, LA, 1999, others; permanent collections include Sierra Club. Spokesperson Coalition for Pet Population Control, San Diego, 1990, 93, Com. Against Proposition C-Pound Animals for Med. Rsch., San Diego, 1990; spokesperson Spay-Neuter Action Project, 1991, steering com., 1991, bd. dir., 1992-93; evaluation subcom. County San Diego Dept. Animal Control Adv. Com.; founder, chair Feral Cat Coalition San Diego County, 1992-93, clinic vol., 2001-04, bd. dirs. 2003-04; chair World Record Feral Cat Fix-athon, 2004, chmn, CEO Preserve Our Wildlife Orgn., 2005—, the environment symposium, New Coll., Sarasota, 2006; Calif. State Humane Officer; vol. in pub. info. San Diego/Imperial Counties chpt. ARC, 1993-2002, chpt. centennial com., 1996-97; pub. info. officers San Diego County Emergency Svc. Orgn., 1993-95; vol. photographer Calif. Wolf Ctr., 1999-2002; others; bd. dirs. Escondido Humane Soc. Found., 1994-99. Finalist Internat. Wildlife Photographer of Yr., Brit. Mus. Nat. History, 2003; recipient Belding award, Advt. Club LA, 1986, 1988, Excellence award, Communication Arts Mag., 1987, Gold award, One Show, 1989, 1st Pl. Mobius Advt. award, US Festivals Assn., 1991, Gold Mercury award, Internat. Acad. Comm. Arts & Sci., 1991, Merit award, PR Club San Diego, 1994, Commendation for disting. humanitarian pub. svc., San Diego County Bd. Supr., 1994, Spl. Commendation for love and concern for all animals, San Diego City Coun., 1994, Gold award, Cmty. Arts Group San Diego, 1986, Best in show, Gold award, 1988, Lifetime Achievement award, U. Nebr., Omaha, 2007. Fellow Royal Photog. Soc. Gt. Britain, Profl. Photographers Am. (Master of Photography award 1985, Photog. Craftsman award 1986), Profl. Photographers of Calif.; mem. PRSA (chmn. So. Tier NY chpt. 1971-72), Soc. Animal Welfare Adminstr., Nat. Soc. Fund Raising Exec. (cert., bd. dir. 1988-89, treas. San Diego chpt. 1990-91, mem. nat. faculty 1992-93), Masons, Sierra Club (Ansel Adams award 2005), The Wilderness Soc., Doris Day Animal League, Defenders of Wildlife, Am. Indian Edn. Fedn., Native Am. Rights Fund, Union Concerned Scientists, Natural Resources Def. Coun., Environ. Def. Action Fund, Ctr. for Biol. Diversity. Republican. Presbyterian. Home: 4238 65th Terr E Sarasota FL 34243 Business E-Mail: allan@ebroadstar.com.

BOERSMA, P. DEE, conservation biologist, educator; b. Mt. Pleasant, Mich., Nov. 1, 1946; d. Henry W. and Vivian (Anspach) B. BS, Ctrl. Mich. U., 1969; PhD, Ohio State U., 1974; DSc (hon.), Ctrl. Mich. U., 2003. From asst. prof. to prof. zoology Inst. Environ. Studies U. Wash., Seattle, 1988—, assoc. dir. Inst. Environ. Studies, 1987—93, acting dir. Inst. Environ. Studies, 1990—91, adj. prof. women's studies, 1993—2007, prof. biology, 2003—, Wadsworth endowed chair in conservation sci., 2006—, acting chair biology, 2005—06; mem. sci. adv. com. for outer continental shelf Environ. Studies Program, Dept. Interior, 1980—83; prin. investigator Magellanic Penguin Project Wildlife Cons. Soc., 1982—. Evans vis. fellow U. Otago, New Zealand, 1995, Pew fellow in marine conservation, 1997-2000; naturalist Lindblad Expdns., 2001-04. Assoc. editor Ecological Applications, 1998-2001; exec. editor Conservation Mag., 2000—; contbr. articles to profl. jours. Mem. adv. U.S. del. to UN Status Women Commn., N.Y.C., 1973, UN World Status Women Commn., N.Y.C., 1973, UN World Population Conf., Romania, 1974; mem. Gov. Lowry's Task Force on Wildlife, 1993; sci. adv. EcoBios, 1985-95; bd. dirs. Zero Population Growth, 1975-82, Washington Nature Conservancy, 1995-98; adv. bd. Walt Disney World Animal Kingdom, 1993—, Island press, 1999—, Compass, 2000-04; bd. dirs. Peregrine Fund, Bullitt Found., 1996-00, Islandwood, 2000-04; mem. scholar diplomatic program Dept. State, 1977. Recipient Outstanding Alumni award Ctrl. Mich. U., 1978, Matrix award Women in Comm., 1983; named to Kellogg Nat. Leadership Program, 1982-85; recipient Top 100 Outsiders of Yr. award Outside Mag., 1987, Outstanding Centennial Alumni award Ctrl. Mich. U., 1993; sci. fellow The Wildlife Conservation Soc., 1982—, Aldo Leopold Leadership fellow, 2000-01. Fellow AAAS, Am Ornithol. Union (regional rep. Pacific seabird group 1981-85); mem. AAAS, Ecol. Soc. Am., Wilson Ornithol. Soc., Cooper Ornithol. Soc., Soc. Am. Naturalists, Soc. Conservation Biology (bd. govs. 1991-94, pres-elect 1995-97, pres. 1997-99, Disting. Svc. award 2006), Ecol. Soc. Am. (mem.-at-large 2003-06), Internat. Union Biol. Scis., Gopher Brokers Club (pres. Seattle chpt. 1982-83). Office: U Wash Dept Biology PO Box 351800 Seattle WA 98195-1800 Business E-Mail: boersma@u.washington.edu.

BOESCH, DIANE HARRIET, retired elementary school educator; b. Erie, Pa., July 3, 1942; d. William Jacob and Dorothy Gertrude (Call) B. BS, Edinboro U., Pa., 1964; MA, Kent State U., Ohio, 1968; postgrad., So. Ill. U., Carbondale, 1969, CUNY, 1972, Norwalk State Tech. Coll., 1979, Northeastern U., Boston, 1982, Fla. State U., 1988. Tchr. math. Iroquois Area Sch. Dist., Erie, 1964-67; grad. asst. Kent State U., 1967-68; tchr., writer Comprehensive Sch. Math. Project, Carbondale, Ill., 1968-70; tchr. math. Weston (Conn.) Pub. Schs., 1970-2000, dept. chmn. math., 1989-2000; math edn. cons., 2000—. Dir. Weston Tchr. Ctr., 1983-84; condr. workshops on math. and writing, Conn., 1970—. Contbr. articles to profl. publs. Vol. nat. elections, Erie, 1960, West Haven, Conn., 1972. Recipient Celebration of Excellence award Conn. State Dept. Edn., 1988, Presdl. award NSF, 1990. Fellow Conn. Acad. for Edn. in Math. and Sci.; mem. NEA, Nat. Coun. Tchrs. Math., Conn. Educator Talent Pool, Conn. Edn. Assn., Weston Tchr. Assn., Coun. Presdl. Awardees in Math., Pi Mu Epsilon, Kappa Delta Pi. Republican. Lutheran. Avocations: genealogy, writing, music, reading, atlanta braves baseball. E-mail: dhb703@aol.com.

BOESCH, FRANCIS THEODORE, electrical engineer, educator; b. NYC, Sept. 28, 1936; s. Victor and Margaret (Wright) B. BS, Poly. Inst. N.Y., 1957, MS, 1960, PhD, 1963. Instr., then asst. prof. elec. engring. Poly. Inst. N.Y., 1957-63; mem. mil. research staff Bell Telephone Labs., 1963-68, mem. research staff, 1969-79; prof. elec. engring. and computer sci., dept. head Stevens Inst. Tech., Hoboken, NJ, 1979-88, dean of faculty, 1988-93, prof. elec. engring., 1993—. McKay prof. elec. engring. and computer sci. U. Calif., Berkeley, 1968-69. Author: Large-Scale Networks, 1976; editor-in-chief: Networks, 1970-81; editor: Graph Theory, 1978-81; contbr. articles to profl. jours. Vice pres. Fair Haven (N.J.) Little League, 1974; scoutmaster Fair Haven council Boy Scouts Am., 1973-78, dist. commnr. Monmouth council, 1978-80. Fellow IEEE, N.Y. Acad. Scis.; mem. Assn. Computing Machinery, Am. Math. Soc., Sigma Xi, Eta Kappa Nu. Home: 16-02 Everett Ter Fair Lawn NJ 07410-2410 Office: Stevens Inst Tech Castle Point Sta Hoboken NJ 07030 Business E-Mail: fboesch@stevens.edu. E-mail: fboesch@aol.com.

BOESE, GIL KARYLE, cultural organization administrator; b. Chgo., June 24, 1937; s. Carl H. and Winifred A. Boese; m. Lillian R. Boese; children: Ann Carroll, Peter Austin, Sara Elisabeth. BA, Carthage Coll., Ill., 1959; MS, No. Ill. U., 1965; PhD; NIMH trainee 1970, Johns Hopkins U., 1973. Instr. biology Thornton Community Coll., Harvey, Ill., 1965-67; asst. prof. biology Elmhurst (Ill.) Coll., 1967-69; dep. dir. Chgo. Zool. Park, Brookfield, Ill., 1971-80; dir. Milw. County Zool. Gardens, Milw., 1980-89; pres. Zool. Soc. Milw. County, Milw., 1989—, Found. for Wildlife Conservation, 1993—. Tech. cons. Belize Zoo and Tropical Edn. Ctr.; founder Birds without Borders Aves Sin Frontera internat. dir., mgr. Runaway Creek Nature Preescree, Belize program; dir. Miller Brewery Friends of the Field. Bd. dirs. Dian Fossey Gorilla Found., chmn. 1998-99, internat. coordinating com., pres., 1997—; bd. dirs. Lewa Conservancy Kenya; improvement assn. bd. dirs. Pewaukee Lake, Wis. Fellow Royal Geog. Soc., Am. Assn. Zool. Parks and Aquariums (bd. dirs.); mem. Hemmingway Soc., Adventurers Club. Office: Zool Soc Milw County 10005 W Bluemound Rd Milwaukee WI 53226-4346 E-mail: boese@zoosociety.org.

BOESE, MICHELLE LYNNE, accountant, consultant; b. Lafayette, Ind., July 19, 1955; d. Robert (Fritz) Lawrence Lowery and Dorothy Jean (Lowery) Toops; m. Stephen Craig Boese, Dec. 26, 1977. Diploma, Ind. Bus. Coll., Ind., 1974; AA in Acctg., Cypress Coll., Calif., 1992; BS in Acctg. cum laude, Colo. Tech. Coll., 2006; MBA in Acctg., Colo. Tech. U., 2008. Internat. Scholar Laureate Program Delegation on Bus., Ctrl. and Eastern Europe 2007. Exec. sec. Sargent Industries, El Segundo, Calif., 1976—79; salesperson Dietzgen Corp., Cerrtios, Calif., 1979—81; sr. acct. Olympic Graphics, Irvine, Calif., 1981—83, Tech. Duplicator Svc., Santa Ana, Calif., 1983—85; contr. Huntington Beach Bus. Svc., Huntington Beach, Calif., 1985—95; owner Boese Consulting, Anaheim, Calif., 1985—2001, Puzzleme Records, Huntington Beach, 1995—97; sr. acct. M.E. Howell & Assocs., Evergreen, Colo., 1997—2002; owner MSB & Assocs., Conifer, Colo., 2001—. Contr. Rancho Westwood Village Homeowners Assn., Anaheim, 1992—96; adminstr. Elizabeth Bowen Childrens Home, Evergreen, 2002. Mem.: Assn. For Ind. Music (AFIM) (assoc.), Ind. State Jr. Bowlers Assn. (assoc.; sec. 1974—75), Wash DC Mus. of Women in Art (assoc.), Nat. Scholars Honor Soc. Achievements include 1996-Letter of Acknowledgement on exemplary service and dedication in my work on Agent Orange Class Assistance Program (National Project for Vietnam Vets and families). Avocations: bicycling, dirt biking, canoeing. Home: PO Box 858 Conifer CO 80433 Office: MSB & Assocs P O Box 838 Conifer CO 80433 Home Phone: 303-816-5594; Office Phone: 303-916-0085. Home Fax: 303-816-5595. Personal E-mail: mboese1@msn.com.

BOESEWETTER, WILLIAM LAWRENCE, elementary school educator, artist; s. Willard William Boesewetter and Monita Louise Low. Student, Bentley Coll., Boston, 1967—68; AA, Cabrillo Coll., Aptos, Calif., 1975. Pottery tchr. Trout Gulch Sch., Aptos, 1975—82, Orchard Sch., Aptos, 1982—; potter Orchard Ash Pottery, Aptos, 1977—; salesman Phoenix Ceramics, Santa Cruz, Calif., 1992—. Ceramics at various art fairs, (Best of Show, 85, others). Educator So. Poverty Law, Atlanta, 1992. With US Army, 1968—71, Vietnam. Recipient Best of Show in ceramics, Triton Mus., Santa Clara, 2002. Mem.: ACLU, Nat. Resource Def., Sierra Club. Green Party. Shinto. Avocations: astronomy, photography, painting. Home: 2120 N Pacific Ave Space 38 Santa Cruz CA 95060-2736 Office: 2288 Trout Gulch Rd Aptos CA 95003 E-mail: oapots@yahoo.com.

BOETTCHER, ROBERT WALTER, civil engineer; b. Gooding, Idaho, Apr. 3, 1931; s. Walter Alfred and Katherine Benedicta (Hansen) B.; m. Margeurite Patricia Warner, Oct. 1, 1960; children: Eric, Edwin, Vanessa. BSCE, Wash. State U., Pullman, 1953. Civil engr. U.S. Bur. of Reclamation, Bismarck, N.D., 1955-56; materials engr. Joseph K. Knoerle & Assocs., Chgo., 1956-59; project engr. Knoerle, Bender, Stone & Assocs., Chgo., 1959-62, project mgr., 1962-73, assoc., 1973-76; sr. assoc. Envirodyne Engrs. Inc., Chgo., 1976—; chief civil engr. O'Hare Assocs., Chgo., 1981-92, MESA Joint Venture, 1992-93; sr. assoc. AOR Joint Venture, Chgo., 1993, Consoer Townsend Envirodyne Engrs., Inc., Chgo., 1994—. With U.S. Army, 1953-55. Mem. ASCE, NSPE, Ill. Soc. Profl. Engrs. Home: 1047 Dell Rd Northbrook IL 60062-3911

BOETTGER, NANCY J., state legislator; b. Chgo., May 1, 1943; m. H. David Boettger; 4 children. BS, Iowa State U., 1965; BA, Buena Vista Coll., 1982. Owner farm, 1965—; spl. edn. tchr., 1965-66; tchr. jr. H.S., 1982-86; dir. edn. Myrtoe Meml. Hosp., 1986-99; mem. Iowa Senate from 41st dist. (now 29th dist.), 1994—2004, asst. majority leader, 1996—2004. Mem. Midwest Legis. Coun., 1996-2000. Mem. First Bapt. Ch., People Who Care; former bd. dirs. Harlan Cmty. Libr.; former mem. dean's adv. bd. Iowa State U. Ext. Mem. PEO, Am. Legis. Exchange Coun., Midwest Coun. State Govts. (chair health and human svcs. 1997-99), Coun. State Govts. (mem. drug task force 1998), Iowa Coun. Internat. Understanding Bd., Shelby County Found. for Edn. (former exec. dir.), Farm Bur., Pork Prodrs. Republican. Home: 926 Ironwood Rd Harlan IA 51537-5308 Office: State Capitol Dist 41 3 9th And Grand Des Moines IA 50319-0001 E-mail: nancy_boettger@legis.state.ia.us.

BOETTINGER, WILLIAM J., metallurgist; BS, Johns Hopkins U., 1968, PhD in Metallurgy, 1972. Metallurgist, fellow Nat. Inst. Stds. & Tech., Gaithersburg, Md., 1974—. Contbr. articles to profl. jours. Recipient Champion H. Mathewson award, 1999, Bruce Chalmers award, 2001, Gold and Silver medals, Dept. Commerce. Mem.: NAE. Office: Nat Inst Stds & Tech Materials Sci and Engring Lab Matls A153 Gaithersburg MD 20899-0001 Office Phone: 301-975-6160. E-mail: wboettinger@nist.gov.

BOETTNER, DAISIE DAWSON, military officer, mechanical engineering educator; b. St. Louis, Mo., Jan. 16, 1959; d. Raymond Turner and Isabel Crichlow Wheeler; m. Brian Lee Boettner, Sept. 10, 1982 (div. Dec. 6, 2001); children: Sarah Leigh, Elizabeth Ann. BS, U.S. Mil. Acad., West Point, NY, 1981; MSE in Mech. Engring., U. of Mich., 1991; PhD, The Ohio State U., 2001. Registered profl. engr., Va., 2005. With U.S. Army, 1981—, advanced through grades to col., 1981—2003; comdr. 89th Ordnance Co., Bremerhaven, Germany, 1983—85; logistics officer 24th Inf. Divsn. (Mech.), Ft. Stewart, Ga., 1986—89; instr., asst. prof. U.S. Mil. Acad., West Point, NY, 1991—94, assoc. prof., 2001—; support ops. officer 524th Corps. Support Bn., Schofield Barracks, Hawaii, 1995—96; chief, ammunition plans U.S. Army Pacific, Ft. Shafter, Hawaii, 1996—98. Dir., aero-thermo group U.S. Mil. Acad., West Point, NY, 2001—03, dir., mech. engring. program, 2003—. Author: (jour. articles) ASME Jour. for Energy Resources Tech., (chpt. in edited volume) Artificial Intelligence in Engring. Design Vol. I: Design Representation and Models of Routine Design. Decorated Army Commendation medal U.S. Army, Army Achievement medal, Meritorious Svc. medal. Mem.: Soc. of Women Engrs., Am. Soc. of Mech. Engrs., Delta Kappa Gamma, Phi Kappa Phi. Avocations: running, sewing, cooking. Office: Dept Civil and Mech Engring US Mi Acad West Point NY 10996

BOFF, KENNETH RICHARD, engineering research psychologist; b. NYC, Aug. 17, 1947; s. Victor and Ann (Yunko) B.; m. Judith Marion Schoer, Aug. 2, 1969 (dec. Apr. 1997); children: Cory Asher, Kyra Melissa; m. Jacque Aelanda Coppler, Aug. 20, 1999. BA, CUNY, 1969, MA, 1972; MPhil, Columbia U., 1975, PhD, 1978. Research scientist Human Resources Lab., Wright Patterson AFB, Ohio, 1977-80; sr. scientist Armstrong Aerospace Med. Rsch. Lab. (now Airforce Rsch. Lab.), Wright Patterson AFB, Ohio, 1980—, dir. design tech., 1980-91, dir. human engring. div., 1991—97; chief scientist, human effectiveness directorate Air Force Rsch. Lab., 1997—2007; Edenfield Exec.-in-Residence Sch. Ind. & Sys. Engring. Georgia Inst. Tech., 2002—04; prin. scientist Tennebaum Inst. Ga. Inst. Tech., Atlanta, 2007—. Project custodian Internat. Air. Standard Coordination Com., Washington, 1984; chmn. com. Tri-Service Human Factors Tech. Adv. Group, Washington, 1984—; chair human factors com. NATO Adv. Group Aerospace R&D, Paris, 1992—; chair human sys. tech. panel Dept. Def., 1994-97; U.S. coord. NATO Rsch. and Tech. Orgn. Human Factors, 1997—. Editor: Handbook of Perception and Human Performance, 1986, Human Engineering Data Compendium, 1988, System Design: Behavioral Perspectives on designers, Tools and Organizations, 1987, Organizational Simulation, 2005; contbr. articles to profl. jours. Travel grantee Rank Prize Found., Cambridge, Eng., 1984; named Air Force Scientist of the Quarter, 1989; recipient Patent award for rap-com display tech., 1989, Human Factors Soc. award for best publ., 1989. Fellow Internat. Ergonomics Assn., Human Factors and Ergonomics Soc.; mem. IEEE (sr.), Human Factors Soc., Am. Psychol. Assn. (div. 21 engring. psychology). Avocations: computers, photography.

BOFFEY, PHILIP M., journalist; b. East Orange, NJ; AB in History magna cum laude, Harvard Coll., 1958. Former reporter, sci., health editor and dep. editl. page editor NY Times, NYC, now editl. writer, and editl. bd. member. Author: The Brain Bank of America, 1975. Co-recipient AAAS-Westinghouse Sci. Journalism award, 1986, Pulitzer prize, 1986, 1987; recipient Robert T. Morse Writers award, Am. Psychiatric Assn., 1987. Mem.: Coun. for Advancement of Sci. Writing (dir.), Nat. Assn. Sci. Writers (past pres.). Office: Editorial Page NY Times 229 W 43rd St New York NY 10036 Office Fax: 212-556-3815.

BOGAARD, JONATHAN HARVEY, lawyer; b. Humboldt, Iowa, Mar. 25, 1957; m. Milena B. Vujovich, Nov. 26, 1983; children: Joseph Daniel, Jonathan Thomas. BBA in Acctg., U. Iowa, 1978, MA in Acctg., 1981, JD, 1981. Bar: Ill. 1981, Iowa 1981, U.S. Dist. Ct. (no. dist.) Ill. 1981, U.S. Tax Ct. 1983, U.S. Ct. Appeals (7th cir.) 1999. Assoc. McDermott, Will & Emery, Chgo., 1981—86, ptnr., 1986—91, Vedder Price, Chgo., 1991—. Bd. dirs. North Suburban YMCA, Northbrook, Ill., 1997—2002. Office: Vedder Price 222 N LaSalle Ste 2600 Chicago IL 60601-1003 Office Phone: 312-609-7651. Business E-Mail: jbogaard@vedderprice.com.

BOGAARD, WILLIAM JOSEPH, mayor, lawyer, educator; b. Sioux City, Iowa, Jan. 18, 1938; s. Joseph and Irene Marie (Hensing) B.; m. Claire Marie Whalen, Jan. 28, 1961; children: Michele, Jeannine, Joseph, Matthew. BS, Loyola Marymount U., LA, 1959; JD with honors, U. Mich., 1965. Bar: Calif. 1966, U.S. Dist. Ct. (ctrl. dist.) Calif. 1966. Ptnr. Agnew, Miller & Carlson, LA, 1970-82; exec. v.p., gen. counsel First Interstate Bancorp, LA, 1982-96; vis. prof. securities regulation and banking Mich. Law Sch., Ann Arbor, 1996-97; lectr. securities regulation and corps. law sch. U. So. Calif., LA, 1997—99; mayor Pasadena, Calif., 1999—. Mem. Calif. Commn. on Jud. Nominees Evaluation, 1997-99. Capt. USAF, 1959—62. Mem. Calif. State Bar, Los Angeles County Bar Assn. (Corp. Counsel of Yr. award 1988). Avocations: jogging, french and spanish languages, hiking. Office: 100 N Garfield Ave Pasadena CA 91101-1726 Office Phone: 626-799-2016. Personal E-mail: w_j_b@msn.com. Business E-Mail: bbogaard@cityofpasadena.net.

BOGAN, ELIZABETH CHAPIN, economist, educator; b. Morristown, NJ, Aug. 22, 1944; d. Daryl Muscott and Tirzah (Walker) Chapin; m. Thomas Rockwood Bogan, June 5, 1965; children: Nathaniel Rockwood, Andrew Allerton. AB, Wellesley Coll., 1966; MA, U. N.H., 1967; PhD, Columbia U., 1971. Mem. faculty Farleigh Dickinson U., Madison, NJ, 1971-92, prof. econs., 1982-92, chmn. merit scholarship com., 1981-82; reviewer univ. press Farleigh Dickinson U., Madison, NJ; mem. faculty Princeton (N.J.) U., sr. lectr. in econs., 1992—. Vis. prof. Princeton U., 1991. Author articles and macroecons. text Recipient Outstanding Tchr. award Fairleigh Dickinson U., 1979, 86, 87, Richard Quandt award for tchg. econs. Princeton U., 1997, 2005; NSF fellow, Pres'. fellow, Earhart fellow Columbia U., 1968-71. Mem. AAUP, Am. Econ. Assn., Ea. Econ. Assn., Atlantic Econ. Soc. Clubs: Wellesley, Beacon Hill. Congregationalist. Home: 41 Windermere Ter Short Hills NJ 07078-2254 Office: Princeton U 109 Fisher Hall Princeton NJ 08544

BOGAN, JOHN C., real estate appraiser; b. June 10, 1944; BBA, U. Memphis, 1972. Lic. affiliate broker Tenn. Commd. officer USN, 1964, advanced through grades to comdr., ret., 1995; sales mgr. W.M. Barr & Co., Memphis, 1978—85; pres. Bogan Enterprises, Inc., Memphis, 1978—; real estate appraiser Shelby County Govt., Memphis, 1992—. Author: Training Manual-U.S. Naval Reserve, 1990, Training Manual-Shelby County Government, 2002. Elder Advent Presbyn. Ch., 1984—. Named Nat. Sales Winner, McKesson Corp., 1984. Mem.: Fisherville Civic Club (pres. 2004—). Home: 2332 N Reid Hooker Eads TN 38028-9307 Office Phone: 901-379-7259. Office Fax: 901-379-7197. Business E-Mail: cdrjcbogan@bellsouth.com.

BOGARD, CAROLE CHRISTINE, soprano; b. Cin. d. Harold and Helen Christina (Whittlesey) Geistweit; m. Charles Paine Fisher, Dec. 30, 1966; children: Christine, Pamela. Student, San Francisco State U. Debuts include: Despina in Cosi fan Tutte (Mozart), San Francisco, 1965, Poppea in Coronation of Poppea (Monteverdi), Netherlands Opera, 1971; other appearances include, Boston Opera, N.E.T., orchs. Boston, Madrid, Minn., Phila., Pitts., San Francisco, summer festivals, Mostly Mozart, N.Y., Tanglewood, Carmel, Aston Magna, Gt. Barrington, Mass., appeared in concerts throughout Europe and with Smithsonian Chamber Players, 1976-; recorded numerous albums including 1st rec. of songs of John Duke for his 80th birthday, 1979, recital of Groupe des Six; premiered songs of Dominic Argento in, Holland, 1978, songs of Richard Cumming (in collaboration with Donald Gramm); regular participant rec. and scholarly projects, Smithsonian Instn.; judge regional auditions, Boston; tchr., with emphasis on technique as taught in last Century; recs. have been re-issued on CDs during the 1990s including Baroque Cantatas and Arias, Mozart C minor Mass, Mozart Coronation Mass., 2 CD collection American Songs, 2000; female lead 3 CD Handel opera Tamerlano, 2002. Mem. Sigma Alpha Iota Home: 161 Belknap Rd Framingham MA 01701-3886 *In my career, I've stuck to old-fashioned principles - trying to use my talent according to the standards which place singing technique on a level with the most taxing instruments. I sing for sincere acclaim and demand for my talent and my music, avoiding repertoire which would abuse my voice. I have refrained from pushing myself through "arranged" magazine articles about my hobbies and insipid appearances on TV talk shows. I have done my best rather than my most - by choice.*

BOGARD, DONALD DALE, planetary geochemist; b. Washington County, Ark., Feb. 6, 1940; s. James A. and Genevieve Bogard. BS, U. Ark., 1962, MS, 1964, PhD, 1966. Rsch. fellow Calif. Inst. Tech., Pasadena, 1966-68; sr. staff scientist NASA, Johnson Space Ctr., Houston, 1968—. Antarctic meteorite curator NASA, 1978-84; discipline scientist planetary program, 1984-92. Contbr. over 130 sci. articles to rsch. jours. Fellow Meteoritical Soc. (sec. 1980-86); mem. Am. Geophys. Union. Office: NASA Johnson Space Ctr Mail Code KR Houston TX 77058 Business E-Mail: donald.d.bogard@nasa.gov.

BOGARD, LAWRENCE JOSEPH, lawyer; b. Champaign, Ill., July 12, 1952; s. Morris Ray and Norma Jean (Shingleton) Bogard; m. Rebecca Lynn Jackson, May 6, 1978 (div. 2003); children: Caitlyn Elizabeth, Peter Jackson; m. Alice A. Medalia, Feb. 24, 2007. AB, Vassar Coll., Poughkeepsie, NY, 1974; JD, Georgetown U., 1977. Bar: D.C. 1977. Atty. U.S. Customs Svc., Washington, 1977-80; assoc. Cladouhos & Brashares, Washington, 1980-84; atty. U.S. Dept. Commerce, Washington, 1984; ptnr. Rose, Schmidt, Hasley & Disalle, Washington, 1984-88, McKenna & Cuneo, Washington, 1988-98, Neville Peterson LLP, Washington, 1998—. Faculty Practicing Law Inst., 1984, 92; mem. U.S.-Can. Free Trade Agreement Ch. 19 Dispute Resolution Roster, 1991-94, panelist, 1992, panel chair 1993; mem. NAFTA Dispute Resolution Roster, 1994—, panel chair, 2001. Author: (with others) Commerce Speaks on Antidumping, 1984, Treatment of Non-Market Economies Under U.S. Antidumping and Countervailing Duty Law: A Petitioner's Perspective, 1992, (with others) Transnational Contracts, 2000—; supervisory editor Customs Law and Administration, 1998—. Mem. ABA, D.C. Bar Assn., Ct. Internat. Trade Bar Assn. Office: Neville Peterson LLP 1400 16th St NW Ste 350 Washington DC 20036 Office Phone: 202-861-2959. Business E-Mail: lbogard@npwdc.com.

BOGARDUS, CARL ROBERT, JR., radiologist, educator; b. Hyden, Ky., June 26, 1933; s. Carl Robert and Jeannette Wanda (Eversole) B.; m. Norma Gail Shields, June 24, 1956; children: Carl Robert III, Cynthia Gail. BA, Hanover Coll., 1955; MD, U. Louisville, 1959. Diplomate: Am. Bd. Radiology, Am. Bd. Nuc. Medicine. Intern Penrose Cancer Hosp., Colorado Springs, Colo., 1959-60, resident, 1960-63; prof. U. Okla. Med. Ctr., 1963—, mem. staff, 1963—. Cons. Okla. hosps.; pres. Bogardus Med. Sys. Inc. Author: Practical Applied Physics of Radiology and Nuclear Medicine, 1969; contbg. author: Benign and Malignant Tumors of the Bladder, 1971, Radiation Biology for the Physician, 1973; contbr. articles to profl. jours. Fellow Am. Coll. Radiology (bd. chancellors, sec.-treas. 1987-91, pres. 1991-92); mem. Okla. Soc. Nuc. Medicine (charter pres. 1966), Am. Soc. Therapeutic Radiology (nat. sec. 1968-70, treas. 1987-88, pres. 1989-90), S.W. Regions Soc. Nuc. Medicine, Okla. Radiol. Soc. (treas. 1970, pres. 1974-75, counselor to Am. Coll. Radiology 1976-85), Okla. County Radiol. Soc. (pres. 1974). Home: 3224 Lamp Post Ln Oklahoma City OK 73120-5621 Office: U Okla Med Ctr 825 NE 101st Oklahoma City OK 73104 Office Phone: 405-271-3577. Business E-Mail: carl-bogardus@ouhsc.edu.

BOGART, MICHELE HELENE, art history educator; b. NYC, Oct. 5, 1952; d. Leo and Agnes Miriam Bogart; m. Philip Joseph Pauly, July 23, 1981; 1 child, Nicholas Bogart Pauly. BA, Smith Coll., Northampton, Mass., 1974; MA, U. Chgo., 1975, PhD, 1979. Asst. prof. U. Ga., Athens, 1979—81, Stony Brook U., 1981—89, assoc. prof., 1989—95, prof., 1995—. Bd. dir. cultural studies U. NC Press, 1998—; mem. adv. conservation group Art Commn. City NY, 1998—, v.p., 1999—2003; bd. dirs. Fine Arts Fedn. NY, NYC, 2005—. Author: (book) Public Sculpture and the Civic Ideal, 1989 (Eldridge prize, 1991), Artists, Advertising and the Borders of Art, 1995, The Politics of Urban Beauty, 2006. Mem. advisory conservation group Art Commn. City NY, 1998—; del. Japanese Assn. Am. Studies, 2000; mem. Art Commn. City NY, NYC, 1998—; bd.dirs. Fine Arts Fedn., NYC, 2005—, v.p., 2007—. Recipient Charles C. Eldridge prize, Smithsonian Inst. Am. Art Mus., 1991; Fellowship, NEH, 1994—95, John Simon Guggenheim Meml. Found., 2001—02. Mem.: Fine Arts Fedn. (bd. dirs. 2005—), Assocs. Art Commn. (treas., exec. com. 1998—). Avocations: running, piano. Office: Stony Brook U Dept Art Staller Ctr Stony Brook NY 11794

BOGDAN, CAROLYN LOUETTA, financial specialist, retired small business owner; b. Wilkes-Barre, Pa., Apr. 15, 1941; d. Walter Cecil and Ethna Louetta (Kendig) Carpenter; m. James Thomas Bogdan, May 5, 1961; 1 child, Thomas James. Head bookkeeper Forty Ft. (Pa.) State Bank, 1959-63, U.S. Nat. Bank, Long Beach, Calif., 1963-65; office mgr. United Parts Exch., Long Beach, 1976-81; contract adminstr. Johnson Controls, Inc., Rancho Dominguez, Calif., 1981-88, credit coord., 1989-98; co-owner, acct. Bogdan Elec. R & D, Lakewood, Calif., 1981—98; ret., 1998. Mem. Radio Amateur Civil Emergency Svc., L.A. County Sheriff Dept., 1974—, records keeper, 1988—93, radio comm. officer, 1994—2002. Mem. Tournament of Roses Radio Amateurs (pin chmn. 1975-2005), Calif. State Sheriffs Assn. (assoc.), Calif. State Office Emergency Svcs. Republican. Avocations: crocheting, gardening, electronics, amateur radio. Home: 3713 Capetown St Lakewood CA 90712-1437

BOGDAN, MICHAEL ANDREW, plastic surgeon; b. Washington, Apr. 12, 1971; s. Victor Michael and Ulla Eva-Maria Bogdan; m. Isidra Veve, Mar. 13, 1999; children: Alexander Michael, Andrew Edwin. BS in Zoology, BS in Chemistry, U. of Md., College Park, 1993; MD, Stanford U., Calif., 1998. Lic. Med. Bd. Calif., Bd. Med. Examiners, Colo., Edn. Dept., NY, Tex. Med. Bd., 2007, diplomate Am. Bd. Plastic Surgery, 2006. Intern in gen. surgery U. Calif.-San Francisco, Stanford Health Care, 1998—99; resident in plastic surgery Stanford U. Med. Ctr., 1999—2003, chief resident in plastic surgery, 2003—04; fellow in aesthetic surgey Manhattan Eye, Ear and Throat Hosp., NYC, 2004—05; cosmetic surgeon Napa Valley Plastic Surgery, Inc., Napa, Calif., 2005—07, Southlake Plastic Surgery, Tex., 2007—. Presenter in field. Author: (book chpt.) Advances in Plastic and Reconstructive Surgery; contbr. articles to profl. jours. and presentations (Tiffany award Am. Soc. of Aesthetic Plastic Surgery, 2004). Mem.: AMA, Am. Soc. Plastic Surgeons, ZedPlast, Napa County Med. Soc., Calif. Med. Assn., Alpha Lambda Delta, Phi Kappa Phi. Office: Southlake Plastic Surgery 900 E Southlake Blvd Ste 100 Southlake TX 76092 Office Phone: 817-442-8900. Office Fax: 817-488-2490. Business E-Mail: drbogdan@drmichaelbogdan.com.

BOGDANICH, WALT, journalist; b. Chgo., Oct. 10, 1950; s. Walter and Helen (Chabraja) B.; m. Stephanie Saul; 1 child, Nicholas Walter. BS in

Polit. Sci., U. Wis., 1975; MA in Journalism, Ohio State U., 1976. Reporter, editor Compass (daily newspaper), Hammond, Ind., 1974-75; reporter Dayton (Ohio) Daily News, 1977, Cleve. Press, 1977-79, Plain Dealer, Cleve., 1980-84; investigative reporter Wall St. Jour., NYC, 1984-88, Washington, 1989-93; TV news prodr. Day One, ABC-TV, NYC, 1993; investigative prodr., 60 Minutes CBS, NYC; investigative editor, bus. and fin. desk NY Times, NYC, 2001—, asst. editor, newly expanded investigative desk. Recipient George Polk award L.I. Univ., 1980, Polk award for health care reporting, 2002, Polk award for natl reporting, 2005, Overseas Press Club award, 1983, Pulitzer prize for newspaper series, 1988, for nat. reporting, 2005; Gerald Loeb award, UCLA Anderson Sch. Mgmt., 2005. Mem. Investigative Reporters and Editors (bd. dirs. 1988-89). Office: NY Times 229 W 43rd New York NY 10036

BOGDANOS, MATTHEW F., lawyer, reserve military officer, writer, boxer; b. NYC, Nov. 1956; m. Claudia T. Bogdanos; 4 children. BA in Classics, Bucknell Univ., 1980; JD, Columbia Univ., 1983, MA in Classical Studies, 1984; MS in Strategic Studies, Army War Coll., 2004. Asst. dist. atty., NYC, 1988—; sr. trial counsel NY Dist. Atty. Office, NYC, 1996. Amateur middle weight boxer. Co-author (with William Patrick): Thieves of Baghdad, 2005. Commd. officer USMC, 1980, with JAGC USMC, 1984—88, reserves USMC, 1988—2001, reserves USMC, 2006—, active duty USMC, 2001—05, col. USMC, 2003. Decorated Bronze Star USMC; recipient Nat. Humanities medal, Iraq Nat. Mus., 2005. Office: NY Dist Atty Office One Hogan Pl New York NY 10013-4311 Office Phone: 212-335-9323.

BOGDANOVICH, PETER, film director, writer, producer, actor; b. Kingston, NY, July 30, 1939; s. Borislav and Herma (Robinson) B.; m. Polly Platt, 1962 (div. 1970); children: Antonia, Alexandra; m. L.B. Straten, Dec. 30, 1988 (div. 2001). Owner The Holly Moon Co., Inc., LA, 1992—. Dir., producer off-Broadway plays: The Big Knife, 1959, Camino Real, Ten Little Indians, Rocket to the Moon, 1961, Once in a Lifetime, 1964; (films) The Wild Angels (2d unit dir., co-writer, actor), 1966; Targets (dir., co-writer, producer, actor), 1968, The Last Picture Show (dir., co-writer, N.Y. Film Critics award, Brit. Acad. award 1971), 1971, Directed by John Ford (dir., writer, interviewer), 1971, What's Up, Doc? (dir., co-writer, producer, Writer's Guild Am. award 1972), 1972, Paper Moon (dir., producer, Silver Shell, Mar del Plata, Spain), 1973, Daisy Miller (dir., producer, Best Dir. Brussels Festival 1974), 1974, At Long Last Love (dir., writer, producer), 1975, Nickelodeon (dir., co-writer), 1976, Saint Jack (dir., co-writer, actor, Pasinetti award, Critics prize Venice Festival 1979), 1979, They All Laughed (dir., writer), 1981, Mask (dir.), 1985, Illegally Yours (dir., producer), 1988, Texasville (dir., producer, writer), 1990, Noises Off (dir., exec. producer), 1992, The Thing Called Love (dir.), 1993; dir.(TV films) Blessed Assurance, 1997, Rescuers: Stories of Courage: Two Women, 1997, Naked City: A Killer Christmas, 1998, A Saintly Switch, 1999, The Mystery of Natalie Wood, 2004, Hustle, 2004; dir. (TV series episode) Fallen Angels, 1995, Painted Word, 1995; Actor Am. Shakespeare Festival, Stratford, Conn., 1956, N.Y. Shakespeare Festival, 1958; (films) Mr. Jealousy, 1997, Highball, 1997, Fifty-Four, 1998, Coming Soon, 1999, The Shoe Store, 1999, Claire Makes It Big, 1999, Rated X, 2000, The Independent, 2000; (TV series) Northern Exposure, 1993, Cybill, 1995, The Sopranos, 1999-; (TV miniseries) Bella Mafia, 1997, Out of Order, 2003; film feature-writer for Esquire, N.Y. Times, Village Voice, Cahiers du Cinema, L.A. Times, N.Y. Mag., Vogue, Variety; author The Cinema of Orson Welles, 1961, The Cinema of Howard Hawks, 1962, The Cinema of Alfred Hitchcock, 1963, John Ford, 1968, Fritz Lang in America, 1969, Allen Dwan: The Last Pioneer, 1971, Pieces of Time: Peter Bogdanovich on the Movies, 1973, The Killing of the Unicorn: Dorothy Stratten: 1960-80, 1984; (with Orson Welles) This Is Orson Welles, 1992; editor: A Year and a Day Engagement Calendar, 1991—; co-dir., writer, interviewer: The Great Professional: Howard Hawks, 1967; weekly network commentator CBS This Morning, 1987-89. Mem. Dirs. Guild of Am., Writers Guild of Am., Acad. Motion Picture Arts and Scis. Address: care Martin Baum and Rick Nicita CAA 9830 Wilshire Blvd Beverly Hills CA 90212-1804

BOGDEN, DANIEL G., former prosecutor; b. Huron, Ohio, 1956; BBA, Ashland U., 1978; JD, U. Toledo. Dep. dist. atty. Washoe County, 1987—90; asst. US atty. dist. Nev. US Dept. Justice, Las Vegas, 1990—2001, US atty., 2001—07. Recipient Outstanding Alumnus award, Ashland U. Alumni Assn., 2005.*

BOGDONOFF, MORTON DAVID, internist, educator; b. NYC, Dec. 8, 1925; s. M. Myron and Minnie (Alpher) B.; m. Jano Segal, July 1, 1951 (div. 1971); children— Reid, Ladd, Jesse, Drue; m. Mary Patton Welt, May 9, 1975. MD, Cornell U., 1948. Diplomate: Nat. Bd. Med. Examiners, Am. Bd. Internal Medicine. Intern, jr. asst. resident, sr. asst. resident dept. medicine N.Y. Hosp., NYC, 1948-50; sr. asst. surgeon USPHS, Nat. Heart Inst., Johns Hopkins U., Balt., 1950-52; sr. asst. resident dept. medicine Duke Hosp., 1952-53, Eli Lilly Research fellow div. endocrinology and metabolism, 1953-54, chief resident dept. medicine, 1954-55; attending physician, chief metabolic div. Durham VA Hosp., 1955-56, cons., 1959-62; asso. prof. clin. medicine Med. Sch. U. Miami, 1956-57; assoc. dept. medicine Duke U., 1955-56, asst. prof. medicine, 1957-59, asso. prof., 1959-62, prof. med., 1962-69, asst. dean grad. med. edn., 1967-69; prof., chmn. dept. internal medicine U. Ill., Chgo., 1970-75; prof. medicine to prof. emeritus Med. Coll. Cornell U., 1975-95, 95—. Cons. Ft. Bragg Hosp., 1959-62, VA Hosps., Fayetteville, Durham, West-Side, Chgo.; mem. study sect. health svcs. rsch. NIH, 1966-70, Commonwealth Fund, 1985-94, Cath. Med. Ctr., 1990-94, Nat. Med. Fellowships, 1987-2002. Editor: Clin. Rsch., 1959—64; chief editor Archives of Internal Medicine, 1967—77, New Developments in Medicine, 1986—90; sci. editor: Drug Therapy, 1978—94; contbr. articles to profl. jours. Fellow Center Advanced Study Behavioral Scis., Stanford, 1977-78 Fellow A.C.P.; mem. Am. Fedn. Clin. Research (past pres.), Am., So., Central socs. clin. investigation, Assn. Am. Physicians, AAAS (chmn. Sect. N 1981-82), Endocrine Soc., Psychosomatic Soc. (past nat. councillor), Soc. Exptl. Biology and Medicine, AMA, Harvey Soc., Alpha Omega Alpha. Office: NY Hosp/Cornell Med Ctr 525 E 68th St New York NY 10021-4885

BOGEN, ANDREW E., lawyer; b. LA, Aug. 23, 1941; s. David and Edith B.; m. Deborah Bogen, Oct. 10, 1970; children: Elizabeth, Michael. BA, Pomona Coll., Claremont, Calif., 1963; LLB, Harvard U, 1966. Bar: Calif. 1966. Assoc. Gibson, Dunn & Crutcher, LA, 1966-73, ptnr. corp. transactions and securities, 1973—. Mem. exec. com. Gibson Dunn & Crutcher, 1991—. Trustee Exceptional Children's Found., LA, 1976-89, Weingart Found., 1999—; bd. dirs. St. Anne's 1990— (chmn.). Office: Gibson Dunn & Crutcher 333 S Grand Ave Ste 4400 Los Angeles CA 90071-3197 Office Phone: 213-229-7000. Office Fax: 213-229-7520. Business E-Mail: abogen@gibsondunn.com.

BOGENSCHUTZ, J. DAVID, lawyer; b. Covington, Ky., May 15, 1944; s. John Francis and Virginia Margaret (Dugan) B.; m. Mary H. McCleary, Oct. 24, 1981; children: Kathleen, Emily. BA, Miami U., Oxford, Ohio, 1966; JD, U. Cin., 1969. Bar: Ohio 1969, U.S. Dist. Ct. (so. dist.) Ohio 1970, U.S. Ct. Appeals (6th cir.) 1971, Fla. 1971, U.S. Dist. Ct. (so. dist.) Fla. 1972, U.S. Ct. Appeals (5th cir.) 1980, U.S. Dist. Ct. (mid. dist.) Fla. 1981, U.S. Ct. Appeals (4th and 11th cirs.) 1981, U.S. Dist. Ct. (ea. dist.) Wis. 1989, U.S. Ct. Appeals (3d cir.) 1999. Instr. Criminal Justice Inst. Nova U., 1977; instr. Broward County Criminal Justice Inst., 1972; asst. solicitor County of Broward, 1971, chief asst. state's atty., 1974-77; ptnr. Bogenschutz & Dutko, P.A., Ft. Lauderdale, Fla. Mem. Gov.'s Com. on Criminal Justice Standards and Goals, 1975-76; mem. bench bar liaison com. U.S. Dist. Ct. (so. dist.) Fla., 1985—, Stephen Booher Inn of Ct. Recipient Harry Gulkin award, 2006. Mem. ATLA, NACDL, Broward County Bar Assn. (criminal law sect. chmn. 1980-81, exec. com. 1981-86, sec., treas. 1985-86), Ohio Bar Assn., Fla. Bar Assn. (criminal law sect., grievance com. 17th jud. cir. 1982-84), Fed. Bar Assn., Greene County Bar Assn., Fla. Pros. Atty.'s Assn., Nat. Dist. Atty.'s Assn., Nat. Assn. Criminal Def. Attys. Democrat. Roman Catholic. Office: Bogenschutz Dutko & Kroll PA 600 S Andrews Ave Ste 500 Fort Lauderdale FL 33301-2851

BOGER, DALE L., chemistry professor; b. Hutchinson, Kans., Aug. 22, 1953; s. Lester W. and Elizabeth (Korkish) B. BS in Chemistry, U. Kans., 1975; PhD in Chemistry, Harvard U., 1980; PhD (hon.), U. Ferrara, 2000. Asst. prof. medicinal chemistry U. Kans., Lawrence, 1979-83, assoc. prof. medicinal chemistry, 1983-85; assoc. prof. chemistry Purdue U., West Lafayette, Ind., 1985-87, prof. chemistry, 1987-91; Richard and Alice Cramer chair chemistry, prof. Scripps Rsch. Inst., La Jolla, Calif., 1991—. Mem. Skaggs Inst. for Chem. Biology, 1996—; Smissman Lectr. U. Kans., 2000; Ross Lectr. Dartmouth Coll., 2002; Alder Lectr. U. Köln, 2005. Founding editor Bioorganic and Medicinal Chemistry Letters, 1990—, exec. editl. bd. mem. Tetrahedron Publications, 1990—. Recipient Career Devel. award NIH, 1983-88, American Cyanamide Academic award, 1989, A. R. Day award, 2000, Paul Janssen award for creativity in organic synthesis, 2002, Adrien Albert medal, Royal Soc. Chemistry, 2003; NSF fellow, 1975-78, Alfred P. Sloan fellow, 1985-89, Japan Promotion of Sci. Fellow, 1993; Searle scholar, 1981-84. Fellow AAAS, Am. Assn. Adv. Sci., Am. Acad. Arts and Scis.; mem. Am. Chem. Soc. (Arthur C. Cope scholar 1989, Aldrich award for creativity in organic synthesis 1999, Ernest Guenther award in chemistry of natural products, 2007, councilor, 1996-99, Medicinal Chemistry Divsn., awards com. mem. 1984-86, Long Range Planning Com., 1981-83), Internat. Soc. Heterocyclic Chemistry (Katritzky award in Heterocyclic Chemistry, 1997). Home: 2819 Via Posada La Jolla CA 92037-2205 Office: Dept Chemistry and Skaggs Inst for Chem Biology 10550 N Torrey Pines Rd BBC 483 La Jolla CA 92037-1000 Office Phone: 858-784-7522. Office Fax: 858-784-7550. Business E-Mail: boger@scripps.edu.

BOGER, DAN CALVIN, science professor, consultant; b. Salisbury, NC, July 9, 1946; s. Brady Cashwell and Gertrude Virginia (Hamilton) Boger; m. Gail Lorraine Zivna, June 23, 1973; children: Gretchen Zivna, Gregory Zivna. BS in Mgmt. Sci., U. Rochester, NY, 1968; MS in Mgmt. Sci., Naval Postgrad. Sch., Monterey, Calif., 1969; MA in Stats., U. Calif., Berkeley, 1977, PhD in Econs., 1979. Cert. cost analyst, profl. estimator. Rsch. asst. U. Calif., Berkeley, 1975-79; asst. prof. econs. Naval Postgrad. Sch., Monterey, Calif., 1979-85, assoc. prof., 1985-92, prof., 1992—, chmn. dept. command, control and comm., 1995—2001, chmn. dept. computer sci., 1997—2001, chmn. dept. info. warfare, 1997—2001, dean divsn. computer and info. scis. and ops., 1997—2001, founding chmn. dept. info. scis., 2002—, dean rsch., 2006—. Cons. econs. and stats. legal matters CSX Corp., others, 1977—; bd. dirs. Evan-Moor Corp. Assoc. editor: Logistics and Transp. Rev., 1981—85, Jour. Cost Analysis, 1989—92; mem. editl. rev. bd. Jour. Transp. Rsch. Forum, 1987—91; contbr. articles to profl. jours. Lt. USN, 1968—75. Flood fellow, Dept. Econs. U. Calif., Berkeley, 1975—76, Dissertation Rsch. grantee, A.P. Sloan Found., 1978—79. Mem.: IEEE, Inst. Ops. Rsch. and Mgmt. Sci. (sec.-treas. mil. aplications soc. 1987—91), Econometric Soc., Am. Statis. Assn., Am. Econ. Assn., Internat. Coun. Sys. Engring., Sigma Xi. Home: 27 Cramden Dr Monterey CA 93940-4145 Office: Naval Postgrad Sch Code IS Monterey CA 93943

BOGER, JOHN CHARLES, law educator, dean; b. Concord, NC, Sept. 8, 1946; s. Charles Edgar Jr. and Mary (Snead) B.; m. Jennifer Lynn Brackenbury, May 13, 1947; children: Gretchen Elisabeth, Peter Grayson. BA, Duke U., 1968; MDiv, Yale U., 1971; JD, U. N.C., 1974. Bar: N.Y. 1975, U.S. Ct. Appeal, U.S. Supreme Ct. Assoc. atty. Paul, Weiss, Rifkind, Wharton & Garrison, NYC, 1974-75, 76-78; law clk. to Justice Samuel Silverman N.Y. Appellate Divsn., NYC, 1975-76; asst. counsel NAACP Legal Def. and Edn. Fund, Inc., NYC, 1978-90; assoc. prof. law U. N.C. Sch. Law, Chapel Hill, 1990-94, prof. law, 1994—, assoc. dean for acad. affairs, 1995—2006, dean, 2006—. Chair Poverty and Race Rsch. Action Coun., Washington, 1989—; dep. dir. Ctr. for Civil Rights at U. N.C., 2002—. Co-editor: Race, Poverty and American Cities, 1996; contbr. articles to profl. jours. Mem.: Order of the Coif, Phi Beta Kappa. Home: 104 Emerywood Pl Chapel Hill NC 27516-8718 Office: U NC Sch Law Cb # 3380 Chapel Hill NC 27599-0001 also: UNC School of Law Van Hecke-Wettach Hall 100 Ridge Road CB #3380 Chapel Hill NC 27599-3380 Business E-Mail: jcboger@email.unc.edu.

BOGER, WILLIAM PIERCE, III, ophthalmologist; b. Phila., Oct. 16, 1945; s. William Pierce Jr. and Mae Elizabeth (Shelton) B.; m. Barbara Crawford, Aug. 10, 1968; children: Matthew, Andrew, John. AB in Biophysics magna cum laude honors, Amherst Coll., 1967; MD, Harvard U., 1971. Diplomate Am. Bd. Ophthalmology. Intern in medicine and pediat. U. Va. Hosp., Charlottesville, 1971-72; resident in ophthalmology Mass. Eye and Ear Infirmary, Boston, 1972-75; clin. fellow in ophthalmology Harvard U., Boston, 1975—76; fellow in pediatric ophthalmology and strabismus Children's Hosp. Med. Ctr., Boston, 1976, assoc. in ophthalmology, mem. full-time staff, 1976-80; pvt. practice specializing in pediatric ophthalmology, Concord, Mass., 1980—. Mem. staff Boston Children's Hosp. Med. Ctr., Boston, Emerson Hosp., Concord, Mass., Winchester Hosp., Mass., Mt. Auburn Hosp., Cambridge, Mass.; instr. Harvard U., 1976—; lectr. in field. Contbr. articles to med. jours., chpts. to book. Capt. M.C., USAR, 1971-81. Pathology grantee Mass. Gen. Hosp., Boston, 1969. Mem. AAAS, Am. Acad. Ophthalmology, Mass. Soc. Eye Physicians and Surgeons, New Eng. Ophthalmol. Soc., Am. Assn. for Pediatric Ophthalmology and Strabismus, Mass. Med. Soc., Rsch. To Prevent Blindness, Phi Beta Kappa, Sigma Xi. Home: 357 Nashawtuc Rd Concord MA 01742-1616 Office: Lexington Eye Assocs John Cuming Bldg 3d Fl Concord MA 01742 Office Phone: 978-369-0713.

BOGERT, JEREMIAH, journalist; Dep. assignment editor, photog. editor The New York Times. Office: NY Times 229 W 43rd St New York NY 10036 Office Phone: 212-556-7371. Office Fax: 212-556-5848.

BOGG, RICHARD ALLAN, sociologist, educator; b. Grosse Pointe, Mich., May 31, 1934; s. Sydney Elmer and Dorothy Marie B. BBA, U. Mich., 1956, PhD, 1971; postgrad., U. Exeter, England, 1957—58; MHA, Washington U., St. Louis, 1960. Asst. adminstr. Port Huron (Mich.) Hosp., 1960-62; rsch. assoc. U. Mich. Sch. Pub. Health, 1965-69; asst. prof. dept. cmty. medicine Faculty Medicine U. Alta., Edmonton, Can., 1969-72; asst. prof. dept. sociology Ball State U., Muncie, Ind., 1972-77, assoc. prof., 1977—; assoc. editor Deviant Behavior, 1992—. Contbr. papers to profl. confs., encys. and jours. USPHS trainee, 1962-65; vol. Planned Parenthood of Delaware County. Mich. Ho. of Reps. spl. rsch. grantee, 1968. Mem. Am. Sociol. Assn., ACLU. Office: Dept Sociology Ball State U Muncie IN 47306-0530 Office Phone: 765-285-7889. Business E-Mail: rabogg@bsu.edu.

BOGGIA, EUGENE STEPHEN, lawyer; b. Glen Cove, NY, Nov. 12, 1946; s. Eugene and Elena Ebbie (Albertelli) B.; m. Suzanne McDonough, Sept. 18, 1982; children: Thomas, Catherine. AB, Georgetown U., 1968; JD, NYU, 1973. Asst. dist. atty. Office of the Dist. Atty., Phila., 1973-88; ptnr. Taylor and Taylor, Phila., 1988-92; claims adminstr., asst. gen. counsel Sch. Dist. of Phila., 1992—. Settlement master, judge pro tem Ct. of Common Pleas, Phila., 1992—. With USN, 1969-71; Vietnam. Mem. Serra Internat. (dist. 28 gov. 1985-86, Phila. chpt. pres. 1980-81, 98-2000, Serran of the Yr. 1989). Democrat. Roman Catholic. Avocations: history, playing piano, golf. Office: Sch Dist of Phila 440 N Broad St 3d Fl Philadelphia PA 19130-4015 Office Phone: 215-400-5182. Business E-Mail: eboggia@phila.k12.pa.us.

BOGGS, BENNETT GIBSON, academic administrator; s. Robert Lee and Barbara Beals Boggs; m. Brenda Sue Spicker, June 11, 1994; children: Brynn Elizabeth, Bethany Grace. BA, Wake Forest U., 1987; M in Edn., Coll. of William & Mary, 1990; PhD, U. Va., 1998. Resident dir. of u. living, learning ctr. U. Ill., Urbana-Champaign, 1990—92; u. area dir. U. NC, Chapel Hill, 1992—94; asst. to the v.p. and provost U. Va., Charlottesville, 1994—96, spl. asst. to the dean, 1996—2000; sr. assoc. academic affairs Ky. Coun. on Postsecondary Edn., Frankfort, 2000—05; exec. asst. to the pres. Muskingum Coll., New Concord, Ohio, 2005—06, Berea Coll., Ky., 2006—. Recipient Ky. Col., Gov. of Ky., 2003; Higher Edn. Inst. scholar, U. Edinburgh, 1998. Mem.: Assn. for the Study of Higher Edn., Phi Delta Kappa, Kappa Delta Pi. Baptist. Home: 169 Lakeside Dr New Concord OH 43762 Office Phone: 839-985-3542. E-mail: boggsb@berea.edu.

BOGGS, BETH CLEMENS, lawyer; b. Dubuque, Iowa, July 28, 1967; d. Theodore Alan and Mary Ann (Fleckenstein) Clemens; m. T. Darin Boggs, Mar. 9, 1991. BA, Govs. State U., 1987; JD, So. Ill. U., 1991. Bar: Ill. 1991, Mo. 1992, US Dist. Ct. (so. dist.) Ill. 1991, US Dist. Ct. (ea. dist.) Mo. 1992, US Dist. Ct. (we. dist.) Mo. 2002, US Dist. Ct. (ctrl. dist.) Ill. 1997. Clk. R. Courtney Hughes & Assocs., Carbondale, Ill., 1990-91; lawyer Sandberg Phoenix & von Gontard, St. Louis, 1991-93; assoc. LaTourette, Schlueter & Byrne, St. Louis, 1993-95; mng. ptnr. Landau, Omahana & Kopka, P.C., St. Louis, 1995-99; mng. and founding ptnr. Boggs, Backer & Bates, LLC, St. Louis, 1999—2002, Boggs, Boggs & Bates, LLC, St. Louis, 2002—. Adj. prof. Webster U., 1995-; former vice-chair A.B.A. Law and Medicine Sect. and Corp. Counsel Com. Editor student articles So. Ill. U. Law Jour., 1991; contbr. articles to profl. jours; speaker and author: insurance and legal/medical topics; published articles in the S.I.U. Law Journal, the Illinois Bar Jour., The Jour. Mo. Bar and the ABA Mag., Contbr. Rights & Remedies and Litig. Settlements. Named one of Lawyers of the Year, Mo. Lawyers Weekly, 2005. Mem. Young Lawyers divsn. of ABA (vice chair corp. counsel com. 1991-92, editor Corp. Counsel Newsletter 1991-92), Women Lawyers Assn., Def. Rsch. Inst., Mo. Orgn. Def. Lawyers; Am. Bar Assn., Tort & Ins. Sect. and Health Care Law Sect., Mo. Bar, Ill. State Bar Assn., Bar Assn. of Metropolitan St. Louis, Lawyers Assn. of St. Louis, St. Clair County Bar Assn., Nat. Assn. Ins. Women, Transp. Lawyers Assn. Avocations: tennis, softball, golf. Office: BBB 7912 Bonhomme Ave Ste 400 Saint Louis MO 63105-3512 Office Phone: 314-726-2310. Office Fax: 314-726-2360. Personal E-mail: bbblawyers@aol.com. Business E-Mail: bboggs@bbblawyers.com.

BOGGS, DANNY JULIAN, federal judge; b. Havana, Cuba, Oct. 23, 1944; s. Robert Lilburn and Yolanda (Pereda) Boggs; m. Judith Susan Solow, Dec. 23, 1967; children: Rebecca, David, Jonathan. AB cum laude, Harvard Coll., Cambridge, Mass., 1965; JD, U. Chgo., 1968; LLD (hon.), U. Detroit Mercy, 1994. Dep. commr. Ky. Dept. Econ. Security, 1969—70; legal counsel, adminstrv. asst. Gov. Ky., 1970—71; legis. counsel to Rep. legislators Ky. Gen. Assembly, 1972; asst. to solicitor gen. US Dept. Justice, Washington, 1973—75; asst. to chmn. FPC, Washington, 1975—77; dep. minority counsel Senate Energy Com., Washington, 1977—79; of counsel Bushnell, Gage, et al., Washington, 1979—80; spl. asst. to Pres. The White House, Washington, 1981—83; dep. sec. US Dept. Energy, Washington, 1983—86; judge US Ct. Appeals (6th cir.), Cin., 1986—2003, chief judge, 2003—. Mem. adv. com. on appellate rules Jud. Conf. US, 1991—94, com. on automation and tech., 1994—2000. Mem. vis. com. U. Chgo. Law Sch., 1984—87, 1999—2002; trustee Lexington Sch., 1999—2005; del. Rep. Nat. Conv., 1972; staff dir. energy subcom. Rep. Platform Com., 1980. Mem.: ABA (chair appellate judges conf. 2001—02), Mont Pelerin Soc., Ky. Bar Assn., Phila. Soc., Phi Delta Phi, Order of Coif. Office: US Ct Appeals US Courthouse 601 W Broadway Ste 220 Louisville KY 40202-2227 Office Phone: 502-625-3900.*

BOGGS, DAVID BRUCE, art educator; b. El Paso, Tex., Nov. 8, 1953; s. William Lee and Mary Carman Dougherty Boggs; m. Patricia Ann Bastion, Dec. 12, 1979; children: Samuel Bastion, Abigail Bastion. BFA, Okla.State U., Stillwater, 1979; MFA in Art & Design, U. Ill., Urbana-Champaign, 1982. Asst. prof. art & art history U. Maine, Machias, 1982—85; prof. art Concordia Coll., Moorhead, Minn., 1985—. Instr. (design competition & exhibition) Artists Call for Justice Competition (Named Illumina Tchr., 2002); exhibitions include National Watercolor Soc., Watercolor USA Honor Soc., one-man shows include Circa Gallery, Mpls., 1999, 2000, 2006; contbr. artwork in pub. and pvt. collections worldwide. Pvt. 1st class US Army, 1972—75, W.Germany. Named to Named to Excellent Tchr. List, U. Ill., 1981; recipient Percent for Art Commn. award, State Maine, 1984; fellow Grad. Tchg. assistantship, U. Ill., 1980—82; Bush fellowship, Bush Found., 1991. Mem.: Nat. Watercolor Soc., Watercolor USA Hon. Soc. Home: 1911 Centre Sq Moorhead MN 56560 Office: Concordia Coll 901 S 8th St Moorhead MN 56560

BOGGS, GEORGE ROBERT, educational association administrator; b. Conneaut, Ohio, Sept. 4, 1944; s. George Robert and Mary (Mullen) B.; m. Ann Holladay, Aug. 8, 1969; children: Kevin Dale, Ian Asher, Micah Benjamin. BS in Chemistry, Ohio State U., 1966; MA in Chemistry, U. Calif., Santa Barbara, 1968; postgraduate student in Ednl. Adminstrn., Natural Scis. and Edn., Calif. State U., 1969—72; PhD in Ednl. Adminstrn., U. Tex., 1984. Cert. std. tchg. specialization in jr. coll., CC supr., CC chief adminstrv. officer. Instr. chemistry Butte Coll., Oroville, Calif., 1968—85, divsn. chmn. nat. sci. and allied health, 1972—81, assoc. dean instrn., 1981—85; pres., supt. Palomar CC Dist., San Marcos, Calif., 1985—2000; pres. Am. Assn. CCs, Washington, 2000—, CEO. Tchg. asst. Ohio State U., 1965-66, U. Calif., Santa Barbara, 1966-68; mem. numerous coms. for colls. and univs., Calif., 1968—; cons. U. Calif., Berkeley, 1995-2000, U. Wis., Madison, 1997-2000, Pellissippi State Tech. Coll., 1995, El Camino Coll., 1994, U. Hawaii CC, 1994, Dept. Nat. Edn., Republic South Africa, 1993, San Joaquin Delta CC Dist., 1986, Marin CC Dist., 1985, Higher Colls. of Tech., United Arab Emirates, 2003; chair pub. mem. com. Accrediting Bd. Engring. and Tech., 2005; bd. dirs. World Fedn. Colls. and Polys., 2002-, bd. chair, 2006-. Contbr. articles to profl. jours. and numerous presentations and publs. on higher edn.; cons. editl. adv. bd. Jour. Applied Rsch. in the CC, 1993-2000; mem. editl. bd. CC Rev., 1997-2000. Named hon. elder, Nat. Coun. Black Am. Affairs, 1993; recipient Pacific Region CEO award, Assn. CC Trustees, Victoria, Brit. Columbia, Can., 1993, Stanley A. Mahr Cmty. Svc. award, San Marcos Coun. C. of C., 1994; Cert. Achievement, Leadership Excellence and Cmty. Svc., Congress of US Ho. Reps., 1994, Harry Buttimer Disting. Adminstr. award, Assn. Calif. CC Trustees, 1994, Recognition award, Nat. Coun. Rsch. and Planning Mgmt., 1997, PBS O'Banion prize for tchg. and learning, 2001, Leadership award, Nat. Inst. Staff and Orgnl. Devel., 2004, Paul Elsner Internat. Excellence in Leadership award, 2004; Richardson fellow, 1982—83. Mem. NSF (adv. com. to directorate for edn. and human resources 1995-97, evaluator 1992, 93, 98), NRC (undergraduate sci. edn. com. 1993-95, chmn. subcommittee tchg. and learning 1993-95), Commn. on 21st Century Edn. in Sci., Tech., Engring. and Math. (mem. nat. sci. bd. 2006), Assn. Calif. CC Tutorial and Learning Assistance (presenter 1984), Calif. Assn. CC (conf. presenter 1984, com. rsch. 1985—), Assn. Calif. CC Adminstrs. (commn. membership devel. 1985), CC League Calif. (bd. dirs. 1990-92, presenter confs. 1990-98), Faculty Assn. Calif. CC, San Diego and Imperial Counties CC Assn., Am. Assn. Cmty. and Jr. Colls. (presenter 1989, 90, 91, 94, 95, bd. dirs. 1990-95, fed. rels. com. 1990-91, 94-95, chair elect 1993—, chair bd. dirs. 1993-94, exec. com. 1993-95, chair bd.

nominating com. 1994-95), So. Calif. CC CEOs Assn. (sec., treas. 1990-2000), Phi Kappa Phi, Upsilon Pi Upsilon (pres. 1965-66), Phi Rho Pi, Rotary (pres. Durham club 1980-81, dist. sec. Calif., 1983-84, various other offices and com. positions held locally and nationally), Phi Theta Kappa (bd. dirs. 2006). Office: Am Assn CCs One Dupont Cir NW Ste 410 Washington DC 20036 Office Phone: 202-728-0200 ext. 235. Business E-Mail: gboggs@aacc.nche.edu.

BOGGS, GEORGE TRENHOLM, lawyer; b. Charleston, SC, Apr. 17, 1947; s. Edwin and Laura (Blair) Boggs; m. Emilie Louise von Thelen, Sept. 6, 1975; children: George T. Jr., Blair M. AB, Princeton U., 1969; JD, U. Va., 1974. Bar: Va. 1974, DC 1975. Tchr. Taft Sch., Watertown, Conn., 1969—71; mem. Dickstein Shapiro LLP, Washington, 1974—, ptnr., 1980—. Editor (with John M. Paxman): The United Nations: A Reassessment, 1973. Mem.: ABA, Va. Bar Assn., Internat. Bar Assn. Republican. Episcopalian. Office: Dickstein Shapiro LLP 1825 Eye St NW Washington DC 20006

BOGGS, GIL, principal ballet dancer; b. Pensacola, Fla. m. Sandra Brown. Student with Robert Barnett, Atlanta Ballet. Prin. Atlanta Ballet, 1977-82; mem. corps be ballet Am. Ballet Theatre, NYC, 1982-84, soloist, 1984-87, 88-91, prin. dancer, 1991—99; dancer Twyla Tharp Dance Co., 1987-88; mgr. Golf Acad. Chelsea Piers, 2001; artistic dir. Colo. Ballet, Denver, 2006—. Repertoire includes La Bayadere, Brief Fling, Coppelia, Drink to Me Only With Thine Eyes, Theme and Variations, Donizetti Variations, Etudes, Fancy Free, Giselle, Manon, The Nutcracker, Rodeo, Romeo and Juliet, Swan Lake, La Sylphide, Tchaikovsky Pas de Deux, Sleeping Beauty, Requiem, Cinderella, BriefFling, Bum's Rush, Nine Sinatra Songs, The Catherine Wheel, Symphonic Variations, Undertow, others; dances works of Paul Taylor, Merce Cunningham, Mark Morris. Office: Colo Ballet 1278 Lincoln St Denver CO 80203 Office Phone: 303-339-1614. E-mail: gil@coloradoballet.org.*

BOGGS, JACK AARON, banker, mayor, publisher, municipal government official; b. Easley, SC, July 4, 1935; s. Walter Benston and Bessie Mae (Jones) B.; m. Isabel Thomas Brown, July 7, 1965; children— James Benston, Renee Chaplin, Edward Cunningham, Donn Lester. BS in Bus. Econs, U. S.C., 1964; grad., Sch. Banking, U. Wis., 1974. Chartered bank auditor certified internal auditor. Sec.-treas. Cedarpoint Farms Corp., Columbia, SC, 1963-67; auditor S.C. Nat. Bank, Columbia, 1967-76; pres. S.C. Automated Clearing House Assn., 1976—2005, pres. emeritus, 2005—07, ret., 2007; sec., treas. Arcadia Publs., 2002—; sec.-treas. E.C. Boggs Law Firm, 2002—. Mem. 5th dist. ops. adv. com. Fed. Res. Bank of Richmond, 1997-99; instr. S.C. Bankers Sch., 1972-80; sec., treas. Five Star Pubs., 1986-88; bd. dirs. NACHA, Inc., 1989-2000; vice chmn. ACH Exec. Dirs. Group, 1989-90, chmn., 1991-93. Mem. town coun., Town of Arcadia Lakes, S.C., 1977-85, mayor, 1985-89, chief of police, 1990-91; treas. S.C. Fedn. Older Ams., 1982-84. With USN, 1952-56, USNR, 1956-60, Air N.G., 1960-63. Mem. Inst. Internal Auditors (bd. govs. 1971-74, pres. 1973-74, internat. rsch. com. 1972-75, internat. membership com. 1976), Bank Adminstrn. Inst. (1st award 1972), S.C. Ducks Unltd. (treas. 1984-92, 98-2002, state chmn. 1992-94), Explorers Club, Sigma Delta Pi, Chi Psi. Democrat. Unitarian Universalist. Home: 804 Arcadia Lakes Dr Columbia SC 29206-1321 Personal E-mail: duckboggs@aol.com.

BOGGS, JAMES DOTSON, lawyer; b. Kansas City, Mo., Aug. 31, 1949; s. William C. and Helen C. (Harbison) B.; m. Vickie R. Boggs, May 27, 1972; children: William Christian, Meghan Raye. BA, U. Mo., Columbia, 1971; JD, U. Mo., Kansas City, 1975. Bar: Mo. 1975, U.S. Dist. Ct. (we. dist.) Mo., U.S. Ct. Appeals (8th cir.), U.S. Supreme Ct. Assoc. Witt and Shafer, Platte City, Mo., 1975-78; ptnr. Witt and Boggs, Platte City, Mo., 1979-81, Witt, Boggs & Shaw, Platte City, Mo., 1982-85, Witt, Boggs, Shaw & Van Amburg, Platte City, Mo., 1985-87; pvt. practice Kansas City, Mo., 1987—. Chmn. Platte County Dem. PArty, 1985-86; commr. Platte County Jud. Commn., 1987-93, 93—. Mem. Mo. Bar Assn. (gov. 1992-97), Mo. Assn. Trial Attys. (govs., 1985—, exec. com. 1994—, v.p. 2000, pres. 2002), Reach Out Am. (dir. 1994—). Office: 6406 N Cosby Ave Kansas City MO 64151-2377

BOGGS, JAMES ERNEST, chemistry professor; b. Cleve., June 9, 1921; s. Ernest Beckett and Emily (Reid) B.; m. Ruth Ann Rogers, June 22, 1948 (dec. 2002); children: Carol, Ann, Lynne. AB, Oberlin Coll., 1943; MS in Chemistry, U. Mich., 1944, PhD, 1953. Rsch. chemist Manhattan Dist. Project, Linde Air Products, Tonawanda, NY, 1944-46; asst. prof. dept. chemistry Eastern Mich. U., Ypsilanti, 1949-52; instr. U. Mich. at Ann Arbor, 1952-53; mem. faculty dept. chemistry U. Tex., Austin, 1953—, assoc. prof., 1958-66, prof., 1966-98; emeritus prof., 1998—; asst. dean Grad. Sch. U. Tex., Austin, 1958-67, dir. Center for Structural Studies, 1969-79, acting dir. Inst. Theoretical Chemistry, 1979-81. Program officer for theoretical and computational chemistry NSF, 1991-94; founder, organizer series Austin Symposia on Molecular Structure, 1966—; chmn. subcom. on theoretical chemistry Internat. Union Pure and Applied Chemistry, 1995-01; internat. lectr. in field. Mem. editl. bd. Jour. Molecular Structure, Structural Chemistry, Asian Jour. of Spectroscopy; contbr. over 305 articles to profl. jours. Mem. Am. Chem. Soc., Am. Phys. Soc., Nat. Acad. Scis. (India), Phi Beta Kappa, Sigma Xi, Phi Lambda Upsilon, Gamma Alpha. Achievements include research in structural chemistry, microwave spectroscopy, quantum chemistry. Office: U Tex Dept Chemistry 1 University Sta A5300 Austin TX 78712 Home Phone: 512-466-9145; Office Phone: 512-466-9145. Business E-Mail: james.boggs@mail.utexas.edu.

BOGGS, JOSEPH DODRIDGE, pediatric pathologist, educator; b. Bellefontaine, Ohio, Dec. 31, 1921; s. Walter C. and Birdella Z. (Coons) B.; m. Donna Lee Shoemaker, June 12, 1964; 1 son, Joseph Dodridge. AB, Ohio U., 1941, Litt.D., 1966; MD, Jefferson Med. Coll., 1945. Intern Jefferson Med. Coll. Hosp., Phila., 1945-46; resident Peter Bent Brigham Hosp., Boston, 1946-48, asso. pathologist, 1947-51; instr. pathology Harvard Med. Sch., Boston, 1948-51; with Children's Meml. Hosp., Chgo., 1951—, dir. labs., 1951—; prof. pathology Northwestern U., Chgo., 1952-92, prof. emeritus, 1992—; dir. BSP Ins. Co., Phoenix. Contbr. articles to profl. jours. Mem. med. adv. bd. Ill. Dept. Corrections, Springfield, 1971-77; bd. dirs. Blood Systems Inc., Phoenix, 1972-94, Community Hosp., Evanston, Ill., 1958-61, Lorretto Hosp., Chgo., 1971-72; chmn. Chgo. Regional Blood Program, 1978-80; bd. dirs. Ben Venue Labs., 1985—. Capt. M.C., U.S. Army, 1948-51. Mem. Am. Soc. Study of Liver Disease, N.Y. Acad. Scis., Midwest Soc. Pediatric Research, Inst. Medicine, Ill. Soc. Pathologists (pres. 1965), Ill. Assn. Blood Banks (pres. 1969-70) Home and Office: 1448 N Lake Shore Dr Chicago IL 60610-6655 Office Fax: 312-488-1873.

BOGGS, JUDITH SUSAN, lawyer, health policy analyst; 3 children. BA cum laude, Bklyn. Coll., 1966; JD, U. Chgo., 1969. Bar: Ky. 1970. Human rights rep. Ky. Human Rights Commn., Frankfort, Ky., 1969; legal counsel Ky. Dept. Mental Health, Frankfort, 1970-73; sr. legal advisor Social and Rehabilitation Service, Washington, 1973-77; dir., health systems div. Health Care Fin. Adminstrn., Washington, 1978-82, special asst. to assoc. adminstr. for policy, 1982-86, spl. asst. to adminstr., 1986-87; sr. policy analyst The White House, Washington, 1987-89; of counsel Alagia, Day, Trautwein & Smith, Louisville, 1989-93; sr. v.p., gen. counsel Ky. Hosp. Assn., 1993-94; pvt. practice, 1994—2002; mem. (judge) Adminstrv. Rev. Bd. US Dept. Labor, 2002—04, mem. (judge) Benefits Rev. Bd., 2004—. Apptd. mem. Ky. Registry Election Fin., 2001—02. Mem. ABA (nat. conf. adminstrv. judiciary), Ky. Bar Assn., Am. Health Lawyers Assn., Louisville Bar Assn. Office: 200 Constitution Ave NW Washington DC Business E-Mail: boggs-judith@dol.gov.

BOGGS, LISA LYNN, biology professor; d. Gary and Patricia Boggs. AA, Ea. Wyo. Coll., Torrington, 1987; BS, Chadron State Coll., Nebr., 1989, MS, 1992; PhD, U. Wyo., Laramie, 2003. Assoc. prof. biology Southwestern Okla. State U., Weatherford, 1992—. Rsch. weed scientist Tex. A&M U., Stephenville, 2005—. Sponsor Zeta Phi Sorority, Weatherford, Okla., 2004. Recipient Outstanding Biology Faculty award, Beta Beta Beta, Biology Club, Southwestern Okla. State U., 2004. Mem.: Western Soc. Weed Sci. (corr.; com. chair 2004—05). Office: Southwestern Oklahoma State University 100 Campus Dr Weatherford OK 73096 Home Phone: 580-772-8948; Office Phone: 580-774-3090.

BOGGS, PAULA ELAINE, lawyer, food service executive; b. Washington, May 2, 1959; d. Nathaniel Boggs Jr. and Janice C. (Anderson) Barber. BA, Johns Hopkins U., Balt., 1981; JD, U. Calif., Berkeley, 1984. Bar: Pa. 1986, DC 1988, Wash. 1992, US Dist. Ct. (we. dist. Wash.) 1988, US Ct. appeals (9th cir.) 1990, US Ct. Appeals (DC and fed. cirs.) 1995. Sr. law clk. Office of Army Gen. Counsel, Arlington, Va., 1984-85; spl. asst. Office of Dep. Under Sec. of Army, Arlington, 1985-86; staff atty. White House Iran-Contra legal task force, Washington, 1987-88; asst. U.S. atty. US Atty.'s Office (we. dist.), Seattle, 1988-93; staff dir. adv. bd. investigative capability dept. def. Dept. Def., Arlington, 1994; ptnr. Preston, Gates & Ellis, Seattle, 1995—97; v.p. legal Dell Computer Corp., 1997—2002; exec. v.p., gen. counsel, sec. Starbucks, Seattle, 2002—. Mem. faculty Nat. Inst. Trial Advocacy, 1995; adj. prof. law U. Wash., Seattle, 1993. Vol. instr. presdl. classroom for young Ams., Washington, 1991; bd. dirs. ctrl. dist. YMCA, Seattle, 1991-93, Greater Seattle YMCA, 1995—; nat. chair Johns Hopkins U. Second Decade Soc., Balt., 1995-96. Recipient Sec. Def. award for Excellence William J. Perry, 1994; Presdl. svc. badge Pres. Ronald Reagan, 1988; Def. Meritorious Svc. award, 1987, Spl. Achievement award Dept. Justice, 1990, 91. Mem. ABA (ho. dels., litig. sect. co-chair bus. torts com., bus. crimes com., criminal justice sect. white collar crimes com., standing com. on constn. and bylaws), Nat. Bar Assn., Wash. State Bar Assn. (corrections com.), King County Bar Assn., Fed. Bar Assn., Wash. Women Lawyers (bd. dirs. 1991-93), Loren Miller Bar Assn. Avocations: running, bicycling, reading. Office: Starbucks 2401 Utah Ave S PO Box 34067 Seattle WA 98124-1067*

BOGGS, STEVEN EUGENE, real estate broker, lawyer; b. Santa Monica, Calif., Apr. 28, 1947; s. Eugene W. and Annie (Happe) B. BA in Econ., U. Calif., Santa Barbara, 1969; D of Chiropractic summa cum laude, Cleveland Chiropractic, LA, 1974; PhD in Fin. Planning, Columbia Pacific U., 1986; JD in Law, U. So. Calif., 1990. Bar: Calif. 1990, U.S. Dist. Ct. (cen. dist.) Calif. 1990, Hawaii 1991, U.S. Ct. Appeals (9th cir.), Colo. 1999; CFP; lic. chiropractor Hawaii, Calif.; lic. radiography X-ray supr. and operator; real estate broker, Colo. Faculty mem. Cleveland Chiropractic Coll., 1972-74; pres. clinic dir. Hawaii Chiropractic Clinic, Inc., Aiea, 1974-87; pvt. practice Honolulu, 1991-99; mem. faculty Hawaii Pacific U., 1997-99; broker, dir. REO/asset mgmt. team (bank foreclosures) Coldwell Banker Walker & Co., 2000—02, RE/MAX Properties, Inc., 2002—. Cons. in field; seminar presenter, 1990—. Contbr. articles to profl. jours. Recipient Formula Atlantic Race Car Champion award, 2003, 2004, 2005, 2006. Fellow Internat. Coll. of Chiropractic; mem. ABA, Am. Trial Lawyers Assn., Consumer Lawyers of Hawaii, Am. Chriopractic Assn., Hawaii State Chiropractic Assn. (pres. 1978, 85, 86, v.p. 1977, sec. 1979-84, treas. 1976, other coms., Valuable Svc. award 1984, Cert. Appreciation 1986, Cert. Achievement 1986, Chiropractor of Yr. 1986, Outstanding Achievement award 1991), Consumer Lawyers of Hawaii (bd. dirs.). Republican. Avocations: bicycling, auto racing. Office: 19050 Archers Dr Monument CO 80132-2807 Personal E-mail: boggs@pcisys.net. Business E-Mail: steve@steveboggs.com.

BOGGS, THOMAS HALE, JR., lawyer, director; b. New Orleans, Sept. 18, 1940; s. Thomas Hale and Corinne (Claiborne) B.; m. Mary Barbara Denechaud, Dec. 27, 1960; children— Hale, Elizabeth, Douglas. AB, Georgetown U., 1961, LL.B., 1965. Bar: D.C. 1965, U.S. Ct. Appeals 1966, U.S. Supreme Ct. 1971. Economist Joint Econ. Com., U.S. Congress, 1961-65; spl. asst. to dir. Office Emergency Planning, 1965-66; ptnr. Patton Boggs LLP, Washington, 1966—, chmn. exec. com. Presdl. Commn. on Exec. Exch., 1979-81; Presdl. del. Independence of Solomon Islands, 1978, Trade Mission to People's Republic of China, 1979. Co-author: Private Trade Barriers in the Atlantic Community, 1964, Corporate Political Activity, 1984. Dem. candidate for U.S. Ho. of Reps. 8th Dist. Md., 1970; mem. Charter Commn., Dem. Nat. Com., 1973; trustee Fed. City Coun., Chesapeake Bay Trust, Univ. Md. Found.; dir. The Keystone Ctr., Congl. Award Found., Suburban Mortgage Assn., 1-800-CONTACTS. Named one of 100 Most Influential Lawyers, Nat. Law Jour., 2006. Mem. Am. Judicature Soc., ABA (com. chmn.), Am. Maritime, Fed. Bar Assns., Delta Theta Phi. Home: 6 E Kirke St Chevy Chase MD 20815-4217 Office: Patton Boggs LLP 2550 M St NW Ste 500 Washington DC 20037-1350 Office Phone: 202-457-6040. Office Fax: 202-457-6315. Business E-Mail: tboggs@pattonboggs.com.

BOGGS, WILLIAM NORMAN, marketing professional, educator; b. Ashland, Ky., Nov. 27, 1956; s. William Norman and Joan Boggs; m. Amelia Rose Vela, Apr. 10, 1976; children: Valerie Boggs Cressman, Benjamin James, Jonathan Andrew, Bradley William. BA, Ind. U., Bloomington, 1978—82. Lic. minister Suburban Bible Ch., Ind., 2002. Line revision mgr. McMaster-Carr, Elmhurst, Ill., 1993—. Instr. Purdue U., Hammond, Ind., 2006—. Mem. Marine Corps League, Hobart, Ind., 2005—. Sgt., grade 5 USMC, 1974—77, Kaneohe Marine Corps Air Station. Decorated Marine Corps Meritorious Mast award 1st Bn., 3d Marines. Mem.: Religious Comm. Assn., Nat. Comm. Assn., Christian Motorcyclist Assn., Am. Mensa. Independent. Avocations: toymaking, computers, juggling, magic. Home: 6811 Ohio Ave Hammond IN 46323 Home Phone: 219-845-3297. Personal E-mail: billboggs@mac.com.

BOGGS, WILLIAM S., lawyer; b. Toledo, May 17, 1946; AB summa cum laude, Wittenberg U., 1968; JD cum laude, Harvard U., 1972. Bar: Calif., US Dist. Ct.(ctrl. & so. dists.) Calif., US Ct. Appeals (9th cir.), US Supreme Ct., All state & fed. cts. Calif. Ptnr. Gray, Cary, Ware & Freidenrich, San Diego, 1979, DLA Piper, San Diego. Spkr. in field. Contbr. articles to. profl. jour. Bd. trustee Found. of La Jolla High Sch.; bd. trustee Museum of Man, bd. dir., pres., 1996—98. Named Best Lawyers, 2007. Mem. ABA, San Diego County Bar Assn., Internat. Assn. Defense Counsel, Assn. Bus. Trial Lawyers, San Diego (emeritus bd mem., bd. of Govs. 1998-2000) San Diego Defense Lawyers, Lincoln's Inn., Assn. So. Calif. Def. Counsel (bd dir. 1997-1998), Big Brothers San Diego County (bd. dir., pres. 1980-82, emeritus bd. mem.), Harvard Club San Diego, Def. Research Inst., master Louis M. Welsh Am. Inns of Ct. Office: DLA Piper 401 B St Ste 1700 San Diego CA 92101 Office Phone: 619-699-2758. Office Fax: 619-699-2101. Business E-Mail: william.boggs@dlapiper.com.

BOGHANI, ASHOK BALVANTRAI, entrepreneur, management consultant; b. Bombay, Aug. 8, 1949; came to U.S., 1970; s. Balvantrai Pranlal and Charusheela (Kapadia) B.; m. Meera Kapadia, May 30, 1977; children: Ami, Amar. B of Tech., Indian Inst. Tech., Bombay, 1970; MS, MIT, 1971, M in Mech. Engring., 1973, ScD, 1974. Staff engr. Foster-Miller, Waltham, Mass., 1974-77, project mgr., 1977-79; sr. cons. Arthur D. Little, Inc., Cambridge, Mass., 1979-90, dir., 1990-2000, v.p., 1994-2000, leader N.Am. transp. and automotive practice, 1998-2000; founder, v.p. bus. devel. IntellectExchange.com, 2000—03; mng. ptnr. FutureAct, LLC, 2003—; dir. Monitor Techs., Monitor Group, 2004—. Mem. transp. hazmat com. Transp. Rsch. Bd., Washington, 1987-94; mem. Benefits, Evaluation and Assessment com., Intelligent Vehicle Hwy. Systems Am., Washington, 1992-96. Contbr. articles to profl. jours. Recipient cert. of recognition NASA, 1976, 78. Mem. ASME, Soc. Automotive Engrs., Indus Entrepreneurs-Atlantic (charter mem.), Democrat. Avocations: photography, travel, hiking, music. Home: 3 Sawmill Rd Acton MA 01720-5835 Office Phone: 617-252-3180. Business E-Mail: ABoghani@alum.mit.edu.

BOGHOSIAN, VARUJAN YEGAN, sculptor, educator; b. New Britain, Conn., June 26, 1926; s. Mesrop and Baidzar (Saylandzian) B.; m. Marilyn Cummins, Sept. 1, 1953; 1 dau., Heidi. Student, Conn. Tchrs. Coll., 1946-48, Vesper George Sch. Art, 1948-50; BFA, Yale U., MFA, 1959; MA (hon.), Brown U., 1965, Dartmouth Coll., 1969. Instr. art U. Fla., 1958-59, Pratt Inst., 1961, Yale U., 1962-64; asst. prof. art Cooper Union Coll., 1959-64; asso. prof. Brown U., 1964-68; artist-in-residence Dartmouth Coll., 1968, prof. art, 1968—, George Frederick Jewett prof. art, 1983—; sculptor in residence Am. Acad. in Rome, 1966-67, 75. Artist woodcut portfolios Orpheus, 1951, The River Styx, 1971; numerous one-man shows including Stable Gallery, NYC, 1963, 64, 65, 66, Cordier and Ekstrom, NYC, 1969, 71, 73, 75, 77-80, 82, 84, 87-89, Berry Hill Galleries, 1997, 99, Arts Club of Chgo., 1970, Claude Bernard Gallery, NYC, 1991, Norton Gallery Art, Palm Beach, Fla., 1993, Washburn Gallery, NYC, 2004, Irving Gallery, Palm Beach, 2006; group shows include Obelisk Gallery, Rome, 1953, Mus. Modern Art, NYC, 1956, Hanover Gallery, London, 1966, retrospective Hood Mus., Hanover, N.H., 1989; represented in numerous permanent collections including, Mus. Modern Art, NYC, Whitney Mus. Am. Art, NYC, Met. Mus. NYC, Addison Gallery Am. Art, Andover, Mass., Worcester Art Mus., Phoenix Art Mus. Chmn. bd. MacDowell Colony. With USN, 1944-46. Recipient award Nat. Inst. Arts and Letters, 1972; Fulbright grantee, Italy, 1953; US Dept. State specialists grantee, 1961; fellow Howard Found., 1966, John Simon Guggenheim Found. fellow, 1985 Mem. NAD, Am. Acad. Arts and Letters (St. Botolph award 1991), Century Assn. (NYC), St. Botolph Club (Boston). Clubs: Century (NYC). Office: Darmouth Coll HB 6081 Visual Studies Office Hanover NH 03755

BOGLE, JANE E., medical transcriptionist; b. Feb. 2, 1944; Cert. med. transcriptionist. Med. transcriptionist St. Joseph Hosp., Concordia, Kans., 1962—99, Spheris, Franklin, Tenn., 1999—. Mem.: Am. Assn. Med. Transcription, Kans. Assn. Med. Transcription.

BOGLE, JOHN CLIFTON, investment company executive; b. Montclair, NJ, May 8, 1929; s. William Yates, Jr. and Josephine (Hipkins) B.; m. Eve Sherrerd, Sept. 22, 1956; children: Barbara, Jean, John Clifton, Nancy, Sandra, Andrew. AB magna cum laude, Princeton U., 1951; LHD (hon.), Widener U., 1997, U. Rochester, 2000, Ea. U., 2000; HHD (hon.), Albright Coll., Immaculata U., 2005; LLD (hon.), U. Del., Susquehanna U., 2001, New School U., 2001, Drexel U., 2003, Pa. State U., 2004, Immaculata U., 2005, Princeton U., 2005, Georgetown U., 2007. With Wellington Mgmt. Co., Phila., 1951-74, asst. to pres., 1954-62, sec., adminstrv. v.p., 1962-66, exec. v.p., 1966-67, pres., CEO, 1967-74; founder, CEO, chmn. Vanguard Group Investment Cos., Valley Forge, Pa., 1974-96; sr. chmn. Vanguard Group, Valley Forge, 1996-99; pres. Bogle Fin. Makerts Rsch. Ctr., Valley Forge, 2000—. Kaufman vis. prof. NYU, 1999-2000; former exec. com. CGU; former chmn. corp. objectives com. Mead Corp. Author: Bogle on Mutual Funds: New Perspectives for the Intelligent Investor, 1993, Common Sense on Mutual Funds: New Imperatives for the Intelligent Investor, 1999, John Bogle on Investing: The First 50 Years, 2000, Character Counts, 2002, The Battle for the Soul of Capitalism, 2005, The Little Book of Common Sense Investing: The Only Way to Guarantee Your Fair Share of Stock Market Returns, 2007; subject of biography: John Bogle and the Vanguard Experiment: One Man's Quest to Transform the Mutual Fund Industry, by Robert Slater, 1996; numerous articles to profl. jours., chpts. to books. Former chmn. bd. trustees Blair Acad.; former chmn. bd. dirs. Nat. Constn. Ctr.; past adv. coun. econs. dept. Princeton U.; past bd. dirs. Independence Standards Bd., Am. Indian Coll. Fund. Recipient Woodrow Wilson medal Princeton U., 1999; named One of Four Investment Giants of the 20th Century Fortune mag., 1999, One of Worlds Most Powerful Influential People Time mag., 2004. Fellow AAAS, Am. Philos. Soc.; mem. Nat. Assn. Securities Dealers (investment cos. com. 1967-74, long-range planning com. 1973-74), Investment Co. Inst. (gov. 1969-81, chmn. 1969-70), Securities and Exch. Commn. (market oversight and fin. svcs. adv. com.), Merion Cricket Club (Haverford), Merion Golf (Ardmore). Office: Vanguard Group PO Box 2600 Valley Forge PA 19482-2600 E-mail: john.c.bogle@vanguard.com.

BOGOSIAN, ERIC, actor, writer; b. Boston, Apr. 24, 1953; s. Henry and Edwina B.; m. JoAnne Bonney, Oct. 1980. Student, U. Chgo., 1971-73; BA, Oberlin Coll., 1976. Founder, dir. The Kitchen, NYC. Actor, writer: (theatre, off-broadway debut) Men Inside, 1982, Voices of America, 1982, (dir., design supr.) FunHouse, 1983, Drinking in America (Drama Desk award for outstanding solo performance 1986), 1986, Talk Radio, 1987, Sex, Drugs, Rock & Roll, 1990, Pounding Nails in the Floor with My Forehead, 1994, SubUrbia, 1994, Griller, 1998, Wake Up and Smell the Coffee, 2000, The Worst of Bogosian, 2007; actor (films) (Cinemax spl.) Drinking in America, 1986, Talk Radio, 1988, Sex, Drugs, Rock & Roll, 1991, Dolores Claiborne, 1995, Under Siege 2, 1995, The Substance of Fire, 1996, Deconstructing Harry, 1997, Office Killer, 1997, Gossip, 1999; TV show appearances: The Twilight Zone, Miami Vice, Law & Order, Larry Sanders Show, Beggars and Choosers; TV movie appearances: The Caine Mutiny Court Martial, 1988, Witchhunt, 1994, A Bright and Shining Lie, 1998, Blonde, 2001; author: Sex, Drugs, Rock & Roll, 1990, Pounding Nails in the Floor with my Forehead, 1994, Notes from Underground, 1993, Wasted Beauty, 2005; (play and film) subUrbia, 1994, Essential Bogosian, 1994, Mall, 2000; author, creator (with Steven Spielberg) (TV series) High Incident, 1996, (voice) Arabian Knight, 1995, (voice) Beavis and Butthead do America, 1996. Recipient Obie, 1986, 90, 94, Drama Critics Circle award; grantee Nat. Endowment for Arts, Berlin Film Fest Silver Bear award, 1988. Mem. SAG, AFTRA, Writer's Guild, Actor's Equity.*

BOGREN, CAROL FERRER, secondary school educator; b. San Diego, Nov. 23, 1954; m. Douglas Edward Bogren, Nov. 25, 2000; 1 child, Leyenda Ann Jacobson. BA, Calif. Polytech. State U., 1981. Cert. in tchg. U. Alaska, Fairbanks, 1984. Elem. tchr. Sacramento City Unified Sch. Dist.; mid. sch. tchr. Santee Unified Sch. Dist., Calif.; acad. instr. Calif. Dept. Correction, Ironwood State Prison, Blythe, 1998—2001; alt. edn. tchr. Riverside County Office of Edn., Calif., 2001—. Owner White Dove Children's Entertainment, San Diego, 1995—97. Vol. Soc. for Prevention of Cruelty to Animals, San Diego, 1996—97; supporter Family Planning, Riverside/San Diego. Mem.: NEA, Riverside County Office Tchrs. Assn., Calif. State Edn. Assn., Calif. Tchrs. Assn.

BOGREN, HUGO GUNNAR, radiology educator; b. Jönköping, Sweden, Jan. 9, 1933; came to U.S., 1970; s. Gunnar Hugo and Signe Victoria (Holmström) B.; m. Elisabeth Faxén, Nov. 1, 1956 (div. 1976); children: Cecilia, Niclas, Joakim; m. Gunilla Lady Whitmore, July 2, 1988. MD, U. Göteborg, Sweden, 1958, PhD, 1964. Diplomate Swedish Bd. Radiology. Resident, fellow U. Göteborg, 1958-64, asst. to assoc. prof. radiology, 1964-69; from assoc. prof. to prof. radiology and internal medicine U. Calif. Davis, Sacramento, 1972—. Vis. assoc. prof. U. San Francisco, 1970-71; vis. prof. U. Kiel, Fed. Republic Germany, 1980, cardiac magnetic resonance unit Royal Brompton Hosp. and Imperial Coll., London, 1986-87, 93-94, 2002-03; participant in med. aid fact finding mission, Bangladesh, 1992. Contbr. numerous articles to profl. jours., chpts. to books. Sr. Internat. Fogarty fellow NIH, London, 1986-87. Fellow Am. Heart Assn., Radiol. Soc., N.Am. Soc. Cardiac Imaging, Soc. Thoracic Radiology, Internat. Soc. Magnetic Resonance in Medicine, Soc. Cardiovasc. Magnetic Resonance, Soc. Cardiovasc. Computed Tomography, Swedish Assn. Med. Radiology; mem. Royal Gothenburg Sailing Club Sweden (hon.), Swedish Cruising Club, Rotary (del.). Lutheran. Avocations: ocean sailing, skiing, classical music. Office: U Calif Davis Med Ctr Div Diagnostic Radiology 4860 Y St Ste 3100 Sacramento CA 95817-2307 Office Phone: 916-734-6535. Personal E-mail: hugobogren@aol.com. Business E-Mail: hugo.bogren@ucdmc.ucdavis.edu.

BOGUE, ALLAN GEORGE, historian, educator; b. London, Ont., Can., May 12, 1921; married; 3 children. BA, U. Western Ont., 1943, MA, 1946; PhD, Cornell U., 1951; LL.D., U. Western Ont., 1973; D.Fil (hon.), U. Uppsala, 1977. Lectr. econs. and history, asst. librarian U. Western Ont., 1949-52; from asst. prof. to prof. history U. Iowa, 1952-64, chmn. dept., 1959-63; prof. history U. Wis.-Madison, 1964-68, chmn. dept., 1972-73, Frederick Jackson Turner prof. history, 1968-91. Mem. hist. adv. com. Math. Soc. Sci. Bd., 1965-71; Scandinavian-Am. Found. Thord-Gray lectr., 1968; mem. Council Inter-Univ. Consortium Polit. Research, 1971-73, 89-91; vis. prof. history Harvard U., 1972; dir. Social Sci. Research Council, 1973-76 Author: Money at Interest, 1955, From Prairie to Corn Belt, 1963, Frederick Jackson Turner: Strange Roads Going Down, 1998, The Earnest Men, 1981, Clio and the Bitch Goddess, Quantification in American Political History, 1983, The Congressman's Civil War, 1989, The Farm on the North Talbot Road, 2001; co-author, editor: The West of the American People, 1970; co-author, contbr.: The Dimensions of Quantitative Research in History, 1972; co-editor, contbr.: American Political Behavior: Historical Essays and Readings, 1974; co-editor: The University of Wisconsin: One Hundred and Twenty Five Years, 1975, The Jeffersonian Dream: Studies in the History of American Law Land Policy and Development, 1996. Lt. Can. Army, 1943—45, capt. Can. Res. Army, 1951—52. Social Sci. Rsch. Coun. fellow, 1955, 66, Guggenheim fellow, 1970, H.E. Huntington Libr. fellow, 1991, 93, Sherman Fairchild Disting. fellow Calif. Inst. Tech., 1975, Ctr. for Advanced Study in the Behavioral Scis. fellow, 1985, NEH fellow, 1985. Fellow Agr. Hist. Soc. (pres. 1963-64); mem. Orgn. Am. Historians (pres. 1982-83), Am. Hist. Assn., Econ. Hist. Assn. (pres. 1981-82), Social Sci. Hist. Assn. (pres. 1977-78), Western Hist. Assn. (hon. life). Avocation: competitive Samoyed dog training. Office: 1914 Vilas Ave Madison WI 53711 Office Phone: 608-255-5643. Business E-Mail: agbogue@wisc.edu.

BOGUS, CARL THOMAS, law educator; b. Fall River, Mass., May 14, 1948; s. Isidore E. and Carolyn (Dashoff) B.; m. Dale Shepard, Sept. 5, 1970 (div. 1987); children: Elizabeth Carol, Ian Troy; m. Cynthia J. Giles, Nov. 5, 1988; 1 child, Zoe Churchill. AB, Syracuse U., 1970, JD, 1972. Bar: Pa. 1973, U.S. Dist. Ct. (ea. dist.) Pa. 1973, U.S. Dist. Ct. Appeals (3d cir.) 1976, U.S. Supreme Ct. 1977. Assoc. Steinberg, Greenstein, Gorelick & Price, Phila., 1973-79, ptnr., 1979-83; assoc. Mesirov, Gelman, Jaffe, Cramer & Jamieson, Phila., 1983-84, ptnr., 1985-91; assoc. prof. Roger Williams U. Sch. Law, Bristol, RI, 1996—2002, prof., 2002—. Vis. prof. Rutgers U. Sch. Law, Camden, 1992—96; mem. bd. visitors Coll. Law, Syracuse (N.Y.) U., 1976—2001; mem. Nat. adv. panel Violence Policy Ctr., 1993—. Author: Why Lawsuits Are Good for America: Disciplined Democracy, Big Business and the Common Law, 2001; editor: The Second Amendment in Law and History, 2001; contbr. articles to profl. jours. Bd. dirs. Handgun Control, Inc., 1987-89, bd. govs., 1992-93; bd. dirs. Ctr. to Prevent Handgun Violence, 1989-92, Lawyers Alliance for Nuclear Arms Control, 1987-89; mem. state governing bd. Common Cause R.I., 1999-2001. Recipient Common Cause Pub. Svc. award, RI, 2002. Mem. ABA (Ross Essay award 1991), Syracuse Law Coll. Assn. (exec. sec. 1979-83, 2d v.p. 1983-85). Democrat. Mem. Soc. Of Friends. Office: Roger William U Sch Law 10 Metacom Ave Bristol RI 02809-5103 Home Phone: 401-247-4743; Office Phone: 401-254-4617. Business E-Mail: cbogus@rwu.edu.

BOGUSKY, ALEX, advertising executive; Art dir. Crispin and Porter Advertising, Miami, Fla., 1989—92, creative dir., 1992—97; ptnr., exec. creative dir. Crispin and Porter Advt. (now Crispin Porter & Bogusky), 1997—2005, CEO, 2005—. Judge Andy Awards, 2005. Work featured in NY Times, Wall Street Journal, USA Today, Newsweek, TIME, Adweek, Brandweek, Advertising Age, and Creativity. Nominee Rave award in Business, WIRED, 2005; named one of 50 Who Matter Now, CNNMoney.com Bus. 2.0, 2006; named to Am. Advt. Fedn. Hall of Achievement, 2002. Office: Crispin Porter & Bogusky LLC 3390 Mary St Ste 300 Miami FL 33133 Office Phone: 305-859-2070.

BOGUT, ANDREW, professional basketball player; b. Melbourne, Australia, Nov. 28, 1984; Attended Univ. Utah, 2003—05. Center Milwaukee Bucks, 2005—. Starting Center Australian Olympic Basketball Team, 2004. Named Player Week (5 times), Mountain West Conf., 2004, Player Yr., 2004, Nat. Player Yr., Basketball Times, 2005, ESPN; named to All-Tournament Team, Great Alaska Shootout, 2004, First-Team All District 13, NABC, 2004, Mountain West Conf., 2004. Office: Milwaukee Bucks 1001 N Fourth St Milwaukee WI 53203

BOGUTZ, JEROME EDWIN, lawyer, educator; b. Bridgeton, NJ, June 7, 1935; s. Charles and Gertrude (Lahn) B.; m. Helene Carole Ross, Nov. 20, 1960; children: Marc Lahn, Tami Lynne BS in Fin., Pa. State U., 1957; JD, Villanova U., 1962. Bar: Pa., U.S. Dist. Ct. (ea. dist.) Pa., U.S. Ct. Appeals (3d cir.), U.S. Supreme Ct. Assoc. Dash & Levy, Phila., 1962—63, Abrahams & Loewenstein, Phila., 1963—64; dep. dir., chief of litigation Community Legal Svcs., Phila., 1964—68, dir., 1968—78; emeritus, 1978—; pvt. practice law Phila., 1968—71; ptnr. Bogutz & Mazer, Phila., 1971—81, Fox Rothschild O'Brien & Frankel, Phila., 1981—98; judge Pro Tem Phila. Ct. Common Pleas, 1992—; ptnr. Christie, Pabarue, Mortensen & Young, P.C., Phila., 1998—. Adj. clin. prof. law Villanova (Pa.) U., 1969-72, lectr., 1987—, bd. consultors Law Sch., 1983—; pres. Internat. Mobile Machines, Phila., 1980-81, Interdigital Comm., 1980-81, also bd. dirs. ABA-JAD Lawyers Conf., 1987-92, mem. exec. coun., 1986-92, vice chmn., 1987-88, chmn., 1989-90, chmn. nominating com., 1989-90, mem. long range planning com., 1989-90; mem. adv. bd. Pa. Med. Profl. Liability Catastrophe Loss Fund, 2000—04; bd. dirs. Jefferson Park Hosp., Phila. Bd. dirs. Am. Friends of Hebrew U., 1988-93, chmn. exec. com., 1991-93, pres., 1993-95, chmn. bd. 1995-98, chair steering com., pres. Pa. Futures Commn. on Justice in the 21st Century, 1993—, chmn. of bd., 1993-97, pres., 1993—; bd. dirs. deMazia Found., 2006—. With USAR, 1956-60. Fellow Am. Bar Found. (life), Pa. Bar Found. (life, pres. 1986-88, bd. dirs. 1983—, lifetime dir. 1991—), Am. Judicature Soc. (life, bd. dirs. 1990-94); mem. ABA (ho. of dels. 1980-84, 86-96, credentials and admissions com. 1987-88, nominating com. 1992, 93, chair ABA/JAD bench bar com., vice chmn. lawyer's conf. 1987-89, chair 1988-90, co-chair mid-yr. meeting com. 1987-88, planning com., conf. sect. officers, 1988-90, bd. mem. consortium on legal svcs. and pub. 1987-91, mem. disaster relief task force, bd. dirs., commr., chmn. ABA Commn. on Advt. 1988-91, adv. coun. ABA Commn. Responsibility 1999—), Pa. Bar Assn. (pres. 1985-86, bd. dirs. 1983-90, chair Governance Com., 1996-98), Phila. Bar Found. (pres. 1981), Phila. Bar Assn. (v.p. 1978, pres.-elect 1979, chancellor 1980, sec. 1975-78, trustee 1979—), Pa. Bar Trust (life mem., chmn. 1993-2001, chmn. emeritus 2001—), Pa. House of Dels. (life; chair governance com. 1996-98), Nat. Met. Bar Leaders (founder, pres. 1979-82, pres. emeritus 1983—), Nat. Conf. Bar Pres. (exec. coun. 1981-84), Phila. C. of C. (bd. dirs. 1980-83). Republican. Jewish. Avocations: golf, sailing. Office: Christie Pabarue Mortensen & Young 1880 JFK Blvd Fl 10 Philadelphia PA 19103-7424 Home: 110 S Somerset Ave Ventnor City NJ 08406 Home Phone: 267-408-5390; Office Phone: 215-587-1692. Business E-Mail: jebogutz@cmpy.com.

BOGY, DAVID B(EAUREGARD), mechanical engineering educator; b. Wabbaseka, Ark., June 4, 1936; s. Jesse C. and Dorothy (Duff) B.; m. Patricia Lynn Pizzitola, Mar. 28, 1961; children: Susan, Rebecca. BS, Rice U., 1959, MS, 1961; PhD, Brown U., 1966. Mech. engr. Shell Devel. Co., Houston, 1961-63; asst. prof. mech. engring. U. Calif., Berkeley, 1967-70, assoc. prof., 1970-75, prof., 1975—, chmn. dept. mech. engring., 1991-99, founder, dir. computer mechanics lab., William S. Floyd, Jr. Disting. prof., 1993—. Cons. IBM Rsch., 1972-83 Contbr. some 300 articles to profl. jours. Served with C.E. U.S. Army, 1961-62. Fellow ASME, IEEE; mem. NAE. Achievements include research in static and dynamic elasticity, fluid jets and mechanics of computer disk files and printers. Home: 8531 Buckingham Dr El Cerrito CA 94530-2533 Office: U Calif 6103 Etcheverry Hall Berkeley CA 94720-1740 Office Phone: 510-642-2570. Business E-Mail: dbogy@berkeley.edu.

BOHAN, GLORIA, travel company executive; BA, Marymount Manhattan Coll., LLD with hon., 2003. With Forbes Mag.; pres. Omega World Travel, Fairfax, Va., 1972—. Bd. dirs. Am. Bus. Conf., Greater Washington Bd. Trade. With Race for the Cure, Suited for Change, Leukemia Lymphoma Soc., Salvation Army; bd. mem. Fairfax County Edn. Found, Enterprising Women Mag, C. of C., Va. Found. Independent Coll. Recipient Woman Yr., Network Entrepreneurial Women, 1990, Entrepreneurial Visionary award, 2003; named Businesswoman of Yr., Office Depot, 2004; named to Enterprising Women Hall of Fame, 2005. Mem. Nat. Assn. Women Bus. Owners, Am. Soc. Travel Agts. (Travel Agt. of Yr. award 2004), Soc. Govt. Travel Profls. (pres. 1986-87). Office: Omega World Travel Inc 3102 Omega Office Park Fairfax VA 22031-2400 Office Phone: 703-359-0200. Fax: 703-350-8880. E-mail: gbohan@owt.net.

BOHAN, LAWRENCE STEWART, retired insurance company executive; b. Memphis, Mar. 26, 1929; s. George Patrick and Mary Stewart Bohan; m. Joan Milas Bohan, July 13, 1984; 1 child, Kimberly. BA, Yale U., 1951; JD, NYU, 1954. Bar: Conn. 1954. Atty. Gumbart, Corbin, Tyler & Cooper, New Haven, 1954—58, Bohan, Hitt, Mihalakos & Sachner, Meriden, Conn., 1960—78; pres., CEO Conn. Attys. Title Ins. Co., Rocky Hill, 1979—2000. Pres. Nat. Assn. Bar-Related Title Insurers, 1980. Pres. Meriden YMCA, 1965—66; bd. chmn. Meriden-Wallingford Hosp., 1978—79. Recipient Outstanding Profl. Svc. award, Conn. Bar Assn., 1991; Root Tilden scholar, NYU Law Sch. Fellow: Conn. Bar Found., Am. Bar Found.; mem.: Phi Beta Kappa. Home: 255 Acorn Dr Middletown CT 06457 Personal E-mail: lsbohan@aol.com.

BOHAN, THOMAS LYNCH, physicist, lawyer; b. Terre Haute, Ind., Feb. 12, 1938; s. Richard Timothy and Anna Elizabeth (Lynch) Bohan; m. Linda Ann Sian, Nov. 26, 1960 (div. Dec. 1981); children: Richard Michael, Cecilia Anne, John Charles; m. Rhonda Beth Berg, July 4, 1987. BS in Physics, U. Chgo., 1960; MS in Physics, U. Ill., 1964, PhD in Physics, 1968; JD, Franklin Pierce Law Ctr., 1980. Bar: Maine 1980, Mass. 1980, U.S. Dist. Ct. Maine 1980, U.S. Patent Office 1980, U.S. Ct. Appeals (1st cir.) 1992, U.S. Ct. Appeals (2nd cir.) 1994, U.S. Supreme Ct. 1996. Rsch. assoc. U. Ill., Urbana, 1968—69; asst. prof. physics Bowdoin Coll., Brunswick, Maine, 1969—76; assoc. Sunenblick, Fontaine and Reben, Portland, Maine, 1980—82; ptnr. Med. and Tech. Cons. (now MTC Forensics), Portland, 1982—86, sole propr., 1986—; propr. Thomas L. Bohan & Assoc., Portland, 1985—2001, Bohan Mathers, Portland, 2002, of counsel, 2003—. Instr. US Dept. Justice, Colombia, 2006—. Editor (with A. Damask): Forensic Accident Investigation: Motor Vehicles-1, 1995; editor: Forensic Accident Investigation: Motor Vehicles-2, 1997; mem. editl. bd.: Jour. Forensic Scis., 2005—; contbr. articles to profl. jours. Chmn. Community Devel. Com., Brunswick, 1976—78; organizer, treas., pres. Peaks Island Land Preserve, Inc., 1994—97; dual citizenship US and Ireland. Fellow, Tex. Instruments, 1965; Rsch. grantee, Am. Heart Assn., 1970—76, The Rsch. Corp., 1972—74, NSF/NATO, 1967, Fulbright scholar, Peru, 1972—73. Fellow: Am. Acad. Forensic Sci. (chair engring. sci. sect. 1997—98, bd. dir. 1999—2005, exec. com. bd. dir. 2000—05, v.p. 2005—06, treas. 2006—); mem.: AAAS, Forensic Specialties Accreditation Bd. (bd. dir. 2005—), Internat. Inst. Forensic Engring. Scis. (bd. dir. 2005—), Maine Patent Practitioners Group, Maine Trial Lawyers Assn., Cumberland County Bar Assn., Am. Phys. Soc., Sigma Xi. Office: MTC Forensics 54 Pleasant Ave Peaks Island ME 04108-1188 also: Bohan Mathers PO Box 17707 Portland ME 04112-8707 Office Phone: 207-766-5184. Personal E-mail: tbohan2@maine.rr.com. Business E-Mail: tlb@mtcforensics.com, tlb@bohanmathers.com.

BOHANAN, DAVID JOHN, management consultant; b. Utica, NY, Dec. 13, 1946; s. Clifton Ralph and Florence Susan Bohanan; m. Judith Ann Petrocci, July 31, 1977; children: Luke, Jacob. BFA in Ceramics and Painting, Alfred U., 1968; BS in Commerce, U. Md., 1979; MBA in Mgmt., Boston U., 1981. Pub. R&R in the Med Mediterranean Pubs. Srl., Vicenza, Italy, 1974-81; pvt. practice fin. cons. Jersey City, 1981-86; bus. cons. S&B Practice Mgmt. Assocs., Greenbrook, NJ, 1986—; fin. planner Fin. Found., Inc., Greenbrook, NJ, 1986-98. Rep. Nathan & Lewis Securities, Inc., N.Y.C., 1982-93, Cadaret, Grant & Co., Syracuse, N.Y., 1994-2000, Nat. Planning Corp., 2001—. Capt. F.A., U.S. Army, 1968-74. Decorated Bronze Star with oak leaf cluster. Republican. Home: 10 Saw Mill Rd Lebanon NJ 08833-4618 Office: S&B Practice Mgmt Assocs 314 Us Highway 22 Green Brook NJ 08812-1700 E-mail: dave@bohanan.com.

BOHANNON, CHARLES TAD, lawyer; b. Dallas, June 25, 1964; s. Charles Spencer and Donna Pauline (Smith) B.; m. Gayle Renee Alston, July 26, 1986. BA, Hendrix Coll., 1986; JD, U. Ark., Little Rock, 1992; LLM, Washington U., St. Louis, 1993. Bar: Ark. 1992, Tex. 1993, U.S. Dist. Ct. (ea. and we. dists.) Ark. 1992, U.S. Dist. Ct. (no. dist.) Tex. 1994, U.S. Ct. Appeals (5th and 8th cirs.) 1994, U.S. Tax Ct. 1994. Staff atty. U.S. Ct. Appeals (8th cir.), St. Louis, 1992-94; assoc. Gill Law Firm, Little Rock, 1994-98; ptnr. Wright, Lindsey & Jennings, LLP, Little Rock, 1998—. Contbr. articles to profl. jours. Mem. ABA, Ark. Bar Assn., Pulaski County Bar Assn., Nat. Transp. Safety Bd., Bar Assn. State Bar of Tex., Nat. Assn. Bond Lawyers, Aircraft Owners and Pilots Assn. Avocations: soccer (player, referee, coach), flying, fly fishing, home renovation. Office: Wright Lindsey & Jennings 200 W Capitol Ave Ste 2300 Little Rock AR 72201-3699 Office Phone: 501-371-0808. E-mail: ctbohannon@wlj.com.

BOHANNON, PAUL M., lawyer; b. Cushing, Okla., May 20, 1950; s. Marvin J. and Marscia (Hughes) Bohannon; m. Cynthia J. James, June 1, 1974; 1 child, Brenton. BA, Okla. State U., 1972; JD, So. Meth. U., 1975. Bar: Tex. 1975, N. Mex. 1976, admitted to practice: US Ct. Appeals (5th Cir.) 1975, US Ct. Appeals (10th Cir.) 1975, US Dist. Ct. (N. Mex.) 1976, US Dist. Ct. (We. Dist.) Tex. 1983, US Dist. Ct. (No. Dist.) Tex. 1983, US Dist. Ct. (So. Dist.) Tex., US Supreme Ct. Ptnr. Hinkle, Cox, Eaton, Coffield & Hensley, Roswell, N.Mex., 1975—83, Midland, Tex., 1983; ptnr., Environ. Practice Group Andrews Kurth LLP, The Woodlands, Tex. Mem.: State Bar N.Mex., N.Mex. Oil & Gas Assn. (founding chmn. environ. affairs com. 1988—91), State Bar Tex. (environ. law com.), Am. Arbitration Assn. (panel arbitrators), Am. Mgmt. Assn., ABA (water quality com. 1980, Environ. Law Sect.), Delta Theta Phi, Order of Coif. Democrat. Episcopalian. Office: Andews Kurth LLP 10001 Woodloch Forest Dr Ste 200 The Woodlands TX 77380 Office Phone: 713-220-4193. Office Fax: 713-238-7180. Business E-Mail: pbohannon@andrewskurth.com.

BOHANNON, SARAH VIRGINIA, personnel professional; b. Roanoke, Va., Mar. 1, 1947; AA in Bus. Adminstrn. Mgmt., Nat. Bus. Coll., 1983. Pers. appointment clk. IRS, Richmond, Va., 1983—84; pers. technician Commonwealth of Va., Richmond, Va., 1985—97, pers. asst., 1997—98, pers. technician, 1999—2000, pers. adminstrv. specialist dept. human resource mgmt., 2001—02; human resources rep. City of Richmond, 2004. Mem. Am. Biog. Inst. (life, dep. gov. 1991, mem. women's inner circle of achievement 1991). Home: 8006 Anoka Rd Richmond VA 23229-3308

BOHANNON-KAPLAN, MARGARET ANNE, non-profit organization executive, lawyer; b. Oakland, Calif., July 6, 1937; d. Thomas Morris and Ruth Frances (Davenport) Bohannon; m. Melvin Jordan Kaplan, Feb. 2, 1961; children: Mark Geoffrey Kaplan, Craig Andrew Kaplan, Stephen Joseph Kaplan, David Benjamin Kaplan, Jonathan Michael Kaplan. Student, Smith Coll., 1955-56, U. Cin., 1956; BA in Philosophy, U. Calif., Berkeley, 1960; LLB, LaSalle Extension U., 1982, Coll. Fin. Planning, 1985. Bar: Calif. 1982; cert. CFP. Engaged in property mgmt., real estate investment Kaplan Real Estate, Berkeley, San Francisco, 1961-77; investment exec. Wellington Fin. Group, San Francisco, 1977—; cons. fin. planning and law San Francisco and Carmel, Calif., 1982—; pres. Wellington Publs., Carmel, 1983—, Exec. Advt., Carmel, 1983—; co-founder, dir. Harry Singer Found., 1987—, Nat. Non-profit 501 C-3 Oper. Found., 1987—. Talk show host Sta. KNRY, KIEZ, 1999. Author (pseudonym Helen P. Rogers): (book) Everyone's Guide to Financial Planning, 1984; author: Social Security: An Idea Whose Time Has Passed, 1985, The American Deficit: Fulfillment of a Prophecy, 1988, The Election Process, 1988, The Deficit: 12 Steps to Ease the Crisis, 1988, (books) Alternatives, 1992, Another Way, 1997, (11 book series) Taking a Stand On, 1991; editor: (books) What Role if Any, Should Government's Role be Regarding Child Care in the United States?, 1991, What if Any, Should Government's Role Be Regarding Health Care in the Untied States?, 1992, What Role Does, And What Role Should Media Play in Choosing Our Candidates for National Office?, 1993, 1997, Doesn't Anyone Care About the Children?, 1994, Responsibility: Who Has It and Who Doesn't and What That Means to the Nation, 1994, 1996—98, White Hats: People Who Try to Make a Difference, 1994, Governments Struggling with Limited Resources, 1995—97, Should Government Intervene to Help Children and Teens in Trouble, If So How?, 1995, Social Security in the Twenty-First Century, 1996, Excerpts from Three 1997 Harry Singer Foundation National High School Essay Contests, 1997, The Budget Process and the National Debt, 1998, The Role of Personal Responsibility in Balancing Individual Liberty and the Common Good, 1999, Kids R Us, 2000, others, (books online) www.singerfoundation.org. Mem.: ABA, Ind. Sector, Fin. Planning Assn., Calif. Bar Assn., Philanthropy Round Table, Commonwealth Club (San Francisco). Office: PO Box 223159 Carmel CA 93922-3159 Home Phone: 831-238-3128; Office Phone: 831-625-4223. Business E-Mail: director@singerfoundation.org.

BOHANON, KATHLEEN SUE, neonatologist; b. Mpls., 1951; BA summa cum laude, U. Minn., 1973, MD, 1977. Diplomate Am. Bd. Pediat., Am. Bd. Neonatal-Perinatal Medicine. Commd. 2d lt. USAF, 1973, advanced through grades to col., 1995; resident in pediats. Case Western Res. U., Cleve., 1977-80; gen. pediatrician USAF, 1980-85; fellow in neonatology Wilford Hall Med. Ctr., San Antonio, 1985-87; neonatologist, dir. neonatal ICU USAF Med. Ctr., Wright-Patterson AFB, Ohio, 1987-95, chmn. dept. pediat., 1995-98, chief med. staff, 1998-2000; ret., 2000; locum tenens neonatologist, 2001—03; staff neonatologist St. Mary's Hosp. and Med. Ctr., Grand Junction, Colo., 2004—06; ret., 2006. Asst. clin. prof. pediat. U. N.D. Sch. Medicine, Grand Forks, 1981-82; assoc. Wright State U. Sch. Medicine, Dayton, Ohio, 1987-2000, Uniformed Svc. U. Health Scis., Washington, 1988-2000; mem. com. Infant Bio-Ethics Com., Dayton, 1990-2000. Fellow Am. Acad. Pediat.

BOHIGIAN, DAVID STEELE, federal agency administrator; b. Mar. 7, 1970; m. Catherine Bohigian. BA cum laude, Washington and Lee U.; JD, Wash. U., Mo. Founder VenCatalyst; mng. dir. Idealab; dir. Jefferson Ptnrs. LLC; asst. to sec. and dir. Office Policy and Strategic Planning US Dept. Commerce, Washington, dep. dir. Office Policy and Strategic Planning, exec. dir. Office of Faith- Based and Cmty. Initiatives, 2004, sr. advisor Office Policy and Strategic Planning, asst. sec. for market access and compliance, Internat. Trade Adminstrn., 2005—. Office: US Dept Commerce Herbert Clark Hoover Bldg 14th St and Constitution Ave, Rm 3868 Washington DC 20230 Office Phone: 202-482-3022. Office Fax: 202-482-5444. E-mail: dbohigian@doc.gov.

BOHLE, SUE, public relations executive; b. Austin, Minn., June 23, 1943; d. Harold Raymond and Mary Theresa (Swanson) Hastings; m. John Bernard Bohle, June 22, 1974; children: Jason John, Christine K. BS in Journalism, Northwestern U., 1965, MS in Journalism, 1969. Tchr. pub. high schs, Englewood, Colo., 1965-68; account exec. Burson-Marsteller Pub. Relations, Los Angeles, 1969-73; v.p., mgr. pub. relations J. Walter Thompson Co., Los Angeles, 1973-79; founder, pres. The Bohle Company, LA, 1979—; pres., CEO The Bohle Co., LA; former exec. v.p. Ketchum Comms., LA. Freelance writer, instr. comm. Calif. State U., Fullerton, 1972—73; instr. writing LA City Coll., 1975—76; lectr. U. So. Calif., 1979—. Contbr. articles to profl. jours. Dir. pub. rels. LA Jr. Ballet, 1971—72; pres. Panhellenic Advisers Coun. UCLA, 1972—73; mem. adv. bd. LA Valley Coll., 1974—75, Coll. Comm. Pepperdine U., 1981—85, Sch. Journalism U. So. Calif., 1987—95, Calif. State U., Long Beach, 1988—93; bd. visitors Medill Sch. Journalism Northwestern U., 1984—. Named charter mem., Hall of Fame; named to Hall of Achievement, Medill Sch. Journalism, 1997, 50 Top Women in PR, PR Week mag., 2001; recipient Alumni Svc. award, Northwestern U., 1995; Univ. scholar, 1961—64, Panhellenic scholar, 1964—65. Fellow: Pub. Rels. Soc. Am. (del. nat. assembly 1980, bd. dirs. LA chpt. 1981—90, v.p. 1983, mem. exec. com. counselors Acad. 1984—86, pres. 1989, co-chmn. long-range strategic com. 1990, sec.-treas. 1990, pres.'s adv. coun. 1991, chmn. 1992, sec. Coll. Fellows 1993, vice chair 1994, del. nat. assembly 1994—96, chmn. 1995, Silver Anvil award 1990, 1994, Best Show award, Sabre award 2000, Best of Show Prisms award 2005, named in Top 100 Women in Gaming 2006); mem.: Accrediting Coun. Edn. Journalism and Mass Comms. (mem. accreditation coun. 2005—07), Women in Comm., World com., Worldcom PR Network, Shai-ai, Kappa Alpha Tau, Delta Zeta (Woman of the Yr. award 1993). Office: 1900 Avenue of the Stars # 200 Los Angeles CA 90067-4301 Office Phone: 310-785-0515 ext. 223. E-mail: sue@bohle.com.

BOHLEN, KENNETH C., multi-industry company executive; BS in Computer Sci., Iowa State U., Ames; MBA, U. Iowa, Iowa City. Various info. and mfg. tech. positions up to head info. svcs. Waterloo ops. Deere & Co.; various sr. positions including v.p. supply chain, chief info. officer Engines, v.p. Six Sigma and dir. supply chain and bus. process improvement AlliedSignal Inc., v.p., chief info. officer Aerospace Group; sr. v.p., chief info. officer Textron, Inc., Providence, 1999—2000, exec. v.p., chief innovation officer, 2000—. Mem. adv. bd. IBM. Named one of Premier 100 Info. Tech. Leaders, Computerworld, 2006. Mem.: Am. Prodn. Inventory Control Soc., Soc. Human Resource Mgmt., Soc. Mfg. Engrs.' Computer and Automated Systems Assn. Office: Textron Inc 40 Westminster St Providence RI 02903 Office Phone: 401-421-2800.*

BOHLENDER, HUGH DARROW, lawyer; b. Sacramento, Oct. 27, 1951; s. Hugh S. and Dorothy Elrene (Darrow) B.; m. Eliese Susanna Wagenseil, June 9, 1973 (div. Feb. 1982); children: Philip Edward, Karen Leslie; m. Ingrid Elizabeth Rieck, Dec. 27, 1997. BS, U.S. Mil. Acad., 1973; MA, Northwestern U., 1982, JD, 1986, postgrad. Bar: Ill. 1986, U.S. Dist. Ct. (no dist.) Ill. 1986. Commd. 2d lt. U.S. Army, 1975, advanced through grades to capt., 1977, resigned, 1981; lectr. Northwestern U., Evanston, Ill., 1984—85; assoc. Lord Bissell & Brook, Chgo., 1986—90; of counsel Allstate Ins. Co., 1990—. Dir. Ala. Ins. Guaranty Assn., 1992-93. Vice chmn. Northbrook (Ill.) Evang. Covenant Ch., 1988-91. Maj. USAR, 1986-93; ret. Mem. ABA, Ill. Bar Assn. Republican. Avocations: running, bicycling, camping, photography, computers. Office: Allstate Ins Co Allstate Plz N Northbrook IL 60062

BOHLIN, DAWN LENORE, electrical engineer; b. Ill., Jan. 13, 1980; m. Bret Bohlin, June 4, 2005. BSEE, U. Ill., Chgo., 2002, MS in Elec. and Computer Engring., 2006. Cert. infrared tech., Ga. Tech U., 2005. EO/IR test and integration engr. Northrop Grumman Corp., Rolling Meadows, Ill., 2002—. Achievements include patents pending for energy on detector measurement method and equipment. Office: 600 S Hicks Rd Rolling Meadows IL 60008

BOHLIN, PETER QUARFORDT, architect; b. Mt. Vernon, NY, Mar. 27, 1937; s. Eric Quarfordt and Ann (Wehmeyer) B.; m. Ann H. Sanders, July 6, 1963 (div.); children: Eve Sanders, Nathaniel Quarfordt; m. Sally Edwards Preate, Sept. 29, 1991. BArch, Rensselaer Poly. Inst., Troy, NY, 1959; MArch, Cranbrook Acad. of Art, Bloomfield Hills, Mich., 1961. Jr. draftsman, designer William Lescaze, FAIA, NYC, 1956; project designer Whitby-Nelson Assocs., Hazleton, Pa., 1960-62, Carl J. Schmidtt & Son, Archs., Wilkes-Barre, Pa., 1962-65; prin. Bohlin Cywinski Jackson, Wilkes-Barre, Pitts., Phila., Seattle, 1965—; Kea prof. architecture U. Md., 1987. Fellow AIA (chair com. on design, Honor award 1981, 84, 90, Gold medal 1987, Honor Award VII Bienal de Arquitectura de Quito, 1990); silver medal Phila. Chpt. AIA, 1992, mem. Pa. Soc. Archs. (Silver medal 1979, 82, 83, 88, 90), Nat. Libr. Bldgs. Design Award of ALA and the AIA, 1991, Grand Award of the Western Red Cedar Lumber Assn., 1992, Soc. Archtl. Historians. Office: Bohlin Cywinski Jackson 307 4th Ave Ste 1300 Pittsburgh PA 15222-2113 also: Bohlin Cywinski Jackson 8 W Market St Ste 1200 Wilkes Barre PA 18701 Office Phone: 570-825-8756. Office Fax: 570-825-3744.*

BOHLINGER, JOHN C., lieutenant governor, former state legislator; b. Bozeman, Mont., Apr. 21, 1936; s. John and Aileen Bohlinger; m. Bette J. Bohlinger (dec. Jan. 2006); 6 children. BA, U. Mont., 1959. Owner women's apparel store, 1961-92; mem. Mon. Ho. Reps. Dist. 14 & 94, 1993—98, Mont. State Senate, Dist. 7, Helena, 1998—2004; mem. local govt. com., pub. health, welfare and safety com.; mem. taxation com., vice chair ethics com.; lt. gov. State of Mont., 2005—. Past pres., chmn. bd. Yellowstone Arts Ctr.; bd. dirs. Billings Symphony Soc., St. Vincent de Paul Soc., Mont. State U. Billings Found., Yellowstone Treatment Ctr. Served with USMC, 1954-61. Mem. Billings Rotary Cub. Republican. Roman Catholic. Office: Office Lt Gov Capitol Station PO Box 200801 Helena MT 59620 Office Phone: 406-444-5665.

BOHM, HENRY VICTOR, physicist; b. Vienna, July 16, 1929; came to U.S., 1941, naturalized, 1946; s. Victor Charles and Gertrude (Rie) B.; m. Lucy Margaret Coons, Sept. 2, 1950 (dec. Oct. 2003); children: Victoria Rie, Jeffrey Ernst Thompson. AB, Harvard U., 1950; MS, U. Ill., 1951; PhD, Brown U., 1958. Jr. physicist GE, 1951, 53-54; teaching, research asst. Brown U., 1954-58, research assoc., summer 1958; staff mem. Arthur D. Little, Inc., Cambridge, Mass., 1958-59; asso. prof. physics dept. Wayne State U., Detroit, 1959-64, acting chmn. physics dept., 1962-63, prof., 1964-93, prof. emeritus Detroit, 1993—, v.p. for grad. studies and research, 1968-71, v.p. for spl. projects, 1971-72, provost, 1972-75, on leave, 1978-83, interim dean Coll. Liberal Arts, 1984-86; pres. Argonne Univs. Assn., 1978-83. Vis. prof. Cornell U., 1966-67, U. Lancaster, Eng., summer 1967, Purdue U., winter, 1977, Rensselaer Poly. Inst., winter 1992; cons.-examiner commn. on instns. higher edn. N. Central Assn. Colls. and Schs., 1971-80, mem. commn., 1974-78. Bd. dirs. Center for Research Libraries, Chgo, 1970-75, chmn., 1973; bd. overseers Lewis Coll., Ill. Inst. Tech., 1980-83. Ltjg. USNR, 1951—53. Fellow Am. Phys. Soc.

BOHM, RICHARD D., lawyer; b. Apr. 8, 1953; BA, Stanford U., 1975; JD, Harvard U., 1978. Assoc. Debevoise & Plimpton LLP, NYC, 1978—86, ptnr., 1986—, co-head Media & Tech. and Private Equity Groups, mem. Mergers & Acquisitions and Securities Groups. Mem.: ABA, Assn. Bar City NY. Office: Debevoise & Plimpton LLP 919 Third Ave New York NY 10022 Office Phone: 212-909-6226. E-mail: rdbohm@debevoise.com.

BOHME, DIETHARD KURT, chemistry professor; b. Boston, June 20, 1941; s. Kurt F. and Maria (Kiesel) B. B.Sc., McGill U., 1962, PhD, 1965. Asst. prof. dept. chemistry York U., Toronto, Ont., 1970-74, assoc. prof. Ont., 1974-77, prof. chemistry Ont., 1977—, disting. rsch. prof. chemistry Ont., 1994—, dir. grad. program in chemistry Ont., 1979-85, chmn. dept. chemistry Ont., 1985—90, Ont., 2000—03, Can. rsch. chair in phys. chemistry tier 1 Ont., 2001; mem. chemistry grant selection com. Nat. Scis. and Engring. Rsch. Coun. of Can., Ottawa, 1983-86. Contbr. articles to profl. jours. NAS-NRC postdoctoral rsch. assoc., 1965-67; A.P. Sloan fellow, 1974, sr. scientist vis. fellow U. Warwick, Eng., 1978, Killam rsch. fellow, 1991-93; recipient Rutherford Meml. medal in chemistry Royal Soc. Can., 1981, A.v. Humboldt rsch. award, 1990, 99, John C. Polanyi award in Phys. and Theoretical Chemistry, 1998, Fred P. Lossing award in mass spectrometry Can. Soc. for Mass Spectrometry, 2002, Gerhard Herzberg award Can. Soc. for Analytical Scis. and Spectroscopy, 2006. Fellow Royal Soc. Can., Chem. Inst. Can. (phys. chemistry divsn. exec. 1980-83, Noranda lectr. in phys. chemistry 1983, medal 2007); mem. Am. Soc. Mass Spectrometry, Am. Chem. Soc. Home: 38 Alberta Dr Concord ON Canada L4K 4X5 Office: York U Dept Chemistry 4700 Keele St Toronto ON Canada M3J 1P3 Home Phone: 905-303-8018; Office Phone: 416-736-2100 ext 66188. E-mail: dkbohme@yorku.ca.

BOHN, DENNIS ALLEN, engineering executive; b. Oct. 5, 1942; s. Raymond Virgil and Iris Elouise (Johnson) Bohn; m. Patricia Tolle, Aug. 12, 1986; 1 child, Kira Michelle. BSEE with honors, U. Calif., Berkeley, 1972, MSEE with honors, 1974. Engring. technician GE Co., San Leandro, Calif., 1964—72; R & D engr. Hewlett-Packard Co., Santa Clara, Calif., 1973; application engr. Nat. Semicondr. Corp., Santa Clara, 1974—76; engring. mgr. Phase Linear Corp., Lynnwood, Wash., 1976—82; v.p. R & D, ptnr. Rane Corp., Mukilteo, Wash., 1982—; founder Toleco Systems, Kingston, Wash., 1980. Editor: We Are Not Just Daffodils, 1975; contbr. poetry to Reason mag.; tech. editor Audio Handbook, 1976; contbr. articles to tech. jours.; columnist Polyphony mag., 1981—83. Suicide and crisis ctr. vol., Berkeley, 1972—74, Santa Clara, 1974—76. With USAF, 1960—64. Recipient Am. Spirit Honor medal, USAF, 1961, Math. Achievement award, Chem. Rubber Co., 1962—63. Mem.: IEEE, Audio Engring. Soc., Tau Beta Pi. Achievements include 3 patents in field. Office: Rane Corp 10802 47th Ave W Mukilteo WA 98275-5098 Business E-Mail: dennisb@rane.com.

BOHN, RALPH CARL, educational consultant; b. Detroit, Feb. 19, 1930; s. Carl and Bertha (Abrams) B.; m. Adella Stanul, Sept. 2, 1950 (dec.); children: Cheryl Ann, Jeffrey Ralph; m. JoAnn Olvera Butler, Feb. 19, 1977 (div. 1990); stepchildren: Kathryn J., Kimberly J., Gregory E.; m. Mariko Tajima, Jan. 27, 1991; 1 child, Thomas Carl; 1 stepchild, Daichi Tajima. BS, Wayne State U., 1951, EdM, 1954, EdD, 1957. Instr. part-time Wayne State U., 1954-55, summer 1956; faculty San Jose (Calif.) State U., 1955-92, prof. div. tech., 1961-92, chmn. dept. indsl. studies, 1960-69, assoc. dean ednl. svc., 1968-70, dean continuing edn., 1970-92, prof. emeritus, 1992—; cons. Calif. State U. Sys., 1992—; cons. quality edn. sys. USAF, 1992-2000; dir. nat. program on non-collegiate sponsored instrn. Calif. State Univ. Sys., 1995—2000, Calif. State U. Inst., 1997—99; pres. Univ. Cons., 1994—. Guest faculty Colo. State Coll., 1963, Ariz. State U., 1966, U. P.R., 1967, 74, So. Ill. U., 1970, Oreg. State U., 1971, Utah State U., 1973, Va. Poly. Inst. & State U., 1973, U. Idaho, 1978; cons. U.S. Office Edn., 1965-70, Calif. Pub. Schs., 1960, Nat. Assessment Ednl. Progress, 1968-79, ednl. div. Philco-Ford Corp., 1970-73, Am. Inst. Rsch., 1969-83, Far West Labs for Ednl. Rsch. Devel., 1971-86; adv. bd. Ctr. for Vocat. and Tech. Edn., Ohio State U., 1968-74; dir. project Vocat. Edn. Act, 1965-67, NDEA, 1967, 68; co-dir. Project Edn. Profession Devel. Act, 1969, 70; mem. commn. coll. and univ. contracts Western Assn. Schs. and Colls, 1976-78, chmn. spl. com. on off-campus instrn. and continuing edn., 1978-88; chmn. continuing edn. accreditation visit U. Santa Clara, 1976; chmn. accreditation team Nellis AFB, Nev., 1992, 2002, U. Nev., Las Vegas, 2000, Nat. U., 2000, Oreg. State U., 2001, Golden Gate U., 2001; chmn. accreditation team to Yokusaka Naval Sta., Japan, 2000, Atsugi Naval Air Facility, Japan, 2000, Yokota Air Base, Japan, 2000, Camp Pendleton Marine Corps Base, 2001, 07, Naval Air Sta., Lamoore, 2002, Dyess AFB, 2003, Twentynine Palms Marine Corps. Base, Calif., 2003, eArmyU web-based degree programs U.S. Army, Washington, 2004, Camp Zama, Army, Tokyo, 2004, Iwakuni Marine Corps Air Sta., Japan, 2005, Osan AFB, Korea, 2005, Junsan AFB, Korea, 2005, Scott AFB, Ill., 2005, Offutt AFB, Nebr., 2005, Misawa AFB, Japan, 2006, US Army Command and Gen. Staff Coll. Coll., Kans., 2006, Sasebo Navel Fleet Base, Japan, 2006, Kitsap Naval Base, Washington, 2007, others; sr. cons. Global Partnership Devel. Calif. State U. Sys., 2000-03. Author: (with G.H. Silvius) Organizing Course Materials for Industrial Education, 1961, Planning and Organizing Instruction, 1976; (with A. MacDonald) Power-Mechanics of Energy Control, 1970, 2d edit., 1983, The McKnight Power Experimenter, 1970, Power and Energy Technology, 1989, Energy Technology: Power and Transportation, 1992; (with others) Basic Industrial Arts and Power Mechanics, 1978, Technology and Society: Interfaces with Industrial Arts, 1980, Fundamentals of Safety Education, 3d edit., 1981, Energy, Power and Transportation Technology, 1986; (with A. MacDonald) Energy Technology, Power and Transportation, 1991; editor (with Ralph Norman) Graduate Study in Industrial Arts, 1961; indsl. arts editor Am. Vocat. Jour., 1963-66; editor Jour. Indsl. Tchr. Edn., 1962-64. Lt. (j.g.) USCGR, 1951-53, capt. Res. ret. Recipient award Am. Legion, 1945; Wayne State U. scholar, 1953. Mem. NEA, Nat. Assn. Indsl. Tech. (bd. accreditation), Am. Indsl. Arts. Assn. (pres. 1967-68, Ship's citation 1971), Am. Coun. Indsl. Art Tchrs. Edn. (pres. 1964-66, Man of Yr. award 1967), Nat. Univ. Continuing Edn. Assn. (chair accreditation com. 1988-91), Nat. Assn. Indsl. Tchr. Educators (past v.p.), Calif. Indsl. Edn. Assn. (State Ship's citation 1971), Am. Drive Edn. Assn., Nat. Fluid Power Soc., Am. Vocat. Assn. (svc. awards 1966, 67), N.Am. Assn. for Summer Sessions (v.p. western region 1976-78), Luth. Acad. Scholarship, Calif. Employees Assn. (pres. San Jose State Coll. chpt. 1966-67), Western Assn. Summer Session Adminstrs. (newsletter editor 1970-73, pres. 1974-75), Calif. C. of C. (edn. com 1969-77), Industry-Edn. Coun. Calif. (bd. dirs. 1974-80), Sci. and Human Values, Inc. (bd. dirs. 1974-2003, chmn. bd. 1976-2002), Tahoe Tavern (bd. dirs. 1987-91, chmn. bd. 1988-90), Seascape Lagoon Homeowners Assn. (bd. dirs. 1988-95, chmn. 1989-95), Nat. Gold Key Honors Soc. (hon. life). Home and Office: 713 Clubhouse Dr Aptos CA 95003-5431 Personal E-mail: rmbohn@cruzio.com.

BOHN, ROBERT G., transportation company executive; Dir. ops. European automotive group Johnson Controls; v.p. ops. Oshkosh (Wis.) Truck Corp., 1992—94, pres., COO, 1994-97, pres., CEO, 1997—2000, chmn., pres., CEO, 2000—. Bd. dir. Graco Inc. Office: Oshkosh Truck Corp 2307 Oregon St Oshkosh WI 54902*

BOHN, ROBERT HERBERT, lawyer; b. Austin, Tex., Sept. 2, 1935; s. Herbert and Alice B.; m. Gay P. Maloy, June 4, 1957; children: Rebecca Shoemaker, Katherine Bernat, Robert H., Jr. BBA, U. Tex., 1957, LLB, 1963. Bar: Tex. 1963, Calif. 1965. Ptnr. Boccardo Law Firm, San Jose, Calif., 1965-87, Alexander & Bohn, San Jose, 1987-91, Bohn, Bennion & Niland, 1992-97, Bohn & Bohn LLP, 1998—. Spkr. Calif. Continuing Edn. of Bar; judge pro tem Superior Ct. of Calif., San Jose, 1975-2006. Named one of Super Lawyers No. Calif., San Francisco Mag., 2005, 2006, Best Lawyers Silicon Valley, San Jose Mag., 1995—2007; named to Best Lawyers in Am., 1995, 2006. Mem. AAJ, Am. Coll. Master Barristers and Advs., Consumer Attys. Calif., Am. Bd. Trial Advocates, Santa Clara County Bar Assn., Calif. State Bar Assn., Santa Clara County Trial Lawyers Assn. (pres. 1999, Trial Lawyer of Yr. 2000), Trial Lawyers Pub. Justice, Roscoe Pound Found., Million Dollar Advocates Forum, Silicon Valley Capital Club, Commonwealth Club, Texas Cowboys Assn., Phi Gamma Delta. Office: 152 N 3rd St Ste 200 San Jose CA 95112-5515 E-mail: bbohn@bohnlaw.com.

BOHNEN, MICHAEL J., lawyer, foundation administrator; b. Buffalo, 1947; m. Joyce B. Oppenheim, 1969; children: Sharon, Deborah. BA, Harvard U., 1968, JD, 1972. Bar: Mass. 1972. Assoc. Nutter, McClennen & Fish, LLP, Boston, 1972-80, ptnr., 1980—2006, of counsel, 2007—; pres. Adelson Family Charitable Found., Needham, Mass., 2007—. Lectr. Boston U. Law Sch., 1981—2001. Co-author: Mass. Corporate Forms, 1990-2006. Pres. Solomon Schechter Day Sch., Newton, 1980—82; chmn. Jewish Coun. for Pub. Affairs, 2002—04; trustee United Jewish Cmtys., 1999—2007; pres. Jewish Cmty. Rels. Coun., Boston, 1991—93; chmn. Combined Jewish Philanthropies, 1993—95, Gann Acad., 1995—2006. Mem. Boston Bar Assn. (chmn. corp. law com. 1997-99). Office: Adelson Family Charitable Found 300 First Ave Needham MA 02494

BOHO, DAN L., lawyer; b. Chgo., Sept. 18, 1952; s. Lawrence M. and Genevieve A. (Zurek) Boho; m. Sheri L. Krisco, Sept. 10, 1977; children: Courtney, Ashely. BA, Loyola U., Chgo., 1974, JD, 1977. Bar: Ill. 1977, US Dist. Ct. (no. dist.) Ill. 1977. Sr. ptnr., leader litig. group Hinshaw & Culbertson, Chgo., 1977—. Fellow: Am. Coll. Trial Lawyers; mem.: ABA, Chgo. Bar Assn. (chmn. professionalism com.), Chgo. Trial Lawyers Club (past pres.), Ill. Bar Assn. (past del. assembly), Advs. Soc., Ill. Def. Coun., Def. Rsch. Inst., Ill. Soc. Trial Lawyers (past bd. dirs.), Fedn. Ins. and Corp. Counsel (past chmn. comml. law sect.), BOMA Chgo., Japan Am. Soc. (past bd. dirs.), Polish Am. Assn. (past chmn. bd. dirs.), Heartland Alliance (past bd. dirs.), Phi Alpha Delta (past pres. Webster chpt.). Avocations: travel, tennis, skiing. Office: Hinshaw & Culbertson 222 N La Salle St Ste 300 Chicago IL 60601-1081 Office Phone: 312-704-3453. Office Fax: 312-704-3001. Business E-Mail: dboho@hinshawlaw.com.

BOHR, MARK T., architectural engineer; b. Chgo., 1953; m. Jean Bohr; children: Russell, Sonja. BS, U. Ill.-Urbana-Champaign, 1976, MS in Elec. Engring., 1978. Joined Intel Corp., Hillsboro, Oreg., 1978, sr. fellow, dir. process architecture and integration Logic Tech. Devel. group, 1994—. Contbr. articles to profl. jours. Fellow: IEEE (Andrew S. Grove award 2003); mem.: NAE. Office: Intel Corp 5200 NE Elam Young Pkwy Hillsboro OR 97124

BOHRMAN, CATHERINE LEUCHS, sculptor; d. Frederick L. Leuchs and G. Marie Bidwell; m. David E. Bohrman, June 9, 1976; children: Amber Bohrman Warrington, Harrison Zerr. Student, Stanford U. Sculpture, Dawn Series, Dubai, United Arab Emirates, Legacy, Constitution Hall, Washington, Joan Scarangelo Found. award. Mem.: Foundry Gallery, DAR, Wash. Sculptors Group, Conn. Women Artists, Nat. Sculpture Soc. (colleague 1996), Greenwich Art Soc. (life; v.p. publicity 1985—2000), Nat. League Am. Pen Women (life; local and nat. bds. 1994). Home Phone: 202-462-8533. Personal E-mail: catherine@bohrman.com.

BOHRMAN, DAVID ELLIS, television news producer; b. Hollywood, Calif., Apr. 30, 1954; s. Stanford Mervyn and Ardelle Joyce (Coleman) B.; m. Catherine Marie Leuchs, June 9, 1976; children— Amber Catherine, Harrison Zerr. B.A. in French, Stanford U., 1976, B.S. in Phys. Sci., 1976; M.S. in Journalism, Columbia U., 1978. Producer KNXT, CBS, Los Angeles, 1978-80; field producer ABC News Nightline, N.Y.C., 1980-81, sr. producer, 1981-82; sr. producer ABC World News Tonight, 1982-84, ABC Polit. Broadcasts and Spl. Events, 1984-88, exec. prodr. ABC News Interactive, 1988-91, creator, exec. prodr. World News Now, 1991-93, combined unit World News Now, World News This Morning, Good Morning America News, 1992-93; exec. prodr. spl. events NBC News, 1993—97, v.p. and exec. in charge of "Moneyline with Lou Dobbs" CNNfn, 1998-99, exec. v.p. CNNfn, 1999, CEO, Pseudo Programs, 2000-01, sr. exec. prodr. NewsNight with Aaron Brown CNN, 2001-2004, v.p. news and prodn./Washington Bur. Chief CNN, 2004-. Patentee in field. Recipient Emmy award Nat. Acad. TV Arts and Sci., 1982, 87, 92, 94. Golden Mike awards Radio TV News Assn., 1979, Los Angeles Press Club award, 1979, Valley Press Club award, Nat. Assn. Working Women award, 1979, Dupont, Peabody, Polk awards for Nightline, Mac World Superstacks award, 1989, 90, Mac User award, 1991, Christopher award, Arthur Ashe award, 1995. Avocation: computers.

BOICE, CRAIG KENDALL, management consultant; b. Portland, Oreg., June 25, 1952; s. Charles A. and Audrey (Larson) B.; m. Jacinta E. Remedios, Nov. 21, 1979. BA summa cum laude, Beloit Coll., 1973; MA, Yale U., 1974, MPhil, 1976, M in Pub. and Pvt. Mgmt., 1979. Instr. fellow philosophy Yale U., New Haven, 1978-79; economist Overseas Pvt. Investment Corp., Washington, 1978; sr. cons. Coopers and Lybrand, Washington and London, 1979-81; v.p. ops. Internat. Licensing Network, NYC, 1981-82; pres., chmn., CEO Boice Dunham Group, NYC, 1983—. Adj. asst. prof. NYU, 1984-99. Cons. Lake Placid (NY) Olympic Organizing Com., 1979, New Haven Homesteading Program, 1979; chmn. edn. com. Automated Meter Reading Mem. Am. Mktg. Assn., Assn. Energy Engrs., Automated Meter Reading Assn., Computer and Automated Sys. Assn., Soc. Mfg. Engrs., Internat. Assn. Energy Econ., World Future Soc. Democrat. Office: Boice Dunham Group 30 W 13th St Apt 3C New York NY 10011-7988 E-mail: bdgbusdevl@msn.com.

BOICE, DANIEL GENE, college librarian; b. Grand Rapids, Mich., June 22, 1957; s. Daniel Grant and Janet Mae Boice; m. Gayla Rae Hibma, Dec. 28, 1977; 1 child, Daniel Francis. BA with honors, Calvin Coll., Grand Rapids, Mich., 1979; MA in History, U. Mich., Ann Arbor, 1982, MA in Libr. Sci., 1982. Asst. to libr. dir. No. Ill. U., DeKalb, 1982—83; reference libr. U. SC, Columbia, 1983—96; coll. libr. Divine Word Coll., Epworth, Iowa, 1996—. Author: The Mitchell Kennerley Imprint, 1997. Sec., trustee Pub. Libr. Bd., Dyersville, Iowa, 2002—; appointee Iowa Commn. Librs., 2006—. Mem.: KC, Cath. Libr. Assn. (bd. dirs. Divsn. II 1996—), Iowa Libr. Assn. Avocations: bicycling, stamp collecting/philately. Home: 404 4th Ave SE Dyersville IA 52040 Office: Divine Word Coll 102 Jacoby Dr SW Epworth IA 52045 Office Phone: 563-876-3353. E-mail: dboice@dwci.edu.

BOIES, DAVID, lawyer; b. Sycamore, Ill., Mar. 11, 1941; Attended, U. Redlands; BS, Northwestern U., 1964; JD, Yale U. Law Sch., 1966; LLM, NYU, 1967; LLD, U. Redlands, 2000. Chief counsel, staff dir. Senate Antitrust Subcom., 1978, Sen. Judiciary Com., 1979; assoc. Cravath, Swaine & Moore, NYC, 1966—72, ptnr., 1973—77, 1980—97; mng. partner Boies, Schiller, & Flexner, Armonk, NY, 1997—. Counsel FDIC, 1991—93; spl. trust counsel U.S. Dept. Justice; lead council Al Gore's presidential campaign, Florida recount, 2000. Author: Public Control of Business, 1977, Courting Justice: From New York Yankees v. Major League Baseball to Bush v. Gore, 1997-2000, 2004. Named Lawyer of the Year, Nat. Law Jour., 1999—2000; named one of 100 Most Influential Lawyers, 2006. Mem. ABA, N.Y. State Bar Assn., Assn. of Bar of City of N.Y; Fellow Am. Coll. of Trial Lawyers, Internat. Acad. Trial Lawyers; Phi Betta Kappa Office: Boies Schiller & Flexner LLP 333 Main St Armonk NY 10504 E-mail: dboies@bsfllp.com.*

BOIES, WILBER H., lawyer; b. Bloomington, Ill., Mar. 15, 1944; s. W. H. and Martha Jane (Hutchison) B.; m. Victoria Joan Steinitz, Sept. 17, 1966; children: Andrew Charles, Carolyn Ursula. AB, Brown U., 1965; JD, U. Chgo., 1968. Bar: Ill. 1968, U.S. Dist. Ct. (no. dist.) Ill. 1968, U.S. Dist. Ct. (ea. dist.) Wis. 1973, U.S. Ct. Appeals (7th cir.) 1974, U.S. Ct. Appeals (5th cir.) 1975, U.S. Ct. Appeals (3d cir.) 1977, U.S. Supreme Ct. 1978, U.S. Ct. Appeals (8th cir.) 1994, U.S. Ct. Appeals (9th cir.) 1995. Assoc. Altheimer & Gray, Chgo., 1968-71; ptnr. McDermott, Will & Emery, Chgo., 1971—. Contbr. articles to profl. jours. Active Internat Inst. for Conflict Prevention and Resolution, panel mem. Fellow Chgo. Bar Found-.(life); mem. ABA, Am. Bar Found., Bar Assn. 7th Fed. Cir., Chgo. Bar Assn. (chmn. class litigation com. 1991-92), Chgo. Coun. Lawyers, Lawyers Club Chgo., Met. Club. Office: McDermott Will & Emery 227 W Monroe St Ste 4400 Chicago IL 60606-5096 Office Phone: 312-984-7686. E-mail: bboies@mwe.com.

BOILER, ELIZABETH ANNE, literature and language educator; b. Washington, Aug. 12, 1974; d. William Fred and Judith Carol Boiler. BA in English and Drama with distinction, U. Va., Charlottesville, 1996, MA in English, 1999. Tutor writing ctr. U. Va., English Dept., Charlottesville, 1997, rsch. asst., 1997; libr. asst. rare books Huntington Libr., San Marino, Calif., 1998; reference and info. svcs. asst. Alderman Libr., Charlottesville, 1998; instr. English Luth. H.S., LaVerne, Calif., 1999, St. Lucy's Priory H.S., Glendora, Calif., 1999—; advanced placement reader Ednl. Testing Svc., Daytona Beach, Fla., 2006. Mem.: Nat. Coun. Tchrs. English, Modern Lang. Assn., Phi Beta Kappa.

BOILLAT, GUY MAURICE GEORGES, mathematical physicist; b. Pontarlier, France, May 18, 1937; s. Georges Paul Charles and Lucie Marguerite Charlotte (Jubin) B. Licence scis., U. Besançon, France, 1959; postgrad., Inst. Henri-Poincaré, Paris, 1959-60, Inst. Theoretical Physics, Copenhagen, 1960-62, Norwegian Tech. U., Trondheim; DSc, Sorbonne U., Paris, 1964. Assoc. prof. dept. math. U. Clermont, Aubière, France, 1966-69, prof., 1969—2004. Lectr., Italy, 1970—; researcher U. Messina, U. Catania, U. Bologna, Italy, 1970—. Co-author: Recent Mathematical Methods in Nonlinear Wave Propagation, 1996; contbr. 100 rsch. articles on nonlinear waves and fields to profl. jours. Dep. mem. Internat. Parliament for Safety and Peace. Recipient Commemorative Millennium Meml. award Albert Einstein Internat. Acad. Found. Mem.: Math. Assn. Am., Internat. Soc. for the Interaction of Mechanics and Math., Internat. Assn. Math. Physics, Am. Math. Soc., Unione Matematica Italiana, French Horological Assn. (bd. dirs. 1983—, sec. gen. 1998—), Acad. M.I.D.I., Maison Internat. Intellectuels (senator), Acad. Peloritana dei Pericolanti (corr.; Messina). Roman Catholic. Home: 16 rue Ronchaux 25000 Besancon France Personal E-mail: boillat@ciram.unibo.it.

BOIME, ALBERT ISAAC, art historian, educator; b. St. Louis, Mar. 17, 1933; s. Max and Dorothy (Rubin) B.; m. Myra Block, June 23, 1964; children: Robert, Eric. AB, UCLA, 1961; MA, Columbia U., 1963, PhD, 1968. Instr. social history of art Columbia U., 1966-67; assoc. prof. SUNY, Stony Brook, 1967-72, prof., chmn. dept. Binghamton, 1972-74, prof., 1974-78; prof. social history of art UCLA, 1978—. Art historian in residence Coll. Creative Studies, U. Calif.-Santa Barbara, 1973; judge NEH, Washington, 1975; mem. adv. council N.Y. Acad. Art, N.Y.C., 1981-. Author: The Academy and French Painting in the 19th Century, 1971, Thomas Couture and the Eclectic Vision, 1981, the Social History of Modern Art: Vol. 1: Art in an Age of Revolution, 1987, Hollow Icons: The Politics of Sculpture in Nineteenth Century France, 1987, Vincent Van Gogh: Sternennacht, 1989, The Art of Exclusion: Representing Blacks in the Nineteenth Century, 1990, The Social History of Modern Art Vol. 2: Art in an Age of Bonapartism, 1990, The Magisterial Gaze: Manifest Destiny and American Landscape Painting (ca. 1830-1865), 1991, The Art of the Macchia and the Risorgimento, 1993, The Odyssey of Jan Stussey in Black and White, 1995, Art and the French Commune, 1995, Violence and Utopia: The Work of Jerome Boime, 1996, The Unveiling of the National Icons: A Plea for Patriotic Iconoclasm in a Nationalist Era, 1998 (Gustavus Myers Outstanding Book award 1999), Art in an Age of Counterrevolution, 1815-1848, 2004, Art in An Age of Civil Struggle, 1848-1871, 2007. Served with AUS, 1955-58. Am. Council Learned Socs. fellow, 1970-71; Guggenheim fellow, 1974-75, 84-85; Regents fellow Smithsonian Institution, 1989-90. Mem. Coll. Art Assn., Soc. Fellows Am. Acad. at Rome Office: UCLA Dept Art 405 Hilgard Ave Los Angeles CA 90095-9000 Business E-Mail: boime@humnet.ucla.edu. *I am grateful for this opportunity to join with my listing the memory of my dear brother, Jerome Philip Boime, whose rare, provocative mind inspired me with the sheer joy of intellectual pursuit. Whatever present success I may have, I owe to my capacity to thoroughly enjoy my work, to exult in ideas and the unboundedness of scholarly activity, and to commit this love to my developing engagement with political, philosophical and social issues.*

BOISE, AUDREY LORRAINE, retired special education educator; b. Hackensack, NJ, Feb. 12, 1933; d. Paul George and Lillian Rose (Goedecker) B. BA, Wellesley Coll., Mass., 1955; MA, Fairleigh Dickinson U., 1977. Cert. tchr. K-8, learning disabilities, supervision. Tchr. Township of Berkeley Heights, N.J., 1958-67; learning cons. Borough of New Providence, N.J., 1978-82, 86-00, ret., 2000; learning cons. Scotch Plains/Fanwood, N.J., 1984-86; instr. Fairleigh Dickinson U., Madison, N.J., 1975-78. Several other short-term tchg. positions; supr. student tchrs., 1968, 1975-78, 2000-02; lectr. on fgn. countries and areas of U.S.; part-time travel agt. Life mem. Rep. Nat. Com. (Pres. club 2003—07); mem. Nat. Rep. Senatorial Com., Washington, Rep. Presdl. Task Force, Washington, Rep. Congl. com., Washington, NJ State Rep. Com., Trenton, Nat. Fedn. Rep. Women, Washington; attended presdl. inauguration, 2005. Recipient Rep. of Yr. Gold medal, Nat. Rep. Com., 2002, 2003, 2006. Mem. NEA, AAUW, N.J. Assn. Learning Cons., Assn. for Children with Learning Disabilities, Hist. Soc. Somerset County, N.J. Edn. Assn., Internat. Platform Assn., Fortnightly Club, Hist. Soc. Summit, Canoe Brook Country Club. Methodist. Avocations: travel, photography.

BOISI, GEOFFREY T., investment company executive; BA, Boston Coll., 1969; MBA, Wharton Sch., U. Pa., 1971. Various positions including chmn. strategic planning, co-chair internat. mgmt. com., ptnr. global fin., head of investment banking svcs. Goldman, Sachs & Co., 1971—93, sr. gen. ptnr.; founding chmn. and sr. ptnr. Beacon Group; co-CEO JPMorgan, 2000—02; chmn. JPMorgan Chase, 2002; chmn. and sr. ptnr. Roundtable Investment Partners LLC, 2003—; gen. ptnr. Rhone Group, LP; ptnr. Tremont Group, LLC. Bd. dirs. Freddie Mac. Chmn., co-founder MENTOR/Nat. Mentoring Partnership, 1990—; overseer Wharton Sch.; trustee Boston Coll., Carnegie Corp.; dir. Brookings Inst.; trustee Joseph P. Kennedy Enterprises; adv. dir. Oxford Analytica; trustee America's Promise, Papal Found. Recipient Humanitarian award, Am. Red Cross of Greater NY, Oliver R. Grace award, Cancer Rsch. Inst. Office: MENTOR 1600 Duke St Ste 300 Alexandria VA 22314

BOISSEAU, RICHARD ROBERT, lawyer; b. Phila., Sept. 6, 1944; s. Robert Bartholomew and Anne Cecilia (Tierney) B.; m. Jo-Ann Elizabeth Tompkins, Jan. 20, 1970; children: Richard Andrew, Thomas, Kristen. BS cum laude, Drexel U., 1968; JD cum laude, Temple U., 1974. Bar: Ga. 1974, U.S. Dist. Ct. (no. dist.) Ga. 1974, U.S. Ct. Appeals (4th cir.) 1980, U.S. Ct. Appeals (11th cir.) 1981, U.S. Supreme Ct. 1984, U.S. Ct. Appeals (9th cir.) 1986. Ptnr. Kilpatrick Stockton LLP, Atlanta, 1974—. Contbg. author: How Arbitration Works, 1987, 93, 97, 2003; contbr. articles to profl. jours. Bd. dirs. Vis. Nurse Health Sys., Atlanta, 1976—. Mem. Ga. Bar Assn., Atlanta Bar Assn. Republican. Roman Catholic. Avocations: golf, running. Office: Kilpatrick Stockton LLP 1100 Peachtree St NE Ste 2800 Atlanta GA 30309-4530 Home Phone: 404-355-2470; Office Phone: 404-815-6317. Business E-Mail: rboisseau@kilpatrickstockton.com.

BOISTURE, ROBERT A., lawyer; m. Mary Margaret Pipkin, 1975; children: Will, John, Jamie. AB, Princeton Univ., 1974; BA, Oxford U., 1976; JD, Yale U., 1979. Bar: DC. Assoc. gen. counsel to dir., public policy YMCA USA, Washington, 1986—92; with Caplin & Drysdale, Washington, 1979—86, mem. firm, 1992—. Co-editor: Jour. Taxation of Exempt Orgns. Mem. Adv. Coun. on Founds.; chmn. Human Svcs. Forum; mem. adv. bd., program on philanthropy and law NYU; bd. dirs. Cmty. Found., Nat. Capital Region, Charity Lobbying in the Public Interest. Marshall scholar, Oxford U., 1974—76. Mem.: ABA. Office: Caplin & Drysdale Ste 1100 One Thomas Cir NW Washington DC 20005-5802 Office Phone: 202-862-5070.*

BOITANO, BRIAN, Olympic athlete; b. Mountain View, Calif., Oct. 22, 1963; Competitive in amateur ice-skating events, 1978—88; Bronze medallist World Figure Skating Championships, 1985; Gold medallist U.S. Nat. Figure Skating Championships, 1985, World Figure Skating Championships, 1986, Silver medallist, 1987; Gold medallist U.S. Nat. Figure Skating Championships, 1988, World Figure Skating Championships, 1988; Silver medallist U.S. Nat. Figure Skating Championships, 1994; U.S. Olympics 6th place, 1994; U.S. Olympic Figure Skating Gold medallist, 1988. Owner White Canvas Prodns. Author (with Suzanne Harper): Boitano's Edge: Inside the Real World of Figure Skating, 1997; performer: (TV films) Carmen on Ice, 1990 (Emmy award, 1990); Nutcracker on Ice, 1995; Skating Romance II, 1996; Skating Spectacular, 2003; Blades of Glory, 2007; featured on cover: Sports Illustrated. Named Role Model of the Yr., Profl. Skaters' Cooperative, 1998; named to U.S. Figure Skating Hall of Fame, 1996, World Figure Skating Hall of Fame, 1996; recipient Gustav Lussi award, Profl. Skaters Assn., 1999.*

BOITER, KEVIN ERNEST, electronics and electrical educator; b. Greenwood, SC, Apr. 9, 1954; s. Fredrick Ernest Boiter and Emma Izora Elledge; m. Virginia Anne Griffin, Apr. 4, 1998. AS, Piedmont Tech. Coll., Greenwood, SC, 1980; BA, Lander U., Greenwood, SC, 1983. Cert. journeyman electrician Musc, SC, 1983. Technician Park-Davis Co., Honea Path, SC, 1979—84; electrician Davis Elec., Eastover, SC, 1984—85; instr. Piedmont Tech. Coll., Greenwood, SC, 1985—, dept. head, 1996—. Office: Piedmont Tech Coll Emerald Rd Greenwood SC 29648 Home Phone: 864-543-3168; Office Phone: 864-941-8467. Business E-Mail: boiter.k@ptc.edu.

BOJSZA, JOAN E., elementary school educator; b. Orange, NJ, Jan. 3, 1949; d. Stephen William and Josephine Rosemary (Sulpy) Horkay; m. Walter Joseph Bojsza, June 20, 1970; children: Elizabeth Joy, Katherine Anne. BS in Early Childhood Edn., U. Md., 1971. Cert. elem. edn. and nursery tchr. N.J. Preschool tchr. Woodyard Rd. Ctr., Clinton, Md., 1971—72, YWCA-Ridgeview Ctr., West Orange, NJ, 1982—91; 2d grade tchr. St. Bernard Sch., Riverdale, Md., 1972—73; title I tchr. Rockaway (N.J.) Twp. Schs., 1973—74, 4th grade tchr., 1974—75; 1st grade tchr. St. Thomas More Sch., Fairfield, NJ, 1975—77; kindergarten tchr. Newton St. Sch., Newark, 1991—99, Quitman St. Sch., Newark, 1999—2002, pre-kindergarten tchr., 2002—03, kindergarten tchr., 2003—. Project, new beginnings tchr. Summer Inst., Newark, 1998; presenter in field. Contbr. chpt. to book. Mem. coun., PTA officer, pres. various, West Orange, 1986—99; PTA officer pres. West Orange HS, 1995—98; active leadership assocs. Montclair State U., 2005—; comitteewoman West Orange Dems., 1991—96; mem. Democratic County Com. Recipient Outstanding Leaders award, Girl Scouts U.S., 1990, Best Practices award, SLT I - Teamwork Colloquim, 2005. Mem.: Nat. Assn. Edn. Young Children, Comer Whole Sch. Reform Model (chairperson mem. parent/staff com. 2000—01), Newark Early Childhood Educators Assn. (v.p. 1993—2001, sec., newsletter editor), Essex Hudson Assn. Edn. Young Children (corr. sec. 2001—, v.p. programs 2004—), Kappa Delta Pi. Avocations: gardening, singing, crafts. Home: 25 Harvard Ter West Orange NJ 07052

BOK, DEREK CURTIS, law educator, former academic administrator; b. Bryn Mawr, Pa., Mar. 22, 1930; s. Curtis and Margaret (Plummer) B.; m. Sissela Ann Myrdal, May 7, 1955; children: Hilary Margaret, Victoria, Tomas Jeremy. BA, Stanford U., 1951; JD, Harvard U., 1954; MA, George Washington U., 1958. Fulbright scholar, Paris, 1954-55; faculty Harvard U. Law Sch., Cambridge, Mass., 1958—, prof., 1961—, dean, 1968-71; pres. Harvard U., Cambridge, Mass., 1971-91, 300th anniversary rsch. U. prof., 1991—, 20interim pres., 2006—07. Editor: (with Archibald Cox) Cases and Materials on Labor Law, 1962; author: (with John T. Dunlop) Labor and the American Community, 1970, Beyond the Ivory Tower: Social Responsibilities of the Modern University, 1982, Higher Learning, 1986, Universities and the Future of America, 1990, The Cost of Talent, 1993, (with William G. Bowen) The Shape of the River, 1998, The Trouble with Government, 2001, Universities in the Marketplace, 2003; contbr.: In the Public Interest, 1980, The State of the Nation, 1997, Universities in the Marketplace, 2003. Bd. overseers Cts. Inst. Music, 1997-2002; chmn. bd. Spencer Found., 2002-; faculty chmn. Hauser Ctr. for Non-Profit Orgs., 2002-. Fellow Ctr. for Advanced Studies in the Behavioral Scis., 1991-92. Fellow Am. Acad. Arts and Scis., mem. Nat. Acad. Edn., Phi Beta Kappa, Am. Philosophical Soc. Office: JFK Sch of Govt Littauer 344 Cambridge MA 02138 Office Phone: 617-495-1502. Office Fax: 617-495-8550; Home Fax: 617-496-6886. E-mail: derek_bok@harvard.edu.

BOK, JOAN TOLAND, utilities executive; b. Grand Rapids, Mich., Dec. 31, 1929; d. Don Prentiss Weaver and Mary Emily Toland; m. John Fairfield Bok, July 15, 1955; children: Alexander Toland, Geoffrey Robbins. AB, Radcliffe Coll., 1951; JD, Harvard U., 1955. Bar: Mass. 1955. Assoc. Ropes & Gray, Boston, 1955-61; pvt. practice Boston, 1961-68; atty. New England Electric Sys., Westborough, Mass., 1968-73, asst. to pres., 1973-77, v.p., sec., 1977-79, vice-chair, 1979-84, pres., CEO, 1988-89, chair, 1984-98, chair emeritus, 1998—. Past pres. bd. overseers Harvard U.; bd. dirs. Boston Adult Literacy Fund, Vt. Hist. Soc., Woods Hole Oceanog. Inst., Mass., The Bold Initiative. Fellow Am. Bar Found.; mem. Boston Bar Assn., Am. Acad. Arts and Scis., Phi Beta Kappa. Unitarian Universalist. Home: 53 Pinckney St Boston MA 02114-4801 Office: 25 Research Dr Westborough MA 01582-0001

BOK, JOHN FAIRFIELD, retired lawyer; b. Boston, Aug. 30, 1930; AB magna cum laude, Harvard U., 1952, LLB magna cum laude, 1955. Bar: Mass. 1955, N.Y. 1982, Pa. 1984. Assoc. firm Ropes & Gray, Boston, 1957-62, 64-69; counsel to devel. adminstr. Boston Redevelopment Authority, 1962-64; ptnr. firm Csaplar & Bok, Boston, 1969-90, Gaston & Snow, Boston, 1990-91; of counsel Foley, Hoag & Eliot, Boston, 1991-2000. Instr. law Boston Coll. Law Sch., part-time 1974-75; lectr. Practicing Law Inst., 1974, New Eng. Law Inst., 1973 Editor Harvard Law Rev., 1954-55. Pres. Cambridge St. Cmty. Devel. Corp., 1972-75, Citizens Housing and Planning Assn., 1968-70, Met. Cultural Alliance, 1973-75, Beacon Hill Civic Assn., 1959-61, Beacon Hill Nursery Sch., 1964-65, Peddock's Island Trust, 1982-85, Mus. Wharf, 1989-94, Boston Ballet, 1991-94, Peter Faneuil Devel. Group, Inc., 1992—2004, Mass. Hort. Soc., 1995-98; v.p. The Cmty. Builders, Inc., 1969-97, pres. or chmn., 1998—2004; chmn. Boston Children's Mus., 1976-78, Mass. Housing Partnership, 1985-92, Social Policy Rsch. Group Inc., 1985-92, Boston Mcpl. Rsch. Bur., 1979-81, bd. dirs. and/or officer Boston Neighborhood Housing Svcs., 1974-76, Boston Waterfront Devel. Corp., 1970-85, Archtl. Conservation Trust for Mass., 1978-92, Wheelock Coll., 1980-95, Strawberry Banke, Inc., 1981-86, Met. Boston Housing Partnership, Inc., 1984-95, Cambridge Coll., 1984-95, Boston Housing Authority monitoring com., 1984-90, The Boston Harbor Assn., 1984-92, Back Bay Assn., 1988-92, Hist. Mass., 1989—, African Am. Meeting House, 1993—2005; mem. Boston Archives and Records Advt. Commn., 1988-95, Cmty. Music Ctr., 1995—, Island Alliance, 1995—, Light Boston!, 1995—. Fulbright-Hays scholar, 1976 Mem. ABA, Mass. Bar Assn., Boston Bar Assn. (chmn. land use com. 1971-74), Phi Beta Kappa. Home: 53 Pinckney St Boston MA 02114-4801

BOKAT, STEPHEN ARTHUR, lawyer, former business association executive; b. Washington, July 30, 1946; s. George and Golda Bokat; m. Karen Gilbert, June 17, 1972; children: Christina Elise, Rebecca Suzanne. BA, Adams State Coll., 1968; JD, George Washington U., 1972. Bar: DC 1973, U.S. Dist. Ct. DC 1974, U.S. Ct. Appeals (DC, 3d, 4th, 5th, 7th, 8th, 9th, 10th, 11th, and fed. cirs.), U.S. Supreme Ct. 1976. Atty., advisor NLRB, Washington, 1972-74, Occupl. Safety and Health Rev. Commn., Washington, 1974-76; appellate atty. solicitors office US Dept. Labor, Washington, 1976-77; sr. labor counsel Nat. Chamber Lit Ctr., Washington, 1977-82; v.p., gen. counsel US C. of C., Washington, 1983-98, sr. v.p., gen. counsel, sec., 1998—2006. V.p. Nat. Chamber Lit. Ctr., Washington, 1985—90, exec. v.p., 1990—. Co-editor in chief: Occupational Safety and Health Law, 1988. Mem.: ABA (co-chmn. occupl. safety and health com. 1983—86), Assn. Corp. Counsel Assn. (bd. dirs. 1983—95, treas. 1987—88, vice chmn. 1988—89, chmn. 1989—90). Avocations: photography, sailing. Office Phone: 202-463-5337. Business E-Mail: sbokat@uschamber.com.

BOKHARI, NAILA QURESHI, mathematician, educational consultant; b. Chelmsford, England, Feb. 1, 1968; arrived in US, 1990; d. Bashir and Shaheen Qureshi; children: Sabrina, Mazin. Degree in Secondary Edn., Roosevelt U., Ill., 1999. Cert. tchr. Ill., 1999. Tchr. math. Quest Acad., Palatine, Ill., 1994—2000; cons. math and gifted edn. Inst. Instrnl. Design, Palatine, 2000—. Dir. curriculum Renaissance Prep. Sch., Franklin Park, Ill., 2003—05. Author: Piece of Pi, 2000. Recipient Tchg. Excellence in Math. Presdl. award, The White Ho., 2000. Mem.: Nat. Assn. Gifted Children, Nat. Coun. Tchrs. Math., Golden Key Nat. Honor Soc. Liberal. Avocations: reading, travel, writing. Office: Institute for Instructional Design Box 2106 Palatine IL 60078 Home Phone: 847-477-4855; Office Phone: 847-776-1517. Business E-Mail: iid4educators@yahoo.com.

BOKHARI, RAZA ALI BABAR, former marketing strategist; b. Shujabad, Punjab, Pakistan, May 29, 1947; arrived in U.S., 1972; s. Syed Mohammad Ali Shah and Syeda Hafeeza (Gilani) Bukhari; m. Sufia K. Durrett, July 23, 1974 (div. 1983); children: Azra Yasmeen, Imran Ali, Amenah Andaleep; m. Syeda Afshan Gilani, Aug. 23, 1983; children: Abdullah Ali, Hammad Ali, Omaima Ali, Mustafa Ali. Student in Engring., Govt. Coll., Lahore, Pakistan, 1965; BS in Mining Engring., U. Engring. and Tech., Lahore, 1969; MS in Indsl. Engring., Wayne State U., 1978; postgrad., Detroit Coll. Law, 1982; postgrad. U.S. Econ. Outlook Conf., U. Mich., 1977-84. Engr., planner Bukhari Elec. Concern, Multan, Pakistan, 1969-70; mgr. mining ops. Felezzate Yazd Co., Iran, 1970-72; salesman Great Books, Inc., Chgo., 1972-73; field underwriter N.Y. Life Ins. Co., 1972-73; indsl. engr. Ellis/Naeyaert Assocs., Inc., Warren, Mich., 1973-74; grad. asst. dept. indsl. engring. and ops. rsch. Wayne State U., Detroit, 1974-75; prin. engr., work leader project svcs. divsn. Generation Constrn. Dept., Detroit Edison Co., 1975-79; tech. advisor Ministry of Prodn., Govt. Pakistan, Islamabad, 1979-80; chmn. dept. bus. adminstrn. Zakariya U., Multan, Pakistan, 1980-83; prin. engr. project controls Enrico Fermi 2 Detroit Edison Co., 1981-82, supr. Fermi 2 rate case task force, 1982-84, spl. projects engr. planning, 1984-88; mgr. econ. support svc. Syndeco, Inc., 1985-88; market planner Detroit Edison Co., 1988-89, sr. mktg. strategist, 1989-90. Dir. global rsch. and intelligence, 1990-92, project dir. bus. customer satisfaction, new products and svcs. rsch., 1992-93, dir. demand side mgmt., 1993-95, dir. customer energy solutions, 1995-96, dir. ethnic mktg., 1996-98, dir. svc. ctr. oper., 1998-2001, mgr. mktg. and sales, 2001-2003; energy cons., pres. Bokhari Enterprises, Inc., 2003—; nat. tech. adv. bd. E-Source; vis. prof. Grad. Sch. Bus. Adminstrn., Wayne State U., 1987—; bd. trustees Asian and Mid. Ea. Am. Coalition; bd. dirs. Asian and Mid. Ea. Am. Forum. Author rsch. papers and articles, presentations in field. Founder Fedn. Engring. Assns. Pakistan, 1969; pres. acad. staff assn., mem. chancellor's com. Zakariya U., Pakistan, 1980-81; pres. Pakistan Cultural Group, Detroit, 1975-76, Pakistan Students Assn., 1975-76; bd. dirs. Detroit Islamic Libr., 1976-77; mem. Econ. Outlook Conf., U. Mich., Ann Arbor, 1977-84, Rep. Presdl. Task Force Honor Roll, Rep. Nat. Com.; charter mem. Rep. Congl Task Force, Rep. Presdl. Legion Merit; vol. planning advisor Cmty. Tng. and Devel. Orgn., Beginning Experience and Mich. Tng. and Resource Ctr.; tchg. cons. applied econs. Jr. Achievement; vol. cons. Detroit Area Agy. on Aging; industry rep. U. Mich. Global Citizenship Program; mem. adv. com. bus. and internat. edn. program Mott C.C.; bd. dirs. Wayne County Foster Care Rev. Bd.; mem. adv. panel Office Tech. Assessment U.S. Congress; mem. bd. dirs. Asian Am. Ctr. for Justice, 1998—; founder Asian and Mid. Eastern Am. Forum, 1996, bd. dirs.; founding mem. Asian & Middle Eastern Cmty Coalition, 1998, trustee; bd. dirs. IAATRADE U.S.A., 1998—. Recipient Pride of Performance medal Engring. U. Pakistan, 1967; Acad. Merit scholar Detroit Coll. Law, 1982. Mem. IEEE, Am. Mgmt. Assn., Am. Mgmt. Assn. Internat., Econ. Club Detroit, Am. Inst. Indsl. Engrs., Am. Assn. Cost Engrs., Engring. Soc. Detroit, ESD Profl. Activities Coun. (co-chmn. civic affairs com., emerging techs. com.), Pakistan Engring. Congress, Pakistan Inst. Mining Engrs., Am. Assn. MBA Execs., Assn. Muslim Scientists and Engrs., Assn. Muslim Social Scientists, Internat. Platform Assn., Islamic Soc. N.Am., Am. Moslem Soc., Islamic Cultural Inst., Islamic Assn. Mich. (chmn. Islamic edn. com., mem. editl. bd. Muslim News), Tanzeem-e-Islami Pakistan and N.Am., Pakistan Assn. of Am., Internat. Assn. Bus. Communicators (bd. dirs., chmn. multicultural communicators com.), Soc. Competitor Intelligence Profls. (steering com.), Assn. Energy Svcs. Profls., Assn. Demand Side Mgmt. Profls., World Future Soc., Internat. Dist. Energy Assn., Bldg. Owners and Mgrs. Assn. Avocations: reading, writing, public speaking, sports, travel. Home: 627 Weybridge Dr Bloomfield Hills MI 48304-1083 Office: PO Box 747 Bloomfield Hills MI 48303-0747 Office Phone: 248-481-6010. Business E-Mail: raviano1@msn.com. E-mail: ravian786@msn.com.

BOKSENBAUM, HOWARD, library director; B. in linguistics, Washington U., St. Louis; MLIS, U. Pitts. Cataloguer U. Pitts. East Asian Libr.; sys. coord. Greene County Libr. System, Pa.; coord. Island Interrelated Libr. System, RI; with RI Office Libr. and Info. Svcs., Providence, 1988—; supr. tech. svcs. RI Office Libr. & Info. Svcs., chief divsn. libr. planning, devel. & info. svcs., libr. program mgr., dir. info. tech. divsn., 1997—2002, chief info. officer, 2002—03, chief libr. officer, 2007—; asst. dir. ctrl. info. mgmt. svcs. RI Divsn. Info. Tech., 2004—06. Mem.: Coalition Libr. Advocates, RI Libr. Assn. Office: RI Office Libr & Info Svcs 2nd Fl 1 Capitol Hill Providence RI 02908-5803 Office Phone: 401-222-3153. E-mail: howardbm@olis.ri.gov.

BOLAND, CHRISTOPHER THOMAS, II, lawyer; b. Scranton, Pa., June 10, 1915; s. Patrick J. and Sarah (Jennings) B.; m. Nora Cusick, Jan. 23, 1943; m. Cornelia Bingham, Mar. 1, 1980. BSS cum laude, Georgetown U., 1937; LL.B., Harvard, 1940. Staff dir. Spl. Senate Com. on Atomic Energy, 1945—47; staff dir., counsel Joint Senate-House Com. on Atomic Energy, 1947; pvt. practice Washington, 1947—; sr. ptnr. Gallagher Boland & Meiburger, Washington, 1955—93, sr. counsel, 1994—. Utility specialist Dept. Energy. Served to lt. col., intelligence USAAF, 1941-45. Mem. ABA, D.C. Bar Assn., Fed. Energy Bar Assn. (pres. 1970), Congressional Country Club (pres. 1974), Harvard Club (Washington), Burning Tree Club (Bethesda, Md.), Rehoboth Beach (Del.) Country Club. Home: 5309 Cardinal Ct Spring Hill Bethesda MD 20816 Office: 818 18th St NW Ste 800 Washington DC 20006 Home Phone: 301-320-4670; Office Phone: 202-289-7200. Business E-Mail: cboland@gbmdc.com.

BOLAND, GERALD LEE, health facility administrator; b. Harrisburg, Pa., Apr. 2, 1946; s. Vincent Harry and Alice Jane (Geiste) Boland; 1 child, Peter Alexander. BS, Lebanon Valley Coll., 1968. Acctg. trainee Armstrong Cork Co., Millville, NJ, 1968, payroll supr., plant ops. acct., 1969—70; sr. fin. acct. Lancaster Gen. Hosp., Pa., 1970—71, mgr. gen. acctg., 1972; mgr. corp. acctg. HMW Industries Inc., Lancaster, 1972; corp. contr. Fleck-Marshall Co. subs. Gable Industries, Lancaster, 1973—74, sec.-treas., 1974—75; contr. Dominion Psychiat. Treatment Ctr., Falls Church, Va., 1975—76; contr., dir. fin. Miller & Byrne Inc., Rockville, Md., 1976—79; v.p. internal auditing Medlantic Healthcare Group, Washington, 1979—88; v.p. ops. Kapner, Wolfberg & Assocs., Van Nuys, Calif., 1988—89; dir. acctg. Providence Hosp., 1989—95, asst. contr., 1995—2001, contr., 2001—. Mem.: Inst. Internal Auditors, Fin. Mgmt. Assn., Healthcare Fin. Mgmt. Assn., Inst. Mgmt. Accts., Am. Acctg. Assn. Home: 246 Grimaldi Way Hedgesville WV 25427-6797 Home Phone: 304-229-4106; Office Phone: 202-269-7039. Business E-Mail: jboland@provhosp.org.

BOLAND, JAMES PIUS, surgeon, educator; b. Phila., Mar. 6, 1931; s. John Patrick and Beatrice Christine (Murphy) B.; m. Kathryn Ann Watts, May 18, 1963; children: Beatrice, James, Kathryn, Sara, Angela, Genevieve. BS, St. Joseph's Coll., Phila., 1948-52; MD, Jefferson Med. Coll., Phila., 1952-56; MPH, U. South Fla., 1998. Diplomate Am. Bd. Surgery, Am. Bd. Thoracic Surgery, Am. Bd. Surg. Critical Care. Asst. prof. to prof. Med. Coll. Pa., Phila., 1964-76; prof. surgery W.Va. U., Charleston, 1976—, chmn. dept. surgery, 1976—. Capt. USNR, ret. Decorated Navy Commendation medal. Fellow ACS. Roman Catholic. Office: W Va U/CAMC 3110 Maccorkle Ave SE Charleston WV 25304-1210 Home: 1108 Kanawha Blvd Charleston WV 25301

BOLAND, JANET LANG, judge; b. Kitchener, Ont., Can., Dec. 6, 1924; d. George William and Miriam Janet (Geraghty) Lang; m. John Brown Boland, Oct. 1, 1949; children: Michael, Christopher, Nicholas; m. Taylor Statten, Oct. 27, 2001. BA, Waterloo Coll., 1946; degree in Law, Osgoode Hall, 1950; LLD (hon.), Sir Wilfred Laurier U. Bar: Ont. 1976, named Queen's counsel 1965. Mem. firm White, Bristol, Beck & Phipps, Toronto, Ont., 1959-69; ptnr. firm Lang Michener, Toronto, 1969-72; county ct. judge Toronto, 1972-76; judge Supreme Ct. of Ont., Toronto, 1976—; mem. Fed. Pension Appeals Bd., 1992—, judge, 1996—. Co-chmn. Penal Reform for Women Joint Com., 1956-58 Mem. Pension Appeal Bd. Mem. Jr. League Toronto (hon. pres.), Can. Women's Sr. Golf Assn. (past pres.). Roman Catholic. Office: 1605 - 33 Harbour Sq Toronto ON Canada M5J 2G2

BOLAND, JOHN KEVIN, bishop; b. Monkstown, Ireland, Apr. 25, 1935; Attended, Catholic Univ., Washington, 1962—64; Master's, Fordham Univ., 1989. Ordained priest Roman Cath. Ch. 1959. Ordained priest, 1959; rector Cathedral of St. John the Baptist, Savannah, Ga., 1970—72; pastor Blessed Sacrament parish, Savannah, Ga., 1972—83, St. Anne parish, Columbus, Ga., 1983—95; vice chancellor Diocese of Savannah, 1965—68, vicar gen., 1973—95, personnel adv., 1976—95, chancellor, 1978—83, bishop, 1995—. Office: Catholic Pastoral Center 601 E Liberty St Savannah GA 31401-5196

BOLAS, GERALD DOUGLAS, museum director, art historian, educator; b. Los Angeles, Nov. 1, 1949; s. Norman Theodore and Elizabeth Louise (Douglas) B.; children: Ellen Claire, John David. BA, U. Calif., Santa Barbara, 1972, MA, 1975; PhD, CUNY, 1998. Tchg. asst. U. Calif., Santa Barbara, 1973-74; NEH mus. intern Yale U. Art Gallery, New Haven, 1975-76, asst. to dir., 1976-77; dir. Washington U. Gallery of Art, St. Louis,

1977-88, Portland Art Mus., Oreg., 1988-92, Ackland Art Mus., U. N.C., Chapel Hill, 1994—. Adj. prof. art history Washington U., 1982-88, U. N.C., Chapel Hill, 1994—; advisor Mo. Arts Coun., St. Louis, 1981-82; field reviewer Inst. Mus. Svcs., Washington, 1980-83; panelist NEA, 1989, NEH, 1990, 95, N.C. Arts Coun., 1995; bd. dirs. Asian Art Soc. of Washington U., 1983-88; mem. No. Calif. adv. com. Archives of Am. Art; active Lake Oswego Arts Commn., 1993-94. Author: Illustrated Checklist of Washington University Collection, 1981; contbr. to books: Ketav: Flesh and Word in Israeli Art, 1996, Paris in Japan: The Japanese Encounter with European Painting, 1987; also contbr. articles to other publs.; numerous catalog forewords. Organizer numerous exhbns. Fellow Winterthur Mus., 1993, Smithsonian Instn., 1993. Mem. Coll. Art Assn., Assn. Art Mus. Dirs. Office: U NC Ackland Art Mus Campus Box 3400 Chapel Hill NC 27599-0001 E-mail: gdbolas@unc.edu.

BOLCAR, KATHERINE ELIZABETH, music educator; b. Pompton Lakes, NJ, Jan. 8, 1981; d. Stephen Bruce and Deborah Pell Bolcar. MusB, Montclair State U., NJ, 2003, MA, 2005. Voice tchr., choir dir. Stokes Forest Music Camp, Brancheville, NJ, 2001—; voice tchr. Music and Performance Studio, Pompton Lakes, NJ, 2005—; choir dir., piano tchr. Dickinson HS, Jersey City, 2006—. Mem. Colonial Musketeers Jr. Ancient Fife and Drum Corps, Hackensack, NJ, 1992—2001, fife instr., arranger, 1999—; brass instr. Sunrisers Drum and Bugle Corps, Rockland City, NY, 2003—06, Fusion Core, Minehill, NJ, 2007—; soprano sect. leader, voice tchr., children's choir asst. St. John's Episc. Ch. in Village, NYC, 2005—; drum and marching technician Hackensack HS, 2006—. Mem.: Nat. Assn. Music Edn., Nat. Assn. Tchrs. Singing, Golden Key Honor Soc., Sigma Alpha Iota. Avocations: skiing, photography, scrapbooks. Home: 52 Woodledge Ave Budd Lake NJ 07828 Office: Dickinson HS Music Dept 2 Palisade Ave Jersey City NJ 07097

BOLCH, CARL EDWARD, JR., oil industry executive, lawyer; b. St. Louis, Feb. 28, 1943; s. Carl Edward and Juanita (Newton) Bolch; m. Susan Bass; children: Carl, Allison, Natalie, Melanie, Jordan. BS in Econs, U. Pa., 1964; JD, Duke U., 1967. Cert. Fla., 1967. CEO, chmn. bd. dirs. RaceTrac Petroleum,Inc., Atlanta, 1967—. Chmn. bd. dir. Nat. Assn. Convenience Stores (NACS), 2000—. Edition editor Close Corporations, 1967. Mem.: Nat. Assn. Convenience Stores (bd. dirs. 1994—), Soc. Ind. Gasoline Marketers (pres. 1987—89), Fla. Bar Assn., ABA. Office: RaceTrac Petroleum Inc PO Box 105035 Atlanta GA 30348-5035 also: Racetrac Petroleum 3225 Cumberland Blvd SE Ste 100 Atlanta GA 30339-6408*

BOLCOM, WILLIAM ELDEN, composer, educator, musician; b. Seattle, May 26, 1938; s. Robert Samuel and Virginia (Lauermann) B.; m. Fay Levine, Dec. 23, 1963 (div. 1967); m. Katherine Agee Ling, June 8, 1968 (div. 1969); m. Joan Clair Morris, Nov. 28, 1975. BA, U. Wash., 1958; MA, Mills Coll., 1961; postgrad., Paris Conservatoire de Musique, 1959-61, 64-65; D of Mus. Art, Stanford U., 1964; D of Music (hon.), San Francisco Conservatory, 1994, Albion Coll., 1995; studied with, Berthe Poncy Jacobson, 1949-58, John Verrall, 1951-58, Leland Smith, 1961-64, Darius Milhaud, 1957-61; George Rochberg, 1966. Acting asst. prof. music dept. U. Wash., Seattle, 1965-66; lectr., asst. prof. music Queens Coll., CUNY, Flushing, 1966-68; vis. critic music theater Drama Sch., Yale U., 1968-69; composer in residence Theater Arts Program, NYU, NYC, 1969-71; asst. prof. U. Mich. Sch. Music, Ann Arbor, 1973-77, assoc. prof., 1973-83, prof., 1983-94, Ross Lee Finney disting. prof. composition, 1949; artist in residence Am. Acad. Rome, 2003; Ernest Bloch composer in residence U. Calif. Berkeley, 2005. Mem. jury Nat. Endowment for Arts, 1976-77, 84, 85. Composer: 6 symphonies, 1957, 64, 79, 86, 89, 97, String Quartets 1-8, 1950-65, String Quartet #9 (Novella), 1972, String Quartet #10, 1988, Décalage for cello and piano, 1961-62, Fantasy-Sonata for piano, 1960-62, Concertante for Flute, Oboe, Violin, and Orch, 1960, cabaret opera Dynamite Tonite, 1960-63, rev., 1966, Octet, 1962, Concerto-Serenade for Violin and Strings, 1964, 12 Etudes for Piano, 1959-66, Fives, Double Concerto for Violin, Piano and Strings, 1966, Morning and Evening Poems (Cantata), 1966, Session I for Chamber Ensemble, 1965, Session II for violin and viola, 1966, Session III for clarinet, violin, cello, piano, percussion, 1966, Session IV for chamber ensemble, 1967, Black Host for organ, percussion and taped sounds, 1967, Piano Rags, 1967-74, cabaret opera Greatshot, 1967-69, Praeludium for vibraphone and organ, 1969, Dark Music for timpani and cello, 1970, Duets for Quintet, 1970, Unpopular Songs, 1969-71, Hydraulis for organ, 1971, Commedia for chamber orch, 1971, Whisper Moon (chamber ensemble), 1971, Frescoes for two pianists, 1971, Seasons for solo guitar, 1974, Open House, song cycle on poems by Roethke, 1975, Piano Concerto, 1975-76, Piano Quartet, 1976, Revelation Studies for Carillon, 1976, Mysteries for Organ, 1976, score for stage works Puntila (Brecht), 1976, Man is Man (Brecht), 1977, Beggar's Opera (posthumous collaboration with Darius Milhaud), 1978, Violin Sonatas, 1956, 78, 92, 94, 12 Gospel Preludes for Organ, 1979, 81, 84, Humoresk for organ and orch., 1969, Brass Quintet, 1979, 24 Cabaret Songs, 1963-96, Aubade for Oboe and Piano, 1982, Songs of Innocence and of Experience (Blake), 1956-82, Violin Concerto in D, 1983, Lilith (saxophone, piano), 1984, Abendmusik, 1977, Little Suite of Dances in E flat for clarinet and piano, 1984, Orphée-Sérénade, 1984, Fantasia Concertante for viola, cello and orch., 1985, Capriccio for Violoncello and Piano, 1985, orchestral dance suite Seattle Slew, 1986, 12 New Etudes for Piano, 1977-86 (recipient Pulitzer Prize, 1988), Spring Concertino for Oboe and Chamber Orch., 1986-87, Five Fold Five for woodwind quintet and piano, 1985-87, Clarinet Concerto, 1990, (musical) Casino Paradise (libretto Arnold Weinstein), 1986-90, Fairy Tales for viola, cello, bass, 1987-88, Sonata for Violoncello and Piano, 1989, (song cycle on Am. women poets) I Will Breathe a Mountain, 1989-90, The Mask (chorus and piano), 1990, Recuerdos for two pianos, 1991, opera McTeague (libretto A. Weinstein and R. Altman), 1990-92, Lyric Concerto for flute and orch., 1993, Trio for clarinet, violin and piano, 1993, Sonata for 2 pianos in one movement, 1993, Suite for play Broken Glass by Arthur Miller, 1994, Let Evening Come (soprano, viola, piano), 1994, A Whitman Triptych, (mezzo-soprano and orchestra), 1995, GAEA Concertos 1-3 for Left Hand and Orch., 1996, Second Piano Quartet, 1995, Briefly It Enters, 1996 (voice and piano), Fanfare for the Detroit Opera House, 1996 (brass), Cabaret Songs, Vol. 3&4 (voice and piano), 1996, Nine Bagatelles, 1996 (piano), Spring Trio, 1996 (piano trio), Turbulence-A Romance, 1996 (2 voices and piano), Sixth Sym., 1997, Collusions (piano written with Curtis Curtis-Smith), 1998, Illuminata (film score written with Arnold Black), 1998, A View From the Bridge (opera), 1998, The Digital Wonder Watch (voice and piano), 1999, The Miracle (male chorus, woodwind quintet, percussion), 1999, Bird Spirits (piano), 2000, Concerto Grosso for Saxophone Quartet and Orch., 1999-2000, From the Diary of Sally Hemings (medium voice and piano), 2000, Piano Quintet (string quartet and piano), 2000, Song (for band), 2001, Naumburg Cycle (baritone and piano), 2001, Borborygm (organ), 2001; pianist in recs: (with Gerard Schwarz) Cornet Favorites, (with Clifford Jackson, baritone) An Evening with Henry Russell, (with mezzo-soprano Joan Morris) Other Songs of Leiber and Stoller, (with Joan Morris and Max Morath) These Charming People, (with Joan Morris) The Girl on the MagazineCover, (with Joan Morris) Songs of Ira and George Gershwin, (with Joan Morris and Lucy Simon) The Rodgers and Hart Album, (with Joan Morris and Max Morath) More Rodgers and Hart, (with Joan Morris) Silver Linings (anthology of Jerome Kern), (with Joan Morris) Blue Skies (anthology of Irving Berlin), (with Joan Morris) Black Max (Bolcom cabaret songs with A. Weinstein poetry), (with Joan Morris) Lime Jello: An American Cabaret, (with Joan Morris) Night & Day (anthology of Cole Porter), (with Joan Morris) Let's Do It, (with Sergiu Luca) Works for Violin and Piano (by Bolcom), (with Joan Morris) After the Ball, Vaudeville, Songs of the Great Ladies of the Musical Stage, Wild About Eubie, (with Joan Morris and Clifford Jackson and chorus) Who Shall Rule This American Nation: Songs of Henry Clay Work, (with Joan Morris and Robert White) Orchids in the Moonlight and The Carioca (songs of Vincent Youmans), (with Joan Morris) Moonlight Bay-Songs As Is and Songs As Was; recs. Bolcom's 4th Symphony (Grammy nominee 1987), Violin Concerto, 5th Symphony, Fantasia Concertante (Am. Composers Orch.), 10th String Quartet (Stanford String Quartet), 1st and 3rd Symphonies, Seattle Slew Suite (Louisville Orch.), Orphée-Sérénade (Grammy nominee 1994), others; solo recordings include Heliotrope Bouquet, Pastimes and Piano Rags, Bolcom Plays His Own Rags, Piano Music of George Gershwin, Piano Music of Darius Milhaud, Bolcom: 12 Etudes, Euphonic Sounds (Scott Joplin anthology); author: (with Robert Kimball) Reminiscing with Sissle and Blake, 1973, Trouble in the Music World, 1988; editor book of essays: The Aesthetics of Survival by George Rochberg, 1982; contbr. to Grove's Dictionary, 6th edit; contbg. editor: Annals of Scholarship. Recipient Kurt Weill award, 1963, William and Noma Copley award, 1960, Marc Blitzstein Award for Excellence Am. Acad. Arts and Letters, 1965, N.Y. State Coun. award, 1971, Nat. Endowment for Arts award, 1974, 79, 82-84, Koussevitzky Found. award, 1974, 93, Henry Russel award, U. Mich., 1977, Mich. Arts Coun. award, 1986, Gov.'s Arts award, 1987, Pulitzer Prize in Music, 1988, Citation of Merit U. Mich. Sch. Music Alumni Assn., 1989, Disting. Achievement award U. Wash., 1993, Alfred I. Du Pont award Del. Symphony Assn., 1994, Henry Russel lectr., U. Mich., 1997, Alumnus Summa Laude Dignatus award U. Washington, 2003, Nat. Medal Arts Nat. Endowment for Arts, 2006; named composer of yr. Am. Guild Organists, 1998, Outstanding Classical Composer Detroit Music Awards, 2006; Guggenheim Found. fellow, 1964, 68; Rockefeller Found. grantee, 1965, 69, 72. Mem. Am. Acad. Arts and Letters, Am. Music Ctr., Am. Composer Alliance, Am. Repertory Theatre (bd. dirs.), Charles Ives Soc. (bd. dirs.), Delta Omicron (nat. patron), Azazels. Home: 3080 Whitmore Lake Rd Ann Arbor MI 48105-9649 Office: U Mich Sch Music 2243 Moore Bldg Ann Arbor MI 48109 E-mail: wbolcom@umich.edu.*

BOLDEN, MARION A., superintendent; b. Apr. 28, 1946; 2 children. BA in Math Edn., Montclair State U., 1968, MA in Tchg., 1982. Tchr. math. Barringer H.S., Newark, 1968—82; dir. Office of Math. Newark Pub. Schs., 1989—96, assoc. supt. tchg. and learning, interim supt. for high schs., 1996—99, supt., 1999—. Avocations: antiques, collecting black memorabilia. Office: Newark Pub Schs 2 Cedar St Newark NJ 07102 Business E-Mail: mbolden@nps.k12.nj.us.

BOLDIN, ANQUAN, professional football player; b. Pahokee, Fla., Oct. 3, 1980; 1 child, Anquan Jr. Studied as Criminology Major, Fla. State Univ. Wide receiver Ariz. Cardinals, 2003—05. Office: Ariz Cardinals PO Box 888 Phoenix AZ 85001-0888

BOLDT, KIMBERLY L., lawyer; b. Jacksonville, Fla. BS, Liberty U., 1988; JD, U. Miami Sch. Law, 1992. Cert.: appellate atty. 1998. Ptnr. Alters, Boldt, Brown, Rash & Culmo, PA. Achievements include practice in the areas of appeals, appellate litigation support and insurance law; handled appeals before the Fla. Supreme Ct., in each of the five dist. courts of appeal, and before the US Ct. of Appeals for the 11th Cir; obtained an affirmance of a $22.5 million jury verdict in a commercial products liability action which was tried in Fed. Ct. in Ft. Lauderdale; provided numerous coverage analyses to both insurance companies and insureds in connection with all types of insurance policies; litigated insurance coverage disputes at the trial level and has handled many appeals involving the interpretation and application of insurance policy language; represented a major US oil company in Fed. Ct. in the US Virgin Islands who was seeking insurance coverage for environmental damage; development of an insurance coverage sub-specialty.

BOLDT, MICHAEL HERBERT, lawyer; b. Detroit, Oct. 11, 1950; s. Herbert M. and Mary Therese (Fitzgerald) B.; m. Margaret E. Clarke, May 25, 1974; children: Timothy (dec.), Matthew. Student, U. Detroit, 1968-70; BA, Wayne State U., 1972; JD, U. Mich., 1975. Bar: Ind. 1975, U.S. Dist. Ct. (so. dist.) Ind. 1975, U.S. Ct. Appeals (7th cir.) 1979, U.S. Supreme Ct. 1980, U.S. Ct. Appeals (D.C. cir.) 1983. Assoc. Ice Miller, Indpls., 1975-81, ptnr., 1982—. Contbr. articles to profl. jours. Bd. dirs. Brooke's Place for Grieving Young People, Inc. Mem. Ind. State Bar Assn., Indpls. Bar Assn., Highland Golf and Country Club (bd. dirs.). Office: Ice Miller LLP Ste 3100 1 American Sq Indianapolis IN 46282-0200 Office Phone: 317-236-2327. Business E-Mail: Michael.Boldt@icemiller.com.

BOLDT, OSCAR CHARLES, construction executive, director; b. Appleton, Wis., Apr. 20, 1924; s. Oscar John and Dorothy A. (Bartmann) B.; m. Patricia Hamar, July 9, 1949; children: Charles, Thomas, Margaret. BSCE, U. Wis., Madison, 1948; degree (hon.), Ripon Coll., Wis., 2001, Lawrence U., Appleton, Wis., 2003, U. Wis., Madison, 2006. Pres. O.J. Boldt Constrn. Co., Appleton, 1950-79, CEO, chmn. bd. dirs., 1979-84; chmn. bd. dirs. The Boldt Group Inc., Appleton, 1984—; sec. W.S. Patterson Co., 1963-89. Trustee Lawrence U., 1981—; emeritus bd. dirs. M&I Bank, L.A., 2002 Chmn. bd. dirs. Cmty. Found. for Fox Valley Region, 1991-93; pres. Appleton YMCA, 1955-57, Appleton Meml. Hosp., 1975-76; bd. dirs. Theda Care (formerly United Health) Wis., 1990-99; co-chmn. fund drive Fox Cities United Way, 1994. 2d lt. USAAF, 1943-45. Named to Paper Industry Internat. Hall of Fame, 2000, Wis. Bus. Hall of Fame, 2003, Jr. Achievement Hall of Fame, 2003, Appleton H.S. Hall of Fame, 1999; recipient Disting. Svc. award, Appleton Jaycees, 1960, Disting. Engr. award, U. Wis., 1985, Walter Rugland Cmty. Svc. award, 1988, Master Entrepreneur award, Ernst and Young, 1991, Renaissance award, 1991, Regent's award, St. Olaf's Coll., 1993, Exec. of Yr. award, N.E. Wis.'s Sales and Mktg. Mag., 1994, Disting. Alumni award, U. Wis. Alumni Assn., 1999, Disting. Contractor award, ASCE, 2000, Wis. Assoc. Gen. Contractor Horizon award, 2003, Walter A. Nushert, Sr. Constructor award, 2005, Samuel C. Johnson Distinction in Corporate Leadership award, Wis. State Hist. Soc., 2007. Mem. Appleton Area C. of C. (pres. 1967), Appleton Rotary (pres. 1975-76, Vocat. Svc. award 1977, Paul Harris fellow, 1979), Riverview Country Club (pres. 1968-69). Republican. Presbyterian. Home: 1715 Reid Dr Appleton WI 54914-5175 Office: The Boldt Group Inc PO Box 373 2525 N Roemer Rd Appleton WI 54911-8623 Office Phone: 920-225-6100. Business E-Mail: oscar.boldt@boldt.com.

BOLDT, WILLIAM GREGORY, academic administrator, consultant; b. Berkeley, Calif., Apr. 22, 1948; s. Alvin M. and Lucille Frances (Keefe) B.; m. Genene Lee Hutchins, Feb. 2, 1974; children: Kim, Kristin, Ryan. BS, U. Oreg., 1971, MS, 1975, EdD, 1980. Asst. prof. Oreg. State U., Corvallis, 1971-76, assoc. prof., 1980-86; asst. prof. U. Oreg., Eugene, 1976-80; dist. dir. Cornell U., Ithaca, N.Y., 1986-89, asst. dean coll. agriculture and life scis., 1989—; pres. Creative Mktg. Assocs., Ithaca, 1984; v.p. for univ. advancement Calif. Polytechnic State U., San Luis Obispo, Calif.; vice chancellor for univ. advancement U. Calif. Riverside, 2004—. Chair Cornell U. Mktg. Com., 1987-90, Oreg. State U. Mktg. Com., 1983-86. Author: Creative Marketing for Higher Education, 1990, Strategic Marketing for Higher Education, 1992, Marketing Your College, 1992, Fund Raising for Higher Education, 1992; editor Jour. of Extension, 1990. Pack master Cub Scouts Am., Cayuga Heights, Ithaca, 1991; trustee Tompkins County Libr., Ithaca, 1992. Recipient Outstanding Profl. award Oreg. Therapeutic Recreation Soc., 1980, Disting. Svc. award Nat. Assn. 4-H Agents, 1985, Excellence award SUNY, 1992. Mem. Epsilon Sigma Phi (Superior Performance award 1991, Nat. Mktg. Chair 1992). Office: Vice Chancellor Univ Adv Univ Calif Riverside 900 Univ Ave Riverside CA 92521

BOLDUC, ERNEST JOSEPH, management consultant, not-for-profit developer; b. Lawrence, Mass., June 11, 1924; s. Ernest Joseph and Ernestine (Mercier) B.; m. Grace Gaydis, June 23, 1945; children: Philip, Richard, Stephen. BS in M.E, Northeastern U., 1948. Cert. Assn. Exec. Market devel. rep. Kawneer Co., Boston and NYC, 1950-55; market devel. rep. Kaiser Aluminum, NYC, 1955-58; exec. sec. Com. Tool Steel Producers Am. Iron and Steel Inst., NYC, 1958-66; exec. dir. Nat. Council Paper Industry for Air and Stream Improvement, NYC, 1966-83; prin. EJB Assocs., Armonk, NY, 1983—. Lectr. in assn. mgmt., meeting planning; coord. program USAID for Mongolian C. of C. trade devel. delegation touring U.S., 1993; cons. to U.S. Dept. Commerce in Albania on assn. mgmt. project, 1995; cons. to World Environment Ctr. projects, Slovakia, Rumania, Bulgaria, Ukraine; cons. USAID-PEM Project, Haiti, 1998. Author: Curtain Wall Do's and Don'ts, 1955, Planning the Successful Meeting, 1959, The Art of Budgeting For Associations, 1980, The Three P's of Running Meetings, 1990; editor Tool Steel Trends, 1961-66. Vol. exec. Internat. Exec. Svc. Corps in Botswana, 1990, in Bulgaria, 1992; trustee No. Castle Hist. Soc., 1990-92; cons. to USAID Mission in Ghana, Africa on assn. mgmt. project, 1992; vol. advisor on assn. mgmt. related projects in Bulgaria for Citizens Democracy Corp in Bulgaria, 1995, Tblisi, Georgia, 1999; vol. speaker Am. Cancer Soc. on prostate cancer, 1998—; vol. advisor ACDI, VOCA and Ctr. for Internat. Pvt. Enterprise, 2001, Romania. Decorated Air medal with 3 oak leaf clusters; recipient Man of Yr. award N.Y. Producers Coun., 1955, W. Erwin Story citation Northeastern U., 1991, Vol. Recognition award Am. Cancer Soc., 1998. Mem. Am. Soc. Assn. Execs. (life; awards com. 1978-80, internat. com. 1992), N.Y. Soc. Assn. Execs. (life; dir. 1979-80, chmn. govt. rels. com. 1979-81, presdl. citation 1987, Disting. Svc. award 1993), Meeting Planners Internat. (bd. dirs. N.Y. chpt. 1979-80), Am. Arbitration Assn. (panel arbitrators). Office: 2 Sunrise Pl Armonk NY 10504-1444 Office Phone: 914-273-4697. Personal E-mail: ejbolduc@aol.com.

BOLEN, DAVID BENJAMIN, former ambassador; b. Dec. 23, 1923; m. Betty Gayden; children: Cynthia, Myra, David. BS, MS, U. Colo., 1950; MPA, Harvard U., 1960; student, Nat. War Coll. Joined Fgn. Service, 1950; adminstrv. asst. Monrovia, Liberia, 1950-52; econ. asst. Karachi, Pakistan, 1952-55; detailed internat. economist Dept. Commerce, Washington, 1955-56, State Dept., 1957-58; desk officer for Afghanistan, 1958-59; detailed advanced econ. studies Harvard, 1959-60; econ. officer Accra, Ghana, 1960-62; staff asst. Washington, 1962-64; officer-in-charge Nigerian affairs, 1964-66; detailed Nat. War Coll., 1966-67; econ. and comml. officer, econ. counselor Bonn, Germany, 1967-72; econ.-comml. counselor Belgrade, 1972-74; ambassador to Botswana, Lesotho, Swaziland, 1974-76; dep. asst. sec. state for African affairs U.S. Dept. State, Washington, 1976-77; ambassador to German Democratic Republic, 1977-80; assoc. dir. internat. affairs E.I. duPont de Nemours & Co., Inc., Wilmington, Del., 1981-89, cons., 1989-94; ret., 1994. Author (collection): Bolen Papers Repository, Hoover Archives, Stanford U.; contbg. editor: World Economic Problems and Policies, 1965. Mem. preliminary investigatory com. Del. Ct. on the Judiciary, 1990-92; mem. polit. sci. vis. com. MIT, 1983-88; trustee U. Del., 1983-92; bd. dirs. Med. Ctr. Del., Del. Coun. Econ. Edn., U.S. Coun. on Internat. Bus., 1981-89, Internat. Mgmt. Devel. Inst., 1981-89, Pacific Basin Trade and Econ. Coun., 1981-89, U.S.-USSR Trade and Econ. Coun., 1981-89, U.S.-German Dem. Republic Trade and Econ. Coun., 1981-89, Coun. Fgn. Rels., U.S.-Yugoslav Econ. Coun., 1986-90, U. Colo. Found., Inc., 1990-96; mem. U. Colo. Bus. Dean's Adv. Coun., 1992-98; dir. Denver Com. on Fgn. Rels., 1994-99; mem. U.S. Olympic track and field team, 1948; advisor Berlin Sculpture Fund, 1997—. Recipient Robert Russell Meml. award, 1948; Norlin Disting. Alumni award U. Colo., 1969; named to Hall of Honor, 1969, Alumni of Century, 1976; recipient Disting. Service award U. Colo., 1983; inducted U. Colo. Athletic Hall of Fame, 2000. Mem. Am. Coun. on Germany (chmn. Denver chpt. 1995-99), Nat. War Coll. Alumni Assn., Fgn. Serv. Assn., Wilmington World Affairs Coun. (dir. 1981-92), Internat. Amateur Athletic Assn., Wilmington Club, U. Colo. Alumni Assn., Harvard Alumni Assn.

BOLEN, M. CHRISTOPHER, lawyer; b. Ft. Worth, Tex., Dec. 26, 1958; BS in Engring. Mgmt. summa cum laude, So. Methodist U., 1981, MBA, JD, So. Methodist U., 1985. Bar: Tex. 1985, NC 1988. Mem. Womble Carlyle Sandridge & Rice PLLC, Durham, NC, co-chair intellectual property practice group. Mem.: Internat. Trademark Assn., Licensing Executives Soc., NC Technologies Assn. (bd. dirs.), NC Bar Assn. Office: Womble Carlyle Sandridge & Rice PLLC PO Box 13069 Research Triangle Park NC 27709 Office Phone: 919-484-2391. Office Fax: 919-484-2089. Business E-Mail: cbolen@wcsr.com.

BOLES, DAVID LAVELLE, lawyer; b. Tulia, Tex., May 22, 1937; s. Jerry Hoytt and Irma Ruth (Walker) B.; m. Kerstin Gunilla Stenrudh, May 25, 1959 (div. 1984); children— David LaVelle Jr., Kerstin Regina Boles Davenport, William Gail-Holger. Student North Tex. U., 1955-57; B.S., Trinity U., 1959; J.D., U. Tex., 1963. Bar: Tex. 1963. Asst. atty. gen. Tex., Austin, 1963-67; sole practice, Denton, Tex., 1967-69; house counsel, corp. officer Sam P. Wallace Co., Inc., Dallas, 1969-73, adminstrv. mgr. contracts, labor, indsl. rels., ins., 1973-85, house counsel, corp. officer MMR/Wallace Group, Inc. and subs., 1985-90; pvt. practice, 1990-2002. Deacon Presbyn. Ch., Austin, Denton, 1963-74, elder, Taos, N.Mex., 1999—. Mem. Tex. Bar Assn., Denton County Bar Assn., Trinity Alumni Assn. (pres. 1965), Denton C. of C. Home and Office: HC 71 Box 100A Taos NM 87571-9501

BOLES, RICHARD GREGORY, clinical geneticist, researcher; b. Pasadena, Calif., Apr. 8, 1961; s. Richard Eugene and Dorothy Mae (Martolio) B.; children: Scott, Philip, Henry. BS in Biochemistry magna cum laude, U. Ariz., 1983; MD, UCLA, 1987. Diplomate Am. Bd. Pediatrics, Am. Bd. Med. Genetics. Pediatric intern, resident Harbor-UCLA Med. Ctr., Torrance, Calif., 1987-90; fellow in genetics Yale U., New Haven, 1991-93; asst. prof. pediatrics Sch. Medicine U. So. Calif., LA, 1993—2004, assoc. prof. pediats. Sch. Medicine, 2004—; attending physician Children's Hosp. of L.A., 1993—, dir. prenatal diagnosis ctr., 1997-99. Mem. sci. adv. bd. United Mitochondria Disease Found., 1996—; mem. profl. adv. bd. Cyclic Vomiting Syndrome Assn. U.S.A./Can., 1998—. English lang. editor Micro Structure Bull., Uppsala, Sweden, 1994-99; contbr. more than 50 articles to sci. jours. Grantee United Mitochondrial Disease Found., 1997, NIH, 2000-03, Nat. Alliance on Rsch. in Schizophrenia and Depression, 2005-06. Mem. Soc. Inherited Metabolic Disease, Am. Soc. Human Genetics, Phi Beta Kappa. Achievements include ongoing research projects in mitochondrial genetics, especially regarding testing modalities; research in mitochondrial disease and cycling vomiting syndrome. Office: Children's Hosp LA Box 90 4650 W Sunset Blvd Los Angeles CA 90027-6062 Office Phone: 323-669-2178. Business E-Mail: rboles@chla.usc.edu.

BOLES, ROGER, otolaryngologist; b. Oakland, Calif., Jan. 13, 1928; s. Albert and Julia B.; m. Marianna (Reeves), June 16, 1956; children: Martin Reeves, Melissa. BA, Stanford U., 1949; post grad., Denver U., 1950—52; MD, George Washington U., 1956. Diplomate Am. Bd. Otolaryngology, Am. Bd. Med. Splty. Intern Fitzsimmons Army Hosp., Denver, 1956—57; asst. resident through sr. clin. instr. Mich. U. Hosp., Ann Arbor, 1959—63, faculty dept. otorhinoloaryngology, 1963—74, prof., 1973—74; prof., chmn. otolaryngology U. Calif. Sch. Medicine, San Francisco, 1974—98; pres. med. staff U. Calif., San Francisco, 1982—83, prof. emeritus otolargyngology, 1998, ret., 1998. Cons. for otolaryngology to Surgeon Gen., USAF, 1975-85; mem. staff San Francisco Gen. Hosp., 1984—, Childrens Hosp. San Francisco (bd. dir. 1987-91); cons. in otolaryngology Va. Hosp., Ann Arbor, Wayne County Hosp., Eloise, Mich., So. Mich. Prison, Jackson Fed. Penitentiary, Milan, Mich., 1963-74, Letterman Gen. Hosp., Presidio of San Francisco, U.S. Naval Hosp., Oakland, Calif., 1974-93, Kaiser Hosp., Oakland, 1975, Va. Hosp., San Francisco; bd. dir. Council Med. Splty. Socs., 1981-82, sec., 1982-83; bd. dir. Am. Acad.

Otolaryngology Head and Neck Surgery, 1981-88, coord. for continuing med. edn., 1980-83, pres., 1987; mem. Accreditation Coun. for Continuing Med. Edn., 1986-92, chmn., 1990; chmn. PEPP com., 1988-89, 90, vice chmn., 1989, residency rev. com. for otolaryngology; Marshall Hale Hosp., San Francisco, 1975-83, bd. dir., 1983-87; mem. Am. Bd. Med. Splty., 1984-89, exec. com., 1988-89; vis. prof. various universities; participant in conferences, conventions, workshops, seminars, inst. Contbg. chapters. to books, numerous reviews, articles, and abstracts to profl. lit. Served in MC, AUS., 1956-59. Fellow ACS (chmn. adv. coun. for otolaryngology 1977-80, adv. com. for continuing med. edn. 1982-83), Am. Laryngol. Assn.; mem. AMA (ho. del. 1975-82, bd. editors archives otolaryngology 1975-85, mem. reference com. on ins. and med. svc. 1978, adv. com. for continuing med. edn. 1981-87), AOA Hon. Med. Soc., Am. Acad. Opthalmology and Otolaryngology (assoc. sec. com. on continuing edn. 1974-80, chmn. manuals editorial com. 1977-80, mem. at large exec. com. div. otolaryngology 1977-78, mem. interspecialty cooperation com. coun. of med. splty. soc. 1986-88), Am. Acad. Facial Plastic and Reconstructive Surgery (co-chmn. standards com. 1977-80, med. edn. com. 1979-81—), Soc. Univ. Otolaryngologists (sec. treas. 1973-80, chmn. com. on under grad. curriculum 1969-74, mem. exec. council 1968-79, pres. 1978, 91), Council Acad. Soc., Assn. Am. Med. Coll., Assn. Acad. Dept. Otolaryngology (vice chmn. sub-com. Nat. Cancer Inst. liaison com. 1977-81, chmn. edn. nominating com. 1978-79), Am. Bronco-Esophagological Assn. (mem. coun. 1981-82), Am. Bd. Otolaryngology(bd. dir. 1974-91, exec. com. 1981-88, mem. various committees 1974-91, chmn. ad hoc com. for nomination process for membership on bd. dir. 1976-77, pres. 1986-88), Am. Council Otolaryngology (mem. sub-com. on hearing 1976-80, rsch. adv. com. 1977-81, pres. 1978-79), Am. Laryngol., Rhinological and Otolaryn. Soc. (mem. editl. bd. transactions 1978-88, mem. coun. 1982-88, pres. 1986-87, historian 1994—), Am. Soc. Neck and Head Surgery, Otosclerosis Study Group, Am. Tinnitus Assn. (sci. adv. bd. 1978-81), Pacific Coast Oto-Opthal. Soc., Soc. Med. Cons. to Armed Forces, Calif. Med. Assn. (program co-chmn. sect. on allergy and otolaryngology, neurology and otolaryngology 1977-78, chmn. adv. council of otolaryngology 1979-80), Calif. Otolaryn. Soc. (pres. 1978-80), U. Calif. San Francisco Sch. Medicine Alumni Faculty Assn. (pres. 1978-79), Am. Otological Soc., Am. Laryngol. Assn. (coun. 1983-84), San Francisco Med. Soc. (bd. dir. 1983-90, treas. 1989-90), Royal Coll. Surgeons in Ireland (hon.), U. Mich. Med. Ctr. Alumni Assn. (bd. gov. 1983), Gold Headed Cane Soc. (hon.), U. Calif. San Francisco Sch. Medicine. Home: PO Box 620203 Woodside CA 94062-0203 Office: Univ Calif San Francisco Dept Otolaryngology 400 Parnassus Ave # A-717 San Francisco CA 94143

BOLEY, BRUNO ADRIAN, engineering educator; b. Gorizia, Italy, May 13, 1924; came to U.S., 1939, naturalized, 1945; s. Orville F. and Rita (Luzzatto) Bolaffio; m. Sara R. Kaufman, May 12, 1949 (dec. Sept. 1983); children: Jacqueline Boley Acquaviva, Daniel L. B.C.E., CCNY, 1943, D.Sc. hon., 1982; M. in Aero. Engring., Poly. Inst. Bklyn., 1945, D.Sc. in Aero. Engring., 1946. Asst. dir. structural research, aero. engring. dept. Poly. Inst. Bklyn., 1943-48; engring. specialist Goodyear Aircraft Corp., 1948-50; assoc. prof. aero. engring. Ohio State U., 1950-52; assoc. prof. civil engring. Columbia U., 1952-58, prof., 1958-68, dir. postdoctoral preceptor program, 1962-68; Joseph P. Ripley prof. engring., chmn. theoretical and applied mechanics Cornell U., Ithaca, NY, 1968-72; dean Technol. Inst., Walter P. Murphy prof. Northwestern U., Evanston, Ill., 1973-86, dean, prof. emeritus, 1986—; prof. civil engring. and engring. mechanics Columbia U., NYC, 1987—. Mem. adv. com. George Washington U., Princeton U., Yale U., Cornell U., FAMU/FSU Inst. Engring., Duke U., Lehigh U., Nat. Cheng Kung U., Republic of China, Istanbul Tech. U., Rowan Coll. N.J.; mem. sci. adv. coun. Internat. Ctr. for Mech. Sics., Udine, Italy, 1980—, Istanbul Tech. U.; chmn. Midwest Program for Minorities in Engring., 1975-82; bd. govs. Argonne Nat. Lab., 1983-86; bd. advisors Who's Who in Sci. and Engring. Author: Theory of Thermal Stresses, 1960, High Temperature Structures and Materials, 1964, Thermoinelasticity, 1970, Crossfire in Professional Education, 1976, Wondering Through Europe: The Story of European Geographical Names, 2007; also articles, numerous tech. papers; editor-in-chief: Mechanics Research Communications; bd. editors Jour. Thermal Stresses, Bull. Mech. Engring. Edn., Internat. Jour. Computers and Structures, Internat. Jour. Engring. Sci., Internat. Jour. Fracture Mechanics, Internat. Jour. Mechs. and Control, Internat. Jour. Mech. Engring. Scis., Internat. Jour. Solids and Structures, Jour. Applied Mechanics, Jour. Structural Mechanics Software, Letters in Applied and Engring. Sci., Nuclear Engring. and Design. Recipient Disting. Alumnus award Poly. Inst. N.Y., 1974, Townsend Harris medal, 1981, commendation Ill. Ho. of Reps., 1986, Theodore von Karman medal ASCE, 1991, Outstanding Scholar award Sigma Xi, 1996, Lagrange Lectr. award Accademia Nazionale dei Lincei, Rome, 1996, Sesquicentennial medal Poly. U., 2005; NATO fellow, 1964-65, NSF fellow, 1965, Japan Soc. Promotion of Sci. Rsch. fellow, 1987. Fellow AIAA, AAAS, Am. Acad. Mechanics (pres. 1974, Disting. Svc. medal 1987), Am. Soc. Engring. Edn.; mem. ASME (hon., exec. com., pres. applied mechanics divsn. 1975, bd. govs. 1984-86, Worcester Reed Warner medal 1991, Daniel C. Drucker medal 2001, Hon. Mem. medal 2007), NAE (life, chmn. task force engring. edn. 1979-80, edn. adv. bd. 1982-86, editl. bd. The Bridge 1986-90, membership com. 1984-88, awards com. 1993-95, chair 1996), Soc. Engring. Scis. (pres. 1975, Disting. Svc. medal 1987, life), Assn. Chairmen Depts. Mechanics (founder, pres. 1970-72), Internat. Assn. Structural Mechanics in Reactor Tech. (chmn. 1977, adv.-gen. 1979—), Thermal Stress Congress (advisor-gen. 1997), Internat. Union Theoretical and Applied Mechanics (sec. Congress com. 1976-96, bur. 1988-96, treas. 1992-96, personal mem. Gen. Assembly 1980—, treas. 1992—), Am. Soc. Engring. Edn. (project bd. 1987, Centennial award 1993), N.Y. Acad. Scis. (Outstanding Educator of Am. 1971), U.S. Nat. Com. Theoretical and Applied Mechanics (chmn. 1975-79, personal mem. Gen. Assembly 1980—), Ill. Coun. Energy Rsch. and Devel. (chmn. 1979-84), Engring. Found. (conf. com. 1986-88). Home: 310 W 106th St New York NY 10025-3429 Office Phone: 212-854-2044.

BOLGER, DAVID P., insurance company executive; b. Aug. 23, 1957; BS in Acctg./Fin., Marquette U., 1979; MM in Fin., Northwestern U., 1980. Credit analyst Am. Nat. Bank & Trust Co., Chgo., 1980-82, comml. banking officer, 1982-89, sr. v.p., CFO, 1989-92, exec. v.p., 1992-93, exec. v.p., treas., 1993-94, pres., 1996-98; exec. dir. Banc One, Chgo., 1998—2001; exec. v.p. fin. and adminstrn. Aon Corp., Chgo., 2003—, CFO, 2003—, chief adminstrv. officer. Dean's adv. coun., Coll. Bus. Adminstrn. Marquette U.; alumni adv. bd., J.L. Kellogg Grad. Sch. Mgmt. Northwestern U.; bd. dir. Mercy Hosp. & Med. Ctr., Impulse Theatre Co., Fist Non-Profit Ins. Co.; active United Way/Crusade of Mercy; bd. dir. Merit Sch. of Music, Lincoln Park Zoo. Mem.: Robert Morris Asscos., Chgo. Hist. Soc., Execs. Club Chgo. Office: Aon Corp 200 East Randolph St Chicago IL 60601*

BOLGER, DOREEN, museum director; BA, Bucknell U., 1971; MA, U. Del., 1973; PhD, CUNY, 1983. Mem. curatorial staff Am. Wing Met. Mus. Art, NYC, 1976—88, curator Am. painting and sculpture, 1989; curator painting and sculpture Amon Ctr. Mus., Ft. Worth, 1989-94; dir. RISD Mus., Providence, 1994-98, Balt. Mus. Art, 1998—. Panelist NEA, NEH; field reviewer Inst. for Mus. and Libr. Svcs.; curator women artists exhbn. for Govt. House, Annapolis, Md.; Ailsa Mellon Bruce vis. sr. fellow Ctr. for Advanced Study in the Visual Arts Nat. Gallery of Art; lectr. in field. Bd. dirs. several orgns. Chester Dale fellow Met. Mus. Art; grantee NEH, Met. Mus. Art Office: Balt Mus Art 10 Art Museum Dr Baltimore MD 21218-3898 Office Phone: 410-396-6460. E-mail: dbolger@arthma.org.

BOLGER, JACQUELINE E., literature and language educator; BA in French, Rosary Coll.; MA in English, Rockford Coll., 1983. Interpreter United Nations; French tchr. Hononegah Cmty. H.S., Rockton, Ill., 1981, and dept. coord. fgn. lang. Named Ill. Tchr. of Yr., 2006; recipient Alumni Award of Distinction, Rockford Coll., 2006. Office: Hononegah High Sch 307 Salem St Rockton IL 61072 Office Phone: 815-624-2070 ext. 208. Business E-Mail: jbolge@hononegah.or. E-mail: jacbol@inwave1.com.*

BOLGER, ROBERT J., JR., lawyer; b. Phila., Apr. 25, 1955; BA with highest distinction, U. Va., JD, 1982. Bar: Md. 1982, US Dist. Ct., Md., DC 1998, US Tax Ct. Ptnr. Venable LLP, Washington, DC, Balt., ptnr. bus. transactions group. Lectr. in field. Mem.: ABA (mem. Tax and Bus. Sect.), D.C. Bar Assn., Md. State Bar Assn., Bar Assn. Balt. City, Fed. Comm. Bar Assn., Phi Beta Kappa. Office: Venable LLP 575 7th St NW Washington DC 20004 also: 1800 Mercantile Bank & Trust Bldg 2 Hopkins Plaza Baltimore MD 21201 Office Phone: 202-344-4902, 410-244-7724. Office Fax: 202-344-8300, 410-244-7742. E-mail: rjbolger@venable.com.

BOLGER, ROBERT JOSEPH, retired trade association administrator; b. Phila., Aug. 9, 1922; s. Harold Stephen and Edna (Adams) B.; m. Helen Siegfried, May 22, 1954; children: Robert, Mary T., Cynthia A., Ann M., Catherine B., David A. BS, Villanova U., 1943; postgrad., Northwestern U., 1945-46, U. Pa., 1946-47, U. Geneva, 1948-49; DS in Pharmacy (hon.), Mass. Coll. Pharmacy, 1983. Salesman Container Corp., Phila., 1947; supr. sales Kraft Food Co., Phila., 1949-52; overseas mgr., dir. retail rels. Smith, Kline Beckman Corp., Phila., 1952-62; asst. to exec. v.p. Nat. Assn. Chain Drug Stores, Inc., Arlington, Va., 1962-67, pres., 1967-87; ret., 1987. Founder, developer Robert J. Bolger Assocs., 1988—; bd. dirs. Barr Labs., Pomona, NY, Am. Pharm. Inst., Washington, Am. Found. Pharm. Edn., Nat. Drug Trade Conf., pres., 1974—82. Co-author: Chain Drug Retailing, 1980. Bd. dirs. Nat. Coun. on Patient Info. and Edn.; hon. bd. dirs. Nat. Assn. Chain Drug Stores Inc.; Nacos Edn. Fedn. Lt. comdr. USNR, 1943—46, PTO. Decorated Air medal; named Man of Yr. Cosmetic and Toiletry sect. United Jewish Appeal, 1972, Chain Exec. of Yr., Chain Drug Rev., 1979; recipient Torch of Learning award Am. Friends of Hebrew U., 1987, Chain Drug Rev. Bd. Lifetime Achievement award, 1988, Robert B. Begley award, 1988. Mem. Am. Pharm. Assn., Com. of 100, U.S. C. of C., Cen. Coun. Nat. Retail Assns. (chmn.), Am. Retail Fedn. (bd. dirs.), Nat. Assn. Cmty. Pharmacists, Joint Commn. Pharmacy Practitioners, Pharmacists Against Drug Abuse (bd. dirs. 1986—), Am. Soc. Assn. Execs. (life), Nat. Assn. Execs. Club (bd. dirs.), Am. Druggist Bd. Advisers, Key Exec. Industry Coun., Alexandria Chief Execs., Belle Haven Country Club. Home and Office: 7705 Maid Marian Ct Alexandria VA 22306-2718 Home Phone: 703-768-8587; Office Phone: 703-660-8473. Office Fax: 703-660-8473. Personal E-mail: helenbolger@cox.net.

BOLHOFNER, BRETT ROBINSON, orthopedist; b. Monterey, Calif., Mar. 12, 1955; BS in Chemistry magna cum laude, Mercer U., 1977; MD, U. South Fla., 1980. Diplomate Am. Bd. Orthopaedic Surgery. Intern USPHS Hosp. and Tulane Affiliates, New Orleans, 1980-81; orthopaedic resident U. South Fla. Coll. Medicine, 1982-86; fellow Assn. for the Study of Internal Fixation Fellowship, Bern, Switzerland, 1986; physician All Fla. Orthopaedic Assocs., St. Petersburg, 1987—. Physician Ctrl. Fla. Migrant and Cmty. Health Ctr., Sanford, Fla., 1981-82; clin. asst. prof. orthopaedic surgery U. South Fla. Coll. Medicine, 1986—; chief orthopaedic surgery Bayfront Med. Ctr., 1990—, mem. stds. and credentials com., 1992—; clin. asst. prof. family practice U. South Fla., 1990—; trustee AO Rsch. Inst. Bd. Dirs. AO/Assn. Study Internal Fixation Lab. for Exptl. Surgery, Davos, Switzerland, 1993; lectr. and presenter in field. Mem. editl. bd. Jour. Orthopaedic Trauma, Orthopaedics Today; contbr. articles to profl. jours., chpts. to books. Staff orthopaedic surgeon Children's Med. Svcs., Pinellas County, Fla., 1987—, St. Petersburg Free Clinic, Pinellas County, 1989—. Commd. USPHS, 1980-81. Fellow Am. Acad. Orthopaedic Surgeons; mem. AMA, ACS (Fla. com. on trauma), Orthopaedic Rsch. and Edn. Found. (Fla. state devel. chmn., Order of Merit), Fla. Orthopaedic Soc. (exec. com. 1996—), Fla. Med. Assn., Orthopaedic Trauma Assn., Pinellas County Med. Soc., Gamma Sigma Epsilon, AO Alumni Assn. Office: All Fla Orthopaedic Assocs 4600 4th St N Saint Petersburg FL 33703-3802

BOLIAN, GEORGE CLEMENT, healthcare executive, psychiatrist; b. New Orleans, May 24, 1930; s. George William and Effie (McQuaid) B.; m. Patricia Ruth Green, July 27, 1957 (div. 1984); children— Mark Geoffrey, Gregory Wayne; m. Patricia Ann Morrison, Mar. 26, 1984; children— Joshua Sean, Zachary Ryan. BA, U. Chgo., 1950, Harvard U., 1952; MD, Tulane U., 1957. Diplomate Am. Bd. Psychiatry and Neurology. Intern Nassau County Med. Ctr., East Meadow, N.Y., 1957-58; resident psychiatry and child psychiatry U. Cin., 1958-62; instr., asst. prof. U. Wash., Seattle, 1965-70; dir. dept. psychiatry Children's Orthopaedic Hosp. and Med. Ctr., Seattle, 1968-70; assoc. prof. U. Hawaii, Honolulu, 1970-86; dir. community mental health ctr. Queen's Med. Ctr., Honolulu, 1971-83, sr. v.p., 1976-83, pres., 1983-86; practice medicine, Nashville, 1986-87; assoc. prof., acting dir. child and adolescent psychiatry Vanderbilt U., Nashville, 1987—2002, prof., 2003—, dir. resident edn., 1988-93, dir. child and adolescent psychiatry, 1999—, vice chmn. dept. psychiatry, 1988—, chmn. Med. Sch. Acad. Programs, 1993—; med. dir. The Psychiat. Hosp. Vanderbilt, Nashville, 1999—. Contbr. numerous articles to profl. jours. Served to capt. U.S. Army, 1962-65 Fellow Am. Psychiat. Assn. (life), Am. Acad. Child Psychiatry, Am. Orthopsychiat. Assn. (life); mem. AMA. Home: 6002 Hickory Valley Rd Nashville TN 37205-1306

BOLICK, KATIE N., elementary school educator; b. Asheville, NC, Nov. 5, 1962; d. Claude F. and Janet S. Norman; m. Charles H. Bolick, May 31, 1997; 1 child, Chandler S. BA in Early Childhood, Lenoir Rhyne Coll., 1985. Cert. lang. arts tchr. grades 7-9 2003. Tchr. grades 3, 5-8 Caldwell County Sch., Lenoir, NC, 1985—97; tchr. 8th grade lang. arts Alexander County Schs., Taylorsville, NC, 1997—. Mem.: English Tchrs. Assn. Episcopalian. Office: West Alexander Mid Sch 85 Bulldog Ln Taylorsville NC 28681-3354

BOLICK, RONNIE LEE, mechanical engineer; b. Hickory, NC, Apr. 23, 1958; s. Hugh Charles and Alma Young Bolick; m. Renee A. Poe, Dec. 7, 1990; 1 child, Rachel Alyssa. BS in Physics, Appalachian State U., Boone, NC, 1988; MME, NC A&T State U., Greensboro, 2003, PhD in Mech. and Materials Engring., 2005. Cert. tech. writer Ctr. Profl. Advancement, 1993. Sr. test engr. Internat. Resistor Corp., Boone, NC, 1988—90; sr. test and reliablity engr. Thomas Built Buses, High Point, NC, 1990—2001; mgr. composites rsch. NC A&T State U., 2001—04, rsch. scientist, 2004—06, dir. rsch. smmart ctr., 2006—. Cons. RRR Technologies, Trinity, NC, 2002—06. Contbr. articles to profl. jours. Golden Leaf grantee, NC, 2006—. Mem.: AIAA (assoc.; reviewer 2006—), ASME (assoc.), ASEE (assoc.; reviewer 2005—06), SAMPE (assoc.; chmn. 2006 materials 2005). American Independent. Achievements include patents pending for. Avocations: kayaking, bicycling, Karate, camping, hiking. Office: North Carolina A&T State U 1601 East Market St Greensboro NC 27411 Home Phone: 336-256-1249; Office Phone: 336-256-1249. Office Fax: 336-256-1247; Home Fax: 336-256-1247. Business E-Mail: rbolick@ncat.edu.

BOLIE, VICTOR WAYNE, molecular biologist, researcher; b. Silverton, Oreg., July 23, 1924; BS in Physics, Iowa State U., 1949, MS in Math., 1950, PhD in Math., Physics, Elec. Engring., 1952; BA in Chemistry, Coe Coll., 1957; MA in Physiology, Stanford U., 1959. Registered profl. engr., Okla., N.Mex. Rsch. adminstr. Collins Radio Co., 1952-57; assoc. prof. Iowa State U., 1957-58, prof., chmn. biomed. engring., 1959-63; rsch. adminstr. Rockwell Internat. Corp., 1963-66; prof. elec. engring. U. Ariz., 1966-67; chaired prof. Okla. State U., 1967-71; chmn. dept. elec. and computer engring. U. N.Mex., Albuquerque, 1971-76, prof. elec. and computer engring., 1976-95, prof. emeritus, 1995—. Team mem. Engring. Coll. Accred. Bd. Engring. & Tech., 1969-76 Author over 90 publs. in field; mem. editorial bd. Biomed. Engring. Trans. IEEE, 1967-70; dir. 33 MS and PhD theses; 38 patents, 2 copyrights. 1st lt., multi-engine pilot, instr., USAF, 1942-47. NSF sr. postdoctoral fellow, 1958-59; recipient Gold Ring Highest Acad. Achievement award USAF, 1944, Rsch. Dir. award Morris Animal Found., 1961, Disting Rsch. Svc. award U. N.Mex., 1988, Cert. Recognition Los Alamos Nat. Lab., 1988. Fellow: IEEE (nat. chmn. joint com. engring. in medicine and biology 1964—65); mem.: Air Force Assn. Res. Officers Assn., Fed. Am. Soc. Exptl. Biology, Am. Soc. Microbiology, Am. Physiol. Soc., Am. Assn. Advancement Sci., Nat. Soc. Profl. Engrs., Portland City Club, Scottish Rite Freemasons, Phi Kappa Phi, Sigma Xi.

BOLIN, BERT RICHARD JOHANNES, atmospheric physicist, meteorologist, researcher; b. Nyköping, Sweden, May 15, 1925; s. Richard and Karin Lovisa (Johansson) B.; m. Ulla Karin Frykstrand, June 7, 1952 (div. 1979); children: Dan, Karina, Göran. BS, U. Uppsala, 1946; MS, U. Stockholm, 1949, PhD in Meteorology, 1956. Assoc. prof. U. Stockholm, 1956-61, prof., 1961-90; sci. dir. European Space Rsch. Orgn., Paris, 1965-67; dir. Internat. Meteorol. Inst., 1961-91; scientific advisor to Swedish Prime min./vice prime min. Stockholm, 1986-91. Chmn. joint orgn. com. GARP WMO, Geneva, 1967-71; vice chmn. Swedish Natural Sci. Rsch. Coun., 1977-80; chmn. intergovtl. panel on climate change WMO/UNEP, Geneva, 1988-97. Contbr. articles to profl. jours. Recipient OMI prize World Met. Orgn., 1981, Tyler prize U. So. Calif., 1988, Grüne Rosette Köber Stiftung, 1990, Milankovic medal European Geophys. Soc., 1993, Blue Planet prize Asahi Glass Found., 1995, Environ. prize U. Lund, 1995, Swedish Royal medal, size 12, 1997, award for sci. co-op AAAS, 1998, Climate Protection award EPA US, 1998, Global Environ. Leadership award GEF, World Bank, 1999, Zayed prize United Arab Emirates, 2004. Mem.: Indian Acad. Sci., Norwegian Acad. Sci., Academia Nazionale delle Scienze Italy, U.S. Nat. Acad. Scis., Russian Acad. Scis., Swedish Acad. Engring. Scis., Royal Swedish Acad. Scis. (Arrhenius gold medal 2000). Mem. Social Dem. Party. Avocations: choir singing, outdoor life. Home: S Åsvägen 51 18452 Österskär Sweden E-mail: bolin.bert@telia.com.

BOLIN, MICHAEL F., state supreme court justice; b. Jefferson County, Ala. m. Rosemary Bolin; 1 child. BS in Bus. Admin. (hon.), Samford U., 1970; JD, Cumberland Sch. of Law, 1973. Atty. pvt. practice, Birmingham, Ala., 1973—88; probate judge Jefferson County, Ala., 1988—2003; justice Ala. Supreme Ct., 2005—. Former chmn. Education and Adoption Com.; former mem. Children's Code Com., Probate Procedures Com., Adoption Com., Paternity Com. Ala Law Inst.; chief election official Jefferson County; chmn. Ala. Electronic Voting Com.; mem. Governor's Commn. on Consolidation, Efficiency, and Funding, Jefferson County Republican Exec. Com. and Steering Com.; campaign coordinator Senator Jeff Sessions, 2002; county party chmn. Jefferson County Republican Party, 2003; mem. Jefferson County Republican Assembly. Mem.: Mid-Ala. Republican Club, Ala. Probate Judges Assn. (pres., sec., treasurer, v.p., pres.). Office: Ala Supreme Ct 300 Dexter Aven Montgomery AL 36104*

BOLIN, RICHARD LUDDINGTON, industrial development specialist, consultant; b. Burlington, Vt., May 13, 1923; s. Axel Birger and Eva Madora (Luddington) B.; m. Jeanne Marie Brown, Dec. 18, 1948; children: Richard Luddington, Jr., Douglas, Judith, Barbara, Elizabeth. BSChemE, Tex. A&M U., 1947; MSChemE, MIT, 1950; Diploma Advanced Mgmt. Program, Harvard U., 1969. Jr. rsch. engr. Humble Oil & Refining Co., Baytown, Tex., 1947-49; staff mem. Arthur D. Little, Inc., Cambridge, Mass., 1950-56, Caribbean office mgr. San Juan, 1957-61; gen. mgr. Arthur D. Little de Mex., Mexico City, 1961-72; pres. Internat. Parks, Inc., Flagstaff, Ariz., 1973-94, chmn., 1995—. Bd. dirs. Parque Indsl. de Nogales, Nogales, Sonora, Mex.; founder, dir. Flagstaff Inst., 1976, dir. World Econ. Processing Zones Assn., 1985-2003, dir. emeritus, 2003, adv. bd. Lowell Obs., Flagstaff, 1993-94, Astrogeology Mus. Preservation, Flagstaff, 1998-02 With US Army, 1942—46. Mem.: Univ. Club of Mex. Office: PO Box 986 Flagstaff AZ 86002-0986 Office Phone: 928-779-0052. Personal E-mail: bolinflag@aol.com.

BOLIN, VLADIMIR DUSTIN, chemist; b. Inglewood, Calif., Feb. 25, 1965; s. Vernon Spencer and Barbara Sue (Chase) B.; m. Elizabeth Lynne Boswood, May 18, 1985; children: Ragnar Spencer, Roark Morgan. BS, U. Ariz., 1987. Chemist, microbiologist Bolin Labs., Inc., Phoenix, 1987-93; bd. dirs., pres. Aerotech Labs., Inc., Phoenix, 1993—, pres., 1993—, Kalmar Labs., Inc., Phoenix, 1993—, also bd. dirs.; v.p. lab ops. Aqualab Inc., Phoenix, 1996—. Bd. dirs., pres. Kalmar Labs., Inc., Phoenix; bd. dirs. Aqualab Inc., v.p., 1996—; bd. dirs. Ariz. Indoor Quality Coun., v.p. 1995—. Mem. ASTM, AAAS, Am. Water Works Assn. (pres.), Assn. Official Analytical Chemists, Am. Soc. Microbiolgy, Am. Chem. Soc., N.Y. Acad. Scis. Office: Aerotech Laboratories 1501 W Knudsen Dr Phoenix AZ 85027-1307

BOLINDER, SCOTT W., publishing company executive; b. 1951; m. Jill Bolinder; children: Jamie, Jesse, Anna. BA in Literature, Wheaton Coll., 1973; MSW, U. Ill., 1975. Adv. sales Huebner Pub. Co., 1979-80; pub. dir. Campus Life Mag., 1980-81, exec. v.p., 1981-82; sr. v.p. Christianity Today Inc., Carol Stream, Ill., 1982-89; v.p., pub. Zondervan Pub. House, Grand Rapids, Mich., 1989—. Bd. dirs. Edn. Assistance Ltd.; active Thornapple Evang. Covenant Ch., Grand Rapids. Capt. US Army, 1975-79. Mem. Acad. Cert. Social Workers. Avocations: music, reading, tennis, biking, Moroccan cooking. Office: Zondervan Pub House 5300 Patterson Ave SE Grand Rapids MI 49512-9512

BOLING, EDWARD JOSEPH, retired academic administrator; b. Sevier County, Tenn., Feb. 19, 1922; s. Sam R. and Nerissa (Clark) B.; m. Carolyn Pierce, Aug. 8, 1950; children: Mark Edward, Brian Marshall, Steven Clark. BS in Accounting, U. Tenn., 1948, MS in Stats., 1950; EdD in Ednl. Adminstrn, Vanderbilt U., 1961; LLD (hon.), U. Richmond, 1984. With Wilby-Kinsy Theatre Corp., Knoxville, Tenn., 1940-41, Aluminum Co. Am., 1941-42; instr. statistics U. Tenn., 1948-50; research statistician Carbide & Carbon Chem. Corp., Oak Ridge, 1950; supr. source and fissionable materials accounting Carbide & Carbon Chem. Corp. (K-25 plant), 1951-54; budget dir. Tenn., 1955-59; commr. finance and adminstrn., 1959-61; v.p. U. Tenn., 1961-70, pres., 1970-88, pres. emeritus, 1988—, univ. prof., 1988-92. Mem. So. Regional Edn. Bd., 1957-61, 70-81, 83-90, 92-96, mem. exec. com., 1974-75, 79-81, vice chmn., 1986-88; mem. Edn. Commn. of States, 1970-82; trustee, chmn. Am. Coll. Testing Program, 1983-85; dir. emeritus Allied Signal Corp., CSX, N.A. Philips, United Foods, Home Fed. Bank. Author: (with D. A. Gardiner) Forecasting University Enrollment, 1952, Methods of Objectifying The Allocation of Tax Funds to Tennessee State Colleges, 1961. Mem. Nat. Govs. Conf. Good Will Tour to Brazil and Argentina, 1960; Mem. com. on taxation Am. Council on Edn. Served with AUS, 1943-46, ETO. Mem. Am. Statis. Assn., Assn. Higher Edn., Nat. Assn. Land-Grant Colls. (com. on financing higher edn.), Am. Coll. Pub. Rels. Assn. (trustee chmn. com. taxation and philanthropy), Am. Coun. on Edn., Knoxville C. of C. (bd. dirs., chmn. bd. 1989-91), Tenn. Resource Valley (dir., chmn. bd. 1991-92, chmn. supr. com. 1992-02, chmn. 21st century jobs initiative), Am. Legion, Phi Kappa Phi (Scholarship award 1947), Beta Gamma Sigma (charter pres. Alpha chpt. 1948), Phi Delta Kappa, Omicron Delta Kappa, Beta Alpha Psi. Democrat. Office: U Tenn System Andy Holt Towers Ste 731 Knoxville TN 37996-0001 Office Phone: 865-974-3500.

BOLING, JOSEPH EDWARD, numismatist, retired military officer; b. San Antonio, Oct. 17, 1942; s. Jack Leroy and Judy Alice B.; m.

Helen-Louise Phelps, June 11, 1964 (div. 1984, m. 2005); children: L. Margaret, David A., Evan J. BS in Metallurgy, MIT, 1964; MBA, U. Wash., 1973; grad., Japanese Nat. Def. Coll., 1984. Commd. 2d lt. U.S. Army, 1964, advanced through grades to col., 1987; dep. chief staff computer architecture U.S. Army, Europe, 1989-92; asst. dep. dir. Worldwide Mil. Command Control System Def. Communications Agy., Reston, Va., 1985-89; retired U.S. Army, 1992. Author: (with others) WWII Military Currency, 1978, WWII Remembered History in Your Hands, A Numismatic Study, 1995, (also editor) Paper Money of the 20th Century: Japan Vol. 1 1979, Japan Vol. 2, 1988; editor: Silent Witnesses: Civilian Camp Money of World War II, 2007. Fellow Am. Numismatic Soc. (life, East Asian coinage com. 1985—); mem. Internat. Bank Note Soc. (life, pres. 1986-90, treas. 1993—, Gold medal for svc. 2001), Am. Numismatic Assn. (life, chief judge 1991-93, 95-2007, dir. judges' familiarization-cert. seminar 1986—, summer seminar instr. 1999—, gov. 2007-, medal of merit 1991, Howland Wood award 1995, Glenn Smedley award 2000, Farran Zerbe Meml. Disting. Svc. award 2005), Pacific N.W. Numismatic Assn. (life, sec. 1994-96, sec.-treas. 1996-2006, Bob Everett Meml. award 2005), Numismatic Lit. Guild, Assn. U.S. Army. Republican. Avocations: Japanese numismatics, theater. Address: PO Box 29344 Indianapolis IN 46229 Personal E-mail: joeboling@aol.com.

BOLIO, JASON S., lawyer; b. Boston, July 16, 1977; s. Stephen M. Bolio; m. Stephanie M. Verenis. BS, U. Mass., Amherst, 1999; JD cum laude, NYU, NYC, 2002. Bar: Mass. 2002, Supreme Ct. Asst. dist. atty. Norfolk Dist. Atty.'s Office, Canton, Mass., 2003—06; spl. asst. dist. atty. Suffolk Dist. Atty.'s Office, Boston, 2004—05; ptnr. Bolio-Fabiono, LLP, Dedham, Mass., 2006—07. Mem.: U. Mass. Alumni Assn., Mass. Bar Assn. Office: Bolio-Fabiano LLP 26 Norfolk St Dedham MA 02026

BOLL, CHARLES RAYMOND, engine company executive; b. Columbus, Ind., Mar. 29, 1920; s. Charles Raymond and Hestella (Snyder) B.; m. Mary Genevieve Lortz, Nov. 6, 1943; children: Charles Raymond III, Cynthia Ann. BS in Elec. Engring, Purdue U., 1941. With Cummins Engine Co., Inc., Columbus, 1941-89, sales engr., 1941-42, asst. regional mgr. Cleve., 1947, mgr. engine sales, 1948-52, gen. sales mgr., 1953-55, v.p. sales, 1955-60, exec. v.p. mktg., 1960-64, pres. Internat. div., 1965-66, exec. v.p., 1966-85, also bd. dirs., 1956-88, dir. emeritus, 1988—. 1st lt., Signal Corps, AUS, 1943-46. Named Outstanding Elec. Engr., Purdue U., 1992. Mem. Soc. Automotive Engrs. Home: 2940 Washington St Columbus IN 47201-2946

BOLLAG, WENDY BOLLINGER, medical educator, scientist; b. Pitts., May 17, 1962; d. Joseph Martin and Carolyn (Cope) Bollinger; m. Roni Jaakow Bollag, June 7, 1986; children, Katherine Amanda, Anna Elizabeth. BS, Pa. State U., 1984; MS, MPhil, Yale U., 1987, PhD, 1990. Coord., lectr. physiology course Yale Physician Assoc. Program, New Haven, 1987-90, Norwalk Hosp./Yale Physician Assoc. Surg. Residency Program, New Haven, 1987-90; postdoctoral rsch. assoc. Hoffmann-La Roche, Nutley, NJ, 1991-92; asst. prof. biology Seton Hall U., South Orange, NJ, 1992-93; from asst. prof. to assoc. prof. medicine Med. Coll. Ga., Augusta, 1993—2004, prof., 2004—. Contbr. articles to profl. jours., chpts. to books. NSF predoctoral fellow, 1984-87. Mem. Soc. Investigative Dermatology, Endocrine Soc., Sigma Xi. Avocations: horseback riding, reading. Office: Med Coll Ga 1120 15th St Augusta GA 30912-0006 Business E-Mail: wbollag@mcg.edu.

BOLLAPRAGADA, RAMESH, information scientist, educator; arrived in U.S., 1991; s. Rajarao and Mangatayaru Dulla Bollapragada; m. Rama Bollapragada, Nov. 24, 1997. BEE, India, 1988, MS Control Systems, Engring., 1989; MBA, Carnegie Mellon U., Pitts., 2003, PhD, 1996. Sr. engr., Bangalore, India, 1989—91; mem. rsch. staff IBM, T.J. Watson Rsch. Ctr., Yorktown Heights, NY, 1994; mem. tech. staff Bell Labs, Lucent Technologies, Holmdel, NJ, 1996—2002; prof. Coll. of Bus., San Francisco State U., 2002—. Vis. prof. Adminstrv. Staff Coll. of India, Bella Vista Campus, Hyderabad, India, 2003, Hyderabad, 04, Ops. Rsch. Dept., Politecnico Di Torino, Italy, 2004, Sch. Computer Sci., Software Rsch. Inst., Carnegie Mellon U., Pitts., 2005, Helsinki Sch. Econs., 2005. Author: (exhibition (conference) INFORMS Conference in Atlanta (Wagner Prize Award presentation, 2003); contbr. articles to profl. jours, numerous exhibits for scientific conferences. Recipient Advanced Technologies Excellence award, Bell Labs, Lucent Technologies, 1999; William Larimer Mellon fellow, Carnegie Mellon U., 1991—96. Mem.: Inst. for Ops. Rsch. and Mgmt. Sci. Achievements include patents for methods and apparatus for analyzing and designing various network configuration scenarios. Home Phone: 707-557-4022; Office Phone: 415-338-7487. Personal E-mail: rbollapragada@yahoo.com.

BOLLE, DONALD MARTIN, retired engineering educator; b. Amsterdam, The Netherlands, Mar. 30, 1933; came to U.S., 1955, naturalized, 1961; s. Maarten C. and Petronella (Kramer) B.; m. Barbara June Girton, Nov. 29, 1957; children— Alan Martin, Thomas Raymond, John Kenneth, Cornelis Adrianus. BS, Durham U., Eng., 1954; PhD, Purdue U., 1961; MA (hon.), Brown U., 1966. Asst. prof. elec. engring. Purdue U., 1961-62; NSF postdoctoral fellow dept. applied math. and theoretical physics Cambridge (Eng.) U., 1962-63; asst. prof. engring. Brown U., 1963-66, assoc. prof., 1966-70, prof., 1970-80; Chandler-Weaver chair elec. engring. Lehigh U., Bethlehem, Pa., 1980-81; dean Lehigh U. (Coll. Engring. and Applied Sci.), 1981-88; interim vice provost info. resources Lehigh U., 1999-2000; sr. v.p. acad. affairs Poly. U., Bklyn., 1988-91, prof., 1991-99, v.p. adminstrn., 1995-96. Richard Merton vis. prof. Technische Hochschule, Braunschweig, Germany, 1967; cons. in field. Fellow IEEE (Richard M. Emberson award 2006), AAAS, IEE (U.K.). Home: 6448 Eichler Cir Coopersburg PA 18036-1382

BOLLENBACH, STEPHEN FRASIER, hotel executive; b. LA, July 14, 1942; s. Walter and Betty (Mason) B.; m. Suzanne Weimer, Apr. 13, 1963 (div. Dec. 1969); m. Barbara May Christeson, Dec. 31, 1970; children: Christopher, Keat. BS in Fin., UCLA, 1965; MBA, Calif. State U., 1968. CFO D.K. Ludwig Group, NYC, 1977-80; chmn., CEO S.W. Savs. & Loan, Phoenix, 1980-82; sr. v.p. fin., treas. Marriott Corp., Washington, 1982-86; sr. v.p., CFO, dir. Holiday Corp., Memphis, 1986-90, Promus Cos., Memphis, 1990; exec. v.p., CFO Marriott Corp., Washington, 1992-93; pres., CEO Host Marriott Corp., Washington, 1993-95; sr. exec. v.p., CFO Walt Disney Co., Burbank, Calif., 1995-96; pres. Hilton Hotels Corp., Beverly Hills, Calif., 1996—2004, CEO, 1996—2004, co-chmn., CEO, 2004—. Non-exec. chmn. KB Home, 2007-; bd. dirs. Harrah's Entertainment Group, Time Warner, Hilton Group PLC, Macy's Inc.; mem. adv. bd. CFO Mag., Boston. Office: Hilton Hotels Corporation PO Box 5567 Beverly Hills CA 90209-5567*

BOLLENDORF, ROBERT FREDRICK, retired education educator, psychologist; b. Kenosha, Wis., Sept. 11, 1946; s. Fred John Bollendorf and Lucile Zeyen; m. Linda Rae Rutcosky; children: Becky Anne Meixensperger, Bryan Robert. BA, St. Joseph's Coll., 1965—68; MS, Southern Ill. U., 1970; EdD, No. Ill. U., 1976. Clinical Psychologist State of Ill., 1977. Counselor Ill. Dept. of Corrections, Geneva, Ill., 1970—71; human services prof. Coll. of DuPage, Glen Ellyn, Ill., 1971—. Author: (novels) Sober Spring, 1988, Flight of the Loon, 1992, Autumn Snow, 2007. Pres. Lisle H.S. Boosters, Ill., 1993—95. Named Tchr. of Yr., Coll. DuPage, 1987; grant, Fund for Post Secondary Edn., 1985—87. Mem.: Am. Counseling Assn. Roman Catholic. Achievements include Grant. Avocations: swimming, bicycling, running, skiing. Office: College of DuPage Fawell Glen Ellyn IL 60137 Office Phone: 630-484-3643. Personal E-mail: bollendorf@sbcglobal.net.

BOLLES, AL, food products executive; B in Microbiology, Mich. State U., East Lansing, M in Food Sci., PhD in Food Sci., Mich. State U., East Lansing. With Gen. Foods, Gerber Products; sr. v.p. global tech. and quality, chief tech. officer Tropicana; head worldwide R & D PepsiCo Beverages and Foods; exec. v.p. R & D and quality ConAgra Foods, Inc., Omaha, 2006—. Achievements include patents in field. Office: ConAgra Foods Inc 1 ConAgra Dr Omaha NE 68102-5001 Office Phone: 402-595-4000.*

BOLLES, DONALD SCOTT, lawyer; b. Buffalo, Dec. 17, 1936; s. Theodore H. and Marie (Heth) B.; m. Jean Waytulonis Oct. 12, 1963 (dec. May 1983); children: Scott, Matthew; m. Geraldine Novinger, Feb. 14, 1988. BA, Alfred U., 1960; JD cum laude, U. San Diego Sch. Law, 1970. Bar: Calif. 1971, U.S. Dist. Ct. (so. and no. dists.) Calif. 1971. Ptnr. Hutton, Foley, Anderson & Bolles, Inc., King City, Calif., 1971-95, Anderson & Bolles, Inc., King City, Calif., 1995-99. Editor lead articles San Diego Law Rev., 1969-70. Chmn. King City Recreation Commn., 1974—77; atty. emeritus Legal Svcs. Srs. Monterrey County, 2004—, dir., 2003—; candidate mcpl. judge primary and gen. election Monterey County, Calif., 1986; trustee Mee Meml. Hosp., King City, 1974—78, chmn., 1978—80; sec., founding mem. bd. dirs. Project Teen Ctr. Inc., 1986—90; bd. dirs. Sun St. Ctrs., 1991—99, Monterey Coll. Law, 1995—2002, pres., 2000—01; dir. Corral de Tierra Homeowners Assn., 1996—98, pres., 2001—05; mem. Camerata Singers, 2000—. Decorated Combat Infantryman's badge, Army Commendation medal. Mem. Monterey County Bar Assn. (exec. com. 1985-86). Clubs: Toastmasters (King City) (pres. 1972-74). Lodges: Lions (pres. 1975-76, sec. 1984-86 King City club). Republican. Avocations: tennis, golf, bridge, choir, computers. Home: 23799-18 Monterey Salinas Hwy Salinas CA 93908-9328 Personal E-mail: dsbolles@sbcglobal.net.

BOLLEY, ANDREA, artist; d. Hildo and Laura Bolley. BFA, U. Windsor, 1975. Tchr. Activity Ctr. Art Gallery Ont., 1979, 80, Arts Sake, Toronto, 1982. One-woman shows include IDA Gallery York U., 1976, Art Gallery Brant, 1977, Pollock Gallery, Toronto, 1977-78, 80, Agnes Etherington Art Ctr., Kingston, 1981, Gallery One, Toronto, 1984-86, Klonaridis Gallery, Toronto, 1989-91, Upper Can. Brewing Co., 1993, Studio Show, 1994-2006, 02, Masterworks Found., Bermuda, 2004, Thames Art Gallery, Ont., 2004; group exhbns. include Grapestake Gallery, San Francisco, 1980, Alta. Coll. Art, Calgary, 1980, Art Gallery Ont., 1981, Art Gallery Hamilton, 1981, Gallery One, 1984-86, Triangle N.Y., 1985, 91, Klonaridis Gallery, 1988, John Schweitzer Gallery, Montreal, 1989, Mississauga Civic Ctr. Art Gallery, 1990, Magnum Books, Ottawa, 1991, Bennington Coll., Vt., 1991, Upper Can. Brewing Co., 1992, Robert Kidd Gallery, Birmingham, Mich., 1999, Group of Ten Corkin-Shopland, Toronto, Can., 2003, McGill U., Montreal, 2003, Guild Hall, London, 2004, Masterworks, Bermuda, 2004, Ocad, Toronoto, 2005, Gibbs Mus., Charleston, James Bard Gallery, Nfld., RW Norton Gallery Gallery, LA, others; represented in permanent collections Can. Coun. Art Bank, Art Gallery Windsor, Labatt's Can. Ltd., Citicorp Ltd., Can., Can. Imperial Bank Commerce, Max Factor Ltd., Chatelaine Mag., J.E. Seagram Ltd., McGill Club, Imperial Oil, Citibank Can., Toronto-Dominion Bank, Casey House, Am. Express, Guaranty Trust, Abitibi Paper, Triangle, Toronto Sund, Arthur Gelgoot and Assoc., Premiere Mag., Bells & Whistles, Masterworks Found., Bermuda, and various pvt. collections. Grantee Ont. Arts Coun., 1975, 76, 78, 79, 84, 85, Can. Coun., 1976, 80; recipient Ont. Soc. Artists Purchase award J.E. Seagram and Son Ltd., 1980. Office: 132 Jarvis St Toronto ON Canada M5B 2B5 Office Phone: 416-955-0660. E-mail: andrea@andreabolley.com.

BOLLIGER, EUGENE FREDERICK, former surgeon; b. Detroit, Sept. 19, 1923; s. Eugene Hans and Julia Frederick (Larson) B.; m. Lois Ann Doan, Dec. 16, 1946; children: Mark, Glen, Cynthia. MD, U. Mich., 1946. Diplomate Am. Bd. Surgery. Intern, then surg. resident Grace Hosp., Detroit, 1947-52; ward surgeon Madigan Army Hosp., Ft. Lewis, Wash., 1952-54; asst. chief surgery 2d Gen. Hosp., Munchweiler, Germany, 1954-55; chief surgery U.S. Army Hosp., Pirmasson, then Wurzburg, Germany, 1955-57; attending surgeon Northwestern Hosp., Mpls., 1957-58; chief of surgery Dickey County Meml. Hosp., Ellendale, ND, 1958-82; surgeon SHARE HMO, Mpls., 1982-87; chief of surgery Mid-Dakota Hosp., Chamberlain, SD, 1988-91, Gregory (S.D.) Community Hosp., 1991-94; retired, 1994. Surg. cons. West Holt Hosp., Atkinson, Nebr., 1992-94, St. Anthony's Hosp., O.Neill, Nebr., 1992-94; real estate cons. Westin-Reid, Mpls., 1987-88. Major U.S. Army, M.C., 1949-57. Fellow ACS; mem. AMA. Republican. Lutheran. Avocations: piano, singing, woodworking, former pilot. Personal E-mail: bolligereugene@comcast.net.

BOLLING, BILL (WILLIAM T. BOLLING), lieutenant governor, former state senator; b. Sistersville, W.Va., June 15, 1957; m. Jean Ann Kineaid; children: Matthew, Kevin. BA, U. Charleston, 1979. 2nd v.p. The Reciprocal Group, 1981—2003; mem. Va. State Senate Dist. 4, 1996—2006, mem. rehab. & social svcs. com., 1996-2000, mem. edn. & health com, 2000—06, mem. agrl., conservation & natural resources com., mem. privileges & elections com., mem. gen. laws com.; comml. ins. cons. RCM&D (Riggs, Counselman, Michaels & Downes), 2003—; lt. gov State of Va., Richmond, 2006—. Mem., chmn. bd. supervisors Hanover County, Va., 1991—95. Republican. Methodist. Office: Office of Lt Governor 102 Governor St Richmond VA 23219 Office Phone: 804-730-4202. Office Fax: 804-786-7514. E-mail: bbolling@billbolling.com.

BOLLING, STEVEN FREDRIC, cardiac surgeon, educator; b. Toronto, July 26, 1955; came to the U.S., 1958; s. Gustaf Fredric and Joan Elizabeth (Small) B.; m. Cheryl Lynn Huey, May 19, 1979; children: Michael Huey, Kathrine Huey. BS, U. Mich., Ann Arbor, 1976, MD, 1979. Diplomate Am. Bd. Surgery, Am. Bd. Thoracic Surgery. Surgical intern John Hopkins Hosp., Balt., 1979—80, surgical resident, 1980—84, cardiac surgery rsch. resident, 1981—82, cardiothoracic surgery resident, 1984—86; asst. prof. thoracic surgery U. Mich., Ann Arbor, 1986-91, assoc. prof. thoracic surgery, 1991—97, prof. thoracic surgery, 1997—99, prof. cardiac surgery, 1999—. Gayle Halperin Kahn Prof. Intergrative Medicine, 2003—, dir., multidisciplinary mitral valve clinic. Adj. staff St. Joseph's Mercy Hosp., Ann Arbor, 1988—; cons. Baxter Healthcare, Inc., 1994—, Medtronic, Inc., 1994—. Contbr. articles to profl. jours. and chpts. to books; patentee in field; mem. editl. bd. Jour. Surg. Rsch. Rsch. grantee NIH, 1987—, Am. Heart Assn., 1990—; recipient Resident Rsch. award, Am. Assn. for Academic Surgery, 1983, George D. Zuidema Rsch. award, 1984, Balt. Acad. Surgery Rsch. award, 1985, Young Investigator award Japan Surg. Soc., 1995; named Disting. Prof. South African Cardiac Soc., 1996, Korean Assn. for Thoracic Surgery, 1997, Japanese Assn. for Thoracic Surgery, 1997. Fellow ACS; mem. Soc. Univ. Surgeons, Am. Assn. for Thoracic Surgery, Soc. Thoracic Surgeons, Internat. Soc. for Heart and Lung Transplantation, Am. Soc. Transplant Surgeons, So. Thoracic Surgical Assn., Cardiothoracic Surgery Network. Co-inventor of heart valve ring, GeoForm ring. Office: Sect Cardiac Surgery Univ Mich Med Ctr 1500 E Medical Center Dr 2120 Taubman Ctr Box 0348 Ann Arbor MI 48109-0348 Office Phone: 734-936-4981. Office Fax: 734-764-2255. Business E-Mail: sbolling@umich.edu.*

BOLLINGER, FRANCES L., elementary school educator; b. Balt., Nov. 19, 1945; d. John and Clara E. Jeskey; m. Kenneth C. Bollinger, Aug. 12, 1972; children: Jennifer C, Garrett R. BS in Edn., Ohio U., Athens, 1967; MEd in Literacy, Lesley U., Cambridge. Mass., 2006. Cert. educator Profl. Standards Commn. Ga., 1997. Tchr. Cleve. City Schs., 1967—78, Sedalia Pk. Elem. Charter Sch., Marietta, Ga., 1997—. Tchr. support specialist Sedalia Pk. Elem. Charter Sch., 2001—; gifted svcs. specialist Cobb County Sch. Dist., Marietta, Ga., 2006—; mem. selection com. Ga. Book Awards. Mem.: ASCD, Nat. Assn. Gifted Children, Nat. Coun. Social Studies, Nat. Coun. Tchrs. English. Presbyterian. Avocations: travel, bridge, reading, needlecrafts. Office: Sedalia Park Elem Charter Sch 2230 Lower Roswell Rd Marietta GA 30068 Home Phone: 770-641-8667; Office Phone: 770-509-5162. Business E-Mail: fran.bollinger@cobbk12.org.

BOLLINGER, LEE CARROLL, academic administrator, law educator; b. Santa Rosa, CA, 1946; m. Jean Magnano Bollinger; children: Lee, Carey. BS, U. Oreg., 1968; JD, Columbia U., 1971. Law clk. to Judge Wilfred Feinberg U.S. Ct. Appeals (2nd cir.), 1971—72; law clk. to Chief Justice Warren Burger U.S. Supreme Ct., 1972—73; asst. prof. law U. Mich., 1973—76, assoc. prof., 1976—78, prof., 1978—94, dean, 1987—94, pres., prof. law, 1997—2002; provost, prof. govt. Dartmouth Coll., 1994—96; pres., prof. law Columbia U., 2002—. Rsch. assoc. Clare Hall, Cambridge U., 1983; bd. dirs. NY Fed. Reserve Bank, 2007—. Co-author (with Jackson): Contract Law in Modern Society, 1980; author: The Tolerant Society: Freedom of Speech and Extremist Speech in America, 1986, Images of a Free Press, 1991; co-editor (with Geoffrey Stone): (essay collection) Eternally Vigilant: Free Speech in the Modern Era, 2001. Bd. dirs. Gerald R. Ford Found., Royal Shakespeare Co.; trustee Kresge Found. Recipient Medal Excellence, Columbia Law Sch. Assn., 2002, Nat. Humanitarian award, Nat. Conf. Cmty. and Justice; fellow, Am. Rockefeller Humanities. Fellow: Am. Acad. Arts and Scis., Clare Hall, Cambridge U. (hon.); mem.: Inst. Internat. Edn. Office: Columbia University 2960 Broadway New York NY 10027-6902 also: 535 W 116th St 202 Low Library Mail Code 4309 New York NY 10027*

BOLLINGER, MICHAEL, artistic director; b. St. Louis, July 1, 1954; s. Rollie Bollinger and Blanche (Bush) Easley; m. Stephanie McClain-Bollinger; children: Tanner Michael, Allison Jeanette. Student, Webster U., 1972-73, U. Mo., 1973-74, U. Mo., St. Louis, 1974-75; BFA, Webster U., 1978. Producing dir., founder Mainstage Theatre, Lake of the Ozarks, Mo., 1978-84; artistic producing dir. Arrow Rock (Mo.) Lyceum Theatre, 1980—2004; exec. dir. Suffolk (Va.) Ctr. for Cultural Arts, 2005—. Dir. Lyceum Airwaves Theatre, 1985-88; guest instr. acting Mo. Baptist Coll., St. Louis, Stephens Coll., Columbia, Mo. Valley Coll., Marshall, mem. theatre adv. panel Mo. Arts Coun., St. Louis, 1987-90; co-prodr. Mo. State Theatre Conf., St. Louis; mem. citizens adv. bd. KBIA-PBS Radio; adv. com. InterAct; Teen to Teen Theatre, Columbia, 1992-93; adjudicator Am. Coll. Theatre Fest, Ruston, La., 1992, Tenn. Arts Commn. Artist Fellowship, Nashville, 1994, Am. Coll. Theatre, 1997. Prodr., dir., actor: nearly 200 plays and musicals, including 6 world premieres and numerous Mo. premieres. Facilities chmn. cultural planning com. Columbia Com. on the Arts, 1993—95; adjudicator Prelude Awards, Indpls., 1993, 1996, Am. Assn. Cmty. Theatre Festival Adjudication, Ill., 1997; judge Mo. State Show Choir Festival, 2003. Recipient Mo. Arts award Mo. Arts Coun., 1983, 94, Outstanding Young Men of Am. award U.S. Jaycees, 1983. Mem. Actors Equity Assn. Liberal. Avocations: photography, travel, animals. Office: Suffolk Ctr Cultural Arts 110 W Finney Ave Suffolk VA 23439-0147 Office Phone: 757-923-0003. Business E-Mail: michael.bollinger@suffolkcenter.org.

BOLLINGER, RALPH RANDAL, surgeon, researcher; b. Dearborn, Mich., Oct. 3, 1944; s. Ralph Perry and Edith Delores (Algren) B.; m. Monika Irmgard Koch, May 1, 1965; children: Christine Laura, Mark Randal. BS in Biology, Tulane U., 1966, MD, 1970, MS in Biochemistry, 1970; PhD in Immunology, Duke U., 1977, MBA with cert. in Health Svc. Mgmt., 1997. Diplomate Am. Bd. Surgery. Stress physiology rsch. physician USAF Sch. of Aerospace Medicine, Brooks AFB, Tex., 1972-74; postdoctoral fellow, instr. in surgery, dept. immunology Duke U., Durham, NC, 1974-76; resident in surgery Duke U. Med. Ctr., 1970—72, 1977—79, chief resident in surgery, 1979—80, asst. prof. surgery, 1980—86, asst. prof. immunology, 1981—86, chief of surg. transplantation, 1983—99, assoc. prof. immunology, 1986—95, assoc. prof. surgery, 1986—91, prof. surgery, 1991—, prof. immunology, 1995—, chief gen. surgery, 1994—2003, vice chair surgery, 2004—06, sr. ednl. advisor, 2006—. Vice councillor United Network for Organ Sharing, Richmond, Va., 1986-88, councillor, 1989-91, v.p., 1991-92, pres., 1992-93; sec. Southeastern Organ Procurement Found., Richmond, 1988-89, v.p., 1989-90, pres., 1990-91; v.p. Carolina Organ Procurement Agy., Greenville, N.C., 1985-87, pres., 1987-89; trustee N.C. Kidney Found., Chapel Hill, 1983-90; pres. elect Durham-Orange County Med. Soc. 2004, pres. 2005. Contbr. numerous articles to profl. jours.; editor: Transplant Management, 1988; mem. editl. bd. Am. Surgeon, 1988, Jour. Surg. Rsch., 1993—96, Jour. ACS, 1996, Graft, 1998, Jour. Investigative Surgery, 2001. Com. chmn. Troop 408, Boy Scouts Am., Durham, N.C., 1982-89; mem. staff/parish rels. com. Duke Meml. Meth. Ch., Durham, 1985-87, chmn., 2003-2004, admin. bd., 2004-06, coun. on ministries, 1983-85. Maj. USAF, 1972—74. Recipient La. Pathology Soc. award Tulane U., 1979, Golden Apple award Duke U., 1984, 89. Fellow ACS; mem. Aerospace Med. Assn. (environ. sci. award 1978), Am. Soc. Transplant Surgeons (membership com. 1988, councillor 1989-93), Transplantation Soc., Soc. Univ. Surgeons, Am. Surg. Assn., So. Surg. Assn., N.C. Assn. Biomed. Rsch. (sec. 2001-03, vice chmn. 2003-05, chmn. 2005-07). Republican. Avocations: scuba diving, gardening, white water canoeing. Home: 1120 Infinity Rd Durham NC 27712-9765 Office: Duke U Med Ctr PO Box 2910 Durham NC 27710-2910 Home Phone: 919-471-2013; Office Phone: 919-681-3889. Business E-Mail: bolli001@mc.duke.edu.

BOLLINGER, WILLIAM ANTHONY, security specialist, educator; s. Robert Louis and Marcella Ceceile Bollinger; m. Coleen J. Petersen, Dec. 22, 1984; 1 child, Christopher. BA, Calif. State U., Long Beach, 1971; MSc, U. So. Calif., LA, 1973. Authorized derivative classifier US Dept. Energy, 1991. Info. specialist Bechtel Power Corp., San Francisco, 1973—78; tech. libr. Saudi Arabian Bechtel Corp., Jubail, Saudi Arabia, 1978; info. mgr. Fluor Engring., Redwood City, Calif., 1978—83; classified security specialist Lawrence Nat. Lab., Livermore, Calif., 1983—. Adj. asst. prof. Golden Gate U., San Francisco, 1985—; adj. instr. U. San Francisco, 1996—2003. Recipient Cold War Svc. Recognition cert., Dept. Def., 2000. Mem.: Export Control Coords. Orgn. (chmn. 2003), Mensa USA (life). Avocations: firearms, astronomy, mountaineering. Home: 1124 Alison Cir Livermore CA 94550

BOLLS, IMOGENE LAMB, English language educator, poet; b. Manhattan, Kans., Sept. 25, 1938; d. Don Q. and Helen Letson (Keithley) Lamb; m. Nathan J. Bolls, Jr., Nov. 24, 1962; 1 child, Laurel Helen. BA, Kans. State U., 1960; MA, U. Utah, 1962. Instr. French Kans. State U., Manhattan, 1959-60; instr. English U. Utah, Salt Lake City, 1960-62; instr. to prof. Wittenberg U., Springfield, Ohio, 1963—. Poet-in-residence, dir. journalism program Wittenberg U.; tchg. poet Antioch Writers' Workshop Antioch Coll., summers, 1992—93; intensive seminar poet Antioch Writers' Workshop Antioch Coll., summer, 1994; poetry tchr. Ohio Poet-in-the-Schs. program, 1972—82; poetry instr. acad. camp; state and nat. poetry judge. Author: (poetry) Glass Walker, 1983, Earthbound, 1989, Advice for the Climb, 1999, works represented in anthologies; contbr. more than 600 poems to mags. Recipient Individual Artist award Ohio Arts Coun., 1982, 90, Poetry prize S.D. Rev., 1983, Poetry award Kans. Quarterly, 1985, Ohioana Poetry award Ohioana Libr. Assn., 1995; finalist Vassar Miller Prize in Poetry, 1994; grantee Ireland, 1986, France, 1990, Am. Southwest. Mem. Acad. Am. Poets (assoc.), Poetry Soc. Am., Women in Comm. Avocations: Native American cultures, hiking, photography, music, travel. Address: PO Box 2917 Taos NM 87571

BOLNICK, HOWARD JEFFREY, insurance company executive, educator, investor; b. Detroit, Oct. 27, 1945; s. Arnold J. and Rebecca (Schuff) B.; m. Kay Zimring, Nov. 29, 1970; children: Lori Ann, Lee Scott. AB with distinction, U. Mich., 1966; MBA, U. Chgo., 1970. Actuary CNA Ins. Cos., Chgo., 1967-76; prin. Coopers & Lybrand, Chgo., 1976-80; pres. bd. dirs. Celtic Life Ins. Co., Chgo., 1980—95; pres. Celtic Health Plans, Chgo., 1994—95; pres., CEO Radix Health Connection, 1997—2001; chmn., CEO InFocus Fin. Group, 2001—06. Adj. prof. Kellogg Grad. Sch., Northwestern U., 1996—; fellow Inst. for Health Svcs. Rsch. and Policy Studies, Northwestern U., 1996-2002. Contbr. articles to profl. and trade publs. Bd. dirs. Schwab Rehab. Ctr., Chgo., 1982-85, Mt. Sinai Med. Ctr., Chgo., 1985-87, Grant Hosp., Chgo., 1991-93, Fla. Small Employer Health Reins. Program, 1992-93; mem. Ill. Comprehensive Health Inst. Plan Bd., Chgo., 1987—, chmn. fin. com., 1989-2002. Fellow Soc. Actuaries (bd. dirs. 1990-92, 94-96, 97-2001, v.p. 1994-96, pres. elect 1997-98, pres. 1998-99); mem. Internat. Actuarial Assn. (chmn. health sect. 2003—), Am. Acad. Actuaries (bd. dirs. 1990-94, 97—, v.p. 1992-94), Health Ins. Assn. Am. (bd. dirs. 1988-90). Jewish. Avocations: scuba diving, travel. Personal E-mail: hbolnick@kellogg.northwestern.edu.

BOLOGNESI, DANI PAUL, virologist, educator; b. Forgaria, Italy, Mar. 19, 1941; s. Carlo and Marina (Iem) B.; m. Sarah Sampson, Aug. 1, 1964; children: James, Michael. BS, Rensselaer Poly. Inst., 1963, MS, 1965; PhD in Virology, Duke U., 1967. Rsch. assoc. dept. surgery Duke U., 1967-68; NIH postdoctoral fellow Max-Planck Institut für Virusforschung, Tübingen, Fed. Republic Germany, 1968-71; asst. prof. surgery, microbiology and immunology Duke U., Durham, N.C., 1971-72, assoc. prof. surgery, assoc. prof. microbiology and immunology, 1972-77, prof. surgery, prof. microbiology and immunology, 1977-84, James B. Duke prof. exptl. surgery, 1984—, dir. AIDS Ctr. for Rsch., 1989—; CEO Trimeris Corp., Durham, N.C., 1998—. Cons., mem. med. and sci. adv. com. Leukemia Soc. Am.; mem. NIH Virology Study Sect.; mem. Bd. Sci. Counselors, chmn. subcom. on AIDS Editor AIDS Research and Human Retroviruses, 1987—; mem. editorial bd.: Cancer Research, 1978— , Virology, 1978—. Mem. Sigma Xi. Office: Trimeris Inc 3500 Paramount Pkwy Morrisville NC 27560-7218

BOLOMEY, ROGER HENRY, sculptor; b. Torrington, Conn., Oct. 19, 1918; s. Henry Albert and Ida (Vurlod) B.; m. Alice Susanne Ryser, June 11, 1948; children: Florence Susanne, Yvonne Marguerite. Student, Acad. Fine Arts, Florence, Italy, 1947, U. Lausanne, Switzerland, 1947-48, Calif. Coll. Arts and Crafts, Oakland, 1948-50. Prof. Herbert H. Lehman Coll., CUNY, 1968-75; prof., chmn. dept. art Calif. State U. at Fresno, 1975-83; painter, 1948-60; sculptor, 1960—. Mem. adv. bd. Mus. No. Ariz. Art Inst., Flagstaff, 1976-78, Nat. Sculpture Conf., U. Kans., Lawrence, 1971-80 Chosen to execute 2 large sculptures for state office bldg., Albany, N.Y., 1967, sculpture for, new Nassau County Supreme Ct. Bldg., 1968, Lehman High Sch., Bronx, N.Y., 1969, Eastridge Mall, San Jose, Cal., 1970, N.Y. State Office Bldg., Hauppauge, N.Y., 1973, others.; one-man shows including, Bolles Gallery, San Francisco, 1960, Royal Marks Gallery, N.Y.C., 1964, 65, numerous group exhbns., 1960— , including, 66th Arm. Exhbn., Chgo. Art Inst., 1962, Salon de Mai, Paris (France) Mus. Art, 1963, 64, Whitney Mus., 1964, Larry Aldrich Mus., Ridgefield, Conn., 1964, Carnegie Inst. Internat. Exhbn., 1964, Whitney Mus., 1964, 66, Highlights, 1964-65, Larry Aldrich Mus., 1965, Quatrieme Expn. Suisse de Sculpture, Bienne, Switzerland, 1966, Amerikanische Kunst aus Schweizer Besitz, St. Gallen, Switzerland, 1966, Contemporary Am. Painting and Sculpture, U. Ill. at Urbana, 1967; represented permanent collections, Mus. Modern Art, San Francisco Mus. Modern Art, Whitney Mus., Slädlische Kunsthalle, Mannheim, W.Ger., Larry Aldrich Mus., Bundy Art Gallery, Waitsfield, Vt., San Francisco Art Inst., Oakland Mus., Los Angeles County Mus., U. Calif. Mus. Art, Berkeley, Chase Manhattan Bank, N.Y.C., also numerous pvt. collections; curator: Forgotten Dimension. Recipient 1st prize, commn. for large mural San Jose (Calif.) State Coll. competition, 1962, 1st prize, purchase award Bundy Art Gallery competition, 1963, Sculpture prize 84th Ann. competition San Francisco Art Inst., 1965 Hon. fellow Royal Acad. Fine Arts (Hague, Netherlands); mem. San Francisco Art Inst., Am. Fedn. Arts. Achievements include being the first to use polyurethane from its fluid form as a medium of art. Address: 6968 Sweetwater Ct Boulder CO 80301-3836 Personal E-mail: bolomey3@comcast.net. *My ultimate goal is to live a fully creative life with the hope that what I do and the way I live will stimulate others to do the same.*

BOLOOKI, HOOSHANG, cardiac surgeon; b. Langeh, Iran, Mar. 28, 1937; came to U.S., 1960, naturalized, 1976; s. Hossein and Fatima (Arjomand) B.; m. C. Joanne McDonald, Aug. 30, 1975; children: Hooshang Michael, Cyrus William, Andrew John. BS cum laude, Alborz Coll., Tehran, 1954; MD, Tehran U., 1960. Intern, resident in surgery Kings County Hosp.; asst. instr. SUNY Med. Center, Bklyn., 1961-67; resident in thoracic and cardiovascular surgery Jackson Meml. Hosp. and U. Miami Sch. Medicine, 1967-69; faculty U. Miami (Fla.) Med. Sch., 1969-77, prof. surgery, 1977—; attending surgeon, dir. adult cardiac surgery Jackson Meml. Hosp., 1969—; dir. cardiopulmonary transplant program U. Miami Jackson Meml. Hosp., 1986-98. Cons. VA Hosp., Miami, 1977-90; mem. adv. panel cardiovascular surgery Ethicon Inc., Davis & Geck Co., Inc., 1974-1995; hon. prof. U. Marón Sch. Medicine, Argentina. Author: Clinical Application of Intra-Aortic Balloon Pump, 1976, 3d edit., 1998, Medical Examination Review, Thoracic Surgery, 2d edit., 1972, 3d edit. Vol. 18, 1981, Cardiovascular Surgery, Vol. 38, 1981; contbr. articles to profl. jours. Recipient Rsch. Career Devel. award NIH, 1972-77, grantee, 1972-75; recipient Grand award U. Tex. Med. Br., 1968, Masterpiece award Transplant Found. South Fla., 1996, Achievement award Iranian-Am. Med. Assn., 1999, award for outstanding svc. 2000, award for contbn. to cardiovasc. surgery Onassis Cardiac Surgery Ctr., 2000, Achievement award Onassis Surg. Found., 2000. Fellow ACS, Royal Coll. Surgeons Can., Am. Coll. Cardiology, Am. Coll. Chest Physicians; mem. AMA (cert. merit), Am. Surg. Assn., Am. Assn. Thoracic Surgery, Soc. Univ. Surgeons, Am. Heart Assn., Fla. Heart Assn. (cert. of merit), Fla. Thoracic Soc., Soc. for Thoracic Surgeons (membership com. 1983-85), So. Thoracic Surg. Assn. (membership com. 1985-87, chmn. 1989, v.p. 1991), Soc. Internat. de Chirugie, Internat. Cardiovascular Soc., Soc. Vascular Surgery, Internat. Soc. Heart and Lung Transplantation, Soc. Acad. Surgeons, David Park Racquet Club, Ski Club. Republican. Muslim. Office: U Miami Sch Med Thoracic Cardio Surgery R-114 Miami FL 33101 Office Phone: 305-585-5271. Business E-Mail: hbolooki@med.miami.edu.

BOLOTOWSKY, ANDREW ILYITCH, flutist, composer; b. NYC, Aug. 20, 1949; s. Ilya Yulevitch and Meta (Cohen) B.; 1 child, Anastasia Elena. Studied with William Kincaid, Phila., 1963—67; studied with Elaine Schaffer, NYC, 1967; studied with Jean-Pierre Rampal, France, 1967; BA, New Sch. Social Rsch., 1971. 1st flute Pan Am. Orch., 1982—; flutist Am. Festival of Microtonal Music, NYC, 1983—99, Downtown Music Ensemble, NYC, 1983—84, 1992—94, 2003, Downtown Music Prodns., 1983—96, 2000—; 1st flute Philharm. Symphony Westchester, 1987—90; baroque flutist Muse, 1987—, Am. Landmark Festival Concerts, 1973—, New Amsterdam Baroque, 1998—, Wood Hill Players, 1999—; founding mem. Brooklyn Baroque, 2000. Performer over 2500 concerts, 1967—; vis. artist Beloit (Wis.) Coll., 1970-73; mime and flute in concert, 1974-84; Delbarton Baroque Ensemble, 1978-81; Criterion Concerts Guggenheim Mus., N.Y.C., 1979; artist N.Y. Com. for Young Audiences, N.Y.C., 1980-87; artist in residence summer mus. theater workshop NYU, 1981; pres. SoHo Baroque Opera Co., N.Y.C., 1983—, Laurel Arts Festival, Jim Thorpe, Pa., 1991-94. Rec. artist (Orion master recording) 6 Serenades by Fernando Carulli, 1978, (Orion master recording) 20th Century Music for Flute and Guitar, 1978, Music for Flute and Mime, 1982, Behavioral Drift by Franz Kamin, 1980, What The Wind Told, 1979, Scribble Music Sampler by Franz Kamin, 1983, Poetry Music Quilts by Beth Anderson, 1982, Mark Steven Brooks: Compositions 1973-87, 1987; recs. include Pitch, Vol. I No. 3, 1988-89, Indian Summer by Tui St. George Tucker, Opus 1 records No. 107, Timepieces by Rita Falbel, 1991, Between the Keys, Newport Classic CD, 1992, Open Secrets (by Jackson Maclow), 1993 XICD, The Music of Frank Wigglesworth, CRI CD 733, Raj Kapoor's CD Kathmandu Embrace, 1997, Crayon (Jackson Maclow issue), 1997, Melody Sumner Carnahan The Time IS Now, Frog Peak Music CD, 1998, Johnny Reinhard's Raven, Stereo Soc. CD, 1999, Judith St. Croix's Vision of Light and Mystery, Sonic Muse CD, 1999, Elodie Lauten's The Deus Ex Machina Cycle, 1999, Lenore Von Stein's I Haven't Been Able to Lie and Tell the Truth (CD), 2002, Daniel Goode's Eight Thrushes in New York Frog Peak Music CD, 2003, Beth Anderson's Swales and Angels New World Records, 2004, JoHann Ludwig Krebs (with Rebecca Pechefsky) Sonatas for Flute and Harpsicord, 2004, Quill Classics CD, Northern Lights, 2005, Quill Classics CD, Jackson MacLow's Doings CD, 2005, Howard Hanson American Classics, 2006, Lenore von Stein's Art and Money CD, 2006, Sudden Sunsets CD, 2006, Jackson and Anne Tardos Roulette Concert, 1999, CD (Tarmac Books and Music CD), 2007, The Pleasures of the French Quill Classics CD, 2007, others; editor Flute Charts for "Pitch", vol. I number 4, 1990; performances on radio and tv including Stas. WBAI, WQXR, WNYC New Sounds, WKCR, WFUV, NBC, CBS, NYC-TV; extra (films) Eyewitness, 1980, Godfather III, 1990 Grantee Carnegie Recital Hall, Tully Hall Criterion Found., 1976-79, Meet the Composer, 1978, 80. Avocations: study of earlier flute systems, walking tours, Russian literature. Office: PO Box 492 New York NY 10276

BOLSTER, ARCHIE MILBURN, retired foreign service officer; b. Ames, Iowa, Apr. 9, 1933; s. Horace Goodwin and Ella Schimpf B.; m. Ann Dorcas Matthews, Mar. 22, 1959; children: Christopher, Matthew, Amy. BA Internat. Rels., U. Va., 1955; MA Pub. Policy and Adminstrn., U. Wis., 1972. Commd. fgn. svc. officer Dept. State, 1958; assigned Phnom Penh, Cambodia, 1959—60, Tabriz, Iran, 1951—63, Tehran, Iran, 1964—66, 1974—76, Bur. Intelligence and Rsch., 1966—68, Office Fuels and Energy, 1969—71; 1st sec. New Delhi, 1972—74; consul gen. Antwerp, Belgium, 1978—81; dep. dir. Divsn. Office Security Assistance and Sales, 1981—83; dep. chief Aviation Negotiations Divsn., 1983—84; spl. projects officer Bur. Refugee Programs, 1984—86. Freedom of Info. Act reviewer, 1984-94, 97-2003, sr. reviewer, 2003-; mem. White House Counsel's Iran-Contra Task Force, 1987-90; mem. staff U.S.-Iran Claims Tribunal, The Hague, Netherlands, 1994-96. Chmn. editl. bd. Fgn. Svc. Jour., 1971. Pres. Williamsburg Civic Assn., Arlington, Va., 1969-70. Served with USNR, 1955-58. Mem. Am. Fgn. Svc. Assn., Assn. Part-Time Profls. (bd. dirs., v.p. 1989-91). Home: 2738 N Lexington St Arlington VA 22207-1437

BOLSTER, ARTHUR STANLEY, JR., history professor; b. Bismarck, ND, Jan. 30, 1922; s. Arthur S. and Gertrude (Pierce) B.; m. Elizabeth Barker Winkfield, Oct. 8, 1949; children: Stephen Clark, Gregory Pierce. AB, Dartmouth, 1943; MA, Harvard, 1947, PhD, 1954. Tchr. history Grosse Pointe (Mich.) High Sch., 1952-57, Pelham (N.Y.) High Sch., 1957-59; mem. faculty Harvard U., Cambridge, Mass., 1959—, prof. edn., 1967-82, prof. emeritus, 1982—. Author: James Freeman Clarke, Disciple to Advancing Truth, 1954. Served to lt. USNR, 1943-46. Mem. New Eng. History Tchrs. Assn. (pres. 1968-69, Kidger award 1970), Phi Beta Kappa. Mem. United Ch. of Christ (deacon). Home: 587 Laconia Cir Lake Worth FL 33467-2662 Office: Harvard U Grad Sch Edn Longfellow Hall Cambridge MA 02138

BOLSTER, JACQUELINE NEBEN (MRS. JOHN A. BOLSTER), communications consultant; b. Woodhaven, NY; d. Ernest William Benedict and Emily Claire (Guck) Neben; m. John A. Bolster, May 8, 1954. Studied, Pratt Inst., Columbia U. Promotion mgr. Photoplay mag., 1949—53; merchandising mgr. McCall's, NYC, 1953—64; dir. promotion and merchandising Harper's Bazaar, 1964—71; dir. advt. and promotion Elizabeth Arden Salons, 1971—76; dir. creative svcs. Elizabeth Arden, Inc., 1976—78; dir. comm. Elizabeth Arden Salons, 1978—87; comm. cons., 1987—. Recipient Art Dir.'s award, 1961, 1966. Mem.: Fashion Execs. Roundtable, Fashion Group, Advt. Women N.Y. (life), Women's Nat. Rep. Club (life). Episcopalian. also: Halsey Neck Ln Southampton NY 11968 Office Phone: 718-849-0975.

BOLSTERLI, MARGARET JONES, English professor, farmer; b. Watson, Ark., May 10, 1931; d. Grover Clevel and Zena (Cason) Jones; m. Mark Bolsterli, Dec. 30, 1953 (div. Dec. 1964); children: Eric, David. BA with honors, U. Ark., 1952; MA, Washington U., St. Louis, 1953; PhD, U. Minn., 1967. Asst. prof. Augsburg Coll., Mpls., 1967-68; prof. English, U. Ark., Fayetteville, 1968-93, prof. emeritus, 1993—, dir. Ctr. for Ark. and Regional Studies, 1984-87. Fulbright lectr., Portugal, 1986; vis. rsch. fellow Yale U., 1997-98; bd. dirs. Ark. Humanities Coun., 1992-94. Author: The Early Community at Bedford Park, 1977, Vinegar Pie and Chicken Bread, 1982, Born in the Delta, 1991, A Remembrance of Eden, 1993; contbr. articles and stories to Jour. Modern Lit., So. Quar., others. NEH Younger Humanist grantee, 1970-71; Ark. Endowment for Humanities grantee, 1980, 81 Mem. MLA (pres. women's caucus), South Cen. MLA. Democrat. E-mail: mbolster@alltel.net.

BOLT, DAWN MARIA, financial planner; b. Bklyn., June 12, 1949; d. Gulick Arthur B. and Georgette Helen (Werner) Bolt-Wiggs; widowed; children: Robert B. Williams, Wesley A. Williams. BA, Bklyn. Coll., 1971. Cert. fin. planner; chartered fin. analyst. Fin. analyst Blyth Eastman Dillon, NYC, 1971—77; rating agy. analyst Fitch Investors Svc., NYC, 1977—78; bank analyst Merrill Lynch, NYC, 1978—80; fin. analyst Moodys Investors Svc., NYC, 1980—86; real estate sales agt. J.R. Silvers Realty, NYC, 1987—95, Coldwell Banker Hunt Kennedy, NYC, 1995—98; pvt. practice fin. planning and coaching, 1998—. Avocations: bowling, tennis, skiing, reading, coaching. E-mail: jodiedawn49@hotmail.com.

BOLT, EUNICE MILDRED DEVRIES, artist; b. Clifton, NJ, Oct. 31, 1926; d. Lambert H. and Cora DeVries; m. Maurice L. Bolt (dec. Nov. 1989); children: Macyn Bolt, Tamsen Bolt, Valerie Bolt Wegner. Grad., Pratt Inst. Art & Design, Bklyn., 1949; BA, Calvin Coll., 1952; MA, Western Mich. U., 1973. Book illustrator Fideler Pubs., Grand Rapids, Mich., 1952-53, Zondervan Pub. Co., Grand Rapids, Mich., 1953-56; prof. Calvin Coll., Grand Rapids, Mich., 1962-67, Grand Rapids C.C., 1968-91. Internat. art study tours coord. and guide, 1978-2005; fine art exhbn. juror, 1987—; lectr. art history, 1991—, presenter watercolor workshops, 1991—; artist-in-residence, 1995—. Exhibited in group shows at Grand Rapids Art Mus., Kalamazoo Inst. Art, U. Mich. Schlusser Gallery, Pitts. Ctr. for the Arts, Westmoreland Mus. Art, Detroit Inst. Art. Home and Studio: 2481 Autumn Ash Dr Grand Rapids MI 49512

BOLTEN, JOSHUA BREWSTER, White House chief of staff; b. Washington, Aug. 16, 1954; BA with distinction, Princeton U., 1976; JD, Stanford U., 1980. Editor Stanford Law Review, 1980; law clk. to Hon. Thelton Henderson US Dist. Ct. (no. dist.) Calif., San Francisco, 1980; pvt. practice Bolten, O'Melveny & Myers, 1980—85; Internat. Trade Counsel US Senate Fin. Com., 1985—89; gen. coun. Office US Trade Rep., 1989—92; dep. asst. to the Pres. for legis. affairs The White House, Washington, 1992—93; tchr., internat. trade Yale Law Sch., 1993; exec. dir., legal & govt. affairs Goldman Sachs Internat., London, 1994—99; policy dir. Bush-Cheney presdl. campaign, 1999—2000; asst. to pres. & dep. chief of staff for policy The White House, Washington, 2001—03; dir. Office Mgmt. & Budget Exec. Office of the Pres., Washington, 2003—06; asst. to Pres., chief of staff The White House, Washington, 2006—. Exec. asst. to dir. Kissinger Commn. on Ctrl. Am. Office: The White House 1600 Pennsylvania Ave NW 1st Fl W Wing Washington DC 20502*

BOLTON, BETTY J., medical/surgical nurse, poet; b. Lusedale, Miss., Sept. 2, 1952; d. Saul Jones and Mary Hurley Fairley; m. Joe N. Bolton, July 28, 1968; children: Terry, Benilda, Timiki; 1 child, Joe Jones. AAS, Miss. Gulf Coast Jr. Coll., 1986; postgrad., Coastal Tng., Pascagoula, Miss., 1989. Libr. ref. aide Pascagoula Libr., Miss., 1986—89; program specialist I Salvation Army Domestic Violence Women, Pascagoula, Miss., 1986—90; owner B&J Vending, Moss Point, Miss., 1990—92; home health nurse Profl. Home Health, Biloxi, Miss., 1992—97; supr. South Miss. Regional Ctr., Long Beach, Miss., 1997—99; pvt. duty nurse Jackson County and South Miss., 2000—03. Author (poetry): Best Poems of 2002, 2002 (Editors Choice award, 2002), Across the Abyss, 2002 (Editors Choice award, 2002), Best Poems of 2003, 2003 (Editors Choice award, 2003). Recipient Pres. award, Iliad Press, 2003. Mem.: Ri Rsch., Acad. Am. Poets, Internat. Soc. Poets. Ch. Of Christ. Avocations: arts and crafts, sewing, walking, creative cooking, poetry. Home: 3809 Jeffery Dr Moss Point MS 39562 Office Phone: 228-325-7040. Personal E-mail: joebet51@bellsouth.net, bettyjoe53@aol.com.

BOLTON, CLAUDE M., JR., civilian military employee, retired military officer; BEE, U. Nebr., 1969; MA in Mgmt., Troy State U., 1978; MA in Nat. Security and Strategic Study, Naval War Coll., 1991. Commd. 2d. lt. USAF, 1969, advanced through grades to major gen., 1998, ret., 2002; pilot McConnell AFB, Ariz., 1971, Ubon Royal Thai AFB, Thailand, 1971-72; various assignments Cannon AFB, N. Mex., 1972-74; pilot, instr. Royal Air Force, Upper Heyford, England, 1974-76; test pilot Eglin AFB, Fla., 1978-82; various assignments Wright-Patterson AFB, Ohio, 1982-85, 88-93, 1996-98, US Dept. Def., Washington, 1986-88, 96, program exec. officer fighter and bomber programs, 1998—2000; comdt. Defense Sys. Mgmt. Coll., Ft. Belvoir, Va., 1993-96; asst. sec. for acquisition, logistics & tech., army acquisition exec., Dept. Army US Dept. Def., Washington, 2001—. Decorated Defense D.S.M., DFC with oak leaf cluster, Legion of Merit, Meritorious Svc. medal with two oak leaf clusters, Air medal with 16 oak leaf clusters, Vietnam Svc. medal with three svc. stars, Rep. Vietnam Gallantry Cross. Office: US Dept Defense Acquisition Logistics and Tech 103 Army Pentagon Washington DC 20310-0103

BOLTON, JOHN ROBERT, former ambassador, federal agency administrator; b. Balt., Nov. 20, 1948; s. Edward Jackson and Virginia (Godfrey) Bolton; m. Gretchen Louise Brainerd, Jan. 1986; 1 child, Jennifer Sarah. BA summa cum laude, Yale U., 1970, JD, 1974. Bar: DC 1975, US Dist. Ct. DC 1975, US Ct. Appeals (DC cir.) 1975, US Ct. Appeals (4th cir.) 1977, US Ct. Appeals (3rd cir.) 1978, US Supreme Ct. 1978, US Ct. Appeals (5th and 11th cirs.) 1981, US Ct. Appeals (10th cir.) 1983, US Ct. Appeals (1st, 6th, 7th, 8th and 9th cirs.) 1988, US Ct. Appeals (2nd cir.) 1989. Assoc. Covington & Burling, Washington, 1974—81, ptnr., 1983—85; legal cons. The White House, Washington, 1981; gen. counsel US Agy. for Internat. Devel., Washington, 1981—82, asst. adminstr. for prog. & policy coordination, 1982—83; exec. dir. com. on resolutions Rep. Nat. Com., Washington, 1983—84; asst. atty. gen. legis. affairs US Dept. Justice, Washington, 1985—88, asst. atty. gen. civil divsn., 1988—89; asst. sec. internat. orgn. affairs bur. US Dept. State, Washington, 1989—93; ptnr. Lerner, Reed, Bolton & McManus (and predecessor firms), Washington, 1993—99; of counsel Kutak Rock LLP, Washington, 1999—2001; under sec. for arms control & internat. security affairs US Dept. State, Washington, 2001—05, permanent US rep. to UN NYC, 2005—06; sr. fellow Am. Enterprise Inst., 2007—. Sr. fellow Manhattan Inst., 1993; adj. prof. George Mason U. Law Sch., 1994-96; pres. Nat. Policy Forum, Washington, 1995-96; sr. v.p. Am. Enterprise Inst., Washington, 1997-2001, commr. US Commn. on Internat. Religious Freedom, 1999-2001; bd. dirs., Project for a New Am. Century, 1989-2001, Subcommittee on Internat. Law, Federalist Soc., 1999-2001 Contbr. articles to profl. jours. Served in US Army Nat. Guard, 1970—74 USAR, 1974—76. Recipient Tree of Life award, No. & So. New Eng. Regions of Hadassah, 1990, Disting. Svc. award, US Dept. State, Edmund J. Randolph award, US Dept. Justice, 1998 Mem.: Pi Sigma Alpha, Phi Beta Kappa. Republican. Lutheran. Home Phone: 301-469-6903.

BOLTON, KENNETH ALBERT, management consultant; b. Mar. 6, 1941; s. Albert and Myrtle (Nelting) B.; m. Maryanne Lavelle; 1 child, Katharine. BS in Indsl. Engring., Pa. State U., 1978; MBA in Environ. Scis., U. Pa.; PhD in Mgmt., Almeda U. Registered profl. engr., Calif. With GE, Allentown, Pa., 1961-63, system mgr. Phila., 1963-72; mgr. MCS Mgmt. Internat., Washington, 1972-80, Coopers & Lybrand, Phila., 1980-82; dir. cons. Worden & Risberg, Phila., 1982-83; v.p. mktg. Laminated, Inc., Hatfield, Pa., 1983-86; pres. Mgmt. Internat., Phila., 1986-90, Wm. P. Bolton, Inc., Phila., 1990—. Contbr. articles to profl. jours. Advisor Jr. Achievement, Media, Pa., 1970; mem. adv. bd. Salvation Army. Mem. NSPE, Am. Arbitration Assn. (panel of arbitrators), Phila. C. of C. (bd. dirs. 1975, lobbyist small bus. coun. 1978), Welcome Soc. Pa., Union League Phila., St. George's Club Bermuda. Republican. Avocations: golf, computers, antiques. Home: 5900 Atlantic Ave Ventnor City NJ 08406-2862 Personal E-mail: mgtintl@aol.com.

BOLTON, MICHAEL, singer, songwriter; b. New Haven, Feb. 26, 1954; s. George and Helen Bolotin; m. Maureen, 1975 (div. 1991); children: Isa, Holly, Taryn. Songwriter for Laura Branigan, Pointer Sisters, Larry Graham, Thelma Houston, Cher, Barbra Streisand, Kenny Rogers; albums include The Hunger, 1987, Soul Provider, 1989, Time, Love & Tenderness, 1991, The Early Years, 1991, Timeless (The Classics), 1992, The One Thing, 1993, Greatest Hits 1985-95, 1995, Michael Bolton - Greatest Hits, 1996, All That Matters, 1997, Merry Christmas From Vienna, 1997, My Secret Passion, 1998, Vol. 2-The Timeless Classics, 1999, Only a Woman Like You, 2002, Joy to the World, 2002, All About Love, 2003, Legends, 2005, Bolton Swings Sinatra, 2006; singles include That's What Love Is All About, 1987, (Sittin' on) the Dock of the Bay, 1988, Fools Game, When a Man Loves a Woman (Best Male Pop Vocal Grammy award 1992); co-songwriter: How Am I Supposed To Live Without You, 1983 (Best Male Pop Vocal Grammy award 1989), Forever, 1989, How Can We Be Lovers, 1989, There's Always Love, 1990; actor (films) Meet Wally Sparks, 1997, Back by Midnight, 2002, Snow Dogs, 2002, High Voltage, 2002; actor & exec. prodr. Offside, 2001, exec. prodr. Good Advice, 2001, (TV films) Terror at Home: Domestic Violence in America, 2005. Founder Michael Bolton Found., 1993. Recipient Lewis Hine award, Nat. Child Labor Com., 1994, Martin Luther King Jr./CORE award, 1996; Hendon fellow, Yale U., 1995. Office: Jive Records 137-139 W 25th St #139 New York NY 10001

BOLTON, ROBIN JEAN, artist, painter; b. Americus, Ga., Sept. 13, 1943; d. Charles Robert and Sara Maude (Sumerford) Ricketson; m. Robert Emory Bolton III, Aug. 20, 1966; 1 child, Robin Jean. BFA, U. Ga., Athens, 1972. Graphic artist Shea/Rustin Pub., Atlanta, 1966-67, Davison's Dept. Store, Atlanta, 1967, Stein Printing Co., Atlanta, 1968, Naylor Assocs., East Point, Ga., 1968, Tucker Wayne & Co., Atlanta, 1968-70, Graphique Ltd., Chgo., 1970-72, Nan Miller Gallery, Rochester, N.Y., 1985—. Instr. Comml. Art Supply, Syracuse, N.Y., pvt. studio Bridgport, N.Y., Liverpool, N.Y.; label designer Persimmon Creek Vineyards, Ga. One-woman shows include The Frog & Peach Gallery, Clayton, Ga., 1997-2000, 2002, Nan Miller Gallery Rochester, N.Y., 2002, Gallery One, San Francisco, Ga. State Botanical Gardens, 2005, Home Expressions Design Ctr., Alpharetha, Ga., 2005; exhibited in group shows at Everson Mus. Art, Syracuse, 1976, The Jacob K. Javits Fed. Bldg., N.Y.C., 1986, Islip (N.Y.) Art Mus., 1989, Kirkpatrick Art Ctr., Oklahoma City, 1989, Nat. Assn. Women Artists Centennial Exhbn., 1989, Wyoming Sem. Juried Regional Exhibit, Kingston, Pa., 1996, U. Ga. State Heritage Botanical Gardens, The Alice Callaway Bldg., 2004, Lagerquist Gallery, Atlanta; permanent collections include the IBM Collection, State of Ga., State Capitol of Ga., Ga. Commn. on Women/Dept. of Labor Bldg. Atlanta, Talullah Falls Sch., Federated

Hall, Talullah Falls, Ga., Farash Coop., Rochester, N.Y.; designer labels for The Persimmon Creek Vineyards Recipient Cooperstown Nat. 1st prize Cooperstown (N.Y.) Art Assn., 1975, Henry Mallory Meml. award, 1978, Arena '76 1st prize, Binghamton, N.Y., 1976, Grand prize Best of Show, Liverpool State Open, 1976, Liquitex-Binney & Smith award for outstanding achievement in field of art, Moravia Coll., Bethlehem, Pa., 1996; named Hon. Youth Art Month Artist, State of Ga., 2001. Mem. Nat. Assn. Women Artists, Liverpool Arts and Crafts Guild, DAR, UDC. Methodist. Avocations: cooking, gardening, reading. Home: 4720 Sharron Point Ct Alpharetta GA 30004-3908 Office Phone: 770-521-1547. Personal E-mail: bbolton1@bellsouth.net.

BOLTON, ROGER, public relations executive; m. Lynne Bolton; 3 children. BA in Journalism, Ohio State U., 1972. Newspaper reporter, Marion, Ohio, 1972—75; press sec. and staff dir. US Congressman Clarence J. Brown, 1975—82; dir. speechwriting Reagan-Bush Re-Rlection Campaign, 1984; asst. US trade rep. pub. affairs Exec. Office of the Pres., 1985—88; spl. asst. to US Pres. Ronald Reagan, 1988—89; asst. sec. of the treasury pub. affairs, 1989—91; dir. corp. media rels., dir. commn. for IBM server and software groups IBM, 1991—95; sr. v.p. commn. Aetna Inc., 1995—2006; sr. counselor APCO Worldwide, 2007—. Pres. Arthur W. Page Soc., 2006—07. Office: APCO Worldwide 51 Madison Ave New York NY 10010

BOLTON, ROGER EDWIN, economist, educator; b. Dover, Pa., Nov. 23, 1938; s. Oscar Jacob and Edna Irene (Hughes) Bolton; m. Julia Carolyn Gooden, June 27, 1964; children: Christopher, Jonathan. AB, Franklin and Marshall Coll., 1959; PhD, Harvard U., 1964. Instr. Harvard U., Cambridge, Mass., 1964-66; asst. prof. econs. Williams Coll., Williamstown, Mass., 1966-69, assoc. prof., 1969-74, prof., 1974—2003, William R. Kenan Jr. prof., 1992-93, Edward Dorr Griffin prof., 1986-92, chmn. dept., 1975-76, 79-81, dir. Ctr. Humanities and Social Scis., 1985-87, chair faculty steering com., 1991-92, William Brough prof., 1994—2003, prof. emeritus, 2003—; rsch. assoc. Ctr. for Environ. Studies, 2003—, coord. self study accreditation, 2006—. Mem. assoc. staff Brookings Instn., 1965—68; sr. economist Curran Assocs., 1973—74; vis. prof. Wellesley Coll., 1977, U. Pa., 1981—82, Clark U., 1993; rsch. assoc. Joint Ctr. Urban Studies, 1979—81; Goerge A. Miller vis. prof. U. Ill., 1988; disting. vis. prof. U. Wis., Madison, 1989; mem. com. placed-based decision making NRC, 2000—02. Author: Defense Purchases and Regional Growth, 1966; editor: Defense and Disarmament, 1966; co-author: Regional Diversity, 1981; co-editor: Internat. Regional Sci. Rev., 1985—89; mem. editl. bd. Internat. Regional Sci. Rev., Annals Regional Sci., Can. Jour. Regional Sci., Growth and Change; mem. editl. bd., book rev. editor: Jour. Regional Sci.; contbr. articles to profl. jours. Mem. Bershire County Regional Planning Commn., Mass., 1980—81, 1982—88, clk., 1983—85, vice-chmn., 1985—87, mem. affordable housing com., 2005—06, mem. clearing ho. rev. com., 2006—; mem. Williamstown Planning Bd., 1983—86, chmn., 1985—86; bd. dirs. No. Berkshire Indsl. Pk. and Devel. Corp., chmn., 1986—88; bd. dirs. Hoosic River Watershed Assn., 2003—, treas., 2004—. Recipient Outstanding Contbn. to Planning award, Bershire County Regional Planning Commn., 1989, David Boyce award, N.Am. Regional Sci. Coun., 2006; Woodrow Wilson fellow, 1959—60, Danforth fellow, 1959—64. Mem.: Western Regional Sci. Assn. (bd. dirs. 2003—), Assn. Am. Geographers, Regional Studies Assn., Regional Sci. Assn. (councillor 1988—91), Am. Econ. Assn. Home: 30 Grandview Dr Williamstown MA 01267-2528 Office: Williams Coll Dept Econs Morey House Williamstown MA 01267 Office Phone: 413-597-2393. Business E-Mail: roger.e.bolton@williams.edu.

BOLTWOOD, RUSSELL LEWIS, lawyer, telecommunications industry executive; b. St. Louis, Apr. 15, 1963; s. Chester McBride and Joan Mary (Schnable) B. AB, U. Calif., Berkeley, 1986; JD, Golden Gate U., 1993. Assoc. atty. Davis, Reno & Courtney, San Francisco, 1993—96; corp. HR, risk mgr. Fritz Companies, Inc., San Francisco, 1996—97; gen. counsel, chief human resources officer UTStarcom, Inc., Alameda, Calif., 1997—. Vol. United Way, Oakland, 1987—. Mem. Am. Mensa, Commonwealth Club Calif., Toastmasters Internat. Avocations: music, backpacking, creative writing, composition of music. Home: 560 Elysian Fields Dr Oakland CA 94605-5010 Office: UTStarcom 1275 Harbor Bay Parkway Alameda CA 94502 Office Phone: 510-846-8800.*

BOMAN, KEITH GREGORY, cardiologist; b. June 1, 1949; BS, U. Calif., Santa Barbara; MD, George Washington U. Sch. Medicine, 1975. Cert. Internal Medicine, Cardiovascular Disease. Asst. prof. clin. medicine U. Nev. Sch. Medicine; practicing medicine Las Vegas, Nev., 1980—; private practice, 1997—. Med. dir. Automated External Defibrillator Program, Boyd Gaming Corp. Co-author: Cardiology for the House Officer (the first handbook and guide for residents and interns entering the field of cardiology), 1982. Bd. trustee Columbia Sunrise Hosp. and Med. Ctr., Donald W. Reynolds Found., 1995—; founder The Meadows Sch., Las Vegas Performing Arts Ctr. Found.; helped relocate Nev. Ballet Theatre; chmn. Las Vegas Performing Arts Ctr. Found. Named Top Doctor, Las Vegas Life. Mem.: Clark County Med. Soc. (past bd. trustee), Alpha Omega Alpha. Achievements include being the first cardiologist to implant a pacemaker in Las Vegas. Office: 601 S Rancho Dr Ste D-28 Las Vegas NV 89106 Office Phone: 702-383-0677.*

BOMAR, MARY AMELIA, federal agency administrator; b. Eng. naturalized, 1977; With U.S. Dept. Def.; supt. Okla. City Nat. Meml. Nat. Park Svc. U.S. Dept. Interior, Okla. state coord., acting supt. Rocky Mountain Nat. Park, asst. supt. San Antonio Missions Nat. Historical Park, supt. Edgar Allan Poe Nat. Park Historic Site, supt. Independence Nat. Historical Park, 2003—05, dir. N.E. region, 2005—06, dir., 2006—. Office: Nat Park Svc US Dept Interior 1849 C St NW Rm 3113 Washington DC 20240 Office Phone: 202-208-4747. Office Fax: 202-219-0910. E-mail: mary_bomar@nps.gov.*

BOMBA, JOHN GILBERT, civil engineer, consultant; b. Yorktown, Tex., Feb. 8, 1932; s. Vincent Englebert and Regina Bertha (Ibrom) B.; m. Jane Killingsworth, June 9, 1958; children: Anne K., Marian R. Thomas, Beatrice J., Norma J. Ohlenbusch. BS in petroleum engr., Tex. A&M, 1954, postgrad. civil, 1959; postgrad. structural, U. Tulsa, 1965. Registered profl. engr. Tex., Okla., La. Jr. engr Collins Construction Co., Port Lavaca, Tex., 1954, 56-61; civil engr. Sigler, Clark & Assocs., Weslaco, Tex., 1961-64; sr. engr. Williams Brothers Co., Tulsa, Okla., 1964-68; dir. of marine svcs. William Brothers Engr. Co., Tulsa, 1968-78; sr. project mgr. R.J. Brown & Assocs., The Hague, The Netherlands, 1978-82; chief engr. R.J. Brown & Assocs. Pty., Ltd., Singapore, 1982-88, R.J. Brown & Assocs. of Am., Houston, 1988-93, Kvaerner R.J. Brown, Houston, 1993-2000, RJ Brown Deepwater, Houston, 2000—01, Technip Offshore Inc., Houston, 2001—. Bd. dirs. Weather Rsch. Ctr., Houston. Editor: Proceedings of Workshop Pipeline Research Needs, 1997; contbr. numerous articles to profl. jours. With Signal Corps US Army, 1954—56. Fellow Am. Soc. Civil Engrs. (chmn. exec. com. pipeline divsn. 1977, 78, chmn. pipeline rsch. com., 1995-97), Houston Marine Tech. Soc. (mem. exec. coun. 1996—, chmn., 2003—). Republican. Roman Catholic. Home: 9834 Moorberry Ln Houston TX 77080-6402 Office: Technip Offshore Inc 11700 Old Katy Rd Ste 150 Houston TX 77079 Personal E-mail: john_bomba@earthlink.net.

BOMBACI, ANTHONY, chef; Grad., Culinary Inst. Am., Hyde Park, 1988. Sous chef Restaurant Chez Philippe, Memphis; demi-chef de partie, garde mgr., entremetier Restaurant La Adrienne, NYC; chef Restaurant le Français; chef de cuisine Lasalle Grill; sous chef The Dining Room, Ritz-Carlton, San Francisco; chef de cuisine Enoteca, Barcelona; exec. chef Nana, Dallas. Named one of Dallas' Rising Stars, StarChefs.com, 2007. Office: Nana Hilton Hotel 2201 N Stemmons Fwy Dallas TX 75207 Office Phone: 214-761-7479. Business E-Mail: anthony.bombaci@hilton.com.*

BOMBACK, FRED M., pediatrician; b. Bklyn., Nov. 11, 1944; s. Milton J. and Florence Bomback; m. Judy S. Bomback, Nov. 23, 1970; children: Mark, David, Andrew, Lawrence. BA, Brandeis U., Waltham, Mass., 1965; MD, NYU, 1969. Pediatrician, 1974—; clin. prof. pediats. Columbia U. Coll. Physicians & Surgeons, NYC, 1975—. Editor: Emergency Office Pediats., 1995—2000. Maj. USAF, 1972—74. Mem.: Alpha Omega Omega, Alpha Omega Alpha. Avocation: languages. Office: Westchester Pediatrics 99 Fieldstone Dr Hartsdale NY 10530

BOMBARA, BETH ANN, insurance company executive; b. Aug. 10, 1967; BBA, Bryant Coll. CPA. Acct. Arthur Andersen LLP, ptnr., 2001—02; sr. mgr. audit practice Deloitte & Touche LLP, 2002—04; v.p. The Hartford Fin. Services Group, Hartford, Conn., 2004—05, v.p., dep. contr., 2005—07, sr. v.p., contr., chief acctg. officer, 2007—. Past. chmn., dir. Foodshare. Mem.: Conn. Soc. CPAs. Office: The Hartford Fin Services Group Hartford Plz 690 Asylum Ave Hartford CT 06115*

BOMBARDELLI, FABIÁN ALEJANDRO, hydraulic engineer, researcher; b. La Plata, Buenos Aires, Argentina, May 12, 1966; s. Reynaldo Julio Bombardelli and Nidia Ethel Michelini. Bachiller, Colegio Nacional Rafael Hernández of La Plata, La Plata, Buenos Aires, Argentina, 1983; BS in Hydraulic Engring., U. de la Plata, Argentina, 1991; Master in Numerical Simulation and Control, U. Buenos Aires, 1999; PhD in Civil and Environ. Engring., U. Ill., 2004. Undergrad. asst. Bur. of Pub. Rds., Buenos Aires Province, La Plata, Buenos Aires, Argentina, 1989—91; rsch. engr. Nat. Inst. for Water, Ezeiza, Buenos Aires, Argentina, 1991—98; rsch. asst. dept. civil and environ. engring. U. Ill., Urbana, Ill., 1999—2003; asst. prof. dept. civil and environ. engring. U. Calif., Davis, 2004—. Cons., Buenos Aires, 1997—98; v.p. and coord. Environ. Inst., Ctr. of Engrs. of Buenos Aires Province, La Plata, Buenos Aires, Argentina, 1994—98. Contbr. articles to profl. jours. Counselor Argentine Cmty. at Urbana-Champaign, Urbana, Ill., 2002—03. Named Outstanding Rschr., Nat. Inst. for Water, Argentina, 1994; recipient Glenn and Helen Stout award, Dept. of Civil and Environ. Engring., U. of Ill. at Urbana-Champaign, 2001. Mem.: Planetary Soc., Am. Phys. SOc., Am. Soc. Civil Engrs., Internat. Assn. Hydraulic Rsch., Internat. Water Resources Assn., Phi Kappa Phi. Avocations: history, literature, classical music, movies, art. Office: Univ Calif Davis Dept Civil and Environ Engring One Shields Ave Davis CA 95616 Office Phone: 530-752-0949. E-mail: fabombardelli@ucdavis.edu.

BOMBARDT, JOHN NICHOLAS, research scientist; b. Phila., Dec. 10, 1942; s. Ruth Mildred Theobald and John Nicholas Bombardt; m. Shirlene Doris Dorsey, June 17, 1967; 1 child, Eric Russell. BA in Physics, Adams State Coll., Alamosa, Colo., 1963; MS in Physics, Am. U., Washington, DC, 1968, PhD, 1972. Gen. physicist Dept. of Army, Ft. Belvoir, Va., 1963—72; supr. physicist US Army, Harry Diamond Lab., Washington, 1972—77; sr. scientist R&D Assoc., Arlington, Va., 1977—82, dep. program mgr. Colorado Springs, 1984—89; program mgr. Jaycor, Colorado Springs, 1989—95; sr. scientist Def. Group Inc., Arlington, 1995—98; rsch. staff mem. Inst. Def. Analysis, Alexandria, Va., 1998—. Nuc. weapons effects divsn. dir., sr. exec. svc. US Army, Harry Diamond Lab., Washington, 1984—86. Fellow, Dept. of Army, 1975—76. Mem.: IEEE (guest editor Transactions on Nuc. Sci. 1979), Am. Phys. Soc., Electromagnetic Pulse Fellows. Avocations: history, running, weightlifting. Office: Inst Def Analyses 4850 Mark Center Dr Alexandria VA 22311-1882

BOMBERGER, RUSSELL BRANSON, lawyer, writer; b. Lebanon, Pa., May 1, 1934; s. John Mark and Viola (Aurentz) B.; divorced; children—Ann Elizabeth, Jane Carmel. BS, Temple U., 1955; MA, U. Iowa, 1956, MA, 1961, PhD, 1962; MS, U. So. Calif., 1960; LLB, JD, LaSalle U.; grad., U.S. Marine Corps Command and Staff Coll., 1987, U.S. Naval War Coll., 1991. Bar: Calif. 1970, U.S. Supreme Ct. 1975. Mem. editorial staff Phila. Inquirer, 1952-54; lectr. U. Iowa, 1955-57, U. So. Calif., 1957-58; asst. prof. U.S. Naval Postgrad. Sch., Monterey, Calif., 1958-62, assoc. prof., 1963-75, prof., 1975-89, prof. emeritus, 1989—; practice law, 1970—. Freelance writer, 1952—, communications cons., 1963—; safety cons. internat. program U. So. Calif. Inst. Safety and Systems Mgmt., 1983—; cons. Internat. Ctr. for Aviation Safety, Lisbon, 1984—; vis. fellow, Oxford U. Author: (novel) The Alternate Candidate, (broadcast series) The World of Ideas, (motion picture) Strokes and Stamps, (stage play) Closely Held; abstracter-editor: Internat. Transactional Analysis Assn. Capt. USNR, 1966-94. Decorated Meritorious Civilian Svc. medal, 1989; Am. Psychol. Found. fellow Columbia U., 1954-55, CBS fellow U. So. Calif., 1957-58, Keith fellow, 2004, Oxford U., 2004 Office: PO Box 8741 Monterey CA 93943-8741 E-mail: rbbomber@excite.com, rbbomber@lawyer.com.

BOMBIERI, ENRICO, mathematician, educator; b. Milan, Nov. 26, 1940; came to U.S., 1977; naturalized 1995; s. Carlo and Luisa (Cambi) B.; m. Susan Russell, Jan. 21, 1967, d 1999; 1 child, Donata. Grad., Trinity Coll., Cambridge; PhD, U. Milan, 1963. Prof. math. U. Cagliari, Italy, 1965, U. Pisa, Italy, 1966-74, Scuola Normale Superiore, Pisa, 1974, Inst. Advanced Study, Princeton, N.J., 1977—. Recipient Fields medal Internat. Math. Union, Vancouver, Can., 1974. Mem. Am. Acad. Arts and Scis., Nat. Acad. Sci., French Acad. Scis., Acad. Nazionale Delle Scienze Italy, Acad. Nazionale dei Lincei (nat. mem.), Swedish Royal Acad. Office: Inst Advanced Study Sch Mathematics Simonyi Hall 213 Einstein Dr Princeton NJ 08540

BOMSE, STEPHEN V., lawyer; b. LA, Dec. 18, 1944; AB, Stanford U., 1964; LLB, Yale U., 1967. Bar: Calif. 1967. Assoc. Heller, Ehrman, White & McAuliffe, San Francisco, 1967—72, ptnr., 1972—, co-chair Antitrust & Trade Regulation Practice Group. Vis. prof. law Stanford U., 1988-89; rep. 9th Cir. Jud. Conf., 1980-82; gen. counsel No. Calif. ACLU, 1980—. Fellow: Am. Bar Found.; mem.: Assn. Bus. Trial Lawyers of No. Calif. (pres. 1994—95), Bar Assn. Calif., State Bar Calif., ABA, Am. Law Inst. Office: Heller Ehrman 333 Bush St San Francisco CA 94104-2878 Office Phone: 415-772-6142. Office Fax: 415-772-6268. E-mail: sbomse@hewm.com.

BONA, FREDERICK EMIL, public relations executive; b. Union City, NJ, Mar. 3, 1939; s. Henry C. and Clementina A. Bona; m. Doris L. Hurlbert, May 27, 1961; children: Lauri Paporello, Dawn Rizzo, Christine Cabana, F.A. (Rick). BS in Mktg., Fairleigh Dickinson U., 1962. Press rels. rep. W.R. Grace & Co., NYC, 1962, mgr. press rels., 1970, dir. press rels., 1980, v.p. corp. communications div., 1983, dep. group exec., 1985, v.p., 1987-94; prin. The Dilenschneider Group, Inc., NYC, 1994-95, LS Comms., Inc., NYC, 1995—. Dep. comms. mgr. Pres.'s Pvt. Sector Survey on Cost Control (Grace Commn.), Washington, 1982-85. Mem. Overseas Press Club (bd. govs. 1988-91, 94-97), Pub. Rels. Soc. N.Y. Roman Catholic. Office: LS Communications Inc 17 Devon Rd Boonton NJ 07005-9305

BONA, JERRY LLOYD, mathematician, educator; b. Little Rock, Feb. 5, 1945; s. Louis Eugene and Mary Eva (Kane) B.; m. Pamela Anne Ross, Dec. 23, 1966 (div. Aug. 2005); children: Rachael Elizabeth, Jennifer Dani'el. BS in Applied Math. and Computer Sci., Washington U., St. Louis, 1966; PhD in Math., Harvard U., 1971; Doctorate (hon.), U. Bordeaux, 2006. Rsch. fellow U. Essex, Colchester, England, 1970-72; L. E. Dickson instr. U. Chgo., 1972-73, from asst. prof. to assoc. prof. to prof., 1973-86; prof. Pa. State U., University Park, 1986-90, Hamilton Shibley prof., 1990-95, acting chmn., 1990-91, chmn., 1991-95; CAM prof. math. and physics U. Tex., Austin, 1995—2002; prof., chmn. U. Ill., Chgo., 2002—07. Rsch. fellow dept. math. Harvard U. 1970, 73; U.K. Sci. and Engring. Rsch. Coun. sr. vis. fellow Fluid Mechanics Rsch. Inst., U. Essex, 1973, 74, 75, 77, 78; vis. rsch. assoc. Brookhaven Nat. Lab., 1976, 77; NAS exch. visitor to Poland, 1977; vis. prof. Centro Brasileiro Pesquisas Fisicas, Rio de Janeiro, 1980, Math. Rsch. Ctr., 1980-81, U. Brasilia, 1982, Lab. Anvendt Matematisk Fysik, Danish Tech. Sch., 1982, Inst. Math. and its Applications, U. Minn., 1985, 88, 90, 91, 2001; rsch. prof. Applied Rsch. Lab., Pa. State U., 1986-95; prof. invité U. Paris-Sud, Ctr. d'Orsay, 1982, 86-87, 92, 2001, 03, l'Inst. Nat. Sci. Rsch.-Oceanology, U. Que., 1982-87, Ecole Normale Superieure de Cachan, 1990-91, dir. rsch. CNRS, 1995, U. Bordeaux, 1995, 2001, 03, 05; invited prof. Inst. Pure and Applied Math., Rio de Janeiro, 1991, 93, 99, 2000, 02, 07, Acad. Sinica, Beijing, 1991, 96, 99, Math. Scis. Rsch. Inst., Berkeley, Calif., 1994, U. de Paris Nord, Math. Lab. Villetaneuse, 1993, 95, 99, 2006, U. Oxford, 1995, UNICAMP Campinas, 1998, 2000, 01, 04, 05, 06, TATA Inst., Bangalore, 1999, 2001, 03-04, vis. adj. prof., 2005—; Inst. Sci. de la Mer, U. Que., vis. adj. prof., 1999-2004; invited prof. U. de Paris Val du Marne, 2007; coll. coun. U. Chgo., 1981-84; task force on undergrad. edn. Pa. State U., 1989-91, hon. degree recepient recommendation com., 1994-95; mem. adv. com. NSF Divsn. Math. Scis., 1990-93, chmn., 1990-92; sci. adv. com. basic rsch. math. scis. U.S. Army Rsch. Office, 1979-82, review com. divsn. math. and computer sci. Argonne Nat. Lab., 1984-90, chmn., 1985-89; rev. panel, site visit team NSF Sci. and Tech. Ctrs., 1988; mem. NATO postdoctoral fellowships rev. panel, 1991; mem. ABET evaluating team, 1992; chmn. proposal rev. panel Dept. Energy, 1993; co-dir. Math. Edn. Reform Network, 1993—2004; vis. com. dept. math. U. Ill., Chgo., 1993, MIT, 1993-97, CUNY Bklyn. Coll., 1994, U. NC, 1996, Howard U., 1999, Fla. State U., 2000, James Franc Inst. U. Chgo., 2000-07, U. Okla., 2004, U. Tenn., 2005, U. Ill., 2005, Purdue U., Ind. U. Indpls., 2005, Ryerson U., 2007; forum post secondary edn. Math. Scis. Edn. Bd., 1994-2004; tchn. nat. vis. com. NY Collab. for Excellence in Tchr. Prep. in Math., Sci., Tech., 1996-2000; spkr., lectr. in field. Mem. editl. bd. SIAM Jour. Math. Anal., 1979—2005, editor-in-chief, 1987-92, 35 others; contbr. articles to profl. jours. Grantee W. M. Keck Found., 1989, NSF, 1972—; NSF grad. fellow Harvard U., 1966-70; Woodrow Wilson fellow Harvard U., 1966-67. Fellow AAAS (nat. com. chair 1994-97, nat. elected office 2001-05); mem. Soc. for Indsl. and Applied Math. (com. mng. editors 1987-92, com. on coms. and appts. 1988-95, vis. lectr. 1992—, rep. to AAAS sect. com. on math. 1994-97, nat. com. chair 1987-92, Am. Math. Soc. (nat. com. chair 1989-96, 99-2005, com. to select Steele prize winner 1984-87, adv. com. on newsletter on collegiate math. edn. 1987-88, bd. judges for Nat. Sci. and Engring. Fair 1990-91, chmn. liaison com. AAAS 1990-92, com. on edn. 1992-96, chmn. subcom. grad. and postdoctoral edn. 1993-95, univ. lectr. series com. 1994—, chmn., 1999-2005, nomination com. 1995-97, chmn. nomination com. 1995-96, com. on coms., chmn. 1998-2002, math. surveys and monographs editl. com. 2003—), Math. Assn. Am. (com. on undergrad. program in math. 1987-91, subcom. on major in math. scis. 1989-90, subcom. on calculus reform and 1st 2 yrs. 1989-91, rep. to AAAS sect. com. on math. 1993-96, program of cons. 1994—2004), Tau Beta Pi. Achievements include setting up a fluid mechanics lab in math. depts.; helping to organize interdisciplinary programs in science, engineering, economics, finance, computer science and mathematics. Office: Univ Ill 851 S Morgan St #249 Chicago IL 60607 Home Phone: 312-946-1406; Office Phone: 312-413-2567. Business E-Mail: bona@math.uic.edu.

BONACORSI, MARY CATHERINE, lawyer; b. Henderson, Ky., Apr. 24, 1949; d. Harry E. and Johanna M. (Kelly) Mack; m. Louis F. Bonacorsi, Apr. 23, 1971; children: Anna, Kathryn, Louis. BA in Math., Washington U., St. Louis, 1971; JD, Washington U., 1977. Bar: Mo. 1977, Ill. 1981, U.S. Dist. Ct. (ea. dist.) Mo., U.S. Dist. Ct. (so. dist.) Ill., U.S. Ct. Appeals (8th cir.), U.S. Supreme Ct. 1995. Ptnr. Thompson Coburn, St. Louis, 1977—. Chairperson fed. practice com. eastern dist., St. Louis, 1987—, eight cir. jud. conf. com., St. Louis, 1987—. Named one of Best Lawyers Am., 2006. Fellow Am. Bar Found.; mem. ABA, ATLA, Mo. Bar Assn., Met. St. Louis Bar Assn., Am. Bd. Trial Advocates (assoc.), Order of Coif. Office: Thompson Coburn LLP One US Bank Plz Saint Louis MO 63101 Office Phone: 314-552-6014. E-mail: mbonacorsi@thompsoncoburn.com.

BONAGURA, VINCENT R., pediatrician, educator, researcher; b. NYC, Mar. 30, 1949; s. Vincent P. and Vivian M. Bonagura; m. Barbara Ann Liskin, June 3, 1962 (dec. Apr. 1994); children: Elizabeth, Vivi, Rebecca, Amy. BA, Columbia U., 1971, MD, 1975. Diplomate Am. Bd. Pediatrics, Am. Bd. Allergy and Immunology (bd. dir. 1999—), Bd. Diagnostic Lab. Immunology. Intern Babies Hosp.-Columbia-Presbyn. Med. Ctr., NYC, 1975-76, resident in pediat., 1976-78; asst. prof. pediatrics Columbia U., NYC, 1981-82, asst. prof. pediatrics and microbiology, 1982-85; chief divsn. allergy, immunology, rheumatology Schneider Children's Hosp./L.I. Jewish Med. Ctr., 1985-99; assoc. prof. pediatrics Albert Einstein Coll. Medicine, Bronx, N.Y., 1989-94, assoc. prof. pediatrics, microbiology and immunology, 1991-94, prof., 1994—; dir. divsn. allergy/immunology North Shore/L.I. Jewish Health Care Sys., 1999—. Adj. asst. prof. microbiology Columbia U.; dir. Am. Bd. Allergy and Immunology, 2000—; appointee allergy and immunology RRC ACGME, 2001—. Contbr. articles to profl. jours. Fellow Am. Acad. Allergy and Immunology (tng. dirs. exec. com., residency rev. com., 2002-); mem. Am. Assn. Immunology, Soc. for Pediatric Rsch., Am. Coll. Rheumatology, Am. Acad. Pediatrics, Alpha Omega Alpha. Avocations: tennis, music, gardening. Office: LI Jewish Med Ctr Dept Pediatrics Schneider Children's Hosp New Hyde Park NY 11040 Office Phone: 516-465-5359. E-mail: bonagura@lij.edu.

BONALDI-MOORE, LORRAINE KAY, nursing educator; d. William Leon and Betty Ann Larsen; m. Louis Anthony Bonaldi (div.); m. Richard Whittier Moore, Dec. 15, 2003; children: Nicholas, Andrew, Anthony. BSN, Pacific Luth. U., 1979; MBA, HCM, U. Phoenix, 2004, MSN, 2005. Nurse U. Calif. San Diego Med. Ctr., 1979—81, Children's Hosp., San Diego, 1981—89, Ctr. for Plastic Surgery, Reno, 1989—2000, Health Insight, Reno, 2001—03, Aesthetic Plastic Surgery, Eugene, Oreg., 2004—05, U. Nev., Reno, 2005—, Washoe Med. Ctr., Reno, 2005—. PALS instr. Mem.: AACN. Avocations: marathon running, volunteer work. Office: Univ Nev Reno NV 89557

BONANNI, FABRIZIO, medical products executive; PhD in Chemistry, U. Florence; grad., Northwestern U. Inst. Internat. Mgmt., J.L. Kelloff Grad. Sch. Mgmt.; grad. Exec. Program in Mfg., Harvard U. Grad. Sch. Bus. Adminstrn. With Baxter Internat. Inc., Italy, 1974, v.p. quality and regulatory affairs Brussels, corp. v.p. regulatory and clin. affairs, corp. v.p. quality systems; sr. v.p. quality and compliance, corp. compliance officer Amgen, Inc., 1999—2003, sr. v.p. mfg., 2003—. Dir. Aastrom Biosciences, Inc. Trustee PR Sci., Tech. and Rsch. Trust, Mus. Contemporary Art, LA; bd. dirs. Calif. Healthcare Inst.; bd. trustees Calif. Sci. Ctr. Found. Office: Amgen Inc 1 Amgen Ctr Dr Thousand Oaks CA 91320-1799 Office Phone: 805-447-1000. Office Fax: 805-447-1010.*

BONANNO, BRUCE BRIAN, emergency physician; b. Irvington, NJ, June 29, 1955; s. Anthony Samuel and Jean Teresa Bonanno; children: Bryan Todd, Danielle Alexandra. BS, Union Coll., Schenectady, NY, 1977; MD, St. George's U., Grenada, 1983. Attending emer. rm. physician Misericordia Hosp., Phila., 1986—87, Monmouth Med. Ctr., Long Branch, NJ, 1987—92, Brick Hosp., NJ, 1992—93, Atlantic City Med. Ctr., 1992—93; attending emergency room physician St. Agnes Med. Ctr., Phila., 1992—93, Helene Fuld Med. Ctr., Trenton, NJ, 1993—95, Centr-aState Med. Ctr., Freehold, NJ, 1994—97, Bayonne Hosp., NJ, 1997—2000, Wilkes-Barre Gen. Hosp., Pa., 1999, Berwick Hosp., Pa.,

1999—2000, Bayshore Cmty. Hosp., Holmdel, NJ, 2000—, Belmond Med. Ctr., Iowa, 2006—, Cmty. Gen. Hosp., Syracuse, 2006—07, Catskills Regional Med. Ctr., Harris, NY, 2006—. Tchr. Hahnemann Sch. Medicine, 1987—92, Robert Wood Johnson Sch. Medicine, 1993, St. George's U. Sch. Medicine, 1993—; med. cons. News RN, 1996—. Host: (TV show) To Your Health, 1996—2006. Mem.: Nat. Assn. Med. Comm. (bd. dirs., sec.-treas.), Am. Coll. Emergency Physicians (chairperson pub. rels. com., sec.-treas., bd.dirs.).

BONAPART, ALAN DAVID, lawyer; b. San Francisco, Aug. 4, 1930; s. Benjamin and Rose B.; m. Helen Sennett, Aug. 20, 1955; children: Paul S., Andrew D. AB with honors, U. Calif., Berkeley, 1951, JD, 1954. Bar: Calif. 1955, US Tax Ct. 1965, US Supreme Ct. 1971. Assoc. Bancroft & McAlister (formerly Bancroft, Avery & McAlister), San Francisco, 1959-62; ptnr. Bancroft & McAlister, San Francisco, 1962-93, Bancroft & McAlister, A Profl. Corp., 1993-99, Bancroft & McAlister LLP, 1999—. Past trustee Bancroft and McAlister Found.; mem. adv. com. Heckerling Estate Planning Inst., U. Miami, Fla., 1974-87, 92—, mem. faculty, 1974, 91-2000; past dir. Myrtle V. Fitchen Charitable Trust. Mem. ABA, Am. Coll. Trust and Estate Counsel, Bar Assn. San Francisco, State Bar Calif. (cert. in estate planning, probate and trust law Bd. Legal Specialization 1991-2006). Office: Bancroft & McAlister LLP Ste 120 300 Drake's Landing Rd Greenbrae CA 94904-3123 Office Phone: 415-464-8855 301. Business E-Mail: abonapart@bamlaw.com.

BONAPARTE, RUDOLPH, engineering company executive; BS in Civil Engring., U. Tex., Austin, 1977; MS in Geotechnical Engring., U. Calif., Berkeley, 1978, PhD in Geotechnical Engring., 1981. Pres., CEO GeoSyntec Consultants, Inc., Atlanta, 1988—. Mem. civil and environ. engring. adv. coun. U. Calif., Berkeley. Contbr. articles to profl. jours., chapters to books. Named Overall Engr. of Yr., Ga. Soc. Profl. Engrs., 2004; recipient Award of Excellence, North Am. Geosynthetics Soc., 1991, IGS award, Internat. Geosynthetics Soc., 1994. Mem.: ASCE (J. James Croes medal 2000), NAE. Office: GeoSyntec Consultants 1255 Roberts Blvd NW Ste 200 Kennesaw GA 30144 Office Phone: 678-202-9500. Office Fax: 678-202-9501.*

BONATZ, EKKEHARD, hand surgeon; s. Edelgard and Hans Bonatz; m. Jill J. Jones, Dec. 21, 1985; children: Thomas, Joseph, Catherine. MD, Medizinische Hochschule Hannover, Germany, 1982. Lic. Orthop. Surgery Am. Bd. Med. Specialties, 2001, cert. Added Qualification in Hand Surgery Am. Bd. Med. Specialties, 2001. Resident in anesthesiology Medizinische Hochschule Hannover, 1982—83; instr. orthop surgery U. Ala., Birmingham, 1988—89; staff surgeon Brooke Army Med. Ctr., San Antonio, 1989—91; surgeon Johnson and Hatchett Orthops., PC, Florence, 1991—92; assoc. prof., faculty and staff surgeon U. Ala. Med. Ctr. Hosps., Birmingham, 1992—2002; surgeon, ptnr. Southlake Orthops., Birmingham, 2002—. Dir. Southlake Orthopaedics Hand Ctr., Birmingham, 2002—. Translator: (book) The Electroencephalogram in Anesthesia. Sponsor Mercedes Marathon, Birmingham, 2004—05. Maj. US Army, 1989—91. Decorated Army Achievement medal US Army. Mem.: Internat. Coll. Surgeons, AMA, ACS, Am. Soc. for Surgery the Hand, Am. Acad. Orthop. Surgeons. Achievements include research in investigated degenerative arthritis of the carpus associated with congenital hypoplastic thumb; conducted prospective study comparing open and endoscopic carpal tunnel release; studied suture anchors versus pull-out buttons for FDP tendon attachment: a biomechanical comparison. Office: Southlake Orthop Hand Ctr 4517 Southlake Pkwy Birmingham AL 35244 Home Phone: 205-969-3484; Office Phone: 205-985-4111. Office Fax: 205-985-4326.

BONAUTO, MARY, lawyer; b. 1961; BA, Hamilton Coll.; JD, Northeastern U. Civil rights project dir. Gay and Lesbian Advs. & Defenders (GLAD), 1990—. Mem. Mass. Atty. Gen. Working Group on Racial Profiling. Mem.: ABA (sub.-com. sexual orientation & gender identity, vice-chair), Boston Bar Assn. (mem. family law steering com.). Office: Gay and Lesbian Advocates & Defenders Ste 800 30 Winter St Boston MA 02108*

BONAVENTURA, CELIA JEAN, biochemist, researcher; b. Silver City, N.Mex., June 19, 1941; d. Rolan James and Ruth (Hale) Taylor; m. Joseph Bonaventura, Aug. 20, 1960; children: Marina Celeste, Michelle Celia. BA, San Diego State U., 1964; PhD, U. Tex., 1968. Rsch. assoc. Duke U. Med. Ctr., Beaufort, N.C., 1972-75, asst. med. rsch. prof., 1975-84, assoc. prof., 1984-90, prof., 1990—; co-dir. Duke U. Marine Biomed. Ctr., Beaufort, 1978—. Mem. Gov.'s Task Force on Aquaculture, 1987-88. Mem. editorial bd. Hemoglobin, 1977-89; contbr. over 100 articles on structure, function and assembly of respiratory proteins to profl. jours. Mem. adv. bd. Vocat. Edn. Program, Carteret County, N.C., 1990—. Rsch. grantee NIH, NSF, Office of Naval Rsch., Nat. Oceanography and Atmospheric Adminstrn., others, 1972—. Mem. AAAS, Am. Chem. Soc., Biophys. Soc. (chmn. human rights com. 1990—). Achievements include development of new concepts in the allosteric control of respiratory proteins; establishment of Marine Biomedical Center to explore the relationships between the marine environment and the human species; research in protein engineering. Office: Duke U Marine Lab Pivers Island Beaufort NC 28516

BONAVIA, PAUL J., energy executive; m. Patricia Sesterhenn; 2 children. BA, Drake U., Des Moines, 1972; law degree, U. Miami, Fla., 1975. Ptnr. Steel Hector & Davis, Miami; v.p., gen. counsel Dominion Resources, Inc., Richmond, Va., 1991, sr. v.p. corp. affairs, 1995; with LeBoeuf, Lamb, Greene & MacRae, LLP; sr. v.p., gen. counsel, pres. Internat. New Century Energies; pres. Energy Markets Xcel Energy (merger of No. States Power Co. and New Century Energies), pres. Comml. Enterprises, pres. Utilities Group. Bd. dirs. Am. Wind Energy Assn., 2007—. Office: Xcel Energy 414 Nicollet Mall Minneapolis MN 55401-1993*

BONAZZI, ELAINE CLAIRE, mezzo soprano; b. Endicott, NY; d. John Dante and Zina (Rossi) Bonazzi; m. Jerome Ashe Carrington, Sept. 21, 1963; 1 child, Christopher Carrington. BM (George Eastman scholar), Eastman Sch. Music. Currently artist-in-residence SUNY, Stonybrook; pvt. voice studio NYC. Past faculty Peabody Conservatory; vis. prof. Eastman Sch. Music, Rochester, NY, 1979; judge nat. and internat. competitions. Singer: Santa Fe Opera, 1958, Opera Soc. Washington, 1960, NYC Opera, 1965, Opera Internacional, 1966, Met. Opera at Forum, 1973, Europe, West Berlin Festival opera, 1961, Spoleto Festival, 1974, Castel Franco Festival Venetian Music, 1975, Berlin Bach Festival, 1976, Pks. Radio TV Difusion, 1980—, Netherlands Opera, 1978, Minn. Opera, 1985, Artpark Festival, 1987, Opera Theater St. Louis, 1988, New Orleans Opera, 1988, 1990, Spoleto-Charleston Festival, 1981, Edmonton Opera, 1990, 1992, Winnipeg Opera, 1993, Libr. Congress concerts, (Operas) Pique Dame, 1989, Vanessa, 1988, Carlson's Midnight Angel, 1993, Glimmergalss Opera La Calisto, 1995, NYC Opera, NY Philharm., Phila. Orch., Boston Symphony, Cleve. Orch., Can. Broadcasting Corp., PBS NET Opera Theatre, NBC, ABC, CBS TV networks, (albums) Candide, Vanguard, Folkways, Grenadilla, The Art of Elaine Bonazzi, 2006 (one of Best Historic Vocal Recs. of Yr., Opera News mag., 1907), over 40 world permier of major works by leading composers with maj. orchs. and opera cos. Named Bonazzi scholar fund in her honor, SUNY Stony Brook, 2005; named one of 6 honored alumni 50th Anniversary Yr., Eastman Sch. Music, 1971; recipient Concert Artists Guild award, 1960; William Matheus Sullivan grantee. Mem.: Mu Phi Epsilon. *In performing great music one tries to be honest as well as inventive-in communicating emotion. And one tries to remain true to the intentions of the composer. It can be a frustrating task requiring infinite patience and infinite care, but what joy for the performer when at last he can touch the heart of the listener.*

BONCEK, JOHN JAMES, mathematics professor; b. Liberty, NY, Jan. 27, 1957; s. Louis and Barbara Boncek. BA, SUNY, Buffalo, 1978; JD, Temple U., Phila., 1981; MS, La. State U., Baton Rouge, 1990; PhD, U. of Cen. Fla., Orlando, 2003. Bar: Pa. 1981. Asst. prof. of math. Troy U., Montgomery, Ala., 2003—. Office: Troy Univ PO Drawer 4419 Montgomery AL 36103-4419 Home Phone: 334-277-8173; Office Phone: 334-241-9789. E-mail: jboncek@troy.edu.

BOND, ALMA HALBERT, psychoanalyst, author; b. Phila., Feb. 6, 1923; BA in Psychology with honors, Temple U., Phila., 1944; MA in Psychology, NYU, 1951; PhD in Devel. Psychology, Columbia U., NYC, 1961. Diplomate Am. Bd. Psychotherapy. Pvt. practice psychoanalysis pvt. practice, NYC, 1953-91; tng. analyst Inst. Psychoanalytic Tng. and Rsch., NYC, 1963—. Author: Who Killed Virginia Woolf, A Psychobiography, 1989, 2000, (with Lucy Freeman) America's First Woman Warrior: The Courage of Deborah Sampson, 1992, Dream Portrait, 1992, Is There Life After Analysis?, 1993, On Becoming a Grandparent, 1994, Profiles of Key West, 1996, the Autobiography of Maria Callas, a Novel, 1998, 2000, I Married Dr. Jekyll and Woke Up Mrs. Hyde, or What Happens to Love, 2000, Tales of Psychology: Short Stories to Make You Wise, 2002, Camille Claudel, a Novel, 2006, Old Age Is a Terminal Illness, 2006; sr. writer CAYO mag.; contbr. Key West Citizen, Solaris Hill, Tropic Keys, Time Out, Remember. Lt. USN, 1944—46. Recipient Honors in Psychology Temple U., 1944, Winner Am. Literary Press Contest, 1993, Runner up First Novel Contest, 1995, Hemingway award, Fla. State awards for fine writing. Mem.: Inst. for Psychoanalytic Tng. and Rsch., Internat. Psychoanalytic Assn., APA. Home and Office: 34 West 11th St Ground Fl New York NY 10011 Home Phone: 212-786-3230; Office Phone: 212-786-3230. Personal E-mail: almahb@aol.com.

BOND, CHRISTOPHER SAMUEL (KIT BOND), senator, lawyer; b. St. Louis, Mar. 6, 1939; s. Arthur D. and Elizabeth (Green) B.; m. Linda Pell; 1 child, Samuel Reid. BA with honors, Princeton U., 1960; LLB, U. Va., 1963. Bar: Mo. 1963, U.S. Supreme Ct. 1967. Law clk. to presiding chief justice U.S. Ct. of Appeals (5th cir.), Atlanta, 1963-64; assoc. Covington & Burling, Washington, 1965-67; pvt. practice law Mexico, Mo., 1968; asst. atty. gen., chief counsel consumer protection div. State of Mo., 1969-70, gov., 1973-77, 81-85; auditor, 1971-73; ptnr. Gage & Tucker, Kansas City, 1985-87; US Senator from Mo., 1987—; chmn. small bus. com. 104th Congress. Mem. appropriations com., 1991—, chmn. subcom. on VA, HUD and ind. appropriations agys., 1991—, subcom. on def., 1993—, subcom. on fgn. ops., 1999—, subcom. on transp., 1995—; budget com., 1989—, environment and pub. works com., 1995—, subcom. on drinking water, fisheries and wildlife, 1995—; chmn. small bus. com., senate Rep. policy com.; pres. Gt. Plains Legal Found., Kansas City, Mo., 1977-80; chmn. Rep. Gov.'s Assn., Midwestern Gov.'s Conf., chmn. con. on econ. and community devel., 1981-83, chmn. con. on energy and environment, 1983-84. Republican. Presbyn. Office: US Senate 274 Russell Senate Bldg Washington DC 20510-0001 also: District Office Ste 204 1001 Cherry St Columbia MO 65201-7931 Office Phone: 202-224-5721, 573-442-8151. Office Fax: 202-224-8149, 573-442-8162.*

BOND, ENRIQUETA CARTER, science administrator; b. Buenos Aires, May 22, 1939; d. James Prescott and Harriette Mortley (Bovard) Carter; m. Langhorne Bond, Aug. 26, 1962; children: Langhorne Carter, Prescott McCook. BA in Zoology and Physiology, Wellesley Coll., 1961; MA in Biology and Genetics, U. Va., 1963; PhD in Molecular Biology and Biochem. Genetics, Georgetown U., 1969. Asst. prof., acting chmn. biology Chatham Coll., Pitts., 1970-73; asst. prof., dept. exec. dept. med. scis. So. Ill. U., Springfield, 1974-78; staff officer Nat. Acad. Scis., Inst. of Medicine, Washington, 1979-80, divsn. dir., 1981-88, exec. officer, 1989-94; pres. Burroughs Wellcome Fund, Durham, NC, 1994—. Bd. regents Nat. Libr. Medicine, Bethesda, Md., 1996—; bd. sci. counselors Nat. Ctr. Infectious Disease Control and Prevention, Atlanta, 1997—; bd. mem. health sci. policy Inst. Medicine, Washington, 1994-97, Nat. Academies' Com. on Sci., Engring., and Pub. Policy Contbr. articles to profl. jours. Bd. dirs. NC Biotech Ctr., Research Triangle Park, NC, 1995—, pres., 1998; bd. dirs. Rsch. Triangle Found., 1996—; mem. leadership coun. Rsch. America!, Alexandria, Va., 1996—. Recipient Profl. Staff award Nat. Acad. Sci., 1985. Mem. AAAS, APHA, Inst. Medicine (mem. coun. 1999—), Am. Soc. Microbiology, Soc. for Advancement of Women's Health Rsch. (sec. bd. dirs. 1995—), Sigma Xi. Episcopalian. Avocations: needlepoint, reading. Office: Burroughs Wellcome Fund PO Box 13901 Research Triangle Park NC 27709-3901

BOND, HALLIE E., curator, historian; b. Denver, Sept. 23, 1955; d. Robert Franklin and Mary Stewart Bond; m. Mason Everett Smith, Sept. 27, 1986; children: Stewart Alexander Smith, Margaret Louise Smith. BA in History, U. Colo., Boulder, 1977; MA in Medieval Studies, U. York, Eng., 1980; MA in History, cert. in History, U. Del., Newark, 1983. Curator Adirondack Mus., Blue Mountain Lake, NY, 1983—, No. Forest Ctr., Concord, NH, 2000—02. Bd. mem. Mus. Small Craft Assn., 1987—91, 1997—2000, 2002—05; adj. instr. St. Lawrence U., Canton, NY, 2004, 05. Author: (books) Boats & Boating in the Adirondacks, 1995; author, editor: A Paradise for Boys & Girls: Childrens Camps in the Adirondacks, 2006. Bd. mem. Adirondack Lakes Ctr. Arts, Blue Mountain Lakes, NY, 1984—90, Ham County Coop. Ext., Lake Pleasant, NY, 1985—88; bd. mem. bd. edn. Long Lake Ctrl. Sch., NY, 1997—. Implementation grant, NEH, 1992, fellowship, Rotary Found., 1978—79, Hagley fellowship, Eleutherian Mills-Hagley Found., 1981—83. Avocation: fiber arts. Office: Adirondack Mus PO Box 99 Blue Mountain Lake NY 12812 Home Phone: 518-624-6398; Office Phone: 518-352-7311 ext 105. Business E-Mail: hebond@adkmuseum.org.

BOND, JAMES MAX, JR., architect, academic administrator; b. Louisville, July 17, 1935; s. James Max and Ruth (Clement) B.; m. Jean Davis Carey, Oct. 11, 1961; children: Carey Julian, Ruth Marion. BA magna cum laude, Harvard U., 1955, MArch., 1958; DHL (hon.), N.J. Inst. Tech., 1993. Registered architect, N.Y., 1963. Archtl. apprentice various offices, Paris, NYC, 1959-64; arch. Ghana Nat. Constrn. Corp., Accra, Ghana, 1964-65; instr. U. Sci. and Tech., Kumasi, Ghana, 1965-67; exec. dir. Architect's Renewal Commn., NYC, 1967-68; asst. prof. to prof. and chmn.Grad. Sch. Architecture and Planning Columbia U., NYC, 1970-85; prof., dean Sch. Architecture and Environ. Studies CCNY, 1985-92; ptnr. Bond, Ryder and Assocs., NYC, 1969-90, Davis Brody Bond, LLP, NYC, 1990—. Favrot chair Tulane U. Sch. Arch., 1999; Charles Moore vis. prof. Taubman Sch. Arch. U. Mich., 2003. Prin. works include Bolgatanga Libr. bldg., Ghana, Schomburg Ctr., N.Y., Studio Mus., Harlem, N.Y.C., Martin Luther King Jr. Ctr. and Tomb, Atlanta, Birmingham Civil Rights Museum; firm selected assoc. arch., World Trade Ctr. Memorial site. Commr. City Planning Commn., N.Y.C., 1980-87; bd. dirs. Mcpl. Arts Soc., N.Y.C., 1986; mem. N.Y. Bldg. Congress, 2002—; bd. dirs. Regional Plan Assn., 2003—. Fulbright grantee, 1958. Fellow AIA (Harry B. Rutkins Meml. award for svc. to profession 1983, Whitney M. Young Jr. Citation award 1987); mem. Am. Acad. Arts and Scis., Nat. Orgn. Minority Architects, Phi Beta Kappa. Democrat. Home: 800 Riverside Dr Apt 5E New York NY 10032 Office: Davis Brody Bond LLP 315 Hudson St New York NY 10013-1009 Office Phone: 212-633-4700. Business E-Mail: mbond@davisbrody.com.

BOND, JULIAN, civil rights association executive; b. Nashville, Jan. 14, 1940; s. Horace Mann and Julia Agnes (Washington) Bond; m. Pamela S. Horowitz, Mar. 17, 1990; children from previous marriage: Phyllis Jane, Horace Mann, Michael, Jeffrey, Julia. BA, Morehouse Coll., 1971; LLD (hon.), Dalhousie U., 1969, U. Bridgeport, 1969, Wesleyan U., Conn., 1969, U. Oreg., 1969, Syracuse U., 1970, Eastern Mich. U., 1971, Tuskegee Inst., 1971, Howard U., 1971, Morgan State U., 1971, Wilberforce U., 1971, Patterson State Coll., 1972, NH Coll., 1973, Detroit Inst. Tech., 1973; DCL (hon.), Lincoln U., Pa., 1970, Bates Coll., 1998, Northeastern U., 1999, Edward Waters Coll., 1995, Gonzaga Sch. Law, 1997, Calif. State U., Monterey Bay, 1998, Washington U., 2000; LLD (hon.), Audrey Cohen Coll., New York, 2001, Williams Coll., 2005, U. Ill., 2006. A founder Com. Appeal for Human Rights, 1960, Student Nonviolent Coordinating Com., 1960, communications dir., 1961-66; reporter, feature writer Atlanta Inquirer, 1960-61, mng. editor, 1963; mem. Ga. Ho. of Reps., from Fulton County, 1965-75, Ga. State Senate, 1975-87. So. corr.: Reporting Racial Equality Wars; narrator Eyes on the Prize, Part 1, Part 2. Chmn. bd. dirs. NAACP, 1998—; mem. adv. bd. Harvard Bus. Sch., Initiative Social Enterprise; bd. dirs. So. Conf. Edn. Fund, So. Poverty Law Ctr., Coun. for a Liveable World; pres. emeritus So. Poverty Law Ctr., bd. dirs.; chmn. Premier Auto Group Diversity Coun. Office Phone: 202-244-1213.

BOND, LINDA GRACE, educational consultant; d. William E. G. and Marjorie Hudson Bond; 1 child, Jessica. BA in Am. Govt., U. Calif., Santa Barbara, 1971; MA in Politics, Rutgers U., New Brunswick, NJ, 1972. Co-dir. student lobby U. Calif., Sacramento, 1972—75; cons. assembly edn. com. Calif. Legislature, Sacramento, 1975—80, sr. cons. senate edn. com., 1983—90; pres. Bond Assocs., Sacramento, 1980—83; sr. cons. Commn. on Tchr. Credentialing, Sacramento, 1990—99, dir. govt. rels., 1999—2005; sr. policy cons. Ctr. for the Future of Tchg. and Learning, Sacramento, 2000—. Sr. edn. cons. Calif. Legislature, Sacramento, 1983—90, Commn. Tchr. Credentialing, Sacramento, 2000—05. Avocations: reading, singing, exercise. Home and Office: Ctr Future Tching and Learning 640 Santa Ynez Way Sacramento CA 95816-3910

BOND, MARC DOUGLAS, lawyer; b. Spokane, Wash., July 3, 1954; s. Richard Milton and Patricia (Hendrickson) B.; m. Cathy Sue Kasner, July 16, 1977; children: Travis Eliot, Carly Mariah, Katie McKenzie, Juli Sierra. BA in Polit. Sci., Willamette U., 1975, JD cum laude, 1978. Bar: Wash. 1978, Alaska 1979, U.S. Dist. Ct. Alaska 1979, U.S. Ct. Appeals (9th cir.) 1984, U.S. Supreme Ct. 1991. Law clk. to presiding judge Alaska Ct. System, Anchorage, 1978-79; assoc. Delaney, Wiles, Hayes, Reitman & Brubaker, Inc., Anchorage, 1979-83; shareholder Delaney, Wiles, Hayes, Gerety, Ellis & Young, Inc., Anchorage, 1983-97; gen. counsel Mount Roberts Tramway Ltd. Partnership, 1995-98; asst. counsel Union Oil Co. of Calif., 1997—2005; gen. counsel Alaska Nitrogen Products, LLC, 1998-2001; sr. counsel Chevron N.Am. Exploration and Prodn., 2005—. Co-founder, bd. dirs. Arctic Power!, 1992—; spl. counsel Alaska Ski Areas Assn., 1992—97. Author: Alaska from Leasing to Production, 2000, Arctic National Wildlife Refuge: America's Serengeti or Big Oil's Playpen, 2003. Legal advisor Alaska div. Nat. Ski Patrol System Inc., Denver, 1982-89, dir. Alaska div., 1988-90, asst. nat. legal counsel, 1990-91, nat. legal counsel, 1991-97; dir. Sourdough Ski Patrol, Girdwood, Alaska, 1983-86; bd. dirs. ARC, Anchorage, 1983-86, Alaska Health Fair, Inc., 2001—06; asst. scoutmaster Boy Scouts Am. Troop 209, 2001—06; USSF cert. soccer referee. Mem. Wash. State Bar Assn., Alaska Bar Assn. (co-chair corp. counsel sect.), Federalist Soc., Asia Pacific Lawyers Assn., South Boys Soccer Booster Found. Republican. Avocations: skiing, hiking, camping, soccer. Office: Chevron 909 W 9th Ave Anchorage AK 99501-3339 Office Phone: 907-276-7600. Business E-Mail: mbond@chevron.com.

BOND, PETER DANFORD, physicist; b. Providence, Jan. 30, 1940; s. Douglas D. and Helen H. (Cannon) B.; m. Sandra E. Salim, Aug. 3, 1968; children: Jennifer, Colin; stepchildren: Anthony Shane, John Shane. BA, Harvard U., 1962; MA, Western Res. U., 1963; PhD, Case Western Res. U., 1969. Rsch. assoc. Stanford U., Palo Alto, Calif., 1969-72; from asst. physicist to acting dir. Brookhaven Nat. Lab., Upton, NY, 1972—97, acting chief info. officer, 2002—03, interim dep. dir. for sci. and tech., 2004—, acting assoc. dir. nuclear and particle physics, 2006—. Chmn. exec. com. Holifield Heavy Ion Rsch. Facility, 1981; mem. program adv. com. Super Heavy Ion Linear Accelerator, 1977-81, chmn., 1981; mem. program com. on heavy ions SUNY, Stony Brook; mem. panel to rev. maj. nuclear physics facilities Dept. Energy, 1987; mem. siting panel for Gammasphere, 1989; reviewer physics program SUNY Grad. Sch.; mem. physics divsn. adv. com. Oakridge Nat. Lab., 1992-97; mem. com. of visitors to NSF Physics Divsn., 1994, 2006; mem. nuclear sci. adv. com. to Dept. Energy/NSF, 1994-97; mem. dean's adv. com. MIT/Lab. Nuclear Sci., 1994-99; sr. policy analyst, Office of Sci. and Tech. Policy, 1999; mem. com. of visitors Dept. Energy High Energy Physics, 2004; mem. com. Nat. Coun. on Radiation Protection, 2002-04; bd. dirs. Nat. Space Biomed. Rsch. Inst., 2005—. Contbr. numerous articles to profl. jours. FOM fellow (the Netherlands), 1983-84. Fellow AAAS (steering com. on physics 2001-03), Am. Phys. Soc. (nuclear physics div. 1977-79, program com. 1989-90, mem. selection com. Tom Bonner Prize 2000-01, chair 2001, panel on pub. affairs 2004-06; chair ad hoc com. on homeland security 2002-04); mem. Sigma Xi. Avocation: athletics. Home: 7 Simpson Pl Stony Brook NY 11790-1744 Office: Brookhaven Nat Lab Directors Office Bldg 460 Upton NY 11973 E-mail: bond@bnl.gov.

BOND, PHILLIP J., technology association executive, former advertising executive; BA in Comm., Linfield Coll., 1978. With Rocky Co., Seattle; spl. asst. to sec. for legis. affairs US Dept. Def., Washington, 1987—90, prin. dep. asst. sec. for legis affairs, 1992—93; chief of staff to Congressman Bob McEwen , rules com. assoc. US Ho. Reps., Washington, 1990—92, chief of staff to Congresswoman Jennifer Dunn, 1993—98; sr. v.p. for govt. affairs, treas. Info. Tech. Industry Coun., 1998—2001; dir. fed. pub. policy Hewlett-Packard Co., 2001; under sec. for tech. adminstrn. US Dept. Commerce, Washington, 2001—05, chief of staff to sec., 2002—03; sr. v.p. govt. rels. Monster Worldwide, 2005—06; gen. mgr. Monster Govt. Solutions, 2005—06; pres., CEO Info. Tech. Assn. Am., Arlington, Va., 2006—. Com. mem. Pres. Nat. Sci. and Tech. Coun.; bus. & sci. bd. advisors NanoDynamics Inc., 2006—. Republican. Office: Info Tech Assn Am 1401 Wilson Blvd Ste 1100 Arlington VA 22209

BOND, RICHARD L., food products executive; BSBA, Elizabethtown Coll., 1969. Bd. dir. IBP, Inc., 1995—2001, pres., COO, 1997—2001; co-COO, Group President, Fresh Meats and Retail Tyson Foods Inc., 2001—03, pres., COO, 2003—06, pres., CEO, 2006—. Bd. dirs. Tyson Foods Inc., 2001—; vice-chmn. Am. Meat Inst. Office: c/o Tyson Foods Inc PO Box 2020 Springdale AR 72765*

BOND, RICHARD LEE, lawyer, state senator; b. Kansas City, Kans., Sept. 18, 1935; s. Clarence Ivy and Florine (Hardison) B.; m. Sue S. Sedgwick, Aug. 23, 1958; children: Mark, Amy. BA, U. Kans., 1957, JD, 1960. City atty., Overland Park, Kans., 1960-62; adminstrv. asst. to Congressman Robert Ellsworth, Washington, 1961-66, Congressman Larry Winn, Washington, 1967-85, Congressman Jan Meyers, Washington, 1986; chmn. bd. dirs. Home State Bank, Kansas City, 1983-94; ptnr. Bennett, Lytle, Wetzler et al, Prairie Village, Kans., 1986-89; senator State of Kans., Topeka, 1985-2001, senate pres., 1997-2001. Vice chmn. Guaranty Bank and Bancshares, Kansas City, Kans., 1995-2002. Mem. Kans. Bd. Regents, 2002—. Named State Legislator of Yr. Governing Mag., 2002. Republican. Presbyterian. Avocations: gardening, tennis, hunting, fishing. Home: 9823 Nall Ave Shawnee Mission KS 66207-2915

BOND, RICHARD RANDOLPH, foundation administrator; b. Lost Creek, W.Va., Dec. 1, 1927; s. Harley Donovan and Marcella Randolph B.; m. Reva Stearns, Apr. 20, 1946; children: David, Philip, Josette, Michael. BS, Salem Coll., 1948, LHD (hon.), 1979, U. No. Colo.; MS, W.Va. U., 1949; PhD, U. Wis., 1955; postdoctoral studies, U. Mich., 1958—59. Various tchg. and fellowship positions, 1949—59; dean of faculty Elmira Coll., NY, 1959—63; dean Coll. Liberal Arts U. Liberia, Monrovia,

1963—64; chief of party Cornell U. Project in Liberia, Monrovia, 1964—66; v.p. acad. affairs Ill. State U., Normal, 1966—71; pres. U. No. Colo., Greeley, 1971—81, pres. emeritus, prof. zoology, 1981—89; state rep. Colo. Gen. Assembly, Denver, 1984—90; interim pres. Front Range C.C., Westminster, Colo., 1991; pres. Morgan C.C., Ft. Morgan, Colo., 1991—96, Cmty. Found., Greeley and Weld County, 1996—2000, Bond Family Found., 1995—. Founder Nat. Student Exch., 1st No. Savs. and Loan; cons., examiner North Ctrl. Accrediting Assn., 1969-82. Author: Colorado Postsecondary Options Act., 1988; contbr. articles to profl. jours. Bd. dirs., chmn. Sunrise Cmty. Health Ctr.; founding mem. Dream Team on Dropout Prevention; Dem. candidate for Col. 4th Congl. Dist., 1990; founder Colo. chpt. Dem. Leadership Coun., 1991—; co-chmn. Clinton Campaign, Colo., 1992; bd. dirs. Colo. chpt. Nat. Multiple Sclerosis Soc., Greeley Habitat for Humanity; chmn. bd. dirs. Univ. Schs. Found.; bd. govs. Univ. Schs., 2003—; bd. of trustee Aims C.C., 2001—. With U.S. Army, 1945-47. Recipient Legislator of Yr. award DAV, 1988, Colo. Acad. Pediat., 1989; Mental Health award, 1990, Polit. Educator of Yr. award, Colo. Edn. Assn., 1991; fellow NSF, 1953-54, Am. Physiol. Soc., 1958, Carnegie Found., 1958-59. Mem. Am. Ornithologists Union, Am. Assn. Colls. and Univs. (bd. dirs. 1979-81), Colo. Assn. Colls. and Univs. (chmn. 1979-81), Rotary (bd. dirs. local chpt.), Habitat for Humanity (bd. dirs. Greeley chpt.), Sigma Xi. Independent. Mem. United Ch. Of Christ. Avocations: gardening, stamp collecting/philately, camping, genealogy. Home and Office: 5601 18th St #51 Greeley CO 80634-2925 Personal E-mail: rrbond@comcast.net.

BOND, VICTORIA ELLEN, conductor, composer; b. LA, May 6, 1945; d. Philip and Jane (Courtl) B.; m. Stephan Peskin, Jan. 27, 1974. B Mus. Arts, U. So. Calif., LA, 1968; M Mus. Arts, Juilliard Sch. Music, 1975, D Mus. Arts, 1977; DFA (hon.), Washington and Lee U., 1992, Hollins Coll., 1995, Roanoke Coll., 1995. Condr., composer. Mem. NY State Coun. Arts Music Panel, 1987-90; bd. dirs. NY Women Composers; pres., artistic dir. Welltone New Music, Inc., 2004. Guest condr. numerous orgns. including most recently Warsaw Symphony, Poland, York Symphony, Pa., Music from Penn's Woods, Pa., 1999-00, NYC Opera Showcasing Am. Composers, 2001, Norwalk Symphony, 2002, Da Corneto Opera Co., 2003, Dallas Symphony Ray Charles Concert, 2003, Central Opera, Beijing, 2004, Ctr. for Contemporary Opera, 2004, 06, Music Festival of the Hamptons, 2004, Chamber Opera, Chgo., 2005, 06, Chamber Opera Chgo., 2006-07; music dir. New Amsterdam Symphony Orch., NYC, 1978-80, Pitts. Youth Symphony Orch., 1978-80, Empire State Youth Orch., 1982-86, Southeastern Music Ctr., 1983-84, Bel Canto Opera, 1983-86, Roanoke Symphony Orch., Va., 1986-95; artistic dir. Bel Canto Opera Co., 1986-88, Harrisburg Opera, 1998-03, Cutting Edge Concerts, NYC, 1999-; artistic adv., Wuhan Symphony, China, 1997-2000; artistic dir. Opera Roanoke, 1989-95; Exxon/Arts Endowment condr., Pitts. Symphony, 1978-80, recs. include Twentieth Century Cello, Two American Contemporaries, The Frog Prince, An American Collage, Live from Shanghai, Victoria Bond: Compositions, The American Piano Concerto, Yes, 2003; commd. by Pa. Ballet, 1978, Jacob's Pillow Dance Festival, 1979, Am. Ballet Theater, 1981, Empire State Inst. Performing Arts, 1983-84, Stage One, Louisville, 1986, Ga. State U., 1986, L'Ensemble, 1990, Renaissance City Winds, 1990, Audubon String Quartet, 1990, Women's Philharm., San Francisco, 1993, Va. Explore Park and The Shanghai Symphony, 1994, D Day Found., 1994, Linda Plaut, 1994, Pianofest, 2005, Duo Gelland, 2005, Ethel, 2005, Am. Piano Concertos, Albany, 2006, Billings Symphony, Mont., Elgin Symphony, Ill., Elements String Quartet, Indpls. Chamber Orch., Composers' Conf., Jade String Trio, Assn., Guido d'Arezzo for Culturale Amici del Convitto Nat. Vittorio Emanuele di Anezzo, 2006, Seduction & Sanctification for Gettysburg Chamber Orch., 2007, bridges for Fontana Chamber Arts, 2006, others; commns. include Gettysburg Chamber Orch., 2006, Fontana Chamber Arts, 2006; composer (albums) Menotti Opera, 2007. Bd. dirs. Am. Music Ctr. Recipient Victor Herbert award 1977, Perry F. Kendig award, 1988, ASCAP Composition award 1973—; Nat. Inst. for Music Theater grantee in opera conducting NYC Opera, 1985, Martha Baird Rockefeller grantee, 1978-79, Meet-The-Composer grantee in Composition, 1973—; Juilliard scholar, 1972-77; Juilliard fellow, 1975-77, Aspen Music Festival fellow, 1973-76; named Exxon/Arts Endowment Conductor, 1978-80, Woman of Yr. in Va., 1990, 91; featured on NBC Today show, 1990, profiled in C.S. Monitor, 1987, Wall Street Jour., 1987, others. Mem. ASCAP (awards 1975—), Am. Symphony Orch. League, Am. Fedn. Musicians, Condrs. Guild (bd. dirs. 1994—98), Internat. Alliance Women in Music, NY Women Composers, Mu Phi Epsilon. Avocations: horseback riding, sailing, hiking. Business E-Mail: victoria@victoriabond.com. *I believe that our life's work is in sharing our talents and gifts with others. Our own happiness and fulfillment are in direct proportion with the amount we give of ourselves.*

BONDANELLA, PETER, literature and language professor, writer; b. Pinehurst, NC, Dec. 20, 1943; m. Julia Conaway Conaway, June 13, 1969. BA, Davidson Coll., NC, 1966; MA, Stanford U., Palo Alto, Calif., 1967; PhD, U. Oreg., Eugene, 1970. Disting. prof. comparative lit. and Italian Ind. U., Bloomington, 1972—. Author: Italian Cinema: From Neorealism to the Present, The Cinema of Federico Fellini (Giovanni Agnelli Found. award Best Book Italian Studies, 1993), Hollywood Italians: Dagos, Palookas, Romeos, Wise Guys and Sopranos. Fellow, NEH, 1980—81, Eli Lilly Found., 1987, Am. Coun. Learned Societies, 1988, Australian Humanities Ctr., 2001. Mem.: Am. Assn. Italian Studies (pres., Pres. award 1983). Home: 2835 S Jolley Cir Saint George UT 84790 Home Phone: 435-673-0322. Home Fax: none. Personal E-mail: bondanella@mac.com.

BONDAREFF, JOAN M., lawyer, retired government agency administrator; b. Utica, NY, Jan. 7, 1944; 1 child. Student, Cornell U., 1961-64; BA in Polit. Sci. cum laude, George Washington U., 1965; JD magna cum laude, Am. U., 1975. Bar: Md. 1975, D.C. 1978, U.S. Supreme Ct. 1979. Clk. Md. Ct. Spl. Appeals, 1975; atty. advisor for legis. and regulation Office Gen. Counsel, Dept. Commerce, Washington, 1975-76, atty. on detail to Dept. Justice, 1976-77; staff atty. NOAA, Washington, 1977-80, sr. counsel to nat. earth satellite svc., 1980-82, asst. gen. counsel for adminstrn., 1981-82, asst. gen. counsel for ocean svcs., 1982-87; sr. counsel Coast Guard and Mcht. Marine group U.S. Ho. of Reps. Mcht. Marine and Fisheries Com., Washington, 1987-94; chief counsel and acting dep. maritime adminstr. Maritime Adminstn., Dept. Transp., Washington, 1994—99; counsel maritime/marine dept. Dyer Ellis & Joseph, Washington, 2001—02; counsel maritime/marine transp. group Blame Rome LLP, Washington, 2003—. Legal counsel Nat. Safe Boating Coun. Contbr. articles to law jours., including Territorial Sea Jour., Coastal Mgmt. Jour., Internat. Ship Registry Rev. Former chmn. Women's Aquatic Network. Mem.: Bar Assn. DC, Md. State Bar Assn., Women's Bar Assn. DC, ABA (marines resouces com. 1989—, vice chair marine resouces com. nat. resources enivronmental law sect. 1994—98). Avocations: hiking, running, music, travel. Office: Blank Rome LLP The Watergate Bldg 600 New Hampshire Ave NW Washington DC 20037

BONDAREFF, WILLIAM, psychiatrist, educator; b. Washington, Apr. 29, 1930; s. Leon and Gertrude Bondareff; children by previous marriage: Hyla, Sarah; m. Rita Haber Kassoy, Jan. 2, 1988. BS in Zoology, George Washington U., 1951, MS in Zoology, 1952; PhD in Anatomy, U. Chgo., 1954; MD, Georgetown U., 1962. Diplomate Am. Bd. Psychiatry and Neurology with added qualifications in geriatric psychiatry. Rsch. assoc., instr. anatomy U. Chgo., 1955; rotating intern USPHS Hosp., Balt., 1962-63; resident in psychiatry Northwestern Meml. Hosp. Inst. Psychiatry, Chgo., 1978-80; asst. prof. anatomy Northwestern U., Evanston, Ill., 1963-65, assoc. prof., 1965-69, prof., 1969-78, chmn. dept. anatomy, 1970-78; prof. psychiatry and gerontology U. So. Calif., LA, 1981—; mem. staff U. So. Calif. Univ. Hosp., LA, 1991—; mem. attending staff L.A. County/U. So. Calif. Med. Ctr., LA, 1981—; mem. Hosp. Good Samaritan, LA, 1981-96; mem. staff Norris Cancer Hosp., 1987—; mem. attending staff Cedars-Sinai Med. Ctr., 2001—, emeritus, 2005—; dir. psychiatry USC Univ. Hosp., 2007—. Physician/cons. VA Hosp., Downey, Ill., 1969-80, Jewish Home for Aged, Reseda, Calif., 1981-90; vis. staff mem. medicine Passavant Pavilion Northwestern Meml. Hosp., 1972-80; dir. div. geriat. psychiatry U. So. Calif., 1981—; dir. U. So. Calif.-St. Barnabas Alzheimer Disease Ctr., 1985-2001; acting dir. dept. Gerontology Research Inst. Andrus Gerontology Ctr.-U. So. Calif., 1982; staff psychiatrist Los Angeles County Hosp., 1981—; past holder various com. offices Northwestern U. Editor Mechanisms of Aging and Devel., 1970—; assoc. editor Am. Jour. Anatomy, 1970-76; mem. editl. bd. Alzheimer Disease and Associated Disorders-An Internat. Jour., 1985-95, Neurbiology of Aging, 1980-94, The Jour. of Gerontology, 1981-84, Internat. Rev. Jour. of Psychiatry, 1988—, Jour. Alzheimer's Disease, 1997-2001; contbr. articles to profl. jours. Mem. sci. adv. bd. Alzheimer's Disease & Related disorders Assn. L.A., bd.dirs., 1989—; mem. rsch. rev. com. treatment, devel. and assessment Nat. Inst. Mental Health, 1987-92. Served with USPHS, 1955-63. USPHS fellow, 1955, U. Cambridge Clare Hall vis. fellow, 1980, Hughes Hall vis. fellow, 1988; scholar Allergy Found., 1960, U. Chgo., 1953; recipient Career Devel. award Nat. Inst. Neurol. Disease and Blindness, 1966-69, Sesquicentennial award Hobart and William Smith Colls., 1972, Sandoz prize Internat. Assn. Gerontology, 1983, Alzheimer Disease and Related Disorders Assn. award, 1984; Fulbright Lectr., U. Goteborg, Sweden, 1967-68. Fellow AAAS (councilor 1970-74), Am. Psychiat. Assn. (geriatrics task force 1981), Gerontol. Soc.; mem. Am. Assn. Anatomists (chmn. local com. ann. meeting 1969), Electron Microscope Soc. Am., Am. Soc. Cell Biology, Am. Acad. Neurology (chmn. neuroanatomical scis. sect. 1971-77), Soc. Neurosci., Assn. Anatomy Chmn. (councilor 1975-77), Am. Assn. Geriat. Psychiatry (program com. 1984-89, bd. dirs. 1985-89), So. Calif. Psychiat. Soc., Internat. Psychogeriat. Assn., Cajal Club, Cosmos Club, Sigma Xi. Office: U So Calif Sch Medicine HCC 4100 1520 San Pablo St Los Angeles CA 90033-1018 Office Phone: 323-442-6016. Business E-Mail: bondaref@usc.edu.

BONDERMAN, DAVID, investment company executive, lawyer; b. Nov. 27, 1942; BA, U. Wash., Seattle, 1963; JD magna cum laude, Harvard U., 1966. Asst. prof. Tulane U. Sch. Law, New Orleans, 1967—68; spec. asst. to Atty. Gen. Civil Rights Divsn., US Dept. Justice, Washington, 1968—69; fellow in fgn. & comparative law Harvard U., 1969—70; ptnr. Arnold & Porter, Washington, 1971—83; COO Keystone Inc. (Robert M. Bass Group), Fort Worth, Tex., 1983—92; founder, prin. & gen. ptnr. Tex. Pacific Group, Ft. Worth, 1993—. Bd. dirs. Ryanair Holdings, CoStar Group Inc., Gemplus Internat. S.A; mem. gov. council Wilderness Soc.; trustee Grand Canyon Trust; bd. dirs. Am. Himalayan Found., Ryanair Holdings, 1996—; dir. & past chmn. U. Wash. Found. Sheldon Fellow. Mem.: Phi Beta Kappa. Office: Tex Pacific Group 301 Commerce St Ste 3300 Fort Worth TX 76102-3128*

BONDERMAN, JEREMY, professional baseball player; b. Kennewick, Wash., Oct. 28, 1982; s. Gene and Dorie Bonderman; m. Amber Bonderman, 2004; 1 child, Mailee Blaize. Pitcher Detroit Tigers, 2003—. Achievements include becoming the youngest Tiger's pitcher to start a game (2003) since Bruce Robbins in 1979; striking out 202 batters in the 2006 season making him the first Tiger since Jack Morris (1987) to strike out at least 200 batters in a season. Mailing: Comerica Pk 2100 Woodward Ave Detroit MI 48201 Office Phone: 313-471-2000.*

BONDI, HARRY GENE, lawyer; b. Sheridan, Wyo., Apr. 3, 1948; s. Gene and Elizabeth (Poynter) B; 1 child, Bert Gene. BS in Fin., Fairfield U., 1970; JD, U. Wyo., 1974; postgrad., Georgetown U. Law Ctr., 1977. Bar: Wyo. 1974, U.S. Dist. Ct. D.C. 1976, U.S. Tax Ct. 1976, U.S. Ct. Claims 1975, U.S. Supreme Ct. 1980, D.C. 1975, Colo. 1988, U.S. Dist. Ct. Wyo. 1977, U.S. Ct. Appeals (10th cir.) 1980. Trial atty. U.S. Renegotiation Bd., Washington, D.C., 1974-77; pub. defender Wyo. State Pub. Defender Office, Casper, 1978-79; pvt. practice Harry G. Bondi, P.C., Casper, 1977—. Author: Wyoming Labor and Employment Law, 1992, Workers Compensation in Wyoming, 1993, Wrongful Discharge Claims Under Wyoming Law, 1994, 95. Chmn. City of Casper Housing and Cmty. Devel. Commn., 1977-81; past pres. Natrona County Meals of Wheels, Inc., 1988-90, Meals on Wheels Found., 1991-94; bd. dirs. Casper Jr. Baseball League, 1994-95. Mem. Wyo. Bar Assn., Natrona County Bar Assn., Am. Trial Lawyers Assn., Wyo. Trial Lawyers Assn., Wyo. Criminal Defense Lawyers Assn., Colo. Bar Assn., D.C. Bar Assn., Federal Bar Assn., Criminal Justice Adminstrn. Panel Dist. Wyo. E-mail: bondilaw@msn.com.

BONDI, JOSEPH CHARLES, JR., education educator, consultant; b. Tampa, Fla., Aug. 15, 1936; s. Joseph C. and Virginia B.; m. Patsy L. Hammer, Aug. 6, 1960; children: Pamela, Beth, Bradley. BS, U. Fla., 1958, M.Ed., 1964; Ed.D., U. Fla, 1968. Tchr., adminstr. Hillsborough County (Fla.) Pub. Schs., 1958-65; instr. U. South Fla., Tampa, 1965-66, asst. prof., 1966-68, assoc. prof., 1968-74, prof. edn., 1974—2003; ptnr. Wiles, Bondi & Assocs. Edn. cons. in field, South Africa, Hong Kong, China, Taiwan, Can., Am. Internat. Schs. Author 28 textbooks including Developing Middle Schools, 1972, Curriculum Development, 1979, 7th edit., 2005, Practical Politics for School Administrators, 1981, The Essential Middle School, 1981, 1993, 2000, 2005, Supervision: A Guide to Practice, 6th edit., 2004, The New American Middle School, 2001. Councilman City of Temple Terrace, Fla., 1970—74, mayor, 1974—78. With USNR, 1958—63. Mem.: Fla. ASCD (pres.). Republican. Lutheran. Personal E-mail: josephbondi@aol.com.

BONDINELL, STEPHANIE, counselor, academic administrator; b. Passaic, NJ, Nov. 22, 1948; d. Peter Jr. and Gloria Lucille (Burden) Honcharuk; m. Paul Swanstrom Bondinell, July 31, 1971; 1 child, Paul Emil. BA, William Paterson U., 1970; MEd, Stetson U., 1983. Cert. elem. educator Fla., guidance counselor grades K-12 Fla. Tchr. Bloomingdale Bd. Edn., NJ, 1971-80; edn. dir. Fla. United Meth. Children's Home, Enterprise, 1982-89; guidance counselor Volusia County Sch. Bd., Deltona, Fla., 1988—. Coord. sch. improvement svcs., Deltona Lakes, 1996—98, Deltona Lakes, 2002—05. Sec. adv. com. Deltona Jr. HS, 1996—98, sec. PTA, 1982; vice-chmn. adv. com. Deltona Mid. Sch., 1988, chmn., 1991—92, 1991—92; mem. adv. com. Deltona HS, 1995—96; secondary sch. task force Volusia County Sch. Bd., 1986—; team leader Volusia County Sch. Accreditation Quality Assurance Team, 2003—07; mem. exec. com. Volusia County Reps.; mem. Rep. Presdl. Task Force; mem. state adv. bd. Fla. Future Educators Am., 1990—92, 2003—07. Named Deltona Lakes Tchr. of Yr., Volusia County Sch., 1991, 1996, Volusia County Sch. Dist. Accreditation Steering Com. Team Leaders, 2003—07, Volusia County Guidance Counselor of Yr., Volusia/Flagler Counseling Assn., 2006; recipient Outstanding Ednl. Partnership award, S.W. Volusia C. of C., 1998, Sunshine State Medallion award, Fla. Pub. Rels. Assn., 1998, award, Volusia/Flagler Alcohol and Drug Abuse Prevention Coun., 1998—2007, Fla. Lottery Creative Tchg. award, 2002; Acad. scholar, Becton, Dickinson & Co., 1966, NJ State scholar, 1966—70. Mem.: AAUW, Am. Counseling Assn., Fla. Edn. Assn., Internat. Platform Assn., Volusia Tchrs. Orgn., NJ Edn. Assn., Fla. Assn. Counseling and Devel., Disvn. Learning Disabilities, Coun. Exceptional Children, Stetson U. Alumni Assn., Deltona Civic Assn., 4 Townes Federated Rep. Women's Club (sec., v.p.), Deltona Rep. Club (v.p. 1991—93). Avocations: painting, creative writing, dance. Home: 1810 W Cooper Dr Deltona FL 32725-3623 Office: Volusia County Sch Bd 222 Adelia Blvd Deltona FL 32725-3976 E-mail: sbondine@mail.volusia.k12.fl.us.

BONDOC, ROMMEL, lawyer; b. June 23, 1938; s. Nicholas Rommel and Gladys Sue (Buckner) Bondoc; m. Ariel Guiberson, Aug. 20, 1960 (div. 1963); m. Alberta Linnea Young, Dec. 13, 1967; children: Daphne, Patience, Margaret, Nicholas. AB, Stanford U., 1959, JD, 1963. Bar: Calif. 1964, U.S. Ct. Appeals (9th cir.) 1965, U.S. Supreme Ct. 1969. Assoc. Melvin Belli, San Francisco, 1964—66, Vincent Hallinan, San Francisco, 1966—69; sole practice San Francisco, 1969—. Mem.: Calif. Attys. for Criminal Justice (bd. dir. 1975—80), No. Calif. Criminal Trial Lawyers Assn. (bd. dir. 1972—, pres. 1978—79), San Francisco Bar Assn. (judiciary com. 1982—85). Democrat. Methodist. Home: 509 Canyon Rd Novato CA 94947-4330 Office: 819 Eddy St San Francisco CA 94109-7701 Home Phone: 415-897-2269; Office Phone: 415-771-6174.

BONDRA, PETER, professional hockey player; b. Luck, Ukraine, Feb. 7, 1968; m. Luba Bondra; children: Petra, David. Right wing Washington Capitals, 1990—2004, Ottawa Senators, 2004—05, Atlanta Thrashers, 2005—06, Chgo. Blackhawks, 2006—. Mem. Team Slovakia, World Cup of Hockey, 1996, Slovakian Olympic Hockey Team, Nagano, Japan, 1998, Torino, Italy, 2006; player NHL All-star game, 1993, 1996—99. Office: Chgo Blackhawk Hockey Team 1901 W Madison St Chicago IL 60612*

BONDS, BARRY LAMAR, professional baseball player; b. Riverside, Calif., July 24, 1964; s. Bobby and Pat Bonds; m. Susann Branco, Feb. 5, 1988 (div. Dec. 1994); children: Nikolai, Shikari; m. Liz Watson, 1998; 1 child, Aisha. BA in Criminal Justice, Ariz. State U., 1986. Outfielder Pitts. Pirates, 1986—92, San Francisco Giants, 1992—. Star: (Reality TV show) Bonds on Bonds, 2006. Founder Barry Bonds Family Found., 1993—. Named Nat. League MVP, Baseball Writers' Assn. of Am., 1990, 1992—93, 2001—04, Maj. League Player of Yr., The Sporting News, 1990, 2001, 2004, Nat. League Player of Yr., 1990, 1991, Player of the Decade (1990's), Male Athlete of Yr., 2001; named to All-Am. Team, Sporting News Coll., 1985, Nat. League All-Star Team, Maj. League Baseball, 1990, 1992—98, 2000—04, 2007; recipient Gold Glove award, 1990—94, 1996—98, Silver Slugger award, 1990—97, 2000—04, Espy award, Best Baseball Player, 1994, 2002, 2004, Espy award, Best Male Athlete, 1994, Philanthropist of Yr. award, Nat. Conf. Black Philanthropy, 1999, Hank Aaron award, 2001—02, 2004. Achievements include holds the record for most home runs in a single season (73), 2001; became third player in MLB to hit 700 career home runs on Sept. 17, 2004; only mem. in 500/500 Club (HR/Steals); became MLB all-time leader in walks with 2,191 on July 4, 2004; led Nat. League in batting average, 2002 (.370), 2004 (.362); oldest player to win Nat. League MVP Award at 40 years old, 2004; holds MLB record with 7 league MVP awards; holds MLB record for consecutive seasons with 30+ Home Runs, 1992-2004; passing Hank Aaron for the all-time home run record by hitting his 756th on August 7, 2007, against the Washington Nationals. Avocations: golf, photography, music. Mailing: San Francisco Giants AT&T Park 24 Willie Mays Plz San Francisco CA 94107*

BONDS, JOHN WILFRED, JR., lawyer; b. Jackson, Tenn., May 6, 1943; s. John Wilfred Sr. and Louise (Robinson) B.; m. Mary Anne Hatchett, July 18, 1969; children: Kathleen Lucile, Mary Julia. BS, U.S. Air Force Acad., 1965; JD, Vanderbilt U., 1973. Bar: Ga. 1973. Commd. 2nd lt. USAF, 1965, advanced through grades to capt. Vietnam, Thailand, 1965-70, resigned, 1970; assoc. Sutherland, Asbill & Brennan, Atlanta, 1973-79, ptnr., 1979—. Editor in chief Vanderbilt Law Rev., 1973. Mem. ABA, Ga. Bar Assn., Atlanta Bar Assn., Lawyers Club Atlanta, Order of Coif. Presbyterian. Office: Sutherland Asbill & Brennan 999 Peachtree St NE Atlanta GA 30309-3996 Home Phone: 404-351-9483; Office Phone: 404-853-8017. Business E-Mail: john.bonds@sablaw.com.

BONDS, MICHAEL P., air transportation executive; Various positions including v.p., contr. and v.p. corp. devel. Continental Airlines, Inc., Houston, 1995—2003, v.p. human resources, 2003—05, sr. v.p. human resources & labor rels., 2005—. Office: Continental Airlines Inc PO Box 4607 Houston TX 77210 Office Phone: 713-324-5000. Office Fax: 713-324-2637.*

BONDURANT, EMMET JOPLING, II, lawyer; b. Athens, Ga., Mar. 16, 1937; s. John Parnell and Mary Claire (Brannon) B.; m. Jane E. Fahey, Aug. 12, 1990; children by previous marriage: Emmet Jopling III, Katherine Elizabeth, Melissa Eileen, Christopher Scott, Miles Stephen. AB cum laude, U. Ga., 1958, LL.B. magna cum laude, 1960; LL.M., Harvard U., 1962. Bar: Ga. 1959. Law clk. to Judge Elbert Haynsworth, Jr. U.S. Ct. Appeals, 4th Circuit, 1960-61; assoc. Kilpatrick, Cody, Rogers, McClatchey & Regenstein, Atlanta, 1962-68, ptnr., 1968-77; ptnr. firm Bondurant, Mixson & Elmore and predecessor, Atlanta, 1977—. Vis. lectr. in antitrust law U. Ga., spring 1971; pres. Atlanta Legal Aid Soc., 1972-73; vice chmn. Ga. Gov.'s Commn. on Criminal Justice Standards and Goals, 1974 Contbr. articles on antitrust and reapportionment, right to counsel, bankruptcy, and local govt. issues to profl. jours.; co-editor: Antitrust Law Developments, 1974. Mem. Joint Atlanta-Fulton County Citizens Adv. Com. on Consolidation, 1969; chmn. Atlanta Charter Commn., 1971-72; co-chmn. Com. for Sensible Rapid Transit, Atlanta, 1971-72; trustee Am. Inns of Ct. Found., 2002-; chmn. Common Cause of Ga., 2002-04; chmn. Ga. Pub. Defender Standards Coun., 2003-; chmn. bd. Ga. Appellate Resource Ctr., 2001-. Named 1 of 5 Outstanding Young Men, Atlanta Jaycees, 1970; recipient Ga. Trial Lawyer of Yr., Am. Bd. Trial Advocates (Ga. chpt.), Good Govt. award, LWV Atlanta-Fulton County, 1980, Dufree award, Calif. Western Sch. Law, 1984, Elbert P. Tuttle Jurisprudence award, 2001, Harold G. Clarke award, Ga. Indigent Def. Coun., 2001. Fellow Am. Bar Found.; mem. ABA (exec. com. Atlanta lawyers com. for civil rights), Ga. Bar Assn., Atlanta Bar Assn. (exec. com. 1975-81, Leadership award 1992), State Bar Ga. (chmn. sect. antitrust law 1972-73, chmn. jud. sys. comm. 1991—), Am. Law Inst., Am. Coll. Trial Lawyers, Am. Acad. Appellate Lawyers, Am. Judicature Soc., Ga. Law Sch. Alumni Assn. (pres. 1996-97), Lawyers Club Atlanta (sec. 1971-72), Phi Beta Kappa, Phi Delta Phi, Phi Kappa Phi, Kappa Alpha. Methodist. Home: 2930 Habersham Rd NW Atlanta GA 30305-2846 Office: Bondurant Mixson & Elmore Ste 3900 1201 W Peachtree St NW Atlanta GA 30309-3417 Office Phone: 678-891-4100, 404-881-4100. Business E-Mail: bondurant@bmelaw.com.

BONDURANT, STUART, physician, educational association administrator; b. Winston-Salem, NC, Sept. 9, 1929; s. Stuart Osborne Bondurant; m. Susan Haughton Ehringhaus, May 5, 1991; children from previous marriage: Stuart, Margaret Lynn, Nancy Vance. BS, Duke U., 1952, MD, 1953; DSc (hon.), Ind. U., 1980. Intern Duke Hosp., Durham, NC, 1953—54, resident in internal medicine, 1954—55; resident Peter Bent Brigham Hosp., Boston, 1958—59; from asst. prof. medicine to prof. Ind. U. Sch. Medicine, Indpls., 1959—67; assoc. dir. Ind. U. Cardiovasc. Rsch. Ctr., 1961—67; chief med. br. artificial heart-myocardial infarction program NIH, Bethesda, Md., 1966—67; prof. medicine, chmn. dept., physician in chief Albany Med. Ctr. Hosp., NY, 1967—74; pres., dean Albany Med. Coll., 1974—79; prof. medicine U. NC, Chapel Hill, 1979—2004, dean Sch. Medicine, 1979—94, interim dean, 1996—97; dir. Ctr. for Urban Epidemiology Studies N.Y. Acad. Medicine, NYC, 1994—96; interim exec. v.p., exec. dean Georgetown U. Med. Ctr., 2004—. Contbr. articles to med. jours. Named Citizen Laureate, Univ. Found., Albany, 1979; recipient Disting. Alumnus award, Duke U. Sch. Medicine, 1974, Merit award, Am. Heart Assn., 1975, Thomas Jefferson award, U. N.C.-Chapel Hill, 1998. Fellow: ACP (regent, pres. 1980), Royal Coll. Physicians London, Royal Coll. Physicians Edinburgh; mem.: Am. Clin. and Climatol. Assn. (pres. 1996), Assn. Am. Med. Colls. (exec. com. 1977, chmn. coun. deans 1979—82, chmn. 1993—94), Inst. of Medicine (interim pres. 1992, David Rall award 2000), Assn. Am. Physicians (pres. 1985—86), Am. Soc. Clin.

Investigation (v.p. 1974). Office: U NC Sch Medicine CB # 7000 Office of Dean Chapel Hill NC 27599-7000 Home: 209 Cedar Berry Ln Chapel Hill NC 27517-7207 Business E-Mail: sbondurant@med.unc.edu.

BONDY, JOANNE, chef; Degree in Banking and Fin., Appalachian State. Tng. Westshore Marritt; sous chef Worthington Hotel, Fort Worth, Tex., bakery chef, mgr.; pvt. caterer; chef Sam's Cafe, Dallas; banquet chef Fairmont Hotel; chef de cuisine Wright's restaurant, Ariz. Biltmore; exec. chef Beau Rivage Resort, Biloxi, Miss.; exec. chef, ptnr. Ciudad D.F., Dallas. Guest chef Am. Harvest Workshop, James Beard House, James Beard Ann. Culinary Awards Ceremony; amb. Dallas Conv. Bur.; chef's coun. Chefs for Humanity, 2005—. Featured on Culinary Trends Mag. cover, guest appearances Food Network, CBS Early Show, (documentaries) A Tribute to Julia Child, PBS. Recipient Mgr. of Yr. award, Fairmont Hotel, 1994. Office: Ciudad D F 3888 Oak Lawn Ave 135 Dallas TX 75219 Office Phone: 214-528-9619. Office Fax: 214-219-3291.*

BONDY, RUPERT, pharmaceutical executive, lawyer; b. 1961; Grad., Cambridge U., Eng., 1983; LLM, Stanford U., Calif. Bar: Eng., Calif. Harkness fellow jurisprudence Harvard U.; tchg. fellow Stanford Law Sch.; atty. Morrison & Foerster, San Francisco, London and NYC, Lovells, London, 1994; pvt. practice atty.; sr. counsel corp. SmithKline Beecham, 1995—98, head. corp. legal and secretarial grp., 1998; head legal ops., global mfg. and supply/corp. GlaxoSmithKline, PLC, 2001, sr. v.p., gen. counsel, mem. corp. exec. team, 2001—. Office: GlaxoSmithKline UK Ltd 980 Great West Rd Brentford TW8 9GS England E-mail: rupert.bondy@gsk.com.*

BONE, HENRY GRADY, III, physician, clinical researcher; b. Seattle, Apr. 4, 1947; s. Henry Grady Jr. and Mary Isabel (Sheehan) B. AB in Biology, Princeton U., 1968; MD with honors, U. Washington, 1972. Diplomate Am. Bd. Internal Medicine, Am. Bd. Endocrinology and Metabolism. Intern Parkland Meml. Hosp., Dallas, 1972-73; resident U. Tex., Southwestern Med. Sch. & Affiliated Hosps., Dallas, 1973-74; clin. rsch. fellow U. Tex., Southwestern Med. Schs. & Affiliated Hosps., Dallas, 1974-76; postdoctoral fellow, clin. instr. U. Calif., San Diego, 1977-78, asst. prof. medicine, 1978-84, NIH clin. investigator La Jolla, 1978-80; rsch. assoc. VA Med., Ctr., La Jolla, 1980-83; dir. clin. rsch. Ciba-Geigy Pharms., Summit, N.J., 1984-87; sr. staff physician Henry Ford Hosp., Detroit, 1987—97; staff physician Cottage/Bonsecours Hosps., Grosse Pointe Farms, Mich., 1994—, St. John Hosp., 1997—, chief endocrinology, metabolism, 2002—. Lectr. grand rounds various med. ctrs., 1977—; adj. prof. medicine U. Mich., 2007—; cons. pharm. industry, 1988—, FDA, 1991—. Contbr. med. articles to profl. jours.; reviewer med. articles for profl. jours. Med. adv. panel Paget's Disease Found., 1988—, dir., sec.-treas., 1990—. Merit scholar Princeton U., 1964-68. Fellow ACP; mem. AMA, AAAS, Am. Soc. for Bone & Mineral Rsch. (Dr. Boy Frame Meml. award 1989), Am. Coll. Endocrinology, The Endocrine Soc., Detroit Inst. Art, Seattle Tennis Club, Princeton Club N.Y., Detroit Yacht Club, Alpha Omega Alpha. Republican.

BONE, LAWSON MITCHELL, songwriter, poet; b. Fayetteville, Tenn., Feb. 13, 1954; s. John Davis and Ester Eugene Bone. BA in Bus. Lit., Ala. A&M U., 1976. 1st asst., mgr. Big K Dept. Stores, Nashville, 1976-90; underwriter Prudential Ins. Co., Huntsville, Ala., 1990-91; songwriter Columbine Records, Hollywood, Calif., 1995—, HillTop Records, Hollywood, 1995—. Songwriter: Hey Writer-Keep It Up, Song Business, Flesh Tight, Got To Be The One; author: (screenplays) Make Bones About It, 1994, Disaster Relief, 1994; author numerous poems. Sponsor Children Internat. Honduras, Kansas City, Mo., 1995—, Childreach, Cali, Colombia, Warwick, R.I., 1995—. Named Famous Poet, Famous Poets Soc., 1996, 98-2003, Poet of Yr., 1999-2003, Internat. Writer of Yr., 2003, Man of Yr., 2004, 2005; named one of Top 100 Communicators, 2006; recipient Poetry Gem award Famous Poets Soc., 2000-02, Poetry award Prometheus Muse of Fire, 2001, Poem of Yr. award, 2002, Shakespeare Trophy of Excellence, 2002-03, Living Legends award, 2004, Medal of Honor, 2004, Decree of Excellence award, 2006. Home: 306 Hamilton St Fayetteville TN 37334-3316

BONE, ROBERT WILLIAM, writer; b. Gary, Ind., Sept. 15, 1932; s. Robert Ordway and Georgia Juanita (Clapp) B.; m. Sara Ann Cameron, Aug. 14, 1965; children: Christina Ann, David Robert. BS in Journalism, Bowling Green State U., 1954. Editor, tng. literature The Armor Sch., Ft. Knox, Ky., 1954-56; reporter, photographer Middletown (N.Y.) Daily Record, 1956-59, San Juan (Puerto Rico) Star, 1959-60; news editor Popular Photography Mag., NYC, 1960-62; editor-in-chief Brazilian Bus. Mag., Rio de Janeiro, 1962-63; picture editor Time-Life Books, NYC, 1963-68; sr. writer Fielding's Travel Guide to Europe, Mallorca, Spain, 1968-71; staff writer Honolulu Advertiser, 1971-84; free-lancer Honolulu, 1984—. Stringer Time-Life News Svc., 1981-86. Author: Maverick Guide to Hawaii, 1977, Maverick Guide to Australia, 1979, Maverick Guide to New Zealand, 1981, Fielding's Alaska and the Yukon, 1989; travel editor Honolulu mag., 1985-88, R.S.V.P. mag., 1988-89. 1st lt., U.S. Army, 1954-56. Named to Journalism Hall Fame Bowling Green State U., 1990. Mem. Soc. Am. Travel Writers, Am. Soc. Media Photographers. Democrat. Home and Office: 1053 Lunaai St Kailua HI 96734-4633 Office Phone: 808-261-1094. E-mail: travelwriter@robertbone.com.

BONEE, JOHN LEON, III, lawyer; b. Hartford, Conn. s. John Leon, Jr. and M. Elaine (Sheridan) B. BA, Trinity Coll., Hartford, 1970; JD, Suffolk U., Boston, 1974; postgrad., Hague Acad. Internat. Law, The Netherlands, 1975. Bar: Conn. 1974, U.S. Dist. Ct. Conn. 1974, U.S. Ct. Appeals (2d cir.) 1975, U.S. Supreme Ct. 1979. Assoc. McCook, Kenyon and Bonee, Hartford, 1974-78; ptnr. Bonee Law Offices, LLP, Hartford, Conn., 1979—. Mem. Estate and Bus. Planning Coun. Hartford, 2003—. Contbr. articles to profl. jours. Mem. bd. edn. Town West Hartford, 1981-83, corp. counsel, 1983, cmty. planning adv. com., 1984, town coun., 1985-89; bd. dirs. world affairs coun., Hartford, 1980-91, estate and bus. planning coun., 2004—; pres. 1892 Club of HFD, 2006—. Mem. ABA (litig. gen. practice and internat. law sects., mem. ho. dels. 1996—), Conn. Bar Assn. (editor-at-large jour. 1978-84, probate, litigation and family law sects., mem. ho. of dels. 1995—, com. on professionalism 2000—), Hartford County Bar Assn. (bd. dirs. 1991-97, treas. 1992-93, sec. 1993-94, pres. elect 1994-95, pres. 1995-96, past pres. 1996-97, co-chair bench/bar leadership conf. com. 1992-93). Office: 1 State St Hartford CT 06103-3100 Office Phone: 860-522-7161. E-mail: boneelaw@aol.com.

BONELLA, MICHAEL J., lawyer; BS cum laude, Villanova U., 1988; JD magna cum laude, Duke U., 1996; LLM in Trial Advocacy, Temple U., 2003. Bar: Pa. 1996, US Ct. Appeals, Fed. Cir., US Dist. Ct., Pa., US Patent and Trademark Office. Ptnr. Woodcock Washburn LLP, Phila. Lt. USN, 1987—93. Mem.: ABA, Phila. Intellectual Property Law Assn. Office: Woodcock Washburn LLP One Liberty Place, 46th Fl Philadelphia PA 19103 Office Phone: 215-564-8987. Office Fax: 215-568-3439. E-mail: bonella@woodcock.com.

BONER, ELEANOR KATZ, lawyer; b. NYC, Jan. 20, 1922; d. Louis and Della (Cherry) Katz; m. Mitchell Boner, June 14, 1942; children: Ethel, Alexander, Lawrence. BA cum laude, Hunter Coll., 1941; LLB, St. Lawrence U., 1943; D in Jud. Sci. cum laude, Bklyn. Law Sch., 1945, JD, 1967; PhD, Columbia U., 1967. Bar: N.Y. 1943, U.S. Dist. Ct. D.C. 1972, U.S. Ct. Appeals D.C. 1972, U.S. Supreme Ct. 1971, U.S. Customs Ct. 1978, U.S. Ct. Internat. Trade 1981. Pvt. practice, NYC, 1943-71; ptnr. Boner & Glod, Washington, 1972-75, Boner, Gold & Oesch, St. Gallen, Switzerland; gen. counsel to Mark Berger, NYC, 1975-80; pvt. practice New Rochelle, N.Y., 1981—. Author: The Hypothetical Question in the Law of Evidence, 1945, Alexander, Child of Love, 1990. Mem. ABA, N.Y. Bar Assn., Assn. Bar of City of N.Y., Westchester County Bar Assn., Phi Beta Kappa. Avocation: art.

BONESIO, WOODROW MICHAEL, lawyer; b. Hereford, Tex., Dec. 27, 1943; s. Harold Andre and Elizabeth (Ireland) B.; m. Michaele Ann Dougherty; children: Elizabeth Eaton, Jo Kristin, William Michael. BA, Austin Coll., 1966; JD, U. Houston, 1971. Bar: Tex. 1971, US Dist. Ct. (we., no., so., and ea. dists.) Tex. 1973, US Ct. Appeals (5th cir.) 1973, US Ct. Appeals (11th cir.) 1981, US Supreme Ct. 2004. Law clk. to US dist. Judge We. Dist. Tex., San Antonio, 1971—73; ptnr. Akin, Gump, Strauss, Hauer & Feld, Dallas, 1973—92, Kuntz & Bonesio LLP, Dallas, 1992—2002, Shackelford, Melton & McKinley LLP, Dallas, 2003—. Spkr. in field. Bd. dirs. Grace Presbytery Devel. Bd., 1986—89; ruling elder First Presbyn. Ch., Dallas, 1999—2001, bd. dirs., 2004—06. Named Tex. Super Lawyer, Tex. Monthly Mag., 2006. Fellow: Dallas Bar Found., Tex. Bar Found.; mem.: ABA, Tex. Mediator Credentialing Assn., Tex. Assn. Mediators, Nat. Assn. Rec. Artists, U. Houston Law Alumni Assn. (chpt. pres. 1982), Austin Coll. Alumni Bd. (mem. bd. 2006—, Disting. Alumni award 2001), Common Cause Tex. (bd. dirs. 1999—2006), Dallas Assn. Def. Counsel, Tex. Bar Coll., Dallas Bar Assn., Am. Judicature Soc., Assn. Atty. Mediators, Am. Arbitration Assn., Fed. Bar Assn., Vocal Majority Chorus (bd. dirs. 1990—, pres. 2002—03), Soc. for Preservation and Encouragement Barber Shop Quartet Singing in Am. (Internat. Chorus champion 1975, 1979, 1982, 1985, 1988, 1991, 1994, 1997, 2000, 2003, 2006), Order of Barons, Phi Alpha Delta. Home Phone: 214-341-4919; Office Phone: 214-780-1400. Business E-Mail: mbonesio@shacklaw.net.

BONESTEEL, MICHAEL JOHN, lawyer; b. LA, Dec. 22, 1939; s. Henry Theodore Samuel Becker and Kathleen Mansfield (Nolan) B.; children: Damon Becker, Kirsten Kathleen; m. Susan Elizabeth Schaaf, June 1, 1980. AB in History, Stanford U., 1961; JD, U. So. Calif., 1966. Bar: Calif. 1967, U.S. Dist. Ct. (ctrl. and so. dists.) Calif, 1967, U.S. Ct. Appeals (9th cir.) 1967, U.S. Dist. Ct. (no. dist.) Calif. 1969, U.S. Dist. Ct. (ea. dist.) Calif. 1983, U.S. Supreme Ct. 1989. Assoc. Haight, Brown & Bonesteel, and predecessors, LA, 1967—71, ptnr., 1972—. Fellow Internat. Acad. Trial Lawyers, Am. Coll. Trial Lawyers; mem. ABA, State Bar Calif., Los Angeles County Bar Assn., Def. Rsch. Inst., Assn. So. Calif. Def. Counsel, Am. Soc. Most Venerable Order of Hospitaller St. John of Jerusalem, Hospitaller Order St. Lazarus of Jerusalem, Grand Priory of Am., Bel Air Bay Club, L.A. Country Club. Office: Ste 800 6080 Center Drive Los Angeles CA 90045-1574 Address: PO Box 45068 Los Angeles CA 90045-0068 Office Phone: 310-215-7100. E-mail: mbonesteel@hbblaw.com.

BONET, FRANK JOSEPH, retired lawyer; b. NYC, Apr. 6, 1937; s. Frank and Alexandra (Roots) B.; m. Mary Ellen Mathews, July 14, 1962; children— Catherine Ann, Frank Joseph, Elizabeth Mary, Jean Marie. BA magna cum laude, St. John's U., 1958, LL.B. (assoc. editor law rev.), 1961. Bar: Tex. 1961. With Horn & Hardart Co., NYC, 1961-72, corp. sec., head corp. legal dept., 1969-72; real estate atty. J.C. Penney Co., Inc., 1972-77, sr. S.W. regional real estate atty. Dallas, 1977-89, mng. atty. real estate dept., 1989-91, also asst. corp. sec.; mng. atty. JCP Realty, Inc., Dallas, 1992-94; chief real estate counsel J.C. Penney Co., Inc., Dallas, 1994-98; pres. Cmty. Care Clinic, Inc., 2004—. Lectr. Internat. Coun. Shopping Ctrs. Contbr. articles profl. jours. Mem. N.Y. State Bar (ret.), State Bar Tex. Home: 1909 Deerfield Dr Plano TX 75023-5110 Personal E-mail: fmeb@verizon.net.

BONFANTE, LARISSA, classics educator; b. Naples, Italy; arrived in U.S., 1939, naturalized, 1951; d. Giuliano and Vittoria (Dompé) B.; m. Peter B. Warren, Sept. 1950 (div. 1962); children: Sebastian Raditsa, Alexandra Bonfante-Warren; m. Leo Ferrero Raditsa, May 2, 1973 (dec. 2001). Student, Radcliffe Coll., 1950, U. Rome, 1951; BA, Barnard Coll., NYC, 1954; MA, U. Cin., 1957; PhD, Columbia U., NYC, 1966. Mem. faculty NYU, 1963—2007, prof., 1978—2007, chmn. dept. classics, 1978—84, 1987—90. Cons. in field; vis. mem. Inst. for Advanced Study, 1980. Author: Etruscan Dress, 1975, paperback, 2003, Out of Etruria, 1981, Reading the Past, Etruscan, 1990; author: (with Giuliano Bonfante) The Etruscan Language (transl. into Italian 1985, into Romanian 1996), 1983, 2d edit., 2002; author: Etruscan Life and Afterlife, 1986, translated into Romanian, 1996, Corpus Speculorum Etruscorum, N.Y. The Metropolitan Museum of Art, 1997; author: (with Judith Swaddling) Etruscan Myths, 2006; editor (with Francesco Roncalli): Antichità dall'Umbria a New York, 1991; editor: (with Judith Sebesta) The World of Roman Dress, 1994; editor: (with Vassos Karageorghis) Italy and Cyprus in Antiquity: 1500-450 BC, 2000; editor: (with Blair Fowlkes) Classical Antiquities at New York U., 2006; translator: Chronology of the Ancient World (E.J. Bickerman), 1967; translator: (with Alexandra Bonfante Warren) The Plays of Hrotswitha of Gandersheim, 1979; contbr. articles to profl. jours. Mem. Archaeol. Inst. Am. (gov. bd. 1982-88), Inst. di Studi Etruschi (fgn., pres. US sect.), German Archaeol. Inst. (corr. mem.). Home: 50 Morningside Dr New York NY 10025-1739 Office: NYU Classics Dept 25 Waverly Pl New York NY 10003-6701 Office Phone: 212-998-8594. Business E-Mail: lb11@nyu.edu.

BONFIELD, ANDREW R.J., pharmaceutical executive; b. London, 1962; B of Commerce, U. Natal, Durban, South Africa. With Price Waterhouse; mem. integration team SmithKline Beecham, 1989—91, dir., v.p. corp. accounts, 1991—97, dep. fin. dir., 1997—99, CFO, 1999—2000; fin. dir. BG Group, PLC, 2000—02; sr. v.p. to exec. v.p., CFO Bristol-Meyers Squibb Co., NYC, 2002—. Bd. dir. BOC Group. Office: Bristol-Meyers Squibb Co 345 Park Ave New York NY 10154-0037*

BONFIELD, ARTHUR EARL, law educator; b. NYC, May 12, 1936; s. Louis and Rose (Lesser) B.; m. Doris (Harfenist), June 10, 1958 (dec. 1995); 1 child, Lauren; m. Eva Tsalikian, Apr. 8, 2000. BA, Bklyn. Coll., 1956; JD, Yale U., 1960, LLM, 1961, post grad. (sr. fellow), 1961-62; DHL (hon.), Cornell Coll., 1999. Bar: Conn. 1961, Iowa 1966. Asst. prof. U. Iowa Law Sch., 1962-65, assoc. prof., 1965-66, prof., 1966-69, Law Sch. Found. disting. prof., 1969-72, John Murray disting. prof., 1972—2003, Alan D. Vestal disting. chair, 2003—, assoc. dean for rsch. Law Libr., 1985—. Vis. prof. law U. Mich., 1970, U. Tenn, 1972, U. NC, 1974, Hofstra U., 1977, Lewis and Clark U., 1984; gen. counsel spl. joint com. state adminstrv. procedure act Iowa Gen. Assembly, 1974-75; spl. counsel adminstrv. procedure exec. br. State of Iowa, 1975; chmn. com. constl. law Nat. Conf. Bar Examiners Multi-State Bar Exam, 1977-2003; reporter 1981 Model State Adminstrv. Procedure Act, Nat. Conf. Commrs. Uniform State Laws, 1979-81; cons. Ark. State Constl. Conv., 1980; chmn. Iowa Governor's Com. State Pub. Records Law, 1983; Iowa commr. Nat. Conf. Commrs. on Uniform State Laws, 1984-2000; chmn. Iowa Gov.'s Task Force on Uniform Adminstrv. Rules, 1985-92; chmn. Iowa Gov.'s Task Force Team on Regulatory Process, Rule Making, and Rules Rev., 1999-2000. Prin. draftsman Iowa Civil Rights Act, 1965; Iowa Fair Housing Act, 1967; Iowa Adminstrv. Procedure Act, 1974; Iowa Open Meetings Act, 1978; Iowa Civil Rights Act, 1978; Amendments to Iowa Pub. Records Law, 1984; Amendments to Iowa Adminstrv. Procedure Act, 1998; author: State Adminstrv. Rule Making, 1986; State and Federal Adminstrv. Law, 1989; contbr. numerous articles to law jours. Recipient Outstanding Svc. to Civil Liberties Award, Iowa Civil Liberties Union, 1974, Hancher Finkbine Outstanding Faculty Mem. Award, U. Iowa, 1980, Faculty Excellence Award, Iowa Bd. Regents, 1995, Outstanding Law Sch. Tchg. Award, U. Iowa, 1996, 2006; Frederick Klocksiem fellow Aspen Inst. Humanistic Studies, 1978. Mem. ABA (chmn. divsn. state adminstrv. law 1976-80, coun. 1980-84, chmn. sect. 1987-88, sect. adminstrv. law and regulatory practice); Am. Law Inst. (life mem.); Iowa State Bar Assn. (chmn. com. adminstrv. law 1971-85, coun. sect. adminstr. law 1990-93, 94-97, 98-99, 2000-03, 05-, reporter and mem., task force on state adminstrv. law reform 1994-96; Pres. Award Outstanding Svc. to Bar and Public 1996); Am. Coun. Learned Soc. (del. from Assn. Am. Law Sch. 1984-94). Avocation: collecting rare 16th-18th century English books. Home: 206 Mahaska Dr Iowa City IA 52246-1606 Office: U Iowa Sch Law Iowa City IA 52242 Business E-Mail: arthur-bonfield@uiowa.edu.

BONFIGLIO, THOMAS ALBERT, pathologist, educator; b. Rochester, NY, Oct. 17, 1942; s. Charles P. and Minnie C. (Argentiere) B.; m. Mary Barat Rice, July 2, 1966; children: Susan Marie, Amy Elizabeth, Megan Lynn. BS magna cum laude, St. John Fisher Coll., 1964; MD, U. Rochester, 1969. Diplomate Am. Bd. Pathology; cert. Nat. Bd. Med. Examiners, Internat. Bd. Cytopathology, N.Y.S. lab. dir.; lic. Ohio, N.Y. Intern in pathology U. Hosps. Cleve., 1969-70, resident in pathology, 1969-71; tchg. fellow pathology Case Western Res. U., 1969-71; chief resident in pathology Strong Meml. Hosp., Rochester, NY, 1971-72; instr., pathology fellow U. Rochester Med. Ctr., 1971-72, asst. prof. pathology, 1972-76, assoc. dir. cytopathology lab., assoc. dir. sch. cytotech., 1973-76, acting dir. surg. pathology, divsn., dir. cytopathology lab., 1975-76; asst. prof. pathology Case Western Reserve U., 1976-77; asst. pathologist, chief divsns. cytopathology and surg. pathology Mt. Sinai Hosp., Cleve., 1976-77; assoc. prof. pathology U. Rochester Med. Ctr., 1977-84, prof. pathology, 1984-89, prof., acting chmn. dept. pathology and lab. medicine, 1989-90, prof., chair dept. pathology and lab. medicine, 1990-97, clin. prof. pathology, 1997—2003, prof. pathology, dir. cytopathology, 2003—. Chmn. Internat. Bd. Cytopathology, 1998—; cons. pathology Rochester Gen. Hosp., 1978-97, Genesee Hosp., 1979-97; attending pathologist, dir. surg./pathology unit, 1984-85, Strong Meml. Hosp., attending pathologist, dir. anatomic pathology divsn., 1985-97, pathologist in chief, 1989-97; sr. attending pathologist, head pathology divsn. Genesee Hosp., 1997-99; dir. pathology divsn. ViaHealth, 1999-2003; sr. attending pathologist Strong Meml. Hosp., 2003—; mem. Cytotechnologist Exam. Com., 1980-83, Biol. Stain Commn., 1981-91, cytopathology exam com. Am. Bd. Pathology, 1984-89, spl. ad hoc com. cytopathology N.Y. State Dept. Health, 1988, others; v.p. Intersoc. Pathology Coun., 1988, pres., 1989; bd. dirs. Univs. Assoc. Rsch. and Edn. in Pathology; presenter papers, abstracts; participant, invited spkr., dir., panelist numerous workshops, meetings, seminars, confs., teleconfs. in field; vis. prof., guest lectr. Med. Coll. Ohio, Toledo, 1980, Dartmouth-Hitchcock Med. Ctr., Hanover, N.H., 1982, William Beaumont Army Med. Ctr., El Paso, 1984, Med. U. N.J., Newark, 1984, New Eng. Deaconess Hosp., Boston, 1985, Henry Ford Hosp., Detroit, 1989, Loyola U. Sch. Medicine, Chgo., 1990, St. Francis Hosp., Hartford, Conn., 1991, Marshall U. Sch. Medicine, Huntington, W.Va., 1991, U. Iowa Sch. Medicine, Iowa City, 1991, U. Mass. Sch. Medicine, 1994. Author: Cytopathologic Interpretation of Transthoracic Fine-Needle Biopsies, 1983, (with others) Histologic Typing of Female Genital Tract, 1994; editor: Gynecologic Cytopathology, 1997, Fine Needle Aspiration of Subcutaneous Organs and Masses, 1996; mem. editl. bd. Human Pathology, 1982-92, Am. Jour. Clin. Pathology, 1985—, Lab. Medicine, 1984-90; mem. N.Am. rev. bd., editl. adv. bd. ACTA Cytologica; contbr. articles to profl. jours.; author video Cytopathology of Fine Needle Biopsies of the Abdomen, 1985. Fellow Am. Soc. Clin. Pathologists (v.p. 1990-91, pres.-elect 1991-92, pres. 1992-93, clin. pathologists commn. on continuing edn., bd. dirs. 1985-94, chmn. nominating com. 1988, 92, rsch. and devel. com. 1985-89, chmn. quality assurance steering com. 1987-92, dep. commr. commn. on continuing edn. 1984-90, chmn. coun. cytopathology 1983-84, coun. on cytopathology 1979-84, Disting. Svc. award 1988, Ward Burdick award 2002), Coll. Am. Pathologists, Internat. Acad. Cytology (sci. program com. 1988-89, terminology com. 1992); mem. AMA, Am. Soc. Cytology (Cert. of Merit for outstanding svcs. 1987, Papanicolaou award 1991, v.p. 1984-85, pres.-elect 1985-86, pres. 1986-87, chmn. sci. program com. 1982-84, exec. com. 1980-88, numerous others), Arthur Purdy Stout Soc. Surg. Pathologists, Assn. Dirs. Anat. and Surg. Pathology (coun. 1989-95), Assn. Pathology chmn., Internat. Soc. Gynecol. Pathologists, Monroe County Med. Soc., N.Y. State Soc. Pathologists, Rochester Area Assn. Pathologists (v.p. 1978-79, pres. 1979-80), U.S. and Can. Acad. Pathology, Papanicoleau Soc. Cytology (Educator of Yr. award 2003), Alpha Omega Alpha. Roman Catholic. Avocations: fishing, boating. Home: 3666 Nibawauka Bch Canandaigua NY 14424-9725 Office: 601 ELmwood Ave Box 626 Rochester NY 14642 E-mail: tabonf@aol.com, tom_bonfiglio@urmc.rochester.edu.

BONGARD, JOSH CLIFFORD, computer scientist, educator; b. Toronto, Can., Apr. 17, 1974; arrived in U.S., 2003; s. Ralph and Carol Bongard. BS summa cum laude in Computer Sci., McMaster U., Hamilton, Ont., Can., 1997; MSc with distinction in Evolutionary and Adaptive Systems, U. Sussex, Brighton, UK, 1999; PhD, U. Zürich, Switzerland, 2003. Postdoctoral rschr. Computational Synthesis Lab. Cornell U., Ithaca, NY, 2003—06; asst. prof. dept. computer sci. U. Vt., Burlington, 2006—. Contbr. articles to profl. jours.; co-author: How the Body Shapes the Way We Think: A New View of Intelligence, 2006. Office: U Vermont Dept Computer Sci 329 Votey Hall 33 Colchester Ave Burlington VT 05405 Office Phone: 802-656-4665. Business E-Mail: josh.bongard@uvm.edu.*

BONGIORNO, JAMES WILLIAM, electronics executive; b. Westfield, NY, Apr. 2, 1943; s. Samuel Salvatore and Marjorie Ruth (Hardenburg) B. Student public schs. Profl. musician, 1961—65; engr. Hadley Labs., Pomona, Calif., 1965—66, Marantz Co., Woodside, NY, 1966—67; chief engr. Rectilinear Rsch. Corp., Bklyn., 1967—68; profl. musician, writer Popular Electronics, also Audio mag., 1968—71; dir. engring. Dynaco Inc., Phila., 1972, S.A.E. Inc., Los Angeles, 1973—74; founder, pres. Gt. Am. Sound Co. Inc., Chatsworth, Calif., 1974—77; founder, 1977; pres. Sumo Electric Co. Ltd., West Hollywood, Calif., 1977—82; ind. electronic cons. Lompoc, Calif., 1982—88; founder, pres. Spread Spectrum Techs., Inc., Lompoc, Calif., 1988—. Ind. electronic cons. Patentee class A audio amplifier, FM IF-detector. Recipient State of Art Design award, Stereo Sound mag., Tokyo, 1976, 1980, 2003, High End Audio Best of CES Show award, 2003. Mem. Audio Engring. Soc., Am. Fedn. Musicians. Republican. Home and Office: 716 N G St Apt 2 Lompoc CA 93436-4530 Home Phone: 805-740-9902; Office Phone: 805-740-9902. Personal E-mail: sstinc@earthlink.net. *Aside from the fact that my lifetime goal has always been to design the world's finest amplifier, I also wanted it to be affordable by as many people as possible. I am happy that I have achieved this goal as there are a lot more poor people than rich people.*

BONGIORNO, JOSEPH JOHN, JR., electrical engineering educator; b. Bklyn., Aug. 3, 1936; s. Joseph John and Mildred Rose (LoPinto) B.; m. Carol Marie Olsen, Nov. 22, 1958; children: James Michael, Peter Joseph, Richard Edward, Cathryn Mary BEE, Poly. Inst. Bklyn., 1956, MEE, 1958, DEE, 1960. Asst. prof. Poly. Inst. N.Y., Bklyn., 1960-64, assoc. prof., 1964-74, prof., 1974-96, prof. emeritus, 1996—. Cons. Unisys (formerly Sperry Systems Mgmt.), Gt. Neck, N.Y., 1963-93. Contbr. articles to profl. jours. Mem. St. Aidan's Parish Sch. Bd., Williston Park, N.Y., 1967-70, 73-76, pres. 1975-76. Rsch. grantee NSF, Washington, 1972, 82, 85, Army Rsch. Office, Durham, N.C., 1993. Fellow IEEE (Control Systems Soc. best paper award 1977) Roman Catholic. Home: 36 Park Ave Williston Park NY 11596-1628 Office: Poly U 105 Maxess Rd Melville NY 11747 Office Phone: 631-755-4214. Business E-Mail: jbongior@rama.poly.edu.

BONGIORNO, WILLIAM J., public relations executive; b. Smithtown, NY, June 26, 1969; s. William J. and Maria Bongiorno; m. Robbin L. Mandarino, July 20, 2002; 1 child, Sarah. BA in Comm., SUNY, Buffalo,

1991. V.p. Mt. & Nadler, Inc., NYC, 1995—2004; pres. Blue Chip Pub. Rels., Inc., South Salem, NY, 2004—. Author: (audio book) Financial Public Relations 101, 2006. Mem.: Pub. Rels. Soc. Am. Office: 14 Canaan Cir South Salem NY 10590

BONGIOVI, STEPHEN, literature and language educator; b. 1950; BA, Le Moyne Coll., 1972; MA, Hofstra Univ. English tchr. Seaford Sch. Dist., 1972—; now also head, Seaford English Dept. and dist. chair. Named NY Tchr. of Yr., 2006; recipient Honorary Patriot award, Seaford Cmty., 2005. Avocation: sports announcer. Office: Seaford High Sch 1575 Seamans Neck Rd Seaford NY 11783 Business E-Mail: steve_bongiovi@mail.seaford.k12.ny.us.*

BONHAG, THOMAS EDWARD, insurance company executive, financial planner, consultant; b. Bronxville, NY, Jan. 19, 1952; s. Herman Arthur and Anne Elizabeth (Sage) B.; m. Noreen Patricia Early, Apr. 24, 1976 (div. Dec. 1981); m. Cornelia Hackett Lyons, Oct. 8, 1983. BS, Fordham U., 1973; MBA, St. John's U., 1979; postgrad., Am. Coll., 1979—84. CLU; cert. fin. planner, chartered fin. cons. Field sales rep. Colgate-Palmolive Co., NYC, 1973-74; employee relations officer Chase Manhattan Bank, NYC, 1974-78; agt., dist. mgr. Equitable Life Assurance Soc., NYC, 1979-83, v.p. northeastern region mktg. Edison, N.J., 1984-90; sr. v.p. Kornreich Life Assocs., Inc., NYC, 1990-94; CEO Winged Keel Group, Inc., NYC, 1994—95; dir. advanced planning/markets Equitable Life, NYC, 1995—98; mng. dir. The deBart Group, Inc., NYC, 1999—2005; exec. dir. Nat. Madison Group, Inc., 2005—. Fin. cons. Am. Geriatrics Soc., NYC, 1983-86; bd. dirs. Fin. Assurance Fed. Credit Union, 2001-07. Mem. Hoboken (N.J.) Environ. Com., 1983-90; mayoral appointee citizens' budget adv. com. Twp. of Cranford, N.J., 1991-92; mem. Cranford Bd. Edn., 1991-94, pres., 1992-94. Mem. Soc. Fin. Svc. Profls., Nat. Assn. Ins. and Fin. Advisors, Fin. Planning Assn., Estate Planning Coun. N.Y.C. Avocations: walking, bicycling, sailing. Home: 406 Monmouth Ave Spring Lake NJ 07762-1131 Office Phone: 212-878-1689. Personal E-mail: tombonhag@msn.com.

BONHAM, HAROLD FLORIAN, research geologist, consultant; b. LA, Sept. 1, 1928; s. Harold Florian and Viola Violet (Clopine) B.; m. Sally Mae Reimer, Sept. 6, 1952 (dec. July 1999); children: Cynthia Jean Kimball, Douglas Craig, Gary Stephen; m. Linda Jean Shipp, June 14, 2000. AA in Physics, U. Calif. Berkeley, 1951; BA in Geology, UCLA, 1954; MS in Geology, U. Nev., 1963. Geologist So. Pacific Co., 1955-61; mining geologist Nev. Bur. Mines and Geology, Reno, 1963-93, acting dir., state geologist, 1993-95; cons. geologist, 1996—. Cons. UN, Can., Australia, Peoples Republic of China, 1980-90; cons. in field. Contbr. articles to profl. jour. V.p. Palomino Valley Gen. Improvement Dist., Nev., 1986-88. With USN, 1946-49, PTO. Fellow Geol. Soc. Am., Soc. Econ. Geologist, Assn. Exploration Geochemists (councillor 1988-94); mem. Geol. Soc. Nev. (hon.). Republican. Avocations: reading, computers, photography, oenology. Home: 265 Mia Dr Sparks NV 89436-7912 Office Phone: 775-424-2806. E-mail: hbonham@sbcglobal.net.

BONHAM-CARTER, HELENA, actress; b. Golders Green, London, Eng., May 26, 1966; 1 child. Student, Westminster. TV appearances include A Pattern of Roses, Miami Vice, A Hazard of Hearts, The Vision, Arms and the Man, Beatrix Potter, Dancing Queen, Fatal Deception, A Dark Adapted Eye; films include Lady Jane, A Room with a View, Maurice, Francesco, The Mask, Getting It Right, Hamlet, Where Angels Fear to Tread, Howard's End, Mary Shelley's Frankenstein, A Little Loving, Mighty Aphrodite, Margaret's Museum, 1994, Portraits Chinois, 1995, Twelfth Night, 1995, Wings of a Dove, 1996, Revengers Comedies, 1996, Keep the Aspidistra Flying, 1997, The Theory of Flight, 1997, Fight Club, 1998, Women Talking Dirty, 1999, Novacaine, 2000, Til Human Voices Wake Us, Planet of the Apes, 2001, Heart of Me, 2001, Live from Baghdad, 2002, Big Fish, 2003, Henry VIII, 2003, (voice) Corpse Bride, 2004, (voice) Wallace & Gromit, 2004, Conversations with Other Women, 2004, Charlie and the Chocolate Factory, 2004. Office: Adam Isaccs United Talent 9560 Wilshire Blvd Beverly Hills CA 90212-2427 also: Conway Van Gelder 18-21 Jermyn St London SW1Y 6HP England

BONHEIM, NELSON ALFRED, gastroenterologist, educator; b. Jackson Heights, Aug. 30, 1942; s. Hans Herman and Sylvia Rosetta Bonheim; m. Carolyn S. Bonheim, June 13, 1965; children: Kimberly, Elizabeth, Michael. BA, Lafayette Coll., Easton, Pa., 1963; MS in Biology, Adelphi U., Garden City, NY, 1965; MD, Chgo. Med. Sch., 1970. Cert. Nat. Bd. Med. Examiners, Am. Bd. Internal Medicine, gastroenterology Am. Bd. Internal Medicine. Intern medicine Bronx Mcpl. Hosp. Ctr., Albert Einstein Coll. Medicine, NY, 1970—71, resident medicine, 1971—72, chief resident medicine, asst. instr., 1972—73; fellow in gastroenterology, asst. physician Cornell Med. Sch., NY Hosp., NYC, 1973—75; attending physician Greenwich Hosp., Conn., 1975—, sect. head dept. gastroenterology, 1976—; ptnr. Greenwich Gastroenterology, Conn., 1978—2000; pres. Ctr. for GI Med., Greenwich, 2000—. Asst. clin. prof. Yale U. Sch. Medicine, New Haven, 1978—. Contbr. articles to profl. jours. Fellow: ACP, Am. Coll. Gastroenterology; mem.: Fairfield County Med. Soc., Conn. State Med. Soc., Am. Gastroenterol. Assn., Am. Soc. for Gastrointestinal Endoscopy, Crohn's and Colitis Found. Am., Inc. (co-founder Fairfield/Westchester chpt. 1975, sci. advisor for chpt. med. adv. com. Fairfield/Westchester chpt. 1975—90, chmn. bd. Fairfield/Westchester chpt. 1990—92, co-pres. Fairfield/Westchester chpt. 1998—, Humanitarian of Yr. award 1988), Alpha Omega. Avocations: golf, opera, reading. Office: Ctr for GI Med 500 W Putnam Ave Greenwich CT 06830 Office Phone: 203-863-2900.

BONICELLI, PAUL J., federal agency administrator; b. 1964; m. Melissa Bonicelli. BA in English, U. Memphis.; MA in Pub. Policy, Regent U.; PhD. in Polit. Sci., U. Tenn. Rschr., analyst, Washington, DC; asst. prof. polit. sci. Grove City Coll., Pa.; dean, assoc. prof. govt. Patrick Henry Coll., Purcellville, 1995—2001; pvt. sector del. UN, 2001—02; profl. staff mem. Internat. Rels. Com. Ho. of Reps., 2001—05; dep. asst. adminstr. Bur. Democracy, Conflict and Humanitarian Assistance US Agy. Internat. Devel., 2005—07, asst. adminstr. Bur. Latin Am. & the Caribbean, 2007—. Chair Governing Justly & Democratically Interagency Com., Dir. Fgn. Assistance, 2005—07. Contbr. articles Jour. of Church and State; author: (novels) Mexico's role in the Contadora process: increasing the deterioration of Mexico-U.S. relations, 1987. Office: US Agy Internat Devel 1300 Pennsylvania Ave NW Washington DC 20523 Office Phone: 202-712-4320.*

BONIFACHO, BRATSA, artist; b. Belgrade, Yugoslavia, 1937; arrived in Can., 1973, naturalized, 1976. Student, Sumatovachka Sch. Art, Belgrade, 1957-59; BArch, MFA, U. Belgrade, 1965; postgrad., Acad. di Belle Arti, Italy, 1966-68, Atelier Kruger, West Germany, 1966-68. Tchr. painting and drawing Sch. Fine Arts, Belgrade, 1967-68; pvt. tutor, 1979-87. One-person shows Gallery Scollard, Toronto, 1978, Contemporary Art Gallery, Vancouver, 1979, Richmond Art Gallery, B.C., 1982, 93, 97, Burnaby Art Gallery, Vancouver, Can., 1982, Heffel Gallery Ltd., Vancouver, 1988, 90, 91, Quan-Schieder Gallery, Toronto, 1989, 90, Fran Willis Art Gallery, Victoria, B.C., Can., 1992, 93, 94, 95, 2000, Patrick Doheny Fine Art Gallery, Vancouver, 1992, 93, 94, Artropolis, 1993, Seattle Art Fair, 1993, Threshold Gallery, Vancouver, 1993, Bau-Xi Art Gallery, Vancouver and Toronto, 1995, 96, 99, 2001, 02, 03, 04, Kimzey Miller Gallery, Seattle, 1996, Mus. History and Art, Anchorage, 1997, Galerija Progres, Belgrade, 2000, Contemporary Art Gallery, Zrenjanin, Yugoslavia, 2001, Gallery of the Matica Srpsick, Novi Sad, Yugoslavia, 2002, Foster/White Gallery, Seattle, 2004, 05, Art Fair, Toronto, 2004, 05, 06, 07, Cologne Art Fair, Germany, 2005, Bau Xi Gallery, Vancouver, B.C., 2006, 2007 Art Fair, Toronto, 2006, Gallery Bau-Xi, Toronto, 2006, 07; exhbn. Richmond Art Gallery, B.C., Foster/White Gallery, Seattle, 2006; juried group exhbns. in B.C., 1974-93; represented in numerous pub. and pvt. collections. Grantee, B.C. Arts Coun., 1996, 1998, 2000, Can. Coun., 1996, 1998, 1999; travel grantee, 2000, 2001, 2002, B.C. travel grantee, 1999. Office: PO Box 549 Sta A Vancouver BC Canada V6C 2N3 Office Phone: 604-254-1405. Business E-Mail: bonifacho@telus.net.

BONIFATI, LOUIS M., music educator; BMus, manhattan Sch. Music, 1974; MMus, Manhattan Sch. Music, 1985; MEd, Columbia U., 1992, EdD, 1997. Cert. tchr. NY, Level III cert. Am. Recorder Soc. Music tchr. Wappingers Ctrl. Sch. Dist., Wappingers Falls, NY, 1986—; classical woodwind instr. State U. at New Paltz, NY, 2001—. Clarinetist Bronx Symphony Orch., Bronx, NY, 1985—. Mem.: Internat. Clarinet Soc., Am. Recorder Soc. Avocation: travel.

BONIFAZ, JOHN CRISTOPHER, lawyer; b. Wilmington, Del., June 22, 1966; s. Cristobal and Deirdre (Cooney) B. BA magna cum laude, Brown U., 1987; JD cum laude, Harvard U., 1992. Bar: Mass., 1993, U.S. Dist. Ct. Mass. 1995. Community liaison Exec. Office of the Mayor, Washington, 1987-88; scheduler/adminstrv. asst. Sen. Kennedy's Re-Election Campaign, Boston, 1988; law clk. DNA People's Legal Svcs., Shiprock, N.Mex., 1990, Fla. Rural Legal Svcs., Lake Worthy, Fla., 1991; staff atty. Ctr. for Responsive Politics, Washington, 1992-93; pvt. practice Boston, 1994—; exec. dir. Nat. Voting Rights Inst., Cambridge, Mass., 1994—, spl. counsel Boston. Lead counsel Coalition of US soldiers, 2003; dem. nominee Sec. of Commonwealth Mass., Mass., 2006. Co-author: The Wealth Primary: Campaign Fundraising and the Constitution, 1994. MacArthur Fellow, Genius award, 1999. Mem. Nat. Lawyers Guild (bd. dirs. Mass. chpt. 1994—), nat. adv. bd. mem. Prog. Demts. Am., Equal Justice Soc. Office: Nat Voting Rights Inst 27 School St Ste 500 Boston MA 02108-4303 Office Phone: 617-624-3900. Office Fax: 617-624-3911.*

BONILLA, FERNANDO J., Puerto Rican government official; Ptnr. Fiddler, Gonzalez & Rodriguez, 1993—97; v.p., gen. adv. Internat. Town, LLC, 1997—; exec. dir., Port Authority Commonwealth of PR, San Juan, 2005, sec. state, 2005—. Office: PR Dept State Box 9023271 San Juan PR 00902 Office Phone: 787-723-4343. Office Fax: 787-725-7303.*

BONILLA, HENRY, former congressman, broadcast executive; b. San Antonio, Jan. 2, 1954; m. Deborah Knapp (div. 2003); children: Alicia, Austin; m. Sheryl Bonilla BA in Journalism, U. Tex., Austin, 1976. Reporter KTVV, Austin, Tex., 1976-78; reporter, prodr. KENS-TV News, 1978-80; asst. press sec. Staff of Gov. Dick Thornburgh, Phila., 1981; news prodr. WABC-TV, NYC, 1982-85; asst. news dir. WTAF-TV, Phila., 1985-86; TV exec. prodr. KENS-TV, San Antonio, 1986-89, exec. prodr. pub. affairs, 1989—92; mem. US Congress from 23rd Tex. dist., 1993—2007, mem. appropriations com., chmn. agr., rural devel., FDA and related agencies subcommittee. Bd. v.p. San Antonio Crimestoppers; mem. adv. bd. United Way Vol. Ctr.; mem. adv. coun. U. Tex. Women's Athletics Dept., San Antonio Mus. Assn. Mex. Splendors Media; bd. dirs. Careers Info. and Referral Svc., San Antonio Pub. Libr. Found. Recipient Leadership award, 1989, Corp. Cmty. Svc. award, 1990, Outstanding Young Tex. Exec. award U. Tex. Ex-Students Assn., 1993, Pres. award US Hispanic C. of C. Tex. Hispanic C. of C., Eagle award Hispanic Heritage Conf., 1993, Award for Legis. Excellence Am. Diabetes Assn., 1994, Golden Bulldog award Watchdogs of the Treas., 1994, Champion of Pvt. Property Rights award League of Pvt. Property Owners, 1994, Golden Flame award Vocat. Home Econ. Tchr. Assn. Tex., 1994, Guardian Small Bus. award Nat. Fedn. Ind. Bus., 1994, Legislator of Yr. Am. Heart Assn Tex., 1994, MLA award for Disting. Pub. Svc., Med. Libr. Assn., 1998, Ground Water Protector award Nat. Ground Water Assn., 2004, Congl. Support for Sci. award Inst. Food Technologies, 2004 Republican. Office Phone: 202-225-4511.*

BONIN, JOHN PAUL, economics professor; b. Lawrence, Mass., Mar. 6, 1945; s. Ralph O. and Mildred May (Kiessling) B.; m. Hélène Boivin, July 26, 1969; children— Corinne, Jennifer BA in Econs., Boston Coll., 1966; MA in Econs., U. Rochester, 1970, PhD, 1973; MA (hon.), Wesleyan U., 1984. Asst. prof. econs. Wesleyan U., Middletown, Conn., 1970-77, assoc. prof., 1977-83, prof., 1983—, Andrews prof. econs., 2000—02, Chester D. Hubbard prof. econs. and social scis., 2002—. Vis. prof. econs. U. B.C., Vancouver, 1977-78, U. Calif.-San Diego, 1974-75, Yale U., 1989, 91; vis. rsch. scholar Birkbeck Coll., London, 1979-80; summer rsch. fellow Internat. Inst. Mgmt., Berlin, 1980; vis. sr. lectr./scholar U. Wash., Seattle, 1985; vis. lectr. Yale Sch. Orgn. and Mgmt., 1989, 91, 93; William Davidson Disting. vis. prof. U. Mich. Sch. Bus., 1998, 99; faculty affiliate, rsch. fellow William Davidson Inst., U. Mich. Bus. Sch., 1996—; cons. World Bank, Inst. for East West Studies, U.S. Dept. Treasury, UN; keynote spkr. various internat. confs. Co-translator (with H. Bonin): Advanced Exercises in Microeconomics, 1983, Economics of Uncertainty & Information, 1989; (with others): Economics of Cooperation & The Labor-Managed Economy, 1985, The Economics of Uncertainty and Information, transl. of Jean-Jacques Laffont Cours de theorie microeconomique, vol. 2, 1989, Banking in Transition Economies: Developing Market Oriented Banking Sectors in Eastern Europe, 1998; editor: Jour. Comparative Econs., 1996—; contbr. articles to profl. jours. NSF postdoctoral fellow, London, 1979-80; rsch. fellow Internat. Inst. Mgmt., Berlin, 1980; rsch. grantee Nat. Coun. for Soviet and Ea. European Rsch., 1992-93. Mem. Am. Econ. Assn., Jour. Comparative Econs. (bd. editors 1983-86, 1992—), Assn. for Comparative Econ. Studies (exec. com. 1989-91, pres. 1996), Nat. Coun. for Eurasian and East European Rsch. (bd. dirs. 1998-2002). Democrat. Roman Catholic. Home: 8 Yellow Wood St Middletown CT 06457-4927 Office: Wesleyan U Dept Of Econs Middletown CT 06457 Office Phone: 860-685-2353. Business E-Mail: JBonin@wesleyan.edu.

BONIN, SUZANNE JEAN, artist; b. Oakland, Calif., Nov. 12, 1955; d. Charles Freeman and Dorice Ruth (Brown) B.; m. John Aime Mearle, Mar. 1976 (div. 1980); m. Donald George Winchester, May 16, 1986 (div. Nov. 1990); m. Joseph Bogusis, Nov. 2, 1996. Owner, mgr. Bonin Gallery, Wolfeboro, NH, 1983-94, Bonin Studio, Wolfeboro, NH, 1994—. Spl. needs art instr. Kingswood Regional Sch. System, Wolfeboro, 1982. Designer logo Audubon Soc. of NH, 1982; exhbn. The Art Place, Wolfeboro; illustrator: The Best Plants for New Hampshire Gardens and Landscapes, 2003; artist, collections at Nat. Mus. Women in Arts, Corcoran Gallery of Art, DC.; illustrator for Nov./Dec. issue ACCENT Home & Garden mag., 2005 Charter mem. Gov. Wentworth Arts Coun., Wolfeboro, 1980, vol., 1980—; donor NH Public TV, Durham; silent auction donor, Am. Lung Assn. NH, Bedford, 2004, 05, Great Waters Music Festival, Wolfeboro, 2005; initiator of art collection for silent auction Hospice, Wolfeboro, 1982—; donor Lakes Region Humane Soc., 1999—; mem. Cmty. Ch. of Alton, 1962—. Mem. League of NH Craftsmen, Washington Area Printmakers, No. NH Arts Alliance. Avocations: gardening, fishing, swimming, cross country skiing, kayaking. Studio: Bonin Studio PO Box 801 Wolfeboro NH 03894-0801 Home Phone: 603-569-5397; Office Phone: 603-569-5397, Business E-Mail: boninstudio@msn.com.

BONINO, FERNANDA, art dealer; b. Torino, Italy, Jan. 5, 1927; arrived in U.S., 1963; d. Francesco Pogliani and Marina Collino; m. Alfredo Bonino, July 29, 1925 (dec. Jan. 1981). M in Art, U. Italy, Torino, 1942. Dir. Galeria Bonino Ltd., NYC, 1963-90, dir., pres., 1981—. Mem. Art Dealers Assn. Am. Office: Galeria Bonino Ltd 48 Great Jones St New York NY 10012-1133 Home Phone: 212-260-2710; Office Phone: 212-598-4262.

BONIS, LASZLO JOSEPH, marketing executive, healthcare professional, chemist; b. Budapest, Hungary, May 31, 1931; came to U.S., 1957; s. Joseph and Ilona (Hunvald) B.; m. Eva Markovich, July 31, 1955 (div. 1981); children: Andrea Christine, Peter Anthony Laszlo; m. Cheryl E. Olsen, Dec. 28, 1985. DM Ing. Mech. Engring., U. Tech. Sci., Budapest, 1953; MSc in Metallurgy, MIT, 1959, postgrad., 1959-60. Registered profl. engr., Calif., Mass.; cert. chemist Nat. Cert. Commn. Assoc. dir. material rsch. Electronics, Inc., Budapest, 1953-56; prof. U. Tech. Sci., 1953-56; rsch. asst. MIT, Cambridge, 1957-60; exec. v.p., tech. dir. Ilikon Corp., Natick, Mass., 1960-62, pres., tech. dir., 1962-74; mgmt. cons. Tech. Fin. and Mktg., Inc., Natick, Mass., 1974—; pres., chmn., tech. dir. Composite Container Corp., Medford, Mass., 1977-88; pres. T.F.M. Cons., Dover, Mass., 1988—. Editor: (4 vols.) Fundamental Phenomena in the Material Science; contbr. articles to profl. jours.; patentee in field. Bd. dirs. The Opera Co., Boston, 1962-85, pres., 1966-85; pres. Boston Opera House, 1991-94. Recipient Muse award Pub. Action for the Arts, 1984, George Washington award Am. Hungarian Found., 1984, Golden Door award Internat. Inst., 1980, Golden Diploma award Tech. U. Sci., Budapest, 2003; named One of Outstanding Young Men of Greater Boston C. of C., 1966. Fellow Am. Inst. Chemists; mem. N.Y. Acad. Scis., MIT Club. Office: TFM Cons 52 Haven St Dover MA 02030-2131 Business E-Mail: dr.bonis@tfmconsultants.com.

BON JOVI, JON (JOHN FRANCIS BONGIOVI JR.), musician, singer, songwriter, actor, professional sports team executive; b. Perth Amboy, NJ, Mar. 2, 1962; s. John and Carol Bongiovi; m. Dorothea Hurley, May, 1989; children: Stephanie Rose, Jesse James Louis, Jacob, Romeo Jon. Grad. high sch., Sayreville. Singer, songwriter band Bon Jovi, 1984—. Co-Owner Phila. Soul Arena Football League Team, 2004—. Mem. various local bands including The Rest, The Wild Ones, Johnny and the Lechers, The Raze, Atlantic City Expressway; singer: (albums with Bon Jovi) Bon Jovi, 1984, 7800 Fahrenheit, 1985, Slippery When Wet, 1986, Bon Jovi Live, 1987, New Jersey, 1988, Keep the Faith, 1992, Crossroad, 1994, These Days, 1995, Bon Jovi, 1999, Crush, 2000, Bounce, 2002, Distance, 2003, This Left Feels Right, 2003, 100,000,000 Bon Jovi Fans Can't Be Wrong, 2004, Have a Nice Day, 2005, Lost Highway, 2007; (solo albums) Blaze of Glory, 1990, Destination Anywhere, 1997; actor (films) The Return of Bruno, 1988, Moonlight and Valentino, 1995, The Leading Man, 1996, Long Time, Nothing New, 1997, Little City, 1997, Homegrown, 1997, Row Your Boat, 1998, U-571, 2000, Pay It Forward, 2000, Vampires: Los Muertos, 2002, Cry Wolf, 2005; guest appearances include Top of the Pops, 1986-2002 (several episodes), The Uncle Floyd Show, 1974, Unsolved Mysteries, 1998, Sex and the City, 1999, Ally McBeal, 2002, MadTV, 2002, Pulse, 2004, Las Vegas, 2005 and several talk shows. Campaigned heavily in 2000 for Al Gore and 2004 for John Kerry. Co-recipient Award of Merit, Am. Music Awards, 2004, with Jennifer Nettles, Collaborative Video of Yr. for the song Who Says You Can't Go Home, CMT Awards (Country Music TV), 2006, with Jennifer Nettles, Best Country Collaboration with Vocals for the song Who Says You Can't Go Home, Grammy Awards, 2007; recipient Diamond Award, World Music Awards, 2005, Favorite Rock Song-Who Says You Can't Go Home, People's Choice Awards, 2007.*

BONNARD, RAYMOND, theater director; b. Chambersburg, Pa., May 13, 1951; m. Ricki Whitacre, Jan. 22, 1977; children: Christopher David, Alexander Whitacre. BS cum laude, Indiana U., Pa., 1973; MFA cum laude, Ohio U., 1976. Prodn. mgr. Mo. Reparatory Theatre, Kansas City, 1978-79; assoc. prodr. Tiffany's Attic Theatre, Waldo Astoria Theatre, Kansas City, 1979-81; prodn. stage mgr. Folly Theatre, Kansas City, 1981; mng. dir. Del. Theatre Co., Wilmington, 1981-84; producing dir. Studio Area Theatre, Buffalo, 1984-95. Asst. prof. U. Mo., Kansas City, 1978-79; respondent Am. Coll. Theatre Festival. Active Buffalo Fin. Planning Commn., Leadership Buffalo. Mem. League Regional Theatres (exec. com. 1988-91), Theatre DIst. Assn. (v.p. 1993—).

BONNEFOUX, JEAN-PIERRE, choreographer, dancer; b. Bourg-en-Bresse, France, Apr. 9, 1943; s. Laurent and Marie-Therese (Noel) Bonnefoux; m. Patricia McBride, Sept. 8, 1973. Student, Paris Opera Sch.; ArtsD (hon.), Goucher Coll., 1987. Tchr. Sch. of Am. Ballet, NYC; choreographer, 1977—80; artistic dir. N.C. Dance Theatre, Charlotte, 1996—, also pres. Ballet artist-in-residence Goucher Coll., Towson, Md., 1984—94; artistic dir. ballet dept. Ind. U., Bloomington, 1985—96. Danseur entoile Paris Opera Ballet, 1958—70; dancer N.Y.C. Ballet, 1970—81. Decorated Officier L'Ordre du Merite France. Office: N Carolina Dance Theatre Ste 113 622 E 28th St Charlotte NC 28205*

BONNELL, BRUNO, information technology executive; Degree in econs. and chemical engring., U. Paris Dauphne. Co-founder, chmn., CEO, chief creative officer Infogrames Entertainment SA (IESA), 1983—; chmn. Atari, Inc., NYC, 2000—, CEO, 2000—04, chief creative officer, 2004—, interim CEO, 2005—06. Bd. dirs. Atari, Inc., 1999—; creator SELL. Shareholder Lyons' UEFA soccer team, the Olympique Lyonnais. Office: Atari Inc 417 Fifth Ave New York NY 10016 Office Phone: 212-726-6500.

BONNELL, VICTORIA EILEEN, sociologist, educator; b. NYC, June 15, 1942; d. Samuel S. and Frances (Nassau) B.; m. Gregory Freidin, May 4, 1971. BA, Brandeis U., 1964; MA, Harvard U., 1966, PhD, 1975. Lectr. politics U. Calif., Santa Cruz, 1972—73, 1974—76, asst. prof. sociology Berkeley, 1976—82, assoc. prof., 1982—91, prof., 1991—. Chair Berkeley Ctr. for Slavic and East European Studies, U. Calif.-Berkeley, 1994-2000, dir. Inst. Slavic, East European, and Eurasian Studies, 2002-04. Author: Roots of Rebellion: Workers' Politics and Organizations in St. Petersburg and Moscow, 1900-1914, 1983; editor: The Russian Worker: Life and Labor Under the Tsarist Regime, 1983, (with Ann Cooper and Gregory Freidin) Russia at the Barricades: Eyewitness Accounts of the August 1991 Coup, 1994, Iconography of Power: Soviet Political Posters Under Lenin and Stalin, 1997, Identities in Transition: Eastern Europe and Russia After the Collapse of Communism, 1996, Beyond the Cultural Turn: New Directions in the Study of Society and Culture, 1999, (with George Breslauer) Russia in the New Century: Stability or Disorder, 2004, (with Thomas Gold) New Entrepreneurs of Europe and Asia: Russia, Eastern Europe and China, 2004; contbr. articles to profl. jours. Recipient Heldt prize in Slavic women's studies, 1991; AAUW fellow, 1979; Regents Faculty fellow, 1978, Fulbright Hays Faculty fellow, 1977, Internat. Rsch. and Exch. Bd. fellow, 1977, 88, Stanford U. Hoover Instn. nat. fellow, 1973-74, Guggenheim fellow, 1985, fellow Ctr. Advanced Study in Behavioral Scis., 1986-87, Pres.' Rsch. fellow in Humanities, 1991-92; grantee Am. Philos. Soc., 1979, Am. Coun. Learned Socs., 1976, 90-91. Mem.: Am. Assn. Advancement Slavic Studies, Am. Sociol. Assn. Business E-Mail: vbonnell@berkeley.edu.

BONNELL-MIHALIS, PAMELA GAY SCOGGINS, library director; b. Monterey, Calif., Feb. 2, 1948; d. Dewey L. and Marlyce I. (Hansen) Scoggins; m. Verneil S. Henerson, June 18, 1966 (div. 1971); 1 child, V. Samuel Henerson III; m. Chrisman E Bonnell, Mar. 2, 1974 (div. 1983); m. Hugh R. McElroy, Nov. 10, 1990 (div. 1996); m. Stephan S. Mihalis, Oct. 5, 2002. BA, Cameron U., Lawton, Okla., 1972; MLS, U. Okla., 1972—73; CPM, S.W. Tex. State U., 1998. Libr. Met. Libr. Sys., Oklahoma City, 1974—75, Office of City Mgr., Dallas, 1977—80; dir. audience devel. Dallas Symphony Orch., 1980—81; libr. Dallas Morning News, 1981—83; libr. mgr. Plano (Tex.) Pub. Libr. Sys., 1983—91; dir. libr. svcs. Waco-McLennan County Libr. System, Waco, Tex., 1992—2001; exec. dir. Elyria (Ohio) Pub. Libr., 2002—05; realtor Scoggins Realty, Lawton, Okla., 2006—. Bd. trustees Lawton Pub. Libr., 2006—. Author: Fund Raising for Small Libraries, 1983; contbr. chapters to books, articles to profl. jours. Gala chair Easter Seal Soc., Dallas, 1988; exec. bd. Am. Heart Assn.,

1997—99; chmn. Lorain County Librs. Coun., 2003—04; trustee Freedom to Read Found., 1999—2003, liaison, 2004—; chmn. Oboler award com. Intellectual Freedom Round Table, 2004—05; program com. Fund, 2004—05; ops. com. Main St. Elyria, 2004—05; bd. dirs. Women's Shelter, Plano, 1991; trustee Dallas Symphony Orch., 1981; bd. dirs. Salvation Army, 2003—05; pres. Townbluff Homeowners Assn., Plano, 1984—90, Hippodrome Theatre Guild, 1996; treas. YWCA, 1995—96. Recipient Telecom. Excellence award, Ctrl. Tex. Edn., 1997. Mem.: ALA (councilor-at-large 1990—99, pres. Intellectual Freedom Round Table 1993—94, constn. and bylaws chair 1994—97, Shirley Olofson Meml. award 1974, cert. of Spl. Thanks 1986, John Phillip Immroth award 1990), Ctrl. Tex. Women's Alliance (bd. dirs. 1992—96), Tex. Libr. Assn. (chmn. Adminstrs. Roundtable 1994—95, trustee Leroy C. Merritt Trust Fund 1997—2000, chair intellectual freedom com. 2000—02, SIRS Intellectual Freedom award 1990), Tex. Mcpl. Librs. Dirs. (pres. 1994—95), Jr. League, Leadership Waco Alumni Assn., Rotary (bd. dirs. 2007—). Avocations: reading, travel. Office: Scoggins Realty Co 1401 W Gore Blvd Lawton OK 73501 Home: 825 NW 44th St Lawton OK 73505 Home Phone: 580-591-0055; Office Phone: 580-357-5700, 580-583-8046. Personal E-mail: pbonnell39@hotmail.com.

BONNELLY, CLAUDE, library director; b. Quebec, Can., Feb. 4, 1946; s. Emmanuel and Gabrielle (Lepine) B.; m. Lise Lebeuf, Dec. 29, 1969; children: Mathieu, Simon. PhB, U Laval, Que., 1966, Lic. Philosophy, 1968; MLS, U. Montreal, 1973. Ref. libr. Libr. U. Laval, Sainte-Foy, Que., 1968-75, head ref. dept., 1975-78, assoc. libr., 1978-88, dir., 1988—2006. Can. Inst. Hist. Microprodns., Ottawa, Can. Initiative on Digital Librs. Contbr. articles to profl. jours. Mem. Assn. Rsch. Librs., Can. Assn. Rsch. Librs. (dir. 1990-91), Assn. Pour l'Avancement des Scis. et des Techniques de la Documentation, Corp. des Bibliothecaires Profls. du Que., Can. Libr. Soc., Internet Soc. Home: 929 Brown Quebec City PQ Canada G1S 2Z6 Office: U Laval Libr Pavillon Bonenfant Quebec City PQ Canada G1K 7P4 Office Phone: 418-656-2131. Business E-Mail: claude.bonnelly@bibl.ulaval.ca.

BONNER, BILLY EDWARD, physics professor; b. Oak Grove, La., Dec. 12, 1939; s. James Wilbur and Julia (Deer) B. BS, La. Tech. U., 1961; MA, Rice U., 1963, PhD, 1965. Prin. scientific officer Rutherford High Energy Lab., Didcot, Berkshire, England, 1966-70; postdoctoral fellow U. Calif., Davis, 1971-72; physicist Los Alamos (N.Mex.) Nat. Lab., 1972-85; scientific assoc. CERN, Geneva, 1983-84; prof. physics Rice U., Houston, 1985—, chmn. dept. physics, 1986-91, dir. Bonner Nuclear Lab., 1987—. Editor 3 books; contbr. articles to profl. jours. Avocations: squash, fishing, cooking. Office: Rice Univ Bonner Nuclear Labs Houston TX 77005-1892 Home Phone: 713-664-5276; Office Phone: 713-348-4897. Business E-Mail: bonner@rice.edu.

BONNER, FRANCIS TRUESDALE, chemist, educator, dean; b. Salt Lake City, Dec. 18, 1921; s. Walter Daniel and Grace (Gaylord) B.; m. Evelyn Hershkowitz, Jan. 17, 1946 (dec. 1990); children: Michael David, Joan Alisa (dec.), Rachel Pearl; m. M. Jane Carlberg, Dec. 31, 1994. BA, U. Utah, Salt Lake City, 1942; MS, Yale U., New Haven, Conn., 1944, PhD, 1945. Chemist Manhattan Project S.A.M. Labs. Columbia U., 1944-46; chemist Clinton Labs., Oak Ridge, 1946-47; scientist Brookhaven Nat. Lab., Upton, NY, 1947-48, research collaborator, 1958-88; asst. prof. chemistry Bklyn. Coll., 1948-54; Carnegie vis. fellow Harvard, 1954-55; research phys. chemist Arthur D. Little, Inc., Cambridge, Mass., 1955-58; prof. dept. chemistry SUNY-Stony Brook, 1958—, founding chmn. dept., 1958-70, dean for internat. programs, 1983-86, prof. emeritus, 1992—. Cons. editor Addison-Wesley Pub. Co., Reading, Mass., 1956-77; Rockefeller Found. adviser on curriculum, instl. devel. Universidad Del Valle, Cali, Colombia, 1961-62, 64, Ford Found. adviser, 1968; Ford Found. adviser to Universidad de Antioquia, Medellin, Colombia, 1962-64; dir. N.Y. Met. Area Ctr. Chem. Edn. Materials Study for NSF 1961-62; mem. com. for chemistry Coll. Entrance Exam. Bd., 1962-63; mem. NSF-sponsored Adv. Coun. on Coll. Chemistry, 1967-70; mem. Coll. Proficiency Exam. Com. Chemistry, N.Y. State Edn. Dept., 1963-64, 66-70; NSF sr. postdoctoral fellow Svc. des Isotopes Stables, Centre d'Etudes Nucleaires de Saclay, Gif-Sur-Yvette, France, 1964-65; vis. scientist Swiss Fed. Inst. for Water Resources and Water Pollution Control, Swiss Fed. Inst. Tech., Zurich, 1973, Kings Coll. U. London, 1987; Nat. Acad. exch. visitor, Romania, 1975; mem. grants adv. panel Fund for Overseas Grants and Edn., 1968-76; bd. dirs. Rsch. Found. State U. N.Y., 1976-88; cons. L.I. Power Authority, 1996-2003. Author: (with Melba Phillips) Principles of Physical Science, 1957, 2d edit., 1971; Contbr. numerous articles profl. jours. Mem. Ind. Rev. Panel for Decommissioning of Shoreham Nuc. Power Sta., 1992-95; mem. bd. edn. Ctrl. Sch. Dist. 6, Huntington, N.Y., 1968-72. Fellow: AAAS; mem.: AAUP, Am. Chem. Soc., Sigma Xi. Home: PO Box 2063 Setauket NY 11733-0707 Office: State U NY Dept Chemistry Stony Brook NY 11794-3400

BONNER, HERBERT DWIGHT, construction management educator; b. Lakewood, Ohio, Sept. 5, 1942; s. Herbert C. and Ruth (H.) B. Bonner; m. Marilyn Anne Seidel, Sept. 18, 1965 (dec.). BArch, Ohio State U., 1969, MArch, 1971. Registered architect, Ohio; cert. profl. constructor. Tng. engr. H.K. Ferguson Co., Cleve., 1961-62, U.S. Steel Corp., Cleve., 1962-64, Hausman Steel Corp., Grandview, Ohio, 1964-65; tng. architect Kellam & Foley Architects, Columbus, Ohio, 1965-68; rsch. assoc. bldg. rsch. lab. Ohio State U., Columbus, Ohio, 1968-71, asst. prof., 1971-74; prof. Columbus State C.C., 1974-95; owner Bonner Constrn. Svcs., Patagonia, Ariz., 1971—. Cons. Aubon Ednl. Svcs., Columbus, 1980-85; adj. faculty mem. Caiptal U., Columbus, 1986-95; exec. dir. Associated Two Yr. Sch. Constrn., Edmonds, Wash., 1989-95. Author: Building Plans and Working Drawings, 1981; editor: Scheduling Construction Projects, 1984, Construction Equipment Operators, 1992; contbr. articles to profl. jours. Trustee Am. Coun. for Constrn. Edn., Monroe, La., 1990-95. Recipient Disting. Svc. award Assn. Bus. and Profl. Women, 1982, Nat. Assn. Women in Constrn., 1984; grantee Dept. of Def., 1970-71, 1st Community Village, 1974, Owens Corning Fiberglass, 1981-82. Mem. AIA, Am. Inst. Constructors, Ohio Horeman's Coun., Tenn. Walking Horse Beaders and Exhibitors Assn., Mid-Ohio Walking Horse Assn., Hocking County Trail Blazers. Avocations: competitive horse riding and showing, endurance riding. Office: Bonner Constrn Svcs PO Box 5724 Valley Spring TX 76885 Home: 6552 CR 403 Valley Spring TX 76885 Office Phone: 325-248-0710. Personal E-mail: d-mbonner@msn.com.

BONNER, JACK WILBUR, III, psychiatrist, educator, administrator; b. Corpus Christi, Tex., July 30, 1940; s. Jack Wilbur and Irldene (Turner) B.; m. Myra Lynn Taylor; children: Jack Wilbur, IV, Katherine Lynn, Shelley Bliss AA, Del Mar Coll., Corpus Christi, 1960; BA with honors, U. Tex., Austin, 1961; MD, S.W. Med. Sch., U. Tex., Dallas, 1965. Diplomate Am. Bd. Psychiatry and Neurology. Intern U. Ark. Med. Center, 1965-66; resident Duke U. Med. Center, 1966-69; assoc. in psychiatry Highland Hosp. divsn. Duke U. Med. Center, Asheville, NC, 1971, asst. prof. psychiatry, 1972-80, dir. outpatient services, 1972-75, med. dir., 1975-81; chmn. bd. dirs., CEO, med. dir. Highland Hosp., Asheville, NC, 1981-92; med. dir. The Oaks Psychiat. Health Sys., Austin, Tex., 1992-93, exec. med. dir., 1993-94; med. dir. Behavioral Health Svcs. Greenville (S.C.) Hosp. Sys. Univ. Med. Ctr., 1994—, adminstr. Behavioral Health Svcs., 1996—2000, acad. chair, 1999—. Asst. clin. prof. Duke U. Med. Ctr., Durham, NC, 1982—87, asst. cons. prof. psychiatry, 1987—; clin. assoc. prof. U. NC Sch. Medicine, Chapel Hill, 1986—92, Quillen-Dishner Coll. Medicine, Johnson City, Tenn., 1989—92, U. Tex. Health Sci. Ctr., San Antonio, 1993—94, U. SC Sch. Medicine, Columbia, 1995—2004, GHS prof. clin. neuropsychiatry and behavioral sci., 2004—. Author: (with others) The Psychology of Discipline, 1983, Unmasking the Psychopath: Antisocial Personality and Related Syndromes, 1986; contbr. articles to profl. jours. Chmn. bd. dirs. The Highland Found., 1980-93; bd. dirs. Western N.C. Med. Peer Rev. Found., 1975-78; trustee La Amistad Found., Maitland, Fla., 1985-95, N.C. Symphony, 1987-92, Cooper Riis Found., Mill Spring, N.C., 2000—. Fellow: APA (trustee 1999—2005, chair fin. and budget com. 2002—, Disting. Life Fellow, Warren Williams award 2002, Nancy C.A. Roeske cert. of recognition for excellence in med. student edn. 2005), Am. Coll. Psychiatrists (treas. 1992—95, 2d v.p. 1999—2000, 1st v.p. 2000—01, pres.-elect 2001—02, pres. 2002—03, sec.-gen. 2006—, E.B. Bowis award 2000), So. Psychiat. Assn. (v.p. 1984—85, chmn. bd. regents 1988—89, pres. 1992—93); mem.: AMA, Group Advancement Psychiatry (treas. 1991—99, pres.-elect 1999—2001, pres. 2001—03), Ctrl. Neuropsychiat. Hosp. Assn. (councillor 1981—85, pres. 1983—84), So. Med. Assn. (sec. sect. on neurology, neurosurgery and psychiatry 1977—80, chmn.-elect 1980—81, chmn. 1981—82), Nat. Anorexic Aid Soc. (nat. anorexia adv. coun. 1979—86), NC Psychiat. Assn. (pres. 1982—83), Buncombe County (NC) Med. Soc. (pres. 1983), Nat. Acads. Practice, Am. Group Psychotherapy Assn., Nat. Alliance on Mental Illness Greenville (bd. dirs. 2005—, v.p. 2006—), Nat. Assn. Psychiat. Health Sys. (trustee 1989—94, 1st v.p. 1990—91, pres.-elect 1991—92, pres. 1992—93), Benjamin Rush Soc. (exec. coun. 2006—), U. Tex. Southwestern Med. Sch. Alumni Assn. (bd. dirs. 1988—95, pres. 1989—91), Phi Theta Kappa. Home: Four Brookside Way Greenville SC 29605-1212 Office: Greenville Hosp Sys Behavioral Health Svcs 701 Grove Rd Greenville SC 29605-5601 Office Phone: 864-455-7834. Business E-Mail: jbonner@ghs.org.

BONNER, JOHN TYLER, biology professor; b. NYC, May 12, 1920; s. Paul Hyde and Lilly Marguerite (Stehil) Bonner; m. Ruth Anna Graham, July 11, 1942 (dec. 2003); children: Rebecca, Jonathan Graham, Jeremy Tyndall, Andrew Duncan. Grad., Phillips Exeter Acad., 1937; BSc, Harvard U., 1941, MA, 1942, PhD (Jr. fellow 1942, 46-47), 1947; DSc, Middlebury Coll., 1970, Princeton U., 2006; LLD, Concordia U., 2003; DLitt, U. Coll. Cape Breton, 2005. Asst. to assoc. prof. Princeton U., 1947-58, prof., 1958-90, emeritus prof., 1990—, chmn. dept. biology, 1965-77, 83-84, 87-88. Lectr. embryology Marine Biol. Lab, Woods Hole, Mass., 1951—52; spl. lectr. U. London, 1957, Bklyn. Coll., 1966; trustee Biol. Abstracts, 1958—63; Arnold Bernhard vis. prof. Williams Coll., 1989; Raman prof. Indian Acad. Scis., 1990. Author: Morphogenesis, 1952, Cells and Societies, 1955, The Evolution of Development, 1958, The Cellular Slime Molds, 1959, The Cellular Slime Molds, rev. edit., 1967, The Ideas of Biology, 1962, Size and Cycle, 1965, The Scale of Nature, 1969, On Development, 1974, The Evolution of Culture in Animals, 1980; author: (with T.A. McMahon) On Life and Size, 1983; author: The Evolution of Complexity, 1988, Researches on Cellular Slime Molds, 1991, Life Cycles, 1993, Sixty Years of Biology, 1996, First Signals, 2000, Lives of a Biologist, 2002, Why Size Matters, 2006; editor: Growth and Form, 1961, Evolution and Development, 1981; assoc. editor: Am. Scientist, 1961—69, mem. editl. bd.: Am. Naturalist, 1958—60, 1966—68, Jour. Gen. Physiology, 1962—69, Growth, 1955—89, Differentiation, 1976—90, Oxford Surveys in Evolutionary Biology, 1982—93; mem. bd. editors Princeton U. Press, 1965—68, 1971, trustee, 1976—82. Staff aero. med. lab. Wright Field, Wright Field, Ohio. Served to 1st lt. USAC, 1942—46. Recipient Selman A. Waksman award for Contbns. to Microbiology, Theobold Smith Soc.; Rockefeller Travelling fellow, France, 1953, Guggenheim fellow, Scotland, 1958, 1971—72, NSF Sr. Postdoctoral fellow, 1963. Fellow: Am. Acad. Arts. and Scis., Indian Acad. Scis. (hon.); mem.: NAS, Am. Philos. Soc., Soc. Growth and Devel., Am. Soc. Naturalists, Sigma Xi, Phi Beta Kappa. Business E-Mail: jtbonner@princeton.edu.

BONNER, JOSIAH ROBINS, JR., (JO BONNER), congressman; b. Selma, Ala., Nov. 19, 1959; s. Josiah Robins Bonner; m. Janée Lambert Bonner; children: Jennifer Lee, Josiah Robins III. JB, U. Ala., 1982. Chief of staff U.S. Rep. Sonny Callahan, press sec., 1984, Congl. press sec., 1985; mem. U.S. Congress from 1st Ala. dist., 2003—. Mem. pres. adv. coun. U. Mobile; mem. bd. cmty. advisors Jr. League Mobile. Named Outstanding Alumnus in Pub. Rels., U. Ala. Coll. Comm., 2000. Mem.: Mobile Area C. of C. (bd. dirs.), U. Ala. Alumni Assn. (Mobile chpt., bd. dirs.), Leadership Mobile (bd. dirs.), Rotary Club (bd. dirs.). Republican. Episcopalian. Office: 315 Cannon HOB Washington DC 20515-0101*

BONNER, ROBERT CLEVE, lawyer; b. Wichita, Kans., Jan. 29, 1942; s. Benjamin Joseph and Caroline (Kirkwood) B.; m. Kimiko Tanaka, Oct. 11, 1969; 1 child, Justine M. BA magna cum laude, Md. U., 1963; JD, Georgetown U., 1966. Bar: D.C. 1966, Calif. 1967, Ct. Appeals (4th, 5th, 9th, 10th cirs.), U.S. Supreme Ct. Law clk. to judge U.S. Dist. Ct., LA, 1966-67; asst. U.S. atty. (ctrl. dist.) Calif. U.S. Dept. Justice, LA, 1971-75, U.S. atty., 1984-89; judge U.S. Dist. Ct. (ctrl. dist.) Calif., LA, 1989-90; ptnr. Kadison, Pfaelzer, et al, Los Angeles, 1975-84; dir. Drug Enforcement Adminstrn., Washington, 1990-93; ptnr. Gibson, Dunn & Crutcher LLP, LA, 1993—2001, 2005—; commr. US Customs Svc., Washington, 2001—03, US Customs & Border Protection, US Dept. Homeland Security, 2003—05. Chair Calif. Commn. on Jud. Performance, 1997-99, co-chair, Calif. Lawyers for Bush-Cheney, 2000. Served to lt. comdr. JAGC, USN, 1967-70 Recipient Medallion of Merit award, Friendly Sons of St. Patrick, 2006. Fellow Am. Coll. Trial Lawyers, Fed. Bar Assn. (pres. Los Angeles chpt. 1982-83); mem. L.A. C. of C. (bd. dirs. 1999-2001), Calif. Bar Assn., DC Bar Assn. Republican. Roman Catholic. Office: Gibson, Dunn & Crutcher LLP 333 S Grand Ave Los Angeles CA 90071 Office Phone: 213-229-7000. E-mail: rbonner@gibsondunn.com.

BONNETT, JAMES W., engineer; b. Milw., Mar. 28, 1949; s. James E. and Carol L. Bonnett. BSEE, Milw. Sch. Engring., 2001. Design engr. Bendix Aerospace Co., Mishawaka, Ind., 1971—73, Cook Electric Co., Morton Grove, Ill., 1973—75; process control engr. GE Med. Sys., Waukesha, Wis., 1976—82, quality control engr. New Berlin, Wis., 1982—2002; quality assurance compliance engr. GE Healthcare Tech., Waukesha, 2002—. Mem.: Am. Soc. for Quality. Avocation: stained glass. Office: GE Healthcare 3000 N Grandview Blvd Waukesha WI 53188

BONNEVILLE, RICHARD BRIGGS, retired gas industry executive; b. Chgo., July 15, 1942; s. Alfred Briggs and Grace Estelle (Burke) Bonneville; m. Mary Ann E. Pittman, July 17, 1976; children: Ann M., John B. BSME, U. Notre Dame, 1964; MBA, Harvard U., 1967. Project engr. Hamilton Std. divsn. United Techs., 1964—65; asst. to pres. Strathmore Paper divsn. Hammermill Paper, Springfield, Mass., 1966; mgr. planning Union Oil Co., Schaumburg, Ill., 1967—72; asst. to exec. v.p. Santa Fe Industries, Inc., Chgo., 1972—77, mgr. planning, 1977—79, dir. planning, 1979—84; corp. sec. Santa Fe So. Pacific Corp., 1984—88; v.p. planning Santa Fe Energy Resources, Inc., Houston, 1988—95; ret., 1995. Mem.: Pi Tau Sigma, Tau Beta Pi. Home: 920 Cranberry Hill Ct Houston TX 77079-5010

BONNEY, HAL JAMES, JR., federal judge; b. Norfolk, Va., Aug. 27, 1929; s. Hal J. and Mary (Shackelford) B.; m. Marie McBee, July 4, 1963 (div. 1979); children: David James, John Wesley. BA, U. Richmond, 1951, MA, 1953; JD, Coll. William and Mary, 1969. Bar: Va. 1969. Instr. Norfolk public schs., 1951-61; supt. Douglas MacArthur Acad., 1961-67; practiced law, 1969-71; law clk. US Dist. Ct., 1969; prof. U. Va., 1964-71, Coll. William and Mary, 1969-71; US bankruptcy judge Norfolk, 1971—96; ret., 1996. Adj. prof. law Regent U. Law Sch., 1987—97; prodr. Hal Bonney Prodns. Author: Overturning Applecarts, 2002. Tchr. Wesleymen Bible Class Sta. WTAR-AM, 1962-98, tchr. emeritus, 1998—; tchr. Good News TV Network, 1989—; treas. Wesleymen Found., Inc., Billy Graham Crusades, 1974-76; pres. adv. coun. CBN U., 1986-95; vice-chmn. Va. Meth. Bd. Edn., Inc., 1991-99; bd. visitors Duke Div. Sch., 1991—; 1st v.p., bd. dirs. Norfolk Union Mission, 1994—; task force on pub. housing City of Norfolk, 1995-96; advisor Film Sch., Regent U., 1996-2000, assoc. prodr. 2000-04; commr. City of Norfolk Parks and Recreation, 2003—, chmn. 2003-07; vice chair rules com. Va. United Meth. conf., 1996-2004; bd. ordained ministry United Meth. Ch., Va; active World Affairs Coun.; pres. coun. Old Dominion U. Recipient S.A.R. Good Citizenship medal, Woodmen of the World History medal, U. Richmond Gold medal, George Washington honor medal Freedoms Found., Alli award Cultural Alliance Greater Hampton Rds., 1998; Judge Hal Bonney Day named in honor by City of Norfolk, Jan. 27, 1998. Mem. Nat. Conf. Bankruptcy Judges (pres. 1983-84, chmn. editl. bd. Am. Bankruptcy Law Jour.), Va. State Bar, Norfolk and Portsmouth Bar Assn., Nat. Film Soc., Am. Film Inst. (Premiere Circle), Brit. Film Inst., Am. Cinematheque (moving picture ball benefit com.), Drama League (NYC), Women in Film (exec. com.), James Kent Inn of Ct. (hon., pres. 1994-96), Phi Alpha Theta, Pi Sigma Alpha, Phi Alpha Delta, Masons, Shriners, Elks, Kiwanis (dir.). Office: The Wesleymen 5100 E Virginia Beach Blvd Norfolk VA 23502 Office Phone: 757-853-4770. Personal E-mail: bonney@cox.net.

BONNEY, JO, theater director; b. Sydney; arrived in US, 1979; m. Eric Bogosian; 2 children. Grad. Fine Arts, Sydney Coll. Arts. Dir. (plays) Funhouse, 1983, Sex, Drugs, Rock & Roll, 1990, Pounding Nails in the Floor with My Forehead, 1994, Some People, 1994, At Midnight and Morning Rain, 1995, Stray Cats, 1997, The Flatted Fifth, 1997, The Fastest Clock in the Universe, 1998, Stop Kiss, 1998, Jails, Hospitals & Hip-Hop, 1998, Look Back in Anger, 1999, Wake Up & Smell the Coffee, 2000, References to Salvador Dali Make Me Hot, 2001, Slanguage, 2001, Good Thing, 2001, Humpty Dumpty, 2002, Fat Pig, 2004, Fifth of July (Lortel award), A Soldier's Play, 2005, The Seven, 2006, All That I Will Ever Be, 2007; directorial cons. (play) House Arrest, 2000; editor: Extreme Exposure: An Anthology of Solo Performance Texts From the 20th Century, 1999. Recipient Obie award, sustained excellence of direction, 1998; grantee Jerome Found., 1980. Mem.: Soc. Stage Dirs. and Choreographers.*

BONNIE, RICHARD JEFFREY, lawyer, educator, consultant; b. Richmond, Va., Aug. 22, 1945; s. Herbert Herman and Helene Selma (Berz) B.; m. Kathleen Ford, June 15, 1967; children: Joshua Ford, Zachary Andrew, Jessica Katherine. BA, Johns Hopkins U., 1966; LLB, U. Va., 1969. Var: Va. 1969, U.S. Dist. Ct. (ea. dist.) Va. 1969; U.S. Ct. Appeals (4th cir.) 1969, U.S. Supreme Ct. 1986. Asst. prof. law U. Va., Charlottesville, 1969—70, assoc. prof., 1973—77, prof., 1977—87, John S. Battle prof., 1987—; dir. Inst. Law, Psychiatry, and Pub. Policy, 1979—, prof. psychiatry, 2001—. Vis. fellow Inst. Criminology, Cambridge U., 1977; vis. prof. Cornell Law Sch., 1993-94, Parsons visitor Sydney Law Sch., 2005; assoc. dir. nat. Commn. Marijuana and Drug Abuse, 1971-73; reporter Nat. Conf. Commrs. on Uniform State Laws, 1972-74; cons. Spl. Action Office for Drug Abuse Prevention Exec. Office of the Pres., 1973-75; spl. asst. to US Atty. Gen., 1975; sec. Nat. Adv. Coun. on Drug Abuse, 1975-80; mem. Com. on Problem of Drug Dependence, Inc., 1979-84; charter fellow Coll. Problems of Drug Dependence, 1992—; cons. Am. Psychiat. Assn., Coun. Psychiatry and Law, 1979—; mem. U.S. State Dept. Del. to investigate psychiat. practices in the Soviet Union, 1989; mem. World Psychiat. Assn. rev. team to investigate Soviet psychiatry, 1991; adv. bd. permanent coordination office Reforms in psychiatry in Ctrl. and Ea. Europe, former Soviet Union, 1993—; bd. dirs. Geneva Initiative on Psychiatry, 1996-2005, Global Initiative on Psychiatry, 2005—; pres. Am. Friends of Geneva Initiatives on Psychiatry, 1997—, mem. MacArthur Found. Network on Mental Health and the Law, 1988-96; bd. dirs. Va. Capital Representation Resource Ctr., 1994-97, 2002—; mem. MacArthur Found. Network on Mandated Treatment, 2000—, MacArthur Found. Network on Neurosci. and Law, 2007—; mem. Max Plank Network on Aging, 2005—; co-chair, bd. dirs. Physicians and Lawyers for Nat. Drug Policy, 2004—; steering com. underage drinking Nat. Inst. Alcohol Abuse and Alcoholism, 2004—; nat. commn. diversion and abuse of prescription Ctr. Addiction and Substance Abuse, 2003-04; chair commn. on mental health law reform Va. Supreme Ct., 2006—; cons. in field Author: The Marijuana Conviction: The History of Marijuana Prohibition in the United States, 1974, 2d edit. 1999, Legal Aspects of Drug Dependence, 1975, Psychiatrists and the Legal Process: Diagnosis and Debate, 1977, Marijuana Use and Criminal Sanctions: Essays in the Theory and Practice of Decriminalization, 1980, Criminal Law: Cases and Materials, 1982, 2d edit., 1986, The Trial of John W. Hinckley, Jr.: A Case Study in the Insanity Defense, 1986, rev. edit., 2000, Criminal Law, 1997, 2d edit., 2004, Growing Up Tobacco Free, 1994, Mental Disorder, Work Disability and the Law, 1997, Reducing the Burden of Injury, 1999, The Evolution of Mental Health Law, 2001, Elder Mistreatment, 2002, Adjudicative Competence, 2002, Reducing Underage Drinking, 2003, Ending the Tobacco Problem, 2007. Chmn. Va. Human Rights Com., Dept. Mental Health and Mental Retardation, 1979-85; chair Commn. on Mental Health Law Reform, Va. Supreme Ct., 2006—; bd. dirs. Coll. on Problem of Drug Dependence, 1996-2000; mem. Steering Com. Underage Drinking, Nat. Inst. Alcohol Abuse and Alcoholism, 2005-, Comm. Increasing Rates of Organ Donation, 2005-. Inst. Criminology fellow Cambridge U., 1977. Fellow: Va. Law Found.; mem.: APA (hon. disting. mem. 2007), NAS (nat. assoc.), ABA (criminal justice-mental health stds. project adv. bd. 1981—87, task force on mental illness and the death penalty 2003—05), Nat. Inst. on Alcohol Abuse and Alcoholism (mem. steering com. on underage drinking 2005—), Inst. Medicine (Yarmolinsky medal 2002), Am. Acad. Psychiat. Law (Amicus award 1994), World Psychiat. Assn. (rev. team to investigate Soviet psychiatry 1991), Va. Bar Assn. (chmn. com. mentally disabled 1981—90, criminal law sect. coun. 1992—96), Am. Psychiat. Assn. (Isaac Ray award 1998, Spl. Presdl. Commendation 2003), Nat. Rsch. Coun. (com. on data and rsch. for policy on illicit drugs 1998—2000, chair com. elder abuse and neglect 2001—02, com. on law and justice 2002—, chair com. underage drinking 2002—, exec. com. divsn. com. behavioral and social scis. and edn. 2003—), Inst. Medicine of NAS (bd. neurosci. and behavioral health 1992—2001, vice chair com. preventing nicotine dependence in children and youth 1993—94, chair com. on opportunities in drug abuse rsch. 1995—96, membership com. 1995—98, chair com. injury prevention control 1997—98, com. to assess sci. base for tobacco harm reduction 1999—2001, com. to assess sys. for protection of human rsch. subjects 2000—02, chair com. to propose strategy to prevent/reduce underage drinking 2002—03, chair com. on reducing tobacco use 2004—, com. on increasing rates of organ donation 2005—). Office: U Va Sch Law 580 Massie Rd Charlottesville VA 22903 Business E-Mail: rjb6f@virginia.edu.

BONNIE, SHELBY W., Internet company executive; b. 1964; married; 3 children. BS in Commerce with distinction, U. Va., 1986; MBA, Harvard U., 1990. With Morgan Stanley & Co.; mng. dir. Tiger Mgmt., 1990—93; co-founder CNET Networks, Inc., San Francisco, 1993, CFO, 1996-97; chmn., CEO CNET Networks Inc., San Francisco, 2000—06; COO CNET: The Computer Network, San Francisco, 1997-99. Bd. dirs. CNET Networks Inc, 1993—; chmn. Interactive Advertising Bur., 2001—03, chmn. emeritus, 2003—. Recipient The NY Ten award, 2003. Office Phone: 415-344-2000. Office Fax: 415-395-9207.

BONNING, KENNETH, retail executive; Assoc. ptnr. Accenture, Ltd., 1996—98; sr. v.p. supply chain Zany Brainy, 1998—2000; sr. v.p. logistics Kohl's Corp., Menomonee Falls, Wis., 2001—04, exec. v.p. logistics, 2004—. Office: Kohls Corp N56 W17000 Ridgewood Dr Menomonee Falls WI 53051-5660 Office Phone: 262-703-7000.*

BONO, ALEXANDER DOMINIC (LEX BONO), lawyer; b. Norristown, Pa., Aug. 13, 1952; s. Stephen C. and Mary A. (Shewchuk) B.; m. Shirley Nay, May 31, 1980; children: Andrew, Alexandra. BA, LaSalle

Coll., 1974; JD, Temple U., 1977. Bar: Pa. 1977, U.S. Dist. Ct. (ea. dist.) Pa. 1978, U.S. Ct. Appeals (3d cir.) 1981, U.S. Ct. Appeals (11th cir.) 1987, U.S. Supreme Ct. 1984. Assoc. Dennis H. Eisman PC, Phila., 1977-78, Blank Rome Comisky and McCauley, Phila., 1978-86, ptnr., 1986—2004; gen. counsel Commerce Bancorp Onc, 2004—. Author: (with others) Audit Committees, 1986, Trial Handbook for Pennsylvania Lawyers, 1982-85; contbr. articles to profl. jours. Vice-chmn. United way Southeast Pa., Phila., 1988; chmn. rev. com. United Way Delaware County, 1989; chmn. CARE, Phila., 1984; com. Cath. Charities Appeal, Bryn Mawr, Pa., 1986-88. Mem. ABA (securities, litigation com. 1988, comml. banking and fin. transaction litigation com. 1988, drafting com. model jury charges for acctg. issues in securities cases, 1989), Phila. Bar Assn., Justinian Soc., St. Alban's Club, Clark's Uptown Club. Republican. Avocations: golf, skiing, softball. Home: 101 Cumberland Pl Bryn Mawr PA 19010-1150 Office: Office of General Counsel 15 South 20th St Birmingham AL 35233

BONO, MARY WHITAKER, congresswoman; b. Cleve., Oct. 24, 1961; d. Clay and Karen Whitaker; m. Sonny Bono, Feb. 1986 (dec.); children: Chesare Elan, Chianna Maria. BFA in Art History, U. So. Calif., 1984. Cert. personal fitness instr. Mem. U.S. Congress from 45th (formerly 44th) Calif. dist., 1998—; mem. energy and commerce com. Bd. dirs. Palm Springs Internat. Film Festival. Active D.A.R.E. Program, Olive Crest Home Abused Children, Tiempos de Los Ninos. Named Woman of the Yr., San Gorgonio (Calif.) chpt. Girl Scouts U.S., 1993. Republican. Avocations: outdoor activities, computer technology. Office: US House of Reps 405 Cannon Ho Office Bldg Washington DC 20515-0545*

BONO, (PAUL DAVID HEWSON), singer, songwriter; b. Dublin, May 10, 1960; m. Alison Stewart, 1982; children: Jordan, Memphis Eve, Elijah, John Abraham. LLD (hon.), Univ. Dublin, Trinity Coll., 2003, U. Penn., 2004. Singer, songwriter U2, 1978—. Mng. dir., co-founder Elevation Partners, Menlo Park, Calif., 2004—. (albums with U2) Boy, 1980, October, 1981, War, 1983, Under a Blood Red Sky, 1983, The Unforgettable Fire, 1984, Wide Awake in America, 1985, The Joshua Tree, 1987 (Grammy award best album, best performance by group), Rattle and Hum, 1988, Achtung Baby, 1991 (Grammy award best rock group vocal, 1993), Zooropa, 1993 (Grammy nomination, Best Alternative album), Pop, 1997, The Best of 1980-1990, 1998, Million Dollar Hotel, 2000, All That You Can't Leave Behind, 2000 (Grammy awards: album of the year, best pop performance, best rock performance, best rock album, 2001), The Best of 1990-2000, 2002, Hasta la Vista Babe!: Live From Mexico City, 2000, How to Dismantle an Atomic Bomb, 2004 (Grammy awards: best rock album, album of yr., best rock group performance & song of yr. for Sometimes You Can't Make it On Your Own, best rock song for City of Blinding Lights, 2006); films/videos: Under a Blood Red Sky: U2 Live at Red Rocks, 1984, Rattle and Hum, 1988; actor in films including U2: Rattle & Hum, 1988, In Darkest Hollywood: Cinema & Apartheid, 1993, Entropy, 1999; composer of film scores including They Call it an Accident, 1982, In the Name of The Father, 1993, Golden Eye, 1995; illustrator (with daughters), Peter and the Wolf, 2003; Co-author (with U2 & Neil McCormick) U2 by U2, 2006 Founder, spokesman, bd. dir. Debt, Aids, Trade in Africa (DATA)-organization officially opened its offices in 2002, 1999—; launched "Red" Campaign, 2006. Named Most Powerful Artist in Music, Q mag., 2002, MusiCares Person of Yr., 2003; named an Honorary Knight Comdr. of the Most Excellent Order of the British Empire, Queen Elizabeth II, 2007; named one of VH1: 100 Sexiest Artists, 2002, Three Persons of Yr., Time Mag., 2005, 100 Most Influential People, 2006; named to Music Hall of Fame, UK, 2004; recipient Freedom award, Nat. Civil Rights Museum, 2004, TED prize, Tech., Entertainment , Design Conf., 2004, Grammy Award for Best Rock Performance by a Duo or Group (Vertigo), 2005, Ambassador of Conscience award, Amnesty Internat., 2005, World's Best-Selling Rock Act, World Music Awards, 2006, Neruda award, Chile, 2006, Chairman's award, NAACP Image Awards, 2007, Liberty medal, Nat. Constitution Ctr., 2007, Bd. Dirs. Spl. Tribute award, Coun. Fashion Designers Am., 2007. Achievements include inducted into Rock and Roll Hall of Fame as mem. of U2, 2005. Office: Regine Moylett Publicity 145A Ladbroke Grove London W10 6HJ England Address: Interscope Records 2220 Colorado Ave Santa Monica CA 90404

BONOMETTI, ROBERT JOHN, technology management and strategy executive; b. NYC, Sept. 29, 1953; s. Joseph Patrick and Fortunata Mary (Barba) B.; m. Virginia Anne Scyphers, Oct. 26, 1997; stepchildren: Jessica, Michael. BS summa cum laude, US Mil. Acad., 1975; MS in Physics, MIT, Boston, 1981, PhD in Physics, 1985; MBA, LI U., 1987. Registered profl. engr., Va. Assoc. prof. physics U.S. Mil. Acad., West Point, NY, 1985-88; program mgr. Def. Advanced Rsch. Projects Agy., Arlington, Va., 1988-93; sr. policy analyst White House Sci. and Tech. Office, Washington, 1993-95; exec. dir. tech. strategy Bell Atlantic Corp., Arlington, Va., 1995-98; pres. MGB Enterprises, LLC, Winchester, Va., 1998—; Byrd prof. info. sys. and computer tech. Shenandoah U., Byrd Sch. Bus., 1999—. Industry adv. bd. Ctr. for Satellite and Hybrid Comm. Networks, U. Md., 1994-2000; chmn. rev. com. commercialization of space NASA, Washington, 1996; exec. dir. info. and comm. R & D com. Nat. Sci. and Tech. Coun., Washington, 1993-95; adj. prof. various univs., 1981—; chmn. Tek-Xam content exec. com. Va. Found. for Ind. Colls., 2000-01 Contbr. articles to profl. jours. Pres. SPCA of Winchester, Frederick and Clarke Counties, 2007-; active animal rights and environ. orgns. Lt. col. US Army, 1975—95. Recipient Laurel award Aviation Week and Space Tech., 1990, Wilkins award, Shenandoah U., 2006, Outstanding Svc. award, Byrd Sch. Bus., 2006; Sci. and Tech. fellow Dept. Commerce, 1993-94; Hertz Found. fellow, 1981-85. Mem. IEEE (sr.), AIAA (sr., Van Allen Conf. award, 1993), Am. Phys. Soc., Am. Astron. Soc. Avocations: music, guitar, weightlifting, tennis, running. Home and Office: Majestik Global Bus Enterprises LLC 260 Golds Hill Rd Winchester VA 22603-3129 Office Phone: 540-545-7272. Personal E-mail: rbonomet@su.edu. Business E-Mail: mgbenterpr@aol.com.

BONOMI, FERNE GATER, public relations executive; b. Council Bluffs, Iowa, July 27, 1923; d. Roy Winfield and Leona Hazel (Bays) Gater; m. Robert Foch Bonomi, Sept. 3, 1949 (div. 1974); children: Robert Duff, David Scott; m. Wayne P. Davis, Apr. 20, 1991. BA magna cum laude, U. Iowa, 1948. Editor Silver City (Iowa) Times, 1940-41; reporter, photographer, Sunday editor Cedar Rapids (Iowa) Gazette, 1943-47; dir. pub. info. Iowa Devel. Commn., Des Moines, 1950-51; pub. info. officer Gov. William S. Beardsley, Des Moines, 1951-53; v.p. Bonomi Assocs. Inc., Des Moines, 1954-72; adminstr. Mid-Iowa Drug Abuse Coun., Des Moines, 1972-74; cons. Plain Talk Pub. Co., Des Moines, 1974-75; communications dir. Iowa Assn. Sch. Bds., Des Moines, 1975-86; owner, operator Bonomi & Co., Des Moines, 1986—. Chmn. pubs. evaluation Am. C. of C. Execs., Washington, 1977-81; mem. Universal Accreditation Bd., 2003-05; co-developer online accreditation course for acad. credit U. Mo., Kansas City, 2007; presenter in field. Author: Show Me A Man, 1969; editor Iowa Sch. Bd. Dialogue, 1975-86; assoc. editor Leader's Mag., 1964-72. Active Gov.'s Com. on Employment Handicapped, 1968—74; chmn. comms. Des Moines Area Religious Coun., 1980—82. Named Iowa Sch. Communicator of Yr., Iowa Sch. Pub. Rels. Assn., 1997. Fellow Pub. Rels. Soc. Am. (developer mentoring program 1994-97, chmn. 1995, pres. Iowa chpt. 1980-82, chmn. accreditation 1982-2001, writer nat. curriculum for accreditation 1998, rev. 2003, Outstanding Contbr. award 1983, commendation for meaningful rsch. Bronze Anvil competition 1997); mem. Nat. Sch. Pub. Rels. Assn. (cert., Gold medallion 1987), Phi Beta Kappa, Alpha Delta Pi (nat. editor 1959-62, Outstanding Alumna award 1977). Mem. United Ch. Christ. Avocations: canoeing, horseback riding, church choir, dance, theater. Office: Bonomi & Co 1003 Kennedy St Ames IA 50010-4247 Office Phone: 515-233-1493.

BONOMI, PHILIP DAVID, physician; b. Chgo., Feb. 22, 1945; s. David Raleigh and Doris Edith (Barron) B.; m. Judith Probst, Mar. 21, 1995; children: Amy, Wendy, David, Thomas, Zachary. MD, U. Ill., 1970, MS in Biochemistry, 1971. Resident Geisinger Med. Ctr., Danville, Pa., 1970-72, 74-75; fellow in oncology Rush U. Med. Ctr., Chgo., 1975-77, asst. prof., 1978-83, assoc. prof., 1983—, dir. sect. med. oncology, 1992—, Alice Pirie-Wirtz prof. med. oncology, 1998—. Contbr. articles to profl. jours. Lt. comdr. USN, 1972-74. Mem. Am. Soc. of Clin. Oncology, Internat. Assn. for the Study of Lung Cancer, Ea. Coop. Oncology Group (chmn. thoracic com. 1985-86). Avocations: gardening, running. Office: 1725 W Harrison St Ste 821 Chicago IL 60612-3828 also: Rush U Med Ctr 1653 W Congress Pkwy Chicago IL 60612*

BONOSARO, CAROL ALESSANDRA, professional society and retired federal agency administrator; b. New Brunswick, NJ, Feb. 16, 1940; d. Rudolph William and Elizabeth Ann (Betsko) B.; m. Donald D. Kummerfeld, Sept. 8, 1962 (div. Jan. 1970); m. Athanasios Chalkiopoulos, Nov. 21, 1976 (div. Dec. 1991); 1 child, Melissa. BA, Cornell U., 1961; postgrad., George Washington U., 1961-62. Analytical statistician Office Mgmt. and Budget, Exec. Office of Pres., Washington, 1961-66; asst. dir. fed. programs div. U.S. Commn. on Civil Rights, Washington, 1966-68, dir. Office Fed. Programs, 1968-69, dir. tech. assistance div., 1969-71, spl. asst. to staff dir., 1972, dir. women's rights program, 1972-79, asst. staff dir. for program planning and evaluation, 1979-80, asst. staff dir. congressional and public affairs, 1980-86; pres. Sr. Execs. Assn., Washington, 1986—. Mem. adv. com. Asian Am. Govt. Execs. Network, 1996—; mem. Nat. Partnership Coun., 1997-2001. Vice chmn. Nat. Com. on Asian Wives of U.S. Servicemen, 1975-85; pres. Catholics for a Free Choice, 1980-83; chmn. bd. dirs. William Jump Found., 2003—. Mem. Exec. Women in Govt., Sr. Exec. Assn. (dir. 1981-86, chmn. bd. dirs. 1983-86) Democrat. Home: 5504 Jordan Rd Bethesda MD 20816-1366 Office: 820 First St NE Washington DC 20002 E-mail: SEAPresident@seniorexecs.org.

BONOW, ROBERT OGDEN, medical educator; b. Camden, NJ, Mar. 11, 1947; m. Patricia Jeanne Hitchens, Sept. 12, 1982; children: Robert Hitchens, Samuel Crawford. BS in Chem. Engring. magna cum laude, Lehigh U., Bethelehem, Pa., 1969; MD, U. Pa., Phila., 1973. Diplomate in internal medicine and cardiovasc. disease Am. Bd. Internal Medicine. Intern in medicine Hosp. U. Pa., Phila., 1973-74, resident, 1974-76; clin. assoc. cardiology br. Nat. Heart, Lung and Blood Inst., Bethesda, Md., 1976-79, sr. investigator, attending physician cardiology br., 1979-92, chief nuclear cardiology sect., 1980-92, dep. chief, 1989-92; Goldberg disting. prof. medicine, Feinberg Sch. Medicine Northwestern U. Med. Sch., Chgo., 1992—; chief divsn. cardiology Northwestern Meml. Hosp., Chgo., 1992—; attending physician dept. medicine VA Lakeside Med. Ctr., Chgo., 1993—2003, Evanston Hosp., Ill., 1994—. Pfizer vis. prof. cardiovasc. medicine Yale U., 1992, U. Mass., 1998; AHA/ACC Task Force on Practice Guidelines Com. on Cardiac Radlonuclide Imaging, 1993-95; chair com. on mgmt. of patents with valvular heart disease, 1996—; vis. prof. various univs., 1982-99; mem. bd. extramural adivsors NHLBI, NIH, 2000—; mem. clin. rsch. roundtable Inst. of Medicine, Nat. Acad. Sci.; working group on methods/technologies Nat. Heart Attack Alert Program, 1994-; co-dir. Bluhm Cardiovascular Inst.; mem. Northwestern Med. Faculty Found.; invited presenter at sci. sessions, symposia and acad. med. ctrs. Mem. editl. bd. Am. Jour. Cardiology, 1983—, Jour. Am. Coll. Cardiology, 1983-87, 91-95, Circulation, 1986—, Cardiovascular Imaging, 1988—, Am. Jour. Cardiac Imaging, 1990-95, Internat. Jour. Cardiac Imaging, 1990-95, Jour. Heart Valve Disease, 1982-95, Jour. Nuclear Cardiology, 1993—, Jour. Nuclear Medicine, 1994-2000, Cardiologia, 1995—, Am. Heart Jour., 1998—; contbr. over 350 publs. in med. jours. and textbooks. Recipient NIH Director's award, 1986, USPHS Commendation medal, 1990, USPHS outstanding svc. medal, 1991; named to The Country's Best Doctor List, Good Housekeeping, America's Top Doctors, Best Doctors in America. Fellow ACP, Am. Coll. Cardiology (exhibits com. 1986-92, 1999-2000, program com. 1991-92, chair extramural edn. com., 1998—, trustee 1999-2004, Disting Fellowship award, 2000, Disting. Svc. award, 2006), Am. Heart Assn. (chmn. sci. session program com. 1998-2000, bd. dirs. 1999-2004, Coun. on Clin. Cardiology, 1999-2001, chmn. Clin. Sci. Com. 2001-2002, pres. 2002-03, bd. dir. greater midwest affiliate, 2000-2006, Nat. Leadership award, 2003, Disting. Achievement award 2005, Golden Heart award, 2007); mem. AAAS, Am. Bd. Internal Medicine (subsplty. bd. cardiovasc. disease 1996-2001), Am. Soc. Clin. Investigation, Assn. Am. Physicians, Am. Heart Assn. Met. Chgo. (bd. govs. 1992-98, rsch. coun. 1992-98, pres. 2001-02), Am. Soc. Nuclear Cardiology (bd. dirs. 1994-98, chmn. edn. com. 1994-2000, nominating com. 1994-96), Assn. Profs. Cardiology (nominating com. 1993—, councillor 1994—, sec., treas. 1996-99, v.p. 1999-2000, pres. 2000-01), Chgo. Cardiology Group (pres. 1994-96), , Am. Fedn. Clin. Rsch., Assn. Am. Physicians, Assn. Univ. Cardiologists, Ctrl. Soc. Clin. Rsch., Alpha Omega Alpha. Office: Northwestern U Med Sch Cardiology Divsn 201 E Huron St Galter 10-240 Chicago IL 60611 Office Phone: 312-695-1105. Office Fax: 312-695-1434.

BONSACK, ROSE MARY HATEM, state legislator, physician; b. Havre de Grace, Md., Oct. 24, 1933; d. Joseph Thomas and Nasma (Joseph) Hatem; m. James P. Bonsack, Aug. 24, 1957; children: Jeanette, Karen, Thomas, David, James J. BS in Chemistry cum laude, Washington Coll., 1955; MD, Med. Coll. Pa., 1960. Intern Easton (Pa.) Hosp., 1961; physician outpatient clinic Kirk Army Hosp., Aberdeen Proving Ground, Md., 1962-74, chief outpatient clinic, 1968-72, chief dept. hosp. clinics, 1972-74; contract physician Harford County Dept. Health, Md., 1975-78; utilization rev. officer Harford Meml. Hosp., Havre de Grace, 1981-82; pvt. practice Aberdeen, Md., 1981—; mem. Md. Gen. Assembly, 1991-99, chmn. house rules and exec. nominations com., 1991-94, mem. house ways and means com., 1995-99. Coord. clinics Hypertensive Coun. Md., 1977-81; reviewer quality assurance for nursing homes in Harford County, Md. Licensing Div., 1977-81; utilization rev. officer Harford Meml. Hosp., Havre de Grace, 1981-82; med. dir. Ashley Alcoholic Rehab., Havre de Grace, 1983-84; mem. Bd. Med. Examiners Md.; mem., exec. sec. Commn. on Med. Discipline, 1985-88. V.p. St. Joan of Arc Home-Sch. Assn., 1968, pres., 1969, mem., 1968-85; v.p. No. Md. Heart Assn., 1969, pres., 1970, bd. dirs., 1973; bd. dirs. Mann House, Bel Air, Md., 1973-82, Harford County Cancer Soc., 1973-86; mem. John Carroll Home-Sch. Assn., 1974—, 1st v.p., 1975, pres., 1975; bd. dirs. John Carroll H.S., 1975—, pres. bd. dirs., 1979-85; mem. Harford County Dem. Cen. Com., 1987-90; mem. chief exec.'s coun. Harford C.C., 1990; trustee Washington Coll., 1992-99, Harford C.C., 1999—. Recipient Outstanding Contbn. to Md. Traffic Safety citation State of Md., 1969, Cert. of Merit for svc. Md. Cancer Soc., 1977, Women Helping Women award Soroptomists Harford and Cecil Counties, 1983-84, V. McCrory award for significant contbn. to enhancement of eye care in Md., Md. Optometric Assn., 1995, Alumni Citation for outstanding achievement and svc. in field of pub. svc. Washington Coll., 2000; named one of Top 100 Women in Md., Daily Record, 1996; named Harford County Living Treasure, 2004. Mem. Am. Acad. Family Physicians (bd. dirs. 1997-99, alt. del. 1990-94, del. from Md. 1994-96, chmn. chpt. affairs com. 1992—, commn. on regulations 1993-96, found. bd. dirs. 1999—), Med. Chirurgical Fac. Md., Hartford County Med. Soc. (sec. 1967, pres. 1968, v.p. 1978, Outstand Cmny. Svc. citation 1979), Md. Acad. Family Physicians (v.p. 1987, pres. 1988, Lifetime Achievement award 2003).

BONSER, CHARLES FRANKLIN, public administration educator; b. Youngstown, Ohio, Feb. 15, 1933; s. William Harley and Anita (Bromley) B.; m. Nancy A. Gebhardt, July 3, 1955; children: Catherine, Jeffrey, Andrew. BA, Bowling Green State U., 1954; MBA, Ind. U., 1961, DBA, 1965. Asst. dir. bus. rsch. Ind. U., Bloomington, 1960-63; dir. Ind. State Tax Policy, 1963-65; assoc. dir. Ind. U., bur. bus. rsch. sch. bus., asst. prof. bus. adminstrn., 1965-69, assoc. prof., 1967-81, prof. bus. adminstrn. and pub. and environ. affairs., 1971-97, assoc. dean sch. bus., 1969-71, spl. asst. to pres., 1971-72, dean sch. pub. and environ. affairs, 1972-88, dir. Inst. Devel. Strategies, 1988-97, Ameritech prof. econ. devel., 1990-97, dean emeritus, 1998—, dir. Arts Adminstrn. program, 2002—. Spl. asst. to sec. HHS, 1986; bus. econs. editor Irving Cloud Pub. Co., Chgo., 1966-91. Gov.'s designee for adminstrn. Fed. Intergovtl. Pers. Act, State of Ind., 1972-82; Ind. rep. Midwest Intergovtl. Pers. Coun., 1972-82; bd. dirs. Nat. Inst. Pub. Mgmt., Washington, 1976-82; bd. dirs. NSF Internat., Ann Arbor, Mich., 1984—. With USAF, 1955-59. Recipient Sagamore of Wabash award Gov. Ind., 1965, 74, Spl. citation U.S. CSC, 1974, 78, Spl. Citation Ind. Gen. Assembly, 1988. Mem. Nat. Assn. Schs. Pub. Affairs Adminstrn. (pres. 1976-77, mem. exec. coun. 1973-78), Am. Soc. Pub. Adminstrn. (mem. exec. coun. 1975-76, 81-82), Nat. Acad. Pub. Adminstrn. (mem. bd. trustees 1989-95), Am. Pub. Works Assn., Ind. Soc. Pub. Adminstrn. (pres. 1975-76), Beta Gamma Sigma, Pi Alpha Alpha (nat. pres. 1980—). Home: 1331 Windfield Rd Bloomington IN 47401-6183 Office: Ind Univ Spea Bldg 201 Bloomington IN 47405

BONSIB, ROBERT CHARLES, lawyer; b. Ft. Wayne, Ind., Dec. 12, 1948; BA, Ind. U., 1971; JD, Cath. U. Am., 1974. Bar: Md. 1974, DC 1990.; admitted to practice US Dist. Ct., Dist. Md., Dist. of Columbia, US Ct. Appeals, DC and Md., 1990. Asst. state's atty. Prince George County State's Atty. Office, Upper Marlboro, Md., 1974—83; asst. US atty. US Atty. Office, Balt., 1983—87; deputy state's atty. Prince George County State's Atty. Office, 1987-90; ptnr. Marcus Bonsib LLC, Greenbelt, Md., 1990—. Apptd. by US Dist. Ct. of Md. to magistrate Judge Selection Com., 1994—; apptd. by US Dist. Ct. Md. to Criminal Justice Act Adv. Com.; elected by Bar Assn. to Gov. Jud. Trial Cts. Nominating Commn., 1990—; counsel Citizen Complaint Oversight Panel, 1990—95; mem. Fed. Criminal Practice Working Group, Joint Bar Assn. Adv. Com., So. Divsn. US Dist. Ct.; apptd. to Md. Pattern Criminal Jury Instructions Com., 1999—. Named Top Lawyer in Criminal Def., Washingtonian Mag., 2004; named one of 75 Best Lawyers in Washington, 2002. Fellow Am. Coll. Trial Lawyers; mem. Nat. Assn. Criminal Defense Attys., Md. Criminal Defense Atty. Assn., Md. Assn. Criminal Law Sect. (chmn. 1986), Prince George County Bar Assn. (bd. dirs. 1988-98, Past Chair, criminal law and federal practice comts.), Md. State Bar Assn. (criminal law sect., past chair), Fed. Bar Assn. Office: Marcus Bonsib LLC 6411 Ivy Ln Ste 116 Greenbelt MD 20770-1405 Fax: 301-441-3003. Business E-Mail: robertbonsib@marcusbonsib.com.

BONTE, FREDERICK JAMES, radiologist, educator, physician; b. Bethlehem, Pa., Jan. 18, 1922; s. Frederick R. and Harriett (Stoudt) B.; m. Cecile Poetzel; children: Frederick W., Stephen J., John A., Therese A., Suzanne M., Ann E. BS, Western Res. U., 1942, MD, 1945. Diplomate: Am. Bd. Radiology, Am. Bd. Nuclear Medicine. Intern Huntington Meml. Hosp., Pasadena, Calif., 1945-46; resident Univ. Hosp., Cleve., 1948-52; practice medicine, specializing in radiology and nuclear medicine Dallas, 1956—; mem. faculty Western Res. U. Sch. Medicine, 1952-56, asst. prof., 1952-56, chief radiotherapy and nuclear medicine, 1954-56; prof. U. Tex. Southwestern Med. Sch., Dallas, 1956—, chmn. dept. radiology, 1956-73, dean, 1973-80; dir. Nuclear Medicine Research Center, 1980—, Effie and Wofford Cain disting. chair in diagnostic imaging; Dr. Jack Krohmer prof. in radiation physics. Mem. bd. Nat. Coun. Radiation Protection and Measurements, 1966-71; radiology tng. com. Nat. Insts. Gen. Med. Scis., USPHS, 1966-70, residency rev. com. radiology AMA, 1966-69, adv. and rev. coms. VA, 1972—; trustee Am. Bd. Radiology, 1969-75; founding trustee Am. Bd. Nuclear Medicine, 1971-73, chmn., 1977-80; internat. cons. on med. edn. Contbr. articles to profl. jours. Capt. M.C., USAAC, 1946-48. Fellow Am. Coll. Radiology, Am. Coll. Nuclear Physicians (Pres.'s award 1997); mem. AMA (del., chmn. grad. med. edn. com., Roentgen Centennial Hartman medal 1995), Soc. Nuclear Medicine (De Hevesy Nuclear Pioneer award 1995), Am. Roentgen Ray Soc. (exec. com.), Radiol. Soc. N.Am., Sigma Xi, Alpha Omega Alpha. Achievements include research on experimental nuclear medicine and radiology. Home: 11138 Wonderland Trl Dallas TX 75229-3943 Office: 5323 Harry Hines Blvd Dallas TX 75390-9061 Home Phone: 214-352-4781; Office Phone: 214-648-2025. Business E-Mail: frederick.bonte@utsouthwestern.edu.

BONTECOU, LEE, artist, sculptor; b. Providence, Jan. 15, 1931; married; 1 child. Student, Art Students League, NYC, 1952—55. Exhibitor Leo Castelli Gallery, NYC, 1960—72. Exhibitions include Leo Castelli Gallery, NYC, 1960—72, David Winton Bell Gallery, Brown Univ., 1962, Fine Arts Mus. San Francisco, 1964, Represented in permanent collections Mus. Modern Art, NYC, Armand Hammer Mus. Art, UCLA, Hirshhorn Mus. and Sculpture Garden, Wash., Mus. Contemporary Art. Recipient First Prize, Nat. Inst. Arts and Letters, 1966; grantee Fulbright Fellowship to Rome, 1957—58. Fellow: Am. Acad. Arts & Scis. Mailing: c/o Knoedler & Co 19 East 70 St New York NY 10021*

BONTOYAN, WARREN ROBERTS, chemist, lab administrator; b. Balt., Aug. 2, 1932; s. Cesario Baron and Dorothy Bertha (Hunter) B.; m. Gladys Frances Daughaday, May 3, 1958; children: Warren Wendel, Suzanne Cheri. BS, U. Md., 1956. Food and drug insp. FDA, Balt., 1956-58; rsch. chemist USDA, Beltsville, Md., 1958-60; head chemist methods devel., tng., standards and quality control lab. EPA, Beltsville, 1960-78, chief chem. and biol. investigation br., 1978-89, also dir. labs., 1978-89; the md. state chemist, chief state chemistry sect. Md. Dept. Agriculture, Annapolis, 1990—. Mem. vector and biol. control expert panel WHO.; U.S. rep. to Collaborative Internat. Pesticide Adv. Coun.; mem. expert panel pesticide chemistry FAO; cons. World Bank, 1987, Chesapeake Rsch. Consortium Inc.; chmn., organizer, participant numerous scientific symposiums. Editor: EPA Manual of Chem. Analysis of Pesticides and Devices, 1975; Contbr. articles to profl. jours. Fellow Assn. Ofcl. Analytical Chemists (pres. 1983, gen. referee pesticide formulation analysis, bd. dirs. 1978-84), Am. Inst. Chemists; mem. Am. Chem. Soc., Assn. Am. Control Ofcls., Am. Oil Chemists Soc., Alpha Chi Sigma. Office: 50 Harry S Truman Pkwy Annapolis MD 21401-8960 Office Phone: 410-841-2721. Business E-Mail: bontoywr@mda.state.md.us.

BONVENTRE, VINCENT MARTIN, lawyer, educator; b. Bklyn., Nov. 11, 1948; s. Martin Victor and Raffaela (Sabella) B.; m. Catherine L. Bonventre; children: Martin Peter, Richard Joseph, Peter John. BS, Union Coll., 1970; JD, Bklyn. Law Sch., 1976; MA in Pub. Adminstrn., U. Va., 1981, PhD, 2002. Bar: N.Y. 1977, U.S. Ct. Mil. Appeals 1977, U.S. Supreme Ct. 1980. Instr. Cochise Coll., Sierra Vista, Ariz., 1978—80; acting asst. prof. govt. U. Va., Charlottesville, 1982-83; law clk. to judge N.Y. State Ct. of Appeals, Albany, 1983-86; supreme ct. jud. fellow U.S. Supreme Ct., Washington, 1986-87; prin. law clk. to judge N.Y. State Ct. Appeals, 1987-90; asst. prof. law Union U. Albany Law Sch., 1990-93, assoc., 1993-96, prof., 1996—. Adj. prof. law Syracuse U., 1993, vis. prof. law, vis. prof. Maxwell Sch. Pub. Affairs, fall 1994; dir. Ctr. for Jud. Process, Albany Law Sch., 2003—; legal commentator local, state and nat. media including N.Y. Times, Nat. Pub. Radio, Fox Newschannel, ABC News, Newsday, N.Y. Law Jour., Gannett, PBS, N.Y.C. Author: Streams of Tendency on the New York Court: Ideological and Jurisprudential Patterns in the Judges' Voting and Opinions, 2003; editor State Constl. Commentary, 1996—; founding editor-in-chief Govt., Law and Policy Jour., 1999-2005, mem. editl. bd., 2005—; contbr. articles to profl. jours Trustee Cath. Charities Archdiocese of Albany, 1996-2005, chair quality improvement, 2005—. Served to capt. U.S. Army Intelligence, 1970-73, JAGC 77-80. U. Va. fellow, 1981-82. Mem. ABA, N.Y. State Bar Assn. Democrat. Roman Catholic. Avocations: pop, classical and opera music, great books, art, travel. Home: 606 Astor Ct Delmar NY 12054-9627 Office: Union U Albany Law Sch 80 New Scotland Ave Albany NY 12208-3434 Office Phone: 518-445-2311. Business E-Mail: vbonv@albanylaw.edu.

BONVILLIAN, WILLIAM BOONE, lawyer; b. Honolulu, Mar. 7, 1947; s. William Doughty and Florence Elizabeth (Boone) B.; m. Janis Ann Sposato, Apr. 12, 1980; children: Raphael William Boone, Marcus Doughty. AB, Columbia U., 1969; MA in Religion, Yale U., 1972; JD, Columbia U., 1974. Bar: Conn. 1975, D.C. 1976, U.S. Supreme Ct. 1983. Law clk. to Hon. Jack B. Weinstein U.S. Dist. Ct. (ea. dist.) N.Y., 1974-75; assoc. Steptoe & Johnson, Washington, 1975-77; dep. asst. sec., dir. congl. affairs, liaison officer U.S. Dept. Transp., Washington, 1977-81; ptnr. Brown, Roady, Bonvillian & Gold, Washington, 1981-85, Jenner & Block, Washington, 1985-89; chief counsel, legis. dir. to Sen. Joseph Lieberman U.S. Senate, Washington, 1989—2006; dir. Washington Office MIT, Washington, 2006—. Bd. editors Columbia Law Rev. 1973-74; contbr. articles to law and sci. jours. Recipient 2 outstanding Performance awards U.S. Sec. Transp., Washington, 1979, 80. Mem. Conn. Bar Assn., D.C. Bar Assn., IEEE (Pub. Svd. award 2007). Democrat. Episcopalian. Home: 930 Hickory Run Ln Great Falls VA 22066-1903 Office: MIT Washington Office Ste 410 820 First St NW Washington DC 20002

BONZAGNI, VINCENT FRANCIS, lawyer; b. Boston, Dec. 10, 1952; s. Augustine Joseph and Augusta M. (Giarla) B.; m. Marie T. Rainville, Aug. 27, 1972 (div. Sept. 1982); 1 child, Gina Theresa; m. Donna J. Bachtell, May 14, 1988; stepchildren: Allison, Neil. BS in Math., Lowell Tech. Inst., Mass., 1974; JD, George Mason U., Fairfax, Va., 1998. Bar: Va. 1998, US Dist. Ct. (ea. and we. dist.) Va., US Ct. Appeals (4th cir.), US Supreme Ct., 2002; notary pub. Claims adminstr. Social Security Adminstrn., 1976-79, quality assurance specialist Boston, 1979-83, disability analyst Arlington, Va., 1983-88, sr. hearings & appeals analyst Falls Church, Va., 1991—2003; program adminstr. Corp. Open Sys., McLean, Va., 1988-91; pvt. practice, 1998—. Profl. rschr. and crossword puzzle constructor, 1982-2003. Author: The Mensa Book of Lists, 1992, The Mensa Book of Lists II, 1997; co-author: A History of Mensa, 1990. Treas. Maplewood Village Condo. Assn., 1989-93, 1998-2001; v.p. High Knob Utilities, Inc., 2005-06, treas., 2006—; bd. dirs. Warren County Coun. on Domestic Violence, Va., 2006—. Mem. ABA, NRA (life), Mensa (local treas. 1986-90, local pres. 1990-91, 2000-2002, nat. historian 1989-2003, nat. SIGs officer 1989-91, internat. archivist 1992-2005, local ombudsman 2003—), Warren County (Va.) Bar Assn., Nat. Orgn. Social Security Claimants' Reps., Nat. Puzzlers League, Phi Alpha Delta. Avocations: crossword puzzles, games, trivia, genealogy. Home: 147 Mountain Top Rd Front Royal VA 22630-6013 Office: Bonzagni Law Firm PC PO Box 2281 Front Royal VA 22630 Office Phone: 540-635-9426. Business E-Mail: bonzlaw@embarqmail.com.

BOO, KATHERINE, newswriter; AB summa cum laude, Columbia U., 1988. Writer, editor Wash. City Paper, 1988—92, Wash. Monthly, 1988—92; staff writer Wash. Post, 1992—; writer New Yorker. Recipient Pulitzer prize, 2000; fellow MacArthur Found. fellow, 2002. Mem.: New Am. Found.

BOOCHEVER, ROBERT, judge; b. NYC, Oct. 2, 1917; s. Louis C and Miriam (Cohen) Boochever; m. Lois Colleen Maddox, Apr. 22, 1943 (dec.); children: Barbara K, Linda Lou, Ann Paula, Miriam Deon; m. Rose Marie Borden, Aug. 31, 2001. AB, Cornell U., 1939, JD, 1941; HD (hon.), U. Alaska, 1981. Bar: N.Y. 1944, Alaska 1947. Law clk. Nordlinger, Riegel & Cooper, 1941; asst. US atty. Juneau, Alaska, 1946—47; ptnr. firm Faulkner, Banfield, Boochever & Doogan, Juneau, 1947—72; assoc. justice Alaska Supreme Ct., 1972—75, 1978—80, chief justice, 1975—78; judge US Ct. Appeals (9th cir.), Pasadena, Calif., 1980; sr. judge US Ct. Appeals, Pasadena, 1986—. Mem. 9th cir. rules com. US Ct. Appeals, 1983—85, chmn. 9th cir. libr. com., 1995—2001; chmn. Ala. Jud. Coun., 1975—78; mem. appellate judges seminar NYU Sch. Law, 1975; mem. Conf. Chief Justices, 1975—79, vice chmn., 1978—79; mem. adv. bd. Nat. Bank of Ala., 1968—72; guest spkr. Southwestern Law Sch. Disting. Lecture Series, 1992. Contbr. articles to profl. jours. Chmn. Juneau chpt. ARC, 1949—51, Juneau Planning Commn., 1956—61; mem. Alaska Devel. Bd., 1949—52, Alaska Jud. Qualification Commn., 1972—75; mem. adv. bd. Juneau-Douglas C.C. Capt. US Army, 1941—45. Named Juneau Man of Yr., Rotary, 1974, The Boochever & Bird Chair for Study and Tchg. of Freedom and Equality, U. Calif. Sch. Law, Davis, 2000; recipient Disting. Alumnus award, Cornell U., 1989. Fellow: Am. Coll. Trial Attys.; mem.: ABA, Am. Law Inst., Am. Judicature Soc. (dir. 1970—74), Juneau Bar Assn. (pres. 1971—72), Alaska Bar Assn. (pres. 1961—62), Alaskans United (chmn. 1972), Juneau C. of C. (pres. 1952, 1955), Altadena Town and County Club, Cornell Club L.A. Office: US Ct Appeals 125 S Grand Ave Rm 205 Pasadena CA 91109-1510 Home Phone: 626-577-9351; Office Phone: 626-229-7200. Business E-Mail: boochever@ca9.uscourts.gov.*

BOOCOCK, STEPHEN WILLIAM, lawyer; b. Wilkinsburg, Pa., Sept. 25, 1948; s. William Samuel and Zelda Elizabeth (Heginbotham) B.; m. Carol Ann Bennett, July 11, 1970; children: Eric Alan, Allison Anne, Megan Leigh. BS in Acctg., Pa. State U., 1970; JD, U. Pitts., 1973. Bar: Pa. 1974, U.S. Dist. Ct. (we. dist.) Pa. 1973. Supervising tax specialist Coopers & Lybrand (now part of PricewaterhouseCoopers), Pitts., 1973-76; tax counsel Incom Internat., Inc., Pitts., 1977-81; asst. treas., dir. tax Allegheny Ludlum Corp., Pitts., 1981—94, asst. v.p. taxes, 1994-96; asst. v.p. taxes, chief tax officer Allegheny Technologies, Inc., Pitts., 1996—2002; dir. tax controversy svcs. Deloitte Tax LLP, Detroit, 2003—. Treas. Meadow Wood Homeowner's Assn., 1990-2001. Served to capt. U.S. Army, 1970-79; with USAR. Mem.: ABA, AICPA, Tax Execs. Inst. (treas. Pitts. chpt. 1985—86, sec. 1986—87, sr. v.p. 1987—88, pres. 1988—89, nat. inst. dir. 1989—91, v.p. region VI 1992—93, 50th ann. task force 1993—95, membership com. 1993—97, mem. IRS adminstrv. affairs com. 1993—2003, nominating com. 1994—95, tax info. sys. com. 1995—97, mem. alternative tax sys. com. 1995—97, nominating com. 1997—98, nat. inst. dir. 1999—2001, mem. nat. exec. com. 1999—2003, nat. treas. 2001—02, nat. sec. 2002—03, vice chmn. and chmn. IRS adminstrv. affairs com. 1995—99), Pa. Inst. CPAs, Allegheny County Bar Assn., Pa. Bar Assn. Republican. Avocations: golf, fishing. Office: Deloitte Tax LLP 600 Renaisance Ctr Ste 900 Detroit MI 48243-1895 Office Phone: 313-396-3520.

BOODEY, CECIL WEBSTER, JR., retired political science professor; b. Yonkers, NY, June 10, 1931; s. Cecil Webster and Dorothy (Mitchell) B.; m. Phyllis Ann Stensland, July 9, 1955 (dec. May 15, 2004); children: William Mitchell, John Barton, Pamela D. Ellen; m. An Ling, July 5, 2005. BA, U. N.H., 1953; postgrad., Princeton U., 1953-54; MA, NYU, 1960. Tng. program Arabian-Am. Oil Co., Dhahran, Saudi Arabia, 1954; with N.Y. Telephone Co., Westchester, 1957-62; instr. polit. sci. Fashion Inst. Tech., NYC, 1964-68, from asst. prof. to prof., 1968-95; ret., 1995; adj. prof. Fashion Inst. Tech., 1996—2005. Chmn. dept. social sci. Fashion Inst. Tech., NYC, 1971—73; vis. prof. fgn. langs. Inner Mongolia U., Huhhot, China, 1989—90, 1996—97, 2001; lectr., China, 2000—. Treas. Richards Boys Club, Yonkers, 1962-63; v.p. Manasquan-Brielle Little League, N.J., 1969; sec. Manasquan Babe Ruth League, 1972-96; Democratic municipal chmn., Manasquan, 1970-78; pres. 11th Ward Democratic Club, Yonkers, 1962; bd. dirs. Manasquan Area Human Rels. Coun., 1973-98, Brookdale C.C., Lincroft, N.J., 1979-88; pres. Squan Soccer Club, 1980. With U.S. Army, 1954-56. Fellow Ford Found., 1953-54; Penfield scholar NYU, 1960. Mem. Am. Polit. Sci. Assn., Assn. Asian Studies, Asia Soc., China Inst. in Am., Am. Profs. for Peace in the Middle East (nat. vice chmn. 1989-90), Phi Beta Kappa, Phi Kappa Phi, Pi Mu Epsilon, Pi Gamma Mu. Methodist. Home: 35 Sherwood Dr Morristown NJ 07960 Personal E-mail: pcboodey@bytheshore.com. *To assist young adults to develop their qualities for critical thinking and to encourage them to participate in extra-curricular activities— these are the goals of my life.*

BOODRO, MICHAEL, editor; With Vogue, 1991—2001; editor-in-chief Garden Design, 2001; style dept. editor NY Times Mag., 2001—04; exec. editor Elle Decor, 2004—06; editor-in-chief Culture & Travel, 2006—07, Martha Stewart Living, 2007—. Office: Martha Stewart Living Omnimedia 11 W 42nd St 25th Fl New York NY 10036*

BOOHER, ALICE ANN, lawyer; b. Indpls., Oct. 6, 1941; d. Norman Rogers and Olga (Bonke) B. BA in Polit. Sci., Butler U., Indpls., 1963; LLB, Ind. U., Bloomington, 1966, JD, 1967. Bar: Ind. 1966, U.S. Dist. Ct. (so. dist.) Ind. 1966, U.S. Tax Ct. 1970, U.S. Ct. Customs and Patent Appeals 1969, U.S. Ct. Mil. Appeals 1969, U.S. Ct. Appeals (D.C. cir.) 1969, U.S. Supreme Ct. 1969; cert. tchr., Ind. Rsch. asst., law clk. Supreme and Appellate Cts. Ind., Indpls., 1966; legal intern, atty., staff legal advisor Dept. State, Washington, 1966-69; staff legal adviser Bd. Vets. Appeals, Washington, 1969-78, sr. atty., 1978—, counsel, 1991—. Former counselor DC Penal Facilities and Shelters, Washington; chair veterans prpgrams Bd. Vets. Appeals, chair exhibits com.; chair exceptional achievement awards Dept. VA, Washington. Author: The Nuclear Test Ban Treaty and the Third Party Non-Nuclear States, also children's books; contbr. articles to various publs., chpts. to Whiteman Digest of International Law; exhibited crafts, needlepoint in juried artisan fairs; originator U.S. postage stamps Women in Mil. Svc., 1980-97, POWs/MIAs, 1986-96. Pres., legal advisor VA Employees Assn.; mem. sec.'s mus. task force Dept. Va; founding sponsor Nat. Mus. of US Army; patron Vietnam Vets. Art Mus.; bd. dirs. cmty. groups including DC Women's Commn. for Crime Prevention, 1980—81, Friends of Nat. Vets. Mus. Named Ky. Col., 1988; recipient various awards, Diisting. Svc. award, Contrbn. of Merit awards. Mem. DAV (life), VFW Aux. (life), D.C. Sexual Assault Coalition (chmn. legal com.), Life Mem. Judge Advocates Assn., U.S. Supreme Ct. Hist. Soc., U.S. Naval Inst., Nat. Mus. Women in Arts, Kennedy Ctr. Stars, Sackler/Freer Galleries (patron), Women in Mil. Svcs. to Am. Found., Bus. and Profl. Women (pres. D.C. 1980-81, nat. UN fellow 1974, nat. bd. dirs. 1980-82, 87-94, Woman of Yr. award D.C. 1975, Marguerite Rawalt award D.C. 1986), USO (DVA sec), Navy League U.S.A. (life), Am. Legion Aux. (life), Women Officers Profl. Assns., Nat. Vets. Mus. Task Force, Nat. Task Force on Women of the Mil. and Women Mil. POWS (chair Esther Peterson Tribute 1995, panel, paper moderator conf. 1997, book reviewer, contbr. to Stars & Stripes, Ex POWs Bull., others), Assn. Former Intelligence Officers (assoc.), Am. News Womens Club, Cons., Saigon Tourist, Inc., Alliance Nat. Def. (editor Advocate), OSS Soc. (assoc.), Nat. Mus. US Army (founding sponsor), Nat. Vietnam Vets. Art Mus., Winterthur.

BOOK, EDWARD RAYMOND, retired trade association administrator; b. Cleve., May 9, 1931; s. Raymond John and Grace Elizabeth Book; m. Inga M. Scheyer, Feb. 14, 1953; children: Sandra Book Liddick, Edward R. Jr., Frederick A. BS in Hotel Adminstrn, Pa. State U., 1954. Mgr. restaurant Howard D. Johnson Co., Harrisburg, 1950-54; mgr. food and beverage, asst. mgr. Hotel Harrisburger, Harrisburg, 1956-60; v.p., gen. mgr. Hotel Bethlehem, Pa., 1960-68; gen. mgr. Hospitality Motor Inn, Cleve., 1968-69, Hotel Hershey, Pa., 1969; mng. dir. Hotel Hershey and Country Club, 1970; dir. hostelry div. HERCO, Inc. (formerly Hershey Estates), 1971, v.p., 1973-74, exec. v.p., asst. to pres., 1974, chmn. bd., pres., CEO, 1974-80, chmn., CEO, 1980-87; vice chmn. bd. dirs. Hershey Trust Co., 1985-87; exec. v.p. Travel Industry Assn. Am., Washington, 1987-89, pres., 1989-94; ret., 1994. Interim pres. USA Nat. Tourism Orgn., 1996-97; mem. travel and tourism industry adv. com. U.S. Senate Commerce Com., 1989-94; mem. adv. com. travel and tourism caucus U.S. Ho. of Reps., 1989-94; charter mem. adv. bd. HRIM program U. Del., 1990-2000; mem. nat. adv. bd. Acad. Travel and Tourism, 1994-97. Chmn. adv. com. Milton S. Hershey Med. Ctr., 1977—82; campaign chmn. Tri-County United Way, 1980, pres., 1982—83; mem. Ams. for Competitive Enterprise Sys., 1977—82; mem. devel. coun. Pa. State U., 1982—89; chair Ctrl. Pa. SCORE, 2004—06; mem. bd. mgrs. Milton Hershey Sch., 1974—87, Milton S. Hershey Found., 1974—87, chmn., 1981—87; trustee Pa. State U., 1977—85, vice chmn. bd., 1982—85; trustee Harrisburg Area YMCA, 1978—87; mem. exec. bd. Keystone Area coun. Boy Scouts Am., 1975—87, Capital Area coun. Boy Scouts Am., 1988—89; bd. dirs. Hwy. Users Fedn., 1993—95; bd. dirs., pres. Palmer Art Mus. Friends, 2005—06. With US Army, 1954—56. Named Pa. Travel Man of Year, 1976, Disting. Alumnus, Pa. State U., 1986; recipient order of achievement Lambda Chi Alpha, 1976; elected to Travel Industry Hall of Leaders, 1986. Mem. VFW (life mem. post 8896), Pa. Travel Industry Adv. Coun. (chmn. 1972-76), Pa. State Hotel and Restaurant Soc. (pres. 1964), Harrisburg Area C. of C. (pres. 1975-76), Am. Hotel and Motel Assn. (industry adv. coun., long range planning com., trustee ednl. inst., resort com. 1975-87), Nat. Inst. for Food Svc. Industry (trustee 1979-82), Travel Industry Assn. Am. (bd. dirs. 1976—, chmn. 1981-82), Pa. State U. Alumni Assn. (life, pres. 1977-79), Pa. Soc. (life), Am. Legion, Lambda Chi Alpha (bd. dirs. 1998-2002). Presbyterian (elder). Home: 305 Village Hts Dr Apt 221 State College PA 16801-7685

BOOK, JOHN KENNETH (KENNY), retail store owner; b. Hillsboro, Ill., June 26, 1950; s. Vern Ray Book and Pearl Iva (Foster) Book Alford Carroll; m. Betty L. Christy, Dec. 23, 1981; children: Elizabeth Marie Dunn Rose, Leslie Michelle Dunn Edge. Assoc. in Acctg., Ky. Bus. Coll., 1974. Laborer Lexington (Ky.) Army Depot, 1968-70; machine operator A.O. Smith, Mt. Sterling, Ky., 1971-72; laborer Irvin Industries, Lexington, Ky., 1973-75; owner Kenny's Signs & Bus. Svcs., Winchester, Ky., 1977-90, Book's Bookkeeping & Tax Svc., Winchester, Ky., 1990—; rsch. bd. advisors ABI, 1990—. Active Winchester Sch. Bd., 1976, 78; candidate for commr. City of Winchester, 1977, 79, 81, 83, 87, elected commr., 1989, re-elected, 1993, 96, 98, 2000, 02, 04, 06, candidate for mayor, 1985; city commr., KLC, DOT; bd. dirs. Blue Grass Rails to Trails. Named to Hon. Order Ky. Cols., 1973; Road scholar Ky. Dept. Transp., 2002, Road Master, 2003; Leadership Fellow Cert., Ky. League Cities, 1999, Leadership Exec. Cert., 2000, Leadership Amb. Cert., 2001, Leadership Bronze Cert., 2003, Leadership Silver Cert., 2003, Leadership Gold Cert., 2004, 05. Mem. Nat. Assn. Tax Profls., Ky. Sheriffs Assn. (hon.), NATP/Am. Inst. Profl. Bookkeepers. Democrat. Office: Book's Bookkeeping & Tax Svc PO Box 840 Winchester KY 40392-0840

BOOKBINDER, RUSS, professional sports team executive; b. Miami Beach, Fla. m. Tammy Bookbinder; children: Josh, Jessy. Grad. in Advt., U. Fla., 1974. Western regional mgr. Profl. Sports Publs., 1976; mgmt. position San Diego Clippers, Denver Nuggets, Dallas Mavericks; dir. corp. devel. Raycom Sports; exec. v.p. bus. ops. Spurs Sports & Entertainment (parent co. of NBA Spurs, Am. Hockey League Rampage and WNBA Silver Stars), San Antonio. Pres. San Antonio Bowl Assn., 1994; bd. dirs. Alamo Bowl, San Antonio Greater C. of C. Mem. adv. bd. Lone Star chpt. Nat. Multiple Sclerosis Soc.; adv. San Antonio chpt. Fellowship of Christian Athletes; bd. dirs. San Antonio Sports Found. Named Multiple Sclerosis Nat. Vol. of Yr., 2003. Office: San Antonio Spurs One AT&T Ctr San Antonio TX 78219*

BOOKER, ALVIN EUGENE, publishing executive, consultant; b. Phila., Jan. 17, 1928; s. Samuel Bear and Yetta (Stein) B.; children: Ellis Carl, Susan Barbara. BA, Temple U. Social worker YMHA, 1950-51; pres. Shopper Publs., Inc., 1952—. Home: Apt 418 1250 Greenwood Ave Jenkintown PA 19046-2957 Personal E-mail: shopperpub@aol.com.

BOOKER, BETTY MAE, poet; b. Allentown, Pa., Nov. 26, 1948; d. Harold George and Bessie (Bealer-Miller) Bartholomew; m. Samuel Efford Booker III, June 27, 1970 (dec. May 1998); children: Liesel Tamarah, Dacey Justin, Jaeson Bartholomew. BA in English, Millersville U., Pa., 1970. Contbr. poetry to jours. and lit. mags., including Plainsong, America, Christian Century, Poetry Now. Home: 27826 Island Dr Salisbury MD 21801-2350 E-mail: sebefford@aol.com.

BOOKER, BRUCE ROBERT, rabbi; b. St. Paul, Dec. 14, 1951; s. Robert Max Booker and Elaine Mae Hinzie; m. Barbara Jean Toelaer, Oct. 28, 1971 (div. Aug. 1982); children: Justin Eric, Rebecca Lynn; m. Patricia Gardner, Nov. 26, 1983; 1 child, David Ray. B in Bibl. Studies, Bibl. Life Coll. & Sem., 1981; MA in Bus. Edn., Columbia Pacific U., 1985, PhD, 1988; postgrad., Union Messianic Jewish Congregations Yeshiva, 1990—93. Ordained rabbi 1989. Tech. instr. Mitel Corp., Irvine, Calif., 1980-85; chief engring. Johnston Telcom., Walnut, Calif., 1985-87; messianic rabbi Beth Shalom Messianic Congregation, Colton, Calif., 1989-91, Etz Chaim Messianic Fellowship, 1991—94, Beth Shalom Messianic Fellowship, Sandpoint, Idaho, 2000—03; mktg. analyst Norstar Telcom., Wilkes-Barre, Pa., 1991-94; pres. Sar Shalom Ministries, Inc., Scranton, Pa., 1991-94, Booker Ednl. Svcs. Corp., Memphis, 1997-98; dir. tng. and tech. support Genesis Comm., Memphis, 1994-97; dir. tng. Hartford Comm., 1998—2002; messianic rabbi Beth Yeshua Messianic Fellowship, Priest River, Idaho, 2003—. Exec. dir. N.E. Pa. Christian Task Force Against Anti-Semitism, Scranton, 1993—94; assoc. prof. Bibl. Life. Coll. and Sem., Marshfield, Mo., 2006—. Author: Mitel ARS Made Easy, 1988, Mitel Generic 1000 Automatic Route Selection Made Easy, 1989, To the Jew First, 1989, Towards a Jewish Evangelism, 1991, The Lie - The Satanic Origins of Anti-Semitism, 1993, A Call to Holiness, 1994, A Merciful Severity - A History of the Christian Persecution Against the Jew, 1995, What If???, 2006. Staff sgt. USMC, 1972—80. Mem.: SAR, DAV (life), NRA (life), Vietnam Vets. Am., Mensa, Jews for Preservation of Firearms Ownership, Messianic Bur. Internat., Internat. High IQ Soc. (life). Republican. Avocation: biblical studies. Home and Office: PO Box 1946 Priest River ID 83856-1946 Home Phone: 208-448-0527. Personal E-mail: brucebooker@msn.com.

BOOKER, CORY ANTHONY, mayor, lawyer; b. Washington, Apr. 27, 1969; s. Cary and Carolyn Booker. BA with honors, Stanford U., 1991, MA in Sociology, 1992; BA with honors, U. Oxford, 1994; JD, Yale U., 1997. Bar: NJ 1998. Staff atty. Urban Justice Ctr., 1997; program coord. Newark Youth Project, 1998; ptnr. Booker, Rabinowitz, Trenk, Lubetkin, Tully, DiPasquale & Webster, PC, West Orange, NJ, 2002—; councilman Ctrl. Ward City of Newark, NJ, 1998—2002, mayor, 2006—. Mem. exec. com. Yale Law Sch.; bd. mem. Columbia U. Tchr.'s Coll. Bd. Trustees, Stanford U. Bd. Trustees, Black Alliance for Ednl. Options, North Star Acad., Integrity Inc., Internat. Longevity Ctr. Contbr. articles to law jours. Founder, dir. Newark Now. Named The Savior of Newark, TIME mag., 2000; named one of Country's 40 Best and Brightest, Esquire mag., 2002, NJ top 40 Under 40, NJ Monthly, Am.'s Most Powerful Players Under 40, Black Enterprise, 2005; Skadden fellow, U. Oxford, 1997, sr. fellow, Rutgers U. Sch. Pub. Policy and Planning, honorary pub. interest fellow, U. Pa. Law Sch. Democrat. Office: City Hall 920 Broad St Ste 200 Newark NJ 07102 E-mail: cabooker@brtlawfirm.com.*

BOOKER, DANIEL I., lawyer; b. Brownsville, Pa., Nov. 14, 1947; s. Harris Taylor and Elizabeth Frances (Hulings) Booker; m. Deborah O'Neil Duff, Nov. 23, 1973; children: Daniel M., Anne R. BA, U. Pitts., 1968; JD, U. Chgo., 1971. Bar: Pa. 1972, DC 1984. Assoc. Reed Smith LLP (formerly Reed Smith Shaw & McClay), Pitts., 1971-73, 77-79, ptnr., 1979—, former head, Antitrust and Trade Regulation Practice, firm mng. ptnr., 1991—2000; trial atty., antitrust divsn. US Dept. Justice, Washington, 1973-77. Chmn. Regional Air Svcs. Partnership; bd. dirs. Allegheny Conf. Cmty. Develop., Pitts. Cultural Trust, RTI Intrnat. Metals, Inc., Océ-USA Holding, Inc.; mem. Jud. Coun. Pa. Contbr. articles to profl. jours. Chmn. bd. Pitts. Civic Light Opera, founding chair Acad. Musical Theater. Mem.: Acad. Trial Lawyers of Allegheny County, Allegheny County Bar Assn., DC Bar Assn. (vice chair antitrust com.), Pa. Bar Assn., ABA. Democrat. Roman Catholic. Avocations: theater, golf. Office: Reed Smith LLP 435 Sixth Ave Pittsburgh PA 15219 also: Reed Smith LLP Ste 1100 East Tower 1301 K St NW Washington DC 20005 Office Fax: 412-288-3063, 202-414-9299. Business E-Mail: dbooker@reedsmith.com.

BOOKER, JAMES DOUGLAS, retired lawyer, government official; b. Columbus, Ohio, June 27, 1933; s. Homer Newton and Grace Bernice (Hermann) Booker; m. Onda Lee Minshall, Aug. 31, 1958; children: Christine E. Booker Garrett, Linda K. Booker Stanek, Molly A. Booker, Andrew W. JD, Ohio State U., 1961. Bar: Ohio 1961, U.S. Dist. Ct. (so. dist.) Ohio 1962, U.S. Ct. Appeals (6th cir.) 1972, U.S. Supreme Ct. 1971. Asst. atty. gen. State of Ohio, Columbus, Ohio, 1961-62; ptnr. Williams, Deeg, Ketcham, Booker & Obetz, Columbus, Ohio, 1962-75; adminstrv. law judge SSA, Columbus, 1975-98, ret., 1998—. Former PTA officer, ch. deacon and Sunday Sch. tchr. Served with U.S. Army, 1953-55. Mem. Ohio State Bar Assn. Republican. Avocations: chess, music, literature. Home: 1290 Smallwood Dr Columbus OH 43235-2503 Personal E-mail: jamesdbooker@prodigy.net.

BOOKER, LEWIS THOMAS, lawyer; b. Richmond, Va., Sept. 22, 1929; s. Russell Eubank and Leslie Quarles (Sessoms) B.; m. Nancy Electa Brogden, Sept. 29, 1956; children: Lewis Thomas Jr., Virginia Frances, Claiborne Brogden, John Quarles. BA, U. Richmond, 1950, LLD, 1977; JD, Harvard U., 1953. Bar: Va. 1953, U.S. Ct. Mil. Appeals 1954, U.S. Supreme Ct. 1958. Assoc. Hunton & Williams, Richmond, Va., 1956-63, ptnr., 1963-95, sr. coun., 1995—; substitute Judge 13th Dist., Va., 1996—. Lectr. in law Seinan Gakuin U., Fukuoka, Japan, 1985; vis. lectr. in law St. Thomas U., Miami, Fla., 1993; maj. gen., sr. mil. aide to Gov. of Va., 1997-2001. Active Va. Coun. on Human Rights, 1987; commr. chmn. Richmond Redevel. and Housing Authority, 1961-70; mem., vice chmn. Richmond Sch. Bd., 1971-80; trustee U. Richmond, 1972-2002, trustee emeritus, 2002—, rector, 1973-77, 81-85, 91-94, vice rector, 1985-87, chmn. exec. commn., 1977-81; trustee Va. Inst. Sci. Rsch., 1981-94, Richmond Symphony, 1987-92, Rouse-Bottom Found., 1989—; pres., 2004-07; active Westminster-Canterbury Found. Richmond, 1995-2001, chmn., 1998-2001; active Robins Found., 1996—, Richmond Symphony Orch. Found., 1999—, Christian Children's Fund, 2000—, ChildFund Internat., 2002—, Richmond Eye and Ear Hosp., 2000—, Homeward, 2001—; chmn. Richmond Eye and Ear Found., 2001-07. With U.S. Army Res., 1959-83, col. ret. Fellow Am. Coll. Trial Lawyers, Am. Bar Found.; mem. ABA, Va. Bar Assn., Va. Law Found. (chmn. fellows coun. 1996-2001), Richmond Bar Assn., Westwood Racquet Club. Democrat. Baptist. Office: Hunton & Williams East Tower Riverfront Pla PO Box 1535 Richmond VA 23218-1535 Home Phone: 804-282-1391; Office Phone: 804-788-8496. Business E-Mail: lbooker@hunton.com.

BOOKER, NANA LAUREL, art gallery owner, honorary consul; b. Waco, Tex., Aug. 5, 1946; d. Karl and Helen Dorothy (Keene) B. BA, Baylor U., 1968; MA, U. Fla., 1970; MBA, Pepperdine U., 1980. Asst. prof. comm. U. New Orleans, 1970-74, 1977-78; pub. rels. cons. New Orleans, 1974-78; dir. pub. rels. Touro Infirmary, New Orleans, 1976-78; dir. comm. Lifemark Corp., Houston, 1978-81; pres. Comm. Alliance, Houston, 1981-82; dir. internat. rels., comm. Mayor's Office, City of Houston, 1982-84; pres. Nana Booker & Assocs. (now Booker/Hancock & Assocs.), Houston, 1984—2004; owner Booker-Lowe Gallery of Australian Aboriginal Art, 2002—. Hon. consul of Australia, State Tex., 1999—. Co-author: Introduction to Theatrical Arts, 1972. Active South Tex. Dist. Export Coun., Houston, 1988-92; press aide campaign K. Whitmire for Mayor, Houston, 1982; exec. adv. bd. coll. bus. adminstrn. U. Houston, 1990-95; bd. dirs. Escape Ctr., 1990-93, YWCA, Houston, 1991-92,

Greater Houston Partnership, 2003—; co-chair Asia-Pacific Arts Cir. Recipient Internat. Assn. Bus. Communicators awards, Women in Comms. awards, Crystal award Am. Mktg. Assn., Outstanding Pub. Rels. Practitioner award Tex. Pub. Rels. Assn., 1996, Vol. of the Yr. award Houston Area Women's Ctr., 1998, Order of Australia, 2005. Mem. Pub. Rels. Soc. Am. (accredited, chairperson internat. sect. 1993-95, Excalibur award 1988, Cert. of Appreciation 1993, 94, 95; mem. U.S. coun. 1994-96), Internat. Pub. Rels. Assn., Houston World Trade Assn. (bd. dirs. 1986—), Houston-Shenzhen Sister City Assn. (bd. dirs. 1987-94), Swiss-Am. C. of C. (bd. dirs. 1987-90), River Oaks Breakfast Club (bd. dirs. 1997), Asia Soc. Tex. (bd. dirs. 1995—). Avocations: photography, design, art. Office Phone: 713-880-1541. Business E-Mail: bookerlowegallery@comcast.net.

BOOKER, SALIH, human rights organization executive; Attended, Wesleyan U., U. Ghana, London Sch. Econ. and Polit. Sci. Legis. asst. TransAfrica, 1980—83; staff mem. com. fgn. affairs U.S. Congress, 1983—86, 1990; assoc. dir. Cath. Relief Svcs. So. Africa, 1991; program officer Ford Found. Ea. and So. Africa, 1986—88; dir. Coun. Fgn. Rels. Africa Studies Program, 1995—99; exec. dir. Africa Action, 2001—06, Global Rights, 2006—. Bd. dirs. Assn. Concerned African Scholars, Africa Access; cons. UN Devel. Program, Ford Found., Carnegie Corp., Bernard van Leer Found., African Devel. Found., Africare. Contbr. articles to profl. jours. Mem.: African Studies Assn. Office: Global Rights 1200 18th St NW Ste 602 Washington DC 20036 Office Phone: 202-822-4600. Office Fax: 202-822-4606.

BOOKHARDT, FRED BARRINGER, JR., architect; b. New Orleans, May 14, 1934; s. Fred B. and Leticia (Chevez) B. BArch, Tulane U., 1959; postgrad., U. Pa., 1960-61. Designer Freret and Wolf, Architects, 1959-60, Kenneth Ripnen, Architect, 1961-63, Francis X. Gina, Architects, 1963-64, Smith, Smith, Haines, Lundberg and Waehler, NYC, 1965; ptnr., v.p. William F. Pedersen & Assocs., NYC and New Haven, 1965-77; prin. Fred B. Bookhardt, Architect, NYC, 1977—. Dir. 28 E. 4th St. Housing Corp.; cons. Engring. Cons. Group, Cairo, Heliopolis and Alexandria, Egypt, 1983—; dir. The Network of Bus. & Profl. Orgns. Contbg. editor Uptown mag., New Orleans; archtl. works include: Superior Cts. Bldg., New Haven, 1974, Hall Minerals and Gems of Am. Mus. Natural History, 1976, Fed. Office Bldg., New Haven, 1978, Restaurant Claire, Key West, Fla., 1978, Woodmere Kingdom of Minerals, 1980, exec. offices So. Container Corp., Hauppauge, N.Y., 1981, Mus. Shop Am. Mus. Natural History, N.Y.C., 1982, renovation of pub. spaces lower level, 1984, employees cafeteria, 1984, Children's Reception Ctr., 1986, Sadowsky residence, Northport, N.Y., 1987, Kaufman residence, N.Y.C., 1987, Grossman residence, Montauk, N.Y., 1983, St. Barts, W.I., 1990, Zweibel residences, N.Y.C., 1983, Ft. Lauderdale, Fla., 1984, exec. offices Bon Temps Employment Agy., N.Y.C., 1984, Dieckmann residence, Manhasset, N.Y., 1985, master plan Am. Mus. Natural History, N.Y.C., 1989, space analysis The Trotting Horse Mus., Goshen, N.Y., 1989, addition and renovation, 1990, De Roy residence, N.Y.C., 1991, Zweibel residence, Boca Raton, Fla., 1993, Kelley residence, St. James, N.Y., 1983, HIV Law Project, 1994, Hinlein residence, 1995, Price/Uribe Residence, East Northport, N.Y., 1996, Branford (Conn.) H.S. with David M. Chin, 1996-97, Mancini Residence, N.Y.C., with Charles Burke, 1998, Fitz Simons Residence, 1999, Cary Grossman Residence, 1999, Bookhardt-Gaskell Residence, New Orleans, 2000. With U.S. Army, 1954-56. Recipient Lumen award Illuminating Engrs. Soc., 1977, 1st pl. award Home Mag. ceramic tile competition. Mem. AIA, N.Y. State Assn. Architects, Architects Coun. N.Y.C., N.Y. Soc. Architects, Am. Assn. Mus., N.E. Mus. Conf., Nat. Cert. Archtl. Rev. Bd. (cert.) Home and Office: 819 Marigny St New Orleans LA 70117-8525

BOOKMAN, ALAN B., lawyer; b. New Orleans, Nov. 28, 1947; BS, Tulane U., 1969, JD, 1971. Bar: La. 1971, U.S. Dist. Ct. (ea. dist.) La. 1971, Fla. 1973, U.S. Dist. Ct. (no. and mid. dist.) Fla. 1975, U.S. Ct. Appeals (5th cir.) 1975, U.S. Supreme Ct. 1977, U.S. Ct. Appeals (11th cir.) 1981. Assoc. to ptnr. Emmanuel, Sheppard & Condon, Pensacola, Fla., 1975—. Adj. prof. Pensacola Jr. Coll. Capt. JAGC US Army, 1971—74. Mem. Escambia-Santa Rosa Bar Assn. (pres. 1992-93), Fla. Bar Assn. (bd. gov, 1996-2004, exec. com., 1999-2000, 2002-, pres.-elect 2004, pres. 2005), Escambia-Santa Rosa Bar Found. (pres. 1987-88, chmn. 1988-89, jud. nomination commn. 1st jud. dist.), Rotary. Avocation: golf. Office: Emmanuel Sheppard & Condon 30 S Spring St Pensacola FL 32502-5612 Office Phone: 850-433-6581. Office Fax: 850-434-5856. Business E-Mail: abookman@esclaw.com.*

BOOKOFF, LESLIE, lawyer; b. Balt., June 18, 1968; BS summa cum laude, U. Md., 1990; JD cum laude, U. Pa., 1993. Bar: Md. 1993, DC 1994, registered: US Patent & Trademark Office. Ptnr. Finnegan, Henderson, Farabow, Garrett & Dunner LLP, Washington, ptnr.-in-charge, Profl. Recruitment. Mem. U. Pa. Law Rev. Office: Finnegan Henderson Farabow Garrett & Dunner LLP 901 New York Ave NW Washington DC 20001-3315 Office Phone: 202-408-4000. Office Fax: 202-408-4400. Business E-Mail: les.bookoff@finnegan.com.

BOOKOUT, JOHN FRANK, JR., oil industry executive; b. Shreveport, La., Dec. 31, 1922; s. John Frank and Lena (Hagen) B.; m. Mary Carolyn Cook, Dec. 21, 1946; children: Beverly Carolyn, Mary Adair and John Frank III (twins). Student, Iowa Wesleyan Coll., 1943, Centenary Coll., 1946-47, LLD (hon.), 1987; BSc, U. Tex., 1949, MA, 1950; DSc (hon.), Tulane U., 1978. Geologist Shell Oil Co., Tulsa, 1950-59, div. exploration mgr., 1959-61, area exploration mgr. Denver, 1961-63, The Hague, Netherlands, 1963-64, mgr. exploration and prodn. econs. dept. NYC, 1965, v.p. Denver exploration and prodn. area, 1966, v.p. Southeastern exploration and prodn. region New Orleans, 1967-70; pres., chief exec. officer, dir. Shell Can. Ltd., Toronto, Ont., 1970-74; exec. v.p., dir. Shell Oil Co., Houston, 1974-76, pres., chief exec. officer, dir., 1976-88; dir., mem. exec. com. Shell Petroleum Inc., 1988—; dir. Royal Dutch Petroleum Co., 1988-93. Bd. dirs. Investment Co. Am., McDermott Internat., Inc.; past chmn. adv. bd. Inst. Bioscis. and Tech.; chmn. Tex. A&M U. Active chancellor's coun., mem. devel. bd. U. Tex.; chmn. bd. dirs. Meth. Hosp., Houston; mem. regional adv. bd. Inst. Internat. Edn.; co-chmn. media com. Econ. Summit, Houston, 1990. With USAAF, 1942-46. Decorated Air medal with 3 oak leaf clusters; comdr. Order of Orange-Nassau (The Netherlands), 1988; recipient Disting. Service award Nat. Assn. Secondary Sch. Prins., John Rogers award Southwestern Legal Fedn., 1986; named Outstanding Chief Exec. Domestic Integrated Oil Co. Wall St. Transcript, 1982-84, Disting. Alumnus U. Tex., 1981; named to Offshore Energy Ctr. Industry Pioneer Hall of Fame, 2001, Tex. Aviation Hall of Fame, 2006. Mem. Am. Assn. Petroleum Geologists (Excellence in Exploration Leadership award 1990), Nat. Petroleum Coun. (former chmn.), Houston C. of C., The Conf. Bd. (bd. dirs.), Am. Petroleum Inst. (life, bd. dirs., past chmn. bd., mgmt. com. Gold Medal award), 25 Yr. Club Petroleum Industry (bd. govs. SW dist.), Coun. on Fgn. Rels. Inc., Bus. Roundtable (mem. policy com.), Am. Coun. on Edn. (bus.-higher edn. forum mem.), The 1001 World Wildlife Fund (life). Office: JKJ LLC One Shell Plz 910 Louisiana Ste 5050 Houston TX 77002

BOOKS, ROBERTA PAULA, real estate finance executive; b. Boston, Apr. 4, 1943; d. Leonard and Mary (Karsh) Books; m. Jay S. Negin, May 20, 1973; children: Martha Alice Books Negin, Samuel Benjamin Books Negin. AB in Math., Bryn Mawr Coll., Pa., 1964, AM in Physics, 1969; MBA, Harvard U., Boston, 1971; postgrad., NYU, NYC, 1966. Acct. mktg. rep. IBM, NYC, 1966-69; v.p. Morgan Stanley, NYC, 1971-81; spl. asst. to comptroller Office of the Comptroller of the Currency, Washington, 1977-79; mng. dir. Prudential Ins. Co. Am., Newark, 1982-86; v.p., co-head real estate capital markets Salomon Bros., NYC, 1986-90; v.p. Citicorp Real Estate, NYC, 1991-94; mng. dir. Chem. Bank, NYC, 1994-96, Landauer Assoc., 1997—99; pres. Books Realty Capital, 1999—. Author pamphlet. Treas., mem. fin., admissions and audit coms. Green Meadow Waldorf Sch., Spring Valley, NY, 2001—; mem. music sch. com. Thurnauer Sch. Music. Mem.: Urban Land Inst. Office: Books Realty Capital 6 Demarest Ct Englewood Cliffs NJ 07632-1904

BOOKSPAN, MARTIN, broadcaster, writer; b. Boston, July 30, 1926; s. Simon and Martha (Schwartz) B.; m. Janet Sylvia Sobel, Oct. 24, 1954; children: Rachel Raissa, David Israel, Deborah Joy. BS, Harvard U., 1947; MusD (hon.), Mannes Coll. of Music, 1991; LHD (hon.), Suffolk U., 1995. Music dir. Sta. WBMS, Boston, 1946—50; concert music dir. Sta. WCOP, 1950—54; exec. dir. New Eng. Opera Theater, 1952—54; media dir. Boston Symphony, 1954—56; program dir. Sta. WQXR, NYC, 1956—67; dir. concerts ASCAP, 1968—83; commentator N.Y. Philharm., 1975—88, Live from Lincoln Ctr., 1976—2006; v.p. Moss Music Group, 1983—88. Cons. The Rockefeller Found., N.Y.C., 1963-67, Madison Sq. Garden, 1984-86, Nat. Westminster Bank, 1987-91; panelist Nat. Endowment for the Arts, Washington, 1978-1986; expert classical music Prodigy on Line Computer Svc., 1990-95; Web moderator Livefromlincolncenter.org, 1997—. Author: 101 Masterpieces Music, 1968, consumer Reports Recs., 1973, (with others) Zubin, 1978, Andre Previn, 1982. Recipient Peabody award, 1948, Letter of Merit Am. Music Ctr., 1977, Medal of Honor, Nat. Arts Club, 1984, Spl. award Concert Artists Guild, 1986, Fine Arts Radio Internat. Lifetime Achievement award, 2002; named to Am. Classical Music Hall Fame, 2006. Mem. AFTRA, ASCAP, Nat. Acad. Records, Screen Actors Guild, The Bohemians, The Dutch Treat. Home and Office: Apt 1414 155 W 68th St New York NY 10023-5819 Office Phone: 212-496-0740. E-mail: shanasima@juno.com.

BOOLBOL, SUSAN K., surgeon; b. NY; MD, George Wahington U., DC. Bd. cert. Am. Bd. Surgery. Breast surgery fellow Meml. Sloan Kettering Cancer Ctr., NYC, 2000—01; surgeon Beth Israel Med. Ctr., NYC, 2001—. Contbr. chapters to books, articles to profl. jours. Recipient Ronald Reagan Gold Medal award, Ronald Reagan Found., 2006. Fellow: ACS (life); mem.: AMA (assoc.), Soc. Surg. Oncology (assoc.), Am. Soc. Clin. Oncology (assoc.), Am. Soc. Breast Disease (assoc.), Am. Soc. Breast Surgeons (assoc.). Office: Beth Israel Medical Center 10 Union Square East Ste 4E New York NY 06831 Home Phone: 917-881-4686; Office Phone: 212-844-6231. Office Fax: 212-844-8954.

BOOMERSHINE, DONALD EUGENE, bureau executive, development official; b. Brookville, Ohio, Oct. 5, 1931; s. Harold Everett and Elsie (Rhoads) B.; m. Marilyn Sullivan, Aug. 29, 1953 (dec.); children: Jeffrey, Alan; m. Patti Watson, May 29, 1985. BS, Bowling Green State U., Ohio, 1953; grad., Northwestern U. Bank Mktg. Grad. Sch., 1965; M in Bank Mgmt., Rutgers U., 1969-72; postgrad., U. Okla. Nat. Comml. Lending Sch., 1974. With jr. exec. program Frigidaire div. Gen. Motors Corp., Dayton, 1955-57; sr. sales rep. IBM, Dayton, 1957-61; bus. devel. rep., asst. cashier Exchange Security Bank, Birmingham, 1961-65; asst. v.p. charge nat. accounts divsn. Birmingham Trust Nat. Bank, 1965-78, v.p., 1968-71, v.p., sales mgr. Circle S div., 1978-80; v.p. community devel. Met. Devel. Bd., 1980-82; pres. Better Bus. Bur. of Cen. Ala., Birmingham, 1982—. Chmn. Bus. Tomorrow Conf. Auburn U., 1975; ednl. chmn. Assoc. Industries Ala., 1975—77; mem. Atlanta-Birmingham br. Fed. Res. Bd., 1990—97, chmn., 1993, 96; bus. adv. coun. Sorrell Coll. Bus., Troy State U. Gen. chmn. US World Youth Games, 1973; v.p. Nat. Vet.'s Day, 1972—; mem. Blue and Gold Bd. US Naval Acad., designated info. officer, 1982—2004; pres. North Ctrl. Ala. chpt. Muscular Dystrophy Found., 1964; trustee Birmingham YWCA, 1972—75; charter mem. Downtown Action Com., 1966; mem. ARC, 1967—, bd. dirs., 1968—80, Birmingham Children's Theatre, 1974—75, Downtown YMCA, Met. YMCA, 1992—97; mem. steering com. Mobile Coll., 1987—90; mem. adv. bd. U. South Ala., 1975—78; chmn. Am. Cancer Crusade, 1976; alumnus Leadership Birmingham, 1991; mem. adv. bd. Ala. State Bd. Edn., 1976—78; bd. govs. Ala. Assn. Ind. Colls. and Univs.; mem. exec. com. Birmingham Cmty. Svc. award; mem. Ala. com. Employers Support of the NG and Res.; bd. dirs., 2d v.p. Birmingham BBB, 1980—82; founding bd. dirs. Ala. Jump Start Coalition, 2002; bd. dirs. Birmingham Zoological Soc., 1972—76. Recipient Comdt. award U.S. Naval Acad., 1994, Comdts. Dir. award, 1999, Outstanding Broadcasters Cooperation award Ala. Broadcasters Assn., 1998, Alumni Cmty. Svc. award Bowling Green State U., 2001; Res. Day proclaimed in his honor, Birmingham, 1983, Donald E. Boomershine Day proclaimed in his honor, 1985; named to Ala. Sr. Citizen Hall of Fame, 2005, BBB, Inc. Hall of Fame, 2006 Mem. Bank Mktg. Assn. (nat. dir. 1971-75, nat. v.p. devel. 1971), Ala. Indsl. Devel. Coun., So. Indsl. Coun., World Trade Assn. Ala., Diplomats of Birmingham (founder, chmn. 1973), Marine Corps Res. Officers Assn. (nat. dir. 1974-76), Ala. Native Sons and Daus. (chmn. 1971-72), Newcomen Soc. of U.S., Birmingham C. of C. (life), Vestavia Country Club, The Club, Touchdown Club (Birmingham, founder, dir., treas), Kiwanis (officer, dir., Birmingham 1971, Hixson fellow 2003, Legion Honor award, 2006), Vestavia Country Club, The Club, Summit Club (founding mem., bd. dirs. 2004), Sigma Chi. Office: Better Bus Bur PO Box 55268 Birmingham AL 35255-5268 Home: 183 Highland Park Drive Birmingham AL 35242

BOON, THIERRY, biomedical researcher; b. Kessel-Lo, Belgium, Dec. 3, 1944; 2 children. Grad., Cath. U. Louvain, Belgium, 1965; PhD, Rockefeller U., NYC, 1970. Rsch. assoc. Rockefeller U., NYC, 1970—71; rsch. charge Nat. Ctr. Sci. Rsch., Paris, 1971—75; charge de cours Cath. U. Louvain, Belgium, 1975—80, prof., 1980—; br. dir. Ludwig Inst. Cancer Rsch., Brussels, 1978—. Mem. sci. com. Fonds National de la Recherche Scientifique, Caisse Generale d'Epargne et de Retraite, Belgian Fedn. Against Cancer; mem. sci. coun. Curie Inst., Paris. Contbr. articles to profl. jours.; mem. editl. bd.: European Jour. Immunology, Immunity, Cancer Cell, Internat. Jour. Cancer, Jour. Exptl. Medicine. Recipient De Voogt Immunology prize, 1986, Rik et Nel Wouters prize, Cancer Rsch., 1986, Award for Rsch. in Immunology, Cancer Rsch. Inst., 1987, Francqui prize, 1990, Dr. Joseph Steiner Cancer prize, 1990, Rabbi Shai Shacknai Meml. prize, Immunology and Cancer Rsch., 1994, Louis Jeantet prize, 1994, Sandoz Immunology prize, 1995, Leopold Griffuel prize, 1999. Mem.: Belgian Cellular Biology Soc., Belgian Immunological Soc., Royal Acad. Medicine Belgium, Pontifical Acad. Scis., Acad. Cancer Immunology (founding mem.), NAS (fgn. assoc.), Am. Assn. Immunologists (hon.), Royal Acad. Scis., Belgium (assoc.). Office: Ludwig Inst Cancer Rsch Cath U Louvain 74 Avenue Hippocrates UCL 7459 B-1200 Brussels Belgium E-mail: Thierry.Boon@bru.licr.org.

BOONE, BILLY WARREN, lawyer, retired judge; b. Perryton, Tex., Feb. 6, 1955; s. Kermit George and Verna Jean (Thomas) B.; m. Celia Trimble, 1990; children: Billy Warren II, Carol Ann. BA with honors, Tex. Tech U., 1977, JD cum laude, 1980. Bar: Tex. 1980, U.S. Dist. Ct. (no. dist.) Tex. 1982, U.S. Ct. Appeals (5th cir.) 1990, U.S. Supreme Ct. 1993. Assoc. David P. Hooper & Assocs., Abilene, Tex., 1980-82; prin. Billy W. Boone, Abilene, 1982—. Part-time U.S. magistrate U.S. Dist. Ct. (no. dist.) Tex., Abilene, 1987-2003; assoc. editor Tex. Tech. Law Sch., 1979-80. Fellow Tex. Bar Found.; mem. Tex. Bar Assn., Tex. Ctr. for Legal Ethics and Professionalism, Abilene Bar Assn. (former dir.), Nat. Coun. U.S. Magistrates (mem. dist. 14D grievance com. 2003—), Order of Coif. Home: 49 Cypress Point St Abilene TX 79606-5130 Office: 104 Pine St #705 PO Box 2797 Abilene TX 79604-2797 Office Phone: 325-695-7460. E-mail: mail@bboone.com.

BOONE, BRET ROBERT, professional baseball player; b. El Cajon, Calif., Apr. 6, 1969; s. Bob Boone. Student, U. So. Calif. Infielder Seattle Mariners, 1992-93, Cin. Reds, 1994-98, Atlanta Braves, 1999-2000, San Diego Padres, 2000—, Seattle Mariners, 2001—05, Minnesota Twins, 2005—. Recipient Am. League Gold Glove Award, 1998, 2001, 2003—04. Achievements include led Am. League in RBI's (141), 2001. Office: Minnesota Twins 34 Kirby Puckett Place Minneapolis MN 55415

BOONE, CHARLES W., physician, pathologist; b. Berkeley, Calif., Dec. 21, 1925; s. Harmon Dunscomb and Florence Celia (Chandler) B.; m. Alexandra Weekes, Dec. 21, 1992. MD, U. Calif., San Francisco, 1951; PhD, U. Calif., LA, 1964. Fellow Coll. Am. Pathologists. Intern gen. practice UCLA, 1954-56, resident pathology, 1956-60, PhD tng. Dept. Biochemistry, 1960-64; post doctoral tng. in Cell Biology Albert Einstein Coll. Medicine, Bronx, NY, 1964-65; chief cell biology sect. Nat. Cancer Inst., NIH, Bethesda, Md., 1965-80; chief pathology Al Hada Hosp., Taif, Saudi Arabia, 1980-84, program dir. chemoprevention branch, Divsn. of Cancer Prevention, 1984-90; divsn. chemoprevention NIH, NCI, Bethesda, 1991—. Author: (book) Cancer Prevention, 1992; contbr. over 140 articles to sci. jours. Ensign USN, 1943-45. Avocations: scuba diving, tennis, history.

BOONE, DEBORAH ANN (DEBBY BOONE), singer; b. Hackensack, NJ, Sept. 22, 1956; d. Charles (Pat) Eugene and Shirley (Foley) Boone; m. Gabriel Ferrer, Sept. 1, 1979; children: Gabriella, Dustin Boone, Tessa Rose, Jordan. Student Calif. schs. Singer: with father, Pat Boone, and family group, 1970—, (albums) You Light Up My Life, 1977, Midstream, 1978, Debby Boone, 1979, Love Has No Reason, 1980, With My Song, 1980, Savin' It Up, 1981, Surrender, 1983 (Dove award, 1983), Choose Life, 1985, Friends For Life, 1987, Be Thou My Vision, 1989, Home For Christmas, 1989, (soundtrack) Reflections of Rosemary, 2005; numerous appearances (TV series) TV talk and variety programs, appeared (ABC-TV Movie of the Week TV films) Sins of the Past, 1984, star children's video Hug Along Songs; author: Debby Boone--So Far, 1988, (children's book) Bedtime Hugs for Little Ones, 1988; co-author: Tomorrow is a Brand New Day, 1989; starred in nat. tour (Broadway plays) Seven Brides for Seven Brothers, 1981—82, nat. tour Sound of Music, 1987—88, The King and I, actress (plays) Camelot, 2005, tribute show Reflections of Rosemary, 2005. Named Singing Star of Yr., Am. Guild Variety Artists, 1978, Working Mother of Yr., 1982; recipient Am. Music award, song of yr., 1977, Grammy award, best new artist, 1977, Grammy award, best inspirational performance, 1980, Grammy award, best Gospel performance for Keep the Flame Burning, 1984, Nat. Assn. Theatre Owners award, best new personality, 1980, Dove award, 1980, Country Music award, best new country artist, 1977. Mem.: Ch. on the Way. Address: 4334 Kester Ave Van Nuys CA 91403-4135

BOONE, DONNA CLAUSEN, physical therapist, statistician, researcher; b. Nebraska City, Nebr., Dec. 12, 1932; d. Otto Ralph and Hallie Rae Clausen; m. Robert William Boone, Apr. 3, 1965. BA in Zoology, U. Wyo., 1954; MS in Phys. Therapy, U. So. Calif., 1980, MS in Biometry, 1983. Lic. phys. therapist, Calif. Phys. therapist Ill. Hosp. Sch., Chgo., 1955—59, Calif. Hosp., LA, 1959—63; hemophilia specialist in phys. therapy Orthop. Hosp., LA, 1963—78, rschr., project dir. Hemophilia Ctr., 1967—78; instr. rsch. methods U. So. Calif., LA, 1982—83, Calif. State U., Long Beach, 1982—83; biostatistician immunology U. So. Calif., LA, 0983—1987, coord., statistician Nat. Clin. Trial, Silicone Study, 1987—93; phys. therapist Huntington Meml. Hosp., Pasadena, Calif., 1993—98; cons. Hemophilia Continuous Quality Improvement, Lompoc, Calif., 1998—. Internat. lectr., cons. World Fedn. Hemophilia, Montreal, Can., 1970-78; cons. biostatis. dentistry and pharmacology U. So. Calif., L.A., 1982-83, cons. orthop., U. Buffalo, 1982-83; continuous quality improvement coach Doheny Eye Inst., L.A., 1990-92, Huntington Meml. Hosp., Pasadena, Calif., 1993-97; cons. phys. therapy working group Nat. Hemophilia Found., 2000—. Editor: Comprehensive Management of Hemophilia, 1976, (internat. newsletter) World Hemophilia AIDS Ctr., 1984-93; contbr. articles to profl. jours. Co-chair United Way Campaign Orthopaedic Hosp., LA, chair, 1975—75; mem. Lompoc Rep. Women, 1998—, legis. chair, 2000—; vol. Rep. Campaign for Ho. of Reps., Glendale, Calif., 1996; recording sec. Santa Barbara County Rep. Women, 2000—01; lay leader St. Mary's Episcopal Ch., 1998—; bd. dirs. World Hemophilia Alliance, sec., 1996—; mem. alumni com. U. Wyo., 1999—; mem. med. adv. bd. Hemophilia Found. So. Calif., LA, 1974—78. Grantee Fed. Govt. Agys., 1967, 73; recipient Dr. Murray Thelin award Nat. Hemophilia Found., 1976, Disting. Alumna award U. Wyo., 1979, Achievement award Alpha Chi Omega, 1980, Spl. Achievement award for treatment advances 50th Anniversary of Nat. Hemophilia Found. 1998, Donna Clausen Boone ann. award Nat. Hemophilia Found. to Phys. Therapist, 1999—. Mem. Antique Automobile Club. Republican. Episcopalian. Avocations: gardening, antique autos, travel, reading, jazz music clubs.

BOONE, J. WILLIAM, lawyer; b. Newnan, Ga., Aug. 31, 1952; s. Daniel Walter Boone Jr. and Winifred Trimble (Glover) Klein; m. Anne Elizabeth Campbell, June 28, 1986. BA cum laude, Wake Forest U., 1974; JD cum laude, Mercer U., 1977. Bar: Ga. 1977, D.C. 1979, U.S. Dist. Ct. (no. dist.) Ga. 1977, U.S. Dist. Ct. (mid. dist.) Ga. 1989, U.S. Dist. Ct. D.C. 1979, U.S. Dist. Ct. Md. 1977. Atty. U.S. Dept. Justice, Washington, 1977-83, asst. U.S. atty. Atlanta, 1983-86; ptnr., bankruptcy, reorganization Alston & Bird LLP, Atlanta, 1986—. Spkr. in field. Mem. Olympic Organizing Com.; active High Mus., Atlanta, 1983—. Capt. USAR, 1974-85. Mem. ABA (internat. sect., chair insolvency com. 2005-06), Internat. Insolvency Inst. (chair corp. governance), Lex Mundi (chair bankruptcy insolvency and reorganization practice group, 2003-06), Ga. Bar Assn. (CLE com. 1987-88), Atlanta Bar Assn. (chmn. bankruptcy sect. 1999-00, bd. dirs. 2001-06), DC Bar Assn., Phi Delta Phi. Presbyterian. Avocations: sports, travel, hunting. Office: Alston & Bird One Atlantic Ctr 1201 W Peachtree St Atlanta GA 30309-3424 Home Phone: 404-350-9331; Office Phone: 404-881-7282. Business E-Mail: bboone@alston.com.

BOONE, JAMES VIRGIL, retired engineering executive, researcher; b. Little Rock, Sept. 1, 1933; s. Virgil Bennett and Dorothy Bliss (Dorough) B.; m. Gloria Marjorie Gieseler, June 5, 1955; children: Clifford B., Sandra J. Smyser, Steven B. BSEE, Tulane U., 1955; MSEE, Air Force Inst. Tech., Ohio, 1959. Assoc. elec. engr. Martin Co., Balt., 1955; R&D engr. USAF, 1955-62; electronics engr. Nat. Security Agy., Ft. Meade, Md., 1962-77, dep. dir. for rsch. and engring., 1978-81; spl. asst. to gen. mgr. mil. electronics divsn. TRW, Inc., San Diego, 1981-83, asst. gen. mgr., 1983-85; dir. program mgmt. and group devel. TRW Electronic Sys. Group, 1985-86, v.p., dir. program mgmt. and group devel., 1986-87, v.p., gen. mgr. def. comm. divsn., 1987-91, v.p. gen. mgr., 1991—93; v.p. requirements and group devel. Sys. Integration Group, 1993-95, v.p. tech. and engring., 1995-96; v.p., gen. mgr. TRW Sys. Svcs. Co., 1994-96. Assoc. dir. Armed Forces Comm. and Electronics Assn., 1991-94, dir., 1994-96; mem. adv. bd. Tulane U. Coll. Engring., 1991-05, pres., 2000-02; adj. prof. sch. information tech. and engring. George Mason U., 1995-96; prin. rsch. scientist C3I Ctr., 1996-98, chair acquisition com. Nat. Cryptologic Mus. Found., Inc., 1997-02; adj. prof. Joint Mil. Intelligence Coll., 2002-03. Author: A Brief History of Cryptology, 2005. Served to capt. USAF, 1955-62. Recipient Exceptional Civilian Svc. award Nat. Security Agy., 1975, Disting. Alumnus award Tulane U. Sch. Engring., 1994. Mem. IEEE (life sr.). Republican. Presbyterian (elder). Home: 4905 Oakcrest Dr Fairfax VA 22030-4548

BOONE, MARY L., library director; b. NC, Dec. 29, 1944; BA, U. NC, Chapel Hill, 1967, MSLS, 1973. Dir. Chapel Hill Pub. Libr., NC, 1978—85; fgn. svc. libr./info. resource officer US Info. Agy./US Dept. State, 1985—2005; state libr. State Libr. NC, Raleigh, 2005—. Founding mem. NC Pub. Libr. Dirs. Assn. Recipient Superior Honor award, USIA, 1998, US Dept. State, 2000, Disting. Alumni award, U. NC Sch. Info. &

Libr. Sci., 2003. Office: State Libr NC 4640 Mail Svc Ctr Raleigh NC 27699-4640 Office Phone: 919-807-7410. Office Fax: 919-713-8748. E-mail: mboone@library.dcr.state.nc.us.

BOONE, MICHAEL MAULDIN, lawyer; b. Henderson, Tenn., Jan. 31, 1941; s. Daniel Lacy and La Nelle Ruby (Stovall) Boone; m. Marla Hays, Aug. 2, 1969; children: Michael Hays, Maryjane Mauldin. BBA, So. Meth. U., 1963, JD, 1967. Bar: Tex. 1967. Assoc. firm Richard D. Haynes, 1967-69; co-founder Haynes & Boone LLP, Dallas, 1970, ptnr., mergers & acquisitions, corp. fin., securities transactions, 1969—, mem. mgmt. com., bd. dir. Adj. prof. law So. Meth. U. Sch. Law, 1972—88. Mem. Dallas Citizens' Coun.; trustee So. Meth. U.; bd. visitors Pepperdine U. Law Sch.; pres. sch. bd. Highland Park Independent Sch. Dist. Named a "Go-To-Lawyer" in Tex. corp./bus. law, Tex. Lawyer Mag.; named one of top corp. fin./mergers & acquisitions lawyers in Dallas, D Magazine, top 10 super lawyers, Tex. Monthly, Law and Politics Mag.; recipient Recipient Disting. Alumni award, So. Meth. U. law Sch., 1990, Next Millennium Award, Freedom's Found., Valley Forge, 1999, Justinian Award for pub. svc., 2004. Mem.: State Bar Tex. (chmn. corp. banking & bus. law sect. 1983—84), Dallas Bar Assn., ABA, Dallas Country Club, City Club, Crescent Club, Phi Delta Phi, Phi Gamma Delta. Mem. Ch. of Christ (elder). Office: Haynes and Boone LLP 901 Main St Ste 3100 Dallas TX 75202-3789 Office Phone: 214-651-5552. Office Fax: 214-200-0369. Business E-Mail: michael.boone@haynesboone.com.

BOONE, MORELL DOUGLAS, information technology educator; b. Londonderry, Northern Ireland, Dec. 15, 1942; arrived in U.S., 1946; s. Paul J. and Margaret (Hill) B.; m. Carolyn June Gallagher, July 6, 1968; children— Ian Charles, Megan Elizabeth BS, Kutztown State Coll., Pa., 1964; MS, Syracuse U., 1968, PhD, 1980. Librarian Pennridge Schs., Perkasie, Pa., 1964-66; reference librarian Hobart and William Smith Colls., Geneva, NY, 1968-70; lectr. Syracuse U., NY, 1970-72; dean learning resources U. Bridgeport, Conn., 1973-80; dir. Ctr. of Ednl. Resources Eastern Mich. U., Ypsilanti, 1980—85, dean learning resources and techs., 1986—2001, prof. interdisciplinary tech., 2001—04, prof., dir. Sch. Tech. Studies, 2004—06, prof., dean College of Tech., 2006—. Presenter at profl. meetings; cons. for internat. ednl. devel. Iran, Swaziland, Yemen, others. Co-author: Training Student Library Assistants, 1991; mem. editl. bd. Libr. Hi Tech.; contbr. articles to profl. jours. Chmn. Community Cablecasting Commn., Ypsilanti, 1981-84, Ypsilanti Ednl. Found., 1988-94; pres. bd. dirs. Meals on Wheels, Ypsilanti, 1998—. Named to Pennridge H.S. Wall of Fame, 2001. Mem. ALA, EDUCAUSE, Soc. Coll. and Univ. Planning, Kiwanis. Democrat. Presbyterian (elder). Avocations: gardening, reading, travel. Home: 5774 Pineview Dr Ypsilanti MI 48197-8983 Office: Eastern Mich U 109 Sill Hall Ypsilanti MI 48197 Home Phone: 734-484-4384; Office Phone: 734-487-0354. Business E-Mail: mboone@emich.edu.

BOONE, STEPHEN CHRISTOPHER, retired neurosurgeon; b. Navasota, Tex., Mar. 18, 1938; s. Berrill Harrison and Joyce (Taylor) Boone; m. Elizabeth Thompson, Apr. 9, 1960 (div. June 1979); children: Stephen, Michael, Laura; m. Susan Pate, Nov. 3, 1979; children: Christopher, Emily. BS, Duke U., 1960, MD, PhD, Duke U., 1965. Diplomate Am. Bd. Neurological Surgery. Surg. intern Duke Hosp., Durham, NC, 1965, resident in neurosurgery, 1967-72; chief neurosurgeon Brooke Army Med. Ctr., 1973-75; asst. chief neurosurgery Walter Reed Army Med. Ctr., Washington, 1975-77; from assoc. prof. to prof. neurosurgery U. NC, 1977-82; neurosurgeon Raleigh Neurosurgery Clinic, NC, 1982—2002; cons. Eastern Neurosurg. & Spine Assocs., Greenville; with United Surg. Assts., Raleigh, NC. Brig. gen. USAR, 1962—89. Republican. Episcopalian. Personal E-mail: scboone38@earthlink.net.

BOONE, TRACY MARIE, mathematics professor; b. Bellefont, Pa., Dec. 7, 1969; d. Donald James and Gloria Jean Koshko; m. David Richard Boone, June 17, 1995; 1 child, Carter David. BS, Lock Haven U., Pa., 1992; MS, Pa. State U., 2001. Tchr. LearnRight, State Coll., Pa., 1992—93; math. tchr. Bedford (Pa.) HS, 1993—2004; adj. faculty Pa. State U., Altoona, Pa., 1995—2004, doctoral student University Park, 2004—. Grade II PSSA adv. com. Pa. Dept. Edn., Harrisburg, 1997—2005. Mem.: Nat. Coun. Tchrs. Math., Pa. Coun. Tchrs. Math., Phi Delta Kappa. Home: 300 Farmstead Lane Unit E State College PA 16803 Personal E-mail: tdboone3@verizon.net.

BOONSHAFT, HOPE JUDITH, public relations executive; b. Phila., May 3, 1949; d. Barry and Lorelei Gail (R ienzi) B. BA, Pa. State U., 1972; postgrad. Del. Law Sch, Kellogg Inst. Mgmt. Tng. Program writer Youth Edn., NYC, 1972; legal aide to judge Phila., 1975; dir. spl. projects Guiffre Med. Ctr., Phila., 1975; senatorial campaign fin. dir. Arlen Specter, Phila., 1975; presdl. campaign fin. dir. Jimmy Carter, Atlanta, 1976; fin. dir. Dem. Nat. Com., 1977—79; dir. devel. World Jewish Congress, NYC, 1978, Yeshiva U., LA, 1979; dir. comm. Nat. Easter Seal Soc., Chgo., 1979-83; CEO Boonshaft-Lewis & Savitch Pub. Rels and Govt. Affairs, LA, 1983-93; sr. v.p. Edelman Worldwide, 1993-95; exec. v.p. external affairs Sony Pictures Entertainement, LA, 1995—. Spl. adv. cmty. rels. The White House, 1977-80; guest lectr. U. Ill., 1982, May Co.'s Calif. Women in Bus. Bd. dirs. L.A. Arts Coun., Los Angeles County Citizens for Economy and Efficiency in Govt. Commn., Calif. Film Commn., Spkrs. Commn. Calif. Initiative. Home: 1967 Mandeville Canyon Rd Los Angeles CA 90049-2235 Office: Sony Pictures Entertainment 10202 Washington Blvd Culver City CA 90232-3119

BOOR, MYRON VERNON, psychologist, educator; b. Wadena, Minn., Dec. 21, 1942; s. Vernon LeRoy and Rosella Katharine (Eckhoff) B. BS, U. Iowa, 1965; MA, So. Ill. U., 1967, PhD, 1970; MS, U. Pitts., 1981. Lic. psychologist, Mo. Research psychologist Milw. County Mental Health Ctr., 1970-72; asst. prof. clin. psychologist Ft. Hays State U., Hays, Kans., 1972-76, assoc. prof., 1976-79; NIMH postdoctoral fellow in psychiat. epidemiology U. Pitts., Western Psychiat. Inst. and Clinic, 1979-81; research psychologist R.I. Hosp. and Butler Hosp., Providence, 1981-84; clin. psychologist Newman Meml. County Hosp., Emporia, Kans., 1985-93, Heartland Health Sys., St. Joseph, Mo., 1994—. Clin. psychologist Ft. Hays State U., 1972-79; asst. prof. psychiatry and human behavior Brown U., Providence, 1981-84; adj. faculty Emporia State U., 1985-94. Contbr. articles to profl. jours. U.S. Pub. Health Service fellow, 1965-67, NIMH fellow 1979-81. Home: 3018 Cambridge St Saint Joseph MO 64506-1164 E-mail: mboor@ccp.com.

BOORAEM, HENDRIK, V, education educator, historian; b. NYC, May 11, 1939; s. Hendrik Booraem, IV and Dorothy Allyn Carr; m. Lynn Francis Allen (div.); children: Dorothy Allen, Hendrik VI, Anna Hollingsworth. BA, U. Va., 1961; MA, Johns Hopkins U., 1974, PhD, 1977. Instr. SUNY, Purchase, 1971—76; tchr. Strom Thurmond H.S., Johnston, SC, 1979—92; assoc. prof. Bucks County C.C., Newtown, Pa., 1992—93, 2003—. Author: The Formation of the Republican Party in New York, 1983, The Road to Respectability, 1989, The Provincial, 1994, Young Hickory, 2002. Mem.: Newtown Hist. Assn., Holland Soc. N.Y., Authors' Guild, N.J. Gay Men's Chorus. Home: PO Box 514 Newtown PA 18940 Office: Bucks County Cmty Coll Swamp Rd Newtown PA 18940

BOORMAN, HOWARD LYON, history professor; b. Chgo., Sept. 11, 1920; s. William Ryland and Verna (Lyon) B.; m. Mary Houghton, Jan. 20, 1972 (dec.); 1 child by previous marriage: Scott A. BA, U. Wis., Madison, 1941; postgrad., Yale U., 1946-47. Divisional asst., divsn. def. materials Dept. of State, Washington, 1942-43; fgn. service officer to Peking, Hong Kong, 1947-54; rsch. assoc. Sch. Internat. Affairs, Columbia U., NYC, 1955-67; prof. history Vanderbilt U., Nashville, 1967-84, prof. emeritus, 1984—. Vis. scholar Univ. Ctr. of Va., 1963. Gen. editor: Biographical Dictionary of Republican China, 4 vols, 1967-71; contbr. articles to profl. jours. Lt. USNR, 1943-46. Recipient Rockefeller Public Service award, 1954-55 Mem.: Assn. Asian Studies, Am. Polit. Sci. Assn., Am. Hist. Assn., Univ. Club (Nashville). Office: Vanderbilt U Dept History Nashville TN 37235

BOORSTEIN, LAURENCE, economist, educator; b. Neuilly, France, Jan. 22, 1951; arrived in U.S., 1951; s. Edward and Regula (Simons) Boorstein. BA, Columbia U., 1972, MS, 1974, CE, 1978, MBA, 1988. Sys. analyst Frederic R. Harris, Inc. engring. divsn. Planning Rsch. Corp., NYC, 1974—77, prin. sys. engr. Frederic R. Harris, Inc. divsn., 1977—79, sr. sys. planner Frederic R. Harris Engring. Divsn., 1979—83, sr. economist Frederic R. Harris, Inc. divsn., 1983—86; sr. economist Soros Assocs., 1988—94; prin. economist DMJM Harris Inc. divsn. AECOM Tech. Corp., 1994—2005, prin. economist, project mgr. DMJM Harris Inc. divsn. Arlington, Va., 2005—. Mem.: Soc. Civil Engrs. Home: 1716 Lake Shore Crest Dr Apt 3 Reston VA 20190-3244 Office: DMJM Harris 3101 Wilson Blvd 4th Fl Arlington VA 22201-4445 Home Phone: 703-437-6881; Office Phone: 703-682-5029. Office Fax: 703-682-5001. Personal E-mail: lboorstein@att.net. Business E-Mail: larry.boorstein@dmjmharris.com.

BOOT, MAX, journalist; BA with high honors, U. Calif., Berkeley, 1991; MA in History, Yale U., 1992. Editor, writer Christian Sci. Monitor, 1992—94; writer & editor Wall St. Jour., 1994—97, editl. features editor, 1997—2002; contbg. editor Weekly Standard, LA Times; sr. fellow nat. security studies Coun. Fgn. Rels., NYC, 2002—. Mem. US Joint Forces Command Transformation Adv. Group. Author: Out of Order: Arrogance, Corruption and Incompetence on the Bench, 1998, The Savage Wars of Peace: Small Wars & the Rise of American Power, 2002 (Gen. Wallace M. Greene Jr. award, Marine Corps Heritage Found., 2003), War Made New: Technology, Warfare, and the Course of History, 2006. Named one of 500 Most Influential People in the US in the field of Fgn. Policy, World Affairs Coun. Am., 2004; recipient Eric Breindel award for Excellence in Journalism, 2007. Office: Coun Fgn Rels 58 E 68th St New York NY 10021 Office Phone: 212-434-9619. E-mail: mboot@cfr.org.*

BOOTH, ANNA BELLE, accountant; b. Homesville, Ohio, Jan. 15, 1912; d. John Wilson and M. Pearl (Toomey) B.; m. Guy DiAmbrosio, Apr. 29, 1930; 1 child, Guy Booth. BA, Taylor Coll., 1930. Office mgr. in charge of mfg. Jacobs Tailored Clothes, Inc., Phila., 1931-41; acct., corp. cashier Lehigh Coal and Navigation Co., Phila., 1941-55; acct. Bishop & Hedberg, Phila., 1955-57; acct., office mgr. The Camax Co., Phila., 1957-60; office mgr., cashier New Eng. Mutual Life Ins. Co., Phila., 1960-67; acct. Wall & Ochs, Inc., Phila., 1967-71; comptr. Bisler Packaging Div./Pet, Inc., Phila., 1971-82; ret. Mem. Am. Soc. Women Accts. (Phila. pres. 1956-58, dir. 1952-54, 62-64, 73-75), LWV (Phila.). Home: 135 S 20th St Apt 1002 Philadelphia PA 19103

BOOTH, BETTY JEAN, retired daycare administrator, poet; b. St. Louis County, Mo., Dec. 27, 1944; d. Richard Augustus and Leoma Thelma (Atchison) Woods; m. Alfred Lee Pope Jr., Aug. 20, 1962 (div. Apr. 14, 1975); children: Wayman Maurice Woods, Audrena Denise Walker-Riffle, Juanita Rosetta Pope-Miller, Victoria Lynn Pope, Daniel Jerome Pope, Alfred Lee III Pope; m. Robert Lee Booth, Mar. 3, 1984 (dec. June 7, 2007); 1 stepchild, David Lee Griffin. Cert., United Bus. Coll., North St. Louis, Mo., 1987. Baby nurse, Ladue, Mo., 1984—89; home care worker and provider Clayton, Mo., 1989; adminstrv. asst. Grateful Home Homeless Shelter, Detroit, 1992; day care asst. Time for Happy Land Care, Detroit, 1999—2004. Author: Traveling on the Wing's of Life's Inner Circle, 2005; contbr. poetry to lit. publs. Recipient numerous awards for poetry. Mem.: Internat. Soc. Poets and POetry. Avocations: writing, gardening, taping, reading, creating. Home and Office: Lafayette Towne Apts 1410 Ohio Saint Louis MO 63104

BOOTH, EDMUND A., JR., prosecutor; BA, U. Ga., 1967; LLD, U. Ga. Sch. Law, 1970. Asst. US atty. (so. dist.) Ga. US Dept. Justice, 1971—86, first asst. US atty (so. dist.) Ga., 1986—, interim US atty (so. dist.) Ga., 2001, acting US atty. (so. dist.) Ga., 2007—; mem. civil justice reform act com. US Dist. Ct. (so. dist.) Ga., 1991—94. Recipient Director's award, Dir. Exec. Office of US Attys., 1994, 2003. Office: US Atty's Office 100 Bull St 2nd Fl Savannah GA 31401 Office Phone: 912-652-4422. Office Fax: 912-652-4388.*

BOOTH, GEORGE KEEFER, corporate financial executive; b. Rockville Centre, NY, July 23, 1943; s. David Conover and Nan (Tracy) B.; m. Jeanne Marie Storey, May 12, 1979; 1 child, Sarah. BA, C.W. Post Coll., 1970; MBA, Fordham U., 1973. Asst. cashier Franklin Nat. Bank, NYC, 1970-74; mgr. facilities leverage leasing Gen. Electric Credit Co., Stamford, Conn., 1974-77; corp. mgr. sales fin. Harris Corp., Melbourne, Fla., 1977-83; exec. v.p. Internat. Capital Equipment Co., NYC, 1983-85; exec. v.p., CFO, bd. dirs. Phoenixcor, South Norwalk, Conn., 1985-94; founder, mng. dir. Black Rock Capital LLC, Ireland, 1994—; dir. Black Rock Capital Ltd., England. Contbr. articles to Leasing Digest, Monitor, ELA. With USN, 1967—69. Mem. Equipment Leasing Assn. (industry future con. 1982-84, captive com. 1981, acctg. com. 1988, mid. market com.), Internat. Assn. Diemaking and Diecutting, Eastern Assn. Equipment Lessors, Middle Market Ind. Bus. Coun., KC, Black Rock Yacht Club (Bridgeport, Conn.; past commodore), Fayerweather Yacht Club, Oronoque Country Club, The Landings. Republican. Roman Catholic. Home: 41 Grist Mill Ln Southport CT 06890 Office: Black Rock Capital LLC PO Box 416 Fairfield CT 06824 Home Phone: 203-259-2022; Office Phone: 203-336-9200. E-mail: gkbooth@blackrockcapital.com.

BOOTH, GORDON DEAN, JR., lawyer; b. Columbus, Ga., June 25, 1939; s. Gordon Dean and Lois Mildred (Bray) B.; m. Katherine Morris Campbell, June 17, 1961; children: Mary Katherine McCormick, Abigail Kilgore Curvino, Sarah Elizabeth, Margaret Campbell, Celecia. BA, Emory U., Atlanta, 1961, JD, 1964, LLM, 1973. Bar: Ga. 1964, D.C. 1977, U.S. Supreme Ct. 1973. Pvt. practice, Atlanta, 1964-96; ptnr. Miller & Martin, Atlanta, 1995—. Bd. dirs., v.p. Stallion Music Inc., Nashville, BAA USA, Inc.; trustee, sec. Inst. for Polit. Econ., Washington. Contbr. articles to profl. jours. Trustee Met. Atlanta Crime Commn., 1977-80, chmn., 1979-80; mem. assembly for arts and scis. Emory Coll., 1971-86, chmn., 1983. Mem. Internat. Bar Assn. (coun. sect. bus. law 1974-88, chmn. aero. law com. 1971-86), State Bar Ga., Capital City Club, Piedmont Driving Club, Univ. Club (NYC), Advocates Club, Sigma Chi. Home: 3226 Paces Mill Rd SE Atlanta GA 30339-3787

BOOTH, HAROLD WAVERLY, lawyer, finance company executive; b. Rochester, NY, Aug. 8, 1934; s. Herbert Nixon and Mildred B. (Anderson) B.; m. Flo Rae Spelts, July 4, 1957; children: Rebecca, William, Eva, Harold, Richard. BS, Cornell U., 1955; JD, Duke U., 1961. Bar: Nebr. 1961, Ill. 1967, Iowa 1974; CLU; chartered fin. counselor; cert. fin. planner. Staff atty. Bankers Life Nebr., Lincoln, 1961-67; pres. First Nat. Bank, Council Bluffs, Iowa, 1970-74; exec. v.p., treas. Blue Cross-Blue Shield Ill., Chgo., 1974-77; pres., chief exec. officer, chmn. Bankers Life Nebr., Lincoln, 1977-84; exec. v.p. Colonial Penn Group, Phila., 1985-87; chmn., chief exec. officer VGVR Cos., 1985—. Served to 1st lt. USAF, 1955-58. Fellow Life Mgmt. Inst. (pres. 1981-84); mem. Ins. Fedn. Nebr. (past pres.) Home: 1000 Stony Ln Gladwyne PA 19035-1128

BOOTH, JANE SCHUELE, real estate company officer, real estate broker; b. Cleve. d. Norman Andrew and Frances Ruth (Hankey) Schuele; m. George Warren Booth, Dec. 6, 1968. AA, Stephens Coll., 1946; student, U. Mo., 1946—47. Lic. real estate broker, Fla. Assoc. J.M. Mathes Inc., NYC, 1947-48; dept. supr. Lord and Taylor, Scarsdale, N.Y., 1948-50; art coord. J. Walter Thompson, Inc., NYC, 1953-58; art buyer SSC&B Inc. Advt., NYC, 1959-80; pres. Jane Schuele Booth Realty, Ocala, Fla., 1982—. Mem. Fla. Thoroughbred Fillies, Ocala, 1980—; charter mem., trustee Royal Dames for Cancer Rsch., Inc., Ocala, 1986—; treas. Ladies Aux. Fla. H.C.H. Inc., Ocala, 1986-90; bd. visitors Fla. Horsemen's Children's Home, Inc., 1983-90. Mem. Ocala/Marion County Assn. Realtors, Ocala/Marion County C. of C. (agribus./equine com.), Nat. Assn. Realtors, Fla. Assn. Realtors. Home: 1771 SW 55th Street Rd Ocala FL 34474-5933 Office: PO Box 5538 Ocala FL 34478-5538 Personal E-mail: janeschuelebooth@aol.com.

BOOTH, JOHN THOMAS, private investor; b. NYC, Oct. 21, 1929; s. John E. and Katherine (Keeler) B.; m. Anne C. Mott, Feb. 26, 1960; children: Alison Booth Cramer, Miven Booth Trageser, Roxanna Booth Cistulli. Grad. cum laude, Deerfield Acad., 1947; BA cum laude, Amherst Coll., 1951; LLB, Harvard U., 1957. Bar: NY 1957. Assoc. firm Dewey Ballantine Bushby Palmer & Wood, NYC, 1957-61; mem. buying dept. Eastman Dillon, Union Securities & Co., NYC, 1961—, ptnr., 1963—; exec. v.p., dir. Blyth Eastman Dillon & Co., Inc., 1972-81; chmn. bd. Eastdil Realty, Inc., 1979-81, Am. Health Capital, Inc., 1982-86, Am. Health Capital Ventures, Inc., 1986-89; chmn. Franklin Venture Capital Inc., 1990-97, Greystone Communities, Inc., 1990—2005, Coleman, Swenson, Booth, Inc., 1997—2005. Bd. dirs. Wells Hill Ptnrs. Ltd., Litchfield Bancorp; former dir. First Charter Fin. Corp., Morse Shoe Inc., SCM Corp; dir., mem. Eli Whitney investment adv. bd. Conn. Innovations, Inc., 1994-2004; asst. to dir. Harvard Def. Studies Program, 1956-57; counsel NY State Assembly Com. on NYC, 1960, Com. on Judiciary, 1961. Trustee, chmn. investment com. Seherr-Thoss Found.; trustee White Meml. Found., Gordie Found.; mem. Litchfield HS scholarship com.; former chmn. Charlotte Hungerford Hosp, Torrington, Conn.; former vestryman Trinity Ch., NY; Lt. (j.g.) USNR, 1951-54. Mem. Delta Kappa Epsilon, Delta Sigma Rho. Clubs: Links, University (NYC); Litchfield (Conn.) Country. Republican. Episcopalian. Office: Box 25 182 Whites Wood Rd Litchfield CT 06759-0025 Office Phone: 860-567-0873.

BOOTH, MARGARET A(NN), communications company executive; b. NYC, Dec. 25, 1946; d. Herbert and Alice (Traum) B.; m. Marvin E. Schechter, Jan. 22, 1984. BS, U. Wis., 1968. Editl. asst. Bantam Books, NYC, 1968-70; publicity asst. Ruder & Finn Inc., NYC, 1970-71, dir. radio and TV, 1971-76, v.p., 1974-76; pres. Pub. Interest Pub. Rels., NYC, 1976—, M. Booth & Assocs., Inc., NYC, 1983—. Author: Promoting Issues and Ideas, 1987; contbr. articles to profl. jours. Bd. govs. Eugene Lang Coll. New Sch. for Social Rsch.; bd. dirs. N.Y. Found. Recipient YWCA Salute to Women Achievers, City of N.Y., 1985. Mem. Pub. Rels. Soc. Am., Women in Comm. (Matrix award for Pub. Rels. 1987), Women Execs. in Pub. Rels.

BOOTH, MITCHELL B., lawyer; b. NYC, June 26, 1927; s. Samuel and Rose (Waxman) B.; m. Barbara C. Ribman, July 13, 1952; 1 son, Brian S. AB, Clark U., 1949; JD, NYU, 1952. Bar: N.Y. 1952. Assoc. I. Moldauer, NYC, 1952—54, Sol A. Rosenblatt, NYC, 1954—67; pvt. practice law NYC, 1967—. Minority counsel joint legis. com. unsatisfied judgments N.Y., 1958-59, joint legis. com. preservation restoration hist. sites N.Y., 1960-64; med. malpractice mediator First Jud. Dept. Supreme Ct. State N.Y., 1980-91; bd. dirs., treas. East Hampton Mews Tenants Corp., Burgos Art Galleries Ltd., Dorolyat Corp. Asst. to chmn. Dem. law com., N.Y. County, 1961-65; rep. admissions for states of N.Y., N.J. and Conn. Clark U., 1968-71. Served to lt. USNR, 1945-46, 49-83. Mem. ABA, N.Y. State Bar Assn., Assn. of Bar of City of N.Y. (com. profl. discipline 1986-89), N.Y. Commandry, Mil. Order Fgn. Wars U.S. (life, judge advocate), Univ. Club. Home: 75 E End Ave New York NY 10028-7909

BOOTH, PENELOPE PARTRIDGE, secondary school educator, writer, principal; b. Niskayuna, NY, Dec. 7, 1943; d. Leonard Charlton and Elizabeth Jane (Russ) Partridge; m. John Robert Booth, Sept. 10, 1966 (div. 1975); children: Elizabeth Ashley, Patricia Anne. BS in Math., Mary Washington Coll., 1965; EdM, Towson State U., 1981. Comml. supr. Chesapeake & Potomac Tel. Co., Washington, 1965-66, Richmond, Va., 1967-68; math. tchr. Havelock (N.C.) H.S., 1966-67, Jack Jouett Jr. H.S., Charlottesville, Va., 1968-70, Baltimore County Pub. Schs., Towson, Md., 1974-81, supr. math., 1987-93; prin. Catonsville (Md.) Mid. Sch., 1993-96; tchr. gifted and talented resource Office Of Math., Towson, 1981-84; chmn. math. dept. Hereford Mid. Sch., Monkton, Md., 1984-87; coord. office of math. Baltimore County Pub. Schs., Md., 1996—2004, new math. cons. Md., 2004—. Instr. Balt. County Pub. Schs., 1976-88, Md. Acad. Scis., Balt., 1984-86, Inst. for Gifted Talented, Towson, 1983-85; cons. Md. State Dept. Edn., Balt., 1981—, Sylvan Learning, 2002-03; adj. prof. Johns Hopkins U., 1996-2004, Coll. Notre Dame, Md., 1997-2003, Loyola Coll., Md., 2002-04, Wake Tech. CC, 2006—; co-owner Conversation Pieces, 1997—; author/cons. Nat. Tng. Network, 2005-06. Author: Essentials of Mathematics, 1988, Consumer Mathematics, 1988, Foundations of Algebra and Geometry, 1998, (booklet) First Book of Testing. Adult leader troop 336, Girl Scouts U.S.A., Towson, 1972-88; mem. Lutherville (Md.) Recreation Coun., 1979-89; cons. Md. Math. League, 1982-87; chmn., co-founder Christa McAuliffe Scholarship Found., 1986—; mem. alumni adv. coun. Towson State U.; mem. adv. bd. MAT Program Johns Hopkins U., 1992-2002. Recipient Presdl. award NSF, 1985, Disting. Alumni award Towson State U., 1989, Educator of Yr. award Md. Coun. Tchrs. of Math., 2002. Mem. ASCD, Nat. Coun. Suprs. Math. (sec.-treas. Md. coun. 2000—), Nat. Coun. Tchrs. Math., Coun. Presdl. Awardees (scholarship chmn.), Nat. Assn. Secondary Sch. Prins., Optimists, Phi Delta Kappa, Delta Kappa Gamma (v.p.). Republican. Presbyterian. Avocations: travel, needlepoint. Home: 5301 Impatiens Ct Holly Springs NC 27540 Office Phone: 919-387-0087. E-mail: pbooth4@nc.rr.com.

BOOTHBY, RICHARD ALFRED, gynecologist, educator; b. Jacksonville, Fla., Mar. 9, 1955; s. Richard Joseph and Louise Frances Boothby; m. Rosemarie Lemanna, Mar. 18, 1978; children: Suzanne, Lauren, Michael, Kristen. BS, Loyola U., New Orleans, 1977; MD, U. S. Fla., Tampa, 1980. Diplomate Am. Bd. Ob-Gyn., 1988, lic. Fla., 1982, Pa., 1985, NY, 1987. Resident in pediat. U. Hosp., Jacksonville, Fla., 1980—81, resident in ob-gyn., 1981—85; fellow in gyn. oncology Hosp. U. Pa., 1985—87; assoc. dir. divsn. gyn. oncology N.Shore U. Hosp., Manhasset, NY, 1987—90; with Orlando Cancer Ctr., 1990—94, M.D. Anderson Cancer Ctr., Orlando, 1994—2003, Fla. Gynecol. Oncology, Bonita Springs, 2004—. Asst. prof. Cornell U. Med. Coll., 1987—90; assoc. dir. med. edn. Arnold Palmer Hosp. for Children and Women, Orlando, Fla., 1987—90; clin. assoc. prof. U. Fla., Coll. Medicine, 1990—; presenter in field. Contbr. scientific papers to profl. jours., chapters to books. Vol. physician Remote Area Medicine, Worldwide, 2007. Mem.: Collier County Med. Soc., Lee County Med. Soc., Fla. Obstetric and Gynecol. Soc., Fla. Soc. Gynecol. Oncologists (immediate past pres. 2006—08, pres. 2004—06), Soc. Gynecol. Oncologists, Am. Soc. Clin. Oncology, Am. Coll. Ob-GYN., Assn. Clin. Rsch. Profls.-Clin. Rsch. Investigators. Avocations: lacrosse, golf, fishing. Office: Fla Gynecologic Oncology 3501 Health Ctr Blvd Ste 2190 Bonita Springs FL 34135

BOOTHBY, WILLIAM MUNGER, retired mathematics professor; b. Detroit, Apr. 1, 1918; s. Thomas Franklin and Florence (Munger) B.; m. Ruth Robin, June 8, 1947; children— Daniel, Thomas, Mark. AB, U. Mich., 1941, MA, 1942, PhD, 1949. Mem. faculty Northwestern U.,

Evanston, Ill., 1948-59; fellow Am.-Swiss Found. for Sci. Exchange, Swiss Fed. Inst. Tech., Zurich, 1950-51; assoc. prof. Washington U., St. Louis, 1959-62, prof. math., 1962-88, ret., 1988—. NSF sr. postdoctoral fellow Inst. for Advanced Study, Princeton, N.J., 1961-62, U. Geneva, Switzerland, 1965-66; professeur associe U. Strasbourg, France, 1971, 77 Author: Introduction to Differentiable Manifolds and Riemannian Geometry; co-editor: Symmetric Spaces; contbr. articles to profl. jours. Served with USAAF, 1942-46. Mem. Am., London math. Socs., Math. Assn. Am., Soc. Indsl. and Applied Math., Sigma Xi. Home: 6954 Cornell Ave Saint Louis MO 63130-3128 Office: Washington U Dept Math Saint Louis MO 63130-4899

BOOTH CORWIN, TAMI, publishing executive; Editor health and medicine category Little Brown, 1994—97; exec. editor health and lifestyle books IDG Books, NYC and Chgo., 1997—2000; dir. new title devel. Rodale, Inc., NYC, 2000, exec. editor Women's Health Books, 2000—01, editor-in-chief Women's Health Books NYC, 2001—, pres., books divsn., 2005—. Named one of 50 Women to Watch, Wall Street Journal, 2005. Office: Rodale Inc 733 3rd Ave 15th Fl New York NY 10017-3204 also: Rodale Inc 33 E Minor St Emmaus PA 18098-0099

BOOTHE, LEON ESTEL, academic administrator emeritus, consultant; b. Carthage, Mo., Feb. 1, 1938; s. Harold Estel and Merle Jane (Hood) B.; m. Nancy Janes, Aug. 20, 1960 (dec. Jan. 1997); children: Cynthia, Diana and Cheri (twins); m. Karen Ball, Nov. 11, 2000. BS (Curators' scholar), U. Mo., 1960, MA, 1962; PhD in History, U. Ill., 1966; LLD, Kyung Hee U., Korea, St. Thomas Inst. Advanced Study, 1985, Hebrew Union Coll., 1994. Tchr. history Valparaiso (Ind.) H.S., 1960-61; asst. prof. history U. Miss., Oxford, 1965-68, assoc. prof., 1968-70; assoc. prof. history George Mason Coll., U. Va. (now George Mason U.), Fairfax, 1970-73, prof. history, 1973-80, assoc. dean, 1970-71, dean, 1971-72, dean coll. arts and scis., 1972-80; provost, v.p. acad. affairs Ill. State U., Normal, 1980-83; pres. No. Ky. U., Highland Heights, 1983—96, pres. emeritus, 1996—, prof. history, 1983—2006, prof. emeritus, 2006—. Bd. dir. Fifth Third Bank No. Ky.; chmn. Am. Assn. of State Colls. and Univs., 1993; bd. dir. Commn. on Internat. Edn. of Am. Coun. Edn.; mem. bd. trustees Am. Classical Music Hall of Fame. Former mem. McLean County Heart Assn., McLean County United Way, INROADS/Cin., Inc., Cin. Music Festival, Cin. Nat. Classical Music Hall Fame, No. Ky. U. Found.; mem. Cin.'s Enjoy the Arts, 1988—90, Sr. Citizens No. Ky., 1996—2005, May Festival, 1998-2003, 1998—2003, Cin. Ballet, 1999—2004; vice chmn. then chmn. No. Ky. United Way, 1988; chmn. Ky. Bicentennial Com., 1990, chmn. steering com., 1992; chmn. Leadership Ky. Class; advisor Cin. Hispanic C. of C.; co-chair blue ribbon econ. devel. study No. Ky. Area Devel. Dist.; lifetime advisor to pres. Nat. Coun. Cmty. and Justice; former mem. adv. bd. Cin. Coun. World Affairs; trustee Cin.-Kharkiv Project, hon. mem., 1995—96; bd. dir. Met. YMCA Cin., 1984—2005, Wood Hudson Cancer Rsch. Lab. Inc., 1987—92, ARC (met. Cin. chpt.), mem. exec. com., vice-chair cmty. edn. svcs., 1989-90, vice-chair cmty. edn. svcs., 1989—90; mem. steering com. Cin. Bicentennial; mem. steering com., exec. com. Cin. Youth Collaborative; bd. dir. Greater Cin. Conv. and Visitors Bur., 1989, Kids Helping Kids, 1998—2003, Merc. Libr., 1998—2004, Festival of Arts, 1998—2002, Nat. Underground Railroad Freedom Ctr., 2000—04, sr. advisor, 1997—2000, exec. com., 2001; trustee Greater Cin. United Way and Cmty. Chest, 1991; steering com. Greater Cin. Summit on Racism, 1994; former bd. dir. Am. Music Scholarship Assn., Cin. Scholarship Found., Leadership Ky. Found.; bd. dir. Sr. Svcs. of No. Ky., 1996, Cetana Found., Ronald McDonald Ho., 2001—05, Cin. Fire Mus., 2006. NEH fellow, 1967-68; scholar Diplomat Seminars Dept. State; recipient Coll. Liberal Arts and Scis. award U. Ill., 1988, Alumni Coun. Pres.'s Spl. Recognition award No. Ky. U., 1989, Alumni award U. Mo., 1989, Walter R. Dunlevey Frontiersman award, 1994, Disting. Citizens Citation award NCCJ, Disting. Pub. Svc. award No. Ky. U. Found., 1995, Character award YMCA, 1997, Kinsman award Urban Appalachian Coun., 1998, Pres. award Pub. Rels. Soc., 2000, Lighthouse Beacon Light award, 2001, Sister Benedict Bunning award, 2003, Excellence award, YMCA, 2005, Lincoln award, Northern Ky. U., 2006. Mem. Soc. Historians Am. Fgn. Rels., McLean County Assn. Commerce and Industry, Am. Assn. State Colls. and Univs. (internat. programs com. 1986-94), No. Ky. C. of C. (Walter R. Dunlevey-Frontierman award 1994), Greater Cin. C. of C. (asst. sec.-treas. 1989-93), Rotary, Masons, Leon Boothe Soc. (svc. award No. Ky. 2002), Sigma Rho Sigma, Omicron Delta Kappa, Phi Alpha Theta, Phi Delta Kappa. Home Phone: 513-232-0981. Business E-Mail: boothel@nku.edu.

BOOTHE, NANCY NANCY, construction executive; b. Kerville, Tex., Oct. 25, 1931; Office asst. Aircarft, San Antonio, John Haward Hosp. Inc., San Antonio; v.p. Booth Nance Family Prodn., San Antonio; pres. Nance Consol. Co., Inc., San Antonio; v.p. Booth Constrn. Inc., San Antonio, Boothe Egg. Co., San Antonio. Mem.: Bexar County Rep. Women, Women's Club San Antonio, Kappa Alpha Theta Alumni Assn., Kappa Alpha Theta Frat. Republican. Presbyterian.

BOOTHROYD, GEOFFREY, industrial and manufacturing engineering educator; b. Radcliffe, Eng., Nov. 18, 1932; arrived in U.S., 1967; s. Arthur and Annie (Fletcher) Boothroyd; m. Shirley Lewis, Apr. 10, 1954; children: Janet Kaye, Lynda Jean. BS in Engring., U. London, 1956, PhD in Engring., 1962, DSc in Engring., 1974. Apprentice Mather & Platt Ltd., Manchester, 1948—56, designer, 1956—57, English Electric Co. Ltd., Leicester, England, 1957—58; lectr., reader Salford (Eng.) U., 1958—67; prof. U. Mass., Amherst, 1967—85, U. R.I., Kingston, 1985—97, prof. emeritus. Vis. prof. Ga. Inst. Tech., Atlanta, 1964—65; cons. mfg. industries U.K. and U.S., also various pubs.; co-founder Boothroyd Dewhurst, Inc. Author: Fundamentals of Metal Machining, 1965; author: (with A.H. Redford) Mechanized Assembly (Japanese edit. 1969), 1968; author: Fundamentals of Metal Machining and Machine Tools (Spanish 1978, internat. student edit. 1979), 1975; co-author: Introduction to Engineering, 1975; author (with C.R. Poli): Applied Engineering Mechanics, 1980; author: (with C.R. Poli, L.E. Murch) Automatic Assembly, 1980; author: Handbook of Feeding and Orienting Techniques for Small Parts; author: (with L. Alting) Manufacturing Engineering Processes, 1982; author: (with P. Dewhurst) Design for Assembly Handbook, Design for Robot Assembly, 1985; author: (with W.A. Knight) Metal Machining and Machine Tools, 1991; author: Assembly Automation and Product Design, 1992; author: (with P. Dewhurst and W.A. Knight) Product Design for Manufacture and Assembly, 1994. Recipient Teaching award, Western Electric, 1969, Sr. Scholar award, U. Mass., 1982, Sci. and Tech. award, R.I. Gov., 1989, Nat. medal of Technology, U.S. Dept. Commerce Technology Admin., 1991, Providence Engring. Soc., 1991, U.K. Mensforth Internat. Gold medal, IEE, 1993, Mcht. Mfg. medal, ASME/SME, 2005; grantee NSF, 1967—87, GE, 1967, 1969, 1981, 1983, AMP Inc, 1978, 1981—84, IBM, 1983—85, AT&T, 1985, Ford Motor Co., 1984, 1986. Fellow: Soc. Mfg. Engrs.; mem.: NAE. Avocation: squash, tennis, golf, painting. Office: Boothroyd Dewhurst Inc 138 Main St Ste 2 Wakefield RI 02879-3574 Office Phone: 401-783-5840. E-mail: gboothroyd@dfma.com.

BOOTHROYD, HERBERT J., insurance company executive; b. Mason City, Iowa, Dec. 23, 1928; s. Herbert L. and Clara (Schmitt) B.; m. Barbara Elizabeth Dunne, Feb. 9, 1961; children: Diane Lea, John Herbert. AB, U. Mich., 1952, AM, 1953. Enrolled actuary, 1976. With Mass. Mut. Life Ins. Co., 1953-57; with New Eng. Mut. Life Ins. Co., Boston, 1957-87, v.p., 1967-77, sr. v.p. pension ops., 1977-82, exec. v.p. group ops., 1983-87; dir. New Eng. Pension and Annuity Co., 1980-87, pres., 1981-87; pres., dir. New Eng. Gen. Life, 1983-85. Dir. New Eng. Mut. Life Ins. Co., 1984-87, New Eng. Variable Life Ins. Co., 1984-97. Contbg. author: (book) Hammett Families, 1983, Cockrill Families of No. Virginia, 2002; contbg. author: Life and Health Insurance Handbook, 1973. Bd. dirs. New Eng. chpt. Am. Diabetes Assn., 1979-84; bd. govs. Handel and Haydn Soc., 1984-94, sec., 1986-94, overseer, 1994—2003; mem. nat. campaign com. U. Mich., 1983-90; bd. dirs. Better Bus. Bur. Ea. Mass., 1980-88, vice chmn., mem. exec. com., 1985-88. With US Army, 1946—47. Fellow Soc. Actuaries; mem. SAR, Am. Acad. Actuaries, Internat. Congress Actuaries, New Eng. Hist. Geneal. Soc., Ky. Hist. Soc., U. Mich. Alumni Assn. (v.p. 1st dist. 1989-91, pres. 1991-93, nat. bd. dirs. 1997-2000, chair nat. clubs coun. 1999-2000), Haile Plantation Golf and Country Club, Phi Beta Kappa, Theta Delta Chi. Home and Office: 4205 SW 96th Dr Gainesville FL 32608 E-mail: herbbooth@aol.com.

BOOTMAN, J. LYLE, pharmacy educator; BS, U. Ariz., 1974; MS, U. Minn., 1976, PhD, 1978; ScD, U. Sci. Phila., 2006. Clin. resident NIH; faculty Coll. Pharmacy, U. Ariz., 1978—, acting dean, 1987—90, dean, 1990—, founding & exec. dir. Health Outcomes and PharmacoEconomic Rsch. Ctr. Cons. and spkr. in field. Contbr. articles to profl. jours. Named one of the 50 most influential pharmacists in Am., The American Druggist, 1997; fellow Am. Found. for Pharm. Edn., Bush Found. Fellow Am. Assn. for Pharm. Scientists; mem. NAS Inst. Medicine, Am. Pharm. Assn. (trustee, pres. 1999-2000). Office: Coll Pharmacy Pulido Ctr PO Box 210202 Tucson AZ 85721 Office Phone: 520-626-1657. Fax: 520-626-4063. E-mail: bootman@pharmacy.arizona.edu.

BOOTON, CAROLYN ANN, mathematics educator; d. Leon Brewer and Ann Johnson; m. Richard Booton, July 29, 2006. BSc, Rensselaer Poly. Inst., Troy, NY, 2004; MA in Tchg., Union Grad. Coll., Schenectady, NY, 2005. Cert. tchr. NY State Dept. Edn., 2005. Tchr. math. Fairport H.S., NY, 2005—. Recipient Principal's Recognition award, Fairport H.S., 2006. Mem.: Assn. Math. Tchrs. NY State, Nat. Coun. Tchrs. Math. Roman Catholic. Avocations: reading, music, bass clarinet.

BOOTY, JOHN EVERITT, retired theology studies educator; b. Detroit, May 2, 1925; s. George Thomas and Alma (Gamauf) B.; m. Catherine Louise Smith, June 10, 1950; children: Carol Holland, Geoffrey Rollen, Peter Thomas, Catherine Jane. BA, Wayne State U., 1952; B.D., Va. Theol. Sem., 1953, DD, 1994, U. of the South, 1997; MA, Princeton U., 1957, PhD, 1960. Ordained to ministry Episcopal Ch., 1953. Curate Christ Episcopal Ch., Dearborn, Mich., 1953-55; asst. prof. ch. history Va. Theol. Sem., 1958-64, assoc. prof., 1964-67; prof. ch. history Episcopal Theol. Sch., Cambridge, Mass., 1967-82; acting dir. Inst. Theol. Rsch., 1974-76; dean Sch. Theology U. of South, Sewanee, Tenn., 1982-85, prof. Anglican studies, 1984-90, prof. emeritus, 1990—, historiographer Episc. Ch., 1988-99. Vis. prof., rsch. Yale Div. Sch., 1985-86; Disting. vis. prof. Episcopal Divinity Sch., 1990-91, prof. emeritus, 1991—; vis. prof. Anglican studies Gen. Theol. Seminary, 1992; Trotter vis. prof. Va. Theol. Sem., 1993, 98. Author: John Jewel as Apologist of the Church of England, 1963, Yearning to be Free, 1974, Three Anglican Divines on Prayer: Jewel, Andrewes, and Hooker, 1978, The Church in History, 1979, 2d edit., 2003, The Spirit of Anglicanism, 1979, The Godly Kingdom of Tudor England, 1981, The Servant Church, 1982, What Makes Us Episcopalians, 1982, Anglican Spirituality, 1982, Meditating on Four Quarters, 1983, 2d edit., 2003, Anglican Moral Choice, 1983, The Christ We Know, 1987, The Episcopal Church in Crisis, 1988, Mission and Ministry: A History of the Virginia Theological Seminary, 1996, An American Apostle: A Biography of Stephen F. Bayne, 1997, Reflections on the Theology of Richard Hooker: An Elizabethan Addresses Modern Anglicanism, 1999; editor: The Book of Common Prayer, 1559: The Elizabeth Prayer Book, 1976, reissued, 2005, John Jewel: The Apology of the Church of England, 1963, 74, 2002, John Donne: Divine Poems, Sermons, Meditations and Prayers, 1990, The Works of Richard Hooker, vol. 4, 1982; co-editor, contbr.: The Study of Anglicanism, 1988; contbr. articles to profl. jours. Chmn. Nat. Youth Commn., P.F. Ch., 1948-50; chmn. bd. St. Luke's Jour. Theology, 1987-91, Sewanee Theol. Rev., 1991-99. Recipient Am. Philos. Soc. award, 1964; Folger Shakespeare Libr. fellow, 1964, NEH fellow, 1978-79 Mem. Soc. for Promoting Christian Knowlege (vice chmn. 1984-87). Home: 612 Mt Israel Rd Center Sandwich NH 03227-3710

BOOZER, CARLOS AUSTIN, JR., professional basketball player; b. Aschaffenburg, Germany, Nov. 20, 1981; s. Carlos Boozer; m. Cindy Boozer. BA in Sociology, Duke U., 2003. Player Cleveland Cavaliers, 2002—04, Utah Jazz, 2004—. Mem. US Olympic Basketball Team, Athens, Greece, 2004, NCAA Nat. Championship Team Duke Blue Devils, 2001. Named to Western Conf. All-Star Team, NBA, 2007. Office: Utah Jazz 301 W South Temple Salt Lake City UT 84101*

BOOZER-BLASCO, CLAUDIA RUTH, family and consumer resources educator; b. St. Louis, Sept. 16, 1950; d. Howard Rae and Frances Kintner Boozer; m. George Blasco Jr., July 30, 1994 (dec. Nov. 15, 2005); stepchildren: Michelle Blasco Smith, Paul Blasco. BS in Home Econs. Edn., U. RI, Kingston, 1972; MEd in Counseling, U. NH, Durham, 1988. Health edn. tchr. St. Joseph's Indian Sch., Chamberlain, SD, 1972—73; home econs. tchr. Guilford Mid.-High Sch., NH, 1974—77; cmty. health educator Manchester Area Family Planning, NH, 1977—83; ext. educator family and consumer resources U. NH Coop. Ext., Brentwood, 1983—. Com. mem. Inst. for Health and Recovery, Cambridge, Mass., 2004—05. Founding mem. Fetal Alcohol Spectrum Disorder Adoptive Parents Support Group, Manchester, 2000—. Recipient Outstanding Family and Consumer Scis. Specialist award, NH Assn. Family and Consumer Scis., 1999. Mem.: Nat. Coun. Family Rels., Am. Assn. Family and Consumer Scis. (cert.), Nat. Ext. Assn. Family and Consumer Scis. (Nat. Comm. award for TV feature 1995, Continued Excellence award 1996, Disting. Svc. award 1995). Unitarian Universalist. Avocations: travel, hiking, miniature dollhouses. Office: U NH Coop Ext 113 North Rd Brentwood NH 03833 Home Phone: 603-429-0072; Office Phone: 603-679-5616.

BOOZMAN, JOHN, congressman; b. Shreveport, La, Dec. 10, 1950; m. Cathy Marley; 3 children. Grad., U. Ark., Fayetteville; OD, So. Coll. Optometry, 1977. Pvt. practice eye clinic, 1977; mem. U.S. Congress from 3d Ark. dist., 2001—; mem. Internat. Relations com., Transp. and Infrastructure com. and Veterans' Affairs com. U.S. Ho. Reps. Served Rogers Sch. Bd.; establisher low vision program Ark. Sch. for Blind for Little Rock; vol. optometrist area clinic. Republican. Office: US Ho Reps 1519 Longworth Ho Office Bldg Washington DC 20515-0403*

BOPP, JAMES, JR., lawyer; b. Terre Haute, Ind., Feb. 8, 1948; s. James and Helen Marguerite (Hope) B.; m. Cheryl Hahn, Aug. 8, 1970 (div.); m. Christine Marie Stanton, July 3, 1982; children: Kathleen Grace, Lydia Grace, Marguerite Grace. BA, Ind. U., 1970; JD, U. Fla., 1973. Bar: Ind. 1973, U.S. Supreme Ct. 1977. Dep. atty. gen. State of Ind., Indpls., 1973-75; ptnr. Bopp & Fife, Indpls., 1975-79, Brames, Bopp, Abel & Oldham, Terre Haute, Ind., 1979-92, Bopp, Coleson & Bostrom, Terre Haute, 1992—. Dep. prosecutor Vigo County, Terre Haute, 1979-86; gen. counsel Nat. Right to Life Com., Washington, 1978—; pres. Nat. Legal Ctr. for Medically Dependent and Disabled, 1984—; gen. counsel James Madison Ctr. Free Speech, 1997—; instr. law Ind. U., 1977-78; mem. com. Nat. Conf. Commrs. Uniform State Laws, 2005—. Editor: Human Life and Health Care Ethics, 1985, Restoring the Right to Life: The Human Life Amendment, 1984; editor-in-chief Issues in Law and Medicine, 1985—. Mem. Pres.'s Com. Mental Retardation, 1984—87, mem. congl. biomed. ethics adv. com., 1987—89; mem. White House Conf. on Families, Washington, 1980, White House Conf. on Aging, Mpls., 1981, Free Speech & Election Law Practice Group The Federalist Soc., former co-chmn. election law subcom., 1996—2005; bd. govs. Rep. Nat. Lawyers Assn., 2002—; alt. del. Rep. Nat. Conv., 1992, 1996, del., mem. platform com., 2000, 2004; mem. Rep. Nat. Com., 2006—; state treas. Ind. Rep. State Party, 2005—06, gen. counsel, 2005—, nat. committeeman, 2006—; chmn. Vigo County Election Bd., 1991—93; del. Rep. State Conv., Indpls., 1980, 1982, 1984, 1986, 1990, 1992, 1994, 1996, 1998, 2000, 2002, 2004, 2006; chmn. Vigo County Rep. Ctrl. Com., 1993—97; mem. nat. com. UNESCO, 2004—06; bd. dirs. Leadership Terre Haute, 1986—89, Alliance for Growth and Progress, Terre Haute, 1993—97; chmn. bd. dirs. Hospice of Wabash Valley, Terre Haute, 1982—88. Mem. Ind. State Bar Assn., Terre Haute Rotary (bd. dir. 1984-86). Republican. Roman Catholic. Home: 1124 S Center St Terre Haute IN 47802-1116 Office: Bopp Coleson & Bostrom 1 S 6th St Terre Haute IN 47807-3510 Home Phone: 812-232-5465; Office Phone: 812-232-2434. Personal E-mail: jboppjr@aol.com.

BOPP, MICHAEL D., lawyer; BA, Brown Univ., 1987; JD, Harvard Univ., 1992. Tax assoc. Price Waterhouse; assoc. Kutak Rock, 1992—95; counsel Permanent Subcommittee Investigations, U.S. Senate, 1995—97, Com. Governmental Affairs, U.S. Senate, 1997—98; sr. investigative counsel Com. Govt. Reform & Oversight, U.S. House Rep.; legislative dir. U.S. Senator Susan M. Collins, 1999—2003; staff dir. & chief counsel Com. Governmental Affairs, U.S. Senate, 2003—06; assoc. dir. gen. govt. programs Office Mgmt. and Budget, 2006—. Office: Office Mgmt and Budget 725 17th St NW Washington DC 20503

BORAH, GREGORY, surgeon, educator; b. NM, Apr. 1950; MD, Harvard U., 1978. Diplomate Am. Bd.Plastic Surgery. Prof., chief of plastic surgery U. Medicine and Dentistry NJ, Robert Wood Johnson Med. Sch., New Brunswick, NJ, 1992—. Pres. Am. Soc. Maxillofacial Surgeons, 1998—99. Contbr. more than 60 articles to profl. jours. Fellow: ACS (trustee 1999—2001); mem.: Am. Soc. Plastic Surgeons. Office: UMDNJ - Robert Wood Johnson Med Sch 1 RWJ Place New Brunswick NJ 08901

BORAS, SCOTT D., professional sports agent; b. Calif., Nov. 2, 1952; m. Jeanette Boras; children: Natalie, Shane, Trent. BS in Chemistry, U. Pacific, 1974, PhD in Indus. Pharmacology, 1976; JD, McGeorge Sch. Law Pacific U., 1982. Bar: Wash. Former infielder outfielder Chgo. Cubs Minor League Org., St. Louis Cardinals Minor League Org.; sports agent, 1981—; founder, owner, talent evaluator Scott Boras Corp.; founder, pres., CEO Impact Mktg. Achievements include representing major clients including Barry Bonds, Alex Rodriguez, Bernie Williams, JD Drew, Johnny Damon, and Daisuke Matsuzaka. Office: Scott Boras Corp 3 San Joaquin Plz Ste 100 Newport Beach CA 92660*

BORAT, See BARON COHEN, SACHA

BORCHARD, WILLIAM MARSHALL, lawyer; b. NYC, Nov. 19, 1938; s. Bernard Philip and Helen (Marshall) B.; m. Myra Cohen, Dec. 13, 1969; children: Jillian, Thomas. BA, Princeton U., 1960; JD, Columbia U., 1964. Bar: NY 1964, U.S. Dist. Ct. (so. and ea. dists.) NY, U.S. Ct. Appeals (2d, 3d, fed. cirs.), U.S. Supreme Ct. Assoc. Kaye, Scholer, Fierman, Hays and Handler, NYC, 1964-74, ptnr., 1974-83, Cowan, Liebowitz and Latman, NYC, 1983—. Author: Trademarks and the Arts, 1999, A Trademark is Not a Copyright or a Patent, 2007; mem. editl. bd. Art and the Law, 1982—, The Trademark Reporter, 1983—99. Staff sgt. USAFR, 1961-67. Stone scholar Columbia Law Sch. N.Y.C., 1962. Mem. ABA (coun. 1987-90), Am. Law Inst. (adv. com. 1986-92), Internat. Trademark Assn. (legal counsel 1988-91). Democrat. Jewish. Avocations: tennis, boating, biking. Office: Cowan Liebowitz & Latman 1133 Ave of Americas New York NY 10036-6799 Home Phone: 914-241-3425; Office Phone: 212-575-0671. Business E-Mail: wmb@cll.com.

BORCHERDING, THOMAS EARL, economist; b. Cin., Feb. 18, 1939; s. Earl Schaff and Vivian Joan (Miller) B.; m. Rhoda Jean Larson, Nov. 23, 1968; children: Matthew James, Benjamin Adam. BA, U. Cin., 1961; PhD, Duke U., 1966. Asst. prof. U. Wash., Seattle, 1966-71; assoc. prof. Va. Polytech Inst., Blacksburg, 1971-73; prof. econs. Simon Fraser U., Burnaby, B.C., Can., 1973-83; prof. law and econs. U. Toronto (Ont., Can.), 1978-79; prof. econs. Claremont (Calif.) Grad. U., 1983—. Editl. bd. CATO Jour., Washington; bd. of advisors Ind. Inst., Oakland, Calif., 1990—. Author: The Egg Board: The Social Cost of Monopoly, 1981; contbr. articles to profl. jours. NDEA fellow Duke U., 1961-64, postdoctoral fellow U. Va., 1965-66, Hoover Instn., Stanford U., 1974-75, Avery fellow Claremont U. Ctr., 1988-97. Mem. Am. Econ. Assn., Western Econ. Assn. (editor 1980-97), Can. Econ. Assn., Pub. Choice Soc., Mont Pelerin Soc., Phi Beta Kappa, Omicron Delta Epsilon, Phi Delta Theta. Home: 889 Connors Ct Claremont CA 91711-6240 Office: Claremont Grad U Sch Politics & Econs Claremont CA 91711 Home Phone: 909-625-4020; Office Phone: 909-621-8783. Personal E-mail: thomas_borcherding@yahoo.com.

BORCHERS, JANET MARISE, elementary school educator, counselor; b. Miami, Fla., July 1, 1955; d. James Hilliard and Janet Marise Cole; m. Kenneth Fred Borchers, May 8, 1976; 1 child, Russell James. AA, Edison C.C., Ft. Myers, Fla., 1989; BA, U. South Fla., Ft. Myers, 1992; MA, Fla. Gulf Coast U., Estero, 2001. Cert. tchr. ESOL Fla., tchr. English 5-9 Fla., primary edn. K-3 Fla., elem. edn. 1-6 Fla., guidance and counseling PK-12 Fla. Tchr. Sch. Dist. of Lee County, Ft. Myers, 1992—2001, sch. counselor, 2001—. Mem. Island Coast FEA Coun., Ft. Myers, 2006—. Named Elem. Sch. Counselor of Yr., Lee County, 2006. Mem.: Fla. Edn. Assn., Fla. Gulf Coast Nat. Writing Project (fellow 2001—, grantee 2006), Tchrs. Assn. Lee County (assoc.; sch. rep. 1992—, Area VII coord. 2002—), Lee County Counselors Assn. (assoc.), Am. Sch. Counselor Assn. (assoc.). Avocation: meditation. Home: 12550 Tower Rd Bonita Springs FL 34135 Office: Spring Creek Elem 25571 Elementary Way Bonita Springs FL 34135 Home Phone: 239-992-7215; Office Phone: 239-947-0001. Office Fax: 239-947-4690. Personal E-mail: jtortures2@aol.com. E-mail: janetmb@leeschools.net.

BORCHERS, ROBERT REECE, physicist, science administrator; b. Chgo., Apr. 4, 1936; s. Robert Harley and Rena Josephine (Reece) B.; m. Mary Bridget Hennessy, Nov. 26, 1960; children: Patrick Joseph, Anne Marie, Robert Edward BS in Physics, U. Notre Dame, 1958; MS in Physics, Math., U. Wis., 1959, PhD in Nuclear Physics, 1962. Prof. physics U. Wis., Madison, 1962—76, vice chancellor, 1976—77, U. Colo., Boulder, 1977—79; dep. assoc., dir. MFE Program Lawrence Livermore (Calif.) Nat. Lab., 1979—83, assoc. dir. computation, 1983—91, asst. to dir. for univ. rels., 1991—93; divsn. dir. advanced sci. computing NSF, Arlington, Va., 1993—2001; chief tech. officer Maui High Performance Computing Ctr., 2001—; CEO R.R. Borchers & Assocs., 2001—04; chief scientist CS Cubed Group, 2004—. Mem. com. NSF, Washington, 1973-93, Nat. Acad. Sci., Washington, 1983-93. Editor Computers in Physics jour., 1987-91, chmn. editorial bd., 1991-95; contbr. numerous chpts. in books, articles on physics and computing. NSF postdoctoral fellow, 1964; A.J. Schmidt Found. fellow and scholar, 1954-60; Sloan Found. fellow, 1964-68; Guggenheim Found. fellow, 1970; recipient W.H. Kiekhofer Disting. Teaching award U. Wis., Madison, 1966; Centennial of Sci. Alumnus award U. Notre Dame, 1966 Fellow Am. Phys. Soc.; mem. IEEE Computer Soc. Avocations: golf, music. Office: MHPCC 550 Lipoa Ste 100 Kihei HI 96753 Business E-Mail: marquis@bborchers.com.

BORCHERT, DONALD MARVIN, philosopher, educator; b. Edmonton, Alta., Can., May 23, 1934; s. Leo Ferdinand and Lillian Violet (Bucholz) B.; m. Mary Ellen Cockrell, Dec. 27, 1960; children: Carol Ellen, John Witherspoon. AB, U. Alta., Edmonton, 1955; BD, Princeton Theol. Sem., 1958, PhD, 1966; ThM, Ea. Bapt. Theol. Sem., 1959. Teaching fellow Princeton Theol. Sem., NJ, 1960-61; asst. prof. Juniata Coll., Huntingdon, Pa., 1966-67, Ohio U., Athens, 1967-71, assoc. prof., 1971-75, prof. philosophy, 1975—2006, assoc. dean Coll. Arts and Scis., 1980-86, chmn.

dept. philosophy, 1987—2002; emeritus prof. philosophy, 2006—. Author: Being Human in a Technological Age, 1979, Introduction to Modern Philosophy, 1981, 7th edit., 2001, Exploring Ethics, 1986, Medical Ethics, 1992, Philosophy of Sex and Love, 1997; editor in chief: Encyclopedia of Philosophy Supplement, 1996, Compendium of Philosophy and Ethics, 1999, Encyclopedia of Philosophy, 10 vols., 2006; contbr. articles to profl. jours. Assoc. Danforth Found. Nat. Humanities Inst. fellow, 1976-77; NEH Implementation grantee, 1981. Mem. Ohio Philos. Assn. (v.p. 1983-85, pres. 1985-90), Ohio Humanities Council (vice chmn. 1981-83, chmn. 1983-85). Presbyterian. Home: 9 Coventry Ln Athens OH 45701-3717 Office: Ohio U Dept Philosophy Ellis Hall Athens OH 45701 Office Phone: 740-593-4588. E-mail: borchert@ohio.edu.

BORCOVER, ALFRED SEYMOUR, journalist; b. Bellaire, Ohio, May 1, 1931; s. Joseph and Kate (Florman) B.; m. Doris E. Wellner, Sept. 13, 1958 (div. 1966); m. Linda A. Gredig, Oct. 11, 1989. BSc in Journalism, Ohio State U., 1953; MSJ, Northwestern U., 1957. Writer Northwestern U., Evanston, Ill., 1957-58; reporter, copy editor Chgo. Tribune, 1959-63, asst. travel editor, 1963-73, assoc. travel editor, 1973-79, editor travel sect., 1979-81, travel editor, columnist, 1981-93; ret., 1994. Freelance travel columnist/writer, 1994—. Author: Dollarwise Guide to Chicago, 1967; contbg. editor Fodor's Chicago, 1985-88; contbr. to Around the World with the Experts, 1970, WGN Travel Show, 1986-93; travel columnist Prodigy On-line Svc., 1990-96. Served to 1st lt. USAF, 1953-55 Recipient spl. citation George Hedmon Awards, 1965, Outstanding Achievement in Travel Writing award N.Y. Travel Writers Assn., 1976, Econ. Impact Writing award Travel Industry Assn. Am., 1983, Lowell Thomas Writing award, 1986; Gold Medal Writing award Pacific Asia Travel Assn., 1987, Cen. States Consumerism Reporting award, 1987, Alumni Svc. award Northwestern U., 1991, Cen. States Best Fgn. Series award, Cen. States Henry E. Bradshaw Meml. Writing award, 1991, Ctrl. States Fgn. Series and U.S. Article awards, 1992, Earl R. Lind Consumer Edn. award Better Bus. Bur. of Chgo., 1993, Ctrl. States Commentary award, 2004, Ctrl. States Consumer Reporting award, 2005. Mem. Soc. Am. Travel Writers (pres. 1973-74), Chgo. Headline Club (pres. 1983-84), Medill Sch. Journalism Alumni Assn. (bd. dirs. 1984-89, pres. 1989-91), Northwestern U. Alumni Assn. (bd. dirs. 1986-90), Soc. Profl. Journalists. Democrat. Jewish. Avocations: tennis, music, photography. Home and Office: 1022 Michigan Ave Evanston IL 60202-1436 Personal E-mail: aborcover@aol.com.

BORDA, RICHARD JOSEPH, retired insurance company executive; b. San Francisco, Aug. 16, 1931; s. Joseph Clement and Ethel Cathleen (Donovan) B.; m. Judith Maxwell, Aug. 30, 1953; children: Michelle, Stephen Joseph. AB, Stanford U., 1953, MBA, 1957. With Wells Fargo Bank, San Francisco, 1957-70, mgr., 1963-66, asst. v.p., 1966-67, v.p., 1967-70, exec. v.p. adminstrn. San Francisco, 1973-85; asst. sec. Air Force Manpower Res. Affairs, Washington, 1970-73; vice chmn., chief fin. officer Nat. Life Ins. Co., Montpelier, Vt., 1985-90; chmn., chief exec. officer Sentinal Group Funds, Inc., 1985-90. Former pres. Air Force Aid Soc., Washington; mem. bd. internat. advisors Monterey Inst. Internat. Studies; govs. coun. Boys and Girls Club Monterey Peninsula; dir. Cmty. Found. Monterey County. Recipient Exceptional Civilian Svc. award, 1973, 95, Stanford Assocs. award. Mem. USMC Res. Officers Assn., Bohemian Club, Old Capital Club, Air Force Aid Soc. (disting. counselor), Phi Gamma Delta, Cypress Point Club. Republican. Episcopalian.

BORDALLO, MADELEINE ZEIEN (MRS. RICARDO JEROME BORDALLO), congresswoman; b. Graceville, Minn., May 31, 1933; d. Christian Peter and Mary Evelyn (Roth) Zeien; m. Ricardo Jerome Bordallo, June 20, 1953; 1 daughter, Deborah Josephine. Student, St Mary's Coll., South Bend, Ind., 1952; AA, St. Katherines Coll., St. Paul, 1953; AA hon. degree for community service, U. Guam, 1968. Presented in voice recital Guam Acad. Music, Agana., 1951, 62; mem. Civic Opera Co., St. Paul, 1952-53; mem. staff KUAM Radio-TV sta., Agana, 1954-63; freelance writer local newspaper, fashion show commentator, coordinator, civic leader, 1963; nat. Dem. committeewoman for Guam, 1964—2004; 1st lady of Guam, 1974-78, 81-85; senator 16th Guam Legislature, 1981-82, 19th Guam Legislature, 1987-88, 20th Guam Legislature, 1989-90, 21st Guam Legislature, 1991-92, 22nd Guam Legislature, 1993-94; Dem. Party candidate for Gov. of Guam, 1990; lt. gov. of Guam, 1994—2002; rep. from Guam to 108th-110th Congresses, 2002—, mem. armed svcs., resources and small bus. coms. Del. Nat. Dem. Conv., 1964, 68, 72, 76, 80, 84, 88-92, 96, 2000-04, pres. Women's Dem. Party Guam, 1967-69; rep. Presdl. Inauguration, Washington, 1965, 77, 85, 2005; del. Dem. Western States Conf., Reno, 1965, L.A., 1967, Phoenix, 1968, conf. sec., 1967-69; del. Dem. Women's Campaign Conf., Wash., 1965, Dem. Inauguration, 1992. Pres. Guam Women's Club, 1958-59; del Gen. Fedn. Women's Clubs Convs., Miami Beach, Fla., 1961, New Orleans, 1965, Boston, 1968; v.p. Fedn. Asian Women's Assn., 1964-67, pres., 1967-69, pres. 1996-98; pres. Guam Symphony Soc., 1967-73, del. convs., Manila, Philippines, 1959, Taipei, Formosa, 1960, Hong Kong, 1963, Guam, 1964, Japan, 1968, Taipei, 1973; chmn. Guam Christmas Seal Drive, 1961; bd. dirs. Guam chpt. ARC, 1963, sec., 1963-67, fund dr. chmn., 2000; pres. Marianas Assn. For Retarded Children, 1968-69, 73-74, 84—; bd. dirs. Guam Theatre Guild, Am. Cancer Soc.; mem. Guam Meml. Hosp. Vols. Assn., 1966—, v.p., 1966-67, pres., 1970-71; chmn. Hosp. Charity Ball, 1966; pres. Women for Service, 1974—, Beauty World Guam Ltd., 1981—, First Lady's Beautification Task Force of Guam, 1983-86; pres. Palace Restoration Assn., 1983—; nominee Dem. party for Gov. of Guam, 1990. Mem. Internat. Platform Assn., Guam Rehab. Assn. (assoc.), Guam Lytico and Bodig Assn. (pres. 1983-98), Spanish Club of Guam, Inetnon Famalaoan Club (pres. 1983-86), Guam Coun. of Women's Club (pres. 1993-95), Nat. Conf. Lt. Govs. (exec. com. 1998—). Democrat. Home: Watergate E 305 N 2510 Virginia Ave NW Washington DC 20037 Office Phone: 202-225-1188. Business E-Mail: madeleine.bordallo@mail.house.gov, roseanne.meno@mail.house.gov.

BORDEAU, CATHERINE, French Professor; BA, MA, PhD, U. Mich. Assoc. prof. French Lyon Coll., Ark. Recipient Nat. Prof. Yr. State of Ark., Carnegie Found. Advancement of Tchg., 2006. Office: Foreign Languages Dept PO Box 2317 Batesville AR 72503

BORDELON, CAROLYN THEW, elementary school educator; b. Shelby, Ohio, Dec. 28, 1942; d. Burton Carl and Opal Mae (Harris) VanAsdale; m. Clifford Charles Spohn, Aug. 28, 1965 (div. Feb. 1982); m. Al Ramon Bordelon, Oct. 26, 1985. BA in History and Polit. Sci., Otterbein Coll., 1966; MA in Edn., Bowling Green State U., 1972; postgrad., Ohio State U., 1986—. Cert. tchr. grades 1-8, Ohio. Elem. tchr. Allen East Schs., Harrod, Ohio, 1966—68, Marion City Schs., Ohio, 1968—78, chpt. I reading tchr., 1978—86, reading recovery tchr., 1986—88, Dublin City Schs., Ohio, 1988—2005; reading specialist Upper Arlington City Schs., Ohio, 2005—. Adj. instr. reading dept. grad. studies Ashland (Ohio) U., 1996. Author: The Parent Workshop, 1992, Octopus Goes to School, 1995. Vol. Am. Heart Assn., Worthington, Ohio, 1991; mem. Rep. Nat. Com., Washington, 1994-95; mem. Royal Scots Highlanders, Mansfield, Ohio, 1976—; deacon Covenant Presbyn. Ch., Upper Arlington, Ohio, 2006—. Recipient Excellence in Edn. award Dublin City C. of C., 1991-93, 96, 97; Dublin City Schs./Ohio Dept. Edn. Tchr. Award grantee, 1993; Martha Holden Jennings Found. scholar, 1978. Mem. Archaeol. Inst. Am., Ohio Edn. Assn., Reading Recovery Coun. N.Am., Columbus Opera Assn., Columbus Mus. Art, Phi Delta Kappa, Phi Alpha Theta. Avocations: bagpiping and scottish activities, archaeology, interior design, harpsichord. Home: 3958 Fairlington Dr Columbus OH 43220-4531 Office: Tremont Elem Sch 2900 Tremont Rd Upper Arlington OH 43221 Personal E-mail: c.bordelonread@aol.com.

BORDELON, SUZANNE MACKIE, writing and rhetoric educator; b. Brampton, Can., Mar. 12, 1962; d. Ian and Eileen Patience (Weaver) Mackie; m. Robert Michael Bordelon, July 16, 1989; 1 child, Nicholas Ian. BA in Journalism and History, U. Wash., 1984; MA in Lit. and Lang., Calif. State U., Chico, 1992; PhD in Rhetoric and Composition, U. Oreg., 1998. Reporter Skagit Valley Herald, Mt. Vernon, Wash., 1986—87, Record Searchlight, Redding, 1987—92; asst. prof. English U. Alaska, Fairbanks, 1998—2002; coord. upper divsn. writing San Diego State U., 2002—. Author: A Feminist Legacy: The Rhetoric and Pedagogy of Gertrude Buck, 2007. Recipient Outstanding Faculty and Staff award, San Diego State U., 2004, Demmert Appreciation and Recognition award, U. Alaska, 2002. Mem.: Modern Lang. Assn., Nat. Women's Studies Assn., Writing Program Adminstrn., Rhetoric Soc. of Am., Nat. Coun. of Teachers of English. Personal E-mail: sbordelon2@cox.net.

BORDEN, DAVID M., state supreme court justice; b. Hartford, Conn., Aug. 4, 1937; BA magna cum laude, Amherst Coll., 1959; LLB cum laude, Harvard U., 1962. Bar: Conn. 1962, U.S. Dist. Ct. Conn. 1962, U.S. Ct. Appeals (2d cir.) 1965, U.S. Supreme Ct. 1969. Pvt. practice, Hartford, Conn., 1962-77; judge Conn. Ct. Common Pleas, 1977-78, Conn. Superior Ct., 1978-83, Conn. Appellate Ct., 1983—90; assoc. justice Conn. Supreme Ct., 1990—; chair rules com. Judges of the Superior Ct., 1992—2001. Chief counsel joint com. on judiciary Conn. Gen. Assembly, 1975-76; lectr. Law U. Conn. Sch. Law, 1968-70, 85-92, 94-; exec. dir. Conn. Commn. to Revise Criminal Statutes, 1963-71; chair Conn. Law Revision Commn. Task Force. Co-author: (books) Connecticut Criminal Jury Instructions, Superior Court Criminal Rules, Connecticut Criminal Law. Recipient Raymond E. Baldwin Public Service award, 1997. Mem. Conn. Bar Assn., Hartford County Bar Assn., Phi Beta Kappa. Democrat. Jewish. Avocations: hiking, reading. Office: Conn Supreme Ct 231 Capitol Ave Hartford CT 06106*

BORDEN, ERNEST CARLETON, oncologist, educator; b. Norwalk, Conn., July 12, 1939; s. Joseph Carleton and Violet Ernette (Lanneau) B.; m. Louise Dise, June 24, 1967; children: Kristin Louise, Sandra Lanneau. AB, Harvard U., 1961; MD, Duke U., 1966. Diplomate Am. Bd. Internal Medicine, Am. Bd. Med. Oncology. Intern Duke U. Med. Ctr., 1966-67; asst. resident in internal medicine Hosp. of U. Pa., 1967-68; med. officer Viropathology Lab., Nat. Communicable Disease Ctr., USPHS/Atlanta, 1968—70; clin. instr. dept. medicine Emory U. Sch. Medicine, Grady Meml. Hosp., 1968-70; postdoctoral fellow oncology divsn. dept. medicine Johns Hopkins U. Sch. Medicine, Balt., 1970-73; asst. prof. divsn. clin. oncology and depts. human oncology and medicine Wis. Clin. Cancer Ctr., Univ. Hosps. and Sch. Medicine, U. Wis.-Madison, 1973-79, assoc. prof., 1979-83, assoc. dir., 1981-90, prof., 1983-90, Am. Cancer Soc. prof. clin. oncology, from 1984; prof. depts. medicine and microbiology Med. Coll. Wis., Milw., 1990-94; also dir. Med. Coll. Wis. Cancer Ctr.; prof. oncology, medicine, microbiology, pharmacology U. Md. Sch. Medicine, Balt., 1994-98; dir. U. Md. Cancer Ctr., 1994-98; dir. ctr. cancer drug discovery and devel. Cleve. Clinic Found., 1998—; prof. molecular medicine Cleve. Clinic Found. Sch. Medicine Case Western Res. U., 2004—. Chief divsn. clin. oncology William S. Middleton VA Hosp., 1977-81; cons. staff Madison Gen. Hosp., 1974-90. Assoc. editor Jour. Interferon Rsch., 1980—, Jour. Biologic Response Modifiers, 1982-90; mem. editl. bd. Cancer Immunology and Immunotherapy, 1981-89, Investigational New Drugs, 1982—, Jour. Nat. Cancer Inst., 1987-91, Jour. Cancer Rsch., 1993-98, Jour. Bioactive and Compatible Polymers, Jour. Biol. Regulators and Homeostatic Agts., 1986, Clin. Cancer Rsch., 1998—; contbr. 300 articles to profl. jours. Recipient Disting. Svc. award Am. Cancer Soc., 1994. Fellow ACP; mem. AAAS, Am. Soc. Microbiology, Am. Assn. Cancer Rsch., Southwest Coop. Oncology Group, Am. Soc. Clin. Oncology, Am. Assn. Immunologists, Am. Fedn. Clin. Rsch., Soc. Biol. Therapy (pres. 1986-88), Internat. Soc. Interferon Rsch. (pres. 1987-89). Unitarian Universalist. Office Phone: 216-444-8183. Business E-Mail: bordene@ccf.org.*

BORDEN, MARK G., lawyer; b. NYC, Feb. 19, 1951; s. Arthur M. and Florence (Smiley) B. BA, Yale U., 1973; JD, Harvard U., 1976. Bar: Mass. 1976. Ptnr. Corp. Dept, mem. mgmt. com. WilmerHale (formerly Wilmer Cutler Pickering Hale & Dorr LLP), Boston. Co-author: Start-up Cos. — Planning, Financing & Operating Successful Bus. Named one of Boston's top lawyers, Boston Mag., 2002. Mem.: Boston Bar Assn., ABA, Tenacre Country Day Sch. (chmn. bd. trustees), Boston Symphony Orchestra (trustee). Office: Wilmer Cutler Pickering Hale & Dorr 60 State St Boston MA 02109-1816 Office Phone: 617-526-6675. Office Fax: 617-526-5000. Business E-Mail: mark.borden@wilmerhale.com.*

BORDERS, WILLIAM ALEXANDER, journalist; b. St. Louis, Jan. 11, 1939; s. William Alexis and Kate (Thompson) B.; m. Barbara D. Burkham, June 17, 1967 (div. 1984); 1 son, William Borders. BA, Yale U., 1960. Staff NY Times, NYC, 1960—, corr. Nigeria, 1970-72, Canada, 1972-75, India, 1975-79, London, 1979-82, dep. fgn. editor, 1982-83, editor Week in Rev. NYC, 1983-89, sr. editor, 1989—2006. Home: 227 E 57th St New York NY 10022-2828 Office: NY Times Co 229 W 43rd St New York NY 10036-3959

BORDIN, CRISTINA STADOLNY, academic administrator; b. Porto Alegre, Brazil, Dec. 18, 1974; d. Regis and Glaci Stadolny Bordin. BA in Bus. Adminstrn., Pontificia U. Catolica, Porto Alegre, Brazil, 1997; MA in Internat. Rels., CCNY, NYC, 2002. Cert. interior designer Brazil. Students job counselor Ctr. Integration Schs. and Companies, Porto Alegre, Brazil, 1993; sales mgr. Sepama Pavimentacoes LTDA, Porto Alegre, Brazil, 1993—96, Tradesign Ctr., Porto Alegre, 1997—99; project mgr. Bildner Ctr. We. Hemisphere Studies CUNY, NYC, 2000—04; asst. to pres. Instnl. Rels. St. Edward's U., Austin, Tex., 2005—. Contbr. Mem.: Soc. U. and Coll. Planning, Assn. Presdl. Assistants. Office: St Edwards University 3001 S Congress Avenue Austin TX 78704 Office Phone: 512-464-8893. Office Fax: 512-448-8687. Business E-Mail: cristinb@stedwards.edu.

BORDLEY, JAMES, IV, surgeon; b. Balt., Nov. 24, 1942; s. James III and Julia (Ross) B.; m. Dianne Redmond; children: Jessica, James V. BA, Yale U., 1965; MD, Columbia U. Physicians/Surgeon, 1970. Surg. intern Bassett Hosp., Cooperstown, NY, 1970-71, surg. resident, 1971-75, att. surgeon, 1978—; staff surgeon Naval Regl. Med. Ctr., Newport, RI, 1975-77; fellow biliary and pancreatic surgery U. Wash., Seattle, 1977; instr. surgery Columbia U., NYC, 1978-80, asst. prof. clin. surg., 1980—. Contbr. articles to profl. jours./publs. Lt. cmdr. USN, 1975-77. Fellow Am. Coll. Surgeons; mem. Soc. Surgery of the Alimentary Tract, Soc. Am. Gastrointestinal Endoscopic Surgeons. Office: Bassett Hosp 1 Atwell Rd Cooperstown NY 13326-1301

BORDNER, PATRICIA ANNE, insurance agent, writer; b. Red Wing, Minn., Mar. 29, 1946; d. Harold Arthur and Cecilia Helen Rodman; m. Thomas Ottis Bordner, May 18, 1981. AA, U. Minn., 1966. Cert. commercial rater U.S. Fidelity and Guaranty Co. Tchr. St. Albert the Great Elem. Sch., Mpls., 1967—68; tchr. Epiphany Edn. Ctr., Coon Rapids, Minn., 1968—70; comml. rater and acctg. clk. U. S. Fidelity and Guaranty Co., Mpls., 1971—85; ind. comml. ins. rater Coon Rapids, 1985—. Author: (poems) Hands of Time, 2000; contbr. poems to poetry contests and mags. Named Internat. Profl. of Yr., Internat. Biographical Ctr., England, 2005; named to Internat. Poetry Hall of Fame, 1996; recipient Golden Poet award, 1990, 1991, 1992, Editor's Choice award, 1993—98, 21st Century award for achiev., Internat. Biographical Ctr., England. Roman Catholic. Home: 1010 94th Ave NW Coon Rapids MN 55433-5501

BORDOGNA, JOSEPH, engineering educator, former science foundation executive; b. Scranton, Pa., Mar. 22, 1933; s. Raymond and Rose (Yesu) B. BSEE, U. Pa., 1955, PhD, 1964; SM, MIT, 1960. With RCA Corp., 1958-64; asst. prof. U. Pa., Phila., 1964-68, assoc. prof., 1968-72, prof., 1972—, assoc. dean engrng. and applied sci., 1973-80, acting dean, 1980-81, dean, 1981-90, dir. Moore Sch. Elec. Engrng., 1976-90, Alfred Fitler Moore prof. engrng., 1979—; dir. engrng. NSF, Washington, 1991-96, COO, acting deputy dir., 1996-99, dep. dir., COO, 1999—2005. Master Stoufer Coll. House, 1972-76; cons. industry, govt., founds.; mem. Nat. Medal of Sci. com., 1989-91; chair adv. com. for engrng. NSF, 1989-91. Author: (with H. Ruston) Electric Networks, 1966, (with others) The Man-Made World, 1971; chmn. editl. bd. Engrng. Edn., 1987-90. With USN, 1955—58. Recipient commendation for first space capsule recovery, 1957, Lindback award for disting. teaching U. Pa., 1967, Centennial medal Phila. Coll. Textiles and Sci., 1988, Am. Indsl. Modernization Leadership award Nat. Coalition for Advanced Mfg., 1993, Chmn.'s award Am. Assn. Engrng. Socs., 1994, Engr. of Yr. award NSPE Phila., 1984, George Washington medal Engrs. Club. Phila., 1997, Gold medal Soc. Mfg. Engrs., 2001, Leadership in Tech. Mgmt. award Portland Internat. Conf. on Mgmt. of Engrng. and Tech., 2003, Leadership award Semiconducter Industry Assn., 2004, Disting. Svc. medal NSF, 2005; named to Engrng. Educators Hall of Fame, 1993. Fellow AAAS (chair engrng. sect. 1998-99), IEEE (chmn. Phila. sect. 1987-88, pres. 1998, Centennial medal 1984), ASME (Johnson and Johnson Diversity medal 2005), Am. Soc. Engrng. Edn. (George Westinghouse award 1974), Internat. Engrng. Consortium; mem. Sigma Xi, Eta Kappa Nu (eminent mem. 2005), Tau Beta Pi, Phi Beta Delta. Achievements include having plateau in Antarctica named Bordogna Plateau, 2005. Office: U Pa Sch Engrng & Applied Sci 610 Levine Hall 200 S 33rd St Philadelphia PA 19104-6314 Office Phone: 215-898-8120. Business E-Mail: bordogna@eniac.seas.upenn.edu.

BORDONARO, KAREN ELIZABETH, school librarian, educator; b. Jamestown, NY, May 21, 1959; d. James Edward Kuechle and Carolyn Elnora Snyder; m. Joseph John Bordonaro, Oct. 8, 1983; children: Matthew William, Katherine Marie. BA in German and Spanish, St. Bonaventure U., Olean, NY, 1981; MA in German, SUNY, Buffalo, NY, 1983, MLS, 1984, EdM in TESOL, 2000, PhD, 2004. Bus. info. specialist The Conf. Bd., NYC, 1984—85; reference libr. Daemen Coll., Amherst, NY, 1985—87; reference libr. I - IV Canisius Coll., Buffalo, 1987—2002; summer faculty mem. English Lang. Inst. SUNY, Buffalo, 2000—04; assoc. dir., libr. for archives and info. literacy Canisius Coll., Buffalo, 2002—05; acad. writing mentor dept. of applied linguistics Brock U., St. Catharines, Ont., Canada, 2005—06, coord. info. literacy svcs., instrn. libr. James A. Gibson Libr., 2005—. Adj. asst. prof. acad. devel. dept. Canisius Coll., Buffalo, 1998—2005. Mem.: Hands-On English (adv. bd. mem. 2000—), Western NY/Ont. Assn. Coll. and Rsch. Librs. (councilor, mem. exec. bd. 2005—07), Can. Libr. Assn., Ont. Libr. Assn. Home: 34 Kohler St Tonawanda NY 14150 Office: Brock Univ James A Gibson Libr Ontario Saint Catharines Canada L2S 3A1 Home Phone: 716-695-9879; Office Phone: 905-688-5550 ext. 4423. Business E-Mail: kbordona@brocku.ca.

BORDY, MICHAEL JEFFREY, lawyer; b. Kansas City, Mo., July 24, 1952; s. Marvin Dean and Alice Mae (Rostov) B.; m. Marjorie Enid Kanof, Dec. 27, 1973 (div. Dec. 1983); m. Melissa Anne Held, May 24, 1987; children: Shayna Robyn, Jenna Alexis, Samantha Falyn. BA, Hamilton Coll., 1974; PhD, U. Kans., 1980; JD, U. So. Calif., 1986. Bar: Calif., 1986, US Dist. Ct. (cen. dist.) Calif., 1986, (so. dist.) Calif., 1987, US Ct. Appeals (9th cir.), 1986. Tchg. asst. biology U. Kans., Lawrence, 1975-76, rsch. asst. biology, 1976-80; post-doctoral fellow Johns Hopkins U., Balt., 1980-83; tchg. asst. U. So. Calif., LA, 1984-86; assoc. Thelen, Marrin, Johnson & Bridges, LA, 1986-87, Wood, Lucksinger & Epstein, LA, 1987-89, Cooper, Epstein & Hurewitz, Beverly Hills, Calif., 1989-93; ptnr. Jacobson, Runes & Bordy, Beverly Hills, 1994-96, Jacobson, Sanders & Bordy, LLP, Beverly Hills, 1996-97, Jacobson White Diamond & Bordy, LLP, Beverly Hills, 1997—2001, White, Bordy & Levey, LLP, LA, 2002—05, Bordy and Levey, LLP, LA, 2005—. Bd. govs. Beverly Hills (Calif.) Bar Barristers, 1988-90, chair real estate law sect. 1998-2000, exec. com. 2000—; bd. govs. Cedars-Sinai Med. Ctr., LA, 1994—; bd. dirs. Sinai Temple, 1998-2003, Jewish Fedn., LA, 2004—; cabinet United Jewish Fund/Real Estate, LA, 1995—; exec. com. Moriah Soc. for U. Judaism, 2002--; planning com. Am. Cancer Soc., 1996-2000; active Guardians of the Jewish Home for the Aging, 1995—, Lawyers Against Hunger, 1995-2002, Fraternity of Friends, 1997-99. Pre-Doctoral fellow NIH, Lawrence, 1977-80, post-doctoral fellow Mellon Found., Balt., 1980-83; named one of Southern Calif. Super Lawyers, 2005—. Mem. ABA, State Bar Calif., LA County Bar Assn., Beverly Hills Bar Assn. (gov., barrister 1988-92, chair real estate sect. 1998-00), Profl. Network Group. Democrat. Jewish. Avocations: running, triathlons, reading. Office: Bordy & Levey LLP 1880 Century Park E Ste 615 Los Angeles CA 90067-1602 Office Phone: 310-551-9700. Business E-Mail: mjbordy@wbllaw.com.

BOREEN, HENRY ISAAC, computer company executive; b. Warsaw, Mar. 7, 1927; came to U.S., 1949; s. Isaac and Grina (Goldstein) B.; m. Lois Adele Golwyn, June 22, 1958; children: Stuart Michael Boreen, Susan Tobey Hailman. BSEE, Drexel U., 1956, MSEE, 1958, DrEngring.Sci (hon.), 2002, D Engring. Sci., 2002. Asst. prof. Drexel U., Phila., 1958; v.p. engr. Vector Mfg. Co., Inc., Trevose, Pa., 1958-64; chmn., CEO Solid State Sci., Inc., Montgomeryville, Pa., 1964-86; chmn. US-Tech, Inc., Valley Forge, Pa., 1987—; chmn., CEO AM Comm., Inc., Quakertown, Pa., 1990-99; chmn. Integrated Circuit Systems Inc., Valley Forge, Pa., 1993-99; with Combex, Inc., Rydal, Pa., 2000—. Bd. trustees Cardiovasc. Found. New Rochelle, NY, 2002—; chmn. Combex, Inc., San Jose. Co-author: Aerospace Telemetry, 1961. Recipient Centennial medal Drexel Univ., 1991. Avocations: gardening, photography, car racing, hiking, bird watching. Office: Combex Inc PO Box 4070 Rydal PA 19046

BOREI, SVEN HANS EMIL, translator, writer, educator; b. Stockholm, Dec. 21, 1941; arrived in US, 1953, naturalized, 1960; s. Hans Georg and Maj Ellen (Österlin) B.; m. Gisela Wilms Möller; children: Bethany, Rolf, Emil. AA, Valley Forge Mil. Acad., 1961; BA in English, U. Pa., 1964; postgrad., Syracuse U. English and writing tchr. Meadowbrook Sch. for Boys, Phila., 1964-65; basic skills instr. adult edn. Syracuse (N.Y.) Pub. Schs., 1965-67; assoc. dir. Ednl. and Cultural Ctr. Onondaga and Oswego Counties, Syracuse, 1966-67; English instr. Maria Regina Jr. Coll., Syracuse, 1967-68; pres., founder, trustee, CEO Ctr. for Literacy, Inc., Phila., 1968-78; literacy project coord. Appalachia Ednl. Lab., Charleston, W.Va., 1980-81; founder, pres., CEO Literacy Inst., Inc., Syracuse, 1981-88; co-prop. H.E.S. Konsult AB, Transförlag, Lerum, Sweden, 1986—; English lang. coord. Språkverket AB, Göteborg, 1987-89. Mem. Nat. Adv. Coun. on Interpreting and Translating, 2001-03; cons., presenter in field. Author: Appalachian Adult Literacy Programs Survey, 2 vols., 1981, LLA Finance Handbook, 1982, A Measure of Freedom, 1995; editor: Quality Thinking, 1998, Translator Rates Survey, Sweden, 2007; translator: Art at Astra, 1997, Jan Johansson, a Visionary Swedish Musician, 1998, Travel Guide for Westmanland, 2000, Jazz Facts, 1999-2002, Lena Mattson, a small fairy tale, 2001, Olle Kåks, Paintings 1970-2002, 2002, Style is Fraud - Carl F. Reutersward, 2003, Sofiero Royal Residence and Glorious Garden, 2005, Norrköping: A History in Textile, 2006; contbr. articles to profl. jours. Supervisory tutor trainer Laubach Literacy Action, Syracuse, 1975, master tutor trainer, 1977, regional trainer cons., 1985, bd. dirs. 1972-80; co-founder, chair Tutors for Literacy in Pa., 1975-76, W.Va. Literacy Coalition, 1980-82, Tenn. Literacy Coalition, 1982-85; mem. Lerum Mcpl. Coun., 1991-98, 2006—, mcpl. exec. com., 1995-98, mcpl. bldg. bd. 1999—; bd. govs. Am.-Swedish Hist. Found., 1973-80, v.p., 1975-77, treas., 1977-78. Mem. Swedish Assn. Profl. Translators (bd. dirs.

1997-2003, vice chmn. 1998-99, chmn. 1999-2003). Avocations: music, local history. Home and Office: PL 3181 Koksås S-443 38 Lerum Sweden Office Phone: 46-302-10987. Personal E-mail: transforlag@heskonsult.com.

BOREL, JAMES CALVIN, chemical company executive; b. Clarion, Iowa, Dec. 26, 1955; s. Ralph Jule and Phyllis Ann Borel; m. Marcia Ann Henderson, Sept. 30, 1978; children: David, Bethany. BS in Agrl. Bus., Iowa State U., Ames, 1978. Product specialist Dupont Agrl. Products, Wilmington, Del., 1981-84; sales mgr. agrl. products Dupont, Stevenage, Eng., 1984-87, mgr. agrl. products Mississauga, Can., 1987-89; gen. supt. Dupont Agrl. Products, Belle, W.Va., 1989-91, mgr. human resources Wilmington, 1991-93; regional dir. Dupont Asia Pacific, Tokyo, 1993-97; bus. dir. N.Am. DuPont Agrl. Products, Wilmington, Del., 1997—, v.p., gen. mgr. crop protection, 1997-98, pres. crop protection, 1998—2004; sr. v.p., Global Human Resources Dupont, 2004—. Trustee Nat. 4-H Council; mem. adv. bd. Ctr. for Human Resource Strategy, Rutgers Univ.; bd. mem. Del. Cmty. Found. Avocations: golf, sailing. Office: duPont Human Resources 9046 DuPont Bldg 1007 Market St Wilmington DE 19898*

BORELLI, FRANCIS J(OSEPH) (FRANK BORELLI), diversified financial services company executive; b. Bklyn., Sept. 2, 1935; s. Anthony and Ida Borelli; m. Madlyn Quadrino, June 25, 1960; children: Frank, Richard. BBA, Baruch Coll. CUNY, 1956. CPA, N.Y. With Deloitte Haskins & Sells, 1956-79, ptnr., 1968-79, mng. ptnr. in charge Bergen County, N.J. office, 1976-79; sr. v.p. fin. and adminstr., dir. Airco, Inc., Montvale, NJ, 1980-84; sr. v.p., CFO, dir. Marsh & McLennan Cos., Inc., NYC, 1984—2000. Bd. dirs. Interpub. Group, Express Scripts, Genworth Fin Bd. dirs. Nat. Multiple Sclerosis Soc., Signal Holdings Inc., Italian Am. Network; trustee St. Thomas Aquinas Coll., Rockland Paramedics Inc.; former dir. Mid Ocean Reinsurance and United Water Resources; former nat. chmn. Fin. Execs. Internat.; chmn. emeritus Nyack Hosp. Mem. Fin. Execs. Inst. (named to Hall of Fame 2006), AICPAs, N.Y. State Soc. CPAs, Ridgewood Country Club, Columbus Found. Home: 13 Patricia Dr New City NY 10956-2008 Personal E-mail: frankcfo@verizon.net.

BOREN, CLARK HENRY, JR., general and vascular surgeon; b. Marinette, Wis., Nov. 23, 1947; s. Clark Henry and Maryon Lillian (Peterson) Boren; children: Jenna Marie, Matthew William, Nathan Clark. BMS, Northwestern U., 1971, MD with distinction, 1973. Diplomate Am. Bd. Surgery. Resident in gen. surgery U. Calif.-H.C. Moffitt Hosp., San Francisco, 1973-79; rsch. fellow in vascular surgery Ft. Miley VA Hosp., 1976-77; vascular fellow Med. Coll. Wis./Milwaukee County Med. Complex, Milw., 1979-80; mem. staff Fox Valley Surg. Assocs., Ltd., Appleton, Wis., 1980—, pres., 1997—. Chmn. bd. United Health Wis., 1995—99. Contbr. articles to profl. jours. Mem.: AMA, ACS, Am. Assn. Vascular Surgery, Wis. Surg. Soc., Midwest Vascular Soc., Peripheral Vascular Surgery Soc., Wis. State Med. Soc., Phi Kappa Psi, Phi Eta Sigma, Phi Beta Pi, Alpha Omega Alpha. Democrat. Home: 330 W River Rd Appleton WI 54915 Office: Fox Valley Surg Assocs 1818 N Meade St Appleton WI 54911-3454 Home Phone: 920-996-0189; Office Phone: 920-731-8131. Business E-Mail: clark.boren@thedacare.org.

BOREN, DANIEL DAVID, congressman; b. Shawnee, Okla., Aug. 2, 1973; s. David L. and Janna L. (Robbins) Boren; m. Andrea Boren. BS in Econs., Tex. Christian U., Ft. Worth, 1997; MBA in Internat. Bus., U. Okla., 2001. Loan processor Banc First Corp.; intern Staff of US Rep. Wes Watkins, field rep.; sr. aide Okla. Corp. Commn.; v.p. Robbins Energy Corp.; intern Ind. Petroleum Assn.; mem. Okla. State Ho. Reps., 2003—04, US Congress from 2nd Okla dist., 2005—, mem. armed svcs. com., mem. natural resources com., mem. fin. svcs. com., mem. Congl. Blue Dog Caucus. Pres., CEO Seminole State Coll. Edni. Found.; chmn. Last Frontier Coun. Boy Scout Campaign; mem. Wewoka Downtown Investment Grp.; bd. dirs. Jasmine Moran Children's Mus., Big Bros. Big Sisters; Knowledge is Power Prog. Found. Mem.: Wewoka C. of C. (bd. dirs.), Seminole Hist. Soc. (pres.), Rotary. Democrat. Office: US House Reps 216 Cannon House Office Bldg Washington DC 20515 Office Phone: 202-225-2701. Office Fax: 202-225-3038.*

BOREN, DAVID LYLE, academic administrator, former senator; b. Washington, Apr. 21, 1941; s. Lyle H. and Christine (McKown) B.; m. Molly Shi, Dec. 1977; children: David Daniel, Carrie Christine. BA summa cum laude, Yale, 1963; MA (Rhodes scholar), Oxford U., Eng., 1965; JD (Bledsoe Meml. prize as outstanding law grad.), U. Okla., 1968. Bar: Okla. 1968. Practiced law in, Seminole, 1968-74; prof. polit. sci., chair divsn. social scis. Okla. Bapt. U., Shawnee, 1969-74; mem. Okla. Ho. of Reps., 1967-75; gov. Okla., 1975-79; mem. U.S. Senate from Okla., 1979-94; pres. U. Okla., Norman, 1994—. Mem. Senate Fin. Com., Senate Agrl. Com.; chmn. Senate Select Com. on Intelligence, govt. dept. Okla. Bapt. U., 1969-74. Trustee Yale U., 1988-97. Named One of 10 Outstanding Young Men in U.S., U.S. Jaycees, 1967. Mem. Assn. U.S. Rhodes Scholars, Phi Beta Kappa. Methodist. Office: U Okla 660 Parrington Oval Rm 110 Norman OK 73019-3003 Office Phone: 405-325-3916. E-mail: dboren@on.edu.*

BOREN, JAMES EDGAR, lawyer; b. New Orleans, Nov. 16, 1949; m. Teresa Anne Berlin; children: Anna Blynn, Katherine Lenore, Rebecca Camille. BA, La. Tech U., 1971; JD, La. State U., 1975. Bar: La. 1975, U.S. Dist. Ct. (mid. dist.) La. 1975, U.S. Ct. Appeals (5th cir.)1975, U.S. Dist. Ct. (we. dist.) La. 1976, U.S. Dist. Ct. (ea. dist.) La. 1977, U.S. Supreme Ct. 1979, U.S. Ct. Appeals (11th cir.) 1981. Asst. dist. atty. Parish of East Baton Rouge, 1975-76; ptnr. Boren, Holthaus & Perez, Baton Rouge, 1976-88; pvt. practice Baton Rouge, La., 1988—. Chair La. Atty. Discipline Bd. Hearing Com., 1994-2000; adj. prof. La. State U. Law Sch., 2002-. Contbr. articles to profl. publs. Mem. ACLU (bd. dirs. 1988-92), La. State Bar Assn. (ho. of dels. 1998—2007, bd. govs. 2007—), La. Assn. Criminal Def. Lawyers (bd. dirs. 1985—, pres. commendation 1986, pres. 1990-91, chair edn. com. 1997—, Tate award 2000), Nat. Assn. Criminal Def. Lawyers (bd. dirs. 1992-95, chmn. death penalty com. 1994-98, indigent def. co-chair 1998-2002). Democrat. Home: 2035 E Lakeshore Dr Baton Rouge LA 70808-1464 Address: 830 Main St Baton Rouge LA 70802-5597 Office Phone: 225-387-5786. Personal E-mail: jimboren@bellsouth.net.

BOREN, LYNDA SUE, gifted education educator; b. Leesville, La., Apr. 1, 1941; d. Leonard and Doris (Ford) Schoenberger; m. James Lewis Boren, Sept. 1, 1961; 1 child, Lynda Carolyn. BA, U. New Orleans, 1971, MA, 1973; PhD, Tulane U., 1979. Prof. Northwestern State U., Natchitoches, La., 1987-89; propr. Colony Country House, New Llano, La., 1992-94; tchr. of gifted Leesville (La.) H.S., 1992—. Vis. prof. Newcomb Coll., Tulane U., New Orleans, 1979-83, U. Erlangen-Nuremburg, Germany, 1981-82, Middlebury (Vt.) Coll., 1983-84, Ga. Inst. Tech., Atlanta, 1985-87, Srinakharinwirot U., Bangkok, 1989-90; mem. planning com. 1st Kate Chopin Internat. Conf., Natchitoches, La., 1987-89; Fulbright lectr. USIA and Bd. Fgn. Scholars, 1981-82, 89-90. Author: Eurydice Reclaimed: Language, Gender and Voice in Henry James, 1989; co-editor, author: Kate Chopin Reconsidered, 1992; contbg. author: Encyclopedia of American Poetry, 1998; contbr. numerous articles to profl. jours. Founding mem. John F. Kennedy libr. Recipient awards for watercolors; Mellon fellow Tulane U., 1977-78; NEH seminar fellow Princeton U., 1986. Mem. MLA, AAUW, DAR, AFT, Fulbright Alumni Assn. Avocations: painting, video film documentaries, photography. Home: 1492 Fords Dairy Rd Newllano LA 71461-4530 Office Phone: 337-239-3464. Personal E-mail: alborn@peoplepc.com, schoenberger@bellsouth.net. Business E-Mail: lboren@vpsb.k12.la.us.

BOREN, WILLIAM MEREDITH, manufacturing executive; b. San Antonio, Oct. 23, 1924; s. Thomas Loyd and Verda (Locke) B.; m. Molly Brasfield Sarver, Dec. 3, 1976; children: Susan, Patricia, Janet, Jenny, Burton, Cliff. Student, Tex. A&M U., 1942-43, Rice U., 1943-44; BS in Mech. Engring., Tex. U., 1949. Vice pres., gen. mgr. Rolo Mfg. Co., Houston, 1949-54; mgr. sales engring. Black, Sivalls & Bryson, Houston, Oklahoma City, 1955-64; vice chmn., dir., mem. exec. com. Big Three Industries, Inc., Houston, 1965—; chmn. Bowen Tool Co., Houston. Bd. dirs. Engring. Adv. Coun., Tex. U.; dir. Air Liquide Am. Corp.; dir. Electric Reliability Coun. Tex. Inventor Classic Bridge game; screenwriter WWII movie Pegasus Bridge. Trustee S.W. Rsch. Inst., San Antonio; bd. dirs. Coun. Econ. Edn.; mem. chancellor's coun. U. Tex. Lt. (j.g.) USN, 1943-46. Named Disting. Grad. Engring. Dept., U. Tex., 1992. Mem. Internat. Oxygen Mfrs. Assn. (chmn.), French-Am. C. of C. (bd. dirs.), Tau Beta Pi, Pi Tau Sigma. Republican. Home: 2906 Midlane St Houston TX 77027-4912

BORENSTEIN, DANIEL BERNARD, psychiatrist, educator; b. Silver City, N.Mex., Mar. 31, 1935; s. Jack and Marjorie Elizabeth (Kerr) B.; m. Bonnie Denice Ulland, June 11, 1967; 1 child, Jay Brian. BSChemE, MIT, 1957; MD, U. Colo., 1962. Diplomate Am. Bd. Psychiatry and Neurology. Intern U. Hosp. U. Ky., 1962-63; resident in psychiatry U. Colo. Med. Ctr., 1963-66; chief resident, psychiatry instr. U. Colo. Sch. Medicine, 1965-66; psychiatry instr. U. So. Calif. Sch. Medicine, 1966-67; asst. clin. prof. psychiatry UCLA Sch. Medicine, 1972-84, assoc. clin. prof., 1984-96, clin. prof., 1996—. Founder, dir. UCLA Mental Health Program for Physicians in Tng., 1980—84; clin. assoc. L.A. Psychoanalytic Soc. and Inst., 1967—71, pres. clin. assocs., 1970—71, faculty, 1973—83, sr. faculty, 1983—2005; pvt. practice medicine specializing in psychoanalysis and psychiatry, West L.A., 1966—; assoc. vis. psychiatrist UCLA Ctr. Health Scis., 1973—90; cons. Medicare Program, 1995—2005; examiner Am. Bd. Psychiatry and Neurology; reviewer various med. and psychiat. jours., 1991—. Author: Manual of Psychiatric Peer Review, 1985, Psychiatric Peer Review: Prelude and Promise, 1985; contbr. articles to profl. jours. Bd. dirs. L.A. Child Devel. Ctr., 1981—85, Found. Advancement Psychiat. Edn. and Rsch., 1991—2005, Coop. Am. Physicians/Mutual Protective Trust, 1994—. Lt. AUS, 1957—58. Recipient Disting. Prof. award, UCLA Sch. Medicine, 2006. Fellow: Am. Coll. Psychiatrists (com. on hon. fellowship 2002—05), Am. Psychiat. Assn. (life; mem. coun. area VI 1977—79, com. to rev. psychiat. news 1979—81, coun. area VI, dep. rep. assembly dist. brs. 1981—82, work group on competition and legis. 1981—83, nominating com. 1982—83, assembly liaison to peer rev. com. 1982—86, assembly rep. dist. brs. 1982—89, assemly liaison to fin. and mktg. com. 1986—87, assembly corr. group on subspecialization 1986—89, assembly liaison to coun. on econ. affairs 1987—89, med. student edn. com. 1987—90, bd. liaison jud. action commn. 1989—91, bd. trustees 1989—, com. managed care 1990—92, com. mem., bd. liaison to managed care com. 1992—99, bd. liaison econ. affairs coun. 1992—99, chmn. bd. ethics appeals, sec. 1995—97, v.p. 1997—99, pres.-elect 1999—2000, pres. 2000—01, chair med. dir. contract negotiating com. 2001, cons. bus. rels. com., chair nominating com. 2001—02, past pres. 2001—, bus. rels. com. 2002—05, fin. and budget com. 2003—06, Disting. fellow); mem.: AMA (ho. dels., alt. 1998—2002, del. 2003—07), Am. Psychoanalytic Assn. (com. on confidentiality 1983—96, com. on govt. rels. and ins. 1983—2000), L.A. Psychoanalytic Soc. and Inst. (co-chmn. ext. divsn. 1973—74, chmn. peer rev. com. 1975—78, curriculum com. 1980—84), Calif. Psychiat. Assn. (exec. coun. 1977—79, 1981—95, chmn. jud. com. 1986—88, bd. trustees 1989—95, Spl. Recognition award 1995), Calif. Med. Assn. (ho. of dels. psychiat. splty. rep. 1979—84, com. on mental health and mental disabilities 1979—85, alt. del. ho. del. 1984—86, del. 1986—88, com. on mental health and mental disabilities 1987—88, bd. trustees 1992—2001, chmn. physicians benevolence oper. com. 1996—2001, chmn. bldg. com. 1999—2001), L.A. County Med. Assn. (chmn. mental health com. Bay dist. 1980—85, com. on substance abuse 1981—86, Bay Dist. bd. dirs. 1981—, Bay Dist. v.p. 1985—86, pres.-elect 1986—87, com. on well-being 1986—89, pres. 1987—88, exec. coun. 1988—91), So. Calif. Psychiat. Soc. (chmn. peer rev. com. 1974—77, exec. coun. 1976—89, ethics com. 1977—85, pres. 1978—79, chmn. fellowship and awards com. 1979—85, chmn. Commn. on Psychiatry and the Law 1980—81, Appreciation award 1979, 1st recipient Disting. Svc. award 1984, Outstanding Achievement award 1993, Outstanding Svc. citation 1975). Office: 151 N Canyon View Dr Los Angeles CA 90049-2721 Office Phone: 310-472-7386.

BORENSTEIN, DAVID GILBERT, internist, writer, rheumatologist; b. Bklyn. s. Murray and Mollie (Koren) B.; m. Dorothy Regina Fait, Aug. 6, 1972; children: Sylvia, Elizabeth, Rebecca. AB, Columbia U., 1969; MD, Johns Hopkins U., 1973. Diplomate Am. Bd. Internal Medicine, Am. Bd. Rheumatology. Intern in medicine Johns Hopkins Hosp., 1973-74, resident in medicine, 1974-76; fellow in rheumatology Johns Hopkins U., 1976-78; asst. prof. medicine George Washington U., Washington, 1978-83, assoc. prof. medicine, 1983-89, prof. medicine, 1989-96, prof. neurosurgery, 1991-96, clin. prof. neurosurgery, 1997-98, clin. prof. medicine, 1997—. Cons. Vaccine Injury Compensation Program, Dept. HHS, Washington, 1993-02, Sulzer Medica, Austin, Tex., 1997-02, Searle, Skokie, Ill., 1997-02, Merck-Medco, Rahway, NJ, 1997-99, OSHA, Dept. Labor, 1998-99, Merck, 1999-04, Pfizer, 2003-04, Epicept, 2004—, Pfizer, 2006-, Biovail, 2006-. Author: Low Back Pain: Medical Diagnosis, 1995, Neck Pain: Medical Diagnosis, 1996, Back in Control! A Conventional and Complementary Prescription for Eliminating Back Pain, 2001, Low Back and Neck Pain: Comprehensive Diagnosis and Management, 3d edit., 2007; contbg. author: Low Back Pain in Rheumatology, 1997; contbg. author Low Back Pain in Rheumatology, 2d edit., 2003, Inflammatory Arthridities and Psoriatic Arthritis in the Lumbar Spine 3d edit., 2004. Mem. Appellate Jud. Nominating Commn., State of Md., 1986-94; med. adv. bd. Arthritis Found. D.C., 1986-88, bd. dirs., 1999—, exec. bd. dirs., 2006—; med. adv. bd. Lupus Found. Greater Washington, 1992-2004. Fellow: ACP, Am. Coll Rheumatology (govt. affairs com. 1998—2004, chmn. govt. affairs com. 2001—04, bd. dirs. 2005—); mem.: Acad. Medicine Washington, Rheumatism Soc. D.C. (pres. 1992—93), Internat. Soc. Study Lumbar Spine (membership com. 1999, chmn. 2002), Cosmos Club. Jewish. Avocations: skiing, squash. Office: Arthritis and Rheum Assocs 2021 K St NW Washington DC 20006-1003 Home Phone: 301-983-2340; Office Phone: 202-293-1470. Personal E-mail: dborenstein715@aol.com.

BORENSTEIN, MARK A., lawyer; b. Bklyn., June 26, 1951; BA, SUNY, Buffalo, 1973; JD, George Washington U., 1976; LLM, Georgetown U., 1978. Bar: Va. 1976, D.C. 1977, Calif. 1978. Law clk. to Hon. Irving Hill U.S. Dist. Ct. (cen. dist.), Calif., 1976-77; mem. Tuttle & Taylor, LA, 1978-2000, Shapiro, Borenstein & Dupont, Santa Monica, Calif., 2000—02, Overland & Borenstein, LA, 2002—. Lectr. U. So. Calif., 1980—82, vis. prof. law, 1997, adj. prof., 1999—. Exec. editor: George Washington Law Review, 1975-76. Inst. for Pub. Interest Representation Law fellow Georgetown U. Law Ctr., 1977-78. Mem. Phi Beta Kappa, Order of the Coif. E-mail: mborenstein@overlandborenstein.com.

BORENSTINE, ALVIN JEROME, search company executive; b. Kansas City, Mo., Dec. 14, 1933; s. Samuel and Ella C. (Berman) B.; m. Roula Alakiotou, Dec. 31, 1976; children: Mana an dSami (twins). BS in Econs., U. Kans., 1956; MBA, U. Pa., 1960. Analyst Johnson & Johnson, New Brunswick, N.J., 1961-62; systems mgr. Levitt & Sons, Levittown, N.J., 1962-66; dir. mgmt. info. svcs. Warren Bros. Co., Cambridge, Mass., 1966-71; mgr. fin. & adminstrv. systems Esmark, Inc., Chgo., 1971-72; pres. Synergistics Assocs. Ltd., Chgo., 1972—. Mem. bus. adv. coun. Program Able, Hellenic Dimensions; mem. civic com. El Valor; mem. North Shore Cultural Ctr. Sys. and Procedures Assn. Systems and Procedures Assn. rsch. fellow, 1959-60, Eddie JAcobson Found. scholar, 1958-60. Mem.: Soc. Info. Mgmt., Assn. Sys. Mgmt. (pres Boston chpt. 1969, Disting. award 1970), Assn. Exec. Search Cons., B'nai B'rith, Carlton Club (mem. exec. svc. corps.). Home: 6033 N Sheridan Rd Chicago IL 60660-3003 Office: Synergistics Assocs Ltd 400 N State St Ste 400 Chicago IL 60610-4624 Home Phone: 773-784-4417. Personal E-mail: ajbsynerg@aol.com.

BORER, JEFFREY STEPHEN, cardiologist; b. Deland, Fla., Feb. 22, 1945; s. Lee Norton and Rita Doris (Feldt) B.; m. Brondi Beth Topchik, Sept. 16, 1978; children: Justine Isolde, Jon Andrew. BA in Govt., Harvard U., 1965; MD, Cornell U., 1969. Diplomate Am. Bd. Internal Medicine, Am. Bd. Cardiovascular Disease; cert. Bd. Nuclear Cardiology. Intern, then resident in medicine Mass. Gen. Hosp., Boston, 1969—71; clin. fellow in medicine Harvard U. Sch. Medicine, Boston, 1969—71; clin. assoc. in cardiology Nat. Heart, Lung and Blood Inst., NIH, Bethesda, Md., 1971—74, chief resident physician, 1973—74, sr. investigator, cardiology br., 1975—79; sr. Fulbright-Hays scholar, Glorney-Raisbeck fellow med. scis Guy's Hosp., U. London, 1974—75; assoc. prof. medicine Cornell U. Med. Coll., NYC, 1979—82, prof., 1982—, Gladys and Roland Harriman prof. cardiovascular medicine, 1983—, prof. cardiovascular med. in radiology, 1990—, prof. cardiovascular medicine in cardiothoracic surgery, 1996—; chief cardiovascular pathophysiology NY Hosp./Cornell Med. Ctr., 1996—; dir. Howard Gilman Inst. for Valvular Heart Diseases Weill Med. Coll. Cornell U., 2000—. Chmn. cardiac and renal adv. com. FDA, Washington, 1981—82, 1983—87, 2001—04, cons., 1989—2000, 2004—, mem., 1977—87, 1999—2004, guest mem. Circulatory Devices Adv. Com., 2003—; mem. life scis. adv. com. NASA, Washington, 1984—88, mem. aero. med. adv. com., 1993—96, life and microgravity scis. and application adv. com., 1996—2001, biol. and phys. rsch. adv. com., 2001—05; chmn. NASA/Mir Peer Rev. adv. com., 1993—95, NASA-NIH Biomed. and Behavioral Rsch. adv. com., 1995—2003; mem. NASA Adv. Coun., 1995—99; vis. prof. Chinese Acad. Med. Scis., Beijing, 1993; chief divsn. cardiovascular pathophysiology NY Hosp.-Cornell Med. Ctr., 1996—. Author 4 books; editor-in-chief Advances in Cardiology, 2001—, Cardiology, 2005-; mem. editl. bds. 11 med. jours.; contbr. more than 350 articles on cardiovascular disease to med. jours.; patentee in field. Sr. surgeon USPHS, 1971—79; trustee NYC Historic Properties Fund, 1984—90; mem. steering com. Assocs. of the Jewish Bd. of Family and Children Svcs., 1989—91; pres. Am. Friends of Israel Nat. Heart to Heart Assn., 1991—2004; adv. com. The NY Pub. Library Dance Collection, 1999—; bd. trustees Glorney Found., 2001—; pres. Corlette Glorney Found., 2004—. Named Thomas W. Smith Meml. lectr., 7th World Cong. on Heart Failure, 2000; recipient Investigator's award prize, European Cardiol. Soc., 1978, spl. award contbns. to cardiology, Assn. Thoracic and Cardiovascular Surgeons of India, 1985, Wiliam A. Johnston award, Internat. Soc. Heart Rsch., 1986, spl. citation contbn. to Mir program, NASA, 1997, Pub. Svc. medal, 1999, Hans-Peter Krayenbeuhl Meml. award, Internat. Acad. Cardiology, 2002; travelling fellow, Am. Physicians Fellowship, 1981, Disting. fellow, Internat. Acad. Cardiol., 2005. Fellow: ACP, NY Cardiol. Soc. (pres. 1990—91), Am. Coll. Chest Physicians (chmn. cardiology forum 1985—86, exec. com. clin. cardiology sect. 1991—95), Am. Heart Assn. (established investigator 1979—84, coun. clin. cardiology and circulation), Argentine Heart Assn. (hon.), Am. Soc. Clin. Investigation, Am. Coll. Cardiology (governing coun. NY chpt. 1991—93, pres. NY State chpt. 1997—98, gov. 1997—2000, bd. govs. 1998—2000, bd. govs. task force on cardiovasc. econs. 1999—2000, steering com., chmn.); mem.: Heart Valve Soc. Am. (pres. 2004—), Cert. Bd. Nuc. Cardiology (bd. trustees 1996—2002, chmn. com. due process and appeals 2002—04), Am. Soc. Nuc. Cardiology (fin. com. 1995—95), Soc. Cardiac Angiography and Interventions (gov. 1995—2000), Soc. Nuc. Medicine (trustee cardiovasc. coun. 1991—94), Harvard Club NYC. Avocations: sports, theater, opera, calligraphy, history. Office: NY Presbyn Hosp Weill Cornell Med Ctr 525 E 68th St New York NY 10021-4885 Office Phone: 212-746-4646.

BORESI, ARTHUR PETER, writer, educator; b. Toluca, Ill. s. John Peter and Eva Boresi; m. Clara Jean Gordon, Dec. 28, 1946; children: Jennifer Ann Boresi Hill, Annette Boresi Pueschel, Nancy Jean Boresi Broderick. Student, Kenyon Coll., 1943—44; BSEE, U. Ill., 1948, MS in Mechanics, 1949, PhD in Mechanics, 1953. Research engr. N. Am. Aviation, 1950; materials engr. Nat. Bur. Standards, 1951; mem. faculty U. Ill., Urbana, 1953—, prof. theoretical and applied mechanics and nuclear engring., 1959-79; prof. emeritus U. Ill. at Urbana, Urbana, 1979; Disting. vis. prof. Clarkson Coll. Tech., Potsdam, NY, 1968-69; NAVSEA research prof. Naval Postgrad. Sch., Monterey, Calif., 1978-79; prof. civil engring. U. Wyo., Laramie, 1979-95, head, 1980-94, prof. emeritus, 1995—. Vis. prof. Naval Postgrad. Sch., Monterey, Calif., 1986—87; cons. in field. Author: Approximate Solution Methods in Engineering Mechanics, 1991, 2d edit., 2002, Elasticity in Engineering Mechanics, 4th edit., 2000, Engineering Mechanics: Statics, 2001, Engineering Mechanics: Dynamics, 2001, Advanced Mechanics of Materials, 6th edit., 2002; contbr. articles to profl. jours. With USAAF, 1943—44, with US Army, 1944—46. Fellow: ASCE, ASME, Am. Acad. Mechanics (founding, treas.); mem.: Am. Soc. Engring. Edn. (Archie Higdon Disting. Educator award 1993). Office: 3310 Willett Dr Laramie WY 82072 Business E-Mail: boresi@uwyo.edu.

BORESI, JOY SUZANNE, pharmacist; b. Breeze, Ill., Sept. 28, 1975; d. Ronald A. and Kathleen F. Venhaus; m. Michael J. Boresi, Sept. 2, 2000. BS in Pharmacy, St. Louis Coll. Pharmacy, 1998, PhD in Pharmacy, 1999. Registered pharmacist Mo., cert. pharmacotherapy specialist Bd. Pharm. Specialties. Pharmacy resident Veterans Affairs Medical Ctr., Cleve., 1999—2000, clin. pharmacy specialist, 2000—02, St. Louis, 2003—; asst. prof. pharmacy St. Louis Coll. Pharmacy, 2002—03. Adj. prof. pharmacy U. Toledo Coll. Pharmacy, 2000—02. Mem.: Gateway Coll. Clin. Pharmacy, Am. Coll. Clinical Pharmacy. Avocations: reading, swimming.

BORETZ, NAOMI MESSINGER, artist, educator; b. Bklyn. BA, Bklyn. Coll.; MA in Fine Arts, CUNY; MA in Art History, Rutgers U.; postgrad., Art Students League N.Y. Exhibitions include Westminster Arts Coun. Arts Ctr., London, 1971, Hudson River Mus., N.Y., 1975, Katonah Gallery, 1976, Condeso-Lawler Gallery, N.Y.C., 1987, Carnegie-Mellon Art Gallery, Pitts., 1989, The Nelson Atkins Mus. of Art, St. Louis, 1994, Westbeth Gallery, N.Y., 1996, Mishkin Gallery, Baruch Coll., 1997, Rutgers (N.J.) U. Art Gallery, 1998, Hillwood Art Mus., N.Y., 2000, Muhlenburg Coll. Art Gallery, 2002, others, Represented in permanent collections Met. Mus. Art, NYC, Solomon R. Guggenheim Mus., Whitney Mus. Am. Art, Mus. Modern Art, DeLand Art Mus., Fla., Brit. Mus., London, Nat. Mus. Am. Art, Washington, Yale U. Art Gallery, Joslyn Art Mus., Omaha, Walker Art Ctr., Mpls., Miami U. Art Mus., Oxford, Ohio, Fogg Art Mus. Harvard U., Cambridge, Mass., Glasgow (Scotland) Mus., San Jose (Calif.) Art Mus., Asheville (N.C.) Art Mus., Princeton U. Graphic Arts Collection, N.J., Mus. S.W., Midland, Tex., Swope Art Mus., Terre Haute, Ind., others; contbr. to arts publs. Artist-fellow Va. Ctr. Creative Arts, 1973, 86, Ossabaw Found., 1975, Tyrone Guthrie Arts Ctr., Ireland, 1987, Writers-Artists Guild Can., 1988; grantee N.J. State Coun. on Arts, 1985-86. Studio: Princeton NJ

BORG, JOSEPH PHILIP, securities association administrator, lawyer; b. NYC, Nov. 20, 1952; s. Philip Joseph and Dorothy Ann (Chircop) B.; 1 child, Chelly. BS in Polit. Sci., CCNY, 1974; JD, Hofstra U., 1977. Bar: N.Y. 1978, Ala. 1978, Fla. 1979, U.S. Dist. Ct. (no. dist.) Ala., U.S. Dist. Ct. (mid. dist.) Ala., U.S. Dist. Ct. (no. dist.) Fla., U.S. Dist. Ct. (mid. dist.) Fla., U.S. Ct. Appeals (5th cir.), U.S. Ct. Appeals (11th cir.), U.S. Supreme Ct. Asst. corp. counsel Hagan Industries, Inc., Montgomery, Ala., 1977-79;

corp. counsel, legal officer First Ala. Bank of Montgomery, 1979-85; ptnr. Capouano, Wampold, Prestwood & Sansone, P.A., Montgomery, 1985-94; dir. Ala. Securities Commn., Montgomery, Ala., 1994—. Adj. prof. law uniform comml. code Faulkner U., 1982-2002; lectr. Jones Bar Review Course, Ala. Continuing Ed. Program. Bd. dirs. Consumer Credit Counseling Svc. of Ala., Inc., 1981-85, pres. , 1982-84; bd. dirs. Ala. Youth Found., 1982-85, programs chmn., 1983-84. Mem. ABA, N.Y. State Bar Assn., Ala. State Bar Assn., Fla. State Bar Assn., Am. Trial Lawyers Assn., N.Y. Trial Lawyers Assn., Montgomery County Bar Assn., Montgomery County Trial Lawyers Assn., Montgomery County Young Lawyers Assn. (sec. 1984, v.p. 1985), N. Am. Securities Administrators Assn., Inc. (pres., 2001-02, 2006-)N.Y. Acad. Sci. Office: N Am Securities Administrators Assn Inc 750 First St NE Ste 1140 Washington DC 20002

BORG, MALCOLM AUSTIN, publishing executive; b. NYC, Jan. 28, 1938; s. Donald Gowen and Flora (Austin) B.; m. Sandra Jean Agemian, Sept. 9, 1961; children— John Austin, Jennifer Ann, Stephen Agemian. BS, Columbia U., 1965; postgrad., Harvard Bus. Sch., 1970; LHD (hon.), Ramapo Coll., NJ, 1985, Fairleigh Dickinson U., 2005. Editl. trainee The Record, Hackensack, NJ, 1959-60, gen. assignment reporter, 1960-62, adminstrv. asst. to pub., 1963-64, asst. pub., 1965-66, v.p., 1967-68, exec. v.p., 1968-70, pres., 1971-78, CEO, 1971—, chmn. bd., 1975—; chmn., CEO North Jersey Media Group, Inc. (including previous co. names), 1971—. Active numerous civic orgns., 1965—; bd. dirs. Wolfeboro (N.H.) Camp Sch., 1970—; mem. Palisades Interstate Park Commn., 1974-2005; chmn. Submarine Meml. Assn., Hackensack, 1974—; mem. adv. bd. Sch. Gen. Studies, Columbia U., 1981—, chmn. 1997—, mem. nat. campaign com. Fund for Columbia, 1983-87, 92-98, mem. alumni adv. bd., 1987-95. Recipient 1st William H. Spurgeon III award Bergen council Boy Scouts Am., 1972, 1st Whitney M. Young award, 1986; Torch of Liberty award Anti-Defamation League, B'nai B'rith, 1973, ann. communications and leadership award Greater N.Y. dist. 46 Toastmasters Internat., 1976, Service to Others award N.J. div. Salvation Army, 1977, ann. community leadership award NO. N.J. Interprofl. Council, 1977, Man of Yr. award Holy Name Hosp., 1977, Editor of Yr. award Nat. Press Photographers Assn., 1985, Owl award Sch. Gen. Studies, Columbia U., 1986, Citizen's award Acad. Medicine N.J., 1986; Alumni Fedn. medal Columbia U., 1991. Mem. Newspaper Assn. Am., Am. Soc. Newspaper Editors, N.J. Press. Assn., Bergen County C. of C. (bd. dirs. 1967-74), N.J. C. of C. (bd. dirs. 1977-79), Hill Sch. Alumni Assn. (pres. 1973-76, trustee 1984-89), Advt. Coun. (bd. dirs. 1978-85), Harvard Bus. Sch. Alumni Assn. (pres. 1976-78), N.J. Srs. Golf Assn., Arcola Country Club (Paramus, N.J.), Columbia Club (N.Y.C.), Englewood Field (N.J.) Club, Mid Ocean Club (Tucker's Town, Bermuda), Harvard Club (N.Y.C.), Bath and Tennis Club (Spring Lake, N.J.), Knickerbocker Country Club (Tenafly, N.J.), Manasquan River Golf Club (Brielle, N.J.), Moselem Springs Golf Club (Fleetwood, Pa.). Avocations: golf, travel. Office: North Jersey Media Group Inc 150 River St Hackensack NJ 07601-7172 Business E-Mail: mac@northjersey.com.

BORG, ROBERT FREDERIC, civil engineer; b. NYC, Jan. 10, 1923; s. Herman Leo and Pauline (Leibman); children: Christina Borg-Gordon, Lisa Borg-Broe, Eric (dec.), Kiri Borg-Henry, Neil (dec.), Dean. B in Civil Engring., NYU, 1944, JD, 1949. Bar: N.Y. 1950; lic. profl. engr., N.Y., 1950. Co-founder, ptnr., founding chmn. Kreisler Borg Florman Gen. Construction Co. & affiliates, Scarsdale, NY, 1955—; co-founder Kensico Construction Co., Scarsdale, 1957, pres., 1966—. Mem. bldg. rsch. adv. bd. Nat. Acad. Engring., Washington, 1963; adj. prof. NYU, 1971-79, Pratt Inst., Bklyn., 1983-86, Columbia U., N.Y.C., 1987-90; mem. US/USSR joint com. on coop. in housing and other forms construction U.S. Dept. Housing and Urban Devel., Washington, 1976-87; mem. Sino-US Trade Delegation to China, 1993. Author (contbg.): (handbook) Building Design and Construction, 1999, Construction Project Management, Temporary Structures in Construction, 1996, Technical and Business Practices; editor (photo): (newspaper) Clinton News, 1940; editor-in-chief (mag.) Quadrangle, NYU Coll. of Engring., 1943; exhibitions include in photography in various locations, 1980—2005, Gallery Show in Soho, N.Y.C., 1985, Show on Cuba, Scarsdale, N.Y., 2001, Show on World Trade Ctr., 2005, Scarsdale Libr., 2004, 2005, Mexico, San Miguel de Allende Then and Now, 2005, Brazil: Salvador da Bahia, 2006, Brazil Carnival, Mardi Gras, 2007, exhibitions include website robertfborg.com. Chmn., founder Garth Woods Conservancy, Scarsdale, N.Y., 1991— co-developer, ptnr. Bethune Tower Apts., N.Y.C., 1970, Heywood Tower Apts., 1972, Univ. Riverview Apts., 1973, Cooper Gramercy Apts., 1975, Marcus Garvey Park Village, 1976, Cove Club Apts., 1992. Served with USN, 1944-46. Finalist Entrepreneur of the Yr. award, So. New Eng., 1996, 1997, 1998, Entrepreneur of the Yr. Inst.; recipient Outstanding Builder Developer award, Associated Builders and Owners Greater N.Y., 1989—90, 1991, Builder of Yr. award, 1996, Emma Lazarus award, 1997, Disting. Alumni Recognition award, DeWitt Clinton H.S., 2001. Fellow: ASCE (mem. com. on contract administrn. 1952, founder, 1st chmn. constrn. group met. sect. 1962, met. sect. bd. dirs. 1962—67, chmn. tech. activities met. sect. 1963, mem. com. on contract administrn. 1963—67, mem. exec. com. nat. constrn. divsn. 1971, chmn., exec. com. nat. constrn. divsn. 1973—74, chmn. com. on social and environ. concerns in constrn. 2001—, master builder, constrn. Inst. ASCE 2003), Am. Arbitration Assn. (mem. nat. panel arbitrators 1957—2006, mem. nat. constrn. industry arbitration com. 1972—2005, chmn. 1974—76, nat. bd. dirs. 1974—84). Office: Kreisler Borg Florman Gen Constrn Co 97 Montgomery St Scarsdale NY 10583-5104 Office Phone: 914-725-4600. Office Fax: 914-725-0346.

BORG, RUTH I., home nursing care provider; d. Axel Gunner and Charlotte (Benston) B. Diploma, West Suburban Sch. Nursing, 1956; tchr.'s degree, Chgo. Conservatory, 1958; BSN, Alverno Coll., 1981. Staff nurse Boath Meml. Hosp., Chgo.; head nurse psychiatry, head nurse long-term medicine VA North Chgo. Med. Ctr.; staff nurse, night supr. intermediate care VA Clement Zabiocki Med. Ctr., Milw.; pool nurse, in-home nursing care provider Milw. County Mental Health Complex; home nurse care provider Dr. Ghonsham Sooknandan, Kenosha, Wis., 1994—99. In-home nursing care provider. Contbr. articles to profl. jours. Recipient Mary D. Bradford Disting. Alumni award, 1998. Mem.: Wis. Nurses Assn. (nominations com.). Avocation: teaching and performing music. Home Phone: 262-652-3281.

BORGATTA, EDGAR F., sociologist, educator; b. Milan, Sept. 1, 1924; came to U.S., 1929, naturalized, 1934; s. Edgar A. and Frances (Zinelli) B.; m. Marie Lentini, Oct. 5, 1946; children: Lynn, Kim, Lee. BA, NYU, 1947, MA, 1949, PhD, 1952. Cert. psychologist, N.Y., Vt., Wis. Instr. NYU, 1949-51, lectr., prof., 1954-59; lectr., rsch. assoc. Harvard U., 1951-54; social psychologist, asst. sec. Russell Sage Found., 1954-59; prof. sociology Cornell U., Ithaca, NY, 1959-61; Brittingham rsch. prof. U. Wis., Madison, 1961-72, chmn. dept. sociology, 1962-65, chmn. divsn. social studies, 1965-68; disting. prof. sociology Queens Coll., CUNY, 1972-77, prof Grad. Ctr., 1972-82, dir. Italian Social Sci. Ctr., 1972-77; rsch. CUNY Case Ctr. for Gerontol. Studies, 1978-81, dir. data svc., 1981-82; prof. sociology U. Wash., Seattle, 1981—93, chmn. dept., 1992—93, prof. emeritus, 1994—; dir Inst. on Aging U. Wash., Seattle, 1981-86. Cons. to bus. and govt., 1953-, Russell Sage Found., 1970-72; lectr., prof., adj. prof. sociology NYU, 1954-59; cons. editor Rand McNally & Co., 1961-74; chmn. bd. F.E. Peacock Pubs., Inc.; Nat. Inst. Gen. Scis.; spl. rsch. fellow, 1972. Editor: Research on Aging, Sociol. Methodology, Sociol. Methods and Research; co-editor: Handbook of Personality Theory and Research; editor-in-chief: Encyclopedia of Sociology, 2d edit.; contbr. articles to profl. jours. Fellow Am. Psychol. Assn., Am. Psychol. Soc.; mem. Psychometric Soc., Sociol. Rsch. Assn., Am. Sociol. Assn. (v.p. 1983), Pacific Sociol. Assn. (pres. 1985), Internat. Inst. Sociology (pres. 1984-89). Office: U Wash Dept Sociology c/o 98 Union St #608 Seattle WA 98101 Office Phone: 206-622-9158. Personal E-mail: efborgat@att.net.

BORGEN, PATRICK IVAN, surgeon; b. Minot, ND, Jan. 7, 1958; s. Ivan M. and Patricia Ann (Padrnoss) B.; m. Elizabeth Claire, Apr. 25, 1987; children: Emily, Charlotte, Patrick, Slater. BS in Biomedical Engring., Tulane U., New Orleans, 1980; MD, La. State U. Med. Sch., 1984. Cert. Surgery, Breast Surgery. Residency Ochsner Clinic, New Orleans, 1984-89; fellow Meml. Sloan-Kettering Cancer Ctr., NYC, 1989-91, attending surgeon, 1991—2006, dir. Breast Cancer Rsch. Lab., 1992, chief breast cancer divsn., dept. surgery, 1994—2006; dir., breast surgery Maimonides Med. Ctr., Bklyn., 2006—; assoc. dir. for breast surgery Maimonides Cancer Ctr., Bklyn., 2006—. Rep. Breast Cancer Screening Panel, 1998—99; Lawson Meml. vis. prof. East Tenn. State U., 2002; mem. steering com. Nat. Surgical Adjuvant Breast and Bowel Project; spkr. in field. Contbr. articles to profl. jours.; mem. editl. bd. Annals Surgical Oncology, 1999-2002; mem. peer-review bd. Journal AMA, 2000-; guest editor Surgery, 2003-, Annals of Surgery, 2003-, Journal ACS, 2003-, Breast Diseases, 2003-, Breast Diseases Quarterly, 2003-, Breast Journal, 2003-, Lancet, 2003-, Archives Surgery, 2003-, Journal Clinical Oncology, 2003-; guest (syndicated radio talk show) Lisa Birnbach Show. Named one of Best Doctors in NY, NY Mag., 1995—2003; Jarrell Meml. Traveling Fellowship award, ACS, 1989, 1998 Found. Fellow, Royal Australasian Coll. Surgeons, Sydney, Australia. Mem.: Am. Soc. for the Study of Breast Diseases (bd. dir.), Tulane Alumni Assn., Am. Soc. Breast Disease, Soc. Tulane Engineers, Soc. Surgical Oncology (chmn., corp. rels. com. 1998—99), NY Metropolitan Breast Cancer Group, Meml. Sloan-Kettering Cancer Ctr. Alumni Found., Am. Surgical Assn., Am. Soc. Clin. Oncology, Am. Assn. Cancer Educators, AAAS. Office: Maimonides Med Ctr 6300 Eighth Ave Brooklyn NY 11220 Office Fax: 718-765-2570, 718-765-2574. E-mail: Pborgen@maimonidesmed.org.*

BORGER, JOHN PHILIP, lawyer; b. Wilmington, Del., Apr. 19, 1951; s. Philip E. and Jane (Smyth) B.; m. Judith Marie Yates, May 24, 1974; children: Jennifer, Christopher, Nicholas. BA in Journalism with high honors, Mich. State U., 1973; JD, Yale Law Sch., 1976. Bar: Minn. 1976, U.S. Dist. Ct. Minn. 1976, U.S. Ct. Appeals (8th cir.) 1979, U.S. Supreme Ct. 1983, N.D. 1988, U.S. Dist. Ct. N.D. 1988, Wis. 1993. Editor-in-chief Mich. State News, East Lansing, 1972-73; assoc. Faegre & Benson, LLP, Mpls., 1976-83, ptnr., 1984—. Bd. dirs. Milkweed Edits., 1995-01; adj. prof. U. Minn. Sch. Journalism and Mass Comm., 1999. Contbr. articles to profl. jours. Named to State News Hall of Fame, Mich. State U., 2007; recipient Freedom of Info. award, Minn. Soc. Profl. Journalists, 2002, First Amendment Award, St. Cloud State U. Dept. Mass. Comms., 2001. Mem. ABA (chmn. media law and defamation torts com. torts and ins. practice sect. 1996-97), Minn. Bar Assn., State Bar Assn. N.D., Wis. Bar Assn., Hennepin County Bar Assn. Office: Faegre & Benson LLP 2200 Wells Fargo Ctr 90 S 7th St Ste 2200 Minneapolis MN 55402-3901 Office Phone: 612-766-7501. Business E-Mail: jborger@faegre.com.

BORGES, FRANCISCO LOPES, venture capitalist; b. Santiago, Cape Verde Islands, Nov. 17, 1951; s. Manuel L. and Maria (Lopes) B. BA, Trinity Coll., 1974; JD, U. Conn., 1978. Bar: Conn. 1979, N.J. 1979. Coun. mem. City of Hartford, Conn., 1981-85, dep. mayor Conn., 1983-85; treas. State of Conn., Hartford, 1989-93; man. dir. of pub. fin. Financial Guaranty Ins. Co., 1993-95; man. dir. FGIC govt. svcs. GE Capital Svcs., Inc., 1995; chmn., ptnr. Landmark Partners, Inc., Simsbury, Conn. Commr. Met. Dist. Commn., Hartford, 1981—; assoc. counsel Travelers Ins. Co., Hartford, 1983; bd. dir. NAACP. Trustee Millbrook (N.Y.) Sch., 1979—; corporator St. Francis Hosp., Hartford, 1981—; vice chmn. steering com. Jr. PTA Hartford, 1984—; active U. Conn. Health Ctr. Adv. Coun., Farmington, 1982—; vice chmn. Capitol Region Coun. Govts., Hartford, 1984—; dir. Hartford Ballet Co., 1985—. Mem. Conn. Bar Assn. Democrat. Office: Landmark Partners Inc 10 Mill Pond Ln Simsbury CT 06070

BORGES, FREDRICK MARIO, lawyer; b. Covina, Calif., Nov. 3, 1960; s. Vincent and Rose Borges. BA, Calif. State U., Fullerton, 1983; JD, Western State U., 1991. Bar: Calif. 1992. Mng. ptnr. Borges, Lauridsen & Sturm, Santa Ana, Calif., 1999—2000; gen. counsel Gateway Med. Group and Pinnacle Health Resources, Anaheim, 1999—2004; ptnr. Beam, Brobeck & West, Santa Ana, 2000—06; sr. ptnr. Beam, Brobeck, West, Borges & Rosa, Santa Ana, Calif., 2006—; regional counsel Concentra Health Svcs., 2000—. Arbitrator, Calif., 1993—. Contbr. articles to profl. jours. Mem.: ABA, Orange County Bar Assn., Am. Health Lawyers Assn. Avocations: stained glass, golf, drums. Office: Beam Brobeck West Borges & Rosa 600 W Santa Ana Blvd Ste 1000 Santa Ana CA 92701 Office Phone: 714-558-3944.

BORGES, WILLIAM, III, management consultant; b. Long Beach, Calif., Nov. 21, 1948; s. William Borges, Jr. and Dorothy Mae (Raymond) Morris; m. Rosalind Denise Marye, Nov. 23, 1968; children: William IV, Blake Austin. BA in Geography, Sonoma State U., Calif., 1973; MBA, U. Phoenix, 1997. Environ. planner Mendocino County Planning Dept., Ukiah, Calif., 1976; project mgr. Engring. Sci., Inc., Berkeley, Calif., 1976-79, Santa Clara County Planning Dept., San Jose, Calif., 1979-81, Internat. Tech. Corp., San Jose, 1985-88; mgr. sales ops. Adac Labs., Milpitas, Calif., 1983-85; prin. WT Environ. Cons., Phoenix, 1988-91; project mgr. Dynamac Corp., Newport Beach, Calif., 1991-93; prin. environ. scientist Midwest Rsch. Inst., Scottsdale, Ariz., 1993-96; gen. mgr. Fitness Care, Inc., Yorba Linda, Calif., 2000—02; bus. process analyst Renown Health, Reno, 2002—07; prin. Eclipse Corp. Devel., Reno, 2007—. Adj. faculty U. Phoenix, Reno, 2003—. Contbr. photographs to mags. Coord. pub. rels. Stellar Acad. Dyslexics, Fremont, Calif., 1988; sr. examiner Nev. Govs. Award Performance Excellence, 2005. With MI US Army, 1967—70. Mem.: Kingsmen Alumni Drum and Bugle Corps., Mensa. Avocations: photography, travel. Personal E-mail: wborges3@clearwire.net.

BORGES-NETO, SALVADOR, radiologist, cardiologist, educator; b. Santa Catarina, Brazil, Aug. 5, 1957; s. Salvador Borges-Filho and Onezir Borges; m. Ana Carvalho, Oct. 22, 1983; children: Nina Borges, Nicholas Borges. BS, Ctr. Ednl. de Niteroi, 1975; MD, U. Fed. Fluminense, Brazil, 1981. Lic. N.C. Med. Bd., 1994. Intern medicine Antonio Pedro U. Hosp., Rio de Janeiro, 1981—82, cardiology tng fellow, 1982—84; rsch fellow medicine cardiovascular divsn. Brigham and Women's Hosp. Harvard Med. Sch., Boston, 1984—85; rsch. fellow cardiology Baylor Coll. Medicine, Houston, 1986; rsch. fellow nuclear cardiology Duke U. Med. Ctr., Durham, NC, 1988—91, nuclear medicine resident, 1992—93; dir. nuc. cardiology Med. Ctr. Duke U., Durham, NC, 2002—, assoc. prof. radiology and medicine Med. Ctr., 2002—. Recipient Young Investigators award, 1992, Tchg. award, Duke U. Dept. Radiology, 1996. Fellow: Am. Coll. Nuclear Physicians, Am. Coll. Cardiology; mem.: Am. Heart Assn., Am. Soc. Nuclear Cardiology (adv. bd.), Am. Soc. Nuclear Cardiology Tng. and Credential Com., Soc. Nuc. Medicine (pres. cardiovasc. coun. 2002—03, mem. cardiovasc. coun. 2006—). Achievements include research in diagnostic cardiac imaging protocols with the use of radionuclides. Office: Duke University Medical Center PO Box 3949 Durham NC 27710 Home Phone: 919-403-6221; Office Phone: 919-684-7857. Office Fax: 919-684-7123; Home Fax: 919-403-6221. Business E-Mail: borge001@mc.duke.edu.

BORGESON, EARL CHARLES, law librarian, educator; b. Boyd, Minn., Dec. 2, 1922; s. Hjalmer Nicarner and Doris (Danielson) Borgeson; m. Barbara Ann Jones, Sept. 21, 1944; children: Barbara Gale, Geoffrey Charles, Steven Earl. BS in Law, U. Minn., 1947, LLB, 1949; BA in Law Librarianship, U. Wash., 1950. Libr. Harvard U. Law Sch. Libr, 1952—70; assoc. dir. Stanford U. Librs., 1970—75; assoc. law libr. LA County Law Libr., Calif., 1975—78; prof., law libr. So. Meth. U., Dallas, 1978—88, prof. law emeritus, 1988—. Lectr. UCLA, 1975—78; adj. prof. Tex. Women's U., 1979—80, U. North Tex., Denton, Tex., 1988—90; libr. AccuFile, Inc., 1992—2001; cons. in field. With USNR, 1943—46. Mem.: Am. Assn. Law Librs. Home: 161 Washington St Sherborn MA 01770

BORGHEI, PEYMAN, medical researcher; b. Tehran, Iran, Aug. 31, 1976; s. Parvindokht Sokhandan and Hebatodin Borghei. MD, Tehran U. Med. Scis., 2003. Diplomate Tehran. Internship Tehran U. Med. Scis., 2000—03, rschr. Amir-Alam Hosp., 2000—05; rschr. U. Calif. Med. Ctr., Orange, 2005—. Recipient Best Poster Presentation, LA Radiol. Soc., 2006; scholar, U. Calif. Irvine Med. Ctr., 2005. Mem.: Internat. Doping Orgn. Achievements include research in MRI in bone marrow disorders; another procedure is recommended instead of invasipre-operative embolization for the resectn of nasopharyngeal angiofibroma for the first time; each stage of the nasopharyngeal angiofibroma, the best surgical approach is recommended; outcome of patients who recieved cohlear implant is dicussed; radiological manifestations of the teratoma of temporal bone is discussed. Home: 32 Weatherby Dr Greenville SC 29615 Office: U Calif Med Ctr 101 The City Dr Orange CA 92868 Personal E-mail: brpayman@yahoo.com.

BORGMAN, GEORGE ALLAN, journalist; b. St. Louis, Jan. 22, 1928; s. Herman Francis and Martha Vivien (Wecker) B.; m. Janet Claire Ferroli, Feb. 27, 1957; children: Carole Elaine (dec.), Paul Allan, Eric Bruno; 1 child by previous marriage, Andrea Vivien Hancock (dec.). Student, U. Mo., 1945-46, 48; MusB in Music History and Lit., St. Louis Inst. Music, 1952; MusM in Musicology, Ind. U., Bloomington, 1953. Cert. in TV Prod. Sch. Radio Tech., NY, 1957. Musician dance bands various locations, 1945-46, 48-50; enlisted bandsman U.S. Army, 1946-48, spl. agent mil. intelligence, 1958-79, advanced through grades to chief warrant officer 3, 1971, ret., 1979; music educator various sch. systems in Colo. and Nev., 1953-57; freelance asst. cinematographer NYC, 1957-58; film editor, TV cameraman Sta. KOMU, Columbia, Mo., 1958; investigator Wackenhut Corp., Boston, 1980-81; personnel security specialist (civilian) U.S. Army, Alexandria, Va., 1981-85; sportswriter Suburban World (newspapers), Needham, Mass., 1988-94; freelance jazz writer, 1988—; New England corr. and jazz writer T-J Today, 1991-92; corr., photographer, contbg. editor, columnist, reviewer Mississippi Rag, 1991—; record reviewer Cadence Mag., 1994-95; reviewer IAJRC jour., 1995—2000, The Jazz Messenger, 1994-96. Contbr. articles to profl. jours. including Joslin's Jazz Jour.; author: notes on jazz CD's. Musician Met. Wind Symphony, Boston, 1981, Fairfax (Va.) City Band, 1982-83, Canton (Mass.) Mcpl. Band/Am. Legion Band, 1980-81; assoc. mem. Westwood (Mass.) Rep. Com., 1988-89. Rated #12 Favorite Jazz Critic, Jazzbeat, 1995. Mem.: Assn. for Recorded Sound Collections, Starr-Gennett Found., Jazz Journalists Assn., Internat. Assn. Jazz Record Collectors, Disabled Am. Vets., Am. Legion. Republican. Home and Office: 158 Burgess Ave Westwood MA 02090-3010 Personal E-mail: algeob@aol.com.

BORGMAN, SYLVIA, artist, activist; b. Clinton, Iowa, Oct. 10, 1952; d. Bernard and Sien (Frik) B.; m. Peter Siczewicz, Oct. 6, 1978 (div. Apr. 1982). BS in Psychology and Sociology, Ill. State U., 1974. Cert. Women in Politics and Government Boston Coll., 1978. Child and family intake worker Ill. Dept. Child and Family Welfare, Springfield, 1973; youth specialist Sangamon County Juvenile Ct., Springfield, 1974; adminstr. asst. MIT, Cambridge, Mass., 1978; ednl. cons. Chrysler Corp., Detroit, 1980, Am. Internat. Tng., San Rafael, Calif., 1984. Lobbyist women's issues, 1975—; art tchr. Salinas and Prundale, Calif. Exhibited art in various group shows. Creator sexual harrassment legis. Alliance Against Sexual Harrassment, Boston, 1978-79; intern Women's Polit. Caucus, Boston, 1977-79; mental health commr. Monterey County, 2006. Democrat. Avocations: art, music. Home: 2294 N Main St Apt 49 Salinas CA 93906-1529 Personal E-mail: borgmanart@comcast.net.

BORIBOONSOMSIN, KANOK, transportation engineer; arrived in U.S., 2002; s. Somboon and Sudarat Boriboonsomsin; m. Punprapai Ongprasert, Dec. 30, 2005. B in Engring., Chulalongkorn U., Bangkok, Thailand, 1999; M Engring. in Infrastructure Engring., Asian Inst. Tech., Pathumthani, Thailand, 2001; PhD in Transp. Engring., U. Miss., Oxford, 2004. Engr. in tng., Calif. Civil engr. Petroleum Authority Thailand, Patun, Chonburi, 2001; rsch. asst. Ctr. Advanced Infrastructure Tech., Oxford, Miss., 2002—04; vis. asst. prof. Ohio No. U., Ada, 2004—05; asst. rsch. engr. Ctr. Environ. Rsch. and Tech., Riverside, Calif., 2005—. Transp. analyst TEMS, Inc., Frederick, Md., 2005. Contbr. articles to profl. jours. (Best paper award Internat. Symposium on Pavement Recycling, 05). Recipient P3 award, US EPA, 2006; fellow, U. Miss., 2004; grantee, Calif. Air Resources Bd., 2007; scholar, Asian Inst. Tech., 1999, Air and Waste Mgmt. Assn., Miss. Chpt., 2003; Rsch. grantee, Ohio Dept. Transp., 2004, Rsch. Grantee, Calif. Dept. Transp., 2005, Tchg. grantee, Ohio No. U., 2004, Summer rsch. fellow, U. Miss., 2003. Mem.: ASCE, Inst. Transp. Engrs., Transp. Rsch. Bd., Chi Epsilon, Phi Kappa Phi. Office Phone: 951-781-5792.

BORIE, BERNARD SIMON, JR., retired physicist, educator; b. New Orleans, June 21, 1924; s. Bernard simon and Ruth (Lastrapes) B.; m. Martine Edith Descamps, May 2, 1957 (div. May 1964); children: Kathleen, Fabienne, Marianne. BS, U. S.W. La., Lafayette, 1944; MS, Tulane U., New Orleans, 1949; PhD, MIT, Cambridge, 1956; Fulbright fellow, U. Paris, 1956-57. Rsch. physicist metall. divsn. Oak Ridge Nat. Lab., 1949-53, group leader x-ray diffraction Metals and Ceramics Divsn., 1957-60, head fundamental rsch. sect., 1960-69, sr. scientist, 1969-85; prof. U. Tenn., 1963—; ret. Vis. prof. Cornell U., 1971-72, U. Calif., Berkeley, 1980. Lt. USNR, 1944-45. Fellow AAAS; mem. AIME, Am. Soc. Metals, Am. Crystallographic Assn., Sci. Rsch. Soc. Am. Achievements include research in diffraction effects of thermal motion, x-ray diffraction studies of imperfect solids; order-disorder effects in solid solutions. Home: 13 Brookside Dr Oak Ridge TN 37830-7616 Personal E-mail: bborie2@comcast.net.

BORISLOW, ALAN JEROME, hospital dental department chairman; b. Phila., Sept. 22, 1936; s. Nathan and Thelma (Kuperstein) B.; m. Susan Marcia Cohen, June 25, 1961; children: Lisa Anne Nadel, Steven Mark, Deborah Lynne. Student, Temple U., 1954-57, DDS, 1961; Cert. in Orthodontics, Albert Einstein Med. Ctr., 1967. Diplomate Am. Bd. Orthodontics. Gen. dentist U.S. Army Dental Corp, Ft. Knox, Ky., 1961-63; dental practice assoc. Dr. Leonard Opack, Marcus Hook, Pa., 1963-64; resident in orthodontics Albert Einstein Med. Ctr., Phila., 1964-67; orthodontic practice assoc. Dr. Joseph Bernstein, Havertown, Pa., 1967-68; dir. dental externships Temple U., Phila., 1969-85; pvt. practice orthodontics Doylestown, Pa., 1969-87; orthodontic program dir. Albert Einstein Med. Ctr., Phila., 1978—, chmn. Maxwell S. Fogel Dept. of Dental Medicine, 1980—. Clin. assoc. prof. Temple U. Sch. Dentistry, Phila., 1986—; adj. assoc. prof. U. Pa. Sch. Dental Medicine, Phila., 1989—. Co-author: (book) A Tradition of Excellence, 1993; contbr. to the book The Combination Technique, 1972; referee, cons. Am. Jour. Orthodontics and Dentofacial Orthopedics, 1995—. Mem. B'nai Brith Svc. Orgn., Montgomery County, Pa., 1972—; exec. bd. Andorra Valley Civic Assn., Whitemarsh Twp., Pa., 1972-82; mem. Citizens Coun., Whitemarsh Twp., 1974-2000; mem. Residents Assn., Whitemarsh Twp., 2001-; bd. dirs. Greater Phila. Health Care Congress, 1991—2004. Recipient Outstanding Resident award Albert Einstein Med. Ctr., 1967, Maimonides Soc. honoree, 2001, Disting. alumnus award Temple U. Dental Alumni Soc., 1994, Physician Leadership award, Albert Einstein Soc., 2002; inducted into Hall of Fame Greater Phila. Health Care Congress, 2001. Fellow Am. Assn. Hosp. Dentists, Am. Coll. Dentists, Internat. Coll. Dentists; mem. Am. Dental Assn., Am. Assn. Orthodontists, Temple U. Dental Alumni Soc. (bd. dirs. 1990—2004), Am. Dental Edn. Assn. Democrat. Avocations: photography, architecture, gardening. Office: Albert Einstein Med Ctr 5501 Old York Rd Philadelphia PA 19141-3018 Personal E-mail: borisloa@einstein.edu.

BORISOFF, RICHARD STUART, lawyer; b. Rochester, NY, May 4, 1945; s. Samuel M. and Ida. B.; m. Risa W. Polgar, Aug. 17, 1967; children: Mindy, Dara. AB, U. Pa., 1967; JD, Columbia U., 1970. Bar: N.Y. 1971, D.C. 1981, U.S. Dist. Ct. (so. dist.) N.Y. 1973, U.S. Ct. Appeals (2nd cir.) 1973. Assoc. Paul, Weiss, Rifkind, Wharton & Garrison, NYC, 1970-78, ptnr., 1978—. Mem.: ABA. Office: Paul Weiss Rifkind Wharton & Garrison LLP Ste 2320 1285 Avenue Of The Americas New York NY 10019-6064 Office Phone: 212-373-3153. Business E-Mail: rborisoff@paulweiss.com.

BORISON, SCOTT CRAIG, lawyer; b. NYC, Feb. 8, 1961; s. E.B. and Joan B. Borison; m. Janet S. Legg, May 22, 1988; children: Ian, Madison. BA in Russian Studies, Fairleigh Dickinson U., 1982; JD, U. Okla., 1987. Bar: Okla. 1987, D.C. 1994, Md. 1995, U.S. Dist. Ct. Md., U.S. Dist. Ct. D.C., U.S. Ct. Appeals (4th and 10th cirs.), U.S. Tax Ct., U.S. Ct. Vets. Appeals. Law clk. Okla. Ct. Appeals, Oklahoma City, 1987-89; counsel Centurion Oil, Inc., Oklahoma City, 1989-93; atty., mem. Legg Law Firm, LLC, Frederick, Md., 1994—. Bd. dirs. Religious Coalition for Emergency Human Needs. Mem. Nat. Assn. Consumer Bankruptcy Attys., Trial Lawyers for Pub. Justice, Frederick County Bar Assn., Bankruptcy Bar Dist. Md. Office: Legg Law Firm LLC 5500 Buckeystown Pike Frederick MD 21703-8331

BORISY, GARY G., molecular biology professor; b. Chgo., Aug. 18, 1942; s. Philip and Mae Borisy; children: Felice, Pippa, Alexis. BS, U. Chgo., 1962, PhD, 1966. Postdoctoral fellow NSF, Cambridge, Eng., 1966-67, NATO, Cambridge, 1967-68; asst. prof. U. Wis., Madison, 1968-72, assoc. prof., 1972-75, prof., 1975-80, Perlman-Bascom prof. life scis., 1980—2000, chmn. lab. molecular biology, 1981—2000; Leslie B. Arey prof. in cell, molecular & anatomical sci. Northwestern U. Feinberg Sch. of Medicine, 2000—, assoc. v.p. rsch., 2003—. Mem. numerous panels NIH and other govt. agys., ACS, HHMI; mem. Marine Biol. Lab. Editor Jour. Biol. Chemistry, 1978-80, Jour. Cell Biology, 1980-82, Internat. Rev. Cytology, 1971-91, Cell Motility and the Cytoskeleton, 1986-94, Jour. Cell Sci., 1988—; contbr. over 200 articles to profl. jours. Recipient Romnes award U. Wis., 1975-80, NIH Merit award, 1989, Zeiss award, 2005; grantee NIH, NSF, ACS. Fellow AAAS, Am. Acad. Arts. & Scis., 2004; mem. Am. Soc. Cell Biology, Am. Soc. Biochemistry and Molecular Biology, Sigma Xi.

BORJA, DAVID M., school system administrator; B in Math, MA in Mgmt., PhD in Bus. Adminstrn.; grad., US Army Command and Gen. Staff Coll., US Army Combined Arms and Services Staff Sch., US Army Corps of Engr. Advanced and Basic Officer Courses, US Army Candidate Sch. Classroom tchr. Marianas HS; sch. prin. Hopwood Jr. High Sch.; assoc. commr. for adminstrn. services; commr. edn. Commonwealth Northern Mariana Islands Pub. Sch. Sys., 2006—. Tchr. repr. Bd. Edn. Commr. Edn., Commonwealth Northern Mariana Islands Pub. Sch. Sys, 1997—2000. Ret. US Army, 1994. Office: Commr Edn Commonwealth Northern Mariana Islands Pub Sch Sys PO Box 501370 CK Saipan MP 96950 Office Phone: 670-664-3798. Office Fax: 670-664-3700.

BORJAS, GEORGE J(ESUS), economics professor; b. Havana, Cuba, Oct. 15, 1950; came to U.S., 1962; s. Juan V. Borjas and Edita F. Diaz; m. Jane Maureen Walsh, Nov. 11, 1989; children: Sarah Jane Irene, Timothy Jorge, Rebecca Kathryn. BS, St. Peter's Coll., Jersey City, 1971; MA, M in Philosophy, PhD, Columbia U., 1975; LHD (hon.), St. Peter's Coll., 2003. Asst. prof. Queens Coll., Flushing, NY, 1975-77; research assoc. Nat. Bur. Econ. Research, Cambridge, Mass., 1983—; prof. econs. U. Calif., Santa Barbara, 1978-90, San Diego, 1990-95; prof. pub. policy Kennedy Sch. Govt., Harvard U., Cambridge, Mass., 1995-97, Pferzheimer prof. pub. policy, 1998—2002, Robert W. Scrivner prof. of econ. and social policy, 2002—. Cons. Unicon Rsch. Corp., Santa Monica, Calif., 1982-94; econs. adv. panel NSF, 1988-90; mem. Gov.'s Coun. of Econ. Advisers, 1993-98 Author: Wage Policy in the Federal Bureaucracy, 1980, International Differences in the Labor Market Performance of Immigrants, 1988, Friends or Strangers: The Impact of Immigrants on the U.S. Economy, 1990, Labor Economics, 1995, Heaven's Door: Immigration Policy and the American Economy, 1999; editor: Hispanics in the United States, 1985, Immigration and the Work Force: Economic Consequences for the United States and Source Areas, 1992, Issues in the Economics of Immigration, 2000, Rev. of Econs. and Statistics, 1998—; mem. editl. bd. Quar. Jour. Econs., 1992-98, Internat. Migration Rev., 1992—, Review of Economics and Statistics, 1997-98; contbr. articles to profl. jours. Fellow Columbia U. Alumni Fund, 1973, NIMH, U. Chgo., 1977; grantee Rockefeller Found., 1983-85, Sloan Found., 1986-93, NSF, 1986—, Russell Sage Found., 1991-93, Smith Richardson Found., 2001—; vis. scholar Harvard U., 1988-89. Fellow Econometric Soc., Soc. Labor Economists; mem. NAS (panel 1984-85, 95-97, Estrada fellow in immigration studies 2000), Am. Econ. Assn., Assn. for Pub. Policy Analysis and Mgmt. (exec. coun. 2000—). Roman Catholic. Office: Kennedy Sch Govt Harvard U 79 Jfk St Cambridge MA 02138-5801 E-mail: gborjas@harvard.edu.

BORK, ROBERT HERON, law educator, retired federal judge; b. Pitts., Mar. 1, 1927; s. Harry Philip and Elizabeth (Kunkle) B.; m. Claire Davidson, June 15, 1952 (dec. 1980); children: Robert Heron, Charles E., Ellen E.; m. Mary Ellen Pohl, Oct. 30, 1982. BA, U. Chgo., 1948, JD, 1953; LLD (hon.), Creighton U., 1975, Notre Dame Law Sch., 1982; LHD, Wilkes-Barre Coll., 1976; JD (hon.), Bklyn. Law Sch., 1984; ThD, DeSales Sch. Theology, 1990; LLD honoris causa, Adelphi U., 1990. Bar: Ill. 1953, D.C. 1977. Assoc., then ptnr. Kirkland, Ellis, Hodson, Chaffetz & Masters, Chgo., 1955-62; assoc. prof. Yale Law Sch., 1962-65, prof. law, 1965-75, on leave, 1973-75; solicitor gen. U.S. Dept. Justice, Washington, 1973-77, acting atty. gen., 1973-74; Chancellor Kent prof. law Yale Law Sch., 1977-79, Alexander M. Bickel prof. pub. law, 1979-81; ptnr. Kirkland & Ellis, Washington, 1981-82; judge U.S. Ct. Appeals (D.C. Cir.), 1982—88; resident scholar Am. Enterprise Inst. for Pub. Policy Rsch., Washington, 1977, adj. scholar, 1977-82, John M. Olin scholar in legal studies, 1988-99, sr. fellow, 2000—03; disting. fellow Hudson Inst., Washington, 2003—; prof. law Ave Maria Sch. Law, 2000—03. Mem., trustee Woodrow Wilson Internat. Ctr. for Scholars, 1973-78; nominated for position assoc. justice U.S. Supreme Ct., 1987, confirmation denied by U.S. Senate; Tad and Dianne Taube Disting. vis. fellow Hoover Instn., 2003. Author: The Antitrust Paradox: A Policy at War with Itself, 1978, 2d edit., 1993, The Tempting of America: The Political Seduction of the Law, 1990, Slouching Towards Gomorrah: Modern Liberalism and American Decline, 1996, Coercing Virtue: The Worldwide Rule of Judges, 2002. With USMCR, 1945-46, 50-52. Recipient Francis Boyer award Am. Enterprise Inst., 1984, Henry Salvatori prize Intercollegiate Svcs. Inst., 1998, Named one of 75 Best Lawyers in Washington, Washingtonian Survey Mag., 2002. Fellow AAAS; mem. Federalist Soc. (co-chmn., bd. trustees). Business E-Mail: rbork@borklaw.com.

BORK, RONALD DALE, academic administrator; b. LeMars, Iowa, Apr. 12, 1948; s. Gladys M. Bork; m. Marilyn J. Schmidt; children: Kristin J., Allison K. Domsch. BSEd, Concordia Tchrs. Coll., Seward, Nebr., 1970, MEd, 1977; EdD, St. Louis U., 1999. Dean, Coll. Edn. Concordia U., Seward, Nebr., 2001—. Thrivent fellow, 2005—06. Mem.: Phi Delta Kappa. Office: Concordia Univ 800 N Columbia Ave Seward NE 68434 Home Phone: 402-646-2174; Office Phone: 402-643-7475. Business E-Mail: ron.bork@cune.edu.

BORKAN, WILLIAM NOAH, electronics executive, biomedical engineer, entrepreneur, venture capitalist, real estate developer; b. Miami Beach, Fla., Apr. 29, 1956; s. Martin Solomon and Annabelle (Hoffman) Borkan; m. Vivienne Eliane; children: Martin, Kenneth. Student, Carnegie Mellon U., 1977. Tech. Dominicks' Radio & TV Co., Miami Beach, 1971-74; computer programmer Mt. Sinai Hosp., Miami Beach, 1973-74; chief studio engr. Sta. WGMA, Hollywood, Fla., 1973-74; disc jockey Sta. WBUS-FM, Miami Beach, 1974; chief rec. engr. Dukoff Recording Studios, Miami, Fla., 1974-75; rec. studio design and constrn. TSI, Hollywood, 1975-77; chief design engr. Lumonics Co., Miami, 1974; svc. mgr. 21st Century Electronics Co., Miami, 1975; lab. tech., mem. curriculum com. elec. engring. dept. Carnegie-Mellon U.; mgr. Tech. Electronics Co., Pitts., 1976; pres. Borktronics Co., Miami, 1974-84; consulting specialist in neurobiometrics St. Barnabas Hosp., NYC, 1978-83; pres., CEO NeuroMed, Inc., 1980-85, Nice Tech., Inc., 1989-96; pres. Master Angler, Inc., 1990—. Dir. Saints Venutres Ltd, 1999—; pres. Electrovest Inc., 1985—; mng. mem. Aloha Investment Group, 2003—; cons. specialist in home automation, home theater and audio. Prodr.: Ho'olina: The Legacy, 2006; contbr. articles to profl. jours. Named Entrepreneur of Yr., Fla. Inc. Mag., 1992; grantee, Carnegie Corp., Carnegie Mellon U. Mem.: AAAS, NY Acad. Scis., Audio Engring. Soc., Assn. Advancement Med. Instrumentation, Refrigeration and Air Conditioning Engrs., Am. Soc. Heating. Achievements include numerous US and foreign patents in field; patents pending in field. Home: 3142 NE 166th St Miami FL 33160-3840 Office: Electrovest 12000 Biscayne Blvd Ste 502 Miami FL 33181-2725 Personal E-mail: bbbillfish@aol.com.

BORKHATARIA, RENA REBECCA, ecologist, researcher; b. Balt., Md., Aug. 12, 1970; d. Navnit Borkhataria and Carmen Virginia Rodriguez; m. Colin James Saunders, Dec. 18, 2001. BS, U. Ariz., Tucson, 1998; MS, NC State U., Raleigh, 2001; postgrad., U. Fla., Gainesville, 2003—. Intern US Fish and Wildlife Svc., Arlington, Va., 1998; biologist, biol. resources divsn. US Geol. Survey, Reston, Va., 1999—2004; rsch. asst. U. Fla., Gainesville, 2003—; biologist, geog. info. sys. specialist Ecostudies Inst., Mt. Vernon, Wash., 2006—. Contbr. articles to profl. jours. Fundraising and grants coord., outreach and edn. horse tng. South Fla. Soc. Prevention Cruelty Animals, Miami, Fla., 2006. Fellow, EPA, 2004—; grantee, US Fish and Wildlife Svc., 2005—; scholar, Morris K. Udall Scholarship Found., 1997, Harry S. Truman Scholarship Found., 1997—2000; Rsch. fellow, NSF, 1998—2001. Mem.: Soc. Field Ornithologists, Waterbirds Soc., Ecol. Soc. Am. Achievements include first to catching adult wood storks. Avocations: conservation, animal welfare. Office: Univ Fla PO Box 110430 Gainesville FL 32611 Home Phone: 786-243-1874. Business E-Mail: rrbork@ufl.edu.

BORKO, HILDA, education educator; BA in Psychology, UCLA, 1971, MA in Philosophy of Edn., 1973, PhD in Ednl. Psychology, 1978. Elem. tchg. credential Calif., specialization in mental retardation U. So. Calif. Asst. and assoc. prof. Coll. Edn., Va. Poly. Inst. and State U., 1980—85; assoc. prof. Coll. Edn., U. Md., College Park, 1985—91, Sch. Edn., U. Colo., Boulder, 1991—94; prof. Sch. Edn. U. Colo., Boulder, 1994—. Co-author (with M. Eisenhart): (book) Designing Classroom Research: Themes, Issues, and Struggles, 1993 (Outstanding article award, 1992); contbr. articles to profl. jours. and chpts. to books. Recipient grants in field. Mem.: APA, Nat. Acad. Edn., Nat. Coun. for Tchrs. of Math., Invisible Coll. for Rsch. on Tchg., Am. Assn. Colls. of Tchr. Edn., Am. Ednl. Rsch. Assn. (pres. 2003—04), Pi Gamma Mu, Phi Beta Kappa, Phi Delta Kappa. Office: U Colo Sch Edn CB249 Boulder CO 80309 Office Phone: 303-492-8399.

BORKOVEC, VERA Z., literature and language professor; b. Brno, Czechoslovakia, Aug. 13, 1926; came to U.S., 1952; d. Josef Zanda and Jarmila (Tuscher) Martinasek; m. Alexej B. Borkovec, Aug. 29, 1951. BA, Charles U., 1949; MA, Hollins Coll., 1961, The Am. U., 1966; PhD, Georgetown U., 1973. Secondary sch. tchr. English, French Montgomery County Pub. Schs., Md., 1961-64; from asst. prof. to assoc. prof. Russian studies The Am. Univ., Washington, 1966-91, prof. emerita. Recipient Artis Bohemiae Amicis medal, Czech Ministry of Culture, 2003. Mem. Czechoslovak Soc. of Arts and Scis. (v.p. 1994—). Avocations: theater, music, poetry. Home: 12013 Kemp Mill Rd Silver Spring MD 20902-1515

BORKOW, MARY P., small business owner, consultant; d. Theodore James Pappas and Assunta Caputo; m. Joel E. Borkow; children: David T., Jason E., Michelle M., K. Andrew, Philip S. Diploma in liberal arts, Sacramento State U., 1973, U. Pitts., 1993. Wth circulation dept. Johnstown Tribune Democrat, Pa., 1962—63; exec. sec. WJAC-TV, Johnstown, 1963—65, Shell Oil Co., Sacramento, 1971—72; adminstr. asst. C. of C., Johnstown, 1983—90; bus. owner Martins Fashions and Footwear, Johnstown, 1990—98; bus. advisor Plastic Surg. Assocs., Johnstown, 1999—. Pres., bd. dirs. YWCA, Johnstown, 1983—89; pres. com. C. of C. Bus. Alliance, Johnstown, 1988—96; pres. bd. dirs. Johnstown Symphony Orch., 1992—2002, pres., 1994—96, aux. mem.; pres. bd. dirs. Main Street Mgr. Program, 1996—98; bd. dirs. Johnstown Area Heritage Assn.; bd. trustees So. Alleghenies Mus. Art; co-founder Tribute to Women Award for YWCA; mem. McCort Sch. Bd., 1988—98; trustee YWCA; pres. Johnstown Symphony Aux.; founder Johnstown Cultural Trust; bd. dirs. Lee Initiatives. Recipient Tribute to Women award, YWCA, 1992, Hall of Fame award, Johnstown C. of C., 2002, Vol. in Arts award, 2005, Dominion People's Vita award, WQED Radio, 2006. Mem.: Meml. Hosp. Aux., Jaha Guild, Roxbury Bandshell Preservation Alliance (pres. 2006), Lee Hosp. Aux., Cultural Affair Com C. of C. (chair 1998—), Pres. Johnstown Investment Club, Johnstown Investment Club (pres. 2005—). Roman Catholic. Achievements include overseeing the building of Johnstown Gazebo in Central Park; responsible for the re-development of the Kernville Revitalization project. Avocations: travel, yoga, golf. Home: 1618 Sunshine Ave Johnstown PA 15905 Office: Plastic Surg Assocs of Johnstown 415 Napoleon Pl Johnstown PA 15901

BORKOWSKI, FRANCIS THOMAS, music educator; b. Weirton, W.Va., Mar. 16, 1936; s. Francis Thomas and Felicia Josephine (Pawlowski) B.; m. Kay Kaiser, Aug. 22, 1959; children: Stanley, Anne-Marie, Christian. BS, Oberlin Coll., Ohio, 1957; M.Mus., Ind. U., 1959; PhD, W.Va. U., 1967; LLD (hon.), St. Leo Coll., Fla., 1989. Clarinetist Indpls. Symphony Orch., 1957-59; music dir. Bishop Kenny High Sch., Jacksonville, Fla., 1959-61; dir. bands W.Va. U., 1961-67; assoc. prof. music edn. Ohio U., Athens, 1967-69, asst. dir. Sch. Music, 1969-70, assoc. dean faculties, 1970-75; prof. music, vice chancellor, dean faculty Ind. U.-Purdue U., Ft. Wayne, 1975-78; v.p. Ft. Wayne Philharmonic Orch., 1976-78; provost U. S.C. System, 1978-83, exec. v.p., provost, 1983-88; pres. U. South Fla., Tampa, 1988-93; chancellor Appalachian State U., Boone, NC, 1993—2003, prof. music, 2003—. Bd. dirs. Fla. Nations Bank. Author articles. Mem. nat. adv. coun. John F. Kennedy Ctr., 1978-80; pres. S.C. Orch. Assn., 1982; bd. dirs. United Way of Columbia, 1981; chmn. Moffitt Cancer Ctr. Bd., United Way Bd., Tampa; mem. urban affairs com. Nat. Assn. Land Grant Colls. Recipient Amicus Poloniae award Poland mag., 1971, award for research Sigma Xi; named Polonian of Yr., 1989, Gold medal with Diamond, INTERPROM, 1997, Commdr. of the Cross of the Rep. of Poland, 2001. Mem. Am. Coun. Edn. (bd. dirs.), Am. Assn. Higher Edn., Music Educators Nat. Conf., Phi Beta Kappa, Mortar Bd., Omicron Delta Kappa, Eta Sigma Gamma, Golden Key, Phi Beta Delta. Roman Catholic. Business E-Mail: borkowskif@appstate.edu.

BORKOWSKI, JOHN JOSEPH, lawyer; b. Detroit, June 30, 1952; s. John Joseph and Virginia Frances (Bergel) B.; m. Carmen Ana Cintron, May 29, 1982 (div. 1993). BA in Govt. and Internat. Studies, U. Notre Dame, 1973; JD, Notre Dame Law Sch., 1976. Bar: Ohio 1976, U.S. Dist. Ct. (no. dist.) Ohio 1976, U.S. Ct. Appeals (6th cir.) 1977, U.S. Ct. Appeals (D.C. cir.) 1985, U.S. Supreme Ct. 1980. Dir. debate U. Notre Dame, Ind., 1974-76; law clk. to justice U.S. Dist. Ct. (no. dist.), Cleve., 1976-78; lawyer FCC, Washington, 1978-80; assoc. Fly, Shuebruk, Gaguine, Boros, Schulkind and Braun, Washington, 1980; lawyer FCC, 1981—; designated fed. officer Pub. Safety Wireless Adv. Com., 1995—96. Asst. for pvt. land mobile radio, 1996-97; chief, policy and rules br. Pub. Safety and Pvt. Wireless divsn. Wireless Telecomm. Bur., 1997-99; asst. divsn. chief Pub. Safety and Pvt. Wireless divsn. Wireless Telecomm. Bur., FCC, 1999-2003, asst. divsn. chief Spectrum Access, Spectrum and Competition Policy Divsn. Wireless Telecomm. Bur., 2003-. Recipient Performance award FCC, 1983, 84, 85, 88, 91, 92, 95, 97, 98, 99, 00, 01, 02, 03, 04, 05, 06. Mem. Train Collectors Assn. Roman Catholic. Avocations: computers, model trains, science fiction. Home Phone: 703-532-3128; Office Phone: 202-418-0626. E-mail: John.Borkowski@fcc.gov.

BORLAND, KATHRYN KILBY, writer; b. Pullman, Mich., Aug. 14, 1916; d. Paul Melbourne and Vinnie (Bensinger) Kilby; m. James Barton Borland, May 16, 1942; children— James Barton, Susan Lee. BS in Journalism, Butler U., 1937. Editor North Side Topics, Indpls., 1938-42. Author: (all with Helen Ross Speicher) Southern Yankees, 1960, Allan Pinkerton, 1962, Miles and the Big Black Hat, 1963, Everybody Laughed, 1964, Eugene Field, 1964, Phillis Wheatley, 1968, Harry Houdini, 1969, Clocks from Shadow to Atom, 1969, Good-Bye to Stony Crick, 1975, The Third Tower, 1974, Stranger in the Mirror, 1974, Good-bye, Julie Scott, 1975, To Walk the Night, 1976, These Tigers' Hearts, 1978, Irena, 1979, Pseudonyms: Alice Abbott, Jane Land. Co-recipient award for most distinguished children's book pub. by Ind. author Ind. U., 1969 Mem.: PEO, Theta Sigma Phi, Kappa Alpha Theta. Home: 1050 S Maish Rd Frankfort IN 46041-3213

BORLAND, VIRGINIA ANN, journalist, fashion specialist, fiber company executive; b. NYC, Mar. 8, 1929; d. Charles Peter and Margaret Elise (Swane) S.; m. J. Nelson Borland, Nov. 13, 1969 (separated 1987). BA, Wells Coll., 1951. Publicist J. Walter Thompson Advt. Agy., 1952-55, Grey Advt., 1956—59; fashion dir. Cunningham & Walsh, NYC, 1960, Avtex Fibers, Inc., NYC, 1961—85; cons. journalist, 1986—. Cons. fashion editor Fashion Galleria mag., KTA, MMI, BASF Fibers; N.Y. corr. Textile World; contbg. editor Style mag., Canada. Vol. pediatric ward Meml. Hosp., 1953-84. Mem. Fashion Group (gov. 1975-77, found. dir. 1983-84), Inner Circle, Color Assn. U.S.A. (chmn. women's apparel color selection com.), Round Table Fashion Execs., Fashion News Workshop, N.Y. Jr. League. Republican. Episcopalian. Home: 110 E End Ave New York NY 10028-7416 E-mail: vborland@nyc.rr.com.

BORLAUG, NORMAN ERNEST, agricultural scientist; b. Cresco, Iowa, Mar. 25, 1914; s. Henry O. and Clara (Vaala) Borlaug; m. Margaret G. Gibson, Sept. 24, 1937 (dec. Mar. 7, 2007); children: Norma Jean, William Gibson. BS in Forestry, U. Minn., Minneapolis, 1937, MS in Plant Pathology, 1940, PhD in Plant Pathology, 1942; ScD (honoris causa), Punjab Agrl. U., India, 1969, Royal Norwegian Agrl. Coll., Norway, 1970, Luther Coll., 1971, Kanpur U., India, 1972, Uttar Pradesh Agrl. U., 1971, Mich. State U., 1971, U. de la Plata, Argentina, 1971, U. Ariz., 1972, U. Fla., 1973, U. Católica de Chile, Chile, 1974, U. Hohenheim, Germany, 1976, Punjab Agrl. U., Pakistan, 1978, Columbia U., 1980, Ohio State U., 1981, U. Minn., 1982, U. Notre Dame, 1987, Oregon State U., 1988, U. Tulsa, 1991, Washington State U., 1995, Andhra Pradesh Agrl. U., India, 1996, Indian Agrl. Rsch. Inst., 1996, De Montfort U., UK, 1997, Emory U., 1999, U. Philippines, 1999; LHD, Gustavus Adolphus Coll., 1971, Iowa State U., 1992; LLD (hon.), New Mexico State U., 1973; D. of Agr. (hon.), Tufts U., 1982; D. of Agrl. Scis. (hon.), U. Agrl. Scis., Godollo, Hungary, 1980, Tokyo U. Agriculture, 1981, U. Nacional Pedro Henríquez Turena, Dominican Republic, U. Cen. del Estes, Dominican Republic, 1983; D. Honoris Causa, U. Mayor de San Simón, Bolivia, U. de Buenos Aires, 1983, U. de Cordoba, Spain, U. Politécnica de Catalunya, Barcelona, Spain, 1986, Colegio Postgraduados, Montecillo, Mexico, 1990; PhD (hon.), U. degli Studi di Bologna, Italy, 1991, Warsaw Agrl. U., Poland, 1993, Bangladesh Agrl. U., 1998, U. LaSalle-Noroeste, Mex., 1999, U. Politécnica de Madrid, Spain, 2000, U. Américas Puebla, Mex., 2000; D. Honoris Causa, U. Autónoma Nuevo León, 2001; PhD (hon.), U. Autónoma de Chapingo, 2001, Rector U. Dubuque, 1992-93; PhD (hon.), U. Studi de Bologna, Italy, 1991, Warsaw Agrl. U., Poland, 1993; ScD (hon.), Dartmouth Coll., 2005. With U.S. Forest Service, 1935—38; instr. U. Minn., 1941; microbiologist E.I. DuPont de Nemours, 1942—44; rsch. scientist in charge wheat improvement Coop. Mexican Agrl. Program, Mexican Ministry Agr. Rockefeller Found., Mexico, 1944—60, assoc. dir. assigned to Inter-Am. Food Crop Program, 1960—63; assoc. dir. CIMMYT, 1964-82; dir. wheat research and prodn. program Internat. Maize and Wheat Improvement Ctr., Mexico City, 1964—79, acting dir., 1981, cons., 1980—; disting. prof. internat. agr. dept. soil & crop scis. Texas A&M U., College Station, Tex., 1984—. Cons., collaborator nst. Nacional de Investigationes Agricolas, Mexican Ministry Agr, 1960—64; cons. FAO, North Africa and Asia, 1960; ex-officio cons. wheat research and prodn. problems to govts. in Latin Am., Africa, Asia, 1960—; mem. Citizen's Commn. on Sci. Law and Food Supply, 1973; mem. Commn. Critical Choices for Am, 1973, Council Agr. Sci. and Tech., 1973—, Presdl. Commn. on World Hunger U.S.A., 1978—79, Presdl. Coun. Advisers Sci and Tech., 1990—93; dir. Population Crisis Com., 1971—92; asesor especial Fundacion para Estudios de la Poblacion A.C., Mexico, 1971—80; mem. adv. council Renewable Natural Resources Found., 1973; A.D. White Disting. prof.-at-large Cornell U., 1983—85; Disting. prof. Internat. Agr., Dept. Soil & Crop Scis. Tex. A&M U., 1984—; adj. prof. dept. biology Emory U., Atlanta, 1991—92; advisor The Population Inst., U.S.A., 1971—78; bd. trustees Winrock Internat. U.S.A.; life fellow Rockefeller Found., 1983—; sr. cons. CIMMYT, 1979—; hon. vis. prof. U. Minn., 1980; adj. prof. dept. biology Emory U., Atlanta, 1991—92. Named Uncle of Paul Bunyan, 1969; named to Hall of Fame, Oreg. State U. Agrl., 1981, Agrl. Nat. Ctr., Bonner Springs, Kans., 1984, Scandinavian-Am., U.S.A., 1986, Nat. Wrestling, 1992; recipient Disting. Service awards, Wheat Producers Assns., and state govts. Mexican States of Guanajuato, Queretaro, Sonora, Tlaxcala and Zacatecas, 1955—60, Recognition award, Agrl. Inst. Can., 1966, Instituto Nacional de Tecnologia Agropecuaria de Marcos Juarez, Argentina, 1968, Sci. Service award, El Colegio de Ingenieros Agronomos de Mexico, 1970, Outstanding Achievement award, U. Minn., 1959, Elvin Charles Stakman award, 1961, Disting. Citizen award, Cresco Centennial Com., 1966, Nat. Disting. Service award, Am. Agrl. Editors Assn., 1967, Genetics and Plant Breeding award, Nat. Council Comml. Plant Breeders, 1968, Star of Distinction, Govt. of Pakistan, 1968, citation and street named in honor, Citizens of Sonora and Rotary Club, 1968, Internat. Agronomy award, Am. Soc. Agronomy, 1968, Distinguished Service award, Wheat Farmers of Punjab, Haryana and Himachal Pradesh, 1969, Nobel Peace prize, 1970, Diploma de Merito, El Instituto Tecnologico y de Estudios Superiores de Monterrey, Mexico, 1971, medalla y Diploma de Merito, Antonio Narro Escuela Superior de Agricultura de la U. de Coahuila, Mexico, 1971, Diploma de Merito, Escuela Superior de Agricultura Hermanos Escobar, Mexico, 1973, award for service to agr., Am. Farm Bur. Fedn., 1971, Outstanding Agrl. Achievement award, World Farm Found., 1971, Medal of Merit, Italian Wheat Scientists, 1971, outstanding Achievement award, Minn. Athletic Club, 1971, Service award for outstanding contbn. to alleviation of world hunger, 8th Latin Am. Food Prodn. Conf., 1972, Nat. award for Agrl. Excellence in Sci., Agri-Mktg. Assn., 1982, Disting. Achievement award, Council for Agrl. Scis. and

Tech., 1982, inaugural lectr., medal, Dr. S.B. Hendrick's Meml. Lectureship., 1981, Henry G. Bennett Disting. Svc. award, 1984, dedicated in his name, Norman E. Borlaug Centro de Capitación y Formación de Agrs., Santa Cruz, Bolivia, 1983, Borlaug Hall U. Minn., 1985, Borlaug Bldg. Internat. Maize and Wheat Improvement Ctr., 1986, Nat. Medal Sci. in Biol. Sciences, 2004, Congl. Gold medal, 2007, numerous other honors and awards from govts., ednl. instns., citizens groups, other honored lectureships. Fellow: Indian Soc. Genetics and Plant Breeding; mem.: NAS, Acad. Nat. Agronomía and Veterinaria Argentina, Chinese Acad. Agrl. Sci., Royal Soc. Eng., Internat. Food Policy Research Inst. (trustee 1976—82), Am. Council on Sci. and Health (trustee 1978—), N.I. Vavilov Acad. Agrl. Scis. Lenin Order (USSR.), Adv. Coun. Renewable Natural Resources Acad. Found. (mem. adv. coun. 1973), Coun. Agrl. Sci. and Tech., Soil Sci. Soc. Am. (hon.), Sociedad de Agronomia do Rio Grande do Sul Brazil (hon.), Royal Agrl. Soc. Eng. (hon.), Royal Soc. Edinburgh (hon.), Hungarian Acad. Sci. (hon.), Indian Nat. Sci. Acad. (hon.), Am. Acad. Arts and Scis. (hon.), Hungarian Acad. Scis. (hon.), Mexican Acad. Scis. (hon.), Am. Assn. Cereal Chemists (hon.; life, Meritorious Service award 1969), Crop Sci. Soc. Am. (hon.), Population Crisis Com., Chinese Acad. Agrl. Scis. (hon. prof. 1994), Sasakawa Africa Assn. (pres. 1986), Academia Nat. de Agronomia y Veterinaria (Argentina), Royal Swedish Acad. Agr. and Forestry (fgn. 1971), India Nat. Sci. Acad., Am. Soc. Agronomy (1st Internat. Svc. award 1960, 1st hon. life), Sigma Xi, Xi Sigma Pi, Alpha Zeta. Office: Tex A&M U 2474 Tamu Dept Soil & Crop Scis College Station TX 77843-2474

BORLING, JOHN LORIN, military officer; b. Chgo., Mar. 24, 1940; s. Edward Gustav and Vivian K. (Strietelmeir) Borling; m. Myrna Lee Holmstedt, June 22, 1963; children: Lauren, Megan. BS, U.S. Airforce Acad., 1963; grad., Armed Forces Staff Coll., 1975, Nat. War Coll., 1980, Harvard U., 1991. Commd. 2d lt. USAF, 1963, advanced through grades to maj. gen., 1989, prisoner of war Vietnam, 1966-73, fighter pilot, comdr., 1974-80, asst. dir. ops. HQ Pentagon Washington, 1981-82, comdr. 86th Combat Support Group Ramstein, Germany, 1982-83, comdr. 86th Fighter Group, 1983-84, exec. officer to COS NATO Mons, Belgium, 1984-86, dep. plans/analysis HQ/SAC Jt. Stategic Target Planning Staff Omaha, 1986-87, comdr. HQ 57th Air Divsn. Minot, ND, 1987-88, dep. ops. HQ SAC Omaha, 1988-91; dir. operational reg(s) HQ Pentagon, 1991-92; dep. chief of staff NATO, Norway, 1992-94, chief of staff, sr. U.S. mil. officer in Scandinavia, 1994-96; pres., CEO United Way, Chgo., 1997-98; dir. The 5th Media, Chgo., 1999—. Chmn. Performance Cons. Group, 2000—; pres., CEO SOS Am., 2000—; advisor AMSAM Biotechnologies Inc.; chmn., CEO, 100 Mission LLC, 2005—; mem. Armed Forces Policy Coun., Chgo., Coun. Fgn. Rels., Chgo., Chgo. Com.; mem. adv. com. Ill. Fatherhood Initiative, Chgo.; mentor Harris Sch., U. Chgo. Founder, charter mem. Ramstein Coun. Internat. Rels., 1983; v.p., bd. dirs. Opera Omaha, 1988—91; treas., bd. dirs. White Ho. Fellow Found., 1991—; adv. bd. Stanton Chase Internat., Maritime Trust Co.; bd. govs. Chgo. Mil. Acad.; bd. dirs. Nat. Jazz Mus., 2000; vice-chmn. Chgo. Meml. Day Parade Com., 2000; dir. Stars & Stripes Relief Fund, 2001; mem. adv. com. Kellog Sch., Northwestern U. Decorated Def. Distin. Svc. medal with oak leaf cluster, Air Force Disting. Svc. medal, Silver Star, Def. Superior Svc. medal, Legion of Merit with oak leaf cluster, DFC with oak leaf cluster, Bronze Star with V device and 2 oak leaf clusters, Air medal with 5 oak leaf clusters, Purple Heart with one cluster; named to Ill. Aviation Hall of Fame, 2004; recipient George Washington medal, Freedom Found., Valley Forge, Pa., 1975, Good Scout award, Boy Scouts Am., Chgo., 1974, Eagle Am. Hero award, Benedictine U., 2001, Patriot's award, City of Chgo., 2001; White Ho. fellow, 1974, Harvard U., 1998. Mem.: VFW, Air Force Assn., Assn. Grads. USAF Acad., Execs. Club Chgo., Comml. Club Chgo., Daedalians. Avocations: music, sports, reading. Office: SOS America Box 1543 Rockford IL 61110-1543 Office Phone: 405-447-2977. Business E-Mail: jlb@pcgok.com, info@sosamerica.org.

BORMANN, MARIE L., medical transcriptionist, small business owner; d. Leonard F. and Patricia E. Ritter; m. Richard D. Bormann, June 24, 1978; 1 child, Stephanie C. Grad., HS, St. Charles, Mo. Med. transcriptionist St. Joseph Health Ctr., St. Charles, 1974—84; office mgr. Monica Minkoff MD, St. Peters, Mo., 1984—86; adminstrv. asst. Baldridge Properties, St. Louis, 1986—88; med. transcriptionist St. Luke's Hosp., Chesterfield, Mo., 1991—2001; pres., CEO Ameriscript LLC, St. Charles, 2000—. Named Internat. Poet of Merit, Internat. Soc. Poetry, 2002—05. Mem.: Assn. Healthcare Documentation Integrity. Avocations: crafts, poetry. Office Phone: 314-750-6901.

BORN, BROOKSLEY ELIZABETH, retired lawyer; b. San Francisco, Aug. 27, 1940; d. Ronald Henry and Mary Ellen (Bortner) Born; m. Alexander Elliot Bennett, Oct. 9, 1982; children: Nicholas Jacob Landau, Ariel Elizabeth Landau, Andrew E. Bennett, Laura F. Bennett, Peter J. Bennett. AB, Stanford U., 1961, JD, 1964. Bar: DC 1966. Law clk. U.S. Ct. Appeals, Washington, 1964—65; legal rschr. Harvard Law Sch., 1967—68; assoc. Arnold and Porter, Washington, 1965—67, 1968—73, ptnr., 1974—96, 1999—2002; chair U.S. Commodity Futures Trading Commn., Washington, 1996—99. Lectr. law Columbus Sch. Law, Cath. U. Am., 1972—74; adj. prof. Georgetown U. Law Ctr., Washington, 1972—73; mem. D.C. Jud. Nominating Commn., 2005—. Pres.: Stanford Law Rev., 1963—64. Chair bd. visitors Stanford Law Sch., 1987; trustee Ctr. Law and Social Policy, Washington, 1977—96; bd. dirs. Nat. Legal Aid and Defenders Assn., 1972—79, Washington Legal Clinic for Homeless, 1993—96, Lawyers Com. for Civil Rights Under Law, 1993—96, Am. Bar Found., 1989—99, Washington Lawyers Com. for Civil Rights and Urban Affairs, 1992—96, ALI-ABA, 2005—; chmn. bd. dirs. Nat. Women's Law Ctr., 1981—96, 2003—. Recipient Lifetime Achievement award, Am. Lawyer mag., 2005. Mem.: ABA (chair sect. ind. rights and responsibilities 1977—78, chair fed. judiciary com. 1980—83, chair consortium on legal svcs. and the pub. 1987—90, bd. govs. 1990—93, chair resource devel. coun. 1993—95, state del. from DC 1994—2005, chair coun. Fund for Justice and Edn. 1995—96), Southwestern Legal Found. (trustee 1993—96), Am. Law Inst., DC Bar (sec. 1975—76, mem. bd. govs. 1976—79), Order of Coif. Office: Arnold & Porter 555 12th St NW Washington DC 20004-1206 Office Phone: 202-942-5832. Business E-Mail: brooksley_born@aporter.com.

BORN, DANA H., dean, career military officer; BS, USAF Acad., 1983; MS, Trinity Univ., 1985; MA, Univ. Melbourne, Australia, 1991; PhD in indsl. & org. psychol., Pa. State Univ., 1994. Commd. 2d lt. USAF, advanced through grades to brig. gen., 2004; job analyst, exec. officer Occupational Measurement Ctr., Randolph AFB, Tex., 1983—86; personnel measurement psychol. USAF Exch. & Liaison office, Australian Royal Air Force, Melbourne, Australia, 1986—89; asst. prof., dept. behavioral sci. USAF Acad., Colo., 1989—91; liaison officer Pa. State Univ., 1991—94; asst. dir., recruiting rsch. & analysis Office of Asst. Sec. of Def. for Force Mgmt. Policy, Washington, 1994—97; policy analyst, aide to Sec. Office of Sec. of the Air Force, Washington, 1997—98; dep. chief, personnel issues team Office of Dep. Chief of Staff for Personnel, Washington, 1998—2000; comdr. 11th Mission Support Squadron, Bolling AFB, DC, 2000—02; prof., head Dept. Behavioral Sci. & Leadership USAF Acad., Colo., 2002—04, dean of the faculty Colo., 2004—. Decorated Def. Meritorious Svc. Medal, Meritorious Svc. Medal with 3 oak leaf clusters, Air Force Commendation medal with oak leaf cluster, Air Force Org. Excellence award, Nat. Def. Svc. medal with bronze star. Office: Dean of the Faculty U S A F Academy CO 80840

BORN, GEORGE HENRY, aerospace engineer, educator; b. Westhoff, Tex., Nov. 10, 1939; s. Henry and Lydia (Schulle) B.; m. Carol Ann Leslie, Mar. 21, 1992. BS, U. Tex., 1962, MS, 1965, PhD, 1968. Engr. Ling-Temco-Vought, Dallas, 1962-63; aerospace technologist Johnson Space Ctr., Houston, 1967-70; mem. tech. staff Jet Propulsion Lab., Pasadena, Calif., 1970-83; sr. rsch. engr. U. Tex., Austin, 1983-85; prof. aerospace engring. U. Colo., Boulder, 1985—, dir. Colo. Ctr. for Astrodynamics Rsch., 1985—. Contbr. articles to profl. jours. Recipient Exceptional Svc. medal NASA, 1980, Pub Svc. medal NASA, 1994. Fellow AIAA (Mechanics and Control of Flight award 1999), Am. Astronautical Soc. (Brouwer award 1998); mem. AAAS, NAE, Am. Geophys. Union, Oceanog. Soc., Inst. Navigation, Am. Meteorol. Soc., Am. Soc. Engring. Educators, Tau Beta Pi. Office: U Colo Campus Box 431 Boulder CO 80309-0431

BORN, ROBERT HEYWOOD, consulting civil engineer; b. LA, Nov. 7, 1925; s. Robert Bogle and Mignon Mary (Heywood) B.; m. Marilyn Alice Simpson, Aug. 15, 1947; 1 child, Stefanie Born. Student, Stanford U., Calif., 1943; BE, U. So. Calif., 1949, MSCE, 1956. Registered civil engr., Calif., Ariz., Nev., Utah, Tenn., Guam; registered agrl. engr., Calif. Assoc. hydraulic engr. Calif. Dept. of Water Resources, LA, 1949-58; chief engr., county hydraulic engr. County Flood Control/Water Conservation Dist., San Luis Obispo, Calif., 1958-70; dir., exec. v.p., regional mgr. CDM, Inc., Pasadena, Calif., 1970-78; v.p., regional mgr. Born, Barrett & Assoc./Barrett Cons. Group, Newport Beach, Calif., 1978-86, Memphis, 1978-86; prin. Robert H. Born Cons. Engrs., Memphis, 1986—88, Irvine, Laguna Niguel, Calif., 1986—88, Asheville, NC, 1997—. Chmn. World Affairs Coun., San Luis Obispo, Calif., 1965. 1st lt. US Army, 1943-47. Decorated Bronze star medal, 1944. Fellow: ASCE (life Engr. of Merit 1994); mem.: Am. Pub. Works Assn. (Floodplain Mgmt. Assn. Calif., cert. outstanding pub. works achievement 1969), US Com. on Large Dams, Am. Water Works Assn. (com. chmn.), Am. Acad. Environ. Engrs. (life; diplomate). Democrat. Presbyterian. Avocations: historical research, travel. Office: Robert H Born Cons Engrs 1658 Ryamar Cove S Memphis TN 38016

BORN, SAMUEL ROYDON, II, retired lawyer, mediator; b. Atwood, Ill., Apr. 19, 1945; s. Samuel Roydon and Mary Elizabeth (Derr) B.; m. Brenda Alice Anderson, June 18, 1988; children: Samuel R. III, Holly Jean, Julie Chamberlain Sipe. Student, Northwestern U., 1963-64, Am. U., fall 1966; BA, Simpson Coll., 1967; JD, Ind. U., 1970. Bar: Ind. 1970, U.S. Dist. Ct. (so. dist.) Ind. 1970, U.S. Ct. Appeals (7th crct.) 1975, U.S. Dist. Ct. (no. dist.) Ind. 1990, U.S. Supreme Ct. 2003. Ptnr. Ice Miller, Indpls., 1970—2006; ret., 2006. Mem. safety com. Associated Gen. Contractors Ind., 1988—2006. Co-author: Safety and Health Guide for Indiana Business, 1999, 5th edit., 2004; mem. bd. editors: Ind. Law Jour., 1969—70; contbr. articles to profl. jours. Mem. bd. visitors Ind. U. Sch. Law, 1988-89, 95-98; chmn. ch. cmty. athletics First Bapt. Ch., Indpls., 1975-78, trustee, 1978-80. Fellow Am. Bar Found., Ind. Bar Found., Indpls. Bar Found.; mem. ABA (mem. nat. conf. bar pres. 1987-99, ho. of dels. 1988-98, labor and employment law sect., ADR sect.), Ind. State Bar Assn. (bd. govs. 1990-99, pres. 1997-98, labor law sect., ADR sect.), Indpls. Bar Assn. (bd. mgrs. 1987-95, pres. 1988, ADR sect.), U.S. C. of C. (occupl. safety and health adminstrv. coun. 1981-86, 2000—06), Ind. C. of C. (past chmn. occupl. safety health com.), Ind. Mfrs. Assn. (pers. labor rels. com. 1982-99), Highland Golf and Country Club, Crooked Stick Golf Club, Univ. Club, Indpls. Lawyers Club, Masons, Shriners, Kiwanis, Phi Eta Sigma, Sigma Alpha Epsilon Presbyterian. Avocations: golf, fly fishing, public speaking, driving. Home: 5202 Grandview Dr Indianapolis IN 46228-1938 Home Phone: 317-255-1985; Office Phone: 317-569-3000. Business E-Mail: cborn@mede8.com.

BORNET, VAUGHN DAVIS, social sciences educator, historian, researcher; b. Phila., Oct. 10, 1917; s. Vaughn Taylor and Florence Davis (Scull) Bornet; m. Mary Elizabeth Winchester, Dec. 28, 1944; children: Barbara Bornet Stumph, Stephen Folwell. BA with honors, Emory U., 1939, MA, 1940; postgrad. fellow, U. Ga., 1940-41; PhD, Stanford U., 1951. Staff Mercer U., 1946; instr. history U. Miami, 1946-48; research assoc. Inst. Am. History, Stanford U., 1951-53; dir. welfare research project Commonwealth Club of Calif., 1953-56; assoc. editor Ency. Britannica, 1958; rsch. assoc. med. econs. AMA, 1958-59; staff RAND Corp., Santa Monica, Calif., 1959-63, 1969; chmn. social scis. div. So. Oreg. U., Ashland, 1963-74, prof. history and social sci., 1963-80. Vis. prof. World Campus Afloat, spring 1969. Author: Struggle for Governmental Power in Georgia, 1754-1757, 1940, Labor and Politics in 1928, 1951, California Social Welfare, 1956, Welfare in America, 1960, The Heart Future, 1961, Labor Politics in a Democratic Republic, 1964, Speaking Up for America, 1975; (with E.E. Robinson) Herbert Hoover: President of the United States, 1975, The Presidency of Lyndon B. Johnson, 1983 (nominee Pulitzer Prize); (juvenile) It's a Dog's Life and I Like It, 1991; (memoir) An Independent Scholar In Twentieth Century America, 1995, Thinking About the Iraq Situation, 2003, Republican, Democrat or Independent.?, 2004, When the Space Race Began, 2005; co-author The Heart Future, 1961; article United States, Ency. Brit. Yearbooks, 1957, 58; contbr. The Federal Campaign of 1864 in East Florida, 1956, Ideas in Conflict, 1958, Herbert Hoover Reassessed, 1981, The Quest for Security, 1982, Essays in Economics and Business History, 1988. Pres. So. Oreg. Symphony Assn., 1973-75; mem. U.S. Com. on Civil Rights, Oreg., 1985—2005. Served to lt. USNR, 1941-45, ret. comdr. Recipient award of merit Am. and Oreg. Heart Assns., 1967, Disting. Svc. award So. Oreg. U. Alumni Assn., 1985, Freedoms Found. award 1986. Mem. Rotary, Sigma Chi. Republican. Home: 365 Ridge Rd Ashland OR 97520-2830 Personal E-mail: bornetvd@ashlandhome.net.

BORNHEIMER, ALLEN MILLARD, lawyer; b. Brewer, Maine, June 10, 1942; s. Millard Genthner and Gertrude Evelyn (Kinney) B.; m. Deborah Russell Hill, June 17, 1967; children: Anneliese, Charles, Elizabeth. Student, Phillips Exeter Acad., 1961; AB, Harvard U., 1965, LLB, 1968. Bar: Mich. 1968, Mass. 1971. Assoc. Dickinson, Wright, McKean & Cudlip, Detroit, 1968-70, Choate, Hall & Stewart, Boston, 1970-76, ptnr., 1976-99, mng. ptnr., 1988-95; principal, gen. counsel Cargex Properties, Inc., Boston, 2000—. Bd. dirs. Cargex Properties, Inc. and affiliated cos., Portland, Maine. Town moderator, Duxbury, Mass., 1982—, chmn. fin. com., 1974-76, mem. capital budget com., 1977; bd. dirs. Jordan Hosp., Plymouth, Mass., 1974-81; trustee North Yarmouth (Maine) Acad., 1976-79. Mem. ABA, Mass. Bar Assn., Boston Bar Assn., Am. Coll. Investment Counsel, Mass. Moderators Assn., Duxbury Yacht Club (bd. dirs. 1982-84), Harvard Club (Boston), Somerset Club (Boston). Republican. Avocations: golf, piano, sailing. Office: 50 Milk St 20th Fl Boston MA 02109-5003 Home Phone: 781-934-2457; Office Phone: 617-338-0181. E-mail: allen.bornheimer@cargex.com.

BORNHOLDT, LAURA ANNA, academic administrator; b. Peoria, Ill., Feb. 11, 1919; d. John and Barbara (Kohl) B. AB, Smith Coll., 1940, MA, 1942; PhD, Yale U., 1945. Asst. prof. history Smith Coll., Northampton, Mass., 1945-52; internat. relations assoc. AAUW, Washington, 1952-57; dean Sarah Lawrence Coll., Bronxville, NY, 1957-59; dean women, adj. prof. history U. Pa., Phila., 1959-61; dean coll., prof. history Wellesley (Mass.) Coll., 1961-64; v.p. Danforth Found., St. Louis, 1964-73; sr. program officer Lilly Endowment Inc., Indpls., 1973-76, v.p. for edn., 1976-84; dir. office univ.-sch. rels. U. Chgo., 1984-94. Nat. adv. com. on black higher edn. and black colls. and univs. Dept. Edn., 1977-82; mem. Yale U. Council, 1977-82; emerita life trustee Coll. of Wooster, Ohio, 1967-77; trustee St. Louis U., 1971-75. Recipient Yale U. Wilbur Cross medal, 1976, Smith Coll. Alumnae medal, 1987. Mem.: Phi Beta Kappa. Home: 925 Juniper Pl Bloomington IN 47408-1285

BORNHORST, KENNETH FRANK, electromagnetics and systems engineer; b. Detroit, Feb. 5, 1929; s. Leo John and Alvina Anna (Laufersweiler) B.; m. Patricia Lucille Drayer, July 3, 1954; children: Kenneth Jr., David L., Patricia A. BEE, U. Dayton, 1951, PhD in Engring., 1985; MEE, Poly. Inst. N.Y., 1954. Project engr. monopulse radar receiver devel. Sperry Gyroscope Co., Great Neck, NY, 1951—54; project engr. autopilot, motor, timer, gyroscope devel. Globe Industries Inc., Dayton, Ohio, 1954—60; project engr. devel. of servo guided shoe machinery United Shoe Machinery Co., Xenia, Ohio, 1960; engring. sect. head mil. equipment divsn. locator and telemetry beacon and automatic direction finder devel. NCR, Dayton, 1960—74; br. chief, analyst electromagnetic threat analysis, radar, advanced weapon sys. Nat. Aeronautical and Space Intelligence Ctr. USAF, Wright-Patterson AFB, Ohio, 1974—94; cons., 1995—. Radar Cross section measurement of troops and vehicles for U.S. Army, 1954-56. Mem. Tau Beta Pi. Achievements include patents for flight control system, UHF bypass capacitor, pulsed carrier radio beacon, UHF radio direction finder, low loss millimeter waveguide.

BORNMANN, WILLIAM GERARD, organic chemist; b. Bklyn., Nov. 16, 1951; s. William Gustof and Martha (Windolf) B.; m. Daria Rae Luth, June 19, 1976. BS, U. Wis., 1975; MS, Mont. State U., 1978; PhD, U. Vt., 1988. Postdoctoral fellow U. Vt., Burlington, 1988-91; lab. mgr. Lab. Bio-Organic Chemistry Meml. Sloan-Kettering Cancer Ctr., NYC, 1991-93, head preparative synthesis core facility, 1993—. Contbr. 25 papers, articles to profl. jours. Mem. AAAS, Am. Chem. Soc., Internat. Soc. Heterocyclic Chemistry, Am. Assn. Pharm. Scientists, Am. Inst. Chemists, Am. Assn. Cancer Rsch., Soc. Medicinal Plant Rsch., Am. Soc. Pharmacognosy, N.Y. Acad. Scis., Royal Soc. Chemistry, Sigma Xi. Achievements include rsch. in the total synthesis of oxo-tabersonine, cephalotaxine, camptothecin, vindoline, catharanthine, tabersonine, vincadifformine and taxol as well as in enantioselective syntheses of vinblastine, leurosidine, vincovaline, organic chemistry. Office: Meml Sloan Kettering Cancer Ctr Preparative Synthesis Core Facility 1275 York Ave # 93 New York NY 10021-6094 Home: 66 Hope Farm Rd Missouri City TX 77459-2480

BORNSTEIN, ELI, artist, sculptor; b. Milw., Dec. 28, 1922; dual citizen, U.S. and Can. m. Christina Girgulis; children: Sarah, Thea. BS, U. Wis., 1945, MS, 1954; student, Art Inst. Chgo., U. Chgo., 1943, Academie Montmartre of Fernand Leger, Paris, 1951, Academie Julian, 1952; DLitt, U. Sask., Can., 1990. Tchr. drawing, painting and sculpture Milw. Art Inst., 1943-47; tchr. design U. Wis., 1949; tchr. drawing, painting, sculpture, design and graphics U. Sask., Canada, 1950-90, prof., 1963-90, prof. emeritus, 1990—, head art dept., 1963-71. Painted in France, 1951-52, Italy, 1957, Holland, 1958; exhibited widely, 1943-; retrospective exhbn. (works 1943-64), Mendel Art Gallery, Saskatoon, 1965, one man shows, Kazimir Gallery, Chgo., 1965, 67, Saskatoon Pub. Libr., 1975, Can. Cultural Ctr., Paris, 1976, Glenbow-Alta. Inst. Art, Calgary, 1976, Mendel Art Gallery, Saskatoon, 1982, York U. Gallery, Toronto, 1983, Confedn. Ctr. Art Gallery, Charlottetown, P.E.I., 1983, Owens Art Gallery, Mt. Allison U., Sackville, N.B., 1984, Fine Arts Gallery, U. Wis.-Milw., 1984, Mendel Art Gallery, Saskatoon, 1996; represented in numerous pvt. collections; executed marble sculpture now in permanent collection, Walker Art Ctr., Mpls., 1947; commns. include aluminum constrn. Sask. Tchr. Fedn. Bldg., 1956, structurist relief in painted wood and aluminum Arts and Sci. Bldg., U. Sask., 1958, structurist relief in enamelled steel Internat. Air Terminal, Winnipeg, Man., Can., 1962, four-part constructed relief Wascana Pl., Wascana Ctr. Authority, Regina, Sask., 1983, six panel structurist relief exterior Synchrotron-Can. Light Source Bldg., U. Sask, 2003, tripart hexaplane constrn. Internat. U., Bremen, Germany, 2006-07; also structurist reliefs exhibited, Mus. Contemporary Art, Chgo., Herron Mus. Art, Indpls., Cranbrook Acad. Art Galleries, Mich., High Mus., Atlanta, Can. House, Cultural Centre Gallery, London, 1983, Can. Cultural Ctr., Paris, 1983, Brussels, 1983, Bonn, 1984, Milw. Art Mus., 1984, Forum Gallery, NY, 2005, 06; model of aluminium construction, 1956 and model version of structurist relief in 5 parts, 1962, now in collection, Nat. Gallery, Ottawa, Ont., model version of Wascana commn. aquired by Can. Ctr. for Arch., Montreal; others in numerous collections.; co-editor: periodical Structure, 1958; founder, editor: The Structurist, ann. publ. 1960-72, biennial, 1972—; contbr. articles, principally on Structurist art to various publ. Recipient Allied Arts medal Royal Archtl. Inst. Can., 1968; hon. mention for 3 structurist reliefs 2d Biennial Internat. Art Exhbn., Colombia, S.Am., 1970. Address: 3625 Saskatchewan Cres S Corman Park SK Canada S7T 1B7 Office: U Sask Box 378 RPO U Saskatoon SK Canada S7N 4J8 Office Phone: 306-966-4198. E-mail: eli.bornstein@usask.ca.

BORNSTEIN, GARY A., lawyer; b. Merrick, NY, Feb. 15, 1973; BA magna cum laude, Yale Univ., 1994; JD magna cum laude, Harvard Univ., 1997. Bar: NY 1998. Law clk., Hon. Amalya L. Kearse US Ct. Appeals, 2nd Cir.; summer assoc. Cravath, Swaine & Moore LLP, NYC, 1996, assoc., 1998—2005, ptnr., litig., 2005—. Notes editor Harvard Law Rev. Mem.: ABA, Phi Beta Kappa. Office: Cravath Swaine Moore LLP Worldwide Plz 825 Eighth Ave New York NY 10019-7475 Office Phone: 212-474-1084. Office Fax: 212-474-3700. Business E-Mail: gbornstein@cravath.com.

BORNSTEIN, GEORGE JAY, literary educator; b. St. Louis, Aug. 25, 1941; s. Harry and Celia (Price) B.; m. Jane Elizabeth York, June 22, 1982; children— Benjamin, Rebecca, Joshua. AB, Harvard U., 1963; PhD, Princeton U., 1966. Asst. prof. MIT, Cambridge, 1966-69, Rutgers U., 1969-70; assoc. prof. U. Mich., Ann Arbor, 1970-75, prof. English, 1975—, C.A. Patrides prof. lit., 1995—. Cons. various univ. presses, scholastic jours., funding agys., 1970—; mem. adv. bd. Yeats: An Annual, 1982-2003, South Atlantic Rev., 1985-88, Rev., 1991—2005, Text, 1993-2006, Paideuma, 2003—, Textual Cultures, 2006—. Author: Yeats and Shelley, 1970, Transformations of Romanticism, 1976, Postromantic Consciousness of Ezra Pound, 1977, Poetic Remaking, 1988, Material Modernism: The Politics of the Page, 2001; editor: Romantic and Modern, 1977, Ezra Pound Among the Poets, 1985, W.B. Yeats: The Early Poetry, vol. 1, 1987, vol. 2, 1994, W.B. Yeats: Letters to the New Island, 1990, Representing Modernist Texts, 1991, Palimpsest: Editorial Theory in the Humanities, 1993, W.B. Yeats: Under the Moon, the Unpublished Early Poetry, 1995, Contemporary German Editorial Theory, 1995, The Iconic Page in Manuscript, Print, and Digital Culture, 1998, W.B. Yeats: Early Essays, 2007. Cubmaster Wolverine council Boy Scouts Am., 1977-79. Recipient good teaching award Amoco Found., 1983, Warner Rice prize for rsch. in humanities, 1988, Rosenthal award for Yeats studies W.B. Yeats Soc., 2000; fellow Am. Coun. Learned Soc., 1972-73, NEH fellow, 1982-83, fellow Old Dominion Found., 1968, fellow Guggenheim Found., 1986-87. Mem. MLA (exec. com. Anglo-Irish 1976-80, exec. com. 20th Century English 1980-85, exec. com. Poetry 1987-92, exec. com. bibliography and textual studies 1993-98, exec. com. methods of rsch. 1998-2003), Soc. Textual Scholarship (program chair 1997, exec. com. 1998-, pres. 2006-07), Am. Conf. on Irish Studies (book prize judge 1991), Racquet Club, Princeton Club (N.Y.C.), Phi Beta Kappa. Home: 2020 Vinewood Blvd Ann Arbor MI 48104-3614 Office: U Mich Dept English Ann Arbor MI 48109-1003 Business E-Mail: georgeb@umich.edu.

BORNSTEIN, LESTER MILTON, retired health facility administrator; b. Boston, Feb. 19, 1925; s. Harry and Celia B.; m. Marilyn Goldstein, Aug. 22, 1948; children: Aura Lynne, Michael Scott, Karen Jane. BS, Boston U., 1948; M.P.H. in Hosp. Adminstrn, Yale U., 1955. Adminstrv. resident Charles S. Wilson Meml. Hosp., Johnson City, NY, 1953-54; asst. dir. Barnert Meml. Hosp., Paterson, NJ, 1954-57, Newark Beth Israel Hosp., 1957-68; pres. Newark Beth Israel Med. Center, Newark, 1968-96. Served with AUS, 1943-45, ETO; to maj., Korean War 1950-53. Decorated Bronze Stars. Fellow Am. Coll. Hosp. Adminstrs., NJ Hosp. Assn. (chmn. bd. trustees 1978-79) Home: 6 Aherne Way West Orange NJ 07052-2102 Personal E-mail: lestb@aol.com.

BORNSTEIN, MORRIS, economist, educator; b. Detroit, Sept. 4, 1927; m. Reva Rice, Apr. 7, 1962; children— Susan, Jane. AB, U. Mich., 1947, A.M., 1948, PhD, 1952. Economist U.S. Govt., 1951-52, 55-58; mem. faculty U. Mich., Ann Arbor, 1958—, prof. econs., 1964—, dir. Center Russian and E. European Studies, 1966-69. Assoc. Harvard U. Russian Rsch. Ctr., 1962-63; vis. rsch. fellow Hoover Instn., Stanford, 1969-70; cons. in field, 1959—; mem. joint com. on Eastern Europe Am. Coun. Learned Socs.-Social Sci. Rsch. Coun., 1977-80. Author: Soviet National Accounts for 1955, 1961, The Soviet Economy, 1962, 4th edit., 1974, Comparative Economic Systems, 1965, 7th edit., 1994, Economia di Mercato ed Economia Pianificata, 1973, Sistemas economicos comparados, 1973, Plan and Market, 1975, Chinese transl., 1980, The Soviet Economy: Continuity and Change, 1981, East-West Relations and the Future of Eastern Europe, 1981, The Transfer of Western Technology to the USSR, 1985, French transl., 1985, contbr. articles to profl. jours.; mem. editorial bd. Jour. Comparative Econs., 1986-88, Problems of Economic Transition, 1987-97, Soviet Economy and Post Soviet Affairs, 1988-2003, Economic Policy in Transitional Economies, 1994—, Communist Economies and Econ. Transformation, 1997-98, Post-Soviet Geography and Econs., 1997-98, Post-Communist Economies, 1999—. With U.S. Army, 1953-55. Ford Found. faculty fellow, 1962-63, Sr. Fgn. Rsch. fellow French Ministry Rsch. and Tech., 1991. Mem. Am. Econ. Assn., Assn. Comparative Econ. Studies (exec. com. 1965-67, 73-75). Office: U Mich Dept Econs Ann Arbor MI 48109-1220

BORNSTEIN, PAUL, medical educator, biochemist; b. Antwerp, Belgium, July 10, 1934; arrived in US, 1947, naturalized, 1952; s. Abraham and Mina (Ginsburg) B. BA, Cornell U., 1954; MD, NYU, 1958. Intern in surgery Yale-New Haven Hosp., 1958-59, intern in medicine, 1959-60, asst. resident in medicine, 1960-62; sr. fellow Arthritis Found. Pasteur Inst., Paris, 1962-63; rsch. assoc. NIH, Bethesda, Md., 1963-65, rsch. investigator, 1965-67; asst. prof. biochemistry and medicine U. Wash., 1967-69, assoc. prof., 1969-73, prof., 1973—, attending physician, 1968—. Mem. editl. bd. Jour. Biol. Chemistry, 1972-78, 80-85, Jour. Cell Biology, 1988-91, 94-97, Matrix Biology, 1993—; assoc. editor Arteriosclerosis, 1980-90, Collagen Related Rsch., 1981-88; contbr. articles to profl. jours. Served to sr. surgeon USPHS, 1963-67. Recipient Lederle Med. Faculty award USPHS, 1968, Rsch. Career Devel. award NIH, 1969, Macy Faculty Scholar award, 1975, Merit award NIH, 1989, Solomon Berson Alumni Achievement award NYU, 2004; Guggenheim fellow, 1985. Mem.: Internat. Soc. Matrix Biology (pres. 2001—03), Am. Soc. Matrix Biology (v.p. 2001—02, pres. 2002—03), Assn. Am. Physicians, Western Soc. Clin. Rsch., Am. Soc. Biol. Chemistry, Am. Soc. Clin. Investigation. Home: 602 34th Ave E Seattle WA 98112-4306 Office: U Wash Sch Medicine Dept Biochemistry PO Box 357350 Seattle WA 98195-7350 Office Phone: 206-543-1789. Business E-Mail: bornsten@u.washington.edu.

BORNSTEIN, STEVEN M., former broadcast executive; b. Fair Lawn, NJ, Apr. 20, 1952; BS, U. Wis., 1974. Mgr. program coordination ESPN, Inc., Bristol, Conn., 1980—81, dir. program planning and qcauisitions, 1981, dir. programming, 1981—83, v.p. programming, 1983—85, sr. v.p. programming and prodn., 1985—88, exec. v.p. programming and prodn., 1988—90, pres., CEO, 1990—98; pres. ABC Sports, NYC, ABC Television, 2001—02, Go.com, The NFL Network, 2005—. Mem.: Cable TV Advt. Bur., European Sports Network (dir. Lafayette Beveer bd.), Nat. Acad. Cable Programming (bd. govs.).*

BOROFF, HENRY JACK, federal judge, educator; b. Boston, May 31, 1951; AB magna cum laude, Boston U., 1972, JD, 1975. Bar: Mass. 1975, U.S. Dist. Ct. Mass. 1976, U.S. Ct. Appeals (1st cir.) 1979, U.S. Supreme Ct. 1987. With Friedman & Atherton, Boston, 1976-81; pvt. practice Boroff & Assocs., 1981—93; bankruptcy judge for Mass., U.S. Bankruptcy Ct., Worcester and Springfield, 1993—. Adj. prof. Western New Eng. Law Sch., 1996—, Northeastern U. Law Sch., 1998—2000; lectr. in field. Mem.: Hampshire County Bar Assn., Hampden County Bar Assn., Mass. Bar Assn., Boston Bar Assn. (chair bankruptcy com. 1987—90). Office: US Bankruptcy Ct Donohue Fed Bldg 595 Main St Worcester MA 01608-2093

BORONICO, JESS STEPHEN, management science educator, dean; b. Bronx, NY, Oct. 23, 1956; s. Stelio and Helen (Michaels) B. BS in Math., Fairleigh Dickinson U., 1978, MS in Math., 1980; PhD in Ops. Rsch., U. Pa., 1992. Prof. mgmt. scis. Rutgers U., Camden, N.J., 1987-88, Phila. Coll. Textiles and Scis., 1988-92, Monmouth U., West Long Branch, NJ, 1993—2001, assoc. dean Sch. Bus., 1998-2000, dean Sch. Bus., 2000-01; prof. mgmt. scis., dean Cotsakis Coll. Bus., William Paterson U., Wayne, NJ, 2001—05; dean Sch. Bus. U. New Haven, 2005—. Cons. United Postal Svc., 1990-92, Reality Techs., 1991, N.J. Hwy. Authority, 1991-92, Kennedy Western U., Calif., 1994-97; mem. adv. bd. to various jours., 1993—. Author: Computer Simulation in Operations Management, 1996; contbg. author: The Service Productivity and Quality Challenge, 1995; editor: Studies in the Strategy and Tactics of Competitive Advantage, 2000; contbr. articles to profl. jours. Fellow U. Pa. Wharton Sch., 1983-87; recipient three Anbar citations of excellence for refereed publs., 1996-98. Mem. Inst. for Ops. Rsch. and Mgmt. Scis., Decision Scis. Inst., Am. Statis. Assn., Mensa. Avocations: softball, computer simulations. Office: U of New Haven School of Business Maxcy Hall 120 300 Boston Post Rd West Haven CT 06516 Business E-Mail: jboronico@newhaven.edu.

BORONOW, RICHARD CARLTON, gynecologist, educator; b. Appleton, Wis., Dec. 18, 1933; children: Robert, Thomas, Amy. BS in Medicine, Northwestern U., 1956, MD, 1959. Diplomate Am. Bd. Ob/Gyn. with cert. in gynecologic/oncology. Intern Cook County Hosp., Chgo., 1959-60; resident in ob/gyn Evanston Hosp., 1960-63; resident in surgery Meml. Hosp. Cancer, NYC, 1963-64; fellow in gynecology Anderson Tumor Inst., Houston, 1964-65; mem. staff Miss. Baptist Med. Ctr., Jackson; clin. prof. gynecology U. Miss. Med. Ctr. Author book; contbr. articles to profl. jours., chpts. to books. Recipient Merit award, Northwestern U. Med. Ctr., 2002, Alum of the Year award, 2002. Fellow ACS, Am. Coll. Ob/Gyn; mem. Am. Radium Soc. (exec. com.), Soc. Gynecologic Oncologists (past pres.), Soc. Surg. Oncologists, Soc. Pelvic Surgeons (past pres.) Office: St Dominic Med West Tower 971 Lakeland Dr Ste 750 Jackson MS 39216 Office Phone: 601-987-3033.

BOROWIEC, ANDREW, art educator, photographer; BA in Russian, Haverford Coll., 1979; MFA in Photography, Yale U., 1982. Instr. Parsons Sch. Design, Paris, 1980-82, 83-84; tchr. photography and art Germantown Acad., Ft. Washington, Pa., 1982-83; instr. New Sch. Social Rsch., NYC, 1982-84; instr. fashion photography Lab. Inst. Merchandising, NYC, 1984; dir. Sch. Art U. Akron, Ohio, 1990-95, prof. art mary Schiller Myers Sch. Art Ohio, 1995—. Guest lectr. contemporary Am. photography U. d'Aix-Marseille, France; vis. assoc. prof. art history Oberlin (Ohio) Coll., 1990. One-man shows include Club House, UN, Geneva, 1978, Galerie Un Moment En Plus, Paris, 1981, Le Poisson Banane, Arles, France, 1981, Galerie Les Arcenaulx, Marseille, France, 1982, Radnor Gallery, Bryn Mawr Coll., Pa., 1983, Perkins Gallery, U. Akron, 1984, Midtown Y Photography Gallery, N.Y.C., 1984, Dishman Gallery, Lamar U., Beaumont, Tex., 1986, Vox Gallery, Akron, 1988, Rose Gallery, St. Edwards U., Austin, Tex., 1988, Dillingham Gallery, Ithaca (N.Y.) Coll., 1988, Exit Gallery, Reno, 1988, Canton (Ohio) Art Inst., 1989, Fla. Internat. U., North Miami, Fla., 1990, Coll. Wooster (Ohio) Art Mus., 1991, Blue Sky Gallery, Portland, Oreg., 1994, Soc. Contemporary Photography, Kansas City, Mo., 1995, 99, Regis U., Denver, 1996, O.K. Harris, N.Y.C., 1997, So. Light Gallery, Amarillo, Tex., 1999, The Print Ctr., Phila., Pa., numerous others; exhibited in group shows at Images Gallery, Cin., 1991, Ea. Mich. U., Ypsilanti, 1992, Photospiva 93, Joplin, Mo., 1993, Contemporary Artists Ctr., North Adams, Mass., 1994, U. Cin., 1995, Blue Sky Gallery, Portland, 1996, Open Space Gallery, Allentown, Pa., 1997, Cleve. Mus. Art, 1998, Silver Eye Ctr. for Photography, Pitts., 2002, numerous others; represented in permanent collections Akron Art Mus., Can. Ctr. Arch., N.Y.C., Montreal, Can., Canton Art Inst., Chgo. Art Inst., Midtown Y. Photography Gallery, N.Y.C., Yale U., New Haven, Smithsonian Am. Art Mus., Cleve. Mus. Art, Libr. Congress, Ctr. for Documentary Studies, Houston Mus. Fine Arts, Hallmark Colection, others; books: Along the Ohio, 2000; staff photographer Internat. Ctr. Photography, N.Y.C., 1979-80; freelance photography The Chronicle for Higher Edn., 1987-93; commn. by Nat. Trust Historic Preservation and Soc. Photographic Edn., 1987, Canton Art Inst., 1988-89; contbr. photography to numerous publs. Recipient Excellence award Kansas City Art Inst., 1987, Hon. Mention and Purchase award Cleve. Mus. Art, 1988, Third prize N.Mex. Photographer, 1994, Purchase prize Nat. Mus. Am. Art, 1996, Fellowship award Soc. Contemporary Photography, 1998; Nat. Endowment Arts/Arts Midwest Photography fellow, 1985; Summer Rsch. fellow U. Akron, 1988, 90, 97, 2000; Individual Artist fellow Ohio Arts Coun., 1988, 98; John Simon Guggenheim Meml. Found. fellow, 1998; Faculty Rsch. grantee U. Akron, 1986; Instl. Support grantee Ohio Arts Coun., 1988; Visual Artists Forums grantee Nat. Endowment Arts, 1988; Folk Endowment grantee U. Akron Sch. Art, 1993; Folk Endowment grantee U. Akron Mary Schiller Myers Sch. Art, 1998. Address: 1062 W Market St Akron OH 44313-7128 Fax: (330) 972-5960. E-mail: borowiec@uakron.edu.

BOROWITZ, ALBERT IRA, lawyer, writer; b. Chgo., June 27, 1930; s. David and Anne (Wolkenstein) B.; m. Helen Blanche Osterman, July 29, 1950; children: Peter Leonard, Joan, Andrew Seth. BA in Classics summa cum laude, Harvard U., 1951, MA in Chinese Regional Studies, 1953, JD magna cum laude, 1956. Bar: Ohio 1957. Assoc. firm Hahn, Loeser, Freedheim, Dean & Wellman, Cleve., 1956-62, ptnr., 1962-83; ptnr. firm Jones, Day, Reavis & Pogue, Cleve., 1983-90, of counsel, 1991-94; cons., 1994—99. Author: Fiction in Communist China, 1954, Innocence and Arsenic: Studies in Crime and Literature, 1977, The Woman who Murdered Black Satin: The Bermondsey Horror, 1981, A Gallery of Sinister Perspectives: Ten Crimes and a Scandal, 1982, The Jack the Ripper Walking Tour Murder, 1986, The Thurtell-Hunt Murder Case: Dark Mirror to Regency England, 1987, This Club Frowns on Murder, 1990, Jones, Day, Reavis & Pogue: The First Century, 1993, Unhappy Endings, 2001, Blood and Ink: An International Guide to Fact-Based Crime Literature, 2002, Terrorism for Self-Glorification: The Herostratos Syndrome, 2005, Crimes Gone By: Collected Essays of Albert Borowitz, 2005; author: (with H.O. Borowitz) Pawnshop and Palaces: The Fall and Rise of the Campana Art Museum, 1991; series editor: True Crime, Kent State Univ. Press, 2001—06. Hon. consul of France in Cleve., 1990-95; v.p. French-Am. C. of C. of No. Ohio, 1993-99; co-founder Borowitz True Crime Collection at Kent State U. Librs. Recipient Cleve. arts prize for lit., 1981, Gold prize for true crime Foreword Mag., 2002. Mem. Am. Law Inst., Rowfant Club (Cleve.), Union Club (Cleve.), Harvard Club (N.Y.C.), Vidocq Soc. Phila. (hon.). Personal E-mail: alborowitz@adelphia.net.

BOROWITZ, JOSEPH LEO, pharmacologist, educator; b. Columbus, Ohio, Dec. 19, 1932; s. Joseph Peter and Anna Louise (Grundei) B.; divorced, 1985; children: Jon Joseph, Peter Joseph, Lynn Anne. BS in Pharmacy, Ohio State U., 1955; MS in Pharmacology, Purdue U., 1957; PhD in Pharmacology (NIH fellow), Northwestern U., 1960. Chief biokinetics br. Sch. Aerospace Medicine, San Antonio, 1960—62; postdoctoral fellow dept. pharmacology Harvard U. Med. Sch., Boston, 1963—64; instr., then asst. prof. pharmacology Wake Forest U. Sch. Medicine, 1964—69; assoc. prof. pharmacology and toxicology Purdue U., 1969—74, prof., 1974—; sabbatical leave to Basel, Switzerland, 1984; vis. prof. sch. pharmacy U. P.R., 2001; sabbatical leave to Cambridge, England, 1976. Adj. prof. pharmacology Ind. Sch. Medicine, 1980—. Contbr. articles to profl. jours. Treas. Tippecanoe County (Ind.) Comprehensive Health Planning Coun., 1971-76. Capt. USAR, 1960. Recipient award for excellence in teaching Bowman Gray Sch. Medicine, 1969, Henry Heine award for excellence in teaching Purdue U. Coll. Pharmacy, 1983; named NIH postdoctoral fellow, 1962-64; grantee NSF, 1965-68, NIH, 1971-74, 86-89, 89-94, 94-98, 1999-2004, 2004—, U.S. Army Med. Rsch., 1989-96, 97-2000. Mem.: Rho Chi. Roman Catholic. Office: Purdue U Dept Med Chem and Molec Pharmacology West Lafayette IN 47907 Home Phone: 765-463-3001. E-mail: borowitz@pharmacy.purdue.edu.

BOROWITZ, SIDNEY, retired physics professor; b. NYC, June 12, 1918; s. Morris and Rose (Cohen) B.; m. Ruth Aaron Meyer, June 20, 1943; children: Michael, Elizabeth. BS, CCNY, 1937; MS, NYU, 1941, PhD, 1948. Physicist David Taylor Model Basin, 1942-43; indsl. engr. Western Electric Co., 1943-45; instr. NYU, NYC, 1946-48, asst. prof., 1950-55, assoc. prof., 1955-59, prof. physics, 1959-84, prof. emeritus, 1984—, dean, 1969-71, chancellor, 1971-77; instr. Harvard U., Cambridge, Mass., 1948-50; chief exec. officer Cistron Biotech., Pine Brook, NJ, 1981-84. Chmn. bd. dirs. Aesculapius Internat. Medicine, N.Y.C., 1987-90, Inst. for Sch. of the Future, N.Y.C., 1987—; cons. NYU, 1987-97; exec. dir. N.Y. Acad. Scis., N.Y.C., 1977-81; mem. investment adv. com. Am. Inst. Physics, 1992-97. Author: Fundamentals of Quantum Mechanics, 1967, Farewell Fossil Fuels, 1998; co-author: Essentials of Physics, 1966, A Contemporary View of Elementary Physics, 1968, Farewell Fossil Fuels, 1999. Avocation: squash. Home: 70 E 10th St New York NY 10003-5102 Office: NYU Physics Dept Washington Sq N New York NY 10003 Office Phone: 212-998-7760. Business E-Mail: sb8@nyu.edu.

BOROWSKY, PHILIP, lawyer; b. Phila., Oct. 9, 1946; s. Joshua and Gertrude (Nicholson) B.; m. Judith Lee Goldwasser, Sept. 5, 1970 (div. 1996); children: Miriam Isadora, Manuel, Nora Jo; m. Victoria Culko Smith, Oct. 17, 2004. BA, UCLA, 1967; JD, U. San Francisco, 1973. Bar: Calif. Pres. and mng. ptnr. Cartwright, Slobodin, Bokelman, Borowsky, Wartnick, Moore & Harris, San Francisco, 1987-95; pres. Law Offices Philip Borowsky, Inc., San Francisco, 1996—2002; mng. ptnr. Borowsky & Hayes LLP, San Francisco, 2002—. Mem. faculty Practicing Law Inst., NYC, 1983-84; mem. adj. faculty Hastings Coll. Law, San Francisco, 1982-83; arbitrator Superior Ct., San Francisco, 1982—, Am. Arbitration Assn., 1982—, Nat. Assn. Securities Dealers, 1994—2003. Co-author: Unjust Dismissal and At-Will Employment, 1985; mem. bd. editl. cons. Bad Faith Law Update, 1986—2004. With US Army, 1968—70, Vietnam. Mem.: Consumer Attys. Calif. Democrat. Office: 1 Market Plz San Francisco CA 94105-1420 Office Phone: 415-896-6800. Business E-Mail: philip.borowsky@borowsky.com.

BORRELLI, JOHN FRANCIS, architect; b. Buffalo, Nov. 6, 1955; s. Peter and Maria (Raimondo) B. BSCE, Columbia U., 1977; postgrad., Pratt Inst., 1977-81. Registered arch., N.Y., N.J., Conn., Vt., Ill., Va., Pa., Fla., Md., Mich., Mass., Calif., Tex. Project coord. C. Raimondo and Sons, Ft. Lee, NJ, 1971-78; project mgr. DAT Cons., NYC, 1978-81, Litchfield Grosfeld Assocs., NYC, 1981-83; project arch. Design Mgmt., Inc., NYC, 1983-87; ptnr. Sys. Collaborative, Inc., NYC, 1987-88, Davis Borrelli Assocs., NYC, 1987-91; exec. v.p. Karco-Davis, Inc., NYC, 1987-91; v.p. Rampart Constrn. Assocs., NYC, 1987-91; prin. Meli Borrelli Assocs., NYC, 1991-94; pres. John Francis Borrelli Arch., P.C., NYC, 1991—; prin. MBA Mcpl., Inc., 1993, MBA Internat., Inc., 1991, SPGA MBA, Inc., 1993, Walter M. Ballard, Ltd., 1993, MBA&A, Inc., 1995, Vici Group, Ltd., NYC, 1995. Prin. works include ING/Barings Securities, Inc.Hdqs., N.Y.C., Credit Suisse Hdqs., Schonfeld Securities LLC (various offices in Chgo., L.A., N.Y.C., Miami Beach, others), Jericho L.I. Hdqs., Netscape Comms. Corp., N.Y., Chgo., Detroit, and Bethesda, Md., HS for Environ. Scis., N.Y.C., Burlington Industries Hdqrs., Walt Disney Book and Product Licensing Offices, Jefferson Ins. Corp. Hdqs., N.J., Western Union Corp. Hdqrs., Parade Publs. Corp. Hdqrs., N.Y.C., Covington Fabrics Corp. Hdqrs., Otterbourg, Steindler, Houston and Rosen, P.C., Lalique, Macromedia, Inc., N.J., Wilson, Elser, Moskowitz, Edelman & Dicker LLP, White Plains, N.Y., Boston, N.Y.C., Va., San Diego, Houston, Albany, Miami, Balt., L.A., Chgo., Las Vegas, San Francisco, Phila. Recipient 1st prize Gabriel Industries, 1976; Columbia U. scholar, 1973-77. Mem. AIA, ASCE, Nat. Trust for Hist. Preservation, World Wildlife Fund, Greenpeace. Avocations: woodworking, antiques, book collecting, gardening, tennis. Office: John Francis Borrelli Architect PC 13 E 37th St New York NY 10016-2821 Home Phone: 201-313-2390; Office Phone: 212-685-7354. Personal E-mail: jfbarchitect@aol.com.

BORROFF, MARIE, English language educator; b. NYC, Sept. 10, 1923; d. Albert Ramon and Marie (Bergersen) B. Ph.B., U. Chgo., 1943, MA, 1946; PhD, Yale U., 1956. Teaching asst. U. Chgo., 1946-47; instr. dept. English Smith Coll., 1948-51, asst. prof., 1956-59, asso. prof., 1959; vis. asst. prof. English Yale U., 1957-58, vis. asso. prof., 1959-6O, asso. prof. English, 1960-65, prof., 1965-71, William Lampson prof., 1971-92, Sterling prof. English, 1992-94; Sterling prof. English emeritus, 1994—; Phi Beta Kappa vis. scholar, 1973-74. Fellow Ezra Stiles Coll., Yale. Author: Sir Gawain and the Green Knight: A Stylistic and Metrical Study, 1962, (with J. B. Bessinger, Jr.); recorded dialogues read in Middle English, 1965, Sir Gawain and the Green Knight: A New Verse Translation, 1967, Pearl: A New Verse Translation, 1977, Language and the Poet: Verbal Artistry in Frost, Stevens, and Moore, 1979, Sir Gawain and the Green Knight, Patience and Pearl: Verse Translations, 2000, Stars and Other Signs: Poems, 2002; essay collection: Traditions and Rewewals Chaucer, the Gawain-Poet, and Beyond, 2003; editor: Wallace Stevens, A Collection of Critical Essays, 1963; videotaped lectures: To Hear Their Voices, Chaucer, Shakespeare and Frost, Assn. of Yale Alumni Great Tchrs. Series, Chapter Headings: Remarks Made at the Annual Initiation Ceremonies of Phi Beta Kappa, Alpha Chapter of Connecticut, 1989-1994, 1996. Bd. Govs. Yale U. Press, 1988-98. Recipient James Billings Fiske poetry prize U. Chgo., 1943; Eunice Tietjens Meml. prize Poetry mag., 1945; Margaret Lee Wiley fellow AAUW, 1955-56; Guggenheim fellow, 1969-70 Fellow Am. Acad. Arts and Scis.; mem. MLA, Acad. Am. Poets, Medieval Acad. Am., Phi Beta Kappa. Home: 311 St Ronan St New Haven CT 06511-2328 Office Phone: 203-432-2233. Business E-Mail: marie.borroff@yale.edu.

BORROR, DOUGLAS G., construction company executive; b. Dayton, Ohio, 1955; m. Kim Borror; children: Danielle, Donald. BA in History, Ohio State U., 1977. Lic. Real Estate Broker. With Huntington Nat. Bank, Columbus, 1977-79, Borror Corp. (now Borror Realty Co. Inc.), Dublin, Ohio, 1979—; pres. Dominion Homes, Inc., Dublin, Ohio, 1987—99, CEO, 1992—; chmn. bd. Dominion Homes, inc., Dublin, Ohio, 1999—. Bd. dir. Ohio Indemnity, Baninsurance Corp., 2004—, Columbia Gas of Ohio, Inc., Huntington Nat. Bank, Capital South Redevelopment Corp., Command Alkon Corp. Edn. chair Young President's Orgn., Columbus Chpt.; adv. bd. Goodwill Industries; bd. dir. Young President's Orgn., Internat., Wellington Sch., Recreation Unlimited; bd. trustee Ohio State U., 2004—; chmn. Columbus Riverfront Commons Corp.; bd. realtors Town of Columbus. Office: Dominion Homes Warranty Services PO Box 5000 Dublin OH 43016-5555

BORSARI, GEORGE ROBERT, JR., lawyer, commentator; b. Wash., July 30, 1940; s. George Robert and Sara Totton (Dunning) B.; m. Regis Ann Herron, Oct. 23, 1964 (div. Jan. 1985); children: George Robert, III, William Grant. BS, Va. Poly. Inst., 1962; LL.B., George Washington U., 1965. Bar: D.C. 1966. Since practiced in, Washington; ptnr. Borsari & Paxson, 1969—. Pres. Local TV Systems, Inc., 1981-89, Outdoor Inst., Inc., 1978—; chmn. Core Group Inc., 1991—. Councilman Town of Glen Echo, Md., 1969-74, mayor, 1977-81, 89-91; mem. Montgomery County (Md.) Muncipality Advisory Bd., 1972-74, Montgomery County CATV Task Force, 1973-74, 80-85, Cable TV Adv. Com., 1979-85; pres. Montgomery County chpt. Md. Mcpl. League. Served to lt. col. JAG USAR. Decorated Army Meritorious Service medal with oak leaf cluster, Army Commendation medal with 2 oak leaf clusters; recipient Presdl. commendation, 1970; St. George award Roman Catholic Archdiocese Washington, 1970; Silver Beaver award Nat. Capital Area council Boy Scouts Am., 1974 Mem. ABA (chmn. cable TV com. sect. sci. and tech. 1982-86, chmn. Broadcast Com. 1986-90, chmn. Mass Media Com. 1990-92, mem. coun. sect. sci. and tech.), D.C. Bar Assn., Fed. Comms. Bar Assn., Isaac Walton League, Kenwood Golf and Country Club (bd. govs. 2004—), Phi Delta Phi. Democrat. Home: 6107 Princeton Ave Glen Echo MD 20812-1125 Office: Borsari & Paxson 4000 Albemarle St NW Ste 100 Washington DC 20016 Business E-Mail: grb@baplaw.com.

BORSCHEL, DEBAROTI MULLICK, internal medicine physician; b. Plainfield, NJ, Oct. 15, 1972; d. Debdas and Sandhya Mullick; m. Gregory Howard Borschel; children: Anjali Mullick, Nikhil Mullick. BS, Emory U., Atlanta, 1989—93; MD, Johns Hopkins U., Balt., 1993—97; MS, U. Mich., Ann Arbor, 2001—03. Cert. internal medicine Am. Bd. Internal Medicine, 2000. Internal medicine resident to chief resident U. Mich. Health Sys., 1997—2001, internal medicine faculty physician, 2001—06; internal medicine faculty physician, hospitalist Wash. U., St. Louis, 2006—. Internal medicine residency assoc. program dir. U. Mich., 2002—05. Contbr. articles to profl. jours. Recipient Young Investigator award, 2002. Mem.: ACP, Assn. Program Dirs. Internal Medicine, Soc. Gen. Internal Medicine. Hindu. Avocations: travel, literature, scuba diving. Home Phone: 314-601-2526.

BORSON, DANIEL BENJAMIN, lawyer, educator, physiologist, researcher; b. Berkeley, Calif., Mar. 24, 1946; s. Harry J. and Josephine F. Borson. BA, San Francisco State Coll., 1969; MA, U. Calif., Riverside, 1973; PhD, U. Calif., San Francisco, 1982; JD, U. San Francisco, 1995. Bar: Calif. 1997, U.S. Dist. Ct. (no. dist.) Calif. 1997, U.S. Patent and Trademark Office 1998; lic. comml. pilot, flight instr. FAA. Musician Composer's Forum, Berkeley, San Francisco, 1961-70; flight instr. Buchanan Flying Club, Concord, Oakland, Calif., 1973-77, pres., 1975-77; physiology U. Calif., San Francisco, 1984-92, asst. rsch. physiologist Cardiovascular Rsch. Inst., 1988-92; assoc. Fliesler Dubb Meyer and Lovejoy LLP, 1997—2003, of counsel, 2003—06; founder Borson Intellectual Property Law Group PC, 2006; pres. Borson Law Group PC, 2006—. Vis. scientist Genentech Inc., South San Francisco, Calif., 1990—92. Contbr. articles, rev. chpts. and abstracts to profl. jours., legal periodicals and law rev. Fellow NIH, 1976-84, grantee, 1988-93; fellow Cystic Fibrosis Found., 1985, grantee, 1989-91; fellow Parker B. Francis Found., 1985-87; grantee Am. Lung Assn., 1985-87. Mem.: ABA, State Bar Calif. (vice chmn. 2003, mem. bd. govs. task force sects. 2003—06, co-chair 2004—05, chair legis. subcom. intellectual property sect. 2006—, patent standing com. 2001—04, exec. com., tchr. domestic and internat. law sect., coun. of sects., intellectual property sect.), No. Calif. Pharm. Discussion Group (bd. dir., chmn. 2000—02, founder and pres. Biosci. Forum 2002—), Fed. Cir. Bar Assn., San Francisco Intellectual Property Law Assn., Am. Intellectual Property Law Assn., Am. Chem. Soc., Am. Soc. Cell Biology, Am. Physiol. Soc. (mem. editl. bd. Am. Jour. Physiology 1990—92), Bay Flute Club (pres. 1978). Avocations: mountain climbing, aviation, music. Office: 1320 Willow Pass Rd Ste 490 Concord CA 94520 Office Phone: 925-395-2060. Business E-Mail: bborson@borsonlaw.com.

BORSTING, JACK RAYMOND, business administration educator; b. Portland, Oreg., Jan. 31, 1929; s. John S. and Ruth B.; m. Peggy Anne Nygard, Mar. 22, 1953; children: Lynn Carol, Eric Jeffrey. BA, Oreg. State U., 1951; MA, U. Oreg., 1952, PhD, 1959. Instr. math. Western Wash. Coll., 1953-54; teaching fellow U. Oreg., 1956-59; mem. faculty Naval Postgrad. Sch., 1959-80, prof. ops. research, chmn. dept., 1964-73, provost, acad. dean, 1974-80; asst. sec. def. (comptroller) Washington, 1980-83; dean Sch. Bus. U. Miami, Fla., 1983-88; Robert Dockson prof. and dean bus. adminstrn. U. So. Calif., Los Angeles, 1988-94; E. Morgan Stanley prof. bus. adminstrn. and exec. dir. Ctr. for Telecomms. Mgmt./U. So. Calif. Marshall Sch. Bus., Los Angeles, 1994—2001, prof., 2002—05. Vis. prof. U. Colo., 1967, 69, 71; vis. disting. prof. Oreg. State U., 1968; bd. visitors Def. Sys. Mgmt. Coll., 1985-91, chmn., 1988-91; trustee Met Life Investor, 2000—, adv. bd. Naval Postgrad. Sch., 1982-86, 98—; bd. overseers Ctr. Naval Analysis, 1984-94; trustee Aerospace Corp., 1986-92, Inst. Def. Analysis, 1990-2003; bd. advisors Elec. Power Rsch. Inst., 1999—; bd. govs., lead gov. Am. Stock Exch., 2005—. Contbr. to profl. jours. Trustee Orthop. Hosp. Found., L.A., 1992—, chmn., 1996-98, chmn. bd. dirs. 1999-2002; trustee Rose Hills Found. 1996—, chmn. 2005; gov. Town Hall of Calif., 1988-94; mem. Army Sci. Bd., 2002—. Recipient Disting. Pub. Service medal Dept. Def., 1980, 82, Disting. Svc. award Oreg. State U., 1982; disting. alumni fellow U. Oreg., 2004. Fellow AAAS, Mil. Ops. Rsch. Soc. (bd. dirs. 1965-72, pres. 1970-71), Internat. Engring. Consortium, Informs; mem. Army Sci. Bd., Inst. Mgmt. Sci., Am. Statis. Soc., Ops. Rsch. Soc. Am. (mem. coun. 1969-79, sec. 1972-74, pres. 1975-76, Kimball medal 1982, Koopmans award 2000), Internat. Fedn. Ops. Rsch. Socs. (treas. 1980-88), Calif. Club, 100 Club LA, Old Capitol Club, Sigma Xi, Pi Mu Epsilon, Beta Theta Pi. Episcopalian. Office: Marshall Sch Bus DCC 217 USC Los Angeles CA 90089-0871 Home Phone: 760-346-5011; Office Phone: 213-740-0982.

BORTH, DAVID E., telecommunications industry executive, researcher; BS, MS, U. Ill. at Urbana-Champaign, PhD in Elec. Engring. Mem. tech. staff Sys. Div. Watkins-Johnson Co., Palo Alto, Calif.; mem. corp. rsch. and devel. Motorola Corp., Schaumburg, Ill., 1980, mgr. Comm. Sys. Rsch. Lab., 1990—98, dir., 1998, head Wireless Access Rsch. Ctr. of Excellence, 2000—05, corp. v.p., chief tech. officer Govt. and Enterprise Mobility Solutions, 2005—. Asst. prof. Sch. Engring. Ga. Inst. Tech., Atlanta. Dan Noble Fellow. Mem.: NAE. Office: Motorola Inc 1303 E Algonquin Rd Schaumburg IL 60196

BORTMAN, DAVID, lawyer; b. Detroit, Sept. 17, 1938; s. Erwin Arne and Miriam Elaine (Shapiro) B. BA, U. Mich., 1962, JD, 1965. Bar: Mich. 1965, Ill. 1971. Asst. prosecutor Wayne County, Detroit, 1965-71; staff atty. Fed. Defender, Chgo., 1971-73; trial atty. SEC, Chgo., 1974-77; sole practice Chgo., 1977-79; ptnr. Bortman, Meyer & Barasa, Chgo., 1980-90; pvt. practice LA, 1990—. Mem. Fed. Ct. Jury Instrns. Com., Chgo., 1984—85; mem. adv. bd. Air Force Office of Pub. Affairs. Chmn. telethon com. Muscular Dystrophy Assn., Chgo., 1984; pres. Met. Chgo. Air Force Comty. Coun., 1985-88; mem. World Affairs Coun. Mem. ABA, ATLA, Acad. of TV Arts and Scis., State Bar Calif., Los Angeles County Bar Assn. (mem. lawyer referral com.), Beverly Hills Bar Assn. (entertainment law steering com.), Fed. Bar Assn. (bd. dirs. Chgo. chpt. 1985-90), Rotary, U. Mich. Club of L.A., U. Mich. Club of Chgo. (bd. govs. 1987-89), Union League of Chgo. (bd. dirs. 1986-89), Variety Club Children's Charities, Jonathan Club, Thalians Charity, West L.A. C. of C. (bd. dirs.), Century City C. of C. (bd. dirs., co-chmn. Entertainment Industry Coun.). Jewish. Home: 11908 Dorothy St Apt 102 Los Angeles CA 90049-5330 Office: 433 N Camden Dr #600 Beverly Hills CA 90210 Home Phone: 310-207-0673; Office Phone: 310-288-1980. Personal E-mail: davesq@earthlink.net.

BORTNICK, DANIEL PHILIP, plastic surgeon; b. Apr. 11, 1963; BS, U. Mo., Kans. City, MD, 1987. Cert. Am. Bd. Plastic Surgery. Internship gen. surgery U. Kans., resident gen. surgery; resident plastic surgery Med. Coll. Ga., 1992—94; surgeon Monarch Plastic Surgery. Post doctoral fellowship molecular genetics & microbiology U. Mo.; clin. asst. prof. dept. surgery U. Kans.; dir. cosmetic aesthetic surgery rotation U. Kans. Med. Ctr.; com. mem. Nat. Plastic Surgery Edn. Found.; bd. dirs. plastic surgery Med. Coll. Ga. Named one of Kansas City Super Dr.'s, Kansas City Mag., 2006. Fellow: ACS; mem.: AMA, Lipoplasty Soc. N.Am., Am. Soc. Aesthetic Plastic Surgery (com. mem.), Am. Soc. Plastic Surgery (com. mem.). Office: Monarch Plastic Surgery 5401 College Blvd Ste 203 Leawood KS 66211 Office Phone: 913-663-3838. Office Fax: 913-663-4434.*

BORTNICK, NEWMAN MAYER, research chemist; b. May 14, 1921; s. Louis Benjamin and Emily Rosa (Roberts) Bortnick; m. Lillian Ulanove, Aug. 29, 1943; children: Karl, Lynn, Wendy. BA magna cum laude, U. Minn., 1941; PhD in Organic Chemistry, 1944. Rsch. chemist Rohm and Haas Co., Phila., 1944—, head high pressure lab., 1959-66, rsch. supr. plastics, 1966-73, mgr., dir. exploratory process rsch., 1973-81, mgr. plastics rsch. dept., 1982-84, corp. rsch. fellow, 1984-90, cons., 1991—. Holder more than 100 patents in organic chemistry, polymers; contbr. articles to numerous profl. jours. Mem. Planning Commn. Springfield Twp., Pa., 1956-66; mem., pres. Bd. Sch. Dirs., Springfield Twp., 1966-73; v.p. intermediate unit 23 Montgomery County Bd. Sch. Dirs., 1971-73; bd. dirs. Carson Valley Sch., Springfield Twp., 1973—, ServiceNet, Inc., 1996—. Recipient Outstanding Achievement award U. Minn., 2000. Fellow AAAS, Am. Inst. Chemists, Royal Soc. Chemistry UK; mem. Am. Chem. Soc. (dir.-at-large 1983-88), Phila. Sect. Am. Chem. Soc. (chmn. 1967, councilor 1968-82, 90-99, Rsch. award 1964, Svc. award 1973), Soc. Plastics Engrs., Phi Beta Kappa, Sigma Xi, Phi Lambda Upsilon. Office: c/o Rohm and Haas Co 100 Independence Mall West Philadelphia PA 19106-2399 E-mail: nbortnick@rohmhaas.com, newm2@aol.com.

BORTON, GEORGE ROBERT, retired airline captain; b. Wichita Falls, Tex., Mar. 22, 1921; s. George Neat and Travis Lee (Jones) B.; m. Anne Louise Bowling, Feb. 5, 1944 (dec.); children: Trudie T., Robert B., Bruce M.; m. Marjorie C. Silvera, May 17, 2006. AA, Hardin Coll., Wichita Falls, 1940. Cert. airline transport pilot, FAA flight examiner. Flight sch. operator Vallejo (Calif.) Sky Harbor, 1947-48; capt. S.W. Airways, San Francisco, 1948-55; check capt. Pacific Airlines, San Francisco, 1955-68, Hughes Air West, San Francisco, 1968-71; capt. N.W. Airlines, Mpls., 1971-82, ret., 1982. Col. USAF, 1943-73, ret. Decorated Air medal. Mem.: Airline Pilots Assn., Air Force Assn., Res. Officers Assn., Model T Club-Phoenix, Model T of Am. Club, Horseless Carriage Club. Republican. Home: Pebble Creek Resort 4053 N 162nd Ave Goodyear AZ 85338

BORTON, JOHN CARTER, JR., (TERRY BORTON), theatrical producer; b. Washington, Aug. 25, 1938; s. John Carter and Mary (Newlin) B.; m. Deborah H. Borton, June 18, 1960; children: Lynn, Mark. BA, Amherst Coll., 1960; MA, U. Calif., Berkeley, 1962; EdD, Harvard U., 1970. Cert. gen. tchr., Calif. Asst. dir. vol. program Berkeley Unified Schs., 1962-63; tchr. English, co-chmn. dept. Richmond (Calif.) Union H.S., 1963-66; cons. Phila. Bd. Edn., 1966-67, acting dir. Office Affective Devel., 1970-71, dir. dual audio TV project, 1971-77; editorial dir. Xerox Edn. Publs., Middletown, Conn., 1977-80, editor in chief, 1980-86; v.p., editor in chief Field Publs. (formerly Xerox Edn. Publs.), Middletown, 1986-91, Weekly Reader Corp. (formerly Field Publs.), Middletown, 1991-92; prodr., lead performer Am. Magic Lantern Theater, 1992—. Lectr. U. Pa., Phila., 1971-76, Phila. Coll. Art, 1976-77; cons. various sch. systems, univ./colls., founds., profl. orgns., govt. agys., 1975-77. Author: Reach, Touch and Teach: Student Concerns and Process Education, 1970, Emotionales und Soziales Lernen in der Schule, 1976; also numerous articles in profl. jours., including Weekly Reader; performer 2 records and tchr.'s manuals introducing poetry to high sch. students; author 20 scripts for The Storyphone, 1976, 80 scripts for Dual Audio, Sta. WUHY-FM, 1972-73, 14 prodns. for Am. Magic Lantern Theater. Bd. dirs. Oddfellow's Theater. Mem. League Hist. Am. Theaters, N.E. Performing Arts Assn., Magic Lantern Soc., Assn. Performing Arts Presenters, Internat. Assn. Performing Arts Young People. Avocations: carpentry, sculpture, writing, gardening. Office: Am Magic Lantern Theater PO Box 44 East Haddam CT 06423-0044 Business E-Mail: tborton@magiclanternshows.com.

BORTS, GEORGE HERBERT, economist, educator; b. NYC, Aug. 29, 1927; s. Elias Alexander and Etta (Silberg) B.; m. Muriel Levenson, Dec. 26, 1948; children: David, Richard, Robert. AB, Columbia U., 1947; AM, U. Chgo., 1949, PhD, 1953; AM (hon.), Brown U., 1957. Prof. econs. Brown U., Providence, 1960—. Mng. editor Am. Econ. Rev., Nashville, 1968-80, World Bus. Adv., Providence, 1990-91; co-author: Economic Growth in a Free Market, 1964. Mem. Am. Econ. Assn., Phi Beta Kappa. Home: 220 Slater Ave Providence RI 02906-3440 Office: Brown U 64 Waterman St Providence RI 02912-9029 E-mail: george_borts@brown.edu.

BORTZ, WALTER M., III, academic administrator; m. Lorraine Bortz; children: Catherine, Walter. BS, Bethany Coll.; PhD in Policy Studies, George Washington U. Dir. admissions Bethany Coll., East Carolina U.; dean admissions Tex. Christian U.; exec. dir. admissions and student fin. assistance U. Hartford, v.p. institutional advancement, acting v.p. adminstrn., acting v.p. student svcs.; v.p. adminstrn. and info. svcs. George Washington U.; pres. Hampden-Sydney Coll., Va., 2000—. Mem. exec. com. Coun. Independent Colls. in Va.; trustee Va, Found. Independent Colls.; head President's coun. Old Dominion Athletic Conf.; mem. commn. on colls. So. Assn. Colls. and Univs. Office: Hampden-Sydney Coll Hampden Sydney VA 23943 Office Phone: 434-223-6110. E-mail: prez@hsc.edu.*

BORUCH, ROBERT FRANCIS, educator, consultant; b. Bayonne, NJ, Oct. 16, 1942; m. Dorothy DeMoya Boruch, June 4, 1989; children: Marc DeMoya, Andre DeMoya. PhD, Iowa State U., Ames, 1968. Prof. Northwestern U., Evanston, Ill., 1970—89; trustee chair prof. U. Pa., Phila., 1989—. Bd. trustees W. T. Grant Found., NYC, 1997—; bd. dirs. Internat. Cambpbell Collaboration, Phila., 2002—. Recipient Donald Campbell award, Policy Studies Orgn., Myrdal award, Am. Evaluation Assn., Rsch. Rev. award, Am. Ednl. Rsch. Assn. Fellow: Am. Statis. Assn., Am. Acad. Arts and Scis.; mem.: NAS (assoc.), Am. Inst. Rsch. (bd.dirs. 1990—). Office: Univ Pa 3700 Walnut St Philadelphia PA 19104 Office Phone: 215-898-0409.

BORUM, OLIN HENRY, retired research scientist; b. Spencer, NC, Nov. 3, 1917; s. Oscar Henry and Marjorie Mae (Leigh) Borum; m. Beatrice Star Comulada, Nov. 14, 1944; children: Pamela Leigh, Robin Olin, Denis Richard. BS, U. N.C., 1938, MA, 1947, PhD, 1949; postgrad., U. Md., 1940—41. Rsch. chemist E.I. du Pont de Nemours & Co., Phila., 1949—50; interim rsch. asst. prof. Cancer Rsch. Lab. U. Fla., 1950; instr., asst. prof. chemistry U.S. Mil. Acad., 1952—55; rsch. adminstr. U.S. Army Chem. Corps R&D Command, Washington, 1956—60, U.S. Army Material Command, Washington, 1964—76; realtor assoc. Unique Properties, Alexandria, Va., 1974—79; realtor, assoc. broker J. Edwards Co., Inc., Alexandria, 1979—82; prin. broker Olin H. Borum Realty, Alexandria, 1982—. Tchr. chemistry U. Va., Arlington, Va., 1966-68 Contbr. articles to profl. jours Leader Nat. Capital Area coun. Boy Scouts Am., 1964-75, unit commr., 1968-75; sec. Mt. Vernon Civic Assn., Va. 1965-66; mem. Com. of 33 (nat. adv. group Nat. Sojourners, Inc.), 1962-71, chmn., 1969-71, Nat. trustee Nat. Sojourners, Inc., 1971-73. Maj. AUS, 1941-46; maj. USAF, 1951-56, lt. col., 1960-64. Recipient cert. Achievement Dept. Army, 1971; Tchg. fellow U. Md., 1940-41, U. N.C., 1946-49 Fellow Am. Inst. Chemists; mem. Am. Chem. Soc., Masons, Shriners, Phi Beta Kappa, Sigma Xi Presbyterian. Home: 9002 Volunteer Dr Alexandria VA 22309-2921

BORUM, RODNEY LEE, corporate financial executive; b. High Point, NC, Sept. 30, 1929; s. Carl Macy and Etta (Sullivan) B.; m. Helen Marie Rigby, June 27, 1953; children: Richard Harlan, Sarah Elizabeth. Student, U. N.C., 1947-49; BS, U.S. Naval Acad., 1953. Design-devel. engr. GE, Syracuse, NY, 1956—57, Cape Kennedy, Fla., 1957—58, missile test condr., 1958-60, mgr. ground equipment engr., 1960-61, mgr. ea. test range engring., 1961-65; adminstr. Bus. and Def. Svcs. Adminstrn.-Dept. Commerce, 1966—68; pres. Printing Industries Am., Arlington, Va., 1968—85, staff cons., 1985-86, mem. exec. com., 1969-85, dir.; pres. W.H. Rigby Cons., 1985-86; exec. v.p. Amasek Inc., Cocoa, Fla., 1986-87; assoc. Fin. Svcs. Orgn., Cocoa, Fla., 1987—89; v.p., CFO Pearl of Va., 1995—; acting COO Somerset Oil, 2007—. Sec. Graphic Arts Show Corp.; dir. Inter-Comprint Ltd., Strangers Cay, Ltd.; mem. governing bd. Comprints Internat.; Rep. candidate 11th dist. U.S. congress, Fla., 1988-90; ops. mgr. COVIX Corp.; mgmt. cons. 1990—; exec. v.p. Pearl of Va., Inc., 1992—. Mem. exec. coun. Cub Scouts Am., 1965; bd. dirs., v.p. Brevard County (Fla.) United Fund, 1964-65; bd. dirs. Brevard Beaches Concert Assn., 1965; mem. edn. coun. bd. dirs. Graphic Arts Tech. Found., Pitts., 1970-86; trustee, founder Graphic Arts Edn. and Rsch. Trust Fund, Arlington, Va., 1978-85; candidate for U.S. Ho. of Reps. from llth dist. Fla., 1988. lst lt. USAF, 1953-56. Named Boss of Yr., C. of C., 1965; recipient Bausch and Lomb Sci. award, 1947, Am. Legion award, 1952. Mem. U.S. Naval Inst., U.S. Naval Acad. Alumni Assn., Graphic Arts Coun. N.Am. (bd. dirs. 1977—), Phi Eta Sigma. Methodist.

BORUS, JONATHAN FREDERICK, psychiatrist, educator; b. Washington, May 4, 1941; s. Joseph B. and Rosalie (Bierman) B.; m. Dixie Lee Nelson, June 13, 1964; children: Joseph S., Joshua S., Daniel A. MD, U. Ill., 1965. Diplomate Am. Bd. Med. Examiners, Am. Bd. Psychiatry and Neurology, Gen. Psychiatry, Forensic Psychiatry. Rotating intern Cook County Hosp., Chgo., 1965-66; resident in psychiatry Neuropsychiat. Inst. U. Ill., Chgo., 1966-69; rsch. psychiatrist Walter Reed Army Inst. Rsch., Washington, 1969-72; cons. psychiatrist Henry Phipps Clinic Johns Hopkins Hosp., Balt., 1972; co-dir., sr. psychiatrist Freedom Trail Clinic Erich Lindemann Mental Health Ctr., Boston, 1972-76; chief psychiat. cons. North End Health Ctr., Boston, 1972-90; dir. tng. Erich Lindemann Mental Health Ctr., Boston, 1974-76; dir. social and community psychiatry Mass. Gen. Hosp., Boston, 1975-83, chmn. com. on teaching and edn., 1983-90, dir. residency and fellowship tng. in psychiatry, 1976-90; prof. psychiatry Harvard Med. Sch., Boston, 1994—; dir. psychiatry Brigham and Women's Hosp., Boston, 1990-92, psychiatrist in chief, 1992—, chmn. dept. psychiatry, 1999—, chmn. edn. com., 2006—; chief of psychiatry Faulkner Hosp., 2001—; Stanley Cobb prof. psychiatry Harvard Med. Sch., 2005—. Founding mem. steering com. psychiat. epidemiology Harvard U., 1979—95, mem. mental health work group, 1982—87; founding mem., sec. Nat. Psychiatry Match Rev. Bd., Washington, 1987—91; appeals bd. Accreditation Coun. for Grad. Med. Edn., Chgo., 1989—99, residing rev. com. in psychiatry, 2007—; adv. com. on mental health NAS, Inst. Medicine, Washington, 1977—79; prin. investigator NIMH, 1975—90; vis. prof. U. Man., 1978, Lettermen Med. Ctr., 1979, U. Conn., 1984, U. South Fla., 1987, USAF Med. Ctr., 1988, Calif. Pacific Med. Ctr., 1990, Tex. A&M, 1993, U. Calif., Davis, 1997—99, 2007; mem. exec. com. dept. psychiatry Harvard U., 1992—, chmn. exec. com., 2003—05, steering com. Ptnrs. Healthcare Psychiatry, 1995—. Assoc. editor Am. Jour. Psychiatry, 1982-90; editor Acad. Psychiatry, 1989-95; edn. editor Harvard Review Psychiatry, 1993—; contbr. numerous articles to profl. jours. Mem. Beacon Hill-West End Mental Health Com., Boston, 1972-76, Lt. Gov.'s Com. for Mental Health Ins., Commonwealth of Mass., 1977-78; disting. cons. Walter Reed Army Med. Ctr., Washington, 1986-89. Maj. U.S. Army, 1969-72. Named Outstanding Psychiat. Educator, Assn. for Acad. Psychiatry, 1992; recipient Vestermark award for psychiat. edn., Am. Psychiat. Assn. and NIMH, 1997, Lifetime Achievement in Mentoring award, Harvard Med. Sch., 1998, Lifetime Achievement award, Assn. for Acad. Psychiatry, 2004. Mem.: Mass. Psychiat. Soc., Am. Assn. Dirs. Psychiat. Residency Tng. (treas. 1979—80, sec. 1981—82), Assn. Acad. Psychiatry (pres. 1986—88), Am. Psychiat. Assn. (Disting. Life fellow). Democrat. Jewish. Office: Brigham and Women's Hosp 75 Francis St Boston MA 02115-6106 Office Phone: 617-732-8140. Business E-Mail: jborus@partners.org.

BORWEIN, DAVID, mathematics professor; b. Kaunas, Lithuania, Mar. 24, 1924; s. Joseph Jacob and Rachel (Landau) B.; m. Bessie Flax, June 30, 1946; children— Jonathan, Peter, Sarah. B.Sc. in Engring, Witwatersrand U., South Africa, 1945, B.Sc. Hons., 1948; PhD, Univ. Coll. London, 1950, D.Sc., 1960. Lectr. St. Andrews U., Scotland, 1950-63; vis. prof. U. Western Ont., London, Can., 1963-64, prof., 1964-89, head math. dept., 1967-89, prof. emeritus, 1989—. Contbr. articles to profl. jours. Served with South African Forces, 1945. NSERC grantee, 1966—2005. Fellow Royal Soc. Edinburgh; mem. London Math. Soc., Am. Math. Soc., Math. Assn. Am., Canadian Math. Soc. (chmn. research com. 1970-73, v.p. 1973-75, pres. 1985-87) Home: 1032 Brough St London ON Canada N6A 3N4 Office: Dept Math U Western Ont London ON Canada N6A 5B7 E-mail: dborwein@uwo.ca.

BORWICK, SUSAN HARDEN, musicologist, educator; d. Clyde and Edythe Brown Harden; m. Douglas Bruce Borwick, Aug. 14, 1976 (div. Apr. 20, 1996); 1 child, John Harden. MusB, MusEdnB, Baylor U., Waco, TX, 1968; PhD, Univ. NC, Chapel Hill, 1972. Asst. prof. music Baylor U., Waco, Tex., 1972—77, Eastman Sch. Music, Rochester, NY, 1977—82; assoc. prof. music Wake Forest U., Winston-Salem, NC, 1982—88, prof. music, 1988—. Chair dept. music Wake Forest U., Winston-Salem, NC, 1982—94, dir. women's studies, 2000—04, 2003—; program devel. and adminstrn. coun. Nat. Women's Studies Assn., 2000—04, chair contemporary curriculum transformation project, 2001—05. Author: (compact disc program notes) American Romantics: Arthur Foote and Amy Cheney Beach; composer: (sacred choral work) Morning Light, Hope: An Advent Choral Introit, (solo for voice, flute, piano) Mary's, Mary's Mary's, (sacred choral work) Benediction, (incidental music) Much Ado about Nothing; contbr. articles to profl. jours., God's Man in Texas, Dark of the Moon. Chair bd. of deacons Knollwood Bapt. Ch., Winston-Salem, NC, 1994—95; sec. Bapt. Women in Ministry, NC, 2000—; pres., v.p., sec. NC Assn. Music Schs., 1987—94. Grantee R. J. Reynolds Rsch. Leave, Wake Forest U., 1996, 1998, 2003—04; Travel to Collections grant, Nat. Endowment for the Humanities, 1986, William C. Archie Rsch. grant, Wake Forest U., 2000—01, 2002—03, 2004—. Mem.: Soc. for Am. Music, Am. Musicological Soc., Coll. Music Soc. (life), Omicron Delta Kappa, Mu Phi Epsilon. Avocations: gardening, travel. Home: 4101 Mill Creek Rd Winston Salem NC 27106-2917 Office: Dept of Music Wake Forest Univ 7345 Reynolda Station Winston Salem NC 27109-7345 Office Phone: 336-758-5953. E-mail: borwick@wfu.edu.

BORYSEWICZ, MARY LOUISE, editor; b. Chgo. d. Thomas J. and Mabel E. (Zeien) O'Farrell m. Daniel S. Borysewicz, June 11, 1955 (dec. 2005); children: Mary Adele, Stephen Francis (dec. 1997), Paul Barnabas. BA, Mundelein Coll., 1970; postgrad. in English lit., U. Ill, 1970—71; grad. exec. program, U. Chgo., 1982. Editor sci. publs. AMA, Chgo., 1971—73; exec. mng. editor Am. Jour. Ophthalmology, Chgo., 1973—95; media cons. Fox-Wahls Design, Chgo., 1999—2004; editl. svc. cons. A.T. Kearney, Chgo., 2004. Asst. sec., treas. Ophthalmic Pub. Co., 1985—95; guest lectr. U. Chgo. Med. Sch., 1979, Harvard U. Med. Sch., 1978, Northwestern U. Med. Sch., 1979, Am. Acad. Ophthalmology, 1976, 81, Northwestern U. Joseph Medill Sch. Journalism, 2002. Editor: Ophthalmology Principles and Concepts, 7th edit., 1992, 8th edit., 1996, Documenta Ophthalmologica History Issue, 1997, 98; contbg. writer Chicago Shops, 2002, 03, 06; contbr. articles to sci. publs. Mem. Coun. Biol. Editors (bd. dirs. 1988-91, fin. com. 1985-88, teller com. 1992-95). Personal E-mail: mbory@aol.com.

BOSCH, JOSEPH A., construction executive; BS, Cornell U., Ithaca, NY. Employee rels. rep. to v.p. employee rels. NE region PepsiCo, 1982—92; with human resources dept. So. divsn. Pizza Hut, Inc., Atlanta, 1992—97, chief people officer, 1997—2004; sr. v.p. human resources Tenet Healthcare Corp., 2004—06, Centex Corp., Dallas, 2006—. Served with US Army. Office: Centex Corp PO Box 199000 Dallas TX 75219-9000 Office Phone: 469-893-2200. Office Fax: 469-893-8600.*

BOSCH, MICHELE C., lawyer; b. Washington, Apr. 29, 1968; BA, U. Va., 1990; JD, Coll. William & Mary, 1993. Bar: Va. 1993, DC 1997, US Patent & Trademark Office. Ptnr. Finnegan, Henderson, Farabow, Garrett & Dunner LLP, Washington, mem. mgmt. com. Mem.: Am. Chem. Soc., Fed. Cir. Bar Assn., DC Bar Assn., Va. Bar Assn., Am. Intellectual Property Assn., ABA. Fluent in French. Office: Finnegan Henderson Farabow Garrett & Dunner LLP 901 New York Ave NW Washington DC 20001-3315 Office Phone: 202-408-4000. Office Fax: 202-408-4400. Business E-Mail: michele.bosch@finnegan.com.

BOSCH COBB, KAREN, library director; Assoc. county libr. Fresno County Pub. Libr., Calif., interim county libr., 2003—05, county libr. Calif., 2005—. Mem. adminstrv. coun. San Joaquin Valley Libr. Sys.; bd. mem. Heartland Regional Libr. Network. Mem.: Calif. Libr. Assn. (Mem. of Yr. award 2005). Office: Fresno County Pub Libr 2420 Mariposa St Fresno CA 93721 Office Phone: 559-488-3185. Office Fax: 559-488-1971. E-mail: Karen.BoschCobb@fresnolibrary.org.

BOSCHERT, THOMAS NEVILLE, historian, educator; b. Memphis, Nov. 5, 1929; s. Thomas Mauldin and Edith Louise Boschert; m. Eva Ann Dickins, Mar. 25, 1952; children: Ann Carter McNeal, Neville Henry, Curtis Dickins. BA, U. Miss., University, 1950, MA, 1985, PhD, 1995. Instr. USAF Tech. Tng. Sch., Keesler Air Force Base, Miss., 1952—55; mgr. Duncan Grain Elevator, AAL, Duncan, 1955—64. Farm owner-operator, Duncan, 1956—83; town clk., tax collector Town of Duncan, 1984—; adj. asst. prof. history Delta State U., Cleveland, 1998—2001, vis. asst. prof. history, 2001—. Contbr. articles to profl. jours. Cmty. committeeman Bolivar County Agrl. and Stblzn. Com., Cleveland, 1960—68; songleader and pianist Duncan Bapt. Ch., 1971—2004; dir. Bolivar County Farm Bur., Cleveland, 1964—76; pres. Bolivar County Hist. Soc., 1976—78. 1st lt. USAF, 1950—55, maj. (ret.) USAF, 1974—89. Recipient George Wash. Honor medal award, Freedoms Found. Valley Forge, 1968. Mem.: So. Hist. Assn., Miss. Hist. Soc. (pres. 1984—84), Am. Hist. Assn. Southern Baptist. Home: 203 Magnolia Hill PO Box 215 Duncan MS 38740 Office: Delta State University West Sunflower Road Cleveland MS 38733 Personal E-mail: thomasn@gmi.net. Business E-Mail: tboschrt@deltastate.edu.

BOSCHETTI, PHILIP J., oil industry executive; b. Yonkers, NY, Apr. 11, 1944; s. Anthony and Santina (Taccetta) B.; m. Linda Marie Liggio, June 11, 1966; children: Keith Philip, Scott Alan. BBA in Mktg., Iona Coll., 1966. Sales mgr. Firestone Tire and Rubber Co., NJ, 1966; fin. adminstr. William S. Paley & Co., NYC, 1969-91; v.p., CFO Burnett Oil Co., Inc., Ft. Worth, 1991—. Asst, sec, treas. The Greenpark Found., Inc., NYC, 1978—91, William S. Paley Found., Inc., NYC, 1978—91; v.p. Burnett Ranches, Inc., Ft. Worth, 1991—, Burnett Aviation Co., Inc., Ft. Worth, 1991—, Exec. Protective Systems, Ft. Worth, 1991—; v.p., CFO Burnett Ranches, Ltd., Ft. Worth, 1992—; v.p., dir. Burnett Svcs., Inc., Ft. Worth, 1992—, Burnett Security Systems, Inc., Ft. Worth, 1994—; v.p. AJJM Capital Corp., Ft. Worth, 1996—; treas., dir. K&M, Inc., Ft. Worth,

1998—2000, Cookworks of Santa Fe, Inc., 1998—2000, Cookworks, Tex., Inc., Ft. Worth, 1998—2002; pres. CW Beverages, Inc., Ft. Worth, 1999—2002, Addison Warehouse Beverages, Inc., Ft. Worth, 1999—2002; mgr. of bd. Burnett Land, LLC; chmn., dir. Club Pro Clearing House Corp., 2000—05. V.p., treas. Westwood Baseball Assn., 1977-88, bd. dirs., 2000-05; v.p. Westwood Babe Ruth, 1985-88; treas. Tommy League, 1984-86; dir. Westwood Recreation Youth Football, 1984-86; mem. Westwood Inds. Club, 1976-80. Decorated Bronze star, Air medal with oak leaf cluster, Vietnamese Honor medal, Vietnamese Svc. medal, Vietnamese campaign medal w/four svc. stars, Nat. Def. Svc. medal. Mem. River Crest Country Club. Office: Burnett Oil Co Inc Burnett Plz Ste 1500 801 Cherry St Unit 9 Fort Worth TX 76102-6881

BOSCHINI, VICTOR JOHN, JR., academic administrator; b. Cleve. m. Megan Boschini; children: Elizabeth, Mary Catherine, Edward Mark, Margaret. B in Sociology and Psychology, Union Coll.; M in Coll. Student Pers., Bowling Green State U.; D in Higher Edn. Adminstrn., Ind. U. Asst. to the dir. of residence life Bowling Green (Ohio) State U., 1978—79; student adviser Western Ill. U., Macomb, 1979—82; asst. dean of students DePauw U., Greencastle, Ind., 1982—84; asst. dean studies Ind. U., Bloomington, 1984—90; assoc. provost Butler U., Indpls., 1990—97; v.p., dean student affairs, edn. prof. Ill. State U., Normal, 1997—99, pres., 1999—2003; chancellor, prof. edn. Tex. Christian U., Ft. Worth, 2003—. Bd. dir. State Farm Mutual Funds Co. Bd..dir. Fort Worth Symphony, Tex.; bd. dir. Van Cliburn Found., Fort Worth, Tex.; bd. trustee Brite Divinity Sch. Office: Tex Christian Univ Box 297080 3861 Bellaire Cir Fort Worth TX 76109 Office Phone: 817-257-7783. Office Fax: 817-927-7518. E-mail: v.boschini@tcu.edu, chancellor@tcu.edu.*

BOSCHMANN, ERWIN, chemistry professor; b. Chaco, Paraguay, Jan. 1, 1939; arrived in U.S., 1959; s. David and Anna Boschmann; m. Priscilla Glee Selzer, Aug. 17, 1962; children: Heidi Kristine Boschmann Amstutz, Tonya Renee, Eric Erwin. PhD, U. Colo., 1968. Asst. prof. Ind. U.-Purdue U., Indpls., 1968-74, assoc. prof., 1974-77, prof. chemistry, 1977—, assoc. dean faculties, 1988—99, assoc. v.p., 1999—2002, Ind. U., 1998—2002; interim vice chancellor acad. affairs Ind. U. E., 2003—04; CEO Plowshares, Indpls., 2004—06; ind. cons., 2006—. Cons. Ford Found., Peru, 1968—73, Asian Devel. Bank, Indonesia, 1985—87. Author: The Electronic Classroom (Fredric Lieber Award, 1985), Ten Teaching Tools, 1987, Foundations of Life, 1991. Recipient Distng. Alumnus award, Bethel Coll., 1998; Lilly Endowment Faculty Open fellow, Indpls., 1988. Mem.: Am. Chem. Soc. Mennonite. Office Phone: 317-278-2511. Business E-Mail: erv@iu.edu.

BOSCIA, JON ANDREW, insurance company executive; b. Pitts., Apr. 15, 1952; s. Louis C. and Stella (Weryha) B.; m. Donna M. Lowar, Aug. 18, 1973; children: Nicole Marie, Brandon Jon. BA, Point Park Coll., 1973; MBA, Duquesne U., 1979. Corp. planner Consolidated Nat. Gas, Pitts., 1974-79; fin. sales rep. Westinghouse, Pitts., 1979-80; asst. v.p. Mellon Bank, Pitts., 1980-83; sr. v.p. Lincoln Nat. Pension, Ft. Wayne, Ind., 1983—98; pres. Lincoln Nat. Life Insurance Co., 1999—2004, Lincoln Fin. Group, Phila., 1998—2001, chmn., CEO, 2001—07. Bd. dirs. Georgia-Pacific Corp. Contbr. articles to profl. jours. Mem. coms. Pitts. Bd. Edn., 1974-79; chmn. coms. Arlington Park, Ft. Wayne, 1983-86; mem. START program Ft. Wayne Community Schs., 1985; bd. dirs. The Phila. Orchestra Assn., Am. Coun. Life Insurers PPC Found. scholar, 1973. Mem. Nat. Assn. Bus. Economists, Planning Forum. Democrat. Methodist. Avocations: jogging, racquetball, playing drums, swimming, reading.*

BOSCO, ANTHONY GERARD, bishop; b. New Castle, Pa., Aug. 1, 1927; s. Joseph M. and Theresa (Pezo) B. BA, St. Vincent Sem., Latrobe, Pa.; juris canonici licentiatus, Lateran U., Rome; LLD (hon.), Duquesne U., 1971; LHD (hon.), St.Vincent Coll., 1988. Ordained priest Roman Cath. Ch., 1952. Asst. chancellor Diocese of Pitts., 1955—65, vice chancellor, 1965—67, chancellor, 1967—85, aux. bishop, 1970—87; bishop Diocese of Greensburg, Pa., 1987—2002; bishop emeritus Diocese of Greensburg, Pa., 2002—. Chmn. chmn. Cath. Comms. Found., 1984—; hon. chmn., trustee Seton Hill Coll., Greensburg, 1987; ex officio mem., bd. regents St. Vincent Sem., Latrobe, Pa., 1987—. Named Pitts.'s Man of Yr. in Religion, Pitts. Jaycees, 1975; recipient Leonardo Da Vinci award for Religion, Order of Italian Sons and Daughter, 1970. Mem.: Christian Assocs. S.W. Pa., Nat. Conf. Cath. Bishops. E-mail: abosco@dioceseofgreensburg.org.

BOSCO, FERNANDO JAVIER, geographer, educator; b. Buenos Aires, Mar. 12, 1971; s. Juan Carlos Bosco and Nilda Ester Visco. BA in Geography, Wittenberg U., Springfield, Ohio, 1994; MA in Geography, Ohio State U., Columbus, 1997, PhD in Geography, 2002. Asst. prof. geography San Diego State U., 2002—. Mem.: Assn. Pacific Coast Geographers (yearbook editl. bd.), Assn. Am. Geographers. Office: San Diego State Univ 5500 Campanile Dr San Diego CA 92182-4493 Office Phone: 619-594-7187. Office Fax: 619-594-4938. Business E-Mail: fbosco@mail.sdsu.edu.

BOSCO, MARY BETH, lawyer; b. Jersey City, Feb. 23, 1956; BA cum laude, Yale Univ., 1978; JD with honors, George Washington Univ., 1983. Bar: DC 1983, US Dist. Ct. (ea. Ark., so. Tex., Wyo. dist.), US Ct. Appeals (8th, 10th & Fed. cir.), US Supreme Ct. Ptnr., head Govt. Contracts & Fed. Marketing practices, mem. mgmt. com. Patton Boggs LLP, Washington. Contbr. articles to profl. jours.; author (contributing): Environ. Law Handbook, 1994. Mem.: ABA. Office: Patton Boggs LLP 2550 M St NW Washington DC 20037-1350 Office Phone: 202-457-6420. Office Fax: 202-457-6315. Business E-Mail: mbbosco@pattonboggs.com.

BOSCO, PHILIP MICHAEL, actor; b. Jersey City, Sept. 26, 1930; s. Philip Lupo and Margaret Raymond (Thek) B.; m. Nancy Ann Dunkle, Jan. 2, 1957; children: Diane, Philip, Christopher, Jennifer, Lisa, Celia, John. BA in drama, Catholic U. Am., 1957. Roles include Brian O'Bannion in Auntie Mame, City Ctr., N.Y.C., 1958; Angelo in Measure for Measure, Belvedere Lake Amphitheatre, N.Y.C., 1960; Heracles in The Rape of the Belt, 1960 (Tony nomination); Will Danaher in Donnybrook, 1961; Hawkshaw in The Ticket-of-Leave Man, 1961; King Henry in Henry IV Part 1, Shakespeare Festival, Stratford, Conn., 1962; Kent in King Lear; Rufio in Antony and Cleopatra: Pistol in Henry V; Aegeon in Comedy of Errors, 1963; Benedick in Much Ado About Nothing; Claudius in Hamlet, 1964; title role in Coriolanus, 1965; Lovewit in The Alchemist, 1967; appeared in Galileo, 1967, Saint Joan, 1968, Amphitryon in 3 Zones, Tiger at the Gates, 1968, Cyrano de Bergerac, 1968, Camino Real, 1970, Operation Sidewinder, 1970, The Playboy of the Western World, 1971, An Enemy of the People, 1971, Antigone, 1971, Mary Stuart, 1971, Narrow Road Into the Deep North, 1972, Twelfth Night, 1972, The Crucible, 1972, Enemies, 1972, The Plough and the Stars, 1973, The Merchant of Venice, 1973, A Streetcar Named Desire, 1973, Mrs. Warren's Profession, 1976, Man and Superman, 1978, Whose Life Is It Anyway?, 1979, A Month In The Country, 1979, Major Barbara, 1980, Inadmissable Evidence, 1981, Hedda Gabler, 1982, Ah! Wilderness, 1983, Misalliance, 1983, Come Back, Little Sheba, 1984, Eminent Domain, 1984, Heartbreak House (Tony nominated), Caine Mutiny, 1984, Be Happy For Me, Masterclass, 1986, You Never Can Tell, 1986 (Tony nominated), A Man For All Seasons, 1986,The Devil's Disciple, 1988, (Broadway) Lend Me A Tenor, 1989, (Antoinette Perry award 1989), The Miser, 1990, Breaking Legs, 1991, (Broadway) An Inspector Calls, 1994, The Heiress, 1995, Moon Over Buffalo, 1995-96 (Tony nomination), Twelfth Night, 1998 Twelve Angry Men (Tony nominated), Chitty Chitty Bang Bang, 2005, Heartbreak House, 2006; films include: Requiem For a Heavyweight, A Lovely Way To Die, The Pope of Greenwich Village, Walls of Glass, Heaven Help Us, The Money Pit, Trading Places, 1983, Children of a Lesser God, 1986, Suspect, 1987, Three Men and a Baby, 1987, The Luckiest Man in the World, 1988, Working Girl, 1988, Dream Team, 1988, Another Woman, 1988, Blue Steel, Quick Change, FX-2, 1990, True Colors, 1990, Straight Talk, 1991, The Return of Eliot Ness, 1991, Shawdows and Fog, 1992, Attica: Line of Fire, 1993, Angie, 1993, Safe Passage, 1993, Milk Money, 1994, Nobody's Fool, 1994, It Takes Two, 1995, The First Wives Club, 1995, My Best Friend's Wedding, 1997, Critical Care, 1997, Deconstructing Harry, 1997, Shaft II, 1998, The Time Machine, 1999, Kate and Leopold, 2000; TV shows include: The Prisoner of Zenda, The Nurses, O'Brien, Hawk, The NET Play of the Month, Tribeca, Grandpa and the Globetrotters, 1987, Echoes in the Darkness, Internal Affairs, 1988, Murder in Black and White, 1989, Return of Eliot Ness, 1991, Law and Order, 1993, 96-98, Cosby, 1998, Spin City, 1999, Criminal Intent, 2001, S.V.U., 2002; (TV movie) Carriers, 1997. Served with U.S. Army, 1951-54. Recipient Critic's Circle award N.Y. Drama Critics, 1960-61; recipient Clarence Derwent award, 1966-67, Tony award nominations, 1961, 84, 87, 96, OBIE award, 1987, Emmy award, 1988, Tony award, Drama Desk award, Outer Critic's Circle award all for best leading actor, 1988-89; inductee Theater Hall of Fame, 1998. Mem. Actor's Equity Assn., Screen Actor's Guild, AFTRA Roman Catholic.

BOSE, AJAY KUMAR, retired chemistry professor; b. Silchar, India, Feb. 12, 1925; arrived in US, 1947, naturalized, 2006; s. Abinash C. and Amita Kumari (Chanda) B.; m. Margaret Lois Logan, Sept. 13, 1950; children: Ryan, Ranjan, Indrani, Indira, Krishna, Rajendra. BS, U. Allahabad, India, 1944, MS, 1946; ScD, MIT, 1950; M in Engring. (hon.), Stevens Inst. Tech., Hoboken, NJ, 1963. Rsch. fellow Harvard U., Cambridge, Mass., 1950-51; lectr., then asst. prof. chemistry Indian Inst. Tech., Kharagpur, 1952-56; rsch. assoc. U. Pa., Phila., 1956-57; rsch. chemist Upjohn Co., Kalamazoo, 1957-59; assoc. prof. Stevens Inst. Tech., 1959-61, prof., 1961-83, George Meade Bond prof. chemistry, 1983-96, prof., 1996—2007; ret., 2007. Founder, dir. Undergrad. Projects in Tech. and Medicine, 1971-2007; cons. various chem. cos. Mem. editl. bd. Jour. Heterocyclic Chemistry, 1980-83; contbr. over 350 articles to profl. jours.; patentee in field. Recipient Outstanding Achievement award Nat. Fedn. Indian Am. Assns., 1990, Ranbaxy Sci. Found. Rsch. award in Pharm. Scis., 1997, Nat. Catalyst award Chem. Mfrs. Assn., 1997, Presdl. award for excellence in sci., math. and engring. mentoring, 1999, Lifetime Achievement award, Indian Chem. Soc., 2006; named N.J. Prof. of Yr., Coun. for Advancement and Support of Edn. and Carnegie Found. for Advancement of Tchg., 1990. Fellow AAAS, Indian Nat. Sci. Acad.; mem. Am. Chem. Soc. (councillor 1964-70, Dreyfus award 1999), Sigma Xi. Avocation: popular sci. writing. Home: 405 Frost Hollow Rd Easton PA 18040-1240 Home Phone: 610-258-8624. Home Fax: 610-438-8232. Personal E-mail: ajaybose@yahoo.com.

BOSE, AMAR GOPAL, electronics executive, electrical engineering educator; b. Phila., Nov. 2, 1929; s. Noni Gopal and Charlotte (Mechlin) B.; children: Vanu Gopal, Maya. SB, SM, MIT, 1952, ScD, 1956. Mem. faculty MIT, Cambridge, 1956—2001, prof. elec. engring.; chmn., CEO Bose Corp., Framingham, Mass., 1964—. Chmn., chief exec. officer Bose Corp., Framingham, Mass. Author: (with Kenneth N. Stevens) Introductory Network Theory, 1965; patentee in acoustics, nonlinear systems and communications. Fulbright fellow India, 1956-57; recipient Baker Teaching award MIT, 1964, Teaching award Am. Soc. Engring. Edn., 1965; named Inventor of Yr., Intellectual Property Owners, 1987; named to Forbes Billionaire List, 2006; Named one of Forbes' Richest Americans, 2006. Fellow IEEE; mem. AASS, Nat. Acad. Engring., Sigma Xi, Tau Beta Pi, Eta Kappa Nu Office: Bose Corp The Mountain Framingham MA 01701-9168

BOSE, ANJAN, electrical engineering educator, academic administrator; b. Calcutta, India, June 2, 1946; s. Amal Nath and Anima (Guha) B.; m. Frances Magdelen Pavlas, Oct. 30, 1976; children: Rajesh Paul, Shonali Marie, Jahar Robert. B Tech with honors, Indian Inst. Tech., Kharagpur, 1967; MS, U. Calif., Berkeley, 1968; PhD, Iowa State U., 1974. Systems planning engr. Con Edison Co., NYC, 1968-70; instr., research assoc. Iowa State U., Ames, 1970-74; postdoctoral fellow IBM Sci. Ctr., Palo Alto, Calif., 1974-75; asst. prof. elec. engring. Clarkson U., Potsdam, N.Y., 1975-76; mgr. EMSD, Control Data Corp., Mpls., 1976-81; prof. elec. engring. Ariz. State U., Tempe, 1981-93; disting. prof. Wash. State U., Pullman, 1993—, dir. Sch. Elec. Engring. and Computer Sci., 1993-98, dean Coll. Engring. and Architecture, 1998—2005, regents prof., 2006—. V.p. Power Math Assocs., Tempe, 1981-84; program dir. power sys. NSF, Washington, 1988-89. Contbr. over 100 articles to engring. jours. Fellow: IEEE; mem.: Nat. Acad. Engring. Home Phone: 509-332-5114. Business E-Mail: bose@wsu.edu.

BOSE, BIMAL KUMAR, electrical engineering educator; b. Calcutta, India, Sept. 1, 1932; came to US, 1971; s. Rajendra and Nirmala (Ghosh) B.; m. Arati Ghosh, June 26, 1961; children: Papia, Amit. BE, Calcutta U., 1956, PhD, 1966; MS, U. Wis., 1960. Asst. engr. Tata Hydro Power Co., Bombay, 1956-59; asst. prof. Bengal Engring. Coll., Calcutta, 1960-71; assoc. prof. Rensselaer Poly. Inst., Troy, NY, 1971-76; rsch. engr. GE R & D Ctr., Schenectady, NY, 1976-87; prof. Condra Chair of Exellence U. Tenn., Knoxville, 1987—. Disting. scientist Power Electronics Appliance Ctr., Knoxville, 1987—; cons. PCI Ozone Corp., NJ, 1971-73, GE, 1971-76, Rsch. Triangle Inst., NC, 1991-95, Bendix Corp., Electric Power Rsch. Inst., Lutron Electronics, UN for tech. devel. in People's Republic China and India; sr. advisor to Beijing Power Electronics R&D Ctr.; lectr. in field; hon. prof. Shanghai U. Tech., 1991, China U. of Mining and Technology, 1996, Xi'an Mining Inst., 1998. Author: Power Electronics and AC Drives, 1986, Modern Power Electronics and AC Drives, 2002; editor: Adjustable Speed AC Drive Systems, 1981, Micro Computer Control of Power Electronics and Drives, 1987, Modern Power Electronics, 1992, Power Electronics and Variable Frequency Drives, 1996, Power Electronics and Motor Drives, 2006; patentee in field; contbr. articles to profl. jours. Recipient Mouat Gold medal Calcutta U., 1967, Publ. award GE, 1982, Silver Patent medal GE, 1983. Fellow IEEE (life, chmn. power electronics, chmn. indsl. power converter com., Trans. Rev. chmn., static power converter com., assoc. editor Trans., neural network coun., Industry Applications Soc. outstanding achievement award 1993, Region 3 outstanding engr. award, 1994, Lamme Gold medal 1996); mem. IEEE Indsl. Electronics Soc. (Eugene Mittlemann Achievement award 1994, chmn. power electronics coun., Cont. Edn. award 1997, Millennium medal 2000, Newell award 2005). Hindu. Avocations: travel, gardening. Home: 404 Dixieview Rd Knoxville TN 37934-2609 Office: Univ of Tenn Dept Elec Engring 419 Ferris Hl Knoxville TN 37996-0001 Office Phone: 865-974-8398. Business E-Mail: bbose@utk.edu, b.bose@ieee.org.

BOSE, MEENA, political science professor; b. Pitts., June 30, 1970; d. Nirmal Kumar and Chandra Bose; m. Colin Churchill Barr, Aug. 7, 1994. BA, Pa. State U., 1990; MA, Princeton U., 1992, PhD in Politics, 1996. Asst. prof. polit. sci. Hofstra U., Hempstead, NY, 1996—2000, acting dir. Honors Program, 1999—2000, Peter S. Kalikow Chair for Presdl. Studies, 2006—; asst. prof. polit. sci. US Mil. Acad., West Point, NY, 2000—01, assoc. prof., 2001—06, dir. Am. Politics Program. Commentator The NewsHour with Jim Lehrer, Rep. Nat. Convention, NYC, 2004. Author: Shaping and Signaling Presidential Policy: The National Security Decision Making of Eisenhower and Kennedy, 1998; co-editor: From Cold War to New World Order: The Foreign Policy of George H.W. Bush, 2002, Making the Grade: Uses and Abuses of Presidential Ratings, 2003. Non-resident fellow, Centre for Pub. Mgmt., Brookings Inst., 1996—97. Mem.: Am. Polit. Sci. Assn. Office: Hofstra U Peter S Kalikow Ctr for Study of Am Pres Hempstead NY 11549-1000 E-mail: Meenekshi.Bose@hofstra.edu.*

BOSE, NIRMAL KUMAR, electrical engineer, mathematics educator; b. Calcutta, West Bengal, India, Aug. 19, 1940; came to U.S., 1961; s. Dhruba Kumar and Roma (Guha) B.; m. Chandra Bose, June 8, 1969; children: Meenekshi, Enakshi. B.Tech., Indian Inst. Tech., Kharagpur, West Bengal, 1961; MS, Cornell U., 1963; PhD, Syracuse U., 1967. Asst. prof. U. Pitts., 1967-70, assoc. prof., 1970-76, prof., 1976-86; Singer prof. elec. engring. Pa. State U., University Park, 1986-91, HRB-Systems prof. elec. engring., 1992—; vis. assoc. prof. U. Calif., Berkeley, 1973-74. Cons. RCA, Meadowland, Pa., 1968-69; spl. lectr. Coll. of Steubenville, Ohio, 1968-70; vis. assoc. prof. Am. U. Beirut, 1971, U. Md., College Park, 1972; vis. fellow Princeton U., 1996; apptd. vis. prof. Israel Inst. Tech., 1996; UN expert in neural networks to instns. and ctrs., India, 1994-95; rschr. Japan Soc. for Promotion of Sci., 1998; Humboldt guest prof. Ruhr U., Bochum, Germany, 2000-03; invited sr. mem. Inst. Math. Scis., Nat. U. Singapore, 2003; invited lectr., rschr. Akita Prefectural U. Japan, 2005. Author: Applied Multidimensional Systems Theory, 1982, Digital Filters: Theory and Applications, 1985, rev. edit., 1993; co-author: Neural Network Fundammentals, 1996; editor: Multidimensional Systems: Theory and Application, 1979, Multidimensional Systems; Progress, Directions and Open Problems, 1985, 2nd edit., 2003; founding editor-in-chief Multidimensional Sys. and Signal Processing, 1990-; co-editor: Handbook of Statistics vol. on Signal Processing and Its Applications, 1993; assoc. editor Cirs., Sys., and Signal Processing Jour., IEEE Trans. of Cirs. and Sys., Jour. Franklin Inst.; adv. com. Internat. Jour. Smart Engring. Sys. Design. Recipient Invitational fellow for rsch. in Japan, Japan Soc. for Promotion of Sci., 1998, Charles H. Fetter Univ. Endowed fellow in elec. engring., 2001—04, Alexander von Humboldt Sr. U.S. Scientist Rsch. award, 1999. Fellow: IEEE (chmn. cirs. and systems tech. com. on edn. 1979—85, Merit award 2000, Circuits and Systems Soc. Edn. award 2007); mem.: Am. Soc. Elec. Engrs., AAAS, NY Acad. Scis., Am. Math. Soc., Sigma Xi. Hindu. Achievements include listed as 1st 15 influential engrs. in 2005 by Registry Pro. Avocations: table-tennis, stamp collecting/philately. Home: 1312 W Park Hills Ave State College PA 16803-3250 Office: Pa State U Dept Elec Engring University Park PA 16802 Office Phone: 814-865-3912. Business E-Mail: nkb1@psu.edu. *Development and cultivation of spiritual and intellectual resources to the best of one's ability supported by parental blessings and encouragement provide the foundation on which the edifice of an individual's contributions to science and society is constructed.*

BOSE, SANTANU, virologist, educator; m. Rumu Bishayee, Nov. 22, 2000. BS, Mt. Olive Coll., NC, 1992; PhD, Med. Coll. Wis., 1998. Rsch. scientist Cleve. Clinic, 1999—2004; asst. prof. health sci. ctr. U. Tex., San Antonio, 2005—. Contbr. chapters to books. Judge NE Ohio Engring. and Sci. Fair, 2001, 2002. Recipient Derieux Rsch. Chemistry award, NC Acad. Scis., 1992; fellow, Med. Coll. Wis., 1993, Morgenthaler Found., 1999; grantee, Am. Lung Assn., 2007. Mem.: Alpha Chi. Achievements include patents for vitamin mediated oral delivery of drugs; patents pending for using virus for cancer treatment; research in immune defense mechanism against respiratory viruses.

BOSH, CHRIS, professional basketball player; b. Dallas, Mar. 24, 1984; s. Noel and Freida Bosh. Student, Ga. Inst. Tech., 2002—03. Forward Toronto Raptors, Ont., Canada, 2003—. Mem. USA Basketball Sr. Men's Prog., 2006—. Founder Chris Bosh Found. Named a McDonald's All-Am.; named to 1st-Team All-Am., Parade, All-Rookie 1st Team, NBA, 2004, Ea. Conf. All-Star Team, 2006, 2007. Mailing: Toronto Raptors Air Canada Ctr 40 Bay St Toronto ON M5J 2X2 Canada*

BOSKEY, BENNETT, lawyer; b. NYC, Aug. 14, 1916; s. Meyer and Janet (Lauterstein) B.; m. Shirley Ecker, July 3, 1940 (dec. 1998). AB, Williams Coll., 1935; LL.B., Harvard U., 1939. Bar: N.Y. 1940, U.S. Supreme Ct. 1943, D.C. 1949. Spl. asst. to Atty. Gen. U.S. Dept. Justice, Washington, 1943; advisor on enemy property U.S. Dept. State, Washington, 1946-47; atty. U.S. Atomic Energy Commn., Washington, 1947-49, dep. gen. counsel, 1949-51; ptnr. firm Volpe, Boskey & Lyons (and predecessors), Washington, 1951-96. Law clk. Judge Learned Hand, 1939-40, Justice Stanley Reed, 1940-41, Chief Justice Harlan F. Stone, 1941-43; trustee Analytic Svcs. Inc., Arlington, Va., 1962-91; adv. bd. internat. legal studies program Am. U., 1987-99. Chmn. bd. trustees Primary Day Sch., Bethesda, Md., 1969—. Served with U.S. Army, 1943-46. Named hon. fellow, Exeter Coll., Oxford U. Mem. ABA, Am. Law Inst. (treas. 1975—, mem. coun., bd. dirs. Am. Law Inst.-ABA continuing profl. edn. 1985—), Am. Soc. Internat. Law (bd. rev. and devel. 1973-88). Office: 5335 Wisconsin Ave NW Ste 930 Washington DC 20015 Office Phone: 202-966-3134. E-mail: bennettbos@aol.com.

BOSKOVICH, NICK F., artist, art educator; b. San Pedro, Calif., June 1, 1949; s. Frank Nick and Frances Boskovich; children: Frank, John. MFA, Calif. State U., Long Beach; 1980. With Saddleback Coll., Mission Viejo, Calif., 1979—2001, Orange Coast Coll., Costa Mesa, Calif., 1979—2003, Calif. State U., Fullerton, Calif., 1996, U. So. Calif., LA, 2001—02, Long Beach City Coll., Calif., 2001—03. Roman Catholic.

BOSL, GEORGE JOSEPH, physician, oncologist; b. Cleve., Oct. 19, 1948; BS in Biology, John Carroll U., 1969; MD, Creighton U., 1973. Diplomate Am. Bd. Medicine, Am. Bd. Oncology. Intern N.Y. Hosp., 1973-74, resident in medicine, 1974-75, Sloan-Kettering Cancer Ctr., 1974-77; fellow in med. oncology U. Minn. Hosp., 1977-79; oncologist Meml. Sloan Kettering Cancer Ctr., NYC, 1979—, dir. oncology, hematology fellow program, 1986-94, head divsn. solid tumor oncology, 1989-97, assoc. physician-in-chief, 1994-97, chmn. dept. medicine, 1997—; prof. medicine Cornell U., NYC, 1991—, Patrick M. Byrne chair clinical oncology. Recipient Award for Excellence in Medicine, Soc. Meml. Sloan-Kettering, 2005. Mem. AMA, Am. Assn. Cancer Rsch., Am. Soc. Clin. Oncology, Alpha Omega Alpha. Office: Meml Sloan Kettering Ctr New York NY 10021

BOSL, PHILLIP L., retired lawyer; b. Feb. 27, 1945; BA, U. Calif., Santa Barbara, 1968; JD, U. So. Calif., 1975. Bar: Calif. 1975. Ptnr. Gibson, Dunn & Crutcher LLP, LA, 1983—2005; ret., 2005. Mem. U. So. Calif. Law Rev., 1973-75. Officer USCG, 1969-72. Mem. ABA, LA County Bar Assn., Assn. Bus. Trial Lawyers, Securities Industry and Fin. Markets Assn. (compliance and legal divsn.), Nat. Futures Assn. (arbitrator), Nat. Assn. Securities Dealers (arbitrator), Order of Coif. Home Phone: 562-597-2600; Office Phone: 213-713-4885. Personal E-mail: pbosl@earthlink.net.

BOSLEY, EDWARD RICHMOND, historical site administrator; b. San Francisco, Apr. 2, 1954; s. Edward Richmond Bosley, Jr. and Phyllis Virginia Bosley; m. Kirby Gray Davis, July 8, 1985 (div. Feb. 15, 2006); children: William Bradford, Julia Gray. BA in Letters and Sci., U. Calif., Berkeley, 1977; MBA, UCLA, 1980. Account exec. Dancer Fitzgerald Sample, NYC, 1980—83, Foote Cone & Belding, San Francisco, 1983—86; assoc. dir. The Gamble House, USC, Pasadena, Calif., 1990—92, dir., 1992—. Sr. warden Episcopal Ch. of Ascension, Sierra Madre, Calif., 2003—05. Recipient Hist. Preservation award, City of South Pasadena, 2003, Calif. Preservation Found., 2005, LA Conservancy, 2005. Mem.: Sigma Phi Soc. (vice-chmn. 1992—96, David S. Brown Disting.

Sigma Phi 2001). Avocation: mountaineering. Office: The Gamble House 4 Westmoreland Pl Pasadena CA 91103 Home Phone: 626-797-1763; Office Phone: 626-793-3334 ext. 26. Office Fax: 626-577-7547. Business E-Mail: bosley@usc.edu.

BOSLEY, KAREN LEE FOLEY, language educator, communications educator; b. Beech Grove, Ind., Sept. 23, 1942; d. Lowell Holmes and Kathryn Gertrude (Drake) Foley; m. Norman Keith Bosley, Dec. 21, 1964; children: Mark Harold, Rachael Kathryn, Keith Lowell, Sidney Clark. AB in Lang. Arts summa cum laude, U. Indpls., 1965; MA in English, Northwestern U., 1967; MA in Journalism, Ball State U., 1984; postgrad. (Newspaper Fund fellow), U. Mo., 1973; postgrad., Ohio U., 1977. Copy editor, reporter Indpls. News, 1963-65; English tchr., yearbook adviser Beech Grove (Ind.) Jr. H.S., 1965-66; English tchr. So. Regional H.S., Manahawkin, N.J., 1967-68; prof. humanities, journalism, and English Ocean County Coll., Toms River, N.J., 1971—, student newspaper adviser, 1971—, student media bd. chmn., 1983—2005, yearbook adviser, 1999—2004. Part-time reporter Daily Times-Observer, Toms River, 1972—77, part-time copy editor, 1993. Contbr. articles to publs. in field. Trustee Long Beach Island Hist. Assn., Friends of Island Libr., 1975-79; pres. Long Beach I PTA; chmn. Long Beach Twp. Dem. Mcpl. Com., 1971-78; Dem. committeeman Long Beach Twp. Dist. 2, 1971-78, 85—; mem. Long Beach Twp. Recreation Commn., 1972-75; bd. dirs. Ocean County Red Cross, 1972-78, Ocean County Family Planning, Inc., 1972-78, bd. dirs. Student Press Law Ctr., 1987-2002, sec., 1998-2000, mem. adv. coun., 2002—; chmn. Cub Scout pack 32, Ocean County Coun. Boy Scouts Am.; founder, bd. dirs. Long Beach I Hist. Assn., Island Dems., Inc.; mem. adminstrv. bd. First United Meth. Ch. Beach Haven Terrace (N.J.); So. Regional H.S. Band Parent Orgn., 1995-96, pres., 1996-97, corr. sec; So. Regional Jazz Band Parents Assn., charter mem., 2001—. Recipient Press Freedom award, Student Press Law Ctr., 2006. Mem. AAUW (pres., dir. Barnegat Light Area br.), NEA, NJ Edn. Assn., Ocean County Edn. Assn., Faculty Assn. Ocean County Coll. (v.p. 1984-85), Coll. Media Advisers, Inc. (disting. newspaper adviser for U.S. 2-yr. colls. 1978, dir., sec., Louis E. Ingelhart First Amendment award 2006, 07, Hall of Fame 2007), Assn. Edn. in Journalism and Mass Comms., CC Journalism Assn. (dir., v.p.), Soc. Profl. Journalists, Soc. Collegiate Journalists (Louis E. Engelhart award 2006), Internat. Platform Assn., Sigma Delta Chi. Home: 9 E Old Whaling Ln Long Beach Township NJ 08008-2930 Office: Ocean CC PO Box 2001 College Dr Toms River NJ 08754-2001 Office Phone: 732-255-0400 ext. 2237. Personal E-mail: kbosley@mac.com.

BOSLEY, TOM, actor; b. Chgo., Oct. 1, 1927; s. Benjamin and Dora (Heyman) B.; m. Jean Eliot, Mar. 8, 1962 (dec. Apr. 1978); 1 dau., Amy; m. Patricia Carr, Dec. 21, 1980. Student, De Paul U., 1946, Radio Inst. Chgo., 1947-48; studied with, Lee Strasberg, 1952. Actor: various roles TV programs Alice in Wonderland, 1953, Arsenic and Old Lace, 1962, Focus, 1961, Naked City, The Right Man, The Nurses, Law and Mr. Jones, Route 66, The Perry Como Show, The Dean Martin Show, Joanie Loves Chachi, The Rebels, Death Trap, Castaways on Gilligan's Island, Return of Mod Squad, For the Love of It, Jessie Owens Story, The Drew Carey Show, ER, Touched by an Angel, One Tree Hill; TV film: Fatal Confession: A Father Dowling Mystery, 1987, The Love Boat, A Valentine Voyage, 1990; regular actor on TV shows Wait Til Your Father Gets Home, Murder She Wrote, 1984-87; star TV series Happy Days, 1974-83, Father Dowling Mysteries, 1989-92, the Parsley Garden, 1993, Legend of the Candy Cane, 2001, Mothers and Daughters, 2002, Returning Mickey Stern, 2002, Mary Christmas, 2002, Christmas at Water's Edge, 2004, The Fallen Ones, 2005, Hidden Places, 2006; also appeared on TV series Profiles in Courage, others; appeared in TV mini-series The Bastard, 1978; narrator TV series That's Hollywood; voice in animated cartoon The Stingiest Man in Town; actor numerous theatrical prodns. in stock companies, also off-Broadway prodns., 1952-56; Broadway debut as Fiorello LaGuardia in Fiorello, 1959 (Tony award best featured actor in musical, 1960); Broadway roles include: musical Nowhere to Go But Up, 1962, plays Natural Affection, 1963, A Murderer Among Us, 1964, The Education of H, Beauty and the Beast, 1994, Cabaret, 2002, On Golden Pond, 2006; film roles include Love with a Proper Stranger, 1963, The World of Henry Orient, 1964, Divorce American Style, 1967, Secret War of Harry Frigg, 1968, Yours, Mine and Ours, 1968, To Find A Man, 1972, Mixed Company, 1974, Gus, 1976, O'Hara's Wife, 1982, Little Bigfoot 2: The Journey Home, 1997, Confession, 2005, Popstar, 2005; indsl. film Perfectly Normal Day. Served with USNR, World War II. Recipient Antoinette Perry award for 1959-60 season as best actor in featured role of musical; Newspaper Guild of Am. Page One award and ANTA award for distinguished contbn. to theatre, 1960; N.Y. Drama Critics award for performance in Fiorello, 1960; Festival of Leadership award Chgo.; Humanitarian award Performing Arts Theater of Handicapped, 1981; Tau award Sacred Heart Rehab. Hosp., Milw. Mem. Actors Equity Assn. (governing council 1961-69), AFTRA, Screen Actors Guild. Office: Shapiro-Lichtman-Stein 8827 Beverly Blvd Los Angeles CA 90048-2405 *I try to go through life by not hurting anyone's feelings, by respecting people for what they are and not what I think they should be; by honoring my heritage and the heritage of others; and by trying to smile at adversity, knowing that if I can, life can be softer and more comfortable than the realities really are.*

BOSMAJIAN, HAIG ARAM, speech communication educator; b. Fresno, Calif., Mar. 26, 1928; s. Aram and Aurora (Keosheyan) B.; m. Hamida Just, Feb. 27, 1957; 1 child, Harlan. BA, U. Calif., Berkeley, 1949; MA, U. of Pacific, 1951; PhD, Stanford U., 1960. Instr. U. Idaho, Moscow, 1959-61; asst. prof. U. Conn., Storrs, 1961-65; prof. speech comm. U. Wash., Seattle, 1965—. Author: Language of Oppression (Orwell award), 1983: editor: Censorship, Libraries and the Law, 1983; Justice Douglas, 1980, Freedom of Speech, 1983, First Amendment in the Classroom Series, 1987: vol. I, The Freedom to Read, 1987, vol. II, The Freedom of Religion, 1987, vol. III, Freedom of Expression, 1988, vol. IV, Academic Freedom, 1989, vol. V, Freedom to Publish, 1989, Metaphor and Reason in Judicial Opinions, 1992, The Freedom Not to Speak, 1999, Burning Books, 2006. Recipient Bicentennial of the Bill of Rights award Western States Communication Assn., 1991. Office Phone: 206-543-2660.

BOSMAN, RICHARD, artist, printmaker; b. Madras, India, 1944; Student, Byam Sch Sch. Painting/Drawing, London, 1964-69, N.Y. Studio Sch., NYC, 1969-71, Skowhegan Sch. Painting, Maine, 1970. Instr. N.Y. Studio Sch., 1972, Skowhegan Sch. Painting and Sculpture, 1982, Sch. Visual Arts, NYC, 1982-84. Tchr. Skowhegan Sch. Painting and Sculpture, Maine, 1982, Sch. Visual Arts, NYC, 1983—85, U. Pa., Phila., 1986, Temple U., Phila., 1987, Columbia U., NYC, 1988—90, Temple U., Phila., 1991, Rhode Island Sch. Design, Providence, 1992, SUNY, Purchase, 1993, Fairfield U., 1993, Yale U., Norfolk, Conn., 1994—98, Vassar Coll., Poughkeepsie, NY, 1995—. Exhibited in one-man shows at Galerie La Maquina Espanola, Madrid, 1990, Galerie Biedermann, Munich, Germany, 1991, Brooke Alexander, 1991, 93, 94, Galleria Toselli, Milan, 1992, Fairfield (Conn.) U. Gallery, 1993, R.I. Sch. Design Print Gallery, 1993, Timmesch Gallery, Mpls., 1993, Brooke Alexander Gallery, NYC, 1994, The Century Assn., 1996, U. Conn., 2000, Vassar Coll., 2002, Elizabeth Harris Gallery, NYC, 2003, Mark Moore Gallery, Santa Monica, Calif., 2004; group shows include Am. Fedn. ARts, N.Y.C., 1989, Walker Art Ctr. from Mpls. to Balt., 1989, U. Maine Mus. Art, Orono, 1989, Galeria La Maquina Espanola, 1989, John Berggruen Gallery, San. Francisco, 1990, Champion Gallery Champion Internat. Group, Stamford, Conn., 1992, Alice Simsar Gallery, Ann Arbor Mich., 1993, Roger Smith Hotel, NYC, 1993, Am. Acad. Arts and Letters, NYC, 1994, U. Ill., 1995, Mus. Modern Art, NYC, 1996, Columbus Mus., Ga., 1996, Walker-Kornbluth Gallery, Fairlawn, NJ, 1998, Snugharbor Cultural Ctr., Staten Island, NY, 2000, Barbara Krakow Gallery, Boston, 2002, Mark Moore Gallery, Santa Monica, Calif., 2004; works included in collections at Albright-Knox Art Gallery, Buffalo, Australian Nat. Gallery, Canberra, Bklyn. Mus., Fogg Art Mus./Harvard U., Nat. Mus. Am. Art, Washington, Weatherspoon Art Gallery, Greensboro, Detroit Inst. Art, Des Moines Art Ctr., Chrysler Mus., Norfolk, Conn., Eli Broad Family Found., L.A., Balt. Mus. Art., Australian Nat. Gallery, Canberra, Australia, others; co-author: Exit the Face, 1982; illustrator: Grasping at Emptiness, 1987, The Captivity Narrative of Hannah Duston, 1987, others. Guggenheim fellow, 1994. Address: c/o Mark Moore Gallery Bergamot Station A1 2525 Michigan Ave Santa Monica CA 90404

BOSOWSKI, EDWARD M., manufacturing executive; BS in Acctg., DePaul U., Chgo., MBA in Fin. With US Gypsum Co., 1976, gen. mgr. materials divsn., v.p. market devel. & planning, exec. v.p. mktg., pres., chief pres., exec. officer, 1999—2000; pres. growth initiatives and internat. USG Corp., 2000—01, v.p., CFO Worldwide Ceilings, v.p. fin. USG Interiors, pres. Growth Initiatives and USG Internat., sr. v.p. mktg. and corp. strategy, exec. v.p. mktg. and corp. strategy, 2004—06, pres. USG Internat., 2004—, exec. v.p., chief strategy officer, 2006—. Office: USG Corp 550 W Adams St Chicago IL 60661-3676 Office Phone: 312-436-4000.*

BOSS, ALAN PAUL, astrophysicist; b. Lakewood, Ohio, July 20, 1951; s. Paul and Marguerite May (Gehringer) B.; m. Catherine Ann Starkie, Aug. 4, 1979; children: Margaret, Nicholas. BS in Physics, U. South Fla., 1973; MA in Physics, U. Calif., Santa Barbara, 1975, PhD in Physics, 1979. Postdoctoral rschr. dept. physics U. Calif., Santa Barbara, 1979; resident rsch. assoc. space sci. divsn. NASA Ames Rsch. Ctr., Moffett Field, Calif., 1979-81; staff assoc. dept. terrestrial magnetism Carnegie Instn., Washington, 1981-83, staff mem., 1983—. Com. mem., chmn. planetary systems sci. working grp. NASA, Washington, 1988-96, com. on planetary and lunar exploration NAS, Washington, 1990-93; panel mem., chmn. origins of solar systems NASA, 1989-96, mem. origins subcom., 1996. Contbr. articles to profl. jours. NASA grantee, 1982—, NSF grantee, 1984—. Fellow: Meteoritical Soc., AAAS, Am. Geophys. Union; mem.: Am. Acad. Arts & Scis., Internat. Astron. Union, Am. Astron. Soc. Democrat. Office: Carnegie Instn Washington Dept Terrestrial Magnetism 5241 Broad Branch Rd NW Washington DC 20015-1305 E-mail: boss@dtm.ciw.edu.

BOSS, AMELIA HELEN, lawyer, educator; b. Balt., Apr. 3, 1949; d. Myron Theodore and Loretta (Oakjones) B.; m. Roger S. Clark, Mar. 3, 1979; children: Melissa, Seymour, Edward, Ashley. Student, Oxford U., Eng., 1968; BA in Sociology, Bryn Mawr, 1970; JD, Rutgers U., 1975. Bar: N.J, Pa., U.S. Dist. Ct. (ea. dist.) N.J., U.S. Dist. Ct. (ea. dist.) Pa., U.S. Supreme Ct., U.S. Ct. Appeals (3d cir.). Law clk. Hon. Milton B. Cranford N.J. Supreme Ct., 1975-76; assoc. Pepper, Hamilton & Scheetz, Phila., 1976-78; assoc. prof. law Rutgers U. Sch. Law, Camden, NJ, 1983-87, Temple U., Phila., 1989-91; prof. law Temple U. Sch. Law, Phila., 1991—, Charles Klein prof. law, 1999—. Vis. prof. law U. Miami Sch. Law, Coral Gables, Fla., 1985—86; Leo Goodwin disting. vis. prof. law Nova U., Sch. Law, 1998; mem. coms. Nat. Conf. Commrs. on Uniform State Laws; U.S. rep. to UN Commn. on Internat. Trade Law; dir. Inst. for Internat. Law and Pub. Policy, 2001—. Author: (books) Electronic Data Interchange Agreements: A Guide and Sourcebook, 1993, ABCs of the UCC: Article 2A, ABCs of the UCC: Article 5; editor-in-chief The Data Law Report, 1993-97, The Business Lawyer, 1998-99, ABCs of the UCC; mem. permanent editl. bd. Uniform Comml. Code; contbr. articles to profl. jours. Named among top 50 women lawyers in U.S. Nat. Law Jour., 1998. Fellow Am. Bar Found.; mem. ABA (chmn. bus. law sect. 2000-01, chmn. sect. officers conf. 2001—), Internat. Bar Assn., Am. Law Inst. (coun. 2000—), Am. Bankruptcy Inst., Am. Coll. Comml. Fin. Lawyers, Nat. Assn. Women Lawyers. Home: 309 Westmont Ave Haddonfield NJ 08033-1714 Office: Temple U Sch Law 1719 N Broad St Philadelphia PA 19122-6002 Office Phone: 215-204-8947.

BOSS, LENARD BARRETT, lawyer; b. Passaic, NJ, Mar. 6, 1960; s. Lawrence Steven and Laura (Ziegler) Boss. BA in Rhetoric, Bates Coll., 1982; JD with high honors, George Washington U., 1985. Bar: Pa. 1985, DC 1986, Md. 1995, US Ct Appeals (4th and 11th cirs) 1986, US Dist Ct DC 1987, US Ct Appeals (DC cir) 1987, US Ct Appeals (3d cir) 1988, US Supreme Ct 1989. Assoc. Asbill, Junkin, Myers & Buffone, Washington, 1986-91; ptnr. Asbill, Junkin & Myers, Washington, 1991-95; asst. fed. pub. defender Fed. Pub. Defender's Office, Washington, 1995-2000; ptnr. Asbill, Junkin, Moffitt & Boss, Washington, 2000—02, Asbill, Moffitt & Boss, Washington, 2002—04; sr. mem., mng. ptnr. Cozen O'Connor, Washington, 2004—. Adj. prof. George Washington U. Law Sch., 1999—; co-chair practitioners adv. group U.S. Sentencing Commn., 2000—04. Author (with Marek): Federal Criminal Practice, 2006. Mem.: ABA (co-chair criminal justice sect. com. on corrections and sentencing 2005—06, co-chair criminal justice sect. com. on sentencing 2006—). Avocations: films, music, sports. Office: 1627 I St NW Ste 1100 Washington DC 20006 Office Phone: 202-912-4818. E-mail: lboss@cozen.com.

BOSS, MARYLIN JEANETTE, elementary school educator; b. Gooding, Idaho, Nov. 11, 1949; d. Don Raymond and Mary Lillian Bauscher; m. Charles Edward Boss, Mar. 22, 1987; 1 child, Jason Job. BA in Elem. Edn., Albertsons Coll. Idaho, Caldwell, 1972. Cert. elem. tchr. Idaho. Tchr. 2d grade Elem. Pub. Sch., Gooding, 1972—76, tchr. phys. edn. Fulton, Ill., 1978, tchr. kindergarten, 1979, 1979—80; tchr. combined first and second grade Cath. Sch., Trinidad, Colo., 1984—85; tchr. fifth grade Elem. Pub. Sch., Hollister, Idaho, 1985—86, tchr. second grade Filer, Idaho, 1986—87, tchr. third grade Hollister, Idaho, 1987—89; tchr. kindergarten Agape Christian Sch., Twin Falls, 1995—96, tchr. 2d grade, 1996—97; tchr. kindergarten-8th grade Three Creek Sch., Rogerson, Idaho, 2003—. Governess Pvt. Family, Mt. Caroll, Ill., 1980—82; substitute tchr. in Wash., Ill. and Iowa, 1976—79; substitute tchr., Colo., 1983—84, Idaho, 1993—95; tutor Labor Camp, Marsing, Idaho, 1968—72. Supporter and vol. helper DAV, 1995—2006. Named Super Servant of Yr., Cornerstone Bapt. Ch., 1994. Mem.: Idaho Farm Bur. (assoc.), NRA (assoc.), Twin Falls Bridge Club (life). Republican. Baptist. Avocations: bridge, visiting and helping the elderly, travel, collecting readings. Home: 2341 US Highway 93 Twin Falls ID 83301 Office: Three Creek School 49909 Three Creek Road Rogerson ID 83302 Home Phone: 208-655-4456.

BOSSARD, ROBERT LEE, biologist, educator; b. Denver, July 22, 1961; s. Randall K. and Dorothy L. Bossard. BS in Biology, U. Utah, Salt Lake City, 1983; MS in Zoology, U. Okla., Norman, 1986; PhD in Entomology, Kans. State U., Manhattan, 1997. Assoc. instr. Westminster Coll., Salt Lake City, 2002—. Adj. instr. Salt Lake CC, Salt Lake City, 2002—. Contbr. articles to profl. jours. Vol. 4-H, Manhattan, 1995—96, Future Farmers Am., Manhattan, 1995—96, Samaritan's Purse, Salt Lake City, 2001—06, Nature Conservancy, Salt Lake City, 1992—93. Mem.: Am. Soc. Parasitologists. Methodist. Office: Westminster Coll 1840 South 1300 East Salt Lake City UT 84105 Business E-Mail: rbossard@westminstercollege.edu.

BOSSART, PAUL NATHANIEL, JR., geologist, geophysicist, consultant; b. Pitts., May 24, 1930; s. Paul Nathaniel and Eugenia Evelyn (Brown) B.; m. Jean Violet Troutman, Feb. 21, 1953; children: Carla B. Kochel, Paula B. DeVore, Victoria. BS in Geology, Pa. State U., 1952; postgrad., U. Pitts., 1952-54. Registerd profl. geologist, Pa. Geophys. trainee Gulf Rsch., Odessa, Tex., 1952-54; asst. supr. seismic interpretation Canadian Gulf Oil, Calgary, Alta., Canada, 1954-56; sys. geophysicist Consolidated Nat. Gas, Pitts., 1956-70; sr. geologist Peoples Nat. Gas., Pitts., 1970-79; pres. Ter-Ex, Inc., Pitts., 1979-85; pres., owner P.N. Bossart & Assoc., Inc., Pitts., 1985—. Cons. in field. Contbr. articles to profl. jours. Chmn. Pine Twp. (Pa.) Authority, 1966-79. Mem. Pitts. Assn. Petroleum Geologists, Pitts. Geological Soc., Soc. Exploration Geophysicists (emeritus). Republican. Lutheran. Home: 115 Mohawk Ln Wexford PA 15090-8831 Office: PN Bossart & Assoc Inc PO Box 55 Wexford PA 15090-0055

BOSSE, MARK THOMAS, social services administrator; b. Portsmouth, NH, Sept. 27, 1962; s. Maurice Claude and Elaine Greta (Hudon) Bosse; m. Lisa Weiss (div.); children: Joshua, Bianca. AA, St. Petersburg Jr. Coll., Fla., 1985; BA, U. South Fla., 1988; MBA summa cum laude, Tampa Coll., 1996. Case mgr. Gulf Coast Cmty. Care, Clearwater, Fla., 1994—96; sales mgr. Spl. Data Processing Inc., Clearwater, 1996—97, Liberti Practice Mgmt., Clearwater, 1997—99; program dir. Assn. for Retarded Citizens, San Bernardino, Calif., 1999—2000; regional program mgr. Wise Sr. Svcs., Santa Monica, Calif., 2000—01; program dir. Bridges Inc., Pomona, Calif., 2001—02; exec. dir. Marian Homes Inc., Brea, Calif., 2002—05; ops. dir. Westview Svcs., Inc., Riverside, Calif., 2005—; CEO, pres. Affordable Elder Solutions, 2006—. Owner, mgr. Final Touch Cleaning Svcs., Clearwater, Calif., 1993—96. Author: Sanity Quest, 2004. Vol. firefighter Americorps, Dunedin, Fla., 1998; HIV educator for lic. facilities. Recipient Disting. Svc. award, State of Fla., 1998, Leadership and Svc. award, Fla. Commn. Cmty. Svc., 1998. Avocations: travel, reading, motorcycling. Office: Westview Svcs 11728 Magnolia Ave Ste D Riverside CA 92503 Office Phone: 818-371-0999. E-mail: markbosse@adelphia.net.

BOSSELMAN, FRED PAUL, law educator; b. Oak Park, Ill., June 14, 1934; s. Fred and Beulah (Chamberlain) B.; m. Kay Wilson, 1956; children: Judith, Carol, Mark. BA, U. Colo., 1956; JD, Harvard U., 1959. Bar: Ill. 1959, Fla. 1985. Assoc. firm Ross & Hardies, Chgo., 1959-67; partner Ross, Hardies, O'Keefe, Babcock & Parsons, 1967-83, Burke, Bosselman & Weaver, Chgo., 1983-91; vis. prof. law Chgo. Kent Law Sch., Ill. Inst. Tech., 1991-92, prof., 1992—2002; prof. emeritus, 2002—. Assoc. reporter Am. Law Inst., 1969-75; dir. Met. Planning Coun. Chgo., 1971-88; commr. Housing Authority Cook County, Ill., 1973-88. Author: (with David Callies) The Quiet Revolution in Land Use Control, 1971, (with David Callies and John Banta) The Taking Issue, 1973, (with Richard Babcock) Exclusionary Zoning, 1974, In the Wake of the Tourist, 1978, (with Craig Peterson and Claire McCarthy) Managing Tourism Growth, 1999, (with Jim Rossi and Jacqueline Lang Weaver) Energy, Economics and the Environment, 2000, (with Peter Orebech) The Role of Customary Law in Sustainable Development, 2005. Dir. Sonoran Inst., 1996—; gov. Santa Lucia Conservancy, 2000—. Mem. ABA (chmn. environ. law com. sect. real property, probate and trust law 1974-77), Am. Soc. Planning Ofcls. (dir. 1977-78), Am. Planning Assn. (sec. 1978-79, pres. 1982-83), Nat. Audubon Soc. (dir. 1985-87). Home: 2715 Woodbine Ave Evanston IL 60201-1565 Office: IIT-Chicago Kent Law Sch 565 W Adams St Chicago IL 60661-3613 Office Phone: 312-906-5351. Business E-Mail: fbosselm@kentlaw.edu.

BOSSEN, WENDELL JOHN, retired financial planner; b. Vienna, SD, Nov. 11, 1933; s. Hans Simonsen and Clara Patrina (Vorseth) B.; m. Jean Davidson, Jan. 6, 1956; children: Mark, Monica. Student, S.D. Sch. Mines, 1952. CLU. Agt. Northwestern Nat. Life Ins. Co., Mpls., 1957-61, dist. mgr., staff mgr., 1961-68, br. mgr., 1968-72, div. v.p., 1972-77; exec. v.p., chief operating officer Inter-Ocean Ins. Co., Cin., 1977-84; exec. v.p. corp. mktg. Mut. Benefit Life Ins. Co., Newark, 1984-92; pres. Internat. Corp. Mktg. Group, Hartford, Conn., 1992-99, retired, 1999. Cons. Newark Performing Arts Corp., 1986. Author: Businessmens Guide to Insurance, 1981; contbr. articles to profl. jours. Chmn. ARC, Waterstown, S.D., 1962, Northeast S.D. chpt. United Way, Waterstown, 1963, Waterstown County Reps., 1963-64; mem. exec. com. S.D. Reps., Pierre, 1964; bd. dirs. Am. Luth. Ch., Cin., 1979, Apostles' House, 1989. Recipient Danforth Found. award, 1952. Mem. Nat. Assn. Life Underwriters (pres. Watertown chpt. 1960-61, v.p. state chpt. 1961-62), Chartered Life Underwriters, Life Ins. Mktg. Research Assn. (com. chmn. 1975). Clubs: Golden Valley Country (Mpls). Lodges: Elks (pres. 1962-63), Lions (pres. 1961, 73), Kiwanis. Avocations: golf, tennis, photography. Home: 111 Sugarberry Ln Hendersonville NC 28739-6933 Office: Internat Corp Mktg Group 100 Campus Dr Florham Park NJ 07932-1006 Personal E-mail: wbossen@aol.com.

BOSSERT, REX THOMAS, editor-in-chief; BA, Carleton Coll., 1979; JD, Northwestern U. Sch. Law, 1986; MA, Stanford U., 1985, PhD in English Lit., 1988. Staff writer L.A. Daily Jour., San Francisco Daily Jour., 1989—97; assoc. editor The Nat. Law Jour., NYC, 1997—99; mng. editor The N.Y. Law Jour., NYC, 1999—2004; editor in chief The Nat. Law Jour., NYC, 2004—. John Henry Wigmore scholar, Stanford U. fellow. Office: The National Law Journal 105 Madison Ave 8th Fl New York NY 10016 Office Phone: 212-313-9083. E-mail: rbossert@amlaw.com.

BOSSES, STEVAN J., mediator, arbitrator; m. Abbye Z. Bosses; children: Donna Lynne, David Keith, Gary Philip. BME, Cornell U., 1960; LLB, Columbia U., 1963. Bar: NY 1963, U.S. Dist. Ct. (so. dist.) NY 1964, U.S. Dist. Ct. (ea. dist.) NY 1964, U.S. Dist. Ct. (ea. dist.) Mich., 1987, U.s. Dist. Ct. (we. dist.) Wis., 1981, U.S. Patent Office 1964, U.S. Ct. Appeals (2d cir.) 1970, U.S. Ct. Appeals (3d cir.) 1979, U.S. Ct. Appeals (fed. cir.) 1982, U.S. Supreme Ct. 1989. Assoc. Watson Leavenworth Kelton & Taggart, NYC, 1963—71, ptnr., 1972—81, Fitzpatrick, Cella, Harper & Scinto, NYC, 1981—2005. Mem. ABA (alternate dispute resolution sect.), ASME, NY State Bar Assn., Am. Intellectual Property Law Assn., Fed. Bar Coun. (trustee 1989-94), Fed. Cir. Bar Assn., NY Intellectual Property Law Assn. Office: 19 Springdale Rd Scarsdale NY 10583-7330 Office Phone: 914-723-9060. Business E-Mail: sbosses@adrpro.net.

BOSSIDY, LARRY (LAWRENCE ARTHUR), pharmaceutical company and former industrial manufacturing executive; b. Pittsfield, Mass., Mar. 5, 1935; m. Nancy Bossidy, 1956; children: Lynn, Larry, Paul, Pam, Nancy, Mary Jane, Lucy, Michael, Kathleen. BA in Econs., Colgate U. With GE, 1957-91; COO GE Credit Corp., 1979—81; pres. GE Services & Materials Sector, 1981—84; exec. v.p. GE, 1981—84, vice chmn., 1984—91; chmn., CEO AlliedSignal Inc., Morristown, NJ, 1991-99; CEO Honeywell Internat. Inc., 1999—2000, 2001—02, chmn., 1999—2000, 2001—02; chmn. exec. com. Merck & Co. Inc., Whitehouse Station, 2005—. Mem. bd. dirs. Merck & Co. Inc., 1992—, JPMorgan Chase, 1998—, Berkshire Hills Bancorp. Co-author: Execution: the Discipline of Getting Things Done, 2002. Mem.: Bus. Roundtable, Bus. Coun., Elfun. Roman Catholic. Office: Merck & Co 1 Merck Dr Whitehouse Station NJ 08889

BOSSON, RICHARD CAMPBELL, state supreme court justice; b. Balt., Mar. 19, 1944; s. Albert D. and Elizabeth S. (Schaeffer) B.; m. Gloria Candelaria, Jan. 9, 1971; children: Christopher, Monica. BA, Wesleyan U., Middletown, Conn., 1966; JD, Georgetown U., 1969; M in Jud. Process, U. Va., 1998. Bar: Conn. 1969, N. Mex. 1970, U.S. Dist. Ct. N. Mex. 1970; cert. soccer referee, 1992—. Atty Legal Aid Soc. of Albuquerque, 1970-73; staff atty. Mexican Am. Legal Def. Fund, 1974, Latin Am. Tchg. Fellow, Fletcher Sch., Bogota, Colombia, 1975; chief of civil div. Atty. Gen. Office, Santa Fe, 1976-78; sr. ptnr. Bosson & Canepa P.A., Santa Fe, 1980—94; judge N.Mex. Ct. of Appeals, 1994—2002; justice N.Mex. Supreme Ct., 2002—, chief justice, 2005—. Mem. constl. revision commn., 1994—95; soccer referee Lead H.S. Candidate Dem. nomination for Atty. Gen of N. Mex., 1978. Reginald Heber Smith fellow. Mem. N.Mex. Trial Lawyers Assn. (bd. dirs. 1980-93), Nat. Assn. Bond Lawyers, Am. Trial Lawyers Assn. Office Phone: 505-827-4892. Business E-Mail: suprcb@nmcourts.com.

BOSSY, MICHAEL, professional sports team executive, retired professional hockey player; b. Montreal, Que., Can., Jan. 22, 1957; m. Lucie Bossy; children: Josieane, Tanya. Right wing Laval Nat. Hockey Club,

1973-77, NY Islanders, 1977—87, exec. dir. corp. rels., 2006—; TV broadcaster Quebec Nordiques, 1987—90. Recipient Calder Meml. trophy, 1978, Conn Smythe trophy, 1982, Lady Byng trophy, 1983. Achievements include being a member of Stanley Cup Champion NY Islanders, 1980-83; NHL single season record for most point and assists by right wing for 1981-82 season; NHL record 9 consecutive 50+ goal seasons 1977-85. Office: NY Islanders Nassau Vets Meml Coliseum 1255 Hempstead Turnpike Uniondale NY 11553

BOST, ERIC M., ambassador, former federal agency administrator; b. Concord, NH; BA in Psych., U. NC, 1974; MA in Spl. Edn., U. South Fla., 1985. Social worker Caswell Ctr., Kinston, NC, 1974—77, dir. mental retardation unit, 1980; dir. mental retardation & devel. disabilities adminstrn. DC Dept. Human Svcs., 1992—93; asst. dir. Ariz. Divsn. Dept. Disabilities, 1993—94; dep. dir. Ariz. Dept. Econ. Security, 1994—97; chief exec. & adminstrv. officer Tex. Dept. Human Services, 1997—2001; under sec. for food, nutrition & consumer svcs. USDA, Washington, 2001—06; US amb. to South Africa US Dept. State, Pretoria, 2006—. Recipient Disting. Svc. award, Food Rsch. & Action Ctr., 2002, Govt. Leadership award, Soyfoods Assn. N.Am., 2003. Office: DOS Amb 9300 Pretoria Pl Washington DC 20521*

BOST, JANE MORGAN, psychologist; b. Corpus Christi, Aug. 20, 1953; d. Clayton Aquilla and Eleanor (Hoving) M.; m. David Edward Bost, June 16, 1984; children: Christopher David, Morgan Jane. BS, Okla. State U., 1976, MS, 1980, PhD, 1984. English tchr. Perry High Sch., Okla., 1976-78; acad. advisor Okla. State U., Stillwater, 1980-82, staff therapist, 1982-83; counseling psychology intern Tex. A&M U., College Station, 1983-84; dir. counseling svcs. Southwestern U., Georgetown, Tex., 1984-92; asst. dir. counseling and mental health ctr. U Tex., Austin, 1992-98, assoc. dir. counseling and mental health ctr., 1998—. Contbr. articles to profl. jours. Mem. collegue status faculty Creative Problem Solving Inst., Buffalo, 1985-86, 88, 91, 92, 93, 94. Named Outstanding Young Women of Am., 1988, 91 Merit award for Outstanding Staff, U. Tex. Parents Assn., 2003-04; grantee Combat Violence against Woman on Campus, U.S. Dept. Justice, 2000, 02, 05. Mem. APA, Am. Coll. Pers. Assn. (mem. directorate commn. psychol. svcs. 2006-07), Tex. Psychol. Assn., Nat. Register Health Service Providers in Psychology. Methodist. Avocations: hiking, photograph, reading, artwork, gardening. Office: U Tex Counseling & Mental Health Ctr Austin TX 78712

BOSTATER, CHARLES R., JR., marine engineer, educator; PhD in Applied Ocean Sci., U. Del., Newark, 1990. Prin. investigator, chief tech. analysis & data mgmt. sect. Md. Dept. Natural Resources, Annapolis, 1976—84; grad. rsch. scientist U. Del., Newark, 1984—87, postdoctoral fellowship applied ocean scis., 1990—92; phys. scientist strategic assessments br. NOAA, Rockville, Md., 1987—89; owner KB Sci., 1989—; asst. prof. dept. marine & environ. systems Fla. Inst. Tech., 1992—98, assoc. prof., 1999—. Contbr. articles to sci. jours. Mem.: IEEE, Am. Soc. Engring. Edn., Estuarine Rsch. Fedn., Internat. Soc. Optical Engring., Am. Soc. Limnology and Oceanography, Am. Geophys. Union, Sigma Xi. Office: Marine and Environ Systems Dept Fla Inst Tech 150 W Univ Blvd Melbourne FL 32901 Office Phone: 321-674-7113. Office Fax: 321-600-9412. E-mail: bostater@probe.pcn.fit.edu.*

BOSTETTER, MARTIN V. B., JR., bankruptcy court judge; b. Balt., Mar. 11, 1926; s. Martin V.B. Bostetter and Louella Jane (Smith) Rice; m. Joanne Rushworth, March 28, 1955; children: Martin III, David W., Jonathan A., Lisa A. BA, U. Va., 1950, LLD, 1952. Bar: Va. 1952, Md. 1953, D.C. 1962. City prosecutor City of Alexandria, Va., 1953-57; chief judge U.S. Bankruptcy Ct. for Ea. Dist. Va., Alexandria, 1985-99. Bd. dirs. Fed. Jud. Ctr., Washington, 1984-87, chmn. edn. com. for all bankruptcy judges, Washington, 1986-89; mem. Fed. State Jud. Rels. Com. of Commonwealth of Va.; chmn. Juvenile Detention Com., Alexandria, 1957-74. Recipient Distinguished Svc. awd. Jr. C.of C., Alexandria, 1959; U.S. Courthouse named Martin V.B. Bostetter U.S. Courthouse by act of Congress, Alexandria, Va., 1998. Office: 200 N Fairfax St Alexandria VA 22314

BOSTIC, JAMES E., JR., paper company executive; b. SC, June 24, 1947; BS in Textile Chemistry, Clemson U., 1969, PhD in Chemistry, 1972. Sr. rsch. scientist Am. Enka Co., 1972; White House fellow, spl. asst. to sec. US Dept. Agr., Washington, 1972—73, dep. asst. sec. agr., 1973—77; corp. regulatory dir. Riegel Textile Corp., 1977—81, pres. Riegel ventures divsn., 1981—82, pres. convenience products divsn., 1982—85; gen. mgr. convenience products divsn. Ga.-Pacific Corp., 1985—87, dir. sales ops. consumer tissue group, 1987—89, gen. mgr. comml. products and sys. divsn., 1989—90, v.p. Butler Paper and Mail-Well, 1991—92, group v.p. comm. papers, 1992—95, sr. v.p. environ., govt. affairs and comm., 1995—2000, exec. v.p. environ., govt. affairs and comm., 2000—03, exec. v.p. environ., govt. affairs and adminstrv. svcs., 2003—05. Bd. dirs. Atlanta Com. for Pub. Edn., Clemson U. Found., Progress Energy Bd., Inc.; bd. dirs., vice chmn. edn. Metro Atlanta C. of C.; trustee Ga. Conservancy, Nat. Parks Conservation Assn., The Westminster Schs.; mem. Pres. Commn. on White House Fellowships; chmn. bd. Project GRAD, Atlanta. Named Outstanding Young Men Am., 1972, 1975; recipient Disting. Svc. award, Greenville (S.C.) Jaycees, 1979, Outstanding Textile Alumnus award, Clemson U., 1983, Outstanding Pub. Servant of Yr. award, S.C. Assn. Minorities for Pub. Adminstrn., 1983, Disting. Alumni award, Clemson U. Alumni Assn., 1990, Vision 300 award, Paper Industry Mgmt. Assn., 1997, Thomas Green Clemson Acad. Engrs. and Scientists award, Clemson U., 2002, G.W. Brumley Project GRAD USA Leadership award, 2005; Doctoral Fellowship for Black Students, Ford Found., 1968. Office: 133 Peachtree St NE Atlanta GA 30303 Personal E-mail: jebostic69@aol.com. Business E-Mail: jebostic@gapac.com.

BOSTICK, CHARLES DENT, retired lawyer; b. Gainesville, Ga., Dec. 28, 1931; s. Jared Sullivan and Charlotte Catherine (Dent) B.; m. Susan Oliver, Sept. 8, 1956; children: Susan, Alan. Student, Emory-at-Oxford U., 1948-49; BA, Mercer U., 1952, JD, 1958. Bar: Ga. 1957, Tenn. 1974, U.S. Dist. Ct. (no. dist.) Ga. 1958, U.S. Ct. Appeals (5th cir.) 1959. Pvt. practice, Gainesville, Ga., 1958-66; asst. prof. law U. Fla., Gainesville, 1966-68, assoc. prof., 1968, Vanderbilt U., Nashville, 1968-71, prof., 1971-92, assoc. dean, dir. admissions, 1975-79, acting dean, 1979-80, dean, 1980-85; ret., 1992. Vis. prof. law U. Leeds, Eng., 1985-86, prof. law emeritus, dean emeritus Sch. Law, 1992. Served to lt. USNR, 1952-55. Mem. Tenn. Bar. Assn. Episcopalian. Office: Vanderbilt U Sch Law 21st Ave S Nashville TN 37240-0001

BOSTICK, RUSSELL M., information technology executive; b. Feb. 4, 1957; BA in Chemistry and Math., Wabash Coll.; MBA in Marketing, U. Chgo. Technology positions IBM, 1979—94, CNA Insurance, 1994—97; chief technology officer Corp. Software & Technology, Norwood, Mass., 1997—98, Chase Ins., 1998—2005; chief information officer Zurich Life US; exec. v.p., chief information officer Conseco, Inc., Carmel, Ind., 2005—. Chmn. bd. gov. IT Resources Ctr. Office: Conseco Inc 11825 N Pennsylvania St Carmel IN 46032 Office Phone: 317-817-2426.

BOSTIN, MARVIN JAY, hospital and health services consultant; came to U.S., 1956; s. Samuel and Rose (Mandel) B.; 1 child, Shepard Craig. BS in Pharmacy, U. Toronto, 1955; MS in Hosp. Adminstrn., Columbia U., 1958; PhD in Pub. Adminstrn., NYU, 1972. Pharmacist New Mt. Sinai Hosp., Toronto, 1953-56; asst. adminstr. L.I. Jewish Hosp., New Hyde Park, NY, 1958-62; assoc. dir. Mt. Sinai Med. Ctr., Miami Beach, Fla., 1962-65; exec. v.p. E.D. Rosenfeld Assocs. Inc., hosp. and health svcs. cons., White Plains, NY, 1965-78; pres. M. Bostin Assocs., Inc., Stamford, Conn., 1979—. Guest scholar Brookings Instn., Washington, 1965; lectr. Sch. Pub. Health and Adminstrv. Medicine, Columbia U., N.Y.C., 1965-78, Grad. Sch. Pub. Adminstrn., 1967; lectr. Grad. Sch. Architecture and Planning, Columbia U., 1975-78; cons. to Bur. of Hearings and Appeals, Social Security Adminstrn., HEW, 1967-68; cons. task force on guidelines for constrn. and equipment of hosp. and med. facilities, USPHS, DHHS, 1987; mem. implementation work group on improving health Nat. Commn. on Children, 1992; spl. cons. to Office of Equal Health Opportunity, Office of Surgeon Gen., USPHS, 1966-67. Mem. Dade County (Fla.) Welfare Planning Coun., Miami, 1962-65; bd. dirs. South Fla. Hosp. Coun., Miami, 1963-65. Fellow APHA, Royal Soc. Health (London), Am. Assn. Healthcare Cons. (chmn. monograph series com. 1970-71, exec. com. 1972-75, profl. standards com. 1974-76); mem. Am. Hosp. Assn. (life), Forum for Health Care Planning (dir. 1982-95, treas. 1988-89, sec. 1989-90), Am. Coll. Healthcare Execs., Can. Coll. Health Svc. Execs. (fgn. affiliate), Internat. Hosp. Fedn. Address: M Bostin Assoc Inc 800 Summer St Ste 315 Stamford CT 06901-1023 Office Phone: 203-961-0511. Business E-Mail: marvin@bostin.com.

BOSTOCK, ROY JACKSON, investment company executive; b. Glen Ridge, NJ, Sept. 25, 1940; s. James Franklin Bostock and Jane (Ritter) Bostock Addis; m. Merilee Huser, 1962; children: Victoria, Matthew, Kate. AB, Duke U., 1962; MBA, Harvard U., 1964. Asst. account exec. Benton & Bowles, NYC, 1964-66, account exec., 1966-68, account supr., v.p., 1968-70, sr. v.p., from 1970, group exec., 1976-81, exec. v.p., gen. mgr., 1981-84; pres. Benton & Bowles, Inc., NYC, 1984-85, D'Arcy Masius Benton & Bowles, Inc., NYC, 1985-88, pres., COO, 1988-89, pres., CEO, from 1989, chmn., CEO, 1990-96, BCom3/McManus Group, NYC, 1996—2001; prin. Sealedge Investments LLC, Greenwich, Conn.; chmn. Northwest Airlines, Saint Paul, Minn., 2007—. Bd. dir. Morgan Stanley, Yahoo! Inc., 2003—, Northwest Airlines, 2005—. Chmn. Partnership for a Drug Free Am. Mem. Am. Assn. Advt. Agys., Phi Beta Kappa. Clubs: Apawamis (Rye, N.Y.); Manursing Island (Rye) (pres. 1983-85); Racquet & Tennis (N.Y.C.). Republican. Presbyterian. Home: S Manursing Island Rye NY 10580*

BOSTON, BETTY LEE, investment company executive, financial planner, consultant; b. Agana, Guam, Dec. 21, 1935; d. Homer Laurence and Bessie Margarete (Leech) Litzenberg; m. Filibert Roth Boston, Aug. 12, 1956; children: William Litzenberg, Beth Boston Tedesco, Brent Litzenberg. BA, U. Mich., Ann Arbor, 1958. CFP®. Stockbroker I.M. Simon & Co., Murray, Ky., 1976—78, 1st of Mich. Corp., Murray, Ky., 1978—86; fin. cons. J.J.B. Hilliard, W.L. Lyons, Inc., Murray, Ky., 1986—2006; v.p. Hilliard Lyons Inc., Murray, Ky., 1998—2006. Instr. adult edn. investment classes Murray State U., 1977—2000; investment commentator Sta. WKMS, Murray, 1987—2006. Author: (fin. columnist) Murray Ledger and Times, 2000—06. Chmn. Inter-Faith Coalition Congregations, Ann Arbor, 1971-73; pres. Need Line Ch. and Cmty. Ministry, Murray, 1981-83; mem. Murray regional bd. Ky. Coun. on Econ. Edn., 1987—. Recipient Woman of Yr. award, Murray Bus. and Profl. Women, 1988. Mem. AAUW (treas. Murray br. 1982-87, pres. 1991-97), Rotary (sec. Murray club 1990-95, pres. 1998-99, Paul Harris fellow). United Methodist. Home: 917 N 16th St Murray KY 42071-1523

BOSTON, BILLIE, costume designer and history educator; b. Oklahoma City, Sept. 22, 1939; d. William Barrett and Margaret Emeline (Townsend) Long; m. William Clayton Boston, Jr., Jan. 20, 1962; children: Kathryn Gray, William Clayton III. BFA, U. Okla., 1961, MFA, 1962. Asst. to designer Karinski of N.Y., NYC, 1966-67; prof. costume history Oklahoma City U., 1987—. Rep. Arts Coun., Oklahoma City, 1987-90, Arts Festival, Oklahoma City, 1972-80; dir. ETC Theater, Oklahoma City SW Coll., 1979-83; actress Lyric Theatre, Oklahoma City, 1979-81; designer Casa Mahara Theatre, Ft. Worth, 1998. Exhibited in group shows at Taos, N.Mex., Santa Fe; represented in permanent collections in Dallas, Taos, Santa Fe, Tulsa, N.Y.C., La Jolla; costume designer Ballet Okla., Oklahoma City, 1979-84, Agnes DeMillie's Rodeo Ballet Okla., 1982, Royal Ballet Flanders, 1983, Pitts. Ballet, 1983, BBC's Childrens Prodn., 1984, 86, Lyric Theatre, Oklahoma City, 1987-95, Red Oak Music Theatre, Lakewood, N.J., 1988, Winter Olympics, 1988, Miss Am. Pageant, 1988, for JoAnne Worley in Hello Dolly, San Francisco Opera Circus, 1991, Jupiter (Fla.) Theatre, 1991-92, Mobile (Ala.) Light Opera, 1992, The Boy Friend, Temple U., Japan, 1995, The Sound of Music, Lyric Stage, Dallas, 1995, Annie Get Your Gun, Guys and Dolls with Vic Damone, 1995, Westbury Flash Valley Forge Music Fair, Oklahoma and Sound of Music, Casa Manana, Theatre, Ft. Worth, 1997, Singing in the Rain, Lone Star Theatre, Galveston, Tex., 1997, Most Happy Fellow, Lyric Stage Dallas, 1997, To Gillian on her 37th Birthday, Watertower Theatre, Dallas, 1998, Carousel, Annie Get Your Gun, Cinderella, Casa Manana, 1998; designer Titanic, Irving, Tex., 2003, Specture Bridegroom, Irving, 2003, Opal, Lyric Stage, Irving, 2003; designer (play) Finian's Rainbow, Lyric Stage, Dallas, Tex., 2004, Ragtime, Lyric Stage, 2004 (Leon Rabin award costume design, 2005). Rep. Speakers Bur. Oklahoma City for Ballet, 1979-85; judge State Hist. Speech Tournament, Oklahoma City, 1985-87; chmn. State of Okla. Conf. on Tchr./Student Relationships, Oklahoma City, 1981. Recipient Gov.'s Achievement award, 1988, Lady in the News award, 1987; Excellence in Costume Design award Kennedy Ctr. Am. Coll. Theatre Festival XXXIV, 2001, Leon Rubin Costume Design award Dallas Theatre League, 2005. Mem. Alpha Chi Omega (house corp. bd. 1986-90). Methodist. Avocation: watercolorist. Home: 1701 Camden Way Oklahoma City OK 73116-5121 Office Phone: 405-521-5050. E-mail: bboston@okcu.edu.

BOSTON, GRETHA, actress, vocalist; b. Crossett, AK; B of Music, N Tex. State U., Denton; vocal study with vocal tech. and coaches, John Wustman, Bill Riley. Carnegie Hall debut Mozart's Coronation Mass, 1991, concert performances Beethoven's Ninth Symphony (Carnegie Hall), Handel's Messiah (Madison, Wis. & Arlington, Tex.), roles (Operas) Carmen in Bizet's Carmen, The Mother in Menotti's The Consul, Ciesca in Puccini's Gianni Schicchi, Delilah in Saint-Saens's Samson et Delilah, Maddalena in Verdi's Rigoletto (N.Y. Grand Opera), Amneris in Verdi's Aida, Azucena in Verdi's Il Trovatore, Queenie in Kern & Hammerstein's Show Boat (Tony award Best Supporting Actress in a Musical, 1995), Maria & Strawberry Woman in Gershwin's Porgy and Bess, 1993, It Ain't Nothin' But The Blues, 1999 (Tony award), appeared (TV series) Law and Order, Rosie O'Donnel, David Letterman, PBS, Today Show. Recipient 3rd place D'Angelo Young Artist Internat. Competition, 1984. Address: 250 W 57th St Ste 2223 New York NY 10107-2210

BOSTON, LLOYD, television personality; b. 1970; V.p. art direction Tommy Hilfiger, event spokesperson; style editor The Today Show, NBC; nat. spokesperson Jones NY. Host (TV series) The Look for Less, Style Essentials, Runway, Full Frontal Fashion; author: (books) Make Over Your Man, Men of Color, Before You Put That On: 365 Daily Style Tips for Her, 2005. Named one of 40 Under 40, Crain's Mag. Office: c/o Jeff Googel William Morris Agy 1325 Ave of Americas New York NY 10019*

BOSTROM, CARL OTTO, physicist, research facility administrator; b. Port Jefferson, NY, Aug. 18, 1932; s. Carl Oscar and Dagmar Ester (Anderson) B.; m. Sara A. Herzog, Sept. 6, 1954; children: Robin I. Bostrom Dagan, Jennifer A. Bostrom Simmons, Carl E. BS in Physics, Franklin & Marshall Coll., 1956; MS in Physics, Yale U., 1958, PhD, 1962; ScD (hon.), Franklin & Marshall Coll., 1992. Physicist space dept. Johns Hopkins U. Applied Physics Lab., Laurel, Md., 1960-68, group supr. space dept., 1968-74, chief scientist space dept., 1974-78, assoc. head space dept., 1978-79, dept. head and asst. dir. space dept., 1979, dep. dir., 1979-80, dir., 1980-92, now dir. emeritus. Mem.-at-large adv. bd. Def. Intelligence Agy., Washington, 1982-87, 92—, chmn. sci. adv. com., 1988-92; ex officio mem. Def. Sci. Bd., Washington, 1988-92; mem. Pres. Com. on Nat. Medal Sci., 1986-91; mem.-at-large Air Force Sci. Adv. Bd., 1983-87; mem. bd. visitors Naval Surface Weapons Systems Engring. Sta. and Naval Ship Systems Engring. Sta., 1982-92; mem. external adv. bd. Ga. Tech. Rsch. Inst., 1988—. Contbr. articles to profl. jours. including Jour. Geophys. Rsch., Geophys. Rsch. Letters, Sci., Space Sci. Rev., others. Mem. BCC chpt. Izaak Walton League, Poolesville, Md., 1974-79. With U.S. Army, 1950-52. Recipient Air Force medal for exceptional civilian svc./, 1987, DOD Medal for Disting. Pub. Svc., 1992, Def. Intelligency Agy. Medal for exceptional civilian svc., 1992, NASA Disting. Pub. Svc. medal, 1992. Fellow Hudson Inst.; mem. AAAS, Am. Phys. Soc., Am. Def. Preparedness Assn., Am Geophys. Union (com. on govtl. and legis. affairs 1975-79, chmn. 1975-77), Am. Soc. Naval Engrs., Internat. Assn. Geomagnetism and Aeronomy, Cosmos Club, Navy League, Phi Beta Kappa, Sigma Xi, Sigma Pi. Personal E-mail: cbostrom@verizon.net.

BOSTROM, ROBERT EVERETT, lawyer, finance company executive; b. Hartford, Conn., Nov. 20, 1952; m. Elizabeth Mitchell Leys, July 14, 1979; children: Leys, Ashley, Allison. BA, Franklin and Marshall Coll., 1974; M in Internat. Affairs, Columbia U., 1976; JD cum laude, Boston Coll., 1980. Bar: N.Y. 1981, U.S. Dist. Ct. (ea., so. dist.) N.Y. Atty. Fed. Res. Bank, NYC, 1980-82; assoc. Windels, Marx, Davies & Ives, 1982-84, Brown & Wood, NYC; ptnr. Winston & Strawn LLP, NYC, 1990—92, 1996—2006, mem. exec. com., head fin. institutions practice; exec. v.p. legal and regulatory, gen. counsel Nat. Westminster Bancorp, 1992—96; exec. v.p., gen. counsel Freddie Mac, McLean, Va., 2006—. Mem. bd. advisors Mergers and Acquistions SNL Securities, 1994—98; mem. faculty Duke Dirs. Edn. Inst. On-Site Dir. Edn. Program; mem. program adv. bd. Brennan Ctr. Justice; mem. law firm adv. com. Met. Corp. Counsel; bd. trustees The Forman Sch.; lectr., moderator, spkr. in field; co-chmn. Strategic Rsch. Inst. Capital Markets Activities of Interant. Banks, 1994, 95. Contbr. articles to profl jours.; editor-in-chief: Boston Coll. Internat. and Comparative Law Review, 1979-80; co-editor: Internat. Practioner's Notebook, 1988-93. Mem. ABA, Internat. Lawyers Assn. (exec. com. Am. br. 1992-94), N.Y. County Lawyers Assn. (banking com.). Office: Freddie Mac 8200 Jones Branch Dr Mc Lean VA 22102 Office Phone: 212-294-4651. Office Fax: 212-294-4700. E-mail: rbostrom@winston.com.*

BOSTROM, SUSAN L., marketing executive; b. 1960; 3 children. BS, U. Ill.; MBA, Stanford U. Acct. exec. AT&T Corp., 1982; with McKinsey & Co., Nat. Semiconductor; sr. v.p. global mktg. and strategic planning FTP Software; with Cisco Systems, Inc., San Jose, Calif., 1997—, v.p. Internet bus. solutions, 1998—2000, sr. v.p., 2000—06, sr. v.p., chief mktg. officer worldwide govt. affairs, 2006—. Exec. sponsor women's initiative Cisco Systems, Inc., 2001—04. Bd. dirs. Varian Med. Systems, 2004—, Stanford Hospitals and Clinics; mem. adv. bd. Stanford Inst. Econ. Policy Rsch. Office: Cisco Systems Inc 170 W Tasman Dr San Jose CA 95134

BOSTWICK, JAMES STEPHEN, lawyer; b. Pasadena, Calif., Jan. 15, 1943; s. Jack Raymond and Rhoda Loraine (Fox) B.; children from a previous marriage: Brenton Reid, Grant Evan, Blake Powell; m. Marti Philips; children: Taylor, Carter. MS, U. Wash., 1965; JD, Hastings Coll. Law, 1968. Bar: Calif. 1968, Hawaii 1981. Pvt. practice, San Francisco, 1968; assoc. Walkup, Downing, Sterns & Poore, 1968-73; ptnr. Walkup, Downing & Sterns, 1973-77, Sterns, Bostwick & Tehin, 1977-79; sr. ptnr. Bostwick & Tehin, 1979-96, Bostwick & Assocs., 1996—. Faculty Coll. Advocacy, 1976—, Hastings seminar on trial practice; lectr. in field. Fellow Internat. Acad. Trial Lawyers (sec. internat. rels. 1997-99, bd. dirs. 1993—, dean 2000—, v.p. 2001, pres.-elect 2002, pres. 2003); mem. Consumer Attys. Calif. (chmn. profl. liability legis. com. 1975-77, bd. dirs. 1978-85, Presdl. Merit award), Inner Circle of Advocates, Am. Bd. of Trial Advocates, Am. Bd. Profl. Liability Attys. (diplomate, founding mem.), Hawaii Acad. Plaintiff's Attys., San Francisco Trial Lawyers Assn. (bd. dirs., chmn. patients litig. fund com., chmn. jud. liaison com., nat. cert. com., Trial Achievement award 1979, Best Lawyer Am. personal injury litg. sect. 1987—). Democrat. Office: 4 Embarcadero Ctr Ste 750 San Francisco CA 94111-4171 Office Phone: 415-421-8300. E-mail: james@bostwickfirm.com.

BOSTWICK, JARRETT T., lawyer; b. Somerville, NJ, July 9, 1973; BA, George Washington U., 1995; JD, Gonzaga U. Sch. Law, 1998; LLM in Taxation, U. Wash. Sch. Law, 1999. Bar: Wash. 1998, Ill. 2004. Assoc. Treacy Law Grp., PLLC, Seattle; dir. wealth planning Nat. Fin. Ptnr. Wealth Design Ctr.; sr. mgr. personal fin. counseling grp. Ernst & Young, LLP; ptnr. wealth planning & philanthropy grp. Gardner, Carton & Douglas, Chgo.; atty. Handler, Thayer & Duggan, LLC, Chgo. Named one of Top 100 Attys., Worth mag., 2005. Office: Handler Thayer & Duggan LLC 191 N Wacker Dr 23rd Fl Chicago IL 60606-1633 Office Phone: 312-641-2100. Office Fax: 312-641-6866. E-mail: jbostwick@htdlaw.com.

BOSTWICK, RANDELL ARMOUR, retired food service executive; b. Niles, Ohio, Oct. 24, 1922; s. Clifton A. and May (Lloyd) B.; m. Jane Elizabeth Foster, Aug. 28, 1948; children: Suzanne Elizabeth, Sherrard, Randell A. Student, U. Mich., Westminster Coll. Asst. traffic mgr. A&P, Youngstown, Ohio, 1948-50, asst. to div. traffic mgr. Pitts., 1952-58, div. traffic mgr., 1958-60, dir. ops., 1960-69, asst. to nat. dir. ops. N.Y. hdqrs., 1969-75; pres. subs. Super Market Service Corp., Montvale, NJ, 1975-88; corp. v.p. The Gt. A & P Tea Co., 1981-88; chmn. Supermarket Service Corp., 1988-91, ret., 1992. Served to capt. Med. Service Corps U.S. Army, 1943-46, 50-52. Presbyterian. Home: 333 River St Apt 513 Hoboken NJ 07030

BOSTWICK, ROBERT OTIS, government agency administrator; b. Mobile, Ala., Apr. 9, 1946; B, U. South Ala., 1967. Supr. Texaco Oil, Mobile, 1979-83; v.p. Midtown Restaurant Corp., Mobile, 1983-85; v.p., CEO, Signs Now, Mobile, 1985-87; v.p., dir. franchising CHECKERS Drive-In Restaurants, Mobile, 1987-89; exec. asst. to mayor Mobile, 1989—. Office: Office of the Mayor Govt Plaza 205 Government St Mobile AL 36602-2613

BOSWELL, ERIC J., federal official; b. Italy, May 31, 1945; s. William O. and Janine (Werner) Boswell; m. Nancy Zucker, 1995; children: Nathaniel, Matthew; stepchildren: Jeremy, Amanda Zucker. BA, Stanford U., 1970. Gen. svcs. officer Fgn. Svc., 1972-75, ops. ctr. spl. asst. to under sec. for mgmt. Washington, 1975-77, consular officer Quebec, 1977—80; officer Bur. of Pers., 1980-83; dep. exec., dir. Bur. European & Can. Affairs US Dept. State, 1983-85, adminstrv. officer Amman, 1985—87, Ottawa, 1987—90, exec. dir. Bur. Near East & South Asian Affairs Washington, 1990-92, exec. asst. to the under sec. for mgmt. Bur. Near East & South Asian Affairs, 1992-93, dir. fgn. missions, 1994—96, asst. sec. for diplomatic security, 1996—98; dir. Pan Am. Health Org. UN, NYC, 1998—2005, sr. advisor for Security Chance Mgmt., 2004; asst. dep. dir. for security Office Dep. Dir. Nat. Intelligence for Mgmt., Washington, 2006—. With U.S. Army, 1967-69. Office: Office Nat Intelligence ADDNI/SEC Rm N-583 DNI-DIAC Washington DC 20511 Business E-Mail: ericjb0@dni.gov.

BOSWELL, G(EORGE) HARVEY, federal judge; b. Medina, Tenn., July 8, 1947; m. Jenny Lynn Butler; one child. BS, U. Tenn., 1969; JD, U. Memphis, 1979. Pvt. practice, Milan, Tenn., 1980-83; atty. Kizer, Bonds, Boswell & Crocker, 1983-93; bankruptcy judge U.S. Bankruptcy Ct. (we.

dist.), Tenn., 1993—. Fellow Tenn. Bar Found.; mem. Nat. Conf. Bankruptcy Judges, Am. Bankruptcy Inst., Tenn. Bar Assn. Office: US Bankruptcy Ct 111 S Highland Ave Ste 324 Jackson TN 38301-6107 Office Phone: 731-421-9370.

BOSWELL, GEORGE MARION, JR., orthopedist, health facility administrator; b. Dallas, May 12, 1920; s. George Marion and Viola (Scarbrough) B.; m. Veta M. Fuller, Oct. 30, 1958; children: Brianna Boswell Brown, Kama Boswell Koudelka, Maia Boswell. BS, Tex. Tech U., 1940; MD, U. Tex., Southwestern Dallas, 1950. Diplomate Am. Acad. Orthop. Surgery. Intern Parkland Hosp., Dallas, 1950-51; resident gen. surgeryand orthopedic surgery Parkland, Baylor and Scottish Rite Hosps., Dallas, 1951-55; practice medicine specializing in orthopedics Dallas, 1955—; v.p. med. affairs Baylor Health Care System, Dallas, 1982-86; dir. orthopaedic clin. studies Baylor U. Med. Ctr., 1995—. Owner Bee Aviation Inc., Dallas, 1968—, Boswell Realty Inc., Dallas, 1971—; lectr., cons. in field. Contbr. articles to profl. jours. Prof. George M. Bowell, Jr. chair in orthopaedic surgery named in his honor Baylor U. Med. Ctr. Fellow ACS; mem. AMA, Am. Acad. Orthopaedic Surgery (Key Man U.S. Congress 1980—), Am. Hosp. Assn., Tex. Hosp. Assn. (Key Man Tex. Legislature 1980—, council on hosp. staffs), Flying Physicians (pres. Tex. 1960-64). Clubs: Cresent (Dallas). Republican. Methodist. Avocations: flying, photography, fishing, saddle making. Home: 7249 Wabash Cir Dallas TX 75214-3535 Office: 10611 Garland Rd Ste 209 Dallas TX 75218 Office Phone: 214-348-8300. Personal E-mail: gmbjr@mac.com.

BOSWELL, GINA R., cosmetics executive; married; 2 children. BS summa cum laude in Bus. Adminstrn., Boston Univ.; M in Pub., Pvt. Mgmt., Yale Univ., 1989. CPA. With Estee Lauder Cos., 1992—99; head, e-bus. to v.p. bus. devel. Ford Motor Co., 1999—2003; v.p. corp. strategy, bus. devel. Avon N.Am., NYC, 2003—05, sr. v.p., COO, 2005—. Bd. dir. Applebee's Internat. Named one of America's Top Women in Bus.-Game Changers, Pink mag. & Forté Found., 2007; grantee Henry Crown Fellowship, Aspen Inst., 2005. Office: Avon Products Inc 1345 Ave of Americas New York NY 10105-0196 Office Phone: 212-282-5623.*

BOSWELL, JAMES DOUGLAS, medical research executive; b. Tulsa, Feb. 12, 1942; m. Pamela Scott; children: Megan, Melanie Student, U. Okla., 1960-61; BA, U. Tulsa, 1964, MA, 1966; PhD, Madison U., 2004. Indsl. relations rep. Trans World Airlines, 1966-68; dir. placement Skelly Oil Co., 1968-72, mgr. employee and pub. relations, 1972-75, gen. mgr. adminstrn., 1975-77; corp. mgr. human resources Getty Oil Co., 1977-81; v.p. employee and pub. relations L.A. Times, 1981-91; CEO House Ear Inst., LA, 1991—, trustee, 1995—. Bd. dirs. Employers Group; pres. Skelly Oil Found., Tulsa, 1974-78, Getty Oil Co. Found., 1978-79. Bd. dirs. L.A. Boys and Girls Club, v.p., 1985; bd. dirs. L.A. Theatre Ctr., 1988-90, L.A. chpt. ARC; bd. dirs. L.A. Jr. Achievement, 1982-91, vice chmn. human resources, 1986; fellow Nat. Health Found., 1992, San Marino Cmty. Ch. Found., 1992-95; mem. Econ. Round Table, 1993, sec.-treas., 1995-96. Mem. Am. Soc. Personnel Adminstrn., Am. Psychol. Assn., Newspaper Personnel Relations Assn., Am. Newspaper Assn. (labor and personnel relations com. 1982-91). Avocations: tennis, skiing, golf. Office: House Ear Inst 2100 W 3rd St 5th Fl Los Angeles CA 90057-1922 Home: 1123 S Orange Grove Blvd Pasadena CA 91105-3314

BOSWELL, LEONARD L., congressman; b. Harrison County, Mo., Jan. 10, 1934; s. Melvin and Margaret B.; m. Dody Boswell; 3 children. BA in Bus. Adminstrn., Graceland Coll., 1969. Commd. 2d lt. U.S. Army, 1956, advanced through grades to lt. col. Vietnam, Germany, Portugal, resigned, 1976; mem. Iowa Senate, 1984-96, pres., 1993-97; mem. U.S. Congress from 3d Iowa dist., 1997—; mem. transp. and infrastucture com., agr. com., select copm. on intelligence, 1999—. Grain and livestock farmer Decatur County, 1976—. Past pres., bd. dirs. local Coop. Elevator, Lamoni. Decorated DFC (2), Bronze Star (2). Mem. VFW, Am. Legion, Cattleman's Assn., Lamoni Lions Club. Democrat. Office: US Ho of Reps 1427 Longworth HOB Washington DC 20515-0001 Business E-Mail: Rep.Boswell.ia03@Mail.house.gov.

BOSWELL, RUPERT DEAN, JR., retired academic administrator, mathematician, educator; b. Marshall County, Miss., Aug. 11, 1929; s. Rupert Dean and Mary Exyah (Ellis) B.; m. Grace Hadaway, Apr. 11, 1952; children: James Elton, Deanna Grace. BS, Miss. State U., 1950, MS, 1951; PhD, U. Ga., 1957. Grad. asst. Miss. State U., Mississippi State, 1950-51; instr. math. Reinhardt Coll., Waleska, Ga., 1951-53; grad. asst. U. Ga., Athens, 1953-56; assoc. prof. math. Miss. State U., 1957-61, prof., 1961-62; prof. math. Monmouth (Ill.) Coll., 1962-77; v.p. acad. affairs Rocky Mountain Coll., Billings, Mont., 1977-85; provost, prof. math. Upper Iowa U., Fayette, 1985-89; prof. math. Jacksonville (Ala.) State U., 1989-94. Mem.: AAUP, Math. Assn. Am. (chmn. com. on vis. lectrs. 1967—69, chmn. Ill. sect.), Am. Math. Soc., Sigma Xi. Presbyterian. Home: 554 Queen Oak St Collierville TN 38017

BOSWELL, WILLIAM PARET, lawyer; b. Washington, Oct. 24, 1946; s. Yates Paret and Mary Frances (Hyland) B.; m. Barbara Stelle Schroeder, Sept. 6, 1969; children: Susan Anne, Sarah Mary, Christina Catherine. BA cum laude, Cath. U., 1968; JD, U. Va., 1971. Bar: Va. 1971, D.C. 1972, U.S. Ct. Mil. Appeals 1972, U.S. Supreme Ct. 1975, Pa. 1978. Atty. Peoples Natural Gas Co., Pitts., 1978-82, asst. sec., gen. atty., 1982-85, sec., gen. counsel, 1985-88, v.p., gen. counsel, sec., 1989-99; gen. counsel Hope Gas, Inc., Pitts., 1998—99; gen. counsel Consol. Natural Gas Co., Pitts., 1999-2000, Dominion Resources, Inc., Pitts., 2000—04; ptnr. McGuireWoods LLP, Pitts., 2000—04; prin. William P. Boswell LLC, 2004—. Exec. com. Gas Industry Stds. Bd., 1994—97, chmn., 2001, N.Am. Energy Stds. Bd., 2002—03, named founding chmn., 2003. Pres. Borough Coun., Osborne, Pa., 1984-97, mayor, 1998—; bd. dirs. Mendelssohn Choir Pitts., 1986-2001, pres. 1997-98; trustee Laughlin Found., 1995—. Capt. JAGC, USAF, 1971-78, col. USAFR, 1978-98, ret. Mem. ABA (chair gas com. 1995-2003, chair infrastructure security com. 2003—), Pa. Bar Assn., D.C. Bar Assn., Va. Bar Assn., Am. Gas Assn. (chair regulatory com. 1996-98), Pa. Gas Assn. (chmn. 1989-90), Am. Corp. Counsel Assn. (pres. Pa. chpt. 1991-92, Excellence in Corporate Practice award 1998), Am. Soc. Corp. Secs., City Club Pitts., Army and Navy Club D.C. Republican. Roman Catholic. Home: 405 Hare Ln Sewickley PA 15143-2050 Office: Dominion Tower 23 Fl 625 Liberty Ave Pittsburgh PA 15222-3142

BOSWORTH, DALE N., former federal agency administrator; b. Altadena, Calif., Dec. 15, 1943; m. Carma J. Bosworth; children: Kristy, Neil. BS in Forestry, U. Idaho. Forest supr. Wasatch-Cache Nat. Forest, Intermountain Region US Forest Svc., USDA, Utah, 1986—90, dep. dir. forest mgmt. Washington, 1990—92, dep. regional forester Pacific S.W. Region San Francisco, 1992—94, regional forester Intermountain Region Ogden, Utah, 1994—97, regional forester No. region Missoula, Mont., 1997—2001, chief Washington, 2001—07. Mem.: Soc. for Range Mgmt., Soc. Am. Foresters.*

BOSWORTH, JAY L., radiation oncologist; b. NYC, Oct. 23, 1945; BS, Bklyn. Coll.; MD, Albert Einstein Coll. Medicine, 1970. Cert. Therapeutic Radiology 1974. Intern Metro Hosp., NYC, 1970—71; resident Bronx Mcpl. Hosp. Ctr., NYC, 1971—74; former chief of divsn. radiation oncology North Shore U. Hosp., Manhasset, NY, attending physician radiation oncology, St. Francis Hosp.; radiation oncologist Nassau Radiologic Group, Manhasset, 1998—. Pres. NY Cancer Soc., 2003—04. Fellow: Am. Coll. Radiology; mem.: Am. Soc. Breast Diseases, Am. Urological Assn., Am. Raium Soc., Am. Soc. Therapeutic Radiology and Oncology. Office: Nassau Radiologic Group 1129 No Blvd Manhasset NY 11030-3801 E-mail: jbosworth@nrad.com.

BOSWORTH, KATE, actress; b. LA, Jan. 2, 1983; Actor: (films) The Horse Whisperer, 1998, Remember the Titans, 2000, The Newcomers, 2000, Blue Crush, 2002, The Rules of Attraction, 2002, Wonderland, 2003, Advantage Hart, 2003, Win a Date with Tad Hamilton, 2004, Beyond the Sea, 2004, Bee Season, 2005, Superman Returns, 2006; (TV series) Young Americans, 2000. Mem.: Nat. Honor Soc. Office: United Talent Agy 5th Fl 9560 Wilshire Blvd Beverly Hills CA 90212

BOSWORTH, STEPHEN WARREN, dean, former ambassador; b. Grand Rapids, Mich., Dec. 4, 1939; s. Warren Charles and Mina (Phillips) B.; m. Christine Holmes, June 7, 1984; children— Andrew, Allison. A.B., Dartmouth Coll., 1961; LLD (hon.), Darmouth Coll., 1986. Vice consul Am. Embassy, Panama City, Panama, 1962—63, prin. officer Colon, 1963—64; Panama desk officer U.S. Dept. State, Washington, 1964—66; econ. officer Am. Embassy, Madrid, 1967—71, Paris, 1971—74; dep. asst. sec. state, 1976-79; ambassador to Tunisia, 1979-81; dep. asst. sec. Inter-Am. affairs, 1981-82; dir. policy planning staff coun. U.S. Fgn. Svc., 1983-84; ambassador Manila, Philippines, 1984-87; pres. U.S.-Japan Found., 1988-96; exec. dir. Korean Energy Devel. Orgn., 1995-97; amb. to Republic of Korea Seoul, 1997-2001; dean Fletcher Sch. Law and Diplomacy, Tufts U., Medford, Mass., 2001—. Adj. prof. Columbia U., 1990-94. Trustee Dartmouth Coll., 1992-2002, chmn. bd. trustees, 1996-99. Recipient Dept. State Disting. Honor award, 1976, 86, Arthur S. Flemming award, 1976; named Diplomat of Yr., Am. Acad. Diplomacy, 1986 Office: Fletcher Sch Law and Diplomacy Tufts Univ Medford MA 02155 E-mail: stephen.bosworth@tufts.edu.

BOSWORTH, THOMAS LAWRENCE, architect, retired educator; b. Oberlin, Ohio, June 15, 1930; s. Edward Franklin and Imogene (Rose) B.; m. Abigail Lumbard, Nov. 6, 1954 (div. Nov. 1974); children: Thomas Edward, Nathaniel David; m. Elaine R. Pedigo, Nov. 23, 1974; stepchildren: Robert Haden Pedigo, Kevin Ian Pedigo. BA, Oberlin Coll., 1952, MA, 1954; postgrad., Princeton U., 1952-53, Harvard U., 1956-57; MArch, Yale U., 1960; PhD Honoris Causa (hon.), Kobe U., Japan, 2003. Draftsman Gordon McMaster AIA, Cheshire, Conn., summer 1957-58; resident planner Tunnard & Harris Planning Cons., Newport, RI, summer 1959; designer, field supr. Eero Saarinen & Assocs., Birmingham, Mich., 1960-61, Hamden, Conn., 1961-64; individual practice architecture Providence, 1964-68, Seattle, 1968—2004; ptnr. Bosworth Hoedemaker, Architecture and Planning, Seattle, 2004—; asst. instr. architecture Yale U., 1962-65, vis. lectr., 1965-66; asst. prof. R.I. Sch. Design, 1964-66, assoc. prof., head dept., 1966-68; prof. architecture U. Wash., Seattle, 1968-98, chmn. dept., 1968-72, dir. multidisciplinary program Rome, 1984-86, prof. emeritus, 1998—; chief architecture Peace Corps Tng. Program, Tunisia, Brown U., summers 1965-66. Vis. lectr. Kobe U., Japan, Oct., 1982, Nov., 1990, Apr., 1993, May, 1995, June, 1998; Pietro Belluschi disting. vis. prof. U. Oreg., 1996; dir. arch. in Rome program U. Wash., Rome, 1996, prof. 2000, 2003. Bd. dirs. N.W. Inst. Arch. and Urban Studies, Italy, 1983-90, pres., 1983-85; dir. Pilchuck Glass Sch., Seattle, 1977-80, trustee, 1980-91, adv. coun., 1993—; mem. Seattle Model Cities Land Use Rev. Bd., 1969-70, Tech. Com. Site Selection Wash. Multi-Purpose Stadium, 1970, Medina Planning Commn., 1972-74, steering adv. com. King County Stadium, 1972-74; chmn. King County (Wash.) Environ. Devel. Commn., 1972-74, King County Policy Devel. Commn., 1974-77; bd. dirs. Arcade Mag., 1988-2002, pres. 1988-2000; bd. mgrs. YMCA Camping Svcs., 1998-2002; adv. bd. U. Wash Rome Ctr., 1999—. With U.S. Army, 1954-56. Recipient 17 design awards; Winchester Traveling fellow Yale U., 1960, Assoc. fellow Ezra Stiles Coll. Yale U., Mid-career fellow in arch. Am. Acad. in Rome, 1980-81; vis. scholar Am. Acad., Rome, spring 1988, fall 2007. Fellow AIA (Seattle medalist 2003); mem. Monday Club (Seattle), Bohemian Club (San Francisco), Tau Sigma Delta. Home: 2411 25th Ave E Seattle WA 98112-2610

BOSWORTH, WILLIAM POSEY, physician, physical education educator; b. Valdosta, Ga., Mar. 23, 1935; s. Paul Brooks and Myra Mae (Posey) B.; m. Wanda Marie Grimm; 1 child, Lynne Marie. BS, U. Tampa, 1957; MEd, Springfield Coll., Mass., 1961; postgrad., Orlando Jr. Coll., Fla., 1968; DO, U. Health Scis., Kansas City, Mo., 1972. Phys. edn. tchr., jr. high sch. tchr. Duval County Sch. Bd., Jacksonville, Fla., 1959—62; intern U.S. Naval Hosp., Phila., 1972—73; gen. practice medicine Jacksonville, 1974—. Physician athletic team, 1975—. Mem. Jacksonville Sports Com., 1981—86, chmn., 1986; mem. Duval County Hosp. Authority, 1982—86, chmn., 1986; mem. Fla. Gov.'s Coun. on Phys. Fitness and Sports, 1985—93, Duval County Sch. Bd., Jacksonville, 1986—90, Fla. Sunshine State Games Found., 1990—99, Sports in Fla. Found., 2000—. With USMCR, 1953—58, with USNR, 1969—99, capt. M.C., 1988—. Decorated Navy Commendation medals (2), Meritorious Svc. medal; named Gen. Practitioner of Yr., Fla. Soc. Am. Coll. Family Physicians, 1982, Health Educator of the Yr., Duval County Coalition Against Tobacco, 1991; recipient Physician's Recognition award, AMA, 1988, 1991, 1994, 1997, 1999, 2002, 2005. Mem.: AAU (pres. Fla. chpt. 1983—87, Life award 1967, Vol. Svc. 35 Yr. Gold Pin award 1988, named Outstanding Vol. 1992), PTA (hon. life-Fla. 2000, Nat. 2001), Freedoms Found. at Valley Forge (pres. Jacksonville chpt. 1995—97, Heart of Gold award 2005, Patriot Spirit of '76 award 2006), Assn. Mil. Surgeons U.S., Duval County Acad. Family Physicians (pres. 1984), Duval County Med. Soc., Fla. Soc. Sons of Am. Revolution (pres. 1980, 2000, Meritorious Svc. medal 1986, Disting. Svc. medal 2001), Fla. Med. Assn., Mandarin Mus. and Hist. Soc. (charter mem. 1992, life mem. 2001), Rotary Club of Mandarin (charter mem. 1975, pres. 1985—86), Rotary Club of San Jose (charter mem. 2003, Outstanding Svc. award 2005), Mandarin Cmty. Club (life; pres. 2002), Am. Legion 40/8 Honor Soc. (Voyageur of Yr. 1990). Office: 9765 San Jose Blvd Jacksonville FL 32257-4402 Office Phone: 904-268-2227.

BOTCHAN, MICHAEL R., molecular biologist, biochemist; b. Bklyn., July 13, 1945; BA in Biology, NYU, 1967; PhD in Biophysics, U. Calif., Berkeley, 1972. Postdoctoral rsch. Cold Spring Harbor Lab., NY, 1972—74, sr. scientist, 1974—80; assoc. prof. dept. molecular biology U. Calif., Berkeley, 1980—94, prof. dept. molecular and cell biology, 1984—. Adj. assoc. prof. dept. microbiol. SUNY, Stony Brook, 1977—79; mem. adv. com. cell biology and microbiol. Am. Cancer Soc., 1978—81, mem. adv. com. nucleic acids and proteins, 1986—90, postdoctoral fellowship com. Calif. divsn., 1986—89; mem. virology study sect. NIH, 1986—91; mem. sci. adv. com. Damon Runyon-Walter Winchell Cancer Rsch. Fund, 1989—92, chmn. sci. adv. com., 1992; mem. sci. rev. bd. Howard Hughes Med. Inst. Contbr. articles to sci. jours.; mem. editl. bd.: Jour. Virology, 1984—90, Molecular and Cellular Biology, 1985—91, Oncogene, 1987—91; editor: Plasmid, 1986. Recipient NIH Merit award, 1987, 2004. Fellow: AAAS, Am. Acad. Arts & Scis. Office: Dept Molecular and Cell Biology U Calif 401 Barker Hall Number 3204 Berkeley CA 94720-3204 Business E-Mail: mbotchan@berkeley.edu.

BOTEACH, SHMULEY, rabbi, television personality, author; b. LA, Nov. 19, 1966; m. Debbie Boteach; 8 children. Studied, Oxford U., England, 1988. Ordained Rabbi NYC Chabad-Lubavitch Hasidic Movement, 1988. Founder Oxford U. L'Chaim Soc.; editor-in-chief Unconventional Wisdom. Host: (TV series) Shalom in the Home; author: Kosher Sex, Wisdom, Understanding, Knowlege, Hating Women: America's Hostile Campaign Against the Fairer Sex, Ten Conversations You Need to Have with Your Children, Parenting With Fire, Shalom in the Home, Kosher Adultery, Dating Secrets of the Ten Commandments, Face Your Fear, Judaism for Everyone, The Private Adam, Why Can't I Fall in Love? (finalist Books for a Better Life award, 2002); TV appearances: Orpah, The View, The Today Show, Good Morning America, The O'Reilly Factor. Named one of The Top 50 Rabbis in America, Newsweek Mag., 2007. Achievements include being first non-christian to be honored with London Times Preacher Yr. award, 2002. Office: PO Box 61 Englewood NJ 07631*

BOTELHO, BRUCE MANUEL, mayor, retired state attorney general; b. Juneau, Alaska, Oct. 6, 1948; s. Emmett Manuel and Harriet Iowa (Tieszen) Botelho; m. Guadalupe Alvarez Breton, Sept. 23, 1988; children: Alejandro Manuel, Adriana Regina. Student, U. Heidelberg, Federal Republic of Germany, 1970; BA, Willamette U., 1971, JD, 1976. Bar: Alaska 1976, U.S. Ct. Appeals (9th cir.) 1976, U.S. Supreme Ct. 1979. Asst. atty. gen. State of Alaska, Juneau, 1976—83, 1987—89, dep. commr., acting commr. Dept. of Revenue, 1983-86; mayor City, Borough of Juneau, 1988—91, 2003—, dep. atty. gen., 1991—94, 2003—; atty. gen. State of Alaska, 1994—2002. Chmn. Alaska Resources Corp., 1984—86; exec. com. Conf. of Western Attys. Gen., 1997—2002. Editor: Willamette Law Jour., 1975—76; contbr. articles to profl. jours. Pres. Juneau Human Rights Commn., 1978—80, Alaska Coun. Am. Youth Hostels, 1979—81, Juneau Arts and Humanities Coun., 1981—83; pres. S.E. Alaska Area Coun. Boy Scouts Am., 1991—93, 2001—05, commr. S.E. Alaska Area Coun., 1993—2000, exec. com. Gt. Alaska Coun., 2006—; pres. Juneau World Affairs Coun., 2000—; chmn. Gov.'s Conf. on Youth and Justice, 1995—96, Gov. Task Force on Confidentiality of Childrens Procs., 1998—2002; trustee Alaska Children's Trust, 1996—2000, Alaska Permanent Fund, 2000—02; co-chmn. Alaska Justice Assessment Commn., 1997—2002; active Commn. for Justice Across the Atlantic, 1999—; chmn. Alaska Criminal Justice Coun., 2000—02; fed. commr. Alaska Rural Jursice and Law Enforcement Commn., 2004—; Assembly mem. Borough of Juneau, 1983—86; chmn. adminstrv. law sect. Alaska Bar Assn., 1981—82; bd. dirs. Alaska Econ. Devel. Coun., 1985—87, Found. for Social Innovations, Alaska, 1990—93, Alaska Mcpl. League, 2003—; bd. mem. Alaska Immigration Justice Project, 2005—; bd. dirs. Tongass Futures Roundtable, 2006—. Named Pro Bono Atty. of Yr., Alaska Bar Assn., 2005; recipient Silver Beaver award, Boy Scouts Am., 2000, Jay Rabinowitz Pub. Svc. award, Alaska Bar Assn., 2007. Mem.: Nat. Assn. Attys. Gen. (exec. com. 1998—). Democrat. Methodist. Avocation: dance. Office Phone: 907-506-5240. Business E-Mail: botelho@gci.net, mayor@ci.juneau.ak.us.

BOTEZ, DAN, physicist; b. Bucharest, Romania, May 22, 1948; arrived in US, 1976, naturalized; s. Emil and Ecaterina (Iacob) B.; m. Lynda Diane Arnold, Sept. 25, 1976; children: Anca, Adrian. BSEE with highest honors, U. Calif., Berkeley, 1971, MSEE, 1972, PhD, 1976; PhD (hon.), U. Politechnica, Bucharest, Romania, 1995. Fellow IBM Thomas J. Watson Rsch. Ctr., Yorktown Heights, NY, 1976-77; tech. staff RCA David Sarnoff Rsch. Ctr., Princeton, NJ, 1977-82, rsch. leader, 1982-84; dir. device devel. Lytel Inc., Somerville, NJ, 1984-86; chief scientist TRW Electro-Optic Rsch. Ctr., Redondo Beach, Calif., 1986, lab dir., 1986-87; sr. staff scientist TRW Rsch. Ctr., Redondo Beach, Calif., 1987-93, TRW tech. fellow, 1990-93; Philip Dunham Reed prof. elec. engring. U. Wis., Madison, 1993—; founder, bd. dirs. AlfaLight Inc., Madison, 2000—. Author: Electro-Optical Communications Dictionary, 1983, Diode-Laser Arrays, 1994; contbr. over 250 articles to profl. jours.; holder 44 U.S. patents. Named Outstanding Young Engr., IEEE Lasers and Electro-Optics Soc., San Jose, 1984, recipient Key to Future award, 1984. Fellow IEEE (chmn. tech. com. on semiconductor lasers 1989-90), Optical Soc. Am.; mem. Phi Beta Kappa. Independent. Eastern Orthodox. Avocations: tennis, travel, photography, skiing. Home: 200 N Prospect Ave Madison WI 53726-4027 Office: U Wis Dept Elec Engring 1415 Engineering Dr Madison WI 53706-1607 Home Phone: 608-231-3432; Office Phone: 608-265-4643. Business E-Mail: botez@engr.wisc.edu.

BOTHFELD, ROBERT, retired industrial engineer, director, retired mechanical engineer, director; b. Sept. 26, 1920; BS, Tufts U., Medford, Mass., 1943; MS in Mech. Engring. Supr. prodn. engring. Fisher Body divsn. GM, 1987; ret., 1998. Mem.: NSPE, Soc. Automotive Engrs. Home and Office: 421 Kenilworth Ave Gulf Breeze FL 32561-4476

BOTHMER, DIETRICH FELIX VON, curator, archaeologist; b. Eisenach, Thuringia, Oct. 26, 1918; came to US, 1939, naturalized, 1944; s. Wilhelm Friedrich Franz Carl and Marie Julie Auguste Karoline (Freiin von und zu Egloffstein) von B.; m. Joyce de la Bégassière, May 28, 1966; children: Bernard Nicholas, Maria Elizabeth Villalba. Student, Friedrich Wilhelms U., Berlin, 1937-38, Wadham Coll., Oxford, 1938-39; diploma classical archaeology, Oxford U., 1939; PhD in Classical Archaeology, U. Calif., Berkeley, 1944; DPhil (hon.), U. Trier, 1997. Asst. curator Greek and Roman art Met. Mus. Art, 1946-51, assoc. curator, 1951-59, curator, 1959-73, chmn., 1973-90, Disting. rsch. curator, 1990—. Adj. prof. NYU, 1966— Book rev. editor: Am. Jour. Archaeology, 1950-57; assoc. editor, 1970-76; author: Amazons in Greek Art, 1957, Ancient Art from New York Private Collections, 1961, An Inquiry into the Forgery of the Etruscan Terracotta Warriors, 1961, Corpus Vasorum Antiquorum, USA fasc. 12, 1963, Greek Vase Painting: An Introduction, 1972, Corpus Vasorum Antiquorum, USA fasc. 16, 1976, Greek Art of the Aegean Islands, 1979, A Greek and Roman Treasury, 1984, The Amasis Painter and His World, 1985, Greek Vase Painting, 1987, Glories of the Past, Ancient Art from the Shelby White and Leon Levy Collection, 1990, Euphronios, Peintre á Athènes au VI siècle avant Jesus Christ, 1990. Mem. Chancellor's Ct. of Benefactors, Oxford U. With AUS, 1943-45. Decorated Bronze Star, Purple Heart; Rhodes scholar Wadham Coll., 1938-39; Internat. House fellow U. Calif., Berkeley, 1940, Alfred B. Jordan fellow, 1940-41, Univ. fellow, 1941-42; Martin Ryerson fellow U. Chgo., 1942-43; Guggenheim Meml. Found. fellow, 1966, hon. fellow Wadham Coll.; Chevalier Légion d'Honneur, 1997. Mem. Archaeol. Inst. Am. (benefactor), Soc. Promotion Hellenic Studies (hon.), Deutsches Archaeol. Inst., Vereinigung der Freunde Antiker Kunst (Basle, Switzerland), Archaeologische Gesellschaft zu Berlin, Institut de France, Académie des Inscriptions et Belles-Lettres (fgn. assoc.), Piping Rock Club. Home: 401 Centre Island Oyster Bay NY 11771-5011 Office: Met Mus Art Fifth Ave at 82nd St New York NY 10028-0198

BOTHNER-BY, AKSEL ARNOLD, chemist; b. Mpls., Apr. 29, 1921; s. Aksel Conrad and Merle Marie (von Hagen) Bothner-B.; m. Christine Treuner, Oct. 15, 1949; children: Peter Ole, Anne Sigrun. Student, U. Nanking, China, 1939; B Chemistry, U. Minn., 1943; MS, NYU, 1947; PhD, Harvard U., 1949. Scientist Brookhaven Nat. Lab., 1949-53; fellow Am. Cancer Soc., Zurich, 1952-53; instr., lectr. Harvard U., 1953-58; cons. Retina Found., 1957-58; staff fellow Mellon Inst., 1958-71, dir., 1960-61, mem. adv. com., 1962-71; prof. chemistry Carnegie-Mellon U., 1967-77, chmn. dept., 1967-70; dean Mellon Inst. Sci., 1971-75, Univ. prof., 1977—, acting head, 1987-91, Univ. prof. emeritus, 1991—. Fulbright lectr. U. Munich, Germany, 1962-63; adj. prof. U. Pitts., 1964—; vis. prof. U. Calif. at San Diego, 1976-77; trustee MPC Corp., 1972-80; Bd. dirs. Pa. Jr. Acad. Scis., 1975-86. Contbr. articles to profl. jours. With AUS, 1943-45. Recipient Disting. Achievement award, U. Minn., 1975, IR-100 award, 1978, Pitts. award, 1988, G. Laukien award, 2002, EAS award for Achievements in Magnetic Resonance, Ea. Analytical Symposium, 2002. Mem.: Am. Soc. Biochemistry and Molecular Biology, Am. Chem. Soc. Achievements include research in theoretical organic chemistry. Home: 6317 Darlington Rd Pittsburgh PA 15217-1835 Business E-Mail: ab6d@andrew.cmu.edu.

BOTHWELL, ANTHONY PEIRSON XAVIER, SR., lawyer, educator; b. Washington, Aug. 12, 1944; s. Frederick Charles Jr. and Catherine Hannon Bothwell; m. Chung Thi Nguyen, Dec. 22, 1973 (div. Nov. 1999); children: Anthony Peirson Xavier Jr., Thomas Theodore Nguyen. BS in Fgn. Svc., Georgetown U., 1966; MS, Boston U., 1968; JD, John F. Kennedy Sch. Law, 1998; LLM with highest honors, Golden Gate U., 2000. Bar: Calif. 1999, US Dist. Ct. (no. dist.) Calif. 2000, US Ct. Appeals D.C. 2003. US Surpeme Ct. 2004. Editor AP, Miami, Fla., 1970-73; comms. coord. Fla. Power and Light Co., Miami, 1973-78; cmty. rels. mgr. Wis. Power and Light Co., Madison, 1978-83; dir. pub. affairs Lawrence Livermore Nat. Lab., Livermore, Calif., 1983-85; cons. Livermore, 1985-88; tax specialist IRS, Oakland, Calif., 1988—2001; pvt. practice San Francisco, 1999—; law prof. John F. Kennedy U. Sch. Law, Walnut Creek, Calif., 2000—. Newsroom clk. The Washington Post, 1969-70; acting news dir. Radio Sta. WBRK-AM, Pittsfield, Mass., 1967; cons. Atomic Indsl. Forum, Washington, 1981-83. Contbr. studies to profl. publs.; asst. editor: Computer World, 1967-68. City campaign chmn. Jesse Jackson for Pres., Livermore, 1988; cons. policy ethics Ams. for Energy Independence, Washington, 1980-82; cons. energy ethics com. Nat. Conf. of Cath. Bishops, Washington, 1981-83; chmn. City Coun. Adv. Com. on Energy and Environment, Livermore, 1985-87; asst. to chmn. Mass. Rep. Fin. Com., 1967-68. Recipient 1st pl. award on Commemoration of 50th Anniversary of Universal Declaration of Human Rights, San Francisco chpt. UN Assn. of USA, 1999. Mem. Internat. Bar Assn., State Bar Calif., Hist. Soc. of U.S. Dist. Ct. for No. Calif., San Francisco Bay Area chpt. Nat. Lawyers Guild (exec. bd. 1995-98), So. Poverty Law Ctr. (leadership coun.), U.S. Holocaust Mus., Rotary Internat. (San Francisco pres. 2007—). Democrat. Avocation: stamp collecting/philately. Office: Law Offices of Anthony P. X Bothwell Ste 100 PMB 314 350 Bay St San Francisco CA 94133 E-mail: attorney@apxbothwell.com.

BOTHWELL, JOHN CHARLES, retired archbishop; b. Toronto, June 29, 1926; s. William Alexander and Anne (Campbell) B.; m. Joan Cowan, Dec. 29, 1951; children— Michael, Timothy, Nancy, Douglas, Ann. BA with honors in Modern History, U. Toronto, 1948; BD, Trinity Coll., Toronto, 1950, DD (hon.), 1972, Huron Coll., U. Western Ont., Wycliffe Coll. U Toronto, 1989; hon. sr. fellow, Renison Coll., U. Waterloo, 1988. Ordained priest Anglican Ch., 1952; curate St. James Cathedral, Toronto, 1951-53, Christ Ch. Cathedral, Vancouver, B.C., 1953-56; rector St. Aidan's Ch., Oakville, Ont., 1956-60, St. James' Ch., Dundas, Ont., 1960-65; canon missioner Niagara Diocese, 1965-69; nat. exec. dir. Anglican Ch. Can., 1969-71; co-adjutor bishop Niagara, 1971-73; bishop Diocese of Niagara, 1973-92, archbishop, 1985-91; Met. of Ont., 1985-91; ret., 1991; chancellor Trinity Coll., U. Toronto, 1991—2003. Hon. sr. fellow Renison Coll., U. Waterloo, 1988. Co-author: Theological Education for the 70's, 1969; author: Taking Risks and Keeping Faith, 1985, Living Faith Day By Day, 1990, Old-Time Religion or Risky Faith?, 1992; contbr. articles to various newspapers. Active numerous nat. and ecumenical coms.; Dir., com. chmn. Hamilton (Ont.) Social Planning Council, 1965-69, 71-75, v.p., 1975-77, pres., 1977-79; v.p. United Way, 1982, 83, pres., 1984-86; bd. dirs. Hamilton Found., 1982, v.p., 1983, pres., 1985 Inducted into City of Hamilton (Ont., Can.) Gallery of Distinction, 1993. Anglican. E-mail: jjcb@sympatico.ca.

BOTICA, MATTHEW J., lawyer; b. Chgo., Jan. 11, 1951; AB summa cum laude, Boston Coll., 1972; JD, Harvard U., 1975. Bar: Ill. 1975, no. dist. Ill. Ptnr. Hopkins & Sutter, Chgo., Winston & Strawn LLP, Chgo., 1998—. Contbr. articles to profl. jours. Recipient The Best Lawyers in Am., 2007; grantee Am. Coll. of Bankruptcy. Mem. ABA, Chgo. Bar Assn., Phi Beta Kappa. Office: Winston & Strawn LLP 35 W Wacker Dr Chicago IL 60601 Office Phone: 312-558-8095. Office Fax: 312-558-5700. Business E-Mail: mbotica@winston.com.

BOTÍN, ANA PATRICIA, bank executive; b. Oct. 1960; BA in economics, Bryn Mawr Coll., 1981. With credit mgmt. and financial analysis dept. J.P. Morgan, Madrid, 1981, with NYC, 1983, v.p. L.Am. divsn., 1985; head banking divsn. capital markets Banco Santander, 1988, bd. dirs., mem. exec. com., 1989—, co-gen. mgr., 1991, gen. mgr. Banco Santander de Negocios, 1991, CEO Banco Santander de Negocios, 1994—99, exec. v.p., 1994—99; founder Suala Tech. Capital Fund, 2000; head, cons. Coverlink, 2000; chmn., Banco Espanol de Credito (Banesto) Banco Santander, 2002—. Bd. dirs. Generali, 2004—. Named one of 50 Women to Watch, Wall St. Jour., 2005, 2006, 50 Most Powerful Women in Global Bus., Fortune mag., 2005, 100 Most Powerful Women, Forbes mag., 2005, 2006. Office: Banesto Avenida Gran Via Hortaleza No 3 28043 Madrid Spain*

BOTKA, BETSY JEAN, industrial arts and career awareness instructor; b. Freeport, NY, Nov. 25, 1956; d. Herman and Ruth Bender Rubenstein; m. Brian Joseph Botka, Aug. 19, 1999. BA, Trenton State Coll., Ewing Twp., NJ, 1979. Cert. Tchr. Idsl. Arts NJ, Elem. Sch. Tchr. NJ. Woodshop instr. Pemperton Twp. HS, Pemberton, NJ, 1979—82; indsl. arts/ career awareness instr. Somerdale Pk. Sch., Somerdale, NJ, 1982—. After sch. sports dir. Somerdale Pk. Sch., Somerdale, NJ, 1995—2005. Mem.: NEA, Somerdale Edn. Assn. (pres. Park Sch. chpt. 1996—98), Camden County Coun. Edn. Assn., NJ Edn. Assn. Avocations: antiques, travel, gardening, interior decorating. Office: Somerdale Pk Sch 301 Grace St Somerdale NJ 08083

BOTKIN, DANIEL BENJAMIN, biologist, environmental scientist, writer; b. Oklahoma City, Aug. 19, 1937; s. Benjamin Albert and Gertrude (Fritz) B.; m. Ellen Chase, Dec. 22, 1962 (div. 1976); children: Nancy, Jonathan; m. Erene Victoria Youngberg, Apr. 7, 1978 (dec. Mar. 1994); m. Jane M. O'Brien (dec. Feb. 2002); m. Diana G. Perez. BA, U. Rochester, 1959; MA, U. Wis., 1962; PhD, Rutgers U., 1968. From asst. to assoc. prof. Yale U., New Haven, 1968-76; assoc. scientist Marine Biol. Lab., Woods Hole, Mass., 1976-78; prof. biology U. Calif., Santa Barbara, 1978-92, chmn. environ. studies program, 1978-85; dir. program on global change biology dept. George Mason U., Fairfax, Va., 1993-97, prof. biology, 1993-99; pres. The Ctr. for the Study of the Environment, 1992—; rsch. prof. biology U. Calif., Santa Barbara, 1999—2004, emeritus, 2004—. Vis. prof. U. Notre Dame, 2003; disting vis. prof. Mich. State U., 2004; Astor lectr. Oxford U., 2007. Author: Discordant Harmonies: A New Ecology for the 21st Century, 1990, paperback edit., 1992, Forest Dynamics: An Ecological Model, 1993, Our Natural History: The Lessons of Lewis and Clark, 1995, reprinted 2004, Passage of Discovery: The American Rivers Guide to the Missouri River of Lewis and Clark, 1999, No Man's Garden: Thoreau and a New Vision for Civilization and Nature, 2001, Strange Encounters: Adventures of a Renegade Naturalist, 2003, Beyond The Stony Mountains: Nature in the American West from Lewis and Clark to Today, 2004; (software) JABOWA, 1970, Timber: model of forest growth, 1983, 87, JABOWA-II, 1992, JABOWA-3 for Windows, 1999 JABOWA-4, 2004; co-author: Forest Succession, 1981, Environmental Studies, 1982, 87, Changing the Global Environment, 1989, Environmental Science: Earth as a Living Planet, 1995, 6th edit., 2007, The Blue Planet, 1999, Essential Environ. Sci., 2007; contbr. articles to profl. jours., popular mags. and newspapers. Trustee Santa Barbara Bot. Garden, 1987-93; bd. dirs. Environ. Literacy Coun., Washington, 2003-06; trustee Am. Folklife Ctr., Libr. Congress, 2004—; commr. US State Dept. to UNESCO; mem. nat. adv. bd. Stetson Kennedy Found., Jacksonville, Fla., 2006—. Recipient 1st Prize, Mitchell Internat. Prize for Sustainable Devel., 1991, Fernow prize for Internat. Forestry, 1995, Texty award, Textbook and Acad. Authors Assn., 2004; Astor Lectureship award Oxford U., 2007, named to Environ. Hall Fame, Calif. Polytechnic U., 1995; grantee EPA, NSF, NASA, NOAA, Mellon Found., New Bedford Whaling Mus., Pew Charitable Trusts, W. Alton Jones Found., World Wildlife Fund, SOHIO Alaska Corp.; fellow Woodrow Wilson Internat. Ctr. for Scholars, Washington, 1977-78, Rockefeller Bellagio Inst., Italy, 1985, East-West Ctr., Honolulu, 1985-87. Fellow AAAS; Cosmos Club, Explorers Club, Sigma Xi (lectr. 1981-83). Avocations: photography, hiking, music. Office: 245 8th Ave #270 New York NY 10011 Home Phone: 212-243-7937; Office Phone: 917-747-3068. Business E-Mail: info@naturestudy.org. E-mail: danielbotkin@rcn.com.

BOTKIN, JAMES W., leadership and executive coach; b. Long Branch, NJ, May 15, 1943; s. Harold M. and Julia (Bishop) B.; m. Karin S. Bartow, Aug. 20, 1999; m. Rosvita Botkin; children: Alexander, Christopher. BA, Harvard U., 1965, MBA, 1968, DBA, 1973; grad., The Coaches Tng. Inst., 2003. Cert. profl. co-active coach 2004. Fellow U. Tex., Austin, 1985—; pres. InterClass, Cambridge, Mass., 1990—2001; founder, chmn. and coach InnerCALL-Internat. Corp. Coaching Alliance, 2004—. Bd. dirs. Lancaster U., England, Internat. Leadership Initiative, Eisenhower Fellowships; internat. advisor New Horizons for Learning, Seattle, 1986—; internat. recognized pub. spkr. Author (with M. Elmandjra and M. Malitza): No Limits to Learning: A Report to the Club of Rome, 1979; author: (with D. Dimancescu and R. Stata) Global Stakes: The Future of High Technology in America, 1982; author: The Innovators: Rediscovering America's Creative Energy, 1984; author: (with D. Dimancescu) The New Alliance: Industry-University Partnerships, 1986; author: (with J. Matthews) Winning Combinations: Entrepreneurial Partnerships Between Large and Small Companies, 1992; author: (with Stan Davis) The Monster Under the Bed: How Business is Mastering the Opportunities of Knowledge for Profit, 1994; author: Smart Business: How Knowledge Communities Can Revolutionize Your Company, 1999. Named Hon. Citizen, Salzburg, Austria, 1977; recipient Innovator award, Rausing Fund, Lund, Sweden, 1990, Alliance award, Carnegie Corp., N.Y.C., 1986. Mem.: Internat. Coaching Fedn., Club of Rome. Avocations: hiking, fishing, travel. Office: 26 Grozier Rd Cambridge MA 02138-3315 Office Phone: 617-661-4536. Personal E-mail: jbotkin@comcast.net.

BOTKIN, MONTY LANE, computer company executive; b. Lubbock, Tex., Mar. 26, 1951; s. Louis A. and Geneva O. (Marlin) B.; 1 child, Nicholas L.; m. Ayami Honda, Oct. 26, 1996. BA, Tex. Tech U., 1975. Supr. Tex. Instruments, Inc., Lubbock, 1976-77, Abilene, Tex., 1977-78; electronic ctr. mgr. Tex. Instruments Supply Co., Palo Alto, Calif., 1978-81; mfg. mgr. home computers Tex. Instruments, Inc., Lubbock, 1981-83, mfg. mgr. calculator, 1983-87, mfg. mgr. ednl. products, 1987-90, Semi-Conductor Grp. photolithography ops. mgr., 1990-91, total quality control mgr. Lubbock Mos Memory, 1991-93; dir. mfg. Brother Industries U.S.A., Bartlett, Tenn., 1993-96, also bd. dirs.; dir. ops. Taiwan Semiconductor Mfg. Co., San Jose, Calif., 1996-2000; v.p. and gen. mgr. LAM Rsch. Corp., 2000—02; oper. officer Fujikin Inc., 2002—; COO U.S.A. and Europe, bd. dirs. Fujikin Am., Santa Clara, Calif., 2002—. Bd. dirs. Carten Controls Inc.; exec. v.p. Fujikin of Europe. Mem. Inst. Indsl. Engrs. (sr.), Am. Soc. for Quality Control (chmn. West Tex. sect.), Am. Prodn. and Inventory Control Soc. Avocations: racquetball, photography, golf.

BOTSAI, ELMER EUGENE, architect, educator, retired dean; b. St. Louis, Feb. 1, 1928; s. Paul and Ita May (Cole) Botsai; m. Patricia L. Keegan, Aug. 28, 1955; children: Donald Rolf, Kurt Gregory; m. Sharon K. Kaiser, Dec. 5, 1981; 1 child, Kiana Michelle. AA, Sacramento Jr. Coll., 1950; AB, U. Calif., Berkeley, 1954; D of Architecture, U. Hawaii, 2000. Registered architect, Hawaii, Calif. Draftsman, then asst. to arch. So. Pacific Co., San Francisco, 1953-57; designer H.K. Ferguson Co., San Francisco, 1955; project arch. Anshen & Allen Arch., San Francisco, 1957-63; prin. Botsai, Overstreet & Rosenberg, Arch. and Planners, San Francisco, 1963—79, Elmer E. Botsai FAIA, Honolulu, 1979—; of counsel Groupe 70 Internat., 1998—; chmn. dept. arch. U. Hawaii, Manoa, 1976-80, dean Sch. Arch., 1980-90, prof., 1990-99, prof. emeritus, 2000—. Lectr. U. Calif., Berkeley, 1976, dir. Nat. Archtl. Accrediting Bd., 1972-73, 79; adminstrv. and tech. cons. Wood Bldg. Rsch. Ctr., U. Calif., 1985-90, mem. profl. preparation project com. at U. Mich., Ann Arbor, 1986-87; co-author water infiltration seminar series for Bldg. Owners and Mgr. Rsch. Ctr., 1986-87; chief investigator effects of Guatemalan earthquake for NSF and AIA, Washington, 1976; steering com. on structural failures Nat. Bur. Standards, 1982-84; chmn., dir. gen. svc. Adv. Com. State of Calif. Co-author: Architects and Earthquake, Rsch. Needs, 1976, ATC Seismic Standards for Nat. Bur. of Standards, 1976, Arch. and Earthquakes: A Primer, 1977, Seismic Design, 1978, Wood-Detailing for Performance, 1990, Wood as a Building Material, 2d edit., 1991; contbr. articles and reports to profl. jour.; prin. works include expansion of Nuc. Weapons Tng. Facility at Lemoore Naval Air Sta., Calif., LASH Terminal Port Facility Archtl. Phase, San Francisco, Incline Village (Nev.) Country Club, 1365 Columbus Ave. Bldg., San Francisco, modernization Stanford Ct. Hotel, San Francisco; monument area constrn. several Calif. cemeteries. With US Army, 1946—48. Recipient Cert. Honor Fedn. Archtl. Coll. Mex. Republic, 1984, Disting. Alumni award U. Hawaii, 2005; named to Wisdom Hall of Fame, 1998; NSF grantee for investigative workshop project, San Diego, 1974-80. Fellow AIA (bd. dir., 1966-71, treas. No. Calif. chpt. 1968-69, pres. 1971, nat. v.p., 1975-76, nat. pres. 1978, pres. Hawaii 1985); hon. fellow Royal Can. Inst. Arch., NZ Inst. Arch. (hon.), Royal Australian Inst. Arch. (1st arch., 1st Am.), La Societe de Arquitectos Mexicano; mem. Archtl. Sec. Assn. (hon.), Soc. Wood Sci. and Tech., Internat. Conf. Bldg. Ofcl. Home: 321 Wailupe Cir Honolulu HI 96821-1524

BOTSFORD, DAVID L., lawyer; b. Phila., Aug. 18, 1952; s. Thomas C. and Lois A. (Yarrison) B. BA, U. Conn., 1974; JD, So. Meth. U., 1977. Bar: Tex., 1977, U.S. Supreme Ct., 1981, U.S. Ct. Appeals (5th & 9th cir.), U.S. Dist. Ct. (all dists.), Tex.; cert. Tex. Bd. Legal Specialization, criminal law. Law clerk Emmett Colvin, Dallas, 1974-77; assoc., ptnr. Emmet Colvin, Dallas, 1978-81; briefing atty. Hon. Truman Roberts Ct. Criminal Appeals Tex., 1977-78; treas. bond trader Chgo. Bd. Trade, 1981-82; assoc. Frank Maloney, Austin, Tex., 1982-88; ptnr. Alvis, Carssow, Cummins, Hoeffner & Botsford, P.C., 1988-93, Botsford & Sauer, L.L.P., 1993-96; pvt. practice Austin, 1996—. Contbr. articles to profl. jours. Tex. Criminal Def. Lawyers Ednl. Inst. fellow, 1990. Mem.: Travis Bar Assn., Tex. Criminal Def. Lawyers Assn. (assoc. dir. 1985, 1986, dir. 1987—91, asst. sec.-treas. 1991—92, sec.-treas. 1992—93, 2d v.p. 1993—94, 1st v.p. 1994—95, pres.-elect 1995—96, pres. 1996—97, Presdl. Excellence award 1989, 1990, 1993, 1994, 1995), Tex. Assn. Bd. Cert. Specialists Criminal Law (pres. 1991—92), State Bar Tex. (criminal law exam. commn. 1985—2005, Coll. State Bar 1991, criminal justice sect.Outstanding Criminal Def. Lawyer of Yr. 1993), Nat. Assn. Criminal Def. Lawyers, Barristers, Order of Coif. Office: 1307 W Ave Austin TX 78701-2948 Office Phone: 512-479-8030. Personal E-mail: dbotsford@aol.com.

BOTSFORD, JON DOUGLAS, lawyer; b. Muskegon, Mich., Aug. 1, 1954; s. Lawrence Wayne and June Arleigh (Hanson) B; m. Joan Elizabeth Nims; children: Jackson, Tess, Matthew. BA, Mich. State U., 1976; JD, UCLA, 1979. Bar: Ill. 1979, U.S. Ct. Appeals (6th cir.) 1980, U.S. Dist. Ct. (no. dist.) Ill. 1981, Calif. 1982, Mich. 1982, U.S. Dist. Ct. (we. dist.) Mich. 1982, U.S. Supreme Ct 1984, U.S. Tax Ct. 1985. Law clk. to Hon. Albert Eagel U.S. Ct. Appeals, 6th Cir., 1979-80; atty. Jenner & Block, Chgo., 1980-82, Warner, Norcross & Judd, Grand Rapids, Mich., 1982-85, Steelcase Inc., Grand Rapids, 1985—87, sr. atty., 1987—92, asst. gen. counsel, 1992—97, gen. counsel, sec., 1997—98, v.p., gen. counsel, sec., 1998—99, sr. v.p., sec., chief legal officer, 1999—. Contbr. articles to profl. jours. Planning commr. Caledonia (Mich.) Township, 1997—99. Mem. ABA, Ill. State Bar Assn., State Bar Calif., State Bar Mich., Grand Rapids Bar Assn. Democrat. Office: Steelcase Inc 901 44th St SE Grand Rapids MI 49508-7575

BOTSFORD, MARY HENRICH, retired ophthalmologist; b. Buffalo, Aug. 22, 1915; d. John William and Margarethe Ingeborg (Kähler) Henrich; m. Daniel Ray Botsford, Feb. 11, 1943 (dec. Dec. 1970); children: Daniel Jr., Janet B. Thrush, William H., Thomas H. BA, Mount Holyoke Coll., 1937; MD, U. Buffalo, 1941. Diplomate Am. Bd. Ophthalmology. Assoc. Ivan J. Koenig M.D., Buffalo, 1943-46, 56-60; pvt. practice Buffalo, 1960-84; retired, 1984. Staff St. Francis Hosp., Buffalo, 1962-72, Vets. Hosp., Buffalo, 1962-72, Gowanda State Hosp., Helmuth, N.Y., 1962-80, Buffalo Children's Hosp., 1943-96, Buffalo Gen. Hosp., 1943-96. Founding bd. dirs., vol. Habitat for Humanity, Buffalo, 1985-2005; vol. Meals on Wheels, Buffalo, 1985-96, Am. Cancer Soc., Buffalo, 1985-96. Recipient Outstanding Achievement in Medicine citation, SUNY, Buffalo, 1984. Mem. Am. Acad. Ophthalmology, Buffalo Ophthal. Club, N.Y. State Ophthal. Soc., Common Cause. Democrat. Lutheran. Avocations: bridge, classical music, travel, theater, reading.

BOTSTEIN, LEON, academic administrator, conductor, historian; b. Zurich, Switzerland, Dec. 14, 1946; s. Charles and Anne (Wyszewianski) Botstein; m. Jill Lundquist, 1970 (div.); children: Sarah, Abigail(dec.); m. Barbara Haskell, 1982. BA (Woodrow Wilson fellow, Danforth Found. fellow, Sloan Found. fellow, Rockefeller fellow), U. Chgo., 1967; MA, Harvard U., 1968, PhD, 1985. Teaching fellow Harvard U., 1968—69; lectr. history Boston U., 1969; asst. to pres. NYC Bd. Edn., 1969—70; pres. Franconia Coll., 1970—75, Bard Coll., Annandale-on-Hudson, 1975—, Leon Levy prof. arts and humanities; pres. Simon's Rock Coll. Bard, Great Barrington, Mass., 1979—; founder, artistic dir. Bard Music Festival, 1990—; music dir. Am. Symphony Orch., NYC, 1992—, Jerusalem Symphony Orch., 2003—; artistic dir. Am. Russian Young Artists Orch., 1995—. Founder, prin. condr. White Mountain Music and Art Festival, NH, 1973—75; condr. Hudson Valley Philharm. Chamber Orch., 1981—92; guest condr. London Philharmonic, Philharmonia Orch., Pro Arte Chamber Orch. of Boston, BBC Symphony Orch., Düsseldorf Symphony, London Symphony Orch., Madrid Opera, NYC Opera; other guest conducting appearances in Korea, Japan, Czech Republic, Philippines, Austria, Brazil, Lithuania, Romania, Scotland, Germany, Switzerland, Russia, Hungary; past chmn. N.Y. Coun. Humanties, Assn. Episc. Colls., Harper's Mag. Found.; vice chair, treas. OSI-NY; mem. bd. OSI-Budapest, Ctrl. European U.; mem. nat. coun. Chamber Music Am.; mem. nat. adv. com. Yale-New Haven Tchrs. Inst.; vis. prof. Hochschule fur angewandte Kunst, Vienna, 1988; vis. faculty Manhattan Sch. Music, 1986; chmn. Salzburg Seminar, 1987; mem. nat. adv. com. Yale-New Haven Tchrs. Inst. Author: Jefferson's Children: Education and the Promise of American Culture, 1997; editor: The Compleat Brahms, 1999, Jour. Musical Quar., 1992—; contbr. articles to profl. publs.; conductor: albums. Decorated Austrian Cross of Honor; nominee Grammy award, 2006; recipient Centennial medal, Harvard Grad. Sch. Arts and Scis., Gold medal, Nat. Arts Club, Disting. Svc. to Arts award, Am. Acad. Arts and Letters; grantee Rockefeller fellow; Berlin Prize fellow. Fellow: Am. Acad. Arts & Scis. Office: Bard Coll Office of Pres Annandale On Hudson NY 12504 Office Phone: 845-758-7423. Business E-Mail: president@bard.edu.*

BOTT, HAROLD SHELDON, accountant, management consultant; b. Chgo., Dec. 12, 1933; s. Harold S. and Mary (Moseley) B.; m. Audrey Anne Connor, May 15, 1964; children: Susan, Lynda. AB, Princeton U., 1955; MBA, Harvard U., 1959; postgrad., U. Chgo., 1960-62. Adminstrv. asst. to exec v.p. Champion Paper, Hamilton, Ohio, 1959-61; mgmt. cons. Arthur Andersen & Co., Chgo., 1961-65, mgr., 1965-71, ptnr., 1971-89. Mng. dir. mgmt. info. cons., ptnr. Andersen Cons., 1988-91; ptnr. Strategic Svcs. Ctr.; vice-chmn. The Assn. Mgmt. Cons., 1982-84; bd. dirs. Harvard Bus. Sch. Assocs.; faculty Grad. Sch. Bus., U. Chgo., 1994-2000; of counsel Omnitech Cons., 1994-2000; pres. H.S. Bott Co., 1994-2003. Officer, pres., dir. Urban Gateways, 1965—90; treas., dir. sch. bd., pres. Kenilworth Caucus, 1990; dir. The Cradle, 2000—03, Kenilworth United Fund, 1983—89; mem. pres.'s vis. com., trustee Chgo. Theol. Sem., 2002—; bd. dirs. Orch. of Ill., 1988—89, The Joseph Sears Found., 2000—04, co-pres., 2001—; commodore Kenilworth Sailing Club, 1987—88; bd. dirs. Alliance Francalle Chi, 1994, 2003, 2004. With USN, 1955—56. Mem. AICPA, Ill. Soc. CPA's, Kenilworth Club (treas., bd. dirs. 1975-79), Kenilworth Hist. Soc. (bd. dirs. 1995—), Indian Hill Club, Chgo. Club. Republican. Congregationalist. Home: 305 Kenilworth Ave Kenilworth IL 60043-1132 Business E-Mail: pete.bott@gsb.uchicago.edu.

BOTT, JAY CORDELL, oncologist, hematologist; b. Salt Lake City, 1947; s. Leroy J. and Blanche T. Bott; m. Julie Christiansen, 1992. BA in Chemistry, U. Utah, 1971, BA in Med. Biology, 1974, MD hons. program in internal medicine, 1975. Cert. internal medicine, hematology, oncology. Intern Naval Regional Med. Ctr., San Diego, 1975—76, resident, 1976—78, fellow in oncology, hematology, 1979—80, 1981—82; fellow in oncology U. Utah Med. Ctr., Salt Lake City, 1980—81; with Utah Valley Regional Med. Ctr., Provo, 1983—, Mountain View Hosp., Payson, Utah, 1983—, Castleview Hosp., Price, Utah, 1984—, Timpanogos Regional Hosp., Orem, Utah, 1998—; founder Oxbow Ranch, Hanna, Utah. Former v.p. Ctrl. Utah Clinic; prior prin. investigator Nat. Surg. Adjuvant Breast Bowel Project, 1995-2004; est. one of the largest found. Quarter Horse breeding programs in U.S.; chmn. dept. hematology & oncology, Utah Valley Reg. Med. Ctr., Provo, 2006-. Mem. Nat. Rep. Com.; missionary LDS Ch., Germany, 1967—69; tchr. Sunday Sch.; with High Cou. and Bishopric, LDS Ch, Cmdr. USNR, 1973—84. Named Utah Rep. Businessman of Yr., 2000, 2001. Fellow: ACP; mem.: Soc. Utah Med. Oncologists (treas. 2007—), Am. Cancer Soc. (past pres. Utah Vly. chpt.), Utah County Med. Assn. (past pres.), S.W. Oncology Group, Am. Soc. Hematology, Am. Soc. Clin. Oncology, Phi Kappa Phi, Phi Beta Kappa. Avocations: ranching, hunting, classical piano, outdoorsports. Office: Ctrl Utah Clinic 1055 N 500 W Provo UT 84604-3305 also: Oxbow Ranch HC 63 Box 324 Hanna UT 84031-0024 Office Phone: 801-374-2367. E-mail: cbott@centralutahclinic.com.

BOTT, SIMON GREGORY, chemistry educator, researcher; b. Leicester, Eng., Oct. 7, 1962; s. Ronald William and Vivienne Mary Bott; m. Angie Rene McGuffey; children: Alexandra McGuffey, Connor. BSc, U. Bristol, Eng., 1983; PhD, U. Ala., 1986. Rschr. Oxford U., Oxfordshire, England, 1987, MIT, Cambridge, Mass., 1988—89; asst. prof. U. North Tex., Denton, 1990—97; assoc. prof. rsch. U. Houston, 1997, advisor, 2002, dir. undergrad. affairs, 2003—. Cons. Rimkus Cons., Houston, 1998. Mem.: Am. Chem. Soc. (pres. local chpt. 2002—04, councillor 2005—), Sigma Xi (local pres. 1995—97). Office: U Houston Dept Chemistry Houston TX 77204 Office Phone: 713-743-2771. Business E-Mail: sbott@uh.edu.

BOTTARI, PAUL J., lawyer; b. NYC, Apr. 26, 1951; BA, U. Notre Dame, 1973; JD, Fordham U., 1976. Bar: NY 1977, US Dist. Ct. So. Dist. NY, US Dist. Ct. Ea. Dist. NY. Ptnr. Wilson, Elser, Moskowitz, Edelman & Dicker LLP, NYC. Mem.: Am. Bd. Trial Advocates, NY State Trial Lawyers Assn. Office: Wilson Elser Moskowitz Edelman & Dicker LLP 23rd Fl 150 E 42nd St New York NY 10017-5639 Office Phone: 212-490-3000 ext. 4103. Office Fax: 212-490-3038. Business E-Mail: bottarip@wemed.com.

BOTTIGLIA, FRANK ROBERT, bank executive; b. S.I., Jan. 12, 1946; s. Hugo and Rose (Renzi) B.; children: Christine Ann, Catherine Rose, Elizabeth Mary, Laura Michele. BBA, CCNY, 1968; MBA, Baruch Coll., 1976. Adv. profl. cert. pub. acctg. Fin. analyst corp. human resources Chase Manhattan Bank, NYC, 1971-73, mgr. fin. controls corp. human resources, 1974-75, mgr. fin. and adminstrn. corp. human resources, 1976-77, sr. fin. mgmt. officer real estate fin., 1978-83, v.p., contr. U.S. regional comml. sector, 1984-89, v.p., budge dir. N.Am. sector, 1990-93, v.p., fin. mgr. global corp. fin., 1994-95, v.p., contr. Mex., 1995-96, v.p., contr. client access Bklyn., 1997-98, v.p., contr. global treasury mgmt., 1998—2004;

dir. Chase Access Svcs. Inc. Bd. mgr. Town and Country Villas Home Owners Assn., S.I., 1991. Sgt. U.S. Army, 1968-70. Mem. Internat. Platform Assn. Roman Catholic. Avocations: tennis, travel, golf. Office: JP Morgan Chase Bank 4 Chase Metrotech Ctr Brooklyn NY 11245-0005 Home: 37 W Francis Ave Morganville NJ 07751-1209

BOTTINI, DAVID WILLIAM, artist, educator; s. Anthony Bottini and Nancy E. Zwart. BA, Mt. St. Mary's U., Emmitsburg, Md., 1983; MFA, Savannah Coll. Art and Design, Ga., 1991. Mem. art faculty Potomac Sch., McLean, Va., 1992—97; adj. faculty mem. Frederick CC, Md., 1994—, Susquehanna U., Selinsgrove, Pa., 2005—; chmn. art dept. Madeira Sch., McLean, 1998—2004. Mem. tchrs.' adv. panel Nat. Gallery Art, Washington, 1994—96. Edn. vol. Kids-In-Design, AIA, Balt., 1994—98. Avocations: walking, architectural history, antiques. Office: For Gabriel 2315 Edgewood Rd Harrisburg PA 17104

BOTTITTA, JOSEPH ANTHONY, lawyer; b. Mar. 9, 1949; s. Anthony S. and Elizabeth (Bellisano) B.; m. Lynda Joan Kloss, Apr. 14, 1979; children: Michelle Emma, Gregory Joseph. BSBA, Seton Hall U., 1971, JD, 1974. Bar: US Dist. Ct. NJ 1974, US Supreme Ct. 1981. Ptnr. Rusignola & Pugliese, Newark, 1974-78; pvt. practice Joseph A. Bottitta, West Orange, NJ, 1979-88; sr. ptnr. Gilbert, Gilbert, Schlossberg and Bottitta, 1988-89; pvt. practice, 1989-95; with Bottitta and Bascelli, 1995-99. Chmn. Supreme Ct. Fee Arbitration Com. Dist. V-B., 1984-85; mem. NJ Uniform Law Commn., 1987-91, NJ Commn. Professionalism in Law, 1997-2000, NJ Supreme Ct. Profl. Responsibility Rules Com., 1999-, Com. on Public Access to Ct. Records, 2006—; pres. NJ Lawyers Svc., 2000—, E-Law.com, 2000—. Fellow: Am. Bar Found.; mem.: ABA, Essex County Bar Assn. (sec. 1983—84, treas. 1984—85, pres.-elect 1985—86, pres. 1986—87), NJ State Bar Assn. (trustee 1988, treas. 1994—95, v.p. 1995—97, pres.-elect 1997—98, pres. 1998—99). Republican. Roman Catholic. Office: c/o NJ Lawyers Svc 2333 Route 22 W Union NJ 07083-8517 E-mail: joeb@njls.com.

BOTTJER, DAVID JOHN, earth science and biology educator; b. NYC, Oct. 3, 1951; s. John Henry and Marilyn (Winter) B.; m. Sarah Ranney Wright, July 26, 1973. BS, Haverford Coll., 1973; MA, SUNY, Binghamton, 1976; PhD, Ind. U., 1978. NRC postdoctoral rsch. assoc. US Geol. Survey, Washington, 1978-79; asst. prof. dept. geol. sci. U. So. Calif., LA, 1979-85, assoc. prof. dept. geol. sci., 1985-91, prof. dept. earth sci., 1991—, prof. dept. biol. sci., 2003—, chair dept. earth sci., 2006—. Rsch. assoc. Los Angeles County Mus. Natural History, 1979—; vis. scientist Field Mus. Natural History, Chgo., 1986; Paleontol. Soc. Disting. lectr., 1992-93; mem. Nat. Sci. Found. panel on earth systems history, 1997-99; sr. fellow UCLA Ctr. for the Study of Evolution and Origin of Life, 2000. Editor Palaios, 1989-96; assoc. editor Cretaceous Rsch., 1988-91; mem. editl. bd. Geology, 1984-89, 95-2000, Hist. Biology, 1988-93; co-editor Columbia U. Press Critical Moments and Perspectives in Paleobiology and Earth History (book series), 1990—; editor-in-chief Palaeo-3, 2000—. Recipient Disting. Scientist award, Ctr. for Study of Evolution and Origin of Life, UCLA, 2002. Fellow AAAS, Geol. Soc. Am., Geol. Soc. London; mem. Paleontol. Soc. (pres. 2004-06), Soc. Sediment Geology (pres. Pacific sect. 2001-02), Internat. Paleontology Assn. Office: U So Calif Dept Earth Scis Los Angeles CA 90089-0740 Office Phone: 213-740-6100. Business E-Mail: dbottjer@usc.edu.

BOTTOLFSON, WAHNITA JOAN, parochial school educator; b. Sharon, Pa., Aug. 23, 1952; d. Jerald Russel and Verlene Estelle Barr; m. Larry Alan Bottolfson, Aug. 30, 2003; children: Corine Hannah Knutson, Christina Joan Cope, James Ryan Cope. BS, Ohio State U., Columbus, 1974. Cert. early and mid. childhood edn. tchr. Ariz., 2001. Tchr. Grace Cmty. Christian Sch., Tempe, Ariz., 1988—. R-Liberal. Christian. Avocations: reading, travel. Home Phone: 480-966-5022; Office Phone: 480-966-5022.

BOTTOM, DALE COYLE, marketing executive, director, management consultant; b. Columbus, Ind., June 25, 1932; s. James Robert and Sarah Lou (Coyle) B.; m. Frances Audrey Wilson, June 6, 1954 (div.); children: Jane Ellen, Steven Dale, Sharon Lynn, Carol Ann; m. Elaine McAuliffe, Aug. 20, 1988. BS, Ball State U., Muncie, Ind., 1954. Admissions counselor Stephens Coll., Columbia, Mo., 1958-61; exec. asst., then staff v.p. Inst. Fin. Edn., Chgo., 1961-67, pres., 1967-92; exec. v.p., chief fin. officer U.S. League Savs. Instns., 1985-89; chmn., dir. SAF-Systems & Forms Co.; sec.-gen. Internat. Union Fin. Instns., Chgo., 1989-95; cons. Resource Strategies Internat., Hinsdale, Ill., 1995—; assoc. v.p., dir. strategic svcs. Inland Real Estate Auctions, Inc. Bd. dirs. Savs. Instn. Ins. Group, Ltd., v.p., CFO; bd. dirs. Edgebrook Bank. Chmn. bd. Barrington (Ill.) United Meth. Ch., 1981; v.p. Chgo. Rotary One, 1967-80. Capt. USAF, 1955-67; comdr. USNR (ret.), 1967-78. Recipient Award of Distinction, Ball State U., 2003. Mem. SAR, Fin. Mgrs. Soc. (dir.), Savs. Instns. Mktg. Soc. Am., Navy League, Ind. Soc. Chgo., Tavern Club (v.p. 1993), Medinah Country Club, Hinsdale Golf Club, Sons of Am. Rev. Republican. Avocations: genealogy, travel, walking. Home and Office: 606 Burr Ridge Clb Burr Ridge IL 60527-5209 Personal E-mail: d.bottom@comcast.net.

BOTTOMLEY, GREGORY E., electrical engineer, researcher; b. Wilmington, Del., June 9, 1961; s. Charles G. and Karen G. Bottomley; m. Laura L. Jones, June 16, 1984; children: James E., Kathleen E. BSEE, Va. Tech, Blacksburg, 1983, MSEE, 1985; PhD, NC State U., Raleigh, 1989. Mem. tech. staff AT&T Bell Labs., Whippany, NJ, 1985—87; rsch. engr. Ericsson Inc., Rsch. Triangle Park, NC, 1991—. Vis. lectr. NC State U., 1990. Named Inventor of Yr., Ericsson, 1997. Fellow: IEEE (Outstanding Svc. award 2004). Methodist. Achievements include more than 70 patents related to wireless communications. Avocations: piano, music, running, swimming. Office: Ericsson Inc PO Box 13905 Research Triangle Park NC 27709 Office Phone: 919-472-7253.

BOTTOMLEY, MICHELLE J., advertising executive; b. Oct. 16, 1964; m. David Bottomley; 2 children. BA Econ., Northeastern U., BS Biology; PhD, Boston U. Corp. rsch. dept. Liberty Mut. Ins. Co.; direct marketer Bronner Slosberg Humphrey; v.p. mktg. Epsilon; joined Ogilvy & Mather, 1998; chief CRM strategist Ogilvy N.Am.; co-mng. dir. OgilvyOne NY, 2005—07; co-pres. Ogilvy N.Am., 2007—. Named a Woman to Watch, Advt. Age, 2007. Office: Ogilvy NY Inc 309 W 49th St New York NY 10019*

BOTTOMLY, (H.) KIM, academic administrator, biology professor, researcher; b. Helena, Mont., Jan. 30, 1946; m. Charles Janeway (dec.); 2 children; m. Wayne Villemez; 1 stepchild. BS, U. Wash., 1969, PhD in Biol. Structure, 1975. Postdoctoral fellow Nat. Inst. Allergy and Infectious Diseases, NIH, Bethesda, Md., 1976—79, adv. counsel mem., 1998; rsch. assoc. Inst. Cancer Rsch., Fox Chase Cancer Ctr., Phila., 1979—80; asst. prof. Dept. Pathology Yale U. Sch. Medicine, New Haven, 1980—86, assoc. prof., 1986, assoc. prof. Immunobiology Sect., 1989—92, prof., 1992, prof. Dept. Dermatology, 1993—, prof. Dept. Molecular, Cellular and Devel. Biology, 2001—, div. dir. biological scis., 2001, acting chair Immunobiology Sect., 2004—05, dep. provost sci., tech., faculty devel., 2005—07; pres. Wellesley Coll., Mass., 2007—. Cons. Bristol Myers-Squibb, 1993, Fuji Pharms., 1994—95, Immunova, Ltd, 1996—97, Boehringer Ingelheim Pharms., 1997—98, Panacea/Seer Pharms., 1998—, Novartis, 2005; mem. sci. adv. bd. La Jolla Inst. Allergy and Immunology, 2005; mem. med. adv. bd. Food Allergy Initiative, 2005—. Editor Immunity, 2000—03, assoc. editor, 2003—05; contbr. articles to profl. jours. Mem.: Fedn. Am. Societies for Experimental Biology, Am. Assn. Immunologists. Office: Wellesley Coll Office of Pres 106 Central St Wellesley MA 02481-8203*

BOTTOMS, ROBERT GARVIN, academic administrator; b. Birmingham, Ala., June 28, 1944; s. Dalton Garvin and Mary Inez (Cruce) Bottoms; m. Gwendolynn Jean Vickers, June 14, 1968; children: David Timothy, Leslie Clair. BA, Birmingham So. U., 1966; BD, Emory U., 1969; D of Ministry, Vanderbilt U., 1972. Chaplain Birmingham (Ala.) So. Coll., 1973—74, asst. to pres., 1974—75; asst. dean, asst. prof. church and ministry Vanderbilt U., Nashville, 1975—78; v.p. for univ. rels. DePauw U., Greencastle, Ind., 1978—79, exec. v.p. external rels., 1979—83, exec. v.p., 1983—86, acting pres., 1985, pres., 1986—. Cons. Arthur Vining Davis Found., Jacksonville, Fla., 1978—79, Luth. So. Sem., Columbia, SC, 1979—80; cons. theol. edn. The Lilly Endowment, Indpls., 1979—82; cons. Fund for Theol. Edn., NYC, 1981—82; chmn. audit com. Centel Cable TV Co., Oak Brook, Ill., 1987—89; Am. ctr. for internat. leadership organizer Edn. Policy Commn. U.S.-USSR Emerging Leaders Summit, Phila., 1988. Author: Lessons in Financial Development, 1982. Chmn. com. on ch. and coll. Episcopal Diocese Ind., 1979—84; bd. advisors Vanderbilt Div. Sch., 1980—93; bd. trustees Seabury-Western Theol. Sem., 2001—; bd. dirs. Joyce Found., 1994—2002, 2004—, G.M. Constrn. Inc., Indpls., 1998—2001, The Posse Found., 2001—, Women in Govt., Washington, 2001—03, Ctr. Leadership Devel., Indpls., 2003—. Recipient CASE V Chief Exec. Leadership award, 2000. Mem.: NCAA (coun. 1989—95, subcom. eligibility appeals), Ind. Colls. Ind. Found. (bd. dirs. 1987—2005, nominating com. 1990—97), Great Lakes Colls. Assn. (bd. dirs. 1987—, chair 1994—96), Ind. Colls. of Ind. (bd. dirs. 1987—, exec. com. 1991—), Am. Coun. Edn. (commn. on women in higher edn. 1990—91), Assn. Governing Bds. Univs. and Colls. (coun. pres. 1997—), Nat. Assn. Schs. and Colls. United Meth. Ch. (bd. dirs. 1987—91), Nat. Assn. Ind. Colls. and Univs. (task force increasing participation of minorities in ind. higher edn. 1989—95), Nat. Coun. Chs. (governing bd. 1985—91), Chgo. Club., Cosmos Club (Washington), Univ. Club of N.Y.C., Columbia Club (Indpls.). Avocation: boating. Home: 125 Wood St Greencastle IN 46135 Office: DePauw Univ Office of Pres 313 S Locust St Greencastle IN 46135-0037 Office Phone: 765-658-4800. Office Fax: 765-658-4224.*

BOTTONE, EDWARD JOSEPH, microbiologist, educator; b. Feb. 18, 1934; BS in Biology, CUNY, 1965; MS, Wagner Coll., 1968; PhD in Microbiology, St. John's U., 1973. Diplomate Am. Bd. Med. Microbiology. Med. technologist 34th Gen. Hosp. U.S. Army, Orleans, France, 1957-59; bacteriology tech. Mt. Sinai Hosp., NYC, 1959-60, assoc. dir. microbiology, 1969—74, dir. microbiology dept., 1975; bacteriology tech. Mt. Vernon (N.Y.) Hosp., 1962; supr. bacteriologist Greenpoint Hosp., Elmhurst Hosp., 1962—69; from assoc. prof. to prof. microbiology, 1975—81; prof. medicine Mt. Sinai Sch. Medicine, NYC, 1994—. From adj. instr. to prof. med. microbiology/pathology Mt. Sinai Sch. Medicine, N.Y.C., 1970—. Mem. editl. bd. Jour. Clin. Microbiology, 1978-89, Manual Clin. Microbiology, 1990-91. Fellow Am. Acad. Microbiology (diplomate, Sonnenwirth meml. award 1996, Profl. Recognition award 2002); mem. Am. Soc. Microbiology (Disting. Achievements in Clin. Microbiology award N.Y.C. br. 1995), Soc. Infectious Diseases, N.Y. Acad. Scis. Office Phone: 212-241-6985. Business E-Mail: edward.bottone@mssm.edu.

BOTTONE, JOANN, health services executive; b. Bklyn., June 20, 1943; d. Anthony and Claire (Bisesti) B.; m. William Recevuto, Feb. 12, 1989; children: Matthew, Sandra. RN, Kings County Hosp. Ctr., Bklyn., 1963; BS, St. Francis Coll., Bklyn., 1980; MPA, Russell Sage Coll., Albany, NY, 1986; PhD in Pub. Adminstrn. magna cum laude, Kensington U., 1995. Bd. cert. Health Care Mgmt. Am. Coll. Health Care Execs., 1997. From staff nurse, head nurse, quality assurance coord. Victory Meml. Hosp., Bklyn., 1961-81; instr. infection control Community Hosp. Bklyn., 1981-82; dir. quality assurance Profl. Stds. Rev. Orgn., Bklyn., 1982-85; devel. and coord. HIV post-test counseling program Greater N.Y. Blood Ctr., NYC, 1985-88; dir. HIV/AIDS programs Health Sci. Ctr. SUNY, Bklyn., 1988—2000. Tchr. SUNY Coll. Health Related Professions; mem. working group to develop statewide policies and procedures for health care workers involved in potential HIV exposures N.Y. State Health Commr., 1990; mem. tech. adv. group to develop guidelines for OSHA's bloodborne pathogen standard Greater N.Y. Hosp. Assn., 1992, N.Y.C. Mayor's HIV and Human Svcs. planning coun., 1999; lectr. in field. Contbr. articles to profl. jours. Mem. Am. Coll. Health Care Execs. (diplomate), Greater N.Y. Hosp. Assn. (tech. adv. group). E-mail: dr.jbr@msn.com.

BOTTORFF, DENNIS C., banker; b. Clarksville, Ind., Sept. 19, 1944; s. Irvin H. and Lucille H. B.; m. Jean Brewington, Aug. 21, 1964; children: Todd, Chad. BE, Vanderbilt U., 1966; MBA, Northwestern U., Evanston, Ill., 1968. Pres. Commerce Union Bank, Nashville; exec. v.p. Commerce Union Corp., Nashville; chmn., CEO Commerce Union Bank and Commerce Union Corp., Nashville, 1984-87; vice chmn., COO Sovran Fin. Corp., Norfolk, Va., 1988-89, pres., COO, 1989-90, C&S/Sovran Corp., Norfolk, Va., 1990—, C&S/Sovran Corp. (merger Citizens & So. Corp. and Sovran Fin. Corp. 1990), 1990—; chmn., CEO First Am. Corp., Nashville, 1991-99; chmn. AmSouth Bancorp., 1999—. Chmn. Tenn. State Lottery Edn. Corp., 2003-; bd. advisors The Jack C. Massey Grad. Sch. Bus., Belmont, Coll., Nashville; bd. dirs. Ingram Industries, Dollar Gen. Corp., TVA, 2006- Bd. dirs. Tenn. Tomorrow; v.p., Vanderbilt Bd. of Trustees, Nashville; trustee Leadership Nashville; bd. dirs. Tenn. Performing Arts Ctr., Nashville Sports Coun. Mem. Hundred Club, Belle Meade Country Club. Presbyterian. Office: TVA 150 2nd Ave N Ste 415 Nashville TN 37201

BOTTS, GREGORY, artist; b. Harrisburg, Pa., 1952; Tchr. various schools; lectr. NY U., NY Studio Sch., Brandeis U. One-man shows include Earl McGrath Gallery, L.A., 1987, Anne Plumb Gallery, NYC, 1989—94, U. Arts Rosenwald-Wolf Gallery, Phila., 1993, Ro Snell Gallery, Santa Barbara, Calif., 1993, Tony Shafrazi Gallery, NYC, 1993, CCS Gallery UCSB, Calif., 1997, others, exhibited in group shows at Robin Lockett Gallery, Chgo., 1986, Mus. Art RISD, Providence, 1988, Richard Green Gallery, L.A., 1990, NY Studio Sch. Art Gallery, NYC, 1991, Cleve. Ctr. Contemporary Art, Ohio, 1994, Deutche Bank Lobby Gallery, NY, 1994, Baruch Coll., 1995, Art Resources Transfer, NYC, 1998, Rotunda Gallery, Bklyn., 1998, others. Recipient award, Am. Acad. Arts and Letters; grantee Adolph and Esther Gottlieb grant. Address: PO Box 164 Abiquiu NM 87510 Office Phone: 505-685-4915. E-mail: botts@cybermesa.com.

BOTVINICK, ELIAS H., nuclear medicine physician, researcher, medical educator; b. Bklyn., Aug. 11, 1942; s. Jacob Botvinick and Mollie Shabansky; m. Carroll L. Lavine, June 28, 1964; children: Matthew M., Jori L. Botvinick-Gnagy. MD, NYU, NYC, 1967. Diplomate Am. Bd. Nuclear Medicine. Fellow in cardiovasc. diseases U. Calif., San Francisco, 1973—75, resident in nuc. medicine, 1975—77, prof. medicine and radiology cardiovasc. divsn. and sect. nuc. medicine, 1975—, co-dir. adult cardiology noninvasive lab., dir. nuc. cardiology, 1990—. Lectr. in field. Contbr. articles to profl. jours. Maj. MC US Army, 1971—73, Vietnam. Decorated Bronze Star; recipient Established Investigator award, AHA, 1981. Master: Am. Soc Nuc. Cardiology (life; bd. dirs. 1995—98). Independent. Achievements include research in medical imaging. Avocations: painting, reading, swimming, music. Office: U Calif San francisco 500 Parnassus Ave San Francisco CA 94143 Office Phone: 415-353-1744. Office Fax: 415-353-8687. Business E-Mail: botvinicke@medicine.ucsf.edu.

BOUBEKRI, MOHAMED, architecture educator; Diploma in Arch., U. Scis. and Tech. Oran, Algeria, 1983; MArch, U. Colo., Denver, 1985; PhD in Arch., Tex. A&M U., 1990. Lic. arch., Algeria, 1983. Jr. archtl. designer Kalik Arch., Mo., 1980—82, Electronic Transcations Assn. U., 1982—83; asst. prof. Concordia U., Montreal, Canada, 1990—93, U. Ill. Sch. Arch., Champaign-Urbana, 1993—99, assoc. prof., 1999—, chair practice and tech. faculty, 2002—. Mem.: Illuminating Engring. Soc. N.Am. (mem. daylighting com. 1995—). Office: Univ Ill Champaign Sch Arch 318 TH Buell Hall MC 621 611 E Lorado Taft Dr Champaign IL 61820

BOUCEK, JENNY, professional basketball coach; b. Nashville, Dec. 20, 1973; B with high honors in Sports Medicine & Sports Mgmt., U. Va., 1997. Guard WNBA Cleve. Rockers, 1997; profl. basketball player Icelandic Basketball League; asst. coach WNBA Washington Mystics, 1999—2000, WNBA Miami Sol, 2000—02, WNBA Seattle Storm, 2003—05; advanced scout NBA Seattle SuperSonics, 2005—06; head coach WNBA Sacramento Monarchs, 2006—. Head coach WNBA Western Conf. All-Star Team, 2007. Named Atlantic Coast Conf. All-Star Team, 1994, GTE Academic All-Am., 1995, 96. Avocations: basketball, volleyball, tennis. Office: Sacramento Monarchs ARCO Arena One Sports Pky Sacramento CA 95834*

BOUCHARD, GILLES, computer company executive; b. 1961; BS in Engring., Ecole Centrale, Lyon, France; M, U. Calif., Berkeley. Joined Hewlett-Packard Co., 1989, gen. mgr. Pavilion Home PC bus. in Americas, 1998—99, v.p. worldwide ops. personal computing orgn., 1999—2001, v.p. and gen. mgr. bus. customer ops., 2001—02, sr. v.p. imaging and printing grp. ops., 2002—03, chief info. officer, 2003—05, exec v.p. global ops., 2003—. Named one of Premier 100 IT Leaders, Computerworld, 2005. Office: Hewlett Packard Co 3000 Hanver St Palo Alto CA 94304-1185*

BOUCHARD, JAMES PAUL, metal products executive; b. Kansas City, Kans., May 2, 1961; s. Robert Clayton and Helen (Clancy) Bouchard; m. Carolyn Keegan, July 19, 1986. BBA, Loyola U., Chgo., 1984. Asst. to dist. mgr. Inland Steel Co., Chgo., 1983-85; sales rep. Denver br. Westinghouse Electric, 1985-87, U.S. Steel (divsn. USX Corp.), Milw., 1987-91, Midwest area sr. rep. Oak Brook, Ill., 1987-94, resident mgr., 1994-97, strategic planning and devel. mgr. Pitts., 1997-98, mgr. mktg., 1998, nat. mgr. pipe, tube, and container group, 1999-2000; v.p. comml. U.S. Steel-Kosice, Pitts., 2000—02; COO Mars Industries, Chgo., 2002—03; founder, chmn., CEO Esmark, Chgo., 2003—, also bd. dirs.; chmn., CEO Wheeling Pittsburgh Corp., Wheeling, W.Va., 2006—. Bd. dirs. Electric Coating Tech., Bouchard Group, LLC, Esmark, Inc., Wheeling Pitts. Steel Corp., Steel Inst., Washington, Am. Iron and Steel Inst., Washington. Co-inventor, patent light weight concrete, 1983. Bd. dirs. Quaker Valley Recreation Assn., Sewickley, Pa.; mem. Evans Scholars Found., Strategic Leadership Forum, Pitts. Named Steel Man of the Yr., ASD; recipient Damen award, Loyola U., 2007, Disting. Alumni award, 2007. Mem.: Art Inst. Chgo., Loyola U. Alumni Assn., Allegheny Country Club, Butler Nat. Golf Club, Whisper Rock Golf Club, Olde Fla. Golf Club, Naples Bath and Tennis Club (bd. dirs.), Edgeworth Club Serwickley (bd. dirs.), Sweickley Heights Golf Club (Pa.), Edgewood Valley Country Club (bd. dirs.), Chgo. Dist. Golf Assn. Republican. Roman Catholic. Avocations: golf, basketball, baseball, football. Home: 3 Beaver St Sewickley PA 15143-1217 Office Phone: 708-756-0400. Personal E-mail: jpbouchard@esmark.com.*

BOUCHARD, THOMAS JOSEPH, JR., psychology professor, researcher; b. Manchester, NH, Oct. 3, 1937; s. Thomas and Florence (Charest) B.; m. Pauline Marina Proulx, Aug. 13, 1960; children: Elizabeth, Mark. BA, U. Calif., Berkeley, 1963, PhD, 1966. Asst. prof. U. Calif., Santa Barbara, 1966-69, U. Minn., Mpls., 1969-70, assoc. prof., 1970-73, prof., 1973—, chmn. dept. psychology, 1985-91. Dir. Minn. Ctr. Twin and Adoption Rsch., U. Minn., 1980—. Assoc. editor: jours. Jour. Applied Psychology, 1977—80, Behavior Genetics, 1982—86; contbr. articles jours. more than 175 articles to profl. jours. With USAF, 1955-58. Fellow AAAS, APA, Am. Psychol. Soc.; mem. Phi Beta Kappa, Sigma Xi. Office: U Minn Dept Psychology 75 E River Rd Minneapolis MN 55455-0280 Home: PO Box 880104 Steamboat Springs CO 80488 E-mail: bouch001@tc.umn.edu.

BOUCHARD, WENDY ANN BORSTEL, language educator; m. Douglas K. Bouchard, Aug. 6, 1983. BA, SUNY, Geneseo, 1978; MA, Hofstra U., Hempstead, NY, 1982. Cert. secondary English tchr. N.Y. English tchr. Oneida (N.Y.) Sr. H.S., 1978—80, Mineola Jr. H.S., 1980—81, Thompson Jr. H.S., Syosset, NY, 1981—83, Roslyn (N.Y.) Jr. H.S., 1983—84, Garden City (N.Y.) Mid. Sch., 1984—2000, Garden City (N.Y.) Sr. H.S., 2000—. Life mem. Girls Scouts Am. Mem.: N.Y. State English Coun., L.I. Lang. Arts Coun., N.Y. State United Tchrs., Nat. Coun. Tchrs. English. Avocations: travel, reading, swimming. Office: Garden City Sr High Sch 170 Rockaway Ave Garden City NY 11530 Business E-Mail: bouchardw@gcufsd.net.

BOUCHER, BRIAN, professional hockey player; b. Woonsocket, RI, Jan. 2, 1977; m. Melissa Boucher; 1 child, Tyler. Goalie Phila. Flyers, 1999—2002, Phoenix Coyotes, 2002—06, Calgary Flames., 2006, Chgo. Blackhawks, 2006—07, Columbus Blue Jackets, 2007, Phila. Phantoms, 2007—. Goaltender Team USA World Jr. Championships, 1997, 98. Charity work Children's Miracle Network. Named to All-Rookie Team, NHL, 2000. Achievements include setting NHL record for most consecutive regular season shutouts (5 games). Avocation: golf. Office: Phila Phantoms Wachovia Spectrum 3601 S Broad St Philadelphia PA 19148*

BOUCHER, BRUCE AMBLER, art historian, art critic; b. Birmingham, Ala., Nov. 5, 1948; arrived in Eng., 1970; s. John Walter and Louise Ambler (Kean) B.; m. Gillian Moore, Aug. 3, 1974 (div. 1981); m. Isabel Ruth Carlisle, Feb. 13, 1982 (div. 1996); children: Venetia, Miranda; m. Diane Michaels, Apr. 17, 1999. AB, Harvard U., 1970; BA, Oxford U., Eng., 1972; MA, U. London, 1974, PhD, 1987. Lectr. U. Coll., U. London, 1976-92, reader, 1992-98, prof. art history, 1998—. Fellow Villa Itatti, Florence, Italy, 1984-85, Humboldt Found. Bonn, Berlin, 1989-90, 94, Leverhulme rsch. fellow. 2001—. Author: Sculpture of Jacopo Sansovino, 1991 (Salimbeni prize 1992), Andrea Palladio, 1994, Italian Baroque Sculpture, 1998. Mem. Internat. Assn. Art Critics, Athenaeum. Anglican. Office: Univ London Univ Coll Dept History Art Gower St London WC1E 6BT England

BOUCHER, JOSEPH W(ILLIAM), lawyer, educator, accountant, writer; b. Menominee, Mich., Oct. 28, 1951; s. Joseph W. and Patricia (Coon) B.; m. Susan M. De Groot, June 4, 1977; children: Elizabeth, Bridget, Joseph William III BA, St. Norbert Coll., 1973; JD, U. Wis., 1977, MBA in Fin., 1978. Bar: Wis. 1978, U.S. Dist. Ct. (we. dist.) Wis. 1978; CPA, Wis. Adminstrv. aide to Senator Wis. Senate, Madison, 1977; from assoc. to ptnr. Murphy, Stolper et al., Madison, 1977-84; ptnr. Stolper, Koritzinsky, Brewster & Neider, Madison, 1985-94; mng. ptnr. Stolper, Koritzinsky, Brewster, Neider, Madison, 1989-92, Neider & Boucher, S.C., 1995—. Lectr. bus. U. Wis., Madison, 1980- Co-author: Organizing a Wisconsin Business Corporation, 1995, 3d edit., 2007, Wisconsin LLCs and LLPs Handbook, 1996, 3d edit., 2007; contbr. articles to Wis. Bar Assn. Bd. dirs. Jackson Found., 1994—99, West Met. Bus. Assn., 1990—95, Dane County United Way, 1986—89, 2006, Wis. Chamber Orch., 1990—94, pres., 1993—94; bd. dirs. St. Coletta's, 1997—2001, Edgewood H.S., 1997—2003, chair, 2001—03; mem. bd. advisors St. Mary's Med. Ctr., Madison, 1989—91. Named One of Outstanding Young

Men of Am., 1979, Wis. Lawyer Adv. of Yr., SBA, 1983, 2005, Disting. Alumni, St. Norbert Coll., 2004. Mem. ABA, AICPA (mem. bd. examiners, mem. bus. law subcom. 1987-90), Am. Bar Found., Wis. Bar Assn., Wis. State Bar Assn. (mem. corp. com. 1991—, co-chairperson interprofl. com. 1992-95, chair ltd. liability co. subcom.), Dane County Bar Assn., Wis. Inst. CPAs, U. Wis. Bus. Alumni Assn. (bd. dirs. 1980-87) Roman Catholic. Avocations: sports, reading. Office: Neider & Boucher SC 440 Science Dr Madison WI 53711-1064 Home Phone: 608-233-4105; Office Phone: 608-661-4500. Business E-Mail: Jboucher@neiderboucher.com.

BOUCHER, RICHARD A., federal agency administrator; b. Bethesda, Md., Dec. 13, 1951; s. Melville J. and Ellen (Kaufmann) B.; m. Carolyn L. Brehm, June 19, 1982; children: Madeleine Brehm, Peter Brehm. BA cum laude, Tufts U., 1973; postgrad., George Washington U., 1976-77. Vol. Peace Corps, Senegal, 1973-75; with Agy. Internat. Devel., Guinea, 1975-76; various positions Fgn. Svc., 1977-84; econ. officer US Consulate Gen., Shanghai, 1984-86; sr. watch officer US Dept. State, 1986-87, dep. dir. polit. affairs office European security and polit. affairs, 1987-89, dep. spokesman, 1989—93, acting spokesman, 1992-93, U.S. amb. to Cyprus Nicosia, 1993-96; consulate gen. US Consulate Gen., Hong Kong, 1996—99; U.S. sr. ofcl. Asia Pacific Econ. Cooperation Forum, 1999—2000; asst. sec. for pub. affairs, dept. spokesman US Dept. State, Washington, 2000—05, asst. sec for South & Ctrl. Asian Affairs, 2006—. Office: US Dept State Harry S Truman Bldg 2201 C St NW Rm 6254 Washington DC 20520

BOUCHER, RICK (FREDERICK C. BOUCHER), congressman, lawyer; b. Abingdon, Va., Aug. 1, 1946; s. Ralph E. and Dorothy (Buck) Boucher; m. Amy Boucher. BA, Roanoke Coll., Salem, Va., 1968; JD, U. Va. Sch. Law, Charlottesville, 1971. Bar: Va. 1971, NY 1972. Assoc. Milbank, Tweed, Hadley, McCloy, NYC, 1971-73; ptnr. Boucher & Boucher, Abingdon, Va.; mem. Va. State Senate, Richmond, 1974—83, US Congress from 9th Va. dist., 1983—, mem. energy and commerce com., ranking minority mem. energy and air quality subcommittee, mem. judiciary com., founder, co-chmn. Internet Caucus, 1996—. Recipient Disting. Svc. award Va. Highlands Cmty. Coll., Abingdon, 1984, Beamer award for Contbns. to Vocat. Edn., 1986, Legislator of Yr. award Vietnam Vets. Am., 1993, Politician of Yr. award, Libr. Jour., 2006. Mem. ABA, Assn. Bar of NYC, Va. Bar Assn. Democrat. Methodist. Office: US Ho Reps 2187 Rayburn Ho Office Bldg Washington DC 20515-4609 Office Phone: 202-225-3861.*

BOUCHER, WAYNE IRVING, policy analyst; b. Bay City, Mich., Dec. 12, 1934; s. Harold Oscar and Mildred Christine (Born) B.; m. Donna Lou Collins, June 12, 1961 (div. 1973); children: Michèle Annette, Robert Alain. BA in English Lang. and Lit., U. Mich., 1956, MA in English Lang. and Lit., 1960; postgrad. in philosophy, U. Mo., 1959-61. Instr. English U. Mo., Columbia, 1958-63; asst. to pres. Rand Corp., Santa Monica, Calif., 1963-69; rsch. assoc. Inst. for the Future, Middletown, Conn., 1969-71; co-founder, v.p. The Futures Group, Glastonbury, Conn., 1971-76; dept. dir., dir. rsch. Nat. Commn. on Electronic Fund Transfers, Washington, 1976-78; sr. rsch. assoc. Ctr. for Futures Rsch., U. So. Calif., LA, 1978—84; exec. v.p. Benton Internat., Torrance, Calif., 1984-93; pres. The Ark. Inst., Little Rock, 1993-94; pres., COO Electronic Funds Transfer Assn., Herndon, Va., 1994—95; co-founder, mng. dir. Strategic Futures Internat., Harpers Ferry, W.Va., 1995—2006; pvt. practice Harpers Ferry, 2006—. Author: (with J.L. Morrison and W.L. Renfro) Futures Research and Strategic Planning, 1984; Spinoza in English, 1991, 2d edit., 1999, Spinoza: 18th and 19th Century Discussions, 6 vols., 1999; editor: (with J.L. Morrison and W.L. Renfro) Applying Methods and Techniques of Futures Research, 1983; author, editor: The Study of the Future, 1977; editor (with E.S. Quade) Systems Analysis and Policy Planning, 1968, W. Hale White's Translation of SPinoza's Ethics, 2007; mem. editorial bd. Technol. Forecasting and Social Change, 1978-82, Futures Rsch. Quar., 1984—; contbr. articles to profl. jours. Home and Office: 87 Lakeside Dr Harpers Ferry WV 25425-4731 Personal E-mail: wboucher@earthlink.net.

BOUCKAERT, CARL M., manufacturing executive; Founder, CEO Beaulieu of Am. Group, 1978—. Republican. Avocation: horseback riding. Office: Beaulieu of Am LLC 1502 Coronet Dr Dalton GA 30720

BOUDART, MICHEL, chemical engineer, consultant, chemist, educator; b. Belgium, June 18, 1924; came to U.S., 1947, naturalized, 1957; s. Francois and Marguerite (Swolfs) B.; m. Marina D'Haese, Dec. 27, 1948; children: Mark, Baudouin, Iris, Philip. BS, U. Louvain, Belgium, 1944, MS, 1947; PhD, Princeton U., 1950; D honoris causa, U. Liège, U. Notre Dame, U. Nancy, U. Ghent. Research asso. James Forrestal Research Ctr., Princeton, 1950-54; mem. faculty Princeton U., 1954-61; prof. chem. engring. U. Calif., Berkeley, 1961-64, adj. prof. chem. engring., 1994—; prof. chem. engring. and chemistry Stanford U., 1964-80, Keck prof. engring., 1980-94, Keck prof. engring. emeritus, 1994—. Co-founder Catalytica, Inc.; Humble Oil Co. lectr., 1958; AIChE lectr., 1961; Sigma Xi nat. lectr., 1965; chmn. Gordon Rsch. Conf. Catalysis, 1962. Author: Kinetics of Chemical Processes, 1968, (with G. Djéga-Mariadassou) Kinetics of Heterogenous Catalytic Reactions, 1983; editor: (with J.R. Anderson) Catalysis: Science and Technology, 11 vols., 1981-96, (with Marina Boudart and René Bryssinck) Modern Belgium, 1990; mem. adv. editl. bd. Catal. Letters, 1989—, Catalysis Rev., 1968—, Jour. Molecular Catalysis, 1995—, Cattech, 1996—. Recipient Curtis-McGraw rsch. award Am. Soc. Engring. Edn., 1962, R.H. Wilhelm award in chem. reaction engring., 1974, Chem. Pioneer award Am. Inst. Chemists, 1991; Belgium-Am. Ednl. Found. fellow, 1948, Procter fellow, 1949; Fairchild disting. scholar Calif. Tech. Inst., 1995. Fellow AAAS, Am. Acad. Arts. and Scis., Calif. Acad. Scis.; mem. NAS, NAE, Am. Chem. Soc. (Kendall award 1977, E.V. Murphee award in indsl. and engring. chemistry 1985), Catalysis Soc., Am. Inst. Chem. Engrs., Chem. Soc., Académie Royale de Belgique (fgn. assoc.), French Nat. Acad. Pharmacy (fgn.). Home: 228 Oak Grove Ave Atherton CA 94027-2218 Office: Stanford U Dept Chem Engring Stanford CA 94305 Office Fax: 650-723-9780.

BOUDIN, MICHAEL, federal judge; b. NYC, Nov. 29, 1939; s. Leonard and Jean Boudin; m. Martha Field, Sept. 18, 1984. BA, Harvard Coll., 1961, LLB, 1964. Bar: NY 1964, DC 1967. Law clk. to Hon. Henry J. Friendly US Ct. Appeals (2d cir.), 1964—65; law clk. to Justice John Harlan US Supreme Ct., Washington, 1965—66; assoc. firm Covington & Burling, Washington, 1966—72, ptnr., 1972—87; dep. asst. atty. gen. anti-trust divsn. US Dept. Justice, Washington, 1987—90; judge US Dist. Ct. (DC dist.), Washington, 1990—92, US Ct. Appeals (1st cir.), Boston, 1992—, chief judge, 2001—. Vis. prof. Harvard Law Sch., 1982—83, lectr., 1983—98, U. Pa. Law Sch., 1984—85. Contbr. articles to profl. jours. Mem.: Am. Law Inst. Office: US Ct Appeals 1st Cir 1 Courthouse Way Ste 7710 Boston MA 02210-3009 Office Phone: 617-748-4431.

BOUDOULAS, HARISIOS, cardiologist, researcher, medical educator; b. Velvendo-Kozani, Greece, Nov. 3, 1935; married; 2 children. MD, U. Salonica, Greece, 1959; D (hon.), U. Salenica; numerous hon. Dr. degrees. Resident in internal medicine Red Cross Hosp., Athens, Greece, 1960-61, U. Salonica First Med. Clinic, 1962-66, resident in internal medicine and cardiology, 1962-66, lectr., 1969-70; postgrad. fellow, instr. div. cardiology Ohio State U. Coll. Medicine, Columbus, 1970-73, asst. prof. medicine, 1975-78, assoc. prof., 1978-80, dir. cardiac non-invasive lab., 1978-80, prof. medicine div. cardiology, 1980—2002, prof. pharmacy, 1984—2002, dir. cardiovascular rsch. div., 1983-86, dir. cardiovascular teaching and rsch. lab., 1992—2002; prof. medicine div. cardiology Wayne State U., Detroit, 1980-82, chief clin. cardiovascular rsch., 1980-82; chief cardiovascular diagnostic and tng. center VA Med. Ctr., Allen Park, Mich., 1980-82; chief sect. cardiology Harper-Grace Hosps., Detroit, 1982. Mem. Antepistelon Athens Acad., 1998—; dir. Ctr. for Clin. Rsch., pres. sci. coun. Found. Biomed. Rsch., Acad. Athens, 2002—. Editor in chief Hellenic Jour. Cardiology, 1990-2000; mem. editl. rev. bd. jours. cardiology; contbr. numerous articles to med. jours. Named Disting. Research Investigator, Cen. Ohio chpt. Am. Heart Assn., Columbus, 1983. Fellow ACP, Am. Coll. Cardiology (trustee Ohio chpt. 1993-97), Am. Heart Assn. (coun. clin. cardiology 1989-93, coun. exec. com. 1991-93, sci. com. 1991-93), European Soc. Cardiology (sci. com. 1991-93, valvular heart disease working group 1993—), Greek Heart Assn., Am. Fedn. Clin. Rsch., Laeneck Soc. (chmn. 1991-93), Hellenic Cardiol. Soc. (pres. 2005-07). Address: 4 Soranou Ephesiou 11527 Athens Greece Home Phone: 30 210 675 34 77. Business E-Mail: boudoulas@bioacademy.gr.

BOUDREAU, DANIEL J., retired state supreme court justice; b. Natick, Mass., 1947; m. Faith Boudreau, 1972. BA, Boston Coll., 1969; MA, Rutgers U., 1972; JD, U. Tulsa, 1976. Pvt. practice, Broken Arrow, Okla., 1976—80; trial judge Tulsa County, Okla., 1980—92; judge, then vice-chief judge Okla. Ct. Civil Appeals, 1992-99; justice Okla. Supreme Ct., Oklahoma City, 1999—, Appellate Ct. on the Judiciary, 2001—04; prof. U. Tulsa Coll. of Law, 2004.

BOUDREAU, DIANE, writer; d. Robert and Gloria Boudreau; m. Robert S. Roberson, Jr.; 1 child, Nicholas Roberson. BA, Boston U., 1992; M in Mass Communication, Ariz. State U., Tempe, 1995. Editl. asst. Nephrology News and Issues, Scottsdale, Ariz., 1994—95; tech. writer, webmaster PLP Digital Systems, Scottsdale, 1995—97; sci. writer, web editor Ariz. State U., Tempe, 1997—. Recipient Copper Quill award for feature writing, IABC Phoenix, 1996, 1997, 1998, 2002, 2005, 2006, EPIC award, Hon. Mention, feature writing, Women in Comm., 1996, Silver Quill award for human interest writing, IABC So. Region, 1996, 2000, 2006, Award of distinction for Web design, Coun. for the Advancement and Support of Edn., 1999, Cactus Quill award for writing, IABC Tucson, 2003, 2005, 2006. Mem.: U. Rsch. Mag. Assn. (bd. mem. 2006—07), Nat. Assn. Sci. Writers. Office: Arizona State University Research Publications Box 873803 Tempe AZ 85287-3803 Home Phone: 480-820-5508; Office Phone: 480-965-7260. Office Fax: 480-965-9684. Business E-Mail: dianeb@asu.edu.

BOUDREAU, THOMAS M., lawyer, health products executive; b. St. Louis, 1951; BA cum laude, Maryville Coll., 1973; JD magna cum laude, St. Louis U., 1979. Bar: Mo. 1979, US Dist. Ct. (ea. dist. Mo.) 1979, US Tax Ct. 1980. Ptnr. Husch & Eppenberger, St. Louis, 1986—94; v.p., gen. counsel Express Scripts Inc., Md. Heights, Mo., 1994, sr. v.p., gen. counsel, sec., 1994—. Co-author: The Law of Lender Liability, 1990; asst. editor St. Louis U. Law Jour., 1978-79. Fellow: Am. Coll. Comml. Fin. Lawyers; mem.: ABA. Office: Express Scripts Inc 13900 Riverport Dr Maryland Heights MO 63043*

BOUDREAUX, JOHN, marketing and public relations executive; b. Franklin, La., July 28, 1946; s. Abel John and Dorothy (Bourgeois) B. BA, La. State U., 1969. Reporter, copy editor Morning Advocate, Baton Rouge, 1969-71; successively reporter, copy editor, asst. city editor Houston Post, 1971-76, city editor, 1976-84; pub. rels. cons., 1984-85; sr. communications specialist IBM, Dallas, 1985-87, comm. mgr. San Francisco, 1987-88, program mgr. Westchester County, NY, 1988-2000; mng. editor IBM.com, 2000—03; pres. EJB Comms., 2003—. Named Outstanding Journalism Grad., La. State U., 1969. Mem. Soc. Profl. Journalists, Sigma Delta Chi (bd. dirs. Houston chpt. 1975, 83).

BOUDREAUX, KENNETH JUSTIN, economist, educator; b. New Orleans, Dec. 22, 1943; s. Aldwin John and Beverly Estelle (Swanton) B.; m. Carole Jean Barnette, May 28, 1966; 1 child, Beau Justin AB, Princeton U., 1965; MBA, Tulane U., 1967; PhD, U. Wash., 1970. Asst. prof. Sch. Bus., Tulane U., New Orleans, 1970-73, assoc. prof., 1973-78, prof., 1978—, assoc. dean faculty, 1981-83. Cons. City of New Orleans Author: Basic Theory of Corporate Finance, 1977, Finance, 1990; editorial bd. Jour. Econs. and Bus., Jour. Fin. Rsch.; contbr. articles to scholarly jours. AACSB fellow, 1969-70; recipient Wissner award Tulane U., 1972, 75, Outstanding Prof., 1972, 75, Disting. Prof., 1973 Fellow Fin. Analysts Fedn.; mem. Am. Econ. Assn., Am. Fin. Assn., Western Fin. Assn., Western Econ. Assn. Clubs: Cannon (Princeton U.), Pickwick, So. Yacht Club. Office: Tulane U Sch Bus New Orleans LA 70118 Office Phone: 504-895-8741.

BOUÉ, DANIEL ROBERT, pediatric pathologist, neuropathologist, educator; b. NYC, June 22, 1958; s. Robert Charles and Dorothea Anna B.; m. Julie Marie Borgerding; children: Rachel Hope, Jenna Elizabeth, AnnaMarie Monique, Sarah Jane, Rebecca Catherine. BA cum laude, Carleton Coll., 1980; PhD, U. Minn., 1988, MD, 1991. Diplomate in anat. and clin. pathology and pediatric pathology Am. Bd. Pathology. Intern U. Calif., San Diego, 1991—92, resident in pathology, 1992—94, chief resident-elect, 1994—95; attending physician U. Calif./San Diego Med. Ctr., 1994—95; clin. instr. U. Calif., San Diego, 1994—95; fellow pediat. pathology Columbus Childrens Hosp., 1995—96; clin. instr. Ohio State U., Columbus, 1995—97, clin. asst. prof. pathology, 1998—2003, clin. assoc. prof. pathology, 2004—; fellow pediat. neuropathology Columbus Childrens Hosp., 1996; staff pathologist, dir. Neuropathology program Childrens Hosp., Columbus, 1997—; dir. surg. and autopsy neuropathology, muscle and nerve biopsy svcs. Interim dir. perinatal pathology and autopsy svc. U. Calif., San Diego, 1994—95; rev. pathologist, investigator Biopathology Ctr. Children's Hosp. Rsch. Found.; presenter in field. Contbr. articles to profl. jours.; referee med. jour. publs. Med. Scientist scholar U. Minn., 1982-91, G.T. Evan scholar Dept. Lab. Medicine and Pathology, 1982-85, Life & Health Ins. Med. Rsch. Fund, scholar, 1985-90; recipient J.T. Livermore Hematology award Minn. Med. Found., 1988, Undergrad. Med. Student Rsch. award 1991, Dr. Vernon D.E. Smith award, 1990; grantee multiple grants. Fellow Am. Coll. Pathology, Am. Soc. Clin. Pathologists (Sheard-Sanford award 1988), Coll. Am. Pathologists; mem. Soc. Pediat. Pathology, Am. Assn. Neuropathologists, Alpha Omega Alpha. Office: Columbus Childrens Hosp Dept Lab Med 700 Childrens Dr Columbus OH 43205-2664

BOUFFORD, JO IVEY, health facility administrator, educator; b. Durham, NC, July 2, 1945; BA in Psychology magna cum laude, U. Mich., 1967, MD with distinction, 1971; DSc (hon.), SUNY, Bklyn., 1992. Diplomate Nat. Bd. Med. Examiners, Am. Bd. Pediats. Resident in social pediats. medicine Montefiore Hosp. and Med. Ctr., Bronx, N.Y., 1971-74, asst. attending physician, 1975-97, co-dir. Inst. for Health Team Devel., 1975-82, dir. residency program in social medicine, 1975-82; adminstrv. dir. Valentine Lane Family Practice, Yonkers, N.Y., 1975-82; v.p. med. ops. N.Y.C. Health and Hosps. Corp., 1982-83, v.p. med. and profl. affairs, 1983-85, exec. v.p., 1985, acting pres., 1985, pres., 1985-89; internat. fellow in comparative health sys. mgmt. King's Fund Coll., London, 1989-91, dir., 1991-93; prin. dep. asst. sec. for health US Dept. Health & Human Services, Washington, 1993-97, acting asst. sec. for health, 1997; dean, Robert F. Wagner Grad. Sch. Pub. Svc. NYU, 1997—2002, clin. prof. peds., 1997—, prof. pub. svc. health policy & mgmt., 2003—; pres. The NY Acad. Medicine, NYC, 2007—. Adj. prof. Lehman Coll. Nursing, Bronx, 1974-80; mem. Nat. Adv. Coun. for Health Professions Edn. US-DHHS, 1976-80; mem. tech. panel on the ednl. environ. Grad. Med. Edn. Nat. Adv. Coun., 1979-80; cons. on manpower programs divsn. medicine bur. Health Professions Edn. HRSA-DHHS, 1980-88; mem. N.Y. State Coun. on grad. med. edn., 1987-89, N.Y. State Commn. on Grad. Med. Edn., 1985-86; rep. of U.S. on exec. bd. WHO, 1994-97; U.S. staff dir. Gore-Chernomyrdin Commn. Health Com., 1994-97; various consulting positions. Mem. editl. bd. Jour. Med. Edn., 1980-86; mem. editl. adv. bd. The New Physician, 1979-89; contbr. articles to profl. jours.; presenter in field. Mem. Nat. Adv. Coun. of Agy. for Healthcare Quality and Rsch., 2000—04; bd. dirs. United Hosp. Fund, 1999—; chair sub-bd. on pub. health, Open Soc. Inst., 1998-2004; mem. N.Y. State Coun. on Grad. Med. Edn., 1987-89. Fellow Am. Acad. Pediats.; mem. APHA, NAS Inst. Med. (coun. mem., fgn. sec.; Robert Wood Johnson health policy fellow 1979-80), Soc. Med. Adminstrs., Med. Adminstrs. Conf. Office: The NY Acad Medicine 1216 Fifth Ave New York NY 10029 Office Phone: 212-998-7410. E-mail: jo.boufford@nyu.edu.*

BOUGAS, JAMES ANDREW, physician, surgeon, educator; b. Bismarck, ND, Jan. 25, 1924; s. Andrew James and Mary (Psaltiras) B.; m. Tiina Parlin, June 27, 1953; children: Karen Louise, Tiina Maria. MD, Harvard U., 1948. Diplomate Am. Bd. Surgery, Am. Bd. Thoracic Surgery. Intern Columbia U. Svc., Bellevue Hosp., NYC, 1948-50, chief resident in surgery, 1952-53; resident Presbyn. Hosp., NYC, 1950-52, chief resident surgery, 1953; fellow Overholt Clinic, Boston, 1953-55, assoc., 1955-65; chief thoracic surgery U. Hosp., Boston, 1965-70; assoc. prof. surgery Boston U. Sch. Medicine, 1965—. Lectr. Tufts U. Sch. Medicine, Boston, 1965-70; chmn. Gordon Rsch. Confs., 1967-68. Contbr. articles to profl. jours. Pres. Heart Assn., Boston, 1967-69; chmn. Mass. Rehab. Commn. Adv. Com.; trustee Boston Tb Assn. With U.S. Army, 1942-44. Fellow AAAS; mem. ACS, Am. Coll. Cardiology, Am. Assn. Thoracic Surgeons, Soc. Thoracic Surgeons, Am. Coll. Cardiology, Am. Heart Assn., Mass. Med. Soc. (legis. com., coun.), Norfolk Dist. Med. Soc. (pres. 1989-90, Tri-State regional planning com.). Achievements include development of combined cardiac catheterization; porous metal prostheses fabrication and cardio-pulmonary physiology. Business E-Mail: jbougas@caregroup.harvard.edu.

BOUGH, KRISTOPHER, pharmacologist; BS, Gettysburg Coll., Pa., 1992; MS with distinction, Georgetown U., DC, 1998; PhD with distinction, Georgetown U., 1999. Tchg. fellow Georgetown U., DC, 1994—99; rsch. fellow U. Wash., Seattle, 1999—2001, Emory U., Atlanta, 2001—05; pharmacologist US Food & Drug Adminstrn., Rockville, Md., 2005—. Adj. asst. prof. Oglethorpe U., Atlanta, 2003; adv. mem., com. on postdoctoral edn. Emory U., 2004, co-instr. neuroscience & behavior, 05, internship, office tech. transfer, 05. Contbr. chapters to books, articles to profl. jours. Recipient Young Investigator award, Am. Epilepsy Soc., 2001—02, Individual Nat. Rsch. Svc. award, NIH, 2002—03; grantee Rsch. grant, Charlie Found., 2002—04; Rsch. Tng. fellowship, Epilepsy Found., 2000—01, MERCK Rsch. scholarship, Emory U., Ctr. Neurodegenerative Disease, 2002—03, Howard Hughes Med. Inst. Tchg. scholarship, Emory U., Howard Hughes Med. Inst., 2003—04. Mem.: AAAS, Am. Assn. Pharm. Scientists, Am. Epilepsy Soc., Soc. Neuroscience, Sigma Xi. Office: US Food & Drug Adminstrn 7520 Standish Pl Rm 1345 Rockville MD 20855 Business E-Mail: kristopher.bough@fda.hhs.gov.

BOUGHAN, ZANETTA LOUISE, music educator; b. Grantham, Eng., Mar. 22, 1959; arrived in U.S., 1964; d. Peter Leonard and Alyda Venita Maria (Bellord) Snowden; m. Robert William Boughan, Nov. 3, 1995. AAS, Cochise Coll., 2003—; BS with honors, Wayland Bapt. U., 2005. Pvt. piano and violin instr., Sierra Vista, Ariz., 1988—. Concertmaster Cochise Coll. Orch., Sierra Vista, 1999—2001, Pima Coll. Orch., Tucson, 2001—02; first violinist Sierra Vista Sym. Orch., 2001—02. Vol. Sierra Vista Police Dept., 2002—06; ct. apptd. spl. adv. vol. State Ariz., 2002—; vol. in Police Svc., 2002—06; mem. Citizens Police Acad. Assocs., 2003—; vol. Cochise County Juvenile Ct., 2003—06, Vol. Interfaith Caregiver Program, 2005—. With USN, 1979—84. Mem.: Ariz. Music Tchrs. Assn., Nat. Music Tchrs. Assn., Cochise Music Tchrs. Assn. (chmn. fundraising com. 1997—, sec. 1998—2000, treas. 2001—03, pres. 2003—05, Profl. Develop. grant 2001), Phi Theta Kappa. Avocations: photography, travel, music, swimming, tennis, walking, reading. Home: 4924 Marconi Dr Sierra Vista AZ 85635 Personal E-mail: zboughan@earthlink.net.

BOUGHTER, BARBARA B., retired mathematics educator; b. Sellersville, Pa., June 16, 1947; d. Luther Thomas and Adele Sterner Barndt; m. Charles Robert Moyer, 1971 (div. 1976); m. Frederick Wayne Boughter (dec. 1994); children: Jonathon Brian, Jeffrey Ryan. BSc, Kutztown State U., Pa., 1969; EdM, Kutztown State U., 1978. Math tchr. Indian Valley Jr. HS, Harleysville, Pa., 1969—71, Mary Potter Mid. Sch., Oxford, NC, 1971—73, Pennridge HS, Perkasie, Pa., 1973—98, Pennridge Ctrl. Mid. Sch., Silverdale, Pa., 1998—2005; ret., 2005. Cheerleading adv. Indian Valley Jr. HS, 1969—71; adv. Class of 1976 Pennridge HS, 1973—76, mentor student tchrs., 1978—87; sub. tchr., 2005—. Deacon on consistory St. Stephen's United Ch. of Christ, 2006—, treas., 2006—; mem. bd. dirs. Harleysville Soccer Assn., 1986—88; officer, coord. Souderton H.S. Soccer Parents Assn., 1994—98. Named to Wall of Tolerance, Southern Poverty Law Ctr., 2005. Mem.: NEA, Pa. Assn. of Sch. Retirees, Southern Poverty Law Ctr., Nat. Coun. of Teachers of Math. Home: 990 Long Mill Rd Telford PA 18969

BOUGHTON, LESLEY D., library director; b. New Haven, Jan. 21, 1945; d. Robert and Marjorie (Anderson) D.; m. Charles E. Boughton, Sept. 5, 1964 (dec. 1991); children: Michael, James, Gregg. AB, Conn. Coll., 1971; MLS, So. Conn. State U., 1978. Dir. Platte County Library, Wheatland, Wyo., 1980-88, Carbon County Library, Rawlins, Wyo., 1988-93, Natrona County Pub. Library, Casper, Wyo., 1993—99; state libr. Wyo. State Libr., Cheyenne, 1999—. Mem. Gov's. Telecommunications Coun., Wyo., 1994—. Mem. ALA (chpt. councilor 1988, 91), Wyo. Library Assn. (pres. 1985, Disting. Svc. award 1991), Chief Officers of State Libr. Agys. Office: Wyo State Libr 516 S Greeley Hwy Cheyenne WY 82002 Office Phone: 307-777-5911. Business E-Mail: lbough@state.wy.us.*

BOUILLIANT-LINET, FRANCIS JACQUES, global management consultant; b. Garches, France, Aug. 20, 1932; came to U.S., 1977; s. Jacques Achille and Virginia Sutton (McKee) B.-L.; m. Carolyn Jeanine Taylor, Nov. 17, 1978. Diploma in sci., Admiral Farragut Acad., 1948; postgrad., Duke U., 1949-50. Mgmt. trainee Harry Ferguson Cos., Europe, 1951-53; sales promotion mgr. Massey-Harris-Ferguson, Paris, 1957-59; gen. programs mgr. Massey Ferguson Ltd., Coventry, Eng., 1959-63, coord. office of pres. Toronto, Ont., Can., 1963-65, group product mgr., 1966-68; dir. internat. logistics Allis Chalmers Corp., Milw., 1968-71; joint mng. dir. LePiol, s.a.r.l., Cannes, France, 1971-77; chmn. bd., chief exec. officer FBL, Inc., Hurtsboro, Ala., 1977—, also bd. dirs. Exec. dir. H.J. Crawley, Ltd., Leamington, Eng., 1961-66; bd. dirs. F.J.B., Inc., Thermal, Calif. Author: (manual) The New Product Process, 1963; trademark registrant for "Rent-a-Boss." Charter founder Ronald Reagan Rep. Ctr., Washington, 1987. With French Armed Forces, 1953-54, 56-57. Mem. Capital City Club (life), Midland (Ga.) Fox Hounds. Office: FBL Inc PO Box 298 Hurtsboro AL 36860-0298

BOUKER, INA B., elementary school educator; b. Manokotak, Alaska; m. John Bouker. BA, Univ. Hawaii, Hilo. Tchr. Dillingham City Schools, Alaska, 1984—; now tchr. Dillingham Elem. Sch., Alaska. Named Alaska Tchr. of Yr., 2007; named one of Summit Educators of Yr., First Alaskans Inst., 2002. Mem.: Bristol Bay Native Corp. Office: Dillingham Elem Sch PO Box 170 Dillingham AK 99576 Business E-Mail: ina@dlgsd.org.*

BOUKNIGHT, LON (J.A. BOUKNIGHT JR.), lawyer, utilities executive; b. Florence, SC, Apr. 9, 1944; s. J.A. and Frances Lea (Huff) B.; m. Deborah Anne Harmon, Jan. 3, 1981; children: Robert Harmon, Amanda Alison. BA in Hist., Wofford Coll., 1965; JD, Duke U., 1968. Bar: NC

1968, DC 1973. Ptnr. Tally, Tally & Bouknight, Fayetteville, NC, 1968-73, Newman & Holtzinger, P.C., Washington, 1973-94, Steptoe & Johnson, LLP, Washington, 1994—2005, chmn., 1998—2004; gen. counsel, exec. v.p. Edison Internat., Rosemead, Calif., 2005—. Contbr. articles to pub. utilities jours. Mem. ABA (chmn. antitrust com. pub. utility law sect. 1985), Fed. Energy Bar Assn. Episcopalian. Avocations: golf, baseball, reading. Office: Edison Internat PO Box 976 Rosemead CA 91770 Office Phone: 626-302-2338.

BOULANGER, VICTOR, director; M, John Marshall Law Sch., Chgo., 2000. Chmn. tech. Josephinum Acad., Chgo., 2001—06. Office: Josephinum Academy 1501 North Oakley Chicago IL 60622 Office Phone: 773-276-1261. E-mail: victor.boulanger@josephinum.org.

BOULDING, ELISE MARIE, sociologist, educator; b. Oslo, July 6, 1920; came to U.S., 1923, naturalized, 1929; d. Joseph and Birgit (Johnsen) Biorn-Hansen; m. Kenneth Boulding; Aug. 31, 1941; children: John Russell, Mark David, Christine Ann, Philip Daniel, William Frederic. BA, Douglass Coll., 1940; MS, Iowa State Coll., 1949; PhD, U. Mich., 1969. Rsch. assoc. Survey Rsch. Inst., U. Mich., 1957-58, Mental Health Rsch. Inst., 1959-60; rsch. devel. sec. Ctr for Rsch. on Conflict Resolution, 1960-63; prof. sociology, project dir. Inst. Behavioral Sci., U. Colo., Boulder, 1967-78; Montgomery vis. prof. Dartmouth Coll., 1978-79, chmn. dept. sociology, 1979-85; prof. emerita, 1985; sec. gen. Internat. Peace Rsch. Assoc., 1989-91; pres. IPRA Found., 1992-96. Mem. program adv. council Human and Social Devel. Program, UN Univ., 1977-80; mem. governing council, 1980-86. Author: (with others) Handbook of International Data on Women, 1976, Bibliography on World Conflict and Peace, 1979, Social System of Planet Earth, 1980, Women and the Social Costs of Economic Development, 1981; author: The Underside of History: A View of Women Through Time, 1975, rev. edit., 1992, Women in Twentieth Century World, 1977, Children's Rights and the Wheel of Life, 1979, Building a Global Civic Culture: Education for an Interdependent World, 1988, 90, One Small Plot of Heaven, 1990, Cultures of Peace: The Hidden Side of History, 2000; (with Kenneth Boulding) The Future: Images and Processes, 1994; editor: Peace Culture and Society: Transnational Research and Dialogue with Clovis Brigagao and Kevin Clements (eds.), 1990; New Agendas for Peace Research: Conflict and Security Reexamined (ed.), 1992; Building Peace in the Middle East: Challenges for States and Civil Society, (ed.), 1993. Internat. chair Women's Internat. League for Peace and Freedom, 1967-70; mem. Exploratory Project on Conditions for Peace, 1984-90; mem. U.S. Commn. for UNESCO, 1978-84; mem. UNESCO Peace Prize jury, 1980-87; chair bd. Boulder Cmty. Parenting Ctr., 1988-92; bd. dirs. Am. Friends Svc. Com., 1990-94, Wayland MA Coun. on Aging, 1988-2000; councillor Interfaith Peace Coun., 1995—. Recipient Disting. Achievement award Douglass Coll., 1973, Ted. Lentz Peace award, 1976, Athena award, 1983, Nat. Women's Forum award, 1985, Inst. of Def., Disarmament, Peace and Democracy award, 1990, Jack Gore Meml. Peace award Denver Am. Friends Svc. Com., 1992, Global Citizen award Boston Rsch. Ctr., 1995, Peacemaker of Yr. award Rocky Mountain Peace and Justice Ctr., 1996, World Futures Studies Fedn. award, 1997, Jane Addams Peace Activist award Women's Internat. League for Peace and Freedom, 2000; named to Rutgers Hall of Disting. Alumni, 1994; Danforth fellow, 1965-67; named Peacemaker Elder, Nat. Conf. on Peacemaking and Conflict Resolution, 1999; chosen as one of 1000 Women for the Nobel Peace Prize, 2005. Mem. Am. Sociol. Assn. (Jessie Bernard award 1982, Peace and War sect. award 1994), Internat. Peace Rsch. Assn. (newsletter editor 1983-87), World Future Studies Fedn., Colo. Women's Forum. Mem. Soc. Of Friends. Home: N Hill 865 Central Ave Apt I 301 Needham MA 02492-1361

BOULE, MICHELLE L., librarian, writer; married. Grad. in English, Tex. A&M U., 2001; MLS, Tex. Woman's U. Social scis. libr. U. Houston Librs. Mem.: ALA, Libr. and Info. Tech. Assn. (co-chair Blogs, Interactive Media, Groupware and Wikis IG 2006—07). Avocations: reading, cooking, baking, camping, mountain biking. Office: U Houston Librs 114 University Libraries Houston TX 77204-2000 Office Phone: 713-743-9776. Office Fax: 713-743-9778. E-mail: mlboule@uh.edu, mboule@gmail.com.

BOULEY, JOSEPH RICHARD, pilot; b. Fukuoka, Japan, Jan. 7, 1955; came to U.S., 1955; s. Wilfrid Arthur and Minori Cecelia (Naraki) B.; m. Sara Elizabeth Caldwell, July 6, 1991; children: Denise Marie, Janice Elizabeth, Eleanor Catherine, Rachel Margaret, David Caldwell, Caroline Minori. BA in English, U. Nebr., 1977; MAS, Embry Riddle Aeronautical U., 1988; grad., Fed. Law Enforcement Tng. Ctr., Artesia, N.Mex., 2003. Cert. nat. level athletics ofcl. U.S.A. Track and Field, 2001. Commd. 2d lt. USAF, 1977, advanced through grades to maj., 1988, F-117A Stealth Fighter pilot Persian Gulf, 1991; ret. lt. col. USAFR, 2000; pilot United Airlines, 1992—. Ct. apptd. spl. advocate Office of Guardian Ad Litem, Salt Lake City, 1996-99. Decorated DFC, Air medal (4), Air Force Commendation medal (3), Air Force Achievement medal; recipient Alumni Achievement award U. Nebr., 1998; inducted into Air Force ROTC Hall of Fame, U. Nebr., 2003. Mem. VFW, Am. Legion, DFC Soc., Airline Pilots Assn., Red River Valley Fighter Pilots Assn., Aircraft Owners and Pilots Assn. Roman Catholic. Avocations: flying, golf, running, photography. Home: 952 E Springwood Dr North Salt Lake UT 84054 Office Phone: 801-309-9149. Personal E-mail: balijo@aol.com.

BOULEZ, PIERRE, composer, conductor; b. Montbrison, France, Mar. 26, 1925; s. Leon and Marcelle (Calabre) Boulez. Student, Olivier Messiaen at Paris Conservatory; D (hon.), Cambridge, 1980; D, Bale, 1980, LA, 1984, Oxford, 1987, Brussels, 1988. Founder Concert du Petit Marigny, 1953—54; apptd. dir. music Jean-Louis Barrault's Theater Co., 1948; tchr., lectr., condr.; musical adviser, prin. guest condr. Cleve. Symphony Orch., 1970—71; chief condr. BBC Symphony Orch., 1970—75; musical dir. N.Y. Philharm. Orch., 1971—77; dir. Inst. de Recherche et de Coord. Acoustique/Musique, 1976—91; prin. guest condr. Chgo. Symphony Orch., 1995—2006, conductor emeritus, 2006—. Vis. prof. Harvard Univ., 1962—63; prof. Coll. de France, 1976; pres. The Ensemble Intercontemporain, 1976—97. Composer: toured Europe, North and South Am.; conducting appearances include: Edinburgh Festival, Bayreuth Festival, Salzburg Festival, Lucerne Festival; composer: Sonatina for flute and piano, 1946, Three Piano Sonatas, 1946, 1950, 1957, Le Soleil des eaux for voice and orchestra, 1947, Structures, 1952, Le Marteau sans maître, 1955, Deux improvisations sur Mallarmé, 1957, Tombeau (on text of Mallarmé), 1959, Pli selon pli, 1960, Structures II, 1962, Eclat, 1964, Domaines, 1968, Eclat/Multiples, 1970, cummings ist der dichter, 1970, explosante-fixe, 1973, Rituel, 1975, Messagesquisse, 1976, Notations I-IV, 1980, Répons, 1981, Dialogue de l'ombre double, 1986, Mémoriale, 1985, Visage nuptial, 1989, Dérive I, 1985, Anthèmes pour violin solo, 1992, explosante-fixe for large ensemble and electronics, 1993, Anthèmes for Violin Solo and Electronics, 1997, sur Incises, 1998, Notations VII, 1999, Déreive 2, 2002; author: Relevés d'apprenti, 1966, Points de Repère, 1981, le pays fertile-Paule Klee, 1989, Jalon-10 ans d'enseignement au Collège de France, 1989; musical criticism and analysis including: Penser la musique aujourd'hui, 1963. Recipient prize of Siemens Found., 1979, Praemium Imperiale, Japan Art Assn., 1989, Grosses Verdienstkreuz RFA, 1990, Polar Music prize, Sweden, 1996, Wolf prize in arts (music), Wolf Found., Israel, 2000, Grawemeyer award, 2001.*

BOULHOSA, MICHAEL L., lawyer; b. Yonkers, NY, June 6, 1960; BA, Fordham U., 1983; JD, Pace U., 1985. Bar: NY 1986, NY Supreme Ct., US Dist. Ct. Ea. Dist. NY, US Dist. Ct. So. Dist. NY. Ptnr. Wilson, Elser, Moskowitz, Edelman & Dicker LLP, NYC. Mem.: NY County Trial Lawyers Assn., Bronx County Bar Assn., NY State Trial Lawyers Assn., NY State Bar Assn. Office: Wilson Elser Moskowitz Edelman & Dicker LLP 23rd Fl 150 E 42nd St New York NY 10017-5639 Office Phone: 212-490-3000 ext 2849. Office Fax: 212-490-3038. Business E-Mail: michael.boulhosa@wilsonelser.com.

BOULLY, LAJUAN BONNIE, minister, religious studies educator; b. Sanford, Fla., Oct. 11, 1930; d. Ira and Charity Pearl (Ellis) Brewer; children: James Robert, Leroy, Olan W., Mildred. Degree, Polk Cmty. Coll. Cert. day care. Sec. tng. dept. Publix Supermarket, Lakeland, Fla.; pastor, tchr. Faith Harbor Ch., Lakeland, Fla.; evangelist Taiwan, 1978, various locations, 2002—. Author: Miracles of Faith Harbor, 2006. Mem.: Morris Cercullo World Evangelism. Home: 4516 Redwood St Winter Haven FL 33880-1633 Office Phone: 863-294-6158. Personal E-mail: lajuanboully@aol.com. E-mail: ljboully@cs.com.

BOULOS, PAUL FARES, civil and environmental engineer; b. Beirut, June 28, 1963; came to U.S., 1983; s. Fares and Marie-Rose (Abou Hadid) B. BS, Beirut U., 1985; BSCE, U. Ky., 1985, MSCE, 1986, PhD, 1989; advanced mgmt. program, Harvard Bus. Sch., 2003. Asst. prof. U. Ky., Lexington, 1990-91; dir. water distbn. tech. Montgomery Watson, Pasadena, Calif., 1991-96; pres., COO MWH Soft Inc., Pasadena, 1996—. Internat. hydraulic expert on over 200 municipal drinking water projects worldwide; cons. in field. Author KYPIPED: Comprehensive Network Analyzer, 1990, H2OMAP, H2ONET and InfoWater Distribution Modeling and Management, 1999, 8 authoritative engrng. textbooks; contbr. over 100 articles to profl. publs. Recipient Best Rsch. Paper award U.S. EPA, 1994, ASCE, 1996, AWWA, 2003; grantee NSF, 1987, Am. Water Works Rsch. Found., 1992. Mem. ASCE (treas. 1992), Am. Water Works Assn., Sigma Xi, Tau Beta Pi, Chi Epsilon (U.S. delegation to NATO Advanced Study Inst. 1993). Achievements include work on computer-assisted water quality and hydraulic network modeling. Home: 9971 Winona St Westminster CO 80031-2528 Office: 380 Interlocken Crescent Ste 300 Broomfield CO 80021

BOULOT, PHILIPPE, chef; b. Apr. 15, 1959; m. Susan Boulot. Grad., Jean Drouant Hotel Sch., Paris, 1978. With The Nikko, Paris, Four Seasons Inn on the Park, London, Four Seasons Cliff Hotel, San Francisco, The Mark Hotel, NYC; exec. chef The Heathman Restaurant, Portland, 1994—. Named Best Chef: Northwest/Hawaii, James Beard Found., 2001. Office: The Heathman Hotel 1001 SW Broadway at Salmon Portland OR 97205*

BOULTBEE, JOHN ARTHUR, former publishing executive; b. Can., July 4, 1943; s. Thomas Edward and Helene Marion (Pattison) B.; m. Eleanor Rose Moore, Nov. 2, 1968 (div. 1985); children: Paul Keith, Leslie Elizabeth; m. Sharon Ann Whitby, Dec. 28, 1985; 1 child, Michael James Edward. B in Commerce, U. Toronto, Ont., Can., 1967, CA, 1970. Mgr. Coopers & Lybrand, Toronto, 1973-77, ptnr., 1977-85, ptnr. in charge of tax group, 1985-86; v.p., CFO Hollinger Inc., Toronto, 1986-98, exec. v.p., CFO, 1999—2002; exec. v.p. Hollinger Internat. Inc., Toronto, 2002—03; pub. Saturday Night Mag., Toronto, 1988-89; pres. Saturday Night Mag. Inc., Toronto, 1989-94; vice-chmn. Saturday Night Mag. Ltd., Toronto, 1994-96, vice-chmn., pres., 1996-98. Bd. dirs. Hollinger Inc., Toronto, Argus Corp. Ltd., Toronto, Consol. Enfield Corp., Toronto, Iamgold Corp., Toronto; bd. govs. Royal St. George's Coll., Toronto. Editor, contbr. Can. Tax Jour., 1980-86. Mem.: Can. Inst. Chartered Accts., Osler Bluffs Ski Club. Avocations: bicycling, tennis, running, skiing, golf.

BOULUD, DANIEL, chef, restaurant owner; b. France, Mar. 25, 1955; Chef, Copenhagen, European Commn., Wash., DC, Polo Lounge, NYC; owner, chef Le Régence, NYC; exec. che Le Cirque, NYC, 1986—92; owner Daniel, NYC, 1993—, Café Boulud, NYC, 1998—, Palm Beach, DB Bistro Moderne, NYC, 2001—, Daniel Boulud Brasserie, 2005, Feast & Fêtes Catering, Daniel Boulud Connoisseur line. Author: Cooking with Daniel Boulud, 1993; author: (with Dorie Greenspan) Daniel Boulud's Cafe Boulud Cookbook: French American Recipes for the Home Cook, 1999; author: Letters to a Young Chef, 2003; author: (with Peter Kaminsky, Martin H.M. Schreiber) Chef Daniel Boulud: Cooking in New York City, 2002; author: (with Margaret Russell) Daniel's Dish: Entertaining at Home With a Four-Star Chef, 2003; author: (with Melissa Clark) Braise, 2006. Named Chef Yr., Bon Appétit mag.; recipient Top Table award, Gourmet mag., Outstanding Restaurateur award, James Beard Found., 2006. Office: Daniel 60 E 65th St New York NY 10021 Office Phone: 212-288-4141.*

BOULWARE, BOBBIE L., music educator; b. Mt. Airy, NC, Feb. 19, 1949; s. Willie James and Annie Mae Teletha (Pearson) Boulware. BA in Music Edn., Montclair State U., NJ, 1971; MA in Music Edn., Jersey City State U., NJ, 1991. Music tchr. Newark Pub. Sch. Dist., 1973—76, Scotch Plains Sch. Dist., 1976—79, Mountain Lakes Sch. Dist., 1979—2006. Adj. prof. Seton Hall U., S. Orange, 1980—; accompanist N.J. Oratorio Soc., Montclair, 1993—2003; bd. mem., performer Assisi Music Festival, Italy, 2000—; lectr. in field. Ch. organist Van Riper Ellis Broadway Bapt. Ch., 1995—. Recipient Dr. Jack Sacher Lctr. Series award, Montclair State U., 2004. Mem.: Music Educator's Nat. Conf., Nat. Assn. Bapt. Musicians, Knights of Malta. Baptist. Avocations: reading, cooking, composing, writing, poetry. Home: 25 New Hampshire St Newton NJ 07860

BOULWARE, MARGARET A., lawyer; b. New Bedford, Mass., Oct. 22, 1947; d. Louis Melvin and Sarah Trezvant (Symmes) Boulware; m. Hartley Hampton. BS, U. Ga., 1969; MS, Clemson U., 1970; JD, U. Houston, 1975. Bar: Tex. 1976, Ct. Appeals Fifth Circuit 1976, 11th Circuit 1981, US Fed. Circuit 1990, US Supreme Ct. 2006. Assoc. Vinson & Elkins, Houston, 1976—81; ptnr. Vaden, Eckenroht & Boulware, Houston, 1981—95; shareholder Fish & Richardson, Houston, 1995—98, Jenkens & Gilchrist, Houston, 1998—2005. Pres. Houston Intellectual Property Law Assn., 1994—95, Am. Intellectual Property Law Assn., 1998—99; chair patent pub. adv. com. US Patent & Trademark Office, 1999—. Bd. trustees Clemson U. Found., SC, 1999—, Houston Grand Opera, 2000—. Recipient Dean's award, U. Houston Law Ctr., 1986, 1991, chair award, State Bar of Tex., I.P. Section, 1997. Fellow: Houston Bar Found., State Bar Tex. Found. Office: Baker Mckenzie 711 LA St Pennzoil Place South Tower Houston TX 77002 Home: 310 Park Laureate Dr Houston TX 77024 Office Phone: 713-427-5003. Office Fax: 713-427-5099. Business E-Mail: meg.boulware@bakernet.com.

BOULWARE, MICHAEL, professional football player; b. Columbia, SC, Sept. 17, 1981; Studied Sports Mgmt., Fla. State Univ. Safety Seattle Seahawks, 2004—. Office: Seattle Seahawks Qwest Field 800 Occidental Ave S Seattle WA 98134

BOUMA, ROBERT EDWIN, lawyer; b. Ft. Dodge, Iowa, July 19, 1938; s. Jack and Gladys (Cooper) B.; m. Susan Lawson, Nov. 26, 1963; children: James, Whitley. BA, Coe Coll., 1960; JD, U. Iowa, 1962. Bar: Iowa 1962, N.Y. 1964, Ill. 1985. Asso. Cravath, Swaine & Moore, NYC, 1962-70; gen. counsel Xerox Data Systems Co., Los Angeles, 1970-73; sr. group counsel Xerox Corp., Rochester, N.Y., 1973-76; asso. gen. counsel Monsanto Co., St. Louis, 1976-78; sr. v.p., gen. counsel Household Internat., Prospect Heights, Ill., 1978-84; ptnr., chmn. firm trial dept. McDermott Will & Emery LLP, Chgo., 1984—. Trustee Coe Coll., Ill. Inst. Continuing Legal Edn. Served with USN, 1962-63, v.p. bd. dir. IA Law Sch. Found. Mem. ABA (co-chmn. com. on corp. counsel lit. sect.), Chgo. Bar Assn. Clubs: Mid-Day (Chgo.); Winter (Lake Forest, Ill.); Onwentsia (Lake Forest, Ill.); Legal of Chgo. Home: 901 Church Rd Lake Forest IL 60045-1457 Office: McDermott Will & Emery LLP 227 W Monroe St Ste 3100 Chicago IL 60606-5096 Office Fax: 312-984-7700, 312-984-7718. Business E-Mail: rbouma@mwe.com.

BOUNDS, HANK M., school system administrator; b. Hattiesburg, Miss. m. Susie Bounds; children: Will, Caroline. BS, U. So. Miss., 1991, MS in Ednl. Adminstrn., 1994; PhD, U. Miss., 2000. Tchr. Petal and Moss Point high schools, Miss.; prin. Forrest County HS, Bklyn., Miss., Lumberton, Miss., Pascagoula HS; supt. Pascagoula Sch. Dist.; state supt. edn. Miss. Dept. Edn., 2005—. Mem. S.E. Regional Adv. Bd US Dept of Edn, mem. Nat. Forum on Edn. Statistics. With Miss. Army Nat. Guard. Named Edn. Alumnus of Yr., U. Miss., 2003; recipient Nat. Reading Renaissance Award, 2003. Mem.: Nat. Assn. of Secondary Sch. Prin.'s (Adminstr. of Yr. for Miss. 2001). Office: Miss Dept Edn / Ctr HS PO Box 771 Jackson MS 39205 Office Fax: 601-359-3513.*

BOUNDS-SEEMANS, PAMELLA J., artist; b. Milton, Del., Nov. 5, 1948; d. James Wilson Bounds and Marguerite Edna (Rickards) Bounds Carey; m. Jeffrey Wayne Seemans, Mar. 20, 1984; children: Misty Autumn, Sterling Hunter, Jordan Windsor. BA, N.Mex. Highlands U., 1971, MA, 1972. Tchr. elem. art Indian River Sch. Dist., Frankford, Del., 1973-79. Lectr. U. Md., 1981, U. Del., 1986, Del. Tech. and C.C., 1988, 75th Del. Women's Day Conf. at U. Del., U. Del. Coll. Arts and Mineralogy, 1999. Exhibited in group shows including Rehoboth (Del.) Art League, 1980, 89, 90, 92, 93, Tideline Gallery, Rehoboth Beach, Del., 1980—, Greenville, Del., 1993, Wicomico Art League, 1980, Del. Tech. and C.C., Georgetown, 1981, U. Md., 1981, Bluestreak Gallery, Wilmington, Del., 1989—, Blue Streak Art Gallery, Wilmington, 1993, Jamison Gallery, Santa Fe, 1993—, Del. Art Mus., 1996, Biennal 96 and 98 Del. Art Mus., U. Del., 1999, Am. Mus. Visionary Arts, Balt., 2000, numerous others; represented in permanent collections including Wilmington (Del.) Trust Co., Del. Nat. Bank, Sussex County Courthouse, Del. Parks and Recreation Bldg., Del. State Folklore Collection, also numerous pvt. collections; poster for mayor's office Clifford Brown Jazz Festival, Wilmington, 1998; mem. cmty. adv. editl. bd. News Jour., Gannett Papers, Wilmington, 1997-98; artist Dino Doys Rennaissance Corp.; author: Delaware Folk Artist Collection Book and Collection, 2006. Donated art work to oncology ctr. Beebe Hosp. Found., 1995, Multiple Sclerosis Found. Del., Ronald McDonald House Del.; mem. cmty. adv. bd. News Jour. editl. Staff, 1997—; mem. Parents Adv. Bd. U. Del., 2004-07. Recipient award for outstanding body of work Torpedo Factory, Alexandria, Va., 1982; fellow State of Del. Divsn. of the Arts, 1995. Mem. Nat. Mus. of Women in the Arts, Del. Art Mus., Tunnel 2d place award for most outstanding work in exhibit 1990, Popular Vote award 1980, 93, 94, 95, 96, 1st place award 1993, hon.), Del. Ctr. for Contemporary Arts, Del. Ctr. for Creative Arts, Newark Arts Alliance, Del. Nature Soc., Mothers Multiple Births (v.p. 1987), Wicomo Art League (hon. mention 1981), Univ. and Whist Club (Wilmington). Avocations: criminology, fashion, psychology, gourmet cooking. Home: 1203 Greenbank Rd Wilmington DE 19808-5842

BOURCIER, RICHARD JOSEPH, retired French language and literature educator; b. New Bedford, Mass., Dec. 25, 1930; s. Adrien and Alida (Richard) B.; m. Florence Rita Michaud, June 17, 1961 (dec. Nov. 26, 1994); children: Michelle, Camille, Jeanine, Normand, Paul. AB, Assumption Coll., 1958; MA in French, Laval U., 1959; PhD in Comparative Lit., SUNY, Binghamton, 1983. Instr. New Bedford (Mass.) Pub. Sch. Sys., 1959-60, Coll. of the Holy Cross, Worcester, Mass., 1961-68; asst. then assoc. prof. U. Scranton (Pa.), 1968—83; prof. U. Scranton, Pa., 1983—97; ret., 1994. Dir. French house U. Scranton, 1989-94. Cantor Ch. St. Gregory, Clarks Green, Pa., 1973—. Sgt. U.S. Army, 1953-55. Decorated Chevalier/Knight Order of Acad. Palms (French govt.). Mem. MLA, AAUP, Am. Assn. Tchrs. French, Institut Français, Assn. des Amis de Georges Duhamel, U.S.A. Dance, Inc. (formerly US Amateur Ballroom Dancers Assn.). Avocations: woodworking, music, dance. Home: 103 Belmont Ave Clarks Green PA 18411-1101 Office Phone: 570-941-4014.

BOURDAIN, ANTHONY, chef, writer; b. NYC, June 25, 1956; m. Ottavia Busia, Apr. 20, 2007; 1 child, Ariane. Attended, Vasser Coll.; grad., Culinary Inst. Am. Chef Supper Club, NYC, One Fifth Ave., Sullivan's; exec. chef Brasserie Les Halles. Author: Bone in the Throat, 1995, Gone Bamboo, 1997, Kitchen Confidential: Adventures in the Culinary Underbelly, 2000, Typhoid Mary: An Urban Historical, 2001, Cook's Tour: In Search of the Perfect Meal, 2001, Cook's Tour: Global Adventures in Extreme Cuisines, 2002, The Bobby Gold Stories, 2003, Anthony Bourdain's Les Halles Cookbook: Strategies, Recipies, and Techniques of Classic Bistro Cooking, 2004, La Cocina de Les Halles: Strategies, Recipes and Techniques of Classic Bistro Cooking, 2005, The Nasty Bits: Collected Varietal Cuts, Usable Trim, Scraps, and Bones, 2006; host: (TV series) A Cook's Tour, 2002; Anthony Bourdain: No Reservations, 2005—.*

BOURDON, CATHLEEN JANE, professional society administrator; b. Sparta, Wis., July 13, 1948; d. Cletus John and Josephine Marie (Bourdon) Scheurich; children: Jill Krzyminski, Jeff Krzyminski. BA in Polit. Sci., U. Wis., 1973, MLS, 1974. Tchr. Peace Corps, Arba Minch, Ethiopia, 1969-72; asst. prof., dir. Alverno Coll. Libr., Milw., 1974-83; dep. exec. dir. Assn. Coll. and Rsch. Librs., Chgo., 1983-93; exec. dir. Ref. and User Svcs. Assn. divsn. ALA Assn. Specialized and Coop. Libr. Agys., Chgo., 1993—2007; assoc. exec. dir. ALA, 2007—. Mem. ALA (pres. Staff Assn. 1987-88). Avocations: movies, reading. Office: ALA 50 E Huron St Chicago IL 60611-5295 Office Phone: 312-280-3217. E-mail: cbourdon@ala.org.

BOURGAIZE, ROBERT G., economist; BA, U. Wash., 1949. Bd. dirs., sr. v.p. Peoples Nat. Bank, Seattle; pres. Central Bank, N.A., Tacoma, University Place Water Co., Epsilon Econ. Inc. Mem. Nat. Assn. Bus. Economists, English-Speaking Union U.S.A. (nat. dir.), Royal Commonwealth Soc., Am. Waterworks Assn. (life), Pacific Northwest Writers Conf., Adam Smith Econ. Found., Adam Smith Soc. (founder 1976), Theta Chi. Office: 4201 B Bridgeport Way W University Place WA 98466-4304

BOURGEAULT, RONALD, art appraiser; Antiques dealer, auctioneer, 1970—; owner antiques shop, Salem, Mass.; founder, prin., chief auctioneer Northeast Auctions, Portsmouth, NH, 1987—. Appraiser Antiques Roadshow, WGBH-PBS. Lectr. in field. Named one of Power Fifty Who Mattered Most, Art & Auction Mag., 2002. Mem.: NH Antiques Dealers Assn., Nat. Auctioneers Assn., Appraisers Assn. Am. Office: Northeast Auctions 93 Pleasant St Portsmouth NH 03801 Office Phone: 603-433-8400. Office Fax: 603-433-0415. Business E-Mail: neainfo@ttlc.net.

BOURGEOIS, LOUISE, sculptor; b. Paris, Dec. 25, 1911; arrived in US, 1938, naturalized, 1953; m. Robert Goldwater, 1938 (dec. 1973); 3 children. Student, Sorbonne U., 1932-35; baccalaureate, Ecole des Beaux Arts, 1936-38; postgrad., Ecole du Louvre, 1936-37, Acad. Grande Chaumiere; D.F.A. (hon.), Yale U., 1977, Calif. Coll. Arts and Crafts, 1988, Moore Coll. Art, Mass. Coll. Art, 1983, Md. Art Inst., 1984, The New Sch., 1987. Instr. Md. Art Inst., Balt., 1984, New Sch. Social Rsch., NYC, 1987. One-woman shows include Norlyst Gallery, 1947, Peridot Gallery, 1949, 50, 53, Allan Frumkin Gallery, Chgo., 1953, White Art Mus., Cornell U., Ithaca, N.Y., 1959, Stable Gallery, 1964, Rose Fried Gallery, 1963, 112 Greene St., N.Y.C., 1974, Xavier Fourcade Gallery, N.Y.C., 1978-80, Max Hutchinson Gallery, N.Y.C., 1980, Renaissance Soc., 1981, Mus. Modern Art, N.Y.C., 1982, retrospective Contemporary Art Mus., Houston, 1983, Daniel Weinberg Gallery, L.A., 1984, Robert Miller Gallery, 1982, 84, 87-89, 91, Serpentine Gallery, London, 1985, Maeght-Lelong, Zurich, 1985, Paris, 1985, Taft Mus., Cin., 1987-89 (travelled to The Art Mus. at Fla. Internat. U., Miami, Fla., Laguna Gloria Art Mus., Austin, Tex., Gallery of Art, Washington U., St. Louis, Henry Art Gallery, Seattle, Everson Mus. Art, Syracuse, N.Y.), Mus. Overholland, Amsterdam, The Netherlands, 1988, Dia Art Found., Bridgehampton, N.Y., retrospective Frankfurter Kunstverein, Frankfurt, Fed. Republic Germany, 1989 (travelled to Städtische Galerie im Lenbachhaus, Munich, 1990, Riverside Studios, London, 1990, Musée d'Art Contemporain, Lyon, 1990, Fondacion Tapies, Barcelona, Spain, Kunstmuseum, Berne, Switzerland, Kröller-Müller Mus., Otterlo, The Netherlands), Linda Cathcart Gallery, Santa Monica, Calif., 1990, Barbara Gross Gallerie, Munich, 1990, Karsten Schubert, London, 1990, Galerie Krinzinger, Vienna, 1990, Karsten Greve Gallery, Cologne, 1990, Ginny Williams Gallery, 1990, Monika Sprüthe Galerie, Cologne, 1990, Robert Miller Gallery 1986, 1987, 1988, 1989, 1991, Galerie Lelong, Zurich, 1991; solo exhbns. include Parrish Art Mus., Southampton, N.Y., Ydessa Hendeles Found., Toronto, 1991, 92, Milwaukee Art Mus., 1992, The Fabric Workshop, Phila., Galerie Karsten Greve, Paris, Linda Cathcart Gallery, Santa Monica, Calif., Second Floor, Reykjavik, Iceland; exhibited in numerous group shows, U.S., Europe including Sculpture Ctr., 1997, Jim Kempner Fine Art, 1997, Steinbaum Krauss Gallery, 1998, Mary Boone Gallery, 1998, Am. Craft Mus., 1998; represented in permanent collections Mus. Modern Art, N.Y.C., Whitney Mus., Met. Mus. Art, Hirshorn Mus., Musée Nat. D'Art Moderne, Paris, R.I. Sch. Design, NYU, Albright-KnAustralian Nat. Gallery, Canberra, Musée d'Art Moderne, Paris, Mus. Fine Arts, Houston, Guggenheim Mus., N.Y.C., Kunstmus. Bern, stmus. Lucerne, Albertina, Vienna, Mus. Modern Art, Vienna, Walker Art Ctr., Mpls., Storm King Art Ctr., Mountainville, N.Y., New Mus. Contemporary Art, N.Y.C., DC Moore Gallery, N.Y.C., Cheim & Read Gallery, N.Y.C., Denver Art Mus., Colo.; appeared in Limited Edition Artists Books 1990; public works include installation sculpture (with Alan Wanzenberg) Hold Me Close, Hat Nopparat Nat. Pk., Thailand, 2007. Recipient Outstanding Achievement award Women's Caucus, 1980, Pres.'s Fellow award R.I. Sch. Design, 1984, Skowhegan medal sculpture Skowhegan (Maine) Sch. Painting, and Sculpture, Gold medal of honor Nat. Arts Club, 1987, Creative Arts Medal award Brandeis U., 1989, Grand Prix Nat. de Sculpture French Ministry of Culture, 1991, Nat. medal arts, 1999, Wolf prize in arts Wolf Found., Israel, 2003; recipient Lifetime Achievement award Coll. Art Assn., 1989, Internat. Sculpture Ctr., 1991; named Officer of Arts and Letters French Ministry of Culture, 1984. Fellow Am. Acad. Arts and Scis.; mem. Am. Acad. and Inst. Arts and Letters, Sculptors Guild, Am. Abstract Artists, Coll. Art Assn. (Disting. Artist award for lifetime achievement 1989). Office: Robert Miller Gallery 524 W 26th St Ground Fl New York NY 10001-5541*

BOURGEOIS, PATRICIA MCLIN, academic administrator, women's health and pediatrics nurse, educator; b. Hammond, La., Mar. 12, 1941; d. Lannie McLin and Mary (Lossett) Nicolay; m. Charles Bourgeois, June 10, 1962; children: Deborah, Cynthia, Terry Kay, Lori, Betsy. BSN, McNeese State U., 1962; MSN, Northwestern State U., Natchitoches, La., 1980. Cert. clin. nurse specialist, nursing child assessment, La. Office nurse pediatrics Green Clinic, Ruston, La., 1962-63; staff nurse ob-gyn. Lincoln Gen. Hosp., Ruston, 1963-64; staff nurse nursery St. Francis Cabrini Hosp., Alexandria, La., 1966-67; prof. maternal/child nursing La. Tech. U., Ruston, 1975—, faculty senate v.p., 2005—, faculty senate pres., 2006. Part-time office nurse Green Clinic, 1975-93; part-time resident nurse Methodist Children's Home, Ruston, 1990-97. Vice chairperson La. Coalition for Maternal/Infant Health, Baton Rouge, 1989-91; pres. Ruston Civic Guild, 1990. Recipient Inst. Regulatory Excellence fellow, Nat. Coun. State Bd. Mem. ANA (del. 1991-93), La. State Nurses Assn. (sec. 1991-93, pres. 1994-95), La. State Bd. of Nursing (apptd. mem., v.p. 2004, pres. 2005). Democrat. Roman Catholic. Office: La Tech Univ PO Box B 152 Ruston LA 71272-3178

BOURGET, EDWIN ROBERT, marine ecologist, educator; b. Senneterre, Que., Can., July 6, 1946; s. Jean-Paul and Myrtle (O'Malley) B.; m. Paule Reny, June 16, 1969; children: Frédéric, Virginie. BSc, U. Laval, Que., 1969, MSc, 1971; PhD, U. Wales, 1974. Oceonology rschr. U. Que., Rimouski, 1974-76; adj. prof. U. Laval, 1976-80, assoc. prof., 1980-84, prof., 1984—, dir. biology dept., 1997-98, vice dean rsch. faculty sci. engring., 1998-2001, vice rector rsch., 2007—, U. Sherbrooke, Que., 2001—07. Author/co-author 6 books or book chpts.; contbr. numerous articles to profl. jours. Recipient Michel-Jurdant prize, Can.-French Assn. Advancement Sci., 1996; grantee in field. Mem. Groupe Interuniversitaire de recherches oceanographiques du Que. (dir. 1993-96), Natural Sci. and Engring. Rsch. Coun. (adv. bds. 1987-91), Fonds pour la Formation de Chercheurs et l'Aide a la Recherche, Nat. Sci. and Engring. Rsch. Coun. Office: Pavilion des Scis de Edn University Laval Laval PQ Canada 1K 7PA Office Phone: 418-656-2599. Business E-Mail: edwin.bourget@ulaval.ca.

BOURGUIGNON, ERIKA EICHHORN, anthropologist, educator; b. Vienna, Feb. 18, 1924; d. Leopold H. and Charlotte (Rosenbaum) Eichhorn; m. Paul H. Bourguignon, Sept. 29, 1950. BA, Queens Coll., 1945; grad. study, U. Conn., 1945; PhD, Northwestern U., 1951; DHL, CUNY, 2000. Field work Chippewa Indians, Wis., summer 1946; field work Haiti; anthropologist Northwestern U., 1947-48; instr. Ohio State U., 1949-56, asst. prof., 1956-60, assoc. prof., 1960-66, prof., 1966-90, acting chmn. dept. anthropology, 1971-72, chmn. dept., 1972-76, prof. emeritus, 1990—; dir. Cross-Cultural Study of Dissociational States, 1963-68. Bd. dirs. Human Relations Area Files, Inc., 1976-79 Author: Possession, 1976, rev. edit., 1991, Psychological Anthropology, 1979, Italian transl., 1983; editor, co-author: Religion, Altered States of Consciousness and Social Change, 1973, A World of Women, 1980; co-author: Diversity and Homogeneity in World Societies, 1973; adv. editor: Behavior Sci. Rsch., 1976-79; assoc. editor Jour. Psychoanalytic Anthropology, 1977-87; mem. editl. bd. Ethos, 1979-89, 97—2005, 2005—, Jour. Haitian Studies, 2000—, Anthropology of Consciousness, 2002—; editor: Margaret Mead: The Anthropologist in America—, Occasional Papers in Anthropology, No. 2, Ohio State U. Dept. Anthropology, 1986; (with Barbara Rigney) Exile: A Memoir of 1939 by Bronka Schneider, 1998; contbr. articles to profl. jours. Fellow Am. Anthrop. Assn.; mem. Ctrl. State Anthrop. Soc. (treas. 1953-56, exec. com. 1995-98), Ohio Acad Sci., World Psychiat. Assn. (transcultural psychiatry sect.), Am. Ethnol. Soc., Current Anthropology (assoc.), Soc. for Psychol. Anthropology (nominations com. 1981-82, bd. dirs. 1991-93, lifetime achievement award 1999), Soc. for the Anthropology of Religion, Phi Beta Kappa, Sigma Xi. E-mail: bourguignon.1@osu.edu. *It is more important to enjoy doing what you do, and to be able to do what you want to do, than to be successful. Success, if it comes, is only a by-product, nothing more.*

BOURI, ANIL K., neurologist, director; arrived in US, 1973; s. Vidya Rattan and Shakuntla D. Bouri; m. Manjeet K. Dhillon, Jan. 17, 1972; 1 child, Anil Jr. MBBS, Panjab U., 1968, MD, 1972. Diplomate Am. Bd. Neurology and Psychiatry, Am. Bd. Sleep Medicine. Neurologist Gundersen Luth. Med. Ctr., Lacrosse, Wis., 1979—; med. dir. Wis. Sleep Disorders Ctr./Gundersen Med. Ctr., Lacrosse, 1986—. Fellow, Am. Assn. Electromyography and Electrodiagnosis. Office: Gundersen Luth Med Ctr 1910 S Ave La Crosse WI 54601

BOURKE-FAUSTINA, MARLENE FRANCES, music educator; b. Honolulu, Mar. 10, 1944; d. Francis Patrick and Violet Kahale Bourke; m. Manuel Edward Faustina, Jan. 3, 1990; children: Aaron Faustina, Christian Faustina, Shane Faustina. B.Mus.Edn., Walla Walla Coll., College Place, Wash., 1970; Profl. Diploma in Music Edn., U. Hawaii, Honolulu, 1973. Music tchr. Umatilla County #31/K-8, Milton-Freewater, Oreg., 1970—72; chorus/band/vocal coach Hawaiian Mission Acad., Honolulu, 1974—76; chorus, music tchr. Hawaiian Mission Elem. Acad. K-12, Honolulu, 1974—76, Waianae Intermediate Sch., Waianae, 1977—84, Highlands Intermediate Sch., Pearl City, Hawaii, 1984—88, Wahiawa Intermediate Sch., 1988—92, Waianae Intermediate Sch., 1992—. Vocalist Royal Hawaiian Band, Honolulu, 1972—77, Ctrl. Union Ch., Honolulu, 1977—84, Kawaihao Ch., Honolulu, 2005—06. Dir., coord. Roses Waianae Charity WIS Campaign for Homeless. Named Outstanding Secondary Educators of Am. award, 1978, Hawaii Leeward State Tchr. of the Yr., 1985, 2003; recipient Outstanding Alumni award, Kamehameha Schs., 1970. Mem.: Am. Choral Dirs. Assn., Music Educators Nat. Conf. Democrat. Seventh-Day Adventist. Avocations: designing Hawaiian floral arrangements, gardening, arranging music. Home: 85-223 C Ala Akau St Waianae HI 96792 Office: Waianae Intermediate Sch 85-626 Farrington Hwy Waianae HI 96792 Business E-Mail: marlene-bourke-faustina@notes.k12.hi.us.

BOURM, ROGER MICHAEL, real estate broker, investor, property manager; b. Bellingham, Wash., May 31, 1954; s. John Milton and Gloria June Bourm; children: Matina Mary June, Allyse Nicole. A in Tech., Point Pierce Coll., 1976. Registered tech. Am. Registry Radiologic Techs., 1976; assoc. broker Wash., 1997. Registered tech St Joseph Hosp., Bellingham, Wash., 1976—79; gen. sales mgr Wilson Motors, 1979—93; assoc. broker Coldwell Banker, 1995—2007; owner Bourm Properties, 1995—. Chair Pacific N.W. chpt. The Arthritis Found., 2001—. With med. corps. dept. def. US Army, 1974—76. Mem.: Am. Registry Radiologic Techs., Nat. Assn. Realtors (assoc.). Home: 516 16th St Bellingham WA 98225 Office: Bourm Properties 516 16th St Bellingham WA 98225 Office Phone: 360-739-5624. Fax: 360-671-8868. Personal E-mail: bourm@aol.com.

BOURNE, CHARLES PERCY, information scientist, educator; b. San Francisco, Sept. 2, 1931; s. Frank Percy and Edith (Dunlap) B.; m. Elizabeth A. Scheidtmann, Aug. 15, 1953; children— Glen Wade, Holly Ann. BS in Elec. Engring., U. Calif., Berkeley, 1957; MS in Indsl. Engring., Stanford, 1963. Sr. research engr. Stanford Research Inst., Menlo Park, Calif., 1957-66; v.p. Information Gen. Corp., Palo Alto, Calif., 1966-70; pres. Charles Bourne & Assos., Menlo Park, 1970—; prof. in residence Sch. Library and Info. Studies; dir. Inst. Library Research U. Calif.-Berkeley, 1971-77; v.p. gen. info. div. Dialog Info. Svcs., Inc., Palo Alto, 1977-92. Research in info. scis. for libraries, schs., acads., including Library of Congress, Nat. Agrl. Library, U.S. Patent Office, Nat. Acad. Sci.; Guest lectr. univs. including U. Calif. at Berkeley, 1963-66; Sarada Ranganathan lectr., Bangalore, India, 1978; cons. corr. Nat. Acad. Sci. com. on sci. and tech. information, 1968-70; mem. adv. bd. Chem. Abstracts, 1965-68, Ency. Library and Information Scis., 1967— , Documentation Abstracts, 1968-69, Ann. Rev. Information Sci. and Tech., 1966; mem. adv. bd. World Affairs Report, 1987-90; U.S. rep. to a com. of Internat. Fedn. for Documentation, 1966-76; UNESCO cons. to Indonesia and Tanzania; Nat. Acad. Scis. cons. to Ghana, 1976; mem. U.S.-Egyptian Task Force on Tech. Info. Problems, 1976, U.S. del. UNESCO Intergovtl. Conf. Sci. and Tech. Info. for Devel., 1979; mem. Network Adv. Com. Library of Congress, 1987-92; delegate -at-large White House Conf. Lib. and Info. Svcs., 1991. Author: Methods of Information Handling, 1963, Technology in Support of Library Science and Information Service, 1980; co-author: A History of Online Information Services, 2003; contbr. articles profl. jours. Served with USMCR, 1950-51. Recipient ann. award of merit Am. Documentation Inst., 1965 Mem. Am. Soc. Information Sci. and Tech. (pres. 1970, Best Info. Sci. Book award 2004), ALA (dir. information scis. and automation div. 1966-67), Nat. Info. Standards Orgn. (bd. dirs. 1987-90). Home: 1619 Santa Cruz Ave Menlo Park CA 94025-5761

BOURNE, HENRY CLARK, JR., electrical engineer, educator, retired academic administrator; b. Tarboro, NC, Dec. 31, 1921; s. Henry Clark and Marion (Alston) B.; m. Margaret Barr Thomas, Aug. 15, 1953; children: Katherine Wimberley, Henry Clark III, Thomas Franklin, Margaret Alston. S.B., MIT, 1947, S.M., 1948, Sc.D., 1952. Registered profl. engr., Calif., Tex. Asst. prof. Mass. Inst. Tech., 1952-54; asst. prof., then assoc. prof. U. Calif. at, Berkeley, 1954-63; prof. elec. engring. Rice U., Houston, 1963-77, chmn. dept., 1963-74; sect. head engring. div. NSF, Washington, 1974-75, div. dir. engring., 1977-79; dep. asst. dir. Directorate Engring. and Applied Sci., 1979-81; v.p. for acad. affairs Ga. Inst. Tech., Atlanta, 1981-86, 87-88, acting pres., 1986-87, prof. elec. engring., 1988-92, prof. elec. engring. emeritus, 1992—. Cons. editor Harper & Row, N.Y.C., 1961-67; cons. elec. engring., 1952— Author tech. papers in field of magnetics. Served to 1st lt. C.E. AUS, 1943-46. Sci. Faculty fellow NSF, 1960-61; hon. research assoc. Univ. Coll. London; Eng., 1961 Fellow IEEE, AAAS; mem. Am. Phys. Soc., Am. Soc. Engring. Edn., Sigma Xi, Tau Beta Pi, Eta Kappa Nu, Phi Kappa Phi, Omicron Delta Kappa, Beta Gamma Sigma, Delta Tau Delta. Episcopalian. Home: 173 Windrush Rd Winston Salem NC 27106

BOURNE, HENRY R., pharmacology professor, department chairman, researcher; b. Danville, Va., Mar. 1, 1940; m.; three children. MD, Johns Hopkins U., 1965. Instr. in medicine U. Calif., San Francisco, 1971—72, asst. prof. medicine and pharmacology, 1972—75, assoc. prof. medicine and pharmacology, 1975—81, chief, div. of clinical pharmacology, 1980—83, sr. staff mem., Cardiovascular Rsch. Inst., 1980—, prof. medicine and cellular and molecular pharmacology, 1981—, prof., chair. dept. pharmacology, 1983—91, acting chair, dept. pharmacology, 1993—94. Editorial bd. Science, 1988—, Molecular Biology of the Cell, 1991—, UCSF Mag., 1992—, Current Biology, 1993—, Current Opinion in Cell Biology, 1994—, Sci. Perspectives, 1996—, Ency. Life Scis., 1997—. Recipient Merit award, NIH, 1990—91. Mem. AAAP, AAAS, NAS, Am. Assn. Cell Biology, Am. Soc. Pharmacology & Exptl. Therapeutics (Rawls-Palmer award, 1985), Am. Soc. Biol. Chemists, Inst. Medicine, Phi Beta Kappa, Alpha Omega Alpha. Office: Bourne Lab UCSF Box 2140 600 16th St San Francisco CA 94107 also: U Calif Box 0450 513 Parnassus Ave Med Sci 1212 San Francisco CA 94143-0450 Office Phone: 415-476-8162. Office Fax: 415-514-0169. E-mail: bourne@cmp.ucsf.edu.

BOURNE, KATHERINE DAY, journalist, educator; b. Lynn, Mass., Sept. 11, 1938; d. Schuyler Vandervort and Elsie Marie (Mayo) Day; m. William Nettleton Bourne; children: William Alexander, Katherine Loring. BS in Edn., Keene Tchrs. Coll., 1960; MEd, Harvard U., 1984. Tchr. Wachusett Regional High Sch., Holden, Mass., 1960-61; arts editor Bay State Banner, Boston, 1966—2006; dir. edn. Suffolk County House of Correction, Boston, 1979-84; edn. coord. Dept. Transitional Asst., Mass., 1984—2002, ret., 2002—; lead critic Kay Bourne Arts Report, 2006—. Adj. scholar Northeastern U., 2006—. Contbr. music revs. to Christian Sci. Monitor. Dir. rels. Crime-out, Boston, 1983; mem. Gov.'s Commn. on Status of Women, 1970-74; co-founder, dir. Harvard-Radcliffe Forum Theatre, Cambridge, 1964-68; bd. dirs., mem. ARC Greater Boston, 1987-95, NAACP Boston, 1978-81. NEH journalism fellow, 1978; recipient Melnea A. Cass award Greater Boston YMCA, 1984. Mem. NAACP (life). Avocations: collecting african-american literature, aerobics, photography, stamps, art relating to black history and life. Home: 52 High St Brookline MA 02445-7707

BOURNE, LYLE EUGENE, JR., psychology professor; b. Boston, Apr. 12, 1932; s. Lyle E. and Blanche (White) H. BA, Brown U., 1953. Asst. prof. psychology U. Utah, 1956-61, assoc. prof., 1961-63; vis. assoc. prof. U. Calif., Berkeley, 1961—62, vis. prof., 1968—69; assoc. prof. psychology U. Colo., Boulder, 1963—65, prof., 1965—2001, prof. emeritus, 2002—, dir. Inst. Cognitive Sci., 1979—83, chmn. dept. psychology, 1983—91; clin. prof. psychiatry U. Kans. Med. Ctr., 1967—90. Vis. prof. U. Wis., 1966, U. Mont., 1967, U. Hawaii, 1969; cons. in exptl. psychology, VA, 1965-93. Author: Human Conceptual Behavior, 1966, Psychology of Thinking, 1971, Psychology: Its Principles and Meanings, rev. edits., 1976, 79 82, 85, Cognitive Processes, 1979, rev. edit., 1986, Psychology: A Concise Introduction, 1988, Psychology: Behavior in Context, 1998; acad. editor: Basic Concept Series, Learning-Cognition Series, Scott, Foresman Pub. Co., 1970-76, Charles Merill Co., 1980-84, Advanced Psychological Texts Series, Sage Publications, 1992—; editor Jour. Exptl. Psychology: Human Learning and Memory, 1975-80; cons. editor Jour. Clin. Psychology 1975-97, Jour. Exptl. Psychology: Learning, Memory and Cognition, 1984-92, Memory and Cognition, 1984-89. Recipient Rsch. Scientist award NIHM, 1969-74. Mem.: APA (coun. editors 1975—80, coun. reps. 1976—79, chmn. early awards com. 1978—79, bd. sci. affairs 1978—81, coun. reps. 1986—89, bd. sci. affairs 1989—92, pres. divsn. 3 1992, publ. and commn. bd. 1995—), Coun. Grad. Depts. Psychology (exec. bd. 1985—89), Soc. Gen. Psychology (pres. 2001), Rocky Mountain Psychol. Assn. (pres. 1987—88), Fedn. Behavioral Psychol. and Cognitive Scis. (v.p. 1994—95, pres. 1995—97), Soc. Exptl. Psychologists (chmn. 1987—88), Psychonomic Soc. (governing bd. 1976—81, chmn. 1980—81), Sigma Xi. Home: 785 Northstar Ct Boulder CO 80304-1088 Home Phone: 303-776-7511; Office Phone: 303-492-4210. E-mail: lbourne@psych.colorado.edu.

BOURNE, MATTHEW, performing company executive, artistic director; BA in Dance/Theatre, Laban Centre, 1985. Dir., choreographer and artistic dir. Adventures in Motion Pictures, London, 1987—2002; founder New Adventures Dance Co., 2004—. Founder mem. Lea Anderson's The Featherstonehaughs, 1988. Stage works include: Overlap Lovers, 1987; Spitfire, 1988; Buck and Wing, 1988; The Infernal Gallop, 1989; Town & Country, 1991; The Nutcracker, 1992; Deadly Serious, 1992; The Percys of Fitzrovia, 1992; Highland Fling, 1994; Swan Lake, 1996; Cinderella, 1997; TV work includes Late Flowering Lust, 1993, Drip-A Narcissistic Love Story, 1993; choreographer As You Like It, 1989, Children of Eden, 1990, A Midsummer Night's Dream, 1991—92, The Tempest, 1991, Show Boat, 1991, Peer Gynt, 1994, Watch With Mother, 1994, Oliver!, 1994, Watch Your Step, 1995, Boutique, 1995, Roald Dahl's Red Riding Hood, 1995, A Play Without Words, 2004 (LA Drama Critics Cir. award for choreography, 2006); dir. & choreographer (plays) Edward Scisssorhands, 2007. Recipient Bonnie Bird award, A Place Portfolio commn. and a Barclays New Stages award for choreography, Hamburg Shakespeare Award for Arts, 2003, Nat. Dance Awards, Critics' Cir., 2004. Mailing: New Adventures Sadler's Wells Theatre Rosebery Ave London EC1R 4TN England*

BOURNE, PETER GEOFFREY, physician, educator, writer; b. Oxford, Eng., Aug. 6, 1939; s. Geoffrey Howard and Gwen (Jones) B.; m. Mary Elizabeth King, Nov. 9, 1974. MD, Emory U., 1962; MA in Anthropology, Stanford U., 1969. Fellow dept. psychiatry Med. Sch.; co-dir. Alcoholism Project, Emory U., 1962-63; intern King County Hosp., Seattle, 1963-64; rsch. psychiatrist Walter Reed Army Inst.; rschr. Washington, 1964-67; chief neuropsychiat. br. U.S. Army Med. Research Team, Vietnam, 1965-66; cons. S.E. Asia Health Br. (AID), Dept. State, 1966-67; resident dept. psychiatry, Stanford U. Med. Center, Palo Alto, Calif., 1967-69; dir. mental health unit Southside Comprehensive Health Center, Atlanta, 1969-71; founder, dir. Atlanta S Ctrl. Cmty. Mental Health Ctr., 1970-71; dir. Ga. Office Drug Abuse, 1971-72; spl. adviser for health affairs to Gov. Jimmy Carter of Ga., 1971-73; asst. dir. White House Spl. Action Office for Drug Abuse Prevention, 1972-74; cons. Drug Abuse Coun., Washington, 1974-76; pres. Found. for Internat. Resources, 1975-76; Mid-Atlantic coord., dep. campaign dir. Jimmy Carter Presdl. Campaign, 1975-76; spl. asst. for health issues to U.S. Pres., Washington, 1976-78; mem. U.S. del. to Exec. Coun. UNICEF, 1977; asst. sec. gen. UN, NYC, 1979-81; pres. Global Water, 1981-98; exec. v.p., pub. Devel. Internat., 1986-90; mem. U.S. Pres. Commn. on White House Fellows; head U.S. del. UN Devel. Program Governing Coun., 1978; emergency rm. physician Casualty Hosp., Washington, 1966-67; emergency room physician Kaiser Permanente Hosp., Santa Clara, Calif., 1967-69; psychiat. cons. Santa Clara County Hosp., 1968-69, San Mateo County Hosp., 1969; cons. WHO, Geneva, 1972, UN Divsn. on Narcotic Drugs, 1976; asst. prof. dept. psychiatry Emory U. Med. Sch., 1969-72, asst. prof. dept. preventive medicine and cmty. health, 1969-72; lectr. dept. psychiatry Harvard U. Med. Sch., 1974; v.p. Nat. Coordinating Coun. on Drug Abuse Edn., 1971-72; prof. psychiatry, chmn. dept. St. Georges Med. Sch., Grenada, 1979-98; pres. Peter Bourne Assocs., Washington, 1985-98. Mem. of jury The Lasker Awards, 1978—79; vice chancellor St. Georges U., Grenada, 1998—2001, vice chancellor emeritus, Grenada, 2001—; chmn. Med. Edn. Coop. with Cuba, 2000—; vis. scholar Green Coll., Oxford, England, 2001—; bd. dir. Inst. Human Virology, Balt., Nat. Grad. U., Wash., Student Partnerships Worldwide, London. Author: Men, Stress and Viet Nam, 1970; editor: Psychology and Physiology of Stress, 1969, (with R. Fox) Alcoholism: Progress in Research and Treatment, 1973, Addiction, 1974, Acute Drug Abuse Emergencies, 1976, Water Resources: Social and Economic Aspects, 1983, Fidel, A Biography of Fidel Castro, 1986, Jimmy Carter: A Comprehensive Biography from Plains to the Post-Presidency, 1997; mem. editorial bd. Psychiatry, 1968— , Am. Jour. Drug Alcohol Abuse, 1973—; contbr. articles to profl. jours. and chpts. to books. Bd. dirs. Save the Children Fedn., Inst. for So. Studies; chmn. global bd. dirs. Hunger Project; chmn., bd. trustees Council on Hemispheric Affairs, 1986—; chmn. bd. dirs. Am. Assn. World Health, 1982-98, Health and Devel. Internat., 1997—, Youth Advocate Program, 1998—, Med. Edn. Collaboration with Cuba, 1998—, Inst. Caribbean and Internat. Studies, Windward Islands Rsch. and Edn. Found. Served to capt. U.S. Army, 1964-67. Decorated Bronze Star medal, Air medal, Combat Medics badge; recipient William C. Menninger award Central Neuropsychiat. Assn., 1967, Pub. Svc. award Nat. Assn. State Drug Abuse Program Coordinators, 1974, Pub. Svc. award Assn. Chinese Ams., 1978; named one of Five Outstanding Young Men in America, Atlanta Jaycees, 1971, one of Five Outstanding Young Men in Ga., Ga. Jaycees, 1972. Fellow Am. Psychiat. Assn. (disting. life, chmn. task force on drugs and drug abuse edn. 1969-73); mem. AAAS, Ga. Psychiat. Assn., Washington Psychiat. Soc., Royal Soc. Medicine, Med. Assn. Ga., Soc. for Internat. Health (pres. 1988-92), Am. Med. Soc. on Alcoholism, Am. Anthrop. Assn., World Fedn. for Mental Health. Democrat. Home and Office: 2119 Leroy Pl NW Washington DC 20008-1848 Home Phone: 202-462-7266; Office Phone: 202-462-7266. Business E-Mail: pbourne@igc.org. *I have always felt that my training as a physician was only a starting point in using my life to touch, for the better, the lives of as large a number of people as possible, whether formulating national health policy for the President of the United States, through the United Nations, through the private voluntary agencies or the academic world. I believe that ultimate gratification can only come from the sense that one has left the world a better place than when one arrived.*

BOURNE, RUSSELL, publisher, author; b. Boston, Oct. 10, 1928; s. Standish T. and Sylvia (Russell) B.; m. Miriam Anne Young, Aug. 22, 1953 (dec.); children: Sarah Perkins, Jonathan, Louise Taber, Andrew Russell; m. Dora Grabfield Flash, Oct. 31, 1992. AB magna cum laude, Williams Coll., 1950. Reporter Life mag., 1950-53, asst. to Henry R. Luce, 1953-56; assoc. editor Archtl. Forum, 1956-59; editor Am. Heritage Jr. Library, 1959-64, Time-Life Books, Great Ages of Man, 1964-69; assoc. chief Nat. Geog. Book Service, 1969-72; partner Bourne-Thompson & Assocs., Washington, 1972-77; sr. editor Smithsonian Exposition Books, Washington, 1977-80; pub. Hearst Gen. Books, NYC, 1980-81; pub., editor Am. Heritage Books, NYC, 1981-83; pub. cons., 1984—. Author: View From Front Street, 1989, Red King's Rebellion, 1990, Floating West, 1992, Best of the Best Sparkman and Stephens Designs, 1995, Americans on the Move, 1995, Invention in America, 1996, Rivers of America, 1998, Gods of War, Gods of Peace, 2002, Cradle of Violence, 2006. Served with CIC, U.S. Army, Berlin, 1950-52. Home and Office: 390 Savage Farm Dr Ithaca NY 14850

BOURQUE, BOYD D., secondary school educator; Secondary tchr. Hahnville High Sch.; instr. TCP/IP and phys. networking La. State U., Baton Rouge. Recipient Tchr. Excellence award Internat. Tech. Edn. Assn., 1992.

BOURQUE, BRUCE JOSEPH, archaeologist, educator; b. Clinton, Mass., Dec. 27, 1943; s. Ellsworth Joseph and Doris Ilona Bourque; life ptnr. Diane Jean Chase; children: Garrett Bruce, Amanda Sarah. PhD, Harvard U., Cambridge, Mass., 1971; BA in Anthropology, U. Mass., 1965. Chief archaeologist Maine State Mus., Augusta, 1972—; sr. lectr. in anthropology Bates Coll., Lewiston, Maine, 1973—. Mem.: Am. Anthrop. Assn., Soc. Am. Archaeology. Office: Maine State Mus State Ho Sta 83 Augusta ME 04333 Home Phone: 207-623-1497; Office Phone: 207-287-6604. Business E-Mail: bruce_bourque@maine.gov.

BOURQUE, LOUISE, film director, film instructor; BA in Comm., Univ. de Moncton, 1986; BFA in Film Prodn., Concordia Univ., 1990; MFA in Filmmaking, Sch. Art Inst. Chgo., 1992. Film instr. Sch. Mus. Fine Arts, Boston. Dir.: (films) The People in the House, 1994, Going Back Home, 2000, Self Portrait Post Mortem, 2002, The Bleeding Heart of it, 2005. Achievements include appearing in Whitney Biennial, Whitney Mus. Art, NYC, 2006. Office: SMFA Boston 230 The Fenway Boston MA 02115

BOUSBIB, ARI, manufacturing executive; M math & mech. engring., Ecole Superieure des Travaux Publics, Paris; MBA, Columbia Univ. Assoc. Booz Allen & Hamilton, 1987—92, ptnr., 1992—97; v.p. strategic planning United Technologies Corp., Hartford, Conn., 1997—99, v.p. corp. strategy & develop., 1999—2000, COO Otis bus. unit, 2000—02, pres. Otis bus. unit, 2002—. Bd. dir. Best Buy Co. Office: United Technologies United technologies Bldg Hartford CT 06101*

BOUSHEK, RANDY L., insurance company executive; b. Mpls., Minn. B in math. with honors, Concordia Coll., 1979; grad., Minn. Mgmt. Acad., Carlson Sch. Mgmt., 1992. Actuarial & fin. mgmt. positions Thrivent Fin. for Lutherans, Mpls., 1981—99, sr. v.p., chief investment officer, 1999—2002, sr. v.p., treas., 2002—04, sr. v.p., CFO, 2004—. Fellow: Soc. Actuaries; mem.: Am. Acad. Actuaries. Office: Thrivent Fin for Lutherans 625 4th Ave S Minneapolis MN 55415*

BOUSSO, RAPHAEL, physicist, educator; PhD, Cambridge U., 1998. Postdoctoral fellow Stanford U., Kavli Inst. Theoretical Physics, Santa Barbara; fellow physics dept. Harvard U., 2002—03; mem. faculty to assoc. prof. physics dept. U. Calif., 2003—. Fellow Radcliffe Inst., 2002—03. Contbr. articles to sci. jours.; author: A Covariant Entropy Conjecture, 1999, The Holographic Principle, 2002, Light Sheets and Bekenstein's Bound, 2003; author: (with J. Polchinski) The String Theory Landscape, 2004; co-author: Quantization of Four Form Fluxes and Dynamical Neutralization of the Cosmological Constant, 2000. Named one of Brilliant 10, Popular Sci. mag., 2002; recipient NSF award, 2004. Office: Ctr Theoretical Physics U Calif Dept Physics 366 LeConte Hall 7300 Berkeley CA 94720-7300 Office Phone: 510-643-9195. E-mail: bousso@lbl.gov.

BOUSTANY, CHARLES W., JR., congressman, surgeon; b. Lafayette, La., Feb. 21, 1956; s. Charles and Madlyn Boustany; m. Bridget Edwards, 1979; children: Erik, Ashley. BS, Univ. Southwestern La., 1978; MD, La. State Univ., New Orleans, 1982. Surgeon, pvt. practice, Lafayette, La., 1990—2004; mem. US Congress from 7th La. dist., 2005—. Mem. Lafayette Parish Rep. exec. com., 1996—2001. Bd. dir. Greater Lafayette C. of C., 2001, v.p. govt. affairs, 2002; mem. tissue adv. bd. La. Organ Procurement Agy.; bd. dir. Lafayette Gen. Med. Ctr. Mem.: Lafayette Parish Med. Soc. (pres. 2000). Republican. Office: US Ho Reps 1117 Longworth Ho Office Bldg Washington DC 20515-1807 Office Phone: 202-225-2031. Office Fax: 202-225-5724.*

BOUTH, MICHAEL T., marketing executive; b. Houston, Mar. 7, 1950; s. James C. Booth and Gertrude L. Sandifer; m. Vivian K. Mitchell (div.); children: Taylor L. Booth, Geoffrey M. Booth; m. Diana V. Krauchenko, Sept. 17, 2004. BA, U. Houston. Programmer, analyst Exxon, Houston, 1978—85; sr. analyst Computer Horizons, Cin., 1985—86; tech. mktg. mgr. Digital Equipment Corp., Nashua, NH, 1986—90; mktg. mgr. Cognos Corp., Schaumburg, Ill., 1990—92; sr. mktg. strategist Software AG, Reston, Va., 1993—96; electronic media mgr. Silvon Software, Westmont, Ill., 1997—99; mktg. dir. SLP Infoware, Chgo., 1999—2000; dir. global mktg. and rsch. Comptia, Oakbrook Terrace, Ill., 2000—02; pvt. practice cons. Naperville, Ill., 2002—06; dir. mktg. and membership AASM, Westchester, Ill., 2006—. Mem.: Mensa. Avocation: golf.

BOUTIN II, BERNIE L., information technology executive; s. Bernard L. and Alice B. Boutin; m. Gay Stern, May 16, 2000; 1 child, Ryan Boutin. AS, NH Tech. Inst., Concord, 1988. Gen. mgr. VDI Techs., Inc., Portsmouth, NH, 1993—2000, EME, Inc., Portsmouth, 2001—. Product cons. TransQuick, Inc., Atlanta, 1996—98. Sec. Springbrook Bd. Dirs., Portsmouth, 1999—2002. Democrat. Roman Catholic. Avocations: golf, travel, swimming. Home: 11 Lynette Ln Fremont NH 03044 Office: EME Inc 1981 Woodbury Ave Portsmouth NH 03801 Home Phone: 603-734-2433; Office Phone: 603-430-9999. Office Fax: 603-430-0700. Business E-Mail: bboutin@allwirelessinfo.com.

BOUTIS, TOM, artist, painter, printmaker; b. NYC, Aug. 25, 1922; s. Athanasios and Olga (Toskos) B.; m. Bertha Peters, Nov. 15, 1953; 1 child, Athanasios. BFA, Cooper Union U. Artist: one-person exhbns. include Drawings, Cooper Union, N.Y.C., 1953, Paintings: Zabriesky Gallery, N.Y.C., 1955, Am. Embassy, Rome, Italy, 1957, Area Gallery, N.Y.C., 1959, 60, Art Ctr. No. N.J., Tenafly, N.J., 1968; Decade on Paper, Landmark Gallery, N.Y.C., 1976, Paper on Paper, 1978, Cylinders, Columns, Circles and Color, 1979, Shadow Drawings, 1989, Monoprints, 1981, Painting, 1972, 75, 77, 81, Paintings and Monoprints, Maurice M. Pine Libr., Fairlawn, N.J., 1985, Works on Paper, Greek Embassy, 1989; 2-man exhbns. (with Alex Katz) Tanager Gallery, N.Y.C., 1958; group exhbns. include Greek Am. artists Noemata, Bklyn. Mus., 1977, Art Callender, Cooper Union Alumni Exhbn., N.Y.C., 1978, Landmark Gallery, N.Y.C., 1972, 82, Contemporary Drawings, Louise Ross Gallery, N.Y.C., 1984, Xmas Invitation, A.I.R., N.Y.C., 1985, Works on Paper, Ann Weber Gallery, Georgetown, Maine, 1987, Gallery Artists and Friends, Am. Acad. Arts & Letters, N.Y.C., 1988, 89, Shapolsky Gallery, N.Y.C., 1988, Arsenal Invitational, Arsenal Gallery, N.Y.C., 1989, Out of the 50's Snyder Fine Art, N.Y.C., 1993, Nat. Acad. Design, N.Y.C., 1992, 93, 95, 97, 99, 2001, 03, 05, Monhegan Island Artists, The Governor's Mansion, Augusta, Maine, 1996, Works on Paper, Bergen Mus., N.J., 1998, Greek Am. Artists Queens Mus., 1999, (drawing show) Nat. Acad., 2003; represented in public collections at NYU, Everson Mus., Syracuse, N.Y., Chem. Bank, N.Y.C., Prudential Bache, N.Y.C., Resource Mgmt., N.Y.C., St. Michel's Hosp., Newark, Calvin Klein Collection, N.Y.C., Calvin Klein Works on Paper, Weisbaden German, Nieully, France, N.Y. Hilton, Broad Nat. Bank of Newark and many others. Recipient scholarship to Skowhegan (Maine) School of Painting, 1951, Fulbright to Rome, 1955-57, Mark Rothko Found. award, 1974; grantee: N.Y. Coun. on Arts, 1975 (painting), 1979 (graphics), Nat. Endowment for the Arts, 1976, Adolf and Esther Gottleib Found., 1983, The Rockefeller Found. Residency, Bellagio, Italy, 1989. Mem. NAD. Home: 162 E 82nd St New York NY 10028-1826 Office: 195 Chrystie St New York NY 10002 Office Phone: 212-529-7303. Personal E-mail: tboutis@aol.com.

BOUTROS, GEORGE F., investment banker; b. Beirut, 1960; married; 3 children. BS in Civil Engring., U. Calif., Berkeley, 1983, MS in Structural Engring., 1984; MBA, UCLA. Various positions to mng. dir., mergers and acquisitions Morgan Stanley, 1986—96; mng. dir., tech. group Deutsche Morgan Grenfell (DMG), 1996—99; co-head, global tech. banking, co-head, global mergers and acquisions Credit Suisse First Boston, San Francisco, mng. dir., co-chmn. global tech. group, 1999—. Named a Top Dealmaker, Dealmaker mag., 2006. Office: Credit Suisse First Boston Global Tech Group 650 California St San Francisco CA 94108 Office Phone: 415-249-2100.*

BOUTROS, LINDA NELENE WILEY, medical/surgical nurse; b. New Orleans, Aug. 31, 1951; d. Robert Vernon and Marye Dell (Adcock) Wiley; m. Eddy Boutros, Dec. 23, 1972; children: Scott, Mark, Natalie. BS in Nursing, U. S.W. La., 1973. Cert. health care risk mgr. RN, relief charge, charge nurse, med./surgical flr. Bap. Hosp., Beaumont, Tex., 1973—76; RN, coord./supr. of nursing Kelsey Seybold Clinic, Missouri City, Tex., 1982-86; RN, head nurse S.W. Pediatric Ctr., Sugarland, Tex., 1986-87; RN, nursing supr. Westshore Hosp., Tampa, Fla., 1988-89; med.-surg. nurse Centurion Hosp., Carrollwood and Tampa, 1989-90, asst. head nurse med., 1990-91, relief supr., 1991, dir. surg. nursing svcs., 1992-93; nurse mgr. surg. floor, relief house supr. Univ. Cmty. Hosp. Carrollwood, Tampa, Fla., 1993-99, RN adminstrv. supr., 1999—2005, relief supr., 2005—. Adj. faculty U. So. Fla. Coll. Nursing; clin. instr. for RN nursing students U. Cmty. Hosp. Carrollwood. Mem. ANA, Fla. Nurses Assn. Office: Univ Cmty Hosp Carrollwood 7171 N Dale Mabry Hwy Tampa FL 33614-2670 Personal E-mail: lwboutros@hotmail.com.

BOUTROS, SEAN, plastic surgeon; b. 1973; m. Heather Boutros. Grad., Tex. A&M U., 1994; MD, Baylor Coll. Medicine, 1998. Lic. NY, 2002, Tex., 2005. Resident gen. surgery NYU Med. Ctr., NYC, 1998—2001, resident plastic surgery Inst. Reconstructive Surgery, 2001—04, craniofacial fellowship, 2004—05; elective in ear reconstruction Clinic George Bizet, Paris, 2003; plastic surgeon Houston Plastic and Craniofacial Surgery, 2005—. Clin. instr. Dept. Surgery NYU Med. Ctr., 1998—2001, 2001—05. Co-editor: Current Therapy in Plastic Surgery, 2005; contbr. Surgical Anatomy Around the Orbit, 2005, Surgical Anatomy of the Face, 2nd edit., 2005; contbr. articles to med. and plastic surgery jours. Mem.: Tex. Soc. Plastic Surgeons, Harris County Med. Assn., Tex. Med. Assn., Houston Soc. Plastic Surgeons, Am. Cleft Palate and Craniofacial Assn., NY Soc. Plastic Surgery, Northeastern Soc. Plastic Surgery, Am. Soc. Plastic Surgeons, Am. Coll. Surgeons, Alpha Omega Alpha, Beta Beta Beta. Avocations: running, fishing, tennis, hunting, travel, woodworking. Office: Houston Plastic and Craniofacial Surgery 6410 Fannin Ste 732 Houston TX 77030 Office Phone: 713-791-0700.

BOUTTERIN, EMMANUEL, public relations executive; b. Paris, Sept. 19, 1957; Degree, U. Aix-Marseille II, 1987. Journalist Le Meridional, Marseilles, France, 1984-86, Ouest-France, Cherbourg, Caen, 1986-88; dir. radio Frequence Mistral, Sisteron, France, 1988-89; dir. communication Jausiers Vacances Timeshare RCI, Marseilles, 1989-93; dir. gen. Agence Intermedia, Phototelem, Marseilles, 1993—; pres. Syndicat Nat. des Radios Libres, 2004—. Lt. French Marines, 1983. Mem.: Tribunal des Prud'hommes de Manosque (juge, pres. 2003—), Union Nat. des Anciens Eleves des Ecoles de Journalisme (pres. 1989—2001). Office: Intermedia 2 rue Grignan 13001 Marseille France Office Phone: (33) 4 91555685. E-mail: intermedia@online.fr.

BOUTWELL, ANNE DIELSCHNEIDER, artist, painter; b. Portland, Oreg., Mar. 12, 1932; d. William Norwood and Edra Anne Dielschneider; m. Burr North Boutwell, Sr., Aug. 22, 1955 (dec. Jan. 20, 1977); children: Burr North Boutwell, Jr., Meade Norwood, Noell Seufert. BFA in Portraiture, Pacific NW Coll. Art, PNCA, 1980; BS in Drawing and Painting, U. Oreg., Sch. Architecture and Allied Arts, 1954. Artist Anne Boutwell Studios, Portland, 1981—86; mktg. support Print Right (now Lazerquick), Willsonville, Oreg., 1986—87; assoc. dir. Argus Fine Arts Corp., Portland, 1987—88. Program editor, various coms., chmn. of Oreg. hist. soc. vol. progam Portland Jr. League, Portland, 1961—72; pres. Womens League, 1972—75; arts and cultural standing com., arts and humanities, land use and zoning, land use study standing committees City Club, 1977—88; visual arts chmn., spl. events com. Art Quake Bd. of Dis., 1982—85; pres. Portland Beautification Assn., 1986—88; regent Mutlnomah Chpt., DAR, 1998—2000; organizing sec. for state of oreg. Oreg. State Soc. DAR, Oreg., 2002—04. Wall mural, Vista St. Claire, 2 wall murals, LazerQuick Corp. Exec. Hdqrs., Willsonville, Represented in permanent collections Oreg. Hist. Soc., Portland, Dr. Francis J. Newton. Collection, Portland Art Mus., Rental Sales. Mem. Rep. Party. Recipient 50 Yr. Pin, Kappa Kappa Gamma, 1951-2001, Order of the Emerald Soc. 50 Yr. Pin, U. Oreg., 2004. Mem.: DAR, Portland Art Mus., Contemporary Art Coun., Jr. League Garden Club, Women's Archtl. League, Trinity Catherdral Iconography Inst. (icon painter 2004—05), Arnold Bennett Hall Soc. Episcopalian. Home: 2309 SW 1st Ave #441 Portland OR 97201-5039 Home Phone: 503-525-0606. Personal E-mail: anneboutwell@aol.com.

BOUVIER, LINDA FRITTS, publishing executive; b. Dover, NJ, Nov. 8, 1946; d. Fletcher Loomis and Dorothy Evelyn (Lukens) Fritts; m. Alan Moylan, May 30, 1971 (div.); m. John Emerson Ross, Dec. 28, 1985 (div.); m. Claude Edward Bouvier, Nov. 12, 1994 (div.); m. Alan Jay Dressler, Oct. 11, 2005 (dec.). BFA in Advt. Design, Visual Comm., Pratt Inst., Bklyn., 1968. Designer MD Med. News Mag., NYC, 1968-71; art dir. Miami (Fla.) Mag., 1973-74; ind. cons. Linda Moylan Design, Miami, 1974-84; prodn. mgr. U. Miami, 1984-85; product devel., sales The Mazer Corp., Dayton, Ohio, 1986-89; sales mgr. TSI Graphics, Cranford, N.J., 1989-92; product mgr., electronic svcs. RR Donnelley and Sons, NYC, Waltham, Mass., 1992-94; v.p. emerging pub. technologies Simon & Schuster, NYC, 1994-95; v.p. prodn., mfg., inventory sch. divsn. Houghton Mifflin Co., Boston, 1995-97; sr. acct. exec. Ames On-Demand, Woburn, Mass., 1998-99; v.p. content devel. and pub. rels. RoweCom, Inc., Cambridge, Mass., 1999-2000; cons. Boston, 2000—. Adv. bd. The Heller Report: Internet Strategies for Education Markets, 1995—. Co-chair N.Y. Book Show, 1989. Enabling technologies com. Am. Assn. Publ., 1995. Recipient award Soc. Pub. Designers, 1970-82. Mem. Bookbuilders of Boston. Avocations: photography, gourmet cooking, art, horticulture. Home Phone: 603-532-4603. Personal E-mail: lbouvier@aol.com.

BOUVIER, MARSHALL ANDRE, lawyer; b. Jacksonville, Fla., Sept. 30, 1923; s. Marshall and Helen Marion B.; m. Zepha Windle, July 11, 1938; children: Michael A., Debra Bouvier Williams, Mark A., Marshall André III, Suzanne, John A. (dec.), Wendy Bouvier Clark, Jennifer Lynn. AB, Emory U., LLB, 1949. Bar: Ga. 1948, Nev. 1960. Commd. USN, 1949; naval aviator, judge advocate; ret., 1959; atty. State of Nevada, 1959-60; pvt. practice, Reno, 1960-82, 88—; dist. atty. County of Storey, Nev., 1982-88, spl. cons. to Nev. Dist. Atty., 1991-95; pres., CEO A.G.E. Corp., 1997—. Mem. Judge Advocates Assn., Am. Bd. Hypnotherapy, Ancient and Honorable Order Quiet Birdmen, Rotary, E Clampus Vitus, Phi Delta Phi, Sigma Chi.

BOUVIER, MONICA RENEE, traffic director; b. Spokane, Jan. 18, 1963; d. Jesse James Oliver and Susie Ann Williams; 1 child, Joshua Dominic Lee Bouvier-Paul. Student, U. Anchorage, 1983—87, U. Phoenix, 2007—. Program coord., PSA dir. KIMO Channel 13 (ABC), Anchorage, 1991—95, traffic mgr., PSA dir., 1995—99, KTVA Channel 11 (CBS), Anchorage, 1999—2001, nat. sales mgr., traffic and PSA dir., 2001—05, KTBY Channel 4 (FOX), Anchorage, 2001—05; traffic and PSA KTVA Channel 11 (CBS), 2005—. Democrat. Avocations: reading, writing, travel, tennis, walking.

BOUYOUCOS, JOHN VINTON, retired research and development company executive; b. Lansing, Mich., Nov. 9, 1926; s. George John and Delia (Bemis) B.; m. Stella Wright, Sept. 29, 1953; children: Anne Stephanie, Peter Johnson, Hope Nicola; m. Kristine Thuesen Hordon, May 26, 1984. Student, U. Mich., 1944; AB, Harvard U., 1949, MS, 1950, PhD, 1955, Harvard Bus. Sch. Smaller Co. Mgmt. Program cert., 1976. Asst. dir. Harvard Acoustics Research Lab., Harvard U., 1955-59; mgr. hydroacoustics dept. Gen. Dynamics Electronics Div., Rochester, NY, 1959-71; pres., chief scientist Hydroacoustics Inc., 1972—2006; ret., 2006. Cons. in field. Patentee in field. Pres., chmn. bd. Soc. Chamber Music, Rochester, 1977-96, chmn. bd. 1996-99, chmn. emeritus, 1999—; bd. dirs., vice chmn. Rochester Philharm. Orch., 1978-89, hon. bd. dirs., 1990—. Served with U.S. Navy, 1944-46. Recipient Rochester Patent Law Assn. Inventors award, 1973. Fellow IEEE, Acoustical Soc. Am. (v.p. 1970-71; disting. svc. citation 2000, Gold cert., 2004, Engring. Acoustics Silver medal, 2004); mem. Soc. Exploration Geophysicists, Audio Engring. Soc., Inst. Noise Control Engrs. Clubs: Harvard Bus. Sch. Rochester (pres. 1984). Home: 11 Elmwood Hill Ln Rochester NY 14610-3445

BOVA, BENJAMIN WILLIAM, writer, editor; b. Phila., Nov. 8, 1932; s. Benjamin P. and Giove (Caporiccio) B.; m. Rosa Cucinotta, Nov. 28, 1953 (div. 1973); children: Michael Francis, Regina Marie; m. Barbara Ellen Berson, June 28, 1974. BS in Journalism, Temple U., 1954; MA in Communications, SUNY Albany, 1987; EdD, Calif. Coast U., 1996. Formerly newspaper reporter; mktg. mgr. Avco Everett Rsch. Lab.; formerly tchr. sci. fiction Harvard U.; formerly tchr. sci. fiction, dir. film courses Hayden Planetarium, N.Y.C.; editor Upper Darby (Pa.) News, 1954-56; tech. editor Project Vanguard, 1956-58; motion picture scriptwriter Phys. Sci. Study Com., Ednl. Svcs., Inc., Watertown, Mass., 1958-60; mgr. mktg. Avco Everett Rsch. Lab., Avco Corp., Everett, Mass., 1960-71; editor Analog Sci. Fiction-Sci. Fact mag. Conde Nast Pub. Co., NYC, 1971-78; fiction editor Omni mag., NYC, 1978-79, exec. editor, 1979-81, v.p., editorial dir., 1981-82. Past mem. panel Office Tech. Assessment, U.S. Congress; lectr. Nat. Geog. Soc., major govt. and corp. exec. groups, univs.; adv. bd. Post Coll.; bd. contbrs. USA Today; publ. Galaxy Online.com, 1999-2000. Author: (fiction) The Star Conquers, 1959, Star Watchman, 1964, The Weathermakers, 1967, Out of the Sun, 1968, The Dueling Machine, 1969, Escape!, 1969, Exiled From Earth, 1971; author: (with George Lucas) THX 1138, 1971; author: Flight of Exiles, 1972, As On a Darkling Plain, 1972, When the Sky Burned, 1972, Forward in Time, 1973; author: (with Gordon R. Dickson) Gremlins, Go Home!, 1974; author: End of Exile, 1975, The Starcrossed, 1975, City of Darkness, 1976, Millennium, 1976, The Multiple Man, 1976, Colony, 1978, Maxwell's Demons, 1978, Kinsman, 1979, The Exiles Trilogy, 1981, Voyagers, 1981, Test of Fire, 1982, The Winds of Altair, 1983, Escape Plus, 1984, Orion, 1984, The Astral Mirror, 1985, Privateers, 1985, Promethians, 1986, Voyagers II: The Alien Within, 1986, Battle Station, 1987, The Kinsman Saga, 1987, Vengeance of Orion, 1988, Peacekeepers, 1988, Cyberbooks, 1989, Voyagers III, Star Brothers, 1990, Orion in the Dying Time, 1990, Future Crime, 1990; author: (with Bill Pogue) The Trikon Deception, 1992; author: Mars, 1992; author: (with A.J. Austin) To Save the Sun, 1992; author: Triumph, 1993, Empire Builders, 1993, Challenges, 1993, Sam Gunn, Unlimited, 1993, Orion and The Conqueror, 1994, Death Dream, 1994; author: (with A.J. Austin) To Fear the Light, 1995; author: Orion Among the Stars, 1995, Brothers, 1996, Moonrise, 1997, Moonwar, 1998, Sam Gunn Forever, 1998, Twice Seven, 1998, Return to Mars, 1999, Venus, 2000, Jupiter, 2001, The Precipice, 2001, The Rock Rats, 2002, Saturn, 2003, Tales of the Grand Tour, 2004, The Silent War, 2004, Powersat, 2005, Mercury, 2005, Titan, 2006, The Green Trap, 2006, The Sam Gunn Omnibus, 2007; fiction, The Aftermath, 2007; author: (nonfiction) The Milky Way Galaxy, 1961, Giants of the Animal World, 1962, Reptiles Since the World Began, 1964, The Uses of Space, 1965, In Quest of Quasars, 1970, Planets, Life and LGM, 1970, The Fourth State of Matter, 1971 (Best Sci. Book award ALA, 1988), The Amazing Laser, 1972, The New Astronomies, 1972, Starflight and Other Improbabilities, 1973, Man Changes the Weather, 1973; author: (with Barbara Berson) Survival Guide for the Suddenly Single, 1974; author: The Weather Changes Man, 1974, Workshops in Space, 1974, Through Eyes of Wonder, 1975, Science: Who Needs It?, 1975, Notes to a Science Fiction Writer, 1975, Closeup: New Worlds, 1977, Viewpoint, 1977, The Seeds of Tomorrow, 1977, The High Road, 1981, Vision of the Future: The Art of Robert McCall, 1982, Assured Survival, 1984, Star Peace, 1986, Welcome to Moonbase!, 1987; author: (with Sheldon Glashow) Interactions, 1988; author: The Beauty of Light, 1988, First Contact, 1990, The Craft of Writing Science Fiction That Sells, 1994, Space Travel, 1997, Immortality, 1998, The Story of Light, 2001, Faint Echoes, Distant Stars, 2004; author: (with Jon Paul) Visions of Lake Tahoe, 2004. Recipient 6 Sci. Fiction Achievement awards for best profl. editor (Hugo), E.E. Smith Meml. award for imaginative fiction, New Eng. Sci. Fiction Soc., 1974, Balrog award, 1983, Inkpot award, 1985, Disting. Alumnus award, Temple U., 1982, Isaac Asimov Meml. award, 1996, Lifetime Achievement award, Arthur C. Clarke Found., 2005, John W. Campbell Meml. award for best sci. fiction novel, Titan, 2006. Fellow AAAS, Brit. Interplanetary Soc.; mem. AIAA, Nat. Space Soc. (pres. 1982-88, pres. emeritus, chmn. bd. 1988-92), N.Y. Acad. Scis., Sci. Fiction Writers Am. (charter, pres. 1990-92), Planetary Soc., Nature Conservancy, Nat. Space Club, Explorers Club, Amateur Fencer's League Am.

BOVA, VINCENT ARTHUR, JR., lawyer, consultant, photographer; b. Pitts., Apr. 25, 1946; s. Vincent A. and Janie (Pope) Bova; m. Breda Murphy, Mar. 20, 1971; 1 child, Kate Murphy Bova. BA in Bus. Adminstrn., Alma Coll., Mich., 1968; MPA, Ohio State U., 1972; JD, Oklahoma City U., 1975. Bar: Okla. 1975, N.Mex 1976, U.S. Dist. Ct. N.Mex 1976, U.S. Tax Ct. 1976, U.S. Ct. Appeals (10th cir.) 1976, U.S. Supreme Ct. 1979. Mktg. and systems rep., computer systems divsn. RCA, 1968-70; rsch. analyst Rsch. Atlanta, 1972-73; assoc. Threet, Threet, Glass, King & Maxwell, 1976-78; ptnr. Lill & Bova, P.A., 1978-81; pvt. practice Albuquerque, 1981—. Past pres. Bare Bulls Investment, 1982, Fumilan Investment, 1983, Toastmasters; rsch. analyst urban affairs Ohio Dept. Urban Affairs, Columbus, 1971; panel mem. N.Mex Med. Rev. Commn., 1981—, N.Mex Legal/Dental/Osteopathic Podiatry Com., 1981—; v.p. Albuquerque Com. Fgn. Rels., 2001—, pres., bd. dirs.; co-owner Albuquerque Photography Gallery. Contbr. articles to profl. jours. Bd. dirs. Rio Grande Nature Ctr.; pres., v.p. spl. projects S.W. Arts and Crafts Festival, Albuquerque, 1986—89; pol. cons. Nov. Group; active N.Mex Estate Planning Coun., 1978—, Edn. Forum; sec.-treas., vice-chmn., pres. adv. bd. Salvation Army, 1987—, bd. dirs., 2005—; contbr. Ctr. Home Prevention Domestic Violence, 1984—85, Ronald McDonald House, 1984; past chmn. N.Mex Workers' Compensation Monthly; advt. com. Supreme Ct. Panel; moot ct. judge Albuquerque. With Air N.G., 1969—75. Named one of Oustanding Young Men of Am., 1975, 1976; recipient Pacesetters award, Ohio State U., 1972. Mem.: ABA, ATLA (advanced grad. Nat. Coll. Advocacy), Collaborative Law N.Mex. (founding mem.), Photog. Soc. Am. (pres. chpt.), Profl. Photography Assn., Internat. Credit Assn. (lectr.), Image Profls. S.W. (bd. dirs., print chmn. 1996—, pres., bd. dirs., Photography award 1996, Best of Show 2000, others), Sole Practitioners Assn., N.Mex Fin. Planning Assn., Albuquerque Bar Assn., Bus. Round Table, Nat. Assn. Social Security Claimants Reps. (past state chmn.), Internat. Assn. Fin. Planners, N.Mex Trial Lawyers Assn., Nat. Def. Lawyers Assn. (staff chmn. 1986), State Bar N.Mex (mem. med. legal panel, med.-dental podiatry legal panel, rep. probate, wills and trusts ann. report), N.Mex Bar Assn. (pres. small firm and solo sect.), Ct. Practice Inst. (advanced diplomate), Profl. Photographers Am. (assoc. 8 awards 1999), Toastmasters (past pres., v.p., edn. chmn., Able Toastmaster award), Ohio State U. Alumni Assn. N.Mex (pres.), Albuquerque Petroleum Club (bd. dirs.), Enchanted Lens Camera Club, Zia Scuba Club, Millionaires Tip Club, Albuquerque Knife and Fork (pres., v.p., sec.-treas., bd. dirs.), Inn of Ct., Sigma Tau Gamma (pres. Albuquerque com. fgn. rels.), Phi Alpha Delta.

Democrat. Presbyterian. Avocations: flower gardening, photography - video and still, computers, investing, reading. Office: 5716 Osuna Rd NE Albuquerque NM 87109-2527 Office Phone: 505-881-5225.

BOVAIRD, BRENDAN PETER, lawyer; b. NYC, Mar. 9, 1948; s. John Francis and Margaret Mary (Endrizzi) Bovaird; m. Carolyn Warren Boyle, Dec. 18, 1971; children: Anne Warren, Sarah Grant. BA, Fordham U., 1970; JD, U. Va., 1973. Bar: N.Y. 1974, DC 1980, Pa. 1983, U.S. Dist. Ct. (so. and ea. dists.) N.Y. 1974, U.S. Ct. Appeals (2d cir.) 1974. Atty. Dewey, Ballantine, Bushby, Palmer & Wood, NYC, 1973—82; asst. gen. counsel Campbell Soup Co., Camden, NJ, 1982—89; sr. v.p., gen. counsel, sec. Orion Pictures Corp., NYC, 1989—92; counsel, mem. exec. com. Wyeth-Ayerst Internat., Inc., St. Davids, Pa., 1992—95; pres. KDH, Inc., 1994—; v.p., gen. counsel UGI Corp., Valley Forge, Pa., 1995—2003, AmeriGas Propane, Inc., Valley Forge, 1995—2003; counsel Hunt & Ayres, LLP, Phila., 2004—. Bd. dirs. Phila. Shakespeare Festival, 2004—, Young Audiences of Ea. Pa., Inc., 2005—, Phila. Vol. Lawyers for the Arts, 2005—. Mem.: The Athenaeum Phila., Motion Picture Export Assn. Am. (bd. dirs. 1990—92), Aircraft Owners and Pilots Assn., Phila. Country Club. Office: 1818 Market St Philadelphia PA 19103 Home Phone: 610-896-8684; Office Phone: 215-557-8500. Business E-Mail: bpbovaird@huntandayres.com.

BOVAY, HARRY ELMO, JR., retired engineering company executive; b. Big Rapids, Mich., Sept. 4, 1914; s. Harry E. and Addibelle (Bentley) B.; m. Sue Goldston, Feb. 1, 1977; children: Mark Benson, Susan Stone. C.E., Cornell U., 1936. Jr. engring. aide U.S. C.E., 1936-37; jr. metal insp., project engr. Humble Oil & Refining Co., Baytown, Tex., 1937-45; cons. engr. Houston, 1946-62; pres. Bovay Engrs., Inc., Houston, 1962-73, chmn. bd., chief exec. officer, 1974-84. Owner Bovista Reel Ranch, Tex.; pres. Mid-South Telecommunications Co., Inc., 1987—; endowed chair Tex. A&M U. and Cornell U., 1997. Editor: Mechanical and Electrical Systems for Buildings. Pres., Sam Houston Area council Boy Scouts Am., 1963-64, exec. com. South Central region, 1973-76, bd. dirs., 1975-79, v.p., 1980-81, pres., 1981-82, mem. nat. exec. bd., 1981-84, chmn. camping/outdoor com., 1983-85, chmn. nat. audit com., 1982-87, mem. nat. adv. coun., 1985-98; mem. nat. adv. coun. Scouts Am., 1985—, nat. properties com., 1990—, mem. nat. high adventure com., 1990—; mem. Houston Forum Sr. Coun. Advisor, 2003—; chmn. Houston Commn. Zoning, 1959-60; bd. dirs. Vis. Nurse Assn., Houston, 1970-75, Retina Rsch. Found., 1998—; active United Fund Houston and Harris County; mem. Houston Adv. Council Naval Affairs, 1959; mem. Tex. Water Resources Adv. Com., 1968-71; mem. adv. com. Coastal Engring. Lab., Tex. A&M U., 1969, also mem. adv. council for Pres.; mem. engring. adv. com. Miss. State U., 1974-77; mem. Alumni Council Cornell U. Coll. Engring.; bd. visitors McDonald Obs., 1985—; mem. demand subpanel Energy Research Adv. Bd., 1985-86; mem. adv. com. rsch. programs Tex. Higher Edn. Coordinating Bd., 1992-95. Recipient Silver Beaver award Boy Scouts Am., 1965, Silver Antelope, 1976, Silver Buffalo, 1986, George Washington Svc. award Paul Carrington chpt. SAR, 1998, Whitney M. Young Jr. Svc. award, 2002, Woodson medal for Outstanding Cmty. Svc. and Leadership, Houston Forum, 2004, Ellis Island medal Honor, 2006; named Disting. Engr., Tex. Engring. Found.; Baden-Powell fellow, World Scouting Orgn.; camping area Bovay Ranch Sam Houston Area Coun. Boy Scouts Am. Fellow ASCE, ASHRAE (ASHRAE-ALCO award); mem. Nat. Soc. Profl. Engrs. (pres. 1976, Achievement award 1987), Tex. Soc. Profl. Engrs. (pres. 1967-68), Am. Inst. Cons. Engrs. (past pres Tex. chpt.), Houston Engring. and Sci. Soc. (past 2d v.p.), Am. Rd. Builders Assn. (exec. com.), Am. Concrete Inst., Am. Wood Preservers Assn., ASTM (councilor 1960-64), Forest Products Research Soc., Tex. Forest Products Mfrs. Assn., SAME (Toulmin medal), Pres.' Assn., Newcomen Soc. N.Am., Nat. Acad. Engring., Houston Livestock Show & Rodeo (life), Knight Order Francis I. Clubs: Houston, Kiwanis, Cosmos, Houston Country, Petroleum, Royal House Bourbon Two Sicilies. Episcopalian. Office: 3355 W Alabama St Ste 1140 Houston TX 77098-1799

BOVE, ALFRED ANTHONY, medical educator; b. Phila., Apr. 28, 1938; s. Alfred Anthony and Adeline Amelia (DeRose) B.; m. Sandra Ann Seltzer, June 25, 1966; children: Jacqueline, Christopher, Andrew. BSEE, Drexel U., 1962; MD, Temple U., 1966, PhD, 1970. Diplomate Am. Bd. Internal Medicine, Am. Bd. Cardiology, Am. Bd. Undersea Hyperb Medicine. Med. intern Temple U. Hosp., Phila., 1966-67, med. resident, 1969-70, postdoctoral fellow, 1967-69, asst. prof. medicine, 1973-81, prof. medicine, 1986—2001, prof. emeritus, 2001—; postdoctoral fellow Mayo Clinic, Rochester, Minn., 1970-71, prof. medicine, 1981-86; chief of cardiology Temple U. Med. Sch., 1986—99, chief cardiology, 2005—, assoc. dean, practice plan affairs, 1999—2001. Author: Diving Medicine, 4th edit., 2004; co-author: Diving Medicine, 1990, Exercise Medicine, 1982; editor: Skin Diver mag., 1981—; editor-in-chief: cardiosource.com, 2002-07; contbr. articles to profl. jours. Capt. USNR, 1971-73, 98, ret. Recipient Established Investigator award Am. Heart Assn., 1975, Paul Dudley White award Assn. Mil. Surgeons of the U.S., 1998, Disting. fellow award, ACC, 2002. Fellow ACP, Am. Coll. Cardiology (state gov. 1989-92); mem. Am. Physiologic Soc., IEEE, Undersea and Hyperbaric Med. Soc. (pres. 1983, ACC bd. trustees 2002-07, v.p., 2007-08, Craig Hoffman award 1988, Stover-Link award 1974). Roman Catholic. Avocations: scuba diving, marathon racing. Office: Temple U Med Ctr Cardiology Sect 3401 N Broad St Philadelphia PA 19140-4105 Home Phone: 610-896-2881; Office Phone: 215-707-9259. Business E-Mail: bovea@tuhs.temple.edu. E-mail: fred@scubamed.com.

BOVE, JOHN LOUIS, chemistry and environmental engineering educator, researcher; b. NYC, Apr. 15, 1928; s. Frank and Bridget (Randazzo) B.; m. June Althea Burns, Dec. 28, 1957; children: Adele, Catherine. BA in Chemistry, Bucknell U., 1949, MSA. in Chemistry, 1954; PhD in Chemistry, Case Western Res. U., 1973. Asst. prof. chemistry Cooper Union, NYC, 1958-67, prof. chemistry and environ. engring., chmn. dept. chemistry, 1970—, dir. environ. program, 1970—; v.p. Cooper Union Research Found., 1974-80; founder, pres., CEO Red Hen Spectra, NYC. Dep. dir. bur. tech. svcs. NYC Air Resources, 1967-70; dir. Mid-Atlantic Consortium Air Pollution, 1970-76; CEO Cu Spectra, Inc Contbr. chpts., articles to profl. publs. Served with M.C. U.S. Army, 1950. Recipient Schweinburg Schweinburg Found., 1964; fellow Dow Chem. Co., 1953—; grantee NSF, 1960— Republican. Achievements include patents for method for identifying organic spectra. Home: 125 Richards Rd Ridgewood NJ 07450-1115 Office: The Cooper Union Cooper Union 51 Astor Pl New York NY 10003-7132 Business E-Mail: bove@cooper.edu.

BOVE, PATRICE MAGEE, elementary school educator; b. Ft. Madison, Iowa, Apr. 29, 1946; d. Claude and Susie T. Magee; m. Roger E. Bove, Aug. 6, 1983; 1 child, Jonna. MusB, U. Iowa, 1968; M of Music Edn., Temple U., 1976. Tchr. elem. instrumental music Birmingham Sch. Dist., Mich., 1968-69; tchr. elem. music T-E Sch. Dist., Berwyn, Pa., 1969—. Co-author: Philadelphia Orchestra Student Concert Books, 1994-06; contbr. MENC (Strategies for Teaching Elementary Music), 1996. Educator, writer edn. adv. com. Phila. Orch., 1994—2006; accompanist chorus, Wayne, Pa., 1995, Suzuki Concerts, Immaculata, Pa., 1994-97. Mem. AAUW, Nat. Assn. Music Therapy, Music Tchrs. Assn., Gordon Inst. Music Learning, Suzuki, Kodaly, Orff, Pa. Music Edn. Assn. (dist. 12 co-host elem. songfest 1995), Music Educators Nat. Conf. Avocations: reading, computers, cooking. Home: 325 Holly Rd West Chester PA 19380-4614

BOVEN, DOUGLAS GEORGE, lawyer; b. Holland, Mich., Aug. 11, 1943; BSE, U. Mich., 1966, JD, 1969. Bar: Calif. 1970. Ptnr. Reed Smith LLP, San Francisco, 1989—. Arbitrator Fed. and Superior Ct. Panel of Arbitrators, 1980—; panelist Superior Ct. Early Settlement Program, 1987-. Mem. ABA (mem. bus. bankruptcy, Chpt. 11 and secured creditors coms.), Am. Bankruptcy Inst., Comml. Law League Am., State Bar Calif. (insolvency law and real estate sects.), Alameda County Bar Assn., Sonoma County Bar Assn., Bay Area Bankruptcy Forum, Bar Assn. San Francisco (comml. law and bankruptcy sect., mem. arbitrator fee disputes com. 1973—), Tau Beta Pi. Office: Reed Smith LLP Two Embarcadero Ctr Ste 2000 San Francisco CA 94111 Office Phone: 415-543-8700. Business E-Mail: dboven@reedsmith.com.

BOVENDER, JACK OLIVER, JR., hospital management company executive; b. Winston Salem, NC, Aug. 16, 1945; s. Jack Oliver Sr. and Eva Louise (Westmoreland) B.; m. Barbara Ann Tuttle; 1 child, Richard Spencer. AB, Duke U., 1967, MHA, 1969. Asst. adminstr. Community Gen. Hosp., Thomasville, NC, 1972-75; assoc. adminstr. West Fla. Regional Med. Ctr., Pensacola, 1975-77; adminstr. Largo Med. Ctr., Largo, Fla., 1977-80, West Fla. Regional Med. Ctr., Pensacola, 1980-85; div. v.p. Hosp. Corp. Am., Atlanta, 1985-87, pres., group ops. Nashville, 1987-91; sr. v.p., operations Hospital Corp. of America, Nashville, exec. v.p., 1992—94, pres., 1997—2001, COO, 1997—2001, chmn., CEO, 2002—. Mem. editorial bd. Jour. of Health Adminstrn. Edn., Washington, 1987—, Health Adminstrn. Press, Ann Arbor, Mich., 1988—. Bd. dirs. United Way, Pensacola, 1984; sr. warden and vestryman Christ Ch., Pensacola, 1982-85. Lt. USN, 1969-72. Fellow Am. Coll. Healthcare Execs.; mem. Pensacola C. of C. (bd. dirs. 1984), Leadership Nashville, Duke U. Hosp. and Health Adminstrn. Alumni Coun. (pres. 1986-87), Duke U. Gen. Alumni Bd., Rotary (Largo, Pensacola). Republican. Episcopalian. Avocations: reading, sports. Office: HCA Health SVCS Virginia 1602 Skipwith Rd Richmond VA 23229-5205 also: Columbia/HCA 1 Park Plaza Nashville TN 37203-6527*

BOVIN, DENIS ALAN, diversified financial services company executive; b. NYC, Nov. 4, 1947; s. Henry and Ruth (Klein) B.; m. Terry Schneider, Dec. 8, 1973; children: Michelle, Andrew. BS, MIT, 1969; MBA, Harvard U., 1971. Assoc. Salomon Bros. Inc., NYC, 1971-76, v.p., 1976-81, mng. dir., 1981-92; vice chmn. Bear Stearns & Co., Inc., NYC, 1992—. Vice chmn. Bus. Execs. for Nat. Security, Intrepid Mus.; bd. dirs. Ctr. for Strategic and Budgetary Analysis. Mem. exec. com. MIT Corp., mem. def. bus. bd.; adv. bd. fgn. intelligence Pres.; mem. Coun. on Fgn. Rels., Inc.; trustee MIT; cons. in field. Recipient Dept. Def. medal for Disting. Pub. Svc., 1995; named Outstanding Investment Banker, Instl. Investor Mag., NYC, 1985, a Top Dealmaker, Dealmaker mag., 2006. Mem. NY Soc. for Security Analysts, Investment Assn. NJ, Bus. Exec. for Nat. Security (bd. dirs.), Bear Stearns (bd. dirs.), MIT Alumni Assn. NY. Office: Bear Stearns & Co 383 Madison Ave New York NY 10179- E-mail: dbovin@bear.com.

BOW, STEPHEN TYLER, JR., business executive; b. Bow, Ky., Oct. 20, 1931; s. Stephen Tyler Sr. and Mary L. (King) B.; m. Kathy O'Connor, July, 1982; children: Jerry, Jon; children by previous marriage: Sandra Bow Morris, Deborah Bow Goodin, Carol, Clara, Lisa. BA in Sociology, Berea Coll., Ky., 1953; grad. exec. program bus. adminstrn., Columbia U., 1976. CLU. With Met. Life Ins. Co., 1953-74, 76-89; agt. Lexington, Ky., 1953-55; sales mgr. Birmingham, Ala., 1955-58; field tng. cons., 1958-59; territorial field supr., 1959-60; dist. sales mgr. Frankfort, 1960-64, Lexington, 1964-66; exec. asst. field tng. NYC, 1966-67; regional sales mgr. NJ, 1967-72; agy. v.p., officer-in-charge Can. hdqrs., 1972-74; exec. v.p., chmn., chief exec. officer Capital Holding Corp., Louisville, 1974-76; officer-in-charge Midwestern hdqrs. Met. Life Ins. Co., Dayton, 1976-83, sr. v.p., officer-in-charge Western Hdqrs., 1983-89; chmn., CEO Southeastern Group, Inc., Louisville, 1993-94; pres., CEO Anthem Life of Ind., Indpls., 1993-95; chmn., CEO Anthem Life Ins. Cos., 1995-96; exec. v.p. Assoc. Ins. Cos., Inc., Indpls., 1993-96; chmn. Acordia of San Francisco, 1993-96; pres., CEO Delta Dental Ky., Louisville, 1989-94, Blue Cross and Blue Shield Ky., Louisville, 1989-93; vice chmn. DeHayes Group, 1996—; pres. Steve Bow and Assocs., Inc., 1996—; chmn. Victory Tech., Inc., 1998—. Past chmn. Dayton Power and Light Audit Com.; chmn. bd. dirs. Advice Co.; chmn. EBridge Techs. Past bd. dirs. San Francisco Visitors and Conv. Bur., 1985-87, Ind. Coll. of No. Calif., Bay Area Coun., Lindsey Wilson Coll.; mem. adv. bd. Hugh O'Brian Youth Found.; bd. dirs. Calif. Legis. Adv. Commn. on Life and Health Ins., Metro United Way, Ky. Health Care Access Found., Greater Louisville Econ. Devel. Coun.; Leadership Ky., Greater Louisville Fund for the Arts, Boy Scouts Am., Bay Area Boy Scouts Am., Bay Area Council, U. San Francisco, Ky. Home Mut., Ky. Forward, Asian Bus. League, McLaren Coll. Bus., My Old Ky. Home Coun.; mem. corp. council San Francisco UN Assn.; past mem. San Francisco Pvt. Industry Council; past chmn. United Negro Coll. Fund of San Francisco, 1985-86; mem. exec. com. bd. dirs., v.p. county ops. United Way of San Francisco Bay Area, 1985-87; vol. chmn. U.S. Savs. Bond Campaign, Bay Area, 1987; trustee Ky. Ind. Coll. Fund, Berea Coll.; chmn. bd. dirs. Advice Co. Recipient Outstanding Sales Mgmt. award N.Y. Sales Congress, 1972, Frederick D. Patterson award United Negro Coll. Fund San Francisco, 1986, Outstanding County Ops. Vol. award United Way of Bay Area, 1987, Bus. Appreciation award Jeffersontown, Ky. C. of C., 1993, Pres.'s award, 1993, Leadership award Internat. Women's Forum, Washington, 1993; named Citizen of Yr. Wright State U. Med. Sch., Dayton, 1982. Mem. Nat. Assn. Life Underwriters, Gen. Agts. and Mgrs. Assn., Calif. Bus. Roundtable, Nat. Assn. Corp. Dirs. (founder, former pres.), Calif. C. of C. (bd. dirs.), Ky. C. of C., Ky. Home Life Exec. Com., Am. Cancer Soc. Clubs: Lincoln of Northern Calif. Republican. Methodist. Avocations: golf, painting, reading. Office Phone: 916-652-7667. Business E-Mail: steve@adviceco.com. *We achieve goals by thinking positively and focusing on objectives, not on problems. We achieve economic success by concentrating on serving our fellow man and finding new ways to satisfy his needs. We achieve personal satisfaction by doing more than is expected of us, and exceeding even our own expectations through determination and persistency. We achieve happiness by becoming so interested and absorbed in our work that we forget selfish, petty matters. We achieve a successful life by living each day as if our entire life is to be judged by that day alone.*

BOWA, LAWRENCE ROBERT (LARRY BOWA), former professional baseball manager; b. Sacramento, Dec. 6, 1945; m. Sheena Bowa; 1 child, Tori. Student, Sacramento City Coll. Player various minor league teams, 1966-69; player with Phila. Phillies, Nat. League, 1970-81, Chgo. Cubs, Nat. League, 1982-85, N.Y. Mets, 1985; mgr. Las Vegas Stars, 1986, San Diego Padres, 1986-88, Phila. Phillies, 2002—04; third base coach N.Y. Yankees, 2005—. Player All-Star games, 1974-76, 78, 79, World Series, 1980. Holder major league record for highest lifetime fielding percentage for shortstop; winner Gold Glove, 1972, 78.

BOWDEN, AISHA L., elementary school educator; d. Charles and Eleanor Bowden. B in Music Edn., Howard U., 2006. Elementary Music DC Pub. Schools. Tchr. music Thomson Elem. Sch., Washington, 2000—. Recipient Key Communicator award, Arts for Every Student Program, 2003; Fulbright Groups Study Abroad grant, Fulbright, 2001. Mem.: Ubiquity, Inc. (life). Avocation: travel. Office: Thomson Elementary Sch 1200 L St NW Washington DC 20001 Home Phone: 240-988-4546; Office Phone: 202-448-8664.

BOWDEN, BOBBY (ROBERT CLECKLER BOWDEN), college football coach; b. Birmingham, Ala., Nov. 8, 1929; s. Robert Pierce and Sunset (Cleckler) Bowden; m. Julia Ann Estock, Apr. 1, 1949; children: Robyn Hines, Steve, Tommy, Terry, Ginger Madden, Jeff. BS, Howard U., 1953; grad. degree, Peabody Coll. Asst. football coach, head track coach Howard Coll., Homewood, Ala., 1954—55, head football coach, 1959—62; head football coach, athletic dir. South Ga. Coll., Douglas, Ga., 1955—58; wide receivers coach Fla. State U., Tallahassee, 1963—65; offensive coord. W.Va. U. Mountaineers, Morgantown, 1966—69, head football coach, 1970—75, Fla. State U. Seminoles, Tallahassee, 1975—. Co-author (with Terry Bowden): Winning's Only Part of the Game: Lessons of Life and Football, 1996; co-author: (with Setve Bowden) The Bowden Way: 50 Years of Leadership Wisdom, 2001; co-author: (with Jim Bettinger) The Book of Bowden, 2001; co-author: (with Steve Ellis) Bobby Bowden's Tales from the Seminole Sidelines, 2004. Named So. Ind. Coach of Yr., 1977, 79, Nat. Coach of Yr., ABC-Chevrolet, 1979, Nat. Coack of Yr. (Bobby Dodd), 1980, Region II Coach of Yr., 1987, Coach of Yr., Walter Camp Football Found., 1991, Atlantic Coast Conf. Coach Yr., 1993, 1997, Gold Medal, Nat. Football Fedn. awards, 2006; named to Fla. Sports Hall of Fame, 1983, Ala. Sports Hall of Fame, 1986; recipient Neyland Trophy; inducted into Coll. Football Hall of Fame, 2006. Baptist. coaching Fla. State U. to the 1993 & 1999 BCS Nat. Championship; won 12 Atlantic Coast Conf. Champioships; the only coach in college football history to win 11 consecutive bowl games, 1985-95. Office: Fla State U 307 Moore Athletic Ctr Stadium Dr Tallahassee FL 32306-1096*

BOWDEN, DAVID, conductor; b. Winston-Salem, NC, Nov. 22, 1953; s. Robert Marshall and Phyllis Bowden; m. Donna Sjaardema, Aug. 17, 1974; children: Kirsten Ruth, Kristi Elisabeth. MusB, Wheaton Coll.; MusM, MusD, Ind. U. Prof. music Huntington (Ind.) Coll., 1976—83; assoc. instr. music Ind. U., Bloomington, 1983—90; dir. worship and music Evang. Cmty. Ch., Bloomington, Ind., 1984—2004; music dir., condr. Columbus Ind. Philharm., 1987—, Terre Haute (Ind.) Symphony Orch., 1997—, Carmel (Ind.) Symphony Orch., 1999—. Music dir., condr. (CD recording) Dupre Complete Music for Organ and Orchestra. Pres. Bloomington (Ind.) Pops, 1990—95; dir. WFIU, local NPR Sta., Bloomington; judge, std. awards panel ASCAP, NYC, 1999—2001. Recipient award for Adventuresome Programming, ASCAP, 1989—96; fellow, Ind. U., 1984; scholar, 1977—78, 1983—85; Nat. Merit scholar, Wheaton Coll., 1972—76. Mem.: Condrs. Guild (nat. conf. spkr. 1995—, chair new music project), Am. Symphony Orch. League (nat. conf. spkr. 1992—96), Pi Kappa Lambda. Achievements include broadcasts of orchestral perfomances on NPR Perfromance Today and PRI's Pipedreams. Avocations: running, travel, reading, basketball. Office: Columbus Ind Philharm 315 Franklin St Columbus IN 47201 Home Phone: 812-336-6488.

BOWDEN, DEREK THOMAS, orchestra director, educator; b. Salisbury, Md., Sept. 1, 1976; s. Ervin Thomas and Donna Kay Bowden; m. Robin Radford; children: Christopher Douglas, Claire Draper-Hamilton. BS, Salisbury U., Md., 2000; MA, U. Del., 2004. Quality control analyst Dewberry & Davis, LLC, Fairfax, Va., 2000—01; instr. U. Del., Newark, 2001—04; mng. dir., instr. Salisbury U., 2001—. Mem. NASM accreditation com. music dept. Salisbury U., 2004—05, mem. cultural affairs com., 2004—05, active Md. Summer Ctr. for the Arts, 2001—03. Mem.: Assn. Am. Geographers, Phi Mu Epsilon. Home: 5037 Holland Rd New Church VA 23415 Office: Salisbury U 1101 Camden Ave Salisbury MD 21801

BOWDEN, DOUGLAS MCHOSE, neuropsychiatric scientist, foundation director; b. Durham, NC, Apr. 7, 1937; s. Daniel Joseph and Charlotte (McHose) B.; m. Vivian Lee Bowden, 1966 (div. 2005); children: Dana, Julie, Carlos, Luis BA, Harvard U., 1959; MD, Stanford U., 1965. Staff assoc. NIMH, Bethesda, Md., 1966-69; asst. prof. psychiatry U. Wash., Seattle, 1969-73, assoc. prof. dept. psychiatry & behavioral scis., 1973-79, prof. psychiatry & behavioral scis., 1979—; core staff sci. Nat. Primate Rsch. Ctr., U. Wash., 1969—; from asst. dir. to assoc. dir. Regional Primate Rsch. Ctr., U. Wash., 1977-88, dir., 1988-94. Adj. assoc. prof. pharmacology U. Wash., 1975-79, adj. prof. pharmacology, 1979-88; rsch. fellow Japan Soc. Promotion of Sci., Japan Assn. Animal Sci., Tokyo, Tsukuba, Inuyama/Kyoto, Japan, 1989. Author: Neuronames (c) Neuroanatomical Nomenclature, 1992; editor: Aging in Nonhuman Primates, 1979; translator Traumatic Aphasia, its Syndromes, Psychology and Treatment, 1970, Primate Models of Human Neurogenic Disorders, 1976 Surgeon USPHS, 1966-69. Fellow Gerontol. Soc. Am.; mem. Am. Soc. Primatologists, Soc. Neurosci., Gerontol. Soc., Internat. Primatological Soc. Office: U Wash Natl Primate Rsch Ct Box 357330 1705 NE Pacific St Seattle WA 98195-7330 Office Phone: 206-543-2456. Business E-Mail: dmbowden@u.washington.edu.

BOWDEN, GEORGE NEWTON, judge; b. East Orange, NJ, Nov. 21, 1946; s. W. Paul and Catherine A. (Porter) B. BA, Bowdoin Coll., Brunswick, Maine, 1971; JD, U. Maine, 1974. Bar: Wash. 1974, Maine 1975, US Dist. Ct. (we. dist.) Wash. 1978, US Ct. Appeals (9th cir.) 1980, US Supreme Ct. 1982. Asst. county atty. Lincoln County, Wiscasset, Maine, 1974; dep. pros. atty. Grays Harbor County, Montesano, Wash., 1974-76, King County, Seattle, 1976, Snohomish County, Everett, Wash., 1976-79; ptnr. Senter & Bowden, Everett, 1979-97; judge Snohomish County Superior Ct., Everett, 1997—. Bd. dirs. Snohomish County Legal Svcs., 2003—. Bd. dirs. Everett Symphony Orch. 1993-2003, pres. 1996-98; v.p. Driftwood Players, Edmonds, Wash., 1978; bd. dirs. Camp Fire USA, 2004—, v.p., 2007, Habitat for Humanity Snohomish County, 2004-, pres., 2006-07; active Leukemia & Lymphoma Soc. Team in Tng., 2007. Sgt. USMC, 1966—68. Mem. ATLA, NADCL, Wash. State Bar Assn. (CLE com., fee arbitration bd., legal aid and pro bono com.), Wash. Assn. Criminal Def. Lawyers (bd. govs., sec. 1993), Wash. State Trial Lawyers Assn., Snohomish County Bar Assn. (pres. 1995), Rotary. Avocations: scuba diving, skiing, bicycling. Office: Snohomish County Courthouse Superior Ct 3000 Rockefeller Ave M/S502 Everett WA 98201-4046

BOWDEN, HELEN FRANCES, psychologist; d. Gary Ronald and Vivian Jane Bowden. BS in Psychology, U. Fla., 1997, MS in Psychology, 2001, PhD in Counseling Psychology, 2005. Tchg. asst. U. Fla., Gainesville, 1998—2001, peer counseling grad. coord., 2001—02, eating disorders grad. coord., 2002—04; intern U. Notre Dame, South Bend, Ind., 2003—04; resident in psychology Clements & Assocs., Lake Mary, Fla., 2005—06; psychologist Salus Behavioral Health, Miami, Fla., 2006—. Anderson scholar, U. Fla., 1996. Mem.: APA, Golden Key, Phi Kappa Phi, Phi Beta Kappa. Democrat. Roman Catholic. Avocations: photography, karaoke, creative writing, movies, reading. Home: 2276 N Brentwood Cir Lecanto FL 34461 Office: Salus Behavioral Health 11900 Biscayne Blvd Ste 780 Miami FL 33181 Personal E-mail: emerald_starr1@yahoo.com.

BOWDEN, HENRY LUMPKIN, JR., lawyer; b. Atlanta, Aug. 2, 1949; s. Henry Lumpkin and Ellen Marian (Fleming) B.; m. Roberta Jeanne Johnson, June 30, 1973; children: Caroline Bruton, Henry Lumpkin III. BA, U. Va., 1971; JD, Emory U., 1974. Bar: Ga. 1974. Law clk. for Hon. Griffin B. Bell U.S. Ct. Appeals (5th cir.), Atlanta, 1974-75; ptnr. King & Spalding, Atlanta, 1975-95; prin. Bowden Law Firm, P.C., Atlanta, 1995—. Trustee Atlanta Ballet, Inc., 1976-85, chmn., 1983-84; trustee Emory U., Atlanta, 1986—; trustee Hist. Oakland Found., Inc., Atlanta, 1987-95, chmn. 1992-95; trustee Westminster Schs., Atlanta, 1995-2000. Fellow Am. Coll. Trust and Estate Counsel (state chair 1991-96), Am. Bar Found.; mem. ABA, State Bar Ga. (chair fiduciary sect. 1990-91), Atlanta Bar Assn., Lawyers Club Atlanta, Piedmont Driving Club (dir. 1996-99), Capital City Club, Nine O'Clocks (pres. 1977-78), Farmington Country Club, Gridiron Secret Soc., Homosassa Fishing Club, The Ten, Phi Beta Kappa, Omicron Delta Kappa, Phi Delta Theta. Methodist. Home: 2542 Habersham Rd NW Atlanta GA 30305-3566 Office: 191 Peachtree St NE Ste 849 Atlanta GA 30303-1741

BOWDEN, HENRY WARNER, religion educator; b. Memphis, Apr. 1, 1939; s. Warner Hill and Jeannette Evelyn (Winn) B.; m. Karin Violet Svensson, June 9, 1962 (div. Aug. 1989); children: Robin Warner, Annika Hillery; m. Michele Clare Cairns, May 1997. AB magna cum laude, Baylor

U., 1961; MA, Princeton U., 1964, PhD, 1966. Instr. faculty of arts and scis. Douglass Coll., Rutgers U., 1964-67, asst. prof., 1967-71, asst. dean acad. affairs, 1969-72, assoc. prof., 1971-79, prof., 1979—2007; ret., 2007. Editor religion books Greenwood Press, 1979—; cons. Funk & Wagnells Revised Ency., 1981—83; cons., author World Book Ency., 1984—94. Author: Church History in the Age of Science: Historiographic Patterns in the United States, 1876-1918, 1971, Church History in an Age of Uncertainty: Historiographical Patterns in the United States, 1906-1990, 1991, American Indians and Christian Missions: Studies in Cultural Conflict, 1981, Dictionary of American Religious Biography, 1977, 2d edit., 1993; author, consulting editor: American National Biography; editor: Religion in America, 1970, Indian Dialogues, 1980, A Century of Church History: The Legacy of Philip Schaff, 1988, Church History: A Centennial Collection of Landmark Studies, 1988; contbr. numerous articles to profl. jours.; assoc. editor Am. Nat. Biography, 1989-99. Bd. dirs. Historical Soc. Episcopal Ch., 1999—2005. Honors fellowship Harvard U. summer session, 1960; religion fellow Princeton U., 1961-62, Roothbert fellow, 1962-64, Lilly Found. fellow, 1964-65, Rutgers Rsch. Coun. fellowship, 1969-70; Rutgers Rsch. Coun. summer grantee, 1967. Mem. Am. Soc. of Ch. History (pres. 1984, exec. sec. 1993-2004), Am. Cath. Hist. Assn., Hist. Soc. of Episcopal Ch. (bd. dirs. 1999-2005). Democrat. Episcopalian. Office: Religion Dept Rutgers Univ New Brunswick NJ 08903 E-mail: bowden1939@yahoo.com.

BOWDEN, JESSE EARLE, editor, writer, cartoonist, journalist, educator; b. Altha, Fla., Sept. 12, 1928; s. Jesse Walden and Earlene (Rackley) B.; m. Mary Louise Clark, Feb. 4, 1951; children: Steven Earle, Randall Clark. BS in Journalism and Polit. Sci, Fla. State U., 1951; DHL, U. West Fla., 1985. Reporter, columnist Panama City (Fla.) News-Herald, 1950; sports editor Pensacola (Fla.) News-Jour., 1953-57, news editor, 1957-65, editl. page editor, 1965-66, editl. cartoonist, 1965—, editor-in-chief, 1966-97, v.p., editor, 1969-97, editor emeritus, 1998—; prof. journalism U. West Fla., 1983—2007; charter mem., chmn. Pensacola Hist. Commn., 1967-2001; chmn. Gulf Islands Nat. Seashore Adv. Com., 1990-93; pres. U. West Fla. Found., 1977-79, Pensacola Hist. Soc., 1978-86. Pres. West Fla. Hist. Preservation, Inc., U. West Fla., 2001—. Author: Always the Rivers Flow, 1979, Fla. Classic edit., 2002, Iron Horse in the Pinelands, 1982, Pensacola: Florida's First Place City, 1989, The Write Way, 1990, When You Reach September, 1990, Fla. Classic edit., 2005, Gulf Islands: The Sands of All Time, 1994, Earle Bowden: Drawing from an Editor's Life, 1996, Look and Tremble: A Novel of West Florida, 2000, Texas Desperado in Florida: The Capture of John Wesley Hardin in Pensacola, 1877, 2002, Embrace an Autumnal Heart, 2003; editor Emerald Coast Rev., Vol. V 1993, Vol. VI, 1995, Vol. VII, 1997, Vol. IX, 1999, Vol. X, 2001. Trustee Pensacola Jr. Coll.; bd. dirs. Fla. Hist. Soc. Served to capt. USAF, 1951-53. U. West Fla. Found. fellow, 1982; recipient Disting. Citizen award Pensacola Jr. Coll., 1966, Nat. Editl. Writing award Freedoms Found. at Valley Forge, 1967, 68, 69, 70, 72, 74, awards for editls. and cartoons, 1967, 68, 69, 72, 86, George Washington Medallion Lifetime award, 2004, DeLuna award Pensacola Founders' Day, 1979, Pensacola Kiwanis Civic award, 1982, award Am. Assn. State and Local History, 1984, Founder's award Inspiring Pensacola Bus. awards, 1992, Bob Graham Hon. AIA Archtl. Awareness award Fla. Assn. Archs., 1992, Malcolm B. Johnson Fellowship award James Madison Inst., 1994, Spirit of Pensacola award, 1998; named Pensacola Profl. Bus. Leader of Yr., 1980, J. Earle Bowden Jr. Historian award named in honor Pensacola Jr. League, 1983, Preservationist of Yr., Fla. Trust Hist. Preservation, 1985, West Fla. Lit. Hall of Honor, 1989, Dorothy Dodd Lifetime Achievement award Fla. Hist. Soc., 2000; Gulf Island Nat. Seashore Hwy. named J. Earle Bowden Way, 1997, Mary Call Darby Collins award, Fla. Sec. of State, 2002, Lifetime Achievement award Pensacola Heritage Found., 2002. Mem. Am. Soc. Newspaper Editors, Nat. Conf. Editl. Writers, Fla. Soc. Newspaper Editors (pres. 1970), Rotary. Achievements include establishment of J. Earle Bowden history endowment U. West Fla. Home: 2220 Mccutchen Pl Pensacola FL 32503-3422 Office: One NewsJour Pla Pensacola FL 32501 Personal E-mail: jeb2220@aol.com.

BOWDEN, M. GABRIELA, biomedical researcher, educator; b. La Plata, Argentina; BS, Univ. Mar del Plata; PhD in Microbiology and Molecular Genetics, Univ. Tex. Houston Health Sci. Ctr. Grad. Sch. Biomedical Sciences, 1999. Rsch. tng., field of molecular pathogenesis of infections Tex. A&M Univ. Inst. Biosciences and Tech., 1999—2004, rsch. asst. prof., Ctr. for Extracellular Matrix Biology, 2004—. Contbr. articles to profl. jours. Recipient NIH Individual Rsch. award, 2001. Office: Tex A&M Univ Inst Biosciences and Tech (IBT 620D) 2121 W Holcombe Blvd Houston TX 77030 Office Phone: 713-677-7572. Office Fax: 713-677-7576. Business E-Mail: gbowden@ibt.tamhsc.edu.

BOWDEN, MARK ROBERT, writer; b. St. Louis, July 17, 1951; s. Richard Houston and Rita Lois (Keane) B.; m. Gail Louise Mclaughlin, July 24, 1955; children: Aaron Keane, William B.J., Anya Rachel, Daniel Mark, Benjamin Houston. BA, Loyola Coll., 1973. Staff reporter Balt. News-Am., 1973-79; staff writer Phila. Inquirer, 1979—2003; nat. corres. The Atlantic Monthly, 2003—. Adj. prof. Loyola Coll., Balt. Author: Doctor Dealer: The Rise and Fall of an All-American Boy and His Multimillion-Dollar Cocaine Empire, 1987, Bringing The Heat: A Pro Football Team's Quest for Glory, Fame, Immortality and a Bigger Piece of the Action, 1994, Black Hawk Down: A Story of Modern War (Hal Boyle award, Overseas Press Club, 2000), 1999, Killing Pablo: The Hunt for the World's Greatest Outlaw (Cornelius Ryan award, Overseas Press Club, 2002) 2001, Roadwork: Among Tyrants, Heroes, Rogues, and Beasts, 2004, Guests of the Ayatollah: The First Battle in America's War with Militant Islam, 2006 Recipient Nat. Sci. Writing award AAAS, 1980, 1st pl. feature article Nat. Assn. Sunday Newspaper Mag. Editors, 1985.

BOWDEN, TOMMY, college football coach; b. Birmingham, Ala., July 10, 1954; m. Linda Joan White; children: Ryan, Lauren. Secondary coach Fla. State Univ., 1978—80, tight ends coach, 1981—83; practice sessions coach Ea. Carolina Univ., 1980; running backs coach Auburn Univ., 1980—81, asst. coach, 1991—97; qb coach and asst. coach Duke Univ., 1983—86; wide receiver coach Univ. Ala., 1987—90; head coach Clemson Univ. Office: Clemson Univ Athletic Dept PO Box 31 Clemson SC 29633

BOWDEN, VIRGINIA MASSEY, librarian; b. Houston, Tex., July 22, 1939; d. Calvin Scott and Juanita Barlow Massey; m. Charles Lee Bowden, July 2, 1960; children: Sharon Scott Bowden Davis, Ellen Maureen Bowden McIntyre. BA, U. Tex., 1960, PhD, 1994; MSLS, U. Ky., 1970. Programmer Texaco Inc., Houston, 1960-64; sr. programmer AMA, Chgo., 1964-65, C.E.I.R. Inc., NYC, 1965-66, Bambergers, Newark, 1967-68; systems analyst, asst. to dir. U. Tex. Health Sci. Ctr., San Antonio, 1970-78, assoc. libr. dir., 1978-85, libr. dir., 1985—2003, libr. dir. emeritus, 2004—. Author: (with others) Handbook of Medical Library Practice, 1983; contbr. articles to profl. jours. Prse. Friends Pub. Libr., San Antonio, 1989-90. Recipient numerous grants Nat. Libr. Medicine, 1982-2003, Julia Grothaus award Bexar Libr. Assn., 1983; fellow Coun. Libr. Resources, 1978-79. Fellow Med. Libr. Assn. (Louise Darling medal 1990); mem. ALA, LWV (bd. dirs. 1983-85, 2004-2005), Acad. Health Info. Profls, Assn. Acad. Health Sci. Libr. Dirs. (bd. dirs. 1995-98), Nat. Network Librs. Medicine (bd. dirs. South Ctrl. region 1995-97), Amigos Bibliographic Coun. (trustee 1986-89), Nat. Libr. Medicine (cons. 1983-88), Tex. Libr. Assn., Coun. Rsch. and Acad. Librs. (pres. 1986-87), Tex. Coun. State Univ. Librs. (pres. 1996-98), Daus. Rep. Tex., Phi Beta Kappa (pres. San Antonio Assn. 1979). Unitarian Universalist. Home: PO Box 2968 Canyon Lake TX 78133-0016

BOWDEN, WILLIAM DARSIE, retired interior designer; b. Palo Alto, Calif., Aug. 11, 1920; s. Edmund Robert and Elisabeth (Darsie) B.; m. Anne Minor Lile, July 29, 1948; children: Darsie Minor, Raleigh Anne, Elisabeth Lile. BA, Stanford U., 1942. Jr. exec. Frederick and Nelson Dept. Store, Seattle, 1946-48; v.p., co-owner William L. Davis Co., Seattle, 1948-84. Trustee Found. for Interior Design Edn. Rsch., Plestcheeff Inst. for Decorative Arts U. Wash. Served to 1st lt. AUS, 1943-46. Fellow Am. Soc. Interior Designers (pres. Wash. chpt. 1966-67, nat. v.p. 1969-71), Furniture History Soc. (London), Phi Beta Kappa, Alpha Delta Phi. Clubs: University, Wash. Athletic. Republican. Episcopalian. Home and Office: 2030 Beans Bight Rd NE Bainbridge Island WA 98110 Office Phone: 206-780-9418. E-mail: bowdbxx@aol.com.

BOWDEN, WILLIAM P., JR., lawyer, finance company executive; b. East Orange, NJ, Feb. 29, 1944; s. W. Paul and Catherine (Porter) B.; m. Margo Redman, June 8, 1968; children: Jennifer Porter, Peter Chandler. AB, Williams Coll., Williamstown, Mass., 1966; JD, Columbia U., NYC, 1969. Bar: NY. Atty. Davis Polk & Wardwell, NYC, 1969-75, 77-80; gen. counsel, sec. Alaska Interstate Co., Houston, 1976-77; assoc. gen. counsel Citicorp, NYC, 1980-85; dep. gen. counsel Marine Midland Banks, Inc., NYC, 1985-91; chief counsel Office of Comptr. of Currency, U.S. Dept. Treasury, Washington, 1991-94; gen. counsel CS First Boston, Inc., NYC, 1994-96, Société Générale Ams., 1997—2001, Willis Group Holdings Ltd., NYC and London, 2001—06; mng. dir. Promontory Fin. Group, LLC, NYC, 2006—07. Mem. ABA, Assn. of Bar of City of NY, Rockaway Hunting Club, Lawrence Beach Club, Univ. Club, The Anglers Club of NY Office Phone: 212-365-6989. Business E-Mail: wbowden@promontory.com.

BOWDISH, JAMES L.S., lawyer; b. Tottenville, NY, July 4, 1944; s. Lewis S. and Margaret E. Bowdish; m. Jenny C. Campbell, Aug. 13, 1966; children: Michelle E., Michael L. BA cum laude, Wake Forest Coll., Winston-Salem, NC, 1966; JD cum laude, Stetson U., St. Petersburg, Fla., 1969. Bar: Fla. 1996, cir. ct. mediator: Supreme Ct. Fla. 1995. Counsel Crary, Buchanan, et. al., Stuart, Fla., 1973—2007; mng. ptnr. Crary, Buchanan, Bowdish, et. al., Stuart, Fla., 2007—. Mem. Fla. 19th Jud. Cir. Jud. Nominating Commn., Stuart, 2001—07, Fla. 4th Dist. Sr. Judge Cert. Commn., West Palm Beach; mem., past pres. United Way of Martin County, Stuart. Capt. judge advocate US Army, 1969—73. Named one of, Fla. Superlawyers, 2006, 2007. Mem.: Am. Arbitration Assn. (mem. panel of neutrals), Am. Assn. for Justice, Martin County Bar Assn. (pres. 1985—86), The Fla. Assn. for Justice, Stuart Rod and Reel Club (past pres.), Kiwanis. Conservative-R. Episcopalian. Avocations: fishing, golf, tennis. Home: 471 NE Town Terr Jensen Beach FL Office: Crary Buchanan Bowdish et al 555 Colorado Ave Stuart FL 34994 Home Phone: 772-223-4304; Office Phone: 772-223-4304. Office Fax: 772-287-9988; Home Fax: 772-287-9988.

BOWDLER, ANTHONY JOHN, internist, educator; b. London, Eng., Oct. 16, 1928; came to U.S., 1967; s. Edward Thomas and Clara (Anthony) B.; m. Eleanor Madeleine Sladen, July 30, 1955; children: Noelle Clare, Jonathan Francis. BSc, U. Coll., London, 1949, MB, BS, 1952, MD (Bilton Pollard fellow), 1962, PhD, 1967; postgrad. (Buswell Sr. fellow), U. Rochester, 1962-64. Intern Univ. Coll. Hosp., London, 1952, casualty med. officer, 1956, registrar and rsch. fellow, 1958-62; intern Dorking Hosp., Surrey, England, 1957, Hammersmith Hosp., London, 1953, Brompton Hosp., London, 1956; sr. instr. U. Rochester, NY, 1962-64; sr. lectr. U. Coll. Hosp. Med. Sch., London, 1964-67; assoc. prof. medicine Mich. State U. Coll. Human Medicine, East Lansing, 1967-70, prof. medicine, 1971-80, Marshall U. Sch. Medicine, Huntington, W.Va., 1980-97, prof. medicine emeritus, 1997—. Hon. cons. Univ. Coll. Hosp., London, 1967. Served as surgeon lt. Royal Navy, 1953-55. Fellow ACP, Royal Coll. Physicians, Royal Coll. Pathologists; mem. AMA, Am. Fedn. Clin. Rsch., Ctrl. Soc. Clin. Rsch. (emeritus), Am. Soc. Hematology (emeritus), Am. Soc. Clin. Oncology (emeritus), Brit. Med. Assn. (life) Researcher in internal medicine. Home: 4609 Sawgrass Dr E Ann Arbor MI 48108-8644 Personal E-mail: abowdler@comcast.net.

BOWE, WILLIAM J(OHN), lawyer; b. Chgo., June 23, 1942; s. William John Sr. and Mary (Gwinn) B.; m. Catherine Louise Vanselow, 1979; children: Andrew M., Patrick D. BA, Yale U., 1964; JD, U. Chgo., 1967. Bar: Ill. 1967, Tenn. 1984. Assoc. Ross, Hardies, O'Keefe, Babcock, McDougall & Parsons, Chgo., 1967—68; assoc., then ptnr. Roan & Grossman, Chgo., 1971—78; v.p., gen. counsel, sec. The Bradford Exch. Ltd., Niles, Ill., 1979—83; asst. gen. counsel, v.p., gen. counsel United Press Internat. Inc., Nashville, 1984—85; v.p. to exec. v.p., gen. counsel, sec. Ency. Britannica, Inc., Chgo., 1986—; sec. William Benton Found., Chgo., 1987—96; pres. Merriam-Webster, Inc., Springfield, Mass., 1995—96, Ency. Britannica Ednl. Corp., Chgo., 1995—99. Part-time faculty Summer Law Inst. Kenneth Wang Law Sch., Soochow U., Suzhou, China, 2005. Mem. bd. editors Intellectual Property Studies, Chinese Acad. Social Studies, Beijing, 1996-99; contbr. articles to legal jours. Mem. The Annenberg Washington Program Anti-Piracy Project, Washington, 1988—89; bd. dirs. Internat. Anticounterfeiting Coalition, Washington, 1993—96, chmn., 1994—96; gen. counsel Gov.'s Task Force on Sch. Fin., Chgo., 1975—76; trustee Hull Ho. Assn., Chgo., 1977—79; pres., bd. dirs. Clarence Darrow Cmty. Ctr., Chgo., 1975—84; mem. bd. overseers Ill. Inst. Tech.-Kent Coll. Law, 1982—86; mem. Gov.'s Task Force on Workforce Preparation, 1991—93, Gov.'s Work Group on Early Childhood Care and Edn., 1994—95, Gov.'s Edn. Summit, 2000—02. With US Army, 1968—71. Mem.: ABA, Software and Info. Industry Assn. (govt. affairs coun. 1999—), Software Publs. Assn. (govt. affairs com. 1997—99), Intellectual Property Assn. Chgo., Chgo. Bar Assn., Ill. Bar Assn., Ill. State C. of C. (bd. dirs. 1989—96, mem. edn. com. 1989—99), Cliff Dwellers Club (bd. dirs. 2004—, pres. 2006—). Office: Ency Britannica Inc 331 N LaSalle St Chicago IL 60610-4707 Office Phone: 312-347-7084. E-mail: wbowe@eb.com.

BOWEN, ANDREA, actress; b. Columbus, Ohio, Mar. 4, 1990; Actor: (TV films) Angelo a New York, Un, 1996; (films) Highball, 1997, (voice) The Longest Journey, 1999, Extreme Skate Adventure, 2003, The Cat in the Hat, 2003, Party Wagon, 2004, Red Riding Hood, 2004, Luckey Quarter, 2005; (TV series, guest appearances) Law & Order, 1996, 1997, Law & Order: Special Victims Unit, 2001, Third Watch, 2001, Arli$$, 2002, Boston Public, 2003, One Tree Hill, 2003, Strong Medicine, 2003, Without a Trace, 2005; (TV series) That Was Then, 2002, Desperate Housewives, 2004— (Screen Actors Guild Award for outstanding performance by an ensemble in a comedy series, 2005, 2006). Office: Desperate Housewives Touchtone Television 100 Universal City Plaza Bldg 2128 Ste G Universal City CA 91608

BOWEN, BRENDA DENISE, literature and language professor; b. Sacramento, Aug. 12, 1964; d. William David Bowen and Patricia Dianne Cowen; m. Robert Charles Bilodeau, Aug. 18, 1988 (div. Nov. 6, 1996). B English, Tex. Tech U., Lubbock, 1994; M English, Ea. N.Mex. U., Portales, 1997. Cert. Inst. Children's Lit., 04. Grad. tchg. asst. Ea. N.Mex. U., 1995—97; English instr. Mesa CC, Ariz., 1997—2000, Sierra Coll., Rocklin, Calif., 2001—. Staff writer, editor Virgo Pub., Phoenix; freelance writer Calif. Job Jour., Sacramento. Contbr. articles to mags. Vol. women and children in need Adventure Christian Ch., Rocklin, 2006. Jack and Blanche Williamson writing scholar, Ea. N.Mex. U., 1996. Mem.: Nat. Coun. Tchrs. English, Am. Studies Assn., Soc. Children's Book Writers and Illustrators. Avocations: Japanese food, reading, writing, tennis. Office: Sierra Coll 5000 Rocklin Rd Rocklin CA 95677 Office Phone: 916-624-3333 ext. 3508.

BOWEN, BRUCE, professional basketball player; b. Merced, Calif., June 14, 1971; m. Yardley Barbon, 2004; children: Ojani, Ozmel. BA, Calif. State U., Fullerton, 1993. Guard Miami Heat, Fla., 1996—97, Fla., 2000—01, Boston Celtics, 1997—99, Phila. 76ers, 1999—2000, San Antonio Spurs, 2001—. Founder Bruce Bowen Found. Named to NBA All-Defensive First Team, 2004, 2005, 2006, 2007. Achievements include winning an NBA Championship as a member of the Spurs, 2005. Office: San Antonio Spurs One AT&T Ctr San Antonio TX 78219*

BOWEN, CHRISTOPHER EDWARD, researcher, director; b. Jamaica, NY, July 24, 1947; s. James Frederick Jr. and Roseanne Marie (McGrath) B.; m. Barbara Francine Heitman, Sept. 11, 1971; children: Melissa, Jason, Heather. BA in English, St. John's U., 1970; MLS, Queen's Coll., 1974; BS in Pharmacy, St. John's U., 1979. Head libr. L.I. Press, Jamaica, 1965-77; asst. head libr. N.Y. Post, NYC, 1977-88; libr. dir. Star Mag., Tarrytown, NY, 1988—2000; rsch. dir. Dark Star Mining, Southbury, Conn., 2000—. Mem. Spl. Librs. Assn. Office: Dark Star Mining PO Box 588 Southbury CT 06488 Personal E-mail: darkstarmining@aol.com.

BOWEN, CLOTILDE MARION DENT, retired military officer, psychiatrist; b. Chgo., Mar. 20, 1923; d. William Marion Dent and Clotilde (Tynes) D.; m. William N. Bowen, Dec. 29, 1945 (dec.). BA, Ohio State U., 1943, MD, 1947. Intern Harlem Hosp., NYC, 1947-48; resident and fellow in pulmonary diseases Triboro Hosp., Jamaica, NY, 1948-50; resident in psychiatry VA Hosp., Albany, NY, 1959-62; asst. resident in psychiatry Albany Med. Ctr. Hosp., 1961-62; pvt. practice NYC, 1950-55; chief pulmonary disease clinic, 1950-55; asst. chief pulmonary disease svc. Valley Forge Army Hosp., Pa., 1955—59; chief psychiatry VA Hosp., Roseburg, Oreg., 1962-66, acting chief of staff, 1964-66; asst. chief neurology and psychiatry Tripler Gen. Hosp., Hawaii, 1966-68; psychiatr. lcons. and dir. Rev. Br. Office Civil Health and Med. Program Uniform Svcs., 1968-70; commd. capt. US Army, 1955, advanced through ranks to col., 1968, neuropsychiat. cons. USA Vietnam Medcom Vietnam, 1970—71, chief dept. psychiatry Fitzsimons Army Med. Ctr., 1971-74, chief dept. psychiatry Tripler Army Med. Ctr., 1974-75, comdr. Hawley Army Clin., post surgeon Ft. Benjamin, Harrison, Ind., 1977-78, chief dept. primary care and cmty. medicine, 1978-83, chief psychiat. consultation svc. Fitzsimons Army Med. Ctr., 1983-85; assoc. clin. prof. psychiatry U. Hawaii, 1974-75; chief psychiatry svc. med./regional office ctr. VA, Cheyenne, Wyo., 1987-90; staff psychiatrist Denver VA Satellite Clin., Colorado Springs, Colo., 1990-96; ret., 1996. Locum Tenens practice psychiatry, 1996—; surveyor Joint Commn. on Accreditation Healthcare Orgns., 1985-92; assoc. clin. prof. psychiatry U. Colo. Med. Ctr., Denver, 1971-2006; spkr. Vietnam Vets. Meml. Wall, 2001. Decorated Legion of Merit, Bronze Star, Vietnam, others; recipient Colo. Disabled Am. Vets. award, 1994-95, Pres.'s 300 Commencement award Ohio State U., 1987, Profl. Achievement award Ohio State U. Alumni Assn., 1998, Cert. of Appreciation, VFW, 2000, Am. Assn. Emergency Psychiat. award, 2001. Fellow Am. Psychiat. Assn. (disting. life), Acad. Psychosomatic Med.; mem. AMA, Nat. Med. Assn., Menninger Found (charter), Ctrl. Neuropsychiat. Assn. (Peter Bassoe fellow), S.W. Assn. of Buffalo Soldiers, Inc. Home: 1020 Tari Dr Colorado Springs CO 80921-2257 *To be successful one must always aspire to a goal just beyond his or her immediate reach.*

BOWEN, DAVID R., science and technology educator, consultant; b. NYC, Sept. 13, 1939; s. Lewis Howard and Nancy (Nichols) B.; m. Joyce Helen Blades, Mar. 12, 1966; children: Peter Scott, Amy Elizabeth Bowen Herhold. BS in Physics, Haverford Coll., 1961; PhD in Physics, U. Pa., 1966. Rsch. assoc. U. Pa., 1967; rsch. assoc., instr. Cornell U., Ithaca, N.Y., 1967-70; asst. prof. Northeastern U., Boston, 1970-73, Nathaniel Hawthorne Coll., Antrim, N.H., 1973-74, assoc. prof., 1974-75, Wayne State U., Detroit, 1975—. Cons. Ford Motor Co., Dearborn, Mich., 1989—. Contbr. chpts. to books, numerous articles to profl. jours. Recipient numerous grants and rsch. awards. Mem. Soc. Of Friends. Avocations: internet and computers, sailing, windsurfing. Home: 4704 Elmhurst Ave Royal Oak MI 48073-1780 Office: Wayne State U 2311 A/AB Detroit MI 48202 Office Phone: 313-577-1498. Business E-Mail: d.r.bowen@wayne.edu.

BOWEN, DEBRA LYNN, state official, former state legislator; b. Rockford, Ill., Oct. 27, 1955; d. Robert Calvin and Marcia Ann (Crittenden) Bowen; m. Mark Nechodom; 1 child. BA, Mich. State U., 1976; JD, U. Va., 1979. Bar: Ill. 1979, Calif. 1983. Assoc. Winston & Strawn LLP, Chgo., 1979-82, Washington, 1985-86, Hughes Hubbard & Reed, LA, 1982-84; sole practice LA, 1984-93; mem. Calif. State Assembly from 53rd dist., Sacramento, 1992—98, Calif. State Senate from 28th dist., Sacramento, 1998—2006; sec. state State of Calif., Sacramento, 2007—. Gen. counsel, State Employee's Retirement System Ill., Springfield, 1980-82; adj. prof. Watterson Coll. Sch. Paralegal Studies, 1985. Exec. editor Va. Jour. Internat. Law, 1977-78; contbr. articles to profl. jours. Mem. mental health law com. Chgo. Coun. Lawyers, 1980-82. Rotary Internat. fellow Internat. Christian U., Tokyo, 1975; Wigmore scholar Northwestern U. Sch. Law, Chgo., 1976; recipient James Madison Freedom of Info. award No. Calif. chpt. Soc. Profl. Journalists, 1995. Mem. Calif. Bar Assn. (exec. com. pub. law sect. 1990-94), Mortar Bd., Phi Kappa Phi. Office: Office Sec State 1500 11th St Sacramento CA 95814*

BOWEN, DONALD EDGAR, physics professor, former academic administrator; b. Bklyn., Apr. 10, 1939; s. Frederick John David and Dorothy (Watson) B.; m. Jamie Andrews, June 5, 1965 (dec. Dec. 1977); 1 child, Meredith; m. Daphne Russell, July 19, 1979; children: Michael Justin, Kristen. BA, Tex. Christian U., 1961, MA, 1963; PhD, U. Tex., 1966. From asst. prof. to full prof. U. Tex., El Paso, 1966-84, chmn. dept. physics, 1972-80, asst. v.p. for acad. affairs, 1980-84; v.p. for acad. affairs S.W. Mo. State U., Springfield, 1984-90; pres. Stephen F. Austin State U., Nacogdoches, Tex., 1990—91, prof. physics, 1990—; rector Am. U., Baku, Azerbaijan, 1997—99; v.p. academic affairs Sharjah Coll., United Arab Emirates, 2003—04. Home: 3402 Ashbury Ct Nacogdoches TX 75965-5868 Office: Stephen F Austin State U Miller Sci Bldg 322E 1936 North St Nacogdoches TX 75961 Office Phone: 936-468-2015. E-mail: dbowen@sfasu.edu.

BOWEN, GILBERT WILLARD, minister; b. Muskegon, Mich., Dec. 30, 1931; s. Bruce Oliver and Beatrice Lillian (Sibley) B.; m. Marlene Mary Michell, July 31, 1954; children: Kathryn Leigh, Mark Kevin, Stephen James. BA, Wheaton Coll., 1955; MDiv, McCormick Theol. Sem., 1957, PhD in Ministry, 1976; cert., Ctr. for Religion and Psychotherapy, 1976; DLL (hon.), Nat. Coll. Edn., 1987. Ordained to ministry Presbyn. Ch., 1956. Minister 1st United Presbyn. Ch., Blue Earth, Minn., 1956-63, Faith United Presbyn. Ch., Tinley Park, Ill., 1963-65, Community Presbyn. Ch., Mt. Prospect, Ill., 1965-70, Kenilworth (Ill.) Union Ch., 1970—. Exchange minister Johanneskirche, Neuwied, Fed. Republic Germany, 1961-62; pres. bd. Ctr. for Religion and Psychotherapy; bd. dirs. McCormick Theol. Sem., Chgo., Anatolia Coll., Thessaloniki, Greece, Presbyn. Home, Evanston. Mem. adv. com. North Shore Sr. Ctr., Winnetka, Ill.; bd. dirs. Hospice of North Shore, Wilmette, Ill., Shelter for Battered Women, Evanston; chmn. Instl. Rev. Bd., Evanston. Mem. Am. Assn. Pastoral Counselors, Acad. Parish Clergy, Am. Waldensian Aid Soc. Clubs: Indian Hill. Republican. Avocations: tennis, golf, vocal music. Home: 2 Arbor Ln # 112 Evanston IL 60201 Office: Kenilworth Union Ch 211 Kenilworth Ave Kenilworth IL 60043-1299 E-mail: gwbowen@aol.com.

BOWEN, HAROLD J. (JAY), III, investment company executive; BA, Univ. NC, Chapel Hill, 1984; attended, London Sch. Econ., 1989. Joined Bowen Hanes & Co., Atlanta, Guam, 1986, pres., chief investment officer.

Bd. mem. Fulton County Taxpayers Assn. Mem.: Nat. Economists Club, Nat. Assn. Bus. Economists, Atlanta Economists Club, Atlanta Soc. Financial Analysts. Office: Bowen Hanes & Co Ste 880 3290 Northside Pkwy Atlanta GA 30327*

BOWEN, JAMES THOMAS, career officer; b. Mason City, Iowa, May 4, 1948; s. Stanley Thomas and Marilyn Louise (Ott) B.; m. Joyce Anne Kermabon, Sept. 10, 1977; 1 child, Steven James. BBA, U. Iowa, 1969; MS, U. So. Calif., LA, 1974. Cert. project mgmt. profl. Commd. 2nd lt. USAF, 1969, advance through grades to col., 1991; student pilot 3575th Pilot Tng. Wing, Vance AFB, Okla., 1969-70; co-pilot 773rd Tactical Airlift Squadron, Clark AFB, Phillipines, 1971; pilot 6594th Test Group, Hickam AFB, Hawaii, 1971-75; acquisition program mgr. Aeronautical Systems Div., Wright-Patterson AFB, Ohio, 1976-82; chief, standoff surveillance and attack systems HQ USAF, Rsch. Devel. and Acquistion, Pentagon, Va., 1984-87; chief, acqusition plans and programs br. Air Force Inspection and Safety Ctr., Norton AFB, Calif., 1988-90; dir. projects joint tactical autonomous weapons Aero. Systems Div., Wright-Patterson AFB, Ohio, 1990-91, dir. devel. and integration F-16, 1991-94; F-16 mgmt. dir. Ogden Air Logistics Ctr., Hill AFB, Utah, 1994-95; custom sys. program mgr. Hewlett Packard and Agilent Tech. Cos., Santa Rosa, Calif., 1996-2001; site mgr. Agilent Techs., Rohnert Pk., Calif., 2001—02, sr. program mgr., 2002—05; owner On Target Program Mgmt. Solutions Consulting Co., 2006—. Decorated Air medal USAF, 1972. Mem. Mil. Officers Assn. Am., Air Force Assn., Def. Systems Mgmt. Coll. Alumni Assn., Am. Mgmt. Assn., Ret. Officers Assn., Project Mgmt. Inst. Methodist. Avocations: skiing, deep sea fishing, golf. Office Phone: 425-585-0903. Personal E-mail: tresbowen@comcast.net. Business E-Mail: jim_bowen@ontargetpmsolutions.com.

BOWEN, JEAN, retired librarian, consultant; b. Albany, NY, Mar. 23, 1927; d. John W. and Grace Lester (Quier) B.; m. Henry F. Bloch, June 26, 1962; 1 child, Pamela A. Bloch. AB, Smith Coll., Northampton, Mass., 1948, AM, 1956; MS, Columbia U., NYC, 1957. Curator Rodgers & Hammerstein Archives of Recorded Sound, NYC, 1962-67; asst. chief music divsn. N.Y. Pub. Libr., NYC, 1967-85, chief music divsn., 1986-96, dir. Humanities and Social Scis. Libr., 1996-2000. Cons. Rockefeller Bros. Found., NYC, 1963, NYC, 67, N.Y. Philharm., NYC, 1984, Schubert Archives, NYC, 1982; mem. faculty Rare Book Sch. Columbia U., NYC, 1984, NYC, 87, NYC, 91; bd. dirs. Amphion Found., NYC; mem. bd. New World Records, NYC. Contbr. articles to High Fidelity, Opera News, Am. Record Guide, Saturday Rev., MLA Notes, New Grove Dictionary of Am. Music. Mem.: Rare Book Sch. (mem. faculty, Columbia U., NYC 1984, 1987, 1991).

BOWEN, JEWELL RAY, chemical engineering professor; b. Duck Hill, Miss., Jan. 9, 1934; s. Hugh and Myrtle Louise (Stevens) B.; m. Priscilla Joan Spooner, Feb. 4, 1956; children: Jewell Ray, Sandra L., Susan E. BS, MIT, 1956, MS, 1957; PhD, U. Calif., Berkeley, 1963. Asst. prof. U. Wis., Madison, 1963-67, assoc. prof., 1967—70, prof. chem. engring., 1970-81, chmn. chem engring. dept., 1971-73, 78-81, assoc. vice chancellor, 1972-76; prof. chem. engring. U. Wash., Seattle, 1981-2000, prof. emeritus, 2001—, dean coll. engring., 1981-96. Cons. in field; adviser NSF, Dept. Def.; vis. prof. Kyoto U. Internat. Innovation Ctr., 2002; bd. dirs. Inst. Dynamics of Explosions and Reactive Sys., 1989-2007, pres., 1989-95, treas., 1995-05. Contbr. articles to profl. jours.; editor: 7th-10th Internat. Colloquia on Dynamics of Explosions and Reactive Systems, 1979, 81, 83, 85, chmn. program com. 18th. Mem. Wash. High Tech. Coordinating Bd., 1983—87; bd. dirs. Wash. Tech. Ctr., 1983—87, interim exec. dir., 1989—91; bd. dirs. U. Wash. Retirement Assn., 2003—07, 1st v.p., 2004—05, pres., 2005—07. Recipient SWE Rodney Chipp award, 1995; NATO-NSF postdoctoral fellow, 1962-63, sr. postdoctoral fellow, 1968; Deutsche Forschungsgemeinschaft prof., 1976-77. Fellow AIAA, AAAS (com. on coun. affairs 1995-97, sect. chmn. 1996-97), Am. Soc. Engring. Edn. (deans coun. 1985-92, chmn. 1989-91, bd. dirs. 1989-94, 1st v.p. 1991, pres.-elect 1992, pres. 1993); mem. AIAA, AIChE, Am. Phys. Soc., Combustion Inst., Sigma Xi, Tau Beta Pi, Beta Theta Pi. Home: 5324 NE 86th St Seattle WA 98115-3922 Office: U Wash Dept Chem Engring PO Box 351750 Seattle WA 98195-1750 Personal E-mail: bowen5324@comcast.net.

BOWEN, LINNELL R., director; b. Orlando, Fla., June 16, 1940; m. Paul Ivan, Jr. Bowen; children: Julia Anne, Paul Ivan III. Student, U. Md., 1962; fundraising and devel. mgmt. program, Goucher Coll., 1990; leadership tng. course, Nat. Trust for Hist. Preserve, 1991. Tchr. U.S. history Annapolis H.S., 1962—65; dir. devel./pub. rels., dir. edn., ednl. cons. Hist. Annapolis Found., 1976—94; adj. tchr. Colonial Md. Experience Anne Arundel C.C., 1989—91; adj. tchr. fundraising for hist. preservation Goucher Coll. Ctr. for Continuing Studies, 1993—95; exec. dir. Annapolis 300, A Capital Celebration, 1994—95, Md. Hall for Creative Arts, 1996—. Bd. pres. Cultural Arts Found. Anne Arundel County, 1995—96, Jr. League Annapolis Adv. Bd., 1995—96; County exec. appt. Scenic and Hist. Rds. Commn., 1986—96; pres. Scholarship for Scholars Inc., 1991—93; steering com. Millennium Legacy Trail Art Competition, City of Annapolis Whitbread Race; active Cultural Heritage Alliance Com.; founder, dir. Annapolis Arts Alliance, 2004—05; bd. dirs. Scholarship for Scholars Inc., 1991—93, Annapolis and Anne Arundel County Conf. and Visitors Bur.; adv. com. Mitchell Gallery at St. John's Coll., 1995—2005. Named one of Md.'s Top 100 Women, 1998, 2001; recipient City of Annapolis award of commendation, Annapolis 300 Celebration, 1995, Cmty. award for Annapolis 300 Celebration, Hist. Annapolis Found., 1996, Leadership Anne Arundel Cmty. Trustee award, 1996, Lifetime Achievement award, Pub. Rels. Soc. Annapolis and Anne Arundel County, 1999; fellow Paul Harris fellow, Rotary Found., 1997. Mem.: Annapolis/Anne Arundel County (chpt. trustee), Pub. Rels. Soc. Am., Annapolis and Anne Arundel County C. of C., Anne Arundel Trade Coun. Office: 801 Chase St Annapolis MD 21401 Home Phone: 410-224-0706; Office Phone: 410-263-5544. Personal E-mail: anna300@aol.com. Business E-Mail: lbowen@mdhallarts.org.

BOWEN, LOWELL REED, lawyer; b. Prince Frederick, Md., Jan. 29, 1931; s. Perry Gray and Melba (Hutchins) B.; m. Marilyn Sack, June 14, 1958; children: Mark Holdsworth, David Stockbridge. BA, U. Md., 1952; LLB, U. Md., Balt., 1957. Bar: Md. 1957, U.S. Dist. Ct. Md. 1958, U.S. Ct. Appeals (4th cir.) 1959, U.S. Supreme Ct. 1964. Law clk. to chief judge U.S. Dist. Ct. Md., Balt., 1957—58; assoc. Miles & Stockbridge, Balt., 1958—65, ptnr., 1966—, mng. ptnr., 1974—91, chmn., 2001—02. Lectr. U. Md. Law Sch., 1958-63, U. Balt. Law Sch., 1965-70. Mem., chmn. various coms. Md. Commn. to Revise Annotated Code Md., Annapolis, 1973—; mem. Standing Com. on Rules of Practice and Procedure, Md. Ct. Appeals, Annapolis, 1980—; trustee, chmn. Balt. Opera Co., Inc., 1977-92; mem. Md. Humanities Coun., 1992-97; trustee, pres. Lyric Found., Inc., 1997-2005. 1st lt. USAF, 1952-54. Mem. ABA, Md. State Bar Assn. Office: Miles & Stockbridge PC One W Pennsylvania Ave Towson MD 21204 Business E-Mail: lbowen@milesstockbridge.com.

BOWEN, MARY LU, ecumencial administrator; b. Wheeling, W.Va., Feb. 14, 1930; d. Walter Philip and Helen Elizabeth (Luthy) Wagenheim; m. Robert Edward Bowen, June 13, 1953; children: Jeanne, Thomas, Robert, David. BS in Edn., Wittenberg U., Springfield, Ohio, 1952; MA in Social Scis., SUNY, Binghamton, 1989. Cert. tchr., Ohio, W.Va., Tex., N.Y. Various teaching positions, 1952-80; coord. ministry with the aging Coun. of Chs., Broome County, NY, 1979-82, adminstrv. asst., 1982-83, asst. dir., 1984-86; assoc. for ecumenical devel. N.Y. State Coun. of Chs., Albany, Syracuse, 1990-94, regional dir. southern tier Albany, 1995-96, dir. of pub. policy, 1997—98, exec. dir., 1998—. Sec. exec. cabinet N.Y. State Coun. Chs., Albany, Syracuse, 1986-91; synodical lay rep. Evang. Luth. Ch. in Am. Region VII Coun., Phila., 1987-91, churchwide leadership team Social Min. Project, Chgo., 1990-91, sec. constituting conv. Upstate N.Y. Synod, Syracuse, 1987. Author: Reclaiming Christianity's Feminist Heritage: Reflections on Patriarchal Teachings and Women's Problems, 1989, Handbook for Clergy on Child Abuse and Neglect, 1995. Mem. Broome County Coordinating Coun. Child Abuse and Neglect, 1986-88, 96-98, treas. 1997; mem. Luth. Statewide Advocacy Exec. Com., Albany, 1982-90, 2000—, chmn. exec. com., 1991-99; regional adv. bd. Citizen Action N.Y., Binghamton, 1994-98; co-chmn. Interreligious Health and Justice Coalition, N.Y. Ctrl. So. Tier Region, 1994-98; Evang. Luth. Ch. in Am. Coalition for Mission in Appalachia, 1996-06, chair, 2000-01. Recipient Citizen Action N.Y. Phoenix award, 1998, Upstate N.Y. Synod Lay Discipleship award, 1999; Sr. Congl. intern, 1997. Mem.: Nat. Assn. Ecumenical Staff. Democrat. Lutheran. Avocations: travel, reading. Home: 14 Overbrook Dr Apalachin NY 13732-4234 Office: NY State Coun Chs 18 Computer Dr W Ste 107 Albany NY 12205 Personal E-mail: marylubowen@aol.com, nyscoc@aol.com.

BOWEN, MICHAEL ANTHONY, lawyer, writer; b. Ft. Monroe, Va., July 16, 1951; s. Harold James and Judith Ann (Carter-Waller) B.; m. Sara Armbruster, Aug. 30, 1975; children: Rebecca Elizabeth, Christopher Andrew, John Armbruster, Marguerite Judith, James Harold. AB summa cum laude, Rockhurst Coll., 1973; JD cum laude, Harvard U., 1976. Bar: Wis. 1976, U.S. Dist. Ct. (ea. and we. dists.) Wis., U.S. Ct. Appeals (4th, 5th, 7th, 8th and 10th cirs.), Wis. Supreme Ct. Assoc. Foley & Lardner, Milw., 1976-84, ptnr., 1984—. Author: Can't Miss, 1987, Badger Game, 1989, Washington Deceased, 1990, Fielder's Choice, 1991, Faithfully Executed, 1992, Act of Faith, 1993, Corruptly Procured, 1994, Worst Case Scenario, 1996, Collateral Damage, 1999, The Fourth Glorious Mystery, 2000; co-author: The Wisconsin Fair Dealership Law 1988, contbr. articles to profl. journs. Recipient Best Lawyers in Am., America's Leading Lawyers for Bus., Chambers USA, Wis. Super Lawyers, Law & Politics Media Inc., 2006. Mem. ABA, Wis. Bar Assn., Milw. Bar Assn., St. Thomas More Lawyers' Soc. (pres. 1983), Milw. Young Lawyers' Assn. (pro bono legal services 1982). Roman Catholic. Avocations: photography, running, cross country skiing. Office: Foley & Lardner 777 E Wisconsin Ave Milwaukee WI 53202-5367 Office Phone: 414-297-5538. Office Fax: 414-297-4900. Business E-Mail: mbowen@foley.com.

BOWEN, OTIS RAY, former secretary of health and human services, former governor; b. Rochester, Ind., Feb. 26, 1918; s. Vernie and Pearl (Wright) B.; m. Elizabeth A. Steinmann, Feb. 25, 1939 (dec. Jan. 1981); children: Richard H., Judith I. McGrew, Timothy R., Robert O.; m. Rose May Hochstetler, Sept. 26, 1981. AB in Chemistry, Ind. U., 1939, MD, 1942, LL.D. (hon.), Anderson Coll., 1973, Valparaiso U., 1973, Butler U., 1973; LL.D., S.C. U. Med. Ctr., 1986; LL.D. (hon.), Vincennes U., Tri-State Coll., Calumet Coll., U. Evansville, Ind. U., 1987, Ind. State U., Ball State U., U. Notre Dame, Rose-Hulman Inst., St. Joseph Coll., Calumet Campus of Purdue U., Manchester Coll., Hanover Coll., St. Mary's Coll., Bethel Coll., Marian Coll.; LL.D.(hon.), U. Md., Balt., 1987; LL.D. (hon.), Baylor U., 1987; LL.D (hon.)degree, Wabash U., 1987, NYU Med. Coll., 1987. Intern, Meml. Hosp., South Bend, Ind., 1942-43; practice gen. medicine Bremen, Ind., 1946-72; past mem. staff Bremen Community Hosp., Parkview Hosp., Plymouth, Ind., St. Joseph's and Meml. Hosp., South Bend, St. Joseph Hosp., Mishawaka, Ind.; clin. prof. family medicine Sch. Medicine, Ind. U., 1976-85; coroner Marshall County, Ind., 1952-56; mem. Ind. Ho. of Reps., 1956-58, 60-72, minority leader, 1965-67, speaker of house, 1967-72; vice chmn. legis. council Ind. (Gen. Assembly), 1967-68, chmn., 1970-72; gov. State of Ind., 1973-81; mem. staff dept. family medicine Long Hosp., Indpls., 1981-85; mem. Council State Govts., 1973-81, mem. exec. com.; sec. US Dept. Health & Human Services, Washington, 1985—89. Mem. Edn. Commn. States, 1973-81, chmn.-elect, 1976-77, chmn., 1977-78; mem. Midwest Govs. Conf., 1973-81, vice chmn., 1977-78, chmn., 1978; mem. Republican Govs. Conf., 1973-81, chmn., 1978; mem. Nat. Govs. Conf., 1973-81, chmn., 1979; past chmn. com. on crime reduction and pub. safety, mem. energy com.; past mem. Pres.'s Commn. Fed. Paperwork, Pres.'s Commn. Sci. and Tech.; mem. Pres.'s Commn. Federalism, 1981-82; past chmn. Interstate Mining Commn.; past med. services dir. Marshall County CD; mem. Midwest Govs. Gt. Lakes Caucus; former mem. adv. com. on curricula Vincennes U.; hon. dir. Center for Pub. Service, Anderson Coll.; chmn. Adv. Council Social Security, 1982; chmn. adv. council BACCHUS, 1979-85 Contbr. articles to med. jours. Past trustee Ancilla Coll.; trustee Valparaiso U., 1978-85; past mem. adv. council United Student Aid Fund; mem. adv. bd. Indpls. chpt. Fellowship Christian Athletes; mem., past chmn. Lutheran Sch. Bd., Bremen; past v.p. congregation, past fin. bd. chmn. St. Paul's Lutheran Ch., Bremen.; bd. govs. Riley Meml. Assn., 1981-85; bd. dirs. Greater Indpls. Council Alcoholism, 1982-85, Lilly Endowment Inc. Served from 1st lt. to capt. M.C., AUS, 1943-46, PTO. Recipient Merit award Ind. Pub. Health Assn., 1971, Presdl. Citation, NYU, Maynard K. Hine award Ind. Dental Assn.; named Alumni of Year, Ind. U. Med. Sch., 1971; Disting. Service award Future Farmers Am., 1976; Public Service award Ind. Soc. Public Adminstrn, George F. Hixson award Kiwanis Internat., 1987. Mem. AMA (Dr. Benjamin Rush award 1973), Ind. Med. Assn. (legis commn. 1958-71, 13th dist. councilor 1965-71), 13th Dist. Med. Assn. (past pres.), Marshall County Med. Assn. (past pres.), Am. Gen. Practice Assn., Ind. Gen. Practice Assn., 13th Dist. Gen. Practice Assn., Farm Bur., Marshall County Tb Soc. (past v.p.), Bremen C. of C., Am. Legion, VFW, Alpha Omega Alpha, Phi Beta Pi, Delta Chi (Delta Chi of Yr. 1986). Clubs: Kiwanis (past pres., George F. Hixon award 1987). Lutheran.

BOWEN, PATRICIA LEDERER, dental educator; b. Evanston, Ill., July 5, 1943; d. John Arthur and Edna Virginia Lederer; m. Clarence Henry Metzner, Jr., June 1, 1963 (div. Feb. 1972); children: Donald Frederick Metzner, John Henry Metzner; m. Steven Casto Bowen, Mar. 31, 1973. Dental Hygienist, U. Louisville, Ky., 1972; B in Health Edn., U. Ky., Ft. Knox, 1982; MPA, We. Ky. U., Bowling Green, 1985. Pvt. practice dental hygienist, various locations, 1972-75; pub. health dental hygienist U.S. Army, Berlin, 1975-78; cmty. health dental hygienist U.S. Army Dental Activity, Ft. Knox, Ky., 1978-95, U.S. Army Health Svcs. Command, Ft. Knox, Ky., 1981-95; pub. health dental hygienist Meade County (Ky.) Sch. Sys., 1995-96, LaRue County (Ky.) Sch. Sys., 1995-96; instr. pub. dental health Elizabethtown (Ky.) C.C., 1996-97; asst. dir. Meade County Tourism, 1996-97, dir., 1997—2004. Reporter Meade County Messenger, 1998, news editor, 1999—2003; lectr. in field. Contbr. articles to profl. jours. Pub. health dental hygienist Lebanon Sch. Sys., Ohio, 1974—75; pub. health dental program presenter Grand Junction, Colo., 1973—74; CPR instr./instr.-trainer Am. Heart Assn., Ft. Knox, 1985—98, ARC, Ft. Knox, 1978—87; vol. libr. and literacy West Point Ind. Sch., 2004—; PR/Edn. chmn. Pets In Need Soc., bd. dirs., 2005—. Decorated Order of Mil. Med. Merit U.S. Health Svcs. Command; recipient Patriotic Civilian Svc. award, Dept. of Army, 1986, award for Excellence, Delta Dental Ins. Co., 1991, 1994. Mem.: Ky. Oral Health Consortium (exec. sec.-treas. 1991—96, chair 1995—96), Ky. Dental Hygiene Assn. (chair pub. health dental hygiene 1980—84), Louisville Dental Hygiene Assn. (chair legislation 1982), Am. Assn. Pub. Health Dentistry, Am. Dental Hygiene Assn. (pub. health cons. Ky. 1979—80), Meade County C. of C. (dir. 1998, Vol. of the Yr. 1998), Assn. U.S. Army (v.p. publicity 1994—2004). Avocations: photography, travel, snorkeling, hiking, reading. Home: 67 Greenbriar Ct Brandenburg KY 40108-9153 E-mail: pbowen@bbtel.com.

BOWEN, PATRICK HARVEY, lawyer, consultant; b. Cin., July 7, 1939; s. Albert Vernon and Elsie Matilda (Harvey) B.; m. Karen A. Hunter; 1 child, Harvey Shaw. BA, Marietta Coll., 1961; JD, Duke U., 1964; MBA, Columbia U., 1975. Bar: N.Y. 1965, Conn. 1990. Assoc. Mudge, Rose, Guthrie & Alexander, NYC, 1964-66; atty. Kennecott Copper Corp., NYC, 1966-71, asst. counsel, 1971-79, asst. gen. counsel, 1979-83, asst. sec., 1980-83; sr. assoc. atty. Allied Stores Corp., NYC, 1983-87, v.p., gen. counsel, sec., 1987-88, v.p., 1988-89; pvt. practice Stamford, Conn., 1990—2003, Bridgeport, Conn., 2004—. Mem. ABA, Conn. Bar Assn., NY State Bar Assn., N.Y.C. Bar Assn., Soc. Corp. Secs. and Governance Profls. Avocation: traditional jazz musician. Office: 602 Courtland Ave Ste 104 Bridgeport CT 06605-3324 Office Phone: 203-366-6750. E-mail: phbowen@aol.com.

BOWEN, PAUL L., information systems and accounting educator; b. Knoxville, June 9, 1951; arrived in Australia, 1993; s. W. L. Paul and Helen (Duboise) B.; m. Christina Wong, Nov. 27, 1999; children: Reece P., Abigail R. BS, Ga. Inst. Tech., 1973; MBA, U. Tenn., 1976, M of Accountancy, 1990, PhD, 1992, MS in Computer Sci., 1995. CPA. Asst. br. mgr. Valley Fidelity Bank, Knoxville, 1973-76; asst. v.p. 3d Nat. Bank, Knoxville, 1976-80; project mgr. Oak Ridge (Tenn.) Nat. Lab., 1980-88; grad. tchg. asst. U. Tenn., Knoxville, 1988-92; asst. prof. Auburn (Ala.) U., 1992-93; assoc. prof. U. Queensland, Brisbane, Australia, 1993—2006, Fla. State U., 2006—. Mem. editl. bd. Jour. Info. Sys., 1994—, Internat. Jour. Acctg. Info. Systems, 2000-, Jour. Database Mgmt., 2002-; contbr. articles to profl. jours. Treas. Gideons Internat., Brisbane, 1994—. Am. Assn. of Collegiate Schs. of Bus. doctoral fellow, 1988. Mem. IEEE, Australian Computer Soc., Assn. for Info. Sys., Am. Acctg. Assn., Beta Alpha Psi, Beta Gamma Sigma. Baptist. Avocations: farming, bush walking, cooking. Office: Fla State Univ Dept Acctg Tallahassee FL 32306-1110 Office Phone: 850-644-4224. Business E-Mail: pbowen@cob.fsu.edu.

BOWEN, PETER GEOFFREY, arbitrator, business educator; b. Iowa City, July 10, 1939; s. Howard Rothmann and Lois Berntine (Schilling) B.; m. Shirley Johns Carlson, Sept. 14, 1968; children: Douglas Howard, Leslie Johns. BA in Govt. and Econs., Lawrence Coll., 1960; postgrad., U. Wis., 1960-61, U. Denver, 1963-64, U. Colo., 1994; PhD, Hamilton U., 2003. Cert.: expert witness, Denver. V.p. Perry & Butler, Denver, 1972-73; exec. v.p., dir. Little & Co., Denver, 1973; pres. Builders Agy. Ltd., Denver, 1974-75; CEO, gen. ptnr. The Investment Mgmt. Group Ltd., Denver, 1975—2005. Arbitrator NASD Dispute Resolution, Inc., 1996-, Am. Arbitration Assn., 1996-, Eagle County Colo. Atty.'s Office, 1997-03, N.Y. Stock Exch., 2004; adj. prof. bus. Colo. Mountain Coll., 1992-00; asst. prof. Regis U., 2000-03; lectr. Daniels Coll. Bus. U. Denver, 2004-; CLE lectr. on real estate syndications, 1983. Author: A Small Business Primer for Displaced Corporate Executives, 2000, Legal and Regulatory Environment of Small Business in Colorado, 2006; contbr. articles to profl. publs. Vice-chmn. Greenwood Village (Colo.) Planning and Zoning Commn., 1983-85; mem. Vail Planning and Environ. Commn., 1992-96; chmn. emeritus Vail Partnership Environ. Edn. Programs, Inc., 1993-2000; elected mem. City Council Greenwood Village, 1985-86, also mayor pro tem, 1985-86; trustee Vail Mountain Sch. Found., 1987-88. Mem.: Colo. Bar Assn. (patron mem., mem. legal fee arbitration com. 2002—), Lawrence U. Alumni Assn. (bd. dirs. 1966—72, 1982—86, 2001—), Acad. of Mgmt. Home: 16006 Double Eagle Dr Morrison CO 80465-9617 Business E-Mail: pbowen2@du.edu.

BOWEN, RAY MORRIS, academic administrator, engineering educator; b. Ft. Worth, Mar. 30, 1936; s. Winfred Herbert and Elizabeth (Williams) B; m. Sara Elizabeth Gibbens, July 5, 1958; children: Raymond Morris, Marguerite Elizabeth. BS in Mech. Engring., Texas A&M U., 1958, PhD in Engring., 1961; MS in Mech. Engring, Calif. Inst. Tech., 1959. Registered profl. engr., Ky. Assoc. prof. Mech. Engring. La. State U., Baton Rouge, 1965-67; prof. Mech. Engring. Rice U., Houston, 1967-83, chmn. dept., 1972-77; dir. divsn. NSF, Washington, 1982-83, from acting asst. dir., engr. to dep. asst. dir., engr., 1990-91; prof. Engring., dean U. Ky., Lexington, 1983-89; v.p. acad. affairs Okla. State U., Stillwater, Okla., 1991-93, interim pres., 1993—94; pres. Tex. A&M U., College Station, 1994—2002, pres. emeritus, 2002—, prof. mech. engring., 1994—. Staff Sandia Corp., Albuquerque, 1966-67, 72, cons., 1970-78; cons. U.S. Army Ballistic Rsch. Lab, Aberdeen Proving Ground, Md., 1970; chmn. budget, NSF Com. Author: Introduction to Continuum Mechanics for Engineers, 1989; co-author: Introduction to Vectors and Tensors, Vols. I and II, 1976; contbg. author: Rational Thermodynamics, 1984; contbr. articles to profl. jours. Capt. USAF, 1961-64. Soc. of Scholars Johns Hopkins U., 1964-65 Soc. Scholars Johns Hopkins U., Nat. Sci. Bd., 2002-, Tau Beta Pi, Phi Kappa Phi, Sigma Xi. Office: Tex A&M Univ Evans Library Annex 252C College Station TX 77843-5000 Office Phone: 979-862-2955. Business E-Mail: rbowen@tamu.edu.

BOWEN, RHYS See QUIN-HARKIN, JANET

BOWEN, RICHARD LEE, retired academic administrator, political scientist, educator; b. Avoca, Iowa, Aug. 31, 1933; s. Howard L. and Donna (Milburn) B.; m. Connie Smith Bowen, 1976; children: James, Robert, Elizabeth, Christopher; children by previous marriage— Catherine, David, Thomas. BA, Augustana Coll., 1957; MA, Harvard, 1959, PhD, 1967. Fgn. service officer State Dept., 1959-60; research asst. to U.S. Senator Francis Case, 1960-62; legis. asst. to U.S. Senator Karl Mundt, 1962-65; minority cons. sub-com. exec. reorgn. U.S. Senate, 1966-67; asst. to pres., assoc. prof. polit. sci. U. S.D., Vermillion, 1967-69, pres., 1969-76, Dakota State Coll., Madison, 1973-76; commr. higher edn. Bd. Regents State S.D., Pierre, 1976-80; Disting prof. polit. sci. U. S.D., 1980-85; pres. Idaho State U., Pocatello, 1985—2005, pres. emeritus, 2005—. Served with USN, 1951-54. Recipient Outstanding Alumnus award Augustana Coll., 1970; Woodrow Wilson fellow, 1957, Congl. Staff fellow, 1965; Fulbright scholar, 1957.

BOWEN, RICHARD LEE, architect; b. Canton, Ohio, Nov. 1, 1935; s. Raymond Leed and Lillian E. (White) Bowen; m. Robin Herrington (div.); children: Richard Lee, David Herrington, Laurel Ann, Sean Andrew, Scott Edward; m. Gail Audrey; children: Tabitha Erin, Colin Leed. BA, Case Western Res. U., 1959. Registered arch., 50 states, DC, P.R., Can., Australia, Nat. Coun. Archtl. Registration Bd.s, Archtl. Registration Coun. U.K. Pvt. practice Richard L. Bowen & Assocs. Inc., Cleve., 1959—, Pompano Beach, 1969—2004, Richard L. Bowen & Assoc., Inc., Naples, Fla., 2004—; pres. Enerwaste, Inc., 1992—99. Apptd. mem. Ohio State Archtl. Registration Bd., 2001—, Nat. Coun. Archtl. Registration Bds., mem. internat. registration com., mem. com. for internat. reciprocity. Prin. works include Western Campus, Cuyahoga CC, Akron Ohio State Office Bldg., West Jr. HS, John Hay HS, John Marshall HS, Cleve. Ctrl. Police Hdqs., Cleve. Hopkins Internat. Airport, FAA Regional Office Bldg., classroom and libr. bldgs. Ashtabula Campus, Kent State U., Wade Park VA Hosp., Westerly Sewage Treatment Facility Cuyahoga Regional Sewer Authority, Cuyahoga CC Manpower Skills Ctr. Ohio, Ravemna Waste Water Treatment Plant, John Hay H.S., Cleve., Ohio, others. Mem. Leadership Cleve.; mem. exec. com. Cuyahoga County Rep. Party, Cleve., 1963—; trustee St. Luke's Hosp. Assn., 1996—2000, Cleve. Internat. Air Show; mem. adv. bd. Cleve. Inst. Art; mem. adv. bd. knights hosp. Sovereign Order St. John Jerusalem, 2004. Recipient Energy Conservation Design award, Fla. Power Winter Garden Shoppint Ctr., 1986, Merit award, Cleve. Restoration Soc., 1992, 2005, Outstanding Achievement award, Cleve. Growth Assn., 1997, Design award, Am. Registered Architects, 2003. Mem.: AIA (design award excellence 1976, award 1979, 2000, 2002, 2003), Am. Arbitration Assn., Urban Land Inst., Am. Assn. Planners, Bldg. Ofcls. Coun. Am., Constrn. Specifications Inst., Internat. Coun. Shopping Ctrs., Guild Religious Architecture, Soc. Archtl. Historians, Am. Soc. Ch. Architecture, Royal Inst. Brit. Archs., Royal Archtl. Inst. Can., Nat. Assn. Indsl. and Office Pks. (awards 1985, 1989, 1992, 1994, 1995, 2000, 2003),

Archs. Soc. Ohio (honor award 1988, 2000, 2001, 2004), Hillbrook Club, Cat Cay Club, Rowfant Club, Ft. Lauderdale Yacht Club, Chagrin Valley Country Club, The Club, Union Club, Phi Gamma Delta. Avocations: sailing, skiing, fly fishing, deep sea fishing. Home: 14926 Hillbrook Dr Chagrin Falls OH 44022-2634 Office: 13000 Shaker Blvd Cleveland OH 44120-2063 Home Phone: 440-893-9110; Office Phone: 216-377-3800. Personal E-mail: r.bowen@rlba.com.

BOWEN, STEPHEN STEWART, lawyer; b. Peoria, Ill., Aug. 23, 1946; s. Gerald Raymond and Frances Arlene (Stewart) B.; m. Joan Elizabeth Logan, June 18, 2005; children: David, Claire. BA cum laude, Wabash Coll., 1968; JD cum laude, U. Chgo., 1972. Bar: Ill. 1972, U.S. Dist. Ct. (no. dist.) Ill. 1972, U.S. Tax Ct. 1977. Assoc. Kirkland & Ellis, Chgo., 1972-78, ptnr., 1978-84, Latham & Watkins, Chgo., 1985—. Adj. prof. DePaul U. Masters in Taxation Program, Chgo., 1976-80; lectr. Practicing Law Inst., N.Y.C., Chgo., L.A., 1978-84, N.Y.C., 1986—. Mem. vis. com. U. Chgo. Div. Sch., 1984—2005, mem. vis. com. Sch. Law, 1991-93; mem. planning com. U. Chgo. Tax Conf., 1985—, chair, 1995-98; trustee Wabash Coll., 1996—. Fellow Am. Coll. Tax Counsel; mem. ABA, Ill. State Bar Assn., Order of Coif, Met. Club (Chgo.), Econ. Club Chgo., Phi Beta Kappa. Office: Latham & Watkins Sears Tower Ste 5800 Chicago IL 60606-6306

BOWEN, TIM, recording industry executive; Mng. dir. CBS Records (name changed to Sony Music UK); pres. Sony Music Publishing Internat., NYC, 1982—86; mng. dir. Columbia Records; sr. v.p. mktg. & bus. affairs Universal Music Internat., 1994, exec. v.p.; COO BMG Europe, 2002—03; chmn. BMG UK & Ireland, 2003—04, Sony BMG UK/Canada/Australia/New Zealand/S. Africa, 2004—06; COO Sony BMG Music Entertainment, 2006—. Office: Sony BMG Music Entertainment 550 Madison Ave New York NY 10022 Office Phone: 212-833-8000. Office Fax: 212-833-4583.

BOWEN, WILLIAM GORDON, foundation administrator, economist; b. Cin., Oct. 6, 1933; s. Albert A. and Bernice (Pomert) B.; m. Mary Ellen Maxwell, Aug. 25, 1956; children: David Alan, Karen Lee. BA, Denison U., 1955; PhD, Princeton U., NJ, 1958. Mem. faculty Princeton U., 1958-88, prof. econs., 1965-88, dir. grad. studies Woodrow Wilson Sch. Pub. and Internat. Affairs, 1964-66, provost, 1967-72, pres., 1972-88, Andrew W. Mellon Found., NYC, 1988—2006, sr. rsch. assoc., pres. emeritus, 2006—; founding chmn., bd. dirs. Ithaka Harbors Inc., NYC. Bd. dirs. Merck and Co., Inc., JSTOR, ARTstor Inc.; bd. overseers Tchrs. Ins. and Annuity Assn.-Coll. Ret. Equities Fund.; Romanes lectr. U. Oxford, 2000; Jefferson lectr. U. Va., 2004. Author: The Wage-Price Issue: A Theoretical Analysis, 1960, Wage Behavior in the Postwar Period: An Empirical Analysis, 1960, Economic Aspects of Education: Three Essays, 1964, (with W. J. Baumol) Performing Arts: The Economic Dilemma, 1966, (with T. A. Finegan) The Economics of Labor Force Participation, 1969, Ever the Teacher, 1987, (with J. A. Sosa) Prospects for Faculty in the Arts and Sciences, 1989, (with Neil L. Rudenstine) In Pursuit of the PhD, 1992, Inside the Boardroom: Governance by Directors and Trustees, 1994, (with T. Nygren, S. Turner, E. Duffy) The Charitable Nonprofits, 1994, (with Derek Bok) The Shape of the River: Long-Term Consequences of Considering Race in College and University Admissions, 1998, (with James L. Shulman) The Game of Life: College Sports and Educational Values, 2001, (with Sarah A. Levin) Reclaiming the Game: College Sports and Educational Values, 2003, (with Martin A. Kurzweil and Eugene M. Tobin) Equity and Excellence in American Higher Education, 2005. Trustee Ctr. for Advanced Study in Behavioral Scis., 1978-84, 89-92, Denison U., 1992-2000; regent emeritus Smithsonian Instn. Recipient Joseph Henry medal Smithsonian Instn., 1996, (with Derek Bok) Gravemeyer award in edn. U. Louisville, 2001. Mem. Am. Econs. Assn., Indsl. Rels. Rsch. Assn., Coun. on Fgn. Rels., Phi Beta Kappa. Office: Ithaka Harbors Inc 151 E 61st St New York NY 10021-8124 Office Phone: 212-826-8114.

BOWEN, WILLIAM HENRY, dental researcher, educator; b. Enniscorthy, Ireland, Dec. 11, 1933; came to U.S., 1956, naturalized; s. William H. and Pauline (McGrath) B.; m. Carole Barnes, Aug. 9, 1958 children: William, Deirdre, Kevin, David, Katherine BDS, Nat. U. Ireland, Dublin, 1955; MSc, U. Rochester, NYC, 1959; PhD, U. London, 1965; DSc, U. Ireland, Dublin, 1974; D Odontologiae (hon.), U. Goteborg, Sweden, 1995, U. Oslo, Norway, 1991; D Odontologiae (honoris causa), U. Umeå, Sweden, 1993; MD (honoris causa), Nat. U. Irleland, 1995, Trinity Coll., Dublin, 1999. Diplomate Am. Bd. Dentistry, Inst. Medicine-NAS. Assoc. pvt. dental practice private dental practice, London, 1955-56; Quinten Hogg fellow Royal Coll. Surgeons, London, 1956-59, Nuffield Found. fellow, 1962-65, sr. research fellow, 1965-69, Sir Wilfred Fish fellow, 1969-73; acting chief caries prevention br. Nat. Inst. Dental Research, NIH, Bethesda, Md., 1973-79, chief, 1979-82; chmn. dental research U. Rochester, N.Y., 1982-95. Dir. Cariology Ctr., Rochester, 1984-95. Fellow AAAS (sect. R-Dentistry, chair elect 1989, chair 1990); mem. ADA (Gold medal 2000), European Orgn. Caries Rsch., Internat. Assn. Dental Rsch. (treas. 1982-88, v.p. 1988, pres. elect 1989, pres. 1990), Fedn. Dentaire Internationale, Inst. Medicine, Lab. Animal Sci. Assn., Zool. Soc. Roman Catholic. Home: 315 County Road 9 Victor NY 14564-9710 Office: U Rochester Ctr for Oral Biology 601 Elmwood Ave Rochester NY 14642-0001 Office Phone: 585-275-0772.

BOWEN, WILLIAM JACKSON, retired gas industry executive; b. Sweetwater, Tex., Mar. 31, 1922; s. Berry and Annah (Robey) Bowen; m. Annis K Hilty, June 6, 1945; children: Shelley Ann, Barbara Kay, Berry Dunbar, William Jackson. BS, U.S. Mil. Acad., 1945. Registered profl engr, Tex. Petroleum engr. Delhi Oil Corp., Dallas, 1949-57; v.p. Fla. Gas Co., Houston, 1957-60, pres. Winter Park, Fla., 1960-74; pres., CEO Transco Cos., Inc., Houston, 1974-81; chmn. Transco Cos., Inc. (name changed to Transco Energy Co.), Houston, 1976-92; CEO Transco Energy Co., Houston, 1981-87; ret., 1992; also bd. dirs. Transco Energy Co., Houston; ret., 1992. Bd. dir. J.P. Poindexter and Co., Inc.; hon. vice chmn. World Energy Coun. Bd. dirs. YMCA, Houston; trustee emeritus bd Baylor Coll. Medicine; trustee emeritus bd. Jesse H Jones Grad. Sch. Bus., Rice U. With AUS, 1945—49. Mem.: U.S. Energy Assn. (past chmn.). Episcopalian. Office: Williams 2800 Post Oak Blvd Level 16 Houston TX 77056-6100 Home Phone: 713-850-0454; Office Phone: 713-215-2301.

BOWEN-FORBES, JORGE COURTNEY, artist, poet; b. Queenstown, Guyana, May 16, 1937; came to U.S., 1966; s. Walter and Margarita V. (Forbes) Bowen. BA, Queens Coll., Eve Leary, Guyana, 1969; MFA, Chelsea (Eng.) Sch. Design, 1972. Comml. artist Guyana Litographic, Georgetown; art dir. Corbin Advt. Agy., Bridgetown, Barbados; tech. advisor Ministry of Info. and Culture, Georgetown. Nat. juror Nat. Arts Club, N.Y.C., 1985, Nat. Soc. Painters in Casein and Acrylic. Major exhbns. include Expo 67, Can., Nat. Acad. Design, N.Y., Frye Mus., El Paso (Tex.) Mus., Wichita (Kans.) Centennial, Caribbean Festival of the Arts, Newark Mus.; one-man shows include Nat. and Colgrain Collections, Guyana, El Paso Mus. Art, Kindercare Internat., Leon Loards Gallery, McCreery Cummings Fine Art Collection, Bomani Gallery, San Francisco; author: Best Watercolors, 1996, Creative Watercolor, 1996, numerous poems; contbr. articles to profl. jours.; published in Best in Watercolor, Best in Oil Painting, Best in Acrylic Painting, Creative Watercolor, Splash 11, Best Contemporary Watercolors, American Poetry Annual. Recipient Silver medal of honor Allied Artists of N.Y., 1978, Gold medal of honor, 1975. Mem. Nat. Watercolor Soc. (signature mem.), Nat. Soc. Painters in Casein and Acrylics, Audubon Artists, Knickerbocker Artists (Gold Medal of Honor 1977, 79), Am. Watercolor Soc. (signature mem., High Winds medal 1984, Elsie and David Wu Ject-Key Meml. award 1998). E-mail: bowenforbes@yahoo.com.

BOWER, DOUGLAS WILLIAM, counseling administrator, psychotherapist, clergyman; b. Niagara Falls, NY, Jan. 6, 1948; s. Charles Henry Bower and Phyllis June (Rank) Ayres; m. Cheryl Stewart, May 25, 1980; children: Katherine Elizabeth, Erin Colleen. AA, Manatee Jr. Coll., Bradenton, Fla., 1969; BS, Oglethorpe U., 1972; PhD, U. Ga., 1989. RN, Ga.; ordained to ministry United Meth. Ch., 1981; cert. counselor, Ga.; life cert. diplomate Am. Psychotherapy Assn. Nurse Northside Hosp., Atlanta, 1970-80; assoc. pastor lst United Meth. Ch., Griffin, Ga., 1980-82; pastor, pastoral counselor Oconee Street United Meth. Ch., Athens, Ga., 1982-86; dir. Counseling Ministeries, Athens, 1986—. Adj. faculty Ft. Valley State U., 1999—2005. Contbr. articles to profl. jours. Commr. Oglethorpe County, Dist. 1, 2002-06; chair spl. needs com. North Ga. Conf. United Meth. Ch.; mem. citizens svc. bd., Advantage Mental Health; bd. mem. Action Inc. Fellow: Am. Psychotherapy Assn.; mem.: Ga. Sheriffs Assn. (hon.). Avocations: music, walking, reading. Office: PO Box 143 Bishop GA 30621-0143 *While we may not make an impact on the world, we can and do make an impact on the immediate world around and within us. Persistence in maintaining faith, even in the face of adversity, makes a powerful impact on our immediate world.*

BOWER, FAY LOUISE, academic administrator, nursing educator; b. San Francisco, Sept. 10, 1929; d. James Joseph and Emily Clare (Andrews) Saitta; children: R. David, Carol Bower Tomei, Dennis James, Thomas John. BS with honors, San Jose State Coll., 1965; MSN, U. Calif., 1966, DNSc, 1978. Cert. pub. health nurse, sch. nurse, Calif. Office nurse Dr. William Grannis, Palo Alto, Calif., 1950-55; staff nurse Stanford Hosp., 1964-72; asst. prof. San Jose (Calif.) State U., 1966-70, assoc. prof., 1970-74, prof., 1974-82, coord. grad. program in nursing, 1977-78, chairperson dept. nursing, 1978-82; dean U. San Francisco, 1982-89, v.p. acad. affairs, 1988-89, dir. univ. planning and instl. rsch., 1989-91; pres. Clarkson Coll., 1991-97; cons. in field, 1997—; chair dept. nursing Holy Names U., 2000—. Vis. prof. Harding Coll., 1977, U. Miss., 1976; lectr. U. Calif., San Francisco, 1975; nat. exec. adv. bd. Nurse Week, 1999—; spkr., cons. in field. Author: Approaches to Teaching Primary Care, 1981, The Newman Systems Model: Application to Nursing Education and Practice, 1982, Managing a Nursing Shortage: A Guide to Recruitment and Retention, 1989, Cracking the Wall: Women in Higher Education Administration, 1993, Nurses Taking the Lead., 2000, Care and Management of Alzheimers, vols. 1-5, 2002, Developing and Managing a Career in Nursing, 2003; (with Em O. Bevis) Fundamentals of Nursing Practice: Concepts, Roles and Functions, 1978, (with Margaret Jacobson) Community Health Nursing, 1978, The Process of Planning Nursing Care, 3d edit., 1982, (with Mae Timmons) Medical Surgical Nursing, 1995, (with others) Concepts & Issues in Nursing, 3d edit., 1996, Creating Nursings' Futures: Issues, Opportunities & Challenges, 1999; contbr. articles to profl. jours. Fellow Am. Acad. Nursing; mem.APHA (Calif. chpt.), Nurses Assn., Western Gerontol. Assn., Jesuit Deans in Nursing (chair 1982-85), Rotary (Omaha), Sigma Theta Tau (internat.pres., 1993-95, magnet appraiser 2006—). Democrat. Roman Catholic. Home: 1457 Indianhead Cir Clayton CA 94517-1239 Office Phone: 510-436-1024. Personal E-mail: fbower1@sbcglobal.net. Business E-Mail: bower@hnu.edu.

BOWER, GLEN LANDIS, judge, lawyer; b. Highland, Ill., Jan. 16, 1949; BA, So. Ill. U., 1971; JD (hon.), Ill. Inst. Tech., 1974. Bar: Ill. 1974, US Ct. Mil. Appeals 1975, US Ct. Appeals (7th cir.) 1976, US Dist Ct. (so. dist.) Ill. 1977, US Dist. Ct. (cen. dist.) Ill. 1992, US Supreme Ct. 1978, US Tax Ct. 1984, US Ct. Claims 1986, US Dist. Ct. (no. dist.) Ill. 1994, US Ct. Veterans Appeals 1995. Sole practice, Effingham, Ill., 1974-83; prosecutor Effingham County, Ill., 1976-79; mem. Ill. House of Reps., Springfield, 1979-83; asst. dir., gen. counsel Ill. Dept. Revenue, Springfield, Ill., 1983-90; Presdl. apptd. chmn. US R.R. Retirement Bd., 1990-97; asst. to Ill. Sec. of State, 1998-99; apptd. dir. revenue State of Ill., 1999—2003; sr. advisor US SBA, Washington, 2004—05; judge US Immigration Ct., Chgo., 2005—. Mil. aide to Gov. of Ill., 1999-2003; liaison mem. Adminstrv. Conf. of US, 1991-95; mem. Nat. Adv. Com. for Juvenile Justice and Delinquency Prevention, Washington, 1976-80, US Econ. Adv. Bd. of US Dept. Commerce, Washington, 1981-85, Ill. Gen. Assembly State Adv. Com. on Cir. Ct. Fin., Springfield, 1984; mem. Revenue Bd. Appeals, Chgo., 1985-87, chmn., 1986-87; mem. Com. of 50 on Ill. Constn., 1987-88; adv. com. on electronic tax adminstrn. IRS, 2000-2003, So. Ill. U. Pub. Policy Inst., 2000. Co-editor: Handbook on State Taxation, 1991; contbr. articles to profl. jour. Bd. dir. Dana-Thomas House Found., Springfield, Ill., 1989-90; trustee McKendree Coll., Lebanon, Ill., 1978-81; chmn. State of Ill. Organ and Tissue Donors Adv. Bd., 1993-98. Lt. col. USAFR, 1974—99, ret. Recipient Disting. Svc. award So. Ill. U., 1971, Recognition citation Am. Legion, 1980, Outstanding Svc. cert. to tchg. profession Ill. Edn. Assn., 1981, Disting. Svc. award Am. Vets., 1980, 82, Presdl. citation Navy League US, 1981, Constitution award Mus. of Our Nat. Heritage, 1988, Silver Good Citizenship medal Ill. Soc. SAR, 1990, Profl. Achievement award Ill. Inst. Tech., 1993, Friend of History award Ill. State Hist. Soc., 1994, Alumni Achievement award So. Ill. U., 1994, Disting. Alumnus award So. Ill. U. Coll. Liberal Arts, 2000, Outstanding Civilian Svc. Medal, Dept. Army, 2003; named Outstanding Freshman Legislator, Ill. Edn. Assn., 1980, Legislator of Yr., Ill. Assn. Rehab. Socs., 1981, 82. Fellow: Am. Bar Found. (life), Ill. Bar Found. (life); mem.: US Capitol Hist. Soc. (charter), Effingham County Mental Health Assn. (pub. affairs com. 1977—78), SBA Adv. Coun., Effingham Regional Hist. Soc. (bd. dir. 1973—77), Ill. State Hist. Soc. (v.p. 1979—81, Ralph C. Francis award 1967), Nat. Assn. Tax Adminstrs. (vice chmn. attys. sect. 1985—86, chmn. 1986—88, vice chmn. attys. sect. 1988—89), Effingham County Bar Assn. (sec. 1976—77, pres. 1983—84), Ill. State Bar Assn. (labor law sect. coun. 1976—77, sec. state taxation sect. coun. 1987—88, vice-chair 1988—89, chair 1989—90, sect. coun. on employee benefits 1991—98, sect. coun. on adminstrv. law 2000, Bd. Gov.'s award 1999), Fed. Tax Adminstrs. (bd. trustees 2001—03), Am. Coun. Young Polit. Leaders (life; One of 10 dels. to China 1988, del. to East Asia-Pacific internat. alumni summit Tokyo 2006), Sons of Am. Revolution, Field Mus. of Natural History, Smithsonian Assocs., Abraham Lincoln Assn., Res. Officers Assn. (life), The Nat. Sojourners (life), So. Ill. Univ. Alumni Assn. (life), Am. Legion (life), Effingham County Old Settlers Assn. (pres., bd. dir. 1983—86), Art Inst. of Chgo., So. Ill. U. Carbondale Found. (bd. dir. 1993—2002), Army and Navy Club Washington D.C., Kiwanis (pres. 1977—78), Shriners (life), Phi Alpha Delta (life). Methodist. Office: US Immigration Ct Ste 1900 55 E Monroe St Chicago IL 60603

BOWER, GORDON HOWARD, psychologist, educator; b. Scio, Ohio, Dec. 30, 1932; s. Clyde Ward and Mabel (Bosart); m. Sharon Anthony, Jan. 30, 1957; children: Lori, Tony, Julia. BA, Western Res. U., 1954; MS, Yale U., 1957, PhD, 1959. Prof. psychology Sch. Humanities and Scis., Stanford U., Calif., 1959—, Albert Ray Lang prof. psychology Calif., 1975—2005, Albert Ray Lang prof. psychology emeritus, 2005—, chmn. psychology dept. Calif., 1978-82, assoc. dean of humanities and scis. Calif., 1983-86. Mem. exptl. psychology rev. bd. NIMH, 1968-71; mem. psychology and ednl. process com. Soc. Sci. Rsch. Coun., 1970-72; grant reviewer NIMH, NSF, Nat. Insts. Edn., Can. Rsch. Coun. Editor: The Psychology of Learning and Motivation: Advances in Research and Theory, 1968; mem. editorial bd. Jour. Comparative and Physiol. Psychology, 1963-70, Jour. Math. Psychology, 1964-70, Jour. Exptl. Psychology, 1965-72, Jour. Exptl. Analysis of Behavior, 1965-69, Jour. Psychology, 1965-72, Jour. Verbal Learning and Verbal Behavior, 1968-88, Cognitive Psychology, 1969-75, Cognitive Therapy and Rsch., 1976-79, Cognition and Emotion, 1987—; contbr. articles to profl. jours. NIMH postdoctoral fellow, 1965; Woodrow Wilson fellow, U. Minn., 1954-55; Ctr. for Advanced Study in Behavioral Scis. fellow, 1973; named one of the 100 Most Eminent Psychologists of the 20th Century, Review General Psychology, 2002; recipient 2005 Nat. Medal Sci., NSF, 2007. Fellow Am. Psychol. Assn. (exec. com. div. exptl. psychology 1974-76, pres. Div. 3 1975, Disting. Sci. contbn. award 1979); mem. Western Psychol. Assn. (pres. 1989-90, 2005), Psychonomic Soc. (bd. govs. 1972-76), chmn. governing bd. 1975-76, chmn. publs. com. 1978), Cognitive Sci. Soc. (bd. govs. 1982-88, pres. 1988), NAS, , Am. Acad. Arts and Scis., Soc. Exptl. Psychologists, Am. Psychol. Soc. (bd. govs. 1989—95), Am. Philos. Soc. Office: Stanford U Dept Psychology Dept Psychology Rm 314 Stanford CA 94305 Home Phone: 650-494-8163. Business E-Mail: gbower@stanford.edu.

BOWER, JAMES MASON, neuroscientist, educator, science administrator; b. Northampton, Mass., Feb. 17, 1954; s. Mason James and Dorothe Gule Bower; m. Carolina Becker Livi, Dec. 11, 1997; children: Katherine Gule, John Hywel, Ian Ferrera, Lucas Pohlman. PhD, U. Wis., Madison, 1981. Prof. biology Calif. Inst. Tech., Pasadena, 1985—2001; prof. computational biology U. Tex., San Antonio, 2001—. Chmn. bd. Numedeon Inc., Pasadena, Calif., 1999—, CEO, 1999—. Prodr.(founder): (ednl. web site) Whyville (named Children's Best Site, iParenting, 2006). Grantee, NIH, 1982—2007, NSF, 1982—2007. Independent. Achievements include research in computational neuroscience; cerebellum as non-motor device; development of GENESIS neural simulation system; patents pending for web use safety technology. Avocations: horse breeding, polo, musician. Home Phone: 210-382-0553; Office Phone: 210-567-8080.

BOWER, JEAN RAMSAY, lawyer, writer; b. NYC, Nov. 25, 1935; d. Claude Barnett and Myrtle Marie (Scott) Ramsay; m. Ward Swift Just, Jan. 31, 1957 (div. 1966); children: Jennifer Ramsay, Julia Barnett; m. Robert Turrell Bower, June 12, 1971 (dec. June 1990). AB, Vassar Coll., 1957; JD, Georgetown U., 1970. Bar: D.C. 1970. Exec. dir. D.C. Dem. Ctrl. Com., Washington, 1969-71; pvt. practice Washington, 1971-78, 94—; dir. Counsel of Child Abuse and Neglect Office D.C. Superior Ct., 1978-94. Mem. Mayor's Com. on Child Abuse and Neglect, 1973-94, vice chmn., 1975-79; mem. Family Div. Rules Adv. Com., 1977-94; pres., bd. dirs. C.B. Ramsay Found., 1984—; cons. child welfare issues, writer. Contbr. poetry to In a Certain Place. Mem. D.C. Child Fatality Rev. Com., 1992-; bd. dirs. Friends D.C. Superior Ct., 1994—, pres. bd. dirs., 2002-05; bd. dirs. Family and Child Svcs., Washington, 1995-2003, bd. dirs., 2004-; bd. mem. Folger Poetry Bd., 1998-, chair, 2002-06, Folger Shakespeare Libr., 1998-. Named Washingtonian of the Yr. Washington Mag., 1978. Mem. Women's Bar Assn. (bd. dirs. 1993-96, found. 1986-91, Woman Lawyer of Yr. 1986), D.C. Bar Assn. (election bd. 1994-96, Beatrice Rosenberg award 1994), Women's Bar Assn. Found. (bd. dirs. 1986-91). E-mail: JBower3714@aol.com.

BOWER, JEFF, professional sports team executive; m. Lisa Bower; 1 child, Lindsey. B in Hist. and Edn., St. Francis Coll., Pa. Asst. coach Pa. State U., 1983—86, Marist Coll., Poughkeepsie, NY, 1986—90, assoc. head coach, 1990—95; advance scout New Orleans/Okla. City Hornets (formerly Charlotte Hornets and New Orleans Hornets), 1995—97, dir. scouting, 1997—2000, asst. coach, 1998—99, 2003—04, asst. gen. mgr., 2000—01, gen. mgr., 2001—02, 2002—03, 2005—, dir. player pers., 2004—05. Office: New Orleans Okla City Hornets Oklahoma Tower 210 Park Ave Ste 1850 Oklahoma City OK 73102

BOWER, JOHN ARNOLD, JR., architect; b. Phila., Apr. 22, 1930; s. John Arnold and Marie Imogene (Siegle) B.; m. Joan Wolfington, Sept. 13, 1952; children: Bradley Clark, Mark Arnold, Craig Newton. Student, Pa. State Coll., 1948-49, Ohio State U., 1949-51; BArch with honors, U. Pa., 1953. Registered architect, Pa., N.Y., N.J., Del., Md., Conn., Ill., La., S.C., N.C., Minn. Draftsman John A. Bower, Sr. Architect, Phila., 1950-51; designer Phila. Planning Commn., 1953-54; sr. designer Vincent G. Kling Architects, Phila., 1954-61; ptnr. Bower and Fradley Architects, Phila., 1961-78, Bower Lewis Thrower Architects, Phila., 1978—. Prof. emeritus architecture U. Pa.; mem. design adv. panel Dept. Housing and Community Devel., Balt., 1964—. Prin. works include Vance Hall, Wharton Grad. Ctr. (gold medal AIA Phila. chpt. 1973, design citation 1968), Internat. House (gold medal AIA Phila. chpt. 1967), Milles Sculpture Group (silver medal AIA Phila. chpt. 1972), Gallery at Market E. (cert. excellence - urban design 1978), Soc. Hill Townhouses (1st honor award Pa. Soc. Architects 1966), Princton Forrestal Village (Merit award Pa. Soc. Architects 1987), Market St. E. Transp. Mall Ctr., One Reading Ctr. Office Tower, Balt. Mus. Art. (restoration, additions), 1234 Market St. Office Bldg., 1500 Walnut St. Office Bldg., Marriott Phila. Conv. Ctr. Hotel. Albert F. Schenk travelling fellow U. Pa., 1954, fellow Fontainbleau Sch. Fine Arts-Music, Paris, 1954. Fellow AIA (nat. urban planning and design com. 1974-75, nat. com. on design 1976-78); mem. NAD (assoc.), Carpenter's Co., Hexagon Honor Soc., Tau Sigma Delta. Clubs: Germantown Cricket. Office: Bower Lewis Thrower Architects 1216 Arch St Ste 9 Philadelphia PA 19107-2835

BOWER, JOHN RICHARD FENN, archaeologist, educator; b. Newton, Iowa, May 5, 1935; s. John Oates and Lillian Keithen Bower; m. Andrea Garcia Montero, Feb. 1961 (div. Aug. 1965); m. Janice Sophie Johnson, Sept. 26, 1966; 1 child, Jennifer Keithen. BA, Harvard U., Cambridge, Mass., 1957; MA, Northwestern U., Evanston, Ill., 1968, PhD, 1973. Editor Rand McNally & Co., Skokie, Ill., 1962—67; asst. prof. Lake Forest Coll., Lake Forest, Ill., 1970—73; from asst. prof. to full prof. Iowa State U., Ames, 1973—92, prof. emeritus, 1992—; part-time lectr. U. Minn., Duluth, 1992—2003; rsch. assoc. anthropology U. Calif., Davis, 2004—. Rsch. fellow Brit. Inst. History and Archaeology in East Africa, Nairobi, Kenya, 1971; dir. archeol. excavations Serengeti Park, Tanzania. Author: In Search of the Past, 1986; co-sr. editor Prehistoric Cultures and Environments in Africa, 1988, Evolution and Ecology of Homo eretus, 1995, co-sr. author A Comparative Study of Prehistoric Foragers in Europe and North America, 2002. Lt. USN, 1957—62. Recipient Wilton Park award for internat. svc., Iowa State U., 1989; fellow Fulbright fellow, 1982. Fellow: Am. Anthropol. Assn.; mem.: AAAS, Soc. for Am. Archaeology, Duluth Cmty. Sailing Assn. (bd. dir. 2000—03), No. Lakes Archaeol. Soc. (bd. dir. 2002—03), Duluth Yacht Club (vice commodore 2002—03). Democrat. Unitarian Universalist. Achievements include research in conduct of first trans-Atlantic archaeological investigations with Polish collaboration. Avocations: sailing, fly fishing, music, poetry. Mailing: PO Box 72006 Davis CA 95617 Personal E-mail: jrfbower@aol.com.

BOWER, JOSEPH LYON, business administration educator; b. NYC, Sept. 21, 1938; s. Morris L. and Florence (Turitz) B.; m. Nancy Milender, Feb. 16, 1958 (dec. Sept. 19, 2006); children: Jonathan, Deborah. AB, Harvard U., 1959, MBA, 1961, D Bus. Adminstrn., 1963. Asst. prof. Grad. Sch. Bus. Adminstrn. Harvard U., Boston, 1963-68, assoc. prof. Grad. Sch. Bus. Adminstrn., 1968-71, Donald K. David prof. bus. adminstrn. Grad. Sch. Bus. Adminstrn., 1972—, sr. assoc. dean for external rels. Grad. Sch. Bus. Adminstrn., 1986-89, chmn. doctoral programs, dir. of rsch. Grad. Sch. Bus. Adminstrn., 1989-95, faculty mem. John F. Kennedy Sch. Govt. Cambridge, Mass., 1969—. Bd. dirs. Anika Rsch. Inc., Woburn, Mass., Brown Shoe Inc., St. Louis, Sonesta Internat. Hotels Corp., Boston, New Am. High Income Fund, Boston, Loews Corp., N.Y.C.; trustee TH Lee, Putnam Emerging Portfolio, Boston; chair gen. mgr. program Grad. Sch. Bus. Adminstrn., 1996—. Author: Managing Resource Allocation Process, 1971 (McKinsey Found. award 1971), Two Faces of Management, 1983, When Markets Quake, 1986; co-author: Public Management: Text and Cases, 1978, Business Policy: Text and Cases, 7th edit., 1991, Business Policy: Managing Strategic Processes, 8th edit., 1995, From Resource Allocation to Strategy, 2005 Life trustee New Eng. Conservatory Music,

Boston, 1984-03, DeCordova and Dana Mus. and Park, Lincoln, Mass., 1987—. Co-recipient (with C.M. Christensen) McKinsey Found. award, 1995. Mem. Am. Econ. Assn., Coun. Fgn. Rels., St. Botolph Club (Boston), Harvard Club (N.Y.C.). Avocations: tennis, boating, golf. Office: Harvard Bus Sch Sch Bus Morgan # 467 Boston MA 02163 Office Phone: 617-495-6282. Business E-Mail: jbower@hbs.edu.

BOWER, PHILIP JEFFREY, cardiologist; b. Kenmore, NY, Nov. 23, 1935; s. Philip Graydon and Evelyn (McLoney) B.; children: Elizabeth Ann, Susan Lynn. BA, U. Va., 1957; MD, Johns Hopkins U., 1961; MBA, Tulane U., 1998. Diplomate Am. Bd. Internal Medicine with supspecialty in cardiology. Intern in medicine U. N.C., Chapel Hill, 1961-62; resident in medicine Johns Hopkins U., Balt., 1962-63, Mayo Clinic, Rochester, Minn., 1965-66, fellow in cardiology, 1966-68; staff physician Ochsner Clinic, New Orleans, 1969—78; dir. cardiology, dir. catheterization lab. East Jefferson Gen. Hosp., Metairie, La., 1978-98; cardiologist Togus VAH, Maine, 1998—2001, acting chmn. dept. medicine Maine, 1999—2001; cardiologist Low Country Cardiology, Walterboro, SC, 2001—06, Coastal Physician Assocs., Varnville, SC, 2006—. Instr. medicine U. Ga. Sch. of Medicine, Augusta, 1963-65; clin. asst. prof. medicine La. State U., New Orleans, 1974—p clin. prof. medicine Tulane U., New Orleans, 1983—; former mem, bd. dirs. Found. East Jefferson Gen. Hosp. Found., Metairie; cons. in field. Contbr. articles to profl. jours.; presenter in field. Capt. U.S. Army, 1963-65. Fellow ACP, Am. Coll. Cardiology, Am. Coll. Chest Physicians, Coll. Clin. Cardiology, Soc. Cardiac Angiography and Interventions, Am. Heart Assn. (bd. dirs. 1979-83); mem. AMA, So. Med. Assn. Avocations: walking, wine, food, travel. Home: 63 Butler Farm Rd Seabrook SC 29940-2816 Office Phone: 803-943-1229. Personal E-mail: pjbower@hughes.net.

BOWER, RICHARD JAMES, minister; b. Somerville, NJ, June 9, 1939; s. Oneil A. and Mildred R. (Goss) B.; m. Helen Ann Cheek, Dec. 29, 1962 (div. 1985); 1 child, Christopher Scott. Student, Sorbonne, Paris, 1959-60; BA, Wesleyan U., 1961; MDiv, Drew U., Madison, NJ, 1965; student, Oxford U., Eng., 1983; DD, Piedmont Coll., 1999. Ordained to ministry, Congl. Christian Ch., 1965. Min. Cmty. Congl. Ch., Kewaunee, Wis., 1965-67; sr. min. Congl. Ch., Bound Brook, NJ, 1967-78, Congl. Ch. of the Chimes, Sherman Oaks, Calif., 1978-95; preaching min. Congl. Ch. Messiah, LA, 1995-96, First Congl. Ch., LA, 2002, 2005. Mem. exec. com., dir. Nat. Assn. Congl. Christian Chs., 1973-77, chmn., 1976-77,asst. moderator, 1981-82, moderator, 1982-83, exec. search com., 1990-91, nominating com., 1991-93, chmn., 1992-93; mem. World Christian Rels. Commn., 1993-97. Appeared on TV programs; contbr. poetry and articles to periodicals. Organizer, pres. Am. Field Svc., Kewaunee, 1966-67; dir. Children's Bur., L.A., 1981-88; bd. fellows Hollywood Congl. Ctr., 1979-82; bd. dirs. Heritage Playhouse, 1986-96. Recipient Citation for Disting. Svc., Nat. Assn. Congl. Christian Chs., 1997. Mem. Cal-West Assn. (dir., moderator 1986-87) Lodges: Bound Brook Rotary (pres. 1975-76). Democrat. Home: 365 W Alameda Ave Apt 302 Burbank CA 91506-3339 E-mail: rijabo@juno.com.

BOWER, RICHARD STUART, retired economist; b. NYC, Aug. 1, 1928; s. Jacob and Elsie (Vander Beugle) Bower; m. Dorothy Ann Hagberg, June 23, 1953; children: Gari Ellen, Laura Jane, Nancy Lynne. AB, Kenyon Coll., 1949; MBA, Columbia, 1955; PhD, Cornell U., 1962. Instr. econs. Kenyon Coll., 1949-50, Alfred U., 1955-57; asst. prof. econs. and bus. Vanderbilt U., 1959-62; prof. bus. econs. Dartmouth, 1962—99; ptnr. Bower Rohr and Assocs., Hanover, 1981—2001; ret., 2001. Author: Investment and Liquidity: A Case Study of Clay Construction Products, 1965; contbr. articles to profl. jours. With USNR, 1951—55. Mem.: Am. Econ. Assn., Phi Beta Kappa, Phi Kappa Phi, Beta Gamma Sigma. Democrat. Jewish. Home: South Esker Hanover NH 03755

BOWER, ROGER HARRISON, endocrinologist, director; b. Rosebud, Mont., June 7, 1942; s. Paul Edgar and Elizabeth Dorothea Bower; m. Rose Ann Grady, Apr. 20, 1963; children: Jeffrey Harrison, Susan Elizabeth Cellini. BS, U. Nebr., Lincoln, 1966; MS, U. Nebr., Omaha, 1968, MD with high distinction, 1970. Cert. Am. Bd. Internal Medicine, 1974, endocrinology and metabolism Am. Bd. Internal Medicine, 1975, fellow Am. Coll. Physicians, 1978. Med. group comdr. 43rd Med. Group, Malmstrom AFB, Mont., 314th Med. Group, Little Rock AFB, Ark., 1993—95, 6th Med. Group, MacDill AFB, Fla., 1995—97, 77th Med. Group, McClellan AFB, Calif., 1997—99; dep. command surgeon USAF Air Materiel Command, Wright Patterson, Ohio, 1999—2001; chief med. officer Vets. Adminstrn. Med. Clinic, Daytona Beach, Fla., 2001—. Contbr. articles to profl. med. jours. Bd. mem. local chpt. ARC, Great Falls, Mont.; chmn. leadership com. Combined Fed. Campaign, Daytona Beach, 2003—06. Col. USAF, 1969—2001. Decorated Legion of Merit USAF, 6 Meritorious Svc. awards; recipient Pfizer Prize, U. Nebr., 1967, Lange award, 1967. Mem.: DAV (life), Am. Legion, Air Force Assn., Mil. Officers Assn., Assn. Mil. Surgeons U.S., Am. Coll. Physician Execs. Independent. Roman Catholic. Achievements include discovery of synthesized four novel amino acids. Avocations: running, exercise, reading, travel. Office: Vets Administration Outpatient Clini 551 Nat Health Care Dr Daytona Beach FL 32114 Home Phone: 386-671-1068; Office Phone: 386-323-7541. Office Fax: 386-323-7570. Business E-Mail: roger.bower@med.va.gov.

BOWER, THOMAS MICHAEL, lawyer; b. NYC, Apr. 6, 1952; s. John Joseph and Marianne Judith (Milch) B.; m. Sharon Misae Nakamoto, Dec. 1, 1979. BA magna cum laude, Cornell U., 1973; JD, Columbia U., 1976. Bar: N.Y. 1977, U.S. Ct. Mil. Appeals 1979, U.S. Dist. Ct. (so. dist. and ea. dists.) N.Y. 1980. Assoc. Bower & Gardner, NYC, 1980-83, ptnr., 1984-91; prin. Newman & Bower, P.C., NYC, 1991-92; of counsel Bickford, Hahn & Haley, 1993-98; ptnr. Shaub Ahmuty Citrin & Spratt, LLP, NYC, 1998—2004; pvt. practice Briarcliff Manor, NY, 2004—. Lt. JAGC, USNR, 1976-80. Mem. Fedn. Def. and Corp. Counsel, Def. Rsch. Inst., Alpha Delta Phi. Office: 245 Hardscrabble Rd Briarcliff Manor NY 10510-1802 Office Phone: 888-842-4922. Business E-Mail: tombower@thomasbower.com.

BOWERFIND, EDGAR SIHLER, JR., internist, educator, retired medical association administrator; b. Cleve., May 7, 1924; s. Edgar Sihler and Edna (Strong) B.; m. Maria Washington Tucker, Apr. 28, 1956; children—Edgar Sihler III, Ellis Tucker, Jane Strong, William Minor Lile Student, Creighton U. Med. Sch., 1945-47; MD, Western Res. U., 1949. Diplomate Am. Bd. Internal Medicine. Intern Univ. Hosps. of Cleve., 1950-51, resident in medicine, 1954-56; practice medicine specializing in internal medicine Cleve., 1957-92; mem. faculty Case Western Res. U. Sch. Medicine, Cleve., 1956-92, asst. prof. medicine, 1965-92, dir. health clinics, utilization rev., 1965-92, asst. prof. emeritus, 1992—; chief med. services Horizon Ctr. Hosp., Cleve., 1981-83. Sec. Citizens Commn. on Grad. Med. Edn., 1964-66 Sub-deacon Episcopal Diocese Ohio, 1970—; trustee The Sihler Mental Health Found. Served with AUS, 1943-46, to capt. USAF, 1951-53. Decorated Bronze Star; Ogelbay fellow in medicine U. Hosps. Cleve., 1955-56 Home: Ste 915 2181 Ambleside Dr Cleveland OH 44106

BOWERING, GEORGE HARRY, writer, consultant, language educator; b. Penticton, BC, Can., Dec. 1, 1936; s. Ewart Harry and Pearl Patricia (Brinson) Bowering; m. Angela May Luoma, Dec. 14, 1962; 1 child, Thea Claire. Student, Victoria Coll., 1953—54; BA, U. B.C., 1960, MA, 1963; postgrad., U. Western Ont., 1966—67. Asst. prof. Am. lit. U. Calgary, Canada, 1963-66; writer in residence Sir George Williams U., Montreal, Que., 1967-68, asst. prof., 1968-71; prof. Simon Fraser U., Burnaby, B.C., 1972—2001; poet laureate of Can. Author: Mirror on the Floor, 1967, Autobiology, 1972, Flycatcher and Other Stories, 1974, Concentric Circles, 1977, A Short Sad Book, 1977, Protective Footwear, 1978, Another Mouth, 1979, Burning Water, 1980, A Place to Die, 1983, Caprice, 1987, Harry's Fragments, 1990, The Rain Barrel, 1994, Shoot!, 1994, Parents From Space, 1994, Piccolo Mondo, 1998, Diamondback Dog, 1998; poetry Points on the Grid, 1964, The Man in Yellow Boots, 1965, The Silver Wire, 1966, Rocky Mountain Foot, 1968, The Gangs of Kosmos, 1969, Touch, 1971, In the Flesh, 1973, The Catch, 1976, Particular Accidents: Selected Poems, 1981, Smoking Mirror, 1984, Kerrisdale Elegies, 1984, 71 Poems for People, 1985, Delayed Mercy, 1986, Sticks & Stones, 1989, Quarters, 1991, Urban Snow, 1992, George Bowering Selected, 1993, The Moustache, 1993, Blonds On Bikes, 1997; (poetry) His Life: A Poem, 2000, Baseball, 2003, Changing on the Fly, 2004, Vermeer's Light, 2006; (essays) The Mask in Place, 1982, A Way with Words, 1982, Craft Slices, 1985, Errata, 1988, Imaginary Hand, 1988, A Magpie Life, 2001, Cars, 2002, Left Hook, 2005; author: (history) Bowering's B.C., 1996, Egotists and Autocrats, 1999, Stone Country, 2003; editor Taking the Field: The Best of Baseball Fiction, 1990, 92, Likely Stories: A Postmodern Sampler, 1992, And Other Stories, 2001, (short stories) Standing On Richards, 2004, Baseball Love, 2006. Served with RCAF, 1954-57. Mem.: Assn. Can. TV and Radio Artists. Home: 4403 W 11th Ave Vancouver BC Canada Personal E-mail: bowering@sfu.ca.

BOWERMAN, ANN LOUISE, writer, secondary school educator, genealogist; b. Branch County, Mich., June 4, 1933; d. George Allen and Mary (Thomas) Hubbard; m. Virgil Lee Bowerman, June 4, 1954 (div. 1977); children: William Lee, Sally Ann; m. Virgil Wayne Dunkel, Jr., May 23, 1987 (div. Dec. 1996). BA, We. Mich. U., 1966, MSLS, 1971, MA, 1976. Cert. tchr. K-8 Mich., libr. sci. Tchr. Bethel #6 Sch. Dist., Coldwater, Mich., 1953—55; tchr. kindergarten Union City Schs., Mich., 1963—64; children's libr. Sturgis Pub. Libr., Mich., 1971—72; libr./media specialist Coldwater H.S., 1972—91; field rep. U.S. Census Bur., 2000—02, 2003—; media specialist libr. Union City Schs., 2002—03; ret., 1991. Mem. programming com., mem. ann. scholarships telethon com., camera staff, video editor Cable TV Channel 31, Coldwater, 1983—90. Author: The Bater Book, 1987, A Bowerman Family History, 1998, Historic Howe, Indiana Walking Tour, 1998, The William Bowerman Family of Conneaut Township, 1998, A Boone Family History, 2007; co-author: Recommendations for High School Media Centers in Michigan, 1980; contbr. articles to profl. jours. Leader All Around 4-H Club, Union City, 1954—74; mem. Sullivan Lady's Aid Soc., Union City, 1955—74, Coldwater Hist. Preservation Assn., 1978—86, Twin Lakes Cmty. Assn., 1997—2004, Mich. Assn. Computer Users in Learning, 1975—91; mem. adv. coun. Calhoun and Branch Counties Regional Ednl. Media Ctr., Marshall, Mich., 1972—91; mem., chair governing bd. Woodlands Libr. Coop., Albion, Mich., 1973—74, 1983—86; chair winter program com. Tibbits Arts Found., Coldwater, 1980—90; com. mem. So. Mich. Region Coop., Albion, 1989—91; mem. cultural arts com., mem. walking tour com. Howe (Ind.) Cmty. Assn., 1996—2005, pres., 2003—05; del. Mich. Rep. State Conv., Detroit, 1986; candidate Branch County Commr., Coldwater, 1988. Recipient cert. of Appreciation, Mich. Assn. Media Edn., 1980, 1991, Golden Apple Retirement award, Coldwater HS, 1991. Mem.: DAR (mem. good citizen selection com., treas. Coldwater br. 1997—2002, registrar 2003—04, regent 2003—05), Coldwater Edn. Assn. (sec. 1980—90), Crawford County Geneal. Soc., Union City Geneal. Soc., Ctrl. N.Y. Geneal. Soc., New Eng. Hist. Geneal. Soc., Soc. Genealogists (London), St. Joseph County Hist. Soc. (advisor to Land Office Mus. com. 1997—2005), Old Brutus Hist. Soc., Schenectady County Hist. Soc., Mich. Assn. Ret. Sch. Pers., Descs. Founders of Ancient Windsor, Beta Phi Mu. Avocations: travel, coin collecting/numismatics, tennis. Home: 1820 W 600 N Howe IN 46746-9406

BOWERS, BEGE KAYE, literature and communications educator, academic administrator; b. Nashville, Aug. 19, 1949; d. John and Yvonne Bowers. BA in English cum laude, Vanderbilt U., 1971; student, U. Mich., 1985; MACT, U. Tenn., 1973, PhD, 1984. Asst. loan officer Ctr. for Fin. Aid and Placement, Baylor U., Waco, Tex., 1975-76; editorial asst. Wassily Leontief, NYU, NYC, 1976-78; instr. bus. English Florence-Darlington Tech. Coll., Florence, SC, 1979-80; tchr. English and French St. John's High Sch., Darlington, SC, 1980-82; teaching asst. dept English U. Tenn., Knoxville, 1982-84; from asst. prof. English to prof. Youngstown (Ohio) State U., 1984—92, prof., 1992—, asst. to dean Coll. Arts and Scis., 1992-93, dir. profl. writing and editing, 1996-2000, assoc. to the dean Coll. Arts and Scis., 2001—02, asst. provost acad. programs and planning, 2002—05, interim provost, 2005, v.p. acad. affairs, 2005, assoc. provost acad. programs and planning, 2005—. Freelance editor MLA, NYC, 1978-80; cons. Project Arete, Youngstown and Mahoning County Pub. Schs., 1984-87, Youngstown Pub. Schs., 1986, 87-88, 90-91, Macmillan Pub. Co., 1986, Trumbull County Schs., Ohio, 1988, Akron Beacon Jour., 1994-95, Ohio Dept. Edn., 1998-2001, Ohio Bd. Regents, 2002—; chair Mahoning Area Consortium Tech. Prep. Governing Bd., 2002—. Co-editor: CEA Critic, 1998—2002, CEA Forum, 1988—2004; co-editor: (with Barbara Brothers) Reading and Writing Women's Lives: A Study of the Novel of Manners, 1991; co-editor: (with Chuck Nelson) Internships in Technical Communication, 1991; co-editor: (with Mark Allen) Annotated Chaucer Bibliography, 1986—96, 2002 (MLA award for disting. bibliography, 2004); mem. editl. bd. South Atlantic Rev., 1987—89; editor: more than 40 pamphlets, 7 children's books, and 1 videoscript. Alumni Found. Rsch. fellow U. Tenn., 1978, dissertation fellow U. Tenn., 1983, Davis editl. fellow U. Tenn., 1984; Grad. Rsch. Coun. grantee Youngstown State U. Mem.: MLA, Gould Soc. (pres. faculty com. 1991—93), No. Ohio Soc. for Tech. Comm., Soc. for Tech. Comm. (Jay R. Gould award for excellence in tchg. tech. comm. 1999, Disting. Chpt. Svc. award 2001, Assoc. fellow award 2002), Assn. Tchrs. Tech. Writing, New Chaucer Soc. (asst. bibliographer 1986—), Coll. English Assn. Ohio, Coll. English Assn. (exec. bd., Disting. Svc. award 1996, Lifetime Achievement award 2005), Phi Beta Kappa, Phi Kappa Phi (web mgr. 2005—, pres. 1991—92, sec. 1994—98, exec. bd. 1998—). Office: Youngstown State U Office of the Provost Youngstown OH 44555-0001 Office Phone: 330-941-1560. E-mail: bkbowers@ysu.edu.

BOWERS, BRENT, editor; m. Barbara Bowers. Vol. Peace Corps, N. Africa; former reporter, editor Wall St. Jour.; small bus. editor, now columnist NY Times. Co-author: The Synergy Myth, 1997, 1,000 Years, 1,000 People, 1998, Synergy & Other Lies, 1999; editor: New York Times Management Reader: Hot Ideas & Best Practices from the New World of Business, 2001; author: If At First You Don't Succeed., 2006, The Eight Patterns of Highly Effective Entrepreneurs, 2007. Avocations: hiking, poker, reading. Mailing: c/o Random House 1745 Broadway New York NY 10019*

BOWERS, CHARLES RICHARD, surgeon; b. Frederick, Md., 1924; MD, Johns Hopkins U., 1947. Diplomate Am. Bd. Surgery. Intern Union Meml. Hosp., Balt., 1947-48; resident in surgery Baylor U. Med. Ctr., Dallas, 1948-49, 50-52, resident in pathology, 1949-50; clin. instr. U. Tex. Sch. Medicine, San Antonio, 1952-54; mem. staff emeritus St. Johns Med. Ctr., Anderson, Ind., 1954-98. Clin. instr. USAF Lackland AFB, San Antonio, 1952-54. Active Vol. Physicians for Vietnam, 1966-72. Capt. M.C. USAF, 1952-54. Fellow Am. Coll. Surgeons; mem. AMA. Home: 8734 Grey Oaks Ave Sarasota FL 34238-4371

BOWERS, CHRISTI C., mediator, lawyer, writer, poet; b. Hagerstown, Md., Nov. 4, 1970; BA in Psychology, BS in Bus., Shepherd Coll., 1993; JD, MS, U. Balt., 1998, MBA, 2000. Bar: Md. 2000, cert.: Md. Inst. Continuing Profl. Edn. Lawyers (mediator), Md. Inst. Continuing Profl. Edn. Lawyers (domestic, custody and visitation mediator), Md. Inst. Continuing Profl. Edn. Lawyers (domestic property, fin. issues mediator) 2000, Md. Inst. Continuing Profl. Edn. Lawyers (advanced transformative mediator) 2002, Md. Inst. Continuing Profl. Edn. Lawyers (worker's compensation mediator) 2002, Dist. Ct. of Md. (advanced mediator) 2002. Pvt. practice, Hagerstown, 2000—; tchr.,presenter co-parenting workshop for adults and children Children of Separation and Divorce (now Nat. Family Resiliency Program), Balt., 2000—; case mgr., staff mediator family divsn. Cir. Ct. for Prince George's County, Upper Marlboro, Md., 2003—. Vol. mediator civil large and small claims cases Dist. Ct. Md., Annapolis, 2000—; vol. faculty critiquer Md. Inst. Continuing Profl. Edn. Lawyers Mediation Tng., Balt., 2001—; substitute tchr. Bd. Edn. Washington County, Hagerstown, 1999—. Author: Mediation In Maryland; editor: Resolving Issues newsletter. Exec. bd.- mem. at large Md. Coun. Dispute Resolution, Balt., 2002; bd. dirs., sec. Washington County Cmty. Mediation Ctr., Hagerstown, 2002—03. Recipient cert. appreciation for vol. mediation, Dist. Ct. of Md., 2002. Mem.: ABA, Assn. Conflict Resolution, Washington County Bar Assn., Md. State Bar Assn., Sigma Iota Epsilon (hon.). Avocations: writing, singing, travel, writing, poetry. Office Phone: 301-730-6244. Personal E-mail: christicbo511@aol.com. Business E-Mail: ccbowers@co.pg.md.us.

BOWERS, CURTIS RAY, JR., chaplain; b. Lancaster, Pa., Feb. 6, 1933; s. Curtis Ray and Oleita (Geisler) B.; m. Doris Jean, June 18, 1955; children: Sharon, William, Stephen. BA, Asbury Coll., 1958; MDiv, Asbury Theol. Sem., 1960. Pastor Methodist Ch., Cynthiana, Ky., 1956-60, Ch. of the Nazarene, Cape May, N.J., 1960-61; chaplain U.S. Army, 1961-84; dir. chaplaincy ministries Ch. of the Nazarene, Kansas City, Mo., 1984-2000. Author: Forward Edge of the Battle Area: A Chaplain's Story. Col. U.S. Army, 1961-84. Decorated Silver Star; named Srs. Double Inter-Svc. Tennis Champion, 1982; named to 327th Infantry Regimental Hall of Fame, 1998; recipient Outstanding Chaplain of Yr. award, Ch. of the Nazarene, 2000. Mem. Ch. Of The Nazarene. Avocation: tennis. Home: 3523 Portland Ave Nampa ID 83686-7993 Home Phone: 208-442-1689. Personal E-mail: crbowers11@juno.com.

BOWERS, FRANCIS ROBERT, educational consultant, literature educator; b. NYC, May 4, 1920; s. William Leo and Catherine (Callahan) B. BA, Cath. U. Am., 1946, PhD, 1959; MA, Fordham U., 1952. Tchr. Ascension Sch., NYC, 1946-48, St. Augustine's HS, Bklyn., 1948-51, St. Peter's HS, Staten Island, 1951-53; instr. De La Salle Coll., Washington, 1953-59; assoc. prof. English and world lit. Manhattan Coll., 1959-70, 85-89, chmn. dept., 1967-70, chmn. grad. English dept., 1961-70, dean arts and scis., 1970-80, provost, 1980-85, acad. advisor to intercollegiate athletes, 1988—2004, acad. advisor to art students, 2004—. Author: Characterization in Narrative Poetry of George Crabbe, 1959. Trustee scholarship Cath. U., 1953-58. Finn grantee, 1962; Manhattan Coll. grantee, 1966 Mem. Phi Beta Kappa. Office: Manhattan Coll Dean Arts Office Bronx NY 10471 Home Phone: 718-543-2402; Office Phone: 718-862-7987.

BOWERS, GLENN LEE, retired professional society administrator; b. York, Pa., May 7, 1921; s. Elmer Frederick and Naomi Mae (Shellenberger) B.; m. Betty June Lehr, Apr. 21, 1943; children— Tina, Timothy BS, Pa. State U., 1946, MS, 1948. Wildlife biologist Pa. Game Commn., various locations, 1948-57, chief div. research Harrisburg, 1957-59, dep. exec. dir., 1959-65, exec. dir., 1965-82. Chmn. bd. dirs. Worldwide Furbearer Conf., Frostburg, Md., 1976-80 Contbr. articles to profl. jours. Served to capt. USMCR, 1942-45, PTO Recipient John Pearce Meml. award N.E. sect. Wildlife Soc., 1982; Nat. Wildlife Conservationist award Nat. Wildlife Fedn., 1982 Mem. Wildlife Soc., Internat. Assn. Fish and Wildlife Agys. (exec. com. 1972-80, pres. 1978-79, gen. counsel 1983-95, Seth Gordon award 1982), N.E. Assn. Fish and Wildlife Agys. (various offices, v.p., pres. 1965-82). Lodges: Masons. Republican. Methodist. Avocations: fishing, hunting. Home: 221 Mountain Rd Dillsburg PA 17019-1514

BOWERS, JANE MEREDITH, retired music educator; b. Mpls., Sept. 17, 1936; B in Music, Wellesley Coll., 1958; MA in Music History, U. Calif., Berkeley, 1962, PhD in Music History, 1971. Instr. U. N.C., Chapel Hill, 1968-72; asst. prof. dept. music history and musicology Eastman Sch. Music, Rochester, N.Y., 1972-73, 74-75; lectr., instr. women's studies, music and continuing edn. Portland (Oreg.) State U., 1977—81; instr. flute Reed Coll., Portland, 1979-81; from asst. prof. dept. music to prof. U. Wis., Milw., 1981—2001, prof., 1993—2001, chmn. music history and lit. area, 1997—2001, mem. faculty senate, 1997—2000, ret., 2000. Lectr. women's studies program Cornell U., Ithaca, N.Y., spring 1979; vis. asst. prof. dept. music Oreg. State U., 1980-81; lectr. in field, 1969—; flutist Am. Wind Symphony, summer 1958, Cabrillo Music Festival, 1963-64; asst. prin. flutist Oakland Symphony Orch., 1962-65; free-lance Baroque flutist, N.Y.C., 1975-77; numerous recitals and chamber music concerts on modern and Baroque flute, 1964-85. Editor: Michel de La Barre: Pieces pour la Flute Traversiere, 1978, Joseph Boden de Boismortier: Petites Sonates pour 2 Flutes Traversieres, 1993, (with Judith Tick) Women Making Music: The Western Art Tradition, 1150-1950, 1986, paperback edit., 1987 (Deems Taylor award ASCAP 1987, Pauline Alderman prize 1987), François Devianne's Nouvelle Méthode Théorique et Pratique pour la Flute, 1999; contbr. articles and revs. to profl. jours. and anthologies. Bd. dirs. Early Music Guild Oreg., 1981, Early Music Now, Milw., 1989-92. Alfred Hertz meml. travel scholar, 1965-66; postdoctoral fellow AAUW, 1973-74, 78-79, fellow Ctr. for 20th Century Studies, U. Wis.- Milw., 1982-83, Humanities Inst., U. Wis.-Madison, 1988-89; grantee NEH, summers 1980, 84. Mem. Am. Mus. Instrument Soc. (rev. editor Jour. 1976-81, bd. govs. 1988-91), Am. Musicological Soc. (coun. 1982-84, chmn. performance com., 1998-2000, mem., chmn. Noah Greenberg award com. 1987-89), Coll. Music Soc. (sec. com. on status of women 1972-74, mem. com. 1992-96, tchr. Summer Inst. 1993), Soc. for Ethnomusicology (coun. 1995-98, chmn. constn. revision com. 1996-2000), Am. Women Composers (editl. bd. 1992-94), Internat. Assn. Women in Music (editl. bd. 1995-2002), Assn. Women in Edn. (vice chmn., chmn. U. Wis.- Milw. 1985-87). Home: 2516 E Stratford Ct Shorewood WI 53211-2634

BOWERS, JOHN EDWARDS, engineering educator; PhD, Stanford U. Prof. elec. and computer engring. U. Calif., Santa Barbara, dir. Multidisciplinary Optical Switching Tech. Ctr. (MOST). Fellow: IEEE (Leos William Streifer Award 1996), American Physical Soc.; mem.: NSF (Presidential Young Investigator 1988), NAE, Sigma Xi. Office: U Calif Dept Elec and Computer Engring Eng Sci Bldg Rm 2221C Santa Barbara CA 93106-9560 Office Phone: 805-893-8447. Office Fax: 805-893-7990. E-mail: bowers@ece.ucsb.edu.

BOWERS, JOHN M., labor union administrator; b. NYC, Nov. 11, 1924; m. Marcy Bowers; children: John, Christine. Exec. v.p. Internat. Longshoremen's Assn., NYC, 1963—87, pres., 1987—. V.p. Internat. Transport Workers Fedn., 1990—2006; founder Internat. Longshoremen's Assn. Civil Rights Com., 1991—, Internat. Longshoremen's Assn. Children's Fund, 1993—. Served in US Army. Named Man of Yr., Irish Am. Labor Coalition, 1992; named to The Internat. Maritime Hall of Fame, Maritime Assn. NY & NJ; recipient Adm. of the Sea award, United Seaman's Svc., 1992, Connie award, Containerization & Intermodel Inst., 1994, Golden Compass award, Seafarer's House. Office: Internat Longshoresmen's Assn 17 Battery Pl Ste 930 New York NY 10004-1207 E-mail: jbowers@ilaunion.org.*

BOWERS, KIM, lawyer, energy executive; b. Ohio; BA, Miami U., Ohio; MA, Baylor U., Waco, Tex.; JD, U. Tex. Sch. Law, Austin. With Kelly, Hart & Hallman, Ft. Worth; corp. counsel to sr. comml. counsel Valero Energy

Corp., San Antonio, 1997—2002, mng. counsel, 2002—03, v.p. legal svcs., 2003, sr. v.p., gen. counsel, 2006—. Office: Valero Energy Corp One Valero Way San Antonio TX 78249*

BOWERS, KLAUS D(IETER), electronics executive, researcher; b. Stettin, Germany, Dec. 27, 1929; s. Franz A. and Elisabeth (Schneider) B.; m. Roswitha U. Rau, June 15, 1964; children: Pamela, Colin. BA, Oxford U., Eng., 1950, MA, PhD, 1953. Research lectr. in physics Christ Ch., Oxford U., 1952-56; with AT&T, 1956-90; researcher Bell Telephone Labs., Murray Hill, NJ, 1956-59, mgr. electronics devel., 1959-66, Allentown, Pa., 1966-71; mng. dir., v.p. Sandia Nat. Labs., Albuquerque, 1971-75; exec. dir. Pa. Labs. Bell Telephone Labs., Allentown, 1975-79, v.p. Murray Hill, 1979-90. Chmn. Semiconductor Rsch. Corp., 1987-88 Author: Non Frangimur: My First Six Decades, 2004; contbr. articles to profl. jours.; patentee in field. Trustee Cedar Crest Coll., 1983-87. Fellow IEEE (Frederik Philips award 1989); mem. Nat. Acad. Engring. Home: 2890 Golf Cir Emmaus PA 18049-1735

BOWERS, MICHAEL THOMAS, chemistry professor; b. Spokane, Wash., June 6, 1939; s. John W. and Fae (Scott) B.; married, Feb. 8, 1964; children: Molly, Shelia, Melissa. BS, Gonzaga U., 1962; MS, U. Ill., 1964, PhD, 1966. Asst. prof. U. Calif., Santa Barbara, 1966-73, assoc. prof., 1973-76, prof. chemistry, 1976—. Faculty rsch. lectr. faculty senate U. Calif., Santa Barbara, 1994. Editor Internat. Jour. Mass Spectrometry, 1986—; contbr. over 300 articles to profl. jours.; editor 3 books in field; assoc. editor Jour. Am. Chem. Soc. 1st lt. U.S. Army, 1966-68. Guggenheim Found. fellow, 1994. Fellow AAAS, Am. Phys. Soc.; mem. Am. Chem. Soc. (assoc. editor jour. 1989—, Nobel laureate signature award 1989, Outstanding Achievement in Mass Spectrometry award 1996), Am. Soc. Mass Spectrometry (Disting. Contbn. award 2004), Internat. Mass Spectrometry Soc. (Thomson gold medal 1997). Roman Catholic. Avocations: golf, running. Office: U Calif Dept Chemistry Santa Barbara CA 93106 Office Phone: 805-893-2893. E-mail: bowers@chem.ucsb.edu.

BOWERS, NELL S., psychologist; b. Mineola, NY, Sept. 23, 1946; d. Phil Bertram and Coleta Barron Shuman; m. R. Dennis Bowers, June 17, 1967; children: K. Shannon Wilson, C. Devon, Sarah G. BS, U. Kans., Lawrence, 1968; MEd, Boston U., 1972. Lic. psychologist Pa. Counselor Montgomery City Schs., Rockville, Md., 1972—73; cons. parent edn. Polk County Juvenile Ct., Des Moines, 1974—76; dir. cmty. career planning Ctr. for Women, Des Moines, 1976—78; dir. continuing edn. for adult students Bucks County C.C., Newtown, Pa., 1979—83; cons. Doylestown, Pa., 1983—89; psychologist, 1989—. Vol. Critical Incident Stress Mgmt., Bucks County Emergency Med. Svcs., Pa., 1994—; vol. cmty. crisis response team NOVA, Bucks County, Pa., 1998—. Troop leader, advisor Girl Scouts of Freedom Valley, Valley Forge, Pa., 1994—2001; badge advisor, troop com. Boy Scouts Am., Bucks County, Pa., 1995—2002; bd. dirs., founding pres. Childrens Cultural Ctr., Bucks County, Pa., 1987—89; bd. dirs., v.p., pres. Dance Theatre of Pa., Doylestown, 1994—2000. Mem.: APA, Ctrl. Bucks C. of C. Methodist. Achievements include founding mem. Bucks County Commrs.' Adv. Coun. on Women, 1979-85; founder "A Day for All Women", 1981. Avocations: needlecrafts, sewing, reading, camping. Office: 350 S Main St Ste 309 Doylestown PA 18901 Office Phone: 215-348-3379. Office Fax: 215-348-8487.

BOWERS, PATRICIA ELEANOR FRITZ, economist; b. NYC, Mar. 21, 1928; d. Eduard and Eleanor (Ring) Fritz. Student scholar, Goucher Coll., 1946-48; BA, Cornell U., 1950; MA, NYU, 1953, PhD, 1965. Statis. asst. Fed. Res. Bank NY, NYC, 1950-53; lectr. Upsala Coll., East Orange, NJ, 1953-59; researcher Fortune mag., NYC, 1959-60; teaching fellow NYU, NYC, 1960-62, instr., 1962-64; mem. faculty Bklyn. Coll., CUNY, 1964-00, prof. econs., 1974-2000, chair dept. econs., 1996-99, prof. emerita, 2000—. Author: Private Choice and Public Welfare, 1974. Sec. Friends of the Johnson Mus., Cornell U., 1989-91; Cornell Fund rep. Class of 1950, Cornell U., 2004—. Mem. Am. Econ. Assn., Econometric Soc., Met. Econ. Assn. (sec. 1963-68, pres. 1974-75), Am. Statis. Assn. (univs. chmn. ann. forecasting confs. 1970-71, 71-72), Cornell Club NY, Kappa Alpha Theta. Home: 145 E 16th St Apt 11-L New York NY 10003-3405

BOWERS, RICHARD PHILIP, manufacturing executive; b. Reading, Pa., July 27, 1931; s. Clarence Philip and Lottie Rose (Linkowski) B.; m. Dolores R. Bowers; children: Richard P., Karen M., Lisa Ann, Julie L. Student, St. Bonaventure U., Olean, NY, 1949-51. Sales engr. Bowers Battery and Spark Plug Corp., Reading, Pa., 1952-57; v.p. sales Gen. Battery Cord, Reading, Pa., 1957-64; v.p. sales and mktg. East Penn Mfg. Co., Lyon Station, Pa., 1964-67, exec. v.p., 1967-95; also bd. dirs. E. Penn Mfg. Co., Lyon Station, Pa. Pres. TBS Systems of Ala., Birmingham, 1986—, Pioneer Auto Parts, Phila., 1980—, electro Battery Co., St. Louis; chmn. bd. Taylor Battery Co., Louisville, 1986—; chmn. bd. Power Battery Toronto, Can. Pres. Green Hills Lake Recreational Assn., Green Hills, Pa., 1984-87. Served with U.S. Army, 1962-64. Named Man of Yr., Automotive Merchandising, Chgo., 1984, 89. Mem. Battery Coun. Internat. (chmn. conv. planning com. 1986-91), Ind. Battery Mfrs. Assn. (past pres., bd. dirs.). Democrat. Roman Catholic.

BOWERS, TERREE A., lawyer; b. Shirley, Mass., Aug. 6, 1954; s. Thomas Allan and Virginia Ann (Wilson) B.; m. Constance Tasulis, Mar. 15, 1987; 3 children. BA with high honors, U. Tex., 1976, JD, 1979. Bar: Calif. 1979, US Dist. Ct. (ctrl. dist. Calif.), US Ct. Appeals (9th cir.). Legal clk. state affairs com. Tex. Senate, 1979; assoc. Adams, Duque & Hazeltine, LA, 1979-82; asst. US atty. Dept. Justice, LA, 1982-92; US atty. Ctrl. Dist. Calif., LA, 1992-94; legal coord. Internat. War Crimes Tribunal Yugoslavia, 1994—99; advisor Internat. War Crimes Tribunal-Rwanda, 1994—99; chief dep. City Atty.'s Office, LA, 1998—2005; ptnr. white collar crime practice grp. Howrey LLP, LA, 2005—. Mem. standing com. on discipline Fed. Dist. Ct. (Ctrl. Dist. Calif.); co-chair human rights subcommittee ABA Internat. Law Com.; bd. mem. Inner City Law Ctr.; adj. prof. internat. crime law seminars UCLA, 2000—02. Recipient Disting. Svc. award Atty. Gen., 1992, Nat. commendation Depts. Justice, Treasury and State. Mem. Phi Beta Kappa, Alpha Phi Omega, Friars, Omicron Delta Kappa, Goodfellow. Office: Howrey LLP Ste 1100 550 S Hope St Los Angeles CA 90071 Office Phone: 213-892-1882, 626-224-3900. Office Fax: 213-892-2300. E-mail: BowersT@howrey.com.

BOWERS, THOMAS ARNOLD, journalism educator, dean; b. Plymouth, Ind., Sept. 27, 1942; s. Merritt Edward and Beulah Irene (Burkhart) Bowers; m. Patricia Mills Shane, July 29, 1966 (div.); children: Matthew, Lisa; m. Mary Ellen McKay Woolley, Jan. 10, 2002. BA in Journalism with distinction, Ind. U., 1964, MA in Journalism, 1969, PhD in Communication Rsch., 1971. Asst. prof. Sch. Journalism U. N.C., Chapel Hill, 1971-76, assoc. prof., 1976-80, prof., 1980-93, assoc. dean, 1980—2005, interim dean, 2005—06; James L. Knight prof. Sch. Journalism and Mass Comm. U. N.C., 1993—2006, dean emeritus, 2006—. Cons. Meredith Coll., Raleigh, N.C., 1973, Inform, Inc., Hickory, N.C., 1981-85, The Coll. Bd., N.Y.C., 1989, bd. regents U. Fla., Am. Univ. Co-author: Fundamentals of Advertising Research, 1979, 4d edit., 1991; editor Journalism Educator, 1983-88; also articles, chpts. in books. Cons. LWV, Chapel Hill, 1973, also various polit. candidates; chmn. com. United Way, Chapel Hill, 1979, 88. Capt. U.S. Army, 1965-68. Recipient Silver medal award, Triangle Advt. Fedn., N.C., 1994, Sanders award Tchg. Excellence, U. N.C., 1997; grantee, Freedom Forum, 1988—95. Mem. Assn. Edn. Journalism and Mass Communication (pres. 1988-89), Am. Advt. Fedn., Am. Acad. Advt., Newspaper Assn. Am., Phi Beta Kappa, Kappa Tau Alpha. Avocation: reading. Home: 17 Dartford Ct Chapel Hill NC 27517-8667 Personal E-mail: tbowers@email.unc.edu.

BOWERS, W. PAUL, utilities executive; b. 1956; Grad., U. West Fla., Pensacola; M in Mgmt. Residential sales rep. Gulf Power Southern Co., 1979, sr. v.p. retail mktg. Ga. Power, 1995—98, pres., CEO Western Power Distbn. Bristol, England, 1998—2000, sr. v.p. Southern Co. Svcs. Inc., chief mktg. officer, 2000—01, exec. v.p. Southern Co. Svcs. Inc., 2001, bd. dirs., pres., CEO Southern Power, 2001—05, pres. Southern Co. Generation, 2001—. Office: Southern Co Generation 30 Ivan Allen Jr Blvd NW Atlanta GA 30308 Office Phone: 404-506-5000.*

BOWERS, WILLIAM CHARLES, lawyer; b. Washington, Sept. 15, 1946; s. Kenneth Victor and Johnlou (Sweet) B.; children by previous marriage: William Che, Lynn Ann; m. JoAnne Kennedy, July 30, 1988; 1 child, Liam Flynn. AB, Princeton U., 1968; JD with distinction, Emory U., 1975. Bar: Ga. 1975, N.Y. 1988. Law clk. to Hon. Griffin Bell, U.S. Ct. Appeals for 5th Circuit, Atlanta, 1975-76; assoc. Sutherland Asbill & Brennan, Atlanta, 1976-82, ptnr., 1982-83, Trotter, Smith & Jacobs, Atlanta, 1983-85; counsel Paul, Hastings, Janofsky & Walker, Atlanta, 1985-88; ptnr. Paul, Hastings, Janifsky & Walker, NYC, 1988-90; gen. counsel GPA Capital, Shannon, Ireland, 1990-93; assoc. gen. counsel GE Capital Aviation Svcs., Stamford, Conn., 1993-95; ptnr. Winthrop, Stimson, Putnam & Roberts, NYC, 1995-2000, Pillsbury Winthrop LLP, 2001—05; ptnr., chmn. structured fin. practice Pillsbury Winthrop Shaw Pittman, NYC, 2005—. Editor (exec. articles): Emory Law Jour. Lt. USN, 1968-72. Mem.: ABA (past chmn. Corp. Tax com.). Democrat. Episcopalian. Office: Pillsbury Winthrop Shaw Pittman 1540 Broadway New York NY 10036 Office Phone: 212-858-1106. Office Fax: 212-858-1500. Business E-Mail: william.bowers@pillsburylaw.com.

BOWERSOCK, GLEN WARREN, retired historian, educator; b. Providence, Jan. 12, 1936; s. Donald Curtis and Josephine (Evans) Bowersock. AB, Harvard U., 1957; BA, Oxford U., Eng., 1959, MA, DPhil, 1962; D (hon.), U. Strasbourg, 1990, Ecole Pratique Hautes Etudes, Paris, 1999, U. Athens, 2005. Lectr. ancient history Oxford U., 1960-62, vis. lectr., 1966; instr. Harvard U., 1962-64, asst. prof., 1964-67, assoc. prof. classics, 1967-69, prof. Greek and Latin, 1969-80, chmn. dept. classics, 1972-77, assoc. dean faculty arts and scis., 1977-80; prof. hist. studies Inst. Advanced Study, Princeton, NJ, 1980—2006, prof. emeritus, 2006—; hon. fellow Balliol Coll., Oxford, 2004—. Sr. fellow Dumbarton Oaks Ctr. for Byzantine Studies, Washington, 1984—93, Ctr. for Hellenic Studies, Washington, 1976—90; cons. Ednl. Svcs., Inc., 1964, NEH, 1971—; mem. sci. com. Scuola Normale Superiore di Pisa, Italy, Istituto di Studi Umanistici, Florence, Italy; chmn. sci. com. Maison de l'Orient Mediterraneen , Lyon, France; mem. Internat. Colloquium on the Classics in Edn., 1964—66; vis. prof. Australian Nat. U., 1972, Princeton U., 1986—87, Coll. France, 1997; Sather prof. U. Calif., Berkeley, 1991; Jerome lectr. U. Mich. and Am. Acad. in Rome, 1989; syndic Harvard U. Press, 1977—81; lectr. Thompson Lectures, Pomona, 1993, Wiles Lectures, Queens U. , Belfast, Northern Ireland, 1993. Author: Augustus and the Greek World, 1965, Pseudo-Xenophon, Constitution of the Athenians, 1968, Greek Sophists in the Roman Empire, 1969, Julian the Apostate, 1978, Roman Arabia, 1983, Hellenism in Late Antiquity, 1990, Fiction as History from Nero to Julian, 1994, Studies on the Eastern Roman Empire, 1994, Martyrdom and Rome, 1995, Selected Papers on Late Antiquity, 2000, Mosaics as History--The Near East from Late Antiquity to Islam, 2006, Lorenzo Valla, Donation of Constantine, 2007, Saggi sulla tradizione classica, 2007; editor: Philostratus' Life of Apollonius, 1970, Approaches to the Second Sophistic, 1974; editor: (with J. Clive and S. Graubard) Edward Gibbon and the Decline and Fall of the Roman Empire, 1977; editor: (with C. P. Jones) L. Robert-Martyre de Pionios, 1994; editor: (with T. J. Cornell) Momigliano-Studies on Modern Scholarship, 1994; editor: (with P. Brown and O. Grabar) Late Antiquity-A Guide to the Postclassical World, 1999; mem. editl. bd.: Arabian Archaeology and Epigraphy, Ancient Civilizations from Scythia to Siberia (Russian Acad. Scis.), Berytus, Am. Jour. Philology, 1987—95, Am. Scholar, 1981—93; editor (gen.): Revealing Antiquity. Trustee Am. Schs. Oriental Rsch., 1984—90; bd. dirs. Met. Opera Guild; adv. dir. Met. Opera Assn.; mem. nat. coun. Glimmerglass Opera, 1994—2004. Recipient James H. Breasted prize, Am. Hist. Assn., 1992, Chevalier de la Légion d' honneur, Chevalier des Arts et des Lettres; Rhodes scholar, 1957—60. Fellow: Accademia Nazionale dei Lincei, Am. Numis. Soc. (coun. 1983—96), Am. Acad. Arts and Scis.; mem.: Acad. des Inscriptions et Belles-Lettres, Russian Acad. Scis. (fgn.), German Archaeol. Inst. (corr.), Soc. Promotion Roman and Hellenic Studies (hon. Am. sec. Roman Soc.), Leschetizky Assn. Am., Am. Philol. Assn., Am. Philos. Soc. (coun. 1992—98), Johnsonians, Century Club (N.Y.C.), Knickerbocker Club (N.Y.C.), Phi Beta Kappa. Office: Inst Advanced Study Sch Hist Studies Einstein Dr Princeton NJ 08540 Office Phone: 609-734-8353. Business E-Mail: gwb@ias.edu.

BOWERSOX, PATRICIA ANNE, social worker; b. Lincoln Park, Mich., Oct. 4, 1974; d. David George and Elizabeth Mary Bowersox. BA in Psychology, U. Mich., Dearborn, 1997; MSW, U. Mich., Ann Arbor, 1999. Sch. social worker Downriver HS, Brownstown, Mich., 1999—2001, The Dearborn Acad., 2001—; group facilitator Henry Ford Hospice, Sandcastles, 2000—01. Group facilitator Maplegrove Children's Program, Bloomfield, Mich., 1999—; social worker Henry Ford Hospice, Mich., 2000—01. Vol. group facilitator Maplegrove Children's Program, Bloomfield, Mich., 1999—, Henry Ford Hospice, Trenton, Mich., 2000—01. Mem.: NASW, Mich. Assn. Social Workers. Avocations: running, reading, cooking. Home: 22446 Olmstead Dearborn MI 48124

BOWERSOX, THOMAS H., lawyer; b. Beatrice, Nebr., May 1, 1941; s. William H. Bowersox and Fairy (Casey) Huff; m. Barbara Mathieson, Aug. 23, 1963; children: William T., Christopher T., Elizabeth A. BBA, U. Houston, 1965, JD, 1969. Bar: U.S. Dist. Ct. (so. and ea. dists.) Tex., U.S. Ct. Appeals (5th and 11th cirs.). Instr. South Tex. Jr. Coll., Houston, 1967-72; assoc. prof. Sam Houston State U., Huntsville, 1972-74; assoc. Baker & Botts, Houston, 1975-76; from assoc. gen counsel to pres. subs. co. Zapata Corp., Houston, 1976-93, exec. v.p., 1993-94; ptnr. Bowersox, Herron & Williamson, Houston, 1996-98; of counsel Hope & Causey, Conroe, Tex., 1998—. Adv. com. energy trade policy, U.S. trade rep. industry sector Dept. of Commerce, 1989-93. Bd. dirs. Offhore Energy Ctr., Houston, 1988-92, mem. adv. bd. 1992-98; mem. adv. com. Sam Houston State U. Coll. Bus., 1985-2001. Mem. Internat. Assn. Drilling Contractors (vice chmn. contracts and risk mgmt. com. 1984-85, chmn. govt. affairs com. 1986-87, v.p. Tex. gulf coast 1989, v.p. offshore 1990-91, chmn., bd. dirs., 1992), Am. Bureau of Shipping. Avocations: golf, camping, reading. Office: Hope & Causey PO Box 3188 Conroe TX 77305-3188 Office Fax: 936-441-4674. Personal E-mail: thbowersox@earthlink.net.

BOWES, FREDERICK, III, publishing executive, consultant; b. Norwalk, Conn., Dec. 20, 1941; s. Frederick Jr. and Mary Priscilla (Herron) B.; m. Margaret Anne Hathaway, Sept. 17, 1966; children: Heather Hathaway Ezzy, Catherine Herron. AB, Dartmouth Coll., 1963; MBA, Columbia U., 1965. Fin. staff Perkin-Elmer Corp., Norwalk, Conn., 1965-70; v.p. ops. and fin. South Shore Pub. Co., North Scituate, Mass., 1970-77; cons. Graphics Mgmt., Inc., Duxbury, Mass., 1977-79; pres. Info-Graphics Inc., Braintree, Mass., 1979-80; v.p. pub. New Eng. Jour. Medicine, Mass. Med. Soc., Waltham, Mass., 1981-90; pres. Macmillan New Media, Cambridge, Mass., 1990-94, Cadmus Digital Solutions, 1995-96; pres., CEO Bowes & Assocs., Inc. dba Publist.com, 1996-2000; cons. Electronic Pub. Assocs., 2000—. Dir. Ctr. for Applied Spl. Tech. CAST, Peabody, Mass., 1999—2000. Sr. warden Parish of St. John the Evangelist, Duxbury, 1981-84; trustee, treas. Soc. St. Margaret, Boston, 1984—; trustee Mass. Bible Soc., Boston, 1983-88. Mem. Soc. Scholarly Pub. (pres. 1998). Episcopalian. Avocation: birdwatching.

BOWES, HENRY EDWARD, retired communications executive; b. Merchantville, NJ, Sept. 7, 1915; s. Henry Joseph and Evaline Sarah (Humphreys) Bowes; m. Lauretta Helen Schultz, July 17, 1965; children from previous marriage: Henry, Shirley. Grad., Valley Forge Mil. Acad., 1932; student, U.S. Naval Acad., 1934-35; DBA (hon.), North Cen. Coll. With Philco Corp., 1936-62, gen. mgr. home radio div., 1955-56, v.p., gen. mgr. TV div., 1956-58, v.p. mktg., 1958-61; v.p., dir. mktg. for N.Am., dir. govt. rels. ITT, 1962-64, v.p. indsl. mktg. worldwide, 1964-66, dir. sales and distbn. ITT System, 1966-67, sr. v.p., 1967; pres., CEO McCall Corp., 1967-68; exec. v.p. Bell & Howell Co., 1969, pres., chief oper. officer, 1970-73, also bd. dirs.; ret., 1973. Chmn. exec. com. Docutel Corp.; bd. dirs. Beloit Mfg. Co., No. Telecom Corp., Embosograph Corp., Norton Simon, Inc., Cartier, Pitts. and Lake Erie RR. Served to col. USAAF, World War II. Decorated Legion of Merit; recipient Disting. Alumni award, Valley Forge Mil. Acad. Mem.: Valley Forge Mil. Acad. Alumni Assn., Lost Tree Club (North Palm Beach, Fla.). Republican. Episcopalian.

BOWICK, SUSAN D., retired computer company executive; b. 1948; Bus. analyst Hewlett-Packard Co., Loveland, Colo., 1972-85, pers. mgr. Lake Stevens instrument divsn. Everett, Wash., 1985-89, group pers. mgr. computer sys. orgn., 1989-93, pers. mgr. San Diego, 1993-95, pers. mgr. computer orgn. Palo Alto, Calif., 1995-98, exec. v.p. human resources, 1998—2004; cons. Nokia Corp., 2006—, Siemens A.G., 2006—. Bd. dirs. Comverse Tech., Inc., 2006—.

BOWIE, E(DWARD) J(OHN) WALTER, hematologist, researcher; b. Church Stretton, Shropshire, Eng., Mar. 10, 1925; came to U.S., 1958; s. Edgar Ormond and Ann Brown (Lorrimer) B.; m. Gertrud Susi Ulrich, Dec. 22, 1948; children— Katherine Ann, Christopher John, John Walter, James Ulrich MA, Oxford U., Eng., 1950, BM, BCh, 1952, DM, 1981; MS, U. Minn., 1961. House physician Univ. Coll. Hosp., London, 1953; sr. house officer Bethlem Royal and Maudsley Hosps., London, 1953-54; pvt. practice medicine Treherne, Man., Canada, 1954; fellow in medicine Mayo Clinic, Rochester, Minn., 1958-60, cons. in internal medicine and hematology, 1961-90, head sect. hematology research, 1971-89; prof. medicine and lab. medicine Mayo Med. Sch., Rochester, Minn., 1974-90, prof. emeritus, 1990-96, ret., 1996. Invited spkr. Gordon Confs., 1973, 76, 78, Royal Soc., London, 1980; chmn. thrombosis coun. Internat. Soc. and Fedn. Cardiology, 1991; internat. dir. Thrombosis Vascular Tng. Ctrs. Co-author 6 books; assoc. editor Jour. Lab. and Clin. Medicine, 1976-80; contbr. chpts. to books, numerous articles to profl. jours. Recipient Judson Daland travel award Mayo Found., 1963, named Disting. Investigator, 1988, Disting. Alumnus Mayo Found., 1996. Fellow ACP, AMA, Royal Coll. Pathology; mem. AAAS, Am. Heart Assn. Internat. Soc. on Thrombosis and Haemostasis (v.p. 1980-81, Disting. Career award 1991), Am. Soc. Hematology, Internat. Com. on Thrombosis and Haemostasis (chmn. 1989-90), Ctrl. Soc. for Clin. Rsch., Am. Fedn. for Clin. Rsch., World Fedn. Haemophilia. Office: Emeritus Section Mayo Clinic Rochester MN 55905

BOWIE, LEE, academic administrator, philosopher, educator; BA in Math., Yale U.; PhD, Stanford U. Joined Mount Holyoke Coll., South Hadley, Mass., 1975, prof. philosophy, founding dir. Speaking, Arguing and Writing Program, founding co-dir. Harriet L. and Paul M. Weissman Ctr. for Leadership, v.p. student affairs, dean, 2003—. Mem. adv. com. on multi-cultural and coll. life Mount Holyoke Coll., mem. academic adminstrv. bd., mem. fellowship com., mem. academic policy com. Co-editor: Thirteen Questions in Ethics and Social Philosophy, 1998, Twenty Questions: An Introduction to Philosophy, 2000. Office: Mount Holyoke College Skinner Hall Rm 213A 50 College St South Hadley MA 01075*

BOWIE, NORMAN ERNEST, university official, educator; b. Biddeford, Maine, June 6, 1942; s. Lawrence Walker and Helen Elizabeth (Jacobsen) B.; m. Bonnie Jean Bankert, June 11, 1966 (div. 1980); children: Brian Paul, Peter Mark; m. Maureen Burns, Sept. 19, 1987. AB, Bates Coll., 1964; PhD, U. Rochester, 1968. Mem. faculty Lycoming Coll., Williamsport, Pa., 1968-69; asst. prof. philosophy Hamilton Coll., Clinton, NY, 1969-74, assoc. prof., 1974-75, U. Del., Newark, 1975-80, prof., 1980-89, dir. Ctr. for Study of Values, 1977-89; Elmer L. Andersen chair corp. responsibility U. Minn., Mpls., 1989—, chair dept. strategic mgmt. and orgn., 1992-95; fellow in ethics and professions Harvard U., 1996-97; Dixons prof. bus. ethics and social responsibility London Bus. Sch., 1999-2000. Lynette S. Autrey vis. prof. bus. ethics Rice U., spring 1986; vis. prof. Sch. Mgmt. U. Scranton, 1986-87, Sch. Bus. Adminstrn., Georgetown U., 1988-89; exec. v.p. seminars The Aspen Inst., 1998-99. Author: Towards a New Theory of Distributive Justice, 1971, Business Ethics, 1982, (with Ronald Duska) 2nd edit., 1990, University Business Partnerships: An Assessment, 1994, Business Ethics: A Kantian Perspective, 1999, Management Ethics, 2005; co-author: The Individual and the Political Order, 1977, 4th edit., 2007, (with Patrick E. Murphy, Gene R. Lazniak and Thomas A. Klein) Ethical Marketing, 2005; editor: Ethical Issues in Government, 1981, Ethical Theory in the Last Quarter of the Twentieth Century, 1983, Making Ethical Decisions, 1985, Equal Opportunity, 1988, Guide to Business Ethics, 2001; co-editor: Ethical Theory and Business, 1979, 7th edit., 2003, Ethics, Public Policy and Criminal Justice, 1982, The Tradition of Philosophy, 1986, Ethics and Agency Theory, 1992; co-editor Bus. and Profl. Ethics Jour., 1981-88; assoc. editor Bus. Ethics Quar., 2005—. Mem. N.Y. Coun. for Humanities, 1974-75. NDEA fellow, 1965-68 Mem. Acad. Mgmt., Am. Philos. Assn. (nat. exec. sec. 1972-77), Am. Soc. for Value Inquiry (pres. 1980-81), Soc. Bus. Ethics (pres. 1988), Phi Beta Kappa. Home: PO Box 508 Trappe MD 21673-0508 Office: Carlson Sch Mgmt 321 19th Ave S Minneapolis MN 55455-0438 Office Phone: 612-625-6807. Business E-Mail: nbowie@umn.edu.

BOWIE, PETER WENTWORTH, judge, educator; b. Alexandria, Va., Sept. 27, 1942; s. Beverley Munford and Louise Wentworth (Boynton) B.; m. Sarah Virginia Haught, Mar. 25, 1967; children: Heather, Gavin. BA, Wake Forest Coll., 1964; JD magna cum laude, U. San Diego, 1971. Bar: Calif. 1972, DC 1972, US Dist. Ct. DC 1972, US Dist. Ct. Md. 1973, US Dist. Ct. (so. dist.) Calif. 1974, US Ct. Appeals (DC cir.) 1972, US Ct. Appeals (9th cir.) 1974, US Supreme Ct. 1980. Trial atty. honors program Dept. of Justice, Washington, 1971-74; asst. U.S. Atty. US Atty.'s Office, San Diego, 1974, asst. chief civil divsn., 1974-82, chief asst. US atty., 1982-88; lawyer rep. US Ct. Appeals (9th cir.) Jud. Conf., 1977-78, 84-87; judge US Bankruptcy Ct., San Diego, 1988—2006, chief judge, 2006—. Lectr. law Calif. Western Sch. Law, 1979-83; exec. com. 9th Cir. Judicial Conf., 1991-94; com. on codes of conduct Jud. Conf. of US, 1995-2003; advisor ABA Joint Commn. to Evaluate Model Code of Jud. Conduct, 2003-. Bd. dirs. Presidio Little League, San Diego, 1984, coach, 1983-84; alumni adv. bd. Sch. Law U. San Diego, 1998-2002. Lt. USN, 1964-68, Vietnam. Recipient Disting. Alumni award, U. San Diego Sch. Law, 2003. Mem. State Bar Calif. (hearing referee ct. 1982-86, mem. rev. dept. 1986-90), Fed. Bar Assn. (pres. San diego chpt. 1981-83), San Diego County Bar Assn. (chmn. fed. ct. com. 1978-80, 83-85), Assn. Bus. Trial Lawyers (bd. govs.), San Diego Bankruptcy Forum (bd. dirs.), Rotary Club, Phi Delta Phi. Republican. Mem. Unitarian Ch. Office: US Bankruptcy Court 325 West F St San Diego CA 92101-6017 Office Phone: 619-557-5158.

BOWKER, LEE HARRINGTON, sociologist, educator, writer; b. Bethlehem, Pa., Dec. 19, 1940; s. Maurice H. Bowker and Blanche E. Heffner; m. Nancy Bachant, 1966 (div. 1973); 1 child, Kirsten Ruth; m. Dee C. Thomas, May 25, 1975; children: Jessica Lynn, Gwendolyn Alice. BA, Muhlenberg Coll., 1962; MA, U. Pa., 1965; PhD, Wash. State U., 1972. Instr. in Sociology Lebanon Valley Coll., Annville, Pa., 1965-66, Allbright Coll., Reading, Pa., 1966-67; assoc. prof. Whitman Coll., Walla Walla,

Wash., 1967-77; prof., assoc. dean U. Wis., Milw., 1977-82; dean grad. sch. and research Ind. (Pa.) U. of Pa., 1982-85; provost, v.p. Augustana Coll., Sioux Falls, SD, 1985-87; dean behavioral and social scis. Humboldt State U., Arcata, Calif., 1987-97, emeritus dean, prof. sociology, 1997—2006. Cons. various pubs., colls., univs. and state agys; expert witness. Author: Prison Victimization, 1980, Humanizing Institutions for the Aged, 1982, Masculinities and Violence, 1997, The Role of the Department Chair, revised edit., 1997, Ending the Violence, rev. edit., 1998; assoc. editor Pacific Sociol. Rev., 1975-78, Justice Quar., 1983-85, Criminal Justice Policy Rev., 1984-95; contbr. articles to profl. jours. Pres. Blue Mountain Action Coun., OEO, Walla Walla, 1969-71; dir. social therapy program, Wash. State penitentiary, Walla Walla, 1971-73; bd. dirs. Milw. Bur. Community Corrections, 1979-81, Sioux Falls Symphony, 1985, United Way of Humboldt County, 1988-91. Grantee NIMH 1973, 79, 81, Washington Arts Commn. 1972, Washington Office Community Devel. 1974, Fulbright Found. 1985, Nat. Retired Tchrs. Assn./Am. Assn. Retired Persons Andrus Found. 1980; Law Enforcement Assistance Adminstrn. co-grantee, 1978. Mem.: Am. Soc. Criminology, Am. Sociol. Assn., Pacific Sociol. Assn. Home: 3513 H St Eureka CA 95503-5358 Personal E-mail: dtbandlhb@cox.net.

BOWKER, RAYANNE SONES, elementary school educator; b. Austin, Tex., Jan. 14, 1955; d. James Ray and Gayle Eugenia-Whitmire Sones; m. Roy Frazier Bowker II, Feb. 24, 1983; children: Rachel Filosa, Randall (Randy) Filosa. MusB, Stephen F. Austin U., Nacogdoches, Tex., 1977; MEd in Curriculum and Instrn., Nat. Louis U., Stuttgart, Germany, 1998. Tchr. elem. music South Athens Elem. Sch. and Bel Air Elem. Sch., Tex., 1977—81, Matzke Elem. Sch., Houston, 1981—82, choral dir. 5th grade, 1981—82; tchr. elem. music Mainz Am. Elem. Sch., Germany, 1982—95; dir. elem. chorus, 1982—95; tchr. elem. music Patch Elem. Sch., Stuttgart, 1995—, dir. elem. chorus, 1995—. Tchr. piano pvt. practice, Athens, Tex., 1977—81. Tchr. Sunday sch. music Internat. Bapt. Ch., Stuttgart, 2005—. Mem.: NEA, European Music Educators Assn., Fed. Edn. Assn. (faculty rep. 2006—). Democrat. Baptist. Avocation: music. Home: Hq Useucom Cmr 480 Box 2443 APO AE 09128 Office: Alexander M Patch Elementary School Unit 30401 APO AE 09107 Office Phone: 049-711-680-5200.

BOWLBY, LEYMOND AMBROSE, linguist, translator; b. Oklahoma City, June 5, 1922; s. Leymond Leroy and Victoria Maria (Bradshaw) B.; m. Eunice Jacquelyn Kelley, Apr. 17, 1949 (div. June 1958); children: Linda Ley, Victoria Lynn. BA in Journalism/Edn., Oklahoma City U., 1950; MEd, Okla. U., 1960; PhD in Applied Linguistics, Pacific Western U., LA, 1986. Cert. tchr., Conn.; cert. tchr., media specialist, Okla. Tchr. Mansfield (Conn.) Ctr. Pub. Schs., 1950-51, Oklahoma City Pub. Schs., 1952-57, audio-visual film libr., 1957-61, instrnl. media cons., 1963-74; grad. asst. Okla. U., Norman, 1961-62; owner, operator nursery Trees 'n Things, Tuttle, Okla., 1975-87; ind. lang. translator Tuttle, 1987—. Author: Audio-Visual: A Manual for Teachers, 1965, Cuffings: Aphorisms and Epigrams Written on a Shirt Sleeve, 2003; photo illustrator: Social Studies for Today's Children, 1964; text contbr. various pamphlets, 1961-73; translator: Disorder and Early Sorrow, 1988, historic German essays for Am. poultry archives. Sgt. ETO US Army, 1942—45. Decorated French Liberation medal. Mem. Nat. Coalition Ind. Scholars (assoc.), Am. Lit. Translators Assn., Nat. Assn. Scholars; mem. Okla. State Retired Tchrs. Assn., Soc. for Preservation Poultry Antiquities, Normandy Vets. Assn. of Gt. Britain (life), Phi Delta Kappa (local v.p.). Republican. Roman Catholic. Avocations: genealogy, mycology, horticulture, arboriculture, culinary arts. Home and Office: 7501 W Britton Rd 105 Oklahoma City OK 73132-1603

BOWLER, MARIANNE BIANCA, federal judge; b. Boston, Feb. 15, 1947; d. Richard A. and Ann C. (Daly) B. BA, Regis Coll., 1967; JD cum laude, Suffolk U., 1976, LLD (hon.), 1994; LD (hon.), Regis Coll., 2003. Bar: Mass. 1978. Rsch. asst. Harvard Med. Sch., Boston, 1967-69; med. editor Mass. Dept. of Pub. Health, Boston, 1969-76; law clk. Mass. Superior Ct., Boston, 1976-77, dep. chief law clk., 1977-78; asst. dist. atty. Middlesex Dist. Atty.'s Office, Cambridge, Mass., 1978; asst. U.S. atty. U.S. Dept. of Justice, Boston, 1978-90, exec. asst. U.S. atty., 1988-89, sr. litigation counsel, 1989-90; magistrate judge U.S. Dist. Ct. Mass., Boston, 1990—2002, chief U.S. magistrate judge, 2002—. Chmn. bd. trustees New England Bapt. Hosp., Boston, 1990-95. Trustee Suffolk U., Boston, 1994—. Discovering Justice, 2003—; bd. dirs. The Boston Found., 1995—; dir. South Cove Nursing Facilities Found., Inc., 1995—; co-pres. Boston Coll. Inn of Ct., 1998—2002; bd. dirs. Discovering Justice, 2003-; overseer U.S.S. Constn. Mus., 2005-. Mem. Jr. League Boston, Suffolk Law Sch. Alumni Assn. (pres. 1979-80), Vincent Club, Isabel O'Neil Found., Save Venice. Democrat. Roman Catholic. Avocations: faux finishing, trompe l'oeil painting. Office: 1 Courthouse Way Ste 8420 Boston MA 02210-3010 Office Phone: 617-748-9219. Business E-Mail: honorable_marianne_bowler@mad.uscourts.gov.

BOWLER, NICOLA, engineering educator; b. Hereford, UK, Dec. 6, 1968; d. Ian and Derette Margaret Dance; m. John Reginald Bowler, June 19, 2000; children: Charlotte Derette, Eliza May. BSc, U. Nottingham, UK, 1990; PhD, U. Surrey, Guildford, UK, 1994. Rsch. fellow U. Reading, UK, 1994, U. Surrey, 1995—98; sr. scientist Def. Evaluation Rsch. Agy., UK, 1999; rsch. assoc. Ctr. for Nondestructive Evaluation, Ames, Iowa, 1999—2001, assoc. scientist, 2001—06; assoc. prof. Iowa State U., Ames, 2006—. Panel mem. NSF, Washington, 2000; adj. assoc. prof. Iowa State U., Ames, 2001—06; com. mem. Internat. Workshop Ende, 2004—. Contbr. articles to profl. jours. Vestry mem. Episcopal Ch., Ames, 2004—06. Recipient Outstanding Mentor, US Dept. Energy, 2006. Mem.: IEEE, Materials Rsch. Soc., Inst. Physics. Avocations: running, bicycling, yoga, sewing. Office: Iowa State Univ Dept Materials Sci & Engring 2220 Hoover Hall Ames IA 50011

BOWLES, BARBARA LANDERS, investment company executive; b. Nashville, Sept. 17, 1947; d. Corris Raemone Landers and Rebecca (Bonham) Jennings; m. Earl Stanley Bowles, Nov. 27, 1971; 1 son, Terrence Earl. BA, Fisk U., 1968; MBA, U. Chgo., 1971. Chartered fin. analyst. From bank official to v.p. First Nat. Bank of Chgo., 1968-81; asst. v.p. Beatrice Cos., Chgo., 1981-84; v.p. investor rels. Kraft Inc., Chgo., 1984—89; pres., founder The Kenwood Group Inc., Chgo., 1989—2005; vice chair The Profit Investment Group, 2006—. Bd. dirs. Black & Decker Corp., Hyde Pk. Bank. Bd. dirs. Children's Meml. Hosp., Wis. Energy, and Dollar Gen. Corp. The Chgo. Urban League; coun. mem. Grad. Sch. Bus. U. Chgo. Scholar United Negro College Fund, 1989. Mem. NAACP (life), Assn. Investment Mgmt. and Rsch., Chgo. Fisk trustee (1998-). Mem. United Ch. of Christ. Avocations: tennis, bridge. Office Phone: 312-828-1600. E-mail: kenwoodg@aol.com.

BOWLES, CRANDALL CLOSE, textiles executive; m. Erskine Bowles. B in Econ., Wellesley Coll.; MBA, Columbia U. Fin. analyst Springs Industries, Inc., 1973—78; exec. v.p. Springs Co., 1978—82, pres., 1982; exec. v.p. growth and devel. Springs Industries, Inc., 1992, exec. v.p. textile prodn., 1993, pres. bath fashions group, 1995, pres., COO, 1997—98, CEO, chmn., 1998—2006; chmn. Springs Industries., Inc., 2006—; co-chmn., co-CEO Springs Global US, 2006—. Bd. dir. Deere & Co., JPMorgan Chase. Bd. trustees African Wildlife Found.; bd. mem. Juvenile Diabetes Rsch. Found., Charlotte Inst. for Tech. Innovation, Maya Angelou Rsch. Ctr. on Minority Health. Mem.: Com. of 200, Palmetto Bus. Forum, Bus. Roundtable, Bus. Coun., Am. Textile Mfrs. Inst., Excellence in Edn. Coun. Office: Springs Global PO Box 70 205 N White St Fort Mill SC 29715-1654*

BOWLES, DAVID STANLEY, engineering educator, consultant; b. Romford, Essex, Eng., June 30, 1949; m. Valerie Rosina Curd; children: Penny, Simon, Amy. BSc, City U., Eng., 1972; PhD, Utah State U., 1977. Registered profl. engr., Utah; cert. profl. hydrologist. Jr. civil engr. George Wimpey & Co., Hammersmith, London, 1967-72; rsch. asst. prof. Utah State U., Logan, 1976-80, rsch. assoc. prof., 1980-81, adj. rsch. assoc. prof., 1981-83, rsch. prof., 1983-85, prof., 1985—, assoc. dir., 1986-91, dir., 1992-96, Inst. for Dam Safety Risk Mgmt., 2000—. Vis. scientist Internat. Inst. Applied Systems Analysis, Laxenburg, Austria, 1979; br. mgr., engr. Law Engring., Denver, 1981-83; prin. Risk Assessment Cons. Engrs. and Economists (RAC), 1986—; mem. Australian Com. on Large Dams. Contbr. numerous articles to profl. jours. Bd. dirs. U.S. Soc. on Dams. Fellow ASCE, Am. Water Resources Assn.; mem. Soc. Risk Analysis, Am. Geophys. Union, Am. Inst. Hydrology, Assn. State Dam Safety Ofcls. Home: 1520 Canyon Rd Providence UT 84332-9431 Office: Utah Water Rsch Lab Utah State Univ Logan UT 84322-8200 Home Phone: 435-753-6004; Office Phone: 435-753-6004. E-mail: bowles@cache.net.

BOWLES, ERSKINE B., academic administrator, former White House chief of staff; b. Greensboro, NC, Aug. 8, 1945; s. Hargrove "Skipper" Bowles; m. Crandall Bowles; 3 children. BS in Bus. Adminstrn., U. N.C., 1967; MBA, Columbia U., 1969. With Morgan Stanley & Co., NYC, Bowles Hollowell Conner & Co., Charlotte, NC, 1975-93; adminstr. Small Bus. Adminstrn., Washington, 1993-94; asst. to the Pres. & dep. chief of staff The White House, Washington, 1994—95, chief of staff to Pres., 1996—98; ptnr. Forstmann Little & Co., NYC, 1999—2001; mng. dir., co-founder Carousel Capital Co., LLC, 1999—2001, sr. adv., 2002—; chmn. Erskine Bowles & Co. LLC, 2003—; dep. spl. envoy for Tsunami Recovery UN, 2005; pres. U. N.C., Chapel Hill, 2006—. Bd. dirs. Merck & Co., 1999—2001, VF Corp., 1999—2001, First Union Corp., 1999—2001, Wachovia Corp., 2001, Krispy Kreme Doughnut Corp., 2003, Cousins Properties, 2003—, Gen. Motors Corp., 2005—, Morgan Stanley, 2005—. Pres. Juvenile Diabetes Found.; Dem. Senate nominee, NC, 2002, 04. Office: U NC 910 Raleigh Rd PO Box 2688 Chapel Hill NC 27515-2688*

BOWLES, NEWTON ROWELL, United Nations executive; b. Chengdu, Szechuan, China, Dec. 4, 1916; Canadian citizen. s. Newton Ernest and Muriel Olive (Wood) B.; m. Augusta Davis, Mar. 29, 1946 (div. July 1969); m. Jean Presley Vaudrin, Dec. 4, 1970 (dec. July 1996). BA, U. Toronto, Ont., Can., 1939, MA, 1940; postgrad., Johns Hopkins U., 1941-42. Chief China desk United Nations Relief Rehab. Adminstrn., Washington, 1945-46, dept. dir. programs China Mission Shanghai, 1946-48; chief China desk UNICEF, NYC, 1948-50, chief Asia sect., 1951-60, dir. program divsn., 1961-76, chief program policy, 1977-85, sr. policy cons., 1986—. Mem. UN Task Force for Child Survival Force, Atlanta, 1986-98, UN rep. Can. UN Assn., Can. Group of 78, Can. Pugwash Group; rep. Sci. for Peace, Internat. Peace Bur. Economists Against Arms Race, NGO Disarmament Com.; mem. Carnegie Coun. Ethics and Internat. Affairs. Author: The Diplomacy of Hope, 2001, rev. edit., 2004. Decorated Order of Can. Mem. Soc. for Internat. Devel., Arms Control Assn., Soc. for Internat. Devel. Office: UNICEF 3 United Nations Plz New York NY 10017-4486

BOWLING, CHARLES BRYAN, legal association administrator; b. Nurnberg, Germany, Dec. 23, 1951; s. Charles Edward and Sieglinde Bowling; 1 child, Erik Bryan. BS, U. Houston, 1995, MA, 1998; PhD canidate in bus. adminstn., N. Ctrl. U., 2005—. Mgmt. trainer Midcap Corp., San Antonio; tch. adv. Motion Industries, Houston; policy procedures officer Ky. Dept. of Corrections, Frankfort, Ky. Coord. Citizens Corps., Bell County, Ky., 2004; Col. USA Vet. Homeland Security Svcs., Johnson City, Tenn., 2004. Named Ky. Col., 2000. Avocations: running, reading, music. Office: Ky Dept of Corrections Frankfort KY 40601

BOWLING, DANIEL S., III, lawyer; b. Atlanta, Oct. 19, 1955; s. Daniel Seymour and Martha (Alexander) B.; m. Elizabeth Grede, July 12, 1983; children: Daniel IV, Edward Alexander, Elizabeth. BA, Millsaps Coll., Jackson, Miss., 1977; JD, Duke U., 1980. Bar: Ga. 1980, U.S. Ct. Appeals (11th cir.) 1981, (5th cir.) 1981, (6th cir.) 1981, U.S. Dist. Ct. (no. dist., so. dist., mid. dist.) Ga. 1981, U.S. Dist. Ct. (ea. dist.) Mich. Assoc. Smith, Currie & Hancock, Atlnata, 1980-85, ptnr., 1985; various positions including labor and employment counsel, group v.p., and gen. mgr. Coca-Cola Enterprises Inc., Atlanta, 1986—2001, sr. v.p. human resources, 2001—. Mem. selection com. Fla. State Bar Pro-Bono award; former pres. Atlanta Coun. Younger Lawyers; sr. lecturing fellow Duke Law Sch. Bd. trustees Millsaps Coll.; Johnston Legacy Scholarship Found. Mem. ABA, State Bar Ga., Atlanta Bar Assn., Am. Corp. Counsel Assn., Lawyers Club Atlanta, Ansley Golf. Republican. Office: Coca-Cola Enterprises-West One Coca-Cola Pla Atlanta GA 30313

BOWLING, JOHN C., academic administrator; Pres. Olivet Nazarene U., 1991—.

BOWLING, LANCE CHRISTOPHER, recording industry executive; b. San Pedro, Calif., May 17, 1948; s. Dan Parker and Sylvia Lois (Van Devander) B. BA in Polit. Sci. and History, Pepperdine U., 1966-70, MPA, 1973. Owner, founder Cambria Master Recordings, Palos Verdes, Calif., 1972—. Editor: Joseph Wagner: A Retrospective of Composer-Conductor 1900-74, 1976, Hazards Pavilion, Jour of Soc for Preservation of South Calif. Mus. Heritage, 1985—; author: Eugene Hemmer: Composer-Pianist, 1983; prodr. over 150 classical records including works by Charles W. Cadman, Madeleine Dring, Mary Carr Moore, John Crown, Ed Bland, Florence Price, Elinor Remick Warren, Miklos Rozsa, Erich W. Korngold, Max Steiner, Ernst Gold, William Grant Still, Arthur Lange, Carlos Chavez, George Gershwin, also classical music radio station documentaries, programs for Taz Libr. Congress; contbr. Opera News, 2003, The Cue Sheet. Active allocation com. Region V, United Way, L.A., 1978-85; bd. dirs. Elinor Remick Warren Found., Film Music Soc., Hollywood, Calif., So. Calif. Music History Resource, L.A. Ballet; bd. dirs., pres. New World Ctr. for Arts, L.A. Recipient Golden Rose award Pi Iota chpt. Phi Beta, 1988. Mem. ASCAP, Nat. Acad. Recording Arts and Scis. (classical com., Hall of Fame com.), Assn. Recorded Sound Collections, Music Libr. Assn., Soc. for Preservation of Film Music, Sonneck Soc., Variety Arts Club (L.A.), Mus. Arts Club (Long Beach, Calif.), Zamorano Club (L.A.). Episcopalian. Avocations: collecting early Calif. books and ephemera, restoration of 78 RPM recordings and antique automobiles. Home: 2625 Colt Rd Palos Verdes Peninsula CA 90275-6578 Office: Cambria Master Recordings 1659 W 7th St San Pedro CA 90732-3421 Office Phone: 310-831-1322. E-mail: cambriamus@aol.com.

BOWLSBY, BOB, athletic director; b. Jan. 10, 1952; m. Candice Bowlsby; children: Lisa, Matt, Rachel, Kyle. BS, Moorhead State U., 1975; MS, U. Iowa, 1978. Asst. athletic dir. No. Iowa U., athletic dir., 1984-91, U. Iowa, Iowa City, 1991—2007, Stanford U., Calif., 2007—. Chair NCAA Divsn. I Mgmt. Coun., 1997-99; mem. NCAA Divsn. I Basketball com., 2000-03, chair, 2004-05. Chmn. Big Ten Championships and awards com., 2002-03; chair NCAA Olympic Sports Liaison Com., NCAA/USOC liaison com., Olympics com. mem; bd. dirs. Iowa Games. Mem. Nat. Assn. Collegiate Dir. of Athletics (exec. com.). Office: Stanford U Stanford CA 94305-6150 Office Phone: 319-335-9435. E-mail: robert-bowlsby@uiowa.edu.

BOWMAN, BRUCE, art educator; b. Dayton, Ohio, Nov. 23, 1938; s. Murray Edgar Bowman and Mildred May (Moler) Elleman; m. Julie Ann Gosselin, 1970 (div. 1980); 1 child, Carrie Lynn. AA, San Diego City Coll., 1962; BA, Calif. State U., LA, 1964, MA, 1968. Tchr. art L.A. City Schs., 1966—, North Hollywood Adult Sch., Calif., 1966—68; instr. art Cypress Coll., 1976—78, West L.A. Coll., 1969—. Seminar leader, 1986—. Author: Shaped Canvas, 1976, Toothpick Sculpture and Ice Cream Stick Art, 1976, Ideas: How to Get Them, 1985, (recording) Develop Winning Willpower, 1986, Waikiki, 1988; one-man shows include Calif. State U., L.A., 1968, Pepperdine U., Malibu, 1978, exhibited in group shows at McKenzie Gallery, L.A., 1968, Trebor Gallery, 1970, Cypress Coll., 1977, Design Recycled Gallery, Fullerton, 1977, Pierce Coll., Woodland Hills, 1978, Leopold/Gold Gallery, Santa Monica, 1980. With USN, 1957—61. Avocation: karate (black belt Tang Soo Do). Home: 2180 Sherborne St Camarillo CA 93010

BOWMAN, BRUCE ALAN, civil engineer; b. Garmisch-Partenkirchen, Bavaria, Germany, Mar. 12, 1959; s. Walter Earl and Ingeborg Marie Bowman; m. Leslie Suzanne Thompson, Sept. 19, 1981; children: Gregory, Douglas. BS Chemistry, Ind. U., 1981; MS Ops. Rsch., USAF Inst. Tech., 1988; PhD Civil Engring., Columbia U., 1995. Analyst Office of the Dep. Chief of Staff for Pers., Hdqs., US Army, Washington, 1990—92; asst. prof. US Mil. Acad., West Point, NY, 1996—99; sect. chief and divsn. chief, joint warfighting analysis divsn. (j8) Office of the Chmn. of the Joint Chiefs of Staff, Washington, 1999—2001; prin. cons. PricewaterhouseCoopers Mgmt. Consulting LLP, Fairfax, Va., 2001—01; sr. profl. staff Johns Hopkins U. Applied Physics Lab., Laurel, Md., 2001—03; sr. scientist Anser, Inc., Arlington, Va., 2003—04; sr. cons. IBM Bus. Cons. Svcs., Fairfax, 2004; dir. sys. engring. SAIC, McLean, Va., 2005; prin. Hilltop Cons. Ptnrs., Oak Hill, Va., 2005—. Co-chmn. sys. dynamics in nat. security conf. Nat. Def. U., Washington, 2000; mem. adv. bd. MobilePro Corp.; profl. lectr. George Washington U., Washington, 2004—05, adj. prof., 2005—07; dean Sch. Engring. Norwich U., Vt., 2007—. Contbr. book Pipeline Risk Management Manual, 1996. Coo and founding exec. dir. The ACE Mentor Program of the Greater Wash. DC Met. Area, Inc., 2000—04; elder Presbyn. Ch. U.S.A., 1991; youth soccer coach Springfield, Va., 1989—91, Rockland County, NY, 1992—95. Lt. col. US Army, 1981—2001. Mem.: ASCE, Mil. Ops. Rsch. Soc. (chmn. weapons of mass destruction nat. symposium 2001—01). Avocations: reading, chess, soccer, jogging. Office Phone: 802-485-2267. Business E-Mail: babowman@norwich.edu.

BOWMAN, C. MICHAEL, physician; married; two children. BS in Chemistry with honors, U. Ill., 1968; PhD in Genetics, U. Wis., 1972, MD, 1975. Diplomate Am. Bd. Pediatrics, Am. Bd. Pediatric Pulmonology. Pediat. resident Vanderbilt U., 1975-78, chief resident, 1978-79; dir. comprehensive cystic fibrosis ctr. Med. U. S.C.; divsn. head Divsn. Pediat. Pulmonolgy, Allergy & Immunology; prof. pediats. Med. U. S.C., Charleston, 2000—. Fellow Am. Acad. of Pediat., mem. Am. Bd. of Pediat., Am. Thoracic Soc. Achievements include research in lung disorders in children. Office: Med U S C Ste 281 PO Box 250561 135 Rutledge Ave Charleston SC 29425 Office Phone: 843-876-1555. Office Fax: 843-876-1583. Business E-Mail: bowmanm@musc.edu.

BOWMAN, CATHERINE MCKENZIE, lawyer; b. Tampa, Fla., Nov. 10, 1962; d. Herbert Alonza and Joan Bates (Baggs) McKenzie; m. Donald Campbell Bowman, Jr., May 21, 1988; children: Hunter Hall, Sarah McKenzie. BA in Psychology and Sociology, Vanderbilt U., 1984; JD, U. Ga., 1987. Bar: Ga. 1987, U.S. Dist. Ct. (so. dist.) Ga. 1987. Assoc. Ranitz, Mahoney, Forbes & Coolidge, P.C., Savannah, Ga., 1987-91; ptnr. Forbes and Bowman, 1991—2007; mem. The Bowman Law Office, L.L.C., 2007—. Bd. dirs. Greenbriar Children's Ctr., 1994-98, exec. com. 1995, pres. 1996-98; mem. distbn. com. Savannah Found., 1994-2002; ball com. Telfair Arts Acad., 2002, Historic Savannah Found., 2002; chmn. Savannah Country Day Sch. Fair, 2004, Savannah Country Day Sch. Party, 2004; sec. Savannah Country Day Sch. Parents Assn., 2005-06, Creative Minds Com., 2005-. Mem. Am. Employment Law Coun., Internat. Assn. Def. Counsel, Ga. Def. Lawyers Assn. (chmn. employment com. 2006-07), Savannah Young Lawyers Assn. (pres. 1996-97), 2000 Club (membership chair 1990-91, pres. 1992), South Atlantic Found. (bd. dirs. 1992). Office: 7505 Waters Ave Ste D3 Savannah GA 31406 Office Phone: 912-401-0121. Business E-Mail: catherine@thebowmanlawoffice.com.

BOWMAN, DANIEL OLIVER, retired psychologist; b. Holly Hill, SC, Feb. 1, 1931; s. John Daniel and Pansy (Mizzell) Bowman. BA in Music, Furman U., 1951; MEd, U. S.C., 1952; PhD, U. Ga., 1963. Lic. psychologist, S.C. Tchr., English, French Summerville (S.C.) H.S., 1952-53; chmn. English dept., sr. guidance counselor Boys H.S., Anderson, S.C., 1955-61; instr. psychology U. Ga., Athens, 1961-63; asst. prof. psychology The Citadel, Charleston, S.C., 1963-66, assoc. prof. psychology, counselor to corps cadets, 1966-69, prof. psychology, dir. grad. studies, 1969-77, prof., head dept. psychology, 1977-91, Arland D. Williams prof. psychology, 1991-96, prof. emeritus, 1996—. Cons. Charleston County Sheriff's Dept., 1985-94, Berkeley County Sch. System, Moncks Corner, S.C., 1977-89. Chmn. Charleston County Mental Retardation Bd., 1988-90. Mem. APA, AAUP, NASP, Am. Psychol. Soc. (charter), Southea. Psychol. Assn., S.C. Psychol. Assn. (pres. 1990-91, Outstanding Contbrs. Psychology 1988), Phi Kappa Phi (pres. 1979-80), Phi Delta Kappa. Home: 6 Fort Royal Ave Charleston SC 29407-6012 E-mail: bowmano@aol.com.

BOWMAN, DAVID FREDERICK, music educator; b. Wausau, Wis., Apr. 17, 1969; s. Stuart Warren and Gloria Jean Bowman; m. Stephanie Jean Stern, Apr. 25, 1992; children: Kylie Jenae, Mara Alexandra. MusB, U. Wis., 1991, M in Sch. Bus., 2002. Music tchr. Marshall Mid. Sch., Janesville, Wis., 1992—93, Parker HS, Janesville, 1993—2002, Lincoln HS, Manitowoc, Wis., 2002—. Instrl. mgr. Janesville Parker HS, 2001—02; dept. chair Manitowoc Music Dept., 2005—. Mem. performance com. Comprehensive Musicianship, 2006—. Recipient Tchr. of Yr., Janesville Parker Sch., Will Schmid award, Wis. Sch. Music, 2004, Carol and Robert Bush Choral Dir. award, 2004, 2007; scholarship, MidAm. Pipeline, 1996. Mem.: Manitowoc Edn. Assn., Am. Choral Dirs. Assn. (singspiel chair 2004).

BOWMAN, DONALD EUGENE, investment advisor; b. Dayton, Ohio, July 9, 1930; s. John Peter and Delia Francis (Sink) B.; m. Mary Louise, Jan. 20, 1984; children: Clark Woodford, Marylouise Chalfant. BA, U. Wis., 1952; MBA, Loyola Coll., Balt., 1982; Exec. Advanced Mgmt. degree, Harvard U., 1974; postgrad., Stanford U., 1976. Chartered investment counselor. CEO, pres. T. Rowe Price Assn., Balt., 1956-79; founder, CEO, pres. Bowman Fin. Mgmt. Co., Balt., 1978—. Chmn. audit com., vice chmn. investment com., mem. budget and fin. com. U. Balt. Found., 1978—, mem. fin. and strategic planning com., 2006—; bd. dirs. Roland Park Girls Sch., 1969-75, U. Wis. Found., Madison, 1978-95, U. Balt. Found., 1978—, 4-H Found., Washington, 1988—, Wis. Alumni Assn., 1995-2000; chmn., bd. dirs. Towson U. Found., Balt., 1989-95; exec. MBA bd. dirs. Loyola Coll., Balt., 1985—; trustee Balt. Opera Co., 1996-2003; chmn. bd. St. Pauls Sch. for Girls, 1992-95; mem. adv. coun. ERISA, 1972-75; bd. govs. Investment Coun. Assn. Am., Washington, 1968-78; mem. No Load Mut. Fund Bd., 1970-78; trustee Alliance for Chesapeake Bay, 2002—; hon. chmn. Md. Nat. Rep. Bus. Adv. Coun., Presdl. Bus. Adv. Coun.; pres. planned giving com. Towson U.; Capt. USNR, 1952-90. Recipient Businessman of Yr. award, Nat. Rep. Congl. Com., 2003, 2005, Republican Leadership US Ho. of Reps., Md., 2005, Congl. Order of Merit, Exec. Coun. Nat. Republican Congl. Com., 2006. Mem.: Navy Mutual Aid Assn. (fin. com., audit com., employee 401K plan com., bd. dirs.). Republican. Avocations: tennis, exercise, golf. Office: Bowman Fin Mgmt Co Inc 1330 Smith Ave F Baltimore MD 21209-3703 Office Phone: 410-433-1900. Personal E-mail: bowmanmgt@verizon.net.

BOWMAN, DOROTHY LOUISE, artist; b. Hollywood, Calif., Jan. 20, 1927; d. Bruce L. and Dorothy L. (Kalkman) B; m. Howard Hugh Bradford, Dec. 30, 1949 (div. 1965); children: Brock, Cyndra, Tal Scott, Heather, Delia, Callia. Student, Chouinard Art Inst., Calif., 1945-48, Jepson Art Inst., LA, 1948-49; BA, Webster U., 1979. One-woman show Ventana Gallery, Big Sur, 1998; serigrapher, printmaker, painter: represented in permanent collections: Immaculate Heart Coll., L.A. County Mus., Bklyn. Mus., Long Beach Mus., Crocker Art Gallery, Mus. Modern Art, Phila., Mus. Fine Arts, San Jose State Coll., De Cordova and Danna Mus., Boston Pub. Libr., Boston Mus. Fine Arts, N.Y. Pub. Libr., Rochester Meml. Gallery, U. Wis., U. Hawaii, U. Ill., U. Kans., Santa Barbara Mus., Achenbach Found. Legion of Honor, Mus. Modern Art, Monterey, Calif., Libr. Congress, Calif. State Libr. Archives, Arquivos Historicos De Arte Contemporanea Museu De Arte Moderna, San Paulo, Brazil, Ch. of Latter Day Saints History Mus., Salt Lake City, 1987, Nat. Mus. of Women in the Arts, Washington, 2000—; twice juried internat. show 27 countries, 1987; creator animation films The Mobius World, 2000, Really O'Reiley, 2002, Never Seen Fox, 2003, Cry Baby Lion!; Traveling show Smithsonian Inst., Nat. Collection of Fine Arts, 1952; movie prodr. hist. film, Big Sur, 2002. Address: Nat Mus of Women in the Arts Archives 1250 New York Ave NW Washington DC 20005-3970 Office Phone: 831-375-5170. E-mail: dorothybowman@redshift.com.

BOWMAN, DOROTHY MARIE, retired librarian; b. North Tazewell, Va., May 20, 1937; d. Roy and Thelma Vivian Ann (Shrader) Brewster; m. John LeRoy Bowman, Dec. 28, 1957; children: Annette Toner, Kathleen Rader, Alice Newell. BS in Edn., Radford Coll., Va., 1958; MLS, Cath. U. Am., 1989. Tchr., librarian Virginia Beach (Va.) Pub. Schs., 1958-59; tchr. Norfolk (Va.) City Schs., 1959-60; librarian Albemarle Pulp & Paper Mfg. Co., Richmond, Va., 1961-64; tchr. Henrico (Va.) Pub. Schs., 1966-67, asst. librarian, 1967-70; librarian Chickahominy Acad., Henrico County, 1972-73, Nasemond-Suffolk Acad., Va., 1975—2000; ret., 2000. Residential campaign chmn. Am. Cancer Soc., Richmond, 1972—73; co-chair evaluation steering com. Nasemond-Suffolk Acad., 1984—85, chair tech. task force, 1992, mem. assessment policy com., 1991, cons. self-study com., 1992—; pres. Highland Springs (Va.) United Meth. Women, 1973—74; co-chair Main St. United Meth. Ch. Coun. on Ministries, Suffolk, 1983—85; mission coord. edn. and interpretation Portsmouth Dist. United Meth. Women, 2006. Mem.: AAUW (br. treas. 1983—87), Kings Fork Women's Club (pres. 2004—), Highland Springs Jr. Women's Club (pres. 1970—71), Sans Souci Lit. Club (pres. Suffolk chpt. 1985—87), Delta Kappa Gamma (chpt. pres. 1986—88). Republican. Avocations: needlecrafts, cooking, reading. Home: 100 Ayers Creek Ln Suffolk VA 23434-7508 Personal E-mail: mbowman@whro.net.

BOWMAN, EUGENE WILLIAM, retired mathematics professor; b. North Powder, Oreg., Mar. 28, 1910; s. Albert Franklin and Helen (Groves) Bowman; m. Ida Jones (dec. 1995); children: Eugene William, Virginia. BS, U. Idaho, Moscow, 1935, MS, 1936. HS prin. cert. Wash., supt. credential Wash. Tchr. pub. schs., Forest Grove, Oreg., 1931—34; instr. Coeur d'Alene Jr. Coll., Idaho, 1936—38; supt. Rockford Pub. Schs., Wash., 1941—46; prof. math. So. Oreg. Coll., Ashland, 1949—75; ret., 1975. Contbr. articles to profl. jours. Fgn. svc. officer US Govt., Quito, Ecuador, 1960—62. Lt. comdr. USN, 1946—49. Mem.: Rotary, Masons, Phi Delta Kappa. Avocations: hunting, boating, fishing. Home: 641 Torringyon Dr Sunnyvale CA 94087

BOWMAN, FRANK LEE (SKIP BOWMAN), retired military officer; b. Chattanooga, Dec. 19, 1944; m. Linda Anne Rich, June 10, 1966; children: Greg, Christy. BS, Duke U., 1966; MS in Nuclear Engring., Naval Arch., MIT, 1973; LHD (hon.), Duke U. Commd ensign USN, 1966, advanced through grades to admiral, 1996; naval officer at sea on USS Simon Bolivar, USS Pogy, USS Daniel Boone, 1966-77; exec. officer USS Bremerton USS Bremerton, 1978-80; comdr. USS City of Corpus Christi USN, 1983-86, comdr. USS Holland, 1988-90, dep. dir. ops. joint staff Washington, 1991-92, dir. polit.-mil. affairs joint staff, 1992-94, dep. chief naval ops., chief naval pers., 1994-96, dir. naval nuclear propulsion, 1996—2004; pres., CEO Nuclear Energy Inst., Washington, 2005—. Decorated Disting. Svc. medal, Defense Disting. Svc. medal, Legion of Merit with 3 gold stars, Meritorious Svc. medal with 2 gold stars, Battle E Efficiency award, four times, Navy Expeditionary medal twice, Humanitarian Svc. medal twice. Office: Nuclear Energy Inst 1776 I St NW Ste 400 Washington DC 20006

BOWMAN, FRANK O., law educator; b. 1955; BA, Colo. Coll., 1976; JD, Harvard U., 1979. Bar: Colo. 1979. Trial atty. criminal divsn. U.S. Dept. Justice, Washington, 1979—82; spl counsel Yates & Crane, P.C., Durango, Colo., 1982—83; dep. dist. atty. Denver, 1983—86; pvt. practice Colo., 1986—87; assoc. Anderson, Campbell & Laugesen, P.C., Denver, 1987—89; dep. chief so. criminal divsn. Fla., 1989—95; spl. counsel U.S. Sentencing Commn., Washington, 1995—96; assoc. prof. law Ind. U., 1999—2002, M. Dale Palmer prof. law, 2002—. Vis. prof. Washington & Lee, 1994—95, Gonzaga, 1996—99; acad. advisor criminal law com. U.S. Jud. Conf., 1998—2001. Co-author: Federal Sentencing Guidelines Handbook; contbr. articles to profl. jours.; mem. editl. bd.: Federal Sentencing Reporter, Criminal Justice Review. Office: Ind Univ Sch Law Lawrence W Inlow Hall Rm 316 530 W NY St Indianapolis IN 46202-3225 Office Phone: 317-274-2862. Office Fax: 317-278-3326. E-mail: frbowman@iupui.edu.

BOWMAN, GEORGE ARTHUR, JR., retired judge; b. Milw., Dec. 1, 1917; s. George Arthur and Edna Oral (Hunter) B.; m. Rose Mary Thorpe, Aug. 8, 1947 (dec. 1980); children: George A. III, Daniel Andrew. Student, U. Wis., 1936-39; JD, Marquette U., 1943. Bar: Wis. 1943, U.S. Supreme Ct. 1943. Asst. dist. atty. Milw. County, 1947-48, children's ct. judge, 1967-72; asst. city atty. City of Milw., 1948-67; adminstrv. law judge Office of Hearing and Appeals Social Security Adminstrn. Dept. HHS, Chgo., 1973-97, adminstrv. law judge emeritus, 1997; pvt. practice, 1997—. Appointed Pres.'s Task Force, Law Enforcement Assistance Adminstrn., 1972; former counsel Milw. Police Dept.; advisor Nat. Council of Juvenile Ct. Judges, Nat. Conv., Atlanta; chmn. conv. com. Nat. Council of Juvenile Ct. Judges, Milw., 1972; chmn. State Task Force on Juvenile Delinquency, 1970-71; legis. com. Wis. Bd. Juvenile Ct. Judges, 1970-71; former mem. numerous legis. coms., Milw.; pioneered Legal Defender System in Children's Ct.; lecturer, Marquette U. Co-author: LEAA Uniform Standards for Police Departments, 1973 (Pres.'s citation). Bd. dirs. Am. Indian Info. and Action Group, Inc. "Project Phoenix", Juneau Acad.; chmn. Milw. County Rep. Party, 1961-62; active supporter numerous community juvenile programs, including Milw. Boys' Club, St. Joseph's Home for Children, Mt. Mary Coll. Proglram for Truant and Delinquent Girls, Operation Outreach, others; Social Security judge. With USN, 1943-46. Recipient Continious Svc. award Office of Hearings and Appeals Soc. Security Adminstr., 1991. Mem. Fed. Assn. Adminstrv. Law Judges, Assn. Office of Hearing and Appeals Adminstrv. Law Judges, Wis. State Bar Assn., Milw. Bar. Assn., Nat. Council Juvenile Ct. Judges, Am. Judicature Soc., Nat. Council of Sr. Citizens, Inc., Internat. Juvenile Officers Assn., Am. Legion (former post comdr.), Nat. Probate Judges Assn., New Trier Rep. Orgn., Committeeman's Club, Hawthorne Turf Club, Sigma Alpha Epsilon. Roman Catholic. Home: 2824 Orchard Ln Wilmette IL 60091-2144

BOWMAN, HAZEL LOIS, retired English language educator; b. Plant City, Fla., Feb. 18, 1917; d. Joseph Monroe and Annie (Thoman) B. AB, Fla. State Coll. for Women, 1937; MA, U. Fla., 1948; postgrad., U. Md., 1961-65. Tchr. Lakeview HS, Winter Garden, Fla., 1939-40, Eagle Lake Sch., Fla., 1940-41; welfare visitor Fla. Welfare Bd., 1941-42; specialist U.S. Army Signal Corps, Arlington Hall, Va., 1942-43; recreation work, asst. procurement officer ARC, CBI Theater, 1943-46; lab. technician Am. Cyanamid Corp., Brewster, Fla., 1946-47; instr., asst. prof. gen. extension divsn. U. Fla., Fla. State U., 1948-51; freelance writer, editor, indexer NY, 1951-55, Fla., 1951—55; staff writer Tampa Morning Tribune, Fla., 1956; staff writer, telegraph editor Winter Haven News-Chief, Fla., 1956-57; registrar, admissions officer U. Tampa, 1957-59; coll. counselor Atlantic States, 1959-60; registrar, freshman advisor Towson State Tchrs. Coll., Balt., 1960-62; dir. student pers., guidance, admissions Harford Jr. Coll., Bel Air, Md., 1962-64; instr., asst. prof. English, journalism York Coll., Pa., 1965-69; tchr. S.W. Jr. HS, Lakeland, Fla., 1969-70; tchr. learning disabled Vanguard Sch., Lake Wales, Fla., 1970-82; libr. asst. Polk County Hist. and Geneal. Libr., Bartow, Fla., 1986-91. Editor Fla. Flambeau, 1936-37, Tampa Altrusan, 1958-60, Polk County Hist. Calendar, 1986-90. Mem. Polk County Hist. Commn., 1992-99. Recipient Mayhall Music medal, 1933, Excellence in Cmty. Svc. award Nat. Soc. DAR, 1994, Outstanding Achievement award Fla. State Geneal. Soc., 2002. Mem.: AAUW (hon. 50 yr. life), Polk County Hist. Assn., Imperial Polk Geneal. Soc., Nat. Geneal. Soc., Mortar Board, Chi Delta Phi, Alpha Chi Alpha. Home: 1001 Fifth St NE Mulberry FL 33860-2608

BOWMAN, JAMES EDWARD, pathologist, educator; b. Washington, Feb. 5, 1923; s. James Edward and Dorothy (Peterson) B.; m. Barbara Taylor, June 17, 1950; 1 child, Valerie June. BS, Howard U., 1943, MD, 1946. Intern Freedmen's Hosp., Washington, 1946-47; resident pathology St. Lukes Hosp., Chgo., 1947-50; chmn. dept. pathology Provident Hosp., 1950-53, Shiraz (Iran) Med. Ctr. Nemazee Hosp., 1955-61; vis. prof., chmn. dept. pathology faculty of medicine U. Shiraz, 1959-61; dir. labs. U. Chgo., 1971-80, prof. dept. pathology, medicine, com. on genetics , biol. scis., collegiate div., 1972-93, dir., 1973-93, prof. emeritus, 1993—. Cons. pathology, div. hosp. and med. facilities HEW, USPHS, 1968; mem. Health and Hosps. Governing Commn., Cook County, 1969-72; mem. exec. com. hemalytic anemia study group NHLI, NIH, Bethesda, Md., 1973-75, Sabbatical fellow Ctr. for Advanced Study in Behavioral Scis., Stanford U., 1981-82, Ethical, Legal & Social Issues, Nat. Human Genome Program NIH/DOE. Contbr. to books and articles to profl. jours. Capt. M.C., AUS, 1953-55. Spl. rsch. fellow NIH Galton Lab., Univ. Coll., London, 1961-62. Mem. Coll. Am. Pathologists, Am. Soc. Clin. Pathologists, Am. Soc. Human Genetics, Cen. Soc. Clin. Rsch., Am. Soc. Hematology, Am. Assn. Phys. Anthropologists, Acad. Clin. Lab. Physicians and Scientists. Home: 4929 S Greenwood Ave Chicago IL 60615-2815 Office: U Chgo Dept Pathology 5841 S Maryland Ave Chicago IL 60637-1463 E-mail: jbowman@uchicago.edu.

BOWMAN, JAMES KINSEY, publishing executive, rare book dealer; b. Strongsville, Ohio, Nov. 1, 1933; s. Benjamin H. and Margaret A. (Kinsey) B.; m. Judith Ann Lofton, Mar. 29, 1957; children: J. Reed, Eustacia L., Todd K. BA, Denison U., Granville, Ohio, 1956. With McGraw-Hill Book Co., NYC, 1956-90, gen. mgr., v.p. coll. div., 1965-68, group v.p. higher edn., 1968-73, v.p. marketing, 1973-82, sr. v.p. adminstrn., 1982-84, sr. v.p. internat., 1984-87, v.p. gen. mgr. bookstores, 1987-90; chief exec. officer Judith Bowman Books, 1990—. Bd. dirs. Catskill Fly Fishing Ctr. and Mus., 1998-2004. Mem. Am. Assn. Pubs. (pres. coll. div. 1971-72), Slagle Trout Club (Mich.), Bedford Chowder and Marching Club (pres. 1976-77), Atlantic Salmon Fedn., Theodore Gordon Flyfishers Club (N.Y.C.), Anglers Club of N.Y., Phi Gamma Delta. Democrat. Presbyterian. Home and Office: 98 Pound Ridge Rd Bedford NY 10506-1241 Office Phone: 914-234-7543. E-mail: jubobo@aol.com.

BOWMAN, JEAN LOUISE, lawyer, civic worker; b. Albuquerque, Apr. 3, 1938; d. David Livingstone and Charlotte Louise (Smith) McArthur; children: Carolyn Louise, Joan Emily, Amy Elizabeth, Eric Daniel. Student, U. N.Mex., Albuquerque, 1956—57, U. Pa., Phila., 1957—58, Rocky Mountain Coll., Billings, Mont., 1972—74; BA in Polit. Sci. with high honors, U. Mont., Missoula, 1982, JD, 1985. Dir. Christian edn. St. Luke's Episcopal Ch., 1979-80; law clk. to assoc. justice Mont. Supreme Ct., 1985-87; exec. v.p. St. Peter's Cmty. Hosp. Found., 1987-91; exec. dir. Harrison Hosp. Found., Bremerton, Wash., 1991-93, St. Patrick Hosp. and Health Found., 1993—2001, Missoula Symphony Bd., 1993-99; pres. Missoula Symphony Assn., 1996-98; dir. devel. Five Valleys Land Trust, 2002—05. Bd. dirs. 1st Bank West. Trustee Rocky Mountain Coll., 1972-80; bd. dirs. Billings (Mont.) Area C. of C., 1977-80; mem. City-County Air Pollution Control Bd., 1969-74, chmn., 1970-71; del. Mont. State Constnl. Conv., 1971-72, sec., 1971-72; chmn. County Local Govt. Study Commn., 1973-76; mem. long range planning com. Billings Sch. Dist., 1978-79; bd. dirs. Billings LWV, 1970-72; pres. Helena LWV, 1988, 2d v.p. Mont. LWV, 1987-91; bd. dirs. Internat. Choral Festival, 1999—, pres., 2007-; bd. dirs. Mont. Justice Found., 1999-2003, Friends of Flagship, 2003-04, Inst. Medicine and Humanities, 2007-; mem. governing bd. Missoula Aging Svcs., 2007-. Recipient Philanthropy Svc. award, 2004; named one of Billings' most influential citizens Billings Gazette, 1977; Bertha Morton scholar, 1982. Mem. Mont. State Bar, Missoula Rotary (pres. 1997-98). Republican. Home: 1911 E Broadway St Missoula MT 59802-4901 Personal E-mail: jmbmsla@montana.com.

BOWMAN, JOHN J., judge; b. Oak Park, Ill., Jan. 13, 1930; 5 children. BS, U. Ill., 1952; JD, John Marshall Law Sch., 1959. Pvt. practice law, 1959-72; state's atty. DuPage County, Ill., 1973—76, circuit judge Ill., 1976-90; presiding judge 2d dist. Ill. Ct. Appeals, Oak Brook Terrace, 1998—2000; justice 2d Dist. Appellate Ct., 1990—. With US Army, 1952—54, Japan. Mem.: Alpha Tau Omega. Office Phone: 630-320-1466.

BOWMAN, JOSEPH PAUL, protective services official, writer, retired military officer; b. Vallejo, Calif., Nov. 8, 1959; s. George William Grokett and Elaine Joyce Santos; m. Maria Felix Brandenburg, July 11, 1981; children: Maria Crystal, Victoria Vanessa. AA, Allan Hancock Coll., Santa Maria, Calif., 1999. Commd. lt. USAF, 1978, advanced through grades to master sgt., 1995, assigned to Gulf War King Khalid Mil. City, Saudi Arabia, 1991, ret., 1999; fed. police officer Dept. Vets. Affairs, Fresno, Calif., 2000—. Author: The Bad Man From Bodie, 2005. Decorated Airman's medal Sec. Air Force, Overseas Short Tour ribbon USAF, Noncommd. Officers Profl. Mil. Grad. Ribbon with one oak leaf cluster, Air Force Achievement medal with three oak leaf clusters, Air Force Commendation medal with three oak leaf clusters, S.W. Asia Svc. medal with two battle stars, Kuwait Liberation medal, Joint Meritorious Unit award with one oak leaf cluster, Air Force Achievement medal with three oak leaf clusters, Kuwait Liberation medal, Humanitarian Svc. medal, Outstanding Vol. Svc. medal, Meritorious Svc. medal with one oak leaf cluster; recipient Overseas Long Tour ribbon with one oak leaf cluster, 1992, 1998, Joint Meritorious Unit award with one oak leaf cluster, 1991, Nat. Def. Svc. medal, Dept. Def., 1991, Armed Forces Expeditionary medal, USAF, 1997, Outstanding Unit award with V device and four oak leaf clusters, 1999, Longevity Svc. award with four oak leaf clusters, 1999, Good Conduct medal with one silver and one bronze oak leaf cluster, 1999. Mem.: VFW (life). Home: 9376 S Claremont Avenue Fowler CA 93625 Home Phone: 559-834-9146. Personal E-mail: joegrokett@aol.com.

BOWMAN, KATHLEEN GILL, academic administrator; BS English & Spanish, U. of Minn., 1964, MA English Edn., 1967, PhD English Edn., 1977. Rsch. assoc. Legis. Adv. Coun. on the Econ. Status of Women, St. Paul, 1976-77; asst. dir. of grad. studies, asst prof. of Edn. Reed Coll., Portland, OR, 1977-79, exec. asst. to the pres., dir. of spl. programs, 1979-82; assoc. dir., program officer Fred Meyer Charitable Trust, Portland, OR, 1982-84; assoc. v.p. for rsch. U. of Oreg., Eugene, OR, 1985-89, vice-provost for internat. affairs, 1989-94; pres. Randolph-Macon Woman's Coll., Lynchburg, VA, 1994—. Fullbright Sr. Scholar award, Japan & Korea, 1993. Office: Randolph-Macon Womans Coll Office of the Pres 2500 Rivermont Ave Lynchburg VA 24503-1555

BOWMAN, LEAH, fashion designer, consultant, photographer, educator; b. Chgo., Apr. 21, 1935; d. John George and Alexandra (Colovos) Murges; m. Veron George Broe, Aug. 31, 1954; 1 child, Michelle; m. John Ronald Bowman, Feb. 28, 1959 Diploma, Sch. of Art Inst., Chgo., 1962. Designer Korach Bros. Inc., Chgo., 1962-65; costume designer Hull House South Theatre, Chgo., 1966-67, Wellington Theatre, Chgo., 1966-67; from instr. to prof. emeritus Sch. of Art Inst., Chgo., 1967—2001, prof. emeritus, 2001—. Prodr. fashion performances and style exhbns.; vis. prof., cons. SNDT Women's U., Bombay, 1980, 85, 92, Ctrl. Acad. Arts and Design, Beijing, People's Republic of China, 1987; faculty sabbatical exhbn. Sch. of Art Inst., 1986, 93. Recipient Fulbright award, Coun. for Internat. Exchange for Scholars, India, 1980, Pres. award, Art Inst. Chgo., 1991, Honoror's award, Sch. of Art Inst., Chgo., 1998, Disting. Faculty award, Sch. Art Inst. Chgo., 2005. Office: Sch of Art Inst Chgo 37 S Wabash Ave Chicago IL 60603-3002

BOWMAN, MARJORIE ANN, physician, educator; b. Grove City, Pa., Aug. 18, 1953; d. Ross David and Freda Louise (Smith) Williamson; m. Robert Choplin; children: Bridget Williamson Foley, Skyler Weston Williamson Choplin. BS, Pa. State U., 1974; MD, Jefferson Med. Coll., 1976; MPA, U. So. Calif., LA, 1983. Intern, then resident in family practice Duke U., Durham, NC, 1976-79; med. officer USPHS, Hyattsville, Md., 1979-82; clin. instr. uniformed svcs. U. Health Scis., Bethesda, Md., 1980-83; dir. family practice residency, prof. Georgetown U. Sch. Medicine, Washington, 1983-86; chmn. dept. family practice, prof. Wake Forest U., Winston-Salem, NC, 1986—96; prof., chmn. dept. family medicine & cmty. health U. Pa., Phila, 1996—. Author: (Book) Stress and Women Physicians, 1985, 1990, Women in Medicine: Life and Career, 2002; editor: Archives Family Medicine, 1992—2000, Jour. Women's Health, 2001—05, Jour. Am. Bd. Family Medicine, 2003—; contbr. articles to profl. jours. Fellow Am. Acad. Family Physicians; mem. AMA, Soc. Tchrs. Family Medicine (bd. dirs. 1984-88, bd. dirs. Found. 1984-99, v.p. 1988-91, pres. 1991-92), Am. Pub. Health Assn. Republican. Unitarian Universalist. Office: Univ Pa 2 Gates 3400 Spruce St Philadelphia PA 19104-4283 Business E-Mail: bowmanm@uphs.upenn.edu.

BOWMAN, PASCO MIDDLETON, II, judge; b. Timberville, Va., Dec. 20, 1933; s. Pasco Middleton and Katherine (Lohr) Bowman; m. Ruth Elaine Bowman, July 12, 1958; children: Ann Katherine, Helen Middleton, Benjamin Garber; m. Katharine Thisher Pitt, Aug. 19, 2006. BA, Bridgewater Coll., 1955; JD, NYU, 1958; LLM, U. Va., 1986; LLD (hon.), Bridgewater Coll., 1988. Bar: N.Y. 1958, Ga. 1965, Mo. 1980. Assoc. firm Cravath, Swaine & Moore, NYC, 1958—61, 1962—64; asst. prof. law U. Ga., 1964—65, assoc. prof., 1965—69, prof., 1969—70, Wake Forest U., 1970—78, dean, 1970—78; vis. prof. U. Va., 1978—79; prof., dean U. Mo., Kansas City, 1979—83; judge US Ct. Appeals (8th cir.), Kansas City, Mo., 1983—2003, chief judge, 1998—99, sr. judge, 2003—. Mng. editor: NYU Law Rev., 1957—58, reporter, chief draftsman: Georgia Corporation Code, 1965—68. Col. USAR, 1959—84. Fulbright scholar, London Sch. Econs. and Polit. Sci., 1961—62, Root-Tilden scholar, 1955—58. Mem.: Mo. Bar, NY Bar. Office: US Ct Appeals 8th Circuit 10-50 US Courthouse 400 E 9th St Kansas City MO 64106-2607 Office Phone: 816-512-5800.*

BOWMAN, PATRICIA LYNN, lawyer; b. Mpls., July 5, 1956; d. Robert Lee and Delores Helen (Roberts) B. BA in History with distinction, Stanford U., 1978; JD cum laude, Harvard U., 1981; MA, Grad. Theol. Union, 1999. Assoc. Perkins Coie, Seattle, 1981-84, Foster, Pepper & Shefelman, Seattle, 1984-89; v.p., assoc. counsel Washington Mut. Bank, Seattle, 1989-97. Pastoral assoc. for social outreach, St. James Cathedral, Seattle, 2000—. Bd. dirs., vice chair Common Ground, Seattle, 1987-93; bd. dirs. Elderhealth Northwest, Seattle, 1994-97. Mem. ABA, Wash. State Bar Assn., Seattle-King County Bar Assn., Seattle Mortgage Bankers Assn. (mem. legal com.), Phi Beta Kappa.

BOWMAN, RICHARD CARL, defense consultant, retired air force officer; b. Chgo., July 5, 1926; s. Carl Elias and Lucile (Rutan) B.; m. Lois Jean Hassenauer, June 10, 1950; children: Mary Bowman Millikin, Kristin Bowman Spencer, Margaret Bowman Flaherty, Victoria Bowman Smoke, Richard Carl. BS, U.S. Mil. Acad., 1949; MS, Okla. State U., 1954; MPA, Harvard U., 1958, PhD, 1964. Enlisted in U.S. Army, 1943; commd. 2d lt. USAF, 1949, advanced through grades to maj. gen., 1975; pilot, flight comdr. Korea, 1951; mem. initial staff Air Force Acad., 1955-57, assoc. prof. polit. sci., 1959-63; mem. staff Nat. Security Council, 1964-66, Nat. War Coll., 1966—67, Office Sec. Air Force, 1967-73; dep. def. adviser to Am. ambassador to NATO, 1973-75; dir. European and NATO affairs Office Sec. Def., 1975-81, ret., 1981. Contbr. to mil. jours. Decorated Def. D.S.M. (2), Air Force D.S.M., Def. Superior Service medal, Legion of Merit (2), D.F.C., Air medal (3), Commendation medal (2); Grand Service Cross with Star W. Ger.; comdr. Order of St. Olaf (Norway, with star). Mem.: Harvard U. Alumni Assn., West Point Assn. Grads., KC (assoc. state marshall, past grand knight). Roman Catholic. Home: 7824 Midday Ln Alexandria VA 22306-2724

BOWMAN, ROBERT A., Internet company executive; BS, Harvard U., 1977; MBA, U. Pa., 1979. With U.S. Dept. Treasury, 1979-81, Goldman Sachs & Co., Investment Banker, 1981-83, State Mich. Treasury, 1983-90; CFO, exec. v.p. ITT Sheraton Corp., NYC, 1991—98; head Outpost.com; found., CEO MLB Advanced Media, LLP, 2000—. Named one of New York's Influentials, New York Mag., 2006. Office: MLB Advanced Media, LP 5th Fl 75 9th Ave New York NY 10011 Office Phone: 212-485-3444. Office Fax: 212-485-3456.*

BOWMAN, ROGER MANWARING, real estate company officer; b. Duluth, Minn., Dec. 3, 1916; s. Lawrence Fredrick and Gladys (Manwaring) B.; m. Judith Claypool, Apr. 10, 1942 (dec. 1993); Ann, David, Mary Bowman Johnson, Lawrence II. Student, U. Mich., 1934—36, Wayne State U., 1937. Pres. North Star Airways, Duluth, 1946-50, North Star Engring. Co., Duluth, 1946-50, Superior (Wis.) Aero, 1946-50, Lawrence F. Bowman Co., Duluth, 1950-70, Gen. Cleaning Corp., Duluth, 1954-92, Bowman Corp., Duluth, 1970-83, Bowman Properties, Duluth, 1983-92; chmn. Deltona Corp., Miami, Fla., 1985-89. Cons. Topeka Group, Duluth, 1985-89; bd. dirs. Parish Corp., Minn. Power, Norwest Bank; chmn. Bowman Properties, 1988-96, Gen. Cleaning Corp., 1985—; mng. gen. ptnr. 6 ltd. partnerships, 1990—. Chmn. St. Louis County Welfare, Duluth, 1964-69, chmn. Govs. Real Estate Adv. Commn., 1968-70; pres. Duluth Devel. Corp., 1960-68; trustee Ordean Found., 1968-92; bd. dirs. Duluth Bd. Realtors, 1958-62; pres. Duluth Bldg. Owners and Mgrs. Assn. Internat., 1963-65. Lt. col. USMCR, 1940-45. Recipient Silver Beaver award Boy Scouts Am., 1959, Mayor's Commendation City of Duluth, 1976. Mem. Duluth Steam Coop. (bd. dirs. 1970-86), Duluth Bldg. Owners and Mgrs. Internat., Duluth Bd. Realtors, Real Property Adminstrs., Kitchi Gammi Club (dir. 1974-78), Northland Country Club, Boca Raton Resort and Club, Delray Beach Yacht Club. Republican. Episcopalian. Avocation: cooking. Office: 575 Wells Fargo Ctr Duluth MN 55802 Home Phone: 561-276-2047. Personal E-mail: rbowman16@aol.com.

BOWMAN, WILLIAM SCOTT (SCOTTY BOWMAN), professional hockey coach; b. Montreal, Can., Sept. 18, 1933; s. John and Jane Thomson (Scott) B.; m. Suella Belle Chitty, Aug. 16, 1969; children: Alicia Jean, David Scott, Stanley Glen, Nancy Elizabeth and Robert Gordon (twins). Student, Sir George Williams Bus. Sch., 1954; LHD (hon.), Canisius Coll.,

Buffalo, 2003. Scout exec. Club de Hockey Canadien, Montreal, 1956-66, coach, 1971-79; coach, gen. mgr. St. Louis Blues Hockey Club, 1966-71; coach, gen. mgr., dir. hockey ops. Buffalo Sabres Hockey Club, 1979-86; TV analyst Hockey Night in Can., 1987-90; dir. player devel. Pitts. Penguins Hockey Club, 1990-91, interim head coach, 1991-92, head coach, 1992-93, Detroit Red Wings Hockey Club, 1993—2002, dir. player pers., 1993—2002. Mem. Hockey Hall of Fame Selection Com.; head coach Team Can., 1976. Recipient Jack Adams award, 1977, 96, Victor award for NHL Coach of Yr., 1993, 96, 2002, Stanley Cup Championship, 1973, 1976-79, 1992, 1997-98, 2002, Lester Patrick award 2001, award Can. Soc. N.Y., 2001, Wayne Gretzky award 2002; named NHL Exec. of Yr. Sporting News, 1979-80, NHL Coach of Yr. Sporting News, 1995-96, Hockey News, 1976-77, 93-97, NHL Exec. of the Yr. Hockey News, 1996-97, NHL Coach of Yr., 1967-68, Hockey News Coach of Yr., 1968, 76, 95-96, Exec. of Yr., 1997; inducted into Hockey Hall of Fame, 1991, Mich. Sports Hall of Fame, 1999, Buffalo Sports Hall of Fame, 2000, Can. Walk of Fame, 2003, Can.'s Sports Hall of Fame, 2004, Quebec Sports Hall of Fame, 2005; holder NHL career regular season records for wins (1,244) and winning percentage (.670); holder NHL career playoffs records for wins (223) and games (353); recipient Stanley Cup as head coach Montreal Canadiens, 1973, 76-79, Pitts. Penguins, 1992, Detroit Red Wings, 1997-98, 2002; only coach in NHL history to win Stanley Cup with 3 different teams. Office: Detroit Red Wings Joe Louis Arena 600 Civic Center Dr Detroit MI 48226-4419

BOWNE, MARTHA HOKE, editor, consultant; b. Greeley, Colo., June 9, 1931; d. George Edwin and Krin (English) Hoke; children: Gretchen, William, Kay, Judith. BA, U. Mich., 1952; postgrad., Syracuse U., 1965. Tchr. Wayne (Mich.) Pub. Schs., 1953-54, East Syracuse and Minoa Cen. Schs., Minoa, NY, 1965-68; store mgr. Fabric Barn, Fayetteville, NY, 1969-77; store owner Fabric Fair, Oneida, NY, 1978-80; prodr., owner Quilting by the Sound, Port Townsend, Wash., 1987—2000, Quilting by the Lake, Cazenovia, NY, 1981—. Organizer symposium Am. Quilters Soc.; founder, pres. Quilter's Quest confs., 1994—. Mem., pres. Minoa Library, 1960-75; mem. Onondaga County Library, Syracuse, 1968-71. Mem.: Am. Quilters Soc. (editor Am. Quilter mag. 1985—95). Avocations: reading, hiking, travel, bridge, Scrabble. Home: 478 Oden Bay Dr Sandpoint ID 83864-6499 E-mail: martyidaho@sandpoint.net.

BOWNE, SHIRLEE PEARSON, credit manager; b. High Shoals Twp., NC, Mar. 11, 1936; d. Lloyd E. Pearson and Parnell (James) Garland; divorced; 1 child, Gregory Charles. Grad. h.s., Gaffney, SC. Various secretarial positions, 1955-64; sales repr., pres. Real Estate Marketers, Inc., Tallahassee, 1964-80; chief exec. officer Shirlee Bowne Mktg. & Devel. Inc., Tallahassee, 1980-91; vice chmn. Nat. Credit Union Adminstrn., Washington, 1991-97. Cons. in field. Treas. Rep. Party Fla., 1988-91. Episcopalian. Avocation: bridge. Personal E-mail: shirleebrowne@earthlink.net.

BOWRON, EDGAR PETERS, art museum curator, administrator; b. Birmingham, Ala., May 27, 1943; s. James Edgar Bowron and Dorothe Peters Lowles; children: James Edgar III, Clara Beatrice, St. John Grenfell. BA, Colgate U., 1965; MA, Inst. Fine Arts, NYU, 1969; PhD, NYU, 1979. Edn. lectr. Met. Mus. Art, NYC, 1969-70; registrar Mpls. Inst. Arts, 1970-73; curator Renaissance and Baroque art Walters Art Gallery, Balt., 1973-78; adminstrv. asst. to dir. and curator Renaissance and Baroque art Nelson Gallery-Atkins Mus., Kansas City, Mo., 1978-81; dir. N.C. Mus. Art, Raleigh, 1981-85; Elizabeth and John Moors Cabot dir., prof. fine arts Art Mus. Harvard U., Cambridge, Mass., 1985-90; sr. curator paintings Nat. Gallery of Art, Washington, 1991-96; Audrey Jones Beck curator of European art Mus. Fine Arts, Houston, 1996—. Art adv. panel IRS, 1994—. Author: Pompeo Batoni and His British Patrons, 1982; European Paintings before 1900 in the Fogg Mus., 1990; Masterworks of European Painting in Museum of Fine Arts, Houston, 2000; editor: Selected Writings of Anthony M. Clark: Studies in Eighteenth Roman Painting, 1981, The North Carolina Museum of Art: Introduction to the Collections, 1983, Anthony M. Clark, Pompeo Batoni, A Complete Catalogue of his Works with an Introductory Text, 1985, Bernard Bellotto and the Capitals of Europe, 2001; co-editor: Art in Rome in the Eighteenth Century, 2000; contbr. articles to profl. jours. Trustee Mus. Fine Arts, Boston, 1988-90; mem. art adv. panel IRS, 1994--. Mem. NEA (arts and artifacts indemnity adv. panel 2000-04), Assn. Art Mus. Dirs. (trustee 1987-90), Master Drawings Assn. (bd. dirs. 1987—) Office: Mus Fine Arts PO Box 6826 Houston TX 77265-6826

BOWSHER, CHARLES ARTHUR, retired government official, financial executive; b. Elkhart, Ind., May 30, 1931; s. Matthew A. and Ella M. (West) B.; m. Mary C. Mahoney, Dec. 14, 1963; children: Kathryn M., Stephen C. BS, U. Ill., 1953; MBA, U. Chgo., 1956; DSc in Bus. Adminstrn. (hon.), Bryant Coll., 1984; D Pub. Svc. (hon.), George Washington U., 1993; DSc (hon.), U. Ill.-Chgo., 1994; Dr. Pub. Svc. (hon.), St. Joseph's U., 1994; DSc in Pub. Svc. (hon.), Am. U., 1996. C.P.A., Ill. Ptnr. Arthur Andersen & Co., Chgo., 1956-67, Washington, 1971-81; asst. sec. of Navy for fin. mgmt. Dept. Def., Washington, 1967-71; comptroller gen. U.S., 1981-96. Bd. dirs. DeVry Inc., Washington Mutual Investors Fund, SI Internat.; bd. govs. NASD trustee Ctr. Naval Analysis, U.S. Navy Meml. Found., Concord Coalition, Com. for a Responsible Fed. Budget. Vis. com. Sch. Bus., selection com. Roger W. Jones award for Exec. Leadership; nat. adv. bd. Pvt. Sector Coun.; active Bus. Execs. for Nat. Security Commn. With U.S. Army, 1953-55 Recipient Enduring Lifetime Achievement award Am. Acctg. Assn., 1996, Integrity award Office of Insp. Gen., 1996; named to Acctg. Hall of Fame, 1996. Mem. AICPA, Nat. Acad. Pub. Adminstrn., Nat. Assn. Govt. Accts., Burning Tree Club (Washington), Met. Club (Washington), Beta Alpha Psi, Pi Kappa Alpha. Home: 4503 Boxwood Rd Bethesda MD 20816-1815 Office Phone: 301-229-5923.

BOW WOW, See MOSS, SHAD

BOX, THADIS WAYNE, university dean emeritus, educator; b. Llano, Tex., May 9, 1929; s. Daniel W. and Mary Madelyn (Hasty) B.; m. Virginia Price, July 16, 1954; children— Dennis, Mary, Paul, Emily. BS, S.W. Tex. State Coll., 1956; MS, Tex. A&M U., 1957, PhD, 1959. Rancher, Burnet, Tex., 1946-51; Welder Wildlife Found. fellow Sinton, Tex., 1956-59; asst. prof. Utah State U., 1959-61; assoc. prof. to prof. Tex. Tech. U., 1962-68; dean Coll. Natural Resources Utah State U., 1970-89; Gerald Thomas prof. N.Mex. State U., 1989-92. Bd. dir. Internat. Ctr. Arid and Semi-Arid Land Studies, 1968-70; cons. FAO, UN (also fgn. govts. and pvt. orgns.). Author articles, books. With AUS, 1951-53. Recipient E. Harris Harbison award for Distinguished Teaching, 1967; Commonwealth Sci. and Indsl. Rsch. Orgn. fellow, Australia, 1968-69. Mem. Soc. Range Mgmt.

BOXER, BARBARA, senator; b. Bklyn., Nov. 11, 1940; d. Ira and Sophie (Silvershein) Levy; m. Stewart Boxer, 1962; children: Doug, Nicole. BA in Economics, Bklyn. Coll., 1962. Aide to Congressman John L. Burton, 1974—76; stockbroker, econ. rschr. N.Y. Securities Firm, NYC, 1962-65; journalist, assoc. editor Pacific Sun, 1972-74; congl. aide to rep. 5th Congl. Dist. San Francisco, 1974-76; mem. 98th-102d Congresses from 6th Calif. dist., mem. armed services com.; select com. children, youth and families; majority whip at large; co-chair Mil. Reform Caucus; chair subcom. on govt. activities and transp. of house govt. ops. com., 1990-93; US Senator from Calif. US Senate, 1993—. Mem. Presdl. Advisory Commn. on Holocaust Assets in the US; mem. com. commerce, sci. and transp. US Senate, com. environment and public works, com. fgn. relations. Author (with Nicole Boxer): Strangers in the Senate: Politics and the New Revolution of Women in America, 1993; (with Catherine Whitney) Nine and Counting: The Women of the Senate, 2000, (with Mary-Rose Hayes) (novels) A Time to Run, 2005. Mem. Marin County Bd. Suprs., 1976-82, pres. 1980-81; mem. Bay Area Air Quality Mgmt. Bd., San Francisco, 1977-82, pres., 1979-81; bd. dirs. Golden Gate Bridge Hwy. and Transport Dist., San Francisco, 1978-82; pres. Dem. New Mems. Caucus, 1983. Recipient Open Govt. award Common Cause, 1980, Rep. of Yr. award Nat. Multiple Sclerosis Soc., 1990, Margaret Sanger award Planned Parenthood, 1990, Women of Achievement award Anti-Defamation League, 1990, Star Legis. award LA Women's Legis. Coalition, 1991, Elected Official of the Year Stonewall Democratic Club, 1997, Edgar Wayburn award Sierra Club, 1997, Demetris Bouhoutsos award Hellenic-Am. Coun. So. Calif., 1998, Pres. award for the Advancement of Women Nat. Assn. Women Lawyers, 1998, Alumnae of the Year, Bklyn. Coll., 1999, Reg. Elected Official of the Year Sacramento Area Coun. Governments., 1999, Vision award Highwood Online Girlsite, 1999, Pub. Servant award Nat. Orgn. on Fetal Alcohol Syndrome, 1999, Every Action Counts Congl. award Hadassah, 1999, Spirit of Achievement Albert Einstein Coll. Med., 2000, Paul E. Tsongas award Lymphoma Rsch. Found. Am., 2000, Peter H. Behr award Friends of the River, 2000, Environmental Leadership award Calif. League of Conservation Voters, 2003. Mem.: Marin Community Video, Marin Nat. Women's Polit. Caucus, Marin Edn. Corps. Democrat. Jewish. Office: US Senate 112 Hart Senate Office Bldg Washington DC 20510-0001 also: District Office Ste 2240 600 B St San Diego CA 92101-4508 Office Phone: 202-224-3553, 619-239-3884. Office Fax: 619-239-5719.*

BOXER, JEROME HARVEY, data processing executive, accountant, management consultant, vintager; b. Chgo., Nov. 27, 1930; s. Ben Avrum and Edith (Lyman) B.; m. Sandra Schaffner, June 17, 1980; children by previous marriage: Michael, Jodi. AA magna cum laude, East L.A. Coll., 1952; AB with honors, Calif. State U., LA, 1954. CPA, Calif.; cert. computing profl. Lab. instr. Calif. State U., LA, 1953-54; staff acct. Dolman, Freeman & Buchalter, LA, 1955-57; sr. acct. Neiman, Sanger, Miller & Beress, LA, 1957-63; ptnr. Glynn and Boxer, CPAs, LA, 1964-68; v.p., sec. Glynn, Boxer & Phillips Inc., CPAs, L.A. and Glendale, Calif., 1968-90; pvt. practice cons., 1990—. Owner Oak Valley Vineyard; instr. viticulture Cuesta Coll.; pres. Echo Data Svcs. Inc., 1978-90; instr. data processing L.A. City Adult Schs.; tchr., lectr., cons. wines and wine-tasting; instr. photography. Contbr. to Wine World Mag., 1974-82. Founding pres. Congregation Ohr Tzafon, spiritual leader, 1998—2003; mem. ops. bd. Evrywoman's Village; bd. dirs. Paso Robles Libr.; bd. dirs., v.p. So. Calif. Jewish Hist. Soc., Paso Robles Art Assn., Calif.; bd. dirs. Calif. Mid-State Fair, Project Theatre Found.; pres. Calif. Mid-State Fair, 2005; v.p. Jewish Hist. Soc. of Ctrl. Coast; co-founder Open Space Theatre; former officer Ethel Josephine Scantland Found.; past post advisor Explorer scouts Boy Scouts Am., Eagle Scout. Recipient Youth Svc. award Mid-Valley YMCA, 1972-73. Mem.: AICPA, Ctrl. Coast Vineyard Team, Paso Robles Wine Festival Steering Com., Clowns of Am., Inc., World Clown Assn., Paso Robles Vintners and Growers Assn., Cellarmasters, Wines and Steins, Ctrl. Coast Winegrowers Assn., Am. Wine Assn., Am. Jewish Hist. Soc., Data Processing Mgmt. Assn., Assn. for Systems Mgmt., Calif. Soc. CPAs, Assoc. Students Calif. State U. L.A. (life) (hon.), Profl. Musicians of Am. (life), Cuesta Coll North County Ambs., Soc. Preservation of Variety Arts, Friends of Photography, L.A. Photog. Ctr., Acad. Model Aeros., Nat. Model Railroad Assn., Maltose Falcons Home Brewing Soc., San Fernando Valley Silent Flyers, San Fernando Valley Radio Control Flyers, Acad. Magical Arts, Internat. Brotherhood of Magicians, L.A.-Bordeaux Sister City Affiliation, Western Region Clown Assn., Paso Robles Shrine Clowns, Scottish Rite Rsch. Soc., Soc. Bacchus Am., Internat. Shrine-Clown Assn., South Coast Corinthian Yacht Club (former dir., officer), German Shepherd Dog Club Am., Pacific Mariners Yacht Club, Exch. Club, Verdugo Club, German Shepherd Dog Club Los Angeles County, Braemar Country Club, The Invisible Lodge, Kiwanis (pres. Sunset-Echo Park 1968), So. Calif. Research Lodge, Shriner, B'nai Brith, Paso Robles Masons (32 degree, master 2004), Blue Key, Alpha Phi Omega. Home and Office: 1660 Circle B Rd Paso Robles CA 93446-9595 E-mail: jhboxer@yahoo.com.

BOXER, LAURENCE ALAN, physician, research educator; b. Denver, May 17, 1940; s. Sam G. and Tillie (Belstock) B.; m. M. Grace Jordison, Aug. 23, 1969; 1 child, David. BA, U. Colo., 1961; MD, Stanford U., 1966. Intern, resident pediatrics Yale U., New Haven, 1966-68; resident pediatrics Stanford Hosp., Palo Alto, Calif., 1968-69; fellow hematology Children's Hosp., Harvard U., Boston, 1972-74; instr. pediatrics Harvard Med. Sch., Boston, 1973-75; asst. prof. to prof. Ind. U. Sch. Medicine, Indpls., 1975-82; prof., dir. pediatric hematology/oncology U. Mich., Ann Arbor, 1982—, assoc. chair pediat., 1996—. Mem. study sect. NIH, Bethesda, Md., 1981—; cons. Amgen, Thousand Oak, Calif., 1988—, Genzymel; established investigator Am. Heart Assn., Dallas, 1978-83; internat. adv. bd. U. Malaysia, Sarawak. Assoc. editor Blood, 1993-98, Jour. Clin. Investigation, 1997-2002; contbr. articles to profl. jours, chpts. to books. Maj. U.S. Army, 1969-72. NIH grantee, Bethesda, 1976—. Fellow ACP, Am. Acad. Pediatrics (E. Mead Johnson rsch. award 1983); mem. Soc. Pediatric Rsch. (pres. 1986), Am. Soc. Hematology (councillor 1988-92), Am. Soc. Clin. Investigation, Am. Soc. Cell Biology, Am. Assn. Pathologists, Am. Assn. Physicians, Am. Clin. Climate Assn. Republican. Jewish. Avocation: swimming. Office: U Mich L2110 Women's Hosp Ann Arbor MI 48109-0238 Home Phone: 734-668-0020; Office Phone: 734-764-7127. Business E-Mail: laboxer@umich.edu.

BOXER, LEONARD, lawyer; b. NYC, Feb. 11, 1939; s. Max Boxer and Sally (Grill) Koffler; m. Enid Feuer, Nov. 24, 1965; children: Michael, Jason, Douglas. BS, NYU, 1960, LLB, 1963. Bar: N.Y. 1963, U.S. Dist. Ct. (so. and ea. dists.) N.Y. 1985, U.S. Supreme Ct. Assoc. Eisenberg & Weiss, Bklyn., 1964-65; ptnr. Olnick, Boxer, Blumberg, Lane & Troy, NYC, 1965-86, Stroock & Stroock & Lavan, NYC, 1987—. Mem. adv. bd. Chgo. Title Ins. Co., NYC, 1980—; mem. exec. com., gov., counsel NY Real Estate Bd.; mem. adv. bd. Valley Nat. Bank, 2003—. Mem. spl. real estate com. Guggenheim Mus., 2004—; trustee NYU Law Sch., 1994—, NYU, 2000—06, Nat. Jewish Ctr. Immunology and Respiratory Medicine, Jewish Assn. Svcs. for the Aged, Children's Hearing Inst., N.Y. Eye and Ear Infirmary, NYU, 2000—, Cancer Rsch. Inst., 2001. Mem. N.Y. State Bar Assn., Bklyn. Bar Assn., Tax Certiorari Bar Assn. (bd. dirs. 1983-97), Beta Alpha Psi. Home: 875 Park Ave New York NY 10021 Office: Stroock & Stroock & Lavan 180 Maiden Ln Fl 17 New York NY 10038-4937

BOXER, LESTER, lawyer; b. NYC, Oct. 19, 1935; s. Samuel and Anna Lena (Samovar) B.; m. Frances Barenfeld, Sept. 17, 1961; children: Kimberly Brett, Allison Joy. AA, UCLA, 1955, BS, 1957; JD, U. So. Calif., 1961. Bar: Calif. 1962; U.S. Dist. Ct. (ctrl. dist.) Calif. 1962. Assoc. Bautzer & Grant, Beverly Hills, Calif., 1961-63; pvt. practice Beverly Hills, 1963-65, 69—; ptnr. Boxer & Stoll, Beverly Hills, 1965-69. Mem. Calif. Bar Assn., LA County Bar Assn., Beverly Hills Bar Assn. Office: 1801 Century Park E Ste 2513 Los Angeles CA 90067-4703 Office Phone: 310-553-3344.

BOXER, MARK L., healthcare insurance company executive; BS in Engring., U. Hartford, BA in Physics; MS in Info. Systems, Drexel U.; MBA, U. Conn. Mem. staff engring. and ops. mgmt. N.E. Utilities; dir. strategic planning Hewlett Packard, global practice dir. bus. process svcs., line of bus. mgr. US and Europe managed svcs., bus. unit chief info. officer; v.p. tech. ops. CIGNA HealthCare, chief info. officer Healthsource, sr. v.p. info. tech. and eCommerce; sr. v.p. eBusiness Anthem, Inc., 2000; sr. mgmt. positions WellPoint, Inc., Indpls., 2000—04, exec. v.p., chief strategy officer, 2004—05, exec. v.p., chief info. officer, 2005—06, exec. v.p. chief ops. and tech. officer, 2006—07, exec. v.p., pres. & CEO ops., tech. & govt. services, 2007—. Dir. FinishMaster, Inc.; sr. adv. Ctr. Health Systems Rsch. Mem. editl. adv. bd.: Ins. and Tech. Mag. Bd. overseers U. Conn. Sch. Bus. Office: Wellpoint Inc 120 Monument Cir Indianapolis IN 46204*

BOXER, SARAH, critic, reporter, writer; BA, Harvard U. Staff writer NY Times, NYC, former editor Book Review, photography critic, internet critic. Contbr. Metropolis, Village Voice, Sports Illustrated. Author: In the Floyd Archives: A Psycho-Bestiary, 2001. Office: NY Times Culture Desk 229 W 43rd St New York NY 10036 Office Phone: 212-556-1891. Office Fax: 212-556-1516.

BOYADZHIEV, KHRISTO NONEV, mathematician, educator, researcher; b. Sofia, Bulgaria, Sept. 4, 1948; came to U.S., 1989; s. Nonio Christoff and Maria I. Boyajieff; m. Irina Assenova Dimitrov, May 8, 1982; children: Marinella, Alexandra M. MS in Math., Sofia U., 1972, PhD in Math., 1978. Sr. rsch. fellow Inst. Math. Bulgarian Acad. Scis., Sofia, 1978-90; prof. math. Ohio No. U., Ada, 1990—. Reviewer Math. Revs., Ann Arbor, Mich., 1980—, Zentralblatt fur Mathematik, Berlin, Germany, 1988—. Contbr. articles to profl. jours. Recipient Badge of Honor, Sofia U., 1971. Mem. Am. Math. Soc., Math. Assn. Am. Achievements include research and theorems in functional analysis, classical analysis and operator theory. Home: 625 W Lima Ave Ada OH 45810-1615 Office: Ohio No Univ Dept Math Ada OH 45810 E-mail: k_boyadzhiev@onu.edu.

BOYAN, NORMAN J., retired education educator; b. NYC, Apr. 11, 1922; s. Joseph J. and Emma M. (Pelezare) B.; m. Priscilla M. Simpson, July 10, 1943; children: Stephen J. (dec.), Craig S., Corydon J. AB, Bates Coll., Lewiston, Maine, 1943; A.M., Harvard U., 1947, Ed.D., 1951. Instr. U.S. history Dana Hall Sch., Wellesley, Mass., 1946-48; research assoc. Lab. Social Relations, Harvard U., 1950-52; asst. prin. Mineola (N.Y.) High Sch., 1952-54; prin. Wheatley Sch., East Williston, N.Y., 1954-59; assoc. prof. edn., dir. student teaching and internship U. Wis., 1959-61; assoc. prof. edn. Stanford U., 1961-67; dir. div. edn. labs. U.S. Office Edn., 1967-68, assoc. commr. for research, 1968-69; prof. edn. Grad. Sch. Edn., U. Calif., Santa Barbara, 1969-90, prof. emeritus, 1990—, dean, 1969-80; assoc. in edn. Grad. Sch. Edn., Harvard U., 1980-81; dir. Ednl. Leadership Inst. U. Calif., 1989-91. Vis. scholar Stanford U., 1974, 86; vis. prof. U. Ark. Program in Greece, 1977, Coll. Edn., Pa. State U., 1981, Faculty Edn. U. B.C., 1983, U. Alta., 1988, UCLA, 1991; cons. in field. Co-author: Instructional Supervision Training Program, 1978; mem. editl. bd. Harvard Edn. Rev, 1948-50, Jour. Secondary Edn, 1963-68, Jour. Edn. Rsch., 1967-82, Urban Edn, 1967-90; cons. editor, contbr. 5th edit. Ency. Ednl. Rsch., 1982; editor, contbr. Handbook Rsch. on Ednl. Adminstrn., 1988; contbr. articles to profl. jours. Served with USAAF, 1943-46. Recipient Shankland award for advanced grad. study in ednl. adminstrn., 1950, Roald F. Campbell Lifetime Achievement award U. Coun. for Ednl. Adminstrn., 1998. Mem. Am. Ednl. Rsch. Assn. (v.p. div. A 1978-80), Phi Beta Kappa, Phi Delta Kappa. Home: 1031A Calle Sastre Santa Barbara CA 93105-4439 Personal E-mail: nboyan@cox.net.

BOYARSKY, ANDREW HAROLD, surgeon, educator; b. Burlington, Vt., Feb. 18, 1952; BA, Rutgers U., 1974, MD, 1980. Diplomate Am. Bd. Surgery, Am. Bd. Surg. Critical Care. Intern U. Medicine and Dentistry N.J.-Rutgers Med. Sch., Piscataway, 1980-81, resident, 1981-85; fellow in vascular surgery Maimonides Med. Ctr., Bklyn., 1985-86; mem. staff Robert Wood Johnson Hosp., New Brunswick, NJ; assoc. prof. surgery U. Medicine and Dentistry N.J.-Robert Wood Johnson, 1993—. Office: UMDNJ-RW Johnson Med Sch Dept Surgery New Brunswick NJ 08903 Office Phone: 732-235-7920.

BOYARSKY, SAUL, urologist, educator; b. Burlington, Vt., July 22, 1923; s. Samuel and Ethel (Kaplan) B.; m. Rose Eisman, June 17, 1945; children: Myer William, Terry Linda Boyarsky, Hannah Gail Boyarsky. BS magna cum laude, U. Vt., Burlington, 1943, MD cum laude, 1946; JD, Washington U., St. Louis, 1981. Bar: Mo. 1983. Surg. intern, urology resident Duke Hosp. and VA Med. Ctr., 1950—54; instr. in physiology NYU, NYC, 1955—56; assoc. prof. urology Albert Einstein Coll., NYC, 1956-63; prof. urology Duke U., Durham, NC, 1963-70, head divsn. genito-urinary surgery, 1970-73; prof. Washington U., St. Louis, 1970-89, head divsn. urology, 1970-73; clin. prof. surgery St. Louis U., 1991—; emeritus urologist Barnes-Jewish-Christian Hosp., Washington Hosp. Med. Ctr., St. Louis; cons. assoc. dept. surgery Duke U. Med. Sch., Durham, NC, 2007—. Chmn. rsch. and tng. com. NIH, Bethesda, Md., 1968; cons. on med. devices FDA, Washington, 1969—; chmn. biomed. engring. com. AUA, Balt., 1975—90; founder Urology Lawyers Coun.; chmn. steering and curriculum com., facilitator Lifelong Learning Inst., U. Coll., Washington U., St. Louis; instr. and facilitator Duke Inst. for Learning in Retirement, Durham, NC, 1999, Durham, 2001—03, mem. curriculum com.; chmn. Duke Intergenerational Forum for Ethical Issues, Durham, NC, 2002—05; sr. rsch. assoc. Kenan Inst. for Ethics; rsch. assoc. Ctr. Jewish Studies, Duke U., Durham, NC; cunsulting assoc. dept. surgery Duke U. Med. Ctr., Durham, NC. Author: The Neurogenic Bladder, 1967; (with others) Hydrodynamics of Micturition, 1971, Urodynamics; Hydrodynamics of the Ureter and Renal Pelvis, 1971, Ureteral Dynamics, 1972, The Care of the Neurogenic Bladder Patient, 1979, Goals in Male Reproductive Research, 1981; mem. editl. bd. Jour. of Legal Medicine. Chmn. steering com. Lifelong Learning Inst., Univ. Coll. Washington U., St. Louis. Capt. U.S. Army, 1943-50. Fellow ACS, Am. Acad. Forensic Sci., Am. Coll. Legal Medicine (former bd. govs.); mem. AAAS, AMA, ABA, AAUP, Am. Urol. Assn. (former chmn. biomed. engring. com.), Am. Assn. Clin. Urologists, Am. Assn. Genitourinary Surgeons, Am Physiologic Soc., Biomed. Urol. Assn., Internat. Continence Soc., Mo. Med. Assn., Mo., Urologic Soc., Pan-Am. Med. Assn., St. Louis Met. Med. Soc., St. Louis Urol. Soc., Societe Internationale D'Urologie, Soc. Univ. Urologists, Urodynamics Soc. (founder, 1st pres.), Am. Arbitration Assn., Am. Coll. Legal Medicine, Mo. Bar Assn., Bar Assn. Met. St. Louis, Mo. Orgn. Def. Lawyers, Urology Lawyers Coun. (founder, pres.). Home: 6412 Mimosa Dr Chapel Hill NC 27514-9059 Personal E-mail: saulboyarsky@gmail.com.

BOYATT, THOMAS DAVID, retired ambassador; b. Cin., Mar. 4, 1933; s. Lynn Craig Haven and Florine (Cloar) B.; m. Maxine Lorraine Shearwood, Dec. 30, 1971; children: Thomas Benton, Christopher Lynn, Jessica Allyn, Alexander Shearwood, Catherine Jordan. BA, Princeton U., 1955, MA, 1956. Vice consul US Dept. State, Antofagasta, Chile, 1960-62; with US Dept. Treasury, 1962-64; 2d sec. Am. Embassy, Luxembourg, 1964-66, 1st sec. Nicosia, Cyprus, 1967-70; dir. Cypriot affairs Near East Bur. US Dept. State, Washington, 1970-74, assigned to Sr. Seminar, 1974-75; dep. chief mission, minister counselor Am. Embassy, Santiago, Chile, 1976-78; US amb. to Upper Volta US Dept. State, Ouagadougou, 1978-80, US amb. to Colombia Bogota, 1980-84; v.p. market devel. Sears World Trade Inc., Washington, 1984-87; ptnr. IRC Group, 1988-96; pres. US Def. Systems, 1990-96; pres., CEO Fgn. Affairs Coun. Trustee Princeton U., 1984-89; bd. dirs. Patterson Sch./U. Ky., Inst. for Study of Diplomacy/Georgetown U.; mem. State Dept. Adv. Com. on Leadership and Mgmt., 2004. 1st lt. SAC, USAF, 1956-59. Decorated Legion d'Honneur (Upper Volta), Gran Cruz Order of San Carlos (Colombia); recipient Meritorious Honor award US Dept. State, 1969, William R. Rivkin award Am. Fgn. Service, 1970, Christian A. Herter award, 1976 Mem.: Am. Fgn. Svc. Assn. (treas.), Washington Inst. Fgn. Affairs (bd. dirs.), Acad. of Diplomacy (bd. dirs.), Am. Fgn. Svc. Assn. (pres. 1971—74, award for post-retirement contbns. to fgn. affairs 1999, Lifetime Achievement award 2001).

BOYCE, BERT ROY, university dean emeritus, library and information science educator; b. Sharon, Pa., Jan. 10, 1938; s. Bert Roy and Julia (Loyd) B.; m. Judith Irene Warren, Aug. 25, 1968; children: Maria Natasha, Gabriel Augustus. BA in History, Marietta Coll., 1959; MS in Libr. Sci., Case Western Res. U., 1968; PhD, Cast Western Res. U., 1972. Asst. dir. Redevel. Authority, Sharon, 1966-67; rsch. analyst info. systems Libr. Congress, Washington, 1968-69; asst. prof. U. Mo., Columbia, 1972-78, chair dept. info. sci., 1976-83; assoc. prof. Sch. Libr. and Info. Sci. La. State U., Baton Rouge, 1983-85, prof. Sch. Libr. and Info. Sci., 1985—, dean Sch. Libr. and Info. Sci., 1990—. Author: Operations Research for Libraries and Information Agencies, 1991, Measurement in Information Science, 1994, Text Information Retrieval Systems, 2d edit., 1999, 3d edit., 2006; contbr. articles to profl. jours. Lt. USN, 1960-66, Vietnam. Sr. Fulbright-Hays scholar, Brazil, 1974. Mem. ALA (Shera Rsch. award 1988), Am. Soc. for Info. Sci. (Outstanding Info. Sci. Tchg. award 1989), La. Libr. Assn., Assn. for Libr. and Info. Sci. Edn. Democrat. Office: La State U Sch Libr and Info Sci 267 Coates Hl Baton Rouge LA 70803-0001 Office Phone: 225-578-3158. Business E-Mail: lsboyc@lsu.edu.

BOYCE, CORRIE MOSBY, music educator; b. Columbia, SC, Apr. 7, 1953; d. Rufus Levi and Emma Jo Mosby; m. W. Ray Boyce, June 21, 1975; 1 child, Ray D'Mitry. BA, Columbia Coll., 1974; MEd, Cambridge Coll., 1995. Tchr. Richland Sch. Dist. 1, Columbia, 1974—; instr. Middle Sch. Sci. Enrichment Program, Benedict Coll., Columbia, 1996—. Cluster leader Keenan Cluster Sch.'s Music Program, Columbia, 1989—90; choral music curriculum com. Richland Sch. Dist. 1, Columbia, 1998; Curriculum Leadership in the Arts participant S.C. State Dept. Edn., Columbia, 2003. Rhomania co-chairperson Beta Epsilon Sigma chpt. Sigma Gamma Rho, 1991—2002. Named Outstanding Club Woman of Yr., S.C. Fedn. of Women and Youth Clubs, Inc., 1990, United Meth. Woman of Yr., I. DeQuincey Newman United Meth. Women, 1995, Living the Legacy honoree, Nat. Coun. Negro Women, Inc., 1998. Mem.: Music Educators Nat. Conf. and affiliates, NEA and affiliates (mem. S.C. del. assembly 1993—98). United Methodist. Home: 204 Torwood Dr Columbia SC 29203 Office: Richland County Sch Dist 1 1616 Richland St Columbia SC 29201 E-mail: corrie0407@aol.com.

BOYCE, DANIEL HOBBS, finance company executive; b. Flint, Mich., Oct. 19, 1953; s. James Edward and Alice Marilyn (Hobbs) B.; m. Suzanne Kay Williams; children: Kenneth C., Geoffrey A., Stephen J. BA, U. Mich., Ann Arbor, 1974; MA, U. Mich., 0979. CFP. Rep. Mut. Svc. Corp., Detroit, 1982-87; br. mgr. Investment Mgmt. & Rsch. Inc., Atlanta, 1987—; co-managing ptnr. Ctr. Fin. Planning Inc., Southfield, Mich., 1988—. V.p. Southworth, Boyce & McFawn Planning Corp., Troy, Mich., 1982-85; owner, fin. planner Daniel H. Boyce Fin. Adv. Svcs., Birmingham, Mich., 1985-88; mem. adj. faculty Coll. Fin. Planning, Denver, 1985-90; mem. adv. coun. cert. program in personal fin. planning Oakland U., Rochester, Mich., 1987-2002; edn. cons. Nat. Ctr. for Fin. Edn., Denver, 1985-2001. Columnist: Money Matters, 1984—86, Personal Fin., 1987—93. Bd. dirs. Great Lakes Chamber Music Festival, 1996-98, Detroit Chamber Winds and Strings, 1992-2003, chmn. bd., 1995-98; trustee Prescott Coll., 2005—, chmn. bd., 2007—; min. music Birmingham Unitarian Ch., 1976-2001, emeritus, 2002—, bd. pres., 2003-04; bd. trustees, Prescott Coll., Ariz., 2005— Named one of Top 200 Fin. Planners in U.S., Money Mag. and Worth Mag., 1987, 1996, 1997, 1998. Mem. Internat. Assn. Fin. Planning (bd. dirs. S.E. Mich. chpt. 1984-87, 89-91), Detroit Soc. Inst. CFPs (pres. 1986-87, chmn. 1987-88). Office: Ctr Fin Planning Inc 40 Oak Hollow St Ste 125 Southfield MI 48033

BOYCE, DAVID S., lawyer; b. Medina, NY, 1949; AB, Cornell U., 1971; MBA, U. Utah, 1973; JD with high honors, U. Fla., 1977; LLM in Taxation, Georgetown U., 1979. Bar: Calif. 1979; cert. tax specialist Calif. Bd. of Legal Specialization. Atty.-adv. Judge Howard A Dawson Jr, US Tax Ct., 1977—79; adj. prof. law Univ. San Diego, 1980—84; now adminstrv. ptnr. LA office Jones Day. Mem.: ABA, Am. Health Lawyers Assn., LA Bar Assn., Order of Coif. Office: Jones Day 555 S Flower St 50th Fl Los Angeles CA 90071 Office Phone: 213-243-2403. Office Fax: 213-243-2539. Business E-Mail: dsboyce@jonesday.com.

BOYCE, DOREEN ELIZABETH, foundation administrator, educator; b. Antofagasta, Chile, Apr. 20, 1934; d. George Edgar and Elsie Winifred Vaughan; m. Alfred Warne Boyce, Aug. 11, 1956; children: Caroline Elizabeth, John Trevor Warne. BA with hons., Oxford U., Eng., 1956, MA with hons., 1960; PhD, U. Pitts., 1983; DHL (hon.), Westminister Coll., 1986, Washington and Jefferson Coll., 1993, Franklin and Marshall Coll., 2005. Lectr. and tutor in econs. U. Witwatersrand, South Africa, 1960-62; provost and dean of faculty, Mary Helen Marks prof. econs. Chatham Coll., Pitts., 1963-79; prof. econs., chmn. dept. econs. and mgmt. Hood Coll., Frederick, Md., 1979-82; pres. Buhl Found., Pitts., 1982—. Dir. and vice chair DQE Duquesne Light Co., Dollar Bank, FSB, Coun. Ind. Colls., Carnegie Mus.; co-founder, dir. Microbac Labs., Inc.; Pa. Gov.'s Sports and Exposition Facilities Task Force, 1995; del. White House Conf. on Small Bus., 1980; mem. Gov.'s Conf. Small Bus., 1979-82; mem. devel. com. Somerville Coll., Eng., 2005—, mem. appeal com. Chmn. bd. dir., emerita trustee Franklin and Marshall Coll., 1982-04, Frick Edn. Commn., 1980-94, Carnegie Sci. Ctr., 1982—, Carnegie Inst., 2005-; mem. Fed.Jud. Nominating Commn., 1977-79, Pa. Gov.'s Commn. on Financing of Higher Edn., 1983-85; bd. dir. World Affairs Coun., 1984-96. Recipient Medallion of Distinction, U. Pitts., 1987, Univ. Laureate, U. Pitts., 2004; named Disting. Dau. Pa., 1996, Hon. Fellow Somerville Coll., U. Oxford, Women Who Make A Difference award, Internat. Women's Forum, 1998. Mem. Am. Econs. Assn., Am. Assn. Higher Edn., Grantmakers of Western Pa. (pres. 1984), Internat. Women's Forum, Assn. Governing Bds. Univ. and Coll. (coun. bd. chairs 2002—), Duquesne Club (bd. dirs. 2000-03, chmn. found. 2005-). Office: Centre City Tower 650 Smithfield St Ste 2300 Pittsburgh PA 15222-3912

BOYCE, EMILY STEWART, retired library and information scientist, educator; b. Raleigh, NC, Aug. 18, 1933; d. Harry and May (Fallon) B. BS, East Carolina U., 1955, MA, 1961; MS in Libr. Sci., U. N.C., 1968; postgrad., Cath. U. Am., 1977. Libr. Tileston Jr. H.S., Wilmington, NC, 1955-57; children's libr. Wilmington Pub. Libr., 1957-58; asst. libr. Joyner Libr. East Carolina U., Greenville, NC, 1959-61, libr. III, 1962-63; ednl. supr. II ednl. media divsn. N.C. State Dept. Pub. Instrn., Raleigh, 1961-62; assoc. prof. dept. libr. and info. scis. East Carolina U., 1964-76, prof., 1976-92, chmn. dept., 1982-89; retired, 1992. Cons. So. Assn. Colls. and Schs., Raleigh, 1975-92. Active Asheville YWCA, Mediation Ctr., Botanical Gardens, Literacy Coun. Buncombe County. Mem. ALA, AAUW, N.C. Libr. Assn., Assn. Libr. and Info. Sci. Educators, Spl. Librs. Assn. Democrat. Home: 3000 Galloway Ridge C107 Pittsboro NC 27312 Personal E-mail: esboyce107@nc.rr.com.

BOYCE, GREGORY H., energy executive; b. 1954; BS in Mining Engring., U. Ariz., 1976; completed advanced mgmt. prog., Grad. Sch. Bus., Harvard U. Exec. asst. to vice chmn. Std. Oil of Ohio, 1983—84; dir. Govt. & Pub. Affairs Kennecott Corp., pres. Kennecott Minerals Co., 1993—94, pres., CEO Kennecott Energy Co., 1994—99; CEO energy Rio Tinto PLC, 2000—03; pres., COO Peabody Energy Corp., 2003—05, pres., CEO, 2006—. Mem. Coal Industry Adv. Bd. Internat. Energy Agy.; past bd. mem. Ctr. Energy & Econ. Devel., Western Regional Coun., Nat. Coal Coun., Mountain States Employers Coun., Wyo. Bus. Coun. Bd. dirs. St. Louis Regional Chamber and Growth Assn. Mem.: Nat. Mining Assn. (past bd. mem.). Office: Peabody Energy Corp 701 Market St Saint Louis MO 63101-1826 Office Phone: 314-342-7574. Office Fax: 314-342-7720. E-mail: gboyce@peabodyenergy.com.*

BOYCE, JOSEPH NELSON, retired journalist, consultant, educator; b. New Orleans, Apr. 18, 1937; s. John and Sadie (Nelson) B.; m. Carol Hill, Dec. 21, 1968; children: Leslie, Nelson, Joel, Beverly. Student, Roosevelt U., Chgo., 1955-65, John Marshall Law Sch., 1965-67. Mem. Chgo. Police Dept., 1961-66; reporter Chgo. Tribune, 1966-70; corr. Time mag., 1970-73, chief San Francisco bur., 1973-79, chief So. U.S. bur., 1979-85, dep. chief Eastern U.S. bur., 1985-87; sr. editor Wall St. Jour., 1987-98, ret., 1998; media rels. cons. Dow Jones/Wall St. Jour., 1998—. Rotating faculty mem., summer program for minority journalists U. Calif., Berkeley, 1986, Berkeley, 87, Berkeley, 88, Berkeley, 89; bd. dirs. Jazzmobile, Inc., NYC; guest lectr. various colls. and univs.; vis. faculty summer program for minority journalists U. Ala.; vis. faculty Poynter Inst., 1993; William Randolph Hearst vis. prof.-in-residence Howard U., 1996; mem. adv. bd. Lyndon B. Johnson Sch. of Public Affairs U. Tex., Austin, 1998—; adj. prof. Sch. Journalism Columbia U., NYC, 1999, Ind. U., Indpls., 2002, 05, 06, 07. Chmn. Marin County Black Leadership Forum, 1974-75; mem. Marin Justice Coun., 1977-78; bd. dirs. Jazzmobile, 1991-95. With USNR. Recipient Outstanding Black Achiever award Met. YMCA, NYC, 1975, Alvin S. Bynum Mentor award IUPUI, 2006; co-recipient Unity In Media award Lincoln U., 1975; Time Mag.-Duke U. fellow, 1981-82. Mem. NAACP, Nat. Assn. Black Journalists, Nat. Assn. Minority Media Execs. (bd. dirs. 1991-93), Soc. Profl. Journalists (Indpls. chpt. bd. dirs., pres. 2003-04). Episcopalian. Personal E-mail: boycevibe@aol.com.

BOYCE, MARIA WYCKOFF, lawyer; b. Houston, Tex., Aug. 30, 1963; BA cum laude, Conn. Coll., 1985; JD, Northwestern Univ., 1988. Bar: Tex. 1988, US Dist. Ct. (so., ea., no., we. dist. Tex., Colo.), US Ct. Appeals 5th cir., US Supreme Ct. Ptnr. litigation dept. & mem. exec. com. Baker Botts LLP, Houston. Editor (in chief): Jour. Criminal Law & Criminology. Mem. adv. bd. Girls Inc. of Greater Houston; bd. dir., Houston chpt. Tex. Gen. Counsel Forum. Mem.: Am. Intellectual Property Law Assn., Houston Bar Assn., Fed. Bar Assn. (pres.elect). Office: Baker Botts LLP One Shell Plz 910 Louisiana St Houston TX 77002-4995 Office Phone: 713-229-1922. Office Fax: 713-229-2722. Business E-Mail: maria.boyce@bakerbotts.com.

BOYCE, RALPH L. (SKIP BOYCE), ambassador; b. Washington, Feb. 1, 1952; married; 2 children. BA, George Washington U., 1974; MPA, Princeton U., 1976. Staff asst. to amb. US Fgn. Svc., Tehran, Iran, 1977—79, comml. attache Tunis, Tunisia, 1979—81, fin. economist Islamabad, Pakistan, 1981—84; spl. asst. to dep. sec. US Dept. State, Washington, 1984—88, polit. counselor Bangkok, 1988—92, dep. chief of mission Singapore, 1992—93, charge d'affaires, 1993—94, dep. chief of mission Bangkok, 1994—98, dep. asst. sec. for East Asia and Pacific Affairs Washington, 1998—2001, US amb. to Indonesia Jakarta, Indonesia, 2001—04, US amb. to Thailand Bangkok, 2004—. Recipient Disting. User of Thai Lang. award, Govt. Thailand, 2007. Fluent in Persian, French, and Thai. Office: DOS Amb 7200 Bangkok Pl Washington DC 20521*

BOYD, ARTHUR BERNETTE, JR., surgeon, clergyman, beverage company executive; b. Durham, NC, June 29, 1947; s. Arthur Bernette and Mammie Lee (Chalmers) B.; m. Delphine Victoria Huffman, Mar. 14, 1981; children: Arthur III, Vicki BA, Fla. A&M U., 1969; postgrad., NYU, 1970; MD, Meharry Med. Coll., 1978; postgrad., U. N.C., Chapel Hill, 1998. Cert. ATLS instr., PALS. Intern surgery Howard U. Hosp., Washington, 1978—80; resident and chief resident surgery St. Luke's Hosp., Cleve., 1981—84; fellow liver transplant U. Pitts., 1984—85; chief surgeon, pres. Phoenix Med. Surg. Svc., Inc., Cleve., Caribbean, 1986—. Adj. prof. anatomy and physiology Cuyhoga C.C., Cleve., 1988—; cons. surgeon other hosps. and physicians, Cleve., 1988—; continuing med. educator dept. surgery Case We. Res. U. Sch. Medicine, Cleve., 1997-98; faculty med. bd. profl. preparation course U. Mo., Kansas City, 1997; chief adminstrv. fellow trauma, surg. critical care R.A. Cowley Shock Trauma Ctr., U. Md. Med. Sys., 1993-94, clin. instr. surgery, sr. trauma fellow, 1994-96; clin. instr. surgery, sr. fellow, traumatologist, Baltimore County, 1994—; co-traumatologist Prince George Cmty. Hosp., Cheverly, Md., 1994-95; pres., CEO Motown Beverage Co. Ohio, Cleve., 1998—, Towne Club Internat. Ohio, Inc., Cleve., 1998—, Nat. Fin. Group, Inc., Cleve., 1997—; pres., CEO, chmn. Star Beverage Corp., Shaker Heights, Ohio, 1997 Inventor: wheelchair with mechanism to raise or lower left or right buttocks of person, hemostat that carries two sutures, synthetic covering with zipper to cover bowel when abdomen unable to be closed after surgery Vol. Cleve. Cmty. Action Against Addiction, 1987-88; mentor Case We. U. Inner City Program, Cleve., 1988—; judge honors sci. projects Shaker Heights Mid. Sch., 1998; mem. Shaker Heights Cmty. Leaders Meetings Fellow ACS (assoc.), Internat. Coll. Surgeons; mem. AAAS, AMA, N.Y. Acad. Scis., Nat. Med. Assn. (mentor 1990—), Assn. Black Cardiologists, Ohio State Med. Soc., Cleve. Surg. Soc., Nat. Assn. Small Bus. Owners, Internat. Assn. Small Bus. Owners, Greater Cleve. Ministers Alliance, Masons, Omega Psi Phi, Alpha Phi Omega Democrat. Methodist. Avocations: reading, sports, golf. Home and Office: Motown Beverage Co 3277 Lee Rd Cleveland OH 44120-3451 Office: Star Beverage 3277 Lee Rd Cleveland OH 44120-3451 Office Phone: 216-991-4799. Personal E-mail: aboydstar@aol.com.

BOYD, BENJAMIN S., lawyer; b. Springfield, Mo., Nov. 1, 1961; BA, BA, Univ. Ark., 1984, JD with high honors, 1987. Bar: Ark. 1987, Va. 1988, DC 1988, Md. 1991, US Dist. Ct. (DC, ea. & we. Va., Md., Colo. dist.), US Ct. Appeals (9th, DC cir.), US Supreme Ct. Ptnr., Nat. Hiring co-chmn. DLA Piper Rudnick Gray Cary, Washington. Office: DLA Piper Rudnick Gray Cary 1200 19th St NW Washington DC 20036-2412 Office Phone: 202-861-3942. Office Fax: 202-223-2085. Business E-Mail: benjamin.boyd@dlapiper.com.

BOYD, CAROLYN PATRICIA, history professor; b. San Diego, June 1, 1944; d. Peter James and Patricia Mae (de Soucy) B.; m. Frank Dawson Bean, Jan. 4, 1975; children: Peter Justin Bean, Michael Franklin Bean. AB with great distinction and with honors in History, Stanford U., 1966; MA, U. Wash., 1969, PhD, 1974. Tchg. asst. dept. history U. Wash., 1970-71; from instr. to prof. dept. history U. Tex., Austin, 1973-95, prof. history, 1995-99, assoc. dean Grad. Studies, 1986-88, 90-92, chair history dept., 1994-99; dir. univ. honors program, assoc. prof. history U. Md., College Park, 1989-90; prof. history U. Calif., Irvine, 1999—, chair history dept., 2004—06, dean Grad. Studies, 2006—. Lectr. in field. Author: Praetorian Politics in Liberal Spain, 1979, La política pretoriana en el reinado de Alfonso XIII, 1990, Historia Patria: Politics, History and National Identity in Spain, 1875-1975, 1997, Spanish edit., 2000, Religion y politica en la Espana contemporanea, 2007; mem. editl. bd. Essays, 1992-95, Ayer, 2005-; author chpts. to books; contbr. articles to profl. jours. Recipient Summer award U. Tex. Rsch. Inst., 1997; Woodrow Wilson hon. fellow, 1966, Fulbright-Hays fellow, 1966-67, NDEA Title IV fellow, 1968-72, AAUW fellow, 1972-73, ACLS fellow, 1985; ACLS Grant-in-Aid, 1977, Am. Philos. Soc. grant, 1978, URI Rsch. grant, 1985, New Del Amo Program grant, 2000-02; fellow Woodrow Wilson Internat. Ctr. for Scholars, 2002-03. Mem. Am. Hist. Assn. (James Harvey Robinson prize com. 1992-94, John Fagg prize com. 2001-03), Soc. Spanish and Portugese Hist. Studies (gen. sec. 2000-04, mem. exec. com. 1978-80, 83-85, 96-98, chair local arrangements, program chmn. conf. 1987), Coun. European Studies, Internat. Inst. in Spain, Assn. Contemporary History. Office: U Calif Irvine Office Grad Studies Irvine CA 92697-0001 Business E-Mail: cpboyd@uci.edu.

BOYD, DANA KRISTIN, elementary school educator; Tchr. to lead tchr. Dolphin Terrace Elem. Sch., El Paso, Tex., 2000—06, asst. prin., 2006—. Named Tex. Tchr. of Yr., 2007. Avocation: running. Office: Dolphin Terrace Elem Sch 9700 Pickerel El Paso TX 79924 Office Phone: 915-434-6502. Office Fax: 915-757-8073. Business E-Mail: dboyd@yisd.net.*

BOYD, DAVID PRESTON, business educator; b. NYC, Oct. 19, 1943; s. David Preston and Mignon (Finch) B.; m. Sally Sparks, Sept. 9, 1989. BA in English Lit., Harvard U., 1965; DPhil in Behavioral Scis., Oxford U., 1973. Asst. headmaster Dedham (Mass.) Country Day Sch., 1965-69; co-owner the Old Cambridge (Mass.) Co., 1973-77; instr. coll. bus. adminstrn. Northeastern U., Boston, 1977-78, asst. prof., 1978-82, assoc. prof., 1982-87, Patrick F. and Helen C. Walsh rsch. prof., 1985-86, chmn. human resources mgmt. dept., 1986-87, prof., 1987—, acting dean, 1987, dean coll. and grad. sch. bus. adminstrn., 1987-94. Author: Elites and Their Education National Foundation for Educational Research, 1973; mem. editl. bd. Internat. Jour. Value-Based Mgmt., Cross-cultural Mgmt.; contbr. articles to profl. jours. Past trustee Pine Manor Coll.; corporator Brookline Bancorp. Recipient Excellence in Teaching award Northeastern U., 1980; Northeastern U. grantee, 1982-84, Control Data Corp., 1983, NYU, 1985. Fellow Mass. Hist. Soc.; mem. Soc. Colonial Wars, S.R., Oxford Soc., Tennis and Racquet Club, Somerset Club, Mass Hort. Soc. (former trustee), Comml. Club, Beta Gamma Sigma, Phi Kappa Phi. Home: 14 Bristol Rd Wellesley Hills MA 02481-2727 Office: Northeastern U 304 Hayden Hall Boston MA 02115-5000 Office Phone: 617-373-4727. Business E-Mail: d.boyd@neu.edu.

BOYD, DEBORAH ANN, pediatrician; b. Urbana, Ohio, Jan. 30, 1955; d. John A. Sr. and Juanita Jean (Routt) B. BA cum laude, Wittenberg U., 1977; MD, U. Cin., 1982. Diplomate Am. Bd. Pediatrics, Nat. Bd. Med. Examiners. Intern Children's Hosp. Med. Ctr., Cin., 1982—83, pediat. resident, 1982—85; pediatrician Nat. Health Svc. Corps, Springfield, Ohio, 1985—89; former pediatrician Cmty. Hosp. Health Care Ctr., Springfield, 1989—97; staff pediat. primary care ctr., clin. faculty Children's Hosp. Med. Ctr., Cin., 1998—. Mem. Continuing med. edn. com. Mercy Med. Ctr., Springfield, 1989—, infection control com., 1987—. Adv. com. Miami Valley Child Devl. Ctr., Springfield, 1985—, New Parents as Tchrs., 1986—. Mem. Assn. of Clinicians for the Underserved, Am. Acad. Pediats., Ambulatory Pediat. Assn. Democratic. Avocations: bicycling, photography, basketball, music, church activities. Home: 12132 S Pine Dr Apt 240 Cincinnati OH 45241-1743 Office: Dept Gen Com Pediatrics Children's Hosp Med Ctr 3333 Burnet Ave Fl 4 Cincinnati OH 45229-3026 Office Phone: 513-636-7594.

BOYD, DERRICK S., lawyer; b. Plainview, Tex., Dec. 18, 1968; m. Cheri Boyd; 2 children. BA, U. Tex., Austin, 1991, JD, 1994. Cert.: Tex. Bd. Legal Specialization (civil trial specialist), bar: Tex. 1994. Ptnr. Simpson, Boyd & Powers, P.L.L.C., Decatur, Tex. Named a Rising Star, Tex. Super Lawyers mag., 2006. Mem.: Million Dollar Advocates Forum, Assn. Trial Lawyers of Am., State Bar Tex. (mem. unauthorized practice of law com., dist. 7), ABA (mem. antitrust sect.), Wise County Bar Assn. Office: Simpson Boyd & Powers PLLC PO Box 957 Decatur TX 76234 Office Phone: 940-627-8308.*

BOYD, DONNA CATHERINE, physical anthropologist, educator; b. Johnson City, Tenn., June 15, 1960; d. Robert Hartsell Markland and Mary Geraldine Hensley Hurd; m. Charles Clifford Boyd, Jr., June 7, 1980; children: Merritt, Emily, Forrest. BA, U. Tenn., Knoxville, 1981, MA, 1984, PhD, 1988. Asst.prof. anthropology Radford U., Va., 1989-95, assoc. prof. Va., 1995—98, prof. anthropology Va., 1998—. Adj. mem. Va. Med. Examiner's Office, We. Dist., 1999—; phys. anthropology cons. Dept. Historic Resources, Richmond, Va., 1991—, James River Inst. for Archaeology, Williamsburg, Va., 1993—, Louis Berger & Assocs., Richmond, 1996—; mem. ann. edits. adv. bd. Dushkin Pub. Group, Sluice Dock, Guilford, Conn., 1992—; guest spkr. in field. Contbr. articles to profl. jours. Recipient Va. Outstanding Prof. Award, State Coun. of Higher Edn. for Va., 2006, US Professors of Yr. Award for Outstanding Master's Universities and Colleges Prof., Carnegie Found. for Advancement of Tchg. and Coun. for Advancement and Support of Edn., 2006; Radford U. Found. grantee, 1990. Mem. Am. Assn. Phys. Anthropologists, Va. Acad. Sci., Sigma Xi, Phi Kappa Phi. Achievements include conducting anthropological research on hundreds of prehistoric and historic human skeletons representing more than 30 different projects, documenting the health, illnesses and demographic characteristics of prehistoric and historic Virginians. Office: Radford U 0212 Young Hall Box 6948 Radford VA 24141 Home: 489 Easter Creek Rd, NW Riner VA 24149 Office Phone: 540-831-5856. E-mail: doboyd@radford.edu.*

BOYD, EARL E., JR., councilman; b. Shoals, Ind., Aug. 29, 1943; s. Earl Ernest and Mary Louise (McCauley) Boyd; m. Barbara Jean Chattin, June 22, 1963; children: Wesley, Theresa, Kevin, Rebecca, Brian. Councilman Town of Shoals, Ind., 1996—; precinct committeeman Martin County Rep. Ctrl. Com., Shoals, Ind., 1993—, county chmn., 1997—. Named Ky. Col., Gov. Ky., 2000. Mem.: Eagles (pres. 1997—98). Home: PO Box 627 8th St Shoals IN 47581 Office: Martin County Rep Ctrl Cm 206 4th Shoals IN 47581

BOYD, F. ALLEN, JR., congressman, farmer; b. Valdosta, Ga., June 6, 1945; m. Cissy Boyd; children: David, John, Suzanne. BA, Fla. State U., 1969. Mem. Fla. Ho. of Reps., 1989—97, US Congress from 2d Fla. dist., 1997—, mem. appropriations com., mem. mil. constrn. and the agr. com., mem. rural devel. com., mem. food and drug adminstrn. Chmn. Fla. House Dem. Conservative Caucus. With US Army, 1969—71. Democrat. Office: US Ho Reps 1227 Longworth Ho Office Bldg Washington DC 20515-0902*

BOYD, JAMES ROBERT, energy executive; b. Nashville, July 29, 1946; s. James Clinton and Mary Avon (Motlow) B.; m. Elise White, June 27, 1970; children: Elizabeth, Mary Franklin. BSEE, U. Ky., 1969; MBA, NYU, 1972. Sales engr. Westinghouse Electric Co., NYC and St. Louis, 1970-75, mgr. generation sales St. Louis, 1975-77, cons. planning Pitts., 1977-79, mgr. div. planning, 1979-81; mgr. strategic planning Ashland (Ky.) Oil Co., 1982-84, dir. corp. planning, 1984-86, sr. v.p., group oper. officer, 1989—2002; sr. v.p. adminstrn. Ashland Exploration, Houston, 1986-87, pres., 1987-89. Chmn. bd. dirs. Arch Coal Inc., 1998—; bd. dirs. Farmers Bank, Halliburton, Inc. Avocations: golf, hunting, swimming. Office: 2333 Alexandria Dr Ste 134 Lexington KY 40504 Office Phone: 859-514-6013.

BOYD, JEFFERY HAWTHORNE, travel company executive, lawyer; b. NYC, Aug. 7, 1956; s. John Scudder and Ann Lewis (Taylor) B.; m. Teresa Mary Gage, June 26, 1982; children: Jeffery Hawthorne Jr., Valerie Gate, Allyson Taylor. BA summa cum laude, St. Lawrence U., 1978; JD summa cum laude, Cornell U., 1981. Bar: N.Y. 1982, Conn. 1988, U.S. Dist. Ct. (so. dist.) N.Y. 1982. Assoc. Sullivan & Cromwell, NYC, 1981-88; resident assoc. Melbourne, Australia, 1983-85; ptnr. Robinson & Cole, Stamford, Conn., 1988—; asst. gen. counsel Lord, Abbett & Co.; exec. v.p., gen. counsel Oxford Health Plans, priceline.com Inc., Norwalk, Conn., 2000, COO, 2000—02, pres., co-CEO, 2002, pres., CEO, 2002—. Article editor Cornell Law Rev., 1980-81. Mem. ABA, N.Y. Bar Assn. (sec. corps. com. 1985-88), Conn. Bar Assn., Stanwich Club, Order of Coif, Phi Beta Kappa. Republican. Episcopalian. Avocations: fly fishing, lacrosse, skiing, tennis, golf. Office: priceline 800 Connecticut Ave Norwalk CT 06854*

BOYD, JOHN W., JR., farmer, association executive; b. NYC; Farmer, 1983—; pres., founder Nat. Black Farmers Assn., 1995—. Named one of 100 Most Influential Black Americans, Ebony mag., 2006. Achievements include founded the association to fight the racism in the USDA loan programs; led class action law suit of 1000 black farmers against the USDA in 1997 that led to a historic agreement in 1999; Staged a protest in 2003 on behalf of black farmers by traveling 200-plus miles from his farm in Virginia to Washington on a wagon pulled by his two mules, Struggle and 40 Acres. Office: Nat Black Farmers Assn 68 Wind Rd Baskerville VA 23915 Office Phone: 434-848-1865.

BOYD, JOSEPH ARTHUR, JR., lawyer; b. Hoschton, Ga., Nov. 16, 1916; s. Joseph Arthur and Esther Estelle (Puckett) B.; m. Ann Stripling, June 6, 1938; children: Joanne Louise Boyd Goldman, Betty Jean Boyd Jala, Joseph Robert, James Daniel, Jane N. Ohlin. Student, Piedmont Coll., Demorest, Ga., 1936-38, LLD, 1963; student, Mercer U., Macon, Ga., 1938-39; JD, U. Miami, Coral Gables, Fla., 1948; LLD, Western State U. Coll. Law, San Diego, 1981. Bar: Fla. 1948, U.S. Supreme Ct. 1959, D.C. 1973, N.Y. 1982. Practice law, Hialeah, 1948-68; city atty., 1951-58; mem. Dade County Commn., Miami, Fla., 1958-68, chmn., 1963; vice mayor Dade County, 1967; justice Fla. Supreme Ct., Tallahassee, 1969-87, chief justice, 1984-86. Mem. Hialeah Zoning Bd., 1946-48; juror Freedoms Found., Valley Forge, Pa., 1971, 73 Bd. dirs. Bapt. Hosp., Miami, 1962-66, Miami Coun. Chs., 1960-64; emeritus trustee Piedmont Coll. Recipient Nat. Top Hat award Bus. and Profl. Women in U.S. for advancing status of employed women, 1967 Mem. ABA, Fla. Bar Assn., Hialeah-Miami Springs Bar Assn. (pres. 1955), Tallahassee Bar Assn., Hialeah-Miami Springs C. of C. (pres. 1956), Am. Legion (comdr. Fla. 1953-54), VFW, Shriners, Masons (33 deg.), Lions, Elks, Iron Arrow, Phi Alpha Delta. Democrat. Baptist (deacon).

BOYD, JOSEPH DON, diversified financial services company executive; b. Muncie, Ind., Jan. 22, 1926; s. Joseph Corneluis and Waneta May (Barrett) B.; m. Cynthia Reiley, Dec. 28, 1957; children— Jane Elizabeth, Craig A., Michael J. AB (Rector scholar), DePauw U., 1948; MA, Northwestern U., 1950, Ed.D., 1955. Ednl. asst. First Meth. Ch., Anderson, Ind., 1948-49; residence hall counselor Northwestern U., Evanston, Ill., 1949-50, univ. examiner, instr. edn., guidance lab. asst., 1952-54, dean men, asst. prof. edn., 1955-61; exec. dir. Ill. Scholarship Commn., 1961-80; dir. instnl. relations and research Nat. Coll. Edn., Evanston, 1981-84; pres. Joseph D. Boyd & Assocs., Deerfield, Ill., 1984—. Residence hall dir., head tennis coach, asst. basketball coach Albion Coll., 1950-52 Mem. Nat. Assn. Adminstrs. State Scholarship Programs, Phi Delta Kappa, Delta Tau Delta, Phi Eta Sigma. Clubs: Rotarian. Methodist. Home: 1232 Warrington Rd Deerfield IL 60015-3145 Office: 600 Deerfield Rd Deerfield IL 60015-3229 Business E-Mail: jboyd@christumcdeerfield.org.

BOYD, KELLY A., lawyer, educator; d. JoAnn M and adopted d. Jerry R Holsbeck, Ralph Potteiger; m. Jeffrey A Boyd, June 16, 1984; children: Amber N, Tiffany M. JD, William Mitchell Coll. of Law, St. Paul, 2000. Bar: Minn. 2000, Wis. 2000. Atty. Soucie & Bolt, Anoka, Minn., 2000—05, Kelly A. Boyd Law Office, LLC, Roseville, Minn., 2005, Henningson & Snoxell, LTD., Maple Grove, Minn., 2006—. Vol. Cross of Hope Luth. Ch., Ramsey, Minn., 2000—. Mem.: ATLA, Hennepin County Bar Assn., Minn. State Bar Assoc, Minn. Trial Lawyers Assoc (chair 2002—04). Office: Henningson & Snoxell LTD 200 6900 Wedgwood Rd Osseo MN 55311 Office Phone: 763-560-5700. Office Fax: 763-560-0119. Business E-Mail: kboyd@hennsnoxlaw.com.

BOYD, LARRY C., information technology executive; married; 2 children. B in Polit. Sci., Stanford U., JD. Ptnr. Gibson, Dunn & Crutcher, 1985—99; sr. v.p. legal svcs. U.S. Ingram Micro Inc., Santa Ana, Calif., 2000—04, sr. v.p., sec., gen. counsel, 2004—. Mem.: ABA, Orange County Bar Assn., State Bar Calif. Office: Ingram Micro Inc 1600 E St Andrew Pl PO Box 25125 Santa Ana CA 92799-5125 Office Phone: 714-566-1000.*

BOYD, LORRAINE ALISON, finance educator; b. St. Stephen, Canada, Sept. 15, 1948; arrived in US, 1995; d. Garnet Allison and Diana Hartley Boyd; m. Ronald Allan Eden (div.); 1 child, Jessica Lynn Eden; m. Charles Frazer Hermann, July 8, 1995. BA with honor in econ., Mount Allison U., Canada, 1970; MA in econ., McGill U., Canada, 1973; PhD with dist. in econ., Dalhousie U., Canada, 1976. Lectr. Mt. St. Vincent U., Dept. of Econ., Halifax, Canada, 1971—74, asst. prof., 1976—80; asst. prof. to assoc. Brock U., Dept. Econ., St. Catharines, 1980—88; assoc. prof. to prof. The Norman Paterson Sch. of Internat. Affairs, Carleton U., Ottawa, 1988—95; vis. prof. Kennedy Sch. Gov., Harvard U., Cambridge, Mass., 1992—93; assoc. prof. Tex. A & M U., Dept. Mgmt., Coll. Station, Tex., 1995—2002; adj. prof. Tex. A&M U., George Bush Sch. of Gov. and Pub. Svc., College Station, Tex., 1997—; prof. Tex. A&M Dept. of Mgmt., College Station, 2002—; adj. rsch. prof. Carleton U., Norman Paterson Sch. of Internat. Affairs, Ottawa, Canada, 1995—2003; vis. prof. U. Tex., Dept. Mgmt., Austin, Tex., 2004—05. Exec. tng. Canada Customs and Revenue Agency, Ottawa, Canada, 1990—; cons. Industry Canada, Ottawa, Canada, 1990—, Bur. of Labor Statistics, US Dept. of Labor, Wash., DC, 1999—; owner, tax transfer pricing cons. firm Eden Cons., Ottawa, Canada, 1988—95, Coll. Station, Tex., 1995—. Co-editor: Multinationals and Transfer Pricing, 1985; editor: Retrospectives on Public Finance, 1991; contbr. articles various profl. jours.; co-editor: Multinationals in the Global Political Economy, 1993; editor: Multinationals in North America, 1994; author: Taxing Mutnationals: Transfer Pricing and Corporate Income Taxation in North America, 1998; co-editor: Growth, Multinationals and Governance, 2005. Founder, pres. Canadian Women Economists Network, 1991; co-founder, sec. Active Learning in Internat. Affairs, 1995; founder, pres. Women in the Acad. of Internat. Bus., 2001. Recipient Gov. General's medal, Gov. Canada, 1966; Doctoral fellowship, Canada Coun., 1974, Killam Found., 1974, Rsch. grant, Social Scis. and Humanities Rsch. Coun., 1984, 1987, Faculty fellowship, Pew Found., 1991, Rsch. grant, Social Scis. and Humanities Rsch. Coun. of Canada, 1991, Canada-US Fulbright Rsch. fellowship, Found. for Edl. Exchange between Canada and The USA, 1992, various other fellowships. Mem.: Internat. Studies Assn., Acad. of Mgmt., Acad. of Internat. Bus., Am. Econ. Assn., Canadian Econ. Assn., Internat. Inst. of Pub. Fin. Office: Tex A&M U Dept Mgmt Tamu 4221 423B Webner Bldg College Station TX 77843-4221 Office Phone: 979-862-4053. E-mail: leden@tamu.edu.

BOYD, MALCOLM, minister, writer; b. Buffalo, June 8, 1923; s. Melville and Beatrice (Lowrie) B.; life ptnr. Mark Thompson. BA, U. Ariz., 1944; B.D., Ch. Div. Sch. Pacific, 1954; postgrad., Oxford U., Eng., 1955; S.T.M., Union Theol. Sem., NYC, 1956; DD (hon.), Ch. Div. Sch. of Pacific, 1995. Ordained to ministry Episcopal Ch., 1955. V.p., gen. mgr. Pickford, Rogers & Boyd, 1949-51; rector in Indpls., 1957-59; chaplain Colo. State U., 1959-61, Wayne State U., 1961-65; nat. field rep. Episcopal Soc. Cultural and Racial Unity, 1965-68; resident fellow Calhoun Coll., Yale U., 1968-71, assoc. fellow, 1971—; writer-priest in residence St. Augustine-by-the Sea Episcopal Ch., 1982-95. Lectr. World Council Chs., Switzerland, 1955, 64; columnist Pitts. Courier, 1962-65; resident guest Mishkenot Sha'ananim, Jerusalem, 1974; chaplain AIDS Commn. Episcopal Diocese L.A., 1989—; poet-in-residence Cathedral Ctr. of St. Paul, L.A., 1996—, hon. canon, 2002; mem. adv. bd. White Crane Inst., 2007. Host (TV) Sex in the Seventies, LA, 1975; author: Crisis in Communication, 1957, Christ and Celebrity Gods, 1958, Focus, 1960, rev. edit., 2001, If I Go Down to Hell, 1962, The Hunger, The Thirst, 1964, Are You Running with Me, Jesus?, 1965, rev. edit., 1990, 40th anniv. rev. edit., 2006, Free to Live, Free to Die, 1967, Book of Days, 1968, As I Live and Breathe: Stages of an Autobiography, 1969, The Fantasy Worlds of Peter Stone, 1969, My Fellow Americans, 1970, Human Like Me, Jesus, 1971, The Lover, 1972, When in the Course of Human Events, 1973, The Runner, 1974, The Alleluia Affair, 1975, Christian, 1975, Am I Running with You, God?, 1977, Take Off the Masks, 1978, rev. edit. 2007, Look Back in Joy, 1981, rev. edit., 2007, Half Laughing, Half Crying, 1986, Gay Priest: An Inner Journey, 1986, Edges, Boundaries and Connections, 1992, Rich with Years, 1993, Go Gentle Into That Good Night, 1998, Running with Jesus: The Prayers of Malcolm Boyd, 2000, Simple Grace: A Mentor's Guide to Growing Older, 2001, Prayers for the Later Years, 2002; plays Boy, 1961, Study in Color, 1962, The Community, 1964, others; editor: On the Battle Lines, 1964, The Underground Church, 1968, (with Nancy L. Wilson) Amazing Grace: Stories of Gay and Lesbian Faith, 1991; (with Chester Talton) Race and Prayer: Collected Voices, Many Dreams, 2003, (with J. Jon Bruno) In Times Like These--How We Pray, 2005; book reviewer: LA Times, 1979-85; contbg. editor, columnist Episcopal News; columnist Modern Maturity, 1990-2000; contbr. articles to popular mags. including Newsday, Parade, The Advocate, also newspapers. Active voter registration, Miss., Ala., 1963, 64; mem. Los Angeles City/County AIDS Task Force. Malcolm Boyd Collection and Archives established Boston U., 1973; recipient Integrity Internat. award, 1978, Union Am. Hebrew Congregations award, 1980, Lazarus Project award, 2002, Louie Crew award for svc. to gay and lesbian people, 2003, Giants of Justice award Clergy and Laity United for Econ. Justice, 2004, Unitas award, Union Theol. Sem., NYC., 2005. Mem. Nat. Council Chs. (film awards com. 1965), P.E.N. (pres. PEN Ctr. U.S. West 1984-87), Am. Center, Authors Guild, Integrity, Nat. Gay Task Force, Clergy and Laity Concerned (nat. bd.), NAACP, Amnesty Internat., Episc. Peace Fellowship, Fellowship of Reconciliation (nat. com.). Episcopalian. Office: PO Box 512164 Los Angeles CA 90051-0164 Business E-Mail: malcolmboyd@ladiocese.org. *The years have taught me the cost of getting involved in life. It is all a risk. One is on stage in an ever-new set without a script. The floor may give way without warning, the walls abruptly cave in. One may die at the hand of an assassin acting on blind impulse. Security, for which men sell their souls, is one of the few real jests in life. Yet the cost of not getting involved in life is higher; one has merely died prematurely. When one has stripped power of its mystique, its robes and artifices, it becomes vulnerable. When you stand up to power, you stand up to one or more individuals. Look an individual, then, in the eye, laugh, if you feel like it. This may be rightly received as a much-needed expression of human solidarity.*

BOYD, MARY FRANCES, retired school nurse, pastor; b. Stockton, Md., Feb. 18, 1944; d. Alonzo Willard and Polly Frances Wilson; m. Eddie Boyd, July 29, 1972; children: Nathanael Ivan, Stephen Eddie. RN Salisbury U., 1965. Staff nurse Peninsula Gen. Hosp., Salisbury, Md., 1965—67; sch. nurse Wicomico City Bd. Edn., Salisbury, 1967—68, 1975—82, Worcester County Bd. Edn., Newark, Md., 1985—2006; indsl. nurse Buddy Bay Processing Plant, Snow Hill, Md., 1968—74, Worcester County Penal Sys., Snow Hill, 1982—85. Pastor First Corinthians Holiness Ch. Inc., 1979—; overseer Glorious Mt. Sinai Holy Ch., 2005—. Mem.: NAACP. Avocations: cooking, sewing, quilting, reading, singing.

BOYD, MICHAEL ALAN, investment company executive, lawyer; b. St. Petersburg, Fla., Aug. 19, 1937; s. Horace Clinton and Celeste Elizabeth (Tarpley) B. AB, Harvard Coll., Cambridge, Mass., 1958; postgrad., Queen's Coll., Oxford, Eng., 1958-61; LLB, Harvard U., Cambridge, 1967. Bar: N.Y. 1968. Assoc. Davis Polk & Wardwell, NYC, 1967-71; sr. v.p., gen. counsel Donaldson, Lufkin & Jenrette, Inc., NYC, 1971—2001; sr. mng. dir. Brock Capital Group LLC, 2002—; ptnr. Brock Ptnrs., LLP, 2002—. With AUS, 1962—64, maj. gen. USAR. Rhodes scholar, 1958. Mem. Civil Affairs Assn. (nat. dir. 1983—), Assn. U.S. Army (bd. govs. N.Y. chpt. 1990—, pres. 1995-97), Oxford Alumni Assn. of N.Y. (pres. 1996-99), Oxford Univ. Soc. (trustee 2002—), Classical Am. Homes Preservation Trust (dir. 1999—), Harvard Law Sch. Assn. N.Y.C. (pres. 2005—). Republican. Home: 33 Greenwich Ave Penthouse 2 New York NY 10014 Office: 622 Third Ave 12th Fl New York NY 10017 Home Phone: 212-989-6971.

BOYD, RALPH F., JR., finance company executive, former federal agency administrator; b. Schenectady, NY, Feb. 7, 1957; BA, Haverford Coll., 1979; JD, Harvard U., 1984; LLD (hon.), Suffolk U., 2001. Law clk. Hon. Joseph H. Young U.S. Dist. Ct. Md.; assoc. Ropes & Gray, Boston, 1987—91; asst. U.S. atty. major crimes unit U.S. Attys. Office, 1992—98; ptnr. Goodwin Procter LLP, 1998—2001; asst. atty. Gen. Civil Rights Divsn. U.S. Dept. Justice, Washington, 2001—03; sr. ptnr. Alston & Bird LLP, 2003—04; exec. v.p., gen. counsel Fed. Home Loan Mortgage Corp. (Freddie Mac), McLean, Va., 2004—05, exec. v.p. community rels., 2005—; chmn. Freddie Mac Found., 2005—. Mem. exec. com. Mass. Jud. Nominating Commn., 1996—2001; mem. U.S. Magistrate Judge Selection and Rev. Panel, 1998. Office: Freddie Mac 8200 Jones Branch Dr Mc Lean VA 22102-3110*

BOYD, THEOPHILUS BARTHOLOMEW, III, publishing company executive; b. Nashville, May 15, 1947; s. Theophilus B. Jr. and Mable (Landrum) B.; m. Yvette Jean Duke, May 5, 1984; children: Theophilus B. IV, LaDonna Yvette, Shalae Shantel, Justin Marriel. BS, Tenn. State U., 1969; DD, Shreveport Bible Coll., 1980; LittD (hon.), Easonian Bapt. Sem., 1983. Pres. dir. R.H. Boyd Pub. Corp., Nashville, 1969-79; pres., chief exec. officer, 1979—. Chmn. Citizens Bank, Nashville, 1982—. Vice chair Meharry Med. Coll. bd. trustees, Nashville, 1989—; trustee Fla. Meml. Coll., Miami, 1984-86; bd. dirs. Nashville Symphone Assn., 1986-87, Nashville chpt. March of Dimes, 1986—; past pres. 100 Black Men of Mid. Tenn.; v.p. fin., treas. 100 Black Men Am., 1992-94; head R.H. Boyd initiative United Way. Named Hon. Citizen, City of Dallas, 1980, Man of Yr., 1990; recipient Key to the City, Denver, 1985, New Orleans, 1986, Great Seal of U.S. award; named man of the yr. 1990 March of Dimes. Mem. Nashville Area C. of C. (exec. bd.), Kappa Alpha Psi, Sigma Pi Phi, Richland Country Club. Democrat. Baptist. Avocations: boating, marathon running. Office: RH Boyd Publishing Corp 6717 Centennial Blvd Nashville TN 37209-1017

BOYD, THOMAS MARSHALL, lawyer; b. Yorktown, Va., Sept. 10, 1946; s. Laurel Barnett and Mildred Warner Wellford (Marshall) B.; m. Torri Carol Tyler, Oct. 2, 1976; children: Brooke Warner, Tyler Randolph. BA in History, Va. Military Inst., 1968; JD, U. Va., 1971. Bar: Calif. 1973, D.C. 1974. Law clk. to Hon. A. Andrew Hauk U.S. Dist. Ct. (cen. dist.) Calif., Los Angeles, 1973-74; trial atty., atty. advisor U.S. Dept. Justice, Washington, 1974-76; assoc. counsel com. on judiciary U.S. Ho. of Reps., Washington, 1976-86; dep. asst. atty. gen. Dept. Justice Office Legis. Affairs, Washington, 1986-88, asst. atty. gen., 1988-89, dir. office policy devel., 1989-91; dep. gen. counsel Kemper Corp., Washington, 1991-93, v.p. and legis. counsel, 1993-96; v.p. for legis. affairs Investment Co. Inst., Washington, 1996-98; ptnr. Ramsey, Cook, Looper & Kurlander LLP, Washington, 1998-99, Alston & Bird, LLP, Washington, 1999—. House counsel Presdl. Transition Com. on Criminal Justice, Washington, 1980-81; pub. mem. Adminstrv. Conf. U.S., 1992-95; mem. adv. com. data privacy Dept. Homeland Security, 2006-. Co-editor U.S. Atty.'s Criminal Trial Manual, 1971; contbr. articles to profl. jours. and editorials to newspapers. Served to capt. USAF, 1968-73. Recipient Nat. Media award Delta Soc., 1985, Edmund J. Randolph award, 1988. Mem. U.S. Supreme Ct. Bar Assn., Calif. Bar Assn., D.C. Bar Assn., Army-Navy Country Club, Leland (Mich.) Country Club, Golf Club of Va. Republican. Episcopalian. Avocations: golf, jogging, writing. Office: Alston & Byrd LLP 950 F St NW Washington DC 20004-1404 Office Phone: 202-756-3372. Business E-Mail: tboyd@alston.com.

BOYD, TODD, cinematic arts educator; BA, Wayne State U., Detroit, 1987; PhD, U. Iowa, Iowa City, 1991. Vis. prof. Ind. U., Dept. of Comparative Lit., Ind., 1992—92; asst. prof. U. So. Calif., Sch. Cinematic Arts, LA, 1992—97, assoc. prof., 1997—2003, prof., 2003—, Katherine and Frank Price endowed chair study race and popular culture, 2005—. Vis. prof. U. Utah, Dept. Comm., Salt Lake City, 1991—92. Author: (book) The Notorious Ph.D's Guide to the Super Fly 70s: A Connoisseur's Journey Through the Fabulous Flix, Cool Sounds, and Hip Vibes That Defined a Decade, Young, Black, Rich, and Famous: The Rise of the NBA, the Hip Hop Invasion and the Transformation of American Culture, The New H.N.I.C.: The Death of Civil Rights and the Reign of Hip Hop; editor: Basketball Jones: America Above the Rim; author: Am I Black Enough for You?: Popular Culture From the 'Hood and Beyond; editor: Out of Bounds: Sports, Media, and the Politics of Identity; writer, associate producer: (film) The Wood; commentator Dennis Miller Show, CNBC, 2004, Classic Now, ESPN Classic, 2005—06, News and Notes with Ed Gordon, NPR, 2005—. Recipient Studies Ctr. Jr. Faculty award, U. So. Calif., 1997, Tchg. and Mentoring award, U. So. Calif. Parents Assn., 2005; fellow, U. So. Calif., 1992—2002, Ind. U., 1992, James Irvine Found./So. Calif. Studies Ctr., USC, 1998—2000; James Irvine Found. Curriculum Enrichment grantee, U. So. Calif., 1993, Patricia Roberts-Harris fellow, U. Iowa, 1988. Office Phone: 213-740-3334.

BOYD, WILLARD LEE, academic administrator, educator, lawyer, museum director; b. St. Paul, Mar. 29, 1927; s. Willard Lee and Frances L. (Collins) Boyd; m. Susan Kuehn, Aug. 28, 1954; children: Elizabeth Kuehn, Willard Lee, Thomas Henry. BS in Law, U. Minn., 1949, LLB, 1951; LLM, U. Mich., 1952, SJD, 1962. Bar: Minn. 1951, Iowa 1958. Assoc. Dorsey & Whitney, Mpls., 1952—54; from instr. to prof. law U. Iowa, Iowa City, 1954—64, assoc. dean Law Sch., 1964, v.p. acad. affairs, 1964—69, pres., 1969—81, 2002—03, pres. emeritus, 1981—; pres. The Field Mus., Chgo., 1981—96, pres. emeritus, 1996—. Chmn. Nat. Mus. Scis. Bd., 1988—96; chair bd. dirs. Harry S Truman Libr. Inst., 1997—2001; past mem. adv. bd. Met. Opera; past adv. bd. Ill. Humanities Coun., Ill. Arts Coun., Chgo. Cultural Affairs Bd., Nat. Arts Coun.; past pres. Nat. Com. Accrediting, Ill. Arts Alliance; adv. com. edn. arts Getty Ctr.; adv. com. cultural property U.S. Dept. State, 2003—. Chmn. Am. Assn. Univs. Recipient Charles Frankel prize, Nat. Endowment for Humanities, 1989. Mem.: ABA (com. social labor and indsl. legislations 1963—65, chmn. 1965—66, coun. 1975—82, sect. legal edn. and admission to bar chmn. 1980—81, chmn. coun. of sect. on legal edn. and admission), Am. Law Inst., Am. Acad. Arts & Sci., Iowa Bar Assn. Home: 620 River St Iowa City IA 52246-2433 Office: Univ Iowa Law Sch Iowa City IA 52242-1113 Home Phone: 319-339-5948; Office Phone: 319-335-9004. Business E-Mail: willard-boyd@uiowa.edu.

BOYD, WILLIAM S., hotel and gaming company executive; s. Sam A. and Mary Boyd; 3 children. JD, Univ. Nev., Las Vegas. Pvt. practice law, 1960—75; co-founder Boyd Gaming Corp., Las Vegas, 1973, now chmn., CEO. Named one of Forbes' Richest Americans, 2006. Mem.: Am. Gaming Assn. (vice chmn.). Office: Boyd Gaming Corp 2950 Industrial Rd Las Vegas NV 89109-1150 Office Phone: 702-792-7200. Office Fax: 702-792-7313.*

BOYD, WILLIAM SPROTT, lawyer; b. San Francisco, Feb. 12, 1943; s. R. Mitchell S. and Mary (Mitchell) B.; children: Mitchell Sagar, Sterling McMicking. AB, Stanford U., 1964, JD, 1971. Bar: Calif. 1972, U.S. Dist. Ct. (no. dist.) 1972, U.S. Ct. Appeals (9th cir.) 1972, U.S. Dist. Ct. (cen. dist.) Calif. 1974, U.S. Dist. Ct. (ea. dist.) Calif. 1976. Assoc. Brobeck, Phleger & Harrison, San Francisco, 1971-77, ptnr., 1977—, of counsel. Mem. Lawyers Com for Urban Affairs, San Francisco, 1979—; bd. dirs. San Francisco Legal Aid Soc., 1980-85. Lt. USNR, 1965-68, Vietnam. Mem. ABA, Calif. Bar Assn., San Francisco Bar Assn.

BOYDA, NANCY, congresswoman; b. St. Louis, Aug. 2, 1955; m. Steve Boyda; 7 children. BS in Chem. & Edn., William Jewell Coll., 1977. Analytical chemist, field inspector EPA, 1978; mgmt. position Marion Laboratories; mem. US Congress from 2nd Kans. dist., 2007—, mem. agrl. com., armed svcs. com. Democrat. Methodist. Office: 1711 Longworth House Office Bldg Washington DC 20515 also: 510 SW 10th Ave Topeka KS 66612

BOYE, ROGER CARL, academic administrator, journalism educator; b. Lincoln, Nebr., Feb. 8, 1948; s. Arthur J. and Matilda J. (Danca) B. BA with distinction, U. Nebr., 1970; MS in Journalism with highest distinction, Northwestern U., 1971. News editor The Quill, Chgo., 1971-73; instr. Medill Sch. Journalism, Northwestern U., Evanston, Ill., 1973-76; vis. prof. journalism Niagara U., Niagara Falls, NY, 1976-78; gen. mgr. The Quill, 1980-84, bus. mgr., 1984-86; asst. dean, asst. prof. Medill Sch. Journalism Northwestern U., 1986-92, asst. dean, assoc. prof., 1992—2004, assoc. prof., 2004—05, assoc. prof. emeritus, 2005—. Judge various journalism awards and contests, 1970s—; master comm. residential coll. Northwestern U., 1989—96, 2004—. Weekly columnist Chgo. Tribune, 1974-93; contbr. Ency. Britannica Book of the Yr. and the Compton Yearbook, 1982-99; contbg. editor The Numismatist, 2001--. Recipient Maurice M. Gould award Numismatic Lit. Guild, 1981, 92; named to Medill Sch. Journalism Hall of Achievement. Mem. Phi Beta Kappa, Kappa Tau Alpha. Office: Northwestern Univ Medill Sch Journalism 1845 Sheridan Rd Evanston IL 60208-0815 Office Phone: 847-491-2069. Business E-Mail: r-boye@northwestern.edu.

BOYER, AURELIA G., information technology executive; M in Nursing, MBA. RN. Project mgr. clinical info. sys. NY Hosp., 1993—96; cons. PriceWaterhouse; dir. NY Hosp., 1996—98, v.p., 1998; sr. v.p. NY Presbyterian Hosp. (formerly NY Hosp.), chief info. officer. Office: NY Presbyterian Hospital 525 East 68th St New York NY 10021 Office Phone: 212-585-6427.

BOYER, CARL, III, not-for-profit developer, retired mayor, municipal official, secondary school educator; b. Phila., Pa., Sept. 22, 1937; s. Carl Boyer Jr. and Elizabeth Campbell Timm; m. Ada Christine Kruse, July 28, 1962. Student, U. Edinburgh, Scotland, 1956-57; BA, Trinity U., 1959; MEd in Secondary Edn., U. Cin., 1962; postgrad., Calif. State U., Northridge, 1964-72. Tchr. Edgewood High Sch., San Antonio, Tex., 1959-60; libr. U. Cin., Cincinnati, Ohio, 1960-61; tchr. Eighth Avenue Elem. Sch., Dayton, Ky., 1961-62, Amelia High Sch., Amelia, Ohio, 1962-63; instr. Kennedy San Fernando Comm. Adult Sch., San Fernando, Calif., 1964-74, Mission Coll., San Fernando, 1971; tchr. San Fernando High Sch., San Fernando, Calif., 1963-98. Faculty chmn. San Fernando High Sch., dept. chmn.; cons. Sofia (Bulgaria) City Coun., 1991, Bandung Regency, Indonesia, 2003; key spkr. World Mayors' Conf., Jaipur, India, 1998. Author: Santa Clarita: The Formation and Organization of the Largest Newly Incorporated City in the History of Humankind, 2005; author, compiler 23 books on genealogy and family history; contbr. articles to profl. jours. Councilman City of Santa Clarita, Calif., 1987-98, mayor pro tem, 1989-90, 94-95, mayor, 1990-91, 95-96; mem. Nat. League Cities Internat. Mcpl. Consortium, 1992-98; mem. revenue and taxation com. League Calif. Cities, 1992-95; sec. Calif. Contract Cities Assn., 1992-93; trustee Santa Clarita C.C. Dist., 1973-81, pres., 1979-81; bd. dirs. Castaic Lake Water Agy., 1982-84, pres. Newhall-Saugus-Valencia Fedn. Homeowners Assn., 1969-70, 71-72; pres. Del Prado Condo. Assn., Inc., Newhall, Calif.; exec. v.p. Canyon County Formation Com.; chmn. Santa Clarita City Formation Com., 1987; pres. Santa Clarita Valley Internat. Program, 1991-97, 04-05, v.p., 2005-; treas. Healing the Children Calif.,

1994-96, pres., 1996-99, 03-05, nat. pres., 1999-00, vol. med. mission adminstr., 2000—. Mem. New Eng. Hist. Geneal. Soc. Democrat. Methodist. Avocations: travel, photography. Home: PO Box 220333 Santa Clarita CA 91322-0333

BOYER, CAROLYN MERWIN, school psychologist; b. New Haven, Conn., Oct. 4, 1936; d. Richard Treat Merwin and Elsie Mae (Donaldson) Schuyler; m. Kenneth Sutton Boyer, Aug. 19, 1961; 1 child, Kenneth Merwin. BA in Spanish, Bucknell U., 1958; MS, So. Conn. State U., 1991. Nat. cert. sch. psychologist Milford Bd. Edn. Claims approver Equitable Life Assurance, NYC, 1961—63; libr. asst. Milford Pub. Libr., Conn., 1973—74; archtl. reporter Dodge/McGraw Hill, 1974—84; sec. Milford Bd. Edn., 1984—92, sch. psychologist, 1992—2003; ret. Reporter neighborhood news Milford Citizen, 1973—76. Exhibitions include oil paintings Firehouse Art Gallery, Milford, 2004—05. Mem. diaconate bd. 1st Ch. Christ, 1980—83, 1999—2002; bd. dirs. Miles Merwin Assn., Milford, 1974—75; bd. dirs., membership chair Nat. Assn. Women Constrn., 1975—78. Mem.: Nat. Assn. Sch. Psychologists, Conn. Assn. Sch. Psychologists. Republican. Avocations: gourmet cooking, tennis, reading, birdwatching, art. Home: 11 Anderson Ave Milford CT 06460

BOYER, HERBERT WAYNE, retired biochemist, biotechnology company executive; b. Pitts., July 10, 1936; m. Grace Boyer, 1959. BS in Biology and Chemistry, St. Vincent Coll., Latrobe, Pa., 1958, DSc (hon.) (hon.), 1981; MS, U. Pitts., 1960, PhD, 1963. Post-grad. study Yale U., 1963—66; mem. faculty U. Calif., San Francisco, 1966—, prof. microbiology, 1966—75, prof. biochemistry and biophysics, 1975—91, prof. biochemistry and biophysics emeritus, 1991—; co-founder, dir. Genentech, Inc., San Francisco, 1976—, v.p., 1976—90. Investigator Howard Hughes Med. Inst., 1976—83; bd. dir. Allergan, Inc., Irvine, Calif., 1994—, chmn. bd. dirs., 1998—2001, vice-chmn. bd. dirs., 2001—; bd. dir. Scripps Rsch. Inst. Mem. several editl. bds.; contbr. articles to profl. jours. Co-recipient Swiss Helmut Horten Rsch. award, 1993; named to Calif. Inventor's Hall of Fame, 1985, Nat. Inventor Hall of Fame, 2001; recipient V.D. Mattai award, Roche Inst., 1977, Albert and Mary Lasker award for basic med. research, 1980, Golden Plate award, Am. Acad. Achievement, 1981, Indsl. Rsch. Inst. Achievement award, 1982, Moet Hennessy-Louis Vuitton prize, 1988, Jerome H. Lemelson-MIT prize for excellence in invention and innovation, 1996, Nat. Tech. medal, 1989, Nat. Sci. medal, 1990, Perkin medal, Soc. Chem. Industry, 2007. Fellow: AAAS, Am. Acad. Arts and Scis.; mem.: NAS, Am. Soc. Biol. Chemists. Achievements include obtaining, with Stanley N. Cohen, first patent in the field of recombinant deoxyribonucleic acid (DNA), 1980.*

BOYER, JAMES LORENZEN, internist, educator; b. NYC, Aug. 28, 1936; s. Ralph R. and Alice M. B.; m. Phoebe Bennet, Feb. 23, 1963; children: Phoebe Christine, Anna Birch. AB, Haverford Coll., Pa., 1958; MD, Johns Hopkins U., 1962. Diplomate: Am. Bd. Internal Medicine. Med. intern N.Y. Hosp., NYC, 1962-63, resident in medicine, 1963-64, Yale-New Haven Hosp., 1966; postdoctoral fellow liver study unit Yale U., 1966-68; mem. faculty U. Chgo. Pritzker Sch. Medicine, 1972-78, prof. medicine, 1976-78, dir. liver study unit, 1972-78; prof. medicine, dir. liver study unit, chief divsn. digestive diseases Yale U. Med. Sch., 1978-96; dir. Yale Liver Ctr., 1984—, Ensign prof. of medicine, 1996—. Treas., bd. dirs. Am. Liver Found., 1976-85, chair Sci. Adv. Com., 2003-04, chmn. bd. dirs., 2004—; dep. chmn. Nat. Digestive Disease Adv. Bd., 1981-84; coun. mem. NIDDK, 1985-90. Contbr. articles to profl. jours. Chmn. bd. trustees Mt. Desert Island Biol. Lab., Salsbury Cove, Maine, 1995-2003. Lt. comdr. USPHS, 1964-66. Josiah Macey faculty scholar, 1976 Mem. Am. Assn. Study Liver Disease (pres. 1980), Am. Fedn. Clin. Rsch., ACP, Am. Gastroenterol. Assn. (councillor 1983-86), Internat. Assn. Study Liver Diseases (v.p. 1982-84, pres.-elect 1986-88, pres. 1988-90), Am. Soc. Clin. Investigation, Assn. Am. Physicians, Soc. Clin. Rsch., Am. Clin. and Climatolgic Assn. Office: Yale U Sch of Medicine 333 Cedar St New Haven CT 06520-8014

BOYER, JAN E., federal agency administrator; BA, Stanford U.; MPA, Harvard U., 1994. Chief exec. Softbank Corp., FleetBoston Fin. Corp., Salomon Barney, Inc.; sr. advisor to pres. Overseas Pvt. Investment Corp.; U.S. alt. exec. dir. Inter-Am. Devel. Bank U.S. Dept. Treasury, 2005—. Vis. fellow internat. fin. and emerging markets Inst. Internat. Economics. Office: US Dept Treasury 1300 NY Ave NW Rm NE1101 Washington DC 20577 Office Phone: 202-623-1031. Office Fax: 202-623-3096.

BOYER, JOHN WILLIAM, history professor, dean; b. Chgo., Oct. 17, 1946; s. William Dana and Mary Frances (Corbley) B.; m. Barbara Alice Juskevich, Aug. 24, 1968; children: Dominic, Alexandra, Victoria. BA, Loyola U., 1968; MA, U. Chgo., 1969, PhD, 1975. From asst. prof. to assoc. prof. U. Chgo., 1975-85, prof., 1985—, Martin A. Ryerson Disting. Svc. prof., 1996—, acting dean divsn. social scis., 1992-93, dean of the coll., 1992—. Author: Political Radicalism in Late Imperial Vienna, 1981, Culture and Political Crisis in Vienna, 1995, Three Views of Continuity and Change at the University of Chicago, 1999; editor: Jour. of Modern History. Capt. USAR, 1968-80. Recipient Theodor Körner prize Theodor Körner Found., 1978, John Gilmary Shea prize Am. Cath. Hist. Assn., 1982, Ludwig Jedlicka Meml. prize Kuratorium des Ludwig-Jedlicka-Gedächtnispreises, 1996, Austrian Cross Hon. Sci. and Art, First Class, 2004, Karl von Vogelsang State History prize Republic of Austria, 2006; Alexander von Humboldt fellow, 1980-81. Mem. Austrian Acad. Scis. (corr.). Roman Catholic. Avocation: cooking. Home: 1428 E 57th St Chicago IL 60637-1838 Office: U Chgo 1126 E 59th St Chicago IL 60637-1580 also: U Chgo Press Jour Divsn 1427 E 60th St Chicago IL 60637 Office Phone: 773-702-8576. Business E-Mail: jwboyer@uchicago.edu.

BOYER, KAYE KITTLE, association management executive; b. Peoria, Ill., July 5, 1942; d. Keith Howard and Evelyn Pearl (Benson) Kittle; m. Jon Frederick Boyer, Mar. 20, 1965; children: Tristan Boyer Binns, Kristine Monique Hitchens. Student, Merrill Palmer Inst., Detroit, 1964; BS in Home Econs., Pa. State U., University Park, 1964; MA in Sociology, Rutgers State U., New Brunswick, 1967. Cert. assn. exec.; cert. in family and consumer scis. Creative rschr. Nat. Inst. Drycleaning, Silver Spring, Md., 1963; extension home economist Md. Coop. Extension Svc., Westminster, 1964-65; coord. human resources N.J. Coop. Extension Svc., New Brunswick, 1966-67; instr. Douglass Coll., Rutgers U., New Brunswick, 1967-70; coord., instr. pilot project Urban Coalition of Met. Wilmington (Del.) Inc., 1972; asst. to chmn. 4-H Youth Devel. Dept., Cook Coll., 1973-74; feasibility study dir. Ocean County Coll., Toms River, N.J., 1975; exec. dir. N.J. Home Economics Assn., Manalapan, 1975-86; pres. Boyer Mgmt. Svcs., Manalapan, NJ, 1984—86, Earleville, Md., 1986—2002, Palm Coast, Fla., 2002—. Mgr. Costume Soc. Am., Palm Coast, Fla., 1984-2006, exec. dir., 2006-; cons. Plumpton Pk. Zool. Gardens Rising Sun, 1988-89, bd. dirs., 1990-92; cons. N.J. White House Conf., Trenton, 1980, Baltimore County Med. Assn., 1995-96, Md. Acad. Family Physicians, 1994, 97, Textile Soc. Am., 1998—; adv. com. Dept. Cmty. Edn. Rutgers U., 1979-84 Editor Exchs. Newsletter; resource dir., N.J. Programs and Svcs. Related to Adolescent Pregnancy. Vol. Soroptomist Internat. of Elkton, Md., 1987-94; bd. dir. Cmty. Libr. Cecilton, 1986-92; player US Pub. Links Amateur, 1986; trustee Cecil County Bd. Libr., 1998-2002. Couples Champion Grand Haven Golf Club, 2005, Sr. Women's Club Champion, 2005. Mem.: AAUW (v.p. program devel. NJ divsn. 1984—86), Profl. Conv. Mgmt. Assn. Edn. Found. (transition team product/svc. 2001, design task force 2000, learning ctr. task force 2000—01, trustee 2000—03), Fla. Assn. Family and Consumer Scis., Profl. Conv. Mgmt. Assn. (edn. and profl. devel. com. 1996—2001, ednl. and profl. devel. working com. 2002), Fla. Soc. Assn. Execs. (edn. com. 2006), Am. Soc. Assn. Execs. (cert.), Am. Assn. Family and Consumer Scis. (cert., Ruth O'Brien project grantee), Pa. State Alumni Assn. (chmn. strategic planning Daytona-Palm Coast chpt. 2003—, chair auction com. 2006—), Kappa Omicron Nu (v.p. fin. 1992—93, chair constn. and bylaws com. 1994—97). Democrat. Avocation: golf. Home and Office: 107 Front St Palm Coast FL 32137

BOYER, LESTER LEROY, JR., architecture educator, consultant; b. Hanover, Pa., Apr. 6, 1937; s. Lester Leroy and Ruth Florence (Kessler) B.; m. Patricia Barbara Hayes, Dec. 28, 1958; children: Douglas Lester, Blane Edward, Darla Mae. B of Archtl. Engring., Pa. State U., 1960, MS in Archtl. Engring, 1964; PhD in Architecture, U. Calif., Berkeley, 1976. Registered profl. engr., Pa. Instr. archtl. engring. Pa. State U., 1960-64; rsch. engr. Armstrong Cork Co., Lancaster, Pa., 1964-68; course dir. Nat. Soc. Profl. Engrs., 1964-74; sr. cons. acoustics and noise control Bolt Beranek and Newman Inc., Cambridge, Mass., 1968-70; faculty Okla. State U., Stillwater, 1970-84, dir. environ. control program, 1970-84, prof. architecture, 1979-84, Tex. A&M U., College Station, 1984—96, chmn. div. design tech. Coll. Arch., 1988-90, prof. emeritus, 1999—. Fulbright scholar U. N.S.W. and U. Queensland, Australia, 1982, Tech. U., Delft, The Netherlands, 1992; dir. daylighting rsch. NSF, 1985-88; vis. researcher Solar Energy Rsch. Inst., Colo., summer 1985; cons. acoustics, environ. comfort and passive energy design, 1970—; dir. earth-sheltered bldg. rsch. Control Data Corp. and U.S. Dept. Energy, 1979-81; chair energy rsch. rev. panel on fenestration Office Energy Rsch., U.S. Dept. Energy, Washington, 1988; gen. chmn. Internat. Conf. Earth Sheltered Bldgs., Sydney, Australia, 1983; tech. chmn. Internat. Conf. Earth Sheltered Bldgs., Mpls., 1986; vis. prof., chair dept. arch. Kuwait U., 1997-98; mem. design team Benham Blair & Affiliates, Oklahoma City. Author: Earth Shelter Technology, 1987; editor: Building Design for Environmental Hazards, 1973, Earth Sheltered Building Design Innovations, 1980, Earth Shelter Performance and Evaluation, 1981, Earth Shelter Protection, 1983, Design in Geotecture, 1986, Proceedings of 5th Internat. Conf. on Underground Space and Earth Sheltered Structures, Tech. Univ. Delft, The Netherlands, 1992; contbg. author Simulating Daylight with Architectural Models, 1987. Recipient 1st Pl. Design award Nat. Energy Design competition Calif. State Office Bldg., Sacramento, 1983. Mem. ASHRAE (nat. daylighting symposium organizer 1988), Am. Solar Energy Soc. (nat. coord. passive earth cooling program 1981), Am. Underground Space Assn. (bd. dirs. 1989-92), Illuminating Engring. Soc. Lutheran. Home: HC 68 Box 19 Fort Garland CO 81133-9702 E-mail: llb@fone.net.

BOYER, NICODEMUS ELIJAH, chemist, consultant; b. Daugavpils, Latgale, Latvia, June 1, 1925; arrived in U.S., 1949; s. Aloizs and Elvira Adele (Buchholz) Bojars. BS in Natural Scis., U. Göttingen, Germany, 1949; PhD in Chemistry, U. Ill., 1955; postgrad., Princeton U., 1955-56. Rsch. chemist Hooker Chem. Corp., Niagara Falls, NY, 1956-61; project leader, lectr. Ill. Inst. Tech., Chgo., 1961-63; rsch. fellow Borg-Warner Chems., Washington, 1964-76; sr. staff mem. Raychem Corp., Menlo Park, Calif., 1976-78; asst. prof. Ind. State U., Terre Haute, 1978-80; sr. rsch. assoc. PPG Industries, Chgo., 1980-88; sr. cons. Delta Sci. Cons., Parkersburg, W.Va., 1988-92, Three Rivers, Mich., 1992—. Lectr. evening sch. U. Buffalo, 1958-60; prof. Glen Oaks Coll., Centreville, Mich., 1995-2001. Vol. abstractor Chem. Abstracts Svc., Columbus, Ohio, 1958-71; editor Cosmology Technikas Apskats, Montreal, Que., Can., 1987-93; author: Organophosphorus Chemistry, Vol. 1, 1957, Vol. 2, 1959, Radiation Chemistry: Monomers and Polymers, 1977, A New Theory of Cosmology, 1983, The Physics of Creation, 2 vols., 1990, Fire Retardants: A Review and Selected Patents, 1991, Cosmogony, 1992, The Baltic Civilization, 2003, The Big Bang: Cosmological Evolution Theory from the Dark Matter, 2003; contbr. over 70 articles to profl. jours.; 180 chemistry patents. Founding mem. Latvian Cath. Students' Assn., Germany, 1946-64; vice chmn. Latvian Acad. Soc. Valdemarija, Ill., Calif., Mich., 1964-; life mem. Rep. Presdl. Task Force, 1989-. With U.S. Army, 1945. Internat. Refugee Orgn. scholar U. Göttingen, 1946-49, Nat. Cath. Welfare Conf. scholar U. Ill., 1949-51; recipient Quality Control & Safety award PPG Industries Inc., 1987. Mem. AAAS, Am. Chem. Soc., N.Y. Acad. Scis. (life), Latvian Acad. Scis., U. Ill. Alumni Assn., Phi Lambda Upsilon, Sigma Xi, Am. Legion (life). Republican. Roman Catholic. Achievements include discovery of extremely stable white coatings to heat and ultraviolet radiation for space applications; patent for the first large-scale fire retardant additive for ABS resins; invented a new theory of cosmology. Office: Delta Sci Cons PO Box 312 Three Rivers MI 49093-0312 E-mail: studeophile@cs.com.

BOYER, PATRICIA W., publishing executive, editor; b. Weaverville, NC, Oct. 12, 1925; d. William Malcolm and Katherine Lotspeich Waters; m. Clyde M. Boyer, June 28, 1946 (dec. Aug. 10, 1997); children: John Gregory, Abigail, Judd Meredith, Clyde Merrill. Co-owner Boyer Ranch, Calif., 1963—97; CEO Got Solar, Inc., Oreg., 2001—; CFO H2Nation Pub. Inc., Brookings, Oreg., 2003—, Nev., 2003—; editor H2Nation Mag., Nev., 2003—. Bd. dirs. H2Nation Pub., Inc., Sparks, Nev., 2003—, Got Solar, Inc., Oreg., 2000—. Author: The Last Free Chief of the Modoc Nation: An Allegory, 2001. Mem.: Women Writing the West, Nat. Mus. of the Am. Indian at the Smithsonian, Toastmasters Internat. Avocations: music, poetry, gardening, writing, history. Office: H2Nation Publishing Inc PO Box 52080 Sparks NV 89435 Office Phone: 775-356-8411. Business E-Mail: pat@h2nation.com.

BOYER, PAUL D., biochemist, educator; b. Provo, Utah, July 31, 1918; s. Dell Delos and Grace (Guymon) Boyer; m. Lyda Mae Whicker, Aug. 31, 1939. BS, Brigham Young U., 1939; MS, U. Wis., 1941, PhD in Biochemistry, 1943; PhD (hon.), U. Stockholm, 1974, U. Minn., 1996, U. Wis., 1998. Asst. rschr. biochemistry U. Wis., 1939—43; Instr., research assoc. Stanford, 1943—45; from asst. prof. to prof. biochemistry U. Minn., 1945—56; Hill research prof. U. Minn. Med. Sch., 1956—63; prof. chemistry UCLA, 1963—89, dir. Molecular Biology Inst., 1965—83, dir. biotech. program, 1985—88, 1985-89, prof. emeritus, 1989—; chmn. biochemistry study sect. USPHS, 1962—67. Mem. U.S. Nat. Com. for Biochemistry, 1965—71. Editor: Ann. Rev. of Biochemistry, 1965—71; assoc. editor:, 1972—88; editor: Biochemical and Biophysical Research Communications, 1969—79, The Enzymes, 1970—; mem. editl. bd.: Biochemistry, 1969—76, Jour. Biol. Chemistry, 1978—83, 1987—; contbr. articles to profl. jours. Co-recipient Nobel prize for chemistry, 1997; recipient McCoy award chem. rsch., 1976, Tolman award, 1984, Rose award, Am. Soc. Chemistry and Molecular Biology, 1989, UCLA medal, 1998; fellow Guggenheim Found., 1955—56. Fellow: AAAS (v.p. biol. scis. 1985—88, council); mem.: NAS, Biophys. Soc., Am. Chem. Soc. (chmn., biochem. divsn. 1959—60, Enzyme Chemistry award 1955), Am. Soc. Biol. Chemists (pres. 1969—70, council mem.). Home: 1033 Somera Rd Los Angeles CA 90077-2625 Office: Dept Chem-Biochem Paul Boyer Hall 639 607 Charles E Young Dr E Box 951569 Los Angeles CA 90095-0001

BOYER, ROBERT ALLAN, finance company executive; b. Detroit, Mar. 2, 1934; s. Robert Allan and Elizabeth (Szabo) B.; children: Jennifer, Stephen, Lorna. MBA, Cornell U., 1959. Alfred P. Sloan fellow Cornell U. Grad. Sch., Ithaca, NY, 1958, 59; exec. asst. to pres. Merck & Co., Inc., Rahway, NJ, 1962-68; dir. fin. TWA Corp., NYC, 1969-72; nat. dir. fin. Coopers & Lybrand, NYC, 1972-79; exec. dir. Sullivan & Cromwell, NYC, 1979—. Chmn., founder Legal Execs. Group, Law Firm Tech. Group, 1979. Mem. congl. support com.; mem. Pres.'s Club Rep. Party, 1990. Fellow Coll. Law Practice Mgmt.; mem. ABA, Assn. Legal Adminstrs. (exec. com. 1986-87), Aircraft Owners and Pilots Assn., Yorktown Bicentennial Com. (bd. dirs., sec.), Echo Lake Country Club (Westfield, N.J.), Cornell Club (N.Y.), Cornell Club (N.J.), India House (N.Y.C.), N.Y. Acad. Scis. Clubs: Echo Lake Country (Westfield, N.J.). Republican. Presbyterian. E-mail: rboyernyc@aol.com.

BOYER, TYRIE ALVIS, lawyer; b. Williston, Fla., Sept. 10, 1924; s. Alton Gordon and Mary Ethel (Strickland) B.; m. Elizabeth Everett Gale, June 9, 1945; children: Carol, Tyrie, Kennedy, Lee. BA, U. Fla., 1953, LLB, JD, 1954. Bar: Fla. Atty. Crawford, May & Boyer, Jacksonville, Fla., 1954-58, Boyer Law Offices, Jacksonville, 1958-60; judge Civil Ct. of Record, Jacksonville, 1960-63; cir. judge 4th Jud. Cir. of Fla., Jacksonville, 1963-67; atty. Dawson, Galant, Maddox, Boyer, Sulik & Nichols, Jacksonville, 1967-73; appellate judge 1st Dist. Ct. Appeal, Tallahassee, 1973-79; chief judge 1st Dist. Ct. Appeals, Tallahassee, 1975-76; atty. Boyer, Tanzler, Blackburn & Boyer, Jacksonville, 1979-84, Boyer, Tanzler & Sussman, Jacksonville, 1984—. Adj. prof. Fla. Coastal Sch. Law, Jacksonville, 1996—, U. North Fla., 1998—; chmn. Supreme Ct. Com. on Standard Conduct Governing Judges, Tallahassee, 1976—79. Contbr. articles to profl. jours. Chmn. Duval County Hosp. Authority, Jacksonville, 1970-73, Jacksonville Bldg. Fin. Authority, 1980-81; pres. Jacksonville Legal Aid Assn., 1954-61; bd. dirs. Jones Coll., Jacksonville, 1978-85; bd. advs. Fla. Coastal Sch. Law, 1996—; adj. prof. U. North Fla., 1998—. With USN, 1942—45, PTO. Mem. ABA, Am. Judicature Soc., Fla. Bar, Amer. Bar Assn., Jacksonville Bar Assn., Fla. Acad. Trial Lawyers, Am. Bd. Trial Advs., SCV (comdr.), Mil. Order Stars and Bars (comdr.), Masons, dir., Safari Club Internat., Fla. Blue Key, Order of Coif, Phi Beta Kappa, Phi Kappa Phi. Methodist. Avocation: big game hunting. Home: 3966 Cordova Ave Jacksonville FL 32207-6019 Office: Boyer Tanzler & Sussman 210 E Forsyth St Jacksonville FL 32202-3320 Office Phone: 904-358-3030.

BOYER, TYRIE WILLIAM, judge, law educator; b. Jacksonville, Fla., Aug. 2, 1948; s. Tyrie Alvis and Elizabeth Gale Boyer; m. Lori Tofflemire Nemeyer, Nov. 6, 1997; children: Kimberly Jane Elizabeth, Kelley Deborah Lee, R. J. Nemeyer. BSBA, U. Fla., Gainesville, 1972, JD, 1976. Cert.: Fla. Bar (civil trial Lawyer) 1983, Nat. Bd. of Trial Advocacy (civil trial advocacy) 1997, bar: Fla. 1976, U.S. Supreme Ct. 1997, U.S. Dist. Ct. (mid. dist.) Fla. 1977, U.S. Ct. of Appeals (5th and 11th cirs.) 1981. Asst. pub. defender Pub. Defender, Jacksonville, 1976—77; assoc. Mathews, Osborne, Ehrlich, McNatt, Gobleman & Cobb, Jacksonville, 1977—79; judge Duval County, Jacksonville, 2001—; ptnr. Boyer, Tanzler & Boyer, Jacksonville, 1979—2000; adj. prof. Fla. Coastal Sch. of Law, Jacksonville, Fla., 1999—; adminstrv. judge Duval County Ct., 2007—08. Chmn. Fla. Bar Com. on Profl. Ethics, Tallahassee, 1986—88, Fla. Bar Civil Procedure Rules Com., Tallahassee, 1998—99; chmn. Law Day Jacksonville Bar Assn., 1978—79. Author: (novels) RETRIBUTION; contbr. articles to legal jours. and outdoor publs. Dist. dir., counselor Boy Scouts of Am., Jacksonville, 2002—04; mem. Jacksonville C. of C., 1998—2000; bd. dirs. Jacksonville Cmty. Coun., Inc., 1980; bd. of advisors pre-law program U. of North Fla., 2003; advisor Family Farm, Jacksonville, 2002—05; bd. dirs. Salvation Army, Orange Park, Fla., 1995—96; bd. mem. YMCA, Jacksonville, 1977—79; bd. dirs March of Dimes, Jacksonville, 1979; chmn. Sportsmen Against Hunger, Safari Club Internat., Jacksonville, 1991; pres. student body U. of Fla., Gainesville, 1973, chief justice traffic ct., 1972. Capt. USAR, 1969—82. Named one of Outstanding Young Men of Jacksonville, Jaycees, Jacksonville, Fla., 1979, Outstanding Young Men of Am., 1980; named to Hall Fame, U. Fla., 1972, 1973; recipient Ethics award, Safari Club Internat., 1995, Svc. award, Filipino Travelers of Fla., 2000—01, President's award, Safari Club Internat., 2002, Fla. Blue Key, U. Fla., 1972, John Marshall Bar Assn. Cert. of Merit, U. of Fla., 1988, Paul Harris fellowship. Fellow: Am. Bd. of Trial Advocates (pres., v.p., sec., treas. Jacksonville chpt. 1989—92), Found. of Am. Bd. of Trial Advocates; mem.: NRA, FBA, ATLA, ABA, Jacksonville Trial Lawyers Assn., Jacksonville Bar Assn., Acad. of Fla. Trial Lawyers, Fla. Bar Assn., Clay County Bar Assn., Fla. Bd. of Trial Advocates (bd. dirs. 1992), Christian Legal Soc., Safari Club Internat. (regional v.p., bd. dirs., pres. Jacksonville chpt. 1982—2005), Nat. Alumni Assn. of the U. of Fla., South Jacksonville Rotary Internat. (bd. dirs.), Jacksonville Hist. Soc. (pres. 2005—07), Am. Legion, Masons, Omnicron Delta Kappa, Sigma Delta Pi (chancellor 1972), Delta Theta Phi (dean 1975). Episcopalian. Avocations: outdoor recreation, bridge. Office: Duval County Courthouse Rm 324 330 E Bay St Jacksonville FL 32202 Home Phone: 904-398-1194; Office Phone: 904-630-2579. Office Fax: 904-630-8358. Personal E-mail: twboyer@coj.net.

BOYER, WILLIAM JOSEPH, food products executive; b. Mcleansboro, Ill., Nov. 19, 1945; s. William Joseph Boyer and Billie Gayle Pobanst; children: William R., Laura M., Jennifer M.; m. Diann Basler; 1 child, Bobbi. BA, Ea. Ill. U., Charleston, 1979. Bd. dirs. Boyer Coffee Co, Denver, 1965—2006, Bros. Coffee Co., Denver, 1990—2000. Served with USN, 1965—68. Mem.: Shriners (corr.; fund raiser). Republican. Avocations: golf, teaching, counseling. Home: PO Box 3955 Carbondale IL 62902 Office: Boyer Coffee Co 7295 N Washington Denver CO 80229 Office Phone: 800-452-5282. E-mail: b4java@aol.com.

BOYERS, ROBERT, literature and language professor; b. NYC, Nov. 9, 1942; s. Paul and Selma (Busell) B.; m. Madelyn Gray Dolen, Aug. 31, 1963 (div. 1975); children: Lowell, Zachary Meyer; m. Margarita A. O'Higgins, Dec. 16, 1975; 1 son, Gabriel Levin. BA, Queens Coll., CUNY, 1963; MA, NYU, 1965. Instr. New Sch. Social Research, NYC, 1967, Baruch Sch., CUNY, 1967-68; asst. prof. English Skidmore Coll., Saratoga Springs, NY, 1969-73, assoc. prof., 1973-80, Tisch Prof. Arts and Letters, 1980—2006. Dir. NY State Summer Writers Inst., 1987—; adj. prof. liberal studies New Sch. for Social Rsch. Grad. Faculty, 1993—. Editor-in-chief: Salmagundi Mag., 1965— , Bennington Rev., 1978-83; author: Excursions: Selected Literary Essays, 1976, Lionel Trilling: Negative Capability and the Wisdom of Avoidance, 1977, F.R. Leavis: Judgement and the Discipline of Thought, 1978, R.P. Blackmur, Poet-Critic: Towards A View of Poetic Objects, 1980, Atrocity and Amnesia: The Political Novel Since 1945, 1985, After the Avant Garde: Essays on Art and Culture, 1988, Excitable Women, Damaged Men, 2005, The Dictator's Dictation. The Politics of Novels and Novelists, 2005; editor: Robert Lowell: A Portrait of the Artist in His Time, 1970, R.D. Laing and Anti-Psychiatry, 1971, The Legacy of the German Refugee Intellectuals, 1972, Psychological Man: Approaches to an Emergent Social Type, 1975, Contemporary Poetry in America, 1975, The Salmagundi Reader, 1983; assoc. editor Rev. of Existential Psychiatry and Psychology, 1973-78. NEH sr. fellow, 1979-80, 90—; Rockefeller Found. grantee Bellagio, Italy, 1980, Cooper Prize for short fiction, Ontario Rev. Democrat. Jewish. Office: English Dept Skidmore Coll Palamountain Hall 325 815 North Broadway Saratoga Springs NY 12886 Home Phone: 518-587-7491; Office Phone: 518-580-5156. Business E-Mail: rboyers@skidmore.edu.

BOYES, PATRICE FLINCHBAUGH, lawyer; b. York, Pa., Aug. 1, 1957; d. Glenn Dale Flinchbaugh and Patricia Ann (Frey) Shultz. BA, Dickinson Coll., 1978; MA, U. Mich., 1980; JD, U. Fla., 1991. Bar: Fla. 1991, Fed. 1994. Law clk. Rakusin & Ivey, Gainesville, Fla., 1989; summer assoc. Hopping, Boyd, Green & Sams, Tallahassee, 1990; gen. counsel GeoSolutions, Inc., Gainesville/Tallahassee, Fla., 1986—2002; pres. Boyes & Assocs., PA, Gainesville, Fla., 1991—, Wildcat Tech. Svc., Inc., 1995-99. Pres. Wildcat Tech. Svcs., Inc., Gainesville, 1995-99. Pres. Hist. Gainesville, Inc.; chair City's Hist. Preservation Adv. Bd.; vol. Kanapha Bot. Gardens; counsel Duckpond Neighborhood Assn., Inc. Recipient Keystone Press award Pa. Soc. Newspaper Editors and Pubs., 1981, City Beautification award, 1994, Hist. Preservation award, 1994, Fla. Trust for Hist. Preservation award, 1996; grad. fellow Modern Media Inst., St. Petersburg, Fla. Mem. Fed. Bar Assn., Fla. Bar Assn. (environ. and land use sect., real property sect.), 8th Jud. Cir. Bar Assn., Fla. Assn. Women Lawyers, Gainesville C. of C., Pi Delta Epsilon, Gainesville Country Club, Rotary. Avocations: golf, historical preservation, photography, gardening, reading. Office: 408 W University Ave Ste PH Gainesville FL 32601 Office Phone: 352-372-2684. E-mail: boyeslaw@bellsouth.net.

BOYETT, JOAN REYNOLDS, performing company executive; b. LA, May 2, 1936; d. Clifton Faris Reynolds and Jean Margaret Hauck; m. Harry William Boyett, Oct. 5, 1956; children: Keven William, Suzanne Marie Boyett. Student, Occidental Coll., 1954-55, Pasadena Playhouse, 1955-57. Mgr. youth activities LA Philharm. Orch., 1970-79; dir., founder edn. divsn. The Music Ctr. LA County, 1979-2001, v.p. edn., 1988-2001. Mem. supt.'s task force on arts edn. Calif. State Dept. Edn., 1997; cons. NEA, Washington; chmn. arts edn. task force Calif. Arts Coun., Sacramento, 1993-95; arts edn. mem. Nat. Working Group, Washington, 1992-95; mem. U.S. Sec. of Edns. Com. on Am. Goes Back to Sch. Active various coms. and task forces, L.A., Sacramento. Named Woman of Yr. L.A. Times, 1976; recipient Labor's award of honor County Fedn. Labor, L.A., 1984, Susan B. Anthony award Bus. and Profl. Women, 1986, Gov.'s award Calif. Arts Coun., 1989, R.O.S.E. Outstanding Svc. to Edn. award, U. So. Calif., 1999, Outstanding Arts Educator award Calif. Arts Coun., 2001, Music Ctr. Club 100 Spl. Tribute award, 2001, Women in Ednl. Leadership award, 2002, Ovation award for cmty. svc. Theatre League Alliance, 2002. Mem. Calif. Art Edn. Assn. (Behind the Scenes award 1985), Calif. Dance Educators Assn. (Svc. award 1985), Calif. Ednl. Theatre Assn. (Outstanding Contbn. award 1990, nominated for Nat. Medal Arts 1996, 97). Republican. Presbyterian. Avocations: reading, attending arts events, gardening, swimming. Home: PO Box 1805 Studio City CA 91614-0805

BOYETTE, RICHARD T., lawyer; b. Fayetteville, NC, Aug. 4, 1952; BA, Univ. NC, Chapel Hill, 1974, JD, 1977. Bar: NC 1977, cert.: mediator. Law clerk, Hon. Walter E. Brock NC Ct. of Appeals, 1977—78; asst. dist. atty. 12th Judicial Dist., 1978—80; ptnr., mediation, comml. litig. Cranfill Sumner & Hartzog, Raleigh, NC. Mem.: Internat. Assn. Def. Counsel, NC Assn. Def. Attys. (pres. 1990—91, Award for Profl. Excellence 2004), NC Bar Assn., Wake County Bar Assn., Def. Rsch. Inst. (bd. dir. 1998—2001, pres. 2004—05). Office: Cranfill Sumner & Hartzog Ste 300 225 Hillsborough St PO Box 27808 Raleigh NC 27611 Office Phone: 919-863-8729. Office Fax: 919-863-3915. Business E-Mail: rtb@cshlaw.com.

BOYKAN, MARTIN, composer, music educator; b. NYC, Apr. 12, 1931; m. Susan Schwalb, 1983. AB summa cum laude, Harvard U., 1951; student, U. Zurich, Switzerland, 1951—52; MusM, Yale, 1953. Asst. prof. music Brandeis U., Waltham, Mass., 1964-67, assoc. prof. music, 1967-76, prof., 1976—, Irving G. Fine prof., 1986—. Composer-in-residence Composer's Conf., Wellesley, Mass., 1987; vis. prof. composition Columbia U., 1988-89, NYU, 1993, 2000; sr. Fulbright lectr. Bar Ilan U., Israel, 1994. Composer: String Quartets, 1949, 1965, Flute Quintet, 1953, Psalm, 1958, Prelude for Organ, 1959, Chamber Concerto for 13 Instruments, 1971, String Quartet No. 2, 1973, Piano Trio, 1975, Elegy for soprano and 6 instruments, part I, 1979, Elegy for soprano and 6 instruments, part II, 1982, String Quartet No. 3, 1984, Epithalamion for baritone, violin and harp, 1985, Shalom Rav, 1985, Fantasy Sonata for Piano, 1987, Sonata for cello and piano, 1988, Symphony for orch. with baritone solo, 1989, Piano Sonata #2, 1990, Nocturne for Cello, Piano and Percussion, 1990, Eclogue for flute, violin, cello, horn and piano, 1991, Echoes of Petrarch for flute, clarinet and piano, 1992, Voyages for Soprano and Piano, 1992, Sea-Gardens for Soprano and Piano, 1993, Impromptu for Solo Violin, 1993, Three Psalms for Soprano and Piano, 1993, Pastorale for Piano, 1993, Sonata for violin and piano, 1994, Ma'ariv Settings for chorus and organ, 1995, String Quartet No. 4, 1996, 3 Shakespeare Songs for Chorus, 1996, City of Gold for solo flute, 1996, 2d Trio for violin, cello and piano, 1997, Psalm 121 for soprano and string quartet, 1997, Usurpations for piano, 1997, Sonata for Solo Violin, 1998, Flume for Clarinet and Piano, 1998, Romanza for Flute and Piano, 1999, A Packet for Susan for Mezzo-Soprano and Piano, 2000, Second Chances Song Cycle for Mezzo Sop and Piano on Texts By Mary Oliver, 2005, Motet for Mezzo-Soprano and Viol Consort, 2000, 2d version for clarinet, viola and cello, 2005, Songlines for flute, clarinet, violin and cello, 2001, Concerto for Violin and Orchestra, 2003, Eulogy for Piano Solo, 2005, Piano Trio No. 3, 2006, Piano Sonata No. 3, 2007; author: Silence and Slow Time, 2004; mem. editl. bd.: Perspectives of New Music; contbr. articles to profl. jours. Nat. winner Jeunesses Musicales, 1967, League-ISCM, 1983; recipient Martha Baird Rockefeller award, 1974, Fromm Found. commn., 1975, award Internat. Soc. Contemporary Music, 1983, Koussevitzky commn., 1985, AAUL, 1986, 88, rec. award Am. Acad. and Nat. Inst. Arts and Letters, 1986, Walter Hinrichsen Publ. award Am. Acad. and Inst. Arts and Letters, 1988; Paine fellow, 1951, Fulbright fellow, 1953-55, Guggenheim fellow, 1984, Sr. Fulbright fellow, 1994; grantee Nat. Endowment for Arts, 1983, and numerous others. Mem. Am. Music Ctr., Phi Betta Kappa. Home: 10 Winsor Ave Watertown MA 02472-1460 Office: Music Dept Brandeis Univ Waltham MA 02454 Office Phone: 781-736-3337. Business E-Mail: boykan@brandeis.edu.

BOYKIN, ANNE JANE, dean; BSN, Alverno Coll., 1966; MSN, Emory U., 1972; PhD, Vanderbilt U., 1981. Asst. prof. Marquette U., Milw., 1973-74; assoc. prof., asst. dir. Valdosta (Ga.) State Coll., 1975-80; in-svc. educator Holy Cross Hosp., Ft. Lauderdale, Fla., 1980-81; assoc. prof. Fla. Atlantic U., Boca Raton, 1984—, dean Coll. Nursing, prof., 1996—. Dir. Christine E. Lynn Ctr. for Caring. Co-author: Nursing as Caring: a Model for Transforming Practice, 1993, 2d edit., 2001; editor: Living a Caring-Based Program, 1993, Power, Politics and Public Policy: A Matter of Caring, 1995; co-editor: Caring as Healing: Renewal through Hope, 1994; contbr. chpts. to books, articles to profl. jours. Mem. Internat. Assn. for Human Caring, Fla. Nurses Assn. (Nursing Educator award 1991), Sigma Theta Tau, Phi Kappa Phi. Office: Fla Atlantic U Christine E Lynn Coll Nursing 777 Glades Rd PO Box 3091 Boca Raton FL 33431-0991 Office Phone: 561-297-3206. Business E-Mail: boykina@fau.edu.

BOYKIN, GLADYS, retired religious organization administrator; b. NYC, Dec. 10, 1929; d. Jacob Allen and Annie Mae (Alston) McClendon; m. Eugene S. Callender (div. 1963); 1 child, Renee Denise; m. John R. Strachan (dec. 1982); m. Elton Boykin, 1996. Student, NYU, 1947-49. Dep. asst. Presbyn. Ch. of East Africa, Nairobi, Kenya, 1964-67; assoc. for women's program Presbyn. Ch. of U.S., NYC, 1970-83; exec. dir. United Presbyn. Women, NYC, 1983-97; ret., 1997. Cons. Peace Corps, Nairobi, 1964-67, Operation Crossroads Africa, Nairobi, 1964-67, Afro-Am. Ednl. Inst., Teaneck, N.J., 1977-79, various women's orgns. in Asia, Australia, Europe, Africa. V.p. Addicts Rehab. Ctr. Bd., N.Y.C., 1957—; mem. N.Y. Coalition of 100 Black Women, N.Y.C., 1972—; v.p., bd. dirs. La. Internat. Cultural Ctr.; bd. dirs. aging resource ctr. Sister Cities of Louisville. Recipient Cert. of citation borough pres. N.Y.C., 1977, Harlem Peacemaking award Harlem Peacemaking Com., 1983, Vol. award Louisville Internat. Culture Ctr., 1996. Mem. La. C. of C., River City Assn. Bus. and Profl. Women., Downtown Resident Assn. (pres.), Jefferson Club (bd. govs.). Avocations: music, reading, travel, needlepoint, theater. Home: 800 S 4th St Apt 2202 Louisville KY 40203-2132

BOYKIN, KEITH O., former government official, writer; b. St. Louis, Aug. 28, 1965; s. William Oliver Boykin and Shirley Ann (Hayes) Parker. BA, Dartmouth Coll., 1987; JD, Harvard U., 1992. Polit. campaign worker Dukakis for Pres., Boston, 1987-88; pub. sch. tchr. Lithonia H.S., DeKalb County, Ga., 1989; mcpl. cons. City of Pine Lawn, Md., 1989; spl. asst. to pres. The White House, Washington, 1993—95. Adj. prof. govt. Am. U., Washington, 1991—2001. Author: One More River to Cross: Black and Gay in America, 1996, Respecting the Soul, 1999, Beyond the Down Low; Sex, Lies and Denial in Black America, 2005; co-editor: 100 Successful College Application Essays; host My Two Cents, BET-TV, 2006. Founding bd. dirs., pres. Nat. Black Justice Coalition, 2003—06. Recipient Young Alumni award Harvard Black Law Students Assn., Cambridge, 1994. Democrat. Mailing: PO Box 1229 New York NY 10037 E-mail: kb@keithboykin.com.

BOYKIN, RICHARD RENARDA, lawyer, former legislative staff member; b. Jackson, Miss., Sept. 9, 1968; s. George Albert and Burnette (Knight) B. BA, Ctrl. State U., 1990; JD, U. Dayton, 1994. Bar: Ill. 1994. Tchg. asst. U. Dayton (Ohio), 1993-94, legal intern, 1994; legis. fellow office of Sen. Carol Moseley Brown (Ill.) U.S. Congress, Washington, 1994-95; contract atty. Attys. Per Diem, Washington, 1995-96, Aspen Sys. Corp., Washington, 1996-97; chief of staff to Rep. Danny K. Davis US Congress, Washington, 1997—2007; ptnr. Barnes & Thornburg LLP, Chgo., 2007—. Assoc. min. Met. Bapt. Ch., motivational spkr. Recipient: Martin Luther King Dream Classic award, Nat. Assn. Community Health Centers Svc. award, the John C. Stennis Leadership Award, ELI Disting. Leadership award, Litigation award, US Dept. Justice, Congl. Black Caucus Fellows award, Am. Jurisprudence award; Stennis fellow Sen. John C. Stennis Fellowship, 1999-00. Mem. ABA, Chgo. Bar Assn., Ill. State Soc. (bd. dirs.). Baptist. Avocations: reading, racquetball, basketball. Office: Barnes & Thornburg LLP One N Wacker Dr Ste 4400 Chicago IL 60606 E-mail: richard.boykin@BTLaw.com.

BOYKIN, ROBERT HEATH, retired banker; b. Carlsbad, N.Mex., Jan. 10, 1926; s. Calvin Clay and Ruby (Heath) B.; m. Camille Inkman, Nov. 26, 1948; 1 child, Robert Heath. BBA, U. Tex., 1950, LL.B., 1953; student, Park Coll., 1943-44; spl. courses, La. State U., Tex. A. and M. Coll., Am. Mgmt. Assn. Bar: Tex. bar 1952. Tabulating supr. Tex. Edn. Agy., 1948-52; with Fed. Res. Bank of Dallas, 1953-91, asst. counsel, 1959-61, asst. counsel, asst. sec. bd., 1961-65, asst. v.p., asst. sec. bd., 1965-67, asst. v.p., sec. bd., 1967-68, v.p., sec. bd., 1968-70, sr. v.p., sec. bd., 1971-75, sr. v.p., 1976, 1st v.p., 1976-80, pres., 1981-91, ret., 1991. Sec. Conf. Pres.'s of Fed. Res. Banks, 1963-64, chmn., 1980; instr. negotiable instruments Dallas chpt. Am. Inst. Banking, 1959-61 Served as lt. (j.g.) USNR, 1943-47. Mem. Tex. Bar Assn., Tex. Bankers Assn., Delta Tau Delta, Phi Alpha Delta. Methodist.

BOYKIN, WILLIAM G. (JERRY BOYKIN), federal agency administrator, career military officer; b. Wilson, NC, Apr. 19, 1948; BA in Edn., Va. Polytechnic & State U., 1971; MA, Shippensburg U.; student, Army War Coll., 1990—91. Commd. U.S. Army, 1971, advanced through grades to lt. gen., 2003; chief spl. ops. divsn., Office Chmn. Joint Chiefs of Staff The Pentagon, 1994—95; dep. dir. ops., readiness & mobilization U.S. Army; dep, dir. spl. activities CIA; comdg. gen. Spl. Forces Command U.S. Army, Ft. Bragg, NC, 1998-2000, commdg. gen. Spl. Warfare Ctr., 2000—03; dep. under sec. intelligence US Dept. Def., Washington, 2003—. Recipient Def. Superior svc. medal with 3 oak leaf clusters, Legion of Merit with 1 oak leaf cluster, Bronze star, Air medal, Purple Heart. Office: US Dept Def 1000 Def Pentagon Washington DC 20301

BOYKINS, MICHAEL L., lawyer; b. Jan. 17, 1965; BS, U. Wis., 1987, JD, 1990. Ptnr., co-chmn. firm racial & ethnic diversity com. McDermott Will & Emery LLP. Fellow: Am. Coll. Investment Counsel; mem.: Chgo. Com. Minorities in Large Law Firms (bd. dir.), Econ. Club Chgo., Wis. Bar Assn., Ill. Bar Assn. Office: McDermott Will & Emery LLP 227 W Monroe St Chicago IL 60606 Office Phone: 312-984-7599. Office Fax: 312-984-7700. Business E-Mail: mboykins@mwe.com.

BOYKO, CHRISTOPHER ALLAN, federal judge; b. Cleve., Oct. 10, 1954; s. Andrew and Eva Dorothy (Zepko) B.; m. Roberta Ann Gentile, May 29, 1981; children: Philip, Ashley. B in Polit. Sci. cum laude, Mt. Union Coll., 1976; JD, Cleve. Marshall Coll. Law, 1979. Bar: Ohio 1979, Fla. 1985, U.S. Dist. Ct. (no. dist.) Ohio 1979, H.S. Ct. Appeals (6th cir.) 1990, U.S. Tax Ct. 1986, U.S. Supreme Ct., 1988. Prin. Boyko & Boyko, Parma, Ohio, 1979—93, 1995; asst. prosecutor City of Parma, 1981-87, prosecutor, 1987—93, dir. of law, 1987-93; exec. v.p., gen. counsel copy Am., Inc., 1993-94; judge Parma Mcpl. Court, 1993, Ct. Common Pleas, Cuyahoga County, Ohio, 1996—2004, Judicial Corrections Bd., 1999—2004; chair Ct. Vet. Svc. Com., 2000—04, policy com., 2003—04; judge U.S. Dist. Ct. (No. dist.) Ohio, 2005—. Guardian ad litem Juvenile Ct., 1979-93; legal advisor spl. weapons and tactics divsn. City of Parma Police Dept., 1984-93; chief counsel S.W. Enforcement Bur., 1991-93; mem. faculty Ohio Jud. Coll., Nat. Jud. Coll., lectr. FBI Nat. Acad. jud. editor Law and Fact Com., 1999-2003. Active Citizens League of Greater Cleve., 1985-2004; former trustee Cops & Kids, Inc., Cleve. Bar Assn., 2000—, County Bar Assn.; mem. Parma Drug Task Force, 1987-1993; mem. adv. com. Parmadale Children's Svcs., 1991—; mem. St. Anthony's Sch. Commn. Mem.: Nat. Inst. Trial Advocacy (steering com. 2003—), Mt. Union Coll. Alumni Assn., Am. Inns of Ct. Found. (William K. Thomas Inn of Ct. 2004), Narcotics Law Officers Assn., Parma Bar Assn. (past pres., past trustee), Cleve. Bar Assn. (former past bd. trustees, lectr. in law), Cuyahoga County Bar Assn., Ohio Bar Assn., Fla. Bar Assn., ABA, Cuyahoga County Police Chiefs Assn. (assoc.), Elks. Byzantine Catholic. Avocations: martial arts, reading, fitness. Office: 801 W Superior Ave Cleveland OH 44113 Office Phone: 216-357-7151. Business E-Mail: christopher_boyko@ohnd.uscourts.gov.

BOYKOFF, THOMAS M., retired lawyer; s. Jules Y. and Frieda Boykoff; children: Jules M., Maxwell, Molly. BA, U. Wis., Madison, 1964; JD, U. Mich., Ann Arbor, 1967. Staff atty. Wis. Legis. Coun., Madison, 1970—75; dir. tech. svc. Wis. Dept. Rev., Madison, 1975—79; commr. Wis. Tax Appeals Commn., Madison, 1979—84, 1999—2004; ret., 2004; gen. coun. Commr. Savings and Loan, Madison, 1984—96, adminstr., 1996—99. Instr., lectr. U. Wis. Law Sch., Madison, 1979—91; hearing examiner Madison Rent Abatement Program, 1988—; apptd. mem. Wis. Supreme Ct. Bd. of Bar Examiners, Madison, 2006—. Author: How to Represent a Client Before the Wis. Tax Appeals Com., 1985; contbr. editor: Community Property in a Nutshell, 2d edit., 1988; contbr. articles to profl. jours. Pres. Friends of Madison Libr., 2006—; bd. dirs. Hist. Madison, Inc., Madison, 1999—, U. Wis. Women's Basketball Team Booster Club, Madison, 2000—05; mem. Miss Madison Pageant Com., 2004—06. Mem.: Jane Austen Soc. N.Am. (treas. Wis. region 2005—), State Bar Wis. (pres. govt. lawyers divsn. 1993—95, conv. com. 1999—), Dane County Bar Assn. (program com. 1984, 2000—), Madison Sherlock Holmes Soc. (facilitator 1988—). Avocations: baseball card collecting, stamp collecting/philately, reading. Home: 221 S High Point Rd #305 Madison WI 53717 Personal E-mail: thomb222@aol.com.

BOYLAN, ELIZABETH SHIPPEE, academic administrator, biologist, educator; b. Shanghai, Nov. 29, 1946; d. Nathan M. and Elizabeth (Little) Shippee; m. Robert J. Boylan, Oct. 2, 1971; children: Elizabeth B., Emily A. AB, Wellesley Coll., 1968; PhD, Cornell U., 1972. Postdoctoral fellow U. Rochester (N.Y.) Sch. Medicine, 1972-73; asst. prof. Queens Coll. CUNY, Flushing, 1973-78, assoc. prof., 1978-82, prof. biology, 1983-95, acting asst. provost, 1988-89, asst. provost, 1989-90, assoc. provost, 1990-92; acting provost Queens Coll. CUNY, Flushing, 1992-93; assoc. provost acad. programs and planning Queens Coll., Flushing, 1994-95; provost and dean of faculty Barnard Coll., NYC, 1995—, prof. biology, 1995—. Chmn. Queens Coll. Acad. Senate, 1985-88; mem. grad. faculty Grad. Ctr. CUNY, N.Y.C., 1977-95; vis. investigator Sloan-Kettering Inst. Cancer Rsch., N.Y.C., 1979-80; trustee N.Y. Met. Ref. and Rsch. Libr. Agy., Manhattan, 1989-97, chmn. fin. com. 1991-97; co-chmn. bd. trustees study com. on secondary edn. CUNY, 1987-88, co-chair vice chancellor's task force on sci., engring., tech. and math., 1988-89; panelist NSF grad. fellowship program, 1992-93; cons. to Nat. Cancer Inst., N.J. Commn. on Cancer Rsch., Endocrine Soc.; mem. breast cancer task force NCI, 1980-84; mem. adv. com. Am. Cancer Soc., 1981-85; Am. Coun. Edn. fellow Pace U., 1993-94; commr. Commn. on Higher Edn., Mid. States Assn. Colls. and Schs., 1999-2004. Contbr. and reviewer articles to profl. publs.; patentee in field. Grantee Nat. Cancer Inst., 1975-83, Am. Inst. Cancer Rsch., 1987-90, Am. Fedn. Aging Rsch., 1988-89. Mem. AAAS, Soc. Devel. Biology, Am. Assn. Cancer Rsch., N.Y. Acad. Scis., Sigma Xi. Office: Barnard Coll Office of Provost 3009 Broadway New York NY 10027-6501 Office Phone: 212-854-2708. Business E-Mail: eboylan@barnard.edu.

BOYLAN, KEVIN BERNARD, neurologist; b. Arlington, Mass., Aug. 20, 1956; s. Charles Vincent and Edith Murial (Aho) B. BA in Social Sci. cum laude, U. Calif., Irvine, 1979, BS in Biology, 1979; MD, U. Calif., San Francisco, 1983. Diplomate Nat. Bd. Med. Examiners, Am. Bd. Psychiatry and Neurology, also Sub.-Bd. Clin. Neurophysiology, Am. Bd. Electrodiagnostic Medicine. Intern Johns Hopkins Hosp., Balt., 1983-84; fellow neurology U. Calif., San Francisco, 1984-87, fellow med. genetics, 1985-87, resident, 1987-90; fellow neuromuscular diseas Johns Hopkins Hosp, 1990-91; instr. neurology Johns Hopkins U., 1991; asst. prof. Mayo Grad. Sch. Medicine, Jacksonville, Fla., 1992—; assoc. cons. Mayo Clinic, Jacksonville, Fla., 1992-94, cons., 1994—, 1994—. Dir. EMG lab. Mayo Clinic, 1994—; dir. Muscular Dystrophy Assn. Clinic N.E. Fla., 1994—. Contbr. numerous articles to profl. jours. Multiple Sclerosis fellow Nat. Multiple Sclerosis Soc., 1984-87, Charles A. Dana fellow Charles A. Dana Found., 1990-91. Mem. AAAS, Am. Soc. Human Genetics, Am. Acad. Neurology, Duval County Med. Assn. Office: Mayo Clinic Dept Neur 4500 San Pablo Rd S Jacksonville FL 32224-3899

BOYLAN, MERLE NELSON, librarian, educator; b. Youngstown, Ohio, Feb. 24, 1925; s. Merle Nelson and Alma Joy (Kepple) B. BA, Youngstown U., 1950; M.L.S., Carnegie-Mellon U., 1956; postgrad., U. Ariz., 1950—51, Ind. U., 1952. Libr., Pub. Health Libr. U. Calif., Berkeley, 1956-58; sci. librarian U. Ariz., Tucson, 1958-59; engring. librarian Gen. Dynamics/Convair, San Diego, 1959-61, Gen. Dynamics/Astronautics, 1961-62; assoc. librarian Lawrence Radiation Lab., U. Calif., Livermore, 1962-64, library mgr., 1964-67; chief librarian NASA Ames Rsch. Ctr., Moffett Field, Calif., 1968-69; asso. dir. libraries U. Mass., Amherst, 1969-70, dir. libraries, Univ. librarian, 1970-72; dir. libraries U. Tex., Austin, 1973-77, U. Wash., Seattle, 1977-89, dir. emeritus, 1989—, prof. Sch. Librarianship, 1982-89; exec. bd. Amigos Bibliographic Council, 1974-77; mem. fin. com., governance com., user's council, computer service council Wash. Library Network, 1978—. Del. Gov.'s Conf. Librs. and Info. Svcs., 1979; sec. Texas State Bd. Libr. Examiners, 1974-77; mem. bibliographic networking and resource sharing advisory group Southwestern Libr. Interstate Coop. Endeavor, 1975-77; sec., chmn. exec. bd. Pacific N.W. Bibliographic Ctr., 1977-83; mem. com. centralzed acquisitions of libr. materials for internat. studies Ctr. for Rsch. Librs.; del. OCLC Users Coun., 1981-86. Sec. bd. trustees Littlefield Fund for So. History, 1974-77, Fred Meyer Charitable Trust; mem. adv. bd. Libr. and Info. Resources for Northwest, 1984-87. Mem. ALA, Assn. Coll. and Rsch. Librs. (legis. com. 1977-81), Assn. Rsch. Librs. (bibliographic control com. 1979-83), Spl. Librs. Assn., Am. Soc. Info. Sci., Beta Phi Mu. Home: 1354 Bellefield Park Ln Bellevue WA 98004-6854 Office: Univ of Wash Librs Suzzallo Libr Seattle WA 98195-0001

BOYLE, ALAN, editor; b. Bernard, Iowa, Aug. 24, 1954; s. Orland and Irma Boyle; m. Tonia Boyle; children: Natalie, Evan. BA in English and Philosophy, Loras Coll., Dubuque, Iowa, 1976; MS in Journalism, Columbia U., NYC, 1977. Features editor Spokesman-Rev., Spokane, Wash., 1978—84; fgn. desk editor Seattle Post-Intelligencer, 1985—96; sci. editor MSNBC, Redmond, Wash., 1997—. Presenter in field. Author: (web coverage) MSNBC Space News (Space Journalism award, 06), (web log) Cosmic Log (Sci. Journalism award AAAS, 02). Mem.: Coun. Advancement Sci. Writing (bd. dirs. 2005—), Nat. Assn. Sci. Writers, Soc. Profl. Journalists (pres. western Wash. pro chpt. 2002—03), NW Sci. Writers Assn. (pres. 2005—). Office: MSNBC 1 Microsoft Way Redmond WA 98052 Office Phone: 425-706-1867.

BOYLE, ANN M., dean, dental educator; BA, Case Western Reserve U., 1971; DMD, Fairleigh Dickinson U., 1975, MA in Ednl. Psychology, 1984. Cert. gen. practice Hackensack Hosp., 1976; managament cert. Harvard U., 1999. Mem. faculty Coll. Dental Med. Fairleigh Dickinson U., 1976—90, chair restorative dept., 1988—90; chair restorative dept. to assoc. dean acad. affairs Sch. Dentistry Case Western Reserve U., Cleveland, 1991—94; assoc. dean Sch. Dental Med. So. Ill. U., 1995—2002, acting dean, 2002—03, dean, prof. restorative dentistry, 2003—. Extramural pvt. practice. Fellow: Pierre Fauchard Acad., Am. Coll. Dentists; mem.: ADA (mem. commn. on Dental Accreditation), Internat. Assn. Dental Rsch., Am. Assn. Dental Rsch., Am. Dental Edn. Assn., Acad. Operative Dentistry. Office: So Ill U Sch Dental Med 2800 College Ave Bldg 273/2300 Alton IL 62002

BOYLE, ANTONIA BARNES, writer, editor; b. Detroit, May 21, 1939; d. James Merriam and Florence (Maiullo) B.; 1 child, Caitlin Merriam Burns. BS in Comm., Northwestern U., Evanston, Ill., 1962. Staff announcer WEFM-FM, Chgo., 1975-78; pres. Boyle Communications, Chgo., 1978-85; exec. producer Nightingale-Conant Corp., Chgo., 1985-90, Cassette Prodns. Unltd., Irwindale, Calif., 1990-92; pres. Antonia Boyle & Co., 1992—; v.p. content acquisition Youachieve.com, Inc., 1997—. Author: The Optimal You, 1990, Taping Yourself Seriously, 1991; co-author (with Jay Gordon): Good Food Today, Great Kids Tomorrow, 1994; co-author: (with Scott McKain) Just Say Yes, 1994; co-author: (with William McCurry) Guerrilla Managing for the Imaging Industry, 1997; co-author: (with William McCurry and Harold Lloyd) It's Your People-.Really!, 2005; co-author: (with K.D. Sullivan) The Gremlins of Grammar, 2005. Chmn., bd. dirs. Horizons for the Blind, Chgo., 1984; bd. dirs. WNUR FM Alumni, Northwestern U., Evanston, 2002-03; mem. Off-Campus Writers Workshop, Winnetka, Ill. Mem. AFTRA. Mailing: 3223 Lake Ave Ste 15C No 349 Wilmette IL 60091-1174 Personal E-mail: aboyleco@earthlink.net.

BOYLE, BARBARA DORMAN, film company executive; b. NYC, Aug. 11, 1935; d. William and Edith (Kleiman) Dorman; m. Kevin Boyle, Nov. 26, 1960; children: David Eric, Paul Coleman. BA in English with honors, U. Calif., Berkeley, 1957; JD, UCLA, 1960. Bar: Calif. 1961, N.Y. 1964, U.S. Supreme Ct. 1964. Atty. bus. affairs dept, corp. asst. sec. Am. Internat. Pictures, LA, 1960-65; ptnr. Cohen & Boyle, LA, 1967-74; exec. v.p., gen. counsel, chief op. officer New World Pictures, LA, 1974-82; sr. v.p. prodn. Orion Pictures Corp., LA, 1982-85; exec. v.p. prodn. RKO Pictures, LA, 1986-87; pres. Sovereign Pictures, Inc., LA, 1988-92, Boyle and Taylor Prodns., 1993-99, Valhalla Motion Pictures, LA, 2000—03; chair film, TV and digital media dept. UCLA, 2003—. Lectr. in field. Exec. prodr. (film) Eight Men Out, 1987, Bottle Rocket, 1995, Campus Man; prodr. (films) Mrs. Munck, 1995, Phenomenon, 1996, Instinct, 1999; exec. prodr. The Hi Line, 1998; co-prodr. Phenomenon II, 2002; contbr. chpts. to books. Bd. dirs. UCLA Law Fund Com., L.A. Women's Campaign Fund; pres. Ind. Feature Project/West; founding mem. entertainment adv. coun. sch. law UCLA, co-chmn. 1979-80, co-chair, 2002-03. Named UCLA Law Sch. Alumni of Yr, 1999, Women in Film Crystal award, 2000. Mem. Acad. Motion Picture Arts and Scis. (exec. com.), Acad. TV Arts and Scis. (exec. com.), Women in Film (pres. 1977-78), Hollywood Women's Polit. Com., Calif. Bar Assn., N.Y. State Bar Assn. Office: UCLA Sch of Theater Film & TV 203 E Melnitz Box 951622 Los Angeles CA 90095-1622 Office Phone: 310-825-7741. Business E-Mail: boyle@tft.ucla.edu.

BOYLE, CANDYACE, psychologist; b. Jackson, Tenn., Dec. 15, 1978; d. Max and Janis Horton; m. LeVarr Boyle, May 12, 2003. BA, Baylor U., 2001; MA, U. Memphis, 2002, Edn. Specialist Degree, 2004. Nat. cert. sch. psychologist NASP, 2004. Sch. psychologist Hardeman County Bd. of Edn., Bolivar, Tenn., 2004—. Mem.: NASP (nat. cert. sch. psychologist), Tenn. Assn. Sch. Psychologists. Office: Hardeman County Board of Education PO Box 112 10815 Old Hwy 64 Bolivar TN 38008 Home Phone: 731-217-4119; Office Phone: 731-658-2510 120. Office Fax: 731-658-2061. Business E-Mail: boylec@k12tn.net.

BOYLE, CHRISTOPHER GEORGE, language educator, counseling administrator; b. Binghamton, NY, July 27, 1930; s. Edward George and Mary Giblyn B.; m. Mary Ella Morris, Dec. 30, 1951; children: Catherine Flowers, Anne Butler, Russell, Elizabeth O'Brien. AB, Amherst Coll., 1952; EdM, Harvard U., 1960. Cert. secondary tchr., Ariz., cmty. coll. tchg. cert., Ariz. English tchr., coach St. Stephen's Sch., Austin, 1952-54, Worcester (Mass.) Acad., 1954-55; English tchr., dept. head, coach St. Andrew's Sch., Middletown, Del., 1955-80; Fulbright tchr. of English U.S. Dept. of State, Helsinki, Finland, 1962-63; English dept. head, dean of studies, tchr., coach, counselor St. Gregory Coll. Preparatory Sch., Tucson, Ariz., 1980-94. Instr. Freshman English U. Del., Newark, 1970-71; part-time coll. counselor, cons. Catalina Foothills H.S., Tucson, 1997-99; advanced placement English lit exam. reader, cons., Coll. Bd./Ednl. Testing Svc., Princeton, N.J., 1965-96, workshop leader for AP English tchrs., San Jose, Calif., 1989-97; reader Scholastic Assessment Test English essays, 1967-2004. Contbr. articles to profl. jours. Mem. Del. Coun. of Tchrs. of English (pres. 1969-71). Episcopalian. Avocations: scuba diving, choral music, reading. Home: 4820-L E Fort Lowell Rd Tucson AZ 85712-1262 E-mail: cboyle727@aol.com.

BOYLE, DANIEL ROBERT, musician, delivery service executive; b. Bowling Green, Ohio, Dec. 5, 1973; s. Robert Theodore Boyle and Linda Marie (Goris) Boyle; 1 child from previous marriage, Frederic Joseph Edward. B magna cum laude, Bowling Green State U., 1996; postgrad., U. Toledo, 1997—98. Choir dir. Evergreen Local Schs., Metamora, Ohio, 1996—2000; mid. sch. choral dir. Maumee City Schs., Ohio, 2000—02; sales rep. Verizon Wireless, Findlay, Ohio, 2002—03; driver FedEx Ground, Toledo, 2003—. Organist, choir dir. St. Louis Cath. Ch., Custar, Ohio, 1981—97, Grace Luth Ch., Elmore, Ohio, 1997—. Advisor 4-H, Portage, Ohio, 1991—97. Recipient Man of Yr., Sigma Alpha Iota, Bowling Green State U., 1994; Pres.'s scholar, Bowling Green State U., 1991—95. Mem.: Am. Soc. Composers, Authors, Publishers, Am. Guild Organists, Evergreen HS Future Farmers Am. (hon.), Phi Eta Mu, Golden Key, Phi Mu Alpha Sinfonia (music/ritual dir. warden 1994—95). Lutheran. Avocations: bicycling, composing music. Home: 6638 N Texas St Whitehouse OH 43571 Personal E-mail: danboyle@wcnet.org.

BOYLE, E. THOMAS, federal magistrate judge; b. Paterson, NJ, Apr. 30, 1939; m. Mary Lou Kelly; two children. BS in English, Holy Cross Coll., 1961; LLB, U. Va., 1964. Bar: N.Y. 1965, U.S. Ct Appeals (2d cir.) 1974, U.S. Dist. Ct. (ea. and so. dists.) N.Y. 1974. Assoc. Mendes & Mount, NYC, 1965-66; trial counsel Legal Aid Soc. Suffolk County, NY, 1966-72; appellate counsel Fed. Defender Svcs., NYC, 1972-75; pvt. practice Smithtown, NY, 1975-88; county atty. Suffolk County, Hauppauge, NY, 1988-92; ptnr. Boyle, Shea & Nornes, Hauppauge, NY, 1992-95; magistrate judge for ea. dist. N.Y. U.S. Dist. Ct., Uniondale, 1995—. Mem. 2d Circuit Conf. Planning Com., 2001—04. Office: 834 Fed Plz Long Island Fed Courthouse 834 Central Islip NY 11722 Office Phone: 631-712-5710.

BOYLE, EDWARD J., lawyer; b. Bklyn., July 3, 1941; BA, St. John's U., 1964, JD, 1967. Bar: NY 1967, US Dist. Ct. So., No., & Ea. Districts NY, US Supreme Ct., US Ct. Appeals 2nd, 7th, & 11th Circuits. Law clk. NY State Ct. Appeals, 1967—69; pvt. practice atty., 1969—75, 1977—83; chief trial counsel NY regional office SEC, 1975—77; ptnr. Wilson, Elser, Moskowitz, Edelman & Dicker LLP, NYC, 1983—. Mng. editor St. John's Law Rev., 1966—67. Mem.: ABA, Assn. of the Bar of the City of NY, NY State Bar Assn. Office: Wilson Elser Moskowitz Edelman & Dicker LLP 23rd Fl 150 E 42nd St New York NY 10017-5639 Office Phone: 212-490-3000 ext. 2392. Office Fax: 212-490-3038. Business E-Mail: boylee@wemed.com.

BOYLE, FRANCIS ANTHONY, law educator; b. Chgo., Mar. 25, 1950; AB in Polit. Sci., U. Chgo., 1971; JD magna cum laude, Harvard U., 1976, AM, 1978, PhD, 1983. Bar: Mass. 1977. Tchg. fellow, assoc. Harvard U. and Ctr. Internat. Affairs, 1976—78; tax atty. Bingham, Dana & Gould, Boston, 1977—78; prof. law U. Ill., Champaign, 1978—. Prof. USSR Summer U. Jurists, 1989; Parhad lectr. U. Calgary, 2001; Bertrand Russell peace lectr. McMaster U., 2007. Author: World Politics and International Law, 1985 (Outstanding Acad. Book, Choice mag. 1985-86), Defending Civil Resistance Under International Law, 1987, The Future of International Law and American Foreign Policy, 1989, The Bosnian People Charge Genocide, 1996, Foundations of World Order, 1999, The Criminality of Nuclear Deterrence, 2002, Palestine, Palestinians and International Law, 2003, Destroying World Order, 2004, Biowarfare and Terrorism, 2005, Protesting Power, 2007; contbr. articles to profl. jours. Mem. bur. polit.-mil. affairs (scholar-diplomat program) U.S. Dept. State, 1981; bd. dirs., coordinating coun. Lawyers Com. on Nuc. Policy, 1981—; cons. Amnesty Internat., 1983—; chmn., panel of jurists IPO Brussels Tribunal on Reagan Adminstrns. Fgn. Policy, 1984; advisor Coun. for Responsible Genetics, 1985—; cons. UN Com. on Exercise of Inalienable Rights of Palestinian People, 1987—; bd. dirs. Amnesty Internat. USA, 1988-92; gen. agent Republic of Bosnia and Herzegovina Internat. Ct. Justice with E&P Powers, 1993-94; atty of record E&P Chechen Republic of Ichkeria, 2000—; Chechen amb. to Norway, 2004-05. Mem. Am. Soc. Internat. Law (ad hoc guidelines com. 1978-80, Lieber group on laws of war 1979—), Phi Beta Kappa, Sigma Xi (cert. of merit and prize in biology). Office: U Ill Coll Law 504 E Pennsylvania Ave Champaign IL 61820-6909 Office Phone: 217-333-7954. Business E-Mail: fboyle@law.uiuc.edu.

BOYLE, GERTRUDE, sportswear company executive; b. Augsberg, Germany, 1924; came to U.S., 1938; d. Paul and Marie Lanfrom; m. Neil Boyle, 1948; children: Tim, Kathy, Sally. BA in Sociology, Univ. Ariz., 1947. Pres., CEO Columbia Sportswear Co., Portland, Oreg., 1970-88, CEO, 1988-94, chmn. bd., 1994—. Named one of Best Mgrs. Bus. Week Mag., 1994, Am.'s Top 50 Women Bus. Owners Working Woman mag., Woman of Yr. Oreg. chpt. Women's Forum, 1987. Office: Columbia Sportswear Co 14375 NW Science Park Dr Portland OR 97229-5418

BOYLE, JACK H., retail executive; With Famous-Barr May Dept. Stores Co.; v.p. mdse. planning and allocation Kohl's Corp., Menomonee Falls, Wis., 1999, divisional mdse. mgr. for jrs., sr. v.p. misses' and sportswear, exec. v.p., gen. mdse. mgr. women's apparel and accessories, 2005—. Office: Kohls Corp N56 W17000 Ridgewood Dr Menomonee Falls WI 53051-5660 Office Phone: 262-703-7000.*

BOYLE, JANE J., federal judge, lawyer; b. Sharon, Pa., Dec. 15, 1954; BS, U. of Tex., Austin, 1977; JD, So Meth. U., Dallas, 1981. Asst. dist. atty. Dist. Atty.'s Office, 1981-87; asst. U.S. atty. U.S. Dist. Ct. (no. dist.) Tex., 1987-90, magistrate judge U.S. Dallas, 1990—2002, U.S. atty., 2002—04; judge US Dist. Ct. (no. dist) Tex., 2004—. Office: US Courthouse 1100 Commerce St Rm 1452 Dallas TX 75242

BOYLE, JOHN HOWARD, history educator; b. Everett, Wash., Aug. 6, 1955; s. Charles Raymond and Nancy Jane Boyle; m. Betsy Anne Burrow; 1 child, McKenzie Rose. BS in History, So. Oreg. U., Ashland, 1977; MS in Geography, U. Oreg., Eugene, 2002. Cert. secondary edn. tchr. Oreg., 1984. Tchr. U. Oreg., Eugene, Jackson Alternative, Ashland, 1984—90, Nyssa Middle Sch., Oreg., 1990—95, Lowell H.S., Oreg., 1996—. Coach varsity girls basketball Lowell H.S., 1998—2002. Advisor Serenity Lane, Medford, Oreg., 1985—90, Spl. Olympics, Ashland, 1988—90, Hi-Q, Eugene, Oreg., 2000—. Mem.: US Golf Assn. (Lifetime Achievement award 2004). Home: 481 Cardinal Way Springfield OR 97477 Office: Lowell HS 45 S Pioneer St Lowell OR 97452

BOYLE, KAMMER, financial planner, investment advisor, research analyst, options trader; b. New Orleans, June 17, 1946; d. Benjamin Franklin and Ethel Clair (Kammer) B.; m. Edward Turner Barfield, July 23, 1966 (div. 1975); children: Darren Barfield, Meloe Barfield. BS in Mgmt. magna cum laude, U. West Fla., 1976; PhD in Indsl./Organizational Psychology, U. Tenn., 1982. Lic. psychologist, Ohio, Tenn.; reg. securities rep. InterSecurities, Inc., Nat Assn. Securities Dealers. Pvt. practice mgmt. psychology, Knoxville, 1978-81; tchg. and rsch. asst. U. Tenn., Knoxville, 1977-81; mgmt. trainer U.S. State Dept., Washington, 1978; cons. PRADCO, Cleve., 1982-83; pres., cons. Mgmt. and Assessment Svcs., Inc., Cleve., 1983-90; pres. Kammer Investment Co., Cleve., 1989-96; fin. asst. advisor O'Donnell Securities Corp., Cleve., 1997-98; registered securities prin., investment advisor rep. and retirement specialist Wealth Charter Group, 1998—2004, asset mgr., options trader, rsch. analyst, 2005—. Mem. editl. rev. bd. Jour. of Managerial Issues, 1987; author and presenter ann. Conf. APA, 1980, Southeastern Psychol. Conf., 1979, ann. Conf. Soc. Indsl./Orgnl. Psychologists, 1987, ann. conf. Am. Soc. Tng. and Devel., 1988. Mem. Jr. League Am., Pensacola, Fla., 1970-75; treas. Bar Aux., Pensacola, 1971. Recipient Capital Gifts Stipend U. Tenn., 1976-80; Walter Bonham fellow, 1980-81. Mem. APA, Cleve. Psychol. Assn., Orgn. Devel. Inst., Acad. of Mgmt., Soc. Advancement Mgmt. (pres. 1974-75), Am. Soc. Tng. and Devel. (chpt. rep. career devel. 1984-86), Cleve. Psychol. Assn. (bd. dirs. 1987-88), Real Estate Investor's Assn. (Cleve., trustee/sec. 1992-94), Mensa. Office: Wealth Charter Group 1154 Castleton Rd Cleveland OH 44121

BOYLE, KEVIN GERARD, historian, educator, writer; b. Detroit, Oct. 7, 1960; s. Kevin C. and Anne Boyle; m. Victoria Lynn Getis, Jan. 4, 1992; children: Abigail Grace, Hannah Claire. BA, U. Detroit, 1982; PhD, U. Mich., 1990. Asst. prof. history U. Toledo, 1990—94; asst./assoc. prof. history U. Mass., Amherst, 1994—2002; assoc. prof. history Ohio State U., Columbus, 2002—. Author: The UAW and the Heyday of American Liberalism, 1945-1968, 1995, Arc of Justice: A Saga of Race, Civil Rights, and Murder in the Jazz Age, 2004 (Nat. Book Award for Nonfiction, 2004); co-author: Muddy Boots and Ragged Aprons: Images of Working-Class Detroit, 1900-1930, 1997; editor: Organized Labor and American Politics, 1894-1994: The Labor-Liberal Alliance, 1998. Fellow, Rockefeller Found., 1990—91, Mary Ball Wash. Chair in Am. History, J. William Fulbright Found., 1997—98, Am. Coun. Learned Socs., 2001—02, NEH, 2001—02, John Simon Guggenheim Found., 2001—02. Home: 173 N Stanwood Rd Bexley OH 43209 Office: Ohio State Univ Dept History Dulles Hall Columbus OH 43210 Office Phone: 614-292-7101.

BOYLE, KEVIN RICHARD, lawyer; s. Richard E. and Janet E. Boyle. BA, Vanderbilt U., 1994; JD 1st in class, U. Ariz., 1997. Bar: Calif. 1997, DC 1999, U.S. Ct. Appeals (9th cir.) 1998, U.S. Dist. Ct. (ctrl., no. and so. dists.) Calif. 2001. Law clk. to Hon. Melvin Brunetti U.S. Ct. Appeals (9th cir.), Reno, 1997—98; assoc. Kirkland & Ellis, Washington, 1998—99; law clk. to Chief Justice William H. Rehnquist U.S. Supreme Ct., Washington, 1999—2000; atty. Greene, Broillet, Panish & Wheeler, Santa Monica, Calif., 2001—05; founding ptnr. Panish, Shea & Boyle, LA, 2005—. Office: Panish Shea & Boyle 11111 Santa Monica Blvd Ste 700 Los Angeles CA 90025 Office Phone: 310-477-1700. Business E-Mail: Boyle@PSandB.com.

BOYLE, LARA FLYNN, actress; b. Davenport, IA, Mar. 24, 1970; m. Donald Ray Thomas, Dec. 18, 2006. Actor: (films) Poltergeist III, 1988, Dead Poet's Society, 1989, How I Got into College, 1989, The Rookie, 1990, The Dark Backward, 1991, Eye of the Storm, 1991, May Wine, 1991, Mobsters, 1991, Wayne's World, 1992, Where the Day Takes You, 1992, Equinox, 1992, The Temp., 1993, Three of Hearts, 1993, Red Rock West, 1993, Threesome, 1994, Baby's Day Out, 1994, The Road to Wellville, 1994, Cafe Society, 1995, THe Big Squeeze, 1996, Red Meat, 1997, Farmer & Chase, 1997, Afterglow, 1997, Happiness, 1998, Susan's Plan, 1998, Chain of Fools, 2000, Speaking of Sex, 2001, Men in Black II, 2002, Land of the Blind, 2006, Fwiends.com, 2006; (TV movies) Terror on Highway 91, 1989, The Preppie Murder, 1989, Past Tense, 1994, Jacob, 1994, Since You've Been Gone, 1998, Crazy, 2005, The House Next Door, 2006, Shades of Black: The Conrad Black Story, 2006; (TV series) Twin Peaks, 1990-91, The Practice, 1997-2003, Huff, 2004-05, Las Vegas, 2005-06; (TV mini-series) Amerika, 1987; (TV appearances) Sable, 1987, The Hidden Room, 1991, Legend, 1995, Ally McBeal, 1998, 2002*

BOYLE, OLABISI ARIYO, manufacturing engineer; m. John Boyle; 1 child, Robert John. BS, Fordham U., Columbia U. Sch. Engring., 1988, MS, 1991. Various engring. position Ford Motor Co., Wayne, Mich., 1995—98, supr. vehicle ops. quality, 1998—2001, mgr. mfg. strategy & bus. planning, 2001—04; sr. mgr. product strategy DaimlerChrysler Corp., Auburn Hills, Mich., 2004—. Recipient Most Promising Engr., Women of Color Tech. Awards, 2005. Office: DaimlerChrysler Corp 1000 Chrysler Dr Auburn Hills MI 48326-2766

BOYLE, RICHARD EDWARD, lawyer; b. Westville, Ill., Mar. 27, 1937; s. Kelley George and Florence (Weisert) B.; m. Janet E. Peskar, Nov. 22, 1968; children: Kevin, Douglas, Leslie. BA, U. Ill., 1959, LLB, 1961. Bar: Ill. 1962, Mo. 1985, U.S. Dist. Ct. (so. dist.) Ill. 1962, U.S. Dist. Ct. (cen. dist.) Ill. 1962, U.S. Dist. Ct. (ea. dist.) Mo. 1991, U.S. Ct. Appeals (7th cir.) 1975, U.S. Supreme Ct. 1985. Assoc. Costello, Wiechert, Roberts & Gundlach, 1962-68; ptnr. Gundlach, Lee, Eggmann, Boyle & Roessler, Belleville, Ill., 1968—. With USAFR. Fellow Am. Coll. Trial Lawyers, Am. Bar Found. (mem. Adv. Group Civil Justice Reform Act 1990—); mem. Am. Bd. Trial Advs., Nat. Assn. R.R. Trial Counsel (pres. 1991-92), St. Clair County Bar Assn. (pres. 1979-80), Am. Bd. Trial Advocates (named one of Best Lawyers in Am.). Home: 13 Oak Knoll Pl Belleville IL 62223-1817 Office: Gundlach Lee Eggmann Boyle & Roessler Box 23560 5000 W Main St Belleville IL 62226-4727

BOYLE, RICHARD JOHN, art historian, author; b. NYC, June 3, 1932; s. James and Gertrude (Eichhorn) B.; m. Patricia Murray, June 19, 1971; 1 son, Eric; stepchildren: Rick, Cheryl, Barbara. BA, Adelphi U., Garden City, NY, 1954; cert. fine art, Oxford U., Eng., 1959; postgrad., Art Students League, NYC, 1962. Profl. painter, 1959-66; curator Internat. Art Found., Newport, R.I., 1962; dir. Middletown (Ohio) Fine Arts Ctr., 1963-65; curator painting and sculpture Cin. Art Mus., 1965-73; dir. Pa. Acad. Fine Arts, 1973-82; lectr. art history Phila. Coll. Art, 1984-86, acting dir. continuing edn., 1986; lectr. art history Phila. Coll. of Textiles, 1990—; assoc. prof. Temple U., Japan, 1991-92. Adviser Nexus Gallery, Artist Coop.; lectr. Tyler Sch. of Art, Temple U., 1987—; coll. art assoc., mem. bd. advisors Creative Artists Network, 1985—; mem. artistic advisors Am. Poetry Rev., 1983—. Author: American Impressionism, 1974, John Twachtman, 1979; co-author: Genius of American Painting, 1973, Willard Metcalf, 1988, Connection With A Place: The Collection of the Brandywine River Museum, 1991; art editor: Ency. Am. History, 1973. Mem. exec. com. Phila. Devel. Corp. Served with U.S. Army, 1954-56. Benjamin Franklin fellow Royal Soc. Arts, 1976 Mem. Nat. Soc. Lit. and Art.

BOYLE, TATIANA GENNADIEVNA, research scientist; b. Khabarovsk, Russia, June 15, 1969; arrived in U.S., 1995, naturalized, 2004; d. Gennadyi Petrovich Sapozhnikov and Tamara Mikhailovna Sapozhnikova; m. David Edward Boyle, Nov. 29, 1997; 1 child, Austin Michael. MS in Biology and Chemistry magna cum laude, Khabarovsk State Pedagogical U., 1991; PhD in Biology, Russian Acad. Scis., Ecology Rsch. Inst., Khabarovsk, 1995. Sr. scientist Russian Acad. Scis., Khabarovsk, 1991—99; rsch. scientist USDA Forest Svc., Sitka, Alaska, 1997—98; sr. scientist North Pacific Mountain Flora Rsch., Portland, Oreg., 1997—. Scientist Tahoe-Baikal Inst., South Lake Tahoe, Calif., 1995—97; sr. scientist Sustainable Ecosystems Inst., Portland, Oreg., 1999—; author and editor TV series Path in the Forest, 1998. Author: Distribution and Preservation of Rare Vascular Plant Species (Khabarovsk Territory, Jewish Autonomous Region), 1994, Rare Plants of Khabarovsk Ter., 1998; contbr. chapters to books. Mem.: AAAS, Am. Inst. Biol. Scis. Achievements include research in new species habitats in Siberia and Alaska; new classification for rare plants species; development of sys. of natural protected areas for rare and endangered species in Russian Far East. Avocations: skiing, photography. Personal E-mail: dr.tatianaboyle@gmail.com. Business E-Mail: postmaster@drboylelab.com.

BOYLE, T.C., writer, literature educator; b. Peeksill, NY, Dec. 2, 1948; married, 1974; 3 children. BA U. Potsdam, 1968; MFA, U. Iowa Writer's Workshop, 1974; PhD in 19th century brit. lit. U. Iowa, 1977; LHD (hon.), SUNY, 1991. Prof. of English, founder, creaitve writing program U. of Southern Calif., 1978—. Author: stories have appeared in The New Yorker, Harper's, Esquire, The Atlantic Monthly, Playboy, The Paris Review, GQ, Antaeus, Granta, (book) Descent of Man, 1979 (St. Lawrence award for fiction, best story collection of the yr., 1980), Water Music, 1982 (Prix Passion publishers prize for best novel of the yr., 1989), Budding Prospects, 1984, Greasy Lake, 1985 (Commonwealth of Calif., Silver medal for lit., 55th ann. awards, 1986), World's End, 1987 (Commonwealth Club of Calif. gold medal for lit., best novel of the yr., 57th ann. awards, 1988, PEN/Faulkner award, best novel of the yr., 1988, Editor's Choice, N.Y. Times Book Review, one of the 16 best books of the yr., 1987), If the River was Whiskey, 1989 (Editor's Choice, N.Y. Times Book Review, one of the best 13 books of the yr., 1989, PEN Ctr. West Literary prize, best short story collection of the yr., 1989), East is East, 1990, The Road to Wellville, 1993, Without A Hero, 1994, The Tortilla Curtain, 1995 (Prix Medicis Etranger, 1997), Riven Rock, 1998, T.C. Boyle Stories, 1998 (Bernard Malamud prize in short fiction from the PEN/Faulkner Found., 1999), A Friend of the Earth, 2000, After the Plague, 2001 (Souther Calif. bookseller's assn. award for best fiction title of the yr., 2002), Drop City, 2003 (Nat. Book award finalist), (other) The Inner Circle, 2004, (book) Tooth and Claw, 2005; co-author: Talk Talk, 2006. Recipient Nat. Endowment for the Arts fellowship, 1977, 1983.

BOYLE, TERRENCE W., federal judge; b. Passaic, NJ, Dec. 22, 1945; married; 3 children. BA, Brown U., 1967; JD, Am. U., 1970. Minority counsel housing subcommittee, banking and currency com. US Ho. Reps., 1970-73; legis. asst. to Senator Jesse Helms US Senate, 1973; judge US Dist. Ct. (ea. dist.) NC, 1984—, chief judge, 1997—2004; nominee US Ct. Appeals (4th cir.), 2005. Office: US Dist Ct PO Box 306 Elizabeth City NC 27907-0306*

BOYLE, TIM, apparel executive; s. Gert Boyle; m. Mary Boyle; 2 children. BS in Journalism, U. Oreg., 1971. With Columbia Sportswear Co., Portland, Oreg., 1970—, pres., CEO, 1989—. Trustee Reed Coll.; mem. Young Presidents' Orgn.; bd. dirs. Pacific Crest Outward Bound Sch., Jesuit H.S. Named one of Sports Industry's 100 Most Influential Players, Sportstyle mag., 1993—96; recipient N.W. Entrepreneur of Yr. award, Inc. Mag., 1992.

BOYLE, WILLIAM CHARLES, engineering educator; b. Mpls., Apr. 9, 1936; s. Robert and Daphne Boyle; m. Nancy Lee Hahn, Apr. 11, 1959; children: Elizabeth Lynn, Michele Jenette, Jane Lynette, Robert William. CE, U. Cin., 1959, MS in Sanitary Engring., 1960; PhD in Environ. Engring., Calif. Inst. Tech., 1963. Registered profl. engr., Wis., Ohio. With Milw. Sewerage Commn., 1955-56; civil engr. O. G. Loomis & Sons, Covington, Ky., 1956-59; asst. engr. Ohio River Valley Water Sanitation Commn., summer 1959; asst. prof. dept. engring. U. Wis., Madison, 1963-66, assoc. prof., 1966-70, prof. dept. civil and environ. engring., 1970-96, chmn. dept. civil and environ. engring., 1984-86, assoc. chair, 1988-96, emeritus prof., 1996—. Vis. prof. Rogaland Distriktshogskole, Stavanger, Norway, 1975-76; vis. prin. engr. Montgomery Engrs. Inc., Pasadena, Calif., 1988-89; cons. Procter & Gamble Co., Monsanto Co., S.B. Foot Tanning Co., Wis. Canners & Freezers Assn., Wis. Concrete Pipe Assn., Oscar Mayer & Co., Bartlett-Snow, Hide Svc. Corp., W.R. Grace & Co., Lake to Lake Dairies, Milw. Tallow, Wausau Paper Co., Packerland Packing Co., Ray-O-Vac, U.S. Army CERL, Owen Ayres & Assocs., Donohue Engrs., Davy Engrs., Carl C. Crane, Green Engring., RSE divsn. Ayres & Assocs., Schreiber Corp. Inc., Sanitaire, J.M. Montgomery, Engrs., Camp, Dresser, McKee, Phila. Mixing Sys., Polkowski, Boyle, & Assocs., Rust E&I Com.; peer rev. panel on environ. engring. EPA; accreditation visitor Accreditation Bd. for Engring. and Tech., 1990—. Contbr. chapters to books, articles to profl. jours. Sr. warden St. Andrews Episcopal Ch., Madison, 1972-74, treas., 1979-85. Recipient Engring. Disting. Alumnus award U. Cin., 1986, Founders award U.S.A. nat. com. Internat. Assn. Water Pollution Rsch. & Control, 1988, commendation EPA, 1989; Mills Found. scholar U. Cin., 1954-59; USPHS trainee, U. Cin., 1959-60; fellow Ford Found., Calif. Inst. Tech., 1960-61, USPHS, Calif. Inst. Tech., 1961-63 Mem. ASCE (life, advisor U. Wis. student chpt. 1968-71, chmn. student affairs com. 1970-72, chmn. profl. activities com. 1972-74, nat., control mem. tech. coun. on codes and standards-environ. standards 1999—, chmn. environ. stds. devel. coun. 1998-2001, chair oxygen transfer standards com., 1975-2002, history and heritage com., vice chair water infrastructure security enhancement stds., reviewer EED Jour., Rudolf Hering medal 1975, Engring. Achievement award Wis. chpt. 1986, Engr. of Yr. award Wis. sect. 1998), Water Environment Fedn. (life, rsch. com., joint task force-pretreatment of wastewater, tech. practice com.-energy in treatment plant design, chmn. program com., bd. control, 1996-98, jour. reviewer, chmn. tech. practice com. task force on aeration, Radebaugh award 1978, Eddy award com. 1992-98, Harrison Prescot Eddy Rsch. medal 1989, chmn. rsch. symposia, editl. bd. 2004—, water environ. rsch. found. 2005—, Gordon Maskew Fair medal for environ. engring. edn., 1992, Arthur Sydney Bedell award 2001), Am. Water Works Assn. (life, chmn. task group on oxygen transfer), Am. Acad. Environ. Engrs. (diplomate, life, accreditation vis. Accreditation Bd. Engring and Tech., chmn. edn. com. 1993, trustee 1994-97, pres. 1999-2000, rep. bd. dir. ABET, 1994-2000, commr. Engr. Accreditation comm. 2001-05, Stanley E. Kappe award 2002), Am. Foundrymen's Soc. (com. on waste disposal, Outstanding Rsch. Paper award environ. cen. div. 1989), Sigma Xi, Theta Tau, Phi Eta Sigma, Chi Epsilon, Tau Beta Pi (advisor U. Wis. student chpt. 1994-96). Episcopalian. Avocations: photography, travel. Home: 105 Carillon Dr Madison WI 53705-4614 Office: Univ Wis 2256 Engineering Hall 1415 Engineering Dr Madison WI 53706-1607 E-mail: boyle@engr.wisc.edu.

BOYLE, WILLIAM LEO, JR., educational consultant, retired academic administrator; b. Utica, NY, July 23, 1933; s. William Leo and Gladys (Kuney) B. AB, Colgate U., 1955; postgrad. in Spl. Mgmt. Program, Cornell U. Law Sch., 1960—61; MA, Columbia U., 1964, Profl. Diploma in Ednl. Adminstrn., 1967, EdD, 1969; LLD (hon.), Hawthorne Coll., 1979; postdoctoral, Harvard U., 1979—81; LHD (hon.), Mercy Coll., 1983; LittD (hon.), Curry Coll., 1992. Participant advanced mgmt. program, recruiter, ednl. adviser Procter & Gamble Co., Cin., 1958-60; legis. aide higher edn. com. N.Y. State Senate, Albany, 1961-62; account exec., ednl. cons. Batten, Barton, Durstine & Osborn, NYC, 1962-64; assoc. dir. devel., presdl. asst. Wesleyan U., Middletown, Conn., 1964-65; program cons. Coun. for Aid to Edn., NYC, 1965-70, asst. v.p., 1970-72, v.p., 1972-75; pres. Keuka Coll., Keuka Pk., NY, 1975—78, Curry Coll., Milton, Mass., 1978—92, pres. emeritus, 1992—; part-time practice as ednl. cons. to pvt. colls. and univs., Utica, 1992—. Pres., trustee 1036 Park Avenue Corp., NYC, 1970—74; ednl. cons. Pres. Ford Com., Washington, 1976. Author: The National Corporate Educational Support Movement, 1954-1966, 1969; contbr. articles to ednl. and profl. jours. Vice chmn. nat. bus. and industry com. Colgate U., Hamilton, NY, 1974—, mem. nat. coun., 1975—, ann. fund exec. com., 1975—, Colgate '55 class agt., 1994—, mem. maj. gifts com., established Boyle Scholarship, 1985, Boyle award in polit. sci., 1997; mem. bd. devel. com. Cmty. Found., Utica, 1992—98; established Boyle Individual Fund, Cmty. Found., Utica, 1991, Boyle Parents Meml. Fund, Cmty. Found., Utica, 2002; bd. dirs. Slocum-Dickson Found., Utica, 1991—, Family Svcs. of the Mohawk Valley, Utica, 1992—, House of the Good Shepherd, Utica, 1992—, Oneida County Hist. Soc., Utica, 1994—. Lt. USAF, 1955—58. Decorated Comdr.'s citation USAF. Mem. various ednl. and profl. orgns., also Colgate Univ. Club (N.Y.C.), Columbia Univ. Club (N.Y.C.), Ft. Schuyler Club (Utica) (bd. mgrs.), Sadaquada Golf Club (Utica), Yahnundasis Golf Club (Utica), Rotary (Paul Harris fellow 2006). Home: 52 Chestnut Hills New Hartford NY 13413-2908

BOYLES, FREDERICK HOLDREN, historian; b. Gainesville, Fla., Nov. 9, 1954; s. Eugene Harry and Frances Louise (Holdren) B.; m. Deborah Anne Beverly, Aug. 21, 1976; children: Cynthia Beverly, Joseph Holdren. A in Edn. and History, Abraham Baldwin Coll., 1974; BS in Edn. and History, U. Ga., 1976; M in Recreation and Parks Adminstrn., Clemson U., 1981. Dir. trail camp Goshen (Va.) Scout Camps, 1975-79; tchr. history and geography Waycross (Ga.) City Schs., 1976-78; instr. grad. students Clemson (S.C.) U., 1978-79; outdoor recreation planner Nat. Park Svc., Atlanta, 1979-81; historian Cumberland Gap Nat. Hist. Park, Middlesboro, Ky., 1981-85; supt. Moores Creek Nat. Battlefield, Currie, NC, 1985-89, Andersonville (Ga.)-Jimmy Carter Nat. Hist. Sites, 1989—. Adj. faculty Lincoln Meml. U., Harrogate, Tenn., 1983-84, U. N.C., Wilmington, 1987. Scoutmaster troop 231 Boy Scouts Am., Americus, Ga., 1994; elder 1st Presbyn. Ch., Americus, 1991—. Comdr. USNR, 1987, comdg. officer navy cargo handling bn. 11, Jacksonville, Fla. Named Supt. of Yr., Nat. Pk. Svc., 1998; recipient Superior Achievement award, U.S. Dept. Interior, 1980, Good Citizenship award, SAR, 1989; scholar Grad. alumni scholar, Clemson U., 1979. Mem. Sumter C. of C. (bd. dirs. 1992—), Americus Rotary Club, Burgaw N.C. Rotary Club (bd. dirs. 1988, 90), Burgaw Area C. of C. (pres. 1989). Home: 200 Webber Rd Americus GA 31719-2136 Office: Nat Park Svc 496 Cemetery Rd Andersonville GA 31711-9707 Office Phone: 229-924-0343. E-mail: fred_boyles@nps.gov.

BOYLES, JAMES KENNETH, retired banker; b. Louisville, Jan. 27, 1916; s. Forrest Lee and Florence (Glenn) B.; m. Hilda Margaret Rose, Sept. 13, 1940; children: Margaret, James, Douglas, Kevin. Student, Columbia U., Am. Inst. Banking, Rutgers U. With Guaranty Trust Co., NYC, 1933-37; loan officer Chem. Bank, NYC, 1937-50; exec. v.p. The Nat. State Bank, Elizabeth, N.J., 1950-83, dir., 1965-88. Trustee emeritus Union Coll., Cranford N.J. Served to 1st lt., inf., U.S. Army, 1942-46, ETO. Decorated Purple Heart. Mem. Robert Morris Assocs. (pres. 1963) Republican. Episcopalian.

BOYLES, WILLIAM ARCHER, lawyer; b. Lakeland, Fla., Aug. 16, 1951; s. Jesse V. and Louise A.; m. Laura M. Rose, June 12, 1977; children: William Archer Jr., John H. BSBA, U. Fla., 1973, JD, 1976, LLM in Taxation, 1978. CPA Fla.; bar: Fla. 1977, U.S. Tax Ct. 1978, U.S. Dist. Ct. (mid. dist.) Fla. 1979. Assoc. Gray, Harris & Robinson, P.A., Orlando, Fla., 1978-82, shareholder, 1982—. Mem. Cen. Fla. Estate Planning Coun. Bd. dirs. Christian Family Svcs., Inc., Gainesville, Fla., 1977-86, Ctrl. Fla. YMCA, Orlando, 1979-81; treas. Univ. Blvd. Ch. of Christ, Orlando, 1979-88; bd. dirs., treas. Orlando Shakespeare Festival, Inc., 1989-97, bd. dirs., 1992, 2d v.p., 1992-95; bd. dirs. Better Bus. Bur. Ctrl. Fla., 1994-02, chair-elect, exec. com. 1994, 95, chmn., 1996-97; Leadership Orlando, Leadership Fla.; mem. Planned Giving Coun. Ctrl. Fla. Mem. ABA, Fla. Bar (exec. coun. tax sect.), Orange County Bar Assn., AICPA, Fla. Inst. CPA's, Am. Assn. Atty.-CPA's, Small Bus. Coun. Am. (polit. action com.), Citrus Club. Republican. Office: Gray Robinson PA 301 E Pine St Ste 1400 Orlando FL 32801-2798 Office Phone: 407-843-8880. Business E-Mail: wboyles@gray-robinson.com.

BOYLL, DAVID LLOYD, retired broadcast executive; b. Terre Haute, Ind., Aug. 17, 1940; s. Lloyd A. and Stella Elizabeth (Ellinger) B.; m. Margie R. Coker, Apr. 14, 1962; children: Elizabeth Marie, Kelli Renae. BS in Edn., Abilene Christian U., 1964. Announcer Sta. KWKC, Abilene, Tex., 1959-64; program dir. Sta. KWKC-AM-FM, Abilene, 1964-68; sta. mgr. Sta. KFMN-FM, Abilene, 1968-74, owner, operator, 1974-80, ptnr., gen. mgr., 1980-82, Sta. KEYJ-AM-FM, Abilene, 1982-92; pres., mgr. Sta. KHXS/EZ106, Abilene, 1992-96; ptnr. KMPC-AM/KWKC-AM, Abilene, 1998—. Part-owner Sta. KYYD (now KWKC-AM), Abilene, 1995—; owner KMPC-EZ 1560, 1997—; ptnr., owner KWKC-AM, KZQQ-AM, 1998—. Pres. Abilene Downtown Assn., 1980-83; pres. Chisholm Trail coun. Boy Scouts Am., 1985-87; chmn. adv. com. Taylor County Juvenile Bd.; chmn. Abilene State Sch. Vols., 1987-90, named Vol. of Yr., 1990; chmn. local emergency planning com. Taylor County. Recipient Silver Beaver award Boy Scouts Am., 1987, Leadership and Comms. award Toastmasters Internat., 2003. Mem. Rotary (past pres., bd. dirs. Abilene club). Republican. Home: 3949 N 9th St Abilene TX 79603-5543 Home Phone: 325-673-5617. Business E-Mail: boyll-david@sbcglobal.net.

BOYNE, WALTER JAMES, writer, retired museum director; b. East St. Louis, Ill., Feb. 2, 1929; s. Walter William and Emily (Campbell) B.; m. Jeanne Quigley, Dec. 26, 1952; children: Mary Louise, Katherine Elizabeth, William James, Margaret Ann. BBA, U. Calif., Berkeley, 1958; MBA, U. Pitts., 1963; PhD (hon.), Salem Coll., 1985. Commd. 2d lt. USAF, 1952, advanced through grades to col., 1971, ret., 1974; asst. curator Nat. Air and Space Mus., Washington, 1974-75, curator, 1975-78, exec. officer, 1978-80, asst. dir., 1980-82, acting dir., 1982-83, dir., 1983-86; ret., 1986. Chmn. bd. dirs. Wingspan TV Channel; aerospace expert in residence Discover Comms.; v.p. Fighter Pilot Prodns.; chmn. Nat. Aeronautic Assn. Author: Boeing B-52, 1981, Messerschmitt Me-262, 1980, Treasures of Silver Hill, 1982, Flying, 1979, Jet Age, 1979, De Havilland DH-4, 1983, McDonnell Douglas F-4, 1983, Vertical Flight, 1983, Leading Edge, 1986, (novel) The Wild Blue, 1986, The Smithsonian Book of Flight, 1987, The Power Behind the Wheel, 1988, Trophy for Eagles, 1989, Weapons of Desert Shield, 1991, Gulf War, 1991, Eagles of War, 1991, Air Force Eagles, 1992, Classic Aircraft, 1992, Art in Flight, 1992, Silver Wings, 1993, Clash of Wings, 1994, Clash of Titans, 1995, Beyond the Wild Blue, 1997, Beyond the Horizons, 1998, Brassey Air Combat Reader, 1999, Aces in Command, 2001, Classic Aircraft, 2001, Best of Wings, 2001, Aviation 100, 2001, Encyclopedia of Air Warfare, 2002, The Two O'Clock War, 2002, Dawn Over Kitty Hawk, 2003, Chronicle of Flight, 2003, The Influence of Air Power on History, 2003, Rising Tide, 2003, Operation Iraqi Freedom, 2003, Today's Best Military Writing, 2003, Roaring Thunder: A Novel of the Jet Age, 2006, Supersonic Thunder, 2007, Collectable Aircraft, 2007, Soaring to Glory, the Air Force Memorial, Beyond The Wild Blue 1947-2007, 2007; prodr., writer: (video) Beyond the Wild Blue; author, host, narrator: (video) Clash of Wings, 1998, The Sculptures of John Safer, 1998. Recipient Best Fgn. Book award Aero Club de France, 1982, Robert A. Brooks award Smithsonian Instn., 1980, Best Fiction and Non-Fiction awards Aviation Space Writers, 1987, Thomas McKean Meml. Cup, 1989, Cliff Henderson Trophy 1986, Gil Robb Wilson award AIA, 1997, President's award lifetime achievement Nat. Aeronautics Assn., 2005, Deacon Lyman award journalistic excellence; named Elder Statesman of Aviation Nat. Aviation Assn., 1998; named to Nat. Aviation Hall of Fame, 2007. Mem. Daedalians, Am. Aviation Hist. Soc. (nat. advisor), Author's Guild, Sons of the Desert, Cosmos Club, Flying Aces Club Home: 20582 Rosewood Manor Sq Ashburn VA 20147 Office Phone: 703-729-8687. Personal E-mail: wboyne@cqi.com, wboyne@verizon.net. *There is a pleasure in work; it is doubled if appreciated by a peer.*

BOYNES, SEAN G., dental anesthesiologist, researcher; b. Wheeling, W.Va., Apr. 19, 1978; s. William and Jennie Boynes; m. Vicki Malush, Apr. 24, 2004. BS, Lipscomb U., 1999; MS, Almeda U., 2003; DMD, U. Pitts., 2003. Diplomate Nat. Dental Bd. Anesthesiology. Faculty clin. rsch. assoc. U. Pitts., 2003—04, residen tin dental anesthesiology, 2003—. Editor-in-chief: The Bull.: The Dental Soc. of Western Pa., 2004—; contbr. articles to profl. jours. Named to, Consumer's Rsch. Coun., America's Guide to America's Top Dentists. Fellow: Am. Dental Soc. of Anesthesiology (assoc. Rsch. Writing award 2004); mem.: ADA (corr.), Pa. Dental Assn. (rep. com. comms.), Am. Dental Edn. Assn., Dental Soc. Western Penn. (dir. commns. publ. relations), Am. Inst. of Biol. Scis. (corr.), Acad. of Gen. Dentistry (corr.), Am. Acad. of Devel. Medicine and Dentistry (assoc.), Am. Soc. of Forensic Odontolgy (assoc.), Am. Soc. of Dental Anesthesiologists (assoc.), Alpha Chi (life), Delta Sigma Delta (life). Achievements include research in the efficacy and clinical anesthetic charactics of 4% articaine with and without epinephrine when administered for dental anesthesia; sedation anesthesia education in dental schools of the United States.

BOYNTON, ALTON L., pharmaceutical executive; PhD in Radiation Biology, U. Iowa, 1972. Dir., med. oncology, Cancer Rsch. Ctr. U. Hawaii, prof. genetics and molecular biology; assoc. dir. Cancer Rsch. Ctr., Hawaii; dir., dept. molecular medicine Northwest Hosp., 1995—2003; co-founder, dir. Northwest Biotherapeutics, Inc., Bothell, Wash., 1996—, chief scientific officer, 1996—, exec. v.p., 2000—03, sec., 2001—, COO, 2001—, pres., 2003—. Office: Northwest Biotherapeutics Inc 18701 120th Ave NE Ste 101 Bothell WA 98011 Office Phone: 425-608-3000.*

BOYNTON, ANDREW C., dean; m. Jane Murphy; children: Owen, Dylan, Ian, Evan. BS, Boston Coll., 1978; MBA, PhD, U. NC, Chapel Hill. Prof. strategy Darden Sch., U. Va.; prof. Kenan-Flager Bus. Sch., 1994—97; prof. strategy Internat. Inst. Mgmt. Devel. (IMD), Lausanne, Switzerland, 1997—2004, dir. MBA program, 1998—2004; dean Carroll Sch. Mgmt., Boston Coll., Chestnut Hill, Mass., 2005—. Contbr. articles to profl. jours. Office: Carroll Sch Mgmt Boston Coll 140 Commonwealth Ave Chestnut Hill MA 02467 Office Phone: 617-552-8420. E-mail: andy.boynton.1@bc.edu.

BOYNTON, FREDERICK GEORGE, lawyer; b. Yokohama, Japan, May 9, 1948; s. Fred Wenderoth and Buelah Eleanor (Nygaard) Boynton; children: Emily Margaret, Charlotte Clayton, Susan Jeanne. BA, The Citadel, 1970; JD, Tulane U., 1973. Bar: S.C. 1973, Ga. 1976, U.S. Dist. Ct. Ga. 1976, U.S. Ct. Appeals (5th and 11th cirs.). Assoc. Smith, Gambrell & Russell, and predecessors, Atlanta, 1976-82, ptnr., 1982-88; sole practice law Atlanta, 1988—2002; of counsel Morris, Hardwick, Schneider, 2002—. Author: Criminal Defense Techniques, 1976; editor articles Tulane Sch. Law Rev. Exec. com. Southside Progress Assn., Atlanta, 1983-84, Leadership Sandy Springs, 1989-90; bd. dirs. Atlanta Union Mission, 1990-97, exec. com., 1991, sec., 1992, adv. bd., 1998—; mem. Local Advisory Coun., Ridgeview Mid. Sch, 2001-03. Served to capt. JAGC, U.S. Army, 1973-76. Fellow Lawyers Found. Ga.; mem. ABA, Fed. Bar Assn. (pres. Atlanta chpt. 1981-82, mem. exec. com. 1982—, dep. chmn. adminstrv. law sect. 1986-87, bd. dirs. younger lawyers divsn. 1981-84, v.p. 11th cir. 1985-87), State Bar Ga. (chmn. adminstrv. law sect. 1987-88), Order of Coif. Office: 7000 Central Pkwy Ste 300 Atlanta GA 30328 Office Phone: 770-392-0500. E-mail: fboynton@closingsource.net.

BOYSE, PETER DENT, academic administrator; b. Saginaw, Mich., Mar. 24, 1945; s. John Wesley and Ellen Elizabeth (Dent) B.; m. Barbra Ann Meehan, Sept. 2, 1972; children: Heather, Cassandra. BA, Albion Coll., 1967; MS, U. Mich., 1969, Oreg. State U., 1973, PhD, 1987. Nuclear scientist Westinghouse, Pitts., 1969-71; dir. student activities Calif. State U., Northridge, 1973-74, epic dir., 1974-76; dir. student devel. Linn-Benton Community Coll., Albany, Oreg., 1976-79, ctr. dir., 1979-82, asst. to pres., 1982-88; exec. v.p., COO Delta Coll., University Center, Mich., 1988—92, pres., 1993—. Facilitator Emerging Leaders Inst., Ann Arbor, Mich., 1990; chair Mich. C. of C. Assn., 2000-01. Contbr. articles to profl. jours. Chair Bd. League Innovation, 2003. Mem. Am. Assn. C. of C. (mem. bd. 2001-04). Avocations: reading, golf, travel. Office: Delta Coll 1961 Delta Dr University Center MI 48710-0001 Home: 6084 Old Hickory Dr Bay City MI 48706-9068

BOYSEN, JONEA GENE, marketing executive, copywriter; d. Robert Dee and Linda Susan Boysen. BS in Mktg., Mgmt. and Psychology, Calif. Luth. U., 2004, MBA in Mktg. and Fin., 2005; grad. Global Bus. Program in Internat. Mgmt., FH-Joanneum, Graz, Austria, 2003. Profl. cert. marketer Am. Mktg. Assn., 2005, cert. bus. communicator Bus. Mktg. Assn., 2005. Mktg. comm. specialist and copywriter UBS Fin. Svcs. Inc., Ventura, Calif., 2003—04; pub. rels. copywriter NBC, Universal and Calif. Luth. U., Burbank, Calif., 2004—04; mgmt. cons., copywriter Jonea Gene Copywriting & Consulting Inc., Myrtle Beach, SC, 1999—; mng. editor The Breeze, Myrtle Beach, 2006—; writer The Weekly Surge, 2006—. Author (copywriter): (mktg. plan) DECA Learn & Earn Project (11th Pl. in Nation, 2000). Mem.: Am. Advt. Fedn., Am. Mktg. Assn., Myrtle Beach C. of C. (amb.), Conway Area C. of C. (bd. dirs.), Sigma Beta Delta, Psi Chi. Achievements include Youngest MBA Grad. at Calif. Luth. U. to date. Avocations: feng shui, time with family, fiance and friends, exercise. Home Phone: 970-667-3051; Office Phone: 843-267-9977.

BOYTER, CALE, film company executive; b. June 28, 1972; m. Melissa Boyter; 1 child. Student, Mont. State U. With Paradigm; asst. to sr. v.p. devel. New Line Cinema, LA. Exec. prodr.: (films) Dumb and Dumberer, 2003, Elf, 2003, Butterfly Effect, 2004, Boy-Next-Door, 2004, A Hist. of Violence, 2005, Wedding Crashers, 2005, Just Friends, 2005, Grilled, 2006, How to Eat Fried Worms, 2006. Office: New Line Cinema 116 N Robertson Blvd Los Angeles CA 90048-3103*

BOYTER, SCOTT M., academic administrator; b. Cedar City, Utah, June 19, 1947; s. Neil K. and Mae (Macfarlane) Boyter; m. Sherrie L. Bowen, Aug. 2, 1974; children: Laura Michelle, Tonia Leigh, Diana Lynn. BS, Brigham Young U., Provo, Utah, 1973, MS with high distinction, 1987. Adminstrv. asst. coll. fine arts and comms. Brigham Young U., Provo, Utah, 1973-76, bus. mgr. Sch. Music, 1976-82, bus. mgr. Coll. Fine Arts and Comm., 1982-94, asst. dean, contr. Coll. Fine Arts and Comm., 1995—. Missionary Ch. Jesus Christ LDS, Ohio, 1967—69. With USAR, 1971—2004. Recipient 1st Sgt. of the Yr. award, 96th Regional Support Command, USAR, 1996. Mem.: Am. Assn. Univ. Adminstrs., Am. Philatelic Soc., Beta Gamma Sigma. Republican. Mem. Lds Ch. Avocations: stamp collecting/philately, WWII history. Home: 331 N 875 E Orem UT 84097-5075 Office: A 501 HFAC Brigham Young Univ Provo UT 84602 Business E-Mail: scott_boyter@byu.edu.

BOZALIS, JOHN RUSSELL, physician; b. St. Louis, Sept. 19, 1939; s. George Sauter and Ruth (Russell) B.; m. Sharon Louise Sabo, June 21, 1963; children: John Jr., David L., Diana. BA, U. Okla., 1961, MD, 1965; MS, U. Mich., 1971. Diplomate Am. Bd. Internal Medicine, Am. Bd. Allergy and Immunology. Intern Henry Ford Hosp., Detroit, 1965-66, resident, 1966-68, chief resident, 1968-69; fellow in allergy-immunology U. Mich., Ann Arbor, 1969-71, instr., 1969-71; clin. asst. prof. U. Tex., San Antonio, 1972-73; pvt. practice Okla. Allergy Clinic, Oklahoma City, 1973—. Clin. instr. Coll. Medicine, U. Okla., 1973, clin. asst. prof., 1977-83, clin. assoc. prof., 1983-89, clin. prof., 1989—; mem. courtesy staff Mercy Hosp., Bapt. Hosp., Deaconess Hosp., St. Anthony Hosp., Presbyn. Hosp., Children's Hosp., Okla. Tchg. Hosp., S.W. Med. Ctr. Trustee Casady Sch., 1977-85, United Way Okla. City, chmn. profl. divsn. 1983, Okla. Health Scis. Found.; bd. dirs. Infant Ctr., 1983-86, Allied Arts Okla. City, 1984-86, 92, Hosp. Hospitality House, 1983-86, United Way Greater Okla. City, 2006; vice chmn. health scis. ctr. U. Okla. Centennial Commn.; bd. trustees McGee Eye Inst., search com. for chmn. dept. ophthalmology and dir., 1991, Okla. City Mus. Art., 2003—, U. Okla. Found., 2003—; active Com. of 100, 1991; bd. trustees Okla. City Pub. Schs. Found., 1989—, Okla. Orthopedic and Arthritis Found., Inc., Bone and Joint Hosp., 1993; trustee Oklahoma City Mus. Arts, 2003—, U. Okla. Found., 2003; chmn. legis. task force for promotion of children's health State of Okla., 2002-06; pres. bd. Schs. Healthy Lifestyles, 1997—. Maj. USAF, 1971-73. Recipient Regents' Alumni award U. Okla., 1992; named Physician of Yr.-Pvt. Practice, U. Okla. Coll. of Medicine Alumni Assn., 1993, recipient dean's award, 1998. Fellow ACP, Am. Coll. Chest Physicians, Am. Acad. Allergy; mem. AMA, Am. Thoracic Soc., Okla. State Med. Assn. (del. 1993—, vice spkr. ho. dels. 1997, trustee 1993—), Okla. Lung Assn., Okla. Thoracic Soc. (pres. 1979), John M. Sheldon Soc., Okla. County Med. Soc. (editor Bull. 1978-83, chmn. orientation com. 1989—, pres. 1996, bd. trustees 1996—), Osler Soc. (pres. 1984), Okla. City Acad. Medicine, Robert M. Bird Soc., U. Okla. Coll. Medicine Alumni Assn. (chmn. rsch. com., pres. 1983-85), Okla. City C. of C. (bd. dirs. 1988-90). Republican. Episcopal. Avocations: hunting, golf, fly fishing, travel, gardening. Office: Okla Allergy and Asthma Clinic PO Box 26827 Oklahoma City OK 73126-0827 Home Phone: 405-843-7115; Office Phone: 405-235-0040. Business E-Mail: jbozalis@oklahomaallergy.com.

BOZDECH, MAREK JIRI, physician, educator; b. Wildflecken, Bavaria, Federal Republic Germany, Oct. 12, 1946; s. Jiri Josef and Zofia Jadwiga (Swiatecka) B.; m. Frances Barclay Craig, Dec. 22, 1967; children: Elizabeth, Andrew, Matthew. AB, U. Mich., 1967; MD, Wayne State U., 1972. Diplomate Am. Bd. Internal Medicine, Am. Bd. Med. Oncology, Am. Bd. Hematology. Intern and resident in internal medicine U. Wis. Hosps., Madison, 1972-75, dir. clin. hematology lab., 1978-82, dir. bone marrow transplantation, 1984-85; asst. prof. medicine U. Wis., Madison, 1978-84, assoc. prof. medicine, 1984-85; clin. fellow in hematology Moffitt Hosp. U. Calif., San Francisco, 1975-76, postdoctoral fellow in hematology Cancer Research Inst., 1976-78, research assoc. Cancer Research Inst., 1977-78, assoc. prof., 1985-89; dir. adult bone marrow transplantation U. Calif. Med. Ctr., San Francisco, 1985-89; chief oncology Kaiser Permanente Med. Ctr., Santa Rosa, Calif., 1989-91; pvt. practice specializing in oncology Hematology Redwood Regional Oncology Ct., Santa Rosa, 1991—. Contbr. articles to profl. jours. Scout leader Boy Scouts Am., Novato, Calif., 1985; bd. trustees Pacific Found. Med. Care, 1995—. Recipient Nat. Research Service award NIH, 1977-78; Wayne State U. scholar, 1971. Mem. ACP, Am. Soc. Hematology, Am. Soc. Clin. Oncology, Assn. No. Calif. Oncologists (bd. dirs. 1994-97), Sonoma County Med. Assn. (bd. dirs. 1994-96). Avocations: skiing, gardening, music, films, theater. Home: 50 La Placita Ct Novato CA 94945-1244 Office: Redwood Regional Oncology 121 Sotoyome St Ste 203 Santa Rosa CA 95405-4822 Personal E-mail: mbozdech@mindspring.com, mbozdech@yahoo.com.

BOZELL, BRENT (L. BRENT BOZELL III), communications executive; b. Washington, July 14, 1955; m. Norma Bozell; 5 children. BA in History, Univ. Dallas, Irving. Founder, pres., chmn. bd. dirs. Media Rsch. Ctr., Alexandria, Va., 1987—; founder, pres., chmn. Parents TV Coun., LA, 1995—2007. Invited spkr. in field; founder Culture and Media Inst., 2006—. Co-editor: And That's the Way It Isn't: A Reference Guide to Media Bias, 1990; author, Weapons of Mass Distortion: The Coming Meltdown of the Liberal Media, 2004; nationally syndicated columnist contbr. articles to newspapers including The Wall St. Journal, The Washington Post, Washington Times, LA Times, Nat. Rev., Investors Business Daily; TV commentator and invited guest on Hannity & Colmes, The O'Reilly Factor, NBC Today Show, CNN Inside Politics, Larry King Live, Good Morning America, C-SPAN, CBN and Entertainment Tonight; guest, guest host (radio shows) ABC Radio, NPR Morning Edition, Michael Reagan Show, Rush Limbaugh Show; launched CNSNews.com, 1998. Founder, pres., Conservative Victory Com.,1987-, now exec. dir.; nat. fin. chmn. Buchanan for President campaign; fin. dir., pres. Nat. Conservative Polit. Action Com., Conservative Comm. Ctr.; mem. Coun. for Nat. Policy Named Pew Meml. Lectr., Grove City Coll., 1998, Alumnus of Yr., U. Dallas, 1998. Office: Media Rsch Ctr 325 S Patrick St Alexandria VA 22314*

BOZEMAN, FRANK CARMACK, lawyer; b. Greenwood, Miss., Oct. 16, 1933; s. Frank Carmack and Mamie Hyatt (Pyle) B.; m. Mary Ireland Callcott, Dec. 29, 1961; children: Frank C. III, William Pyle, Thomas Anderson. BA, U. of South, 1955; MA, U. Va., 1956; JD, Washington and Lee U., 1960. Bar: Fla. 1960, Va. 1960. Assoc. Beggs and Lane, Pensacola, Fla., 1960-65; ptnr. Harrell, Wiltshire, Bozeman, Clark & Stone, Pensacola, 1965-75, Carlton, Fields, Ward, Emmanuel, Smith & Cutler, P.A., Pensacola, 1975-93, Bozeman, Jenkins & Matthews, Pensacola, 1993—. Editor Washington and Lee Law Rev., 1960. Chmn. Eagle Scout rev. com. Boy Scouts Am., Pensacola, 1961-63; trustee U. of the South, 1990-96. Capt. USAF, 1956-57. Mem. Am. Bd. Trial Advs. (pres. Pensacola chpt. 1989-90), Fla. Def. Lawyers Assn., Fedn. Ins. and Corp. Counsel, Register of Pre-Eminent Lawyers, Def. Rsch. Inst., Order of Coif, Phi Beta Kappa, Phi Delta Phi (Grad. of Yr. award 1960). Republican. Episcopalian. Avocations: sailing, gardening, civil war history and research. Home: 122 W Lloyd St Pensacola FL 32501-2637 Office: Bozeman Jenkins & Matthews PO Box 13105 Pensacola FL 32591-3105 Office Phone: 850-434-6223.

BOZEMAN, THEODORE D., religion educator; b. Gainesville, Fla., Jan. 27, 1942; s. Simuel Bozeman and Kathleen Ford; m. Hannelore Bozeman, July 29, 1973. BA, Eckerd Coll., 1964; BD, Union Theol. Sem., NYC, 1968; ThM, Union Sem., Richmond, Va., 1970; PhD, Duke U., 1974. Prof. U. Iowa, 1974—. Author: Protestants in an Age of Science, 1977, To Live Ancient Lives, 1988, The Precisionist Strain, 2004. NEH fellow, 1982, 95; recipient James Henley Thornwell award Presbyn. Hist. Assn., 1975. Mem. Am. Soc. Ch. History, Orgn. Am. Historians, So. Hist. Assn., Am. Hist. Assn. Office: U Iowa Dept Religious Studies Iowa City IA 52242 Business E-Mail: d-bozeman@uiowa.edu.

BOZINOVSKI, STEVO, computer science educator, researcher; s. Misko and Goluba Bozinovski; m. Liljana Bulakovska Bozinovska; children: Nevena, Adrian. BEE in Computer Sci., U. Zagreb, Croatia, 1973; MSc in Electronics, U. Zagreb, 1975, PhD in Computer Sci., 1982; diploma in Robotics and FMS, State Acad. Sci., Krems, Austria, 1993. Vis. rschr. U. Mass., Amherst, 1980—81; prof. U. Cyril and Methodius, Skopje, Macedonia, 1983—2001; assoc. prof. S.C. State U., Orangeburg, 2001—. Vis. scholar Kanazawa Inst. Tech., Japan, 1984, U. Mass., Amherst, 1995—96; vis. rschr. German Info. Tech. Ctr., Sankt Augustin, 1999, 2000; conf. organizer Biocybernetics Soc., Skopje, 1978—84; session organizer on genetics, metabolics and flexible mfg. SCI Multiconf., Orlando, Fla., 2001;

guest editor Jour. Automatika, Zagreb, 1985. Author: Consequence Driven Systems, 1995; book cover pages; contbr. articles to profl. jours. Recipient Award for best paper in robotics, ETAN (Electronics, Telecommunications, Automation, and Nuclear Engineering Soc.), Nis, Yugoslavia, 1985; Fulbright Found. grantee, 1980, 1995. Mem.: IEEE, N.Y. Acad. Sci., Macedonian Biocybernetics Soc. Achievements include first to control robots using EEG and EOG signals; solve delayed reinforcement learning problem using neural network; introduce a neural feeling-based self-reinforcement learning mechanism; recognize that DNA is the cell real-time database operating system; introduce robotics metaphor in molecular genetics. Avocations: Macedonian history, comic arts. Home: 241 Wannamaker St Orangeburg SC 29115 Office: South Carolina State Univ 300 College St Orangeburg SC 29117 E-mail: sbozinovski@scsu.edu.

BOZIWICK, GEORGE E., music librarian, composer; b. Rockville Centre, NY, Aug. 23, 1954; s. George Emil Boziwick and Jean Constance Kuch; m. Stephanie Doba, July 26, 1986; children: Anna, Emily. BA, SUNY, Oneonta, 1976; MA in Music Composition, Hunter Coll., 1981; M in Libr. Svc., Columbia U., 1987. Music libr. circulating collections The N.Y. Pub. Libr. for the Performing Arts, NYC, 1986—88, music libr. music divsn., 1988—91, curator Am. Music Collection, 1991—2006, chief music divsn., 2006—. Author: Magnificat, 2005; composer: Opus One Records #135, 162; contbr. articles to profl. jours. Sec. parish adv. coun. Oratory Ch. of St. Boniface, Bklyn., 2000—02, composer, musician, performer, 2003—. Mem.: Am. Music Ctr., Music Libr. Assn. (coord. Music Publs. Assn./Music Libr. Assn./Maj. Orch. Libr joint com., bd. dirs.), Soc. for Am. Music (bd. dirs. 2001—04). Avocation: blues harmonica player. Home: 614 10th St Brooklyn NY 11215 Office: NY Pub Libr for the Performing Arts Music Divsn 40 Lincoln Center Plaza New York NY 10023 Office Phone: 212-870-1647.

BOZOYAN, SYLVIA, elementary school educator; b. Aleppo, Syria, Feb. 18, 1953; arrived in U.S., 1953; d. Edward Yervant and Takouhi (Knnablian) B. BA, St. Peter's Coll., 1975; MEd, William Paterson Coll., 1978. Cert. elem. tchr. NJ, nursery sch. tchr. NJ. 1st grade tchr. Thomas A. Edison Sch., Union City, NJ, 1975—. Armenian sch. tchr. Holy Cross Armenian Ch., Union City, 1972—80, Sunday sch. tchr., 1969—. Named Outstanding Tchr. Govs. Tchr. Recognition Program, N.J., 1987-88, Outstanding Young Woman of Am., Ala., 1982, 87. Mem. Armenian Gen. Benevolent Union of Am. (sec. N.Y./N.J. Met. chpt. 1985-1995, sec., dancer ANTRANIG Dance Ensemble/exec. com. 1979—), N.J. Edn. Assn., Hudson County Edn. Assn., Union City Edn. Assn., Kappa Delta Pi, Pi Lambda Theta. Home: 1812 West St Union City NJ 07087-3311

BOZOZUK, MICHAEL, civil engineer; b. Poland, Nov. 10, 1929; married Marcelle F. M. Daoust, July 20, 1957; children: Lyne, Sylvie, Camille. BSc in Civil Engring., U. Man., Winnipeg, Can., 1952, MSc in Soil Mechanics, 1954; PhD in Geotechnical, Purdue U., 1972. Rsch. officer geotechnical section, divsn. building rsch. Nat. Rsch. Coun. Can., 1953-89; pvt. practice, 1989—96; exec. dir. Engring. Inst. Can., 1994-99. Com. soil and rock instrumentation Transp. Rsch. Bd., 1972-81, com. on founds. of bridges and other structures, 1972-81; chmn. adv. com. civil tech. Algonquin Coll., Ottawa, 1972-76; adv. com. Beaufort Sea artificial island Dept. Indian and No. Affairs, Govt. Can., 1981-84; rsch. com. silo founds. Ont. Silo Assn., 1978-82; Can. Gen. Stds. Bd. Geotextiles, 1980-85; chmn. adv. com. environ./geotechniques Sir Sanford Fleming Coll., Lindsay, Ont., 1983-87; tech. com. on founds. Can. Stds. Assn., 1983-90; mem. Can. Geosci. Coun., 1985-91; S.E. China Tour Lectr., 1986; hon. prof. Chengdu U., China, 1986; sci. advisor various orgns. and univs. Assoc. editor: Can. Geotech. Jour., 1982—86. Recipient Hon. award Caisse Populaire St. Genevieve, Ottawa, Can. Engring. Centennial Silver Medal, 1987, Cert. Citizenship City Calgary, 1987. Fellow Engring. Inst. Can. (Can. Paper award 1960, John B. Stirling medal 1990, Svc. award, 1999, Can. Pacific Railway Engring. medal, 2003), Can. Soc. Civil Engrs., Can. Acad. Engring., Can. Soc. Sr. Engrs., NRC Can. (assoc. com. geotech. rsch., tech. advisor 1985-89, sec. 1989-91); mem. Geocontbns. (founding v.p. 1993-95, pres. 1999-2000), Can. Found. for Geotechnique (pres. 2001-05), Assn. Profl. Engrs. Ont., Can. Geotech. Soc. (cross Can. tour lectr. 1979, pres. 1986-88, chmn. award com. 1986-90, Best Paper prize 1973, Svc. award 1988, R. F. Legget Medal award 1994, A.G. Stermac award, 2006), Ottawa Geotech. Group (sec. 1957-59, chmn. 1976-78), Internat. Soc. Soil Mechanics and Found. Engring., Can. Geotech. Fund (treas. 1985-88), Ottawa Lapsmith Club (pres. 1995). Roman Catholic. Home and Office: 691 Sandra Ave Ottawa ON Canada K1G 2Z7

BOZZELLI, RICHARD, publishing executive; b. Apr. 15, 1958; m. Shannon T. Bozzelli; m. Nelson R., Heather L., Carter M. BS in Acctg. with honors, U. Ala., Birmingham, 1980, postgrad., NYU, 1990. CPA, Ala. Audit supr. Peat Marwick & Mitchell, 1980-84; asst. treas., dir. internal audit Bruno's Inc., 1984; audit mgr., co-dir. small bus. practice Ernst & Young (Ernst & Whinney), 1984-87; v.p., dir. Alabama Bancorp, Birmingham, 1987—; v.p., CFO EBSCO Industries, Inc., Birmingham, 1987—. Bd. dirs. PsychPartners, LLC, Primary Care Physicians Clinics, Inc.; dir. steering com. MBA program U. Ala., Birmingham. Mem. Norton bd. Birmingham So. Coll.; mem. steering com. U. Ala.-Birmingham $20mm Capital Campaign; mem. Young Bus. Leaders of Birmingham; vol. mem. Jefferson County Commn.-Operation New Birmingham; mem. pub. affairs com. Birmingham C. of C. Recipient Class of 1994 Leadership award Nat. Multiple Sclerosis Soc., Outstanding Alumni award U. Ala. Birmingham Sch. Bus., 2003. Mem. AICPAs, Ala. Soc. CPAs (taxation com., ethics com.), U. Ala. Birmingham Nat. Alumni Soc. (bd. dirs., exec. com.), Nat. Assn. Accts. (past bd. dirs. Birmingham Magic City chpt.), Nat. TRIO Alumni Soc. (Ala. chpt.), Metro Sertoma (past mem. bd. dirs.), Beta Alpha Psi (past pres.), Omicron Delta Kappa, Alpha Lambda Delta. Home: 1205 S Cove Ln Birmingham AL 35216-3867 Office: EBSCO Industries Inc 5724 Highway 280 East Birmingham AL 35242 Office Phone: 205-991-6600.

BRAASCH, JOHN WILLIAM, retired surgeon, consultant; b. Rochester, Minn., Dec. 11, 1922; s. William Frederick and Nellie (Stinchfield) B.; m. Nancy Wheeler King, Mar. 21, 1946; children: William Frederick, Elizabeth King, Nancy Kathryn, Peggy Stinchfield. BS, Yale U., 1944; MD, Harvard U., 1946; MS in Physiology, U. Ill., 1948; PhD in Surgery, U. Minn., 1955. Diplomate Am. Bd. Surgery (bd. dirs. 1979-85). Intern St. Luke's Hosp., Chgo., 1946-47; resident in gen. surgery Mayo Clinic, Rochester, Minn., 1950-55; mem. attending staff Mpls. Gen. Hosp., 1955-57, Northwestern Hosp., Mpls., 1955-57; surg. staff New England Bapt. Hosp., Boston, 1957-80, New England Deaconess Hosp., Boston, 1957-80, Lahey Clinic Found., Boston, 1957-96, chmn. dept. surgery, 1971—83; sr. cons. dept. surgery Lahey Clinic, Burlington, Mass., 1983-96, ret., 1996. Asst. clin. prof. surgery Harvard Med. Sch., Boston, 1975—. Author 3 books, several book chpts.; also numerous articles. Capt. U.S. Army, 1948-50. Recipient Balfour award for rsch. Mayo Clinic Found., Rochester, 1955, Mayo Clinic Disting. Alumnus, 2007. Mem. Am. Surg. Assn., Soc. for Surgery Alimentary Tract (v.p. 1987-88), Internat. Soc. Surgery, So. Surg. Soc., New England. Surg. Soc. (pres. 1984-85), Boston Sur. Soc. (pres. 1982), Internat. Hepato-Pancreato-Biliary Surgery Assn. (hon.), Surgeons Travel Club. Republican. Avocations: tennis, gardening, duplicate bridge.

BRAATZ, RICHARD DEAN, chemical engineer; b. Millington, Tenn., July 18, 1966; s. Richard Dean and Loralee Ann (Cota) B. BS, Oreg. State U., 1988; MS, Calif. Inst. Tech., 1991, PhD, 1993. Rsch. engr. Chevron Rsch. Co., Richmond, Calif., 1988; vis. rsch. scientist U. Trondheim, Norway, 1993, DuPont Co., Wilmington, Del., 1993-94; from asst. prof. to assoc. prof. U. Ill., Nat. Ctr. Supercomputing Applications, Urbana, 1994—2002, prof., 2002—, millennium chair, 2006—, sr. rsch. scientist, 1997—2002, prof., 2002—. Vis. prof. MIT, Cambridge, Mass., 2002—03; mem. adv. bd. Indsl. and Engring. Chemistry Rsch., 2005—07. Mem. editl. bd.: Control Sys. Soc., Jour. Process Control, Automatica; contbr. articles to profl. jours. Active Boy Scouts Am., 1983—. Recipient Young Faculty award, DuPont, 1995, Xerox award, 1999; fellow, Hertz Found., 1991. Fellow IEEE (Antonio Ruberti Young Rschr. prize 2005); mem. AIChE (session chair 1995-99, CAST Young Rshr. award 2005, Excellence in Process Devel. Rsch. award 2006), Am. Automatic Control Coun. (session chair 1994-98, Presentation award 1993, Donald P. Eckman award 2000), Am. Soc. Engring. Edn. (Curtis W. McGraw Rsch. award 2004) Avocations: hiking, nordic and alpine skiing, wine tasting. Home: 2310 E Shurts Cir Urbana IL 61801-6748 Office: Univ Ill 293 Roger Adams Lab 600 S Mathews Ave # C-3 Urbana IL 61801-3602

BRABECK, MARY MARGARET, dean, psychology professor; BA, U. Minn., 1967, PhD, 1980; MS, St. Cloud U., 1970. Tchr. Bryant Jr. H.S., 1968—71; instr. U. Minn., 1971—75; instr. psychology Salve Regina Coll., Newport, RI, 1976—80; asst. prof., coord. The Human Devel. Program Boston Coll., Chestnut Hill, 1980—86, assoc. prof., 1986—92; assoc. prof., divsn. dir. Lynch Sch. Edn., Boston Coll., 1988—90, prof., chair dept. counseling, devel. psychology and rsch. methods, 1990—92, assoc. dean, 1992—95, dean, 1996—2003, prof., 1996—2003; dean The Steinhardt Sch. Edn., NYU, 2003—, prof. psychology, 2003—. Vis. prof. Brown U. Ctr. Human Devel., 1995—96; chmn. bd. Am. Assn. Colls. Tchr. Edn. Recipient Kuhmerker award, Assn. Moral Edn., 1996, Boston Higher Edn. Partnership Svc. award, 2002, Alumni Achievement award, U. Minn., 2006. Fellow: APA (bd. ednl. affairs 2004—06, com. on women leadership award 2006, Presdl. citation 2006, Presdl. award 2005). Office: Steinhardt Sch Edn Joseph & Violet Pless Hall NYU 82 Washington Sq E New York NY 10003 Business E-Mail: mary.brabeck@nyu.edu, mmb7@nyu.edu.

BRACCO, LORRAINE, actress; b. Bklyn., Oct. 2, 1954; m. Daniel Guerard, 1979 (div. 1982); 1 child, Margaux; m. Harvey Keitel, 1982 (div. 1993); 1 child, Stella; m. Edward James Olmos, Jan. 28, 1994 (dec. Mar. 1, 2002). Studied, Actors Studio; studied with Stella Adler, Ernie Martin, John Strasberg. Acttress: (films) Duos sur canape, 1979, What Did I Ever Do to the Good Lord to Deserve a Wife Who Dinks in Cafes with Men?, 1980, Commissaire Moulin, 1980, Fais gaffe a la gaffe, 1981, A Complex Plot About Women, Alleys and Crimes, 1986, The Pick-Up Artist, 1987, Someone to Watch Over Me, 1987, Sing, 1989, The Dream Team, 1989, As Long as It's Love, 1989, Sea of Love, 1989, Goodfellas, 1990 (Acad. award nominee for best supporting actress 1990, LA Film Critics Assoc. award for best sup. actress, 1990), Talent for the Game, 1991, Switch, 1991, Medicine Man, 1992, Radio Flyer, 1992, Traces of Red, 1992, Being Human, 1994, Even Cowgirls Get the Blues, 1994, The Basketball Diaries, 1995, Hackers, 1995, Les Menteurs, 1996, Silent Cradle, 1997, Ladies Room, 1999, Tangled, 2000, Your Aura is Throbbing, 2000, Riding in Cars With Boys, 2001, Tangled, 2001, Death of a Dynasty, 2003, Max and Grace, 2004, My Suicidal Sweetheart, 2005; (TV movies) Scam, 1993, Getting Gotti, 1996, Lifeline, 1996, The Taking of Pelham One Two Three, 1998, Custody of the Heart, 2000, Sex in our Century, 2001, Dinner with the FoodFellas, 2006; (TV series) The Sopranos, 1999-2007,(SAG award for Outstanding Performance by an Ensemble in a Drama Series, 2000); (TV appearances) Crime Story, 1986, Law & Order: Trial By Jury, 2005; (off-Broadway plays) Goose and Tom-Tom; (Broadway plays) The Graduate, 2002; dir. (films) AutoMotives, 2000; Author: On the Couch, 2006 Mem.: bd. of dir. Riverkeeper, NY Council for the Humanities. Office: First Artists Assoc 12 W 57th St #PH New York NY 10019-3900

BRACE, FREDERIC F. (JAKE BRACE), air transportation executive; married; 3 children. B in Indsl. Engring., U. Mich.; MBA, U. Chgo. Various fin. mgmt. positions Am. Airlines, Dallas; mgr. oper. budgets United Airlines, Elk Grove Village, Ill., 1988, v.p., contr., 1991—93, v.p. corp. devel., 1993—94, v.p., contr., corp. devel., 1994—95, v.p. fin. analysis, contr., 1995—98, v.p. fin., 1998—99, sr. v.p. fin., treas., 1999—2001; sr. v.p., CFO UAL Corp. and United Airlines, Elk Grove Village, Ill., 2001—02, exec. v.p., CFO, 2002—. Chmn. bd. dirs. United Airlines Employees' Credit Union; bd. dirs. Equant, GetThere.com, Galileo. Trustee Mus. Sci. and Industry, Chgo. Office: UAL Corp 1200 E Algonquin Rd Elk Grove Village IL 60007*

BRACERAS, ROBERTO M., lawyer; AB, Dartmouth Coll., 1991; JD, Yale Univ., 1994. Bar: Mass. 1994. Law clerk, Hon. Nathaniel M. Gorton US Dist. Ct., Dist. of Mass.; trial atty., criminal divsn., fraud sect. US Dept. Justice; ptnr., litig. dept. Goodwin Procter LLP, Boston, mem., diversity com. Bd. dir. Discovering Justice; Goodwin Procter liaison Boston Lawyer's Group. Mem.: Mass. Judicial Nominating Commn. Office: Goodwin Procter LLP Exchange Pl 53 State St Boston MA 02109 Office Phone: 617-570-1895. Office Fax: 617-523-1231. Business E-Mail: rbraceras@goodwinprocter.com.

BRACH, PAUL HENRY, artist; BFA, U Iowa, 1948, MFA, 1950. Tchr. U. Mo., Columbia, 1950-51, New Sch. Social Rsch., NYC, 1952-55, NYU, 1954-67, 86-90, Parsons Sch. Design, 1956-67, The Cooper Union, 1960-62, 79-82, Cornell U., 1965-67; chair dept. visual arts. U. Calif., San Diego, 1967-69; dean Sch. Art Calif. Inst. Arts, Valencia, 1969-75; chair divsn. arts Fordham U., NYC, 1975-79, Empire State Coll., NYC, 1979—95; Milton Avery disting. prof. Bard Coll., NYC, 1993; represented by Flomenhaft Gallery, NYC. Vis. artist U. N.Mex, Albuquerque, 1965; guest critic U. Minn., Mpls., Sarah Lawrence Coll., Bronxville, N.Y., Montclair (N.J.) State Coll., Art Forum Mag., 1976; vis. critic N.Y. studio program Empire State Coll., 1976—; cons. Rutgers U., New Brunswick, 1977; guest critic Bard Coll., Empire State Coll., N.Y.C., 1977; contbg. critic Art Forum Mag., 1977; vis. artist Banff (Can.) Art Ctr., 1979; contbg. critic Art in Am., 1979-2002; guest lectr. Pratt Inst., N.Y.C., 1980, Tuscon Mus. Art, 1992; vis. artist Litho Workshop, Ariz. State U., Tempe, 1981, U. N.Mex., Albuquerque, 1981; guest lectr. Tuscon Mus. Art, 1992. One-man shows at Leo Castelli, N.Y.C., 1957, 59, Cordier Ekstrom Gallery, N.Y.C., 1961-63, Kornble Gallery, N.Y.C., 1971, Andre Emmerich Gallery, N.Y.C., 1974, Jean Millant Gallery, L.A., 1974, Benson Gallery, Bridgehampton, N.Y., 1975, Lerner Heller Gallery, N.Y.C., 1978, 80, Yares Gallery, L.A., 1979, Janus Gallery, L.A., 1980, Yares Gallery, Scottsdale, Ariz., 1981, Bernice Steinbaum Gallery Ltd., N.Y.C., 1983, 85, 87, 90, 91, Elaine Horwitch Galleries, Palm Springs, Calif., 1987, Benton Gallery, Southampton, N.Y., 1987, Vered Gallery, East Hampton, N.Y., 1989, Rancho Linda Vista Gallery, Oracle, Ariz., 1992, Steinbaum Krauss Gallery, N.Y.C., 1994, McAllen (Tex.) Internat. Mus., 1995, Tucson (Ariz.) Mus. Art, 1995, Guild Hall, East Hampton, 1995, Bernice Steinbaum Gallery, Miami, Fla., 2000, others; exhibited in group shows at Wake Forest U. Art Gallery, Winston-Salem, N.C., 1988, Rose Art Mus., Brandeis U., Waltham, Mass., 1988, Anderson Gallery, Va. Commonwealth U., Richmond, 1988, Temple U., Phila., 1988, Alexandra Monet Fine Arts, New Orleans, 1989, Bernice Steinbaum Gallery, N.Y., 1990, Guild Hall Mus., East Hampton Ctr. Contemporary Art, 1990, Weatherspoon Art Gallery, Greensboro, N.Y.C., 1990, Tyler Art Gallery, Oswego, N.Y., 1990, Albright-Knox Art Gallery, Buffalo, 1990, LewAllen/Butler Gallery, Sante Fe, N.Mex., 1993, Vered Gallery, East Hampton, 1993, Steinbaum Krauss Gallery, N.Y.C., 1993, Kent (Conn.) Gallery, 1994, Andre Zarre Gallery, N.Y.C., 1995, U. Iowa, Iowa City, 2002, Flomenhaft Gallery, N.Y.C, 2005, Whitney Mus. Am. Art, 2006; others; represented in permanent collections at Mus. Modern Art, N.Y.C., Whitney Mus. Am. Art, N.Y.C., L.A. County Mus. Art, St. Louis Art Mus., Smith Coll. Mus., Nebr. Art Mus., Albuquerque Mus. Art, Mus. Fine Art, Santa Fe, Phoenix Art Mus., NYU, U. Iowa, others; contbr. articles to profl. jours. Fellow Djerassi Found., Woodside, Calif., 1987, 90.

BRACH, RICHARD S., lawyer; b. Mexico City, 1948; AB, Princeton U., 1969; JD, Columbia U., 1972; attended, Hague Acad. Internat. Law, Netherlands. Bar: N.Y. 1973, England & Wales (registered fgn. lawyer) 1994. Ptnr., head global project fin. group & mem. Latin Am. practice group Milbank, Tweed, Hadley & McCloy, NYC. Mem. ABA, N.Y. State Bar Assn., Assn. Bar City N.Y. Office: Milbank Tweed Hadley & McCloy 1 Chase Manhattan Plz Fl 47 New York NY 10005-1413 Office Phone: 212-530-5350. Office Fax: 212-530-5219. Business E-Mail: rbrach@milbank.com.

BRACHMAN, RON, research and development company executive; BSEE, Princeton U.; MS, PhD, Harvard U. Rsch. v.p. AT&T Labs, 1986—2002; dir. info. processing tech. office U.S. Def. Advanced Rsch. Projects Agy., 2002—05; v.p. worldwide rsch. ops. Yahoo! Inc., NYC, 2005—. Co-author (with Hector Levesque): (textbook) Knowledge Representation and Reasoning, 2004. Fellow: Am. Assn. Artificial Intelligence (past pres.). Office: Yahoo Inc 701 1st Ave Sunnyvale CA 94089

BRACHNA, GABOR (SAMUEL), elementary school educator; b. Cleve, May 14, 1941; s. Gabor and Ethel Brachna; m. Susan Chamberlin, Dec. 24, 1987; children: Christopher, Jonathan. BA, Kent State U., 1963; postgrad., London Sch. Econs., 1964—65; grad. elem. sch. adminstrn., Case Western Reserve State U., Cleve., 1973; moral devel. cert., Harvard U., 1983. Tchr. Cleve. Pub. Sch., 1966—71, adminstrv. intern, 1971—74, peer advisor, 1994—96; rschr. Cleve. C. of C., 1998. Advisor Tchr. Adv. Bd. for Natural History Mus., Cleve., 1988—89; rschr. Intellicor, NYC, 1977; curriculum developer Cleve. Lang. Arts Curriculum Devel. Com., 1971—74. Author (contbg. author): (novels) Whatever Happened to the Paper Rex Man?, 1993, (encyclopedia) Encyclopedia of Cleveland History, 1987, World East Pubs., 1999. V.p. Cleve. Cultural Gardens, 1993; liason rep. Buckeye Woodland Sch. Cmty. Coun., Cleve., 1971—74; moderator Great Decisions Coun. on World Affairs, Lakewood, Ohio. With U.S. Army Nat. Guard, 1965—71. Recipient cert. of appreciation, Kiwanis Club, 1979. Mem.: Knights of St. John of the Hosp. of Jerusalem (Malta). Republican. Lutheran. Avocations: tropical fish, stamps. Home: 2954 Eaton Rd Shaker Heights OH 44122-2516

BRACK, O. M., JR., language educator; b. Houston, Nov. 30, 1938; s. O. M. and Olivia Mae (Rice) B.; 1 child, Matthew Rice; m. Cynthia Alison Burns, May 22, 2004. Student, U. Houston, 1956-57; BA, Baylor U., Waco, Tex., 1960, MA, 1961; PhD, U. Tex., Austin, 1965. Asst. prof. William Woods Coll., 1964-65; asst. prof. English lit. U. Iowa, Iowa City, 1965-68, assoc. prof., 1968-73, dir. center textual studies, 1967-73; prof. English lit. Ariz. State U., Tempe, 1973—. Chmn. 18th Century Short Title Catalogue Com., 1970-73; pres. Arete Publs., Ltd., 1976-81; Albert H. Smith Meml. lectr. bibliography Birmingham Bibliog. Soc., Eng., 1983; vis. fellow U. Oxford Wolfson Coll., 1986-87; mem. adv. bd. 18th-Century Brit. Periodical Subject Index, 1996—, Soc. for Textual Scholarship, 1998; bd. dirs. 18th-Century Short-Title Catalogue, Inc., 1999-2000. Author: Bibliography and Textual Criticism, 1969, Samuel Johnson's Early Biographers, 1971, Hoole's Death of Johnson, 1972, Henry Fielding's Pasquin, 1973, A Catalogue of the Leigh Hunt Manuscripts, 1973, The Early Biographies of Samuel Johnson, 1974, American Humor, 1977, Twilight of Dawn, 1987, Writers, Books and Trade, 1994, Samuel Johnson in New Albion, 1997, The Macaroni Person and the Concentrated Mind, 2004, A Commentary on Mr. Pope's Principles of Morality, or Essay on Man, 2004, The Devil Upon Crutches, 2005, Tobias Smollett, Scotland's First Novelist, 2007; textual editor: Works of Tobias Smollett, 1966—; gen. editor: Works of Tobias Smollett, 1973-86; editor: English Literature in Transition, 1981-82, mem. editl. com., 1982—91; editor: Studies in Eighteenth Century Culture, 1981-86; mem. editl. com.: Yale edit. Works of Samuel Johnson, 1977—; editl. cons. The Literature of England, Scott, Foresman & Co., 1977-79, Works of David Hume, Princeton U. Press, 1990-91, Oxford U. Press, 1995-97; asst. editor: Eighteenth-Century Bibliography, 1964-73, Books at Iowa, 1966-73; editor Eighteenth Century: A Current Bibliography, 1983-90; mem. editl. com.: Age of Johnson, 1985-2003, Rocky Mountain Rev. of Lang. and Lit., 1980-98, Clarissa Project, 1987-2000. Mem. Salvation Army Coun., South Mountain Corps, 1996-2002, chair, 1999-2002. Named Grad. Coll. Outstanding Mentor, 2000; recipient Grad. Coll. Disting. Rsch. award, 1981—82, Rocky Mountains MLA Huntington Libr. award, 1986, Humanities Rsch. award, 1989—90, Faculty Achievement award, Ariz. State U. Alumni Assn., 1991; fellow, Huntington Libr., 1978, Am. Coun. Learned Soc., 1979—80, Newberry Libr., 1982, Andrew W. Mellon Fund, Huntington Libr., 1994, Huntington Libr., 1996, 1997; grantee, Am. Philos. Soc., 1967, NEH, 1993—95, 1995—98; scholar Disting. scholar, Phi Kappa Phi, 1975. Mem. MLA, Am. Soc. 18th Century Studies, East-Ctrl. Soc. 18th Century Studies, South Central 18th Century Soc. (pres. 1982-83), Western Soc. for 18th Century Studies (pres. 2000-01), Brit. Soc. 18th Century Studies, Rocky Mountain MLA, Bibliog. Soc. Am., Bibliog. Soc. U. Va., Bibliog. Soc. (London), Printing Hist. Soc., Am. Printing History Assn., Assn. for Scottish Literary Studies, Samuel Johnson Soc. So. Calif. (bd. dirs. 1989—, pres. 1994-95), The Lichfield Johnson Soc., The Johnson Soc. London, The Johnson Soc. Australian, Grolier Club, The Johnsonians (pres. 2001-02). Episcopalian. Office: Ariz State U Dept English Tempe AZ 85287-0302 Business E-Mail: om.brack@asu.edu.

BRACKEN, HARRY MCFARLAND, philosophy educator; b. Yonkers, NY, Mar. 12, 1926; s. Harry S. and Grace M. (McFarl) B.; m. Eva Maria Laufkotter, Dec. 24, 1949 (div.); children— Christopher, Timothy; m. Elisabeth van Gelderen, June 19, 1985 BA, Trinity Coll., Hartford, Conn., 1949; MA, Johns Hopkins, 1954; PhD, U. Iowa, 1956. Instr. U. Iowa, Iowa City, 1955-57, asst. prof., 1957-61; asso. prof. U. Minn., Mpls., 1961-63; prof. Ariz. State U., Tempe, 1963-66; prof. philosophy McGill U., Montreal, Que., Canada, 1966-91. Prof. U. Calif., San Diego, 1970; vis. prof. Trinity Coll., U. Dublin, Ireland, 1972-73, 79-80; vis. prof. metaphysics U. Coll., Nat. U. Ireland, Dublin, 1972-73, 79-80; adj. faculty philosophy Erasmus U., Rotterdam, 1988-95, Rijksuniversiteit Groningen, 1990-95; adj. prof. philosophy Ariz. State U., 1995—. Author: The Early Reception of Berkeley's Immaterialism: 1710-1733, 1959, 2d edit., 1965, Berkeley, 1974; Mind and Language: Essays on Descartes and Chomsky, 1984, Freedom of Speech: Words Are Not Deeds, 1994, Descartes, 2002; mem. bd. edit. cons. History Philos. Quar., 2005—. Served with USNR, 1943-46, PTO. Recipient Acad. Freedom award Ariz. Civil Liberties Union, 1965; Edn. award J. I. Segal Found. for Jewish Culture, 1972 Mem. Am. Philos. Assn., Internat. Berkeley Soc., The Hume Soc., USS Lauderdale Assn. Home: 9107 E Avenida Las Noches Apache Junction AZ 85218-4676

BRACKEN, (MYRA) JEANNE MUNN, librarian, writer; b. Poughkeepsie, NY, Apr. 15, 1946; d. Richard Earl Munn and Laura Inez Prentice Munn; m. Raymond Ronald Bracken, May 16, 1970; children: Lisa Jeanne, Mollie Howland. BA, U. N.H., Durham, 1968; MS, Simmons Coll., Boston, 1971; student, Philips U., Marburg, Germany, 1966—67. Circulation libr. Boston U. Sch. of Medicine, 1968—69; reference libr. Arthur D. Little, Inc., Cambridge, Mass., 1969—76; asst. reference libr. Acton (Mass.) Meml. Libr., 1978—93; corr., commentator Littleton (Mass.) Ind., 1979—; reference libr. Lincoln (Mass.) Pub. Libr., 1993—. Author: (nonfiction book) Children with Cancer, It All Began With An Apple; editor: The Shot Heard 'Round the World, Women in the American Revolution; author: Someday We'll Laugh About This. Named Libr. of the Yr., N.Y. Times, 2005; recipient Best Editl. award, Mass. Press Assn., 1980, Best Column award, Nat. Newspaper Assn., 1989, Excellence in Cancer Comm. award, Mass. divsn. Am. Cancer Soc., 1983. Mem.: ALA, Sisters in Crime, New Eng. Libr. Assn., Soc. of Children's Book Writers and Illustrators. Congregational/United Church Of Christ. Avocations: mystery lovers' conventions, reading, knitting, travel, swimming. Home: P

O Box 308 Littleton MA 01460 Office: Lincoln Pub Libr 3 Bedford Rd Lincoln MA 01773 Office Phone: 781-259-8465. Personal E-mail: jmbracken@verizon.net. E-mail: jbracken@minlib.net.

BRACKEN, LINDA DARLENE, medical/surgical nurse; b. Muncie, Ind., May 7, 1948; d. Russell Lloyd and Ina Fern (Blaich) Enyeart; m. Norman Harold Bracken, Apr. 15, 1972; children: Aaron Lee, Dana Lynn. ADN, Ind. U., 1968. RN, Ind. Staff nurse, night charge Meth. Hosp., Indpls., 1968-69; office nurse ob/gyn Muncie Clinic, 1969-70; asst. supr. OR Marion (Ind.) Gen. Hosp., 1970-72; staff nurse OR and float Anderson (Ind.) Community Hosp., 1972-83, staff nurse, OR, cardiac cath. lab., 1987-88; office nurse, surgeon Robert McCurdy, Anderson, 1983-84; staff nurse, crit. care McPherson Hosp., Howell, Mich., 1984-87; staff nurse Favorite Nurse, Indpls., 1988-90; staff nurse OR St. John's Health Systems, Anderson, 1992—, Daybreak and Vis. Nurse Care, 2003—, Progressive Homecare Svcs., 2003—05. Pres.: Talking Tours, 1990—. Republican. Avocations: reading, music. Home: 2016 N 900 W Anderson IN 46011-9121 Office Phone: 765-620-2507.

BRACKEN, PAUL, political science professor; b. Phila., Mar. 12, 1948; s. John Joseph and Gertrude (Logue) B.; m. Nanette Elizabeth Beattie, May 25, 1974; children: Kathleen, James, Margaret. BS, Columbia U., 1971, MS, 1976; PhD, Yale U., 1982. Rsch. asst. Fels Ctr. Govt., U. Pa., Phila., 1971-72; sr. staff Ketron, Inc., Arlington, Va., 1972-74; dir. rsch. Hudson Inst., Croton-on-Hudson, NY, 1974-83; asst. prof. Yale U., New Haven, 1983, assoc. prof., 1984-85, prof., 1986—. Lectr. various univs. and colls.; cons. in field. Author: Command and Control of Nuclear Forces, 1983, Fire in the East, 1999; contbr. articles to profl. jours. Mem. Commn. of Conn.'s Future, 1981-85, Inst. Social and Policy Studies, Yale U. Mem. Internat. Inst. Strategic Studies, Yale Ctr. for Internat. Studies, Coun. Fgn. Rels. Avocations: skiing, golf, amateur radio. Home: 22 Green Ln Ridgefield CT 06877-3017 Office: Yale U PO Box 1A New Haven CT 06520 E-mail: bracken7@snet.net.

BRACKEN, PEG, writer; b. Filer, Idaho, Feb. 25, 1918; d. John Lewis and Ruth (McQuesten) B.; m. John Hamilton Ohman, June 15, 1991; 1 child from previous marriage, Johanna Bracken. AB, Antioch Coll., 1940. Author: The I Hate to Cook Book, 1960, The I Hate to Housekeep Book, 1962, I Try to Behave Myself, 1963, Peg Bracken's Appendix to The I Hate to Cook Book, 1966, I Didn't Come Here to Argue, 1969, But I Wouldn't Have Missed It for the World, 1973, The I Hate to Cook Almanack - A Book of Days, 1976, A Window Over the Sink, 1981, The Compleat I Hate to Cookbook, 1986, On Getting Old for the First Time, 1996. Office Phone: 503-294-0443. Personal E-mail: akafeller@aol.com.

BRACKEN, RICHARD M., healthcare company executive; b. Richmond, Va., 1977; m. Judith Bracken; 4 children. B, 1974; M, Med. Coll. Va., 1977. Various exec. positions HCA Inc., 1981—95, pres. Pacific divsn., 1995—97, pres. western group, 1997—2001, CEO, 2001, pres., COO Nashville, 2002—. Mem.: Fedn. Am. Hosps. (bd. dirs.), Calif. Hosp. Assn. (bd. dirs.). Office: HCA Inc 1 Park Plz Nashville TN 37203*

BRACKEN, THOMAS ROBERT JAMES, real estate investment executive; b. Spokane, Wash., Jan. 1, 1950; s. James Lucas and Frances (Cadzow) B.; m. Linda Jacobson, Sept. 9, 1972; children: Karl Forest, David Erskine. BS, Yale U., 1971; MBA, Columbia U., 1972. Sr. appraiser Prudential Ins., NYC, 1972-74, mgr. real estate NYC and Newark, 1974-76, assoc. gen. mgr. Seattle, 1977-78; v.p. First City Investments, Seattle, 1978-80; pres. Fenix, Inc., Seattle, 1980-86; v.p. Washington Mortgage Corp., Seattle, 1982-85, exec. v.p., 1986-88; sr. v.p. Pioneer Bank, Lynwood, Wash., 1985-86; pres.real estate financing USL Capital, San Francisco, 1988-97; sr. v.p. real estate fin. group Orix, USA, San Francisco, 1997-98; pres. Presidio Interfunding Corp., San Francisco, 1998-99; dir. L.J. Melody & Co., San Jose, Calif., 2000—03; mem. Crossbow Capital, LLC, Los Altos, Calif., 2000—; mng. dir. The Broe Cos., San Francisco, 2003—05; sr. v.p. Capmark Fin. Inc., San Francisco, San Jose, 2005—. Mem. Nat. Assn. Indsl./Office Parks (v.p. Seattle chpt. 1981-83), Yale Assn. Western Wash. (pres. 1984-86), Urban Land Inst., Mortgage Bankers Assn. Presbyterian. Avocations: running, sports. Office: Capmark Fin Inc 601 Montgomery St 15th Fl San Francisco CA 94111 Office Phone: 415-646-7712. Personal E-mail: tombracken@msn.com. E-mail: tom.bracken@capmark.com.

BRACKENBURY, JAMES M., manufacturing executive; B, M, Mich. State U. Product engr. Lear Corp., 1983, v.p. interior products divsn. Europe, pres. DaimlerChrysler divsn., 2004, pres. Mex. ops., 2004, sr. v.p., pres. Mex./Ctrl. Am. Regional Group, 2005—06, sr. v.p., pres. North Am. Seating Systems, 2006, sr. v.p., pres. European ops., 2006—. Office: Lear Corp 21557 Telegraph Rd PO Box 5008 Southfield MI 48086 Office Phone: 248-447-1500. Office Fax: 248-447-1722.*

BRACKENRIDGE, N. LYNN, not-for-profit developer; b. Youngstown, Ohio, Sept. 9, 1957; d. John Bruce and Mary Ann (Rossi) Brackenridge; m. Harry Lee Carrico, July 1, 1994. BA, Lawrence U., 1978; MS, Georgetown U., 1980. Tchg. asst. Georgetown U., Washington, 1979-81, admissions officer, 1984-85, editor, writer devel., 1985-87, asst. dir. devel., 1987-89; dir. devel. Cath. Charities U.S.A., Washington, 1989-91, Johns Hopkins U. Bologna (Italy) Ctr., 1991-92; dir. devel. and pub. rels. Nat. Ctr. for State Cts., Williamsburg, Va., 1993-97; v.p. for devel. Gateway Homes Greater Richmond (Va.), Inc., 1998-99, pres., 1999—2004; exec. dir. John Marshall Found., 2004—. Vol. Richmond Ballet, 1993-95, Leukemia Soc. Am., Hampton, Va., 1996—; bd. dirs. Ctrl. Va. chpt. Nat. Alliance for Mentally Ill, 2005. Georgetown U. fellow, 1979-81; recipient diplome d'etudes Inst. d'Etudes Francaises de Touraine, 1976. Mem.: Nat. Soc. Fund Raising Execs. (cert. fund raising exec., chair program com., pres. 1997). Democrat. Avocations: flying small aircraft, running, reading, films, languages. Home: 9303 Cragmont Dr Richmond VA 23229-7610 Office: John Marshall Found 209 W Franklin St Richmond VA 23220 Home Phone: 804-740-8693; Office Phone: 804-775-0861. Business E-Mail: lynnb@johnmarshallfoundation.org.

BRACKETT, COLQUITT PRATER, JR., judge, lawyer; b. Norfolk, Va., Feb. 24, 1946; s. Colquitt Prater Sr. and Antoinette Gladys (Cacace) B.; 1 child, Susan Elizabeth Brackett Brooks. BS, U. Ga., 1966, MA, 1968, JD, 1973, LLM, 1976; travel mktg. profl. diploma, S.E. Tourism Soc. Mktg. Coll., 1999. Bar: Ga. 1973, U.S. Dist. Ct. (so. dist.) Ga. 1974, U.S. Dist. Ct. (mid. dist.) Ga. 1977, U.S. Supreme Ct. 1980, Tenn. 1987. Assoc. Surrett & CoCroft, Augusta, Ga., 1972-74; ptnr. Surrett & Brackett, Augusta, 1974-76; faculty Sch. Law, U. Ga., Athens, 1977-82; mng. ptnr. Brackett, Prince & Neufeld, Athens, 1982-90; adminstrv. law judge Ga. Dept. Med. Assistance, Athens, 1990-98. Hearing officer Ga. State Bd. Edn., 1979-91; v.p. Mus. Dolls & Gifts, Inc., Watkinsville, Ga., 1983—; pres. Bear Country Lodge and Conf. Ctr., Pigeon Forge, Tenn., 1996— Am. Toy Mus. Assoc., 2003-; chmn. bd. Adventures in Toy Land, 1999-00; exec. dir. Soc. Preservation of Am. Childhood Effects, 2002-; curator Toy Mus., Natural Bridge, Va., 2002-; bd. dirs. Va. Hospitality and Travel Assn., 2003-. Author: Court Administration, 1972; (monograph) The Security Inventors Protection Corporation and the Operations of SIPC, 1976; (musical play) Americanization of Mary Poppins, 1995. Pres. Athens/Clarke Mental Health Assn., 1985; chmn. bd. dirs. N.E. Ga. Mental Health Assn., 1989-90; officer of Election-Commonwealth of Va., 2002-04; bd. dirs. Coalition for The Blue Ridge Pkwy., 1994-00, Oconee Cultural Arts Found., 1995-97, Blue Ridge Pkwy. Assn., 1997-01. Fellow Paul Harris fellow, Buchanan Rotary Club; Nat. scholar, Phi Alpha Delta fraternity, 1973. Mem.: NRA, KC (4th deg.), ABA, Sevier County Bar Assn., Ga. Trial Lawyers Assn., Ga. Assn. Adminstrv. Law Judges (bd. dir. 1990—91), Ga. State Bar Assn., Blue Ridge/ Shenandoah Travel Mktg. Group (chmn. bd. 2004—), Blue Ridge Pkwy. Assn., Shenandoah Valley Travel Assn. (bd. dir. 2003—04), Internat. Platform Assn., S.E. Tourism Soc., Ea. Nat. Parks Assn., Soc. Am. Poets, 300 Club Roanoke, Magna Carta Barons, Cotillion Club Roanoke, Rotary Internat. (pres. elect Buchanan chpt. 2004—05, pres. 2005—, Paul Harris fellow), Phi Alpha Delta. Roman Catholic. Avocations: reading, music, golf, cross country skiing. Office Phone: 540-291-9920. Business E-Mail: smokymts@ntelos.net, curator@awesometoymuseum.com.

BRACKETT, MARTIN LUTHER, JR., lawyer; b. Charlotte, N.C., Feb. 23, 1947; s. Martin Luther and Helen Virginia (Smith) B.; m. Lisa Nichol; children— Martin Hunter, Alexander Jones, Amelia Kathleen, Lauren Hart. B.A., Davidson Coll., 1969; J.D., U. N.C., 1972. Bar: N.C. 1972, U.S. Dist. Ct. (we. dist.) N.C. 1973, U.S. Ct. Appeals (4th cir.) 1975. Ptnr. Bailey, Brackett & Brackett, P.A., Charlotte, N.C., 1973-83, Brackett & Sitton, Charlotte, 1983-85, Robinson, Bradshaw & Hinson, P.A., 1985—. Mem. Auditorium-Coliseum-Conv. Ctr. Authority, Charlotte, 1981-87, chmn., 1985-87. Served to capt. U.S. Army, 1972-73. Recipient Van Hecke-Wettach award U. N.C., 1972. Fellow Am. Coll. Trial Lawyers; mem. N.C. Acad. Trial Lawyers (bd. govs. 1980-86, 88-95, v.p. 1984-86). Democrat. Presbyterian. Office: 1900 Independence Ctr 101 N Tryon St Charlotte NC 28246-0100 Office Phone: 704-377-8347.

BRACKETT, MARY VIRGINIA, language educator, writer; b. Fort Riley, Kans. d. Edmund C. Roberts Jr. and Helen W. Kost, Robert F. Ferranti (Stepfather); m. Edmund C. Brackett, July 27, 1991; children: Lisa P. Lamb, Shandra R. Chapman, William W. Meredith. BS in Med.Tech., U Ark. Med Ctr., Little Rock, 1973; BSBA in Mktg. and Mgmt., Mo. So. State Coll., Joplin, 1989; MA in English, Pittsburg State U., Kans., 1991; PhD in English, U. Kans., Lawrence, 1998. Registered med. Technologist Am. Soc. Clin. Pathologists, 1974. Bus. mgr. Joplin Ophthalmology, Mo., 1978—89; tchg. asst. U. Kans., Lawrence, 1991—94; asst. prof. English East Ctrl. U., Ada, Okla., 1994—99; chmn. dept. English Triton Coll., River Grove, Ill., 1999—2006, dir. scholars program, 2001; asst. prof. English, asst. dir. honors program Pk. U., Parkville, Mo., 2006—. Author: (research) Facts on File Companion to the British Novel: Beginnings to the Nineteenth Century, 2006 (recommended in jour. Choice, 2006), (reference) Encyclopedia of Classic Love and Romance Literature, (biography) Elizabeth Cary: Woman of Conscience (NY Pub. Libr. list of recommended reading for teens, 1997), Restless Genius: The Story of Virginia Woolf (recommended feminist book for youth by Amelia Bloomer Project, 2005), A Home in the Heart: The Story of Sandra Cisneros. (PSLA YA Top Forty Nonfiction, 2004), Menachem Begin, Steve Jobs: Computer Genius of Apple, F. Scott Fitzgerald: Writer of the Jazz Age, Jeff Bezos, (creative non-fiction) The Contingent Self: One Reading Life; actor: (play) No Place Like Home. Dir scholars program svc. learning initiative Triton Coll., 2002—06; vol. Platte County Dem. Steering Com., Kansas City, Mo., 2006. Named Outstanding Faculty Mem., Ill. CC Tchg. Assn., 2006; grantee Angie Debo: Am. Indian Champion, Okla. Humanities Found., 1999, Park U.; Salute to Arts grantee, Ill. Arts Coun., 2003—05. Mem.: MLA, Nat. Coun. Rsch. on Women, Soc. Children's Book Writers and Illustrators. Office: Park U 8700 NW River Park Dr Parkville MO 64152 Home Phone: 816-587-8167; Office Phone: 816-584-6818. Business E-Mail: virginia.brackett@park.edu.

BRACKETT, RONALD E., investment company executive, lawyer; b. Rockford, Ill., May 10, 1942; s. F. Earl Brackett and Anne (Christenberry) Townsend; m. Susan Catherine Stichnoth, May 31, 1975; 1 child, Charles William. BA, Trinity Coll., 1964; JD, U. Mich., 1967. Bar: N.Y. 1968. Assoc. Rogers & Wells, NYC, 1968-74, ptnr., 1974-91, mng. ptnr., 1984-85, cons., 1992-94; founder, prin. Associated Growth Investors, L.P., Babylon, NY, 1992—. Bd. dirs. King Kullen Grocery Co., Inc., Westbury, NY. Mem.: N.Y. State Bar Assn., Phi Beta Kappa. Office: Associated Growth Investors LP 1801 House Argyle Square Babylon NY 11702-2711

BRACKMANN, DERALD E., otolaryngologist; b. Buckley, Ill., Feb. 13, 1937; s. Otto Henry Brackmann and Anna Mina Abraham; m. Charlotte Joyce Boyden, June 21, 1959; children: David, Douglas, Mark, Steven. Student, U. Ill., 1958, MD, 1962. Diplomate Am. Bd. Otolaryngology. Intern Ill. Ctrl. Hosp., Chgo., 1962—63; resident ob-gyn. Ill. Rsch. Hosp., Chgo., 1963—64; resident Otolaryngology Los Angeles County/U. So. Calif. Med. Ctr., 1966—70, chief otology, 1981—98; staff physician House Ear Clinic, LA, 1970—85, pres., 1985—. Chief ENT svc. St. Vincent Med. Ctr., 1971—98; clin. prof. otolaryngology U. So. Calif., clin. prof. neurologic surgery; clin. instr. House Ear Inst. Editor: Otologic Surgery, Neurotology, Neurological Surgery of the Ear & Skull Base; editl. bd.: jour. Advances in Otolaryngology-Head and Neck Surgery, Laryngoscope, Neurotology; co-author (chpt.): Electrocochleography, 1976, Hearing Disorders, 1976, Acoustic Tumors: Diagnosis and Management, 1979, Acoustic Tumors Vol. 1 Diagnosis, 1979, Otolaryngology, 1980, Controversy in Otolaryngology, 1980, Butterworth International Medical Reviews: Otology, 1982, Disorders of the Facial Nerve, 1982, Essential Otolaryngology Head & Neck Surgery, 3d edit., 1983; author: Surgery of the Skull Base, 1983, Meniere's Disease: A Comprehensive Appraisal, 1983; contbg. editor: Neurological Surgery of the Ear and Skull Base, 1982; co-author: Gerald M. English Otolaryngology, Sensory Evoked Potentials, 1984, Cochlear Implants, 1985; author: The Facial Nerve, 1986; co-author: Ear and Skull Base, 1986, Conn's Current Therapy, 1988, Otologic Medicine and Surgery, 1988, Advances in Otolaryngology-Head and Neck Surgery, 1989; author: Operative Challenges in Otolaryngology Head and Neck Surgery, 1990, Neurosurgery Update 1: Diagnosis, Operative Technique and Neuro-Otology, 1990, Operative Techniques in Otolaryngology-Head and Neck Surgery, 1991, Surgery of Cranial Base Tumors, 1993; author: Handbook of Intraoperative Monitoring, 1994; co-author: Essential Otolaryngology, 1995, Otolaryngology, 1996; author: Atlas of Head & Neck Surgry-Otolaryngology, 1996, Disorders of the Vestibular System, 1996, Head and Neck Surgery Volume 2: Ear, 1996; co-author: Acoustic Tumors Diagnosis and Management, 2d edit., 1997, Diseases of the Ear. 6th edit., 1998, Essential Otolaryngology, 1998, Head and Neck Surgery-Otolaryngology, Vol. 2, 1998, Surgery of the Skull Base, 1998, Textbook of Clinical Neurology, 1998, Cranial Base Surgery, 1999; author: The Facial Nerve, 2000; co-author: Operative Techniques in Neurosurgery, 2001, Controversies in Otolaryngology, 2001, Surgery of the Ear, 5th edit., 2002, Essential Otolaryngology, 2003; editor: Neurologic Surgery of the Ear and Skull Base, 1982; contbg. editor: Otologic Surgery, 1994, 3d edit., 2001; co-editor: Neurotology, 1994; contbr. over 200 articles to profl. jours. Capt. USAF, 1964—66. Recipient Alumni Achievement award, U. Ill., 1997, Gold medal, Prosper Meniere's Soc., 2000; fellow, House Ear Inst. and Clinic, 1970—71. Fellow: AMA, Am. Laryngol. Rhinol. Otol. Soc., Am. Acad. Olotaryngology Head and Neck Surgery (pres. 1988, com. facial nerve disorders, pres. 1987—88); mem.: ACS, Asian Conf. Neurol. Surgeons, N.Am. Skull Base Soc. (pres. 1995—96), Rsch. Study Club, LA Soc. Otolaryngology (pres. 1986—87), Otolaryngology Soc. Australia (hon.), Royal Soc. Medicine (hon.), LA County Med. Assn., Calif. Med. Assn., Am. Otol. Soc. (task force sub-certification, pres. 1995—96), Am. Neurotology Soc. (exec. coun., pres. 1984—85), Centurion Club, Alpha Omega Alpha. Republican. Achievements include research in neurotology; cochlear implant; auditory brainstem implant. Avocations: fishing, hunting. Office: House Ear Clinic 2100 W 3rd St Los Angeles CA 90057 Office Phone: 213-483-9930. Business E-Mail: dbrackmann@hei.org.

BRADBEER, CLIVE, biochemistry educator; b. Tynemouth, Northumberland, Eng., Feb. 20, 1933; came to U.S., 1962, naturalized, 1994; s. Joseph Walter and Mary (Hall) B.; m. Wilma Jean Youngert, Sept. 1, 1960; children: Suzanne Mary, Thomas Clive. BSc with first class honors, Durham U., Newcastle Upon Tyne, Eng., 1954, PhD, 1957. Jr. rsch. biochemist U. Calif., Berkeley, 1957-59, Davis, 1959; postdoctoral fellow U. Wis., Madison, 1959-60; lectr. Queen Mary Coll., London U., 1960-62; asst. prof. Sch. Medicine, U. Va., Charlottesville, 1964-69, assoc. prof., 1969-79, prof., 1979—. Vis. scientist NIH, Bethesda, Md., 1962-64, ad hoc mem. study sect., 1980-84; vis. prof. U. Otago, Dunedin, New Zealand, 1982-83, 93. Contbr. articles to profl. jours. Mem. Am. Soc. for Biochemistry and Molecular Biology. Episcopalian. Achievements include contbns. in elucidation of the molecular mechanisms involved in utilization of vitamin B12 in microbial and animal cells. E-mail: cb7f@virginia.edu.

BRADBURN, NORMAN M., behavioral science educator; b. Lincoln, Ill., July 21, 1933; s. Hubert Benjamin and Mary Celeste (Marshall) B.; m. Wendy McAneny, Dec. 15, 1956; children: Isabel Stuart, Andrew Marshall, Laura Humphreys. BA, U. Chgo., 1952, Oxford U., Eng., 1955; MA, Harvard U., 1958, PhD in Social Psychology, 1960. From asst. prof. to assoc. prof. behavioral sci. U. Chgo., 1960-67, prof., 1967—, chmn. dept. behavioral sci., 1973-79, Tiffany and Margaret Blake Disting. Service prof., 1977-99, provost, 1984-89, prof. emeritus, 1999—. Sr. study dir. Nat. Opinion Rsch. Ctr., Chgo., 1961— , dir., 1967-71, 79-84, 89-92, rsch. dir., 1992-2000, sr. fellow, 2004—; asst. dir. NSF, 2000—04. Author: (with D. Caplovitz) Reports on Happiness, 1967, The Structure of Psychological Well-Being, 1970, (with S. Sudman, G. Gockel) Side by Side: A Study of Integrated Neighborhoods, 1971, (with S. Sudman) Response Effects in Surveys, 1974, Asking Questions: A Practical Guide to Questionnaire Construction, 1982, revised edit. (with Sudman and Wansinik), 2004, Polls and Surveys: Understanding What They Tell Us, 1988, (with others) Improving Questionnaire Design and Interview Method, 1979, (with S. Sudman and N. Schwarz) Thinking About Answers, 1996. Alexander von Humboldt scholar U. Cologne (Germany), 1970-71 Fellow AAAS, Am. Statis. Assn.; mem. Internat. Statis. Inst., World Assn. Pub. Opinion Rsch., Am. Assn. Pub. Opinion Rsch. (pres. 1991-92), Am. Acad. Arts and Scis.

BRADBURY, BETTY MARIE, history and music educator; b. Madison, Ind., Mar. 5, 1933; d. Lawrence Allen and Elsie Margret (Spivey) Bladen; m. Robert Lesley Bradbury, Aug. 23, 1952; children: Robert A., Jonathan R., Randall E., Daryl R., Robert II. Diploma, Sherwood Music Sch., 1966; Assoc. in Gen. Studies, Ind. U., Kokomo, 1989, B Gen. Studies with distinction, 1990, MS in Edn., 1995. Cert. tchr., adminstr. Tchr. Malta (Ohio) Christian Sch., 1971-73, Beaver Valley Wesleyan, Vanport, Pa., 1973-77; pvt. piano tchr. Madison, Ind., 1977-80; tchr. Bible Wesleyan Acad., Crab Orchard, W.Va., 1980-82, Beckley (W.Va.) Pentecostal Acad., 1983-84; tchr., prin. Bible Wesleyan Acad., Crab Orchard, 1984-87; tchr. Union Bible Acad., Westfield, Ind., 1989-90, prin., 1990-92; prof. Union Bible Coll., Westfield, 1992—. Seminar leader-tchr. Evang. Bible Mission, Haiti, 1993, 95, 98, 2000; mem. exec. com. Union Bible Coll., Westfield, 1990-92; chmn. Union Bible Coll. edn. dept., 2000-04 Author: The Walls Talk, 1993. Jr. ch. leader Pilgrim Holiness Ch., Indpls., 1993-94; sec.-treas. Pilgrim Holiness Ch., Muncie, Ind., 1969-71; den mother Cub Scouts, Middletown, Ind., 1966-69; missionary pres. Bible Wesleyan Ch., Crab Orchard, 1984-86. Mem. Alpha Chi. Republican. Avocations: reading, music, puzzles. Home: 507 S Walnut St Westfield IN 46074-8956

BRADBURY, BILL (WILLIAM CHAPMAN BRADBURY III), state official; b. Chgo., May 29, 1949; s. William L. and Lorraine (Patterson) B.; m. Betsy Harrison (Sept. 1984); children: Abby, Zoe; m. Kathleen P. Eymann, June 7, 1986. Student, Antioch Coll., 1967-69. News reporter KQED-TV Newsroom, 1969-70; dir. pub. affairs Sta. KMPX-FM, San Francisco, 1970; mem. video prodn. group Optic Nerve, San Francisco, 1970-73; project dir. Coos Country TV, Bandon, Oreg., 1973-75; reporter, anchor Sta. KVAL-TV, Eugene, Oreg., 1975-76; news dir. Sta. KCBY-TV, Coos Bay, Oreg., 1976-78; prodr., writer, editor video news feature svc. Local Color, Langlois, Oreg., 1978-79; field prodr. PM Mag., Sta. KGW-TV, Portland, Oreg., 1979-80; mem. Oreg. Ho. of Reps., Salem, 1980-84, Oreg. State Senate, Salem, 1984-95, pres., 1993-95; exec. dir. Sake of the Salmon, Gladstone, Oreg., 1995-99; sec. state State of Oreg., Salem, 1999—. Chmn. Western Legis. Conf., Coun. State Govs., 1991, mem. ocean resources com.; founder, former chmn. Pacific Fishery Legis. Task Force. Prodr. documentaries Gorda Ridge—Boom or Bust for the Oregon Coast?, The Tillamook Burn—From Ruin to Rejuvenation, Not Guilty by Reason of Insanity, Child as Witness, Local Color, Salmon on the Run, The First Perennial Poetic Hoohaw, TV Town Hall Meetings, Common Sense, also prodr. mktg. videos and commls. for polit. candidates, hosp. Democrat. Mem. Soc. Of Friends. Avocation: kayaking. Office: Office Sec of State 141 State Capitol Bldg Salem OR 97310-0722 Office Phone: 503-986-1523. Office Fax: 503-986-1616. E-mail: bill.bradbury@state.or.us.*

BRADBURY, RAY DOUGLAS, writer; b. Waukegan, Ill., Aug. 22, 1920; s. Leonard Spaulding and Esther Marie (Moberg) B.; m. Marguerite Susan McClure, Sept. 27, 1947 (dec. Nov. 24, 2003); children: Susan Marguerite, Ramona, Bettina, Alexandra. DLitt, Whittier Coll., 1979. First pub. short story, 1941; stories pub. pulp mags., 1941-45. Author: (short story collections) Dark Carnival, 1947, The Illustrated Man, 1951, The Golden Apples of the Sun, 1953, Fahrenheit 451, 1953 (Commonwealth Club Calif. gold medal 1954), The October Country, 1955, A Medicine for Melancholy, 1959 (pub. in Eng. as The Day It Rained Forever, 1959), The Ghoul Keepers, 1961, The Small Assassin, 1962, The Machineries of Joy, 1964, The Vintage Bradbury, 1965, The Autumn People, 1965, Tomorrow Midnight, 1966, Twice Twenty-Two, 1966, I Sing The Body Electric!, 1969, Harrap, 1975, Long After Midnight, 1976, The Best of Bradbury, 1976, To Sing Strange Songs, 1979, The Stories of Ray Bradbury, 1980, Dinosaur Tales, 1983, A Memory of Murder, 1984, The Toynbee Convector, 1988, Kaleidoscope, 1994, Quicker Than the Eye, 1996, Driving Blind, 1998, One More For the Road, 2002, Bradbury Stories: 100 of His Most Celebrated Tales, 2003, The Cat's Pajamas: Stories, 2004, A Sound of Thunder and Other Stories, 2005; (with Robert Bloch) Bloch and Bradbury: Ten Masterpieces of Science Fiction, 1969 (pub. in Eng. as Fever Dreams and Other Fantasies, 1970), Whispers From Beyond, 1972; (novels) The Martian Chronicles, 1950 (pub. in Eng. as The Silver Locusts, 1951), Dandelion Wine, 1957, Something Wicked This Way Comes, 1962, Death is a Lonely Business, 1985, A Graveyard for Lunatics, 1990, Green Shadows, White Whale, 1992, From the Dust Returned, 2001, Let's All Kill Constance, 2003, Farewell Summer, 2006; (juvenile novels) Switch on the Night, 1955 (Boys Club Am. Jr. Book award 1956), R is for Rocket, 1962, S is for Space, 1966, The Halloween Tree, 1972, The April Witch, 1987, The Other Foot, 1987, The Foghorn, 1987, The Veldt, 1987, Fever Dream, 1987, The Smile, 1991, With Cat for Comforter, 1997, Dogs Think That Every Day Is Christmas, 1997; (non-fiction) Teacher's Guide: Science Fiction, 1968, Zen and the Art of Writing, 1973, Mars and the Mind of Man, 1973, The Mummies of Guanajuato, 1978, Beyond 1984: Remembrance of Things Future, 1979, Los Angeles, 1984, Orange County, 1985, The Art of Playboy, 1985, Zen in the Art of Writing, 1990, Yestermorrow: Obvious Answers to Impossible Futures, 1991, Ray Bradbury On Stage: A Chrestomathy of His Plays, 1991, Journey to Far Metaphor: Further Essays on Creativity, Writing, Literature, and the Arts, 1994, The First Book of Dichotomy, The Second Book of Symbiosis, 1995, Bradbury Speaks: Too Soon From the Cave, Too Far From the Stars, 2005; (plays) The Meadow, 1960, Way in the Middle of the Air, 1962, The Anthem Sprinters, and Other Antics, 1963, The World of Ray Bradbury, 1964, Leviathan 99, 1966, The Day It Rained Forever, 1966, The Pedestrian, 1966, Dandelion Wine, 1967, Christus Apollo, 1969, The Wonderful Ice-Cream Suit and Other Plays, 1972, Madrigals for the Space Age, 1972, Pillar of Fire and Other Plays for Today, Tomorrow, and Beyond Tomorrow, 1975, That Ghost, That Bride of Time: Excerpts from a Play-in-Progress, 1976, The Martian Chronicles,

1977 (5 L.A. Drama Critics Circle awards), Farenheit 451, 1979, A Device Out of Time, 1986, Falling Upward, 1988;(poetry) Old Ahab's Friend, and Friend to Noah, Speaks His Piece: A Celebration, 1971, When Elephants Last in the Dooryard Bloomed: Celebrations for Almost Any Day in the Year, 1973, That Son of Richard III: A Birth Announcement, 1974, Where Robot Mice and Robot Men Run Round in Robot Towns, 1977, Twin Hieroglyphs That Swim the River Dust, 1978, The Bike Repairman, 1978, The Author Considers His Resources, 1979, The Aqueduct, 1979, The Attic Where The Meadow Greens, 1979, The Last Circus, 1980, The Ghosts of Forever, 1980, The Haunted Computer and the Android Pope, 1981, The Complete Poems of Ray Bradbury, 1982, The Love Affair, 1983, Forever and the Earth, 1984, Death Has Lost Its Charm for Me, 1987, They Have Not Seen the Stars: The Collected Poetry of Ray Bradbury, 2002; prodr. one-act plays, Royal Shakespeare Festival Theatre, The Pandemonium Theatre Co., 1963; screenwriter: (films) It Came from Outer Space, 1953, The Beast from 20,000 Fathoms, 1953, Moby Dick, 1956, Icarus Montgolfier Wright, 1962 (Academy award nomination best short film 1963), An American Journey, 1964, Picasso Summer, 1972, Something Wicked This Way Comes, 1983; (TV scripts) Alfred Hitchcock Presents, Jane Wyman's Fireside Theatre, steve Canyon, Trouble Shooters, Twilight Zone, Alcoa Premiere, Curiosity Shop, Ray Bradbury Television Theatre; editor: Timeless Stories for Today andTomorrow, 1952, The Circus ofDr. Lao and Other Improbable Stories, 1956, A Day in the Life of Hollywood, 1992. Mem. adv. bd. Science Fiction Mus. and Hall of Fame. Recipient O. Henry prize, 1947, 48, Benjamin Franklin award best story, 1954, Nat. Inst. Arts and Letters award, 1954, Golden Eagle award, 1957, Mrs. Ann Radcliffe award Count Dracula Soc., 1965, 71, Writers Guild award 1974, World Fantasy award for lifetime achievement, 1977, Balrog award best poet, 1979, Aviation and Space Writers award, 1979, Gandalf award, 1980, PEN Body of Work award, 1985, Medal for Disting. Contribution to Am. Letters Nat. Book Found., 2000, Presdl. Nat. Medal of Arts, 2004; Pulitzer Prize Special Citation, 2007. Mem. Screen Writers Guild, Sci. Fantasy Writers Am., Pacific Art Found. (v.p.), Writers Guild Am. (mem. screen writers bd.) Office: Bantam Doubleday Dell 1540 Broadway New York NY 10036-4039 Mailing: c/o Avon Books 1350 Avenue Of The Americas New York NY 10019-4702*

BRADBURY, STEVEN G., federal agency administrator; b. 1958; s. Edward T. Bradbury; m. Hilde Elisabeth Kahn, Oct. 16, 1988. BA, Stanford U., 1980; JD, U. Mich., 1988. Bar: DC. Atty., advisor, Office Legal Counsel US Dept. Justice, Washington, 1991—92; law clk. to Hon. James L. Buckley US Ct. Appeals (DC cir.), Washington, 1990—91; law clk. to Justice Clarence Thomas US Supreme Ct., Washington, 1992—93; ptnr. Kirkland & Ellis LLP, Washington; prin. dep. asst. atty. gen. Office of Legal Counsel, US Dept. Justice, Washington, acting asst. atty. gen., 2005—. Mem.: Federalist Soc.*

BRADDOCK, DONALD LAYTON, retired lawyer, accountant, real estate broker, investor; b. Jacksonville, Fla., Dec. 14, 1941; s. John Reddon and Harriet Braddock; children: Stella Helene Taylor, Leslie Ann Meshad, Donald Layton Jr. BS in Bus. Adminstrn., U. Fla., 1963; JD, 1967. Bar: Fla. 1968, U.S. Supreme Ct. 1976, U.S. Tax Ct. 1970; CPA; registered real estate broker. With Coopers and Lybrand, CPAs, 1964-65, Keith C. Austin, CPA, 1965-67, Kent, Durden & Kent, attys. at law, 1967-71; sole practice, 1971-73; ptnr. Howell, Kirby, Montgomery, D'Aiuto & Dean, attys. at law, 1974-76; pres., dir. Howell, Liles, Braddock & Milton, attys. at law, Jacksonville, Fla., 1976-88; ret., 1988. Bd. dirs., mem. audit, exec. com. Fla. Lawyers Mutual Ins. Co.; bd. dirs. Lawyers Reinsurance Co., 2003—; pres., dir. Donald L. Braddock Chartered dba Mandarin Realty, 1970—. Bd. dirs. Jacksonville Vocat. Edn. Authority, 1971-75; mem. Jacksonville Bicentennial Commn., 1976; bd. govs. Fla. Bar Found., 1984-86, sec.-treas., 1986-88. Served with Air N.G., 1963-69. Mem.: Jacksonville Bar Assn. (bd. govs. 1978—84, pres. 1983—84), Jacksonville C. of C. (com. of 100), Fla. Bar (bd. govs. young lawyers sec. 1972—77), U. Fla. Alumni Assn. (pres. 1975, bd. dirs. 1968—75), Friars Club, Fla. Blue Key, Alpha Tau Omega, Phi Delta Phi. Republican. Office: PO Box 57385 Jacksonville FL 32241-7385

BRADDOCK, RICHARD S., Internet company executive; s. Robert L. and Mary Alice (Krueger) B.; m. Susan Schulte, Feb. 14, 1978; 1 child, Christina; children by previous marriage: Jennifer, Richard, Derek BA, Dartmouth Coll., 1963; MBA, Harvard Bus. Sch., 1965. Mem. mktg. staff General Foods, White Plains, NY, 1965-73; mem. staff Citicorp, NYC, 1973-92, sector exec. in charge of worldwide consumer fin. svcs., info. bus., investor rels., corp. pub. affairs, customer affairs, corp. advt., 1985-90, also bd. dirs.; pres. Citibank/Citicorp, NYC, 1990-92; chief exec. officer Medco Containment Svcs., Montvale, NJ, 1992; spl. advisor Gen. Atlantic Ptnrs. LLC, 1996-97; non-exec. chmn. True North Communications Inc., 1997; CEO Priceline.com, 1998—2002, chmn., 1998—2004. Bd. dirs. Eastman Kodak, Lotus Devel. Corp.; chief exec. officer Medical Mktg. Group, Synetics. Bd. dirs. Cancer Rsch. Inst., N.Y.C., Lincoln Ctr., N.Y.C. Partnership; mem. Coun. on Fgn Rels. Mem. N.Y. C. of C. (bd. dirs.).

BRADDOM, RANDALL LEE, physiatrist, educator; b. Monarch, Va., Oct. 29, 1942; s. Audy Lee and Ruth Janet Braddom; m. Diana Verdun, 2001; children from previous marriage: Eric C., Steven R., Karen L. BA, DePauw U., 1964; MD, Ohio State U., 1968, MS, 1971. Diplomate Am. Bd. Electrodiagnostic Medicine, Am. Bd. Phys. Medicine and Rehab. Rotating intern Mt. Carmel Hosp., Columbus, Ohio, 1968-69; resident in phys. medicine and rehab. Ohio State Univ. Hosps., Columbus, 1969-72; physiatrist, electromyographer Rancocas Valley Hosp., Willingboro, NJ, 1972-74, Phila. Naval Med. Ctr., 1972-74; asst. prof. phys. medicine and rehab. U. Cin., 1974-75, assoc. prof., dir. phys. medicine and rehab., 1975-81; med. dir. phys. med. and rehab. St. Francis-St. George Hosp., Cin., 1987-89, Providence Hosp., Cin., 1982-89; assoc. prof., dep. chmn. rehab. medicine Temple U., Phila., 1989-91; chmn. rehab. medicine Albert Einstein Hosp., Phila., 1989-91; v.p. med. affairs Moss Rehab. Hosp., Phila., 1989-91; practitioner Rehab. Assocs., Indpls., 1991-96; med. dir. Hook Rehab. Ctr., Indpls., 1991-98; prof., chmn. phys. medicine and rehab. Ind. U. Sch. Medicine, Indpls., 1991-98. Dir. Wishard Health Svcs., Indpls., Ind.; physiatrist Albert Einstein Med. Ctr. N., Phila., 1973; clin. instr. rehab. medicine Thomas Jefferson Coll. Med., Phila., 1972-74; assoc. in medicine Jewish Hosp., Cin., 1974-89; cons. phys. medicine and rehab. VA Hosp., Cin., 1975-81; dir. phys. med. and rehab. U. Hosps., U. Cin., 1975-81; assoc. clin. prof. phys. med. Ohio State U., Columbus, 1984-90; clin. assoc. prof. phys. medicine and rehab. U. Cin., Coll. Medicine, 1982-89; cons. St. Francis Hosp., Indpls., 1991-97; phys. med. and rehab. svc. chief Wishard Meml. Hosp., Indpls., 1991-2000; dir. phys. medicine and rehab. svc. Richard Roudebush VA Hosp., Indpls., 1991-97; vis. prof. Dept. Phys. Medicine and Rehab. U. Ark., 1992, U. Ky. Dept Phys. Medicine and Rehab., 1992, Dept. Internal Medicine Divsn. Phys. Medicine & Rehab. La. State U. Sch. Medicine, New Orleans, La., 1994, Baylor Coll. Medicine Dept. Phys. Medicine & Rehab., 1994, N.J. Sch. Medicine and Dentistry Dept. P.M. & R.; presenter in field; lectr. in field. Author: (with others) Physical Medicine & Rehabilitation Review, 1980; editor: Sports Medicine and Rehabilitation: A Sport-Scientific Approach, 1994, Physical Medicine and rehabilitation, 1996; contbr. articles to profl. jours. Founder, med. dir. ECCO Family Health Ctr., Inc., Columbus, 1970-72; bd. dirs. Nat. Paraplegia Found., 1975-80; med. adviser Easter Seals Soc. Southwestern Ohio, 1980-82; asst. scoutmaster Troop 291, Boy Scouts Am., 1982-84; chmn. Citizens for Our Schs. Tax Levy Campaign, Forest Hills Sch. Dist., Cin., 1985; trustee Total Living Concepts, Inc., Cin., 1977-85, Disability Svcs. Group, Inc., Cin., 1985-89; bd. examiners The Henry B. Betts award, 1991-94. Lt. comdr. USNR, 1972—74. Recipient Kiwanis Club Citizenship award, Dayton, 1960, Rsch. award Am. Paralyzed Vets. Assn., 1968, Am. Therapeutic Soc., 1968, Landacre Soc. award Ohio State U., 1978, Sidney Licht Lectureship Ohio State U., 1985, Alumni Achievement award Ohio State U., 1993, Sidney Licht Lectureship U. Minn., 1993, Randy Braddom award U. Cin. Coll. Medicine, 1989, Landwerlen award, Muscular Dystrophy Found. Ind., 1994, Lifetime Achievement award, AANEM, 2004; named Man of Yr. Columbus Citizen-Jour., 1970. Mem. Am. Acad. Phys. Med. and Rehab. (med. edn. com. 1983-86, membership recruitment group 1987, career brochure devel. group 1987, joint ann. meeting planning subcom. 1987-88, chairperson continuing med. edn. subcom. 1982-86, sci. program com. 1982-86, mktg. and comm. com. 1987-89, chairperson med. edn. com. 1986-88, sec. bd. govs. 1988-90, third-mem.-at-large 1990-91, 2nd mem.-at-large 1991-92, 1st mem.-at-large 1992-93, chair awards com. 1992-93, v.p. 1994-95, fin. com. 1994-95, chair annual meeting task force 1994-95, pres. elect 1994-95, pres. 1995-96, past pres. 1996-97, Disting. Clinician award 1997), Am. Assn. Electrodiagnostic Medicine (com. on edn. 1974-76, exam. com. 1975-76, liaision to assn. of acad. physiatrists 1988, chairperson courses com. 1986-89, pres.-elect 1989-90, bd. dirs. 1989-92, pres. 1990-91, immediate past pres.-chairperson long-range planning com. 1991-92, chmn. long range planning com. 1991-92, alt. del. AMA House of Dels. 1993-95, nominating com. 1993-94, chmn. 1994-95), Am. Assn. Electrodiagnostic Medicine, Assn. Acad. Physiatrists, Ohio State Med. Alumni Assn., AMA, Am. Bd. Electrodiagnostic Medicine (bd. dirs. 1994, long-range planning com. 1994, treas. 1995-98), Cin. Soc. of Phys. Medicine and Rehab. (pres., founder 1987-88), Internat. Med. Med. Assn. (U.S. counselor 1986-95). Presbyterian. Avocations: bicycling, writing, tennis. Office: 80 Oak Hill Rd Red Bank NJ 07701 Home Phone: 215-699-5035; Office Phone: 732-741-2313. Personal E-mail: rbraddom@earthlink.net.

BRADEMAS, JOHN, retired academic administrator, former congressman; b. Mishawaka, Ind., Mar. 2, 1927; s. Stephen J. and Beatrice Cenci (Goble) B.; m. Mary Ellen Briggs, July 9, 1977. BA magna cum laude (Vets. nat. scholar), Harvard, 1949; PhD in Social Studies(Rhodes scholar), Oxford U., Eng., 1954, DCL (hon.), 2003; LLD (hon.), U. Notre Dame, Middlebury Coll., Tufts U. (others); LHD, Brandeis U., CCNY (and 46 other hon. degrees). Legis. asst. US Senator Pat McNamara; adminstrv. asst. US Rep. Thomas L. Ashley, 1955; exec. asst. to presdl. nominee Stevenson, 1955-56; asst. prof. polit. sci. St. Mary's Coll., Notre Dame, Ind., 1957-58; mem. 86th-96th Congresses from 3d Ind. Dist., 1959—81; chief dep. majority whip 93d-94th Congresses, 1973—77; majority whip 95th-96th Congresses, 1977—81; mem. com. house adminstrn., com. on edn. and labor, joint com. Libr. Congress; pres. NYU, 1981-92, fundraising campaign initiator, 1984, pres. emeritus, 1992—, founder John Brademas Ctr. for Study of Congress, 2005—; mem. NY State Bd. Regents, Albany, 2004—. Chmn. bd. dirs. Fed. Res. Bank NY; dir. RCA/NBC, Columbia Pictures, Loew's Corp., Scholastic, Inc., NY Stock Exch., Rockefeller Found., Oxford U. Press-U.S.A.; past mem. bd. visitors John F. Kennedy Sch. Govt.; bd. overseers Harvard U.; mem. overseers' com. to visit Grad. Sch. Edn.; past mem. Nat. Hist. Publs. Commn., Nat. Commn. on Financing Post-Secondary Edn.; mem. Nat. Commn. Student Fin. Assistance, 1981-83, chair grad. edn. subcom., Study Nat. Needs Biomed. and Behavioral Rsch. NRC, Nat. Acad. Sci. Com. Rels. between Univs. and Govt., Nat. Commn. Financing Postsecondary Edn., Nat. Hist. Publs. and Records Commn.; bd. dirs. Am. Coun. Edn., mem. Commn. Nat. Challenges to Higher Edn., 1986-87; chmn. NY State Coun. on Fiscal and Econ. Priorities; bd. dirs. Comfidex Corp., InsurBanc, Kos Pharms., NYNEX, Texaco Inc., Alexander S. Onassis Pub. Benefit Found., Ctr. Nat. Policy, DC, Soc. Preservation Greek Heritage, Queen Sofia Spanish Inst., US-Japan Found., World Conf. Religions for Peace, Am-European Cmty. Assn.; pres. King Juan Carlos I Spain Ctr., NYU Found.; adv. bd. mem. mental illness prevention ctr., NYU Med. Ctr.; vice chmn. adv. coun. Ams., UNESCO; twentieth century fund task force mem. presdl. appointments, 1996. Author: Anarcosindicalismo y revolución en España, 1930-37, 1974, Washington, D.C. to Washington Square, 1986; co-author (with Lynne P. Brown) The Politics of Education: Conflict and Consensus on Capitol Hill, 1978. Bd. dirs. Aspen Inst., Ams. for Arts., Berlitz Internat. Inc., Carnegie Internat. Endowment Nat. Commn. on Am. and the New World, Nat. Endowment for Democracy, 1993-2001, Carnegie Commn. on Sci., Tech. and Govt., chmn. com. on Congress; mem. Nat. Commn. Pub. Svc., Nat. Adv. Coun. on Pub. Svc., US adv. coun. Transparency Internat., internat. adv. coun., mem. Ctrl. Com. World Coun. Chs., fifth assembly del. United Meth. Ch, Nairobi, 1975; bd. dirs Ctr. for Nat. Policy, chmn. exec. com.; chmn. Nat. Adv. Com. of Fighting Back, chmn. Pres.'s Com. Arts and Humanities, 1994-2001, Am. Ditchley Found., gov. Ditchley Founds.; life trustee U. Notre Dame; bd. dirs. Am. Coun. for the Arts, Acad. for Edni. Devel., Athens Coll. (Greece), Coun. to Aid Edn.; trustee Com. for Econ. Devel., nat. commn. mem. jobs and small bus., 1986; mem. Cons. Panel to Comptr. Gen. of US, Bd. of Advisors of The Carter Ctr. Emory U., Carnegie Coun. on Ethics and Internat. Affairs, Trilateral Commn., Coun. on Spain and US, Internat. Coun., Ctrl. European U., Budapest, Am. Assocs. St. Catherine Found., Pilgrims Soc. Great Britain, Pilgrims Soc. US, VSA/arts, Internat. Adv. Coun. Pharos Trust, Cyprus; founding bd. mem. Ctr. Democracy and Reconciliation in S.E. Europe, Salonika, Greece, sr. advisor; chmn. nat. adv. com., Fighting Back, Robert Wood Johnson Found., adv. coun. David Rockefeller fellowships, NYC Partnership; hon. patron Fundación Residencia de Estudiantes, Madrid, mem. accreditation com. Red Latinoamericana de Cooperación Universitaria; dir. Am. Friends Girona Mus. and Inst., Spain; nat. adv. bd. mem. instns. democracy, Annenberg Pub. Policy Ctr., U. Pa.; first congl. delegation chair, China, 1977, first Chinese-US univ. pres. seminar attendee, Beijing, 1985; co-chmn. ind. commn., Nat. Endowment Arts, 1990. With USNR, 1945—46. Decorated chevalier of Legion of Honor, France, High Knight Comdr. of Honor Order of the Phoenix, Greece, Grand Cross of Alphonse X, Min. Edn. and Culture, Spain, 1997, Commendatore Order of Merit, Pres. Italy, 2000; recipient Disting. Svc. award Inst. Internat. Edn., 1966, Disting. Svc. award NEA, 1968, Disting. Svc. award Tchrs. Coll., Columbia U., 1969; Merit award Nat. Coun. Sr. Citizens, 1972; Disting. Svc. award Coun. of State Adminstrs. of Vocat. Rehab., 1973; Disting. Svc. award Conservation Edn. Assn., 1974; Caritas Soc. award for Outstanding Contbns. in Field of Mental Retardation, 1975, Gold medal St. Barnabas, Pres. Makarios, Cyprus, 1975; Gold Key award Am. Congress Rehab. Medicine, 1976; Disting. Svc. to Arts award AAAL, 1978; one of three recipients George Peabody award for Outstanding Contbn. to Music in Am., 1980, Town Hall Friend of Arts award, NYC, 1981, Hubert H. Humphrey award Am. Polit. Sci. Assn., 1984, Ann. Gold medal, Spanish Inst., NYC, 1985, Charles Evan Hughes Gold medal, Nat. Conf. Christians and Jews, 1985, Ellis Island medal of Honor, 1986, Nat. Govs. Assn. award, 1988, Athenagoras award for Human Rights, 1990, Gold medal of Honor City of Athens, 1991, Ann. Am. Assembly Svc. to Democracy award, 1992, Dwight D. Eisenhower medal, 1992, Disting. Svc. award, Am. Coun. Arts, 1996, Lifetime Achievement award, Ind. Coun. Humanities, 1997, Lifetime Achievement award, Cyprus Fedn. Am., 1998, Benjamin Rush award, Dickinson Coll., 1999, Nat. Svc. award, Anderson Ranch Arts Ctr., Colo., 1999, Ann. Fulbright award, Metro Internat., 2000, Lifetime Achievement award for Leadership in Arts award, Ams. Arts and US Conf. Mayors, 2000, Democracy Svc. award, Nat. Endowment Democracy, 2001, Albert Gallatin medal, NYU, 2001, Disting. Svc. award, Nat. Hist. Publs. Records Commn., 2002, Global Edn. Achievement award, Fairleigh Dickinson U., 2004, Ann. Cultural award, Recording Industry Am., Disting. Svc. award, Am. Assn. U. Presses, Disting. Svc. medal, Columbia U., Disting. Svc. award in Internat. Edn., Inst. Internat. Edn., James Bryant Conant Disting. Svc. Edn. award, Edn. Commn. States, Gold Key award Am. Congress Rehab. Medicine, Disting. Svc. award, Coun. State Adminstrs. Vocat. Rehab., Humanist of Yr. award, Nat. Assn. Humanities Edn.; Named One of Top Four Most Important People in Am. Higher Edn., Change Mag., 1975; Named Humanist of Year, Nat. Assn. Humanities Edn., 1978, Pres. Constantine Karamanlis, Greece, 1981, Grand Comdr. Knights of Holy Sepulchre, Patriarch Diodoros, Jerusalem, 1982, Friend of Barcelona, Mayor Pasqual Maragall, 1993, Disting. Friend Oxford U., 1998, Post Office Named in His Honor, South Bend, Ind., 2002; Hon. fellow Brasenose, Oxford U., 1972. Fellow Am. Acad. Arts and Scis. (coun. mem., mem. European acad., 1999), Nat. Acad. Edn. (corr. mem. acad. Athens, corr. mem. acad. Argentina, 1998); mem. Phi Beta Kappa (Senator, dir.), Am. Assn. Museums (named to Centennial Honor Roll, 2006) Methodist. Office: NY State Edn Dept Bd Regents Rm 110 EB Albany NY 12234 also: NYU 53 Washington Sq S Rm 304 New York NY 10012

BRADEN, BERWYN BARTOW, lawyer; b. Pana, Ill., Jan. 10, 1928; s. George Clark and Florence Lucille (Bartow) B.; m. Betty J.; children—Scott, Mark, Mathew, Sue, Ralph, Ladd, Brad Student, Carthage Coll., 1946-48, U. Wis., 1948-49, JD, 1959. Bar: Wis. 1959, U.S. Supreme Ct. 1965. Ptnr. Genoar & Braden, Lake Geneva, Wis., 1959-63; individual practice law Lake Geneva, Wis., 1963-68, 72-74; ptnr. Braden & English, Lake Geneva, Wis., 1968-72, Braden & Olson, Lake Geneva, Wis., 1974—2002, Gagliardi Braden Olson and Capelli, Lake Geneva, 2002—06, Braden Olson Drapler, Lake Geneva, 2007—. City atty. City of Lake Geneva, 1962-64, 2006—; tchr. Law Sch., U. Wis., 1977 Bd. dirs. Lake Geneva YMCA. Mem. ABA, Walworth County Bar Assn. (pres. 1962-63), State Bar Wis. (chmn. conv. and entertainment com. 1979-81, chmn. adminstrn. Justice and Judiciary com., 1986-87, bench bar rels. com., 1987-90, mem. exec. com. Wis. Bicentennial Com. on Constn.), Wis. Acad. Trial Lawyers (sec. 1975, treas. 1976, dir. 1977-79) Office: 716 Wisconsin St Lake Geneva WI 53147-1826 also: PO Box 940 Lake Geneva WI 53147-0940 Home: 41 Golf Pkwy Madison WI 53704 Office Phone: 262-248-6636. Business E-Mail: BBraden@bodlaw.net.

BRADEN, GREGORY C., lawyer; b. Cleve. BA in Mathematical Economics, with honors, U. Wis., 1979, JD with honors, 1982. Bar: Wis. 1982, Ga. 1986. Assoc. Reinhart Boerner, 1983—84; ptnr. Alston & Bird LLP, Morgan, Lewis & Bockius, Washington, 2007—. Lectr. in field; adj. prof. Emory U. Law Sch. Pro-bono counsel Cath County Clean Commn., 1986—. Fellow: Am. Coll. Employee Benefits Counsel; mem.: Southern Employee Benefits Conf. (sec., steering com.), ESOP (Employee Stock Ownership Plan) Assn., State Bar Wis., Atlanta Bar Assn., State Bar Ga., ABA (Tax Sect., Labor Sect.), Order of Coif. Office: Morgan Lewis & Bockius 1111 Pennsylvania Ave NW Washington DC 20004 Office Phone: 202-739-5217. Office Fax: 202-739-3001. Business E-Mail: gbraden@morganlewis.com.

BRADEN, JAMES DALE, former state legislator; b. Wakefield, Kans., Aug. 2, 1934; s. James Wesley and Olive (Reed) B.; m. Naomi Carlson, July 3, 1952 (div. Jan. 1983); children: Gregory, Michael, Ladd, Amy; m. Margie Clark Tidwell, Sept. 17, 1983; stepchildren: Richard, Lon, Dale. Grad. high sch., Wakefield. CLU, The Am. Coll. Meat cutter, Wakefield, 1952-64; ins. agt., securities broker Braden Fin. Svcs., Clay Ctr., Kans., 1964—; state rep. Kans. Ho. of Reps., Topeka, 1974-91, house majority leader, 1985-87, speaker of the house, 1987-91. Past chmn. econ. devel. com. Nat. Conf. State Legislatures, legis. coordinating council, calendar and printing com.; past chmn. assessment and taxation com.; mem. Council of State Govts. intergovtl. affairs com.; past chmn. taxation task force of Midwestern Conf. of Council State Govts.; chmn. Interstate Cooperation Commn.; former mem. State Fin. Council, Kans. Inc.; past chmn. Legis. Commn. on Kans. Econ. Devel.; past mem. Kans. Pub. Agenda Commn. Active St. Paul's Episcopal Ch., Clay Ctr.; mem. Rep. Party Exec. Com. Mem. NALU, Kans. Assn Ins. and Fin. Advisors (past pres.), Million Dollar Round Table (life), Rotary, Masons, Shriners, Elks. Episcopalian. Avocations: hunting, fishing, flying, sailing. Home: PO Box 58 Clay Center KS 67432-0058 Office: Braden Fin Svcs 1101 5th St # 58 Clay Center KS 67432-2021 Office Phone: 785-632-3601. E-mail: jbraden@eaglecom.net.

BRADEN, THOMAS WARDELL, news correspondent; b. Greene, Iowa, Feb. 22, 1917; s. Thomas Wardell and Louise (Garl) Braden; m. Joan E. Ridley, Dec. 18, 1948 (dec.); children: David, Mary, Joan, Susan, Nancy, Elizabeth, Thomas Wardell III(dec.) , Nicholas. BA, Dartmouth Coll., 1940, MA, 1964; LittD, Franklin Coll. Ind., 1979. Newspaperman, instr. English Dartmouth, 1946, asst. to pres. and asst. prof., 1947—48; exec. sec. Mus. Modern Art, NYC, 1949; dir. Am. Com. on United Europe, 1950; editor, pub. Blade Tribune, Oceanside, Calif., 1954—68; columnist Los Angeles Times Syndicate, 1968—86; commentator CNN, CBS, NBC, 1978—89. Author (with Stewart Alsop): Sub-Rosa, 1946; author: Eight is Enough, 1975. Mem. Calif. Bd. Edn., 1959—67; past pres. Trustee Calif. State Coll., 1961—64, Dartmouth, 1964—74, Carnegie Endowment, 1970—82. With King's Royal Rifle Corps Brit. Army, 1941—44, Africa and Italy, trans. to inf. AUS, 1944, served as a parachutist office of Strategic Svc.

BRADFORD, BARBARA TAYLOR, writer, journalist; b. Leeds, Eng. arrived in U.S., 1964; d. Winston and Freda (Walker) Taylor; m. Robert Bradford, Dec. 24, 1963. Student pvt. schs., Eng.; LittD (hon.), Leeds U., Eng., 1990, U. Bradford, West Yorkshire, Eng., 1995; LHD (hon.), Teikyo Post U., Waterbury, Conn., 1996. Women's editor Yorkshire (Eng.) Evening Post, 1951-53, reporter, 1949-51; editor Woman's Own, 1953-54; columnist London Evening News, 1955-57; exec. editor London Am., 1959-62; editor Nat. Design Center Mag., 1965-69; syndicated columnist Newsday Spls., LI, 1968-70; nat. syndicated columnist Chgo. Tribune-N.Y. (News Syndicate), NYC, 1970-75, LA Times Syndicate, 1975-81. Author: Complete Encyclopedia of Homemaking Ideas, 1968, A Garland of Children's Verse, 1968, How to Be the Perfect Wife, 1969, Easy Steps to Successful Decorating, 1971, Decorating Ideas for Casual Living, 1977, How to Solve Your Decorating Problems, 1976, Making Space Grow, 1979, Luxury Designs for Apartment Living, 1981, (novels) A Woman of Substance, 1979, Voice of the Heart, 1983, Hold the Dream, 1985, screen adaptation, 1986, Act of Will, 1986, To Be the Best, 1988, The Women in His Life, 1990, Remember, 1991, Angel, 1993, Everything to Gain, 1994, Dangerous to Know, 1995, Love in Another Town, 1995, Her Own Rules, 1996, A Secret Affair, 1996, Power of a Woman, 1997, A Sudden Change of Heart, 1999, Where You Belong, 2000, The Triumph of Katie Byrne, 2001, Three Weeks in Paris, 2001, Emma's Secret, 2003, Unexpected Blessings, 2004, Just Rewards, 2005, The Revenscar Dynasty, 2007, The Revenscar Heir, 2007. Recipient Dorothy Dawe award, Am. Furniture Mart, 1970, 1971, Matrix award, N.Y. Women in Comm., 1985, Spl. Jury prize for body of lit., Deauville Festival Am. Film, 1994, Just award. Mem.: Am. Soc. Interior Designers, Authors Guild Am. (mem. coun. 1989—), Nat. Soc. Interior Designers (Disting. Editl. award 1969, Nat. Press award 1971), Coun. Authors Guild. Office: Bradford Enterprises 450 Park Ave New York NY 10022-2605 Office Phone: 212-308-7390. Personal E-mail: bradford.ent@att.net.

BRADFORD, CARL O., judge; b. Dallas, Nov. 16, 1932; s. Montie Leroy and Vivian Ila (Milan) B.; m. Claire Solange Chaloux, Jan. 15, 1955 (dec. 1972); children: Timothy, Kathleen, Elizabeth; m. Mary Ellen Sanborn, July 7, 1973; children: Bethany, Michael. Student, U. Detroit, 1956-59; JD, U. Maine, Portland, 1962. Bar: Maine 1963, U.S. Dist. Ct. Maine 1963, U.S. Ct. Appeals (1st cir.) 1963, U.S. Supreme Ct. 1978. Asst. atty. gen. State of Maine, Augusta, 1963-64, justice Superior Ct., 1981-98, active-ret. justice Superior Ct., 1998—. Ptnr. Powers & Bradford, Freeport, Maine, 1964—81; commr. Uniform State Laws, 1972—76; mem. drafting com. Uniform Exemptions Act, 1974—76. Bd. dirs. Nat. Ctr. State Cts., Williamsburg, Va., 1997—2000; trustee Nat. Jud. Coll., Reno, 2001—, sec. bd. trustees, 2004—, chair, 2006—. With USN, 1951—55. Fellow Am. Bar Found., Maine Bar Found.; mem. Maine Bar Assn. (bd. govs. 1970-78, pres. 1977-78), Maine Trial Lawyers Assn. (bd. govs., sec. 1970-81), ABA (ho. of dels. 1978-81, 90-95, state bar del. 1978-81, bd. govs. 1st dist. 1990-93, bd. lisiaon to Nat. Conf. Spl. Ct. Judges 1990-91, liaison to Criminal Justice Sect. 1990-93, liaison to Nat. Conf. State Trial Judges 1991-93, chair subcom. nominations and awards com. 1991-93, bd. govs. program com. 1990-91, mem. oper. com. 1991-93, project 2000 subcom. 1991-93, bd. govs. chair compensation com. 1993, bd. govs. exec. com. 1993, bd. govs. exec. dir. search com. 1990, mem. comm. on multi-disciplinary practice 1998-2000), Nat. Conf. State Trial Judges (del. 1982-97, jud. immunity com. 1984-97, chair 1991-96, conf. vice chair 1993, chair-elect 1994-95, chair 1995-96), Am. Judicature Soc. Home: 225 Sea Meadows Ln Yarmouth ME 04096-5523 Office: Superior Ct PO Box 287 Portland ME 04112-0287 Office Phone: 207-822-4174.

BRADFORD, DANA GIBSON, II, lawyer; b. Coral Gables, Fla., Sept. 29, 1948; s. Dana Gibson and Jeanette (Ellis) B.; m. Mary E. Bradford, June 20, 1970 (div. Jan. 1982); 1 child, Jeffrey Dana; m. Donna P. Bradford, Apr. 14, 1984; 1 child, Shannon Claire. BA, U. Fla., 1970; JD, Duke U., 1973. Bar: Fla. 1973, U.S. Dist. Ct. (mid. dist.) Fla. 1974, U.S. Dist. Ct. (so. and no. dists.) Fla. 1979, U.S. Ct. Appeals (5th cir.) 1974, U.S. Ct. Appeals (11th cir.) 1982, U.S. Supreme Ct. 1977. Lawyer, ptnr. Mahoney, Hadlow & Adams, Jacksonville, Fla., 1973-82, Baumer, Bradford & Walters, Jacksonville, 1982—2000, Smith, Gambrell & Russell, LLP, Jacksonville, 2000—. Mem. Fla. Bd. Bar Examiners, 1989-94, chmn. bd., 1992-93; mem. Fla. Supreme Ct. Commn. on Professionalism, 1996-98; seminar lectr. Contbr. chpt. to book, articles to profl. jours. Mem. Leadership Jacksonville, 1982; spl. counsel Jacksonville Sports Authority. Capt. U.S. Army Res., 1972-80. Mem. ABA, ATLA, Jacksonville Bar Assn. (bd. govs. young lawyers sect. 1976-78, chmn. trial sects. 1989-90), Jacksonville Assn. Def. Counsel (pres. 1978-79), Am. Bd. Trial Advocates. Republican. Methodist. Office: Smith Gambrell & Russell LLP 50 N Laura St Ste 2600 Jacksonville FL 32202-3625 Office Phone: 904-598-6100. Business E-Mail: dgbradford@sgrlaw.com.

BRADFORD, DAVID S., surgeon; b. Charlotte, NC, Oct. 15, 1936; m. Sharon Hale; children: David Mackay, Jennifer Sutherland, Tyler Speir. BA, Davidson Coll., 1958; MD, U. Pa., 1962. Diplomate: Am. Bd. Orthopaedic Surgeons. Intern in surgery Columbia-Presbyn. Med. Center, NYC, 1962-63, resident in gen. surgery, 1965-66; resident in orthopaedic surgery N.Y. Orthopaedic Hosp., Columbia-Presbyn. Med. Center, NYC, 1966-68, jr. Annie C. Kane fellow orthopaedic surgery, 1968-69; research trainee orthopaedics Nat. Inst. Arthritis and Metabolic Diseases, 1969-70; prof. orthopaedic surgery U. Minn. Hosps., Mpls., 1970-90, chief of spine surgery, 1984-90; dir. Twin Cities Scoliosis Spine Ctr., Mpls., 1984—90; prof., chmn. dept. orthopaedic surgery U. Calif., San Francisco, 1991—. Mem. bd. editors: Spine, Spine Journal, Spine Letter, AOA News, Clinical Orthopaedics and Related Rsch., Journal of Am. Academy of Orthopaedic Surgeons, Journal of Pediatric Orthopaedic Rsch.; contbr. articles to profl. jours. Mem. AMA, Am. Acad. Orthopaedic Surgeons, Am. Orthopaedic Assn., Assn. Bone and Joint Surgeons (past pres.), Orthopaedic Rsch. Soc., Scoliosis Rsch. Soc. (past pres.), British Scoliosis Soc., European Spine Deformity Soc., Internat. Soc. Orthopaedic Surgery and Traumatology, N. Am. Spine Soc., Orthopaedic Rsch. & Educational Found., Scoliosis Rsch. Soc., Spine Arthroplasty Soc. Office: U of Calif San Francisco Dept Orthopedic Surgery MU-320W Box 0728 San Francisco CA 94143-0728 Office Phone: 415-476-2280.

BRADFORD, DENNIS DOYLE, real estate broker and developer; b. Tulsa, Sept. 5, 1945; s. Doyle Earl and Elta (Price) B.; m. Richie Deloris Dawson BSBA Econs., U. Tulsa, 1969. Sales and mktg. rep. Xerox Corp., Oklahoma City, 1969—72; comml. loan officer Mager Mortgage Co., Oklahoma City, 1973—74; pvt. practice real estate Oklahoma City, 1973—; pres., owner Bradford Oil Co., Oklahoma City, 1977—80; pres. Blazer Oil Co., Oklahoma City, 1980—; v.p. Petro So., Inc., Tampa Fla., 1983—84; ptnr. Coachman Inns, Oklahoma City, 1981—86; chmn., CEO Coachman Inc., Oklahoma City, 1985—98; dir. Coachman Inc, San Juan, 1998—2002; pres., CEO Olympic Mills Corp., Guaynabo, PR, 1995—97; pres. West Coast Ptnrs., Inc., Okla. City, 1997—; prin. Genesis Group, Bradenton, Fla., 2005—. Mem. nat. adv. coun. to US SBA, Washington, 1982-92; del. to White House Conf. on Small Bus., 1986; adv. bd. Nat. SBDC, Washington, 2003—, vice chmn., 2005-06, chmn., 2006-; prin. Genesis Group, Bradenton, Fla., 2006- Bd. dirs. Okla. Med. Ctr. Found., 1989-94, Salvation Army of P.R., 1996-97; bd. dirs., sec. Okla. Air and Space Mus., 1989-95, v.p. 1991-92, pres. 1992-93; mem. Local Selective Svc. Bd., Oklahoma City, 1988-94, Rep. Eagles, 1979-92, Rep. Presdl. Round Table Mem. Nat. Cowboy Hall of Fame, Okla. Heritage Assn., Okla. County Hist. Soc., Air Force Assn., Navy League, Young Pres.'s Orgn. (chmn. 1993-94, N.Am. spl. projects officer 1993-94), World Pres.'s Orgn. (chmn. Oklahoma City chpt. 2002-04, 2005—), Oklahoma City C. of C., Balloon Fedn. Am., Oklahoma City Golf and Country Club, Summit Club Tulsa, Bradenton Country Club Republican. Methodist. Office: West Coast Ptnrs Incn 301 NW 63rd St Ste 500 Oklahoma City OK 73116-7989 Home: 4305 17th Ave West Bradenton FL 34209 Business E-Mail: ddb@westcoastpartners.com.

BRADFORD, JAMES C., JR., brokerage house executive; b. Nashville, July 25, 1933; s. James C. and Eleanor (Avent) B.; m. Lillian Frances Robertson, Nov., 1967; children: Jay, Bryan. BA, Princeton U., 1955. Trainee Lehman Bros., NYC, 1958; ptnr. J.C. Bradford & Co., Nashville, 1959-2000; sr. mng. dir. U.B.S. PaineWebber, Nashville, 2001—. Chmn. dist. com. Nat. Assn. Securities Dealers, Atlanta, 1970-73; dir. Securities Industry Assn., N.Y.C., 1972-75; gov. Am. Stock Exch., 1986-87; bd. dirs. N.Y. Stock Exch., 1987-93, Nat. Assn. Securities Dealers Regulation. Trustee Mongomery Bell Acad., Nashville, 1968—; pres. Nashville Symphony Assn., 1969-70; pres. bd. trustees Ensworth Sch., Nashville, 1988-89. 1st lt. USAF, 1955-57. Mem. Belle Meade Country Club (bd. dirs. 1987-89), Nat. Assn. of Securities (gov. Washington 1996). Republican. Episcopalian. Office: UBS 3102 West End Nashville TN 37203 Business E-Mail: jimmy.bradford@ubs.com.

BRADFORD, JAMES WARREN, JR., dean, finance educator; b. Newport News, Va., May 3, 1947; s. James Warren and Blanche B.; m. Susan Garrision; children: Geoffrey, Emily, Alexander, Laura. BA in Polit. Sci., U. Fla., 1969; JD, Vanderbilt U., 1973. Pvt. practice, 1973; ptnr. Hunter, Smith & Davis, Kingsport, Tenn., 1973-84; v.p., gen. counsel AGF Industries, Inc., Kingsport, 1984-92, pres., CEO, 1992—99, United Glass Corp., 1999—2001; clin. prof. mgmt. Owen Grad. Sch. Mgmt., Vanderbilt U., Nashville, 2002—04, assoc. dean corp. rels., 2002—04, acting dean, 2004—05, dean, 2005—, Ralph Owen prof. practice of mgmt., 2005—. Mem. ABA, Tenn. Bar Assn., Kingsport Bar Assn. Avocations: golf, running, bicycling, gardening. Office: Vanderbilt U Owen Grad Sch Mgmt 401 21st Ave S Nashville TN 37203 Home: 101 Savoy Cir Nashville TN 37205 Office Phone: 615-343-5705. Office Fax: 615-343-7177. E-mail: jim.bradford@owen.vanderbilt.edu.

BRADFORD, JANE TURNER, librarian; b. Indpls., July 10, 1946; d. Roy Orlando and Ruthann (Vandivier) Turner; m. Bruce Carlton Bradford, Sept. 1, 1968 (div. 1985); 1 child, Amanda Elizabeth. BA, Stetson U., 1968; MA, Pa. State U., 1970; MS, U. Ill., 1987. Instr. Stetson U., De Land, Fla., 1976-85, asst. prof., ref. libr., 1987-92, women's advocate, 1995—98, assoc. prof., 1992—2006, prof., 2006—. Co-author: LibrarY Handbook: A Guide to Research, rev. edit. 1998 Pres. ParentCraft, De Land, 1979-81; mem. intellectual freedom com. Fla. Libr. Assn., 1988-90, chair publs. com., 1992-93, Brit. coun. exchange, No. Ireland, 1998; participant libr. exch. Paedagogische Hochschule, Freiburg, Germany, 2007. Libr. Exchange-Moscow, Stetson U., 1992, China, 1988. Mem. ALA, AAUW (univ. liaison 1987-95), Am. Assn. of Coll. and Rsch. Librs., Fla. Libr. Assn., Assn. of Coll. and Rsch. Librs. Fla., Beta Phi Mu, Sigma Tau Delta. Office: PO Box 8418 421 N Woodland Blvd Deland FL 32723-3760 Office Phone: 386-822-7190. Business E-Mail: jbradfor@stetson.edu.

BRADFORD, JAY TURNER, insurance company executive, state legislator; b. Little Rock, Apr. 30, 1940; s. Turner and Chrystal (Jacobs) B.; 1 child, Chrystal. BA, Henderson Coll., 1963. Cert. ins. counselor. Ins. agent Metropolitan Life Co., Pine Bluff, Ark., 1963-65, McLellan Ins. Co., Pine Bluff, 1968-76; pres. Pine Bluff Ins. Exchange, 1976—. Alderman City of Pine Bluff, 1981-82; mem. Ark. State Senate, 1983—; mem. chmn. Health Labor Com., 1983—; chmn. Senate Efficiency Com.; pres. pro temArk. State Senate, Pro team Ho. of Reps., 2005—, chmn. health com., 2005—. Named Small bus. Man of Yr., 1988; recipient leadership award Leadership Pine Bluff, 1987. Mem. Soc. Ins. Agts. (cert. ins. counselor), Ind. Ins. Agts. Ark. (pres. 1981—), Subiaco Alumni Assn. (pres. 1977), Pine Bluff Civitan (pres. 1967). Democrat. Episcopalian. Office: First Ark Ins Group PO Box 72225 Little Rock AR 72225 Office Phone: 501-666-0653.

BRADFORD, JOANNE K., computer software company executive; married; 2 children. BA in Journalism and Advertising, San Diego State U. Mgmt. tng. RH Macy, 1986; dist. sales mgr. Engring. News Record; acct. mgr. BusinessWeek mag. McGraw-Hill Cos., 1989, tech. mktg. mgr. BusinessWeek mag., v.p. sales Western region BusinessWeek mag., 1997, v.p. sales N. Am. Mktg. BusinessWeek mag.; v.p., chief media revenue officer MSN, Redmond, Wash., 2001—06; corp. v.p. global sales & trade mktg Microsoft Corp., Redmond, Wash., 2006—. Named one of Media Up-and-Comers, BusinessWeek, Women to Watch, Advertising Age, 2003. Mem.: Interactive Advertising Bureau (bd. dirs.). Office: Microsoft Corp 1 Microsoft Way Redmond WA 98052-6399 Office Phone: 425-882-8080. Office Fax: 425-936-7329.*

BRADFORD, LOUISE MATHILDE, social work administrator; b. Alexandria, La., Aug. 3, 1925; d. Henry Aaron and Ruby (Pearson) B. BS, La. Poly. Inst., 1945; cert. in social work, La. State U., 1949; MS, Columbia U., 1953; postgrad., Tulane U., 1962-64, La. State U., 1967; cert., U. Pa., 1966. Diplomate NASW, Am. Bd. Clin. Social Work; cert. social worker Acad. Cert. Social Workers; La. Bd. Approved Clin. Suprs. With La. Dept. Pub. Welfare, Alexandria, 1945-78, welfare caseworker, 1950-53, children's case supr., 1957-59, child welfare cons., 1959-73, social svcs. cons., 1973-78, state cons. day care, 1963-66; dir. social svcs. St. Mary's Tng. Sch., Alexandria, 1978-2000; adoption splst. Vols. of Am., 2000—07. Del. Nat. Day Care Conf., Washington, 1964; mem. early childhood edn. com. So. States Work Conf., Daytona Beach, Fla., 1968; mem. La. adv. com. 1970 White House Conf. on Children, also del.; mem. So. region planning com. Child Welfare League Am., 1970-73; mem. profl. adv. com. Cenla chpt. Parents Without Partners, 1970-95; adj. asst. prof. sociology La. Coll. Pineville, 1969-85; lectr. Kindergarten Workshop, 1970-72; mem. La. 4-C Steering Com.; social svcs. cons. La. Spl. Edn. Ctr., Alexandria, 1980-86; del. Internat. Conf. on Social Welfare, Nairobi, 1974, Jerusalem, 1978, Hong Kong, 1980, Brighton, 1982, Montreal, 1984; del. White House Conf. on Children. Bd. dirs. Cenla Cmty. Action Com., Alexandria, 1966-68; mem. kindergarten bd. Meth. Ch., 1967-87, ofcl. bd., 1974-75, 77-81, 83-85, 96-98, 2000-03. Recipient Social Worker of Yr. award, Alexandria br. NASW La. Conf. Social Welfare, 1974, Lifetime Achievement award, La. Chpt. Nat. Assn. of Social Workers, 2003. Mem.: DAR, NASW (Lifetime Achievement award, La. chpt. 2003), Ctrl. La. Pre-Sch. Assn. (dir. 1967—70), Am. Assn. on Mental Retardation (La. social work chair 1989—94, Meritorious Contbn. award 1999, La. chpt. Svc. award 2001, Region V Svc. award 2001), Internat. Coun. on Social Welfare, La. Conf. Social Welfare (George Freeman award 1987, Hilda C. Simon award 1987), So. La. Assn. Children Under Six, Acad. Cert. Social Workers, Alexandria Golf and Country Club, Lions.

BRADFORD, MARIAH, elementary school educator, consultant; b. Bay Springs, Miss., Sept. 23, 1929; d. Glasco Hunter Bender and Georgianna Holloway; m. Demond Bradford, Sr., Apr. 15, 1960 (div. Sept. 1984); children: Anita, Demond Jr., Kelvin. BS in Home Econs., Jackson Coll., 1953; MS in Edn., Ind. U., 1973; LHD (hon.), Martin U., Indpls., 1994. Cert. tchr. Miss., 1953, Ind., 1962, Ariz., 1997. Tchr. Scott County Pub. Schs., Forest, Miss., 1953—57, Meridian Mcpl. Separate Schs., 1957, 1959—61; county ext. agent Coop. Ext. Dept., Kosciusko, 1958—59; tchr. Indpls. Pub. Schs., 1963—92; sub. tchr. Peoria Unified Schs., Ariz., 1997—2001, Dysart Unified Schs., Surprise, 1997—. Sec., bd. dirs. Martin U., Indpls., 1989—94. Contbr. poems to literary publs. and jours. (Editors' Choice award, 1996). Commr. Planning and Zoning, Surprise, Ariz., 1997—99; big sister Big Brothers/Big Sister, Indpls. and Phoenix, 1987—2003; supt. Sunday sch. Gideon Missionary Bapt. Ch.; cons. Zion Rest Dist. Ch. Nurses Auxiliary. Recipient Sagamore of the Wabash, State of Ind., Gov. Evan Bayh, 1994, Golden Apple award, Indpls. Power and Light Co. and Cmty. Leaders Allied for Superior Schs., 1992, Special Human Rights award, Indpls. Edn. Assn. Human Rights Com., 1993, Human Rights award, Indpls. Edn. Assn., 1983; grantee, Indpls. Pub. Schs. Found., 1986, DePauw U. and Dept. of Health Edn. and Welfare, 1977. Mem.: NAACP (life), Assn. Negro Bus. and Profl. Women's Clubs (founder, pres. Madame Walker chpt. 1979—89, Sojourner Truth award 1982), Household of Ruth (#6851, Grand United Order of Oddfellows). Democrat. Baptist. Avocations: writing, reading, travel, volunteering, sewing. Home: 18019 N 145th Dr Surprise AZ 85374-4222 Personal E-mail: bradfordsurp@aol.com.

BRADFORD, MARLENE KAY, history educator, writer; b. Chgo., Oct. 19, 1946; d. Johnnie Lofton and Beatrice Edna (McManus) Cooper; m. Willie Farrell Bradford, Aug. 1, 1970; children: Meredith, Todd. BS in Chemistry, Union U., Jackson, Tenn., 1968; MA in History, Southwest Tex. State U., San Marcos, 1991; PhD in History, Tex. A&M U., College Station, 1998. Cert. tchr. Tex. Lectr. history Tex. A&M U., 1998—2001; tchr. govt. and history Garland Ind. Sch. Dist. (Naaman Forest H.S.), Tex., 2001—. Academic decathlon coach Garland Ind. Sch. Dist., 2004—. Author: (book) Scanning the Skies, 2001; editor: (multi-vol.) Natural Disasters, 2000. Mem.: Tex. Coun. Social Studies, Am. Hist. Assn. Avocations: quilting, accordion, singing.

BRADFORD, MICHELLE M., social studies educator; children: Rebecca, Amy. BA in Elem. Edn., Social Studies, State U. Coll., Buffalo, 2002, MA in Ednl. Computing, 2005. Tchr. social studies grade 7 Amherst Mid. Sch., NY, 2002—, dept. chair social studies, 2005—. Tchr. rep. Amherst Mid. Sch. Leadership Team, 2005—, Literacy Coun., Amherst, 2006—. Mem.: NY State Coun. Social Studies, Nat. Coun. Social Studies. Office: Amherst Mid Sch 55 Kings Hwy Amherst NY 14226-4398

BRADFORD, MONICA M., editor; BS in chemistry, St. Mary's Coll., Notre Dame, Ind. Publ. divsn. Am. Chem. Soc., 1981—89; staff Science mag., 1989—, now exec. editor. Vice chair Am. Heart Assn. Sci. Pub. Com. Mem.: Coun. Sci. Editors (dir. and pres.), Soc. Scholarly Pub. Office: Science/AAAS 1200 NY Ave NW Washington DC 20005

BRADFORD, STEVEN PAUL, film educator, department chairman; b. Phoenix, Jan. 28, 1960; s. Paul Everett and Janett May Bradford. BA in Cinema TV Prodn., U. So. Calif., LA, 1982. Video prodr. CompuSave, Irvine, Calif., 1984—85; dir. photography Bradford Comm., Seattle, 1985—2003; digital video prodr. Sierra Online, Bellevue, Wash., 2000—01; media arts program chair Collins Coll., Tempe, Ariz., 2004—, dir. Sch. Film, 2006—. Prodr.: (short film) Satellites and You; dir. photography (short video) The Last Bough, (short 16mm film) Stonewash, (feature film) FLO$$. Outreach vol. Seattle Monorail Project, 2000—04; bd. mem. USC Cinema Alumni Assn., LA, 1985—86, Wash. Film Video Assn., Seattle, 1995—97, 2005—. Mem.: Media Comm. Assn. Internat. D-Liberal. Achievements include invention of automated system for creating personalized children's videos from a single master, in real time, 1987. Home: 700 W University Dr #237 Tempe AZ 85281 Office: Collins Coll 1140 S Priest Dr Tempe AZ 85281 Home Phone: 480-540-8144. Personal E-mail: bradford@seanet.com. E-mail: sbradford@collinscollege.edu.

BRADFORD, SUSAN ANNE, management consultant, writer; b. Pasadena, Calif., Dec. 2, 1969; d. Wesley Gene and Nancy Cornelia (Dixon) B. Student, Coll. Cevenol, 1985, St. Andrews U., 1989—90; BA in English, U. Calif., Irvine, 1992; MA in Internat. Rels., Essex U., 1996, postgrad. Editor-in-chief Gandalf's Gazette, Irvine, 1987—88; news editor New Univ., Irvine, 1987—88; intern Sta. CBS-TV News, LA, 1989; host, exec. prodr. Witness the News TV show, Irvine, 1990—92; prodn. asst. PBS Red Car Film Project, LA, 1982—83; intern in news writing Sta. KNX News, LA, 1993; reporter City News Svc., LA, 1994—95; founder/editor European Rev., 1995—98; coord. VA media outreach Kerry-Edwards Presdl. Campaign, 2004; prin., owner Bradford Consulting, 2005—. Sr. rsch. fellow, polit. cons., councillor Atlantic Coun. U.K., 1996—2002; speechwriter U.K. Shadow Fgn. Sec. Michael Howard, 1998; prodr. Fox News Channel, 2000; speechwriter Korean Amb. Sung Chul Yang, 2002—03; Va. pub. rels. dir. Clark presdl. campaign, 2003—04; cons., 2005; pres., CEO Bradford Con., 2005—. Author poems; contbr. articles to profl. jours. Mem., spkr., media liaison UN Assn., 2000—; mem. adv. com. NATO U., 1996—99. Recipient Writing awards Palos Verdes Nat. Bank, 1987, AFL-CIO, 1987, 3d Pl. award Nat. Fedn. Press Women, 1992. Mem. Calif. Press Women (pub. rels. chair 1991-92), Hollywood Women's Press Club (bd. dirs. 1989-94, bd. dirs. Scholarship Found., 1992-93), European Movement (com., London strategy group media coord. 1995-98), Irvine Women's Crew (founder, pres.), English Speaking Union, Federalist Soc. (internat. law com.), UN Assn. (media cons., spkr., writer), Creative Coalition, Federalist Soc. Mem. United Ch. Of Christ. Office Phone: 705-659-1499. Personal E-mail: susanbradford7@aol.com. Business E-Mail: susan@susanbradford.info.

BRADFORD, TUTT SLOAN, retired publisher; b. Apr. 30, 1917; s. Tutt S. and Zula (Bowen) B.; m. Elizabeth Hendley, June 30, 1941 (dec.); children: Nancy, Debbie; m. Mercedes F. Bradford, Dec. 14, 2001. Student, Wofford Coll., Spartanburg, SC, 1934; LLD, Maryville Coll., Tenn., 2005. Pub. Cleve. Daily Banner, 1948-51; asst. to pres. Gen. Newspapers, 1951; pub. Bristol (Va.) Herald Courier, 1951-55, Maryville (Tenn.) Alcoa Daily Times, 1955-85. Bd. dir. humanities, Tenn., 1971-73; mem. devel. coun. U. Tenn., 1980-83; bd. dirs. Maryville Coll., 1974-79, 81-2003, Knoxville Symphony, Knoxville Mus. of Art, Thompson Ctr. for Cancer Survival, Lakeshore Mental Hosp., Tenn. Tech. Found.; Tenn. Resource Valley, 1988-91, 92-95, East Tenn. Found.; pres. Blount Meml. Hosp. Found., Boy's Club Found., Blount Hearing and Speech Found., 1991, Blount County Libr. Found., 1999. Pres. Blount County Indsl. Devel. Bd., 1970-72. With 9th AF AUS, 1943-45, ETO. Recipient Disting. Svc. award Bristol Jr. C. of C, 1952, Maryville-Alcoa Jr. C. of C., 1958, 73, Sequoyah Literacy award Tenn. Hist. Com., 1995, Tenn. Vol. Cmty. award Gov. Don Sunquist, 2003; named to East Tenn. Hall of Fame, Jr. Achievement, 1990; named Vol. Yr., U. Tenn., 1994, Outstanding Philanthropist Nat. Soc. Fund Raising Execs., 1991. Mem. So. Newspaper Pubs. Assn. (bd. dirs. 1968-70), Tenn. Press Assn. (pres. 1974), Knox Arts Coun. (award 1988), E.Tenn. Soc. Profl. Journalists (award 2006), Blount County C. of C. (pres. 1960), Kiwanis (pres. Maryville 1967, 1987). Home: 805 Shannondale Way 131 Maryville TN 37803-5972

BRADFORD, WILLIAM DALTON, pathologist, educator; b. Rochester, NY, Nov. 2, 1931; s. William Leslie and Lenora Dee (Dalton) B.; m. Anne Bevington Harden, July 8, 1961; children— Scott Harden, Lisa Graham BA, Amherst Coll., 1954; MD, Western Res. U., 1958. Diplomate Am. Bd. Pediatrics, Am. Bd. Anatomic Pathology. Intern in pathology Boston Children's Med. Ctr., 1958-59, resident in pediatrics, 1959-61; teaching fellow in pathology Harvard Med. Sch., 1963-64; asst. prof. pathology Duke U., Durham, NC, 1966-70, assoc. prof., 1970-81, prof., 1981—, assoc. dean, 1970-71, 74-78, 84-87, asst. to chancellor for health affairs, 1987-89, dir. pediatric pathology, 1966—, dir. pathology tng. program, 1974-2001. Pres. Durham YMCA, 1978, bd. dirs., 1976-83, 90-95; mem. bd. visitors YMCA Camps Sea Gull/Seafarer, chair, 2002-07; faculty chmn. athletics Duke U., 1979-85. Lt. comdr. USN, 1961-63. Recipient Golden Apple award Student Med. Assn., 1969, 93, 95, 98, Layman of Yr. award YMCA, 1974, 78, Disting. Tchr. award Duke Med. Alumni Assn., 1989; Mead Johnson fellow, 1963-64. Mem. Internat. Acad. Pathology, Am. Assn. Pathologists, Soc. Pediatric Research, Group for Rsch. in Pathology Edn., Soc. for Pediatric Pathology (pres. 1987-88), Nat. Collegiate Athletic Assn. Council, Nat. Faculty Athletics Reps. Forum (chmn. 1985), Atlantic Coast Conf. (pres. 1982-83), Duke Med. Alumni Coun. (pres. 2000-01, exec. com. med. sch. admissions, vice-chmn. 2007—). Office: Duke U Med Ctr PO Box 3712 Durham NC 27710-0001 Home Phone: 919-489-4937; Office Phone: 919-684-5112. Business E-Mail: bradf001@mc.duke.edu.

BRADFORD, WILLIAM EDWARD, oil field equipment manufacturing company executive; b. Dallas, Jan. 8, 1935; m. JoDeane Browning, Aug. 18, 1955; children: William B., A. Kathleen, Jon E. BS in Geology, Centenary Coll., 1958; grad., Tex. A&M U., 1975. Salesman Hycalog, Inc., 1958-61; v.p., gen. ptnr. Analytical Logging, Inc., 1961-70; product mgr. Oilfield Products Group Dresser Industries, Inc., Dallas, 1970-72, mgr. Mid-cont. Oilfield Products Group, 1972-73, mgr. Europe, Africa, Middle East Oilfield Products Group, 1973-76, v.p. Security Divsn., 1976-78, pres. Security Divsn., 1980-83, group pres. Oilfield Products Group, 1983-84, v.p. ops., 1984-92, sr. v.p., 1988-92; pres. CEO Dresser-Rand Co., Corning, NY, 1992-95; pres., COO and dir. Dresser Industries, Inc., Dallas, 1995-96, pres., CEO, dir., 1996-98, chmn. pres., 1998-2000; chmn. Halliburton Co. (formerly Dresser Industries, Inc.), Dallas, 2000—. Bd. dirs. Valero Energy Corp. Mem.: Petroleum Equipment Suppliers Assn., Am. Assn. Petroleum Geologists, Soc. Petroleum Engrs., Dallas Country Club, Rolling Rock Club, Northwood Country Club (Dallas). Office: Two Turtle Creek Village 3838 Oak Lawn Ave Ste 224 Dallas TX 75219

BRADIE, PETER RICHARD, lawyer, engineer; b. Bklyn., Feb. 19, 1937; s. Alexander Robert and Blanche Isabelle Bradie; m. Anna Barbara Corcoran, Jan. 22, 1960; children: Suzanne J., Barbara L., Michell S. BSME, Fairleigh Dickinson U., 1960; JD, South Tex. Coll. Law, 1978. Registered profl. engr., Ala.; bar: Tex. 1978, U.S. Dist. Ct. (so. dist.) Tex. 1981. Performance engr. Pratt & Whitney Aircraft, West Palm Beach, Fla., 1961-63; sr. engr. Hayes Internat. Corp., Huntsville, Ala., 1963—68, Lockheed Missiles and Space, Huntsville, 1964—69; fluidics engr. Double A Products Co., Manchester, Mich., 1969—70; cons. Spectrum Controls, Montvale, NJ, 1970—74; sr. project mgr. Materials Rsch. Corp., Orangebury, NY, 1974—85; sr. contracts adminstr. Brown & Root Inc., Houston, 1974-85; sole practice Houston, 1985-91; ptnr. Bradie, Bradie & Bradie, Houston, 1991—. Counsel Inverness Forest C.A, Houston., 1978-80; sr. counsel Raymond-Brown & Root-Molem, J.V., Houston, 1982-84. Contbr. articles on fluidic controls to mags.; patentee. Dem. committeeman Bergen County, Haworth, N.J., 1959; del. Harris County Reps., Houston, 1984; officer, bd. dirs. Inverness Forest Civic Assn., Houston, 1975-78. Served to 2d lt. USMCR, 1958-61. Mem.: Comml. Law League Am., Houston N.W. Bar Assn. (treas. 1986, bd. dirs. 1988, pres.-elect 1988—89, pres. 1990—91), Tex. Bar Assn., Champions Sunrise Rotary Club, Montvale Rotary Club (bd. dirs. 1973—74), Rotary Internat., Am. Inn of Ct. Republican. Jewish. Avocations: classical music, history, computers.

Home: 7011 Evergreen Magnolia TX 77354 Office: Bradie Bradie & Bradie 6606 FM 1488 STe 148-363 Magnolia TX 77354 Home Phone: 936-273-0993; Office Phone: 936-271-2580. Business E-Mail: bradiex3@bradie-law.com.

BRADLEE, BENJAMIN CROWNINSHIELD, former editor; b. Boston, Aug. 26, 1921; s. Frederick J. and Josephine (deGersdorff) B.; m. Jean Saltonstall, Aug. 8, 1942; 1 son, Benjamin Crowninshield; m. Antoinette Pinchot, July 6, 1956; children: Dominic, Marina; m. Sally Quinn, Oct. 20, 1978; 1 son, Josiah Quinn Crowninshield. AB, Harvard U., 1943; LHD (hon.), Georgetown U., 2006. Reporter N.H. Sunday News, Manchester, 1946- 48, Washington Post, 1948-51; press attachè embassy Paris, France, 1951-53; European corr. Newsweek mag., Paris, 1953-57, reporter Washington bur., 1957-61, sr. editor, chief bur., 1961-65; mng. editor Washington Post, 1965-68, v.p., exec. editor, 1968-91, v.p. at large, 1991—. Author: That Special Grace, 1964, Conversations with Kennedy, 1975, A Good Life--Newspapering and Other Adventures, 1995. Served to lt. USNR, 1942-45. Home: 3014 N St NW Washington DC 20007-3404 Office: care Washington Post 1150 15th St NW Washington DC 20071-0001

BRADLEY, AMELIA JANE, lawyer; b. Columbia, SC, Apr. 18, 1947; d. Hugh Wilson and Amelia Jane Bradley; m. Richard Bancroft Hovey, Apr. 1, 1977. BA, U. Va., 1968; MA, George Washington U., 1971. Bar: Va. 1976, D.C. 1985. Analyst budget and mgmt. NLRB, Washington, 1968—71, 1972; clk. Cohen and Vitt, PC, Alexandria, Va., 1972—76; assoc. Cohen, Vitt & Annand, PC, Alexandria, 1976—80; White House fellow USDA, Washington, 1980—81, Office U.S. Trade Rep., Exec. Office of Pres., Washington, 1981, asst. gen. counsel, 1981—82, assoc. gen. counsel, 1982—84; prin. dep. gen. counsel Office U.S. Trade Rep., Exec Office of Pres., Washington, 1989—92; asst. U.S. trade rep. for dispute resolution Office U.S. Trade Rep., Exec. Office of Pres., Washington, 1994, legal advisor to U.S. GATT del. Geneva, 1984—87; assoc. dir. for global environment White House Office on Environ. Policy, Washington, 1994—95; assoc. dir. internat. trade and devel. Coun. on Environ. Quality, Washington, 1994—95; asst. U.S. trade rep. for monitoring, enforcement Office U.S. Trade Rep., Exec. Office of Pres., Washington, 1996—2002; dep dir. Inst. Internat. Econ. Law, Georgetown U. Law Ctr., Washington, 2004—. Chief negotiator U.S. GATT Uruguay Round Dispute Settlement Negotiating Group, 1986-87, 89-93; chmn. interagy. Sect. 301 Com., Washington, 1988-92; vis. rsch. assoc. Fletcher Sch. Law and Diplomacy, Tufts U., Medford, Mass., 1987-88; vis. rschr. Harvard U. Law Sch., Cambridge, Mass., 1988; adj. prof. Georgetown U. Law Ctr., 2003—. Mem. editl. adv. bd.: Jour. Internat. Econ. Law, 2004—06. Mem., chmn. Alexandria Human Rights Commn., 1975-80; pres., trustee Alexandria Law Libr., 1978-80; founding mem. Lawyer Referral Svc., Alexandria, 1978. NEH fellow, 1978. Mem. ABA, Va. State Bar (chmn. com. on legal edn. and admission to bar 1977-84), D.C. Bar (chmn. internat. trade com. 1989-90). Episcopalian.

BRADLEY, ANN WALSH, state supreme court justice; b. Richland Center, Wis. married; 4 children. BA, Webster Coll., 1972; JD, U. Wis., 1976. Former high school tchr.; atty. priv. practice, 1976—85; judge Marathon County Circuit Ct., Wausau, Wis., 1985—95; justice Wis. Supreme Ct., Madison, Wis., 1995—. Former assoc. dean and faculty mem. Wis. Judicial Coll.; former chair Wis. Jud. Conference; lecturer ABA Asia Law Initiative; commr. Nat. Conference on Uniform Laws. Bd. of visitors U. Wis. Law Sch. Fellow: Am. Bar Found.; mem.: ABA, State Bar of Wis. (Bench Bar Com.), Am. Law Inst., Am. Judicature Soc. (Harley award 2004). Office: Wis Supreme Ct PO Box 1688 Madison WI 53701-1688*

BRADLEY, APRIL RAIN, psychology professor; d. Bernis Bradley and Cynthia Sabelhaus. BA in Spanish, U. Ariz., 1992, BS in Psychology, 1992; MA in Clin. Psychology, U. Tex., El Paso, Tex., 1995; PhD in Clin. Psychology, U. Nev., 2004. Psychotherapist Ariz. Children's Home, Tucson, 1995—97; intern Ann Arbor VA Hosp., Mich., 2002—03; asst. prof. U. N.D., Grand Forks, ND, 2003—. Forensic investigator Psychol. Health Assocs., Reno, 2000—02. Contbr. articles to profl. jours. Grantee, Psychol. Health Assocs., 2001—02. Mem.: APA, ACLU, Midwestern Psychol. Assn., N.D. Psychol. Assn. Avocations: travel, poker, reading. Office: Univ North Dakota Psychology Box 8380 Grand Forks ND 58202

BRADLEY, BILL (WILLIAM WARREN BRADLEY), former senator; b. Crystal City, Mo., July 28, 1943; s. Warren W. and Susan (Crowe) B.; m. Ernestine Schlant, Jan. 14, 1974; 1 dau., Theresa Anne. BA, Princeton U., 1965; MA, Oxford U., Eng., 1968. Player N.Y. Knickerbockers Profl. Basketball Team, 1967-77; U.S. senator from N.J., 1979-96; mem. fin., energy coms., spl. com. on aging, 1997—98; Disting. leadership scholar, chair U. Md., College Park; Payne Disting. prof. Inst. for Internat. Studies, Stanford U., 1997-98; campaigned for Dem. Presdl. Nomination, 1999-2000; mng. dir. Allen & Co., LLC, 2000—; chief outside advisor non-profit practice McKinsey & Co., 2000—04. Essayist CBS TV Weekend Evening News, 1997-98; sr. advisor, vice chair internat. coun. J.P. Morgan and Co., Inc., 1997-99; bd. dirs. Willis Ins. Group, Seagate Tech., 2003-, Starbucks Coffee Co. Gather.com, 2006-; vis. prof. pub. affairs Univ. of Notre Dame, 1998; bd. trustees Princeton U., 1998-2002; mem. Coun. Fgn. Rels. Author: Life on the Run, 1976, The Fair Tax, 1984, Time Present, Time Past: A Memoir, 1996, Values of the Game, 1998, The Journey From Here, 2000, The New American Story, 2007; host (radio talk show) American Voices, 2005-. Chmn. Nat. Civic League, 1997-98. 1st lt. USAFR, 1967-78. Rhodes scholar, 1965-67; named three-time basketball All-Am.; recipient Sullivan award as the country's outstanding amateur athlete. Democrat. Achievements include being a mem. of NBA championship team, 1970, 73, Gold medal team Tokyo Olympics. Office: Allen & Co 711 Fifth Ave Fl 9 New York NY 10022

BRADLEY, BOB, professional soccer coach; b. Montclair, NJ, Mar. 3, 1958; B.History, Princeton U.; M.Sports Adminstrn., Ohio U. Head coach soccer Ohio U., Athens, 1980-81; asst. coach U. Va., 1982-83; head coach Princeton U., 1984-95; asst. coach D.C. United, 1995-97; head coach Chgo. Fire, 1997—, New York MetroStars, USA Soccer, 2006—. Named Major League Soccer's 1998 All Sport Coach of the Yr., NCAA Divsn. I Men's Coach of the Yr., 1993, winningest coach MLS history. Office: MetroStars Third Fl One Hammon Plz Secaucus NJ 07094

BRADLEY, CHARLES MACARTHUR, retired architect; b. Chgo., Sept. 26, 1918; s. Harold Smith and Helen Francis (MacArthur) B.; m. Joan Marie Daane, July 27, 1946; children: Mary Barbara, Nancy Ann, Sally Joan, William Charles (dec.). BS in Architecture, U. Ill., 1940. With Holabird & Root, architects, Chgo., 1940-41, Giffels & Vallet, architects and engrs., Detroit, 1941-44; ptnr., corp. pres. Bradley & Bradley, architects and engrs., Rockford, Ill., 1947-2001; ret., 2001. Pres. Bradley Bldg. Corp., 1962—. Prin. works include North Sheboygan (Wis.) High Sch. and addition, 1960-68, J.F. Kennedy Middle Sch., Rockford, 1968, Singer Health Clinic, Rockford, 1964, Jacobs H.S., Algonquin, Ill., 1976, Atwood plant, Rockford, 1977, Admiral Home, Chgo., 1978, Bushnell (Ill.) Jr. H.S., 1980, Bloom H.S., 1983, Evenglow Lodge, 1984, East Aurora H.S. addition, 1992, Erie H.S., 1994; author papers on life cycling old schs., roofing procedures. Active Blackhawk coun. Boy Scouts Am. Served with C.E., U.S. Army, 1945-46. Decorated Bronze Star; recipient Meritorious Svc. award Ill. Assn. Sch. Bds., 1976. Mem. AIA (pres. No. Ill. chpt. 1962, treas. Ill. coun. 1973-74), Ill. Soc. Architects (pres. 1974), Edn. Facilities Planners Inst., Ill. Assn. Sch. Bd. Officers, Rotary, Union League, Univ. Club, Midday Club (Chgo.), Shriners, Moose, Rockford Country Club, Quail Creek Country Club, Naples Sailing & Yacht Club, Lauderdale Lakes Sailing Club, Meridian Club. Republican. Congregationalist. Home and Office: Meridian Club 1103 4901 Gulfshore Blvd N Naples FL 34103

BRADLEY, CHARLES WILLIAM, podiatrist, educator; b. Fife, Tex., July 23, 1923; s. Tom and Mary Ada (Cheatham) B.; m. Marilyn A. Brown, Apr. 3, 1948 (dec. Mar. 1973); children: Steven, Gregory, Jeffrey, Elizabeth, Gerald. Student, Tex. Tech., 1940-42; D. Podiatric Medicine, Calif. Coll. Podiatric Medicine U. San Francisco, 1949, MPA, 1987, D.Sc. (hon.). Pvt. practice podiatry, Beaumont, Tex., 1950-51, Brownwood, Tex., 1951-52, San Francisco, San Bruno, Calif., 1952—; assoc. clin. prof. Calif. Coll. Podiatric Medicine, 1992-98. Chief of staff Calif. Podiatry Hosp., San Francisco; mem. surg. staff Sequoia Hosp., Redwood City, Calif.; mem. med. staff Peninsula Hosp., Burlingame, Calif.; chief podiatry staff St. Luke's Hosp., San Francisco; chmn. bd. Podiatry Ins. Co. Am.; cons. VA; assoc. prof. podiatric medicine Calif. Coll. Podiatric Medicine. Mem. San Francisco Symphony Found.; mem. adv. com. Health Policy Agenda for the Am. People, AMA; chmn. trustees Calif. Coll. Podiatric Medicine, Calif. Podiatry Coll., Calif. Podiatry Hosp.; mem. San Mateo Grand Jury, 1989. Served with USNR, 1942-45. Mem. Am. Podiatric Med. Assn. (trustee, pres. 1983-84), Calif. Podiatry Assn. (pres. No. div. 1964-66, state bd. dirs., pres. 1975-76, Podiatrist of Yr. award 1983), Nat. Coun. Edn. (vice-chmn.), Nat. Acads. Practice (chmn. podiatric med. sect. 1991-96, sec. 1996—), Am. Legion, San Bruno C. of C. (bd. dirs. 1978-91, v.p. 1992, bd. dir. grand jury assoc. 1990), Olympic Club, Commonwealth Club Calif., Elks, Lions. Home: 2965 Trousdale Dr Burlingame CA 94010-5708 Office: 560 Jenevein Ave San Bruno CA 94066-4408 E-mail: bradlee2@aol.com.

BRADLEY, DONALD EDWARD, lawyer; b. Santa Rosa, Calif., Sept. 26, 1943; s. Edward Aloysius and Mildred Louise (Kelley) B.; m. Marianne Stark, Apr. 22, 1990; children: Evan Patrick, Matthew Jordan, Andrea Phelps. AB, Dartmouth Coll., 1965; JD, U. Calif., San Francisco, 1968; LLM, N.Y.U., 1972. Bar: Calif. 1968, U.S. Dist. Ct. (no. dist.) Calif. 1968, U.S. Ct. Appeals (9 cir.) 1968, U.S. Tax Ct. 1972, U.S. Ct. Claims 1973, U.S. Supreme Ct. 1981. Assoc. Pillsbury, Madison & Sutro, San Francisco, 1972-77, ptnr., 1978-84; mem. Wilson Sonsini Goodrich & Rosati, Palo Alto, Calif., 1984—, gen. counsel, mem. exec. mgmt. com. Mng. dir. Wilson Sonsini Goodrich & Rosati, Palo Alto, 1995—; adj. prof. Golden State U., San Francisco, 1973-82; pres., chmn. bd. dirs. Atty.'s Ins. Mut. Risk Retention Group, Honolulu, 1986—. Capt. U.S. Army, 1969-70. Recipient Charles M. Ruddick award N.Y.U., 1972, award Bureau of Nat. Affairs, Washington, 1968. Mem. ABA, Internat. Bar Assn., Santa Clara Bar Assn., San Francisco Bar Assn., Internat. Tax Club, Peninsula Tax Club. Office: Wilson Sonsini Goodrich & Rosati 650 Page Mill Rd Palo Alto CA 94304-1050 Office Phone: 650-493-9300. Office Fax: 650-493-6811. E-mail: dbradley@wsgr.com.

BRADLEY, DONDEENA G., consumer products company executive; b. Dec. 28, 1964; m. Allen Bradley; children: Madison, Keaton. Prin. Health Bus. Partners Consulting; founder Conceptual Ventures; dir., applied innovation and strategy McNeil Nutritional, LLC, a Johnson & Johnson Co., New Brunswick, NJ. Mem. editl. bd. Nutraceuticals World. Named one of 25 Masters of Innovation, BusinessWeek. Office: McNeil Nutritionals LLC 501 George St New Brunswick NJ 08903 Business E-Mail: dbradley1@mcnus.jnj.com.

BRADLEY, E. MICHAEL, lawyer; b. NYC, Apr. 13, 1939; s. Otis Treat Bradley and Marian Booth (Alling) Ward; m. Judith Allen Thompson, June 29, 1962; children: Jennifer Treat, Michael Thompson, Thomas Alcott, Samuel Allen. BA, Yale U., 1961; LLB, U. Va., 1964. Bar: NY 1965. Assoc. Davis, Polk & Wardwell, NYC, 1964-72, Brown & Wood, NYC, 1972-73, ptnr., 1974-95, mem. policy com., 1981-94, mem. exec. com., 1989-94; ptnr. Jones Day, NYC, 1995—2004, Katten Muchin Rosenman LLP, NYC, 2004—. Lectr. Practicing Law Inst., NYC, 1970-79; 86, Am. Law Inst.-ABA, Phila., 1977-78; arbitrator Am. Arbitration Assn., NYC, 1975—. Contbg. editor: The Use of Experts in Corporate Litigation, 1978, Securites Law Techniques, 1985, 05. Bd. dirs. Bennett Coll. Found., NYC, 1984—, Inst. of Ams., La Jolla, Calif., 2001—; trustee Salisbury (Conn.) Sch., 1987—. Mem. ABA, NY State Bar Assn., Fed. Bar Coun., Assn. Bar City of NY, Union Club, Coral Beach Club, Quogue Field Club, Shinnecock Yacht Club, Nat. Golf Links of Am., L.I. Wyandanch Club. Republican. Presbyterian. Office: Katten Muchin Rosenman LLP 575 Madison Ave New York NY 10022 Office Phone: 212-940-8570. Business E-Mail: em.bradley@kattenlaw.com.

BRADLEY, EDWARD JAMES, state official, computer programmer and analyst; b. Syracuse, NY, Jan. 3, 1946; s. Robert Carroll and Hazel Irene (Malone) B.; m. Gwen Eileen Coats, Sept. 3, 1977 (div. 1984); 1 child, Edward James II. BA cum laude, SUNY, Albany, 1971, MPA, 1980; grad., Citizens Police Acad., 1992. Specialist N.Y. State Dept. Social Svcs., 1973-78; pub. adminstr. N.Y. State Dept. Transp., Albany, 1978-81; pub. mgmt. intern N.Y. State Dept. Civil Svcs., 1981-82; personnel adminstr. N.Y. State Dept. Taxation & Fin., 1982-83; computer programmer, analyst N.Y. State Dept. Transp., 1983—2005; ret., 2005. Commr. City of Albany Mcpl. Civil Svc. Commn., 1992-93, chmn., 1992-93. Author: Child and Family Genealogy Reporting System. Pres. Child and Family Enterprises, Inc., Albany, 1978-84, Traditional Am. Values, Albany, 1984-2003, Books Unbound, 1991-2003, V.O.T.E.S., 1992-2003; fundraiser United Way Am./Northeastern N.Y., Inc., 1976-78, Capital Are Coun. Chs., 1978, Birthright of Albany, Inc., 1984-88; mem. Albany County Dem. Com., 1985-93; active Pro-life Dems., Inc., 1984-94, Nat. Right-to-Life Com., Inc., 1984—, N.Y. State Right-to-Life, 1984—, Human Life Internat., 1992—; mem. nat. nominating com. Outstanding Young Ams., 1997—. With USN, 1963-66. Named one of Outstanding Young Men Am., 1982. Mem. DAV, ASPA, Am. Mgmt. Assn., Am. Pub. Welfare Assn., N.Y. State Forum for Info. Resources Mgmt., Vietnam Era Vets., Am. Legion, N.Y. Assn. Transp. Engrs., Capital Dist. Geneal. Soc. (pres. 1982-84), Nat. Spkrs. Assn., Toastmasters, Elks. Roman Catholic. Home: 1941 Western Ave Apt 1403 Albany NY 12203-7014 E-mail: jiggsmalone@msn.com.

BRADLEY, EDWARD JOSEPH, JR., electrical engineer; b. St. Louis, July 19, 1962; s. Edward Joseph and Marie Agnes (Stuchlik) B. BSEE, U. Mo., Rolla, 1984; MBA, St. Louis U., 1989. Registered profl. engr., Mo., Ill. Asst. engr. T&D spl. studies Union Elec. Co. (now Ameren Corp.), St. Louis, 1985-87, asst. engr. T&D stds., 1987-88, engr. T&D stds., 1988-92, engr. T&D svc. test operating, 1992-95, customer svc. engr. metro. underground dist., 1995-97, engr. distbn. standards, 1997-98, Ameren Corp., Saint Louis, 1998—. Scout leader Boy Scouts Am., St. Louis, 1980—, Explorer Venturing leader, 1988—. Recipient Bronze Pelican and St. George awds., Cath. Com. of Boy Scouts Am., 1994, 2001, Dist. Award of Merit, 1995, William Spurgeon award Exploring, 1997, Silver Beaver award Boy Scouts Am., 2002, Venturing Leadership award, 2005. Mem. IEEE (sr.), NSPE, Engrs. Club of St. Louis. Roman Catholic. Avocations: outdoors, collections. Home: 4365 Kensington Manor Dr Saint Louis MO 63128-2355 Office Phone: 314-554-3177. Business E-Mail: ebradley@ameren.com.

BRADLEY, ELIZABETH CLAY, financial planner, educator; b. Dayton, Ky., Feb. 6, 1948; d. Glenn Washington and Margaret Elizabeth Clay; m. James D. McPhail, Aug. 16, 1970 (dec. Sept. 1990); m. Julian Bradley, May 4, 1996. BS in Home Econs., U. Ky., 1970; MS in Family Econs., Kans. State U., 1977. CFP. Tchr. Bourbon County Jr. HS, Paris, Ky., 1970—71, Manhattan HS, Kans., 1974—84; investment rep. Edward Jones, Cary, NC, 1984—2001; ret., 2001; cons. Wachovia Sec., Raleigh, NC, 2002—. Bd. dirs. Wake Tech. C.C. Found. Author: (workbook) Motivation Plus, 1982, The Good Life, 2001. Chair Expanding the Circle-Glenaire, Cary, 2001—04; trustee Glenaire Presbyn. Home, Cary, 2002—04; mem. 5th Ave. Presbyn. Ch.; bd. dirs. Glenaire Found., Triangle Fin. Planning Assn., 2003—04, Wake Tch. Cmty. Coll. Found., 2005—. Named Young Educator, Kans. Assn. Vocat. Home Econs. Tchrs., 1984, Small Businessperson of Yr., Cary C. of C., 1988. Mem.: Cary C. of C. (named Small Bus. Person of Yr. 1988). Avocations: walking, writing, designing clothes, quilting. Office Phone: 919-571-2830. Personal E-mail: eclaybradley@nc.rr.com.

BRADLEY, JAMES EDWIN, religious studies educator; b. Portland, Oreg., Oct. 3, 1944; s. Clarence Jefferson Bradley and Phyllis Claire Hartzog; m. Diane Ellen Ball, June 25, 1966; children: Rachel Anne Harshbarger, Daniel James, Matthew Ellis. BA, Pasadena Nazarene Coll., Calif., 1968; BD, Fuller Theol. Sem., Pasadena, 1971; PhD, U. of So. Calif., LA, 1978. Prof. of ch. history Fuller Theol. Sem., Pasadena, 1976—. Author: Popular Politics and the American Revolution in England, 1986, Religion, Revolution, and English Radicalism, 1990, Church History: An Introduction to Research, Reference Works, and Methods, 1995; editor: Church, Word, and Spirit, 1987, Religion and Politics in Enlightenment Europe, 2001; book rev. editor: American and Episcopal History, 1989—2007, religion sect. editor: The Eighteenth Century: A Current Bibliography, 1979—87, editor, adv. editor: Studia Biblica et Theologica, 1971—87, bd. adv. editors: Eighteenth-Century Studies, 1992, mem. editl. bd.: Christian History, 1994—97. Recipient summer fellowship, Inst. of Humane Studies, 1980, summer stipend, NEH, 1981, Issues Rsch. grant, Assn. of Theol. Schs., 1987, Lilly-Endowment grant for theol. edn. in the Evang. tradition, Lilly, 1992, Pew Evang. Scholars grant for rsch. on religion in the English Enlightenment, Pew, 1994. Mem.: North Am. Conf. on Brit. Studies, Am. Soc. for Eighteenth-Century Studies, Am. Hist. Assn., Am. Soc. of Ch. History. Office: Fuller Theological Sem 135 N Oakland Ave Pasadena CA 91182 Home Phone: 909-621-5422; Office Phone: 626-584-5242. Business E-Mail: bradley@fuller.edu.

BRADLEY, JAMES P., orthopedist; b. Feb. 15, 1953; BS, Pa. State U., 1975; MS in Cell Biology, Fla. Inst. Tech., 1978; MD, Georgetown U. Sch. Medicine, 1982. Diplomate Nat. Bd. Med. Examiners; cert. Am. Bd. Orthopaedic Surgery. Gen. surgery resident U. Tenn., Chattanooga, 1982-84; orthop. surgery resident U. Health Ctr. Pitts., 1984-87; sports medicine fellow Kerlan-Jobe Orthop. Clinic, Inglewood, Calif., 1987-88; orthopedist Pitts., 1988—, Oakland Orthop. Assocs., Pitts., Burke & Bradley Assocs., Pitts. Active staff U. Pitts. Med. Ctr., 1988—, Mercy-Providence Hosp., Pitts., 1992—, Passavant Hosp., Pitts., 1993—; asst. staff St. Margaret's Hosp., Pitts., 1988—; assoc. staff St. Francis Med. Ctr., Pitts., 1988—, Allegheny Valley Hosp., Natrona Heights, pa., 1988—; courtesy staff Shadyside Hosp., Pitts., 1988—, Citizens Gen. Hosp., New Kensington, Pa., 1988—; attending staff Allegheny Gen. Hosp., Pitts., 1994—; med. dir. Tennis Tng. and Mgmt. Group, 1993; chmn. Tutorials of the AOSSM, 1994; team physician Fox Chapel Area H.S. Football Team, 1990—, Dapper Dan Round Ball Classic, 1991-, Shadyside Acad. Football Team, 1991—, Pitts. Steelers Profl. Football Club, 1991-, Born 2 Run All Star Basketball Game, LaRoche Coll., 1995, LA Dodgers (when in town); orthop. cons. to local HS and coll. athletic teams; dir. sports medicine dept. St. Margaret's Meml., Pitts., 1992—; clin. preceptor residency program St. Francis Med. Ctr., Pitts., 1992—; med. dir. Oakland Rehab., Pitts., 1993—; sports medicine fellowship program Tuckahoe Orthopaedic Assocs., Ltd., Richmond, Va., 1993—; clin. asst. prof. dept. orthopaedic surgery U. Pitts. Sch. Medicine, 1994—; serves on Nat. Football League injury and safety panel; presenter in field. Consulting reviewer Arthroscopy: The Journal of Arthroscopic and Related Surgery, 1991—, The Physician and Sports Medicine, 1992—; contbr. articles to profl. jours. Named one of Golf Digest Top 250 Golfer Doctors in Am., 2006. Fellow Am. Acad. Orthopaedic Surgeons; mem. AMA, Am. Orthopaedic Assn. Med. Honor Soc., Am. Orthopedic Soc. for Sports Medicine (edn. com.), Am. Shoulder and Elbow Surgeons, Arthroscopy Assn. N.Am., Ea. Orthpaedic Assn., Nat. Football League Physicians Soc. (past pres.), Pa. Med. Soc., Pa. Orthopaedic Soc., Pa. Athletic Trainers Soc., Allegheny County Med. Soc., 20th Century Orthop. Assn., Georgetown U. Alumni Assn., Herodicus Soc., Alpha Omega Alpha. Office: Burke & Bradley Orthop 200 Medical Arts Bldg 200 Delafield Rd Ste 4010 Pittsburgh PA 15215 Address: U Pitts Med Ctr Ctr for Sports Medicine 3200 S Water St Pittsburgh PA 15203 Office Phone: 412-784-5770.*

BRADLEY, JEAN IRENE, elementary school educator; d. Lawrence Carl and Mildred Eleanora Stuehringer; m. Danforth Tremain Bradley, Dec. 31, 1977. BS Edn., Cleve. State U., 1966, MS Edn., 1970; post grad., U. Pitts., 1970—72. Tchr. math Bonita Mid. Sch., Bonita Springs, Fla., 1989—96, Gulf Mid. Sch., Cape Coral, Fla., 1983—89, 1996—2005. Mem. budget com. Gulf Mid. Sch., Cape Coral, 1996—, mem. sch. leadership com., 1996—, facilitator focus group, 2005—06, leader 7th grade team, 2005—, coach math team, 1988—89, mem. safety com., 2005—; mem. sch. steering com. Bonita Mid. Sch., Bonita Springs, 1989—96, mem. budget & curriculum committees, 1989—96. Migrant tutor Lee County Schs., Ft. Myers, Fla., 1990—93, mentor drop out prevention program, 1997—2000. Nominee Golden Apple Tchr. Recognition award, Student Nominations, 1995—2006; named Mid. Sch. Math. Tchr. of Yr., Lee County Math. Coun., 1999. Mem.: Tchrs. Assn. Lee County (sch. rep. 1983—2006), Lee Sci. Edn. Assn., Fla. Coun. Tchrs. Math., Lee County Math Coun. Avocations: sudoku, crossword puzzles. Home: 1446 Medoc Lane Fort Myers FL 33919 Office: Gulf Middle Sch 1809 SW 36th Ter Cape Coral FL 33914 Home Phone: 239-481-4100. Personal E-mail: dtbdl@earthlink.net.

BRADLEY, JEB (JOSEPH E. BRADLEY), former congressman; b. Rumford, Maine, Oct. 20, 1952; m. Barbara Bradley; children: Jan, Ramona, Urs, Sebastian BA in Sociology, Tufts U., Mass., 1974. Painter, contractor; owner-operator Evergain Natural Foods, Wolfeboro, NH; mem. NH State Ho. Reps. from Dist. 8, 1991—2003, US Congress from 1st NH Dist., 2003—07, mem. armed svcs. com., small bus. com., veterans affairs com., budget com. Mem. Wolfeboro Planning Bd., 1986-90, Wolfeboro Budget Com., 1989; mem. Champlain Lakes Region Conservation Trust, 1989-90; v.p. Carpenter Sch. PTO, 1989-90; bd. dirs. Harbor Ho. children's shelter, Wolfeboro, Vis. Nurse Assn.-Hospice of So. Carroll County and Vicinity Named NH Leader for 21st Century, Bus. NH Mag.; recipient Gov. George D. Aiken award, N.E. Assn. Electric Cooperatives, Legislator of Yr., Ski NH, 2000. Republican. Protestant. Avocation: rock climbing.*

BRADLEY, JENNETTE B., former state official, lieutenant governor; b. Oct. 2, 1952; m. Michael C. Taylor. BA in Psychology, Wittenberg U. Lic. registered rep. Nat. Assn. Securitites Dealers. Exec. dir. Columbus Met. Housing Authority; sr. v.p. pub. fin. banker Kemper Securities; sr. v.p., pub. funds mgr. Huntington Nat. Bank; councilwoman Columbus (Ohio) City Coun., 1991—2002, chair parks and recreation com., chair utilities and energy generation coms., chair safety com., mem. safety and judiciary com., mem. adminstrn. com., mem. recreation and parks com., mem. health, housing and human svcs. com., mem. zoning com.; lt. gov. State of OH, 2003—05, treas., 2005—06; dir. OH Dept. Commerce, 2003—05. Mem. fin., adminstrn. and intergovernmental rels. steering and policy coms. Nat. League Cities. Grad. Leadership Columbus; trustee Wittenberg U.; bd. mem., former chair Joint Columbus and Franklin County Housing Adv. Bd. Recipient Woman of Achievement award, YWCA. Republican. Achievements include being the first African-American woman to be elected as Lt. Governor in Ohio and in the nation's history.*

BRADLEY, JERRY ALAN, psychologist, consultant; b. LA, Apr. 25, 1946; s. Norman Aaron and Kate Bradley; m. Barbara Ann Adams/Rohr, June 26, 1971; 1 child, John Nathan. BA summa cum laude, San Jose State U., 1976; postgrad., Claremont Grad. Sch., 1977—79; PhD, Am. Commonwealth U., 1993. Diplomate clinical and substance abuse psychology Am. Bd. Psychol. Specialties. Program dir. Sierra Vista, Highland, Calif.,

1978—85, Vista Pacifica, Riverside, 1982—85; dir. Montclair Child Care Ctr., Montclair, 1987—89, Regency Oaks, Riverside, 1987—89; cons., staff psychologist Ea. LA Regional Ctr., Alhambra, 1989—; clin., forensic psychologist Ctr. Integral Psychology, Ventura, 1996—. Psychologist, counselor Wellspring Project, Ch. Foothills, Ventura, 1996—2005. Fellow: Am. Coll. Forensic Examiners Internat., Internat. Coll. Advanced Practice Psychologists, Internat. Coll. Prescribing Psychologists, Prescribing Psychologists Register; mem.: AAAS, APA, Nat. Assn. for Mentally Ill, Am. Assn. Mental Retardation, LA County Psychol. Assn., Ventura County Psychol. Assn., Calif. Psychol. Assn. Avocation: music. Office: Ctr Integral Psychology 1746F S Victoria Ave #344 Ventura CA 93003 Home Phone: 805-639-4094; Office Phone: 805-639-4093. Office Fax: 805-639-4092. E-mail: ishecal@sbcglobal.net.

BRADLEY, JERRY WAYNE, language educator, department chairman; b. Jacksboro, Tex., Aug. 24, 1948; s. Carmon Jackson and Beatrice Zella Bradley; m. Kathryn Rose Coffield (div.). BA, Midwestern U., 1969; MA, PhD, Tex. Christian U., Ft. Worth, 1975. Asst. prof. Boston U., 1975—76; prof., dean Ind. U. SE, New Albany, 1993—94; assoc. prof., dept. head N.Mex. Inst. Mining and Tech., Socorbo, 1976—93; prof., dept. head West Tex. A&M U., Canyon, 1994—2001; prof., grad. dean, assoc. v.p. rsch. Lamar U., Beaumont, Tex., 2001—. Editor N.Mex. Humanities Rev., 1978—93; lit. panelist N.Mex. Arts Divsn., 1986—89; mem. lit. arts panel Tex. Commn. on Arts, 2004—; councilor Tex. Inst. Letters, 2002—06; poetry editor Concho River Rev., 1999—; bd. of directors Amarillo Bay, 1999—; editl. bd. New Tex., 1998—2004. Author: Simple Versions of Disaster, 1991, The Movement: British Poets of the 1950s, 1993, Popular Writers in America and England, 1997, Famous Writers of American Literature, 1997. Recipient Outstanding Alumnus, Coll. of Liberal Arts, Midwestern State U., 2002, Joe D. Thomas Scholar Tchr. Yr. award, Tex. Coll. English Assn., 2000, Boswell Poetry prize, Tex. Christian U., 1980, 1984, 1988, 1996; grantee, N.Mex. Arts Divsn., 1980, Coordinating Coun. of Lit. Magazines, 1979, Austin Writers League, 1996—98, 2000, Witter Bynner Poetry Found., 1990—94, N.Mex. Inst. Mining and Tech., 1991, Nat. Endowment for Arts, 1982—84, N.Mex. Arts Divsn., 1982, 1990; Astrophysics and Poetry grantee, N.Mex. Humanities Coun., 1982, Book Distbn. grantee, Nat. Endowment for Arts, 1979—82, Einstein celebration grantee, N.Mex. Humanities Coun., 1979, Program Support grantee, Meadows Found., 1995, U. Tchg. fellow, Tex. Christian U., 1970—75. Mem.: Tex. Assn. Creative Writing Tchrs. (pres. 1995—97, Poetry Award 1976), South Ctrl. MLA, Popular Culture Assn., Nat. Assn. Fgn. Students Advisors, Conf. Coll. Tchrs. English (Frances Hernandez Teacher-Scholar award 2005), Am. Acad. Poets, SW Tex. Popular Culture Assn. (pres. 1998—2000), Coll. English Assn., Tex. Inst. Letters (coun. 2002—05), Pi Kappa Delta, Phi Beta Delta, Sigma Tau Delta (hon.). D-Liberal. Avocations: golf, tennis, guitar. Home: 1085 Monterrey Drive Beaumont TX 77706 Office: Lamar U Box 10078 Beaumont TX 77710 Home Phone: 409-860-0447; Office Phone: 409-880-8229. Office Fax: 409-880-1723; Home Fax: 409-880-1723. Business E-Mail: jerry.bradley@lamar.edu.

BRADLEY, JOHN A., career military officer; b. Lebanon, Tenn. BS in Math., U. Tenn., Knoxville, 1967; postgrad., Indsl. Coll. Armed Forces, 1978, Harvard U., 1996, Syracuse U., 2000. Commd. 2d lt. USAF, 1967, advanced through grades to lt. gen., 2004; mathematician, program analyst Hdqrs. Strategic Air Command, Offutt Air Force Base, Nebr., 1967—69; pilot combat tng. Sheppard Air Force Base, Tex., 1969—70; fighter pilot 8th Spl. Ops. Squadron, Bien Hoa Air Base, Vietnam, 1970—71; instr. pilot 50th Flying Tng. Squadron, Columbus Air Force Base, Miss., 1971—73, 47th Tactical Fighter Squadron, Barksdale Air Force Base, La., 1973—78; chief standardization and evaluation 917th Tactical Fighter Group, Barksdale Air Force Base, La., 1978—81; asst. ops. officer, ops. officer 47th Tactical Fighter Squadron, Barksdale Air Force Base, La., 1981—83; dep. commdr. ops. 917th Tactical Fighter Group, Barksdale Air Force Base, La., 1983—85; comdr. 924th Tactical Group, Bergstrom Air Force Base, Tex., 1985—88; dep. chief of staff ops. 10th Air Force, Bergstrom Air Force Base, Tex., 1988—89; comdr. 442d Fighter Wing, Richard-Gebaur Air Force Base, Mo., 1989—93; dep. to chief of Air Force Res. Hdqrs. USAF, Washington, 1993—98; comdr. 10th Air Force, Naval Sta. Joint Res. Base, Ft. Worth, 1998—2002; dep. comdr. Joint Task Force-Computer Network Ops., U.S. Space Command, Arlington, Va., 2002; asst. to the Chmn. of the Joint Chiefs of Staff, reserve matters The Pentagon, 2002—04; chief Air Force Reserve, Washington, 2004—; comdr. Air Force Reserve Command, Robins AFB, Ga., 2004—. Decorated DSM, Def. Meritorious Svc. medal, Meritorious Svc. medal with oak leaf cluster, Legion of Merit, DFC, Air medal with 3 silver oak leaf clusters, Air Force Commendation medal, Air Force Achievement medal; recipient Def. Superior Svc. medal, Joint Meritorious Unit award with oak leaf cluster, Air Force Outstanding Unit award with "V" device & silver & bronze oak leaf cluster, Air Force Orgnl. Excellence award. Office: Hq USAF/RE 1150 Air Force Pentagon Washington DC 20330-1150

BRADLEY, JOHN ANDREW, health facility administrator; b. Hammond, Ind., Aug. 3, 1930; s. Andrew C. and Florence (Wolfe) B.; m. Judith E. Salmi, June 1, 1955; children: John Michael, Kerry Kathleen, Kelly Ann. BS, Loras Coll., 1952; MHA, St. Louis U., 1955, PhD, 1962. Asst. adminstr. Incarnate Word Hosp., St. Louis, 1958-61; from assoc. adminstr. to administr. Santa Rosa Med. Ctr., San Antonio, 1961-69; from v.p. to sr. v.p. Am. Medicorp, Inc., San Antonio, 1969-78; with Am. Healthcare Mgmt., Dallas, 1978-89, pres., 1978-84, chmn., CEO, 1985-89, Chancellor Health Systems Inc., Dallas, 1989—. Capt. AUS, 1953-57. Home: 4228 Winding Way Ct Dallas TX 75287-2767 Office Phone: 972-733-3231. Personal E-mail: jack3231@att.net.

BRADLEY, JOHN FRANCIS, financial services company executive; b. Pittsfield, Mass., Oct. 30, 1960; s. George Joseph and Marion S. Bradley; m. Kristine Lee Savary, Oct. 12, 1986; stepchildren: Nashunda Dowdell, Kisha Dowdell. BS in Indsl.-Labor Rels., Cornell U., 1982, MBA, 1983. Employee rels. asst. J.P. Morgan & Co. Inc., NYC, 1983-86, staff rels. officer, 1986-88, asst. v.p., 1988-89, v.p. human resources policy and consulting, 1989—. Staff mediator Bklyn. Mediation Ctr., 1983-86. Mem. alumni adv. bd. N.Y. State Sch. Indsl. and Labor Relations, Cornell U., Ithaca, N.Y., 1969—. Named Bus. Coord. of Yr. INROADS, 1988. Mem. Am. Soc. for Personnel Adminstrn., Nat. Assn. Banking Affirmative Action Dirs. (bd. dirs. 1985—). Democrat. Roman Catholic. Avocations: camping, swimming, outdoor activities. Office: JP Morgan & Co Inc 23 Wall St New York NY 10005-1962

BRADLEY, LAURENCE ALAN, psychologist; b. Cleve., Sept. 13, 1949; s. Irving and Jeanne (Weil) B.; m. Gifford Weary, Dec. 28, 1974 (div. 1979); m. Elizabeth Wrenn, Oct. 3, 1981 (div. 1991), Virginia Wadley, March 26, 2007. *Father, Irving Bradley, is an engineer, inventor, and management consultant with 26 product and process patents. Mother, Jeanne Weill Bradley, was an Executive Security and homemaker. Paternal grandfather, David Bradley built homes and apartment complexes in New Haven, Connecticut and Cleveland, Ohio and was elected to the Shaker Heights, Ohio 100 in recognition of his community contributions. Maternal grandfather, Leo Weill, was a prominent Attorney and prosecutor in Cleveland, Ohio who also served as commissioner of purchases and supplies for the City of Cleveland. I am married to Dr. Virginia Wadley, Assistant Professor of Medicine at University of Alabama at Birmingham and mother of Mallory Wadley Rushing, an Interior Designer, and Rachel Wadley, manager of a surgical practice in Birmingham, Ala.* BA cum laude in Psychology with honors, Vanderbilt U., Nashville, 1971, PhD in Psychology, 1975. Clin. intern Duke U. Med. Ctr., Durham, NC, 1975-76; asst. prof. U. Tenn., Chattanooga, 1976-77, Fordham U., Bronx, 1977-80, Bowman Gray Sch. Med., Winston-Salem, NC, 1980-82, assoc. prof., 1982-89, adminstrv. head sect. med. psychology, 1981-89; assoc. prof., dir. epidemiology, edn. & health svcs. rsch. Multipurpose Arthritis & Musculoskeletal Disease Ctr U. Ala., Birmingham, 1989-92, prof., dir. epidemiology, edn. & health svcs. rsch., 1992-99; prof., dir. neuro-behavioral medicine rsch. Multidisciplinary Clin. Rsch. Ctr., Birmingham, 1999—. Adj. assoc. prof. U. NC, Greensboro, 1983-89; vis. behavioral scientist Orebro Med. Ctr. Hosp., Sweden, 1986-92. Co-author: Health Psychology: Clinical Methods and Research, 1991; co-editor: Medical Psychology: Contributions to Behavioral Medicine, 1981, Coping with Chronic Disease: Research and Applications, 1983; assoc. editor: Clin. Psychology, Pain, 1995—2000, editl. bd.: Health Psychology, 1999—2001, Arthritis Care and Rsch., 1995—2004, Jour. Back and Musculoskeletal Rehab., 1999—. Rsch. grantee Robert Wood Johnson Found., 1983-86, Am.-Scandinavian Found., 1986, Am. Fibromyalgia Syndrome Assoc., 1996, Fetzer Inst., 2000-05, NIH, 1989— Fellow APA, Soc. Personality Assessment; mem. Internat. Assn. Study of Pain, Am. Pain Soc., Soc. Behavioral Medicine, Am Coll. Rheumatology, Arthritis Health Professions Assoc. (Disting. scholar, 1992), Sigma Xi, Phi Beta Kappa. Democrat. Achievements include research to determine that relaxation training and psychological therapy reduces pain behavior and number of painful joints among patients with rheumatoid arthritis, and that functional brain activity abnormalities are associated with chronic pain. Office: U Ala Divsn Clin Immunol and Rheumatol 178A Shelby Rsch Bldg 1825 Univ Blvd Birmingham AL 35294-0001 Office Phone: 205-934-8550. Personal E-mail: painsensation@aol.com. Business E-Mail: braddog@uab.edu.

BRADLEY, LAWRENCE D., JR., lawyer; b. Santa Monica, Calif., Feb. 19, 1920; s. Lawrence D. Bradley and Virginia L. Edwards; m. Joan Worthington, Feb. 1, 1945; children: Gary W., Brooks, Eric Scott. BS, USCG Acad., 1942; LLB, Stanford U. Law Sch., 1950. Bar: Calif. 1950, U.S. Dist. Ct. (ctrl. dist.) Calif. 1950, U.S. Dist. Ct. (so. dist.) Calif. 1967. Assoc. Pillsbury, Madison & Sutro, LA, 1950-59, ptnr., 1959—90; ret. ptnr. Pillsbury Winthrop Shaw Pittman LLP, 1990—. Lectr. admiralty and ins. law U. So. Calif., 1952-80. Pres. Stanford Law Rev., 1949-50; assoc. editor Am. Maritime Cases, 1990-2000. Mem. adv. bd. Tulane Admiralty Law Inst., 1990—. With USN, 1942-48; served to lt. comdr. Res. Mem. ABA, Calif. Bar Assn., Maritime Law Assn. U.S. (mem. exec. com. 1974-78, chmn. cruise line com. 1991-94), Inst. Navigation, Order of Coif, Calif. Club, Chancery Club, Calif. Yacht Club, San Diego Yacht Club, Propeller Club, Transpacific Yacht Club, Tutukaka South Pacific Yacht Club. Office: Pillsbury Winthrop Shaw Pittman LLP 725 S Figueroa St Ste 2800 Los Angeles CA 90017-5443 Home Phone: 310-472-4639; Office Phone: 213-488-7256.

BRADLEY, MARILYNNE GAIL, advertising executive, educator; b. Rockford, Ill., Apr. 12, 1938; d. Sherwin S. and Lillian (Leopold) Gersten; m. Charles S. Bradley, 1959 (div. Feb., 1994); children: Suzanne, Scott. BFA, Washington U., St. Louis, 1960; MAT, Webster U., St. Louis, 1975; MFA, Syracuse U., 1981; postgrad., St. Louis Tchrs. Acad., 1990. With Essayons Studio, St. Louis, 1968-69; tchr. Webster Groves (Mo.) H.S., 1970-98; instr. Webster Univ., Webster Groves, 1973-82, 97—, supr., 2002—; instr. U. Mo., 1980—, St. Louis U., 1978-99, Washington U., St. Louis, 1984-87. Sec. Mo. Art Edn., State of Mo., 1986-87; mem. Tchrs. Acad., 1990-92. Author, illustrator: Arpens and Acres, 1976, Packets on Parade, 1980, illustrator: St. Louis Silhouettes, 1977; editor: (videos) 12 Water Color Lessons, 1987, Techniques of American Watercolor, 1990, The Santa Fe Trail Series, 1993, Over Gauguin's Shoulder, 1994, Aboriginal Art Techniques, 1994, City of Century Homes, 1995, Australian Dreamings, 1996, Aboriginal Art - Past, Present and Future, 1996, Drawing and Painting Techniques, 1997, Line, Shape, Value, 1998, Molas, Snip and Sew: The Kuna Indians, Molas: Panamanian Traditions, 1999, The Katy Trail Series, 2000, Art Along the Katy Trail, 2000, Apre's Paris, 2001, Lewis and Clark Trail, 2001, It's Somewhere in St. Louis, 2002, St. Louis World's Fair, 2004, The Mathematics of Moorish Mosaics, 2004, Sidewalks of St. Louis, 2005, World Travels, 2006. Bd. govs. Webster Groves Hist. Soc., 1965-72, 94—; mem. St. Louis Philharm. Soc., 1956-72; commr. City of Webster Groves, 1995—; co-chair Hist. Preservation Com., 2002, v.p., 2002—06; active Arts Commn., 2005—. Named Tchr. of Yr., 1987, Best of Show, Mo. Watercolor Soc., 2000, Educator of Yr. award Mo. Art Edn. Assn., 2006, Humana Found. award, 2006. Mem.: Mo. Watercolor Soc. (bd. mem. 2001—), St. Louis Artist Guild (sec. 1985—86, pres. 1989—92, v.p. pres.'s coun. 1995—, treas. 2004, Disting. Woman 1987), St. Louis Woman Artists, So. Watercolor Soc. (life; sec. 1978—80, v.p. 2002—04, pres. 2004—, chair 26th ann. exhibit, chair 28th ann. exhibit, Silver Brush award, Exceptional Salute to the Masters award), Monday Club (chmn. 1979—83). Avocations: music, art, travel. Home and Office: Bradley & Assocs 817 S Gore Ave Saint Louis MO 63119-4023 Office Phone: 314-968-1439. Personal E-mail: mgbrad@aol.com.

BRADLEY, MELVIN LEROY, communications executive; b. Texarkana, Tex., Jan. 6, 1938; s. S.T. and David Ella (Garth) B.; m. Ruth Ann Terry, Mar. 3, 1958; children: Cheryl, Eric, Jacqueline, Tracy. Student, Los Angeles City Coll., 1955, Compton Coll., 1965; BS, Pepperdine U., 1973; LLD (hon.), Shaw U., 1982, Bishop Coll., 1984, Lane Coll., 1986. Real estate broker, Los Angeles, 1960-63; dep. sheriff Los Angeles County, 1963-70; asst. to Gov. Ronald Reagan, 1970-75; dir. public relations Drew Med. Sch., Los Angeles, 1975-77; asst. v.p. United Airlines, 1977-81; sr. policy advisor to Pres. U.S., White House, 1981-82, asst. to Pres. U.S., 1982-89; pres. Garth & Bradley Assocs., Washington, 1989—. Bd. dirs. Essex Bancorp, LoanCare Servicing Ctr., SMA MicroSys. Republican. Baptist. Office: 1405 Palm St Houston TX 77004 Office Phone: 301-237-7043. Personal E-mail: garthbrad@yahoo.com.

BRADLEY, MURRAY L(EE), librarian; b. Balt., July 20, 1941; s. Howard Lee and Isabel (Biggs) B. BS in Social Sci., Loyola Coll., Balt., 1963; MSLS with honors, Cath. U. Am., 1969; MBA with honors, Bryant Coll., 1983. Reference and circulation libr. U.S. Naval Acad., Annapolis, Md., 1964-68, asst. acquisitions libr., 1968-70, sci. and tech. libr., 1970-72, acquisitions libr., 1972-77; head readers svc. divsn. U.S. Naval War Coll. Libr., Newport, R.I., 1977-91; head rsch. reports sect. Naval Rsch. Lab., 1991-96, dep. chief libr., head info. svcs. br., 1996-99; chief of info. Patrick Henry br. Fairfax County Pub. Libr., Vienna, Va., 1999—2004; libr. Reston Regional Pub. Libr., Fairfax County Pub. Libr., Reston, Va., 2004—. Assoc. editor Criarl Newsletter, 1988-91. Mem. ALA, Spl. Librs. Assn. (R.I. chpt. treas. 1978-79, D.C. chpt. nominating com. 1994, co-chair mil. librs. group 1995-98, awards com. 1997), Am. Soc. Info. Sci. (sec. Chesapeake Bay chpt. 1973-74, program chmn. 1974-75, chmn. 1975-76, award of merit jury 1977-78, treas. Potomac Valley chpt. 1993-94), Beta Phi Mu. Office: Reston Regional Pub Libr 11925 Bowman Towne Dr Reston VA 20190 Home: 19375 Cypress Ridge Terr Unit 607 Leesburg VA 20176-5187 Personal E-mail: mbradley0720@comcast.net.

BRADLEY, NOLEN EUGENE, JR., retired personnel executive, educator; b. Memphis, Nov. 29, 1925; s. Nolen Eugene and Anice Pearl (Luther) B.; m. Eloise Mullins, Jan. 7, 1947; children: Sharon (Mrs. Edward W. Vanderpool), Diana (Mrs. Wiley M. Rutledge), Nolen Eugene III, David Lee. BS, Memphis State U., 1951, MA, 1952; EdD, U. Tenn., 1966. Instr. polit. sci. Memphis State U., 1951-52; tchr. English Messick High Sch., Memphis, 1952-56; asst. dean admissions Memphis State U., 1956-64; dir. State Agy. for Title I, Higher Edn. Act, 1965, Div. Continuing Edn., U. Tenn., 1966-70; dean instrn. Vol. State Community Coll., Gallatin, Tenn., 1970-78; tutor, ednl. cons., 1978-79; pers. asst. Hoeganaes Corp., Gallatin, 1979-80, pers. mgr., 1980-82; dir. pers. Music Village U.S.A., Hendersonville, Tenn., 1984—; ret., 1981. Contbr. articles to profl. jours. Deacon Bapt. ch., 1966—. With AUS, 1944-46, ETO. Mem. Am. Assn. Sch. Adminstrs., Tenn. Adult Edn. Assn., Tenn. Edn. Assn., Omicron Delta Kappa, Pi Delta Epsilon, Phi Delta Kappa, Phi Kappa Phi. Democrat. Lion. Avocations: writing, travel, movies, reading. Home: 907 Harris Dr Gallatin TN 37066-3462 E-mail: geneloise@bellsouth.net.

BRADLEY, PAULA E., former state legislator; b. New Haven, Oct. 11, 1924; d. Richard Travis and Harriett (Bogenhagen) Elliott; m. William L. Bradley, 1947; children: James R. Choukas-Bradley, Dwight C., Paul W. BA, Hiram Coll., 1945; postgrad., Middlebury Coll., 1946, Hartford Seminary, 1963-64. Ret. rsch. assoc. univ. devel. Yale U.; mem. N.H. Ho. of Reps., 1992—98, 2000—02. Treas. Coos County Dem. Com., 1992—2006, Randolph Dem. Party, 1992—2004; chair bd. adjustment Town of Randolph, 2000—01, mem. planning bd., 2003—06; mem. Gorham (N.H.) Congregational Ch.; bd. dirs. Coos County Family Health Svcs., Berlin, NH, 1993—2001, 2004—06, Weeks Meml. Hosp., Lancaster, NH, 1993—95, No. Forest Heritage Park, Berlin, NH, 2001—06, No. Country Coun., 2003—06. Mem.: Randolph Mountain Club (bd. dirs. 1986—91, treas. 1989—91, bd. dirs. 1992—97, pres. 1995—96). Democrat. Avocations: walking, gardening, choral singing. Home and Office: 33 Christian Ave #18 Concord NH 03301

BRADLEY, RICHARD (RICHARD BLOW), writer; b. 1964; BA, Yale Coll.; MA in Am. History, Harvard Univ. Reporter-researcher New Republic Mag., Washington; staff writer, columnist Regardie's Mag., Washington, editor-in-chief, 1992—95; co-founding editor, sr. editor George Mag., NYC, 1995—97, Washington affairs editor, 1997—99, exec. editor, 1999. Exec. editor Yale's New Jour. Mag.; author (as Richard Blow): (non-fiction) American Son: A Portrait of John F. Kennedy Jr., 2002 (#1 NY Times bestseller list, 2002); author: Harvard Rules: The Struggle for the Soul of the World's Most Important University, 2005; contbr. articles to numerous publs., online websites. Mailing: c/o Author Mail HarperCollins Pub 10 E 53rd St New York NY 10022

BRADLEY, RICHARD EDWIN, retired academic administrator; b. Omaha, Mar. 9, 1926; s. Louis J. and Betsy (Winterton) B.; m. Doris I. McGowan, June 8, 1946; children— Diane, Karen, David. Student, Creighton U., 1946-48; BSD., U. Nebr., 1950, D.D.S., 1952; MS, State U. Iowa, 1958. Instr. State U. Iowa, 1957-58; asst. prof. Creighton U., 1958-59; asst. prof., chmn. dept. periodontics U. Nebr., 1959-62, assoc. prof., 1962-65, prof., 1965-67; assoc. dean Coll. Dentistry, 1967-68, dean, 1968-80; pres., dean Baylor Coll. Dentistry, 1980-90, pres., dean emeritus, 1990—; clin. prof. Coll. Dentistry U. Nebr. Med. Coll., Lincoln, 1990—; cons. dental edn., 199-93. Mem. Commn. A, Coun. on Dental Edn., 1986-93; pres. Am. Assn. Dental Schs., 1977-78; mem. nat. adv. com. on health professions edn. Dept. Health and Human Resources, 1982-86; pres. Am. Fund for Dental Health, 1986-87; mem. bd. of vis. Temple Univ. Sch. of Dentistry, 2001—. Editor: The New Dentist, 1992-94; contbg. editor Orban's Textbook of Periodontics, 1963; contbr. Clark's Clin., 1980. Mem. bd. visitors Temple U. Sch. Dentistry, 2003-. With USNR, 1944—46. Established Dr. Richard and Doris Endowed Fund periodontics U. Nebr. Found., 2006. Fellow AAAS, Internat. Coll. Dentists; mem. ADA, Am. Acad. Peridontology Found. (bd. dirs., pres. 1994-96), Am. Coll. Dentists (regent 1992-96, v.p. 1997-98, pres. Found. 2001-02), Sigma Xi, Omicron Kappa Upsilon. Office: U Nebraska Coll Dentistry Lincoln NE 68583-0740

BRADLEY, SLATER, artist; b. San Francisco, Calif., 1975; BA, UCLA, 1998. One-man shows include, Taka Ishii Gallery, Tokyo, 2005, Matrix 216: Year of the Doppelganger, U. Calif. Berkeley Art Mus. & Pacific Film Archive, 2005, Blum & Poe, LA, 2004, Stoned & Dethroned, Team Gallery, NYC, 2004, Annandale-on-Hudson, NY, Ctr. Curatorial Studies Mus., Bard Coll., NY, 2003, Armory Photography Show, 2002, Here are the Young Men, Team Gallery, 2002, Universitatsstadt Kaiserslautern, Germany, 2002, Art + Pub., Geneva Switzerland, 2002, Arndt & Ptnr., Berlin, Germany, 2002, Video Cube, FIAS, Paris, 2001, Trompe Le Monde, Galerie Yvon Lambert, 2001, Home Town Hero, Refusalon, San Francisco, 2001, Spl. Projects Series, P.S.1, NY, 2000, Charlatan, Team Gallery, NYC, 2000, Fried Liver Attack, 1999, exhibited in group shows at Whitney Biennial, Whitney Mus. Am. Art, 2004, Premieres, Mus. Modern Art, NYC, 2004, Harlem Postcards, Studio Mus. Harlem, NYC, 2004, Statemate, Mus. Contemporary Art, Chgo., 2004, Playlist, Palais de Tokyo, 2004, When Darkness Falls, Gallery 400, U. Ill., Chgo., 2003, What am I doing Here?, ESSO Gallery, NYC, 2003, Someone to Watch Over Me, Smart Project Space, Amsterdam, Netherlands, 2003, The Passing, Galeria Helga de Alvear, Madrid, 2002, burst, Team Gallery, NYC, 2002, Art & Wellbeing-Aesthetics of Recreation, Kunsthaus Meran-Merano Arte, Italy, 2001, Dear Dead Person, Momenta, Bklyn., 2001, Friction Fiction, Echo Park Projects, LA, 2000, SoCal Car Culture, Irvine Fine Arts Ctr., Calif., 1999, Text & Numbers, Remba Gallery, LA.

BRADLEY, THOMAS A., insurance company executive; With St. Paul Cos., Inc., St. Paul, sr. v.p. fin., CFO, 2001—04, Zurich North America, 2004—. Office: Zurich No America 550 W Washington Blvd Chicago IL 60661 Office Fax: (651) 310-8294.

BRADLEY, (R.) TODD, communications and computer company executive; b. Balt., Nov. 29, 1958; BSBA, Towson State U., Balt. V.p. Fed. Express; v.p., mng. dir. EMEA ops. AC Nielsen; various exec. positions to pres. NCH Promotional Svcs. subsidiary Dun & Bradstreet Corp., 1993—97; pres., CEO Transport Internat. Pool subsidiary of GE Capital Svcs., 1997—98; sr. v.p. Europe, Mid. East and Africa region Gateway Inc., San Diego, 1998—2001, sr. v.p. US consumer bus., 1999—2001, exec. v.p. global ops., 1999—2001; exec. v.p., COO Solutions Grp. Palm Inc., 2001—02, pres., COO Solutions Grp., 2002, CEO, Solutions Grp., 2001—03; CEO palmOne, Inc., Milpitas, Calif., 2003—05, adv., 2005; exec. v.p. personal systems grp. Hewlett-Packard Co., Palo Alto, Calif., 2005—. Bd. visitors Towson U. Office: Hewlett-Packard Co 3000 Hanover St Palo Alto CA 94304 Office Phone: 408-503-7000.*

BRADLEY, WALTER D., lieutenant governor, real estate broker; b. Clovis, N.Mex., Oct. 30, 1946; s. Ralph W. and M. Jo (Black) B.; m. Debbie Shelly, Sept. 17, 1977; children: Tige, Lance, Nicole, Kristin. Student, Eastern N.Mex. U., 1964—67. Supr. Tex. Instruments, Dallas, 1967—73; mgr., salesman Nat. Chemsearch, Irving, Tex., 1973—76; real estate broker, owner Colonial Real Estate, Clovis, 1976; real estate broker Realtors Assn. N.Mex., Clovis, N.Mex., 1976—; state senator Curry County, State of N.Mex., 1990—92; lt. gov. State of N.Mex., Santa Fe, 1995—2003; dir. comml. divsn. N.Mex. State Land Office, 2004; dir. bus. and govt. affairs Dairy Farmers Am., 2005—. V.p., bd. dirs. Clovis Indsl. Commn., 1983—86, pres. econ. devel., 1987; bd. dirs. United Way, Clovis, 1984—86, Curry County Blood Adv. Bd., Clovis, 1980—85; chmn. Curry County Reps., Clovis, 1984—88, Cosmos Soccer, Clovis, 1984. Named Man of Yr., Progressive Farmer Mag., 1998; recipient Leadership award, Albuquerque NAACP, 1997, Disting. Svc. award, N.Mex. Farm and Livestock Bur., 1997, Leadership Beautification award, Keep N.Mex. Beautiful, 2000, Mark Weidler Disting. Pub. Servant award, N.Mex. Petroleum Marketers Assn., 2000, Outstanding N.Mex. Small Bus. Supporter, N.Mex. Small Bus. Devel. Ctr., 1997, Outstanding Leadership award, N.Mex. Cattle Growers' Assn., 1996. Mem.: N.Mex. Jaycees, Curry County Jaycees, Clovis C. of C., Clovis Bd. Realtors (pres. 1982, 1993), Realtors Assn. N.Mex. (v.p., bd. dirs. 1982—85, v.p. 1987—88), Lions. Republican. Baptist. Home: 917 B Norris St Clovis NM 88101 Office Phone: 505-763-4528. E-mail: wbradley@dfamilk.com.

BRADLEY, WANDA LOUISE, librarian; b. Havre de Grace, Md., June 6, 1953; d. William Smith and Josephine Viola (Miller) B. BA, U. Md., 1975; MSLS, Atlanta U., 1976; postgrad., Cath. U.; MPA (scholar), U.

Balt., 1986. Libr. Harford County Pub. Libr., Bel Air, Md., 1976, Harford County Bd. Edn., Bel Air, Md., 1977-81, Nat. Grad. U., Arlington, Va., 1982, Md. State Dept. Edn., Balt., 1982-83, U.S. Dept. Labor, Washington, 1984, Balt. Gas and Electric Co., 1984-85, Morgan State U., Balt., 1985, Coppin State Coll., Balt., 1985-86, Montgomery County Pub. Sch. System, Rockville, Md., 1985-86, Community Coll., Balt., 1987-88; grant adminstr. Howard County Pub. Libr., 1988; libr., media specialist Balt. City Pub. Sch. System, 1992—. Acad. advisor George Mason U., Fairfax, Va., 1981-82. Dept. Edn. fellow, 1983-84; U. Balt. Merit scholar, 1984, Atlanta U. scholar, 1976, U. Md. scholar, 1971; Howard County Pub. Libr. grantee, 1988. Mem. ALA, ASIS, Md. Libr. Assn., Spl. Librs. Assn., Med. Libr. Assn. Methodist. Office: Diggs Johnson Mid Sch 1300 Herkimer St Baltimore MD 21217 Office Phone: 410-396-8700.

BRADLEY, WILLIAM BRYAN, cable television regulator; b. Charleston, W.Va., Feb. 12, 1929; s. Floyd England and Florence Clara (O'Bryan) B.; m. Virginia Vanderhoof Logan, Oct. 27, 1951; children: Christopher, Thomas, Michael, John, Mary Clare (dec.), Mary Ellen, Ann. BA in Journalism cum laude, U. Notre Dame, 1950. Supr., indsl. engr. Martin Co., Denver, 1958-61, 62-65; cons. Reynolds, Ward & Carey, Denver, 1961-62; analyst Denver City Coun., 1965-69, staff dir., 1969-82; dir. Office of Telecommunications, Denver, 1982-94; sr. assoc. Media Mgmt. Svcs., Inc., 1994-99. Co-founder, dir., vice-chmn. Greater Metro Cable Consortium, 1992; initiated joint city-industry cable TV Tech. Stds., 1987, adopted by FCC, 1992. Participant Japanese-Am. conf. on Globalization and Cable TV, Suwa, Japan, 1991. Co-founder Nat. Assn. Telecomm. Officers and Advisors, Washington, 1980, bd. dirs., 1983-88, pres., 1985-87; chmn. telecomm. subcom. Colo. Mcpl. League, Denver, 1985-86; bd. dirs. Denver Cmty. TV, 1996-98; charter mem. The Cable Ctr., 1998. Line Officer USN, 1950-53. Roman Catholic. Avocations: chess, books.

BRADLEY GARDNER, JANICE, federal agency administrator; BA, Wake Forest U.; MA, American U. Econ. officer U.S. Embassy to Japan, 1990—92; br. chief Persian Gulf Office Leadership Analysis, 1993—95; dir. ctrl. intelligence rep. to nat. sec. coun. Exec. Office of Pres., 1995—96; spl. advisor internat. affairs Office of V.P., 1996; chief East Asia group Fgn. Broadcast Info. Svc., dep. dir.; sr. intelligence liaison US Dept. Treasury, dep. asst. sec. intelligence and analysis, asst. sec. intelligence and analysis, 2005—. Office: Dept of Treasury 1500 Pennsylvania Ave NW Washington DC 20220 Office Phone: 202-622-1841. Office Fax: 202-622-1829.

BRADSHAW, CONRAD ALLAN, retired lawyer; b. Campbell, Mo., Dec. 22, 1922; s. Clarence Andrew and Stella (Cashdollar) B.; m. Margaret Crassous Sanderson, Dec. 31, 1959; children: Dorothy A., Lucy E., Charlotte L. AB, U. Mich., 1943, JD, 1948. Bar: Mich. 1948. With Warner, Norcross & Judd, LLP, ret., 2005. Lt. USNR, 1943—46. Mem. ABA, State Bar Mich. (chmn. corp., fin. and bus. law sect. 1976), Grand Rapids Bar Assn. (pres. 1970) Office: 900 Fifth Third Ctr 111 Lyon St NW Grand Rapids MI 49503 Office Phone: 616-752-2344.

BRADSHAW, DENIS JAMES, engineer, graphic designer; b. Franklin, Va., Dec. 31, 1948; s. Lonnie August and Marion Bradshaw; children: Matthew James, Mary Suzanne, Kimberly Lynn. BS in Indsl. Engring. and Ops. Rsch., Va. Poly. Inst. and State U., 1971, M of Engring., 1973. Instr. Va. Poly. Inst. and State U., Blacksburg, 1971—72; various engr., br. head, and divsn. dir. positions Naval Aviation Depot, Norfolk, 1973—92, prodn. engring. dept. head, 1992—94; facilities, safety and environ. office head Atlantic Ordnance Command, Yorktown, 1994—97, explosives safety dept. head, 1997—2000; gen. engr. Navy Region, Mid-Atlantic, Regional Safety Office, Virginia Beach, 2000—. Founder, owner, graphic designer Accents Media, Virginia Beach, 2002—; tchg. asst. Va. Poly. Inst. and State U., 1971—73. Photographer, Fire Hydrant on Fire. Vol. Am. Cancer Soc., Am. Heart Assn., Neighborhood Watch, Va., Virginia Beach Soccer Club; mgmt. advisor Jr. Achievement, Norfolk; min. adminstrn. Christ Cmty. Ch., Chesapeake, 1999—2004; trustee, treas., Sunday sch. tchr. various churches; team mem. Jamaica Mission Trip, 1996; bd. chmn. Tidewater Emmaus, 1998—98; bd. mem. Naval Air Rework Facility NORVA Assn., Norfolk; mem. Nat. Assn. Superintendents U.S. Naval Shore Establishments, Norfolk; com. chmn. Inst. Indsl. Engineers, Virginia Beach. Recipient Cost Reduction Diamond award, Naval Aviation Depot, 1979—87, Spl. Act award Environ. Cleanup, 1986, tchg. assistantship, Va. Poly. Inst. and State U., 1971—73; scholarship, State of Va., 1968—71. Republican. Baptist. Achievements include Naval Air Systems Command Senior Executive Management Development Program Graduate (1989); Naval Air Systems Command nominee for Arthur S. Flemming Award, sponsored by downtown Jaycees of Washington, DC granted annually to 10 career federal employees or members of the Armed Forces (1988); Developed safety sofware program that was approved for Navy-wide use (2003). Avocations: christian service, graphic design, skiing, bicycling, photography. Home: 2238 Oak Street Virginia Beach VA 23451-1312

BRADSHAW, DOVE, artist; b. NYC, Sept. 24, 1949; d. David Nelson and Jean Kathryn (Cormack) B. BFA, Boston Mus. Sch. Fine Arts, 1973. Co-artistic advisor The Merce Cunningham Dance Co., NYC, 1984—. Artist in residence Pier Ctr., Orkney, Scotland, 1995, Niels Borch Jensen, Copenhagen, 1999, 2000, 05, Sirius Art Ctr., Cork, Ireland, 2000, Statens Vaerksteder for Kunst, Copenhagen, 2000, Pont-Aven, France, 2007. One-man shows include Alan Stone Gallery, NYC, 1979, Graham Gallery, NY, 1979, Ericson Gallery, 1982, NY Wave Hill, NY, 1983, Sandra Gering Gallery, N.Y., 1988, 89, 91, 93, 95, 98, PSI Mus., NYC, 1991, Mattress Factory Mus., Pitts., 1990, 99, Pier Ctr., Orkney, Scotland, 1995, Stalke Gallery, Copenhagen, 1995, 96, 98-99, 2001, 03-04, Barbara Krakow Gallery, 1997, Mus. Contemporary Art, LA, 1998, Larry Becker Contemporary Art, Phila. 2000, 05, Stark Gallery, NY, 2001, Baruch Coll., CUNY, 2003, Diferenca Gallery, Lisbon, 2003, Volume Gallery, NY, 2004, SolwayJones, LA, 2005, Spirit of Discovery, Trancoso, Portugal, 2006-07, Radio Rocka, Bolognano, Italy, 2006, Gallery 360 degree, Tokyo, 2006, 6th Gwangju Biennale, Republic of Korea, 2006, Pierre Menard Gallery, Cambridge, Mass., 2007, Björn Ressle Fine Art, NY, 2007, others; exhibited in group shows at Am. Ctr., Paris, Science Mus., Tokyo, 1982, Mus. Modern Art, NYC, 1989, Carnegie Internat., Pitts., 1991, Met. Mus. NY, 1992, Art Inst. Chgo., 1992, 96, Aldrich Mus., Ridgefield, Conn., 1993, 2004, Phila. Mus., 1993, 98, 2000, Swiss Inst., NYC, 1995, Baumgartner Gallery, Washington, 1998, Carnegie Mus. Art, 1997, Whitney Mus. Am. Art, NY, 1997, Millennium Film Theatre, 1998, Mus. Contemporary Art, LA, 1998, U. Calif., San Diego, U. Mass. Amherst, 1999, UBU Gallery, NYU, Univ. Art Mus., U. Va., Charlottsville, 2000, 05, Anastasi Bradshaw Cage Mus. Contemporary Art, Roskilde, Denmark, 2001, 04, Rooseum Contemporary Art Ctr., Malmo, Sweden, Nikolaj Contemporary Art Ctr. Copenhagen, 2002, Baruch Coll., NY, Volckers and Freunde Gallery, Berlin, Tanya Bonakdar, NY, 2003, Stalke Gallery, Copenhagen, 2004, Anastasi Bradshaw Cage Cunningham, Shering Fine Art, Berlin, 2005, Salt Mountain, 2006, Marine Maritime Mus., Staten Island, NY, Missing Peace, Rubin Mus., NY, 2007, others; represented in permanent collection at Met. Mus. Art, NYC, Mus. Modern Art, NYC, Bklyn. Mus. Art, Whitney Mus. Am. Art, Art Inst. Chgo., Phila. Mus. Art, Ark. Art Ctr., Little Rock, Fogg Art Mus., Cambridge, Mass., Harvard U., Getty Ctr., LA, Mus. Contemporary Art, LA, Nat. Gallery, Washington, Carnegie Mus Art, Pitts., Mattress Factory Mus., Pitts., Birmingham Mus. Art., Ala., Bowdoin Coll. Art Mus., Brunswick, Maine, Internat. Le Pompidou Ctr., Paris, Pier Ctr. Orkney, Scotland, Mus. Art, Bilboa, Spain, Kunst Mus., Dusseldorf, Germany, Modern Mus., Stockholm, Russian State Mus., St. Petersburg, Self Interest and Radio Rocks, 1999, Six Continents, 2003, Angles 12 Rotatiions, 2003, One of the Boys, 2004, And So And All, 2004, They Were and Went, 2004, (outdoor sculpture) Material/Immaterial, 2005, (photography) One of the Boys, And So And All, Angles 12 Rotations, 2003; prodr., dir., artist: (film) Indeterminacy, 1995; self prodr. Met. Mus. postcard, 1976, 92, Met. Mus. guerilla postcard, 1978, (outdoor sculpture) Indeterminancy, 1993, Passion, 1993, (paintings) Boundary, Full, 1991, Contingency, 1984—, others; artist, prodr. handmade books, including Plain Air (installation with live birds 1969, 88, 91. Recipient Pollock-Krasner award, 1985; grantee Nat. Endowment Arts, 1975, NSF, 2002, 2006. Mem.: Larry Becker Contemporary Art, Pierre Menard Gallery, Björn Ressle Fine Art, Stalke Gallery. Avocations: meditation, yoga, running, reading, gardening, landscape gardening. Home and Studio: 924 W End Ave New York NY 10025-3534 Office Phone: 212-666-4133. Personal E-mail: dbradshaw1@nyc.rr.com.

BRADSHAW, GLENN RAYMOND, art educator; b. Peoria, Ill., Mar. 3, 1922; s. Elza Raymond and Hilda Catherine (Johnson) B.; m. Inez Ellen Payne, June 5, 1947; children: Kristen, Todd, Lisa, Adam, Scott. BS, Ill. State U., 1947; MFA, U. Ill., 1950. Critic tchr. U. Ill., Urbana, 1947-50, prof. art, 1952-86, prof. emeritus; asst. prof. art Iowa State Tchrs. Coll., Cedar Falls, 1950-52. Master classes Springmaid Watercolor Workshop, Myrtle Beach, SC, 1986—. One-man shows include Ill. State Normal U., 1947, 50, 61, Cedar Falls Art Assn., 1951, Schermerhorn Gallery, Beloit, Wis., 1956, 57, 59, Millikin U., Decatur, Ill., 1955, Flint Art Ctr., Mich., 1957, Old Orchard Bank, Skokie, Ill., 1960, Gilman Gallery, Chgo., 1963, 65, Jane Haslem Gallery, Madison, Wis., 1966, 70, St. Louis Gallery, 1967, The Canal House, Indianapolis, 1969, Wustum Mus., Racine, Wis., 1969, Ill. State Mus., Springfield, 1972, Krannert Art Mus., Champaign, Ill., 1972, Tower Park Gallery, Peoria Hghts., Ill., 1973, 76, 78, 81, 85, Fanny Garver Gallery, Madison, Wis., 1976, 81, U. Wis., 1976, MacNider Mus., Mason City, Iowa, 1976, Prairie House, Springfield, Ill., 1980, Bicentennial Mus., Paris, Ill., 1980, Neville-Sargent Gallery, Evanston, Ill, 1980, 84, 87, 89, 91, U. San Diego, 1981, House of Art, Champaign, 1982, Humewood II Gallery, Toronto, Can., 1988, Ctr. for Vis. Arts, Wausau, Wis., 1997; group shows include Royal Watercolor Soc., London, Eng., 1962, Met. Mus. Art, N.Y.C., 1996-67, Clev. Inst. of Art, 1968, U. Colo., 1970, Am. Watercolor Soc. Invitational, Australia, 1975, Mexico City, 1989, Akron Art Inst., 1976, U. Ill. Faculty Exhibitions, Taiwan, 1981, Hong Kong, 1982, Tokyo, 1983, Albuquerque Mus. Art, 1985, June Kelly Gallery, N.Y.C., 1988, Galeri Hartl and Klier, Tubingen, Germany, 1988, L.A. County Century Gallery, 1993, Tex. Women's U., Denton, 1994, Nat. Taiwan Art Edn. Inst., 1994, Springfield Mus., 1997, Jenkins-Johnson Gallery, San Francisco, 2007, Cluerna Gallery, Urbana, Ill., 2007, Burroughs CharpinMus., Myrtle Beach, SC, 2007; represented in numerous permanent collections. With U.S. Army, 1942-45. Recipient John Young Hunter award Am. Watercolor Soc., N.Y.C., 1973, Ed Whitney Prize, 1974, Arches Paper Co. prize Long Beach Mus. Art, 1974, 1st prize Nat. Watercolor Soc., 1977, Dr. David Soletsky Memorial award Nat. Soc. of Painters in Caseinand Acrylic, N.Y.C., 1978, John J. Newman Medal and prize, 1996, William A. Paten prize Nat. Acad. Design, 1987, Schweitzer prize, 1993, Whitaker prize, 1996, 2001, Lifetime Achievement award Watercolor USA Honor Soc., 2000, others. Mem. Nat. Acad., Nat. Watercolor Soc., Am. Watercolor Soc. Studio: 6403 Pine Point Dr Mc Naughton WI 54543 Home Phone: 715-277-2401.

BRADSHAW, JEAN PAUL, II, lawyer; b. May 12, 1956; married; children: Andrew, Stephanie. BJ, JD, U. Mo., 1981. Bar: Mo. 1981, U.S. Dist. Ct. (we. dist.) Mo. 1982, U.S. Dist. Ct. (so. dist.) Ill. 1988, U.S. Ct. Appeals (8th cir.) 1986, U.S. Supreme Ct. 1987. Assoc. Neale, Newman, Bradshaw & Freeman, Springfield, Mo., 1981-87, ptnr., 1987-89; U.S. atty. we. dist. Mo. U.S. Dept. Justice, Kansas City, 1989-93; of counsel Lathrop & Gage, Kansas City, 1993-99, mem., 2000—, chair dept. health law, 2000—05. Named Spl. Asst. Atty. Gen. State of Mo., 1985-89; mem., chmn. elect U.S. Atty. Gen.'s adv. com., office mgmt. and budget subcom., sentencing guidelines subcom.; mem. com. infractions NCAA Divsn. II, 2005—. Chmn. Greene County Rep. cen. com., 1988-89; pres. Mo. Assn. Reps., 1986-87; bd. dirs. Greene County TARGET, 1984-89; mem. com. on resolutions, family and community issues and del. 1988 Rep. Nat. Conv.; mem. platform com. Mo. Reps., 1988; chmn. Greene County campaign McNary for Gov., 1984, co-chmn. congl. dist. Dole for Pres., 1988, regional chmn. Danforth for Senate, 1988, co-chmn. 7th congl. dist. Webster for Atty. Gen., 1988; county chmn. U. Mo.-Columbia Alumni Assn., 1985-87; bd. dirs. Springfield Profl. Baseball Assn., Inc.; past mem. Mo. Adv. Coun. for Comprehensive Psychiat. Svcs., former bd. dirs. Ozarks Coun. Boy Scouts Am.; pres. bd. trustees St. Paul's Episcopal Day Sch., 1997-2002. Named Outstanding Recent Grad. U. Mo.-Columbia Sch. Law, 1991. Mem. ABA, NCAA (divsn. II com. Infractions, 2005—), Mo. Bar Assn., Kansas City Met. Bar Assn., U. Mo.-Columbia Law Sch. Alumni Assn. (v.p. 1988-89, pres. 1990-91), Law Soc. U. Mo.-Columbia Law Sch. Office: 2345 Grand Blvd Ste 2800 Kansas City MO 64108-2612 Office Phone: 816-460-5507. Business E-Mail: jpbradshaw@lathropgage.com.

BRADSHAW, JERALD SHERWIN, chemistry educator, researcher; b. Cedar City, Utah, Nov. 28, 1932; s. Sherwin H. and Maree (Wood) Bradshaw; m. Marilyn Barrus Bradshaw, July 2, 2005; children: Donna M. Webster, Melinda C. Waterman. BS, U. Utah, 1955; PhD, UCLA, 1963. Postdoctoral Calif. Inst. Tech., Pasadena, 1962—63; chemist Chevron Rsch., Richmond, Calif., 1963—66; from asst. prof. to assoc. prof. chemistry Brigham Young U., Provo, Utah, 1966—74, prof., 1974-93, asst. chmn. chemistry dept., 1980-86, Reed M. Izatt prof., 1993-2000, emeritus prof., 2000—. Vis. prof. Nat. Acad. Sci., U. Ljubljana, Yugoslavia, 1972-73, 82, U. Sheffield, England, 1978, James Cook U., Townsville, Australia, 1988. Author 2 books; contbr. more than 400 articles to profl. jours.; patentee in field. Served with USNR, 1955-59. Recipient Utah Gov.'s medal in sci. and tech., 1991. Mem. Am. Chem. Soc. (Utah award 1989, nat. award for separations sci. and tech. 1996), Internat. Soc. Heterocyclic Chemistry (bd. advisors 1980-82), Utah Acad. Sci., Sigma Xi (ann. lectr. 1988). Republican. Mem. Lds Ch. Avocations: stamp collecting/philately, church activities. Office: Brigham Young U Dept Chemistry-Biochemistry Provo UT 84602 Business E-Mail: jerald_bradshaw@byu.edu.

BRADSHAW, JOHN ROBERT COVINGTON, III, Internet company executive; b. Carthage, NY, Aug. 4, 1942; s. John Covington and Selma Pauline Bradshaw; children: Sean C., Heather Hodgson. BS, U. Mo., 1968, MBS, 1970. Pres., CEO UniGlobe Fin. Inc., Clearwater, 1998—, UniGlobe Leasing., UniGlobe Multimedia; pres., owner ATM Nat. Svcs., Clearwater, Fla., 1989—. Mem. Clearwater C. of C. (chmn. resource com.), Rotary, SCORE. Avocations: boating, travel, model trains.

BRADSHAW, MURRAY CHARLES, musicologist, educator; b. Hinsdale, Ill., Sept. 25, 1930; s. Murray Andrew and Marie (Novak) Orth; m. Doris Hogg (div.); children: Jean Marie, Murray Edward, Thomas Andrew; m. Sharon Ann Slitton, Apr. 19, 1997. MusM in Piano, Am. Conservatory Music, Chgo., 1955, MusM in Organ, 1958; PhD in Musicology, U. Chgo., 1969. Prof. UCLA, 1966—2004. Music critic Gary Post Tribune, Ind., 1962—64; chair dept. musicology UCLA, 1993—95. Author: The Origin of the Toccata, 1972, The Falsobordone, 1978, Francesco Severi, 1981, Girolamo Diruta The Transylvanian, 1984, Giovanni Luca Conforti, 1985, Gabriele Fattorini, 1986, Emilio d' Cavalieri, 1990, Conforti, "Breve et facile", 1999, Emilio de' Cavalieri, Rappresentatione di Anima, et di Corpo (1600), 2007; gen. editor: Musicological Studies and Documents and Miscellanea, 2000—; contbr. articles to profl. jours. Organist, choirmaster various chs., Ill., Ind., Calif., 1948—. With US Army, 1954—56. Grantee, Am. Philos. Soc., 1987; Travel grantee, NEH, 1994. Mem.: Am. Guild Organists, Am. Musicol. Soc. (pres. local chpt. 1979—81), Ctr. Medieval and Renaissance Studies. Avocations: walking, dance, bridge, languages. Home: 17046 Burbank Blvd Apt 3 Encino CA 91316-1830 Office: UCLA Dept Musicology 405 Hilgard Ave Los Angeles CA 90095-9000 Personal E-mail: mbrads3486@aol.com.

BRADSHAW, RICHARD EUGENE, science and technology government relations consultant; b. Rocky Mount, NC, Jan. 15, 1950; s. Harvey Edmond and Grace Darling (Cowley) B.; m. Pamela Anne Lacey, June 3, 1989. BA in Polit. Sci., U. N.C., 1974; MA in Internat. Rels., East Carolina U., 1977; postgrad., U. S.C., 1977-78. Fgn. svc. officer U.S. Dept. of State, Washington, Paris, 1978-82; dir. rsch. North Am. Telecomm. Assn., Washington, 1982-83; R&D policy cons. Washington Nichibei Cons., Washington, 1983-87; asst. prof. George Mason U., Fairfax, Va., 1987—93; sr. S & T policy analyst NSF, Washington, 1988—92; v.p. North Atlantic Rsch., Inc., Washington, 1993—94; asst. to sec. IMF, Washington, 1995—96; spl. asst. to Sec. Energy U.S. Dept. Energy, Washington, 1997—2001; v.p. Columbus Newport LLC, Arlington, Va., 2001; ptnr. Dykema Gossett PLLC, Washington, 2001—04; prin. Stirling Strategic Svcs. LLC, Washington, 2004—. Vis. fellow George Mason U., Arlington, Va., 1996-98. Policy coord. for sci. and tech. issues Bill Clinton for Pres. Campaign, 1992; campaign staff, Clinton/Gore '96; fin. com. staff, 1997 Presdl. Inaugural. Office: Stirling Strategic Svcs LLC 1120 G St NW Ste 830 Washington DC 20005 Office Phone: 202-783-0048. Business E-Mail: rbradshaws3@earthlink.net.

BRADSHAW, RICHARD ROTHERWOOD, engineering executive; b. Phila., Sept. 12, 1916; s. Joseph Rotherwood and Rosanna (Jones) B.; m. Audrey Grace Skinn, Oct. 3, 1940 (dec. Jan. 1981); children— Linda M., Barbara A., Vicki; m. Chanin Hale, Feb. 14, 1986. BS, Calif. Inst. Tech., 1939; MS, U. So. Calif., 1950. Pres. Richard R. Bradshaw, Inc., Van Nuys, Calif., 1946—, pres. br. office Honolulu. Contbr. articles to tech. jours., Important works include, Disneyworld Hotels, Orlando, Fla., U.S. embassy, Warsaw, Poland, U.S. Exhbn. Bldg., Moscow USSR, Taraara Hotel, Tahiti, Gulf Life Bldg., Jacksonville, Fla., Los Angeles City Airport. Recipient Alfred Lindau award Am. Concrete Inst., 1968, many others for structural design. Mem. ASCE, Internat. Assn. Bridges and Structural Engring., Am. Seismol. Soc., Cons. Engrs. Assn., Internat. Assn. Thin Shells, Am. Concrete Inst., Am. Arbitration Assn. Office: Richard R Bradshaw Inc 17300 Ballinger St Northridge CA 91325-2005 Office Phone: 818-772-1810.

BRADSHAW, ROD ERIC, personnel consultant; b. Washington, May 29, 1957; s. Howard Vernon and Ona A. (Joyce) Bradshaw; m. Rebecca Lynn Bell, Mar. 20, 1974 (div. Jan. 1981); m. Pierrette A. Newman, Dec. 2, 2000. BS, U. Md., 1973; M in Human Resource Mgmt. with honors, Pepperdine U., 1981. Pers. cons. Career Devel. Corp., Atlanta, 1977-79, regional office mgr., 1979-82, prin., mgr., 1982-93; pres. Bradshaw & Assocs., 1993—. Envoy to attending countries Atlanta Olympic Games, 1996; asst. to pres. Christopher's Corner Cmty. Assn., Marietta, Ga., 1978—79, chmn. planning com., 1979; rep. Gov.'s Environ. Symposium Smithsonian Inst., 1971; fund raiser, charter mem. High Mus. Art, Atlanta, 1979—; sponsor, adv. bd. rep. Sch. Bd. Coop. Bus. Edn. Adv. Bd.; merit badge counselor Boy Scouts Am.; nominating com. bd. mem. Buckhead Bus. Assn., Young Bucks, Outstanding Ams.; dir. cmty. affairs Atlanta Games Legacy Orgn., 1998—2000; pres. bd. dirs. Jefferson Twp., 1998—; mem. Pub. Schs. Work Bd. Learning Adv. Bd.; v.p. Windsor Gate Governance. Named One of Outstanding Young Men of Am., Atlanta C. of C., 1985; recipient J.P. Rice Scholarship, 1971. Mem.: Am. Mgmt. Assn., Nat. Assn. Pers. Cons. (v.p. Windsor gate governance), Am. Legion, Internat. Platform Assn., Atlanta Ski Club, Delta Tau Delta, Omicron Delta Kappa. Republican. Avocation: Avocations: yachting, home improvement projects, sports, politics. Home: 5717 Windsor Gate Ln Fairfax VA 22030- Office: Bradshaw & Assocs 400 Galeria Pkwy Ste 1500 Atlanta GA 30339-

BRADSHAW, SHELDON, lawyer; BA, Brigham Young U., 1991; JD, George Washington U., 1996. Law clk. to Hon. Karen J. Williams US Dist. Ct. (4th Cir.); prin. dep. asst. atty. gen. Civil Rights Divsn. US Dept. Justice, Washington; asst. gen. counsel Food & Drug Adminstrn., Washington, chief counsel. Office: Food and Drug Administration 605 Parklawn Bldg 5600 Fishers Ln Rockville MD 20857 Office Phone: 301-827-1137. E-mail: sheldon.bradshaw@fda.hhs.gov.

BRADSHAW, TERRY (TERRY PAXTON BRADSHAW), sports announcer, former professional football player; b. Shreveport, La., Sept. 2, 1948; m. Melissa Babich, 1972 (div. 1973); m. Jo Jo Starbuck, 1976 (div. 1983); m. Charlotte Hopkins, 1983 (div. 1999); children: Rachael, Erin. Grad., La. Tech. U. Quarteback Pitts. Steelers, 1970-84; sports analyst CBS Sports Inc NFL Today, 1987-94, Fox Sports, 1995—. Author, country and western singer, entertainer, appears in numerous commls., pub. speaker; author: It's Only a Game, 2001 (NY Times Best Selling Book), Keep It Simple, 2002 (NY Times Best Seller); actor: (films) Hooper, 1978, Smokey and the Bandit II, 1980, Cannonball Run, 1981, (voice) Robots, 2005, Failure to Launch, 2006, (TV series) Home Team with Terry Bradshaw, 1997; special guest appearances include Hardcastle and McCormick, 1985, The Sinbad Show, 1994, Blossom, 1994, Married with Children, 1995, 1996, Everybody Loves Raymond, 1997, (voice) King of Hill, 2000, Malcolm in the Middle, 2002, 8 Simple Rules.for Dating My Teenage Daughter, 2002, The Simpsons, 2005, Mad TV, 2005, several talk shows and others. Named Most Valuable Player, Super Bowl XIII, 1978, Super Bowl XIV, 1979, Most Favorite TV Sportscaster TV Guide, 1999; named to Pro Bowl, 1978, 79; inducted into Pro Football Hall of Fame, 1989; recipient Emmy award for sports studio analyst, 2000, 02; named Father of Yr. L.A., 2000; recipient Star on Hollywood Walk of Fame, 2001. Achievements include being the quarterback in Super Bowl wins of 1974, 75, 78, 79. Office: care Fox Network PO Box 900 Beverly Hills CA 90213-0900 Address: 1925 N Pearson Ln Roanoke TX 76262-9018

BRADSHER, KEITH VINSON, journalist; m. Danielle Downing, 2005. BA in Econs. with highest honors, U. N.C., 1986; MPA in Econs., Princeton U., 1989. Bus. reporter The N.Y. Times, NYC, 1989-91, Washington corr., 1991-95, Detroit bur. chief, 1996—2001, Hong Kong bureau chief, 2002—. Morehead scholar, 1986; recipient George Polk award for nat. reporting, 1998. Mem. Fgn. Correspondents Club (1st v.p. 2006—), Phi Beta Kappa. Office Phone: 212-556-7415.

BRADT, HALE VAN DORN, physicist, x-ray astronomer, educator; b. Colfax, Wash., Dec. 7, 1930; s. Wilber Elmore and Norma (Sparlin) B.; m. Dorothy Ann Haughey, July 19, 1958; children— Elizabeth, Dorothy Ann. AB in Music, Princeton U., 1952; PhD in Physics, MIT, 1961. Mem. dept. physics MIT, 1961—, prof., 1972-2001, prof. emeritus, 2001—; sci. investigator Small Astronomy Satellite, NASA, 1975-79; co-prin. investigator High Energy Astronomy Obs., 1977-79; prin. investigator Rossi x-ray timing explorer ASM, 1995—2001. Co-editor: X and Gamma Ray Astronomy, 1973, The Active X-ray Sky, 1998; mem. editl. bd. Astrophys. Jour. Letters, 1974-77; author: Astronomy Methods, 2004. With USNR, 1952—54. Recipient Exceptional Sci. Achievement medal NASA, 1978, Buechner Tchg. prize MIT, 1990, Outstanding Advisor award MIT, 2004. Mem. Am. Astron. Soc. (sec.-treas. high energy astrophysics divsn. 1973-75, chmn. 1981, Rossi prize HEAD divsn. 1999), Am. Phys. Soc., Internat. Astron. Union, Sigma Xi. Office: MIT 37-587 Cambridge MA 02139

BRADTKE, ROBERT A., ambassador; b. Chgo., 1947; married. Attended, U. Notre Dame, U. Va. With Fgn. Svc., 1973—; am. polit. sci. assn. congl. fellow Office East European Affairs, 1978—83; with Bur. Legis,

Affairs US Dept. State, 1990—94, dep. asst. sec. for legis. affairs, 1992—93, exec. asst. for legis affairs., 1994—96; dep. chief of mission Am. Embassy, London, 1996—99; exec. sec. NSC, 1999—2001; dep. asst. sec. for European & Eurasian Affairs US Dept. State, 2001—04, prin. dep. asst., 2004—06, US amb. to Croatia Zagreb, 2006—. Recipient Presdl. Meritorious Svc. Award, 2001. Office: US Embassy 5080 Zagreb Pl Washington DC 20521*

BRADWAY, JOHN KENT, orthopedist; b. July 13, 1957; BA (cum laude) in Biology, Whitman Coll., Walla Walla, 1979; MD, U. Ariz. Coll. Medicine, Tucson, 1983. Lic. Ariz., cert. Am. bd. Orthop. Surgery. Resident, orthop. surgery Mayo Grad. Sch. Medicine, Rochester, Minn., 1983—88; private practice Scottsdale, Ariz. Hosp. affiliations Piper Ctr. Out Patient Surgery, Scottsdale Healthcare-North (Shea), mem. joint adv. com.; bd. and exec. com. mem. Ariz. Sci. Ctr., 1996—2002; orthop. surgeon cons. Ariz. Diamondbacks, 2002—04; Order of Merit contbr. to Orthop. Rsch. and Edn. Found.; pres. Orthop. Surgeons Network Ariz., P.C., 1994—; examiner Am. Bd. Orthop. Surgery. Named to numerous Top Doctor recognitions, local and nat. Fellow: Am. Acad. Orthop. Surgeons; mem.: Ariz. Orthop. Soc., Maricopa County Med. Soc., Western Orthop. Assn., Am. Assn. of Hip and Knee Surgeons, State Orthop. Soc., State Med. Soc. Avocations: golf, alpine skiing, fly fishing. Office: 10213 N 92nd St Ste 101 Scottsdale AZ 85258 Office Phone: 480-860-6005. Office Fax: 480-860-1882.*

BRADWAY, ROBERT, medical products executive; BA in Biology, Amherst Coll., Mass.; MBA, Harvard U. Positions through mng. dir. healthcare practice Europe Morgan Stanley, NYC & London, 1988—2006; v.p. ops. strategy Amgen, Inc., Thousand Oaks, Calif., 2006—07, exec. v.p., CFO, 2007—. Office: Amgen Inc 1 Amgen Ctr Dr Thousand Oaks CA 91320-1799 Office Phone: 805-447-1000. Office Fax: 805-447-1010.*

BRADY, ADELAIDE BURKS, public relations agency executive, giftware catalog executive; b. NYC, June 27, 1926; d. Earl Victor and Audrey Calvert Burks; m. James Francis Brady, Jr., June 22, 1946 (div. 1953); 1 child, James Francis. BS, Boston U., 1994. Exec. v.p. Media Enterprises, 1952—55; dir. group rels. Save the Children Fedn., NYC, 1955-59; dir. pub. affairs divsn. Girl Scouts U.S.A., NYC, 1959-69; pres. Comm. Internat., Inc., Washington, 1969-73, Burks Brady Comm., Washington, 1972—, Adelaide's Angel Shopper Catalog Inc., Wilton, Conn., 1976—. Exec. v.p. Arts in Parks Inc., Washington, 1971—. Past bd. dirs. Lenox Hill Hosp., N.Y.C., Achievement Rewards for Coll. Scientists Found.; pres. Animal Lovers Inc. Decorated comdr. Order of St. John of Jerusalem (Eng.); recipient Silver Reel award for film The Children of Now, Save the Children Fedn. Mem. NAFE, NEA, AAUW, Nat. Assn. Women Bus. Owners, Pub. Rels. Soc. Am., Am. Women in Radio and TV, Nat. Ednl. Broadcasters Assn., Am. Soc. Profl. and Exec. Women, Women Execs. in Pub. Rels., N.Y. Press Women, Nat. Fedn. Press Women (state pres.),Women's Econ. Roundtable, DAR, Capitol Hill Club (Washington), Yacht and Country Club (Fla.), MDW Officers Club (Washington). Republican. Episcopalian. also: Yacht Country Club 3664 SE Fairway E Stuart FL 34997-6116 Office: 785 Park Ave New York NY 10021-3552

BRADY, BRUCE MORGAN, lawyer; b. Oakland, Calif., Oct. 9, 1950; s. Alfred Foster and Anne Felton (Hazlewood) B.; m. Barbara Jean Gehrett, June 8, 1974; children: Morgan G., Evan L.G. BA in Anthropology, Columbia Coll., 1972; JD, Boston U., 1975. Asst. dist. atty. King's County Dist. Atty., Bklyn., 1975-81, dep. chief criminal ct., 1980-81; assoc. Gabrini & Scher, P.C., NYC, 1981-84, ptnr., 1984-90; sr. ptnr. Callan, Koster, Brady, & Brennan, LLP, NYC, 1990—. Lectr. NY State Trial Lawyers Inst. Legal adv., vice-chmn. Children's Aid an Family Svcs., Paramus, N.J., 1990-2005; pres. Ridgewood (N.J.) Lacrosse Assn., 1993-99. Mem.: ATLA, ABA (litig. sect., tort, trial, ins. sect.), NJ State Bar Assn., NY County Lawyers Assn., NYC Med. Def. Bar Assn. (charter mem.), NY State Trial Lawyers Assn. Avocations: golf, snow sports, theater, personal computing. Office: Callan Koster Brady & Brennan LLP 1 Whitehall St New York NY 10004-2109 E-mail: bbrady@ckbblaw.com.

BRADY, CHRISTINE ELLEN, education coordinator; b. Manchester, NH, Feb. 23, 1943; d. George Lewis and Lucy Eleanor (Broderick) B. BA in English, Manhattanville Coll., 1964; MA in English, U. Pa., 1966; EdD in Curriculum and Instrn., No. Ariz. U., 1987. Cert. tchr., NY, Ariz., Mass.; cert. adminstr., NY, Ariz. English instr. Bryn Mawr (Pa.) Coll., 1966-67; lang. arts tchr. Tuba City (Ariz.) H.S., 1978-82; asst. dir. Reading/Learning Ctr., Flagstaff, Ariz., 1982-83; supervisory home living specialist Apache Agy. Dept. Indian Affairs, Whiteriver, Ariz., 1983-85; English and edn. lectr. Cortland (NY) State Coll., 1988-89; asst. dir. Tchr. Ctr. Broome County, Binghamton, NY, 1990-91; English instr. Broome C.C., Binghamton, 1989-91; labor svc. rep. NY State Dept. Labor, Ithaca, 1992-94; Title I lang. arts tchr. Highland Residential Ctr. NY State Office Children and Family Svcs., Highland, 1994-98, edn. coord. S.I. Residential Ctr., 1998—2003; edn. supr. Arthur Kill Correctional Facility NY State Dept. Corrections, SI, 2003—. Adj. faculty Met. Coll., NYC, 2004—. Mem.: Corrections and Youth Svcs. Assn., Phi Delta Kappa (exec. bd. 1998). Office: Arthur Kill Correctional Facility NY State Dept Correctional Svcs Staten Island NY 10309 Home Phone: 718-987-6469; Office Phone: 718-356-7333 ext. 4330. E-mail: bradyceb@aol.com.

BRADY, DONNA ELIZABETH, sales, marketing and performing company executive; d. Frank A. and Dorothy Eleanor (Munden) B. BA, Knox Coll., 1976. Stage mgr., lighting designer Dance Edn. Svcs., Inc., Northport, NY, 1973—86; coord. Am. Dance Festival Tech. Assistance Project, NYC, 1981—85; exec. dir. Performing Arts Resources, Inc., NYC, 1986—, also pres., bd. dirs.; fiscal/mktg. specialist Monterey Bay Aviation, 2002—05, dir. sales and mktg., 2005—07; dir. ops. OfficeStar Computer Tng. Ctr., 2007—. Project staff Tech. Assistance Group/TAG Found., Ltd., NYC, 1980-81; treas. NY Tech. Assistance Providers Network, 1995, 96, co-chair 1997; lighting designer, stage mgr. Solomons Co. Dance, 1978-81; asst. stage mgr. Pilobolus, 1978. Bd. dir. Artists Cmty. Fed. Credit Union, 1992-2001, sec., 1993-2000; bd. dir., treas. Acanthus Dance, 1997—. Mem. Am. Dance Guild (bd. dirs. 1980-87, treas. 1983-87). Office Phone: 831-324-0794. Personal E-mail: dbradypar@aol.com.

BRADY, EDMUND MATTHEW, JR., lawyer; b. Apr. 24, 1941; s. Edmund Matthew and Thelma (McDonald) B.; m. Marie Pierre Wayne, May 14, 1966; children: Edmund Matthew III, Meghan, Timothy. BSS, John Carroll U., 1963; JD, U. Detroit, 1966; postgrad., Wayne State U., 1966—69; DHL (hon.), U. Detroit, 1998. Bar: Mich. 1966, US Dist. Ct. (ea. dist.) Mich. 1966, US Ct. Appeals (6th cir.) 1973, US Supreme Ct. 1974. Sr. ptnr. Vandeveer & Garzia, 1973—90, Plunkett & Cooney, P.C., 1990—2003; ptnr. Garan Lucow Miller P.C., Detroit, 2003—04. Village clk. Grosse Pointe Shores, Mich., 1975-80; trustee St. John Hosp. and Med. Ctr., Detroit, 1992-2000, chmn., 1994-2000, Grosse Pointe Acad., Mich., 1977-83, adv. trustee, 1983-89; vice chmn. St. John Physicians Hosp. Orgn., 1994-95; supr. Grosse Pointe Twp., 1994-2000, trustee, 1989-2000; pres., dir. Grosse Pointe Hockey Assn., 1969-70; bd. dirs., chmn. maj. gifts divsn. 1st Fund, St. John Hosp. Guild; bd. dirs., pres. Friends of Bon Secours Hosp.; trustee, mem. exec. com., mem. fin. com. St. John Health Sys., 1998-2000. Recipient award of distinction U. Detroit Law Alumni, 1981, Michael Franck award State Bar of Mich. Rep. Assembly, 1998, Respected Advocate award Mich. Trial Lawyers Assn., 1998; named U. Detroit Mercy Law Sch. Alumnus of Yr., 2003. Fellow Am. Bar Found. (life), Mich. State Bar Found. (life); mem. ABA, Am. Coll. Trial Lawyers, Inter. Soc. Barristers, Am. Bd. Trial Advocates, Assn. Def. Trial Counsel (dir. 1975-80, pres. 1980-81), Mich. Def. Trial Counsel (dir. 1980-81), Def. Rsch. Inst. (Exceptional Performance citation 1981), Cath. Lawyers Soc., Soc. Irish-Am. Lawyers (founding dir. 1979-81), Detroit Bar Assn. (dir. 1986-91, sec.-treas. 1988, pres.-elect 1989-90, pres. 1990-91), State Bar Mich. (commr. 1991-98, treas. 1994, v.p. 1995, pres.-elect 1996, pres. 1997-98), Mich. Super Lawyers, Country Club of Detroit, Detroit Athletic Club, Delta Theta Phi. Republican. Roman Catholic. Personal E-mail: edmundbrady@comcast.net.

BRADY, EDWARD THOMAS, state supreme court justice; b. Bklyn., Nov. 1, 1943; s. Thomas and Virginia (Briggs) Brady; m. Dianne Downing; children: Thomas Robert, Ryan Ashley. Grad., Officer Candidate Sch., 1966; BA in Criminal Justice, U. Nebr., 1972; MA in Criminal Justice, CUNY, 1977; JD, U. Calif., San Diego, 1978. Bar: N.C., Ga., D.C., U.S. Supreme Ct., U.S. Ct. Appeals (4th cir.), U.S. Ct. Appeals (5th cir.), U.S. Ct. Appeals (D.C. cir.), U.S. Army Ct. Mil. Rev., U.S. Ct. Mil. Appeals. Enlisted pvt. US Army, 1965; ret. as col. USAR, 1995; pvt. practice in law Fayetteville, NC, 1978—; spl. agt., criminal investigator Dept. Treas., Bur. Alcohol, Tobacco and Firearms; assoc. justice NC Supreme Ct., Raleigh, 2002—. Decorated DFC, Bronze Star medal, Air Medal with Valor Device for heroism and 2d-18th oak leaf cluster, Vietnam Cross of Gallantry with Bronze Star. Office: Justice Bldg PO Box 1841 Raleigh NC 27602*

BRADY, EDWARD THOMAS, JR., lawyer, writer; b. Somerville, Mass., May 11, 1940; s. Edward Thomas Brady and Marie Florence Cashman; m. Margaret Alice Linehan, Oct. 28, 1963 (div. Dec. 1979); children: Sharon Lynn, Keith Andrew. BA in Bus Adminstrn., Northeastern U., 1963; JD, Suffolk U., 1968. CPCU, CLU. Underwriter Lumber Mut. Fire Ins. Co., Boston, 1962—67; trial atty. Continental Ins. Co., Boston, 1969—72; atty., govt. affairs and law, property-casualty dept. Travelers Ins. Co., Hartford, Conn., 1972—76; gen. counsel Shelby Mut. Life Ins. Co., Shelby, Ohio, 1977—79; atty. Self-employed Sole Practioner, Somerville, Mass., 1979—2001; author Self-Employed Free Lance Author, Winchester, Mass., 2001—. Author: Last In My Class, 2001 (Cert., 2002), (short stories) Good Grief! About Relationships. And Other Short Stories That Make You Wish They Were Shorter, 2004 (Cert., 2004), (novel) Georgie! My Georgie! The First Greek-American To Win The Medal Of Honor, 2005 (Summer 2005 Scheduled Publ.), (guest columnist) Winchester Star. Tchr. Ch., Winchester, Woburn and Somerville, Mass., 1965—2001; coach Little League, Avon, Conn., 1972—76. Mem.: VFW (hon.; non-serving mem. 2003—05). Roman Catholic. Avocations: reading, writing, walking, music, travel. Home Phone: 781-721-4694; Office Phone: 781-721-4694. Personal E-mail: ponythruns@aol.com.

BRADY, JAMES JOSEPH, labor arbitrator; b. Jersey City, Mar. 2, 1936; s. James and Anna (Shine) B.; m. Sheila Hartney, July 24, 1965; children: Matthew, Michael, James. BA, U. Notre Dame, 1959, MA in Econs., 1963, PhD in Econs., 1969. Profl. baseball player Detroit Tigers, 1955-60; asst. prof. econs. Ind. U., South Bend, 1965-69; asst. prof., assoc. prof., prof. econs. Old Dominion U., Norfolk, Va., 1969-79; dean Coll. Arts and Scis. Jacksonville (Fla.) U., 1979-83, dean Coll. Bus., 1983-84, v.p. acad. affairs, 1984-88, pres.-elect, 1988-89, pres., 1989-95, prof. econs., 1995—. Spl. magistrate Fla. Pub. Employees Rels. Commn., Tallahassee, 1985—; pvt. labor cons., Jacksonville, 1978-88; mem. Fed. Mediation and Conciliation Svc. Labor Panel, 1985—; perm. arbitrator State Fla. dept. mgmt. svcs., 1999— Author: Arbitration Principles: Layoffs, 1989; co-author: Transportation Noise Pollution, 1970. With U.S. Army, 1959-61. NASA grantee, Norfolk, Va., 1970. Mem. Am. Arbitration Assn. (labor arbitrator 1965—, comml. arbitrator 1987-89), Indsl. Rels. Rsch. Assn., Soc. Profls. in Dispute Resolution, Jacksonville C. of C. (bd. dirs. 1989—). Avocations: fishing, cooking, tennis. Home: 1072 Meadow View Ln Saint Augustine FL 32092-1055 Personal E-mail: jimbrady@sjcgcc.com.

BRADY, JAMES WINSTON, commentator, writer, editor; b. NYC, Nov. 15, 1928; s. James Thomas and Marguerite Claire (Winston) B.; m. Florence Kelly, Apr. 12, 1958; children: Fiona, Susan. BA, Manhattan Coll., 1950. Pub. Women's Wear Daily, NYC, 1964-71; editor, pub. Harper's Bazaar, NYC, 1971-72; editor N.Y. mag., NYC, 1977; syndicated columnist N.Y. Post, NYC, 1980-83; news commentator WCBS-TV, NYC, 1981-87; editor-at-large Advt. Age, NYC, 1977—2005. Author: Superchic, 1974, Paris One, 1976, Nielsen's Children, 1978, The Press Lord, 1981, Holy Wars, 1983, Designs, 1986, The Coldest War, 1990, Fashion Show, 1992, The House That Ate the Hamptons, 2000, Warning of War: A Novel of the North China Marines, 2002, The Marines of Autumn: A Novel of the Korean War, 2000, The Marine: A Novel of War from Guadalcanal to Korea, 2003, The Scariest Place in the World: A Marine Returns to North Korea, 2005; weekly columnist Parade mag., NYC, 1986—, Forbes.com, 2006. Served to 1st lt. USMC, 1951-52. Recipient Emmy award N.Y. TV Acad., 1975 Mem.: University (N.Y.C.). Democrat. Roman Catholic. Home: PO Box 1584 East Hampton NY 11937-0704 Business E-Mail: in_step_with@parade.com.

BRADY, JEAN STEIN, retired librarian; b. Concord, Mass., Nov. 4, 1930; d. Walfred and Mary Selina (Jussila) Stein; m. Maurice Goodrich Klein, Feb. 22, 1957 (div. 1982); 1 child, Audrey Elaine; m. Lawrence Kevin Brady, Oct. 15, 1988. BS, Simmons Coll., 1952; cert. d'Etudes, U. Grenoble, France, 1954; MA, Northwestern U., 1957. Cert. pub. libr., N.Y. Sr. libr. N.Y. Pub. Libr., 1952-53, 57-60; cataloger Columbia U., NYC, 1954-55; reference asst. Northwestern U., Evanston, Ill., 1955-57; cataloger U. W.Va., Morgantown, 1960-61; book reviewer ALA, Chgo., 1961-63; sr. cataloger Cleve. Pub. Libr., 1964-70; sr. catalog libr. Yale U. Libr., New Haven, Conn., 1970-92; cataloger Columbia U., NYC, 1993-95; ret., 1995. Revision asst. Bibliographical Guide to Romance Langs. and Lits., 1956-57; reviewer: Booklist and Subscription Books Bulletin, 1961-63. Mem.: Simmons Coll. Club Cape Cod. Democrat. Episcopalian. Avocations: reading, travel, walking, swimming.

BRADY, JOHN PATRICK, JR., electronics educator, consultant; b. Newark, Mar. 20, 1929; s. John Patrick and Madeleine Mary (Atno) B.; m. Mary Coop, May 1, 1954; children: Peter, John P., Madeleine, Dennis, Mary G. BSEE, MIT, 1952, MSEE, 1953. Registered profl. engr., Mass. Sect. mgr. Hewlett-Packard Co., Waltham, Mass., 1956—67; v.p. engring. John Fluke Mfg. Co., Inc., Mountlake Terrace, Wash., 1967—73, Dana Labs., Irvine, Calif., 1973—77; mgr. engring., tech. advisor to gen. mgr. Metron Corp., Upland, Calif., 1977—78; ptnr. Resource Assocs., Newport Beach, Calif., 1978—86; prof. electronics Orange Coast Coll., Costa Mesa, Calif., 1977—99, emeritus, 1999, faculty fellow, dean tech., 1983—84, chmn. electronics tech. dept., 1994—96, chmn. acad. rank com., 1988—98. Instr. computers and elec. engring. Calif. State U., Long Beach, 1982-84; dir. measurement sci. conf. MIT, L.A., 1982-83. Contbr. articles to profl. jours. Mem. evaluation team Accrediting Commn. for Cmty. and Jr. Colls., 1982-92; mem. blue ribbon adv. com. on oversees tech. transfer U.S. Dept. of Commerce, 1974-76. With USN, 1946-48. Mem. Eta Kappa Nu, Tau Beta Pi, Sigma Xi. Office: Orange Coast Coll Costa Mesa CA 92626

BRADY, JOSEPH VINCENT, behavioral biologist, educator; b. NYC, Mar. 28, 1922; s. James J. and Mary F. (Michaelson) B.; m. Nancy Heaton; children: Barbara Ann, Michael Joseph, Kathleen Theresa, Nancy Marie, Joanne Cecelia, Jessica Lea, Margaret Mary. BS, Fordham U., 1943; PhD, U. Chgo., 1951. Dep. dir. div. neuropsychiatry Walter Reed Inst. Research, 1951-71; prof. psychology U. Md., 1955-69; prof. behavioral biology Johns Hopkins Sch. Medicine, Balt., 1967—, prof. neurosci., 1982—; dir. Behavioral Biology Rsch. Ctr. Johns Hopkins U., Balt., 1992—; pres., chmn. bd. trustees Inst. for Behavior Resources, Balt., 1988—. Cons. pres. sci. adv. com. Merck Inst. for Therapeutic Rsch., U.S. Army Med. Rsch. and Devel. Command, NASA; assoc. chmn. Nat. Commn. for Protection Human Subjects of Biomed. and Behavioral Rsch., 1974-79; chmn. sci. adv. com. New Eng. Regional Primate Rsch. Ctr., Harvard Med. Sch., Boston, com. on problems of drug dependence NRC, com. on space biology and medicine, com. on toxicology NAS; mem. adv. com. NASA/NIH; mem. space medicine com. NAS Inst. Medicine. Contbr. articles to profl. jours. Col. M.C., U.S. Army. Fellow AAAS, APA (pres. divsn.), Am. Coll. Neuro-psycho-pharmacology, Coll. Problems Drug Dependence (pres.), Acad. Behavioral Med. Rsch.; mem. Eastern Psychol. Assn. (pres.), Assn. Behavior Analysis, Soc. Behavioral Medicine (pres.), Pavlovian Soc. (pres.), Behavioral Pharmacology Soc. (pres.), Am. Soc. Pharmacology and Exptl. Therapeutics, Nat. Space Biomedical Rsch. Inst., Federated Am. Socs. Exptl. Biology. Home: Unit 610 1000 Fell St Baltimore MD 21231-3554 Office: Johns Hopkins U Behavioral Biology Rsch Ctr 5510 Nathan Shock Dr Baltimore MD 21224-6823 Office Phone: 410-550-2779. Business E-Mail: jvb@jhmi.edu.

BRADY, KEVIN PATRICK, congressman; b. Vermillion, SD, Apr. 11, 1955; m. Cathy Patronella Brady; 2 children. BS in Mass Comm., U. SD, 1990. Pres. South Montgomery County-Woodlands C. of C., 1985—96; mem. Tex. State Ho. Reps., 1990-96, US Congress from 8th Tex. dist., 1997—, dep. whip, mem. ways and means com., mem. joint econ. com., mem. ho. policy com. Active Saints Simon and Jude Cath. Ch. Named Outstanding Young Texan, Tex. Jaycees, Legis. Standout, Dallas Morning News; named one of 10 Best Legislators for Families and Children, State Bar Tex.; recipient Achievement award, Tex. Conservative Coalition, Friend of the Farm Bur., Am. Farm Bur. Montgomery County, Tex. chpt., 2005, Scholars Achievement award, Excellence in Pub. Svc., North Harris Montgomery Cmty. Coll. Dist., Support for Family Issues award, Tex. Ext. Homemakers Assn., Victims Rights Equalizer award, Texans for Equal Justice Ctr. Mem.: Rotary. Republican. Roman Catholic. Office: US Ho Reps 428 Cannon Ho Office Bldg Washington DC 20515-4308 Office Phone: 202-225-4901.*

BRADY, LAWRENCE PETER, lawyer; b. Jersey City, July 26, 1940; s. Lawrence Peter and Evelyn (Mauro) B.; div; children: Deegan, Tara, Kerry, Melissa, James; m. Mary Helen Reynolds, Mar. 28, 1984. BS in Acctg., St. Peters Coll., 1961; JD, Seton Hall U., 1964; LLM, Bklyn. Law Sch., 1966. Bar: N.J. 1964, U.S. Dist. Ct. N.J. 1964, U.S. Supreme Ct. 1969, U.S. Ct. Appeals (3rd cir.) 1972, N.Y. 1991; cert. civil trial atty. State of N.J. 1982; cert. Nat. Bd. Trial Advocacy 1989. Asst. prosecutor Hudson County, Jersey City, 1964-70; prosecutor Town of Kearny, N.J., 1971-74; sr. ptnr. Doyle & Brady, Kearny, 1974—2006, Brady & Brady, 2006—. Dir., founding incorporator Growth Bank, New Vernon, NJ. Named a NJ Super Lawyer, New Jersey Mag., 2007. Mem. ATLA, Nat. Bd. Trial Advocacy, N.J. State Bar Assn., Hudson County Bar Assn., West Hudson Bar Assn. (sec. 1980, treas. 1981, v.p. 1982, pres. 1983), Am. Trial Lawyers N.J. (bd. govs.), Roxiticus Golf Club (Mendham, N.J.), Sandalfoot Country Club (Boca Raton, Fla.), Ocean Reef Club (Key Largo, Fla.), Ocean Reef Yacht Club. Roman Catholic. Avocations: golf, tennis, travel, fishing, boating. Office: Doyle & Brady 377 Kearny Ave Kearny NJ 07032-2600 Office Phone: 201-997-0030.

BRADY, LUTHER W., JR., radiologist, educator; b. Rocky Mount, NC, Oct. 20, 1925; s. Luther W. and Gladys B. AA, George Washington U., 1944, AB, 1946, MD, 1948, DFA (hon.), 2003, Colgate U., 1988; DSc (hon.), Lehigh U., 1990; MD (hon.), Toyama U., Japan, 1996; D (hon.), U. Heidelberg, Germany, 1997. Diplomate Am. Bd. Radiology (treas. 1980-82, v.p. 1982-84, pres. 1984-86). Intern Jefferson Med. Coll. Hosp., Phila., 1948-50, resident in radiology, 1954-55; resident radiology Hosp. U. Pa., Phila., 1955-56; fellow Nat. Cancer Inst., 1954-57; practice medicine, specializing in radiation oncology Phila. Asst. instr. radiology Jefferson Med. Coll. Hosp., 1954-55, U. Pa., Phila., 1955, instr., 1956-57, assoc. radiology, 1957-59; asst. prof. radiology Coll. of Physicians and Surgeons, Columbia U., NYC, summer, 1959; assoc. prof. radiology Hahnemann Med. Coll. and Hosp., Phila., 1959-62, prof., 1963—97, Disting. Univ. prof., 1997-, chmn. dept. radiation oncology, 1970—97; asst. prof. radiology Harvard Med. Sch., Boston, 1962-63; mem. med. radiation adv. com. Bur. Radiation Health, HEW, 1971-74; cons. radiation therapy various hosp.; mem. US del. to Interam. Congress Radiology, 1975, Internat. Congress of Radiology, 1981; sec. gen. Internat. Congress Radiology, 1985; med. adv. radiation therapy, med. affairs com., 1984-97; dir. Pa. Blue Shield, Camp Hill; chair Pa. Cancer Control Bd., 1989-97. Author: Tumors of the Nervous System, 1975, Cancer of the Lung, Clinical Applications of the Electron Beam; editor Cancer Clin. Trials (Am. Jour. Clin. Oncology), (with C. Perez) Principles and Practice of Radiation Oncology; editorial bd. Cancer; assoc. editor: Gynecologic Oncology, Am. Jour. Roentgenology, Cancer Research; sr. editor: Internat. Jour. Radiol. Oncology; contbr. articles on radiation therapy to profl. jour. Bd. dirs. Assn. Artists Equity of Phila., Welcome House, 1974-94, Settlement Music Sch., 1973—, Phila. Art Alliance, 1977-84; mem. oriental art com., trustee Phila. Mus. Art, 1974— , chmn. friends exec. com., 1968-72, mem. print, contemporary art and Indian art coms., 1974—; trustee Fleisher Art Meml., 1997-, Founders Award, 2003; trustee Curtis Inst. Music, 1997-, The Phillips Collection, 2003. Served to lt. M.C. USN, 1950-54. Recipient Grubbe award Chgo. Radiol. Soc., 1977, Gold medal Gilbert Fletcher Soc., 1984, Albert Soiland Gold medal U. So. Calif., 1985, del Regato Gold medal, 1986, Disting. Alumni award George Washington U., 1991, Padro Pio medal, 1993. Fellow Am. Coll. Radiology (Gold medal 1983); mem. AMA (Gold medal Disting. Svc. award 1999, Am. Roentgen Ray Soc., Am. Radium Soc. (Gold medal 1981), Am. Cancer Soc., Am. Fedn. Clin. Rsch., Am. Bd. Radiology, Am. Soc. Clin. Oncology, Am. Coll. Radiation Oncology (Gold medal 1996), Am. Soc. for Therapeutic Radiology and Oncology (Gold medal 1987), Am. Assn. for Cancer Rsch., Soc. Chmn. Acad. Radiation Oncology Program, Soc. Chmn. Acad. Radiology Dept., Assn. Pendergrass Fellows, Internat. Soc. for Radiation Oncology, Internat. Skeletal Soc., Internat. Club Radiotherapists, James Ewing Soc., Radiation Rsch. Soc., Soc. Surg. Oncology, Assn. Univ. Radiologists, Radiation Rsch. Soc., Radiol. Soc. N.Am. (Gold medal 1989), Del. Med. Soc., Med. Soc. State Pa., Pa. Radiol. Soc., Phila. County Med. Soc.(Stristmater award 1999), Phila. Roentgen Ray Soc. Clubs: Merion Cricket; Racquet, Union League (Phila.), Phila., Peale. Office: 230 N Broad St Philadelphia PA 19102-1121 also: Hahnemann U Hosp Broad & Vine MS-200 Philadelphia PA 19102 Office Phone: 215-762-1998. Business E-Mail: Lbrady@drexelmed.edu.

BRADY, MARY ROLFES, music educator; b. St. Louis, Nov. 26, 1933; d. William Henry and Helen Dorothy (Slavick) Rolfes; m. Donald Sheridan Brady, Aug. 29, 1953; children: Joseph William, Mark David, Douglas Sheridan, John Rolfes, Todd Christopher. Student, Stanford U., 1951—54, UCLA, 1967, U. So. Calif., 1972—73; pvt. studies with, Roxanna Byers, Dorothy Desmond, and Rudolph Ganz. Pvt. piano tchr., LA, 1955—; TV and radio performer. Pres. Jr. Philharm. Com. L.A., 1975-76; legis. coord., bd. dirs. Philharm. Affiliates, L.A., 1978-80. Life mem. Good Samaritan Hosp., St. Vincent Med. Ctr., L.A.; trustee St. Francis Med. Ctr., 1984-88; bd. dirs. Hollygrove-L.A. Orphans Home, Inc. Mem. Am. Coll. Musicians Club, Stanford Women's Club (past bd. dirs., pres. L.A. chpt. 1977—), The Muses, Springs Country Club.

BRADY, M(URIEL) JANE, judge, former state attorney general; b. Wilmington, Del., Jan. 11, 1951; d. William Henry Brady Jr. and Edith Brady; m. Michael E. Neal, 1989. BA, U. Del., 1973; JD, Villanova U., 1976. Dep. atty. gen. State of Del., 1977—90; chief prosecutor Sussex County, 1987—90; solo law practice, 1990—94; atty. gen. State of Del., Wilmington, 1994—2005; judge Del. Superior Ct., Wilmington, 2005—. Bd. dirs. Nat. Dist. Attys. Assn., Kent/Sussex Industries. Past chair Rep Attys. Gen. Assn.; bd. dirs. Nat. Org. Victim Assistance; founder KINfolk; bd. dirs. Del. Children's Trust Fund; advisory bd. Big Bros./Big Sisters Sussex County. Named Delaware's Top Fraud Fighter, AARP Del., 1998;

recipient Del. Humane Assn. award, Kent County SPCA's Animal Kindness award, Woman of the Yr. award, Del. Federation of Bus. and Professional Women, Leadership and Excellence award, Coordinating Council Against Sexual Assault in Del. Mem.: Nat. Assn. Attys. Gen. (exec. com.). Republican.

BRADY, NICHOLAS FREDERICK, investment company executive, former secretary of the treasury; b. NYC, Apr. 11, 1930; s. James C. and Eliot (Chace) B.; m. Katherine Douglas, Sept. 5, 1952; children: Nicholas Frederick, Christopher D., Anthony N., Katherine C. BA, Yale U., 1952; MBA, Harvard U., 1954. With Dillon Read & Co. Inc., NYC, 1954-82, former chmn., CEO, 1982; chmn., CEO Purolator Courier Corp. Inc., Basking Ridge, 1983; US Senator from NJ, 1982; sec. US Dept. Treasury, Washington, 1988-93; founder, chmn. Darby Overseas Investments, Ltd, Washington, 1994—. Dir. Bessemer Securities Corp., Doubleday & Co., Ga. Internat. Corp., Wolverne World Wide Inc., ASA Ltd., Media Gen. Inc., NCR Corp. Trustee assoc. Boys' Club Newark.; Reagan appointee MX missile devel. options panel, Central Am. Study Commn., 1983. Mem.: Bond (N.Y.C.), Lunch (N.Y.C.) (bd. govs.), Links (N.Y.C.).*

BRADY, PHILLIP DONLEY, lawyer; b. Pasadena, Calif., May 20, 1951; s. Donley L. and Evelyn M. (Dorweiler) B.; m. Kathleen Ryan; children: Ryan Donley, Conor Phillip, Sean Patrick. BA cum laude, U. Notre Dame, 1973; JD cum laude, Loyola U., Los Angeles, 1976. Bar: Calif. 1976, U.S. Ct. Appeals (D.C. cir.) 1978, U.S. Supreme Ct. 1980, U.S. Ct. Mil. Appeals 1990. Assoc. atty. Spray, Gould & Bowers, LA, 1976-78; dep. atty gen. State of Calif., LA, 1978-79; legis. counsel U.S. Rep. Daniel E. Lungren, Washington, 1979-81; regional dir. ACTION Agy., San Francisco, 1981-82; dir., Congl. Affairs, Immigration and Naturalization Svc. Dept. of Justice, Washington, 1982-83, assoc. dep. atty. gen., 1983-84, acting asst. atty. gen., 1984-85; dep. asst. to V.P. The White House, Washington, 1985-88, dep. counsel to Pres., 1988-89; gen. counsel Dept. Transp., Washington, 1989-91; asst. to Pres. and staff sec. The White House, Washington, 1991-93; v.p, gen. counsel Am. Automobile Mfrs. Assn., Washington, 1993—99; COO ind. rels. Nat. Automobile Dealers Assn., McLean, Va., 1999—2001, pres., 2001—. Mem. Coun. of the Adminstrv. Conv. of the U.S., 1988-93. Mem. ABA, Calif. State Bar Assn., FBA (chair gen. counsels sect. 1989-91, nat. coun. 1989—). Home: 5916 Colfax Ave Alexandria VA 22311-1024 Office: Nat Automobile Dealers Assn 8400 Westpark Dr Mc Lean VA 22102-3522

BRADY, ROBERT A., congressman; b. Phila., Apr. 7, 1945; m. Debra Brady; 2 children: Robert, Kimberly. Grad. H.S., Phila. Carpenter, Phila., 1963-65; ofcl. Carpenter's Union, Phila., 1965-98; mem. US Congress from 1st Pa. dist., 1998—, sr. whip, chmn. House adminstrn. com. Mem. Pa. Dem. State Com., Dem. Nat. Com.; instr. Organizational Dynamics course, U. Pa. Mem. 34th Ward Dem. Exec. Com., 1967; elected 34th Ward leader, 1980, chmn. Phila. Dem. Party, 1986; appointed asst. sgt.-at-arms Phila. City Coun., 1975-83, Phila. dep. mayor for labor in the W. Wilson Goode adminstrn.; cons. to the Pa. State Senate; Pa. Turnpike commr.; bd. dirs. Phila. City Redevel. Authority. Named Friend of the Nat. Pks., Nat. Pks. Conservation Assn. Democrat. Office: US House Reps 206 Cannon House Office Bldg Washington DC 20515-3801 Office Phone: 202-225-4731. Office Fax: 202-225-0088.*

BRADY, RODNEY HOWARD, diversified financial services and broadcast company executive, retired academic administrator, federal official; b. Sandy, Utah, Jan. 31, 1933; s. Kenneth A. and Jessie (Madsen) B.; m. Carolyn Ann Hansen, Oct. 25, 1960; children: Howard Riley, Bruce Ryan, Brooks Alan. BS in Acctg. with high honors, U. Utah, MBA with high honors, 1957; DBA, Harvard U., 1966; postgrad., UCLA, 1969-70; PhD (hon.), Weber State Coll., 1986, Snow Coll., 1991, Univ. Utah, 1997. Missionary Ch. Jesus Christ of Latter-day Saints, Great Britain, 1953-55; teaching assoc. Harvard U. Bus. Sch., Cambridge, Mass., 1957-59; v.p. Mgmt. Systems Corp., Cambridge, 1962-65, Center Exec. Devel., Cambridge, 1963-64, v.p., dir. Boston, 1964-65; v.p. Tamerand Reef Corp., Christiansted, St. Croix, V.I., 1963-65; v.p., dir. Am. Inst. Execs., NYC, 1963-65; v.p., mem. exec. com. aircraft div. Hughes Tool Co., Culver City, Calif., 1966-70; asst. sec. adminstrn. and mgmt. Dept. HEW, Washington, 1970-72; chmn. subcabinet exec. officers group of exec. br., 1971-72; exec. v.p., chmn. exec. com., dir. Bergen Brunswig Corp., Los Angeles, 1972-78; chmn. bd. Uni-mgrs. Internat., Los Angeles, 1974-78; pres. Weber State Coll., Ogden, Utah, 1978-85; pres., CEO Bonneville Internat. Corp., Salt Lake City, 1985-96, also dir.; pres., CEO Deseret Mgmt. Corp., Salt Lake City, 1996—. Bd. dirs. Amerisource Bergen Corp., 1st Security Bank Corp., 1985-2000, Mgmt. and Tng. Corp., Deseret Mut. Benefit Assn., chmn.; bd. dirs. Maximum Svc. Television, Inc., Intermountain Health Care Found., Nat. Assn. Broadcasters TV Bd., 1993-96; bd. advisors Mountain Bell Telephone, 1983-87; chmn. Nat. Adv. Com. on Accreditation and Instl. Eligibility, 1984-86, mem., 1983-87; chmn. Utah Gov.'s Blue Ribbon Com. on Tax Recodification, 1984-90; cons. Dept. Def., Dept. State, Dept. Commerce, HEW, NASA, Govt. of Can., Govt. of India (and indsl. firms), 1962—. Author: An Approach to Equipment Replacement Analysis, 1957, Survey of Management Planning and Control Systems, 1962, The Impact of Computers on Top Management Decision Making in the Aerospace and Defense Industry, 1966, (with others) How To Structure Incentive Contracts— A Programmed Text, 1965, My Missionary Years in Great Britain, 1976, An Exciting Start Along an Upward Path, 1978; contbr. articles to profl. jours. Mem. exec. com. nat. exec. bd. Boy Scouts Am., 1977—; chmn. nat. Cub Scout comm., 1977-81, pres. Western region, 1981-83, chmn. nat. ct. of honor, 1984-88; mem. adv. com. program for health sys. mgmt. Harvard U., 1973-78, mem. nat. adv. coun. U. Utah, 1971—, chairperson, 1974-76, nat. adv. bd. Coll. Bus., 1985—, chmn., 1989-93, mem. adv. com. Brigham Young U. Bus. Sch., 1972—; mem. dean's round table UCLA Grad. Sch. Mgmt., 1973-78; trustee Ettie Lee Homes for Boys, 1973-79; mem. gov. bd. McKay Dee Hosp., Ogden, Utah, 1979-87; bd. dirs. Utah Endowment for Humanities, 1978-80, Nat. Legal Ctr. for the Pub. Interest, 1991—, vice chmn., 1994-95, chmn., 1995-97, Utah Shakespeare Festival, 1992-2001, Ogden C. of C., 1978-83; bd. dirs. Utah Opera Co., 1997—, Utah Symphony Orch., 1985--. 1st lt. USAF, 1959-62. Recipient Silver Antelope award Boy Scouts Am., 1976; recipient Silver Beaver award Boy Scouts Am., 1979, Silver Buffalo award Boy Scouts Am., 1982, Disting. Alumni award U. Utah, 1990. Mem. Nat. Assn. TV Broadcasters (bd. dirs.), Am. Mgmt. Assn. (award 1969), L.A. C. of C. (tax structure com. 1969-70), Salt Lake Area C. of C. (bd. dirs. 1985-88), SAR (pres. Utah chpt. 1986-87), Sons of Utah Pioneers, Freedoms Found. at Valley Forge (nat. bd. dirs. 1986—), L.A. Country Club, Alta Club, Rotary, Phi Kappa Phi, Tau Kappa Alpha, Beta Gamma Sigma. Mem. LDS Ch. (past pres. L.A. stake). Office: Deseret Mgmt Corp Eagle Gate Tower 60 E South Temple Ste 575 Salt Lake City UT 84111-1016

BRADY, ROSCOE OWEN, neurogeneticist, educator; b. Phila., Oct. 11, 1923; s. Roscoe O. and Martha (Roberts) Brady; m. Bennet Carden Manning, 1972; 2 children. Student, Pa. State U., 1941-43; MD, Harvard U., 1947; postgrad., U. Pa., 1948-49. Intern Hosp. U. Pa., 1947-48; NRC fellow U. Pa., 1948-50, USPHS spl. fellow, 1950-52; sect. chief Nat. Inst. Neurol. Diseases and Blindness, NIH, 1954-67, asst. lab. chief neurochemistry Bethesda, Md., 1967-72; chief developmental and metabolic neurology br. Nat. Inst. Neurol. Disorders and Stroke, 1972—; pres., CEO Targeted Techs., Inc., Rockville, Md., 2006—. Professorial lectr. George Washington U. Sch. of Medicine, 1963—73; mem. faculty Georgetown U. Sch. of Medicine, 1965—; mem. med. staff Children's Hosp., Washington, 1992—; chmn. sci. adv. bd. Therascope, A.G., Heidelberg, Germany. Author (with Donald B. Tower): Neurochemistry of Nucleotides and Animo Acids, 1960; author: Basic Neurosciences, 1975; author: (with John A. Barranger) Molecular Basis of Lysosomal Storage Disorders, 1984; author: numerous articles. Recipient award, Gairdner Found., 1973, Lasker Found., 1982, Passano Found., 1982, Warren Alpert Found. award, 1992, Myrtle Wreath award, Hadassah, 1993, Exec. Excellence award, Sr. Execs. Assn., 1993. Mem.: NAS (J.S. Kolvenko medal 1991), Inst. of Medicine, Am. Soc. Human Genetics, Am. Soc. Clin. Investigation, Am. Acad. Mental Retardation, Am. Acad. Neurology (Kotzias award 1980), Am. Soc. Biol. Chemists. Achievements include development of biosynthesis of myelin sheath lipids, nature of metabolic defects in Gaucher's disease, Neimann-Pick disease, Fabry's diseases and Tay-Sachs disease; enzyme replacement and gene therapy for lipid storage diseases; discovery of aberrant metabolism of sphingolipids in neoplastic diseases; role of antigenic sphingolipids in neurological diseases. Home: 6026 Valerian Ln Rockville MD 20852-3410 Office: NIH 9000 Rockville Pike Bethesda MD 20892-1260 Office Phone: 301-496-3285. Business E-Mail: bradyr@ninds.nih.gov.

BRADY, RUPERT JOSEPH, retired lawyer; b. Washington, Jan. 24, 1932; s. John Bernard and Mary Catherine (Rupert) B.; m. Maureen Mary MacIntosh, Apr. 20, 1954; children: Rupert Joseph Jr., Laureen Zegowitz, Kevin, Warren, Jeanine Hartnett, Jacqueline Rada, Brian, Barton. BEE, Cath. U. Am., Washington, DC, 1953; JD, Georgetown U., Washington, DC, 1959. Bar: Md. 1961, US Ct. Appeals (DC cir.) 1964, US Patent Trademark Office 1961, DC 1962, US Supreme Ct. 1969, US Ct. Appeals (fed. cir.) 1961. Elec. engr. Sperry Gyroscope Co., LI, 1953-56; patent specifications writer John B. Brady, patent atty., 1956-59; patent atty. B.P. Fishburne, Jr., Washington, 1959—61; pvt. practice Washington, Md. and Va., 1961—2004, Md., 1961; sr. ptnr. Brady, O'Boyle & Gates, Washington & Chevy Chase, Md., 1963-95; of counsel Birch, Stewart, Kolasch & Birch, LLP, Va., 1996—2004, ret., 2004. V.p. Ministr-O-Media Inc. Patentee crane booms, moldboard support assembly. Mem. ABA, Am. Intellectual Property Law Assn., Md. Patent Law Assn., Senator's Club Alumni. Republican. Roman Catholic. Home: 7201 Pyle Rd Bethesda MD 20817-5623 Office: 8110 Gatehouse Rd Ste 100E Falls Church VA 22042-1210

BRADY, SHARON, engineering executive; BA in Edn., Benedictine Coll., Atchison, Kans. V.p. human resources Home Svcs. divsn. Sears, Roebuck & Co.; v.p., chief human resource officer Snap-On Inc., Pleasant Prairie, Wis.; sr. v.p. human resources Ill. Tool Works (ITW), Glenview, 2006—. Mem.: Human Resources Mgmt. Assn. Chgo. Office: Ill Tool Works 3600 W Lake Ave Glenview IL 60026-1215 Office Phone: 847-724-7500. Office Fax: 847-657-4572.*

BRADY, STEPHEN R. P. K., physician; b. New London, Conn., Oct. 13, 1955; s. Richard Harris and Jeanne Margaret (Halpin) Brady; m. Marsha Anne Erickson, June 18, 1978 (div. Jan. 1993); 1 child, Ericka Anuhea; m. Elizabeth Ada Rewick, Dec. 27, 1994 (div. Nov. 2006). AB cum laude, Harvard U., Cambridge, Mass., 1977; MPH, U. Hawaii, 1978, postgrad., 1979; MD, U. Pa., Phila., 1982. Diplomate Am. Bd. Internal Medicine. Intern U. Hawaii, 1982-83, resident in internal medicine, 1983-85, clin. instr. Sch. Medicine, 1986-99, clin. asst. prof. Sch. Medicine, 1999—2003, assoc. prof. Sch. Medicine, 2003—, vice-chair Dept. Native Hawaiian Health, Sch. Medicine, 2003—06; physician Kaiser Clinics, Honolulu, 1985-86; physician, med. dir. Kokua Kalihi Valley, Honolulu, 1986-89; physician Waianae (Hawaii) Coast Health Svc., 1989-94; asst. med. dir., physician Am. Hawaii Cruises, Honolulu, 1989-95; physician Straub Clinic and Hosp., Honolulu, 1984—. Founding chair Hawaii Consortium Continuing Med. Edn. U. Hawaii Sch. Medicine, 1993—; mem. com. rev. and recognition Accreditation Coun. Continuing Med. Edn., 2004—, bd. dirs., 2007—. Host (TV series) Health in Paradise, 2001—03, UH on Call, 2005—06; editor: Hawaii Med. Jour., 2005—. Cubmaster Boy Scouts Am., Kailua, Hawaii, 1995—2000; trustee St. Louis Sch., 2006—. Comdr. US Mcht. Marine, 1989—. Named Scot of the Yr., State of Hawaii, 1999, Physician of the Yr., Honolulu County Med. Soc., 2002; named one of Best Drs. in Am., 2001—06; recipient Po'okela award, 1991, 1993, 1995, 1999, Guy Milnor award, 1999, Cub Scouter award, Aloha coun. Boy Scouts Am., 1999, Cubmaster award, 2000; Rsch. grantee, Kuakini Med. Rsch. Inst., Honolulu, 1971, Pacific Health Rsch. Inst., Honolulu, 1972—78, Children's Hosp., Phila., 1979, Paul Harris fellow, 1995. Fellow: ACP-Am. Soc. Internal Medicine; mem.: APHA, AMA, ACP, Ahahui O Na Kauka (pres. 2004—06), Soc. Epidemiologic Rsch., Hawaii Med. Assn. (chair cont. med. edn. com. 1987—, councillor, named Physician of Yr. 2007), Plaza Club, Rotary, Kaneohe Yacht Club, Soroptimist (pres. 1998—99), Elks, Delta Omega. Congregationalist. Avocations: singing, running, sailing, scuba diving, music. Home: 758 Kapahulu Ave PMB 309 Honolulu HI 96816-1196 Office: Dept Native Hawaiian Health 677 Ala Moana Blvd # 1016B Honolulu HI 96813 Office Phone: 808-587-8559. Personal E-mail: kaukaoli@hotmail.com.

BRADY, TERRENCE JOSEPH, mediator, arbitrator, retired judge; b. Chgo., Dec. 24, 1940; s. Harry J. and Othele R. Brady; m. Debra René, Dec. 6, 1969; children: Tara René, Dana Rose. BA cum laude, U. St. Thomas, St. Paul, 1963; JD, U. Ill., 1968. Bar: Ill. 1969, U.S. Dist. Ct. (no. dist.) Ill. 1970, U.S. Ct. Appeals (7th cir.) 1971. Pvt. practice, Crystal Lake, Ill., 1969-70, Waukegan, 1970-77; assoc. judge 19th Jud. Cir., 1977—2004, ret., 2004; mediator, arbitrator pvt. practice, 2004—. Lectr. Ann. Ill. Assoc. Judge Seminars, Statewide Ill. Traffic Conf., 1982, Lake County Bar Assn. Seminar, 1983, 88, others; invited participant Law and Econs. Seminar, U. Kans., 2000, Judicial Faculty Development, Ill. Judicial Conf., 2000; vis. jud. faculty Nat. Jud. Coll., U. Nev. Reno, 1997, condr. seminar civil mediation, 1999; materials author and lectr. in field, 1997; author, presenter, lectr. in field, 1998-; long range planning com. 19th Jud. Circuit, Lake County, Ill., 1999; alt. faculty mem., Chancery and Miscellaneous Remedies, 2000, Settlement Techniques, 2002; mem. delegation of Am. judges, Mexican Govt. Jud. Visitation Program, Mex.,2001. Author: Settle It, The Docket, 1998, The Six Steps of a Jury Trial, 1999, Civil Discovery-Rule 213-Keys to Compliance, 1999; author and lectr., SCR 213-2000 Update, The Docket, 2000; mem. editl. bd. The Docket; contbr. articles to profl. jours. With US Army, 1963—64, with US Army, 1968—69. Mem. ISBA (bench and bar sect. coun., adv. polls com., assembly mem. 2000-), LCBA (civil trial, med., legal coms.), Ill. Bar Assn. (com. on jud. adv. polls 1994—, vice-chair adv. polls 1998, task force on domestic violence 1998—, chair jud. adv. polls, 1999, sec. com. on jud. adv. polls 1997-99, bench and bar coms., jud. evaluating com.), Ill. Judges Assn. (bd. govs.), Ill. Bar Found., Lake County Bar Assn., Libertyville Racquet Club. Avocations: tennis, golf, writing, reading. Office Phone: 847-362-7885, 847-840-3044. Business E-Mail: tjbrady63@yahoo.com. *Notable cases include: Wiegman vs. Hitch-Inn Post, 721 N.E. 2d 614, 2d Dist, 1999, affirmed in allowing case to go to jury on strong circumstantial evidence of wet floors and stairs in motel swimming pool and recreational areas; Benitez vs. KFC Nat. Mgmt. Co., 714 N.E., 2d 1002, 2d Dist, 1999, affirmed in entering judgment for three pls-waitresses, and against for df-employees and mgrs. of KFC; Nowak vs. Coghill, 695 N.E., 2d 532, 2d Dist., 1998, affirmed trial ct. of df's motion of summary judgment in its finding no evidence of unnatural accumulation of snow, nor such accumulation as a proximate cause of pl's fall and injuries; Gantz vs. McHenry County Sheriff, 694 N.E., 2d 1078, 2d Dist, 1998, petition for leave to appeal denied at 699 N.E., 2d 1031, Ill. S. Ct., 1998, affirmed trial courts dismissal of pl's complaint on essential grounds of courts lack of subject matter jurisdiction via the preemption of collective bargaining issues under the Illinios Public Labor Relations Act; Koules vs. Euro-American Arbitrage, Inc., 689 Ill. 2d 411 2d Dist., 1998, affirmed trial court's grant of df'a motion for summary judgment against pl's employment contract claims of payment of guaranteed salary and vacation benefits; Lenz vs. Julian, 657 Ill. 2nd 712 2d Dist., 1995, affirmed trial ct. allowing the jury to decide pl's automobile negligence claims against a state trooper although the defendant claimed bars of sovereign immunity and public official immunity; Adams vs. Adams, 133 Ill. 2d 457 S. Ct., 1989, which involved the Ill. Appellate Ct., in a divided opinion, affirmed, Adams vs. Adams, 174 Ill. App. 3d 595 2d Dist., 1988. The Ill. Supreme Ct. reversed and remanded, holding the issues of paternity and consent must be determined under Fla. law; Agazim vs. Agazim, 176 Ill. App. 3d 225 2d Dist., 1988, which affirmed the trial ct.'s distbn. of marital property requiring the husband to pay off substantial marital debts which he had incurred of his own purposes; Chapman vs. Chapman, 162 Ill. app. 3d 308 2d Dist., 1987; which affirmed trial ct.'s denial of husband's motion to vacate a marital property settlement agreement, without an evidentiary hearing; Peppers vs. FNB of Lake Forest, 151 Ill. App 3d 909 2d Dist., 1987, which affirmed trial ct.'s enjoining the defendant bank, as trustee, from seeking forfeiture of a real estate purchase installment contract; People ex. rel. Foreman vs. Sojourner's Motorcycle Club Ltd., 134 Ill. App. 3d 448 2d Dist., 1985, which affirmed trial ct.'s denial of defendant's motion to quash adminstrv. search warrant processed by sheriff's dep. on behalf of, and executed by, the County Zoning officer.*

BRADY, TOM (THOMAS EDWARD PATRICK BRADY JR.), professional football player; b. San Mateo, Calif., Aug. 3, 1977; s. Thomas and Galynn (Johnson) Brady; 1 child, John Edward Moynahan. BA, U. Mich., 2000. Quarterback New Eng. Patriots, 2000—. Named MVP, Super Bowl XXXVI, 2002, Super Bowl XXXVIII, 2004, Sportsman of Yr., Sports Illus. mag., 2005; named to Pro Bowl, 2001, 2004—05; recipient Espy Award for Breakthrough Athlete of Yr., ESPN, 2002. Achievements include being the youngest starting quarterback in NFL history to win a Super Bowl, 2002; member, Super Bowl Champion New England Patriots, 2002, 2004, 2005; drafted as a catcher by the Montreal Expos (MLB), 1995. Office: New England Patriots 60 Washington St Foxboro MA 02035*

BRADY, UPTON BIRNIE, editor, literary agent; b. Washington, Apr. 17, 1938; s. Francis Ignatius and Sue (Birnie) B.; m. Sally Ryder, Nov. 17, 1962; children— Sarah Schenck, Andrew Upton Birnie, Nathaniel Francis Ryder, Alexander Childs. AB, Harvard Coll., 1959. Coll. field editor Random House, NYC, 1961-63; editor McGraw Hill, NYC, 1963-65; mng. editor Atlantic Monthly Press, Boston, 1965-72, assoc. dir., 1972-79, dir., 1979-84, exec. editor, 1984-88; free-lance editor, cons., literary agt., 1988—. Served to lt. (j.g.) USNR, 1959-61 Mem.: PEN. Roman Catholic. Home and Office: PO Box 164 81 Town Farm Hill Rd Hartland Four Corners VT 05049-0164

BRADY-BORLAND, KAREN, retired reporter, columnist; b. Buffalo, Mar. 13, 1940; d. Charles A. and Mary Eileen (Larson) B.; m. Gregg Robinson Borland, Sept. 6, 1969 (div. July 1985); children: Caitlin Luise, Kristin Robinson, Leila Nell. BA in English, Daemen Coll., 1961; MS in Journalism, Columbia U., 1962. Summer reporter Buffalo News, 1961, reporter, 1965-68, columnist, 1968-81; editor Prentice-Hall, Inc., Englewood, NJ, 1962-65; press officer for Rep. Max McCarthy U.S. Ho. Reps., Washington, 1967; gen. assignment & features reporter Buffalo News, 1981—91, higher education reporter, 1991—2002; ret., 2002. Book reviewer Buffalo News, 2006—. Recipient numerous awards Buffalo Newspaper Guild, 1969-79, N.Y. State award for Major Dailies Mag. Writing AP, 1982, numerous community awards, Hilbert Coll. medal, 2002.

BRAENDEL, DOUGLAS ARTHUR, hotel executive; b. Highland Park, Mich., Dec. 9, 1939; s. Helmuth Gunther and Constance Leah (Drysdale) B.; m. Cameron Lawry, Nov. 30, 1968; children: Jennifer Braendel Miller, Eric, Heike Lawry Batluck. BSBA, Lehigh U., 1961, MBA, 1971; Grad., Army Command and Gen. Staff, Coll., Army War Coll. Commd. U.S. Army, 1966, advanced through grades to col., 1989; bn. supply officer 24th Med. Bn., Fed. Republic of Germany, 1966-68; patient adminstr., detachment comdr. 3d Mobile Army Surg. Hosp., Vietnam, 1968-69; CFO Noble Army Community Hosp., Ft. McClellan, Ala., 1972-75; asst. prof. health adminstrn. Baylor U. Grad. Sch., San Antonio, 1975-79; exec. officer 45th Med. Battalion, Hanau, Fed. Republic Germany, 1980-82; adminstr. Army Regional Med. Lab., Landstuhl, Fed. Republic Germany, 1982-84; comdr. 10th Mobile Army Surg. Hosp., Ft. Meade, Md., 1984-86; dir. programs and evaluation Army Surgeon Gen., Washington, 1986-89; spl. asst. Office Managed Care, Health Care Fin. Adminstrn., Washington, 1989-90; CFO U.S. Army Health Svcs. Command, San Antonio, 1990-93; dir. capitation financing Office Asst. Sec. Def., Falls Church, Va., 1993-96; ret. U.S. Army, 1996; health care mgmt. cons., 1996—2000; bus. mgr. White Sulphur Springs Hotel, 2000—. Adj. instr. Park Coll., San Antonio, 1976—79, Gadsdon (Ala.) State Jr. Coll., 1973—74, Allegany (Md.) Coll., 1997—98. Vol. income tax asst. IRS, Falls Church, Va., 1986-90, Bedford, Pa., 1996—; unit commr. Boy Scouts Am., Kaiserslautern, Fed. Republic Germany, 1982-84, scoutmaster, Rochester, N.Y., and Augsberg, Fed. Republic Germany, 1965-68; pres. Bedford County Citizens' Concerned for Human Life, 2004—. Col. U.S. Army, 1966—. Decorated Def. Superior Svc. medal, Legion of Merit with oak leaf cluster, others; recipient Outstanding Author award Am. Soc. Mil. Comptrollers, 1994. Fellow Am. Coll. Healthcare Execs. (Regents award for leadership in health care 1994); mem. Assn. U.S. Army, Beta Gamma Sigma. Avocations: sailing, skiing. Office: White Sulphur Springs Hotel 4499 Milligans Cove Rd Manns Choice PA 15550 Office Phone: 814-623-5583. E-mail: braendel@bedford.net.

BRAEUTIGAM, RONALD RAY, economics professor, educational association administrator; b. Tulsa, Apr. 30, 1947; s. Raymond Louis and Loys Ann (Johnson) B.; m. Janette Gail Carlyon, July 27, 1975; children: Eric Zachary, Justin Michael, Julie Ann. BS in Petroleum Engring., U. Tulsa, 1969; MSc in Engring.-Econ. Systems, Stanford U., 1971, PhD in Economics, 1976. Petroleum engr. Standard Oil Ind., Tulsa, 1966—70; staff economist Office of Telecomm. Policy, Exec. Office of Pres., Washington, 1972—73; from asst. to prof. econs. Northwestern U., Evanston, Ill., 1975—, dir. bus. instns. program, 1995—2004, Harvey Kapnick prof. Bus. Instns. dept. econs., 1990—, Charles Deering McCormick prof. tchg. excellence, 1997—2000, assoc. dean, 2004—06, assoc. provost, 2006—. Vis. prof. Calif. Inst. Tech., Pasadena, 1978-79, sr. rsch. fellow Internat. Inst. Mgmt., Berlin, 1982-83, 91. Co-author: The Regulation Game, 1978, Price Level Regulation for Diversified Public Utilities, 1989, Microeconomics: An Integrated Approach, 2002; assoc. editor Jour. Indsl. Econs., Cambridge, Mass., 1987-90; mem. editorial bd. MIT Press Series on Regulation, Cambridge, 1980-90, Jour. Econ. Lit., 1987-91, Rev. Indsl. Orgn., 1991—2004, Microeconomics, 2005. Coach Skokie (Ill.) Indians Little League, 1985-91, Evanston Youth Baseball Assn., 1991-96. Grantee, Dept. Transp., NSF, Ameritech, Sloan Found., Mellon Found. Mem. Am. Econ. Assn., Econometric Soc., Internat. Telecommunications Soc. (bd. dirs. 1990-97), European Econ. Assn., European Assn. for Rsch. in Indsl. Econs. (exec. com. 1992—, pres. 1997-99), Soc. Petroleum Engrs. Avocations: travel, music, languages. Home: 731 Monticello St Evanston IL 60201-1745 Office: Northwestern U Office of the Provost Evanston IL 60208-0001

BRAFF, ZACH, actor, director, scriptwriter; b. South Orange, NJ, Apr. 6, 1975; s. Hal and Anne Braff. BA in Film, Northwestern U., Evanston, Ill. Actor: (films) Manhattan Murder Mystery, 1993, Getting to Know You, 1999, Blue Moon, 2000, The Broken Hearts Club: A Romantic Comedy, 2000, Endsville, 2000, (voice) Chicken Little, 2005, The Last Kiss, 2006, The Ex, 2007; actor, dir., writer (films) Garden State, 2004 (Grammy Award for Best Compilation Soundtrack, 2005); actor: (TV series) Scrubs, 2001—; (TV films) My Summer as a Girl, 1994, (theatre) Macbeth, 1998, Romeo & Juliet, Twelfth Night, 2002. Achievements include directing and writing several short films including Lionel on a Sun Day; directing commercials and public service announcements.*

BRAFFORD, WILLIAM CHARLES, lawyer; b. Pike County, Ky., Aug. 7, 1932; s. William Charles and Minnie (Tacket) B.; m. Katherine Jane Prather, Nov. 13, 1954; children— William Charles III, David A. JD, U. Ky., 1957; LLM (fellow), U. Ill., 1958. Bar: Ky. 1957, Ga. 1965, Tax Ct. U.S 1965, Ct. Claims 1965, Ohio 1966, U.S. Ct. Appeals 1966, U.S. Supreme Ct. 1970, Pa. 1973. Trial atty. NLRB, Washington and Cin., 1958-60; atty. Louisville & Nashville R.R. Co., Louisville, 1960-63, So. Bell Telephone Co., Atlanta, 1963-65; asst. gen. counsel NCR Corp., Dayton, Ohio, 1965-72; v.p., sec., gen. counsel Betz Dearborn, inc., Trevose, Pa., 1972-97, ret., 1997. Former dir. Betz Process Chems., Inc., Betz, Ltd. U.K., Betz Paper Chem. Inc., Betz Energy Chems., Inc., Betz S.A. France, B.L. Chems., Inc., Betz GmbH, Germany, Betz Entec, Inc., Betz Ges. GmbH, Austria, Betz NV Belgium, Betz Sud S.p.A., Italy, Betz Internat. Inc., Betz Europe Inc., Primex Ltd., Barbados; arbitrator, NASD. Served as 1st lt. C.I.C. AUS, 1954-56. Mem. Am. Soc. Corp. Secs., Nat. Assn. Corp. Dirs. Republican. Presbyterian.

BRAFMAN, BENJAMIN, lawyer; b. NYC, July 21, 1948; s. Sol and Rose (Friedman) B.; m. Lynda J. Bienenfeld, June 23, 1971; children— Jennifer, David. BA, Bklyn. Coll., 1971; JD with distinction, Ohio No. Coll. Law, 1974; LLM. in Criminal Justice, NYU, 1979. Bar: NY 1975, US Ct. Appeals (2d cir.) 1975, US Supreme Ct. 1978.manuscript editor, Ohio Northern U. Law Review, 1973-74, assoc., McGuire & Lawler, NYC, 1974-76; asst. dist. atty. NYC, 1976-79, mem., Brafman & Ross P.C., NYC, 1979—. Mem. ABA, Assn. Trial Lawyers Am., Nat. Assn.Criminal Defense Lawyers, NY Coun. of Criminal Def. Lawyers (Norman Ostrow award), bd. dirs., NY Criminal Bar Assn, 1990-92 (Outstanding Pvt. Criminal Def. Practitioner award, 2005); Fellow, Am.Coll. of Trial Lawyers; named "Best Criminal Defense Lawyer", NY Mag., 1997. Office: Brafman & Ross PC 26th Fl 767 Third Ave New York NY 10017*

BRAGA, STEPHEN LOUIS, lawyer; b. Newport, RI, Nov. 29, 1955; s. Manuel Louis and Nancy Rose (Lincourt) B. BA cum laude, Fairfield U., 1978; JD magna cum laude, Georgetown U. Law Ctr., 1981. Bar: D.C. 1982, U.S. Supreme Ct., U.S. Ct. Appeals (D.C., 1st, 2d, 3d, 7th, 9th and D.C. cirs.), U.S. Dist. Ct. D.C., U.S. Tax Ct. Law clk. U.S. Dist. Ct. D.C., Washington, 1981-82; atty. Miller, Cassidy, Larroca & Lewin, Washington, 1982—2000; ptnr. litigation dept. & hiring ptnr. Washington office Baker Botts LLP, Washington, 2000—. Adj. prof. Georgetown U. Law Ctr., Washington, 1993—. Democrat. Roman Catholic. Avocation: sports. Office: Baker Botts LLP The Warner 1299 Pennsylvania Ave NW Washington DC 20004-2400 Office Phone: 202-639-7704. Office Fax: 202-585-1066. Business E-Mail: stephen.braga@bakerbotts.com.

BRAGDON, LYNN LYON, library administrator; b. Kansas City, Mo., Dec. 22, 1944; d. Chester Willard and Frances Helen (Bechtold) Lyon; m. James Albert Bragdon, Jr., June 16, 1969. BS in Edn., Ctrl. Mo. State U., Warrensburg, 1967; MLS, U. Okla., Norman, 1968. Rsch. libr. E.I. DuPont de Nemours, Wilmington, Del., 1968-72; asst. libr. North Cobb H.S., Marietta, Ga., 1972-74; head cataloging U. Miss. Med. Ctr., Jackson, 1975-76, assoc. dir. libr. ops., 1976-77; mgr. reference svcs. Miss. R & D Ctr., Jackson, 1977-79; chief libr. svc. VA Med. Ctr., Grand Junction, Colo., 1980-96, mgr. libr. sect., 1997—. Mem. governing bd. Pathfinders Regional Libr. System, 1985-2004; mem. regional adv. com. Midcontinental Regional Med. Libr. Program, Omaha, 1988-92; mentor new chiefs libr. svc. Dept. Vets. Affairs, Washington, 1992—. Mem. Jr. Svc. League, Grand Junction, 1984—, bd. dirs., 1986-94, 2002-05, sec., 1988-90, coord. park, 1991-94; active Western Colo. Mus., 1984-2000; asst. lay leader Meth. Ch., 1996-2000, chmn. evangelism com., 2004-06, mem. ch. coun., 2004-06, mem. lay leadership com., 2007—; mem., ex-officio Va. libr. adv. coun. Dept. Vet. Affairs, 2001-06. Recipient Med. Informatics fellowship Nat. Libr. Medicine, 2002. Mem. Acad. Health Info. Profls. (disting.), Med. Libr. Assn., Colo. Coun. Med. Librs., Colo. Nat. Monument Assn. (v.p., bd. dirs. 1986-87, mem. bd. dirs. 1986-92), Grand Junction Gem and Mineral Soc. (libr. 1983), Western Colo. Botanic Soc. Methodist. Avocations: travel, cross country skiing, music, golf, boating. Home: 610 Broken Spoke Rd Grand Junction CO 81504-5270 Office: Library 142D VA Med Ctr 2121 North Ave Grand Junction CO 81501-6428 Business E-Mail: lynn.bragdon@va.gov.

BRAGDON, PAUL ERROL, retired academic administrator, educator; b. Portland, Maine, Apr. 19, 1927; s. Errol Freemont and Edith Lillian (Somerville) B.; m. Nancy Ellen Horton, Aug. 14, 1954; children: David Lincoln, Susan Horton, Peter Jefferson. BA magna cum laude, Amherst Coll., 1950, DHL (hon.), 1980; JD, Yale U., 1953; LLD (hon.), Whitman Coll., 1985; DLitt. (hon.), Pacific U., 1988; DHL (hon.), Reed Coll., 1989; DHL (hon.), Lewis & Clark Coll., 2005; DSc (hon.), Oreg. Health Scis. U., 2004. Bar: N.Y. 1954. With firm Dewey, Ballantine, Bushby, Palmer & Wood, NYC, 1953-58, Javits, Trubin, Sillcocks, Edelman & Purcell, NYC, 1961-64; counsel Tchrs. Ins. and Annuity Assn. Coll. Retirement Equities Fund, NYC, 1958-61; asst. to mayor City of NY, 1964-65, exec. sec. to mayor, 1965, exec. asst. to pres. City Council, 1966-67; v.p. NYU, 1967-71; pres. Reed Coll., Portland, Oreg., 1971-88; pres. emeritus, 1988—; asst. for edn. to gov. State of Oreg., 1988-91; dir. Office Edn. Policy and Planning Oreg., 1990-91; pres. Med. Rsch. Found. Oreg., Portland, Oreg., 1991-94, Oreg. Grad. Inst. Sci. and Tech., Portland, Oreg., 1994-98; interim pres. Lewis & Clark Coll., Portland, Oreg., 2003—04. Trustee Amherst Coll., 1972-78. Recipient Torch of Liberty award Anti-Defamation League of B'nai B'rith, 1985, Presdl. Leadership award Marylhurst U., 1988, award of excellence Kaul Found., 1994, Aubrey Watzek award Lewis and Clark Coll., 1999, Simon Benson award Portland State U., 1999, Libr. Leadership award Libr. Found. Multnomah County, 2001. Mem. Phi Beta Kappa, Phi Beta Kappa Assocs., Beta Theta Pi, Arlington Club, Univ. Club. Home: 7535 SE 31st Ave Portland OR 97202-8532 Personal E-mail: bragdonp@reed.edu.

BRAGG, CHERYL FULLER, psychologist; b. Warrenton, Va., July 21, 1956; d. Stanley Ralph and Jane Lanham Fuller; m. Jeffrey Phillip Bragg, May 11, 1975; children: Jonathan, Katharine. BA, U. Va., 1978; MA, Boston U., 1982, PhD, 1986. Cert. sch. psychol. Va. Psychologist Lang. and Cognitive Devel. Ctr., Boston, 1984—88; therapist Phillips Program for Children and Families, Annandale, Va., 1990—. Cons., sch. psychologist Fairfax Co., Loudoun Co. Pub. Schs., Va., 1989—90; adj. prof. George Mason U., Fairfax, Va., 1989—90; vis. prof. Tufts U., Boston, 1988. Human relations com. Thomas Jefferson HS Sci. and Tech., 1997—2001, bd. officer, 1998—2000. Pre-Doctoral Rsch. fellowship, NIMH, 1982—83, Pre-Doctoral Tchg. fellowship, 1979—82. Mem.: Assn. Psychol Sci., Nat. Assn. Sch. Psychologists, Tchg. Tolerance. Buddhist. Achievements include research in cognitive devel. treatment of autistic, asperger; emotionally disturbed, neurologically impaired, and attachment disturbed children. Avocation: painting. Office: Phillips Program for Children and Families 7010 Braddock Rd Annandale VA 22003

BRAGG, ELLIS MEREDITH, JR., lawyer; b. Washington, Jan. 30, 1947; s. Ellis Meredith Sr. and Lucille (Tingstrum) B.; m. Judith Owens, Aug. 18, 1968; children: Michael Andrew, Jennifer Meredith. BA, King Coll., 1969; JD, Wake Forest U., 1973. Bar: N.C. 1973, U.S. Dist. Ct. (we. and mid. dists.) N.C. 1974, U.S. Ct. Appeals (4th cir.) 1980, U.S. Supreme Ct. 2002. Assoc. Bailey, Brackett & Brackett, P.A., Charlotte, N.C., 1973-76; ptnr. Howard & Bragg, Charlotte, 1976-77, McConnell, Howard, Johnson, Pruitt, Jenkins & Bragg, Charlotte, 1977-79; pvt. practice, , Charlotte, 2002—. Dist. chmn. Mecklenburg County Dems., Charlotte, 1978; coach youth soccer program YMCA, Charlotte, 1982-83; mem. Headstart Policy Council, Charlotte, 1985. Mem. ABA, N.C. Bar Assn., N.C. Acad. Trial Lawyers. Presbyterian. Avocations: reading, jogging, gardening. Home: 6407 Honegger Dr Charlotte NC 28211-4718 Office: 500 E Morehead St Ste 210 Charlotte NC 28202-2694 Office Phone: 704-334-0888. Personal E-mail: Bragglaw@aol.com.

BRAGG, LAWRENCE D., III, lawyer; b. 1948; BA cum laude, Yale U., 1970; JD magna cum laude, Harvard U., 1974. Bar: Mass. 1974. Law clk. Judge Edward T. Gignoux, US Dist. Ct. (Maine), 1975—76; ptnr. corp. dept. Ropes & Gray, Boston, 1983—, co-head pub. fin. practice group. Mem.: Nat. Assn. Bond Lawyers, Boston Bar Assn. Office: Ropes & Gray LLP One International Pl Boston MA 02110-2624 Office Phone: 617-951-7427. Office Fax: 617-951-7050. Business E-Mail: lawrence.bragg@ropesgray.com.

BRAGG, MICHAEL ELLIS, lawyer, insurance company executive; b. Holdrege, Nebr., Oct. 6, 1947; s. Lionel C and Frances E (Klinginsmith) Bragg; m. Nancy Jo Aabel, Jan. 19, 1980; children: Brian Michael, Kyle Christopher, Jeffrey Douglas. BA, U. Nebr., 1971, JD, 1975. ChFC, CPCU, CLU; bar: Alaska 1976, Nebr 1976, U.S. Supreme Ct. 2001. Assoc. White & Jones, Anchorage, 1976-77; field rep. State Farm Ins., Anchorage, 1977-79, atty. corp. law dept. Bloomington, Ill., 1979-81, sr. atty., 1981-84, asst. counsel, 1984-86, counsel, 1986-88; asst. v.p., counsel gen. claims dept. State Farm Fire and Casualty Co., Bloomington, 1988-94; v.p., counsel, gen. claims dept. State Farm Ins. Co., Bloomington, Ill., 1994-97, assoc. gen. counsel corp. law dept., 1997—2006. Lectr, contbr legal seminars. Contbr, ed: articles to legal and ins. jour. Pres. McLean County Crime Detection Network, 1988—95. With USNG, 1970—76. Recipient Disting. Legal Svc. Award, Corp. Legal Times, 1998, 2003, Tort, Trial and Ins. Com. award, Am. Bar Assn., 2005. Fellow: Am. Bar Found.; mem.: ABA (various offices tort, trial and ins. practice sect. 1981—2004, vice-chmn property ins law com. 1986—91, chmn. ins. coverage litigation com. 1991—92, chmn. task force on ins. staff counsel 2000—02, coun. 2000—03, standing com. on ethics and profl. responsibility 2001—04, Staff Coun. Excellence award Tort, Trial and Ins. Practice sect. 2005), Assn. Profl. Responsibility Lawyers, Soc. Fin. Svc. Profls., Internat. Assn. Def. Counsel, Fedn. Def. and Corp. Counsel, Def. Rsch. Inst., Assn. Corp. Counsel. Republican. Avocations: golf, tennis. Home Phone: 309-829-6778. Personal E-mail: buck.bragg@verizon.net.

BRAGG, ROBERT HENRY, physicist, researcher; b. Jacksonville, Fla., Aug. 11, 1919; s. Robert Henry and Lilly Camille (McFarland) B.; m. Violette Mattie McDonald, June 14, 1947; children: Robert Henry, Pamela. BS, Ill. Inst. Tech., Chgo., 1949, MS, 1951, PhD, 1960. Assoc. physicist rsch. lab. Portland Cement Assn., Skokie, Ill., 1951-56; sr. physicist physics div. Armour Rsch. Found. Ill. Inst. Tech., Chgo., 1956-61; sr. mem., mgr. phys. metallurgy dept. Lockheed Palo Alto Rsch. Lab., Palo Alto, Calif., 1961-69; prof. materials sci. U. Calif., Berkeley, 1969-87, chmn. dept. materials sci. and mineral engring., 1978-81, prof. emeritus, 1987—. Faculty sr. scientist Lawrence Berkeley Lab., 1969-87, emeritus 1987—; mem. materials rsch. adv. com. NSF, 1982-86; program dir. div. materials rsch. U.S. Dept. Energy, 1981-82; cons. IBM, Siemens-Allis, NASA, NIH, NSF, NRC; vis. prof. Musashi Inst. of Tech., Tokyo, 1989, Howard U., 1979; del. 2d Edward Bouchet Internat. Conf., Accra, Ghana, 1990; rschr. Mich. U., Howard U., AT&T Collaborative Access Team, 1999. Contbr. articles to profl. jours. Pres. Palo Alto NAACP, 1967-68. With U.S. Army, 1943-46. Decorated Bronze star (2); recipient Disting. award No. Calif. sect. Am. Inst. Mining and Metall. Engrs., 1970, citation U. Calif., Berkeley, 1996; J. William Fulbright rsch. fellow, Nigeria, 1992-93. Fellow Nat. Soc. of Black Physicists; mem. AAUP, AAAS, Am. Phys. Soc., Am. Ceramics Soc. (chmn. No. Calif. sect. 1980), AIME (chmn. No. Calif. sect. 1970), Am. Carbon Soc., No. Calif. Coun. Black Profl. Engrs., Am. Crystallographic Assn., Sigma Xi, Tau Beta Pi. Democrat. Home: 2 Admiral Dr Ste 373 Emeryville CA 94608-1502 Office: U Calif Dept Materials Sci & Engring Berkeley CA 94720-0001 Personal E-mail: petebragg@aol.com.

BRAGINSKY, VLADIMIR BORISOVICH, physics professor, department chairman; b. Moscow, Aug. 3, 1931; s. Michail Michaiovich Zavialov and Anna Stepanovna (Kot) Braginskaya; stepfathre Boris Nicolaevich Braginsky; m. Rogneda Enverovna Schikhlinskaya, May 2, 1958; childrenP Olga, Oleg. MS in Physics, Moscow State U., 1954, PhD in Physics, 1959, DSc in Physics, 1967. Sr. worker dept. physics Moscow State U., 1954-56, asst. prof., 1956-64, sr. rsch. fellow, 1964-68, prof., 1968—, chmn. dept., 1986—. Vis. assoc. Calif. Inst. Tech., Pasadena, 1994—; advisor to pres. M. Planck Soc., Germany, 1995—. Author: Physical Experiments with Test Bodies, 1972, Measurements of Weak Forces in Physics Experiments, 1977, Systems with Small Dissipation, 1985, Quantum Measurement, 1992. Recipient Lebedev gold medal Presidium of Soviet Acad. Scis., 1975, Schiller medal U. Jena, Germany, 1980, Fairchild award Calif. Inst. Tech., 1990, A. von Humboldt award Humboldt Found., 1993. Mem. Russian Acad. Scis. (corr.), Acad. Europaea, Am. Acad. Arts & Sciences (hon. fgn.); fgn. assoc. NAS. Avocation: history. Office: Moscow State U Faculty of physics Vorobjovy Gory 119899 Moscow Russia

BRAHA, THOMAS I., oil industry executive; b. Austin, Tex., Sept. 3, 1947; s. Jacob and Valentine (Capone) B.; m. Nancy Elizabeth Rowe, Mar. 31, 1973 (div.); children: Nancy Elizabeth, Jeanne Valentine, Travis Ian. BSME, U. Tex., 1969; MBA, Temple U., 1971; postgrad., NYU, 1971-73. Engr. Davis Electronics, Inc., Austin, 1967, Whirlpool Corp., Evansville, Ind., 1968; project engr. ITE Imperial Corp., Phila., 1969-71; sr. supply analyst Mobil Oil Corp., NYC, 1971-74; pres. Western Hemisphere Bulk Oil (U.S.A.), Inc., NYC, 1974-75. Chmn. bd., CEO Braha Holding Corp., Braha Oil Corp. and Subs., Braha Estates, Inc., Braha Farms, Braha Profit and Pension Trusts; adj. faculty The Wharton Sch., U. Pa., 1996-2002; chmn. Molecular Valley Initiative of Greater Phila. Region, 2003—. Active Bryn Mawr Presbyn. Ch. Mem. ASME, Am. Mgmt. Assn., Am. Petroleum Inst., Inst. Petroleum (U.K.), Nat. Petroleum Refining Assn., Phila. Country Club. Office: Braha Holding Co PO Box 390 Bryn Mawr PA 19010-0390 Personal E-mail: tombraha@aol.com.

BRAHAM, RANDOLPH LEWIS, political science professor; b. Bucharest, Romania, Dec. 20, 1922; came to U.S., 1948, naturalized, 1953; m. Elizabeth Sommer, Dec. 15, 1954; children: Steven, Robert. BA, CCNY, 1948, MS, 1949; PhD, New Sch. for Social Research, 1952. Research assoc. YIVO-Inst. for Jewish Research, NYC, 1954-59; faculty CCNY, NYC, 1959—, prof. polit. sci., 1971—, disting. prof., 1987—, disting. prof. emeritus, 1992—, chmn. dept. polit. sci., 1971-81. Dir. Inst. for Holocaust Studies, Grad. Ctr. CUNY, 1980—; faculty Fairleigh Dickinson U., Hofstra U., Hunter Coll., 1956-59 Author: The Politics of Genocide, 2 vols., 1981, 2d rev. edit., 1994, The Hungarian Labor Service System, 1977, Hungarian Jewish Studies, 3 vols., 1966-73, Soviet Government and Politics, 1965, Human Rights, 1979; writer, editor, contbr. to books in field. Democrat. Home: 11407 Union Tpke Flushing NY 11375-6850 Office: CUNY Graduate Ctr New York NY 10016

BRAHMA, CHANDRA SEKHAR, civil engineering educator; b. Calcutta, India, Oct. 5, 1941; came to U.S., 1963; s. Nalinia Kanta and Uma Rani (Bose) B.; m. Purnima Sinha, Feb. 18, 1972; children: Charanjit, Barunashish. B in Engring., Calcutta U., 1962; MS, Mich. State U., 1965; PhD, Ohio State U., 1969. Registered profl. engr. Calif., Utah, N.H., Tex., Wis. Asst. engr. Pub. Works Dept., Calcutta, 1962-63; rsch. asst. Mich. State U., East Lansing, 1963-65; teaching and rsch. assoc. Ohio State U., Columbus, 1965-69; project engr. Frank H. Lehr Assocs., East Orange, N.J., 1969-70; sr. soils engr. John G. Reutter Assocs., Camden, N.J., 1970-72; asst. prof. Worcester (Mass.) Poly. Inst., 1972-74; prin. soils engr. Daniel, Mann, Johnson & Mendenhall, Balt., 1974-79; sr. engr. Sverdrup Corp., St. Louis, 1979-80, cons., 1980—; prof. Calif. State U., Fresno, 1980—2002, prof. emeritus, 2002—. Cons. Expert Resources, Inc., Peoria Heights, Ill., 1981—, The Twining Labs., Inc., Fresno, 1982—, Law Offices Marderosian and Swanson, Fresno, 1985—, Law Offices Hurlbutt, Clevenger, Long and Vortmann, Visalia, Calif., 1988—, Tech. Adv. Svcs. for Attys., Blue Bell, Pa., 1992—. Author: Fundaciones y Mechanica de Suelos, 1986; contbr. articles to profl. jours. Head sci. judge Calif. Cen. Valleys Sci. and Engring. Fairs, Fresno, 1988-2002. Recipient Outstanding Prof. of Yr. award Calif. State U., 1989, Halliburton award Calif. State U., 1991, Calif. Ctrl. Valley Outstanding Profl. Engr. award Calif. Soc. Profl. Engrs., 1993, Disting. Svc. award, 1994, Claude C. Laval Jr. award Innovative Tech. and Rsch. Calif. State U., 1991, 92, Portrait of Success award KSEE 24, Fresno, Calif., 1997, Std. of Excellence award Tau Beta Pi, 1997, Outstanding Prof. award Tau Beta Pi, 1998, Outstanding Prof. award NSPE, 1998; Brahma St. named in City of Bakersfield, Calif., 1989; Fulbright scholar, 1984; Hugh B. William fellow, Assn. Drilled Shaft Contractors, 1986, others. Fellow ASCE (v.p. 1983-84, pres. 1984-85, Outstanding Engr. award 1985, Disting Svc. award, 1986, Outstanding Prof. award 1985, Edmund Friedman Profl. Recognition award 1993); mem. ASTM, Am. Soc. Engring. Edn. (AT&T Found. award 1991, Outstanding Tchg. award 1997, AT ANDT Found. award for excellence in tchg. and rsch. 1991), Rotary (chair Clovis club 1986—, chair pub. rels. 1987, chair youth svcs. 1989, bd. dirs. 1989). Democrat. Hindu. Avocations: swimming, tennis, music, reading. Home and Office: 561 Houston Ave Clovis CA 93611-7032 Home Phone: 559-323-0316; Office Phone: 559-323-0316. E-mail: chandrab@csufresno.edu, csbconsultant@netscape.net, chandrab.1@netzero.net.

BRAHMS, WILLIAM BERNARD, librarian, publisher, writer; b. Camden, NJ, Oct. 1, 1966; s. William Arthur and Jane Dilks Brahms; m. Gina-Marie Lugo, Dec. 7, 1996; children: Matthew Frederick, Giovanna Elizabeth. BA with honors in Econs., Rutgers U., New Brunswick, NJ, 1989; MLS, Rutgers U., 1993; student in Law, Rutgers Sch. Law, Camden, NJ, 1990—91. Cert. profl. libr. NJ State Dept. Edn., 1993. Libr. intern South Brunswick Pub. Libr., 1992—93; refrence libr. Franklin Twp. Pub. Libr., Somerset, NJ, 1993—95, sr. reference libr., 1995—99, head adult svcs. (reference), 1999—2004; chief libr. Camden County Libr. Sys., 2004, Voorhees br. mgr., 2004—, mgr. M. Allan Vogelson Regional br.; pres., CEO Reference Desk Press, Inc., 2004—. Adv. com. mem. NJ Digitization Hwy., Trenton; com. mem. Highlands Regional Libr. Coop. Info. Svcs. Com., Denville, NJ, 1995—2004; twp. historian Twp. of Franklin, Somerset, 1999—2004; bd. mem., web master Haddon Twp. Hist. Soc., NJ, 2004—; project coord., co-creator, mgr. Shelf Life, Camden Libr. Sys., 2005—06; presenter in field. Author: (book) Images of America: Franklin Township, 1997 (Mayor's Commendation, Franklin Twp., 1998), Franklin Township, Somerset County, NJ: A History, 1998 (Mayor's Commendation, Franklin Twp., 1999); editor: Cap & Skull Centennial History and Biographical Directory, 2000; compiler: Notable Last Facts: A Compendium of Endings, Conclusions, Terminations and Final Events Throughout History, 2005, Brent J. Donaway's The Grand Old Lady: A Book Celebrating the Premiere of the Film, the History of the Westmont Theatre and Her Supporters, 2007 (Cmty. Support award, Footstep Films LLC, 2007); actor: (films) Brent J. Donaway's The Grand Old Lady, 2007. Bd. mem. Friends of the Franklin Twp. Pub. Libr., Somerset, 1993—2003; mem. Meadows Found., Somerset, 1998—2004, Raritan-Millstone Heritage Alliance, Somerset, 1998—2004, Friends of Camden County Libr. Sys., Voorhees, NJ, 2004—; bd. mem., hist. Cap and Skull Soc. Alumni Assn., New Brunswick, NJ, 1994—; bd. mem. February 1st 1845 Found., New Brunswick, NJ, 2006—. Named Author of Yr., Marconi Found., 1999; recipient High Skull, Cap & Skull Soc., Rutgers Coll., 1989, Profl. Leadership award, Rutgers U. Sch. Commn. Info. and Libr. Sci., 1999; Henry Rutgers scholar, Rutgers Coll., 1989. Mem.: ALA, Ind. Book Pubs. Assn., Small Pubs. Assn. N.Am., NJ Libr. Assn., Green Press Initiative, Phi Eta Sigma, Omicron Delta Epsilon, Phi Beta Kappa, Beta Phi Mu, Delta Phi (bd. mem., Hist. Alumni Assn., Epsilon Chpt.). Achievements include pioneering early web-based public library-hosted local history collection image and full-text searchable newspaper and photographic databases with Franklin Photo Archive. Avocations: history, genealogy, book mark collecting. Home: 305 Briarwood Ave Haddonfield NJ 08033 Office: Camden County Libr Sys 203 Laurel Rd Voorhees NJ 08043 Office Phone: 856-772-1636 ext. 3308. Office Fax: 856-858-1134. Personal E-mail: gmandwb@comcast.net. Business E-Mail: wbrahms@camden.lib.nj.us, info@referencedeskpress.com.*

BRAID, RALPH M., economics professor; b. Princeton, NJ, Oct. 1, 1953; s. Thomas H. and Mary D. Braid; m. Ann D. Harrison, June 1, 1991 (div. Mar. 22, 2002); 1 child, Julia M. AB in Physics, U. Chgo., 1975; PhD in Econs., MIT, Cambridge, Mass., 1979. Asst. prof. econs. Columbia U., NYC, 1979—88; vis. asst. prof. econs. Princeton U., 1986; assoc. prof. econs. Wayne State U., Detroit, 1988—93, prof. econs., 1993—. Mem. editl. bd. Jour. Urban Econs., 1989—2007, Am. Econ. Rev., 2006—; assoc. editor Jour. Regional Sci., 1990—, Regional Sci. and Urban Econs., 1991—2004. Contbr. articles to profl. jours. Recipient Pres.'s award for Excellence in Tchg., Wayne State U., 1992;, NSF grad. fellow, 1975—77, 1978—79. Mem.: Am. Econ. Assn., Phi Beta Kappa. Office: Wayne State U Dept Econs Detroit MI 48202 Office Phone: 313-577-2540. Office Fax: 313-577-9564. Business E-Mail: rbraid@wayne.edu.

BRAILER, DAVID J., federal agency administrator; b. Kingwood, W. Va., July 16, 1959; 1 child. M in mgmt. sci., PhD in mgmt. sci., Wharton Sch., U. Pa.; MD, W. Va. U. Sch. Medicine, 1986. Bd. cert. internal medicine 1989. Resident Hosp. at U. Pa.; founder CareScience, Inc. (formerly Care Mgmt. Sci.), Phila., 1993, chmn., CEO, 1993—2003; sr. fellow info. tech. and quality care Health Tech. Ctr. (HealthTech), San Francisco, 2003; nat. health info. tech. coord. US Dept. Health and Human Svc. (HHS), Washington, 2004—06, vice-chair, Am. Health Info. Cmty., 2006—. Recipient Charles A. Dana Scholar, U. Pa. Sch. Medicine, Robert Wood Johnson Clinical Scholar, U. Pa., Martin Eipstein award, Nat. Libr. Medicine. Achievements include first med. student to serve on bd. trusttes for AMA. Office: US Dept Health and Human Svc 200 Independence Ave SW Washington DC 20201 Office Phone: 202-690-7151. Business E-Mail: david.brailer@hhs.gov.

BRAIMAN, MARK STEPHEN, biomedical educator, researcher; b. Rochester, NY, Oct. 27, 1956; s. Alex and Pauline Dieter (Pommerenke) B. AB summa cum laude in Chemistry, Harvard U., 1977; PhD in Chemistry, U. Calif., Berkeley, 1983. Postdoctoral fellow dept. chemistry MIT, Cambridge, 1983-86; postdoctoral fellow dept. physics Boston U., 1986-87, rsch. asst. prof. dept. physics, 1987-88; asst. prof. dept. biochemistry U. Va., Charlottesville, 1988-94, assoc. prof., 1994—. Contbr. articles to profl. jours., chpts. to books. Mem. candidate selection com. All-Berkeley Coalition, 1981. NSF Grad. fellow, 1977, U. Calif. Regents fellow, 1980, Helen Hay Whitney fellow Helen Hay Whitney Found., 1983-86; Lucille P. Markey scholar Lucille P. Markey Charitable Trust, 1986-92. Mem. AAAS, Biophys. Soc., Am. Chem. Soc. Democrat. Unitarian Universalist. Achievements include use of vibrational spectroscopy to analyze the mechanisms of light-driven proton transport by bacteriorhodopsin and of chloride transport by halorhodopsin. Office: Syracuse University Chemistry Department CST 1014 Syracuse NY 13244

BRAIN, JOSEPH DAVID, biomedical researcher, educator; b. Paterson, NJ, Jan. 20, 1940; married, 1961; 3 children. SM, Harvard U., 1962, SMHyg, 1963, SDHyg, 1966. Rsch. assoc. in physiology Harvard U., Boston, 1966—68, from asst. prof. to assoc. prof., 1968—78; prof. physiology Harvard Sch. Pub. Health, Cambridge, Mass., 1978—, Cecil K. and Philip Drinker prof. environ. physiology, dir. Harvard Pulmonary

Specialized Ctr. Rsch., 1977—96, dir. respiratory biol. program, 1981—93, dir. physiology program, 1993—98, chair dept. environ. health, 1990—2005. Mem. com. Cardiovasc. and Pulmonary Study Sect. NIH, 1975-79, program project rsch. rev. com. Nat. Heart, Lung and Blood Inst., 1980-83; bd. sci. counsellors Nat. Inst. Occupl. Safety and Health, 1992-96; dir. Ctr. Environ. Health/Nat. Inst. Environ. Health Scis. Bd. trustees Taylor U., 1984—. Fellow AAAS, Am. Physiol. Soc., Am. Thoracic Soc., Reticuloendothelial Soc., Sigma Xi. Office: Harvard U Sch Pub Health 665 Huntington Ave Boston MA 02115-6021 Office Phone: 617-432-1272. E-mail: brain@hsph.harvard.edu.

BRAINARD, MELISSA, accountant; b. Buffalo, Jan. 11, 1969; d. Peter Anthony and Mary Agnes (Lazarus) Arena; m. Kevin Joseph Brainard, Sept. 25, 1993; children: Jacob Leon, Zachary Martin. BS, SUNY, Buffalo, 1991. CPA, N.Y., 1993. From staff mem. to mgr. KPMG, Buffalo, 1991-97; CFO Goodwill Industries Western N.Y., 1997-98; mgr. Deloitte & Touche, Buffalo, 1999—2002; contr. Albright-Knox Art Gallery, Buffalo, 2002—. Avocation: running marathons and ultra marathons. Personal E-mail: runningfreak@verizon.net. Business E-Mail: mbrainard@albrightknox.org.

BRAINERD, CHARLES J(ON), psychologist, mathematics professor; b. Lansing, Mich., July 30, 1944; emigrated to Can., 1971; s. Charles Donald and Geraldine Elaine (Leffler) B.; m. Susan Haske, Jan. 18, 1964 (div.); 1 dau., Tereasa Gail; m. Valerie Reyna, Oct. 5, 1985; 1 son, Bertrand. BS, Mich. State U., 1966, MA, 1968, PhD, 1970. Asst. prof. psychology U. Alta., Edmonton, Can., 1971-73, assoc. prof., 1973-76, H.M. Tory prof. social sci., 1983-86; prof. U. Western Ont., London, 1976-83, U. Ariz., Tucson, 1987—2004, U. Tex., Arlington, 2004—. Vis. prof. U. Minn., Mpls., 1980-81, So. Meth. U., Dallas, 1986-87. Author: Piaget's Theory of Intelligence, 1978, Origins of the Number Concept, 1979; editor: Alternatives to Piaget, 1978, Recent Advances in Cognitive-Developmental Theory, 1983, Springer-Verlag Series in Cognitive Development, 1979—, Devel. Rev., 2000—; assoc. editor: Behavioral and Brain Scis., 1980—. Fellow Am. Psychol. Assn., Can. Psychol. Assn. (pres. devel. psychology sect. 1986-87); mem. Psychonomic Soc., Soc. for Research in Child Devel. (assoc. editor Child Devel. 1977-80). Office: Univ Texas Psychology Dept Arlington TX 76019 Home Phone: 817-468-0449; Office Phone: 817-272-1202. Business E-Mail: brainerd@uta.edu.

BRAINERD, RICHARD CHARLES, human resources executive, consultant, educator; b. LA, Dec. 22, 1944; s. Calvin Richard and Charlotte Louise (Roethe) B.; m. Phyllis Jean Cottingham Wentzel, July 14, 1966, (div. Dec. 1980); children: Bret, Staci; m. Mary Keith Knopp, Mar. 31, 1984; children: Andrew, Mary Angela. BS in Bus. and Econs., U. Wis., 1968; grad. leadership devel. program, Ctr. for Creative Leadership, Greensboro, NC, 1985. Pers. analyst Wis. Bur. Personnel, Madison, 1968-74; dir. pers., asst. adminstr. for adminstrn. Wis. Dept. Justice, Madison, 1974-80; dep. commr. pers. Minn. Dept. Employee Rels., St. Paul, 1980-85; dir. pers. Ramsey County, St. Paul, 1985-97; human resources dir. Met. Coun., St. Paul, 1997—2004; dir. human resources Am. Red Cross, St. Paul, 2004—05; cons. project CPS-HR, Washington, 2004—. Instr. U. Minn. Carlson Sch. Mgmt. Employer Edn. Svc., Mpls., 1985-2003; co-chair, mem. exec. bd. Twin Cities Area Labor-Mgmt. Coun., Mpls., 1994—; advisor Inst. for Labor Mgmt. Studies, White Bear Lake, Minn., 1997; speaker on human rels., expert witness, 1985—; cons. Qualified Neutral Alt. Dispute Resolution, 2005— Coach Mahtomedi (Minn.) Youth Baseball Assn., 1992-97; vice chair Bd. of Pub. Works, Madison, Wis., 1979-80; vice chair, mem. fin. com. City of Mahtomedi, 1994—, city coun., 2004—; pres. Riverside Lions, St. Paul, Minn., 1995-98; bd. dir. ARC North Ctrl. Blood Svcs., St. Paul, Minn., 2003—; bd. dirs. Minn. State Colls. and Univs. Found., 2006—. Mem. Pub. Employer Labor Rels. Assn., Minn. Pub. Employer Labor Rels. Assn., Internat. Pub. Mgmt. Assn. Human Resources (pres. 1990, bd. dirs.; hon. life, Stockberger award), St. Paul Human Resource Dirs. Assn. (pres., v.p., sec.-treas.), Nat. League of Cities (human devel. policy and adv. com. 2006), League Minn. Cities (bd. dirs. 2007—). Lutheran. Avocations: skiing, hunting, birdwatching, swimming, reading. Home: 1823 Park Ave Mahtomedi MN 55115-1932 E-mail: richardbrainerd@comcast.net.

BRAININ, STACY L., lawyer; b. Houston, Jan. 3, 1959; BA with high honors, U. Tex., 1981, JD with high honors, 1984. Bar: Tex. 1984, admitted to practice: US Dist. Ct. (No. Dist.) Tex. 1986, US Ct. Appeals (5th Cir.) 1986, US Dist. Ct. (Ea. Dist.) Tex. 1987, US Supreme Ct. 1991. Ptnr., antitrust & white collar criminal defense Haynes and Boone LLP, Dallas. Assoc. editor Tex. Law Rev., 1983—84. Mem.: Dallas Bar Assn. (Antitrust & Trade Regulation Sect.), ABA (Litig. Sect., Criminal Justice Sect. white collar crime com. healthcare fraud subcom), Phi Beta Kappa, Order of Coif. Office: Haynes and Boone LLP 901 Main St Ste 3100 Dallas TX 75202-3789 Office Phone: 214-651-5584. Office Fax: 214-200-0373. Business E-Mail: stacy.brainin@haynesboone.com.

BRAISTED, MARY JO, elementary school educator; b. Rochester, Minn., July 28, 1957; d. George Richard and Maxine Helen Hays; 1 child from previous marriage, Jennifer. BBA, Fla. Atlantic U., Boca Raton, 1981, BA in Elem. Edn., 2001, MEd in Ednl. Leadership, 2007. Mgr. mktg. adminstrn. IBM Corp., Boca Raton, 1982—84, mgr. product scheduling, 1985—88; vol. St. Joan of Arc, Boca Raton, 1989—96; tchr. Boca Raton Elem. Sch., 2001—. Sch. adv. com. chair, mem. profl. devel. com., PTA/faculty liaison Boca Raton Elem. Sch., 2003—06; instr. Sci. IDEAS, Boca Raton, 2005. Mem. Rep. Women's Club, 2003—06. Named Tchr. of the Yr., Rotary, 2006. Mem.: Nat. Sci. Tchrs. Assn. (presenter 2005). Roman Catholic. Avocations: travel, reading, walking. Home: 1100 Pepperidge Ter Boca Raton FL 33486 Office: Boca RatonElem Sch 103 SW 1st Ave Boca Raton FL 33432 Office Phone: 561-338-1454.

BRAITERMAN, THEA GILDA, economics professor, state legislator; b. Balt., Sept. 11, 1927; d. Isaac E. and Clara (Fink) Bloom; m. Marvin Braiterman, Mar. 21, 1948; children: Kenneth, Marta, David. BS, Johns Hopkins U., 1949; MA, U. Md., 1966; PhD, Union Inst., 1977. Assoc. prof. econs. Balt. Coll. of Commerce, 1973—93; prof. econs. New England Coll., Henniker, NH, 1973—, prof. emeritus, 1992—; mem. NH Ho. of Reps., 1988-94. Cons. on retirement, 1988—; selectman Town of Henniker, 1997-2005. Author: Workbook on Economic Theory, 1966; contbr. articles to profl. jours. Sec., bd. govs. United Way of Merrimack County, Concord, N.H., 1984-90; v.p., bd. govs. Cmty. Svcs. Coun., Concord, 1980-84. Jane Addams Peace Assn. grantee, 1976-77; Gilmore grantee New Eng. Coll., 1988-90. Mem. Am. Econ. Assn., Ea. Econ. Assn. Home: PO Box 686 Henniker NH 03242-0686 Office: New England Coll Henniker NH 03242 E-mail: theabrait@tds.net.

BRAITHWAITE, BARBARA JO, retired secondary school educator; BA, Ctrl. Mich. U., 1959; MA, U. Mich., 1960. Geography tchr. Pocono Mountain Sch. Dist., Swiftwater, Pa., 1980—2001; ret., 2001. Recipient 1st Place award Am. Express geography competition for tchrs., 1990, Outstanding Secondary Level Tchr. of the Year award Pa. Coun. Social Studies, 1992, Innovative Tchg. award State Farm Ins. Co., 1995, US, Russia, Ukraine Tchr. Excellence award Am. Couns. for Internat. Edn., US State Dept., 1997, Pa. Tchr. of Yr. award Dept. Edn., 1999. Mem.: Pa. Assn. Sch. Retirees (life), Nat. State Tchrs. of Yr. Pa. (life). Home: 65 Garnet Ln Stones Throw East Stroudsburg PA 18301 Personal E-mail: bjb65@aol.com.

BRAITHWAITE, WILFRED JOHN, physics professor; b. Ferndale, Wash., Apr. 11, 1940; s. John Alfred and Joyce Elinor (Gunderson) B.; m. Wanda Pearl Chism, June 3, 1961 (div. 1975). BS in Physics with honors, Seattle Pacific U., 1962; MS in Physics, U. Wash., 1965, PhD in Physics, 1971; postgrad., U. Tex., 1988-89. Instr. physics Princeton (N.J.) U., 1970-72; asst. prof. physics U. Tex., Austin, 1972-79, rsch. scientist faculty, 1979-81; tech. and sci. cons. Austin, 1981-89; assoc. prof. physics U. Ark., Little Rock, 1989-95, prof. physics, 1995—. Vis. staff mem. Los Alamos (N.Mex.) Nat. Lab., 1975-76, 78-79; vis. scientist Ind. U., Bloomington, 1990-96; affiliate prof. physics U. Wash., Seattle, 1991-96; sci. assoc. PPE divsn. CERN, Geneva, Switzerland, 1992—; guest scientist Brookhaven Nat. Lab., Upton, N.Y., 1992—; lectr. in field; grant referee Ark. Sci. and Tech. Authority, 1990—; cons. for GE Corp. R&D, 2002—. Numerous unedited contbns.; jour. referee Phys. Rev. C and Phys. Rev. Letters, 1970—, Found. Physics, Assoc. Ed. Ark. Acad. Sci., 2000—. U.S. Dept. Energy rsch. grantee, 1992-95, 99—, Ark. Sci. and Tech. Authority rsch. grantee, 1993-94, 96-98; numerous grants from NSF, Dept. of Energy, Robert A Welch Found. Mem. IEEE, Am. Phys. Soc., Nat. Assn. for Rsch. in Sci. Teaching, N.Y. Acad. Sci., Ark. Acad. Sci. Achievements include rsch. of time reversal invariance; high excitation neutron particle-hole states; charge-dependent matrix elements in light nuclei; method for determining rotational symmetries of nuclear states using heavy ions; multiply-excited atomic states in helium-like and lithium-like oxygen; strength of the 3-alpha process in stellar helium burning; method for identifying antimatter stars; large isospin mixing in light nuclei via scattering comparisons of positive and negative pions near the pion-nucleon resonance; measurement limits on source sizes formed in symmetric collisions of ultra-relativistic heavy nuclei; method for separating charged kaons and pions in Time Projection Chambers via in-flight decays; instrument design for high-energy nuclear physics. Home: 1 Broadmoor Dr Little Rock AR 72204-4818 Office: Univ of Ark at Little Rock Dept Physics and Astronomy 2801 S University Ave Little Rock AR 72204 E-mail: wjbraith@comcast.net.

BRAKAS, NORA JACHYM, education educator; b. Schenectady, NY, Aug. 9, 1952; d. Thaddeus Michael and Theresa Mary (Patnode) J.; m. Jurgis Brakas, June 15, 1996. BS in Elem. Edn., Plattsburg State U. Coll., 1974; MS in Reading, SUNY, Albany, 1977, Cert. Advanced Study in Reading, 1986, PhD in Reading, 1990. Cert. elem. sch. tchr., reading tchr. Elem. sch. and reading tchr. Lee (Mass.) Ctrl. Sch., 1976-82; reading specialist Guilderland (N.Y.) Sch. Dist., 1988-89; rsch. asst., tchg. asst. SUNY, Albany, 1985-88, instr. reading dept., 1989-90; asst. prof. tchr. edn., reading specialist Southeastern La. U., Hammond, 1990-91, Marist Coll., Poughkeepsie, NY, 1991—. Presenter, spkr. in field. Contbr. articles to profl. jours. Student Literacy Corp. grantee U.S. Dept. Edn., 1991, IBM/Marist Joint Study Project grantee, 1992. Mem. Internat. Reading Assn., Soc. Children's Book Writers and Illustrators. Avocations: drawing, writing children's books, collecting antique children's books. Home: PO Box 176 Rhinecliff NY 12574-0176 Office: Marist Coll 388 F Dyson Poughkeepsie NY 12601 E-mail: Nora.Brakas@Marist.edu.

BRAKE, CECIL CLIFFORD, retired diversified manufacturing executive; b. Ystrad, Mynach, Wales, Nov. 14, 1932; came to U.S., 1967; s. Leonard James and Ivy Gertrude (Berry) B.; m. Vera Morris, Aug. 14, 1954; children— Stephen John, Richard Colin, Vanessa Elaine Chartered engr.; B.Sc. in Engring., U. Wales, 1954; M.Sc., Cranfield Inst., Bedford, Eng., 1957; grad. A.M.P., Harvard U. Sch. Bus., 1985. Mgr. research and devel. Schrader Fluid Power, Wake Forest, NC, 1968-70, engring. mgr., 1970-75; mng. dir. Schrader U.K. Fluid Power, 1975-77; v.p., gen. mgr. Schrader Internat., 1977-78; group v.p. Schrader Bellows, Fluid Power, Akron, Ohio, 1978-82; exec. v.p. Scovill, Inc., Waterbury, Conn., 1982-86; pres. Yale Security, Inc. subs. Scovill, Inc.; group exec. Eagle Industries, Inc., Chgo., 1986—; retired, 1997. Chief oper. officer Mansfield (Ohio) Plumbing Products Inc., Hart and Cooley Inc., Holland, Mich., Caron Internat., Inc., Rochelle, Ill., Caron Internat., Inc., Rochelle, Ill., Chemineer Inc., Dayton, Ohio, Pulsafeeder Inc., Rochester, N.Y., Clevaflex Inc., Cleve., Equality Specialties Inc., N.Y.C., De Vilbiss Co., Toledo, Hill Refrigeration, Trenton, N.J., Air-Maze Corp., Bedford Heights, Ohio, Burns Aerospace Corp., Winston Salem, N.C., Atlantic Industries, Inc., Nutley, N.J., Stimsonite Products, Niles, Ill.; ptnr., owner Prince of Wales Inc.; bd. dirs. CFI Industries. Avocations: sailing, golf. Office: Eagle Industries Inc 2 N Riverside Plz Chicago IL 60606-2600 Home: 1461 Sabal Palm Dr Boca Raton FL 33432 also: 112 Melville Ave Fairfield CT 06825-2005 E-mail: cecilcliffb@aol.com.

BRAKE, WILLIE EDWARD, computer company executive, educator; b. Farmington Hills, Mich., Dec. 25, 1973; s. Frances Helen and Willie Edward Brake; 1 child, Olivia Madison Zeigler-Brake. B in Interdisciplinary Studies, Wayne State U., Detroit, 1996; M in Bus. Adminstrn./Tech. Mgmt., U. Phoenix, Southfield, Mich., 1999. Microsoft Certified Profl. Microsoft Corp., Wash., 2001, Microsoft Office Specialist Microsoft Corp., Wash., 2001, CompTIA A+ Certified Ill., 2001, Certified Netware Adminstr. Novell Corp., Mass., 2001. Network adminstr. Wayne State U., Detroit, 1991—95; systems analyst Ford Motor Co., Dearborn, Mich., 1995—96; bus. analyst DaimlerChrysler Corp., Auburn Hills, Mich., 1996—99, EDS Corp., Troy, Mich., 1999—2000; sr. bus. systems analyst Sony Corp., San Diego, 2000—00; systems adminstrn. mgr. KMart Corp., Atlanta, 2001—01; systems analyst Ford Motor Co., 2001—02; adj. prof. U. Phoenix, 2001—; pres., CEO All About Tech., Inc., Detroit, 2001—. Counselor Svc. Corps of Ret. Execs., Detroit, 2004—. Vol. Jr. Achievement, Detroit, 1996—2005; mem. Bus. Adv. Coun., Washington, 2005—05; chmn. bd. Ctr. For Creative Arts, Inc., Detroit, 2001—05. Recipient Nat. Rep. Leadership award, Nat. Rep. Congl. Com., 2005, Presdl. Acad. Fitness award, The White House, 1989, 1990, 1991; grantee Small Bus. award, Mich. Dept. Labor and Econ. Growth, 2005; Robert O. Cork Scholarship, 1995. Mem.: IEEE, NAACP (assoc.), Computing Tech. Industry Assn., BBB, Nat. Assn. of the Self Employed, Local Bus. Network, Booker T. Wash. Bus. Assn., Detroit Regional C. of C., Big Bros. and Big Sisters of Southeastern Mich., United Way of Southeastern Mich., Nat. Honor Soc. (hon.), Alpha Phi Alpha Frat., Inc. (life). R-Liberal. Pentecostal. Avocations: travel, camping, reading, cooking, physical fitness. Home: 19785 W 12 Mile Rd Southfield MI 48076 Office: All About Technology Inc 2727 Second Ave Ste 131 Detroit MI 48201 Office Phone: 313-218-4888. Office Fax: 313-962-2429. Personal E-mail: wbrake@wayne.edu, wbrake@all-about-technology.com.

BRAKE, YVONNE MARIE, not-for-profit developer; b. Youngstown, Ohio, Sept. 5, 1953; d. John Allen and Pearl Jean McMillan; m. Darryl Arlan Brake, May 12, 1979; children: Michael E. Forney II, Daren A. BA in Mgmt., Malone Coll, Canton, Ohio, 1998; MA, Case Western Res. U., Cleve., 2001; grad. in Ch. Theilogy, Ashland Theol. Seminary, Ohio, 2002. With devel. dept. Haven Rest Ministries, Akron, Ohio, 1989—98, dir. devel., 1998—; exec. dir. Because He Cares, Inc., Akron, 1980—. Cons. East Akron Com. Ho., 2002—05, EANDC, Akron, 2002—05; presenter in field. Author: (plays) No Choices Left, 1984; co-author Experience In Pride, 1986, (learning module) Teaching Children To Give, 2003. Exec. dir., founder; bd. mem. Jubilee Temple Ch., Akron, 2004—, ABC, Inc., Akron, 1995—98. Recipient Black Woman Excellence award, Summit County YWCA, Akron, 1996, Woman Excellence, Akron Black Woman Leadership Caucas, Akron, 2004. Mem.: Akron Urban League, Akron Cmty. Svc. Ctr., Assn. Gospel Rescue Missions, Christian Cmty. Devel. Assn., Assn. Fundraising Profls. (bd. mem. 2005), Nat. Ctr. Black Philanthropy, Ohio Assn. Family and Consumer Sci. (Friends and Family award 2003). Avocations: writing, singing, dance, weightlifting, walking. Office: Haven Rest Ministries 175 E Market St Akron OH 44308

BRAKELEY, GEORGE ARCHIBALD, JR., fundraising consultant; b. Washington, Apr. 18, 1916; s. George Archibald and Lillian (Fay) B.; m. Roxana Byerly; children: George Archibald III, Deborah Fay, Joan Keller. BA, U. Pa., 1938. V.p., dir. John Price Jones Co., Inc. (fund-raising counsel), NYC; pres., treas. John Price Jones Co. (Can.), Ltd., 1950-52; chmn., CEO G.A. Brakeley & Co., Ltd., 1952-61, G.A. Brakeley & Co., Inc., LA, 1956-69; chmn., chief exec. officer Brakeley, John Price Jones Inc., 1972-83; chmn. Brakeley, John Price Jones, Inc., 1983-87, sr. cons., 1987—. Author: Tested Ways to Successful Fund Raising. Trustee Ctr. for the Study of the Presidency. Capt. C.E. AUS, WWII. Mem. Mayflower Soc., Anglers Club (N.Y.C.), Montreal Racket Club (hon.), Wee Burn Golf Club (Darien, Conn.), Royal Poinciana Golf Club (Naples, Fla.). Episcopalian.

BRAKEMAN, LOUIS FREEMAN, retired university official; b. Kalamazoo, Nov. 9, 1932; s. Louis Freeman and Ruth Adelaide (Parsons) B.; m. Lori Mallett, Aug. 16, 1953; children: David, Mark, Peter, Paul, Amy. BA, Kalamazoo Coll., 1954; MA, Fletcher Sch. Diplomacy, Tufts U., 1955, PhD, 1963; LHD, Denison U., 1985. Lectr. history Brown U., 1958-59; asst. prof. polit. sci. Carroll Coll., Waukesha, Wis., 1959-62; mem. faculty Denison U., Granville, Ohio, 1962-85, prof. polit. sci., 1968-85, chmn. dept., 1965-70, dean Coll., 1970-73, provost, 1973-85, acting pres., 1974-75; dir. research project faculty devel. Gt. Lakes Colls. Assn., 1985-86; provost Stetson U., DeLand, Fla., 1987-93. Vis. prof. polit. sci. Kalamazoo Coll., 1987; vis. scholar center for Study of Higher Edn. U. Mich., 1980; dir. Regional Council Center for Internat. Students, summers 1966-68; chmn. regional selection com. Danforth Found. Assocs. Program, 1971-73; mem. Common Cause, 1972—. Co-author: Research Problems in American Politics, 1969, What One Has Within, What the Context Provides, 1989; contbr. articles to profl. jours. Pres. Volusia County Arts Coun., 1994-96, West Volusia Habitat for Humanity, 1996-98; sec. DeLand Mus. Art, 2000-01. Fulbright scholar India, 1957-58; Danforth grad. fellow, 1954-57 Mem. ACLU, Nature Conservancy, Audubon Soc., Public Radio, Phi Beta Kappa. Presbyterian (elder). Avocation: birdwatching. Home: 10 Northlake Dr Orange City FL 32763 Personal E-mail: lbrakema@earthlink.net.

BRAKER, GREGORY S., lawyer; b. Beaver Dam, Wis., June 19, 1962; BA magna cum laude, Evangel Coll., 1984; MA with honors, U. Md., 1987; JD, Georgetown U., 1992. Bar: Md. 1992, DC 1995, admitted to practice: US Dist. Ct. (Dist. Md.), US Dist. Ct. (DC), US Dist. Ct. (Ea. Dist.) Va., US Ct. Appeals (4th Cir.). Ptnr., Corp. Def. Dept. & Environ. Dept. Venable LLP, Washington. Lectr. in field. Co-author: The Knock on the Door: Preparing for, and Responding to, a Criminal Investigation, 1999; contbr. Mem.: Environ. Law Inst., Bar Assn. DC, ABA (Natural Resources, Environment & Energy Law Sects.), Md. State Bar Assn. Avocation: coaching youth sports teams. Office: Venable LLP 575 7th St NW Washington DC 20004 Office Phone: 202-344-4807. Office Fax: 202-344-8300. Business E-Mail: gsbraker@venable.com.

BRAKER, WILLIAM PAUL, retired aquarium executive, ichthyologist; b. Chgo., Nov. 3, 1926; s. William Paul and Minnie (Wassermann) B.; m. Patricia Reese, Sept. 2, 1950. BS, Northwestern U., 1950; MS, George Washington U., 1953; student, U. Chgo., 1955—60. Mem. staff John G. Shedd Aquarium, Chgo., 1953—94, dir., 1964—93, hon. trustee, 2005; asst. sec. Shedd Aquarium Soc., 1960-65, sec., 1965-94; ret., 1994. Served with AUS, 1950-52. Named to Centennial Honor Roll, Am. Assn. Museums, 2006. Mem.: Am. Assn. Zool. Parks and Aquariums, Assn. Zoos and Aquariums (bd. mem. 1968—75, 1991—93, pres. 1973—74, President's award, Outstanding Svc. award, Disting. Svc. award, R. Marlin Perkins award 1999), Nature Conservancy, Ill. chpt., Soc. Marine Mammalogy, Am. Fisheries Soc., Am. Soc. Icthyologists and Herpetologists, Internat. Union Dirs. Zool. Gardens.*

BRAKER, WILLIAM PAUL, music educator; b. Harvey, Ill., June 10, 1957; s. William Paul and Patricia Reese Braker; m. Joan Miller, Oct. 6, 1957; children: Sydney Ann, Calvin James. MusB in Edn., Nothern Ill. U., 1980; MusM in Edn., VanderCook Coll. Music, 1990. Band dir. Odell Schs., Ill., 1980—81; music tchr. Chadwick Schs., Ill., 1981—84; band dir. Forrestville Valley #221, Forreston, Ill., 1984—. Music adv. com. Ill. HS Assn., Bloomington, 2003—05. Pres., bd. deacons North Grove Ch., Forreston, 2005—07. Named Tchr. of Yr., Forrestville Valley #221, 1990. Mem.: Nat. Band Assn. (assoc.), Ill. Music Educators Assn. (assoc.; bd. dirs. 1992—97). Achievements include IHSA music sweepstakes Class C state champions, 1993, 2000-07. Avocations: hunting, outdoor activities. Home: 14264 W Coffman Rd Forreston IL 61030 Office: Forrestville Valley #221 601 E Main St Forreston IL 61030 Home Phone: 815-938-2245; Office Phone: 815-938-2195. Business E-Mail: cbraker@fvdistrict221.org.

BRAKKE, MYRON KENDALL, retired research chemist, educator; b. Fillmore County, Minn., Oct. 23, 1921; s. John T. and Hulda Christina (Marburger) B.; m. Betty-Jean Einbecker, Aug. 16, 1947; children: Kenneth Allen, Thomas Warren, Joan Patricia, Karen Elizabeth. BS, U. Minn., 1943, PhD, 1947; DSc (hon.), U. Nebr., 1996. Rsch. assoc. Bklyn. Bot. Garden, 1947-52; rsch assoc. U. Ill., 1952-55; rsch. chemist U.S. Dept. Agr., Lincoln, Nebr., 1955-86. Prof. plant pathology U. Nebr., Lincoln, 1955-86. Editor: Virology, 1960-66; contbr. articles to profl. jours. Fellow AAAS, Am. Phytopath. Soc. (Award of Distinction 1988); mem. Am. Chem. Soc., Nat. Acad. Scis., Sigma Xi, Phi Lambda Upsilon, Gamma Sigma Delta, Alpha Zeta. Home: 4429-103 Columbine Dr Bellingham WA 98226 E-mail: mkbrakke@mac.com.

BRAKKEN, WILLIAM, construction executive; Grad., Wash. State Univ. CPA. Mgmt. positions Weyerhaeuser Co., American-Strewell; fin. mgmt. positions Lanoga Corp., Redmond, Wash., 1982—88, v.p., then exec. v.p., CFO, 1988—2006; exec. v.p., CFO Pro-Build Holdings Inc., So. Plainfield, NJ, 2006—. Office: Pro-Build Holdings Inc 1 Cragwood Rd South Plainfield NJ 07080 Office Fax: (426) 882-2959.*

BRALEY, BRUCE, congressman; b. Grinnell, IA, Oct. 30, 1957; m. Carolyn Kalb, 1983; children: Lisa, David, Paul. BA, Iowa State U., 1980; JD, U. Iowa, 1983. Atty. Dutton, Braun, Staack and Hellman, PLC; mem. US Congress from 1st Iowa dist., 2007—, mem. oversight & govtl. reform com., small bus. com., transp. & infrastructure com. Mem., Bd. Dirs. Iowa Legal Aid. Pres. Waterloo Dollars for Scholars prog., Big Brothers/Big Sisters of Northeast Iowa; mem., Platform Com. 2nd Congl. Dist. Dem. Party, 1998, Black Hawk County Dem. Party, 1998—2004, 1st Congl. Dist. Dem. Party, 2004; vol. Kerry Edwards Campaign, 2004; precinct coord. John Edwards for Pres. Campaign, 2004. Co-recipient Couple of Yr., Big Brothers/Big Sisters of Northeast Iowa; recipient Vol. Performance award, Cedar Valley Mayor, 1998. Mem.: Vis. Nurses Assn., Iowa Trial Lawyers Assn. Democrat. Presbyterian. Office: 1408 Longworth House Office Bldg Washington DC 20515 also: 501 Sycamore St Ste 623 Waterloo IA 50703*

BRALEY, OLETA PEARL, community health nurse, writer; b. Rochester, NY, July 19, 1944; d. Horace Everet and Ruby Doris Sullivan; m. Edward Walter Plow, June 24, 1967 (div. Jan. 10, 1990); children: James Edward Plow, John Patrick Plow; m. Franklin John Braley, Mar. 17, 1990 (dec. 1992). Lic. in cosmetology, Continental Sch. Beauty, 1966; student, Sch. Visual Arts, NYC, 1963. Prodn. Kodak Park, Rochester, 1964—66; hairdresser local salons Rochester, 1966—80; money room oper. AMSA, Rochester, 1986—90; home health aide Tender Loving Care, Rochester, 1990—97; home health caretaker Via Health II, Rochester, 1992—2004, Home Care Plus, 2004—. Author: (poetry book) Best of the 90's, 1996,

Best Poetry and Poets, 2002; composer: (songs) Remember, 1997, Wondering, 1997, Here to Stay, A Country Letter; featured (on-air interview) with Brian Jobel, N.Y.C., 1999, author various poems in field; lyricist: Our American Vet, 2005, staff writer: Countrywine Pub., 2005—. Recipient Editor's Choice award, Internat. Soc. Poetry, 1995—98, 2002. Avocations: music, art, writing, playing piano and cello. Home: 91 B Green Leaf Meadows Rochester NY 14612-4347

BRALY, ANGELA FICK, health insurance company executive, lawyer; b. July 2, 1961; married; 3 children. BBA, Tex. Tech. U., 1983; JD, So. Meth. U., 1985. Bar: Mo. 1985. Ptnr. Lewis Rice & Fingersh LC, St. Louis, 1987—99; interim gen. counsel RightCHOICE Managed Care Inc., St. Louis, 1997—98, exec. v.p., gen. counsel., corp. sec., 1999—2003; pres., CEO Blue Cross Blue Shield of Mo., St. Louis, 2003—05; exec. v.p., gen. counsel, chief pub. affairs officer WellPoint, Inc., Indpls., 2005—07; pres., CEO Wellpoint, Inc., Indpls., 2007—. Bd. dirs. Wellpoint, Inc., 2007—. Named one of The 25 Most Influential Women in Bus., St. Louis Bus. Jour., 2000, The Top 25 Women in Healthcare, Modern Healthcare mag., 2007. Mem.: ABA, Am. Health Lawyers Assn., State Bar Mo., Bar Assn. Met. St. Louis, St. Louis Health Lawyers Network. Office: WellPoint Inc 120 Monument Cir Indianapolis IN 46204 Office Phone: 317-488-6000.

BRAM, LEON LEONARD, publishing company executive; b. Chgo., Sept. 20, 1931; s. Samuel and Rose Bram; m. Doris A. Hebel, Apr. 29, 1961 (div. 1972); children: Mark James, Alexander Anton; m. Joanne Frances Casino, Sept. 30, 1978 (div. 1990); 1 child, Victoria Lynn. B.Sc., DePaul U., 1967. Various positions Chgo. Pub. Library, 1949-55, F.E. Compton Co., Chgo., 1955-63; dir. editorial rsch. Standard Ednl. Corp., Chgo., 1963-69; exec. editor F.E. Compton Co., Chgo., 1969-74; v.p., editorial dir. Primedia Reference Corp., Mahwah, NJ, 1974-97, arts adminstr., 1998, non-profit mktg. mgr., 1999—. Mem. ALA.

BRAMAN, NORMAN, automotive and former sports team executive; b. West Chester, Pa., Aug. 22, 1932; s. Harry and Katie (Rappaport) B.; m. Irma Miller, Sept. 30, 1956; children: Debra Braman Shack, Susan Lynn. BA, Temple U., 1955. With mktg. and sales dept. Seagrams Distbrs., NYC, 1955-57; founder Keystone Stores, Phila., 1957-72; pres. Braman Enterprises, Miami, Fla., 1972—; owner Phila. Eagles, 1985—94; chmn. ARCONA, Miami, 1985-87. Mem. U.S. Holocaust Meml. Council; campaign chmn. United Jewish Appeal, Miami; bd. govs. U. Miami Med. Sch.; bd. dirs. Am. Israel Pub. Affairs Com., Miami; mem. Dade County Planning and Adv. Bd.; founder, trustee Mt. Sinai Med. Ctr., Miami; bd. govs. Tel Aviv U.; trustee United Israel Appeal Named one of Top 200 Collectors, ARTnews Mag., 2004. Mem. Greater Miami C. of C. Republican. Avocation: Collecting modern and contemporary art, especially Am. Office: Braman Enterprises 2060 Biscayne Blvd Fl 2 Miami FL 33137-5024

BRAMANTI, FRANK J., insurance company executive; CPA. Mgmt. positions through exec. v.p., CFO, interim pres. HCC Ins. Holdings, Houston, 1980—2001, bd. dir., 2001—, CEO, 2006—. Office: HCC Insurance Holdings 13403 Northwest Fwy Houston TX 77040*

BRAMBLE, JAMES HENRY, mathematician, educator; b. Annapolis, Md., Dec. 1, 1930; s. Charles Clinton and Edith (Rinker) B.; m. Margaret Hospital Hays, June 25, 1977; children: Margot, Tamara, Mary, James; 1 stepchild, Myron A. Hays. AB, Brown U., 1953; MA, U. Md., 1955, PhD, 1958; D.Sc. (hon.), Chalmers U. Tech., Göteborg, Sweden, 1985. Mathematician Gen. Electric Co., Cin., 1957-59, Naval Ordnance Lab., White Oak, Md., 1959-60; asst. prof., assoc. prof., prof. U. Md., 1960-68; prof. Cornell U., Ithaca, N.Y., 1968-94, prof. emeritus, 1994; prof. Tex. A&M U., College Station, 1994-99, disting. prof., 1999—. Dir. Center Applied Math., 1974-80; cons. Brookhaven Nat. Lab., 1976-94; vis. prof. Chalmers U. Tech., Göteborg, 1970, 72, 73, 76, 86, U. Rome, 1966-67, Ecole Poly., Paris, 1978, Lausanne, Switzerland, 1979; vis. prof. U. Paris, 1981; lectr. in field. Chmn. editorial bd. Mathematics of Computation, 1975-84; contbr. articles profl. jours. Mem. Am. Math. Soc., Soc. Indsl. and Applied Math. Office: Cornell U Dept Of Math Ithaca NY 14853 also: Tex A&M U Dept Math College Station TX 77843-0001 E-mail: bramble@math.tamu.edu.

BRAMBLE, LAURA, library director; b. Wis. BA, U. Wis.; MLS, U. Ill. With Ctrl. Libr. Indpls.-Marion County Pub. Libr., 1970—80, dir. tech. svcs. and collection devel., dir. collection mgmt. and dir. Ctrl. Libr. and COO, 1992—, interim CEO, 2007—; temp. spl. projects libr. corp. libr., Houston; br. mgr. Harris County Pub. Libr., Houston; dir. Avon-Washington Twp. Pub. Libr., Hendricks County, Ind., 1986—92. Office: Indpls Marion County Pub Libr Interim Ctrl Libr 202 N Alabama St Indianapolis IN 46204

BRAMBLE, RONALD LEE, lawyer, consultant; b. Pauls Valley, Okla., Sept. 9, 1937; s. Homer Lee and Ethyle Juanita (Stephens) Bramble; m. Kathryn Louise Seiler, July 2, 1960; children: Julia Dawn, Kristin Lee. AA, San Antonio Coll., 1957; BS, Trinity U., 1959, MS, 1964; JD, St. Mary's U., 1975; DBA, Ind. No. U., 1973. Cert. lay spkr. Meth. Ch. Mgr., guyer Fed-Mart, Inc., San Antonio, 1959—61; tchr. bus. San Antonio Ind. Sch. Dist., 1961—65, edn. coord., bus. tng. specialist, 1965—67; assoc. prof., chmn. dept. mgmt. San Antonio Coll., 1967—73; prin. Ron Bramble Assocs., San Antonio, 1967—77; pres. Adminstrv. Rsch. Assocs., Inc., 1977—82; v.p. PIA, Inc., 1982—83; v.p. fin. Solar 21 Corp., 1983—84; sr. staff Ausburn, Astoria & Seale (formerly Ausburn, O'Neill & Assocs.), San Antonio, 1984—89; pvt. practice, 1990—. Cons., comptr. TEL-STAR Sys., Inc., 1993—95; v.p. MegaTronics Internat. Corp., 1995—2003; pres. Freight Mate, San Antonio, 2003—; lectr. bus., edn. and ch. groups, 1965—. Cons. editor: Prentice-Hall, Inc., 1969—71; contbr. articles to profl. jours. Mem.: ABA, Adminstrv. Mgmt. Soc. (pres. 1966—68, Merit award 1968), Comml. Law League, Christian Legal Soc., Acad. Mgmt., Nat. Assn. Bus. Economists, Internat. Assn. Cons. to Bus., Internat. Platform Assn., Sales and Mktg. Execs. San Antonio (bd. dirs. 1967—68, Disting. Salesman award 1967), Bus. Edn. Tchrs. Assn. (pres. 1964), San Antonio C. of C., World Affairs Coun. of San Antonio, Am. Soc. Trial Cons., Toastmasters, Lions, Phi Delta Phi. Republican. Home: 127 Palo Duro St San Antonio TX 78232-3026 Personal E-mail: rlbramble@aol.com.

BRAMBLETT, GEORGE, JR., lawyer; b. Dallas, May 28, 1940; BA, So. Meth. U., 1963, LLB, 1966. Bar: Tex. 1966. Ptnr., Litig. Haynes and Boone LLP, Dallas. Spkr. in field; contbr. articles to profl. jour. Named Trial Lawyer of Yr., Dallas Bar Assn., 2001. Fellow: Am. Bar Found., Tex. Bar Found., Internat. Soc. Barristers, Am. Bd. Trial Advocates, Internat. Acad. Trial Lawyers, Am. Coll. Trial Lawyers; mem.: Tex. Assn. Def. Counsel, ABA, Phi Delta Phi. Office: Haynes and Boone LLP 901 Main St Ste 3100 Dallas TX 75202-3789 Office Phone: 214-651-5574. Office Fax: 241-200-0374. Business E-Mail: george.bramblett@haynesboone.com.

BRAME, JOSEPH ROBERT, III, lawyer; b. Hopkinsville, Ky., Apr. 18, 1942; s. Joseph Robert and Atwood Ruth (Davenport) B.; m. Mary Jane Blake, June 11, 1966; children: Rob, Blake, Virginia, John, Thomas. BA with high honors, Vanderbilt U., 1964; LLB, Yale U., 1967. Bar: Va. 1968, D.C. 2001. Assoc. McGuire, Woods, Battle & Boothe, Richmond, Va., 1967-72, ptnr., 1972-97; mem. NLRB, 1997-2000; shareholder Ogletree, Deakins, Nash, Smoak & Stewart, P.C., Washington, 2000—02, McGuire Woods, LLP, 2002—. Adj. lectr., U. Va. Law Sch., 2006; lectr. in field. Contbr. articles to profl. jours. Mem. adv. bd. Salvation Army, Richmond, 1980-97, chmn., 1989-91; troop com. chmn. Robert E. Lee coun. Boy Scouts Am., 1980-91; chair 10th Amendment Litig. com., Gov.'s Adv. Coun. on Federalism and Self Determination, 1994-97; gen. counsel Rep. Party Va., 1993-96. Mem. Am. Bar Found., Am. Coll. Labor and Employment Lawyers, Va. State Bar, Phi Beta Kappa. Presbyterian. Office: McGuire Woods LLP Washington Sq 1050 Conneticut Ave NW Ste 1200 Washington DC 20036-5317 Office Phone: 202-857-1718. Business E-Mail: rbrame@mcguirewoods.com.

BRAMHALL, ROBERT RICHARD, management consultant; b. Oct. 30, 1927; s. Richard Marion and Ima Lucille (Stovall) Bramhall; m. Mary Margaret Bundy, Aug. 10, 1957; children: Robert Richard Jr., Laura Bramhall Wolf. AB in Social Rels., Harvard U., 1951, MBA, 1960. CPA Ill. With GE, Fairfield, Conn., 1954—66, Philco-Ford subs. Ford Motor Co., Phila., 1966—68, Warwick Electronics subs. Whirlpool Corp., Niles, Ill., 1968—70; prin. Bramhall Assocs., Lake Forest, Ill., 1970—. Cons. Rockwell Internat., Bunker-Ramo Corp., Dan River Inc., Molex, Spartan Mills, Rollins, Inc., Lubrizol Corp., Sears (Can.) Ltd., Northrop Corp.; lectr. bus. Barat Coll., Coll. Lake County, Ill. With US Army, 1946—48. Recipient Winner Singles and Doubles, Vt. State Tennis Championship, 1956, runner-up, U.S. Clay Ct. Doubles' Championships (with Bobby Riggs). Mem.: Harvard Chgo. Club. Republican. Presbyterian. Home and Office: Bramhall Assocs 855 Buena Rd Lake Forest IL 60045-0783 Office Phone: 847-370-1027. E-mail: robtrbramhall@sbcglobal.net.

BRAMLETT, PAUL KENT, lawyer; b. Tupelo, Miss., May 31, 1944; s. Virgil Preston and McDuff (Goggans) B.; m. Shirley Marie Wilhelm, June 14, 1966; children: Paul Kent II (dec.), Robert Preston. AA with honors, Itawamba Jr. Coll., Fulton, Miss., 1962-64; BA, David Lipscomb Coll., 1966; postgrad., George Peabody Coll., 1966; JD, U. Miss., 1969. Bar: Miss. 1969, U.S. Dist. Ct. (no. dist.) Miss. 1969, U.S. Ct. Appeals (5th cir.) 1974, U.S. Supreme Ct. 1974, U.S. Dist. Ct. (we. dist.) Tenn. 1976, Tenn. 1980, U.S. Dist. Ct. (mid. dist.) Tenn. 1980, U.S. Ct. Appeals (6th cir.) 1980, U.S. Ct. Appeals (11th cir.) 1981, U.S. Dist. Ct. (so. dist.) Miss. 1983, U.S. Dist. Ct. (ea. dist.) Tenn. 2003. Pvt. practice, Tupelo, Miss., 1969-80, Nashville, 1980—. Mem. Million Dollar Advs. Forum, 1998. Mem. ABA, Miss. Trial Lawyers Assn. (bd. govs. 1976-79), Tenn. Bar Assn., Miss. Bar Assn. (pub. info. com. 1979-81), Nashville Bar Assn. (fed. ct. com. 1980-81, 2005-06), Am. Arbitration Assn. (comml. panel), Civitan Club (past gov. and legal counsel no. dist. Miss.). Mem. Ch. of Christ. Avocation: music. Office: PO Box 150734 Nashville TN 37215-0734 Office Phone: 615-248-2828.

BRAMLETTE, DAVID C., III, retired federal judge; b. New Orleans, Nov. 27, 1939; BA, Princeton U., 1962; JD, U. Miss., 1965. Assoc., then ptnr. Adams, Forman, Truly, Ward & Bramlette, Natchez, Miss., 1975-91; spl. cir. judge Dist. Ct. (6th dist.) Miss., 1977, 79; judge US Dist. Ct. (so. dist.) Miss., Jackson, 1991—2006, sr. judge, 2006—. Trustee Miss. Nature Conservancy, 1990—; pres. BBCHA, 1989-90; active Arcole Hunting Camp, Ducks Unlimited, Nat. Wild Turkey Fedn.; mem. adv. bd. Natchez Lit. Celebration. Office: US Dist Ct PO Box 928 Natchez MS 39121-0928 Office Phone: 601-442-3006.*

BRAMMELL, STEPHEN HARRISON, lawyer; b. Ardmore, Okla., Dec. 5, 1957; m. Allison Brammell. BBA with distinction, U. Okla., 1979; JD, Georgetown U. Law Ctr., 1982. Bar: Okla. 1982, Tenn. 1988, Nev. 2003. Assoc. Conner & Winters, Tulsa, 1982—84; corp. staff atty. Harrah's Entertainment Inc., Las Vegas, 1984—87, sr. staff atty., 1987—97, v.p., assoc. gen. counsel, 1997—99, sr. v.p., gen. counsel, 1999—. Office: Harrah Entertainment Inc Legal Dept One Harrahs Ct Las Vegas NV 89119 Office Phone: 702-407-6000. Office Fax: 702-407-6037. E-mail: sbrammell@harrahs.com.*

BRAMMER, J. WILLIAM, JR., judge, lawyer; b. Des Moines, Iowa, Sept. 15, 1942; s. James W. and Mary Virginia (Steck) Brammer; m. Donna Crosby, June 20, 1964; children: Jill S., James W. III. BS, U. Ariz., 1964, JD, 1967. Bar: Ariz. 1967, U.S. Dist. Ct. Ariz. 1968, U.S. Ct. Appeals (9th cir.) 1970, U.S. Supreme Ct. 1970. Law clk. to judge Ariz. Ct. Appeals, Tucson, 1967—68; asst. atty. City of Tucson, 1968; from assoc. to ptnr. DeConcini, McDonald, Brammer, Yetwin & Lacy PC, Tucson, 1968—97; judge Ariz. Ct. of Appeals, Tucson, 1997—. Mem. com. exams. Ariz. Supreme Ct., Phoenix, 1977-84, chmn. 1982-84; mem. Commn. on Jud. Conduct, 2003—, chair, 2005—; mem. bd. govs. State Bar Ariz., 1995-97. Bd. visitors U. Ariz. Coll. Law, Tucson, 1981-84, 88—. Fellow: Ariz. Bar Found.; mem.: ABA, Law Coll. Assn. U. Ariz. (pres. 1990—91), Pima County Bar Assn. (pres. 1993—94), Morris K. Udall Inn of Ct. (pres. 2001—02). Office: Ariz Ct Appeals 400 W Congress St Ste 302 Tucson AZ 85701-1353 Office Phone: 520-628-6945. Business E-Mail: brammer@appeals2.az.gov.

BRAMMER, LAWRENCE MARTIN, psychologist, educator; b. Crookston, Minn., Aug. 20, 1922; s. Martin G. and Edna L. (Thiesen) B.; m. Marian S. Sjolin, Feb. 11, 1945; children: Karin Marie, Kristen Lenore. BS, St. Cloud State U., 1943; MA, Stanford U., 1948, PhD, 1950. Diplomate: Am. Bd. Prof. Psychology. Psychologist Stanford U. Counseling and Testing Ctr., 1948-50; assoc. dean students Sacramento State Coll., 1950-64; prof. ednl. psychology U. Wash., Seattle, 1964-88, prof. emeritus, 1988—. Author: Therapeutic Psychology, 6th edit., 1993, Helping Relationships, 8th edit., 2002, Outplacement and Inplacement Counseling, 1984, How to Cope with Life Transitions, 1991, Caring for Yourself While Caring for Others: A Caregiver's Survival and Renewal Guide, 1999. Lt. M.S.C. AUS, 1944-46. Fulbright fellow, 1961-62 Fellow APA; mem. ACA, Queen City Yacht Club, Elks. Democrat. Lutheran. Home: 8005 Sandpoint Way NE A23 Seattle WA 98115

BRAMNIK, ROBERT PAUL, lawyer; b. NYC, Nov. 17, 1949; s. Abe and Ruth (Richman) B.; m. Sheryl Ann Kalus, Aug. 12, 1973; children: Michael Lawrence, Andrew Martin. BA, CCNY, 1970; JD, Bklyn. Law Sch., 1973. Bar: N.Y. 1974, Ill. 1980, U.S. Dist. Ct. (so. and ea. dists.) N.Y. 1974, U.S. Dist. Ct. (no. dist.) Ill. 1980, U.S. Dist. Ct. (ctrl. dist.) Ill. 1982, U.S. Ct. Appeals (2d cir.) 1974, U.S. Ct. Appeals (4th cir.) 1987, U.S. Ct. Appeals (3d and 7th cirs.) 1992, U.S. Ct. Fed. Claims 1994, U.S. Supreme Ct. 1977. Sr. trial atty. NYSE, Inc., NYC, 1973-75; asst. gen. counsel E.F. Hutton & Co., Inc., NYC, 1975-77, Nat. Securities Clearing Corp., NYC, 1977-79; with Arvey, Hodes, Costello and Burman, Chgo., 1979-86, ptnr., 1982-86, Wood, Lucksinger & Epstein, Chgo., 1987-88, Altheimer & Gray, Chgo., 1988-97, Wildman, Harrold, Allen & Dixon, Chgo., 1997—2003, Duane Morris LLP, Chgo., NYC, 2003—. Lectr. Securities Industry Assn. Compliance and Legal div., N.Y.C., 1980-91, 95-2001. Vice chmn. Ill. Adv. Com. on Commodity Regulation, Chgo., 1985-89, chmn., 1989-95. Fellow: Ill. Bar Found.; mem.: ABA (com. on futures and derivatives regulation, com. on fed. regulation of securities), Nat. Futures Assn. (arbitrator 1991—, hearing com. 2001—), Nat. Assn. Sec. Dealers (arbitrator 1981—), Assn. of Bar of City of N.Y. Jewish. Office: Duane Morris LLP 227 W Monroe St Ste 3400 Chicago IL 60606 Office Phone: 312-499-0121. Business E-Mail: rpbramnik@duanemorris.com.

BRAMS, MARVIN ROBERT, economist, mental health counselor, interfaith minister, educator; b. Boston, Apr. 16, 1937; s. Leo and Sarah Brams; m. Myrna Berlin, May 15, 1960; children: Adam, Aaron. BS, Northeastern U., 1959, MBA, 1962; PhD, Clark U., 1967; M in Counseling, U. Del., 1984; postgrad., Carl Rogers Inst. Psychotherapy, 1985, Inst. Rational Emotive Therapy, 1987; MS in Spiritual Therapy, New Sem., 1990. Diplomate Am. Bd. Med. Psychotherapists; ordained as interfaith min. Columbia U., 1989; cert. Nat. Bd. Cert. Counselors; lic. mental health counselor; cert. in clin. pastoral edn. Instr. econs. Northeastern U., 1965-67; economist, prof. urban affairs and pub. policy U. Del., Newark, 1967—97, clin. psychotherapist Employee Wellness Program, 1995—97; fellow in psychoanalytic psychotherapy Harvard U., 2002—03. Econ. cons. to legal profession; vis. scholar Harvard U. Divinity Sch., 1997-99; psychiatry intern Med. Ctr. Del., 1996-97; clin. psychotherapist, VA Hosp., 1999-2001, Beth-Isreal-Deaconess Hosp., 2000-02. Contbr. chpts. to books and articles to jours. and newspapers. Mem. Gov.'s Com. Del. State Fins., 1969, Gov.'s Econ. Adv. Coun., 1969-72; adv. com. property tax exemption policy Cities of Newark and Wilmington, 1972-75; mem. Del. Revenue Study Comm., 1973, Citizens Task Force on Housing, 1975, Del. Tomorrow Commn., 1974-76, New Castle County Water Supply Adv. Coun., 1975-81, Del. Revenue Study Com., 1977; fed. revenue sharing adv. com. City of Newark, 1976-78; advisor Del. Dept. Natural Resources, 1979. 1st lt. ordinance AUS, 1959-60. Fellow in urban econs. and pub. policy MIT, 1970, NSF fellow Stanford U., 1971. Mem. ACA, Assn. Humanistic Psychology, Am. Mental Health Counselors Assn., Am. Men and Women of Sci., Mass. Inst. for Psychoanalysis, Northeastern Soc. for Group Psychotherapy, Boston Psychomalytic Soc. Home: PO Box 440412 Somerville MA 02144-0005 Office Phone: 617-666-3780. Personal E-mail: brams02140@yehoo.com.

BRAMS, STEVEN JOHN, political science professor; b. Concord, NH, Nov. 28, 1940; s. Nathan and Isabelle (Tryman) B.; m. Eva Floderer, Nov. 13, 1971; children: Julie Claire, Michael Jason. BS, MIT, 1962; PhD, Northwestern U., 1966. Research assoc. Inst. Def. Analyses, Arlington, Va., 1965-67; asst. prof. polit. sci. Syracuse U., 1967-69; asst. prof. NYU, 1969-73, assoc. prof., 1973-76, prof., 1976—. Vis. prof. U. Rochester, U. Pa., U. Mich., Yale U., U. Calif.-Irvine, U. Haifa, Inst. Advanced Studies, Vienna; cons. in field; mem. coun. Game Theory Soc., 2004-06, Soc. of Social Choice and Welfare, 2004-05. Author: Game Theory and Politics, 1975, rev. edit., 2004, Paradoxes in Politics: An Introduction to the Nonobvious in Political Science, 1976, The Presidential Election Game, 1978, Biblical Games: Game Theory and the Hebrew Bible, 1980; author: (with Peter C. Fishburn) Approval Voting, 1983;: rev. edit., 2007, Superior Beings: If They Exist, How Would We Know?, 1983, Superpower Games: Applying Game Theory to Superpower Conflict, 1985, Rational Politics: Decisions, Games and Strategy, 1985; author: (with D. Marc Kilgour) Game Theory and National Security, 1988; author: Negotiation Games: Applying Game to Bargaining and Arbitration, 1990;: rev. edit., 2003, Theory of Moves, 1994; author: (with Alan D. Taylor) Fair Division: From Cake-Cutting to Dispute Resolution, 1996, The Win-Win Solution: Guaranteeing Fair Shares to Everybody, 1999; co-editor: Applied Gamed Theory, 1979, Modules in Applied Mathematics: Political and Related Models, 1983; mem. editl. bd.: Pub. Choice, 1973—90, 2003—, Am. Polit. Sci. Rev., 1978—82; mem. editl. bd. Jour. Politics, 1968—73, 1978—82, 1991—, Math. Social Scis., 1980—, Theory and Decision, 1982—, Jour. Behavioral Decision Making, 1987—90, Jour. Theoretical Politics, 1988—, Group Decision and Negotiation, 1991—, Control and Cybernetics, 1993—, Rationality and Society, 1999—; mem. editl. bd.: Internat. Studies Quarterly, 1999—2003. Social Sci. Rsch. Coun. fellow, 1964-65, Guggenheim fellow, 1986-87; Russell Sage Found. vis. scholar, 1998-99, grantee NSF, 1968-71, 73-75, 80-91, Social Sci. Rsch. Coun., 1968, Ford Found., 1984-85, Sloan Found., 1986-89, U.S. Inst. Peace, 1988-89. Fellow AAAS; mem. Pub. Choice Soc. (pres. 2004-06), Am. Econ. Assn., Am. Polit. Sci. Assn., Internat. Studies Assn. (Susan Strange award 2002), Policy Studies Orgn., Peace Sci. Soc. (pres. 1990-91). Democrat. Jewish. Achievements include patents in field. Home: 4 Washington Square Vlg Apt 17I New York NY 10012-1910 Office Phone: 212-998-8510. Business E-Mail: steven.brams@nyu.edu.

BRAMSON, JAMES B., dentist, dental association administrator; DDS, U. Iowa Coll. Dentistry, 1979. Pvt. practice, Mass.; exec. dir. Mass. Dental Soc., 1997—2001, ADA, Chgo., 2001—. Grantee Hillenbrand Fellowship. Mem.: Mass. Dental Soc., ADA (dir. Coun. on Dental Practice 1990—97, sec./treas. Endowment and Assistance Fund Inc. 1990—97, dir. Commn. on Relief Fund Activities). Office: ADA 211 E Chicago Ave Chicago IL 60611 also: ADA Ste 1200 1111 14thSt NW Washington DC 20005

BRAMSON, LEON, social scientist, educator; b. Chgo., Dec. 6, 1930; s. William and Sophie (Dudowitz) B.; m. Mary Elizabeth Hamlin, Mar. 12, 1960 (div. 1982); children: Rachel, Ruth; m. Nathalie Hubbard Bonsal, 1984; 1 child, Samuel Appleton. AB, U. Chgo., 1950, MA, 1953; PhD, Harvard, 1959. Instr. social relations Harvard, 1959-61, asst. prof., 1961-65; assoc. prof., chmn. dept. sociology and anthropology Swarthmore Coll., 1965-77, prof. sociology, 1971-78; program officer Exxon Edn. Found., NYC, 1978-80; coordinator social analysis, corp. planning dept. Exxon Corp., NYC, 1980-82; asst. dir. div. gen. programs NEH, Washington, 1982-85, sr. program officer, 1985—. Vis. prof. sociology U. Calif. at San Diego, 1972; cons. Peace Corps Agy., 1965; edn. cons. Trustee Nat. Service Secretariat, 1967-74, Good Hope Sch., Frederiksted, St. Croix, U.S. V.I., 1972-78; policyholder-elected trustee Tchrs. Ins. and Annuity Assn., N.Y.C., 1973-78, Coll. Retirement Equities Fund, 1978-79 Author: The Political Context of Sociology, 1961; Asso. editor: Am. Sociol. Rev, 1967-69; editor: Robert MacIver: On Community, Society and Power, 1970, (with G. W. Goethals) War: Studies from Psychology, Sociology, Anthropology, 1964. Served with AUS, 1953-55. Fulbright scholar Netherlands, 1957-58 Office: NEH Divsn Research Programs Rm 318 1100 Pennsylvania Ave NW Washington DC 20506

BRAMSON, ROBERT SHERMAN, lawyer; b. NYC, Nov. 11, 1938; s. Oscar David and Gertrude (May) B.; m. Ruth Schaffer, June 27, 1942; children: Jonathan, Jennifer, James, Julia. B.M.E., Rensselaer Poly. Inst., 1959; JD, Georgetown U., 1963; postgrad., U. Chgo. Sch. Bus., 1963-64. Bar: Ill. 1963, Pa. 1968, NY 1984. Patent examiner US Patent Office, Washington, 1959-60; patent agt. Stevens, Davis, Miller & Mosher, Washington, 1960-63; atty. Abbott Labs., North Chgo., Ill., 1963-66, Scott Paper Co., Phila., 1966-68; ptnr., head computer and tech. law group Schnader, Harrison, Segal & Lewis, Phila., 1968-89; v.p., gen. patent and tech. counsel Unisys Corp., Blue Bell, Pa., 1989-90; founder Bramson and Pressman, Conshohocken, Pa., 1991, 95—; pres., CEO InterDigital Tech. Corp., King of Prussia, Pa., 1992-95; pres. VAI Patent Mgmt. Corp., Conshohocken, Pa., 1995—2004. Adj. prof. Temple U. Law Sch., Phila. Mem. ABA, Internat. Bar Assn., Am. Law Inst., Am. Patent Law Assn., Phila. Patent Law Assn., Phila. Bar Assn. Home: 112 Booth Ln Haverford PA 19041-1752 Office: Bramson & Pressman 1100 Hector St Ste 410 Conshohocken PA 19428-2378 Office Phone: 610-260-4444. Business E-Mail: rbramson@b-p.com.

BRAMWELL, HENRY, federal judge; b. Bklyn., Sept. 3, 1919; s. Henry Hall and Florence Elva (MacDonald) B.; m. Ishbel W. Brown, Jan. 29, 1966. LLB, Bklyn. Law Sch., 1948, LLD (hon.), 1979. Bar: N.Y. bar 1948. Asst. U.S. atty., Bklyn., 1953-61; asso. counsel N.Y. State Rent Commn., 1961-63; judge Civil Ct., NYC, Bklyn., 1966, 69—; asst. adminstrv. judge Kings County, Bklyn., 1974—; judge U.S. Dist. Ct., Bklyn., 1975—; U.S. Sr. Dist. judge, 1987—. Mem. Community Mayors N.Y. State; trustee Bklyn. Law Sch., 1978— Active Bklyn. Old Times Found., Inc. Served with AUS, 1942-44. Profiled in Black Judges on Justice, 1994. Mem. ABA, Nat. Bar Assn. (life), N.Y. State Bar Assn., Bklyn. Bar Assn. (trustee), Fed. Judges Assn. (founding mem.). Home: 101 Clark St Brooklyn NY 11201-2746 Office: US Dist Ct 225 Cadman Plz E Brooklyn NY 11201-1818

BRANAGAN, JAMES JOSEPH, lawyer; b. Johnstown, Pa., Mar. 5, 1943; s. James Francis and Caroline Bertha (Schreier) B.; m. Barbara Jeanne Miller, June 19, 1965; children: Sean Patrick, Erin MacKay, David Michael. BA in English Lit. with honors magna cum laude (Woodrow Wilson fellow), Kenyon Coll., Gambier, Ohio, 1965; LLB cum laude,

Columbia U., 1968. Bar: Ohio 1968. Assoc. Jones, Day, Reavis & Pogue, Cleve., 1968-72; with Leaseway Transp. Corp., Cleve., 1972-81, gen. counsel, 1975-80, sec., 1979-81, v.p. corp. affairs, 1980-81; also officer, dir. Leaseway Transp. Corp. (subsidiaries); v.p. Premier Indsl. Corp., Cleve., 1981-82; sr. counsel TRW Inc., 1982-88; pvt. practice Cleve., 1988—; treas., gen. counsel, sec. Biomec Inc., 1998—2003. Mem. ABA, Ohio Bar Assn., Cleve. Bar Assn., Phi Beta Kappa. Business E-Mail: bizlaw2@oh.rr.com.

BRANAGH, KENNETH, actor, film director; b. Belfast, Northern Ireland, Dec. 10, 1960; m. Emma Thompson, Aug. 1989 (div. 1996); m. Lindsay Brunnock, May 2003. Grad., Royal Academy of Dramatic Art, 1981; LittD (hon.), Queens U., Belfast, 1990. Co-founder Renaissance Theater Co., Eng., to 1994. Actor: (films) Coming Through, 1985, A Month in the Country, 1987, High Season, 1987, Dead Again, 1991, Swing Kids, 1993, Othello, 1995, The Gingerbread Man, 1998, The Proposition, 1998, Celebrity, 1998, The Theory of Flight, 1998, The Dance of Shiva, 1998, The Periwig-Maker (voice), 1999, Wild Wild West, 1999, How to Kill Your Neighbor's Dog, 2000, The Road to El Dorado (voice), 2000, Schneider's 2nd Stage, 2001, Alien Love Triangle, 2002, Rabbit-Proof Fence, 2002, Harry Potter and the Chamber of Secrets, 2002, Five Children and It, 2004; (TV films) Too Late to Talk to Billy, 1982, Easter 2016, 1982, A Matter of Choice for Billy, 1983, To the Lighthouse, 1983, A Coming to Terms for Billy, 1984, Ghosts, 1986, The Lady's Not for Burning, 1987, Strange Interlude, 1988, Look Back in Anger, 1989, Shadow of a Gunman, 1995, Big Al Uncovered, 2000, Conspiracy, 2001, Shackleton, 2002, Warm Springs, 2005; (TV miniseries) Maybury, 1981, Boy in the Bush, 1984, Fortunes of War, 1987; (TV series) Thompson, 1988; dir. (films) Dead Again, 1991, Swan Song, 1992, (TV films) Twelfth Night, or What You Will, 1988, dir., writer (films) In the Bleak Midwinter, 1995, Listening, 2003, actor, dir., writer Henry V, 1989, Hamlet, 1996, actor, dir., prodr. Peter's Friends, 1992, actor, dir., co-prodr. Frankenstein, 1994, actor, dir., prodr., writer Much Ado About Nothing, 1993, Love's Labour's Lost, 2000; dir., prodr., writer: (films) As You Like It, 2006; dir., prodr. The Magic Flute, 2006; Sleuth, 2007. Decorated Order of Arts and Letters (France).

BRANAND, CLAIRE DIANE, advertising executive, writer; d. Frank X. Dostal and Clara A. Weidmann; m. David C. Branand, May 12, 1990 (dec. Sept. 29, 2001); 1 child, Wendy C. Student, Chamberlayne Jr. Coll., 1962—63; BFA, Parsons Sch. Design, 1966; student, Sch. Visual Arts, 1966—67. Layout artist R.H. Macy & Co., NYC, 1966—70; freelance art dir. and writer Washington, 1974—77; prin., owner Halpert & Assocs. Advt., Washington, 1978—90; owner Branand & Assoc., Washington, 1990—. Pres. Skye Pub., Annapolis, Md., 1996—. Author: Overboard! A Provocative History of the U.S.S. J.P. Kennedy, Jr., 2000, Here's To Your Health! Cooking With Red Wine, 2002, Getting Off, 2006, Nat. Assn. Post-Polio Syndrome Newsletter. Sec. bd. dirs. Nat. Assn. Post Polio Syndrome, Washington, 1991—96. Recipient Citation, Assn. for Help of Retarded Children, 1967. Mem.: U.S. Navy League (assoc.), U.S. Naval Inst. (assoc.). Avocations: painting, writing, poetry, cooking, nutrition. Office: Skye Publishing PO Box 4562 Annapolis MD 21403 Office Phone: 410-340-2680.

BRANCA, JOHN GREGORY, lawyer, consultant; b. Bronxville, NY, Dec. 11, 1950; s. John Ralph and Barbara (Werle) B. AB in Polit. Sci. cum laude, Occidental Coll., 1972; JD, UCLA, 1975. Bar: Calif. 1975. Assoc. Kindel & Anderson, Los Angeles, 1975—77, Hardee, Barovick, Konecky & Braun, Beverly Hills, Calif., 1977—81; ptnr. Ziffren, Brittenham, Branca, Fischer, Gilsert, Lurie, Stiffelman, Cook, Johnson, Lande & Wolf LLP, LA, 1981—. Cons. N.Y. State Assembly, Mt. Vernon, 1978-82, various music industry orgns., L.A., 1981—. Editor-in-Chief UCLA-Alaska Law Rev., 1974-75; contbr. articles to profl. jours. Cons., bd. trustees UCLA Law Sch. Com., UCLA Athletic Dept., Occidental Coll., Musician's Assistance Program, 1995. Recipient Bancroft-Whitney award; named Entertainment Lawyer of Yr. Am. Lawyer mag., 1981. Mem. ABA (patent trademark and copyright law sect.), Calif. Bar Assn., Beverly Hills Bar Assn. (entertainment law sect.), Phi Alpha Delta, Sigma Tau Sigma. Avocations: art, antiques, music, real estate. Office: Ziffren Brittenham Branca Fischer Gilsert Lurie Stiffelman Cook Johnson Lande & Wolf LLP 1801 Century Park W Fl 9 Los Angeles CA 90067-6406

BRANCATO, LEO JOHN, manufacturing executive; b. NYC, Oct. 27, 1922; s. Leo and Josephine (Abbruscato) B. B in Mech. Engring, Cooper Union, 1950; MS, Columbia U., 1952. Registered profl. engr., Conn. Design engr. Ermold Co., NYC, 1946-51; with Heli-Coil Corp., Danbury, Conn., 1952-70, exec. v.p., 1963-70, pres., 1970; v.p., dir. Mite-Corp., merger co. including Heli-Coil Co., Danbury, 1970-74; pres. Mite-Corp., 1974-88. Incorporator Union Savs. Bank, Danbury, 1967-92. Patentee in field of fastener tech. Trustee Danbury Hosp., 1961-2005, Union Savs. Bank Found. Inc., 1998-2005; chmn. Housatonic Regional Mental Health Council, 1965-68; commr. conservation, Danbury, 1974-79; mem. bd. visitors U. Conn. Sch. Bus. Adminstrn., 1977-89. Lt. C.E., AUS, 1943-46 Fellow ASME; mem. Princeton Club (N.Y.C.), Port Washington Yacht Club (N.Y.), Tau Beta Pi.

BRANCH, BRENDA SUE, library director; b. Buffalo, Apr. 27, 1947; BS in Edn., SUNY, Cortland, 1969; MLS, postgraduate student, SUNY, Buffalo, 1972, Stephen F. Austin State U., 1975—76, SW Tex. State U., 1973—74, MPA in Pers. Adminstrn., 1985. Tchr. Kenmore Ind. Sch. Dist., 1969—70; asst. health scis. libr. SUNY, Buffalo, 1971—73; br. mgr. Austin Pub. Libr., 1973—75, prog. devel. coord., 1977—80, supr. br. svcs., 1980—86, assoc. dir. pub. svcs., 1986—91, dir. librs., 1991—; acquisitions libr. Tex. Ea. U., 1975; humanities libr. Stephen F. Austin State U., 1975—76; dist. libr. coord. Longview Ind. Sch. Dist., 1976—77. Project mgr. reduction-in-force project City of Austin, 1988, co-chair customer svc. task force, coord. creativity prog., 1990; mem. long range planning com. svcs. spl. populations Tex. State Libr., 1992. Mem. Austin Travis County Continuing Edn. Adv. Bd., Austin, 1981, Tex. Mcpl. League, Mayor's Coalition Workplace Literacy, 1990, Literacy and Fundamental Edn. Spkr.'s Bur., 1991-93, Leadership Austin, 1991, chair kids prog., 1993; tutor, trainer Travis County Adult Literacy Coun., 1986-89; chair City of Austin Workplace Literacy Task Force, 1989; mem. spkr.'s bur. United Way, 1990-92; mem. MPA adv. coun. SW Tex. State U., 1993; bd. dirs. Big Bros./Big Sisters, 1986-90, chair pub. rels. com., 1986-90, fundraiser, 1986-90, com. co-chair, 1986-90. Recipient Outstanding Achievement for Govt. Svc. award YWCA, 1991. Mem. ALA, Tex. Libr. Assn. (treas. dist. V 1976-77, mem. continuing edn. com. 1978-79, mem. membership com. 1986-89, mem. ann. conf. placement ctr. 1989, mem. literacy com. 1990, chair 1990-93, mem. resource sharing com. 1990, mem. ad hoc property com. 1992, mem. minority recruitment com. 1992-93, co-chair legis. day 1992-93, chair-elect pub. libr. divsn. 1994-95, chair 1995-96), Austin Soc. Pub. Adminstrn. (chair membership com. 1984-89, newsletter editor 1984-89), Toastmasters (v.p., pres., newsletter editor). Office: Austin Public Library PO Box 2287 800 Guadalupe St Austin TX 78701-2314 Office Phone: 512-974-7444. E-mail: brenda.branch@ci.austin.tx.us.

BRANCH, FELECIA ANN-SELDON, elementary school educator; d. Willie George and Doris Juanita Seldon; 1 child, Justin Michael Alexander. BA in Liberal Arts, U. Detroit, 1991. Cert. provisional tchg. U. Detroit, 1995, profl. tchg. 7-12 in speech & English U. Detroit, 2001. Lang. arts tchr. Hutchins Mid. Sch., Detroit, 1991—. Debate coach Detroit Pub. Schs., 1992—2001; narrative contest judge Area D, 1997; tchr. liason Mid-East/West Fest, 1997—2001, mem. planning com., 1997—2001; tchr. participant Inside Out, 1997—; leader Reading for Real Tchr., 1999—2000, Jr. Great Books, 2000—02, Soar to Success, 2001; accelerated reader tchr. leader Renaissance Reading, 2005. Mem. planning com. Mid East/West Fest, 1997—2001; participant W.K. Kellogg Found. Youth Initiative, 1998—99; mem. Site-based Mgmt. Com. Hutchins Mid. Sch., 1999—; vol. donor Great Book Leader for Reading Detroit Pub. Libr., 2000—02; asst. girl scout troop leader Girl Scouts Am., 1997—; leader Jr. Great Books Detroit Pub. Libr., 2000—02; tchr. Wednesday Night Children's Bible Study, 2004—. Recipient Cert. Recognition, Detroit Middle Schs. Debate League, 1992—2001. Avocations: reading, writing, poetry, skating, weight-lifting. Home Phone: 248-399-4993; Office Phone: 313-873-2787.

BRANCH, JASON, lawyer; b. Columbus, Ga., Feb. 28, 1973; BA cum laude, Davidson Coll., 1995; JD magna cum laude, Univ. Ga., 1998. Bar: Ga. 1998, Supreme Ct. Ga., Middle, No. Dists. Ga., U.S. Dist. Ct., U.S. Ct. Appeals Eleventh Circuit. Spkr. in field. Contbr. articles to numerous profl. jours. Named Ga. Rising Star, SuperLawyer Mag., 2006. Office: Phillips-Branch 1415 Wynnton Road Columbus GA 31902 Office Fax: 706-571-0765.

BRANCH, JOHN CURTIS, biology professor, lawyer; b. Buffalo, Okla., Oct. 1, 1934; s. Ernest Samuel and Ethel Imogene (Parsons) B.; m. Jacqueline Joyce Davis, July 20, 1960; children: Kim Renee, Karla Jean, Kay Lynn. BS, Northwestern Okla. State U., 1959; MS, U. Okla., 1963, PhD, 1965; JD, Okla. City U., 1980. Bar: Okla. 1980. Asst. prof. biology dept. Okla. City U., 1964-67, assoc. prof. biology dept., 1967-75, prof. biology dept., 1975—. With U.S. Army, 1955-57. Mem. Okla. County Bar Assn., Okla. Acad. Sci., Okla. Bar Assn., Beta Beta Beta. Methodist. Avocations: reading, sports, travel. Home: 2705 Abbey Rd Oklahoma City OK 73120-2702 Office: Okla City U Dept Biology 2501 N Blackwelder Ave Oklahoma City OK 73106-1402 also: 1525 SW 89th St Oklahoma City OK 73159 Office Phone: 405-634-7600.

BRANCH, JOSEPH C., lawyer; BA, Marquette U., 1967, JD magna cum laude, 1971. Bar: Wis. 1971. Ptnr. Foley & Lardner LLP, Milw., mem. ins. industry practice group. Editl. rev. bd. Jour. Ins. Regulation, 1985—; bd. dirs. Fedn. Regulatory Counsel. Co-author: Insurers Operating Under Assumed or Fictitious Names: When, How &.What?!, LLC Bandwagon: Insurers Beware. Mem.: Internat. Assn. Ins. Law, Defense Research Inst., Inc., Milw. Bar Assn., ABA (tort & ins. practice sect., com. lawyers profl. liability), State Bar Wis. (chmn. ins. com. 1980—86, bd. gov., exec. com.). Office: Foley & Lardner LLP 777 E Wisconsin Ave Milwaukee WI 53202-5306 Office Phone: 414-297-5837. Business E-Mail: jbranch@foley.com.

BRANCH, MARY FLETCHER COX, secondary school educator; b. Jackson, Tenn., May 20, 1938; d. John Fletcher and Helen Wood (Henderson) Cox; m. William Terrell Branch, 1964; 1 child, Ashley Tucker. BA in Biology and Chemistry, Lindenwood U., St. Charles, Mo., 1960; MS in Microbiology, U. Bombay, 1962, U. Ark., Little Rock, 1965. Cert. HS tchr. State of Ark. Blood chemistry rschr. Barnes Hosp., St. Louis, 1960—61; tchr. Elston Sr. H.S., Michigan City, Ind., 1962—63; biology and chemistry tchr. Little Rock Ctrl. H.S., 1965—70; tchr., dept. chair sci. and math St. Mary's Episcopal Day Sch., Tampa, Fla., 1977—92; sci. tchr. Berkeley Prep. Sch., Tampa, 1992—99; tchr., dept. chair math St. John's Episcopal Day Sch., Tampa, 1999—2004; tchr., dept. chair sci. Holy Trinity Luth. Sch., Tampa, 2004—. Mem. adv. hon. bd. Berkeley Prep. Sch., 1992—99, sci. Olympics chairperson, 1992—95. Vol. Tampa Gen. Hosp., 1970—77; mem. Golf View Civic Assn., Tampa, 1978—; vol. Mus. Sci. and Industry, Tampa, 1978—85, bd. dirs., 1978—85. Named disting. faculty soc., charter mem., St. Mary's Episcopal Day Sch., Tampa, 2006. Office: Holy Trinity Luth Sch 3712 W El Prado Blvd Tampa FL 33629-8700

BRANCH, MICHAEL LEE, social studies educator, consultant; b. Parkersburg, W.Va., Sept. 30, 1955; s. Jarratt Carlton and Erma Geraldine Branch; m. Karen Florence Allio; 1 child, Amanda Nicole. BA in Edn., Glenville State Coll., W.Va., 1981. Cert. tchr. W.Va. Dept. Edn., 1981. Educator Wood County Schs., Parkersburg, W.Va., 1983—. Cons. W.Va. State Dept. Edn., Charleston, W.Va., 1994—. Min. United Meth. Ch., Parkersburg, W.Va., 2003—06. Recipient Tchg. award, Ashland Oil, 1994, NASDAQ, 2000; grantee, W.Va. Edn. Alliance, 2001, 2004; scholar, W.Va. U., 1978. Mem.: Am. Fedn. Tchrs. (licentiate), Nat. Coun. Social Studies (licentiate), Global Assn. Econ. Educators (life). Republican. Achievements include design of curriculum for career clusters, civis, personal financial responsibility. Avocations: travel, coin collecting/numismatics, music. Home: 233 Oakbrook Dr Mineral Wells WV 26150 Office: Wood County Schools 1210 13th Street Parkersburg WV 26101 Home Phone: 304-489-1968; Office Phone: 304-420-9663. Personal E-mail: mlbranc@hotmail.com.

BRANCH, MICHELLE (MICHELLE JAQUET DESEVREN BRANCH), musician; b. Flagstaff, Ariz., July 2, 1983; d. David and Peggy Branch; m. Teddy Landau, May 23, 2004; 1 child, Owen Isabelle. With Maverick Records, Beverly Hills, Calif., 2001—. Musician: (albums) Broken Bracelet, 2000, The Spirit Room, 2001, Breathe - The Remixes, 2002, Hotel Paper, 2003; musician: (with The Wreckers) Stand Still, Look Pretty, 2006; musician: (singles) Everywhere, 2001, All You Wanted, 2001, Goodbye to You, 2003, Are You Happy Now?, 2003, Breathe, 2003; (with Santana) (singles) The Game of Love, 2002 (Grammy award for Best Pop Collaboration with Vocals, 03), (with The Wreckers) Leave the Pieces, 2006. Recipient Grammy award for Best New Artist, 2003. Office: Maverick Recording Co 3300 Warner Blvd Burbank CA 91505-4632*

BRANCH, TAYLOR, writer; b. Atlanta, Jan. 14, 1947; s. Franklin T. and Jane (Worthington) B.; m. Christina Macy; 2 children. AB, U. N.C., 1968; postgrad., Princeton U., 1968-70. Staff member Washington Monthly mag., Washington, D.C., 1970-73, Harper's mag., NYC, 1973-75, Esquire mag., NYC, 1975-76. Author: (with Bill Russell) Second Wind: The Memoirs of an Opinionated Man, 1979, The Empire Blues, 1981, (with Eugene M. Propper) Labyrinth, 1982, Parting the Waters: America in the King Years, 1954-63, 1988 (Pulitzer Prize for history 1989, Nat. Book Critics Circle award for non-fiction 1988, Christopher award 1988, Nat. Book award nomination 1989), Pillar of Fire: America in the King Years, 1963-65, 1999, At Canaan's Edge: America in the King Years, 1965-68, 2006; editor, contbr.: (with Charles Peters) Blowing the Whistle: Dissent in the Public Interest, 1972. Recipient Nat. Humanities medal. Address: Author Mail Simon & Schuster 1230 Ave of the Americas New York NY 10020

BRANCH, THOMAS BROUGHTON, III, lawyer; b. Atlanta, June 5, 1936; s. Thomas Broughton Jr. and Alfred Iverson (Dews) B.; m. Trudi Schroetter, Dec. 27, 1963; children: Maria Barbara, Thomas B. IV. BA cum laude, Washington and Lee U., 1958, JD, 1960. Bar: Ga. 1960, U.S. Dist. Ct. (no. dist.) Ga. 1960, U.S. Ct. Appeals (5th cir.) 1960, U.S. Dist. Ct. (mid. dist.) Ga. 1980, U.S. Ct. Appeals (11th cir.) 1980, U.S. Dist. Ct. (so. dist.) N.Y. 1984, U.S. Ct. Appeals (2d cir.) 1984, U.S. Supreme Ct. 1991. Assoc. Kilpatrick & Cody, Atlanta, 1960-63; ptnr. Greene, Buckley et al, Atlanta, 1963-79, Wildman, Harrold, Allen, Dixon & Branch, Atlanta, 1979-89, Branch, Pike & Ganz, Atlanta, 1990-95, Holland & Knight, Atlanta, 1995—. Asst. prof. Woodrow Wilson Law Sch., Atlanta, 1964-68; trustee Washington and Lee U., Lexington, Va., 1979-90, trustee emeritus, 1991—; trustee, chmn. Atlanta Lawyers Found., Atlanta, 1980-81, Atlantis Aurora, Inc., 1970-74. Mem. Citizens Adv. Council on Urban Devel., Atlanta, 1977; trustee The Children's Sch., Inc., Atlanta, 1980-85; elder, clk., trustee First Presbyn. Ch., Atlanta, 1967-79, 81-85, 97—. Fellow Am. Bar Found.; mem. ABA, Ga. Bar Assn., Atlanta Bar Assn. (mem. jud. selection and tenure com. 1988—), Am. Jud. Soc., Atlanta Lawyers Club (pres. 1976-77), Bleckley Inn of Ct. (master), Ansley Golf Club (pres., bd. dirs. 1976-87). Home: 85 Montgomery Ferry Dr NE Atlanta GA 30309 Office Phone: 404-898-8106. E-mail: tbranch@hklaw.com.

BRANCH, WILLIAM BLACKWELL, playwright, producer; b. New Haven, Sept. 11, 1927; s. James Matthew and Iola (Douglas) B.; m. Marie Louise Foster, Aug. 19, 1956 (div.); 1 dau., Rochelle Ellen. BS, Northwestern U., 1949; M.F.A., Columbia U., 1958; ABC fellow, Yale U., 1965-66. Prof. Cornell U., 1985-94. Vis. scholar, lectr. numerous univs.; vis. prof. U. Md., Baltimore County, 1979-82; U. Calif. Regents lectr., spring, 1985; vis. Luce fellow Williams Coll., fall, 1983; vis. disting. prof. William Paterson Coll. N.J., Wayne, 1994-96. Actor appearing in: Anna Lucasta, 1945, Detective Story, 1951; playwright for theatre, TV and motion pictures, 1951—; assoc. in film, Columbia Sch. of Arts, 1968-69; staff writer-producer, Channel 13, Ednl. TV, N.Y.C., 1962-64; dir. The Jackie Robinson Show, NBC, 1958-60; co-author: The Jackie Robinson Column N.Y. Post and syndication, 1959-61; screenwriter Universal Studios, 1968-69, producer, NBC News, 1972-73, pres., William Branch Assos., 1973—; works include (theatre) A Medal for Willie, 1951, In Splendid Error, 1954, A Wreath for Udomo, 1960, To Follow the Phoenix, 1960, Baccalaureate, 1975; (TV) Light in the Southern Sky, 1958 (Robert E. Sherwood TV award 1958), A Letter From Booker T., 1987; TV documentary Still a Brother: Inside the Negro Middle Class, 1968 (Emmy award nominee 1969, Blue Ribbon award Am. Film Festival 1969); documentary TV series Afro American Perspectives, 1974-83; screen Together for Days, 1971; exec. producer: Black Perspective on the News, Pub. Broadcasting System, 1978-79; author: Fifty Steps Toward Freedom, 1959; author, editor: Black Thunder: An Anthology of Contemporary African American Drama, 1992 (Am. Book award 1992), Crosswinds: An Anthology of Black Dramatists in the Diaspora, 1993. Bd. dirs. Am. Soc. African Culture, 1963-70; treas. Nat. Conf. African Am. Theatre, 1987-91; bd. dirs. Nat. Citizens Com. for Broadcasting, 1969-71; mem. nat. adv. bd. Ctr. for Book, Library of Congress, 1979-83, W.E.B. DuBois Found., 1987—. Served with AUS, 1951-53. John Guggenheim fellow, 1959-60; recipient Hannah B. Del Vecchio award Columbia, 1958 Address: 53 Cortlandt Ave New Rochelle NY 10801-2032 Office Phone: 914-235-1809.

BRANCH, WILLIAM TERRELL, urologist, educator; b. Paragould, Ark., Dec. 7, 1937; s. William Owen and Mary Rose (Dempsey) B.; m. Lauinia McClure; children: Ashley Tucker, William T., Steven K. BS, Ark. State U., 1964, MD, 1971. Diplomate Am. Bd. Urology. Adminstrv. asst. mental retardation planning project State of Ark., Little Rock, 1964-66; intern U. South Fla. Sch. Medicine Affiliated Hosps., Tampa, 1971-72, resident in surgery, 1972-73, resident in urology, 1973-75, chief resident in urology, 1975-76; practice medicine specializing in urology Tampa, 1976—; mem. staff, sec. urology Tampa Gen. Hosp., 1976-78, vice chief urology, 1978-80, chief urology, 1980-82; mem. staff, co-chief surgery Meml. Hosp., Tampa, 1978-80, vice chief med. staff, 1980-82, chief med. staff, 1982-84, trustee, 1983-88, bd. dirs.; clin. prof. urology U. South Fla. Coll. Medicine, Tampa, 1994—. Mem. adv. bd. Suncoast Ednl. Telecommunications Systems, 1982; vice chmn., bd. dirs. Meml. Hosp., 1987-88; cons. in urology James A. Haley VA Hosp., Tampa, 1978—; mem. staff St. Joseph's Hosp., Tampa, 1976—, Tampa Gen. Hosp.; cons. staff Women's Hosp., Tampa; adv. bd. Glendale Fed. Savs., 1983-85, Beneficial Harbour Island Savs. Bank, 1985-87, South Trust Bank, 1988-2000, also bd. dirs., exec. com., chair audit com.; chief urology, bd. mem. Tampa Outpatient Surgery Facility, 2000—; chmn. vol. faculty com. Dept. Surgery U. South Fla. Coll. Medicine; chmn. bd. dirs. Shriners Hosp. for Children, Tampa. Author: (with others) Mental Retardation in Arkansas, 1964-66; A Demographic Study, 1966; cons. editor Jour. Fla. Med. Assn., 1978-93. Bd. dirs. Tampa Ballet, 1980, Tampa Charity Horse Show Bd. Dirs. Assn., 1985-87, Shriners Hosp. for Children, Tampa, 2000, Tampa Outpatient Surg. Facility,United Way, Tampa, 1983-90, mem. exec. com., 1984-88; mem. med. adv. bd. Nat. Kidney Found. of Fla., Inc., 1983-90; mem. Tampa Bay Super Bowl XXV Task Force, Super Bowl XXXV Task Force; mem. adv. bd. dirs. Salvation Army; founding chmn. Kettle com., vice chmn. adv. bd. dirs., chmn., 1998-2000. Recipient Disting. Alumnus award Ark. State U., 1986, named to Dunklin County Hall Honor, 2006. Fellow ACS (credit com. region IV, Fla. chpt. 1982-98, exec. com. Fla. chpt. 1985-92, sec., treas. 1987-88, pres.-elect 1989-90, pres. 1990-92, gov. 1990-96, bd. gov. chpt. activities com. 1991-96, alt. 1993, chmn. nomination com. 1995, chmn. applications com. region IV); mem. Am. Urol. Assn., Royal Soc. Medicine (affiliate), Fla. Med. Assn. (del. 1983, 88-96), Fla. Urol. Soc. (Milton Copeland award 1976, exec. com. 1978-82), Hillsborough County Med. Assn. (exec. com. 1978-81, treas. 1981-82, sec. 1983-84), Fla. Quality Med. Assurance, Inc. (bd. dirs., treas., chmn. exec. com. 1995, chmn. bd. govs.), Southeastern Surg. Congress, Greater Tampa C. of C. (dir. 1982-86, 87-90, chmn. med. meetings task force 1983-84, Super Star award 1983), Tampa Bay Surg. Soc. (founding mem., sec., bd. dirs. 1998, pres. 1999-2001), Tampa Hist. Soc., Hillsborough County Med. Soc. (pres. polit. action com. 1986-87, 88-89), Tampa Yacht and Country Club (gov. 1984-87), Centre of Tampa Club (founding mem. 1988-93, bd. dirs., chmn. mem. com., leading man ROJ Count #89), Univ. Club (treas. 1998-99, sec. 1999-2000, bd. dirs. 1998-99), Ye Mystic Krewe of Gasparilla (bd. dirs. 1991-2000, 1st lt. 1988-89, lord chamberlain 1994-95, chmn. exec. com. 1995-96, capt. 1996-98), King Gasparilla LXXXVI. Office: 2919 W Swann Ave Ste 303 Tampa FL 33609-4051 Office Phone: 813-877-0463.

BRAND, CHARLES MACY, history professor; b. Stanford, Calif., Apr. 7, 1932; s. Carl F. and Nan (Surface) B.; m. Mary Jane Shorrock, Aug. 7, 1954; children: Catharine, Stephen. BA, Stanford U., 1953; MA, Harvard U., 1954, PhD, 1961. Asst. prof. history San Francisco State Coll., 1962-64; asst. prof. Bryn Mawr Coll., Pa., 1964-69, assoc. prof., 1969-75, prof. history, 1975-99, chmn. dept. history, 1978-81, 96-97, prof. emeritus, 1999—. Author: Byzantium Confronts the West, 1180-1204, 1968, 2d edit., 1992; editor: Icon and Minaret, 1969; translator: Deeds of John and Manuel Comnenus (by J. Kinnamos), 1976. Served with U.S. Army, 1955-57. Dumbarton Oaks Center for Byzantine Studies fellow, 1961, 1988; Fulbright research fellow, 1968; Gennadius fellow, 1968; Guggenheim fellow, 1972 Mem. U.S. Nat. Com. for Byzantine Studies (1961), Medieval Acad. Am., Am. Hist. Assn., Byzantine Studies Conf. Home: 508 Montgomery Ave Haverford PA 19041-1409

BRAND, DONALD ALBERT, medical researcher, educator; b. New Rochelle, NY, Dec. 3, 1945; s. Charles Salmon and Norma Ruth Brand; m. Catherine L. Learned, Apr. 10, 1993; m. Gabriella Maresca, Sept. 12, 1964 (div.); children: Jeffrey Charles Brand-Ballard, Thomas Russell. BS, Antioch Coll., Yellow Springs, Ohio, 1968; MA, U. Wis., Madison, 1970; MPhil, Yale U., New Haven, Conn., 1975, PhD, 1976. Asst. prof., pub. health Yale U., New Haven, 1976—83, rsch. scientist, 1983—87, sr. rsch. scientist, 1987—89; sr. rschr. United Healthcare Corp., Minnetonka, Minn., 1990—95; assoc. prof., medicine N.Y. Med. Coll., Valhalla, 1996—2004, prof., medicine, 2004—07; adj. prof. medicine and pediatrics NY Med. Coll., Valhalla, 2007—. Mem., extremity radiography panel FDA, U.S. Pub. Health Svc., Rockville, Md., 1984—85; mem., site visit and spl. rev. com., trauma and burn program, nat. inst. gen. med. scis. NIH, U.S. Pub. Health Svc., Bethesda, Md., 1985; dir., primary care rsch. N.Y. Med. Coll., Valhalla, 1995—2007; dir. health outcomes rsch. Winthrop U. Hosp., Mineola, NY, 2007—; mem. rev. com. divsn. ind. rev. health resources and svcs. adminstrn. US Dept. Health and Human Svcs., 2005; cons. in field. Contbr. articles to profl. jours. Grantee, Nat. Ctr. for Health Svcs. Rsch., U.S. Pub. Health Svc., 1979—80, Nat. Fund for Med. Edn., 1979—80, The John A. Hartford Found., 1983—87, Mar. of Dimes Birth Defects Found., 1989—90, Am. Coll. Gastroenterology, 1999—2000, Health Resources and Services Adminstrn., USPHS, 2000—07. Mem.: Soc. for Med. Decision Making. Achievements include development of several diagnostic decision aids for physicians in pediatrics, internal medicine, and trauma. Avocation: photography. Office: Winthrop U Hosp Office Health Outcomes Rsch 222 Station Plz N Mineola NY 11501 Home Phone: 914-831-5417; Office Phone: 516-663-2914. Business E-Mail: dbrand@winthrop.org.

BRAND, EDWARD CABELL, retail executive; b. Salem, Va., Apr. 11, 1923; s. William F. and Ruth (Cabell) B.; m. Shirley Hurt, June 20, 1964; children: Sylvia, Miriam, Liza, Richie (dec.), John, Edward (dec.), Marshall (dec.), Caroline. Grad., Va. Mil. Inst., 1944; HHD (hon.), Roanoke Coll., 1997, Washington and Lee U., 1999, Ferrum Coll., 2005, Va. Western Coll., 2005. Dept. of State econ. analyst, intelligence office Berlin Mil. Govt., 1947-49; v.p. Ortho-Vent Shoe Co., 1949-62; pres. Brand Edmonds Assocs. Advertising, 1962-66, chmn. bd., 1962-81; founder, pres. Stuart McGuire Co., Salem, Va., 1962-85, chmn. bd., chief exec. officer, 1973-85; chmn. emeritus, cons. Stuart McGuire Co. (merged with Home Shopping (TV) Network), 1985-86; pres. Recovery Systems, Inc., Salem, Va., 1986—2005. Rsch. assoc., former instr. bus. adminstrn. and sales mgmt. Roanoke Coll. Chmn. Va. State Bd. Health, 1989-93; pres., founder, chmn. Cabell Brand Ctr. for Internat. Poverty and Resource Studies; dir. Southeast Rural Assistance Project Inn; cons. Rainwater Mgmt. Solutions; former mem. Bus. Leadership Adv. Council.; founder, pres. Total Action Against Poverty, Roanoke Valley, 1965-95; pres. Pvt. Sector Commn. Va. Community Action Agys., 1986-88; mem. Gov.'s Commn. on Fed. Funding of State Domestic Program, 1986-88; trustee Council on Religion and Internat. Affairs, Ethics Resource Ctr., Heinz Ctr. Sci., Econs. and Environ.; bd. dirs. Roanoke Coun. Cmty. Svcs., Woodlands Conf. divsn. Woodlands Ctr. for Future Research and the Houston Area Research Ctr., Global Water, Washington, Va. Health Care Found., Richmond, Va., 1993-2000, Va. Found. for the Humanities and Pub. Policy, Charlottesville, 1993-99, Blue Ridge Pub. TV, Roanoke, Va., 1993—, Action Alliance for Va. Children and Youth, Richmond, 1994-2000, Va. Conservation Network, Richmond, 1996—; bd. trustees Western Va. Land Trust, Roanoke, Va., 1995-2000; assoc. World Resources Inst., Washington, 1985. Served from pvt. to capt. AUS, 1942-46, ETO. Decorated Bronze Star. Named Businessman in U.S. who has done most to help disadvantaged people, Vista, 1980; recipient LBJ Humanitarian nat. award, 1989, Outstanding Citizen Rotary Club, 1999. Mem. NAS (coun., pres. cir.), Social Venture Network, Direct Selling Assn. (past dir., chmn. named to Hall of Fame), U.S. C. of C., Conf. Bd. (exec. coun.), World Pres. Assn. (past dir., chmn. Argentina Conf. 1988), Newcomen Soc. N.Am., Roanoke Touchdown Club (past pres.), Valley Torch Club (past pres.), Roanoke Sales Execs. (past dir.), Rotary (past. pres. Salem). Home: 701 W Main St Salem VA 24153-3513 Office: PO Box 429 Salem VA 24153-0429 Personal E-mail: scbrand25@comcast.net. *In addition to trying to do the best job I could— whether in school, business, public service, or in my family— I have felt a continuing need to improve our system and society. This has led to extensive study, travels, and a variety of extra-curricular activities. Today I have great confidence in the future of the United States and the world, but see urgent need for dramatic changes in our value systems, and need for long range planning. Our Center focuses on inter-relationship between poverty and resource limitation for sustainable development with specific focus on water problems locally and globally.*

BRAND, GEORGE EDWARD, JR., retired lawyer; b. Detroit, Oct. 25, 1918; s. George Edward and Elsie Bertie (Jones) B.; m. Patricia Jean Gould, June 7, 1947; children— Martha Christine, Carol Elsie, George Edward. BA, Dartmouth Coll., 1941; postgrad., U. Minn., Harvard U., 1941; JD, U. Mich., 1948. Bar: Mich. 1948, U.S. Supreme Ct. 1958. Mem. firm George E. Brand, Detroit, 1948-63, Butzel, Long, Gust, Klein & Van Zile, P.C., Detroit, 1963—; ptnr., dir., pres. Butzel, Long, Gust, Klein & Van Zile, 1974-89; ret. Served with USNR, 1942-46. Recipient Individual citation as fighter dir. officer in Solomon Islands, 1943. Fellow Am. Bar Found., Am. Coll. Trial Lawyers; mem. ABA, Am. Judicature Soc., Detroit Bar Assn., VFW. Clubs: N.S.S.C. Home: 1233 Kensington Ave Grosse Pointe Park MI 48230-1101 Office: 150 W Jefferson Ave Ste 900 Detroit MI 48226-4416

BRAND, JASON, diversified financial services company executive; Grad., Cornell U. Cert. CFA 1997. Derivative marketer Fixed Income Divsn. Merrill Lynch, NYC, mng. dir., head corp. fin. grp., head Am. debt sales, COO global investor client grp., head Pacific rim global markets, sr. v.p., co-head Pacific rim global markets & investment banking. Office: Merrill Lynch 4 World Trade Ctr 250 Vesey St New York NY 10080

BRAND, JEFFREY S., dean, law educator; AB, U. Calif., Berkeley, 1966, JD, 1969. Pub. defender Contra Costa County, Calif.; adminstrv. law judge Agricultural Labor Rels. Bd.; ptnr. Farnsworth, Saperstein and Brand, Oakland; prof. law U. San Francisco Sch. Law, dean, 1999—. Chmn. USF Center for Law and Global Justice. Former editor-in-chief Federal Litigator. Office: U San Francisco Sch Law 2130 Fulton St San Francisco CA 94117 Office Phone: 415-422-6304.

BRAND, MICHAEL, museum director; b. Australia, 1958; m. Tina Gomes Brand; 2 children. BA in Asian Studies, with honors, Australian Nat. U., Canberra, 1979; MA, Harvard U., 1982, PhD, 1987. Rsch. fellow Arthur M. Sackler Gallery Smithsonian Instn., 1987, co-dir. Mughal Garden Project Lahore, Pakistan, 1988—93; curator Asian art Mus. Art Rhode Island Sch. Design, 1985—87, Nat. Gallery of Australia, 1988—96; asst. dir. Queensland Art Gallery, Brisbane, Australia, 1996—2000; dir. Va. Mus. Fine Arts, Richmond, 2000—05, J. Paul Getty Mus., LA, 2005—. Co-author (with Glenn D. Lowry): Akbar's India: Art from the Mughal City of Victory, 1985. Office: J Paul Getty Mus 1200 Getty Ctr Dr Ste 1000 Los Angeles CA 90049-1679 E-mail: mbrand@getty.edu.

BRAND, MYLES, sports association and former academic administrator; b. NYC, May 17, 1942; s. Irving Philip and Shirley (Berger) B.; m. Wendy Hoffman (div. 1976); 1 child: Joshua; m. Margaret Zeglin, 1978. BS, Rensselaer Poly. Inst., Troy, NY, 1964; PhD, U. Rochester, 1967; PhD (hon.), Rensselaer Poly. Inst., Troy, NY, 1991. Asst. prof. philos. U. Pitts., 1967—72; assoc. prof. to prof., dept. chmn. U. Ill., Chgo., 1972—81; prof., dept. head U. Ariz., Tucson, 1981—83, dir. cognitive sci. prog., 1982—85, dean social & behavioral scis. Tucson, 1983—86; provost, v.p. acad. affairs Ohio State U., Columbus, 1986—89; pres. U. Oreg., Eugene, 1989—94, Ind. U., Bloomington, 1994—2002, NCAA, Indpls., 2003—. Author: Intending and Acting, 1984; editor: The Nature of Human Action, 1970, The Nature of Causation, 1976, Action Theory, 1976. Bd. dirs. Ariz. Humanities Coun., 1984-85, Am. Coun. Edn., Washington, 1992-97. Recipient rsch. award NEH, 1974, 79. Mem. Clarion Hosps. Assn. of Am. Phi, Assn. Am. Univs. (pres. 1999). Office: NCAA Travel Svc 111 Water St New Haven CT 06511-5759*

BRAND, OSCAR, folk singer, writer, educator; b. Winnipeg, Man., Can., Feb. 7, 1920; s. Isadore and Beatrice (Shulman) B.; m. Rubyan Saber (div.); children: Jeannie, Eric, James; m. Karen Lynn Grossman, June 14, 1970; 1 child, Jordan. BA, Bklyn. Coll., 1942; Polit. Sci. Laureate, Fairfield U., 1972; PhD (hon.), U. Winnipeg, 1987. Host, performer Folksong Festival, Sta. WNYC-AM, NYC, 1945—. Pres. Harlequin Prodns., Inc., Gypsy Hill Music, Inc.; trustee Newport Festival Found.; mem. faculty Hofstra U., New Sch., 1970-80; music adviser nat. bd. YWCA; mem. creative bd. Sesame Street, Pres.'s Com. on Nutrition; cons. Bill Moyers, PBS-TV, 1983; curator Songwriters Hall of Fame. Host: (TV show) World of Folkmusic, H.E.W., 1962-68, Oscar Brand's Am. Odyssey, 1970-72, Treasure Chest, The First Look, 1965-68, (radio show) Voices in the Wind, 1974-80, 13 of Segovia, First Person Am.; star: (TV series) Let's Sing Out, Can., 1962-68, Brand New Scene, Can., 1966; artistic dir. Project America, 92d St. Y, 1998-2001; music dir. (TV series) Nat. Geog. Bicentennial, 1974, Sunday, Exploring; music advisor: (TV series) Nuclear Age, 1986-87, (PBS) Liberty, 1998; writer, dir.: (TV spl. and show) Sing, America, Sing, Kennedy Ctr. Bicentennial Celebration, 1975; composer, lyricist: (broadway show) Joyful Noise, 1966, HYMAN KAPLAN, 1968, (off-broadway show) In White America, 1965, How to Steal an Election, 1969, 2003, It's a Jungle, Bridge of Hope for lit. conf., 1969, Celebrate for N.Y. Presbytery, 1970, (off broadway show) Thunder Bay, Fun and Games, Protest, 1999, Ready Aim Sing, 1999, Ballads and Ballots, 2000, Me and Woody, 2000, (songs for film) The Fox, Sybil, The Long Riders, Blue Chips, 1994; author: Singing Holidays, 1957, Bawdy Songs, 1960, Folksongs for Fun, 1961, The Ballad Mongers, 1964, Songs of '76, 1974, When I First Came to This Land, 1975, Party Songs, 1983; rec. artist 100 albums; performer (video) At Home, 1988, Campaigns for Smithsonian, 1999; editor: Words About Music, 1980-2002; prodr. "Campaigns in Cotton", N.Y. Hist. Soc., 2004. Program coord. Nat. Hadassah, 1989-98; trustee BMI Found., 1995—; music dir. Rukeyser Guide, 1996. Served as sgt. M.C. AUS, 1942-45. Recipient Radio Pioneers of Am. award, 1986, Edinburgh, Valley Forge and Film Festival awards for documentary and ednl. films, 1946, numerous other awards include Emmy, Peabody, Freedoms Found., Scholastic for radio, TV and films, 1962-86, Lifetime Achievement award World Folk Music Assn., 1996, Peabody Personal award, 1996, citation Can. Songwriters Hall of Fame, 2006; honoree Coalition Against Domestic Violence (adv. bd. 1993—), United Cmty. Fund, 1997; named Illustrious Alumnus Bklyn. Coll., 2001. Mem. Nat. Acad. Popular Music (bd. dirs. 1969—, host longest running radio show in history Guinness Book World Records). Avocations: sailing, carpentry. Office: Gypsy Hill Music PO Box 1362 Manhasset NY 11030-6362 Office Phone: 516-487-5979. E-mail: oscarbrand@oscarbrand.com, oscrbrand@aol.com. *I need more time.*

BRAND, RACHEL L., federal agency administrator, lawyer; BA, U. Minn., 1995; JD, Harvard U., 1998. Law clk. to Justice Charles Fried Mass. Supreme Judicial Ct., 1998—99; law clk. to Justice Anthony Kennedy U.S. Supreme Ct.; assoc. Cooper, Carvin & Rosenthal; assoc. counsel to Pres. The White House, Washington; prin. dep. asst. atty gen. Office of Legal Policy, U.S. Dept. Justice, Washington, 2003—05, acting asst. atty. gen., 2005, asst. atty. gen., 2005—. Editor-in-chief Harvard Jour. Law and Pub. Policy. Office: Office Legal Policy Rm 4234 Main Justice Bldg 950 Pennsylvania Ave NW Washington DC 20530-0001 Office Phone: 202-514-4601.*

BRAND, STEVE AARON, lawyer; b. St. Paul, Sept. 5, 1948; s. Allen A. and Shirley Mae (Mintz) B.; m. Gail Idele Greenspoon, Oct. 9, 1977. BA, U. Minn., 1970; JD, U. Chgo., 1973. Bar: Minn. 1973, U.S. Dist. Ct. Minn. 1974, U.S. Supreme Ct. 1977. Assoc. Briggs & Morgan, St. Paul, 1973-78, ptnr., 1978-91, Robins, Kaplan, Miller & Ciresi, LLP, 1991—. Pres. Jewish Vocat. Svc., 1981—84, Sholom Found., 1996—99; bd. dirs. Friends of the St. Paul Libr., 1997—2005; pres. Mt. Zion Hebrew Congregation, 1985—87. Mem. ABA, Minn. Bar Assn. (chmn. probate and trust law sect. 1984-85), Hebrew Union Coll.-Jewish Inst. Religion (bd. overseers 1987—, vice-chmn. 1996—), Am. Coll. Trust and Estate Counsel (Minn. chair 1991-96, regent 1998-2004), Ramsey County Bar Found. (pres. 1995-2000), Phi Beta Kappa, B'nai Brith. Democrat. Home: 1907 Hampshire Ave Saint Paul MN 55116-2401 Office: Robins Kaplan Miller & Ciresi LLP 2800 LaSalle Plz 800 Lasalle Ave Minneapolis MN 55402-2015 Home Phone: 651-698-8211; Office Phone: 612-349-8731. Business E-Mail: sabrand@rkmc.com.

BRAND, VANCE DEVOE, astronaut, director; b. Longmont, Colo., May 9, 1931; s. Rudolph William and Donna (DeVoe) B.; m. Joan Virginia Weninger, July 25, 1953; children: Susan Nancy, Stephanie, Patrick Richard, Kevin Stephen; m. Beverly Ann Whitnel, Nov. 3, 1979; children: Erik Ryan, Dane Vance. BS in Bus., U. Colo., 1953, BS in Aero. Engring., 1960; MBA, UCLA, 1964; grad., U.S. Naval Test Pilot Sch., Patuxent River, Md., 1963; DSc (hon.), U. Colo., 2000. With Lockheed-Calif. Co., Burbank, 1960-66, flight test engr., 1961-62, traveling engr. rep., 1962-63, engrng. test pilot, 1963-66; astronaut NASA Johnson Space Ctr., Houston, 1966-92, command module pilot Apollo-Soyuz mission, 1975, comdr. STS-5 Mission, 1982, comdr. STS 41-B Mission, 1984, comdr. STS-35 Mission, 1990; chief plans Nat. Aero-Space Plane Joint Program Office, Wright-Patterson AFB, Ohio, 1992-94; asst. chief flight ops. directorate DFRC NASA, Edwards, Calif., 1994-98, dep. dir. aerospace projects, 1998—2002, acting dir. aerospace projects, 2002—04, dep. assoc. ctr. dir. for programs, 2004—. With USMCR, 1953-57. Decorated 2 Disting. Svc. medals NASA, 2 Exceptional Svc. medals, 3 Space medals; inducted into Internat. Space Hall of Fame, 1996, U.S. Astronaut Hall of Fame, 1997, Internat. Aerspace Hall of Fame, 2001. Fellow AIAA, Am. Astron. Soc., Soc. Exptl. Test Pilots. Office: M/S D2332 DFRC PO Box 273 Edwards CA 93523-0273

BRANDAU, CHRISTIE PEARSON, librarian; b. Boone, Iowa, May 7, 1949; d. Ingemar Nils and Elsa Pearson; m. John Alan Brandau, Dec. 20, 1968; children: Jennifer Brandau Carlson, Kara Brandau Califf, Benjamin John. MA in Libr. sci., U. of Iowa, 1988; BA in Polit. sci., Iowa State U., 1975. Asst. state libr. State Libr. of Iowa, Des Moines, 1991—2000; state libr. Libr. of Mich., Lansing, 2000—05, State Libr. Kans., Topeka, 2005—. Recipient President's award, Mich. Assn. Media in Edn., 2003. Mem.: ALA (SCAS chair 2001—02), Kans. Libr. Assn., Chief Officers of State Libr. Agencies (legis. co-chair, exec. com.), Mich. State Hist. Records Adv. Bd., Mich. Humanities Coun. Office: State Libr Kans Rm 343 N 300 SW 10th Ave Topeka KS 66612-1593 Office Phone: 785-296-5466. E-mail: christieb@kslib.info.

BRANDEIS, BARRY, retired apparel executive; b. May 3, 1946; s. Norman and Jennie (Yousin) B.; m. Renee Riesenberg, Apr. 4, 1971; children: Adam, Marisa. BS in Psychology, Pa. State U., 1968, MBA in Mgmt., 1970; MBA in Fin., CUNY, 1974, postgrad., 1975. Account exec. Meridian Securities Co., Bala Cynwyd, Pa., 1968-70; instr. Baruch Coll. Pace U. Grad. Sch., 1971, assoc. prof., 1975—99; asst. to chmn. Wasko Gold Products Corp., NYC, 1975—77, v.p. fin., 1977—80, exec. v.p., 1980—83; group exec. Holding Capital Group, 1984—85; CEO Budoff, Inc., 1985—88; v.p. Craftex Creations, Inc., 1988—90; prin. Twin Era Ltd., 1991—2005; ret., 2005. Mem. U.S. Senate Bus. Adv. Bd.; alumni bd. Pa. State U., Abington; pres. Orgn. of Student Assn., 1967, Penna Assn. of Coll. Students, 1968. Mem. AAUP, Internat. Precious Metals Inst. (charter), Assn. MBA Execs., PR C. of C. in U.S. (bd. dirs.), Internat. Platform Assn., NY Acad. Scis., Parmi Nous, Omicron Delta Kappa, Psi Chi.

BRANDEL, ROLAND ERIC, lawyer; b. Chgo., Nov. 30, 1938; s. Eric John and Louise Catherine (Covich) B.; m. Catherine Terry, July 3, 1963 (div. July 1970). BS in Econs., Ill. Inst. Tech., 1960; JD, U. Chgo., 1966; postgrad., Columbia U., 1970. Commd. ensign U.S. Navy, 1960, advanced through grades to lt. comdr., ret., 1970; clk. to chief justice Calif. Supreme Ct., San Francisco, 1966-67; sr. counsel, ptnr. Morrison & Foerster, 1967—. Vis. prof. law U. Calif., Berkeley, 1974-75; consumer adv. council Fed. Res. Bd., Washington, 1976-80; vis. com. U. Chgo. Law Sch., 1983-86, Golden Gate Law Sch., San Francisco, 1983—; study groups of EFT and Negotiable Instruments Sec. of State Adv. Commn., Washington, 1983-90; chmn. San Francisco Com. on Fgn. Relations, 2002-. Co-author: Law of EFT Systems, 1988, TIL: 4 Comp. Guide plus supplement, 1981-87, Community Reinvestment Act Manual, 1978, Financial Privacy Comp. Manual, 1979. Mem. Planning Comm. City of Berkeley, 1972-74; chmn. Waterfront Adv. Bd., Berkeley, 1973. Recipient Lifetime Achievement award, Calif. Bankers Assn., 2000, Am. Coll. Consumer Fin. Svcs. Lawyers, 2004. Mem. ABA (chmn. consumer fin. svcs. com. 2006, coun. bus. law 1982-86, 2002—06, chmn. ad hoc com. payment systems 1983-88), Inst. Marine Resources (adv.bd. 1983-86), Nat. Ctr. Fin. Svcs. (chmn. legal adv. com. 1985—, mng. com. 1983—), State Bar Calif. (chair bus. law sect., 1993-94, mem. 2006), Am. Coll. Consumer Fin. Svcs. (pres. 1999-2001), U. Chgo. Law Sch. Alumni (pres. 1968-94). Home: 58 Roble Rd Berkeley CA 94705-2838 Office: Morrison & Foerster 425 Market San Francisco CA 94105 Office Phone: 415-268-7093. E-mail: rbrandel@mofo.com.

BRANDENBURG, DAVID SAUL, gastroenterologist, educator; b. Linz, Austria, Apr. 12, 1948; arrived in US, 1948; s. Mayer and Syda Brandenburg; m. Bette Ellen Hirschberg, Aug. 8, 1971; children: Stacey, Mark, Marci. BA, Rutgers U., 1968; MD, Georgetown U., 1972. Bd. cert. internal medicine; bd. cert. GI. Intern, resident R.I. Hosp.-Brown U. Affiliated, Providence, 1972-75; gastroenterology fellow Emory U., Atlanta, 1975-77; pvt. practice Atlanta Digestive Diseases and Internal Medicine, 1977-82, Brandenburg and Kramer M.D., P.C., Atlanta, 1983-97; clin. asst. prof. medicine Emory U. Sch. Medicine, Atlanta, 1977—; with Atlanta Gastroenterology Assocs., 1997—. Med. dir. North Atlanta Endoscopy Ctr., Atlanta, 1986-2002; sec., v.p., pres. Ga. Soc. GI Endoscopy, Atlanta, 1980-86; chmn., med. adv. com. Ga. chpt. Crohn's and Colitis Found., Atlanta, 1995-97. Bd. trustees Temple Emmanuel, Dunwoody, Ga., 1985-91, 95-96, treas., 1988-89, v.p., 1990-91. Fellow Am. Coll. Gastroenterology (gov. 1991-95); mem. Am. Gastroenterol. Assn., Am. Soc. Gastrointestinal Endoscopy. Office: 5671 Peachtree Dunwoody Rd Ste 600 Atlanta GA 30342-2311 Office Phone: 404-257-9000.

BRANDENSTEIN, DANIEL CHARLES, astronaut, retired military officer; b. Watertown, Wis., Jan. 17, 1943; s. Walter C. and Agnes (Holzworth) B.; m. Jane A. Wade, Jan. 2, 1966; 1 dau., Adelle. BS, U. Wis., River Falls, 1965; postgrad., U.S. Naval Text Pilot Sch., Patuxent River, Md., 1971. Commd. officer U.S. Navy, 1965, advanced through grades to capt., 1984, ret., 1993, student aviator Pensacola, Fla., 1965-67, aviator Whidbey Island, Wash., 1967-71, test pilot Patuxent River, Md., 1971-74, aviator Whidbey Island, Wash., 1974-78; astronaut NASA Johnson Space Ctr., Houston, 1978-93, chief astronaut office, 1987-93; dir. program development Loral Space Info. Sys., Houston, 1993-96; exec. v.p. Kistler Aerospace Corp., Kirkland, Wash., 1996-99; v.p. Lockheed Martin Space Ops., 1999—. Decorated Legion of Honor (France), 34 medals and awards USN, 1968-93; recipient Disting. Alumnus award U. Wis., 1982, Yuri Gagarin Gold medal Fedn. Aeronautique Internationale, 1990, Laurel Award, Space/Missiles, Aviation Week & Space Tech., 1993, Haley Space Flight award Am. Inst. of Aeronautics and Astronautics, 1993; named to Astronaut Hall Fame, 2003. Mem. AIAA (Haley Space Flight award 1993), Soc. Exptl. Text Pilots (Ivan C. Kinchloe award 1992), U.S. Naval Inst., Assn. Space Explorers. Office: PO Box 58980 Houston TX 77258-8980 Home Phone: 281-303-0132; Office Phone: 281-853-3314. E-mail: dan.brandenstein@lmco.com.

BRANDES, CHARLES H., investment company executive; BA, Bucknell U. Founder Brandes Investment Ptnrs., 1974, chmn. exec. com., mem. investment oversight com. Author: Internat. Value Investing: Making the Right Choice at the Right Price, 1996, Value Investing Today, 1997. Named one of 400 Richest Ams., Forbes mag., 2006. Office: Brandes Investment Ptnrs 11988 El Camino Real, Ste 500 PO Box 919048 San Diego CA 92191-9048

BRANDES, JOANNE, lawyer; BA, U. Wis., Eau Claire; JD, Willamette U. Assoc. Herz, Levin, Teper, Chernof & Sumner, SC, 1978—81; with S.C. Johnson & Son, Inc., 1981—96; sr. v.p., gen. counsel S.C. Johnson Comml. Markets, Inc., 1997—2002; exec. v.p., chief adminstrv. officer, gen counsel JohnsonDiversey, Inc. (formerly Johnson Wax Profl.), Sturtevant, Wis., 2002—. Dir. JohnsonFamily Funds, Inc., Andersen Corp. Inc., Bright Horizons Family Solutions Inc., Watertown, Mass., 1998—. Regent emeritus U. Wis., Wis., 1996—; past mem. Gov.'s Commn. on Glass Ceiling; chmn. Wis. Child Care Coun.; past president Racine Area United Found. Named Working Mother of Yr., Working Mother mag., 1994; named to Eau Claire Alumni Hall of Honor, U. Wis., 1995, 2002; recipient Bus. Jour. Women of Influence award, 2002. Office: JohnsonDiversey, Inc 8310 16th St PO Box 902 Sturtevant WI 53177-0902

BRANDES, RAYMOND STEWART, historian, educator, dean; b. San Diego, Jan. 2, 1924; s. Theodore C. and María Rosario (Peters) B.; m. Irma Dolores Montijo, Jan. 28, 1961; children: Elena María, Elisa Anne, Laura Raquel, Claudia Reneè, Ramón Antonio, Marta Denise, Paula Nicole. BA, U. Ariz., 1961, PhD, 1965. Asst. prof. history U. San Diego, 1966-67, assoc. prof., 1967-71, prof., 1971-98, univ. archivist, 1992-98, chmn. dept., 1967-73, grad. dean, 1973-91; ret., 1998. Dir. several grants related to hist. preservation and hist. site archaeology in San Diego area. Author: Diario of Miguel Costanso, 1969, Troopers West: Military and Indian Affairs on the American Frontier, 1970, Frontier Military Posts of Arizonia, 1960, San Diego: An Illustrated History, 1982; editor Brand Book 1, San Diego Corral of Westerners, 1970, Masterplanner for Old Town State Historical Park, 1973-74, Old Town San Diego, 1821-1974, 1976, History and Archaeology of New Town, San Diego, 1985, Coronado: The Enchanted Island, 1987, 3d edit., 1999, Coronado: We Remember, 1993, The Pacific Coast League San Diego Padres, 2 vols., 1936-1957, 1997. Mem. Gaslamp Quarter Project Area Com., 1977—, chmn., 1980; v.p. San Diego Sci. Found., 1978-87, Internat. Am. Heritage Found., 2000—. With U.S. Army, 1943-46, USAR, 1950-53. Recipient medal of San Diego de Alcala, U. San. Diego, 1997; NDEA grantee, 1961-64; CETA grantee, 1978, 79; named Outstanding Prof. Social Sci. U. San Diego, 1968, 69, Disting. Historian medal U. Ariz., 1989. Mem. Mex.-Am. Educators, Nat. Coun. Pub. History, Soc. Am. Baseball Rschrs., Pacific Coast League Baseball Hist. Soc., San Diego Baseball Hist. Soc. (1st pres.), Coronado Hist. Soc. & Mus. (bd. dir.). Democrat. Roman Catholic. Home: 230 W Laurel St Apt 406 San Diego CA 92101-1464 Office Phone: 619-702-7137. E-mail: raybrandes@sbcglobal.net.

BRANDES, STANLEY HOWARD, anthropology educator, writer; b. NYC, Dec. 26, 1942; s. Emanuel Robert and Annette (Zalisch) B.; m. Jane Brandes; children: Nina Rachel, Naomi Clara. BA, U. Chgo., 1964; MA, U. Calif., Berkeley, 1969, PhD, 1971. Asst. prof. anthropology Mich. State U., East Lansing, 1971-75; asst. prof. anthropology U. Calif., Berkeley, 1975-78, assoc. prof., 1978-82, prof. anthropology, 1982—, chmn. dept., 1990-93, 97-99. Dir. Barcelona Study Ctr., U. Calif. and Ill., Spain, 1981-82, Mexico City Study Ctr., 1995-96, U. Calif. Author: Migration, Kinship and Community, 1975, Metaphors of Masculinity, 1989, Forth: The Age and the Symbol, 1985, Power and Persuasion, 1988, Staying Sober in Mexico City, 2002; co-editor: Symbol as Sense, 1980. NIH fellow, 1967-71; NICHD Rsch. fellow, 1975-77; fellow John Carter Brown Libr., 1994; Am. Council Learned Socs. grantee, 1977 Fellow Am. Anthrop. Assn.; mem. Am. Ethnological Soc., Soc. for Psychol. Anthropology Office: U Calif Dept Anthropology Berkeley CA 94720-0001 Office Phone: 510-642-6945. Business E-Mail: brandes@berkeley.edu.

BRANDEWIE, RICHARD ANTHONY, laser and optics consultant; b. Sidney, Ohio; s. Leo Peter and Mary Agnes (Doorley) B.; m. Arlene Therese Warner, Aug. 29, 1959; children: Leo Peter, Frances Brandewie Geoffrion. BEE, U. Detroit, 1959; MS, Carnegie Inst. Tech., Pitts., 1960, PhD, 1963. Mem. tech. staff N.Am. Aviation, Anaheim, Calif., 1963-67; supr. lasers Rockwell Autonetics, Anaheim, 1967—79; mgr. lasers Rockwell Rocketdyne, Canoga Park, Calif., 1979-80, dir. rsch., 1980-84, program mgr., 1984-92; ind. cons. Monte Nido, Calif., 1992—. Contbr. articles to profl. jours. Dir. Edenwild Property Owners Assn., L.A., 1983, sec., 1983, pres., 1984. Recipient Esso fellowship Esso Corp., Carnegie Inst. Tech., 1961-63; recipient Nat. Sci. and Tech. award Iris Active

Systems Group, 1992. Mem. IEEE, Am. Phys. Soc., Carnegie Mellon U. L.A. Alumni Assn. (dir., sec. 1980, pres. 1995-96), Sigma Xi, Eta Kappa Nu, Tau Beta Pi. Achievements include recognition as a founding father of laser radar and a major early contributor to the field of adaptive optics. Mailing: PO Box 201 Woodland Hills CA 91365-0201 Personal E-mail: richbrand@ieee.org.

BRANDHORST, WESLEY THEODORE, retired library and information scientist; b. Portland, Oreg., May 9, 1933; s. Wesley Theodore and Mary Margeurite (LaRouche) B.; m. Jane Smythe, Sept. 1, 1962; children— Tristan, Thea BA, U. Calif.-Berkeley, 1955, M.L.S., 1957. Spl. intern Libr. Congress, Washington, 1957-59; libr. Documentation Inc., Washington, 1959-61; asst. dir. NASA Sci. and Tech. Info. Facility, Washington, 1962-69; dir. ERIC Processing and Reference Facility, Washington, 1970-2000; ret., 2000. Chmn. Z39 Nat. Info. Stds. Orgn., 1985-87. Contbr. articles to profl. jours. Mem. ALA, AAAS, Spl. Librs. Assn., Am. Soc. Info. Sci. Unitarian Universalist. Avocations: tennis, running, bicycling, chess, reading. Home: 3346 Yonge Ave Sarasota FL 34235 Personal E-mail: tbrandho@verizon.net.

BRANDIS, BERNARDINE, lawyer; b. San Francisco; d. Sidney Norman and Sheva Diane (Braunstein) B.; m. Jeffrey Peter Alperin, Mar. 27, 1982; 1 child, Shaun Lee Alperin. BA, UCLA, 1975, JD, 1978. Bar: Calif. 1978. Counsel 20th Century Fox, LA, 1981-83; dir. bus. affairs Universal Pictures, Universal City, Calif., 1983-85; v.p. bus. affairs Walt Disney Pictures and TV, Burbank, Calif., 1985-88; sr. v.p. bus./legal affairs Hollywood Pictures Co., Burbank, 1988; exec. v.p. bus. and legal affairs Walt Disney Studios. Named one of 100 Most Powerful Women in Entertainment, Hollywood Reporter, 2006. Mem. Phi Beta Kappa. Office: Walt Disney Studio TD202F 500 S Buena Vista St Burbank CA 91521-0006*

BRANDLER, JONATHAN M., lawyer; b. LA, Jan. 8, 1946; AB, U. Calif., Berkeley, 1967; JD, U. So. Calif., 1970. Bar: Calif. 1971. Ptnr. Hill, Farrer & Burrill LLP, LA. Lectr. Inst. Bus. Law, 1981-92. Mem. State Bar Calif. (labor law sect.), L.A. County Bar Assn. (labor law sect.). Office: Hill Farrer & Burrill LLP 1 California Plaza 300 S Grand Ave Ste 37 Los Angeles CA 90071-3110 E-mail: jbrandler@hfbllp.com.

BRANDMAIER, JEFF, diversified financial services company executive; MS in Info. Sys., Stockton State Coll.; MBA in Fin., Pace U. Mgmt. IBM; sr. mgr. KPMG Nolan, Norton & Co.; chief info. officer The Money Store, 1995—2001; sr. v.p., chief info. officer H&R Block, Inc., Kans. City, Mo., 2001—. Avocation: amateur competitive equestrian. Office: H&R Block 4400 Main St Kansas City MO 64111

BRANDON, DAVID A., food service executive; b. 1952; m. Jan Brandon. AB, tchg. cert., U. Mich., 1974. With Procter & Gamble Distbg. Co., 1974-79, GFV Comm., Inc., 1979-83, COO, exec. v.p., dir., 1983-86; COO, exec. v.p., pres., dir. Valassis Inserts, Inc., Livonia, Mich., 1986—99; pres., CEO Valassis Communication, Inc., Livonia, Mich., 1989—99, chmn., 1997—98; chmn., CEO Domino's Pizza, Inc., Ann Arbor, Mich., 1999—. Bd. dirs. TJX Cos., Burger King Corp., 2003—, Kaydon Corp. Bd. regents U. Mich., 1999—2006; bd. dirs. Detroit Renaissance, Purple Rose Theatre Co. Office: Dominos Pizza Inc 30 Frank Lloyd Wright Dr PO Box 997 Ann Arbor MI 48106-0997 Business E-Mail: brandod@dominos.com. E-mail: dabran@umich.edu.*

BRANDON, ELVIS DENBY, JR., financial planner; b. Nov. 28, 1927; s. Elvis Denby and Hazel Ione (Davidson) Brandon; m. Helen Holt Deupree, Apr. 25, 1953; children: Elvis Denby III, Raymond Wilson. BA with honors, Rhodes Coll., Memphis, 1950; MA, Duke U., 1952. CLU; CFP, chartered fin. cons., registered prin. NASD. Chmn. Brandon Fin. Planning Inc./Brandon Investments, Inc., Memphis, 1952—. Prodr., moderator (TV) Your Future Unlimited, 1955 (Sylvania TV award). Tchr. Shady Grove Presbyn. Ch., Memphis, 1989—; mem. pres.'s coun. and heritage soc. Rhodes Coll.; coord. Great Millennium Reunion. Mem.: Fin. Planners Assn. (P. Kemp Fain Jr. award honoree 2007), CFP Bd. Stds. (chmn. 1989—90, 1st chmn. internat. coun. 1992), Rotary, Racquet Club Memphis, Phi Beta Kappa. Home: 505 West Racquet Club Pl Memphis TN 38117 Office: 5101 Wheelis Rd Ste 112 Memphis TN 38117 Home Phone: 901-683-5614; Office Phone: 901-324-6600. Business E-Mail: edenbybrandonjr@brandonplanners.com.

BRANDON, ELVIS DENBY, III, financial planner; b. Memphis, Aug. 11, 1954; s. Elvis Denby Jr. and Helen (Deupree) B.; m. Sarah Louise Buntin, Mar. 15, 1980; children: Elizabeth Holt, William Denby, Mary Buntin. BBA, So. Meth. U., 1976; MBA, Memphis State U., 1979. Cert. fin. planner; CLU; chartered fin. cons. Mgmt. candidate First Tenn. Bank, NA, Memphis, 1979-80; sr. credit analyst Banc Texas/Dallas NA, 1980-82; asst. v.p., comml. loan officer Banc Texas/Sherman NA, 1982; pres. Brandon Investments, Inc., Memphis, 1982—; v.p. Brandon Fin. Planning, Inc., Memphis, 1982—. Adj. faculty Coll. for Fin. Planning, Denver, 1984-85. Elder Idlewild Presbyn. Ch. Mem.: NASD (registered prin.), Fin. Planning Assn. Presbyterian. Home: 5953 Brierdale Ave Memphis TN 38120-2345 Office: Brandon Fin Planning Inc 5101 Wheelis Rd Ste 112 Memphis TN 38117 Business E-Mail: denbybrandon@brandonplanning.com.

BRANDON, LIANE, filmmaker, educator; Student, St. Lawrence U., U. Edinburgh, Scotland; exchange student, U. Moscow; AB, MEd, Boston U. Ski instr., Mt. Tremblant, Que., Canada; actress Children's Theatre, Cambridge, Mass.; film project dir. English dept. Quincy pub. schs., Mass.; prof. film-TV prodn. and media studies Sch. Edn. U. Mass., Amherst, 1973—2006, prof. emeritus, 2007—; co-founder, mem. New Day Films, 1971—, Filmwomen of Boston, 1974—; co-dir. UMass Ednl. TV, U. Mass., Amherst, 1994—2004; dir. Sch. Edn. Ednl. Tech. Program, U. Mass., 1998—. Film cons. Mass. Gov.'s Commn. Status Women, 1974, Smith Coll., 2007; cons. Mass. Artists Found., 1975, 82, Sta. WGBH-TV, 1992—97; judge Regional Student Acad. Awards, 1991, New Eng. Regional Emmy Awards, 1992; trustee Theaterworks, 1981—83; bd. dirs. Boston Film-Video Found., 1983—87, ACLU Mass., 1986—97; mem. adv. bd. Children's Media Found. Boston, 1993—97; guest lectr. various confs. edn. and film, colls. and art schs. Exhibitions include Mus. Modern Art, Whitney Mus. Am. Art, Chgo. Art Inst., Nat. Film Theatre, London, Internat. Women's Film Festival, Paris, Mus. Fine Arts, Boston, Libr. Congress, Washington, John F. Kennedy Ctr. Performing Arts; dir., prodr.: (films) Anything You Want to Be, 1971 (Blue Ribbon Am. Film Festival); Betty Tells Her Story, 1972; Once Upon a Choice, 1980 (Silver medal Houston Internat. Film Festival); How to Prevent a Nuclear War, 1987 (Blue Ribbon Am. Film Festival, 1988); prodr.: (video) Goodnight Amherst, 1995, Fine Print, 1995, Try This at Home, 1998 (Judge's Choice award Hometown Video Festival, 1999), Fresh Ink, 1998, Try This at Home: Nature Series, 2000 (award of Distinction, Communicator award); photographer Murder at Harvard, 2002, Act Your Age, 2002, The Most Dangerous Woman in America, 2005, The Powder and the Glory, 2006. Recipient Creative Artist award, AAUW, 1975, Disting. Alumni award, Boston U., 1985; Careth Found. grantee, 1988, Funding Exch. grantee, 1989, Mass. Found. Humanities and Pub. Policy grantee, 1975, Film Fund grantee, 1985. Mem.: Women in Film and Video New Eng. (founding mem. 1981—), Assn. Ind. Video and Filmmakers, New Eng. Screen Edn. Assn. (v.p. 1972—83). E-mail: brandon@educ.umass.edu.

BRANDON, RAYMOND WILSON, financial planner, securities principal; b. Memphis, Mar. 11, 1959; s. Elvis Denby Jr. and Helen (Deupree) B.; m. Dana Stallings, Sept. 21, 1996. BA, Vanderbilt U., 1981; MBA, U. Tex., 1983. CFA; CLU; cert. fin. planner; chartered fin. cons. Pres., chmn. investment com. Brandon Fin. Planning, Inc., Memphis, 1983—; v.p. ops. Brandon Investments, Inc., Memphis, 1983—. V.p. Brandon Underwriting Specialists, Inc., Memphis. Sord scholar U. Tex., 1983. Mem. Fin. Planning Assn. (pres. Memphis chpt. 1988-89), Am. Soc. Fin. Svc. Profls., Memphis Inst. Cert. Fin. Planners (bd. dirs.), CFA Inst., Rotary (Paul Harris fellow, treas., bd. dirs., v.p. 2007), Racquet Club Memphis, Phi Beta Kappa. Presbyterian. Avocations: swimming, running, travel, magic, public speaking. Office: 5101 Wheelis Rd Ste 112 Memphis TN 38117 Office Phone: 901-324-6600. Business E-Mail: RayBrandon@BrandonPlanning.com.

BRANDON, WALTER WILEY, JR., retired physicist, retired aerospace engineer; b. Gainesville, Ga., Dec. 1, 1929; s. Walter Wiley and Nancy (Logan) Brandon; m. Patricia Donham, May 18, 1957; children: Dean Corbly, Miles Logan, Nancy Lynn. BA, Emory U., 1952, MS, 1953. Scientist Rohm and Haas Co., Huntsville, Ala., 1953—64, 1967—71; aerospace engr. Boeing Co., Huntsville, 1964—67; analyst U.S. Army Missile Command, Huntsville, 1972—87; aerospace engr. NASA Marshall Space Flight Ctr., Huntsville, 1987—98, ret., 1998. Tech. cons. detonation U.S. Army Missile Command, Huntsville, 1988, Morton-Thiokol Corp., Huntsville, 1988. Fellow: AIAA (assoc.); mem.: Sigma Pi Sigma (Emory U. chpt. pres. 1952—53), Sigma Xi (assoc.). Methodist. Avocations: photography, model building. Home: 1902 Colice Rd SE Huntsville AL 35801-1640

BRANDOW, STEPHEN JON, priest; b. Olean, NY, Dec. 25, 1960; s. David Arden and Jacqueline Delores (Johns) B. BA, Northwestern State U. La., 1983, BA in Social Work, 1985; MDiv, Notre Dame Sem., 1996. Ordained to ministry, Cath. Ch., 1996. Social worker Woodview Regional Hosp., Pineville, La., 1986; med. clk. VA Med. Ctr., Alexandria, La., 1986-91; assoc. pastor St. Rita Cath. Ch., Alexandria, La., 1996-97, Immaculate Heart of Mary Cath. Ch., Tioga, La., 1997-2000. Chaplain Ctrl. La. State Hosp., Pineville, 1997—2000, Christus St. Frances Cabrini Hosp., Alexandria, 1997—, 1997—2001, VA Med. Ctr., Alexandria, 1998—; mem. com. continuing formation of clergy Diocese of Alexandria, 1996—, sec., 1996—97. Mem. Cath. Commn. on Scouting, 1997—; bd. dir. Girl Scout Coun. of Ctrl. La., 2001—02; v.p. Attakapas Coun. Boy Scouts of Am., cmty. adv. bd. Achita Valley Coun., 2003—. Recipient Whitney Young Svc. award, Boy Scouts Am., 2002, Pelican award, Cath. Com. on Scouting, Diocese of Alexandria, 2003; James E. West fellow, Boy Scouts Am., 2002. Mem.: United Assn. Christian Counselors, La. Chaplains Assn. (bd. dirs. 1999—2002). Avocation: yoga. Home: PO Box 39 Tioga LA 71477 Office: VA Med Ctr PO Box 69004 Tioga LA 71306 Fax: 318-483-5053. E-mail: sbran62261@aol.com.

BRANDOW, THEO, architect; b. Phila., Nov. 18, 1925; s. Ralph and Minnie (Weinstock) B.; m. Selma Koss, July 22, 1945; children: Jonathan, Rinna, Shanna. Student, Girard Coll., 1935—43; BArch, U. Pa., 1949. Assoc. Oskar Stonorov, Phila., 1949-52; pvt. practice architecture Phila., 1952-78; project dir. Rochlin & Baran & Assocs., West Los Angeles, Calif., 1978-81; pres. Brandow Design Assocs., 1982-87; pvt. practice architecture Ambler, Pa., 1987—. Cons. urban renewal; vis. speaker sch. system Wellspring Ecumenical Ctr., Phila., 1966—. Prin. works include houses, apt. and office buildings, churches; design architect Benjamin Franklin House; works pub. in various mags. including Life, House and Home, Am. Home; author: Closer to Saturday, 1971, Michla, A Trilogy; also articles and lectures on Israel's Day of Atonement War of 1973; group shows include Chestnut Hill Fine Arts Festival, Phila., 1995 (1st place prize 1995), New Hope Art Festival, Pa., 1995 (award of excellence 1995), Lansdale Festival of the Arts, Pa., 1995 (most unique craft award 1995), Woodmere Art Mus., Phila., 1996, 97, 98, 2d Fl. Gallery, Mechanicsburg, Pa., 2005; juried shows include Susquehanna Art Mus., Harrisburg, Pa., 2004, W.M. Riis Gallery, Camp Hill, Pa., 2005. V.p. Erdenheim PTA, Pa., 1956; active Whitemarsh Valley Fair Housing Coun., 1966—; cubmaster local coun. Boy Scouts Am.; bd. dirs. local Jewish synagogue. With USNR, 1943-46. Recipient award World Traveling Exhibit Art in Arch., 1949, Homes for Better Living, 1957, 59, state citation Am. Home mag., 1957, nat. citation, 1958, spl. award Am. Builder mag., 1959, McCall's Congress for Better Living award, 1959, awards Nat. Assn. Home Builders, 1961, Bronze Plaque of Appreciation, Temple Beth Shalom, Mechanicsburg, 2005. Mem. AIA (awards 1957, 61). Home: 2601 #1 Market St Camp Hill PA 17001 E-mail: ted@brandow.com.

BRANDRETH, ELIZABETH ANNE, library director; b. NYC, July 8, 1937; d. John Joseph and Edith M. (Mayer) B. AA, Mount Aloysius Jr. Coll., Cresson, Pa., 1957; BA, Coll. Misericordia, 1961; MSLS, Cath. U. Am., 1963; MS in Human Resources Adminstrn., U. Scranton, 1988. Mem. Sisters of Mercy. Asst. libr. Coll. Misericordia, Dallas, Pa., 1963-64; libr. Bishop McCort H.S., Johnstown, Pa., 1964-67; reference libr. Mount Aloysius Jr. Coll., Cresson, Pa., 1967-71, libr. dir., 1971-79; dir. libr. svcs. Mercy Hosp., Scranton, Pa., 1979-95; regional dir. libr. svcs. Mercy Health Ptnrs., Scranton, 1995—. Sec.-treas. bd. dirs. Catherine McAuley Ctr., Scranton, 1986-95; sec. bd. dirs. N.E. Pa. chpt. Susan G. Komen Breast Cancer Found., Scranton, 1989-93; bd. trustees Coll. Misericordia, Dallas, 1990-93. Mem. Med. Libr. Assn., Pa. Libr. Assn. (bd. mem. N.E. chpt. 1985-87), Beta Phi Mu. Roman Catholic. Avocation: reading. Office: Mercy Hosp 746 Jefferson Ave Scranton PA 18510-1697 Home Phone: 570-348-2059. Personal E-mail: ebrandreth@hotmail.com.

BRANDRUP, DOUGLAS WARREN, lawyer; b. Mitchell, SD, July 11, 1940; s. Clair L. and Ruth M. (Wolverton) B.; m. Patricia R. Tuck, Dec. 20, 1986; children: Kendra, Monika, Peter. AB in Econs., Middlebury Coll., 1963; JD, Boston U., 1966. Bar: N.Y. 1969, U.S. Dist. Ct. (so. dist.) N.Y. 1970, U.S. Ct. Appeals (2d cir.) 1970. Assoc. Donovan, Leisure, Newton & Irvine, NYC, 1968-72; ptnr. Griggs, Baldwin & Baldwin, NYC, 1972-80, sr. ptnr., 1980—. Mem. disciplinary com. first dept. appellate divsn. Supreme Ct. State of N.Y., 2003. Mem. Govs. Security Adv. Com., State of N.J., 1975-90. Capt. U.S. Army, 1966-68. Recipient Ellis Island medal of Honor, 1999, Order of St. John, 2002. Mem. ABA, N.Y. County Bar Assn., N.Y. State Bar Assn., Met. Club (N.Y.C., pres.), Mashomack Preserve Club. Republican. Episcopalian. Office: 57 Old Post Rd No 2 Greenwich CT 06830 Office Fax: 203-629-7983.

BRANDS, JAMES EDWIN, medical products executive; b. Lebanon, Ind., July 5, 1937; s. Edwin Herman and Pearl Irene (Brown) B.; m. Gail Marian Knight, Sept. 12, 1959; children: Jeffrey, Scot, Alan, Susan. AB, Wesleyan U., Middletown, Conn., 1959; MBA, U. Chgo., 1961; JD, Kennedy-Western U., Boise, Idaho, 1992. CPA, Mo. Staff acct., mgr. Arthur Andersen, Chgo., 1961-71, ptnr. St. Louis, 1971-82; sr. v.p. Scherer-Storz, Inc., St. Louis, 1982-86, bd. dirs.; vice chmn., CFO Scherer Healthcare Inc., Atlanta, 1982-95; exec. v.p. Scherer Sci. Ltd., Atlanta, 1986-95; chmn., CEO Marquest Med. Products, Inc., Denver, 1993-95; CFO Wilson Pest Control, Inc., Atlanta, 1997-99; sr. exec. v.p. Able Telcom Holding Corp., Atlanta, 1999—2001. Bd. dirs., pres. BodyCare Inc., Atlanta; pres. Brands & Co, 1981—, Throwleigh Tech. LLC, Atlanta, 2000—. Mem. AICPA, Mo. Soc. CPAs, Bellerive Country Club (St. Louis), Country Club of the South (Atlanta). Home: 4330 Bancroft Valley Alpharetta GA 30022-5175 Personal E-mail: brandsj@bellsouth.net.

BRANDT, CARL DAVID, research virologist; b. Bridgeport, Conn., Jan. 19, 1928; s. Carl August and Hildur (Wedberg) B.; m. Elsa Lund Erickson, Apr. 25, 1964; children: Karen, Erik. BS, U. Conn., 1949; MS, U. Mass., 1951; PhD, Harvard U., 1958. Rsch. instr. dept. vet. sci. U. Mass., Amherst, 1949-52, 54; rsch. virologist Charles Pfizer & Co., Inc., Ind. and Conn., 1958—62; assoc., dept. epidemiology Pub. Health Rsch. Inst., NYC, 1962—66; rsch. assoc. virology rsch. Children's Nat. Med. Ctr., Washington, 1966-79, sr. rsch. assoc., 1979-86, sr. scientist, 1986-94; ret., 1994. Instr. Georgetown U. Med. Sch., Washington, 1966-69; asst. prof. pediat. George Washington U. Med. Sch., Washington, 1969-74, assoc. prof., 1974-94, emeritus prof., 1994. Contbr. over 125 articles to profl. jours. 1st lt. USAF, 1952-54. Fellow Am. Acad. Microbiology, Infectious Diseases Soc. Am., Am. Coll. Epidemiology; mem. N.Y. Color Slide Club (bd. dirs. 1965-66), Silver Spring Camera Club (pres. 1970-71), Rock Creek Amateur Radio Assn. (pres. 1985-89). Avocations: photography, amateur radio. Home: 819 E Franklin Ave Silver Spring MD 20901-4709

BRANDT, CAROLE, theater educator, department chairman; b. Lincoln, Ill., Oct. 22, 1937; d. Clifton Perry and Mary Helen (Mitchell). BS in Speech Edn., U. Ill., 1959, MA in Theatre Art, 1962; postgrad., U. Iowa, 1968-69; PhD in Directing and Dramatic Lit., So. Ill. U., 1976. Tchr. speech and drama, play dir. pub. schs., Oak Lawn, Joliet, Maywood, Ill., 1959-65, 66-68; teaching asst. in speech U. Ill., Urbana, 1961-62; teaching asst. in rhetoric, then instr. edn. play prodn. U. Iowa, Iowa City, 1968-69; asst. prof. theatre Ill. State U., Normal, 1969-74; assoc. prof. drama Ill. Wesleyan U., Bloomington, 1975-82, dir. Sch. Drama, 1977-82; artistic dir. Cen. Sta. Dinnner, Bloomington, 1982-83, Co. ONSTAGE, Bloomington, 1983-84; prof., chmn. dept. theatre U. Fla., Gainesville, 1984-88; prof., head dept. theatre arts, exec. producer, artistic dir. Pa. State U. and Pa. Centre Stage, University Park, 1988-94; dean Meadows Sch. of the Arts, So. Meth. U., Dallas, 1994—, prof. Vis. artist, prof. Idaho State U., Pocatello, 1984; critic Am. Coll. Theater Regional and State Festivals; guest critic numerous univs. and theatres; mem. Pa. Adv. Coun. for Arts in Edn., 1990-92; exec. producer, bd. dirs. Pa. Centre Stage, 1988-92; mem. nat. com. Am. Coll. Theatre Festival, Kennedy Ctr. for Performing Arts, Washington, 1978-89, 91-93, mem. nat. exec. com., 1982-89, 91-93, nat. chmn., 1985-87. Co-author: (video tape) Adjudication 1987; dir. Nat. Evening of Scenes, Kennedy Ctr. for Performing Arts, 1986, A Chorus Line, Hippodrome State Theatre, 1987. Convener Nat. Think Tank for Change, Washington, 1990; trustee Twin Cities Ballet, Bloomington, 1982; panel mem. Ill. Arts Coun., Chgo., 1978-81; mem. reading panel Nat. Endowment for Arts, 1991-92. Recipient Theatre Educator of Yr. award Fla. Assn. for Theatre Edn., 1988; AMOCO medal of excellence Am. Coll. Theatre Festival, 1981, Kennedy Ctr. medal, 1989, 91, 93, Disting. Alumni awrd Dept. Theatre/So. Ill. U., 1996, Coll. Arts and Scis./So. Ill. U., 1997, Encomienda de la Orden de Isabel La Catolica, King Juan Carlos, 2001, Creative Arts award for excellence Dallas Hist. Soc., 2002. Fellow Coll. Fellows Am. Theatre (former dean); mem. Assn. for Theatre in Higher Edn. (founding, bd. govs. 1991—, pres. 1993-95), Nat. Assn. Schs. Theatre (panelist, evaluator 1987, 89-92, bd. dirs. 1991—, treas., v.p., pres.), Soc. for Stage Dirs. & Choreographers, Nat. Theatre Conf. (life, v.p., pres.), Fla. Theatre Conf. (pres.), Ill. Theatre Assn. (pres.). Avocations: reading, listening to music, cultural events. Office: Meadows Sch Arts/So Meth U Offfice of the Dean PO Box 750356 Dallas TX 75275-0001 Home Phone: 972-387-0940; Office Phone: 214-768-2880. Business E-Mail: cbrandt@mail.smu.edu.

BRANDT, ELSA LUND ERICKSON, music educator; b. Bklyn., Oct. 3, 1932; d. Ernst Ansgar Erickson and Astrid Osestad; m. Carl David Brandt, Apr. 25, 1964; children: Karen, Erik. BMus, Manhattan Sch. Music, NYC, 1953; MMus, Manhattan Sch. Music, 1963; BMusE, Hartt Coll. Music, Hartford, Conn., 1957. Violinist Hartford Symphony Orch., 1954—57; instrumental instr. pub. schs., New Rochelle, NY, 1958—60; violinist New Orleans Symphony Orch., 1960—61; violin tchr., prep. dept. Manhattan Sch. Music, NYC, 1961—63; freelance musician Washington, 1967—89; asst. prof. music Howard U., Washington, 1968—90; pvt. studio Silver Spring, Md., 1985—. Founder Maggini String Quartet, Silver Spring; past adjudicator string festivals Md. State Tchrs. Assn.; tape audition com. Johansen Internat. String Competition, 1997, 2000, 03. Performer: (violin solo recital) Carnegie Recital Hall, 1966. Mem.: Friday Morning Music Club (soloist, violin and viola 1967—), Am. String Tchrs. Assn. (curriculum com. Am. String Tchrs. Assn. Md.-DC chpt., pres. Md. DC chpt., Outstanding Tchr. of Yr. Am. String Tchrs. Assn. Md.-DC chpt. 2000), Coll. Music Soc. (life), Photographic Soc. Am. Home and Studio: 819 E Franklin Ave Silver Spring MD 20901-4709 Personal E-mail: ElsaBrandt@aol.com.

BRANDT, FREDERIC SHELDON, dermatologist; b. June 26, 1949; BA, Rutgers U., 1971; MD, Hahnemann Med. Coll., 1975. Diplomate Am. Bd. Internal Medicine, Am. Bd. Dermatology, lic. physician N.Y., 1979, Fla., 1982, Calif., 1982. Intern NYU, NYC, 1975—76, resident in internal medicine, 1976—78; resident in dermatology U. Miami, Fla., 1978—81; pvt. practice dermatology Coral Gables, Fla. Clin. assoc. prof. dept. dermatology U. Miami, Fla.; clin. rsch. investigator Collagen Corp., 2003—; lectr. in field; mfr. Dr. Brandt Skin Care Products. Contbr. articles to profl. jours. Mem.: AMA, Miami Soc. for Dermatology and Cutaneous Surgery, Internat. Soc. Cosmetic Laser Surgeons, Internat. Soc. for Dermatologic Surgery, Fla. Soc. Dermatology, Fla. Med. Assn., Dermatology Found. Leaders Soc., Dade County Med. Assn., Am. Soc. Dermatologic Surgeons, Am. Acad. Dermatology, Phi Beta Kappa. Office: 4425 Ponce De Leon Blvd Ste 200 Coral Gables FL 33146 also: 317 E 34th St Sixth Fl New York NY 10016 Office Phone: 305-443-6606, 212-889-7096. Office Fax: 305-443-4890.*

BRANDT, HOWARD EDWARD, physicist; b. Emerado, ND; s. Howard Edward and Mamie Luella (Franklin) B.; m. Marilyn Kay McKinstry, Mar. 25, 1972; children: Karen, Sonja. BS in Physics, MIT, 1962; MS in Physics, U. Wash., 1963, PhD in Physics, 1970. Engr., physicist Boeing Co., Seattle, 1958-64; predoctoral rsch. asst. U. Wash., Seattle, 1964-70; physics tchr. Seattle Prep. Sch., 1971-72; physicist U. Md., College Park, 1972-73, Lulejian and Assocs., Falls Church, Va., 1973-76, Sci. Applications, Inc., McLean, Va., 1976-77, Army Rsch. Lab., Adelphi, Md., 1977—. Editor various books/conf. procs. in field, including Selected Papers on Nonlinear Optics, 1991; contbr. articles to profl. jours. Sloan Found. scholar, 1958-62; recipient Siple Silver medallion U.S. Army, 1980; Fellow US Army Rsch. Lab., 2004. Mem. Am. Phys. Soc., Am. Optical Soc., Am. Math. Soc., Math. Assn. Am., Am. Assn. Physics Tchrs. Presbyterian. Avocations: mathematics, philosophy. Home: 2713 Shanandale Dr Silver Spring MD 20904-1633 Office: Army Rsch Lab 2800 Powder Mill Rd Adelphi MD 20783-1138 Office Phone: 301-394-4143. Business E-Mail: hbrandt@arl.army.mil.

BRANDT, IRA KIVE, pediatrician, geneticist; m. Dorothy Godfrey; children: Elizabeth, Laura, William, Rena. AB, NYU, 1942; MD, Columbia U., 1945. Diplomate Am. Bd. Pediatrics, Am. Bd. Med. Genetics. Intern Morrisania City Hosp., NYC, 1945-46; resident Lincoln Hosp., NYC, 1948-50; fellow pediatrics Yale U., New Haven, 1955-57, asst. prof., 1957-61, assoc. prof., 1961-68; chmn. dept. pediatrics Children's Hosp., San Francisco, 1968-70; clin. prof. pediatrics U. Calif., San Francisco, 1970; prof. pediatrics and med. genetics Ind. U. Sch. Medicine, Indpls., 1970-89, prof. emeritus, 1989—. Served to capt. U.S. Army, 1946-47, 52 Mem. Am. Pediatric Soc., Am. Acad. Pediatrics, Soc. Pediatric Rsch., Soc. Inherited Metabolic Disorders, Am. Soc. Human Genetics, Am. Coll. Med. Genetics. Office: Ind U Sch Medicine Dept Pediatrics 702 Barnhill Dr # 0907 Indianapolis IN 46202-5128 Business E-Mail: ibrandt@iupui.edu.

BRANDT, JENNIFER ANNE, lawyer; b. Perth Amboy, NJ, July 26, 1969; d. Sanford D. and Joan M. (Klein) B. BA highest honors, Rutgers U., 1991; JD, U. Pa., 1994. Bar: Pa. 1994, N.J. 1994, D.C. 1996. Assoc. Dilworth, Pakson, Kalish & Kauffman, LLP, Phila., 1994—98; mem. Cozen O'Connor, Phila., 1998—. Editor (sr.): Jour. Internat. Bus. Law, 1994. Named one of Lawyers on the Fast Track, Am. Lawyer Media, 2004;

Arthur Littleton Fellowship, U. Pa. Mem.: ABA, N.J. Bar Assn., Pa. Bar Assn., Phila. Bar Assn. (co-chair, mem. comm.). Office: Cozen O'Connor 1900 Market St Philadelphia PA 19103

BRANDT, JOHN HENRY, physician; b. Cleve., July 30, 1940; s. Harold Paul and Dorothy Helen (Kern) B.; m. Jon Ellison, July 30, 1963 (div. 1971); children: Sylvia Ann, Laura Ann; m. Marilyn Ruth Brandt, July 25, 1980. BA, Yale U., 1962; postgrad., Cambridge U., Eng., 1962—64; MD, Harvard U., 1970. Asst. to dir. Harvard Ctr. for Cmty. Health, Boston, 1968—69; clin. fellow Med. Sch. Harvard U., Boston, 1970—73, instr. psychiatry Med. Sch., 1973—74, 1974—99; resident psychiatrist McLean Hosp., Belmont, Mass., 1970—73, dir. Waverley House, 1973—74, attending psychiatrist, 1974—90, Mass. Mental Health Ctr., 1991—99; staff psychiatrist med. dept. MIT, Cambridge, 1979—99. Active Mass. Hist. Soc., New Eng. Hist. Geneal. Soc.; mem. Trinity Ch., Boston, 1988—. Mem.: Internat. Inst., N.Y. Acad. Medicine, Mass. Med. Soc., World Boston, Lincoln Land Conservation Trust, Gore Pl., Bostonian Soc., Yale Mory's Assn., Guild St. Luke, English Speaking Union, Clare Assn., Am. Friends Cambridge U., Harvard Musical Assn. (dir. 1990—93), Russell Trust Assn., Colonial Soc., Nichols House Mus., Trustees Reservations, Soc. for Preservation New Eng. Antiquities, Chief Execs. Club Boston, Cosmos Club, Yale Club Boston (sec. 1988—90, dir. 1990—93), Harvard Faculty Club, Boston Athenaeum, Harvard Club Boston (chmn. Ho. com. 1989—91, v.p. 1991—93), Yale Elizabethan Club, Thursday Evening Club, Phi Beta Kappa. Republican. Avocation: music. Home and Office: PO Box 530 Lincoln MA 01773-0530

BRANDT, JOHN REYNOLD, editor, journalist; b. Amarillo, Tex., Aug. 25, 1959; s. Reynold Francis Jr. and Patricia Levonne (Wallace) B.; m. Svetlana Stevovich, May 28, 1989; children: Emma Evangeline Stevovich Brandt, Aidan Reynold Stevovich Brandt. BA, Case Western Reserve U., Cleve., 1981. Sales rep. Merrell Dow Pharmaceuticals, Cleve., 1982-84, Miles Pharmaceuticals, Cleve., 1984-88, Tokos Perinatal Nursing Svcs., Cleve., 1988-89; sr. assoc. M. Zunt Assocs., Cleve., 1989-90; dir. mgmt. devel. CSA Health System, Cleve., 1990-91; assoc. editor Corp. Cleve. Mag., 1991-94; from exec. editor to pub. IndustryWeek Mag., Cleve., 1994—2000; chief editl. dir. Exec. Mag., 2000—03, pres., pub., 2001—03; pres. John R. Brandt, Inc., 2000—; CEO MPI Group, Inc., 2003—. V.p. Inst. Environ. Edn., Cleve., 1990-91. Bd. dirs. Work in N.E. Ohio Coun., 1997—; judge Workforce Excellence Awards of Nat. Assn. Mfrs., 1997-2000, Am. Bus. Media Neal awards, 2000. Recipient numerous awards in field from Am. Bus. Press, Assn. of Area Bus. Publs., The Press Club of Cleve., March of Dimes, Am. Soc. Bus. Press Editors. Mem. Press Club of Cleve. (dir. 1994-2001, v.p. 1996-98, pres. 1998-99). Office: 2835 Sedgewick Rd Cleveland OH 44120-1837 Office Phone: 216-991-8390. Personal E-mail: jbrandt@mpi-group.net.

BRANDT, KATHLEEN See WEIL-GARRIS BRANDT, KATHLEEN

BRANDT, KEITH E., plastic surgeon, educator; b. San Antonio; s. Melroy and Valeria Brandt; m. Tina Garza Brandt; children: Taylor, Travis. BS, Tex. A&M U., College Station, 1979; MD, U. Tex., Houston, 1983. Cert. Am. Bd. Plastic Surgeons, 1995, Am. Bd. Surgeons, 1999, added qualification in surgery of hand 1995. Instr. surgery Washington U., St. Louis, 1991—92, assoc. prof., 1999—2005, William G. Hamm prof. surgery, 2006—; asst. prof. U. Tex., Houston, 1993—95, assoc. prof., 1996—99. Unit commr. Boy Scouts Am., Chesterfield, Mo., 2006. Named one of Am.'s Top Doctors, Castle Connolly Med., Inc., 2006, Am.'s Top Doctors Cancer, 2006. Mem.: Am. Soc. Reconstructive Microsurgery, Am. Bd. Plastic Surgery, Am. Soc. Plastic Surgeons. Avocation: running. Office: Washington U Divsn Plastic Surgery 660 S Euclid Box 8238 Saint Louis MO 63110

BRANDT, KIMBERLY GLANZ, recreational facility executive, director; BA, Truman State U., Kirksville, Mo., 2000. Dir. mktg. The Walt Disney Co.; dir. membership and mktg. Glen Echo Country Club, St. Louis, 2004—. Mem. com. SSM Rehab Found., St. Louis; mem. fundraising com. St. Louis Ballet; mem. sports commn. City of St. Louis; mem. diamond ball com. Nat. Leukemia and Lymphoma Soc., St. Louis, 2006. Named one of 30 Under 30, St. Louis Bus. Jour., 2006. Mem.: Nat. Profl. Club Mktg. Assn. (pres. St. Louis chpt. 2007). Office: Glen Echo Country Club 3401 Lucas and Hunt Rd Saint Louis MO 63121 Home Phone: 636-532-9199; Office Phone: 314-383-1500. Office Fax: 314-383-3209. Business E-Mail: kim@gecc.org.

BRANDT, LAWRENCE JAY, internist, gastroenterologist, educator; b. May 20, 1944; BS in Biology cum laude, CCNY, 1965; MD, SUNY, Bklyn., 1968. Diplomate Am. Bd. Internal Medicine, Am. Bd. Gastroenterology; lic. physician, N.Y. Intern Mt. Sinai Hosp., NYC, 1968-69, resident, chief resident in medicine, 1969-72, fellow in gastroenterology, 1971-72; physician divsn. gastroenterology, dept. medicine Montefiore Med. Ctr., NYC, 1974—, assoc. dir. divsn. gastroenterology, 1980-85; dir. div. gastroenterology Moses divsn. Montefiore Med. Ctr., North Ctrl. Bronx Hosp., 1985-99; from instr. to assoc. prof. medicine Albert Einstein Coll. Medicine, Bronx, NY, 1974-85, prof. medicine, 1985—, prof. surgery, 1999—; acting dir. clin. gastroenterology Montefiore Med. Ctr./Albert Einstein Coll. Medicine, 1999—2001, dir. Gastroenterology, 2001—. Contbr. numerous articles to profl. jours. Maj. U.S. Army, 1972-74. Fellow ACP, Am. Acad. Physicians and Patients, Am. Gastroenterol. Assn.; master Am. Coll. Gastroenterology; mem. Am. Soc. Gastrointestinal Endoscopy, N.Y. Soc. Gastroenterol. Assn., N.Y. Soc. Gastrointestinal Endoscopy, Phi Beta Kappa. Office: Montefiore Hosp and Med Ctr 111 E 210th St Bronx NY 10467-2401 Home Phone: 914-472-6850; Office Phone: 718-920-4846. Business E-Mail: lbrandt@montefiore.org.

BRANDT, RICHARD PAUL, communications and entertainment company executive; b. NYC, Dec. 6, 1927; s. Harry and Helen (Satenstein) Brandt; m. Helen H. Kogel, May 31, 1975; children: Claudia, David, Matthew, Thomas, Jennifer. BS with high honors, Yale U., 1948; PhD of Comm. Arts (hon.), Am. Film Inst., 2002. With Trans-Lux Theatres Corp., 1950-54, v.p., 1952-54; with Trans-Lux Corp., Norwalk, Conn., 1950—59, v.p., 1959-62, pres., 1962-80, chmn. bd., 1974—2003, CEO, 1974-92, chmn. emeritus, 2003—; dir. Am. Book-Stratford Press, Inc., 1962-87, Brandt Theatres, 1950—85, Presdl. Realty Corp., 1972—; founding gov. Ind. Film Importers & Distbrs. Am., 1959-63, bd. dirs., 1959-69; v.p., mem. exec. com. Theatre Owners Am., 1965—78; mem. bill of rights com. Council Motion Picture Orgns., 1963-65; bd. dirs. Film Soc. Lincoln Ctr., 1968-71; mem. N.Y. State Bus. Adv. Com. on Mgmt. Improvement, 1966-70. Bd. dirs. Trans-Lux Corp.; chmn. bd. Univ. Settlement Soc., 1964-66, hon. pres., bd. dirs., 1966-77; dir. Am. Theatre Wing, 1970-99, United Neighborhood Houses, 1968-73; bd. dirs., treas. Settlement House Employment Devel., 1969-72; trustee, mem. exec. com. Am. Film Inst., 1971—, vice chmn., 1980-83, chmn. bd., 1983-86, chmn. emeritus 1986—; trustee Mus. Holography, 1979-82; mem. Tony awards mgmt. com., 1986-98; founder Live Poets Soc., 1991—. Vice chmn. bd. Coll. of Santa Fe, 1987-98; trustee Maritime Ctr., Norwalk, 1991-92; treas. bd., exec. com. Coll. of Santa Fe, 1999-2004; bd. dirs. Taos Talking Pictures Festival, 1998-2003. Recipient Disting. Svc. award Coll. Santa Fe, 2004; named Exhibitor of Yr., ShoWest, 1984. Mem. Nat. Assn. Theatre Owners (dir. 1957-78, exec. com. 1965-78, Sherrill Corwin award 1983), Phi Beta Kappa, Sigma Xi. Office: Trans Lux Corp 2209 Miguel Chavez Rd Bldg A Santa Fe NM 87505

BRANDT, ROBERT FREDERIC, III, retired editor, journalist; b. Louisville, Sept. 17, 1946; s. Robert Frederic Jr. and Dorothea (Burton) B.; m. Annette Floyd, Aug., 1968 (div.); m. Walda Ruth DuPriest, Sept., 1980. Student, Ea. Ky. U., 1964-66; BA, U. Ky., 1968. Copy editor The Hartford (Conn.) Courant, 1968-69, The Tampa (Fla.) Tribune, 1971-72; news editor The Miami (Fla.) Herald, 1972-78; asst. mng. editor The Washington Star, 1978-81, Newsday, LI, NY, 1981-87, v.p., mng. editor, 1987—2001; ret., 2001. Bd. dirs. Guide Dog Found. for Blind, Inc., Smithtown, N.Y. Mem.: Talbot County Humane Soc. (bd. dirs.). Presbyn. Office Phone: 410-829-3737. E-mail: bbrandt1@verizon.net.

BRANDT, RONALD STIRLING, retired editor, researcher; b. Neligh, Nebr., Aug. 14, 1932; s. Ferdinand B. and Ruth G. (Thornton) B.; m. Dorothy May Rice, May 13, 1951; children: Rhonda, Rebecca, Bonita. BS, U. Nebr., 1955; MA, Northwestern U., Evanston, Ill., 1960; EdD, U. Minn., 1970. Tchr. Racine (Wis.) Pub. Schs., 1957-62, prin., 1962-64; tchr., cons. No. Nigeria Tchr. Edn. Project, Maiduguri, 1965-66; program coord. Upper Midwest Regional Edn. Lab., Mpls., 1966-68; dir. staff devel. Mpls. Pub. Schs., 1968-70; assoc. supt. Lincoln (Nebr.) Pub. Schs., 1970-78; exec. editor Ednl. Leadership, Alexandria, Va., 1978-96; asst. exec. dir. ASCD, Alexandria, 1995-97; adj. faculty George Mason U., Fairfax, Va., 2003—05. Co-author: Dimensions of Thinking, 1986, Dimensions of Learning, 1992, the Language of Learning, 1997; editor: Content of the Curriculum, 1988, Assessing Student Learning, 1998, Education in a New Era, 2000; author: Powerful Learning, 1998. 1st lt. U.S. Army, 1955-57. Inductee EdPress (Ednl. Press Assn.) Hall of Fame, Apr. 1996. Home Phone: 703-765-4779; Office Phone: 703-765-4779. E-mail: ronbrandt@cox.net.

BRANDT, WILLIAM ARTHUR, JR., consulting executive; b. Chgo., Sept. 5, 1949; s. William Arthur and Joan Virginia (Ashworth) B.; m. Patrice Bugelas, Jan. 19, 1980; children: Katherine Ashworth, William George, Joan Patrice, John Peter. BA with honors, St. Louis U., 1971; MA, U. Chgo., 1972, postgrad., 1972-74. Asst. to pres. Pyro Mining Co., Chgo., 1972-74; commentator Sta. WBBM-AM, Chgo., 1977; with Melaniphy & Assocs., Inc., Chgo., 1975-76; pres., cons. Devel. Specialists, Inc., Chgo., 1976—. Mem. adv. bd. Sociol. Abstracts, Inc., San Diego, 1979-83. Contbr. articles to profl. jours. Life trustee Fenwick H.S.; trustee Comml. Law League of Am., Internat. Coun. Shopping Ctrs., Nat. Assn. Bankruptcy Trustees, Ill. Sociol. Assn., Midwest Sociol. Soc., Urban Land Inst., Am. Bankruptcy Inst.; mem. Fla. del. to Dem. Nat. Conv., 1996, also mem. Dem. Party Platform Com., 2000. LaVerne Noyes scholar, 1971-74. Mem. Am. Bankruptcy Inst., Am. Sociol. Assn., Amelia Island Plantation Club, Union League Club Chgo., City Club of Miami, gov. mem. Chicago Symphony, Clinton/Gore '96 Natl. Finance Bd., mnging. trustee Democratic Natl. Comm., maj. trust mem. Democratic Senatorial Campaign Comm., Zoological Soc. Miami Metro Zoo (life), Mich. Shores Club. Democrat. Roman Catholic. Office: 333 S Grand Ave Ste 4070 Los Angeles CA 90071-1544 also: 26 Broadway New York NY 10004 also: 345 California St Ste 1150 San Francisco CA 94104 Office Phone: 312-263-4141.

BRANDT, WILLIAM PERRY, lawyer; b. Phoenix, July 1, 1953; s. Joseph A. and Dorothy L. (Perry) B.; m. Elizabeth Sprague, May 16, 1987; 1 child, Elizabeth Hundley. BA, Vanderbilt U., 1974, JD, 1977. Bar: Mo. 1977, U.S. Dist. Ct. (ea., we. dist. Mo., Kans.), U.S. Ct. Appeals (8th cir. 1992), U.S. Supreme Ct. 1992. Assoc. to ptnr. Stinson, Mag & Fizzell, Kansas City, Mo., 1977—97; ptnr. Berkowitz Stanton Brandt Shaw & Williams, Kansas City, Mo., 1997—2005; ptnr., comml. litig., securities enforcement & compliance practices Bryan Cave LLP, Kansas City, Mo., 2005—. Mem. merit selection commn. US Dist Ct., 1990—91. Editor (exec.): Vanderbilt Law Rev.; contbr. chapters to books, articles to profl. jours. Ward committeeman Jackson County Rep. Party, 1988-92. Named one of Best Lawyers in Am., 2001—; named to Best of the Bar, Kansas City Bus. Jour., 2002—06; recipient Morgan Prize, Vanderbilt Univ. Law Sch., 1977. Fellow: Am. Bar Found.; mem.: ABA, Internat. Assn. Def. Counsel, Def. Rsch. Inst., legal & compliance div. Securities Industry Assn., US Supreme Ct. Hist. Soc. (no. Mo. chmn. 1997—98), Kansas City Met. Bar Assn. (chmn. securities law com. 2000), Lawyers Assn. Kansas City (pres. 1999—2000). Episcopalian. Office: Bryan Cave LLP Ste 3500 1200 Main St Kansas City MO 64105-2100 Office Phone: 816-374-3206. Office Fax: 816-374-3300. Business E-Mail: perry.brandt@bryancave.com.

BRANDT-SOETERMANS, VALERIE LOUISE, dancer, educator; b. Rockford, Ill., Feb. 14, 1966; d. Lloyd Walter Brandt and Carol Louise Tinsley; m. Jay Scott Joseph, July 10, 1999; children: Joseph Lee, Audrey Louise. BFA in Musical Theatre and Dance, Millikin U., 1988. Back-up singer, dancer Louise Mandrell Rd. Show, Hendersonville, Tenn., 1991—97, The Grand Palace with Louise Mandrell, Branson, Mo., 1992—94; singer, dancer Nashville (Tenn.) Now, 1991—92; actress Family Matters Warner TV, 1998; actress Breastman HBO TV, 1998; singer, dancer Radisson Diamond Cruise Line, 1998—99; tchr. tap, choreographer Progressive Movement Acad., Cherry Valley, Ill., 2002—05, Barnabas Acad., Rockford, Ill., 2004—. Recipient Young Am. award, Rockford (Ill.) Register Star, 1984, Most Entertaining Dance Piece award, Dance Xplosion Talent Tour, 2004, Outstanding Choreography award, 2004. Mem.: Ill. Christian Home Sch. Educators, Sigma Alpha Iota (hon. musician). Republican. Avocations: singing, painting, cooking, decorating, reading.

BRANDWEIN, RUTH ANN, social welfare educator, social services administrator, writer; b. Bklyn., Apr. 24, 1940; d. Charles and Kate (Berkowitz) Solin; divorced; children: Lorena Lisa Epstein, Garth Whitman. BA magna cum laude, Bklyn. Coll., 1960; MSW, U. Wash., 1970; PhD, Brandeis U., 1978. Libr. trainee Bklyn. Pub. Libr., 1960—61; substitute tchr. N.Y.C. Bd. Edn., 1961—63; recreation dir. Seattle Park Dept., 1964—66; exec. dir. Ctrl. Seattle Commn. Coun., 1967—69; rsch. assoc. Harvard U./Lab. Comm. Psychiatry, Boston, 1971—72; asst. prof., chair, comm. org. Boston U. Sch. Social Work, 1973—78; dir., assoc. prof. U. Iowa Sch. Social Work, Iowa City, 1978—81; dean Sch. Social Welfare SUNY, Stony Brook, 1981—89, prof. Sch. Social Welfare, 1981—, dir. Social Justice Ctr., 2001—; commr. Suffolk County Dept. Social Svcs., Hauppauge, NY, 1989—93; holder Spafford Endowed chair U. Utah Sch. Social Work, 1994—96. Vis. prof. U. Wash. Sch. Social Work, 2000-01; co-founder Women's Rsch. Ctr. of Boston, 1971-78; co-dir. Women's Com. of 100, 1995—; cons. U.S. Senate Subcom. on Vets.' Affairs, 1971; guardian ad litem Family Ct., Middlesex County, Mass.; expert witness Grevatt vs. U. Minn., Duluth; vis. assoc. Inst. Policy Studies, 1986-87; lead reviewer Nat. Inst. Justice, 1997-98; presenter in field. Author: Battered Women, Children and Welfare Reform: The Ties That Bind, 1999; editor: Affilia; founding editor, mem. corp. bd. Affilia: Jour. Women and Social Work, 1985—, mem. editl. bd., book rev. editor, 2004—; contbr. articles to profl. jours. and chpts. to books. Mem. Nat. Adv. Coun. Violence Against Women, 1997—2000; mem. steering com. LI Fund for Women and Girls, 1993—2000; mem. alumni bd. Heller Sch. Brandeis U., 2003—; mem. adv. bd. LI Housing Svcs., 2004—; bd. dirs., v.p. Kehillath Shalom Synagogue, Cold Spring Harbor, NY, 1987—90, bd. dirs., 2001—06, chair social action com., 2001—06; bd. dirs. mental health coun. Gov., NY, 1990—2002, chmn. mental health coun., 1992—95; chmn. exec. task force family violence Suffolk County, 1988—94; bd. dirs. United Way LI, Melville, NY, 1982—88, mem. allocations com., 2002—05; bd. dirs. Suffolk Cmty. Coun., Islandia, NY, 1981—97; bd. dirs., mem. exec. com. Am. Jewish Congress, LI, 1989; bd. dirs. NY Civil Liberties Union, 1994—98; adv. bd. LI Progressive Coalition, 1998—; bd. dirs. LI Cmty. Found., 1994—96, Hudson- Peconic Planned Parenthood, 1997—2005; mem. action fund bd. Hudson-Peconic Planned Parenthood, 2003—; bd. dirs. LI Health and Welfare Coun., 1996—2001, Suffolk Coalition Against Domestic Violence, 2003—, v.p., 2006—. Recipient Disting. Alumnus award U. Wash. Sch. Social Work, Seattle, 1989, Congrl. award Congressman Mrazek, Suffolk County, N.Y., Hon. Supporter award Women on the Job; Vol. Svc. award, Suffolk County Human Rights Commn., 2003, Stony Brook Hillel Found. award, 2005, Jewish Reconstructionist Fedn. award, 2005. Mem.: NASW (bd. dirs. 1991—96, 2d v.p. 1994—96, pres.-elect NY state chpt. 1997—98, pres. 1998—2000, nat. com. on women's issues 2000—03, Suffolk County Social Worker of Yr. 1989, Lifetime Achievement award 2003), Huntington NY NOW (bd. dirs. 1982—91, chair 1988—91), Coun. Social Work Edn. (chair women's commn. 1980—83, bd. dirs. 1987—89, chair internat. commn. 1988—89), NY Pub. Welfare Assn. (bd. dirs. 1990—93), Phi Beta Kappa. Office: SUNY Stony Brook Sch Social Welfare Health Sci Ctr Level 2 Rm 093 Stony Brook NY 11794-0001

BRANEGAN, JAMES AUGUSTUS, III, journalist; b. Phila., June 6, 1950; s. James Augustus, Jr. and Emmeline Elizabeth (McBurney) B.; m. Stefania Pittaluga, Feb. 4, 1992. BA, Cornell U., 1972; MS in Journalism, Northwestern U., 1973. Reporter Chgo. Today, 1973-74, Chgo. Tribune, 1974-81; with Time Mag., 1981—2001, chief econs. corr. Washington bur., 1986-87, Hong Kong corr., 1987-93, European econ. corr. Brussels, 1993-97, State Dept. corr. Washington, 2001, White House corr., 1997-2001; adj. prof. Georgetown U, 2002—03, Northwestern U., 2002—03; profl. staff mem US Senate Com. on Fgn. Rels., Washington, 2003—. Co-recipient Pulitzer prize for spl. local reporting, 1976 Office: c/o Senate Fgn Rels 450 Dirksen Senate Office Bldg Washington DC 20510

BRANHAM, C. MICHAEL, lawyer; b. Columbia, SC, Nov. 6, 1957; s. Mack C. and Jennie Louise (Jones) B.; m. Teresa Barrett; children: Anthony, Mark. BS, Auburn U., Montgomery, Ala., 1979; JD, U. S.C., 1983. CPA; bar: S.C., cert.: (tax law specialist). Acct. Wilson, Price, Barranco & Billingsley, CPAs, Montgomery, 1979-80; law clk. Atty. Gen.'s Office, State of S.C., Columbia, 1981-82; acct. Price, Waterhouse, Columbia, 1983-86; tax lawyer Young Clement Rivers, LLP, Charleston, SC, 1986—; chmn. tax, estate planning and probate group Young Clement Rivers LLP, Charleston, SC, 1999—, firm mgmt. com., 1999—, asst. mng. ptnr., 1999—2001, mng. ptnr., 2002—. Chmn. taxation law specialization adv. bd. S.C. Supreme Ct., 1995—97; pres. Charleston Tax Coun., 1993—94; active Charleston Estate Planning Coun.; dean's adv. bd. Med. U. S.C. Nursing Sch., 1994—97, chmn. planned giving adv. coun., 1993—97; S.C. case reporter ABA sect. real property, probate and trust law, 1997—2002; mem. Bishop Gadsden Estate Planning Adv. Coun., Charleston, 1998—2002. Coach Hungryneck Internat. Soccer Assn., Mt. Pleasant, SC, 1989—99, James Island/Trident United Soccer Assn., Charleston, 1999—2000; sec., bd. dirs. S.C. Youth Soccer Assn., 2000—02; mem. Frances P. Bunnelle Found., 2000—04, chmn., 2003—04; mem. bd. dirs. Trident United Way, 2004—. Mem. ABA, AICPA, S.C. Assn. CPAs, S.C. Bar Assn., Charleston Breakfast Rotary. Avocations: soccer coaching, weightlifting. Home: 225 Dovewood Ln Vance SC 29163 Office: Young Clement Rivers LLP 28 Broad St Charleston SC 29401-3070 Office Phone: 843-724-6683. Business E-Mail: mbranham@ycrlaw.com.

BRANHAM, GREGORY HARRIS, facial plastic surgeon; b. Columbia, SC, Mar. 28, 1957; s. Clarence Stevenson and Theodocia (Hearon) B.; m. Cynthia Lynn Nowell, June 7, 1986; children: Allison, Matthew, Grace. BS in Biology, U. S.C., 1979, MD in Medicine, 1983. Asst. prof. St. Louis U., 1990-96, assoc. prof., 1996—2004, assoc. dean, 1995—2004; instr. Washington U., St. Louis, 1989-90, assoc. prof., dir. facial plastic surgery & reconstructive surgery, sch. of medicine, 2004—, assoc. prof. otolaryngology-head & neck surgery, chief, divsn. plastic reconstructive surgery. Exec. com. mem. St. Louis U. Governing Coun., 1995—2004. Fellow Am. Coll. Surgeons, Am. Acad. Facial Plastic & Reconstructive Surgery (bd. examiner 1994—), Am. Acad. Otolarngology (award of honor, 1998). Office: Washington Univ Sch Medicine Dept Otolaryngology Box 8115 660 S Euclid Ave Saint Louis MO 63110 Office Phone: 314-432-7760, 314-432-7760. Business E-Mail: branhamg@ent.wush.edu.*

BRANHAM, JENNIE JONES, artist; d. Charles Alfonzo and Louise Kilgo Jones; m. Mack Carison Branham, Dec. 17, 1953; children: Kenneth Gary, Charles Michael, Keith Robert, Laurie Lynn. BA in Art and Art Mgmt., Columbia Coll., 1986. Art gallery dir. Columbia Coll., Columbia, 1986—90; supt. of fine arts S.C. State Fair, Columbia, 1997—2000. Exhibitions include, Crooked Creek Art League, Trenholm Artists Guild, Hilton Head Art League, SC State Fair, Sumter Gallery Art, Carolina Gallery, McKissick Mus, Gallery at Nonnah's, represented in corporate and private collections. Com. mem. Endorsing Com. for Luth. Chaplains of, Washington, 1975—81; mem. Religion & Art, Salisbury, NC, 1983—89; pres. Officers Wives Assn., Air University (Maxwell AFB), Ala., 1971—72. Mem.: Crooked Creek Art League (founding pres. 1995, Mem. of the Yr. 1995). Republican. Lutheran. Avocations: travel, reading, aerobics. Home: 109 Laurent Way Irmo SC 29063 Office: Circa Art 109 Laurent Way Irmo SC 29063 Home Phone: 803-234-5188. Personal E-mail: jennie2839@hotmail.com.

BRANHAM, MACK CARISON, JR., retired religious organization administrator, minister; b. Columbia, SC, Apr. 20, 1931; s. Mack Carison and Laura Pauline (Sexton) Branham; m. Jennie Louise Jones, Dec. 17, 1953; children: Kenneth Gary, Charles Michael, Keith Robert, Laurie Lynn. BS, Clemson U., 1953; MDiv, Luth. Theol. Sem., 1958, STM, 1963; MS, George Washington U., 1968; PhD, Ariz. State U., 1974; DD (hon.), Newberry Coll., 1990; LLD (hon.), Clemson U., 1991. Ordained to ministry Luth. Ch., 1958. Commd. 2d lt. USAF, 1953, advanced through grades to col., 1959; pastor Providence Nazareth Luth. Ch., Lexington, SC, 1958-59; adminstrv. asst., registrar Luth. Theol. So. Sem., 1979-81, v.p. adminstrn., 1981-82, pres., 1982-92, pres. emeritus, 1992—. Instr., counselor in field. Editor: Air Force Chaplain newsletter, 1975—77. Decorated Bronze Star, Legion of Merit; named to Order of Palmetto (S.C.). Mem.: Greater Chapin C. of C. (bd. dirs. 1998—2000, pres. 2000), Rotary (dist. gov. 2004—05). Lutheran. Home: 109 Laurent Way Irmo SC 29063 Personal E-mail: mbranham@hotmail.com.

BRANIN, JOSEPH J., library director; b. Phila., Mar. 26, 1947; s. Harry J. and Margaret (Daley) B.; m. Anita Anker, Oct. 8, 1988; children: Kathleen, Sara. BA, LaSalle Coll.; MA in English Lit., U. Pitts., MLS. Br. libr. Kent State U., Salem, Ohio, 1975-77; asst. dir. librs. U. Ga., Athens, 1977-86; assoc. u. libr. U. Minn., Mpls., 1986-96; dean librs. SUNY, Stony Brook, 1996-99; dir. Ohio State U. Librs., Columbus, 2000—. Cons. librs., pvt. corps., 1985—. Editor: various books; Contbr. articles, book revs. to profl. pubs. Intern Coun. Libr. Resources Columbia U., 1984-85. 1st lt. US Army, 1969—71, Germany, Vietnam. Sr. fellow UCLA, 1991. Mem. ALA (chair numerous coms.), Assn. Coll. & Rsch. Librs. (editor-designate Coll. & Rsch. Librs. Jour., 2007-08), Rsch. Librs. Group (mem. com.). Home: 376 W 6th Ave Columbus OH 43201-3135 Office: Ohio State U Librs 1858 Neil Ave Mall Columbus OH 43210-1286 Office Phone: 614-292-6154. E-mail: branin.1@osu.edu.*

BRANKER, ANTHONY DANIEL JOHN, music educator, researcher, composer; b. Elizabeth, NJ, Aug. 28, 1958; s. Daniel C. and Joan P. Branker; m. Lisa A. Parris, Dec. 12, 1992; 1 child, Parris Jolean. BA in Music, Princeton U., NJ, 1980; MusM in Jazz Pedagogy, U. Miami, Coral Gables, Fla., 1983. Prof. and chair dept. of music Ursinus Coll., Collegeville, Pa., 1986—96; prof. and dir. jazz studies Hunter Coll. CUNY, NYC, 1996—2000; sr. lectr. and dir. jazz studies Princeton U., NJ, 1989—. Vis. prof. music Manhattan Sch. of Music, NYC, 2003—05. Composer: Spirit Song and J.C.'s Passion (Commn. from The Commn. Project, 2004), One for Dawud (Internat. Assn. Jazz Edn. Composition prize, 1986), Each On

Teach One (Internat. Assn. Jazz Edn. Composition prize, 1989). Recipient Disting. Tchg. award, Inst. Arts and Humanities Edn., 1992, Presdl. Scholars Tchr. Recognition award, US Dept. Edn., 1999, Lifting Up the World with a Oneness-Heart award, Sri Chinmoy, 2003, Alumni award, Assn. Black Princeton Alumni, 2004; fellow, NEH, 1989; Fulbright Scholar, Coun. Internat. Exch. of Scholars, 2005—. Mem.: Princeton Symphony Orch. (hon.; trustee 2004—). Office: Princeton Univ Dept Music Woolworth Ctr Princeton NJ 08544 Office Phone: 609-258-2219. Office Fax: 609-258-6793.

BRANN, DONALD LEWIS, JR., school superintendent; b. LA, Nov. 1, 1945; s. Donald Lewis and Shirley June (Scott) B.; m. m. Sari Ellen Donohoe, June 17, 1967; children: Shanonn, Rebecca. AA in Bus. Adminstrn., El Camino Coll., 1966; BS, U. So. Calif., LA, 1968, EdD in Ednl. Adminstrn., 1982; MA in Elem. Edn., Calif. State U., LA, 1972. Cert. tchr., sch. adminstr., Calif. Tchr. El Segundo (Calif.) Unified Sch. Dist., 1970-72, reading specialist, 1972-76, program coord., 1976-79; prin. Wilsona Sch. Dist., Lancaster, Calif., 1979-81, supt., 1981-84, Old Adobe Union Sch. Dist., Petaluma, Calif., 1984-91, Mother Lode Union Sch. Dist., Placerville, Calif., 1992-93, Wiseburn Sch. Dist., Hawthorne, Calif., 1993—. Bd. dirs. Schs. Committed To Reducing Utility Bills, Sacramento, 1983—; mem. State Supts. Small Sch. Adv. Com.; coord. El Segundo Jr. Olympics, 1972; bd. dirs. Antelope Valley Fedn. Tchrs. Credit Union, Lancaster, 1983; v.p., bd. dirs. Friends of Antelope Valley Indian Mus., Lancaster, 1982. Named One of Top 100 Sch. Execs. in N.Am., Exec. Educator, 1985. Mem. Am. Assn. Sch. Adminstrs., Sonoma County Supts. Gang of 13, Assn. Calif. Sch. Adminstrs., Small Sch. Dist. Assn. (founder, pres., treas. 1983—), Alpha Kappa Psi. Home: 640 California St El Segundo CA 90245-3216 Office: Wiseburn Sch Dist 13530 Aviation Blvd Hawthorne CA 90250-6498 Office Phone: 310-643-3025. E-mail: dbrann@wiseburn.k12.ca.us.

BRANN, EVA TONI HELENE, philosophy educator; b. Berlin, Jan. 21, 1929; came to U.S., 1941; d. Edgar and Paula (Sklarz) B. BA, Bklyn. Coll., 1950; MA, Yale U., 1951, PhD, 1956; HHD (hon.), Whitman Coll., 1995, Middlebury Coll., 1999, Iona Coll., 2006. Instr. archaeology Stanford (Calif.) U., 1956-57; tutor St. John's Coll., Annapolis, Md., 1957—, dean, 1990-97; mem. Inst. for Advanced Study, 1958. Mem. U.S Adv. Commn. for Internat. Edn., 1975-77; vis. prof. Whitman Coll., Walla Walla, Wash., 1978-79; honors prof. U. Del., Newark, 1984-86. Author: Protoattic Pottery from the Athenian Agora, 1962, Paradoxes of Education in a Republic, 1979, The World of the Imagination, 1991, The Past Present, 1997, What, Then, Is Time, 1999, The Ways of Naysaying, 2001, Homeric Moments, 2002, The Music of the Republic, 2004, Open Secrets, 2004; translator: Greek Mathematics and the Origin of Algebra, 1968; co-translator: Plato's Sophist, 1996, Plato's Phaedo, 1998. Mem. state adv. com. U.S. Commn. on Civil Rights, Md., 1988-96. Recipient Pres. Nat. Humanities medal, 2005, medal, Yale Alumni Assn., 2006, Bklyn. Coll. Alumni Assn.; grantee, NEH, 1987; Woodrow Wilson Ctr. fellow, 1976. Mem. Phi Beta Kappa. Democrat. Jewish. Office: St John's Coll 60 College Ave Annapolis MD 21404-2800 Home Phone: 410-268-0445; Office Phone: 410-263-2371.

BRANN, RICHARD ROLAND, lawyer; b. Olney, Ill., June 9, 1943; s. Roland John and Margaret (McVay) B.; m. Penny Sue Farrington, June 5, 1965; children: Wesley R., Patrick T. BA, Miss. State U., 1965; JD, U. Tex., 1968. Bar: Tex. 1968, U.S. Dist. Ct. (so., no., ea. and we. dists.) Tex. 1970, U.S. Ct. Appeals (5th and 11th cirs.) 1973, U.S. Supreme Ct. 1973; bd. cert. in labor and employment law Tex. Bd. Legal Specialization. Assoc. Baker Botts, Houston, 1968—76, ptnr., 1976—. Chmn. fed. judiciary rels. com. State Bar Tex., 1996-98, pattern jury charges oversight com., 2005—07; chmn. Houston Mgmt. Lawyers Forum, Houston, 1981. Editor: Tex. Assn. of Bus. and C. of C. Labor Law Quar. Rev., Tex. Labor Letter; chmn. bd. editors Tex. Bd. Legal Specialization, 2000-2003. With USMC, 1961-66. Fellow Coll. Labor and Employment Lawyers; mem. ABA, Tex. Bar Assn., Tex. Bar Coll., Houston Bar Assn. (chmn. labor and employment law sect. 1997-98), Def. Rsch. Inst., Am. Employment Law Coun., Houston Club, Order of Coif, Phi Kappa Phi. Republican. Methodist. Avocations: fitness activities, reading. Home: 13 Stonegate Dr Houston TX 77024-2703

BRANNAN, CLEO ESTELLA, retired elementary school educator; b. Turon, Kans., Feb. 22, 1924; d. Jesse Logan and Nancy Elma (Cox) Zink; m. Raymond Eugene Brannan, Aug. 4, 1946 (dec.); children: Raymond Eugene Jr., Nancy Estelle, Tricia Elaine. BS, Ft. Hays State U., 1964. Cert. elem. edn. educator Kans. Elem. tchr. Pretty Prairie (Kans.) Schs., 1943—45, Meade (Kans.) Elem. Sch., 1945—48, 1958—60, 1961—87, substitute secondary sch. tchr., 1987; ret., 1987. Contbr. articles to propular mags. Trustee Meade Pub. Libr., 1961—65, 1990—96, trustee, treas., 1990—; state bd. dirs. Friends of Kans. Librs., 1990—96. Named Kans. State Libr. Friend of the Yr., 2002. Mem. AAUW (local pres. 1985-86), Kans. Ret. Tchrs. Assn. (bd. dirs. 1991-99, state pres. 1996-97), Delta Kappa Gamma. Avocations: collecting china, travel, reading, arranging flowers. Home: PO Box 13 Meade KS 67864-0013

BRANNAN, EULIE ROSS, educational consultant; b. Norwood, Ohio, Sept. 6, 1928; s. Olin Hiram and Bernice Cleo (Beall) Brannan; m. Ruby Merle Moore, Dec. 16, 1945 (dec.); children: Stephen Earl, Deborah Brannan Watkins, Rebecca Brannan Hagan, Julie Ross Brannan-Williams; m. Willie Metta Strong, Mar. 7, 1981. AA, Ala. Christian Coll., 1947; BA, Huntingdon Coll., 1949; MS, Auburn U., 1953, EdD, 1960; postgrad., Harding Grad. Sch., 1960—63, Oxford U., Eng., 1981; LHD, Faulkner U., 2005. HS tchr., Montgomery, Ala., 1949-51; guidance counselor Montgomery Bible HS, 1951-53; prin. Ala. Christian HS, Montgomery, 1953-55; prof. Ala. Christian Coll., Montgomery, 1953-55, asst. to pres., 1955-56, acad. dean, 1956-69, acad. v.p., 1969-73, pres., 1973-81; field dir. Nat. Edn. Program, Huntsville, Ala., 1981-82; pres. Jefferson Christian Acad., Birmingham, Ala., 1982-90; assoc. J. Robert Clark & Assocs., 1990-91; spl. counsel to pres. Faulkner U., Montgomery, 1991—2004; involvement min. Madison (Ala.) Ch. of Christ, 2004—. Chaplain Madison Police Dept., 1996—; bd. trustees Faulkner U., 2005—. Mem.: Phi Delta Kappa. Home: 103 Manningham Dr Madison AL 35758-7419 Office: Madison Ch of Christ 556 Hughes Rd Madison AL 35758 Office Phone: 256-772-3911. E-mail: eulieb@bellsouth.net.

BRANNEN, JEFFREY RICHARD, lawyer; b. Tampa, Fla., Aug. 27, 1945; s. Jackson Edward and Tobiah M. (Lovitz) B.; m. Mary Elizabeth Strand, Nov. 24, 1972; 1 child, Samuel Jackson. BA in English, U. N.Mex., 1967, JD, 1970. Bar: N.Mex. 1970, U.S. Dist. Ct. N.Mex. 1970, U.S. Ct. Appeals (10th cir.) 1976, U.S. Supreme Ct. 1978. Law clk. N.Mex. State Supreme Ct., Santa Fe, 1970-71; from assoc. to pres., shareholder Montgomery & Andrews, pa, Santa Fe, 1972-93; pres. Jeffrey R. Brannen, P.A., Santa Fe, 1993—; of counsel Comeau, Maldegan, Templeman & Indall (formerly known as Carpenter, Maldegan, Templeman & Indall), Santa Fe, 1995—. Faculty Nat. Inst. Trial Advocacy, Hastings Ctr. for Trial & Appellate Advocacy, 1980-93; co-chmn. Pers. Injury Inst., Hastings, 1992. Mem. ABA, Am. Bd. Trial Advocates (N.Mex. pres. 1998), Assn. Def. Trial Attys. (state chmn. 1992—), Def. Rsch. Inst. (Exceptional Performance Citation 1989), N.Mex. Def. Lawyers Assn. (pres. 1989). Democrat. Avocations: skiing, soccer, fly fishing, travel. Office: 325 Pesco de Heralta Santa Fe NM 87501 Office Phone: 505-983-4429. Fax: (505) 982-4611. Business E-Mail: jrb@brannenlaw.net.

BRANNON, GUY EMILIO, psychiatrist; b. Bossier City, La., June 19, 1968; s. Guy Winfred and Ruby Rangel Brannon; m. Shelley Marie Lawson, Apr. 20, 1996; children: Dechlin Adair children: Grayson Alarich. BS, La. State U., Shreveport, 1991; MD, La. State U., Health Sci. Ctr., Shreveport, 1995. Diplomate La. State Bd. Med. Examiners, 1996. Intern La. State U. Med. Ctr., Shreveport, 1995—96, resident, 1996—99, chief resident, 1998—99; dir. adult psychiatric unit Brentwood-A Behavioral Health Co., Shreveport, 1999—. Asst. clin. prof. psychiatry La. State U. Health Scis. Ctr., Shreveport, 1999—; adj. prof. psychology La. State U., Shreveport, 2002—; pres., CEO PharmaComm., LLC, LaPharma, LLC, 2005. Contbr. chapters to books, articles to profl. jours. Fellow: Am. Assn. Integrated Medicine; mem.: AMA, Am. Assn. Psychiat. Medicine (diplomate), Assn. Clin. Rsch. Profls., Am. Soc. Clin. Pharmacology, La. Group Psychotherapy Soc., Am. Group Psychotherapy Assn., Am. Soc. Addiction Medicine, Am. Med. Polit. Action Com., La. Psychiat. Med. Assn. (N.W. La. chpt. v.p. 2000—01, N.W. La. chpt. pres. 2002—04, Dr. John M Bick award 1995), Am. Psychiat. Assn., So. Med. Assn., Am. Psychotherapy Assn., Am. Acad. Pain Mgmt., Mental Health Assn. Caddo - Bossier (bd. mem. 2000—05). Achievements include research in clinical drug trials. Office: Brentwood - A Behavioral Health Company 1002 Highland Ave Shreveport LA 71101 Personal E-mail: docbrannon@aol.com. E-mail: brentwoodoffice@aol.com.

BRANNON, RONALD ROY, retired minister; b. Aberdeen, SD, Apr. 16, 1928; s. Walter Carlos and Mary Erma (Snyder) B.; m. Rosalee Vernela Carry, July 20, 1949; children: Rhonda Lee Storer, Rodney Vaughn, Randall Roy. BA, Okla. Wesleyan U., 1950; DD, Southern Wesleyan U., 1987. Ordained to ministry Wesleyan Ch., 1951. Pastor Heber Wesleyan Ch., Miltonvale, Kans., 1949-52, First Wesleyan Ch., Wichita, Kans., 1952-68; dist. supt. Kans. Dist. of the Wesleyan Ch., 1968-83; gen. sec. Internat. Ctr.-The Wesleyan Ch. Hdqtrs., Indpls., 1982-2000; ret., 2000. Co-founder, coord. police chaplaincy, Wichita. Trustee/sec. bd. dirs. Miltonvale Wesleyan Coll., 1967-72, Okla. Wesleyan U., 1968-84, So. Wesleyan U., 1984-92; mem., sec. bd. dirs. Hephzibah Children's Home, 1983-92, chair bd. dirs., 1992—; bd. dirs. Wesleyan Investment Found., 1983—2003. Mem. Nat. Assn. Evangelicals (bd. dirs. 1970-72), Christian Holiness Assn. (treas. 1984-88). Republican. Mem. Wesleyan Ch. Home: 1707 Prospect View Dr Lawrenceville GA 30043

BRANNON-PEPPAS, LISA, chemical engineer, researcher; b. Houston, Sept. 19, 1962; d. James Graham and Patricia Ann (Hightower) Brannon; m. Nicholas A. Peppas, Aug. 10, 1988. BS, Rice U., 1984; MS, Purdue U., 1986, PhD, 1988. Sr. formulations chemist Eli Lilly & Co., Indpls., 1988-91; pres., founder Biogel Tech., Indpls., 1991—2002; rsch. prof. dept. biomed. engrng. U. Tex., Austin, 2002—, dir. Ctr. of Biol. and Med. Engrng., 2003—. Author, editor: Absorbent Polymer Technology, 1990, mem. editl. bd.: Jour. Applied Polymer Sci., 1995—2001, Jour. Controlled Release, 1997—2001, Jour. Nanoparticle Rsch., 1998—, Biomaterials, 1999—2003, Drug Development and Industrial Pharmacy, 2003—. Vol. Indpls. Mus. Art, 1990—98, Humane Soc. Indpls., 1990—98, Indpls. Zoo, 1994—2000; trustee Chem. Engrng. Found., 1999—2000. Recipient Harold B. Lamport award Biomed. Engrng. Soc., 1989; named Outstanding Young Alumna, Kinkaid Sch., 1998. Fellow Am. Inst. of Med. and Biol. Engrng.; mem. AIChE (dir. 1998-2000, exec. bd. programming coun., dir. materials divsn., chmn. subcom. biomaterials divsn. 1990-93, dir.-at-large food, pharm. and bioengrng. divsn. 1992-94, 2d vice chair materials divsn. 1994-95, 1st vice chmn. materials divsn. 1995-96, chmn. 1996-97, bd. dirs. 1998-2000), Am. Chem. Soc. (membership com. 1990—), Controlled Release Soc. (treas. 1995-98, internat. planning com. 1991, bd. govs. 1992-95), Jr. League Indpls. (bd. dirs. 1992-94). Avocations: fine art, dance, travel. Office: U Tex Austin CPE 3-168a Austin TX 78712 E-mail: peppas@mail.utexas.edu.

BRANSCOMB, HARVIE, JR., lawyer; b. Dallas, Mar. 24, 1922; s. Bennett Harvie and Margaret (Vaughan) B.; m. Mary Josephine Goodearle, Dec. 28, 1951; children: Mary Margaret, Bennett Hill, Richard Lee. AB, Duke U., 1943; LL.B., Yale U., 1948. Bar: Tex. 1948, D.C. 1980, CPA, Tex. Shareholder Branscomb P.C., Attys.-at-Law, Corpus Christi, Tex., 1948—. Contbr. articles to profl. jours. Trustee emeritus Southwestern Legal Found.; trustee, chmn. Una Chapman Cox Found. Served with USNR, 1943-46. Fellow Am. Coll. Tax Counsel; mem. ABA, (chmn. tax sect. 1979-80), State Bar Tex. (chmn. sect. taxation 1961-62), Am. Law Inst., Am. Inst. CPA's, Phi Beta Kappa, Phi Delta Phi. Episcopalian. Home: 4500 Ocean Dr Apt 8B Corpus Christi TX 78412-2500 Office: 802 N Carancahua St Ste 1900 Corpus Christi TX 78470-0102 Home Phone: 361-853-6032; Office Phone: 361-888-9261.

BRANSCOMB, LEWIS MCADORY, physicist, researcher; b. Asheville, NC, Aug. 17, 1926; s. Bennett Harvie and Margaret (Vaughan) B.; m. Margaret Anne Wells, Oct. 13, 1951 (dec. Oct. 1997); children: Harvie Hammond, Katharine C. Branscomb Kelley; m. Constance Mullin, July 3, 2005. AB summa cum laude, Duke U., 1945, DSc (hon.); MS, Harvard U., 1947, PhD, 1949; DSc (hon.), Poly. Inst. N.Y., Clarkson Coll., Rochester U., U. Colo., Western Mich. U., Lycoming Coll., U. Ala., Pratt Inst., Rutgers U., Lehigh U., U. Notre Dame; DEng (hon.), Colo. Sch. Mines, 1999; D Pub. Politics, Carnegie Mellon U., 2000; DSc (hon.), SUNY, Binghamton; LHD (hon.), Pace U. Instr. physics Harvard U., 1950-51; lectr. physics U. Md., 1952-54; vis. staff mem. Univ. Coll., London, 1957-58; chief atomic physics sect. Nat. Bur. Standards, Washington, 1954-60, chief atomic physics div., 1960-62; chmn. Joint Inst. Lab. Astrophysics, U. Colo., 1962-65, 68-69; chief lab. astrophysics div. Nat. Bur. Standards, Boulder, Colo., 1962-69; prof. physics U. Colo., 1962-69; dir. Nat. Bur. Standards, 1969-72; chief scientist, v.p. IBM, Armonk, NY, 1972-86, mem. corporate mgmt. bd., 1983-86; dir. sci. and tech. policy program Kennedy Sch. Govt., Harvard U., Cambridge, Mass., 1986-96, Albert Pratt pub. service prof., 1988-94; Aetna prof. pub. policy and corp. mgmt. Harvard U., Cambridge, Mass., 1994-96, prof. emeritus, 1996—; dir. Belfer Ctr. for Sci. and Internat. Affairs, 2001—; adj. prof. Sch. Internat. Rels. and Pacific Studies, U. Calif., San Diego, 2005—. Mem.-at-large Def. Sci. Bd., 1969-72; mem. high level policy group sci. and tech. info. Orgn. Econ. Coop. and Devel., 1968-70; mem. Pres.'s Sci. Adv. Com., 1965-68, chmn. panel space sci. and tech., 1967-68; mem. Nat. Sci. Bd., 1978-84, chmn., 1980-84; mem. Pres.'s Nat. Productivity Adv. Com., 1981-82; mem. standing com. controlled thermonuclear rsch. AEC, 1966-68; mem. adv. com. on sci. and fgn. affairs Dept. State, 1973-74; mem. U.S.-USSR Joint Commn. on Sci. and Tech., 1977-80; chmn. Com. on Scholarly Communications with the People's Republic of China, 1977-80; mem. tech. assessment adv. coun. Office of Tech. Assessment, U.S. Congress, 1990-95; chmn. Carnegie Forum Task Force on Teaching as a Profession, 1985-86; dir. Lord Corp., 1987-; mem. pres.'s bd. visitors U. Okla., 1968-70; mem. astronomy and applied physics vis. coms. Harvard U. 1969-83, bd. overseers, 1984-86; mem. physics vis. com. M.I.T., 1974-79; mem. Pres.'s Com. Nat. Medal Scis., 1970-72; bd. dir. Am. Nat. Standards Inst., 1969-72; trustee Carnegie Instn., 1973-90, mem. Carnegie Commn. on Sci., Tech. and Govt., 1988-93; trustee Poly. Inst. N.Y., 1974-78, Vanderbilt U., 1980-2003, Nat. Geog. Soc., 1984-01, Woods Hole Oceanographic Instn., 1985-92, 93-98, LASPAU, 2002-2003; chmn. Nat. Info. Infrastructure-2000 steering com. NRC, 1994-95; Harvie Branscomb disting. vis. prof. Vanderbilt U., 1999-2000; rsch. assoc. Scripps Instn. Oceanography U. Calif., San Diego, 2005—. Author: Empowering Technology, 1993, Confessions of a Technophile, 1995, Korea at the Turning Point, 1996, Investing in Innovation, 1998, Industrializing Knowledge, 1999, Taking Technical Risks, 2001, Making America Safer, 2002, Seeds of Disaster, Roots of Response, 2006; editor Rev. Modern Physics, 1968-73. Trustee Telluride Inst., 1996-97; mem. Commn. on Global Info. Infrastructure, 1995—. USPHS fellow, 1948-49; Jr. fellow Harvard Soc. Fellows, 1949-51; recipient Rockefeller Pub. Service award, 1957-58, Gold medal exceptional service Dept. Commerce, 1961, Arthur Flemming award D.C. Jr. C. of C., 1962, Samuel Wesley Stratton award Dept. Commerce, 1966, Career Service award Nat. Civil Service League, 1968, Vannevar Bush award, nat. Sci. Bd., 2001, Proctor prize Rsch. Soc. Am., 1972, Okawa prize in Info. and Telecomm., 1998, prize for Info. and Telecomms. Ohkawa Found., 1998, Centennial medal, Harvard U., 2002. Fellow Am. Phys. Soc. (chmn. divsn. electron physics 1961-68, pres. 1979), AAAS (dir. 1969-73, 99-2003), Am Acad. Arts and Scis.; mem. NAS (coun. 1972-75, 98-2001), Nat. Acad. Engring. (Arthur Bueche award), Engring. Acad. Japan (fgn. assoc.), Russian Acad. Sci., Washington Acad. Scis. (Outstanding Sci. Achievement award 1959), Nat. Acad. Pub. Adminstrn., Am. Philos. Soc., Phi Beta Kappa, Sigma Xi (pres. 1985-86). Office: U Calif San Diego Grad Sch Internat Rels Pac Studies 9500 Gilman Dr #0519 La Jolla CA 92093-0519 Business E-Mail: ibranscomb@branscomb.org. *No achievement is entirely one's own nor is there satisfaction without sharing.*

BRANSCOME, ERIC EUGENE, music educator, writer; s. Ken M. and Darlene J. Branscome; m. Devyn Michelle Raef, July 24, 1999; children: Hope E., Meg K. MusB, Stephen F. Austin State U., Nacogdoches, Tex., 1995; MusM in Horn Performance, Northwestern U., Evanston, Ill., 1996; postgrad., U. North Tex., 2003—. Adj. prof. music Dallas (Tex.) Bapt. U., 2002—06; instr. music edn. and brass East Tex. Bapt. U., 2006—. Tchg. fellow music U. North Tex., Denton, Tex., 2003—06; sponsor Tau Beta Sigma (Iota Beta chpt.); cons. in field. Named Tchr. of Yr., High Pointé Elem. Sch., 1998—99. Mem.: Nat. Assn. for Music Edn., Tex. Music Educators Assn., Approved Workmen Are Not Ashamed Club (citation 2000), Phi Kappa Phi, Pi Kappa Lambda. Republican. Avocations: camping, canoeing, music. Office: East Tex Bapt U 1209 N Grove St Marshall TX 75670

BRANSFORD-YOUNG, ANGHARAD ANN, counselor, educator; d. Byron Everett and Frankie C. Bransford; children: Alison Koi Howard, Stephanie Ann Parker. BA, N. Tex. U., Denton, 1965; MA, Northeastern State U., Tahlequah, Okla., 1968; EdD, U. Tulsa, Okla., 1982. Sr. Diplomate Am. Bd. Disability Analysts, lic. Profl. Counselor Okla. Dept. Health, Family Therapist Okla. Dept. Health. Counselor Oral Robert U. U. Counseling, Tulsa, 1981—84, asst. dir., 1984—86; counselor Tulsa CC, 1986—87; counselor, dir. Counseling Care Assn., 1987—90; dir. Oral Roberts U. U. Counseling, 1990—98; counselor/cons., pvt. practice Tulsa, 1996—; assoc. prof. Oral Roberts U., 1998—. Address: PO Box 52492 Tulsa OK 74152

BRANSKI, RYAN KAYE COMFORT, research scientist; b. Neenah, Wis., Aug. 8, 1974; s. Sharon Kaye Sarazin; m. Sarah Wyeth Forrest, Aug. 11, 2001; 1 child, Thomas Raymond Forrest. BA, U. Fla., 1996, MA, 1998; PhD, U. Pitts., 2005. Clin. fellow U. Pitts. Voice Ctr., 1998—99; asst. attending scientist Meml. Sloan-Kettering Cancer Ctr., NYC, 2005—. Office: Meml Sloan-Kettering Cancer Center Box 104 1275 York Ave New York NY 10021 Home Phone: 973-783-7487; Office Phone: 212-639-3095. Office Fax: 212-717-3015. Business E-Mail: branskir@mskcc.org.

BRANSOME, EDWIN DAGOBERT, JR., internal medicine educator; b. NYC, Oct. 27, 1933; s. Edwin Dagobert and Margaretta De Witt (Homans) B.; m. Janet Grace Williams, June 27, 1959; children: Edwin D. III, April Grace. AB, Yale U., 1954; MD, Columbia U., 1958. Intern, resident, rsch. fellow Peter Bent Brigham Hosp., Harvard Med. Sch., Boston, 1958-62; rsch. assoc. Columbia U. Coll. Physicians and Surgeons, NYC, 1962-64; assoc. Scripps Clinic and Rsch. Found., LaJolla, Calif., 1964-66; from asst. prof. to assoc. prof. MIT, Cambridge, Mass., 1966-70; prof. medicine, endocrinology and physiology Med. Coll. Ga., Augusta, 1970—2000, chief sect. endocrinology and metabolism, 1999—2000, prof. emeritus, 2000—. Com. mem. US Pharmacopoeia, Rockville, Md., 1976-90, trustee, 1990-2000, pres., 1999-2000, past pres., 2000-05; cons. Accelerated Pharm., Inc., 1999—2006, cons. in endocrinology and metabolism, 2000—, sci. advisor. Mem. editl. bd. Diabetes Care, 2003-06; contbr. articles to profl. jours. Bd. dirs. TriDevel. Commn., Aiken, SC, 1987-91, treas., 1989-90; bd. dirs. Am. Diabetes Assn., Alexandria, Va., 1986-88. Postdoctoral rsch. fellow NIH, 1959-61, Am. Cancer Soc., 1962-64; recipient Pub. Policy award Ga. affiliate Am. Diabetes Assn., 1990. Fellow Am. Coll. Endocrinology; mem. Am. Cancer Soc. (faculty rsch. assoc. 1976-70), Endocrine Soc., others. Achievements include patent (with others) in method of predicting biological activity of compounds by DNA models. Home and Office: 621 Magnolia St SE Aiken SC 29801-4903 Office Phone: 803-649-5150. Personal E-mail: bransomejr@gforcecable.com.

BRANSON, BRANLEY ALLAN, biology professor; b. San Angelo, Tex., Feb. 11, 1929; s. Branley Allan and Era Elizabeth (Rogers) B.; m. Mary Louise Lewis, June 3, 1964; 1 son, Rogers McGowan. AA, Northeastern Okla. A. and M. Coll., 1954; BS, Okla. State U., 1956, MS, 1957, PhD, 1960. Asst. prof. biology Kan. State Coll., Pittsburg, 1960-64; prof. biology Eastern Ky. U., Richmond, 1964—, found. prof., 1989-90. Contbr. articles to mags. Recipient Sci. award Okla. A. and M. Coll., 1953; named Disting. Scientist of Ky., 1984 Fellow Okla. Acad. Sci., AAAS; mem. Southwestern Assn. Naturalists (bd. govs. 1965—), Am. Malacological Union, Soc. for Study Evolution, Kan. Acad. Sci., Ky. Acad. Sci. (editor transactions), Soc. Systematic Zoologists, Am. Soc. Zoologists, Am. Soc. Ichthyologists and Herpetologists, Sigma Xi, Phi Theta Kappa, Phi Kappa Phi. Achievements include research and numerous publs. on description several species unknown animals; described structural workings lateral-line system in various fishes; olfactory system, geog. distbn. fishes and mollusks. Home: 100 Walnut Hill Dr Richmond KY 40475-3620 Personal E-mail: scribe11@earthlink.net. *I've had a long-term love affair with the nature of things, and the fervor doesn't seem to be lessening any with the passage of time. And strongly supported by the very real love affair with my wife and son, I've simply had the best of conditions for being creative.*

BRANSON, HARLEY KENNETH, finance company executive; b. Ukiah, Calif., June 10, 1942; s. Harley and Clara Branson; 1 child, Erik Jordan. BS in Acctg. and Fin., San Jose State U., 1965; JD, Santa Clara U., 1968. Bar: Calif. 1969-98. Law clk. to judge US Ct. Appeals (9th cir.), San Diego, 1968-69; pvt. practice San Diego, 1969-78; div. counsel Ralston Purina Co., San Diego, 1978-83; group gen. counsel Castle & Cooke, Inc., San Diego, 1983-85; exec. v.p., gen. counsel, corp. sec. Bumble Bee Seafoods, Inc., San Diego, 1985-89; pres., CEO Flying Palms LLC, San Diego, 1995—.

BRANSON, TIMOTHY E., lawyer; b. 1960; BA in Polit. Sci. and Econ. with honors, U. Wis., Madison, 1983; JD with distinction, U. Iowa, 1986. Bar: Minn. 1986. Assoc. Dorsey & Whitney LLP, Mpls., 1986—93, ptnr., trial group, co-chair, ERISA litig., 1994—. Adj. prof. Hamline Law Sch., 1993. Office: Dorsey & Whitney LLP Ste 1500 50 S Sixth St Minneapolis MN 55402-1498 Office Phone: 612-343-7920. Office Fax: 612-340-8856. Business E-Mail: branson.tim@dorsey.com.

BRANSTETTER, ANN DYCHE, psychology professor; b. Springfield, Mo., Sept. 2, 1971; d. William Calvin and paulene May Dyche; 1 child, Margaret May. BS magna cum laude in Psychology, Southwest Mo. State U., Springfield, 1993; MS in Clin. Psychology, ND State U., Fargo, 1995; PhD in Clin. Psychology, U. Kans., Lawrence, 2001. Tchg. asst. Dept. Psychology U. Kans., 1996—97, instr. Dept. Psychology, 1998; resident psychology U. Ill. Med. Ctr., Chgo., 1999—2000; clin. health psychology intern U. Ill., 2000—01; instr. in medicine Wash. U. Sch. Medicine, St. Louis, 2000—03; prin. investigator ACS, 2001—03, Wash. U. Med. Sch., 2000—02; asst. prof. Mo. State U., Springfield, 2003—. Guest reviewer Jour. Abnormal Psychology, 2001; editl. bd. mem. Online Behavior Analyst, 2005—07; guest lectr. various sch., 1999—2005. Recipient Excellence in Psychology award, Southwest Mo. State U., 1991, Winner Rsch. Competition, Mo. Psychological Assn., 1993; Grad. Study Rsch. Enhancement award, ND State U., 1995, Presidential award, Assn. for

Advancement Behavior Therapy, 2000, Citation award, Soc. Behavioral Medicine, 2004. Mem.: ACS (chair 2005—, ambassador 2006), Am. Psychological Assn., Am. Pain Soc., Assn. Behavioral and Cognitive Therapies, Assn. Behavior Analysis, Clin. Behavior Analysis Spl. Interest Group (pres. 2003—06), Golden Key, Phi Kappa Phi, Psi Chi. Office: Mo State U Dept Psychology 901 S Nat Ave Springfield MO 65897-0001 Office Phone: 417-836-5406. Business E-Mail: annbranstetter@missouristate.edu.

BRANSTETTER, CECIL DEWEY, SR., lawyer; b. Deer Lodge, Tenn., Dec. 15, 1920; s. Miller Henry and Lillie Mae (Adams) B.; m. Charlotte Virginia Coleman, Aug. 5, 1944; children: Kay Frances Johnson, Linda Charlotte Mauk, Kathy Jane Stranch , Cecil Dewey Jr. BA, George Washington U., 1947; JD, Vanderbilt U., 1949. Bar: U.S. Supreme Ct. 1957, U.S. Ct. Appeals (6th cir.) 1963. Ptnr. Branstetter, Kilgore, Stranch & Jennings, Nashville, 1990—. Chmn. Bd. Profl. Responsibility Supreme Ct. Tenn. Contbr. articles to profl. jours. Mem. Gen. Assembly Tenn., Nashville, 1950-53; chmn. Charter Commn. and Charter Revision Commn., Nashville, 1957-62, 78-90; mem. Met. Action Commn., Nashville, 1964-68; pres. Coun. Community Agys. and Tenn. Environ. Coun., Nashville, 1970, 71-73. Sgt. U.S. Army, 1943-46, lt. Res., 1946-52, ETO. Mem. ACLU (bd. dirs.), ABA, Met. Human Rels. Commn., Am. Judicature Soc., Tenn. Conservation League (Carter Patten award), Am. Trial Lawyers Assn., Tenn. Bar Assn., Tenn. Trial Lawyers Assn., Nashville Bar Assn., Davidson County Sportsman Club, Order of Coif. Democrat. Baptist. Avocations: farming, fishing, hunting, raising angus cattle.

BRANT, HENRY, composer; b. Montreal, Que., Can., Sept. 15, 1913; s. Saul and Bertha (Dreyfuss) B.; children: Piri, Joquin, Linus; m. Katu Wilkovska, 1989. Student, Juilliard Sch. Music, NYC, 1930-34; DFA (hon.), Wesleyan U., 1998. Mem. faculty Juilliard Sch. Music, 1947-55; dept. music Columbia U., 1943-53; mem. faculty Bennington (Vt.) Coll., 1957-80. Composer, condr. documentary films, U.S. Govt. OWI, State Dept., Dept. Agr. 1940-47; composer, condr. various radio network program series for NBC, CBS, ABC, 1942-46; large ensemble works include Angels and Devils, 1931, Origins: Percussion Symphony, 1952, Signs and Alarms, 1953, Antiphony 1, 1953, Millenium 2, 1954, Encephalograms 2, 1954, Ceremony, 1954, Galaxy 2, 1954, December, 1954, spatial opera Grand Universal Circus, 1956, Hieroglyphics, 1957, The Children's Hour, 1958, Mythical Beasts, 1958, Atlantis, 1960, Concerto with Lights, 1961, Barricades, 1961, Headhunt, 1962, Voyage 4; Total Antiphony, in 83 Parts, 1963, Odyssey-Why Not?, 1965, Kingdom Come, 1970, Crossroads, 1971, Immortal Combat, 1972, American Requiem, 1973, Prevailing Winds, 1974, Solomon's Gardens, 1974, Homage to Ives, 1975, A Plan of the Air, 1975, Spatial Piano Concerto, 1976, Antiphonal Responses, 1977, Trinity of Spheres, 1978, Orbits: 80 Trombones, 1979, The Secret Calendar, 1980, The Glass Pyramid, 1980, Meteor Farm, 1982, Western Springs, 1984, Fire in the Amstel, 1984, Desert Forests, 1985, Northern Lights Over the Twin Cities, 1986, Ghost Nets, 1988, Rainforest, 1989, 500: Pathways to Security, 1990, Prisons of the Mind, 1990, Hidden Hemisphere, 1992, Fourscore, 1993, Homeless People, 1993, Trajectory, 1994, Plowshares and Swords, 1996, Mergers, 1998, Ice Field, 2001 (Pulitzer prize in music 2002), Crystal Antiphonies, 2000, Glossary, 2000, Prophets, 2000, others; recs: Columbia, Desto, CRI, New World, Nonesuch, Sonic Arts, AmCam, Newport Classic. Recipient Prix Italia, 1955, Alice M. Ditson award, 1962, 64, ASCAP/Nissim award 1985, Mcpl. citations: Boston, 1983, N.Y.C., 1992; Guggenheim fellow 1946, 55, Thorne fellow, 1972; grantee: Inst. Arts and Letters, 1955, Copley, 1960, Huber, 1960, Dollard 1966, N.Y. State Coun. for Arts, 1974, NEA, 1976, ASCAP/Nissim 1984, Fromm, 1992, Koussevitzky Found., 1996. Mem. Am. Acad. Arts and Letters (life) Achievements include pioneering in development of spatial-antiphonal music. Office: c/o Carl Fischer LLC 65 Bleecker St New York NY 10012 *Undoubtedly, the answer to the riddle of existence must be: perpetual discovery.*

BRANT, JAMES WILLIAM, educational consultant, mathematician, educator; b. Indpls., Ind., Mar. 3, 1941; s. Frederick Merle Brant and Ellen Adelaide Lloyd, Harold Anthony Nelson (Stepfather); m. Nancy Kay Dreher, Jan. 3, 1962; children: James Eric, Kelly Michael, Christie Diane Barnes. BS, Ind. State, Terre Haute, 1964; MA in Liberal Studies, Valparaiso U., Ind., 1972; PhD in Arts and Sci., Columbia Pacific U., San Rafael, Calif., 1992. Tchr. secondary math. Hardin County Sch. Dist., Vine Grove, Ky., 1961—65, Duneland Sch. Sys., Chesterton, Ind., 1965—93; edn. cons., k-12 math. Nev. Dept. of Edn., Carson City, 1994—. Projects dir. math. edn., standards, assessments, and profl. edn. Nev. Dept. of Edn., Carson City, 1994—2004; conf. chair western regional conf. Nat. Coun. Tchrs. of Math., Reno, 1996—98, publicity chair ann. conf., Las Vegas, 2000—02; devel. cons.: k-3 informal assessments project W.Va. Dept. Edn., Charleston, 2002—03; dir. profl. edn., leadership, outreach svcs. and edn. programs Nev. Math. Coun., Carson City, 1994—. Project designer and editor: W.Va. Informal Assessment Program for K-3 Math., 2004 (W.Va. Dept. Edn. commendation, 2003). Recipient Achievement award, Nat. Coun. of Teachers of Math., 1998, Leadership award, Nev. Math. Coun., 2002. Episcopalian. Avocations: grant writing, golf. Home: 1707 Jamie Way Carson City NV 89701 Office Phone: 775-885-1437. E-mail: drjimbrant@msn.com.

BRANT, PETER M., magazine publishing executive, real estate developer; m. Stephanie Seymour, 1995; 4 children. Chmn., CEO White Birch Paper Co., Conn.; co-owner Brant Publications (Interview Art in Am., The Mag. Antiques), NY. Co-founder Greenwich Polo Club, Conn., 1985—. Exec. prodr.: (films) Basquiat, 1996; exec. prodr.: (films) Pollock, 2000. Bd. trustees Solomon R. Guggenheim Mus., NYC. Office: White Birch Paper Co 80 Field Pt Rd Greenwich CT 06830 Office Phone: 203-661-3344. Office Fax: 203-661-3349.

BRANT, SANDRA J., magazine publisher; m. Peter M Brant. Pub., pres. Brant Publs., NYC, 1985—. Publisher, Art in America, The Magazine Antiques, Interview. Office: Brant Publs 575 Broadway New York NY 10012-3230

BRANTINGHAM, ANDRYA J., special education educator; b. Libertyville, Ill., May 27, 1965; d. John David and Betsy Ann Luther; m. Eric Lawrence Brantingham, May 24, 1997; children: Kade Pierre, JD Luke. BS, Fla. State U., 1987; MA, U. No. Colo., 1994; PhD in Curriculum Instrn., U. Wyo., 2001. Tchr. Littleton Pub. Schs., Colo., 1989—94; tchr. spl. edn. North Park Schs., Walden, Colo., 1994—96; tchr. Ouray R-1, Ridgway, Colo., 2001—03; staff devel. contractor pvt. practice, Norwood, 2004—. Bd. dirs. Wright's Mesa Ctr., Norwood; mem. exec. bd. Voyager Youth Program, Ridgway, 2003—04. Coach Spl. Olympics, Ft. Collins, Colo., 1985—87. Mem.: ASCD, Colo. Assn. Sch. Bds. Avocations: horseback riding, skiing. Home: PO Box 451 Norwood CO 81423

BRANTINGHAM, PAUL JEFFREY, criminologist, educator; b. Long Beach, Calif., June 29, 1943; s. Charles Ross and Lila Carolyn (Price) Brantingham; m. Patricia Louise Matthews, Aug. 26, 1967; 1 child, Paul Jeffrey Jr. BA, Columbia U., 1965, JD, 1968; Diploma in Criminology, Cambridge U., 1970. Bar: Calif. 1969. Asst. prof. Fla. State U., Tallahassee, 1971-76, assoc. prof., 1976-77, Simon Fraser U., Burnaby, BC, Canada, 1977-85, prof., 1985—2005, Royal Can. Mounted Police Univ. prof. crime analysis, 2005—, assoc. dean faculty interdisciplinary studies, 1980-82; dir. spl. revs. Pub. Svc. Commn. Can., Ottawa, Ont., 1985-87. Editor: Juvenile Justice Philosophy, 1974, 2d edit., 1978, Environmental Criminology, 1981, 2d edit., 1991; author: Patterns in Crime. Recipient Eisenhower Watch award, Columbia U., 1966; Ford Found. fellow, 1969—70, Western Soc. Criminology fellow, 1996, Sr. fellow, Fraser Inst. Mem.: ABA, Western Soc. Criminology (v.p. 2000—01, pres. 2001—02, J.D. Lohman award 2003, Pres. award 2006), Soc. Reform Criminal Law, Can. Criminal Justice Assn., Acad. Criminal Justice Scis., Am. Soc. Criminology (chmn. nat. program 1978), Calif. Bar Assn. Home: 4680 Eastridge Rd North Vancouver BC Canada V7G 1K4 Office: Simon Fraser U Sch Criminol 8888 University Dr WMC 1632 Burnaby BC Canada V5A 1S6 Home Phone: 604-929-6910; Office Phone: 778-782-4175. Business E-Mail: branting@sfu.ca.

BRANTLEY, ANDY (ANTHONY G.), educational association administrator; Dir. human resources U. NC, Asheville, Davidson Coll.; assoc. v.p. human resources U. Ga.; CEO Coll. and Univ. Profl. Assn. Human Resources, Knoxville, Tenn., 2005—. Mem.: Coll. and Univ. Profl. Assn. Human Resources (chair host com. So. Regional Conf. 1994—95, sec., treas. So. Region Bd. 1995—96, chair-elect 1996—97, chair 1997—98, pres.-elect 1999—2000, mem. nat. bd. 1997—2002, pres. 2000—01, Donald A. Dickason award 2004). Office: Coll and Univ Profl Assn Human Resources 2607 Kingston Pike Ste 250 Knoxville TN 37919 Office Phone: 865-637-7673 ext. 121. E-mail: abrantley@cupahr.org.*

BRANTLEY, BENJAMIN DAVID, theater critic; b. Durham, NC, Oct. 26, 1954; s. Russell Harold and Elizabeth Ann Brantley. BA, Swarthmore Coll., 1977. Reporter, editor Women's Wear Daily/W, NYC, 1978-83; European editor, pub. Women's Wear Daily/W/M, Paris, 1984-85; writer, contbg. editor Vanity Fair mag., NYC, 1987-92; film critic Elle mag., NYC, 1988-93; staff writer New Yorker mag., NYC, 1992-93; chief theater critic NY Times, NYC, 1993—. Host Theater Review WQXR. Office: NY Times Culture Desk 229 W 43rd St New York NY 10036-3959 also: WQXR 122 Fifth Ave New York NY 10011 Office Phone: 212-556-7669. Office Fax: 212-556-1516.

BRANTLEY, JEFFREY GARLAND, health science association administrator; b. Rocky Mount, NC, Nov. 4, 1949; s. Roy Garland and Irene (Cockrell) B.; m. Mary Mathews, Nov. 21, 1981. BA in History, Davidson Coll., 1971; MD, U. N.C., 1977. Diplomate Am. Bd. Psychiatry. Resident in psychiatry U. Calif., Irvine, 1981; pvt. practice psychiatry Laguna Niguel, 1981-82, Durham, NC, 1985-87; med. dir. Hospice Orange County, Laguna Niguel, Calif., 1982; clin. dir. Durham County Mental Health Ctr., NC, 1982-89; freelance cons., educator, 1990—; dir. mindfulness-based stress reduction program Duke Ctr. for Integrative Medicine, 1998—. Clin. assoc. dept. psychiatry U. Calif., Irvine, 1981-82; consulting assoc. Dept. Psychiatry Duke U., 1983—. Author: Calming Your Anxious Mind, 2003, 2nd edit., 2007, Five Good Minutes in the Evening, 2006, Five Good Minutes at Work, 2007; co-author: Five Good Minutes: 100 Morning Practices to Help You Stay Calm and Relaxed All Day Long, 2005. Mem.: N.C. Psychiat. Assn., Am. Psychiat. Assn. Democrat. Buddhist. Avocations: sports, golf, jogging, music. Home and Office: 1109 Huntsman Dr Durham NC 27713-2370 Office Phone: 919-660-6741. Business E-Mail: brant006@mc.duke.edu.

BRANTLEY, JEFFREY HOKE, baseball analyst, retired professional baseball player; b. Florence, Ala., Sept. 5, 1963; Student, Miss. State U. With San Francisco Giants, 1988-93; pitcher Cin. Reds, 1994-97, St. Louis Cardinals, 1997-98, Phila. Phillies, 1999—2000, Tex. Rangers, 2001; baseball analyst ESPN, 2002—. Selected to Nat. League All-Star Team, 1990. Achievements include member of Nat. League Championship Team, 1989. Office: ESPN 935 Middle St Bristol CT 06010

BRANTON, JAMES LAVOY, lawyer; b. Albany, Tex., Apr. 19, 1938; s. George Lyndon Branton and Oletha Imogene (Westerman) Johnson; m. Molly Branton, May 18, 1968; children: Christina, Victoria, Claudia. BA, U. Tex., 1961, LLB, 1962. Bar: Tex., U.S. Dist. Ct. (we., so, ea. and no. dists.) Tex., U.S. Ct. Appeals (5th cir.). Ptnr. Hardberger, Branton & Herrera, Inc., San Antonio, 1974-78, Branton & Mendelsohn, Inc., San Antonio, 1978-83, Branton, Warncke, Hall & Gonzales, P.C., San Antonio, 1983-88, Branton & Hall, P.C., San Antonio, 1988—. Co-author: Trial Lawyer's Series, 1981-91. Capt. USAF, 1962—65. Named one of Top 100 Lawyers, 2003, Tex. Super Lawyers, Tex. Monthly, 2003—06. Fellow Am. Coll. Trial Lawyers (state com. 1993-95, chair 1996-98), Internat. Soc. Barristers, Internat. Acad. Trial Lawyers, Tex. Bar Found. (chair 1989-90); mem. Tex. Trial Lawyers Assn. (pres. 1975-76), State Bar Tex. (pres. 1994-95), Am. Bd. Trial Advocates (pres. San Antonio chpt. 1990-91, Tex. Trial Lawyer of Yr. 1994). Avocations: flying, scuba diving. Home: 127 E Lynwood Ave San Antonio TX 78212 Office: Branton & Hall PC One Riverwalk Pl Ste 1700 700 N St Mary's St San Antonio TX 78205 Office Phone: 210-224-4474. Business E-Mail: jimbranton@branton-hall.com.

BRANTZ, GEORGE MURRAY, retired lawyer; b. Phila., Oct. 19, 1930; s. Louis Paul and Jeannette (Vinitz) B.; m. Joan Nadler, Mar. 29, 1953; children: Nancy Brantz Ginsberg, Amy L. Brantz Bedrick. AB, Princeton U., 1952; LLB magna cum laude, Harvard U., 1957. Bar: Pa. 1957. Ptnr. Wolf, Block, Schorr and Solis-Cohen, Phila., 1966-93; ret., 1993. Pres. Council Migration Service, Phila., 1971-73; bd. dirs. Phila. Port Corp., 1982-84. With U.S. Army, 1952-54. Mem.: Am. Law Inst., Jane Austen Soc. (treas. 1993—98). E-mail: jbrantz@comcast.net.

BRAS, RAFAEL LUIS, engineering educator; b. San Juan, Oct. 28, 1950; s. Rafael and Amalia Antonia (Muniz) B.; m. Patricia Ann Brown, June 29, 1974; children: Rafael Edmundo, Alejandro Luis. BSCE, MIT, 1972, MSCE, 1974, DSc in Water Resources and Hydrology, 1975; Laurea (hon.), U. Perugia, Italy, 1991. Registered profl. engr., Mass., PR. Asst. prof. U. PR, Mayaguez, 1975—76; from asst. prof. hydrology to assoc. prof. MIT, Cambridge, 1976—82, prof., 1982—, head water resources and environ. engring. divsn., 1983—91, dir. Ralph M. Parsons Lab., 1983—91, dir. Minority Intro. to Eng. and Sci., 1987, William E. Leonhard prof. engring., 1988—95, Bacardi and Stockholm Water Founds. prof., 1995—2004, Edward A. Abdun-Nur prof., 2004—, head dept. civil and environ. engring., 1992—2001, chair faculty, 2002—05; assoc. dir. Ctr. for Global Change Sci., 1990—, dir. Terrascope Program, 2006—. Vis. assoc. prof. U. Simon Bolivar, Caracas, Venezuela, 1982-83; vis. scholar Internat. Inst. Applied Sys. Analysis, Vienna, 1983; vis. prof. Iowa Inst. Hydraulic Rsch., U. Iowa, 1989-90; mem. adv. bd. engring. divsn. NSF, 1988-91; earth scis. and applications divsn. adv. subcom. NASA, 1990, sci. team TRMM mission, 1991-94, chair Earth Sys. Sci. and Applications Adv. Com., 1998-2002; sci. steering group GCIP-Global Energy and Water Cycle Experiment, 1991-95; adv. coun. for com. Nat. Insts. for Environment; mem. adv. com. civil engring. dept. Rensselaer Poly. Inst., 2000-02, Johns Hopkins U., 1998—,dept. civil and environ. engring. Cornell U., 2001—; mem. adv. coun. Princeton U., 1999—; mem. nominating com. Stockholm Water Prize, 1996-2004; mem. exec. com. Clarke Prize, 2002-04; mem. sci. com. Inter Poly. Sch., Milan, Italy, 2003-2006; vis. prof. Harvard U., 2001-2002; mem. com. New Orleans regional hurricane protection program, NAS, 2005—; mem. rels. com. UCAR, 2006—; cons. in field; lectr. in field. Author: (with I. Rodriguez-Iturbe) Random Functions and Hydrology, 1985, 94, Hydrology: An Introduction to Hydrologic Science, 1990; editor: The World at Risk: Natural Hazards and Climate Change, 1993; editor Nonlinear Processes in Geophysics, 1996-2000; contbr. articles to profl. jours.; assoc. editor Water Resources Rsch., 1980-88, Jour. Geophys. Rsch.-Atmospheres, 1996-98; mem. editl. bd. Jour. Hydrology, Internat. Jour. Environ. Tech.; mem. editl. adv. bd. SERRA, 1998—. Recipient Walter L. Huber Civil Engring. prize, 1993, Giants in Sci. award Quality Edn. for Minorities Math., Sci. and Engring. Network, 2001, Albert Baez Jr. award and Outstanding Educator award Hispanic Engr. Nat. Achievement Awards Conf., 1999, MLK-MIT Leadership award, 2000, Clarke prize, 1998, Hispanic Engr. Nat. Achievement award hall of fame, 2003, AGU Lorenz Lecture, 2003; named to Top 100 Most Influential Hispanics, Hispanic Bus., 1997; Guggenheim fellow, 1982; P.R. Econ. Devel. Adminstrn. fellow; Horton lectr. AMS, 1999, Kisiel Disting. lectr., 2002, William Mong Disting. lectr. U. Hong Kong, 1999-2000, Boussinesq-KNAW lectr., 2005; NASA Pub. Svc. medal, 2002. Fellow: AMS, AAAS (mem. electorate nominating com. engring. sect. 2007—), ASCE (task com. 1996—97, Huber prize 1993), Am. Meteorol. Soc. (Robert E. Horton lectr. award 1999), Am. Geophys. Union (chmn. bd. jous. editors 1984—88, chair budget and fin. 1990—94, pres. Hydrology sect. 2003—06, statutes and bylaws com. 2006—, assoc. editor, Horton award 1981, James B. Macelwane award 1982, Lorenz lectr. 2003, Hydrology Days award 2006); mem.: Internat. Water Acad., U.S. Nat. Acad. Engring., Nat. Acad. Engring. Mex. (corr.), Soc. Presdl. Fellows Lectrs., Boston (Mass.) Soc. Civil Engrs., MIT Alumni Assn. (Bronze Beaver award 2005), Tau Beta Pi, Sigma Xi, Chi Epsilon. Roman Catholic. Office: MIT Rm 48-213 Dept Civil Environ Engring Cambridge MA 02139 Home Phone: 781-862-1436; Office Phone: 617-253-2117. Business E-Mail: rlbras@mit.edu.

BRASEL, JO ANNE, pediatrician, educator; b. Salem, Ill., Feb. 15, 1934; d. Gerald Nolan and Ruby Rachel (Rich) B. BA, U. Colo., 1956, MD, 1959. Diplomate in pediatrics and pediatric endocrinology Am. Bd. Pediatrics. Pediatric intern, resident Cornell U. Med. Coll.-NY Hosp., NYC, 1959-62; fellow in pediatric endocrine Johns Hopkins U. Sch. Medicine, Balt., 1962-65, asst. prof. pediats., 1965-68; asst. prof., then assoc. prof. pediatrics Cornell U. Med. Coll., NYC, 1969-72; assoc. prof., then prof. pediats. Columbia U. Phys. and Surg., NYC, 1972-79; prof. pediats. Harbor-UCLA Med. Ctr./UCLA Sch. Medicine, 1979—, program dir. Gen. Clin. Rsch. Ctr., 1979-93, prof. medicine, 1980—2005; Joseph W. St. Geme, Jr. prof. pediats. UCLA Sch. Medicine, 1999—2005, prof. emeritus pediatrics, 2005—. Mem. adv. com. FDA, Rockville, Md., 1971-75; mem. nutrition study sect. NIH, Bethesda, Md., 1974-78; mem. select panel for promotion of child health HEW, Washington, 1979-80; mem. life scis. adv. screening com. Fulbright-Hays program, Washington, 1981-84; mem. digestive disease and nutrition grant rev. group NIADDK, 1985-89; mem. US Govt. Task Force on Women, Minorities and the Handicapped in Sci. and Tech., 1987-89. Recipient Rsch. Career Devel. award NIH, 1973-77, Irma T. Hirschl Trust Career Sci. award, 1974-79, Sr. Fulbright Sabbatical Rsch. award, 1980. Mem. Soc. Pediatric Rsch. (sec.-treas. 1973-77, v.p. 1977-78, pres. 1978-79), Am. Fedn. Clin. Rsch., Endocrine Soc., Am. Soc. Clin. Nutrition, Am. Inst. Nutrition, Western Assn. Physicians, Lawson Wilkins Pediatric Endocrine Soc. (bd. dirs. 1972-74, v.p. 1991-92, pres. 1992-93), Western Soc. Pediatric Rsch., Phi Beta Kappa, Alpha Omega Alpha. Office: Harbor-UCLA Med Ctr Box 446 1000 W Carson St Torrance CA 90509-2910 Office Phone: 310-222-1971. Business E-Mail: brasel@labiomed.org.

BRASFIELD, EVANS BOOKER, lawyer; b. Richmond, Va., Sept. 21, 1932; s. George Frederick and Minna (Booker) B.; children: Evans Booker, John McDonald, Elizabeth Lee; m. Anne Dobbins Heilig, June 28, 1980; stepchildren: J. Randall Heilig, Mollie H. Storey. BA, U. Va., 1954, LLB, 1959. Bar: Va. 1959. Pvt. practice, Richmond; ptnr. Hunton & Williams, Richmond, 1965-99; gen. counsel Va. Electric & Power Co., Richmond, 1976-94, Dominion Resources, 1983-91. Pres. Children's Home Soc. Va., 1972-73, bd. dirs., 1965-91; chmn. Cen. Va. Ednl. TV Corp., 1978-84, bd. dirs., 1965-2004; bd. dirs. Richmond Cmty. Action Program, 1974-76, Richmond Area Cmty. Coun., 1973-75, Big Bros. Richmond, 1970-75, Sheltering Arms Hosp., 2001—. With USNR, 1954-56. Fellow Am. Bar Found., Va. Law Found.; mem. ABA (chmn. sect. pub. utility law 1996-97), Va. Bar Assn. (exec. com. 1981-86, pres. 1985), Richmond Bar Assn., , Va. State Bar, Phi Beta Kappa (pres. Richmond chpt. 1982-83). Clubs: Country of Va., Commonwealth, (Richmond). Presbyterian. Home: 2 Ampthill Rd Richmond VA 23226-2233

BRASH, SUSAN KAY, principal; b. Valparaiso, Ind., June 17, 1950; d. Loren Lewis and Naomi Louise (Mundy) Betz; m. Richard Allen Brash, July 8, 1970; children: Jennifer Lea, Julie Christine, Jill Reneé. BS, Ind. U., 1972, MS, 1976, Edn. Specialist, 1989. Cert. adminstrn. and supervision, elem. edn. grades K-8, reading grades K-12, gifted and talented grades K-12. Tchr. grade 1 Portage (Ind.) Twp. Schs., 1971-72; adult basic edn. El-Tip-Wa Vocat., Logansport, Ind., 1976-79; reading tchr. grades 6-8 Ea. Pulaski Schs., Winamac, Ind., 1979-80, reading tchr. grades 9-12, 1980-84, gifted/talented coord., 1984-87, elem. prin., 1987-89, Met. Sch. Dist. Lawrence Twp., Indpls., 1989—. Advisor St. Vincent's Stress Ctr., Indpls., 1993—; presenter and cons. in field. Named Adminstr. of Yr., Ind. Assn. Learning Disabilities, 1990; recipient City Coun./Mayor award, 1994. Mem. ASCD, Nat. Assn. Elem. Sch. Prins. (Nat. Disting. Prin. 1995), Ind. Assn. Sch. Prins. (Ind. Prin. of Yr. 1994), Phi Delta Kappa. Office: Met Sch Dist Lawrence Twp 7601 E 56th St Indianapolis IN 46226-1310

BRASHARES, ANN, writer; b. Chevy Chase, Md. m. Jacob Collins; children: Sam, Nathaniel, Susannah. B in philosophy, Barnard Coll. With Daniel Weiss Associates, NYC, editor-in-chief; co-pres., editor-in-chief 17th St. Productions, NYC. Author: Steve Jobs: Thinks Different, 2001, Linus Torvalds: Software Rebel, 2001, The Sisterhood of the Travelling Pants, 2001, The Second Summer of the Sisterhood, 2003, Girls in Pants: The Third Summer of the Sisterhood, 2005 (Quills award for young adult/teen book, 2005). Office: c/o Random House Inc 1745 Broadway New York NY 10019

BRASHEAR, KAREN KATHLEEN, elementary school educator; b. Pendelton, Oreg., Dec. 14, 1951; d. Elvin William and Ruby Ina (Klein) Sievers; m. Kenneth George Brashear, Sept. 1, 1973; children: Melanie Lynn, Bryan Keith. Degree in applied arts and scis., Columbia Basin Coll., 1985; BA in elem. edn., Ea. Wash. U., 1990. Cert. Am. Assn. of Christian Counselors. Loan sec. Baker Boyer Nat. Bk., Walla Walla, Wash., 1975—77; sci. specialist Richland Sch. Dist., Richland, Wash., 1982—2004, ednl. asst., 1988—90, thcr., 1990—2005. Sci. specialist Richland Schs., Richland, Wash., 1992—2005. Women's min. dir. SDA Ch., Richland, Wash., 2003—05; ropes course facilitator Columbia Basin Challenge Course, Wash. Recipient SEPAC Golden Cir. award, Richland Sch. Dist., 1996—97. Mem.: Am. Assn. of Christian Counselors. Avocations: skiing, boating, knitting, reading, travel. Home: 334 Columbia Point Dr Unit 301 Richland WA 99352 Office Phone: 509-371-2680. E-mail: kbrashear@bossig.com.

BRASHER, TERRIE WALKER, secondary school educator; b. Leeds, Ala., June 20, 1960; d. Ernest Hershel and Ellen Imojean Walker; m. Donald Ray Brasher, July 19, 1986; children: Trey Donald, Cody Ray. MA in Edn., U. Ala., Birmingham, 1998; MS in Biology, Samford U., Birmingham, 1982. Lab technician Samford U., Birmingham, 1980—82, U. Ala., Birmingham, 1982—83; lab instr. Samford U., Birmingham, 1983—91; sci. tchr. Moody (Ala.) H.S., 1997—. Grantee, St. Clair County Ednl. Assn., 2005, St. Clair Ednl. Assn., 2006. Home: 2738 Sunrise Dr Moody AL 35004 Office: Moody High Sch 714 High School Dr Moody AL 35004 Home Phone: 205-640-4755; Office Phone: 205-640-5127.

BRASHIER, KENNETH E., humanities educator; BA, U. Mo., 1987, U. Oxford, 1990; MA, Harvard U., 1993; PhD, U. Cambridge, 1998. Faculty mem. Reed Coll., Portland, Oreg., 1998—2003, assoc. prof. religion and humanities, 2003—. Recipient US Professors of Yr. Award for Outstanding Baccalaureate Coll. Prof., Carnegie Found. for Advancement of Tchg. and Coun. for Advancement and Support of Edn., 2006; granted NEH Fellowship; Rhodes Scholar, Harry S Truman Scholar. Office: Reed Coll 3203 SE Woodstock Blvd Portland OR 97202-8199 Office Phone: 503-517-5065. E-mail: brashiek@reed.edu.*

BRASKET, CURT JUSTIN, systems analyst; b. Tracy, Minn., Dec. 7, 1932; s. Curt John and Mary Ann (Jenniges) B.; m. Rita Ann Bronk, July 20, 1963; children: Monica, Barbara, Rebecca. Student, U. Minn., 1950—51; BA in Math, St. John's U., Collegeville, Minn., 1954. Systems analyst Unisys (Sperry, Univac), St. Paul, 1957-88. Served with AUS, 1955-57. Mem. U.S. Chess Fedn. (life master, life mem.), Internat. Chess Fedn. (master 1983—) Achievements include being U.S. Chess master, 1953—; U.S. jr. champion, 1952; 16 times Minn. champion, 4 times North Ctrl. champion. Home: 220 Spring Valley Dr Minneapolis MN 55420-5540

BRASS, ERIC PAUL, internal medicine and pharmacology educator, academic administrator; b. Bklyn., Sept. 3, 1952; s. Edward A. and Barbara B.; m. Kathy E. Sietsema, Sept. 3, 1994; children: Carl, Courtney, Alexander. BSChemE, Case Western Res. U., 1974, MSChemE, 1975, PhD in Pharmacology, 1979, MD, 1980. Diplomate Am. Bd. Internal Medicine. Resident in internal medicine U. Wash., Seattle, 1980-82, fellow in clin. pharmacology, 1982-83; asst. prof. medicine and pharmacology U. Colo., Denver, 1983-89; assoc. prof. medicine and pharmacology Case Western Res. U., Cleve., 1989-93; asst. dir. Calif. Clin Trials, 1993-94; prof., chair dept. medicine Harbor-UCLA Med. Ctr., 1994—2000; dir. Harbor-UCLA Ctr. Clin. Pharm., 2000—; prof. medicine David Geffen Sch. Medicine, UCLA, 1994—. Mem., chair FDA Nonprescription Drug Adv. Com., 1993—2001. Contbr. more than 130 articles to sci. jours. Recipient Faculty Devel. award Pharm. Mfrs. Assn. Found., 1985; NIH rsch. grantee, 1985, 88, 93. Mem. Am. Fedn. Clin. Rsch., Am. Soc. Pharmacology and Exptl. Therapeutics, Am. Soc. Clin. Pharmacology and Therapeutics (Young Investigator award 1987), Am. Soc. Clin. Investigation. Office: Harbor-UCLA Med Ctr 1124 W Carson St Torrance CA 90502-2004 Office Phone: 310-222-4050. Business E-Mail: ebrass@ucla.edu.

BRASSEAUX, CARL ANTHONY, historian, educator, academic administrator, curator; b. Opelousas, La., Aug. 19, 1951; s. Ferdinand and Odile Valajean (Johnson) B.; m. Glenda M. Melancon, July 21, 1973; children: Ryan Andre, David Marc, Aimée Elizabeth. BA in Polit. Sci. cum laude, U. Southwestern La., 1974, MA in History, 1975; PhD summa cum laude, U. Paris, 1982. Asst. dir. Ctr. La. Studies U. La. at Lafayette, 1975—2000, mem. grad. faculty, 1987—, mgr. info. sys. Ctr. La. Studies, 1985—, curator colonial records collection Ctr. La. Studies, 1980—, asst. prof. dept. history, 1991-94, assoc. prof. dept. history, 1994-98, disting. univ. prof., 1995—, dir., 2003—, U. La. at Lafayette, Ctr. Cultural and Eco Tourism, 2001—; prof. dept. history U. La. at Lafayette, 1998—. Cons. La. Park Svc., Baton Rouge, 1984, Nat. Park Svc., Washington, 1987-88, U.S. Corps. Engrs., New Orleans, 1995; adj. asst. prof. dept. history U. Southwestern La., 1987-90; vis. prof. U. Laval, Que., summer 1994. Bd. editors U. La. at Lafayette, 1975—; freelance editor Scribner's Ref. Divsn., N.Y.C., 1991-92; author: Denis-Nicolas Foucault and the New Orleans Rebellion of 1768, 1987, The Founding of New Acadia: Beginnings of Acadian Life in Louisiana, 1765-1803, 1987, In Search of Evangeline: Origins and Evolution of the Evangeline Myth, 1989, Lafayette, Where Yesterday meets Tomorrow: An Illustrated History, 1990, The Foreign French: French Immigration into the Mississippi Valley, 1820-1900, Vol. I, 1990, Vol. II, 1992, Vol. III, 1993; Scattered to the Wind: Dispersal and Wanderings of the Acadians, 1755-1809, 1991, Acadian to Cajun: Transformation of a People, 1803-1877, 1994, A Refuge for All Ages: Immigration in Louisiana History, 1996, France's Forgotten Legion: Service Records of French Military and Administrative Personnel Stationed in the Mississippi Valley, 1699-1769, 2000; co-author: The Courthouses of Louisiana, 1977, A Bibliography of Acadian History, Literature and Genealogy, 1955-85, 1986, A Bibliography of Scholarly Literature on Colonial Louisiana and New France, 1992, Crevasse: The 1927 Flood in Acadiana, 1994, Creoles of Color in the Bayou Country, 1995, France's Forgotten Legion: Service Records of French Military and Adninstrative Personnel Stationed in the Mississippi Valley, 1699-1769, 2000, (with Keith P. Fontenot) Steamboats on the Louisiana's Bayous, 2004, (with Ryan Brasseaux and Marcelle Bienvenu) Stir the Pot: A History of Cajun Cuisine, 2005; co-editor: A Franco-American Overview: Louisiana, Vol. V, 1981, Vol. VI 1981, Vol. VII: The Postbellum Period, 1982, Vol. VIII: French Louisiana in the Twentieth Century, 1982; mng. editor La. History, 1993—, La. History Newsletter, 1993—; translator, editor, annotator, compiler many other works; mng. editor Louisiana History, 1993—; contbr. more than 100 articles to profl. jours., chpts. to books. Mem. Southeastern Columbus Quincentenary Comm., 1987-92. Recipient Kemper Williams prize, 1979, manuscript hon. mention, 1975, Robert L. Brown prize, 1980, Spl. Lifetime Achievement award LDS Ch., 1987, Golden Achievement award Breaux Bridge Hist. Soc., 1989, Chevalier, l'Ordre des Palmes Académiques, diploma, 1991, medal, May 1994, Nat. Daus. of Am. Revolution award, 1995; named Univ. Disting. Prof. of History, U. Southwestern La., 1995, La. Writer of Yr., La. Ctr. for the Book, 2003, La. Humanist of Yr., La. Endowment for the Humanities, 2005. Fellow La. Hist. Assn. (Pres.'s Meml. award 1986), French Colonial Hist. Soc. (book prize 1987, La. Writer of Yr., 2003, Literary award, 2005, La. Humanist of Yr., 2005). Avocations: photography, bicycling, travel, computers. Office: Ctr La Studies 302 E Saint Mary Blvd Lafayette LA 70503-2038 Business E-Mail: cab6944@louisiana.edu.

BRASWELL, DANIEL EDWIN, military officer; b. New Orleans, Apr. 16, 1960; s. Buford Wallace and Patricia Gail Braswell; m. Patricia Walker, Nov. 29, 1986; children: Benjamin Daniel, Charles Walker, Madelyn Elise. BS, US Naval Acad., Annapolis, Md., 1983. Commd. officer USN, 1978, advanced through grades to capt., exec. officer Helicopter Combat Support Squadron Four Sigonella, Sicily, Italy, 1999—2001, commdg. officer Helicopter Combat Support Squadron Four, 2001—02, Ea. Europe and Eurasia divsn. chief Joint Staff Washington, 2004—05; Am. Legation US Naval Attache US Embassy, Islamabad, Pakistan, 2006—. Scout leader Boy Scouts Am., Dumfries, Va., 2002—. Decorated Def. Superior Svc. medal Office of the Sec. of Def. Republican. Home Phone: 703-221-6164.

BRASWELL, JACKIE BOYD, state agency administrator; b. Leon County, Fla., Feb. 15, 1938; d. Chalmer Parks and Kathryn Iris (Johnson) Boyd; m. Fletcher Braswell, Nov. 28, 1957; children: Flecia Lori, Carmen Ethelee. BS, Fla. State U., 1964; M in Ednl. Adminstrn., 1976. Cert. educator Valdosta State Coll., 1968, lic. real estate sales assoc. Fla., 2005, cert. Rayner Real Estate, Tallahassee, Fla. Lic. tchr., adminstr. Fla. single mgr., ammunition, base clothing fund, security clearance USAF, Moody AFB, 1958-61; tchr. bus. edn. Berrien H.S., Nashville, Ga., 1966-69, Rickards H.S., Tallahassee, 1970-75; bus.-vocat. tchr., chmn. dept. career edn. Lincoln H.S., 1975—99; dir. ednl. affairs and policy Fla. Lottery, 1999—2005; real estate assoc. Rayner Real Estate, 2005—. Co-owner, fin. mgr. Rundown Farms, Tallahassee, 1969—; pres. Eight Out Investment Group, 1993-2003; mem. Gov.'s Mentoring Initiative Lottery Mentoring Program, 1999-2005. Editor: In Touch, 1979-80; contbr. articles to profl. jours. Apptd. Fla. State Bd. Pub. Schs., Gov. Fla., 1987-90, vice chmn., 1990-91; chmn.; apptd. mem. by Spkr. House of Reps. to Fla. Commn. Edn. Reform and Accountability, Spkr. Fla. House Reps., 1991-93; invited del. Citizens Amb. Program People Internat., Beijing, Hangzhou, Shanghai, China, 1995; fundraising chmn. Dist. Sch. Supts. Campaign, 1996; sponsorship chair Capital Cultural Ctr., Chukker Challenge, 1997-98; mem. fundraising com. Boys and Girls Club Big Bend, mem. fundraising com. ann. dinner, 2005-06; mem. ann. fundraiser com. Pace Ctr. Girls, 2005, 06. Recipient Merit award Future Farmers Am., 1974; selectee Harvard Inst., 1991. Mem. Nat. Mus. Women in the Arts (charter), Nat. Bus. Edn. Assn., Fla. Vocat. Assn., Fla. Bus. Edn. Addn., Leon Vocat. Assn. (pres. elect 1987-88, pres. 1988-89), Leon Classroom Tchrs. Assn. (sec.-treas. 1987-88, chair pub. rels., parliamentarian 1988-89, govtl. rels. 1991), Dance Arts Guild, Leon County Farm Bur., Capital Gains Club (treas., 2000), Quill and Scroll, Phi Kappa Phi. Republican. Home and Office: 7006 N Meridian Rd Tallahassee FL 32312-8017

BRASWELL, LOUIS ERSKINE, lawyer; b. Selma, Ala., Mar. 11, 1937; s. Erskine McKinley and Leota (Grubb) B.; m. Moren, Nov. 4, 2005; children by previous marriage: Margaret, Anne, Helen. AB, Birmingham So. Coll., 1959; JD, Harvard U., Cambridge, Mass., 1962. Bar: Ala. bar 1962. Assoc. firm Hand, Arendall, Bedsole, Greaves & Johnston, Mobile, Ala., 1963-68; ptnr. Hand Arendall LLC, Mobile, 1968—2006. Participant Nat. Conf. on Discovery Reform, U. Tex. Law Sch., 1982; program participant 11th Cir. Jud. Conf., 1984, others Bd. dirs. Children's Dental Clinic, Mobile, 1965-75; past pres. Friends of Mobile Publ. Libr.; bd. dirs. Jr. Achievement of Mobile; past pres. YMCA Roskies Alumni Assn.; bd. dirs. Kidney Found. South Ala., 1978-85, Ecumenical Ministries, Inc., 2001-04. With US Army, 1962-63. Mem. Athelstan Club, Rotary Internat., Point Clear Rotary Club (bd. dirs. 1997-2000, pres. 1998-99). Presbyterian. Home: 250 N Bayview St Fairhope AL 36532 Office: PO Box 123 Mobile AL 36601-0123

BRASWELL, MARK K., lawyer; b. Memphis, Dec. 16, 1963; BA with high honors, U. Tenn., 1986; JD with honors, U. Tenn. Coll. Law, 1990. Bar: Pa. 1990, Tenn. 1993. Branch chief, Enforcement Divsn. SEC; assoc. Kirkpatrick & Lockhart LLP, Washington; ptnr., Securities Regulation & Enforcement Dept. Venable LLP, Washington. Author: Conservative Pragmatism versus Liberal Principles: Warren E. Burger on the Suppression of Evidence, 1956-1986, 1987. Mem.: ABA, Tenn. Bar Assn., Phi Delta Phi, Pi Sigma Alpha. Office: Venable LLP 575 7th St NW Washington DC 20004 Office Phone: 202-344-8231. Office Fax: 202-344-8300. Business E-Mail: mkbraswell@venable.com.

BRASWELL, ROBERT M., state agency administrator; m. Amy Braswell; children: Nathan, Jessica. BBA in Fin., Ga. So. Coll., 1984. Fin. examiner Ga. Dept. Banking and Fin., supervisory examiner NW region, dir. NW dist. 1, dep. commr. mortgage, 2003—05, commr., 2005—. Office: Ga Dept Banking and Fin 2990 Brandywine Rd Ste 200 Atlanta GA 30341-5565 Office Phone: 770-986-1628. E-mail: robertb@dbf.state.ga.us.

BRATCHER, JUANITA, journalist; b. Columbus, Ga. d. Benjamin Pickens and Tommie (English) Forte; m. Neal Archie Bratcher; children: Pamela, Angela, Sonya, Neal Jr. AA, Olive Harvey Coll.; BA in Journalism, Columbia Coll., 1976. News reporter South End Rev., Chgo., Roseland Rev., Chgo., Chgo. Defender; editor, publ. Southeast Alliance, Chgo., Copyline Mag., Chgo., 1990—. Bd. dirs. Provident Found.; host cable talk show One on One; host Internet talk show PCC Network. Author: Harold: The Making of a Big City Mayor, 1993, I Cry for a People: In Their Struggle for Justice, 1996, Crooked Curves: The Last of the Red Hot Mamas, 1999, A Celebration of Love, 2001, Love Me One More Time, 2001, The Best Poems and Poets of 2001, The Best Poems and Poets of 2002, The Best Poems and Poets of 2003, Sound of Poetry, 2003, Chasing the Good Times, 2003, Noble House: Theatre of the Mind, 2004, Noble House: Colours of the Heart, 2004; works appear in Nat. Libr. of Poetry Best Poems of 1997, A Celebration of Poets, 1998, The Best Poems and Poets of 2001, The Best Poems and Poets of 2003, Noble House Theatre of the Mind, 2004, Under a Quick Silver Moon, 2002, Great Poems of the Western World, 2004, Best Poems & Poets of 2005, recordings include Too Many Memories, 1996, Everything But Love, 1996, I'm Here for You, 1997, You've Been Gone Too Long, 1997, God Can Ease the Pain, 1999, Glorious Day in Heaven, 1999, America, The Land of Freedom, 1999, Freedom, Our Birthright, 1999, That Twinkle In Your Eyes, 2001, Overdose of Love, 2001, CD recordings include God Can Ease the Pain, 1999, A Glorious Day in Heaven, 1999, The Sound of Poetry, album recordings include America, The Land of Freedom, 1999, Freedom, Our Birthright, 1999, Everything But Love, 2001, That Twinkle in Your Eyes, 2001, An Overdose of Love, 2001, A Toast To Christmas, 2001, Can't Make It Without Him, 2001, CD recordings include The Sound of Poetry, 2002, mem. editl. com. One City, Chgo. Coun. Urban Affairs, The Sound of Poetry, 2004, guest panelist, guest host for numerous TV and radio programs. Mem. Regional Aux. Coun. Atlas Ctr.; press aide Cook County bd. campaign John S. Stroger, Alderman Lorraine Dixon; press sec. Cook County Bd. Pres. John H. Stroger campaign, 2006. Named Black Bus. Woman of Yr., Pky. Cmty. Ho., 1993; named to Internat. Poetry Hall of Fame, Probation Challenge's Hall of Fame, 1991, Portrait of Achievers Hall of Fame, 2006; recipient certs. of merit, Chgo. Pub. Schs., Everyday Hero award, Ill. Sec. State George Ryan, 1993, award, The Kizzy Found., 1983, Probation Challenge Portraits of Achievers award, 1983, 1987, Editor's Choice award (6), Nat. Libr. Poetry, Svc. award, Boy Scouts Am., US Dept. Edn. Region V Outstanding Suppport of Human Rights award, Ill. Dept. Human Rights, 1985, Cmty. Svc. award, Ada Park Adv. Coun., 1990, Exemplary Civic Svc. award, Dorcas Care Ctr., 1988, Excellence in Achievement award, Zeta Phi Beta, Outstanding Svc. in Media and Telecomm. award, Delta Sigma Theta, Press award, Chgo. and No. Dist. Assn. of Club women, Inc., Par Excellence Journalism award, Coalition for United Cmty. Action, 1987, Dedicated Svc. to Cmty. award, Firefighters for Justice and Equality, 1987, The Good Spirit of Excellence award, 2000, From Whence We Came award, Allstate Ins., 2002, Editor's Choice award, Internat. Libr. Poetry, 2006. Mem. Internat. Soc. Poets. Baptist. Home: 9026 S Cregier Ave Chicago IL 60617-3533 Office Phone: 773-375-8127. Fax: 773-375-7461. E-mail: JuanitaBratcher@yahoo.com.

BRATER, DONALD CRAIG, dean, educator; b. Oak Ridge, Tenn., 1945; m. Stephanie Brater; 1 child, Aimee. BA in chemistry, Duke U., 1967; MD in pharmacy, Duke U. Med. Sch., 1971. Intern Duke U., 1970—71; resident in medicine U. Calif., San Francisco, 1971—73, fellow in clin. pharmacology, 1973—76; mem. faculty Southwestern Med. Sch.; joined faculty Ind. U. Sch. Medicine, 1986, chmn. dept. medicine, John B. Hickam prof. medicine, prof. pharmacology and toxicology, 1990—2000, Walter J. Daly prof., 2000—, dean, 2000—. Pres. U.S. Pharmacopoeia; bd. mgrs. Inproteo, Indpls.; adj. faculty mem. Purdue U. Sch. Pharmacy; active with Indpls. U. Sch. Medicine program in Kenya. Recipient Duke Med. Alumni Award, 2000, Friends of Pharmacy Award, Purdue U. Sch. Pharmacy, 2003. Mem.: Assn. Profs. Medicine, Am. Soc. Clin. Pharmacology and Therapeutics, Assn. Am. Physicians, Am. Soc. Clin. Investigation. Office: Ind U Sch Medicine 1120 W South Dr Fesler Hall Indianapolis IN 46202-5114

BRATHWAITE, EDWARD KAMAU (KAMAU BRATHWAITE, LAWSON EDWARD BRATHWAITE), poet, educator; b. Bridgetown, Barbados, May 11, 1930; s. Hilton Edward and Beryl (Gill) B.; m. Doris Monica Welcome, Mar. 26, 1960; 1 child, Michael. Student, Harrison Coll., Barbados; BA with honors in History, Pembroke Coll., U. Cambridge, Eng., 1953, diploma in edn., 1954; DPhil, U. Sussex, UK, 1968. Edn. officer Ministry of Edn., Ghana, 1955-62; tutor dept. extra mural studies U. West Indies, Kingston, Jamaica, 1962-63, univ. lectr., 1963-72, sr. lectr. in history, 1972-76, reader, 1973-83, prof. social and cultural history, 1982—; prof., comparative lit. NYU. With Plebiscite Office for UN in Trans-Volta Togoland, 1956-57. Writings include: The People Who Came, 3 vols., 1968-72, Folk Culture of the Slaves in Jamaica, 1970, The Development of Creole Society in Jamaica 1770-1820, 1971, Caribbean Man in Space and Time, 1974, Contradictory Omens: Cultural Diversity and Integration in the Caribbean, 1974, Our Ancestral Herigage: A Bibliography of the Roots of Culture in the English-Speaking Caribbean, 1976, Wars of Respect: Nanny, Sam Sharpe and the Struggle for People's Liberation, 1977, The Colonial Encounter: Language, 1984, History of the Voice: The Development of Nation Language in Anglophone Caribbean Poetry, 1984; (poetry) Rights of Passage, 1967, Masks, 1969, Panda No. 349, 1969, The Arrivants: A New World Trilogy, 1973, Days and Nights, 1975, Other Exiles, 1975, Blacks and Blues, 1976, Mother Poem, 1977, Word Making Man: A Poem for Nicolas Guillen, 1979, Sun Poem, 1982, Third World Poems, 1983, X/Self, 1987, DreamStories, 1994, Words Need Love, Too, 2000, Born to Slow Horses, 2005 (Griffin Internat. Poetry prize, 2006); (plays) Four Plays for Primary Schools, 1961, Odale's Choice, 1972; editor: Iouanaloa: Recent Writing from St. Lucia, 1963, Barbados Poetry 1661-1979, 1979, New Poets from Jamaica, 1979, Jamaican Poetry: A Checklist, 1979; recs. include The Poet Speaks 10, 1968, Rights of Passage, 1969, Masks, 1972, Islands, 1973, The Poetry of Edward Kamau Braithwaite, 1976, Poemas, 1976. Guggenheim fellow, 1972, City of Nairobi fellow, 1972, Fulbright fellow, 1982; recipient Arts Coun. Gt. Britain bursary, 1967, Camden Arts Festival prize, 1967, Cholmondeley award, 1970, Bussa award, 1973, Casa de las Americas prize, 1976, Musgrave medal Inst. Jamaica, 1983. Mem. Caribbean Artists Movement (founding sec. 1966—). Office: NYU Dept Comparative Lit MC 6723 19 University Pl Fl 4 New York NY 10003-4556 also: U West Indies Dept History Mona Kingston 7 Jamaica Mailing: Author Mail Wesleyan Univ Press 215 Long Lane Middletown CT 06459 Office Phone: 212-998-3845. Business E-Mail: kb5@nyu.edu.

BRATHWAITE, FRANK B., education educator; b. June 4, 1947; BA in Polit. Sci., Waterloo Luth. U., Ont., Can., 1971; MEd in Curriculum, Ont. Inst. Studies in Edn., Toronto, 1973; PhD in Edn., Walden U., Mpls., 1989. Cert. supervisory officer Ont., 1977, prin. Ont., 1978, tchr. Alta., 1978. Prin. Oilfields HS, Foothills Sch. Dist. # 31, High River, Alta., Canada, 1979—87; supt. schs. York Region Dist. Sch. Bd., Aurora, Ont., 1987—99; asst. prof. edn. D'Youville Coll., Buffalo, 2000—. Presenter in field. Mem.: Ont. Coll. Tchrs., Ont. Supervisory Officers Assn., Am. Ednl. Rsch. Assn., Nat. Coun. Tchrs. English. Office: D'Youville Coll 320 Porter Ave Buffalo NY 14201

BRATHWAITE, ORMOND DENNIS, chemistry professor; b. Parish Land, Barbados, Jan. 19, 1956; s. Dennis Berisford and Erin Eulene (Forde) B.; m. Maria Roslyn Alleyne, May 28, 1983; children: Marcus, Shayna. BS in Med. Tech., York Coll., 1982; MA in Biochemistry, CCNY, 1985; PhD in Biochemistry, CUNY, 1991. Phlebotomy technician, med. technologist intern Brookdale Hosp. Med. Ctr., Bklyn., 1981—84; adj. instr. CCNY, NYC, 1985—91; asst. rsch. scientist Borough Manhattan CC, NYC, 1991—94; asst. prof. chemistry and biology Cuyahoga CC, Highland Hills, Ohio, 1994—. Adj. instr. Bklyn. Coll., 1982-83; adj. prof. biology Kean Coll. NJ, Union, 1988-89; vis. scientist dept. cancer biology Cleve. Clinic Found., 1994-95. Recipient US Prof. of Yr. award, Carnegie Found. for Advancement of Tchg. and Coun. for Advancement and Support of Edn., 2006. Avocations: ping pong/table tennis, running, swimming, gardening, reading. Office: Cuyahoga CC 4250 Richmond Rd Highland Hills OH 44122-6104 Office Phone: 216-987-2401. E-mail: Ormond.Brathwaite@tri-c.edu.

BRATT, BENJAMIN, actor; b. San Francisco, Dec. 16, 1963; m. Talisa Soto, Apr. 13, 2002; children, Sophia Rosalinda, Mateo Bravery. BFA, U. Calif., Santa Barbara, 1986. Actor: (film) Bright Angel, 1991, One Good Cop, 1991, Bound by Honor, 1993, Demolition Man, 1993, The River Wild, 1994, Clear and Present Danter, 1994, Follow Me Home, 1997, The Next Best Thing, 2000, The Last Producer, 2000, Red Planet, 2000, Miss Congeniality, 2000, Traffic, 2000, Peniro, 2001, After the Storm, 2001, Abandon, 2002, The Woodsman, 2004, Catwoman, 2004, Thumbsucker, 2005, The Great Raid, 2005; (TV) Police Story: Gladiator School, 1988, Nasty Boys, 1989, Chains of Gold, 1991, Shadowhunter, 1993, Texas, 1994, Woman Undone, 1996, Exiled, 1998, After the Storm, 2001, (TV series) Knightwatch, 1988, Nasty Boys, 1990, Law & Order, 1995-99, E-Ring, 2005-; prodr.: Follow Me Home, 1997; TV guest appearances include: Homicide: Life on the Street, 1993. Winner ALMA award as best lead actor in a TV series for Law & Order, 1998, 99.

BRATT, NICHOLAS, investment and research and development company executive; b. Gerrards Cross, Eng., June 6, 1948; came to U.S., 1976; s. Guy Maurice and Francoise Nelly (Girardet) B.; m. Kuniko Matsui, Aug. 10, 1976; 1 child, Emi Margaret Matsui. Degree in politics, philosophy, econs., Oxford U., 1970; MIA, Columbia U., 1972. Rsch. analyst Morgan Grenfell & Co. Ltd., London, 1972-75; portfolio mgr. Morgan Grenfell S.A., Geneva, 1976, Scudder, Stevens & Clark, NYC, 1976—2002, mng. dir., 1984—2002, Deutsche Asset Mgmt., NYC, 2002—03; portfolio mgr. Lazard Asset Mgmt. LLC, 2003—. Pres. Scudder Internat. Fund, N.Y.C., 1982, Korea Fund, N.Y.C., 1984-2003, Scudder New Asia Fund, N.Y.C., 1987-2003, Brazil Fund, N.Y.C., 1988-2003, Scudder New Europe Fund, N.Y.C., 1990, Argentina Fund, N.Y.C., 1991-98, First Iberian Fund, N.Y.C., 1991-98, Scudder Greater Europe Fund, 1994—. Mem. N.Y. Assn. for Fgn. Investment (chmn. 1978-80), Japan Soc., Korea Soc. (bd. dirs.). Avocations: mountain climbing, skiing, tennis, paddle tennis, sailing, golf. Business E-Mail: nicholas.bratt@lazard.com.

BRATTEN, MILLIE MARTINI, editor-in-chief; m. John Bratten. With merchandising dept. Mademoiselle mag., 1975; assoc. editor Bride's mag. Conde Nast Pubs., NYC, fashion coord. menswear Bride's mag., editor accessories, fashion and beauty assoc. Bride's mag., exec. editor Bride's mag., 1991—94, editor-in-chief Bride's mag., 1994—; editl. dir. Conde Nast Bridal Group, 2002—. TV appearances in Weekend Today, Good Morning Am., Good Day N.Y., Network News, Family Values, Weddings of a Lifetime; host Romance Classics A Day of Diana; interviewed in USA Today, N.Y. Times, Washington Post, Wall Street Journal, Boston Globe, Forbes, ABC Radio Network. Mem. Am. Soc. Mag. Editors (bd. dir.), Fashion Group Internat., NY Women in Comms., Inc. (program coun. NY, past bd. dirs., v.p. membership). Office: Conde Nast Pubs 4 Times Sq 6th Fl New York NY 10036 Business E-Mail: editorinchief@bridesmag.com.*

BRATTON, CHRISTOPHER ALAN, academic administrator, videographer, art educator; b. Akron, Ohio, July 3, 1959; s. William Raymond and Barbara Jean (Yerkey) B.; m. Dalida Maria Benfield, Oct. 7, 1994; children, Isadora and Joaquin BFA, Atlanta Coll. of Art, 1982; student, Whitney Ind. Study Program, 1984-86; MFA, U. Wis., Milw., 1994. Project dir. Rise and Shine Prodns., NYC, 1988-89; guest lectr. Sch. of Visual Arts, NYC, 1990, Sch. of the Art Inst., Chicago, Ill., 1990; vis. prof. ctr. for modern culture and media Brown U., Providence, 1991-92; faculty mem. Sch. of Art Inst., Chgo., 1992—2004, chmn. dept. video, 1993-95, chmn. dept. video, com. on exhbns. and events, instn-wide tech. initiative, 1997—98, chair dept. of film, video, and new media Chicago, Ill., 2000—01, dean undergraduate studies, 2002—04; pres. San Francisco Art Inst., Calif., 2004—. Guest lectr. in video prodn. SUNY at Old Westbury, 1986, Channel Four workshop, Derry Northern Ireland, 1986, seminars N.Y.U., panelist N.Y. Marxist Sch., Video, Edn. and Culture, N.Y.C., 1989, Literacy on the Table seminar, Video and Literacy, Bronx (N.Y.) Coun. on the Arts, 1989, Columbus in Context, Union Theol. Sem., N.Y., Mediactive Conf. Low Format Video and Media Edn., 1990; curator Teaching TV, Artists' Space, N.Y., 1990, vis. artist Hallwalls, Buffalo, Ednl. Video Ctr., N.Y.C., 1991, R.I. Sch. of Design, Providence, 1992, Gallery 400, Univ. Ill., Chgo., 1994; coord. producer Teaching TV, Deep Dish TV, 1992; presenter Hunter Coll. Roundtable on Media and Culture, N.Y.C., 1992, The Ctr. for 20th Century Studies, U. Wis., Milw., 1992; grants panelist NEA Regional fellowships, Film in the Cities, Mpls., 1993; panelist Guerilla TV, Ctr. for New TV, N.Y.C., 1993. Editor, curator: (videotape) Teaching TV, 1991; dir. (videotapes), Counterterror The North of Ireland, 1990, (Best Advocacy Work, The Atlanta Film and Video Festival 1991, Silver Apple, Oakland, Calif. Nat. Ednl. Film and Video Festival, Finalist Athens (Ohio) Festival) Framing the Panthers in Black and White (Am. Film Fest Red Ribbon, New Eng. Film and Video Fest Best Social

Documentary, Australian Video Festival finalist, Hallwalls Festival of New Journalism, Buffalo, Jurors' award, Peoples Choice award The Global Africa Festival, Oakland, Calif., Spl. Jurors' award Black Maria Film and Video Fetival, East Orange, N.J., others), A Small War: The United States in Puerto Rico, 1995. Recipient fellowship in sculpture NEA, 1988, Citation Nat. Ednl. Film and Video Festival for Brooklyn, 1989, Bronze Apple for Walls and Bridges, 1990, Grand prize Internat. Youth Film and Video Festival, Warsaw for Brooklyn, 1990, Artist's Residency fellowship, Wesner Ctr. for Contemporary Art, Columbus, Ohio, 1993; grantee, Checkerboard Found., 1989, N.Y. State Coun. on the Arts, 1989, 91, J. Roderick MacArthur Found., 1989, NEA, 1990. Office: San Francisco Art Inst 800 Chestnut St San Francisco CA 94113 E-mail: president@sfai.edu.*

BRATTON, JAMES HENRY, JR., lawyer; b. Pulaski, Tenn., Oct. 9, 1931; s. James Henry and Mabel (Shelley) B.; m. Alleen Sharp Davis, Oct. 15, 1960; children: Susan Shelley McGonigle, James Henry III, Margaret Alleen Schilling. BA optime merens, valedictorian, U. South, 1952; BA, Oxford U., Eng., 1954, MA, 1978; LL.B., Yale U., 1956. Bar: Tenn. 1956, Ga. 1957. With antitrust div. Dept. Justice, summer 1955; since practiced in Atlanta; sr. ptnr. Smith, Gambrell & Russell. Vis. lectr. U. Ga. Law Sch., 1967; adj. prof. law Emory U., 1984-2001. Editor Yale Law Jour.; contbr. articles to profl. jours. Mem. Gov.'s Citizens Adv. Council on Environ. Affairs, 1970-74, U. South Sch. Theology Visiting Com., 2004-; trustee Pembroke Coll. Found., Inc., Trust Fund for Sibley Park, Ga. chpt. Multiple Sclerosis Soc., U. of the South, 1984-87, 95-98, Peachtree Rd. United Meth. Ch., 1997-2000, chmn. bd. trustees; bd. dirs. Soccer in the Streets, Buckhead Christian Ministry, pres., 1996; pres. Peachtree Heights West Civic Assn., 1984-99; co-chmn. Sewanee Parents Council, 1987-88; v.p. Pembroke Coll. Soc. of N.Am.; mem. Williams Parents' Fund, 1984-86; mem. parents adv. coun. Hamilton Coll., 1988-91. Named Alumnus of Yr., Sewanee Club Atlanta, 1990; John R. Crawford Disting. Svc. Award, U. of South, 2003. Fellow Lawyers Found. Ga., Am. Law Inst.; mem. ABA (standing com. on aero. law 1962-84, chmn. 1977-80), State Bar Ga. (founding chmn. environ. law sect. 1970-73), Fed. Bar Assn., Atlanta Bar Assn., Lawyers Club Atlanta, Old Warhorse Lawyers Club, Am. Acad. Polit. and Social Scis., Am. Judicature Soc., Associated Alumni U. of South (v.p. admissions 1993-95, pres. 1995-97), Yale Law Alumni Assn. (exec. com. 1976-79), Pembroke Coll. Found., Inc. (treas. 2003-), Phi Beta Kappa, Phi Delta Phi, Pi Gamma Mu, Gridiron. Democrat. Methodist. Home: 63 N Muscogee Ave NW Atlanta GA 30305-3542 Office: 1230 Peachtree St NE Atlanta GA 30309-3592 Office Phone: 404-815-3510. Business E-Mail: jbratton@sgrlaw.com.

BRATTON, WILLIAM EDWARD, electronics executive, management consultant; b. Dallas, Oct. 25, 1919; s. William E. and Edna (Walker) B.; m. Betty Thume, May 30, 1942; children: Dale, Janet, Donna. AB in Econs., Stanford U., 1940; MBA, Harvard U., 1945. From v.p. to pres. Librascope, Glendale, Calif., 1947-63; v.p., gen. mgr. Ampex, Culver City, Calif., 1963-66; pres. Guidance Tech., Santa Monica, Calif., 1967-68; v.p. electronics div. Gen. Dynamics, San Diego, 1969-72; pres. Theta Cable T.V., Santa Monica, 1974-82; pres., chief exec. officer Stagecoach Properties, Salado, Tex., 1959-99, ret., 1999. Served to lt. (j.g.) USNR, 1944-46. Mem.: El Niguel Country (Laguna, Calif.) (pres. 1978-79). Republican. Episcopalian. Avocations: golf, skindiving.

BRATTON, WILLIAM J., police chief, former commissioner; m. Cheryl A. Fiandaca, 1986 (div.); 1 child, David; m. Rikki Jo Klieman, April 30, 1999 B, B, postgrad., Boston State Coll.; grad. Sr. Execs. and Sr. Exec. Fellows Program, Harvard U.; grad., FBI Nat. Exec. Inst., New Eng. Inst. Law Enforcement Mgmt. Command Program, Police Exec. Rsch. Forum Sr. Mgmt. Inst. for Police. Various positions to exec. supt. Boston Police Dept., 1970-83, police commr., 1992-94; chief of police Mass. Bay Transp. Authority, 1983-86; supt. Met. Police Dept., Boston, 1986-90; chief N.Y.C. Transit Police Dept., 1990-92; police commr. N.Y.C. Police Dept., 1994-96; exec. v.p. First Security Consultants, NYC, 1996—98; pres., COO Carco Group Inc, St. James, NY, 1998—2001; chief of police L.A. Police Dept., 2002—. Mem. exec. session of policing Kennedy Sch. Govt. Harvard U., 1985-92 mem. policing in 21st century work group Nat. Inst. Justice, Washington. Mem. Internat. Assn. Chiefs of Police (major cities chiefs group), Police Exec. Rsch. Forum (pres. 1994—). Office: Office of the Chief of Police 150 N Los Angeles St Los Angeles CA 90012

BRATTSTROM, BAYARD HOLMES, biology professor; b. Chgo., July 3, 1929; s. Wilber LeRoy and Violet (Holmes) B.; m. Cecile D. Funk, June 15, 1952 (div. May 1975); children: Theodore Allen, David Arthur.; m. Martha Isaacs Marsh, July 8, 1982. BS, San Diego State Coll., 1951; MA, UCLA, 1953, PhD, 1959. Dir. edn. Natural History Mus., San Diego, 1949-51, asst. curator herpetology, 1949-51; assoc. zoology UCLA, 1954-56; research fellow paleoecology Calif. Inst. Tech., Pasadena, 1955; instr. biology Adelphi U., Garden City, NY, 1956-60; asst. prof. Calif. State U., Fullerton, 1960-61, assoc. prof., 1961-66, prof., 1966-94, prof. emeritus, 1994—. Co-owner Horned Lizard Ranch, Horned Lizard Press; rschr., author publs. in osteology, ecology, conservation, zoogeography of vertebrates, social behavior; hon. rsch. assoc. herpetology, vertebrate paleontology Los Angeles County Mus., 1961—; pres. Fullerton Youth Mus. and Natural Sci. Ctr., 1962-64, dir., 1962-66; assoc. prof. zoology UCLA, summers 1962-63; vis. prof. zoology Sydney U., Australia, 1978, U. Queensland, Brisbane, Australia, 1984; vis. rschr. James Cook U., Townsville, Australia, 1993-94; ecol. cons. to numerous govtl. agys. and pvt. corps. Author: The Talon Digs Deeply Into My Heart, 1974; author: (with M.A. Brattstrom) Aussie Slang, 2000. Recipient Disting. Teaching award Calif. State U., Fullerton, 1968, Dean's award for Outstanding Teaching and Rsch., 1992; Am. Philos. Soc. grantee to Mex., 1958, to Panama, 1959; NSF grantee, 1964-66; NSF fellow Monash U., Australia, 1966-67. Fellow AAAS (mem. coun. 1965-90), Herpetological League; mem. Am. Soc. Ichthyologists and Herpetologists (bd. govs. 1962-66, v.p. western div. 1965), Orange County Zool. Soc. (mem. bd. 1962-65, pres. 1962-64), So. Calif. Acad. Sci. (dir. 1964-67), Ecol. Soc. Am., Soc. for Study Evolution, Soc. Systematic Zoology, San Diego Soc. Natural History, Soc. Vertebrate Paleontology, Am. Soc. Mammalogists, Cooper Ornithol. Soc., Am. Ornithol. Soc., Am. Soc. Zoologists, Sigma Xi. Home: Horned Lizard Ranch PO Box 166 Wikieup AZ 85360 *My life and research has been based on an insatiable curiosity about the natural world, especially as seen in the evolutionary adaptations of animals to their environment and their interactions with each other.*

BRAUCHLI, MARCUS WALKER, editor; b. Boulder, Colo., June 19, 1961; s. Christopher R. and Margot L. Brauchli; m. Maggie Farley. AB, Columbia U., 1983. Nat. copy editor AP-Dow Jones & Co., 1984; Scandinavia corr. The Wall St. Jour., Dow Jones & Co., 1987—88, economics & fin. reporter Tokyo, 1988—92, Asia corr., Hong Kong bur. chief, 1992—95, China bureau chief, 1995—99, news editor, 1999—2000, nat. news editor, 2000—03, global news editor, 2003—05, deputy mng. editor NYC, 2005—07, mng. editor, 2007—. Commentator CNBC, Asia Bus. News. Office: The Wall St Jour 200 Liberty St New York NY 10281*

BRAUDE, MICHAEL, commodities trader, researcher; b. Chgo., Mar. 6, 1936; s. Sheldon and Nan B.; m. Linda Rae Miller, Aug. 20, 1961; children— Peter, Adam BS, U. Mo., Columbia, 1957; MS, Columbia U., NYC, 1958. Vice pres. Commerce Bank, Kansas City, Mo., 1960-73; vice pres. Mercantile Bank, Kansas City, Mo., 1966-73; exec. v.p. Am. Bank, Kansas City, Mo., 1973-84; pres., CEO Kansas City Bd. Trade, Mo., 1984—2001. Bd. dirs. Midwest Trust Co., Kansas City, Mo., Kansas City Life Ins. Co., Kansas City, Mo., MGP Ingredients, Atchison, Kans., Hodgdon Corp., Shawnee Mission, Kans. Author: Managing Your Money, 1975, also 12 childrens books Pres. Metr. Cmty. Coll. Found., Kansas City, Mo., 1982-84; mayor City of Mission Woods, Kans., 1982-84; trustee Kans. Pub. Employee Retirement Sys., 2001—, Baker U., 2006—. Mem. U. Mo. Alumni Assn. (bd. dirs. 1985-87). Jewish. Avocations: running, public speaking. Home: 5319 Mission Woods Ter Shawnee Mission KS 66205-2013 Personal E-mail: cmbraude@aol.com.

BRAUDE, ROBERT MICHAEL, retired medical librarian; b. LA, Sept. 27, 1939; s. Aaron and Dorothy (Lishner) B.; children— Michael, Daniel, Julianne. BA, UCLA, 1962, MLS, MA, 1964; PhD, U. Nebr., 1987. Reference librarian Biomed Library Ctr. for Health Scis., UCLA, Los Angeles, 1964-65, head Medlars search sta., 1965-68; assoc. dir. U. Colo. Med. Library, Denver, 1968-75, dir., 1975-77, U. Nebr. Med. Library, Omaha, 1978-86; asst. dean for info. resources, Frances and John Loeb librarian Weill Med. Coll./Cornell U., 1986—; ret., 2001. Adj. faculty U. Denver, 1972-78; vis. assoc. prof. Sch. Libr. Sci., Pratt Inst., 1988—; del. White House Conf. on Libraries and Info. Services, 1979; mem. biomed. library rev. com. Nat. Library Medicine, Bethesda, Md., 1980-84, mem. panel on med. informatics long range planning project, 1985-86, mem. planning panel on outreach programs, 1988-89. Author: (continuing edn. syllabus) Planning: Strategic and Tactical, 1983, also articles and book chpts.; mem. editorial adv. bd. Bibliography of Bioethics; mem. editorial bd. ann. Statis. of Med. Sch. Librs. and U.S. and Can., 19887-93; mem. editorial bd. Jour. Am. Med. Informatics Assn. Sec.-treas. Children's Chorale, Denver, 1974-75, trustee, 1975-77 Fellow N.Y. Acad. Medicine, Med. Libr. Assn. (sec., bd. dirs. 1972-75, Janet Doe lectr. 1996, chmn. numerous coms. N.Y.-N.J. chpts., Outstanding Achievement award Mid-continental chpt. 1986, Noyes award 2002), Am. Coll. Med. Informatics; mem. ALA, Acad. Health Info. Profls. (disting.), Health Scis. Libr. Dirs. (stds. and practices com. 1980-83), Assn. Western Hosps. (chmn. hosp. librs. sect. 1976-77, membership com. 1976-77), Am. Med. Informatics Assn. (mem. editl. bd.). Personal E-mail: bobbraude@lycos.com.

BRAUDY, SUSAN ORR, writer; b. Phila. d. Bernard and Blanche (Malin) Orr. BA cum laude, Bryn Mawr Coll.; postgrad., U. Pa., Yale U. Editor, writer The New Jour. Yale U., New Haven; assoc. editor Newsweek Mag., NYC; editor, writer Ms. Mag., NYC; freelance writer N.Y. Times, Vanity Fair Mag., NYC; v.p. Warner Bros., NYC, L.A., Michael Douglas Prodns., NYC, L.A. Author: (memoir) Between Marriage and Divorce, 1975, (novels) Who Killed Sal Mineo, 1984, What the Movies Made Me Do, 1984, (nonfiction) This Crazy Thing Called Love, 1991, Family Circle: The Boudins and the Aristocracy of the Left, 2003; screenwriter: (films) Scorsese Co.; Am. Zeotrope; Ixtlan; Disney. Mem.: NOW, Authors' Guild, Writers Guild of Am., PEN Club Internat., Vet. Feminists Am. Home: 240 Central Park S Apt 16B New York NY 10019-1413

BRAUER, HARROL ANDREW, JR., broadcast executive; b. Oct. 17, 1920; s. Harrol Andrew and Bertie (Gregory) B.; m. Elizabeth Anne Hill, May 18, 1946; children: Harrol Andrew III, William Lanier, Gregory Hill. BA, U. Richmond, 1942; LLD, Christopher Newport U. Chief announcer, program dir., account exec. various radio stas. in Va., 1939—42, various radio stas in Va., 1945—49; v.p. Sta. WVEC Radio, Hampton, Va., 1949—80; v.p., dir. sales Sta. WVEC-TV, Hampton, 1953—82; v.p. Peninsula Cable Corp., 1966—82; chmn. Wyatt Bros., 1983—90. Pres. Hampton Cmty. Chest, 1951-52; crusade chmn. Peninsula unit Am. Cancer Soc., 1960—; mem. Hampton Sch. Bd., 1963—, vice-chmn., 1964-68, chmn., 1968-70; pres. Hampton Parking Authority, chmn., 1988—; bd. dirs. YMCA, Va. USO; bd. dirs., vice-chmn. Va. Pub. Telecomms. Bd., chmn., 1985—; chmn. Soc. Founders of Mace Christopher Newport U., 1989—; chmn. bd. trustees Hampton Roads Ednl. TV Assn., 1965-70; rector Christopher Newport U., 1976-82; co-chmn. for 375th Anniversary Celebration City of Hampton, 1985. Lt. USNR, 1942-45. Recipient Thomas P. Chisman award Va. Air and Space Ctr., Disting. Svc. medallion Christopher Newport U., NCCJ award, Am. Advt. Fedn. Silver Medal award, Disting. Citizen award City of Hampton, Outstanding Man of Yr. award Peninsula Ad Club, 1993. Mem. Hampton Retail Mchts. Assn. (past pres., bd. dirs.), Chesapeake Acad. Found. (vice-chmn. 1988—), Jamestowne Soc., Peninsula C. of C. (past bd. dirs.), Broadcast Pioneers, James River Country Club, Hampton Yacht Club, Peninsula Exec.'s Club (past pres., bd. dirs.), Town Point Club, Kiwanis (past bd. dirs., pres., lt. gov.), Sigma Alpha Epsilon. Home: 35 N Boxwood St Hampton VA 23669-2401 Personal E-mail: ehb24@aol.com.

BRAUER, RHONDA LYN, publishing executive, lawyer; b. Gary, Ind., Nov. 23, 1959; d. Hugh Donald and Charlotte Gloria (Danzig) B.; m. Gregory John Holch, Sept. 7, 1989; children: Jillian Brauer Holch, Justin Brauer Holch. BA magna cum laude, Cornell U., 1981; JD magna cum laude, Ind. U., 1984. Bar: N.Y. 1985, U.S. Dist. Ct. (so. and ea. dist.) N.Y. 1991, U.S. Supreme Ct. 1992. Assoc. Cleary, Gottlieb, Steen & Hamilton, NYC, 1984-86, 89-92, Brussels, 1986-88; counsel The N.Y. Times Co., NYC, 1992—94, sr. counsel, 1994—2006, asst. sec., 1996—2002, corp. sec., 2002—, corp. governance officer, 2006—. Contbr. articles to profl. jours. Pro bono work Lawyers Com. for Human Rights, NYC, 1984-86, ACLU, 1989-90, Vol. Lawyers for the Arts, NYC, 1989-92, NY Lawyers for the Pub. Interest, 1992-95. Recipient Anne MacIntyre Litchfield prize of history Cornell U. Coll. Arts and Scis., 1981; Salzburg (Austria) Seminar fellow, 1988. Mem. Assn. Bar City N.Y., N.Y. Women's Bar Assn., Soc. Corp. Secs. and Governance Profls. (chmn. corp. practices com. 2006—). Avocations: swimming, hiking, films, jogging, sculling.

BRAUER, STEPHEN FRANKLIN, diplomat, manufacturing company executive; b. Sept. 3, 1945; s. Arthur John, Jr. and Jane (Franklin) B.; m. Camilla Cary Thompson, June 12, 1971; children: Blackford Fitzhugh, Rebecca Randolph, Stephen Franklin, Jr. Student, Washington and Lee U., 1963-64; BA, Westminster Coll., 1967; LLD (hon.), 1997. Sales and mktg. ofcl. Hunter Engring. Co., St. Louis, 1971-78, exec. v.p., 1978-81, pres., 1981-2001; U.S. amb. to Belgium, 2001—03. Bd. dirs. Boatmen's Trust Co., St. Louis, 1986-96; ptnr. St. Louis Cardinals baseball club, 1996—2003; pvt. client bd. Bank of Am., 1996—. Civilian aide Sec. Army, 1991-95; trustee Mo. Bot. Garden, 1988—; trustee Washington U., St. Louis, 1991—; mem. Mo. 21st Jud. Dist. Commn., 1992-96; hon. consul Govt. Belgium, 1987-2001; mem. nat. bd. Smithsonian Instn., Washington, 1993-99. 1st lt. C.E., AUS, 1968-70. Recipient St. Louis Regional Commerce Growth Assn. Tech. award, 1993, Recognition of Outstanding Bus. Leadership award U.S. Ho. of Reps., 1993, Dean's award Washington U. Sch. Engring., 1998, Spirit of Enterprise award Mo. Rep. Party, 1999, Henry Shaw Medal, M. Bot. Gardens, 2003. Mem. St. Louis Consular Corps., St. Louis (Mo.) Civic Progress, St. Louis Country Club, Everglades Club (Palm Beach). Republican. Episcopalian. Home: 9630 Ladue Rd Saint Louis MO 63124-1311 Office: 11250 Hunter Dr Saint Louis MO 63044-2306 Personal E-mail: sfbrauer@hunter.com.

BRAULT, GERARD JOSEPH, French language educator; b. Chicopee Falls, Mass., Nov. 7, 1929; s. Philias J. and Aline E. (Rémillard) B.; m. Jeanne Lambert Pepin, Jan. 23, 1954; children: Francis Gerard, Anne-Marie Welsh, Suzanne Eveline Dannenmueller. AB, Assumption Coll., Worcester, Mass., 1950, DLitt, 1976; AM cum laude, Laval U., 1952; PhD, U. Pa., Phila., 1958. Teaching fellow U. Pa., 1954-56, assoc. prof. Romance langs., 1961-65, vice dean Grad. Sch., 1962-65; instr. French Bowdoin Coll., Brunswick, Maine, 1957-59, asst. prof. French, 1959-61; prof. French Pa. State U., University Park, 1965-90, Disting. prof. French and medieval studies, 1990, Edwin Erle Sparks prof. French and medieval studies, 1990-97, head dept. French, 1965-70, Edwin Erle Sparks prof. emeritus French and medieval studies, 1998—. Fellow Inst. Arts and Humanistic Studies, 1976—; dir. NDEA Summer Insts., Bowdoin Coll., 1961, 62, Assumption Coll., 1964; Fulbright fellow, Strasbourg, France, 1956-57, Fulbright rsch. scholar and Guggenheim fellow, Strasbourg, 1968-69; sr. fellow in Can. studies, Quebec City, 1984, Camargo Found. fellow, Cassis, France, 1987, 94. Author: Celestine: A Critical Edition of the First French Translation (1527) of the Spanish Classic La Celestina, 1963, Cours de langue française destiné aux jeunes Franco-Américains, 1963, rev. edits., 1965, 69, Early Blazon, 1972, rev. edit., 1997, Eight Thirteenth-Century Rolls of Arms in French and Anglo-Norman Blazon, 1973 (prix Paul Adam-Even), The Song of Roland: An Analytical Edition (named outstanding book Choice 1979), 2 vols., 1978, La Chanson de Roland: Student Edition, 1984; The French-Canadian Heritage in New England, 1986, Rolls of Arms of Edward I (1272-1307) (Aspilogia III), 2 vols., 1997 (Bickersteth medal, Riquer prize); mem. editl. bd. French Forum, 1975— , Purdue U. Monographs, 1978—; contbr. articles to profl. jours. Mem. Cath. Commn. on Intellectual and Cultural Affairs, also, Comité de Vie Franco-Américaine, Société Historique Franco-Américaine. Served with CIC, U.S. Army, 1951-53. Decorated Palmes Académiques French Ministry Edn., 1965, officer, 1975; officer, Ordre National du Mérite, 1980, Ordre des Francophones d'Amérique, 1980; recipient Faculty Scholar medal Pa. State U., 1981, Class of 1933 Humanities award, Pa. State U., 1987 Fellow Soc. Antiquaries of London, Heraldry Soc. London, Medieval Acad. Am. (adv. bd. Speculum 1972-75), Académie Internationale d'Héraldique; mem. MLA, Société Rencesvals pour l'étude des épopées romanes (pres. 1985-88, pres. Am.-Canadian br. 1970-73, editorial bd. Olifant 1975—), Am. Assn. Tchrs. French, Middle Atlantic Conf. Canadian Studies (pres. 1981-83), Internat. Arthurian Soc., Harleian Soc. (council 1987-98). Home: 705 Westerly Pky State College PA 16801-4227 Home Phone: 814-238-3862. Business E-Mail: gjb2@psu.edu.

BRAULT, JAMES WILLIAM, physicist; b. New London, Wis., Feb. 10, 1932; s. Lucian Joseph and Alvina Lucy (Boville) B.; m. Margueritte Elaine Bryan, June 29, 1952 (div. May 1986); children: Stephen Michael, Lisa Lynn, Jennifer Elaine; m. Lynda Margaret Harris Faires, July 5, 1992. BS in Physics, U. Wis., 1953; student, Cornell U., 1953-55; PhD in Physics, Princeton U., 1962. Research staff member project Matterhorn Princeton U., NJ, 1955-57, instr. NJ, 1961-64; asst. physicist Kitt Peak Nat. Obs., Tucson, 1964-68, assoc. physicist, 1969-70; physicist Nat. Solar Obs., Tucson, 1971-94; rsch. assoc. U. Colo., Boulder, Colo., 1994—. Contbr. articles to profl. jours. Recipient Alexander von Humboldt award (Rep. of Germany), 1986-87. Fellow Optical Soc. Am.; mem. Am. Phys. Soc., Am. Geophysical Union. Democrat. Address: 1006 Honeysuckle Ln Louisville CO 80027-1096

BRAUMAN, JOHN I., chemist, educator; b. Pitts., Sept. 7, 1937; s. Milton and Freda E. (Schlitt) B.; m. Sharon Lea Kruse, Aug. 22, 1964; 1 dau., Kate Andrea. BS, MIT, 1959; PhD (NSF fellow), U. Calif., Berkeley, 1963. NSF postdoctoral fellow UCLA, 1962-63; asst. prof. chemistry Stanford (Calif.) U., 1963-69, asso. prof., 1969-72, prof., 1972-80, J.G. Jackson-C.J. Wood prof. chemistry, 1980—, chmn. dept., 1979-83, 95-96, cognizant dean phys. scis., 1999—2003. Cons. in phys. organic chemistry; adv. panel chemistry divsn. NSF, 1974-78; adv. panel NASA, AEC, ERDA, Rsch. Corp., Office Chemistry and Chem. Tech., NRC; coun. Gordon Rsch. Confs., 1989-95, trustee, 1991-95. Mem. editl. adv. bd. Jour. Am. Chem. Soc., 1976-83, Jour. Organic Chemistry, 1974-78, Nouveau Jour. de Chimie, 1977-85, Chem. Revs., 1978-80, Chem. Kinetics, 1987-89, Accts. Chem. Rsch., 1995-97, 98-2001; bd. trustees Ann. Revs., 1995—, mem. editl. adv. bd.; dep. editor for phys. scis. Sci., 1985-2000, chair sr. editl. bd., 2000—. Alfred P. Sloan fellow, 1968-70, Guggenheim fellow, 1978-79; Christensen fellow Oxford U., 1983-84, Nat. Medal of Science award, 2002. Fellow AAAS (chmn. sect. 1996-97, mem.-at-large sect. 1997-99), Calif. Acad. Scis. (hon.); mem. NAS (home sec. 2003-07, 07-, Award in Chem. Scis. 2001), Am. Acad. Arts and Scis., Am. Philos. Soc., Am. Chem. Soc. (award in pure chemistry 1973, Harrison Howe award, 1976, R.C. Fuson award, 1986, James Flack Norris award 1986, Arthur C. Cope scholar, 1986, Linus Pauling medal 2002, J. Willard Gibbs medal 2003, exec. com. phys. chemistry divsn., com. on sci. 1992-97), Sigma Xi, Phi Lambda Upsilon. Home: 849 Tolman Dr Palo Alto CA 94305-1025 Office: Stanford U Dept Chemistry Stanford CA 94305-5080

BRAUMILLER, ALLEN SPOONER, gas industry executive, geologist; b. Texarkana, Tex., Feb. 1, 1934; s. Jack and Jenie (Spooner) B.; m. Patsy Lois McCoy, Dec. 23, 1955; children: Allen Spoonr, Dana Ruth Braumiller Nance, Adrienne Brevard, Colin McCoy. Student, Tulane U., 1952-53; BS, U. Miss., 1955; MS, U. Ill., 1957. Sr. exploration geologist Carter Oil Co. (merged into Humble Oil & Refining Co. 1961), 1957-69; v.p., exploration geologist Helmerich & Payne, Inc., Tulsa, 1969-96, ret., 1996; pres. Braumiller & Braumiller, Inc., Tulsa, 1995—; mgr. Est Tex. Seismic Data, LLC, Tulsa, 1996—. Geol. cons. No. Ill. Natural Gas, Urbana, 1956-57. Elder area Presbyn. ch.; mem. Philbrook Mus. Art, Tulsa, Thomas Gilcrease Mus., Tulsa. Mem. Am. Assn. Petroleum Geologists, Geol. Soc. Am., Am. Assn. Profl. Landmen, Ill. Geol. Soc., Oklahoma City Geol. Soc., Tulsa Geol. Soc., Soc. Petroleum Engrs., Archaeol. Inst. Am., Internat. Assn. Energy Advs., Internat. Platform Assn., Internat. Wine and Food Soc., Tulsa C. of C., U.S. C. of C., Nat. Trust for Historic Preservation, Knife and Fork Club, Petroleum Club (bd. dirs. 1989-92). Republican. Avocations: reef diving, cycling, swimming, gardening, music. Home: 4979 E 113th St Tulsa OK 74137-7607 also: Braumiller & Braumiller Inc Philtower Bldg 427 S Boston Ave Ste 500 Tulsa OK 74103-4118 Address: 5105 E Belle Fontaine Beach Rd Ocean Springs MS 39564 Office Phone: 918-582-2300. Personal E-mail: patbrau@cs.com.

BRAUN, ANNA M., music educator; d. Robert F. and Virginia R. Fultz; m. Steven J. Braun, July 9, 1988; children: Robert J., Jonathan S., Stefanie J. BA in Music Edn., Coll. of NJ, Trenton, 1981—85; MA in Tchg., Marygrove Coll., Detroit, Mich., 1996—98; EdD in Tchr. Leadership, Walden U., Minneapolis, Minn., 2004—07. Cert. Teacher of Music, K-12 NJ, 1986. Orch. dir. East Brunswick Pub. Schools, Hammarskjold Mid. Sch., East Brunswick, NJ, 1987—; music tech. workshop presenter East Brunswick Pub. Sch., East Brunswick, NJ, 2003—06; part time lectr. Mason Gross Sch. of the Arts, Rutgers U., New Brunswick, NJ, 2005; music tech. workshop presenter Ednl. Tech. Tng. Ctr., East Brunswick, NJ, 2005. Webmaster Princeton Chpt. Nat. Soc. DAR, Princeton, NJ, 2002—07. Recipient Spl. Recognition for Vol. Info. Specialists, NJ Chpt. Nat. Soc. of the DAR, 2004; grantee Improving Student Music Performance through the use of Advanced Audio Tech., East Brunswick Pub. Schools, 2003, Creation of a Music Audio Libr., 2004. Mem.: East Brunswick Band Boosters Assn., Ctrl. Jersey Music Educators Assn., NJ Music Edn. Assn. (Master Tchr. Award 2006), Nat. Music Educators Assn., Princeton Chpt. Nat. Soc. of the DAR (vol. info. specialist 2002—07). Achievements include NJ Governor's award in Leadership in Arts Edn., 2006. Office: Hammarskjold Middle School 200 Rues Lane East Brunswick NJ 08816 Office Phone: 732-613-6890. E-mail: abraun@ebnet.org.

BRAUN, DAVID A(DLAI), lawyer; b. NYC, Apr. 23, 1931; s. Morris and Betty Braunstein; m. Merna Feldman, Dec. 18, 1955; children: Lloyd Jeffrey, Kenneth Franklin, Evan Albert. AB, Columbia U., NYC, 1952, LLB, 1954. Bar: N.Y. 1955, Calif. 1974. Assoc. Ellis, Ellis and Ellis, NYC, 1954—56, Davis and Gilbert, 1956—57; ptnr. Pryor, Braun, Cashman & Sherman, 1957—73, Hardee, Barovick, Konecky & Braun, NYC, 1973, LA, 1974—81; pres., CEO Polygram Records, Inc., N.Y.C., 1980—81; counsel Wyman, Bautzer, Rothman, Kuchel & Silbert, LA, 1982—85; ptnr. Braun, Margolis, Burrill & Besser, LA, 1985—87; counsel Silverberg, Rosen, Leon & Behr, 1987—89, Silverberg, Katz, Thompson & Braun, 1989—91; spl. counsel Proskauer, Rose, Goetz & Mendelsohn, 1991—93; ptnr. Monasch Plotkin & Braun, 1993—94; pvt. practice, 1994—98; sr. counsel Akin, Gump, Strauss, Hauer & Feld, LLP, LA, 1998—2006. Adj. prof. U. So. Calif. Sch. Cinema-TV; guest lectr. UCLA Ext.; adv. com. Ctr.

for Law, Media and the Arts, Columbia U. Sch. Law; internat. adv. bd. Nat. Inst. Entertainment and Media Law, Southwestern U. Sch. Law. Co-prodr.: (off-Broadway play) A Woman of Will, 2005. Bd. visitors Columbia Coll., 1980-86, Columbia Law Sch., 1992-94; bd. dirs. Reprise! Broadway's Best in Concert, Musician's Assistance Program, 1994-98, Tu 'Um EST Cmty. Drug Rehab. Ctr., Rock and Roll Hall of Fame, 1985-93. Mem. Assn. of City of NY, LA County Bar Assn., Beverly Hills Bar Assn., Nat. Acad. TV Arts and Scis. (pres. NY chpt. 1972-73), NATAS, Am. Arbitration Assn., Hollywood Radio and TV Soc. (bd. dirs. 1983-86), Sigma Chi, Phi Alpha Delta. Jewish. Home and Office: 1035 Alston Rd Montecito CA 93108-2407 E-mail: dbraun423@cox.net.

BRAUN, GUSTAV MILAN, otolaryngologist, surgeon; b. Mar. 8, 1938; BA in Chemistry, Wayne State U., 1962; MS, U. Iowa, 1971; MD, U. Mich., 1965. Diplomate Am. Bd. Otolaryngology. Intern UCLA Affiliated Hosps., 1965-66; resident in surgery Wadsworth VA Hosp., LA, 1966-67; resident in ear, nose, throat and facial plastic surgery U. Iowa Hosps., Iowa City, 1967-71; asst. prof. facial plastic surgery and otolaryngology Sch. Medicine U. Calif., San Diego, 1974-76; pvt. practice Calif., 1977-78, Harlingen, Tex., 1979—90, Houston, 1991—2000, Mineral Wells, Tex., 2001—06, Palo Pinto Gen. Hosp., Mineral Wells, 2001—06. Clin. asst. prof. Baylor Coll. Medicine, Houston, 1991-2001. Maj. U.S. Army, 1966-73. Fellow ACS, Am. Acad. Facial Plastic and Reconstructive Surgery, Am. Acad. Otolaryngology-Head and Neck Surgery; mem. Tex. Med. Assn, Rotary Internat. (Paul Harris fellow). Mailing: PO Box 1527 Mineral Wells TX 76068-1527 Personal E-mail: gusbraun@cox-internet.com.

BRAUN, HARLAND W., lawyer; b. NYC, Sept. 21, 1942; BA, U. Calif., LA, 1964, JD, 1967. Bar: Calif. 1967, U.S. Dist. Ct. (Ctrl. Dist. Calif.) 1967, cert.: specialist in pvt. practice 1973. Dep. dist. atty., LA County, 1968—73; pvt. practice, 1973—. Mem. UCLA Law Rev., 1965—67. Mem. UCLA Law Review, 1965—67. Mem.: Am. Inn of Ct. (mem., criminal justice sect. organizing com.), LA County Bar Assn., Calif. Attys. Criminal Justice, Criminal Courts Bar Assn. Office: Harland W Braun PC 1880 Century Park E Ste 710 Los Angeles CA 90067-1608 Office Phone: 310-277-4777. Office Fax: 310-277-4045. E-mail: Harland@braunlaw.com.*

BRAUN, JEFFREY LOUIS, lawyer; b. NYC, Oct. 2, 1946; s. Arthur and Berta (Freimark) B.; m. Beth Essig, June 6, 1982; children: Arthur Paul, Emily Claire. BA, Rutgers U., 1968; JD, Yale U., 1971. Bar: N.Y. 1974, U.S. Dist. Ct. (so. and ea. dists.) N.Y., U.S. Tax Ct., U.S. Ct. Appeals (2d cir.), U.S. Ct. Appeals (9th cir.), U.S. Supreme Ct. Law clk. to Judge Harry Pregerson US Dist. Ct. (cen. dist.) Calif., LA, 1971—72; assoc. Paul, Weiss, Rifkind, Wharton & Garrison, NYC, 1972—74, Rosenman & Colin LLP, NYC, 1974—80, ptnr., 1980—2002; coun. Kramer Levin Naftalis & Frankel LLP, NYC, 2002—06, ptnr., 2006—. Mem. N.Y. State Bar Assn. (co-chmn. com. on real estate litigation 2005—), Assn. of the Bar of the City of N.Y. (com. on internat. human rights 1985-88, com. on mcpl. affairs 1988-91, com. on recruitment and retention of lawyers 1992-94, long-range planning com. 1994-97), Fed. Bar Coun. (com. on cts. of the second cir. 1995—). Home: 15 Park Rd Irvington NY 10533-2008 Office: Kramer Levin Naftalis & Frankel LLP 1177 Ave of Americas New York NY 10036 Office Phone: 212-715-7830. Business E-Mail: jbraun@kramerlevin.com.

BRAUN, JEROME IRWIN, lawyer; b. St. Joseph, Mo., Dec. 16, 1929; s. Martin H. and Bess (Donsker) B.; children: Aaron, Susan, Daniel; m. Dolores Ferriter, Aug. 16, 1987. AB with distinction, Stanford U., 1951, LLB, 1953. Bar: Mo. 1953, Calif. 1953, U.S. Dist. Ct. (no. dist.) Calif., U.S. Tax Ct., U.S. Ct. Mil. Appeals, U.S. Supreme Ct., U.S. Ct. Appeals (9th cir.). Assoc. Long & Levit, San Francisco, 1957-58, Law Offices of Jefferson Peyser, San Francisco, 1958-62; founding ptnr. Farella, Braun & Martel (formerly Elke, Farella & Braun), San Francisco, 1962—. Instr. San Francisco Law Sch., 1958-69; mem. U.S. Dist. Ct. Civil Justice Reform Act Adv. Com., 1991—; spkr. various state bar convs. in Calif., Ill., Nev., Mont.; request moderator/participant continuing edn. of bar programs; past chmn. 9th Cir. Sr. Adv. Bd., past chmn. lawyer reps. to 9th Cir. Jud. Conf.; mem. appellate lawyers liaison com. Calif. Ct. Appeals 1st dist.; jud.conf. U.S. Com. Long Range Planning; founder Jon Samuel Abramson Scholarship Endowment Stanford U. Law. Revising editor: Stanford U. Law Rev.; contbr. articles to profl. jours. Mem. Jewish Community Fedn. San Francisco, The Peninsula, Marin and Sonoma Counties, pres., 1979-80; past pres. United Jewish Community Ctrs. 1st lt. JAGC, U.S. Army, 1954-57, U.S. Army Res., 1957-64. Recipient Lloyd W. Dinkelspiel Outstanding Young Leader award Jewish Welfare Fedn., 1967, Professionalism award 9th cir. Am. Inns of Ct., 1999, John P. Frank Professionalism award, 2005. Fellow Am. Acad. Appellate Lawyers, Am. Coll. Trial Lawyers (teaching trial and appellate advocacy com.), Am. Bar Found.; mem. ABA, Calif. Bar Assn. (chmn. adminstrn. justice com. 1977), Bar Assn. San Francisco (spl. com. on lawyers malpractice and malpractice ins.), San Francisco Bar Found. (past trustee), Calif. Acad. Appellate Lawyers (past pres., mem. U.S. Dist. Ct. Civil Justice Reform Act adv. com., Calif. Ct. of Appeals 1st Dist. Appellate Lawyers liaison com., jud. conf. of the U.S., com. on long-range planning, panelist 1994), Am. Judicature Soc. (past dir.), Stanford Law Sch. Bd. of Visitors, U.S. Dist. Ct. of No. Dist. Calif. Hist. Soc. (past pres., bd. dirs.), 9th Cir. Ct. of Appeals Hist. Soc. (past. pres.), Mex.-Am. Legal Def. Fund (honoree), Order of Coif. Personal E-mail: jbraun@fbm.com.

BRAUN, JOSEPH J., lawyer; b. Cin., Aug. 6, 1973; BA, U. Ky., 1994; JD, U. Toledo, 1998. Bar: Ohio 1998, US Dist. Ct. Southern Dist. Ohio 2000. Prosecutor Mayor's Ct., Wyoming, Ohio; assoc. Strauss & Troy. Mem. Clermont County Mental Health Bd., 1998—99; trustee Clermont County Pub. Libr., 1999—. Named one of Ohio's Rising Stars, Super Lawyers, 2006. Mem.: Assn. Trial Lawyers Am., Ohio Trial Lawyers Assn., Cin. Bar Assn., Ohio State Bar Assn., ABA. Office: Strauss & Troy Federal Reserve Bldg 150 E 4th St Cincinnati OH 45202-4018 Office Phone: 513-621-2120. Office Fax: 513-241-8259.

BRAUN, LILIAN JACKSON, writer; Author: The Cat Who Could Read Backwards, 1966, The Cat Who Ate Danish Modern, 1968, The Cat Who Turned On And Off, 1968, The Cat Who Saw Red, 1986, The Cat Who Played Brahms, 1987, The Cat Who Played Post Office, 1987, The Cat Who Knew Shakespeare, 1988, The Cat Who Sniffed Glue, 1988, The Cat Who Had Fourteen Tales, 1988, The Cat Who Went Underground, 1989, The Cat Who Talked to Ghosts, 1990, The Cat Who Lived High, 1990, The Cat Who Knew A Cardinal, 1991, The Cat Who Wasn't There, 1992, The Cat Who Moved A Mountain, 1992, The Cat Who Went Into The Closet, 1993, The Cat Who Came to Breakfast, 1994, The Cat Who Blew the Whistle, 1995, The Cat Who Smelled a Rat, 2001, The Cat Who Went Up the Creek, 2002, The Cat Who Talked Turkey, 2004, The Cat Who Went Bananas, 2005.

BRAUN, LLOYD, Internet company executive; b. Long Island; Grad., Vassar Coll.; JD, U. Calif. Hastings Sch. Law. Atty. corp. transactions Stroock & Stroock & Lavan, 1983—84; entertainment atty. Silverberg, Rosen, Leon & Behr, 1985—89; pres. Brillstein-Grey Entertainment, 1994—98; chmn. Buena Vista TV Prodns., 1998—99; co-chmn. ABC TV Entertainment Group, 1999—2002, chmn., 2002—04; head, media group Yahoo! Inc., 2004—. Vice chmn. Lauri Strauss Leukemia Found.; bd. trustees Vassar Coll. Recipient LA Free Clinic's highest honor for personal commitment to the clinic's philosophy that health care is right for all, 2000.*

BRAUN, LUDWIG, retired engineering educator; b. Bklyn., May 14, 1926; s. Ludwig and Wetie (Schmidt) B.; m. Eva Margaret Taylor, Sept. 7, 1947; children: Barbara Ann, Edith Elizabeth, Anne Catherine, John Ludwig. BEE, Poly. Inst. Bklyn., 1950, MEE, 1955, DEE, 1959. Elec. engr. Allied Control Co., NYC, 1950-51; head electronics dept. Anton Electronics Labs., Inc., Bklyn., 1951-55; from instr. elec. engring. to prof. sys. and elec. engring. Poly. Inst. Bklyn., 1955-72; prof. engring. SUNY, Stony Brook, 1972-82, dir. bioengring. program, 1976-79, dir. personal computers in edn. lab., 1979-82; prof. computer sci., dir. acad. computing lab. N.Y. Inst. Tech., Central Islip, 1982-87; rsch. prof. NYU, NYC, 1987-89; ret., 1989. Sr. fellow C.W. Post Campus, L.I.U., 1998-2004; dir. Nat. Inst. Microcomputer Based Learning, 1981-87, Intercounty Tchr. Resource Ctr., 1985-87, Mecklenburger Group, 1993-96; lectr., med. scientist Downstate Med. Ctr., 1970-82; cons. ednl. tech., 1990—, Vertol divsn. Boeing Co., GE, Ford Found., NSF, Nat. Inst. Edn., IBM, NET Schs., Inc.; tech. advisor Orton Soc., Suffolk. Author: (with E. Mishkin) Adaptive Control Systems, 1961; contbg. author: Signals and Systems in Electrical Engineering, 1962, Perry's Chemical Engineering Handbook, 1961, System Engineering Handbook, 1965, Computer Techniques in Biomedicine and Medicine, 1973, Vision Test Recommendations for American Education Decision Makers, 1990, Celebrating Success, 1995. Mem. Women's Action Alliance, 1985-88; bd. dirs. Playing To Win, Inc., 1983-90, Internat. Coun. for Computers in Edn., 1987-89. With AUS, 1944-46. First recipient Paul Pair award for contbns. to edn. through tech., 1995, Nat. Ednl. Computing Assn. Pioneer award in Ednl. Tech., 1999; fellow Global Village Schs. Inst., 1996-98. Mem. IEEE (sr. 1990), Internat. Soc. for Tech. in Edn. (bd. dirs. 1989-90), Sigma Xi, Tau Beta Pi, Eta Kappa Nu. Home: 11 Parsons Dr Dix Hills NY 11746-5217 Home Phone: 631-423-6269. E-mail: ludbraun@optonline.net.

BRAUN, MARY LUCILE DEKLE (LUCY BRAUN), psychotherapist, consultant, counseling administrator, educator; b. Tampa, Fla. d. Guthrie "Gus" J. and Lucile (Culpepper) Dekle; children: John Ryan, Matthew Joseph, Jeffrey William, Douglas Edwin. AB, Brenau Coll.; MA, U. Cen. Fla.; EdD, U. Fla. Cert. disability mgmt. specialist, rehab. counselor, victim advocate; lic. mental health counselor; lic. marriage and family therapist; nationally cert. counselor. Coord. Orange County Child Abuse Prevention, Orlando, Fla., 1983-88; cons. Displaced Homemaker Program, Orlando, 1989-94, DCS, Oviedo, Fla., 1990-92. Adj. prof. U. Ctrl. Fla., Orlando, Troy State U.; clin. dir. Response Sexual Abuse Treatment Program, 1993—95; mem. adv. bd. Fla. Hosp. Women's Ctr., Orlando, 1989—95; bd. dirs. Parent Resource Ctr., Orlando, Children With Attention Deficit Disorders, Orlando, 1989—91; cons. program devel. for children and adolescent treatment svcs., 1997—98; dir. clin. svcs. Rehab. and Indsl. Counseling, 1997—; cons., counselor contractor VA; counselor Share the Care Program. Author: Someone Heard, 1987, Humor Us Soup, 1989, Child Abuse and Neglect: Resource Guide for Orange County Schools, 1985, 2d edit., 1987; contbg. author: Death from Child Abuse, 1986, Personality Types of Abusive Parents, 1993, Why Children Fight, 1992. Sustaining mem. Jr. League of Greater Orlando. Recipient Cmty. Svc. award Walt Disney World, 1987, Outstanding Alumna award Brenau U., 2006. Mem. ACA, Am. Acad. Marriage and Family Therapists, Fla. Counseling Assn., Nat. Bd. Cert. Counselors, Phi Kappa Phi, Kappa Delta Pi, Chi Sigma Iota, Alpha Delta Pi. Avocations: scuba diving, sailing, puzzles, travel.

BRAUN, MICHAEL ANDREW, radiologist; b. Shorewood, Wis., Sept. 30, 1959; s. Roger John and Mary Braun; m. Theresa Maria Dimitsopoulos, Sept. 17, 1994; children: Katherine Nicole, Alexander Joseph. BS, Marquette U., 1982; MD, U. Wis., 1986. Resident in diagnostic radiology Albany (NY) Med. Ctr., 1987—91; fellow in interventional radiology Northwestern U., Chgo., 1991—92; asst. prof. radiology Northwestern Meml. Hosp., Chgo., 1992—95; pvt. practie St. Mary's Radiologists, Milw., 1995—2000, pres., CEO, 1998—2000; med. dir. radiology St. Mary's Hosp., Milw., 1998—2002; chief interervention radiology Wis. Radiology Specialists, Milw., 2000—. Author: Interventional Radiology Procedure Manual, 1997; contbr. articles to profl. publs. Fellow: Am. Coll. Chest Physicians; mem.: Milw. Roentgen Ray Soc. (sec.-treas. 2000—02, v.p. 2003—), Soc. Interventional Radiology. Avocations: Alpine skiing, bicycling. Office: Wis Radiology Specialists 1045 Glen Oaks Ln Mequon WI 53092

BRAUN, ROBERT CLARE, retired association and advertising executive; b. Indpls., July 18, 1928; s. Ewald Elsworth and Lila (Inman) B. BS in journalism-advtg., Butler U., 1950; postgrad., Ind. Univ., 1957-66. Reporter Northside Topics Newspaper, Indpls., 1949; advt. mgr., 1950; asst. mgr. Clarence E. Crippen Painting Co., Indpls., 1951; corp. sec. Auto-Imports, Ltd., Indpls., 1952-53; pres. O.R. Brown Paper Co., Indpls., 1953-69; pres., chief exec. ofcr. Robert C. Braun Advt. Agy., 1959-70; with Zimmer Engraving Inc., Indpls, IN, 1964-69; former chmn. bd. O.R. Brown Paper, Inc. Advtg. cons. Rolls Royce Motor Cars, 1957-59, exec. dir., CEO Historic Landmarks Found., Ind., 1969-73, exec. v.p. Purchasing Mgmt. Assn., Indpls., 1974-85, Midwest Office Systems abd Equipment Show, 1974-85, Grand Valley Indsl. Show, 1974-85; Evansville Indsl. Show, 1982-85, Ind. Bus. Opportunity Fair, 1985-88. Author: The Mr. Eli Lilly That I Knew, 1977. Editor: Historic Landmarks News, 1969-74; Hoosier Purchaser mag., 1974-85, I.R.M.S.D.C. News, 1985-88. Contbr. articles to profl. jours. Chmn. Citizens' Adv. Com. to Marion County Met. Planning Dept., 1963; pres. museum com. Indpls. Fire Dept., 1966-76; mem. adv. com. Historic Preservation Commn. Marion County, 1967-73; Midwestern artifacts cons. to curator of White House, Wash., 1971-73; mem. chmn. Mayor's Contract Compliance Adv. Bd., 1977-91; mem. Mayor's subcom. for Indpls. Stadium, 1981-83; adv. bd., exec. com. Indpls. Office Equal Opportunity 1982—; mem. Ind. Minority Bus. Opportunity Counc., 1985-88; mem. Met. Mus. Art, Indpls. Mus. of Art bd. dirs. Historic Landmarks Found. Ind., 1960-69; dir., sec. Ind. Arthritis and Rheumatism Found., 1960-67, pres., 1969, dir., 1970-90, hon. lifetime dir., 1992—, dir. Assoc. Patient Svcs., 1976-91, dir. emeritus, 1992; pres. Amanda Wasson Meml. Trust, 1961-72. Recipient Meritorious Svc. awd. St. Jude's Police League, 1961; citation for meritorious svc. Am. Legion Police Post 56, 1962; Tafflinger-Holiday Park appreciation awd., 1973; Nat. Vol. Svc. Citation, Arthritis Found., 1979; Margaret Egan Meml. awd. Ind. Arthritis Found., 1980; Indpls. Profl. Fire Fighters meritorious svc. awd., 1982. Mem. Marion County Hist. Soc. (dir. 1964—, pres. 1965-69, 74-76, 1st v.p. 1979), Am. Guild Organists (mem. Indpls. chpt., charter mem. Franklin Coll. br.), Indpls. Humane Soc., Ind. Mus. Soc. (treas., dir. 1967-74), Internat. Fire Buff Assocs., Indpls. Second Alarm Fire Buffs (sec.-treas. 1967, pres. 1969), Ind. Hist. Soc., Nat. Hist. Soc., Nat. Trust Historic Preservation, Smithsonian Assn., Friends of Cast Iron Architecture, Soc. Archtl. Historians, Am. Heritage Soc., N.A.P.M. Editors Grp. (nat. sec. 1979-81, nat. chmn./pres. 1981-84), Am. Assn. State and Local History, Decorative Arts Soc. Indpls., Ind. Soc. Assn. Execs., Nat. Assn. Purchasing Mgmt. (W.L. Beckham internat. pub. rels. awd. 1983), purchasing Mgmt. Assn. Indpls. (dir. 1974—), Victorian Soc. Am. (nat. sec. 1971-74), Lambda Chi Alpha, Alpha Delta Sigma, Sigma Delta Chi, Tau Kappa Alpha. Club: Indpls. Press, Rolls-Royce Owners. Home: 1415 W 52nd St Indianapolis IN 46228-2316 Personal E-mail: rbraun1@comcast.net.

BRAUN, ROBERT DAVID, aerospace engineer, educator; BS in Aerospace Engring., Pa. State U., 1987; MS in Astronautics, George Washington U., 1989; PhD in Aeronautics and Astronautics, Stanford U., Calif., 1996. With NASA Langley Rsch. Ctr.; David and Andrew Lewis assoc. prof. space tech. Ga. Inst. Tech., 2003—, co-dir. Space Systems Design Lab. Mem. aircraft design grp. Stanford U., Calif., 1991—96; chief engr. NASA Intelligent Synthesis Environment Prog., 2000—01; mission arch. Aerial Regional-scale Environ. Survey Mars Scout mission, 2001—03. Contbr. articles to sci. jours. Fellow: AIAA (Disting. lectr. 2003—06, mem. multidisciplinary optimization tech. com. 2004—06, mem. space systems tech. com. 2006, Lawrence Sperry award 1999). Office: Dept Aerospace Engring Ga Inst Tech 270 Ferst Dr Atlanta GA 30332-0150 Office Phone: 404-385-6171. E-mail: robert.braun@ae.gatech.edu.*

BRAUN, STANLEY, orthodontist, educator; s. Max and Sarah Braun; m. Constance Ann Belle, June 25, 1955; children: Lory Susan Wasserman, Stephen Mitchell, Mark Charles. B of Mech. Engring., NYU, 1951, MME, 1952; DDS summa cum laude, Ohio State U., 1963. Lic. Bd. Dentistry Ohio, Ind., Ill., Ky. Asst. chief engr. Master Vibrator Co., Dayton, Ohio, 1956—58; assoc. prof. of orthodontics Ind. U., Indpls., 1965—69; pvt. practice in splty. orthodontics Indpls., 1965—96; clin. prof. of orthodontics U. of Louisville, 1976—95, Vanderbilt U. Med. Ctr., Nashville, 1994—2004, U. of Ill., Chgo., 1995—98, Marquette U., Milw., 1998, St. Louis U., 1999—2001. Rsch. fellow NIH, Washington, 1963—65; cons. in orthodontics to the surgeon gen. Dept. of Health, Washington, 1965—67; editl. bd. Jour., Angle Orthodontic Soc., Edina, Minn., 1995—; guest editor seminars in orthodontics. Contbr. chpt. to textbook; mem. editl. bd.: Am. Jour. Orthodontics and Dentofacial Orthopedics, Jour. Angle Orthodontic Soc., 1995—2005; contbr. articles to profl. jours.; editl. bd. Med. Sci. Monitor, 2004—. 1st lt. USAF, 1952—54. Recipient Don Shusterman Meml. award, Ohio State U., 1963, Cert. of Recognition, NYU Orthodontic Soc., 1970, Disting. award, Am. Soc. of Dentistry for Children, 1963, Cert. of Recognition, Chgo. Dental Soc., 1965, Award of Recognition, Am. Acad. of Dental Medicine, 1975, Callahan Meml. Commn. award, Ohio State U., 1963. Mem.: Tau Beta Pi, Omicron Kappa Epsilon, Pi Tau Sigma. Achievements include Member of Engineering Team that Developed Fusing System for the First U.S. Intercontinental Ballistics Missile; design of Concrete Automatic Troweling Machine. Avocations: travel, stained glass creations, painting.

BRAUN, STEPHEN BAKER, academic administrator; b. Cleve., Nov. 3, 1942; s. William B. and Louise M. (Baker) B.; m. Retta F. Kriefall, June 16, 1974; children: Elizabeth Rachel, Christopher Baker. BS, Xavier U., 1964; MBA, Fairleigh Dickinson U., 1976; postgrad., Imperial Coll., U London, 1996; PhD, Portland State U., 2007—. Regional mgr. Northwest Airlines, Inc., St. Paul, 1967-72; v.p. Inflight Motion Pictures, Inc., NYC, 1972-78; v.p., gen. mgr. Columbia Pipe & Supply, Inc., Portland, 1978-79; exec. v.p. Golby Mfg. Co., Portland, 1979-80; v.p. fin. Timberline Software, Inc., Portland, 1980-82; pres., founder Computer Systems Supplyware, Inc., Portland, 1982-87; dean Sch. Mgmt., Concordia U., Portland, 1987—92, exec. v.p., 1993—2001; COO Concordia U. Found., Portland, 1993-2000, vice chmn., dir., 1985-2000. Mem. bd. regents Concordia U., 1986-87, 92-2000; bd. dir. Alameda Resources Co., Tigard, Oreg., BioReaction Industries; vis. scholar grad. sch. bus. U. Wash., 2000—; adv. faculty Harvard Bus. Sch. Pub., 2005—; founder, chmn. CEO Roundtable, 1994—; mem. adv. bd. Oreg. Bus. mag., 2002—; nat. keynote spkr., Defense Contract Mgmt. Agy, 2004; exec. panelist McKinsey & Co.'s Quar. Rsch. Publ., 2004—; cmty. leader Fed. Res. Bank San Francisco, 2005—. Com. chmn. United Way, Boston, 1966; bd. dirs. German Am. Found., 1990-2000. With USN, 1964-67. Mem. Oreg. Ctr. Entrepreneurship (pres., founder, 1986), Oreg. Enterprise Forum, Am. Mktg. Assn. (panelist 1985-88), Nat. Assn. Corp. Dirs., Assn. Data Processing Systems Orgn., Rotary (long-range planning com. 1985-96, judge Oreg. Enterprise Forum, Entrepreneur of Yr. award 1998, moderator, major league baseball debate, 2003). Lutheran. Office: Concordia U 2811 NE Holman St Portland OR 97211-6099 also: Imperial Coll/Mgmt Sch 53 Princes Gate Exhibition Rd London SW7 2PG England Office Phone: 503-288-9371. Business E-Mail: sbraun@cu-portland.edu.

BRAUN, THOMAS W., dean, academic administrator; b. Pitts. BS in Biology, U. Pitts., 1969, DMD summa cum laude, 1973, MS in Pharmacology, 1973, PhD in Anatomy, 1977. Resident in oral and maxillofacial surgery Presbyn. U. Hosp., Pitts.; instr. in anatomy at Sch. Dental Medicine U. Pitts., 1975—90, assoc. prof. , chmn. dept. oral and maxillofacial surgery, 1990—93, assoc. dean hosp. affairs, 1991—96, prof., 1993—, sr. assoc. dean, 1996—99, interim dean Sch. Dental Medicine, 1999—2000, dean Sch. Dental Medicine, 2000—. Contbr. articles to profl. jours. Mem.: Pa. State Dental Bd., Great Lakes Soc. of Oral and Maxillofacial Surgeons (past pres.), Pa. Soc. Oral and Maxillofacial Surgeons (past pres.), Am. Assn. Oral and Maxillofacial Surgery (mem. ho. of dels.), Am. Bd. Oral and Maxillofacial Surgery (past pres.). Office: 3501 Terrace St Pittsburgh PA 15261 Office Phone: 412-648-1938. Office Fax: 412-648-1008. Business E-Mail: twb3@dental.pitt.edu.

BRAUND-ALLEN, JULIANNA ELISE, librarian; b. Anchorage, Nov. 11, 1953; d. Melvin Arnold and Gertrude Evelyn Johansen Braund; m. George Robert Allen, Sept. 9, 1978; stepchildren: Quentin Christine, Shelley Leigh, Cindy Elaine, Kathleen Diane 1 child, Missa Melaina. BA cum laude, U. Alaska, Fairbanks, 1977; MLS summa cum laude, La. State U., 1986. Ref. libr. Anchorage Mcpl. Librs., 1986—88; rsch. libr. Environment & Natural Resources Inst. U. Alaska, 1988—2006, program mgr., arctic environ. info. & data ctr. Environment & Natural Resources Inst., 1993—2006, reference libr., assoc. prof., consortium libr., 2000—06, acting program mgr., Alaska St. Climate Ctr., Environ. & Natural Resources Inst., 2002—04, reference libr., prof., consortium libr., 2006—; mgmt. team libr. Alaska Resources Libr. & Info. Svcs., 1997—. Editor Vizual Dog, Anchorage, 1994—2003; spl. librs. rep. Gov.'s Libr. Adv. Coun., 1998—2002. Editor: The Health of the Inuit of North America: A Bibliography from the Earliest Times through 1990, 1993, Icebreakers: Alaska's Most Innovative Artists, 1999; contbr. articles to profl. jours. Recipient Hammer award, Nat. Performance Rev., V.P. Gore, 1997, cert. of Appreciation, U.S. Dept. of Interior, 1997, Nat. award Libr. Svc., U.S. Inst. Mus. & Libr. Svcs., 2001, citation Exceptional Svc. Citizens of Alaska, Alaska State Legis., 2002. Mem.: ALA, United Acads., Alaska Libr. Assn., Polar Librs. Colloquy (bulletin editor 2006—), Beta Phi Mu, Phi Kappa Phi. Office: Univ Alaska Consortium Libr 3211 Providence Dr Anchorage AK 99508 Home Phone: 907-561-6635; Office Phone: 907-786-7666. Business E-Mail: anjb1@uaa.alaska.edu.

BRAUNER, GARY JULES, dermatologist, cosmetic laser surgeon; b. Bridgeport, Conn., Sept. 14, 1941; s. Charles and Frances (Rabitz) B.; m. Judith Susan Schlosser, Aug. 29, 1965; children: Lisa Michelle, Wendy Ellen. BA magna cum laude, Yale Coll., 1963; MD, Harvard U., 1967. Diplomate Am. Bd. Dermatology and Am. Bd. Pathology in Dermatopathology. Intern Jewish Hosp. of St. Louis, 1967-68; resident in dermatology Mass. Gen. Hosp., Boston, 1968-70, chief resident dermatology, 1970-71; asst. to assoc. clin. prof. dermatology Albert Einstein Coll. of Medicine, Bronx, NY, 1971-87; assoc. clin. prof. dermatology NY Med. Coll., Valhalla, 1987-93, Mount Sinai Sch. of Medicine, NYC, 1993—. Chief dermatology Morrisania Hosp., Bronx, 1975-76, North Ctrl. Bronx Hosp., 1976-82; chief dermatology svc. Rikers Island Health Ctr., East Elmhurst, NY, 1975-79; provisional attending physician Englewood Hosp., NJ, 1975-78, assoc. attending physician, 1978-81, attending physician, dermatology, 1981—, chief dept. dermatology, 1992-03; attending physician Hackensack U. Med. Ctr., 1982—; asst. attending Westchester County Med. Ctr., 1987-91, Met. Hosp., NYC, 1987-93; attending physician, dermatology Pascack Valley Hosp., Westwood, NJ, 1992-, Mt. Sinai Med. Ctr., provisional attending dept. dermatology 1993-95, asst. attending, 1995-97; attending Mt. Sinai Med. Ctr., 1997-; lectr. in field. Contbg. editor Hosp. Physician, 1978—, Health Practitioner and Physician's Asst., 1978—; assoc. editor Dialogues in Dermatology, 1978-92, 95—, Jour. of the Am. Acad. of Dermatology, 1988-93, Laser Medicine and Surgery News and Advances, 1988-96; editor The Schoch Letter, 2003—; contbr.

numerous articles to profl. jours. Maj. U.S. Army, 1971-74. Fellow Am. Acad. Dermatology (dir. 1992-97), Am. Soc. Dermatol. Soc.; mem. Am. Soc. of Laser Medicine and Surgery, Dermatol. Soc. Greater NY (pres. 1990-91), NY State Dermatol. Soc. (dir.), NJ State Med. Soc., Soc. for Investigative Dermatology, Assn. for Mil. Dermatologists, Internat. Soc. Tropical Dermatology, Bergen County Med. Soc., NJ Dermatol. Soc., Soc. for Pediatric Dermatology, Internat. Soc. for Dermatol. Surgery (dir. 1997-99, treas. 2000-04, sec. 2004—), Internat. Soc. for Pediatric Dermatology, Med. Coun. Skin Cancer Found., NY State Med. Soc., NY County Med. Soc. Avocations: gardening, travel, photography. Office: 125 E 63rd St New York NY 10021-7310 Office Phone: 212-421-5080. Personal E-mail: dermlaser@aol.com.

BRAUNER, RONALD ALLAN, theology studies educator; b. Phila., Aug. 5, 1939; s. Samuel Joseph Brauner and Ann Ruth (Soloner) Levin; m. Marcia Faith Silver, Sept. 9, 1962; children: Yaakov Baruch, Miriam Aliza. Cert. in tchg., Greenberg Inst., Jerusalem, 1960; BS in Edn., Temple U., 1962; PhD, Dropsie Coll., 1974. Cert. tchr., Pa. Assoc. prof. Gratz Coll., Phila., 1967—78; acad. dean Reconstructionist Rabbinical Coll., Phila., 1972—83; dir. Brandeis-Bardin Inst., LA, 1983—85; exec. dir. Hebrew Inst. Pitts., 1985—91; pres. Found. for Jewish Studies, Inc., Pitts., 1991—. Prof. Jewish studies Siegal Coll. Jewish Studies, 1994—. Editor Jewish Civilization: Essays and Studies, 1979-85, Straightalk, 1991—; author: Being Jewish in a Gentile World: A Survival Guide, 1995, Thinking Jewish: The Art of Living in Two Civilizations, 2001. Democrat. Office: Found for Jewish Studies 1531 S Negley Ave Pittsburgh PA 15217-1419 Office Phone: 216-464-4050. Personal E-mail: rbrauner@att.net. Business E-Mail: rbrauner@siegalcollege.edu.

BRAUNESREITHER, LORI JEAN, environmental services administrator; b. Yankton, SD, Jan. 8, 1965; BS, U. SD, Vermillion, 1988; cert. in Solid Waste Mgmt., U. Calif., Berkeley, 1997. Registered environ. health specialist Calif. Dept. Health Svcs., 1991, cert. landfill inspector Solid Waste Assn. N.Am., 1996. Environ. chemist, Santa Paula, Calif., 1988—89; environ. health specialist ii Ventura County Environ. Health, Calif., 1989—93; environ. health officer City Pitts., Calif., 1993—94; sr. environ. health specialist Contra Costa County Environ. Health, Concord, Calif., 1994—. Trainer solid waste Contra Costa County Environ. Health, Calif. Integrated Waste Mgmt. Bd., 2000—. Vol. fundraiser Food Bank Contra Costa and Solano, 2003—07. Nominee Gina Martin Employee of Yr. award, Contra Costa County, 2006; named Most Creative, Graphics Queen & Most Elegant Fundraiser, Food Bank Contra Costa and Solano, 2006; recipient Heart and Soul award, Food Bank of Contra Costa and Solano, 2005. Mem.: Nat. Environ. Health Assn. (bd. dels. 1997—98), Calif. Environ. Health Assn. (life; sec. 1992—95, v.p. 1995—96, pres. elect 1996—97, pres. 1997—98, bd. dirs. 1990—99). Home: 250 Chilpancingo Pkway #25 Pleasant Hill CA 94523 Office: Contra Costa County Environ Health 2120 Diamond Blvd Ste 200 Concord CA 94520 Home Phone: 925-687-5435; Office Phone: 925-646-5225 232. Office Fax: 925-646-5130. Personal E-mail: llorijb@aol.com. Business E-Mail: lbraunes@hsd.cccounty.us.

BRAUNGART, RICHARD GOTTFRIED, political scientist, educator; b. Balt., Apr. 21, 1935; s. Paul Peter and Jean Mary (Stanton) B.; m. Margaret Lombard Mitchell, Aug. 29, 1964; children— Julia, Katherine, Elizabeth. BA, U. Md., 1961, MA, 1963; PhD, Pa. State U., 1969. Rsch. asst. Bur. Social Sci. Rsch., Washington, 1964; instr. sociology Pa. State U., State College, 1966-69; asst. prof. sociology U. Md., College Park, 1969-72; assoc. prof. sociology Syracuse U., NY, 1972—76, prof. sociology, 1976—2002, prof. internat. rels., 1993—2002, prof. polit. sci., 1998—2002, prof. emeritus, 2003—. Rsch. dir. President's Commn. on Campus Unrest, 1970; vis. lectr. USIA, 1971; prof. assoc. East-West Ctr., Honolulu, 1978; lectr., cons. Nat. U. Mex., 1980, USSR Acad. Scis., Moscow, 1989; German Marshall Fund U.S., Berlin and Fed. Republic Germany, 1990, China Youth Coll. for Politics, Beijing Acad. Social Scis., Shanghai Ctr. Youth Rsch., Shanghai Acad. Social Scis., Ewha U., Seoul, Han Nam U., Taejon, Republic of Korea, 1991, Vista U., U. Pretoria, Potchefstroom U., U. Orange Free State, U. Port Elizabeth, Witwatersrand U., South Africa, 1992, UN, N.Y.C., 1995, 98. Author: Family Status, Socialization and Student Politics, 1979; editor: Society and Politics, 1976, Jour. Polit. and Mil. Sociology, 1983; editor: (assoc.), 1984—; editor: Life Course and Generational Politics, 1984, 1993, The Political Sociology of the State, 1990, Critical Issues in the U.S., 1997—98; editor: (series) Research in Political Sociology, 1985—89; mem. editl. bd.:, 1989—; editor (assoc.): Western Sociol. Rev., 1976—82, Sociol. Spectrum, 1980—83; editor: (book rev.) Jour. Polit. and Mil. Sociology, 1977—84; mem. editl. bd.: Sociol. Symposium, 1972—77, Polit. Behavior, 1978—84, Micropolitics, 1980—84, Quar. Jour. Ideology, 1983—90, Bangladesh e-Jour. Sociology, 2004—. With US Army, 1954—56, with USAR, 1956—62. Mem. Am. Sociol. Assn. (polit. sociology sect. co-founder, treas. 1982-84, sect. coun. 1985-88, collective behavior sect. coun. 1984-86), Internat. Soc. Polit. Psychology (nominating com. 1983-84, chmn. nominating com. 1989-90. governing coun. 1989-91, chmn. search com. 1990-91), Internat. Sociol. Assn. (v.p. rsch. com. 1982-90, 98-2002, pres. com. polit. sociology 1994-98), Soc. Study Social Problems (chmn. internat. conflict and coop. divsn. 1984-86, chmn. com. stds, rsch., tchg. 1996-98), Internat. Polit. Sci. Assn. (pres. com. on polit. sociology 1994-98, v.p. rsch. com. 1998-2002). Democrat. Avocations: gardening, jogging, travel. Home: 4783 Armstrong Rd Manlius NY 13104-1418 Office: Syracuse U Dept Sociology Syracuse NY 13244-1090 E-mail: rgbraung@maxwell.syr.edu, rbraung1@twcny.rr.com.

BRAUNISCH, HENNING, electronics engineer, researcher; b. Hanover, Germany, Nov. 16, 1969; s. Karl-Heinz and Ilse Braunisch; m. Monica Haladyna, July 25, 1998; 1 child, Isabel. PhD, MIT, Cambridge, Mass., 2001. Sr. packaging engr. Intel Corp., Chandler, Ariz., 2001—. Mem. editl. bd. Jour. of Electromagnetic Waves and Applications, Cambridge; mem. tech. program com. Progress in Electromagnetics Rsch. Symposium, Cambridge, 2002—. Contbr. articles to profl. jours. Recipient travel grant, Dept. of State Fgn. J. W. Fulbright Grad. Student Program, 1994—95; fellow, German Acad. Exch. Svc., 1997—98, German Nat. Merit Found., 1992—96. Mem.: IEEE (sr.; chair standing com. on confs. Phoenix sect. 2004—), Inst. of Physics. Achievements include patents for Microelectronics; patents pending for Microelectronics; research in Microelectronics. Office: Intel Corp Mail Stop CH5-166 5000 W Chandler Blvd Chandler AZ 85226-3699 Home Phone: 480-664-8656.

BRAUNSDORF, PAUL RAYMOND, lawyer; b. South Bend, Ind., June 18, 1943; s. Robert Louis and Marjorie Braunsdorf; m. Margaret Buckley, June 18, 1966; children: Christopher, Mark, Douglas, Amy. BA magna cum laude, U. Notre Dame, 1965; LLB, U. Va., 1968. Bar: NY 1968, US Dist Ct (we. dist.) NY 1969, US Dist Ct (no. dist.) NY 1980, US Ct Appeals (2d cir) 1975, US Supreme Ct 1980. Assoc. Harris Beach LLP, Rochester, 1968-75; ptnr., 1976—. Instr Nat Inst Trial Advocacy, Rochester, 1988; lectr in field. Author (contbg auth): (book) Antitrust Health Care Handbook II, 1993, Antitrust Law in New York, 1995, 2d edit., 2002. Bd dirs McQuaid Parent's Club, 1984—90, pres, 1986—87; bd dirs Mercy Parent's Club, 1989—90, Brighton Baseball, 1987—90. Mem.: NY State Bar Assn. (exec. com. antitrust sect. 2006, sec. exec. com. antitrust sect. 2007). Avocations: tennis, photography, music. Office: Harris Beach LLP 99 Garnsey Rd Pittsford NY 14534 Office Phone: 585-419-8603. Business E-Mail: pbraunsdorf@harrisbeach.com.

BRAUNSTEIN, DIANE KAREN, non-profit association executive, government administrator, government relations professional; b. Bklyn., Feb. 20, 1956; d. Elliott Bernard and Barbara (Stadin) B. Grad. in polit. sci., Kenyon Coll., 1977. Constituent aide Congressman Bill Green, NYC, 1978, legis. aide Washington, 1979-80; social ins. planning specialist Social Security Adminstrn., Balt., 1981-84; staff asst. soc. security subcom. US House Ways and Means Com., Washington, 1983; legis. analyst Office of Asst. Sec. for Legis. HHS, Washington, 1984-86, 88-89, acting dep. asst. sec. human svc. legis. Office of Asst. Sec. Legislature, 1990; Congl. affairs advisor Social Security Adminstrn., Washington, 1987-88; dep. staff dir. U.S. Senate Com. on Aging, Washington, 1990-91; dir. rsch. and policy devel. White House Conf. on Aging, Washington, 1991-92; dir. Mich. Office of Svcs. to Aging, Lansing, Mich., 1993-95; sr. assoc. APCO Assocs., Inc., Washington, 1996—; program dir. aging and long term care Nat. Govs. Assn., Washington, 2000—04; dir. tech. assistance and sys. change Alzheimer's Assn., Washington, 2005—; mem. nat. adv. panel Social Work Leadership Inst. NY Acad. Medicine. Mem. steering com. Inst. Gerontology, Wayne State U., Detroit, 1993-01. Contbr. articles to profl. jours. Selected goodwill exch. mission Konrad Adenhaver Found., B'nai Brith, Germany, 1994. Named 1995 honoree Mich. Assn. of Foster Grandparents/Sr. Companions Program. Mem. Nat. Acad. Social Ins.

BRAUNSTEIN, DOUGLAS, bank executive; BS in Econs., Cornell U., 1983; JD, Harvard U., 1986. With Merrill Lynch; head mergers and acquisitions Chase Securities, Inc. Chase Manhattan Corp., NYC, 1997—. Office: Chase Manhattan Corp 270 Park Ave Fl 12 New York NY 10017-2036

BRAUNSTEIN, GLENN DAVID, physician, educator; b. Greenville, Tex., Feb. 29, 1944; s. Mervin and Helen (Friedman) B.; m. Jacquelyn D. Moose, July 5, 1965; children: Scott M. Braunstein, Jeffrey T. Braunstein. BS summa cum laude, U. Calif., San Francisco, 1965, MD, 1968. Diplomate Am. Bd. Internal Medicine, subsplty. endocrinology, diabetes, metabolism. Intern, resident Peter Bent Brigham Hosp., Boston, 1968-70; clin. fellow in medicine Harvard U. Med. Sch., Boston, 1969-70; clin. assoc., reproduction rsch. br. NIH, Bethesda, Md., 1970-72; chief resident in endocrinology Harbor Gen. Hosp. UCLA, 1972-73; dir. endocrinology Cedars-Sinai Med. Ctr., LA, 1973-86, chmn. dept. medicine, 1986—; asst. prof. medicine UCLA Sch. Medicine, 1973-77, assoc. prof., 1977-81, prof., 1981—, vice chair dept. medicine, 1986—. Cons. for AMA drug evaluations, 1990—; mem. internat. adv. com. Second World Conf. on Implantation and Early Pregnancy in Human, 1994; mem. endocrinologic and metabolic drugs adv. com. FDA, 1991-95, chmn., 1994-95, spl. advisor, 1995-2001, 04-, chmn., 2001-04; bd. mem. Am. Bd. Internal Medicine Endocrinology, Diabetes, Metabolism Subsplty., 1991-99, chmn., 1995-99, bd. dirs., 1995-99; bd. dirs. Am. Bd. Emergency Medicine 2002-06. Mem. editl. bd. Mt. Sinai Jour. Medicine, 1984-88, Early Pregnancy: Biology and Medicine, 1998, Am. Family Physician, 1995—, The Am. Jour. Medicine, 1996—, Clin. Endocrinology & Metabolism, 1978-80; assoc. editor Integrative Medicine: Integrating Allopathic, Alternative and Complementary Medicine, 1997-2000. Bd. dirs. Israel Cancer Rsch. Fund, 1991-94, Cedars-Sinai Med. Ctr., 1997-2003; mem. Jonsson Comprehensive Cancer Ctr., 1991—. Recipient Gold Headed Cane Soc. award U. Calif. San Francisco Med. Ctr., 1968, outstanding achievement and cmty. svc. award Anti-Defamation League, 1997, James R. Klinenberg Chair in Medicine, 2000—, Sherman M. Mellinkoff Faculty award UCLA Sch. Medicine, 2002; Merck scholar, 1968, Mosby scholar, 1968. Fellow ACP (mem. adv. com. to gov., So. Calif. region 1989—, credentials com. So. Calif. region 1993); mem. AAAS, Cross Town Endocrine Club (chmn. 1982-83), Endocrine Soc. (publs. com. 1983-89, long range planning com. 1986-87, recent progress hormone rsch. com. 1993-98, ann. meeting steering com. 1993-98, spl. programs com. 1998—, media adv. com. 1999-2005, chmn. 2002-05, Disting. Physician award 2006), Pacific Coast Fertility Soc. (pres. 1988), Western Soc. for Clin. Rsch., Am. Fedn. for Clin. Rsch., Am. Thyroid Assn., Am. Fertility Soc., Western Assn. Physicians (pres. 1998-99), North Am. Menopause Assn., Assn. Am. Physicians, Am. Soc. Clin. Investigations (mem. nominating com. 1989), Univ. Calif. San Francisco Sch. Medicine Alumni Faculty Assn. (regional v.p. so. Calif., mem. bd. dirs. Israel Cancer Rsch. Fund 1991-94), Phi Delta Epsilon, Alpha Omega Alpha. Office: Cedars Sinai Med Ctr Dept Med Pla Level Rm 2119 8700 Beverly Blvd Los Angeles CA 90048-1865 Office Phone: 310-423-5140. Business E-Mail: braunstein@cshs.org.

BRAUNWALD, EUGENE, physician, educator; b. Aug. 15, 1929; m. Nina H. Starr (dec.); m. Elaine R. Smith, 1993; children: Karen G., Allison, Jill. AB, NYU, 1949, MD, 1952; AM (hon.), Harvard U., 1972; MD (hon.), U. Lisbon, 1984; ScD (hon.), Mt. Sinai Med. Ctr., 1991; MD (hon.), U. Rome, 1991, U. Portg, 1992, U. Vienna, 1995, U. La Plata, Argentina, 1995, U. Rio de Janeiro, 1998, Carol Davila U., 2002, U. Athens, 2003, U. Padua, 2003, Bates Coll., 2003, Comenius U., Bratislava, 2004, U. Modena, 2005. Diplomate Am. Bd. Internal Medicine, Am. Bd. Cardiovascular Disease. Intern, fellow Mt. Sinai Hosp., NYC, 1952—54; research fellow Columbia U. Coll. Physicians and Surgeons, NYC, 1954—55; clin. assoc. cardiovascular physiology lab. Nat. Heart Inst., Bethesda, Md., 1955—57; asst. resident Osler Med. Service, Johns Hopkins Hosp., Balt., 1957—58; chief cardiology sect., chief cardiology br., clin. dir. Nat. Heart and Lung Inst., Bethesda, 1958—68; prof., chmn. dept. medicine U. Calif.-San Diego, 1968—72; Hersey prof. of theory and practice of medicine Harvard U. Med. Sch., Boston, 1972—96, Herrman Blumgart prof. Medicine, 1980—89, chmn. study group, 1984—, Disting. Hersey prof., 1996—; faculty dean for acad. programs Harvard U., Boston, 1996—2003. Chmn. dept. medicine Brigham and Women's Hosp., 1972—96, Beth Israel Hosp., 1980—89; lectr. physiology George Washington U., 1959—62; from asst. clin. prof. to clin. prof. Georgetown U. Sch. Medicine, 1960—68; lectr. medicine Johns Hopkins U., 1960—68; trustee McLear Ptnrs., 1993—96; vis. prof. numerous U.S. and fgn. univs.; lectr. in field. Co-editor: Year Book of Cardiovascular and Renal Diseases, 1965—72, Year Book of Medicine, 1973—93, Harrison's Principles of Internal Medicine, 1967—; editor: Heart Disease, 1980—; mem. editl. bds.: Ciculation, Jour. Clin. Investigation, 1964—71, Jour. Cardiovascular Pharmacology, Am. Jour. Medicine, Am. Jour. Cardiology, New Eng. Jour. Medicine, numerous others. Bd. visitors Rockefeller U., 1978—82; mem. vis. com. MIT, 1979—85, Technion U., 1979. Recipient Arthur S. Fleming award, 1965, Superior Svc. award, HEW, 1967, Disting. Achievement award, Modern Medicine, 1968, Gustav Nylin award, Swedish Med. Soc., 1970, Williams award Outstanding Chmn. and Medicine, 1987, Bristol Myers Squibb Excellence in Cardiovascular Rsch. award, 1993, J. Allyn Taylor Internat. prize, Robarts Rsch. Inst., 1993, Gold medal, European Cardiac Soc., 2004. Master: Am. Coll. Cardiology (v.p. 1967, trustee 1967, 1970—75, Disting. Scientist award 1987); fellow: ACP (Phillips award 1991), Am. Acad. Arts and Scis.; mem.: NAS, Internat. Soc. Cardiology, Royal Soc. Medicine, Harvey Soc., Am. Heart Assn. (bd. dirs. 1966—75, v.p. 1966—70, Rsch. Achievement award 1972, Herrick award 1981), Am. Soc. Pharmacology and Exptl. Therapeutics (John Jacob Abel award 1965), Am. Physiol. Soc., New Eng. Cardiovascular Soc. (pres. 1987—88), Assn. Univ. Cardiologists, Western Soc. for Clin. Rsch. (pres. 1971—72), Am. Fedn. Clin. Rsch. (pres. 1969—70), Am. Soc. Clin. Investigation (pres. 1974—75), Western Assn. Physicians, Assn. Am. Physicians (Kober medal 1998), Assn. Profs. Medicine (pres. 1974—75), Johns Hopkins Soc. Scholars, Alpha Omega Alpha. Office: TIMI Study Group 350 Longwood Ave 1st Fl Boston MA 02115 Office Phone: 617-732-8989. E-mail: ebraunwald@partners.org.

BRAUS, IRA L., music educator, researcher; b. New York, Sept. 10, 1951; s. Harold A. and Elaine Braus. MusB, Oberlin Conservatory Music, 1974; MusM, SUNY Stony Brook, 1976; PhD, Harvard U., 1988. Instr. New Eng. Conservatory, Boston, Mass., 1985—86; vis. asst. prof. Bates Coll., Lewiston, Maine, 1991—92; asst. prof. Hartt Sch., West Hartford, Conn., 1998—2004, assoc. prof., 2004—. Wulsin fellow, Tanglewood Music Ctr., 1973. Avocations: hiking, cooking. Office: The Hartt School 200 Bloomfield Ave West Hartford CT 06117 Office Phone: 860-768-4124. E-mail: braus@hartford.edu.

BRAVARD, JEAN-LOUIS, diversified financial services company executive; MBA, Cornell U. Johnson Sch. of Mgmt.; degree in acctg. & fin., Ecole Supérieure de Commerce, Paris. Dir. U.S. fixed income rsch. and global tech. rsch. VICOR Inc.; various positions in corp. fin. J.P. Morgan & Co.; co-founder IFusion Com Corp., 1996—97; CEO Arbinet Comm., NYC, 1997—99; mng. dir., global fin. svcs. industry EDS, Plano, Tex., 1999—. Mem. Internat. Chamber of Commerce Commn. on Banking and Insurance. Mem.: Futures and Options Assn. Avocations: skiing, tennis, golf, scuba diving. Office: EDS 5400 Legacy Dr Plano TX 75024

BRAVERMAN, ALAN CHARLES, cardiologist, educator; b. Columbia, SC, Nov. 2, 1960; married. MD, U. Mo., Kansas City, 1985. Diplomate Bm. Bd. Internal Medicine, Am. Bd. Cardiovasc. Disease. Resident in internal medicine Brigham and Women's Hosp., Boston, 1985-88, fellow in cardiology, 1988-90, chief resident in internal medicine, 1990-91; dir. Marfan Clinic Barnes-Jewish Hosp., St. Louis, 1993—, cardiologist, dir. cardiology firm, 2001; assoc. prof. medicine Washington U. Sch. Medicine, St. Louis. Mem. profl. adv. bd. Nat. Marfan Found. Fellow Am. Coll. Cardiology; mem. ACP, AMA, Am. Heart Assn., Alpha Omega Alpha. Office: Washington U Cardiology Cons 16419 East Pavilion 1 Barnes Hospital Plz Saint Louis MO 63110-1036 Business E-Mail: abraverm@imgate.wustl.edu.*

BRAVERMAN, ALAN N., lawyer; b. Mass. BA, Brandeis U., 1969; JD, Duquesne U., 1975. Bar: D.C. 1976. Assoc. Wilmer, Cutler & Pickering, 1976-82, ptnr., 1983-93; exec. v.p., gen. counsel ABC, Inc., NYC, 1993-2000; deputy, gen. counsel The Walt Disney Co., Burbank, Calif., 2000—03, sr. exec. v.p. & gen. coun., 2003—. Office: ABC Inc 500 S Buena Vista St Burbank CA 91521-0922 Office Phone: 818-560-7896.*

BRAVERMAN, HERBERT LESLIE, lawyer; b. Buffalo, Apr. 24, 1947; s. David and Miriam P. (Cohen) B.; m. Janet Marx, June 11, 1972; children: Becca Danielle, Benjamin Howard. BS in Econs., U. Pa., Phila., 1969; JD, Harvard U., Cambridge, Mass., 1972. Bar: Ohio 1972, US Dist. Ct. Ohio 1972, US Supreme Ct. 1975, US Ct. Appeals (6th cir.) 1980, US Ct. Claims 1980. Assoc. Hahn, Loeser, Freedheim, Dean & Wellman, Cleve., 1972-75; sole practice Cleve., 1975-87; ptnr. Porter, Wright, Morris & Arthur, Cleve., 1987—96, Walter & Haverfield LLP, Cleve., 1996—. Councilman Orange Village, Ohio, 1988—, pres., 1998-01. Capt. USAR, 1970—82. Fellow Am. Coll. Trust and Estate Counsel; mem. ABA, Ohio Bar Assn., Bar Assn. Greater Cleve. (former chmn. estate planning trust and probate sect.), Suburban East Bar Assn. (pres. 1978-80), Rotary (Cleveland Heights pres. 1980), B'nai Brith (local pres. 1978-84), Wharton Club Cleve. (pres. 1991—), Am. Jewish Congress (Ohio pres. 1992—). Avocations: golf, symphony, reading. Home: 3950 Orangewood Dr Cleveland OH 44122-7406 Office: Walter & Haverfield LLP Ste 3500 1301 E 9th St Cleveland OH 44114-1821 also: 2000 Auburn Dr Ste 200 Beachwood OH 44122 Office Phone: 216-928-2903. Business E-Mail: hbraverman@walterhav.com.

BRAVERMAN, IRWIN MERTON, dermatologist, educator; b. Boston, Apr. 17, 1929; s. Morris and Molly (Singer) B.; m. Muriel Stella Freedman, June 5, 1955; children: Paula, David, Michael. AB in Biology summa cum laude, Harvard U., 1951; MD, Yale U., 1955. Diplomate: Am. Bd. Med. Examiners, Am. Bd. Dermatology, Am. Bd. Pathology. Practice medicine specializing in dermatology New Haven; asst. prof. dermatology Yale U., New Haven, 1962-68, assoc. prof., 1968-73, prof., 1973—. Author: Skin Signs of Systemic Disease, 1970, 3d edit., 1997; contbr. articles to profl. jours. Served to capt. U.S. Army, 1956-58. Recipient Mr. and Mrs. J.N. Taub Internat. Meml. award for research in psoriasis Baylor Med. Coll., 1980 Mem. AMA, New Eng. Dermatol. Soc. (v.p. 1990-91, pres. 1991-92), Am. Dermatol. Assn., Am. Acad. Dermatology (dir. 1980-83, Sulzberger Internat. lectr. 1989, Master of Dermatology 1993, Everett C. Fox Meml. lectr. 2001), Soc. Investigative Dermatology (bd. dirs. 1982-87, pres. elect 1991-92, pres. 1992-93, David M. Carter award for mentorship 1999), Am. Fedn. Clin. Rsch., Am. Assn. Physicians. Office: Yale U Med Sch 333 Cedar St New Haven CT 06510-3289 Home Phone: 203-795-9301; Office Phone: 203-785-4092. Business E-Mail: irwin.braverman@yale.edu.

BRAVERMAN, JORDAN, columnist; b. Boston, July 4, 1936; s. Morris and Molly (Singer) B. BA, Harvard Coll., 1958; MPH, Yale U., 1963; MS of Fgn. Svc., Georgetown U., 1968. Urban planner, economist City Govt. of Quincy, Mass., 1959-61; adminstr. Nat. Blue Cross Assn., Chgo., 1963-65; economist U.S. Dept. Health Edn. and Welfare, Pub. Health Svc., Washington, 1965-67; mgmt. cons. EBS Mgmt. Cons., Washington, 1967-69; asst. to the exec. dir. Am. Pharm. Assn., Washington, 1969-72; dir. pub. policy rsch. Pharm. Mfrs. Assn., Washington, 1972-74; mng. editor Topics in Health Care Financing, Rockville, Md., 1974-75; dir. legis., policy analysis divsn. Health Policy Ctr., Georgetown U., Washington, 1975-77; cons. editor, author Washington, 1978—. Appeared numerous TV and radio shows; speech writer, lectr., pub. spkr., jour./mag. book reviewer, cons. editor VA, Washington, 1986-88, FMAS, Inc., Rockville, 1990—, others; columnist The Balt. Sun, 1990, Am. Weekly News, Washington, 1988—, Capital Jester, Washington, 1993, Internat. Med. News Svc., Washington, 1982—, Consumer Health Reporter, Washington, 1983-84, World Media Reports, 2001—, others; manuscript book referee, reviewer U. Press Am., 1982—, Rowman & Littlefield Publs. Inc., 1995—. Author: Pharmaceutical Payment Plans: An Overview, 1973, Crisis in Health Care, 1978, rev. 1980, The Consumer's Book of Health: How to Stretch Your Health Care Dollar, 1982, The Education of the Osteopathic Physician, 1985, Health Maintenance Organizations: New Choices for Paying and Receiving Medical Care, 1986, Nursing Home Standards: a Tragic Dilemma in American Health, 1970, State Health Insurance Plans: Is Anyone Listening?, 1977, To Hasten the Homecoming: How Americans Fought World War II Through the Media, 1996, Your Money and Your Health, 2006, others; (cassette) The Sound of Poetry, 1995-2004, Sound of Poetry, 2005, Sound of Poetry, 2007; (photog. anthologies) Cherished Moments in Time, 1997, Candid Captures, 2001, Shadows of Thought, 2001, Best Photos of 2005; photogs. exhibited in World Sci., Washington, 1997, Internat. Photo. Hall of Fame Mus., 1997-2001; photogs. included in Editor's Choice Desk Calendar, Internat. Libr. Photograpy, 1999, Internat. Libr. Photography Desk Calendar, 1999 (Editor's Choice award 1998-99), Reflections from the Past, 1998, America at the Millennium: The Best Photos of the 20th Century, 1999, The Best Photos of 2000, Hidden Treasures, 2000 (Poetry's Elite award, 2000, Editor's Choice award, 2001), Best Photos of 2003; contbr. articles to profl. jours. William Stoughton scholar Harvard U., 1958-59; recipient Editors Choice award N.Am. Open Poetry Contest, 1994, 97, candidate Robert F. Kennedy Journalism award 1994, John H. Dunning prize in US History, Am. Hist. Assn., 1997, Albert J. Beveridge award in Am. History Am. Hist. Assn., 1997, Short Story award, PEN/Amazon.com, 2000; nominated Pulitzer Prize in Letters, 1996; named one of enscribed names National Wall of Tolerance, Montgomery, Alabama, 2001. Mem. Internat. Soc. Poets (Poet of Yr. 1996, Internat. Poet of Merit, 1997, 99- 2000, elected Hall of Fame 1997, Editor Choice award, 2004, 06, Outstanding Achievement Poetry award 2007), Internat. Soc. Photographers (disting. mem., Silver Bowl award 2004), Am.-Indian Ednl. Found. (scholarship com.), Friends of Statue of Liberty and Ellis Island, Inc. (charter), Harvard Club of Washington, Yale Club of Washington, Georgetown Club of Washington. Achievements include poem "Taps" was accepted into the historcial records of Arlington Nat. Cemetery, Va. Avocations: trumpet, old time radio collector, theater, sports. Home: 2401 H St NW Washington DC 20037-2564 E-mail: jbrvrman@aol.com.

BRAVERMAN, RAY HOWARD, secondary school educator; b. Bklyn., Feb. 28, 1947; s. Irving Leonard and Josephine (Segan) B.; divorced; 1 child, Christopher Marc; m. Barbara Diane Braverman, July 30, 1994. BA in History, U. Del., 1969; MA in History, Wash. Coll., 1979; postgrad., U. Del., 1979-85. Cert. tchr., Del. Chmn. history dept., history instr. Dover (Del.) H.S., 1970—. Chmn. history dept. Dover H.S. Recipient Cert. of Appreciation, U. Del., 1987, Nat. Coun. History Edn., 1991; Advanced Placement Tchr. Recognition award Coll. Bd., 2006. Mem. NEA, Nat. Coun. for the Social Studies, Del. Coun. for Social Studies, Nat. Coun. for History Edn., World History Assn., Del. Edn. Assn., Capital Educators Assn., Orgn. of Am. Historians, Am. Hist. Assn. Home: 33 Elizabeth Ave Dover DE 19901-5803 Office: Dover HS One Pat Lynn Dr Dover DE 19904-2853 Office Phone: 302-672-1551 ext. 2551. E-mail: rbraver@capital.k12.de.us.

BRAVERMAN, ROBERT JAY, management consultant, educator; b. NYC, Mar. 4, 1933; s. Arthur and Ruth Edith (Beck) B.; m. Alice Glantz, Dec. 24, 1954; 1 son, John Nachum; m. Claire Hurney, Dec. 31, 1964; children: Sam, Amy. AB with honors and distinction, Columbia U., 1954; postgrad., Harvard U. Sch. Law, 1956-57, Sch. Bus., 1963. With Harbridge House, Inc. (Mgmt. Cons.), Cambridge, Mass., 1957-66; with ITT, NYC, 1966-86; sr. v.p., CEO ITT Coins Inc., NYC, 1986—. Chief exec. officer Braverman Adv. Svcs., 1986—91; prof. practice of pub. policy studies Duke U.; adj. prof. NYU, 1999—2002. Served with U.S. Army, 1954-56. Mem. Phi Beta Kappa. Home and Office: 345 W 88th New York NY 10024 Personal E-mail: robertbraverman@msn.com.

BRAVERMAN, STANLEY DEEMS, ophthalmologist; b. Miami, Fla., Oct. 10, 1950; s. Nathan and Rosalina Braverman; m. Jennifer Juliane Rimel-Braveman, July 2, 2000; 2 children. MD, U. Miami, 1972—76. Lic. Am. Bd. Ophthalmology, 1981. Internship Tulane U., New Orleans, 1976—77; resident ophthalmology Duke U. Eye Ctr., Durham, NC, 1978—80; gen. practice Claiborne Health Clinic, New Orleans, 1979; ophthalmologist, owner Braverman Eye Ctr., Hallandale Beach, Fla., 1981—. Asst. prof. ophthalmology Bascom Palmer Eye Inst. U. Miami Sch. Medicine; adj. assoc. prof. Sch. Optometry U. Houston, 1995—; clin. assoc. prof. Nova Southeastern Coll. Optometry, 1995—; adj. clin. assoc. prof. New Eng. Coll. Optometry, 1995—; presenter, guest lectr. in field. Manuscript reviewer Am. Jour. Ophthalmology; contbr. articles to profl. jours., chapter to book. Com. mem. Broward County Sch. Adv. Bd., Fla., 1987—98; bd. dirs. Hallandale Symphonic Orchestra, 1990—94, Am. Cancer Soc. S.Broward Unit, 1990—94; mem. Hallandale C. of C. Fellow: Internat. Coll. Surgeons, Am. Coll. Surgeons, Am. Acad. Ophthalmology; mem.: AMA, Internat. Soc. Refractive Surgery, Anterior Segment Laser Soc., Am. Soc. Cataract & Refractive Surgery, Refractive Surgery Interest Grp., Fla. Med. Assn., Rotary (dir. 1984—86), Omicron Delta Kappa, Big Brother's Am., Zeta Beta Tau (social chmn. 1969—70). Office: Braverman Eye Ctr 1935 E Hallandale Beach Blvd Hallandale FL 33009

BRAVO, ADELE, elementary school educator; b. Calif. married; 2 children. BA in Social Work, Azusa Pacific Univ.; MEd student, Regis Univ. Tchr., 1990—, Whittier, Calif., Boulder Valley, Colo., Louisville (Colo.) Elem. Sch. Site coord. Summer Literacy Acad., 2000—, ESL Summer Sch., 2000—. Named Colo. Tchr. of Yr., 2006. Mem.: Luiseno Shoshone Indians. Office: Louisville Elem Sch 400 Hutchinson St Louisville CO 80027 Business E-Mail: adele.bravo@bvsd.org.*

BRAVO, IRENE MARIA, psychologist, educator; b. Bayamo, Cuba, Jan. 24, 1949; arrived in U.S., 1966; d. Edmundo Pedro Bravo and Irene Manuela Castro; m. Robert Quintero, Feb. 14, 1968 (div. Oct. 27, 1987); children: Robert Francis Quintero, Giselle Christine Quintero, Marguerite Irene Quintero. B in Psychology, Fla. Internat. U., 1990, M in Psychology, 1994, PhD in Psychology, 1998. Lic. psychologist Fla., mental health counselor Fla., hypnotherapist. Crisis counselor Miami Mental Health Ctr., 1994; mental health therapist South Shore Hosp., Miami, 1994—96; clin. intern Miami Heart Inst. and Cedars Med. Ctr., Miami, 1996—97; clin. coord. Adult Day Treatment Ctr., Miami, 1997—98; asst. prof. Carlos Albizu U., Miami, Fla., 1999—2003; pvt. practice Miami, 1998—; assoc. prof. Carols Albizu Univ., 2003—. Adj. instr. Fla. Internat. U., Miami, 1994—2001; presenter in field; coord. Child Psychology Concentration, 2005. Contbr. articles to profl. jours. Mem.: APA, Florida Psychol. Assn., Soc. Child and Adolescent Psychology. Roman Catholic. Avocations: classical music, interior decorating, films. Office: Carlos Albizu U 2173 NW 99th Ave Miami FL 33172 Business E-Mail: ibravo@albizu.edu.

BRAVO, KENNETH ALLAN, lawyer; b. Cleve., July 27, 1942; BS, Rutgers U., 1964; JD cum laude, Ohio State U., 1967. Bar: Ohio 1967, D.C. 1967. Trial atty. Criminal Divsn., U.S. Dept. Justice, 1967-69, spl. atty., 1969-79; ptnr. Benesch, Friedlander, Coplan & Aronoff, Cleve., 1979-94; of counsel Ulmer & Berne LLP, Cleve., 1994-96, ptnr., 1997—. Mem. ABA, Ohio Bar Found. (life), Ohio State Bar Assn. (coun. of dels. 1992—, bd. govs. 2001—04), Fed. Bar Assn. (bd. trustees No. dist. Ohio chpt. 2002—), Cleve. Bar Assn. (chmn. fed. ct. com. 1984-85, trustee 2001-02), Cuyahoga County Bar Assn. (chmn. fed. ct. com. 1980-82, chmn. cert. grievance com. 1986-88), Nat. Assn. Criminal Def. Lawyers, Lawyer-Pilots Bar Assn., Jud. Conf. 8th Dist. Ohio (life), Jud. Conf. 6th Cir. U.S. Ct. Appeals (life), Ohio State U. Law Alumni Soc. (pres.). Office: Ulmer & Berne LLP 1660 W 2nd St Ste 1100 Cleveland OH 44113-1454 Home Phone: 216-381-5910; Office Phone: 216-583-7102. Business E-Mail: kbravo@ulmer.com.

BRAVO, LUIS FERNANDO, investment banker; s. Fernando Ismael Bravo and Ivonne Ulrica Bianchi. BA in Econs., Wash. and Lee U., 1996, BS in Physics-Engring., 1996; MBA, U. Pa., 2003. Lic. Series 7, Series 3, and Series 63 Nat. Assn. Securities Dealers. Asst. v.p. UBS Securities, Inc., NYC, 1996—98; assoc. Bear, Stearns & Co. Inc., NYC, 1998—2001; summer assoc. Goldman, Sachs & Co., NYC, 2002; assoc. Goldman Sachs, NYC, 2003—. Recipient Wharton Way award, Wharton Student Coun., 2003; Elizabeth B. Garrett scholar, Wash. and Lee U., 1995. Mem.: Wharton Alumni Club Peru (dir., founder 2003—04), Omicron Delta Epsilon, Phi Beta Kappa, Pi Kappa Phi (treas. 1995—96, Rho chpt.). Office: Goldman Sachs 85 Broad St New York NY 10004 Home Phone: 212-945-2737; Office Phone: 212-902-4886. Office Fax: 212-428-9187. Personal E-mail: fernando.bravo@gs.com.

BRAVO, ROSE MARIE, apparel executive; b. NYC, Jan. 13, 1951; d. Biagio and Anna (Bazzano) LaPila; m. William Selkirk Jackey, Oct. 9, 1983. BA in English, Fordham U., 1971. Exec. trainee, dept. mgr. A&S, Bklyn, 1971—74; assoc. buyer Macy's, NYC, 1974—75, buyer, 1975—79, councilor, 1979—80, adminstr., 1980—84, group v.p., 1984—85, sr. v.p., 1985—88; chmn., CEO I. Magnin, San Francisco, 1988—92; pres. Saks Fifth Ave., Inc., NYC, 1992—97; CEO Burberry Group plc, London, 1997—2006, vice chmn., 2006—. Bd. dirs. Tiffany & Co., Burberry Group plc. Named one of the Most Powerful Women in Bus., Forbes mag., 2005, 50 Most Powerful Women in Global Bus., Fortune mag., 2005. Office: Burberry Group plc 18-22 Haymarket London SW1 4DQ England

BRAWNER, GERALD ANDRE, paralegal; b. Washington, May 12, 1965; s. Gerald Andre and Alberta Katherine Brawner; m. Joanne Smith (div.); children: DeRoy Andre, Gerald Andre III. Grad. HS, Washington, 1984. Paralegal asst. to criminal investigator, 1984—95; paralegal, bd. dirs. Half-Way There, Washington, 1995—2004. Cons. Washington Connection, Washington, 2000—04. Democrat. Achievements include invention of water backpack and gun assembly; Captain Hydro cartoon character and trademark design; Project Hydro Force and Hydro Force trademark design. Avocations: reading, writing, fishing, chess.

BRAXTON, EDWARD K., bishop; b. Chgo., June 28, 1944; s. Cullen L. and Evelyn Braxton. Studied, Quigley Preparatory Sem., Niles Coll. Sem.; MA, STL, St. Mary of the Lake Sem., Mundelein, Ill.; PhD in Religious Studies, Cath. U., Louvain, Belgium, 1975, STD in Systematic Theology, 1975; post-doctoral fellowship, U. Chgo. Div. Sch., 1975—76. Deacon St. Raymond De Penafort Parish, Mt. Prospect, Ill.; ordained priest Archdiocese of Chgo., 1970; assoc. pastor Holy Name Cathedral, Chgo., 1970—71, Sacred Heart Parish, Winnetka, Ill., 1971—73, St. Felicitas Parish, Chgo., 1975—76; William A. Coolidge Chair of Ecumenical Thought Harvard U., 1976—77; pastoral ministry St. Paul's Parish, Cambridge, Mass., 1976—77; vis. prof. U. Notre Dame, 1977—78; chancellor for theol. affairs to Bishop James A. Hickey, Cleveland, 1978—80; spl. asst. for theol. affairs to Archbishop James A. Hickey, Washington, 1980—83; scholar in residence N.Am. Coll., Rome, 1983; dir. Calvert House Cath. Student Ctr. U. Chgo., 1983—86; ofcl. theol. cons. to William H. Sadlier Inc., NYC, 1986—92; pastor St. Catherine of Siena Parish, Oak Park, Ill., 1992—95; ordained bishop, 1995; aux. bishop Archdiocese of St. Louis, 1995—2001; bishop Lake Charles, La., 2001—05, Belleville, Ill., 2005—. Contbr. numerous articles to journals including Harvard Theological Review, Theological Studies, Louvain Studies, Irish Theological Quarterly, The New Catholic Encyclopedia, Origins, Commonweal, America, The National Catholic Reporter. Mem. US Conf. Cath. Bishops. (chmn. com. on Am. Coll. Sem. at U. Louvain; mem. com. on liturgy, com. on evangelization) Roman Catholic. Office: Diocese of Belleville The Chancery 222 S Third St Belleville IL 62220 Office Phone: 618-277-8181. Fax: 618-277-0387.

BRAXTON, FREDERICK, music educator; b. Richmond, Va., June 19, 1945; s. Frederick and Mary Louise Braxton; 1 child, Hannah Pheobe Baxton Marks. BA in Music Edn., Va. Union U., 1978. Lic. tchr. State Bd. Edn., Va., 2004. Music tchr. Rehab. Sch. Authority, Beaumont, Va., 1979—83, Richmond Pub. Schs., 1984—; caseworker Youth Devel. Ctr., Richmond, Va., 1978. Pvt. piano tchr., Richmond, 1973—92, Richmond, 2000—; mentor Carver Elem. Sch., Richmond, 2004—05. Composer: (songs) Bee Rax's Musical Collection. Minister Mt. Sinai Holy Ch., 1995—. Specialist US Army, 1965—67. Recipient Loyal Svc. award, Rehabilitative Sch. Authority Commonwealth of Va., 1981. Mem.: Va. Edn. Assn., Richmond Edn. Assn., Bus. Assn. Network Coun. Avocations: redesign old lamps, genealogy. Home Phone: 804-231-3481; Office Phone: 804-780-6247. Personal E-mail: beerax@aol.com.

BRAXTON, HERMAN HARRISON, JR., lawyer, jduge; b. Durham, NC, May 15, 1936; s. Herman Harrison and Anne (Grimm) B.; AB in Polit. Sci., U. NC, 1958; JD, U. Va., 1961; m. Patricia Gail Galway, June 26, 1965; children: Herman Harrison III, Grace Anne, William Marshall. Bar: Va., 1961; Ptnr. Willis, Braxton, Ashby & Bass, Fredericksburg, 1965—96; commonwealth atty. City of Fredericksburg, 1974-82; gen. dist. judge 15th Dist., 1996-2005; cir. judge 15th Jud. Cir., Stafford, Va., 2005-07, Fredericksburg, Va. Pres. Fredericksburg chpt. Va. Mus. Fine Arts, 1970-72. Served to capt. JAGC, USAF, 1961-64. Recipient Disting. Svs. award Fredericksburg Jr. C. of C. Mem. Fredericksburg C. of C. (pres. 1972-73), Va. Bar Assn., 15th Jud. Circuit Bar Assn., Fredericksburg Area Bar Assn. (pres. 1980), Pi Kappa Alpha, Phi Alpha Delta. Episcopalian. Home: 1204 Charles St Fredericksburg VA 22401-3706 Personal E-mail: hhblaw@aol.com.

BRAY, DALE IRVING, civil engineering educator; b. Moncton, Can., June 1, 1940; s. Ivan Simeon and Marion Estella (Irving) B.; m. Carol Velma Cox, June 27, 1964; children: Marnie, Mark. BS in Civil Engring., U. N.B., Fredericton, Can., 1963, MS in Civil Engring., 1965; PhD, U. Alta., Edmonton, Can., 1972. Asst. prof. U. N.B., Fredericton, 1965-72, assoc. prof., 1972-78, prof., 1978-98, chmn. dept. civil engring., 1994—98, mem. groundwater studies group, 1988—98, prof. emeritus, 2004. Contbr. articles to profl. jours. Mem. Can. Water Resources Assn. (Disting. Svc. award 1995), Can. Soc. Civil Engring. (Camille A. Dagenais award 1998). Baptist. Avocations: hiking, canoeing. Office: Dept Civil Engring U New Brunswick PO Box 4400 Fredericton NB Canada E3B 5A3 Business E-Mail: dalebray@nbnet.nb.ca.

BRAY, GEORGE AUGUST, internist, researcher, educator; b. Evanston, Ill., July 25, 1931; s. George A. and Mary H. B.; m. Martha, Aug. 8, 1959 (div. July 1983); children: George, Thomas, Susan, Nancy; m. Marilyn Rice, Jan. 1, 1984. BA summa cum laude, Brown U., 1953; MD magna cum laude, Harvard U., 1957. Diplomate Am. Bd. Internal Medicine; cert. Nat. Bd. Med. Examiners, Mass. Bd. Registration Medicine, Calif. Bd. Med. Examiners, La. Bd. Med. Examiners. Intern Johns Hopkins Hosp., Baltimore, Md., 1957-58; rsch. assoc. NIH, Bethesda, Md., 1958-60; resident U. Rochester, NY, 1960-61; rsch. assoc. Mill Hill Nat. Inst. Med. Rsch., London, 1961-62; asst. prof. medicine Tufts U., Boston, 1964-69, assoc. prof., 1969-70, UCLA, 1970-72, prof., 1972-81, U. So. Calif., Los Angeles, 1981-89, prof. medicine and physiology, 1983-89, chief of Diabetes and Nutrition Los Angeles County USC Med. Ctr., 1981-89; prof. medicine, vice chancellor Med. Ctr. La. State U., Baton Rouge, 1989-99; exec. dir. Pennington Biomed. Rsch. Ctr., Baton Rouge, 1989-99; prof., chief clin. sci., 1999—; Boyd prof. La. State U., Baton Rouge, 1999—. Vis. prof. U. Ill., 1981; cons. FDA, 1971, 95, Can. Dept. Health and Welfare, Ottawa, Ont., 1974, Nat. Inst. on Aging; mem. adv. coun. Nat. Inst. Diabetes, Digestive and Kidney Diseases, 1985-90; lectr. Furth meml. lectr. East Carolina U., 2006; Sommer meml. lectr., Portland, 2004. Author: Obese Patient, 1976; editor: Obesity in America, 1979, Obesity in Perspective, 1976, Treatment of Obesity, 1985, 89, Obesity: Basic Aspects and Clinical Applications, 1989; contbr. articles to profl. jours. Recipient Travel award Am. Thyroid Assn., 1970, Sam E. Roberts award Kans. Nutrition Soc., 1977, Wellcome Vis. Prof. award Mich. State U., 1978, U. Chgo., 1985, Alumni Day spkr. Harvard Med. Sch., Boston, 1982, Osborne and Mendel award Am. Inst. Nutrition, 1989, E.V. McCollum award Am. Soc. Clin. Nutrition, 1989, Joseph Goldberger award in Clin. Nutrition AMA, 1994, TOPS award NAASO, 1999, W. Henry Sebrell award Weight Watchers Found., 2000, Bristol-Myers Squibb/Mead Johnson Nutrition award, 2000, Stunkard Lifetime Achievement award, NAASO, 2003; grantee NIH, 1965—, Weight Watchers Found., 1979-81, Kroc Found., 1980-81; fellow NSF, 1961-62, NIH, 1962-64. Master: Am. Coll. Endocrinology (pres. 1993—95, editor Endocrine Practice 1993—95), ACP, APC (chmn.-elect con. med. spltys. 1987—88, bd. regents 1987—91, chmn. 1988—91); fellow: AAAS, Am. Inst. Nutrition (Osborne-Mendal award 1988), Am. Dietetic Assn. (hon.), Am. Soc. Nutrition Sci.; mem.: Johns Hopkins U. Sch. Scholars, Internat. Assn. Study Obesity (pres.-elect 1990—94, pres. 1994—98, Willendorf award 1980), Am. Soc. Clin. Investigation (hon.), Assn. Am. Physicians (hon.), N.Am. Assn. Study Obesity (chmn. organizing com. 1980—82, councilor 1984—88, pres.-elect 1988—89, pres. 1989—90, editor Internat. Jour. Obesity 1974—91, Obesity Rsch. 1991—97, TOPS award 1999, Stunkard Lifetime Achievement award 2003), Am. Fedn. Clin. Rsch., Am. Diabetes Assn. (bd. dirs. So. Calif. 1984—88, 1988—89), Endocrine Soc., Am. Soc. Clin. Nutrition (councilor 1982—84, v.p. 1985—86, pres.-elect 1986—87, pres. 1987—88, McCollum award 1989), Am. Assn. Clin. Endocrinology (bd. dirs. 1990—96), Peripatetic Club (hon.), Alpha Omega Alpha, Sigma Xi, Phi Beta Kappa. Avocations: medical history, travel. Office: Pennington Ctr 6400 Perkins Rd Baton Rouge LA 70808-4124

BRAY, RICHARD DANIEL, librarian; b. Albany, NY, June 19, 1945; s. Harry and Sylvia Jeanette (Weiss) B.; m. Suzannah Guidos, Aug. 17, 1980. AA, Pasadena City Coll., 1966; BA, San Francisco State U., 1969; MLS, San Jose State U., 1994. Mgr. Guild Books, Inc., Chgo., 1979-88; instr. English Columbia Coll.; lit. panelist L.A. Dept. Cultural Affairs, 1989-90, Calif. Arts Coun., 1989-92, NEA, 1992-94; mgr. sr. svcs. Alameda County Libr. Sr. Svcs., Fremont, Calif., 2000—. Judge, Carl Sandburg award Friends of Chgo. Pub. Library, 1985-86. Mem. lit. adv. bd. Ill. Arts Coun., 1985-87, multi-arts adv. com. Chgo. City Arts Program, 1985-87; bd. dirs. Friends of Chgo. Pub. Libr., 1985-87, Coun. Literary Mags. and Presses, 1987-92. Named one of the Movers & Shakers, Libr. Jour., 2007. Mem. ALA, Am. Booksellers Assn. (edn. com. 1987-89), Nat. Writers Union, Am. Writers Congress (exec. 1981-82), Calif. Libr. Assn., Multicultural Review (mem. bd. advs.), Calif. Poets and Writers (mem. bd. advs.), Am. Soc. on Aging. Office: Alameda County Library 2450 Stevenson Blvd Fremont CA 94538-2326 Office Phone: 510-745-1499. E-mail: rbray@aclibrary.org, richardbray@yahoo.com.

BRAY, TIM (TIMOTHY WILLIAM BRAY), computer company executive, software developer; b. Can., June 21, 1955; married; 1 child. BSc in Math. and Computer Sci. with honors, U. Guelph, Ont., Can., 1981. Freelance stage mgr., Guelph, Ont., Waterloo, Ont., Canada, 1976—79; software specialist Digital Equipment Corp., Toronto, Ont., Canada, 1981—83; sys. software group leader, computer support tech. leader, digital products group Microtel Pacific Rsch., Vancouver, B.C., Canada, 1983—87; mgr. New Oxford English Dictionary Project U. Waterloo, Ont., Canada, 1987—90; part-time CEO Waterloo Maple Software, 1989—90; mng. dir. Open Text Corp., Waterloo, 1989—91, sr. v.p. tech. Waterloo, Ont., Vancouver, 1991—96; prin. Textuality Svcs., Vancouver, 1996—99; founder, CEO Antarctica Sys., Inc., Vancouver, 1999—2002, CTO, 1999—2004; dir. web technologies Sun Microsystems, Inc., Santa Clara, Calif., 2004—. Part-time lectr. Simon Fraser U., Vancouver, 1984; appointee for W3C Tech. Architecture Group, 2001—04; co-chair Internet Engring. Task Force AtomPub Working Group; expert in field; spkr. in field. Contbr. articles to profl. jours.; written many software applications including Bonnie, 1989—96, Lark, 1997, Genx, 2004; co-editor: Namespaces in XML, 1996—99; publishes blog tbray.org. Achievements include co-creator XML (Extensible Markup Language); contributor to Atom web standards. Office: Sun Microsystems Inc 4150 Network Cir Santa Clara CA 95054

BRAZDIL, JAMES FRANK, chemist, researcher; b. Cleve., July 21, 1953; BS in Chemistry summa cum laude, John Carroll U., 1975; MS in Phys. Chemistry, Case Western Res. U., 1978, PhD in Phys. Chemistry, 1979. Project assoc. Standard Oil, Cleve., 1975-79, rsch. project leader, 1980-82, sr. rsch. specialist, 1982-83; group leader Standard Oil/Brit. Petroleum, Cleve., 1983-89; rsch. sci., rsch. group leader Brit. Petroleum, Cleve., 1989-92; sr. rsch. assoc. BP Chems., Cleve., 1992—. Lectr. various profl. orgns. and assns. Co-contbr. numerous articles to profl. jours. Recipient Lubrizol Corp. award in chemistry, 1975, Scholastic Achievement award Am. Inst. Chemists, 1975, Tech. Achievement award Cleve. Tech Socs. Coun., 1989, Pitts.-Cleve. Catalysis Soc. award, 1990. Mem. Am. Chem. Soc. (local treas. 1984-86, chmn. 1988, trustee 1994—, petroleum divsn. chmn. 1995-96), Catalysis Soc. N.Am., Pitts.-Cleve. Catalysis Soc. (sec. 1984-85, pres. 1985-86, Soc. award 1990), Sigma Xi. Achievements include 67 U.S. patents in field. Office: BP Chems 4400 Warrensville Center Rd Cleveland OH 44128-2837

BRAZEAL, AURELIA ERSKINE, former ambassador; b. Chgo., Nov. 24, 1943; BS, Spelman Coll., 1965; M of Internat. Affairs, Columbia U., 1967; postgrad., Harvard U., 1972. With Foreign Svc., 1968; consular and econ. officer U.S. Embassy, Buenos Aires, 1969-71; econ. reports officer Econ. Bureau U.S. State Dept., 1971-72, watch and line officer Office of Secretariat, 1973-74, desk officer Uruguay, Paraguay, 1974-77; review officer Office of Secretariat U.S. Dept. Treasury, 1977-79; econ. officer Tokyo, 1979-82; officer ECON Bur. U.S. Dept. State, 1982-84; dep. dir. Econ. Office Japan, 1984-86; mem. sr. seminar, 1986-87; min. counselor econ. affairs U.S. Embassy, Tokyo, 1987-90; U.S amb. to Micronesia, 1990-93; U.S. amb. to Kenya, 1993-96; deputy asst. sec. East Asian & Pacific Affairs, 1996-98; dean sr. seminar Fgn. Svc. Inst., Arlington, Va., 1998-99, dean leadership and mgmt. sch. and sr. seminar, 1999—2002; U.S. amb. to Ethiopia, 2002—05; diplomat-in-residence Howard U., Washington, 2005—07, spl. advisor, 2007—. Office: Howard Univ 2218 6th St NW Washington DC 20059

BRAZELL, KAREN WOODARD, literature educator; b. Buffalo, Apr. 25, 1938; d. Charles Cary and Josephine Mary (Bordonaro) Woodard; m. James Reid Brazell, Aug. 27, 1961 (div. 1978); children: Katherine Ann Brazell Rivera, Stephen Reid. Student, Coll. Wooster, 1956—58, Internat. Christian U., Tokyo, 1958—60; BA, U. Mich., 1961, MA, 1962; PhD, Columbia U., 1969; D Lit (hon.), U. Puget Sound, 1993. Asst. prof. Japanese lit. Princeton U., 1969—74; assoc. prof. Cornell U., Ithaca, NY, 1974—79, prof., 1979—2000, Goldwin-Smith prof. Japanese lit. and theatre, 2000—, chmn. dept. Asian studies, 1977—82, dir. East Asia program, 1987—91, dir. Global Performing Arts Consortium, 2000—. Vis. prof. U. Calif., Berkeley, 1984, Nat. Inst. Japanese Lit., Tokyo, 1988-89, Kyoto Ctr. Japanese Studies, 2001-02; vis. Shinchôsha prof. Japanese Lit., Columbia U., 1996; disting. vis. prof., Nat. U. Singapore, 2000; dir. Global Performing Arts Consortium, 2000-. Author: Confessions of Lady Nijo, 1973 (Nat. Book award 1974), Noh as Performance, 1977, Dance in the Noh Theater, 1981; editor: Twelve Plays of the Noh and Kyôgen Theaters, 1988, re-printed edit., 1997, Traditional Japanese Theater: An Anthology of Plays, 1998; assoc. editor: Jour. Japanese Studies, 1978—; contbr. articles and book revs. to profl. jours. Trustee Cornell U., 1979-83; bd. dirs. U.S.-Japan Soc. Ithaca, N.Y., Japan Soc. N.Y.C. Performing Arts Adv. Com., 1993-2005, Japan-U.S. Partnership for Performing Arts Inc., N.Y.C., 1994-98 Fulbright-Hayes fellow, 1972-73, NEH fellow, summer 1974, Cornell U. Soc. Humanities fellow, 1976-77, Japan Found. fellow, 1978, 85, Nat. Inst. Japanese Lit. rsch. fellow, Tokyo, 1988-89. Mem. Assn. Asian Studies, Assn. Tchrs. of Japanese (exec. com. 1981-83, bd. dirs. 1989-92), Phi Beta Kappa (senator at large 1976-82, trustee found. 1977-82). Office: Cornell U Dept Asian Studies Ithaca NY 14853 Business E-Mail: kwb3@cornell.edu.

BRAZELTON, THOMAS BERRY, pediatrician, educator; b. Waco, Tex., May 10, 1918; s. Thomas Berry and Pauline (Battle) B.; m. Christina Lowell, Dec. 3, 1949; children: Catherine Bowles, Pauline Battle, Christina Lowell, Thomas Berry. AB, Princeton U., 1940; MD, Columbia U., 1943; DSc (hon.), Russell Sage Coll., 1987, Wheaton Coll., 1991, Tufts U., 1994, Loyola U., Chgo., 1994, U. Mass., 1995; causa (hon.), U. Lisbon, Portugal, 1992; LHD (hon.), Northeastern U., 1990; EdD (hon.), Wheelock Coll., 1991; D in Pub. Svc. (hon.), Cedar Crest Coll., 1992; LLD (hon.), Boston Coll., 1996. pres. Nat. Ctr. Clin. Infancy Programs, 1988-1990. Intern Roosevelt Hosp., NYC, 1944; resident Mass. Gen. Hosp., Boston, 1945-47, Children's Hosp., Boston, 1947; resident in child psychiatry Putnam Children's Ctr., Roxbury, Mass., 1947-50; prof. Psychiatry & Human Devel. Brown U., 1988—; clin. prof. emeritus pediatrics Children's Hosp., Boston, 1999—. Instr. pediatrics Harvard U. Med. Sch., 1951-72, assoc. prof., 1972-1986, clin. prof. pediatrics emeritus, 1988-; dir. child devel. unit Children's Hosp. Med. Ctr., Boston, 1972-92; researcher in child devel. Putnam Children's Ctr. and Harvard Ctr. Cognitive Studies, 1968-88; sch. physician Shady Hill Sch., 1966-76, Cambridge Nursery Sch., 1967-70; pres. Nat. Ctr. for Clin. Infant Programs, 1988-91; mem. Nat. Commn. on Children, 1989-92; founder, Brazelton Touchpoints Ctr., 1993; pres. & chmn., Brazelton Found., 1996-. Author: over 200 scholarly articles, (books) Infants and Mothers: Individual Differences in Development (Child Study Assn. Ann. award 1970), 1969; Toddlers and Parents, 1974; Neonatal Behavioral Assessment Scale, 1974; The Family— Can It Be Saved?, 1975; Doctor and Child, 1976; The Family: Setting Priorities, 1979; On Becoming a Family, 1981, To Listen to a Child, 1984, Working and Caring, 1984; Affective Development in Infancy, 1986, What Every Baby Knows, 1988, Families Crises and Caring, 1989, The Earliest Relationship, 1990, Touchpoints: Your Child's Emotional and Behavioral Development, 1992, Going to the Doctor, 1997 (syndicated columns) Families Today, NY Times. Contbr. editor, Family Circle mag. Contbr. articles to Family Circle mag., profl. jours. Appeared Lifetime Cable TV show What Every Baby Knows 1984-1998 (Emmy award for Daytime Host, 1994) Served with USNR, 1944-45 Recipient Gold Medal, Excellence in Clin. Medicine, Alumni Assoc., Columbia U. Coll. Physicians & Surgeons, Hero award, Robin Hood Found., 2000, Children's Care award, Cardinal Health, 2002. Mem. Am. Acad. Pediatrics (chmn. child devel. sect. 1970), Soc. Rsch. in Child Devel. (pres. 1987-90), Mass. Med. Soc., New England Pediatric Soc., Am. Assn. Child Care in Hosps., Nat. Assn. Edn. of Young Children, Zero to Three (Washington) (pres. 1989-91), Barnstable (Mass.) Yacht Club. Achievements include development of Neonatal Behavioral Assessment Scale. Office: Children's Hosp Ste 320 1295 Boylston St Boston MA 02215-3407

BRAZELTON, WILLIAM THOMAS, chemical engineer, educator, dean; b. Danville, Ill., Jan. 22, 1921; s. Edwin Thomas and Gertrude Ann (Carson) B.; m. Marilyn Dorothy Brown, Sept. 23, 1943; children— William Thomas, Nancy Ann. Student, Ill. Inst. Tech., 1939-41; BS in Chem. Engring, Northwestern U., 1943, MS, 1948, PhD, 1952. Chem. engr. Central Process Corp., 1942-43; instr. chem. engring. Northwestern U., 1947-51, asst. prof., 1951-53, assoc. prof., 1953-63, prof., 1963-91, prof. emeritus, 1991—, chmn. dept., 1955-56, asst. dean Technol. Inst., 1960-61, assoc. dean, 1961-94, acting asst. dean, 1994-96, ret., 1996. Engring. and ednl. cons., 1949— Mem. Prospect Heights (Ill.) Bd. Edn., 1957-61; bd. dirs., exec. com. Chgo. Area Pre-Coll. Program. Recipient Vincent Bendix Minorities in Engring. award ASEE, 1986. Mem. Am. Inst. Chem. Engrs. (chmn. Chgo. sect. 1966-67), Am. Chem. Soc., Am. Soc. Engring. Edn. (chmn. Ill.-Ind. sect. 1963-64, 73-74, Vincent Bendix Minorities in Engring. award, 1986), Soc. for History of Tech., Soc. for Indsl. Archeology, Sigma Xi, Tau Beta Pi, Phi Lambda Epsilon, Alpha Chi Sigma, Triangle. Home: 10 E Willow Rd Prospect Heights IL 60070-1332 Office: Northwestern U Technol Institute Evanston IL 60208-0001 Business E-Mail: wtb@northwestern.edu.

BRAZIL, HAROLD EDMUND, political science professor; b. Bearden, Ark., Aug. 24, 1920; s. Paul Brazil and Lavenia (Govenor) Pullen; children: Leslie, Christopher, Susan, Paul, Ernest, Harold, Michael. BS, Tuskegee U., 1942; MA, Ohio State U., 1957; PhD, Ohio State U., Columbus, 1961. Placement officer VA, Columbus, 1946-49; dir. civil personnel Internat. Refugee Orgn., Fed. Republic of Germany, 1949-50; personnel officer USAF, Philippines, 1955-57, dir. research and community relations, 1957-59, command historian Philippines and S.E. Asia, 1959-62; attaché Am. Embassy, Cairo and Monrovia, Liberia, 1962-66; prof., chmn. dept. polit. sci. Sienna Coll., Loudonville, N.Y., 1966-70; co-dean sch. humanities and social sci. Rensselaer Poly. Inst., Troy, N.Y., 1970-72, prof., chmn. dept. history and polit. sci., 1972-75, prof. polit. sci., 1975-90, prof. emeritus, 1990—. Instr. Indsl. Coll. of Armed Forces, Washington, 1964, Fgn. Service Inst. of Dept. of State, Washington, 1965. Author: The Taiwan Straits Crisis of 1958, 1959, The Politics of Philippine Economic Development, 1962, A World Apart: America Military Diplomacy in S.E. Asia, 1976, The Law of the Oceans: Pursuing Order in the Twenty-First Century, 1988, The Third World, Multinationals, and the Law of the Sea Treaty, in Papers in Public Law and Comparative Political Science, 1989. Served as capt. USAF, 1942-46. Mem. Am. Internat. Polit. Sci. Assn., African Studies Assn., Inter-Univ. Seminar on Armed Forces and Soc. Home: PO Box 1560 Troy NY 12181-1560 Office: Rensselaer Poly Inst Dept Sci and Tech Studies Sage Hall Troy NY 12181

BRAZILE, DONNA, advocate; b. New Orleans; B, La. State U. Regional dir. Hands Across Am., 1985; nat. coord. housing Housing Now, 1989; founder, exec. dir. Nat. Polit. Congress Black Women; chief staff to Eleanor Holmes Norton, DC del. to US House Reps.; former host, prodr. A View From the Hill, Radio One News; campaign mgr. for Al Gore presdl. campaign, 2000; founder, mng. dir. Brazile and Assocs., LLC. Adj. prof. Georgetown U.; sr. fellow James MacGregor Burns Acad. Leadership, U. Md.; at-large mem. Dem. Nat. Com.; polit. commentator CNN; columnist Roll Call Newspaper; contbg. writer Ms. mag. Nat. student coord. Martin Luther King, Jr. Holiday Com., 1981; nat. mobilization dir. 20th Anniversary Commemoration 1963 March on Wash., 1983; nat. chair Voting Rights Inst., 2003. Named one of Outstanding Young Achievers, Ebony mag., 100+ Most Influential Black Americans, 2006, 100 Most Powerful Women in Wash., Washingtonian mag., 2001; recipient Congl. Black Caucus Youth award, Nat. Women's Student Leadership award. Office: Acad Leadership Univ Md College Park MD 20742-7715 Office Phone: 301-405-6100. Office Fax: 301-405-6402. Business E-Mail: dbrazile@academy.umd.edu.

BRAZILE, FRANCISCO LARUE, management consultant; b. Phoenix, May 2, 1972; s. Robert Pershing and Marihelen Brazile. BA, U. Tex., Austin, 1993; BS, MS, Tex. State U., San Marcos, 1995; D Natural Sci., U. Zurich, Switzerland, 2000. Geographer US Geol. Survey, Austin, 1992—96; rschr. U. Zurich, 1996—2000; software engr. Union Bank Switzerland, Zurich, 2000—01; chief tech. arch. Redsafe Bank, Swisslife, Zurich, 2001—02; tech. cons. Fidelity eBusiness, Boston, 2002—03; chief tech. arch. Zions Bancorporation, Salt Lake City, 2003—05; sr. cons. Von Neumann Tech., San Francisco, 2005—. Vol. Bd. Suprs., San Francisco, 2006—07. Grantee, EU Esprit Program, 1997—2000. Mem.: IEEE, Armed Forces Comm. and Electronics Assn., Assn. Am. Geographers, Silicon Valley Assn. Startup Entrepreneurs. Achievements include research in cartographic generalization. Avocations: flying, bicycling, engineering, languages. Home Phone: 415-863-8824.

BRAZILE, ORELLA RAMSEY, library director; b. Leesville, La., May 28, 1945; d. Dave Ramsey and Lue Bertha Harris; m. Rodgers Henry Brazile, June 4, 1966. BS, Grambling State U., 1967; M in Libr. Sci., U. North Tex., 1973; MEd, So. U., La., 1976; MS, U. North Tex., 1982, PhD, 1991. Libr. Caddo Parish Sch. Bd., Shreveport, La., 1968—68; circulation libr. So. U. at Shreveport, La., 1968—78, interim vice chancellor, 1993—94, libr. dir., 1978—. Bd. of trustees Shreve Meml. Libr., Shreveport, 1985—2004; bd. mem. YMCA, 1986—88; site evaluator So. Assn. Colls., Atlanta, 1987—2003. Mem. NAACP, 1985—2005, Am. Legion Women Aux., Shreveport, 1975—2005, YWCA, 1980—2005. Fellow, Nat. Assn. of U. Women, 1988; grantee, La. Edn. Quality Support Fund, 1992. 1995. Mem.: Nat. Assn. of U. Women (life; sponsor 1990—2005), Delta Sigma Theta Sorority (life; journalist 1985—86). Baptist. Avocations: bowling, walking, aerobics. Home: 4396 Worth Cir Shreveport LA 71109 Office: So Univ at Shreveport 3050 Martin Luther King Jr Drive Shreveport LA 71107 Home Phone: 318-635-1676; Office Phone: 318-674-3401. Office Fax: 318-674-3403. E-mail: 318 674-3403.

BRAZINSKI, FRANK WILLIAM, composer, educator; b. May 8, 1932; B of Music-in-Composition, Oberlin Conservatory, Ohio, 1958; MusM in Composition, U. So. Calif., L.A., 1962. Cert. music K-12 NY. Tchr. vocal music Copiague Jr. HS, NY, 1968—71, Oceanside Schs., NY, 1971—96; adj. vocal music Jericho Middle Sch., NY, 1997—99, Oyster Bay HS, NY, 1999—2004. Mem., keyboardist Big Bay Band, 1994—; composer-in-residence 23d St. Madison Sq. Constituency, 1993, Britten-on-the-Bay Concert Series, 1995—97. Composer: (choral symphony) Frontier Symphony: Legend of Sacajawea, 1964, Five Ways of Looking at King's Weston, 1965, Nonet for Woodwind Quintet and String Quartet, 1966, Evocations for String Quartet, 1964, (commn.) Introduction, Toccata and Arioso for Violin Solo, String Orchestra and Timpani, 1993, A Day at the Circus, 1995, Pritschka's Honor, 1996, Eggg, 1997, Song for St. Cecilia's Day, 1996, Seven Songs of Langston Hughes, 2001. Nominee Pulitzer award for Sonata for Clarinet and Piano: In Memoriam, 1995, nominee Pulitzer award for Concerto for Brass Quintet: A Regal Universe, 1996; recipient Ford Found. grant, Edmonds Washington, 1964—65, 1965—66, US Fed. Title 6 grant, 1967—68; grantee, BMI, U. So. Calif., LA, 1961—62, 1962—63. Mem.: Music Educators Nat. Conf., Pi Kappa Lambda.

BRAZINSKY, IRV(ING), chemical engineering educator, department chairman; b. NYC, Oct. 27, 1936; s. Israel and Rebecca (Singer) B.; m. Rosalie Seligson, June 14, 1959; children: Howard, Michael. BSChemE, Cooper Union, 1958; MS, Lehigh U., 1960; ScD, MIT, 1967. Chemist Freeport Sulfur Co., Port Sulfur, La., 1957; rsch. engr. NASA, Cleve., 1958, 59-61, Polaroid Corp., Waltham, Mass., 1966-69; sr. rsch. engr. Celanese Corp., Summit, NJ, 1969-76; sr. R & D engr. Halcon Internat., NYC, 1976—81; process devel. mgr. Foster Wheeler Energy Corp., Livingston, NJ, 1981-85, cons., 1985-88; adj. prof. N.J. Inst. Tech., Newark, 1971-81; assoc. prof. chem. engring. Cooper Union, NYC, 1985-91, prof., 1991—, chmn. dept., 1989—. Cons. Gen. Foods Inc., Philip Morris Inc., N.Y.C. Dept. of Pers., 1985-92. Pioneer, patentee processes for heat stabilizing microporous plastic film, improving melt strength of polyester and nylon melts, and rapid chilling of beverages; contbr. articles to profl. jours. Mgr., coach Matawan Little League, 1975-81; active YMCA Indian Guides Program, 1972-80; coach Aberdeen-Matawan Basketball League, 1979-85; v.p. Matawan High Sch. Parents Athletic Assn., 1986-90. Schweinburg scholar, 1954-55; Petroleum Rsch. Fund fellow, 1958-59, A.D. Little fellow, 1963-64, Proctor & Gamble fellow, 1964-66; N.Y. State Regents scholar, 1954-58, Campbell, Reilly, Schiff and O'Rourke scholar, 1955-58. Mem. AIChE, Am. Soc. Engring. Edn., Am. Chem. Soc., Soc. Plastics Engrs., Cooper Union Fedn. of Coll. Tchrs. (v.p. 1997-2003, pres. 2003—,) Cooper Union Rsch. Found. (bd. 2001—), Soc. Rheology, N.Y. Acad. Scis., Sigma Xi. Home: 6 Rustic Ln Matawan NJ 07747-2865 Office: Cooper Union 51 Astor Pl New York NY 10003-7132 Office Phone: 212-353-4373. E-mail: rosingrustic@msn.com.

BREADY, RICHARD LAWRENCE, manufacturing executive; b. Brookline, Mass., July 7, 1944; s. John Norbert and Catherine Rosalie B.; m. Loretta Lipman, July 16, 1971; 1 child, Barrett Wynn. BA in Econs, St. Anselm's Coll., Manchester, NH, 1965; MS in Acctg, Northeastern U., Boston, 1966; DBA (hon.), Johnson and Wales Coll., 1986. CPA Mass. With Arthur Andersen & Co., C.P.A.'s, Boston, 1966-74, audit mgr., 1969-74; ind. cons., 1974-75; treas. Nortek, Inc., Cranston, RI, 1975—77, exec. v.p., COO, 1975—77, pres., 1979—90, chmn., CEO, 1990—, also bd. dirs. Bd. dirs. Syenergy Methods, Inc., R.I. Hosp., Profl. Facilities, Mgmt., Inc. Mem. U. R.I. Found.; bd. dirs. Nat. Corp. Theatre Fund, Jr. Achievement, R.I. Philharm., Coalition for Cmty. Devel.; mem. nat. coun., bd. overseers, bd. visitors Northeastern U.; corp. mem., mem. fin. com., mem. audit com. Northeastern U.; bd. overseers Moses Brown Sch.; trustee Providence Performing Arts Ctr., Trinity Repertory Co., First Night Providence, NCCJ. With USAR, 1966-67. Mem. AICPA, Nat. Assn. Mfrs., Am. Mgmt. Assn., Greater Providence C. of C., R.I. Commodores. Office: Nortek Inc 50 Kennedy Plz Ste 1700 Providence RI 02903-2393*

BREAKSTONE, JOSHUA SCOTT, musician, educator, composer; b. Elizabeth, NJ, July 22, 1955; s. Arthur L and Priscilla Breakstone; m. Nathalie Laure Guarracino, Oct. 10, 2001. BA in Jazz Studies, New Coll., 1975. Guitarist, composer: recording Wonderful!, Oh! Darling, Remembering Grant Green, Sittin' On The Thing with Ming, Let's Call This Monk, This Just In, Japanese Songs, The Music of Bud Powell, Tomorrow's Hours: Joshua Breakstone Plays The Music of Wes Montgomery, A Jamais, Memoire, Four Over Four Equals One, Echoes, Evening Star, Self Portrait In Swing, Nine By Three, Walk Don't Run, I Want To Hold Your Hand. Business E-Mail: jzguitar@compuserve.com.

BREAKSTONE, MARC L., lawyer; b. NYC, Feb. 16, 1959; BA, U. Mich., 1981; JD, Northeastern U. Sch. Law, 1986. Bar: Mass. 1986, US Dist. Ct., Dist. Mass. 1987, US Ct. Appeals, First Circuit 1987. With Sugarman & Sugarman, 1986—92; principal Breakstone, White-Lief & Gluck, 1992—. Named Mass. Lawyer Yr., Mass. Lawyer Weekly, 2002. Mem.: Mass. Bar Assn., Mass. Acad. Trial Atty., ATLA. Office: Breakstone White-Lief & Gluck PC Two Ctr Plz Ste 530 Boston MA 02108 Office Phone: 617-723-7676. Business E-Mail: breakstone@bwglaw.com.

BREAKSTONE, ROBERT ALBERT, information technology executive, consumer products company executive, consultant; b. NYC, Feb. 20, 1938; s. Morris and Minnie B.; m. Eileen Fogel, Nov. 5, 1966; children: Warren, Ron, David. BS in Math., CCNY, 1960, MBA in Mgmt., 1964. Sys. engring. mgr. IBM, NYC, 1960-64; dir. mgmt. sys. Continental Copper & Steel Industries, Inc., NYC, 1964-68; v.p., CFO Sys. Audits, Inc., NYC, 1968-70; v.p., group exec. Chase Manhattan Bank, NYC, 1970-74; group v.p., bd. dirs. Chesebrough-Pond's, Inc., Greenwich, Conn., 1974-85; pres., CEO Health-Tex Inc., NYC, 1985-88; exec. v.p., COO GTech Corp., West Greenwich, RI, 1988-95; pres., CEO Landmark Internat. Group, Inc., Boca Raton, Fla., 1995—. Adj. asst. prof. Pace U. and NYU, 1964-71; adj. prof. Mercy Coll. Grad. Sch. of Bus., 1997—; bd. dirs. State of Conn. Conix Program, OSF, Inc., By Design Internat. Ltd.; bd. advisors Hoffinger Industries; spkr. in field. Bd. dirs. Stamford Mus. and Nature Ctr., Bi-Cultural Sch.; pres. United Jewish Fedn. of Stamford, 1996-98. Mem. N.Am. Soc. Corp. Planning, Am. Apparel Mfrs. Assn. (dir.), Mu Gamma Tau (pres.). Mem. N.Am. Soc. Corp. Planning, Am. Apparel Mfrs. Assn., Mu Gamma Tau (pres.). Office: Landmark International Group Inc 2432 NW 62nd St Boca Raton FL 33496 also: 95 Lynam Rd Stamford CT 06903-4527 Office Phone: 203-322-3679, 561-893-0500. Business E-Mail: rab@landmarkinternational.com.

BREATHED, BERKELEY, cartoonist; b. Encino, Calif., June 21, 1957; s. John William Breathed and Martha Jane (Martin) de Varennes; m. Jody Boyman, May 10, 1986; children: Sophie, Milo. BA, U. Tex., 1980. Syndicated cartoonist Washington Post Writer's Group, Washington, 1980-95. Cartoonist: Bloom County, 1980-89, Outland, 1989-95; author: (compilations) Loose Trails, 1983, Toons for Our Times,1984, Penguin Dreams and Stranger Things, 1985, Bloom County Babylon: Five Years of Basic Naughtiness, 1986, Billy and the Boingers Bootleg, 1987, Tales Too Ticklish To Tell, 1988, Night of the Mary Kay Commandos, 1989, Classics of Western Literature, 1990, Politically, Fashionably and Aerodynamically Incorrect, 1992, His Kisses Are Dreamy But Those Hairballs Down My Cleavage., 1994, One Last Peek: The Final Hits, The Special Hits, The Inside Tips, 1995, (children's books) A Wish for Wings that Work (also TV spl., home video), 1991, The Last Basselope, 1992, Goodnight Opus, 1993, Red Ranger Came Calling, 1994, Edwurd Fudwupper Fibbed Big, 2000, Flawed Dogs, 2003, Opus: 25 Years of His Sunday Best, 2004. Recipient Pulitzer prize for editorial cartooning Columbia U., 1987. Avocations: travel, motorcycling.

BREATHITT, LINDA K., energy advisor, former federal energy commissioner; b. Hopkinsville, Ky. BA in Edn., U. Ky., 1975; cert. state-local govt. exec. mgmt. pro., Harvard U. Exec. dir. Washington Office, Commonwealth of Ky., 1980-92; commr. Ky. Pub. Svc. Commn., 1993-95, chmn., 1996-97; commr. FERC, 1997—2002; sr. energy advisor Thelen Reid Brown Raysman & Steiner, LLP, Washington, 2002—. Bd. dirs. Martin Sch. Pub. Policy, U. Ky., Tata Energy Rsch. Inst. Regulatory Studies and Governance, New Delhi. Mem.: U. Ky. Alumni Assn. Methodist. Avocations: photography, scuba diving, gardening. Office: Thelen Reid Brown Raysman & Steiner, LLP 701 8th St NW Washington DC 20001 Office Phone: 202-508-4063. Office Fax: 202-654-1880.

BREAULT, KEVIN D., social studies educator, researcher; b. NYC, May 24, 1954; s. Roland E. and Vera A. Breault; m. Joy Dworkin, June 27, 1982 (div. Sept. 1985); m. Lynn E. Egan, July 30, 1988; 1 child, Lucy. BA, Reed Coll., 1978; MA, U. Wash., 1983; PhD, U. Chgo., 1986. Asst. prof. U. Cin., 1985-87, Washington U., St. Louis, 1988-91, U. Ill., Chgo., 1991-92; assoc. prof. Austin Peay State U., Clarksville, Tenn., 1993-97; assoc. prof. sociology Mid. Tenn. State U., Murfreesboro, 1997-98, prof., 1998—. Author: (monograph) Four Hundred Years of Social Thought, 1986, (children's book) With Wings To Fly, 2000; contbr. articles and book revs. to profl. jours., including Am. Jour. Sociology, Jour. Interpersonal Violence, jour. Quantitative Criminology, Social Forces, Brit. Jour. Sociology, Contemporary Sociology, Sociol. Focus, Am. Sociol. Rev., Jour. Marriage and Family, Sociol. Quar., Social Sci. Rsch., also chpts. to books. Grantee U. Cin., 1986, Austin Peay State U., 1994, G.H. Weems Ednl. Found., 1997, Mid. Tenn. State U., 1999; fellow Ctr. for Advanced Study in Behavioral Scis., Ogburn-Stouffer fellow U. Chgo., 1987-88. Mem. Am. Sociol. Assn., Am. Birding Assn. Avocations: birding, travel, chess, writing young adult books. Office: Middle Tenn State U Dept Sociology Murfreesboro TN 37132 Home: 9413 Atherton Ct Brentwood TN 37027-8700 Office Phone: 615-221-5113. Personal E-mail: kbreault@bellsouth.net.

BREAULT, ROBERT LEE, music educator; s. Leon and Michaelene Breault; m. Julia L. Haywood, May 31, 1991. B in Music, St. Norbert Coll., 1985; M in Music, U. Mich., 1987, D in Musical Arts, 1991. Prof., dir. opera U. Utah, Salt Lake City, 1992—. Recipient Alumni award, St. Norbert Coll., 1998, Outstanding Tchr. award, U. Utah, Coll. Fine Arts, 2001, Kolozsvar award, NYC Opera, 2007. Mem.: AGMA, NATS. Avocations: photography, dachshunds, golf. Home Phone: 801-278-9815.

BREAULT, THEODORE E(DWARD), lawyer; b. NYC, Mar. 7, 1938; m. Gretchen S. Clements, Dec. 10, 1966; children: Victoria Ann, Theodore Edmund, Heidi Sherwin, Edmund Clements. BS, Manhattan Coll., NYC, 1960; JD, Cath. U. Am., Washington, DC, 1963. Bar: DC 1964, Va. 1964, Pa. 1970, US Ct. Appeals (DC cir.) 1964, (4th cir.) 1969, US Supreme Ct. 1967. Assoc. Seltzer & Suskind, Washington, 1964-69, Egler & Reinstadtler, Pitts., 1969-77; pvt. practice Fairfax, Va., 1967-69, Pitts., 1977—2006; with Welch Gold & Siegel, PC, Pitts., 2006—. Lectr. Cath. U. Am. Sch. Nursing, 1968, Robert Morris Coll., 1973-74; mem. Pa. Workmen's Compensation Sect.; spl. master Allegheny County Ct. of Common Pleas; arbitrator US Dist. Ct.; med. malpractice mediator Beaver County, Pa. Pres. Sewickley Symphony Orch., Pa., 1974-75. Fellow: Pa. Bar Found. (life); mem.: Am. Coll. Legal Medicine (assoc. in law), Am. Arbitration Assn. (arbitrator accident and comml. claims), Pa. Def. Inst., Am. Soc. Law and Medicine, Allegheny County Bar Assn. (health law sect., chmn. workmen's compensation sect. 2001—02), D.C. Bar Assn., Va. State Bar Assn., Pa. Bar Assn. (civil litigation sect.), Matrimonial Inns of Ct. (master). Home: 108 Claridge Dr Moon Township PA 15108-3204 Office: Welch Gold & Siegel PC 1240 Lawyers Bldg 428 Forbes Ave Pittsburgh PA 15219 Home Phone: 412-262-1441; Office Phone: 412-391-1014.

BREAUX, JOHN BERLINGER, lawyer, communications professor, former senator; b. Crowley, La., Mar. 1, 1944; s. Ezra H., Jr. and Katherine (Berlinger) B.; m. Lois Gail Daigle, Aug. 1, 1964; children: John B., William Lloyd, Elizabeth Andre, Julia Agnes. BA in Polit. Sci, U. Southwestern La., 1964; JD, La. State U., 1967. Bar: La. 1967. Ptnr. Brown, McKernan, Ingram & Breaux, 1967-68; legis. asst. to Congressman Edwin W. Edwards, 1968-69, dist. asst., 1969-72; mem. US Congresses from 7th Dist. La., 1072—1987; U.S. Senator from La. Washington, 1987—2005; mem. fin. com., 1990—2005; chief dep. whip, 1993—2005; sr. counsel Patton Boggs LLP, Washington, 2005—; Disting prof. comm. Manship Sch. Mass Comm. La State U., Baton Rouge, 2005—, sr. fellow Reilly Ctr. Media & Pub. Affairs, 2005—. Chmn. Nat. Water Alliance, 1987-88, Nat. Dem. Senatorial Campaign Com., 1989-90, founder and past chair, Dem. Leadership Coun., 1991-93; co-chmn. Nat. Bipartisan Commn. on Future of Medicare, 1998-99; co-chmn. Nat. Commn. on Retirement Policy, 1997-98; mem. Senate Rules Com.; mem. bd. dirs, CSX Corp., 2005- Co-chair senate Centrist Coalition; mem. Senate New Dems. Recipient Am. Legion award; Moot Ct. finalist La. State U., 1966; Neptune award Am. Oceanic Orgn., 1980 Mem. La. Bar Assn., Crowley Jr. C. of C., La. Jr. C. of C., Pi Lambda Beta, Phi Alpha Delta, Lambda Chi Alpha. Democrat. Office: Patton Boggs LLP 2550 M St NW Washington DC 20037 also: The Manship Sch 211 Journalism Bldg La State U Baton Rouge LA 70803

BREAUX, PAUL JOSEPH, lawyer, pharmacist; b. Franklin, La., Mar. 11, 1942; s. Sidney J. and Irene (Bodin) B.; m. Marilynn Anne Jones, Aug. 21, 1965; children: Jason E., James P. BS in Pharmacy, Northeast La. U., 1965; JD, La. State U., 1972. Bar: La. 1972, U.S. Supreme Ct. 1975. Pharmacist Belanger's Pharmacy, Morgan City, La., 1965-66, Clinic Pharmacy, Morgan City, La., 1966-69; pvt. practice of law Lafayette, La., 1972-73, 93—; assoc. Allen, Gooch, Bourgeois, Breaux, Robison, Theunissen Attys., Lafayette, 1973-75; ptnr. Allen, Gooch, Bourgeois, Breaux, Robison & Theunissen, Lafayette, 1975-93. Sec., bd. dirs. Bank of Lafayette. Bd. dirs. Lafayette Community Health Care Clinic, Inc., 1992-05, vice chmn., 1996-2002; bd. dirs. Hospice of Acadiana, Inc., 1996-, v.p., 1999-2003, pres. 2003-04; bd. dirs. The Hospice Found., pres. 1998-2000; mem. Gov.'s Universal Health Care Law Reform Commn., 1992-; active Boy Scouts Am., 1984-92. Named Vol. of Yr., Lafayette Cmty. Health Care Clinic, Inc., 2000. Mem.: ABA, Soc. Hosp. Attys. of La. Hosp. Assn., Acad. Hosp. Attys. of Am. Hosp. Assn., Am. Health Lawyers Assn., Am. Soc. Pharmacy Law, Am. Soc. Law & Medicine, Nat. Assn. Retail Druggists, Am. Compliance Inst., La. Pharmacists Assn. (bd. dir. 1991—99, 2001—04, Pharmacist of Year award 1992), Am. Pharm. Assn., La. Bankers Assn. (La. banking code legis. revision com. 1983, mem. bank counsel com. 1983—85, 1988—90), Lafayette Parish Bar Assn., La. Bar Assn., Lafayette C. of C., Phi Eta Sigma, Kappa Psi. Republican. Roman Catholic. Office: 600 Jefferson St Ste 503 Lafayette LA 70501-6998 Home Phone: 337-984-0379; Office Phone: 337-266-2270.

BREAZEALE, MACK ALFRED, research scientist, educator; b. Leona Mines, Va., Aug. 15, 1930; s. Carl Samuel and Maude Ella (Moore) Breazeale; m. Joanne Morton O'Dell, Oct. 4, 1952 (dec. Nov. 1989); children: Jennifer Lee, David Mark, William Carl; m. Louise Hanna Scott, Nov. 10, 1990. BA, Berea Coll., Ky., 1953; MS, U. Mo., Rolla, 1954, degree (hon.) in Physics, 2004; PhD, Mich. State U., East Lansing, 1957. Asst. rsch. prof. Mich. State U., 1957-62; assoc. prof. U. Tenn., 1962-67, prof. physics and astronomy, 1967—95; cons. solid state div. Oak Ridge Nat. Lab., 1962-71, cons. health and safety research div., 1985-87; cons. Naval Rsch. Labs., 1971-75; prin. investigator contracts Office Naval Rsch., AEC, 1963—95; disting. rsch. prof. U. Miss., 1988—; prin. scientist Nat. Ctr. for Phys. Acoustics, Miss., 1988—. Guest Inst. Basic Tech. Problems, Warsaw, Poland, 1972; vis. prof. Tech. U. of Denmark, 1977; guest U. Paris, 1977; mem. program com. Internat. Symposium on Nonlinear Acoustics, 1975, 76, 78, 81, 84, 87, 90, 93, 96, 99, 2002, 05. Contbr. articles to profl. jours. Recipient U. Mo. Alumni Merit award, 1990; Fulbright rsch. fellow Tech. U., Stuttgart, Fed. Republic Germany, 1958-59; Fulbright travel grantee, 1977-78, NATO rsch. grantee, 1978-81, 92-2001, 2004-06, NSF US-Italy program grantee, 1982-86 Life fellow IEEE (adminstrv. com. ultrasonics, ferroelectrics and frequency control soc. 1987-89, program com. 1979—, pres. lectr., 1987, co-chair Atlanta Meeting Ultrasonics Symposium 2001, named Disting. Lectr. 1987-88);

fellow Inst. Acoustics (UK), Acoustical Soc. Am. (assoc. editor Nonlinear Acoustics 1977-2001, Silver medal in phys. acoustics 1988); mem. AAUP, Acoustical Soc. Am., Am. Phys. Soc., Sigma Xi, Phi Kappa Phi, Sigma Pi Sigma. Office: National Center for Physical Acoustics Rm 1027 Coliseum Dr University MS 38677 Office Phone: 662-915-7490. Business E-Mail: breazeal@olemiss.edu. *Scientific progress ultimately depends upon absolute integrity and honesty. A scientist therefore must pursue Truth in such a manner that the path between himself and his goal can never be so totally obstructed by any other human being.*

BREBBIA, CARLOS ALBERTO, engineering educator, consultant; b. Rosario, Argentina, Dec. 13, 1948; came to U.S., 1969; s. Carlos Alejandro and Elda (Eiris) B.; m. Carolyn Susan Stones, Oct. 30, 1971; children: Alexander Carlos, Isabel Elena. BS in Civil Engring., U. Litoral, Rosario, 1968; PhD in Civil Engring., U. Southampton, Eng., 1970; PhD (hon.), U. Bucharest, 1994. Lectr. U. Southampton, 1970-75, reader, 1976-79; assoc. prof. Princeton (N.J.) U., 1975-76; prof. U. Calif., Irvine, 1979-81; dir. Wessex Inst. Tech., Southampton, 1981—; pres. Computational Mechanics Inc., Billerica, Mass., 1984—. Mem. several adv. bds. Author 13 books; editor over 300 books; editor 3 profl. jours. Recipient Ville France medal; freeman City of London. Fellow Inst. Mech. Engring. UK, Royal Soc. Arts; mem. ASCE, Liverymen of Co. of Sci. Instrument Makers (mem. Prigogine award com.). Roman Catholic. Achievements include development of the main concept of the boundary element method, of innovative computational techniques, of an industrial computer aided design code based on boundary element methods; founder of Computational Mechanics Internat., LTD, Wessex Institute of Technology. Office: WIT Ashurst Lodge Ashurst Southampton SO407AA England Business E-Mail: carlos@wessex.ac.uk.

BRECHER, ARMIN GEORGE, lawyer; b. Prague, Czechoslovakia, July 7, 1942; s. Gerhard and Eleanor Brecher; m. Elizabeth Pardue Rountree, July 2, 1966; children: Lindsay Brecher Cobb, Stefan Ryan, Alden Kelsey. BA summa cum laude, Emory U., Atlanta, 1966; LLB, U. Va., 1969. Ptnr., chair exec. com. and bd. ptnrs. Powell, Goldstein, Frazer & Murphy, Atlanta, 1969—. Mem. The ESOP Assn. Presbyterian. Office: Powell Goldstein LLP 1201 W Peachtree St NW Fl 14 Atlanta GA 30309-3488

BRECHER, AVIVA, physicist, researcher; b. Bucarest, Romania, July 4, 1945; came to U.S., 1965; d. Reuven and Melita (Hecht) Schwartz; m. Kenneth Brecher, Aug. 18, 1965; children: Karen Iris, Daniel Isaac. Student, Technion, Haifa, Israel, 1964-65; BS in Physics, MS in Physics, MIT, 1968; PhD in Applied Physics, U. Calif., San Diego, 1972. Postdoctoral rsch. scientist MIT, Cambridge, Mass., 1972-75, rsch. scientist, lectr., 1975-80; asst. prof. Physics Wellesley (Mass.) Coll., 1977-80; sr. tech. cons. A. D. Little, Inc., Cambridge, 1980-85; dir. academic/ind./govt. rels. Boston U., 1985-86; sr. tech. & policy analyst Nat. Transp. Sys. Ctr. U.S. Dept. Transp., Cambridge, 1986-2000. Nat. tech. expert in transp. safety, health & environment, 2000—. Contbr. articles to profl. jours. and tech. papers. Bd. dirs MIT Hillel. Collamore fellow MIT, 1967; Amelia Earhardt fellow U. Calif., San Diego, 1969-70, PhD Dissertation fellow, 1971; fellow Japan Soc. Promotion Sci., 1980. Fellow: AAAS (com. sci., engring. & pub. policy 1990-95); mem. NRC (Transp. Rsch. Bd. 1995—), IEEE (stds. com., ICES 1997—, COMAR 2002—), Am. Phys. Soc. (Congress Sci. fellow, 1983, panel on pub. affairs 1995-98, 2001—, chair Forum on Physics and Soc., 1999-2000, APS fellow, 1999), NAS (Transp. Rsch. Bd., com. Applications Emerging Tech.1995-2000), Internat. Astron. Union, Union Concerned Scientists, MIT Alumnae Assn. Democrat. Jewish. Avocations: piano, languages, travel, archaeology. Home: 35 Madison St Belmont MA 02478-3535 Office: US Dept Transp Nat Transp Sys Ctr 55 Broadway Cambridge MA 02142-1093 Personal E-mail: avivabrecher@hotmail.com. Business E-Mail: brecher@volpe.dot.gov.

BRECHER, BERND, management consultant; b. Germany, Oct. 2, 1932; arrived in U.S., 1940; s. Jacob and Betty (Lewinsohn) B.; m. Helen Edith Casel, Feb. 1, 1959; children: Jacalyn Naomi, Alison Fay, Daniel Evan. BA, Columbia U., 1954, MS in Journalism, 1955. Dir. devel., pub. rels. and alumni affairs Coll. Physicians and Surgeons, Sch. Dentistry, Columbia U., NYC, 1954-57; campaign dir., supr. John Price Jones Co., Inc., NYC, 1958-67; v.p. Hamilton Coll. and Kirkland Coll., Clinton, N.Y., 1967-69; exec. v.p. John Price Jones Internat., Inc., NYC, 1969-71; sr. v.p. Brakeley, John Price Jones, Inc., NYC, 1971-73; pres. Bernd Brecher & Assocs., Inc., NYC and Scarsdale, 1973-93, Instl. Advancement Programs Inc., NYC, Tuckahoe, Becket, Mass., 1979—. Cons., strategic planner for arts, health, edn., youth, religious, cmty., environ. and other not-for-profit instns.; exec. dir. The Grad. Ctr. Found., NYC, 1994—97, Lehman Coll. Found., 2000—; cons. Lilly Endowment, Indpls., 1994—2006. Pres. Bd. Edn., Greenburgh, N.Y., 1977-78, Woodlands Scholarship Fund, Hartsdale, N.Y., 1965-66, Sec. Columbia Grads., 1980-85; mem. exec. com. Columbia Journalism Sch. Alumni, 1981-89; trustee Berkshire Children's Mus., 1998-2000; bd. dirs. Columbia U. Club Found., 1983—, v.p. 2003—; With U.S. Army, 1957-58. Recipient alumni medal for svc. Columbia U., 1983, Pres.'s Cup, 1981, Lion Awards, 1979, 80, 94, 99, Genesis award as a founder Alzheimer's Assn., 2005. Mem. Coun. for Advancment and Support of Edn. (Quarter Century Svc. award 1981), Assn. Fundraising Profls. (v.p. N.Y. chpt. 1987-89), Am. Assn. Cmty. and Jr. Colls., Am. Hosp. Assn., Am. Assn. Mus., Princeton Univ. Club, Univ. Club of Chgo. Avocations: theater, tennis, travel, fine dining. Home: 35 Parkview Ave Bronxville NY 10708-2953 Office: Instl Advancement Programs Inc 65 Main St Tuckahoe NY 10707-2908 Office Phone: 914-779-4092. Business E-Mail: BrecherServices@aol.com.

BRECHER, JOHN, columnist; m. Dorothy J. Gaiter, Apr. 17, 1979; 2 children. BA in Journalism, Columbia U. With The Miami Herald, Newsweek, 1980—84; city editor The Miami Herald, 1984; sr. special writer Page One Wall Street Jour., 1990, page one editor NYC, 1992—2000, co-author (with Dorothy Gaiter) Tastings column. Appearances Martha Stewart Living, Today. Co-author (with Dorothy Gaiter): The Wall Street Journal Guide to Wine, 1999, The Wall Street Journal Guide to Wine New and Improved, 2002, Love by the Glass: Tasting Notes From a Marriage, 2003. Office: Dow Jones & Co 200 Liberty St Fl 11 New York NY 10281-1099

BRECHER, KENNETH, astrophysicist, educator; b. NYC, Dec. 7, 1943; s. Irving and Edythe (Grossman) B.; m. Aviva Schwartz, Aug. 18, 1965; children: Karen, Daniel. BS, MIT, 1964, PhD, 1969. Research physicist U. Calif., San Diego, 1969-72; asst. prof. physics MIT, Cambridge, 1972-77, assoc. prof., 1977-79; assoc. prof. astronomy and physics Boston U., 1979-81, prof., 1981—, dir. Sci. and Math. Edn. Ctr., 1990—. Author, editor: (with G. Setti) High Energy Astrophysics and Its Relation to Elementary Particle Physics, 1974, (with M. Feirtag) Astronomy of the Ancients, 1979; contbr. numerous articles to profl. jours. Mem. Mass. Cultural Coun., 1989-91. Guggenheim fellow, 1979—80, W.K. Kellogg fellow, 1985—88, NRC sr. rsch. assoc., 1983—84, Exploratorium Osher fellow, 2001. Fellow Am. Phys. Soc. (chmn. astrophysics div. 1990-91); mem. Am. Aston. Soc., Internat. Astron. Union, Am. Assn. Physics Tchrs., Optical Soc. Am., Sigma Xi. Home: 35 Madison St Belmont MA 02478-3535 Office: Boston U Dept Astronomy 725 Commonwealth Ave Boston MA 02215-1401

BRECHER, MICHAEL, political science professor; b. Montreal, Mar. 14, 1925; s. Nathan and Gisela (Hopmeyer) B.; m. Eva Danon, Dec. 7, 1950; children: Leora, Diana, Seegla. BA, McGill U., 1946; MA, Yale U., 1948, PhD, 1953. Mem. faculty McGill U., Montreal, 1952—, prof. polit. sci., 1963—, R.B. Angus prof. polit. sci., 1993—. Founder Shastri Indo-Can. Inst., 1968, pres., 1969, 70; vis. prof. U. Chgo., 1963; vis. prof. internat. rels. Hebrew U., Jerusalem, 1970-75, U. Calif., Berkeley, 1979, Stanford U., 1980. Author: The Struggle for Kashmir, 1953, Nehru: A Political Biography, 1959, The New States of Asia, 1963, Succession in India, 1966, India and World Politics, 1968, Political Leadership in India, 1969, The Foreign Policy System of Israel, 1972, Israel: The Korean War and China, 1974, Decisions in Israel's Foreign Policy, 1975, Studies in Crisis Behavior, 1979, Decisions in Crisis, 1980, Crisis and Change in World Politics, 1986, Crises in the 20th Century: Vol. 1, Handbook of International Crises, Vol. 2, Handbook of Foreign Policy Crises, 1988, Crisis, Conflict and Instability, 1989, Crises in World Politics, 1993, A Study of Crisis, 1997, 2000, Millennial Reflections on International Studies, 2002; contbr. over 80 articles in field to profl. jours. Recipient Watumull prize, Am. Hist. Assn., 1960, Killam awards, Can. Coun., 1970—74, 1976—79, Woodrow Wilson Found. award, Am. Polit. Sci. Assn., 1973, Fieldhouse tchg. award, McGill U., 1986, Disting. Scholar award, Internat. Studies Assn., 1995, Léon-Gérin Quebec Prize for Human Scis., 2000, Disting. Rsch. award, McGill U., 2000; Nuffield fellow, 1955—56, Rockefeller fellow, 1964—65, Guggenheim fellow, 1965—66, rsch. grantee, Can. Coun. and Soc. Sci. and Humanities Rsch. Coun. of Can., 1960, 1965, 1968, 1969—70, 1975—76, 1980—87, 1990—92, 1993—96, 2002—05. Fellow Royal Soc. Can.; mem. Internat. Studies Assn. (pres. 1999-2000), Brit. Internat. Studies Assn., World Assn. Internat. Relations, Internat., Am., Can., Israeli polit. sci. assns. Home: 5 Dubnov St Jerusalem 91043 Israel Office: McGill U Dept Pol Sci 855 Sherbrooke St W Montreal PQ Canada H3A 2T7 Office Phone: 514-398-4800. Business E-Mail: michael.brecher@mcgill.ca.

BRECHKA, FRANK TILSON, retired librarian, historian; b. NYC, Sept. 30, 1930; s. Frank August and Marjorie Tilson (Connell) B. AB, Columbia U., 1952, MS, 1954, AM, 1958; PhD, U. Calif., Berkeley, 1968. Libr. N.Y. Pub. Libr., NYC, 1954-57, sr. libr., 1959-61; head libr. S.I. C.C., NYC, 1958-59; reference libr. Wagner Coll., NYC, 1961-63, U. Calif., Berkeley, 1967-71, history libr., 1971-91, retired, 1991. Instr. history and librarianship U. Calif., Berkeley, 1970-77; cons. San Francisco Towers Libr., 1996—. Author: Gerard Van Swieten and His World, 1700-1772, 1970; contbr. articles to profl. jours. Rsch. grantee Librs. Assn. Univ. Calif., Berkeley, 1982; scholar Columbia Univ. Sch. Libr. Svc., N.Y.C., 1952-53, Fulbright, Netherlands and Austria, 1965-66. Mem. Am. Hist. Assn., Inst. for Hist. Study. Avocations: collecting books and antique maps, writing letters, travel. Home: 1661 Pine St Apt 823 San Francisco CA 94109-0409

BRECHT, WARREN FREDERICK, retired business executive; b. Detroit, May 21, 1932; s. August F. and Margaret (Roos) B.; m. Barbara Boone, July 31, 1983; children: Amy E., Stephen F., David C., Peter J. BA, DePauw U., 1954; postgrad., U. Mich., 1955; MBA, Harvard U., 1959. Systems analyst W.R. Grace & Co., Cambridge, Mass., 1959—61; v.p., treas. Mgmt. Systems Corp., Cambridge, 1961—65; ptnr. in charge adminstrn. Peat, Marwick, Livingston & Co., Boston, 1965—69; prin. in charge profl. practice, mgmt. cons. dept. Peat, Marwick, Mitchell & Co., NYC, 1969—71; dep. asst. sec. for mgmt. and budget U.S. Dept. Interior, Washington, 1971—72; asst. sec. for adminstrn. U.S. Dept. Treasury, 1972—77; v.p. acctg. and mgmt. info. systems Northeast Utilities, Hartford, Conn., 1977—85; sr. v.p. N. Am. Holding Corp. and Subs., East Hartford, Conn., 1985—89; sr. v.p., sec. Butler Internat. (formerly N.Am. Ventures Inc.), Montvale, NJ, 1985—2001; sr. v.p. adminstrn. and sec. Butler Svc. Group., Inc., Montvale, 1990—2001. Mem. panel deregulation govt. mgmt. Nat. Acad. Pub. Adminstrn., 1982—83. Exec. bd. coun. BSA, Bergen County, NJ, 1997—98; bd. dirs., treas. Nyack Cmty. Ctr., 1999—2006; Trustee Conn. Pub. Expenditure Coun., 1978—84; vice chmn. ch. coun., treas., trustee Riverside Ch., NYC, 1993—2000, 2002—06. With USAF, 1955—57. Recipient Outstanding Young Man award Lexington (Mass.) Jaycees, 1968; Exceptional Service award Dept. Treasury, 1976; Alumni citation DePauw U., 1976; Rector Scholar 25th Anniversary Achievement award DePauw U., 1979. Mem. Phi Beta Kappa. Home: 23 Tallman Ave Nyack NY 10960-1605 Personal E-mail: wbbrecht@optonline.net.

BRECHTEL, UNDA JURKA, retired library director; b. Riga, Latvia, Mar. 3, 1935; came to US, 1951; d. Aleksanders and Irene (Stesingers) Jurka; m. Philipp Jack Brechtel Jr., Sept. 3, 1960 (div. Aug. 1986); children: Philipp Jack III, Peter Kevin. BS in Psychology, St. Thomas Aquinas, 1981; MLS, LI U., 1982. Reference libr. Haverstraw Pub. Libr., NY, 1982-83; libr. dir. Sloatsburg Pub. Libr., NY, 1983-85, Wanaque Pub. Libr., NY, 1985-88, Oakland Pub. Libr., NJ, 1988-2000; libr. LI U., Sparkill, NY, 2000—06; ret., 2006. Mem. NJ Libr. Assn., NY Libr. Assn. Lutheran. Avocations: ballroom dancing, travel, gardening.

BRECKENRIDGE, JAMES G., dean, consultant; s. Robert C. and Nola T. Breckenridge; m. Mary B. Barrett, Oct. 22, 1977; children: Catherine E., Annemarie J., Christine C. BA, Va. Tech, Blacksburg, 1976; MA, U. Va., Charlottesville, 1987; MBA, Gannon U., Erie, Pa., 1999. Advanced from commd. 2d lt. to lt. col. US Army, 1976—98, ret. lt. col., 1998; dir. admissions Mercyhurst Coll., Erie, 1998—2000, chmn. dept. intelligence studies, 2002—06, dean Walker Sch. Bus., 2006—. Asst. prof. dept. history US Mil. Acad., West Point, NY, 1987—90; pres. sch. bd. Fairview Sch. Dist., Pa., 2001—; pres. Applied Intelligence Assocs., Erie, 2004—. Decorated Legion of Merit US Army. Mem.: Assn. Former Intelligence Officers (corr.), Internat. Assn. for Intelligence Edn. (assoc.; bd. dirs. 2004—06), Assn. of the US (life), Phi Kappa Phi. Office: Mercyhurst Coll 501 E 38th St Erie PA 16546 Home Phone: 814-835-4170; Office Phone: 814-824-2458. Personal E-mail: breckenridge.james@gmail.com. Business E-Mail: jbreckenridge@mercyhurst.edu.

BRECKINRIDGE, JAMES BERNARD, optical engineer; s. Albert Coles and Catherine Rose (Wengler) B.; m. Ann Marie Yoder, July 24, 1965; children: Douglass E., John Brian. BS in Physics, Case Inst. Tech., 1961; MS in Optical Sci., U. Ariz., 1970, PhD in Optical Sci., 1976. Rsch. asst. Lick Obs., Mt. Hamilton, Calif., 1961-64; electron tube engr. Rauland Corp., Chgo., 1967; rsch. asst. Kitt Peak Nat. Obs., Tucson, full time, 1964-66, 68, 75-76, part time, 1969-74; mem. tech. staff Jet Propulsion Lab., Calif. Inst. Tech., 1976—, part-time faculty in applied physics, 1981—97, mgr. optics sect., 1981-94; program mgr. for innovative imaging tech. and sys. Def. Program Office, 1994—99; leader NASA Team to Assess Optics Tech. in Former Soviet Union, 1992-97; program dir. advanced tech. and instrumentation, program dir. Nat. Radio Astronomy Obs., NSF, 1999—2002; chief technologist Astron. Search for Origins, NASA, 2002—. Co-investigator NASA Spacelab 3; adv. com. NASA, NSF, Dept. Def.; staff mem. Hubble Space Telescope Failure Bd., 1990, tech. mgr. Hubble Space Telescope Camera Optics Repair. Contbr. articles to jours. in field; 5 patents in field. Scoutmaster Boy Scouts Am.; trustee United Ch. of Christ; mem. Soc of the Cin. in NJ. Fellow Optical Soc. Am. (bd. dirs.), Royal Astron. Soc., Internat. Soc. Optical Engring. (bd. govs., pres. 1994, George W. Goddard award 2003); mem. Am. Astron. Soc., Coun. Sci. Soc. Pres.'s (bd. dirs. 1996), Internat. Astron. Union, Internat. Congress on Optics (U.S. chair 1999-2001), Breckinridge Family Assn. (pres. 1999—2006). Achievements include research in space-based remote optical and infrared sensing instrumentation, interferometry, spectroscopy, image intensifiers and image analysis. Office: 4800 Oak Grove Dr Pasadena CA 91109 Home: 985 E California Blvd Ste 203 Pasadena CA 91106 Office Phone: 818-354-6785.

BRECKNER, WILLIAM JOHN, JR., retired military officer; b. Alliance, Ohio, May 25, 1933; s. William John and Frances P. (Bertchey) B.; m. Cheryl V. Carmell, Aug. 30, 1963; children: William R., Kristen C. BA, SUNY, 1976; postgrad., Harvard U., 1980. Commd. 2d lt. USAF, 1955, advanced through grades to maj. gen., 1983, various pilot and command positions worldwide, 1955-72; comdr. USAF Interceptor Weapons Sch., 1973-75; vice commandant cadets USAF Acad., Colo., 1976-79; comdr. 82d Flying Tng. Wing Williams AFB, Ariz., 1979-80; dep. chief staff logistics Hdqrs. Air Tng. Commd., Tex., 1980-83; chief staff Hdqrs. USAF Europe, 1983-84; commdr. 17th Air Force, Sembach AFB, Germany, 1984-86; ret., 1986. Commr. Colo. Springs Airport Adv. Commn., 2003-; bd. dirs., trustee Falcon Found.; Prisoner of war, Vietnam, 1972-73. Decorated D.S.M., 1986, Silver Star, 1972, Legion of Merit, 1973, Bronze Star medal, 1973, Air medal, 1968, 72, Purple Heart, 1972, 73, Republic of Vietnam Cross of Gallantry with palm, 1973 Mem. Nat. War Coll. Alumni Assn., Order Daedalians (bd. dirs.), Air Force Assn., Nam Prisoners of War Inc., Red River Valley Fighter Pilots Assn., C. of C. (chmn. mil. affairs coun. 1994-95). Lutheran. Avocations: golf, skiing, tennis. Home: 17865 Fairplay Way Monument CO 80132-8581 Office: 590 Hwy 105 Ste 266 Monument CO 80132 Office Phone: 719-481-6000. E-mail: brexgroup@earthlink.net.

BRECKON, DONALD JOHN, academic administrator; b. Port Huron, Mich., June 11, 1939; s. Robert Joseph and Margaret Elizabeth (Wade) B.; m. Sandra Kay Biehn, Sept. 4, 1959; children: Lori E., LeeAnne M., Lisa C., Lynanne U. AA, St. Clair County C.C., 1959; BS, Central Mich. U., 1962, MA, 1963; postgrad., U. Wis., 1965-66, Western Mich. U., 1968; MPH, U. Mich., 1968; PhD, Mich. State U., 1977; D of Pub. Svc. (hon.), Ctrl. Mich. U., 2001. Instr. hrealth edn. Central Mich. U., Mt. Pleasant, 1963-68, asst. prof., 1968-72, assoc. prof., 1972-81, prof. health edn., 1978-81, asst. dean health, phys. edn. and recreation, 1981-82, assoc. dean edn., health and human svcs., 1982-86, dean grad. studies/assoc. provost for rsch., 1986-87; pres. Park Coll./Park U., Parkville, Mo., 1987—2001. Author: Hospital Health Education: A Guide to Program Development, 1982, Community Health Education: Setting, Roles and Skills, 1985, 3d rev. edit., 1994, Microcomputer Applications to Health Education and Health Science, 1986, Matters of Life and Death, 1987, Managing Health Promotion Programs: Leadership Skills for the 21st Century, 1997; contbr. articles to profl. jours. Bd. dirs. St. Lores Northland Hosp. Recipient Central Mich. U. Tchg. Effectiveness awrd, 1975, Disting. Svc. award Mich. Alcoholism and Addiction Assn., 1977, Disting. Alumni award St. Clair County, 1988, Centennial award Ctrl. Mich. U., 1992, Northlander of Yr. award Kans. City Northland regional C. of C.; Mich. Dept. Edn. scholar, 1971, Yale U. Drug Dependence Inst. scholar, 1973, Midwest Inst. Alcohol Studies, Mich. Dept. Pub. Health scholar, 1974; Am. Coun. on Edn. Leadership dEvel. program fellow, 1979. Mem. Mich. Pub. Health Assn. (pres. 1976-77), Am. Pub. Health Assn., Soc. Pub. Health Edn. (pres. 1978-79), Am. Hosp. Assn. (coun. govs.). Home: 7320 NW Katie Cir Kansas City MO 64152-1988 Office: Park Coll Office of Pres Parkville MO 64152

BREDA, JOHN ALEXANDER, physician, musician; b. Boston, Sept. 9, 1954; s. Alexander John and Eda (Feroli) B.; m. Karen Schultz, Aug. 14, 1988; 1 child, Joseph Samuel. MusB, MusM, New England Conservatory Music, Boston, 1972-78; postgrad., Harvard U., Cambridge, Mass., 1990; MD, U. Mass., Worcester, 1996. Diplomate Am. Bd. Internal Medicine, 2000; cert. instrument rated pilot. Symphonic musician Oreg. Symphony, Portland, 1982-89; med. rschr. Harvard Sch. Pub. Health, Boston, 1989-90, Harvard Med. Sch., Boston, 1990-91; intern, resident Metro West Med. Ctr., Framingham, Mass., 1996-97; resident Miriam Hosp., R.I. Hosp., Brown U. Program, Providence, 1997-99; physician internal medicine Harvard Vanguard Med. Assocs., Medford, Mass., 1999—2001; physician internal medicine primary, urgent care Harvard U. Health Svcs., Cambridge, Mass., 2001—04; med. examiner Bridgewater Goddard Pk. Med. Assocs., 2004—. Instr. medicine Harvard Med. Sch., 2001—; woodwind instrument builder, cons. clarinet design, Boston, 1978—; guest lectr. New Eng. Conservatory Music, Boston, 1981. Performed with numerous musical orgns. including San Francisco Opera, 1980, Santa Fe (N.Mex.) Opera, 1980, Boston Symphony, 1978-81. Betty Lea Stone fellow Am. Cancer Soc., 1992, Tanglewood fellow Berkshire Music Ctr., 1982, Symphony Orch. Inst. fellow, 1996. Mem. AMA, Mass. Med. Soc. (Charles River dist. scholar 1992), Worcester Med. Soc. Avocations: flying, skiing, bicycling. Business E-Mail: jbreda@massmed.org.

BREDAR, JAMES KELLEHER, judge; b. Omaha, Feb. 6, 1957; BA, Harvard U., 1979; JD, Georgetown U., 1982. Bar: Colo. 1983, Md. 1995, U.S. Supreme Ct. 1993. Nat. park ranger U.S. Dept. Interior, Estes Park, Colo., 1976-80; jud. law clk. U.S. Dist. Judge R. Matsch, Denver, 1983; dep. dist. atty. State of Colo., Craig, 1984; asst. U.S. atty. U.S. Dept. Justice, Denver, 1985-89; asst. fed. pub. defender U.S. Courts, Denver, 1989-91, fed. pub. defender Balt., 1992-98; project dir. Vera Inst. Justice, London, 1991-92; U.S. magistrate judge Balt., 1998—. Vis. scholar Yale U., New Haven, 1981-82. Author/editor: Justice Informed, 1992. Office: US Magistrate Judge 8C US Courthouse 101 W Lombard St Baltimore MD 21201-2605

BREDE, ANDREW DOUGLAS, science administrator, botanist; b. Pitts., Feb. 4, 1953; s. James Faris and Adele Katherine (Konefal) Brede; m. Linda Davis Rudd, Jan. 11, 1992; children from previous marriage: Loralee Elizabeth, Michael Douglas. BS, Pa. State U., 1975, MS, 1978, PhD, 1982. Asst. golf course supt. Valley Brook Country Club, McMurray, Pa., 1975-76; grad. rsch. asst. Pa. State U., University Park, 1976-82; assoc. prof. Okla. State U., Stillwater, 1982-86; dir. rsch. Simplot Turf & Horticulture, Post Falls, Idaho, 1986—. Chmn. variety rev. Lawn Inst., Marietta, Ga., 1990—96; bd. dirs. Nat. Turfgrass Evaluation Program; golf course supr. Assn. Am. Rsch. Com., 1996—97; organizer Turfgrass Conf., China. Author: Turfgrass Maintenance Reduction Manual, 2000; assoc. editor: Agronomy Jour., 1993—99; contbr. articles to profl. jours. and mags.; prodr.: 15 ednl. videos. Recipient Genetics and Plant Breeding award for industry, Nat. Coun. Comml. Plant Breeders, 2005; Rsch. grantee, 1983—86. Fellow: Crop Sci. Soc. Am. (Fred V. Grau Turfgrass Sci. award 2005), Am. Soc. Agronomy. Republican. Achievements include patents in field; development of 60 plant varieties. Avocation: amateur radio operating. Office: Simplot Turf & Horticulture 5300 W Riverbend Rd Post Falls ID 83854-9456

BREDEHOFT, ELAINE CHARLSON, lawyer; b. Fergus Falls, Minn., Nov. 22, 1958; d. Curtis Lyle and Marilyn Anne (Nesbitt) Charlson; m. Keenan P. Frank; children: Alexandra Charlson, Michelle Charlson. BA, U. Ariz., 1981; JD, Cath. U. Am., 1984. Bar: Va. 1984, DC 1994, admitted to practice: US Ct. Appeals (4th Cir.) 1984, US Bankruptcy Ct. (Ea. Dist.) Va. 1987, US Ct. Appeals (DC Cir.) 1994. Assoc. Walton and Adams, McLean, Va., 1984-88, ptnr., 1988-91, Charlson Bredehoft, PC (now Charlson Bredehoft & Cohen PC), Reston, Va., 1991—. Spkr. Fairfax Bar Assn. CLE, 1992—, spkr. VB Assn., 1993—; spkr. Labor and Employment Law Update, 1993—, Va. Women's Trial Lawyers Assn. Ann. Conf., 1998, Va. Bar Assn. Labor and Employment Conf., 1994—97, 1999—, Va. Trial Lawyers Assn., 1995, 97, Va. Law Found., 1995—, 1995—, Va. Assn. Def. Attys., 1996, 2001; mem. faculty Va. State Bar Law Student Professionalism Com.2, 2001—; invitee 4th Cir. Jud. Conf., 1997—99, permanent mem., 1999—; invitee Boyd Graves Conf., 1999—; substitute judge 19th Jud. Dist., 1998—. Bd. dir. Va. Commn. on Women and Minorities in the Legal Sys., 1987—90, sec., 1988—90. Named an 12 top Employment Lawyers in the Washington Met. Area, Legal Times, 2004; named one of The Best Lawyers in America, 1997, 50 Best Lawyers in Washington, Washingtonian mag., 1997, 40 Top Lawyers Under 40, 1998, 75 Best Lawyers in Washington, 2002, top employment lawyers, 2004; recipient The Best Lawyers in America, 1998, 1999, 2000, 2001, 2002, 2003, 2004. Fellow: Internat. Acad. Trial Lawyers, Am. Coll. Trial Lawyers; mem.: Fairfax Bar Assn. (chair diversity taskforce 1998—99, co-chair subcom. on minorities, Pres.'s Vol. award 1998, 1999), Minn. State Soc., Va. Trial Lawyers Assn. (mem. com. on long-range planning 1996—97, vice chmn.

ann. conv. 1996—98), Va. Bar Assn. (spkr. 1995, 1997, mem. exec. com. young lawyers sect., mem. litig. com., mem. nominating com., chmn. model jud. com.), George Mason Inns of Ct. (master 1996—). Office: Charlson Bredehoft & Cohen PC 11260 Roger Bacon Dr Ste 201 Reston VA 20190-5252 Home Phone: 703-444-0805; Office Phone: 703-318-6800. E-mail: ebredehoft@charlsonbredehoft.com.

BREDEHOFT, JOHN MICHAEL, lawyer; b. NYC, Feb. 22, 1958; s. John William and Viola (Struhar) B.; m. Ivana Terango; children: Alexandra Charlson, Michelle Charlson , John Paris. AB magna cum laude, Harvard Coll., 1980, JD cum laude, 1983. Bar: D.C. 1983, U.S. Dist. Ct. D.C. 1985, U.S. Ct. Appeals (D.C. cir.) 1985, U.S. Ct. Appeals (1st cir.) 1986, U.S. Supreme Ct. 1987, U.S. Ct. Appeals (9th cir.) 1988, U.S. Ct. Appeals (3rd and 5th cir.) 1989, U.S. Tax Ct. 1989, U.S. Ct. Appeals (4th Cir.) 1990, U.S. Dist. Ct. Mont. 1991, Va. 1992, U.S. Dist. Ct. (Ea. Dist.) Va. 1992, US Bankruptcy Ct. (Ea. Dist.) Va., 1992. Assoc. Cleary, Gottlieb, Steen & Hamilton, Washington, 1983-91; prin. Charlson & Bredehoft, Fairfax, Va., 1991-98; ptnr. Venable LLP, McLean, Va., 1998; ptnr., Labor & Employment Dept. Venable LLP, Vienna, Va. Contbg. editor Employment Law in Virginia, 1997. Bd. dirs. Falls Brook Assn., Herndon, Va., 1988-91; nat. class 1983 reunion gift chmn. Harvard Law Sch. Fund, Cambridge, 1988, class agt., 1994—; mem. Harvard Debate Centennial Com., 1992. Named Lawyer of Yr., Met. Washington Employment Lawyers Assn., 1996, Va. Legal Elite, Va. Bus., 2000-2004. Mem. ABA (sect. on litigation), Va. Bar Assn. (sect. on labor and employment law, governing coun. mem., vice chair), Va. Trial Lawyers Assn. (founding officer, employment law sect.), Fairfax Bar Assn. (sect. on employment law, vice chmn. 1997-98, chmn. 1998-99), Def. Rsch. and Trial Inst. (appellate advocacy com.), Va. Law Found./Va. CLE (employment law com.), Va. Women Attys. Assn. Office Phone: 703-760-1629. Office Fax: 703-821-8949. Business E-Mail: jmbredehoft@venable.com.

BREDESEN, PHILIP NORMAN, governor; b. Oceanport, NJ, Nov. 21, 1943; s. Philip Norman and Norma (Walborn) B.; m. Andrea Conte, Nov. 22, 1974; 1 child, Benjamin. AB in Physics, Harvard U., 1967. Computer programmer Itek Corp., Lexington, Mass., 1967-70; dir. systems devel. Searle Medidata, Lexington, 1970-73, div. mgr. London, 1973-75; dir. spl. project Hosp. Affiliates Internat., Nashville, 1975-78; v.p. internat. div. INA Health Care Group, Nashville, 1978-80; chmn. and chief exec. officer HealthAmerica Corp., Nashville, 1980-86; chmn., co-founder Coventry Corp., Nashville, 1986-90; chmn. Clin. Pharms., Nashville, 1986-93; mayor Met. Govt. Nashville and Davidson County, 1991-99; pres. Bredex Corp., Nashville, 2000—02; gov. State of Tenn., Nashville, 2003—. Bd. dirs. Nashville Symphony, 1985-91, Univ. Sch. Nashville, 1986-95, United Cerebral Palsy, 1988-92, United Way of Middle Tenn., 1985-90, Tenn. State U. Found., Nashville Pub. Libr. Found., 1997—07; chmn., founder The Land Trust for Tenn., 1999-2001; trustee Frist Ctr. for Visual Arts, 1998-03, chair fin. com., 2000-03; founder Nashville's Table, 1989, bd. dirs., 1989-91. Democrat. Presbyterian. Avocations: skiing, reading, computers. Home: 1724 Chickering Rd Nashville TN 37215-4908 Office: State Capitol Office Governor Nashville TN 37243-0001 Office Phone: 615-741-2001. Office Fax: 615-532-9711. Business E-Mail: phil.bredesen@state.tn.us.

BREDFELDT, JOHN CREIGHTON, economics educator, writer, retired military officer; b. Oct. 31, 1947; s. Willis John and Geraldine Elizabeth (Creighton) Bredfeldt; m. Janice Elizabeth Hamilton; children: Jason Caulter, Bryan Thomas. BBA, Wichita State U., 1969, MA in Econs., 1971; PhD in Pub. Adminstrn., La Salle U., 1995; grad., Air Command and Staff Coll., 1984, Nat. Security Mgmt. Coll., 1987. Dir. Brennan Halls Wichita State U., 1969-71; commd. 2d lt. USAF, 1971, advanced through grades to lt. col., 1987, ret., 1993; budget/cost analyst Aero. Sys. Divsn., Dayton, Ohio, 1971-76; insp. Air Force IG, Andrews AFB, Md., 1976-79; chief economist Dir. Programs AF/PRP, Pentagon, Va., 1979-83; chief cost analyst divsn. USAF Europe, 1985-87, dep. dir. program control, engine program office Dayton, 1987-89; dir. program control spl. ops. forces USAF, 1989-93; project leader for econs./fin. analyst Modern Techs. Corp., Warner Robins, Ga., 1993—. Instr. econs. Wichita State U., 1969-71; bus. prof. Bowie State Coll., 1980-83; econs. instr. European divsn. U. Md., Germany, 1985-87, Sinclair C.C., Dayton, 1988-93, Macon (Ga.) State Coll., 1994—; adj. prof. Mercer U., 1996, Wesleyan Coll., 1998. Contbr. articles to profl. jours. Rep., Sunday sch. tchr. Ramstein Protestant Parish Coun. Germany, 1984-86; asst. scoutmaster Ramstein coun. Boy Scouts Am., 1984-87, den leader, 1998, charter rep., 1999—; v.p. St. Timothy Lutheran Ch., Dayton, 1989-91; prayer team leader Wesley United Meth. Ch., Macon, 2004, chmn. fin. com., 2005-. Mem. Assn. Govt. Accts., Soc. Cost Estimating and Analysis, Am. Soc. Mil. Comptrollers, Nat. Eagle Scout Assn. Personal E-mail: jeb15@cox.net.

BREE, MARLIN DUANE, publisher, author; b. Norfolk, Nebr., May 16, 1933; s. George F. and Luile Bree; m. Loris Bree; 1 child, William Marlin. BA, cert. in journalism, U. Nebr., 1955. Mng. editor Davidson Pub. Co., 1958-61; editor Greater Mpls. mag., 1962-63; pub. rels. specialist Blue Shield, 1964-67; editor Sunday Mag., Star and Tribune, Mpls., 1968-72; columnist Corp. Report, Mpls., 1973-77; publs. cons., 1978-83; co-founder, ptnr., editorial dir. Marlor Press, Inc., St. Paul, 1983-91, co-owner, pub., 1992—. Chmn. Midwest Book Awards, St. Paul, 1992; judge Boating Writers Internat. Writing Contest, 2005-07. Author: In the Teeth of the Northeaster: A Solo Voyage on Lake Superior, 1988, Call of the North Wind: Voyages and Adventures on Lake Superior, 1996, Wake of the Green Storm: A Survivor's Tale, 2001, Broken Seas: True Tales of Extraordinary Seafaring Adventures, 2005; co-author: Alone Against the Atlantic, 1981, Kid's Travel Fun Book, 2007. Dir. comm. Mpls. Bicentennial Celebration, 1976. With US Army, 1955—57. Named Pub. of Yr., Midwest Ind. Pubs. Assn., 1994; recipient Golden Web award, 2003-04, Writing award Boating Writers Internat., 2003, 07, Grand Prize, Boating Writers Internat., 2004. Mem.: St. Paul Sail and Power Squadron (hon.). Avocation: sailing. Office: Marlor Press Inc 4304 Brigadoon Dr Saint Paul MN 55126-3100 Business E-Mail: marlin.marlor@minn.net.

BREECE, ELLIOTT, network administrator, Internet entrepreneur; b. 1984; Grad., Brown U., 2006. Co-founder & chief exec. Amie, Inc./AmieStreet.Com, Providence, 2006—. Named one of Best Entrepreneurs Under 25, Bus. Week, 2006; recipient Bronze medal for Computer Sci., NAACP Academic, Cultural, Technol. & Sci. Olympics, 2000. Home and Office: 168 Williams St Providence RI 02906 Office Phone: 401-437-6708. E-mail: elliott@amiestreet.com.

BREECE, ROBERT WILLIAM, JR., lawyer; b. Blackwell, Okla., Feb. 5, 1942; s. Robert William Breece Sr. and Helen Elaine (Maddox) Breece Robinson; m. Elaine Marie Keller, Sept. 7, 1968; children: Bryan, Justin, Lauren BSBA, Northwestern U., 1964; JD, U. Okla., 1967; LLM, Washington U., St. Louis, 1970. Bar: Oklahoma 1967, Mo. 1970. Pvt. practice, St. Louis, 1968—. Pres., chmn. bd. dirs. Crown Capital Corp., St. Louis. Mem. ABA, Internat. Bar Assn., Mo. Bar Assn., Phi Alpha Delta, Beta Theta Pi, Forest Hills Country Club (pres. 1978), St. Louis Club, Club at Meditterra, Assocs. for Corp. Growth. Personal E-mail: awbreece@comcast.net.

BREECHER, MAURY MARTIN, writer, small business owner; b. Jersey City, Nov. 7, 1954; s. Maurice I. and Marie Breecher; m. Connie Ray (div.); children: Martin Ray, Christopher Craig; m. Anne Boudreau (div.); 1 child, Michael. BA in Liberal Arts, SUNY, Albany, 1987; MPH, U. Ala., Birmingham, 1990; PhD in Mass Comm., U. Ala., 1996. Contract writer, reporter WebMD, Atlanta, 1999—2001; writer Breecher Enterprises, San Diego, 2001—04; exec. editor UCLA Diabetes Perspective Newsletter, 2003—04; owner, operator A Life to Remember: Memoirs & Autobiographies, Corpus Christi, Tex., 2004—; owner, editor Breecher Enterprises, Corpus Christi, 2005—. Author: (non-fiction) Healthy Homes in a Toxic World, 1992; co-author (with Peter Brooksmith): Dr. Anderson's Antioxidant, Antiaging Health Program, 1996, Live Longer Better, 1997, BioHazard: The Hot Zone and Beyond, 1997, Future Plagues: Mankind's battle for survival, 1997; contbr. articles to profl. jours. Past bd. dirs. Unitarian Universalist Ch., Tuscaloosa, Ala. Fellow, Nat. Assn. Sci. Writers, 2006. Mem.: Nat. Assn. Sci. Writers, Assn. Personal Historians, Am. Med. Writers Assn., Authors Guild, Am. Soc. Journalists and Authors. Home: PO Box 331235 Corpus Christi TX 78463 Office: Breecher Enterprises 1719 Third St Ste 1 Corpus Christi TX 78464 Home Phone: 361-299-5648. Office Fax: 206-984-2763; Home Fax: 206-984-2763. Personal E-mail: bookwriter@nasw.org. E-mail: drbreecher@diabetesreviews.com.

BREED, ALLEN FORBES, social services administrator; b. Wisconsin Rapids, Wis., Oct. 1, 1920; s. Noel Jerub and May Belle (Forbes) B.; m. Virginia Mae Plaskett, June 24, 1945; children: Marla, Eleanor, Carol. BA cum laude, U. Pacific, 1942. With Dept. Youth Authority, Calif., 1945-76, supt. correctional schs., 1947-65, chief div. instns., 1965-67; chmn. Youth Authority Bd., Calif., 1967-76; dir. Dept. Youth Authority, Calif., 1967-76; vis. fellow Dept. Justice, 1976-77; spl. master U.S. Dist. Ct., RI, 1977-78; dir. Nat. Inst. Corrections, Dept. Justice, Washington, 1978-83; chmn. bd. Nat. Council Crime and Delinquency, Washington, 1983-91, 98-99; spl. master to fed. and state cts. on prison litigation issues, 1983—. Chmn. Task Force on Corrections and mem. Joint Commn. on Juvenile Justice Standards, ABA and Inst. Judicial Adminstrn.; mem. nat. adv. com. on Juvenile Justice and Delinquency Prevention; mem. U.S. del. UN Congress on Prevention of Crime and Treatment of Offenders, Caracas, Venezuela, 1980; mem. UN Congress on Prevention Crime and Treatment of Offenders, Milan, Italy, 1985; del. Internat. Conf. on Criminology, Hamburg, Federal Republic of Germany, 1988, Internat. Conf. on Future of Corrections, Ottawa, Can., 1991—; leader del. on juvenile justice to Russia, 1989—; lectr. 1st Sino-Am. Criminal Justice Inst., People's Republic China, 1986; criminal and juvenile justice del. People's Republic China, 1992; del. Internat. Conf. Corrections, Warsaw, 1993. Contbr. articles to profl. jours., newspapers, mags. Mem. justice programs adv. com. Edna McConnel Clark Found., 1983-89; chmn. Calaveras County Libr. Commn., 2000—; mem. Calaveras County Juvenile Justice Commn., 2002-, past chair; mem. Calaveras Cmty. Found., 2004—; mem. Am. Justice Inst., 2000—; mem. Calaveras County Delinquency Prevention Comm., past chair; bd. dir. Calaveras Cmty. Found.; v.p. Am. Justice Inst.; mem. Calaveras County Libr. Comm. Served to maj. USMC, 1942-45. Decorated Purple Heart. Mem. Nat. Assn. State Correctional Adminstrs. (state and nat. awards), Nat. Assn. State Juvenile Delinquency Program Adminstrs. (past pres.), Interstate Compact on Probation and Parole (past pres.), Am. Correctional Assn. (v.p. 1984-86, bd. govs. 1986-91), Am. Arbitration Assn., Nat. Coun. Crime and Delinquency (chmn. emeritus bd. dirs.), Calif. Probation, Parole and Correctional Assn. Episcopalian. Home: PO Box 698 San Andreas CA 95249-0698

BREEDEN, DOUGLAS TOWER, finance educator, consultant, former dean; b. Leavenworth, Ind., Sept. 29, 1950; s. Russell E. and Annabelle (Tower) B.; m. Josie Chao-Chih Pian, June 4, 1972; children: Jennifer, Laurel, Mark, David. BS in mgmt. sci., MIT, 1972; postgrad., Harvard U., 1973—74; MA in econs., Stanford U., 1976, PhD in fin., 1978. Asst. prof. fin. U. Chgo., 1978—79, Stanford U., 1979—81, assoc. prof. fin., 1981—85; vis. assoc. prof. fin. Yale U., 1981—82, Sloan Sch. Mgmt., MIT, 1984-85; area coord. for fin. and econs. Fuqua Sch. Bus., Duke U., Durham, NC, 1985—86, 1987—88, assoc. prof. fin., 1985—89, co-dir. Futures and Options Rsch. Ctr., 1987-90, prof. fin. Durham, NC, 1989—91, rsch. prof. fin., 1991—99, dean, 2001—07, William W. Priest prof. fin., 2001—; vis. prof. fin. Kenan Flagler Bus. Sch., U. NC, Chapel Hill, 2000, Dalton McMichael Prof. Fin., 2000-01; co-founder Smith Breeden Assocs., Chapel Hill, NC, 1982—, chmn. bd., 1982—2005, chmn. emeritus, 2005—, pres., 1988-2000; chmn. bd. Smith Breeden Mut. Funds, 1992-2000; chmn. bd., prin. shareholder Harrington Fin. Group, 1988—2001. Chmn., owner Wyandotte Cmty. Corp., 1989—; co-owner, Old Capital Golf Course, Corydon, IN, 1998-; chmn. bd., prin. shareholder, Cmty. First Fin. Group, 1986-; cons. Chgo. Bd. Trade, 1977-82; exec. tchr. Nomura Sch. Adv. Mgmt., Tokyo, 1987, 89-92. Editor Jour. Fixed Income, 1990-2001; assoc. editor Jour. of Fin., 1988-91, Rev. of Fin. Studies, 1987-89, Jour. Fin. Quantitative Analysis, 1985-87, Jour. Fin. Econs., 1982-88, Jour. Money, Credit and Banking, 1980-83; contbr. articles to profl. jours. Bd. dirs. Chapel Hill-Carrboro City Schs., 1989-93, Chapel Hill-Carrboro Pub Sch. Found., 1987-89; chmn. Breeden Family Found., 1989—; bd. dirs. Fund for Human Possibilities, 1995—; bd. visitors Fuqua Sch. Bus., Duke U., 1995-99; mem. deans adv. coun. Sloan Sch. Mgmt., MIT, 1999—, mem. vis. com., 1999—, mem. Pres. adv. com., 2000-01; donor Smith Breden prize Jour. of Fin., 1989—. Rotary Internat. Grad. Fellow in Bus., 1972-73, Batterymarch Fin. Mgmt. Fellow, 1981-82, Dean Witter Fellow in Fin., 1981-82. Mem. Am. Fin. Assn. (bd. dirs. 1988-91), Western Fin. Assn., Applied Capital Markets Group of Nat. Bur. Econ. Rsch. Methodist. Avocations: golf, skiing, basketball. Office: Duke U Fuqua Sch Bus One Towerview Dr Box 90120 Durham NC 27708-0120*

BREEDEN, MIMI, bank executive; B in English and French, Fla. State U.; MBA, Ga. State U. Analyst R & D dept. SunTrust Banks, Inc., mgr. Ga. In-Store Banking unit, with retirement svcs. area of instl. trust, 2001, mgr. instl. trust, 2002—05, mgr. pvt. wealth mgmt. line of bus., 2005—06, corp. exec. v.p., dir. human resources, mem. mgmt. com., 2006—. Office: SunTrust Banks Inc PO Box 4418 Atlanta GA 30302-4418 Office Phone: 404-588-7711. Office Fax: 404-827-6173.

BREEDEN, RICHARD C., investment company executive, former federal agency administrator; b. Dec. 6, 1949; m. Holly Breeden; 3 children. BS, Stanford U., 1972; JD, Harvard U., 1975. Law tchr., 1975-76; ptnr. Cravath, Swaine & Moore LLP, NYC, 1976-81; exec. asst. to under sec. US Dept. Labor, 1981-82; exec. dir. White House Regulatory Task Force; dep.counsel to v.p. The White House, Washington, 1982—85; ptnr. Baker & Botts LLP, Houston, 1985-89; chmn. SEC, Washington, 1989—93; chmn. internat. fin. services Coopers & Lybrand, LLC, 1993—96; chmn. Richard C. Breeden & Co., Greenwich, Conn., 1996—; corp. monitor WorldCom, Inc., 2002; founder, CEO Breeden Capital Mgmt., Greenwich, Conn., 2006—; mng. ptnr., chief investment officer Breeden Partners, Greenwich, Conn., 2006—. Bd. dirs. BBVA. Contbr. articles to profl. jours. Named one of 100 Most Influential Lawyers, Nat. Law Jour., 2006. Office Phone: 203-618-0065. Business E-Mail: rcb@breedenco.com.

BREEDIN, BERRYMAN BRENT, journalist, consultant, historian, public relations executive; b. Beaufort, SC, Nov. 3, 1925; s. Berryman Brent Breedin and Jane Cunningham Dixon; m. Allain Crenshaw, Sept. 1959 (div. Jan. 1978); children: David Singleton, Sarah Breedin Chase, Amelia Breedin Twargowski; m. Catherine McCuen Muller, Sept. 2006. BA, Washington and Lee U., 1947. Reporter Caller-Times, Corpus Christi, Tex., 1947-48; sports editor, columnist Daily Mail, Anderson, SC, 1949-52; publicist, editor Clemson U., SC, 1952-55, 64-66; resident mgr. Hunt Internat. Oil Co., Pakistan, 1955—58, Hunt Energy and Mineral Co. Australia, 1996—97; press sec. U.S. Senator Strom Thurmond, Washington, 1958-59; info. specialist DuPont Co., Wilmington, Del., 1960-63; editor Am. Coll. Pub. Rels. Assn., Washington, 1966-71, Coun. Libr. Resources, Washington, 1972-75; dir. pub. rels. Georgetown U., Washington, 1977-79, Rice U., Houston, 1981-87; pvt. practice Columbia, SC, 1988—; historian White House Weekly, Washington, 1998—2003. Adv. Washington D.C. Libr., 1972-76, Houston Zoo, 1981-87. Founding mem. Capital Hill Montessori, Washington, 1964, Field Sch., Washington, 1972. With USN, 1944-45. Mem. Nat. Press Club, Sigma Delta Chi. Episcopalian. Avocations: sports history, movie history. Home and Office: 1829 Senate St Apt 18-B Columbia SC 29201-3837 Home Phone: 803-771-7832; Office Phone: 803-237-9410. Personal E-mail: bbreedin@bellsouth.net.

BREEDLOVE, JAMES (JIM BREEDLOVE), lawyer; b. Danville, Va. BA, Harvard, 1972; JD, Harvard Law Sch., 1975. Bar: Mass., DC, NY. With Davis Polk & Wardell Law, NYC, 1975—78; corp. gov., fin. atty. Phillip Morris Cos., Inc., 1978—90; asst. to atty. gen. US Dept. Justice, Wash., DC, 1990—92; v.p., chief gen. coun. GE Electrical Corp., 1992—94, sr. v.p., gen. coun., corp. sec., 1994—2004; v.p., gen. counsel, corp. sec. Praxair, 2004—, now sr. v.p., 2006—. Mem.: ABA. Office: Praxair 39 Old Ridgebury Rd Danbury CT 06810-5113

BREEN, EDWARD DEVEAUX, manufacturing executive; b. Mar. 14, 1956; married; 3 children. BS in Bus. Adminstrn. and Econs., Grove City Coll. With Gen. Instrument, 1978—88, sr. v.p. sales terrestrial products worldwide sales orgn., 1988—94, exec. v.p. terrestrial sys., 1994—96, sr. v.p. sales Broadband Networks Group, 1996—97, chmn., pres., CEO, 1997—2000; exec. v.p., pres. broadband comms. sector Motorola, 2000—01, exec. v.p., pres. networks sector, 2001—02, pres., COO Schaumburg, Ill., 2002, also bd. dirs.; chmn., CEO Tyco Internat., Portsmouth, NH, 2002—. Bd. dirs. McLeod USA Inc., Tyco Internat. Ltd. Named one of Top 15 CableFAX Mag.'s 100 most influential people in cable, 1999; recipient Vanguard award, Nat. Cable TV Assn., 1998. Office: Tyco Intl 273 Corporate Dr 100 Portsmouth NH 03801-6807

BREEN, JOHN EDWARD, civil engineer, educator; b. Buffalo, May 1, 1932; s. Timothy J. and Alice C. (Keenan) B.; m. Marian T. Killian, June 20, 1953; children: Mary L., Michael T., Dennis P., Sheila A., Sean E., Kerry T., Christopher D. B.C.E., Marquette U., Milw., 1953; DSc (hon.), Marquette U., 2004; MS in Civil Engring., U. Mo., 1957; PhD, U. Tex., Austin, 1962. Registered profl. engr., Tex., Mo. Structural designer Harnischfeger Corp., Milw., 1952-53; asst. prof. U. Mo., Columbia, 1957-59; mem. faculty U. Tex., Austin, 1959—, prof. civil engring., 1969—, J.J. McKetta prof. engring., 1977-81, Carol Cockrell Curran chair engring., 1981-84, Nasser I. Al-Rashid chair civil engring., 1984—; dir. P.M. Ferguson Structural Engring. Lab., Balcones Research Center, 1967-85. Cons. in field. Contbr. articles to profl. jours. Served to lt. USNR, 1953-56. Recipient Tchg. Excellence award Gen. Dynamics Corp., 1971, Tchg. Excellence award U. Tex. Student Assn., 1963, Teaching Excellence award Std. Oil Found. Ind., 1968, Fedn. Internat. Precontrainte medal, 1990, Internat. award of merit in structural engring. Internat. Assn. Bridge and Structural Engring., 2000, Freyssinet medal Internat. Assn. for Structural Concrete, 2002, Caquot medal French Assn. Civil Engring., 2004, John A. Roebling medal Engrs. Soc. Western Pa., 2005. Mem.: ASCE (T.Y. Lin medal 1985, 1989, 1991, A.J. Boase Reinforced Concrete Rsch. Coun. award 1987, Croes medal 1999), Swiss Acad. Engring., Nat. Acad. Engring., Am. Concrete Inst. (hon.; bd. dirs. 1974—77, Wason medal 1972, 1983, Raymond C. Reese Rsch. medal 1972, 1979, Kelly medal 1981, Anderson medal 1987, Raymond Davis lectr. 1978, Bloem award 1989, Alfred E. Lindau award 1994, Structural Engring. award 2002), Austin Yacht Club (commodore 1977), Sigma Xi. Democrat. Roman Catholic. Home: 8603 Azalea Trl Austin TX 78759-7501 Office: Univ Tex Ferguson Lab 10100 Burnet Rd PRC Bldg 177 Austin TX 78758-4445 Office Phone: 512-471-4578. Business E-Mail: jbreen@mail.utexas.edu.

BREEN, KATHERINE ANNE, speech and language pathologist; b. Chgo., Oct. 31, 1948; d. Robert Stephen and Gertrude Catherine (Bader) Breen. BS, Northwestern U., 1970; MA, U. Mo., Columbia, 1971. Cert. speech pathologist. Speech/lang. pathologist Fulton (Mo.) Pub. Schs., 1971-73; co-dir. Easter Seal Speech Clinic, Jefferson City, Mo., summer 1972, 73; speech/lang. pathologist Shawnee Mission (Kans.) Pub. Schs., 1973-96; staff St. Joseph's Hosp., Kansas City, Mo., 1978-81, Midwest Rehab. Ctr., Kansas City, 1985; pvt. practice speech therapy Deborah A. King & Assocs., 2003—. Cons. East Ctrl. Mo. Mental Health Center; guest lectr. Fontbonne Coll., St. Louis. Vol., Mid Am. Rehab. Hosp. Mem. NEA, Am. Speech and Hearing Assn., Kans. Speech and Hearing Assn., Mo. State Tchrs. Assn., Kansas City Alumni Assn. of Northwestern U. (dir. alumni admissions coun., Outstanding Leadership award 1981, Svc. award 1991), Friends of Art Nelson/Atkins Art Gallery and Mus. (vol.), Nat. Trust Historic Preservation, Kansas City Hist. Found., Zeta Phi Eta. Methodist. Home: 8318 Mackey St Shawnee Mission KS 66212-2728

BREEN, KENNETH MICHAEL, lawyer, former prosecutor; b. Buffalo, Dec. 15, 1966; BA cum laude, Boston Coll., 1989, JD, 1992. Bar: NY, U.S. Dist. Ct. NY (ea. and so. dist.), U.S. Ct. Appeals (2d cir.). Prosecutor US Dept. Justice, Washington, 1995—99, asst. US atty. criminal divsn. (Ea. dist.) NY, 1999—2003, dep. chief bus. and securities fraud sect., 2003—05; ptnr. Fulbright & Jaworski, LLP, NYC, 2005—07, Paul, Hastings, Janofsky & Walker LLP, NYC, 2007—. Coord. capital markets unit Terrorist Financing Task Force, Washington, 2001; spkr. in field. Recipient Svc. award, US Secret Svc., 1997, Outstanding Atty. award, US Dept. Justice Tax Divsn., 1997, Svc. award, IRS Criminal Investigations Divsn., 1997, FBI, 2000, 2003, 2005, NY Police Dept. Detectives Endowment Assn., 2000, FDA Office of Criminal Investigations, 2000, Honorary award, Recording Industry Assn. Am., 2002, Svc. award, US Postal Inspection Svc., 2005. Mem.: ABA, Nat. Assn. Criminal Def. Lawyers, Nat. Bar Coun. Office: Paul Hastings Janofsky & Walker LLP Park Ave Tower 75 E 55th St 1st Fl New York NY 10022 Office Phone: 212-318-3000. Office Fax: 212-318-3400. E-mail: kennethbreen@paulhastings.com.

BREEN, RICHARD F., JR., law librarian, educator; b. Providence, Aug. 1, 1940; s. Richard F. and Elizabeth (Hurlin) B.; children: Stephanie, Jonathan. AB in Econs., Dartmouth Coll., 1962; LLB, U. Maine, Portland, 1967; MLS, U. Oreg., 1973. Bar: Maine, N.H. Asst. dean U. Maine Sch. Law, Portland, 1967-70; with firm Tesreau and Gardner, Lebanon, NH, 1970-72; assoc. law libr., assoc. prof. law U. Maine Sch. Law, Portland, 1974-76; law libr., assoc. prof. law Willamette U. Coll. Law, Salem, Oreg., 1976-80, law libr., prof. law, 1980—, interim adminstrv. dean., law libr., 1986-87. Legal specialist to Albania for ABA Ctrl. and East European Law Initiative, 1995. Mem. U.S. Olympic Biathlon Tng. Team, 1963. Capt. USAR, 1962—64. Mem. Am. Assn. Law Librs., Casque and Gauntlet Sr. Soc. Democrat. Congregationalist. Avocations: cross country skiing, hiking. Office: Willamette U Law Libr 245 Winter St SE Salem OR 97301-3916 Office Phone: 503-370-6386. Business E-Mail: dbreen@willamette.edu.

BREEN, STEPHEN P., editorial cartoonist; b. LA, 1970; m. Cathy Breen; 2 children. Grad., U. Calif., Riverside, 1992. Editl. cartoonist Asbury Park Press, Neptune, NJ, 1994—2001, San Diego Union-Tribune, 2001—. Caricatures, Sunday Celebs page, comic strip, Grand Avenue, hundreds of newspapers and nat. mags. Copley News Svc. Recipient John Locher Meml. award, Assn. Am. Editl. Cartoonists, Charles M. Schulz award, Scripps Howard, Pulitzer prize, 1998, hon. mention, best cartoons on internat. affairs., Overseas Press Club. Office: San Diego Union-Tribune 350 Camino de la Reina92 PO Box 120191 San Diego CA 92112-0191

BREES, DREW (DREW CHRISTOPHER BREES), professional football player; b. Austin, Tex., Jan. 15, 1979; s. Chip Brees; m. Brittany Brees. BA in Indsl. Mgmt. & Mfg., Purdue U., West Lafayette, Ind., 2001. Quarterback San Diego Chargers, 2001—06, New Orleans Saints, 2006—. Co-founder Brees Dream Found. Named Big Ten Player of Yr., 1998, 2000,

NFL Comeback Player of Yr., AP, 2004, Sports Illus., 2004, Dallas Morning News, 2004, Most Improved Player of Yr., Pro Football Weekly, 2004, Pro Football Writers of Am., 2004, CBSSportsline.com, 2004, FoxSports.com, 2004; named to NFL Pro-Bowl Team, 2004, NFC Pro Bowl Team, NFL, 2007, NFL All Pro Team, 2007; recipient Maxwell award, 2000, Socrates award. Mem.: Sigma Chi. Office: New Orleans Saints 58 Airline Dr Metairie LA 70003*

BREESKIN, MICHAEL WAYNE, lawyer; b. Washington, Dec. 25, 1947; s. Nathan and Sylvia (Raine) B.; m. Frances Cox Lively, May 29, 1982; children: Molly Louise, Laura Rose. BA cum laude, U. Pitts., 1969; JD, Georgetown U., Washington, DC, 1975. Bar: DC 1975, Colo. 1983, US Dist. Ct. DC 1977, US Dist. Ct. Colo. 1983, US Ct. Appeals (DC cir.) 1978, US Ct. Appeals (10th cir.) 1984, US Supreme Ct. 1995. Mng. atty. Tobin & Covey, Washington, 1977-79; assoc. Donald M. Murtha & Assocs., Washington, 1979-80; counsel NLRB Office Rep. Appeals, Washington, 1980-83; trial atty. NLRB Denver Regional Office, 1983-88; assoc. Wherry & Wherry, Denver, 1989-91; sr. atty. The Legal Ctr. for People with Disabilities and Older People (formerly The Legal Ctr. Serving Persons with Disabilities), Denver, 1991—98; gen. counsel Assn. Cmty. Living Boulder County, Inc. (formerly the Assn. for Retarded Citizens in Boulder County, Inc.), 1998—2000; counsel Fox & Robertson, PC, Denver, 2000—02, Arc of Denver, Inc., 2002—. Presenter, lectr. in field. Adv. com. Domestic Violence Initiative for Women with Disabilities, 1997—. Recipient Outstanding Work for People with Disabilities acknowledgement Very Spl. Arts Colo., 1996; named Profl. of Yr., The Arc of Adams County, 1997; recipient Adv. of the Year award Assn. Cmty. Living in Boulder County Inc., 1996, Schenkein award Arc of Denver, Inc., 1997, award Disability Ctr. Ind. Living and Colo. Cross-Disability Coalition, 1999, Colo. Cross-Disability Coalition Meml. award for Civil Rights Legal Advocacy, 2000. Mem. ABA, Colo. Bar Assn. (disability law sect.), Colo. Coun. Spl. Edn. Lawyers, Arapahoe County Bar Assn., Disability Rights Roundtable. Avocations: bicycling, skiing, reading. Office: Arc of Denver 1905 Sherman St Ste 300 Denver CO 80203 Office Phone: 303-831-7733. Business E-Mail: mbreeskin@arcofdenver.org.

BREEZE, WILLIAM HANCOCK, academic administrator; b. Cin., Nov. 25, 1923; s. William T. and Nancy (Hancock) B.; m. JoAnne Robertson Watson, Oct. 8, 1949 (dec. Jan. 1983); 1 child, Nancy Louise Breeze; m. Barbara L. Hall, Dec. 15, 1990. Student, Berea Coll., 1943-44; AB, Centre Coll., Danville, Ky., 1945; MA, U. Ky., 1948. Various actuarial positions Ohio Nat. Life Ins. Co., Cin., 1948-56, actuary, 1956-65, asst. to pres., 1965-67, sr. v.p., 1967-72, exec. v.p., 1972-86; v.p., gen. sec. Centre Coll., Danville, Ky., 1987-88, 89-91, acting pres., 1988-89, spl. asst. to pres. for endowment, 1991—. Bd. dirs. Ohio Nat. Life Ins. Co., 1966-88. Bd. dirs. Jr. Achievement Greater Cin., 1974-84; trustee Centre Coll., 1980-86. Served to lt. (j.g.) USNR, 1943-46, PTO. Fellow: Soc. Actuaries. Republican. Presbyterian. Avocations: reading, classical music. Home: 468 W Broadway St Danville KY 40422-1420 Office: Centre Coll Danville KY 40422 Home Phone: 859-236-1816; Office Phone: 859-238-5207. Business E-Mail: breeze@centre.edu.

BREGA, CHARLES FRANKLIN, lawyer, director; b. Callaway, Nebr., Feb. 5, 1933; s. Richard E. and Bessie (King) B.; m. Betty Jean Witherspoon, Sept. 17, 1960; children: Kerry E., Charles D., Angie G. BA, The Citadel, 1954; LLB, U. Colo., 1960. Bar: Colo. 1960. Assoc. firm Hindry & Meyer, Denver, 1960-62, partner, 1962-75, dir., 1975; dir. firm Roath & Brega, Denver, 1975-89, Brega & Winters, Denver, 1989—2003, Lindquist & Vennum PLLP, Denver, 2004—. Lectr. in field; guest prof. U. Colo., U. Denver, U. Nev., others. Trustee Pres.'s Leadership Class, U. Colo., 1977—. Served with USAF, 1954-57. Named Colo. Super Lawyer, 2005—; named one of Best Lawyers in Am., Best Lawyers in Colo. Mem. Colo. Trial Lawyers Assn. (pres. 1972-73), Assn. Trial Lawyers Am. (gov. 1972-79), ABA, Am. Law Inst., Am. Bd. Trial Advs., Internat. Acad. Trial Lawyers, Internat. Soc. Barristers, Cherry Hills Country Club, Denver Athletic Club. Episcopalian. Home: 4501 S Vine Way Englewood CO 80110-6027 Office: Lindquist & Vennum PLLP 600 17th St Ste 1800s Denver CO 80202-5441 Home Phone: 303-761-2077; Office Phone: 303-454-0525. Business E-Mail: cbrega@lindquist.com.

BREGA, KERRY ELIZABETH, physician, researcher; b. Denver, Sept. 8, 1961; d. Charles Franklin and Betty Jean Brega. BA, U. Colo., 1983, MD, 1989. Diplomate Am. Bd. Spine Surgery, Am. Bd. Neurol. Surgery. Resident in neurosurgery U. Colo., Denver, 1990-95, asst. prof. neurosurgery, 1995—; dir. neurosurgery Littleton Adventist Hosp., Denver, 1998—; asst. prof. neurosurgery U. Colo., Denver, 1995—2005, assoc. prof. neurosurgery, med. dir. Stroke Ctr., 2006—, assoc. dir. neurosurg. residency tng. program, 2006—. Bd. dirs. Donor Alliance, Denver, 1994—. Mem. Am. Coll. Spine Surgery, Am. Assn. Neurol. Surgeons, Congress Neurol. Surgeons, Colo. Neurol. Soc., Alpha Omega Alpha. Office: 4200 @ 9th Ave Denver CO 80262 Office Phone: 303-315-1429.

BREGE, DORANCE CHARLES, biologist; b. Alpena, Mich., Nov. 20, 1946; s. Alfred Charles and Effie M. (Claus) Brege; m. Donna L. Hupp, Jan. 17, 1976; children: Paul, Robert, Matthew. BS, Mich. State U., East Lansing, 1968, MS, 1969. Fishery tech. Mich. Dept. Nat. Rsch., Gaylord, 1968—72, US Fish & Wildlife Svc., Marquette, Mich., 1973—76, fishery biologist Olympia, Wash., 1976—78, Marquette, Mich., 1979—82, Ludington, Mich., 1983—86, Marquette, 1987—. Control unit task force Great Lakes Fishery Comm., Ann Arbor, Mich., 1996—2007. Author: Reduction of the Lampricide, TFM, in the Great Lakes, 2003. Trustee, head trustee Redeemer Luth. Ch., Marquette, 1998—2005. Sgt. US Army, 1969—71, Korea. Recipient Vernon Applegate award, Great Lakes Fishery Comm., 2002. Mem.: Am. Fishery Soc. (rivers & streams com. 2004—07). Avocation: fishing. Home: 1108 Cleve Marquette MI 49855 Office: US Fish and Wildlife Svc 3090 Wright Marquette MI 49855 Business E-Mail: dorance-brege@fws.gov.

BREGLIO, JOHN F., lawyer; b. NYC, June 5, 1946; s. John N. and Sylvia V. (Calucci) B.; m. Nan K. Proctor, May 22, 1976; children: Eliza Mason, Nola Breglio Heller. BA, Yale U., 1968; JD, Harvard U., 1971. Bar: N.Y. 1972, U.S. Dist. Ct. (ea. and so. dists.) 1974, U.S. Ct. Appeals (2d cir.) 1975, U.S. Ct. Appeals (D.C. cir.) 1982. Ptnr. Paul, Weiss, Rifkind, Wharton & Garrison, NYC, 1971—, chair, Entertainment Dept. Adj. prof. Sch. of Arts, Columbia U.; chmn., lectr. on entertainment industry N.Y. Law Jour. Seminars, NYC, 1984—88, Practising Law Inst. Bd. dirs. Acting Co., NYC, 1982-92, Golden Fund, NYC, 1989—, Alliance for Arts, Inc., 1989—, Am. Found. for AIDS Rsch., NYC, 1994—, Young Playwrights Inc., 1995—; chmn. bd. Theater Devel. Fund, NYC, 1982-2005; mem. adv. com. Theatre Collection Coun., Mus. of City NY. Mem. ABA, NY State Bar Assn., Assn. of Bar of City of NY, Am. Arbitration Assn. (panel arbitrators), The Century Assn. (NYC), Yale Club (NYC), Phelps Assn. (New Haven), League of Am. Theatres and Producers. Home: 1120 5th Ave New York NY 10128-0144 also: 41 School House Rd Waccabuc NY 10597 also: 52 W Miacomet Rd Nantucket MA 02554-4369 Office: Paul Weiss Rifkind Wharton & Garrison LLP 1285 Avenue Of The Americas New York NY 10019-6064 Office Phone: 212-373-3391. Business E-Mail: jbreglio@paulweiss.com.

BREGMAN, ARTHUR RANDOLPH, lawyer, educator; b. Phila., Dec. 9, 1946; s. Nathan and Stella (Husock) B.; m. Patrice Rosalie Gancie, May 30, 1980. BA, Columbia U., 1968; MA, Yale U., 1969; JD, Georgetown U., 1985. Bar: DC 1985, US Ct. Appeals (DC cir.) 1985, US Dist. Ct. DC 1985, US Claims Ct. 1985. Treas. Nat. Coun. for Soviet and E. European Rsch., Washington, 1981-83; law clk. Washington Lawyers' Com. for Civil Rights, 1983-84; assoc. Klores, Feldesman and Tucker, Washington, 1985-86; dir. Soviet and E. European Svcs. APCO, Washington, 1988-91; of counsel Steptoe & Johnson, Washington, Moscow, 1991-92, ptnr. Washington and Moscow, 1992-99, Squire, Sanders & Dempsey, Washington, 1999—2003, Salans, Washington, NY, 2003—. Adj. prof. Georgetown U. Law Ctr., Washington, 1986-89; program dir. Internat. Law Inst., Washington, 1986-91; chmn. bd. adv. US-Russia Bus. Law Report, 1990—. Editor: U.S.-Soviet Contract Law, 1987. Recipient Civil Procedure prize Lawyers Coop. Pub. Co., Balt., 1982. Mem. ABA (internat. bar sect.), DC Bar Assn. Home: 3059 Porter St NW Washington DC 20008-3272 Office: 1330 Connecticut Ave NW Washington DC 20036 also: 620 Fifth Ave New York NY 10020 Office Phone: 202-457-8305. Business E-Mail: rbregman@salans.com.

BREGMAN, MARK, information technology executive; BS in Physics, Harvard Coll.; MS in Physics, PhD in Physics, Columbia U. Sr. mgmt. positions IBM Rsch. and IBM Japan, 1984—2000; CEO Airmedia Inc., 2000—01; exec. v.p. product ops. Veritas Software Corp., Mountain View, Calif., 2002—04, chief tech. officer, 2004, acting mgr., application and svc. mgmt. group, 2004; chief tech. officer Symantec Corp., Cupertino, Calif., 2004—06. Bd. overseers Fermi Nat. Accelerator Lab. Mem. vis. com. Harvard U. Lib. Mem.: Am. Physical Soc., IEEE (sr.). Office: Symantec Corp 20330 Stevens Creek Blvd Cupertino CA 95014 Office Phone: 800-327-2232. Office Fax: 650-527-2908.

BREHL, JAMES WILLIAM, lawyer; BS in Engring., U. Notre Dame, 1956; JD, U. Mich., 1959. Bar: Minn. and various fed. cts. Lawyer Maun & Simon, St. Paul, 1963-2000; law practice and mediation/arbitration Nuetral Svcs., 2000—; of counsel Martin & Squires, St. Paul, 2006—. Contbr. articles to law jours. Mem. Minn. Bar Assn. (exec. com. 1996-97), Ramsey County Bar Assn. (exec. coun. 1977-80, 87-90, pres. 1993-94). Home Phone: 651-275-3549; Office Phone: 651-767-3745. Personal E-mail: jdbrehl@aol.com.

BREHM, JOAN M., social sciences educator; b. Burlington, Wis., Nov. 17, 1967; d. Bernard T. and Coletta J. Brehm. BA, U. Minn., Mpls., 1991; MA, U. Mont., Missoula, 1998; PhD, Utah State U., Logan, 2003. Coord. program tng. USDA/Fgn. Agr. Svc., Washington, 1991—96; asst. prof. sociology Ill. State U., Normal, 1996—. Contbr. articles to profl. jours. Sec., operational k-9 handler Ill. Search Dogs Inc., Talulah, Ill., 2003—06; pres. bd. Land Connection, Congerville, 2005—06. Recipient Utah State U. Rsch. Asst. Yr., Coll. Arts and Humanities, Utah State U., 2000—01; grantee, Ill. State U., 2003, 2006; Lowry Nelson fellow, Utah State U., 1999, Joseph and Grace Geddes Rsch. scholar, 2000—02. Mem.: Internat. Assn. Soc. and Natural Resources (coun. mem. 2005—), Rural Sociol. Soc. (Natural Resources Rsch. Group co-chair 2005—06). Avocations: backpacking, bicycling, skiing, gardening, cooking. Office: Illinois State Univ Campus Box 4660 Normal IL 61790-4660 Office Phone: 309-438-7177.

BREHM, LORETTA PERSOHN, retired art educator, librarian, consultant; b. New Orleans, Jan. 31, 1954; d. Edwin Joseph and Loretta (Persohn) B. BA, Nicholls State U., Thibodaux, La., 1975, MEd, 1979, postgrad., 1980. Cert. tchr., La. Substitute tchr. Jefferson Parish Sch. Bd., Gretna, La., 1971-74; tchr. art John Ehret Sch., John Ehret High Sch., Marrero, La., 1974-95; art tchr., libr. Westbank Cathedral Acad., 1995-98; cons. Ventures Edn. Sys., 1998—; pub. rels. rep. Jefferson West Higher Edn. Ctr., 1999—. Trustee, chmn. bd. emeritus Jefferson Parish Coun. on Aging; assessor La. State Dept. Edn., 1997—. Ladies Aux. Westwego Vol. Fire Co.; historian Westwego Bicentennial; vol. Westwego Com. on Aging, Gumbo Festival, Bridge City, La., ARC, Operation Mainstream, others; founding mem. Jefferson Parish Cmty. Arts Commn.; alumni pres., former sch. advisor Jefferson Parish 4-H Clubs; art dir. Knights of King Arthur Mardi Gras Orgn.; libr. asst. Westbank Cathedral Acad.; choir, set designer Holy Guardian Angels Ch.; trustee Jefferson Parish Coun. on Aging, 1993—; bd. dirs. Westwego Hist. Soc., Jefferson Parish Hist. Soc.; commnr. Westwego Law Enforcement Commn., Westwego Zoning Commn., treas. Westwego Tourist Commn.; vice-chmn. Bridge City Cmty. Com. on Aging, chmn., 2007—. Recipient awards from Jefferson Parish Sch. Bd., 1978, Westwego Vol. Fire Co., 1982, 4-H Club, 1983, Am. Automobile Assn. Nat. Sch. Traffic Safety Program, 1987-92, others. Mem. Nat. Art Edn. Assn., La. Art Edn. Assn., Internat. Reading Assn. (chmn. Jefferson Parish coun.), Jefferson Parish Hist. Soc. (charter), New Orleans Mus. Art, La. Children's Mus., Nicholls State U. Alumni Assn., Delta Kappa Gamma (pres. Epsilon State), Kappa Kappa Iota, Phi Delta Kappa. Democrat. Avocations: travel, gardening, social work, freelance art work. Home: 250 Louisiana St Westwego LA 70094-4114

BREHM, SHARON STEPHENS, psychology professor, former academic administrator; b. Roanoke, Va., Apr. 18, 1945; d. John Wallis and Jane Chappel (Phenix) Stephens; m. Jack W. Brehm, Oct. 25, 1968 (div. Dec. 1979) BA, Duke U., 1967, PhD, 1973; MA, Harvard U., 1968. Clin. psychology intern U. Wash. Med. Ctr., Seattle, 1973-74; asst. prof. Va. Poly. Inst. and State U., Blacksburg, 1974-75, U. Kans., Lawrence, 1975-78, assoc. prof., 1978-83, prof. psychology, 1983-90, assoc. dean Coll. Liberal Arts and Scis., 1987-90; prof. psychology, dean Harpur Coll. of Arts and Scis. SUNY, Binghamton, 1990-96; prof. psychology and interpersonal comm., provost Ohio U., Athens, 1996—2001; v.p. acad. affairs Ind. U., 2001—03, sr. advisor to pres., 2004—05; chancellor Ind. U. Bloomington, 2001—03, prof. dept. psychology, 2001—. Vis. prof. U. Mannheim, 1978, Istituto di Psicologia, Rome, 1989; Fulbright sr. rsch. scholar Ecole des Hautes Etudes en Sciences Sociales, Paris, 1981-82; Soc. for Personality and Social Psychology rep. APA's Coun. of Reps., 1995-2000; chair governing bd. Ohio Learning Network, 1998-99 Author: The Application of Social Psychology to Clinical Practice, 1976, (with others) Psychological Reactance: A Theory of Freedom and Control, 1981, Intimate Relationships, 1985, 2d edit., 1992, (with others) Social Psychology, 1990, 4th edit., 1999, also numerous articles, and chpts. Mem. APA (fin. com. 1999-2001, 2002-04, pres. elect, 2005-). Office: Ind U 1101 E 10th St Bloomington IN 47405-7000 Personal E-mail: sbrehm@indiana.edu.

BREHM-HEEGER, PAULA, library director, library association executive; MLS, Ind. U., 1995. Children's services libr. Anderson Pub. Libr., Ind.; youth services libr., asst. br. mgr. Kans. City Pub. Libr.; children's libr. North Ctrl Br. libr.; teen coord. Pub. Libr. Cin. and Hamilton County, Ohio, 2002—. Recipient Pat Beuhler Call to Conf. award, Mo. Libr. Assn., 1998, Econo-clad Outstanding Lit. Prog. award, Assn. Libr. Svc. to Children, 2000. Mem.: Cath. Libr. Assn., Young Adult Action Coun., Ohio Libr. Coun., Young Adult Libr. Services Assn. (pres.-elect 2006—07, pres. 2007—, mem. bd. dirs.). Office: Pub Libr of Cin and Hamilton County 800 Vine St Cincinnati OH 45202-2009 Office Phone: 513-369-6941. Business E-Mail: paulabrehmheeger@fuse.net.*

BREIDEGAM, DELIGHT EDGAR, JR., battery company executive; b. Fleetwood, Pa., Oct. 3, 1926; s. DeLight Daniel and Helen Mamie (Fenstermacher) B.; m. Helen Merkel, Feb. 28, 1948; children: Daniel, Sally. LLD (hon.), Kurtztown U., 1997; attended, Gettysburg Coll., 1944-45; LLD (hon.), Moravian Coll., 1995. Chmn., CEO East Penn Mfg. Co., Inc., Lyon Sta., Pa.; mem. Battery Coun. Internat. Trustee Moravian Coll.; bd. dir. Kutztown U. Served with USAF. Recipient Grow with Berks award Reading Assn. Reators, 1994, Richard J. Caron award of excellence, 1997; named Entrepreneur of Yr., Ea. Pa./Delaware Valley, 1990, Outstanding Bus. Leader Northwood U., 2004; named to Jr. Achievement Hall of Fame, 1994, Moravian Coll. Hall of Fame. Mem. Reading-Berks C. of C. (Bus. Person of Yr. 1984), Moselem Springs Golf Club, Bonita Bay Country Club, Longleff Golf and Country Club, Saucon Valley Country Club, Huguenot Lodge, Shriners, Mason, lifetime mem. BCI Lutheran. Office: East Penn Mfg Co Inc Deka Rd Lyon Station PA 19536 Home: 214 Deysher Rd Fleetwood PA 19522

BREIDENBACH, WARREN CONRAD, plastic surgeon, hand surgeon; b. June 21, 1946; Grad., U. Calgary, Can.; MD, Harvard Med. Sch., 1975. Cert. Plastic Surgery, Hand Surgery. Postgraduate tng. in plastic surgery McGill U., Montreal; microsurgery fellow Eastern Vir. Med. Sch., Norfolk; Christine M. Kleinert hand fellow; ptnr. Kleinert, Kutz and Associates Hand Care Ctr., PLLC; asst. clin. prof. surgery (plastic and reconstructive) U. Louisville. Author of several articles. Recipient Clin. Rsch. Scholarship award, Am. Soc. Plastic Surgery and Reconstructive Surgery, Senior award. Mem.: Am. Soc. for Peripheral Nerve (sec.), Am. Soc. for Surgery of the Hand. Achievements include being appointed the first hand scholar with the Louisville Institute for Hand and Microsurgery; being the lead surgeon in all three successful hand transplant surgeries that took place in the US in 1999, 2001 and 2006. Office: Kleinert Kutz and Associates Hand Care Ctr PLLC Ste 700 225 Abraham Flxner Way Louisville KY 40202 Office Phone: 502-561-4263.*

BREIGER, RONALD LOUIS, social sciences educator; b. NYC, Mar. 19, 1948; s. Lazarus H. and Lillian E. (Berman) Breiger; m. Linda Ruth Waugh, May 20, 1984; 1 child, David Luis Waugh-Breiger. AB, Brandeis U., 1966—70; PhD, Harvard U., 1970—75. Asst. prof. of sociology Harvard U., 1975—79, assoc. prof. of sociology, 1979—81; prof. of sociology Cornell U., Ithaca, 1981—95, dept. chmn., 1988—93, Goldwin Smith prof. sociology, 1995—2000; prof. of sociology U. of Ariz., 2000—. Vis. prof. U. of Lille-1, France, 2002. Editor: (jour.) Social Networks, 1998—2006; author: (collected works) Explorations in Structural Sociology (Harvard Studies in Sociology series); chair (symposium) Nat. Acad. Scis. workshop on Dynamic Network Models and Analysis. Fellow Ctr. for Advanced Study in the Behavioral Scis., 1985—86. Mem.: Nat. Sci. Found. (mem. sociology panel 1988—90), Sociol. Rsch. Assn., Internat. Network for Social Network Analysis (exec. bd. mem. 2003, mem. exec. bd. 2003—, Simmel award 2005), Am. Sociol. Assn. (exec. com., sect. on math. sociology 2000—02). Office: U Ariz Dept of Sociology Tucson AZ 85721-0027 Office Phone: 520-621-3297.

BREIMAYER, JOSEPH FREDERICK, patent lawyer; b. Belding, Mich., May 4, 1942; s. Ronald and Crystal Helen (Reeves) B.; m. Margaret Anne Murphy, Aug. 26, 1967; children: Kathleen A., Deborah L., Elizabeth L. BEE, U. Detroit, 1965; JD, George Washington U., 1969. Bar: D.C. 1970, N.Y. 1973, Minn. 1975. Cooperative engr. Honeywell Inc, Mpls., 1962-65; patent examiner U.S. Patent and Trademark Office, Washington, 1965-70; patent atty. Eastman Kodak Co., Rochester, NY, 1970-73; sr. patent counsel Medtronic Inc., Mpls., 1973-90; assoc. Fredrikson & Byron, Mpls., 1990-93. Pres. Good Shepherd Home and Sch. Assn., 1984; precinct chmn. Dem. Farmer Labor Party, 1980-82. Mem. Minn. Intellectual Property Law Assn. (treas. 1986). Avocations: boating, skiing, travel. Home: 4700 Circle Down Golden Valley MN 55416-1101 Home Phone: 763-374-9684; Office Phone: 763-528-2831. Personal E-mail: jfbpatent@aol.com.

BREININ, GOODWIN M., physician; b. NYC, Dec. 10, 1918; s. Louis and Mary (Mirsky) B.; m. Rose-Helen Kopelman, June 22, 1947; children: Bartley James, Constance. BS, U. Fla., 1939; A.M., Emory U., 1940, MD, 1943. Diplomate Am. Bd. Ophthalmology (dir., vice chmn., cons.). Intern U.S. Marine Hosp., Stapleton, NY, 1944; resident ophthalmology N.Y. U.-Bellevue Med. Ctr., 1947-51, sr. Heed fellow ophthalmology, 1954, Daniel B. Kirby prof. research ophthalmology, 1957; Daniel B. Kirby prof. ophthalmology Bellevue and U. Hosps., 1959—2007, prof. emeritus, 2007—; chmn. dept. ophthalmology N.Y. U.-Bellevue Med. Ctr., 1959—2000; dir. eye svc. Bellevue and U. Hosps., NYC, 1959—2000; chmn. med. bd. N.Y. U.-Bellevue Med. Ctr., 1975-77. Mem. vision commn. NRC, 1960-65; hon. rsch. assoc. with Sir Andrew Huxley, U. Coll., London, 1966-67; chmn. vision rsch. tng. com. Nat. Insts. Neurol. Diseases and Blindness, 1963-64; chief cons. Manhattan VA Hosp.; cons. Manhattan Eye, Ear and Throat, St. Vincent's, Beth Israel hosps., Lenox Hills Hosp.; surg. gen. USPHS; chmn. Nat. Res. Rev. Com., 1976-77; vis. prof., cons. Hailie Selassie I Univ. Found., Ethiopia, 1972; lectr. Mem. various adv. coms. relating to field, mem. med. adv. bd. Nat. Coun. to Combat Blindness; pres. Council for U.S./USSR Health Exch., 1977; mem. Am. com. Internat. Agy. for Prevention of Blindness, 1980—; pres. 2d Internat. Symposium in Visual Optics, Tucson, 1982; lectr. in field. Author: The Electrophysiology of Extraocular Muscle, 1962; editor: Advances in Diagnostic Visual Optics, 1983; mem. editorial bd. Investigative Ophthalmology, Archives of Ophthalmology; Contbr. articles to profl. jours. Mem. bd. advisors for medicine Emory U., Atlanta; mem. coun. visitors Marine Biol. Labs., Woods Hole, Mass.; mem. vis. com. for drawings and prints Met. Mus. Art, N.Y.C., 2005— Capt. US Army, 1944—46. Named Wright lectr., U. Toronto, 1972, Lloyd lectr., Bklyn. Ophthal. Soc., 1971, May lectr., NY Acad. Medicine, 1974, guest of honor, Australian Coll. Ophthalmologists, 1974, Japanese Congress Neuro-Ophthalmology, 1979, Scobee lectr., 1977; recipient Knapp medal for contbn. ophthalmology, AMA, 1957, Edward Lorenzo Holmes lectr. citation and award for contbns. to med. sci., Inst. Medicine Chgo., 1959, Gifford lectr. and award, Chgo. Ophthal. Soc., 1970, Heed Ophthalmic Found. award, 1968, Emory U. medal, 1993, Disting. Svc. award, NYU Sch. Medicine, 2003. Fellow Am. Acad. Ophthalmology and Otolaryngology (v.p. 1979, Sr. Honor award 1984), ACS, N.Y. Acad. Medicine (sec. sect. ophthalmology 1962-63, chmn. sect. 1967-68); mem. AAAS, AMA (sec. sect. on ophthalmology 1966-69, chmn. 1970-71, Knapp medal, 1957), Rsch. Ophthalmology, Am. Ophthal. Soc. (Gifford award Chgo. chpt. 1970), N.Y. Ophthal. Soc. (pres. 1980), Harvey Soc., Am. Commn. for Optics and Visual Physiology (chmn. 1970—), Am. Orthoptic Coun., Assn. Univ. Profs. Ophthalmology, Pan. Am. Assn. Ophthalmology, Century Assn., Practitioners Club, Charaka Club (N.Y.C.), Sigma Xi, Alpha Omega Alpha. Home: 912 Fifth Ave New York NY 10021-4159 Business E-Mail: gb7@nyu.edu.

BREISACH, ERNST A., historian, educator; b. Schwanberg, Austria, Oct. 8, 1923; came to US, 1953; s. Otto and Maria (Eder) B.; m. Herma E. Pirker, Aug. 2, 1945; children: Nora Sylvia, Eric Ernst. PhD in History, U. Vienna, Austria, 1946; D in Econs., Wirtschafts U., 1950. Prof. Realgymnasium Vienna XIV, Austria, 1946-52; assoc. prof. Olivet Coll., Mich., 1953-57; prof. Western Mich. U., Kalamazoo, 1957-96. Author: Introduction to Modern Existentialism, 1962, Caterina Sforza: A Renaissance Virago, 1967, Renaissance Europe, 1300-1517, 1973, Historiography: Ancient, Medieval, and Modern, 1983, 2d edit., 1994, American Progressive History, 1993, On the Future of History: The Postmodernist Challenge and Its Aftermath, 2003; editor: Classical Rhetoric and Medieval Historiography, 1985. Nat. Found. for Humanities fellow, 1989-90. Mem. Am. Hist. Assn. Home: 1700 Bronson Way Apt 145 Kalamazoo MI 49009-9108 Office: Western Mich U Dept History Kalamazoo MI 49008 Personal E-mail: ebreisach@sbcglobal.net.

BREIT, WILLIAM, economist, educator, writer; b. New Orleans, Feb. 13, 1933; s. Murray and Sylvia (Shor) Breit. BA, U. Tex., 1955, MA, 1956; PhD, Mich. State U., 1961. Asst. prof. La. State U., Baton Rouge, 1961—63, assoc. prof., 1964—65, U. Va., 1965—70, prof., 1970—83; E.M. Stevens disting. prof. econs. emeritus Trinity U., San Antonio, 1983—89, Vernon F. Taylor disting. prof. econs., 1999—2002. Contbr. articles to profl. jours.; author (with others): The Antitrust Penalties, 1976; author: Murder at the Margin, 1978, 1993, The Academic Scribblers, 1982, 1998, The Fatal Equilibrium, 1985, 1986, The Antitrust Casebook, 1982, 1996, A Deadly Indifference, 1998, Lives of the Laureates: Eighteen Nobel

Economists, 2004. Recipient Disting. Alumni award, Mich. State U., 1998, San Antonio Coll., 2006—07, Disting. Achievement award, S.W. Social Sci. Assn., 2002. Mem.: Am. Econ. Assn., So. Econ. Assn. (v.p. 1980—81, pres. 1985—86), Mystery Writers Am., Phi Beta Kappa (book prize 1977). Home: 438 E Hildebrand Ave San Antonio TX 78212-2501 Office: Trinity Univ 1 Trinity Pl San Antonio TX 78212-7200

BREITBARTH, S. ROBERT, manufacturing executive; b. Newark, July 15, 1925; s. Jacob and Rose (Brandman) B.; m. Laurel Patricia Stroh, Oct. 30, 1949 (dec. Jan. 1998); children: Meredith Jane, Jill Gretchen. BEE, Cornell U., 1949. V.p. Gen. Cable Corp., Greenwich, Conn., 1966-77, exec. v.p., 1976-78; pres. Gen. Cable Internat., Inc., 1978-85, also bd. dirs.; v.p. GK Technologies, Inc., 1979-82. Cons. UN Centre on Transnat. Corps., 1989-90. Treas. Stony Point Assn., Westport, Conn., 1973-75, pres., 1975-76, 87-88. Served with USAAF, 1944-46. Decorated Venezuela-Orden al Merito en el Trabajo Primera Clase, govt. Venezuela. Mem. IEEE, Spain-U.S. C. of C. (bd. dirs.), Wire Assn., Cornell Soc. Engrs., Cornell Club of N.Y. Home: 2 Stony Point Rd Westport CT 06880-5921 Personal E-mail: r.breitbarth@sbcglobal.net.

BREITENBACH, MARY LOUISE MCGRAW, psychologist, chemical dependency counselor; b. Pitts., Sept. 26, 1936; d. David Evans McGraw and Louise (Schoch) Neel; m. John Edgar Breitenbach, Apr. 15, 1960 (dec. 1963); m. Joseph George Piccoli III, Aug. 15, 1987; children: Cary Plumer Frye and Douglas Plumer (twins), Kirstin Amethyst Gretchen Leticia Piccoli. Postgrad., Oreg. State Coll., 1960-61; BA, Russell Sage Coll., Troy, NY, 1958; MEd, Harvard U., Cambridge, Mass., 1983. Lic. profl. counselor, chem. dependency specialist, Wyo.; cert. addiction specialist, level III; cert. addiction counselor II, master addiction counselor. Paraprofl. psychologist St. John's Episc. Ch., Jackson, Wyo., 1963—94; pvt. practice Wilson, Wyo., 1983—. Counselor Curran/Seeley Found. Addiction Svcs., Jackson, 1989-91, Van Vleck House/Tri-County Group Home, Jackson, 1986-89, others; provider multiple employee assistance programs local and nat. cos.; adv. com. Learning Ctr., 1997—. Trustee Teton Sci. Sch., Kelly, Wyo, 1960-76; pres. bd. govs. Teton County Mus., 1989-91, Jackson; vestry mem. St. John's Ch., Jackson. Mem.: APA, LWV, Wyo. Psychol. Assn., Wyo. Assn. Counseling and Devel., Wyo. Assn. Addiction Specialists, Nat. Assn. Alcohol and Drug Addiction Counselors. Democrat. Episcopalian. Avocations: horseback riding, reading, gardening. Home and Office: 3625 N Cheney Ln Wilson WY 83014 Office Phone: 307-733-0310.

BREITENFELD, FREDERICK, JR., retired educational consultant, broadcast executive; b. NYC, Sept. 26, 1931; s. Frederick and Dorothy (Falk) B.; m. Mary Ellen Fitzgerald, Dec. 27, 1954 (dec. 1998); children: Ann Clark, Kathleen Ellen. BS in Engring., Tufts U., 1953, MEd, 1954; MS in TV-Radio, Syracuse U., 1960, PhD, 1963; LHD (hon.), U. Md., 1976, Salisbury State Coll., 1982, Phila. Coll. Textiles and Sci., 1987, Wesley Coll., 1992. Tchr. physics and chemistry pub. H.S., North Creek, NY, 1958-59; program adminstr. U. Coll., Syracuse U., 1960-61; asst. dean Syracuse U., 1961-63; resident cons. in comm. U.S. Air Force, Cape Canaveral, Fla., 1963-64; rsch. project dir. Nat. Assn. Ednl. Broadcasters, Washington, 1964-65, assoc. dir. ednl. TV stas. divsn., 1965-66; exec. dir. Md. Center for Pub. Broadcasting, Owings Mills, Md., 1966-83; CEO, pres. WHYY Inc., 1983-97. Chmn. Ea. Ednl. TV Network, 1974-76; founding chmn. Am. Program Svc., 1991, vice-chmn., 1993; vice-chmn. bd. mgrs. PBS, 1973; cons., lectr. in field; adj. prof. Cath. U. Am., 1967-72, Am. U., 1972-74; vis. prof. Syracuse U., 1976, Johns Hopkins U., 1978-83; charter mem., chmn. Nat. Univ. Consortium for Telecomms. in Tchg. Trustee Thomas Jefferson U., 1988-2006, Valley Forge Mil. Acad. and Coll., 1992-2007, Bucks County C.C., 1994—; bd. dirs. Nat. Bd. Med. Examiners, 1995-99; active Lower Makefield Twp. Zoning Hearing Bd., Bucks County, Pa., 1998-99, Pennsbury Bd. Sch. Dirs., 1998-2001. Naval aviator USNR, 1954-58. Recipient Disting. Alumnus award Radio TV dept. Syracuse U., 1967; Andrew White medal Loyola Coll., Balt., 1979; Lord Baltimore medal St. Mary's Coll., 1980; Man of Yr. award Boys and Girls Club of Phila., 1987; Globe and Anchor award USMC Scholarship Found., 1991; Williamson award for excellence in cmty. svc. Williamson Free Sch., 1993. Mem.: AFTRA, Screen Actors Guild. Home: 1525 Harvest Dr Yardley PA 19067-4234 E-mail: ricbreit@aol.com. *To live is both to care and to laugh.*

BREKHUS, MELVIN G., construction executive; b. ND; BS in Engring. Sci., Univ. Mont., 1972. V.p., cement prodn. Tex. Industries (TXI), Dallas, 1989, exec. v.p., COO, cement, aggregates and concrete, pres., CEO, 2004—. Bd. dir. Portland Cement Assn. (chmn. 2001-2002); past pres. Am. Portland Cement Alliance; chmn. Innovative Paving Rsch. Found. Office: TXI 1341 W Mockingbird Ln Dallas TX 75247 Office Fax: 972-647-6700.

BREKKE, ALAN LEE, industrial engineer; b. Havre, Mont., Aug. 6, 1946; s. Knute Charles Brekke and Doris Emily Allen. Degree in indsl. and mgmt. engring., Mont. State U., 1974. Constrn. worker Brekke & sons, Harlem, Mont., 1959-70; deliverer and stockperson Merry Mkt., Harlem, 1962-64; intern Western Interstate Commn. for Higher Edn., Sydney, Mont., 1971; indsl. engr. Mont. State U., Bozeman, 1973; indsl. engr., with program planning dept. The Boeing Co., Seattle, 1974-83; constrn. mgr. Harlem H.S., 1986-87; indsl. engr. in pvt. practice Harlem, 1983—. Staff writer (centennial book) Thunderstorms and Tumbleweeds, 1989; author: Kid Curry, 1989. With EMS Blaine County III Ambulance, Harlem, 2000—. Avocations: mining, genealogy, ancient history, art. Home and Office: PO Box 635 Harlem MT 59526-0635 Office Phone: 406-353-2730.

BREKKE, STEWART ERNEST, retired chemistry and physics educator; b. Chgo., Dec. 28, 1941; s. Herbert and Rebecca Brekke. BA, U. Ill., 1965; MA, Wayne State U., 1971; MS in Edn., Purdue U., 1987. Cert. tchr. Ill. Physics and chemistry tchr. Chgo. Pub. Schs., 1975—2001; ret., 2001. Presenter in field. Contbr. articles to profl. jours., scientific papers. Mem.: Am. Assn. Physics Tchrs. (emeritus mem.), Am. Phys. Soc. Achievements include invention of mathematical theory of parallelism, divergence and convergence; nuclear vibration: the determinant of nuclear barrier heights, Quark oscillaton and nuclear barrier height as an irregular wave; research in oscillating nuclear cross sections and impact parameters making them variables; reduced mass calculation must include effects of nuclear vibration; electron orbits as oscillating mechanical cloud; reconstruction (partial) of the prometheia; gravitational anomalies: an attribute of each heavenly body galaxy and galactic group; physics and chemistry literacy indicate it must be mathematical; development of approximate best fit modeling teaching strategy; modification of Einstein Photoelectric Effect equation. Avocations: chess, tennis. Home: 2900 Maple Ave Apt 17D Downers Grove IL 60515-4134 Personal E-mail: stewabruk@aol.com.

BRELAND, JAMES ANDREW, minister; b. McDonald, Miss., Feb. 10, 1927; s. Luther Clifton Breland and Onie Mae Rice; m. Billie A. Wasson, June 8, 1954; 1 child, Brenda Carol. AA, East Ctrl. Jr. Coll., Decatur, Miss., 1949; BS in Edn., Delta State U., Cleveland, Miss., 1950, MEd, 1970; postgrad., New Orleans Bapt. Theol. Sem., 1953. Ordained min. Bapt. Ch., 1950. Math. tchr. West HS, Miss., 1950—51; dir. Bapt. Campus Ministry, Delta State U., 1951—91; pastor Pace Bapt. Ch., Miss., 1991—97; interim pastor Bapt. chs., Cleveland area, 1997—. Moderator Bolivar Bapt. Assn., Cleveland, 1979—81. Editor: Breland Family History, 1977. Cpl. US Army, 1945—46. Mem.: Mid-Delta Bapt. Mins.' Conf., Golden Cir. Alumni Club (pres. 2003—05). Republican. Home: 200 Sostes Dr Cleveland MS 38732 Personal E-mail: jbreland@tecinfo.com.

BRELAND, SANDY ANN, broadcast executive, director; b. New Orleans, Sept. 7, 1962; d. John Jerry and Betty Joy (Johnson) B.; m. John David McNamara, Apr. 10, 1992; 1 child, Ryan David. BA in Comms., Loyola U., 1983. Prodr., assignment editor WWL Radio, New Orleans, 1984-88; asst. editor WWL-TV, New Orleans, 1989-94, news dir., 1994—2006, KTVK/KASW-TV, Phoenix, 2006—. Recipient George Foster Peabody award for coverage of Hurricane Katrina, 2006, Edward R. Murrow award for coverage of Hurricane Katrina, 2006, Alfred I. duPont-Columbia U. award for coverage of Hurricane Katrina, 2007. Mem. Loyola U. Pres. Coun., RTNDA, CBS News Dir. Caucus. Avocations: boating, reading to child, camping. Office: KTVK/KASW-TV 5555 N 7th Ave Phoenix AZ 85013*

BRELAND-NOBLE, ALFIEE MATIESE, psychologist, researcher; b. Annapolis, Md., Mar. 14, 1969; d. Allen Eugene and Mattie McLeod Breland; m. Richard Noble, III, Aug. 17, 2002. BA, Howard U., 1991; MA, NYU, 1993; PhD, U. of Wis., 1997; M of Health Scis., Duke U., 2003—. Counselor U. Settlement, NYC, 1991—93, Young Adult Learning Acad., NYC, 1992—93; cultural diversity specialist Madison Inner City Coun. on Substance Abuse, Inc., Madison, Wis., 1994—96; asst. prof. Mich. State U., East Lansing, 1997—2002; staff psychologist Meridian Profl. Psychol. Cons., East Lansing, 2000—02; nat. rsch. svc. award postdoctoral fellow Duke U. Med. Ctr., Durham, NC, 2002—03, Nat. Rsch. Svc. postdoctoral rsch. fellow dept. psychiatry, 2003—. Cons. Okemos (Mich.) Pub. Schs., 2001, Flint (Mich.) Pub. Schs., 2001, Iowa City (Iowa) Pub. Schs., 2001; editl. bd. mem. Jour. of Black Psychology, 2002—, Dimensions of Counseling: Rsch., Theory and Practice, Kalamazoo, 1998—2002, Jour. of Multicultural Counseling and Devel., 1998, assoc. editor, 1997—98. Co-author: (book chpt.) Elementary School Counseling in the New Millennium, Violence in American Schools: Practical Guidelines for Counselors; contbr. articles to profl. jours. Named one of Young Leaders Under 30, Ebony Mag., 1999; recipient Outstanding Undergraduate Student scholarship, Delta Sigma Theta, 1987, dissertation fellowship, U. of Wis., 1996; fellow R25 Mentoring and Edn. for Mental Health Svcs. Rsch., NIMH, Yale U. and UCLA, 2001—02, Leopold Scheep Found., 1993. Mem.: ACA (clin. rsch. network com. 2002—), APA, Soc. for Rsch. on Adolescence, Soc. for Rsch. on Child Devel., Kappa Delta Pi, Alpha Kappa Alpha (Kappa Psi Omega chpt. pres. 1993—94). Democrat. Roman Catholic. Achievements include Created model that addresses mental health disparities of African American adolescents with depressive disorders under-utilization of mental health services; research in color consciousness. Avocations: step aerobics, reading, weightlifting, travel. Office: Duke U Med Ctr Box 3527 Durham NC 27710 Home: 1728 Ravenwing Dr Fuquay Varina NC 27526-5314 Office Phone: 919-416-2432. Personal E-mail: alfieeb@hotmail.com. E-mail: abreland@psych.mc.duke.edu.

BRELSFORD, THEODORE WILLIAM, JR., theology studies educator; b. Flemington, NJ, Apr. 21, 1960; s. Theodore W. Brelsford, Sr. and Linda Claire Brelsford; m. Donna C. Sheeley, Sept. 24, 1983; children: Carmina C., Natalie H. BA, Slippery Rock U., Pa., 1983; MDiv, Princeton Theol. Sem., NJ, 1988; PhD, Emory U., Atlanta, Ga., 1999. Asst. prof. religion and edn. Emory U., 1998—, dir. religious edn. program Candler Sch. Theology, 2002—. Author: We Are the Church Together, 1996; co-author: Religions of Atlanta, 1996; contbr. articles to profl. jours. Bd. dirs. Atlanta United Div. Ctr., 2001—06. Fellow, Princeton Theol. Sem., 1988, Emory U., 1991—96; grantee, Wabash Ctr. Tchg. and Learning in Theology and Religion, 2002. Mem.: United Meth. Assn. Scholars of Christian Edn. (corr.; adv. bd. 2005—06), Assn. Practical Theology (corr.), Am. Acad. Religion (corr.), Religious Edn. Assn. (corr.; bd. dirs. 2000—04, gen. editor 2000—04), Internat. Seminar Religious Edn. and Values (assoc.). Avocations: gourmet cooking, poetry, writing. Office: Emory University 1380 Oxford Road Atlanta GA 30322

BREM, HENRY, neurosurgeon, educator, researcher; b. Paterson, NJ, Aug. 14, 1952; s. Jacob and Adele (Machabanski) B.; m. Rachel Frydman, Jan. 28, 1978; children: Andrea, Alisa, Sarah. BA, NYU, 1973; student, Harvard U., 1973-74, MD, 1978. Diplomate Am. Bd. Neurosurgery. Intern in surgery Peter Bent Brigham Hosp., Boston, 1978-79; fellow in neurosurgery Johns Hopkins Hosp., Balt., 1979-80; resident in neurosurgery Neurol. Inst. N.Y. Columbia Presbyn. Med. Ctr., NYC, 1980-84; neurosurgeon Johns Hopkins U. Sch. Medicine, Balt., 1984—, prof. neurosurgery, ophthalmology and oncology, 1991—, dir. Hunterian Neurosurg. Lab., 1995—, assoc. dir. dept. neurosurgery, 1995—, Harvey Cushing profl, chmn. dept. neurosurgery, 2000. Office: Johns Hopkins Hosp Meyer 7-113 600 N Wolfe St Baltimore MD 21287-0005

BREMENSTUHL, DAVID P., elementary school educator; b. Englewood, NJ, Aug. 10, 1942; s. V. Burton and Elsie M. (Dutcher) Bremenstuhl; m. Mary Ann K. Warnock, Sept. 13, 1973; 1 child, Heather-Erin. BS in Edn., SUNY, New Paltz, 1964, postgrad., 1967—73, U. Md., 1967—73. Cert. tchr. NY State Dept. Edn., advanced profl. cert. Md. Bd. Edn. Elem. tchr. Middletown Pub. Schs., NY, 1964—66, White Plains Pub. Schs., NY, 1966—70, Irvington Pub. Schs., Irvington-on-Hudson, NY, 1971—73, Montgomery County Pub. Schs., Rockville, Md., 1973—2003, Edn. Cons. Svc., 2003—. Mem. Am. Friends Svc. Com.; founding sponsor Martin Luther King, Jr. Nat. Meml.; invited mem. Arturo Schomburg Soc.; founding mem. Nat. Campaign for Tolerance, Prog. Patriots Fund; active Pub. Concern Found.; mem. US Holocaust Meml. Mus.; mem. leadership coun. So. Poverty Law Ctr.; creator Autographs in Excellence awards; contbg. mem. Government Accountability Project. Nominee to Zachor (Cir. of Remembrance), US Holocaust Meml. Mus.; named Wilson Assoc., Woodrow Wilson Internat. Ctr. Scholars, Press Assoc., Columbia Journalism Review; named to Founder's Roll of Honor, Martin Luther King Jr. Nat. Meml. Found., Wash.; recipient Lifetime Achievement award, George Washington Elem. Sch. PTA, 1970, honor Wall of Tolerance Meml., Ala. Master: William J. Clinton Presdl. Ctr.; mem.: NAACP, ACLU, NEA, Union of Concerned Scientists, Assn. Psychohistory, Montgomery County Edn. Assn., Md. State Tchrs. Assn., Arturo Schomburg Soc., Human Rights Watch, Wilderness Soc., Amnesty Internat., Interfaith Alliance, Nation Assoc. (The Nation Inst.), Nat. Resources Def. Coun., Oxfam Am., Doctors Without Borders, Common Cause, Nation Assoc., Smithsonian Instn. Found. Hist. Preservation, Spl. Olympics, Ptnr. of Consci./Amnesty Internat., The Jimmy Carter Ctr., Native Am. Rights Fund, Earth Justice, Sierra Club. Unitarian Universalist. Achievements include name inscribed on Wall of Tolerance civil rights memorial in Montgomery, Alabama. Avocations: poetry, composing music, landscape gardening, reading. Home: 9601 Brink Rd Gaithersburg MD 20882 Personal E-mail: mbremenstu@aol.com.

BREMER, CELESTE F., judge; b. San Francisco, 1953; BA, St. Ambrose Coll., 1974; JD, Univ. of Iowa Coll. of Law, 1977; EdD, Drake U., 2002. Asst. county atty. Scott County, 1977-79; asst. atty. gen. Area Prosecutors Div., Iowa, 1979; with Carlin, Liebbe, Pitton & Bremer, 1979-81, Rabin, Liebbe, Shinkle & Bremer, 1981-82; with legal dept. Deere and Co., 1982-84; corp. counsel Economy Forms Corp., 1985-89; magistrate judge U.S. Dist. Ct. (Iowa so. dist.), 8th cir., Des Moines, 1984—; ed. D. Drake U. Sch. of Edn., 2002. Instr. Drake Univ. Coll. of Law, 1985—88, 2005—06. Mem. ABA, Fed. Magistrate Judge Assn., Nat. Assn. Women Judges, Am. Judicature Soc., Iowa State Bar Assn. (bd. govs., 1987-90), Iowa Judges Assn., Iowa Supreme Ct. Coun. on Jud. Selection (chmn. 1986-90), Iowa Orgn Women Attys., Polk County Bar Assn., Polk County Women Attys. Office: US Courthouse Ste 435 123 E Walnut St Des Moines IA 50309-2036 Office Phone: 515-284-6200.

BREMER, GABRIEL, chef; b. Concord, NH, 1977; life ptnr. Analia Verolo. Chef Fore Street Restaurant, Portland, Maine; owner, chef Gabriel's, Portland, Maine; sous chef Rialto, Cambridge, 2000; chef Le Soir, Newton, Mass.; co-owner, exec. chef Salts, Cambridge, 2004—. Named one of Boston's Rising Stars, StarChefs.com, 2006, Best New Chefs, Food & Wine Mag., 2007. Avocation: classical percussion. Office: Salts Restaurant 798 Main St Cambridge MA 02139 Office Phone: 617-876-8444.*

BREMER, HOWARD WALTER, lawyer, consultant; b. Milw., July 18, 1923; s. Walter Hugo and Lydia Martha (Schmidt) B.; m. Caryl Marie Faust, May 28, 1948; children: Katharine, William (dec.), Thomas, Timothy, Margaret. BSChemE, U. Wis., 1944, LLB, 1949. Bar: Wis. 1949, US Patent and Trademark Office 1954, US Supreme Ct. 1957, US Ct. Appeals (fed. cir.) 1959, US Dist. Ct. (so. dist.) Ohio 1960. Patent atty. Procter & Gamble Co., Cin., 1949-60; patent counsel Wis. Alumni Rsch. Found., Madison, 1960-88; cons., Madison, 1988—. Mem. adv. com. Coun. on Govtl. Rels., Washington, 1975-93; panel mem. Office Tech. Assessment, Washington, 1981-83; mem. adv. commn. patent law reform Washington, 1991-92; bd. dirs. rsch. found. U. Iowa, 2006-07. Internat. adv. bd. Industry and Higher Edn. Jour., 1996—; contbr. articles to profl. jours. Pres. Edgewood Campus Sch. PTA, Madison, 1967-69; mem. adv. bd. Edgewood H.S., 1971-80, chmn. adv. bd., 1973-74. With USN, 1944-46. Recipient Alumni Appreciation award, Edgewood H.S., 1990, Hon. Recognition award, U. Wis. Coll. Agrl. and Life Scis., 2000. Mem. ABA (chmn. com. 1993-2001), Intellectual Property Law Assn. (chmn. com. 1996-99, Jefferson medal), NJ Intellectual Property Law Assn., State Bar Wis. (chmn. intellectual property sect. 1967-68, 79-80), Wis. Intellectual Property Law Assn. (pres. 1989-90), Assn. Univ. Tech. Mgrs. (trustee 1977-78, 80-82, pres. 1978-80, com. chmn. 1985-93, mem. editl. bd. jour. 1990—, Birch award 1980, 5 scholarships in his name 2003). Avocations: building furniture, home maintenance, model railroading, travel, reading. Home: 1106 Brookwood Rd Madison WI 53711-3116 Office Phone: 608-263-2831. Business E-Mail: hwbremer@warf.org.

BREMER, JOHN M., lawyer; b. 1947; BA, Fordham U., 1969; JD, Duke U., 1974. Bar: Wis. 1974. From atty. law dept. to sr. exec. v.p. Northwestern Mut. Life Ins., Milw., 1974—2002, COO, 2002—. Office: Northwestern Mutual Life Ins Co 720 E Wisconsin Ave Milwaukee WI 53202-4703

BREMER, KAREN INGRID, food service executive; b. Montreal, Que., Can., Jan. 16, 1959; d. Horst T. and Ingrid Alice (Simon) B.; m. Thomas Pattison, July 21, 1981 (div. Mar. 1989). AA in Liberal Arts, HCC, 1976. Regional svc. supr. JoJo's Restaurants Inc., Irvine, Calif., 1979-81, unit mgr., 1981-82; gen.mgr. Ginger Jar Restaurants Inc., Orange, Calif., 1982-83; unit mgr. W.R. Grace Restaurant Co., Irvine, 1983-84; gen. mgr. Peasant Restaurants Inc., Atlanta, 1984-95; area mgr. Peasant Restaurants, Inc., Atlanta, 1995-96, regional mgr., 1996-98, pres., 1998—2000; founder Great Hospitality, LLC, Atlanta, 2000—. Instr. in time mgmt. Peasant Restaurants Mgmt., Atlanta, 1988; speaker Cobb County Sch. Bd., Marietta, 1989; mgr. City of Atlanta Br. for Dem. Conf., 1988; pres. food svc. 9HTA, bd. dirs. ACVB, Team 9A, 9HTA, Nat. Restaurant Assn., 2002-, Rewards Network Inc., 2007- Editor, author: Opening Manual, 1980, Management Training Manual, 1985. Treas. Downtown Atlanta Restaurant Assn.; mem. pub. safety task force Ctrl. Atlanta Progress. Recipient 9H7A Food Svc. Industry Leader award, 1999, State Leadership award Nat. Restaurant Assn., 1998—. Mem. Am. Bus. Women's Assn. (exec. v.p.), Cobb County C. of C. Lutheran. Avocations: travel, cooking, water sports. Office: Great Hospitality LLC 17 Internat Blvd NE Atlanta GA 30303

BREMER, (L.) PAUL (LEWIS PAUL BREMER III), former diplomat; b. Hartford, Conn., Sept. 30, 1941; s. L. Paul and Nina (Struthers) B.; m. Frances Winfield, June 11, 1966; children: Paul, Leila. BA, Yale U., 1963; cert., Inst. d'etudes Politiques, U. Paris, 1964; MBA, Harvard U., 1966. With Diplomatic Svc., 1966; exec. asst. to sec. state US Dept. State, Washington, 1974-76, dep. exec. sec., 1979-81, exec. sec., spl. asst. to sec. of state, 1981—83; dep. amb., chief of mission Am. Embassy, Oslo, 1976—79; US amb. to The Netherlands US Dept. State, The Hague, 1983—86, amb.-at-large for counter-terrorism, 1986—89; mng. dir. Kissinger Assocs., 1989—2000; chmn. Nat. Commn. on Terrorism, 1999—2001; chmn. polit. risk bus. Marsh Inc., 2000—, chmn., CEO crisis consulting practice, 2001—03; mem. Homeland Security Adv. Coun., 2002—04; presdl. envoy to Iraq The White House, 2003; dir. Office of Reconstruction and Humanitarian Assistance Coalition Provisional Authority, Baghdad, Iraq, 2003—04. Bd. dirs. Air Products and Chems. Inc., Akzo Nobel NV, Netherland-Am. Found.; chmn. adv. bd. GlobalSecure Corp. Co-author (with Malcom McConnell): My Year in Iraq: My Struggle to Build a Future of Hope, 2006. Recipient Superior Honor award US Dept. State, 1974, Presdl. Merit Pay award, 1983, Presdl. Medal of Freedom, 2004, Joseph H. Sherick award, US Dept Def., 2004, Victory of Freedom award, Nixon Library Mem. Internat. Inst. Strategic Studies, Coun. on Fgn. Rels. (bd. dirs.), Netherlands-Am. Found., Conner Peripherals Inc., Air Products and Chems. Inc. Republican. Roman Catholic. Avocations: skiing, jogging, history.

BREMER, RONALD ALLAN, genealogist, editor; b. Southgate, Calif., May 2, 1937; s. Carl Leonard and Lena Evelyn (Jury) B.; childen: Blindy, Ron, Trina, Rebecca, Jim, Melinda, Aaron, Serena, Lorrie, Jennie, Elizabeth, Hans, Adam, Rachel. Student, Los Angeles Trade Tech., Cerritos Coll., Am. U., Brigham Young U.; grad., Nat. Inst. Geneal. Rsch., 1961. Prof. genealogist, 1959—; research specialist Fam. Hist. Libr., Salt Lake City, 1969-72; profl. lectr. on genealogy Salt Lake City, 1973—; pres. The Rsch. Inst. Lectr. in field. Author: World's Funniest Epitaphs, 1983; Compendium of Historical Sources, 1983; (with Bill Dollarhide) America's Best Genealogy Resource Centers, 1998; editor Genealogy Digest mag., Salt Lake City, 1983-84, Roots Digest, 1984-85 *Money and things don't matter. Position and education mean little. Genius and slow-normal have the same opportunity. Happiness is achieving your greatest potential. Go for the goose-bumps!.*

BREMER MARTINO, JUAN JOSE, former ambassador; b. Mexico City, 1944; Law degree, Nat. Autonomous U. Mex., 1966. Pvt. sec. to Pres. Govt. of Mex., 1972—75; dep. sec. Ministry of Presidency, 1975—76; head Nat. Fine Arts Inst., 1976—82; dep. sec. cultural affairs Ministry Edn., 1982; pres. Cervantino Internat. Festival, 1983; pres. fgn. affairs com. Chamber of Deps., 1985—88; amb. to Sweden Mexican Embassy, 1982, amb. to USSR, 1988—90, amb. to Fed. Rep. Germany, 1990—98, amb. to Spain, 1998—2000, amb. to U.S. Washington, 2001—04. Co-chair Mexican delegations XXVI Mex.-U.S. Interparliamentary Commn., Colorado Springs, Colo., 1986, XVII Mex.-U.S. Interparliamentary Commn., New Orleans, 1988; participant Commn. to Study Future of Mexican-Am. Rels., 1988; lectr. in field.

BREMNER, JAMES DOUGLAS, psychiatrist, researcher, education educator; b. Topeka, Kans., June 5, 1961; s. James Douglas and Linnea Bremner; m. Laura Viola Vaccarino, Aug. 1, 1991; children: Sabina Francesca, Dylan Vittorio. BS, U. Puget Sound, 1983; MD, Duke U. Sch. Medicine, 1987. Cert. Am. Bd. of Psychiatry and Neurology, 1996, Am. Bd. of Nuc. Medicine, 2001. Prof. psychiatry and radiology Emory U. Sch. Medicine, 2000—; dir. Emory Ctr. for Positron Emission Tomography, 2000—06. Asst. and assoc. prof. of psychiatry Yale U. Sch. of Medicine, 1992—2000. Author: (book) Does Stress Damage the Brain?. Achievements include research in brain imaging and neurobiology of mood and anxiety disorders. Home: 2125 Ponce de Leon Ave NE Atlanta GA 30307 Office: Emory Univ 306 E Mailstop 1256/001/AT 1256 Briarcliff Rd NE Atlanta GA 30306 Office Phone: 404-712-9569. Business E-Mail: jdbremn@emory.edu.

BREMNER, JOHN MCCOLL, agronomy and biochemistry educator; b. Dumbarton, Scotland, Jan. 18, 1922; came to U.S., 1959; s. Archibald Donaldson and Sarah Kennedy (McColl) B.; m. Eleanor Mary Williams, Sept. 30, 1950; children: Stuart, Carol. BS, Glasgow U., 1944, DSc, 1987; PhD, U. London, 1948, DSc, 1959. With chemistry dept. Rothamsted Exptl. Sta., Harpenden, Eng., 1945-59; assoc. prof. Iowa State U., Ames, 1959-61, prof. agronomy and biochemistry, 1961-75, C.F. Curtiss disting. prof. agriculture, prof. agronomy, biochemistry, 1975-93; disting. prof. emeritus, 1993—; ret., 1986. Tech. expert IAEA, Austria, 1964-65, Yugoslavia, 1964-65. Author or co-author over 300 publs. including 30 chpts in sci. monographs. Recipient Outstanding Research award First Miss. Corp., 1979, Alexander Von Humboldt medal Alexander Von Humboldt Found., Fed. Republic of Germany, 1982, Gov.'s Sci. medal State of Iowa, 1983, Harvey Wiley award U.S. Assn. Ofcl. Analytical Chemists, 1984, Spencer medal Am. Chem. Soc., 1987, Burlington No. Found. Faculty Achievement award for Research, Gamma Sigma Delta award of merit for disting. service to agriculture, Regents award for faculty excellence, 1992, Award for Advancement of Agrl. & Food Chemistry, Am. Chem. Soc.; fellow Rockefeller Found., 1957, Guggenheim Found., 1968. Fellow AAAS, Am. Acad. Microbiology, Am. Soc. Agronomy (Agronomic Rsch. award 1985, Environ. Quality Rsch. award 1990), Soil Sci. Soc. Am. (Achievement award 1967, Bouyoucos Disting. Career award 1982, Disting. Svc. award 1993), Iowa Acad. Sci. (disting.); mem. NAS, Am. Soc. Microbiology, Brit. Soc. Soil Sci., Internat. Soil Sci. Soc., Phi Kappa Phi (centennial medalist 1997), Sigma Xi, Gamma Sigma Delta. Achievements include patent for nitrification inhibitor; development and evaluation of nitrification and urease inhibitors for control of adverse transformations of fertilizer nitrogen in soils; development of methodology for research on the nitrogen cycle and environmental problems related to agriculture; research on microbial, enzymatic, and chemical processes responsible for nitrogen transformations in soils, such as nitrification, denitrification, chemodenitrification, and urease activity. Personal E-mail: jmbremner@earthlink.net.

BREMS, DAVID PAUL, architect; b. Lehi, Utah, Aug. 10, 1950; s. D. Orlo and Gearldine (Hitchcock) B.; m. Johna Devey Brems; children: Stefan Tomas Brems, Beret Alla Brems. BS, U. Utah, 1973, MArch, 1975. Registered arch., Utah, Calif., Colo., Ariz., Wyo., N.Mex., Idaho, Mont., Tex., Wash., HCARB. Draftsman Environ. Assocs., Salt Lake City, 1971-73; draftsman/architect intern Environ. Design Group, Salt Lake City, 1973-76; architect/intern Frank Fuller AIA, Salt Lake City, 1976-77; prin. Edward & Daniels, Salt Lake City, 1978-83; pres. David Brems & Assocs., Salt Lake City, 1983-86; prin. Gillies, Stransky, Brems, Smith P.C., Salt Lake City, 1986—. Mem. urban design com. Assist, Inc., Salt Lake City, 1982—85, Salt Lake County Planning Commn., 1991—97, chmn., 1992—96; mem. Emigration Twp. Planning Commn., 1997—, chmn., 1997—99; mem. Emigration Masterplan Adv. Com., 1997—99; invited lectr. Wyo. Soc. Archs., 1992, sch. engring. U. Utah, 1993, 95, VA, 1993, Utah Soc. Archs., 1994, Utah Power and Light, 1994, WMR, 2006, others; juror U. Utah Grad. Sch. Architecture, 1975—, adj. prof., 1990—93, mem. adv. com., 2000—; juror Utah Soc. Am. Planning Assn., 1994—, Sunstone Symposium, 1995, Contemporary Arts Group, 1995—, others. Pub. Firm Profile Intermountain Architecture, 1996, Web Mag., 1997; prin. works include solar twin homes Utah Holiday (Best Solar Design award), Sun Builder, Daily Jour., Salt Lake Tribune, Brian Head Day Lodge, Easton Aluminum, Four Seasons Hotel, Gore Coll. Bus., CMF Tooele, utah Regional Corrections Facility, St. Vincents De Paul Ctr., Steiner Aquatic Ctr., U. Utah Football Support Facility, Sports Medicine West, West Jordan Cmty. Water Park, Utah N.G. Apache Helicopter Hangar & Armory, Kashmitter I Residences, St. Thomas More Cath. Ch., Spanish Fork Cmty. Water Park, Natures Herbs, ABC Office Bldg. Divsn. of Natural Resources Bldg., Kashmitter II Residence, Litton Residence, Elliott Emigration Residence, Elliott Boulder Residence, Utah Olympic Speed Skating Oval for 2002 Olympics, Vis. Ctr. Grand Staircase Escalante Nat. Monument, Bennett Fed. Bldg., and others; ALTA Club mem., Great Salt Lake Yacht Club mem., Bear Lake Yacht Club mem., mem. Leadership Utah; mem. 2002 Olympic Energy and Water subcom., 1996—; mem. State of Utah Divsn. of Facilities Mgmt. Com. on Energy Efficient Architecture. Mem. Salt Lake City Bus. Advisory. Recipient awards Am. Concrete Inst., 1993, Chief Engrs. Honor award U.S. Army Corps Engrs., 1994; Bronze medalist Utah Summer Games, 1991, Silver medalist, 1992, Gold medalist, 1994, Design award Dept. Def., 1995, Blue Seal award, 1995, Outstanding Project award U.S. Dept. Def., 1995, Western Mountain Region Hon. Mention St. Thomas More, 1996, Solar Today award Sun award, Energy Uses News award Dept. Natural Resources, 1996, Western Mountain Region Merit award Bennet Fed. Bldg., 2003, Western Mountain Citation award, 2003, Jewish Cmty. Ctr. Holocaust Meml., 2003 ,Utah Heritage Found. award, others; named Best Pvt. Project by Intermountain Architecture, 1994, Salt Lake County Vol. of Yr. Salt Lake County Planning Commn., 1995, Best Recreation Project Intermountain Arch., 1995, award for Sahara Office Bldg., Ceramic Tiles of Italy, 2004, award Utah Masonry Coun. Fellow: AIA (chmn. Western Mountain Regiona honor awards 1983, pres. Salt Lake chpt. 1983—84, chmn. Western Mountain Region conf. 1986, pres. Utah Soc. 1987, chmn. Western Mountain Regional honor awards 1988, com. on design 1990—, juror Colo. West awards 1992, chmn. com. on environment AIA Utah 1993, chmn. Design for Life Workshop at Sundance 1993, Utah concrete masony assoc. Emigration Canyon home 2003, chair com. on design 2006, Honor awards 1983, Merit awards 1983, 1985, Honor awards 1988, PCI award 1988, IFRAA award 1988, Merit awards 1988, 1993, IFRAA award 1994, Merit awards 1999, Steel Inst. award 2002, Honor award 2002, Sarnafil award 2002, Merit award 2003, Honor awards 2003, Nat. Concrete Masony award of excellence 2003, Heritage Found. awards 2003, Utah Bronze medal 2006, award Utah sect. IES for St. Thomas More, Utah 25 Yr. award for Emigration Passive Solar Twin Home, Sustainable Design Excellence Honor award 2007); mem.: Utah Energy Forum, Am. Solar Soc., Am. Solar Energy Soc., Utah Soc. Architects, Black Builder Mesa Water Assn. (sec.), Acorn Hills Water Assn. (trustee), Am. Planning Assn. (juror awards 1994), Illuminating Engring. Soc. (assoc.), Utah Open Lands (S.W. Utah br.), Salt Lake Olympic Com. (environ. adv. com.), Hobie Fleet 67 (commodore 1985—86). Home: 119 N Young Oak Rd Salt Lake City UT 84108-1601

BREMSER, GEORGE, JR., electronics executive; b. Newark, May 26, 1928; s. George and Virginia (Christian) B.; m. Marie Sundman, June 21, 1952 (div. July 1979); children: Christian Fredrick II, Priscilla Suzanne, Martha Anne, Sarah Elizabeth; m. Nancy Kay Woods, Oct. 27, 1983 (div. Feb. 1989); m. Betty Glover Lohse, Oct. 8, 1997 (dec. Mar. 2001). BA, Yale U., 1949; postgrad., U. Miami, 1959; MBA, NYU, 1962. With McCann-Erickson Inc., NYC, 1952-61, asst. gen. mgr. Bogota, Colombia, 1955, gen. mgr., 1955-57, account supr. NYC, 1958, v.p., mgr. Miami, Fla., 1959-61; with Gen. Foods Corp., White Plains, NY, 1961-71; v.p., gen. mgr. internat. div. Gen. Foods Europe, White Plains, NY, 1967; pres. Gen. Foods Internat., White Plains, 1967-71; group v.p. Gen. Foods Corp., White Plains, 1970-71; chmn., pres., chief exec. officer Texstar Corp., Grand Prairie, Tex., 1971-81; exec. v.p. Shaklee Corp., San Francisco, 1981-82; chmn., pres., chief exec. officer Etak Inc., Menlo Park, Calif., 1983-88, 96, chmn., 1989-96, 97—; chmn., pres., CEO Etak, Inc., Menlo Park, Calif., 1996-97, chmn., 1997-2000, CEO, 2000-01; bd. dir. Tele Atlas N.A., Inc., 2000—, chief adminstrv. officer, 2001—02. Bd. dirs. PBI Industries Inc Trustee Union Ch., Bogota, 1956-57; Dem. county committeeman, Ridgewood, N.J., 1962-63; mem. New Canaan (Conn.) Town Council, 1969-73; founder, past pres. Citizens Com. for Conservation, New Canaan; mem. coun. Save the Redwoods League, 1987—. Served to 2d lt. USMC 1950-52, capt. Res. Mem. New Canaan Country Club, Brook Club, Yale Club (N.Y.C.), Block Island Club, Casino Club (Nantucket, Mass.), Explorers Club, Phi Beta Kappa, Beta Gamma Sigma, Beta Theta Pi. Home: Apt 3317 131 Embarcadero West Oakland CA 94607-3768 also: Mansion Beach Rd Block Island RI 02807 Office: Tele Atlas NA Inc 1700 Seaport Blvd Ste 150 Redwood City CA 94063 Office Phone: 650-385-2300 x2306. Business E-Mail: george.bremser@teleatlas.com.

BREN, DONALD L., real estate company executive; b. LA, 1932; married; 7 children. BA in Bus. Admin., Econ., U. Wash., 1958, MBA. Founder, pres. Bren Company (later renamed California Pacific Homes), Newport Beach, 1958—, Mission Viejo (Calif.) Co., Newport Beach, 1963—67; CEO Irvine Co., Newport Beach, 1977—, chmn. bd., 1998—. Established Donald Bren Sch. of Environmental Sci. & Mgmt., U. Calif., Irvine Ranch Land Reserve Trust, 2005, Excellence in Edn. Enrichment Fund, 2006. Chmn. Donald Bren Found.; trustee Orange County Museum of Art, Los Angeles County Museum of Art, Calif. Inst. of Tech., U. Calif., Irvine Found., Uncommon Alliance Nature Conservancy, 1996—. Officer USMC, 1954—57. Named one of 50 Most Generous Philanthropists, Fortune Mag., 2005, BusinessWeek mag., 2006, World's Richest People, Forbes Mag., 2001—, Forbes Richest Americans, 1999—, 100 most influential people in Southern Calif., LA Times, 2006; recipient U. Calif. Irvine Medal, 1989, Semper Fidelis Award, Marine Corps U. Found., 1998, Gen. Leonard F. Chapman Medallion, 2003, U. California Presdl. Medal, 2004. Fellow: Am. Acad. Arts & Scis. Avocations: sailing, skiing, tennis. Office: The Irvine Co 550 Newport Center Dr Newport Beach CA 92660-7011*

BRENCHLEY, JEAN ELNORA, microbiologist, researcher, science administrator; b. Towanda, Pa., Mar. 6, 1944; d. John Edward and Elizabeth (Jefferson) B.; m. Bernard Asbell, July 21, 1990 (dec. Feb. 2001). BS, Mansfield U., 1965; MS, U. Calif., San Diego, 1967; PhD, U. Calif., Davis, 1970; degree (hon.), Lycoming Coll., 1992. Rsch. assoc. biology dept. MIT, Cambridge, 1970-71; from asst. prof. to assoc. prof. microbiology Pa. State U., Univ. Pk., 1971-77, head. dept. molecular and cell biology, dir. Biotech. Inst. University Park, 1984-87, prof. microbiology, dir. Biotech. Inst., 1984-90, prof. microbiology and biotech., 1990—; assoc. prof., then prof. biology Purdue U., West Lafayette, Ind., 1977-81; research dir. Genex Corp., Gaithersburg, Md., 1981-84. Mem. Nat. Biotech. Policy Bd., 1990-93; trustee Biosis, 1983-88; vis. scholar NIH, 1991. Editor Applied and Environ. Microbiology, 1981-85; mem. editorial bd. Jour. Bacteriology, 1974-84, Butterworth Biotech. Series, 1988-92; editor Microbiol. Revs., 1992-97. Recipient Outstanding Alumni award Manfield U., 1983; Waksman award Theobald Smith Soc., 1985; named to Pa. Hall of Fame, 1988. Fellow AAAS (nominating com. 1990-92), Am. Acad. Microbiology; mem. NAS (bioprocess com.), Am. Soc. Microbiology (pres. 1986-87, ASM Found. lectr. 1975, Alice Evans award 1996), Assn. Women in Sci., Am. Soc. Biol. Chemists, Am. Chem. Soc., Found. for Microbiology (trustee 1988-95), Sigma Delta Epsilon (hon.). Office: Pa State Univ Frear Lab University Park PA 16802

BRENDEL, BETTINA, abstract artist; b. Lueneburg, Germany; d. Robert and Xenia (Bernstein) Brendel; m. Arthur Spitzer, Mar. 4, 1949 (div. July 1965); 1 child, Violet Spitzer Lucas. Abiturium, Oberlyceum, Hamburg, Germany, 1940; student, Kunstschule, Hamburg, Germany, 1941—42; cert., Staatliche Hochschule fur Bildende Kunste, Hamburg, Germany, 1945—47; postgrad., U. So. Calif., 1955—58, New Sch. for Social Rsch., NYC, 1968—69. Instr. UCLA Extension, 1958—61; lectr. Coll. Art Assn., Chgo., 1971, Inst. Optics, Rochester, NY, 1971; instr. UCLA Extension, 1976; lectr. U. So. Calif., 1980. Conf. participant Gulbenkian Found., Paris, Lisbon, Portugal. One-woman shows include Santa Barbara (Calif.) Mus., 1966, Spectrum Gallery, N.Y., 1967, Artcore Gallery, L.A., 1984, Long Beach Mus., 1998, Galerie Wosimsky, Germany, 1999, David Lawrence Gallery, Beverly Hills, 2000, exhibitions include nat. and internat. group shows; author: book of poems, 1977; contbr. articles to publs., to profl. publs.; exhibitions include computer art, 1982— (prize Palm Springs, Calif., 1997, 1998), Gallery Wosimsky, Giessen, Germany, 2003, Represented in permanent collections Armand Hammer Mus., L.A. County Mus. Art, Long Beach Mus., Mus. Konkrete Kunst, Ingolstadt, Germany, Werner Heisenberg Inst., Munich. Recipient 1st prize, La Jolla (Calif.) Art Mus., 1958—59, Long Beach Mus. Art, 1960, Purchase prize, San Francisco Mus., 1966. Mem.: UCLA Alumni Assn., Friends of the Ctr. for History of Physics, YLEM Artists Using Sci. and Tech. (contbr. newsletter), L.A. Printmaking Soc., Archives Am. Art, Mus. Contemporary Art, L.A. County Mus. Art. Democrat. Home: 1061 N Kenter Ave Los Angeles CA 90049-1313 Home Phone: 310-476-5860; Office Phone: 310-476-5860. Personal E-mail: bb4art@yahoo.com.

BRENDEL, JOHN S., lawyer; b. McKeesport, Pa., May 6, 1951; BA with distinction, Cornell U., 1973; JD cum laude, Harvard U., 1976. Bar: Pa. 1977. Assoc., ptnr. Buchanan Ingersoll P.C., Pitts., 1977-95; ptnr. Cohen & Grigsby P.C., 1995-97; v.p., gen. counsel Mastech Corp., Oakdale, Pa., 1997-2000; sr. v.p. iGATE Capital Corp., Pitts., 1997—2003; dir. Cohen & Grigsby P.C., Pitts. Adj. prof. immigration law U. Pitts. Sch. of Law., Duquesne U. Sch. Law. Fulbright-DAAD fellow, 1976-77, Best Lawyers Am. (immigration Law) 2005-2006. Mem. Am. Immigration Lawyers Assn., former chair Immigration Policy Com., Info. Tech. Assn. Am. (ITAA).,founding mem. Pitts. chpt., Dept. Labor Liaison Com., Immigration and Nationality Com., bd. dirs. Jefferson Memorial Park and Funeral Home, Chair bd. dirs. Cystic Fibrosis Found. Western Pa. Office: Cohen & Grigsby PC 11 Stanwix St 15th Fl Pittsburgh PA 15222-1319 Office Phone: 412-297-4987. Business E-Mail: jbrendel@cohenlaw.com.*

BRENDLER, CHARLES BURGESS, urologist, educator; b. Charlottesville, Va., June 20, 1944; s. Herbert and Virginia Burgess B.; m. Lucretia Cattley Rock, June 18, 1966; children: Christopher, Amy, Emily, Peter. AB, Harvard Coll., 1966; MD, U. Va., 1974. Instr. urology Johns Hopkins U., Balt., 1980-81, asst. prof. urology, 1981-85, assoc. prof. urology, 1985-93; chief urology Balt. City Hosps., 1981-84; prof., chief urology U. Chgo., 1994—96; prof. urology Northwestern U./Feinberg Sch. Medicine, 2006—; vice-chmn. surgery Evanston Northwestern Healthcare, Ill., 2006—. Surg. exec. com. U. Chgo. Med. Ctr., 1994-2006, surgery edn. com., 1994-2006. Assoc. editor: Glenn's Urologic Surgery, 1998; co-author: Campbell's Urology, 1985, 5th edit., 2007; co-author Operative Urology 1990, 3rd edit., 2002; contbr. articles to profl. jour. Capt. USAF, 1967-71. Mem. Am. Urol. Assn. (2d prize clin. rsch. 1983, 1st prize clin. rsch. Mid-Atlantic sect. 1991, 92), Am. Assn. Genito-Urinary Surgeons, Nat. Urol. Forum, Soc. Basic Urol. Rsch., Soc. Urol. Oncology, Am. Joint Commn. on Cancer (advisor task force on urol. cancer 1997), Alpha Omega Alpha. Democrat. Unitarian Universalist. Avocations: skiing, hiking, jogging, travel. Home: 434 W Arlington Pl Chicago IL 60614 Office: Evanston Hosp 2650 Ridge Ave Walgreen Bldg Ste 2507 Evanston IL 60201 Home Phone: 773-248-5138; Office Phone: 847-570-1090. Business E-Mail: cbrendler@enh.org.

BRENDLINGER, LEROY R., academic administrator; b. Frederick, Pa., Dec. 14, 1918; s. Claude R. and Elsie May B.; m. Virginia Steltz, Dec. 28, 1941; children: Dawn, Brian, Craig. BS, West Chester State Coll., 1946; MS, U. Pa., 1949; Ed.D., Temple U., 1959. Former tchr., East Greenville, Pa.; Ordnance Officer Candidate Sch., Aberdeen, Md.; former prin. Pottsgrove (Pa.) Schs.; former asst. supt. Montgomery (Pa.) Schs.; pres. Montgomery County Community Coll., now pres. emeritus. Chmn. SCORE, chpt. 594 Tri County area. Author: The Brendlinger Family History 1660-1994, 1995. Past pres. Montgomery County (Pa.) Health and Welfare Coun.; bd. dirs. Montgomery Hosp., Lutheran Children and Family Svc.; pres. Tri-County Area local chpt. Score 594, Pottstown, Pa. With U.S. Army, 1942-46, ETO. Recipient Outstanding Alumnus award West Chester U., 1984. Mem. Am. Assn. Jr. and C.Cs. (past pres. Pa. Commn. C.Cs.). Clubs: Brookside Country (treas. bd. govs.). Office: 340 Dekalb Pike Blue Bell PA 19422-1412

BRENDTRO, LARRY KAY, psychologist; b. Sioux Falls, SD, July 26, 1940; s. A. Kenneth and Bernice (Matz) B.; m. Janna Agena, July 14, 1973; children: Daniel Kenneth, Steven Lincoln, Nola Kristine. BA, Augustana Coll., 1961; MS, S.D. State U., 1962; PhD, U. Mich., 1965. Prin. Crippled Children's Hosp. and Sch., Sioux Falls, 1962-63; psychology intern Hawthorn Ctr., Northville, Mich., 1964-65; instr. U. Mich., 1965; asst. prof. U. Ill., Urbana, 1966-67; pres., CEO Starr Commonwealth, Albion, Mich., 1967-81; prof. Augustana Coll., Sioux Falls, S.D., 1981-99; founder Reclaiming Youth Internat., Lennox, SD, 1997—. Mem. U.S. Coordinating Coun. on Juvenile Justice and Delinquency Prevention, 1997—. Co-author: The Other 23 Hours, 1969, Positive Peer Culture, 1974, 1985, Re-educating Troubled Youth, 1983, Reclaiming Youth at Risk, 1990, 2002; co-editor: Reclaiming Children and Youth, 1992—, Reclaiming Our Prodigal Sons and Daughters, 2000, Troubled Children and Youth, 2004, No Disposable Kids, 2005, Kids Who Outwit Adults, 2005, The Resilence Revolution, 2006. Lutheran. Home and Office: Reclaiming Youth Internat PO Box 57 Lennox SD 57039-0057 Office Phone: 605-647-2532. E-mail: courage@reclaiming.com.

BRENES, JEREMY, homeopath, researcher; b. Oklahoma City, Dec. 18, 1973; s. Alvaro and June Brenes. BS in Math., U. Okla., Norman, 1996; D in Homeopathy, British Inst. Homeopathy, London, 2003. Processing geophysicist Western Geophys., Houston, 1997—2001; pres., treas., cons., founder Homeopathic Village, Inc., Houston, 2003—. Author: (website) homeopathicvillage.com, 2002; author, pub. (books) Homeopathic Repertory of Heavy Elements, 2006; author: (books) Dice Roll Probability Tables, 2007, (newsletter) Homeopathic Village Electronical Newsletter, 2003—. Mem.: History Channel Club, Folio Soc. Avocations: reading, gardening, computers, arms and armor collecting.

BRENNAN, CARRIE, principal; b. 1967; BA, Darthmouth Coll., Hanover, NH; MA, U. Ariz. Founding faculty mem. Catalina Foothills High Sch.; prin. City High Sch., Tucson. Co-dir. Southern Ariz. Writing Project's Tchr. Inst.; workshop instructor curriculum design and collaborative profl. devel.; chair Symposium on Sch. Improvement. Involved with Tucson Small Sch. Project. Named one of 40 Under 40, Tucson Bus. Edge, 2006. Office: City High School PO Box 2608 Tucson AZ 85702 Office Phone: 520-623-7223. Office Fax: 520-547-0680. Business E-Mail: carrie@cityhighschool.org.

BRENNAN, DAVID R., pharmaceutical executive; BBA, Gettysburg Coll. From sales rep. (US Divsn.) to gen. mgr. Merck and Co., Inc. and Chibret Internat. (subs. of Merck and Co., Inc.), 1975—92; joined Astra Merck Inc. (joint venture between Astra AB and Merck, then Astra Merck merged in 1998 with Astra USA of Boston to create Astra Pharm.); v.p. mktg. and bus. planning and develop. Astra Merck Inc. and Astra Pharma. LP, 1992—99; sr. v.p., commercialization and portfolio mgmt. AstraZeneca Pharma. LP, 1999—2001; sr. v.p., bus. planning and develop. Astra Pharm. L.P. (merged with Astra AB and Zeneca PLC); pres., CEO AstraZeneca LP, Wilmington, Del., also bd. dir.; exec. v.p., N.Am. AstraZeneca PLC, 2001—06, CEO London, 2006—. Mem. exec. bd. Pharma. Rsch. and Manufactures Am. Chmn. bd. dirs. Am. Heart Assn. (Southeastern Pa.); bd. dir. CEO Roundtable on Cancer. Office: Astrazeneca PLC 15 Stanhope Gate London W1K 1LN England Office Phone: 302-886-3000, 800-456-3669.

BRENNAN, DONALD A., retail executive; Sr. v.p., gen. mdse. mgr. men's and children's Burdines divsn. Federated Dept. Stores; exec. v.p. mdse. planning and allocation Kohl's Corp., Menomonee Falls, Wis., 2001—04, exec. v.p., gen. mdse. mgr. men's and children's, 2004—. Office: Kohls Corp N56 W17000 Ridgewood Dr Menomonee Falls WI 53051-5660 Office Phone: 262-703-7000.*

BRENNAN, DONNA LESLEY, public relations company executive; b. Washington, Mar. 13, 1945; d. Don Arthur and Louise (Tucker) B.; m. James L Bergey, Mar. 6, 1999. BA, Denison U., 1967. Tchr. Souderton Area H.S., Pa., 1967—69; mgr. media rels. Ins. Co. N.Am., Phila., 1969—72; dir. press rels. Colonial Penn Group, Phila., 1972—75, 1975—81, dir. comm., 1981—83; v.p. corp. comm. Norstar Bancorp, Albany, NY, 1983—85; v.p. comm. Meritor Fin. Group, Phila., 1986—87; pres. Donna Brennan Assocs., Chester Springs, Pa., 1988—. Bd. dirs. A Chance to Heal, 2005—, French & Pickering Creeks Conservation Trust, 2006—, Forum Found., 2006—. Mem. Pub. Rels. Soc. Am. (pres. Phila. chpt. 1988), Phila. Women's Network (founder, bd. dirs.), Pathways Pa. (vice-chmn. 1995—, bd. dirs.), Forum of Exec. Women (pres. 1992-93, bd. dirs. 1989-97). Home Phone: 610-469-8746; Office Phone: 610-469-8765. E-mail: db@brennanpr.com.

BRENNAN, EDWARD A., air transportation and former retail executive; b. Chgo., Jan. 16, 1934; s. Edward and Margaret (Bourget) B.; m. Lois Lyon, June 11, 1955; children: Edward J., Cynthia Walls, Sharon Lisnow, Donald A., John L., Linda Thode. BS, Marquette U., 1955. With Sears, Roebuck and Co., 1956—95, asst. gen. mgr., NY group retail stores, 1969—72, gen. mgr., western NY group, 1972—75, adminstrv. asst. to the v.p., Ea. terr., 1975, gen. mgr., Boston group, 1976, exec. v.p. So. terr. Atlanta, 1977-80, pres. merchandise group Chgo., 1980-81, chmn., CEO merchandise group, 1981-84, corp. pres., COO merchandise group, 1984-86, chmn., pres., CEO, 1986—95; exec. chmn. AMR Corp. and Am. Airlines, 2003—. Bd. dirs. Minn. Mining & Mfg. Co., AMR Corp., 1987-, Allstate Corp., 1993-, 3M, Exelon Corp., McDonald's Corp. Chmn. bd. trustees Marquette U.; trustee De Paul U., Rush-Presbyn.-St. Luke's Med. Ctr. Mem. Bus. Roundtable, Bus. Coun. Office: AMR Corp 4333 Amon Carter Blvd Fort Worth TX 76155

BRENNAN, FRANCIS PATRICK, banker; b. Somerville, Mass., Jan. 9, 1917; s. John Joseph and Bridget (Sullivan) B.; m. Mary J. Gilhooly, July 23, 1949; children: Mary Ann, Eileen, John, Thomas. AB cum laude, Boston Coll., 1939; postgrad., Bentley Coll. Accounting and Finance, 1941. Loan officer Reconstrn. Finance Corp., Boston, 1941-42, 46-53; exec. v.p. Mass. Bus. Devel. Corp., Boston, 1954-61; chmn., chief exec. officer Union Warren Savs. Bank, Boston, 1961-87; vice-chmn. Home Owners Savs. Bank (merger Union Warren Savs. Bank), Boston, 1987-90. Bd. dirs., trustee, chmn. audit com. Boston Co. Funds, Inc.; chmn., pres., treas. Laurel Mut. Funds, 1993—; bd. dirs., exec. and fin. coms., chmn. audit and salary com. Boston Mut. Life Ins. Co., chmn. Dreyfus/Laurel Mutual Funds. Former trustee vice chmn. exec. com., chmn. fin. com. Stonehill Coll.; chmn. Mass. Bus. Devel. Corp.; mem. Sidney Farber Cancer Inst., Boston; mem. Mass. Hist. Soc.; past bd. dirs. Boston Mcpl. Research Bur., Greater Boston Real Estate Bd., Boston met. chpt. ARC. 2d lt. AUS, 1942-45, ETO. Decorated Bronze Star. Mem. Savs. Banks Assn. Mass. (pres. 1972-73), Mass. Bankers Assn. (dir.-at-large), Greater Boston C. of C. (v.p., admitted to Acad. of Disting. Bostonians 1992), Algonquin Club (Boston), Clover Club (Boston), Winchester Country Club, Madison Sq. Garden Club, Knights of Malta, Knights of Holy Sepulchre. Roman Catholic. Home: 36 Central St Winchester MA 01890-2630 Office Phone: 781-928-1103.

BRENNAN, GERALD D. (JERRY), biotechnology company executive; BSBA in Acctg. and Bus. Economics, Marquette U.; JD, University of Ill. CPA Ill.; bar: Ill. Tax mgr. Coopers & Lybrand; tax counsel Premark; v.p. distributor operations and admin. Tupperware N. Am.; pres. Tupperware

Canada; gen. counsel Tupperware Worldwide; CFO, COO Capcom Coin-Op, Inc.; CFO, Great Lakes fine chem. div. and Monsanto Pharma Tech Great Lakes Chem. Corp., dir. new ventures; v.p. admin. and financial operations, CFO Aastrom Biosciences Inc., 2005—.

BRENNAN, HENRY HIGGINSON, architect; b. Chgo., Nov. 25, 1932; s. Henry D. and Ann (Higginson) Brennan; m. Margaret Butler, 1960; children: Henry Higginson Jr., Kathryn Ann Brennan Smith, Martin Timothy, Jennifer M. B.Arch., U. Ill., 1958. Registered arch., 12 states. Draftsman Westchester Constrn., White Plains, NY, 1958—59; job capt. Ketchum & Sharp, NYC, 1959—61, project architect, dir. prodn., 1961—73; sr. v.p., dir. N.Y. office Welton Becket, 1973—84; ptnr. Brennan Beer Gorman/Archs., 1984—. Prin. works include master plan and design of maj. office bldgs., hotels, retail and mixed-use complexes. Mem.: AIA, Apawamis Club (Rye, NY). Office: Brennan Beer Gorman Architects 515 Madison Ave New York NY 10022-5403 E-mail: hankbrennan@bellsouth.net.

BRENNAN, JAMES JOSEPH, lawyer, bank executive; b. Chgo., July 14, 1950; s. John Michael and Rosemary (Rickard) Brennan; m. Donna Jean Blessing, June 2, 1973; children: Michael James, Laura Jessica. BS, Purdue U., 1972; JD, Indiana U., 1975. Bar: Ind. 1975, U.S. Dist. Ct. (so. dist.) Ind. 1975, U.S. Tax Ct. 1975, U.S. Ct. Appeals (6th cir.) 1976 U. S. Ct. Appeals (4th cir.) 1977, Ill., 1978, U.S. Dist. Ct. (no. dist.) Ill. 1978, U.S. Ct. Appeals (7th cir.) 1978, U.S. Supreme Ct. 1981. Law clk. to judge U.S. Dist. Ct. (ea. dist.), Tenn., 1975-77; ptnr. Pope, Ballard, Shepard & Fowle, Ltd., Chgo., 1977-87, Hopkins & Sutter, Chgo., 1987-91; ptnr., co-chmn. fin. svcs. group Barack, Ferrazzano, Kirschbaum & Perlman, Chgo., 1991-99; exec. v.p. corp. affairs, gen. counsel BankFinancial Corp., 2000—. Chmn. legal affairs com. Ill. Bankers Assn., Chgo., 1986, chmn. bank counsel sect., 1987; lectr. programs for bankers, bank examiners, accts. and bank counsel; participant drafting of various Ill. banking laws; adj. prof. grad. sch. bank law Ill. Inst. Tech. Kent Coll. Law, 1992-2000. Articles editor Ind. Law Rev., 1974—75; editor: Ill. Bankers Assn. Law Watch, 1988—94; contbr. articles to profl. jours. 1st recipient Disting. Bank Counsel award, Ill. Bankers Assn., 1989. Mem. Riverside Golf Club (bd. dirs. 1992-2000, sec.-treas. 1995-98), Western Golf Assn. (bd. dirs. 1998—, Evans Scholars (Purdue chpt. 1968-72, pres. 1970-71). Business E-Mail: jbrennan@bankfinancial.com.

BRENNAN, JOHN JOSEPH, mutual fund company executive; b. Boston, July 29, 1954; s. Francis Patrick and Mary Josephine (Gilhooley) B.; m. Catharine Barbara Joyce, May 17, 1980; children: William Thomas, Kara Boggs, Conor Hewette Bruen. AB, Dartmouth U., 1976; MBA, Harvard U., 1980. Planner N.Y. Bank for Savs., 1976-78; fin. mgr. S.C. Johnson & Son, Inc., Racine, Wis., 1980-82; asst. to the chmn. The Vanguard Group, Inc., Valley Forge, Pa., 1982-85, sr. v.p., chief fin. officer, 1985-86, exec. v.p., 1986-89, pres., 1989—96, CEO, 1996—, chmn., 1998—. Bd. dirs. ICI Mut. Ins. Co. Mem. Fin. Exec. Inst., Mut. Fund Edn. Alliance (gov. 1985—, exec. v.p. 1986—). Roman Catholic. Office: Vanguard Group Investment PO Box 2600 Valley Forge PA 19482-2600

BRENNAN, JOHN JOSEPH, lawyer, administrator; b. Troy, NY, Nov. 1, 1958; s. James Patrick and Grace Marie (Bartolomeo) B. AAS, Schenectady CC, NY, 1978; BA cum laude, Siena Coll., 1981; JD cum laude, Union U., 1985. Bar: N.Y. 1986, U.S. Dist. Ct. (no. dist.) N.Y. 1986, U.S. Supreme Ct. 1999. Law clk. to Appellate Divsn. Justice 4th Dept., Herkimer, N.Y., 1985-86; assoc. law ck. to justice State Supreme Ct., Herkimer, 1986-90; law clk. to U.S. Magistrate-Judge, Utica, N.Y., 1991-92; assoc. law clk. to justice N.Y. Supreme Ct., Utica, 1992—2001, 2002—. Adj. prof. Herkimer County CC, 2003—; mem. panel Surrogate Decision Making Program, 2002—. Bd. dirs. Mohawk Valley Red Cross, Utica Zoo. Mem. ABA, N.Y. State Bar Assn., Oneida County Bar Assn. (bd. dirs.), Herkimer County Bar Assn. (treas. 1990), KC, Pi Gamma Mu. Roman Catholic. Avocations: running, skiing. Home: 119 Court St Herkimer NY 13350-1923 Office: Herkimer County Ct House Utica NY 13350

BRENNAN, JOSEPH, lawyer; m. Molly Tschida Brennan; 2 children. Grad., Vanderbilt U.; JD, Ind. U. Ind. contractor Miller, Faucher, Chertow, Cafferty & Wexler, Chgo.; dep. purchasing agent, dir. contracts, asst. corp. counsel City of Chgo.; corp. counsel BlueMeteor Inc., 1999—2001; gen. counsel, sec. T-Systems N.Am. Inc., 2001—05; v.p. external affairs, gen. counsel The Field Mus. of Natural History, 2005—. Office: The Field Mus of Natural History 1400 S Lake Shore Dr Chicago IL 60605-2496 Office Phone: 312-922-9410.

BRENNAN, LAWRENCE EDWARD, retired electronics engineer; b. Oak Park, Ill., Jan. 29, 1927; s. Lawrence John and Lillian Irene (Day) B.; m. Mary Ellen Green, Aug. 9, 1947; children: Kathleen, Marianne, Teresa, James. BSEE, U. Ill, 1948; PhD in Elec. Engring., U. Ill., 1951. Mem. tech. staff Rand Corp., Santa Monica, Calif., 1957-67; chief scientist Tech. Svc. Corp., Santa Monica, 1967-80; v.p. Adaptive Sensors, Inc., Santa Monica, 1980-93; cons. pvt. practice, Orange Beach, Ala., 1993—99; ret., 1999—. Served with USN, 1944-46. Fellow: IEEE. Home Phone: 251-987-1526. E-mail: lbrennan@gulftel.com.

BRENNAN, MAUREEN, lawyer; b. Morristown, NJ, Aug. 7, 1949; BA magna cum laude, Bryn Mawr Coll., 1971; JD cum laude, Boston Coll., 1977. Bar: Pa. 1977, U.S. Dist. Ct. (ea. dist.) Pa. 1978, Ohio 1989. Atty. U.S. EPA, Washington, 1977-80; asst. dist. atty. Phila. Trial and Appellate Divs., 1980-84; in-house environ. counsel TRW Inc., 1985-87; assoc. Baker & Hostetler LLP, Cleve., 1987-91, ptnr., 1991—. Adj. prof. Case Western Res. U., Cleve., 1990-92, 00-06. Active Cleve. Tree Commn., 1991-96, co-chair, 1993-95; trustee Clean-Land Ohio, 1990-2000; rep. Canal Heritage Corridor Com., 2000—; mem. Cuyahoga County Greenspace Working Group, 1999-2002; bd. dirs. Crown Point Ecology Ctr., 2001--. Recipient Bronze Medal for Achievement, U.S. EPA, 1980. Mem. ABA (natural resources and environ. sect., standing com. environ law 1996-98), Pa. Bar Assn. (environ. law com.), Ohio State Bar Assn. (environ. law com.), Cleve. Bar Assn. (environ. law sect., chair wetlands com. 1991-92, sect. chair 1996-97, mem. steering com. adv. OEPA on Brownfield regulations 1995-97). Office: Baker & Hostetler LLP 3200 Nat City Ctr 1900 E 9th St Ste 3200 Cleveland OH 44114-3475 Office Phone: 216-861-7957. Business E-Mail: mbrennan@bakerlaw.com.

BRENNAN, MICHAEL J., lawyer; b. Mountain Lakes, New Jersey, Oct. 16, 1956; AB cum laude, with distinction in Govt., Dartmouth Coll., 1978; JD cum laude, Georgetown U. Law Ctr., 1983. Bar: Md. 1983. Ptnr., Real Estate Dept. Venable LLP, Towson, Md. Lectr. in field. Assoc. editor The Tax Lawyer, 1982—83. Bd. mem. Literary Works Inc., Chesapeake Habitat for Humanity; mem. Balt. County Leadership Program, Balt. County Loan Rev. Bd. Mem.: Dartmouth Lawyers Assn., ABA, Md. State Bar Assn., Balt. County Bar Assn. Fluent in Spanish. Office: Venable LLP 210 Allegheny Ave PO Box 5517 Towson MD 21204 Office Phone: 410-494-6271. Office Fax: 410-821-0147. Business E-Mail: jmbrennan@venable.com.

BRENNAN, MURRAY FREDERICK, surgeon, oncologist; b. Auckland, New Zealand, Apr. 2, 1940; came to U.S., 1970; m. Susan Chambers, May 26, 1973; children: Sean, Ryan, Meghan, Patrick. BSc, U. New Zealand, 1961; B Medicine B Surgery, U. Otago, New Zealand, 1964, ChM, MD, U. Otago, New Zealand, 1983, DSc (hon.), 1997; MD (hon.), U. Goteborg, Sweden, 1991. Surg. intern and resident U. Otago, 1965-69; clin. rsch. fellow Harvard Med. Sch., Boston, 1970-72; sr. resident, clin., rsch. fellow Peter Bent Brigham Hosp., Boston, 1972—75; sr. investigator, vis. scientist Nat. Cancer Inst., Bethesda, Md., 1975-81; prof. surgery, attending surgeon N.Y. Hosp./Cornell Med. Ctr., NYC, 1981—; vis. physician Rockefeller U., NYC, 1981-93; attending surgeon Meml. Sloan-Kettering Cancer Ctr., NYC, 1981—, chmn. dept. surgery, 1985—. Fellow ACS, Royal Australian Coll. Surgeons, Brazilian Coll. Surgeons (hon.), Royal Coll. Surgeons in Ireland (hon.); mem. Inst. Medicine NAS, Royal Coll. Surgeons Edinburgh (hon.), Royal Coll. Physicians and Surgeons Glasgow (hon.), Asian Surg. Soc. (hon.), Assn. Surgeons of Gt. Britain and Ireland (hon.), Royal Coll. Surgeons Eng. (hon.), Royal Australasian Coll. Surgeons (hon.), Royal Coll. Physicians and Surgeons in Can. (hon). Office: Meml Sloan-Kettering Cancer Ctr 1275 York Ave New York NY 10021-6094

BRENNAN, NOELLE C., lawyer; JD, DePaul U., 1995. Assoc. Katten Muchin & Zavis; trial atty., supervisory atty. Equal Employment Opportunity Commn.; ptnr. Brennan & Monte Ltd. Adj. prof. employment discrimination; ct. apptr. monitor overseeing hiring practices and compliance with ct. orders City of Chgo. Named one of 40 Under 40, Crain's Chgo. Bus., 2005. Office: Brennan & Monte Ltd Ste 1530 20 South Clark St Chicago IL 60603 Office Phone: 312-422-0001. Office Fax: 312-422-0008. E-mail: nbrennan@brennan-monte.com.

BRENNAN, NORMA JEAN, professional society administrator, director; b. Helena, Mont., Apr. 16, 1939; d. Harland Sanford Herrin and Elizabeth (Wardlaw) Brumfield; m. Anthony E. Brennan, Dec. 4, 1964 (div. Mar. 1986); children: Christopher E., Kimberly A. BA, U. Pacific, 1960. Editl. asst. Am. Rocket Soc., NYC, 1961-62, asst. mng. editor, 1962-65; mng. editor AIAA, NYC, 1978-80, publs. divsn. dir. NYC, Washington, Reston, Va., 1980—. Mem. Young Republicans, Stockton, Calif., 1958-60; vol. Mt. Sinai Hosp., N.Y.C., 1962-64. Fellow: AIAA (Space Shuttle Flag award); mem.: Washington Women's Info. Network, N.Am. Serials Interest Group, Coun. Engring. and Sci. Soc. Execs., Assn. Am. Pubs., Coun. Sci. Editors, Soc. for Scholarly Pub. (bd. dirs.). Avocations: reading, travel, gardening. Home: 11551 Links Dr Reston VA 20190-4820 Office: AIAA 1801 Alexander Bell Dr Reston VA 20191-4344 E-mail: normab@aiaa.org.

BRENNAN, PATRICK J., lawyer; b. Bronx, NY, Oct. 28, 1963; BA, Fordham U., 1984; JD, St. John's U., 1987. Bar: NY 1988, US Dist. Ct. So. Dist. NY, US Dist. Ct. Ea. Dist. NY. Asst. dist atty., Bronx County, NY, 1987—92; ptnr. Wilson, Elser, Moskowitz, Edelman & Dicker LLP, NYC. Mem.: NY State Bar Assn., Assn. of the Bar of the City of NY. Office: Wilson Elser Moskowitz Edelman & Dicker LLP 23rd Fl 150 E 42nd St New York NY 10017-5639 Office Phone: 212-490-3000 ext. 2302. Office Fax: 212-490-3038. Business E-Mail: brennanp@wemed.com.

BRENNAN, ROBERT LAWRENCE, educational director, psychometrician; b. Hartford, Conn., May 31, 1944; BA, Salem State Coll., 1967; M of Art in Tchg., Harvard U., 1968, EdD, 1970. Rsch. assoc., lectr. Grad. Sch. Edn., Harvard U., Cambridge, Mass., 1970-71; asst. prof. edn. SUNY, Stony Brook, 1971-76; sr. rsch. psychologist Am. Coll. Testing Program, Iowa City, 1976-79, dir. measurement rsch. dept., 1979-84, asst. v.p. for measurement rsch., 1984-92, disting. rsch. scientist, 1990-94. Dir. Iowa Testing Programs, 1994-2002; adj. faculty Sch. Edn. U. Iowa, 1979-94, E.F. Lindquist prof. edn. measurement, 1994—, dir. ctr. for advanced studies in measurement and assessment, 2002—. Author: Elements of Generalizability Theory, 1983, Test Equating Methods and Practices, 1995, Generalizability Theory, 2001, Test Equating, Scaling and Linking Methods and Practices, 2004; editor: Methodology Used in Scaling the Act Assessment and P-ACT, 1989, Cognitively Diagnostic Assessment, 1995, Educational Measurement, 4th edit., 2007; assoc. editor Applied Psychological Measurement, 1982—, Jour. Ednl. Measurement, 1978-83, 96—; contbr. articles to profl. jours. Harvard U. prize fellow, 1967. Fellow: APA; mem.: Iowa Acad. Edn. (pres. 1996—99), Psychometric Soc., Nat. Coun. Measurement Edn. (bd. dirs. 1987—90, v.p. 1995, pres. 1997—98, Tech. Contbn. award 1997, Career Contbn. award 2000), Am. Statis. Assn., Midwestern Ednl. Rsch. Assn. (pres. 1987—88), Am. Ednl. Rsch. Assn. (v.p. 1994—96, Divsn. D award 1980, E.F. Lindquist Career Contbn. award 2004). Home: 1925 Liberty Ln Coralville IA 52241-1071 Office: Univ Iowa 210D Lindquist Ctr Iowa City IA 52242-1533 Office Phone: 313-335-5405. Business E-Mail: robert-brennan@uiowa.edu.

BRENNAN, ROBERT WALTER, association executive; s. Walter R. and Grace A. (Mason) B.; m. Mary J. Engler, June 15, 1962; children: Barbara, Susan (twins). BS Edn., U. Wis., 1957. Tchr., coach Waukesha HS, Wis., 1959-63; asst. track coach U. Wis.-Madison, 1963-69; head track coach, 1969-71; exec. asst. to mayor City of Madison, 1972-73; pres. Greater Madison C. of C., Madison, 1973-2004; cons. U. Wis.-Madison Chancellor's Office, Corp. Rels., 2004—. Mem. adv. council U. Wis.-Madison Sch. Edn., 1984—; mem. Madison Urban League, 1971—; bd. dirs. Cherokee Park, Inc., Wis. Nordic Sports Found.; dir. Wis. C. of C. Execs., 1974-76, Very Slp. Arts-Wis., 1983-2000, World Dairy Ctr. Authority, 1993-95, Wis. Exec. Residence Found., 1993-, Wis. Sesquicentennial Commn., 1998, U. Wis.-Madison Bus. Sch. Weinart Applied Ventures Program, 1997-; chmn. bd. dirs. Wis. Innovation Network, 1987-; sec., treas. Wis. Tech. Coun., 2000-. Second lt. US Army. Named Madison's Favorite Son, 1971; recipient Pen & Mic Club award, 1971, Know Your Madisonian award, 1975, Religious Heritage of Am. award, 1978, Nat. award Family Found. of Am., 1980. Mem. Wis. Alumni Assn. (nat. bd. dirs. 1981-2000, pres. 1985-86, chmn. bd. 1986-87), "W" Club (life, cert. of merit), Downtown Rotary Club (dir. 1974-76), Phi Epsilon Kappa, Theta Delta Chi (life). Home: 5514 Comanche Way Madison WI 53704-1026 Office: Greater Madison C of C 615 E Washington Ave Madison WI 53703-2952 Home Phone: 608-249-1848; Office Phone: 608-263-1394. Personal E-mail: rwbrennan@charter.net. Business E-Mail: rwbrennan@bascom.wisc.edu.

BRENNAN, THOMAS EMMETT, lawyer; b. Detroit, May 27, 1929; s. Joseph Terence and Jeannette Frances (Sullivan) B.; m. Pauline Mary Weinberger, Apr. 28, 1951; children: Thomas Emmett, Margaret Ann and John Seamus (twins), William Joseph, Marybeth, Ellen Mary. LL.B., U. Detroit, 1952; LL.D., Thomas M. Cooley Law Sch., 1976. Bar: Mich. 1953. Assoc. Kenny, Radom, Rockwell & Mountain, Detroit, 1952-53; ptnr. Waldron, Brennan & Maher, Detroit, 1953-61; judge Detroit Ct. Common Pleas, 1962-63, Wayne County Circuit Ct., 1963-66; justice Mich. Supreme Ct., 1967-73, chief justice, 1969-70; adj. prof. polit. sci. U. Detroit, 1970-72; founder, dean emeritus Thomas M. Cooley Law Sch., Lansing, 1972—. Mem. Mich. Commn. Law Enforcement and Criminal Justice, 1969-70; bd. dirs. Motor Wheel Corp., 1987-89. Author: Judging the Law Schools, 1997, The Bench, 2000. Founder, commr. Am. Golf League, 2000; bd. dir. Cath. League for Religious & Civil Rights, 1993—. Fellow Am. Bar Found., Mich Bar Found.; mem. ABA, Ingham County Bar Assn., State Bar Mich. (bd. commrs. 1979-83), Mich. Assn. of Professions (Disting. Citizens award 1982), Assn. of Ind. Colls. and Univs. Mich. (bd. dirs., exec. com., sec. 1990, chmn. 1991), Cath. Lawyers Soc. (Thomas More award 1987), Am. Jurisprudence Soc., Inc. Soc., Irish Am. Lawyers, Cooley Legal Author's Soc. (charter), Mich. State C. of C. (bd. dirs. 1988-94), Walnut Hills Country Club (bd. dirs. 1992-95), KC, Delta Theta Phi. Roman Catholic. Home: 12953 Grand Traverse Dr Dade City FL 33525 Office: American Golf League 12953 Grand Traverse Dr Dade City FL 33525-8251 Personal E-mail: thosbrennan@aol.com.

BRENNAN, THOMAS JOHN, city and state official, consultant, educator; b. Bklyn., Mar. 23, 1923; s. Thomas Joseph and Violet Emma (Jurgens) B.; m. Margaret Karen Jensen, Sept. 18, 1948; children: Debra Gail, Mark Kevin, Laurie Kathleen. AB, Wittenberg Coll., 1949; MGA, U. Pa., 1950. Cons. Pub. Adminstrn. Svc., Chgo., 1950—56; dep. sec. for adminstrn. Dept. Welfare Commonwealth Pa., Harrisburg, 1957—59; dep. sec. for state properties Pa. Dept. Property and Supplies, 1959—64; exec. officer Del. Dept. Mental Health, Dover, 1965—67; v.p. Exec. Mgmt. Svc., Arlington, Va., 1967—76; exec. dir. Gov.'s Justice Commn. Pa. Commn. on Crime and Juvenile Delinquency, 1976—79; dir. water utility City of New Brunswick, NJ, 1983—91, chief labor negotiator, 1988—91, pers. mgr., 1988—91, exec. officer police dept., 1989—91, pub. mgmt. cons., 1991—. Adj. instr. U. Del., 1965—67; adj. assoc. prof. Rider Coll., Lawrenceville, NJ, 1983—84, Lawrenceville, 1984—85; hearing officer N.J. Dept. Civic Svc., Trenton, 1976—2002; cons. exam. constrn., 1985—2000; cons. to staff com. UN, 1982—84; cons. various municipalities and agys.; presenter papers to profl. orgns. Bd. dirs. Bucks County Opera, Pa., 1975-80, Bucks County Play House, New Hope, Pa., 1970s; elected mem. alumni coun. Wittenberg U., 1989—; mem. Merrill's Mauraders, WWII. Decorated Silver Star, Bronze Star with 2 oak leaf clusters, Combat Infantry badge; recipient various plaques; Fels scholar U. Pa., 1948. Mem. VFW, Internat. Personnel Mgmt. Assn., Am. Pub. Works Assn. (dist. rep. Eastern Pa. bldg. and grounds com.), Am. Water Works Assn., Internat. Chief of Police Assn., Nat. Conf. State Justice Planning Adminstrn. (regional chmn., exec. com.), Criminal Justice Tng. Inst. (chmn. planning com. 1978-79), Huntington Valley Hunt (Bucks County, bd. dirs. 1975-80), Am. Legion, Upper Makefield Hist. Soc. (bd. dirs.), Wharton Alumni (Phila.), U. Pa. Emeritus Soc. (steering com. 2004—), Fraternal Order of Police. Avocations: fox hunting, pleasure riding. Home: 327 Pineville Rd Newtown PA 18940-3111

BRENNAN, TODD, information technology executive; BSEE, Cornell Univ.; MS in Elec., Computer Engring, PhD in Elec., Computer Engring, Univ. Wis. Software engr., VLSI Adv. Methodology group Digital Equipment Corp.; rsch. staff, satellite comm. divsn. MIT Lincoln Lab.; founder Okena (acquired by Cisco 2003); founding chmn., chief tech. officer Bit 9, Inc., Cambridge, Mass. Named one of Top 25 Chief Tech Officers, InfoWorld mag., 2006. Office: Bit 9 Inc Ten Canal Pk Ste 201 Cambridge MA 02141 Office Phone: 617-393-7400. Office Fax: 617-393-7499.*

BRENNAN, TROYEN A., insurance company executive, physician, educator, lawyer; m. Wendy Warring; 2 children. MA philosophy & politics, Oxford U.; MD, JD, MPH, Yale U., 1984. Intern, resident Mass. Gen. Hosp.; internist Brigham & Womens Hosp., Boston, 1987—2006; pres., CEO Brigham & Women's Physicians Org., Boston, 1997—2005; prof. law & pub. health Harvard U. Sch. Pub. Health, 1992—2006; prof. medicine Harvard U. Med. Sch., 1995—2006; sr. v.p., chief medical officer Aetna Inc., Hartford, Conn., 2006—. Trustee Am. Bd. Internal Medicine Found., Philadelphia; bd. govs. ACP. Contbr. chapters to books, articles to scholarly & scientific journals; author: (books) Just Doctoring: Medical Ethics in the Liberal State, 1991; co-author: A Measure of Malpractice: Medical Injury, Malpractice Litigation, & Patient Compensation, 1993, New Rules: Regulation, Markets, & the Quality of American Health Care, 1995, Health Care & Policy: Readings, Notes, & Questions, 1998. Mem.: Inst. Medicine. Office: Aetna Inc 151 Farmington Ave Hartford CT 06156*

BRENNAN, WILLIAM JOSEPH, manufacturing executive; b. Buffalo, Feb. 11, 1928; s. Laurence J. and Mary Julia (Scherer) B.; m. Rita Jeanne Brooks, Dec. 27, 1947; 1 dau., Susan. BA, Bryant and Stratton Coll., 1949. With Fedders Corp., 1949—, asst. controller corp., 1962-64, dir. distbn. brs., 1965-67, v.p., dir. sales, 1967-74, v.p., dir. adminstrn., 1974-77; pres. Fedders Fin. Corp., 1977-78, group v.p. diversified products, 1978-80, v.p. fin., chief fin. officer, 1980; exec. v.p., chief fin. officer, dir. Fedders Corp., Peapack, NJ, 1986-87; pres. NYCOR Inc., Peapack, 1987-88; fin. cons. Fedders Corp., NYCOR Inc., 1988—. Bd. dirs. Fedders Corp.; chmn. bd. dirs. CSM Environ.; arbitrator NYSE. Served with AUS, 1946-47. Republican. Roman Catholic. Home and Office: 224 Whispering Woods Ct Little Silver NJ 07739 Personal E-mail: bb842@aol.com.

BRENNAN, WILLIAM P. (BILL BRENNAN), computer company executive; B in Econs., U. Ill. Various positions IBM Corp., 1979—93; ind. bus. cons., 1993—2003; v.p. sales and product ops. Forsythe Technology, Inc., Skokie, Ill., 2003—05, pres., 2005—. Bd. dirs. Forsythe Solutions Group, Inc., Forsythe Technology, Inc. Mem.: Soc. Info. Mgmt. Office: Forsythe Technology Inc 7770 Frontage Rd Skokie IL 60077 Office Phone: 847-213-7000.

BRENNAN-BERGMANN, BRIDGET CATHERINE, special education educator; b. San Antonio, June 10, 1955; d. Eugene Anthony and Evelyn Joyce Brennan; m. Ernest Bergmann, Jr., Dec. 29, 1997. BS, Stephen F. Austin State, Nacogdoches, Tex., 1978; MEd, North Tex. State U., Denton, 1981. Cert. tchr. for life in areas ednl. diagnostician, physically handicapped, elem. and psychology tchr. Tchr. Stoneleigh Day Sch., Denton, 1978, Hartford County, Md., 1987—90; tchr., diagnostician Lewisville I.S.D., Tex., 1978—84, diagnostician, 1985—87; tchr., counselor Am. Sch., Guadalajara, Mexico, 1984—85; tchr., spl. edn. dept. chair Randolph Field Elem. Sch., Randolph AFB, 1990—. Vol. Therapeutic Horseback Riding, San Antonio, 2003—05; leader support group Alzheimer's Assn., Schertz, Tex., 2004—. Named Tchr. of Game, San Antonio Spurs/Rampage, 2003; recipient Carol Gray award tchr. outstanding students, Future Horizons, Arlington, Tex., 2004. Mem.: Assn. Tex. Profl. Educators, Phi Delta Kappa, Alphi Chi. Avocations: doll collecting, antiques, gardening. Office: Randolph Field Elem Sch Bldg 146 Randolph Afb TX 78148 Office Fax: 210-357-2346.

BRENNECKE, ALLEN EUGENE, lawyer; b. Marshalltown, Iowa, Jan. 8, 1937; s. Arthur Lynn and Julia Alice (Allen) B; m. Billie Jean Johnstone, June 12, 1958; children: Scott, Stephen, Beth, Gregory, Kristen BBA, U. Iowa, 1959, JD, 1961. Bar: Iowa 1961. Law clk. U.S. Dist. Judge, Des Moines, 1961—62; assoc. Mote, Wilson & Welp, Marshalltown, Iowa, 1962—66; ptnr. Harrison, Brennecke, Moore, Smaha & McKibben, Marshalltown, 1966—2000; of counsel Moore, McKibben, Goodman, Lorenz & Ellefson, LLP, Marshalltown, 2000—. Contbr. articles to profl. jours. Bd. dirs. Marshalltown YMCA, 1966-71; mem. bd. trustees Iowa Law Sch. Found., 1973-86, United Meth. Ch., Marshalltown, 1978-81, 87-89; fin. chmn. Rep. party 4th Congl. Dist., Iowa, 1970-73, Marshall County Rep. Party, Iowa, 1967-70. Fellow ABA (chmn. ho. of dels. 1984-86, bd. govs. 1982-86), Nat. Jud. Coll. (bd. dirs. 1982-88), Am. Coll. Trusts and Estates Counsel, Am. Coll. Tax Counsel, Am. Bar Found., Iowa Bar Assn. (pres. 1990-91, award of merit 1987); mem. Masons, Shriners, Promise Keepers. Republican. Methodist. Avocations: golf, travel, sports. Office: Moore McKibben Goodman Lorenz & Ellefson LLP 302 Masonic Temple Marshalltown IA 50158 Office Phone: 641-752-4271. Personal E-mail: blackbear703@marshallnet.com. Business E-Mail: attorneys@marshalltownlaw.com.

BRENNEIS, ANNE SCHAACK, religious studies educator; b. El Monte, Calif., Mar. 1, 1961; d. Richard Allen and Bonnie Rae Schaack; m. Martin Robert Brenneis, Nov. 10, 2002. Student, Excelsior Coll., Albany, NY. Med. transcriptionist Transcriptions, Ltd., Mt. Laurel, NJ, 1989—99; tchr., tutor St. John San Francisco Orthodox, 1994—. Vol. tutor San Rafael Sch. Vols., Calif., 2005—; treas. Marin Rep Women. Fedn., 2006; choir mem. Holy Virgin Russian Orthodox Cathedral, San Francisco, 1994—. With USN, 1981—87. Avocations: music, history, languages.

BRENNEMAN, DELBERT JAY, lawyer; b. Albany, Oreg., Feb. 4, 1950; s. Calvin M. and Velma Barbara (Whitaker) B.; m. Caroline Yorke Allen, May 29, 1976; children: Mark Stuart, Thomas Allen. BS magna cum laude, Oreg. State U., 1972; JD, U. Oreg., 1976. Bar: Oreg. 1976, U.S. Dist. Ct. Oreg. 1977, U.S. Ct. Appeals (9th cir.) 1977. Assoc. Schwabe, Williamson, and Wyatt, Portland, Oreg., 1976-83, ptnr., 1984-92, Hoffman, Hart &

Wagner, Portland, Oreg., 1993—. Spkr. Oreg. Self-Ins., 1978, 90; seminar instr. U. Oreg. Law Sch., Eugene, 1980. Mem. ABA, Oreg. State Bar Assn., Multnomah County Bar Assn. (spkr. 1983-84), Order of Coif, Multnomah Athletic Club, Propeller Club of U.S. (bd. dirs. 1983-85), Phi Kappa Phi, Beta Gamma Sigma. Office: Hoffman Hart & Wagner 1000 SW Broadway Fl 20 Portland OR 97205-3072 Home Phone: 503-292-4667; Office Phone: 503-222-4499. Personal E-mail: brennemans@hotmail.com. Business E-Mail: djb@hhw.com.

BRENNEMAN, GREGORY D., food service executive; b. Newton, Kans., Nov. 26, 1961; m. Ronda K. Brenneman; 3 children. BA in Acctg. and Fin., Washburn U., Topeka, Kansas; MBA with distinction, Harvard Bus. Sch. V.p. Bain & Co., Inc., 1987—93; founder, chmn., CEO TurnWorks, Inc., 1994, 2001—04, 2006—; cons. Continental Airlines Inc., Houston, 1993—95, COO, 1995—2001, pres., 1996—2001; CEO PricewaterhouseCoopers Consulting, 2002, Burger King Corp., Miami, 2004—06, chmn., 2005—06; pres., CEO Quiznos Combined Entity LLC, Denver, 2007—. Bd. dirs. Continental Airlines, Inc., 1995—2001, Home Depot, Inc., 2000—, Automatic Data Processing, Inc., 2001—. Office: TurnWorks Inc 1330 Lake Robbins Dr Ste205 The Woodlands TX 77380 also: Quiznos 1475 Lawrence St Ste 400 Denver CO 80202*

BRENNEMAN, HUGH WARREN, JR., judge; b. Lansing, Mich., July 4, 1945; s. Hugh Warren and Irma June Brenneman; m. Catherine Brenneman; 2 children. BA, Alma Coll., 1967; JD, U. Mich., 1970. Bar: Mich. 1970, D.C. 1975, U.S. Dist. Ct. (we. dist.) Mich. 1974, U.S. Dist. Ct. Md. 1973, U.S. Ct. Mil. Appeals 1971, U.S. Ct. Appeals (6th cir.) 1976, U.S. Ct. Appeals (D.C. cir.) 1981, U.S. Supreme Ct. 1980. Law clk. Mich. 30th Jud. Cir., Lansing, 1970-71; asst. U.S. atty. Dept. Justice, Grand Rapids, Mich., 1974-77; assoc. Bergstrom, Slykhouse & Shaw PC, Grand Rapids, 1977—80; magistrate judge US Dist. Ct. (we. dist.) Mich., Grand Rapids, 1980—. Instr. Western Mich. U., Grand Valley State U., 1989-92. Active Gerald R. Ford coun. Boy Scouts Am., 1984—, v.p., 1988—92, pres., 2006—; mem. Grand Rapids Hist. Commn., 1991—97, pres., 1995—97; dir. Cmty. Reconciliation Ctr., 1991; past bd. dirs. Welcome Homes for the Blind; pres. Rotary Charities Found., Grand Rapids, 2006—. Capt. JAGC US Army, 1971—74. Recipient Disting. Alumnus award Alma Coll., 1998. Fellow Mich. State Bar Found.; mem. FBA (pres. Western Mich. chpt. 1979-80, nat. del. 1980-84), U.S. Dist. Ct. Hist. Soc. (pres. 2002-04), State Bar Mich. (rep. assembly 1984-90), D.C. Bar Assn., Grand Rapids Bar Assn. (chmn. U.S. Constn. Bicentennial com., co-chmn. Law Day 1991), Fed. Magistrate Judges Assn., Am. Inns of Ct. (master of bench Grand Rapids chpt., pres.), Phi Delta Phi, Omicron Delta Kappa, Rotary (past pres., Paul Harris fellow), Econ. Club of Grand Rapids (past bd. dirs.). Congregationalist. Office: US Dist Ct West Mich 110 Michigan St NW Rm 580 Grand Rapids MI 49503-2313 Office Phone: 616-456-2568.

BRENNEMAN, TAMI K., not-for-profit fundraiser; d. Carol J. and Jon C. Eggert (Stepfather); m. Jeremy J. Brenneman; children: Laura K., Amy L. BBA (hon.), Am. InterContinental U., Ill., 2006. Legal sec. Barker, Cruise, Kennedy, Houghton & Foster Law Office, Iowa City, 1987—94; legal asst., office mgr. Davis Foster Law Firm, Iowa City, 1994—2000; charitable and events coord. Iowa Donor Network, North Liberty, Iowa, 2001—. Mem.: Assn. Fund Raising Profls. (treas. Ea. Iowa chpt. 2007—), Donor Family Coun. Mennonite. Office: Iowa Donor Network 550 Madison Ave North Liberty IA 52317 Home Phone: 319-646-2300; Office Phone: 319-665-3787.

BRENNEN, STEPHEN ALFRED, management consultant; b. NYC, July 07; s. Theodore and Margaret (Pembroke) B.; m. Yolanda Alicia Romero, Sept. 28, 1957; children: Stephen Robert, Richard Patrick. AB cum laude, U. Americas, Mexico City, 1956; MBA, U. Chgo., 1959. Supr. Montgomery Ward, Chgo., 1956; credit mgr. Aldens, Chgo., 1956-59; gen. mgr. Purina de Guatemala, 1964-66; pres. Purina Colombiana, Bogotá, 1967-69; founding pres. Living Marine Resources, Inc., San Diego, 1969-70; mng. dir. Central and S. Am. Ralston Purina, Caracas, Venezuela, Coral Gabels, Fla., 1970-74; pres. Van Camp Seafood Co., San Diego, 1974-79; chmn. P.S.C. Corp., Buena Park, Calif., 1979-81; pres. Inter-Am. Cons. Group, San Diego, 1981-85; chmn. Beta Enterprises Inc., 1986-91. Advisor Nat. Productivity Exch.; spl. asst. C.A.O., County of San Diego, Calif., 1987-95; mng. ptnr. Interam. Cons. Group, 1983-95; ptnr. Acad. Interpreting & Translations, Internat., 1995; assoc., owner the Montgomery Group, Inc., La Jolla. Author: Successfully Yours. Past mem. adv. bd. Mexican-Am. Found. Served with USAF. Mem. U. Chgo. in San Diego (past pres.). Roman Catholic. Office Phone: 858-354-2508. Personal E-mail: ybrennen@aol.com.

BRENNER, BARRY MORTON, physician; b. Bklyn., Oct. 4, 1937; s. Louis and Sally (Lamm) B.; m. Jane P. Deutsch, June 12, 1960; children: Robert, Jennifer. BS, L.I. U., 1958; MD, U. Pitts., 1962; MA (hon.), Harvard U.; DSc (hon.), Long Island U.; D.M.Sc. (hon.), U. Paris, (Pierre et Marie Curie); diploma (hon.), Charles U., Prague; fellow (hon.), Royal Coll. of Physicians, London; MD (hon.), U. Complutense, Madrid. Asst. prof. medicine U. Calif.-San Francisco, 1969-72, asso. prof. medicine and physiology, 1972-75; prof. medicine and physiology U. Calif., San Francisco, 1975-76; Samuel A. Levine prof. medicine Harvard Med. Sch., Boston; with Peter Bent Brigham Hosp., Boston, 1976—; dir. renal div. Brigham and Women's Hosp., Boston, 1979-2001, dir. emeritus, 2001—. Dir. physician-scientist program, Harvard Med. Sch., 1984-90, Harvard Ctr. for Study of Kidney Diseases, 1987-2000; cons. NIH. Editor: The Kidney, 2 vols., 1976, 7th edit., 2004, Renal Pathology, 2 vols., 1989, 2d edit., 1994, Textbook of Hypertension, 2 vols., 1990, 2d edit., 1995; Acute Renal Failure, 1985, 3d edit., 1994; co-editor Contemporary Issues in Nephrology, 1978-90; founding editor Current Opinion in Nephrology and Hypertension, 1992—; contbr. numerous articles to profl. jours. Recipient Homer W. Smith award N.Y. Heart Assn., 1984, George E. Brown award Am. Heart Assn., 1983, Merit award NIH, 1984, SKF Disting. Scientist award 1985, Donald W. Seldin and David Hume awards Nat. Kidney Found., 2003, Am. Acad. Arts and Scis., 1995, Philip S. Hench Disting. Alumnus award, U. Pitt., 1995, Novartis award Coun. High Blood Pressure Rsch. Am. Heart Assn., 2005, rsch. grantee NIH, 1969-2000. Fellow AAAS, Molecular Med. Soc.; mem. Am. Soc. Cell Biology, Am. Physiol. Soc., Assn. Am. Physicians (councillor), Am. Soc. Clin. Investigation (councillor, v.p.), Am. Soc. Nephrology (councillor, pres., John P. Peters award), Am. Soc. Hypertension (exec. com., pres., Richard Bright award), Internat. Soc. Nephrology (councillor, Jean Hamburger award, Amgen Internat. prize), Western Assn. Physicians, Salt and Water Club, Interurban Clin. Club, Alpha Omega Alpha, Phi Sigma. Office: 75 Francis St Boston MA 02115-6110 Office Phone: 617-732-5850. Business E-Mail: bbrenner@partners.org.

BRENNER, BETH FUCHS, publishing executive; Grad., U. Vt., 1980. Sales promotion coordinator Chanel, Inc., 1980-83; promotion mgr. M mag., 1983-86; adv. sales rep. New York mag., 1986-91, adv. dir., 1991-93, SELF mag., 1993-94, pub., 1994-2001, v.p., pub., 2001—04; v.p., pub. domino mag., 2004—. Office: Domino Mag 4 Times Sq New York NY 10036-6562 E-mail: Beth_Brenner@condenast.com.

BRENNER, EDGAR H., legal association administrator; b. NYC, Jan. 4, 1930; s. Louis and Bertha B. (Guttman) B.; m. Janet Maybin, Aug. 4, 1979; children from previous marriage— Charles S., David M., Paul R. BA, Carleton Coll., 1951; JD, Yale U., 1954. Bar: D.C. 1954, U.S. Ct. Claims 1957, U.S. Supreme Ct. 1957. Mem. 2d Hoover Commn. Legal Task Force Staff, Washington, 1954; trial atty. U.S. Dept. Justice, Washington, 1954-57; assoc. Arnold & Porter, Washington, 1957-62, ptnr., 1962-89. Co-dir. Inter Univ. Ctr. for Legal Studies, 1999—. Co-editor: Legal Aspects of Terrorism in the United States, Terrorism and the Law, U.S. Federal Legal Responses to Terrorism, The United Kingdom's Legal Responses to Terrorism; contbr. articles to profl. jours. Commr. Fairfax County Econ. Devel. Corp., Va., 1963—78; trustee emeritus Insts. Behavior Resources; bd. dirs., treas. Stella and Charles Guttman Found., NYC; bd. dirs. Ams. for Med. Progress, Arlington, Va. Recipient Disting. Achievement award Carleton Coll., 2001; fellow Coll. Problems of Drug Dependency. Mem. D.C. Bar Assn., Yale Club, Explorers Club (N.Y.C.). Democrat. Home: 340 Persimmon Ln Washington VA 22747-1845 Office: 4620 Lee Hwy Ste 216 Arlington VA 22207-3400 Office Phone: 703-524-0880. Personal E-mail: edgarhbrenner@email.com.

BRENNER, EGON, academic administrator, consultant; b. Vienna, July 1, 1925; s. Aaron and Margarethe (Adler) B.; m. Rhoda Greenberg, Dec. 24, 1950; children: Dorothy, Claudia. B.E.E., CCNY, 1944; M.E.E., Poly. Inst. Bklyn., 1949, D.E.E., 1955. Mem. faculty CCNY, 1946-81, prof. elec. engring., 1966-81, dean engring., 1971-73, acting provost, 1973-74, provost, v.p. acad. affairs, 1974-76; acting vice chancellor for acad. affairs CUNY, 1976-77, dep. chancellor, 1978-81; exec. v.p. Yeshiva U., 1981-93, prof. emeritus. Vis. prof. Tex. Tech. U., summer 1965, U. Okla., 1966 Author: (with M. Javid) Analysis of Electric Circuits, 1959, 2d rev. edit., 1967, Analysis, Transmission and Filtering of Signals, 1963. Served with AUS, 1944-46. Decorated Bronze Star. Fellow IEEE, AAAS; mem. Am. Soc. Engring. Edn., Sigma Xi, Eta Kappa Nu, Tau Beta Pi. Address: 1601 Abaco Dr Coconut Creek FL 33066 Personal E-mail: egonb25@gmail.com.

BRENNER, ELIZABETH (BETSY BRENNER), publishing executive; b. Bellevue, Wash. m. Steven Ostrofsky. BJ, MBA, Northwestern U. City news reporter The Chgo. (Ill.) Tribune, 1977, bus. news reporter, columnist, 1978; with mktg. dept. The New York Times; with retail advt. and circulation posts Miami Herald, Rocky Mountain News, Denver, sr. v.p. sales and mktg., 1994—96; pub. Bremerton (Wash.) Sun, 1996—98, The News Tribune, Tacoma, 1998—2004; pres. & pub. Milw. Jour. Sentinel, 2004—; v.p. Journal Comm. Inc., 2004—06, exec. v.p., 2006—; COO Journal Comm. Inc. Pub. Businesses, 2006—. Bd. dirs. Econ. Devel. Bd, Tacoma, Mus. Glass, Greater Tacoma Cmty. Found., exec. coun.; mem. Tacoma adv. coun. U. Wash.; co-chmn. campaign Olympic Coll. Libr. Kitsap County; bd. dirs. United Way of Greater Milw., Boys & Girls Club, Greater Milw. Com. Named to Hall of Achievement, Northwestern U. Medill Sch. Journalism, 2006. Mem.: Audit Bur. Circulations (Liason com.), Newspaper Assn. Am. (Mktg. com.). Office: Milwaukee Journal Sentinel PO Box 371 Milwaukee WI 53201 Office Phone: 414-224-2954. E-mail: betsy.brenner@mail.tribnet.com, bbrenner@journalsentinel.com.*

BRENNER, FRANK, lawyer; b. NYC, Oct. 26, 1927; s. Jack and Betty (Teifer) B.; children: Jay Marlow, Matthew Adam, Amy Rebecca, Diane Rachel. BA cum laude, Lehigh U., 1948; JD, Harvard U., 1951. Bar: N.Y. 1951, U.S. Supreme Ct. 1955, U.S. Tax Ct. 1975. Asst. dist. atty., NY County, 1951-55; pvt. practice NYC, 1955—2003; judge N.Y.C. Criminal Ct., 1983-84. Mng. dir. InterEquity Capital Corp., 1991-98; adminstrv. judge Waterfront Commn. N.Y. Harbor, 1994-98; jud. hearing officer N.Y. State Supreme Ct., 2000-03; arbitrator Nat. Assn. Securities Dealers, 2001—, Nat. Arbitration Forum, 2006—; spl. referee appellate divsn. Supreme Ct., 2002-03. Mem. mediation and arbitration panel JAMS/Endispute, 1993-99. With USNR, 1945-46. Recipient commendation Brit. Royal Commn. on Capital Punishment, 1950. Fellow Am. Acad. Matrimonial Lawyers; mem. ABA (litig. sect. com. on trial complex crimes 1977-2003, criminal justice sect. com. on def. function 1979-2003, RICO subcom. on white collar crime 1982-84), N.Y. State Bar Assn. (ho. dels. 1978-83, 85-90, 92-96, fellow, bar found. 1992-2003, com. on unlawful practice law 1984-89, criminal justice sect. com. on criminal discovery 1985-2002), Assn. Bar City N.Y. (spl. com. on legal aid inquiry 1971-2, com. on penology 1972-77, com. profl. discipline 1982-85, criminal cts. com. 2002-03), N.Y. County Lawyers Assn. (dir. 1977-83, pres. coun. of assn. 1992-2002, jud. com. 1991-2002, chmn. Pres. adv. com. criminal law, 1990-2003, chmn. com. criminal law 1968-70, 80-83, com. matrimonial law 1975-80, spl. com. on selection and tenure of judges 1975-77, spl. com. to review jud. discipline 1979-80), Fund for Modern Cts. (com. on ct. facilities 1985-2002), Harvard Club (N.Y.C., Sarasota). Home: 7958 Royal Birkdale Cir Bradenton FL 34202

BRENNER, FREDERIC JAMES, biology professor, ecologist, consultant; b. Warren, Ohio, Dec. 25, 1936; s. Frederick James and Katherine Louise (Newberry) B.; m. Patricia Elaine Gavin, Aug. 27, 1967; children: Elaine, Cheryl. BS, Thiel Coll., Greenville, Pa., 1958; MS, Pa. State U., University Park, 1960, PhD, 1964. Teaching intern Denison U., Granville, Ohio, 1964-65; asst. prof. biology Thiel Coll., 1965-69, Grove City Coll., Pa., 1969-70, assoc. prof. Pa., 1970-86, prof. Pa., 1986—. Pres. Brenner Ecol. Svc., Grove City, 1974—. Editor: (with others) Species Spl. Concern Pa., 1985, Endangered and Threatened Species Program in Pa., 1986, Environ. Consequences of Energy Prodn., 1987, Wetlands Ecology and Conservation Emphasis in Pa., 1989, Biological Diversity: Problems and Consequences, Environmental Contaminants, Ecosystems and Human Health, 1995, Forests: A Global Perspective, 2005, Wildlife Disease: Landscape Epidemiology Spatial Distribution and Utilization Remote Sensing Technology, 2005; contbr. over 300 articles to profl. jours. Chmn. Mercer County Solid Waste Authority, 1988—; sec.-treas. Mercer County Conservation Dist., 1975—; treas., vice chmn., chmn. Mercer County Regional Planning Commn., 1989-93, sec., 1990; mem. exec. bd. Shenango Conservency; mem. exec. bd. French Creek Coun., Erie, 1972, coun. pres. 2007-; dir. Woodbadge Course Boy Scouts Am., 1973-89 (Silver Beaver award 1973, Dist. award merit 1976). Recipient Nat. Conservation award DAR, 1989, Cmty. Svc. award Grove City United Way, 1993, Disting. Alumni Svc. award Alpha Phi Omega, 1994, 2004, Disting. Citizen award Boy Scouts Am., 2004. Fellow AAAS, Ohio Acad. Sci.; mem. Ecol. Soc. Am. (exec. coun. 1978-82), Pa. Acad. Sci. (editor newsletter PAS 1966, pres.-elect 1992-94, pres. 1994-96, exec. coun. 1986—, Lifetime Achievement award), Nat. Assn. Acad. Scis. (sec. 1995-98, pres.-elect 1998-99, pres. 1999-2000), Wildlife Soc. (pres. Pa. chpt. 1975-77), Nat. Assn. of Acad. of Sci. (pres. 1999-2000), Rotary (dist. gov. 2007—), Beta Beta Beta (v.p. 1993—, Yokley Faculty Svc. award). Republican. Episcopalian. Avocations: hunting, fishing, hiking, camping. Office: Grove City Coll Dept Biol Grove City PA 16127 Office Phone: 724-458-2113. Personal E-mail: brenecol@zcominternt.net. Business E-Mail: fjbrenner@gcc.edu.

BRENNER, HOWARD, chemical engineering educator; b. NYC, Mar. 16, 1929; s. Max and Margaret (Wechsler) B.; children: Leslie, Joyce, Suzanne; m. Lisa Glucksman, Sept. 8, 1995. BChemE, Pratt Inst., 1950; MChemE, NYU, 1954, D in Engring. Sci., 1957. Instr. chem. engring. NYU, 1955-57, asst. prof. chem. engring., 1957-61, assoc. prof., 1961-65, prof., 1965-66, Carnegie-Mellon U., 1966-77; prof., chmn. dept. chem. engring U. Rochester, NY, 1977-81; W.H. Dow prof. chem. engring. MIT, Cambridge, Mass., 1981—. Sr. vis. fellow Sci. Rsch. Coun. Gt. Britain, 1974; Fairchild Disting. scholar Calif. Inst. Tech., 1975-76, Chevron vis. prof., 1988-89; Gulf vis. prof. Carnegie-Mellon U., Pitts., 1991; Lady Davis fellow, Israel, 1995-96; vis. prof. U. Calif., Berkeley, 1996. Author: (with J. Happel) Low Reynolds Number Hydrodynamics, 1965, 2d edit., 1973, Russian edit., 1976; (with D.A. Edwards and D.T. Wasan) Interfacial Transport Processes and Rheology, 1991; (with D. A. Edwards) Macrotransport Processes, 1993; contbr. articles to profl. jours.; co-editor in chief Physico-Chem. Hydrodynamics, 1988-89. Recipient Bingham Medal Soc. Rheology, 1980, Disting. Alumni award Pratt Inst., 2001, Caribbean Congress Fluid Dynamics award, 2001; Guggenheim fellow, 1988. Fellow AAAS, NAE, AIChE (Alpha Chi Sigma award 1976, Walker award 1985, Warren K. Lewis award 1999), Am. Acad. Mechanics; mem. NAS, Am. Acad. Arts and Scis., Soc. Rheology (Bingham medal 1980), Am. Phys. Soc. (Fluid Dynamics prize 2001), Am. Chem. Soc. (Kendall award 1988, 11th ann. Honor Scroll Indsl. Engring. Chemistry Divsn. 1961), Am. Soc. Engring. Edn. (Gen. Electric Sr. Rsch. award 1996). Office: MIT Dept Chem Engring Rm 66 562 77 Massachusetts Ave Cambridge MA 02139-4307 Office Fax: 617-258-8224. Business E-Mail: hbrenner@mit.edu.

BRENNER, JANET MAYBIN WALKER, lawyer; b. Arkansas City, Kans. d. D. Arthur and Maybin (Gardner) Walker; children: Margaret Maybin Potthast, Theodore Kimball Jonas, Amanda Nash Freeman; m. Edgar H. Brenner, Aug. 4, 1979. AB, U. So. Calif.; JD, George Washington U., 1978. Bar: D.C. 1978, U.S. Dist. Ct. (D.C. cir.), U.S. Supreme Ct. Sponsor Brenner Women's Leadership com.; mem. women's com. Corcoran Gallery Art, Washington, 1969—. Mem. women's com. Found. for Preservation of Hist. Georgetown; trustee Phillips Collection. Mem. D.C. Bar Assn., Sulgrave Club (Washington). Home: 3325 R St NW Washington DC 20007-2310 also: Shadow Ridge Farm Washington VA 22747

BRENNER, JOEL F., federal agency administrator; b. 1947; BA, U. Wis.; PhD, London Sch. Economics; JD, Harvard U. Atty. U.S. Dept. Justice; inspector gen. Nat. Security Agy., 2002—06; exec., mission mgr. counterintelligence Nat. Counterintelligence, Washington, 2006—. Office: Nat Counterintelligence Exec NCIX CS5 Rm 300 Washington DC 20505 Office Phone: 703-682-4500. Fax: 703-682-4510.

BRENNER, MARK LEE, academic administrator, physiologist, educator; b. Boston, June 19, 1942; s. Harry D. and Beatrice (Price) B.; m. Ruth Abramson, Aug. 30, 1964; children: Jonathan, Tamara. BS, U. Mass., 1964, MS, 1965; PhD, Mich. State U., 1970. From asst. prof. to prof. horticultural scis. U. Minn., St. Paul, 1970—98, assoc. dean Grad. Sch., 1989-94; assoc. v.p. rsch., 1992-94; v.p. rsch. and dean Grad. Sch., 1994-98; vice chancellor rsch. and grad. edn. Ind. U.-Purdue U., Indpls., 1998—; assoc. v.p. rsch. Ind. U., Bloomington, Ind., 1998—. Cons. Abbott Labs., Chgo., 1988-89, Monsanto Corp., St. Louis, 1982-86, 88; bd. dir. Coun. Govt. Rels., ETS-GRE; v.p. bd. dirs. Assn. Accreditation Human Rsch. Protection Programs, Inc.; mem. Coun. Rsch. Policy and Grad. Edn., 1999—. Contbr. articles to profl. jours. Fellow Am. Soc. Horticultural Scis. (Outstanding Grad. Educator award 1993); mem. Am. Soc. Plant Physiologists (exec. com. 1986-89), Internat. Plant Growth Substance Assn. (sec.-treas. 1988-91), Minn. Chromatography Forum (pres. 1980-81, Palmer award 1986). Home: 8070 Lynch Ln Indianapolis IN 46250-4222 Office: Office of Vice Chancellor Rsch and Grad Edn Admin Bldg 122 355 N Lansing St Rm 122 Indianapolis IN 46202-2596 Office Phone: 317-274-1020. Business E-Mail: mbrenner@iupui.edu.

BRENNER, MICHAEL BARRY, rheumatologist, educator; BS magna cum laude, Washington U., St. Louis, 1971; MD, Vanderbilt U., 1975. Intern, resident, chief resident in internal medicine Vanderbilt U. Hosp., Nashville, 1975—79; rsch. assoc. dept. pathology Dana-Farber Cancer Inst., Boston, 1982—84, investigator divsn. tumor virology, 1984—85; asst. prof. medicine dept. rheumatology and immunology Harvard Med. Sch. and Brigham and Women's Hosp., Boston, 1986—89; chief lab. immunochemistry Dana-Farber Cancer Inst., Boston, 1988—92; assoc. prof. medicine dept. rheumatology and immunology Harvard Med. Sch. and Brigham and Women's Hosp., Boston, 1990—91; K. Frank Austen prof. medicine dept. rheumatology and immunology Harvard Med. Sch., Boston, 1991—2006, Theodore Bevier Bayles prof. medicine, 2006—, chief lymphocyte biology sect., 1991—; chief divsn. rheumatology, immunology and allergy Brigham and Women's Hosp., Boston, 1995—, sr. physician; fellow in rheumatology UCLA, 1979—81. Mem.: NAS. Office: Harvard Med Sch/Brigham and Women's Hosp Dept Medicine One Jimmy Fund Way Boston MA 02115*

BRENNER, RAYMOND ANTHONY, priest; b. Evansville, Ind., Feb. 12, 1943; s. George Frederick and Marie Catherine (Gries) B. BA, St. Meinrad Coll., Ind., 1965; MDiv, St. Meinrad Sch. Theology, 1969. Ordained priest Roman Cath. Ch., 1969. Deacon Nativity Ch., Indpls., 1968; assoc. pastor St. John's Ch., Loogootee, Ind., 1969-74, Sts. Peter and Paul Ch., Haubstadt, Ind., 1974-78; pastor St. Mary's Ch., Sullivan, Ind., 1978-86, St. Joan of Arc Ch., Jasonville, Ind., 1982-86, Resurrection Ch., Evansville, 1986—2002, St. Joseph Ch., Jasper, Ind., 2002—. Mem. Cath. Charities Bd., Evansville, 1972-75; v.p. Ministerial Assn., Sullivan, 1985-86; pres. Coun. of Priests, Evansville, 1989; diocesan chaplain St. Vincent de Paul Soc., Evansville, 1990-94. Mem. Wabash Valley Human Svcs., Vincennes, Ind., 1982-86, Sullivan Housing Authority, 1983-85, Fed. Emergency Mgmt. Agy., Sullivan, 1984-86, Emergency Food Bank, Sullivan, 1984-86; spiritual advisor Evansville Cath. Cursillo, 1994—; chaplain German Twp. Vol. Fire Dept., 1998-2002, Cmty. Marriage Builders, 1997—2006. Mem. Optimists (chaplain Evansville Westside club 1990-2002, dist. chaplain Ind. South 2006-07), Elks. Democrat. Address: St Joseph Cath Ch 1020 Kundek St Jasper IN 47546-1917 E-mail: rbrenner@evansville-diocese.org. *It takes so little time to offer a smile, and the rewards are beyond imagining. Somehow they know you care and that God cares too.*

BRENNER, ROBIN E., librarian; BA in Creative Writing, with honors, Bryn Mawr Coll., 1999; MS in Libr. and Info. Sci., U. Ill., Urbana-Champaign, 2003. Circulation desk asst. Canaday Libr., Bryn Mawr, Pa., 1997—99; libr. technician Cary Meml. Libr., Lexington, Mass., 1999—2006; reference and teen services libr. Brookline Pub. Libr., Brookline, Mass., 2006—. Judge Will Eisner Comics Industry Awards, 2007; lectr. in field. Author: Understanding Manga and Anime, 2007; creator, editor-in-chief: No Flying, No Tights. Named one of Top 20 Most Powerful People in Japanese Manga Publishing, ICv2 mag., 2006, also named one of the Movers & Shakers, Libr. Jour., 2007; recipient Disting. Leadership award, U. Ill. Grad. Sch. Libr. and Info. Sci. Alumni Assn., 2007. Mem.: Young Adult Libr. Services Assn. (popular paperbacks for young adults com. 2003—06, graphic novel task force 2003—05, great graphic novels for teens com. 2005—08), ALA. Office: Brookline Public Library 361 Washington St Brookline MA 02445 Office Phone: 617-730-2370. E-mail: robin@noflyingnotights.com.

BRENNER, SYDNEY, molecular biologist, researcher; b. Germiston, South Africa, Jan. 13, 1927; naturalized, British citizen; s. Morris and Lena (Blacher) B.; m. May Woolf Balkind, 1952; 3 children; 1 stepchild. MSc, U. Witwatersrand, Johannesburg, South Africa, 1947, MB, BCh, 1951; DPhil, Oxford U., 1954; 10 hon. degrees. Postdoctoral fellow U. Calif. Berkeley; mem. sci. staff Med. Rsch. Coun., Cambridge, England, 1957-92, dir. lab. molecular biology, 1979-86, dir. molecular genetics unit, 1986-91; fellow King's Coll., Cambridge U., 1959—; hon. fellow Exeter Coll., Oxford U., 1985; rsch. scientist dept. medicine U. Cambridge Sch. Clin. Medicine, 1992-96; mem. staff Scripps Rsch. Inst., La Jolla, Calif., 1992-94; pres., dir. The Molecular Scis. Inst., La Jolla & Berkeley, Calif., 1996—; disting. rsch. prof. The Salk Inst., La Jolla, Calif., 2000—. Carter-Wallace lectr. Princeton U., 1966, 77; Gifford lectr. U. Glasgow, Scotland, 1978-79; Dunham lectr. Harvard U., 1984; hon. prof. genetic medicine U. Cambridge Clin. Sch., 1989-96; lectr. in field. Contbr. articles to sci. jours. Recipient Warren Triennial prize, 1968, William Bate Hardy prize Cambridge Philos. Soc., 1969, Albert Lasker Med. Rsch. award, 1971, Royal medal Royal Soc., 1974, Charles-Leopold Mayer prize French Acad., 1975, Gairdner Found. ann. award, 1978, Krebs medal FEBS, 1980, CIBA medal Biochem. Soc., 1981, Feldberg Found. prize, 1983, Rosenstiel award Brandeis U., 1986, Prix Louis Jeantet de Medecine, Switzerland, 1987, medal Genetics Soc. Am., 1987, Harvey prize Technion-Israel Inst. Tech., 1987, Hughlings Jackson medal Royal Soc. Medicine, 1987, Waterford Bio-Med. Sci. award Rsch. Inst. Scripps Clinic, 1988, Kyoto prize Inamori Found., 1990, Gairdner Found. Internat. award, Can., 1991, King Faisal Internat. prize, 1992, Disting. Achievement award Bristol-Myers Squibb, 1992, Albert Lasker award for Spl. Achievement in Medicine, 2000, Novartis Drew award in Biomed. Sci., 2001, Nobel Prize in Physiology or Medicine, 2002. Fellow Royal Soc. (Croonian lectr. 1986, Royal medal 1974, Copley medal 1991), AAS, IASc (hon.) RSE (hon.), Royal Coll. Physicians (Neil Hamilton Fairley medal 1985) Royal Coll. Pathologists (hon.); mem. Max-Planck Soc., Deutsche Acad. Natural Sci. Leopoldina (Gregor Mendel medal 1970), Am. Philos. Soc. (fgn.), Real Acad. Ciencias (Spain), Am. Acad. Arts and Scis. (fgn. hon.), NAS (U.S., fgn. assoc.), Royal Soc. South Africa (fgn. assoc.), Acad. Europa, Chinese Soc. Genetics (hon.), Assn. Physicians Gt. Brit. and Ireland (hon.); associé étranger, Académie des Scis.; corr. Scientifique Emérite de l'INSERM. Office: Molecular Scis Inst 2168 Shattuck Ave Berkeley CA 94704-1307 E-mail: sbrenner@salk.edu.

BRENNER, THEODORE ENGELBERT, retired trade association administrator; b. NYC, Apr. 18, 1930; s. Engelbert F.J. and Julie M. (Kierschner) B.; m. Maria T. Finn, Sept. 12, 1953; children— John Finn, Elisabeth Ann, Christopher. BCE, Manhattan Coll., 1951; MS, Johns Hopkins, 1954. Registered profl. engr., Pa., N.J. Diplomate Am. Acad. Environ. Engrs. Mgr. waste treatment dept. Permutit div. Sybron Corp., Paramus, NJ, 1959-62; prin. Hydroscience, Inc., Ft. Lee, NJ, 1963; with Soap and Detergent Assn., NYC, 1963-93, v.p., tech. dir., 1970, v.p., dir. govt. affairs, 1971, pres., 1972-93; ret., 1993. Exec. dir. Joint Industry Govt. Task Force Eutrophication, 1968-70; mem. Dept. Interior Water Resources Sci., Info. Center Adv. Group, 1969-70; mem. spl. adv. com. N.Y. Temp. State Commn. on Water Resources Planning, 1964-67 Contbr.: chpt. to Advances in Environmental Sciences, Vol. II, 1969; articles to profl. jours. Mem. Rumson Bd. Edn., 1968-74, 1st v.p., 1973-74; mem. Rumson-Fair Haven Regional Bd. Edn., 1974-77, v.p., 1976-77. Served to capt. USAF, 1952-59; lt. col. ret. Mem. ASCE, AIChE, Am. Soc. Assn. Execs., Union League (N.Y.C.), Seabright (N.J.) Beach Club. Home: 5 Tyson Ln Rumson NJ 07760-1912

BRENT, DAVID A., psychiatrist, medical educator; b. Rochester, NY; BS, Pa. State U., 1972; MD, Jefferson Med. Coll., Phila., 1974; MSHyg, Univ. Pitts. Grad. Sch. Pub. Health, 1987. Pediat. intern U. Colo. Med. Ctr., Denver, 1974—75, psychosocial pediat. fellow, 1975—76; acting med. dir. Las Animas-Huerfano County Health Dept., Trinidad, Colo., 1976—77; psychiat. resident Psychiat. Dept., Univ. Pitts. Sch. Med., Western Psychiat. Inst. & Clinic, 1978—82, post-doctoral fellow, 1982—85, asst. prof. child psychiatry, 1982—89, assoc. prof., 1989—94, prof., 1994—, chief of child & adolescent psychiatry, 1990—98, academic chief, child & adolescent psychiatry, 1998—; co-founder, co-dir. Svcs. for Teens at Risk (STAR), Western Psychiat. Inst. & Clinic, Pitts., 1986—89, dir., 1989—. Dir. Advanced Ctr. for Intervention & Svcs. Rsch. for Early-Onset Mood & Anxiety Disorders; endowed chair in suicide studies Univ. Pitts. Sch. Med., 2002. Recipient Clin. Investigator award, NIMH, 1985, Beatrice Cummings Mayer award, Am. Acad. Child & Adolescent Psychiatry, 1993, Children's Mental Health Alliance Psychotherapy award, 1999, Rsch. award, Am. Found. Suicide Prevention, 1998, Dublin award, Am. Assoc. Suicidology, 2000, Beck Inst. award for Excellence in Cognitive Therapy, 2003, Blanche F. Ittleson award, APA, 2003, Simon Gratz Rsch. award, Jefferson Med. Coll., 2003, Voice of Mental Health award, Jed Found., 2004. Mem.: Inst. Medicine. Office: Western Psychiatric Inst & Clinic 3811 O'Hara St Pittsburgh PA 15213 Office Phone: 412-246-5596. Office Fax: 412-246-5344. E-mail: brentda@upmc.edu.

BRENT, PATRICIA LEE, health facility administrator, writer; d. Charles Robert and Marion Helen Brent; m. George Dewey Sorenson, Mar. 12, 1988. BS, Vt. Coll., 1968; MPH, Emory U., 1981; JD, Vt. Law Sch., 1997. Cert. med. technologist Am. Soc. Clin. Pathology, 1968. Dir. profl. svcs. Alice Peck Day Meml. Hosp., Lebanon, NH, 1981—87, v.p., strategic planning, 1987—94; pres. Morgan Hill Assocs., Meriden, NH, 1998—; rsch. asst. Dartmouth Med. Sch., Hanover, NH, 1968—70, rsch. assoc., 1972—79, Stanford U. Sch. Medicine, Palo Alto, Calif., 1970—72. Mem. editl. adv. bd. compliance CCH, Inc., Chgo., 2003—. Author: (book-medicare hosp. financing policy) Inside Medicare Outliers: Keys to Policy, Payment and Compliance, (book-medicare reimbursement policy) Understanding Reimbursement for Investigational Drugs and Devices, (web-based book) Critical Access Hospitals: The Application Process, 2005; content editor, cons. (web-based ednl. product) Medicare and Medicaid Now; contbr. articles to profl. jours. and newsletters. Mem. med. ethics com. Alice Peck Day Meml. Hosp., Lebanon, 1996—; chair rev. and allocations com. United Way Upper Valley, Lebanon, 1992—94, bd. mem., 1992—95, Am. Lung Assn., Manchester, 1984—92; pres. Human Svc. Coun. Upper Valley, 1988—92. Mem.: Healthcare Fin. Mgmt. Assn., Healthcare Compliance Assn. (region 1 planning com. 2000—05), Am. Health Lawyers' Assn. Episcopalian. Avocations: downhill skiing, birdwatching, hiking, antiques. Office: Morgan Hill Assos PO Box 176 Meriden NH 03770 Home Phone: 603-469-3600; Office Phone: 603-469-3536.

BRENT, ROBERT LEONARD, medical educator; b. Rochester, NY, Oct. 6, 1927; s. Charles and Rose (Katz) Brent; m. Lillian H. Hoffman, Aug. 21, 1949; children: David A., James R., Lawrence H., Deborah A. AB, U. Rochester, 1948, MD with honors, 1953, PhD, 1955, DSc (hon.), 1988. Fellow Nat. Found., Strong Meml. Hosp., 1953-54; intern pediatrics Mass. Gen. Hosp., Boston, 1954-55; chief radiation biology Walter Reed Army Inst. Rsch., 1955-57; mem. faculty Jefferson Med. Coll., 1955—, prof. radiology, 1962—, also prof. pediatrics, Louis and Bess Stein prof. pediatrics, 1985—, emeritus chmn. pediats., 1999—; apptd. Disting. prof. Thomas Jefferson U., 1989. Mem. human embryology study sect. NIH, 1970—74; hon. prof. Norman Bethume U. Med. Sci., China, 1992, W. China U. Med. Scis., Chengdu, 1992; chmn. med. adv. bd. Nat. Found.; mem. fertility and maternal health com. FDA; trustee Health and Environ. Sci. Inst., 1991—94; pres. First Internat. Congress Birth Defects, China, 1994; Taylor lectr. Nat. Coun. Radiation Protection and Measurements, 2006. Editor in chief: Teratology, 1976—93. With US Army, 1955—57. Recipient Med. Sch. award, Alpha Omega Alpha, 1952, Richie Meml. prize, U. Rochester Med. Sch., 1953, Lindback Found. award for Disting. Tchg., 1968, Burlington Internat. award, 1990, Landauer award, Health Physics Soc., 1995, Robley D. Evans Commemorative medal, 2001, Dean's medal, Thomas Jefferson U., 2007; fellow, Royal Soc. Medicine, 1971—72, FitzWilliam Coll., Cambridge, 1971—72; Lady Davis scholar, Hadassah Med. Ctr., Jerusalem, 1983—84. Mem.: AAAS, Ambulatory Pediat. Assn., European Teratology Soc., Japan Teratology Soc., Nat. Acad. Sci. (elected Inst. Medicine 1996), Nat. Coun. Radiation Protection, Soc. Devel. Biology, Am. Assn. Immunology (emeritus), Phila. Pediat. Soc., Phila. Coll. Physicians, Soc. Exptl. Biology and Medicine, Am. Acad. Pediat. (Merit citation 2001), Am. Pediat. Soc., Soc. Pediat. Rsch., Am. Soc. Exptl. Pathology, Radiation Rsch. Soc., Internat. Life Sci. Inst., Teratology Soc. (pres. 1967—68), Inst. Medicine NAS, Sigma Xi. Home Phone: 610-719-1996; Office Phone: 302-651-6880. E-mail: rbrent@nemours.org.

BRENT, ROBERT LEWIS, urologist; b. Detroit, May 27, 1936; s. Morris S. Brent and Anne Anita Fuller; m. Dasi Sosnick, June 9, 1957; children: Carol, Thomas, David, Gregg. BA, Wayne U., 1956; MD, Wayne State U., 1960. Diplomate Am. Bd. Urology. Intern Sinai Hosp. Detroit, Detroit, 1960—61, resident in gen. surgery, 1961—62, USAH Ft. Ord, 1962—64; resident in urology Phila. Gen. Hosp., 1964—67, sr. resident in urology, 1966—67; pvt. practice urology Detroit, 1967—93; assoc. prof. urology Wayne State U. Coll. Medicine, Detroit, emeritus, 1993—, William Beaumont Hosp., Royal Oak, Mich., 1993—, St. John's Hosps., Troy and Warren, Mich., 1993—. Cons. urologist Detroit Med. Ctr., 1968—93. Capt. US Army, 1962—64. Fellow: ACS; mem.: Am. Urology Assn. Jewish. Avocations: marathons, tennis, bridge. Home: 2721 Glenbrooke Ct Bloomfield Hills MI 48302 Office Phone: 248-335-0326. Personal E-mail: rbrent3696@aol.com.

BRENTLINGER, PAUL SMITH, venture capital executive; b. Dayton, Ohio, Apr. 3, 1927; s. Arthur and Welthy Otello (Smith) B.; m. Marilyn E. Hunt, June 23, 1951; children: Paula, David, Sara. BA, U. Mich., 1950, MBA, 1951. With Harris Corp., Melbourne, Fla., 1951-84, v.p. corp. devel., 1969-75, v.p. fin., 1975-82, sr. v.p. fin., 1982-84; ptnr. Morgenthaler Ventures, Cleve., 1984—. Former chmn., bd. dirs. Hypres, Inc., Elmsford, NY; former chmn., bd. trustees Cleve. Inst. Art, 1992—98. Mem. Union Club, Phi Beta Kappa. Home: 2755 Eaton Rd Cleveland OH 44122-1800 Office: Morgenthaler 50 Public Sq Ste 2700 Cleveland OH 44113-2236

BRENTLINGER, WILLIAM BROCK, college dean; b. Flora, Ill., Aug. 21, 1926; s. Arthur Kenneth and Frances (Maxwell) B.; m. Barbara Jean Weir, Dec. 29, 1946; children: Gregory, Gary, Rebecca Anne, Garth, Barbara Sue. Student, Washington U., 1946-47; AB, Greenville Coll., 1950; MA, Ind. State U., 1951; PhD, U. Ill., 1959. Instr. speech Greenville Coll., 1951-59, chmn. dept., 1959-62, dean of coll., 1962-69, dean coll. fine arts and comm., 1969-92; interim pres. Lamar U., Beaumont, Tex., 1992-93, asst. to pres., 1993—. Cons. higher edn. Served with USNR, 1944-46. Recipient tchr. study award Danforth Found., 1957 Mem. Internat. Council Fine Arts Deans, Speech Communication Assn. Am., Tex. Speech Assn., Tex. Assn. Coll. Tchrs., Tex. Council Arts in Edn. (pres.), Phi Kappa Phi. Clubs: Rotary (Beaumont). Baptist. Home: 6530 Salem Cir Beaumont TX 77706-5552 Office: Lamar U PO Box 10001 Beaumont TX 77710-0001 *I have always attempted to treat people as subjects, not objects, as fellow creatures of God, and thus to be worked with not worked upon.*

BRENZEL, JEFFREY, dean; m. Sally Brenzel; children: Paul, Sarah. BA, Yale U., 1975; PhD in philosophy, U. Notre Dame, 1992. With Nat. Assn. Securities Dealers, Ky. C. of C.; v.p. membership, edn. and svcs. Mich. C. of C.; founder InterLearn Inc., 1992; dir. undergraduate admissions Yale U., New Haven, 2005—. Mem.: Assn. Yale Alumni (exec. dir. 1997—2005). Office: Yale U Dean of Undergrad Admissions PO Box 208234 New Haven CT 06520-8234 Office Phone: 203-432-9321. E-mail: jeff.brenzel@yale.edu.*

BREON, APRIL MICHELLE, music educator; b. Shakopee, Minn., May 3, 1978; d. John Lee and Patricia Joan Hissink; m. Daniel Spencer Breon, Apr. 2, 2004. MusB in Ch. Music, S.W. Bapt. U., 1999; MusM in Piano Pedagogy, Mo. State U., 2007. Pvt. piano tchr., Springfield, 1998—; intern First Bapt. Ch., Springfield, 1999; music sec. Ridgecrest Bapt. Ch., Springfield, 2000—03. Coord. medals and chartering Nat. Royal Ranger Ministries, Springfield, 2003—06; sec. Greene County Bapt. Assn., Springfield, 2006—. Recipient Ronald Howard Surrette Meml. Ch. Music award, S.W. Bapt. U., 1999; scholar, 1996—99, 1997—99. Mem.: Music Tchrs. Nat. Assn., Piano Tchrs. Guild of Am., Springfield Piano Tchrs. Forum, Mo. (treas. 2000—07), Nat. Scholars Honor Soc. Southern Bapist.

BRERETON, TODD RICHARD, history professor; s. Thomas Frederick Brereton and Alma Lillian Hammond. BA, W.Va. Wesleyan Coll., 1977; MA, SW Tex. U., 1989; PhD, Tex. A&M U., 1994. Adj. prof. Blinn Coll., College Station, Tex., 1994—97; vis. asst. prof. U. Louisville, 1997—99, Georgetown Coll., Ky., 1999—2002; assoc. prof. Iowa Wesleyan Coll., Mount Pleasant, Iowa, 2002—. Contbr.: The Oxford Companion to American Military History, 1999; author: Educating the U.S. Army: Arthur L. Wagner and Reform, 1875-1905, 2000; contbr. Reader's Guide to Military History, 2001; contbr. Recipient West Point Mil. History Summer Seminar award, US Mil. Acad., 2000; Coll. of Liberal Arts Rsch. grant, Tex. A&M U., 1992, Office of Grad. Studies Rsch. grant, 1993. Mem.: Soc. for Mil. History, Orgn. of Am. Historians, Am. Hist. Assn. Office: Iowa Wesleyan Coll 601 N Main St Mount Pleasant IA 52641 Office Phone: 319-385-6336.

BRESANI, FEDERICO FERNANDO, manufacturing executive; b. Lima, Peru, Apr. 27, 1945; came to U.S., 1964; s. Federico L. and Beatriz (Ferrer) B.; m. Patricia Anne Grannis, Aug. 26, 1972; children: Christina Anne, Vianna Clarissa. BS in Elect. Engring., Milw. Sch. of Engring., 1970; MBA, Fairleigh Dickinson U., 1980. Engr. Cerro Corp., Lima, Peru, 1973-76; supr. Cerro Corp./CMP, NYC, 1976-77, mgr., 1978, purchasing mgr., 1979-80; product mgr. Schumag, Inc., Norwood, NJ, 1980-82, v.p., 1982; sales, mktg. mgr. EVG, Inc., NYC, 1983-85; v.p. EVG, NYC, 1986-92, pres., 1992—. Mem. Wire Assn. Internat., Wire Reinforcement Inst., Latin Am. Iron and Steel Inst., Am. Concrete Inst., Concrete Reinforcing Steel Inst., Rowayton Yacht Club, Omicron Delta Epsilon. Avocations: sailing, amateur radio. Office: EVG 220 E 42nd St New York NY 10017-5806 Office Phone: 212-697-0770. Business E-Mail: f.bresani@evg-usa.com.

BRESCHER, JOHN B., JR., lawyer; b. Elizabeth, NJ, July 8, 1947; BS, Lehigh U., 1969; JD, Georgetown U., 1972, LLM, 1976. Bar: N.J. 1973, D.C. 1975. Atty. McCarter & English, Newark. Adj. prof. law Seton Hall U., 1980—84. Mem.: ABA, N.J. State Bar Assn., Essex County Bar Assn. Office: McCarter & English PO Box 652 Four Gateway Ctr 100 Mulberry St Newark NJ 07102-4004 Office Phone: 973-639-2012. E-mail: jbrescher@mccarter.com.

BRESKY, STEVEN J., agricultural products executive; b. Apr. 2, 1953; s. H. Harry Bresky. V.p. Seaboard Corp., Mission, Kans., 1989—2001, sr. v.p. internat. ops., 2001—06, pres., CEO, 2006—07, chmn., pres., CEO, 2007—. Office: Seaboard Corp 9000 W 67th St Mission KS 66202*

BRESLAUER, KENNETH J., science educator, researcher; BS, Wis. U., 1968; MPhil, Yale U., 1970, PhD, 1972. With Rutgers, The State U. NJ, Piscataway, NJ, 1974—, prof., dean life sciences, 1996—, Linus C. Pauling prof. chemistry and chemical biology, v.p., Health Sci. Partnership, 2005—. Contbr. articles to profl. jours.; editor-in-chief Nucleic Acid Sciences, 1995—98, mem. editorial bd. Biopolymers, 1990—. Named one of 2007 People to Watch, Sunday Star-Ledger; recipient Wolfgang prize, 1970, Sunner Medal awards, 1985, Johnson & Johnson Rsch. Discovery award, 1987, Huffman Meml. award, 1995; Humboldt Fellow, 1981—82. Mem.: AAAS. Achievements include producing the first thermodynamic database that permits scientists to predict the stability of DNA; expert in the field of biocalorimetry. Office: Rutgers U Chemistry & Chemical Biology Wright Labs 610 Taylor Rd Office WL-155 Piscataway NJ 08854 Office Phone: 732-445-3956. Office Fax: 732-445-3409. Business E-Mail: kjbdna@rutchem.rutgers.edu.*

BRESLAWSKI, JAMES P., health products executive; CPA. Controller, v.p. fin., CFO Henry Schein Inc., Melville, NY, 1980—90, pres. Sullivan Schein Dental subs., 1990—2005, exec. v.p., 1992—2005, pres., COO, 2005—. Past chmn. Dental Trade Alliance. Trustee Long Island Univ. Office: Henry Schein Inc 135 Duryea Rd Melville NY 11747*

BRESLIN, ABIGAIL KATHLEEN, actress; b. NYC, Apr. 14, 1996; d. Michael and Kim Breslin. Actress (films) Signs, 2002, Raising Helen, 2004, The Princess Diaries 2: Royal Engagement, 2004, Keane, 2004, Chestnut: Hero of Central Park, 2004, Air Buddies, 2006, Little Miss Sunshine, 2006 (Best Young Actress, Critics Choice Award, Broadcast Film Critics Assn., 2007, Outstanding Performance by a Cast in a Motion Picture, SAG, 2007), The Ultimate Gift, 2006, The Santa Clause 3: The Escape Clause, 2006, No Reservations, 2007, (TV films) The Family Plan, 2005, (TV appearances) Hack, 2002, What I Like About You, 2002, Law & Order: Special Victims Unit, 2004, Navy NCIS: Naval Criminal Investigative Service, 2004, Ghost Whisperer, 2006, Grey's Anatomy, 2006, The View, 2006, MTV Video Music Awards, 2006, The Tonight Show with Jay Leno, 2006.*

BRESLIN, EILEEN MARY, lawyer; b. NYC; d. Hugh Edward Breslin Jr. and Eileen Edith Whalen; m. Joseph Amedeo Rocca, Sept. 4, 1983; children: Andrew Amedeo, Adriana Eileen, Stephanie Elizabeth. BA, SUNY, NYC, 1981; JD, Yale U., 1984. Bar: N.Y., U.S. Dist. Ct. (so. dist.) N.Y., U.S. Dist. Ct. (ea. dist.) N.Y. Assoc. corp. and banking dept. Milbank, Tweed, Hadley & McCloy LLP, NYC, 1984—95; ptnr. Greenberger & Forman, 1995—97; ptnr., mem. mgmt. com. Jaspan Schlesinger Hoffman, LLP, Garden City, 1997—2005; assoc. gen. counsel NBTY, Inc., Bohemia, 2006—. Asst. prof. SUNY, Farmingdale, 2007—. Mem. Nat. Assn. Women Bus. Owners (pres. L.I. chpt.), Am. Arbitration Assn. (mem. comml. panel), Assn. Bar NYC (mem. com. corp. law), L.I. Software & Tech. Network. Avocation: young astronauts program. Office: NBTY Inc 90 Orville Dr Bohemia NY 11716 Personal E-mail: embreslin@aol.com. Business E-Mail: ebreslin@nbty.com.

BRESLIN, MICHAEL JOSEPH, III, social services administrator, educator; b. Fountain Springs, Pa., Feb. 5, 1949; s. Michael Joseph Jr. and Barbara Ellin (Mellet) B. BS in Sociology, U. Scranton, 1971; MS in Adminstrn., Shippensburg U., Pa., 1984. Tchr. aide Selinsgrove (Pa.) Ctr., 1968, 69, 70; caseworker Northumberland County Children and Youth Agy., Sunbury, Pa., 1971-73; juvenile probation officer Northumberland County Juvenile Ct., 1973-74, supr., 1974-75, dir., 1976-87; dir. human svcs. Northumberland County Human Svcs., 1987-91; exec. dep. sec. Dept. Pub. Welfare, Harrisburg, Pa., 1992-95; v.p. Northwestern Corp., Harrisburg, Pa., 1995-97; sr. v.p. Northwestern Human Svcs., Harrisburg, 1997—. Adminstr. Northumberland County Mental Health and Mental Retardation Program, 1984-87; mem. adj. faculty Susquehanna U., Selinsgrove, 1989-91; cons. Tng. & Mgmt. Systems, Gibsonia, Pa., 1983-85; mem. Youth Svcs. Tng. Ctr., 1986-90. Mem. adv. bd. White Deer Run Treatment Ctr., Allenwood, Pa., 1975-77; advisor Explorer Pres. Assn., Netami dist. Boy Scouts Am., 1980-81, tng. coord. Explorer program, 1982-86, scouting coord. Explorer Post 2312, 1986-91; coord. high sch. youth program St. Michael's Ch., Sunbury, 1981-91, pres. parish coun., 1989-91; vice chmn. SSS, Sunbury, 1982-89; chmn. Sunbury Govt. Study Commn., 1989-90; bd. dirs. Hemlock coun. Girls Scouts U.S.A., 1990-95; bd. dirs. Pa. Partnerships for Children, 1996-2001, treas., 2001-2005, vice chmn., 2005, chmn., 2006—; mem. parish coun. St. Patrick Cathedral, Harrisburg, 1997-2000, mem fin. com., 2005—; bd. dirs. Found. for Preservation of St. Lawrence Chapel, 2005—; chair citizen rev. panel United Way Capitol Region, 1998-2000, bd. dirs., 2003—; chair Early Childhood Initiative Steering com. United Way, 1999-2005; bd. dirs. United Way Capital Region, 2003-, chmn. elect, 2006, chmn., 2007. Named Chief Probation Officer of Yr., Juvenile Ct. Judges Commn., Harrisburg, Pa., 1985, Profl. of Year, 2006; recipient Liberty Bell award Northumberland County Bar Assn., 1986, Meritorious Svc. award Pa. Foster Parents, 1988, affiliate award Pa. Assn. County Commrs., 1990, Citizen of Yr., City of Sunbury, 1992, Pres.'s award Pa. Assn. County Human Svc. Dirs., 1994, Disting. Svc. award Juvenile Detention Ctr. Adminstrs. Pa., 1994; named Profl. of Yr., Nat. Alliance Mental Illness Pa., 2006. Mem. Nat. Juvenile Ct. Svcs. Assn. (regional rep. 1989-93), Nat. Coun. Juvenile and Family Ct. Judges (awards com.), Nat. Juvenile Detention Assn., Nat. Juvenile Ct. Svcs. Assn., Mental Health and Mental Retardation Program Adminstrs. Assn., Mental Health and Mental Retardation Adminstrs. Assn. Pa. (chmn. 1989-91). Democrat. Office: Northwestern Human Svcs 1320 Linglestown Rd Harrisburg PA 17110-2822 Home: 4515 Laurelwood Dr Harrisburg PA 17110-2829 Office Phone: 717-441-9502. Personal E-mail: mikebreslin@comcast.net. Business E-Mail: mbreslin@nhsonline.org.

BRESLOW, ESTHER MAY GREENBERG, biochemistry professor, researcher; b. NYC, Dec. 23, 1931; d. Harry Daniel and Lillian (Solomon) Greenberg; m. Ronald Charles David Breslow, Sept. 4, 1955; children: Stephanie Ruth, Karen Ann. BS with distinction, Cornell U., Ithaca, NY, 1953; MS in Biochemistry, NYU, NYC, 1955, PhD in Biochemistry, 1959; postgrad., Radcliffe Coll., Cambridge, Mass., 1954-55. Postdoctoral fellow Cornell U. Med. Coll., NYC, 1959-61, rsch. assoc., 1961-64, asst. prof., 1964-72, assoc. prof., 1972-78, prof. biochemistry, 1978—2006, prof. emeritus, 2007—, acting chmn. dept. biochemistry, 1992-95. Mem. rev. panels NIH, Bethesda, Md., 1973—77, Bethesda, 1994—97, NSF, Bethesda, 1981—84. Mem. editl. bd. Jour. Biol. Chemistry, 1982-87, Internat. Jour. Peptide and Protein Rsch., 1981-97; contbr. articles to profl. jours. Mem. Englewood Bd. Health, NJ, 1986-94; mem. Dem. Mcpl. Com., Englewood, 1985-91. Fellow, Eli Lilly, 1954—55, USPHS, 1959—61; grantee, NIH, 1961—. Fellow AAAS; mem. Am. Soc. for Biochemistry and Molecular Biology, Am. Chem. Soc. (sec. divsn. biol. chemistry 1972-76), Harvey Soc., Sigma Xi. Home: 44 W 77th St New York NY 10024 Office: Joan and Sanford I Weill Med Coll Cornell U 1300 York Ave New York NY 10021-4805 Office Phone: 212-746-6428. Business E-Mail: ebreslow@med.cornell.edu.

BRESLOW, LESTER, public health physician, educator; b. Bismarck, ND, Mar. 17, 1915; s. Joseph and Mayme (Danziger) Breslow; m. Devra J.R. Miller, 1967; children: Norman, Jack, Stephen. BA, U. Minn., 1935, MD, 1938, MPH, 1941, DSc (hon.), 1988. Diplomate Am. Bd. Preventive Medicine and Public Health. Intern USPHS Hosp., Stapleton, NY, 1938—40; dist. health officer Minn. Dept. Health, 1941—43; preventive medicine officer U.S. Army, 1943—45; chief bur. chronic diseases Calif. Dept. Pub. Health, Berkeley, 1946—60, chief divsn. preventive medicine, 1960—65, dir. dept., 1965—68; lectr. U. Calif. Sch. Pub. Health, Berkeley, 1950—68; prof. pub. health UCLA Sch. Pub. Health, 1968—, chmn. dept. preventive medicine and social medicine, 1969—72, dean, 1972—80, mem. divsn. cancer control, 1980—, dir. health promotion ctr., 1988—91, dean, prof. emeritus, 1980—; dir. study Pres.'s Commn. Health Needs of Nation, 1952. Cons. Office of Technology Assessment, Nat. Heart, Lung, Blood Inst., 1977, Nat. Cancer Inst., 1981—, chmn. bd. sci. counsellors divsn. cancer prevention and control, 1982—84; chmn. Nat. Com. on Vital and Health Stats., 1979—81; mem. US- China health scis. com. US Dept. HHS, 1982; bd. dirs., chmn. Calif. Ctr. Health Improvement, 1998—. Editor: Ann. Rev. Pub. Health, 1979—90, Encyclopedia Pub. Health, 2002; editorial cons. in field:. Active LA County Pub. Health Commn., 1996—, chmn., 1997—98, 2007. Capt. US Army, 1943—45. Decorated Bronze Star; recipient Lasker award, Mary Lasker Found., 1960, Porter prize, 1998, Outstanding Achievement award, U. Minn., 1970, Thomas Francis, Jr. Meml. award, U. Mich. Fellow: AAAS, ACP, Am. Coll. Preventive Medicine (Disting. Svc. award 1976); mem.: APHA (past pres., Sedgwick medal 1977, Dana award, Charles A. Dana Found. 1988, Healthtrac Found. Prize 1995, 1997), NY Acad. Medicine (Stephen Smith Achievement in Public Health award 2005), Inst. Medicine NAS (council 1978—80, chmn. bd. health promotion and disease prevention 1980—82, Lienhard award 1997), Assn. Schs. Public Health (pres. 1973—74), Am. Cancer Soc. (nat. dir., Calif. dir., chmn. adv. com. on rsch. etiology), Internat. Epidemiol. Assn. (past pres.), Am. Epidemiol. Soc., Public Health Cancer Assn. (past pres.), Am. Heart Assn. (fellow epidemiology sect.). Home: 10926 Verano Rd Los Angeles CA 90077-2224 Office Phone: 310-825-1388. Business E-Mail: breslow@ph.ucla.edu.

BRESLOW, NORMAN EDWARD, biostatistics educator, researcher; b. Mpls., Feb. 21, 1941; s. Lester and Alice Jane (Philp) Breslow; m. Gayle Marguerite Bramwell, Sept. 7, 1963; children: Lauren Louise, Sara Jo. BA, Reed Coll., 1962; PhD, Stanford U., 1967; Doctorate (honoris causa), U. Bordeaux II, 2001. Trainee Stanford U., 1965—67; vis. research worker London Sch. Hygiene, 1967—68; instr. U. Wash., Seattle, 1968—69, asst. prof., 1969—72, assoc. prof., 1972—76, prof., 1976—, chmn. dept. biostats., 1983—93; statistician Internat. Agy. Research Cancer, Lyon, France, 1972—74. Mem. Hutchinson Cancer Ctr., Seattle, 1982—; statistician Nat. Wilms' Tumor Study, 1969—2003; cons. Internat. Agy. Rsch. Cancer, Lyon, 1978—79; assoc. prof. U. Geneva, 1994—2006. Co-author: (Scientific publ. nos. 32 and 82 on statistics in cancer rsch.) IARC, ISI (most highly cited publication in mathematical sciences for 1993-2003). Named sr. U.S. Scientist, Alexander Humboldt Found., Fed. Republic of Germany, 1982; recipient Spiegelman Gold medal, APHA, 1978, Preventive Oncology Acad. award, NIH, 1978—83, Snedecor award, Com. of Pres.'s on Statis. Socs., 1995, R.A. Fisher lectr. award, 1995; fellow sr. Internat., Fogarty Ctr., 1990; grantee rsch., NIH, 1984—. Fellow: AAAS, Royal Statis. Soc., Am. Statis. Assn. (com. on fellows 1996—2000, N. Mantel award 2002); mem.: Internat. Biometric Soc. (regional com. 1975—78, coun. 1994—2000, v.p. 2001, 2004, pres. 2002—03), Inst. Medicine-Nat. Acad. Scis., Internat. Statis. Inst. Avocations: ski mountaineering, hiking, bicycling. Office: Univ Wash Dept Biostatistics Seattle WA 98195-7232 Business E-Mail: norm@u.washington.edu.

BRESLOW, RONALD CHARLES, chemist, educator; b. Rahway, NJ, Mar. 14, 1931; s. Alexander E. and Gladys (Fellows) Breslow; m. Esther Greenberg, Sept. 7, 1955; children: Stephanie, Karen. AB summa cum laude, Harvard U., 1952, MA, 1953, PhD, 1955. NRC fellow Cambridge (Eng.) U., 1955—56; mem. faculty Columbia U., NYC, 1956—, prof. chemistry, 1962—66, S.L. Mitchell prof., 1966—, univ. prof., 1992—. Cons. to industry, 1958—; editor Benjamin, Inc., 1962—; mem. medicinal chemistry panel NIH, 1964—; mem. adv. panel on chemistry NSF, 1971—; centenary lectr. London Chem. Soc., 1972; mem. sci. adv. com. GM Corp., 1982—; A.R. Todd vis. prof. Cambridge U., 1982; hon. prof. U. Sci. & Tech., China. Author: Organic Reaction Mechanisms, 1965, 2d edit., 1969; editl. bd. Organic Syntheses, 1964—, Jour. Organic Chemistry, 1969—, Jour. Bio-organic Chemistry, 1972—, Tetrahedron, 1975—, Tetrahedron Letters, 1975—, Procs. NAS, 1984—; contbr. articles to profl. jours. Trustee Rockefeller U., 1981—; bd. sci. advisers Alfred P. Sloan Found., 1978—85. Recipient Fresenius award, Phi Lambda Upsilon, 1966, Mark Van Doren award, Columbia U., 1969, Great Tchr. award, 1981, Roussel prize, 1978, T.W. Richards medal, 1984, A.C. Cope award, 1987, G.W. Kenner award, U. Liverpool, Eng., 1988, Paracelsus prize, Swiss Chem. Soc., 1999, Arthur Day award, 1990, Nat. medal of Sci., NSF, 1991, Paracelsus award, New Swiss Chem. Soc., Royal Soc. London, 1990, Mayor's award in Sci., N.Y.C., 2000, Welch award in Chemistry, Welch Found., 2003, Othmer medal, Chem. Heritage Found., 2006. Fellow: Indian Acad. Scis. (hon. fgn.), Am. Acad. Arts and Scis., Korean Chem. Soc. (hon.); mem.: NAS (chmn. chemistry divsn. 1974—77, award in chemistry 1989), European Acad. Sci., Royal Soc. Chemistry (London, hon.), Chem. Soc. Japan (hon.), Royal Soc. London (hon.), New Swiss Chem. Soc. (Paracelsus award 1990), Am. Chem. Soc. (pres.-elect 1995—96, pres. 1996, chmn. divsn. organic chemistry 1970, Pure Chemistry award 1966, Baekeland medal 1969, Harrison Howe award 1974, Remsen award 1977, J.F. Norris award 1980, N.Y. sect. Nicholas medal 1989, Priestley medal 1999, Bioorganic Chemistry award 2002, Willard Gibbs medal 2004, Paul Gassman award 2006), Am. Philos. Soc. (coun. 1987—), Phi Beta Kappa (1st marshall 1952). Home: 44 W 77th St New York NY 10024 Office: Columbia U Dept Chemistry 116th St & Broadway New York NY 10027

BRESLOW, STEPHANIE R., lawyer; b. NYC, June 20, 1960; d. Ronald and Esther Breslow. BA cum laude, Harvard U., 1981; JD, Columbia U., 1984. Bar: Ohio 1984, NY 1986. Assoc. Cleary Gottlieb Steen & Hamilton, NYC, 1985-93; ptnr., corp. dept. Schulte Roth & Zabel LLP, NYC, 1993—, hiring ptnr., recruiting com. Spkr. in field; co-author: New York Limited Liability Companies and Partnerships, NY & Del. Business Entities: Choice Formation Operation Financing and Acquisitions. Bd. trustees The Joyce Theater, NY. Harlan Fiske Stone Scholar, 1982—84. Mem.: Pvt. Investment Fund Forum (founding mem.), Wall St. Hedge Fund Forum (steering com.), Assn. Bar City NY. Office: Schulte Roth & Zabel LLP 919 Third Ave New York NY 10022-4774 Office Phone: 212-756-2542. Office Fax: 212-593-5955. Business E-Mail: stephanie.breslow@srz.com.

BRESLOW, TINA, public relations executive; b. Phila., Feb. 18, 1946; d. Harry and Doris (Stein) Horowitz; m. Alan Breslow, Aug. 28, 1965 (div. 1970); children: Peter, Jennifer, Brett. Office mgr. Temple U. Ctr. City, Phila., 1976-79; publicist Temple U. Theater, Phila., 1979-81; mgr. pub. rels. Hershey Phila. Hotel, 1981-83; dir. pub. rels. Franklin Plaza Hotel, Phila., 1983-84; account mgr. Sommers Rosen, Inc., Phila., 1984-85; prin. Breslow Partners, Phila., 1985—. Pub. rels. cons. Dock St. Beer, Phila., 1986-87, Sheraton Soc. Hill Hotel, Phila., 1985-86. Chmn. pub. rels. com. Phila. Convention and Vis. Bur., 1985; pub. rels. cons. Phila. City Planning Commn., 1988, Phila. Commn. on AIDS, 1988. Recipient Super Communicator award Women in Communication, 1984, Best New Bus. Intro. award Phila. Better Bus. Bur., 1986, Community Svs. award Hotel Sales and Mktg. Assoc. Internat., 1988, Golden Bell award, 1988, Breakfast for Champions and Olymic Fundraiser The Alexander Hotels, 1988, Woman of Distinction award, 2002; named to Wall of Fame. N.E. H.S., 2002. Mem. Phila. Pub. Rels. Assn., Pub. Rels. Soc. Am. Jewish. Office: Tina Breslow Pub Rels 2042 Rittenhouse Sq Philadelphia PA 19103-5621

BRESNAHAN, PAMELA ANNE, lawyer, mediator, arbitrator; b. Washington, Ohio, Nov. 21, 1954; d. Richard and Margaret (McBride) Bresnahan; m. Theda Sersen, Sept. 6, 1941. Student, Wayne State U., 1946—47; LLB, Detroit Coll. Law, 1950; BA magna cum laude, U. Md., 1976; post grad, 1976—77, JD (hon.), 1980. Bar: Md. 1980, US Dist. Ct./Md 1980, DC 1982, US Supreme Ct. 1984, NY 1988. Atty. Dearborn Twp., Mich., 1956—62; corp. counsel Town Dearborn Heights, Mich., 1962—63; mcpl. judge, 1963—69; judge 20th Dist. Ct. Mich., Dearborn Heights, 1969—75, 3d Jud. Cir. Mich., Wayne County, 1975; chief judge, 1977—87; exec. chief judge Wayne Cir. Ct., 1981—87; prin. Seidenman & Bresnahan, PA, Balt., 1980—82; assoc. Finley, Kumble et al, Washington; ptnr. Laxalt, Washington, Perito and Dubuc, Semmes, Bowen & Semmes, Washington, 1991—95, Vorys, Sater, Seymour and Pease, Washington, 1995—; mediator/arbitrator DC and Md. ct. and pvt. arbitrations; adj. prof. U. San Diego Law Sch., Calif., 2006. Named one of 100 Most Influential Lawyers, Nat. Law Jour., 2006, The 50 Most Influential Women Lawyers in Am., 2007; recipient Gov. and Mayor Citations for Pub., Svc., 1988; fellow Am. Bar Found., Md. Bar Found. Mem.: Anne Arundel County Bar Assn., Md. State Bar Assn. (exec. com., bd. gov. 1986—87, chair jud. appointments 1991—92), Women's Bar Assn. Md. (pres. 1987—88), Young Lawyers Md. State Bar Assn. (chmn. 1986—87), Young Lawyers Exec. Coun. (Dist. 7 rep. 1987—88), ABA (chair tellers com. 1994—96, chair 1995—97, chair house com. on membership 1996—97, select com. of The House 1997—98, lawyers responsibility for client protection com., select com. of The House 2000—), Am. Judicature Soc., Mich. Judges Assn., Conf. Met. Ct., Detroit Assn. Def. Counsel, Mich. Assn. Trial Lawyers, Mediation Tribunal Assn., Detroit Coll. Law, Jud. Dispute Resolutions, Inc., Sponsor US Naval Acad. Plebe Sponsor Program, United Fund, Eastport Yacht Club, Elks, Washtenaw Country Club, Phi Kappa Phi, Alpha Omicron Pi, Phi Beta Kappa. Roman Catholic. Office: Vorys Sater Seymour and Pease LLP 1828 L St NW Ste 1111 Washington DC 20036-5109*

BRESNICK, MARTIN, composer, educator; b. NYC, Nov. 13, 1946; BA in Music Composition, U. Hartford, 1967, MA, 1968, DMA, 1972; student in music composition, Stanford U., Acad. für Musik, Vienna. Prof. San Francisco Conservatory of Music Coll., 1971—72, Stanford U., 1972—75; Valentine prof. music Amherst Coll., 1993; Mary Duke Biddle prof. music Duke U., 1998; Cecil and Ida Green vis. prof. composition U. British Columbia, Canada, 2000; composer-in-residence Australian Youth Orch. Nat. Music Camp, 2001, 04; vis. prof. competition Eastman Sch. Music, 2002—03; vis. prof. New Coll., Oxford, 2004; Housewright eminent scholar and featured guest composer Fla. State U., 2005; vis. composer Royal Acad. Music, London, 2005; prof. composition Yale Sch. Music, coord. Composition Dept. Compositions include Trio for Two Trumpets and Percussion, 1966, Introit, 1969, Ocean of Storms, 1970, 3 intermezzi, 1971, Musica, 1972, B's Garlands, 1973, Wir Weben, Wir Weben, 1978, Conspriacies, 1979, Der Signal, 1982, High Art, 1983, String Quartet 2 Bucephalus, 1984, Bread and Salt, 1984, Tent of Miracles, 1984, Bag o'Tells, 1984, 3 Choral Songs, 1985, Just Time, 1985, One, 1986, Lady Neils Dumpe, 1987, Trio, 1988, Pontoosuc, 1989; other symphonic ensembles include (orch.) Opere della Musica Povera, Angelus Novus, 1991, 9', Opere dell Musica Povera, Sinfonia, 1992, 15', (orch., mezzo soprano solo) Falling, 1994, 20'; other large chamber ensembles Opere della Music Povera, 8 movements, many versions, 1990-95, 10', On an Overgrown Path, 1996, 25'; other small chamber ensembles include String Quartet #3, 1992, 20',(mezzo soprano, piano) Falling, 1994, 20'; other choral works include Opere della Musica Povera, New Haven, Woodstock, NY, 1993, 5'; author: How Music Works; contbr. articles to profl. jours. Fulbright fellow, 1969, Nat. Endowment for Arts grantee, 1975, 79, Conn. Commission on Arts grantee, 1982, Guggenheim fellow, 2003; recipient Rome prize, 1976, Premio Ancona, 1980, Sinfonia Music prize, 1982, Composers Inc. 1st prize, 1985, 89, Elise L. Stoeger prize Chamber Music Soc. Lincoln Ctr., 1996, Berlin prize Am. Acad. Belin, 2001. Mem. ASCAP (Aaron Copland prize tchg. 2000), Conn. Composers Inc. (bd. dirs.), Am. Music Ctr., AAAL (Charles Ives Living award 1998). Office: Composition Dept Yale School Music PO Box 208246 New Haven CT 06520-8246

BRESS, MICHAEL E., retired lawyer; b. Mpls., Aug. 23, 1933; s. Michael J. and Anna (Tema) B.; m. Grace Billings, June 3, 1966; 1 child, Anne Ruth. BA, U. Minn., 1954, LLB, 1957. Bar: NY 1958, Minn. 1959. Assoc. Donovan Leisure Newton & Irvine, NYC, 1957-59, Dorsey & Whitney LLP, Mpls., 1959-64; ptnr. Dorsey & Whitney LLP, Mpls., 1964-91, of counsel, 1992-97, ret., 1998. Trustee St. Vladimir's Orthodox Theol. Sem., Crestwood, N.Y. Mem. Minn. Bar Assn., Hennepin County Bar Assn., Phi Beta Kappa. Home: 2007 W Franklin Ave Minneapolis MN 55405-2422 Personal E-mail: mbress@comcast.net.

BRESSAN, PAUL LOUIS, lawyer; b. Rockville Centre, NY, June 15, 1947; s. Louis Charles Bressan and Nance Elizabeth Batteley. BA cum laude, Fordham Coll., 1969; JD, Columbia U., 1975. Bar: N.Y. 1976, Calif. 1987, U.S. Dist. Ct. (so., ea. and no. dists.) N.Y. 1976, U.S. Dist. Ct. (no. and ctrl. dists.) Calif. 1987, U.S. Ct. Appeals (2d cir.) 1980, U.S. Supreme Ct. 1980, U.S. Ct. Appeals (1st and 4th cirs.) 1981, U.S. Ct. Appeals (11th cir.) 1982, U.S. Ct. Appeals (9th cir.) 1987, U.S Ct. Appeals (7th cir.) 1991, U.S. Dist. Ct. (ea. dist.) Calif. 1995; U.S. Dist. Ct. (so. dist.) Calif. 1997. Assoc. Kelley, Drye & Warren, NYC, 1975-84, ptnr. NYC and Los Angeles, 1984—2003; shareholder Buchalter Nemer, LA, 2003—. Served to lt. USNR, 1971-72. Named One of Outstanding Coll. Athletes of Am., 1969; Harlan Fiske Stone scholar Columbia Law Sch. Mem. ABA, Calif. Bar Assn., Phi Beta Kappa. Republican. Roman Catholic. Office: Buchalter Nemer 1000 Wilshire Blvd Ste 1500 Los Angeles CA 90017-2457 Office Phone: 213-891-5220. Business E-Mail: pbressan@buchalter.com.

BRESSE-RODENKIRK, ROBERT FRANCIS, journalist; b. Evanston, Ill., Apr. 28, 1952; s. Robert Francis and Joan Marie (Wolter) Rodenkirk. BA in History and Journalism, Ind. U., 1974; postgrad., Northwestern U., 1976. Program dir., pub. affairs dir. WIUS Radio, Bloomington, Ind., 1972-74; reporter City News Bur. of Chgo., 1974-77; news dir. WNUR Radio, Evanston, Ill., 1977; announcer WDHF Radio, Chgo., 1977; news dir. WMET Radio, Chgo., 1977-78; Chgo. corr. AP Radio Network, 1978-79; reporter, anchor WINS Radio, NYC, 1984-88, WMAQ Radio, Chgo., 1979-84, 88-00; reporter WBBM Radio, Chgo., 2000—. Recipient Nat. Broadcast awards AP, 1998, UPI, 1979, 81, 83, 90, 98, Nat. award Sigma Delta Chi, 1996, Max Karant award Aircraft Owners & Pilots Assn., 1997, others. Mem.: Chgo. Headline Club (bd. dirs. 1993—, pres.-elect 1995—96, pres. 1996—97, v.p. 1998—2003, Peter Lisagor award 1988, 1996, 2000, 2001, 2002, 2003, 2004, 2005), Radio-TV News Dirs. Assn. (Edward R. Murrow Regional award 1998, 2002), Soc. Profl. Journalists, Ill. News Broadcasters Assn. (bd. dirs. 1988—, v.p. 1994—96, pres. 1996—97), Shore Line Interurban Hist. Soc. (sec. 2002—), Fox River Trolley Mus. (publicity dir.), Ill. Rlwy. Mus., Branford Electric Rlwy. Assn. Roman Catholic. Avocations: railroading, bicycling. Home Phone: 847-729-6397; Office Phone: 800-784-6397. Personal E-mail: borowmaq@aol.com.

BRESSLER, BARRY E., lawyer; b. Phila., Apr. 7, 1947; s. Joseph and Shirley M. (Eiseman) B.; m. Risé Sharon Cohen, June 14, 1970 (dec.); children: Allison Ivy, Michelle Amy. AB, Franklin and Marshall Coll., Lancaster, Pa., 1968; JD, U. Pa., 1971. Bar: Pa. 1971, U.S. Dist. Ct. (ea. dist.) Pa. 1973, U.S. Ct. Appeals (3d cir.) 1977, U.S. Supreme Ct. 1988, U.S. Dist. Ct. (mid. dist.) Pa. 1990, U.S. Dist. Ct. Colo. 2005. Law clk. to judge Superior Ct. Pa., Phila., 1971-73; assoc. Meltzer & Schiffrin, Phila., 1973-79, ptnr., 1979-86, Fox, Rothschild, O'Brien & Frankel, Phila., 1987-88, Schnader, Harrison, Segal & Lewis, LLP, Phila., 2000—; mem., sr. lawyer real estate litig. and creditors' rights Pelino & Lentz, P.C., Phila., 1988-2000. Adj. instr. landlord-tenant law Delaware County CC, Media, Pa., 1985—, Montgomery County CC, Blue Bell, Pa., 1987—; spl. counsel in bankruptcy to atty. gen. State of Ohio, 1993-96. Mem. English Ceramic Study Group, Phila.; v.p., sec. Temple Sinai, Dresher, Pa., 1991-97, 2003-04; grad. Leadership, Inc., Phila. Mem. ABA (litigation sect.), Pa. Bar Assn. (corp. banking and bus. sect.), Phila. Bar Assn. (real property sect.), Bankruptcy Conf. Ea. Dist. Pa. (treas. 1995-2000), Am. Arbitration Assn., Louis D. Brandeis Law Soc., Tau Epsilon Rho. Republican. Jewish. Avocations: tennis, ceramics, bridge. Office: Schnader Harrison Segal and Lewis LLP 1600 Market St Ste 3600 Philadelphia PA 19103-7286 Office Phone: 215-751-2050. Business E-Mail: bbressler@schnader.com.

BRESSLER, BARRY LEE, physicist, systems analyst; b. Reading, Pa., Feb. 16, 1936; s. Kenneth Russell and Lillian Mary (Good) B. BS in Physics, Ursinus Coll., 1957; MS in Physics, Va. Poly. Inst. State U., 1979, PhD in Physics, 1986. Tchr., curator insect collection Reading Pub. Mus., 1954-55; data-processing technician Philco Corp., Phila., 1956, jr. engr. Spring City, Pa., 1957-58; physicist Naval Surface Warfare Ctr., Dahlgren, Va., 1958-94, group leader, 1983-89, fellow, 1983-85, sr. scientist, 1989-94; prin. scientist EG&G Tech. Svcs., Inc., Dahlgren, 1994-95, sr. prin. scientist, 1995—2004; prin. engr. MagnaCom, Inc., Dahlgren, 2005—. Cons. Windy Knoll Enterprises, Inc., Magnolia, Tex., 1994-2003; adj. prof. physics Va. Poly. Inst. State U., Blacksburg, 1994-2005. Scholar Bryn Mawr Coll., 1957. Mem. Am. Phys. Soc., Coleopterists Soc. (jour. referee 1991-95), Sigma Pi Sigma, Sigma Xi. Achievements include mathematical modeling, simulation, and computation of trajectories for ballistic missiles, reentry vehicles, and interceptor missiles; determination of guidance commands for flight tests of maneuvering reentry vehicles; analysis of simulated engagements between evasively maneuvering reentry vehicles and interceptor missiles; design and optimization of reentry maneuvers; threat analysis; analysis of advanced strategic and tactical weapons systems; formulation of theoretical models for the electromagnetic pulse produced by a high-altitude nuclear burst, and for various other weapons effects; research in the quantum mechanics of many-particle systems, particularly of fermion-boson systems. Avocations: econophysics, training Shetland sheepdogs, natural history. Home: PO Box 1345 Fredericksburg VA 22402-1345 Office: MagnaCom Inc 16156 Dahlgren Rd Dahlgren VA 22448

BRESSLER, RICHARD J., investment company and former entertainment company executive; married; two children. Grad. summa cum laude, Adelphi Coll., 1979. CPA. Ptnr. Ernst & Young, Inc., 1979-88; from asst. controller to exec. v.p., CFO Time Warner, Inc., NYC, 1988—95, CEO, sr. v.p., 1995—98; sr. v.p., CFO Viacom Inc., NYC, 2001—05; mng. dir., head strategic resources group Thomas H. Lee Partners L.P., Boston, 2006—. Bd. dirs. Prep for Prep, Outward Bound; mem. Chase Nat. Adv. Bd., CFO Adv. Coun.; trustee Citizen's Budget Commn. Mem. Am. Inst. CPAs, N.Y. State Soc. Cert. CPAs. Office: Thomas H Lee Partners LP 100 Federal St 35th Fl Boston MA 02110

BREST, PAUL A., law educator, foundation administrator; b. Jacksonville, Fla., Aug. 9, 1940; s. Alexander and Mia (Deutsch) B.; m. Iris Lang, June 17, 1962; children: Hilary, Jeremy. AB, Swarthmore Coll., 1962; JD, Harvard U., 1965; LLD (hon.), Northeastern U., 1980, Swarthmore Coll., 1991. Bar: N.Y. 1966. Law clk. to Hon. Bailey Aldrich U.S. Ct. Appeals (1st cir.), Boston, 1965-66; atty. NAACP Legal Def. Fund, Jackson, Miss., 1966-68; law clk. Justice John Harlan, U.S. Supreme Ct., 1968-69; prof. law Stanford U., 1969—, Kenneth and Harle Montgomery prof. pub. interest law, Richard E. Lang prof. and dean, 1987-99; pres. William and Flora Hewlett Found., Menlo Park, Calif., 1999—. Author: Processes of Constitutional Decisionmaking, 1992. Mem. Am. Acad. Arts and Scis. Home: 814 Tolman Dr Palo Alto CA 94305-1026 Office: William and Flora Hewlett Found 2121 Sand Hill Rd Menlo Park CA 94025 Business E-Mail: pbrest@hewlett.org.

BRESTLE, DANIEL J., cosmetics executive; m. Cathy Brestle; 2 children. BA, Villanova U., 1967. With Johnson & Johnson, 1973—78; distbn. mgr. Estée Lauder Cos., Oakland, NJ, 1978—79, plant mgr., 1979, dir. mfg., warehousing and distbn., 1979—83, regional mktg. dir. Aramis NYC, 1983—84, v.p., nat. sales mgr. prescriptives, 1984—88, pres. prescriptives, 1988—92, pres. Clinique Labs., 1992—98, pres. Estée Lauder U.S. and Can., 1998—2001, group pres., 2001—05, COO, 2005—. Mem. adv. coun. Coll. Commerce & Fin. Villanova U. With USAF. Mem.: Cosmetic, Toiletry, and Fragrance Assn. (bd. dirs.). Office: Estee Lauder Co Inc 767 5th Ave New York NY 10153*

BRETT, ARTHUR CUSHMAN, JR., banker; b. Bronxville, NY, Mar. 23, 1928; s. Arthur Cushman and Mary Kathryn (Clark) B.; m. Mary Elizabeth Cunliffe, Aug. 21, 1954; children: Margaret Brett Uzarski, Catherine Brett Main, John, Patricia, Matthew BS, Fordham U., 1953; MBA, NYU, 1959. Asst. v.p. Bowery Savs. Bank, NYC, 1950-68; instl. registered rep. Salomon Bros., NYC, 1968-71, 73-75, Blyth Eastman Dillon, Boston, 1971-73; v.p. Mut. Am. Life Ins. Co., NYC, 1975-78; v.p. investments, sec. East River Savs. Bank, NYC, 1978-80; sr. v.p., treas., chief investment officer Apple Bank for Savs., NYC, 1980-92. Mem. investment com. Social Sci. Rsch. Coun., 1976-86, NYU Fed. Credit Union, 1983-89. Mem.: NY Soc. Security Analysts. Roman Catholic. Home: 2514 Redding Rd Fairfield CT 06824-1745

BRETT, BARRY J., lawyer; b. NY, Dec. 25; m. Leslie Brett; children: Jessica, Marisa Brett-Fleegler. BA, City Coll., NY, 1961; LLB cum laude, Columbia U., NY, 1964. Ptnr. Troutman Sanders LLP, NYC, 2005—, Parker Chapin LLP, NYC, 1973—2000, Jackson & Gilchrist Parker Chapin, 2000—05. Pres. Coll. Alumni Assn., NYC, life mem. Mem.: ABA, NY State Bar Assn. (Antitrust Sect. Svc. award). Office: Troutman Sanders LLP Chrysler Building 405 Lexington Ave New York NY 10174 Home Phone: 212-535-7510; Office Phone: 212-704-6216. Office Fax: 212-704-6288. E-mail: barry.brett@troutmansanders.com.

BRETT, GEORGE HOWARD, baseball executive, former professional baseball player; b. Glen Dale, W.Va., May 15, 1953; s. Jack Francis and Ethel (Hansen) B. Student, Longview C.C., Mo., El Camino Coll., Torrance, Calif. Former third baseman Kansas City (Mo.) Royals Profl. Baseball Team, v.p. baseball ops. Player Am. League All-Star Game, 1976—88. Named Am. League batting champion, 1976, 80, 90, Am. League Most Valuable Player, 1980; player Am. League All-Star Game, 1976-88; Inductee Baseball Hall of Fame, Cooperstown, N.Y., 1999. Address: care Kansas City Royals attn: vp ops PO Box 419969 Kansas City MO 64141-6969

BRETT, HARRY P., lawyer; b. Bklyn., June 8, 1950; BA, SUNY, Stony Brook, 1971; JD, NY Law Sch., 1978. Bar: NY 1979, US Dist. Ct. So., Ea., We., & No. Districts NY 1979, US Supreme Ct. 1993, US Ct. Appeals 2nd Cir. Criminal investigator, 1974—78; joined Wilson, Elser, Moskowitz, Edelman & Dicker LLP, NYC, 1978, now ptnr., chmn. firm hiring com., co-chmn. general liability practice group. Mem.: Am. Soc. Indsl. Security, NY State Trial Lawyers Assn. Office: Wilson Elser Moskowitz Edelman & Dicker LLP 23rd Fl 150 E 42nd St New York NY 10017-5639 Office Phone: 212-490-3000 ext. 2282. Office Fax: 212-490-3038. Business E-Mail: bretth@wemed.com.

BRETT, JAMES CLARENCE, retired journalism educator; b. Watertown, NY, July 28, 1931; s. Clarence Richard and Justina Leone (Cleland) B. BA, Notre Dame U., 1953. With Watertown Daily Times, 1955-71, author series on Frederick Exley, 1968; chmn. Times Editl. Assn., 1970; adj. assoc. prof. Oswego (N.Y.) State U. Coll., 1970-71, asst. prof., 1971-96; ret., 1996. Mem. organizing com. SUNY Colls. in the North Country, Fort Drum, Watertown, N.Y., 1985; organizer, dir. student internship program New York Times, 1972. Pvt. first class U.S. Army, 1953-55. Mem. Royal Hort. Soc., Am. Hort. Soc., Jefferson County Hist. Soc., Master Gardeners Am., Nature Conservancy, N.Y. State Ret. Tchrs. Assn., Oswego Emeriti Assn., Am. Legion, Ives Hill Country Club, Black River Valley Club. Republican. Roman Catholic. Avocations: gardening, travel, reading. Home and Office: 146 Ward St Watertown NY 13601-4616 Office Phone: 315-782-1138. E-mail: jimbrett1@aol.com.

BRETT, JAN CHURCHILL, illustrator, author; b. Hingham, Mass., Dec. 1, 1949; d. George and Jean (Baxter) Brett; m. Daniel Bowler, Feb. 27, 1970 (div. Jan. 1979); 1 child, Lia Bowler; m. Joseph Hearne, Aug. 18, 1980. Student, Colby Jr. Coll., 1968-69, Boston Mus. Fine Arts Sch., 1970; DHL (hon.), Fitchburg State Coll., 1996. Author, illustrator Fritz and the Beautiful Horses, 1981 (Parent's Choice award, 1981), Good Luck Sneakers, 1981, Annie and the Wild Animals, 1985, The First Dog, 1988, Beauty and the Beast, 1989, The Wild Christmas Reindeer, 1990, The Twelve Days of Christmas, 1990, The Mitten, 1990, Goldilocks and the Three Bears, 1990, The Owl and the Pussycat, 1991, Berlioz the Bear, 1991, The Trouble With Trolls, 1992, Christmas Trolls, 1993, Town Mouse, Country Mouse, 1994, Armadillo Rodeo, 1995, Comet's Nine Lives, 1996, The Hat, 1997 (Am. Booksellers Abby award, 1998), The Night Before Christmas, 1998, The Gingerbread Baby, 1999, Hedgie's Surprise, 2000, illustrator Woodland Crossings, 1978, Inside a Sand Castle and Other Secrets, 1979, The Secret Clocks Time Senses of Living Things, 1979, St. Patrick's Day in the Morning, 1980 (Parent's Choice award, 1981), Young Melvin and Bulger, 1981, In the Castle of the Cats, 1981, Some Birds Have Funny Names, 1981 (Amb. Honor award English Speaking Union U.S., 1983), I Can Fly, 1981, Prayer, 1983, The Valentine Bears, 1983, Some Plants Have Funny Names, 1983, Where Are All the Kittens, 1984, Old Devil is Waiting, 1985, The Mother's Day Mice, 1985, Scary, Scary

Halloween, 1986, Noelle of the Nutcracker, 1986, The Enchanted Book, 1987, Happy Birthday, Dear Duck, 1988, Hedgre's Surprise, 2000, Daisy Comes Home, 2002. Mem. bd. overseers Boston Symphony Orch., 1991—99, trustee, 1999—, Thayer Acad., Braintree, Mass. Mem.: Nat. Soc. Colonial Dames Am., Chilton Club. Office: 132 Pleasant St Norwell MA 02061-2523 E-mail: janbrett@janbrett.com.

BRETT, JOHN BRENDAN, JR., retired advertising and public relations executive; b. Mar. 28, 1944; s. John Brendan and Vera Mae (Locke) Brett; m. Alyene Maybeth Wales, Apr. 30, 1966; children: Heather Allyson, Sean Timothy. Student, U. Md., 1964-65, U. So. Miss., 1965-66; BS in Advt., U. Fla., 1969. Advt. supr. Armstrong Cork Co., Lancaster, Pa., 1969-72; mgr. advt. K-D Mfg. Co., Lancaster, 1972-75; dir. mktg. comm. Brodart Inc., Williamsport, Pa., 1975-78; mktg. comm. supr. E. I. duPont de Nemours & Co., Wilmington, Del., 1978-80, group mgr. mktg. comm., carpet fibers, 1980-85, mgr. corp. advt., 1985-87, group mgr. mktg. comm. electronics, 1987-91, sr. cons. external affairs, 1991-92; mgr. mktg. commn. and pub. affairs Sontara Tech./Dupont Nonwovens, Old Hickory, Tenn., 1992-99, global brand mgr., 1999—2001; dir. alumni rels. and grant programs Aquinas Coll., Nashville, 2001—07; ret., 2007. Mem. Idea98 com., mem. Idea2001 com. INDA Nonwovens Assn., 1997—99; mem. advt. adv. coun. U. Fla., 1984—87. Mem. editl. sounding bd. Advertising Age mag., 1985—87. Vice chmn. Del. all-star football game com. Del. Found. Retarded Children, 1982—83, chmn., 1984, trustee, 1989—92; chmn. bldg. com. Country Hills Homeowners Assn., 1994—2000, sec. bd. dirs., 2000—02; mem. vestry St. Thomas Episc. Ch., Lancaster, 1974—75, St. David's Episc. Ch., Wilmington, 1989—92, sr. warden, 1991—92; treas. N.E. Missionary Convocation Diocese of Mid. Tenn., Diocesesan Conv. Del., 1995; mem. stewardship com. St. Timothy Luth. Ch., Hendersonville, Tenn., 2003—07, asstg. min., 2007—; bd. govs. Automotive Advertisers Coun., 1975. Recipient Oustanding Advt. Campaign award, Am. Bus. Press/Bus.-Profl. Advt. Assn., 1974. Mem.: Assn. Nat. Advertisers (mem. corp. advt. com. 1985—86), Antique Automobile Club Am., Mid-Tenn. Classic Chevy Club (v.p. 2002, treas. 2003—04), Hendersonville Optimist (bd. dirs.), Kappa Tau Alpha, Alpha Delta Sigma. Avocations: photography, gardening, antique autos. Home: 170 Woodlake Dr Gallatin TN 37066 Home Phone: 615-452-0655.

BRETT, THOMAS RUTHERFORD, federal judge; b. Oklahoma City, Oct. 2, 1931; s. John A. and Norma (Dougherty) B.; m. Mary Jean James, Aug. 26, 1952; children: Laura Elizabeth Brett Tribble, James Ford, Susan Marie Brett Crump, Maricarolyn Swab. BBA, U. Okla., 1953, LL.B., 1957, JD, 1971. Bar: Okla. 1957. Asst. county atty., Tulsa, 1957; mem. firm Hudson, Hudson, Wheaton, Kyle & Brett, Tulsa, 1958-69, Jones, Givens, Brett, Gotcher, Doyle & Bogan, 1969-79; judge U.S. Dist. Ct. (no. dist.) Okla., Tulsa, 1979—2003; of counsel Crowe and Dulany, 2003—. Bd. regents U. Okla., 1971-78; mem. adv. bd. Salvation Army; trustee Okla. Bar Found. Col. JAG, USAR, 1953-83. Named to Okla. Heritage Assn. Hall of Fame, 2000. Fellow Am. Coll. Trial Lawyers, Am. Bar Found.; mem. Okla. Bar Assn. (pres. 1970), Tulsa County Bar Assn. (pres. 1965), U. Okla. Coll. Law Alumni Assn. (bd. dirs.), Order of Coif (hon.). Democrat.

BRETTHAUER, ERICH WALTER, chemist, educator; b. Denver, Sept. 12, 1937; s. Walter V. and Lucy E. B.; m. Sharlene Marie Stimpson, Oct. 10, 1966; children: Terrance Magee, Anthony Magee, Heidi, Erich Walter II. BS, U. Nev., 1960, MS, 1962. Various sci. rsch. and mgmt. positions Pub. Health Svc. and EPA, 1962-68; dir. monitoring ops. div. EPA, Las Vegas, 1978-79, dir. nuclear radiation assessment div., 1979-80, detail to U.S. radiation policy coun. Washington, 1980-81, lab. dir. Office Rsch. Devel. Environ. Monitoring Systems Lab. Las Vegas, 1985-89, asst. administr. Office Rsch. & Devel. Washington, 1990-93; rsch. prof. U. Nev., Las Vegas, 1993-95. Congl. fellow U.S. Senate Com. on Environ. and Pub. Works, 1982—; recipient Gold medal for directing and monitoring outreach program at Three Mile Island EPA, 1979. Mem. Am. Chem. Soc., Am. Water Works Assn., Sigma Xi.

BRETT-MAJOR, DAVID MICHAEL, physician, military officer; b. Lima, Ohio, Aug. 11, 1970; s. Lawrence Elliott Major and Lin Brett; m. Sherry Michelle Williams, June 12, 1993; 1 child, Olivia Margaret. BS, US Naval Acad., Annapolis, 1992; MD, Uniformed Svcs. U., Bethesda, 2002. Diplomate Internal Medicine Am. Bd. Internal Medicine, 2005. Commd. lt. USN, advanced through grades to lt. commdr., 1988—, surface warfare officer Newport, RI, 1992—98, coord. course US naval acad., 1996—98. Decorated Commendation medal with star and Achievement medal USN; fellow, Nat. Capitol Consortium, 2005—07. Mem.: AMA, Infectious Diseases Soc. Am., Am. Coll. Physicians, Assn. Mil. Surgeons the US (life), US Naval Inst. (life), Alpha Omega Alpha (life). Home Phone: 301-563-3315.

BRETTSCHNEIDER, RITA ROBERTA FISCHMAN, retired lawyer; b. Bklyn., Nov. 12, 1931; d. Isidore M. and Augusta T. (Singer) Fischman; m. Bertram D. Brettschneider, June 25, 1950 (dec. Nov. 17, 1986); children: Jane Brettschneider, Joseph Brettschneider; m. Bertram D. Cohn, June 30, 1991 (dec. July 2002). BA, CUNY, 1953; JD, Bklyn. Law Sch., 1956; postgrad., NYU, 1968-69, Nat. Inst. Trial Advocacy, 1976. Bar: N.Y. 1961, U.S. Dist. Ct. N.Y. 1971. Pvt. practice, Huntington, NY, 1961—2004; ret., 2004. Instr. women and the law C.W. Post Coll., Brookville, N.Y., 1969-70; spl. assoc. prof. philosophy and law New Coll. Hofstra U., Hempstead, N.Y., 1974-76; faculty N.Y. Law Jour. Conf. Changing Concepts in Matrimonial Law, 1976; legal advisor Am. Arbitration Assn., 1977-84. Contbr. numerous articles to profl. jours. Pres., bd. dirs. For Our Children and Us, 1992—2001. Mem. N.Y. Bar Assn. (civil rights com.), Nassau-Suffolk Women's Bar Assn. (chair judiciary com. 1974-80, pres. 1980-81, Suffolk chpt. bd. dirs., chmn. reproductive and health rights com. 2005—). Home: 2 Crosby Pl Cold Spring Harbor NY 11724-2403 Office: Brettschneider & Brettschneider 83 Prospect St Huntington NY 11743-3306 Home Phone: 631-367-9088; Office Phone: 631-367-3111. Personal E-mail: vember@aol.com.

BRETZFELDER, DEBORAH MAY, retired museum staff member; b. Hazelton, Pa., Sept. 21, 1932; d. Joseph and Rose (Smulyan) Hirsh; m. Robert Bretzfelder, Dec. 24, 1955; children: Karl, Marc. Student, Syracuse U., NY, 1950-53. Textile colorist, designer Cohn-Hall-Marx, NYC, 1954-55; fashion coord. Hecht's Dept. Store, Washington, 1956; freelance artist Washington, 1956-58; exhibits technician Smithsonian Instn., Washington, 1958-59, supr. exhibits prodn., 1959-63, exhibits specialist Nat. Mus. Am. History, 1963-75, visual info. specialist, project mgmt. officer, 1975-83, acting chief design, 1983, chief design, 1983-87, assoc. asst. dir. exhibits and pub. spaces, 1987-88; ret., 1988. Cons. various firms., orgns., mus. personnel; instr. mus. programs; freelance photographer and exhibit designer; project dir. Contbr. works to various publs.; musician: violin sect. Capital Symphony Orch. (formerly George Washington U. Orch.), 1965—2003, violin sect. Georgetown Symphony Orch., 2003—, violin sect. Capital Symphony Orch., 2005—. Mem.: Am. Craft Coun., Fiber Arts Study Group, Nat. Mus. Women in Arts, Nat. Soc. Hist. Preservation, Am. Assn. Mus., Tau Sigma Delta. Jewish. Home: 2748 Woodley Pl NW Washington DC 20008-1517 Office Phone: 202-232-7665. Personal E-mail: drbretzfelder@hotmail.com.

BREUER, JOANN GREEN, theater director; d. Louis A. and Mathilde Soloff; m. Miklos M. Breuer; children: Shoshanna, Jonas. BA, Wellesley Coll., 1959; MA in Tchg., Harvard U., 1960. Artistic dir. Cambridge (Mass.) Ensemble, 1970—79; instr. Harvard U., Cambridge, 1979—84; play dir. Am. Repertory Theatre, Cambridge, 1981—84; artistic assoc. Boston Shakespeare, Boston, 1985—86, Am. Nat. Theater, Washington, 1986—87, Vineyard Playhouse, Tisbury, Mass., 2000—. Play dir., adaptor short stories numerous cos., including Theatre of the Deaf, 1970—. Author: The Small Theatre Handbook, 1970 (Best Play awards). Recipient award, Boston Critics' Cir., 1970—80, Continued Excellence in Directing award, 1999. Mem.: Soc. Stage Dirs. and Choreographers. Jewish. Avocation: social service. Home: 1501 Beacon St # 804 Brookline MA 02446 Office: Vineyard Playhouse 24 Church St Vineyard Haven MA 02568 Office Phone: 508-693-6450. Personal E-mail: jgbreuer@comcast.net.

BREUER, STEPHEN ERNEST, religious organization administrator, consultant; b. July 14, 1936; came to U.S., 1938, naturalized, 1945; s. John Hans Howard and Olga Marion (Haar) B.; m. Gail Fern Breitbart, Sept. 4, 1960 (div. 1986); children: Jared Noah, Rachel Elise; m. Nadine Bendit, Sept. 25, 1988. BA cum laude, UCLA, 1959; gen. secondary credential, 1960. Tchr. L.A. City Schs., 1960-62; dir. Wilshire Blvd. Temple Camps, LA, 1962—84; instr. Hebrew Union Coll., LA, 1965-76, 1992—, field instr., 1977-81; dir. Edgar F. Magnin Religious Sch., LA, 1970-80; field instr. San Francisco State U., 1970-80; exec. dir. Wilshire Blvd. Temple, LA, 1980—2004; instr. U. Judaism, 1991; field instr. Calif. State U., San Diego; prin. Steve Breuer Assocs., LA, 2005—. Exec. dir. Progressive Assn. of Reform Day Schs., 2005—. V.p. L.A. Youth Programs Inc., 1967-77; youth advisor L.A. County Commn. Human Rels., 1969-72, bd. dirs. Cmty. Rels. Conf. So. Calif., 1965-85; bd. dirs. Alzheimer's Disease and Related Disorders Assn., 1984-95, v.p. L.A. County chpt., 1984-86, pres., 1986-88, nat. exec. com., 1987-95, nat. devel. chair, 1992-95, Calif. state coun. pres. 1987-92, chmn. of Calif. gov.'s adv. com. on Alzheimer's disease, 1988-97; mem. goals program City of Beverly Hills, Calif., 1985-91; bd. dirs. Pacific S.W. regional Union Am. Hebrew Congregations, 1985-88, nat. bd., exec. com., 1993-97; bd. dirs. Echo Found., 1986-88, Mazon-Jewish Response to Hunger, 1993-97, 2003-, Wilshire Stakeholders exec. com., 1987-94, Internat. Rescue Com. West Coast Bd., 1999-2005; treas. Wilshire Cmty. Prayer Alliance, 1986-88; active United Way; founded Steve Breuer Consulting for Non Profits, 2005—; v.p. Century City Homeowner's Alliance, 2007—. Recipient Svc. award L.A. County Bd. Suprs., 1982, 87, Ventura County Bd. Suprs., 1982, 87, L.A. City Coun., 2005, Weinberg Chai Lifetime Achievement award Jewish Fed. Coun. L.A., 1986, Nat. Philanthropy Day L.A. medallion, 1993, Recognition award L.A. County Redevel. Agy., 1994, award L.A. Bus. Coun., 1997, award L.A. City Coun., 2005, Sherut L'am Svc. to People award Hebrew Union Coll., 2005; Steve Breuer Conference Ctr. named in his honor at Wilshire Blvd. Temple Camps, Malibu, 1990. Mem.: ASCD, NATA, Nata Breuer Leadership Fund, Progressive Assn. Reform Day Schs. (exec. dir. 2005—), Jewish Profl. Network, So. Calif. Conf. Jewish Communal Workers, Am. Mgmt. Assn., Jewish Communal Profls. So. Calif., Profl. Assn. Temple Adminstrs. (pres. 1985—88), L.A. Assn. Jewish Edn. (bd. dirs.), Nat. Assn. Temple Educators (Kaminker curriculum award 1973), Nat. Assn. Temple Adminstrs. (nat. bd. dirs. 1987—, v.p. 1991—93, pres. 1993—97, Svc. to Judaism award 1989, Svc. to the Cmty. award 1990, Svc. award 1994, Steve Breuer Leadership Fund established 2004), So. Calif. Camping Assn. (bd. dirs. 1964—82), Century City Homeowners' Alliance, Assn. Reform Zionists Am. (bd. dirs. 1993—98), People for the Am. Way, Los Angeles County Mus. Contemporary Art, Maple Mental Health Ctr. of Beverly Hills, Living Desert, Wildlife Fedn., Ctr. for Environ. Edn., Wilderness Soc., UCLA Alumni Assn, World Union for Progressive Judaism, Jewish Resident Camping Assn., Amnesty Internat. Office: 3663 Wilshire Blvd Los Angeles CA 90010-2798 Home Phone: 310-556-3386; Office Phone: 213-388-2401. Personal E-mail: sebwbt@aol.com. Business E-Mail: seb@wbtla.org.

BREUER, WILLIAM BENTLEY, author; Frequent keynote spkr.; guest numerous radio shows and TV programs; former guest lectr. salesmanship, publicity and promotion seminars. Author: An American Saga, 1982, Bloody Clash at Sadzot, 1982 (transl. into Belgian), Captain Cool, 1983, They Jumped at Midnight, 1983, Drop Zone Sicily, 1984 (transl. into Japanese and French), Hitler's Fortress Cherbourg, 1984, Agony at Anzio, 1985 (transl. into Czechoslovakian), Storming Hitler's Rhine, 1985 (transl. into Serbo-Croatian), Death of a Nazi Army, 1985, Operation Torch, 1986, Retaking the Philippines, 1987, Devil Boats, 1987 (transl. into Japanese), Operation Dragoon, 1988 (transl. into French), The Secret War with Germany, 1988, Sea Wolf, 1989, Nazi Spies in America, 1989, Geronimo!, 1990, Hoodwinking Hitler, 1993, Race to the Moon, 1993 (transl. into Burmese, Choice award ALA 1995), The Great Raid on Cabanatuan, 1994 (made into film The Great Raid 2005), J. Edgar Hoover and His G-Men, 1995, MacArthur's Undercover War, 1994 (transl. into Polish), Feuding Allies, 1995 (trans. into Polish), Shadow Warriors, 1996, War and American Women, 1997, Unexplained Mysteries of World War II, 1997 (transl. into Polish, Czech and Chinese), Vendetta: Castro and the Kennedy Brothers, 1997 (transl. into Polish), Undercover Tales of World War II, 1998, Top Secret Tales of World War II (transl. into Japanese), 1999, Secret Weapons of World War II (trnasl. into Arabic and Chinese), 2000, Daring Missions of World War II, 2001 (transl. into Polish and Chinese), Deceptions of World War II, 2002 (transl. into Polish), The Air-Raid Warden Was a Spy, 2002, The Spy Who Spent the War in Bed, 2003, Guts!, 2005. Recipient numerous awards. Hon. mem. numerous vets. assns.

BREVERMAN, HARVEY, artist; b. Pitts., Jan. 7, 1934; s. Theodore and Sarah (Haffner) B.; m. Deborah Dobkin, June 26, 1960. BFA, Carnegie Mellon U., 1956; MFA, Ohio U., 1960. Tchr. Carnegie Mellon U., summer 1959; tchr. drawing Ohio U., Athens, 1960-61, Ill. State U., Normal, summer 1969, Falmouth Art Sch., England, 1969; prof. art U. at Buffalo, 1961—99, SUNY disting. prof., 1999—. Resident painter State Acad. Fine Arts, Amsterdam, 1965-66, vis. painter Kalamazoo Inst. Art, summer 1972, 73, vis. artist Oxford U., 1974, 77, U. Mich., 1978, Md. Inst. Coll. Art, 1984, 92d St. Y, NYC, 1989, Coll. William and Mary, 1990, Skidmore Coll., 1990, Pont Aven Sch. Art, France, 1995, Jagiellonian U., Poland, 1997; one man shows include Albright-Knox Art Gallery, Buffalo, 1967, 89, U. Oreg., U. Ill., 1970, Canton Art Mus., Ohio, 1971, 87, Middlebury Coll., 1973, FAR Gallery, NYC, 1974, 79, Gadatsy Gallery, Toronto, 1975, 76, 79, 80, 87, Kalamazoo Inst. Art, 1976, Muskegon Mus. Art, Muskegon, Mich., 1977, Grand Rapids Art Mus., Mich., 1977, Gadatsy Gallery, Toronto, 1978, 81, 84, U. Mich., 1978, Nardin Galleries, NYC, 1980, U. NH, 1981, Art Gallery of Hamilton, 1981, Hollins U., 1982, Niagara U., 1984, Miami U. Art Mus., Ohio, 1987, Meml. Art Gallery, Rochester, NY, 1988, Wenniger Gallery, Boston, 1988, St. Lawrence U., 1989, Taller Galeria Ft., Cadaqués, Spain, 1990, Babcock Galleries, NYC, 1990, 91, Brigham Young U., 1993, Nina Freudenheim Gallery, Buffalo, 1994, Butler Inst. Am. Art, 1997, Yeshiva U. Mus., NYC, 1997, 02, Milton Weill Gallery, NYC, 1997, Gertrude Herbert Inst. Art, Augusta, Ga., 2000, Ind. U. Sch. Fine Arts Gallery, Bloomington, 2001; group shows at Corcoran Biennial, Wash., 1963, Bklyn. Mus., 1964, Assn. Am. Artists, NYC, 1965, Rijksakademie, Amsterdam, 1968, Boston Mus. Fine Arts, 1968, NAD, 1968, Pa. Acad. Fine Arts Biennial, 1969, Brit. Internat. Bienniale, Bradford, Eng., 1970, 72, FAR Gallery, 1972-74, Whitechapel Gallery, London, 1973, Pushkin Mus., Moscow, 1972, 2d Norwegian Internat. Biennial, 1974, Mus. Modern Art, Oxford, 1974, Honolulu Acad. Fine Arts, 1975, 8th Internat. Art Fair, Basel, Switzerland, 1977, Auslands Institut, Dortmund, W. Ger., 1977, Arte Fiere '78, Bologna, 1978, Art Gallery Ont., Toronto, 1979, Am. Acad. and Inst. Arts and Letters, NYC, 1980, 81, NYU, 1980, Jewish Mus., NYC, 1982, Queens Mus., NYC, 1983, Rose Art Mus., Brandeis U., 1985, Minn. Mus. Art, St. Paul, 1985, Roger Ramsay Gallery, Chgo., 1986, Va. Mus. Fine Arts, Richmond, 1986, Lever House Gallery, NYC, 1986, Albright-Knox Art Gallery, 1987, Harvard U., Carpenter Ctr., 1987, Mus. Art, San Juan, P.R., 1987, Contemporary Arts Ctr., Cin., 1988, Mus. of Fine Arts, Houston, 1988, Oakland Mus., Calif., 1988, 8th Print Internat., Barcelona, 1988, 4th Internat. Print Biennal, Taipei Fine Arts Mus., 1989, Inst. Contemporary Art, Boston, 1990, La Jolla Mus. Contemporary Art, 1990, Grand Palais, Paris, 1990, Yurakucho Art Forum, Tokyo, 1991, Denver Art Mus., 1991, Scottsdale Ctr. for the Arts, 1991, NAD, NYC, 1992, Internat. Print Triennal, Krakow, Nüremberg, 1994, 97, 2000, 03, Mus. Applied Arts, Belgrade, 1995, XIII Premio Internat. Per L' Incisione, Biella, Torino, 1997, Bermuda Nat. Gallery, 1997, 9th Internat. Print Biennale, Varna, Bulgaria, 1997, Beijing Internat. Ex-Libris Exhbn., China, 1998, Embassy of France, La Maison Française, Washington, 1998, Florean Mus., Baia Mare, Romania, 1999, 2001, 02, Mus. Civico Di Grafica, Brunico, Italy, 1999, Chateau du Puget, Alzonne, France, 1999, 12th Deutsche Internat. Grafik Triennale, Frechen, Germany, 1999, De Mini Gravura, Vitoria, Brasil, 2000, Bankside Gallery, London, 2000, Quingdao Internat. Print Biennial, China, 2000, Lahti Art Mus., Finland, 2000, Temple Gallery, Rome, 2002, Inst. for Advanced Art and Culture, Aix-en-Provence, France, 2002, 4th Egyptian Internat. Triennial, Cairo and Alexandria, 2003, 1er Concours Internat. d'Exlibris, Ankara and Istanbul, Turkey, 2003, Zeichen der Gegenwart, Vienna Art Gallery, Austria, 2003, L'Espace Melanie, Riec-Sur-Belon, Brittany and Mona Bismark Found., Paris, 2003, Internat. Print and Drawing Exhbn., Silpakorn U. Art and Culture Ctr., Bangkok, 2003, Gracefield Arts Ctr., Dumfries, Scotland, 2003-04, Adam Mickewicz U., Poznan, Poland, 2005, Lefkas, Greece, 2005, Inst. ZacatecanoCultura, Guadelupe, Zacatecas, Mex., 2005, 5th Egyptian Internat. Triennial, Cairo and Alexandria, 2006, Concorso Internat. Exhibit, Tripotea Italiana Found., Cornuda, Italy, 2006, Saga-Hollar Soc. Gallery, Prague, Czechoslovakia, 2006, 5th Internat. Graphics Triennial, Nat. Inst. and Mus. Bitola, Republic of Macedonia, 2006, Internat. Envraving Exhbn., Civic Mus., Cremona, Italy, 2007; also traveling exhibits in US, Europe, Ctrl. Am., Japan, paintings for US embassies, 1976; represented in permanent collections Mus. Modern Art, NYC, Whitney Mus., Art Gallery of Windsor, Ontario, Can., Albright-Knox Art Gallery, Phila. Mus., Butler Inst. Art, Youngstown, Ohio, Nat. Mus. Am. Art, Washington, Libr. of Congress, Israel Mus., Jerusalem, Bradford City Art Mus., St. Catharines Dist. Arts Coun., Ont., Can., Victoria and Albert Mus., London, Balt. Mus. Art, Nat. Portrait Gallery, Washington, Brit. Mus., London, Hunterian Art Gallery, Glasgow, Met. Mus. Art, NYC, Smithsonian Inst., Washington, others. Served with AUS, 1956-58, Korea. Grantee Louis Comfort Tiffany Found., 1962, Netherlands Govt., 1965, NY Coun. Arts, 1972; named fellow NEA, 1974-75, 80-81, Va. Ctr. for the Creative Arts, 1992; elected mem. Nat. Acad. Design, NYC, 1992; recipient Hassam-Speicher award Am. Acad. Arts and Letters, 1990, 91, Nat. Alumni Assn. medal of merit Ohio U., 1992, Disting. Tchg. Art award Coll. Art Assn. NYC, 2003, Individual Artist award, Buffalo Arts Coun. and Erie County Niagara Partnership, 2005. Address: 76 Smallwood Dr Snyder NY 14226-4027

BREWER, AIDA M., state official; BS in Bus., LeMoyne Coll., Syracuse. With Key Bank, 1976—83; investment officer, asst. investment officer Treasury Divsn., NY, 1983—2000; dep. treas. State Dept. Taxation and Fin., NY, 2000—02, dep. commr. NY, 2002—. treas. NY, 2002—. Recipient First Woman Treas., N.Y., 2000. Mem.: Nat. Assn. State Treas., Assn. for Fin. Profls. Office: NY State Dept of Taxation and Fin Divsn Treasury PO Box 22119 Albany NY 12201-2119 E-mail: aida-brewer@tax.state.ny.us.*

BREWER, ANGELA SUE, middle school educator; b. Knoxville, Tenn., Nov. 13, 1962; d. Fred David and Constance Sue Wyrick; m. Mark Alan Brewer, July 27, 1985; children: Ashley Michelle, Destiny Cheyenne. BS, U. Tenn., Knoxville, 1985, MS, 1988. Tchr., dept. head Knox County Schs., Knoxville, 1985—88, Cobb County Schs., Marietta, Ga., 1988—91; tech. writer, trainer Roane State Coll., Oak Ridge, Tenn., 1992—93; tech trainer sampling and environ. group Sci. and Tech. Inc., 1993—94; tchr. Cobb County Schs., 1994—96, Paulding County Schs., Dallas, 1996—98, tchr., dept. head, 1998—. Recipient Tchr. Yr., Paulding County Schs., 2003. Avocations: travel, reading, photography, cooking. Office Phone: 770-443-7028.

BREWER, BARBARA BAGDASARIAN, nursing administrator; b. Providence, Apr. 18, 1950; d. Bagdasar and Grace (Sarkisian) Bagdasarian; m. Timothy F. Brewer III, May 28, 1983. BSN, U. R.I., 1972; MA in Liberal Studies, Conn. Wesleyan U., 1986; MSN, Yale U., 1988; MBA, Columbia U., 1992; PhD, U. Ariz., 2002. RN, Ariz., Conn., R.I., Ind. Staff nurse Miriam Hosp., Providence, 1972; head nurse orthopeds. unit Frisbie Meml. Hosp., Rochester, NH, 1973-76; staff nurse St. Francis Hosp. and Med. Ctr., Hartford, Conn., 1976; clin. coord. continuing care unit Middlesex Meml. Hosp., Middletown, Conn., 1976-86; dir. cardiology svcs. Lawrence and Meml. Hosp., New London, Conn., 1988-92, v.p. ambulatory svcs., 1992-95; adminstrv. leader emergency svcs. Tucson Med. Ctr., 1996-97; rsch. assoc. U. Ariz., Coll. of Nursing, 1998—2001; predoctoral fellow NIH, 1999—2002; project dir. U. Ariz., 2001—03; v.p. quality Clarian Health Ptnrs., 2003—05; dir. profl. practice John C. Lincoln North Mountain Hosp., 2005—. Rschr. in field. Co-author: Improving Your Skills in 12-Lead ECG Interpretation, 1990. Mem.: ANA, Ariz. Nurses Assn., Am. Orgn. Nurse Execs., Sigma Theta Tau (treas. chpt. 2001—03). Office Phone: 602-331-5882. E-mail: barbara.brewer@jcl.com.

BREWER, BRENDA NEAL, assistant principal, educator; d. Roy F. and Mae Neal; m. Thomas M. Brewer, June 3, 1967; children: Tracey Lynn Curtin, Melissa Morgan Rueping. AB in History, Ga. State U., Atlanta, 1973, MEd, 1975. Cert. adminstr. Ga., 2003, tchr. gifted Ga., 1995, ednl. specialist Tenn., 2003. Tchr. DeKalb County Bd. Edn., Decatur, Ga., 1973—96; tchr., dept. chair Gwinnett County Bd. Edn., Suwanee, Ga., 1996—2005, asst. prin., 2005—. Named Tchr. of Yr., Stone Mountain HS, 1992, Star Tchr., 1992, Collins Hill HS, 2002. Mem.: Nat. Assn. Secondary Prins. (assoc.), Nat. Social Studies Assn. (assoc.), Ga. Nat. Honor Soc. (assoc.; elected bd. advisor 1992—97), Alpha Delta Kappa (hon.; sec. 1997—2002). Avocations: travel, reading, tennis. Office: Collins Hill High Sch 50 Taylor Rd Suwanee GA 30024 Home Phone: 770-965-6300; Office Phone: 770-682-4100. Business E-Mail: brenda_brewer@gwinnett.k12.ga.us.

BREWER, BRUCE WILLIAM, plastic surgeon; b. Queens, NY, Apr. 13, 1949; s. Charles William and Viola Marjorie Brewer; m. Susan Elaine Welshonce; children: Reid, Todd. BA, Brown U., 1971; MD, SUNY, Downstate, 1975. Diplomate Am. Bd. Plastic Surgery. Resident in plastic surgery Duke Med. Ctr., 1980—83; Christine Kleinert hand surgery fellow Louisville, 1981. Named Top Surgeon, Consumer Rsch. Coun. Am. Fellow: ACS; mem.: Am. Soc. Plastic Surgeons. Avocations: fishing, sailing, tennis. Office: Long Island Plastic Surgical Group 999 Franklin Ave Garden City NY 11530 Office Phone: 516-742-3404.

BREWER, CAREY, retired academic administrator; b. Lynchburg, Va., July 8, 1927; s. James Allen and Esther Goode (Leftwich) B.; m. Betty Ann Brighton, Sept. 3, 1949; children— Mary Elizabeth, Robert Allen, Ruth Ann, Catherine Lee. BA, Lynchburg Coll., 1949; student, Am. U., 1951; M.P.A., Harvard U., 1952, PhD, 1956. Analyst with legislative reference service Library of Congress, 1949-56; sr. def. specialist mil. ops. subcom. Ho. of Reps., 1956-60; mem. staff joint com. atomic energy U.S. Congress, 1960-61; various positions Office Emergency Planning, Exec. Office of Pres., 1961-64; pres. Lynchburg Coll., 1964-83. Lectr. Am. U., 1954-56; Mem. bd. higher edn., also mem. gen. bd., ch. fin. council Christian Ch. (Disciples of Christ); mem. Pres.'s Civil Def. Adv. Council, 1970-72; Bd. dirs. Nat. Lab. for Higher Edn.; pres. Va. Found. Ind. Colls., 1978-80 Author: Civil Defense in the United States, 1951, Implications of a National Service Program, 1952, Science and Defense, 1956, also numerous articles. Served with USNR, 1945-46. Littauer fellow Harvard, 1951-53 Mem. Council Ind. Colls. Va. (pres. 1972-74), Greater Lynchburg C. of C. (past pres.) Mem. Christian Ch. Clubs: Sphex, Waterfront Golf.

BREWER, CAROL A., biology professor; BA in Biology, Calif. State U., Fullerton, 1981; BS in Sci. Edn., U. Wyo., 1985, MS in Zoology and Physiology, 1986, PhD in Botany, 1993. Cert. sr. ecologist Ecol. Soc. Am., 2000. Prof. divsn. biol. scis. U. Mont., Missoula, assoc. dean Coll. Arts and Scis. Bd. dirs. Mont. Natural Hist. Ctr., 1995—2000, Ecol. Soc. Am., 2000—06, Biomimicry Inst., 2007—; mem. sr. mgmt. team Nat. Ecol. Obs. Network, 2005—; mem. exec. adv. bd. Earth and Sky Radio Series, 2006—; mem. nat. adv. bd. Long Term Ecol. Rsch. Network, 2006—. Contbr. articles to sci. jours.; assoc. editor: Conservation Biology, 2001—, mem. editl. bd.: Frontiers in Ecology and the Environment, 2005—. Recipient Fulbright Sr. Scholar award, Argentina, 1998; Inst. Internat. Edn. fellowship, 1986—87. Mem.: Soc. Conservation Biology, Brit. Ecol. Soc., Am. Inst. Biol. Scis. (Edn. award 2007), Ecol. Soc. Am. (life; v.p. edn. and human resources 2000—06), Phi Delta Kappa. Office: U Mont Coll Arts and Sci LA 136 Missoula MT 59812 Office Phone: 406-243-6013. Office Fax: 406-243-4184. Business E-Mail: carol.brewer@umontana.edu.*

BREWER, CLAIR HERBERT, JR., retired minister; b. New Brighton, Pa., July 14, 1930; s. Clair Herbert, Sr. and Ethel Viola (McKee) Brewer; m. Janis Avery Ashdown, Aug. 24, 1954; children: Carol Louise Kopkas, John Stuart, Linda Jean Wilt, Mary Patricia Pitman, Susan Elizabeth Gainous. BA, Muskingum Coll., New Concord, Ohio, 1952; MDiv, Pitts. Theol. Sem., 1955, ThM, 1959; MPA, U. Pitts., 1969. Ordained to ministry United Presbyn. Ch. N.Am., 1955. Asst. min. E. Whittier United Presbyn. Ch., Calif., 1955—57; staff asst. radio-tv Cleve. Area Ch. Fedn., Cleveland, Ohio, 1957—59; pastor First Presbyn. Ch., Freedom, Pa., 1960—64, interim pastor Huron, Ohio, 1992—94, Sandusky, Ohio, 1995—97, stated supply pastor Willard, Ohio, 2004—05, parish assoc. Norwalk, Ohio, 2006—; asst. prof. bus. and religion Tarko Coll., Mo., 1965—72; assoc. dean Acad. Christian Thought and Svc. Tarkio Coll., Mo., 1965; asst. to dir. and projects coord. Sys. Rsch. Ctr. Case Western Res. U., Cleve., 1973—77; interim pastor Presbyn. Chs. in N. Ctrl. Ohio, 1977—83; assoc. pastor nurture and pastoral care Fairmount Presbyn. Ch., Cleveland Heights, Ohio, 1983—92; coord. hunger, health and housing ministries Mauamee Valley Presbytery, Findlay, Ohio, 2005—. Cons. Cmty. Coun. United Way, St. Joseph, Mo., 1967—69; pres. bd. dirs. Emerging Patterns Interdependent Cmty., Inc., Lakewood, Ohio, 1978—84; chmn. Ohio Presbyns. Pub. Policy Advocacy, Maumee, 2000—07; vice moderator Maumee Valley Presbytery, 2000, moderator, 01, chair bd. trustees, 02, past moderator, mem. coun., 2002—03. Singer (bass-baritone): A Cappella Choir, Muskingum Coll. (Ann. Tuition Scholarship, 1949). Coord. mobile health fairs Maumee Valley Presbytery and Ohio Migrant Edn. Ctr., Fremont, 2003—07; v.p. Elder Coll. Bowling Green State U., Huron, 2005—07. Fellow, U. Pitts., 1963—65, Case Western Res. U., 1972—73. Mem.: Maumee Valley Presbytery, Presbyn. Ch. (USA). Democrat. Presbyterian. Avocations: woodworking, gardening, music. Home: 1032 Main St Huron OH 44839-2324 Office: First Presbyterian Ch 21 Firelands Blvd Norwalk OH 44957 Home Phone: 419-433-6313; Office Phone: 419-668-1923.

BREWER, CLINT, editor; b. Knoxville, Tenn. m. Amy Brewer; children: Emma Grace, Davis Clinton. Music critic Knoxville (Tenn.) Jour.; staff reporter Lebanon (Tenn.) Democrat, mng. editor, 2002—06; editor Gannett Corp. Middle Tenn. Newspaper Group, 2000; owner Mt. Juliet (Tenn.) News, 2000—02; exec. editor City Paper, Nashville, 2006—. Recipient Malcolm Law Meml. award for Investigative Reporting (4-time winner), Tenn. AP Mng. Editor's Contest. Mem.: Tenn. Press Assn., Soc. Profl. Journalists (pres. elect). Office: City Paper Ste 28 624 Grassmere Park Nashville TN 37221 Office Phone: 615-301-9229. E-mail: cbrewer@nashvillecitypaper.com.*

BREWER, COREY WAYNE, college basketball player; b. Portland, Tenn., Mar. 5, 1986; s. Ellis and Glenda Brewer. Student, U. Fla., Gainesville, 2004—. Forward U. Fla., 2004—. Named a McDonald's All-Am., 2004; named Tenn. Player of Yr., Gatorade, 2004, Class AA Mr. Basketball, 2004, Mid-State Player of Yr., The Tennessean, 2004, Co-Defensive Player of Yr., Southeastern Conf., 2006, Most Outstanding Player, NCAA Tournament, 2007; named to All-Southeastern Conf. Second Team, 2006. Achievements include winning the NCAA Championship with Florida, 2006, 07, Southeastern Conference Tournament, 2006. Mailing: U Fla Basketball Office PO Box 14485 Gainesville FL 32604-2485 E-mail: cb2@ufl.edu.*

BREWER, DAVID L., III, school system administrator, retired military officer; b. Farmville, Va., May 19, 1946; m. Richardene Brewer; 1 child, Stacey. BS in Biology, Prairie View A&M U.; MA in Nat. Security & Strategic Studies, Naval War Coll. Enlisted USN, 1970, advanced through grades to vice adm., 2002, ret., 2006; elec. warfare officer USS Little Rock; minority recruiting officer Naval Recruiting Dist., Memphis, 1972—75; combat info. ctr. officer USS Calif., 1975; weapons officer USS William H. Standley, 1978—80; engring. officer USS Okinawa, 1981—83; exec. officer USS Fresno, 1983—84; enlisted cmty. mgr. combat sys. ratings Office of Chief of Naval Ops., Washington, 1985—86; comdr. USS Bristol County, 1986—88; spl. asst. equal opportunity Chief Naval Ops., 1988; comdr. USS Mount Whitney, 1991—92, US Naval Forces Marianas, 1994—96, Amphibious Group THREE, 1997—99; vice chief naval edn. and tng. Pensacola, Fla., 1999—2001; comdr. Military Sealift Command (MSC), 2001—06; supt. LA Unified Sch. Dist., 2006—. Head David and Mildred Brewer Found. Decorated Def. Superior Svc. medal, Legion of Merit with gold star, Meritorious Svc. medal with gold star, Navy Achievement medal; recipient Disting. Grad. Leadership award, Naval War Coll., Navy League of US Vincent T. Hirsch Maritime award Office: LA Unified Sch Dist Office of Supt PO Box 3307 Los Angeles CA 90051 Office Phone: 213-241-7000. Office Fax: 213-241-8442. E-mail: superintendent@lausd.net.*

BREWER, EDWARD CAGE, III, law educator; b. Clarksdale, Miss., Jan. 20, 1953; s. Edward Cage Brewer Jr. and Elizabeth Blair (Alford) Little; m. Nancy Corr Martin, Dec. 27, 1975 (div. Sept. 1985); children: Katherine Martin, Julia Blair; m. Laurie Carol Alley, June 27, 1993 (div. Dec. 1999); 1 child, Caroline Elizabeth McCarty; m. Karlyn Ann Schnapp; children: Matthew Karl Schnapp, Andrew Cage Schnapp. BA, U. of the South, 1975; JD, Vanderbilt U., 1979. Bar: Ala. 1980, U.S. Ct. Appeals (5th and 11th cirs.) 1981, U.S. Dist. Ct. (so. dist.) Ala. 1981, Ga. 1982, U.S. Dist. Ct. (no. dist.) Ga. 1982, U.S. Dist. Ct. (so. dist.) Ga. 1988, U.S. Ct. Appeals (3d and 8th cirs.) 1983, U.S. Dist. Ct. (mid. dist.) Ga. 1992, U.S. Supreme Ct. 1996. Law clk. to Hon. Virgil Pittman U.S. Dist. Ct. (so. dist.) Ala., Mobile, 1979-81; law clk. to Hon. Albert J. Henderson U.S. Ct. Appeals (5th and 11th cirs.), Atlanta, 1981-82; pvt. practice Atlanta, 1982-96; instr. Coll. of Law Ga. State U., Atlanta, 1992, 94; adj. prof. legal writing Emory U., Atlanta, 1994-96; asst. prof. law No. Ky. U., Highland Heights, 1996-2000, assoc. prof. law, 2000—02, prof. law, 2002—. Co-author: Railway Labor Act of 1926: Legislative History, 1988, Georgia Appellate Practice, 1996, 2d edit., 2002; author: Powerpoint Materials for Morgan and Rotunda, Professional Responsibility, 1997, 2d edit., 2003; contbr. articles to profl. jours. Mem.: Omicron Delta Kappa, Phi Beta Kappa. Episcopalian. Avocations: choral music, guitar, bicycling, hiking, canoeing. Home: 4851 Open Meadow Dr Independence KY 41051-8510 Office Phone: 859-572-6943. Business E-Mail: brewerec@nku.edu.

BREWER, ERIC A., computer science educator; BS in Computer Sci., U. Calif., Berkeley; D in Computer Sci., MIT. Rsch. asst. MIT, 1989-94; prof. computer sci. divsn. U. Calif., Berkeley; dir. Inktomi, 1996, interim pres., CEO, 1996, chief tech. officer, 1996-97, chief scientist, 1997. Contbr. articles to profl. jours. Founder Fed. Search Found., 2000. Named a Global Leader for Tomorrow, World Econ. Forum; named Most Influential Person on the Architecture of the Internet, Industry Std.; named one of Top 10 Innovators, InfoWorld, Top 100 Young Innovators Under 35, Tech. Rev., 1999, Top 100 Most Influential People for the 21st Century, 12 e-Mavericks, Forbes mag. Mem.: NAE. Office: Computer Sci Divsn U Calif Berkeley 623 Soda Hall Berkeley CA 94720-1776 Office Phone: 510-642-8143. Office Fax: 510-642-5775. E-mail: brewer@cs.berkeley.edu.*

BREWER, JAMES TIMOTHY, music educator, director; b. Mullins, SC, Feb. 26, 1960; s. James Thomas and Morrie Grace Brewer; m. Sheryl Lynn Hundley; children: Audrey Denise, Justin Timothy. AA, Emmanuel Coll., Franklin Springs, Ga., 1980; MusB, Berry Coll., Mount Berry, Ga., 1982; MusM in Edn., Winthrop U., Rock Hill, SC, 1993. CLU N.C. Dept. Ins., 2003; cert. music educator Assn. Christian Schs. Internat., 2005. Dir. bands Swainsboro (Ga.) H.S., 1982—84, Parkwood H.S., Monroe, NC, 1984—95; ednl. rep. Brook Mays Music Co., Dallas, 1995—2004; dir. athletic bands U. N.C., Charlotte, NC, 1997—99; dir. bands Metrolina Christian Acad., Indian Trail, NC, 2004—. Band adjudicator, clinician NC. and S.C. Bands, NC, 1984—. Composer (arranger): (songs) Christmas March, Saint Nick Meets the Good King, His Grace is Sufficient For Me. Dir. orch. Ft. Mill (S.C.) Ch. God, 2004—06. Mem.: Am. Sch. Bandmasters Assn., Music Educators Nat. Conf. (assoc.). Achievements include development of music education curriculum. Avocations: golf, amateur radio, carpentry, auto restoration. Home: 7928 Charter Oak Lane Charlotte NC 28226 Office: Metrolina Christian Academy PO Box 1460 Indian Trail NC 28079 Home Phone: 704-759-8310. Personal E-mail: tbrewer2@carolina.rr.com. Business E-Mail: tim.brewer@fbcit.org.

BREWER, JANICE KAY, state official; b. Hollywood, Calif., Sept. 26, 1944; d. Perry Wilford and Edna Clarice (Bakken) Drinkwine; m. John Leon Brewer, Jan. 1, 1963; children: Ronald Richard, John Samuel, Michael Wilford. HHD (hon.), LA Chiropractic Coll., 1970. Cert med. asst. Valley Coll., Burbank, Calif., 1963, practical radiol. techician cert. Valley Coll., Burbank, Calif., 1963. Pres. Brewer Property & Investments, Glendale, Ariz., 1970—; mem. Ariz. Ho. Reps., Phoenix, 1983—86, Ariz. State Senate, Phoenix, 1987—96, majority whip, 1993—96; mem. Maricopa County Bd. Supr., 1997—2002; sec. state State of Ariz., Phoenix, 2003—. State com. woman Rep. Party, Phoenix, 1970, Phoenix, 83; legis. liaison Arrowhead Republic Women; treas. Nat. Assn. Lt. Gov., 2004; bd. dir. Motion Picture & TV Commn. Named Woman of Yr., Chiropractic Assn. Ariz., 1983, Legislator of Yr., Behaviour Health Assn. Ariz., 1991, NRA, 1992; recipient Freedom award, Vets. of Ariz., 1994. Mem.: Am. Legis. Exch. Coun., Nat. Fedn. Rep. Women, NOW. Republican. Lutheran. Office: Office Sec State 7th Fl State Capitol 1700 W Washington Phoenix AZ 85007-2808 Office Phone: 602-542-3012. Office Fax: 602-542-1575.*

BREWER, JOHN CHARLES, journalist; b. Cin., Oct. 24, 1947; s. Harry Marion and Barbara Ann (Burrier) B.; m. Adeline Laude, Dec. 22, 1973 (div. 1994); children: Andrew John, Jeffrey Joseph; m. Ann Hagen Kellett, 1997 (dec. Mar. 2005). BS, Calif. State Poly. U., Pomona, 1970. Newsman, photographer Daily Report, Ontario, Calif., 1967-69; newsman AP, LA, 1969-74, news editor, 1974-75, asst. chief bur. Seattle, 1975-76, chief of bur., 1976-82, LA, 1982-86, gen. exec. membership dept. NYC, 1986-88; exec. editor news svc. The N.Y. Times, 1988-90, editor in chief news svc., 1990-97; pres. N.Y. Times Syndication Sales Corp., 1990-97; publisher, editor Peninsula Daily News, Port Angeles, Wash., 1998—. Bd. dirs. Port Angeles C. of C., Olympic Meml. Hosp. Found., Port Angeles Downtown Assn. Mem. Fedn. of Fly Fishers, Northwest Steelheaders-Trout Unlimited, Nat. Steelhead Trout Assn., Rotary Internat., Kiwanis. Republican. Roman Catholic. Office: Peninsula Daily News 305 W 1st St Port Angeles WA 98362-2205 Home Phone: 360-452-4639; Office Phone: 360-417-3500. Business E-Mail: john.brewer@peninsuladailynews.com. *I enjoy very much being a journalist and newspaper executive. Nothing can compare with it. As for finding time for everything— the news and photo reports, relations with advertisers and subscribers, my family, my personal, problems—always the problems—I am reminded of a woman who had eleven children. She was asked how she had time to take care of all of them. She replied that when she had one child it took 100 percent of her time, and eleven could not take more. I think there's an analogy in this.*

BREWER, LEWIS GORDON, judge, educator; b. New Martinsville, W.Va., Sept. 6, 1946; s. Harvey Lee and Ruth Carolyn (Zimmerman) B.; m. Kathryn Anne Yunker, May 25, 1985. BA, W.Va. U., 1968, JD, 1971; LLM, George Washington U., 1979. Bar: W.Va. 1971, Calif. 1978. Commd. 2d lt. USAF, 1968, advanced through grades to col., 1988, dep. staff judge adv. Travis AFB, Calif., 1976—78, chief civil law San Antonio Air Logistics Ctr. Kelly AFB, Tex., 1979-83, staff judge adv. MacDill AFB, Fla., 1983—86, chief Air Force Cen. Labor Law Office Randolph AFB, Tex., 1987-88, dep. staff judge adv. Air Tng. Command, 1988-89, staff judge adv. 7th Air Force Osan AFB, Korea, 1989-91, 45 Space Wing Patrick AFB Fla., 1991-93; adminstrv. law judge W.Va. Edn. and State Employee Grievance Bd., Charleston, 1993-2000, mediator, 1994—; legal counsel W.Va. Ethics Commn., Charleston, 2000, exec. dir., 2004—. Instr. bus. law No. Mich. U., Marquette, 1972, Solano Coll., Suisun City, Calif., 1978; instr. labor law Webster U., Ft. Sam Houston, 1983. Decorated Air Force Commendation medal, Meritorious Service medal, Legion of Merit. Mem. ABA, Assn. for Conflict Resolution, W.Va. Bar Assn., State Bar Calif., W.Va. U. Alumni Assn., George Washington U. Alumni Assn. Roman Catholic. Home: 528 Sheridan Cir Charleston WV 25314-1063 Office: 210 Brooks St Ste 300 Charleston WV 25301-1826 Office Phone: 304-558-0664. Business E-Mail: lbrewer@wvadmin.gov. E-mail: mede8wv@abanet.org.

BREWER, LOUIE GEORGE, JR., blood bank specialist; b. Big Spring, Tex., Oct. 8, 1946; s. Mary Belle Stice; m. Linda May Allen, Aug. 30, 2003; children: John Joseph Campbell, David Edward Campbell. BS in Chemistry, U. Tex., Austin, 1969. Cert. specialist in blood bank technology Am. Soc. Clin. Pathologists, 1982, med. technologist Am. Soc. Clin. Pathologists, 1971. Processing shift supr. Gulf Coast Regional Blood Ctr., Houston, 1979—80, reference lab. specialist, 1980—84; tech. dir. United Blood Svcs., Ft. Smith, Ark., 1984—85; blood bank supr. Hosp. Corp. Am. Med. Ctr. Plano, Tex., 1986—96; mgr. reference and transfusion svc. Carter BloodCare, Dallas, 1996—98; tech. supr. Lake Pointe Med. Ctr., Rowlett, Tex., 1998—2001; lab. shift supr. Baylor Med. Ctr., Garland, Tex., 2002—03; ret., 2003. Contbr. articles to profl. jours. 1st lt. USAF, 1969—75. Mem.: Am. Guild Organists, Pi Kappa Lambda. Methodist. Achievements include discovery of previously unknown Rh blood haplotype. Avocation: organist. Home: 2137 Savannah Trail Denton TX 76205 Home Phone: 940-387-8761. Home Fax: 940-381-6741. Personal E-mail: louiebrewer@hotmail.com.

BREWER, MARK COURTLAND, lawyer; b. Hammond, Ind., Apr. 1, 1955; s. Harold Russell and Carol Joan (Odell) B. BA, Harvard U., 1977; JD, Stanford U., 1981. Bar: U.S. Dist. Ct. (ea. and we. dist.) Mich. 1983, U.S. Ct. Appeals (6th cir.) 1983. Law clk. U.S. Ct. Appeals (5th cir.), Austin, 1981-82; law clk. to justice Mich. Supreme Ct., Lansing, 1982-83; assoc. Sachs, Waldman, O'Hare, P.C., Detroit, 1983-89; mem. Sachs, Waldman & O'Hare, Detroit, 1989-95. Pres. Stanford Pub. Interest Law Found. Palo Alto, Calif., 1980-81; bd. dirs. Mich. Protection and Adv. Svc., Lansing, Mich. Contbr. articles on AIDS discrimination, drug testing, and employee privacy to profl. publs. Mem. Macomb County Dem. Com., Mich., 1982—, 12th Congl. Dist. Dem. Com. Macomb County, 1983-93, 10th Congl. Dist. Dem. Com. Macomb County, 1993—2003; chmn. Mich. Dem. Party; vice chair Dem. Nat. Com. Mem. ATLA, ABA, FBA (pres. ea. dist. Mich., bd. dirs. 1999-2000), State Bar Mich. (Outstanding Young Lawyer 1988), Mich. Trial Lawyers Assn., Assn. State Dem. Chairs (pres.), Sierra Club. Democrat. Lutheran. Office: Mich Democratic Party 606 Townsend St Lansing MI 48933-2313 Office Phone: 517-371-5410.

BREWER, PAUL HUIE, advertising executive, artist, portrait painter; b. Jan. 24, 1934; s. Ralph Wright and Margot (Riviere) Brewer; m. Anita Hines, May 16, 1953 (div. 1971); children: Anita Joy(dec.) , Launa Riviere; m. Carole Lynn Kuhrt, July 8, 1972; children: Nicole Renee, Brett Kuhrt. BA, La. Coll., Pineville, 1956; degree in advt. design, Famous Artists Schs., Westport, Conn., 1959. Artist Ralph Brewer's Studio and Engraving Co., Alexandria, 1952—54; art dir. Sta. KALB-TV, Alexandria, 1954—56; designer New Orleans Pub. Svc. Co., 1956; artist King Studio, Chgo., 1957; asst. art dir. Continental Casualty Co., Chgo., 1957—58; designer, art dir. Field Enterprises divsn. Chgo. Sun-Times, then dir. design; art dir. State Farm Ins. Cos., Bloomington, Ill., 1973, dir. art and design, 1973—77; prodn. mgr., exec. art dir. U.S. Savs. and Loan League, Chgo., 1977—, corp. v.p., 1983—. Cons. Johns Byrne Co., 1991, Darwill, 1992—93; instr. Wilmette (Ill.) Park Dist., 1997—, Glencoe (Ill.) Park Dist., 1997—, Winnetka (Ill.) Park Dist., 1997—, Deerpath (Ill.) Art League, 2003—, Suburban Fine Arts Ctr., 2003—. One-man shows include La. Coll., 1963, Chgo. Pub. Libr., Chgo. Press Club, Who Am I?, 1973, Represented in permanent collections Union League Club, Chgo., Ill. Bell Telephone Co., Standard Rate & Data, Krantzen Studio, Red Buttons, Lee Bolivier, Edward P. Morgan, others, Jack Benny, Danny Kaye, Danny Thomas, Pablo Picasso, Mrs. Marshall Field IV, Phil Silvers, David Susskind, Leonard Bernstein, Chuck Connors, Merve Griffin, Bob Newhart, Mike Singletary, Carol Kuhrt, others, New in the City, Count a Lonely Cadence, Who Am I?. Advt. dir. Artists Guild Bull., 1965; chmn. Artist Guild Chgo. Watercolor Show, 1967; bd. dirs. Artists Guild Chgo. Credit Union, House of Wray Corp. Ill., North Shore Art League, Lake County Art Commn., Deerpath Art League; elder Presbyn. Ch. Recipient award, Am. Newspaper Guild, Artists Guild Chgo., Famous Artists Sch., Graphic Arts Coun. Chgo., Hartford Illustrationaward, 1968, Chgo. III award, 1970, Nat. award, Louisville Rotogravure Assn., 1975, 3 SIMSA nat. awards, 1977, 2 SIMSA nat. awards, 1979, award, Union League Chgo., award of excellence, Hopper Paper Co., 1978, 1979, 2 Addy awards, State of Iowa, 1980, Nat. Merchandising awrad, P.O.P.I.A., 1980, 2 nat. awards, Fin. Insts. Mktg. Assn., 1984, award, Internat. Paper Co., 1984, Fima award, 1989, 1990, award, Chgo. Fin. Advertisers, 1990, awards of excellence in painting for In View exhbn., Highland Park, Ill., 2004—06. Mem.: La. Coll. Alumni Assn., North Shore Art League, Chgo. Soc. Typographic Arts, Chgo. Soc. Communicating Arts (bd. dirs.), Deerpath Art League, Am. Soc. Portrait Artists, Famous Artists Sch. Alumni Assn., Artists Guild Chgo., Am. Watercolor Soc. (assoc.). Home: 1160 S Green Bay Rd Lake Forest IL 60045-4065 also: 3630 Lee St Alexandria LA 71302-3929 also: 1400 S Shore Dr Delavan WI 53115-3627 Office Phone: 847-295-4119. Personal E-mail: paulbrewerart@aol.com.

BREWER, PETER GEORGE, ocean geochemist; b. Ulverston, Eng., Dec. 30, 1940; came to U.S., 1967, naturalized, 1982; s. Frederick and Irene (Clarkson) B.; m. Hilary Williams, Mar. 29, 1966; children: Jillian Anne, Alastair Michael, Erica Christine. BSc, Liverpool U., Eng., 1962, PhD, 1967. From asst. scientist to sr. scientist Woods Hole Oceanog. Inst., Mass., 1967—78, sr. scientist, 1978—91; program dir. marine chemistry NSF, 1981—83; exec. dir. Monterey Bay Aquarium Rsch. Inst., Pacific Grove, Calif., 1991—96, sr. scientist, 1996—. Leader of ocean sci. expeditions; mem. Environ. Task Force, 1992-93, NAS Ocean Studies Bd., 1986-94, Com. on Climate Change and the Ocean, 1987-90; convenor NATO A.R.I. on Chem. Dynamics of Upper Ocean, Jouy en Jossas, France, 1983; mem. NAS panel on policy implications of greenhouse gas warming: mitigation, 1989-91; mem. NAS carbon dioxide adv. com., 1982-83; vis. prof. U. Wash., 1979; mem. GEOSECS sci. adv. com., 1972-78. Assoc. editor: Geophys. Rsch. Letters, 1977-79, Jour. Marine Rsch., 1974-81, Deep-Sea Rsch., 1984-87, Jour. of Oceanography, 1994—; contbr. over 130 articles to sci. publs. Chmn. Gordon Rsch. Conf. on Chem. Oceanography, 1980; vice-chmn. Joint Global Ocean Fluxes Com., SCOR, 1987-90; mem. adv. bd. Applied Physics Lab., U. Wash., 1991-96. Grantee NSF, NASA, Office Naval Rsch., Dept. Energy. Fellow AAAS, Am. Geophys. Union. Office: Monterey Bay Aquarium Rsch Inst 7700 Sandholdt Rd Moss Landing CA 95039-0628 Business E-Mail: brpe@mbari.org.

BREWER, RALPH WRIGHT, JR., lawyer, writer; b. Alexandria, La., Jan. 9, 1928; s. Ralph Wright and Margot (Marguerite) (Riviere) B.; m. Barbara Ann Els, Dec. 27, 1952; m. 2d Peggy Alice Knapps, Aug. 29, 1968; children: David, Daniel, Ralph, William, Margo, Stacie. BA in Journalism, La. State U., 1950, JD, 1955. Bar: La. 1955, US Dist. Ct. (ea. dist.) La. 1956, US Dist. Ct. (we. dist.) La. 1958, US Dist. Ct. (mid. dist.) La. 1963, US Ct. Apls. (5th cir.) 1959, US Supreme Ct. 1971. Sole practice, Baton Rouge, 1955—. Served with USN, 1946-47, 50-52. Newspaper columnist, 1981—; contbr. in field. Mem. ABA, La. State Bar Assn., Baton Rouge Bar Assn., Assn. Trial Lawyers Am., La. Trial Lawyers Assn., Sigma Delta Chi. Democrat. Presbyterian. Avocations: running, road racing, marathoning, lay preaching. Home: 1023 Waverly Dr Baton Rouge LA 70806-1914 Office: 1157 Laurel St Baton Rouge LA 70802-4643 Home Phone: 225-926-8649; Office Phone: 225-387-0293.

BREWER, RICHARD B., biotechnology company executive; m. Debbie Brewer (div.). BS in Biology, Va. Poly. Inst. and State U.; MBA, Northwestern U. With Genentech, Inc., 1984—95; sr. v.p. U.S. sales and mktg. Genentech Europe Ltd. and Genentech Can., Inc.; exec. v.p. ops. Heartport, Inc., 1996—98, COO; pres., CEO, dir. Scios Inc. ($2.4 billion merger with Johnson & Johnson), Sunnyvale, Calif., 1998—2004; mng. ptnr. Crest Asset Mgmt. Mem. adv. bd. Kellogg Grad. Sch. Mgmt., Ctr. for Biotech., Northwestern U., 2001—; mem. corp. roundtable Am. Heart Assn., 1993—94, chmn. pharm. roundtable, 1994—95; bd. dirs. Dendreon Corp., Agensys, Inc., Corus Pharma, Corgentech Inc., Faster Cures, SRI Internat., 2006—. Office: Corgentech 650 Gateway Blvd South San Francisco CA 94080

BREWER, ROBERT ALLEN, physician; b. Inpls., Jan. 29, 1927; s. Robert Dewayne and Viola Mae (Grant) Brewer; m. Mildred Noreen Barnett, Jan. 1, 1950 (dec. May 1997); children: Robert A. Jr., Raymond, Richard, Brian, Andrew. AA, St. Petersburg Jr. Coll., Fla., 1949; AB, Ind. U., 1952; MD, Ind U., Inpls., 1955. Emergency dept. staff physician Mound Park Hosp., St. Petersburg, Fla., 1960; staff physician Pinellas Hosp., Largo, Fla., 1961-68; pvt. practice Logansport, Ind., 1969—. Mem. Cass County Rep. Com., Logansport, Ind.; candidate for city coun., 1995. Capt. US Army, 1957—59. Mem.: AMA, Cass County Med. Assn., Ind. Med. Assn., Am. Acad. Family Practitioners (bd. cert. diplomate). Republican. Avocations: stamp collecting/philately, coin collecting/numismatics. Office: PO Box 119 803 E Broadway Logansport IN 46947-0119 Home: 3415 W 296th St Kirklin IN 46050

BREWER, ROBERT H., consumer products company executive; Dir. audit Praxair Inc., W.R. Grace & Co.; v.p. global corp. audit svcs. Office Depot, Inc., Delray Beach, Fla., sr. v.p., chief compliance officer. Chmn. bus. & industry com. and nominations com. AICPA; v.p. student rels. Inst. Internal Auditors. Office: Office Depot Inc 2200 Old Germantown Rd Delray Beach FL 33445*

BREWER, ROY EDWARD, lawyer; b. Atlanta, Dec. 22, 1949; s. Roy Mullins and Martha JoAnn (Still) Brewer; m. Catherine Elizabeth Schindler, May 5, 1979; children: Garrett Edward, Alex Winston. BA in Polit. Sci., U. Fla., 1971, MA in Polit. Sci., 1973; JD, U. Pacific, 1982. Bar: Calif. 1984, U.S. Dist. Ct. (ea. dist.) Calif. 1984, U.S. Supreme Ct. 1990. Regional planner North Cen. Fla. Regional Planning Council, Gainesville,

Fla., 1975-78; dir. met. affairs Sacramento Met. C. of C., 1978-79; dir. land planning Raymond Vail and Assocs., Sacramento, 1979-84; pvt. practice Sacramento, 1984-89; ptnr. Hunter McCray Richey & Brewer, Sacramento, 1989-95, Hunter, Richey, DiBenedetto & Brewer, Sacramento, 1995—2000, mng. ptnr., 1993—2000; ptnr. Brewer Law Firm, 2000—06, Brewer Lofgren LLP, 2006—. Bd. dirs. Am. River Natural History Assn., 1986—90, pres., 1988—89; bd. dirs. No. Calif. Rugby Football Union, 1985—88, pres., 1985—88; chmn. Sacramento Ad-hoc Charter Comm., 1988—90; bd. dirs. Healthcare, 1987—90, chmn., 1988—89; bd. dirs. Sacramento Met. C. of C., 1985—91, 2007—, pres., 1990; trustee ARC, 1989—90; chmn. Local Govt. Reorgn. Com., 1988; chair Leadership Sacramento, 2000, co-chair, 2001—03; sr. fellow Am. Leadership Forum, Mt. Valley Chpt., 2005—; bd. dirs. Sacramento Symphony Assn., 1987—95, Am. Lung Assn., 1988—92, Sacramento Downtown Partnership, 1997—99. Named among Best and Brightest, Sacramento Mag., 1985; recipient Sacramento Regional Pride award for cmty. devel., 1991, Exceptional Performers award, Air Force Assn., 1991, Sacramentan of the Yr. award, 1991. Mem.: Am. Inst. Cert. Planners. Avocations: rugby, karate, scuba diving, snowboarding. Office Phone: 916-944-8896.

BREWER, SCOTT, law educator; b. NYC; BA in Philosophy and Religious Studies, SUNY, Stony Brook, 1979; MA in Philosophy, Yale U., 1980, JD, 1988; PhD in Philosophy, Harvard U., 1997. Law clk. to Judge Harry T. Edwards US Ct. Appeals DC Cir., 1989—90; law clk. to Justice Thurgood Marshall US Supreme Ct., 1990—91; lectr. law Harvard Law Sch., Cambridge, Mass., 1988, asst. prof., 1991—98, prof., 1998—. Office: Harvard Law Sch 1563 Massachusetts Ave Cambridge MA 02138 Office Phone: 617-495-3147. Office Fax: 617-496-4866. Business E-Mail: sbrewer@law.harvard.edu.

BREWER, THOMAS BOWMAN, retired university president; b. Ft. Worth, July 22, 1932; s. Earl Johnson and Maurine (Bowman) B.; m. Betty Jean Walling, Aug. 4, 1951; children: Diane, Thomas Bowman Jr.; m. Tyra King Thomas, Nov. 10, 2005. BA, U. Tex., 1954, MA, 1957; PhD, U. Pa., Phila., 1962. Instr. St. Stephens Episcopal Sch., Austin, Tex., 1955-56, S.W. Tex. State Coll., San Marcos, 1956-57; from instr. to asso. prof. North Tex. State U., Denton, 1959-66; asst. prof. U. Ky., 1966-67; asso. prof. Iowa State U., 1967-68; prof. history, chmn. dept. U. Toledo, 1968-71; dean Tex. Christian U., Ft. Worth, 1971-72, vice chancellor, dean univ., 1972-78; chancellor East Carolina U., Greenville, NC, 1978-82; v.p. acad. affairs Ga. State U., Atlanta, 1982-88; pres. Met. State Coll. of Denver, 1988-93; interim provost U. Alaska, Anchorage, 1995-97. Editor: Views of American Economic Growth, 2 vols, 1966, The Robber Barons, 1969; gen. editor: Railroads of America Series. Home: 104 Javelin Dr Austin TX 78734-5016 Personal E-mail: TBBSR@alumni.utexas.net.

BREWER, TIMOTHY FRANCIS, III, retired cardiologist; b. Hartford, Conn., Oct. 30, 1931; s. Timothy F. Brewer Jr. and Catherine Marie (Sullivan) Brewer; m. Norma Rae Flicker, June 14, 1954 (div. Jan. 1980); children: Raymond, Donna, Timothy, Kevin, William; m. Barbara Grace Bagdasarian, May 28, 1983. BA, Yale Coll., 1953; MD, N.Y. Med. Coll., 1957. Diplomate Bd. Internal Medicine Cardiovasc. Diseases. Intern St. Francis Hosp., Hartford, 1957-58; resident in internal medicine VA Ctr., LA, 1958-60; spl. fellow in cardiovascular diseases Cleve. (Ohio) Clinic, 1960-62; pvt. practice St. Francis Hosp., Hartford, 1962-64; assoc. dir. clin. rsch. Pfizer Inc., Groton, Conn., 1964-71; dir. Clin. Pharmacology Miles Lab., West Haven, Conn., 1971-74; pvt. practice Middlesex Hosp., Middletown, Conn., 1974-96, ret., 1996. Pres. med. staff Middlesex Hosp., Middlesex, Conn., 1981—83, chief cardiology sect., 1988—95. Fellow: ACP, Coun. on Clin. Cardiology, Am. Coll. Chest Physicians (emeritus), Am. Coll. Cardiology (emeritus); mem.: AMA (pres. South Ctrl. Conn. chpt. 1982, bd. dirs. 1980), Am. Heart Assn. (Conn. affiliate). Avocation: golf. Personal E-mail: tfb3@earthlink.net.

BREWER, WILLIAM THOMAS, theater educator, theater director; b. McAlester, Okla., Aug. 31, 1949; s. Kathryn Naomi and Jewel Archibald Brewer; m. Lou Ellen Allen, July 21, 1949; children: Brandon Thomas, Grant Irvin. MA, U. Ark., Fayetteville, 1984. Speech, drama instr. Eufaula HS, Okla., 1971—80; bus. mgr. dept. drama U. Ark., 1980—81; tv prodn. coord., drama instr. McAlerster HS, 1982—83; dir. theatre Hutchinson C.C., Kans., 1984—2006, chmn. fine arts dept., 2000—, Delos V. Smith endowed chair performing arts, 2000—. Actor: The Death of a Salesman, Never Let 'em Catch You At It, (one-man play) A History of the Oklahoma Federal Theatre Project, 1935-39, An Evening With Milburn Stone; contbr. articles to profl. jours. Sgt. 1st class Mil. Police Co., Okla., 1970—77. Named Dragon Educator of Yr., Student Govt. Assn., Hutchinson C.C., 2003. Mem.: Assn. Arts Agencies Kans. (bd. dirs. 1983—2000), Kans. Nat. Edn. Assn. Democrat. Methodist. Avocations: woodworking, painting, soccer. Home: 1407 W 14th Hutchinson KS 67501 Office: Hutchinson Cmty Coll 1300 N Plum Hutchinson KS 67501 Home Phone: 620-960-3681; Office Phone: 620-665-3471. Personal E-mail: wtbrewer@gmail.com. Business E-Mail: brewerb@hutchcc.edu.

BREWERTON, TIMOTHY DAVID, psychiatrist; b. Baton Rouge, Mar. 26, 1953; s. John Lee and Helen (Bouy) B.; m. Therese Kathleen Killeen, June 16, 1990. BS, La. State U., 1974; MD, Tulane U., 1979. Diplomate Am. Bd. Psychiatry and Neurology, Am. Bd. Child and Adolescent Psychiatry, Am. Bd. Forensic Psychiatry. Intern, resident psychiatry U. Calif., San Francisco, 1979—82; staff psychiatrist Hawaii State Hosp., Kaneohe, 1982—84; med. staff fellow NIMH, Bethesda, Md., 1984—87, guest rschr., 1987—95; asst. prof. psychiatry and behavioral scis. Med. U. S.C., Charleston, 1987—90, assoc. prof. psychiatry and behavioral scis., 1990—97, fellow in child and adolescent psychiatry, 1994—96, prof. psychiatry and behavioral scis., 1997—2002, clin. prof. psychiatry and behavioral sci., 2002—. Dir. Eating Disorders Program, Inst. Psychiatry, Charleston, 1987—2002; med. cons. Nat. Crime Victims Rsch. and Treatment Ctr., 1996—2002. Contbr. articles to profl. jours.; editor: Clinical Handbook of Eating Disorders: An Integrated Approach, 2004. Recipient Award for Creative Achievement Dept. Psychiatry U. Calif. San Francisco, 1982. Fellow Am. Psychiat. Assn. (disting.), Acad. Eating Disorders (bd. dirs. 2000-02); mem. Soc. Biol. Psychiatry, Am. Acad. Clin. Psychiatrists (Clin. Rsch. award 1989, bd. dirs. 1993-97), Eating Disorders Rsch. Soc. (pres.-elect 2000-01, pres. 2001-02, past pres. 2002-03), Am. Acad. Child and Adolescent Psychiatry, Internat. Soc. for the Study of Dissociation, S.C. Coun. Child and Adolescent Psychiatry (pres.-elect 2003, pres. 2004-05, past pres. 2005-06) Office: 216 Scott St Mount Pleasant SC 29464 Personal E-mail: tbrewerton1@comcast.net.

BREWINGTON, ARTHUR WILLIAM, retired English language educator; b. Bklyn., Nov. 10, 1906; s. Oscar and Julia (Wenisch) B.; m. Thelma Sherman, Aug. 18, 1955. AB, Asbury Coll., 1928; MA, Cornell U., 1931; PhD, Vanderbilt U., 1941. Head English dept. Tenn. Wesleyan Coll., Athens, 1929-31; instr. English Pa. State U., State College, 1932-33; prof. English and speech Memphis State U., 1940-43; inspector quality control Glenn Martin Co., Balt., 1943-45; head speech dept. Towson State U., Balt., 1945-71. Dir. drama and theater Towson State U., 1946-69. *Sent to India by the Fulbright Committee of the State Department and engaged by the Indian Ministry of Education at the time of developing Indian independence following the separation from England. At the time some Indian political leaders were set to remove the English language from India and replace it with Hindu. Helped to save the English language for India. Sent to lecture at colleges and universities in many Indian states and to work with many leaders of Indian public education. First speech educator employed by Towson State University in 1945. Introduced and developed a program of speech education, theater and dramatics, speech and hearing.* Contbr. rsch. to profl. publs. Fund-raiser, bd. dirs. Am. Heart Assn., Green Valley, 1995-96. Fulbright grant US State Dept., 1955-56, Danforth grant, 1963. Mem. Fulbright Assn. (pres. U. Ariz. chpt. 2001-02), Kiwanis (com. chmn. 1971-95), Masons (chaplain lodge 171 1972-75), Cornell Club., Green Valley Shrine Club (pres. 1974), Creativity, Mental Illness and Crime, 2007. Democrat. Episcopalian. Avocations: theater, movies, TV, opera, symphony. Home: 69 W Cedro Dr Green Valley AZ 85614-4203 Personal E-mail: art1110@cs.com.

BREWSTER, CARROLL WORCESTER, former academic administrator; b. NYC, Mar. 26, 1936; s. Carroll Harwood and Blandina (Worcester) Brewster; m. Ursula Mary Orange, Mar. 9, 1968 (div. Apr. 1996); children: Abraham Carroll, Ursula Constant, Clandina Worcester. BA, Yale, 1957, LL.B., 1961; L.H.D. (hon.), Hollins Coll., 1981, Hobart and William Smith Coll., 1991; postgrad., Kings Coll., Cambridge U., 1957-58. Bar: Conn. 1962. Law clk. to chief judge U.S. Dist. Ct., Conn., 1961-62; legal asst. to Hon. Mohamed Ahmed Abu Rannat, Chief Justice of the Sudan, Khartoum, 1962-64; assoc. Tyler, Cooper, Grant, Bowerman & Keefe, New Haven, 1965-69, also U.S. commr., 1966-69; lectr. Yale Law Sch., 1967-69; coll. dean Dartmouth Coll., 1969-75; pres. Hollins Coll., Va., 1975-81, Hobart and William Smith Colls., NY, 1982-91; exec. dir. Hole in the Wall Gang Fund, New Haven, 1991-98. Trustee Phillips Exeter Acad., 1970—80, Anatolia Coll., 1990—, U. New Haven, 1995—2005; chmn. bd. dirs. Presiding Bishop's Fund World Relief, 1986—91, Episcopal Ch. Found., 1985—93. Editor: Sudan Law Jour. and Reports, 1961—65. Sr. Fulbright scholar, U. Khartoum, Sudan, 1981—82. Home: 126 Lounsbury Rd Ridgefield CT 06877-4730

BREWSTER, DARYL G., food products executive; b. Newark, Nov. 14, 1956; s. Robert E. and Margery Fleming (Frank) B.; m. Renee' Lynn Rice, July 11, 1981; children: Hallyn Rice, Jordan Rice, Keeler Rice, Meade Rice. BA, U. Va., 1979; MBA, U. N. Carolina, 1982. Asst. service bur. dir. Atlantic Coast Conf., Greensboro, NC, 1979-80; asst. dir. mktg. U. N. Carolina, 1980-82; asst. product mgr. Gen. Foods, White Plains, NY, 1982-83, assoc. product mgr., team leader, product mgr., team leader, 1984-85, sr. product mgr. NY, 1985-87, grocery sales mgr. Scottsdale, Ariz., 1987; with Campbell Soup Co.; pres. Planters & Specialty Foods Co. Kraft Foods / Nabisco, 1997—2000; pres. Nabisco Biscuit Co., 2000—02; pres. Canada, Mexico, Puerto Rico Kraft Foods, 2002—03, pres. No. Am. snacks & cereals sector, 2003—06; pres., CEO Krispy Kreme Doughnuts Inc., Winston-Salem, NC, 2006—. Bd. dir. E*Trade Fin. Corp. Coach Offl., Various Youth League Sports. Recipient Raven Socitey award Univ. Va., Charlottesville Va. 1979. Mem.: Phi Beta Kappa. Avocations: raising kids, sports. Mailing: Krispy Kreme Doughnuts PO Box 83 Winston Salem NC 27102

BREWSTER, ELIZABETH WINIFRED, literature educator, poet, writer; b. Chipman, NB, Can., Aug. 26, 1922; d. Frederick John and Ethel May (Day) Brewster BA, U. N.B., 1946, DLitt, 1982; MA, Radcliffe U., 1947; BLS, U. Toronto, 1953; PhD, Ind. U., 1962. Cataloger Carleton U., Ottawa, Ont., 1953—57, Ind. U. Libr., Bloomington, 1957—58, N.B. Legis. Libr., 1965—68, U. Alta. Libr., Edmonton, Canada, 1968—70; mem. English dept. Victoria U., B.C., 1960—61; reference libr. Mt. Allison U. Libr., Sackville, N.B., 1961—65; vis. asst. prof. English U. Alta., 1970—71; mem. faculty U. Sask., Saskatoon, Canada, 1972—, asst. prof. English, 1972—75, assoc. prof., 1975—80, prof., 1980—90, prof. emeritus, 1990—. Author: East Coast, 1951, Lillooet, 1954, Passage of Summer, 1969, Sunrise North, 1972, In Search of Eros, 1974, Sometimes I Think of Moving, 1977, The Way Home, 1982, The Sisters, 1974, It's Easy to Fall on the Ice, 1977, Digging In, 1982, Junction, 1982, A House Full of Women, 1983, Selected Poems 1944-1984, 1985, Visitations, 1987, Entertaining Angels, 1988, Spring Again, 1990, The Invention of Truth, 1991, Wheel of Change, 1993, Away from Home, 1995, Footnotes to the Book of Job, 1995, Garden of Sculpture, 1998, Burning Bush, 2000, Jacob's Dream, 2002, Collected Poems, 2003, 2004, Bright Centre, 2005. Recipient E.J. Pratt award for poetry, U. Toronto, 1953, Pres. medal for poetry, U. We. Ont., 1980, Lit. award, Can. Broadcasting Corp., 1991, Lifetime award excellence in arts, Sask. Arts Bd., 1995, Short List award, Gov. Gen., 1996, Sask. Book award for poetry, 2003, Sask. Centennial medal, 2005. Mem. League Can. Poets (life), Writers' Union Can., Assn. Can. Univ. Tchrs. English, Order of Can.

BREWSTER, JAMIE SUSAN, theater educator; b. Appleton, Wis., Mar. 6, 1961; d. James H. and Peggy A. Brewster; m. James Tyra, Oct. 1, 1959. BA in Oral Comm. Edn., U. Ctrl. Okla., Edmond, 1982, BA in English, 1983; M in Gifted Edn., Okla. City U., 1994. Cert. Tchr. Okla. Dept. Edn., 1982. Tchr. Capitol Hill HS, Oklahoma City, 1987—92; drama tchr. Summit Mid. Sch., Edmond, 1993—. Dir. Korean Student Exch. Program, Edmond, 2000—03. Actor: (cmty. theatre) Lost in Yonkers (Best Actress, 1998); founding mem. (profl. theater) CityRep Theatre Co. Recipient Educator of Yr., Teen Ink Mag., 2001—02, Tchr. of Yr., Capitol Hill HS, 1992, Summit Mid. Sch., 2004, Dr. Pepper Educator of Yr., 1992; scholar, Quartz Mountain Arts Program, 1992. Mem.: OEA. Democrat. Avocations: reading, crafts, writing, theater. Home Phone: 405-858-0873. Personal E-mail: jamesnjamie6@aol.com.

BREWSTER, MARY MOORHEAD, retired educational association administrator; b. Fitzgerald, Ga., May 11, 1924; d. Henry Augustus and Grace Haynes Moorhead; m. Joseph Screver Brewster, June 28, 1947 (dec.); children: Linda Brewster Ayers, Joseph S. Jr., John G. II. BS in Edn., West Ga. Coll., Carrollton, 1962; M in Adminstrn., West Ga. U., 1990; M in Bus. Edn., Ga. State U., Atlanta, 1970. Semi profl. War Dept., South Eastern States, 1943—45; exec. sec. Polk County Tuberculosis Assn., Cedartown, Ga., 1952—55; tchr. Polk County Bd. Edn., 1962—78, asst. supt., 1978—89. Mem. State Textbook Com., 1970—75. Pres. Polk Ret. Educators, Cedartown, Ga., 1991—92, Polk Hist. Soc., Cedartown, 1989—90; mem. sec. Jury Selection Comm., Cedartown, 1985—90; tchr. First Bapt. Ch. Sun. Sch., Cedartown, 1980—. Recipient Outstanding Educator, Ga. Vocat. Assn., 1975—76. Mem.: Resaissance Honors Program. Avocations: travel, gardening, reading.

BREWSTER, OLIVE NESBITT, retired librarian; b. San Antonio, July 19, 1924; d. Charles Henry and Olive Agatha (Nesbitt) Brewster. BA, Our Lady of Lake Coll., 1945, BS in LS, 1946. Asst. librarian aeromed. library U.S. Air Force Sch. Aviation Medicine, Randolph AFB, Tex., 1946-60; chief cataloger aeromed. library Sch. Aerospace Medicine, Brooks AFB, Tex., 1960-83, chief tech. processing, 1983-88; ret., 1988. Mem.: ALA, Mensa. Anglican. Home: 1906 Schley Ave San Antonio TX 78210-4332

BREWSTER, ROBERT CHARLES, diplomat, consultant; b. Beatrice, Nebr., May 31, 1921; s. Charles Lee and Lillian Asenath (French) B.; m. Mary Virginia Blackman, Feb. 22, 1951. Student, Grinnell Coll., 1939-41; AB, U. Wash., 1943; postgrad., U. Mex., 1946, George Washington U., 1947, Columbia U., 1946-48. Fgn. affairs analyst State Dept., Washington, 1948-49, fgn. service officer, 1949-81; 3d sec. Am. Embassy, Managua, Nicaragua, 1949-51, 2d sec., 1951-52; vice consul Am. consulate gen. Stuttgart, Germany, 1952-55; policy briefing officer ICA, staff asst. to under sec. of state for econ. affairs, 1958, spl. asst. to under sec. of state, 1959-60; assigned Nat. War Coll., 1960-61; fgn. service insp., 1961-63; counselor Am. Embassy, Asuncion, Paraguay, 1964-66; dep. exec. dir. Bur. of European Affairs, 1966-67, exec. dir., 1967-69; dep. exec. sec. Dept. State, 1969-71, dir. personnel, 1971-73; amb. Ecuador, 1973-76; coord. for Law of Sea Dept. State, 1976, dep. asst. sec. for oceans and internat. environmental and sci. affairs, 1977-78, insp. gen., 1979-81, cons., 1981-89. Mem. D.C. Commn. on Aging, 1984-85; bd. dirs. Nat. Defense Univ. Found., 1984-87; mem. Com. on Research for Security of Future U.S. Embassy Bldgs. Nat. Acad. Scis., 1985-86. With USNR, 1943-46. Mem. Nat. War Coll. Alumni Assn. (pres. 1981-83), Foggy Bottom Assn. (v.p. 1984-85, pres. 1985-87), Diplomatic and Consular Officers Ret. Clubs: Cosmos (Washington). Home: 3050 Military Rd NW 410 Washington DC 20015 E-mail: rbrewster2@earthlink.com.

BREWSTER, RUDI MILTON, judge; b. Sioux Falls, SD, May 18, 1932; s. Charles Edwin and Wilhemina Therese (Rud) B.; m. Gloria Jane Nanson, June 27, 1954; children: Scot Alan, Lauri Diane (Alan Lee), Julie Lynn Yahnke. AB in Pub. Affairs, Princeton U., 1954; JD, Stanford U., 1960. Bar: Calif. 1960. From assoc. to ptnr. Gray, Cary, Ames & Frye, San Diego, 1960-84; judge U.S. Dist. Ct. (so. dist.) Calif., San Diego, 1984—98, sr. judge, 1998—. Capt. USNR, 1954-82 Ret. Fellow Am. Coll. Trial Lawyers; mem. Am. Bd. Trial Advs., Internat. Assn. Ins. Counsel, Am. Inns of Ct. Republican. Lutheran. Avocations: skiing, hunting, gardening. Office: US Dist Ct Ste 4165 940 Front St San Diego CA 92101-8902 Office Phone: 619-557-6190. Business E-Mail: Rudi_Brewster@casd.uscourts.gov.

BREWSTER, WILLIAM HOWARD, lawyer; b. Takoma Park, Md., Nov. 10, 1962; s. William and Maridell (Baker) B.; m. Karen McCue, Aug. 16, 1986; children: Kristina Baker, William Howard, Katherine Marie. BA, MA, Emory U., 1984; JD, U. Va., 1987. Bar: Ga. 1987, U.S. Dist. Ct. (no. dist.) Ga. 1988, U.S. Dist. Ct. (mid. dist.) Ga. 1992, U.S. Ct. Appeals (11th cir.) 1989, U.S. Ct. Appeals (4th cir.) 1992, (9th cir.), 2004, U.S. Supreme Ct. 1992. Assoc. Kilpatrick & Cody, Atlanta, 1987-94, ptnr., 1994—97, Kilpatrick Stockton, LLP, Atlanta, 1997—2001, 2007—, mng. ptnr., 2001—06. Barrister Lumpkin Am. Inns of Ct., Atlanta, 1989—; adj. prof. U. Va. Sch. Law, 2000, Emory U. Sch. Law, 2001—. Bd. dirs., chair Special Olympics, Ga.; bd. dirs. Metro Atlanta C. of C.; bd. visitors Emory U. Mem.: U. Va. Sch. Law (bd. advisors), State Bar Ga. (antitrust, intellectual property and sports & entertainment secs.), Am. Intellectual Property Law Assn. (trademake litig. com.), Internat. Collegiate Licensing Assn., Internat. Trademark Assn., Commerce Club (operating bd.), Lawyers Club Atlanta. Office: Kilpatrick Stockton LLP 1100 Peachtree St NE Ste 2800 Atlanta GA 30309-4530 E-mail: BBrewster@KilpatrickStockton.com.

BREWTON, WESLEY HOPKINS (WES BREWTON), retired chef, retired real estate manager; b. St. Louis, Sept. 1, 1932; s. Alton Beverly Brewton and Arlene Bessie Gina Wesley; m. Dorothy Mae Lottie-Brewton (div.); children: Wesley Hopkins Jr., Wesley Andre Harris. AA in Drafting, Trade Tech., LA, 1961; AA in Architecture, East Los Angeles, 1963. Sr. aircraft engine mechanic Republic Aviation, Long Island, NY, 1954; sr. jet engine mechanic Curtiss Wright, NJ, 1955—56, machinist, 1956—57; electromech. draftsman Douglas Aircraft, LA, 1962—63; electromech. draftsman Saturn SIV-B project Missile and Space Divsn. McDonnell Douglas, Huntington Beach, Calif., 1963—65; co-owner, archtl. draftsman Vanguard Builders, Compton, Calif., 1965—67; sr. electromech. draftsman Electronic Memories, El Segundo, Calif., 1967—68; drafting rm. supr., mgr. Microdata Corp., Huntington Beach, 1968, design svcs. mgr., 1968—70, Calif. Data, Huntington Beach, 1970—76, Data 100, Warwick, RI, 1976; founder, chef Original Ho. of BBQ, Providence, 1976—83, Wes' Rib Ho., Olneyville, RI, 1983—86, Wes Brewton's Original BBQ, Providence, 1989—90; cook Virginia Mason Hosp., Seattle, 1990—91; chef, kitchen mgr. East Side Mental Health, Redmond, Wash., 1991—2000; apt. ho. mgr. Capitol Hill Housing Improvement Program, Seattle, 2004. Author: Into the Wind, 1995, Wilma, 1996. Civil rights plaintiff Brewton Versus Bd. Edn., St. Louis, 1949—50; blockwatch capt. Neighborhood Watch, Seattle, 2001. Served with USAF, 1950—54. Democrat. Baptist. Avocations: aircraft models, cooking, calligraphy, fishing. Home: 955 W 5th Ave Apt F4 Kennewick WA 99336 Office Phone: 206-860-4816.

BREY-CASIANO, CAROL A., library director; BSc in Music, Ill. State U., Normal, 1979; MLS, U. Ill., Urbana-Champaign, 1980; PhD student, U. Tex., Austin, 1995—96. Bookmobile svcs. libr. Ozark Regional Libr., Ironton, Mo., 1980—82; dir. Muskogee Pub. Libr., Okla., 1982—87, Oak Pk. Pub. Libr., Ill., 1991—95, Thomas Branigan Meml. Libr., Las Cruces, N.Mex., 1996—2000; assoc. dir. Ea. Okla. Dist. Libr. Sys., 1984—87; asst. dir. Decatur Pub. Libr., Ill., 1987—91; pres. VISIONS, El Paso, Tex., 1994—; dir. librs. El Paso Pub. Libr., 2000—. Adj. prof. Rosary Coll. Grad. Sch. Libr. and Info. Sci., River Forest, Ill., 1994—95; doctoral asst. Grad. Sch. Libr. and Info. Sci. U. Tex., Austin, 1995—96; adj. prof. Universidad Autónoma de Chihuahua, Mexico, 1997; part-time instr. Libr. Tech. Prog. Doña Ana Br. CC, Las Cruces, 1997—. Contbr. articles to profl. jours. Named Boss of Yr., Am. Bus. Women's Assn. Indian Capital Chpt., 1983; named one of Outstanding Young Women of Am., 1984. Mem.: ALA (past pres.), REFORMA, Border Regional Libr. Assn., Tex. Libr. Assn., Pub. Libr. Assn., Rio Grande Rotary Club, Beta Phi Mu. Office: El Paso Pub Libr 501 N Oregon St El Paso TX 79901-1103 Office Phone: 915-541-4098. Office Fax: 915-541-4945. E-mail: breycx@elpasotexas.gov.

BREYER, JAMES WILLIAM, venture capitalist; b. New Haven, July 26, 1961; s. John Paul and Eva Breyer; m. Susan Zaroff, June 20, 1987. BS, Stanford U., 1983; MBA, Harvard U., 1987. Sr. bus. analyst McKinsey & Co., NYC, 1983-85; assoc. Accel Ptnrs., San Francisco, 1987-90, gen. ptnr., 1990-95, mng. gen. ptnr., 1995—. Bd dirs. RealNetworks, Inc., 1995-, Wal-Mart Stores, Inc., 2001-, TechNet, Silicon Valley Cmty. Ventures, Harvard Bus. Sch. Calif. Rsch. Ctr. Baker scholar Harvard U., 1987. Mem. Nat. Assn. Venture Capitalists (bd. dirs.), Western Assn. Venture Capitalists (bd. dirs.), Harvard Bus. Sch. Club of No. Calif. Office: Accel Ptnrs 428 University Ave Palo Alto CA 94301-1812

BREYER, K. JON, lawyer; b. NYC, July 24, 1974; BA, Lehigh U., 1996; JD, William Mitchell Coll. Law, 2000. Bar: Minn. 2000, US Dist. Ct. (dist. Minn.). Law clk. Minn. Ct. Appeals, Hennepin County Dist. Ct., 2000—01; assoc. Fruth, Jamison and Elsass, P.A., Mpls. Named a Rising Star, Minn. Super Lawyers mag., 2006. Mem.: Douglas Amdahl Inns of Ct., ABA, Fed. Bar Assn. (mem. Minn. chpt.), Minn. State Bar Assn., Hennepin County Bar Assn. Office: Fruth Jamison & Elsass PA 3902 IDS Ctr 80 S 8th St Minneapolis MN 55402 Office Phone: 612-344-9700. E-mail: jbreyer@fruthlaw.com.*

BREYER, STEPHEN GERALD, United States supreme court justice; b. San Francisco, Aug. 15, 1938; s. Irving G. and Anne R. Breyer; m. Joanna Hare, Sept. 4, 1967; children: Chloe, Nell, Michael. AB, Stanford U., 1959; BA (Marshall scholar), Oxford U., 1961; LLB, Harvard U., 1964; LLD (hon.), U. Rochester, 1983. Bar: Calif. 1966, D.C. 1966, Mass. 1971. Law clk. to Hon. Arthur J. Goldberg U.S. Supreme Ct., Washington, 1964—65; spl. asst. to asst. atty. gen. (antitrust) Donald Turner U.S. Dept. Justice, Washington, 1965—67; asst. prof. law Harvard U., 1967—70, prof., 1970—81, lectr., 1981—94, prof. John F. Kennedy Sch. Govt., 1978—81; asst. spl. prosecutor Watergate Spl. Prosecution Force, 1973; spl. counsel U.S. Senate Judiciary Com., 1974—75, chief counsel, 1979—81; judge U.S. Ct. Appeals (1st cir.), Boston, 1980—90, chief judge, 1990—94; Oliver Wendell Holmes lectr. Harvard Law Sch., 1992; assoc. justice U.S. Supreme Ct., Washington, 1994—. Mem. U.S. Sentencing Commn., 1985—89, Jud. Conf. of U.S., 1990—94; mem. bd. dirs. Dia Art Found, 1985—86; vis. lectr. Coll. Law, Sydney, 1975, Salzburg (Austria) Seminar, 1978, 93; vis. prof. U. Rome, 1993; Jud. Conf. rep. to Adminstrv. Conf. U.S., 1981—94. Author (with Paul MacAvoy): The Federal Power Commission and the Regulation of Energy, 1974; author: (with Richard Stewart) Administrative Law and Regulatory Policy, 1979, Administrative Law and Regulatory Policy, 3rd edit., 1992; author: Regulation and its Reform, 1982, Breaking the Vicious Circle, 1993, Active Liberty: Interpreting Our Democratic Constitution, 2005; contbr. articles to profl. jours. Trustee U. Mass., 1974—81; bd. overseers Dana Farber Cancer Inst., Boston, 1977—94. US Army, 1957. Recipient Annual award for Scholarship in Adminstrv. Law, ABA, 1987. Mem.: ABA, Coun. Fgn. Rels., Am. Acad. Arts and Scis., Am. Law Inst., Am. Bar Found. Office: US Supreme Ct One First St St NE Washington DC 20543-0001*

BREYTSPRAAK, JOHN, JR., management consultant; b. Chgo., May 24, 1929; s. John and Grace Willets (Merrick) B.; m. Charlotte Helfand, Dec. 27, 1958 BA Econs., Lake Forest Coll., Ill., 1950. Mgr. mktg. comm. fibers divsn. Am. Cyanamid, NYC, 1964—67; mgr. merchandising Vectra Fiber, Std. Oil Co. N.J., NYC, 1967—69; account supr. Doyle Dane Bernbach, NYC, 1969—73; mgr. mktg. svcs. Formica Corp., Am. Cyanamid, Cin., 1973—76; pres. Sanitas Wallcoverings, Am. Cyanamid, Wayne, NJ, 1976—80; gen. mgr. Chem. Light, Am. Cyanamid, Wayne, 1980—81; pres. Simmons Wallcoverings, Gulf & We., NYC, 1981—84; cons. New Bern, NC, 1984—96; pres. Composers Music Co., New Bern, 1987—97; cons. Lacey, Wash., 1996—, South Sound Sr. Svcs., 2000—. Composer 12 musical works, 1985-89 Pres., Craven Concerts Inc., Craven County, N.C., 1987-89; instr. U.S. Power Squadron, Craven County, 1985-87; mem. New Bern Hist. Soc., 1986-89, contbr. articles to jour., 1988-89 Avocation: landscape design. Home and Office: 1414 Sleater Kinney Rd SE Lacey WA 98503-2537

BRIACH, GEORGE GARY, lawyer, consultant; b. Youngstown, Ohio, Apr. 11, 1954; s. George William and Donna Jean (Phillips) B.; m. Loretta Ann Lepore, May 17, 1985; 1 child, Rachel Renee. BS magna cum laude, Youngstown State U., 1976; JD, U. Akron, Ohio, 1982. Bar: Ohio 1983, Mahoning County, 1983. Assoc. Flask & Policy, Youngstown, 1983-91; asst. atty. gen. State Atty. Gen.'s Office, Youngstown, 1984-90; solicitor Poland Village, Ohio, 1988-89; cons., dir. Mahoning County Auditor, Ohio, 1990—, asst. pros. atty. Ohio, 2000—; ptnr. White & Briach, Youngstown, 1991—. Fundraiser United Way, Youngstown, 1989-92; bd. dirs., treas., pres. D&E Counseling Ctr., Youngstown, 1992-98, 2000-06; trustee, treas. Children' Challenge Found., Inc., 1998-2000, 2002—; trustee Children's Cir. Friends Found.; bd. dirs. Interfaith Home Maintenance, 1999-2005. Mem. Ohio Bar Assn., Mahoning County Bar Assn., Youngstown State U. Alumni Assn., Tippecanoe Country Club. Avocations: aerobic and weight training, golf, reading, travel. Home: 45 Russo Dr Canfield OH 44406-9666 Office: White & Briach 755 Boardman Canfield Rd Ste K4 Youngstown OH 44512-4300 Office Phone: 330-758-0080.

BRIAN, BRAD D., lawyer; b. Merced, Calif., Apr. 19, 1952; BA, U. Calif., Berkeley, 1974; JD magna cum laude, Harvard U., 1977. Bar: Calif. 1977, U.S. Ct. Appeals (3d cir.) 1978, U.S. Dist. Ct. (ctrl. dist.) Calif. 1978, U.S. Ct. Appeals (9th cir.) 1980. Law clk. to Hon. John J. Gibbons U.S. Ct. Appeals (3d cir.), 1977-78; asst. U.S. atty. Office U.S. Atty. (ctrl. dist.) Calif., 1978-81; hearing examiner L.A. City Police Commn., 1982; atty., ptnr. Munger, Tolles & Olson, LA, 1981—. Lectr. in law U. So. Calif. Law Ctr., 1983; instr. Nat. Inst. Trial Advocacy, 1986; guest instr. Harvard Law Sch. Trial Advocacy Program, 1983; past pres. & mem. bd. dir. Legal Aid Found. Los Angeles; mem. bd. dir. Western Justice Ctr; mem. Indigent Def. Panel & chmn. Pro Se panel, U.S. Dist Ct. Los Angeles. Co-editor, Internal Corporate Investigations, 2d ed. 2002; bd. editors Harvard Law Rev., 1975-77, mng. editor and treas., 1976-77. Mem. bd. dir. Los Angeles County Music Ctr.; vice chmn. bd. dir. Joffrey Ballet, 1990—91. Named one of Top 50 Trial Lawyers in Los Angeles, Los Angeles Bus. Jour., 1999, 100 Most Influential Lawyers in Calif., Los Angeles Daily Jour., 1998—2002. Fellow, Am. Coll. Trial Lawyers; mem. ABA (chmn. pre-trial practice and discovery, litigation sect. 1987-89, liaison with fed. jud. confs. 1989-91, chair task force on civil justice reform act of 1990), Fed. Bar Assn. (past pres. L.A. chptr.), State Bar Calif., L.A. County Bar Assn. (mem. fed. practice standards com. 1980-82). Office: Munger Tolles & Olson LLP 355 S Grand Ave Fl 35 Los Angeles CA 90071-1560 Office Phone: 213-683-9280. Business E-Mail: brianbd@mto.com.

BRIANT, CLYDE LEONARD, metallurgist, educator; b. Texarkana, Ark., May 31, 1948; s. Clyde Leonard and Bonnie Barbara (Green) B.; m. Jacqueline Louise Duffy, July 16, 1977; children— Paul, Judith, Bonnie. BA, Hendrix Coll., Conway, Ark., 1971; BS, Columbia U., 1971, MS, 1973, Eng. Sc.D., 1974. Postdoctoral fellow U. Pa., Phila., 1974-76; staff metallurgist Gen. Electric Co., Schenectady, NY, 1976—94; prof. engring. Brown U., Providence, 1994—, Otis Randall prof., 2000—, dean engring., 2003—06, v.p. rsch., 2006—. Vis. scientist Rsch. Inst. for Tech. Physics, Hungarian Acad. Scis., Budapest, 1991. Editor: Embrittlement of Engineering Alloys, 1983; contbr. articles to profl. jours. Recipient Alfred Noble prize, 1980; named one of 100 Most Outstanding Young Scientists in U.S.A., Sci. Digest, 1984; overseas fellow Churchill Coll., Cambridge, Eng., 1987-88. Fellow Am. Soc. Metals; mem. AIME (Robert Lansing Hardy gold medal Metall. Soc. 1977, Rossiter W. Raymond 1979). Democrat. Office: Brown Univ Office VP Rsch Box 1937 Providence RI 02912 Home: 89 Power St Providence RI 02906 Office Phone: 401-863-7408. Business E-Mail: Clyde_Briant@brown.edu.

BRICCETTI, ALBERT B., physician, consultant; b. Mt. Kisco, NY, Sept. 22, 1940; s. Thomas Bernard and Joan Theresa Briccetti; m. Mary K. Campbell, June 2, 1984; children: Mark Thomas, Christine Elaine. AB, Johns Hopkins U., Balt., 1962; MD, Georgetown U., Washington, 1966. Diplomate Am. Bd. Internal Medicine, 1971, in rheumatology Am. Bd. Internal Medicine, 1972, Am. Bd. Med. Mgmt. Am. Coll. Physician Execs., 1992. Intern 2nd Med. (Cornell) Divsn., Bellvue Hosp., NYC; resident 2nd Med. Divsn. and Beth Israel Hosp., Boston; fellow Boston U. and Boston City Hosp.; commd. maj. USAF, 1971, advanced through grades to col., 1978; chmn. dept. medicine Malcolm Grow USAF Med. Ctr., Washington, 1971—81; command surgeon USAF Acad., Colorado Springs, Colo., 1981—84; comdr. USAF Hosp. Torrejon Air Base, Spain, 1984—85; dep. command surgeon USAF Europe, Ramstein Air Base, Germany, 1985—87; dir. med. plans and resources Hdqrs. USAF, Bolling AFB, Washington, 1987—92; med. dir. Beaver Med. Group and EPIC Mgmt., Redlands, Calif., 1992—97; CEO, med. dir. Corona Regional Med. Group, Calif., 1997—99; prin. cons. Med. Directions LLC, Colorado Springs, 1999—. Dir. Air Force Village West, Riverside, Calif., 2006. Decorated Meritorious Svc. medal USAF, Legion of Merit; Jimmie Doolittle fellow, Aerospace Edn. Found., 1979. Master: ACP (gov. 1988—92, Laureate award 1992); fellow: Am. Coll. Rheumatology, Aerospace Med. Assn.; mem.: Flying Physicians Assn. (dir. 2003). Avocation: flying. Home Phone: 719-302-5129; Office Phone: 719-302-5129.

BRICE, CHARLES STEVEN, airline executive; b. Columbus, Ohio, Feb. 13, 1951; s. Charles Simonton Jr. and Rita Eva (Kuder) B.; m. Darlene Lynn Call, Sept. 13, 1978 (div. June 1986); m. Sally Ann Minard, Sept. 20, 1997; children: Marissa Kay and Jessica Victoria (twins). BA, San Francisco State U., 1974. Lic. FAA airframe and power plant. Ops. mgr. Lockheed Aircraft Co., San Francisco, 1979-83; mgr. ramp svcs. Northwest Airlines, San Francisco, 1983-88, mgr. passenger svcs., 1988-92, dir. customer svc. and ground ops., 1992—. Vice-chmn. bd. dirs. San Francisco Fgn. Flag Carriers, 1997—; chmn. Sta. Mgrs. Am. Transport/SFO, San Francisco, 1994, chmn. security com., 1995. Bd. dirs. March of Dimes, San Mateo County, Calif., 1994-95; mem., airline advisory bd. Calif. Dept. Agr., Sacramento, 1991-92; mem. adv. bd. San Francisco City Coll., 1988—. Mem. Commonwealth Club. Avocations: skiing, hiking, golf, tennis. Office: NW Airlines San Francisco Inter Airport San Francisco CA 94128 Home: 502 Silver Ave Half Moon Bay CA 94019-1564

BRICE, JACQUELINE (JACKIE BRICE), landscape artist; b. Miami, July 11, 1935; d. Alvin Fletcher and Limmie Claudie Holliday; m. Herman Wood Brice, Feb. 27, 1954; children: Debra Lynn Corry, Herman Jr.(dec.). Exhibitions include The Mus. Sci., Miami, A.E. Bean Backus Gallery & Mus, Ft. Pierce, Fla., The Riviera Country Club, Coral Gables, Fla., Rod & Reel Club, Hibiscus Island, Miami Beach, Fla., Govs. Club, West Palm Beach, Fla., Governmental Ctr., West Palm Beach, Northwood U., Loxahatchee Hist. Mus., Jupiter, Fla., State Capitol Bldg., Tallahassee, Richard B. Russell Senate Bldg., Washington, Ann Norton Sculpture Gardens, West Palm Beach, Ct. Ho. Cultural Ctr. Galleries, Stuart, Fla., Govs. Office, State Capitol Bldg., Tallahassee, Hart Senate Bldg., Washington, Jupiter Town Hall Gallery, Lighthouse Ctr. Arts, Tequesta, Fla., Represented in permanent collections Palm Beach County, Mcpl. Juno Beach, Fla., Town of Jupiter, Barry U., Miami, Bascom-Palmer Eye Inst., Palm Beach, Jupiter Med. Ctr., Allen Morris Corp., Hill-York Corp., Hav-A-Tampa/Phillies Corp., Barnett Banks, Cmty. Savs., Coconut Grove Bank, Comerica, Burt Reynolds, Greg Norman, U.S. Senator and Mrs. Bob Graham, U.S. Congressman and Mrs. E. Clay Shaw, The White House; contbr. to covers of mags. Mem. Palm Beach Cultural Coun., Fla. History Ctr. and Mus., Norton Mus. Art. Mem.: Nat. Mus. Women in Arts, Nat. Assn. Women Artists. Office Phone: 561-575-2499. E-mail: jhbric@msn.com.

BRICE, ROGER THOMAS, lawyer; b. Chgo., May 7, 1948; s. William H. and Mary Loretta (Ryan) B.; m. Carol Coleman, Aug. 15, 1970; children: Caitlin, Coleman, Emily. AB, DePaul U., 1970; JD, U. Chgo., 1973. Bar: Ill. 1973, Iowa 1973, U.S. Ct. Appeals (10th, 4th, 6th and 7th cirs.) 1975, U.S. Dist. Ct. (no. and ctrl. dists.) Ill. 1977, 1995, U.S. Trial Bar (no. dist.) 1982, U.S. Supreme Ct. 1978. Staff atty. Office of Gen. Counsel NLRB, Washington, 1974-76; assoc. Kirkland & Ellis, Chgo., 1976-79, Reuben & Proctor, Chgo., 1979-80, ptnr., 1980-86, Isham, Lincoln & Beale, Chgo., 1986-88, Sonnenschein, Nath & Rosenthal LLP, Chgo., 1988—. Legal counsel, bd. dirs. Boys and Girls Clubs Chgo., 1991—. Fellow Coll. Labor and Employment Lawyers. Roman Catholic. Home: 3727 N Harding Ave Chicago IL 60618-4026 Office: Sonnenschein Nath & Rosenthal LLP 233 S Wacker Dr Ste 7800 Chicago IL 60606-6409 Home Phone: 773-463-5048; Office Phone: 312-876-3112. E-mail: rbrice@sonnenschein.com.

BRICHFORD, MAYNARD JAY, archivist; b. Madison, Ohio, Aug. 6, 1926; s. Merton Jay and Evelyn Louise (Graves) B.; m. Jane Adair Hamilton, Sept. 15, 1951; children— Charles Hamilton, Ann Adair Brichford Martin, Matthew Jay, Sarah Lourena. BA, Hiram Coll., Ohio, 1950; MS, U. Wis., Madison, 1951. Asst. archivist State Hist. Soc. Wis., 1952-56; methods and procedures analyst Ill. State Archives, 1956-59; records and space mgmt. supr. Dept. Adminstrn. State of Wis., Madison, 1959-63; archivist U. Ill., Urbana, 1963-95, asso. prof., 1963-70, prof., 1970—. Contbr. articles to profl. jours. Mem. gen. commn. on archives and history United Meth. Ch., 1988-96; bd. chmn. U. Ill. YMCA, 1987-89. With U.S. Navy, 1944-46. Council on Library Resources grantee, 1966-69, 70-71; Nat. Endowment for the Humanities grantee, 1976-79; Fulbright grantee, 1985; Am. Phil. Soc. grantee, 1992. Fellow Soc. Am. Archivists (pres. 1979-80); mem. Ill. Archives Adv. Bd. (chmn. 1979-84) Republican. Methodist. Home: 409 Eliot Dr Urbana IL 61801-6725 Office: 106A Arch Rsch Ctr 1707 S Orchard St Urbana IL 61801-3607 Business E-Mail: brichfor@uiuc.edu. E-mail: brich2@prairienet.org.

BRICK, ARLINE ROTH, education educator; d. Irving K. and Elizabeth S. Roth; m. Lawrence Samuel Brick, Nov. 3, 1974; children: Jason, Sheri, Adam. BA, U. Hartford, West Hartford, Conn., 1969, MEd, 1972. Cert. tchr. Conn. Rsch. assoc. U. Hartford, West Hartford, 1968—69; biology and psychology tchr. Bulkeley HS, Hartford, Conn., 1969—2003; adj. tchr. Goodwin Coll., East Hartford, Conn., 2003, Capital CC, Hartford, 2003—. Bd. dirs. West Hartford Bd. Edn., 1981—89, 1991—95, chmn. bd., 1986—89, 1993—95. Named Citizen of Yr., West Hartford Edn. Assn., 1989—90. Personal E-mail: lonbrick@yahoo.com.

BRICK, DONALD BERNARD, software company executive; b. Bklyn., Oct. 1, 1927; s. Maxwell B. and Edna (Newman) B.; m. Phyllis Madeline Hahn, Oct. 19, 1952; children: James Laurence, Susan Carol Weinbaum, Howard Andrew. Student, Newark Coll. Engring., 1945-46; AB cum laude, Harvard U., 1950, S.M., 1951, PhD, 1954. Registered profl. engr., Mass. Teaching fellow, research asst., fellow Harvard U., 1950-55; sr. scientist, sci. dir. GTE Sylvania, Waltham, Mass., 1955-65; tech. mgmt. cons. Lexington, Mass., 1954-55, 65-75; founder, pres., chmn., tech. dir. Info. Research Assoc.-Infoton Inc., Burlington, Mass., 1965-71; v.p. Addressograph-Multigraph Corp., 1972-73; tech. dir., dep. for devel. plans Elec. Systems div. U.S. Air Force, Bedford, Mass., 1975-83; pres. D.B. Brick and Co., Inc., Lexington, 1983-99; v.p. Aetna Telecommunications Cons., Centerville, Mass., 1983; CEO 1D Vehicle.Com, Inc., Burlington, Mass., 1999-2000; pres. Donald B. Brick & Assocs., Inc./Hi-Tech Solutions USA, 2002—. Cons. in field , 2001—. Contbr. articles to profl. jours.; patentee in field. V.p., bd. dirs. Temple Emunah, Lexington, 1970; assoc. campaign chmn. Combined Jewish Philanthropies of Greater Boston, 1974-78, life trustee, 1985—, mem. exec. bd., 1980-89, chmn. cash collections, 1982-84, chmn. high tech. team, 1984-87; chmn. fundraising Am. Technion Soc., N.E. Region, 1989-93. With U.S. Army, 1946-47. Fellow: IEEE (life; chmn. 1969—70); mem.: N.E. Israel C. of C. (exec. bd. 1993—99). Home and Office: 39 Solomon Pierce Rd Lexington MA 02420-2536 Office Phone: 781-861-1286. E-mail: pmbdbb@earthlink.net. *Not compromising ideals or moral standards for easy gain. Striving to produce quality work that I am proud of.*

BRICK, MICHAEL, journalist; Bklyn. Bur. reporter New York Times, 2005. Author: (articles) Permit Denial for Central Park Adds to Push for Protests There, 2004, Returning to Neighborhoods that are no Longer Homes, 2005. Office: The New York Times 229 W 43rd St New York NY 10036

BRICKELL, CHARLES HENNESSEY, JR., marine engineer, retired military officer; b. Memphis, Apr. 13, 1935; s. Charles Hennessey and Mary Ellen (Viau) B.; m. Barbara Virginia Davis, Jan. 4, 1958; children: David Brian, Patricia Ellen, Susan Elizabeth, Timothy Paul, Joel Howard. BS in Marine Engring., U.S. Merchant Marine Acad., 1957; MA in Bus. Mgmt., Cen. Mich. U., 1980. Enlisted USN, 1953, commd. ensign, 1957, advanced through grades to rear adm., 1984; dir. research and devel. Undersea and Strategic Warfare, and Nuclear Energy, 1984-87; dir. USN Strategic Def. Initiative Program, 1984-88; dep. dir. Navy Rsch. Devel., Test and Evaluation, 1987-88; ret. USN, 1988; gen. mgr. advanced technologies Stone & Webster Engring. Corp., Boston, 1988-91; dir. Ops. ea. region N.Am. Energy Svcs., Issaquah, Wash., 1991-93; dir. fluids and structural mechanics Applied Rsch. Lab. Pa. State U., State Coll., 1993—. Mem. bd. advisors Applied Rsch. Lab Pa. State U., 1988-93; cons. NAS. Decorated Def. Superior Service Medal, Legion of Merit with three Gold Stars, Meritorious Service Medal with two Gold Stars. Mem. Sigma Iota Epsilon. Roman Catholic. Avocations: baseball, basketball sports officiating. Office Phone: 814-863-9900.

BRICKER, HARVEY MILLER, retired anthropology educator; b. Johnstown, Pa., June 29, 1940; s. George Harry and Florence Helen (Miller) B.; m. Victoria Evelyne Reifler, Dec. 27, 1964. BA, Hamilton Coll., 1962; MA, Harvard U., 1963, PhD, 1973. Successively instr., asst. prof., assoc. prof. to prof. anthropology Tulane U., New Orleans, 1969—2005. Co-author: The Analysis of Certain Major Classes of Upper Palaeolithic Tools, 1969, Excavation of the Abri Pataud: The Perigordian VI Assemblage, 1984; co-editor: Hunting and Animal Exploitation in the Later Palaeolithic and Mesolithic of Eurasia, 1993; editor: La Paléolithique Supérieur de l'abri Pataud (Dordogne), 1995; contbr. articles on French prehistory and Maya archaeoastronomy to profl. jours. Decorated Order Palmes Académiques (France). Fellow AAAS; mem. Soc. Am. Archaeology, Soc. French Prehistory. Office Phone: 504-865-5336. E-mail: hbricker@tulane.edu.

BRICKER, JOHN TIMOTHY, pediatric cardiologist; b. East Liverpool, Ohio, Dec. 20, 1952; s. John Franklin and Rebecca Jane (Skidmore) B.; m. Janet Lynn Pearch, Aug. 25, 1973; children: Valarie, John, Susan. BA, Malone Coll., 1974; MD, Ohio State U., 1976; MBA, U. Chgo., 2002. Intrn, resident, fellow Baylor Coll. Medicine, Houston, 1976-83; asst. prof. pediatrics Baylor Coll. Medicine, Tex. Children's Hosp., Houston, 1983-88, assoc. prof. pediatrics, 1988; chief cardiology Tex. Children's Hosp., Houston, 1992—2003; chief pediatric cardiology Tex. Heart Inst., Houston, 1992—2003, vice chair pediatrics, 2003—05; chair pediats. U. Ky. Dept. Pediats., Lexington, 2005—. Editor: Current Practice of Pediatric Cardiology, 1988, The Science and Practice of Pediatric Cardiology, 1990, 2d edit., 1998, Cardiac Toxicity after Treatment for Childhood Cancer, 1993. Fellow Am. Acad. Pediatrics, Am. Coll. Cardiology, Am. Coll. Chest Physicians. Mem. Soc. Of Friends. Office: Univ Ky Dept Pediats 740 South Limestone J-406 Lexington KY 40536 Home Phone: 859-296-9504; Office Phone: 859-323-5481. Business E-Mail: tim.bricker@uky.edu.

BRICKER, NEAL S., physician, educator; b. Denver, Apr. 18, 1927; s. Eli D. and Rose (Quiat) B.; m. Miriam Thalenberg, June 24, 1951 (dec. 1974); children: Dusty, Cary, Susan, Daniel Baker; m. Ruth T. Baker, Dec. 28, 1980. BA, U. Colo., 1946, MD, 1949. Diplomate Am. Bd. Internal Medicine (bd. govs. 1972-79, chmn. nephrology test com. 1973-76). Intern, resident Bellevue Hosp., NYC, 1949-52; sr. asst. resident Peter Bent Brigham Hosp., Boston, 1954-55, asso. dir. cardio-renal lab., 1955-56; instr. Harvard, 1955-56; fellow Howard Hughes Med. Inst., 1955-56; from asst. prof. to prof. Washington U., 1956-72, dir. renal div., 1956-72; Mem. sci. adv. bd. Nat. Kidney Found., 1962-69, chmn. research and fellowship grants com., 1964-65, mem. exec. com., 1968-71; prof. medicine, chmn. dept. Albert Einstein Coll. Medicine, 1972-76; prof. medicine U. Miami, Fla., 1976-78, vice chmn. dept., 1976-78; Disting. prof. medicine UCLA, 1978-86; disting. prof. medicine, dir. sci. and tech. planning Loma Linda (Calif.) U., 1986-92; exec. v.p. Naturon Pharm., Riverside, Calif., 1992; clin. prof. medicine UCR/UCLA Program in Biomed. Scis., UCR, 1996—. Cons. NIH, 1964-68, chmn. gen. medicine study sect., 1966-68, chmn. renal disease and urology tng. grants com., 1969-71; vis. investigator Inst. Biol. Chemistry, Copenhagen, 1960-61; investigator Mt. Desert Island Biol. Labs.; advisor on behalf Inst. Medicine to Sen. Lowell Weicker. Assoc. editor: Jour. Lab. and Clin. Medicine, 1961-67, Kidney Internat, 1972; editorial com.: Jour. Clin. Investigation, 1964-68, Physiol. Revs, 1970-76, Am. Heart Assn. Publs. Com., 1974-79, Calcified Tissue Internat., 1978-86, Proc. Soc. Exptl. Biology and Medicine, 1978-86; editor: Supplements, Circulation and Circulation Research, 1974-79; contbr. articles to profl. jours., chpts. to books. Served with USNR, 1944-45; Served with U.S. Army, 1952-54. Recipient Gold-Headed Cane award U. Colo., 1949, Silver and Gold Alumni award, 1975; USPHS Research Career award, 1964-72; Skylab Achievement award NASA, 1974; Pub. Service award, 1975; George Norlin Silver medal award U. Colo. 1982, citation Kidney Found. So. Calif., 1984; honoree 50th Ann. Wash. U. Med. Sch. Renal Divsn., 2004. Fellow A.C.P.; mem. Am. Fedn. for Clin. Research, Central Soc. Clin. Research (council 1970-73), Assn. Am. Physicians, Am. Soc. for Clin. Investigation (pres. 1972-73, chmn. com. nat. med. policy 1973-77, Disting. Service award 1969), Internat. Soc. Nephrology (exec. com. 1966-81, v.p. 1966-69, treas. 1969-81, history honoree, video legacy honoree 2004), Internat. Congress Nephrology (pres. 1981-84), Am. Soc. Nephrology (1st pres., John Peters medal 1991), Am. Physiol. Soc., Soc. for Exptl. Biology and Medicine, Western Soc. Clin. Research, So. Soc. Clin. Investigation, Nat. Acad. Scis. (com. on space biology and medicine, ad hoc panel on renal and metabolic effects space flight 1971-72, mem. drug efficacy com. 1966-68, com. space biology, chmn. medicine in space sci. bd. 1972-81, com. chmn. 1978-81, chmn. com. renal and metabloic effects space flight 1972-74, chmn. study com. on life scis. 1976-81, mem. space sci. bd. 1977-81), Internat. Soc. nephrology, (hon.), Inst. Medicine of NAS, Internat. Soc. Nephrology, Sigma Xi, Alpha Omega Alpha. Home: 4240 Piedmont Mesa Claremont CA 91711-2332 Office: UCR/UCLA Riverside CA 92521-0121

BRICKER, RUTH, national foundation administrator, real estate developer; b. Oak Park, Ill., Mar. 23, 1930; m. Neal S. Bricker; children: Daniel Baker, Cary, Dusty, Suzanne. Student, UCLA, 1945; postgrad. in Art, U. So. Calif.; BA in Urban Planning, Antioch U., MA in Urban Planning, 1978. Cert. mediator. Staff Artforum Mag., LA, 1966—69; we. dir. Experiments in Art and Tech., LA, 1969—75; owner Empire Real Estate and Devel., LA, 1975—76; mng. gen. ptnr. Orchard Pk. Devel., Loma Linda, Calif., 1988—; prodr. , "Headline", "The Doc. are in" Inland Empire, Cable Sys., Calif., 2000—. Designer Trade-Off; developed programs in art and tech. for Calif. State Coll.-Long Beach, U. So. Calif., UCLA; designer laser light wall Calif. Inst. Tech.; lectr. and cons. in field. Author: Getting Rich in Real Estate Partnerships, 1983; editor, contbg. author: Experiments in Art and Technology/L.A. Jour., 1974-79; prodr. (monthly TV program) Headline; publr. Warner Books. Mem. Mayor's Housing Task Force, L.A.; Internat. Inst. Kidney Diseases; founding mem. exec. com. Sav. and Preserving Archtl. and Cultural Environment; bd. mem. Am. Found. for Pompidou Mus., Paris, Getty Mus., Archival Sec. Achievements include development of art and technology programs for the first moon landing in 1969. E-mail: ruthbricker@comcast.net.

BRICKER, VICTORIA REIFLER, anthropologist, educator; b. Hong Kong, June 15, 1940; arrived in US, 1947, naturalized, 1953; d. Erwin and Henrietta (Brown) Reifler; m. Harvey Miller Bricker, Dec. 27, 1964. AB, Stanford U., 1962; A.M., Harvard U., 1963, PhD, 1968. Vis. lectr. anthropology Tulane U., 1969-70, asst. prof., 1970-73, assoc. prof., 1973-78, prof., 1978—2005, chmn. dept. anthropology, 1988—91, 2003—05. Author: Ritual Humor in Highland Chiapas, 1973, The Indian Christ, The Indian King: The Historical Substrate of Maya Myth and Ritual, 1981 (Howard Francis Cline meml. prize Conf. Latin Am. History), A Grammar of Mayan Hieroglyphs, 1986, (with Gabrielle Vail) Papers on the Madrid Codex, 1997, (with Eleuterio Po'ot Yah and Ofelia Dzul de Po'ot) A Dictionary of the Maya Language as Spoken in Hocaba, Yucatan, 1998, (with Helga-Maria Miram) An Encounter of Two Worlds: The Book of Chilam Balam of Kaua, 2002; book rev. editor: Am. Anthropologist, 1971-73; editor: Am. Ethnologist, 1973-76; gen. editor: Supplement to Handbook of Middle American Indians, 1977—. Guggenheim fellow, 1982; Wenner-Gren Found. Anthropol. Rsch. grantee, 1971; Social Sci. Rsch. Coun. grantee, 1972; NEH grantee, 1990. Fellow Am. Anthrop. Assn. (exec. bd. 1980-83); mem. NAS, Am. Philos. Soc., Am. Soc. Ethnohistory (exec. bd. 1977-79).

BRICKEY, KATHLEEN FITZGERALD, law educator; b. Austin, Tex., Sept. 16, 1944; d. Robert Bernard and Ina Marie (Daw) Fitzgerald; m. James Nelson Brickey, Aug. 22, 1969. BA, U. Ky., 1965, JD, 1968. Criminal law specialist/cons. Ky. Crime Commn., Frankfort, Cin., 1968-71; exec. dir. Ky. Judicial Conf. and Coun., Frankfort, 1971-72; adj. prof. law U. Ky., Lexington, 1972; asst. to assoc. prof. law U. Louisville, 1972-76; assoc. prof. to prof. law Washington U., St. Louis, 1976-89, George Alexander Madill prof. law, 1989-93, James Carr prof. of criminal jurisprudence, 1993—, Israel Treiman faculty fellow, 2001—02. Cons. U.S. Sentencing Commn., 1988, 91; witness U.S. Senate Com. on Judiciary, Washington, 1986. Author: Kentucky Criminal Law, 1974, Corporate Criminal Liability, 1984, 2d edit., 1992-94, Corporate and White Collar Crime, 1990, 4th edit., 2006; contbr. articles to profl. jours. Mem. Am. Law Inst., Soc. for Reform of Criminal Law, Assn. Am. Law Schs. (sect. on criminal justice chair 1989, exec. com. 1985-91, 94-95). Office: Washington U Sch Law Campus 1120 Saint Louis MO 63130 E-mail: brickey@wulaw.wustl.edu.

BRICKHILL, WILLIAM LEE, international finance consultant; b. Rahway, NJ, Oct. 13, 1937; s. William Welch and Wilma Eloise (Gay) Mumford; m. Margaret A. Stempel, June 16, 1961 (div. 1971); children: William L., Barbara A., Cynthia A., Robert L.; m. Joan Marie Ward, May 19, 1988. Student, U. Ga., 1957, Sophia U., Tokyo, 1958-60; BBA, George Washington U., 1970. Lic. comml. and instrument rated pilot. Internat. specialist Am. Security & Trust Co., Washington, 1960-62; loan officer Export-Import Bank of U.S., Washington, 1962-90, dep. mgr. contract adminstrn., 1990-91, dep. v.p. contract adminstrn., 1991-94, ret., 1994; cons. internat. fin., 1994—. Contbr. articles to profl. jours. Vol. archeology divsn. Fairfax County Park Authority. With U.S. Army, 1956-58, Germany. Mem. Nat. Capital Bromeliad Soc. (1st v.p. 1991—), Nat. Capital Orchid Soc., Gem, Mineral and Lapidary Soc. (bd. dirs., v.p. 1965-75), Archeol. Soc. Va. Roman Catholic. Avocations: aviation, botany, woodworking, archaeology, flintknapping. Home and Office: 6338 Phyllis Ln Alexandria VA 22312-6402 E-mail: brickhillb@aol.com.

BRICKLER, JOHN WEISE, lawyer; b. Dayton, Ohio, Dec. 29, 1944; s. John Benjamin and Shirley Hilda (Weise) B.; m. Marilyn Louise Kuhlmann, July 2, 1966; children: John, James, Peter, Andrew, Matthew. AB, Washington U., St. Louis, 1966; JD, Washington U., 1968. Bar: Mo. 1968, US Supreme Ct. 1972, US Dist. Ct. (ea. dist.) Mo. 1974, US Ct. Appeals (8th cir.) 1974. Assoc. Peper, Martin, Jensen, Maichel and Hetlage, St. Louis, 1973-77, ptnr., 1978-98, Blackwell Sanders Peper Martin LLP, St. Louis, 1998—2003, Spencer Fane Britt & Browne LLP, 2003—. Chmn. Concordia Pub. House, St. Louis, 1998-2001, Green Park Lutheran Sch., St. Louis, 2006-. Bd. dirs. Luth. Family and Children's Svcs. Mo., St. Louis, 1988-93, vice chmn., 1988-89, Green Pk. Luth. Sch., 2003—, chmn., 2006—. Capt. JAGC, U.S. Army, 1969-73. Mem. ABA, Nat. Assn. Bond Lawyers, Bar Assn. Met. St. Louis. Office: Spencer Fane Britt & Browne LLP 1 N Brentwood Blvd Ste 1000 Saint Louis MO 63105-3925 Office Phone: 314-333-3930. Business E-Mail: jbrickler@spencerfane.com.

BRICKLEY, RICHARD AGAR, retired surgeon; b. Bluffton, Ind., Aug. 15, 1925; s. Harry Dwight and Ina (Agar) B.; m. Suzanne Slusser, Nov. 28, 1964; children: Dinah B. Olson, Sarah Jane, Richard Agar II, Laura Brickley Wakeley, Andrew John. Student, Ind. U., 1943-44; BS, B.M., Northwestern U. Med. Sch., 1947, MD, 1948. Diplomate: Am. Bd. Surgery. Intern Cook County Hosp., Chgo., 1947-49, surg. resident, 1955-56; gen. practice Bluffton, 1949-50; surg. preceptorship with Drs. Gatch and Owen, Indpls., 1950-51, 54; pvt. practice medicine, specializing in surgery Indpls., 1957-86; chmn. gen. surgery div. Meth. Hosp., Indpls., 1962-66, Winona Meml. Hosp., Indpls., 1971-73, chief of med. staff, 1974-75, bd. dirs., 1977-84. Served with M.C. USAF, 1951-53. Fellow ACS; mem. AMA, Ind. Med. Assn., Aerospace Med. Assn., Marion County Med. Soc. (chmn. bd. dirs. 1976-77), Seven-Up Club (Hillman, Mich.) (owner), Beta Theta Pi, Nu Sigma Nu. Home: 4530 Crooked Creek Ridge Dr Indianapolis IN 46228-2859 Office Phone: 317-293-0907. Personal E-mail: rbrickley211@comcast.net.

BRICKLIN, DANIEL, software designer, consultant; b. 1951; BS in Electrical Engring. and Computer Sci., MIT, 1973; MBA, Harvard U., 1979; LHD (hon.), Newbury Coll., 2001. Project leader, sr. software engr. Digital Equipment Corp., 1973—76; sr. systems programmer FasFax Corp., 1976—77; market researcher Prime Computer, Inc., 1977—79; co-founder Software Arts, Inc., Wellesley, Mass., 1979, chmn. bd. dirs., exec. v.p., 1979—85; founder Software Garden, Inc., Newton Highlands, Mass., 1985, pres., 1985—89, 1994—95, 2004—; co-founder State Corp., Newton, Mass., 1990—94; founder Trellix Corp. (acquired by Interland, Inc.), 1995—2003; chief tech. officer Interland, Inc., Corcord, Mass., 2003—04. Spkr. in field; cons. in field; founding trustee Mass. Software Coun. Developer Dan Bricklin's Demo Program, 1986 (Software Publishers Assn. award for Best Programming Tool, 1986), Dan Bricklin's Demo II Program, 1987 (Software Publishers Assn. award for Best Programming Tool, 1987), Dan Bricklin's PageGarden Program, 1989, Dan Bricklin's OverAll Viewer, 1994, Dan Brinklin's demo-it!, 1994. Co-recipient with Bob Frankston, Washington award, Western Soc. Engineers, 2001; named Fellow award inductee, Computer History Mus., 2004; recipient IEEE Computer Soc. Computer Entrepreneur award, awards from, Assn. Computing Machinery, Boston Jaycees, MIT and from publs. Computer Reseller News and PC Mag. Mem.: NAE, Boston Computer Soc. (bd. dir.), Software Publishers Assn. (bd. dir., Lifetime Achievement award). Achievements include being co-creator with Bob Frankston of VisiCalc, the first electronic spreadsheet in 1979; helped develop one of the first word processing systems in the mid-1970's; programmed the most popular prototyping tool of the MSDOS world; helped introduce the world to the capabilities of electronic ink on pen computers, and introduced new types of easy web site authoring. Office: Software Garden Inc PO Box 610369 Newton Highlands MA 02461 Office Phone: 617-332-2240.

BRICKLIN, MARK HARRIS, magazine editor, publisher; b. Phila., Apr. 13, 1939; s. Arthur Benjamin and Rose (Gaurd) Bricklin; m. Alice Goddard Terry, Apr. 26, 1963 (div.); children: Deirdre, Brendon. BA, Temple U., 1960; postgrad., Boston U., 1961, Temple U., 1962. Teaching fellow English Boston U., 1960—61; city editor Phila. Tribune, 1962—71; freelance writer, photographer, 1962—71; with Rodale Press, Emmaus, Pa., 1971—, v.p., 1975—; exec. editor Prevention mag., 1974—97; founding editor, editorial dir. Spring mag., 1982—84; edit. dir. Men's Health mag., Emmaus, 1980—, Heart & Soul mag., Emmaus, 1994—; editor-in-chief Pets: Part of the Family, 1997—, founding editor, 1998. Journalism preceptor Pkwy. Exptl. Program Phila. Sch. Dist.; cons. book pub. Author: The Practical Encyclopedia of Natural Healing, 1976, Lose Weight Naturally, 1979, Natural Healing Cookbook, 1981, Rodale's Encyclopedia of Natural Home Remedies, 1982; co-author: Positive Living and Health, 1990, Secrets of Executive Success, 1991. Founder Prevention Walking Club, 1986. Home: 5218 W Hopewell Rd Center Valley PA 18034-9607 Office: Prevention 33 E Minor St Emmaus PA 18098-0001 E-mail: mark.bricklin@rodale.com.

BRICKMAN, KENNETH ALAN, state agency administrator; b. Hannibal, Mo., Sept. 10, 1940; s. Roy Frederick and Nita Wilma (Swearingen) B.; m. Mildred Darlene Myers, Aug. 10, 1963; children: Heather Katherine, Erik Alan. BS in Bus. and Econs., Culver-Stockton Coll., Canton, Mo., 1963; JD, U. Mo., 1970. Bar: Ill. 1970, Mo. 1970, US Supreme Ct. 1975. Ptnr. firm Scholz, Staff & Brickman, Quincy, Ill., 1970-78; pres. real estate brokerage Landmark of Quincy, Inc./Better Homes & Gardens, 1978-79; counsel, chief counsel Ill. Dept. Commerce and Cmty. Affairs, Springfield, 1980—85; gen. counsel, dep. dir. Ill. State Lottery, Springfield, 1986-91; sec.-treas., exec. v.p. La. Lottery Corp., Baton Rouge, 1991-95; exec. v.p. Iowa Lottery, Des Moines, 1995—. Served as capt. USAF, 1963-67. Mem. Culver Stockton Coll. Alumni Assn. (pres. 1979). Office: Iowa Lottery 2323 Grand Ave Des Moines IA 50312-5307

BRICKNER, STEVEN J., chemist; BS in Chemistry, Miami Univ., 1976; MS in Organic Chemistry, Cornell Univ., 1978, PhD in Organic Chemistry, 1981; postdoctoral rsch., NIH, 1982. Rsch. scientist Upjohn (now Pfizer), 1982—96; rsch. adv. Pfizer Inc., Groton, Conn., 2001—. Forum on Emerging Infections mem. Inst. Medicines. Co-recipient Fred Kagan Lead Finding award, 1995. Mem.: Am. Chem. Soc. (31st Northeast Regional Indsl. Innovation award 2003, Award for Team Innovation 2007). Achievements include recipient 21 US patents, inc. being co-inventor linezolid, which became the basis of Zyvox.*

BRICKSON, RICHARD ALAN, lawyer; b. Madison, Wis., Feb. 10, 1948; s. William Louis and Nancy May (Gay) B.; m. Marilyn Joan Serenco, June 20, 1971; children: Jennifer Lynne, Katherine Anne, Evan Leigh. BA, Wabash Coll., Crawfordsville, Ind., 1970; JD, Georgetown U., Washington, DC, 1973. Bar: Mo. 1973. Staff atty. The May Dept. Stores Co., St. Louis, 1973-77, assoc. gen. counsel, 1977-79, asst. gen. counsel, 1979-81, counsel, 1981-82, counsel, sec., 1982-88, sr. counsel, sec., 1988—2005; divsnl. v.p. law Macy's Inc., 2006—. Office: Macy's Inc 611 Olive St Saint Louis MO 63101-1721

BRICKWEDDE, RICHARD JAMES, lawyer; b. Bklyn., Dec. 12, 1944; s. George L. and Rose M. (McCarthy) B.; m. June Minsch Gamber, Sept. 2, 1978; stepchildren: Stephanie, Karen, Frances. AB, Syracuse U., 1966; JD, Fordham U., 1969. Bar: NY 1970, DC 1971, US Tax Ct. 1972, US Supreme Ct. 1991. Staff asst. Syracuse office Senator Robert F. Kennedy, NY, 1965-66; adminstrv. asst. US P.O. and OEO/VISTA, Washington, 1966; mgmt. cons. Washington, 1969-71; gen. counsel The Student Vote, Washington, 1971; pvt. practice law Syracuse, 1971-80; regional counsel NY State Dept. Environ. Conservation, Syracuse, 1980-91, acting regional dir., 1984; with Green, Seifter Attys. PLLC, Syracuse, 1992—2003, Brickwedde Law Firm, Syracuse, 2003—. Assoc. counsel to majority leader NY State Assembly, 1975, asst. counsel to spkr., 1976-77. Author: The Student's Right to Vote, 1971, Duke's Tale, 1991, Interstate Garbage: The Carbone Case and the Commerce Clause, 1994, The Superfund Recycling Equity Act of 1999, 2000; contbg. editor Network, 1975-76; reviewer in field; contbr. articles to profl. jours. and trade publs. Treas. Legal Svcs. Ctrl. NY, Inc., 1980—81, pres., 1981—82; Goodwill amb. Internat. Ctr. Syracuse, 2000; chmn. voting rights task force Dem. Nat. Com., 1970—71; bd. dirs. Legal Svcs. Ctrl. NY, Inc., 1978—83, Huntington Family Ctrs., Inc., Syracuse, 1971—89, NY Alpha Tau Omega Student Aid Fund, Inc., Syracuse, 1972—2000, Onondaga County Child Care Coun., Inc., NY, 1978—80; v.p. Huntington Family Ctrs., Inc., Syracuse, 1980; bd. dirs. Internat. Ctr. of Syracuse, 1992—2000, bd. dirs., pres., 1998—99; bd. dirs. Appleseed Trust, 2000—, The Nature Conservancy of Ctrl. and Western NY, 2001—. Named Hon. Citizen State of Tex., 1976; recipient Pub. Citizenship award NY Pub. Interest Rsch. Group 1980. Mem.: ABA (vice chair spl. com. on solid waste 1998—2002, state and local govt. vice-chair environ. com. 1998—2000, 2005—), Nat. Solid Waste Mgmt. Assn. (steering com. NY chpt. 1992—2001), Onondaga County Bar Assn. (co-chair CLE com. 1999—2000, bd. dirs. 2000—04), NY Bar Assn. Democrat. Office: Brickwedde Law Firm One Park Pl Ste 400 300 S State St Syracuse NY 13202-2060 Home Phone: 315-449-2117; Office Phone: 315-423-3302. Business E-Mail: rbrickwedde@brickwedde.com.

BRIDE, NANCY J., lawyer; b. Oct. 7, 1970; BA, Bowdoin Coll., 1992; JD, Notre Dame Law Sch., 1997. Bar: Ohio, US Dist. Ct. Southern Dist. Ohio, US Ct. of Appeals, Sixth Cir. Team in tng. mentor Leukemia & Lymphoma Soc.; vol. The Point, Wills for Heroes Prog.; mentor Cin. Youth Collaborative; orgnaizer Am. Breast Cancer Soc.; hostess Bacchanalian Soc. Wine Tasting Fundraiser. Named one of Ohio's Rising Stars, Super Lawyers, 2006. Mem.: Cin. Bar Assn. (Ct. Common Pleas Com.), Ohio State Bar Assn., ABA, Notre Dame Club of Cin. Office: Greenebaum Doll & McDonald PLLC 2800 Chemed Ctr 255 E 5th St Cincinnati OH 45202-4728 Office Phone: 513-455-7600. Office Fax: 513-455-8500.

BRIDEGAM, WILLIS EDWARD, JR., retired librarian; b. Pottstown, Pa., Oct. 15, 1935; s. Willis Edward and M. Emma (Eberhart) B.; m. Nathalie J. Bridegam; 1 child, Martha Ann. BMus, Eastman Sch. Music, 1957; MS, Syracuse U., NYC, 1963; MA (hon.), Amherst Coll., 1985. Med. librarian U. Rochester (N.Y.) Sch. Medicine, 1966-69, asso. dir. univ. libraries, 1969-72; dir. libraries State U. N.Y., Binghamton, 1972-75; librarian Amherst (Mass.) Coll., 1975—2004. Mem. founding com. Oberlin Group. Author: A Collaborative Approach to Collection Storage: The Five College Library Depository, 2001. Trustee, treas. Jones Libr., Amherst, 2005—. With US Army, 1957. Mem. ALA, Assn. Coll. and Rsch. Libraries. Clubs: Grolier (N.Y.C.). Home: 53 Memorial Dr Amherst MA 01002-2533

BRIDENSTINE, LOUIS HENRY, JR., lawyer; b. Detroit, Nov. 13, 1940; s. Louis and Mary Ellen (O'Keefe) B.; m. Lucia Elizabeth Pucci, June 18, 1966; 1 child, Lucia McMullin. BS, John Carroll U., 1962; MA, U. Detroit, 1966, JD, 1965. Bar: Mich. 1966, U.S. Dist. Ct. (ea. dist.) Mich. 1966. Trial atty., atty.-advisor FTC, Washington, 1966-72; sr. legal counsel, v.p. dir. comms. Motor Vehicle Mfrs. Assn. U.S., Inc., Detroit, 1972-81; sr. v.p., gen. counsel, sec. Campbell-Ewald Co., Warren, Mich., 1981—. Exec. dir. Motorists Info., Inc., Detroit, 1977; legal affairs com. Am. Assn. Advt. Agys., N.Y.C., 1990—, chair, 2000—. Youth allocations panelist United Way Cmty Svcs., Detroit, 1991-98, chair, 1993-98, fund distbn. panelist, 1994-98, admissions compliance com. panelist, 2001-02; trustee, bd. dirs. Catholic Youth Orgn., Detroit, 1981-97, 99-2000, chair bd. dirs., 1990-92. Fellow Mich. State Bar Found. (life); mem. Mich. Bar Assn., Am. Corp. Counsel Assn., Alpha Sigma Nu, Blue Key, Detroit Athletic Club. Avocations: travel, reading. Office: Campbell Ewald Co 30400 Van Dyke Ave Warren MI 48093-2368 E-mail: libridens@campbell-ewald.com.

BRIDESTOWE, Lord See MOORE, THOMAS

BRIDGE, BOBBE JEAN, state supreme court justice; b. 1944; m. Jonathan J. Bridge; children: Rebecca, Don. BA magna cum laude, U. Wash; MA, U. Mich., PhD in Polit. Sci.; JD, U. Wash., 1976. Superior Ct. judge King County, Wash., 1990-1999; chief judge King County Juvenile Ct., Wash., 1994-97, asst. presiding judge Wash., 1997-98, presiding judge Wash., 1998-99; justice Wash. State Supreme Ct., 1999—. Chmn. Judicial Info. Sys. Comm, Legislative Comm.; co-chmn. Unified Family Ct. Bench-Bar Task Force. Bd. dirs. YWCA, Becca Task Force, State Commr. on Children in Foster Care, Seattle Children's Home, Catalyst for Kids Youth Care, Tech. Adv. Com. Female Juvenile Offenders, Adv. Com. Adolescent Life Skills Program, Street Youth Law Program, Northwest Mediation Svc., Woodland Pk. Zoological Soc., Wash. Coun. Crime and Delinquency, Women's Funding Alliance, Alki Found., Privacy Fund, Seattle Arts Commn., U. Wash. Arts and Sci. Devel., Greater Seattle C. of C., Metrocenter YMCA, Juvenile Ct. Conf. Com.; mem. King County Task Force on Children and Families, Wash. State's Dept. Social and Health Svcs. Children., Youth, Family Svcs. Adv. Com., Child Protection Roundtable, Govs. Juvenile Justice Adv. Com.; chmn. State Task Force on Juvenile Issues, Coun. Youth Crisis Work Group, Families-at-Risk subcom., Bd. Dirs. Ctr. Career Alternatives, Candidate Evaluation Com. Seattle-King Mcpl. League, Law and justice Com. League Women Voters; co-chmn. Govs. Coun. on Families, Youth, and Justice; pres. Seattle Women's Commn., Seattle Chpt. Am. Jewish Com.,bd. dirs., asst. sec.-treas. Jewish Fedn. Greater Seattle, chmn., vice chmn. Cmty. Rels. Coun. Named Judge of Yr. Wash. Women Lawyers, 1996; recipient Hannah G. Solomon award Nat. Coun. Jewish Women, 1996, Cmty. Catalyst award Mother's Against Violence in Am., 1997, Women Making a Difference award Youthcare, 1998, Annual Family Advocate award, 2002; honored "woman helping women" Soroptimist Internat. of Kent, 1999. Mem. Nat. Kidney Found., Ctr. Women and Democracy, Phi Beta Kappa. Office: Wash Supreme Ct PO Box 40929 Olympia WA 98504-0929*

BRIDGE, HERBERT MARVIN, retail executive; b. Seattle, Mar. 14, 1925; s. Ben and Sally (Silverman) B.; m. Shirley Selesnick, Jan. 25, 1948; children: Jonathan J., Daniel E. BA in Polit. Sci., U. Wash., Seattle, 1947. Pres. Ben Bridge Jeweler Inc., Seattle, 1955—76, chmn., 1977—. Pres. Downtown Seattle Assn., 1980-81; past pres., Am. Jewish Com.; bd. dirs. Naval Acad. Found., Naval Undersea Mus., Alliance for Edn.; past chmn. Puget Sound USO; chmn. sr. adv. bd. Goodwill Games of 1990; co-chmn. King County chpt. United Way, 2000-01. Rear adm. USNR, 1942-85. Decorated Legion of Merit with Gold Star in lieu of 2d award; recipient Israel Bonds Masada award, 1974, Am. Jewish Com. Human Rels. award, 1978, Navy League scroll hon., 1980, 96, Alumni Legend award U. Wash., 1987, Vol. of Yr. award Jewish Fedn., 1991, Humanitarian award Privacy Fund, 1991, Heritage award Mus. History and Industry, 1993, A.K. Guy Cmty. Svc. award YMCA, 1995, Cmty. Svc. award Sea 1st, 1998, Citizen of Yr. award Seattle-King County, 2001, Achievement medal Fred Hutchinson Cancer Ctr., 2003, Lifetime Achievement award Jewelry Info. Ctr., 2005; named to Nat. Jewelers Hall of Fame, 1998, Puget Sound Bus. Hall of Fame, 1999, Maritime Supporter of Yr., Navy League and Seattle Yacht Club, 2007. Mem.: Greater Seattle C. of C. (past pres.), Pacific N.W. Jewelers (past pres.), Am. Gem. Soc. (head trustee 1993—2000, Cert. Gemologist, Triple Zero award 2001, Shipley award 2003), Rotary, City Club (founder), Wash. Athletic Club (past pres.), Naval Res. Assn. (past pres.), Shriners. Democrat. Office: PO Box 1908 Seattle WA 98111-1908 Office Phone: 206-239-6868. Personal E-mail: hmbridge1@aol.com.

BRIDGE, JONATHAN JOSEPH, lawyer, retail executive; b. Seattle, Mar. 19, 1950; s. Herbert Marvin and Shirley Geraldine (Selesnick) B.; m. Bobbe Jean Chaback, May 20, 1978; children: Donald, Rebecca. BA with honors, U. Wash., 1972, JD, 1976. Bar: Wash. 1976, U.S. Dist. Ct. (we. dist.) Wash. 1976, U.S. Ct. Mil. Appeals 1977, U.S. Ct. Appeals (9th cir.) 1979, U.S. Supreme Ct. 1980. Legal service officer USN, Oak Harbor, Wash., 1976-79, staff judge adv. Bremerton, Wash., 1979-81; exec. v.p. Ben Bridge Jeweler, Inc., Seattle, 1981-90, gen. counsel, co-chief exec. officer, 1990—. Bd. dirs. Ben Bridge Corp., Seattle, Jewelers Am., N.Y.C., Jewelers Vigilance Com., N.Y., Wis., Assn. Wash. Bus., KUOW Pub. Radio, Seattle, Assn. Wash. Bus., Wash. Cts. Hist. Soc.; v.p. bd. dirs. Ctr. Children and Youth Justice. Bd. dirs. King County Mental Health Bd., Seattle, 1984, Wash. Retail Assn., 1985-94, Evergreen Children's Assn., 1998—, Seattle Police Found., 2001-04; vice chmn. Seattle Urban League, 1986-88, chmn., 1988-89; pres. Am. Jewish Com., Seattle, 1986-88; counsel Pacific Northwest Jewelers Assn., 1988-2000, treas., 1990, pres., 1995-97; bd. dirs. Alliance for Edn., 1990—, chair, 2007-; mem. bd. Ctr. for Career Alternatives, 1981—; precinct committeeman, 1990-96; bd. dirs. U. Wash. Law Sch. Found., 1994-, pres., 2003-05; v.p. Ctr. for Children and Youth Justice, 2006-, sec., 2006-. Served to lt. comdr. USN, 1972-81, Vietnam, to capt. Res., 1981-2003. Mem. ABA, Wash. State Bar Assn. (vice chair legal svcs. to the armed forces sect. 2006—), Seattle/King County Bar Assn., Judge Advocates Assn., Greater Seattle C. of C., U. Wash. Alumni Assn. (bd. dirs. 1986-93), U. Wash. Law Sch. Alumni Assn. (pres. 1989-91), Wash. Athletic Club, Columbia Tower Club, City Club. Democrat. Jewish. Office: Ben Bridge Jeweler Inc PO Box 1908 Seattle WA 98111-1908 Home Phone: 206-283-4860. E-mail: jbridge@benbridge.com.

BRIDGE, THOMAS PETER, psychiatrist, researcher; b. Nashville, June 2, 1945; s. Thomas Gale and Hilma Elizabeth (Hartzler) B.; m. Mary L. Matthews, Dec. 15, 1969 (div. Sept. 1974); m. Beth J. Soldo, Sept. 20, 1975. BA, Duke U., 1967; MD, Med. Coll. Va., 1971. Diplomate Am. Bd. Psychiatry and Neurology. Rsch. fellow Duke U., Durham, NC, 1972-74; clin. staff fellow NIMH, Bethesda, Md., 1977-79, chief unit on geriatrics Washington, 1980-83; sci. advisor Alcohol, Drug, and Mental Health Adminstrn., Rockville, Md., 1983-86, AIDS coord., 1986-90; chief clin. trials br. Nat. Inst. on Drug Abuse, Rockville, 1990—2000; dir. benefit risk mgmt. Johnson & Johnson, 2001—04; dir. licensing and early devel., CNS and oncology products Hoffman La Roche, 2004—. Editor: AIDS Neuropsychiatry, 1989; contbr. more than 75 articles to profl. jours. Named J.D. Lane Outstanding Investigator, USPHS, 1984; recipient New Investigator award Am. Geriatrics Soc., 1985, Sec.'s Disting. Svc. award Dept. Health & Human Svcs., 2000. Fellow Coll. Internat. Neuropsychopharmacology; mem. AAAS, Am. Coll. Neuropsychopharmacology. Achievements include patents for novel pharmacologic treatments for cognitive enhancement, chronic fatigue, and psoriasis. Home: 210 W Rittenhouse Sq Philadelphia PA 19103 Office: 340 Kingsland St Nutley NJ 07110 Home Phone: 215-985-4947. Business E-Mail: peter.bridge@roche.com.

BRIDGEFORD, GREGORY M., consumer products company executive; BS in Psychology, U. Va.; MBA, Wake Forest U. Various pos., including exec. asst. to chmn., v.p. corp. devel. Lowe's Cos., Inc., Wilkesboro, NC, sr. v.p. merchandising/gen. merchandising mgr., 1996—98, sr. v.p. mktg., 1998—99, sr. v.p. bus. devel., 1999—2004, exec. v.p. bus. devel., 2004—. Office: Lowes Cos Inc 1605 Curtis Bridge Rd Wilkesboro NC 28697*

BRIDGER, BALDWIN, JR., electrical engineer; b. Savannah, Ga., Sept. 18, 1928; s. Baldwin and Helen Bush (Stubbs) B.; m. Wilma Grace Martz, Mar. 21, 1953; children: Ruth Carson, John Wesley, Mary Gere. BS in Engring., Emory U., 1948; postgrad., U. Iowa, 1966-68. Registered profl. engr., Tex., Pa. Test engr. GE, Lynn, Mass., Trenton, N.J., Ft. Wayne, Ind., Schenectady, NY, 1948-50, design engr. Phila., 1953-65, engring. mgr. Burlington, Iowa, 1965-68, Phila., 1968-71, product planner, 1972-73; chief engr. Powell Elec. Mfg. Co., Houston, 1973-83, mgr. engring., 1983-85, mgr. application and new products engring., 1985-90, tech. dir., 1990-96; pres. Bridger Engring. Co., 1996—. Contbr. articles to tech. jours. With USN, 1951-52. Fellow IEEE (dept. chmn. 1987-88, soc. treas. 1989-90, soc. sec. 1991, soc. v.p. 1992, pres. 1993, editor tech. jour. 1997-2006); mem. Phi Beta Kappa. Republican. Methodist.

BRIDGER, BEVERLY MARIA, historic site director; b. New Orleans, La., Aug. 10, 1946; d. George William and Elizabeth Louise Bridger; m. Michael Sinclair Wilson, Nov. 25, 1982; children: Andrew Bridger Wilson, Leigh Kathryn Wilson. BA, Kent State U., Ohio, 1968; AS, Okla. State U., Oklahoma City, 1977; Master of Liberal Arts, Alaska Pacific U., Anchorage, 1979. Cert. in tchg. Kent State, 1968. Head libr. Regional Campus Kent State U., Salem, Ohio, 1969—74; info. officer VISTA, Oklahoma City, 1974—77; pub. info. officer State Dept. Natural Resources, Anchorage, 1977—80; dir. pub. affairs Alaska Pacific U., Anchorage, 1980—84; exec. dir. Sagamore Inst. Adirondacks, Raquette Lake, NY, 1989—. Bd. mem. Young Arts Assn., Saranac Lake, NY, 1999—2004; bd. dir. St. Eustace Episcopal Ch., Lake Placid, NY, 2001—04. Mem.: Upstate History Alliance. Avocations: gardening, reading. Office: Sagamore Sagamore Rd POBox 40 Raquette Lake NY 13436 Office Phone: 315-354-5311 22. Business E-Mail: sagamore@telenet.net.

BRIDGES, ALAN J., physician; s. Jay and Dolores Bridges; m. Peggy Kelley, July 3, 1981; children: Chris, Jeff, Kelly. BA, Augustana Coll., Rock Island, Ill., 1979; MD, U. Ill., Peoria, 1983. Lic. Internal Medicine Am. Bd. Internal Medicine, 1986, Rheumatology Am. Bd. Internal Medicine, 1989. Asst. prof. medicine U. Mo., Columbia, 1989—92; prof. medicine, sr. vice-chair dept. medicine U. Wis., Madison, 1992—; chief staff Madison VA Hosp., 2005—. Fellow: ACP, Am. Coll. Rhuematology. Office: U Wis Hosp 600 Highland Ave Madison WI 53792 Office Phone: 608-280-7094. Business E-Mail: ajb@medicine.wisc.edu.

BRIDGES, ALAN LYNN, physicist, researcher, application developer, computer scientist; BS in Physics, Ga. Inst. Tech., 1972, MS in Physics, 1974, postgrad., 1975—78, postgrad., 1994—95. Cert. C-130J R&M HUD, BIU, MC, FMECA. Asst. rsch. scientist Ga. Tech. Rsch. Inst., Atlanta, 1975—78; asst. mgr. product Humphrey Instruments Inc., San Leandro, Calif., 1978; pres., cons. ETC West Ltd., 1979—; with Lockheed Aero Sys. Co., 1983—88; sr. prin. engr. new bus. devel. Lockheed Electronics Co., Atlanta, 1988—90; sr. engr., program mgr. Flat Panel & Graphics Display Sys. SCI Tech., Inc., Hunstville, Ala., 1990—92; software engr. specialist life cycle software support and F22 & C130JRM & S sys. engring. Lockheed Martin Aero. Sys. Co., Marietta, Ga., 1992—2001, sr. S.W. software specialist, 1998—; reliability, supportability and safety staff engr., lead engr. visiona display server Barcoview LLC, 2001—03; staff reliability/safety engr. L-3 Comm. Display Sys., Alpharetta, Ga., 2003—, reliability and safety mgr. joint strike fighter panoramic cockpit display, supportability mgr. and system, software safety engr., 2005—, common criteria NIAP vulnerability testing and certification JSF PCD, PCD system/sub system safety, 2007—. Mem. Lockheed Software Process Std. ISO 9000/SEI CMM software and sys. engring. CMM process action team, ACM stds. com. tech. adv. group ISO 9241 Contbg. editor Computer Tech. Rev., PC Graphics & Video Mag.; bi-monthly columnist Hardcopy, 1983-93; contbr. articles to profl. jours Mem. IEEE (sr., dir. Atlanta sect., 1987-88, sec. 1988-89, treas. 1989-90, chmn. student activities com. 1985-87, sec.-treas. computer soc. chpt. 1985-86, chmn. computer soc. chpt. 1986-89, vice-chmn. 1987-88, gen. chmn. Atlanta software tech. conf. 1987, P1226 ABBET com., P1498/12207 stds. com., SW stds. com.), Assn. for Computing Machinery, Optical Soc. Am., Soc. Photo-Optical Instrumentation Engrs., Nat. Security Indsl. Assn. (integrated diagnostic working group, co-chair integrated avionics task group), Soc. for Tech. Comm., Computer Press Assn., Soc. for Info. Display, Nat. Telesys. Conf., Control and Displays Session Orgn., Am. Nat. Stds. Inst./Internat. Stds. Orgn., Sigma Pi Sigma Avocations: amateur radio, woodworking. Home: 8523 Colony Club Dr Alpharetta GA 30022-5407 Office: L-3 Comm Display Sys 1355 Bluegrass Lakes Pkwy Alpharetta GA 30004-8458 Office Phone: 770-752-5135. Personal E-mail: alan.bridges@1-3com.com.

BRIDGES, B. RIED, lawyer; b. Kansas City, Mo., Oct. 20, 1927; s. Brady R. and Mary H. (Nieuwenhuis) B.; 1 son, Ried George. BA, U. So. Calif., 1951, LLB, 1954. Bar: Calif. 1954. Ptnr. Bonne, Bridges, Mueller & O'Keefe, L.A. and Las Vegas, 1958—. Fellow Am. Coll. Trial Lawyers, Internat. Acad. Trial Lawyers; mem. Calif. Bar Assn., Am. Bd. Trial Advs. (diplomate), Pacific Corinthian Yacht Club, Balboa of Mazatlan (Sinaloa, Mex.). Republican. Avocation: sportfishing. Home: 1001 Kensington Ct Carson City NV 89703-5431 Office: Bonne Bridges Mueller O'Keefe & Nichols 3441 S Eastern Ave Ste 402 Las Vegas NV 89109-3314 Office Phone: 775-841-0118. Personal E-mail: brb2551@aol.com.

BRIDGES, BEAU (LLOYD VERNET BRIDGES III), actor; b. Hollywood, Dec. 9, 1941; s. Lloyd Vernet and Dorothy (Simpson) B.; m. Julie Landifield, 1964 (div. 1984); 2 children; m. Wendy Treece Bridges, Apr. 10, 1984; 3 children. Attended, U. Calif. at Los Angeles. Film appearances include The Incident, For Love of Ivy, 1968, Gaily, Gaily, 1969, The Landlord, 1970, Adam's Woman, The Christian Licorice Store, 1971, Hammersmith is Out, 1972, Child's Play, 1972, Your Three Minutes Are Up, 1973, Lovin' Molly, The Other Side of the Mountain, 1975, Swashbuckler, 1976, Two-Minute Warning, 1976, Dragon Fly, 1976, Greased Lightning, 1977, Norma Rae, 1979, The Fifth Musketeer, 1979, The Runner Stumbles, 1979, Honky Tonk Freeway, 1980, Night Crossing, 1982, Love Child, 1982, Heart Like a Wheel, 1983, The Hotel New Hampshire, 1984, Iron Triangle, 1987, The Fabulous Baker Boys, 1989, (also dir.) Seven Hours to Judgment, 1988, The Wizard, 1989, Daddy's Dying.Who's Got the Will?, 1990, Married to It, 1993, Sidekicks, 1993, Nightjohn, 1996, Losing Chase, 1996, Jerry Maguire, 1996, Rocket Man, 1997, Meeting Daddy, 1998, White River Kid, 1999, Sordid Lives, 2000, Meeting Daddy, 2000, Boys Klub, 2001, Debating Robert Lee, 2004, The Ballad of Jack and Rose, 2005, Smile, 2005, I-See-You.Com, 2006, The Good German, 2006, (voice) Charlotte's Web, 2006; TV appearances include The Man Without a Country, 1973, The Stranger Who Looks like Me, 1974, The Whirlwind, 1974, Medical Story, The President's Mistress, 1978, The Four Feathers, 1978, The Child Stealer, 1979, United States, 1980, The Kid from Nowhere, 1982, Dangerous Company, 1982, Witness for the Prosecution, 1982, The Red-Light Sting, 1984, A Fighting Choice, Outrage, 1989, Wildflower, 1991; TV films include Wildflower, 1991, Million Dollar Babies, 1994, Kissenger and Nixon, 1995, Hidden In America, 1996, The Second Civil War, 1997, Inherit the Wind, 1999, The White River Kid, 1999, Common Ground, 2000, Songs in Ordinary Time, 2000, The Christmas Secret, 2000, The Agency, 2001, We Were the Mulvaneys, 2002, Sightings: Heartland Ghost, 2002, Out of the Ashes, 2003 Evil Knievel, 2004, 10:5 Apocalypse, 2006; TV mini-series Space, 1985, Without Warning: The James Brady Story, HBO, 1992 (Emmy award leading actor, 1992), The Positively True Adventures of the Alleged Texas Cheerleader-Murdering Mom, HBO, 1993 (Emmy award, Outstanding Supporting Actor in a Miniseries or Special, 1993, Golden Globe Award, Best actor in a mini-series or movie made for television, 1994), P.T. Barnum, 1999, Voyage of the Unicorn, 2001, 10.5, 2004; T.V.(also prodr.), The Defenders: payback, 1997; The Defenders: Choice of Evils, 1998; T.V. Series, Maximum Bob, 1998, The Agency, 2002-03, Stargate SG-1, 2005-2007. Office: Creative Artists care Steve Tellez 9830 Wilshire Blvd Beverly Hills CA 90212-1825

BRIDGES, CHRIS See **LUDACRIS**

BRIDGES, CONSTANCE ROSE, communications educator; b. Omaha, Dec. 13, 1951; d. David Jerome and Rose Marie Daley; m. David Lynn Bridges, Aug. 17, 1973; children: Jeremy, Ryan, Christian. BJ, Creighton U., Omaha, 1973; MA in Mass. Communication, Bowling Green State U., Ohio, 2000, PhD in Communication Studies, 2004. Pub. rels. & info. dir. Midland Luth. Coll., Fremont, Nebr., 1975—78; pub. rels. & devel. dir. Meml. Hosp. Dodge County, Fremont, 1981—87; reporter Ft. Benning Bayonet, Ga., 1991—93; bus. mgr., pub. rels. Ft. Knox Guest Housing, Ky., 1995—97; rsch. asst. Bowling Green State U., 1998—2004; lectr. St. Charles CC, St. Peters, Mo., 2004—06, U. Mo., Kansas City, Rockhurst U., Kansas City, 2006—. Co-author: Communication & Terrorism, 2002. Mem. choir Cure Ars Ch., Leawood, Kans., 2006—07. John H. Walker scholar, Bowling Green State U., 2002. Mem.: Cntl. State Communication Assn., Internat. Communication Assn. Office: U Mo 103J Manheim 5100 Rockhill Rd Kansas City MO 64110

BRIDGES, DAVID MANNING, lawyer; b. Berkeley, Calif., May 22, 1936; s. Robert Lysle and Alice Marion (Rodenberger) B.; m. Carmen Galante de Bridges, Aug. 16, 1973; children: David, Stuart. AB, U. Calif., Berkeley, 1957, JD, 1962. Assoc. Thelen, Marrin, Johnson & Bridges, San Francisco, 1962-70, ptnr., 1970-94, mng. ptnr. Houston, 1981-91. Served as lt. (j.g.) USN, 1957—59. Mem. ABA, State Bar of Tex., Tex. Bar Assn., Houston Bar Assn., Internat. Bar Assn., Houston Club, Coronado Club, Pacific-Union Club. Office: 700 Louisiana St Ste 4600 Houston TX 77002-2732 Home Phone: 713-524-9090; Office Phone: 713-655-0022. Personal E-mail: dbridhou@aol.com.

BRIDGES, GEORGE S., academic administrator, sociology educator; m. Kari Tupper; children: Anna, James, Lauren, Seth. BA cum laude, U. Wash., 1972; MA in Criminology, U. Pa., 1973, PhD in Sociology, 1979. Social scientist Office of Policy and Planning Office of Atty. Gen., US Dept. Justice, 1976, asst. adminstr. Fed. Justice Rsch. Program, 1977—81; adj. prof. Inst. Criminal Justice and Criminology, U. Md., 1980—81; asst. prof. Dept. Sociology and Legal Studies Program Case Western Reserve U., 1981—82; asst. prof. Dept. Sociology U. Wash., Seattle, 1982—88, assoc. prof., 1989—97, prof., 1998—2005, acting dir. Soc. and Justice Program, 1988—89, 1992, dir., 1996—98, assoc. dean, assoc. vice provost Office of Undergraduate Edn., 1998—2001, acting dean, 2001—02, vice provost, 2001—05, dean, 2002—05; pres., prof. Whitman Coll., Walla Walla, Wash., 2005—. Dep. editor Criminology, 1984—87; author: Inequality, Crime, and Social Control, 1994; co-author: Crime and Society: Criminal Justice, 1996, Crime and Society: Crime, 1996, Crime and Society: Juvenile Delinquency, 1996, Teaching and Learning in Large Classes, 2000; contbr. articles to profl. jours. Recipient J. Francis Finnegan Meml. Prize in Criminology, U. Pa., 1974, Award for Outstanding Achievement by Scholar, Wash. Coun. on Crime and Delinquency, 1995. Mem.: Soc. Study of Social Problems, Law and Soc. Assn., Am. Soc. Criminology, Am. Sociological Assn., Am. Assn. Higher Edn., Alpha Kappa Delta, Phi Eta Sigma. Avocations: hiking, skiing. Office: Whitman Coll Memorial Bldg 303,304 345 Boyer Ave Walla Walla WA 99362 Office Phone: 509-527-5132. Business E-Mail: bridges@whitman.edu.*

BRIDGES, JEFF, actor; b. Los Angeles, Dec. 4, 1949; s. Lloyd Vernet (dec. 1998) and Dorothy (Simpson) B.; m. Susan Bridges, 1977; 3 children Made acting debut at age 8 in Sea Hunt TV series; appeared in films Halls of Anger, 1970, The Last Picture Show, 1971, Fat City, 1972, Bad Company, 1972, The Iceman Cometh, 1973, Lolly-Madonna XXX, 1973 The Last American Hero, 1973, Thunderbolt and Lightfoot, 1974, Hearts of the West, 1975, Rancho Deluxe, 1975, King Kong, 1976, Stay Hungry, 1976, Somebody Killed Her Husband, 1978, Winter Kills, 1979, The American Success Company, 1979, Heaven's Gate, 1980, Cutter's Way, 1981, Tron, 1982, The Last Unicorn (voice only),1982, Kiss Me Goodbye, 1982, Starman, 1984, Against All Odds, 1984, Jagged Edge, 1985, The Morning After, 1986, 8 Million Ways To Die, 1986, Nadine, 1987, Tucker, 1988, See You In The Morning, 1989, The Fabulous Baker Boys, 1989, Texasville, 1990, The Fisher King, 1991, American Heart(also prod.), 1992, The Vanishing, 1993, Fearless, 1993, Blown Away, 1994, Wild Bill, 1995, White Squall, 1996, The Mirror Has Two Faces, 1996, The Big Lebowski, 1998, Arlington Road, 1999, Forever Hollywood, 1999, The Muse, 1999, Simpatico, 1999, The Contender, 2000, Scenes of the Crime, 2001, K-Pax, 2001, Masked and Anonymous, 2003, Seabiscuit, 2003, Stick It, 2006; TV movies: Silent Night, Lonely Night, 1969, In Search of America, 1971, The Girls in Their Summer Dresses and Other Stories by Irwin Shaw, 1981, Hidden in America (also prod.), 2002; (TV, voice) Raising the Mammoth, 2000, Lewis & Clark: Great Journey West, 2002. Office: Creative Artists Agency care Rick Nicita 9830 Wilshire Blvd Beverly Hills CA 90212-1825

BRIDGES, JOHN FRANCIS PATRICK, healthcare educator, researcher; b. Orange, NSW, Australia, Dec. 20, 1973; arrived in U.S., 1999; s. Terrence Allen and Margaret Myree Bridges; m. Coatney Charlene Rene, Dec. 27, 2003; 1 child, John Patrick Ryan. B Econs. with honors, Australian Nat. U., Canberra, 1996; M Econs. with honors, U. Sydney, Australia, 1997; PhD, CUNY, 2002. Rsch. asst. Nat. Bur. Econ. Rsch., NYC, 1999—2002, rsch. economist, 2004—; asst. prof. Case Western Res. U., Cleve., 2002—04; health economist dept. tropical hygeniene and pub. health U. Heidelberg, Germany, 2004—06; asst. prof. Johns Hopkins Bloomberg Sch. Pub. Health, Balt., 2006—. Robert E. Gilleece fellow CUNY, 1999—2002. Recipient Bernie O'Brien New Investigator award, ISPOR, 2006. Mem.: Internat. Soc. Pharmacoecons. and Outcomes Rsch. Roman Catholic. Office: 689 N Broadway Rm 451 Baltimore MD 21205 Home Phone: 410-529-2918; Office Phone: 410-614-9851. E-mail: jbridges@jhsph.edu.

BRIDGES, JUDY CANTRELL, gifted and talented education educator; b. Dallas, Feb. 17, 1947; d. William and Jewel Alexandria (Autrey) C.; m. Gary L. Bridges, Aug. 17, 1969; children: John Drewry, Judith Alexandria. BA, Tex. Tech. U., 1969; gifted/talented endorsement, Sul Ross State U., Alpine, Tex., 1992, MEd, 1993; cert. in mid-mgmt., Sul Ross State U., 1994. Lic. secondary edn. math. and English. Tchr. New Deal (Tex.) Ind. Sch. Dist., 1969—70, Indpls. Pub. Schs., 1970, USDESEA, Zweibruecken, Germany, 1971—73, Lubbock (Tex.) Ind. Sch. Dist., 1973—76, Ector County Ind. Sch. Dist., Odessa, Tex., 1976-85, 87-90, tchr. gifted spl. edn., 1990—92, gifted/talented coord., 1992—97, dir. advanced acad. svcs., 1977—2001; ednl. cons., self employed Odessa, 2001—02; prin., dir. enchanced academic programs Midland Ind. Sch. Dist., 2002—. Acct. Walter Smith CPA, Odessa, 1977—82; real estate appraiser Appraisal Assocs., Odessa, 1985—87; vis. lectr. Sul Ross State U., Alpine, 1994, Alpine, 1997—98, Alpine, 2001; mem. gifted/talented adv. com. Region 18 Edn. Svc. Ctr., Midland, Tex., 1993—; adv. dir. Ptnrs. for Excellence, 2002—. Author: (poem) Paradigm Shifts in the West Texas Sand, 1991. Advisor, officer Jr. League of Odessa, Inc., 1980—, treas./treas. elect, 1986—88; active State Bd. for Educator Cert. Math. Stds. Com., 2000; chair math. Gifted/Talented Performance Stds. Com. Tex., 2000; treas. Campaign to Elect County Judge, Odessa, 1991; mem. bd. Permian H.S. Football Booster Club, 1993; dir. region I Tex. Acad. Decathlon, 1999, 2000; bd. dirs. ECISD Edn. Found., 2002—03, Odessa Symphony Guild, 1996—2004, 2005—; mem. Tex. Edn. Agy. Commr.'s Adv. Coun. on Gifted and Talented Edn., 2004—. Recipient Dept. of Def. Commendation, U.S. Dependent Edn. System, Zweibruecken, 1973, Cert. of Appreciation-Stop of Felony Odessa Police Dept., 1992. Mem. ASCD, NEA, Nat. Assn. Gifted Children, Tex. State Tchrs. Assn. (treas. Ector County unit 1991-92), Tex. Assn. Gifted and Talented (bd. dirs. 1999-2001, sec.-treas. 2002, pres.-elect 2003, pres. 2004, immediate past pres., 2005—), Am. Creativity Assn., Nat. Coun. Tchrs. Math, Ptnrs. for Excellence (bd. dirs. 2002—), West Tex. Reading Coun. Baptist. Avocations: skiing, floral design, reading, travel. Office: 1300 E Wall St Midland TX 79701 E-mail: jcbridges@sbcglobal.net.

BRIDGES, LEONARD HAL, retired history educator, writer; b. Luling, Tex., Nov. 10, 1918; s. Leonard Harold and Lyda Lois (King) B.; m. Alice Miskjian, Aug. 21, 1949; children: Lois Alice, Stephanie Ann. BJ, U. Tex., 1940; MA, Columbia U., 1947, PhD, 1950. Instr. history U. Ark., Fayetteville, 1950-53; asst. prof. U. Colo., Boulder, 1953-55, assoc. prof., 1955-60, prof., 1960-64, U. Calif., Riverside, 1964-79, prof. emeritus, 1979—. Author: Iron Millionaire: Life of Charlemagne Tower, 1952, Lee's Maverick General: Daniel Harvey Hill, 1961, reprinted, 1991, American Mysticism: From William James to Zen, 1970. Maj. U.S. Army, 1940-45, MTO. Sr. faculty fellow U. Calif., 1965; rsch. grantee Am. Philos. Soc., U. Colo., U. Calif. Avocations: writing, walking, reading.

BRIDGES, LEWIS DAVID, elementary school educator; b. Jan. 2, 1949; AA, City Coll. Chgo.; BS, S. Ill. U., Carbondale; M, Trevecca N. U., Nashville. 1st sgt. US Army, Port Campbell, Ky., 1978—98; project mgr. Tenn. Housing Dept., Nashville, 1998—2004; tchr. John F. Kennedy Middle Sch., Nashville, 2004—06. Decorated Accommodation medals US Army, Germany, Meritous Svc. award US Army, Ft. Roley, Kans. Mem.: Profl. Educators Tenn., Am. Legion. Home: 1460 Wexford Downs Ln Nashville TN 37211-8591 Personal E-mail: lewisb51@yahoo.com.

BRIDGES, ROGER DEAN, historian; b. Marshalltown, Iowa, Feb. 10, 1937; s. Floyd F. and Beatrice Andrea (Pipher) B.; m. Karen Maureen Buckley, June 4, 1960; children: Patrick Sean, Kristin Joy, Jennifer Lynn. BA, Iowa State Tchrs. Coll., 1959; MA, State Coll. of Iowa, 1962; PhD, U. Ill., 1970; LHD, Lincoln Coll., Ill., 1987, Tiffin U., 1994. Tchr., libr. Keokuk (Iowa) Pub. Schs., 1959—62; instr. in history Bradley U., Peoria, Ill., 1967; asst. prof. history U. S.D., Vermillion, 1968—69; asst. editor Papers of Ulysses Grant, Carbondale, Ill., 1969—70; dir. rsch. Ill. State Hist. Libr., Springfield, 1970—76, head libr., 1976—85; dir. Ill. State Hist. Libr./Ill. Hist. Preservation Agy., Springfield, 1985—87; dir., editor Lincoln legal papers project, asst. state historian Ill. Hist. Preservation Agy, Springfield, 1987—88; exec. dir. Rutherford B. Hayes Presdl. Ctr., Fremont, Ohio, 1988—2003, exec. dir. emeritus, 2004—. Instructional asst. prof. Ill. State U., Normal, 1974—84, Normal, 2005—06, asst. prof., 2005—07, adj. prof. history, 2006—; adj. prof. Sangamon State U., Springfield, 1985—88, Bowling Green State U., Ohio, 1989—2003. Author, editor: Illinois: Its History and Legacy, 1984; asst. editor: Papers of Ulysses S. Grant, vol. 4, 1972. Bd. dir. Springfield Urban League, 1976-82, Gt. Am. People Show, New Salem, Ill., 1978-85, McLean County Hist. Soc., 2005-; bd. dir. and pres. Conv. and Visitors Bur. Sandusky County, Fremont, 1988-99; bd. dir., sec. and v.p. Birchard Pub. Libr. Sandusky County, 1988-2003, 1996-99; active Abraham Lincoln Bicentennial Commn. McLean County, Ill., 2006—. Nat. Hist. Publs. Commn. fellow, 1969-70; recipient Disting. Svc. awrd Springfield Urban League, 1977. Mem. Am. Hist. Assn., So. Hist. Assn., Abraham Lincoln Assn. (bd. dirs. 1985-, pres. 2004-06), Orgn. Am. Historians, Soc. for Historians of Gilded Age and Progressive Era (sec./treas. 1989-2003, mem. coun. 2004-06, sec. 2006—, Dist. Svc. award 2007), Ill. State Hist. Soc. (bd. dirs. 2003-06, bd. adv. 2006—07, Disting. Svc. award 1988), Ohio Acad. History (exec. coun. 1996-98), trustee Ohioana Library Assn., 1998-2003), McLean County Hist. Soc. (bd. dirs. 2005—), C. of C. Sandusky County (bd. dirs. 1999-2002), David Davis Mansion Found. (bd. dirs. 2003-). Democrat. Baptist. Home: 2804 Mockingbird Ln Bloomington IL 61704 Home Phone: 309-664-5476; Office Phone: 309-664-5476. Personal E-mail: rdbridges@insightbb.com. Business E-Mail: rdbridg@ilstu.edu.

BRIDGES, ROY DUBARD, JR., former federal agency administrator; b. Atlanta; m. Benita Louise Allbaugh; children: 2. BS in Engring. Sci., USAF Acad., 1965; MS in Astronautics, Purdue U., 1966. Commd. 2d lt. USAF, advanced through grades to maj. gen., comdr. 6510th Test Wing Edwards AFB, Calif., 1986-89, comdr. Ea. Space and Missile Ctr. Patrick AFB, Fla., 1989-90, comdr. Air Force Flight Test Ctr. Edwards AFB, 1991-93, dir. requirements Air Force Materiel Command Wright-Patterson AFB, Ohio, 1993-96, ret., 1996; dir. John F. Kennedy Space Ctr. NASA, 1997—2003; dir. Langley Rsch. Ctr., NASA, 2003—06; dir. ops. Northrop Grumman Tech. Svcs., Herndon, Va., 2006—. Achievements include being a NASA astronaut, piloted Space Shuttle Challenger July and August, 1985. Office: Northrop Grumman Tech Svcs 2411 Dulles Corner Pkwy Herndon VA 20171 Office Phone: 703-713-4378. E-mail: roy.bridges@ngc.com.

BRIDGES, SHIRLEY WALTON, air transportation executive; BA in math., Clark Atlanta U.; M in project mgmt., George Washington U. Positions with Bridgehaus Inc., Norfolk So. R.R.; sr. project mgr. Delta Air Lines, Inc., 1990; v.p. airline ops. systems Delta Tech., Inc., sr. v.p. ops., now COO; chief info. officer Delta Air Lines, Inc., 2006—. Named one of the Premier 100 IT Leaders, Computerworld, 2005. Office: Delta Tech Inc 1001 Internat Blvd Atlanta GA 30354-1801

BRIDGES, WILLIAM BRUCE, electrical engineer, educator, researcher; b. Inglewood, Calif., Nov. 29, 1934; s. Newman K. and Doris L. (Brown) Bridges; m. Carol Ann French, Aug. 24, 1957 (div. 1986); children: Ann Marjorie, Bruce Kendall, Michael Alan; m. Linda Josephine McManus, Nov. 15, 1986. BEE, U. Calif., Berkeley, 1956, MEE (GE Rice fellow), 1957, PhD in Elec. Engring. (NSF fellow), 1962. Assoc. elec. engring. U. Calif., Berkeley, 1957-59, grad. rsch. engr., 1959-61; mem. tech. staff Hughes Rsch. Labs. divsn. Hughes Aircraft Co., Malibu, Calif., 1960-77, sr. scientist, 1968-77, mgr. laser dept., 1969-70; prof. elec. engring. and applied physics Calif. Inst. Tech., Pasadena, 1977—2002, Carl F Braun prof. engring., 1983—2002, Carl F Braun prof. engring. emeritus, 2002—, exec. officer elec. engring., 1978-81. Lectr. U. So. Calif., LA, 1962—64; Sherman Fairchild Disting. scholar Calif. Inst. Tech., 1974—75; bd. dirs. Access Laser Corp. Author (with C. K. Birdsall): (book) Electron Dynamics of Diode Regions, 1966; contbr. articles to profl. jours.; assoc. editor: IEEE Jour. Quantum Electronics, 1977—82, Jour. Optical Soc. Am., 1978—83. Mem. sci. adv. bd. USAF, 1985—89. Named Disting. Engring. Alumnus, U. Calif., Berkeley, 1995, Hon. Alumnus, Calif. Inst. Tech., 2003; recipient L. A. Hyland Patent award, 1969, Lifetime Achievement award for excellence in tchg., Assoc. Students of Calif. Inst. Tech., 2003. Fellow: IEEE (Quantum Electronics award 1988), Laser Inst. Am. (Arthur L. Schawlow award 1986), Optical Soc. Am. (objectives and policies com. 1981—86, 1989—91, bd. dirs. 1982—84, v.p. 1986, pres.-elect 1987, pres. 1988, past pres. 1989); mem.: Am. Acad. Arts and Scis., Am. Radio Relay League (life), Nat. Acad. Scis., Nat. Acad. Engring., Tau Beta Pi, Sigma Xi, Phi Beta Kappa, Eta Kappa Nu (One of Outstanding Young Elec. Engrs. 1966). Achievements include invention of noble gas ion laser; patents in field. Avocation: amateur radio. Office: Calif Inst Tech Moore Bldg 136-93 Pasadena CA 91125-9300 Office Phone: 626-395-4809. Business E-Mail: w6fa@caltech.edu.

BRIDGEWATER, BERNARD ADOLPHUS, JR., retired retail executive; b. Tulsa, Mar. 13, 1934; s. Bernard Adolphus and Mary Alethea (Burton) Bridgewater; m. Barbara Paton, July 2, 1960; children: Barrie, Elizabeth, Bonnie. AB, Westminster Coll., Fulton, Mo., 1955; LLB, U. Okla., 1958; MBA, Harvard, 1964. Bar: Okla. 1958, U.S. Ct. Claims 1958, U.S. Supreme Ct. 1958. Asst. county atty., Tulsa, 1962; assoc. McKinsey & Co., mgmt. cons. Chgo., 1964-68, prin., 1968-72, dir., 1972-73, 75; assoc. dir. nat. security and internat. affairs Office Mgmt. and Budget, Exec. Office Pres., Washington, 1973-74; exec. v.p. Baxter Travenol Labs., Inc., Chgo. and Deerfield, Ill., 1975-79, dir., 1975-85; pres. Brown Group, Inc., Clayton, Mo., 1979-87, 90-99, CEO, 1982-99, chmn., 1985-99, also dir.; now ret.; cons. TIAA-CREF, NYC. Adv. dir. Schroder Venture Ptnrs. LLC, NYC. Author (with others): Better Management of Business Giving, 1965. Trustee Rush-Presbyn. St. Luke's Med. Ctr., 1974—84, Washington U., St. Louis, 1983—94, 1995—2003, 2004—, Barnes Hosp., St. Louis, 1987—90; bd. visitors Harvard U. Bus. Sch., 1987—93. Served to lt. USNR, 1958—62. Recipient Rayonier Found. award, Harvard U., 1963; George F. Baker scholar, 1964. Mem.: Indian Hill Country Club, Log Cabin Club, St. Louis Country Club, Phi Alpha Delta, Omicron Delta Kappa, Beta Theta Pi. Office: 7701 Forsyth Blvd Ste 1000 Saint Louis MO 63105-1841

BRIDGEWATER, HERBERT JEREMIAH, JR., radio personality; b. Atlanta, July 3, 1942; s. Herbert Bridgewater and Mary Sallie (Clark) Bridgewater-Hughes. BA, Clark Coll., Atlanta, 1968; postgrad., Atlanta U.; L.H.D., Faith Coll., 1978; LL.D., Heed U., 1978. Cert. ordained min. in theology Interdenominational Theol. Ctr. CITCO, Atlanta, 2004; ordained minister Gospel, 2005; apptd. First Chaplain , City of East Point Police Dept. Tchr. bus. edn. and English Atlanta Pub. Sch. System, 1964-67; relocation and family svcs. cons. Atlanta Housing Authority, 1967-70; columnist, writer Atlanta Daily World, 1968—, Lovely Atlanta; consumer protection specialist FTC, Atlanta, 1970-83; pres. Bridgewater's Personnel Service, 1971—; assoc. prof. bus. edn. and mass communication Clark Coll., instr., 1983-86, Atlanta Jr. Coll., 1986—, The Univ. System of Ga., 1986—; with reservations sales Delta Airline Inc., Atlanta, 1984—. Host program Enlightenment Radio Sta. WGKA-AM, 1975-79; host pub. affairs program Confrontation Radio Sta. WZGC FM and WIGO AM, 1975-79, WYZE AM, 1979—; TV talk show host Bridging the Gap Mem. Epilepsy Found. Am., Nat. Urban League, Big Bros. Council of Atlanta, Met. Boys Clubs of Atlanta, YMCA, NAACP; active So. Christian Leadership Conf., Ga. and nationwide civil rights movements; bd. dirs. Atlanta Dance Theater, Ralph C. Robinson Atlanta Boys Club, Proposition Theater Co., Am. Cancer Soc., Just-Us Theatre Task Force. Recipient Pres.'s award Clark Coll. United Negro Coll. Fund, 1960, 61, Best Citizens award Delta Sigma Theta, 1962, Humanitarian award Future Soc. Orgn., 1975, award Atlanta Dance Theatre, 1978-79, also; Met. Atlanta Boys Club; FTC Superior service medal, 1978; Bronner Bros. Nat. Beauticians Conv. Excellence in Communication award, 1978; named One of Most Outstanding Young Men in Am., Nat. Jr. C. of C., 1969, One of Most Eligible Bachelors in Am., 1970, One of 1,000 Successful Black Americans, 1973; both Ebony Mag.; One of 10 Outstanding Young People of Atlanta, 1977-78; One of 20 Most Progressive Young People in Atlanta, 1977; Herbert Bridgewater Day proclaimed in his honor Atlanta. Mem. Atlanta Jr. C. of C., Young Men on the Go, Clark Coll. Alumni Assn., Clark Coll. Assn., Heritage Valley Community Civic Orgn., Hungry Club Forum, Internat. Assn. for African Heritage and Black Identity (founding) Baptist (founder, chmn. bd. jr. deacons). Home: 2963 Duke Of Windsor East Point GA 30344-5606 Personal E-mail: HerbertBridgewater@yahoo.com. *Any* *success which I may have achieved is attributed to my deeply rooted religious rearing which impels me to put God first in all my undertaking. Applying myself to the task with diligence, being prayerful in all my endeavors, and having a mother who is not only my backbone, but who has also stood steadfastly by my side, are the essential factors which I deem vital in my life's achievement.*

BRIDGEWATER, RACHEL, library and information scientist; BA in Biology, Simon's Rock Coll. of Bard, 1994; MLS, Emporia State U., 2004. Circulation supr. Sherman Art Libr. Dartmouth Coll., Hanover, NH, 1996—97; programmer and analyst Strategic Interactive Group, Boston, 1998, sr. tech. analyst, 1998—99, tech. mgr., 1999—2000; dir. web develop. Virtuous Inc., Portland, Oreg., 1999—2002, v.p., 1999—; asst. circulation services mgr. Vancouver Cmty. Libr., Vancouver, Wash., 2002—04; reference libr. Washington State U., Vancouver, 2004—05, reference coord., 2005—. Asset keyworder Veer.com, Calgary, 2004—05; web developer PORTALS, Portland, Oreg., 2004—05; developer and webmaster NWCentral, Portland, 2005—; lectr. in field. Named one of the Movers & Shakers, Libr. Jour., 2007; recipient Achievement award, Beta Phi Mu, 2004. Mem.: Libr. Instruction Roundtable, Oreg. Libr. Assn., Assn. Coll. & Rsch. Libr., Social Responsibilities Roundtable, Intellectual Freedom Roundtable, ALA. Office: Washington State Univ Library 14204 NE Salmon Creek Ave Vancouver WA 98686 Office Phone: 360-546-9694. E-mail: bridgewa@vancouver.wsu.edu.

BRIDGFORTH, ROBERT MOORE, JR., aerospace engineer; b. Lexington, Miss., Oct. 21, 1918; s. Robert Moore and Theresa (Holder) Bridgforth; m. Florence Jarnberg, Nov. 7, 1943; children: Robert Moore, Alice Theresa. At, Miss. State Coll., 1935—37; BS, Iowa State Coll., 1940; MS, MIT, 1948; post grad., Harvard U., 1949. Asst. engr. Standard Oil Co., Ohio, 1940; teaching fellow M.I.T., 1940—41, instr. chemistry, 1941—43, rsch. asst., 1943—44, mem. staff divsn. indsl. cooperation, 1944—47; assoc. prof. physics and chemistry Emory and Henry Coll., 1949—51; rsch. engr. Boeing Airplane Co., Seattle, 1951—54, rsch. specialist, 1954—55, sr. group engr., 1955—58; chief propulsion sys. sect. Sys. Mgmt. Office, 1958—59, chief propulsion rsch. unit, 1959—60; founder and chmn. bd. Rocket Rsch. Corp., 1960—69, Explosives Corp. Am., 1966—69. Fellow: AIAA (assoc.), Brit. Interplanetary Soc.; mem.: AAAS, Combustion Inst., N.Y. Acad. Scis., Soc. for Leukocyte Biology, Tissue Culture Assn., Am. Assn. Physics Tchrs., Am. Inst. Physics, Am. Ordnance Assn., Am. Rocket Soc. (pres. Pacific N.W. chpt. 1955), Am. Chem. Soc., Am. Astronautical Soc. (dir.), Am. Inst. Chemists, Sigma Xi. Achievements include patents for rocket tri-propellants and explosives. Home: 4325 87th Ave SE Mercer Island WA 98040-4127 Office Phone: 206-232-4065.

BRIDGMAN, GEOFF, lawyer; b. Seattle, July 2, 1967; BA magna cum laude, Ctrl. Wash. Univ., 1988; JD summa cum laude, Seattle Univ., 1995. Bar: Wash. 1995. Gen. litig. atty. Ogden Murphy Wallace P.L.L.C., Seattle. Contbr. articles to numerous profl. jours. Named Seattle Rising Star, SuperLawyer Mag., 2006. Mem.: ABA, Wash. State Trial Lawyers Assn., Wash. State Bar Assn. Office: Ogden Murphy Wallace Ste 2100 1601 Fifth Ave Seattle WA 98101-1686

BRIDGMAN, G(EORGE) ROSS, lawyer; b. New Haven, Dec. 27, 1947; s. George Ross Bridgman and Betty Jean (Soderquist) Burrows; m. Patricia Hess; children: Taylor Wilson, Katharine June, Elizabeth Honey. BA cum laude, Yale U., 1970; JD, Northwestern U., 1973. Bar: Ohio 1973, U.S. Dist. Ct. (so. dist.) Ohio 1974, U.S. Dist. Ct. (no. dist.) Ohio 1976, U.S. Ct. Appeals (6th cir.) 1984, U.S. Supreme Ct. 1990. Assoc. Vorys, Sater, Seymour & Paese, Columbus, Ohio, 1973-80, ptnr., 1980—. Mem. editorial bd. Northwestern U. Law Rev., Chgo., 1972-73. Trustee Columbus Jr. Theatre of the Arts, 1976-80, pres., 1978-80; trustee, v.p. London (Ohio) Pub. Libr., 1979-84; bd. dirs. Ctrl. Ohio Regional Coun. on Alcoholism, Columbus, 1987-89; trustee Kidscope, Columbus, 1988-89, Recovery Alliance, Columbus, 1989-97, Ohio Parents for Drug-Free Youth, 1991-99; mem. exec. bd. Simon Kenton coun. Boy Scouts Am., 1996—; mem. Columbus Symphony Chorus, 1999—; bd. dirs. Ohio Drug Assistance Program, 2005—, Ohio Lawyers Assistance Program, 2005. Fellow: Coll. Labor and Employment Lawyers; mem.: ABA, Nat. Assn. Coll. and Univ. Attys., Ohio Bar Assn., Columbus Bar Assn., Columbus Country Club, Capital Club. Republican. Episcopalian. Office: Vorys Sater Seymour & Pease PO Box 1008 52 E Gay St Columbus OH 43215-3161 E-mail: grbridgman@vssp.com.

BRIDGMAN, THOMAS FRANCIS, retired lawyer; b. Chgo., Dec. 30, 1933; s. Thomas Joseph and Angeline (Gorman) B.; m. Patricia A. McCormick, May 16, 1959; children: Thomas, Kathleen Ann, Ann Marie, Jane T., Molly. BS cum laude, John Carroll U., 1955; JD cum laude, Loyola U., Chgo., 1958. Bar: Ill. 1958, U.S. Dist. Ct. 1959. Assoc. McCarthy & Levin, Chgo., 1958, Baker & McKenzie, Chgo., 1958—96, ptnr., 1962—96. Trustee John Carroll U., 1982-88. Fellow Am. Coll. Trial Lawyers, Am. Bd. Trial Advs. (adv.), Internat. Acad. Trial Lawyers (past pres.), Union League Club, Beverly Country Club (Chgo., pres. 1983). Democrat. Roman Catholic. Home: 9400 S Pleasant Ave Chicago IL 60620-5646 Office: Baker & McKenzie 1 Prudential Plaza 130 E Randolph St Ste 3700 Chicago IL 60601-6342

BRIDSTON, PAUL JOSEPH, strategic management consultant; b. Grand Forks, ND, May 28, 1928; s. Joseph and Anna (Pederson) B.; m. Peggy C. Cullen, Aug. 26, 1955; children: Peter, Rebecca, Sarah BA magna cum laude, Yale U., 1950; MBA, Stanford U., 1952. Sec.-treas. First Fed. Savs. & Loan Assn., Grand Forks, ND, 1955-61, pres., 1962-81, chmn. bd., 1961-82; pres. J.B. Bridston Ins. Co., 1963-80; cons. Bridston Co., 1990—. Chief Housing Guaranties Program Latin Am., AID, Washington, 1964-65; cons. U.S. Dept. State, 1968-70; asst. insp. gen. fgn. assistance, 1970; mem. N.D. Ho. Reps., 1972-74; chmn. Pioneer Mortgage Co., 1980-84; vis. prof mgmt. U. Okla., 1988-92 Pres. Grand Forks YMCA, 1959-60, GrandForks United Fund, 1961-62; bd. dirs. Tyrone Guthrie Theatre, Mpls., 1963-69, Boys Club Am., 1963-69; chmn. Martin County Atlantic-Pacific Housing, Inc., Fla., 1984-86. With USNR, 1952-55. Mem. Nat. Savs. and Loan League (bd. dirs. 1981), U.S. Savs. League (chmn. internat. devel. com. 1968-69), Yale U. Alumni Assn., Stanford Alumni Assn., Augusta Nat. Club. Lutheran. Home: 6843 Tall Pines Rd NE Bemidji MN 56601-7095 Personal E-mail: pbridstn@paulbunyan.net.

BRIDWELL, KEITH HAPP, orthopedic surgeon; b. St. Louis, May 4, 1953; s. James Robert and Shirley (Happ) B.; m. Mala Gusman, Dec. 21, 1978 (dec. Jan., 2001); 1 child, Grace Marie. AB in Biology and Psychology, Washington U., St. Louis, 1973, MD, 1977. Diplomate Am. Bd. Orthopaedic Surgery, Am. Acad. Orthopaedic Surgeons. Clin. asst. prof. orthopedic surgery U. Ky., Lexington, 1983-84; asst. prof. orthopedic surgery, dir. spine surgery U. Cin. Med. Ctr., 1983-84; asst. prof. orthopedic surgery Washington U., St. Louis, 1984-90, assoc. prof. orthopedic surgery, 1990-95, prof., 1995-97, Asa C. and Dorothy W. Jones prof. orthopedic surgery, 1997—; chief, adult, pediatric spinal surgery Washington Univ. Sch. Medicine, St. Louis. Staff mem. Barnes-Jewish Hosp., fellow, 1993—, St. Louis Children's Hosp., transfusion com., 1985—, children's adv. com., 1986-92, Shriners Hosp. for Children, VA Hosp Associate editl. bd. Spine, 1989-95, dep. editor, 1995—; editl. bd. Jour. Spinal Disorders, SpineUniverse; co-editor in chief The Textbook of Spinal Surgery, 1991, 2d. edit., 1997; reviewer Jour. Bone and Joint Surgery, 1996—; section editor Principles of Orthopaedic Practice, 2d edit., 1997; contbr. articles to profl. jours. Grantee NIH, 1999—. Mem. Acad. Orthopaedic Soc., Am. Acad. Orthopaedic Surgeons, Clin. Orthopaedic Socl, Mid-Am. Orthopaedic Assn., Mo. State Orthopaedic Assn., N.Am. Spine Soc. (subcom. resident core curriculum 1995—, Outstanding Paper award 1999), St. Louis Orthopaedic Soc., Scoliosis Assn., Scoliosis Rsch. Soc. (Russell L. Hibbs award 1987, 91, Walter P. Blount award 1987, John H. Moe award 1995, bd. dirs. 1995-97, 2000—, grantee 1998—, 1st v.p. 2000—, pres. elect 2001, pres. 2002—), Am. Orthopaedic Assn. (internat. travelling fellowships subcom. 1998—, chmn. 1999-2000, editl. bd. AOA News 1999—), Fedn. Spine Assns. (chmn. program com. 1999, sec.-treas. 2000—), Eliot Soc. Washington U. Office: Washington U Sch Med Dept Orthop Surgery Box 8233 660 S Euclid Ave Saint Louis MO 63110 E-mail: bridwellk@msnotes.wustl.edu.*

BRIEANT, CHARLES LA MONTE, federal judge; b. Ossining, NY, Mar. 13, 1923; s. Charles La Monte and Marjorie (Hall) B.; m. Virginia Elizabeth Warfield, Sept. 10, 1948. BA, Columbia U., 1947, LL.B., 1949. Bar: N.Y. 1949. Mem. firm Bleakley, Platt, Schmidt & Fritz, White Plains, 1949-71; water commr. Village of Ossining, 1948-51; town justice, 1952-58; town supr., 1960-63; village atty. Briarcliff Manor, N.Y.; also spl. asst. dist. atty. Westchester County, 1958-59; asst. counsel N.Y. State Joint Legis. Com. Fire Ins., 1968; judge U.S. Dist. Ct. (so. dist.) N.Y., NYC, 1971-86, U.S. Dist Ct. So. Dist. N.Y., White Plains, 1993—; chief judge U.S. Dist. Ct. (so. dist.) N.Y., NYC, 1986-93. Adj. prof. Bklyn. Law Sch.; mem. Jud. Conf. U.S., 1989-95, mem. exec. com., 1991-95. Mem. Westchester County Republican Com., 1957-71; mem. Westchester County Legislature from 2d Dist., 1970-71. Served with AUS, World War II. Mem. ABA, N.Y. State Bar Assn., Westchester County Bar Assn., Ossining Bar Assn. Episcopalian (vestryman). Club: SAR. Office: US Dist Ct US Courthouse 300 Quarropas St White Plains NY 10601-4140

BRIEGER, GEORGE, lawyer; b. Hungary, Apr. 30, 1966; came to the US, 1977; s. Jenö and Miriam Brieger. BS in Computer Sci. cum laude (hon.), Bklyn. Coll., 1988; JD, Cardozo Sch. Law, 1993; LLM in Patent and Intellectual Property Law, George Washington U., DC. Bar: NY 1994, DS 2002, US Dist. Ct. (so. and ea. dists.) NY 1995, US Ct. Internat. Trade, 1999, registered patent atty. Fellow in Medieval European History Revel Grad. Sch., NYC, 1988—90; internat. counsel Bacher & Ptnrs. Atty. at Law, Budapest, Hungary, 1996-98; atty. Internat. Trade Litig. US Customs Svc., NYC, 1998-2000; atty. Sughrue Mion, Washington, 2001—05, Ostrolenk, Faber, Gerb & Soffen, NYC, 2006—. Editor New Europe Law Rev. Cardozo Sch. Law, NYC, 1992-93, Sughrue Rev., 2001-03; contbr. chpt. to book. Adv. bd. Budapest-NY Sister City Com., NYC, 1996—. Mem. Am. Intellectual Property Law Assn. Avocations: linguistics, philosophy, computer technology, tai chi, swimming. Office: 1180 Avenue of the Ams New York NY 10036-8403 Business E-Mail: gbrieger@ostrolenk.com.

BRIEGER, GERT HENRY, medical educator; b. Hamburg, Germany, Jan. 5, 1932; arrived in U.S., 1938, naturalized, 1943; s. Carl Helmuth and Ylse (Fuchs) Brieger; m. Katharine Crenshaw, July 2, 1955; children: Heidi E., William N., Benjamin C. AB, U. Calif., Berkeley, 1953; MD, UCLA, 1957; MPH, Harvard U., 1962; PhD, Johns Hopkins U., 1968. Intern UCLA Med. Ctr., 1957—58; asst. prof. history of medicine Johns Hopkins U. Sch. Medicine, Balt., 1966—70; assoc. prof. cmty. health scis., assoc. prof. history Duke U., Durham, NC, 1970—75; prof. history of health scis., chmn. dept. U. Calif., San Francisco, 1975—84; William H. Welch prof., dir. Inst. History of Medicine Johns Hopkins U., Balt., 1984—2001, chair dept. hist. sci. med. and tech., 1993—2001, disting. svc. prof., 2002—. Author (with A.M. Harvey, S.L. Abrams and V.A. McKusick): A Model of Its Kind, A Centennial History of Johns Hopkins Medicine, 1989; editor: Medical America in the Nineteenth Century, 1972, Theory and Practice in American Medicine, 1976; co-editor Bull. of the History of Medicine, 1990—2004. Served to capt. US Army, 1958—61. Mem.: Inst. Medicine, Am. Assn. History of Medicine (pres. 1980—82). Home: 10 E Lee St Baltimore MD 21202-6003 Office: Johns Hopkins U Welch Med Library Rm 320 1900 E Monument St Baltimore MD 21205-2167 E-mail: gbrieger@jhmi.edu.

BRIER, BONNIE SUSAN, lawyer; b. Oct. 19, 1950; d. Jerome W. and Barbara (Srenco) B.; m. Bruce A. Rosenfield, Aug. 15, 1976; children: Rebecca, Elizabeth, Benjamin. AB in Econs. magna cum laude, Cornell U., 1972; JD, Stanford U., 1976. Bar: Pa. 1976, U.S. Dist. Ct. (ea. dist.) Pa., U.S. Tax Ct., U.S. Ct. Appeals (3d cir.), U.S. Supreme Ct. Law clk. to chief judge U.S. Dist. Ct. Pa. (ea. dist.), Phila., 1976-77, asst. U.S. atty. criminal prosecutor, 1977-79; from assoc. to ptnr. Ballard, Spahr, Andrews & Ingersoll, Phila., 1979-90; gen. counsel Children's Hosp. of Phila., Phila., 1990—. Legal counsel Womens Way, 1979—1999; mem. legal framework work group, panel on non-profit sector, 2005—, lectr. U. Pa. Law Sch., 1988-95; lectr., speaker various orgns. and seminars. Editor Stanford Law Rev., 1974-76; contbr. articles to profl. jours. Bd. dirs. U.S. Com. for UNICEF, 1994—2000, vice chmn., 1998-2000; adv. bd. Exempt Orgn. Tax Review (1998—), Nat. Ctr. on Philanthrophy and the Law, NYU, 1999-2001; mem. IRS Adv. Com. on Tax Exempt and Govt. Entities (2006—), Form Exec. Woman, 1998—. Recipient Woman of Achievement award, March of Dimes, 2003, Leadership award, Women's Way, 2004. Fellow Am. Coll. Tax Counsel, Am. Law Inst. (adv. to principals of law of non-profit orgn. 2003—), Am. Health Lawyers Assn. (bd. dirs. 1991-96); mem. ABA (exempt orgn. com. on tax sect., chair 1991-93, mem. health law sect., bd. dirs. 1997-2005, chair 2003-05), Pa. Bar Assn. (tax sect., health law sect., mem. com. charitable orgn., children's rights), Phila. Bar Assn. (tax sect., health law com.). Home: 132 Fairview Rd Narberth PA 19072-1331 Office: Children's Hosp of Pa 34th St and Civic Ctr Blvd Philadelphia PA 19104 Office Phone: 267-426-6131.

BRIERE, DANIEL, professional hockey player; b. Gatineau, Que., Can., Oct. 6, 1977; m. Sylvie Briere; children: Caelan, Carson, Cameron. Attended, Coll. Saint-Alexandre. Center Phoenix Coyotes, 1998—2003, Buffalo Sabres, 2003—07, co-captain, 2004—07; center Phila. Flyers, 2007—. Player NHL All-Star Game, 2007. Recipient Dudley Garret Meml. Trophy, Am. Hockey League, 1998. Office: Phila Flyers Wachovia Ctr 3601 S Broad St Philadelphia PA 19148*

BRIERLEY, JAMES ALAN, biohydrometallurgy consultant; b. Denver, Dec. 22, 1938; s. Everette and Carrie (Berg) B.; m. Corale Louise Beer, Dec. 21, 1965 BS in Bacteriology, Colo. State U., 1961; MS in Microbiology, Mont. State U., 1963, PhD, 1966. Research scientist Martin Marietta Corp., Denver, 1968-69; asst. prof. biology N.Mex. Inst. Mining and Tech., Socorro, 1966-68, from asst. prof. to prof. biology, chmn. dept. biology, 1969-83; research dir. Advanced Mineral Techs., Golden, Colo., 1983-88; chief microbiologist Newmont Metall. Svcs., Englewood, Colo., 1988-2000; chief rsch. scientist biohydrometallurgy Newmont Mining Corp., 2000-01; cons. Brierley Consultancy, LLC, Highlands Ranch, Colo., 2001—. Vis. fellow U. Warwick, Coventry, Eng., 1976, vis. prof. Catholic U., Santiago, Chile, 1983; adj. prof. dept. metallurgy U. Utah. 1994-96; cons. Mountain State Mineral Enterprises, Tucson, 1980, Sandia Nat. Lab., Albuquerque, 1976, Bechtel Civil and Minerals, Scottsdale, Ariz., 1984, Newmont Gold Co., 1988, Newmont Mining Corp., 2001-06, Smith-Pachter Attys. at Law, 2002-03, Barrick Gold Corp., 2005. Contbr. numerous articles to profl. jours.; patentee in field. Served to staff sgt. Air N.G., 1956-61. Recipient Wadsorth Extractive Metall. award, Soc. Mining, Metall. & Exploration, 2000, Honor Alumnus award, Colo. State U., 2001; grantee 32 rsch. grants. Fellow: AAAS; mem.: Nat. Acad. Engring., Mining and Metall. Soc. Am. Avocations: travel, gardening, hiking, exercise. Home: 2074 East Terrace Dr Highlands Ranch CO 80126-2692 Office: Brierley Consultancy PO Box 260012 Highlands Ranch CO 80163-0012 E-mail: j.brierley@worldnet.att.net.

BRIERTON, CHERYL LYNN, lawyer; b. Hartford, Conn., Nov. 11, 1947; d. Charles Greenwood and Elizabeth (Grechko) Wootton; m. David Martin Black, Oct. 12, 1968 (div. 1978); m. John Thomas Brierton, Sept. 6, 1982 (div. 1988); 1 child, John Greenwood. BA, Wellesley Coll., 1969; JD, U. San Diego, 1982. Bar: Calif. 1983. Tchr., libr. Anglican High Sch., Grenada, West Indies, 1972-74; dep. dir. Transalpino Student Travel, Paris, 1975-76; asst. dir. adminstn. Project OZ, YMCA, San Diego, 1976-78; asst. coord. policy and advocacy Community Congress San Diego, 1978-81; field dir. Calif. Child, Youth and Family Coalition, San Diego, 1981-83; asst. exec. dir. Community Congress San Diego, 1984-85; exec. dir. Calif. Child, Youth and Family Coalition, Sacramento, 1985-86; gen. atty. Def. Logistics Agy., Def. Depot Tracy, Calif., 1986-88; atty.-advisor Dept. of the Navy, Mare Island Naval Shipyard, Vallejo, 1988-89; staff atty. San Diego Superior Ct., 1989—. Mem. faculty Nat. Juvenile Judges Conf. Dispositional Alternatives Serious Offenders, 1982, 6th and 7th Nat. Confs. Juvenile Justice, 1979-80; cons. San Diego Youth Involvement Project, 1983-84, San Diego Youth and Community Svcs., 1983-84, South Bay Community Svcs., Chula Vista, 1983. Mem. Juvenile Justice Commn., Golden Hill Neighborhood Justice Cen. Planning Bd.; mem. com. jud. process Regional Criminal Justice Planning Bd. Scholar U. San Diego 1979. Mem. MENSA. Avocations: yachting, travel. Home: 1329 Bancroft St San Diego CA 92102-2429

BRIGDEN, ANN SCHWARTZ, mediator, educator; b. East Aurora, NY, Oct. 15, 1932; d. John G. and Mildred (Glaser) Schwartz; m. John Kraig Brigden, June 17, 1953 (div. Nov. 1974); children: Nancy Brigden, Barbara Brigden Victor; m. Steve Nemeth, Dec. 31, 1983 (div. Nov. 1996); children: Kyra Nemeth Akins, Abel Nemeth. BS in Human Ecology, Cornell U., 1954; MA in Behavioral Scis., Calif. State U., Dominguez Hills, 1977, grad. cert. in negotiation/conflict res., 1991, MS in Marriage and Family Counseling, 1993. Cert. mediator, L.A. County. Dist. dir. Girl Scouts of Erie County, Buffalo, 1954-55; recreation leader City of Phila., 1955-56; field dir. Angeles Girl Scout Coun., LA, 1956-58, 69-79; dir. vols. Children's Home Soc. Calif., LA, 1979-84, dir. Human Maturity Program, 1984-90; counselor-intern Dolores St. Sch., Carson, Calif., 1990-95; developer and dir. Conflict Resolution Programs Dolores and Catskill Schs., Carson, Calif., 1994—. Adv. bd. L.A. Unified Sch. Dist. Health Edn., 1985-87; chair Maternal, Child & Adolescent Health Coun. L.A. County West, L.A., 1988-93. Author (textbooks): Maturing as Humanly as Possible, 1986, Becoming a Teenager, 1988; co-author (jr. h.s. curriculum) Curriculum in Human Maturity, 1980, revised 1986, 94. Aux. mem. Children's Hosp. San Diego, 1962-68; Girl Scout leader, bd. mem. Girl Scout Coun. San Diego, 1964-68; com. chair Peninsula Action for Youth, Palos Verdes, Calif., 1971-76; vol. mediator L.A. County, 1992—; bd. dirs. Dispute Resolution Ctr. Calif. State U. Dominguez Hills/L.A. County, 1987—. Grantee Soc. Psychol. Study of Social Issues, 1994-96, L.A. County Dept. Edn., 1996—. Mem. So. Calif,. Mediation Assn., Calif. State U. Dominguez Hills Marriage, Family and Child Counseling Alumni Assn. Avocations: volunteering, piano, friends. Home: 3162 Crownview Dr Palos Verdes Estates CA 90275-6414

BRIGDEN, JOHN, lawyer; b. 1964; BS in Elec. Engring. with honors, Purdue U.; JD with honors, Georgetown U. Lic.: Va., Wash., DC, US Paten and Trademark Office. Dir. intellectual property Silicon Graphics, Inc., 1997—2000; v.p. bus. devel., gen. counsel Shutterfly, Inc., 2000—01; v.p., gen. counsel, sec. VERITAS Software Corp., Mountain View, Calif., 2001—03, sr. v.p., gen. counsel, sec., 2003—. Mem.: Calif. Bar Assn. Office: VERITAS Software Corp 222 Casbian Dr Sunnyvale CA 94089

BRIGGLE, GARY LEE, singer, actor, director, educator; b. Moorhead, Minn., Oct. 31, 1953; s. Leland Wilson and Harriet Maxine (Dickerson) B.; m. Christine Helen Maloney, Dec. 10, 1977 (div. Apr. 1982); life ptnr. Wendy Lehr, Feb. 14, 1983. MusB, St. Olaf Coll., Northfield, Minn., 1975. Resident artist Minn. Opera Co., Mpls., 1977-82, Children's Theater Co. & Sch., Mpls., 1979-82; artistic assoc. Seaside Music Theater, Daytona Beach, Fla., 1979—, Ariz. Theater Co., Tuscon, Phoenix, 1991-94, Lyric Opera Cleve., 1984-98, artistic dir., 1995-98; tchr. The Artist's Crossing. Guest dir. Nat. Theater of Hungary, 1999, Boston U., 1998-99, Valparaiso Univ., 1998, Baldwin-Wallace Conservatory, 1999, St. Olaf Coll., 2000, U. Ohio, Miami, 2005, U. Iowa, 2006-07. Actor: Noel & Gertie, Oh Coward!, Sweeney Todd, The Three Penny Opera, (PBS-TV Skylight Opera Theater) The Mikado, Iolanthe, Patience (Carbonell award S. Fla. Critics Assn., 1983), Pirates of Penzance, Yeoman of the Guard, A Talent to Amuse, 2005—06, The Gondoliers, H.M.S. Pinafore. Irene Ryan scholar, Am. Coll. Theater Festival, 1975. Avocations: aquatics, painting, drawing, hiking, camping. E-mail: arlecchino@juno.com.

BRIGGS, ALAN LEONARD, lawyer; b. Dayton, Ohio, Oct. 1, 1942; s. Donald M. and Helen (Barker) B.; m. Linda Ann Dobie, Sept. 10, 1966 (div. 1991); children: Jason, Aimee, Anna; m. Christine M. McCormick, 1991; 1 child, Caitlin. AB, Miami U., Oxford, Ohio, 1964; JD, Ohio State U., 1967; LLM in Patent/Intellectual Property Law, George Washington U., 1998. Bar: Ohio 1967, Calif. 1970, Fla. 1989, D.C. 1995, Va. 1995, Md. 1995. Ptnr. Murphey, Young & Smith, Columbus, Ohio, 1970-88, Squire, Sanders & Dempsey, Columbus, 1988-91, Miami, Fla., 1991-94, Washington, 1994—. Trustee Legal Aid Soc. Fellow Am. Coll. Trial Lawyers; mem. ABA, Ohio State Bar Assn. (coun. of dels. 1980-86, chmn. screening com. coun. dels. 1983-84, sect. litigation bd. govs. 1986-90), Columbus Bar Assn. (pres. 1985, chmn. litigation practice inst. 1987-90), Am. Arbitration Assn. Office: Squire Sanders & Dempsey 1201 Pennsylvania Ave NW Washington DC 20004-2491

BRIGGS, ALICE, clinical child psychologist; d. Wash Briggs and Katie Briggs-Charles. AS in Applied Sci., SUNY, 1979, BS, 1982; MA, Seton Hall U., 1985; profl. diploma, Fordham U., 1992; PhD, Walden U., 2003. Lic. sch. psychologist NY, 1992, NJ, 2002. Psychiat. counselor The Residential Social Svc. Program, Jersey City, 1985; therapeutic technician Jersey City Med. Ctr., 1988; applied behavioral specialist Assn. Children with Retarded Mental Devel. Inc., NYC, 1988—89; substitue tchr. Jersey City Bd. Edn., 1990; tchr. spl. edn. NYC Bd. Edn., 1991, sch. psychologist, 1992—2002; cert. sch. psychologist Jersey City Bd. of Edn., 2002—05, psychologist, 2005—, referral specialist preschool intervention, 2005—. Adj. prof. Coll. New Rochelle, NYC, 1995—2006; cons. in field. Mem. coll. ministry Met. Bapt. Ch., Newark, 2005—07, mem. counseling ministry, 2005—07; chairperson leadership devel. curriculum com Met. Coll. Ministry, 2007; union rep. Jersey City Edn. Assn., 2003—06. Mem.: APA (del. People to People Amb. Program's Psychology Profl. Del. 2006), NY Assn. Sch. Psychologist, Psi Chi (life). Baptist. Avocations: reading, interior decorating, dance, Broadway shows, ballet. Home: 14 River Street Extension 234 Little Ferry NJ 07643 Personal E-mail: briggsdr@verizon.net.

BRIGGS, CHAD MICHAEL, political science professor; b. Iowa City, Dec. 29, 1972; s. Dennis and Carol Briggs; m. Tracy Walstrom, Oct. 4, 1997. BA, U. Wis., Madison, 1994; MA, U. Limerick, Ireland, 1996; PhD, Carleton U., Ottawa, Can., 2001. Rsch. fellow, geography U. Coll. London, 1999—2000; budget and policy analyst TEACH Wis., Madison, 2001—02; asst. prof. polit. sci. Calif. State U., Fullerton, 2002—05; fulbright prof. Corvinus U., Budapest, Hungary, 2005—06; asst. prof. internat. rels. Lehigh U., Bethlehem, Pa., 2006—. Contbr. articles to profl. jours. Polit. advisor Hungarian Free Dem. Party, Budapest, 1993—94. Vis. scholar, U. Coll. London, 1999—2000. Mem.: IEEE (assoc.), Soc. Risk Assessment (assoc.), Golden Key Honor Soc. (hon.), Phi Beta Kappa (hon.). Achievements include research in environmental health risk in post-conflict societies; assessment of perchlorate public health risks; remediation of post-Soviet military sites in Eastern Europe. Avocations: bicycling, travel, book collecting. Home: 118 S 6th St Coplay PA 18037 Home Phone: 610-262-8075; Office Phone: 610-758-3388. Personal E-mail: chad.briggs@lehigh.edu.

BRIGGS, DEREK ERNEST GILMOR, science educator; b. Dublin, Jan. 10, 1950; arrived in US, 2003; s. John Gilmor and Olive Evelyn Briggs; m. Jennifer Olive Kershaw, Sept. 1, 1972; children: Adam D.M., Brian D.J., John A.G. BA, Dublin U. Trinity Coll., 1972; PhD, Cambridge U., Eng., 1976. Lectr. Goldsmiths Coll., London, 1977—85; lectr., reader, prof. Bristol U., England, 1985—2002; prof. Yale U., New Haven, 2003—. Dir. Yale Inst. for Biospheric Studies Yale U., New Haven, 2004—; curator invertebrate paleontology Peabody Mus. Natural History, New Haven, 2003—. Contbr. articles to profl. jours.; author (with D.H. Erwin and F.J. Collier): The Fossils of the Burgess Shale, 1994; author: (with C. Bartels and G. Brassel) The Fossils of the Hunsrück Slate-Marine Life in the Devonian, 1998; author: (with N.H. Barton, J.A. Eisen, D. Goldstein and N.H. Patel) Evolution, 2007; editor (with K.C. Allen): Evolution and the Fossil Record, 1989; editor: (with P.A. Allison) Taphonomy: Releasing the Data Locked in the Fossil Record, 1991; editor: (with P.R. Crowther) Palaeobiology - A Synthesis, 1990, Palaeobiology II, 2001. Recipient Boyle medal, Royal Dublin Soc./Irish Times, 2001. Fellow: Royal Soc. London, Geol. Soc. London (Lyell medal 2000), Paleontol. Soc.; mem.: Palaeontological Assn., Royal Irish Acad. (hon.). Home: 10 Lincoln St New Haven CT 06511 Office: Yale University Geology and Geophysics PO Box 208109 New Haven CT 06520 Home Phone: 203-624-2488; Office Phone: 203-432-8590. Business E-Mail: derek.briggs@yale.edu.

BRIGGS, DICK DOWLING, JR., physician, educator; b. Electric Mills, Miss., Jan. 28, 1934; s. Dick Dowling and Anita (Carnathan) B.; m. Susan Hunt Davis, June 20, 1959; children: Adrienne Davis, Dick Dowling, III, Daniel Roth. BS, U. of South, 1956; MD, Washington U., 1960. Resident, fellow, chief resident U. Ala. Hosp., Birmingham, 1960-62, 64-68; prof. medicine U. Ala., Birmingham, 1964-95, prof., 1971—92, dir. divsn. pulmonary critical care, 1971-92, vice chmn. dept. medicine, 1981-95, eminent scholar chair in pulmonary diseases, 1989-95, emeritus eminent scholar chair, 1995—; pres., CEO, med. dir. U. Ala. Health Svc. Found., P.C., Birmingham, 1988-92; corp. med. dir. Complete Health, 1985—88, Triton Health Sys., Birmingham, 1995-97; chief med. officer Best Drs. Worldwide Health Svcs., Boston, 1997—2005. Cons. VA Med. Ctr., Birmingham, 1966-2003; trustee AmSouth Funds, Birmingham, 1992-2005. Assoc. editor (CDROM) UpToDate, 1994—; sr. editl. bd. Archives Internal Medicine, 1985-97; contbr. articles to profl. publs. Bd. dir. Am. Bd. Emergency Medicine, 1994—2002. Recipient Pulmonary Acad. award NIH, 1972-77, Breath of Life award Cystic Fibrosis Found., 1994; named to Ala. Tennis Hall Fame, 2003. Master: ACP (Laureate award 1995), Am. Coll. Chest Physicians (pres. 1984—85, master fellow 2002); mem.: Am. Bd. Pulmonary Disease (chmn. 1988—90), So. Med. Assn. (chmn. sect. medicine 1973—74), Am. Thoracic Soc. (pres. Ala. chpt. 1978—79), Assn. Pulmonary and Critical Care Medicine Program Dirs. (founding mem. 1984, pres. 1986—87), Newcomen Soc., US Tennis Assn. (Ala. Tennis Hall of Fame 2003), Rotary Club. Episcopalian. Avocations: tennis, music, travel, wine. Home: 2925 Southwood Rd Birmingham AL 35223-1232 Office: Univ Ala Birmingham Sch Medicine 1808 7th Ave S Birmingham AL 35294-0012 Office Phone: 205-934-6015. Business E-Mail: ddbjr@uab.edu.

BRIGGS, EDWARD SAMUEL, naval officer; b. St. Paul, Oct. 4, 1926; s. Charles William and Lois Ione (Johnson) B.; m. Nanette Parks, June 7, 1949; 1 child, Jeffrey Charles. BS, U.S. Naval Acad., 1949. Commd. ensign U.S. Navy, 1949; advanced through officer ranks to vice admiral; naval aviator U.S. Navy, 1951—61, surface warfare officer, 1961—84; commanding officer USS Turner Joy, USS Jouett; asst. chief of staff plans, chief of staff U.S. 7th Fleet, 1972-73; fleet ops. officer, asst. chief staff ops. U.S. Pacific Fleet, Makalapa, Hawaii, 1973-75; comdr. Crusier-Destroyer Group 3, San Diego, 1975-77, Navy Recruiting Command, Arlington, Va., 1977-79, Naval Logistics Command, U.S. Pacific Fleet, Naval Base, Pearl Harbor, Hawaii, 1979-80; dep. comdr.-in-chief U.S. Pacific Fleet, Pearl Harbor, 1980-82; comdr. Naval Surface Force U.S. Atlantic Fleet, 1982-84; ret., 1984. Decorated Bronze Star with combat device and one star, Air medals (2), Navy Commendation medal with combat device and two stars, Legion of Merit with combat device and four stars, D.S.M.; Vietnamese Navy Gallantry medal. Mem. Surface Navy Assn., U.S. Naval Acad. Alumni Assn., Naval Inst., Navy League, San Diego Mil. Adv. Coun. Home: 3648 Lago Sereno Escondido CA 92029-7902 *Dedication to our nation and devotion to its ideals are the responsibilities of citizenship.*

BRIGGS, ETHEL DELORIA, federal agency administrator; BA, N.C. Ctrl. U., 1971; M in Counseling, U. N.C., 1972. Dir. adult svcs. Nat. Coun. Disability, Washington, 1985—, dep. dir., acting exec. dir., exec. dir. Named one of Top 100 African Am. Bus. and Profl. Women, Dollars and Sense Mag., 1989. Office: Nat Coun Disability 1331 F St NW Ste 850 Washington DC 20004-1138 Business E-Mail: ebriggs@ncd.gov.

BRIGGS, FRANKLIN HENRY, retired naval officer; b. Council Bluffs, Iowa, Mar. 7, 1933; s. Edwin Charles Briggs and Anna Maud Brandt; m. Chizuko Imaoka, Aug. 28, 1960. Student, U. Colo., Boulder, 1951; BA, U. Nebr., Lincoln, 1955. Commd. ensign USN, 1955, advanced through grades to capt., 1976; deck and gunnery USS Essex (CVA-9), San Diego, 1955—58; asst. plans officer Comdr. Naval Forces, Yokosuka, Japan, 1958—61; ops. officer USS Paul Revere (APA-248), San Diego, 1961—63; CIC instr. Anti-Air Warfare Def. Ctr., Dams Neck, Va., 1963—66; ship employment officer Amphibious Force, Pacific, Subic Bay, Philippines, 1966—68; comdg. officer Naval Res. Ctr., Scotia, NY, 1968—70; exec. officer USS Anchorage, San Diego, 1970—72; manpower dir. Comdr. 6th Naval Dist., San Diego, 1970—72; dep. comdr. Naval Res. Readiness Command, Washington, 1974—78; Comdr. Cleve. Readiness Command, 1978—79. Decorated Vietnam Campaign medal with 10 stars, Navy Commendation medal with Combat V, Gold star, Cross of Gallantry, Expeditionary medal, Quemay-Matsu. Mem. Ikenobo Internat., Dicken's Fellowship. Conservative. Avocations: reading, history, travel, opera. Home: 890 Buen Tiempo Dr Chula Vista CA 91910-6555

BRIGGS, HAZEN SPENCER PINGREE, III, air traffic controller, educator; b. Pontiac, Mich., June 25, 1957; s. Hazen Spencer Pingree Briggs, II and Reva Macy; m. Barbara Elaine Weigle, Sept. 25, 1962. BA in Theology and Computer Sci., Andrews U., Berrien Springs, Mich., 1982. Software cons. Zenith Data Systems, St. Joseph, Mich., 1981—86; air traffic contr. FAA, Louisville, 1986—87, Jackson, Miss., 1987—92, computer specialist Nashville, 1992—96, Memphis, 1996—2001, instr. Oklahoma City, 2001—07, sys. support Atlanta, 2007—. Mem.: Mensa. Independent. Seventh Day Adventist. Office Phone: 404-305-5576. Personal E-mail: hazenbriggs@bellsouth.net.

BRIGGS, HENRY PAYSON, JR., headmaster; b. Boston, Apr. 14, 1932; s. Henry Payson Sr. and Eleanor Temple (Smith) B.; m. Charlin Shoenberger Devanney, Nov. 28, 1987; children from previous marriage: Payson Stewart, Heather Kavanagh. BA, Harvard U., 1954, MAT, 1959. Dir. admissions and fin. aid Harvard Coll., Cambridge, Mass., 1956-66; headmaster Western Res. Acad., Hudson, Ohio, 1966-76, Seven Hills Sch., Cin., 1976—95; interim head St. James' Episcopal Sch., LA, 1995—96; dir. major gifts Cin. Opera, 1996-99; interim head The Potomac Sch., McLean, Va., 1999-2000, The Norfolk (Va.) Acad., 2000-01, The Ft. Worth CDS, 2001—02, St. Timothy's Sch., Balt., 2002—03, Episcopal H.S., Baton Rouge, 2004—05. Numerous pro-bone affiliations, 2006—07. Bd. dirs. Queen City Found.; former vestryman, warden Christ Episcopal Ch. Cathedral, Cin. 1st lt. U.S. Army, 1954-56. Recipient Dist. Grad. award, Noble and Greenough Sch., 2005. Mem. Headmasters Assn. (former officer), Country Day Sch. Headmasters Assn.(former v.p.), Literary Club, Univ. Club, Tennis Club Cin. (former pres.). Avocations: education, sports, outdoors, politics. Home: 7937 Bar Harbor Dr Cincinnati OH 45255-4430 Personal E-mail: hbriggs@cinci.rr.com.

BRIGGS, JOHN MANCEL, III, lawyer; b. Muskegon, Mich., May 24, 1942; s. John M. Jr. and Margaret Jane (Wren) B.; m. Janice R. Dykema, May 20, 1967; children: Jennifer Anne, Jill Margaret. BS, U. Mich., 1964, JD, 1967. Bar: Mich. 1968, U.S. Dist. Ct. (we. dist.) Mich. 1968, U.S. Ct. Appeals (6th cir.) 1974, U.S. Supreme Ct. 2000. Assoc. Parmenter, Forsythe, Rude, Van Epps, Briggs & Fauri and predecessors, Muskegon, 1967-70, ptnr., 1970-92; shareholder Parmenter O'Toole, Muskegon, Mich., 1992—. Active Muskegon United Appeal, 1968-73; bd. dirs. Big Bros., Muskegon, 1969-74; bd. dirs. Muskegon YMCA, 1970-80, 81-83, 2005—, 1st v.p., 1973-76, pres., 1977-78; bd. dirs. Muskegon-Oceana Legal Aid Soc., 1970-73, pres., 1972-73; bd. dirs. Berean Ch., 1985-86, 88-90, 93-94, 99-01, 2004—, sec., 1988-90, v.p., 1993, pres., 1994, 99, 2000, 07. With USAR, 1967-73. Recipient Disting. Svc. award, Muskegon Jaycees, 1977. Fellow Mich. State Bar Assn.; mem. ABA, Muskegon County Bar Assn. (sec. 1970-71, v.p. 1974-75, pres. 1975-76), Rotary (bd. dirs. 1981-85, pres.-elect 1982-83, pres. 1983-84, Presdl. citation, Paul Harris fellow 2004). Republican. Office: Parmenter O'Toole PO Box 786 601 Terrace St Muskegon MI 49443-0786 Office Phone: 231-722-5410. Business E-Mail: jmb@parmenterlaw.com.

BRIGGS, KERRI LAYNE, federal agency administrator; b. Midland, Tex., 1967; BA, Stephen F. Austin State U., 1989; MA, U. So. Calif., PhD in Edn. Policy & Orgnl. Studies. Rsch. assoc., dir. evaluation U. Tex. Ctr. for Reading and Language Arts, Austin; sr. policy adv. Office Elem. & Secondary Edn. US Dept. Edn., Washington, 2001, sr. policy adv. Office Dep. Sec., acting asst. sec. for planning, evaluation & policy devel., 2006—07, acting asst. sec. for elem. & secondary edn., 2007, asst. sec. for elem. & secondary edn., 2007—. Co-author (with Sharon Vaughn): Reading in the Classroom: Systems for Observation of Teaching and Learning, 2003. Bd. mem. Aged Women's Home of Georgetown. Mem.: Jr. League of Washington (chair Literacy Partnerships Com. 2006—). Office: US Dept Edn 400 Maryland Ave SW Rm 3W315 Washington DC 20202 Office Phone: 202-401-0113. E-mail: kerri.briggs@ed.gov.*

BRIGGS, PHILIP, insurance company executive; b. Paris, Feb. 28, 1928; s. Robert E. and Madeleine (Boell) B. (parents Am. citizens); m. Jean M. Sloan, July 9, 1949; children: Karen, Heather, Peter. AB, Middlebury Coll., 1948. With Met. Life Ins. Co., NYC, 1948-93, v.p., gen. mgr., 1971-73, sr. v.p., 1973-77, exec. v.p., 1977-86, vice chmn. bd. dirs., CFO NYC, 1986-93; chmn. Wellchoice, Inc. (formerly Empire Blue Cross and Blue Shield), NYC, 1993—2004. Fellow: Am. Acad. Actuaries, Soc. Actuaries.

BRIGGS, PHILIP JAMES, political science professor, writer; b. NYC, July 28, 1938; m. Candace Rae Kohn, Jan. 30, 1971; children: Nicola Fulham, Adam Kohn. BS, SUNY, Oswego, 1960; MA, Maxwell Sch. Citizenship and Pub. Affairs, Syracuse U., 1962, PhD, 1969. Asst. prof. social sci. SUNY Coll. Tech., Delhi, 1963-65; part-time admissions counselor Syracuse (N.Y.) U., 1967; assoc. prof. polit. sci. East Stroudsburg (Pa.) U., 1968-72, prof. polit. sci., 1972-99, dept. grad. coord.and chmn., 1977-95, faculty Fulbright adviser, 1981-82, disting. prof., faculty emeriti, 2000—. Foxhowe lectr., 1980; Commonwealth spkr. Pa. Humanities Coun., 1984—86, 1996—99; invited del. Sci. Rsch. Coun., Acad. Sci. USSR, 1979; invited participant seminar Georgetown U., 1983; invited scholar Presdl. Conf. Com., Hofstra U., 1984, 85, 87; panel co-chmn. Internat. Polit. Sci. World Congress, Paris, 1985, panel chmn., Berlin, 94; panel chmn. annual meetings Pa. Polit. Sci. Assn., 1993—99; manuscript referee Armed Forces and Soc., Chgo., 1979, Chgo., 93; cons. McGraw-Hill Book Co., NYC, 1981; spkr. in field. Author: Making American Foreign Policy, President-Congress Relations from the Second World War to Vietnam, 1991, 1992, Making American Foreign Policy, President-Congress Relations from the Second World War to the Post-Cold War Era, 1994, 1995, 1997; contbg. author: series The Congress of the United States, 1789-1989; editor: Politics in America, Readings and Documents, 1972; contbr. articles and revs. to profl. publs.; (TV appearances on) C-Span, 1987, Blue Ridge Cable and Pennarama, 1991, Action News 24, Erie, Pa., 1999. Exec. dir. Rsch. Com. on Armed Forces and Soc. Internat. Polit. Sci. Assn., 1990-99; panel chmn. rsch. com. Fundacion Jose Ortega y Gasset, Madrid, 1990; panel participant Ctr. for Study of Presidency, 1995-96. With USCG, 1962, USCGR, 1962-70.

BRIGGS, REX, marketing executive, writer; Dir. Yankelovich Ptnrs.; dir. rsch. Wired/HotWired; exec. v.p. Millward Brown; founder, CEO Mktg. Evolution, Inc., NYC, El Dorado Hills, Calif. Co-author: What Sticks: Why Most Advertising Fails and How to Guarantee Yours Succeeds, 2006. Named one of Best and Brightest in Media and Tech., Ad Week; recipient Atticus Award, Tenagra Award, Fernanda Monti award. Office: Mktg Evolution Inc 4364 Town Center Blvd Ste 320 El Dorado Hills CA 95762 also: 107 Grand St, Ste 600 New York NY 10013 Office Phone: 916-933-7500, 212-965-8690. Office Fax: 916-941-6134, 212-965-8691.*

BRIGGS, STEVE CLEMENT, lawyer; b. Vernon, Tex., Jan. 26, 1947; s. Galen Pierce and Virginia Irene (Sebert) B. BA, U. Mich., 1970; postgrad., U. Calif., Berkeley, 1970; JD, U. Colo., 1975. Bar: Colo. 1975, U.S. Dist. Ct. Colo. 1975, U.S. Ct. Appeals (10th cir.) 1976, U.S. Ct. Claims 1984. Law clk. to chief judge U.S. Dist. Ct. Colo., Denver, 1975-76; asst. atty. gen. anti-trust sect. State of Colo., Denver, 1976-78; ptnr. Hutchinson, Black, Hill & Cook, Boulder, Colo., 1978—92; judge Colo. Ct. Appeals, 1992—2000; mediator, arbitrator Jud. Arbiter Group, Inc., 2000—. Chair dean's club U. Colo. Law Sch., Boulder, 1985; bd. dirs. Vol. and Info. Ctr., Boulder, 1979-80, United Way, Boulder, 1980, Boulder Philharm., 1990—; v.p. bd. dirs. Counseling Ctr., Boulder, 1983-86. Recipient Outstanding Vol. Legal Svcs. award Eco-Cycle, 1984, Disting. Alumni award U. Colo Sch. Law, 2003. Mem. Colo. Bar Assn. (bd. govs. 1988—, exec. coun. 1990—, pres. 2004-05), Boulder County Bar Assn. (pres. 1986-87). Avocations: golf, travel, movies, reading. Office: Judicial Arbiter Group 1601 Blake St #400 Denver CO 80202 Office Phone: 303-572-1919. Fax: 303-571-1115. Business E-Mail: sbriggs@jaginc.com.*

BRIGGS, WARD WRIGHT, classics educator; b. Riverside, Calif., Nov. 26, 1945; s. Ward Wright and Madge Elizabeth (Ravenscroft) B. BA, Washington & Lee U., 1967; MA, U. N.C., 1969, PhD, 1974. Instr. classics U. S.C., Columbia, 1973-74, asst. prof., 1974-80, assoc. prof., 1980-86, prof. classics, 1986—, Carolina disting. prof. classics, 1996—, Louise Fry Scudder prof. humanities, 1996—, interim assoc. provost, 1996-97. Vis. prof. U. Va., Charlottesville, 1988, U. Colo., 1988; fellow Inst. for Advanced Study, Princeton, 1999-2000. Author: Narrative and Simile from the Georgics in the Aeneid, 1980; editor: Letters of B.L. Gildersleeve, 1987; editor: Biographical Dictionary of North American Classicists, 1994, Soldier and Scholar, 1998; co-editor: Classical Scholarship, 1990; editor Vergilius, Jour. of Vergilian Soc. Am., 1986-95. Mem. Am. Philol. Assn., Classical Assn. Middle West and South (pres. 1988-89), Cambridge Philol. Soc., Phi Beta Kappa. Episcopalian. Home: 1904 Pendleton St Columbia SC 29201-3906 Office: U SC Dept French and Classics Columbia SC 29208-0001 Office Phone: 803-777-2765. Personal E-mail: wbriggs7@bellsouth.net. Business E-Mail: wardbriggs@sc.edu.

BRIGGS, WILLIAM BENAJAH, retired aerospace engineer; b. Okmulgee, Okla., Dec. 13, 1922; s. Eugene Stephen and Mary Betty (Gentry) B.; m. Lorraine Hood, June 6, 1944; children— Eugene Stephen II, Cynthia Anne, Julia Louise, Spencer Gentry BA in Physics, Phillips U., 1943, DSc (hon.), 1977; MSME, Ga. Inst. Tech., 1947. Aero. scientist NACA, Cleve., 1948-52; propulsion engr. regulus II, scout l.v., dynasoar, Washington rep. Chance Vought Aircraft/LTV, Dallas, 1952-64; mgr. advanced planning Marsviking, Jupiter probe McDonnell Douglas Co., St. Louis, 1964-80, dir. program devel. fusion energy, 1980-87. Planetary quarantine adv. panel NASA. Contbr. articles on aero. engring. and energy to profl. jours.; patentee in field Chmn. Disciples Coun. Greater St. Louis, 1969-73; chmn. bd. Christian Bd. Publs., St. Louis, 1974-91; bd. dirs. Joint Cmty. Ministries, 1987-92, Emergency Childrens Home, 1994-2000; chmn. arrangements gen. assembly/synod Disciples of Christ/United Ch. of Christ, 1993; trustee Phillips U., Enid, Okla., 1996—. With USNR, 1943-46, Atlantic and West Pacific. Recipient Svc. award, Emergency Childrens Home, 2003. Assoc. fellow AIAA (dir. region 5 1974-77, v.p. mem. svcs. 1978-79); mem. VFW, Am. Nuclear Soc., Navy League. Mem. Disciples of Christ Ch. Home: 13676 Armstead Dr Saint Louis MO 63131-1513 *Facing a problem, size up the situation, determine what needs to be done, then take action. Steadfastly working your plan does produce results; just give serendipity a chance to happen.*

BRIGGS, WINSLOW RUSSELL, plant biologist, educator; b. St. Paul, Apr. 29, 1928; s. John DeQuedville and Marjorie (Winslow) B.; m. Ann Morrill, June 30, 1955; children: Caroline, Lucia, Marion. BA, Harvard U., 1951, MA, 1952, PhD, 1956; D in Natural Sci. (hon.), U. Freiburg, Germany, 2002, D (hon.) in Plant Biology, 2002. Instr. biol. scis. Stanford (Calif.) U., 1955-57, asst. prof., 1957-62, assoc. prof., 1962-66, prof., 1966-67; prof. biology Harvard U., 1967-73, Stanford U., 1973—; dir. dept. plant biology Carnegie Instn. of Washington, Stanford, 1973-93. Author: (with others) Life on Earth, 1973; mem. editl. bd. Ann. Rev. Plant Physiology, 1961-72; contbr. articles on plant growth and devel. and photobiology to profl. jours. Vol. Calif. State Pk. sys. Recipient Alexander von Humboldt U.S. Sr. Scientist award, 1984-85, Sterling Hendricks award USDA Agrl. Rsch. Svc., 1995, DeWitt award for partnership Calif. State Pks., 2000, Finsen medal Assn. Internat. Photobiology, 2000; John Simon Guggenheim fellow, 1973-74, Deutsche Akademie der Naturforscher Leopoldina, 1986. Fellow AAAS, Am. Soc. Plant Physiologists (pres. 1975-76, Stephen Hales award 1994, Adolph Gude award, 2007); mem. NAS, Calif. Bot. Soc. (pres. 1976-77), Am. Acad. Arts and Scis., Am. Inst. Biol. Scis. (pres. 1980-81), Am. Soc. Photobiology, Bot. Soc. Am., Nature Conservancy, Sigma Xi. Avocation: Chinese cooking. Home: 480 Hale St Palo Alto CA 94301-2207 Office: Carnegie Inst Washington Dept Plant Biology 260 Panama St Stanford CA 94305-4101 *With gifted students, remarkable things are possible.*

BRIGGUM, SUE MARIE, corporate executive; b. Harrisburg, Pa., Apr. 8, 1950; d. John Gehring and Blanche Faye (Hess) B.; m. Martin Rose, Jan. 6, 1984; 1 child, Lauren. BA, U. Pitts., 1972; MA, U. Wis., 1973, PhD, 1979; JD, Harvard U., 1980. Bar: DC 1980. Lectr. U. Wis., Madison, 1973-77; assoc. Wald, Harkrader & Ross, Washington, 1980-86, Piper & Marbury, Washington, 1986-87; dir. govt. affairs Waste Mgmt., Wash., 1987. Co-author: Concordance to Almayer's Folly, 1980, Hazardous Waste Regulation Handbook, 1983, rev. edit 1985; co-editor: Modernism in Literature, 1976. Office: Waste Mgmt Ste 300 601 Pennsylvania Ave NW Bldg Washington DC 20004-2601 Office Phone: 202-628-3500. Office Fax: 202-628-0400. Business E-Mail: sbriggum@wm.com.

BRIGHAM, HENRY DAY, JR., retired lawyer; b. Pittsfield, Mass., Dec. 12, 1926; s. Henry Day and Gladys M. (Allen) B.; m. Catherine T. Van't Hul, Dec. 16, 1961; children: Henry Day, Johan Van't Hul, Alexander Frederick. BA, Yale U., 1947, JD, 1950. Bar: N.Y. 1951, Mass. 1966. Assoc. Milbank, Tweed, Hope & Hadley, NYC, 1951-52, 54-56, Simpson Thacher & Bartlett, NYC, 1956-66; v.p., gen. counsel, dir. Eaton & Howard, Inc., Boston, 1966-73, pres., 1973-79; v.p., chmn. exec. com. Eaton & Howard, Vance Sanders, Inc., Boston, 1979-81, Eaton Vance Corp., Boston, 1981—96; ret., 1996. Former trustee Eaton Vance Cash Mgmt. Fund, Boston; former v.p., trustee Eaton Vance Tax Free Reserves, Boston; former sec., clk., dir. Investors Bank & Trust Co., Boston; v.p., sec., trustee Wright Managed Income Trust, Boston, Wright Managed Equity Trust, Boston. Pres. Trustees of Donations of Episc. Diocese Mass., 1984-89; sr. warden Ch. of the Redeemer, Chestnut Hill, 1975-79; sec., bd. dirs. Chestnut Hill Assn. (Mass.), 1969—. Lt. USNR, 1952-54. Mem.: Soc. of the Cin., Assn. Yale Alumni (bd. govs.), Investment Counsel Assn. Am. (bd. govs.), Somerset Club, Longwood Cricket Club, Downtown Club, The Country Club, Tennis & Racquet Club, Harvard Club, Tarratine Club, Soc. Colonial Wars, Phi Delta Phi, Phi Beta Kappa. Episcopalian.

BRIGHAM, LAWSON WALTER, oceanographer, researcher; b. Greenport, NY, June 5, 1948; BS in Ocean Sci., US Coast Guard Acad., New London, Conn., 1970; MS in Mgmt., Rensselaer Poly. Inst., Troy, NY, 1979; diploma in naval & strategic studies with distinction, US Naval War Coll., Newport, RI, 1982; MPhil in Polar Studies, Cambridge U., Eng., 1996, PhD in Polar Oceanography, 2000. Coast guard liaison officer to the chief of naval ops. The Pentagon, Washington, 1985—86; first commdg. officer USCGC Escanaba, Boston, 1986—89; commdg. officer polar icebreaker USCGC Polar Sea, Seattle, 1993—95; rsch. fellow Marine Policy Ctr. Woods Hole Oceanog. Instn., Mass., 1989—90; chief strategic planner USCG Hdqs., Washington, 1990—93; office of naval rsch. arctic chair, assoc. prof. Naval Postgraduate Sch., Monterey, Calif., 1996—97; rsch. scientist Scott Polar Rsch. Inst. Cambridge U., 1998—2000, rsch. assoc. Scott Polar Rsch. Inst., 2000—; dep. dir., Alaska office dir. US Arctic Rsch. Commn., Anchorage, 2001—. Chmn. arctic marine shipping assessment Arctic Coun., Tromso, Norway, 2004—, vice-chmn. protection of the arctic marine environment working group, 2005—; bd. govs. Arctic Inst. N.Am., Fairbanks, Alaska, 1991—; corp. mem. Woods Hole Oceanog. Instn., Woods Hole, Mass., 1995—99; bd. dirs. North Pacific Rsch. Bd., Anchorage, 2002—06; adj. scientist Office of Naval Rsch. Europe, London, 1996—2002. Author: The Soviet Maritime Arctic, 1991; mem. editl. bd.: Polar Record, 1995—; contbr. chapters to books. Decorated Legion of Merit Sec. of Transp., Meritorious Svc. medals USCG and USN, Arctic & Antarctic Svc. medals. Fellow: Arctic Inst. N.Am., Royal Geog. Soc., Explorers Club (Citation of Merit 1996); mem.: Am. Geophys. Union, NY Yacht Club, Sigma Xi. Achievements include first to Captain a US polar icebreaker to the North Pole and first surface ship crossing of the Arctic Ocean in 1994. Avocations: sailing, fishing. Office: US Arctic Rsch Commn 420 L St Ste 315 Anchorage AK 99501-1971 Office Phone: 907-271-4577. Office Fax: 907-271-4578. Business E-Mail: usarc@acsalaska.net.

BRIGHAM, NICOLETTE BAINBRIDGE, special education services professional; b. St. Albans, Eng., Sept. 29, 1965; d. Roland Everard Bainbridge, Kathleen Treacy Bainbridge; m. Michael J. Brigham, Sept. 24, 2005. BA in Psychology, Wichita State U., Kans., 1989; MS in Edn., U. Kans., Lawrence, 1999; PhD in Spl. Edn., Vanderbilt U., Nashville, 2006. Early childhood spl. edn. tchr. Rainbows United, Wichita, Kans., 1994—96; infant-toddler program dir. Spl. Svcs. Coop., Wamego, Kans., 1996—2000; rsch. asst. Vanderbilt U., Nashville, 2000—04; edn. cons. Vanderbilt Children's Hosp., 2004—05; coord. outreach program Vanderbilt Kennedy Treatment Rsch. Inst. Autism Spectrum Disorders, 2005—. Chair Interagency Coordinating Coun., Wamego, 1996—2000; mem. Parents as Teachers Adv. Bd., Wamego, 1996—2000; autism cons. Spl. Svc. Coop., Wamego, 1998—2000; adj. instr. Highland C.C., Wamego, 2000. Contbr. articles to profl. jours. Chair Interagency Coord. Coun., Wamego, Kans., 1996—2000; mem. United Way Pottawatomie and Wabaunsee Counties, Wamego, 1998—2000, Parent as Tchrs: Adv. Bd., Wamego, 1996—2000; Member Graduate Student Council of Vanderbilt University, Nashville, 2000—00. Recipient Grad. Rsch. assistantship, Vanderbilt U., 2000, 2001, 2002, 2003. Mem.: Autism Soc. Am. Independent. Roman Catholic. Avocations: travel, literature. Office: Vanderbilt Kennedy TRIAD 1207 18th Ave S Nashville TN 37212 Office Phone: 618-936-2163. Business E-Mail: nicolette.l.bainbridge@vanderbilt.edu.

BRIGHI, ROBERT J., principal; Prin. Arthur W. Erskine Elem. Sch., Cedar Rapids, Iowa. Recipient Elem. Sch. Recognition award U.S. Dept. Edn., 1989-90. Office: Arthur W Erskine Elem Sch 600 36th St SE Cedar Rapids IA 52403-4314

BRIGHT, BRUCE FREDERICK, lawyer; b. Washington, Sept. 1, 1966; s. Stanley Joseph and Pamela Stanley Bright; m. Arlette Kelly Bright, June 1, 1996; children: Abigail Elizabeth, Wyatt Lee, Colin Stanley. BA, U. Del., Newark, 1988; JD, Widener U., Wilmington, Del., 1994. Atty. Ln. & Waterman, Davenport, Iowa, 1994—95; lawyer LeBoeuf, Lamb, Greene & MacRae LLP, Washington, 1995—99, Hyatt, Peters & Weber, Annapolis, Md., 1999—2001, Ayres, Jenkins, Gordy & Almand, P.A., Ocean City, Md., 2001—. Exec. com. mem. United Way of Lower Ea. Shore, Salisbury, Md., 2006—07, dir., 2006—07. Mem.: Phi Kappa Phi, Phi Delta Phi, Moe Levine Trial Adv. R-Consevative. Episcopalian. Avocations: sailing, golf, tennis, travel. Home: 10477 Golf Course Rd Ocean City MD 21842 Office: Ayres Jenkins Gordy & Almand PA 6200 Coastal Hwy Ocean City MD 21842 Home Phone: 410-213-1014; Office Phone: 410-723-1400. Office Fax: 410-723-1861. Personal E-mail: bbabright@comcast.net. Business E-Mail: bbright@ajgalaw.com.

BRIGHT, CRAIG BARTLEY, lawyer; b. Mineola, NY, May 23, 1931; s. Herbert Lester and Gertrude Lillian (Smith) Bright; m. Judith Alice Pollard, July 31, 1955 (dec. Aug. 1956); m. Ann Sharpe, July 18, 1959. BA summa cum laude, Colgate U., 1952; JD magna cum laude, Harvard U., 1955. Bar: N.Y. 1956, U.S. Dist. Ct. (so. and ea. dists.) N.Y. 1961, U.S. Dist. Ct. Conn. 1961, U.S. Ct. Appeals (2d cir.) 1961. Staff judge adv. Judge Adv. Gen.'s Group, 1955—57; assoc. Patterson, Belknap, Webb & Tyler, NYC, 1957—64, ptnr., 1965—92. Co-author: The Law and the Lore of Endowment Funds, 1969, The Developing Law of Endowment Funds, 1974; contbr. articles to law jours. Capt. USAF, 1955—57. Mem.: ABA, Assn. of Bar of City of N.Y., N.Y. State Bar Assn. (chmn. com. on profl. ethics 1981—84), Hermitage Club Goochland, Va. Republican. Presbyterian. Home and Office: 21 Hunting Ridge Rd Manakin Sabot VA 23103-2614 Personal E-mail: cbbasb@comcast.net.

BRIGHT, DAVID FORBES, academic administrator, classicist, educator; b. Winnipeg, Man., Can., Apr. 13, 1942; s. John Hamilton and Pauline Murray (Forbes) B.; m. Marlene Joanne Mayercik, Feb. 20, 1965; children: Jennifer, Sarah. BA (hons.), U. Man., 1962; AM, U. Cin., 1963, PhD, 1967. Asst. prof. classics Williams Coll., Williamstown, Mass., 1967—70; from asst. to assoc. prof. classics U. Ill., Urbana-Champaign, 1970—85, prof. classics and comparative lit., 1985—89, chmn. dept. classics, 1977-81, 85-88, dir. comparative lit. dept., 1986—88, acting dean Coll. Liberal Arts and Scis., 1988—89; dean Coll. Liberal Arts and Scis. Iowa State U., Ames, 1989—91; dean, v.p. for arts and scis. Emory U., Atlanta, 1991—97, prof. classics and comparative lit., 1991—, chmn. dept. classics, 1999—2005, dir. comparative lit., 1999—2001. Author: Haec mihi fingebam. Tibullus in his World, 1978, Elaborate Disarray: The Nature of Statius' Silvae, 1980, Miniature Epic in Vandal Africa, 1987, The Academic Deanship, 2001; editor: Classical Texts and Their Traditions, 1984. Bd. dirs. Atlanta Ballet Co., Savoyards Light Opera, Atlanta Baroque Orch., Coun. Colls. Arts and Scis., pres. 1996-97. Woodrow Wilson Found. fellow, 1962, U. Cin. travel fellow Am. Acad. in Rome, 1965-66, Am. Council Learned Socs. fellow, 1981-82; Rsch. scholar Delmas Found., 1987. Mem. Am. Philol. Assn., Classical Assn. Middle West and South (exec. com. 1985-89, pres. 1989), Vergilian Soc. (trustee 1983-86), Soc. of Fellows Am. Acad. Rome. Episcopalian. Home: 2646 Ramgewood Dr NE Atlanta GA 30345-1516 Office: Emory U Dept Classics 221F Candler Libr Atlanta GA 30322-0001 Office Phone: 404-727-4404. Business E-Mail: david.bright@emory.edu.

BRIGHT, KEVIN S., producer; b. 1954; Dir. prodn. Bright-Kauffman-Crane Prodns., Burbank, Calif. Creator, exec. prodr. Dream On, 1990-96 (Cable Ace award), Friends, 1994-2004 (Emmy nominee 1995, 96), Veronica's Closet, 1997-2000, Jesse, 1998-2000; exec. prodr. Ron Reagan Show, 1990; prodr. The Adventures of Brisco County, Jr., 1993-94; exec. prodr. Joey, 2004—. Office: Bright-san Prodns 16030 Ventura Blvd Ste 380 Encino CA 91436

BRIGHT, MARGARET, sociologist; b. Bentonville, Ark., Nov. 19, 1918; d. William Ray and Edna May (Woolwine) B.; m. Herman Binder, 1983. AB, U. Calif., Berkeley, 1941; MA, U. Mo., 1944; PhD, U. Wis., 1950. Lectr. rural sociology U. Mo., 1944-47; asst. project dir. U. P.R., 1950-51; acting assoc. prof. Cornell U., 1951-52; social affairs officer population br. UN, NYC, 1952-54; research assoc. Bur. Applied Social Research Columbia U., NYC, 1954-57; sociologist-demographer UN Tech. Assistance, Bombay, India, 1957-59; asst. prof. chronic diseases Johns Hopkins U., Balt., 1959-63, assoc. prof., 1963-68; dir. research Center for Urban Affairs, 1968-72, assoc. prof. behavioral scis., 1968-70, prof., 1970-83, prof. emerita, 1983—. Mem. U.S. Mission Coop. Health and Sanitation to, Brazil, 1960. Author: Cooperativas de Consumo de Puerto Rico: Análisis Socio-Económicó, 1957; co-author: Graduates of American Schools of Public Health, 1976; contbr. articles to profl. jours. Mem. Balt. Mayor's Task Force on Polit. Redistricting, 1971; mem. Rockefeller Commn. on Population and the Am. Future, 1970-72. Mem. Am. Pub. Health Assn. Democrat. Office: 624 N Broadway Baltimore MD 21205-1900 Home: 105 W 39th St Apt P-1 Baltimore MD 21210

BRIGHT, MYRON H., federal judge; b. Eveleth, Minn., Mar. 5, 1919; s. Morris and Lena A. Bright; m. Frances Louise Reisler, Dec. 26, 1947; children: Dinah Ann, Joshua Robert. AA, Eveleth Junior Coll, 1939; BSL, U. Minn., 1941, JD, 1947. Bar: N.D. 1947, Minn. 1947. Assoc. Wattam, Vogel, Vogel & Bright, Fargo, ND, 1947—49, ptnr., 1949—68; judge US Ct. Appeals (8th cir.), Fargo, 1968—85, sr. judge, 1985—; disting. prof. law St. Louis U., 1985—88, emeritus prof. of law, 1989—95. Lectr. Thomas Jefferson Sch. of Law, 2003—. Capt. USAF, 1942—46. Recipient Francis Rawle award, ALI-ABA, 1996, Lifetime Achievement award, U. N.D. Law Sch., 1998, Herbert Harley award, AJS, 2000. Mem.: ABA, Fed. Judges Assn., Cass County Bar Assn., Bar Assn. Met. St. Louis, US Jud. Conf. (com. on adminstrn. of probation sys. 1977—83, adv. com. on appellate rules 1987—90, com. on internat. jud. rels. 1996—2003), N.D. Bar Assn. Office: US Ct Appeals 8th Cir 655 1st Ave N Ste 340 Fargo ND 58102-4952 also: Thomas F Eagleton US Courthouse 111 S 10th St Rm 26 325 Saint Louis MO 63102*

BRIGHT, WILLARD MEAD, retired manufacturing executive, director; b. NYC, Mar. 26, 1914; s. William Van Horn and Bernice Hartwell (Reynolds) B.; m. Martha Norris Land, May 15, 1944 (dec.); 1 child, Willard Mead; m. Virginia L. Jones, Mar. 14, 1981 (div. Aug. 1996). BS, U. Toledo, 1936, MS, 1937; postgrad., U. Pitts., 1937-38; A.M., Harvard U., 1941, PhD, 1942. Research chemist Kendall Co., Boston, Chgo., 1942-52; asst. lab. dir. Kendall Co. (Bauer & Black div.), 1944-48; lab. dir. (Theodore Clark Lab. div.), Cambridge, Mass., 1948-52; asst. research dir. Lever Bros. Co., 1952-54, research dir., 1954-60, v.p. research and devel., 1960-64; chmn. bd. W. H. Norris Lumber Co., Houston, 1957-64; treas. Border Lumber Co., Weslaco, Tex., 1957-64; v.p. R.J. Reynolds Tobacco Co., 1964-68; sr. v.p., pres. profl. products group Warner-Lambert Pharm. Co., 1968-70; pres., chief exec. officer Kendall Co., Boston, 1970-73; pres. Curtiss-Wright Corp., 1973-74, Boehringer Mannheim Corp., 1974-81; chmn. Zoll Med. Corp, 1982-96; ret., 1996. Bd. dirs. Zoll Med. Corp.; mem. adv. com. on patents U.S. Dept. Commerce, 1966-69; mem. bd. visitors dept. chemistry Boston U. Recipient Gold T award U. Toledo, 1960 Mem. N.A.M. (chmn. sci. tech. com. dir. 1970-73), Am. Chem. Soc., N.Y. Acad. Scis., Assn. Rsch. Dirs., Indsl. Rsch. Inst. (dir. 1963-69, pres. 1967-68), Dirs. Indsl. Rsch., Sigma Xi, Phi Kappa Phi, Harvard Club (Boston), Comml. Club (Boston), The Country Club (Brookline, Mass.), Bent Pine Golf Club (Vero Beach, Fla.). Home: 105 Prestwick Cir Vero Beach FL 32967-7514

BRIGHTBILL, DAVID JOHN, lawyer, former state legislator; s. Johnathan McMichael and Verda (McGill) Brightbill; m. Donna J. Long; children: J. David, Jonathan D., Andrew J., Christian M. BA, Pa. State U., 1964; JD, Duquesne U., 1970. Sch. dir. Lebanon (Pa.) Sch. Dist., 1965-67; dist. atty. Lebanon, Pa., 1977-81; mem. Pa. Senate, Dist. 48, Harrisburg, Pa., 1982—2007, majority leader, 2001—06, chmn. environ. resources & energy com., 2000—06; of counsel Stevens & Lee P.C., Reading, Pa., 2007—. Office: Stevens & Lee PC 111 N Sixth St PO Box 679 Reading PA 19603 E-mail: djb@stevenslee.com.

BRIGHTON, GERALD DAVID, retired finance educator; b. Weldon, Ill., May 14, 1920; s. William Henry and Geneva (Ennis) B.; m. Lois Helen Robbins, June 7, 1949; children: Anne, William, Joan, John, Jeffrey. BS, U. Ill., 1941, MS, 1947, PhD, 1953. CPA Ill. Instr. accountancy U. Ill., Urbana, 1947-53, prof., 1954-83, Ernst & Whinney Disting. prof., 1983-88, prof. emeritus, 1988—, dir. undergrad. acctg. program, 1978-86; staff acct. Touche, Niven, Bailey & Smart, Chgo., 1953-54. Cons. G.D. Brighton, C.P.A., Urbana, 1954—; vis. prof. U. Tex.-Austin, 1973; program specialist Dept. HUD, Washington, 1979; vice chmn. U. Ill. Athletic Assn., Urbana, 1982-86 Contbr. articles to profl. jours. Alderman City of Urbana, 1967-69; officer, bd. dirs. U. Ill. YMCA, Champaign, 1959-81, 89-95, trustee, 2002—; bd. dirs. Wesley Found., U. Ill., 1986—; treas. John Gwinn for Congress, Urbana, 1982-83, Green Meadows coun. Girl Scouts U.S., 1981-83. Served to maj. U.S. Army, 1941-46. AACSB Faculty fellow, 1978-79; recipient Bronze Tablet for high honors U. Ill., 1941 Mem. AICPA (hon.), Ill. Soc. CPAs (disting.), Am. Acctg. Assn., Assn. Govt. Accts., Govtl. Fin. Officers Assn., Nat. Tax Assn., Tax Inst. Am. Democrat. Methodist. Home: 501 Evergreen Ct Urbana IL 61801-5928 Office: U Ill 1206 S 6th St Champaign IL 61820-6978 Personal E-mail: gbrighton@sbcglobal.net. *Happiness comes very indirectly. "Seek and ye shall find." That is at best a half truth. If we rely on direct rewards for our happiness we are in trouble. At best, the string of treats will be irregular. The key is to widen one's circle. Try to rejoice in the good fortunes of your colleagues. Sometimes, jealousy gets in the way. What is the greatest satisfaction I have had from teaching? It is the occasional glimpses that I see that former students are doing well.*

BRIGHTON, JOHN A., mechanical engineer, academic administrator; b. Gosport, Ind. BS in mech. engring., Purdue U., 1959, MS in mech. engring., 1960, PhD in mech. engring., 1963. Design draftsman Schwitzer Corp., Indpls., 1952—55; instr. mech. engring. Purdue U., 1960—62; tech. staff Aerospace Corp., El Segundo, Calif., 1962; asst. prof. mech. engring. Carnegie-Mellon U., 1963—65; asst. prof. mech. engring Pa. State U., 1965—67, assoc. prof. mech. engring., 1967—77; chmn. dept. mech. engring. Mich. State U., 1977-82; dir. Sch. Mech. Engring. Ga. Inst. Tech., 1982-88; dean Coll. Engring. Pa. State U., 1988-91, exec. v.p., provost, 1991—99, U. Prof., chair Tchg. and Learning Consortium, 1999—2002; provost Nat.-Louis U., Chgo., 2002—03; asst. dir. for engring. NSF, 2003—. Named Disting. Engring. Alumni, Purdue U., 2004; recipient Rodney D. Chipp Meml. Award, Soc. Women Engineers, 1992. Fellow: Am. Soc. Engring. Edn., ASME. Office: NSF 4201 Wilson Blvd Arlington VA 22230 Office Phone: 703-292-8300. E-mail: jbrighto@nsf.gov.

BRIGHTON, LOUIS ANDREW, religious studies educator; b. Saskatoon, Sask., Can., Oct. 30, 1927; s. Louis Frederick Brighton and Helen Ester Frinke; m. Mary Belle Williams; children: Stephan Louis, Anne Louise, Christine Marie, Mary Helen, Mark Andrew. BA, Concordia Coll., 1950; MDiv, Concordia Sem., 1952, STM, 1964; PhD, St. Louis U., 1991; grad., N.Y. Inst. Photography, 1965. Clergyman Holy Trinity Luth. Ch., London, 1952—58, Our Redeemer Luth. Ch., Decatur, Ill., 1958—68, St. John Luth. Ch., Lexington, Ky., 1968—74; prof. NT and bibl. langs. Concordia Sem., St. Louis, 1974—. Author: Commentary on Revelation, 1999; contbr. articles to profl. jours. Luth. chaplain London Prisons, 1957; juvenile chaplain Decatur Jail, 1958—68. Staff sgt. US Army, 1946—48, Korea. Named Ky. col., Gov. Louie B. Nunn, 1970. Avocation: photography. Home: 2541 Belmont Dr High Ridge MO 63049 Office: Concordia Seminary 801 DeMun Ave Saint Louis MO 63105 Office Phone: 314-505-7127. Personal E-mail: mbrighton@sbcglobal.net.

BRIGHTON, RUTH LOUISE, lay worker, educator; b. Harrisburg, Pa., Apr. 18, 1931; d. Paul Gerhard and Ruth Genevieve (Lee) Krentz; m. Carl T. Brighton, July 27, 1954; children: David, Susan, Andrew, Joel. BA, Valparaiso U., 1953; MS in Math., U. Wis., 1955. Cert. tchr. Tchr. Sunday sch., adult Bible class Christ Meml. Luth. Ch., Malvern, Penn., 1969—; coord. adult edn., Ea. dist. Luth. Ch.-Mo. Synod, Buffalo, 1986-89, bd. dirs., 1988-90. Bd. dirs. Concordia Pub. House, St. Louis, 1989—2001. Teaching fellow in math. U. Wis., 1953. Home: 14 Flintshire Rd Malvern PA 19355-1108

BRILES, JUDITH, writer, consultant; b. Pasadena, Calif., Feb. 20, 1946; d. James and Mary Tuthill; children: Shelley, Sheryl, Frank (dec.), William (dec.). MBA, Pepperdine U., 1980; PhD, Nova U., 1990. Brokers asst. Bateman, Eichler, Hill, Richards, Torrance, Calif., 1969-72; account exec. E. F. Hutton, Palo Alto, Calif., 1972-78; pres. Judith Briles & Co., Palo Alto, 1978-85, Briles & Assocs., Palo Alto, 1980-86; ptnr. Briles Group, Inc., Aurora, Colo., 1987—, Colo. Book Shepherd, 2007. Instr. Menlo Coll., 1986-87, Skyline Coll., 1981-86, U. Calif.-Berkeley Sch. Continuing Edn., U. Calif.-Santa Cruz Sch. Continuing Edn., U. Hawaii; mem. adv. coun. Miss Am. Pageant, 1989-95, No-nonsense Panty Hose, 1989-92, Colo. Women's News, 1993-97; founder Colo. Authors Hall of Fame, 2005-. Author: The Woman's Guide to Financial Savvy, 1981, Money Phases, 1984, Woman to Woman: From Sabotage to Support, 1987, Dollars and Sense of Divorce, 1988, Faith and Savvy Too!, 1988, When God Says No, 1990, The Confidence Factor, 1990 (Bus. Book of Yr, 2003), Money Guide, 1991, The Workplace Factor, 1990, Money Guide, 1991, The Workplace: Questions Women Ask, 1992, Financial Savvy for Women, 1992, The Briles Report on Women in Healthcare, 1994, Money Sense, 1995, Gender Traps, 1996, Raising Money Wise Kids, 1996, When God Says No, 1997, The Dollars and Sense of Divorce, 1998, Woman to Woman 2000, 1999 (chgo. Tribune Bus. Book of Yr.), 10 Smart Money Moves for Women, 1999(Book of Yr., 2002), Smart Money Moves for Kids, 2000 (Best How to Parenting, 2001), The Confidence Factor—Cosmic Goose Lay Golden Eggs, 2001, Stop Stabbing Yourself in the Back, 2001, Zapping Conflict in the Healthcare Workplace, 2003, Money Smarts, 2005; columnist Colo. Woman News, Denver Bus. Jour., MsMoney.com, Men in Nursing. Pres., v.p., sec., bd. dirs. foothill-DeAnza Coll. Found., Los Altos Hills, Calif., 1979-90; bd. dirs. Col. Nurses Task Force, Col. League Nursing, 1994-95; mem. adv. bd. Flint Ctr., Cupertino, Calif. Mem. NAFE (adv. bd. bus. woman's mag. 1981-86), Peninsula Profl. Women's Network, Nat. Speaker's Assn. (bd. dirs.), WISH List (bd. dirs. 1998-2002), Colo. Ind. Pubs. Assn. (bd. dirs. 2000-, pres. 2002-05), Gilda's Club (Denver bd. dirs. 2001-04, pres., v.p.). Independent. Office Phone: 303-627-9179. Personal E-mail: drjbriles@aol.com. Business E-Mail: judith@briles.com.

BRILEY-SAEBO, KAREN CATHERIN, physics professor; b. Oxford, Ohio, Oct. 27, 1964; d. Nancy Magrum and Mike Briley; m. Jan-Eystein Saeboe, July 1, 1989; children: Alexander Saebo, Lisa Saebo, Magnus. BSc, Ohio State U., 1987; PhD in Med. Physics, U. Uppsala, Sweden, 2004. Sr. rsch. scientist Amersham Health Care, Oslo, 1989—2004; fellow Mt. Sinai Sch. Medicine, NYC, 2005—. Contbr. articles to profl. jours. Mem.: Am. Heart Assn., NY Acad. Sci. Achievements include patents for external calibration standards for MRI; use of USPIOs to determine in vivo blood oxygenation levels; use of MRA agents to evaluate both renal function and morphology; use of MRA agents during induced passive catheter tracking; use of Mn chelates for evaluation cardiac perfusion; sodium shift agents for determination of intracellular sodium. Office: Mt Sinai Sch Medicine PO Box 1234 One Gustave Levy Pl New York NY 10029 Office Phone: 1-212-241-6858. Business E-Mail: k_saeboe@yahoo.com.

BRILL, AARON BERTRAND, nuclear medicine educator; b. NYC, Dec. 19, 1928; s. Louis And Cecile (Sroge) B.; m. Joan Booth Morrison, Sept. 1, 1950; children: Paul, David, Laurie. AB, Grinnell Coll., 1949; MD, U. Utah, 1956; PhD in Biophysics, U. Calif., Berkeley, 1961. Statistician Contra Costa County Health Dept., Martinez, Calif., 1949—50; res. asst. U. Calif., Donner Lab, 1950—52; biophysicist U. Utah Pediatrics Dept., Salt Lake City, 1952-56; intern Salt Lake City Gen. Hosp., 1956-57; USPHS officer Div. of Radiol. Health, Rockville, Md., 1957-64; asst. prof. radiology dept. radiology scis. Johns Hopkins Hosp. and Sch. of Hygiene, 1961-64; assoc. prof. radiol. Vanderbilt U. Sch. Medicine, Nashville, 1964-72; assoc. prof. medicine, biomed. engring. and physics, 1964-79; prof. radiology Vanderbilt U. Sch. Medicine, Nashville, 1972-79, SUNY, Stony Brook, 1979-87; sr. scientist, nuc. medicine coord. Brookhaven (N.Y.) Nat. Lab., 1979-87; prof. nuclear medicine U. Mass. Sch. Medicine, Worcester, 1987—97. Rsch. affiliate MIT, Cambridge, 1993-2005; affil. prof. Worcester Poly. Inst., Worcester, 1995-97; rsch. prof. radiol. sci. Vanderbilt U. Sch. Medicine, Nashville, 1997—, rsch. prof. physics, adj. prof. biomed. engring. Editor: Low Level Radiation Fact Book, 1st edit. 1982, 2d edit., 1985; editor: IEEE Trans Med. Imaging, 1986-92. Med. dir. USPHS, 1957-64, U. Calif. at Berkeley fellow, 1959-61. Fellow IEEE, Am. Coll. Nuclear Physicians, Am. Inst. Med. and Biol. Engring.; mem. NAS (com. on atomic casualties 1964-70, com. on biol. effects of ionizing radiation 1978-80; com.to assess sci. info. for radiation exposure and edn. program 2004-06, com. on assessment of CDC and prevention radiation studies from DOE contractor sites 2002-04, nat. coun. on radiation protection and measurement 1972-82, 92-97). Avocations: tennis, sailing, skiing. Office: Vanderbilt U Med Sch Dept Radiol Sci Mcn S1314 Nashville TN 37232-2675 Office Phone: 615-322-3190. Business E-Mail: aaron.brill@vanderbilt.edu.

BRILL, ALAN RICHARD, entrepreneur; b. Evansville, Ind., July 5, 1942; s. Gregory and Bernice Lucille (Froman) B.; children: Jennifer Leigh, Katherine Anne, Alison Elizabeth. AB, DePauw U., 1964; MBA, Harvard U., 1968. Mgmt. cons. Peace Corps, Ecuador, 1964-66; sr. acct., cons. Arthur Young & Co., NYC, 1968-71; v.p. ops. Charter Med. Mgmt. Co., Inc., 1972-73; v.p. controller Hosp. Investors, Atlanta, 1972-73; v.p., treas., dir. Worrell Newspapers, Inc., Worrell Broadcasting, Inc., Charlottesville, Va., 1973-79; pres. Brill Assocs., Evansville, Ind., 1979—, Brill Media Co., Inc., Evansville, Ind., 1980—. Bd. visitors U. So. Ind. Sch. Bus. Mem. AICPA, N.Y. State Soc. CPAs, Evansville C. of C. (bd. dirs.), Jobs for S.W. Ind. (bd. dirs.), Beacon Group, Farmington Country Club (Charlottesville), Safari Internat. Club. Republican. Methodist. Home: PO Box 3517 Evansville IN 47734-3517 Office: Brill Media Co Inc PO Box 3353 Evansville IN 47732-3353

BRILL, DONALD MAXIM, researcher, educator; b. Elk Mound, Wis., Sept. 8, 1922; s. John James and Grace Darling (Mayo) B.; m. Meredith Joy Wright, June 25, 1955; children: John Richard, Rebecca Jean, Linda Marie, Susan Elizabeth. BS, Stout State U., 1947; MA, U. Minn., 1949; PhD, U. Wis., Madison, 1973. Tchr. Mpls. Pub. Schs., 1949-50, Eau Claire (Wis.) Pub. Schs., 1950, Chippewa Valley Tech. Coll., 1951-58; supr. Wis. Tech. Colls., Madison, 1958-65; coord. Great Cities Program for Sch. Improvement Rsch. Coun., Chgo., 1965-67; supr. rsch. Wis. Tech. Colls., Madison, 1967-70, asst. state dir., 1970-83. Adj. prof. U. Wis., Stout, 1983-86. Mem. State Com. Employer Support Guard and Res., 1983-86; mem. Eau Claire Area Sch. Bd., 1989-92; founding bd. dirs. Fourth Dimension, Inc., WHEM-FM, 1994-98; primary candidate 3d Congl. Dist., Wis., 1994. With U.S. Army, 1942-45, ETO Mem. DAV (life), VFW (life), SAR (chpt. pres.), Am. Vocat. Assn. (life), The Mayflower Soc. (life). Republican. Baptist. Avocations: writing, genealogy, poetry, travel. Home: W2745 Mitchell Rd Eau Claire WI 54701-8603 E-mail: dmb316@charter.net.

BRILL, KENNETH C., federal official, former ambassador; b. Ft. Hood, Tex., Oct. 13, 1947; m. Mary Lee Pfeifer; children: Katherine, Christopher BS, Ohio U., 1969; MS, U. Calif., Berkeley, 1973. With US Fgn. Svc., 1975—, posted Accra, 1976-78, staff asst. African Bur., 1978-79, desk officer, 1979-81; spl. asst. to under sec. for polit. affairs US Dept. State, 1981-82, dep. dir., then dir. Office of Egyptian Affairs, 1982-84, counselor for polit. affairs Amman, 1984-86, consul gen. Calcutta, 1986-89, exec. asst. to under sec. for polit. affairs Washington, 1989-91, dep. chief of mission, charge d'affaires New Delhi, 1991-94, exec. dept. sec. & spl. asst. to sec. Washington, 1994, U.S. amb. to Republic of Cyprus Nicosia, 1996—99, prin. dep. asst. sec. for oceans, internat. environment & scientific affairs Washington, 1999—2001, acting asst. sec. for oceans, internat. environment & scientific affairs, 2001, U.S. rep. to the IAEA Vienna, 2001—04, U.S. rep. to the UN, 2001—04; internat. affairs advisor to the comdt. Industrial Coll. of the Armed Forces, 2004—05; dir. Nat. Counterproliferation Ctr. Office Nat. Intelligence, Washington, 2005—. With U.S. Army, 1970-72. Recipient Disting., Superior and Meritorious Honor award U.S. Dept. State.

BRILL, LAURA W., lawyer; d. Charles B. and Paula W. Brill; life ptnr. Ellen Evans; children: Sophie, Benjamin. AB, Brown U., Providence, RI, 1987; JD, Columbia U., NYC, 1994. Bar: N.Y. 1995, Calif. 1998, U.S. Dist. Ct. (so., ea. and we. dists.) N.Y. 1998, U.S. Dist. Ct. (so., ctrl., no. dists.) Calif. 2001, U.S. Ct. Appeals (3d, 4th, 5th, 9th and fed. cirs.), U.S. Supreme Ct. Law clk. to Hon. Wilfred Feinberg, U.S. Ct. Appeals (2d cir.), NYC, 1994—95; assoc. Howard Darby & Levin, LLP, NYC, 1996; law clk. to Hon. Ruth Bader Ginsburg, U.S. Supreme Ct., Washington, 1996—97; assoc. Irell & Manella, LLP, LA, 1997—2000, ptnr., 2001—. Mem. com. State Bar Calif. Com. on Appellate Cts., 2003—06; mem. bd. visitors Columbia U. Sch. Law, 2005—. Book rev. editor: Columbia Law Review, 1993—94; contbr. articles to profl. jours. Named So. Calif. Super Lawyer, L.A. Mag., 2005, 2006; named one of Top 75 Women Litigators in Calif., L.A. and San Francisco Daily Jour., 2006; recipient James Kent scholarship, Columbia U. Sch. Law, 1992, 1994, Harlan Fiske Stone scholarship, 1993, John Ordroneaux prize, 1994, Emil Schlesinger Labor Law prize, 1994, Defender of Democracy award, People for the Am. Way, 2000. Mem.: ABA (sect. litigation co-chair com. on pro bono and pub. interest litigatio 2005—), Fed. Bar Assn. (LA. chpt. bd. dirs. 2005—). Office: Irell and Manella LLP 1800 Avenue of the Stars Los Angeles CA 90067 Office Phone: 310-277-1010. Office Fax: 310-203-7199. Business E-Mail: lbrill@irell.com.

BRILL, LESLEY, literature and film studies educator; b. Chgo., Sept. 3, 1943; s. Walter Henry and Fay (Trolander) B.; m. Megan Parry, Jan. 18, 1970; children: Benjamin, Calista. BA, U. Chgo., 1965; MA, SUNY, Binghamton, 1967; PhD, Rutgers U., 1971. Asst. prof. English U. Colo., Boulder, 1970-80, assoc. prof., 1981-89, chmn. dept. English, 1981-85, grad. dir., 1985-87; prof. English dept. Wayne State U., Detroit, 1989—, prof. and chmn. dept. English, 1989-94. Vis. lectr. U. Kent, Canterbury, Eng., 1978-79; vis. prof. U. Paul Valery, Montpellier, France, 1984, U. de Nantes, France, 1995. Author: The Hitchcock Romance: Love and Irony in Hitchcock's Films, 1988, John Huston's Filmmaking, 1997, Crowds, Power and Transformation in Cinema, 2006; contbr. articles on lit. and film to profl. jours. Rockefeller Found. fellow, 1977-78. Mem. Soc. Cinema Studies. Office: Wayne State U Dept English Detroit MI 48202 E-mail: aa4525@wayne.edu.

BRILL, MICHAEL HENRY, physicist, editor; b. Bay Shore, NY, Jan. 26, 1949; s. Henry and Wenonah (Beale) B. BA in English and Physics, Case Western Res. U., Cleve., 1965—69; MS in Physics, Syracuse U., 1969—71, PhD in Physics, 1971—76. Postdoctoral fellow MIT, Cambridge, 1974—77; physicist Perception Tech. Corp., Winchester, Mass., 1977—79; chief scientist Solotest Corp., Framingham, Mass., 1979; sr. scientist Jaycor, Alexandria, Va., 1980—83; sr. staff scientist Sci. Applications Internat. Corp., McLean and Falls Church, Va., 1983—94; mem. tech. staff Sarnoff Corp., Princeton, NJ, 1994—2001; ind. cons., 2001—03; book-review editor Physics Today, College Park, Md., 2002—03; prin. color scientist Datacolor, Lawrenceville, NJ, 2003—07, mgr. sci. and tech., 2007—. Pres. Inter-Soc. Color Coun., 1998-2000; chmn. tech. com. 1-56 improved color matching functions Internat. Illumination Commn., 1999—; chmn. color appearance analysis subcom. Am. Soc. Testing and Materials Internat., 2005-. Co-author: Dimensional Analysis through Perspective, 1990, 2d edit., 2004; assoc. editor Physics Essays, 1995—, mem. editl. bd. Color Rsch. and Application, 1990—; contbr. articles to profl. jours.; reviewer in field:. 2d lt. USAF, 1972. Co-recipient Emmy award for outstanding tech. achievement Nat. Acad. TV Arts and Scis., 2000. Mem. ASTM Internat. (chair tech. subcom. color and appearance analysis 2005—), Optical Soc. Am., Soc. for Info. Display, Soc. for Imaging Sci. and Tech., Inter-Soc. Color Coun. (Macbeth award 1996), Phi Beta Kappa Achievements include development of a retina model with adaptive contrast sensitivity and receptor; volumetric theory of color constancy; broken-mirror model of acoustic rough-surface scattering; formulation of theories of perspective invariance in images; patents in field. Avocations: poetry writing, ping pong/table tennis, recreational mathematics. Home: PO Box 465 14 Basin St Kingston NJ 08528 Office: Datacolor 5 Princess Rd Lawrenceville NJ 08468 Office Phone: 609-895-7432. Business E-Mail: mbrill@datacolor.com.

BRILL, RICHARD C., physical science educator; b. Sacramento, July 25, 1946; MS, U. Hawaii, 1975. Rsch. asst. geochronology U. Hawaii, Manoa, Honolulu, 1970—72, tchg. asst., 1972—74, rsch. assoc. geochemistry dept. oceanography, 1976—78, premed. advisor Coll. Arts and Scis., 1979—84; lectr. Honolulu CC, 1974—76, prof. phys. sci., 1984—; lectr. Kapiolani CC, Honolulu, 1977—79. Rschr. NSF, Mc Murdo, Antarctica, None, 1978—79; cons., mem. liberal arts program coun. Western Gov.'s U., Salt Lake City, 1997—; fellow Lawrence Berkeley (Calif.) Lab., 1992. Prodr.(prodr., writer, talent): (TV production) Introduction to Geology: Earth Revealed; graphic artist, web page designer: online textbook The Nature of Physical Science, newspaper columnist: Facts of the Matter; actor: (live theater) Inherit the Wind, Miss Firecracker Contest, Alone Together; prodr.(prodr. camera operator, editor, title designer): (video production) Archival productions of live theater; columnist: Professor Science, Honolulu Advertiser; prodr., director, writer, graphic artist, talent: (TV production) The Nature of Physical Science. Mem. Govs. Hawaii Innovation Coun., 2007—. With US Army, 1966—69. Avocations: photography, videography, travel, kayaking, computer software. Office: Honolulu CC 874 Dillingham Blvd Honolulu HI 96817-4598 Office Phone: 808-845-9488. Business E-Mail: rickb@hcc.hawaii.edu.

BRILL, STEVEN, magazine editor; b. Queens, NY, Aug. 22, 1950; married; 2 children. BA summa cum laude, Yale U., 1972, JD, 1975. Asst. to the Mayor N.Y.C., 1972-73; contbg. editor, columnist New York mag., 1974-76; law columnist and writer Esquire mag., NYC, 1977-79; founder, editor-in-chief American Lawyer mag., NYC, 1978-82; exec. v.p. AM-LAW Pub. Corp., NYC, 1978-82; pres., CEO, editor-in-chief Courtroom TV Network, Am. Lawyer Media, L.P., 1982; founder Brill's Content mag., 1997—2001; contbg. editor, columnist NBC, 2001; lectr. Yale U., New Haven. Author: Firearms Control--A Research and Policy Report, 1976, The Teamsters, 1978; freelance writer Harper's mag., 1974-76. Recipient John Hancock award for Bus. Journalism, 1976, Nat. Mag. award for Essays and Criticism, 1983, Nat. Mag. award, 1991. Mem. Phi Beta Kappa. Office: Yale U 63 High St Rm 109 PO Box 208302 New Haven CT 06520-8302 Office Phone: 203-432-2233. Office Fax: 203-432-7066.

BRILL, STEVEN CHARLES, financial planner, lawyer; b. Miami, Fla., Aug. 21, 1953; s. Arthur W. and Joan K. (Caveretta) B. AB, Boston U., 1975; JD, Western New Eng. Coll., 1978; LLM, NYU, 1986. Advanced underwriting cons. Equitable Life Assurance Soc., NYC, 1978-79; sr. advanced underwriting cons. Met. Life Ins. Co., NYC, 1979-85; asst. v.p. personal fin. planning group Dean Witter Reynolds, NYC, 1985-87; v.p., dir. asset allocation group Chase Pvt. Bank, NYC, 1987-98; prin. Spielberger, Dampf, Brill & Levine, LLC, 1998—. Chmn. Cmty. Housing Innovations, Inc.; past pres., dir. Wychwood Owner's Corp., Great Neck, NY, Realty of Bay Terr. Inc., Bayside, NY; pres. Hillpark Columns Housing Corp., Great Neck NY. Contbr. articles to Mature Outlook Mag. Avocations: skiing, tennis, golf. Home: 7 Hillpark Ave Unit E Great Neck NY 11021 Office Phone: 516-870-0024. Personal E-mail: brilladvis@aol.com.

BRILL, YVONNE CLAEYS, engineer, consultant; b. St. Norbert, Manitoba, Can., Dec. 30, 1924; d. August and Julienne (Carette) Claeys; m. William Franklin Brill, Dec. 15, 1951; children: Naomi, Matthew, Joseph. BS, U. Manitoba, Canada, 1945; MS, U. So. Calif., 1951. Mathematician Douglas Aircraft, Santa Monica, Calif., 1945-46; research analyst Rand Corp., Santa Monica, 1946-49; group leader Marquardt Corp., Van Nuys, Calif., 1949-52; staff engr. UTC Research, East Hartford, Conn., 1952-55; project engr. Wright Aeronautical, Wood Ridge, NJ, 1955-58; mgr. propulsion systems RCA AstroElectronics, Princeton, NJ, 1966-81, staff engr., 1983-86; mgr. solid rocket motor NASA Hdqrs., Washington, 1981-83; with space engring segment Internat. Maritime Satellite Orgn., London, 1986-91; cons. Brill Assocs., Skillman, NJ, 1991—. Mem. USAF Sci. Adv. Bd., Washington, 1982-83, Nat. Acad. Engring.; Com. on Internat. Orgns. and Programs, 1992-96; apptd. mem. aerospace safety adv. panel NASA, 1994-2001. Contbr. articles to sci. jours.; patentee in field. Recipient Engr. of Yr. award, Ctrl. Jersy Engring. Couns., 1979, Diamond Superwoman award, Harpers Bazaar/DeBeers Corp., 1980, Disting. Pub. Svc. medal, NASA, 2001, Judith A. Resnik award, IEEE, 2002. Fellow AIAA (Marvin C. Demlar award 1983, WYLD award in rocket propulsion 2002), Soc. Women Engrs. (dir. student affairs 1979-80, 83-84, treas. 1980-81, Engring. Achievement award 1986, Resnik Challenger medal 1993); mem. Nat. Acad. Engring., Internat. Astronautical Acad. (academician, edn. com. 1983-85), Sigma Xi, Tau Beta Pi. Home and Office: 914 Route 518 Skillman NJ 08558-2616

BRILLIANT, ASHLEIGH ELLWOOD, cartoonist, writer; b. London, Dec. 9, 1933; came to the U.S., 1956, naturalized, 1969; s. Victor and Amelia (Adler) B.; m. Dorothy Low Tucker, June 28, 1968. BA with honors, Univ. Coll., London, 1955; MA in Edn., Claremont Grad. Sch., 1957; PhD in Am. History, U. Calif., Berkeley, 1964. Tchr. English Hollywood H.S., LA, 1956-57; tchg. asst., reader in history U. Calif., Berkeley, 1960-63; asst. prof. history Ctrl. Oreg. Coll., Bend, 1964-65, Floating Campus divsn. Chapman Coll., Orange, Calif., 1965-67; entertainer in coffeehouses, outdoor spkr. San Francisco, 1967-68; syndicated cartoonist, dir. Brilliant Enterprises, pub. and licensing, San Francisco, Santa Barbara, Calif., 1967—. Creator Pot-Shots postcards, T-shirts, cocktail napkins, tote-bags, other items; mem. faculty Sonoma State U., Santa Barbara City Coll.; vis. scholar Ctrl. Oregon Cmty. Coll., 2002. Author: I May Not Be Totally Perfect, But Parts of Me Are Excellent, And Other Brilliant Thoughts, 1979, I Have Abandoned My Search for Truth and Am Now Looking for a Good Fantasy, 1980, Appreciate Me Now and Avoid the Rush, 1981, I Feel Much Better Now That I've Given Up Hope, 1984, All I Want Is A Warm Bed and A Kind Word, and Unlimited Power, 1985, I Try to Take One Day At A Time, But Sometimes Several Days Attack Me At Once, 1987, The Great Car Craze: How Southern California Collided With The Automobile in the 1920's, 1989, We've Been Through So Much Together and Most of It Was Your Fault, 1990, Be A Good Neighbor and Leave Me Alone, 1992, I Want to Reach Your Mind.Where is it Currently Located, 1994, I'm Just Moving Clouds Today-Tomorrow I'll Try Mountains, 1999; illustrator: The Illimuniated Life, 1995, Adult Development and Aging, 1995, Give Yourself the Unfair Advantage!, 1995, Designing Effective Organizations, 1995, The Baby Boomers' Guide to Living Forever, 2000, Multiple Streams of Internet Income, 2001, Breaking Free From Boomerang Love, 2004; founder, leader Ban Leafblowers and Save Our Town, 1996. Recipient Raymond B. Bragg award, 1987, Disting. Alumnus of Yr. award Claremont Grad. U., 2000; Claremont Grad. Sch. scholar, 1956; Haynes fellow, 1962, Panama-Pacific fellow, 1963; nominated Poet Laureate, City Santa Barbara, Calif., 2007. Mem. Newspaper Comics Coun., No. Calif. Cartoonists Assn., Mensa. Home and Office: 117 W Valerio St Santa Barbara CA 93101-2927 E-mail: ashleigh@west.net.

BRILLIANT, ELEANOR LURIA, retired social work educator; b. Bklyn., Nov. 25, 1930; d. Joseph and Leah (Cohen) Luria; m. Richard Brilliant, June 24, 1951; children: Stephanie, Livia, Franca, Myron. BA, Smith Coll., Northampton, Mass., 1952; MS, Bryn Mawr Coll., Pa., 1969; DSW, Columbia U., NYC, 1974. Asst. in prodn. course Harvard Bus. Sch., Cambridge, Mass., 1952—54; instr. Bryn Mawr Coll., 1969—71; adminstr., dir. Lower East Side Family Union, NYC, 1974—75; dir. planning/evaluation United Way of Westchester, White Plains, NY, 1975—78, assoc. exec. dir., 1978—80; asst. prof. Columbia U., NYC, 1980—84, assoc. prof., 1984—85; assoc. prof. social work Rutgers U., New Brunswick, NJ, 1986—95, dir. BSW program Livingston Coll., 1987—89, mem. women's studies faculty, 1992—2006, chair, adminstr. policy and planning area MSW program Sch. Social Work, 1992—97, prof., 1995—2006, prof. emeritus, 2006. Cons. United Way of Westchester, White Plains, 1980, Family Info. and Referral Svc. Teams, Inc., White Plains, 1980-83, 87, James Bell Assoc., 1994-96. Author: The Urban Development Corporation: Private Interests and Public Authority, 1975, The United Way: Dilemmas of Organized Charity, 1990, Private Charity and Public Inquiry: A History of the Filer and Peterson Commissions, 2000; assoc. editor: Signs: Jour. of Women in Culture and Society, 2005—, mem. editl. bd.: Nonprofit and Vol. Sector Quar., 2004—. Mem. rsch. com. Women's Philanthropy Inst., 2003—05. U.S. Fulbright grantee, 1972-73, NIMH grantee 1968-69; fellow Douglass Coll., Rutgers U., 1992—. Mem. NASW (rep. to del. assembly 1987, 90, nat. treas. 1989-91), Assn. for Rsch. on Non-Profit Orgns. and Vol. Action (v.p. adminstrn./sec. 1997-99, bd. mem.-at-large 1999-01), Internat. Soc. for Third-Sector Rsch., Assn. for Cmty. Orgn. and Social Adminstrn. Avocations: travel, reading, swimming. Home: 10 Wayside Ln Scarsdale NY 10583-2908 Office: Rutgers U Sch Social Work 536 George St New Brunswick NJ 08901-1167 Personal E-mail: elbrillian@aol.com.

BRILLIANT, LARRY (LAWRENCE BRILLIANT), preventive medicine physician, epidemiologist, technology pioneer, writer, educator, entrepreneur, social venture capitalist; b. May 5, 1944; m. Girija Brilliant; 3 children. Student, U. Mich., 1965; MD, Wayne State U., 1969; MPH, U. Mich., 1977; DSc (hon.), Knox Coll., 2004. Cert. Preventive Medicine and Pub. Health. Med. officer, smallpox eradication and epidemiol. adv. Inter Country Team WHO (regional office-South East Asia, New Delhi), 1973—77; asst. prof., Internat. Health and Epidemiology, Sch. Pub. Health U. Mich., 1977—80, assoc. prof., dept. epidemiology, Sch. Pub. Health, 1981—88; co-founder, CEO The WELL (Whole Earth 'Lectronic Link), 1985—; co-founder, chair Seva Found., Berkeley, 1979, bd. dir., 1979—; mem. GBN network; exec. dir. Google.org, 2006—. Co-founder, CEO of a series of tech.-based companies Network Technologies Inc. and SoftNet Systems; co-founder, CEO Cometa Networks (joint venture with AT&T, IBM and Intel), 2004; epidemiologist, survey mgr. WHO Prevention of Blindness Prog., Katmandu, Nepal, 1980—81; staff mem. WHO Global Commn. to certify smallpox eradicated in Burma, India, Nepal and Iran; last UN WHO med. officer to visit Iran in search of hidden smallpox; vol. first responder for smallpox bioterrorism response effort Ctrs. for Disease Control; spkr. in field. Contbr. articles to profl. jours.; co-author: The Management of Smallpox Eradication in India, 1985; co-author: (with R.P. Pokhrel, N. Grasset, G. Brilliant) The Epidemiology of Blindness in Nepal, 1988; author: Boffa Newsletters. Bd. dir. Wavy Gravy Camp Winnarainbow; volunteered in Sri Lanka for tsunami relief, 2005; worked in India with WHO polio eradication program; established Pandefense; mem. Dean's adv. bd. Berkeley Sch. Pub. Health; mem. adv. bd. Grateful Dead-created Rex Found., Presidio World Coll. MBA program in sustainable bus., Future in Review (FiRe). Named Internat. Pub. Health Hero, U. Calif., Berkeley Sch. Pub. Health; recipient Best Online Pub. award for WELL, Computer Press Assn., 1990, several awards from WHO and Govt. India for work in smallpox eradication, Peacemaker prize, Ctr. for Peace and Conflict Resolution, Wayne State U., Detroit, 2005, Ted prize (awards-a wish to change the world), 2006. Achievements include helping manage the WHO smallpox eradication program in South Asia; served as physician to members of the Grateful Dead. Mailing: Google 1600 Amphitheatre Pky Mountain View CA 94043

BRILLIANT, RICHARD, art historian, educator; b. Boston, Nov. 20, 1929; s. Frank and Pauline (Apt) B.; m. Eleanor Luria, June 24, 1951; children: Stephanie, Livia, Franca, Myron. BA magna cum laude, Yale U., 1951, MA, 1957, PhD, 1960; LLB, Harvard U., 1954. Bar: Mass. 1954. From asst. prof. to prof., chmn. dept. art history U. Pa., Phila., 1962-70; prof. art history and archaeology Columbia U., NYC, 1970—, Anna S. Garbedian prof. in the humanities, 1990—2004, emeritus, 2004—; vis. Mellon prof. fine arts U. Pitts., 1971; vis. prof. Princeton U., 1986. Vis. prof. Scuola Normale Superiore, Pisa, Italy, 1974, 80, 88; chmn. governing bd. Soc. Fellows Columbia U., 1981-84; cons. Sta. WNET-TV, N.Y., 1984-89, N.Y. Hist. Soc., 2004-05; dir. Italian Acad. for Advanced Studies in Am., Columbia U., 1996-00. Author: Gesture and Rank in Roman Art, 1966, Arch of Septimius Severus in the Roman Forum, 1967, The Arts of the Ancient Greeks, 1973, Roman Art, 1974, Pompeii: A.D. 79, 1979, Visual Narratives, 1984, Portraiture, 1991, Commentaries on Roman Art, 1994, Facing the New World, 1997, My Laocoon, 2000, Un Americano a Roma, 2000; co-author: (film) The Fayum Portraits, 1988, editor Art Bull., 1990-94; co-curator exhbn. Ctr. for African Art, N.Y.C., 1990; guest curator, exhibitor Jewish Mus., N.Y.C., 1997; guest curator (exhbn.) Mpls., Inst. Arts, 2003-04, NY Hist. Soc., 2006. Fulbright grantee Rome, Italy, 1957-59; fellow Am. Acad. in Rome, 1960-62; Guggenheim fellow, 1967-68; NEH sr. fellow, 1972-73. Mem.: Am. Acad. Arts and Scis., N.Y. Acad. Sci., Conn. Acad. Arts and Scis., Am. Sch. Classical Studies (mng. com. 1974—2007), Coll. Art Assn. (Disting. Scholar award 2005), German Archaeol. Inst. (corr.), Phi Beta Kappa. Democrat. Avocations: reading, travel, wine. Home: 10 Wayside Ln Scarsdale NY 10583-2908

BRILLSTEIN, BERNIE J., producer, talent manager; b. NYC, Apr. 26, 1932; s. Moe and Tillie Brillstein; m. Deborah Ellen Koskoff, 1975; children: Leigh, David Koskoff, Nick Koskoff, Michael, Kate. BS in Advt., NYU. Mailroom/talent rep. William Morris Agy., NYC, 1955-64; talent rep. Mgmt. III, NYC, 1964-69; packager, owner, producer The Brillstein Co., LA, 1969—; CEO Lorimar Film Entertainment, LA, 1996—; co-chair Brillstein-Grey Entertainment, Beverly Hills, Calif., 1991-96. Exec. producer (TV) Alf, 1986, The Boys, 1989, Politically Incorrect, 1997-98, 2000-01, It's The Garry Shandling Show, The Days and Nights of Molly Dodd, The Naked Truth, 1995, Mr. Show, 1995, The Steve Harvey Show, 1996, The Dana Carvey Show, 1996, Just Shoot Me, 1997, The Martin Short Show, 1999, Primetime Glick, 2001, The Wayne Brady Show, 2001; exec. producer (films) Dangerous Liaisons, Up the Academy, 1980, Blues Brothers, 1980, Neighbors, 1981, Continental Divide, 1981, Doctor Detroit, 1983, Ghostbusters I 1984, Summer Rental, 1985, Spies Like Us, 1985, Dragnet, 1987, Ghostbusters II, 1989, Larry Sanders Show, Celluloid Closet, 1995, Cat and Mouse, Happy Gilmore, 1996, The Cable Guy, 1996, Bulletproof, 1996, What Planet Are You From? 2000, Run Ronnie Run, 2002, exec.cons. The Real Ghostbusters, 1986. Served with U.S. Army, 1953-55. Recipient Peabody awards, Emmy nominations, Cable Ace award; honoree L.A. Free Clinic, 1987. Mem. N.Y. Friars Club, Beverly Hills C. of C. (bd. dirs.), Acad. Motion Picture Arts and Scis., TV Acad. Office: Brillstein-Grey Entertainment 9150 Wilshire Blvd Ste 350 Beverly Hills CA 90212-3453

BRILMAYER, R. LEA, lawyer, educator; b. 1950; BA, U. Calif.-Berkeley, 1970, JD, 1976; LLM, Columbia U., 1978. Bar: Tex. 1978. Assoc. in law Columbia U, 1976—78; asst. prof. law U. Tex., 1978—79, U. Chgo., Chgo., 1979—81, prof., 1991; vis. prof. Yale U., New Haven, 1981—82, Nathan Baker prof., 1986—91, Howard M. Holtzmann prof. Internat. Law, 1998—; Benjamin F. Butler prof. NYU, NYC, 1991—97. Author: Justifying International Acts, 1989, American Hegemony: Political Morality in a One Superpower World, 1994, Conflict of Laws: Foundation and Future Directions, 1995. Office: Yale U Dept Law PO Box 208215 New Haven CT 06520 E-mail: lea.brilmayer@yale.edu.

BRIM, ORVILLE GILBERT, JR., former foundation administrator, writer; b. Elmira, NY, Apr. 7, 1923; s. Orville G(ilbert) and Helen (Whittier) B.; m. Kathleen J. Vigneron, May 30, 1944; children: John G., Scott W., Margaret L., Sarah M. BA, Yale U., 1947, MA, 1949, PhD in Sociology, 1951. Instr. sociology U. Wis., 1952-53, asst. prof., 1953-55; sociologist Russell Sage Found., NYC, 1955-64, asst. sec., 1959-64, pres., 1964-72, trustee, 1964-72, cons., 1972-74; pres. Found. for Child Devel., 1974-85; mem. core study group MacArthur Found. Rsch. Program Successful Aging, 1985-89; dir. MacArthur Found. Rsch. Network on Successful Mid Life Devel., 1989—2002; pres. Life Trends, Inc., 1991—2002; vis. scholar Russell Sage Found., 1985-86; interim pres. Social Sci. Rsch. Coun., 1998-99. Vice chmn. Am. Inst. for Rsch., 1971-88, chmn. 1988-91; chmn. bd. dirs. Automation Engring. Lab., 1959-67; dir. Consumer Behavior, Inc., 1957-61; chmn. environ. panel U.S. Office Edn., 1962-64; mem. drug rsch. bd. NAS., 1964-66, adv. com. on child devel., 1971-76; mem. mental health tng. com. NIMH, 1959-62; chmn. commn. social scis. NSF, 1968-69; nat. adv. food and drug coun. HEW, 1967-69; chmn. com. on work and personality in mid. years Social Sci. Rsch. Coun., 1972-79; trustee Found. for Child Devel., 1972-85, Ctr. for Creative Leadership, 1972-78, Mental Health Law Project, 1973-77, William T. Grant Found., 1975-84, Greenwich Hosp., 1972-77 Author: Sociology and the Field of Education, 1958, Education for Child Rearing, 1959, Personality and Decision Processes, 1962, Intelligence: Perspectives 1965, 1966, Socialization after Childhood: Two Essays, 1966, American Beliefs and Attitudes Toward Intelligence, 1969, The Dying Patient, 1970, Learning to Be Parents, 1980, Ambition: How We Manage Success and Failure Throughout Our Lives, 1992; editor: Lifespan Development and Behavior, Vol. 2-6, 1979-83, Constancy and Change in Human Development, 1980, How Healthy Are We? A Nat. Study of Well-Being at Midlife, 2004; cons. editor Child Devel., 1958-61, Sociology of Edn., 1963-69, Sociometry, 1959-62; mem. publ. com. The Public Interest, 1967-75. Served as 1st lt. USAAF, 1943-46. Recipient Wilbur Lucius Cross medal Yale Grad. Sch. Assn., 1975; Kurt Lewin Meml. award Soc. Psychol. Study Social Issues, 1979, Disting. Career Contbns. to the Sci. Study of Life Span Devel., Soc. for the Study of Human Devel., 2005. Fellow APA, AAAS, Am. Sociol. Assn., Am. Acad. Arts and Scis., Am. Orthopsychiat. Assn. (pres. 1974-75), Ea. Sociol. Soc. (pres. 1971-72); mem. Inst. Medicine of NAS, Soc. Rsch. Child Devel. (Disting. Sci. Contbns. award, 1985).

BRIMÉE, JEAN-MICHEL, physical therapist, educator; s. Jean-Marie Brismée and Josette Jacobs; life ptnr. Roxanne Michelle Lloyd; children: Kita Ashley Lloyd, Nicholas Colten Brismée-Lloyd, Aimée Alexis Brismée-Lloyd, Marcus Ashton Brismée-Lloyd, Zoé Mikayla Brismée-Lloyd, Ashley Michelle Brismée-Lloyd. BS, Cath. U. Louvain-la-Neuve, Belgium, 1977—85; MS, Tex. Tech U., Lubbock, 1990—96, ScD, 2000—03. Lic. orthopaedic clinical specialty Am. Phys. Therapy Assn., 1998. Asst. prof. Tex. Tech U. Health Scis. Ctr., 1997—. Phys. therapy cons. U. Med. Ctr., Lubbock, 1997—; dir. rsch. com. Internat. Acad. Orthopaedic Medicine, Tucson, 2000—, dir. fellowship program, 2004—. Contbr. articles to profl. jours. Recipient Ball Dynamic award, 2002. Fellow: Am. Phys. Therapy Assn., Am. Acad. Orthopaedic Manual Phys. Therapists (assoc.). Office: Tex Tech Univ Health Scis Ctr 3601 4th St Lubbock TX 79430 Home Phone: 806-746-5557.

BRIMMER, ANDREW FELTON, economist, consultant; b. Newellton, La., Sept. 13, 1926; s. Andrew and Vellar (Davis) B.; m. Doris Millicent Scott, July 18, 1953; 1 dau., Esther Diane. BA, U. Wash., 1950, MA, 1951; postgrad. (Fulbright fellow), U. Bombay, India, 1951—52; PhD, Harvard U., 1957; LLD, Nebr. Wesleyan U., 1968, Marquette U., 1968, L.I. U., 1969, Oberlin Coll., 1969, Tufts U., 1970, Colgate U., 1970, Atlanta U., 1970, Middlebury Coll., 1971, U. Notre Dame, 1971, Bishop Coll., 1971, Upsala Coll., 1972, U. Md., 1976, U. Mich., 1979, U. So. Calif., 1980, Washington U., 1982, Ind. U., 1991, New Sch. U., 1999, Harvard U., 1999; D.Soc.Sc., Boston Coll., 1971, Temple U., 1974; D.C.L., U. Miami, 1971, U. of the South, 1984; D.H.L., DePaul U., 1975. Economist Fed. Res. Bank, NYC, 1955—58; asst. prof. Mich. State U., 1958—61, Wharton Sch. Finance and Commerce, U. Pa., 1961—66; dep. asst. sec. Dept. Commerce, Washington, 1963—65, asst. sec. for econ. affairs, 1965—66; mem. Fed. Res. Bd., 1966—74; Thomas Henry Carroll Ford Found. vis. prof. Grad. Sch. Bus. Adminstrn. Harvard U., 1974—76; pres. Brimmer & Co., Inc., Washington, 1976—; Wilmer D. Barrett prof. econs. U. Mass.-Amherst. Bd. govs., vice chmn. Commodity Exchange, Inc.; bd. dirs. Bank of Am., Am. Security Bank, MNC Fin., Inc., Du Pont Co., Gannett Co., Inc., BellSouth Corp., Conn. Mut., Navistar Internat. Corp., Blackstone Investment Income Trust, Carr-Am. Realty, Black Rock Investment Income Fund; mem. Fed. Res. Central Banking Mission to Sudan, 1957; cons. SEC, 1962-63; chmn. Washington DC Fin. Control Bd., 1995-98; mem. Trilateral Commn.; trustee Coll. Retirement Equities Fund. Author: Survey of Mutual Funds Investors, 1963, Life Insurance Companies in Capital Market, 1962, Economic Development: International and African Perspectives, 1976, The World Banking System: Outlook in a Context of Crisis, 1985, International Banking and Domestic Economic Policies, 1986; Contbr. articles to profl. jours. Chmn. bd. trustees Tuskegee U., Com. for Econ. Devel.; bd. dirs. Interracial Council for Bus. Opportunity; mem. internat. panel UN Mgmt. and Decision Making Project, 1986-88; panel on fgn. trade stats. NAS. With AUS, 1945-46. Named Govt. Man of Year Nat. Bus. League, 1963; recipient Arthur S. Flemming award, 1966, Russworm award, 1966, Capital Press Club award, 1966, Golden Plate award Am. Acad. Achievement, 1967, Alumnus Summa Laude Dignatus U. Wash. Alumni Assn., 1972, Nat. Honoree Beta Gamma Sigma, 1971, Horatio Alger award, 1974, Equal Opportunity award Nat. Urban League, 1974, One Hundred Black Men and N.Y. Urban Coalition award, 1975, Disting. Svc. award Interracial Coun. Bus. Opportunity, 1986, Pub. Svc. award North Adams State Coll., 1987, George Washington U., 1998, Shenandoah U., 2004. Fellow Am. Acad. Arts and Scis., Nat. Assn. Bus. Economists,

Ea. Econ. Assn. (v.p. 1989, pres.-elect 1990-91, pres. 1991-92), N.Am. Econ. and Fin. Assn. (v.p. 1995, pres.-elect 1996, pres. 1997, vice chair exec. com. 2004—); mem. Am. Econ. Assn. (Richard T. Ely lectr. 1982, v.p. 1989), Am. Fin. Assn., Assn. for Study Afro-Am. Life and History (pres. 1970-73, 89—), Coun. Fgn. Rels., Nat. Economists Club, Am. Statis. Assn., Soc. Govt. Economists (Disting. lectr. on econs. in govt. 1988), Omicron Delta Epsilon. Office: Brimmer & Co Inc 4400 Macarthur Blvd NW Washington DC 20007-2521 Home Phone: 202-686-5828; Office Phone: 202-342-6255. E-mail: afbrimmer@aol.com.

BRIMMER, CLARENCE ADDISON, federal judge; b. Rawlins, Wyo., July 11, 1922; s. Clarence Addison and Geraldine (Zingsheim) B.; m. Emily O. Docken, Aug. 2, 1953; children: Geraldine Ann, Philip Andrew, Andrew Howard, Elizabeth Ann. BA, U. Mich., 1944, JD, 1947. Bar: Wyo. 1948. Pvt. practice law, Rawlins, 1948-71; mcpl. judge, 1948-54; U.S. commr., magistrate, 1963-71; atty. gen. Wyo. Cheyenne, 1971-74; U.S. atty., 1975; chief judge U.S. Dist. Ct. Wyo., Cheyenne, 1975-92, dist. judge, 1975—. Mem. panel multi-dist. litigation, 1992-2000; mem. Jud. Conf. U.S., 1994-97, exec., 1995-97. Sec. Rawlins Bd. Pub. Utilities, 1954-66; Rep. gubernatorial candidate, 1974; trustee Rocky Mountain Mineral Law Found., 1963-75. With USAAF, 1945-46. Mem. ABA, Wyo. Bar Assn., Laramie County Bar Assn., Carbon County Bar Assn., Am. Judicature Soc., Masons, Shriners, Rotary. Episcopalian. Office: US Dist Ct 2120 Capitol Ave Rm 2603 Cheyenne WY 82001

BRIN, FOSTER BLAKE, psychiatrist; b. Springfield, Mass., May 23, 1948; s. Henry Brin and Gertrude Gail Scholl; m. Deborah Lynn Wood, Mar. 29, 2003; 1 stepchild, Sean Kendrick McCann; m. Martha Lynne Ehlers (dec.); 1 child, Andrew Victor. BS, U. Fla., Gainesville, 1970; MD, U. Miami, 1978. Psychiatry intern Tripler Army Med. Ctr., Honolulu, 1979—80, psychiatry resident, 1980—83; staff psychiatrist Wynn Army Comty. Hosp., Ft. Stewart, Ga., 1983—85, Cen. State Hosp., Milledgeville, Ga., 1990—2003, River Edge Behavioral Health Ctr., Macon, Ga., 2003—. Assoc. prof. dept. psychiatry Mercer U. Sch. Medicine. Physician local troop Boy Scouts Am., Warner Robins, Ga., 1995—. Capt. US Army, 1979—85. Mem.: AMA, Am. Psychiat. Assn. Methodist. Avocations: stamp collecting/philately, music, album collecting. Personal E-mail: fsbrin@cox.net.

BRIN, ROYAL HENRY, JR., lawyer; b. Dallas, Oct. 9, 1919; BA, JD, U. Tex., 1941. Bar: Tex. 1941. Postgrad. fellow Harvard U., 1941—42; atty. OPA, Washington, 1942; assoc. firm Strasburger & Price, Dallas, 1946-56, ptnr., 1956—. Editor-in-chief Tex. Law Rev., 1940-41; contbr. articles to profl. jours. Fellow Am. Bar Found. (life); mem. ABA, Am. Acad. Appellate Lawyers, State Bar Tex., Tex. Assn. Def. Counsel (pres. 1981-82), Dallas Bar Assn., Dallas Assn. Def. Counsel, Def. Rsch. Inst., Internat. Brotherhood Magicians (pres. 1969-70), The Chancellors (grand chancellor 1940-41), Order of Coif, Phi Beta Kappa, Phi Eta Sigma. Home: 6506 Lupton Dr Dallas TX 75225-2323 Office: 4300 Bank of Am Plz 901 Main St Dallas TX 75202-3714 Home Phone: 214-368-8110; Office Phone: 214-651-4604. Business E-Mail: royal.brin@strasburger.com.

BRIN, SERGEY MIHAILOVICH, information technology executive; b. Moscow, Aug. 21, 1973; s. Michael and Genia Brin; m. Anne Wojcicki, May 2007. BS in Math. and Computer Sci. with honors, U. Md., College Park, 1993; MS, Stanford U., 1995; MBA (hon.), Instituto de Empresa. Co-founder Google, Inc., Mountain View, Calif., 1998, pres., 1998—2001, pres. tech., 2001—, also asst. sec., dir. Bd. dirs. Google, Inc., 1998—; spkr. World Econ. Forum and the Technol., Entertainment and Design Conf.; spkr. in the field. Author: (Articles) Extracting Patterns and Relations from the World Wide Web; Scalable Techniques for Mining Casual Structures; Beyond Market Baskets: Generalizing Association Rules to Correlations; co-author (with Larry Page): Dynamic Data Mining: A New Architecture for Data with High Dimensionality; guest appearence on Charlie Rose Show, CNBC, CNNfn. Co-recipient (with Larry Page) Marconi prize, 2004; named one of Persons of the Week (with Larry Page), ABC World News Tonight, 2004, World's 100 Most Influential People, Time Mag., 2005, Forbes Richest Americans, 2006—, 50 Who Matter Now, CNNMoney.com Bus. 2.0, 2006, 2007; recipient Business Leader of Yr. for Google, Inc., Scientific American 50, 2005; fellow NSF. Office: Google Inc 1600 Amphitheatre Pkwy Mountain View CA 94043 Office Fax: 650-618-1499.*

BRINBERG, HERBERT RAPHAEL, publishing executive; b. NYC, Jan. 27, 1926; s. Henry and Anna (Stambler) B.; m. Blanche Leiman, July 15, 1945; children: Amy Lynn, Todd Michael. AB, Cornell U., 1947; MS, Columbia U., 1948; PhD, NYU, 1955; DSc (hon.), Syracuse U., 1989. Research economist Conf. Bd., 1948-50; cons. economist Boni Watkins, 1951-54; asst. dir. research Licensed Beverage Industries, 1954-55; mgr. econ. research and planning Canco div. Am. Can Co., 1956-61, dir. comml. research, 1961-66, v.p. planning, 1966-71, v.p. info. tech., 1971-78; pres., chief exec. officer Aspen Systems, Rockville, Md., 1978-85, Panel Pubs., Inc., Greenvale, NY, 1982-85; mng. dir. Wolters Kluwer U.S. Corp., NYC, 1978-85, pres., chief exec. officer, dir., 1986-89; pres., CEO Parnassus Assocs. Internat., Inc., 1990—; chmn. Assoc. Info. Mgrs., 1988-90. Bd. dirs. K&F Industries, 1988-2004, Brill Acad. Pub., 1988-2004; chmn. bd. dirs. The Associated Blind; adj. prof. Baruch Coll., 1988—, chmn. bus. adv. coun. Bernard L. Schwartz Comm. Inst., 1998—; chmn. bd. visitors Sch. Info. Studies, Syracuse U., 1996—. Mem. coun. Cornell U., 1998-2003. With USAAF, 1944-45. Mem. Info. Industry Assn. (past chmn., vice chmn. 1994-98), Software and Info. Industry Assn.(bd. dirs. 1999-2001), Cornell Club N.Y.C. Business E-Mail: hrbrinberg@parnassusassociates.com.

BRIND, DAVID HUTCHISON, lawyer, judge; b. Albany, NY, Feb. 4, 1930; s. Charles Albert and Laura Stuart (Hutchison) B.; m. Shirley Jean Hodgins, Mar. 6, 1954; children: Susan Brind Morrow, Charles. AB, Union Coll., 1951; LLB, Albany Law Sch., 1954, JD, 1968; LHD, N.Y. Inst. Tech., 1971. Bar: N.Y. 1954, U.S. Supreme Ct. 1970. Atty. law divsn. N.Y. State Dept. Edn., Albany, 1954—55; with U.S. Army Ctr. Intelligence Corps, 1955—57; ptnr. Chacchia & Brind, Geneva, NY, 1957—64; sole practice Geneva, 1964—95; presiding judge Geneva City Ct., 1974—96; ret., 1995; apptd. jud. hearing officer N.Y. State Supreme Ct., 1995—. Hearing officer N.Y. State and Local Ret. Sys., 1997—; counsel real estate N.Y. State Dormitory Auth., 1970-86; gen. counsel Geneva Gen. Hosp., 1966-85; local counsel Conrail; spl. counsel N.Y. Tchrs. Retirement Sys., 1959-72. Bd. dirs. Geneva United Way, 1965-89; campaign chmn. United Way Greater Rochester (N.Y.), 1966-69, pres., 1969-71; trustee Geneva Gen. Hosp., 1962-73; pres., 1969-71; trustee Geneva Hist. Soc., 1963-90, pres., 1968-70; chmn. Geneva Hist. Commn., 1969-89; mem. exec. bd. Finger Lakes coun. Boy Scouts Am., 1965—; bd. dirs. 7 Lakes Coun. Girl Scouts U.S.A., 1966-73; bd. dirs. Geneva Gen. Hosp. Nursing Home, pres., 1969-71; v.p. Geneva Bd. Edn., 1962-67; mem. pres.'s coun. Eisenhower Coll., 1972-79, Hobart & William Smith Colls., 1967—. Recipient Geneva Cmty. Chest/Red Cross Svc. citation, 1969, named Man of Yr., Geneva C. of C., 1971. Mem. Am. Assn. Homes for Aging, NY State Sch. Bds. Assn. (law revisions com. and constnl. conv. com. 1964-68), Monroe County Jud. Com., 1976-80, Ontario County Bar Assn., NY State Bar Assn. (jud. coun.), Fedn. NY State Judges, NY State Assn. Jud. Hearing Officers (treas. 1995—), NY Assn. Supreme Ct. Justices by Appt., NY State Ct. Judges (pres. 1988-90), St. Andrews Soc. Albany, Rotary (pres. 1967-68, Paul Harris fellow 2005), Finger Lakes Forum (pres. 1991-2005, chair Fingerlakes inquiry com. 1995—). Republican. Presbyterian. Home: 43 Delancey Dr Geneva NY 14456-2809 Office: 37 Seneca St Geneva NY 14456-0409 Office Phone: 315-789-9191. Personal E-mail: judge@novocon.net.

BRIND'AMOUR, ROD, professional hockey player; b. Ottawa, Ont., Can., Aug. 9, 1970; married; 3 children. Grad., Mich. State U. With St. Louis Blues, 1988—91; left wing/center Phila. Flyers, 1991—99, Carolina Hurricanes, 1999—, capt., 2005—. Mem. CCHA All-Rookie Team, 1988—89; player NHL All-Star Game. Recipient CCHA Rookie of Yr. award, 1988—89, Frank J. Selke Trophy, 2006, 2007. Achievements include being a member of Stanley Cup Champion Carolina Hurricanes, 2006. Office: Carolina Hurricanes RBC Ctr 1400 Edwards Mill Rd Raleigh NC 27607-3624*

BRINEGAR, CLAUDE STOUT, retired oil industry executive; b. Rockport, Calif., Dec. 16, 1926; s. Claude Leroy Stout and Lyle (Rawles) B.; m. Elva Jackson, 1950 (div.); children: Claudia, Meredith, Thomas; m. Mary Katharine Potter, 1983 (dec. 1993); m. Karen Bartholomew, 1995. BA, Stanford U., 1950, MS, 1951, PhD, 1954; LLD (hon.), Elmira Coll., 1997. V.p. econs. and planning Union Oil (now Unocal), LA, 1965, pres. Pure Oil divsn. Palatine, Ill., 1965-69, sr. v.p., pres. refining and mktg. LA, 1969-73; U.S. Sec. of Transp. Washington, 1973-75; sr. v.p. adminstr. Unocal Corp., LA, 1975-85, mem. exec. com., 1968-73, 75-92, exec. v.p., CFO, 1985-91, vice chmn. bd., 1990-95. Founding dir. Conrail, Inc., 1974-75, 90-98; vis. scholar Stanford U., 1992-97; bd. dir. CSX Corp., 1998-2002. Author: monograph on econs. and price behavior, 1970; contbr. articles to profl. jours. Chmn. Calif. Citizens Compensation Commn., 1990-2002; mem. regional selection panel White House Fellows Program, 1976-83, chmn., 1983; head transp. transition team Pres. Ronald Reagan, Washington, 1980-81. Mem. Am. Petroleum Inst. (bd. dir. 1976-85, 88-91, hon. life dir. 1992), Georgetown Club, Boothbay Harbor Yacht Club, Phi Beta Kappa, Sigma Xi. Avocation: collecting first editions of Mark Twain. Home and Office: 2444 Sharon Oaks Dr Menlo Park CA 94025

BRINEY, ALLAN KING, retired radiologist; b. Wilkinsburg, Pa., Nov. 17, 1921; s. Alonzo Tripp and Helen Marie (Hardman) B.; m. Gayle Diane Briney, July 4, 1986; children: Ronald A., Nancy E., Barbara A., Douglas C. BS summa cum laude, U. Pitts., 1943, MD, 1945. Diplomate Am. Bd. Radiology; lic. real estate salesperson Ariz. Intern Pitts. Hosp., 1945-46; fellow in radiology Hosp. U. Pa., Phila., 1948-51; radiologist Topeka Med. Ctr., 1951-53, Murphy Meml. Hosp., Whittier, Calif., 1953-62, Whittier Radiology Med. Group, 1953-94, Memrad Med. Group, Whittier, 1995-97; chief of staff Presbyn. Intercommunity Hosp., Whittier, 1979, radiologist, 1959-97; ret., 1997. Capt. USAF, 1946-48. Fellow Am. Coll. Radiology. Libertarian. Deist. Avocations: skiing, bicycling, hiking, swimming, sailing. Home: 220 Cayuse Trl Sedona AZ 86336-9797 Personal E-mail: allanking@earthlink.net.

BRING, MURRAY H., retired lawyer; b. Denver, Jan. 19, 1935; s. Alfred Alexander and Ida (Molinsky) B.; m. Constance Brooks Evert, Dec. 30, 1963 (div. June 1989); children: Beth, Catherine, Peter; m. Kathleen Delaney, May 19, 1990. BA, U. So. Calif., 1956; LLB, NYU, 1959. Bar: N.Y. 1960, D.C. 1963, U.S. Supreme Ct. 1966. Law clk. to Chief Justice Earl Warren U.S. Supreme Ct., Washington, 1959-61; spl. asst. to asst. atty. gen. civil div. Dept. Justice, Washington, 1961-62; spl. asst to dep. undersec. state Dept. State, Washington, 1962-63; dir. policy planning anti-trust divsn., 1963-65; ptnr. Arnold & Porter, Washington, 1965-87; sr. v.p., gen. counsel Philip Morris Cos., Inc., NYC, 1988-94, exec. v.p. external affairs and gen. counsel, 1994-97, vice chmn., gen. counsel, 1997-2000; ret., 2000. Editor-in-chief N.Y. Law Rev., 1958-59. Bd. dirs. Guild Hall East Hampton, NYU Law Sch. Found. Mem. ABA, Order of Coif, Phi Beta Kappa, Phi Kappa Phi. Avocations: fishing, photography, art. Office: Altria Group Inc 120 Park Ave New York NY 10017-5592

BRINGARDNER, JOHN MICHAEL, lawyer, clergyman; b. Columbus, Ohio, Nov. 7, 1957; s. John Krepps and Elizabeth (Evans) B.; m. Emily Presley, June 19, 1982; children: John Taylor, Michael Steven, Malee Elizabeth. BA, U. Central Fla., Orlando, 1979; postgrad., Mercer U., 1979; JD, Fla. State U., 1981. Bar: Fla. 1982, Calif. 1994, U.S. Dist. Ct. (mid. dist.) Fla., U.S. Dist. Ct. (no. dist.) Fla., U.S. Ct. Appeals (11th cir.). Assoc. McFarlain, Bobo, Sternstein, Wiley & Cassidy, Tallahassee, Fla., 1982-87, Finley, Kumble Wagner, Tallahassee, 1987; minister Boston Ch. of Christ, 1987-90; evangelist Bankok Christian Ch., 1990-92, Metro Manila Christian Ch., 1992-93; gen. counsel Internat. Chs. of Christ, LA, 1993—. Bd. dirs. Eye Care Corp., Orlando, Fla., Quality Coffee Corp., Tallahassee. Mem. ABA, Fla. Bar Assn. Avocations: football, baseball, triathlons, hiking, music. Office: La International Church of Christ 3731 Wilshire Blvd Ste 810 Los Angeles CA 90010-2850

BRINGHURST, ROBERT, poet; b. LA, Oct. 16, 1946; s. George Heber and Marion Jeanette B.; 1 child, Piper Laramie. Student, MIT, 1963—64, student, 1970—71, U. Utah, 1964—65; BA in Comparative Lit., Ind. U., 1973; MFA, U. B.C., Vancouver, Can., 1975; DLitt, U. Coll. Fraser Valley, Abbotsford, Can., 2006. Vis. lectr. dept. creative writing U. B.C., Vancouver, 1975-77, lectr. dept. English, 1979-80; adj. lectr. Simon Fraser U., Burnaby, B.C., Canada, 1983-84; writer-in-residence U. Winnipeg, Man., Canada, 1986; Can./Scotland exch. fellow U. Edinburgh, Scotland, 1989-90; Ashley Fellow Trent U., Peterborough, Canada, 1994; writer in residence U. Western Ont., 1998-99; adj. prof. Simon Fraser U., 2000—03. Conjunct prof. Trent U., 1998—; Ralph Gustafson chair in poetry Malaspina Coll., 2003. Author: Shipwright's Log, 1972, Cadastre, 1973, Stonecutter's Horses, 1974, Deuteronomy, 1974, Eight Objects, 1975, Bergschrund, 1975, Jacob Singing, 1977, Tzuhalem's Mountain, 1982, Beauty of the Weapons: Selected Poems 1972-82, 1982, Ocean/Paper/Stone, 1984, Tending the Fire, 1985, Shovels, Shoes and the Slow Rotation of Letters, 1986, Blue Roofs of Japan, 1986, Pieces of Map, Pieces of Music, 1987, Conversations with a Toad, 1987, The Black Canoe: Bill Reid and the Spirit of Haida Gwaii, 1991, 2d edit., 1992, The Elements of Typographic Style, 1992, 3d edit., 2004, The Calling: Selected Poems 1970-95, 1995, Elements, 1995, A Story as Sharp as a Knife: The Classical Haida Mythtellers and Their World, 1999, The Book of Silences, 2001, Ursa Major, 2003, Prosodies of Meaning: Literary Form in Native North America, 2004, The Solid Form of Language: An Essay on Writing and Meaning, 2004, New World Suite No. 3, 2005, The Old in Their Knowing, 2005, Wild Language, 2006, The Tree of Meaning, 2006; editor (translator): Nine Visits to the Mythworld, 2000, Being in Being: Collected Works of Skaay of the QQUUNA Qiighawaay, 2001, The Fragments of Parmenides, 2003; editor: (with others) Visions: Contemporary Art in Can., 1983; co-author: The Raven Steals the Light, 1984, 1996; co-author: (with others) Part of the Land, Part of the Water: A History of the Yukon Indians, 1987; co-author: A Short History of the Printed Word, 1999, Carving the Elements: A Companion to the Fragments of Parmenides, 2004, author numerous poems, stage prodns., works for multiple voices, Everywhere Being Is Dancing, 2007. Guggenheim fellow in poetry, 1988, Philips fellow Am. Philos. Soc., 2000; recipient Edward Sapir prize, 2004 Home: Box 51 Heriot Bay BC Canada VOP 1HO

BRINGMAN, JOSEPH EDWARD, lawyer; b. Elmhurst, NY, Jan. 31, 1958; s. Joseph Herman and Eileen Marie (Sheehy) B.; m. Laurie Lynn Cunningham, July 11, 1992; children: Joseph Edward Jr., Elizabeth Grace. BA, Yale U., 1980; JD, Stanford U., 1983. Bar: N.Y. 1984, Wash. 1985, U.S. Dist. Ct. (we. dist.) Wash. 1986, U.S. Ct. Appeals (9th cir.) 1986, U.S. Ct. Appeals (fed. cir.) 1988, U.S. Dist. Ct. (ea. dist.) Wash. 2000. Acting asst. prof. U. Wash. Law Sch., Seattle, 1983-85; assoc. Perkins Coie, Seattle, 1985-91, of counsel, 1992—. Dir. Perkins Coie Cmty. Fellowship, Seattle, 1990-96, chair assoc. tng. com., 1997-2000. Editor: Stanford Jour. Internat. Law, 1980-83; author Fed. Trial Practice chpt. Washington Lawyers' Practice Manual, 2002-03. Mem. Yale Alumni Schs. Com., 1980—. Nat. Merit scholar, 1976; recipient Pro Bono Publico award Trumbull Coll. (Yale U.), 1980. Mem. ABA, Wash. State Bar Assn., King County Bar Assn. (jud. screening com. 1993-96, chair fair campaign practices com. 1997-99, 2006-, judiciary and cts. com. 1999-2003, sec. 2003-2004, trustee 2003-06, membership com. 2003-, CLE com. 2003-2004, chair audit com. 2005, Pres.'s award 2006). Democrat. Roman Catholic. Office: Perkins Coie LLP 1201 3rd Ave Fl 48 Seattle WA 98101-3099 Office Phone: 206-359-8501. Business E-Mail: jbringman@perkinscoie.com.

BRININSTOOL, DAVID, architect; Grad., U. Mich., MArch, 1976. With Skidmore, Owings and Merrill, Chgo., 1980—84; sr. project arch. Pappageorge/Haymes, 1984; prin. Brininstool+Lynch, Ltd., Chgo. AIA rep. Archtl. Record Editl. Adv. Bd.; adj. prof. Grad. Sch. Architecture Ill. Inst. Tech. Mem.: AIA (bd. mem., v.p. Chgo. chpt., past chmn. design com. Chgo. chpt.). Office: Brininstool+Lynch Ltd 230 W Superior St 3rd Fl Chicago IL 60610 Office Phone: 312-640-0505. Office Fax: 312-640-0217. E-mail: db@brininstool-lynch.com.*

BRINK, DAVID RYRIE, lawyer; b. Mpls., July 28, 1919; s. Raymond Woodard and Carol Sybil (Ryrie) B.; m. Irma Lorentz Brink; children: Anne Carol, Mary Claire, David Owen, Sarah Jane. BA with honors, U. Minn., 1940, BSL with honors, 1941, JD with honors, 1947; LLD, Capital U., 1981, Suffolk U., 1981, Mitchell Coll. Law, 1982. Bar: Minn. 1947, U.S. Dist. Ct. Minn. 1947, U.S. Tax Ct. 1967, U.S. Supreme Ct. 1980, U.S. Ct. Appeals (D.C. Cir.) 1982. Assoc. firm Dorsey & Whitney, Mpls., 1947-53, ptnr., 1953-89, head Washington office, 1982-84, ret. ptnr. Trustee Lawyers Com. Civil Rights Under Law, 1978—; bd. dirs. Nat. Legal Aid and Defender Assn., 1978-80; U.S. panelist for Dispute Resolution under Free Trade Agreement with Can.; bd. visitors U. Minn. Law Sch., 1978-81; chmn. trust and estates dept. Dorsey & Whitney, 1956-82 Mem. editl. bd. U. Minn. Law Rev, 1941-42; contbr. articles to profl. jours. Bd. govs. Am. Coll. Trust and Estate Counsel Found., 1987-95. Served to lt. comdr. USNR, 1943-46. Recipient Outstanding Achievement award U. Minn., 1982 Fellow Coll. Law Practice Mgmt. (hon.), Am. Coll. Trust and Estate Counsel (regent, exec. com.); mem. ABA (gov. 1974-77, 80-83, pres. 1981-82), Ctrl. and Ea. European Legal Initiative, Com. on Law and Nat. Security, Com. on Substance Abuse, Adv. Com. to Commn. on Lawyers Assistance Programs 2000-2003, Com. on Specialization, chmn. 1977-80, Fund Pub. Edn. ABA (pres. 1981-82), Am. Bar Found. (state chmn. 1977-80, gov. 1980-83), Am. Bar Retirement Assn. (pres. 1976-77), Am. Judicature Soc. (bd. dir. 1988—), Nat. Conf. Bar Pres., Inst. Jud. Adminstrn., Am. Arbitration Assn. (trustee 1981—), Can.-U.S. Law Inst. (adv. bd. 1987—), Minn. Bar Assn. (pres. 1978-79), Internat. Mgmt. and Devel. Inst., Hennepin County Bar Assn. (pres. 1967-68), Street Law (nat. adv. bd. 1982-85, chmn. 1983-84), Lawyers Concerned Lawyers (bd. dir. 2003—), N.W. Athletic Club, Sr. Tennis Players Club, Inc. Office: Dorsey & Whitney # 50 S 6th St Minneapolis MN 55402

BRINK, MARION FRANCIS, trade association administrator; b. Golden Eagle, Ill., Nov. 20, 1932; s. Anton Frank and Agnes Gertrude B. BS, U. Ill., 1955, MS, 1958; PhD, U. Mo., 1961. Rsch. biologist U.S. Naval Radiol. Def. Lab., San Francisco, 1961-62; assoc. dir. div. nutrition rsch. Nat. Dairy Council, Chgo., 1962-65, dir. div. nutrition rsch., 1965-70, pres., 1970-85; exec. v.p. ops. United Dairy Industry Assn., Rosemont, 1985-88, chief exec. officer, 1988-91. Vice chmn. human nutrition adv. com. USDA, 1980-81. Contbr. articles to profl. jours. Recipient citation of merit U. Mo. Alumni Assn. Mem. Am. Soc. for Nutritional Scis., Am. Soc. Clin. Nutrition, Am. Dietetic Assn., Dairy Shrine Club, Soc. for Nutrition Edn., Chgo. Nutrition Assn., Alpha Tau Alpha, Gamma Sigma Delta. Home: 444 Highcrest Dr Wilmette IL 60091-2358

BRINKEMA, LEONIE MILHOMME, federal judge; b. NJ, June 26, 1944; d. Alexander Juste and Modeste Leonie Milhomme; m. John Robert Brinkema, Dec. 22, 1966; children: Robert Aaron, Eugenie Alexandra. BA with honors, Douglass Coll., 1966; MLS, Rutgers U., 1970; JD with honors, Cornell U., 1976. Bar: D.C. 1976, Va. 1978. Trial atty. U.S. Dept. Justice, Washington, 1976-77, 1983-84; asst. U.S. atty. U.S. Atty's Office Ea. Va., Alexandria, 1977-83; prin. Leonie M. Brinkema Atty., Alexandria, 1984-85; U.S. magistrate judge U.S. Dist. Ct. (ea. dist.) Va., Alexandria, 1985-93, U.S. dist. judge, 1993—. Legal lectr. Va. State Bar Professionalism Faculty, 1990-92, No. Va. Criminal Justice Acad., 1984-85; guest lectr. Alexandria Bar Assn., Alexandria Women Attys. Assn., Va. Women Attys. Assn., U.S. Dept. Justice Advocacy Inst., Va. Law Found. Active Fairfax Choral Soc., Alban Chorale. Woodrow Wilson grad. fellow, 1966, Danforth Found. grad. fellow, 1966. Mem. ABA, Va. State Bar, D.C. Bar, Nat. Assn. Women Judges, Va. Women Attys. Assn., George Mason Inn of Ct. (master), Phi Beta Kappa. Avocation: singing. Office: US Dist Ct 401 Courthouse Sq Alexandria VA 22314-5704

BRINKER, CHARLES JEFFREY, chemistry and chemical engineering educator; b. Easton, Pa., Nov. 28, 1950; BS in Ceramic Sci. with honors, Rutgers U., 1972, MS in Ceramic Sci., 1975, PhD in Ceramic Sci., 1978. Mem. tech. staff inorganic materials chemistry Sandia Nat. Labs., Albuquerque, 1979—; disting. mem. technical staff to sr. scientist Sandia Nat. Labs, Albuquerque, 1991—; prof. chemistry and chem. engring. U. N.Mex., Albuquerque, Disting. Nat. Lab. Prof. Chemistry and Chem. Engring., 1991—, co-dir. ctr. micro-engineered materials. Co-editor: Better Ceramics Through Chemistry, 1984, 6th edit., 1994; assoc. editor Jour. Am. Ceramic Soc.; mem. editl. bd. Chemistry of Materials, Jour. Sol-Gel Sci. and Tech., Jour. Porous Materials, Current Opinion in Solid State and Materials Sci.; author: Sol-Gel Science, 1990; contbr. articles to profl. jours. Recipient Basic Energy Scis. award Dept. Energy, 1986, 92, 94, 95, Zachariasen award, 1988 Jour. Non-Crystalline Solids, 1985-87, Ralph K. Iler award in chemistry of colloidal materials Am. Chem. Soc., 1996, NOVA award Lockheed Martin, 1996, R&D 100 award, 1996, E.O. Lawrence award, 2002. Fellow Am. Ceramic Soc.; mem. Materials Rsch. Soc. (founder, co-organizer), Keramos, Nat. Academy Engring. Office: Advanced Materials Lab 1001 University Blvd SE Albuquerque NM 87106-4325

BRINKER, NANCY GOODMAN, social services administrator, former ambassador; b. Peoria, Ill., 1946; m. Norman Brinker; 1 child, Eric. B in Sociology, U. Ill., 1968; PhD (hon.), Southern Meth. U. Founder Susan G. Komen Breast Cancer Found., 1982—, Race for the Cure fitness/walk fundraising event, 1983—; founder, chair, CEO In Your Corner, Inc., 1994—98; US amb. to Hungary US Dept. State, Budapest, 2001—03. Spkr. in field; advocate for women's health issues in Congress; collaborating ptnr., Nat. Dialogue on Cancer; bd. dirs. LHC Group, Inc., 2006-Author: The Race is Run One Step at a Time, 1995; co-author: 1000 Questions About Women's Health; articles published in nat. and internat. media. Bd. dirs. Physicians Reliance Network, Harvard Sch. Pub. Health, NYU Med. Sch. Found., Nat. Surg. Adjuvant Breast Project, Susan Komen Breast Cancer Found., Palm Beach Fellowship of Christians and Jews, Manpower, Inc., 2004-, US Oncology, Inc., Netmarket, Inc., Meditrust Corp.; mem. Nat. Cancer Adv. Bd.; bd. govs. Nat. Jewish Coalition.; mem. adv. bd. Harvard Ctr. for Cancer Prevention, Women's Health Initiative, Nat. Coalition of Cancer Suvivorship, Nat. Cancer Inst. Recipient Jefferson award for Hero award Coping Mag., 1996, Pub. Svc. award Oncology Nursing Soc., 1996, Greatest Pub. Svc. by a Pvt. Citizen, Am. Inst. Pub. Svc., 1997, Lifetime Achievement award Nat. Breast Cancer Awareness Month, 1997, Albert Einstein's Sarnoff Vol. award, Humanitarian of Yr. award Mt. Sinai, James Ewing Layman's award, Soc. Surg. Oncology, Humanitarian of Yr. award Rep. Women's Leadership Forum, Healthcare Humanitarian award, Global Conf. Inst., Tex. Gov. award, outstanding nat. svc., the first Salomon Smith Barney Extraordingary Achievement award, Champion of Prevention award, Nat. Found. for Ctrs. for Disease Control, internat. achievements in support of breast cancer rsch., Sword of Ignatius

Loyola award, St. Louis Univ., Spl. Recognition award, Am. Soc. Clin. Oncology, Caring award, 1999, Cino del Duca award, 2000, Toastmasters Internat. Top Five Speakers award, 2001, Lifetime Achievement award, Sisters Network, 2001, Mary Woodward Lasker Pub. Svc. award in Support of Med. Rsch. & the Health Sciences, Lasker Found., 2005, Global Pathfinder award, Am. Soc. Breast Disease, 2006; named EVIE Profl. of the Yr., Profl. & Bus. Forum, 2005, Centennial Medal for Disting. Pub. Svc., Am. Assn. Cancer Rsch., 2007; named one of 100 Most Important Women of 20th Century, Ladies Home Jour., 25 Most Powerful Women in Am., Biography Mag., Top 10 Champions of Women's Health, Ladies Home Jour.; named to Cancer Rsch. and Treatment Fund, Inc. Cancer Survivors Hall of Fame. Mailing: Susan G Komen Breast Cancer Foundation PO Box 650309 Dallas TX 75265-0309

BRINKER, NORMAN E., restaurant company executive; BS, San Diego State U. Chmn., CEO Steak & Ale Restaurants, 1966-72; restaurant group pres. Pillsbury; chmn., CEO Burger King S&A Restaurant Group, Chili's Inc., Dallas, 1983-91; chmn. Brinker Internat. Inc., Dallas, 1991—. Office: Brinker Internat Inc 6820 LBJ Fwy Dallas TX 75240

BRINKER, THOMAS MICHAEL, finance company executive; b. Phila., Sept. 8, 1933; s. William Joseph and Elizabeth C. (Feeley) B.; m. Doris Marie Carlin, Oct. 11, 1958; children: Thomas Michael, James E., Joseph F., Diane M. Student, St. Joseph's U., U. Pa.; MS in Fin. Svcs., Am. Coll., 1980; DBA, Heed U., 1990; BA in Orgnl. Mgmt., Ea. Coll., 1991. Registered investment advisor; CLU, ChFC, CFP, AEP. With Ice Capades, 1951-52, 56; with Casa Carioca, Garmisch, Fed. Rep. Germany, 1954-56; profl. ice skating tchr. and mfrs. rep. Ridley Park, Pa., 1956-60; agt., div. mgr. Prudential Ins. Co., Phila., 1960-65; gen. agt. Mut. Trust Life Ins. Co., 1965-70; pres., founder Fringe Benefits Inc., Havertown, Pa., 1970—, Fin. Foresight Ltd., Havertown, Pa., 1983—. Adj. prof. Pa. State U., 1984—, St. Joseph's U., 1985—. Host: (radio) Financial Forum, Sta. WWDB-FM, 1982-90, Sta. WCZN-AM, 1990-91, daily report on fin. foresight Sta. WFLN-FM, 1992-, WCZN-AM, 1994-, children's fin. reports on Dr. Tom on Money Matters, WPWA-AM, 1994-, WWCN, Estero, Fla., 1997, others; co-host: (radio) Fin. Foresight, Sta. WFIL-AM, Phila., 1998-2000, WWDB-AM Phila., 2001-, WPEN-AM Phila., 2003-; author: HI, I'm Tom Brinker, You're on WWDB, 1987; columnist: Financially Yours, 1983-, Dollars and $ense, 1999-; ghostwriter: Nat. Assn. Life Underwriter's Fin. Fitness campaign, 1985; columnist Dollars and $ense, 1999-; contbr., author, condr. of seminars on fin. planning; contbr. articles to profl. jours. Pres., Delaware County Estate Planning Coun., 1979-80, Pipeline Inc., Springfield, Pa., 1970-71; dir. nat. coun. Invest-in-Am., 1986; bd. dirs. Pacific Advisors Fund, Inc., 1992—, Cypress Benefit Svcs., Inc., 1997—. Recipient Nat. Quality award Nat. Assn. Life Underwriters, 1966-2002, Nat. Sales Achievement award, 1970-2000, TransAmerica Fin. Advisors award, 2003. Mem. CLU, Delaware County Life Underwriters (pres. 1975-76, 82-83), Am. Coll. Life Underwriters, Nat. Assn. Life Underwriters, Internat. Platform Assn., Nat. Assn. Ins. and Fin. Advisors (inducted into Hall of Fame, 2003), Internat. Assn. Fin. Planners (v.p. Delaware Valley chpt. 1986-88, pres. 1989-, chmn. 1990-), Million Dollar Round Table (mem. Ct. of the Table 1986-, Top of the Table 1991, 93-95, Twenty-Five Million Dollar Internat. forum 1992-93), Lake Naomi Club (v.p., mem. bd. govs. 1982, pres. 1986), KC, Manor Club, Tom Brinker's Op. Christmas Baskets (pres.), Kingsport Club, Inc. (bd. dirs., treas. 1997-). Roman Catholic. Home: 115 Locust Ave Springfield PA 19064-1619 Office: 1 N Ormond Ave Havertown PA 19083-5010 E-mail: jbrinker@brinkerorg.com.

BRINKLEY, ALAN DAVID, provost, historian; b. Washington, June 2, 1949; s. David and Ann (Fischer) B.; m. Evangeline Morphos, June 3, 1989; 1 child, Diane Elizabeth. AB, Princeton U., 1971; PhD, Harvard U., 1979. Asst. prof. history MIT, Cambridge, 1978—82; Dunwalke assoc. prof. history Harvard U., Cambridge, 1982—88; prof. history grad. sch. CUNY, 1988—91; prof. history Columbia U., NYC, 1991—98, Allan Nevins prof. history, 1998—, provost, 2003—; Harmsworth prof. Am. history Oxford (Eng.) U., 1998—99. Author: Voices of Protest: Huey Long, Father Coughlin, and the Great Depression, 1982 (Nat. Book award 1983), The Unfinished Nation: A Concise History of the American People, 1993, The End of Reform: New Deal Liberalism in Recession and War, 1995, Liberalism and its Discontents, 1998. Trustee Century Found., NYC, 1996—, chmn. bd. trustees, 1999—; trustee The Dalton Sch., NYC, 1999-05, Nat. Humanities Ctr., 2004—. Guggenheim Found. fellow, 1984-85, Woodrow Wilson Ctr. Internat. Scholars fellow, 1985, Nat. Humanities Ctr. fellow, 1988-89; Media Studies Ctr. fellow, 1993-94; Russell Sage Found., 1996-97. Fellow Am. Acad. Arts and Scis.; mem. Century Assn. Home: 435 Riverside Dr # 52 New York NY 10025 Office: Columbia U 205 Low Libr New York NY 10027 Business E-Mail: ab65@columbia.edu.

BRINKLEY, AMY WOODS, bank executive; b. Franklin, Va., Jan. 19, 1956; d. Samuel Baker and Iris (Lankford) Woods; m. Robert Gentry Brinkley, Jan. 2, 1988; 2 children. BA, U. NC, Chapel Hill, 1978. Credit analyst NCNB, Charlotte, NC, 1978-79, internat. banking officer, 1979-80, comml. banking officer Greensboro, NC, 1981-84, credit policy officer, 1985-87; sr. consumer credit policy exec. NationsBank (formerly NCNB), Greensboro, 1988—93; exec. v.p., sr. consumer credit policy exec. NationsBank, 1990—99, mktg. grp. exec., 1993—99; pres. consumer products. Bank Am. (formerly NationsBank), 1999—2001; chmn. risk policy Bank Am., 2001—02, dep. head risk mgmt., 2001—02, global risk exec., 2002—. Bd. dirs. Carolinas HealthCare Sys., Pvt. Export Funding Co.; bd. trustees Princeton Theol. Sem. Bd. trustees Princeton Theol. Seminary; bd. advisors Partners in Out-of-Sch. Time, NC Dance Theatre, former chmn., bd. trustees; mem. U. NC bd. visitors. Named one of The 25 Most Powerful Women in Banking, US Banker mag., 2004, 2005, Most Powerful Women in Bus., Fortune mag., 2005, 50 Most Powerful Women in Bus., 2006, 25 Most Powerful Women in Banking, US Banker, 2006, 50 Women to Watch, Wall St. Jour., 2006. Mem. Women's Profl. Forum, Risk Mgmt. Roundtable, RMA Consumer Credit Execs., Phi Beta Kappa. Office: Bank Am 100 N Tryon St 18th Fl Charlotte NC 28255*

BRINKLEY, CHRISTIE, model, spokesperson, designer; b. LA, Feb. 2, 1954; d. Don and Marge B.; m. Jean François Allaux, 1974 (div. 1981); m. Billy Joel, 1985 (div. 1994); 1 child, Alexa Ray; m. Ricky Taubman, 1995 (div. 1995) 1 child Jack Paris; m. Peter Cook, 1996 (separated 2006); 1 child Sailor Lee. Attended, U. Calif., Northridge, La Grande Chaumiere. Model Elite Model Mgmt., Ford Models Inc., 1982—; co-owner Christie Brand Cosmetics, 1995—. Spokeswoman Nuskin Internat. Modeled for over 500 mag. covers incl. Sports Illustrated's annual swimsuit issue, 1979, 80, 81; product promotions incl. longest cosmetic contract with Cover Girl, Prell, Chanel No. 19 perfume; pub. Christie Brinkley's Outdoor Beauty and Fitness Book, 1983; appearance (film) National Lampoon's Vacation, 1983, Vegas Vacation, 1997, (video) Billy Joel's "Uptown Girl", River of Dreams, Keepin the Faith, Matter of Trust, (TV) Mad About You, 1994; designed album cover Billy Joel's "River of Dreams"; active infomercials Total Gym; past host Living in the 90's with Christie Brinkley CNN, others. also: William Morris Agy 1325 Avenue Of The Americas New York NY 10019-6026

BRINKLEY, DOUGLAS G., historian, writer, educator; b. Atlanta, Dec. 14, 1960; married; 3 children. BA, Ohio State U., 1982; MA, Georgetown U., 1983, PhD in military and diplomatic hist., 1989; PhD (hon.), Trinity Coll., Hartford, Conn. U., NOVA Southeastern U. Prof. US Navel Acad., Princeton U., Hofstra U.; Stephen E. Ambrose prof. history, dir. Eisenhower Ctr. for Am. Studies U. New Orleans; prof. history, dir. Theodore Roosevelt Ctr. for Am. Civilization Tulane U., New Orleans, 2005—07, dir. Theodore Roosevelt Ctr. for Am. Civilization; prof. history, fellow James A. Baker III Inst. Pub. Policy Rice U., Houston, 2007—. Author: Dean Acheson: The Cold War Years, 1953-1971, 1992, The Majic Bus: An American Odyssey, 1993, The Unfinished Presidency: Jimmy Carter's Journey Beyond the White House Years, 1998, Rosa Parks: A Biography, 2000, The New York Times Living History: World War II: The Axis Assault, 1939-1942, 2003, Voices of Valor: D-Day, June 6, 1944, 2004, Tour of Duty: John Kerry and the Vietnam War, 2004, The World War II Memorial: A Grateful Nation Remembers, 2004, Wheels for the World: Henry Ford, His Company, and a Century of Progress, 2005, The Boys of Pointe du Hoc: Ronald Reagan, D-Day, and the Heroic Feats of the U.S. Army Rangers, 2005, The Great Deluge: Hurricane Katrina, New Orleans and the Mississippi Gulf Coast, 2006 (Robert F. Kennedy Book Award, 2007); co-author (with Townsend Hoopes): Driven Patriot: The Life and Times of James Forrestal, 1992, Franklin Roosevelt and the Creation of the United Nations, 1997; co-author: The Mississippi and the Making of a Nation, 2002; Theodore Roosevelt, the U.S. Navy, and the Spanish-American War, 2003; co-author: (with Julie M. Fenster) Parish Priest: Father Michael McGivney and American Catholicism, 2006; editor: Dean Acheson and the Making of US Foreign Policy, 1993, John F. Kennedy and Europe, 1997, Strategies of Enlargement: The Clinton Doctrine and US Foreign Policy, 1997, Hunter S. Thompson: The Proud Highway: Saga of a Desperate Southern Gentleman 1955-1967, 1997, Hunter S. Thompson: Fear and Loathing in Ameica, 2001, Windblown World: The Journals of Jack Kerouac 1947-1954, 2004; co-editor (with Clifford P. Hackett): Jean Monnet: The Path to European Unity, 1991; co-editor: (with Gable and Naylor) Theodore Roosevelt: The Many-Sided American, 1993; co-editor: (with D. Facey-Crowther) The Atlantic Charter, 1994; co-editor: (with Stephen Ambrose) Witness to America: An Illustrated Documentary History of the United States from the Revolution to Today, 1999; co-editor: (with Andrew Carroll) War Letters: Extraordinary Correspondence from Wars, 2001. Recipient Stessin award Disting. Scholarship, Hofstra Univ., 1993, Theodore and Franklin Roosevelt Naval History award, 1993, Notable Book award, NY Times, 1993, 1998, Bernath Lecture prize, 1996. Office: James A Baker III Inst for Pub Policy Baker Hall, Ste 120 6100 Main St Houston TX 77005*

BRINKLEY, JACK THOMAS, lawyer, retired congressman; b. Faceville, Ga., Dec. 22, 1930; s. Lonnie Elester and Pauline (Spearman) B.; m. Alma Lois Kite, May 29, 1955; children: Jack Thomas Jr., Fred Alen II. Student, Young Harris Coll., 1947-49, Okla. A. and M. Coll., 1952; LL.B. cum laude, U. Ga., 1959. Bar: Ga. 1958, DC 1973. Sch. tchr., Ga., 1949-51; assoc. firm Young, Hollis & Moseley, Columbus, Ga., 1959-61; ptnr. firm Coffin & Brinkley, Columbus, 1961-66; mem. Ga. Ho. Reps., 1965-66; sr. ptnr. Brinkley and Brinkley, 1983-95, of counsel, 1996-2000, of counsel emeritus, 2001—; mem. 90th-97th Congresses from 3d Ga. dist.; chmn. mil. facilities and installations subcom. 97th Congress. Mem. Ga. Ho. Rep., 1965-66. Trustee Young Harris Coll. Mem. Ga. Bar Assn., Columbus Bar Assn., Young Lawyers Club of Columbus (pres. 1963-64), Blue Key, Muscogee Civitan Club (pres., 2005), Masons. Democrat. Baptist. Office: Corporate Ctr Ste 901 Columbus GA 31902 Office Phone: 706-576-5322. Personal E-mail: jtbrink@bellsouth.net.

BRINKMAN, DALE THOMAS, lawyer; b. Columbus, Ohio, Dec. 10, 1952; s. Harry H. and Jean May (Sandel) B.; m. Martha Louise Johnson, Aug. 3, 1974; 3 children: Marin Veronica, Lauren Elizabeth, Kelsey Renee. BA, U. Notre Dame, 1974; JD, Ohio State U., 1977. Bar: Ohio 1977, U.S. Dist. Ct. (so. dist.) Ohio 1979. Assoc. Schwartz, Shapiro, Kelm & Warren, Columbus, 1977-82; asst. tax counsel Am. Elect. Power, Columbus, 1982; gen. counsel Worthington Industries, Inc., Columbus, 1982-99, v.p. adminstrn., gen. counsel, sec., 1999—, corp. sec., 2000—. Author: Ohio State U. Law Jour.,1975-76, editor, 1976-77. Trustee, officer Friends of Dahlberg Ctr., Columbus, 1980-86; dir., officer Assn. for Developmentally Disabled, Columbus, 1986-94. Mem. ABA, Ohio State Bar Assn., Columbus Bar Assn. Republican. Roman Catholic. Office: Worthington Industries 200 W Old Wilson Bridge Rd Worthington OH 43085-2247 E-mail: dtbrinkm@worthingtonindustries.com.*

BRINKMAN, FIONA SUSAN, bioinformaticist, educator, molecular biologist; BSc with honors, U. Waterloo, 1990; PhD, U. Ottawa, 1996. Chemistry technician Ministry of Environ.-Air Resources Br., Toronto, Ontario, Canada, 1987, ORTech Internat., Mississauga, Ontario, Canada, 1988; rsch. technician III, Connaught Labs., Toronto, Ontario, Canada, 1989—89; rsch. technician Lab. Ctr. for Disease Control, Health Can., Ottawa, Ontario, 1990—90; postdoctoral fellow and rsch. assoc. U. of BC, Vancouver, Canada, 1996—2001; prof. Simon Fraser U., Burnaby, British Columbia, Canada, 2001—; coord. Pseudomonas Aeruginosa Cmty. Genome Annotation Project, 2001—; rsch. dir. bioinformatics Genome Can. Pathogenomics Project, 2003—. Contbr. over 100 articles to profl. jours. Named one of World's Top 100 Young Innovators Under Age 35, MIT, 2002, Can.'s Top 40 Under 40, Caldwell Partners Internat., 2004; recipient Entrance scholarship, U. Ottawa, 1990, Scholar Career award, Michael Smith Found. for Health Rsch., 2001, Young Innovator award, Sci. Coun. of BC, 2003, New Investigator award, Can. Insts. of Health Rsch., 2005, Senior Scholar Career award, Michael Smith Found. for Health Rsch., 2007, Fisher award, Canadian Soc. Microbiologists, 2007; Postdoctoral fellowship, Can. Cystic Fibrosis Found., 1996, Discovery grants, Natural Scis. and Engring. Rsch. Coun. of Can., 2001—, Spl. Rsch. Projects grant, US Cystic Fibrosis Found., 2001—, Establishment grant, Michael Smith Found. for Health Rsch., 2001—03, Tng. Program grant, Can. Insts. of Health Rsch., 2002—, Large Scale Rsch. Projects grant, Genome Can., 2003—, Equipment grant, Inimex Pharms., 2003—05, Spl. Funds grant, IBM Can., 2004—05. Mem.: Soc. for Can. Women in Sci. and Tech., Internat. Soc. for Computational Biology, Am. Soc. for Microbiology, Can. Soc. of Microbiologists. Achievements include development of PSORTb, the world's most precise computer program for the ID of bacterial protein locations (used in the ID of potential new drug and vaccine targets against infectious diseases). Office: Simon Fraser Univ MBB Dept 8888 University Dr Burnaby BC Canada V5A1S6

BRINKMAN, JOHN ANTHONY, historian, educator; b. Chgo., July 4, 1934; s. Adam John and Alice (Davies) B.; m. Monique E. Geschier, Mar. 24, 1970; 1 son, Charles E. AB, Loyola U., Chgo., 1956, MA, 1958; PhD, U. Chgo., 1962. Rsch. assoc. Oriental Inst., U. Chgo., 1963, dir. inst., 1972-81, asst. prof. Assyriology and ancient history, 1964-66, assoc. prof., 1966—70, prof., 1970—84, Charles H. Swift disting. svc. prof., 1984—2001, chmn. dept., 1969—72, Charles H. Swift disting. svc. prof. emeritus, 2001—. Ann. prof. Am. Schs. Oriental Rsch., Baghdad, 1968-69; chmn. Baghdad Schs. Com., 1970-85, chmn. exec. com., 1973-75, trustee, 1975-90; chmn. vis. com. dept. Near Ea. langs. and civilizations Harvard U., 1995-2001. Author: Political History of Post-Kassite Babylonia, 1968, Materials and Studies for Kassite History, Vol. I, 1976; Prelude to Empire, 1984; editorial bd. Chgo. Assyrian Dictionary, 1977—, State Archives Assyria, 1985—; editor in charge Babylonian sect. Royal Inscriptions of Mesopotamia, 1979-91; contbr. numerous articles to profl. jours. Fellow Am. Research Inst., in Turkey, 1971; sr. fellow Nat. Endowment Humanities, 1973-74; Guggenheim fellow, 1984-85, Emeritus fellow, Mellon Found., 2005—. Fellow Am. Acad. Arts and Scis.; mem. Am. Oriental Soc. (pres. Middle West chpt. 1971-72), Am. Schs. of Oriental Rsch., Brit. Sch. Archaeology in Iraq, Deutsche Orient Gesellschaft, Brit. Inst. Archaeology at Ankara. Roman Catholic. Home: 1321 E 56th St Apt 4 Chicago IL 60637-1762 Office: U Chgo 1155 E 58th St Chicago IL 60637-1569 Office Phone: 773-702-9545.

BRINKMAN, MICHAEL, neuropsychologist, researcher; b. Lima, Ohio, Feb. 20, 1974; s. Arthur and Mary Brinkman; m. Deirdra Murphy, May 11, 2002. D of Psychology, Va. Consortium Program in Clin. Psychology, Virginia Beach, Va., 2005. Case mgr. CRI, Inc., Cin., 1999—2001; clin. psychology intern VA Ann Arbor Health Sys., Mich., 2004—05; postdoctoral fellow clin. neuropsychology U. Mich. Health Sys., Ann Arbor, 2005—. Vol. Alzheimer's Assn., Ann Arbor Chpt., 2006. Vis. fellowship, APA, 2003. Mem.: Internat. Neuropsychol. Soc. (assoc.), Sigma Xi, Phi Kappa Phi, Psi Chi. Liberal. Achievements include research in the neuropsychology of depression using functional magnetic resonance imaging. Avocations: golf, hiking, travel, camping. Office: Univ Mich Health Sys Ann Arbor MI Home Phone: 734-646-2199. Personal E-mail: mbrinx@med.umich.edu.

BRINKMAN, MICHAEL OWEN, health care consultant, educator; b. Chgo., May 15, 1936; s. Adam John and Alice Corrine (Davies) B.; m. Mary Judith Zeitz, Jan. 18, 1958; children: Stephen, Daniel, Julie, Amy, Carl, Mary Alice. BEE magna cum laude, Marquette U., 1958. Instr. Marquette U., Milw., 1957-59; engr. Wis. Electric Power, Milw., 1958-59, A.C. Electronics, Oak Creek, Wis., 1959-62; svc. engr. Nuclear-Chgo. Corp., Des Plaines, Ill., 1962-63, dir. of svc., 1963-66, plant mgr., 1966-67; gen. mgr. Electrovac, Melrose Park, Ill., 1968; mktg. analyst A.C. Electronics, Oak Creek, Wis., 1969-70; pres. On-Call Nat., Barrington, Ill., 1970-72, Hosp. Maintenance Cons., Columbus, Wis., 1972—. Co-author: (books) Clinical Engineering, 1975, Managing Your Medical Equipment, 1978, 82; contbr. numerous articles to profl. jours. Dep. committeeman Schaumburg Twp. Rep., Hoffman Estates, Ill., 1964-67; supt. Country Christian Schs., Nashotah, Wis., 1978-90, bd. dirs., 1990-95; bd. dirs. Victory Christian H.S., Neosho, Wis., 1991-2003, vol. tchr., 1991-2005; mem. Oconomowoc Bible Fellowship, elder, 1996—. Mem. Med. Equipment Repair Assocs. (exec. dir. 1973—), Triangle Fraternity, Eta Kappa Nu, Pi Mu Epsilon, Tau Beta Pi, Alpha Sigma Nu. Avocations: bible teaching, golf, stamp collecting/philately, antique glassware. Home: 443 W Prairie St Columbus WI 53925-1349 Office: Hosp Maintenance Cons Inc PO Box 309 Columbus WI 53925-0309 Office Phone: 920-623-4481. Personal E-mail: mobrinkman@sbcglobal.net. Business E-Mail: mbrinkman@meraserv.net.

BRINKMAN, PAUL DEL(BERT), retired foundation administrator, journalist, educator; b. Olpe, Kans., Feb. 10, 1937; s. Paul Theodore and Delphine Barbara (Brown) Brinkman; m. Evelyn Marie Lange, Aug. 5, 1961 (dec. June 1988); m. Carolyn L. Backer, July 27, 1990; children: Scott Michael, Susan Lynn Moeser stepchildren: Debra, Cynthia, Jeffrey. BS, Emporia State Coll., 1958; MA in Journalism (Newspaper Fund fellow), Ind. U., 1963, PhD in Mass Comm. (Scripps-Howard fellow), 1971. Editor, reporter Emporia (Kans.) Gazette, 1954-59; instr. journalism Leavenworth (Kans.) High Sch., 1959-62; lectr. Ind. U., Bloomington, 1962-65, 68-70; asst. prof. Kans. State U., Manhattan, 1965-68; prof., dean Sch. Journalism U. Kans., Lawrence, 1970-86, vice chancellor for acad. affairs, 1986-93; dir. journalism programs John S. and James L. Knight Found., Miami, 1993-2001; dean U. Colo. Sch. Journalism and Mass Comm., Boulder, 2001—02, mem. adv. bd., 2002. Balt. Sun disting. lectr. Coll. Journalism, U. Md., 1993. Bd. dirs. William Allen White Found., 1974; chmn. Big Eight Athletic Conf., 1980-81, 87-88; faculty rep. Nat. Collegiate Athletic Assn., 1978-93; press fellowship adv. com. Knight Internat.; adv. bd. Journalism Sch. U. Colo.; coun. on accreditation of law schs. ABA, 1998-2004; bd. govs. Kinsey Inst., 2002—, v.p., 2007—. Named Trayes Prof. of Yr. Mass Comm. Soc. divsn. Assn. Edn. Journalism, 1990; recipient Disting. Alumni award Emporia State Coll., 1978, Disting. Svc. award Ind. U., 1986. Mem. Am. Assn. Schs. and Depts. Journalism (pres. 1977-78), Inland Daily Press Assn. (chmn. edn. com. 1980-83), Assn. Edn. Journalism (chmn. publs. com. 1974-75, pres. 1980-81), Soc. Profl. Journalists, Lawrence C. of C. (v.p. 1987-88), Rotary (pres. Lawrence chpt. 1987-88), Bloomington Press Club (bd. dirs. 2002—, v.p. 2007—), Indiana U. Sch. Journalism Alumni (bd. dirs. 2003-), Ernie Pyle Soc., Sigma Delta Chi, Kappa Tau Alpha. Home: 3112 Coppertree Drive Bloomington IN 47401 Personal E-mail: del.brinkman@insightbb.com.

BRINKMAN, WILLIAM FRANK, physicist, research and development company executive; b. Washington, Mo., July 20, 1938; s. William F. and Mildred A. (Bocklege) Brinkman; m. Sybille Zeldin, Sept. 17, 2001; children: David, Curtis. BS, U. Mo., 1960, PhD, 1965. Postdoctoral fellow Oxford U., 1966; mem. staff Bell Labs., Murray Hill, NJ, 1966-72, dept. head, 1972-74, dir., 1974-84; v.p. rsch. Sandia Nat. Lab., Albuquerque, 1984-87; v.p. phys. scis. rsch. Lucent Techs./Bell Labs., Murray Hill, NJ, 1987-2000, v.p. rsch., 2000—01; sr. rsch. physicist dept. physics Princeton U., NJ, 2002—. Contbr. articles to profl. jours. Fellow AAAS, Am. Phys. Soc. (pres. 2002, George E. Pake prize 1994); mem. Am. Acad. Arts and Scis., Nat. Acad. Sci. (chmn. 8-vol. report Physics Through the 1990s), Am. Philos. Soc. Achievements include research in theoretical physics. Home: 20 Constitution Hill W Princeton NJ 08540 Office: Princeton Univ Dept Physics 328 Jadwin Hill Princeton NJ 08542 Business E-Mail: wfb@princeton.edu.

BRINKMANN, ROBERT JOSEPH, lawyer; b. Cin., Dec. 25, 1950; s. Robert Harry and Helen R. (Streuwing) B.; children: Christopher, Julia. BA, U. Notre Dame, Ind., 1972; postgrad., Alliance Française, 1974-75; AM, Brown U., Providence, 1977; JD, Loyola U., Los Angeles, 1980. Bar: Calif. 1980, DC 1981, US Ct. Appeals (DC and 9th cirs.) 1981, US Supreme Ct. 1984, US Ct. Appeals (6th cir.) 1987. Tchr. secondary schs., Los Angeles and Paris, 1974-77; assoc. Hedrick & Lane, Washington, 1980-82; gen. counsel Nat. Newspaper Assn., Washington, 1982-92; exec. dir. Red Tag News Publs. Assn., 1990-92; v.p., counsel postal and regulatory affairs Newspaper Assn. Am., Reston, Va., 1992—2003; ptnr. Olive, Edwards & Brinkmann, LLC, Washington, 2003—05; atty. Law Offices of Robert J. Brinkmann, LLC, Washington, 2005—. Mem. faculty Am. Press. Inst., Reston, 1982-92; adj. faculty U. Md., 1996—. Mem. ABA (chmn. postal affairs com.), Fed. Communications Bar Assn. Roman Catholic. Home: 204 Lynn Manor Dr Rockville MD 20850-4431 Office: 1730 M St NW Ste 200 Washington DC 20036 Business E-Mail: robertbrinkmann@rjbrinkmann.com.

BRINKMEYER, SCOTT S., lawyer; b. Chgo., Sept. 27, 1949; BA, DePauw U., 1971; JD, St. Louis U., 1975. Bar: Mich. 1975, cert.: Am. Arbitration Assn. Nat. Panel (civil neutral arbitrator) 2004, US Dist. Ct., Western Dist. Mich. (mediator) 2005. Atty. Mika, Meyers, Beckett & Jones, PLC, Grand Rapids, Mich. Jud. law clk. Mo. Ct. appeals, 1974. Assoc. editor St. Louis U. Law Jour., 1974. Pres. Grand Rapids Rotary Dist. 290, 1997—98. Fellow: Mich. State Bar Found., Am. Bar Found.; mem.: ABA (Ho. Del. 2003—04), Grand Rapids Bar Assn., Def. Rsch. Inst., Mich. Def. Trial Counsel, State Bar Mich. (rep. assembly 1992—2004, bd. commrs. 1995—2004, exec. com. 1996—98, chair 2003—04, pres. 2003—04, sects. on environ. law, litigation, negligence law, dispute resolution, exec. com. 1999—2004). Office: Mika Meyers Beckett and Jones 900 Monroe Ave NW Grand Rapids MI 49503-1423

BRINN, LOUIS BERNARD, radiologist; b. NYC, Oct. 19, 1934; s. Joseph and Mollie Brinn; m. Rosalie Harriet Kesten; children: Elissa, Joshua, Deborah. BS, NYU, NYC, 1954; MD, NYU, 1958. Cert. diagnostic radiology and therapeutic radiology Am. Bd. Radiology. Asst. attending radiologist Mt. Sinai Hosp., NYC, 1964—67; sr. attending radiologist Good Samaritan Hosp., West Islip, NY, 1967—2000; pvt. practice radiology South Shore Radiology, West Islip, 1967—2000; radiologist Zwanger and Pesiri Radiology, Plainview, NY, 2000—04; attending radiologist North Shore Hosp., Plainview, 2002—04; ret. Contbr. articles to profl. jours. Capt. med. corp US Army, 1960—62. Mem.: Suffolk County Med. Soc., LI Radiology Soc.

BRINSMADE, AKBAR FAIRCHILD, chemical engineering consultant; b. Puebla, Mex., May 31, 1917; s. Robert Bruce and Helen Steenbock Brinsmade; m. Juanita Phillips, June 16, 1944; children: Anne Hudson Brinsmade, Robert Bruce P., Charlotte Lynn Brinsmade. BS in Chemistry, U. Wis., Madison, 1939; MSChemE, MIT, Cambridge, 1942; postgrad., Poly. Inst. Bklyn., 1945—46, NYU, 1947—49, Tulane U., New Orleans, 1967—73. Registered profl. engr., N.C., La. Gen. mgr. Cia. Minera SnFrancisco y Anex., San Luis Potosi, Mexico, 1939—40; sr. rsch. engr. Shell Oil Co. Inc., Houston and NYC, 1942—48; project mgr. Internat. Indsl. Cons., NYC and Caracas, 1949—50; mng. dir. Promotora Nacional de Indsl., Caracas, 1952—57; R&D engr. Hercules Powder Co., Rocket Center, W.Va., 1959—64; rsch. engring. specialist Chrysler Space Divsn., New Orleans, 1966—69; chem. engring. cons. to maj. U.S. and fgn. corps., 1969—. Author: Travel to the Stars, 1996; contbr. chapters to books. Chmn. Citizens for Goldwater, Allegany County, Md., 1964. Fellow Am. Inst. Chemists; mem. NSPE, AIChE, Am. Chem. Soc., La. Engring. Soc. (profl. engr.), Phi Eta Sigma, Phi Lambda Upsilon, Sigma Alpha Epsilon. Republican. Lutheran. Achievements include patents for Gravity Module. Avocations: books, history, languages, travel, tennis. Home: 486 Channel Mark Dr Biloxi MS 39531

BRINSMADE, LYON LOUIS, retired lawyer; b. Mexico City, Feb. 24, 1924; s. Robert Bruce and Helen (Steenbock) B. (Am. citizens); m. Susannah Tucker, June 9, 1956 (div. 1978); children: Christine Fairchild, Louisa Calvert; m. Carolyn Hartman Lister, Sept. 22, 1979 (dec. 2003). Student, U. Wis., 1940-43; BS, Mich. Technol. U., 1944; JD, Harvard U., 1950. Bar: Tex. 1951. Assoc. Butler, Binion, Rice, Cook & Knapp, Houston, 1950-58, ptnr. in charge internat. dept., 1958-83, Porter & Clements, Houston, 1983-91; sr. counsel Porter & Hedges (formerly Porter & Clements), Houston, 1991-99. Bd. dirs. Houston br. English-Speaking Union of U.S., 1972-75. Served with AUS, 1946-47. Mem. ABA (chmn. com. internat. investment and devel. of sect. internat. law and practice 1970-76, council 1972-76, 81-82, vice chmn. 1976-79, chmn.-elect 1979-80, chmn. 1980-81, co-founder and co-chmn. com. Mex. 1982-85), Internat. Bar Assn., Inter-Am. Bar Assn. (co-chmn. sect. oil and gas laws, com. natural resources 1973-76, council 1984-87), Houston Bar Assn., State Bar Tex. (chmn. internat. law com. 1970-74, mem. council sect. internat. law 1975-78), Am. Soc. Internat. Law (exec. council 1984-86), Houston World Trade Assn. (sec., dir. 1967-70), Houston World Trade Assn. (chmn. legis. com. 1967-72), Houston C. of C. (chmn. legis. subcom. internat. bus. com. 1970-72), SAR, Allegro of Houston, Harvard Club (Houston), Sigma Alpha Epsilon. Episcopalian. Home: PO Box 1149 Wimberley TX 78676-1149 Home Phone: 512-847-2576; Office Phone: 512-847-2576.

BRINSON, GAY CRESWELL, JR., retired lawyer; b. Kingsville, Tex., June 13, 1925; s. Gay Creswell and Lelia (Wendelkin) B.; m. Bette Lee Butter, June 17, 1979; children from former marriage: Thomas Wade, Mary Kaye. Student, U. Ill., Chgo., 1947-48; BS, U. Houston, 1953, JD, 1957. Bar: Tex. 1957, U.S. Dist. Ct. (so. dist.) Tex. 1959, U.S. ct. Appeals (5th cir.) 1962 U.S. Dist. Ct. (ea. dist.) Tex. 1965, U.S. Supreme Ct. 1974; U.S. Dist. Ct. (no. dist.) Tex. 1990; diplomate Am. Bd. Trial Advocates, Am. Bd. Profl. Liability Attys. Spl. agt. FBI, Washington and Salt Lake City, 1957-59; trial atty. Liberty Mut. Ins. Co., Houston, 1959-62; assoc. Horace Brown, Houston, 1962-64, Vinson & Elkins, Houston, 1964-67, ptnr., 1967-91; of counsel McFall, Sherwood & Sheehy, Houston, 1992-2000. Lectr. U. Houston Coll. Law, 1964-65; mem. staff Tex. Coll. Trial Advocacy, Houston, 1978-86; prosecutor Harris County Grievance Com.-State Bar Tex., Houston, 1965-70 With AUS, 1943—46, ETO. Fellow Tex. Bar Found. (life); mem. Tex. Acad. Family Law Specialists (cert.), Tex. Assn. Def. Counsel, Tex. Bd. Legal Specialization (cert.), Fedn. Ins. Counsel, Nat. Bd. Trial Advocacy (cert.), Houston Ctr. Club, Phi Delta Phi. Home: 3740 Del Monte Dr Houston TX 77019-3018 Personal E-mail: gbrinson@houston.rr.com.

BRINSTER, RALPH LAWRENCE, biologist, educator; BS, Rutgers U., 1953; VMD, U. Pa., 1960, PhD in Physiology, 1964; D honoris causa, U. Basque Country, Spain, 1994; DSc (hon.), Rutgers U., 2000. Tchg.fellow U. Pa., Phila., 1961-64, instr. Sch. Medicine, 1964-65, asst. prof., then assoc. prof. Sch. Vet. Medicine, 1965-70, prof. physiology Sch. Vet. Medicine, 1970—, Richard King Mellon prof. reproductive physiology, 1975—. Lectr. Harvey Soc., 1984, Juan March Found., Madrid, 1992. Recipient Charles-Leopold Mayer prize, French Acad. Scis., 1994, March of Dimes prize, Devel. Biology, 1996, Bower award and prize, Sci., 1997, Disting. Svc. award, USDA, 1989, John Scott award, City Trusts Phila., 1997, Ernst W. Bertner award, 2001, Wolf prize in medicine, 2003, Gairdner Found. internat. award for achievement in med. rsch., 2006. Fellow: Am. Acad. Arts. and Scis.; mem.: AVMA, NAS, Inst. Medicine. Office: Univ Pa Sch Vet Medicine Philadelphia PA 19104

BRIONES, DAVID, judge; b. El Paso, Tex., Feb. 26, 1943; m. Delia Garcia; 4 children. BA, U. Tex., El Paso, 1969; JD, U. Tex., Austin, 1971. Ptnr. Moreno & Briones, 1971-91; judge El Paso County Ct. No. 1, El Paso, 1991-94; dist. judge U.S. Dist. Ct. (we. dist.) Tex., El Paso, 1994—. Mem. Jud. Conf. Com. Adminstrn. Magistrate Judges Sys., 2003—. With US Army, 1964—66. Fellow: Tex. Bar Found.; mem.: Mex.-Am. Bar Assn., El Paso Bar Assn., State Bar Tex. Office: US Courthouse Courtroom 1 511 E San Antonio Ave El Paso TX 79901-2401 Office Phone: 915-534-6744. Business E-Mail: David_Briones@txwd.uscourts.gov.

BRIONES, TERESITA LANDICHO, medical researcher, educator; d. Milagros Landicho and Carlos Briones. PhD, U. Mich., 1997. RN Mich., 1989. Clin. nurse specialist U. of Mich., Ann Arbor, Mich., 1989—95, rsch. asst., 1994—97; postdoctoral fellow Beckman Inst., Urbana, Ill., 1997—2000; assoc. prof. U. of Ill., Chgo., 2000—. Rsch. cons. Harbor -UCLA Med. Ctr., LA, 1988—89; edn. cons. Santa Monica Hosp., Santa Monica, Calif., 1985—86. Grantee Rsch., NIH, 2000 to present. Mem.: NY Acad. of Sci., Nat. Neurotrauma Soc., Am. Physiol. Soc., Soc. for Neuroscience. Achievements include research in Midwest Nursing Research Society New Investigator Award. Office: Univ Illinois 845 S Damen Ave M/C 802 Rm 750 Chicago IL 60612 Home Phone: 312-787-4457; Office Phone: 312-355-3142. Office Fax: 312-996-4979. E-mail: tbriones@uic.edu.

BRIOSO-MESA, MAUREEN DIANE, mental health services professional; b. Queens, NY, Aug. 24, 1975; d. Esther Estela and Hugo Alberto Brioso. MSc with distinction, Carlos Albizu U., Miami, 2002. Lic. mental health counselor, cert. nat. counselor. Outpatient counselor Children's Psychiat. Ctr., Miami, 2001—02; counselor Family Resource Ctr., Miami, 2002—03; child therapist The Village, Miami, 2003—04; behavioral health therapist Family Counseling Svcs., Miami, 2004, clin. supr., 2005—06; care mgr. Magellan Behavioral Health Svcs., Doral, Fla., 2006—. Mem.: Nat. Bd. Cert. Counselors, Fla. Assn. Play Therapy (corr.; Miami-Dade chpt. chair profl. devel. 2006), Assn. Play Therapy (corr.), Fla. Mental Health Counselor Assn. (corr.), Am. Mental Health Counseling Assn. (corr.). Office: Magellan Behavioral Health Svcs Doral FL Home Phone: 305-274-5263; Office Phone: 800-424-1693.

BRISBANE, ARTHUR SEWARD, newspaper publisher; b. NYC, Sept. 30, 1950; s. Seward Scatcherd and Doris Mae (Fauser) B.; m. Jo Ellen Hull, Oct. 16, 1982; children: Allison Faith, Madeline Mariah, Laura Calista. AB, Harvard Coll., 1973. Child care worker McLean Hosp., Belmont, Mass., 1973-74; freelance musician, 1974-76; reporter Glen Cove (N.Y.) Guardian, 1976-77, Kansas City (Mo.) Star & Times, 1977-79, columnist, 1979-84; reporter Washington Post, 1984-87, asst. city editor, 1987-89; columnist Kansas City Star, 1990-92, editor, v.p., 1992-97, pub., pres., 1997—2004; sr. v.p. Knight Ridder, Inc., 2005—06. Author: Arthur Brisbane's Kansas City, 1982. Avocations: tennis, reading.*

BRISCOE, ANNE M., retired science educator; b. NYC, Dec. 1, 1918; m. William A. Briscoe, Aug. 20, 1955 (dec. Dec. 1985); m. Theodore H. Heinly Sr., Jan. 21, 1989 (dec. Dec. 2002). MA, Vassar Coll., 1945; PhD, Yale U., 1949. From rsch. assoc. to asst. prof. Cornell U. Med. Coll., NYC, 1950-56; faculty Columbia U. Coll. Physicians and Surgeons, NYC, 1956—, prof. emeritus, 1987. Spl. lectr., 1987-89; lectr. Harlem Hosp. Center Sch. Nursing, 1968-77; adj. asst. prof. Hunter Coll., 1951-64, 73-75; mem. N.Y.C. Commn. on Status of Women, 1979-93, vice chair, 1982-93; non-govtl. orgn. del. to UN; adv. coun. Inst. Nuc. Power Ops., 1979-84. Contbr. articles to profl. jours. Sterling Jr. fellow, USPHS fellow, Yale U., 1949; recipient Yale medal, 1986, Susan B. Anthony award, 1989, Wilbur Cross medal Yale Grad. Sch. Sesquicentennial Convocation, 1997, Yale Fund Chmns. award, 2000. Fellow: AAAS (mem. coun. 1982—85, chmn.'s award Yale Alumni Fund 2001), Assn. Women in Sci. (editor newsletter 1971—74, nat. pres. 1974—76), N.Y. Acad. Sci. (chair women in sci. com. 1978—92, bd. govs. 1981), Am. Inst. Chemists (sec. N.Y. chpt. 1981—83); mem.: ACS, Assn. Women in Sci. Ednl. Found. (pres. 1978—82), Fedn. Orgns. for Profl. Women (treas. 1978—80), Harvey Soc., Am. Fedn. Clin. Rsch., Am. Soc. Clin. Nutrition, Yale Grad. Sch. Alumni Assn. (pres. 1981—86), Assn. Yale Alumni (assembly rep. 1978—, bd. govs. 1982—85). Home: 2116 Sea Cres Ruskin FL 33570-6128 E-mail: drannieb@aol.com.

BRISCOE, DAVID MICHAEL, physician, scientist, researcher; b. Dublin, Aug. 26, 1959; came to U.S., 1986; s. Joseph Henry and Deborah Briscoe; m. Carol J. Briscoe, Apr. 26, 1991; children: Adam, Leah. MB, Roycal Coll. Surgeons, Ireland, 1982, MRCP, 1985. Resident in medicine Eastern Health Bd., Ireland, 1982-86; resident in pediatrics U. Colo., Denver, 1986-88; fellow in nephrology Harvard Med. Sch., Boston, 1988-91, fellow in nephrology rsch., 1989-93, instr. medicine, 1993-95, asst. prof. medicine, 1995—. Dir. transplant immunology lab. Children's Hosp., Boston. Contbr. more than 30 articles to profl. jours. Mem. Am. Soc. Transplantation (Roche Basic Sci. Investigator award (assoc. prof. level), 2007), Am. Soc. Nephrology, Am. Soc. Pediatric Nephrology, Pediatric Acad. Soc. Office: Childrens Hosp 300 Longwood Ave Boston MA 02115-5737*

BRISCOE, JACK CLAYTON, lawyer; b. July 23, 1920; s. Park Harry and Elsie Gertrude (Woodward) B.; m. Dorothy Lillian Shaw, Sept. 3, 1949; children: Jacqueline Kamp, Jeffrey S., Ryd Joan. BS in Econs., U. Pa., 1943; LLB, Harvard U., 1948. Bar: Pa. 1950. Assoc. Robert C. Duffy, Phila., 1966—85; ptnr. Briscoe, Haggerty & Howard, Phila., 1966—85, Briscoe & Howard, Phila., 1986—90, Jack C. Briscoe & Assocs., Phila., 1990—. Instr. U. Pa., 1950—56; bd. dirs. Prime Inc.; chmn. bd. dirs. Master's Plan Fin. Svcs., Inc., Zoe Consulting Inc., Cmty. Capital Adivsors Inc. Elder United Presbyn. Ch. Manoa; active Fellowship Christian Athletes; mem. Rep. Presdl. Task Force; dir., pres. emeritus Pa. Bible Soc.; mem. bd. dirs. Faith Theol. Sem.; People for People, Inc.; bd. dirs. Prime, Inc., Urban Youth Racing Sch., Inc. With USAF, 1943—46. Recipient Branch Ricky Assocs. award, Cert. Achievement award, Compulsory Arbitration Divsn. Phila. County Ct. Fellow: Harry S. Truman Libr. Inst.; mem.: ABA, Chapel of Four Chaplains (legion hon. mem.), World Affairs Coun., Gideons Internat., Friendly Sons of St. Patrick, Pa. Soc. Harvard Law Sch. Assn., Phila. Bar Assn., Pa. Bar Assn., Emeritus Club Harvard Law Sch., Union League Club, Lawyers Club, Harvard Club. Office: Land Title Bldg Ste 2226 100 South Broad St Philadelphia PA 19110 Office Phone: 215-564-6025. Office Fax: 215-557-7651. Personal E-mail: jcblaw@juno.com.

BRISCOE, JOHN, lawyer; b. Stockton, Calif., July 1, 1948; s. John Lloyd and Doris (Olsen) B.; m. Carol E. Sayers; children: John Paul, Katherine JD, U. San Francisco, 1972. Bar: Calif. 1972, U.S. Dist. Ct. (no., ea. and ctrl. dists.) Calif. 1972, U.S. Supreme Ct. 1978, U.S. Ct. Appeals (9th cir.) 1981, Permanent Ct. Arbitration (The Hague) 2005. Dep. atty. gen. State of Calif., San Francisco, 1972—80; ptnr. Washburn and Kemp, San Francisco, 1980—88, Washburn, Briscoe & McCarthy, San Francisco, 1988—2002, Stoel Rives LLP, San Francisco, 2002—05, Briscoe Ivester and Bazel LLP, San Francisco, 2005—. Author: Surveying the Courtroom, 1984, rev. edit., 1999, Falsework, 1997, Tadich Grill, 2002; editor: Reports of Special Masters, 1991; contbr. articles to profl. and lit. jours Mem.: ABA, Am. Soc. Internat. Law, San Francisco Bar Assn. Roman Catholic. Office: Briscoe Ivester & Bazel LLP 155 Sansome St 7th Fl San Francisco CA 94104 Home Phone: 415-994-5701; Office Phone: 415-402-2700. Business E-Mail: jbriscoe@briscoelaw.net.

BRISCOE, MARY BECK, federal judge; b. Council Grove, Kans., Apr. 4, 1947; m. Charles Arthur Briscoe. BA, U. Kans., 1969, JD, 1973; LLM, U. Va., 1990. Rsch. asst. Harold L. Haun, Esq., 1973; atty.-examiner fin. divsn. ICC, 1973—74; asst. U.S. atty. for Wichita and Topeka, Kans. Dept. Justice, 1974—84; judge Kans. Ct. Appeals, 1984—95, chief judge, 1990—95; judge US Ct. Appeals (10th cir.), Topeka, 1995—. Named to Women's Hall of Fame, Univ. Kans., 2001; recipient Univ. Kans. Law Soc. Disting. Alumnus award, 2000. Fellow: Kans. Bar Found., Am. Bar Found.; mem.: ABA, Women Attys. Assn. Topeka, Kans. Bar Assn. (Outstanding Svc. award 1992), Topeka Bar Assn., Nat. Assn. Women Judges, Am. Judicature Soc., U. Kans. Law Soc., Kans. Hist. Soc., Washburn Law Sch. Assn. (hon.). Office: US Ct Appeals 10th Cir 645 Massachusetts Ste 400 Lawrence KS 66044-2235 also: US Ct Appeals 10th Cir Byron White US Courthouse 1823 Stout St Denver CO 80257*

BRISENO, KATHLEEN, education educator; d. Dominick Joseph and Rose Clare Tomaino; m. Jack Richard Briseno, Oct. 21, 1995; children: Matthew, Megan Knops. AA, Wright Coll., Chgo., 1972; BE, Northeastern Ill. Univ., Chgo., 1974; MEd, Northern Ill. Univ., Dekalb, Ill., 1979; EdD, Northen Ill. Univ., Dekalb, Ill., 2001. Cert. tchng. special and elem. edn. Ill. Spl. edn. tchr. Union Ridge Sch. Dist., Harwood Heights, Ill., 1974—79, Roselle Sch. Dist., Ill., 1979—80; asst. dir. spl. edn. intern Wheaton Sch. Dist., Ill., 1980—81; lectr. Elgin C.C., Ill., 1981; adj. faculty Nat. Coll. of Edn., Evanston, Ill., 1983, Northeastern Ill. Univ., Chgo., 1983—84, Nat. Louis U.; supr. student tchrs. Univ. Iowa, Iowa, 1989, Lewis Univ., Romeoville, Ill., 1989; field svc. coord., supr. student tchrs. Loyola Univ. of Chgo., Chgo., 1981—91; faculty North Ctrl. Coll., Naperville, Ill., 1990—93; supr. student tchrs., instr. No. Ill. Univ., Dekalb, Ill., 1991—92, grad. asst., 1992—93; sub. tchr. Woodridge Sch. Dist., Ill., 1992—94; resident supr. of student tchr. Western Ill. Univ., Macomb, Ill., 1993—94; program coord. Dekalb County Special Edn. Assn., Dekalb, Ill., 1994—97; asst. prof. U. Mo., 1996; asst. dir. student svcs. and spl. edn. Naperville Sch. Dist #203, Naperville, Ill., 1997—. Part time faculty Coll. DuPage, Glen Ellyn, Ill., 1987—; reviewer and editor Merrill/Macmillan Publ. Co., Columbus, Ohio, 1990—; adj. faculty Nat. Lois U., 2006. Author: Fall, 1993, Mandates as Reform: Who's Kidding Whom?, 2001, Grabbintg a Bully By the Horns, 2007. Chair cmty. and residential svcs. authority Ill. House of Reps. Mem.: ASCD, Coun. Exceptional Children, Assn. Tchr. Educators, Ill. Whole Language, No. Ill. Reading Coun., Internat. Reading Assn., Field Experience Supr. Network, Ill. Alliance of Adminstr. of Spl. Edn., Misericordia, Little City Found., Ray Graham Assn. for People with Disabilities, March of Dimes Birth Defects Found., YMCA, Little Friends, Ronald Mcdonald House, Boys and Girls Clubs of Chgo. Avocations: music, travel, reading. Home: 1821 Princeton Cir Naperville IL 60565 Office: Naperville Cmty Unit Sch Dist #203 203 Hillside Naperville IL 60540 Office Phone: 630-420-6389. Business E-Mail: kbriseno@naperville203.org.

BRISKIN, JACQUELINE ELIZABETH, author; b. London; came to U.S., 1938, naturalized, 1944; d. Spencer and Marjorie Orgell; m. Bert Briskin, May 9, 1948; children— Ralph, Elizabeth, Richard. Author: (novels) California Generation, 1970; Afterlove, 1974; Rich Friends, 1976; Paloverde, 1978; The Onyx, 1982; Everything and More, 1983; Too Much Too Soon, 1985, Dreams Are Not Enough, 1987, The Naked Heart, The Other Side of Love, 1991, The Crimson Palace, 1995. Recipient LMV Peer award, 1985. Mem. Authors Guild, PEN.

BRISKIN, MADELEINE, oceanographer, paleontologist; b. Paris, Sept. 4, 1932; came to U.S., 1951, naturalized, 1956; d. Michel and Mina B. BS, CCNY, 1965; MS, U. Conn., 1967; PhD, Brown U., 1973. Prof. geology Geology-Physics Bldg., U. Cin., 1980—. Recipient award Rsch. Support, 1971-72, Support award NSF, 1978. Mem. AAAS, Am. Geophys. Union, Am. Quaternary Assn., Climap, Cin. Engrs. and Scientists Soc., Planetary Soc., Soc. Sci. Exploration, Woods Hole Oceanographic Instn., Lamont-Doherty Geol. Obs., N.Y. Acad. Scis., Sigma Xi. Achievements include discovery of 430,000 plus years astronomical cycle in deep-sea sediments; development of pulsating earth model. Office: U Cin Dept Geology Cincinnati OH 45221-0001

BRISKMAN, LOUIS JACOB, lawyer, broadcast executive; b. Jan. 13, 1949; m. Maureen Frances O'Shaughnessy (dec. Mar. 18, 2001). BA, U. Pitts., 1970; JD, Georgetown U., 1973. Bar: Pa. 1973. With Westinghouse Electric Corp., 1975, chief counsel, 1978-81, assoc. gen. counsel energy and advanced tech. & broadcasting divsn., 1986-87, dep. gen. counsel, 1987-92, sr. v.p., gen. counsel, 1993-98; v.p., sec., gen. counsel Group W Cable, Inc. (subs. Westinghouse), 1981-83; v.p., sec., chief legal officer Group W Broadcasting Co., 1983-86; exec. v.p., gen. counsel CBS Corp., NYC, 1998-2000, 2005—, CBS TV, NYC, 2000—02; sr. v.p., gen. counsel Aetna Inc., Hartford, Conn., 2004—05. Bd. regents Georgetown U. Office: CBS Corp 51 W 52nd St New York NY 10019-6188 Office Phone: 212-975-4321.*

BRISKMAN, ROBERT DAVID, engineering executive; b. NYC, Oct. 15, 1932; s. Nathan S. and Rose L. (Fishman) B.; m. Lenora Heffner, Mar. 30, 1957; children: Laura G., Sharon L., Robert D. Jr., Douglas E. BSE, Princeton U., 1954; MS, U. Md., 1961. Registered profl. engr., D.C. Devel. engr. IBM, Poughkeepsie, NY, 1954-55; analyst Army Security Agy., Washington, 1956-58; chief of program support tracking and data acquisition NASA, Washington, 1959-63; asst. v.p. domestic systems Communication Satellite Corp., Washington, 1964-72; asst. v.p. space and info. systems Comsat Gen. Corp., Washington, 1973-76; dir. pre-operational program Satellite Bus. Systems, McLean, Va., 1977-79; v.p. systems implementation Comsat Gen. Corp., Washington, 1980-85; sr. v.p. engring. and ops. Geostar Corp., Washington, 1986—90; co-founder, exec. v.p. engring. Sirius Satellite Radio Inc., NYC, 1991—2001, tech. exec., 2001—. Contbr. articles on satellite systems and applications, 1956—; telecommunications editor: McGraw-Hill Ency. Sci. and Tech., 1985—; patentee in field. Capt. U.S. Army, 1955-57. Recipient Founders award Electronics and Aerospace Sys. Conf., 1980, Apollo Achievement award, NASA, 1963; named to Soc. Satellite Profls. Internat. Hall of Fame, 2001, Space Found. Technology Hall of Fame, 2002. Fellow AIAA (Aerospace Comm. award, 2007), IEEE (v.p. tech. activities, sec.-treas., 1976-78, Centennial medal, 1984), Washington Acad. Sci., Washington Soc. Engrs. (pres. 1988-89); mem. Old Crows, Internat. Acad. Astronautics, Armed Forces Comm. and Electronics Assn., Internat. Astron. Fedn. (mem. space comm. and navigation com. 1989—, chmn. 2004—), Cosmos Club, Union League Club. Republican. Office: Sirius Satellite Radio Inc 1221 Ave of the Americas New York NY 10020

BRISSETTE, MARTHA BLEVINS, lawyer; b. Salisbury, Md., Apr. 30, 1959; d. Reuben Wesley and Miriam Rebecca (Walters) Blevins; m. Henry Joseph Brissette III, May 24, 1980; children: Madeline Rose, William Roy. BA, U. Richmond, 1981, JD, 1983. Bar: Va. 1983, US Supreme Ct. 1987. Law clk. Supreme Ct. Va., Richmond, 1983-84; atty. Dept. Justice, Washington, 1984-88; staff atty. Office of the Exec. Sec., Supreme Ct. Va., Richmond, Va., 1988; asst. atty. gen. Office of the Atty. Gen. of Va., Richmond, 1989-92; v.p. counsel Lawyers Title Ins. Corp., Richmond, 1992-97; asst. counsel State Farm Ins. Cos., 1997-99; asst. atty. gen. Office of Atty. Gen. of Va., Richmond, 1999—2001; pvt. practice Richmond, 2002—05; assoc. Ukrops Supermarkets, Inc., 2004—05; atty. Va. Divsn. Legis. Svcs., Richmond, 2005—07; policy analyst Va. State Bd. Elections, Richmond, 2007—. Mem.: Richmond Bar Assn. Roman Catholic. Avocation: cake decorating. Home: 8307 Forge Rd Richmond VA 23228-3127 Office Phone: 804-864-8925. Personal E-mail: marthabrissette@aol.com. Business E-Mail: marthabbrissette@justice.com, mbrissette@leg.state.va.us.

BRISSON, STEVEN CHARLES, curator; b. Marquette, Mich., Mar. 4, 1967; s. William LeRoy Sr. and Eleanor Ann Brisson; m. Elizabeth Ann Craig, May 17, 1997; children: Emma, Matthew, Andrew. BS, Northern Mich. U., Marquette, 1989; MA, Cooperstown Grad. Program, NY, 1992. Curator State Hist. Soc. Wis., Madison, 1992—95; curator collections Mackinnel Island State Pk. Comm., Mich., 1996—2003, chief curator, 2003—. Author: (book) Wish You Were Here, 2002, Picturesque Mackinac, 2005 (Mich. Mus. Assn. award, 2006). Bd. dirs. Assn. for Great Lakes Maritime History, Green Bay, 2003—; bd. mem. Bishop Baraga Cath. Sch., Cheboygam, Mich., 1990—; cursillo secretariat Diocese Gaylord, Mich., 1996—99. Democrat. Roman Catholic. Home: 410 Cuyler St Cheboygan MI 49721 Office: Mackinac Island State Park Comm 207 W Sinclair PO Box 873 Mackinaw City MI 49701

BRISTER, BILL H., lawyer, former bankruptcy judge; b. Sieper, La., Mar. 5, 1930; s. Clayton Houston and Era (Price) B.; m. Carolyn Lee McDowell, June 11, 1955; children— Jeff, Julie. B.S. in Chemistry, Northwestern State U. Natchitoches, La., 1948; J.D., U. Tex., 1958. Bar: Tex. 1957, U.S. Dist. Ct. (no. dist.) Tex. 1959, U.S. Ct. Appeals (5th cir.) 1971, U.S. Supreme Ct. 1971. Pvt. practice, Lubbock, Tex., 1958-79; bankruptcy judge U.S. Dist. Ct. (no. dist.) Tex., 1979-85; of counsel Winstead, Sechrest & Minick and predecessor firm, 1986—. Served to col. USMCR, 1951-52. E-mail: billbrist@aol.com. E-mail: billbrist@aol.com.

BRISTER, SCOTT ANDREW, state supreme court justice; b. Waco, Tex., Jan. 8, 1955; s. Miller Robbins and Annette Josephine (Scott) B.; m. Julia Upton Brister, 4 children. BA summa cum laude, Duke U., 1977; JD cum laude, Harvard U., 1980. Bar: Tex. 1980, U.S. Dist. Ct. (so. dist.) Tex. 1981, U.S. Ct. Appeals 1981 (5th cir.), U.S. Supreme Ct. 1986. Briefing atty. to presiding justice Tex. Supreme Ct., Austin, 1980-81; atty. Andrews & Kurth, Houston, 1981-89; judge 234th Dist. Ct., Harris County, Houston, 1989—2000; justice First Dist. Ct. of Appeals, Houston, 2000—01; chief justice 14th Dist. Ct. of Appeals, 2001—03, justice, 2003—. Former mem. Jud. Panel on Multidistrict Litigation, Supreme Ct. Advisory Com., Supreme Ct. Jury Task Force. Co-author Texas Pretrial Practice; author law review articles in Baylor Law Review, St. Mary's Law Jour. Fellow Houston Bar Found., Tex. Bar Found. Office: Tex Supreme Ct 201 W 14th St PO Box 12248 Austin TX 78711*

BRISTOL, MURRAY L., lawyer; b. Oak Park, Ill., May 5, 1966; BBA in Fin. and Entrepreneurship, Baylor U., Waco, Tex., 1988; JD, U. Tulsa Coll. Law, 1992. Bar: Tex. 1993, Okla. 1995, US Dist. Ct. (no. and we. dists. Tex.), US Dist. Ct. (ea., no. and we. dist. Okla.). Asst. dist. atty. 34th Jud. Dist. Atty.'s Office; ptnr. Bristol & Dubiel, LLP, Dallas. Mem. Dallas Vol. Atty. Prog. Mem.: Tulsa County Criminal Def. Assn., Okla. Trial Lawyers Assn., Tulsa County Bar Assn., Assn. Trial Lawyers of Am., Tex. Trial Lawyers Assn., Tex. Criminal Def. Lawyers Assn., Okla. Bar Assn., State Bar Tex., Dallas County Bar Assn., North Dallas Bar Assn. (dir. 1999—2000), Travis County Bar Assn. Office: Bristol & Dubiel LLP 3333 Lee Pk y Ste 600 Dallas TX 75219-5117 Office Phone: 214-880-9988. Office Fax: 214-292-9466. E-mail: mlb@bristoldubiel.com.*

BRISTOL, NORMAN, lawyer, arbitrator, retired food products executive; b. Bronx, NY, June 14, 1924; s. Lawrence and Bell (Allchin) B.; m. Doreen Kingan, Mar. 28, 1952 (dec. June 2001); children: Charles L., Norman, Alexander, Barnaby; m. Sally Hume, May 28, 2004. Grad., Phillips Exeter Acad., 1941; AB, Yale, 1944; LLB, Columbia Law Sch., 1949. Bar: N.Y. bar 1950, Mich. bar 1954. Atty. Root, Ballantine, Harlan, Bushby & Palmer, NYC, 1949-53; with Kellogg Co., Battle Creek, Mich., 1954-78, asst. gen. counsel, 1958-64, sec., 1960-78, gen. counsel, 1964-78, sr. v.p., 1968-75, dir., 1972-78, exec. v.p., 1975-78; atty. Howard & Howard, Kalamazoo, 1979-93. Mem. Gull Lake Comty. Schs. Bd. Edn., 1963-70, pres., 1965-67; trustee Kalamazoo Symphony Soc., Inc., 1983-94, pres., 1990-91; bd. dirs. Southwest Mich. Land Conservancy, Inc., 1996-2001. Lt. (j.g.) USNR, 1943-46. Mem. State Bar Mich., Kalamazoo Bar Assn. Home and Office: 2962 Sylvan Dr Hickory Corners MI 49060-9319

BRISTON, HEATHER IRENE, archivist; d. David William and Emma Jean Briston. BA with honors, Mich. State U., 1992; MS in Info. (Archives and Records Mgmt.), U. Mich., 1999; JD, Syracuse U., 1995. Collections processor and reference asst. Bentley Hist. Libr., U. of Mich., Ann Arbor, 1997—99; supervising project archivist U. of Calif., Berkeley, 1999—2001; u. archivist U. of Oreg., Eugene, 2001—04, Corrigan Solari U. historian and archivist, 2004—. Tchg. fellow, Oreg. Humanities Ctr., 2006—07, Corrigan-Solari Libr. Faculty fellow, U. Oreg. Libr., 2006—07. Mem.: Soc. of Calif. Archivists, Internat. Coun. on Archives, Soc. of Am. Archivists. Office: U Oreg Librs 1299 University of Oregon Eugene OR 97403-1899 Home Phone: 541-684-0714; Office Phone: 541-346-1899. Office Fax: 541-346-1882. E-mail: hbriston@uoregon.edu.

BRISTOW, CYNTHIA LYNN, immunologist; b. Altus, Okla., Aug. 19, 1951; d. Robert O'Neil Bristow and Gaylon Eva Walker; children: Charlie, Bo, Rachel, Mary Ann, Rudy. BA, Winthrop U., 1972; MS, Med. U. SC, Charleston, 1979, PhD, 1986. Postdoctoral assoc. biochemistry Med. U. SC, Charleston, 1986-88; postdoctoral assoc. dental rsch. ctr. U. NC, Chapel Hill, 1988-94, rsch. asst. prof., 1994-98; clin. immunologist pathology and lab. medicine U. NC Hosp., Chapel Hill, 1999-2001; faculty cellular physiology and immunology Rockefeller U., NYC, 2001—03; asst. prof. dept medicine Mount Sinai Sch. Medicine, NYC, 2003—, dir. rsch. Inst Human Genetics and Biochemistry, 2003—. Contbr. articles to profl. jours., chapters to books. Recipient Elsa Pardee Found. award, 1990; grantee, NIH, 1994. Mem.: NY Acad. Sci., Assn. Med. Lab. Immunologists, Am. Diabetes Assn., Am. Chem. Soc., Am. Assn. Immunologists, Am. Soc. Microbiology, Sigma Xi. Episcopalian. Achievements include patents for biotechnology. Avocations: running, music, poetry, art, tennis. Office: Inst Human Genetics and Biochemistry 227 E 19th St Rm D477 New York NY 10003 Home: 312 A Main St Roslyn NY 11576 Home Phone: 917-301-3292; Office Phone: 212-995-6992. Business E-Mail: cynthia.bristow@mssm.edu.

BRISTOW, ROBERT O'NEIL, writer, educator; b. St. Louis, Nov. 17, 1926; s. Jesse Reuben and Helen Marjorie (Utley) Bristow; m. Gail Hamiter Rosen, Aug. 25, 2003; children from previous marriage: Cynthia Lynn, Margery Jan Wu, Gregory Scott, Kelly Robert. BA in Journalism, U. Okla., 1951, MA in Journalism, 1965. Asst. advt. mgr. Altus (Okla.) Times Democrat, 1951-53; freelance writer Altus, 1951-60; prof. English Winthrop Coll., Rock Hill, SC, 1960-87, prof. emeritus, 1987—. Author: Time for Glory, 1968, Night Season, 1970, A Faraway Drummer, 1973, Laughter in Darkness, 1974. With USNR, 1944—45. Recipient award for Lit. Excellence, U. Okla., 1969, award for novel, Friends of Am. Writers, 1974. Mem.: Alpha Tau Omega. Home: 613 1/2 Charlotte Ave Rock Hill SC 29730-3648 Personal E-mail: bobbristow@comporium.net.

BRISTOW, WALTER JAMES, JR., retired judge; b. Columbia, SC, Oct. 14, 1924; s. Walter James and Caroline Belser (Melton) Bristow; m. Katherine Stewart Mullins, Sept. 12, 1952; children: Walter James III, Katherine Mullins(dec.). Student, Va. Mil. Inst., 1941-43; AB, U. NC, 1947; LLB cum laude, U. SC, 1949; LLM, Harvard U., 1950. Mem. Marchant, Bristow & Bates, 1953-76, SC Ho. of Reps., 1956-58, SC Senate, 1958-76; resident judge 5th Cir. Ct. SC, 1976-88; ret., 1988. Nat. pres. Conf. Ins. Legislators, 1974—75. Trustee Elvira Wright Fund Crippled Children, 1963—76; mem. bd. visitors ex officio The Citadel, Charleston, SC, 1967—76. With US Army, 1943—45, ETO, brig. gen. SC Army N.G. Decorated Meritorious Svc. medal; recipient Order of Palmetto, 1999, Order of Cypress, 1999. Mem.: ABA, SC Law Inst., SC Coun. Holocaust, Columbia Ball Club, Palmetto Club, Cotillion Club, Capital City Club, Forest Lake Club, Sertoma, Wig and Robe, Alpha Tau Omega. Democrat. Office: PO Box 1147 Columbia SC 29202-1147

BRISTOW, WILLIAM HARVEY, JR., psychiatrist; b. Harrisburg, Pa. s. William H and Rosa Leah (St Clair) Bristow; m. Lillian H Heise; children: Jill Virginia, Lisa Ann, William H III. AB, Harvard U., 1949; MD, NYU, 1953. Diplomate Am Bd Psychiat and Neurology. Intern 4th Med. divsn. Bellevue Hosp., NYC, 1953—54, resident 4th Med. divsn., 1954—55; resident dept. psychiatry N.Y. VA Hosp., NYC, 1957—60; VA fellow Bellevue Psychiat. Hosp., NYC, 1959—60; pvt. practice Ridgewood, NJ, 1960—. Chmn. dept. psychiat. Bergen Pines County Hosp., Paramus, NJ, 1961; former chmn. dept. psychiat. St. Joseph's Hosp., Wayne, NJ, former pres. med. bd.; former pres. med. bd., clin. dir. Ramapo Ridge Psychiat. Hosp., 1985—98, attending psychiatrist; staff psychiatrist Bergen Regional Med. Ctr., 1998—; mem. emeritus staff Valley Hosp. Fellow: Am. Psychiat. Assn. (life; disting.); mem.: AMA, Med. Soc. N.J., NYU-Bellevue Psychiat. Soc., Assn. Convulsive Therapy, N.J. Psychiat. Assn., Bergen County Med. Soc. Congregationalist. Office Phone: 201-967-4000 ext. 5712.

BRITCHER, MICHAEL, music educator; s. Lester and Martha Britcher; m. Michele Hassell, July 17, 1993. BS in Instrumental Music Edn., West Chester U., PA, 1993; MS in Music, So. Oreg. U., 2003. Drill instr. Upper Darby (Pa.) H.S., 1990, Milton Hershey H.S., Hershey, Pa., 1990—91, Pennsville (N.J.) Sr. H.S., 1991; music tchr. James McHenry Elem. Sch., Lanham, Md., 1994, Magnolia Elem. Sch., Seabrook, Md., 1994; band and chorus dir. Thomas Johnson Mid. Sch., Lanham, 1994—95; music tchr. Springfield Elem. Sch., Rileyville, Va., 1995—98, Luray (Va.) H.S., 1995—98, Phoenixville (Pa.) Area H.S., 1998—; music instr. Downingtown (Pa.) Sr. H.S., 1992. Asst. dir. Chester County Concert Band, West Chester, 2000—03; dir. Page Valley Concert Band, Luray, 1996—98; drill designer and music arranger Phoenixville Area H.S., 1989—93. Nominee Am. Tchr. award, Disney, 2003; named Tchr. of Yr., Page Country Pub. Schs., 1997, Dir. of Yr., Cavalcade of Bands Assn., 2003—04; recipient Ray A. Kroc Tchr. Achievement award, McDonald's, 1998, citation of commendation, Pa. Ho. of Reps., 2000, 2001, 2003, 2004. Mem.: Music Educators Nat. Conf., Nat. Educators Assn., Pa. Music Educators Assn. (Dist. 12 v.p. 2003—05), Pa. State Educators Assn., Phoenixville Area Educators Assn., Kappa Kappa Psi (life; pres. and v.p. 1990—92). Avocations: reading, golf, tennis, Aikido, music. Home: 201 Parkview Blvd Spring City PA 19475 Home Phone: 610-792-0932.

BRITCHFORD, See ALLEN, FRANCES

BRITO, DAGOBERT LLANOS, economics professor; b. Mex., Apr. 6, 1941; came to U.S., 1945, naturalized, 1958; s. John L. and Guadalupe G. (Llanos) B.; m. Patricia Ann Kendrick, June 29, 1968. BA, Rice U., 1967, MA, PhD, Rice U., 1970. Asst. prof. econs. U. Wis., Madison, 1970-72; asso. prof. econs. and polit. sci. Ohio State U., Columbus, 1972-75, prof., 1976-79; dir. Murphy Inst. Polit. Economy; chmn., prof. econs. Tulane U., New Orleans, 1979-84; Peterkin prof. polit. econs. Rice U., Houston, 1984—. Cons. Dept. State, Dept. Def. Author: A Dynamic Model of the Armaments Race, 1972, Strategic Nuclear Weapons and the Allocation of International Rights, 1977, Conflicts and Outbreak of War, 1985, Stock Externalities, Pigovian Taxation and Dynamic Stability, 1987, Richardsonian Arms Race Models, 1989, On the Limits of Economic Control, 1990, Externalities and Compulsory Vaccinations, 1991, The Economic and Political Incentives to Acquire Nuclear Weapons, 1993; (with M.D. Intriligator) The Economics of Disarmament, Arms Races and Arms Control, 1993, Minimizing the Risks for Accidental Nuclear War: An Agenda for Action, 1993; (with P.R. Hartley) Consumer Rationality and Credit Cards, 1995, Proliferation and the Probability of War: A Cardinality Theorem, 1996, Pricing Natural Gas in Mexico, 2002; editor: Strategies for Managing Nuclear Proliferation, 1983; assoc. editor Jour. Optimization Theory and Applications. Served with U.S. Army, 1963-66. NSF grantee, 1972, 74, 77, 78, 81; Mershon Center grantee, 1973, 78; Rice scholar Baker Inst. Mem. Econometric Soc., Public Choice Soc., Houston Philo. Soc. Office: Rice U PO Box 1892 Houston TX 77251-1892 Office Phone: 713-348-5792. Business E-Mail: brito@rice.edu.

BRITT, BILLY JEAN, retired elementary school educator, economic education specialist; b. Pine Bluff, Ark., Oct. 19, 1952; s. Billy Jean and Charlene Faver Britt. BA in Elem. Edn., U. Ark., Monticello, 1973; MEd, U. Ark., Fayetteville, 1983. Cert. gifted and talented edn. tchr. Ark., 1986. Tchr. Woodlawn Elem. Sch., Rison, Ark., 1973—87, Monticello Elem. Sch., 1987—2004; econ. edn. specialist Little Rock br. Fed. Res. Bank St. Louis. Master economics tchr. Ark. Coun. Econ. Edn., Little Rock, 1993—2004; adj. prof. U. Ark., Monticello, 1994—97, math sci. ctr. coord., 1998—99. Author: teacher guides Economics of the Forest (Bessie B. Moore Econ. Edn. award, 2004). Co-chmn. Ark. Jump$tart Fin. Literacy, Little Rock, 2004—; mem. Pulaski County Juvenile Svcs. Bd., Little Rock, 2004—, Ark. Coun. Econ. Edn., Little Rock, 2002—04. Recipient Ark. Math. Tchr. award. Mem.: Global Assn. Tchrs. (bd. dirs. 2004—). Republican. Methodist. Avocations: music, travel, writing, reading. Office: Fed Res Bank Little Rock Br PO Box 1261 Little Rock AR 72203 Home Phone: 870-357-2574; Office Phone: 501-324-8368. Office Fax: 501-324-8200. Business E-Mail: billy.j.britt@stls.frb.org.

BRITT, DAVID VAN BUREN, retired educational communications executive; b. Needham, Mass., July 30, 1937; s. Paul and Ellen Britt; m. Marjorie Joan Britt, Feb. 15, 1958 (div. 1984); children: Pamela Britt-Schneider, Barbara B. Schaefer, Paul David; m. Sue Cushman, July 22, 1989. AB, Wesleyan U., 1959; MPA, Harvard U., 1967. Ops. mgmt. staff No. Trust Co., Chgo., 1959-62; legis. chief U.S. AID, Washington, 1962-68; chief programs and plans U.S. EEOC, Washington, 1968-69; dep. dir. policy planning U.S. Overseas Pvt. Investment Corp., Washington, 1969-70; ind. cons. Washington, 1970-71; from v.p. to COO Sesame Workshop, NYC, 1971-90, CEO, trustee, 1990-99. Mem. Coun. on Fgn. Rels.; mem. adv. bd. Initiative on Social Enterprise, Harvard Bus. Sch., Hauser Ctr. for Non-Profit Orgns., Kennedy Sch. Govt., Harvard U.; trustee New World Found., NYC, 1978—86, Wesleyan U., Middletown, Conn., 1989—92, Edn. Trust, 2005—; bd. dirs. Inmed Partnerships Children, 2005—. Recipient Disting. Alumnus award Wesleyan U., 1994. Episcopalian. Home: 20 River St Guilford CT 06437 Personal E-mail: david@britt-cushman.com.

BRITT, EARL THOMAS, lawyer; b. Phila., July 14, 1940; s. Earl Francis and Marie Rita (Lawless) B.; m. Maureen Wong, Dec. 26, 1964; children: Denise, Karen, Eileen, Mary, Kevin, Stephen. AB, St. Joseph's U., Phila., 1961; JD, U. Pa., 1964. Bar: Pa. 1964, U.S. Dist. Ct. (ea. dist.) Pa. 1964, U.S. Ct. Appeals (3rd cir.) 1964, U.S. Dist. Ct. Appeals (D.C. cir.) 1981, U.S. Supreme Ct. 1982. Atty. Pa. Mfrs. Assn. Ins. Co., Phila., 1964—67; assoc. Swartz Campbell & Detweiler, Phila., 1967—68; assoc., then ptnr. Duane Morris & Heckscher, Phila., 1968—92; founder, ptnr., chmn. Britt Hankins & Moughan, Phila., 1992—; judge pro tem Ct. Common Pleas, Phila., 1991—. Lectr. Comey Inst. Indsl. Rels. St. Joseph's U., 1961-92; adj. faculty Temple U. Sch. Law-Acad. Advocacy, 1994—. Mem. adv. bd. Norwood-Fontbonne Acad., 1997-2002. Mem. ABA, Pa. Bar Assn., Phila. Bar Assn. (trustee campaign for qualified judges 1989, hon. trustee 1990-91), Phila. Assn. Def. Counsel (bd. dirs. 1983-89, 93-94, pres. 1988-89), Pa. Def. Inst. (lectr. Trial Acad. 1990—), Internat. Assn. Def. Counsel, Def. Rsch. Inst., Lawyer's Club Phila. (bd. dirs. 1988-90). Republican. Roman Catholic. Home: 106 Sparango Ln Plymouth Meeting PA 19462-1115 Office: Britt Hankins & Moughan 11 E Airy St Norristown PA 19401 Office Phone: 610-277-9633. Business E-Mail: ebritt@britthankins.com.

BRITT, GLENN ALAN, media company executive; b. Hackensack, NJ, Mar. 6, 1949; s. Walter E. Britt and Helen Crupi; m. Barbara Jane Little, Oct. 25, 1975. AB, Dartmouth Coll., 1971, MBA, 1972. Contr.'s asst. Time, Inc., NYC, 1972-74, fin. dir. Iran project, Time-Life Books Alexandria, Va., 1976-78, dir. video group new bus. devel. NYC, 1980-81, sr. v.p. fin. video group, 1984, v.p., treas., 1986-88, v.p., CFO, 1988-90; sr. v.p., treas. Time Warner Inc., NYC, 1990; exec. v.p. Time Warner Cable Group, Stamford, Conn., 1990-92; pres. Time Warner Cable Ventures, Stamford, Conn., 1992-99, Time Warner Cable, Stamford, 1999—2001, chmn., CEO, 2001—; v.p., treas. Manhattan Cable TV, NYC, 1974-76; v.p. network and studio ops. HBO Inc., NYC, 1978-80, sr. v.p., CFO, 1984-86; sr. v.p. fin. Am. TV and Comm. Corp., Stamford, Conn., 1981-84. Mem. Fin. Exec. Inst., Woodway Country Club, Eastward Ho, Cape Cod National Golf Club and Country Club, Univ. Club. Avocations: skiing, gardening, golf. Office: Time Warner Cable Group 290 Harbor Dr Stamford CT 06902-7475

BRITT, JOHN ROY, banker; b. LA, Oct. 9, 1937; s. Roy Arthur and Virginia Alice (Vaughn) B.; children: Jeffrey John, Belinda Lynn, Gregory Scott. BA, Claremont McKenna Coll., 1959; grad., Pacific Coast Banking Sch., U. Wash., 1973, Managerial Policy Inst., U. So. Calif., 1978. Diplomate Am. Bd. Forensic Examiners. With Security Pacific Nat. Bank, 1959-83, regional v.p. Los Angeles, 1972-74, sr. v.p., 1974-83, adminstr. Mid City-Eastern div., 1978-83; instr. Essentials of Banking Sch., U. Notre Dame, 1979; sr. v.p. Coast Savs. and Loan, Los Angeles, 1983-85; exec. v.p., chief operating officer Pacific Inland Bank, Anaheim, Calif., 1985-86, pres., chief exec. officer, 1986-89; pres. JRB Assocs., 1990—; pres., chief exec. officer United Citizens Nat. Bank, LA, 1992. Mem. pres.'s adv. coun. Claremont McKenna Coll., 1993; past chmn. bd. dirs., mem. exec. com. Commuter Transp. Svcs., Inc., L.A. Capt. USAR, 1959-67. Mem.: Risk Mgmt. Assn., Am. Coll. Forensic Examiners (bd. cert.). Republican. Methodist.

BRITT, JOSEPH JOHN, religious studies educator; b. Balt., July 13, 1948; s. Joseph John and Lottie Elizabeth (Zielinski) Britt. AB in History, Boston Coll., 1970; MA, Northeastern U., Boston, 1972. Tchr. Malden Cath. H.S., Mass., 1970—72, 1976—81, 1983—93, Notre Dame H.S., Utica, NY, 1973—76, St. Joseph Regional H.S., Montvale, NJ, 1981—83, 1993—97, Paltarokas Sch., Panucyzs, Lithuania, 1997—2002; hist. rschr. Xaverian Bros. Generalate, Balt., 2003—04; dir. ednl. programs, curator Pope John Paul II Cutural Ctr., Washington, 2004—. Author: (book) Xaverian Brothers in East Africa, 2004. Bd. dirs, minutemen Boston coord. Boy Scouts Am., Boston, 1985—93. Recipient Silver Beaver award, Boy Scouts Am., 1987. Roman Catholic. Avocations: photography, camping, science fiction, history.

BRITT, KENT A., lawyer; b. Indpls., Nov. 27, 1970; BS, Ind. U., 1994; JD, U. Cin., 1997. Bar: Ohio 1997, US Dist. Ct. Southern Dist. Ohio 1997. Assoc. Vorys, Sater, Seymour and Pease LLP, Cin. Mem. Greater Cin. Chamber of Commerce Bus. Retention Com. Named one of Ohio's Rising Stars, Super Lawyers, 2006. Mem.: FBA, ABA (mem., Litig. Sect. 1997—), Ohio State Bar Assn., Cin. Bar Assn., Phi Alpha Delta. Office: Vorys Sater Seymour and Pease LLP Ste 2000 Atrium Two PO Box 0236 221 E Fourth St Cincinnati OH 45201-0236 Office Phone: 513-723-4488. Office Fax: 513-852-7818.

BRITT, RONALD LEROY, retired manufacturing company executive; b. Abilene, Kans., Mar. 1, 1935; s. Elvin E. and Lona H. Britt; m. Judith Ann, June 29, 1957; children: Brett G., Mark D., Melissa A. BSM.E., Wichita State U., 1963. From product engr. to product planner Hotpoint divsn. G.E. Co., Chgo., 1963-68; product planner Norge Co., Chgo., 1968; product mgr., asst. dir. engirng. Leigh Products Inc., Coopersville, Mich., 1968-74; mgr. rsch. and devel. Miami Carey divsn. Jim. Walter Corp., Monroe, Ohio, 1974-84; sr. v.p. mfg. and engring. Belvedere USA Corp., Belvidere, Ill., 1984-2001, ret., 2001. Industry rep. for electric fans Underwriters Labs. Active Boy Scouts Am., 1970-73, PTA, 1973-78; exec. adviser Jr. Achievement, 1984-85, Boone County chmn., 1968-88; bd. dirs. YMCA, Belvidere, 1990-96, vice-chmn., chmn. fin. com., 1991, v.p., 1992; trustee Dickinson County Hist. Soc., 2003—, v.p., bd. dirs. 2004-06, pres. geneology group, 2004-05; dir. on adv. bd. St. Joseph Hosp., 1990-95, 97-99, chmn. long range planning com., 1991; bd. dirs. Boone County Dist. 100 Edn. Found., 1991-95, Abilene Kans. Airport, 2003-06, Abilene City Econ. Devel. Coun., 2003-07; bd. dirs. Abilene City Heritage Commn., 2003—, chair, 2005-06. With U.S. Army, 1958-60 Recipient Inventor's award Gen. Electric Co., 1967. Mem. ASME, Home Ventilation Inst. (engring. com. 1975-84), Belvidere C. of C. (bd. dirs. 1986-89), Air Capital Corvette Club, Air Capital Carnival Glass Club, Rotary (v.p. 1999-2000, sgt.-at-arms 2001-04, v.p. 2003-04, pres.-elect 2004-05, pres. 2005-06, bd. dirs., asst. dist. gov. 2006—, dist. gov. elect 2007—). Republican. Methodist.

BRITT, STEPHEN THOMAS, medical educator; s. Albert Edward and Mary Jean Britt; 1 child, Joy Elizabeth. Instrnl. ranking of Sifu, Wu's Tai Chi Chuan Acad., Hong Kong, 1997. Instr. Wu's Tai Chi Chuan Acad., Toronto, 1975—87, tech. dir., sr. instr. Royal Oak, Mich., 1987—2005; pres., chief instr. Mich. Wu Style Tai Chi Chuan and Chi Kung Inst., 2005—. Cons. in alternative medicine various hosps., Detroit, 1997—; lectr. in field. Mem.: Mensa (assoc.). Achievements include development, in association with Western medical professionals, of Tai Chi Chuan training techniques for the benefit of patients in rehabilitative environments and occupational therapy; training and preparation of demonstration teams of US students; development of programs with geriatric specialists in the utilization of Tai Chi Chuan training techniques for the benefit of senior citizens; programs utilizing Tai chi Chuan training techniques for specialized support groups such as Parkinsonism, autism and mutiple sclerosis. Office: Mich Wu Style Tai Chi Chuan Inst 3915 Crooks Rd Unit 22 Royal Oak MI 48073 Office Phone: 248-549-9217. E-mail: sifubritt@wustyledetroit.com.

BRITT, TIMOTHY, mathematics professor; b. Lexington, Tenn., July 17, 1960; s. Gerlean Britt. M, U. Memphis, 1996. Systems/ops. mgr. Am. Ordnance, Milan, Tenn., 1982—98; assoc. prof. math. Jackson State CC, Tenn., 1998—. Bd. dirs. Lighthouse United Pentecostal Ch., Jackson, 2005—. Recipient Tchg. Excellence award, NISOD, 2004. Mem.: Mensa. Republican. Avocations: computers, reading, piano. Home: 25 Golden Pond Cove Jackson TN 38305 Office: 2046 North Pky Jackson TN 38301 Home Phone: 731-668-7226; Office Phone: 731-425-2645. Personal E-mail: timbritt@charter.net. Business E-Mail: tbritt@jscc.edu.

BRITTAIN, JAMES EDWARD, science and technology educator, researcher; b. Mills River, NC, May 20, 1931; s. Randall Francis and Velma Hassie (Gillespie) B.; m. Louise Mary Lambert, March 29, 1969 (dec. Mar. 27, 1972); m. Jo Ann Layne, Apr. 14, 1973. BS, Clemson U., 1957; MS, U. Tenn., 1959; MA, Case Western Res. U., 1969, PhD, 1970. Jr. rsch. engr. U. Tenn., Knoxville, 1958-59; asst. prof. elec. engring. Clemson (S.C.) U., 1959-66; asst. prof. history of sci. and tech. Ga. Inst. Tech., Atlanta, 1969-71, assoc. prof., 1972-91, prof., 1992-94; prof. emeritus, 1994—. Author: Engineering the New South, 1985, Alexanderson: Pioneer in American Electrical Engineering, 1992, Scanning The Past: A History of Electrical Engineering and Its Pioneers, 1999, Gun Fights, Dam Sites and Water Rights, 2001; editor: Turning Points in American Electrical History, 1977. With USAF, 1950-54. Smithsonian Instn. rsch. fellow, 1972-73; recipient rsch. contract Nat. Park Svc., 1974-75; grantee NSF, 1979. Fellow IEEE (chmn. history com. 1978-79, 88-89, assoc. editor proceedings 1990-, Centennial medal 1984), Royal Soc. Arts, Radio Club Am. (Batcher Meml. prize 1989); mem. Soc. History of Tech. (mem. exec. coun. 1978-80, 89-91, Usher prize 1971). Baptist. Avocations: trout fishing, hiking, photography of historical industrial sites. Home: 189 Mountain Valley Dr Hendersonville NC 28739-9723

BRITTAIN, LARA MICHELLE, music educator; b. Augsburg, Germany, June 21, 1971; d. Frank William and Gwen (Frutchey) Brittain. BMus, James Madison U., 1993; MusM, Ithaca Coll., 1998. Dir. choir C.D. Hylton H.S., Woodbridge, Va., 1993—2000, Forest Park H.S., Woodbridge, 2000—. Dir. choir Ebenezer United Meth. Ch., Stafford, Va., 1999—; guest condr. Stafford County Choir, 2003, Dist. VI Choir, Appomattox, Va., 2004, Dist VIII Choir, Virginia Beach, Va., 2004, Henry All County Choir, Bassett, Va., 2005, Rappahannock Summer Music Camp, 2005, Miss. Jr. High Summer Music Camp, 2006, Dist. XV Sr. High SSAA Choir, Fredericksburg, 2007. Grantee, Va. Commn. Arts, 2004. Mem.: Music Educators Nat. Conf. (chair Dist. IX 1995—97, Va. state sec. 2000—02), Am. Choral Dirs. Assn. (Va. state treas. 1998—2007, Va. jazz choir chairperson 2007—), Sigma Alpha Iota. Methodist. Avocations: piano, Mary Kay beauty consultant. Home: 10 Pin Oak Ct Stafford VA 22554 Office: Forest Park HS 15721 Forest Park Dr Woodbridge VA 22193

BRITTEN, ROY JOHN, biophysicist; b. Washington, Oct. 1, 1919; s. Rollo Herbert and Marion Hale B.; m. Jacqueline Reid, 1986 (dec. Sept. 2001); children: Gregory, Kenneth. BS, U. Va., 1941; PhD, Princeton U., 1951. Staff mem. dept. terrestrial magnetism Carnegie Instn., Washington, 1951-89; sr. research assoc. Calif. Inst. Tech., Corona del Mar, 1973-81, disting. Carnegie sr. rsch. assoc. biology, 1981-99, emeritus, 1999—. Adj. prof. U. Calif., Irvine, 1991—; discoverer repeated DNA sequences in genomes of higher organisms. Inventor in field. Named Disting. Carnegie Sr. Research Assoc. in Biology, 1981-99. Fellow Am. Acad. Arts and Scis., AAAS; mem. Nat. Acad. Scis. Office: Calif Inst Tech Kerchkhoff Marine Lab 101 Dahlia Ave Corona Del Mar CA 92625-2814 Business E-Mail: rbritten@caltech.edu.

BRITTEN, THOMAS ANTHONY, history professor; b. Lansing, Mich., Feb. 22, 1964; s. Norman Dennis and Jean Ellen Britten; m. Connie Ruth Thornton, Dec. 19, 1987; children: Lydia Ruth Li children: Zachary

Thomas, Reuben Scott, Gabriel John, Asa Benjamin. PhD, Tex. Tech U., Lubbock, 1994. Asst. prof. history U. Tex., Brownsville, 2003—. Author: (book) American Indians in World War One; editor: Jour. South Tex., 2007—. 2d lt. US Army. Independent. Roman Catholic. Home: 2802 Pine Valley Dr Harlingen TX 78550 Office: U Tex 80 Fort Brown Brownsville TX 78520 Home Phone: 956-428-1127; Office Phone: 956-882-7379. Business E-Mail: thomas.britten@utb.edu.

BRITTEN, WILLIAM HARRY, editor, publisher; b. Aug. 25, 1921; s. Harry William and Gertrude Alice (Lehman) B. BA, Western Union Coll., 1943; postgrad., Iowa State Coll., summer 1942; MA, State U. Iowa, 1948. Reporter Worcester (Mass.) Telegram, 1948-55; landscaper John F. Keenen, Leicester, Mass., 1956; sales dept. clk. Reed & Prince Mfg. Co., Worcester, 1957-63, inventory control clk., 1964, chief expeditor, 1965; state editor Marshalltown (Iowa) Times-Rep., 1965-66, staff writer, 1966-67; news editor Denison (Iowa) Bull. and Rev., 1967-68; city editor Boone News Rep., 1968; editor, pub., owner The Tri-County News, Zearing, 1968-89, editor emeritus, 1990—. Editor, pub. Hubbard (Iowa) Rev., 1969-72. Sec. Young Men's Rep. Club, Worcester, 1957; corr. sec. Young People's Rep. Club, 1958; mem. Ward 8 Rep. Com., Worcester, 1960-65; Rep. candidate Mass. state legislature, 1960; ward chmn. to elect Edward W. Brooke atty. gen. Mass., 1962, 64; bd. dirs. Story County (Iowa) Cancer Soc., 1976-81; chmn. Story County, Lincoln Twp. Reps., 1992, 94; active Ch. of Christ, United Meth. Ch. With AUS, 1943-45. Mem. Iowa Newspaper Assn., Nat. Newspaper Assn., Am. Legion (post comdr. 1982-83), U. Iowa Alumni Assn. Office: E Custer St Zearing IA 50278 Home: 66684 110th St Mc Callsburg IA 50154-8014

BRITTON, CLAROLD LAWRENCE, lawyer, consultant; b. Soldier, Iowa, Nov. 1, 1932; s. Arnold Olaf and Florence Ruth (Gardner) B.; m. Joyce Helene Hamlett, Feb. 1, 1958; children: Laura, Eric, Val, Martha. BS in Engring., U. Mich., Ann Arbor, 1958, JD, 1961, postgrad. Bar: Ill. 1961, U.S. Dist. Ct. (no. dist.) Ill. 1962, U.S. Ct. Appeals (7th cir.) 1963, U.S. Supreme Ct. 1970, Mich. 1989. Assoc. Jenner & Block, Chgo., 1961-70, ptnr., 1970-88; pres. Britton Info. Sys., Inc., 1991—2006, Britton Data Sys. Inc., 2006—. Lectr. DePaul U., 1988. Author: Computerized Trial Notebook, 1991, Trial By Notebook, 2002; asst. editor Mich. Law Rev., 1960. Comdr. USNR, 1952-57. Fellow Am. Coll. Trial Lawyers; mem. ABA (litigation sect., antitrust com., past regional chmn. discovery com. 1961), Ill. State Bar Assn. (chmn. Allerton House Conf. 1984, 86, 88, chmn. rule 23 com. 1985-87, chmn. civil practice and procedure coun. 1987-88, antitrust com.), Chgo. Bar Assn. (past chmn. fed. civil procedure com., mem. judiciary and computer law coms., civil practice com.), 7th Cir. Bar Assn., Def. Rsch. Inst. (com. on aerospace 1984), Mich. Bar Assn., Ill. Assn. Trial Lawyers, Order of Coif, Law Club (Chgo.), Racine Yacht Club (Wis.), Macatawa Yacht Club (Mich.), Masons, Alpha Phi Mu, Tau Beta Pi. Republican. Lutheran. Office: 8463 Pawnee Trail Pinckney MI 48169 Home Phone: 810-231-4894; Office Phone: 810-231-3572. Personal E-mail: cbritton@brittonis.com. Business E-Mail: Britton@ic.net.

BRITTON, JANET LYNN, lawyer; b. Portland, Maine; d. Janet Vivar; m. Douglas Britton, Sept. 20, 1997; 1 child, Zachary Douglas. BA, U. So. Maine, Portland, 1993; MA, Muskie Sch. Pub. Svc., Portland, 1999; JD, U. Maine, Portland, 1998. Assoc. counsel Hannaford Bros. Co., Scarborough, Maine, 2002—. Bd. mem. Immigrant Legal Advocacy Project, Portland. Office: Hannaford Bros Co 145 Pleasant Hill Rd Scarborough ME 04070 Office Phone: 207-885-7475. E-mail: jbritton@hannaford.com.

BRITTON, LOUIS FRANKLIN, lawyer; b. Terre Haute, Ind., Mar. 5, 1953; s. Charles J. and Deneta (Reichert) B.; m. Debra Lynne Brown, May 15, 1977; children: Louis J., Laura Elizabeth, Leslie Lynne. BA cum laude, Ind. U., 1974, JD magna cum laude, 1977. Bar: Ind. 1977, U.S. Dist. Ct. (so. dist.) Ind. 1977, U.S. Ct. Appeals (7th cir.) 1997. Assoc. Cox, Zwerner, Gambill & Sullivan, Terre Haute, 1977—81, ptnr., 1981—. Bd. dirs. Regional Mfrs. Coop., 1995—2002. Active Friends of The Woods, St. Mary of the Woods Coll., 1998—; mem. steering com. Vigo County Comprehensive Plan, 2004; sec. Vigo County Taxpayers Assn., 1995—; v.p. agy. rels., bd. rels., bd. dirs. United Way, 1981—84; mem. parish coun. Sacred Heart Ch., 1978—81, St. Benedicts Ch., 1998—2002; bd. dirs. Terre Haute YMCA, 1985—88, Leadership Terre Haute, 1987—90, pres., 1989—90; v.p., bd. dirs. Terre Haute Humane Soc., 1982—84; bd. dirs. Woods Day Care, 1993—98, Greater Terre Haute C.C., 1998—2004, treas., 2000—03, v.p., 1999; pres., bd. dirs. Leadership Terre Haute Alumni Assn., 1984—85, Vigo Preservation Alliance, 1985—95, pres., 1993; youth chmn., bd. dirs. local YMCA, 1987—88. Ira C. Batman fellow, 1976-77; named one of Outstanding Young Men Am., 1982; recipient Outstanding Svc. award Leadership Terre Haute, 1987. Mem. ABA, Ind. Bar Assn., Terre Haute Bar Assn., Order of Coif, Phi Beta Kappa. Home: 2206 N 7th St Terre Haute IN 47804-1802 Office: Cox Zwerner Gambill & Sullivan PO Box 1625 Terre Haute IN 47808-1625

BRITTON, M(ELVIN) C(REED), JR., rheumatologist; b. San Francisco, Apr. 11, 1935; s. Melvin Creed and Mathilda Carolyn (Epeneter) B.; m. Mary Elizabeth Phillips, Nov. 2, 1957; children: Elizabeth Carolynne, Lisa Marie. AB, Dartmouth Coll., 1957, MS, 1958; MD, Harvard U., 1960. Diplomate Am. Bd. Internal Medicine, Am. Bd. Rheumatology, Am. Bd. Quality Assurance. Resident Dartmouth Coll. Sch. Medicine, Hanover, NH, 1964-67; fellow Harvard U. Sch. Medicine, Boston, 1967-69; ptnr. Palo Alto (Calif.) Med. Clinic, 1969—, chmn. dept. medicine, 1990-97. Pres. med. staff Stanford (Calif.) U. Med. Ctr., 1985-87, mem. med. staff bd., 1969-87; bd. dirs. Hosp. Conf. No. Calif., 1988-92, Inst. for Med. Quality, 1998—, treas., 1999-2003, chmn. bd., 2003—; mem. Relative Value Update Commn., 1996— Contbr. articles to med. jours. Pres. Found. for Med. care Santa Clara county, Campbell, 1983-89; mem. Bay Area Lupus Found., 1978—, chmn., 1987-88, 94-95; v.p. Calif. Founds. for Med. Care, 1996, pres., CEO, 1999-2001. Fellow ACP, Am. Coll. Rheumatology (bd. dirs. 1986-89, Paulding Phelps medal 1994, mastership 2000, Disting. Svc. award 2004), Calif. Acad. Medicine (exec. com. 1996-2000, pres. 2001-03); mem. AMA (alt. del. 1988-2003, del. 2003——, chair governing coun., sply. and svcs. soc. 2004-05), Calif. Med. Assn., Santa Clara County Med. Soc. (pres. 1980-81, Bd. Svc. award 1988), Arthritis Found. No. Calif. (chmn. bd. dirs. 1984-87, Disting Svc. award 1985), Vintners Club (San Francisco, v.p. 1975-78), Cosmos Club (Washington). Republican. Episcopalian. Avocations: skiing, travel, enology. Office: Palo Alto Med Clinic 795 El Camino Real Palo Alto CA 94301-2726 Home Phone: 650-326-0856; Office Phone: 650-853-6056. Personal E-mail: rheumdc@aol.com.

BRITTON, THOMAS WARREN, JR., retired management consultant; b. Pawhuska, Okla., June 16, 1944; s. Thomas Warren and Helen Viola (Haynes) Britton; m. Jerlyn Kay Davis, 1964 (div. 1970); 1 child, Natalie Dawn; m. Deborah Ann Mansour, Oct. 20, 1973; 1 child, Kimberly Ann. BSME, Okla. State U., 1966, MS in Indsl. Engring. and Mgmt., 1968. Cons. Arthur Young & Co., LA, 1968—72, mgr., 1972—76, prin., 1976—79, ptnr., 1979—88, office dir. mgmt. svcs. dept. Orange County, Calif., 1979—88; ptnr. Price Waterhouse, LA, 1988—95, ptnr.-in-charge West Coast Nat. Aerospace and Def. Industry practice, 1988—95, west coast mfg. and logistics practice, 1988—95; ptnr., chmn. US MCS Tech. Industry Practice PricewaterhouseCoopers, LA, 1995—2000, chmn. Global MCS Tech. Industry Practice, 1995—2000, COO MCS west bus. unit, chmn. global MCS tech. industry practice, 2000—02; ret., 2002. Lectr. in field. Mem. creative growth bd. City of San Dimas, Calif., 1976—77, chmn. Planning Commn., 1977—83; trustee World Affairs Coun. Orange County, 1980; v.p. ann. fund, pres., chmn. long range planning, bd. pres. South Coast Repertory Theater, 1982—92; trustee Providence Speech and Hearing Ctr., 1985—90, Spl. Olympics So. Calif., 1995—97; mem. devel. com. U. Calif.-Irvine Med. Sch.; chmn. Costa Mesa Arts Coun., 1984. Capt. USAR, 1971—86. Mem. LA Inst. CPAs, Mgmt. Adv. Svcs. Com., Am. Prodn. and Inventory Control Soc., Am. Inst. Indsl. Engrs., Greater Irvine Indsl. League, Okla. State U. Alumni Assn., Jonathan Club, Ridgeline Country Club, Santa Ana Country Club, Kappa Sigma. Home: 9881 Orchard Ln Villa Park CA 92861-3105 Personal E-mail: tom_britton@msn.com.

BRITZ LOTTI, DIANE EDWARD, investment company executive; b. York, Pa, June 15, 1952; d. Everett Frank and Billie Jacqueline (Sherrill) Britz; m. Marcello Lotti, Sept. 9, 1978 (dec. Apr. 1990); children: Ariane Elizabeth Lotti, Samantha Alexis Lotti. BA, Duke U., 1974; MBA, Columbia U., 1982. Asst. mgr. Columbia Artists, NYC, 1974-76; gen. mgr. Ea. Music Festival, Greensboro, NC, 1977-78; v.p. Britz Cobin, NYC, 1979-82; pres. Pan Oceanic Mgmt., Inc., 1983-90, Pan Oceanic Advisors, Ltd., 1988-94; chair Pan Oceanic Mgmt. Ltd., 1994-2001; mng. dir. Am. Capital Ptnr., Ltd., 1996—, Erafo Ltd., 2000—; chmn. Trinity Investors Fund Inc.; founding ptnr. Circle Fin. Group LLC, 2003—, vice chmn., 2003—. Bd dirs Trinity Investors Fund Inc, Cir. Fin. LLC. Bd. advisors Turtle Bay Music Sch.; pres. Marcello Lotti Found.; bd. dirs. exec. com. Am. Acad. in Rome; chair Trinity bd. visitors Duke U. Mem.: Explorers Club, Columbia Bus Sch Club NY. Mem. Soc. Of Friends. Office: Circle Financial 17th Fl 650 Madison Ave New York NY 10022 Personal E-mail: britzlotti@gmail.com.

BRIXIOVA, ZUZANA, economist; b. Teplice, Czech Republic, June 11, 1966; arrived in US, 1988; d. Oldrich Brixi and Marie Brixiova. BA, Prague Coll. Econs., Czech Republic, 1988; PhD, U. Minn., Mpls., 1996. Economist IMF, Washington, 1996—2002, resident rep. Vilnius, Lithuania, 2003—04, sr. economist Washington, 2005—. Rsch. fellow William Davidson Inst., U. Mich., Ann Arbor, 2001—. Recipient Citation of Merit, Assn. Women in Sci., 1995; Dissertation fellow, Inst. Study World Politics, 1995—96, Dissertation Improvement grantee, NSF, 1995. Mem.: Woman's Nat. Dem. Club. Office Phone: 202-623-7138.

BRIZEL, MICHAEL ALAN, retail executive, lawyer; b. Monticello, NY, Jan. 6, 1957; s. Irving and Ruth (Marcus) B.; m. Judith Schwartz, Nov. 1, 1992, 2 children BS in Indsl. and Labor Relations, Cornell U., 1977, JD, 1980. Bar: N.Y. 1981, U.S. Dist. Ct. (ea. and so. dists.) N.Y., U.S. Ct. Appeals (6th cir.). Assoc. Burns, Summit, Rovins & Feldesman, NYC, 1980-83; labor atty. Gen. Foods Corp., White Plains, NY, 1983-84, sr. labor atty., 1984-86, labor counsel, 1986-87, counsel external devel., 1987-89; sr. atty. Reader's Digest Assn., Inc., Pleasantville, NY, 1989-90, assoc. gen. counsel, 1990-96, v.p. U.S. legal affairs, assoc. gen. counsel, 1996—98, v.p., gen. counsel, 1998—2002, sr. v.p., gen. counsel, 2002—07; exec. v.p., gen. counsel Saks, Inc., 2007—. Arbitrator small claims ct. City of White Plains, 1985-87; vis. bd. mem. Pace Law Sch., 2002-. Bd. dirs., pres. 510 E 86th St. Owners, Inc., 1985-86. Mem. ABA, N.Y. State Bar Assn. Office: Saks Inc 12 E 49th St New York NY 10017*

BRIZENDINE, ELLANOR N. (BODIE), headmaster; b. Baltimore, Md. BA in English, Towson State U.; MLA, Johns Hopkins U. Dean of students San Francisco U. HS; English tchr. Bryn Mawr Sch., Baltimore, class dean, dir. admissions and fin. aid, dir. Outreach, interim head of sch., 1994; head of sch. Marin Acad., San Rafael, Calif., 1995—2007, The Spence Sch., NY, 2007—. Faculty mem. Inst. for New Heads Nat. Assn. Independent Sch. Trustee Hamlin Sch., San Francisco; bd. dirs. Calif. Assn. Independent Schools. Mem.: Nat. Assn. Principals of Schools for Girls. Office: The Spence School 22 E 91st St New York NY 10128-0657 Office Phone: 212-289-5940. Office Fax: 212-996-5689.*

BRIZIO-MOLTENI, LOREDANA, surgeon, educator; d. Luigi Brizio and Lina Rossi; m. Agostino Molteni, Sept. 5, 1963; children: Claudio-Enrico, Ronald Stephen Louis. MD, U. Bologna, Italy, 1951. Resident in surgery U. Bologna, 1951—57, asst. prof. surgery, 1957—60; resident in plastic surgery, chief resident Roswell Park Meml. Inst., Buffalo, 1959—62; plastic surgeon Cook County Hosp., Chgo., 1961—62; resident in plastic surgery Christ Hosp., Cin., 1962—63; asst. prof. plastic surgery SUNY, Buffalo, 1965—70; pvt. practice Chgo., 1970—; asst. prof. plastic surgery U. Mo. Sch. Medicine, Kansas City, 1971—76; assoc. prof. plastic surgery Loyola U., Chgo., 1977—85. Adj. prof. pathology Northwestern U., Chgo., 1977—96; presenter in field. Author, editor: Endocrinology of Thermal Trauma, 1990; contbr. articles to profl. jours. Fellow: ACS; mem.: Internat. Burn Assn.

BRIZZOLARA, CHARLES ANTHONY, lawyer, director; b. Chgo., Nov. 20, 1929; s. Ralph D. and Florence H. (Hurley) B.; m. Audree Doyle, Aug. 24, 1968. BA, Lake Forest Coll., Ill., 1951; JD, Ill. Inst. Tech., 1957. Bar: Ill. 1959. Practiced law, Chgo., 1959-67; with Walter E. Heller & Co., also Walter E. Heller Internat. Corp. (later Amerifin Corp.), Chgo., 1967-85; v.p., sec., gen. counsel Walter E. Heller & Co., also Walter E. Heller Internat. Corp., 1974-85, sr. v.p., 1980-85; v.p. Chgo. Bears Football Club, Inc., 1975-88; mem. firm Chadwell & Kayser Ltd., 1985-90; ptnr. Michael Best & Friedrich, LLC, Chgo., 1990—2002; of counsel Berger, Newmark and Fenchel P.C., Chgo., 2003—04, Kane, Carbonara & Mendoza, Chgo., 2004—06, Fioretti, Lower & Carbonara, Chgo., 2007—. Bd. dirs. Abacus Real Estate Fin. Co., Walter E. Heller & Co. S.E., Heller Factoring (Hong Kong) Ltd., Factoring Serfin, S.A., Chandler Leasing Corp., 1975-80; lectr. seminars Am. Mgmt. Assn. Editor: Chgo.-Kent Law Rev, 1956. Bd. dirs. Cath. Charities Archdiocese of Chgo., 1978-99, sec., 1991-94; bd. dirs. Ill. Inst. Tech. Chgo. Kent Alumni Assn., 1980-89. Served with AUS, 1952-54. Mem. Internat. Bar Assn., Ill. Bar Assn. Roman Catholic. Home: Apt 20G 253 E Delaware Pl Chicago IL 60611-1758 Office: 222 S Riverside Plaza Chicago IL 60606

BRO, RUTH HILL, lawyer; b. Brookings, SD, July 9, 1962; BA, Northwestern U., 1984; JD, U. Chgo., 1994. Atty. McBride Baker & Coles (now Holland & Knight), 1994—99, Baker & McKenzie LLP, Chgo., 1999—2001, ptnr., 2001—. Editor: The E-Bus. Legal Arsenal: Practitioner Agreements and Checklists, 2004; co-author: Online Law, 1996, 6th edit., 2000; mem. editl. bd.: SciTech Lawyer, ABA, 2004—, Internet Law & Strategy, Am. Lawyer Media, 2005—, exec. editor, chair bd. dir.: Privacy & Data Protection Legal Reporter, Am. Lawyer Media, 2005—06; contbr. articles to profl. jours. Mem.: ABA (founder e-privacy law com., chair-elect sci. and tech. law sect., mem. info. security com.), Ill. Bar Assn., Chgo. Bar Assn. (computer law com.). Office: Baker & McKenzie LLP One Prudential Plz 130 East Randolph Dr Chicago IL 60601 Home Phone: 630-734-3950; Office Phone: 312-861-7985. Business E-Mail: bro@bakernet.com.

BROAD, ELI, foundation administrator, art collector; b. NYC, June 6, 1933; s. Leon and Rebecca (Jacobson) B.; m. Edythe Lois Lawson, Dec. 19, 1954; children: Jeffrey Alan, Gary Stephen. BA in Acctg. cum laude, Mich. State U., 1954; LLD (hon.), Southwestern U., 2000; HHD (hon.), Mich. State U., 2002. CPA Mich., 1956. Cert. public acct., 1954-56; asst. prof. Detroit Inst. Tech., 1956; co-founder, chmn., pres., CEO SunAmerica Inc. (formerly Kaufman & Broad, Inc.), LA, 1957-2001; chmn. SunAmerica Inc. (formerly Kaufman & Broad, Inc., now AIG Retirement Svcs. Inc.), 2001—05, Kaufman and Broad Home Corp., LA, 1989-93, chmn. exec. com., 1993-95; founder, chmn. Kaufman and Broad Home Corp. (now KB Home), LA, 1993—. Mem. exec. com. adv. bd. Fed. Nat. Mortgage Assn., 1972-73; active Calif. Bus. Roundtable, 1986-2000; co-owner Sacramento Kings and Arco Arena, 1992-99; trustee Com. for Econ. Devel., 1993-95; mem. real estate adv. bd. Citibank, N.Y.C., 1976-81; bd. dirs. Sacramento Kings and ARCO Arena; co-owner Sacramento Kings & Arco Arena, 1992-99. Mem. bd. dirs. LA World Affairs Coun., 1988-2003, chmn., 1994-97, DARE Am., 1989-95, hon. mem. bd. dirs. 1995—; founding trustee Windward Sch., Santa Monica, Calif., 1972-77; bd. trustees Pitzer Coll., Claremont, Calif., 1970-82, chmn. bd. trustees, 1973-79, life trustee, 1982—, Haifa U., Israel, 1972-80, Calif. State U., 1978-82, vice chmn. bd. trustees, 1979-80, trustee emeritus, 1982—, Mus. Contemporary Art, LA, 1980-93, founding chmn., 1980, Archives Am. Art, Smithsonian Instn., Washington, 1985-98, Am. Fedn. Arts, 1988-91, Leland Stanford Mansion Found., 1992-2000, Calif. Inst. Tech., 1993—, Armand Hammer Mus. Art and Cultural Ctr. UCLA, 1994-99; pres. Calif. Non-Partisan Vote Registration Found., 1971-72; chancellor's assoc. UCLA, 1971—, mem. vis. com. Grad. Sch. Mgmt., 1972-90, trustee UCLA Found., 1986-96, exec. com. bd. visitors Sch. of the Arts & Architecture, 1997—; assoc. chmn. United Crusade, LA, 1973-76; chmn. Mayor's Housing Policy Com., LA, 1974-75; del., spkr. Fed. Econ. Summit Conf., 1974, State Econ. Summit Conf., 1974; mem. contemporary coun. LA County Mus. Art, 1973-79, bd. trustees acquisitions com., 1978-81, trustee, 1995—; bd. fellows, mem. exec. com. The Claremont (Calif.) Colls., 1974-79; nat. trustee Balt. Mus. Art, 1985-91; mem. adv. bd. Boy Scouts Am., 1982-85, LA Bus. Jour., 1986-88; mem. adv. coun. Town Hall of Calif., 1985-87; trustee Dem. Nat. Com. Victory Fund, 1988, 92, 96; mem. painting and sculpture com. Whitney Mus., NYC, 1987-89; chmn. adv. bd. ART/LA, 1989; bd. overseers The Music Ctr. of LA County, 1991-92, mem. bd. govs., 1996-98, hon. gov. 1998—; mem. contemporary art com. Harvard U. Art Mus., Cambridge, Mass., 1992-2004; mem. internat. dirs. coun. Guggenheim Mus., NYC, 1993-98; trustee Mus. Modern Art, NYC, 2004—; active Nat. Indsl. Pollution Control Coun., 1970-73, Maeght Found., St. Paul de Vence, France, 1975-80, Mayor's Spl. Adv. Com. on Fiscal Adminstrn., LA, 1993-94; bd. dirs. UCLA/Armand Hammer Mus. Art And Cultural Ctr., 1994-1999; co-founder Broad Found., 1999—; bd. regents Smithsonian Inst., 2004—. Recipient Man of Yr. award, City of Hope, 1965, Golden Plate award, Am. Acad. Achievement, 1971, Housing Man of Yr. award, Nat. Housing Coun., 1979, Humanitarian award, NCCJ, 1977, Am. Heritage award, Anti Defamation League, 1984, Pub. Affairs award Coro Found., 1987, Honors award, visual arts, L.A. Arts Coun., 1989, Lifetime Achievement award, LA C. of C., 1999, Visionary award, Harvard Bus. Sch. Assn. So. Calif., 1999, Visionary award, KCET, 1999, Julius award, U. So. Calif. Sch. Policy, Planning and Devel., 2001, Chmn.'s award, Asia Soc. So. Calif., 2000, Teach for Am. Ednl. Leadership award, 2001, Exemplary Leadership in Mgmt. award, UCLA, The Anderson Sch., 2002, Alexis de Tocqueville award, United Way, 2002, Brass Ring award United Friends the Children, 2003, Civic Medal Hon. LA C. of C., 2004, Earl Warren Outstanding Pub. Svc. award Am. Soc. Pub. Adminstrn. LA Metro. Chpt., 2004, Frederick R. Weisman award Ams. for the Arts, 2005, Svc. to Cmty. award Am. Inst. to Architects LA Chpt., 2005, Louise T. Blouin Found. award, 2006; named one of Top 200 Collectors, ARTnews Mag., 2004, World's Richest People, Forbes Mag., 1999—, Forbes Richest Americans, 1999—; Eli Broad Coll. Bus. and Eli Broad Grad. Sch. Bus. named in his honor, Mich. State U., 1991; Edythe and Eli Broad Art Ctr. named in his honor, UCLA; knighted Chevalier in Nat. Order Legion of Honor, France, 1994. Fellow: AAAS; mem.: Calif. Club, Hillcrest Country Club (LA), Regency Club, Beta Alpha Psi. Avocation: Collecting contemporary art. Office: Broad Found Ste 1200 10900 Wilshire Blvd Los Angeles CA 90024 Office Fax: 310-954-5051.

BROAD, MATTHEW, lawyer; m. Cathy Broad; children: Ben, Sarah. BA bus. econ., U. Calif. Santa Barbara, 1981; JD, Hastings College of Law, 1984. Counsel-leg. dept. Boise Cascade Corp., Boise, Ill., 1984—89, assoc. gen. counsel, 1989—2004; corp. sec. OfficeMax Inc. (formerly Boise Cascade Corp.), 1989—, exec. v.p., gen. counsel, 2004—. Office: OfficeMax Inc 263 Shuman Blvd Naperville IL 60563*

BROAD, MOLLY CORBETT (MARGARET CORBETT BROAD), retired academic administrator; b. Wilkes-Barre, Pa., Feb. 22, 1941; d. Stanley A. and Margaret (Kelly) Corbett; m. Robert William Broad, Aug. 25, 1962; children: Robert W. Jr., Matthew David. BA in Econs., Syracuse U., 1962, postgrad., 1971; MA in Econs., Ohio State U., 1965. Rsch. assoc. to comptr., v.p. finance Ohio State U., Columbus, 1963—65; budget & planning officer Syracuse U., NY, 1971—76; dep. dir. State Commn. Future of Postsecondary Edn. in N.Y., Albany, 1976—77; v.p. govt. & corp. rels. Syracuse U., 1977—85; exec. dir., chief exec. officer Ariz. Bd. Regents, Phoenix, 1985—92; sr. vice chancellor adminstrn. & fin. Calif. State U., 1992—93, exec. vice chancellor, COO, 1993—97; chair bd., CEO Calif. State U. Inst., 1994—97; pres. U. N.C., Chapel Hill, 1997—2005, pres. emeritus, 2006—. Mem. bd. trustees Nat. Humanities Ctr., Research Triangle Park; hon. mem. Chapel Hill Preservation Soc., 1997; mem. bd. advisors NC Blumenthal Performing Arts Ctr.; 2000 campaign chairperson Rsch. Triangle United Way, Morrisville, NC. Named Disting. Alumna, Syracuse U.; recipient Woman of Achievement award, Syracuse, 1979, 1990 Leadership Am. award, Leadership Am., 1990, Ann. award, Leadership Calif., 1996, Arents award, Syracuse U., 1999, Tar Heel of Yr. award, U. (Chapel Hill) NC, 2001, Woman of Achievement award, Gen. Fedn. Women's Clubs (Raleigh) NC, Inc., 2003, Alexander Meiklejohn award, AAUP, 2003, Univ. award, U. N.C., 2006; fellow, Ohio State U., Syracuse U.; GM scholar. Mem.: Beta Gamma Sigma (coun. pres.), Phi Beta Kappa. Roman Catholic. Avocations: tennis, bicycling, gardening. Office: U NC Gen Adminstrn Bldg 910 Raleigh Rd Chapel Hill NC 27514-3916 Business E-Mail: mbroad@northcarolina.edu.*

BROAD, WILLIAM J., science writer; b. Milw. married; 3 children. BA, Webster Coll., 1973; M in History of sci., Univ. Wis. High sch. sci. teacher, Milwaukee; writer Science mag.; with NY Times, 1983—. Author: (books) Betrayers of the Truth: Fraud and Deceit in the Halls of Science, 1983, Claiming the Heavens, 1988, Teller's War: The Top-Secret Story Behind the Star Wars Deception, 1992, Star Warriors: A Penetrating Look into the Lives of the Young Scientists Behind Our Space Age Weaponry, 1993, The Universe Below, 1993, Alien Lair, 2002, The Oracle: The Lost Secrets and Hidden Message of Ancient Delphi, 2006; co-author: Germs: Biological Weapons and America's Secret War, 2001. Co-recipient two Pulitzer Prizes; finalist Pulitzer Prize, 2005, James Wright Brown Pub. Svc. award, Deadline Club, 2005; recipient Westinghouse Sci. Journalism award, AAAS, 1986, Disting. Svc. award, Univ. Wis.-Madison, 1995, Alfred I. duPont-Columbia U. award, 2007. Office: Science Writer NY Times 229 W 43rd St New York NY 10036*

BROADBENT, AMALIA SAYO CASTILLO, graphic arts designer; b. Manila, May 28, 1956; came to U.S., 1980, naturalized, 1985; d. Conrado Camilo and Eugenia de Guzman (Sayo) Castillo; m. Barrie Noel Broadbent, Mar. 14, 1981 (div. Apr. 1999); children: Charles Noel Castillo, Chandra Noel Castillo. BFA, U. Santo Tomas, 1978; postgrad., Acad. Art Coll., San Francisco, Alliance Francaise, Manila, Karilagan Finishing Sch., Manila Computer Ctr.; BA, Maryknoll Coll., 1972. Designer market rsch. Unicorp Export Inc., Makati, Manila, 1975-77; asst. advt. mgr. Dale Trading Corp., Makati, 1977-78; artist, designer, pub. rels. Resort Hotels Corp., Makati, 1978-81; prodn. artist CYB/Young & Rubicam, San Francisco, 1981-82; freelance art dir Ogilvy & Mather Direct, San Francisco, 1986; artist, designer, owner A.C. Broadbent Graphics, San Francisco, 1982—. Faculty graphic design and advt. depts. Acad. Art U., San Francisco. Works include: Daing na Isda, 1975, (Christmas coloring) Pepsi-Cola, 1964 (Distinctive Merit cert.), (children's books) UNESCO, 1973 (cert.). Pres. Pax Romana, Coll. of Architecture and Fine Arts, U. Santo Tomas, 1976-78, chmn. cultural sect., 1975; v.p. Atelier Cultural Soc., U. Santo Tomas, 1975-76; mem. Makati Dance Troupe, 1973-74; vol. spl. events San Francisco Mus. of Modern Art. Recipient Merit cert. Inst. Religion, 1977. Mem. Alliance Francaise de San Francisco. Roman Catholic. Office: 4380A Eagle Peak Rd Concord CA 94521-3427 Personal E-mail: amybroadbent@comcast.net.

BROADBENT, J. STREETT, engineering executive; b. Balt., Nov. 15, 1942; s. Walter Scott and Mabel Naomi (House) B.; children: Kenneth Streett, Sandra Lynn. AB in Physics, Western Md. Coll., Westminster, 1964; postgrad., Johns Hopkins U., 1969-75. Applied rsch. engr. Black & Decker, Towson, Md., 1964-67, instrumentation engr., 1967-68, test supr., test mgr., 1969-76, resident engring. mgr. Hampstead, Md., 1976-79, engring. mgr., 1979-84; real estate sales rep. Broadbent Realty, Reisterstown, Md., 1972-76; engring. mgr. Black & Decker, Towson, Md., 1985-94, sr. tech. mgr., 1994-96, sr. support sys. mgr., 1996-97; dir. Engring. Tech., 1997—2003; pres./owner Easy Streett Enterprises, LLC, Reisterstown, Md., 2003—; ptnr. Advancing Partnerships Consortium, Reisterstown, Md., 2003—04; sales rep. Bankers Life & Casualty, 2004. Treas. Greenbrier Improvement Assn., 1967—89, pres., 1969—70; fund raising com. Western Md. Coll., 1968—72; sec. Reisterstown Jaycees, 1976; com. Reisterstown Revitalization, 1976—77; treas. Md. Jr. Miss Scholarship Program, 1979—83, state chmn., 1983—92, chmn. bd., 1992—95; advancement chmn. Boy Scouts Am., Reisterstown, 1985—87; adv. bd. Essex C.C., 1988—89; steering com., sub-chair logistics Partnering 2K Conf., Morgan State U., 1999—2000, IMIE external adv. com., 2002—03; adv. com. Md. Boat Act, 2005—, officer at large, 2007—; bd. dirs. Advancing Minorities Interest in Engring., 2003. Mem. NSPE, Instrumentation Soc. Am. (sr.), Am. Soc. for Metals, Computer and Automated Sys. Assn., Soc. Exptl. Mechanics, Soc. Plastic Engrs., U.S. Power Squadrons (Dunalk instr. 1990—), Bull/Bear Investment Club (treas. 1985-91). Avocations: boating, skiing, hunting, skeet and trap shooting, tennis. Home: PO Box 508 Reisterstown MD 21136-1324 Office: Easy Streett Enterprises LLC PO Box 508 Reisterstown MD 21136 Office Phone: 410-598-0833. Business E-Mail: streett@easystreett.com.

BROADBENT, PETER EDWIN, JR., lawyer; b. Richmond, Virginia, May 16, 1951; s. Peter Edwin and Nancy Talbot (Norris) B.; m. Mary Anna (Toms), June 5, 1976; children: Peter Edwin III, Christopher Toms, Elizabeth Talbot. BA, Duke U., 1973; JD, U. Va., 1976. Bar: Va. 1976, US Dist. Ct. (ea. dist.) Va., 1976, US Ct. Appeals (fourth cir.), 1976. Assoc. Christian, Barton, Epps, Brent, and Chappell, Richmond, Va., 1976-84; ptnr. Christian and Barton LLP., Richmond, Va., 1984—. Bd. dir. James Monroe Meml. Found. Mem. Richmond City Rep. Com., 1973—; nat. committeeman Young Rep. Nat. Com., Washington, 1974-75; mem. state ctrl. com. Rep. Party of Va., 2001-03, Va. Presdl. elector, 2004, pres. Va. Elector College, 2004; former v.p., dir. Richmond Teams for Progress; former deacon First Presbyn. Ch.; former chmn., bd. dir. Libr. of Va.; bd. dir. Friends of Va. State Archives. Mem. Va. State Bar Assn. (pub. info. com. 1977-82, 1993-2003, chmn. 1982-85, bd. chmn. Bus. Law Sect., 2005—, editor Va. Bus. Law, 1995-98), Va. Bar Assn., Richmond Bar Assn., Greater Richmond Intellectual Property Law Assn., Geneal. Rsch. Inst. Va. (past pres., dir. 1984—), Va. Geneal. Soc. (bd. dirs., pres.), Soc. Colonial Wars in Va. (gov.), Nat. Geneal. Soc. (bd. dirs. 2003—). Republican. Presbyterian. Avocations: genealogy, politics. Office: Christian & Barton LLP 1200 Mutual Bldg 909 E Main St Richmond VA 23219-3095 Home: 4804 Cary Street Rd Richmond VA 23226-1618 Home Phone: 804-285-4313; Office Phone: 804-697-4109. E-mail: pbroadbent@cblaw.com.

BROADHURST, JEROME ANTHONY, lawyer; b. Cleve., Feb. 4, 1945; s. William and Estelle M. (Bozak) B.; m. Annette Lou Wilt, Sept. 3, 1966; children: Stephanie Ann, Jerome A., Elizabeth Marie. BS in Bus., U. Akron, 1967, JD, 1971. Bar: Ohio 1973, Tenn. 1987. Acctg. supr., fin. analyst B.F. Goodrich Co., Akron, Ohio, 1971-73, corp. counsel, 1973-76; counsel, asst. sec. The Weatherhead Co., Cleve., 1976-77; asst. counsel Gen. Tire and Rubber Co., Akron, 1977-80; sr. corp. atty. Holiday Inns, Inc. (subs. Holiday Corp.), Memphis, 1980-81, sec., sr. corp. atty., 1981-84; sec., assoc. gen. counsel Holiday Corp., Memphis, 1984-87, v.p., sec., assoc. gen. counsel, 1987-88; v.p., gen. counsel, sec. Perkins Family Restaurants, L.P., Memphis, 1989-91; pvt. practice law, 1991—; ptnr. Armstrong Allen, PLLC, 2000—06, Apperson Crump and Maxwell PLC, 2006—. Mediator Tenn. Mediation/Arbitration Svc., 1994-95; adj. prof. MBA program Christian Brothers U. Sch. Bus., Memphis, 1997-99. Bd. dirs. Memphis Urban League, 1987-94; trustee Memphis Urban League Endowment Fund, 1987—. Mem. ABA (bus. law sect. com. bus. and corp. litigation 2001—, intellectual property law sect. com. on unfair comp.-trade identity 1996-2006, corp. gov. 2004—, small bus. 2004-, fed. regulation securities 2004-), Tenn. Bar Assn., Memphis Bar Assn., Am. Soc. Corp. Secs. (corp. practices com. 1981-97, 99-2001, 2004—, pub. co. affairs com. 2003-04). Republican. Roman Catholic. Avocations: photography, jogging, racquetball. Office: Apperson, Crump & Maxwell 6000 Poplar Ave Ste 400 Memphis TN 38119-3972 Office Phone: 901-756-8211. Business E-Mail: jbroadhurst@appersoncrump.com.

BROADIE, RICHARD R., history professor; b. Estherville, Iowa, Oct. 7, 1953; s. Maurice R. and Louise K. Broadie; m. Peggy Broadie, July 20, 1991; 1 child, Leah. MA, U. No. Iowa, Cedar Falls, 1977. Lectr. history U. No. Iowa, Cedar Falls, 1977—. Newspaper columnist Cedar Falls Record, 1982—83; pub. radio commentator KUNI Radio, Cedar Falls, Iowa, 1984—2004. Contbr. author: Historic U.S. Court Cases, 2003; contbr. articles to profl. jours., book reviews. Vice-chmn. Black Hawk County Dems., Waterloo, Iowa, 1981—84. Recipient 1st Pl. Editl. Commentary award, Iowa AP Broadcasters Assn., 1992. Mem.: Iowa State Hist. Soc., Orgn. Am. Historians. Home: 1507 W 12th St Cedar Falls IA 50613

BROADNAX, WALTER D., university president, educator; b. Starcity, Ark., Oct. 21, 1944; s. Walter and Mary Lee (Cotton) B.; m. Angel LaVerne Wheelock; 1 child, Andrea Alyce. BA, Washburn U., 1967; MPA, Kans. U., 1969; PhD, Syracuse U., 1975; Hon. Degrees, Washburn U., Topeka; Hon. Degree, Ctrl. State U. Ohio. Dir. Svc. Children, Youth and Adults, Kans., 1979-80; prin. dep. asst. sec. US Dept. HHS, Washington, 1980-81, dep. sec., 1993-96; lectr. pub. mgmt. and pub. policy John F. Kennedy sch. govt. Harvard U., 1981-87, dir. innovations state and local govt., 1985-87; pres. NY State Civil Svc. Commn., 1987-90; commr. NY State Dept. Civil Svc., 1987-90; pres. Ctr. Govtl. Rsch., Inc., Rochester, NY, 1990-93; prof. school of pub affairs Univ of Md, Coll. Pk., Md., 1996-99; dean Coll. Pub. Affairs Am. U., 1999—2002; pres. Clark Atlanta U., 2002—. Bd. dirs. Keycorp, Medecision, Inc., CNA Corp. Contbr. articles to profl. jours. Trustee Syracuse U., Coun. Ind. Colls., Ga. Found. Ind. Colls., Atlanta Regional Coun. Higher Edn., also vice chair bd. Recipient Maxwell Sch. of Citizenship and Pub. Affairs Spirit of Pub. Svc. award, Whiting scholar Washburn U., Pioneer award, Syracuse U. Fellow Nat. Acad. Pub. Adminstrn.; pres. ASPA (Outstanding Pub. Svc. award Nat. Capital Area chpt.), Nat. Acad. Pub. Adminstrn. (Nat. Pub. Svc. award), Nat. Assn. Ind. Colls. and Univs. (trustee). Avocations: reading, jogging, music. Home: 691 Beckwith St SW Atlanta GA 30314- Office: Clark Atlanta U Office of Pres Atlanta GA Office Phone: 404-880-8502. Office Fax: 404-880-8500. Business E-Mail: wbroadnax@cau.edu.

BROADRICK-ALLEN, SANDRA CAROL, retired city manager, civic worker, consultant; b. St. Louis, May 5, 1940; d. Charles Albert Jr. and Verna Catherine (Yount) Allen; m. King Woodard Broadrick, July 4, 1975. BS, Lindenwood Coll., 1962; MA, U. Denver, 1965; PhD, U. Ill., 1975. Cert. tchr. Ill., Mo. Tchr. home econs. Princeville HS, Ill., 1962—65, guidance counselor, 1965—68; dean faculty, dean students Garland Jr. Coll., Boston, 1971—75, pres., 1975—76; adminstr. Office Arms Control, Disarmament and Internat. Security, Urbana, Ill., 1981—82; campaign mgr. for state rep. from 103d legis. dist. Ill. Ho. of Reps., 1982—84; city mgr. Village of Savoy, Ill., 1985—91; adminstrv.-exec. cons., Champaign, Ill., 1992—. Editor: County Banners of the Illinois Association for Home and Community Education, 2000; mem. editl. rev. bd. Nat. Assn. for Women Deans, Adminstrs. and Counselors Jour., 1972-74. Pres. Princeville H.S. PTA, 1968; moderator Princeville Cmty. Coun., 1966—68; bd. dirs. U. YWCA, Champaign, 1983—89; mem. home econs. coun. Champaign County Coop. Ext. Svc., 1985—87, treas. unit coun., 1991—92; vice chmn., pres. Ext. Edn. Found., 1992—99; mem. president's coun. U. Ill., 1998—, Busey Bank, 1998—2005; pres. Ill. Assn. Home and Cmty. Edn., 1997—2000; mem. Carle Found., 2005—; mem. precinct com. Champaign County Dem. Com, 1982—85; sr. h.s. youth fellowship adv. Princeville Presbyn. Ch., 1965—68. Recipient Leadership award Univ. YWCA, 1985, Outstanding Vol. award United Way Champaign County, 1986, cert. of recognition, Ill. Ho. of Reps., 1991; citizens lay advisor scholar Ritenour Sch. Dist., 1958-62, honors scholar Lindenwood Coll., 1958-62; grantee U.S. Office Edn., 1968-70. Mem. Assoc. Country Women of World (vice chmn. UN com. 1998-2001, chmn. 2001-04, bd. dirs. 2001-04), Scroll Soc., Carle Found., Rotary (charter pres. Savoy 1989-91, gov. dist. 6490 2001-02, coord. task force and adminstrv. coord. 2000-01, dir. youth programs 2002-03, chair RI centennial com. 2003-05, dist. trainer 2005-06, chair dist. family rotary com. 2006-, dir. dist. adminstrv. svcs. 2007-, Paul Harris fellow 1993, multiple Spirit of Paul Harris awards, others), Phi Delta Kappa, Kappa Omicron Phi. Avocations: travel, archaeology, gardening. Personal E-mail: sandyba@net66.com.

BROADWATER, DOUGLAS DWIGHT, lawyer; b. Preston, Minn., May 31, 1944; s. George and Marion Elaine (Gleason) B.; m. Beatrice (Kinney), July 8, 1978; children: Ian Dwight, George Francis, Mark Fowler. BA, Harvard U., 1966; JD, Columbia U., 1969. Bar: NY 1969. Staff atty. employment project Ctr. Social Welfare Policy and Law, NYC, 1969—71; assoc. Cravath, Swaine & Moore LLP, NYC, 1971—78, ptnr., litig., 1978—. Bd. dirs. Vis. Nurse Svc., NY, 1991—, chmn., 1998—. Office: Cravath Swaine & Moore LLP Worldwide Plz 825 8th Ave 41st Fl New York NY 10019-7475 Office Phone: 212-474-1553. Office Fax: 212-474-3700. Business E-Mail: dbroadwater@cravath.com.

BROADWATER, JAMES E., publisher; b. Tacoma, Nov. 5, 1945; s. Robert L. and June J. B.; m. Diane K. Plummer, Apr. 22, 1967; children: James Tegan, Kelly Diane, Robert Charles, Krista Dawn. BS in Journalism, U. Fla., 1967. Acct. mgr. Young & Rubicam, Inc., Detroit, Kansas City, NYC and Houston, 1968-73; assoc. pub. Tex. Monthly Mag., Austin, 1973-78; pres., pub. Saturday Rev. Mag., NYC, 1978-80; regional pub. dir. Baker Publs., Houston, 1980-85; pres. HBC, Inc. , Houston, 1985-87; assoc. pub. Tex. Sportsworld Mag., 1985-86; pub. Washington Journalism Rev., 1987-92; pres. The Broadwater Co., Houston, 1993—. Mem. Mag. Pub. Assn., Nat. Press Club, Am. Mgmt. Assn., Direct Mail Mktg. Assn., Lambda Chi Alpha. Baptist. Personal E-mail: jbroadwater@sbcglobal.net. *All things are possible through Christ. Success requires that one deal in results and not succumb to the desire to rationalize excuses.*

BROATCH, ROBERT E., insurance company executive; married; 2 children. BS, Trinity Coll.; MBA, Dartmouth Coll. CPA. With Arthur Andersen & Co., Hartford Ins. Group, Primerica; sr. v.p. fin. Aetna Life & Casualty Co., until 1996; with UNUM Corp., Portland, Maine, 1996—2000, sr. v.p., CFO, 1997-2000; exec. v.p., CFO Gab Robins Group, Parsippany, NJ, 2000—02, Guardian Life Ins., 2002—. Active United Way Portland; past chmn. Conn. Policy and Econ. Coun. Office: Guardian Life Ins H-26-E 7 Hanover Square New York NY 10004 Office Phone: 212-598-8000.*

BROBECK, JOHN RAYMOND, physiology educator; b. Steamboat Springs, Colo., Apr. 12, 1914; s. James Alexander and Ella (Johnson) B.; m. Dorothy Winifred Kellogg, Aug. 24, 1940; children: Stephen James, Priscilla Kimball, Elizabeth Martha, John Thomas. BS, Wheaton Coll., 1936, LL.D., 1960; MS, Northwestern U., 1937, PhD, 1939; MD, Yale U., 1943. Instr. physiology Yale, 1943-45, asst. prof., 1945-48, asso. prof. physiology, 1948-52; prof. physiology, chmn. dept. U. Pa., Phila., 1952-70, Herbert C. Rorer prof. med. scis., 1970-82, prof. emeritus, 1982—. Editor: Yale Jour. Biology and Medicine, 1949-52; chmn. editorial bd.: Physiol. Revs, 1963-72. Fellow Am. Acad. Arts and Scis.; mem. Am. Physiol. Soc. (pres. 1971-72), Am. Inst. Nutrition, Nat. Acad. Scis., Am. Soc. Clin. Investigation, Halsted Soc., Phila. Coll. Physicians, Sigma Xi, Alpha Omega Alpha. Home: 1343 W Baltimore Pike # C118 Media PA 19063-5519

BROBECK, STEPHEN JAMES, consumer advocate; b. New Haven, Sept. 15, 1944; s. John Raymond and Dorothy Winifred (Kellogg) B.; m. Susan Cheney Williams, May 9, 1971. BA, Wheaton Coll., 1966; PhD, U. Pa., 1972. Asst. prof. Case Western Res. U., 1970-79; exec. dir. Consumer Fedn. Am., Washington, 1980—. Vis. assoc. prof. Cornell U., 1989; adj. assoc. prof. U. Md., 1990-92. Author: The Product Safety Book, 1983, The Bank Book, 1986, The Modern Consumer Movement, 1990, Encyclopedia of the Consumer Movement, 1997; contbr. articles to profl. jours. Bd. dirs. Citizens for Tax Justice, 1980—, Coalition Against Ins. Fraud, 1993—, Alliance to Save Energy, 1994—, Jump Start Coalition, 2002—, Ctr. Study Svcs., 1998—. Mem. Am. Council Consumer Interests. Home: 4700 Connecticut Ave NW Washington DC 20008-5629 Office: Consumer Fedn Am 1620 Eye St NW Ste 200 Washington DC 20006-4030 Office Phone: 202-387-6121. Business E-Mail: sbrobeck@consumerfed.org.

BROBST, PETER JOHN, history professor; b. Livermore, Calif., July 2, 1967; s. Peter and Renee Robinson Brobst. BA, U. Kans., Lawrence, 1989; PhD, U. Tex., Austin, 1997. Vis. asst. prof. Franklin and Marshall Coll., Lancaster, Pa., 1998—99; asst. prof. Ctrl. Mo. State U., Warrensburg, Mo., 1999—2000, Ohio U., Athens, Ohio, 2000—05, assoc. prof., 2005—. Author: The Future of the Great Game: Sir Olaf Caroe, India's Independence, and the Defense of Asia, 2005; contbr. articles to profl. jours. Roman Catholic. Avocation: travel. Office: Ohio Univ History Dept Athens OH 45701 Home Phone: 740-594-9600; Office Phone: 740-593-4334. Business E-Mail: brobst@ohio.edu.

BROBSTON, STANLEY HEARD, music educator, writer; b. Jacksonville, Fla., Apr. 28, 1937; s. Stanley Prentiss and Elizabeth Lawrence Brobston; m. Sandra Holloway, Aug. 22, 1964; children: Stanley Holloway, Stephen Henry. BS in Edn., Ga. So. U., Statesboro, 1958; MusM, U. Ga., Athens, 1967; PhD, NYU, 1977. Music educator Syosset Pub. Schs., NY, 1969—98. Zone 13 rep. NY State Sch. Music Assn., Nassau County, NY; spkr. in field. Author: (book) Daddy Sang Lead, The History and Performance Practice of White Southern Gospel Music, 2006. Chmn. Heritage Ctr., Baxley, Ga. Lt. jet carrier pilot USNR, 1959—65, Vietnam. Decorated Vietnam Svc. medal USNR; recipient Builder Brotherhood award, Nat. Conf. Christians and Jews, LI, NY, 1974, Cmty. Svc. award, DAR, 2005. Mem.: Ret. Educators, Lions Club, Vietnam Vets. Am. (life), Gospel Music Assn. (life), Kappa Phi Kappa, Phi Delta Kappa, Phi Mu Alpha Sinfonia. Avocations: flying, church choir. Home Phone: 912-367-0262. Personal E-mail: shbrobston@yahoo.com.

BROCA, LAURENT ANTOINE, aerospace scientist; b. Nov. 30, 1928; arrived in U.S., 1957, naturalized, 1963; s. Paul L. and Paule Jeanne (Ferrand) Broca; m. Leticia Garcia Guerra, Dec. 18, 1972; 1 child, Marie-There Yvonne. BS in Math., U. Bordeaux, 1949; lic. es Scis. in Math. and Physics, U. Toulouse, 1957; grad., Inst. Technique Profl. France, 1980; PhD of Elec. Engring., Calif. We. U., 1979; postgrad., Boston U., 1958, MIT, 1961, Harvard U., 1961. Tchg. fellow physics dept. Boston U., 1957—58; spl. instr. dept. physics N.J. Inst. Tech., Newark, 1959—60; sr. staff engr. advanced rsch. group ITT, Nutley, NJ, 1959—60; examiner math. and phys. scis. U. Paris and Caen Exam Ctr., NYC, 1959—69; sr. engr. surface radar divsn. Raytheon Co., Waltham, Mass., 1960—62, Hughes Aircraft Co., Culver City, Calif., 1962—64; asst. prof. math. Calif. State U., Northridge, 1963—64; prin. engr. astrionics lab. NASA, Huntsville, Ala., 1964—65; fellow engr. Def. and Space Ctr. Westinghouse Electric Corp., Balt., 1965—69; cons. and sci. adv. electronics, phys. scis. and math. indsl. firms and broadcasting stas., 1969—80; head engring. dept. Videocraft Mfg. Co., Laredo, Tex., 1974—75; asst. prof. math. Laredo State U., 1975; engring. specialist dept. sys. performance analysis ITT Fed. Electric Corp., Vandenberg AFB, Calif., 1980—82; engring. mgr. Ford Aerospace and Comm. Corp., Nellis AFB, Nev., 1982—84, Arcata Assocs., Inc., North Las Vegas, Nev., 1984—85; sr. sci. specialist engring. and devel. EG&G-JT3, Las Vegas, 1985—2005, consulting scientist, 2005—. With French Army, 1951—52. Recipient Published Paper award, Hughes Aircraft Co., 1966; Fulbright scholar, 1957. Mem.: IEEE, Am. Def. Preparedness Assn., Am. Nuc. Soc. (vice chmn. Nev. sect. 1982—83, chmn. 1983—84), Air Force Assn., Armed Forces Comm. and Electronics Assn. Home: 5040 Lancaster Dr Las Vegas NV 89120-1445 Personal E-mail: lab_lv@att.net.

BROCCARD, ALAIN FRANSOIS, pulmonologist; MD, U. Geneva, Switzerland, 1985. Diplomate in pulmonary medicine Am. Bd. Internal Medicine, in critical care medicine Am. Bd. Internal Medicine. Intern Hosp. Morles, Switzerland, 1985—86; resident U. Hosp., Geneva, 1986—90; fellow in pulmonary and critical care medicine U. Minn., Mpls., 1994—97, prof. of medicine; critical care fellow Mayo Clinic, Rochester, Minn., 1997—98; micu dir. Regions Hosp., St Paul, Minn. Contbr. articles to profl. publs., chpts. to books. Recipient Cecil J. Watson award, Minn. Med. Found., U. Minn., 1997; grantee Cecil Lehman Mayer rsch. finalist award, Am. Coll. Chest Physician, 2000. Achievements include research in ventilator-induced lung injury; pulmonary circulation, hypercapnia, nitric oxide, ARDS, mechanical ventilation; shock. Office: Regions Hosp 640 Jackson St Saint Paul MN 55101-2595 Office Phone: 651-254-5529. Office Fax: 651-254-3098.

BROCCHINI, RONALD GENE, architect; b. Oakland, Calif., Nov. 6, 1929; s. Gino Mario and Yoli Louise (Lucchesi) B.; m. Myra Mossman, Feb. 3, 1957; 1 child, Christopher Ronald BA in Architecture with honors, U. Calif., Berkeley, 1953, MA in Architecture with honors, 1957. Registered architect, Calif., Nev. Architect, designer SMP, Inc., San Francisco, 1948-53, designer, assoc., 1956-60; assoc. architect Campbell & Wong, San Francisco, 1961-63; prin. architect Ronald G. Brocchini, Berkeley, Calif., 1964-67, Worley K Wong & Ronald G Brocchini Assocs., San Francisco, 1968-87, Brocchini Architects, Berkeley, 1987—. Lectr. Calif. Coll. Arts and Crafts, Oakland, 1981-83; commr. Calif. Bd. Archtl. Examiners, 1961-89; mem. exam. com. Nat. Coun. Archtl. Registration Bds., 1983-85. Author: Long Range Master Plan for Bodega Marine Biology, U. Calif., 1982; prin. works include San Simeon Visitor Ctr., Hearst Castle, Calif., Mare Island Med.-Dental Facillity, IBM Ednl. and Data Processing Hdqrs., San Jose, Calif., Simpson Fine Arts Gallery, Calif. Coll. Arts, Ceramics and Metal Crafts, Emery Bay Pub. Market Complex, Analytical Measurement Facility, U. Calif., Berkeley, Bodega Marine Biology Campus, U. Calif., Berkeley, Fromm & Sichell (Christian Bros.) Hdqrs., The Nature Co., Corp. Offices, Berkeley, Merrill Coll., Athletic Facilities, U. Calif., Santa Cruz, Coll. III Housing, U. Calif., San Diego, Ctr. Pacific Rim Studies, U. San Francisco, married student housing Escondido II, III, IV, Stanford (Calif.) U. With U.S. Army, 1953-55. Recipient Bear of Yr. award U. Calif., Berkeley, 1987, Alumni Citation, 1988; recipient 22 Design Honor awards for architecture, Design award State of Calif. Dept. Rehab., 1995. Fellow AIA (bd. dirs. Calif. coun., pres. San Francisco chpt. 1982); mem. Bear Backers Club (bd. dirs. U. Calif.-Berkeley athletic coun.), Berkeley Breakfast Club (bd. govs.), Order of the Golden Bear, Chi Alpha Kappa. Republican. Roman Catholic. Avocations: auto restoration, photography, sports, art. Office: Brocchini Architects Inc 1600 Shattuck Ave Ste 224 Berkeley CA 94709 E-mail: arcbro@pacbell.net.

BROCHIN, ROBERT M., lawyer; b. May 14, 1955; m. Cristina E. Brochin. BA, U. Fla., 1977; JD, U. Fla. Law Sch., 1980. Bar: Fla. 1981. Dep. gen. counsel Fla. Gov. Office, 1991—92, Fla. Chief Inspector Gen., 1992—93; ptnr., litig. practice group Morgan, Lewis & Bockius LLP, 1993—, chmn. recruiting com-Miami Office. Mem.: Fla. Partnership Am. (chmn.), Dade County Bar Assn., Fla. Bar Assn., Fla. Constn. Revision Commn. (1997-1998). Office: Morgan Lewis & Bockius LLP 5300 Wachovia Fin Ctr 200 S Biscayne Blvd Miami FL 33131-2339 Office Phone: 305-415-3456. Office Fax: 305-415-3001. Business E-Mail: rbrochin@morganlewis.com.

BROCK, CAROLYN PRATT, chemist, educator; b. Chgo., July 25, 1946; d. Charles Stebbings and Grace (Goodman) Pratt; m. Louis Milton Brock, July 22, 1972. BA, Wellesley Coll., Mass., 1968; PhD, Northwestern U., 1972. Asst. prof. chemistry U. Ky., Lexington, 1972-78, assoc. prof. chemistry, 1978-87, prof., 1987—. Vis. scientist organic chemistry lab. Swiss Fed. Inst. Tech., Zurich, 1980—81, Zurich, 1988—89; bd. govs. Cambridge Crystallographic Data Centre, 2001—, vice chmn., 2003—05, chmn., 2005—07. Co-editor: Acta Crystallographica, 1993; editor: Sect. B of Acta Crystallographica, 2002—; contbr. articles to profl. jours. Mem. Am. Chem. Soc., Am. Crystallographic Assn., U.S. Nat. Com. for Crystallography (sec.-treas. 1989-91), Phi Beta Kappa, Sigma Xi. Home: 133 Sycamore Rd Lexington KY 40502-1841 Office: U Ky Dept Chemistry Lexington KY 40506-0055 Home Phone: 859-266-2414; Office Phone: 859-257-1959. Business E-Mail: cpbrock@uky.edu.

BROCK, CHARLES LAWRENCE, lawyer, diversified financial services company executive, investment banker; b. Ottumwa, Iowa, Mar. 7, 1943; s. Charles Harlan and Betty Arlene (Ream) B.; m. Mary Jane Hipp, June 17, 1978; children: William Walker, Susanna Lawrence. BA with highest distinction, Northwestern U., 1964; JD, Harvard U., 1967; postgrad. (Rotary Found. fellow), U. Delhi and India Law Inst., India, 1967-68; grad., Advanced Mgmt. Program, Harvard Bus. Sch., 1979. Bar: N.Y. 1968. Asso. firm Sullivan & Cromwell, NYC, 1969-74; v.p., corp. sec., gen. counsel Scholastic Mags., Inc. (now Scholastic, Inc.), NYC, 1974-80; interim CFO and COO Scholastic Mags., Inc., 1975-76, pub. internat. div., 1976-80; pres. Scholastic Tab Publs. Ltd., Can., 1976-80, Ashton-Scholastic Pty. Ltd., Australia, 1976-80, Ashton-Scholastic Ltd., New Zealand, 1976-80; chmn. Scholastic Publs. Ltd., U.K., 1976-80; sr. v.p., mgmt. dir. Compton Communications, 1980-82; mgr. subsidiaries Compton Advertising, 1980-82; counsel Drinker, Biddle & Reath, NYC, Phila., Washington, 1982-84; ptnr. Carter, Ledyard & Milburn, 1984-95, Brock Ptnrs. and predecessor firms, 1995—; chmn., CEO Brock Capital Group LLC, 2002—. Bd. dirs., chmn. audit coms. B&H Bulk Carriers Ltd., B&H Ocean Carriers Ltd., B&H Maritime Carriers Ltd., Excel Maritime Carriers, 2002-; mem. Harvard Coll. Bd. Overseers Com. on Univ. Resources, 1992—, chmn. Harvard Bd. Overseers Nominating Com. 1996—, coun. Harvard Law Sch. Assn., 1983-85, sec., 1988-90, treas., 1990—92, exec. com., 1986—, chmn. membership com., 1987—, internat. sect., 1991—, 1st v.p., 1994-96, pres. 1996-98; bd. advisors Coll. Arts and Scis., Northwestern U., 1989—, Campaign for Gt. Tchrs. Com., 1989-90, John Evans Club, Northwestern U. 1989—; guild hall trustee Acad. of the Arts, 1990—, mem. exec. com., chmn. nominating com., 1986-90, chmn. bd., 1990-92, trustee, treas. Family Dynamics, 1981-88. Mem. editl. adv. bd. Minority Law Jour. Reunion gift chmn. Harvard Law Sch. Fund, 1967-68, vice chmn., 1975-77, 40th reunion gift co-chmn., 2006-, vice chair, 1978-82; trustee Harvard Law Sch. Assn. NYC, 1982-85, chmn. placement com., 1983-86, v.p., 1985-96, originator, chmn. summer reception, 1982-; chmn. Harvard Community Ptnrs., 1984-86; co-chmn. ann. giving St. Barnard's Sch., 1989-95; mem. adv. bd. Minority Atty. Reporter; deacon Brick Presbyn. Ch., NYC, 1973-76, regent Cathedral St. John The Divine, 1997-. Recipient Mentor award for pioneering efforts creating opportunities for minorities and women award for outstanding svc. Harvard U., 2005, award for outstanding svc. to Harvard U. Mem. ABA, N.Y. State Bar Assn., N.Y. County Lawyers Assn., Assn. Bar City of N.Y., Harvard Alumni Assn. (bd. dirs. 1989—, sec. 1998-2001, 1st v.p. 2001-02, pres. 2002-03, chmn. grad. schs. com. 1992-95), Assn. Am. Pubs., Century Assn., Harvard Bus. Club of N.Y. (v.p. 1984-86), Union Club, N.Y. Yacht Club, Down Town Assn., The Pilgrims, Piping Rock (Locust Valley, N.Y.), Maidstone Club (East Hampton, N.Y.), Ogeechee Golf Club, Phi Beta Kappa, Kappa Sigma. Home: 765 Park Ave New York NY 10021-4254 Office: 622 Third Ave New York NY 10017 Office Phone: 212-209-3000. Business E-Mail: brock@brockcapital.com.

BROCK, DEE SALA, television executive, educator, writer, consultant; b. Covington, Okla., June 7, 1930; d. Lester Edward and Vera Mae (Bowers) Sala; m. Robert Wesley Brock, June 8, 1952 (div. 1979); children: Baron Sala, Bishop Chapman, Bevin Bowers. BA, U. North Tex., 1950, MA, 1956, PhD, 1985. Tchr. high sch. Dallas Ind. Sch. Dist., 1952-66; dir. Dallas Cowboy Cheerleaders, 1960-75; mem. faculty, adminstr. Dallas County Community Coll. Dist., 1966-74, telecourse writer, producer, adminstr., 1974-75, dir. mktg. info., 1975-80; dir., v.p. PBS, Washington, 1980-89, sr. v.p. edn. Alexandria, Va., 1989-90; pres. Dee Brock & Assocs., Plano, Tex., 1991-98; pub. FAQs Press, 1999—. Bd. dirs. Pub. Svc. Satellite Consortium, U.S. Basics; adv. bd. Learning Link, 1987-90, Telcon Industry, 1990-91; chair exec. coun. U. of the World, 1989-91; adv. coun. Triangle Coalition, 1989-91; spkr. in field. Author: Writing for a Reason: Study Guide, 1974; author: (with Jeriel Howard) Writing for a Reason, 1978; author: (with Laura Derr) The World of F. Scott Fitzgerald, 1980; author: (with Deborah Burkett and Carole Wilson) Troup Goes to War: World War II, A Collection of Memories, 1999; author: (with Linda Resnik) Food FAQs: Substitutions, Yields & Equivalents, 2000; author: (with JoAnna Lewis) 100 Great Fundraising Ideas Celebrating 100 Years of Texas Library, 2002; mem. editl. bd.: Am. Jour. Distance Edn., 1987—90; prodr.: (internat. teleconf.) Out of the Red, 1991; prodr., writer: TV series and workbook Communicating in English in the Healthcare Workplace, 1994; contbr. articles to profl. jours. Trustee Coun. for Adult and Experiential Learning, 1989—99; chair spl. task force Mcpl. Libr. Friends of Libr., 1996, pres., 1997—; lay rep. N.E. Tex. Libr. Sys., 1996—, chair planning to plan com., 1997—98, adv. coun., 1998—, vice chair, 1998—2000, chair, 2000—04; chmn. Strategic Planning Com., 1999; fundraising co-chair Komen Tyler Race for the Cure, 1999; active PTA, Dallas; pres. Littera, 2002—04, Friends of the Troup Libr., 1998—; chair Libr. Friends, Trustees and Advs., 2001—03; bd. dirs. Tyler Civic Theatre Ctr., Coalition for the Advancement of Citizenship, 1988—90. Reynolds Econ. fellow U. N.C., 1966; Literacy award N. Tex. Reading Coun., 1980, Nat. Person of Yr. award Nat. Coun. on Community and Continuing Edn., 1985, Award for Excellence in TV Programming NEA, 1986; recipient Outstanding Career Achievement award ITC Am. Assn. Community and Jr. Colls., 1990. Mem. NEH (nat. bd. cons. 1980-85), LWV (bd. dirs., v.p. cmty. rels. Tyler chpt. 2002-03, pres. 2003—), U.S. Distance Learning Assn. (bd. dirs. 1989-91, adv. bd. 1989), So. Assn. Colls. and Schs. (project 1990 task force 1984-86), Nat. Assn. Ednl. Broadcasters (steering com. 1979-81), Assn. Ednl. Comms. Tech., Nat. Coun. Tchrs. English (pres. S.W. regional coun. 1972-74), Tex. Libr. Assn. (legis. com. 1999—, chair roundtable 2001-2003, chair pub. rels. com. 2005—). Methodist. Achievements include being co-patentee video indexing system; design of and management of PBS Adult Learning Service and PBS Adult Learning Satellite Service. Home and Office: 3529 Woods Blvd Tyler TX 75707

BROCK, GREGORY E., editor; With Charlotte Observer, NC, San Francisco Examiner, Calif., Washington Post, NY Times, 1995—, asst. fgn. editor, news editor, Washington bur., 2002—06, sr. editor, 2006—. Office: NY Times Washington Bur 7th Fl 1627 I St Washington DC 20006 Office Phone: 202-862-0446. Office Fax: 202-862-0340. E-mail: brockg@nytimes.com.

BROCK, HELEN RACHEL MCCOY, retired mental health and community health nurse; b. Cromwell, Okla., Dec. 10, 1924; d. Samuel Robert Lee and Ire Etta (Pounds) McCoy; m. Clois Lee Brock, Sept. 29, 1963; children: Dwayne, Joyce, Peggy, Ricki, Stacey. AS, Southwestern Union Coll., Keene, Tex., 1968; BS in Nursing, Union Coll., Lincoln, Nebr., 1970; postgrad., Vernon Regional Jr. Coll., Tex., 1972—76; MPH, Loma Linda U., Calif., 1983. Cert. ARC nurse. Dir. nursing Chillicothe (Tex.) Clinic-Hosp., 1970-77, Pike County Hosp., Waverly, Ohio, 1977-79, Marion County Hosp., Jefferson, Tex., 1979-81; nurse III, nursing unit supr, patient health educator Vernon State Hosp., Maximum Security for Criminally Insane, 1981-96; retired, 1996; nurse, admissions and assessments Texhoma Community Health Svcs., 1987-94. Mem.: ANA, Tex. Nurses Assn. Home: PO Box 238 Chillicothe TX 79225-0238

BROCK, HOLLY MELINDA, marketing professional; b. Terceria, Azores, Portugal, Aug. 28, 1973; d. Edwin L. Cox Jr. and Mary Elizabeth Cox; 1 child, Taylor Robert. Degree in Human Svc. Mgmt. (hon.), U. Phoenix, 2003. Cert. alcohol and drug counseling State of Nev., 2003, HIPAA regulations State of Nev., 2004, HIV/AIDS educator ARC, 2000. Recreation and activity leader Clark County Pk. and Recreation, Las Vegas, 1993—96; activity asst. Desert Ln. Care Ctr., Las Vegas, 1996; domestic violence, children's adv. SAFEHouse, Henderson, Nev., 1996—98; case mgr. Lighthouse Compassionate Care, Las Vegas, 1999—2000; housing coord. Caminar, Inc., Las Vegas, 2000—03; counselor Ctr. Behavioral Health, Las Vegas, 2003; case mgmt. supr. State of Nev. Bur. Cmty. Health, Las Vegas, 2003—04; mktg. dir. The Plz. at Sun Mountain, Las Vegas, 2004—. Mem. So. Poverty Law Ctr., Montgomery, Ala., 2003—04; bd. mem. City of Henderson, Cmty. Devel. Bldg. Grant Adv. Bd., 2003—05; mem. MADD, Las Vegas, 2003—05; edn. chair Susan G. Komen Breast Cancer Found., Las Vegas, 2003—05. Achievements include Name added to the Wall of Tolerance at the Civil Rights Memorial Center in Montgomery, Alabama. Office: The Plaza at Sun Mountain 6031 W Charleston Las Vegas NV 89108 Home Phone: 702-897-0263; Office Phone: 702-658-5882. Office Fax: 702-658-5842.

BROCK, HORACE RHEA, finance educator; b. Leggett, Tex., Aug. 26, 1927; s. Hobby B. and Winona (Epperson) Brock; m. Frances Euline Williams, May 24, 1955; children: Alan Howard, Mary Ann, Charles. BS, Sam Houston State U., 1946, BBA, MA, Sam Houston State U., 1951; PhD, U. Tex., 1954. Prof. U. Ark., 1954-55; disting. prof. North Tex. State U., Denton, 1965-93, chmn. dept. accounting, 1966-74, acting dean Coll. Bus. Adminstrn., 1983-85; dir. Chief Execs. Round Table U. North Tex., Denton, 1993—99. Adviser AID, Istanbul, Turkey, 1967—69; cons. taxation and fin. reporting. Author: Accounting for Oil and Gas Producers, 1960, Intermediate and Advanced Accounting, 1966, Introduction to Taxation, 1972, 17th edit., 1988, Cost Accounting, 1970, 8th edit., 2006, College Accounting, 1974, 11th edit., 2005, Accounting for Oil and Gas Producing Companies, 1982, 6th edit., 2006. With USAF, 1946—49. Mem.: AICPA, Tex. Soc. CPAs, Beta Gamma Sigma. Home: 1900 Westridge St Denton TX 76205-6925 Office: U North Tex 302 Marquis Hall Denton TX 76203 Personal E-mail: brocks3@verizon.net. Business E-Mail: brock@unt.edu.

BROCK, ISAAC, musician; b. Issaquah, Wash., July 9, 1975; Guitarist & lead singer Modest Mouse, 1993—, Ugly Casanova. Singer: (albums) (with Modest Mouse) This is a Long Drive for Someone with Nothing to Think About, 1996, Lonesome Crowded West, 1997, The Fruit That Ate Itself, 1997, The Moon & Antarctica, 2000, Sad Sappy Sucker, 2001, Good News for People Who Love Bad News, 2004, We Were Dead Before the Ship Even Sank, 2007, (with Ugly Casanova) Sharpen Your Teeth, 2002; prodr. (for Wolf Parade) Apologies to the Queen Mary, 2005, Wolf Parade, 2005; actor: (films) Christmas on Mars, 2005. Office: c/o Up Records Box 21328 Seattle WA 98111 also: c/o Epic Records 550 Madison Ave New York NY 10022 Office Phone: 206-320-9004. Office Fax: 206-320-9075.*

BROCK, JAMES RUSH, chemical engineering professor; b. Mission, Tex., Dec. 31, 1930; s. Jerome Dalton and Elizabeth (Beeler) B.; m. Mary Lou Waghorn, July 4, 1964; children: Ianthe, Alison. BA, Rice U., 1952, BS, 1953; MS, U. Wis., 1954, PhD, 1960. Registered profl. engr., Tex. Rsch. engr. Humble Oil & Refining Co., Houston, 1954-55; asst. prof. chem. engring. dept. U. Tex., Austin, 1959-62; postdoctoral fellow at Svc. de Chimie Physique II Université Libre de Belgique, Brussels, 1962-63; asst. prof. chem. engring. dept. U. Tex., Austin, 1963-65, assoc. prof., 1965-69, prof., 1969-73, 73-80, K.A. Kobe prof., 1980—2001, K.A. Kobe prof. emeritus, 2000—; vis. prof. U. Paris VI Faculty Scis., Paris, 1973, Tokyo Inst. Tech., 1988. Mem. rsch. grants adv. com. EPA, Washington, 1970—; v.p. ONG Producing Inc., Austin, 1986-2000; cons. to govt. agys. Co-author: The Dynamics of Aerocolloidal Systems, 1970; co-editor Internat. Revs. in Aerosol Physics and Chemistry, 1971-73; assoc. editor Jour. Environ. Sci. and Health, 1978—, Jour. Aerosol Sci., 1986-88; mem. editorial bd. Jour. Colloid Sci., 1965-66, Aerosol Sci. and Tech., 1984-88; contbr. more than 150 articles to profl. jours.; holder 20 patents in field. Recipient Disting. Svc. award U.S. Army Rsch. Devel. Engring. Ctr., 1987; grantee NSF. Mem. Am. Chem. Soc., Am. Assn. Aerosol Rsch. (Sinclair award 1992), Gesellschaft fur Aerosol Forschung, Tau Beta Pi, Alpha Chi Omega, Phi Lambda Upsilon. Home: 1801 Lavaca St #6E Austin TX 78701-1304

BROCK, JOHN F., beverage company executive; m. Mary Brock. BS chem. engring., MS chem. engring., Ga. Inst. Tech. Positions in product develop. Proctor & Gamble, 1972—83; sr. v.p. ops. & tech. Cadbury Schweppes USA, 1983—90; pres. Cadbury Beverages Internat., 1990—92, Cadbury Beverages Europe, 1992—93, Cadbury Beverages No. Am., 1993—96; mng. dir. global beverages Cadbury Schweppes plc, 1996—2000, COO, 2000—02; CEO Interbrew, 2003—04, InBev, Brussels, 2004—06; pres., CEO Coca-Cola Enterprises, Atlanta, 2006—. Bd. dir. Reed Elsevier plc, 1999—2005, Campbell Soup Co., 2004—06. Office: Coca-Cola Enterprises Inc 2500 Windy Ridge Pkwy Atlanta GA 30339*

BROCK, KARENA DIANE, dancer, educator; b. LA, Sept. 21, 1942; d. Orville DeLoss and Sallie Alice (Anderson) B.; m. Ted Kivitt, Apr. 16, 1965 (div. 1978); m. John Robert Carlyle, June 28, 1985; 1 child, Timothy John. Grad. H.S., Kansas City, Mo. Tchr. master classes Radford (Va.) Coll., U. Louisville, U. Tampa; staff tchr. Bklyn. Coll.; mem. faculty SUNY-Purchase; artistic dir., choreographer, tchr. and founder Hilton Head Dance Theater and Sch., Hilton Head Island, SC, 1985—. Guest tchr. S.C. Dance Inst., Columbia, 1993-94, Walnut Hill Sch., Boston, Savannah Ballet, Cleve. Ballet; tchr. master classes Florence, S.C., Columbia; guest choreographer Towson (Md.) U., 2000, 05, Carolina Ballet Theatre, Greeville, S.C., 1998, Island Dance Theatre Ga., 2005, Ron Jones Dance, Ga., 2004. Dancer, David Lichine Concert Group, L.A., 1960-61, Netherlands Nat. Ballet Co., Amsterdam, 1961-62, mem. corps, Am. Ballet Theatre, N.Y.C., 1963-68, soloist, 1968-73, prin. ballerina, 1973-79, artistic dir., prima ballerina, choreographer, Savannah (Ga.) Ballet Co., 1979-85; co-artistic dir. and choreographer Ballet South, Savannah, 1992-96; guest artist, Miami (Fla.) Civic Ballet, Macon (Ga.) Civic Ballet, Tampa (Fla.) Civic Ballet, U. Ill. Ballet Co., Champaign, San Jose (Calif.) Civic Ballet, Ballet de San Juan, P.R., Gala Ballet, Amarillo (Tex.) Civic Ballet, Maywood Ballet Co., Phila., U. Wis., Milw. Civic Ballet, Stars of Am. Ballet, various TV shows, White House, 1966, 69. Mem. adv. bd. S.C. Arts Commn., Columbia, 1988—; hon. mem. bd. dirs. Columbia City Ballet. Mem.: AFTRA, AGVA, Am. Guild Mus. Artists. Office: Hilton Head Dance Theater and Sch 24 Palmetto Business Park Rd Hilton Head Island SC 29928-3234 Office Phone: 843-785-5477. Personal E-mail: balletkbc@yahoo.com.

BROCK, LOUIS MILTON, JR., engineering educator, researcher; b. Davenport, Iowa, Apr. 16, 1943; s. Louis Milton and Mary Elizabeth (Creech) B.; m. Carolyn Starbuck Pratt, July 22, 1972. BS, Northwestern U, 1966, MS, 1967, PhD, 1972. With Black and Veatch, Kansas City, Mo., 1962, Gen Dynamics/Convair, San Diego, 1963-64, Sargeant-Welch Co., Skokie, Ill., 1964, Am. Can Co., Barrington, Ill., 1965; prof. mech. engring. U. Ky., Lexington, 1971—. Contbr. articles to profl. jours. NSF grantee; USN/Am. Soc. Engring. Edn. fellow, 1983, 85, 87, 90; recipient rsch. award Rsch. Found. U. Ky., 1977, rsch. prof. award, 1986. Fellow ASME; mem. ASCE (corr. award 1989), Sigma Xi, Chi Epsilon. Avocations: hiking, classical music, riding, history. Home: 133 Sycamore Rd Lexington KY 40502-1841 Office: U Ky Dept Mech Engring Lexington KY 40506-0503 Office Phone: 859-257-6336 80656.

BROCK, MACON F., SR., retail company executive; Pres., COO K&K Toys; pres., CEO Dollar Tree Stores Inc., Chesapeake, Va., 1991—. Office: Dollar Tree Stores Inc 500 Volvo Pkwy Chesapeake VA 23320

BROCK, MACON F., JR., retail company executive; BA, Randolph-Macon Coll., 1964. Chmn. Dollar Tree Stores. Past chmn., dir. Va. Beach Found.; past pres., trustee Va. Beach Ctr. for Contemporary Art; chmn. Randolph-Macon Coll.; dir. Greater Norfolk Corp., Hampton Roads Econ. Develop. Alliance, Va. Bus. Coun. Capt. USMC, Vietnam Vet., spl. agt. US Naval Intelligence. Named Entrepreneur-in-Residence, Christopher Newport U., Sch. Bus., 2003. Office: Dollar Tree Stores 500 Volvo Pkwy Chesapeake VA 23320

BROCK, NANCY JEANNE, music educator, writer; b. Cedar Falls, Iowa, Jan. 11, 1951; d. Elmo Calvin Boone and Mable Audry Taylor-Boone; m. Sean Anson Brock, Oct. 3, 1986. BA, U. of No. Iowa, 1974, MA in Comm., 1981. Piano tchr. Wash. Pk. Sch. of Music, Waterloo, Iowa, 1976—79; tv program dir. Ottumwa Courier Channel 11, Ottumwa, Iowa, 1982—84. Composing freelance, Falmouth, Mass., 1991—; prodn. asst. documentary Iowa Pub. TV. Writer/illustrator (storybook, poetry, illustrations) True Things Not Forgotten. Vol. Dem. party, Mass., 2000—06. Recipient Good Citizenship award, ARC - Ottumwa, Iowa, 1984. Mem.: Nat. Guild of Piano Tchrs. Achievements include prodr., editor 45 minute TV documentary FLOOD 47for O. Courier; prodr., dir., editor The People of the Patriot State TV documentary; prodr. Mattakeesett Mag. Out And About In Bourne (Mass.), Our Town (Ottumwa, Iowa) live weekly TV mag. programs. Avocations: raising Italian spinoni, hiking, painting, music. Home: 70 Cloverfield Way Falmouth MA 02536 Home Phone: 508-563-5398.

BROCK, RANDALL J., poet; b. Colfax, Wash., Nov. 24, 1943; s. Homer Clarence and Roberta Mildred (Keith) B. Student, Wash. State U., 1962-68; BA in History, BA in Edn., Ea. Wash. U., 1970; MFA, U. Oreg., 1973. Tchr. Christian Action Ministry, Chgo., 1967; mailman Yellowstone (Wyo.) Park Co., 1968; janitor Spokesman-Rev., Spokane, Wash., 1978-79. Pockets of Origin, 1983; author: numerous poems; contbr. articles to profl. jours., chapters to books. Poetry scholar Centrum, Port Townsend, Wash., 1977. Mem.: Poets and Writers, Spokane Open Poetry Assn., Slatz & Co. Poetry Group, Centerstage. Avocations: mysteries, history, anthropology. Home: PO Box 1673 Spokane WA 99210-1673

BROCK, THOMAS DALE, retired microbiology professor; b. Cleve., Sept. 10, 1926; s. Thomas Carter and Helen Sophia (Ringwald) B.; m. Mary Louise Louden, Sept. 13, 1952 (div. Feb. 1971); m. Katherine Serat Middleton, Feb. 20, 1971; children: Emily Katherine, Brian Thomas. BS, Ohio State U., 1949, MS, 1950, PhD, 1952. Research microbiologist Upjohn Co., Kalamazoo, 1952-57; asst. prof. Western Res. U., Cleve., 1957-59, Ind. U., Bloomington, 1960-61, assoc. prof., 1962-64, prof., 1964-71; E.B. Fred prof. natural scis. U. Wis., Madison, 1971-90, prof. emeritus, 1990—, chmn. dept. bacteriology, 1979-82; pres. Sci. Tech. Pubs., Madison, 1990-94, Savanna Oak Found., 2000—. Found. for Microbiology lectr., 1971-72, 78-79 Author: Milestones in Microbiology, 1961, Principles of Microbial Ecology, 1966, Thermophilic Microorganisms, 1978, Biology of Microorganism, 7th edit., 1994, Basic Microbiology with Applications, 3d edit., 1986, A Eutrophic Lake, 1985, Thermophiles: General, Molecular and Applied Microbiology, 1986, Robert Koch: A Life in Medicine and Bacteriology, 1988, The Emergence of Bacterial Genetics, 1990, Shorewood Hills: An Illustrated History, 1999. Recipient Rsch. Career Devel. award NIH, 1962-68, Waksman award Soc. Indsl. Microbiology, 2003, Aldo Leopold award in Restoration Ecology, 2006, Invader Crusader award State of Wis., 2007. Fellow AAAS; mem. Am. Soc. for Microbiology (hon. mem., chmn. gen. div. 1970-71, Fisher award 1984, Carski award 1988) Home and Office: 1227 Dartmouth Rd Madison WI 53705-2213

BROCK, WILLIAM ALLEN, III, economist, educator; b. Phila., Oct. 23, 1941; s. William and Margaret Brock; m. Joan Brock, Aug. 31, 1962; 1 child, Caroline. AB in Math. with honors, U. Mo., 1965; PhD, U. Calif., Berkeley, 1969. Asst. prof. econs. U. Rochester, NY, 1969-71; assoc. prof. U. Chgo., 1972-75, prof., 1975-81; from assoc. prof. to full prof. Cornell U., 1974-77; Romnes prof. econs. U. Wis., Madison, 1981—, F.P. Ramsey prof. econs., 1984—, W.F. Vilas rsch. prof., 1990—. Vis. assoc. prof. U. Rochester, 1973; cons. U.S. Dept. Justice, SBA, EPA, FTC. Assoc. editor: Jour. Econ. Theory, Internat. Econ. Rev., 1972—99; contbr. articles to profl. jours.; co-author (with A. Malliaris): (book) Differential Equations, Stability and Chaos in Dynamic Economics, 1989; co-author: (with D. Hsieh, B. LeBaron) Nonlinear Dynamics, Chaos and Instability: Statistical Theory and Economic Evidence, 1991. Recipient Roger F. Murray 3d Pl. prize, Inst. Quantitative Rsch. Fin., 1989; NSF grantee, 1970—2003, Sherman Fairchild Disting. scholar, Calif. Inst. Tech., 1978, Guggenheim fellow, 1987—88. Fellow: Am. Econs. Assn. (disting.), Econometric Soc.; mem.: AAAS, NAS. Office: U Wis Dept Econs 1180 Observatory Dr Madison WI 53706-1320

BROCK, WILLIAM EMERSON, former secretary of labor; b. Chattanooga, Nov. 23, 1930; s. William E. and Myra (Kruesi) B.; m. Laura Handly, Jan. 11, 1957 (dec. 1985); children: William, Oscar, Laura, John; m. Sandra Schubert Mitchell, Dec. 5, 1986. BS, Washington and Lee U., 1953. V.p. Brock Candy Co., 1957-62; mem. U.S. Congress from Tenn., 1963-70, U.S. Senate from Tenn., 1971-77; chmn. Rep. Nat. Com., Washington, 1977-81; U.S. trade rep. Washington, 1981-85; sec. U.S. Dept. Labor, Washington, 1985-87; chmn. The Brock Group, Washington, 1987—; founder, chmn. Bridges Learning Systems Inc., Richmond, Tex., 1996—. Co-chmn. Nat. Commn. on Skills of Am. Workforce; chmn. Sec. Commn. on Achieving Necessary Skills, Wingspread Group on Higher Edn.; bd. dir. HealthExtras, On Assignment, ResCare Inc., Strayer Univ. Trustee, counselor Ctr. Strategic and Internat. Studies; vice chmn. Nat. Acad. Found.; chmn. emeritus Nat. Endowment for Democracy. Episcopalian.

BROCKELSBY, JEFFREY LIND, investment executive; b. Rapid City, SD, Oct. 20, 1954; s. Earl John Brockelsby and Maude (Wagner) B. BS in Radio/TV summa cum laude, Bradley U., 1976; MS in Mass Comm., S.D. State U., 1983; Cert. in Biblical Studies, Columbia Biblical Sem., 1996. Reporter KEVN/TV, Rapid City, SD, 1976-77; press aide/campaign press sec. Se. George McGovern, Washington, 1979-81; press sec. Rep. Byron Dorgan, Washington, 1981; program dir. S.D. Democratic Party, Pierre, 1983-85; correspondent Huron Daily Plainsman, Pierre, 1985-86; congl. field rep. Tim Johnson, Rapid City, 1986-87; investment executive Brockelsby Family Trusts, Columbia, S.C., 1993—; corp. treas. Black Hills Reptile Gardens, Inc., Rapid City, 1991—. Bd. dirs. Black Hills Reptile Gardens, Inc., 1993—; polling dir. O'Connor for Gov., Sioux Falls, S.D., 1982; CFO Block Hills Pertie Gardens Inc., 2007—. Author: The Brockelsbys of Crawford County Iowa-A Family History, 1991. State campaign treas. Gary Hart for Pres., 1984; field operative Paul Simon for Pres., Rapid City, 1988; cons. several polit. campaigns. Mem.: Depression and Bipolar Support Alliance. Democrat. Avocations: music, running, genealogy. Home: 164 Heritage Village Ln Columbia SC 29212-3512 Office: Brockelsby Fam Trusts 164 Heritage Village Ln Columbia SC 29212-3512

BROCKENBROUGH, HENRY WATKINS, lawyer; b. Richmond, Va., Aug. 28, 1923; s. Benjamin Willard and Kathleen Reading (Watkins) B.; m. Mary Lane Williams, Oct. 30, 1948; children: Henry Watkins, Rebecca Lane, John Reading, Willson Williams. BA cum laude, Hampden-Sydney Coll., 1944; LLB, U. Va., 1948; grad. degree, Rutgers U., 1957. Bar: Va. 1949. With Crestar Bank, Richmond, 1948-88, v.p., trust officer, 1963-67, sr. v.p., trust officer, 1967-88, spl.counsel and trust cons. to Crestar Bank, 1988-91; ptnr.unsel Taylor, Hazen, Kauffman & Pinchbeck, Richmond, 1991—2003; of counsel Pinchbeck, P.C., Richmond2003. Chmn. trust com. Va. Bankers Assn., 1970-71. Past pres. Estate Planning Coun., Richmond; chmn. bd. dirs. Tuckahoe YMCA, 1975. Lt. (j.g.) USNR, 1943-46. Mem. The Cohoke Club (West Point, Va., past pres.), Lambda Chi Alpha, Delta Theta Phi. Presbyterian. Home: 802 Horsepen Rd Richmond VA 23229-6725 Office: 6932 Forest HIll Ave Richmond VA 23225 Office Phone: 804-320-2439.

BROCKERT, JOSEPH PAUL, government executive, writer, editor, designer; b. Tipp City, Ohio, Sept. 17, 1954; s. Paul Edwin and Mary (Aten) B.; m. Deborah Sue Schaefer, Apr. 10, 1976; children: Jonathan Andre, Jason Anthony. BS in Journalism with honors, Ohio U., 1975. Sr. editor Linn's Stamp News, Sidney, Ohio, 1976—84; sr. stamp program specialist US Postal Svc., Washington, 1984—87, program mgr. stamp design, 1987—93, coord. Citizen's Stamp Adv. Com., 1985, art dir. US stamps and stationary, 1986—, designer, 1988—, mgr. Stamps OnLine website, 1999, head speechwriter, 2001, sr. writer, editor, 2002, curator spl. collections, 2003—06, stamp mfg. specialist, 2007—. Guest curator Smithsonian Nat. Postal Mus., 2005—; agy. rep. Commn. Bicentennial of U.S. Constn., 1986-91. Author: Basic Knowledge for the Stamp Collector, 1978, 4th rev. edit., 1983 (Silver medal Am. Philatelic Soc. 1979, Internat. Bronze medal 1986), (with Elaine Durnin Boughner) Stamp Collecting Made Easy, 1984, 3d rev. edit., 1986; editor: The Postal Service Guide to U.S. Stamps, 20th-22d edits., 1993-95, Stamps etc., 1993-1996, USA Philatelic, 1996-98; composer Mass of the Good Shepherd, 2000, Good Shepherd Celebrates!, 2001; contbr. articles to profl. and hobby jours. Chmn. publicity Gunston (Va.) Elem. PTA, 1985, pres., 1986-87; budget chmn. Fairfax County (Va.) Coun. PTA, 1988-92, sec., 1992; pres. Newington Forest (Va.) Elem. PTA, 1989-91; coach Lorton Little League, 1987-88. Mem.: Am. Philatelic Soc. Roman Catholic. Avocations: music, collecting stamps, photography, composing, bowling. Home and Office: 34652 Crew Rd Pomeroy OH 45769-8907 Office Phone: 703-292-3818. Business E-Mail: joseph.p.brockert@usps.gov.

BROCKETT, FRANCESCA L., retail executive; BA, Harvard U., 1982; MBA, Stanford U., Calif., 1986. Cons. Booz-Allen and Hamilton, Atlanta, 1982—85, McKinsey and Co., Houston, 1986—92; with PepsiCo, New Eng., 1994—95, Irvine, Calif., 1995—97, Tricon Global Restaurants, Louisville, 1997—98; from sr. v.p. strategic planning and bus. devel. to exec. v.p. Toys "R" Us, Inc., Wayne, NJ, 1998—2000, exec. v.p. strategic planning and bus. devel., 2000—. Office: Toys R Us Inc 1 Geoffrey Way Wayne NJ 07470-2030 Business E-Mail: brocketf@toysrus.com.

BROCKETT, OSCAR GROSS, theater educator; b. Hartsville, Tenn., Mar. 18, 1923; s. Oscar Hill and Minnie Dee (Gross) B.; m. Lenyth

Spenker, Sept. 4, 1951; 1 dau., Francesca Lane. BA, Peabody Coll., 1947; MA, Stanford U., 1949, PhD, 1953. Instr. English U. Ky., 1949-50; asst. instr. drama Stanford U., 1950-52; asst. prof. drama Stetson U., DeLand, Fla., 1952-56; from asst. to assoc. prof. U. Iowa, 1956-63; from prof. to distinguished prof. Ind. U., 1963-78; Ashbel Smith prof. drama U. Tex., Austin, 1978-80; dean U. Tex. Coll. Fine Arts, 1978-80; DeMille prof. drama U. So. Calif., LA, 1980-81; Waggener prof. fine arts U. Tex., Austin, 1981-87, Virginia L. Murchison Regents prof., 1987-88, holder Z.T. Scott Family Chair in drama, 1988-99, Univ. Disting. Tchg. prof., 1996—. Author 10 books; contbr. articles to profl. jours. With USNR, 1943-46. Recipient Fulbright award, 1963-64, Medallion of Honor Theta Alpha Phi, 1977, Am. Coll. Theatre Festival Gold Medallion, 1978, Career Achievement award Assn. for Theatre in Higher Edn., 1991, Spl. Citation award U.S. Inst. TheatreTech., 2001; Guggenheim fellow, 1970-71. Mem. Am. Theatre Assn. (past pres., Merit award 1979), Coll. Am. Theatre Fellows (dean. 2002-04), Am. Soc. Theatre Rsch., Internat. Fedn. Theatre Rsch., Nat. Theatre Conf., Nat. Comm. Assn., Shakespeare Assn. Am., Lit. Mgrs. and Dramaturgs of the Americas. Democrat. Episcopalian. Home: 901 W 9th St #903 Austin TX 78703 Office: U Tex Theater and Dance Dept Austin TX 78712 Business E-Mail: obrockett@mail.utexas.edu.

BROCKETT, RAMONA, criminologist, educator; b. Bklyn., Sept. 25, 1962; d. William Edwin and Virginia Mae Brockett. BA, Coll. St. Elizabeth, Convent Station, NJ, 1985; JD, Boston Coll., Newton Centre, Mass., 1989; PhD, Rutgers U., Newark, 1998. Lectr. justice studies Kent State U., Ohio, 1997—98, asst. prof. justice studies, 1998—2000; asst. prof. criminal justice No. Ky. U., Highland Heights, 2001—04, U. Md. Ea. Shore, Princess Anne, 2004—06, assoc. prof. criminal justice, 2006—, chair dept. criminal justice, 2006—. Talk show host (Legal Talk with Dr. Ramona Brockett) Nat. Pub. Radio, WEMS, 2006—; contbr. chapters to books, articles to profl. jours. Broadcast cons. Nat. Pub. Radio/ WHYY, Phila., 1995—96; contbr. Black Issues in Higher Edn., Washington, 2002—05; cons., presenter African Criminology Conf. Columbia U., Manhattan, NY, 2003; contbr., broadcast cons., commentator CBS, News-Makers, Cin., 2003; inspirational/motivational spkr. Ea. Correctional Facility, Princess Anne, 2004—06; trustee bd. mem., exec. bd. mem. Media Bridges, Cin., 2001—04, exec. bd. mem., 2001—04. Named Woman of Yr., Black Cultural League, Rowan U., 1996, Alpha Rho Chpt., Zeta Phi Beta, No. Ky. U., 2004; recipient Outstanding Contbns. in the Field of Drug Law Enforcement award, Drug Enforcement Adminstrn., 1993, 1994, 1995; grantee Law Forum for Pre Law Students, Law Svcs. Admission Coun., 2005. Mem.: Phi Alpha Delta (assoc.; pre law advisor U. Md. Ea. Shore 2004—, Advisor award U. Md. Ea. Shore chpt. 2005, 2006, mini-grant 2005), Acad. Criminal Justice Scientists (assoc.; nat. exec. counselor 2004—, Evelyn Gilbert Unsung Hero award 2006), Am. Soc. Criminology (assoc.; vice chair 2000—02, nat. exec. counselor 2003—05, Outstanding Svc. award 2004, Outstanding Contbns. in Field of Drug Law Enforcement, Divsn. People of Color on Crime 2003), Am. Soc. Criminologists (assoc.; chair membership divsn. people of color on crime 2004—). Conservative. Avocations: bicycling, beaches, travel, music, theater. Office: Univ Maryland Eastern Shore 1 Backbone Rd Princess Anne MD 21853 Home Phone: 410-251-5392; Office Phone: 410-651-8914. Office Fax: 410-651-8098. Business E-Mail: rbrockett@umes.edu.

BROCKHAUS, ROBERT HEROLD, SR., business educator, consultant; b. St. Louis, Apr. 18, 1940; s. Herold August and Leona M. (Stutzke) B.; m. Joyce Patricia Dees, June 13, 1970; children: Cheryl Lynn, Robert Herold BSME, U. Mo.-Rolla, 1962; MSIA, Purdue U., 1966; PhD, Washington U., St. Louis, 1976. Mgr. Ralston-Purina, St. Louis, 1962—69; pres. Progressive Mgmt. Enterprises, Ltd., St. Louis, 1969—; asst. prof. mgmt. sci. St. Louis U., 1972—78, assoc. prof., 1978—84, prof., 1984—2004, chair entrepreneurship Coleman Found., 1991—2004, dir. Small Bus. Inst., 1976—86, dir. Inst. Entrepreneurial Studies, 1987—90, exec. dir. Jefferson Smurfit Ctr. for Entrepreneurial Studies, 1990—2004; state adminstr. Mo. Small Bus. Devel. Ctr., St. Louis, 1982—86; state dir. Mo. Small Bus. Devel. Ctrs., St. Louis, 1987—89. Schoen prof. entrepreneurship Baylor U., 1981; McAninch prof. entrepreneurship Kans. State U., 1985—87; vis. scholar So. Cross U., Australia, 1995; del. White House Conf. on Small Bus., 1986, 95; alderman City of Sunset Hills, 1998—2006; bd. dirs. U. Croatia, 2004—. Co-author: Encyclopedia of Entrepreneur, 1982, Building a Better You, 1982, Nursing Concepts for Health Promotion, 1979, Art and Science of Entrepreneurship, 1985, Entrepreneurship in the 1990's, 1991, The State of the Art of Entrepreneurialship, 1992; editor: Jour. Consulting, 1988-90; co-editor: Frontiers of Entrepreneurship Research, 1990, Advances in Entrepreneurship, Firm Emergence and Growth, 1993, 2d edit., 1995, Entrepreneurship Education, 2001; assoc. editor: Family Bus. Rev., 1993-97; contbr. articles to profl. jours. Bd. dirs. City Venture, St. Louis, 1982—86; troop com. chmn. Boy Scouts Am., 1990—93, vice-chmn. Gravois Trl. coun., 2000—; chmn., pres. Ea. Mo. Small Bus. Week, 2002, bd. dirs., 2002—, African Family Bus. Assn. U.S., 2004—; nat. entrepreneurship rsch. advocate US SBA, 2003; active Nat. Coun. Youth and Religion, 1994—, treas., 2000—06; coun. mem. St. Lucas United Ch. Christ, v.p., 1991—92, pres., 1992—93. Named Extraordinary prof., Potchefstroom U., South Africa, 2000—03, Lindbergh Leader, 2001, Citizen of the Yr., Crestwood-Sunset Hills, 2004, Disting. Alumnus, Lindbergh HS, 2007; recipient Outstanding Svc. award, Boy Scouts Am., 1994, Disting. Svc. award, Gravois Trl. coun. Boy Scouts Am., 2002, Excellence award, NASDAQ, 2002; Fulbright fellow, U. Waikato, New Zealand, 1985. Fellow Internat. Coun. Small Bus. (life, sr. v.p. 1981-83, internat. pres. 1983-84, bd. dirs. 1983, v.p. 1986, exec. dir. 1987-2003), Nat. Small Bus. Inst. Dirs. Assn. (nat. v.p. 1980-82, 96-97, nat. pres. 1982-83, Disting. Mentor award 2000), US Assn. Small Bus. Entrepreneurship (nat. entrepreneurship adv. 2005); mem. Assn. Collegiate Entrepreneurs (internat. bd. dirs., exec. com. 1991-93, Outstanding Entrepreneurship Educator award 1992), Acad. Mgmt. (nat. program chmn. 1977-78, exec. com. 1993-95), Inventors Assn. St. Louis (bd. dirs. 1989-94, 1st v.p. 1991), Family Firm Inst. (internat. conf. chair, 1995, Internat. Svc. award, 2005), Fenton Jaycees (treas.), Exec. Club St. Louis (moderator 1973-86), Pi Kappa Alpha (dist. pres. 1969-74, faculty adv. 1990-2004, pres. house corp. 2006—, Disting. Svc. award 1972), Internat. Coun. Small Bus. (hon. life), Nat. Small Bus. Inst. Dirs. Assn., US Assn. Small Bus. and Entrepreneurship, Family Firm Inst., Futura Yacht Club Marina Assoc. (treas. 2006—), Pi Kappa Alpha, Beta Gamma Sigma, Alpha Phi Omega, Alpha Kappa Psi. Avocations: swimming, sailing, camping. Home: 10000 Hilltop Dr Saint Louis MO 63128-1512 Office Phone: 314-843-5713. Personal E-mail: bob@brockhausgroup.net.

BROCKMANN, WILLIAM FRANK, retired health facility administrator; b. South Bend, Ind., Nov. 14, 1942; s. Ervin William and Elizabeth Marie (Casaday) B.; m. Ellen Meier, June 10, 1967; children: William Edward, Rebecca Jayne. BS in Mgmt., Ind. U., 1966; MHA, St. Louis U., 1968. Administrv. asst. St. Anthony Hosp., Okla. City, 1968; asst. hosp. adminstr. Caylor-Nickel Med. Ctr., Bluffton, Ind., 1972-77, hosp. adminstr., 1977-86, pres., 1986-89, CEO, 1989—2000, mem. exec. com., 1985—2000; pres. River Ter. Estates Retirement Cmty., Bluffton, Ind., 2000—; CEO Bluffton Regional Med. Ctr., 2000—02; ret., 2002. Bd. dirs. Old First Nat. Bank. Gen. campaign mgr. Wells County United Way, 1973; past pres. Bluffton United Meth. Ch., Wells County Found.; pres., bd. dirs. Wells County Coun. on Aging; spkr. in field. Capt. M.S.C. US Army, 1969—71, vietnam vet. Life fellow Am. Coll. Healthcare Execs. (Regents award 2001); mem. Ind. Hosp. Assn. (chmn. bd. 1990-91, Disting. Svc. award 2001), Am. Hosp. Assn. (ho. dels. 1991-93), Ind. Chi Phi Alumni Assn. (pres. 2002-), Chi Phi (Alumnus of Yr. award). Republican. Methodist. Achievements include leading a successful merger of Wells Cmty. Hosp. and Caylor-Nickel Med. Ctr. into Bluffton Regional Med. Ctr. in 2000. Avocations: scuba diving, pool, reading, golf. Home: 1127 Ridgewood Ln Bluffton IN 46714-3827 Personal E-mail: billbrockmann@mchsi.com.

BROCKMEYER, MICHAEL F., lawyer; BA with high distinction, Univ. Ariz., 1974; JD, Univ. Md., 1977. Bar: Md. 1977. Asst. atty. gen., Md., 1978—84; chief, antitrust div. State of Md., 1984—90; ptnr., chmn. Antitrust practice group DLA Piper Rudnick Gray Cary, Balt. Adj. prof. Univ. Md. Sch. Law, 1999—; faculty mem. ALI-ABA, 1987—. Contbr. articles to profl. jours. Sch. bd. mem. Archbishop Curley High Sch. Mem.: ABA, Md. Bar Assn. Office: DLA Piper Rudnick Gray Cary 6225 Smith Ave Baltimore MD 21209-3600 Office Phone: 410-580-4115. Office Fax: 410-580-3115. Business E-Mail: michael.brockmeyer@dlapiper.com.

BROCKOVICH-ELLIS, ERIN, legal researcher; b. Lawrence, Kans., June 22, 1960; d. Frank and Betty Jo Pattee; m. Shawn Brown, 1982 (div. 1987); children: Matthew, Katie; m. Steven Brockovich, 1989 (div. 1990); 1 child, Elizabeth; m. Eric A. Ellis, Mar. 1999. Student, Kans. State U.; MA (hon.), Jones Internat. U.; LLD (hon.), Lewis A. Clark Law Sch., 2005; LHD, Loyola Marymount U., 2007. Management trainee K-Mart, Calif.; electrical engineer trainee Fluor Engineers and Constructors; sec. E.F. Hutton, Reno; former file clerk Masry & Vititoe, Westlake Village, Calif., dir. rsch., exec. cons.; pres. Brockovich Rsch. and Cons., 2006—. Lectr. in field. Co-author (with Marc Eliot): Take It From Me: Life's a Struggle, But You Can Win, 2001; actor: (films) Erin Brockovich, 2000; (TV series) Challenge America, 2001, Final Justice, 2003. Named Ms. Pacific Coast, 1981; recipient Scales of Justice award, Ct. TV, Spl. Citizen award, The Children's Health Environmental Coalition, Mothers & Shakers award, Redbook mag., Lifesaver award, Lymphoma Rsch. Found. Am., World Social Nominations award, 2004, 2005, Julius B. Richmond award, Harvard Sch. Pub. Health, 2005, Profiles in Courage award, Santa Clara Trial Lawyers Assn. Achievements include spearheaded largest toxic tort injury settlement in US history, 1996; settled second case for $335 million, 2006; subject of hit movie "Erin Brockovich", 2000. Office: c/o William Morris Agy 151 El Camino Dr Beverly Hills CA 90212 Office Phone: 818-991-8900. Personal E-mail: erin@bokovich.com.

BROCKS, ERIC, ophthalmologist, surgeon; b. NYC, Apr. 24, 1946; s. William Benjamin and Muriel (Welk) B.; m. Irene Loretta Kraut, Dec. 19, 1970; children: Jason Matthew, Daniel Charles. BA with high honors, U. Rochester, 1968, MD, 1972. Diplomate Am. Bd. Ophthalmology, Nat. Bd. Med. Examiners. Intern medicine NYU Sch. Medicine, NYC, 1973, resident, chief resident ophthalmology, 1973-76; chief resident ophthalmology Bellevue Hosp., NYU Hosp., Manhattan VA Hosp., NYC, 1975-76; attending physician St. Francis Hosp., Beacon, NY, 1976-89; asst./assoc. attending physician Vassar Bros. Med. Ctr., Poughkeepsie, NY, 1976-80, attending physician, 1980—; clin. asst. ophthalmology Tisch (NYU) Hosp., NYC, 1976—2005; clin. asst. attending physician Bellevue Hosp. Ctr., NYC, 1976—2005; eye physician and surgeon Hudson Valley Eye Surgeons, P.C., Fishkill, NY, 1976—, pres., 2000—; med. dir. laser vision correction LCA Vision Laser Assocs., Mt. Kisco, NY, 1996—98; bd. dirs. Fishkill Ambulatory Surgical Ctr., NY, 2001—; med. dir. The Eye Inst., Vassar Brothers Med. Ctr., Fishkill, NY, 2005—. Cons. ophthalmology Julia Butterfield Hosp., Cold Spring, NY, 1981—94, West Point Mil. Acad., Keller Army Hosp., West Point, NY, 1989—96; chief surgery St. Francis Hosp., Beacon, 1988—89, dir. ophthalmology sect., 1981—88, chief of staff, 1979—81; dir. dept. ophthalmology, mem. med exec. com. Vassar Bros. Med. Ctr., 1992—2000, mem. peer rev. com., 1994—; clin. asst. prof. ophthalmology NYU Sch. Medicine, NYC, 1983—2005, course dir. ophthalmology elective, 1976—91; so. NY coord. Nat. Eye Care Project, San Francisco, 1985—; adj. clin. asst. prof. ophthalmology Mt. Sinai Sch. Medicine, NYC, 1993—; mem. adv. bd. Fishkill Ambulatory Surgery Ctr., 2000—. Contbr. articles to profl. jours. Vol. admissions network U. Rochester, 1986-2000, co-chmn. 25th reunion com., 1993. Recipient 25 Yr. faculty svc. citation, NYU Sch. Medicine, 2001, Practice of Excellence, Laser Vision Ctr., 2001, 30 Yr. Svc. award, Vassar Bros. Med. Ctr., 2006, Physician honoree, 2006. Fellow ACS, Am. Acad. Ophthalmology (media coord. N.Y. state Nat. Eye Care projects 1978—, mem. pub. info. coun. 1985—, mem. refractive surgery interest group 1996—); mem. AMA, Am. Soc. Cataract and Refractive Surgery, Med. Soc. State N.Y. (mem. ho. dels. 1984-89, 93-96, mem. subcom. officers and adminstrv. matters 1994, mem. govt. affairs subcom. 1987, mem. fed. legis. com. 1993—), Dutchess County Med. Soc. (mem. exec. com. 1992-96, chmn. legis. liaison com. 1990-92, pres. 1990-91), Boca West Club. Avocations: tennis, golf, reading. Office: Hudson Valley Eye Surgeons Vassar Bros Med Plz 200 Westage Bus Ctr Dr Fishkill NY 12524 Office Phone: 845-896-9280. E-mail: eyes@hves.com.

BROD, FRANK H., computer company executive, accountant; B in Industrial Mgmt., Ill. Inst. Tech. Corp. v.p., controller The Dow Chemical Co.; corp. v.p. fin. and adminstrn., chief accounting officer Microsoft Corp., Redmond, Wash., 2006—. Mem. Emerging Issues Task Force, Fin. Accounting Standards Bd.; immediate past chair Tech. Com. on Corp. Reporting, Fin. Execs. Internat.; mem. Standards Adv. Group, Pub. Co. Accounting Oversight Bd. (PCAOB), Standards Adv. Coun., Internat. Accounting Standard Bd. Recipient Sells Award, Am. Inst. of CPAs, Allred Award, Tex. Soc. of CPAs for Profl. Excellence. Office: Microsoft Corp One Microsoft Way Redmond WA 98052-6399*

BROD, STANFORD, graphics designer, educator; b. Cin., Sept. 29, 1932; s. Morris and Rebecca (Mitman) B.; m. McCrystle Wood; children: Deborah, Daniel, Michael. BS in Design, U. Cin., 1955. Graphic designer Rhoades Studio, Cin., 1955-62; tchr. exptl. typography Art Acad. Cin., 1960-75; graphic designer Lipson, Alport & Glass Assocs., Inc. and predecessor firm Lipson Jacob, Assocs. Inc., Cin., 1962-94, Wood/Brod Design, Cin., 1994—; prof. graphic design U. Cin., 1962—. Tchr. illustration and packaging Art Acad. Cin., 1991-92, 94, 96-98, 2001-05, 07, tchr. corp. identity, 1992-97, 2002-05, 06, tchr. advt. design, corp. design, 1994-97, tchr. visual comms., 1997-98, exhbn. design, 1999, 2002, 2007. Exhibited in group shows at Mus. Modern Art, N.Y.C., 1966, Urban Walls, Cin., 1972, City Banners, Sao Paulo, Brazil, 1975, ITC Ctr., N.Y.C., 1981, Tel Aviv Mus., 1982, Internat. Art Exhbn., Dusseldorf, Germany, 1982, Calligraphia U.S.A./USSR, 1990-96, UN, 1994; one-man shows include Skirball Mus. Hebrew Union Coll., Cin., 1989. Recipient Communications Arts awards, 1959, 64, 66, 70, 73, 76, Creativity on Paper awards, 1960-67, Internat. Typographic awards, 1965, 70, N.Y. Type Dirs. Club award, 1968, Typographic Composition Assn. awards, 1970-76. Office: 3662 Grandin Rd Cincinnati OH 45226-1117 Personal E-mail: stan_brod@excite.com. *The more I design and paint the more I am sensitive to the movement of my pen, computer and brush, and am able to transmit the image of the subject in my head by way of my arm into my hand, and so to my work. I have become aware that pressure demands counter-pressure, and the difference between order and chaos. This points out the importance of the smallest detail, and that order is the basis of all creative work.*

BRODA-HYDORN, SUSAN, entomologist; b. Newton, NJ, Sept. 2, 1947; d. William E. and Margaret G. Hydorn. BS in Entomology with honors, U. Mass., Amherst, 1969; MS in Entomology with honors, U. Fla., Gainesville, 1971; PhD in Entomology, U. Calif., Berkeley, 1977. Tchg. asst. dept. entomology U. Calif., 1973, rsch. asst. biol. control, 1974—76; rsch. assoc. dept. entomology U. Maine, 1977—79; adj. prof. dept. entomology U. Fla., 1979; instr. entomology, preventive medicine divsn. U.S. Army Acad. Health Sci., San Antonio, 1979—82; nematologist, quarantine officer, plant protection and quarantine Animal Plant Health Inspection Svc., USDA, West Hampton Beach, NY, 1984—87, identifier, entomology, 1987—95, nat. thysanoptera specialist, 1995—. Mem.: Am. Arachnological Soc., Md. Entomol. Soc., Entomol. Soc. D.C., Fla. Entomol. Soc. (hist. com. 1993—95), Entomology Soc. Am. (student awards com. 1993—96, internat. affairs com. 1997—2000). Avocations: music, organ. Home: 8319 Snowden Oaks Pl Laurel MD 20708 Office: USDA APHIS PPQ 2200 Broening Hwy Ste 140 Baltimore MD 21224 Office Phone: 410-631-0073. Office Fax: 240-568-0433. Business E-Mail: susan.broda@aphis.usda.gov.

BRODBECK, WILLIAM JAN, marketing professional; b. Platteville, Wis., Feb. 14, 1944; s. Richard W. and Helen (Stoneman) B.; m. Janet Piwonka, Feb. 4, 1967; children: Allison S., Courtney K., Stephanie L. BA, Hillsdale Coll., Mich., 1966; PhD (hon.), Hillsdale Coll., 2004. Asst. to v.p. Hillsdale Coll., 1966-68; mgr. advt. Brodbeck Enterprises, Inc., Platteville, 1968-72, v.p., 1972-79, pres., CEO, 1980-96; pres. Relationship Mktg., Sanibel, Fla., 1996—. Gov. Uniform Product Code Coun., Dayton, Ohio, 1977—86; chmn. First Nat. Bank, Platteville, 1986—92; bd. dirs. Pegasus Holding Group, Inc., Irvine, Calif., 2004—, Noodles and Co., Boulder, Colo., 1997—. Contbr. articles to profl. jours Nat. adv. coun. Heritage Found., Washington, 2003—; pres. Platteville Area Indsl. Devel., 1976—79; bd. govs. The Sanctuary, 1999—2004, v.p., 2001—03, pres., 2003—04; chmn. 3d Congl. Dist. Reagan Campaign, 1976; bd. dirs. Thursday's Child, Madison, Wis., 1983—96, Wis. Shakespeare Festival, Platteville, 1986—96, CROW (Care and Rehab. of Wildlife), 1999—2002, Neenah Springs, Inc., Oxford, Wis., 1997—2006; trustee Hillsdale Coll., 1991—, chmn. presdl. search com., 1999—2000, vice chmn., 2000—03, chmn., 2003—. Mem. Nat. Grocers Assn. (bd. dirs. 1977-85), Food Mktg. Inst. (bd. dirs. 1982-96, mem. efficient consumer response exec. com. 1993-96), U. Wis. Platteville Found. (pres. 1980-81), Platteville C. of C. (pres. 1972-73), Omicron Delta Kappa (chpt. v.p. 1966). Office: Relationship Mktg The Cliffs at Keowee Vineyards 124 Wood Sage Ct Sunset SC 29685 Personal E-mail: wjbrod@aol.com.

BRODEN, THOMAS FRANCIS, III, French language educator; b. South Bend, Ind., Nov. 19, 1951; s. Thomas F. and Joanne Marjorie (Green) B.; m. Marcia C. Stephenson, Oct. 14, 1989. AB, U. Notre Dame, Ind., 1973; AM, Ind. U., 1976, PhD, 1986; postgrad., Coll. France, Paris, 1979-80. Asst. d'anglais Lycee Henri IV and Inst. Nat. Telecomm., Paris, 1979-80, Lycee St.-Louis and Inst. Nat. Agronomique, Paris, 1981-82; lectr. French U. Notre Dame, Ind., 1984-87; vis. asst. prof. Tulane U., New Orleans, 1987-88; asst. prof. French U. Nebr., Lincoln, 1988-91, Purdue U., West Lafayette, Ind., 1991-97, assoc. prof. French, 1997—, chmn. French sect., 1999—2001. Editor Newsletter for Paris-Greimassian Semiotics, 1990-92, 97, La Mode en 1830, 2000. Decorated chevalier Ordre Palmes Academiques; Notre Dame scholar, 1969-73; Rotary fellow, 1973-74, French Govt. fellow, 1981-82, Purdue Ctr. for Humanistic Studies fellow, 2006, Camargo Found. fellow, 2007; grantee NEH, 1990; named Coll. Tchr. of Yr., Ind., 2005. Mem. MLA, Am. Assn. Tchrs. French, (Tchr. of Yr. for Ind. 2005), Ind. Fgn. Lang. Tchrs. Assn. (Coll. Tchr. of Yr. 2005), Semiotic Soc. Am. (exec. bd. 1992-94), Toronto Semiotic Cir., Can. Semiotic Assn., Assn. Internat. de Semiotique Visuelle. Avocations: jogging, biking, gardening. Office: Purdue U Fgn Langs Stanley Coulter Hall West Lafayette IN 47907 Office Phone: 765-494-3828. Business E-Mail: broden@purdue.edu.

BRODER, DAVID SALZER, reporter, writer; b. Chicago Heights, Sept. 11, 1929; s. Albert I. and Nina M. (Salzer) B.; m. Ann Creighton Collar, June 8, 1951; children: George, Joshua, Matthew, Michael. BA, U. Chgo., 1947, MA, 1951; LittD (hon.), Denison U., 1975, Gov.'s State U., 1994; LLD (hon.), Wabash Coll., 1977, Kenyon Coll., 1980, Cleve. State U., 1981, Wittenberg Coll., 1982, Yale U., 1984, Ind. U., 1985, Kalamazoo Coll., 1988, Rider Coll., 1989, Dartmouth Coll., 1990, Colby Coll., 1990, Lawrence U., 1991, Bates Coll., 1992, Stetson U., 1993, U. Mich., 1994, Coll. of William & Mary, 1995, Am. U., 1997, North Central Coll., 2002; D in Polit. Sci. (hon.), DePauw U., 2003; D (hon.), Ctrl. Mich. U., 2003; LHD, Clark U., 2005. Reporter Pantagraph, Bloomington, Ill., 1953-55, Congressional Quar., Washington, 1955-60, Washington Star, 1960-65, Washington bur., NY Times, 1965-66, Washington Post, 1966-75, named assoc. editor, 1975, now nat. polit. correspondent; syndicated columnist The Washington Post Writers Group. Prof. Philip Merrill Coll. Journalism, U. Md., 2001—; regular appearances on Meet the Press & Washington Week in Rev., NBC. Author: The Party's Over: The Failure of Politics in America, 1972, Changing of the Guard: Power and Leadership in America, 1980, Behind the Front Page: A Candid Look at How the News is Made, 1987, Democracy Derailed: Initiative Campaigns and the Power of Money, 2000; co-author (with Stephen Hess) The Republican Establishment: The Present and Future of the GOP, 1967, (with Bob Woodward) The Man Who Would be President: Dan Quayle, 1992, (with Haynes Johnson) The System: The American Way of Politics at the Breaking Point, 1996; contbr. numerous articles on pub. affairs to magazines and books. Former mem. U. Chgo. Alumni cabinet. Served with AUS, 1951-53. Named one of 25 most influential Washington journalists, Nat. Jour., 1997; recipient Pulitzer Prize for Disting. Commentary, 1973, White Burkett Miller Presdl. Award, 1989, 4th Estate Award, Nat. Press Found., 1990, Disting. Contributions to Journalism Award, 1993, Elijah Parrish Lovejoy Award, Colby Coll., 1990, Award for Disting. Achievement in Journalism, William Allen White Found., 1997, Lifetime Achievement Award, Nat. Soc. Newspaper Columnists, 1997, Alumni medal, U. Chgo., 2005; fellow Inst. Politics, JKF Sch. Govt., Harvard U., 1969—70, Inst. Policy Sciences and Pub. Affairs, Duke U.; Poynter Fellow, Yale U. & Ind. U., 1973. Fellow Am. Acad. Arts and Scis., Sigma Delta Chi; mem. Am. Polit. Sci. Assn. (adv. bd. Congrl. Fellows Program 1964—, Carey McWilliams Award 1983), Am. Soc. Pub. Adminstrn., Nat. Press Club, Gridiron Club. Home: 4024 27th St N Arlington VA 22207-5207 Office: Washington Post 1150 15th St NW Washington DC 20071-0002 Office Phone: 202-334-7414. Business E-Mail: broderd@washpost.com.

BRODER, DOUGLAS FISHER, lawyer; b. Cleve., Sept. 30, 1948; s. Harry M. and Peggy (Fisher) B.; m. Rebecca Northey, Jan. 24, 1976; 1 child, Julia N. BA, Vassar Coll., 1970; JD cum laude, Boston U., 1977. Bar: NY 1978, US Dist. Ct. (so. and ea. dists.) NY 1978, US Ct. Appeals (2d cir.) 1983, US Ct. Appeals (6th cir.) 1986, US Ct. Appeals (4th cir.) 1987, US Dist. Ct. (ea. dist.) Mich. 1987, US Supreme Ct. 1993, US Ct. Appeals (9th cir.) 1997. Assoc. Lord, Day & Lord, NYC, 1977-86; ptnr. Coudert Bros. LLP, NYC, 1986—2002; ptnr., head antitrust practice Nixon Peabody LLP, NYC, 2002—05; ptnr. Kirkpatrick & Lockhart Preston Gates Ellis LLP, NYC, 2005—, CEO, head antitrust practice, 2006—. Spkr. and lectr. on continuing legal edn. Author: Antitrust Law Desk Book, 2001, A Guide to US Antitrust Law, 2005, Inside the Minds: Antitrust Laws, 2006; lead editor: International Joint Ventures, Professional Information Publishing Ltd., 1996; U.S. law reporter and mem. editl. bd. European Competition Law Rev.; contbr. chpts. to books and articles to profl. publs. Mem. pro bono panel US. Ct. Appeals (2nd cir.). Named NY Super Lawyer, 2007. Mem.: ABA, Internat. Bar Assn., Assn. Bar City NY. Home: 300 Central Park W New York NY 10024-1513 Office: Kirkpatrick & Lockhart Preston Gates Ellis LLP 599 Lexington Ave New York NY 10022 Home Phone: 212-362-3056; Office Phone: 212-536-4808. Business E-Mail: douglas.broder@klgates.com.

BRODERICK, ANTHONY JAMES, air transportation executive; b. NYC, Feb. 23, 1943; s. Anthony James and Geraldine (Cummings) B.; m. Sylvia Fantasia, May 30, 1967; children: Sean, Pia. BS in Physics, St. Bonaventure U., 1964. Project mgr. pvt. industry, various locations, 1964-71; physicist U.S. Dept. Transp., Cambridge, Mass., 1971-76; staff chief environment and energy FAA, Washington, 1976-79, tech. advisor, aviation standards dept., 1979-82, dep. assoc. adminstr. aviation standards dept., 1982-85, assoc. adminstr. aviation standards dept., 1985-88, assoc.

adminstr. regulation and cert., 1988-96; ind. aviation safety cons., 1996—. Author numerous sci. and tech. articles; patentee in field. Recipient Arthur S. Fleming award Jaycees, 1979, Presdl. Meritorious Exec. Rank award, 1982, Sr. Exec. Svc. awards U.S. Govt., 1983-87, 89-90, 92-95, Presdl. Disting. Exec. Rank award, 1991, Aviation Week Laurel award, 1992, 2000, Flight Internat. Aerospace Personality of Yr. award, 1995, Disting. Career Svc. award Aviation Week/Flight Safety Found., 1996, RTCA achievement award, 1999, ATW Joseph S. Murphy Industry Svc. award, 2000. Fellow: Royal Aero. Soc. Roman Catholic. Home: 4711 Dumfries Rd PO Box 119 Catlett VA 20119-0119 Office Phone: 202-331-2234. Business E-Mail: tonyb@compuserve.com.

BRODERICK, B. MICHAEL, JR., state legislator, banker; Banker, Canton, S.D.; mem. S.D. Ho. of Reps., Pierre, S.D. Mem. agr., nat. resources and transp. coms. S.D. Ho. of Reps.

BRODERICK, DENNIS JOHN, lawyer, retail executive; b. Pitts., Dec. 7, 1948; m. Marian Kinney. BA, U. Notre Dame, 1970; JD, Georgetown U., 1976. Bar: Ohio 1976. Assoc. Hahn, Loeser, Freidheim, Dean & Wellman, Cleve., 1976-81; staff atty. Firestone Tire & Rubber Co., Akron, Ohio, 1982—84, sr. atty., 1984—85, asst. gen. counsel, 1985—87; v.p., dep. gen. counsel for regions Macy's Inc. (formerly Federated Dept. Stores, Inc.), Cin., 1987-88; v.p., gen. counsel Macy's Inc., Cin., 1988-90, sr. v.p., gen. counsel, 1990—, sec., 1993—. Served USN, 1970—73. Mem.: Black Lawyers' Assn. of Cin., Cin. Bar Assn., Am. Corp. Counsel Assn. (dir N.E. Ohio Chpt. 1986). Avocations: motorcycling, motorboating, horseback riding, golf. Office: Macy's Inc 7 W 7th St Cincinnati OH 45202-2424*

BRODERICK, JAMES ALLEN, painter, art educator, etcher; b. Chgo., July 25, 1939; s. James Broderick and Catherine (Cahill); m. Alice Moehelenhof, Aug. 24, 1963 (div. June 1977); children: Brian, Mark; m. Cindy Gambell, Dec. 21, 1978; children: Victoria, Catherine, Maureen. BA, St. Ambrose Coll., Davenport, Iowa, 1962; MA, U. Iowa, 1966. Asst. prof. N.W. Mo. U., Maryville, 1966-76, dir. art gallery, 1967-76, chmn. art dept., 1970-76; prof. art Tex. Tech U., Lubbock, 1976-83, chair art dept., 1976-83; prof. art U. Tex., San Antonio, 1983—2003, dir. visual arts divsn., 1983—2002, chmn. dept. art and art history, prof. emeritus, 2003—. One-man shows include, Iowa, Colo., Tex., Mo., Peru. Mem.: Nat. Coun. Art Adminstrs. (bd. dirs. 1994—), Nat. Assn. Schs. Art and Design (accreditation reviewer 1977, v.p. 1996—99, pres. 1999—2002). Democrat. Home Phone: 830-229-5335. E-mail: jbroderick@utsa.edu, jbrod1@mac.com.

BRODERICK, JOHN CARUTHERS, retired librarian; b. Memphis, Sept. 6, 1926; s. John Patrick and Myrtle Vaughn (Newson) Broderick; m. Kathryn Price Lynch, Sept. 10, 1949; children: Kathryn Price, John Caruthers Jr. AB, Rhodes Coll., 1948; MA, U. N.C., 1949, PhD, 1953. Instr. English U. Tex., Austin, 1952—57; asst. prof. Wake Forest U., Winston-Salem, NC, 1957—58, assoc. prof., 1958—63, prof., 1963—65; with Libr. of Congress, Washington, 1964—88, specialist, 1964—65, asst. chief, 1965—74, chief manuscript divsn., 1975—79, asst. libr. rsch. svcs., 1979—88; ret., 1988. Adj. prof. English George Washington U., 1964—84; vis. prof. U. Va., 1959, U. N.C., 1968, Cath. U. Am., 1990—91. Author: Past Imperfect, Present Tense, 2000; compiler Whitman the Poet, 1961; editor: The Journal of Henry David Thoreau, 1981—90; contbr. articles to profl. jours., Ency. of the Libr. of Congress. Mem. adv. com. U.S. Senate Hist. Office, 1974—78; mem. Nat. Hist. Publs. and Records Commn., 1978—82, Columbus Quincentennial Jubilee Commn., 1986—88. With US Army, 1945—46. Fellow, Coun. Libr. Resources, 1971; grantee, Danforth Found., 1960, Am. Coun. Learned Socs., 1962—63. Mem.: Lit. Soc. Washington, Am. Antiquarian Soc., Acad. Am. Poets, Cosmos Club, Omicron Delta Kappa, Sigma Alpha Epsilon. Home: 415 Russell Ave #511 Gaithersburg MD 20877

BRODERICK, JOHN T., JR., state supreme court chief justice; BA magna cum laude, Coll. Holy Cross, 1969; JD, U. Va., 1972. Atty. Devine, Millimet, Stahl & Branch, Manchester, NH, 1972-89; shareholder Broderick & Dean (formerly Merrill & Broderick), Manchester, 1989-95; assoc. justice NH Supreme Ct., Concord, 1995—2003, chief justice, 2004—. Chmn. ct. accreditation com. NH Supreme Ct., 2004—; mem. Legal Svcs. Corp., 1993—2003; adj. prof. Tuck Sch. Bus., Dartmouth Coll., 2000—. Fellow Am. Coll. Trial Lawyers, Am. Bar Found., NH Bar Found. (bd. dirs. 1985-91); mem. ABA (standing com. on jud. independence 2004-), Mass. Bar Assn., NH Bar Assn. (bd. govs. 1985-91, pres. 1990-91), NH Trial Lawyers Assn. (bd. govs. 1977-82, pres. 1982-83), Nat. Conf. Chief Justices (bd. dirs. 2006-). Office: NH Supreme Ct 1 Charles Doe Dr Concord NH 03301

BRODERICK, MATTHEW, actor; b. NYC, Mar. 21, 1962; s. James and Patricia (Biow) B.; m. Sarah Jessica Parker, May 19, 1997, 1 child: James Wilke Broderick. Student high sch., NYC. Actor: (stage prodns.) Valentine's Day, 1980, Torch Song Trilogy, 1982 (Villager award 1982, Outer Critics Circle award 1982), Brighton Beach Memoirs, 1983 (Los Angeles Critics award 1983, Drama League award 1983, Theatre World award 1983, Antoinette Perry award 1983), Biloxi Blues, 1985, The Widow Claire, 1986-87, How to Succeed in Business Without Really Trying, 1995 (Tony award Lead Actor in a Musical, Outer Critics Cir. award, Drama Desk award), The Producers, 2001-02, 2003, The Odd Couple, 2005; (films) Max Dugan Returns, 1983, WarGames, 1983, Ladyhawke, 1985, 1918, 1985, Ferris Bueller's Day Off, 1986, On Valentine's Day, 1986, Project X, 1987, Courtship, 1987, Biloxi Blues, 1988, Torch Song Trilogy, 1988, Glory, 1989, Family Business, 1989, The Freshman, 1990, Out on a Limb, 1992, The Night We Never Met, 1993, The Lion King (voice), 1994, The Road to Wellville, 1994, Mrs. Parker and the Vicious Circle, 1994, Arabian Night (voice), 1995, The Cable Guy, 1996, Addicted to Love, 1997, Godzilla, 1998, Walking to the Waterline, 1998, Election, 1999, Inspector Gadget, 1999, You Can Count on Me, 2000, Good Boy! (voice), 2003, Marie and Bruce, 2004, The Stepford Wives, 2004, The Last Shot, 2004, The Producers, 2005 (Hollywood Supporting Actor of Yr., Hollywood Film Festival Bd. Adv., 2005), Deck the Halls, 2006; (TV movies) Master Harold.and the Boys, 1985, A Life in the Theater, 1993 (Emmy nomination for best supporting actor miniseries or spl., 1994), The Music man, 2003; prodr., dir., actor: (film) Infinity, 1996. Named to Hollywood Walk of Fame, 2006. Mem. Actors' Equity Assn., SAG. Address: care Creative Artists Agy 9830 Wilshire Blvd Beverly Hills CA 90212-1804*

BRODERSON, THELMA SYLVIA, retired marketing professional; b. St. Louis, Feb. 6, 1932; d. Harry and Lillian (Fishman) B. BA, U. Denver, 1953; postgrad., Washington U., St. Louis, 2001—. Marketer Marsh & McLennan, Inc., St. Louis, 1966—85; account exec. Daniel & Henry Co., St. Louis, 1985—87; marketer G. Steven DeMaster, Inc. at Crane Agy., St. Louis, 1987—99; ret., 1999. Prodr. Harry Fender Program Sta. KMOX-CBS, St. Louis, 1968-74; columnist The Oil Can, 1972-75. Tchr. religious sch. United Hebrew Temple, St. Louis, 1956—63. Donor Harry Fender Memorabilia to St. Louis Pub. Libr. Media Archives and Rare Books Collection, 1997. Mem.: Phi Beta Kappa. Avocations: theater, arts.

BRODEUR, MARTIN, professional hockey player; b. Montreal, Que., Can., May 6, 1972; s. Denis and Mireille Brodeur; m. Melanie Dubois, 1995 (div.); children: Anthony, William, Jeremy, Anabelle. Selected 1st round NHL entry draft NJ Devils, 1994, goalie, 1991—. Mem. Team Can., Olympic Games, Nagano, Japan, 1998, Salt Lake City, 2002, Torino, Italy, 06, Team Can., World Cup of Hockey, 1996, 2004; player NHL All-Star Game, 1996—2004, 2007. Co-author (with Damien Cox): Brodeur: Beyond the Crease, 2006. Named to All-Rookie Team, NHL, 1994, Second All-Star Team, 1997, 1998, 2006, First All-Star Team, 2003, 2004, 2007; recipient Calder Meml. Trophy, 1994, Vezina Trophy, 2003, 2004, 2007, William M. Jennings Trophy, 1998, 2003, 2004. Achievements include being the first goaltender in history to record 11 consecutive 30 win seasons; setting NHL record with 7 playoff shutouts, 2003; setting NHL record for most wins in a single season with 48, 2007; being a member of Stanley Cup Champion NJ Devils, 1995, 2000, 2003; being a member of gold medal Canadian Hockey team, Salt Lake City Olympic Games, 2002; being a member of World Cup Champion Team Canada, 2004. Office: c/o NJ Devils Nat Newark Bldg 744 Broad St, 33rd Fl Newark NJ 07102*

BRODEUR, MICHAEL STEPHEN, dean; b. Jacksonville, Fla., Oct. 15, 1949; s. Victor Edward Jr. and Amy (Ropke) B.; m. Deborah Crystal Cazalas, Aug. 9, 1975 (div. Oct. 1979); m. Cheri Anne Winton, Apr. 10, 1982; children: Trey, Aaron, Dana, Margaret. BA in Econs., U. South Fla., 1972, BA in Fin., 1972; MPA, U. North Fla., 1989. Cert. coll. bus. mgr. Acctg. mgr. Raymond James Fin., St. Petersburg, Fla., 1974-78; asst. OMB dir. Pinellas County, Fla., Clearwater, 1978-79; dir. OMB Alachua County, Gainesville, Fla., 1979-83; treas. City of Orlando, Fla., 1983-84; dir. OMB Orange County, Fla., Orlando, 1984-86; dir. of fin. State of Fla., Gainesville, 1986-91; mgmt. analyst v.p. adminstrv. affil. U. Fla., 1991-93; chief of staff U. Fla. Coll. of Pharmacy, Gainesville, 1994-98, asst. dean fin. and adminstrv. affairs, 1999—2006, sr. assoc. dean fin. and adminstrv. affairs, 2006—. Exec. v.p. COP Faculty Practice Assn., Inc., Gainesville. Recipient Davis Productivity award Davis Found. Fla. Taxwatch, Inc., 1993, 98, Disting. Svc. Alachua County Bd. Commrs., 1983. Democrat. Presbyterian. Avocations: watch collecting, golf, target shooting. Home: 4818 NW 37th Way Gainesville FL 32605-1034 Office: U Fla Coll of Pharmacy PO Box 100484 101 S Newell Dr Gainesville FL 32610-0484 E-mail: brodeur@ufl.edu.

BRODHEAD, DAVID CRAWMER, lawyer; b. Madison, Wis., Sept. 16, 1934; s. Richard Jacob and Irma (Crawmer) B.; m. Nancie Christensen, Aug. 17, 1963; children: Compton, Peter, Christoffer. BS, U. Wis., 1956, LLB, 1959. Bar: N.Y. 1960, Wis. 1959, D.C. 1979. Assoc. firm Paul, Weiss, Rifkind, Wharton & Garrison, NYC, 1959-68, ptnr., 1969—. Bd. dirs. Centennial Industries, Inc., NYC. Editor-in-chief: Wis. Law Rev, 1958-59. Trustee Collegiate Sch., N.Y.C., 1978-85; vestryman Christ and St. Stephen's Episcopal Ch., 1972-82. Mem. N.Y. State Bar, Assn. of Bar of City of N.Y., Wis. Bar. Assn., D.C. Bar Assn., ABA, Westside C. of C. of City of N.Y. (dir. 1970-83), Order of Coif, Delta Theta Phi Clubs: Washington (Conn.); Holland Soc. of N.Y. Office Phone: 212-373-3000. *Take life one day at a time. Yesterday is gone forever and tomorrow is not here. That leaves only today to deal with.*

BRODHEAD, JAMES E(ASTON), actor, writer; b. St. Louis, Jan. 30, 1932; s. James Easton II and Martha Pusey (Mithoefer) B.; m. Sue Hawes, June 21, 1963; children: William James Pusey, Daniel Alexander Hawes. BA in Speech, U. Mich., Ann Arbor, 1954. Announcer/news editor Sta. WNOP, Newport, Ky., 1954-55; actor stage and TV NYC, 1955-62; copywriter/reporter Time Mag., NYC and Calif., 1963-69; pub. rels. account exec. Laurie & Assocs. and Mahoney & Assocs., LA, 1971-74; actor Querencia Prodns., L.A. and Santa Barbara, 1974—. Bd. dirs. Western Adv. Bd., Actor's Equity, L.A., 1978-83, ANTA West, L.A., 1978-80, Western Coun. Actor's Fund Am., 1993-95, Santa Barbara Symphony, 1998-2005. Author: Inside Laugh-In, 1969; appeared in 17 films including Leadbelly, First Monday in October, Frances, Mame, Piranha, 3 Disney comedies; TV films include War & Remembrance, Helter Skelter, Gideon's Trumpet; TV series include The Judge, General Hospital, Here's Lucy, Kraft TV Theatre; more than 100 stage prodns. including Inherit the Wind, First Monday in October. Mem. Ensemble Theatre Co., Pacific Pioneer Broadcasters, Actors' Fund (life), Edwin Forrest Soc. (founding) Am. Atheists, Freedom from Religion Found., Santa Barbara Club, Sakonnet Point Club. Democrat. Avocations: reading, cooking, travel, languages. Home and Office: Querencia Prodns 506 Yankee Farm Rd Santa Barbara CA 93109-1060 Home (Summer): 6 Taylors Ln N Little Compton RI 02837-1144

BRODHEAD, RICHARD H., academic administrator; b. Dayton, OH, Apr. 17, 1947; m. Cynthia Degnan Brodhead; 1 child, Daniel. BA in English summa cum laude, Yale U., 1968, MPhil, 1970, PhD in English, 1972. Asst. prof. English Yale U., 1972—77, assoc. prof. English, 1977—85, prof. English, 1985—90, Bird White Housum Prof. English, 1990—95, chair dept. English, 1988—93, dean Yale Coll., 1993—2004, A. Bartlett Giamatti prof. English, 1995—2004; prof. English Duke U., 2004—, pres., 2004—. Vis. prof. Ecole Normale Superieure, Paris, 1989, 91; faculty mem. Yale-New Haven Tchrs.' Inst., 1982; summer faculty Bread Loaf Sch. English, 1975—76, 1978, 80, 1989—92. Bd. dirs. J. William Fulbright Fgn. Scholarship Bd., 2002—05; trustee Carnegie Corp., 2004—. Recipient Bicentennial medal, Middlebury Coll., 1998, DeVane Outstanding Scholarship and Tchg. medal, Yale U., 1979, Wilbur Lucius Cross medal, 2006. Fellow: Am. Acad. Arts and Scis. Office: Duke U Office of the Pres 207 Allen Bldg Box 90001 Durham NC 27708

BRODIE, ALICE VELMA, health and ethics advocate; b. Akron, Ohio, June 20, 1924; d. Charles Alvin and Lillian Snowden (Twentyman) Keller; m. Milton John Brodie, Dec. 8, 1980 (dec. 1983). Student, U.S. Nurse Cadet Corps, 1944-47; grad., Mt. Sinai Sch. Nursing, Cleve., 1947; BSN in Pub. Health Nursing, Western Res. U., 1952; postgrad., U. Wash., 1963-64, U. Calif., Berkeley, 1969-70, 81, 86, U. San Francisco, 1987-89, Calif. State U., Dominguez Hills, 1997—. RN, Ohio, Calif.; cert. pub. health nurse. Nursing supr. Mt. Sinai Hosp., Cleve., 1952-54; sch. nurse Renton (Wash.) Sch. Dist., 1958-60; pub. health nurse, vis. nurse, sch. nurse King County Health Dept., Seattle; with Ministry of Health, England, Ireland, Germany, France, Italy, Switzerland, Netherlands, Can., Mex., 1967; ship nurse numerous voyages to Australia, New Zealand, South Sea Island, Suva, 1968. Rschr. No. State Hosp., Wash., 1963-64. Vol. BSF Internat., 1968-74, 93-99, ARC, Seattle, 1958-67, Buck Ctr. for Rsch. in Aging, Marin County, Calif., 1989, 90, Family Radio Tours to China, Hong Kong, Taiwan, 1985, Siberia, Mongolia, 1990s, Argentina, Brazil; mem. Vision for Progress, Vallejo, Calif., 1996—, Calif. Lawyers for Arts, San Francisco, 1996—; amb. People-to People citizen amb. UN Internat. Red Cross Ministry of Health, U.K., Eng., Germany, Italy, Switzerland, Ireland, Holland, Netherlands, France; family radio tours to China, Siberia, Hong Kong, Taiwan, Argentina, Brazil, 1985-94. Mem. APHA, ANA (founding mem. Calif. chpt. 1996), AAUW, Calif. Nurses Assn. (former del. to ANA conv. Detroit), Nat. Coun. for Aging, Calif. Lawyers for Arts, Vallejo C. of C. Avocations: health policy analysis, world travel, education, health legislation.

BRODIE, ANGELA M., biomedical researcher, educator; b. Manchester, Lancashire, Eng., Sept. 28, 1934; d. Herbert Kent and Ann (Hargreaves) Hartley; m. Harry Joseph Brodie, Apr. 25, 1928; children: Mark, John. BS in Biochemistry with honors, Sheffield U., Eng., 1956, MS in Biochemistry, 1958; PhD in Chem. Pathology, Manchester U., Eng., 1961. Jr. scientific officer Nat. Blood Transfusion Svc., Manchester, 1956-57; rsch. asst. dept. hormone rsch. Christie Hosp. and Holt Radium Inst., Manchester, 1957-59; predoct. fellow Med. Rsch. Coun., Eng., 1959-61; postdoctorate tng. program in steroid biochemistry Clark U./Worcester Found. Exptl. Biology, Shrewsbury, Mass., 1961—62; staff scientist Worcester Found. for Expt. Biology, Shrewsbury, 1962—78, sr. scientist, 1978-79; res. assoc. prof. dept. pharmacology and exptl. therapeutics U. Md. Sch. Medicine, Balt., 1979-83, assoc. prof. dept. pharmacology and exptl. therapeutics, 1983-86, prof., 1986—; prof. divsn. reproductive endocrinology dept. physiology U. Md., 1985—. Invited presenter Am. Assn. Cancer Rsch., 1987; program leader prostate cancer divsn. oncology dept. medicine The Marlene and Steart Greenebaum Cancer Ctr. U. Md., 1988—; mem. ad-hoc biochem. endorcrinology study sect. NIH, 1982, 83, 85, spl. cons. social scis. and population dynamics, 1982, 84-88, 91, reproductive endocrinology, 1998—; mem. selection com. Roussel Prize, 1985-92; mem. nominating com. Women in Endocrinology, 1991-94, 97-99; chmn. liaison com. Am. Soc. Andrology, 1988-91; site visitor Cancer Rsch. Campaign Program Projects, Eng., 1993, 94, 95; reviewer Nat. Action Plan on Breast Cancer, 1995; mem. integration panel breast cancer program U.S. Army, 1998; chmn. numerous symposia; cons. in field. Editor, contbr. Jour. Enzyme Inhibition, 1990, proceedings 3rd Internat. Aromatase Conf., 1992, Breast Cancer Rsch. and Treatment, 1994; co-editor: Clin. and Biol. Rsch., 1986; rev. Endocrinology, Sci. Steroids, Biology of Reproduction, Cancer Rsch., Jour. Clin. Endocrinology and Metabolism, numerous others; mem. editl. bd. Steroids, 1964-66, 95—, Jour. Steroid Biochemistry, 1985—, Jour. Enzyme Inhibition, 1992—2006; abstractor Biol. Abstracts, 1968-70; assoc. editor Cancer Rsch., 2005—. Recipient Pharmacia Upjohn Internat. award for excellence in clin. rsch., 1998, Brinker Internat. award for breast cancer rsch. The Susan Co. Komen Breast Cancer Found., 2000, Kettering prize Gen. Motors, 2005, Regent's Gold medal U. Md., 2006, Sloan-Kettering C.C. Stock award, 2006, Dean's medal for rsch. U. Med. Sch., 2006, Landon award Am. Assn. Cancer Rsch., 2006; named Rsch. Lectr. of Yr., U. Md., Balt., 2006. Mem. AAAS (mem. program com. 1988-89, membership com. 1997—98, program com. 2007), Internat. Soc. Comparative Oncology, Soc. Study Reproduction (mem. pubs. com. 1985, membership com. 1987, nominations com. 1990, awards com. 1995-97), Endocrine Soc., Soc. Andrology, Soc. for Basic Urologic Rsch. (Coffey Lecture 2007). Achievements include 4 patents; research, development of formestane aromatase inhibitor, first selective aromatase inhibitor specifically designed for treatment of breast cancer; research in new treatments for prostate cancer, steroid biochemistry, endocrinology of breast and prostate cancer and other estrogen mediated diseases, reproductive endocrinology. Office: U Md Sch Medicine 655 W Baltimore St Baltimore MD 21201 Office Phone: 410-706-3137. Business E-Mail: abrodie@umaryland.edu.

BRODIE, HARLOW KEITH HAMMOND, psychiatrist, educator; b. Stamford, Conn., Aug. 24, 1939; s. Lawrence Sheldon and Elizabeth White (Hammond) B.; m. Brenda Ann Barrowclough, Jan. 26, 1967; children: Melissa Verduin, Cameron Keith, Tyler Hammond, Bryson Barrowclough. AB, Princeton U., 1961; MD, Columbia U., 1965; LLD hon., U. Richmond, 1987; LHD (hon.), High Point U., 1992. Diplomate Am. Bd. Psychiatry and Neurology. Intern Ochsner Found. Hosp., New Orleans, 1965-66; resident in psychiatry Columbia-Presbyn. Med. Center, NYC, 1966-68; clin. assoc. intramural research program NIMH, 1968-70; asst. prof. psychiatry, dir. gen. clin. research center Stanford U. Med. Sch., 1970-74; prof. psychiatry, chmn. dept. Duke U. Med. Sch., 1974-82, James B. Duke prof. psychiatry and behavioral scis., 1981—, prof. dept. psychology, prof. law, 1980—; psychiatrist-in-chief Duke U. Med. Center, 1974-82; chancellor Duke U., 1982-85, pres., 1985-93, pres. emeritus, 1993—. Mem. Pres. Biomed. Rsch. Panel, 1975; mem. Carnegie Coun. on Adolescent Devel., 1986-97; trustee Com. for Econ. Devel., 1986-93, subcom. on edn. and child devel., 1990; trustee Nat. Humanities Ctr., 1988-93; nat. rev. and adv. panel for improving campus race rels. Ford Found., 1990-94; bd. dirs. Mental Health and Behavioral Medicine, 1981-83, chmn., 1981-82; chmn. Com. on Substance Abuse and Mental Health Issues in AIDS Rsch., 1992-95; mem. Com. on Leadership Devel., Am. Coun. on Edn., 1990-93. Co-author: The Importance of Mental Health Services to General Health Care, 1979, Modern Clinical Psychiatry, 1982; co-editor: American Handbook of Psychiatry, vols. 6, 7 and 8, 1975, 81, 86, Controversy in Psychiatry, 1978, Psychiatry at the Crossroads, 1980, Critical Problems in Psychiatry, 1982, Signs and Symptoms in Psychiatry, 1983, Consultation-Liaison Psychiatry and Behavioral Medicine, 1986, AIDS and Behavior: An Integrated Approach, 1994, Keeping an Open Door: Passages in a University Presidency, 1996, The Research University Presidency in the Late Twentieth Century, 2005; assoc. editor Am. Jour. Psychiatry, 1973-81. Recipient A.E. Bennet Rsch. award, 1970, Soc. Biol. Psychiatry, Strecker award Inst., Pa. Hosp., 1980, Disting. Alumnus award Ochsner Found. Hosp., 1984, Disting. Med. Alumni award Columbia U., 1985, N.C. award for sci., 1990, William C. Menninger Meml. award ACP, 1994. Fellow: Royal Soc. Medicine; mem.: NAS, Soc. Biol. Psychiatry, Inst. Medicine, Internat. Soc. Sport Psychiatry, Royal Coll. Psychiatrists, Am. Psychiat. Assn. (sec. 1977—81, pres. 1982—83). Home: 63 Beverly Dr Durham NC 27707-2223 Office: Devonwood Co 3211 Shannon Rd Ste 603 Durham NC 27707

BRODIE, KEVIN STUART, social studies educator; b. San Diego, Nov. 22, 1967; s. Angus and Jerry Dean Brodie; m. Valerie Ann Hamilton, July 15, 2000. BA in Philosophy and Religion, U. Calif., Santa Cruz, 1992; MA in Philosophy, U. Conn., 1995; MA in Tchg., Quinnipiac U., 1997; grad., Dov Simens Film School, 2002. Cert. grade 7-12 social studies tchr. Conn. Social studies tchr. intern Hillhouse H.S., New Haven, 1996—97; social studies tchr. Lyman Meml. H.S., Lebanon, Conn., 1997—. Author: (screenplays) Ashes, 2003 (Writer's Digest Writing Competition, 2004), Ravine, 2005, Season of Mists, 2007. Mem. edn. com. Curbstone Press, Willimantic, 2000—02; mem. edn. adv. com. The Nation mag., NYC, 2003—04; mem. adv. bd. Willimantic (Conn.) Food Co-op, 1995—97; mem. Thread City Bread, Willimantic, 1996—98. Recipient Coca-Cola Outstanding Tchr. award, Coca-Cola Edn. Found., 2001, Pushcart prize, Small Press Publishers Assn., 2001—02, Prize, Windham Area Poetry Project, 1999—2000; Japan fellow, Fulbright Meml. Fund, 1999. Mem.: Lebanon Edn. Assn. (mem. profl. resource com. 2002—05), Bertrand Russell Soc., Coventry Hist. Soc., Conn. Authors and Publishers Assn. (assoc.), Still River Writers (life). Independent. Avocations: travel, camping, hiking, cooking. Office: Lyman Meml HS 917 Exeter Rd Lebanon CT 06249 Home Phone: 860-742-5971; Office Phone: 860-642-7576. Personal E-mail: ksbrodie@charter.net. Business E-Mail: kevin.brodie@lebanonct.org.

BRODIE, MENASHA JACOB (JAY), architect, city planner, government executive; b. Balt., Sept. 25, 1936; s. Meyer and Sarah (Rachliss) B.; m. Georgene Ann Gonzales, May 30, 1958; children: Kimberly Brodie-Hopkins, Ellen Maria Jarrett. B.Arch., U. Va., Charlottesville, 1958; M.Arch, Rice U., Houston, 1960. Registered architect, Md. Arch, prin. city planner, chief planner Balt. Urban Renewal and Housing Agy., Md., 1967-69; dep. commr. Dept. Housing and Comm. Devel., Balt., 1969-77, commr., 1977-84; exec. dir. Pa. Ave. Devel. Corp., Washington, 1984-93; sr. v.p. RTKL Assoc., Inc., Washington, 1993-95; pres. Balt. Devel. Corp., Md., 1996—. Mem. Urban Land Inst., 1980—; mem. Gov.'s Task Force on Housing, Annapolis, Md., 1981-83; real estate adv.; spkr. in field. Past trustee Balt. City Life Mus's.; past mem. Presidio Coun., San Francisco; past chair adv. bd. U. Va. Sch. Arch.; former trustee 1st Unitarian Ch. of Balt. Fellow AIA (bd. dir. Balt. chpt. 1977-78, Thomas Jefferson award 1994): mem. Am. Inst. Cert. Planners, Citizens Planning and Housing Assn. (bd. dir. 1976-77), Am. Planning Assn., Lambda Alpha, Nat. Trust for Historic Preservation. Unitarian Universalist. Avocations: ice dancing, writing, music. Home: 609 Craycombe Ave Baltimore MD 21211-2239 Office: Balt Devel Corp 36 S Charles St Fl 16 Baltimore MD 21201-3020 Home Phone: 410-243-7612; Office Phone: 410-243-7612. Business E-Mail: jbrodie@baltimoredevelopment.com.

BRODIE-BALDWIN, HELEN SYLVIA, retired college and human services administrator; d. Adolphus T. and Myrtilla Brodie; m. Wilmer Baldwin, Sept. 6, 1966; 1 child, Trevor Adolphus Avery Baldwin. BA, Hunter Coll., 1956; MA, Columbia U., 1963. Asst. prof. Queensborough C.C., Bayside, NY, 1965—82, dir. counseling-student pers.; asst. prof. CUNY, 1965—82; exec. dir. Minisink Town Ho. and Camp, NYC,

1979—91; asst. to the pres. York Coll. CUNY, Jamaica, NY, 1993—94; exec. dir. The Harlem Cmty. Inc., NYC, 1995—97; pres., ceo Catalyst Consulting Group Internat., NYC, 1999—. Cons. Nat. Conf. of Black Mayors, Atlanta, 2001—; bd. dirs. Louis Aug. Jonas Found., Rhinebeck, NY; cons. Murphy Fine Arts Ctr. Morgan State U., Balt., 2002—; adv. coun. N.Y. Women's Found., NYC, 1988—94. Prodr.: (films) Lucky Devil, 2002; editor (founder): UPTOWN: The Voice of Ctrl. Harlem, 1979—84; prodr.: (plays) Show of Shows. Bd. dirs. Cmty. Bd. 10, NYC, 1989—97; chmn. NYCMS Cadet Corps, Bronx, NY, 1970—79; com. chmn. N.Y.C. Mission Soc., The Cathedral Sch. of St. John the Divine, NYC, YWCA-West Side, NYC, 1970—74; nat. v.p. Am. Camping Assoc., 1988—90, 1992—94. Grantee, Hart Found., 1970, Am. Forum For African Studies, 1970; scholar, NYC Mission Soc., 1952—56. Mem.: NAFE, Nat. Assn. Fgn. Student Advisors (com. chmn. 1970—77), Internat. Women's Club, Delta Sigma Theta (life; v.p.rho chpt. 1954—56). Democrat. Avocations: writing, travel. Home and Office: Catalyst Consulting Group International POBox 250786 Columbia Univ Station New York NY 10025-1509 E-mail: hsbbest@msn.com.

BRODINE, CHARLES EDWARD, physician; b. Sioux City, Iowa, May 10, 1925; s. Ivar and Dorothy B.; m. Lois Bliss, June 26, 1949; children: Stephanie Kay, Jennifer Leah, Charles Edward. BS, Iowa State U., Ames, 1948, research fellow malaria project, 1948-49; MD, Washington U., St. Louis, 1953. Intern St. Louis County Hosp., 1953-54, resident in internal medicine, 1954-55, U.S. Naval Hosp., Oakland, Calif., 1957-59; fellow in hematology, clin. instr. medicine U. Cin. and Cin. Gen. Hosp., 1955-57; head hematology svc. U.S. Naval Hosp., Oakland, 1959-61, Bethesda, Md., 1961-62, cons. in hematology, 1962-73; head divsn. rsch. hematology Naval Med. Rsch. Inst., Bethesda, 1962-66, chmn. dept. clin. investigation, 1966-70, exec. officer, 1970-73; program mgr. Navy frozen blood and trauma rsch. program research div. Bur. Medicine and Surgery U.S. Dept. Navy, Washington, 1962-71, dir. rsch. divsn., 1973-74; spl. asst. med. rsch. and devel. to Surgeon Gen. U.S. Navy, 1974-77; comdg. officer Naval Med. Rsch. and Devel. Command, Nat. Naval Med. Center, Bethesda, 1974-77; asst. med. dir. environ. health and preventive medicine Office Med. Svcs. Dept. State, Washington, 1977-90; mem. Agt. Orange Working Group, 1982-90; exec. com. Nat. Council Internat. Health, 1982-90. Bd. dirs. Gorgas Meml. Inst. Tropical and Preventive Medicine, 1973-89; mem. Bur. Medicine and Surgery Policy Council, 1974-77; med. adviser ARC, 1975-79; adv. com. Nat. Sickle Cell Disease, NIH, 1974-77; mem. com. on biomed. rsch. U.S.-Egypt Joint Working Group, 1975-77; mem. White House Working Group on Internat. Health, 1977; clin. asso. prof. dept. medicine Georgetown U., Washington, 1971—; Dept. State mem. Nat. Council for Internat. Health, 1978-89. Contbr. articles to profl. jours. Mem. exec. com. Gorgas Meml. Inst., 1978-88. Decorated Legion of Merit for blood rsch. project, 1968; recipient Meritorious Service medal for work at Naval Med. Rsch. Inst. U.S. Dept. Navy, 1973; Robert Dexter Conrad award for outstanding sci. achievement Sec. of Navy, 1977 Mem. AMA, Assn. Mil. Surgeons (sustaining membership award 1967), Acad. Medicine of Washington (bd. dirs. 1992—), Soc. for Cryobiology (editorial bd. 1964-66), Soc. Fed. Med. Agys., Western Soc. Clin. Investigation, Soc. Med. Cons. Armed Forces. Home: 211 Russell Ave Apt 57 Gaithersburg MD 20877 Personal E-mail: chuckandlois@gmail.com.

BRODKEY, ROBERT STANLEY, chemical engineering educator; b. LA, Sept. 14, 1928; s. Harold R. and Clara (Goldman) B.; m. Martha Mahr, Dec. 22, 1958 (div. Nov. 1971); 1 son, Philip Arthur; m. Carolyn Patch, Dec. 6, 1975. AA in Chemistry, San Francisco City Coll., 1948; BS with highest honors, U. Calif.-Berkeley, 1950, MS in Chem. Engring, 1950; PhD in Chem. Engring. (Gulf Oil fellow), U. Wis., 1952. Rsch. chem. engr. Esso Rsch. & Engring. Co., Linden, NJ, 1952-56, Esso Std. Oil Co., Bayway, NJ, 1956-57; asst. prof. chem. engring. Ohio State U., Columbus, 1957-60, assoc. prof., 1960-64, prof., 1964-92, prof. emeritus, 1992—. Cons. on turbulent motion, mixing kinetics, rheology, 2-phase flow, fluid dynamics, image processing and analysis; expository lectr. GAMM Conf., 1975; vis. prof. Japan Soc. Promotion Sci., 1978; Clyde chair engring. U. Utah, fall 1994. Author: Transport Phemomena, A Unified Approach, 1988, reprint edit., 2004, The Phenomena of Fluid Motions, 1967, reprint edit., 1995, 2004; editor: Turbulence in Mixing Operations, 1975; contbr. articles to profl. jours. Recipient Outstanding Paper of Yr. award Can. Jour. Chem. Engring., 1970; NATO sr. fellow in sci. Max Planck Institut für Strömungsforschung, Göttingen, Fed. Republic Germany, 1972; Alexander Von Humboldt Found. sr. U.S. scientist award, 1975, 83; sr. rsch. award Coll. Engring. Ohio State U., 1983, 86; Disting. Sr. Rsch. award Am. Soc. Engring. Edn., 1985; Chem. Engr. lectureship award Am. Soc. Engring. Edn., 1986; North Am. Mixing Forum award, 1994. Fellow AAAS, AIChE, Am. Phys. Soc., Am. Inst. Chemists, Am. Acad. Mechanics; mem. Am. Chem. Soc., Am. Soc. Engring. Sci., Soc. Rheology, Sigma Xi, Phi Lambda Upsilon, Alpha Gamma Sigma, Phi Beta Delta. Achievements include patents in field. Office: Ohio St Univ 140 W 19th Ave Columbus OH 43210-1110 Home Phone: 614-262-3967; Office Phone: 614-292-2609. Business E-Mail: brodkey.1@osu.edu.

BRODKIN, ADELE RUTH MEYER, psychologist; b. NYC, July 8, 1934; d. Abraham J. and Helen (Honig) Meyer; m. Roger Harrison Brodkin, Jan. 26, 1957; children: Elizabeth Anne Brodkin Brauer, Edward Stuart. BA, Sarah Lawrence Coll., 1956; MA, Columbia U., 1959; PhD, Rutgers U., 1977. Lic. psychologist N.J. Sch. psychologist pub. schs., 1961—73; assoc. dir. Infant Child Devel. Ctr. St. Barnabas Med. Ctr., Livingston, NJ, 1977-79; clin. asst. prof. dept. psychiatry U. Medicine and Dentistry N.J., Newark, 1979-90, clin. assoc. prof., 1990-2001. Vis. scholar Hasting Ctr. for Life Scis., NY, 1979; sr. child devel. cons.; cons. Scholastic, Inc., 1988—. Author: Between Teacher and Parent, Supporting Young Children As They Grow, 1994, The Lonely Only Dog, 1998, Fresh Approaches to Working with Problematic Behavior, 2001, Raising Happy and Successful Kids, 2006; co-author (with A.T. Jersild and E.A. Lazar): The Meaning of Psychotherapy in the Teacher's Life and Work, 1962; author, prodr.: (documentaries) Competing Commitments, 1984 (Best Ednl. Videotape award N.J. Cable); co-author, prodr.: (ednl. videos) Passage to Physicianhood, 1985; The Insidious Epidemic, 1986; columnist Between Tchr. and Parent, Pre-K Today mag., 1988—93, Early Childhood Today, 1993—, Scholastic Parent and Child mag., 1990—, You and Today's Child, Instr. mag., 1992—93, Kids in Crisis, 1993—96, Ask Dr. Brodkin, Scholastic.com, 1997—, E-Scholastic, 1995—, Instr. mag., 1990—; contbr. articles to profl. jours. Fellow, NIMH, 1962; Adelaide M. Ayer fellow, Columbia U., 1962—63, Louis Bevier fellow, Rutgers U., 1976—77. Mem.: APA, Am. Sociol. Assn., N.J. Psychol. Assn. Home and Office: 84 Pine St Chatham NJ 07928 Personal E-mail: brodkina@earthlink.net.

BRODKIN, ROGER HARRISON, dermatologist, educator; b. Newark, July 31, 1932. A.B. Lafayette Coll., Easton, Pa., 1954; M.D., Jefferson Med. Coll., 1958; M.M.S. in Dermatology, NYU, 1967. Diplomate Am. Bd. Dermatology, Am. Bd. Med. Examiners. Intern, Lenox Hill Hosp., N.Y.C., 1958-59; resident in dermatology NYU and Bellevue Hosp., N.Y.C., 1959-62; teaching asst. NYU, 1962-64, instr. dermatology, 1964-66; clin. asst. prof. U. N.J. Med. and Dental Sch., Newark, 1966-69, clin. assoc prof., 1969-79, clin. prof., 1979—; pres. Ctr. Dermatology, West Orange, N.J. Fellow ACP, N.Y. Acad. Medicine; mem. Am. Acad. Dermatology, Am. Soc. Dermatologic Surgery, N.Y. Acad. Sci., Internat. Soc. Tropical Dermatology, Royal Soc. Medicine, Soc. Investigative Dermatology, Sigma Psi. Office: Ctr Dermatology 101 Old Short Hills Rd West Orange NJ 07052-1000 Office Phone: 973-736-9535.

BRODLAND, DAVID G., dermatologist, surgeon; s. Gene Arthur and Mary Annette Brodland; m. Laura Harmon; children: Michelle, Daniel, Mary, Rachel. BA in Physiology, So. Ill. U., Carbondale, 1981; MD, So. Ill. U., Springfield, 1985. Diplomate Am. Bd. Dermatology. Assoc. prof. Mayo Clinic, Rochester, Minn., 1990—97; pvt. practice Pitts., 1997—; asst. prof. dept. dermatology U. Pitts., 2000—, asst. prof. dept. otolaryngology, 2001—. Co-author: Dermatology, 2003, 2d edit., 2007, Comprehensive Dermatologic Drug Therapy, 2007. Fellow: Am. Acad. Dermatology, Am. Coll. Mole Micrographic Surgery Cutaneous Oncology (pres. 2006—); mem.: Am. Soc. Dermatology (bd. dirs. 1999—2002). Office: 575 Cool Valley Rd Ste 360 Clairton PA 15025

BRODLEY, JOSEPH F., lawyer, consultant, dean; b. Washington, Sept. 22, 1926; s. Joseph and Barbara (Gross) B.; m. Angeli B. Brodley, June 4, 1960; children: Barbara Joanna, Carla Elizabeth. BA, UCLA, 1949; LLB, Yale U., 1952; LLM, Harvard U., 1953. Bar: Calif., NY. Assoc. Dewey, Ballantine, NYC, 1956-61; assoc. ptnr. Richards, Watson & Hemmerling, LA, 1961-68; prof. law Ind. U., Bloomington, 1968-79; prof. law and econ., Kenison disting. scholar of law, prof. econs. Boston U., 1986—, interim dean Law Sch., 1989-90. Cons. Ford Motor Co., Dearborn, Mich., 1984, UN Devel. Project People's Republic of China, Beijing, 1992—; vis. prof. U. So. Calif., 1973, U. Mich., Ann Arbor, 1982; vis. fellow Wolfson Coll., U. Oxford, Eng., 1985; pub. testifier Ho. Subcom. Monopolies, 1977, Senate Jud. Com., Washington, 1986, 87, 90, FTC Hearings Global Competition, 1995, FTC/DOJ Hearings Antitrust and Intellectual Property, 2002; life fellow Clare Hall, U. Cambridge, Eng., 1993—; vis. scholar FTC, 2001; bd. advisors Am. Antitrust Inst., 2002-. Contbr. articles to profl. scholarly jours. 1st lt. JAG USAF, 1953—56, Korea. Mem. Harvard Club (Boston), Yale Club, Phi Beta Kappa. Office: Boston U Sch of Law 765 Commonwealth Ave Boston MA 02215-1401 Business E-Mail: brodley@bu.edu.

BRODMAN, MICHAEL LEWIS, gynecologist, educator; b. NYC, June 11, 1953; MD, Mt. Sinai U., 1982. Cert. in ob-gyn. Resident in ob-gyn. Mt. Sinai Hosp., NYC, 1982-86, fellow in pelvic surgery, 1986-87, dir. gynecology, 1993—. Asst. prof. Mt. Sinai Hosp., N.Y.C., 1987-94, assoc. prof., 1994—, chmn., 2003-. Office: 5 E 98th St New York NY 10029-6501 Office Phone: 212-241-7952.

BRODSKY, ALLEN, retired biophysicist; b. Balt., Nov. 5, 1928; s. Nathan Michael and Gertrude Devera (Silberman) Brodsky; m. Paula Fishman, June 17, 1951 (div. 1983); children: Richard, Karen, Jay; m. Phyllis Levin, Mar. 16, 1984. BS in Engring., Johns Hopkins U., 1949, MA in Physics, 1960; ScD in Biostatistics, U. Pitts., 1966. Diplomate Am. Bd. Health Physics, Am. Bd. Indsl. Hygiene, Am. Bd. Radiology. Radiol. physics fellow Oak Ridge (Tenn.) Nat. Lab., 1950; head health physics unit U.S. Naval Rsch. Lab., Washington, 1950-52; physicist region 2 FCDA, Olney, Md., 1956-57; health physicist AEC, Washington, 1957-61; rsch. assoc. Grad. Sch. Pub. Health U. Pitts., 1961-71, assoc. prof., 1966-71; radiation physicist Mercy Hosp., Pitts., 1971-75; sr. health physicist U.S. Nuc. Regulatory Commn., Washington, 1975-86; sr. scientist Sci. Applications Internat. Corp., McLean, Va., 1997—2006; ret., 2006. Radiation sci. fellowship bd. Oak Ridge Associated Univs., 1967—70; adj. prof. Sch. Pharmacy Duqesne U., Pitts., 1971—75; cons. CD, NAS, Washington, 1975; pvt. cons., adj. prof. radiation sci. Georgetown U., Washington, 1986—. Author, editor-in-chief: Radiation Measurement and Protection vol. I, 1979, vol. II, 1982, vol. III, 1982, vol. IV, 1986; author: Review of Radiation Risks and Uranium Toxicity, 1996; editor: Public Protection from Nuclear, Chemical and Biological Terrorism, 2004; contbr. to regulatory guides, chapters to books, articles to profl. jours. Witness radiation effects U.S. Ho. of Reps., Washington, 1978; witness radiation studies U.S. Senate, Washington, 1978—81; expert witness U.S. Dept. Justice, Washington, 1983—84; pres. Western Pa. Profs. for Peace in Mid. East, Pitts., 1970—71. Lt. CE US Army, 1952—54. Named W. H. Langham lectr., U. Ky., 1979, Failla Meml. lectr., Radiol. And Med. Physics Soc., Health Physics Soc., NY, NYC, 1987; recipient Leadership and Sci. Contbns. cert., Conf. Bioassay, Environ., and Analytical Radiochemistry, 1986, Disting. Grad. award, U. Pitts. Grad. Sch. Pub. Health, 2004. Mem.: APHA, Am. Indsl. Hygiene Assn., Am. Assn. Physicists Medicine, Am. Nuc. Soc. (Radiation Sci. and Tech. award 1993), Health Physics Soc. (life; chmn. stds. com. 1959—61, pres. Western Pa. chpt. 1967—68, chmn. stds. com. 1967—70, bd. dirs. 1967—70, pres. chpt. 1982—83, sec.-treas. govt. sect. 1988—92, Disting. Svc. award Western Pa. chpt. 1966, Founder's award 1986, Fellow award 1992, interviewed on video for history file 2000, Robley D. Evans medal 2001). Avocations: tennis, piano, composing songs, singing, politics. Home: 121 Windjammer Rd Berlin MD 21811-1902 Office Phone: 410-641-6523. Personal E-mail: albrodsky@aol.com.

BRODSKY, BEVERLY ANNE, writer, consultant, editor; b. Phila., June 23, 1950; d. Lewis and Florence Elaine Singer; m. Bruce Brodsky, Aug. 17, 1980; 1 child, Lauren Fay. BA in Psychology cum laude, with gen. and departmental honors, Vassar Coll., Poughkeepsie, NY, 1977. Ordained to ministry L.A. Cmty. Ch. Religious Sci., 2003. Inventory, systems, & computer analyst ASO/NAVICP, Phila., 1978—98; bus. analyst NATEC, San Diego, 1998—2002; freelance book editor & writer El Cajon, 2003—; founder and propr. All One Light, 2004—; co-founder Wisdom, Wealth, Wellness, Vista, 2004—. Pres., v.p. Del. Valley Near-Death Studies, Ardmore, Pa., 1992—98. Dir. LA Cmty. Ch. Religious Sci., 2006—; cmty. group leader, conf. planner Inst. Noetic Scis., Petaluma, 2003—06. Scholar, Vassar Coll., 1975—76. Mem.: Internat. Assn. Near-Death Studies (leader, media cons. and spokesperson 1992—), Seattle Internat. Assn. Near-Death Studies (newsletter editor 2002—, bd. dirs. 2002—), Internat. Found. Survival Rsch. (donor 2004—, bd. dirs. 2004—), Phi Beta Kappa (assoc.; sec. 2001—01). Achievements include near-death experience was highlighted in Dr. Kenneth Ring's 1998 book Lessons from the Light as the concluding account; first person ever interviewed on the subject of near-death experiences on Israeli Public Radio in June 2003; near-death experience and insights were featured in McCall's magazine in 1993 and the BBC documentary, The Human Body: An Intimate Universe, in 1998; featured in Arvin Gibson's They Saw Beyond Death, 2006; featured in feature story Jerusalem Post, 2006. Home Phone: 619-660-5106. Personal E-mail: beverly.brodsky@gmail.com.

BRODSKY, DAVID MICHAEL, lawyer; b. Providence, Oct. 16, 1943; s. Irving and Naomi (Richman) B.; m. Stacey J. Moritz; children: Peter, Isabel, Nell. AB cum laude, Brown U., 1964; LLB, Harvard U., 1967. Bar: N.Y. 1968, U.S. Dist. Ct. (so. dist.) N.Y. 1969, U.S. Ct. Appeals (2d cir.) 1974, U.S. Dist. Ct. (ea. dist.) N.Y. 1977, U.S. Supreme Ct. 1977, U.S. Ct. Appeals (D.C. cir.) 1981, U.S. Ct. Appeals (3d cir.) 1984, U.S. Tax Ct. 1984, U.S. Dist. Ct. (no. dist.) Tex. 1986. Law clk. to U.S. Dist. judge U.S. Dist. Ct. (so. dist.) N.Y., 1967-69; asst. U.S. atty. So. Dist. N.Y., 1969-73; assoc. Guggenheimer & Untermyer, NYC, 1973-75, ptnr., 1976-80; ptnr., chmn. litig. dept. Schulte Roth & Zabel, NYC, 1980-99; mng. dir., gen. counsel-Ams., Credit Suisse First Boston, 1999—2002; ptnr., co-chair securities and profl. liability litigation group Latham & Watkins LLP, 2002—. Lectr. in field. Co-author: Federal Securities Litigation: A Deskbook for the Practitioner, 1997. Chmn. N.Y. Lawyers for Pub. Interest, Inc., 1991-94; bd. dirs. Equal Justice Works, N.Y. Lawyers for the Pub. Interest. Recipient Pathways to Justice award; named one of Leading Litigators in U.S., Chambers, USA. Fellow Am. Coll. Trial Lawyers (mem. access to justice com., criminal procedure com.); mem. ABA, Assn. of Bar of City of N.Y., Am. Law Inst., N.Y. County Lawyers Assn., Fed. Bar Coun., Harvard Club, Univ. Club, Scarsdale Golf Club. Jewish. Office: Latham & Watkins LLP 885 Third Ave New York NY 10022 Office Phone: 212-906-1628. Business E-Mail: david.brodsky@lw.com.

BRODSKY, DONALD W., lawyer; b. NYC, Mar. 5, 1948; BA, Duke U., 1970; JD, U. Tex., 1973. Bar: Tex. 1973, US Ct. Appeals 5th Cir., US Dist. Ct. So. Dist. Tex. Law clk. to Hon. Adrian A. Spears US Dist. Ct. We. Dist. Tex., 1973-74; shareholder Jenkens & Gilchrist, P.C., Houston, firm leader corp. & securities/energy/health practice groups. Mem. ABA, Am. Soc. Hosp. Attys., Fed. Bar Assn., State Bar Tex., Houston Bar Assn. Office: Jenkens & Gilchrist PC 5 Houston Ctr 1401 McKinney Ste 2600 Houston TX 77010 Office Phone: 713-951-3341. Office Fax: 713-951-3314. Business E-Mail: dbrodsky@jenkens.com.

BRODSKY, MARC HERBERT, physicist, research and publishing executive; b. Phila., Aug. 9, 1938; m. Vivian Harriet Simon, Nov. 24, 1966; children: Alexander, Emily. BA in Physics, U. Pa., 1960, MA in Physics, 1961, PhD in Physics, 1965. Rsch. staff mem. IBM T.J. Watson Rsch. Ctr., Yorktown Heights, NY, 1968-80, mgr. semicondr. physics and devices, 1980-87, program dir. Advanced Gallium Arsenide Tech. Lab., 1987-89, dir. tech. planning, 1989-91; mgr. consumer electronics, 1992-93; IEEE Tech. Adminstrn., Fellow U.S. Dept. Commerce, 1991-92; exec. dir., CEO Am. Inst. Physics, College Park, Md., 1993—2007. Mem. adv. coms. U. Pa. Engring. Schs., 1985—93, U.S. Dept. Energy, 1986-89; mem. liaison com. to Internat. Union of Pure and Applied Physics, 1994—; mem. exec. coun. Am. Assn. Pubs. Profl. and Scholarly Pub. Divsn., 1998—, chair, 2004-06. Editor: Amorphous Semiconductors, 1979, 2d edit., 1985; co-editor: Tetrahedrally Bonded Amorphous Semiconductors, 1974; contbr. numerous articles to profl. jours.; patentee in field. Trustee Mt. Kisco (N.Y.) Pub. Libr., 1986-91. Capt. U.S. Army, 1966-68. Fellow IEEE (mem. competitiveness com. 1993-94), Am. Phys. Soc. (exec. com. condensed matter div. 1981-84, edn. com. 1985-88, undergrad. prize com. 1987-88, advisor to coun. 1994—); mem. AAAS (physics nomination com. 1989-91), Am. Assn. Physics Tchrs., Am. Geophys. Union. Avocations: photography, biking, hiking, music, boating.*

BRODSKY, RICHARD EUGENE, lawyer; b. Providence, Nov. 15, 1946; s. Irving and Naomi (Richman) B.; m. Margaret Anne Stone, May 14, 1972; children: Jane, Benjamin. BA magna cum laude, Brown U., 1968; JD cum laude, Harvard U., 1971. Bar: DC 1971, US Supreme Ct. 1980, Fla. 1981, US Dist. Ct. (so. dist.) Fla. 1981, US Ct. Appeals (11th cir.) 1981, US Dist. Ct. (mid. dist.) Fla. 1988, US Dist. Ct. Dist. Colo., US Dist Ct. (ea. dist.) Mich. Legal asst. to commr. FCC, Washington, 1971-72; legis. asst U.S. Ho. of Reps., Washington, 1973; atty. div. enforcement SEC, Washington, 1973-81; ptnr. Paul, Landy, Beiley & Harper, P.A., Miami, Fla., 1981—; counsel Squire, Sanders & Dempsey L.L.P, Miami, Fla. Adj. prof. St. Thomas U. law sch., U. of Miami law sch. Author: (with others) Interstate Commerce Ommission, 1970, Accountants Malpractice, 1988; contbr. articles to profl. jours. Mem. exec. com. U. Miami Citizens Bd. Recipient Fla. Super Lawyer, 2006. Mem. ABA, Bankers Club, Phi Beta Kappa, DC Bar Assn. Democrat. Jewish. Avocations: reading, softball. Home: 6200 SW 92nd St Miami FL 33156-1831 Office: Squire Sanders & Dempsey LLP 200 S Biscayne Blvd Ste 4000 Miami FL 33131 Office Phone: 305-577-7028. Office Fax: 305-577-7001. Business E-Mail: rbrodsky@ssd.com.

BRODSKY, ROBERT FOX, aerospace engineer, educator, author; b. Phila., May 16, 1925; s. Samuel H. and Sylvia (Fox) Brodsky; m. Patricia Wess, Jan. 24, 1959; children: Bette W., Robert D., David V., Jeffrey M. BME, Cornell U., 1947; MAero. Engring., NYU, 1948, DSc in Engring, 1950; MS in Math., U. N.Mex., 1957. Registered profl. engr., Calif., Iowa. Instr. NYU, 1948-50; supr. theoretical aerodynamics Sandia Corp., Albuquerque, 1950-56; chief aerodynamics Convair/Pomona, 1956-59; with Aerojet-Gen. Corp., 1959-71; chief engr. Space-Gen., El Monte, Calif., 1963-67; corp. mgr. european ops. Aerojet-Gen., Paris, 1969-70; mgr. systems test Aerojet ElectroSystems Co., 1970-71; prof., head dept. aerospace engring. Iowa State U., Ames, 1971-80; on faculty improvement leave with space and communications group Hughes Aircraft Co., 1978-79; sr. systems engr. TRW Space and Tech. Group, Redondo Beach, Calif., 1980-83, dir. technol. planning, 1982-86, program mgr., 1986-88; chief engr. Microcosm, Inc., Torrance, Calif., 1988-98. Adj. prof. aerospace engring. U. So. Calif., 1982—96, Nat. Technol. U., 1994—96; vis. prof. The Technion, Haifa, Israel, 1989—90, Haifa, 1994; lectrs. on remote sensing from space, Turin, Italy, 88, Paris, London, Munich, 91, Washington, 1992—94, Washington, 1996, Albuquerque, 95, LA, Cocoa Beach, 1996—98, Cocoa Beach, 2000, Israel, 1999; cons. in field. Author: On the Cutting Edge, 2006; contbr. articles to profl. jours., chapters to books; expert Alien Engineering, History Channel, 2006. With USN, 1944—46. Recipient Ednl. Achievement award, AIAA/Am. Soc. Engring. Edn. Aerospace Divsn., 1978; NSF/NATO Sr. fellow in sci., 1973. Fellow: AIAA (mem. deceleration tech. com. 1963—65, mem. ednl. activities com. 1972—97, mem. spacecraft sys. tech. com. 1978—82, mem. space transp. tech. com. 1985—88, mem. editl. adv. bd. A&A 1977—81, chmn. LA sect. 1986—87, Sustained Svc. award 2000), Inst. Advancment Engring.; mem.: NSPE, Am. Soc. Aerospace Edn. (v.p. 1979—81, Educator of the Yr. 1979), Am. Soc. Engring. Edn. (Centennial citation 1993), Am. Astronautical Soc., Internat. Coun. Sys. Engring., Rotary, Sigma Xi. Achievements include invention of space lifeboat. Home: 110 The Village Unit 410 Redondo Beach CA 90277-2546 Office Phone: 310-937-1811. Personal E-mail: rfoxbro@aol.com.

BRODSKY, SAMUEL, lawyer; b. Kansas City, Mo., June 12, 1912; s. Abraham and Anne (Brodsky) B.; m. Margery J. Bach, Oct. 17, 1944; children: Joan E., Alice E. BA, U. Tulsa, 1933; LL.B., Harvard U., 1936. Bar: N.Y. 1937. Since practiced in, NYC; law clk. to Fed. Circuit Ct. Judge Julian W. Mack, 1936-37; asst. U.S. atty. So. Dist. N.Y., 1937-43, 46, charge civil div., 1942-43, 46; partner firm Aranow, Brodsky, Bohlinger, Einhorn & Alter, 1947-79, Botein, Hays & Sklar, 1979-89; counsel Robinson, Brog, Leinwand, Greene, Genovese & Gluck, NYC, 1989-97. Lectr. taxation NYU Law Sch., 1953, 56-64, Inst. on Fed. Taxation, NYU, Practicing Law Inst. Contbr. articles to profl. jours. Served to lt. USNR, 1943-46. Mem. ABA, N.Y. State Bar Assn. (past chmn. tax sect.), Harvard Law Sch. Assn. N.Y. Jewish (past pres., trustee synagogue). Home: 55 Grasslands Rd Apt B224 Valhalla NY 10595 Office: care Robinson Brog Leinwand Greene Genovese & Gluck 1345 Avenue Of The Americas New York NY 10105-0302 Office Phone: 212-586-4050.

BRODSKY, STANLEY JEROME, physics educator, consultant; b. St. Paul, Jan. 9, 1940; s. Sidney Charles and Esther (Levitt) Brodsky; children: Stephen Andrew, David Jonathan; m. Judith Ellen Preis, June 29, 1986. BS in Physics, U. Minn., 1961, PhD in Physics, 1964. Rsch. assoc. Columbia U., NYC, 1964-66, Stanford Linear Accelerator Ctr., Stanford U., Menlo Park, Calif., 1966-68, mem. permanent staff theoretical physics, 1968-75, assoc. prof., 1975-76, prof., 1976—, head theoretical physics grp., 1996—2002. Vis. AVCO assoc. prof. physics dept. Cornell U., 1970; vis. prof. natural scis. Inst. Advanced Study, Princeton, 1982; mem. sci. and ednl. adv. com. Lawrence Berkeley Lab., U. Calif., 1986-92; vis. prof. Max Planck Inst. Nuc. Physics, Heidelberg, Germany, 1987-88, Coll. William and Mary, 2003; lectr., disting. spkr. colloquium series U. Minn., 1989, Duke U., 1997; mem. prog. adv. com. Gesellschaft für Schwerionenforschung mbH, Darmstadt, Germany, 2004-, Brookhaven Nat. Lab., 2003-06; Disting. fellow Thomas Jefferson Lab., 2003; mem. sci. adv. bd. Hadron Physics Integrated Infrastructure Initiative of European Commn., 2006-. Co-author: Lectures on Lepton Nucleon Scattering and Quantum Chromodynamics, 1982, Quarks and Nuc. Forces, 1982, Nuclear Chromodynamics, 1989; mem. bd. referees, editl. bd. Phys. Rev., Jour. Am. Physics, 1987—; assoc. editor Particle Physics, Nuc. Physics, 1993—. Mem. com. on fundamental cons. NRC, NAS, 1972-75; mem. exec. bd. Weizmann Inst. of Sci. Forum, 1977—; chmn. rev. panel for theoretical physics NSF, 1980-81. US/Israel Binational Found. grantee Weizmann Inst., 1986-90;

recipient Sr. Disting. US Scientist award Alexander von Humboldt Found., 1987—. Fellow Am. Phys. Soc. (particles and fields divsn., J.J. Sakurai prize for Theoretical Particle Physics, 2007), Max Planck Inst. Nuc. Physics (external sci. mem.). Achievements include theoretical developments in elementary particles physics, especially exclusive processes in quantum chromodynamics, two photon processes and nuclear chromodynamics. Office: Stanford Linear Accelerator Ctr 2575 Sand Hill Rd Menlo Park CA 94025-7015 Business E-Mail: sjbth@slac.stanford.edu.

BRODSKY, WILLIAM J., investment company executive; b. NYC, 1944; AB, Syracuse U., 1965, JD, 1968. Bar: N.Y. 1969, Ill. 1985. Atty. Model, Roland & Co., 1968-74; with Am. Stock Exch., 1974-82, exec. v.p. ops., 1979-82; exec. v.p., COO Chgo. Merc. Exch., 1982-85, pres., CEO, 1985-97; chmn., CEO Chgo. Bd. Options Exch., 1997—. Mem. internat. adv. com. Fed. Res. Bank N.Y.; mem. adv. coun. J.L. Kellogg Grad. Sch. Mgmt.; bd. dirs. Peoples Energy Corp. Bd. trustees Northwestern Meml. Healthcare, chair investment com.; trustee Syracuse U. Recipient inclusion, Jr. Achievement Chgo. Bus. Hall of Fame, 2001, Lifetime Achievement award, Anti-Defamation League, 2003. Mem. N.Y. State Bar Assn., Swiss Futures and Options Assn. (bd. dirs.), Econ. Club Chgo., Comml. Club Chgo.; chair, Northwestern Memorial Hosp. Investment Com.; Coun. on Foreign Relations in New York City Achievements include: selection for inclusion into Derivatives Hall of Fame, 2000, Jr. Achievement Chgo. Bus. Hall of Fame, 2001. Office: Chgo Bd Options Exch LaSalle at Van Buren Chicago IL 60605-7413 Office Phone: 312-786-5600.

BRODT, BURTON PARDEE, retired chemical engineer, writer, researcher; b. Evanston, Ill., June 3, 1931; s. Harry Snowden and Marjorie Florence (Pardee) B.; m. Virginia Faye Futch, June 20, 1954 (div. Dec. 1999); children: Howard A., Stephen R., Cynthia A., Phillip D.; m. Gail Elizabeth Clark, June 1, 2001. BS in Chem. Engring., U. Fla., 1954, MS in Chem. Engring., 1958. Devel. engr. DuPont Elastomers, Louisville, 1958-62, sr. rsch. engr. Wilmington, Del., 1962-66, tech. supr. Deepwater, NJ, 1966-69; rsch. supr. polymers div. E.I. DuPont de Nemours and Co., LaPlace, La., 1969-83, sr. supr. rsch. Wilmington, 1983-89, sr. rsch., assoc. LaPorte, Tex., 1989-91, tech. fellow LaPlace, 1991-96; tchg. fellow, sr. scientist DuPont Dow Elastomers, LLC, LaPlace, 1996-98; pres. Brodt Engring., 2003—. Tech. cons., Wilmington, Del., 1999—2002; cons. in field. Author: Scientists and Engineers: Achieving Success in Industry, 2003, Kevlar Technology, 2002, Advances in Neoprene Technology, Four Little Old Men, 2005; also novels, short stories and travel books; contbr. articles to profl. jours. Chmn. Citizens for Goldwater, Wilmington, 1964; founder, pres. Del. Conservative Union, Wilmington, 1965-69; pres. Homeowners Assn., Chadds Ford, Pa., 1988; hs track coach, 2002—. Lt. USAF, 1954-56. Mem.: AIChE. Republican. Achievements include development of chemical processes now in commercial use, Brodt equation for phase transfer catalysis; patents in field. Home and Office: 6051 Canterbury Dr Easton MD 21601-8555 Home Phone: 410-822-0183; Office Phone: 410-770-4372. Personal E-mail: bbrodt@atlanticbb.net.

BRODY, AARON LEO, food and packaging consultant; b. Boston, Aug. 23, 1930; s. Nathan and Lillian (Gorman) Brody; m. Carolyn Goldstein, Apr. 11, 1953; children: Stephen, Glen, Robyn. BS, MIT, Cambridge, 1951, PhD, 1957; MBA, Northeastern U., Boston, 1970. Head food rsch. labs. Whirlpool Co., St. Joseph, Mich., 1957-61; packaging and product devel. mgr. Mars, Inc., Hackettstown, NJ, 1961-66; packaging coord. Arthur D. Little, Inc., Cambridge, Mass., 1967-73; new ventures mgr. Mead Packaging, Atlanta, 1973-81; mgr. mktg. devel. Container Corp. Am., Oaks, Pa., 1981-85; v.p. strategic studies Schotland Bus. Rsch. Inc., Princeton, NJ, 1985-91; mng. dir. Rubbright/Brody, Inc., Duluth, Ga., 1991-2001; pres., CEO Packaging/Brody, Inc., 2001—. Course dir. Mich. State U., East Lansing, 1959—61; instr. Emory U., 1979; adj. assoc. prof. dept. food sci. U. Del., Newark, 1983—86; vis. prof. St. Joseph's U., Phila., 1990; adj. prof. Spring Garden Coll., Phila., 1990, U. Ga., 1995—; sr. instr. Keller Grad Sch. Mgmt., 1996—. Mem. Nat. Def. Exec. Res., 1978—88; mem. food svc. adv. com. USN, 1958—62; mem. optimal program edn., sec. DeKalb County, Ga., 1975; active Kerry for Congress campaign, 1972, Levitas for Congress campaign, 1974; mem. pres.'s coun. Spring Garden Coll., Phila., 1984—89. With US Army, 1952—54. Named Packaging Man of the Yr., Nat. Inst. Packaging, Handling and Logistics Engrs., Carolyn and Aaron Brody Fund for Packaging Rsch. and Edn. in their honor, Mich. State U. Sch. Packaging, 2005, Aaron Brody disting. lectureship in food packaging named in honor, Mich. State U., 2007; named to Packaging Hall of Fame, 1995; recipient Willis H. Carrier award, ASHRAE, 1960, Braverman Meml. award, Israel Inst. Tech., 1976, Outstanding Alumnus award, Northeastern U., 1982; William Underwood fellow, 1955—56. Fellow: AAAS, Inst. Food Technologists (Indsl. Achievement award 1964, Riester-Davis Food Packaging Achievement award 1988, Inds. Scientist award 1994, Nicholas Appert award 2000), Packaging Inst. (v.p. 1973—79); mem.: Product Devel. and Mgmt. Assn., NY Acad. Scis., Inst. Packaging Profls. (hon. Mem. of the Yr. 1994—95, lifetime cert. profl), Planning Execs. Inst., League Internat. Food Edn., Soc. Packaging Profls., Mich. State U. Beaumont Tower Soc., Toastmasters, MIT Club (pres. 1977—79, mem. exec. com., v.p. ednl. coun.), Sigma Xi. Achievements include patents in field. Home: 4981 Trevino Cir Duluth GA 30096-6072 Office: PO Box 956187 Duluth GA 30095 Home Phone: 770-263-6535; Office Phone: 770-613-0991. Personal E-mail: aaronbrody@aol.com.

BRODY, ADRIEN, actor; b. NYC, Apr. 14, 1973; s. Elliot Brody and Sylvia Plachy. Student, Am. Acad. of Dramatic Arts, NYC, HS for the Performing Arts. Actor: (plays, off-Broadway) Family Pride in the '50s, 1986; (TV series) Annie McGuire, 1988; (TV films) Home at Last, 1988, Jailbreakers, 1994; (films) New York Stories, 1989, The Boy Who Cried Bitch, 1991, King of the Hill, 1993, Angels in the Outfield, 1994, Solo, 1996, Bullet, 1996, The Last Time I Committed Suicide, 1997, Nothing to Lose/Ten Benny, 1998, Six Ways to Sunday, 1997, The Undertaker's Wedding, 1997, Restaurant, 1998, The Thin Red Line, 1998, Oxygen, 1999, Summer of Sam, 1999, Liberty Heights, 1999, Bread and Roses, 2000, Harrison's Flowers, 2000, Love the Hard Way, 2001, The Affair of the Necklace, 2001, Dummy, 2002, The Pianist, 2002 (Acad. Award for best actor, 2003, French César, 2003), The Singing Detective, 2003, The Village, 2004, The Jacket, 2005, King Kong, 2005, Hollywoodland, 2006.

BRODY, ALAN JEFFREY, investment company executive; b. Newark, Apr. 19, 1952; s. Robert and Marcia (Ostroff) B.; m. Miriam Kahan, May 22, 1977 BA, Northwestern U., 1974; JD, Rutgers U., 1977. Bar: N.Y. 1978, N.J. 1978. Assoc. Baer Marks & Upham, NYC, 1977-80; v.p. counsel Commodity Exch. Inc., NYC, 1980-81, pres., chief exec. officer, 1981-89, chmn., 1987-88; v.p. Commodities Exch. Ctr. Inc., NYC, 1981-84, alternate dir., 1984-89; sr. v.p. futures div. Lehman Bros., NYC, 1990-96; mng. dir. Lehman Bros. Futures Asset Mgmt. Corp., NYC, 1991-96; sr. v.p. internat. divsn. Prudential Securities, Inc., NYC, 1997-2000; regional dir. Europe/Middle East/Asia Pacific Prudential-Bache Internat. Ltd., London, 2001—04. Mem. commodity policy adv. com. to U.S. trade rep.; past mem. coun. Found. Internat. Futures and Commodities Inst., Geneva. Mem. ABA, N.J. Bar Assn., Assn. of Bar of City of N.Y. (commodities regulation com.), New York County Lawyers Assn., Nat. Futures Assn. (bd. dirs., exec. com. 1986-89), Futures Industry Assn. (past mem. exec. com. law and compliance div.), Am. Copper Council (past bd. dirs.), Copper Club (past bd. dirs.), Swiss Commodities & Futures Assn. (bd. dirs.) Home: 1365 York Ave Apt 33D New York NY 10021-4039

BRODY, BARUCH ALTER, medical educator, academic administrator; b. Bklyn., Apr. 21, 1943; s. Lester and Gussie (Glass) B.; m. Dena Grosser, Aug. 15, 1965; children: Todd, Jeremy, Myles. BA, Bklyn. Coll., 1962; PhD, Princeton U., 1967. Asst. prof. MIT, Cambridge, 1967-75; assoc. prof. Rice U., Houston, 1975-77, prof., 1977—, Andrew Mellow prof. humanities; prof. Baylor Coll. Medicine, Houston, 1982—, dir. Ctr. for Med. Ethics & Health Policy, 1982—, Leon Jaworski prof. biomedical ethics; dir. ethics program Methodist Hosp., Houston. Cons. NASA, 1990-91, 94—. Author: Abortion and the Sanctity of Human Life, 1975, Identity and Essence, 1981, Life and Death Decision Making, 1988, Ethical Issues in Drug Testing Approval and Pricing, 1994, The Ethics of Biomedical Research, 1998, Taking Issue, 2003. Chmn. bd. dirs. Hebrew Acad., Houston, 1976-98; pres. Soc. Health and Human Values, 1995-96. Named Disting. Svc. Prof., Baylor Coll. Medicine, 2002; recipient Disting. Alumnus award Bklyn. Coll., 1991, Michael E. DeBakey rsch. award, 2002. Mem.: Inst. Medicine. Jewish. Office: Ctr Med Ethics & Health Policy Rm 310D 1 Baylor Plz Houston TX 77030 also: Rice U PO Box 1892 6100 South Main Houston TX 77251 E-mail: bbrody@bcm.tcm.edu.

BRODY, BERNARD B., internist, educator; b. NYC, June 24, 1922; s. Abraham and Sarah (Berman) B.; m. Ruth M. Miller, Jan. 15, 1954; children: Sarah, Rachel. BS, U. Wis., 1943; MD, U. Rochester, 1951. Diplomate Am. Bd. Internal Medicine, Nat. Bd. Med. Examiners. Rsch. chemist U. Chgo. and Monsanto, Dayton, Ohio, 1943-47; resident U. Rochester, NY, 1951-53, clin. prof. pathology and medicine NY, 1981-90, prof. emeritus NY, 1990—; resident Genesee Hosp., Rochester, 1955-56, dir. clin. labs., 1967-81, sr. v.p. med. affairs, 1975-87; pvt. practice internal medicine Rochester, 1956-67. Cons. Eastman Kodak Co., 1971-92, Robert Wood Johnson Found., 1975-80, EDMAC Assocs., Inc., 1976-83; trustee Freedom Forum, 1980-98, 2006—; mem. adv. bd. Freedom Forum Media Studies Ctr., N.Y.C., 1985-98, adv. trustee Freedom Forum, 1998—2006. Bd. dirs. Rochester Mus. and Sci. Ctr., 1994-2003, hon. bd. dirs., 2003—; bd. dirs. Genesee Valley Med. Care, Rochester, 1962-68, Crestwood Children's Ctr., 1985-97, hon. bd., 1998—; chmn. med. adv. bd. St. Ann's Home, 1964-67; corp. mem. United Way, Rochester, 1980-87; mem. Citizens Com. Human Rels., 1980-85; v.p., mem. exec. bd. Otetiana coun. Boy Scouts Am., 1981-91; bd. dirs. Via Health Rochester Gen. Hosp., 2001-05; chmn. stewardship cabinet Lifespan, 2003—. 1st lt. U.S. Army, 1953-55. Mem. AMA, ACP, Am. Soc. Internal Medicine, Acad. Clin. Lab. Physicians and Scientists, Am. Assn. Clin. Chemistry, Sigma Xi, Alpha Omega Alpha Home and Office: 12 Huntington Brk Rochester NY 14625-1811 Home Phone: 585-381-6786; Office Phone: 585-381-6786. E-mail: Bbrody@rochester.rr.com. *Stay open-minded and flexible in thinking. It helps to recognize and take advantage of opportunities for adjuncts to or career enhancements or changes. It also makes for an interesting and exciting journey through life.*

BRODY, CATHERINE TYLER, archivist, historian, writer; d. Albert Vincent and Catherine Veronica Tyler; m. Stanley Joseph Brody (dec.); 1 child, S. Laurence. BA, Rosary Coll., River Forest, Ill., 1949; MLS, Pratt Inst., Bklyn., 1966; MA, CUNY, 1976; cert. in archival adminstrn., Nat. Archives, Washington, 1987. Cert. archivist Soc. Am. Archivists. Libr., archivist NYC Tech. Coll., Bklyn., 1966—78, prof., dept. chair, 1978—87, prof., dir. archives, 1987—98; cons., rschr., 1998—; cons. Columbia County Town of Gallatin, NY, 2006—. Sec. CUNY Coun. Chief Librs., 1978—81, chair, 1983—85; mem. panel of judges So. Books Competition, 1979, Carey-Thomas Book Awards, 1990; pres. Acad. Librs. Bklyn., 1980—84; chair Hist. Records and Archives Adv. Coun., NYC, 1992—95; chair printing industry adv. com. NY State Archives and Records Adminstrn., NYC, 1994—98; cons. Am.-Irish Hist. Soc., NYC, 1995—98. Contbg. editor: Printing News, 1977—90; author: Reminiscences of Horace Hart, 1910-1991, 1991, John DePol and the Typophiles, 1998, Checklist: Stone House Press Books and Ephemera, 1978-1988, 1989 (Outstanding Book award Am. Inst. Graphic Arts, 1989), John DePol, A Catalog Raisonee, 2001; asst. editor: Hellmut Lehmann-Haupt, A Bibliography, 1975, Long Island Printing, 1791-1830, 1979; contbr. articles to profl. jours. Town historian Town of Gallatin, NY, 1993—98; mem. interactive video com. Assn. of Bar/NY State Supreme Ct., NYC, 1994—98; mem. com. on ct. facilities Office of Ct. Adminstrn., NYC, 1995; coord. NY State Tech-Prep Material Clearinghouse, 1993—98; bd. dirs. The Fund for Modern Cts., NYC, 1995—, sec. bd. dirs., 2000—04. Recipient Richter award for excellence in grad. scholarship, CUNY Hunter Coll., 1976, Fellowship award, NY Club of Printing Ho. Craftsmen, 1989, Cmty. Svc. award, NY State United Tchrs., 2001; tchg. fellow, St. Louis U., 1949—52. Mem.: ALA, The Soc. of Scribes, Soc. for History of Authorship, Reading and Pub., The Manuscript Soc., Printing Hist. Assn. (London), Pvt. Librs. Assn., Fine Print Book Assn., The Bibliog. Soc. (London), Am. Printing History Assn. (v.p. 1974—78, editor APHA Letter 1974—85, pres. 1978—83, Extraordinary award for disting. svc. 1996), The Alcuin Soc. (Can.), Soc. Am. Archivists, Mid-Atlantic Regional Archives Conf., Archivists Round Table of Met. NY, The Typophiles (sec.-treas. 1973—90, exec. com. mem., archivist 1990—), Acad. Cert. Archivists, Nat. Trust Hist. Preservation, Friends of Clermont, Columbia County Hist. Soc., NY Hist. Soc., Roe-Jan Hist. Soc., Friends of Elmendorf, Columbia Land Conservancy, NY Libr. Club, The Grolier Club, Book Club of Calif., Beta Phi Mu (pres. Theta chpt. 1972—76). Avocations: book collecting, local history. Home: 649 E 14th St Apt 11A New York NY 10009-3115 Personal E-mail: ctbrody@taconic.net.

BRODY, EUGENE BLOOR, psychiatrist, educator, editor; b. Columbia, Mo., June 17, 1921; s. Samuel and Sophie B.; m. Marian Holen, Sept. 23, 1944; children: Julie Anne, James Clarke, John Holen. AB, MA, U. Mo., 1941, DSc (hon.), 1991; MD, Harvard, 1944; grad., N.Y. Psychoanalytic Inst., 1957. Resident Yale Med. Sch., 1944-46, 48-49, from instr. to assoc. prof., 1949-57; prof. psychiatry U. Md. Sch. Medicine, Balt., 1957-76; chmn. dept., also dir. Inst. Psychiatry and Human Behavior, 1959-76, prof. psychiatry and human behavior, 1976-87, prof. emeritus, 1987—; sr. assoc. sch. of hygiene and pub. health Johns Hopkins U., 1986—. Vis. prof. U. Brazil, 1965-68, U. W.I., Kingston, Jamaica, 1972-75, U. Otago, New Zealand, 1981, James Cook U., No. Queensland, Australia, 1992; vis. prof. psychiatry Harvard Med. Sch., 1997-99; fellow Center for Advanced Studies in Behavioral Scis., Stanford, 1975-76, Inst. for Advanced Studies, Tel Aviv U., 1986; mem. adv. bd. Inst. Social Psychiatry, U. San Marcos, Peru, 1968-70; mem. nat. profl. adv. bd. psychiatry, psychology and neurology service VA, 1963-67; cons. WHO (Pan Am. Health Orgn. and Geneva, Switzerland), 1965-95; program dir. Interam. Mental Health Studies Program, 1967-69; mem. exec. bd. World Fedn. Mental Health, 1969-83, adminstrv. mem., 1972-74, mem.-at-large, 1979-81, pres., 1981-83, sec. gen., 1983-99, sr. cons., 1999—; mem. epidemiol. studies rev. com. NIMH, 1975-79, cons. clin. infant devel. program, 1979-81, hosp. rev. com., 1979-86, AIDS grant rev. com. 1987-92; mem. internat. adv. bd. Peruvian Nat. Inst. Mental Health, 1984-94, mem. editl. bd. jours., 1985-94; mem. adv. coun. Hogg Found., 1986-89; mem. sci. com. Internat. Social Sci. Coun., 1989, exec. com. 1989-91, 92-95; cons. UNESCO, 1986-93; sr. advisor Harvard Program Refugee Trauma, 1989-2004; cons. Balt. VA Med. Ctr., 1990-2004. Author: The Lost Ones, Social Forces and Mental Illness in Rio de Janeiro, 1973, Sex, Contraception and Motherhood in Jamaica, 1981, Psychoanalytic Knowledge, 1990, Biomedical Technology and Human Rights, 1993, The Search for Mental Health: A History and Memoir of WFMH, 1948-1997, 1998; editor: (with F.C. Redlich) Psychotherapy with Schizophrenics, 1952, (with R. Monroe and G. Klee) Psychiatric Epidemiology and Mental Health Planning, 1967, Minority Group Adolescents in the United States, 1968, Behavior in New Environments, 1970; cons. editor Jour. Nervous and Mental Disease, 1959-67, editor in chief, 1967—; adv. editor: Tice Med. Ency., 1967-80, Harper & Row Med. Ency., 1980-86; mem. editorial bd. Psychiatry Digest, 1967-71, Mental Hygiene, 1968-70, Social Psychiatry, 1970-81, Internat. Jour. Psychosomatic Obstetrics and Gynecology, 1984-92, Population and Environment, 1987-92; contbr. numerous articles to profl. jours. Chmn. adv. bd. Balt. chpt. Internat. Students Council, ARC, 1964-67; bd. dirs. Md. Partners of Alliance for Progress, 1965-66, Nat. Assn. Mental Health, 1964-66, mem. profl. adv. bd., 1967-71; mem. adv. bd. Inst. for Victims of Trauma, 1988-97; chiaf NP Svc. West Haven, Va., 1953-57. Served to capt. M.C. AUS, 1946-48. Fellow Am. Psychiat. Assn. (life; chmn. com. transcultural psychiatry 1966-68, rep. interam. council 1965-71, trustee 1968-71, chmn. task force family planning 1973-75, Human Rights award 1999), Am. Coll. Psychiatrists (charter), Am. Coll. Psychoanalysts (charter); mem. Assn. Behavioral Sci. and Med. Edn. (pres. 1981), Am. Psychoanalytic Assn. (life), Internat. psychoanalytic assns., Internat. Coll. Pediatrics (senate 1978-86), Internat. Assn. Psychosomatic Ob-Gyn (exec. bd. 1977-86), Peruvian Psychiat. Assn. (hon.), Peruvian Assn. Psychiatry, Neurology and Neurosurgery (hon.), Cosmos Club (Washington), 14 W. Hamilton St. Club (Balt.). Home: 70 Olmsted Green Ct Baltimore MD 21210-1508 Office: Jour Nervous/Mental Disease care Sheppard & Enoch-Pratt Hosp PO Box 6815 Baltimore MD 21285-6815 Personal E-mail: ebbrody@aol.com.

BRODY, EUGENE DAVID, investment company executive; b. Bklyn., Feb. 6, 1931; s. Leon K. and Ruth (Parkoff) B.; m. Jacqueline Galloway, Apr. 5, 1959; children: Jessica, Leslie. BS, U. Pa., 1952; MBA, NYU, 1963. Gen. ptnr. A.W. Jones Assocs., NYC, 1965-70; v.p., bd. dirs. Downe Communications, NYC, 1970-74; chief exec. officer Founders Mut. Depositor Corp., Denver, 1970-74; pres. Beekman Capital, Inc., NYC, 1974—78; sr. v.p., ptnr. Oppenheimer & Co. Inc., NYC, 1978—86; mng. dir. Oppenheimer Capital, 1986-96; pres. Picanet, Inc., NYC, 1997—. Pub. Print Collectors Newsletter, 1971—96; trustee Manhattan Inst. for Policy Rsch., NYC. Author: Odds-On Investing, 1978. Lt. USNR, 1952-55. Mem. N.Y. Futures and Options Soc. (founding dir., pres. 1978-79), University Club N.Y.C., Stamford Yacht Club, East Hampton Tennis Club. Home and Office: 2765 Deerfield Rd Sag Harbor NY 11963 E-mail: genebrody@optonline.net.

BRODY, GERALD DAVID, academic administrator; b. Haverhill, Mass., Apr. 10, 1945; s. Ned and S. Hazel Brody, Helen Brody (Stepmother); m. Abby Goldman, Feb. 12, 1990; children: Hallie Rose, Benjamin Forrest. BA, Brown U., 1968; MEd, U. NH, 1977. Dir. career planning and placement Kent (Ohio) State U., 1977—79; interim v.p. student affairs, assoc. v.p. student affairs, dir. career planning and placement San Jose (Calif.) State U., 1979—93; v.p. student affairs, dean of students Alfred (NY) U., 1993—2004; v.p. student life Southwestern U., Georgetown, Tex., 2004—. Faculty mem. grad. career devel. program John F. Kennedy U., Orinda, Calif., 1983—88; cons. in field. Mem.: Nat. Assn. Student Pers. Adminstrs. (assoc.), Omicron Delta Kappa (assoc.), Phi Kappa Phi (assoc.). Office: Southwestern University 1001 E University Avenue Georgetown TX 78626 Office Phone: 512-863-1582.

BRODY, HAROLD, neuroanatomist, gerontologist, educator; b. Cleve., May 15, 1923; s. Julius and Esther (Barowitz) Brody; m. Anne Pertz, Mar. 24, 1951; children: David Andrew, Evan Barrett. Student, LI U., 1941-43; BS, Western Res. U., 1947; PhD, U. Minn., 1953; MD, U. Buffalo, 1961. Instr. anatomy U. Minn., Mpls., 1949-50; asst. prof. U. ND, Grand Forks, 1950-54, U. Buffalo, 1954-59; assoc. prof. SUNY (merger with U. Buffalo 1961), 1959-63, prof., 1963-95; asst. dean SUNY, 1968-69; assoc. dean SUNY (merger with U. Buffalo 1961), 1969-70, Buswell rsch. fellow, 1970—, chmn. dept. anat. scis., 1971-92, disting. tchg. prof., 1995—. Vis. prof. neurophthalmology St. Mary's Hosp., Rochester, NY, 1965—75; mem. sci. bd. Buffalo Otol. Found., Buffalo, 1968—73; mem. biology coun. Canisius Coll., 1969; mem. com. rsch., demonstration White House Conf. on Aging, Washington, 1971; mem. nat. adv. coun. Nat. Inst. on Aging, NIH, 1975—79; acting dir. Ctr. Study Aging, SUNY, Buffalo, 1977—80; vis. prof. neurophthalmology U. Copenhagen, Copenhagen, 1987; disting. lectr. Anthes Wilson Abernathy, U. Toronto, Ont., Canada, 1987; vis. prof. neurophthalmology U. Copenhagen, Copenhagen, 1990—93; organizer, curator Mus. Neuroanatomy, 1994—; vis. prof. neurophthalmology U. Copenhagen, Copenhagen, 1995. Editor: Jour. Gerontology, 1975—80, Neurobiology Aging, 1981—; mem. editl. bd. Jour. Gerontology, 1973—75, Gerontology and Geriatrics Edn., 1980—; contbr. articles to profl. jours. Pres. Friends Health Scis. Med. Libr., SUNY, Buffalo, 1999; trustee Erie County Meals on Wheels Legal Svcs. for Elderly. With USMC, 1943—46. Co-recipient Lyn Millane Cmty. Svc. award, Amherst Sr. Citizens' Found., NY, 1998—99; recipient travel award, NSF, 1957, Robert W. Kleemeier Rsch. award in gerontology, Gerontol. Soc. Am., 1978; scholar Fulbright sr. rsch. scholar, Copenhagen, 1963. Mem.: AAAS, Buffalo Neuropsychiat. Soc. (pres. 1967—68), Gerontol. Soc. Am. (mem. exec. com. 1961—63, 1968—71, pres. 1974—75), Am. Aging Assn. (trustee 1970—77), Am. Geriat. Soc., Am. Assn Anatomy Chmn., Am. Assn. Anatomists, Roswell Park Med. Club (pres. 1978—79), Alpha Omega Alpha. Achievements include research in the effects of aging on the human central nervous system. Home: 50 Stahl Rd Apt 301 Getzville NY 14068-1554 Office: SUNY Buffalo Main St Campus Dept Pathology and Anat Scis Rm 204 Sherman Hall Buffalo NY 14214 Office Phone: 716-829-2912. Business E-Mail: hbrody@acsubuffalo.edu.

BRODY, JACQUELINE, editor; b. Utica, NY, Jan. 23, 1932; d. Jack and Mary (Childress) Galloway; m. Eugene D. Brody, Apr. 5, 1959; children: Jessica, Leslie. AB, Vassar Coll., 1953; postgrad., London Sch. Econs., 1953-56. Assoc. editor Crowell Collier Macmillan, NYC, 1963-67; writer Coun. Fgn. Rels., NYC, 1968-69; mng. editor Print Collector's Newsletter, NYC, 1971-72, editor, 1972-96, art writer, 1996—; dir., v.p. Picanet, Inc., NYC, 1996—. Office: 2765 Deerfield Rd Sag Harbor NY 11963

BRODY, JANE ELLEN, journalist, researcher; b. Bklyn., May 19, 1941; d. Sidney and Lillian (Kellner) B.; m. Richard Engquist, Oct. 2, 1966; children: Lee Erik and Lorin Michael Engquist (twins). BS, N.Y. State Coll. Agr., Cornell U., 1962; MS in Journalism, U. Wis., 1963; HHD (hon.), Princeton U., 1987; LHD (hon.), Hamline U., 1993, SUNY Hlth. Sci. Ctr., 1999; LHD U. Minn. (hon.), 2000. Reporter Mpls. Tribune, 1963-65; sci. writer, personal health columnist N.Y. Times, NYC, 1965—; mem. adv. council N.Y. State Coll. Agr., Cornell U., 1971-77. Author: (with Richard Engquist) Secrets of Good Health, 1970; (with Arthur Holleb) You Can Fight Cancer and Win, 1977, Jane Brody's Nutrition Book, 1981, Jane Brody's The New York Times Guide to Personal Health, 1982, Jane Brody's Good Food Book, 1985, Jane Brody's Good Food Gourmet, 1990; (with Richard Flaste) Jane Brody's Good Seafood Book, 1994, Jane Brody's Cold and Flu Fighter, 1995, Jane Brody's Allergy Fighter, 1997, The New York Times Book of Health, 1997, The New York Times Book of Women's Health, 2000, The New York Times Guide to Alternative Health, 2001. Recipient numerous writing awards including Howard Blakeslee award Am. Heart Assn., 1971, Sci. Writers' award ADA, 1978, J.C. Penney-U. Mo. Journalism award, 1978, Lifeline award Am. Health Found., 1978 Jewish. Office: NY Times 229 W 43d St New York NY 10036-3913

BRODY, JANE L., lawyer; b. Newark, Mar. 12, 1958; AB in English Lang. and Lit., Smith Coll., 1980; JD cum laude, Boston U., 1983; LLM in Taxation, NYU, 1990. Bar: Mass. 1983, US Dist. Ct. (dist. Mass.) 1984, NJ 1986, US Dist. Ct. (dist. NJ) 1986. Named one of Top 100 Attys., Worth mag., 2005. Mem.: ABA, NJ State Bar Assn. Office: Marcus Brody Ford Kessler & Sahner LLC 5 Becker Farm Rd Roseland NJ 07068 Office Phone: 973-232-0600. E-mail: jlbrody@marcusbrodylaw.com.

BRODY, JOHN, sports association executive; b. 1973; married; 1 child. BA in Polit. Sci., Tufts Univ., Mass., 1995. Exec. v.p. mktg. Boston Celtics, 2002—04; with corp. mktg. dept. Major League Baseball, NYC, 1998—2002, exec., sr. v.p. corp. sales mktg., 2004—. Named one of 40

Under 40, Sports Bus. Jour., 2005—06. Achievements include bringing MLB corp. sponsorship deals above $110 mill. for first time, 2005. Office: Major League Baseball 31st Fl 245 Park Ave New York NY 10167

BRODY, KENNETH DAVID, investment banker; b. Phila., June 30, 1943; s. Herbert Brody and Esther (Forman) Brody Shimberg; m. Judy E. Donahue, Feb. 5, 1964 (div. Feb. 1974); m. Helen M. Tandler, Apr. 6, 1974 (div. Oct. 1978); m. Carolyn J. Schwenker, June 26, 1987. BSE.E. with high honors, U. Md., 1964; MBA with high distinction, Harvard U., 1971. Foreman and staff asst. Chesapeake & Potomac Telephone Co., Washington, 1964-66; with Goldman, Sachs & Co., NYC, 1971-91, ptnr., 1978-91; chmn., pres. Export-Import Bank of US, Washington, 1993-96; co-founder Taconic Capital Advisors, 1999—. Bd. dirs. Telerate, 1983-85, Alex Brown, 1996-97, Yurie Systems, 1996-98, Fed. Realty Investment Trust, 1997-2002, Quest Diagnostics, 1997-2004; chmn. U. Md. Found., 2004—. Bd. dirs. Alvin Ailey Am. Dance Theater, NYC, 1981-93, ARC, 1994-2000, St. John's Coll., 1996-97; chmn. Presdl. Commn. US-Pacific Trade and Investment Policy, 1996-97; chmn. U. Md. Investment Com., 2004-. Capt. US Army, 1966-69. Baker scholar, 1970; Loeb Rhoades fellow, 1971 Mem. Coun. Fgn. Rels., Harvard Club, Tau Beta Pi, Eta Kappa Nu, Omicron Delta Kappa, Alpha Tau Omega. Democrat. Unitarian Universalist. Office: Taconic Capital Advisors 450 Park Ave New York NY 10022 Address: 2401 Kalorama Rd NW Washington DC 20008

BRODY, LAWRENCE, lawyer, educator; b. St. Louis, Aug. 12, 1942; s. Max and Jeannette (Cohen) B.; m. Janice Dobinsky, Dec. 25, 1967; 1 child, Michael Allen. BS in Econs., U. Pa., 1964; JD, Washington U., St. Louis, 1967; LLM in Tax, NYU, 1968. Bar: Mo. Assoc. atty. Husch, Eppenberger, Donohue, Elson & Cornfeld, St. Louis, 1968-74, ptnr., 1974-86, Bryan Cave, LLP, St. Louis, 1986—, group leader Pvt. Client. Adj. prof. Washington U. Sch. Law, 1968—. Author: Missouri Estate Planning, 1988; author, editor Life Insurance Counsellor Series, 1990, 91. Fellow Am. Coll. of Trust and Estate Counsel, Am. Coll. Tax Counsel; mem. Adv. Bd. of Tax Mgmt. Office: Bryan Cave LLP One Metropolitan Square 211 N Broadway Ste 3600 Saint Louis MO 63102-2733 Office Phone: 314-259-2652. E-mail: lbrody@bryancave.com.

BRODY, MARTIN, hotel executive; b. Newark, Aug. 8, 1921; s. Leo and Renee (Kransdorf) B.; m. Florence Gropper, Nov. 22, 1946; children: Marc, Renee. BA, Mich. State U., 1943. Pres. Indsl. Feeding Co., Newark, 1951-61; pres., dir. A.M. Capital Corp., NYC, 1961-71. Chmn. bd., dir. Waldorf System Inc., Boston, 1963-66, Restaurant Assocs., Inc., N.Y.C., 1964-66; chmn. bd., CEO Restaurant Assocs. Industries Inc., 1966-99; chmn. bd. St. Barnabas Corp.; dir. Jaclyn Inc., several Smith Barney mut. funds, Washington Nat. Life Ins. Co. of N.Y.; bd. dirs. Regional Planning Assn. Trustee St. Barnabas Med. Ctr.; bd. dirs. N.J. Transit Corp. Served to capt. AUS, 1943-45. Mem. Orange Lawn Tennis, Greenbrook Country (North Caldwell, N.J.), Boca Raton Hotel and Resort Club. Home: 1 Pine Valley Rd Livingston NJ 07039-8210

BRODY, PETER MARTIN, lawyer; b. Bethlehem, Pa., Aug. 24, 1958; s. Arthur L. and Janice A. (Rossin) B.; m. Jenny A. Sternbach, Dec. 7, 1986; children: Sarah E., Anna E., Daniel E. AB magna cum laude, Princeton U., 1980; JD cum laude, Harvard U., 1984. Bar: Pa. 1985, D.C. 1986, Md. 1992, U.S. Dist. Ct. D.C., U.S. Ct. Appeals (D.C. cir.) 1986, U.S. Ct. Appeals (4th cir.) 1992, U.S. Supreme Ct. 1992. Law clk. to Hon. Carl McGowan U.S. Ct. Appeals, D.C. Cir., Washington, 1984-85; assoc. Rogovin, Huge & Lenzner, Washington, 1984-89, Ropes & Gray, Washington, 1989-93, ptnr. litigation dept., 1993—, co-head intellectual property practice litig. group. Chmn. legal adv. com. Nat. Capital Multiple Sclerosis Soc., Washington, 1990—; mem. adv. com. on Criminal Justice Act procedures U.S. Ct. Appeals, Washington, 1994—. Contbr. articles to profl. jours. Mem. ABA (intellectual property sect.), Internat. Trademark Assn. (geographical indications com.), D.C. Bar Assn., Internat. Wine Lawyers Assn. Avocations: swimming, bicycling, skiing, travel. Office: Ropes & Gray One Metro Ctr Suite 900 700 12th St NW Washington DC 20005-3948 Office Phone: 202-508-4612. Office Fax: 202-508-4650. Business E-Mail: peter.brody@ropesgray.com.

BRODY, RICHARD ALAN, political science educator, researcher; b. NYC, Mar. 2, 1930; s. Lee and Felice Auslander; m. Marjorie Jean Brody, Aug. 23, 1964; children: Gordon Christopher, David Eric, Aaron Jed. BA, San Francisco State U., 1956, MA, 1959; PhD, Northwestern U., 1963. Asst. prof. Stanford (Calif.) U., 1962-66, assoc. prof., 1966-70, prof., 1970-95, chmn. dept., 1972-73, 74-77, prof. emeritus, 1995—. Fulbright prof. U. Leiden, The Netherlands, 1970-71; bd. overseers Am. Nat. Election Study, 1980-87. Author: Simulation Internat., 1963, Assessing the President, 1991; co-author: Reasoning and Choice, 1991 (Woodrow Wilson prize 1992); co-editor: Political Persuasion and Attitude, 1996; editor Polit. Behavior jour., 1990-97. Fellow, Ctr. Advanced Study in Behavioral Sci., 1967-68, Am. Acad. Arts and Scis., 1992; Parthemos fellow U. Ga., 1998. Mem. Am. Polit. Sci. Assn. (coun. 1977-79), Western Polit. Sci. Assn. (pres. 1987-88), Midwest Polit. Sci. Assn. Democrat. Avocations: wines, food, travel, birding. Home: 1636 Edgewood Dr Palo Alto CA 94303-2820 Office: Stanford Univ Dept Polit Sci Stanford CA 94305-6044 E-mail: Brody@Stanford.edu.

BRODY, RICHARD ERIC, lawyer; b. NYC, Sept. 9, 1947; s. Harold I. and Lillian C. (Albert) B.; m. V. Jane Cohen, May 25, 1974; children: Lauren, Erica. BA, Washington and Jefferson Coll., 1969; JD, Boston U., 1975. Bar: Mass. 1975, US Dist. Ct. Mass. 1975, US Ct. Appeals (1st cir.) 1975, US Supreme Ct. 1987. Law clk. Mass. Superior Ct., Boston, 1975-76, chief law clk., 1976-77; assoc. Sisson, Lee & Bloomenthal, Boston, 1977-78; asst. dist. atty. Atty.'s Office Middlesex County Dist., Cambridge, Mass., 1978-82; assoc. Morrison, Mahoney & Miller, Boston, 1982-85, ptnr., 1985-95, Brody, Hardoon, Perkins & Kesten, Boston, 1995—. Lectr. Nat. Inst. Trial Advocacy, trial practice series Harvard U., Mass. Continuing Legal Edn., Def. Rsch. Inst.; evaluator Middlesex Multi-Door Courthouse, Cambridge, 1989—; mediator Arbitration Forums, Inc., Tarrytown, NY, 1989—, cons. Liability Cons., Inc., Sudbury, 1988—; mem. nat. adv. bd. Govtl. Liability Ins., Richmond, 1985—. Trustee Mass. Civil Liability Ins., Boston, 1983-89. Named a Mass. Super Lawyer, 2004, 2005, 2006; named, 2007. Mem. Mass. Bar Assn. (civil litigation sect. coun.), Mass. Assn. Trial Lawyers, Boston Bar Assn., Def. Rsch. Inst., City Solicitors and Town Counsel Assn. Office: Brody Hardoon Perkins & Kesten 1 Exeter Plz Fl 12 Boston MA 02116-2848 Home Phone: 781-449-4487. Business E-Mail: rbrody@bhpklaw.com.

BRODY, ROBERT, dermatologist; b. Cleve., June 15, 1948; s. Melvin and Nancy Elizabeth Brody; m. Mary Ann Conn, July 23, 1988; children: Ian Hamilton Conn, Hartley Messing Conn, Matthew Grant Hutchinson. AB with distinction, Stanford U., 1970; MD, U. Mich., 1974. Intern in internal medicine, Cleve. Clinic, 1974-75, resident in dermatology, 1975-78; practice medicine specializing in dermatology, Cleve., 1978—; staff physician Kaiser-Permanente Med. Center, 1978-82, mem. profl. edn. com., 1978-82, chmn., 1980-82, also sec. exec. com., 1980; pvt. practice, 1982—; asst. clin. prof. Case Western Res. U. Med. Sch., 1978-80, 83—, clin. instr., 1980-83, dermatology dept. rep. to gen. faculty, 1980-82; asst. physician Univ. Hosps. Cleve., 1979—; chief dermatology divsn. St. Luke's Hosp., Cleve., 1999—. Sec., Cleve. Play House Men's Com., 1979-82; mem. ann. fund com. Stanford U., 1978—, regional co-chmn., 1981-82. Diplomate Am. Bd. Dermatology. Mem. Am. Acad. Dermatology, Cleve. Acad. Medicine. Contbr. articles to med. jours. Club: Cleve. Skating, Rowfant. Home: 2870 Glengary Rd Cleveland OH 44120-1731 Office: 3461 Warrensville Ctr Rd Cleveland OH 44122-5227

BRODY, ROBERTA, information science educator; m. Zeb Blackman. PhD, Rutgers U., New Brunswick, NJ, 1996. Assoc. prof. Queens Coll. CUNY, Flushing, 1996—. Editor: Jour. Competitive Intelligence Mgmt. Fellow: Soc. Competitive Intelligence Profls. (pres. 1989—90); mem.: IEEE Soc. on the Social Implications of Tech. (conf. chair internat. symposium on tech. and soc. 2006), Spl. Librs. Assn. (Cox award 1999, Karen J. Switt Leadership award 2003), Beta Phi Mu. Office: Queens College of the City Univ of NY 65-30 Kissena Blvd Flushing NY 11367 Office Phone: 718-997-3790. Business E-Mail: roberta.brody@qc.cuny.edu.

BRODY, WILLIAM RALPH, academic administrator, radiologist, educator; b. Stockton, Calif., Jan. 4, 1944; m. Wendy Brody; 2 children. BSEE, MIT, 1965, MSEE, 1966; MD, Stanford U., 1970, PhD in Elec. Engring., 1975. Intern to resident and fellow dept. cardiovasc. surgery Stanford U. Sch. Medicine, Calif., 1970—73, tng. med. fellow cardiovasc. surgery, resident diagnostic radiology, 1975—77, assoc. prof. to prof. dept. radiology, dir. rsch. labs., 1977—86; with USPHS Nat. Heart, Lung, and Blood Inst., Balt., 1973—75; prof. Stanford U., 1982—84; founder, pres., CEO Resonex, Inc., 1984—87, chmn. bd. dirs., 1987—89; radiologist-in-chief Johns Hopkins Hosp., Balt., 1987—94; mem. staff depts. elec., computer engring., biomedical engring. Johns Hopkins U. Sch. Medicine, 1987—94, Martin Donner prof., dir. dept. radiology, 1987—94; prof. radiology, provost U. Minn. Acad. Health Ctr., 1994—96, spl. asst. to pres., 1996; pres. Johns Hopkins U., 1996—. Bd. dir. Medtronic Inc., Merc. Bankshares; mem. Pres.'s Fgn. Intelligence adv. bd. Contbr. articles to profl. jours. Mem. sci. adv. com. Whitaker Found., 1992—97, governing com., 1997—; fellow coun. cardiovasc. radiology Am. Heart Assn.; mem. internat. adv. bd. Nat. U. Singapore Inst. Sys. Sci., 1994—97; trustee Goldseker Found., 1996; mem. internat. acad. adv. panel, 1997; bd. dirs. Greater Balt. Com., 1997; trustee Balt. Mus. Art, 1997. Recipient Established Investigator award, Am. Heart Assn., 1980—84. Fellow: NAS (Inst. Medicine), IEEE, Am. Acad. Arts & Scis., Am. Inst. Med. and Biomedical Engring., Am. Coll. Cardiology, Am. Coll. Radiology; mem.: NAE, Internat. Soc. Magnetic Resonance in Medicine. Achievements include patents in field. Office: Johns Hopkins U Office of the Pres 242 Garland Hall 3400 N Charles St Baltimore MD 21218-2680 Office Phone: 410-516-8068. Office Fax: 410-156-6097. E-mail: wrbrody@jhu.edu.*

BRODY-LEDERMAN, STEPHANIE, artist; b. NYC; d. Maxwell and Ann Brody. BS in Design, Finch Coll., 1961; MA in Painting, LI U., 1975. One-person exhbns. include James Yu Gallery, 1976, Nassau County Mus. Fine Arts, Roslyn, NY, 1978, Harriman Coll., 1979, Franklin Furnace, NYC, 1979, 55 Mercer Gallery, NYC, 1979, Kathryn Markel Fine Arts, NYC, 1979, 81, 83, Anderson Gallery, Va. Commonwealth U., 1980, Bengt Torvall, Stockholm, 1982, Katzen/Brown Gallery, NYC, 1988, 89, Real Art Ways, Hartford, Conn., 1984, San Francisco Internat. Airport, 1986, Rastovski Gallery, NYC, 1987, Hal Katzen Gallery, NYC, 1988-89, 1991, Alfred U., 1990, Queensboro CC, NY, 1990, Hillwood Art Mus., LI U., Brookville, NY, 1992, Casements Mus., Ormond Beach, Fla., 1994, Broward CC, Ft. Lauderdale, Fla., 1994, Renee Fotouhi Gallery, East Hampton, NY, 1994, Hebrew Home for the Aged, Riverdale, NY, 1994, Galerie Caroline Corre, Paris, 1995, La. State U., Shreveport, 1995, Marc Miller Gallery, East Hampton, NY, 1996, Pierogi 2000, Bklyn., 1996, Arlene Bujese Gallery, East Hampton, NY, 1997, 2001-03, 123 Watts Gallery, NYC, 1998, Edison CC, Fort Myers, Fla., 2001, Hudson Opera House, NY, 2001, Cleary, Gottlieb, Steen & Hamilton Artists Program, NYC, 2003, OK Harris Fine Arts, NYC, 2004, 06, Guild Hall Mus., East Hampton, NY, 2004; exhibited in numerous group shows including Cont Art Mus., 1976, Mus. Modern Art, NYC, 1976, 78, 80, 86, Cooper Hewett Mus., NYC, 1978, Susan Caldwell Gallery, NYC, 1978, Phila. Coll. Art, 1979, Alex Rosenberg Gallery, NYC, 1980, U. Colo., 1981, Freedman Gallery, Albright Coll., Reading, Pa., 1981, Franklin Furnace, NYC, 1981, Galerie Bar de l'aventure, Paris, 1982, Newark Mus., 1983, U. Gallery, U. Mass., 1984, Holly Solomon Gallery, NYC, 1984, OH State U., 1986, The Clocktower, NYC, 1986, Henry Street Settlement, NYC, 1987, 2000, Blum Helman Gallery, NYC, 1989, Queens Mus., 1989, Basel Art Fair, 1989, Ctr. Cultural de boulogne-Billancourt, France, 1989, Pub. Sch. 1 Mus., Queens, NY, 1989, So. Alleghenies Mus. Art, Loretto, Pa., 1990, RI Sch. Design-Mus. Art, Providence, 1990, Libr., Mus. Modern Art, NYC, 1990, Midtown Payson Gallery, NYC, 1990, Hillwood Art Mus., Brookville, NY, 1991, 2001, Sculpture Ctr., NYC, 1992, Heckscher Mus., Huntington Mus., 1992, Am. Acad. Arts and Letters, NYC, 1992, Guild Hall Mus., East Hampton, NY, 1993, 2004, Ind. U., Terre Haute, 1993, Jewish Mus., NYC, 1994, Nat. Mus. Women in Arts, Washington, 1994, 2003, Ronald Feldman Gallery, NYC, 1995, Alt. Mus., NYC, 1995, 1997, Eugenia Cucalon Gallery, NYC, 1995, Rotunda Gallery, Bklyn., 1995, Redfern Gallery, London, 1995, Espace Eiffel-Branly, Paris, 1996, Fotouhi Cramer Gallery, NYC, 1996, 123 Watts Gallery, NYC, 1996, Mediateque, Les Mureaux, France, 1996, San Francisco State U., 1997, Bklyn. Mus., 1997, Weatherspoon Gallery, U. NC, 1997, Gasworks Gallery, London, 1997, HarperCollins Exhbn. Space, NYC, 1997, Parrish Art Mus., Southampton, NY, 1998, Neuburger Mus., Purchase, NY, 1998, Librairie Nicaise, Paris, 1998, Conn. Coll., 1998, Arlene Bujese Gallery, East Hampton, 1998, 2000, 05, Generous Miracles Gallery, NYC, 1999, Montclair Art Mus., NJ, 1999, Minn. Ctr. BA, 1999, Mpls. Coll. Art, 1999, Musee Bourdelle, Paris, 1999—, U. of the Arts, Phila., 1999, Limn Gallery, San Francisco, 1999, Bklyn. Mus., NYC, 2000, Nassau CC, Garden City, NY, 2000, Ctr. Artistique, Verderonne, France, 2000, 02, U. Bridgeport, 2000, Hungarian Consulate, NYC, 2001, Coll. Art and Design, Bristol, Eng., 2001; Ctr. Book Arts, NYC, 2001, 04, 06, Sevran Svc. Culturel, France, 2001, Metaphor Contemporary Art, Bklyn., 2002, Meridian Inernat. Ctr., Washington, 2002, Topkapi Mus, Istanbul, 2002, Gracie Mansion Gallery Chelsea, NYC, 2002, Robert Wilson-Byrd Hoffman Waterill Ctr., Bridgehampton, NY, 2002, Rotunda Gallery, Bklyn., 2002, Ind. State U., 2002, Bradley U., Ill., 2002, Brussels Art Fair, 2002, Snug Harbor, Staten Island, NY, 2002, Kentler Internat. Drawing Space, Bklyn., 2002, 06, 450 Art Gallery, NYC, 2002, Gracie Mansion Booth, Javits Galleria, NYC, 2003, Chelsea Art Mus., NY, 2003,Berliner Kunstproject,Berlin, 2003, OK Harris Gallery, NYC, 2003, Bklyn. Pub. Libr., Kentler Internat. Drawing Space, NYC, 2003, Mus. Biblioteque Forney, Paris, 2004, Mediateque F. Mitterand, Argentan, France, 2005, OK Harris Booth, Chelsea Piers, NY, 2005, Pratt Inst., Skylight Gallery, Bklyn., 2005, Gilbert Pavilion, HHR, Riverdale, NY, 2006, Ctr. Artistique de Verderonne, Manoir du Boulanc, France, 2006, Bklyn. Arts Coun., 2006, St. Joseph's Coll., Bklyn., 2007, Spanierman Gallery, East Hampton, NY; represented in permanent collections including Newark Mus., Mus. Modern Art, Prudential Ins., Bertelsmann Music Group, Guild Hall Mus., East Hampton, LI, Cooper Hewitt Mus., NYC, Grafikhuset Futura, Stockholm, Sweden, Atlanta Coll. Art, Art Gallery of Peale, Brampton, Ont., Yale U. Libr. Art and Arch., New Haven, Conn., The Jewish Mus., NYC, Carnegie Mellon Libr., Pitts., Archive Concrete & Visual Poetry, Miami Bech., Chase Manhattan Bank, NY Health and Hosp. Corp., Newark Mus., NJ, Victoria & Albert Mus., London, Doubleday Books, Saks 5th Ave. Corp., Vero Beach Ctr. for the Arts, Fla., Bklyn. Mus., Montclair Art Mus., NJ, Librairie Arcade, Osaka, Japan, ArmsteaCentre Du Livre D'Artiste, Verderonne, France, Hancock Info. Group, Orlando, Fla., 2002, others; represented in public collections including the Edward Albee Found., Montauk, NY, Am. Womans Econ. Devel. Corp., NYC, Amherst Coll, Mass., Archive Concrete & Visual Poetry, Miami Beach, Fla., Art Gallery Peale, Brampton, Ontario, Can., ASCAP, NYC, Atlanta Coll. Art., Barnes Hosp., St. Louis, Bass Mus. Art Mus. Shop, Miami Beach, Bertelsmann Music Group, NYC, Bklyn. Mus. Art, Bklyn. Union Gas, Carnegie Mellon Lib., Pitts., Ctr. for Arts, Vera Beach, Fla., Ctr. du Livre d'Artiste, Verderonne, France, Chase Manhattan Bank, NYC, Cooper Hewitt Mus., NYC, Cumberland Health Facility, Bklyn., Doubleday Books, Garden City, NY, Erasmus Haus, Basel, Switzerland, Harvard Bus. Sch., Boston, Grafikhuset Futura, Stockholm, Sweden, Guild Hall Mus., East Hampton, NY, Hebrew Home for Aged, Riverdale, NY, Ins. N.Am., NYC, Libraire Arcade, Osaka, Japan, The Jewish Mus., NYC, Med. Coll. Va., Richmond, Montclair Art Mus., NJ, Mus. Fine Art, RI Sch. Design, Providence, Mus. Contemporary Art, LA, Mus. Modern Art, NYC, Nat. Mus. Women in Arts, DC, Nelson-Atkins Mus., Kansas City, Mo., Newark Mus., Print Divsn., NY Pub. Lib., NY Health & Hosps. Corp., Prudential Ins. Co., Newark, Saks 5th Ave. Corp. Collection, Troy, Mich., SUNY-Cortland, Sydney U., Australia, Tate Mus., London, Tesseract Early Sci. Instruments, NY, Paris, Victoria & Albert Mus., London, Wadsworth Athenium Lib., Hartford, Conn., WPA Bookstore, DC, Yale U. Lib. Arts & Architecture, New Haven, Conn.; contbg. artist: Postcards, Series II, JM Kaplan Fund and Pub. Art Fund, 1978, Paris Rev., 1979, ArtistMultiplesProject, 1980, WhiteWalls Mag., 1983, L'Oreil Mag., 1983, Huess House Project, Lower Manhattan Cultural Coun., 1992, Arts in the Hosps., MCV Program, Richmond, 1994, Neuberger Mus., Purchase, NY, 1998, Pub. Art, Cowparade NY, 2000, Project Purgatory Pie Press, NYC, 2001, UNFRAMED Artists Respond to Aids, powerHouse Books, NY, 2002, NUTUREart Multiple Project, 2002, Cover for Paris Rev. 2002, Gastronomica, Jour. Food and Culture, 2003; (paintings for TV) (film) The Heidi Chronicles, 1995, The Apprentice, 2004. Recipient Hassam and Speicher Purchase award Am. Acad. and Inst. Arts and Letters, 1988, Purchase award Arts in Hosps., Richmond, Va., 1994, Ann. award Guild Hall Mus., 1997, Exhbn. award, 2003; grantee Creative Artists Pub. Svc. NYS Coun. Arts, 1979, Ariana Found. for Arts, 1983, LINE grant NYS Coun. Arts, NEA, 1984, Poster Commn. NEA InterArts Program and Alt. Mus., NYC, 1984, Artists grant Artists Space, 1987, Project grant E.D. Found., 1991, USA Commn. award Lancaster Group, 1991, Spl. Opportunity stipend NY Found. Arts and East End Arts Coun., 1992, Drawing Commn., CRIA, 1999. Home: 822 Madison Ave Fl 4 New York NY 10021 Office Phone: 212-570-2519, 718-782-0310. Personal E-mail: sbrodyl@aol.com.

BRODZIK, LESTER LEONARD, artist, retired occupational therapist; b. Chgo., Apr. 7, 1950; s. Frank Chester Brodzik and Rose Baldyga. Grad., Chgo. Acad. Find Arts, 1970, Art Inst. Chgo., 1971; BA, Northeastern Ill. U., 1978. With State Ill., 1970—78, activity therapist, 1978—2001; ret., 2001. Exhibitions include Body Politic Theatre, Gallery 1370, Body Politic Festival and St. Fair, Covenant Club, Beverly Art Ctr., Bernard Horwich Gallery, Art Expo, Navy Pier, Randolph St. Gallery, Artful Dodger, U. Chgo., ARC Invitational Gallery, Objects d'Art, Unique Freaque, Hunters on Clark, Theatre Bldg., Dai Ichi Kangye, Corsh Gallery, NEO, Limelight Exhbns., performance artist, DAS Machine, Ludwigshafen, Germany, X meets Y; performer: (films) How the 8-Track Works, Vanity Ugly Vanity, The Lester Film, (TV show) Is It Art; contbr. articles to profl. jours.

BROECKER, WALLACE S., geophysicist, educator; b. Chgo., Nov. 29, 1931; Attended Wheaton Coll., Wheaton, IL; AB in Physics, Columbia Coll., NYC, 1953; PhD in Geology, Columbia, NYC, 1958. Asst. prof. Columbia U., NYC, 1959—61, assoc. prof., 1961—64, prof., 1964—, Newberry prof. geology, Lamont-Doherty Earth Observatory, 1977—. Contbr. articles to scholarly jours.; author: (textbook) Chemical Equilibria in the Earth, 1971, Chemical Oceanography, 1974, Tracers in the Sea, 1982, How to Build a Habitable Planet, 1985, Glacial World According to Wally, 1992, Greenhouse Puzzles, 1994. Recipient A.G. Huntsman award, Bedford Inst. Oceanography, 1985, Vetlesen prize, Columbia U., 1987, Priestley award, Dickinson Coll., 1990, Nat. medal of Sci., 1996, Blue Planet prize, Asahi Glass Found., Tokyo, 1996, Tyler prize for Environ. Achievement, 2002, Crafoord prize in Geosciences, Royal Swedish Acad. Sciences, 2006. Fellow: Geol. Soc. Am. (Arthur L. Day medal 1984, Don J. Easterbrook Disting. Scientist award 2000), Geol. Soc. London (Wollaston medal 1990), European Geophys. Union (Urey medal 1986, Roger Revelle medal 1995), Am. Geophys. Union (Maurice W. Ewing medal 1979); mem.: NAS (Alexander Agassiz medal 1986), Royal Soc. UK (fgn.), Geochem. Soc. (chmn. 1979, V.M. Goldschmidt award 1986), Am. Acad. Arts and Scis. Achievements include research on the operation of the global carbon cycle within the ocean, atmosphere, biosphere system, and its interaction with climate; development of the theory of large-scale ocean currents and matching it with the interactive Earth System. Office: Columbia U Lamont-Doherty Earth Obs PO Box 1000 61 Rt 9W Palisades NY 10964-8000 E-mail: broecker@ldeo.columbia.edu.*

BROEKER, JOHN MILTON, lawyer; b. Berwyn, Ill., May 27, 1940; s. Milton Monroe and Marjorie Grace (Wilson) B.; m. Linda J. Broeker, Dec. 9, 1983; children: Sara Elizabeth, Ross Goddard; stepchildren: Terrance Mercil Jr., Johnny Mercil, Veronica Mercil. BA, Grinnell Coll., 1962; JD cum laude, U. Minn., 1965. Bar: Minn. 1965, Wis. 1982, U.S. Ct. Appeals (8th cir.) 1966, U.S. Dist. Ct. Minn. 1967,. U.S. Tax Ct. 1969, U.S. Ct. Appeals (5th cir.) 1971, U.S. Dist. Ct. (we. dist.) Wis. 1982, U.S. Supreme Ct. 1984. Law clk. to presiding judge U.S. Ct. Appeals (8th cir.), 1965-66; ptnr. Gray, Plant, Mooty, Mooty & Bennett, Mpls., 1966-71, Broeker, Geer, Fletcher & LaFond and predecessor firms, Mpls., 1971-91; v.p., gen. counsel NordicTrack, Inc., Mpls., 1991-94; founder Broeker Enterprises, 1992—; pres. Legal Mgmt. Strategies, Inc., Mpls., 1994—; of counsel Popham, Haik, Schnobrich & Kaufman, Ltd., Mpls., 1995-96, Halleland, Lewis, Nilan, Sipkins & Johnson, Mpls., 1996-97; pvt. practice, 1997—. Instr. U Minn. Law Sch., 1967-72; lectr. convs. and seminars, 1969—; lectr. U. Minn. Ctr. for Long Term Care Edn., 1972-77, Gt. Lakes Health Congress, 1972, Sister Kenney Inst., 1972. Contbr. articles to legal jours. Bd. dirs. Minn. Environ. Scis. Found., Inc., 1971-73; bd. dirs. Project Environ. Found., 1977-83, chmn., 1980-82; mem. alumni bd. Grinnell Coll., 1968-71; chmn. MInnetonka Environ. Quality and Natural Resources Commn., 1971-72; trustee The Writers Project, Inc., 1999-2001. Recipient Outstanding Alumni award Grinnell Coll., 1973. Mem. ABA (forum com. on health law 1978-91), Minn. Bar Assn. (chmn. environ. law com. 1970-72), State Bar Wis., Hennepin County Bar Assn. (chmn. environ. law com. 1976-77, legis. com. 1972-76, health law com. 1977-79), Am. Soc. Hosp. Attys., Minn. Soc. Hosp. Attys., Am. Health Care Assn. (legal coordinating com. 1970-75, labor com. 1973-74), Nat. Health Lawyers Assn., Minn. Thoroughbred Assn. (bd. dirs. 1991-92), Minn. Quarterhorse Racing Assn. (bd. dirs. 1994—2003, pres. 1997-99), Sierra Club (nat. dir. 1974-76, chmn. chpt. 1971-72, regional v.p. 1973-74). Home: 11402 Burr Ridge Ln Eden Prairie MN 55347-4717 Office: 8120 Penn Ave S Ste 151Q Bloomington MN 55431-1326 Office Phone: 952-886-0435. Business E-Mail: jbroeker@msn.com.

BROENING, WALTER STEPHENS, JR., journalist, history educator; b. Balt., Aug. 15, 1935; s. Walter Stephens and Evelyne (Powers) B.; m. Christine Zucker, Feb. 3, 1962; children: Alexander (dec.), John, Benjamin, Thomas. BA in Polit. Sci., Johns Hopkins U., 1959. Reporter AP, Balt., 1963-65, corr. Paris, 1965-70, Moscow, 1970-74, Lisbon, Portugal, 1974-76; asst. city editor Balt. Sun, 1976-77, op-ed page editor, 1977-85, diplomatic corr., 1985-90; news editor Internat. Herald-Tribune, Paris, 1990-96; vis. scholar in history Johns Hopkins U., Balt., 1996—. With U.S. Army, 1954-56. Mem. Johns Hopkins Club. Home: 5701 Greenleaf Rd Baltimore MD 21210-1319 Office: Johns Hopkins U Dept History 3400 N Charles St Baltimore MD 21218-2608 Personal E-mail: wsb1@verizon.net.

BROERS, LORD ALEC NIGEL, engineering educator; b. Calcutta, India, Sept. 17, 1938; s. Alec William and Constance Amy (Cox) B.; m. Mary Therese Phelan, Dec. 27, 1965; children: Mark, Christopher. BSc, Melbourne U., 1959; BA in Mech. Scis., Cambridge U., 1962, PhD in Elec. Engring., 1965, ScD, 1990; D of Engring. (hon.), Glasgow U., 1996; DSc (hon.), Warwick U., 1997, U. Manchester Inst. Tech., 2002; D in Tech. (hon.), Greenwich U., 2000; LLD (hon.), Melbourne U., 2000; D in Univ. (hon.), Anglia Poly. U., 2000; Fellow (hon.), U. Wales, 2002; D of Engring.

(hon.), Peking U., 2002; DSc (hon.), U. Manchester, 2002; LLD (hon.), U. Cambridge, 2004; DSc (hon.), Trinity Coll., Dublin, 2006. Mem. rsch. staff IBM Thomas J. Watson Rsch. Ctr., Yorktown Heights, NY, 1965-81, mgr. electron beam tech., 1967-72, mgr. photo and electron optics, 1972-81; mgr. advanced tech. IBM East Fishkill Devel. Lab., Hopewell Junction, NY, 1981-84; mem. corp. tech. com. IBM Hdqrs., Armonk, NY, 1984; prof. elec. engring., head elec. div. dept. engring. Cambridge U., 1984-92, head dept. engring., 1992-96, vice chancellor, 1996—2003; mem. rsch. staff IBM Thomas J. Watson Rsch. Ctr., Yorktown Heights, NY, 1965-81. Fellow Trinity Coll., Cambridge, 1985-90; master Churchill Coll., Cambridge, 1990-96; mem. Royal Acad. Engring. Coun., 1994-96, Engring. and Phys. Scis. Coun. U.K., 1992-00; non-exec. dir. gen. bd. Lucas Industries, 1995-96; non-exec. dir. Vodafone Group, L.J. Mears LLC, Plastic Logic Ltd.; chmn. Ho. Lords Sci. and Tech. Select Com., 2004—; sr. advisor Warburg Pincus; mem. Coun. Sci. and Tech. Contbr. numerous articles to profl. jours., chpts. to books; patentee in field. Recipient Am. Inst. of Physics prize for indsl. applications of physics, 1982, Cledo Brunetti award IEEE, 1985; hon. fellow Gonville and Caius Coll., Trinity Coll., Cardiff U., Imperial Coll., St. Edmund's Coll. Fellow Instn. Elec. Engrs. (hon.), Instn. Mech. Engrs. (hon.), Inst. Physics, Royal Acad. Engring. (coun. 1992-96, 00-, v.p. 2000-01, pres. 2001—, Prince Philip medal 2000), Royal Soc.; mem. U.S. Nat. Acad. Engring. (fgn. assoc.), Australian Acad. Technol. Scis. and Engrs. (hon.), Am. Philos. Soc. (fgn. mem.). Avocations: music, skiing, sailing. Home: Saint George Wharf Apt 429 London SW8 2LZ England also: 32 Mount Hope Ave Jamestown RI 02835-1466 Office: Royal Acad Engring 29 Great Peter St Westminster SW1P 3LW England Office Phone: +44207 222 2688. E-mail: president@raeng.co.uk.

BROFFITT, JAMES DRAKE, statistician, educator; b. Indpls., Apr. 8, 1941; s. Wilgus Stanley and Virginia Elizabeth (Drake) B.; m. Barbara Helen Alford, Dec. 20, 1975; children: Daniel James, Virginia Lea. BA in Math., DePauw U., 1963; MS in Stats., Colo. State U., 1965, PhD in Stats., 1969. Statis. analyst Computer Technology, Inc., Dallas, 1969-70; asst. prof. stats. and actuarial sci. U. Iowa, Iowa City, 1970-75, assoc. prof., 1975-85, 86-88, prof., 1988—, chmn. stats. and actuarial sci., 1993—2004. Vis. prof. U. Western Ont., Can., 1985-86; cons. Soc. Actuaries Part 2 Actuarial Exam., Am. Coll. Testing, 1984-85, Iowa Med. Svcs., 1988. Conducted presentations in field at various univs. and confs. in the U.S. and Can.; contbr. numerous articles to profl. jours. Mem. Am. Statis. Assn., Inst. Mathematical Stats., Internat. Actuarial Assn., Soc. of Actuaries (assoc.; acad. cons. to com. which constructs compound interest exam. 1993-95), Sigma Xi, Phi Kappa Phi. Baptist. Home: 1078 Tamarack Trail Iowa City IA 52245-3557 Office Phone: 319-335-0820. Business E-Mail: james-broffitt@uiowa.edu.

BROFFITT, JOYCE CASSANDRA, judge; b. Covington, Tenn., Sept. 20, 1955; d. Dorothy Blanche Broffitt. BA in Psychology, Rhodes Coll., 1977; JD, U. Memphis, 1986. Bar: Tenn. 1987. Dist. prenatal coord. Tenn. Dept. Health, Covington, 1980—82; counselor Shelby County Pretrial Svcs., Memphis, 1983—89; asst. dist. atty. gen. Shelby County Dist. Atty. Gen., Memphis, 1989—96; judge gen. sessions criminal court Shelby County Govt., Memphis, 1996—, judge Frayser Cmty. Ct., 2000—04. Judge Tenn. Ct. of Judiciary, 1999—; v.p. western divsn. Tenn. Gen. Sessions Judges Conf., 1997—98. Trustee Rhodes Coll., Memphis, 1997—2003; bd. dirs. Youth Villages, Memphis, 2002—. Named Alumnus of Yr., Rhodes Coll. Black Student Assn., 1998; recipient Cmty. Svc. award, Frayser Exch. Club, Memphis, 2005. Mem.: Tenn. Bar Assn., Nat. Bar Assn., Am. Judges Assn. Episcopalian. Avocations: reading, needlecrafts. Office: Shelby County Gen Sessions Judges 201 Poplar Ave LL-56 Memphis TN 38103 Office Phone: 901-545-5193.

BROG, DAVID, former air force officer, consultant; b. Manchester, Conn., Aug. 11, 1933; s. Israel and Pesha (Blonstein) B.; m. Verda Anna Raney, Nov. 9, 1959; children: Kai Ling, Tov Binyamin. BA, U. Pitts., 1955; MS, U. So. Calif., 1967. Commd. 2d lt. USAF, 1956, advanced through grades to col., 1978, dir. readiness and electronic combat, Hdqrs. Europe, from 1981, dep. chief staff ops. for command control and communications countermeasures, until 1982, ret., 1982; pres. IRD, Inc. (internat. R & D), domestic and internat. cons. on def. issues, Silver Spring, Md., 1982—. Contbr. articles to profl. jours. Decorated D.F.C., Legion of Merit, Air medal with 12 oak leaf clusters; named Disting. Grad. USAF Air War Coll. Mem. Red River Valley Fighter Pilots Assn. (pres.), Assn. Old Crows, Air Force Assn. Jewish. Home: 9200 Three Oaks Dr Silver Spring MD 20901-3362 Office: PO Box 877 Silver Spring MD 20918-0877 Home Phone: 301-332-8240; Office Phone: 301-588-3283. E-mail: davebrog@comcast.net.

BROGAN, FRANK T., academic administrator, former lieutenant governor; m. Courtney Strickland; 1 child, Colby John. BA magna cum laude, U. Cin.; M in Ednl. Leadership, Fla. Atlantic U. Supt. schs. Martin County Sch. Dist., Fla., 1988-94; commr. edn. Fla. Dept. Edn., Tallahassee, 1994-99; lt. gov. State of Fla., Tallahassee, 1999—2003; pres. Florida Atlantic U., 2003—. Former tchr., dean of students, asst. prin., prin. Martin County Sch. Dist.; chair task force Fla. Classrooms First; mem. development team Tech Prep program. Named Supt. of yr., Fla. Legislature, 1992. Republican. Office: Florida Atlantic Univ / Off of Pres Adminstrn Bldg, Rm # 339 777 Glades Rd Boca Raton FL 33431-0991 Office Phone: 561-297-3450. Office Fax: 651-297-2777.

BROGAN, MICHAEL SPENCER, physical therapist, educator; s. Robert Frederick and Iris Brogan; m. Victoria Murphy, 1978; children: Kelly, Michael. MS in Health Behavioral Scis., SUNY, Buffalo, 1989, PhD, 2005; D in Phys. Therapy, Daemen Coll., 2004. Cert. wound specialist Am. Acad. Wound Mgmt., 1998. Asst. prof. Daemen Coll., Amherst, NY, 1985—89, assoc. prof. phys. therapy, 1989—, chair phys. therapy, 2000—04, dean health and human services, 2005—. Clin. specialist Cath. Health Systems, Buffalo, 2002—. With N.Y. Air Nat. Guard, 1976—82. Grantee, Dept. Def., 2005—. Fellow: Coll. Cert. Wound Specialists; mem.: Am. Phys. Therapy Assn. (licentiate Robert Salant Rsch. award 1996, 2002). Achievements include patents for antifungal device. Office: Daemen College 4380 Main St Amherst NY 14226 Home Phone: 716-825-1730; Office Phone: 716-839-8413. Office Fax: 716-839-9314; Home Fax: 716-839-8314. Business E-Mail: mbrogan@daemen.edu.

BROGAN, STEPHEN (STEVE) J., lawyer; b. NYC, 1952; AB, Boston Coll., 1974; JD, Univ. Notre Dame, 1977. Bar: DC 1977. Dep. asst. atty. gen. US Dept. of Justice, Washington, 1981—83; ptnr.-in-charge Jones Day, Washington, 1989—2002, mng. ptnr., 2003—, and chair adv. com. and partnership com. Chair, adv. com. Jones Day, chair, partnership com. Exec. editor Law Rev., Univ. Notre Dame, 1977. Office: Jones Day 51 Louisiana Ave NW Washington DC 20001-2113

BROGDEN, STEPHEN RICHARD, library director; b. Des Moines, Sept. 26, 1948; s. Paul M. and Marjorie (Kueck) B.; m. Melinda L. Raine, Jan. 1, 1983; 1 child, Nathan. BA, U. Iowa, 1970, MA, 1972. Caretaker Eya Fechin Branham Ranch, Taos, N.Mex., 1970-72; dir. Harwood Found. U. N.Mex., Taos, 1972-75; vis. lectr. U. Ariz., Tucson, 1975-76; rd. mgr. Bill and Bonnie Hearne, Austin, Tex., 1976-79; head fine arts Pub. Libr. Des Moines, 1980-90; dep. dir. Thousand Oaks (Calif.) Libr., 1990-99, dir., 1999—. Chair Met. Coop. Libr. Sys., 2001; bd. mem. Pacific Pioneer Broadcasters, 2005—. Author book revs., Annals of Iowa, 1980; columnist Taos News, 1973. V.p. Hospice of the Conejo, 2004—05; bd. dirs. Thousand Oaks Libr. Found., 1999—; bd. mem. Pacific Pioneer Broadcasters, 2005—. Mem. ALA, Calif. Libr. Assn., Films for Iowa Librs. (pres. 1983-86), Metro Des Moines Libr. Assn. (pres. 1980). Office: Thousand Oaks Libr 1401 E Janss Rd Thousand Oaks CA 91362-2199 Office Phone: 805-449-2660. Business E-Mail: sbrogden@mx.tol.lib.ca.us.

BROGDEN-STIRBL, SHONA MARIE, writer, researcher; b. Tuscaloosa, Ala., Sept. 3, 1948; d. Edward Henry Jr. and Esther Ruth (Coleman) Brogden; m. Robert Clark Stirbl, Mar. 30, 1990. BA, U. South Ala., Mobile, 1972; MA in English (Poetics), NYU, 1982, postgrad. Adult protective social worker Mobile County Dept. Pensions and Security, 1972-74; child protection social worker Cumberland County Child Protective Svcs., Fayetteville, NC, 1975-76; cmty. placement specialist S.I. Devel. Ctr., 1976-78, Manhattan Borough Devel. Svc., NYC, 1978-80; adminstr. Coun. on Internat. Ednl. Exch., NYC, 1981, Office of Univ. Devel., Advt. and Pub. Affairs, NYU, NYC, 1982-85; dir. advt. Office of Advt. and Pub. Affairs, NYU, NYC, 1986; cons. Meml. Sloan-Kettering, NDRI, NYU, NYC, 1986-97. Voice recorder Book on Tape, Jewish Braille Inst., NYC, 1996; adminstrv. support Gay Men's Health Crisis, NYC, 1986; vol. Serendipity Sch. for Emotionally Disturbed Children, Sacramento, 1975; Strasberg Theatre Inst., 1977-78; founding mem. Tell It Like It Was, 1999, Ft. Bragg Semi-Reperatory Theatre Co., 1975-76, Dixie Darlings, 1966-67. Scholar NYU, 1978-82, U. So. Miss., 1966-68. Mem.: Caltech Women's Club. Christian. Achievements include patent photographic films with multiple ASA and associated camera. Avocations: poetry, art, acting, baroque violin, options trading. Home and Office: 465 S Madison #109 Pasadena CA 91101 Business E-Mail: s.brogden.1@alumni.nyu.edu.

BROGDON, BYRON GILLIAM, radiologist, educator; b. Ft. Smith, Ark., Jan. 22, 1929; s. Paul Preston and Lela Florence (Gilliam) B.; m. Barbara Walkow Schreiber, June 23, 1978; 1 child, David Pope; stepchildren: William and Diane Schreiber. BS, U. Ark., 1951, BS in Medicine, 1951, MD, 1952. Intern Univ. Hosp., Little Rock, 1952-53, resident, 1953-55; resident in radiology N.C. Bapt. Hosp., Winston-Salem, 1955-56; asst. prof. radiology U. Fla., 1960-63; assoc. prof. radiology and radiol. scis., radiologist-in-charge diagnostic radiology div. Johns Hopkins U. and Hosp., 1963-67; prof., chmn. dept. radiology U. N.Mex., 1967-77; from prof. chmn. radiology to prof. emeritus U. South Ala., Mobile, 1978—96, prof. emeritus, 1996—. Sabbatical leave Univ. Coll., Galway, Ireland, 1988; cons. in forensic radiology Office Med. Exam. State Ala., 1989—; coord. internat. diagnostic course in Davos, 1984-96; trustee Forensic Sci. Found., 2001—, vice-chair, 2003-04; mem. adv. bd. The Virtopsy Found., Bern, Switzerland, 2006-. Author: Opinions, Comments and Reflections on Radiology, 1983, Forensic Radiology, 1998, a Radiologic Atlas of Abuse and Torture, Terrorism, and Inflicted Trauma (winner Highly Commended Med. Book Competition award 2003); contbr. articles to med. jours. Mem. adv. bd. Vintopsy Found., Bern, Switzerland, 2006—. Maj. USAF, 1953—60. Finalist Ann. Telly awards, 2004; recipient Disting. Alumnus award U. Ark., 1978, Ark. Travelers Commn. award Gov. of Ark., 1985, Disting. Achievement award Wake Forest U. Med. Alumni Assn., 1990, medal from city of Brescia, Italy, 1991, Joint Resolution of Commendation for outstanding profl. achievement Ala. Legis., 1994, Medal of Honor Leopold-Franzens U., Innsbruck, Austria, 1997, Republic of Austria Cross of Honor for Sci. and Arts 1st class, 2002, Highly Commended award, Brit. Med. Assn., 2003. Fellow Am. Coll. Radiology (pres. 1978-79, gold medal 1987), Am. Acad. Forensic Scis. (John B. Hunt award 1995, Disting. Fellow award 2001), Assn. Forensic Radiographers Gt. Britian (patron); mem. AMA (ho. of dels. 1988-95, Physician-Spkr. award 1979), Am. Roentgen Ray Soc. (life, exec. coun. 1974-75, 77-80, 84-90, 2d v.p. 1979-80, gold medal 1996), So. Radiol. Conf. (life hon., pres. 1967-68, sec. 1984-96, Eskridge lectr. 1994), Radiol. Soc. N.Am., Am. Assn. Acad. Chief Residents in Radiology (faculty advisor 1979-2002, nat. sponsor 1983-93, Malcolm Jones orator 1996), Soc. Pediat. Radiology, Assn. Univ. Radiologists (pres. 1973-74, gold medal 1985), Soc. Chmn. Acad. Radiol. Depts. (sec.-treas. 1969-70), Swiss Soc. Med. Radiology (hon., Schinz medal 1992), Internat. Skeletal Soc. (medal 2001), Country Club Mobile, Sigma Xi, Alpha Omega Alpha, Sigma Chi (Significant Sig 1999). Office: Dept Radiology Univ S Ala Med Ctr 2451 Fillingim St Mobile AL 36617-2238 Home: 149 Batre Ln Mobile AL 36608 Home Phone: 251-344-3069; Office Phone: 251-471-7868. Business E-Mail: gbrogdon@usouthal.edu. *For the physician-scientist-educator, the mere transference of knowledge or the acquisition of new data is not enough. He must participate fully in the affairs of the larger community and has a duty to help others to think about, or form an opinion on, issues they otherwise might not have considered.*

BROGDON, W.M., lawyer; b. Columbia, SC, Oct. 14, 1953; s. Wallace M. and Helen (Deloach) B.; m. Cynthia S. Brogdon, Feb. 28, 1987; 1 child, Emily Elizabeth. BS in Biology magna cum laude, Ga. So. U., 1976; JD cum laude, Mercer U., 1982. Bar: Ga. 1982. Law clk. to Hon. B. Avant Edenfield U.S. Dist. Ct. (so. dist.) Ga.; ptnr. Smith & Brogdon Attys., Savannah, Ga., 1983-87, Brannan & Brogdon Attys., Claxton, Ga., 1987-93, Franklin, Taulbee, Rushing & Brogdon, P.C., Statesboro, Ga., 1994-2000; sole practitioner, 2000—. Contbr. articles to profl. jours. Chmn. bd. trustees Bulloch Acad. Sch., Statesboro, 1998—; bd. govs. Mercer U. Law Sch., 1979-81. Named to Rosa Parks Wall of Tolerance, 2005; State of Ga. law scholar, 1980. Mem. ATLA, Am. Bd. Trial Advocates, Ga. Trial Lawyers Assn. (chmn. Amicus com. 1996-98, v.p. mid. cir. 1996-97), Atlantic Cir. Bar Assn. (pres. 1991-92), Ogeechee Cir. Bar Assn. (pres. 1996-97), Nat. Bd. Trial Advocacy (cert.), Am. Bd. Trial Advocates, Rotary (treas. 1992-93), Phi Delta Phi. Methodist. Avocation: fishing. Home: 4599 Country Club Rd Statesboro GA 30458-9007 Office: PO Box 189 Statesboro GA 30459-1002 Home Phone: 912-489-2038; Office Phone: 912-764-6668. Personal E-mail: rowebrog@frontiernet.net.

BROGLIATTI, BARBARA SPENCER, retired television and motion picture executive, consultant; b. LA, Jan. 8, 1946; d. Robert and Lottie Spencer; m. Raymond Haley Brogliatti, Sept. 19, 1970. BA in Social Scis. and English, UCLA, 1968. Asst. press. info. dept. CBS TV, LA, 1968-69, sr. publicist, 1969-74; dir. publicity Tandem Prodns. and T.A.T. Comm. (Embassy Comm.), LA, 1974-77, corp. v.p., 1977-82; sr. v.p. worldwide publicity, promotion and advt. Embassy Comm., LA, 1982-85; sr. v.p. worldwide corp. comm. Lorimar Telepictures Corp., Culver City, Calif., 1985-89; pres., chmn. Brogliatti Co., Burbank, Calif., 1989-90; sr. v.p. worldwide TV publicity, promotion and advt. Lorimar TV, 1991-92; sr. v.p. worldwide TV publicity, promotion and pub. rels. Warner Bros., Burbank, 1992-97; sr. v.p. corp. comm. Warner Bros., Inc., 1997-2000; sr. v.p., chief corp. comm. officer Warner Bros. Entertainment Inc., 2000—04; exec. v.p., chief corp. comm. officer Warner Bros., 2004—05. Pub. rels. cons. Alliance of Motion Picture and Television Prodr., 1980—; advisor com. acad. advanced program UCLA, 2002—; bd. govs. UCLA Found., 2003—; adj. prof. comm. Bradley U., Peoria, Ill., 2006—; cons. pub. rels. Alliance of Motion Picture and TV Prodrs., 1980—. Mem. bd. govs. TV Acad., LA, 1984-86, UCLA Found., 2003—; bd. dir. Nat. Acad. Cable Programming, 1992-94; mem. Hollywood Women's Polit. Com., 1992-93; mem. steering com. LA Free Clinic, 1997-98. Recipient Gold medal Broadcast Promotion and Mktg. Execs., 1984. Mem. Am. Diabetes Assn. (bd. dir. LA chpt. 1992-93), Am. Cinema Found. (bd. dir. 1994-98), Dir. Guild Am., Publicists Guild, Acad. TV Arts and Scis. (vice chmn. awards com.); adv. com. UCLA Acad. Advancement Prog.

BROHN, WILLIAM DAVID, conductor, orchestrator, arranger; b. Flint, Mich. BA in Music, Mich. State U., 1955; MMus, New Eng. Conservatory Music. Played with local ensembles and performed on double bass Boston Pops Orch.; played string bass and piano with numerous musical orgns. including classical, theatrical and jazz groups; condr. nat. tours Robert Joffrey Ballet, Royal Ballet; commd. to adapt and arrange program piece for ann. Christmas concert Cleve. Orch., 1961; recreated sound track for 1938 Russian classic film Alexander Nevsky, 1987; vis. lectr. Oxford U., England. Orchestrated score Miss Saigon, 1991—2001, The Secret Garden, 1991—93, Crazy for You, 1992—96, Carousel, 1994—95, Show Boat, 1994—97, Ragtime, 1998—2000, High Society, 1998, Minnelli on Minnelli, 1999—2000, Sweet Smell of Success, 2002, Wicked, 2003—, ballet orchestration for Agnes de Mille, Twyla Tharp, Lar Lubovich, Am. Ballet Theatre, movie score for Blue Thunder, Endless Love, War Games, Whose Life is it Anyway?, rec. for James Galway Wind Beneath My Wings, rec. for Placido Domingo The Broadway I Love, rec. for Jerry Hadley Golden Days, rec. for Marilyn Horne The Men in My Life, orchestrator West End revival of Lionel Barts Oliver. Recipient Tony award for orchestrations for Ragtime, N.Y. Drama Desk award for Miss Saigon, N.Y. Drama Desk award for The Secret Garden. Office: c/o Gershwin Theatre 222 W 51st St New York NY 10019

BROIDE, MACE IRWIN, public information officer; b. Burlington, Vt., May 21, 1924; s. Abraham A. and Ida (Rosenberg) B.; m. Gloria Leah Goldsholl, Dec. 24, 1943; children: Cheryl Ruth Broide Light, Beverly Elaine Broide Frye, Sandra Pat Broide Banas. AB (Ernie Pyle scholar 1946), Ind. U., 1947. Polit. editor Evansville (Ind.) Press, 1947-58; chief staff U.S. Senate, 1959-68; co-owner DeHart and Broide, Inc.; public affairs cons. Washington, 1968-78; chief staff budget com. U.S. Ho. Reps., 1978—86; pub. affairs cons., 1986-99; ret., 1999. Adj. prof. George Washington U., 1986, 87; lectr. in field. Co-author: Inside the New Frontier, 1963; contbr. articles to newspapers, mags. Sec. Nat. Dem. Senatorial Campaign Com., 1961-62; past bd. dirs. Jewish Community Coun. Evansville; past bd. govs. Nat. Dem. Club. With AUS, 1943-46. Decorated Silver Star, Bronze Star. Mem. Assn. Adminstrv. Assts. U.S. Senate (past pres.), B'nai B'rith (past pres.). Home: 4450 S Park Ave Apt 1111 Chevy Chase MD 20815-3641 Personal E-mail: glomace25@msn.com.

BROIDO, ARNOLD PEACE, music publishing company executive; b. NYC, Apr. 8, 1920; s. Samuel S. and Ruth (Lewis) B.; m. Lucille Janet Tarshes, Mar. 5, 1944; children: Jeffrey, Laurence, Thomas. BS magna cum laude, Ithaca Coll., 1941, DMus (hon.), 1990; MA, Columbia U., 1954. Tchr. instrumental music East Jr. H.S., Binghamton, NY, 1941—42; editor, prodn. mgr. Boosey & Hawkes Inc. (music pub.), 1945—55; v.p., gen. mgr. Century Music & Mercury Music Corp., 1955—57; edn. dir. Edward B. Marks Music Corp., 1957—62; dir. publs. and sales Frank Music Corp., 1962—69; v.p. Boston Music Co., 1968—69; pres. Theodore Presser Co., 1969—95, chmn., 1995—; also dir.; chmn. Elkan-Vogel Inc., 1970—. Pres. Music Industry Coun., 1966-68, v.p., 1969-70; dir., sec. Harry Fox Agy., 1989-2000, sec.-treas., 2000—. Co-author: Music Dictionary, 1956, Invitation to the Piano, 1959; assoc. editor: Univ. Soc. Ency. of Piano Music; contbr. articles to profl. jours. Mem. Nassau County (NY) Dem. Com., 1952-63; bd. dirs. NY Citizens Com. for Pub. Schs., 1963-68, Am. Music Ctr., 1968-72, 78-83, 85-91, Am. Music Conf., 1979-80, Nat. Music Coun., 1979-85, 93—, Music Educators Nat. Conf., 1966-68; trustee ASCAP Found., 1976—, treas., 1990—; trustee Union Free Sch. Dist. 21 Bd. Edn., Rockville Centre, NY, 1963-69, sec., dist. clk., 1966-67, v.p., dist. clk., 1967-69. With USCGR, 1942-45. Recipient Disting. Alumnus award Ithaca Coll., 2001; Lowell Mason fellow MENC, 2003. Mem. ASCAP (bd. dirs. 1972—, bd. rev. 1980-82, asst. treas. 1989-90, treas. 1990—), Music Pubs. Assn. U.S. (pres. 1972-74, 80-82, bd. dirs. 1980-82, 83-92, 96-2005), Nat. Music Pubs. Assn. (bd. dirs. 1980—, sec. 1989—, treas. 2000—), Internat. Pubs. Assn. (v.p. sect. music 1972-73), Internat. Confederation Music Pubs. (v.p. 1978-88, bd. dirs. 1992-07, pres. 1993-94, chmn. 1994-96, pres. 1996-98, chmn. 1998-2003, v.p. 2003-07), Internat. Fedn. Serious Music Pubs. (v.p. 1978-93, 2003-07, pres. 1993-2003), Music Industry Mfrs. Assn. (dir. 1980-82), Charles Ives Soc. (bd. dirs. 1985-2003), Phi Mu Alpha Sinfonia. Office: 588 N Gulph Rd King Of Prussia PA 19406 Home: 3300 Darby Rd Apt C101 Haverford PA 19041-1094 Office Phone: 610-592-1222 ext 218. Personal E-mail: broidoa@aol.com.

BROITMAN, SELWYN ARTHUR, microbiologist, educator, assistant dean; b. Boston, Aug. 30, 1931; s. Julius Z. and Sara (Sallus) B.; m. Barbara Merle Shwartz, June 13, 1953; children: Caryn Beth, Jeffrey Z. BS, U. Mass., 1952, MS, 1953; PhD, Mich. State U., 1956. Dir. Biotech. Assocs., 1959—62; rsch. instr. dept. pathology Boston U. Sch. Medicine, 1963—64, asst. prof. dept. microbiology, 1965—69, assoc. prof. dept. microbiology, 1969—75, prof., 1975—, prof. pathology and lab. medicine, 1983—, asst. dean med. sch. admissions, 1983—, asst. dean divsn. grad. med. sci., 2007—; assoc. prof. nutritional scis. Henry Goldman Sch. Grad. Dentistry Boston U., 1974—. Assoc. medicine dept. medicine Harvard Med. Sch., 1969-74; spl. sci. staff pathology Boston Med. Ctr., 2000-; rsch. assoc. Mallory Inst. Pathology, Boston City Hosp., Gastro Intestinal Rsch. Lab., 1956-71; assoc. in medicine Thorndike Meml. Lab., 1969-74; chair, co-chair of various admission programs Boston U. Sch. Medicine; adv.-at-large Acad. of Advisors, 2003 Contbr. articles to profl. jours. Founding mem. Digestive Disease Found. Served with USAR 373d Gen. Hosp., 1952-66. Recipient Outstanding Teaching award Boston U. Sch. Medicine 1st Yr. Class, 1976 Fellow Am. Coll. Gastroenterology; mem. AAAS, NAS (com. diet, nutrition and cancer 1980-83), Am. Soc. Investigative Pathology, Am. Soc. Nutritional Scis., Am. Assn. Cancer Rsch., Am. Fedn. Med. Rsch., Am. Soc. Microbiology, Soc. Exptl. Biology and Medicine, Nutrition Today Soc. (founding), Am. Gastroent. Assn., Boston Gastroent. Soc., N.Y. Acad. Scis., Boston Bug Club (pres. 1976), Sigma Xi. Achievements include development of post grad program, MA in med. scis., leading to MD, DMD or PhD degree 1986; research in adverse effects of prophylactic antibiotics on human gut flora; role of gut endotoxin in development of liver cirrhosis; rare variant of systemic mastocytosis in a female patient; lactase deficiency following Salmonella infection; protocol for the management of massive small bowel resection; relationship of intestinal absorption of dietary disaccharides to gut enzyme disaccharidase levels; pathogenicity of parasitic disease Giardiasis; toxin mediated Clindamycin Colitis in experimental animals. Office: Boston U Sch Medicine Divsn Grad Med Scis L 317 715 Albany St Boston MA 02118 Office Phone: 617-638-5255. Personal E-mail: sabroitma@hotmail.com. *When problems cannot be resolved by the minds of this generation, the solutions must be sought in the minds of the next. The challenge is to find these young people, encourage them, and wherever possible, remove all obstacles to their learning.*

BROKAW, CLIFFORD VAIL, III, investment banker; b. NYC, Sept. 17, 1928; s. Clifford Vail and Audrey (Stransom Joel) B.; m. Elizabeth Stokes Rogers, June 29, 1960; children: Clifford Vail IV, George Rogers BA, Yale U., 1950; JD, U. Va., 1956. Bar: NY 1957, U.S. Dist. Ct. 1959, U.S. Supreme Ct. 2002. Assoc. White & Case, NYC, 1956-59; assoc. Blyth & Co., Inc., NYC, 1959-61; assoc., then gen. ptnr. W.E. Hutton & Co., NYC, 1961-67; gen. ptnr., sr. v.p. Eastman Dillon Union Securities & Co. and successor firm Blyth, Eastman, Dillon & Co., Inc., NYC, 1967-77; chmn., CEO Invail Capital, Inc., NYC, 1977-95; CEO IRT Corp., San Diego, 1977-95, chmn. bd., 1986-94. Bd. dirs., chmn. fin. com. Brazos River Gas Co., Mineral Wells, Tex., 1962-91; chmn. bd. Cayman Resources Corp., Tulsa, 1977-88, bd. dirs., 1992-95. Bd. advisors Marine Mil. Acad., Harlingen, Tex., 1985-91; mem. alumni assn. coun. U. Va. Sch. Law, 1976-79; founder Brokaw chair corp. law U. Va. Sch. Law, 1985, mem. dean's coun., 1990—, bus. adv. coun., 1995—; mem. indsl. adv. com. Sch. Engring and Applied Sch. U. Va., 1987-94; vestryman French Ch. du St. Espirit, 1986-88, treas., 1988-92, warden, 1989-93. Lt. col. USMCR, 1950-73. Decorated Purple Heart Mem. ABA, Suffolk County Bar assn., Pilgrims U.S., Mil. Order Carabao, Mil. Order World Wars, Mil. Order Fgn. Wars U.S., Mil. Order of Purple Heart, Nat. Inst. Social Scis. (bd. dirs. 1991-94, pres. 1992-94), Nat. Gavel Soc., Ends of Earth, Huguenot Soc. Am. (coun. 1974-80, v.p. 1986-89, pres. 1989-92), Am. Soc. Order of St.

John (comdr.), U. Va. Lawn Soc., Brook Club, Burning Tree Club, The Meadow Club, Bathing Corp. of Southampton, Union Club (N.Y.C.), Masons, Shriners, Yale Club (N.Y.C.), Delta Theta Phi. Republican. Episcopalian. Avocations: tennis, golf. Office: PO Box 5002 Southampton NY 11969-5002

BROKAW, NORMAN ROBERT, talent agency executive; b. NYC, Apr. 21, 1927; s. Isadore David and Marie (Hyde) B.; children: David M., Sanford Jay, Joel S., Barbara M., Wendy E., Lauren Quincy. Student pvt. schs., Los Angeles. With William Morris Agy., Inc., Beverly Hills, Calif., 1943—, sr. agt. and co. exec., 1951-74, v.p. world-wide ops., 1974-80, exec. v.p., dir., 1980—, co-chmn. bd., 1986-91, pres., CEO, 1989-91, chmn. bd., CEO, 1991-97, chmn. bd. worldide, 1997—. Pres. Betty Ford Cancer Ctr., Cedars-Sinai Med. Ctr., L.A., 1978—; bd. dirs. Cedars-Sinai Med. Ctr.; industry chmn. United Jewish Welfare Fund, 1975. With U.S. Army, World War II. Mem. Acad. Motion Picture Arts and Scis., Hillcrest Country Club (L.A.). Clients, past and present, include former Pres. and Mrs. Gerald R. Ford, Bill Cosby, Gen. Alexander Haig Jr., Gen. Claudia Kennedy, Tony Randall, Donald Regan, Senator John Edwards, Senator James Jeffords, Attorney David Boies, C. Everett Koop, Kim Novak, Priscilla Presley, Andy Griffith, Juliette Lewis, Marcia Clark, Christopher Darden; former clients included Marilyn Monroe, Barbara Stanwyck, Susan Hayward. Office: William Morris Agy 1 William Morris Pl Beverly Hills CA 90212-2775 also: William Morris Agy Inc 1325 Avenue Of The Americas New York NY 10019-6026

BROKAW, TOM (THOMAS JOHN BROKAW), former network news anchor; b. Webster, SD, Feb. 6, 1940; s. Anthony Orville and Eugenia (Conley) B.; m. Meredith Lynn Auld, Aug. 17, 1962; children— Jennifer Jean, Andrea Brooks, Sarah Auld. BA in Polit. Sci, U. SD, 1962, degree (hon.), Washington U., St. Louis, Syracuse U., Hofstra U., Boston Coll., Emerson Coll., Simpson Coll., Duke U., 1991, Notre Dame U., 1993, U. Pa., Fairfield U., Brandeis U., Dartmouth Coll., Fla. State U.; DHL (hon.), Dartmouth Coll., 2005. Radio reporter, 1959—62; morning news editor Sta. KMTV, Omaha, 1962-65; news editor, anchorman Sta. WSB-TV, Atlanta, 1965-66; reporter, corr., anchorman Sta. KNBC-TV, Los Angeles, 1966-73; White House corr. NBC, Washington, 1973-76; anchorman Sat. Night News, NYC, 1973-76; host Today show, NYC, 1976-82; anchorman, editor NBC Nightly News with Tom Brokaw, 1982—2004. Corr. NBC coverage US Presdl. elections, 1976, 80, anchor, 84, 88, 92, 96, 2000, 04; corr. Exposé, 1991; anchor The Brokaw Report, 1992—93; co-anchor Now with Tom Brokaw and Katie Couric, 1993—94. Corr. numerous NBC News specials, including To Be A Teacher, 1987, Wall Street: Money Greed and Power, 1987, A Conversation with Mikhail S. Gorbachev (Alfred I. DuPont award), 1987, Home Street Home, 1988, To Be An American (George Foster Peabody award), Tom Brokaw Reports: Why Can't We Live Together, 1997 (Alfred I. duPont - Columbia U. award); Author: The Greatest Generation, 1998, The Greatest Generation Speaks, 1999, An Album of Memories, 2001, A Long Way From Home, Growing Up in the American Heartland in the Forties and Fifties, 2003. Trustee Norton Simon Mus. Art, Pasadena, Calif., U. SD Found., Am. Mus. Natural History; adviser Asia Soc.; mem. bd. vistors, Howard U., Sch. Comm.; bd. dir. Coun. Fgn. Relations; mem. Com. to Protect Journalists Named to TV Hall of Fame, 1997, Acad. TV Arts & Sciences Hall of Fame, 2006; recipient Peabody award, Emmy award for reporting on floods in the Midwest, 1992, Emmy award for Internat. Coverage of the Kosovo conflict, 1999, 7 Emmy awards, Nat. Headliner award, Nat. Conf. Christians and Jews, 1990, Dennis Kauff Meml. award for Lifetime Achievement in Journalism, Boston U., 1995, Lowell Thomas award, Marist Coll., 1995, U. Mo.-Columbia Sch. Journalism Honor medal for Distinguished Svc. in Journalism, 1997, Fred Friendly First Amendment award, 1998, Am. Legion award for Distinguished Pub. Svc. in the field of Comm., 1998, "Tex" McCrary Excellence in Journalism award, Congl. Medal of Honor Soc., 1999, Four Freedoms medal: Freedom of Speech and Expression, 2005, Edward R. Murrow Sch. Comm. Lifetime Achievement in Broadcasting award, Washington State U., 2006, Sylvanus Thayer award, Assn. Graduates of the US Military Acad., West Point, NY, 2006. Mem.: AFTRA (dir. 1968—72), Am. Acad. Arts and Sciences, Reporters Com. for Freedom of Press (mem. adv. com.), Sigma Delta Chi.

BROKKE, CATHERINE JULIET, retired mission executive; b. Mpls., Dec. 25, 1926; d. Emil John and Alma (Brye) Eliason; m. Harold Joseph Brokke, Sept. 9, 1949; 1 child, Daniel. Diploma in nursing, Luth. Deaconess Hosp., Mpls., 1947; student, Concordia Coll., Moorhead, Minn., 1948-49, Bethany Coll. Missions, Mpls., 1949-51. RN, Minn. Sch. and occupational nurse Bethany Fellowship, Mpls., 1951-75; missions sec. Bethany Fellowship Missions, Mpls., 1963-86, dir., 1986-96, retired, 1996. Instr. Bethany Coll. Missions, 1950-88. Mng. editor Message of Cross, 1990-97; composer hymns. Organist Bethany Missionary Ch., Bloomington, Minn., 1956-89; trustee STEM Ministries, 1995-2000, bd. dirs. Mem. Evang. Fellowship of Mission Agys. (trustee 1987-93), Evang. Missions Info. Svc. (bd. dirs. 1994-96). Avocations: piano, organ. Personal E-mail: cathybrokke@att.net.

BROLIN, JAMES (JAMES BRUNDERLIN), actor; b. Los Angeles, July 18, 1940; m. Jane Cameron Agee, 1966 (div. 1984); children: Josh, Jess; m. Jan Smithers, 1986 (div. 1995); 1 child, Molly; m. Barbra Streisand, 1998. Student, UCLA. Regular in TV series The Monroes, 1964-65, Marcus Welby M.D, 1969-76, Hotel, 1983-88, Extreme, 1995, (also exec. prodr.) Pensacola: Wings of Gold, 1997, The West Wing, 2002; host Beyond Belief: Fact of Fiction, 1997, Body Human 2000: Love, Sex and the Miracle of Birth, 1999; TV movie appearances include Marcus Welby M.D, 1969, Short Walk to Daylight, 1972, Class of '63, 1973, Trapped, 1973, Steel Cowboys, 1978, The Ambush Murders, 1982, Mae West, 1982, White Water Rebels, 1983, Cowboy, 1983, Beverly Hills Cowgirl Blues, 1985, Hold the Dream, 1986, Intimate Encounters, 1986, Deep Dark Secrets, 1987, Finish Line, 1989, Voice of the Heart, 1990, Nightmare on the 13th Floor, 1990, And the Sea Will Tell, 1991, Visions of Murder, 1993, Gunsmoke: The Last Ride, 1993, Parallel Lives, 1994, Hijacked: Flight 285, 1996, Marriage of Convenience, 1998, To Love, Honor & Betray, 1999, Skyscrapers: Going Up, 2000, Children of Fortune, 2000, The Reagans, 2003, Widow on the Hill, 2005, Category 7: The End of the World, 2005, Wedding Wars, 2006; film appearances include Take Her, She's Mine, 1963, Goodbye, Charlie, 1964, Von Ryan's Express, 1965, Morituri, 1965, Our Man Flint, 1966, The Boston Strangler, 1968, Skyjacked, 1972, Westworld, 1973, Gable and Lombard, 1976, The Car, 1977, Capricorn I, 1978, Night of the Juggler, 1978, Amityville Horror, 1978, The Gringos, 1980, Pee Wee's Big Adventure, 1985, Indecent Behavior II, The Expert, 1994, Tracks of a Killer, 1995, Terminal Virus, 1995, Last Chance, 1995, Blood Money, 1996, (also dir.) My Brother's Way, 1997, Haunted Sea, 1997, Goodbye America, 1997, Lewis & Clark & George, 1997, Traffic, 2000, The Master of Disguise, 2002, Catch Me If You Can, 2002, A Guy Thing, 2003, The Alibi, 2006. Named Most Promising Actor of 1970 Fame mag., Photoplay mag.; recipient Emmy award. Avocations: licensed pilot, horse breeding, designed and built several homes, a restaurant and a bookstore. Office: Metropolitan Talent Agency 4500 Wilshire Blvd Fl 2 Los Angeles CA 90010-3858*

BROLIN, ROBERT EDWARD, physician, surgeon; b. Holland, Mich., Apr. 12, 1948; s. Edward Magnusson Brolin and Louise A. Mann; children: Lucinda, Brian. BA, DePauw U., Greencastle, Ind., 1970; MD, U. Mich., Ann Arbor, 1974. Diplomate Am. Bd. Surgery. Asst. prof. surgery U. Medicine & Dentistry N.J.-Robert Wood Johnson Med. Sch., New Brunswick, 1980-84, assoc. prof. surgery, 1984-89, prof. surgery, 1989-2000, U. Pitts. Med. Sch., 2001—. Mem. Am. Coll. Surgeons, Am. Soc. Bariatric Surgery (pres. 2000-01), Am. Soc. Clin. Nutrition, N.Am. Assn. Study of Obesity, Soc. Univ. Surgeons, Soc. Surgery of Alimentary Tract. Avocations: jogging, stamp collecting/philately, duplicate bridge. Office: NJ Bariatrics Ste 1 4250 US Rte 1 Monmouth Junction NJ 08852 Office Phone: 732-274-3434. Business E-Mail: rbrolin@njbariatricspc.com.

BROM, ROBERT H., bishop; b. Arcadia, Wis., Sept. 18, 1938; Student, St. Mary's Coll., Winona, Minn., Gregorian U., Rome. Ordained priest Roman Cath. Ch., 1963, consecrated bishop Roman Cath. Ch., 1983. Bishop of Duluth, Minn., 1983—89; coadjutor bishop Diocese of San Diego, 1989—90, bishop, 1990—. Office: Diocese of San Diego Pastoral Ctr PO Box 85728 San Diego CA 92186-5728

BROMAN, PER FREDRIK, education educator; b. Norrkoping, Sweden, July 26, 1962; s. Allan Fredrik and Marianne Elsa Gunvor Broman; m. Nora Anne Engebretsen, Apr. 22, 1968. M in Music Edn., Ingesund Coll. of Music, Sweden, 1987; Post-Grad. Diploma, Royal Coll. of Music, Stockholm, 1992; MA, McGill U., Can., 1995; PhD, Gothenburg U., 1999. Asst. prof. Lulea U. of Tech., Pitea, Sweden, 1992—97, Butler U., Indpls., 1999, Bowling Green State U., 2003—. Author: (scholarly articles) Jour. of the Swedish Musicological Soc., Grove Dictionary of Music and Musicians, (scholarly book) Back to the Future: Towards and Aesthetic Theory of Bengt Hambraeus; editor: (book) Crosscurrents and Counterpoints, (scholarly book) What Kind of Music Theory?. Sgt. Marines, 1982—83, Sweden. Grantee, Sweden Am. Found., 1990, 1991, 1994. Mem.: Swedish Musicological Soc., Coll. Music Soc., Can. U. Music Soc., Soc. for Music Theory (bd. mem., midwest chpt. 2002—), Am. Musicological Soc. Business E-Mail: pbroman@bgsu.edu.

BROMBACHER, BRUCE E., mathematics educator; b. Bucyrus, Ohio, July 3, 1948; s. Willard W. and Aurelia R. (Beisheim) B.; m. Marcia L. Mertz, June 9, 1973; children: Ryan E., Erin E. BS, Heidelberg Coll., 1970; MS, Ohio State U., 1975. Tchr. Upper Arlington (Ohio) Schs., 1976—. Sgt. U.S. Army, 1970-72, Vietnam. Named Nat. Tchr. Yr., 1982. Mem. NEA, Ohio Edn. Assn., Upper Arlington Edn. Assn., Nat. Coun. Tchrs. Math., Ohio Coun. Tchrs. Math., Ohio Mid. Sch. Assn., Sch. Sci. and Math. Assn., Columbus and Suburban Coun. Tchrs. of Math., Math. Assn. Am., Nat. State Tchrs. of Yr., Nat. Mid. Sch. Assn., Phi Delta Kappa, Kappa Delta Phi. Methodist. Home: 291 Electric Ave Westerville OH 43081-2676*

BROMBERG, ALAN ROBERT, lawyer, educator; b. Dallas, Nov. 24, 1928; s. Alfred L. and Juanita (Kramer) B.; m. Anne Ruggles, July 26, 1959. AB, Harvard U., 1949; JD, Yale U., 1952. Bar: Tex. 1952. Assoc. firm Carrington, Gowan, Johnson, Bromberg and Leeds, Dallas, 1952-56, atty., cons., 1956-76; of counsel firm Jenkens & Gilchrist, P.C., 1976—2007. Asst. prof. law Southern Meth. U., 1956-58, assoc. prof., 1958-62, prof., 1962-83, mem. presdl. search group, 1971-72, disting. prof., 1983—; faculty advisor Southwestern Law Jour., 1958-65; counsel Internat. Data Systems, Inc., 1961-65, sec., dir., 1963-65; mem. Tex. Legis. Council Bus. and Commerce Code Adv. Com., 1966-67; vis. prof. Stanford U., 1972-73; mem. adv. bd. U. Calif. Securities Regulation Inst., 1973-78, 79-87. Author: Supplementary Materials on Texas Corporations, 3d edit, 1971, Partnership Primer-Problems and Planning, 1961, Materials on Corporate Securities and Finance— A Growing Company's Search for Funds, 2d edit, 1965, Securities Fraud and Commodities Fraud, Vols. 1-7, 1967-93, 2nd edit., 2000-06, Crane and Bromberg on Partnership, 1968, Bromberg and Ribstein on Partnership, Vols. 1-4, 1994-2007, Bromberg and Ribstein on Limited Liability Partnerships and the Revised Uniform Partnership Act, 1997-2007; mem. ednl. publs. adv. bd., Matthew Bender & Co., 1977-95, chmn., 1981-94; contbr. articles and revs. to law and bar jours.; adv. editor: Rev. Securities and Commodities Regulation, 1969—, Securities Regulation Law Jour, 1973—, Jour. Corp. Law, 1976—, Derivatives: Tax, Regulation, Finance, 1995-97, SMU Law Rev., 1978-. Sec., bd. dirs. Cmty. Arts Fund, 1963-73; gen. atty. Dallas Mus. Contemporary Arts, 1956-63; bd. dirs. Dallas Theater Center, 1955-73, sec., 1957-66, fin. com., 1957-65, mem. exec. com., 1957-70, 79-85, life, 1973— , v.p., trustee endowment fund, 1974-85; trustee Found. for the Arts, 1996—. Served as cpl. U.S. Army, 1952-54. Sr. fellow, Yale U. Law Faculty, 1966—67. Mem. ABA (coms. commodities, partnerships, fed. regulation securities), Dallas Bar Assn. (chmn. com. uniform partnership act 1959-61, libr. com. 1981-83), Tex. Bar Assn. (chmn. sect. corp. banking and bus. law 1967-68, vice chmn. 1965-67, com. corps. 1957—, mem. com. securities 1965—, chmn. 1965-69, mem. com. partnerships 1957—, chmn. 1979-81), Am. Law Inst. (life), Southwestern Legal Found. (co-chmn. securities com. 1982-85), Tex. Bus. Law Found. (bd. dirs. 1988—, co-chmn. legis. com. 1994—). Office: So Meth U Dedman Sch Law Dallas TX 75275-0116 also: 1445 Ross Ave Ste 3200 Dallas TX 75202-2785

BROMBERG, DEBRA, financial analyst, investment advisor; BA, Hunter Coll.; MBA, NYU. Dir. Standard & Poor's Debt Rating Div.; securities analyst PaineWebber; sr. analyst Goldman Sachs; v.p., mem. elec. utility rsch. group Jefferies & Co., NYC, 2000—. Named an All-Star Analyst, Wall St. Jour.; named one of Top Stock Pickers, Forbes Mag. Mem.: Wall Street Utility Group, NY Soc. Security Analysts. Office: Jefferies & Co 520 madison Ave New York NY 10022*

BROMBERG, JOHN E., lawyer; b. Dallas, May 9, 1946; s. Edward S. and Mildred J. (Rosenberg) B.; children from previous marriage: Spencer Harkness, Whitney Payne, Kemp Howitt, Campbell Wynne; m. Beth Jenkins; children: Susan Elizabeth, Melissa Anne. BA, Columbia U., 1968; JD, U. Tex., 1972. Bar: Tex. 1972. Atty. Johnson, Bromberg, Leeds & Riggs, Dallas, 1972—83; chmn. Stutzman, Bromberg, Esserman & Plifka, P.C., Dallas, 1984—. Dir. Tex. Commerce Bank, Dallas, 1983—92; adv. dir. Dallas Adv. Bd. Dir. Chgo. Ins. Co., 1985—94; dir. subs. Tchr. Ins. Annuity Assoc., Tex., 1989—2001. Past pres. Preston Hollow Pk. Assn., pre-sch. playground, Dallas. Named one of Best Lawyers in Dallas, D Mag., 2005. Mem.: State Bar Tex., ABA, Am. Contract Bridge League (past pres. Dallas Unit). Office: Stutzman Bromberg Esserman & Plifka 2323 Bryan St Ste 2200 Dallas TX 75201-2655 Office Phone: 214-969-4923. Office Fax: 214-969-4999. E-mail: bromberg@sbep-law.com.*

BROMBERG, LEE CARL, lawyer; b. Chgo., Sept. 25, 1943; s. Alex Roscoe and Gertrude (Markey) B.; m. Pamela Starr, 1969; children: Sarah, Katherine. BA, U. Mich., 1965; MA, Cornell U., 1966; JD, Harvard U., 1969. Bar: N.Y. 1970, Mass. 1972. Assoc. Rosenman & Colin, NYC, 1969-72; clin. assoc. prof. law Boston U., 1972-75; gen. counsel Mass. Dept. Correction, Boston, 1975-79; spl. asst. atty. gen. Mass. Dept. Atty. Gen., Boston, 1979-95; ptnr. Bromberg & Sunstein, Boston, 1979—. Mem. ABA, Mass. Bar. Assn., Boston Bar Assn., Boston Patent Law Assn. (pres. 2007). Office: Bromberg & Sunstein LLP 125 Summer St Boston MA 02110-1618 Office Phone: 617-443-9292. Business E-Mail: lbromberg@bromsun.com.

BROMBERG, MYRON JAMES, lawyer; b. Paterson, NJ, Nov. 5, 1934; s. Abraham and Elsie (Baker) B.; m. Lisa Murtha, Nov. 28, 1987; children— Kenneth Karl, Eric Edward, Bruce Abraham. BA, Yale U., 1956; LLB, Columbia U., 1959. Bar: N.J. bar 1960, N.Y. bar 1981. Law asst. to dist. atty., NY County, 1958; law asst. U.S. atty. So. Dist. N.Y., 1958-59; assoc. mem. firm Ralph Porzio, Morristown, NJ, 1960-61; ptnr. Porzio, Bromberg & Newman, Morristown, 1962—97, mng. prin., 1980-96. Atty. Morris County Bd. Elections, 1963-64; town atty., Town of Morristown, 1965-67; lectr. trial practice Rutgers Inst. CLE, 1965-94; mem. faculty Kraft-Eidson trial techniques seminar Emory U., 1997-2003. Chmn. fund and membership Morristown chpt. ARC, 1965; chmn. retail div. Cmty. Chest Morris County, 1963; chmn. Keep Morristown Beautiful Com., 1963; mem. Morris Twp. Com., 1970-72; committeeman Morris County Dem. Com., 1962-63, 72-77; lay trustee Delbarton Sch., Morristown, 1972-75; trustee Morris Mus., 1973-79; mem. bd. visitors Columbia Law Sch., 2005-07. Fellow Am. Coll. Trial Lawyers (chmn. com. on admission to fellowship 1986-91, com. on complex litigation 1992-98, com. on tchg. of trial and appellate advocacy 1998-2004), Am. Law Inst. (cons. group product libility), Am. Bar Found. (life); mem. ABA, Internat. Acad. Trial Lawyers (chair NJ 1997-99, regional chair 3d jud. cir. 1997-2000, bd. dirs. 2002-07), NJ Bar Assn. (named outstanding young lawyer 1970, chmn. joint conf. com. with NJ Med. Soc. 1970-72), Morris County Bar Assn., Am. Judicature Soc., Trial Attys. NJ (pres. 1976-77, Trial Bar award 1989), Internat. Soc. Barristers (NJ State chmn., bd. govs., sec.-treas. 1996-97, v.p. 1998-00, pres. 2000-01), Found. Internat. Soc. Barristers (pres. 2002-07), Internat. Assn. Def. Counsel (chair com. on toxic and hazardous substances 1994-96, dir. Def. Counsel Trial Acad. 1996), Andover Alumni Assn. NYC, Columbia U. Law Sch. Assn. NJ (bd. dirs. 1986-95, 2001—), Phillips Acad. Alumni Coun., Yale Club (NYC and ctrl. NJ), Chi Phi, Phi Delta Phi Home: 9 Thompson Ct Morristown NJ 07960-6326 Office: PO Box 1997 100 Southgate Pkwy Morristown NJ 07962-1997 Home Phone: 707-785-3910; Office Phone: 973-538-4006. E-mail: mjbromberg@pbnlaw.com.

BROMBERGER, ALLEN RICHARD, lawyer; b. Princeton, NJ, May 1, 1955; s. Sylvain and Nancy (Lilienthal) Bromberger; m. Lauren Goldstein; children: Michael Barrows, Abigail Florence, Eliza Lee. BA, U. Calif., Berkeley, 1978; JD, U. Calif., San Francisco, 1982. Bar: Calif. 1982, N.Y. 1983. Dir. legal assistance Coun. N.Y. Law Assocs., NYC, 1983-85, assoc. dir., 1985-88, dir. nonprofit law program, 1988-90; exec. dir. Lawyers Alliance for N.Y., NYC, 1990-99; pres. Power of Attorney, NYC, 1999—2005; of counsel Perlman & Perlman, Esq., NYC, 2005—. Bd. dirs. Lawyers Com. Against Violence, N.Y.C., 1996-98, Interlegal USA, N.Y.C., 1994—, Cause Effective, N.Y.C., 1994-2000, Coalition for the Homeless, N.Y.C., 1994-96; mem. IRS Exempt Orgns. Liaison Com., 1993-99. Editor, author: Getting Organized, 1986, 5th edit., 2000, Advising Nonprofits, 1988, 4th edit., 1995. Mem. ABA, Assn. Bar City N.Y., Nat. Assn. Pro Bono Coords. (exec. com. 1996-98), N.Y. State Advisory Task Force on Corps., 1997-99. Office: Perlman & Perlman LLP 41 Madison Ave New York NY 10001-5010 Office Phone: 212-889-0575. Business E-Mail: allen@perlmanandperlman.com.

BROMBERT, VICTOR HENRI, literature educator, author; b. Germany, Nov. 11, 1923; came to U.S., 1941, naturalized, 1943; s. Jacques and Vera B.; m. Beth Anne Archer, June 18, 1950; children: Lauren Nora, Marc Alexis. BA, Yale U., 1948, MA, 1949, PhD, 1953; postgrad., U. Rome, 1950-51; HHD (hon.), U. Chgo., 1981, U. Toronto, 1997. Faculty Yale U., New Haven, 1951-75, from assoc. prof. to prof., 1958-75, Benjamin F. Barge prof. Romance lits., 1969-75, chmn. dept. Romance langs. and lit., 1964-73; Henry Putnam univ. prof. romance and comparative lit. Princeton (N.J.) U., 1975—99, dir. Christian Gauss seminars in criticism, 1984-94, chmn. Coun. Humanities, 1989-94. Summer prof. Middlebury Coll., 1951-53, Institut d'Etudes Françaises, Avignon, 1962, 64, 73, U. Colo., 1965; Christian Gauss Seminar in criticism Princeton U., 1964; vis. prof. Scuola Normale Superiore, Pisa, Italy, 1972, U. Calif., 1978, Johns Hopkins U., 1979, Columbia U., 1980, NYU, 1980-81, U. P.R., 1983, 84, U. Bologna, Italy, 1984, Yale U., 1985; Phi Beta Kappa vis. scholar, 1986-87, 89-90; lectr. Alliance Française, humanities U. Kans., 1966; lectr. Collège de France, 1991; mem. Fulbright screening com., 1965; dir. fellowships in residence NEH, Princeton U., 1975-76, dir. summer seminar, 1979, 82, 84, 86, 88; adv. com. for humanities Libr. of Congress, 1976; mem. Yale U. Coun., 1977-83; ednl. adv. bd. Guggenheim Found., 1982—2005. Author: (Literary Critiques) The Criticism of T. S. Eliot, 1949, Stendhal et la Voie Oblique, 1954, The Intellectual Hero, 1961, The Novels of Flaubert, 1966, Stendhal: Fiction and the Themes of Freedom, 1968, Flaubert par lui-même, 1971, La Prison Romantique, 1976, The Romantic Prison: The French Tradition, 1978, Victor Hugo and the Visionary Novel, 1984, The Hidden Reader, 1988, In Praise of Antiheroes, 1999, Trains of Thought: Memories of a Stateless Youth, 2002, Les Trains du Souvenir: Paris-New York-Omaha Beach-Berlin, 2005; editor: Stendhal: A Collection of Critical Essays, 1962, Balzac's La Peau de Chagrin, 1962, The Hero in Literature, 1969, Flaubert's Madame Bovary, 1969; contbg. author: Literary Critiques The World of Lawrence Durrell, 1962, Ideas in the Drama, 1964, Malraux, 1964, Instants Premiers, 1973, Romanticism, 1973, Literary Criticism, 1974, Die Romanische Novelle, 1977, The Author in His Work, 1978, Essais sur Flaubert, 1979, Writers and Politics, 1983, Flaubert and Postmodernism, 1984, Writing in a Modern Temper, 1984, Literary Theory and Criticism, 1984, Hugo le Fabuleux, 1985, 19th Century Literary Criticism, 1985, Charles Baudelaire, 1987, Albert Camus, 1989, André Malraux, 1989, Gustave Flaubert, 1989, Dilemmes du Roman, 1989, Nineteenth Century French Poetry, 1990, Literature, Culture and Society in the Modern Age, 1991, Literary Generations, 1992, Dix Etudes sur Baudelaire, 1993, George Sand et son temps, 1994, Pratiques d'écriture, 1996, Stendhal et le comique, 1999, 500 Years of Theater History:, 2000, Le Metamorfosi del Ritratto, 2002, Les Modernités de Victor Hugo, 2004, Le bonheur de la littérature, 2005; contbr. articles to profl. jours. Served with M.I. AUS, 1943-45. Decorated comdr. Ordre des Palmes Académiques; recipient Harry Levin prize in comparative lit., 1978, Howard T. Behrman award for disting. achievement in humanities, 1979, Wilbur Lucius Cross medal for outstanding achievement, Yale Univ., 1985, Médaille Vermeil de la Ville de Paris, 1985, The Pres. award for disting. tchg., 1999; fellow Fulbright fellow, 1950—51, Guggenheim fellow, 1954—55, 1970, sr. fellow, NEH, 1973—74, Rockefeller found. resident fellow, Bellagio, Italy, 1975, 1990; grantee Am. Coun. Learned Socs., 1966. Fellow Am. Acad. Arts and Scis.; mem. MLA (editl. adv. comm. 1979-83, pres. 1989), Am. Assn. Tchrs. French, Am. Comparative Lit. Assn., Am. Philos. Soc., Soc. des Etudes Françaises, Soc. des Etudes Romantiques, Acad. Lit. Studies (pres. 1983), Soc. d'Histoire Littéraire de la France, Soc. U. per gli Studi di Lingua e Letteratura Francese, Inst. Romance Studies, Elizabethan Club (pres. 1968-70), Yale Club, Phi Beta Kappa. Home: 49 Constitution Hill W Princeton NJ 08540-6774

BROME, THOMAS REED, lawyer; b. NYC, Aug. 24, 1942; s. Robert Harrison and Mary Elizabeth (Reed) B.; m. Marie Olszewski, June 5, 1971; children: Clinton Reed, Bethan, Heather. AB, Harvard Coll., 1964; LLB, NYU, 1967. Bar: DC 1967, NY 1968. Law clk. to hon. Warren E. Burger U.S. Ct. Appeals, Washington, 1967-68; assoc. Cravath, Swaine & Moore LLP, NYC, 1968-75, ptnr., 1975—. Dir. Legal Aid Soc., NYC, 1989-98, pres., 1994-96. Mem. sch. bd., Ridgewood, NJ, 1989—92, pres., 1991—92; trustee NYU Law Ctr. Found., NY, 1992—, The Valley Hosp., Ridgewood, NJ, 2005—; pres. Ridgewood Pub. Edn. Found., NJ, 1993—96; vice chair NYU Law Ctr. Found., NY, 2001—. Mem. ABA, NY State Bar Assn., Assn. Bar of City of NY Republican. Episcopalian. Office: Cravath Swaine & Moore LLP Worldwide Plz 825 8th Ave New York NY 10019-7475 Office Phone: 212-474-1307. Office Fax: 212-474-3700. Business E-Mail: tbrome@cravath.com.

BROMLEY, BENJAMIN C, physics professor; m. Isabel Dulfano; children: Sarah, Maia, Rebecca, Isaac. BA, Middlebury Coll., Vt., 1982; MS, U. Vt., Burlington, 1997; PhD, Dartmouth Coll., Hanover, NH, 1994. Postdoctoral rschr. Los Alamos Nat. Lab., N.Mex., 1994—96; postdoctoral fellow Harvard U., Cambridge, Mass., 1996—98; from asst. prof. to prof. U. Utah, Salt Lake City, 1998—. Grad. Student Rschrs. Program scholar, NASA, 1994—94. Mem.: Am. Phys. Soc. Achievements include research in planet formation, astrophysical black holes, physical cosmology. Home:

3245 E Oakcliff Dr Salt Lake City UT 84124 Office: Univ Utah Dept Physics 115 S 1400 E Salt Lake City UT 84112 Home Phone: 801-558-2605; Office Phone: 801-581-8227. Business E-Mail: bromley@physics.utah.edu.

BROMLEY, BRUCE DITMAS, language educator, writer; b. NYC, Sept. 23, 1956; s. Stephen Baldwin and Patricia Ann B. Student, Berklee Coll. Music, 1976-80; BA in English with honors, Columbia U., 1995; postgrad., NYU, 1995—. Poetry workship asst. dir. Phillips Brooks House Harvard U., Cambridge, Mass., 1976-80; instr. in compositional analysis Berklee Coll. Music, Boston, 1978-84; poetry reading supr. Shakespeare and Co., Paris, 1985-92; instr. English lit. Columbia U., NYC, 1993-95; instr. expository writing program NYU, 1996—2003, lang. lectr. in expository writing, 2003—. Mentor in expository writing program NYU, 2000—03, lectr., 2003—. Author: (play) Sound for Three Voices, 1986, poems; composer (score and piano) Hamlet; composer, playwright in residence Oxford U. Theatre Troupe, Edinburgh Theatre Festival, Scotland, 1986-87; contbr. poems to Gargoyle Mag. Instr. Earl Hall G.E.D. program Columbia U., N.Y.C., 1995—. Recipient Master Tchr. award NYU, 2000-03, award of excellence, 2003-07, Golden Dozen award for tchg. excellence NYU, 2006; Mohlberger fellow in English Lit., 2000-01. Mem. Princeton Club, Phi Beta Kappa. Home: PO Box 1573 East Hampton NY 11937-0704 Office Phone: 212-998-8861. Business E-Mail: bdb4945@nyu.edu.

BROMLEY, MARILYN MODLIN, librarian; b. Cleve., Mar. 14, 1951; d. Robert A. and Helen F. (Hicks) Modlin; m. Haworth P. Bromley, Nov. 7, 1987. BA magna cum laude, Randolph-Macon Woman's Coll., 1973; MSLS, Cath. U. Am., 1978. Librarian ICF Inc., Washington, 1978-83, Bur. Nat. Affairs Inc., Washington, 1983—94, libr. dir., 1994—. Editor: Direct-Line Distances: U.S. Edition, 1986, Direct-Line Distances: International Edition, 1986, BNA's Directory of State Courts, Judges and Clerks, 1986. Recipient Dialog Corp. Infostar award, 2002. Mem. Spl. Librs. Assn. (treas. Washington chpt. 1984-87, 96-99, bd. dirs. 1988-90, v.p., pres.-elect 1991-92, pres. 1992-93, bylaws com. 2001-03, legal divsn. program planning, Denver, 2007), Phi Beta Kappa, Beta Phi Mu. Episcopalian. Office: Bur Nat Affairs Inc 1801 Bell St Arlington VA 22202 Office Phone: 703-341-3303. Business E-Mail: mbromley@bna.com.

BROMLEY, RICHARD, lawyer; b. Rosetown, Sask., Feb. 8, 1944; s. Arthur Amos and Elsie Anna Freda (Frerichs) B.; m. Marilyn Kay Bill, Aug. 12, 1966; children: Douglas Arthur, Shannon Kimberly, Lindsay Erin. BA, U. Iowa, 1966, JD, 1968. Bar: Iowa 1968, Ill. 1969, US Tax Ct., US Ct. Claims, US Ct. Appeals (5th, 7th, 8th, 10th, fed. cirs.), US Supreme Ct. Ptnr. Foley & Lardner LLP, Chgo. Lectr. Law Sch., DePaul U., Chgo., 1984-89; adj. prof. Kent. Coll. Law, Ill. Inst. Tech., Chgo., 1987-89; sr. v.p., bd. dirs. Ins. Tax Conf. Editor: Iowa Law Rev., 1967-68; bd. advisors Ins. Tax Law Rev., 1989—. Vice chmn., bd. dirs. Chgo. Crime Commn., 1993-2007; sec., bd. dirs. Lookingglass Theatre. Mem. ABA (chmn. com. on taxation of ins. cos.), Fed. Bar Assn. (ins. co. tax com.), Chgo. Bar Assn. (exec. coun. fed. tax com.), Legal Club Chgo., Union League Club, Waushara Country Club (Wautoma, Wis.), Order of Coif. Lutheran. Office: Foley & Lardner LLP 321 N Clark St Ste 2800 Chicago IL 60610-4764 Office Phone: 312-832-4517. Business E-Mail: rbromley@foley.com.

BROMLEY, STEPHEN C., zoology educator; b. LA, Aug. 31, 1938; s. Karl F. and Fae Christensen Bromley; m. Wendy McGarry, Oct. 1968 (div. Oct. 1995); children: John Axel, Anna Ruth, Joseph Jacob, James Asa, Jane Alexis, Stephen Calder. BS, Brigham Young U., Provo, Utah, 1960; AM, Princeton U., NJ, 1962, PhD, 1965. Instr. dept. biology Princeton U., 1964-65; asst. prof. dept. zoology U. Vt., Burlington, 1965-69; rsch. assoc. dept. zoology Mich. State U., East Lansing, 1969-70, assoc. prof. dept. zoology, 1970-76, prof. dept. zoology, 1976—, dir. biol. sci. program, 1970-91, dir. The Conservatory, 1988-90. Mem.: AAAS. Avocations: handball, wood working, music, athletic conditioning, target shooting. Office: Dept Zoology Mich State Univ East Lansing MI 48823 Home: 684 W 3430 South Logan UT 84321 Business E-Mail: sbromley@msu.edu.

BROMSTAD, ANGELA, broadcast executive; married; 2 children. B, U. So. Calif. Asst. Telepictures Productions; dir. creative affairs Freyda Rothstein Productions, 1988—91, v.p. creative affairs, 1991—94; dir. miniseries & motion pictures for television NBC Entertainment, 1994—96, v.p. miniseries & television, 1996; v.p. miniseries & motion pictures for television NBC Studios, 1997—99, v.p. primetime series, 1999—2000, v.p. drama devel., 2000, sr. v.p. drama devel., 2000—03, exec. v.p., 2003—04; co-pres. NBC Universal TV Studio (name changed to Universal Media Studios, 2007), 2004—05, pres., 2005—07. Named one of 100 Most Powerful Women in Entertainment, Hollywood Reporter, 2006. Office: NBC Universal Studios 100 Universal City Plz Universal City CA 91608 Office Phone: 818-777-1000.*

BROMUND, ALICE A., retired elementary school educator; b. Mar. 24, 1943; d. Frank and Louise Vobora; m. Henry A. Cannon, Feb. 14, 1969 (div. July 1979); 1 child, Tracy Ann Young. BA in Humanities, Biola U., 1966. Primary grades tchr., Allendale, 1967—68; tchr. grades 1-2 San Ysidro Sch. Dist., Calif., 1968—70; tchr. sch. dist. grades 1-8 Gorman, Calif., 1970—76; tchr. grade 2 Alpharetta, Ga., 1976—77; kindergarten tchr. Menifee Sch. Dist., Sun City, Calif., 1980—96, 1997—2001; kindergarten tchr., bilingual resource tchr. North Sacramento Sch. Dist.; kindergarten tchr. San Bernardino (Calif.) Unified Sch. Dist., 2001—03; instrnl. tutor K-5, Natomas Sch. Dist., Sacramento, 2006. Nominee Walt Disney Tchr. Am., 1999. Mem.: Calif. Ret. Tchrs. Assn. Personal E-mail: alice_bromund@yahoo.com.

BROMWELL, LINDA ANNE, librarian, writer; BA in Recreation Adminstrn., Calif. State U., 1974; BA in Edn., Western Wash. U., 1977; MA in Nonprofit Mgmt., Regis U., 2003. Cert. tchr. Wash., 1977. Tchr. Archdiocese Seattle, Mount Vernon, Wash., 1977—81; academic instr. Cascades Job Corps Ctr., Sedro-Woolley, Wash., 1988—91; adminstr. Skagit Valley Regional Ministry, Mount Vernon, Wash., 1994—98; coord. tng. ChildCare Resource & Referral, Everett, Wash., 1999—2001; libr. JD Ross Libr., Rockport, Wash., 2002—05; ind. writer Soap Lake, Wash., 2005—. Author: English Grammar Basics, 2005. Chmn. Girl Scouts - Totem Coun., Mt. Vernon, W.Va., 1988—94; liturgy chair Immaculate Heart of Mary Ch., Sedro-Woolley, Wash., 1990—96. Mem.: Alpha Sigma Nu. Independent. Roman Catholic. Avocations: reading, outdoors, travel, theater.

BROMWICH, MICHAEL RAY, lawyer; b. LA, Dec. 19, 1953; s. Leo and Rose (Meyer) B.; m. Felice B. Friedman, Dec. 27, 1980; children: Daniel R., Jonah E., Kira A. AB summa cum laude, Harvard Coll., 1976; MPP, JD, Harvard U., 1980. Assoc. Foley & Lardner, Washington, 1980-83; asst. U.S. atty. U.S. Attys. Office, (so. dist.) N.Y., NYC, 1983-87; assoc. counsel Office of Ind. Counsel, Iran-Contra, Washington, 1987-89; spl. counsel Office Ind. Counsel, Iran-Contra, Washington, 1990, 91; ptnr. Mayer, Brown & Platt, Washington, 1989-93; insp. gen. Dept. Justice, Washington, 1994-99; ptnr. Fried, Frank, Harris, Shriver & Jacobson, Washington and NYC, 1999—. Mem. Pres. Coun. on Integrity and Efficiency, 1994-99. Mem. Phi Beta Kappa. Jewish. Office: Fried Frank Harris Shriver & Jacobson 1001 Pennsylvania Ave NW Ste 800 Washington DC 20004 also: One New York Plz New York NY 10004 Office Phone: 202-639-7297. Personal E-mail: mrbromwich@hotmail.com. Business E-Mail: michael.bromwich@friedfrank.com.

BRON, GUILLERMO (BILL BRON), lending company executive; b. Costa Rica; BS, MIT, 1973; MBA, Harvard U., 1975. Mng. dir. corp. fin. and mergers & acquisitions Drexel Burnham Lambert; founder United PanAm Fin. Corp., 1994, now chmn.; also founder Bastion Capital Fund, 1994. Office: United PanAm Fin Corp Ste 200 3990 Westerly Pl Newport Beach CA 92660

BRONAUGH, EDWIN LEE, retired electrical engineer; b. Salina, Kans., July 22, 1932; s. Edwin and Violet Mary (Dryden) B.; m. Geraldine Kelley, Dec. 10, 1955: children: Cecilia Ann Bronaugh Snodgrass, Dana Lea Bronaugh Weinberg. BA in Physics, Math. and Language, Tex. A&M U., Commerce, 1955. Commd. USAF, 1955, advanced through grades to capt., 1961, various comm. and ops. assignments, 1955-68; major USAFR, 1968; rsch. scientist Southwest Rsch. Inst., San Antonio, 1968-70, sr. rsch. scientist, 1970-76, rsch. dir., 1976-82; dir. R & D, tech. dir. Electro-Metrics Divsn. Penril, Amsterdam, NY, 1982-89; prin. electromagnetic compatibility scientist Electro-Mechanics Co., Austin, Tex., 1989-92, v.p. engrng., 1992-94; prin. EdB EMC Cons., Austin, 1994—2004; lead engr. comm. devices divsn. Siemens Info. and Comm. Products, LLC, Austin, 1997-2000; ret., 2005. Author: Electromagnetic Interference Test Methodology and Procedures, 1988; contbr. over 150 articles to profl. jours.; patentee in field. Decorated Bronze Star, Air Force Commendation medal. Fellow IEEE (life; Third Millennium medal 2000); mem. IEEE Stds. Assn. (life), Electromagnetic Compatibility Soc. of IEEE (stds. com. 1980—, dir. tech. svcs. 1981-87, v.p. 1988-90, pres. 1990-92; Cert. of Appreciation 1979, Cert. of Achievement 1983, Cert. of Acknowledgement 1985, Richard R. Stoddart award 1985, Stds. Medallion 1992, Lawrence G. Cumming award 1992), Am. Nat. Stds. Inst. (vice chmn. accredited stds. com. C63 on electromagnetic compatibility 1986-2002, mem. emeritus C63 2002—), Electromagnetic Compatibility Soc. (hon. life.). Avocations: music, model railroads, engineering history, learning additional languages. Home and Office: 10210 Prism Dr Austin TX 78726-1364 Home Phone: 512-258-6687. Business E-Mail: ed.bronaugh@ieee.org.

BRONFIN, FRED, lawyer; b. New Orleans, Nov. 30, 1918; children: Daniel R., Kenneth A. BA, Tulane U., 1938, JD, 1941. Bar: La. 1941, U.S. Dist. Ct. (ea. dist.) La. 1941, U.S. Ct. Appeals (5th cir.) 1951, U.S. Supreme Ct. 1973. Assoc. Rittenberg & Rittenberg, New Orleans, 1946-50; ptnr. Rittenberg, Weinstein & Bronfin, New Orleans, 1950-60, Weinstein & Bronfin, New Orleans, 1960-63, Bronfin, Heller, Steinberg & Berins, Bronfin & Heller, New Orleans, 1963-91; of counsel Bronfin & Heller, 1991-98, Heller, Draper, Hayden, Patrick & Horn, 1998—. With USN, 1942-46. Mem. ABA, La. Bar Assn., New Orleans Bar Assn., Order of Coif, Phi Beta Kappa. Office: Heller Draper Hayden Et Al 650 Poydras St Ste 2500 New Orleans LA 70130-6175 Office Phone: 504-568-1888. Business E-Mail: fbronfin@hellerdraper.com.

BRONFMAN, CHARLES ROSNER, philanthropist, former distillery executive; b. Montreal, Que., Can., June 27, 1931; s. Samuel and Saidye (Rosner) B.; m. Andrea Morrison (dec. Jan. 23, 2006), 1982; children: Stephen Rosner, Ellen Jane. Student, McGill U., 1948-51; PhD (hon.), Hebrew U. Jerusalem, 1990; LLD (hon.), McGill U., 1990, Concordia U., 1992, U. Waterloo, 1995, U. Toronto, 2000; LHD (hon.), Brandeis U., 1992. With Seagram Co., Ltd., 1951—97, v.p., dir., 1958-71, exec. v.p., 1971-75, pres., 1975-79, dept. chmn., 1979-86, chmn. exec. com., 1975—97, co-chmn., 1986—97; chmn. Koor Industries Ltd., 1997—2002. Owner Montreal Expos, 1968-90; chmn. bd. Claridge-Israel Inc., CRB Found.; bd. dirs. Power Corp. Can.; trustee Brandeis U., Mt. Sinai Med. Ctr., Inc., NYC. Past pres. Allied Jewish Community Svcs., Montreal; life bd. govs. Jewish Gen. Hosp.; bd. dirs. Can. Coun. Christians and Jews; hon. chmn. Can.-Israel Securities Ltd. (State of Israel Bonds Can.); co-founder & chmn. Andrea & Charles Bronfman Philanthropies, Inc., 1986-; co-founder & vice-chmn. Birthright Israel, 2000-; co-founder Charles Bronfman Prize, 2002-. Inductee Can. Baseball Hall of Fame, 1985; named an Hon. Citizen, City of Jerusalem, 2002; named one of NY Influentials, NY Mag., 2006; recipient Officer, Order of Can., 1981, Companion, 1992, Queen's Privy Coun. Can., 1992 Mem. Montefiore (Montreal) Club, Mt. Royal (Montreal) Club, Saint-Denis (Montreal) Club, Elm Ridge Golf and Country (Montreal) Club, Palm Beach Country Club. Office: Brandeis U 415 South St Waltham MA 02454-9110 also: Mt Sinai Med Ctr Inc 1 Gustave L Levy Pl New York NY 10029*

BRONFMAN, EDGAR MILES, SR., retired liquor company executive; b. Montreal, June 20, 1929; naturalized, U.S., 1959; s. Samuel and Saidye (Rosner) Bronfman; m. Ann Loeb, Jan. 10, 1953 (div. 1973); children: Sam, Edgar Jr., Matthew, Holly, Adam; m. Lady Caroline Townshend (annulled Nov. 21, 1974). Student, Williams Coll., 1946—49; BA, McGill U., 1951; LHD (hon.), Pace U., 1982; LLD (hon.), Williams Coll., 1986. Chmn. Metro Goldwyn Mayer, 1969; chmn. adminstrv. com. Joseph E. Seagram & Sons, Inc., 1955-57, pres., 1957-71; chmn., CEO, pres. Distillers Corp.-Seagram Ltd., Montreal, 1971-75; chmn. The Seagram Co. Ltd. and Joseph E. Seagram & Sons Inc., 1975—94; co-founder Scandent Group (parent company, Cambridge Integrated Svcs. Group, Inc.), Cranbury, NJ, 1994—. Bd. dirs. Vivendi Universal, 2000—03, Am. Technion Soc.; pres. World Jewish Congress, 1979—2007. Author: (memoir) The Making of a Jew, 1996. Mem. citizens com. for N.Y.C. U.S.-USSR Trade and Econ. Coun.; chmn. Samuel Bronfman Found.; pres. N.Am. Consortium for Free Mkt. Study; mem. exec. com. Am. Jewish Congress, Am. Jewish Com.; mem. Bus. Com. for Arts United Jewish Appeals; hon. chmn. Fedn. Jewish Philanthropies; dir. Am. com. Weizmann Inst. Sci.; mem. fin. com. Nat. Urban League; mem. internat. adv. bd. Sch. Internat. and Pub. Affairs, Columbia U.; chmn. Anti-Defamation League, NYC; bd. dels. Union Am. Hebrew Congregation; bd. dirs. Am. Com. Weizmann Inst. Sci., Israel. Named Chevalier de la Légion d'Honneur, French Govt.; named one of World's Richest People, Forbes Mag., 1999—, Richest Americans, 1999—; recipient Presdl. Medal of Freedom, The White House, 1999. Mem.: Fgn. Policy Assn., Com. for Econ. Devel., Ctr. Inter-Am. Rels., B'nai B'rith (bd. overseers), Hundred Yr. Assn. N.Y., Coun. Fgn. Rels. Jewish.*

BRONFMAN, EDGAR MILES, JR., recording industry executive; b. NYC, May 16, 1955; With Seagram Co., 1983—2000, pres., 1989—2000, CEO, 1994—2000; vice chmn. Vivendi Universal, 2000—03; chmn., CEO Warner Music Group, 2004—. Gen. ptnr. Accretive Tech. Ptnrs., LLC; trustee NYU Medical Ctr.; bd. dir. IAC/InterActiveCorp, Fandango.com; bd. govs. U. Pa. Joseph H. Lauder Inst. Mgmt. & Internat. Studies. Prodr. films The Blockhouse, 1973, The Border, 1982; prodr. Broadway play Ladies of the Alamo, 1977. Chmn. bd. dirs. Endeavor Global. Office: Warner Music Group 75 Rockefeller Pl New York NY 10019*

BRONIAK, LYNN MARGUERITE, gifted and talented educator, technology educator; d. William Vincent Dapkus and Margaret Patricia Paralis; children: Jennifer, Sarah, Rachel, Theresa, Rebecca. BBA in accounting, U. Mich., 1976; MBA, Ind. U., 1980. Prof. Madonna U., Livonia, Mich., 1995—99; talented and gifted instr. Schoolcraft Coll., Livonia, Mich., 2001—; instr. Henry Ford CC, Dearborn, Mich., 2002—; program chair Coll. Bus. ITT Tech. Inst., Canton, Mich., 2003—. Substitute tchr. Our Lady of Good Counsel Sch., Plymouth, Mich., 2001—. Lectr., eucharistic minister Our Lady of Good Counsel Ch., Plymouth, Mich., 1990—. Republican. Roman Catholic. Avocations: jogging, golf, swimming. Home: 13565 Westbrook Plymouth MI 48170 Office: ITT Tech Inst 1905 S Haggerty Canton MI 48188 Office Phone: 734-397-7800 ext. 327. Personal E-mail: lmbroniak@aol.com. Business E-Mail: LBroniak@itt-tech.edu.

BRONIS, STEPHEN JAY, lawyer; b. Miami, Fla., Feb. 23, 1947; s. Larry and Thelma (Berger) B.; children: Jason Michael, Tyler Adam, Kenneth Lawrence. BSBA, U. Fla., Gainesville, 1969; JD, Duke U., Durham, NC, 1972. Bar: Fla. 1972, DC 1973, US Dist. Ct. (so. dist.) Fla. 1973, US Ct. Appeals (5th cir.) 1977, US Supreme Ct. 1978, US Ct. Appeals (11th cir.) 1981, US Dist. Ct. (mid. dist.) Fla. 1989, Colo. 1994, US Dist. Ct. Colo. 1996, US Ct. Appeals (10th cir.) 1996, US Tax Ct. 1998, US Dist. Ct. (no. dist.) Fla. 2006. Asst. pub. defender 11th Jud. Cir. Fla., Miami, 1972-75; ptnr. Rosen & Bronis, P.A., Miami, 1975-77, Rosen, Portela, Bronis, et al, Miami, 1977-82, Bronis & Potela, P.A., Miami, 1982-90; pvt. practice Miami, 1990-93; ptnr. Davis, Scott, Weber & Edwards, Miami, 1993-95, Zuckerman, Spaeder, LLP, Miami, 1996—. Mem. faculty Nat. Inst. of Trial Adv., U. NC, Yeshiva U, Nova Sch. Law; appointed to Fla. Supreme Ct. Commn. on Professionalism, 2000—; Fla. Bar rep. to 11th Cir. Jur. Conf., 2001-04. Contbr. articles to profl. jours. Recipient Am. Jurisprudence award Bancroft-Whitney Co., 1972. Mem. ABA (ho. of dels. 1999—, Fla. rep. 2000—, chmn. def. function com. of criminal justice sect. 2001-04, chmn. white collar crime com., 2004-06, exec. dir. white collar crime divsn. 2006-, criminal justice sect. coun. 2006-), ATLA, Nat. Criminal Def. Attys. Assn., Am. Bd. Criminal Lawyers (v.p. 1981-82), Fla. Criminal Def. Attys. Assn. (Outstanding Svc. award 1981), Calif. Attys. Criminal Justice, Acad. Fla. Trial Lawyers (criminal law sect. dir.). Democrat. Office: 201 S Biscayne Blvd Ste 900 Miami FL 33131-4326 Home: 1 Grove Isle Dr Apt 1707 Miami FL 33133-4106 Office Phone: 305-358-5000. Business E-Mail: sbronis@zuckerman.com.

BRONKAR, EUNICE DUNALEE, artist, educator; b. New Lebanon, Ohio, Aug. 8, 1934; d. William Dunham and Helen Kate (Hypes) Connor; m. Charles William Bronkar, Jan. 26, 1957; 1 child, Ramona. BFA, Wright State U., 1971, M in Art Edn., 1983, postgrad. art studies, 1989, Dayton Art Inst., 1972. Cert. art tchr., Ohio. Part time tchr. Springfield Mus. Art, Ohio, 1967—77; adj. instr. Clark State C.C., Springfield, 1974—84, lead tchr., 1984—94, adj. asst. prof., 1998—2000, asst. prof., 1989—94; ret., 1994; artist Urbana, Ohio, 1995—. Edn. chmn. Springfield Mus. Art, 1973-74; image banks participant, Ohio Arts Coun., Columbus, Visual Arts Network, Dayton, Ohio, 1994—; affiliated with The Art Ctr. of St. Augustine, Fla. Art Scene, Little Gallery, Springfield, Ohio, The Frame Haven Gallery and Frame Craft Gallery, Springfield, Ohio. One-woman shows include, Springfield, Ohio, Polo Club, Upper Valley Mall Cinema, Security Nat. Bank, Mr. C's Beauty Salon, Lakewood Beach, Clark State C.C., Dayton, Ohio, Miami Valley Hosp., High St. Gallery, Stoeffer's Restaurant, Wegerzyn Garden Ctr., Meml. Hall, Wright State Univ., Urbana, Ohio, Champaign County Arts Coun., Urbana Cinema, South Charleston, Ohio, Cmty. Park Dedication, Phillip Caldwell spl. guest spkr., exhibited in group shows at Springfield Mus. Art, 1999, Zanesville Ohio Art Ctr., 2000, accepted in over 100 area, state, regional, and nat. juried exhbns. including Wilson Gallery, Sidney Ohio and Ohio Water Color Soc. Ann. Travelling shows, 1983—84, 1986—87, We. Ohio Watercolor Soc. (Hon. Mention, 1983, 2001, Chase Patterson award, 1985, Spl. Merit award, 1990, 1st Pl., 1995, 3d Pl., 2005, 1st Pl., 2000, Merit award, 1997, 1998), Dayton Soc. Painters and Sculptors (Best of Show, 1974, 2000, 1st Pl. painting, 2d Pl. painting, 3d Pl. drawing, 1978, Hon. Mention, 1979, 3d Pl. graphic, 1980, Best of Show drawing, 1981, 1st Pl. pastel, 1981, 1st Pl. drawing, 1991, 3rd painting, 1993, 2nd drawing, 1993, Spl. Merit award for balance, 2001, Merit award, 2001, 2003), Champaign County Fair (Best of Show drawing, 1968, 1st pastel, 1968), 1st Painting, Miamisburg, Ohio, 2003 (1st Pl. Oil, 2003, Best of Show Drawing, 2003), Springfield Art Mus. Juried Annual Show, Represented in permanent collections, drawings and paintings in Am. Artist Renown, 1981, Shades of Gray, 1983, 1984, 1986, 1987, 1990, 1991, 1993, 1994, 1997. Cleaned and restored art collections at Springfield Pub. Schs., Hist. Soc. in Springfield, Logan County Hist. Soc., Champaign County Hist. Soc., Warder Pub. Libr., Foos Manor Bed & Breakfast, Masonic Temple, Penn House, Mus. Art in Springfield, 1970-2006, and Calumet Antiques, Yellow Springs, Ohio, other groups and numerous pvt. collections, 1970—; mem. adv. com. comml. art, Clark County JVS Sch., Springfield, 1991-2003; judge more than 10 pub. h.s. art shows, 1970s-90s; judge Logan County Fair Fine Art Show Ohio profl. and amateur, 1998, Champaign County Fair Art Show, 2001. Recipient awards Springfield Mus. of Art, Ohio, 1965, 68, 2d pastel, 1972, 2d pastel, 1st drawing, 1976, Juror's award pastel 1979, 1st drawing 1986, 3d drawing 1987, 2d drawing 1989, 1st drawing 1990, 91, 2d painting 1991, 2d painting 1991, 1st drawing 1992, 2d pastel 1998, 1st drawing 2000, medal Bicentennial Com. of Clarke County and 4H Found. of Ohio, Springfield, 1976, Outstanding Tchr. award Clark State Cmty. Coll., 1992, commd. to paint 2 past pres. Generals of atl. Soc. Daus. Am. Revolution, Continental Hall, Wash. Mem. Western Ohio Water Color Soc, Springfield Mus. of Art (Ohio), Dayton Soc. Painters and Sculptors, Cin. Art Club, Ohio Water Color Soc., Nat. Mus. Women in Arts, Ohio Plein Air Painters, Audubon Artists Soc., Pastel Soc., St. Augustine Art Assn. (Fla.), Portrait Soc. Ames, others. Avocations: swimming, walking, sewing, flower arranging, travel.

BRONKESH, ANNETTE CYLIA, public relations executive; b. Vineland, NJ, Dec. 18, 1956; d. Manasha and Miriam (Kutlan) B.; m. Steven Silver Schwartz, Aug. 18, 1985; children: Sarah, Emily, Julie. BA, NYU, 1979. Sr. editor Instnl. Investor, NYC, 1979; chief editor McGraw-Hill, NYC, 1980-85; dir. Am. Stock Exchange, NYC, 1985-87; v.p. pub. rels. Nikko Securities, NYC, 1987-90; pres. Bronkesh Assocs., Clifton, NJ, 1990—. Mem. 100 Women in Hedge Funds. Mem. Securities Industry Assn. (pub. rels. roundtable), Fin. Women's Assn. N.Y., Phi Beta Kappa. Avocation: piano. Office: Bronkesh Assocs 23 Virginia Ave Clifton NJ 07012-1222

BRONNER, FELIX, physiologist, biophysicist, educator, painter; b. Vienna, Nov. 7, 1921; arrived in U.S., 1937, naturalized, 1943; s. Maurice and Lotte (Vogler) B.; m. Leah Horowitz, Oct. 12, 1947; children: Deborah Rachel, Ethan Samuel. BS, U. Calif., Berkeley and Davis, 1941; PhD (Quaker Oats fellow 1950-52), MIT, 1952; student, Kans. State Coll., 1938; postgrad., U. Minn., 1943, U. Va., 1946; D (hon.), Ecole Pratique des Hautes Etud, Paris, 1996. Rsch. assoc. MIT, 1952-54; Helen Hay Whitney fellow, Arthritis and Rheumatism fellow, Rockefeller Inst. Med. Rsch., NYC, 1954-56, asst., 1956; dir. lab. mineral metabolism Hosp. for Spl. Surgery, NYC, 1957-63; asst. prof. Cornell U. Med. Coll., 1961-63; assoc. prof. physiology U. Louisville Sch. Medicine, 1963-69; prof. oral biology U. Conn., 1969-86, prof. nutritional scis., 1976-89, prof. biostructure and function, 1986-89, prof. emeritus, 1989—. Vis. scientist Weizmann Inst., Israel, 1965, 76, Varon vis. prof., 1988; vis. scientist Pasteur Inst., Paris, 1977, U. Cape Town Med. Sch., 1984, 88, MRC disting. vis. scientist, 1991; guest scientist INSERM, Paris, 1972, Lyon, France, 1988; cons. USPHS, 1965-68, 70-71, USDA, 1978-79, 2001—; vis. prof. Tel Aviv U. Sch. Medicine, 1976. Editor: (with C.L. Comar) Mineral Metabolism: An Advanced Treatise, 1960-69; (with A. Kleinzeller) Current Topics in Membranes and Transport, 1970-90; (with J. Coburn) Disorders of Mineral Metabolism, 1981-82; (with M. Peterlik) Calcium and Phosphate Transport Across Biomembranes, 1981; Epithelial Calcium and Phosphate Transport: Molecular and Cellular Aspects, 1984; Cellular Calcium and Phosphate Transport in Health and Disease, 1988; (with W.D. Stein) Cell Shape Determinants, Regulation, and Regulatory Role, 1989; (with D. Pansu) Calcium Transport and Intracellular Calcium Homeostasis, 1990; Intracellular Calcium Regulation, 1991; (with R V. Worrell) A Basic Science Primer in Orthopaedics, 1991; (with M. Peterlik) Extra- and Intracellular Calcium and Phosphate Regulation: From Basic Research to Clinical Medicine, 1992; Nutrition and Health-Topics and Controversies, 1996; Nutrition Policy in Public Health, 1997; (with R.V. Worrell) Orthopaedics: Principles of Basic and Clinical Science, 1999; Nutritional Aspects and Clinical Management of Chronic Disorders and Diseases, 2003, Nutritional and Clinical Management of Chronic Conditions and Diseases, 2005; (with Mary C. Farach-Carson) Bone Formation, vol. 1, Topics in Bone Biology, 2003, Bone Resorption, vol. 2, 2005, Functional Engineering of Skeletal

Tissues, vol. 3, 2006, Bone and Osteoarthritis, vol. 4, 2007; mem. editl. bd. Am. Jour. Clin. Nutrition, 1968-76, Am. Jour. Physiology, 1985-97, Jour. Nutrition, 1986-95; contbr. articles to profl. jours.; exhibited in one-man shows, numerous juried shows, reviewed in July, 2003 ARTnews. Pres. Bur. Jewish Edn., Louisville, 1968-69. Served with AUS, 1942-46. Recipient André Lichwitz prize, Nat. Inst. Health and Med. Rsch., France, 1974. Fellow AAAS, Am. Soc. Nutrition; mem. Am. Physiol. Soc., Biophys. Soc., Harvey Soc., Soc. Exptl. Biology and Medicine, Orthop. Rsch. Soc., Am. Fedn. Clin. Rsch., N.Y. Acad. Scis., Am. Soc. Bone and Mineral Rsch., Austrian Bone Soc. (hon.). Home: 33 Ferncliff Dr West Hartford CT 06117-1013 Office: U Conn Health Ctr Farmington CT 06030-6125 Office Phone: 860-679-2136. Business E-Mail: bronner@neuron.uchc.edu. *The past century has been bloody, one where entire peoples were murdered. But it has also been a period of great intellectual and artistic advances. I feel privileged to have survived and to have participated in the science and art of our time.*

BRONSON, MERIDITH J., lawyer; b. NYC, Dec. 4, 1958; d. Ira D. and Carolyn Bronson; children: Logan Alexa, Jordan Alanna. BA, Drew U., 1980; JD, Seton Hall U., 1984. Cert. matrimonial law atty., Supreme Ct. N.J. Jud. law clk., Newark, N.J., 1984-85; ptnr. Stern Steiger Croland, Paramus, 1985-95, Shapiro & Croland, Hackensack, N.J., 1995—. Master Family Law Inns of Ct., N.J., 1996-2004. Mem. ABA, ATLA, N.J. Bar Assn., Phi Beta Kappa. Office: Shapiro & Croland 411 Hackensack Ave Fl 6 Hackensack NJ 07601-6365 Office Phone: 201-488-3900.

BRONSON, MICHAEL J., lawyer; b. Cin., May 14, 1976; BA in Polit. Sci., Denison U., 1998; JD, Vanderbilt U. Law Sch., 2001. Bar: Ohio 2001. Clerk Chief Judge, US Dist. Ct. Eastern Dist. NC; assoc. Vorys, Sater, Seymour and Pease LLP, Cin. Mng. editor Vanderbilt Law Review. Named one of Ohio's Rising Stars, Super Lawyers, 2006. Office: Vorys Sater Seymour and Pease LLP Ste 2000 Atrium Two PO Box 0236 221 E Fourth St Cincinnati OH 45201-0236 Office Phone: 513-723-4492. Office Fax: 513-852-7807.

BRONSTEIN, ALVIN J., lawyer; b. Bklyn., June 8, 1928; LLD, N.Y. Law Sch., 1951, LLD (hon.), 1990. Bar: NY 1952, Miss. 1967, La. 1971, US Ct. Appeals (DC, 1st, 2d, 3d, 4th, 5th, 9th, 10th and 11th cirs.), US Supreme Ct. 1961. Ptnr. Bronstein & Bronstein, Bklyn., 1952-63; pvt. practice Elizabethtown, NY, 1963-64; chief staff counsel Lawyers Constl. Def. Com., Jackson, Miss., 1964-68; fellow Inst. Politics, Kennedy Sch. Govt. Harvard U., Cambridge, Mass., 1968-69, assoc. dir. Inst. Politics, Kennedy Sch. Govt., 1969-71; ptnr. Elie, Bronstein, Strickler & Dennis, New Orleans, 1971-72; exec. dir. Nat. Prison Project, Nat. Jail Project ACLU Found., Washington, 1972-96, cons. nat. legal dept., 1996—. Cons., trial counsel CORE, NAACP, NAACP Legal Def. Fund, SCLC, SNCC, Miss. Freedom Dem. Party, Black Panther Party, Nat. Inst. for Edn. in Law and Poverty, and others; guest lectr. various law schs., 1964—; cons. various state corrections depts., 1972—; adj. prof. Am. U. Law Sch., 1973; expert witness in various prison litigs., 1978—; apptd. mem. Fed. Jud. Ctr. Adv. Com. on Experimentation in the Law, 1978-81. Contbg. author: The Evolution of Criminal Justice, 1978, Prisoners' Rights Sourcebook, Vol. II, 1980, Confinement in Maximum Custody, 1980, Sage Criminal Justice Annual, Vol. 14, 1980, Readings in the Justice Model, 1980, Our Endangered Rights, 1984, Prisoners and the Courts: The American Experience, 1985; author: (with Rudovsky and Koren) The Rights of Prisoners, 1988; author, editor: Representing Prisoners, 1981; editor: Prisoners' Self-Help Litigation Manual, 1977; contbr. articles to profl. jours. MacArthur Found. fellow, 1989; named one of the 100 most influential lawyers in Am., Nat. Law Jour., 1985, 88, 91, 94; recipient Roscoe Pound award Nat. Coun. on Crime and Delinquency, 1981, Karl Menninger award Fortune Soc., 1982, Pa. Prison Soc. award, 1991. Office: Penal Reform Internat 1025 Vermont Ave NW Washington DC 20005 Office Phone: 202-686-6578. E-mail: alvbron@aol.com.

BRONSTEIN, ERIC H., surgeon; b. Bronx, NY, Jan. 26, 1962; BS with honors, SUNY, Stony Brook, 1983, MD with distinction, 1987. Diplomate Am. Bd. Surgery, Am. Bd. Thoracic Surgery, Nat. Bd. Med. Examiners, lic. physician N.J., N.Y., D.C. Resident in gen. surgery SUNY Health Sci. Ctr., Bklyn., 1987—93, rsch. fellow dept. surgery, 1989—91, chief resident in gen. surgery, 1993—94; fellow in cardiothoracic surgery George Wasjington U. Hosp., Washington, 1995—97; cardiothoracic surgery attending The Valley Hosp., Ridgewood, NJ, 1997—; asst. clin. prof. surgery Columbia U. Med. Ctr., NYC, 2003—. Contbr. articles to profl. jours. Recipient Golden Apple Tchg. award, Med. Student Assn.; James S. Mountain Meml. scholar. Fellow: Am. Coll. Surgeons; mem.: Bergen County Med. Soc., Soc. Thoracic Surgeons. Office: Valley Hosp 223 No Van Dien Ave Ridgewood NJ 07450 Home: 301 Lynn Dr Franklin Lakes NJ 07417 Office Phone: 201-447-8377. Office Fax: 201-447-8658. E-mail: broner@valleyhealth.com.

BRONSTEIN, LAURA, social worker, educator; b. NYC, Feb. 20, 1955; life ptnr. Chuck Schwerin; children: Aria Bronstein-Moffly, Alexander Bronstein-Moffly, Evan Bronstein-Moffly. BA, Union Coll., Schenectady, NY, 1977; MSW, U. Albany, NY, 1981; PhD, Barry U., Miami Shores, Fla., 1999. LCSW NY, 1981. Chair. assoc. prof. Binghamton U., NY, 1999—. Parent coun. Northfield Mt. Hermon, Mass., 2001—. Mem.: NASW (assoc.). Office: Binghamton Univ Box 6000 Binghamton NY 13902 Office Phone: 607-777-2351. Business E-Mail: lbronst@binghamton.edu.

BRONSTEIN, PETER E., lawyer; b. NYC, Oct. 27, 1943; AB cum laude, Harvard U., 1965; JD, U. Va., 1968. Bar: Va. 1968, NY 1968, US Dist. Ct. (So. Dist. NY) 1973. Ptnr. Bronstein, Van Veen & Bronstein LLC, NYC. Lectr. in field; law commentator Nightline, ABC News, The Oprah Winfrey Show. Fellow: Internat. Acad. Matrimonial Lawyers (mem. bd. governors 2000—05, founding fellow), Am. Acad. Matrimonial Lawyers (mem. bd. managers NY chpt. 1989—92); mem.: Am. Coll. Family Trial Lawyers, NY State Bar Assn. (chmn. family law sect. 1974—76, mem. exec. com. 1976—), Va. Bar Assn., ABA, Assn. Bar City NY (mem. com. matrimonial law). Office: Bronstein Van Veen & Bronstein LLC Floor 40 152 W 57th St New York NY 10019-3310 Office Phone: 212-956-8300. Office Fax: 212-956-1452. E-mail: pbronstein@bvvb.com.*

BRONSTEIN, PHIL, publishing executive; m. Sharon Stone, Feb. 4, 1998 (div. 2004); 1 adopted child, Roan. Reporter Sta. KQED-TV, San Francisco; reporter, fgn. corr. San Francisco Examiner, 1980-90, mng. editor-news, 1990—91, exec. editor, 1991—2000, sr. v.p., exec. editor, 2000—03, exec. v.p., editor, 2003—. Mem.: Am. Soc. Newspaper Editors (chmn. Internat. com. 2003—04). Office: San Francisco Chronicle 901 Mission St San Francisco CA 94103 E-mail: pbronstein@sfchronicle.com.*

BRONSTER, MARGERY S., retired state attorney general, lawyer; b. NY, Dec. 12, 1957; married; 1 child. BA in Chinese Lang., Lit. and History, Brown U., 1979; JD, Columbia U., 1982. Bar: N.Y. 1983, Hawaii 1988, U.S. Dist Ct. (So. & Ea. N.Y. & Hawaii dist.), U.S. Tax Ct., U.S. Ct. Appeals (Ninth & Eleventh cir.). Assoc. Sherman & Sterling, NY, 1982—87; ptnr. Carlsmith, Ball, Wichman, Murray, Case & Ichiki, Honolulu, 1988—94; atty. gen. State of Hawaii, 1994—99; ptnr. Bronster Crabtree & Hoshibata, Honolulu, 1999—. Co-chair planning com. Citizens Conf. Jud. Selection, 1993; chair State of Hawaii Tobacco Prevention & Control Adv. Bd. Author: Litigating a Class Action Suit in Hawaii, 2001. Mem. nat. gov. bd. Common Cause. Recipient Fellow of the Pacific award, Hawaii Pacific Univ., 2000, Profiles in Courage award, SW Bell Conf. We. Atty. Gen., 2000, Advocate of the Year, Hawaii Cancer Soc., 1999, Kelley-Wyman Atty. Gen. of Yr. award, Nat. Assn. Atty. Gen., 1999, Top Cop award, State of Hawaii Law Enforcement Coalition, 1999, Hawaii Woman Lawyer of the Year, Hawaii Women Lawyers, 1998, Tommy Holmes award, Sex Abuse Treatment Ctr., 1998; scholar Harlan Fisk Stone. Office: Bronster Crabtree Hoshibata Suite 2300 Pauahi Tower 1001 Bishop St Honolulu HI 96813 Home Phone: 808-739-2513; Office Phone: 808-524-5644. Business E-Mail: mbronster@bchlaw.net.

BRONZINO, JOSEPH DANIEL, electrical engineer; b. Bklyn., Sept. 29, 1937; s. Joseph Rocco and Antoinette (Saporito) B.; m. Barbara Louise McGrath, Dec. 2, 1961; children: Michael J., Melissa J., Marcella J. BSEE, Worcester Poly. Inst., 1959, PhD in Elec. Engring, 1968; MSEE, U.S. Naval Postgrad. Sch., 1961. Registered profl. engr., Conn. Instr. elec. engring. U. N.H., 1964-66, asst. prof. elec. engring., 1966-67; NSF faculty fellow Worcester Found. for Exptl. Biology, Shrewsbury, Mass., 1967-68, mem. cooperating staff, 1968-94; assoc. prof. engring. Trinity Coll., 1968-75, prof., 1975—, Vernon Roosa prof. applied sci., 1977—, chmn. dept. engring., 1981-91. Adj. faculty Boston U. Med. Sch., 1987—98; dir. and chmn. biomed. engring. program Hartford (Conn.) Grad. Ctr., 1969-97; clin. assoc. dept. surgery U. Conn. Health Ctr., Farmington, 1971-77; rsch. assoc. Inst. for Living, Hartford, 1968-97; reviewer NSF; panelist NSF Rsch. Initiation Grants; dir. Biomed. Engring. Alliance for Conn., 1997—2000; pres. Biomed. Engring. Alliance and Consortium, 2000—; lectr., spkr. in field. Author: Technology for Patient Care, 1977, Computer Application in Patient Care, 1982, Biomedical Engineering Basic Concepts and Instrumentation, 1986, Medical Technology: Economic and Ethical Issues, 1990, Expert Systems: Basic Concepts, 1990, Management of Medical Technology: A Primer for Clinical Engineers, 1992, Biomedical Engineering Handbook, 1995, 3d edit., 2005, Introduction to Biomedical Engineering, 1999, 2d edit., 2005; contbr. articles to profl. publs. Mem. Simsbury (Conn.) Planning Commn., 1977-82. Served to 1st lt. Signal Corps U.S. Army, 1961-63. Recipient Goddard award for profl. achievement, Worcester Poly. Inst., 2004. Fellow: AAAS, IEEE (sr.; regional dir. group engring. in medicine and biology 1973—78, v.p. tech. activities 1982—85, pres. 1985—86, chmn. health care engring. policy com. 1986—90, vice chmn. tech. policy coun. 1990—91, chmn. tech. policy coun., Millenium award 2000), Conn. Acad. Sci. and Engring. (v.p. 2000—02, sec. 2002—04, editor-in-chief Acad. Press Biomed. Engring. Book Series), Biol. Psychiatry, Neurosci. Soc., Am. Soc. Engring. Edn. (exec. com. divsn. biomed. engring. 1973—82, vice chmn. career devel. 1974—76, vice chmn.profl. devel. 1976—77, divisional newsletter editor 1977—79, chmn.-elect divsn. 1979—80, exec. com. 1990—91, chmn. tech. policy coun. 1992—94), Am. Inst. Med. and Biol. Engrs., Rotary (pres. Simsbury club 1971—89, Hartford Club 1989—91, pres. Simsbury club 1991—93). Republican. Roman Catholic. Achievements include rsch. in signal analysis concepts and applications, basic neurophysiol. concepts involved in identifying specific neural circuits associated with specific functions of the brain. Office: Trinity Coll Dept Engring Hartford CT 06106 Home: 1 West St Unit 316 Simsbury CT 06070 Office Phone: 860-547-1995. E-mail: jdbblb@comcast.net, joseph.bronzino@beaconalliance.org.

BRONZO, NEAL A., consumer products company executive; BA in Econs. and Computer Sci., Boston Coll. Various engring. positions Sprint; with PepsiCo, 1990; v.p. field systems Yum! Brands, Inc. (formerly Tricon Global Restaurants); sr. v.p., chief info. officer Pepsi Bottling Group, Inc., 2002—. Office: Pepsi Bottling Group Inc 1 Pepsi Way Somers NY 10589-2201 Office Phone: 914-767-6000.*

BROOK, ADRIAN GIBBS, chemistry professor; b. Toronto, May 21, 1924; s. Frank Adrian and Beatrice Maud (Wellington) B.; m. Margaret Ellen Dunn, Dec. 18, 1954; children— Michael A., Katherine M., David L. BA, U. Toronto, 1947, PhD, 1950, DSc honoris causa, 2006. Lectr. chemistry U. Sask., 1950-51; research fellow Imperial Coll., London, 1951-52, Iowa State Coll., 1952-53; lectr. chemistry U. Toronto, 1953-56, asst. prof., 1956-60, assoc. prof., 1960-62, prof., 1962-87, univ. prof., 1987-89, univ. prof. emeritus, 1989—, chmn. dept. chemistry, 1969-74. Vis. prof. U. Sussex, 1974-75, Cambridge (Eng.) U., 1982, Ind. U., 1988. Contbr. articles to profl. jours. Nuffield Overseas fellow, 1951; recipient Izaak Walton Killam Meml. prize for Sci., 1994. Fellow Royal Soc. Can., Chem. Inst. Can. (CIC medal 1985); mem. Am. Chem. Soc. (Frederic Stanley Kipping award 1973) Home: Apt 202 7 Thornwood Rd Toronto ON Canada M4W 2R8 Office: U Toronto Dept Chemistry 80 St George St Toronto ON Canada M5S 3H6 Home Phone: 416-920-8383. Business E-Mail: abrook@chem.utoronto.ca.

BROOK, DOUGLAS ALAN, former civilian military employee; b. Chgo., Jan. 15, 1944; s. Donald Lee and Dorothe Mae (Johnson) B.; m. Mariana Proctor, Aug. 8, 1974. BA, U. Mich., 1965, MPA, 1967; Ph.D, George Mason U., 2002. Dir. pub. fin. Nat. Assn. Mfgs., NYC, 1971-74, asst. v.p., pub. affairs Washington, 1974-76; dir. pub. affairs Libbey-Owens-Ford Co., Washington, 1976-79, v.p., 1979-82; pres. Brook Assocs. Inc., Washington, 1982-90; asst. sec. (fin. mgmt.) Dept. Army, US Dept. Def., Washington, 1990—92; acting dir. US Office Pers. Mgmt., Washington, 1992—93; v.p. govt. affairs The LTV Corp., 1993—2002; dean Grad. Sch. Bus. & Pub. Policy, Monterey, Calif., 2002—05, prof., dir. Ctr. Def. Mgmt. Reform, 2005—. Mem. vis. com., Gerald R. Ford Sch. Pub. Policy, U. Mich., 1993—2002, MPA adv. com. George Mason U., 2000—02. Trustee U.S. Naval Acad. Found., Annapolis, Md., 1993-2004 Supply corps officer USNR, 1968—98. Recipient Joseph L. Fisher Doctoral award, George Mason U. Sch. Pub. Policy, 2001. Office: Naval Postgraduate Sch Public Affairs Office-Code 004 1 University Cir Monterey CA 93943 E-mail: dabrooks@nps.edu.

BROOK, ROBERT HENRY, public health service officer, internist, educator; b. NYC, July 3, 1943; s. Benjamin and Elizabeth (Berg) Brook; m. Susan Jean Weiss, June 26, 1966 (div. 1980); children: Rebecca, Daniel; m. Jacqueline Barbara Kosecoff Plaut, Jan. 17, 1982; children: Rachel, Davida. BS, U. Ariz., 1964; MD, Johns Hopkins U., 1968, ScD, 1972. Diplomate Am. Bd. Internal Medicine. Intern Balt. City Hosp., 1968—69, resident in medicine, 1969—72; project officer Nat. Ctr. Health Svcs. Rsch., HEW, Washington, 1972—74; vice-chmn. medicine UCLA, 1990—92, dir. clin. scholar program, 1974—, prof. of medicine and pub. health, Ctr. for Health Svcs., 1974—; dir. health program RAND Corp., Santa Monica, Calif., 1990—, v.p., 1998—, corp. fellow. Mem. editl. bd.: Health Adminstrn. Press, 1986—92, Jour. Gen. Internal Medicine, 1987—89, Health Policy, 1986—; published (article) Defining and Measuring Quality Care: A Perspective from US Researchers (Peter Reizenstein prize, 2000); contbr. articles to profl. jours. Dir. Robert Wood Johnson Clin. Scholars Program; chair of panel to advise Statewide Health Planning and Develop., Calif. office, 2002. Asst. surgeon USPHS, 1972—76. Named one of one of 75 pub. health heroes of Johns Hopkins U., 1991; recipient Rsch. prize, Baxter Found. Health Svcs., 1988, Robert J. Glaser award, Soc. Gen. Internal Medicine, Gustav O. Lienhard award for the advancement of personal health services, Inst. Medicine, 2005; fellow Lita Annenberg Biomed. fellow, Inst. Humanistic Studies, 1981. Fellow: ACP (Richard and Hinda Rosenthal Found. award); mem.: Western Assn. Physicians, Johns Hopkins Soc. Scholars, Assn. Am. Physicians, Assn. Health Svcs. Rsch. (bd. dirs. 1982—89, Disting. Health Svc. Rschr. award), Am. Soc. Clin. Investigation, Inst. Medicine NAS. Democrat. Jewish. Home: 1474 Bienveneda Ave Pacific Palisades CA 90272-2346 Office: Rand Corp 1700 Main St Santa Monica CA 90401-3297 Office Phone: 310-393-0411 ext. 7368. Business E-Mail: robert-brook@rand.org.

BROOK, SCOTT JONATHAN BRADLEY, mayor, lawyer; b. Bronx, NY, Apr. 3, 1964; s. Seymour and Marcia Marion (Handelman) B.; m. Brenda Post-Brook, Dec. 14, 1997; 5 children. BS in Psychology, Tulane U., 1985, MBA, 1987; JD, U. Miami, Coral Gables, Fla., 1992. Sr. advisor Tulane U., New Orleans, 1985-87, tchr. asst., 1987; rsch. asst. Howard, Weil, Labouisse, Friedrichs, Inc., New Orleans, 1986-87; career cons. Bus.Week Careers, NYC, 1987; securities legal asst. Milberg Weiss Bershad Specthrie & Lerach, NYC, 1988-89; pres. Brook Cons., Forest Hills, N.Y., 1989; law clk. Faber & Gitlitz, Coral Gables, Fla., 1989-90, Traveller's Insur., 1990-91, Conroy Simberg & Lewis, Hollywood, Fla., 1991—2000; pres. Scott J. Brook, P.A., Coral Springs, Fla., 2000—, Premier Networking Alliance, Inc.; commr. City of Coral Springs, 2002—, mayor, 2006—. Chair affordable housing task force Broward County Planning Coun., 2005—; mayor City Coral Springs, 2006—. Named Freeman fellow, 1985-87; recipient Merit scholarship, Tulane U., 1981-85, Best Brief award State Workers Compensation Competition, 1991. Mem. ABA (founder, chmn. ABA/LSD informational interview network), Soc. Bar and Gavel (pres.), U. Miami Student Bar Assn. (treas.). Office Phone: 954-757-5551. Business E-Mail: scottbrook@scottjbrookpa.com.

BROOKE, AVERY ROGERS, publisher, writer; b. Providence, May 28, 1923; d. Morgan Witter and Lucy Avery (Benjamin) Rogers; m. Joel Ijams Brooke, Sept. 14, 1946; children— Witter, Lucy, Sarah. B.F.A., R.I. Sch. Design, 1945, Union Theol. Sem., 1970. Founder Vineyard Books, Inc., Noroton, Conn., 1971-88; pub., v.p. Seabury Press, NYC, 1980-83. Mentor Annand Program in Spiritual Growth, Yale/Berkeley Div. Sch., 1991—96. Author: Youth Talks with God, 1959, Doorway to Meditation, 1973, How To Meditate without Leaving the World, 1975, Plain Prayers for a Complicated World, 1975, 93, Roots of Spring, 1975, As Never Before, 1976, Hidden in Plain Sight, 1978, Cooking with Conscience (under pseudonym Alice Benjamin), 1975, The Vineyard Bible, 1980, Celtic Prayers, 1981, Trailing Clouds of Glory, 1985, Finding God in the World, 1989, 2d edit., 1994, Plain Prayers in a Complicated World, 1993, Healing in the Landscape of Prayer, 1996, 2d edit., 2004; contbr. articles to religious jours. Mem. The Author's Guild, Oblate Order of the Holy Cross, Spiritual Dirs. Internat. Democrat. Episcopalian. Home: 27 Pasture Ln Darien CT 06820-5618 Office Phone: 203-655-6102. Personal E-mail: AveryRBR@aol.com.

BROOKE, EDWARD WILLIAM, III, lawyer, retired senator; b. Washington, Oct. 26, 1919; s. Edward W. and Helen (Seldon) B. BS, Howard U., 1940; LLB, Boston U., 1948, LLM, 1949; LLD, Howard U., 1967, George Wash. U., 1967; DSc, Lowell Tech. Inst., 1967; LLD, Boston U., 1968, Skidmore Coll., 1969, U. Mass., 1971, Amherst Coll., 1972. Bar: Mass. 1948, D.C. Ct. Appeals 1979, D.C. Dist. Ct. 1982, U.S. Supreme Ct. 1962. Chmn. Boston Fin. Com., 1961-62; atty. gen. State of Mass., Boston, 1963-66; US Senator from Mass., 1967-79; chmn. Nat. Low-Income Housing Coalition; former ptnr. O'Connor & Hannan, Washington; formerly of counsel Csaplar & Bok, Boston. Former pub. mem. Adminstrv. Conf. U.S.; chmn. bd. dirs. Boston Bank Commerce; bd. dirs. Meditrust, Inc., Wellesley, Mass., Grumman Corp., Bethpage, N.Y. Author: The Challenge of Change: Crisis in Our Two-Party System, 1966, Bridging the Divide: My Life, 2007. Chmn. Boston Opera Co.; former commr. Pres.'s Commns. on Housing and of Wartime Relocation and Internment of Civilians; bd. dirs. Washington Performing Arts Soc. Served as capt. inf. AUS, World War II, ETO. Decorated Combat Infantryman's Badge; recipient Disting. Svc. award Amvets, 1952, Charles Evans Hughes award NCCJ, 1967, Springarn medal, NAACP, 1967, Presdl. Freedom medal, 2004. Fellow Am. Bar Assn., Am. Acad. Arts and Scis.

BROOKE, FRANCIS JOHN, III, retired academic administrator; b. Charleston, W.Va., Mar. 4, 1929; s. Francis John Jr. and Elizabeth (Baird) B.; m. Helen Holmes Morgan, Dec. 20, 1958; children: Francis John, Haynes Morgan, David Tucker. BA, Hampden-Sydney Coll., 1949; MA, U. Chgo., 1951; PhD, U. N.C., 1954. Instr. German Roanoke Coll., Salem, Va., summers 1950-52; teaching fellow, part-time instr. U. N.C., Chapel Hill, 1951-54; mem. faculty, to assoc. prof. German U. Va., Charlottesville, 1956-65, asst. dean. Coll. Arts & Scis., 1959-62, acting chmn. dept. modern langs., 1962-63; exec. dean, prof. German Centre Coll., Danville, Ky., 1965-68; v.p. acad. affairs Va. Commonwealth U., Richmond, 1968-74, provost, acad. campus, 1973-79, spl. asst. to pres., 1979-80, prof. German, 1968-80; pres. Columbus (Ga.) Coll., 1980-87; spl. asst. to chancellor Univ. System of Ga., Atlanta, 1988; Pacific N.W. regional rep. Presbyn. Ch. Found., Seattle, 1989-99, ret., 1999. Vice chmn. So. Humanities Conf., 1965; pres. South Atlantic region Am. Assn. Tchrs. German, 1965-67; exec. com. South Atlantic chpt. MLA, 1963-66. Mem. gen. assembly com. on theol. edn. Presbyn. Ch., 1988-90. With AUS, 1954-56. Old Dominion Found. grantee, 1960; intern acad. adminstrn. Ellis L. Phillips Found., Cornell U., 1963-64. Mem. Assn. State Colls. and Univs. (com. on humanities 1984-86, com. on urban affairs 1986-87), Omicron Delta Kappa.

BROOKE, JOHN L., history professor; b. Mass., May 19, 1953; m. Sara C. Balderston, July 31, 1979. BA in History and Anthropology, Cornell U., 1976; MA in History, U. Pa., 1977, PhD in History, 1982. Vis. asst. prof. Amherst (Mass.) Coll., 1982-83; asst. prof. to prof. Tufts U., Medford, Mass., 1983-2001; dept. chair, 1996-97; prof. Ohio State U., Columbus, 2001—. Author: The Heart of the Commonwealth: Society and Political Culture in Worcester County, Massachusetts, 1713-1861, 1989, The Refiner's Fire: The Making of Mormon Cosmology, 1644-1844, 1994; contbr. articles to scholarly jours. Recipient award Nat. Soc. Daus. Colonial Wars, 1989, E. Harold Hugo Meml. Book prize Old Sturbridge Village Rsch. Libr. Soc., 1989, Merle Curti award for intellectual history, 1991, book prize for Am. history Nat. Hist. Soc., 1991, Bancroft prize Columbia U., 1995, ann. book prize Soc. for Historians of Early Am. Republic, 1995, ann. book award New Eng. Hist. Assn., 1995; S.F. Haven fellow Am. Antiquarian Soc., 1982, faculty rsch. fellow Tufts U., 1983, 88, Charles Warren fellow Harvard U., 1986-87, jr. fellow NEH, 1986-87, sr. fellow Commonwealth Ctr., 1990-91, fellow Am. Coun. Learned Socs., 1990-91, NEH fellow 1997-98, Guggenheim fellow, 1997-98. Mem. AAUP, Am. Antiq. Soc., Am. Hist. Assn., Orgn. Am. Historians, Mass. Hist. Soc. Democrat. Home: 1097 Wyandotte Rd Columbus OH 43212-3245

BROOKE, LINDA HUNDLEY, retired human resources specialist; b. Chattanooga, Aug. 9, 1943; d. Howard Derwent and Leola Ruth (Taylor) Hundley; m. James Edmondson Brooke, Feb. 21, 1970. BS, U. Tenn., 1965. Buyer trainee Foley's, Houston, 1965—66; adminstrv. asst. Cameron Iron Works, Houston, 1966—67; placement dir. M. David Lowe, Houston, 1968—69; employment cons. Met. Life Ins. Co., NYC, 1969—73; EEO cons., 1973—78; v.p., dir. affirmative action Chem. Bank, NYC, 1978—87, v.p. human resources subs. liaison, 1987—89; v.p. human resources Creditanstalt, NYC, 1989—94, Sunkyong Am., NYC, 1995—98, Nat. Audubon Soc., NYC, 1999—2007; ret., 2007. Mem.: DAR, Player's Club. Home: 44 Gramercy Park N # 14D New York NY 10010-6310 Personal E-mail: lbrooke@nyc.rr.com.

BROOKE, PETER A., corporate financial executive; m. Anne Brooke; 3 children. Grad., Harvard U.; MBA, Harvard Bus. Sch., 1954. Lending officer First Nat. Bank Boston, founder High Tech. Lending Grp., 1956; head venture capital dept. Bessemer Securities Corp., NYC; head corp. fin. and venture capital Tucker, Anthony & RL Day, Boston, 1963—68; founder TA Associates, 1968, mng. ptnr.; co-founder Sofinnova S.A., Paris, 1973; founder Advent International Corp., 1984, CEO, 1984—96, chmn. Overseer Harvard U.; bd. dirs. Excello Corpn., New Eng. Bus. Svc. Inc., Unitrode Corpn., Wang Labs. Co. Inc.; trustee Colgate U., Middlesex Sch., Eisenhower Exch. Fellowship, Mass. Eye & Ear Infirmary; bd. trustees

Boston Symphony Orch. Served in US Army. Named one of Greater Boston's 100 Most Influential Bus. People of 20th Century, Boston Bus. Jour.; named to Pvt. Equity Hall of Fame, 1996; recipient Lifetime Achievement in Venture Capital award, Nat. Venture Capital Assn. Fellow: Am. Acad. Arts & Scis. Office: Advent Internat Corpn 75 State St Boston MA 02109 E-mail: pbrooke@adventinternational.com.

BROOKE, RALPH IAN, dental educator; b. Leeds, Eng., Apr. 25, 1934; s. Michael and Jeanette (Cohen) B.; m. Lorna Ruth Shields; children: Michael Jeremy Richard, Andrew Timothy. Baccalaureus Chirurgiae Dentium, Licentiate in Dental Surgery, Leeds U., England, 1957. Licentiate Royal Coll. Physicians, 1963. Sr. lectr. Leeds U., 1970-72; prof., chmn. dept. oral medicine U. Western Ont., London, Can., 1972-82, dean dentistry faculty, 1982-97, vice provost health scis., 1987-97. Chief dentistry Univ. Hosp., London, 1973-92. Contbr. articles to profl. jours.; mem. editl. bd. Can. Pain Jour., 1990. Named Hon. Alumnus Distinction, U. Western Ontario, 2006. Fellow Acad. Dentistry Internat. (hon.), Royal Coll. Dentists Can., Royal Coll. Surgeons; mem. Nat. Dental Exam Bd. (past chmn. Can. commn. on dental accreditation), Can. Faculties Dentistry (past pres.), Can. Acad. Oral Medicine (past pres.), Can. Dental Assn. (hon.), Can. Acad. Oral and Maxillofacial Pathology and Oral Medicine (hon.), Ont. Dental Assn. (bd. dirs.). Avocations: music, hiking. Business E-Mail: rbrooke@uwo.ca.

BROOKE, SANDRA LEE, painter; b. Bremerton, Wash., Oct. 9, 1947; d. Milton John and Alberta Marguerite Griffith; m. James William Brooke; 1 child, Christen Michelle Brooke Gladu; m. Henry Marshall Sayre, Nov. 3, 1990; stepchildren: Robert F. Sayre, John P. Sayre. BFA, U. Oreg., 1972, MFA, 1993. Art instr. Oreg. State U., Corvallis, 1990—2000; asst. prof. Oreg. State U.-Cascade, 2001—. Author: Drawing as Expression, 2003, 2d edit., 2007, Techniques and Concepts, Hooked on Drawing, 2003, Hooked on Painting, 2003; exhibitions include Portland Art Mus., Shelley Hall, Bend, Avenida. Bd. dirs. High Desert Jour., Bend, 2005, Arts Ctrl., Bend, 2001—05. Mem.: Nat. Mus. for Women in the Arts (charter), Coll. Art Assn. Democrat. Buddhist. Avocations: skiing, bicycling, golf. Office: Oreg State Univ Cascade Hall 2600 NW College Way Bend OR 97702 Business E-Mail: sandy.brooke@osucascades.edu.

BROOKE, TAL (ROBERT TALIAFERRO), writer; b. Washington, Jan. 21, 1945; s. Edgar Duffield and Frances (Lea) B. BA, U. Va., 1969; M in Theology/Philosophy, Princeton U., NJ, 1986. V.p. pub. rels. nat. office Telecom Inc., 1982-83; pres., chmn. Spiritual Counterfeits Project, Inc., Berkeley, 1989—; founder End Run Pub., 1999—. Guest lectr. Cambridge U., Eng., 1977, 86, 97, 99, Oxford and Cambridge U., 1979, 84. Author: Lord of the Air: The International Edition, 1976, The Other Side of Death, Lord of the Air: The International Edition, 1979, Riders of the Cosmic Circuit, 1986, Millennial Edit., 2002, Avatar of Night, 1987, When the World Will Be As One, 1989, Lord of the Air, 1990, Virtual Gods, 1997, Conspiracy to Silence the Son, 1998, One World, 2000, The Mystery of Death, 2001. Mem. Internat. Platform Assn., Authors Guild, Soc. of The Cincinnati. Office: SCP Inc PO Box 4308 Berkeley CA 94704-0308 Business E-Mail: scp@scp-inc.org.

BROOKENS, CARL, psychologist; b. Chgo., June 13, 1943; s. John William Barnes and Alice Lee Brookens; m. Donna Joyce Helem, Aug. 28, 1966; children: Dionna Cherese, Caron Yvonne. AA, Chgo. City Coll., 1973; BA, DePaul U., 1980; MS, Spertus Coll., 1983; MA, Roosevelt U., 1999. Lic. profl. counselor Ill., cert. counselor Nat. Bd. Cert. Counselors, forensic addictions examiner Nat. Assn. Forensic Counselors. Mgr. spl. programs State of Ill., Chgo., 1975—85, adjudicator Arlington Heights, Ill., 1985—2003, spl. agt. Chgo., 2003—. Mem.: APA, Ill. Mental Health Counselors Assn. Achievements include language competency in Russian, Mandarin Chinese, French and Arabic, American Sign language. Avocations: travel, hapkido (black belt). Office: State of Ill 33 S State St Chicago IL 60603 Personal E-mail: carlbrookens43@sbcglobal.net.

BROOKER, CHIP, lawyer; s. Eugene Brooker and Donna Sims, Henry Sims (Stepfather) and Alice Brooker (Stepmother); m. Rebekah Steely Brooker, July 7, 2001. BS, Tex. A&M U., College Sta., 2001; JD, So. Meth. U., Dallas, 2004. Atty. Haynes & Boone, LLP, Dallas, 2004—05, Payne Mitchell Law Grp., Dallas, 2006—. Recipient Tex. Rising Star, Tex. Monthly & Law & Politics Mag., 2007. Mem.: Dallas Assn. Young Lawyers (dir. 2007—). Office: Payne Mitchell Law Grp 2911 Turtle Creek Blvd Ste 1400 Dallas TX 75219 Office Fax: 214-252-1889. Business E-Mail: chip.brooker@paynemitchell.com.

BROOKER, JEFF ZEIGLER, retired cardiologist; b. Columbia, SC, Nov. 1, 1941; s. Jefferson Zeigler and Virginia (Ligon) B.; m. Rhoda Arrowsmith, June 12, 1966; children: Jeff III, John, Rhoda. BS, U. S.C., Columbia, 1962; MD, Med. U. S.C., 1966. Cert. in interventional cardiology, clin. cardiac electrophysiology, cardiovasc. disease and internal medicine Am. Bd. Internal Medicine. Intern, resident Hosp. U. Pa., Phila., 1966-68; resident internal medicine Stanford U. Med. Ctr., Palo Alto, Calif., 1970-71, rsch. fellow cardiology, 1971-73; staff cardiologist Tex. Heart Inst., Houston, 1973-74; assoc. dir. cardiology Providence Hosp., Columbia, S.C., 1974-81; pvt. practice cardiology Columbia, 1981—2006; ret., 2006. Cons. peer rev. Jour. AMA, Chgo., 1976-77; local and regional rsch. com. Am. Heart Assn., Dallas., 1977-86. Mem. editl. bd. Jour. SC Med. Assn., Columbia, 1991—; editl. reviewer: Essentials of Echocardiography, 1977. Legis. liaison S.C. Med. Assn., Columbia, 1991-92. Lt. comdr. USN, 1968-70. Recipient Best Sci. Article award Roe Found., Columbia, 1991. Achievements include improved method for oral dipyridamole testing for ischemic heart disease; devising a percutaneous method for inserting pacing lead into the internal jugular vein yet still implant and pulse generator on the anterior chest wall, solving for mortality rate in terms of survival rate and disease prevalence. Office: 1625 Bernardin Ave Columbia SC 29204-2003 Office Phone: 803-771-0212.

BROOKER, RICHARD I., architect; b. Boston, June 9, 1927; s. Bernard and Esther (Friedman) Brooker; m. Maria Rivalta, Sept. 3, 1966; 1 child, Niccolo. BArch, Ill. Inst. Tech., 1953. Registered arch., Colo., cert. Nat. Coun. Archtl. Registration Bds. Prin., arch. Archs. Collaborative, Cambridge, Mass., 1953-95, Boston Design Assocs., Waltham, Mass., 1995—2002. Prin. works include Schneider Children's Hosp., LI Jewish Hillside Med. Ctr., New Hyde Park, NY, new constrn. and replacement project Temple U. Hosp., Phila., US Postal Svc. gen. mail and bulk mail and vehicle maint. facilities, Springfield, Mass., Ctrl. Mass. Mail Processing Ctr., Shrewsbury, Mass., US Postal Svc. Westchester Mail Processing/Distbn. Ctr., vehicle maint. facility, Harrison, NY, new facilities and renovations Cabot Corp., Billerica, Mass., hdqrs. facilities, Waltham, Mass., electron microscope lab., Billerica, Al-Hasa campus King Faisal U., Saudi Arabia, U. Baghdad, Iraq, U. Tunis Sch. Law, Econ./Polit. Sci., Tunisia, Sch. Agri., Chott Maria Sousse, Ctrl. Vet. Lab., Sotuba, Mali, Higher Tchr. Tng. Coll., Bamako, Mali, Saudi Arabian Mil. Assistance Program, Three New Military Towns, clin. labs., med. office bldg., maternity ctr. New Eng. Meml. Hosp., Stoneham, Mass., Essex County Ho. Correction, Middleton, Mass., Kuwait Postal Svcs. complex, Kuwait City, Mass. Correctional Instn., Shirley, Mass., exec. meeting, dining rms., urology oper. rms., outpatient recovery area, patient site renovations, dialysis, cardiology, cardia oper. ste., med. office conversion, fit-up, new emergency generator plant St. Vincent Hosp., Worcester, Mass., St. Mary's Hosp., master devel. plan, major additions and various renovations, Kansas City, Mo., Weehawken Waterfront Consultancy, NJ, Roc Harbour Master Plan and Condominium Devel., North Bergen, NJ, numerous other projects. With US Army, 1945—46. Mem.: AIA, Boston Soc. Archs. Home: 265 The Valley Rd Concord MA 01742-4924

BROOKER, ROBERT ELTON, JR., retired manufacturing company executive; b. LA, Apr. 12, 1937; s. Robert Elton and Sarah (Smith) B.; m. Katherine Jones, Mar. 21, 1964; children: Robert III, Carolyn, Christopher, Alison. BS, MIT, 1959; MBA, Harvard U., 1965; PhD, Brown U., 2005. With Cummings Engine Co., 1965-81, gen. mgr. Great Lakes Foundry divsn. South Bend, Ind., 1966-69, pres. fleetguard Dallas, 1970-77, v.p. Latin Am. Miami, Fla., 1977-80, v.p. components group Columbus, Ind., 1981; pres. info. svcs. group N.L. Industries, Houston, 1981-86; pres., COO Lord Corp., Erie, Pa., 1987-90, CEO, 1990-91; pres., COO Connell Ltd. Partnership, Boston, 1993-95; dir. Dura Automotive Sys., 1995-98; ret., 1998. Dir. FCI, 1991—, Innovative Components Inc., 1998—, Dura Automotive Sys., 1995—. Author: British Military Pistols, 1603-1887, 1978, Parole Sachen, 1990; contbr. articles to profl. jours. Mem. Sea Space Symposium. Capt. USMC, 1959-63.

BROOKER, ROBERTA L., library director; Grad., U. Indpls.; MLS, Ind. U. With libr. devel. office Ind. State Libr., Indpls., with Ind. divsn., coord. Ind. state data ctr., assoc. dir. pub. services, 2004—06, interim dir., 2006—. Mem. customer svc. team Ill. State Libr., Indpls., mem. pub. rels. team. Mem.: U. Indpls. Alumni Assn. (bd. mem.). Office: Ind State Library 140 N Senate Ave Indianapolis IN 46204-2296 Business E-Mail: rbrooker@statelib.lib.in.us.*

BROOKER, THOMAS KIMBALL, oil industry executive; b. LA, Oct. 1, 1939; s.Robert Elton and Sally Burton Harrison (Smith) B.; m. Nancy Belle Neumann, 1966 (dec. 2003); children: Thomas Kimball Jr., Isobel, Vanessa. BA in French Lit., Yale U., 1961; MBA, Harvard U., 1968; MA in Art History, U. Chgo., 1989, PhD in Art History, 1996. Assoc. in corp. fin. Morgan Stanley & Co., Inc., NYC, 1968—73, v.p., 1973—75, mng. dir., 1976—88, head Chgo. office, 1978—88; pres. Barbara Oil Co., Chgo., 1989—, bd. dirs. Bd. dirs. Arthur J. Gallagher & Co., Miami Corp., Cutler Oil & Gas Corp.; bd. govs. Midwest Stock Exch., 1980-88, vice chmn., 1986-88. Contbr. articles to profl. jours. Mem. vis. com. libr. U. Chgo., mem. vis. com. visual arts dept.; mem., chmn. com. libr. Yale U. President's Coun., 1980-84; trustee Pierpont Morgan Libr., Gov. John Carter Brown Libr., Yale U. Libr. Assn., Newberry Libr.; bd. dirs. Lyric Opera Chgo. Recipient Sir Thomas More medal U. San Francisco, 1992; assoc. fellow Saybrook Coll., Yale U. Mem. Pres. Adminstrv. Coun., Assn. Internat. de Bibliophilie (pres.), Bibliotheca Wittockiana (sci. com., pres.), Bandar-Log, Caxton Club, Chgo. Club, Comml. Club, Econ. Club, River Club (NYC), Knickerbocker Club (NYC), Grolier Club (NYC), The Casino, Saddle and Cycle Club, Edgartown (Mass.) Yacht Club, The Reading Room (Edgartown), Quadrangle Club, Racquet Club, Rockaway Hunt Club, Wayfarers Club. Home: 1500 N Lake Shore Dr Chicago IL 60610-6657 Office: Barbara Oil Co 21 S Clark St Ste 3990 Chicago IL 60603-2000

BROOKES, LESLIE JOAN, retired maternal/surgical nurse; b. Summit, NJ, Oct. 8, 1941; d. Joseph Mahood and Mildred Evelyn Thompson; m. Robert Arthur Brookes (dec.); children: Timothy Scott, Todd Jonathan. BS, Elmira Coll., NY, 1963; diploma in Nursing, Rapid City Regional Hosp. Sch. Nursing, SD, 1977. RN SD. 1st grade tchr. Meriden Sch. Dist., Conn., 1963—68; substitute elem. tchr. Waterford Sch. Dist., Conn., 1968—69; organist 2d Congl. Ch., New London, Conn., 1969—71; staff nurse Rapid City Regional Hosp., 1977—2003; office asst. Kolbach & Assocs. Investigations, Inc., 2003—05. Asst. organist 1st Congl. Ch., Rapid City, 2002—. Flute player New Horizons Band, 1997—; bd. dirs. Westside Presch., Rapid City, 1976. Republican. Avocations: music, reading, walking, crossword puzzles, crafts. Home: 4115 Sunset Dr Rapid City SD 57702-3277 Personal E-mail: lbrookes@rap.midco.net.

BROOKHART, MAURICE S., chemist; b. Cumberland, Md., Nov. 28, 1942; married, 1965; 2 children. BA, Johns Hopkins U., 1964; PhD in Organic Chemistry, U. Calif., LA, 1968. NATO fellow U. Southampton, 1968-69; assoc. prof., 1969-76; prof. organic chemistry U. NC, Chapel Hill, 1976—. Vis. prof. Oxford U., 1982-83. Fellow Am. Acad. Arts and Scis.; mem. Am. Chem. Soc. (award in Organometallic Chemistry 1992, Arthur C. Cope Scholar award 1994). Achievements include research in mechanistic and synthetic organometallic chemistry; applications of transition metal complexes in organic synthesis and catalysis. Office: U North Carolina Dept Chemistry Chapel Hill NC 27514

BROOKMAN, MARC D., lawyer; b. Phila., Dec. 10, 1942; BS, Temple U., 1964, JD, 1968. Bar: Pa. 1968, US Dist. Ct. Ea. Dist. Pa., US Ct. Appeals 3rd Cir. Ptnr. Duane Morris LLP, Phila., 1979—, chair firm real estate practice group & dept., mem. firm partners bd., 1991—. Past pres. dist. coun. Urban Land Inst.; pres. Del. Valley Smart Growth Alliance; exec. com. Ctrl. Phila. Devel. Corp., 1994—, treas., 1995—96, v.p., 1996—. Mem. ABA (mem. urban, state & local govt. law sect., real property, probate & trust law sect.), Pa. Bar Assn. (mem. real property, probate & trust law sect.), Phila. Bar Assn., Urban Land Inst., Cmty. Associations Inst. (founder, past. pres. Delaware Valley Chpt.) Office: Duane Morris LLP United Plz 30 S 17th St Philadelphia PA 19103-4196 Office Phone: 215-979-1300. Office Fax: 215-979-1020. Business E-Mail: brookman@duanemorris.com.

BROOKNER, ELI, electrical engineer; b. NYC, Apr. 2, 1931; s. Angel and Fanny Brookner; m. Ethel Bobick, Nov. 20, 1955; children: Lawrence, Richard. BEE, CCNY, 1953; MEE, Columbia U., 1955, DSc, 1962. Jr. engr. radar div. Rome (N.Y.) Air Devel. Ctr., summer 1952; rsch. engr. Columbia U. Electronics Rsch. Lab., NYC, 1953-57, sr. rsch. engr., 1960-62; project engr. Fed. Sci. Corp. (name now Nicolet), NYC, 1957-60; prin. fellow Raytheon Co., Sudbury, Mass., 1962—. Internat. lectr. in radar tech.; served on coms. for Nat. Acad. Sci., DARPA, Air Force Sci. Adv. Bd., Air Force Mil. Space Systems Tech. Workshops. Author, editor: Radar Technology, 1977, Aspects of Modern Radar, 1988, Practical Phased-Array Antenna Systems, 1991, Tracking and Kalman Filtering Made Easy, 1998; achievements include conception and lead technical engr. for the wake measurements radar, first pulse doppler travelling wave tube radar put into space, radar system engring. for active phase array RADARSAT II-Plus. Recipient Jour. Premium award Franklin Inst., 1966. Fellow AIAA, IEEE (Centennial medal 1984, third millenium medal, 2000, IEEE Region I award for continuing edn. course devel. 1986, Meritorious Achievement award edn. activities bd. 1990, Centennial medal 2000, Warren White award for excellence in radar engring., 2003, Dennis J. Picard medal for radar techs. and applications 2006); mem. IEEE Aerospace and Electronics Systems Soc. (chmn. Boston chpt. 1972—, Outstanding Chpts. award 1977-78, 83-84, Disting. lectr. 1988—), IEEE Antennas and Propagation Soc. (Disting. lectr. 1983-85, Wheeler Best Applications paper award 1999, chair internat. symposium on phased array systems and tech. 1996, 2003), Internat. Union Radio Sci. (commns. B and C, invited session chmn. 1973), Tau Beta Pi, Eta Kappa Nu. Avocations: dance, classical music, comedy, photography. Home: 282 Marrett Rd Lexington MA 02421-7009 Office Phone: 978-440-4007. Business E-Mail: Eli_Brookner@raytheon.com.

BROOKS, A. TAEKO, historian; d. Mitsuo and Haruko Oshiro; m. E. Bruce Brooks, July 23, 1964; 1 child, E. Clement. BA, U. Hawaii, 1958, MA, 1961. Rsch. assoc. Warring States Project/U. Mass., Amherst, Mass., 1993—. Co-author: The Original Analects, 1998; contbr. chapters to books, articles to profl. jours. Mem.: Soc. for the Study of Early China, Assn. for Asian Studies, Am. Hist. Assn. Office: Warring States Project/U Mass 201C Goodell Amherst MA 01003-9272 Business E-Mail: atbrooks@research.umass.edu.

BROOKS, AARON LAFETTE, professional football player; b. Newport News, Va., Mar. 24, 1976; BA in Anthropology, U. Va. Football player New Orleans Saints, 2000—06, Oakland Raiders, 2006—07. Named NFC Player Wk. (four times); named to All-Madden Team, 2000. Avocations: basketball, reading. Office: Oakland Raiders 1220 Harbor Bay Pkwy Alameda CA 94502

BROOKS, ALFRED R., bank executive; BBA in Acctg., Calif. State U. With Sanwa Bank Calif., Calif. Fed. Mortgage, Bank of Am., Wells Fargo, Union Bank Calif., Washington Mut., Inc., 1998—, divsn. exec. multifamily lending bus., chief lending officer Comml. Group, pres. Comml. Group, 2005—. Office: Washington Mut Inc 1301 Second Ave Seattle WA 98101 Office Phone: 206-461-2000.*

BROOKS, ANDRÉE AELION, journalist, educator, writer; b. London, Feb. 2, 1937; d. Leon Luis and Lillian (Abrahamson) Aelion; m. Ronald J. Brooks, Aug. 16, 1959 (div. Aug. 1986); children: Allyson, James. Journalism cert., N.W. London Poly., 1958. Reporter Hampstead News, London, 1954—58; story editor Photoplay mag., NYC, 1958—60; N.Y. corr. Australian Broadcasting Co., NYC, 1961—68; elected rep. Elstree, England, 1973—74; contbr. columnist N.Y. Times, NYC, 1978—95; freelance journalist, 1978—. Adj. prof. journalism Fairfield U., Conn., 1983—87; assoc. fellow Yale U., 1989—, founder, pres. Women's Campaign Sch., 1993—96; v.p. Minuteman Media, 1995—96; coord., dir. Out Spain hist. curriculum, 2000. Author: Children of Fast Track Parents, 1989 (Best Non-Fiction Book award, 1990), The Women Who Defied Kings: The Life and Times of Dona Gracia Nasi, 2002 (Mark Twain award, 2003, finalist Nat. Jewish Book awards, 2003), Russian Dance, 2004 (1st pl. Nat. Fedn. Press Women, 2005), Spanish lang. edit., 2006. Exec. bd. Am. Jewish Com., 1987—91; trustee Temple Israel, Westport, Conn., 1991—97. Named one of Am. Women Achievement, Am. Jewish Com., 1989; recipient 1st pl. news writing, Conn. Press Women, 1980, 1983, 1985—86, 1987, 1994, Outstanding Achievement award, Nat. Fedn. Press Women, 1981, 1st pl. award mag. writing, 1983, 1st pl. award, Fairfield County chpt. Women Comm., 1982—83, 1986—87, 1992, 1993, 1997, 2d pl. award in mag. writing, Nat. Assn. Home Builders, 1983, Spl. Svc. award, Conn. chpt. Am. Planning Assn., 1983, Mark Twain award, Conn. Press Club, 2003, Pioneer award, Gomez House Found., 2003, honor, Am. Sephardi Fedn., 2001. Mem.: Conn. Press Women (chmn. nominating com. 1983—86), Women Comm. (contest co-chmn. 1983—84). Office Phone: 203-226-9834. Personal E-mail: andreebrooks@hotmail.com. *Keep true to what you believe and don't become cynical or full of hate - for hate only breeds more hate.*

BROOKS, BABERT VINCENT, publisher; b. NYC, Sept. 2, 1926; s. Babert Vincent and Florence (Goodwin) B.; m. Audrey Stephenson, Dec. 6, 1952 (div.); children: Torrey, Scott, Wendy; m. Kathryn Frazer, May 23, 1987. AB magna cum laude, Dartmouth Coll., 1947, MBA with distinction, 1949. Security analyst Arnold Bernhard & Co., NYC, 1952-56; cons. Booz, Allen & Hamilton, NYC, 1956-58; v.p. finance Schine Enterprises, NYC, 1958-61; v.p., treas. Murray Corp. Am., NYC, 1961-62; pres. Brooks, Torrey & Scott, Inc., Westport, Conn., 1962—, Westport Travel Svc., Inc., 1963, chmn., 1988-92; pres. Brooks Community Newspapers, 1974-82, chmn., 1982-99; pub. Westport (Conn.) News, 1964-99, Darien (Conn.) News-Rev., 1973-99, Fairfield (Conn.) Citizen-News, 1973-99, Norwalk Citzen News, 1997-99, Greenwich (Conn.) News, 1983-96, Inside Fairfield County, Westport, 1993-99. Sec.-treas. Airspur Corp., NYC, 1969-70; trustee King Indsl. Properties, Boston, 1965-82; bd. dirs. Westfair, Inc., Westport, Warner Investing Corp., Westport; trustee Am. Inst. Econ. Rsch., Great Barrington, Mass., 1997-2004, vice-chmn., 2002, chmn. bd. dirs., 2003-2004. Bd. dirs., treas. Dartmouth in Greenwich, 1972-81; trustee Conn. Policy and Econ. Coun. Inc., 1989-99, Norwalk Hosp., 1988-93, 95-00, Norwalk Health Svcs., Inc., 1994-2004, U. Bridgeport, 1991—, Media Rsch. Ctr., Washington, 2002—. With USNR, 1945-47. Mem. Riverside Yacht Club, Phi Beta Kappa. Office Phone: 203-847-2616.

BROOKS, BEN A., lawyer; b. Dallas, May 31, 1949; BBA, U. Tex., 1971; JD, So. Meth. U., 1974. Bar: Tex. 1974. Ptnr., co-head Pub. Fin. Sect Vison & Elkins LLP, Dallas. Mem.: Nat. Assn. Bond Lawyers. Office: Vinson & Elkins LLP Trammell Crow Ctr 2001 Ross Ave, Ste 3700 Dallas TX 75201 Office Phone: 214-220-7921. E-mail: bbrooks@velaw.com.

BROOKS, BURKE JAY, JR., oncologist; b. New Orleans, La., Feb. 17, 1954; MD, La. State U. Sch. Medicine, 1979. Cert. Am. Bd. Internal Medicine, Am. Bd. Internal Medicine, Med. Oncology. Intern, internal medicine Charity Hosp./La. State U., New Orleans, 1979—80, resident, med. oncology, 1979—83; fellow, Warren Grant Magnuson Clin. Rsch. Ctr. Nat. Cancer Inst., Bethesda, Md., 1983—86; hosp. appointment Ochsner Health Sys., La., 1987—, chief medicine La., chief med. specialties La., chmn. rsch. com. La., mem. rsch. advisory com. La., chmn., dept. hematology/oncology Baton Rouge; clin. asst. prof. medicine La. State U. Bd. gov. Ochsner Clinic Found. Contbr. articles to med. publications, chapters to books. Office: Ochsner Health Ctr Bluebonnet 9001 Summa Ave Baton Rouge LA 70809*

BROOKS, CHARLES LEE, III, computational biophysicist, educator; b. Detroit, May 14, 1956; married; 2 children. BS in Chemistry and Physics, Alma Coll., Mich., 1978; PhD in Physical Chemistry, Purdue U., 1982. Postdoc. fellow Harvard U., Boston, 1982-85, NIH, 1983-85; from asst. prof. to prof. Carnegie Mellon U., 1985—94, prof., 1994—; prof. molecular biology Scripps Rsch. Inst., 1994—. Mem. spl. rev. panels, site visit coms., mem. reviewers reserve Cell Biology & Biophysics Divsn. A study section, NIH; reviewer, mem. cellular and molecular biophysics panel, NSF; mem. adv. bd. Nat. Biomed. Computation Resource Inst., San Diego Supercomputing Ctr., sr. fellow, 1997; presenter in field. Mem. editl. bd. Proteins, 1995—, Biochimica et Biophysica Acta, 2000—, Physical Chemistry Chemical Physics, 2000—; editor: Jour. Computational Chemistry, 2004; contbr. over 200 articles to profl. jours.; author 1 book, several book chpts. A.P. Sloan fellow, 1990-93, AAAS, 2000; grantee Swedish Rsch. Coun., 1992. Office: Scripps Rsch Inst Dept Molecular Biology TPC6 10550 N Torrey Pines Rd La Jolla CA 92037-1000 Business E-Mail: brooks@scripps.edu.

BROOKS, DANIEL TOWNLEY, lawyer; b. NYC, Apr. 15, 1941; s. Robert Daniel and Mary (Lee) B.; m. Barbara Ann Badertscher, June 16, 1973; children: Daniel Townley, Jr., Andrei Matthew. BS in Engring. cum laude, Princeton U., 1963; LLB, Stanford U., 1967, MS in Engring., 1968. Bar: Calif. 1968, U.S. Dist. Ct. (no. dist.) Calif. 1968, U.S. Ct. Appeals (9th cir.) 1968, N.Y. 1970, U.S. Ct. Appeals (2d cir.) 1972, Va. 1982, D.C. 1998. Assoc. Cadwalader, Wickersham & Taft, NYC, 1968-79; atty. U.S. SEC, Washington, 1979-81; with Computer Law Advisers, Springfield, Va., 1981-85; ptnr. Cadwalader, Wickersham & Taft, Washington, 1985-98, sr. counsel, 1998-2000; sr. v.p., gen. counsel Trading Edge, Inc., Washington, 2000—. Cons. and lectr. in computer law. Mem. ABA, IEEE, Calif. Bar Assn. (inactive), N.Y. State Bar Assn., Va. Bar Assn., D.C. Bar Assn., Computer Law Assn. Inc. (bd. advisors), Assn. Computing Machinery. Home: 6106 Lorcom Ct Springfield VA 22152-1320 Office: Trading Edge Inc 140 Broadway Fl 42 New York NY 10005-1114 E-mail: dbrooks@tradingedge.com.

BROOKS, DARIUS, music company executive; s. Ethel Brooks; m. Deborah Brooks, Sept. 2, 2000; 1 child, Dasha Lyric. Grad. H.S., Chgo. Pres. Journey Music Group. Musical dir. Rainbow Push, Chgo., 1995—. Prodr., songwriter and vocalist: CD My Soul. Recipient multiple Grammy, Stellar and Dove awards. Office Phone: 708-366-9770.

BROOKS, DAVID BARRY, resource economist; b. Easton, Mass., Feb. 15, 1934; s. Abraham and Mae (Fox) B.; m. Toby Judith Haftka, Sept. 11, 1955; children: Michael Jan, Naomi Sara. S.B. in Geology, MIT, 1955; MS in Geology, Calif. Inst. Tech., 1956; PhD in Econs., U. Colo., 1963. Geologist U.S. Geol. Survey, 1956-59; research assoc. Resources for the Future, Washington, 1961-66; asst. prof. econs. Berea Coll., 1966-67; chief div. mineral econs. Bur. Mines, Dept. Interior, 1967-70; chief Mineral Econs. Research div. Can. Dept. Energy, Mines and Resources, 1970-73; dir. Office Energy Conservation, 1974-77; dir. Ottawa office Energy Probe, 1977-82; bd. dirs. Can. Friends of the Earth, pres., 1977-81, 85-88; prin. Marbek Resource Cons. Ltd., Ottawa, Ont., Canada, 1983-88; sr. advisor Internat. Devel. Rsch. Ctr., Ottawa, 1988—2002; dir. rsch. Friends of the Earth, Canada, 2002—. Mem. study team on non-renewable materials, environ. studies bd. Nat. Acad. Scis., 1972-73; mem. study team on environ. Fed. Task Force and Program Rev.; energy options adv. com. Office of Ministry of Energy, Ottawa, 1986-88; exec. dir. Beaufort Sea Rsch. Coalition; bd. dirs. Ont. Hydro; spkr. in field; cons. in field. Author: Supply and Competition in Minor Metals, 1965, Peaceful Use of Nuclear Explosives: Some Economic Aspects, 1969, Minerals: an Expanding or a Dwindling Resource?, 1973, Zero Energy Growth for Canada, 1981; co-author: Life After Oil: A Renewable Energy Policy for Canada, 1983, Watershed: The Role of Fresh Water in the Israeli-Palestinian Conflict, 1994, Water: Local-Level Management, 2002, Fresh Water in the Middle East and North Africa, 2007, Integrated Water Resource Management and Security in the Middle East, 2007; also monographs on environ. problems of mining, water and energy conservation, water and internat. devel.; also articles. Chmn. No. Va. chpt. Congress Racial Equality, 1963-65; sec. Fed. Employees for a Democratic Soc. Served with AUS, 1957. Ashley fellow Trent U., Can., 1992. Mem.: Internat. Water Acad. Home: 1-202 Flora St Ottawa ON Canada K1R 5R7 Office: Friends of the Earth Can 300-260 St Patrick St Ottawa ON Canada K1N 5K5 Office Phone: 613-241-0085 ext. 27. Business E-Mail: dbrooks@foecanada.org.

BROOKS, DAVID EUGENE, lawyer; b. Chickasha, Okla., Apr. 14, 1953; s. Shirley Sherman and Joyce Faye Brooks; m. Victoria Lynn Ward, Aug. 11, 1973; children: Kristina Kaye, Leah Kathene, Stephen Sherman. BA, Southwestern Okla. State U., 1975; JD, U. Tulsa, 1978. Bar: Okla. 1978, U.S. Dist. Ct. (we. dist.) Okla. 1979. Pvt. practice, Chickasha, 1978-81; assoc. dist. judge State of Okla., Mangum, 1981-91, asst. dist. atty. Sayre, 1991-92; pvt. practice Sayre, 1992—. Pres. bd. Beckham County Law Libr., Sayre, 1996—. Mem. Beckham County Bar Assn. (pres. 1993, 2005), Kiwanis of Mangum (pres. 1984), Masons (master, 33 degree). Methodist. Office: Brooks and Israel 119 E Main St Sayre OK 73662-2913 Office Phone: 580-928-5593 ext 104. Personal E-mail: davidbrooks@cableone.net.

BROOKS, DAVID H., manufacturing executive; Founder, co-chmn., chmn. DHB Industries Inc., Westbury, NY, 1992—, CEO, 2000—. Chmn. bd., pres., dir. Brooks Industries of LI, Inc. Office: DHB Industries, Inc Ste 303 400 Post Avenue Westbury NY 11590 Office Phone: 516-997-1155. Office Fax: 516-997-1144.

BROOKS, DEBORAH W., foundation administrator; married; 2 children. BA in Economics, Coll. William & Mary; MBA, Dartmouth Coll., Amos Tuck Sch., 1986; MS in Marital, Family Therapy, Northwestern Univ. V.p., fixed income, asset mgmt. divsn. Goldman, Sachs & Co.; mgr. Harvard Eating Disorders Ctr. nonprofit, Boston, Bill T. Jones/Arnie Zane Dance Co. nonprofit, NYC; pres., co-founder Michael J. Fox Found. for Parkinson's Rsch., NYC, 2000—, CEO, 2000—07. Former mem. Nat. Adv. Environ. Health Scis. Coun., NIH. Bd. dir. Parkinson's Action Network; external adv. bd. Emory Univ. Collaborative Ctr. Parkinson's Disease Environ. Rsch.; bd. overseers Univ. Pa. Sch. Social Policy and Practice; MBA adv. bd. Tuck Sch. Bus., Dartmouth Coll.; adv. bd. FasterCures Philanthropy Adv. Svc. Named one of America 's Top Women in Bus.-Game Changers, Pink mag. & Forté Found., 2007. Office: Michael J Fox Found Church St Sta PO Box 780 New York NY 10008-0780*

BROOKS, DEBRA L., healthcare executive, neuromuscular therapist; b. Cedar Rapids, Iowa, Dec. 10, 1950; children: Brei, Benjamin, Bryan. BA, Coe Coll., 1973; MS, Clayton Coll., 1999, PhD, 2000. Cert. neuromuscular therapy Fla., natural therapeutics specialist N.Mex. Tchr. Cedar Rapids Cmty. Sch. Dist., Iowa, 1973—92; COO NeuroMuscular Therapy Ctr., Walford, Iowa, 1994—. Educator Helping Hands Seminars, Cedar Rapids, 1992—2000, Debra Brooks' Seminars, Walford, 1993—; bus. and ednl. cons. Brooks Consults, Cedar Rapids, 1990—; mem Iowa Bd. Examiners, 2001—03; chair adv. bd. ABLE, 2001—02; mem., chair Nat. Alliance State Bds., 2001—02; editl. bd. Momentum Media. Contbr. articles to profl jours and newsletters. Fundraiser, performer in musicals St Luke's Hosp, Cedar Rapids, 1978—91; fundraiser, performer in Follies Cedar Rapids Symphony, 1981—99; fundraiser, performer in telethons Variety Clubs Am, Cedar Rapids, 1989—91; mem Walford Cmty. Devel., 1994—98; editl. bd. Tng. and Conditioning Mag.; bd. dirs. Cedar Rapids Concert Chorale, 2005—, chmn. fundraising, 2006—. Named Outstanding Mentor of Yr., YWCA, 2001; recipient First in Nation Edn. Award, State of Iowa, 1991, Tribute Women of Achievement award, YWCA, 2001. Mem.: Iowa NeuroMusculary Therapy Ctr., Am. Coll. Healthcare Execs., Am. Massage Therapy Assn. (state v.p., edn. dir. 1992—94, nat. trustee Found. 1994—98, nat. bd. dirs. 1994—2002), Profl. Women's Network (chmn. 2002—03). Avocations: singing, painting, pianist, power walking, philosophy. Office: NeuroMuscular Therapy Ctr PO Box 277 Walford IA 52351-0277 Personal E-mail: drdebrabrooks@yahoo.com.

BROOKS, DERRICK DEWAN, professional football player; b. Pensacola, Fla., Apr. 18, 1973; m. Carol Brooks; children: Derrick Jr., Brianna Monai, Darius. Degree, Fla. State U., 1994, M degree, 1999. Linebacker Tampa Bay Buccaneers, 1995—. Co-hosts weekly minute radio call-in show. Active March of Dimes, D.A.R.E., Audley Evans Ctr.; host Brooks Bunch; founder Derrick Brooks Charities Found. Named Number One on The Sporting News Good Guys List for cmty. work, NFL Man of Yr., 2000, Defensive Player of Yr., 2002; named to NFL Pro-Bowl, 1997-2005, Pro-Bowl MVP, 2005 Mem.: Florida State University board of trustees. Achievements include member of Super Bowl XXXVII Champion Tampa Bay Buccaneers, 2002. Office: Tampa Bay Buccaneers 1 W Buccaneer Pl Tampa FL 33607-5797

BROOKS, DONNA JEAN, counselor, educator; b. San Francisco, Apr. 26, 1935; d. Carter Oswell and Doris Elizabeth (Birt) Garver; children: Deborah Gay Marston, Nancy Jean Littlewood, Paula Sue Giles, Jerry Wayne Brooks, Barry Glenn Brooks. BA in Bus. and Psychology, Webster U.; MA in Counseling, Parks U.; postgrad., Ariz. State U. Cert. tchr. Ariz. Career counselor Maricopa County Health Dept., 1977—97. Instr. Park U., Williams AFB. Author: Celebrate Your Choices, 1986. Clk. governing bd. Chandler Unified Sch. Dist., Ariz., 1990-91, pres. governing bd., 1991-92; chair Chandler United Way, East Valley Charity Ball Benefit, Chandler Hist. Soc., Assn. Human Action for Chandler, Orgn. Celebration of Women in Chandler Cmty.; vol. Desert Caballeros Western Mus., Elks Club, Retired Activities Tchrs. Assn. Recipient Chandler Chamber Club award, 1989; named Woman of the Yr. City of Chandler Celebration, 1989. Home: PO Box 21036 Wickenburg AZ 85358-6036

BROOKS, DOUGLAS H., food service executive; From asst. mgr. to sr. v.p. ops. Chili's Grill & Bar, 1978—92, pres., 1994—99; COO Brinker Internat., Dallas, 1998—2004, pres., 1999—2004, chmn., pres., CEO, 2004—. Office: Brinker Internat 6820 LBJ Freeway Dallas TX 75240*

BROOKS, ELLYN HERSH, retired special education educator; b. Bklyn., Mar. 25, 1943; d. Leonard and Midge Roth Hersh; m. John William Brooks, Aug. 14, 1999; children: Ross Benjamin Hochen, Allison Dawn Israel. BA, U. Fla., 1964; MEd., Trinity Coll., 1975. Cert. advanced spl. edn. tchr. Md. Spl. edn. tchr. Montgomery County Pub. Schs., Rockville, Md., 1975—2005; ret., 2005. Editor, newspaper advisor to HS journalism students. Author: children's literature. Mem.: Montgomery County Ret. Tchrs. Home: 303 Renaissance Ct Chattanooga TN 37419 Home Phone: 301-216-0776.

BROOKS, ERNIE L., lawyer; b. Dayton, Ohio, Dec. 8, 1942; BSEE, Gen. Motors Inst., 1967; MSEE, Purdue U., 1967; JD summa cum laude, Georgetown U. and Wayne State U., 1972. Bar: Mich. 1972, registered: US Patent and Trademark office. Pres. Brooks Kushman, P.C., Southfield, Mich. Note and comment editor: Wayne Law Rev., 1971—72. Named one of Top 10 Trial Lawyers in Am., Nat. Law Jour., 2006. Mem.: ABA, Mich. Intellectual Property Law Assn., Ill. State Bar Assn. Office: Brooks Kushman PC 1000 Town Ctr 22nd Fl Southfield MI 48075 Office Phone: 248-358-4400. Office Fax: 248-358-3351. E-mail: ebrooks@brookskushman.com.*

BROOKS, FREDERICK PHILLIPS, JR., computer scientist, educator; b. Durham, NC, Apr. 19, 1931; s. Frederick Phillips and Octavia Brooks; m. Nancy Lee Greenwood, June 16, 1956; children: Kenneth Phillips, Roger Greenwood, Barbara Brooks LaDine. AB in Physics, Duke U., 1953; SM, Harvard U., 1955, PhD, 1956; D Tech. Sci. (hon.), ETH-Zurich, 1991. Engr. IBM, Poughkeepsie, NY, 1956—59, Yorktown Heights, NY, 1959—60, mgr. devel. computer System/360 Poughkeepsie, 1960—64, mgr. devel. Operating System/360, 1964—65; founder computer sci. dept. U. N.C., Chapel Hill, 1964, prof., 1964—75, chmn. dept. computer sci., 1964—84, Kenan prof., 1975—. Bd. dirs. Triangle U. Computation Ctr., 1966—84, chmn., 1975—77, N.C. Ednl. Computing Svc., 1965—; active Def. Sci. Bd., 1982—86, Nat. Sci. Bd., 1987—92. Author: The Mythical Man-Month-Essays on Software Engineering, 1975, 1995; author: (with K.E. Iverson) Automatic Data Processing, 1963, Automatic Data Processing System/360 Edition, 1969; author: (with G.A. Blaauw) Computer Architecture: Concepts and Evolution, 1997; contbr. articles to profl. jours.; inventor (with D.W. Sweeney) program interruption system, alphabetical read-out device. Trustee Durham Acad., pres., 1977—80; trustee, chmn. Trinity Sch. Durham and Chapel Hill, 2003—; chmn. exec. com. Ctrl. Carolina Billy Graham Crusade, 1972—73; mem. corp. Inter-Varsity Christian Fellowship, 1968—77. Recipient McDowell award, IEEE Computer Soc., 1970, Man of Yr. award, Data Processing Mgmt. Assn., 1970, Bower award and prize for achievement in sci., Franklin Inst., 1975, Nat. Medal Tech., 1985, Harry Goode Meml. award, Am. Fedn. Info. Proc. Socs., 1989, Fellow award, Computer History Mus., 2001; fellow Guggenheim Found., 1975; grantee, NSF, AEC, NIH, NASA, Def. Advanced Projects Rsch. Agy. Fellow: IEEE (John von Neumann medal 1993, Eckert-Manchly award 2004), Brit. Computer Soc. (disting.), Assn. Computing Machinery (coun. mem.-at-large 1966—70, Disting. Svc. award 1987, Allen Newell award 1994, Alan M. Turing award 1999), Am. Acad. Arts and Scis.; mem.: NAE, NAS, Royal Acad. Engring. (U.K.), Royal Netherland Acad. Arts and Scis. Methodist. Home: 413 Granville Rd Chapel Hill NC 27514-2723 Office: Univ NC Dept Computer Sci Sitterson Hall CB# 3175 Chapel Hill NC 27599-3175 Home Phone: 919-942-2529; Office Phone: 919-962-1931. Business E-Mail: brooks@cs.unc.edu.

BROOKS, GAIL DENISE, school system administrator, consultant; b. Camden, NJ, Oct. 24, 1951; d. Russel John and Marie Alverta (Jenkins) Brooks; 1 child, Adrienne. BA, Hofstra U., 1973; MEd, U. Pa., 1983, EdD, 1997. Tchr. Camden Bd. Edn., 1973—87, asst. prin., 1987—93, dir. curriculum & assessment, 1993—98; asst. supt. Monroe (N.J.) Twp. Bd. Edn., 1998—2004; supt. Pleasantivlle (N.J.) Bd. Edn., 2004—. Adj. prof. Rowan U., Glassboro, NJ, 1987—93, Rutgers U., Camden, 2004—. Mem.: Pi Lambda Theta, Phi Delta Kappa. Methodist. Home: 1596 Ormond Ave Camden NJ 08103-2941

BROOKS, GARTH (TROYAL GARTH BROOKS), musician, singer; b. Tulsa, Okla., Feb. 7, 1962; s. Troyal Raymond and Colleen Carroll Brooks; m. Sandy Mahl, 1986 (div. 2001); children: Taylor Mayne Pearl, August Anna, Allie Colleen; m. Trisha Yearwood, Dec. 10, 2005. BS in Avtg. and Journalism, Okla. St. Univ., 1984. Recording artist (albums) Garth Brooks, No Fences (Album of Yr. Acad. Country Music, 1991), Ropin' The Wind, 1991, Beyond the Season, The Chase, 1992, In Pieces, 1993 (Grammy nomination, Best Country Male Vocal for Ain't Goin' Down (Til the Sun Comes Up), The Hits, 1994, Fresh Horses, 1995, Sevens, 1997, The Limited Series, Double Live, 1998, In the Life of Chris Gaines, 1999, Scarecrow, 2001, (songs) The Dance (Video of Yr. award Country Music Assn., 1991, Song of Yr. and Video of Yr. awards Acad. Country Music, 1991), Friends in Low Places (Single Record of Yr. Acad. Country Music, 1991, Grammy award nomination), If Tomorrow Never Comes (Am. Music award for Country Song of Yr., 1991), The Thunder Rolls, We Shall Be Free (Video of Yr., Acad. Country Music), Somewhere Other Than The Night, Learning to Live Again, (TV spls.) This is Garth Brooks, 1992, This is Garth Brooks, Too, 1994, (TV Spls.) Garth Brooks: The Hits, 1995, Garth Brooks Live in Central Park, 1997. Named Best Male Country Music Performer, 1992, 1993, Best Male Musical Performer, People's Choice Awards, 1992, 1993, 1994, Artist of Decade, Acad. Country Music Awards, 1999; named to Grand Ole Opry; recipient Entertainer of Yr. award Acad. Country Music, 1991, 1992, 1993, 1994, Male Vocalist of Yr. award, 1991, Horizon award, Entertainer of Yr. award, Country Music Assn., 1991, 1992, Grammy award for Best Male Country Vocalist, 1992, Grammy award for Best Country Collaboration with Vocals, 1998, Best Male Musical Performer, People's Choice Awards, 1995, Am. Music Awards, Favorite Country Artist & Favorite Country Album, 2000.

BROOKS, GARY, crisis management and family business consultant; BS in Biochem. Engring. and Ind. Mgmt., MIT, 1955; MSChemE and Ops. Rsch., U. Rochester, 1959. Cert. mgmt. cons., turnaround profl. With GE Co., 1955-56, Eastman Kodak Co., 1956-64; mgr. Technomic Cons. Inc., 1968-71; divsn. exec. Scott Paper Co., 1971-76; mng. prin. turnaround cons. firm New Eng., 1976-85; founder, chmn., CEO, Allomet Ptnrs., Inc., NYC, 1985—. Bd. dirs. Diomed Holdings, Inc., VRSim, Inc.; cons. in field; lectr. in field. Contbr. articles to profl. jours. Mem.: Family Firm Inst., Assn. Cert. Turnaround Profls. (1st pres.), Turnaround Mgmt. Assn. (founding mem., former bd. dirs., chair certification com.). Office: Allomet Ptnrs Ltd 510 E 23d St Ste 5G New York NY 10010 Office Phone: 917-690-0823. Business E-Mail: allometny@aol.com.

BROOKS, GENE (LESLIE GENE BROOKS), cultural organization administrator; b. Fletcher, Okla., June 15, 1936; s. Frank and Ethel E. (Spears) Brooks; m. Nancy E. Carman, Aug. 17, 1970; 1 child, Steven Frank. B in Music Edn., Okla. Bapt. U., 1959; M in Music Edn., U. Okla., 1962, D in Music Edn., 1968; postgrad., U. Colo. Chmn. music dept. Cameron U., Lawton, Okla., 1962-69, Midwestern State U., Wichita Falls, Tex., 1969-75, U. Ark., Little Rock, 1975-77; exec. dir. Am. Choral Dir. Assn., Oklahoma City, 1977—. Sec. gen. Internat. Fedn. Choral Music, 1982—85; dir. numerous choral festivals adn convs.; guest condr., clinician, adjudicator, spkr.; mem. juries 25th Internat. Choir Competition, Varna, Bulgaria, 38th Internat. Choral Competition, Gorizia, Italy, 1999, Gorizia, 2000, Nat. Choir Competition, New Zealand, 2000, 6th Internat. Choral Competition, Riva del Garda, Italy, 2000, World Choir Olympics, 2000, 02, Linz, Austria, World Choir Olympics, Busan, Republic of Korea, others. Recipient Disting. Alumni award, Okla. Bapt. U., 1985, Disting. Alumni award in Music, 1996, Disting. Alumni award, U. Okla., 1997. Mem.: Music Tchrs. Nat. Assn. (nat. choral chmn. 1972—75, chmn. music higher edn. 1975—77), Am. Choral Dir. Assn. (life), Coll. Music Soc. (life), Music Educators Nat. Conf. (life). Southern Baptist. Avocations: travel, skiing. Home: 18816 Woody Creek Dr Edmond OK 73003-4108 Office: Am Choral Dir Assn PO Box 2720 Oklahoma City OK 73101 Home Phone: 405-844-2161; Office Phone: 405-232-8161. Business E-Mail: executivedir@acdaonline.org.

BROOKS, GERALDINE, writer, reporter, news correspondent; b. Sydney, Sept. 14, 1955; arrived in Eng., 1989; d. Lawrie and Gloria (Van Boss) B.; m. Anthony Lander Horwitz, Dec. 15, 1984. BA with honors, U. Sydney, 1979; MS in Journalism, Columbia U., 1983. Reporter Sydney Morning Herald, 1979-82, The Nat. Times, NSW, Australia, 1985-86; Australasian corr. Asian Wall Street Jour., NSW, 1986-87; reporter Wall Street Jour., Cleve., 1983-84, Mid. East corr. Cairo and London, 1987—. Author: Nine Parts of Desire, Foreign Correspondence Year of Wonders, 2001, March, 2005 (Pulitzer Prize for fiction, 2006); contbr. articles to mags. Recipient Montague Grover award Australian Journalists Assn., 1979; Hal Boyle award for print reporting Overseas Press Club, N.Y.C., 1990, citation, 1991; Greg Shackleton scholar Australian Fgn. Corrs. Award Com., 1982.

BROOKS, GLENN ELLIS, political science professor, educational association administrator; b. Kerrville, Tex., Aug. 6, 1931; s. Glenn Ellis and Ellen (Mason) B.; m. Ann Rankin, May 31, 1953 (div. Apr. 1992); children: Elizabeth Lee, Amy Mason, Celia Brooks Brown. BA magna cum laude, U. Tex., Austin, 1953, MA, 1956; PhD with distinction, Johns Hopkins U., 1960. Sales mgr. Univ. Tex. Press, Austin, 1953-55; research assoc. Com. on Govt. and Higher Edn., Balt., 1957-59; instr. to prof. polit. sci. Colo. Coll., Colorado Springs, 1960-96, prof. and dean emeritus, faculty asst. to pres., 1968-70, chmn. dept. polit. sci., 1973-76, dean of coll. and faculty, 1979-87, dir. strategic planning, 1991-93. Rockefeller vis. lectr. U. Nairobi, Kenya, 1967-68; acad. visitor London Sch. Econs., 1972; NEH faculty fellow-in-residence Princeton (N.J.) U., 1978-79; bd. dirs. Am. Conf. Acad. Deans, 1982-85; cons. Nat. U. Lesotho, 1990, Am. Coun. Edn. Miver Program, 1992—; chief of party Fenix project Autonomous U. Puebla, Mex., 1994-96. Author: When Governors Convene: The Governors' Conference and National Politics, 1961; (with Frances E. Rourke) The Managerial Revolution in Higher Education, 1966. Contbr. chpts. to books, articles, essays to profl. publs. Mem. Phi Beta Kappa, Phi Eta Sigma. Democrat. Home: 526 Observatory Dr Colorado Springs CO 80904-3970 Personal E-mail: gbrooks@coloradocollege.edu.

BROOKS, H. ALLEN, architectural educator, author, lecturer; b. New Haven, Nov. 6, 1925; s. Harold Allen and Mildred (McNeill) B. BA, Dartmouth Coll., 1950; MA, Yale U., 1955; PhD, Northwestern U., 1957; D Engring. (hon.), Dalhousie U., 1984. Asst. prof. U. Ill., 1957-58; lectr. U. Toronto, 1958-61, asst. prof., 1961-64, assoc. prof., 1964-71, prof., 1971-86; vis. prof. Dartmouth Coll., 1969; Mellon chair Vassar Coll., 1970-71; vis. prof. Archtl. Assn., London, 1977-82, 2003. Author: The Prairie School: Frank Lloyd Wright and His Midwest Contemporaries, 1972 (recipient Alice Davis Hitchcock Book award 1973), Frank Lloyd Wright and the Prairie School, 1984, Le Corbusier's Formative Years: Charles-Edouard Jeanneret at La Chaux-de-Fonds, 1997 (Assn. Am. Pubs./Scholarly Pub. Divsn. Ann. award 1997); editor: Prairie School Architecture, 1975, Writings on Wright, 1981, The Le Corbusier Archive, 32 vols, 1982-85, Le Corbusier, 1987; editl. cons. Le Corbusier Sketchbooks, 1981-82; contbr. to numerous books and jours. With U.S. Army, 1946-47. Guggenheim Found. fellow, 1973-74; Can. Coun. fellow, 1975-76; Social Scis. and Humanities Rsch. Coun. Can. fellow, 1977-79, 83-85; Victoria U. fellow; receipent Wright Spirit award, Frank Llyod Wright Bldg. Conservency, 2002. Fellow Soc. Archtl. Historians; mem. Internat. Coun. Mus., Internat. Com. Monuments and Sites, Soc. Archtl. Historians U.S. (past pres., dir.), Soc. Archtl. Historians Gt. Britain, Soc. Study Architecture Can., Frank Lloyd Wright Bldg. Conservancy. Address: 80 Lyme Rd Hanover NH 03755-1910

BROOKS, HELEN BOUSKY, literature and language professor, performing arts educator; b. Tulsa; d. Richard Isadore and Mary Presley Bousky; m. William Richard Brooks, Sept. 6, 1952; children: James Richard, Andrew Thomas, Steven William. BA in English, San Francisco State U., Calif., 1968, MA in English, 1971; PhD in English and Humanities, Stanford U., Calif., 1980. Sr. lectr. English Stanford U., Calif., 1994—2002, assoc. dir. Interdisciplinary Studies in Humanities, 2000—, prof. (acting) English, 2002—. Guest lectr. English dept. U. St. Louis, Madrid, 2005; del. Oxford Round Table, 2004, 05; invited spkr. and presenter in field. Co-contributing editor: The Variorum Edition of the Poetry of John Donne: The Holy Sonnets, vol. 7, 2005; mem. editl. adv. bd. Forum on Pub. Policy Jour.; contbr. to books and essays. Del. Citizens' Diplomacy Tours, 1989; lector St. Mark's Episcopal Ch., Palo Alto, Calif., 1980—. Recipient Dinkelspiel award, Stanford U., 1994. Mem.: MLA, No. Calif. Renaissance Soc., John Donne Soc. (sec.-treas., mem. exec. bd. 2005—06). Office: Stanford U Interdisciplinary Studies in Humanities Bldg 240 Rm 108 Stanford CA 94305-2152 Office Phone: 650-723-3413.

BROOKS, JACK BASCOM, former congressman; b. Crowley, La., Dec. 18, 1922; s. Edward Chachere and Grace Marie (Pipes) B.; m. Charlotte Collins, Dec. 15, 1960; children: Jack Edward, Katherine Inez, Kimberly Grace. AA, Lamar Jr. Coll., Beaumont, Tex., 1941; BJ, U. Tex., 1943, JD, 1949. Bar: Tex. 1949. Mem. Tex. Legislature, 1946-50, 83rd-89th Congresses from 2nd Tex. dist., 1952-67, 90th-103rd Congresses from 9th Tex. dist., Washington, 1967-95. Author, Lamar Coll. bill, 1949. Lst lt. USMCR, 1942-46; col. Res. ret. Mem. ABA, State Bar Tex., Am. Legion, VFW, Sigma Delta Chi. Home and Office: 1029 East Dr Beaumont TX 77706-4738 Office Phone: 409-896-5552.

BROOKS, JAMES ELWOOD, geologist, educator; b. Salem, Ind., May 31, 1925; s. Elwood Edwin and Helen Mary (May) B.; m. Eleanore June Nystrom, June 18, 1949 (dec.); children: Nancy, Kathryn, Carolyn. AB, DePauw U., Greencastle, Ind., 1948; MS, Northwestern U., Evanston, Ill., 1950; PhD, U. Wash., Seattle, 1954. Research assoc. Ill. Geol. Survey, 1950; geologist Gulf Oil Corp., Salt Lake City, summers 1951-53; instr. geol. scis. So. Meth. U., Dallas, 1952-55, asst. prof., 1955-59, assoc. prof., 1959-62, prof., 1962-95, chmn. dept., 1961-70, dean, assoc. provost univ., 1969-72, provost, v.p., 1972-80, interim pres., 1980-81, prof. emeritus, 1995—, provost emeritus, 1995—; pres., trustee Inst. for Study Earth and Man, Dallas, 1981-97, vice chmn., trustee, 1997—, pres. emeritus. Chmn., trustee ISEM Found., Dallas, 2000—; cons. geologist firm DeGolyer & MacNaughton, Dallas, 1954-59. Contbr. articles to profl. jours. Trustee Hockaday Sch., 1982-88, Dallas Mus. Natural History Assn., 1984—, v.p., 1986-88, pres., 1988-90, hon. life trustee, 1990—; founding mem. Dallas Com. on Fgn. Rels.; hon. life mem. bd. Dallas Ft. Worth Coun. on Fgn. Affairs; mem. exec. bd., internat. rep. Circle Ten coun. Boy Scouts Am., 1982—, internat. com., chmn. 1984—; bd. vis. DePauw U., 1979-83, chmn., 1983; mem. Mayor's Task Force on Fair Park, 1992; chmn. Coun. Fair Park Instns., 1992-94. Fellow AAAS, Geol. Soc. Am., Tex. Acad. Sci., Explorers Club; mem. Am. Assn. Petroleum Geologists, Dallas Geol. Soc., Sigma Xi, Sigma Gamma Epsilon, Sigma Phi. Home: 7055 Arboreal Dr Dallas TX 75231-7315 Office: Inst Study Earth and Man PO Box 750274 Dallas TX 75275-0274 Home Phone: 214-348-1055; Office Phone: 214-768-2325. Business E-Mail: jebrooks@smu.edu.

BROOKS, JAMES L., film producer, director; b. North Bergen, NJ, May 9, 1940; s. Edward M. and Dorothy Helen (Sheinheit) B.; m. Marianne Catherine Morrissey, July 7, 1964 (div.); 1 child, Amy Lorraine; m. Holly Beth Holmberg, July 23, 1978; children: Chloe, Cooper. Student, N.Y. U., 1958-60. Writer CBS News, NYC, 1964-66; writer-producer documentaries Wolper Prodns., LA, 1966-67; founder & owner Gracie Films, 1984. Guest lectr. Stanford Grad. Sch. Communications. Creator TV series Room 222, 1968-69 (Emmy award for outstanding new series 1969); co-creator, prodr. TV series Lou Grant (Peabody award 1978); exec. prodr., co-creator TV series Mary Tyler Moore Show, 1970-77 (Emmy award for comedy writing 1971, 74-77, Outstanding Comedy Series 1975-77, Peabody award, 1977, Writers Guild Am. winner best teleplay The Last Show, nominated best teleplay in episodic comedy, 1972, 77, TV Critics Achievement in Comedy award 1977, Achievement in Series award 1977, Humanitas 1977); writer, prodr. TV series Paul Sand in Friends and Lovers, 1974; co-creator, co-exec. prodr. TV series Rhoda show, 1974-75 (Emmy awards for outstanding writing in drama 1978-80, outstanding drama 1979, 80, 2 Humanitas for 1977, 82); writer TV show The New Lorenzo Music Show, 1976; co-writer, co-prodr. TV film Thursday Game, from 1971; co-creator, exec. prodr. TV series Taxi, 1978-80 (Emmy award for best show, best writing, 1978-79, 79-80, 80-81, TV Film Critics Circle award for achievement in comedy and in a series, 1976-77, Golden Globe awards for best comedy series, 1978, 79, 80, Humanitas prize for episode entitled Blind Date, 1979); co-exec. prodr., co-writer TV series Cindy, 1978 (Writers Guild nomination for outstanding script 1978); co-creator, exec. prodr. TV series The Associates, 1979; exec. prodr., co-exec. prodr., co-creator The Tracey Ullman Show, 1986-90 (Emmy awards Outstanding Variety or Comedy series 1987, 88, 90, winner Emmy awards Outstanding Writing Variety or Music Show 1988-89), The Simpsons, 1990— (winner Emmy awards Outstanding Animated Spl., Outstanding Animated Program, winner Outstanding Animated Program); writer, co-prodr. film Starting Over (Writers Guild nomination for Best Screen Comedy Adaption 1979); actor film Modern Romance, 1981; prodr., writer, dir. film Terms of Endearment, 1983 (Gloden Globe Best Screenplay award 1983, Acad. awards for best film, best dir., best screenplay 1984, Best Dir. award Dirs. Guild Am. 1983, winner comedy based on material from another medium, 1983, Nat. Bd. Rev. Best Picture, 1983, Golden Globe award Best Picture 1983, N.Y. Film Critics Best Picture; writer, dir., prodr. film Broadcast News, 1987 (winner best picture, best. dir., best screenplay N.Y. Film Critics Awards, Dirs. Guild nomination for best dir., Acad. award nomination for Best Picture and Best Screenplay); exec. prodr. film Big, 1988 (Peoples Choice award for favorite comedy motion picture), The War of the Roses, 1989, Say Anything, 1989; exec. prodr. (TV series) The Critic, 1994, What About Joan, 2001; writer, co-prodr. I'll Do Anything, 1994; dir. (play) Bklyn. Laundry; prodr. films Bottle Rocket, 1996, Jerry Maguire, 1996, As Good As It Gets, 1997, Riding in Cars with Boys, 2001; writer, dir. films Spanglish, 2004; writer, prodr. film The Simpsons Movie, 2007. Mem. Dirs. Guild Am., Writers Guild Am., TV Acad. Arts and Scis., Screen Actors Guild, Acad. Motion Picture Arts and Scis. Office: Gracie Films/Columbia Pictures/Sony Pictures Ent Poitier Bldg 10202 Washington Blvd Culver City CA 90232-3119*

BROOKS, JANE K., real estate agent, educator; b. NYC, Feb. 5, 1921; d. Louis B. Kochmann and Nesta Bell Weicker; m. Samuel Hutchison Beer, June 3, 1989; children: Alison Spence, Roger Angus, Camilla Jane; m. Robert Angus Brooks, 1943 (dec.). BA, Smith Coll., Mass., 1942, MA, 1943. Cert. tchr. Mass., 1950, lic. real estate DC, Md., 1979. Rsch. asst. Dept. English Edn., GS English, Harvard U., Cambridge, 1958—61; coll. tchr. Dept. English., Pine MAN Coll., Wellesley, Mass., 1962—65; lectr. Dept. Literature, Am. U., Washington, 1967—69, 1979—88; sales agt. real estate HA Gill, Washington, 1979—2004; ret., 2004. Exec. interviewer Lewis Harris Poll, NYC, 1976—78; editor, publicity dir. Textile Mus., Washington, 1978—79. Editor: Smith College Handbook, 1941—42, Audience Mag., 1959—62, Guide to Part-time Study and Employment in Washington, 1967. Mem.: Literary Soc. of Wash. (corr. sec.), Smithsonian Women's Com. (steering com. 1973—). Avocations: reading, singing, writing, poetry, theater. Home: 2912 - 32 St NW Washington DC 20008

BROOKS, JEFFREY JAMES, environmental services administrator, educator; b. Bay City, Mich., 1967; s. James Edwards and Carol Ruth Brooks; life ptnr. Robin S. Mueller. AS, Delta Coll., University Center, Mich., 1988; BS, Saginaw Valley State U., University Center, 1990; MS, U. Ga., Athens, 1998; PhD, Colo. State U., Ft. Collins, 2003. Water-borne disease control specialist US Peace Corps, Cotonou, Benin, 1990—93; wildlife biology technician U. Ga., Athens, 1993—95, grad. rsch. asst., 1996—98; wildlife biology technician SCA Americorps, Ochopee, Fla., 1995—96; grad. rsch. coord. dept. natural resource recreation and tourism Colo. State U., 2001—03, rsch. assoc. dept. journalism and tech. comm., 2003—04, faculty affiliate, 2005—; social sci. analyst Rocky Mountain Rsch. Sta. US Forest Svc., Ft. Collins, 2004—06, cmty. forestry specialist Internat. Programs Office Washington, 2006—07; environ. planner, recreation Tetra Tech EC, Inc., Bothell, Wash., 2007—. Peace Corps campus recruiter Office Internat. Programs Colo. State U., 2000—03, co-author, cons. rsch. grant proposal Office Internat. Programs, 2002—03; cons., team mem. tech. assistance mission to Nigeria, Internat. Programs Office, US Forest Svc., Washington, 2006—07; cons. rsch. grant proposal Tetra Teach EC, Inc., Bothell, Wash., 2007—. Contbr. articles to profl. jours. Student rep. HIV/AIDS awareness task force Delta Coll., University Center, 1986—87; group leader Habitat for Humanity ho. constrn. project U. Ga., Athens, 1997—98; participant ann. walk/fundraiser Am. Diabetes Assn., Ft. Collins, 2005; counselor/leader for HS youth group St. Peter Evang. Luth. Ch., Ft. Collins, 1999—2001, coord. establishment of presch., 2005—, presch. ministry team leader, 2005—. Recipient Disting. Internat. Involvement and Svc. award, Colo. State U., Office Internat. Programs, 2002—03; travel grantee, Colo. State U., 2001—02, G.F. and H.A. Baggley fellow, Colo. State U., Dept. Natural Resource Recreation and Tourism, 2001—02, 2002—03. Mem.: Internat. Assn. Wildland Fire (assoc.), Nat. Peace Corps Assn. (assoc.). Achievements include development of a conceptual model for building collaborative capacity in natural resources management for communities of stakeholders. Avocations: hiking, cooking, camping, fishing, travel. Office Phone: 970-407-8379. Business E-Mail: jeffrey.brooks@tteci.com.

BROOKS, JEFFREY MARTIN, marketing and sales executive; b. Charlotte, NC, Oct. 14, 1958; s. Jack M. and Margaret Anne (Reap) B.; m. Kim Marke Whitaker, Sept. 26, 1981; 2 children: Justin Jeffrey Whitaker, Evan Martin Whitaker. BSBA in Acctg., East Carolina U.; MS in Econs., N.C. State U. Staff acct. Ernst & Whinney, Raleigh, N.C., 1980-82; acct. rep. Data Gen. Corp., Charlotte, 1982-85; mgr. systems mktg. AT&T, Charlotte, 1985-86; pres. Fastfly Corp., 1985-89; v.p. sales and distbn. Vanguard Cellular Systems, Inc., Greensboro, N.C., 1989-94; v.p. mktg. and sales So. Comm. (subs. So. Co.), Atlanta, 1994—97; asst. v.p. corp. mktg. BellSouth, Atlanta, 1997—2001; v.p. N.Am. channel Vigilinx, 2001—03; exec. v.p. mktg. and sales W.V. Fiber, 2003—04; CEO Ulanji, Charleston, SC, 2004—. Cons. Charlotte Hornets, GTE. Vol. Jr. Achievement, Habitat for Humanity, YMCA Youth Sports; mem. Mt. Pisgah United Meth. Ch., Alpharetta, Ga. Mem. AICPA, Aircraft Owners and Pilots Assn., Nat. Bus. Aircraft Assn., U.S.A. Soccer, Nat. Youth Coaches Assn. Office: 140 N Main St Ste 202 Summerville SC 29483 Office Phone: 843-553-6132. Business E-Mail: jbrooks@ulanji.com.

BROOKS, JERRY CLAUDE, safety engineer, educator; b. College Park, Ga., Apr. 23, 1936; s. John Bennett and Mattie Mae (Timms) B.; m. Peggy Sue Thornton, Feb. 26, 1961; children: Apryll Denise, Jerry Claude, Susan Vereen. BS, Ga. Inst. Tech., 1958. Safety engr. Cotton Prodrs. Assn., Atlanta, 1959-64, dir. safety and loss control, 1964-70; dir. corp. protection Gold Kist, Inc., Atlanta, 1970-81; dir. corp. safety J.P. Stevens, 1981-84, dir. safety and security, 1984-86, dir. health and safety, 1986-88; dir. loss control Am. Yarn Spinners Assn., 1988-89; dir. safety Spring Industries, Inc., 1989-2000; cons. Occupational Safety Cons., 2000—. Instr., Ga. Safety Inst., Athens, Ga., 1971-78. Bd. dirs. Greater Lithonia (Ga.) Homeowners Assn., Ga. Soc. Prevention of Blindness, Ga. Safety Coun. Served with AUS, 1958-59. Mem. Am. Soc. Safety Engrs. (chpt. pres. 1968-69, regional v.p. 1974-76), Nat. Safety Coun. (gen. chmn. fertilizer sect. 1969-70, gen. chmn. textile sec. 1985-87, Disting. Svc. to Safety award 1989, Palmetto chpt. pres. 1994), So. Safety Conf. (v.p. bus. and industry 1968-74, pres. 1974), Am. Textile Mfrs. Inst. (chmn. safety and health com. 1991-93, Donald B. Hayes lifetime achievement award 2000), Am. Soc. Indsl. Security, S.C. Occupl. Safety Coun. (bd. mem. 1994-99), Ga. Bus. and Industry Assn. (dir., named outstanding mem. 1981), Internat. Assn. Hazard Control Mgrs. (chpt. pres. 1979-80), Masons, Rosicrucians, Exch. Club (pres. 1969-70, Book of Golden Deeds award 1981) (Lithonia). Home: 100 Woodmere Ln Columbus NC 28722-4408

BROOKS, JERRY ROBERT, small business owner; b. Gainesville, Tex., Dec. 28, 1925; s. Clay Younger and Mary Irene (Simmons) Brooks. BS in Econs., U. North Tex., 1948, MS in Econs., 1950. Lic. pvt. pilot 1946. Tool designer Nat. Supply divsn. ARMCO Stl., Inc., Gainesville, 1955—82; owner, mgr. Brooks Engrng. Co., Gainesville, 1982—. Contbr. articles to profl. jours. Mem. Gainesville Arts Coun., 1981—84. With USAAF, 1944—45. Recipient Internat. award merit, Internat. Inventors Exhbn., 1965—66, Gold Medal award, 1967, Bronze medal, Internat. Exhbn. New Inventions and Products, 1971. Mem.: AIAA, Planetary Soc., Nat. Space Soc. Achievements include nine patents in diverse fields. Avocations: music, trumpet. Home: 1716 Merrywood Way Gainesville TX 76240-5142 Office: Brooks Engrng Co 921 N Grand Ave Gainesville TX 76240

BROOKS, JOAE GRAHAM, psychiatrist; b. Boston, June 14, 1926; d. Collins and Hannah Slade (Benton) Graham; m. Bernard Charles Brooks, Jan. 11, 1976; children by previous marriage: Anne Benton Millman, Jane Graham Selzer. Nursing degree, Mass. Gen. Hosp. Sch. Nursing, 1947; AB with distinction, U. Rochester, 1950, MD, 1954. Diplomate Am. Bd. Psychiatry and Neurology. Intern in medicine Duke Hosp., Durham, N.C., 1954-55; resident in psychiatry Mass. Mental Health Ctr., Boston, 1955-57; resident in child psychiatry Beth Israel Hosp., Boston, 1957-59, mem. staff, 1959-97; pvt. practice Brookline, Mass., 1959-97. Cons. New Eng. Home for Little Wanderers, Boston, 1959-75, Kimberly Clark Corp., 1983-97; asst. clin. prof. psychiatry Harvard U. Med. Sch., Boston, 1978-97; vol. psychiatrist Sr. Friendship Ctr. Health Clinic, Naples, Fla., 1998-2007; mem. Bd. Registration in Medicine of Mass., 1991-95. Author: No More Diapers! A Guide to Toilet Training, 1971, 2d edit., 1991, When Children Ask About Sex-A Guide for Parents, 1975, I'm A Big Kid Now! A Guide to Toilet Training for Children and Parents, 1989. Distinguished fellow APA (life), Acad. Child and Adolescent Psychiatry (life); mem. Mass. Psychiat. Soc., New Eng. Coun. Child Psychiatry (bd. dirs. 1979-82, pres. 1987-89). Home: 3 Crosslands Dr Kennett Square PA 19348 Office Phone: 239-263-4725.

BROOKS, JOHN EDWARD, college president; b. Boston, July 13, 1923; s. John Edward and Mildred (McCoy) B. BS in Physics, Coll. Holy Cross, 1949; postgrad. in geophysics, Pa. State U., 1949-50; MA in Philosophy, Boston Coll., 1954, MS in Geophysics, 1959; S.T.D. in Dogmatic Theology, Gregorian U., Rome, Italy, 1963; H.H.D. (hon.), St. Ambrose Coll., 1976; D.Sc. (hon.), Worcester Poly. Inst., 1980; D Humanities, Assumption Coll., 1990; HHD (hon.), St. Anselm Coll., 1993; D Humanities (hon.), U. New England, 1994, Anna Maria Coll., 1994, Coll. of the Holy Cross, 1994. Joined Soc. of Jesus, 1950; ordained priest Roman Catholic Ch., 1959; instr. math. and physics Coll. of Holy Cross, Worcester, Mass., 1954-56, instr. theology, 1963-64, asst. prof., 1964-67, assoc. prof. religious studies, 1967-93, chmn. dept. theology, 1964-69, Loyola prof. humanities, 1993—, v.p., dean coll., 1968-70, pres., trustee, 1970-94, pres. emeritus, 1994—, sec. com. ednl. policy, 1968-70, chmn., 1970-94. Participant bibl. and archeol. consortium Jewish Inst. on Religion, Hebrew Union Coll., 1968; inst. acad. deans Am. Coun. Edn., St. Louis U., 1968; trustee St. Peter's Coll., Jersey City, 1969-75, Canisius Coll., Buffalo, 1974-80, Spring Hill Coll., Mobile, Ala., 1981-94, Anna Maria Coll., Paxton, Mass., 1998—, St. Sebastian's Sch., Needham, Mass., 1998-; mem. Mass. Postsecondary Edn. Commn., Mass. 1202 Commn., 1974-77; mem. exec. com. New Eng. Colls. Fund, 1974, 78; mem. Mass. Pub./Pvt. Forum; mem. Worcester Downtown Devel. Corp., Mass. Biotech. Rsch. Inst., 1985—; bd. visitors Air U., 1978-86; bd. dirs. Worcester Mcpl. Rsch. Bur., Inc. Community trustee United Way Cen. Mass.; consortium dir. Social Svcs. Corp., Worcester; bd. dirs. Worcester Mechanics Hall Assn.; mem. commn. govtl. rels. Am. Coun. on Edn., 1989-92. With U.S. Army, 1942-46. Mem. Assn. Jesuit Colls. and Univs. (bd. dirs. 1970-94), Assn. Ind. Colls. and Univs. in Mass. (v.p. 1972-73, chmn. coms., exec. com.), New Eng. Assn. Schs. and Colls. (sec.-treas. 1985-92, pres.-elect 1993, pres. 1994), Econ. Club (pres. Worcester chpt. 1977-78, exec. com. 1978-86), Delta Epsilon Sigma, Alpha Sigma Nu. Office: Coll of Holy Cross Ciampi Hall Worcester MA 01610 Home Phone: 508-793-2258; Office Phone: 508-793-3656. Business E-Mail: jbrooks@holycross.edu.

BROOKS, JOHN SAMUEL JOSEPH, pathologist, researcher; b. Phila., Feb. 2, 1948; BS in Biology, St. Joseph's Coll., Phila., 1970; MD, Thomas Jefferson U., 1974. Diplomate Am. Bd. Pathology. Resident in pathology U. Pa., Phila., 1974-78, chief resident, 1978, asst. prof., 1979-84, assoc. prof., 1984-88, prof., 1988-93, prof. pathology, 2002—, vice-chmn. pathology, 2004—; chmn. dept. pathology Roswell Pk. Cancer Inst., Buffalo, 1993—2002, chmn. dept. lab. medicine, 1997—2002, pres. med. staff, 1997-98; prof., vice chmn. pathology Med. Sch. SUNY, Buffalo, 1993—2002; chmn. dept. pathology Pa. Hosp., 2004—. Vis. prof. Royal Marsden Hosp./Inst. Cancer Rsch., London, 1987; expert in immunohistochemistry. Author: Pathology, 1989; contbr. articles to New Eng. Jour. Medicine, Jour. of AMA, Jour. Urology, Internat. Jour. Ob.-Gyn. Pathology, Am. Jour. Pathology; editor Internat. Jour. Surg. Pathology, 1993-99; mem. bd. editors: Jour. Modern Pathology, Am. Jour. Surg. Pathology, and reviewer; contbr. over 140 articles to profl. jours. Fellow Royal Coll. Pathology; mem. AAAS, Am. Assn. Cancer Rsch., Pathology Soc. Phila. (pres. 1988-90), Ea. Coop. Oncology Group (chmn. sarcoma pathology com. Madison chpt. 1988-95), Internat. Acad. Pathology (edn. com. Atlanta chpt. 1989—), U.S.-Can. Acad. Pathology (coun. mem. 1993-96), Am. Soc. Clin. Pathologists (chair anat. pathology coun. 1995-97, dep. commr. 1997—, bd. dir. 2000—, v.p. 2004-2005, pres.-elect, 2005-2006, pres., 2006-), Arthur Purdy Stout Soc. Surg. Pathologists (coun. mem. 1994), Am. Assn. Clin. Rsch., Fedn. Am. Soc. Exptl. Biology, Medicine Coverage Adv. Com. Lab. Diagnostics Panel, Nat. Internat. Reputation in Diagnostic Surg. Pathology Democrat. Roman Catholic. Achievements include research in significance of double phenotypes in sarcomas, growth factors in sarcomas, in immunohistochemistry; posthumous diagnosis of Pres. Cleveland's tumor. Office: Dept Pathology 6 Preston Bldg Pa Hosp 800 Spruce St Philadelphia PA 19107 Business E-Mail: john.brooks@uphs.upenn.edu.

BROOKS, JOHN WHITE, lawyer; b. Long Beach, Calif., Sept. 3, 1936; s. John White and Florence Belle (O'Grady) B.; m. Elizabeth Ann Bellmore, June 21, 1958; children: Stephen Sanford, John Tinley. AB, Stanford U., 1958, LLB, 1966. Assoc. Luce, Forward, Hamilton and Scripps, San Diego, 1966-71, ptnr., 1971-81, sr. ptnr., 1981—2004, sr. internat. counsel, 2004—; founding chmn. Internat. Svcs. Group, 1989—. Mem. Internat. Coun. Inst. Ams., Pacific Coun. Internat. Policy. 1996-98; panelist Ctr. for Internat. Comml. Arbitration, 1987—; bd. dirs. Union of Pan-Asian Communities, , 1989-98, Ctr. for Dispute Resolution, 1986—; chmn. Pacific Rim Adv. Coun., 1984-91. Author: Passport Pal, The Pacific Rim, 1996-2000, The Heads Up Report; contbr. articles to profl. jours. Mem. Commn. of the Californias, 1977—79; chmn. San Diego Regional Yr. 2000 Working Group, 1998—2000; dir. Corp. Fin. Coun. of San Diego, 1977—82, chmn., 1980—81; bd. visitors Stanford Law Sch., 1978—80. Lt. USN, 1958—63. Alfred P. Sloan scholar, Stanford U., 1958, Rocky Mountain Mineral Law Found. Research scholar, 1966. Mem. ABA (bus. law sect., com. on internat. commercial transactions, subcom. on Asia-Pacific law and internat. bus. structures and agreements, com. on negotiated transactions, internat. law sect., subcom. on multinat. corps., com. on internat. comml. Transactions, com. on corp. compliance, subcom. on compliance set-up and structure, subcom. on developing codes of conduct and compliance policies), Calif. Bar Assn. (bus. law sect. com. on corps. 1977, vice chmn. com. on internat. practice 1986-87, exec. com. internat. law sect. 1987), San Diego County Bar Assn., Internat. Bar Assn. (com. on issues and trading in securities 1980-89, com. on procedures for settling disputes 1980—, com. on bus. orgns. 1989—), Inter-Pacific Bar Assn. (com. on internat. trade), Am. Arbitration Assn. (panel of arbitrators 1975-96), State Bar Calif. Avocations: greenhouse gardening, horse competitions, helicopters, wine, food. Office: Luce Forward Hamilton & Scripps 600 W Broadway Ste 2600 San Diego CA 92101-3372 Office Phone: 619-699-2410. Business E-Mail: jwbrooks@luce.com.

BROOKS, JOYCE MARIA, music educator; b. Scranton, Pa., Jan. 17, 1966; d. James Anthony Geroulo and Mary Joyce (Emmel) Geruolo; 1 child, James M. MusB, Wilkes U., 1988; M Piano Performance, SUNY, Binghamton, 1990. Music tchr. Pocono Mount Sch. Dist., Swiftwater, Pa., 1990—. Mem.: Am. Coll. Musicians, Music Educators Nat. Conf. Office: Swiftwater Elem Ctr PO Box 200 Swiftwater PA 18370 Personal E-mail: JMBTrebleclef@peoplepc.com.

BROOKS, KATHLEEN, journalist; b. Atlanta, Jan. 25, 1957; d. William Chesley and Sara (Brooks) Howton. BA, Stephens Coll., Columbia, Mo., 1978. Mktg. asst. The Laitram Corp., New Orleans, 1978-79; reporter Daily Home, Talladega, Ala., 1979-80, copy editor, 1980-81; asst. wire editor, reporter Gastonia Gazette, NC, 1981, wire editor, 1981-84; asst. wire editor Comml. Appeal, Memphis, 1984-88, Washington editor, 1988-91, nat. editor, 1991—2005; comm. advisor FedEx Freight, 2006. Methodist.

BROOKS, KENNETH N., forestry educator; m. Pamela Naylor; children: Marianne, Robin, Cherie, Nicole. BS in Range Sci., Utah State U., 1966; MS in Watershed Mgmt., U. Ariz., 1969, PhD in Watershed Mgmt., 1970. Hydrologist North Pacific Divsn. Corps of Engrs., Portland, Oreg., 1971-73, Tng. and Methods br. Hydrologic Engrng. Ctr., Davis, Calif., 1973-75; asst. prof. dept. forest resources U. Minn., St. Paul, 1975-79, assoc. prof., 1979-85, prof., 1985—, dir. grad. studies in natural resources sci. and mgmt., 1987—; fellow Environment and Policy Inst. East-West Ctr., Honolulu, 1983—84. Cons. nat. and internat. agencies and firms including Food and Agrl. Orgn. of UN, U.S. Agy. for Internat. Devel., World Bank; condr. workshops in field; Fulbright lectr., Taiwan, 1997-98. Co-author: Guidelines for Economic Appraisal of Watershed Management Projects, 1987, Watershed Management Project Planning, Monitoring and Evaluation: A Manual for the ASEAN Region, 1989, Hydrology and the Management of Watersheds, 1991, 3d edit. 2003, Challenges in Upland Conservation: Asia and the Pacific, 1993, Dryland Forestry, 1995; contbr. articles to profl. jours. Am. Inst. Hydrology (chmn. bd. registration 1995-2003, sec. 1992), Soc. Am. Foresters (chmn. water resources working group 1991-93), Am. Water Resources Assn. (dir. West North Ctrl. dist. 1987-90), Western Snow Conf., Internat. Soc. Tropical Foresters, Xi Sigma Pi, Sigma Xi, Phi Kappa Phi. Business E-Mail: kbrooks@umn.edu.

BROOKS, KEVIN M., multimedia researcher, technology storyteller; BS in Comm., Drexel U., 1982; MA in Film Prodn., Stanford U., Calif., 1985; PhD in Media Arts and Scis., MIT, Cambridge, 1999. Tech. writer, computer systems mgr., video writer/dir. ASK Computer Systems, Mountain View, Calif., 1986—87; audio visual/media specialist, multimedia instrnl. designer, systems specialist Apple Computer, Cupertino, Calif., 1987—91; tech. instr., rsch. asst. MIT Media Lab., Cambridge, Mass., 1991—99; principle staff rschr., tech. storyteller Motorola, Inc. - Motorola Labs./Human Interface Labs., Lexington, Mass., 1999—. Contbr. articles to profl. publs., chapters to books. Named to The Ebony Power 150, Ebony mag., 2007. Home: 33 Grace St Malden MA 02148 Home Phone: 781-324-1758. E-mail: brooks@media.mit.edu, Kevin.Brooks@motorola.com.*

BROOKS, KIX (LEON ERIC BROOKS), musician; b. Shreveport, La., May 12, 1955; m. Barbara Brooks; children: Molly, Eric. Grad., La. Tech. Staff songwriter Tree Pub.; songwriter Highway 101, The Nitty Gritty Dirt Band; with Brooks & Dunn, 1988—; rec. artist Arista, 1991—. Prodr. clothing line "Panhandle Slim Western Wear" with Ronnie Dunn. Singer: (albums) (with Ronnie Dunn) Brand New Man, 1991 (Acad. Country Music award Album of Yr., 1992), Hard Workin' Man, 1993 (Grammy award Best Country Vocal Performance by Duo or Group for Hard Workin' Man, 1993), Waitin' on Sundown, 1994, Borderline, 1996 (Grammy award Best Country Vocal Performance by Duo or Group for My Maria, 1996), Greatest Hits Collection, 1997, If You See Her, 1998, Tight Rope, 1999, Super Hits, 1999, Steers and Stripes, 2001, It Won't Be Christmas Without You, 2002, Red Dirt Road, 2003, Greatest Hits Collection: Volume II, 2004, Hillbilly Deluxe, 2005 (Single of Yr., Song of Yr., & Music Video of Yr. for Believe, Country Music Assn. Awards, 2006, Song of Yr. for Believe, Acad. Country Music, 2006), Kix Brooks, 1993, Common Thread: The Songs of the Eagles, 1994 (Country Music Assn. Album of Yr., 1994), (singles) Boot Scootin' Boogie, 1992, We'll Burn That Bridge, 1993, Rock My World (Little Country Girl), 1993, (songs) (8 Seconds (soundtrack) Ride 'Em High, Ride 'Em Low, 1994, (with Hank Thompson) Hooked on Honky Tonk, 1997, (with Reba McEntire) If You See Him, If You See Her, 1998. Co-recipient Top New Vocal Duo or Group award, Acad. Country Music, 1991, Entertainer of Yr. award, 1995, 1996, 2001, Top Vocal Duo award, 1991—97, 2000—03, 2005—07, Vocal Event of Yr. award, 2007, Home Depot Humanitarian award, 2007, Vocal Duo of Yr. award, Country Music Assn., 1992—99, 2001—06, Entertainer of Yr. award, 1996, Favorite Country Group award, Am. Music Awards, 2004, 2005. Office: Brooks and Dunn PO Box 120669 Nashville TN 37212-0669

BROOKS, LARRY ROGER, judge; b. Oklahoma City, Mar. 8, 1949; s. Stanley James and Dorothy Marguerite (Miller) B.; m. Rebecca Jean Nix, June 5, 1971. BS in Agronomy, Okla. State U., 1971, MS in Agronomy, 1973; JD, U. Okla., 1976. Bar: Okla. 1976. Pvt. practice law, Idabel, Okla., 1977; asst. dist. atty. Craig County Dist. Attys. Office, Vinita, Okla., 1978, Logan County Dist. Attys. Office, Guthrie, Okla., 1979-94; assoc. judge Dist. Ct., Logan County, Okla., 1995—. Ch. bd. mem. Guthrie (Okla.) Ch. of the Nazarene. Mem. Okla. Bar Assn., Guthrie Lions Club (pres. 1991-92), Train Collectors Assn., Nat. Ry. Hist. Soc. Avocations: toy train and railroad memorabilia, railroad history, riding trains. Home: 324 N Capitol St Guthrie OK 73044-3640 Office: Assoc Dist Judge Logan County Courthouse Guthrie OK 73044

BROOKS, LILA, animal rights activist, retired hotel executive; b. Budapest, Hungary; d. Jack Brooks and Lilly Risser. Student, U. Budapest, Marymount Coll., London, UCLA. Hotel exec. Knickerbocker Hotel, 1953—63, banquet mgr. Founder Calif. Wildlife Defenders, 1967—. Author articles, brochures and pamphlets. Vol. Air Force Intelligence, LA, US Army Comm. Corps. Recipient award, LA City Coun., 1975, St. Francis of Assisi Humane award, Mayor Tom Bradley, 1976, award, City of Glendale, 1980, LA County, 1982, Former Councilman Zev Yaroslavsky, 1988. Office: PO Box 2025 Hollywood CA 90078 Home Phone: 323-662-9281; Office Phone: 323-663-1856.

BROOKS, LILLIAN DRILLING ASHTON (LILLIAN HAZEL CHURCH), adult education educator; b. Grand Rapids, Mich., May 27, 1921; d. Walter Brian and Lillian Church; m. Frederick Morris Drilling, 1942 (div. Apr. 1972); children: Frederick Walter, Stephen Charles, Lawrence Alan, Lynn Anne; m. Richard Moreton Ashton, Aug. 25, 1973 (dec. 1990); m. Ralph J. Brooks, May 21, 1994. Student, Grand Rapids Jr. Coll., 1939-41, Wayne State U., 1941-42, Grand Rapids Art Inst., 1945-49, UCLA, 1964-69, Loyola Marymount Coll., Westchester, Calif., 1970-73; life tchg. credential, U. So. Calif., Long Beach, 1973. Life teaching credential, Calif. Decorator John Widdicomb Furniture Co., 1945-49; tchr. art Inglewood Sch. Dist., Calif., 1965-73; tchr. adult edn. art Downey Unified Sch. Dist., 1973-95; tchr. art Assn. Retarded Citizens and Mentally Disadvantaged Students Downey Cmty. Health Ctr., 2003—04. Art tchr. institutionalized adults ages 18 to 60, 2000-2004; lectr. Downey Art League, 1990-92, Whittier (Calif.) Art Assn., 1991, h.s. and mid. sch. lectr., 1994-95; judge Children's Art Exhibit, Downey, 1992; participant Getty Found., San Francisco, 1993, Getty Found., Cranbrook, 1994, Getty Conf. on Aesthetics, 1995, Cin. U., 1992, El Segundo, 1994; mem. state accreditation com. Inglewood and Downey United Sch. Dists., 1966-70, 75-80, 85—; owner A & B Furniture Svc. Ctr., 1995—. One-woman shows include El Segundo Mcpl. Libr., 1965, Pico Rivera Art Gallery, 1978, Downey Art Mus., 1999; exhibited in group shows at Fairlane Show, Dearborn, Mich., 1959, Jane Lessing Art Gallery, 1966, Westchester Mcpl. Libr., 1971, Inglewood City Hall, 1973, Aegina Sch., Greece, 1973, Downey Mus. Art, 1992, 99-2000; represented in permanent collection U. Mich., Calif. Senate Bldg. Pres. bd. dirs. Downey Art Mus., 1996-2002, dir. Mus., 1998, vol. dir., 1999, bd. dirs. 1998-2000; art commr. City of Dearborn, Mich., 1954-59; former pres. Dearborn Art Inst., Pacific Art Guild; pres. Downey Art League, 1991-94, v.p., 1999-2000; pres. Exhbn. Ch., 1995, v.p. 1996-98; vol. dir. Art Mus., 1998-99; lectr. on art as a career local Downey high and mid. schs.; juried children's art shows; vol. tchr. basic art; judge art shows. Recipient Certs. of Appreciation for contbn. of leadership Coord. Coun. Downey, Downey Governing Bd., Downey Bd. Edn., 1997, 2002, Cmty. Svc. award for Outstanding Svc. Downey Rotary, 1994, Cert. of Recognition Calif. State Assembly, 1999, Downey Coord. Coun., 1998-99, award 2002; named Tchr. of Yr., Masons, Downey, 1986; painting chosen to represent dist. in state capital, 1999-2001. Mem. Calif. Coun. on Art Edn. (parliamentarian Downey 1990-92, Calco Excellence in Tchg. award 1991, various certs.). Avocations: reading, hiking, international travel, photography, painting. Home: 9318 Fostoria St Downey CA 90241-4020

BROOKS, LINTON FORRESTALL, former federal agency administrator; b. Boston, Aug. 15, 1938; m. Barbara Julius; children: Julie, Kathryn. BS in Physics, Duke U., 1959; MA in Govt. and Politics, U. Md., 1972; disting. grad., USN War Coll., 1979. Commd. ensign USN, 1959, advanced through grades to capt., 1979; dir. arms control NSC, 1986—89; head US del. on nuc. and space talks, chief strategic arms reductions negotiator US Dept. State, 1989—92; asst. dir. strategic and nuc. affairs US Arms Control and Disarmament Agy., 1992—93; v.p., asst. to Pres. for policy analysis Ctr. Naval Analyses, Alexandria, Va., 1993—2001; dep. adminstr. def. nuc. nonproliferation US Dept. Energy, Washington, 2001—02, acting under sec. of for nuclear security, 2002—03, under sec. for nuclear security, 2003—07, acting adminstr. Nat. Nuclear Security Adminstrn. Washington, 2002—03, adminstr., 2003—07. Cons. strategic arms reductions Clinton Adminstrn. Contbr. articles to profl. jours. Mem.: Phi Beta Kappa. Personal E-mail: linton.brooks@cox.net.

BROOKS, LORRAINE ELIZABETH, retired music educator; b. Port Chester, NY, Mar. 10, 1936; d. William Henry Brooks and Marion Elizabeth Brooks. BS in Music Edn., SUNY, Potsdam, 1958; M of Performance, Manhattan Sch. Music, 1970; cert. in Religion EPS, Trinity Coll., 2001. Dir. Camp Spruce-Mountain Lakes, North Salem, N.Y., 1964-73; youth adviser St. Peter's Episcopal Ch., Port Chester, N.Y., 1964-65, St. Andrew's-St. Peter's Ch., Yonkers, N.Y., 1970-73; v.p. South Yonkers Youth Council, 1970-76; assoc. Sisters Charity of N.Y., Scarsdale, 1978—; eucharistic min., lector Our Lady of Victory Ch., Mt. Vernon, NY, 1981-93, 1981—93; asst. chaplain White Plains Hosp. Ctr., NY, 1981—2000. Cons. Quincy Tenants Assn., Mt. Vernon, 1986—; Cath. spiritual dir., 1986—; choral dir. Elem. Middle Sch.; cons. in field; workshop presenter in kidney hemodialysis transplant; workshop presenter in aging actively St. Denis Roman Cath. Ch., Hopewell Junction, NY, 2006. Soloist Greenhaven Correctional Facility retreat, N.Y., 1994; recital St. Mary's Ch. Outreach Program, 1994. Vestrywoman St. Andrew's Episc. Ch., Yonkers, 1971-75; contralto soloist St. Peter's Episc. Ch., Port Chester, 1959-69, Cape Cod Roman Cath. Charismatic Conf., 1993; mem. Collegiate Chorale, NYC, 1958-68; svc. team mem. Charismatic Cmty., Scarsdale, 1975-91; v.p. Willwood Tenant Assn., Mt. Vernon, 1981-82, pres., 1982-84; vol. speaker NY Regional Transplant Program, 1992—; active Montefiore Med. Ctr. TRIO, 1991—, presenter kidney transplant program, 1995; active Teen/Twenty Encounter Christ, 1995-97; soloist concert Holy Spirit Episcopal Ch., Orleans, Mass.; facilitator Our Lady of the Cape, Brewster, Mass.; inspirational spkr. St. Joan of Arc, Orleans, Mass., 2002; lector, eucharistic min., workshop presenter, leader of prayer group, cons. St. Mary's Roman Cath. Ch., 1993—, facilitator RENEW program, 1994—, CORE team mem., 1996, coord. prayer group Day of Reflection, elected leader prayer group, 1998—, adviser young adults ministry, 1998-2002; asst. coord. RENEW, St. Mary's Ch., Mt. Vernon, NY, leader Charismatic Prayer Group, 1998-2000, cons. to Charismatic group, 2000—; coord. Life in the Spirit Program, 1997; trustee Edn. Parish Svc. Program, Trinity Coll., 2000; vol. chaplain for renal patients St. Joseph's M.C., Yonkers, NY, 2001—; team mem. Women's Cursillo-English, NY Archdiocese; active Christopher Leadership course Gabriel Richard Inst., NY, 2000; dir. EPS Local Task Force, 2003-; mem. Assn. Christian Therapist, McLean, Va., 2003—. Mem. Westchester County Sch. Music Assn. (exec. bd.), Scarsdale Tchrs. Assn. (exec. bd.), Music Educators Nat. Conf., West Cmty. Sch. Music Assn (exec. bd. 1967-70). Democrat. Roman Catholic. Avocations: swimming, reading, walking, organic cooking, concerts. Personal E-mail: brookhem@aol.com.

BROOKS, LYNDA BARBARA, psychologist; b. Seattle, May 4, 1953; d. James Spiro and Anna Lois David; m. Steven Lawrence Brooks, Aug. 25, 1974; children: Joseph Steven, Bryan James. BA cum laude, San Diego State U., 1994, MA in Devel. Psychology, 1996; MA in Clin. Psychology, Calif. Sch. Profl. Psychology, 1998, PhD, 2001; cert., Nat. U., San Diego, 2003. Diplomate Am. Bd. Psychology. Intern Bayview Hosp., Chula Vista, Calif., 2000—01; counselor, therapist Bio-Psyco-Social Rehab., Vista, Calif., 2001—02, The EYE, San Marcos, Calif., 2001—02; counselor Cmty. Rsch. Found., Oceanside, Calif., 2002—04; intern Oceanside Unified Sch. Dist., 2002—03; counselor crisis, referrals United Health Group, San Diego, 2004—05; psychologist Psychiatric Ctrs. at San Diego, Escondido, Calif., 2005—. Tchg. asst. intelligence testing Calif. Sch. Profl. Psychology, 1997—98; presenter in field. Editor: Calif. Sch. Profl. Psyh-newspaper, 1997—98; mem. editl. bd.:, 1996—97; contbr. chapters to books. Vol. Trauma Intervention Program, Fallbrook, 2003—05; vol., counseling ministry St. Peter's Cath. Ch., Fallbrook, Calif., 1999—2003. Recipient Poster Presentation award, Psi Chi, 1995. Nat. Honor Soc. in Psychology, 1995; scholar, Phi Theta Kappa. 1991. Mem.: APA, San Diego Psychol. Assn. Democrat. Roman Catholic. Avocations: art, theater.

BROOKS, MARTHA FINN, consumer products company executive; BA in Econs., Polit. Sci., Yale Univ., MA in Pub., Pvt. Mgmt. V.p. Cummins, Inc.; v.p. engr. bus., global mktg., sales and engring. Alcan, Inc., 2002, pres., CEO, rolled products, Americas, Asia bus. group; COO Novelis, Inc. (spinoff from Alcan), Atlanta, 2005—. Bd. dir. Internat. Paper Co.; bd. trustees Manufacturer's Alliance. Trustee Keep Am. Beautiful, Hathaway Brown Sch. Named one of Next 20 Female CEOs, Pink Mag. & Forté Found., 2006. Office: Novelis Inc Ste 1500 3399 Peachtree Rd NE Atlanta GA 30326 Office Phone: 404-814-4200. Office Fax: 404-814-4219.*

BROOKS, MARTIN, electronic media company executive; b. NYC, Aug. 26, 1950; s. Kenneth and Ruth (Schubert) Brooks; m. Stacey Savage, May 30, 1973 (div. 1980); 1 child, Kerin. BFA, NYU, 1973; cert., Bklyn. Coll., 1975; cert. in bus. sch. prof. devel., U. Warwick, 1985. Sr. prodn. engr. Cinema Sound, NYC, 1971—78; chief rec. engr. G&T Harris, NYC, 1978; mgr. rec. ops. CBS Pub., NYC, 1978—81, mgr. audio visual devel., 1981—83, mgr. software devel., 1983—84, dir. software devel., 1984—86; exec. editor, electronic publ. R.R. Bowker/Reed Reference Pub., NYC, 1986—90, v.p. New Providence, NJ, 1991—95; sr. v.p. electronic pub. Reed Reference Pub., New Providence, NJ, 1995—96; id. cons. NY Intermedia Authority, 1996—98, 2002—; dir. front end devel. and ops. Bol.Com Bertelsman, NYC, 1998—2002. Engr., prodr. radio program Crawdaddy Rock Rev., 1978; ind. cons. films, theater evaluation svc. Dolby Distbr. Svcs. (divsn. Dolby Labs.), 2002—06; owner, developer various web sites; v.p. profl. svcs. RSG Sys., Inc., NYC, 2006—. Editor (and designer): (cd-rom) Books in Print Plus, 1986, Books in Print with Book Reviews Plus, 1987, Variety's Video Directory Plus, 1986, Enviro Energyline Abstracts Plus, 1991, Library Reference Plus, 1992, Children's Reference Plus, 1992, Global Books in Print Plus, 1994, Libros en Venta, 1995, ABMS Medical Specialists Plus, 1995, Advertiser and Agency Red Books Plus, 1995, Corporate Affiliations Plus, 1995, Martindale-Hubbel Law Directory, 1995; prodr.(and designer): (software) Class II, 1984, Adventures in Science Series, 1985; contbr. 77-WABC radio spl., 2002. Mem.: Optical Pub. Assn. (bd. dirs.), Soc. Motion Picture and TV Engrs., Audio Engring. Soc. Home: 11220 72nd Dr Forest Hills NY 11375-5661 Office Phone: 917-887-6450. E-mail: mbrooks@nyintermedia.com.

BROOKS, MEL, film producer and director, actor, scriptwriter; b. June 28, 1926; Author: sketch Of Fathers and Sons in New Faces of 1952, 1957, sketch Shinbone Alley; co-author: sketch All American, 1962; writer (TV series) Your Show of Shows, also Caesar's Hour, The Sid Caesar, Imogene Coca, Carl Reiner, Howard Morris Special, 1967 (Emmy award for outstanding writing achievement in a comedy-variety), co-creator Get Smart, recordings include 2000 Years, 2000 and One Years, 2000 and Thirteen Years, 2000 Year Old Man in the Year 2000, 1997 (Grammy award for Best Spoken Word Album Comedy, 1998), writer, dir. (motion pictures) Producers, 1968 (Acad. award for Best Original Screenplay), writer, dir., star The Twelve Chairs, 1970, co-writer, dir., star Blazing Saddles, 1974, Silent Movie, 1976, co-writer, dir. Young Frankenstein, 1974, co-writer, dir., prodr., star Robin Hood: Men In Tights, 1993, Dracula: Dead and Loving It, 1995, prodr., dir., co-writer and star High Anxiety, 1977, Spaceballs, 1987, Life Stinks, 1991, writer, dir., prodr., star History of the World-Part I, 1981, writer, narrator The Critic, 1964 (Acad. award for best animated short subject); actor: (films) (voice) Robots, 2005; actor, prodr. To Be or Not To Be, 1983; prodr.: 84 Charing Cross Road, 1987; prodr.: The Elephant Man, 1980, Frances, 1982, My Favorite Year, 1982, Fly I, 1986, Fly II, 1989; guest actor (TV series) Mad About You (Emmy award for outstanding guest actor in a comedy series, 1997, 1998, 1999), co-writer, composer, prodr. (Broadway musical) The Producers, 2001—07 (3 Tony awards, Grammy nomination for best song written for motion picture, 2005). Office: c/o The Culver Studios 9336 Washington Blvd Culver City CA 90232-2628

BROOKS, MICHAEL PAUL, retired urban planning educator; b. Topeka, June 13, 1937; s. Paul Edward and Gladys Leora (Nansen) B.; m. Shirley Birdeen Rhoad, June 8, 1958 (div. Aug. 1983); children: David, Timothy, Susan.; m. Ann DeWitt Watts, Feb. 18, 1984. BA magna cum laude, Colgate U., 1959; M in City Planning, Harvard U., 1961; PhD, U. N.C., 1970. Dir. rsch. The N.C. Fund, Durham, 1963-66, dir. planning and program devel., 1966-67; lectr. dept. city and regional planning U. N.C., Chapel Hill, 1967-70, assoc. prof., 1970-71; prof. dept. urban and regional planning U. Ill., Urbana, 1971-78, head dept., 1971-78; dir. Bur. Urban and Regional Planning Rsch., 1971-77; dean Coll. Design, Iowa State U., Ames, 1978-84, Sch. Architecture and Environ. Design, SUNY, Buffalo, 1984-87, Sch. Community and Pub. Affairs, Va. Commonwealth U., Richmond, 1987-91, spl. asst. to provost for strategic planning, 1991—93, prof. dept. urban studies and planning, 1993—2003, ret., 2003. Cons. in field. Commr. Research Triangle Regional Planning Commn., Chapel Hill, N.C., 1969-71 Mem. Am. Planning Assn. (pres. 1979-80), Am. Inst. Cert. Planners, Assn. Collegiate Schs. Planning (pres. 1976-77) Democrat. E-mail: mkbrks@comcast.net.

BROOKS, PATRICK WILLIAM, lawyer, researcher; b. May 11, 1943; s. Mark Dana and Madge Ellen (Walker) B.; m. Mary Jane Davey, Dec. 17, 1966; children: Carolyn Walker, Mark William. BA, State Coll. Iowa, 1966; JD, U. Iowa, 1971. Bar: Iowa 1971, U.S. dist. Ct. (so. dist.) Iowa 1972, U.S. Sup. Ct. 1974, U.S. Ct. apls. (8th cir.) 1979. Tchr. Waterloo (Iowa) Cmty. Schs., 1966-68; mem. staff Donahue & Brooks, West Union, Iowa, 1971-72; ptnr. Mowry, Irvine, Brooks & Ward, Marshalltown, Iowa, 1972—84, Brooks, Ward & Trout, Marshalltown, Iowa, 1992—2005; ret. Active Fayette County Republican Ctrl. Com., Iowa, chmn. platform resolutions com., 1971-72; pres. Marshall County Young Reps., 1974; trustee Iowa Law Sch. Found., 1970-71; bd. dirs. Iowa Hist. Found., 1991-96; active Marshall County Dem. Ctrl. Com. 2005—, Marshall County Bd. Supr., 2007—, Adv. Commn. on Intergovtl. Rels.; bd. dirs. Mid-Iowa Cmty. Action, Second Judicial Dist. Dept. Corrections, Ctrl. Iowa Juvenile Detention Commn., Area Agy. on Aging, Region VI Planning Commn., Regional Workforce Invetment Bd. Mem. Am. Judicature Soc., Iowa Bar Assn., Marshall County Bar Assn. (pres. 1985-86), Iowa Trial Lawyers Assn., Iowa Def. Counsel Assn., Buick Am. Club (bd. dirs. 2001-07, pres. 2003-05). Lutheran. Avocation: international road rally driver and mechanic. Office Phone: 641-753-9134. E-mail: brooker50158@hotmail.com.

BROOKS, PETER (PRESTON), literature educator, department chairman, writer; b. NYC, Apr. 19, 1938; s. Ernest and Mary Caroline (Schoyer) B.; m. Margaret Elisabeth Waters, July 18, 1959 (div. 1995); 3 children; m. Rosa Ehrenreich, May 15, 2001. BA, Harvard U., 1959, PhD, 1965; postgrad., U. Coll. London, 1959-60, U. Paris, 1962-63; MA (hon.), Yale U., 1975; Doctor (hon.), Ecole Normale Supérieure, 1997; MA (hon.), U. Oxford, 2001. From instr. French to prof. French and comparative lit. Yale U., 1965—75, Chester D. Tripp prof. humanities, 1980-2001, dir. The Lit. Major, 1974-79, dir. Whitney Humanities Ctr., 1980-91, 96-01, chmn. dept. French, 1983-88, chmn. dept. comparative lit., 1991-97, Sterling prof. comparative lit. and French New Haven, 2001—04, 2006—; prof. English and law U. Va., Charlottesville, Va., 2004—06, dir. program in law and humanities, 2005—06. Eastman vis. prof. U. Oxford, 2001—02. Author: The Novel of Worldliness, 1969, The Child's Part, 1972, The Melodramatic Imagination, 1976, Reading for the Plot, 1984, Body Work, 1993, Psychoanalysis and Storytelling, 1994, World Elsewhere, 1999, Troubling Confessions, 2000, Realist Vision, 2005, Henry James Goes to Paris, 2007; co-editor: Law's Stories, 1996, Whose Freud?, 2000; contbg. editor Partisan Rev., 1972-88; mem. editl. bd. Yale French Studies, 1966—; chmn. Yale Jour. Criticism, 1987—. Acad. advisor Marlboro Co., 1975—; regional chmn. Mellon Fellowships in Humanities, 1982-84; trustee Hopkins Sch., New Haven, 1983-88; mem. adv. coun. West European program The Wilson Ctr.; mem. adv. bd. Stanford Humanities Ctr., 1996-2001; mem. humanities adv. coun. N.Y. Pub. Libr. Decorated Officier des Palmes Académiques, 1986; Marshall fellow, 1959, Morse fellow, 1967, Guggenheim fellow, 1973, Am. Coun. Learned Socs. fellow, 1980, NEH fellow, 1988. Fellow Am. Acad. Arts and Scis.; mem. MLA (exec. coun. 1993-97), Am. Phil. Soc., Yale Club, Elizabethan Club (New Haven), Century Assn. Democrat. Office: Yale Univ Comparative Lit PO Box 208299 New Haven CT 06520-8299 Office Phone: 203-432-2765. Business E-Mail: peter.brooks@yale.edu.

BROOKS, PHILIP COOLIDGE, JR., archivist, curator, historian; b. Dec. 1, 1940; s. Philip Coolidge and Dorothy Hamilton (Holland) Brooks; m. Susan Mary Fox, Dec. 21, 1965; 1 child, Anthony Franklin Coolidge. BA, U. Kans., 1962, MA, 1966; Exchange fellow, U. Reading, Eng., 1962—63, postgrad., 1964—65, Stanford U. Law Sch., 1963—64. Mus. specialist polit. history Smithsonian Instn., Washington, 1967—71; asst. to exec. dir. Nat. Archives, Washington, 1971—74, asst. to asst. archivist, pub. programs, 1974—83, also curator archives reception room, acting dir., dir. edn. divsn., 1979—83, sr. archives specialist, records centers, 1983—96, devel. officer, 1986—87; ret., 1996. Historian archivist Pres. Inaugural Com., 1968, 89, 93. Contbr. articles on history to profl. jours. Mem. Gadsby's Tavern Acquisitions Commn., Alexandria, Va., 1974—78, Historic Records Adv. Com., Alexandria, 1975—77, Historic Alexandria Restoration and Preservation Com., 2001—06; vice chmn. Historic Alexandria Resources Com., 1983—97, chmn., 1995—97; mem. Alexandria Libr. Co., 1989—; vice chmn. Alexandria Assn., 1976—78; chmn. Alexandria Ad Hoc Lyceum Com., 1981—82, The Lyceum Co., 1983—87, vice chmn., 1987—91; mem., vice chmn. Alexandria Bicentennial Commn., 1972—83; chmn. Alexandria Mus. Task Force, 1979—80, Alexandria 250th Anniversary Com., 1997—2000; dir. RROC Found., 1984—92; pres. Rolls-Royce Found., 2000—03; mem. adv. bd. Coun. Internat. Nontheatrical Events, 1989—97. Recipient Commendable Service award, Nat. Archives, 1976, Archivist's Achievement awards, 1985, 1996, Appreciation cert., City Alexandria, 1976, 1981, 1984, Va. Senate Joint Resolution of Commendation, 2000, Rolls-Royce Found. Commendation, 2003. Mem.: Nat. Trust Historic Preservation, Am. Assn. State and Local History, Rolls Royce Owners Club (dir. 1978—84, editor The Flying Lady 1986—89, v.p. regions 1992—94), Bentley Drivers Club (rep. 1968—), Lambda Chi Alpha. Home: 102 Carnoustie Williamsburg VA 23188

BROOKS, PHILIP RUSSELL, chemistry educator, researcher; b. Chgo., Dec. 31, 1938; s. John Russell and Louise Jane B.; children: Scott, Robin, Christopher, Steven. BS, Calif. Inst. Tech., 1960; PhD, U. Calif., Berkeley, 1964. Rsch. assoc. physics dept. U. Chgo., 1964; from asst. to assoc. prof. chemistry Rice U., Houston, 1964-75, prof., 1975—. Editor: State-to-State Chemistry, 1977. Vol. Boy Scouts Am., Houston, 1970—. Recipient Humboldt prize Alexander von Humboldt Found., 1985; predoctoral fellow NSF, 1960-63, postdoctoral fellow, 1963-64, Alfred P. Sloan fellow, 1970-74, John Simon Guggenheim fellow, 1974-75, Vis. Erskine fellow U. Canterbury, 1991, JSPS fellow Japan Soc. Promotion Sci., 1992. Fellow Am. Phys. Soc.; mem. Am. Chem. Soc. Achievements include research on chemical reaction dynamics. Home: 1026 Glourie Cir Houston TX 77055-7504 Office: Rice U Chemistry Dept MS60 6100 Main St Houston TX 77005-1892 E-mail: brooks@python.rice.edu.

BROOKS, PHILLIP, advertising executive; b. 1955; With Affiliate of Excellence Co., Mpls., 1976—, now pres.; with Excellence Co., Mpls., pres., CEO. Office: The Excellence Co 600 Lakeview Point Dr Saint Paul MN 55112-3494

BROOKS, RENANA ESTHER, clinical psychologist, business and political consultant, researcher; b. Bethesda, Md., July 18, 1956; d. David Abraham and Harriet (Kahn) B.; m. Robert Benjamin Rovinsky, Jan. 1, 1989. Student, Princeton U., 1978; BA, Barnard Coll., 1980; PhD, George Washington U., 1989. Clin. fellow Harvard Med. Sch., Cambridge, Mass., 1985-88; dir. psychol. svcs. Skyline Psychiat. Assocs./Commonwealth Mental Health Assocs., Va., 1989-91; founder, dir. Sommet Inst. for the Study of Power and Persuasion, Washington, 1990—. Author: Breaking the Cycle of Intergenerational Rage, Blame and Shame, 1996, A Nation of Victims, 2003, Character Myth, 2003; contbr. articles to profl. jours. Diplomate, Fellow Am. Bd. Med. Psychotherapy (also div. of cons. psychologists, clin. psychologists); mem. Am. Assn. Marriage and Family Therapy (clin.). Home: 3547 Brandywine St NW Washington DC 20008-2912 Office Phone: 202-783-0775. Personal E-mail: renanabrooks@starpower.net.

BROOKS, RICHARD C., electrical engineer, federal official; b. Phila., Aug. 31, 1945; BEE with honors, U. Va., Charlottesville, 1967; MSE, Johns Hopkins U., 1970; PhD, U. Mo., Columbia, 1973; MBA, Va. Poly. Inst., 1978. Registered profl. engr., Va., 1972. Chief, integrated systems lab. Nat. Weather Svc./NOAA, Silver Spring, Md., 1989—96; dep. dir., systems acquisition office Nat. Oceanic & Atmospheric Adminstrn. (NOAA), Silver Spring, 1996—2002; dir., satellite & ground systems program NESDIS/Nat. Oceanic & Atmospheric Adminstrn. (NOAA), Suitland, Md., 2002—. Troop com. Boy Scouts Am., Arlington, Va., 1984—2003. Lt U.S. Pub. Health Svc., 1968—70, Baltimore, Maryland, Lcdr U.S. Pub. Health Svc. Reserve, 1970—99. Mem.: IEEE (sr.). Achievements include research in image processing and pattern recognition. Avocation: skiing. Office: NOAA Dept Commerce 4401 Silver Hill Rd FB4 Rm 3301 Suitland MD 20746 Office Phone: 301-457-5277. Business E-Mail: richard.brooks@noaa.gov.

BROOKS, RICHARD DICKINSON, lawyer; b. Daytona Beach, Fla., Sept. 17, 1944; m. Betty Jane Huba, Aug. 28, 1971; children: Hillary Ann, Richard Jason. BA, Marietta Coll., Ohio, 1967; JD, Case Western Res. U., 1972. Bar: Ohio 1972, U.S. Dist. Ct. (so. dist.) Ohio 1975, U.S. Ct. Appeals (6th cir.) 1993. Atty. Bridgewater Robe Brooks & Keifer, Athens, Ohio, 1972-87, Arter & Hadden, Columbus, Ohio, 1987—2003, Bailey Cavalieri LLC, Columbus, 2003—. Coach Upper Arlington Cub Scout Baseball, Columbus, 1989-90; pres. A.T.C.O. Inc. Sheltered Workshop, Athens, 1986; bd. dirs. Athens C. of C., 1984-87. Sgt. U.S. Army, 1968-70, Vietnam. Fellow Am. Bar Found., Ohio Bar Found. (pres. 1988); mem. ABA, Ohio Bar Assn. (exec. com. 1979-83), Columbus Bar Assn. (environ. law com.), Athens County Bar Assn. (pres. 1978-79), Ohio CLE Inst. (bd. dirs. 1989-90), Ohio State Legal Svcs. Assn. (bd. dirs. 1982—). Avocations: basketball, tennis, fishing, furniture restoration. Office: Bailey Cavalieri LLC 10 W Broad St Ste 2100 Columbus OH 43215-3422 Office Phone: 614-229-3285. E-mail: richard.brooks@baileycavalieri.com.

BROOKS, ROBIN C., food products executive; b. 1955; 1 child, Nara. BA in Econ., Smith Coll.; M in Fin. and Econ., J.L. Kellogg Grad. Sch. Mgmt. Northwestern U. With Williamette Mgmt. Associates, Deloitte & Touche, Arthur D. Little Valuation, Inc.; chmn., CEO Brooks Food Grp., Inc., 1999—. Dir. United Enterprise Fund, mem. exec. com.; mem. bd. dirs. MultiCultural Foodservice and Hospitality Alliance, treas., 2002—04; mem. bd. dirs. Com. of 200; treas. Commonwealth Inst. South Fla.; appointee SBA Nat. Adv. Coun. Featured in Ebony mag., 2007. Recipient Va. Entrepreneur of Yr. award, Ernst & Young, 2001. Mem.: Women's Foodservice Forum (mem. fin. com., 2003 Entrepreneur of Yr.). Office: Brooks Food Grp 940 Orange St Bedford VA 24523 Office Phone: 540-586-8284.*

BROOKS, RODNEY ALLEN, information technology executive, educator; b. Australia; BSc in Pure Math., Flinders U., South Australia, 1974, MSc in Pure Math., 1977; PhD in Computer Science, Stanford U., 1981. Founder Lucid, 1984, Artificial Creatures (now a subsidiary of iRobot), 1991—; rsch. scientist Carnegie Mellon U., 1983, Artificial Intelligence Lab, MIT, 1983; co-founder ISRobotics (now iRobot Corp.), Burlington, Mass., 1990—; prin. arch., chief tech. officer iRobot Corp., Burlington, Mass.; joined computer sci. faculty MIT, 1984, Fujisu prof. computer sci.

and engring., elec. engring. and computer sci. dept.; dir. MIT Computer Sci. and Artificial Intelligence Lab. (MIT CSAIL). Cray lectr. U. Minn.; Mellon lectr. Dartmouth Coll.; Hyland lectr. Hughes; Forsythe lectr. Stanford U.; vis. lectr. Cornell U., Free U. of Brussels, NEC Rsch. Lab., Princeton, NJ, Electro Tech. Lab., Tsukuba, Japan; bd. dir. Intelligent Inspection Corp. Frequently profiled and quoted in articles and news stories for Good Morning America, Scientific American, Discover, Learning Channel shows, and Nightline for expertise in Artificial Intelligence; contbr. articles in profl. jours.; co-founding editor International Journal of Computer Vision, mem. editl. bds. for Adaptive Behavior, Artificial Life, Applied Artificial Intelligence, Autonomous Robots and New Generation Computing, appeared in "Fast, Cheap and Out of Control", 1996; co-editor (with Pattie Maes): Artificial Life IV: Proceedings of the Fourth International Workshop on the Synthesis and Simulation of Living Systems, 1994; co-editor: (with Luc Steels) The Artificial Life Route to Artificial Intelligence: Building Embodied Situated Agents, 1995; author: Model-Based Computer Vision, 1984, Programming in Common LISP, 1985, Cambrian Intelligence: The Early History of the New AI, 1999, Flesh and Machines: How Robots Will Change Us, 2002. Recipient Computers and Thought award, Internat. Joint Conf. on Artificial Intelligence. Fellow: AAAS, Am. Acad. Arts & Scis.; mem.: NAE, Am. Assn. for Artificial Intelligence (founding fellow). Office: MIT CSAIL The State Ctr 32 Vasser St 32-G430 Cambridge MA 02139 also: iRobot Corp 63 South Ave Burlington MA 01803 Office Phone: 617-253-5223, 781-345-0200. Office Fax: 617-253-0039, 781-345-0201. Business E-Mail: brooks@csail.mit.edu.*

BROOKS, ROGER G., lawyer; b. Poughkeepsie, NY, Dec. 25, 1961; AB, Princeton Univ., 1984; MA, JD, Univ. Va., 1987; MDiv, Regent Coll., Vancouver, BC, 1995. Bar: NY 1989. Law clk., Hon. John D. Butzner, Jr. US Ct. Appeals, 4th Cir.; assoc. Cravath, Swaine & Moore LLP, NYC, 1988—92, 1995—99, ptnr., litig., 1999—. Articles editor Va. Law Rev. Mem.: Assn. Bar of City of NY. Office: Cravath Swaine & Moore LLP Worldwide Plz 825 Eighth Ave New York NY 10019-7475 Office Phone: 212-474-1072. Office Fax: 212-474-3700. Business E-Mail: rgbrooks@cravath.com.

BROOKS, ROGER KAY, insurance company executive; b. Clarion, Iowa, Apr. 30, 1937; s. Edgar Sherman and Hazel (Whipple) B.; m. Marcia Rae Ramsay, Nov. 19, 1955 (div. Sept. 1989); children: Michael, Jeffrey, David; m. Saulene Richer, Mar. 17, 1990. BA in Math., magna cum laude, U. Iowa, 1959. Actuarial asst. Central Life Assurance Co., Des Moines, 1959—64, asst. sec., 1964-68, v.p., 1968-70, exec. v.p., 1970-72, pres., COO, 1972—94; CEO AmerUs (merger of Central Life and American Mutual), 1994—, chmn. emeritus, 2006—. Mem. Des Moines Devel. Com. Named to Iowa Bus. Hall of Fame, Iowa Ins. Hall of Fame; recipient Alexis de Toqueville Soc. award, United Way, Ctrl. Iowa, 2004. Fellow Soc. Actuaries; mem. Greater Des Moines C. of C. (past chmn.), Actuaries Club of Des Moines (past pres.), Phi Beta Kappa. Presbyterian (elder). Club: Des Moines (past pres.). Office: AmerUs Group PO Box 1555 Des Moines IA 50306-1555 Office Phone: 515-362-3660. Business E-Mail: rbrooks@doextra.com.

BROOKS, ROGER LEON, retired academic administrator; b. El Dorado, Ark., Apr. 14, 1927; s. Roger Spurgeon and Lumae (Jackson) B.; m. Martha Edwina Withers, Aug. 25, 1950; children:Leslie, Roger, Geoffrey, Stephen, Douglas. BA, Baylor U., 1949; MA, U. Ill., 1950; PhD, U. Colo., 1959. Instr. English U. Colo., 1955-57, 58-60; prof. Tex. Tech U., Lubbock, 1960-64, assoc. dean Grad. Sch., 1964-67; dean Coll. Arts and Scis. Tex. A&M U., Commerce, 1967-72; pres. Howard Payne U., Brownwood, Tex., 1972-79; v.p. adminstrv. affairs Houston Bapt. U., 1979-87; dir. Armstrong Browning Libr., Baylor U., 1987-96. Cons. Victorian Studies, 1967, Choice, 1970, Can. Coun., 1971. Editor: Studies in Browning and His Circle, 1987-96, Robert Browning and Victorian Culture, 1992, Elizabeth Barrett Browning and Victorian Culture, 1994; contbr. articles to profl. jours. Pres., bd. advs. Baylor U., 2000-02, libr. fellow, 2002—. With USNR, 1945-51; lt. col. USMC, 1972-87, ret. Rsch. grantee U. Colo. at Oxford and Brit. Mus., 1957-58, Tex. Tech. U. at Bibliotheque Nationale, Paris, 1964, Am. Philos Soc. at N.Y. Public Libr., 1963, Brit. Mus., 1980, the Suratt-Lewis Libr. award, 1997. Mem. London Browning Soc., Grolier Club (N.Y.C.), Westlake Club (Houston). Office: Baylor U Armstrong Browning Lib Waco TX 76798

BROOKS, SEAN CHRISTOPHER, criminologist; b. Mexico, Mo., Apr. 23, 1981; s. Lewis William Brooks, Jr. BS in Cell and Molecular Biology and Chemistry, Mo. State U., Springfield, 2003, MS in Chemistry, 2004. Criminalist ii Mo. State Hwy. Patrol, Jefferson City, 2004—. Contbr. articles to profl. jours. Eagle scout Boy Scouts Am., 1997. Mem.: Am. Chem. Soc., Am. Acad. Forensic Sci. (trainee affiliate05 2006), Midwestern Assn. Forensic Scientists (mem. electronic comm. newsletter com. 2006—). Office: Missouri State Highway Patrol Crime Lab 1510 E Elm St Jefferson City MO 65101 Office Phone: 573-526-6134.

BROOKS, SUSAN W., prosecutor; Grad., Miami U.; JD, Ind. U., 1985. Ptnr. McClure, McClure & Kammen, 1985—97; dep. mayor City of Indpls., 1998—99; of counsel Ice Miller Law Firm, Indpls., 2000—01; US atty. (so. dist.) Ind. US Dept. Justice, 2001—. Mem. Atty. Gens. Adv. Com., 2002—03, 2005—, vice chair, 2006—. Chair United Way's Violence and Safety Impact Coun.; protocol chair World Police & Fire Games, Indpls., 2001; nominating com. Hoosier Capitol Girl Scouts Coun.; adv. bd. Marion County Commn. on Youth; mem. Ind. Fed. Cmty. Defender Bd.; bd. mem. Jr. League of Indpls., Little Red Door Cancer Agy., Marion County Commn. on Youth, Network of Women in Bus., Greater Indpls. Progress Com. Named Influential Woman of Indpls, Indpls. Bus. Jour., 1999, Who's Who in Law, 2002; named to 40 under 40 list; recipient Alumnae of Year, Ind. U. Sch. Law, 2006. Office: US Attys Office 10 W Market St Ste 2100 Indianapolis IN 46204 Office Phone: 317-226-6333.*

BROOKS, THOMAS V., energy executive; m. Jean Brooks; 3 children. BS, Yale Univ., M in mgmt. Founding ptnr. AERX Inc., 1989—92; dir. capital & trade resources Enron, 1992—97; v.p. Goldman Sachs, 1997—2001; v.p. bus. develop. Constellation Energy, Balt., 2001; pres. Constellation Commodities Group, 2001—05, chmn., 2005—; vice-chmn. Constellation Energy, 2005—. Bd. mem. Kennedy Krieger Inst., College-bound Found., Hippodrome Found., Balt. Freedom Acad., Bus. Volunteers Unlimited. Office: Constellation Energy 750 E Pratt St Baltimore MD 21202*

BROOKS, TIMOTHY H., broadcast executive; b. Exeter, NH, Apr. 18, 1942; s. John W. R. and Olive P. (Bradbury) B. BA, Dartmouth Coll., 1964; MS, Syracuse U., 1969. Promotion asst. Sta. WTEN-TV, Albany, NY, 1966-68; sales promotion supr. Sta. WCBS-TV, NYC, 1969-70; sr. rsch. analyst NBC Owned Stas. Div., NYC, 1970-72; mgr. ratings rsch. NBC-TV Network, NYC, 1972-76, dir. TV network rsch., 1978-82, dir. program rsch., 1982-88; asst. dir. rsch. and mktg. TV Advt. Reps., Inc., NYC, 1976-77; sr. v.p., media rsch. dir. N.W. Ayer Inc., NYC, 1989-90; v.p. rsch. USA Networks, NYC, 1991-94, sr. v.p. rsch., 1994-99, Lifetime TV, NYC, 2000—03, exec. v.p. rsch., 2003—. Adj. prof. communications L.I. Univ., Greenvale, N.Y., 1979-88. Author: The Complete Directory to Prime Time TV Stars, 1987, Lost Sounds: Blacks and the Birth of the Recording Industry, 1890-1919, 2004 (Deems Taylor award ASCAP 2005, Irving Lowens award Soc. Am. Music 2006), Lost Sounds: Blacks and the Birth of the Recording Industry, 2006 (Grammy award 2007); co-author: The Complete Directory to Prime Time Network and Cable TV Shows, 1946-2007, 1979 (Am. Book award 1980, Broadcast Preceptor award San Francisco State U. 1981), TV's Greatest Hits, 1985, TV in the '60s, 1985, The Columbia Master Book Discography, 1999 (Assoc. Recorded Sound Collections award for Excellence 2000); contbr. articles to profl. jours. Capt. US Army, 1964—66, Vietnam, capt. USAR, 1966—74. Recipient Jack Hill award for excellence and integrity in media rsch., CableTV Advt. Bur., 1995. Mem. Assn. for Recorded Sound Collections (bd. dirs. 1979-97, pres. 1982-84, contbg. editor jour. 1986—, compiler Current Bibliography 1979—, founder ARSC awards for excellence in pub. rsch. on recs., chmn. awards com. 1989-97, Lifetime Achievement award 2004, award for excellence 2005), Media Rating Coun. (exec. com., chmn. cable comm. 1993-96, chmn. 1997-99), Advt. Rsch. Found. (bd. dirs. 1995-2000, chmn. video electronic media coun. 1995—, chmn. 1998-99), Radio-TV Rsch. Coun., Cable and Telecomms. Assn. for Mktg. (chmn. rsch. com. 2003-06, bd. dirs. 2006-), Cabletelevision Advt. Bur. (mem. rsch. com. 1991—), Record Rsch. Assocs., City of London Phonograph and Gramophone Soc., TV Assn. Progammers L.Am. (founding mem.). Avocations: hiking, camping. Office: Lifetime TV Worldwide Plaza 309 W 49th St New York NY 10019-7316 Business E-Mail: brooks@lifetimetv.com.

BROOKS, W. ABDULLAH, pediatrician, researcher; s. Wilburt and Johney Brooks; m. Vanessa Jayne Clark, Oct. 5, 1955; children: Mona Catherine, Alexander Abdullah. BA in Political Sci., U. Calif., 1979; MD, Stanford U., Calif., 1991; MPH, Johns Hopkins U., Balt., 1995. Lic. Md. Dept. Health and Mental Hygiene, 1994. Pediat. residency Cornell Med Ctr., NY Hosp., NY, 1991—94; preventive medicine residency John Hopkins U., Balt., 1994—97, chief resident, preventive medicine residency, 1996—97; sr. scientist, head infectious diseases unit Internat. Ctr. Diarrhoeal Disease Rsch., Bangladesh, 1997—, Ctr. Health and Population Rsch., Dhaka, Bangladesh, 1997—. Faculty mem. Bloomberg Sch. Pub. Health, Johns Hopkins U., Balt., 1997—; mem. governing and tech. advisory bd. Health Resource Ctr., London. Contbr. articles to profl. jours. Governing and tech. adv. bd. Health Resource Ctr., London, 2003—06. Recipient MedScholars award, Stanford Med. Sch., 1986—87; grantee, NIH, 2002—03, Thrasher Rsch. Fund, 2004—06, Bill and Melinda Gates Found., 2004—06, PneumoADIP/Global Alliance for Vaccine Intro., 2004—06, Dept. Health and Human Svcs., 2006; Health and Child Survival scholar, USAID, 1994—95, Health and Child Survival fellow, 1997—2001. Mem.: APHA, Am. Soc. Tropical Medicine and Hygiene. Baha'I Faith. Achievements include research in childhood pneumonia and the role of zinc; childhood pneumonia and mortality and the role of zinc; childhood pneumonia in South Asia; typhoid fever. Office: ICDDR B Centre for Health & Population GPO Box 128 Mohakhali Dhaka 1000 Bangladesh Home Phone: 410-325-9286; Office Phone: 88 02 8826891. Personal E-mail: abrooks@jhsph.edu. Business E-Mail: abrooks@icddrb.org.

BROOKS, WALTER S., dermatologist; b. Cleve., July 16, 1956; s. John R. and Christel W. (Plogsties) B.; m. Debra A. Hart, Aug. 29, 1981; children: Aaron S., David J.H., Arielle N. BA magna cum laude, U. Rochester, 1978, MD, 1982. Resident in internal medicine Rochester Gen. Hosp., NY, 1982-85; resident in dermatology U. Pitts., 1985-88; clin. instr. dermatology to clin. asst. prof. dermatology U. Rochester, 1989—; dermatologist pvt. practice, Rochester, 1988—. Trustee Rochester Acad. Medicine, 1996—99; vice-chair campaign Leadership Soc. Dermatology Found., 1997, chair Upstate NY, 2002—. Del. People to People Internat., 2003, Global Peace Initiative, 2003; amb. People to People, China, 2000; del. People to People Amb., Jordan, 2005, People to People, 2005. Recipient Leadership award Dermatology Found. Soc., 1995; named one of America's Top Physicians, 2003-05 Fellow Am. Acad. Dermatology; mem. Nat. Bd. Med. Examiners, Buffalo-Rochester Dermatol. Assn. (pres. 1995-96), Rochester Dermatol. Soc. (pres. 1996-98). Conservative. Avocation: photography. Home: 22 Silver Fox Dr Fairport NY 14450-8666 Office: 730 Weiland Rd Rochester NY 14626-3919 Home Phone: 585-377-8295; Office Phone: 585-719-9600. Business E-Mail: wbrooks@rochester.rr.com.

BROOKS-GORDON, ELIZABETH FAYE, history educator; b. July 20, 1958; BA, Wake Forest U., Winston-Salem, NC, 1980; JD, Campbell U., Buies Creek, NC, 1988. Legal asst. Curtis O. Harris, Atty.-at-Law, Gastonia, NC, 1989—2000, Office Pub. Defender, Gastonia, 1988; tchr. history Charlotte-Mecklenburg Schs., NC, 1993—. Adj. prof. law York Tech. Coll., Rock Hill, SC, 2005; student-tchr. supr. U. S.C. Upstate, Spartanburg, 2006—07; adj. prof. law Gardner Webb U., Boiling Springs, ND, 2007—. Bench-to-bar editor: Campbell Law Observer. Mem. Gaston County Orgn. for Cmty. Concerns, Inc. Recipient Am. Jurisprudence Book award, Campbell U. Sch. Law, Nat. Educator Apple award, 2006. Mem.: Jr. League Gaston County, Inc., Links, Inc. (past pres. Piedmont chpt.), Alpha Kappa Alpha (past pres. Zeta Mu Omega chpt.), Delta Theat Phi. Office: Kennedy Mid Sch 4000 Gallant Ln Charlotte NC 28273-3208

BROOKSHIRE, BRUCE G., retail grocery store executive; b. Dec. 1928; married. Grad., U. Tex., 1950. With Brookshire Grocery Co. Inc., Tyler, Tex., 1950—, also chmn., CEO. Office: 1600 SW Loop 323 PO Box 1411 Tyler TX 75710-1411

BROOKS SHOEMAKER, VIRGINIA LEE, librarian; b. Oklahoma City, Sept. 16, 1944; d. Leo B. and Eloise Gilreath; m. Phil Ashley Brooks, Aug. 10, 1972 (dec. Oct. 1982); 1 child, Philip Brooks; m. Gene Darrel Shoemaker, Feb. 16, 1986; children: Rob Shoemaker, Julie Shoemaker, Donna Shoemaker, Gary Shoemaker. Student, Oklahoma City C.C., 1980; BS, U. Ctrl. Okla., 1988, M in Sch. Media, 1991, postgrad., 2000—; attended, Okla. State U. With Dept. Human Svcs., Oklahoma City, 1970-75, State Dept. Librs., Oklahoma City, 1980-87; substitute tchr. Oklahoma City Schs., 1989-91, 1995; vol. libr. Children's Libr., Children's Hosp., Oklahoma City, 1992—; libr. vol. Corpus Christi Sch. Libr., 1998—; vol. children's sect. First Bapt. Libr.; vol. Libr. for Blind. Sponsor World Vision, Seattle, 1994—; active cub scouts Boy Scouts Am.; vol. Habitat for Humanity, Vista Care Hospice; dir. project transformation summer reading program First Bapt. Good Shepherd Children's Dental Clinic; vol. Vista Care Hospice, 2002—; project transformation reading program Wesley Meth.; reading sch. libr. tutor First Bapt. Good Shepherd Children's Dental Clinic; active, life mem. Meth. Ch. of the Servant; women mission groups Wesley Meth., First Bapt. Ch.; vol. children's sect. First Bapt. Libr. Recipient Adopt-a-Park award, 1985, 1986, 1987, Oklahoma City Beautiful award, 1985—88, Omniplex Sci. Mus., Oklahoma City, 1986—89. Mem.: Omniplex Sci. Mus. (Adpot-a-Park award 1986—89), Internat. Reading Assn. (reading tutor city schs.), Coun. Exceptional Children, Zool. Soc., Classen Alumni Assn., U. Ctrl. Okla. Alumni Assn. Baptist. Avocations: piano, reading, creative writing, making greeting cards. Office Phone: 405-171-4947. Personal E-mail: doggytown14@webtv.net.

BROOKS-TURNER, MYRA, music educator; b. Knoxville, Tenn., Jan. 13, 1933; d. Paul David and Lilli Ray Brooks; m. Ronald J. Turner, June 11, 1960; children: Stacy Turner Steele, Cheryl Turner Walker, Teresa Turner Basler. Student of piano, voice and composition, Juilliard Sch. Music, 1945—51; BMus in Piano, So. Meth. U., 1955, MusM in Theory and Composition, 1956, postgrad. in Piano, 1957—58. Educator Dallas Indep. Schs., Tex., 1956—60; choral music specialist Knoxville City Schs., Tenn., 1960—65; composer-in-residence Birmingham Children's Theatre, Ala., 1965—68; music instr. Mercer U. Music Prep. Sch., Atlanta, 1975—77; instr. composition Maryville Coll. Prep. Sch. of the Arts, Tenn., 1978—80; music instr. U. Tenn., Knoxville, 1990—92; owner Myra Brooks-Turner Studio of Music, Knoxville, Tenn., 1992—. Freelance writer, pub. MBT Prodns., Knoxville, 1993—; French instr. Ossoli Cir., 2004—; composer Schaum Pub., Inc., 2000—, FJH Music Co. Inc., 2005—. Composer, prodr.: (musicals) Make Way for Love, 1955; Uh-Uh, 1956; Javaho Junction, 1958; composer, dir. The Green Dragon, 1965—68 (Seattle Nat. Playwriting First Place award); over 500 music pieces, 1993—2006; contbr. columns to mags., articles to profl. jours. Music worship leader Epis. Ch. of Ascension, Knoxville, Tenn., 1992—93. Recipient Cultural Arts award, Tenn. Arts Commn., 1982. Mem.: Chopin Soc. (dir. 1993—), Beethoven Soc. (dir. 1993—), Tenn. Fedn. Music Clubs (officer, state bd. 1978—89, Ea. Tenn. divsn. jr. counselor 2002—05, Ea. Tenn. divisional v.p. 2002—, officer, state bd. 2002—, editor State Piano Competition Book 2003, editor state piano competition book 2004—, state jr. counselor 2005—), Nat. Fedn. Music Clubs (jr. festivals bulletin advisor 1982—90), Knoxville Music Tchrs. Assn. (sec., bd. dirs 2000—01, Composer of Yr. 1978, 2001), Tenn. Music Tchrs. Assn., Nat. Music Tchrs. Assn., Ossoli Circle (bd. dirs. 2005—, lang. dept. chmn. 2005—), Knoxville Writers Group (exec. bd., sec. 2005—, editor directory 2007—), Camelot Fine Arts Club, Camelot Fine Arts Club (pres. 2005—,), U. Tenn. Faculty Women's Club, Tuesday Morning Musical Club (pres. 1990—91), Pi Kappa Lambda, Mu Phi Epsilon (pres. 1973—74, pres. Atlanta Alumnae, Music Therapy award 1974), Alpha Delta Pi. Republican. Episcopalian. Avocations: study of French, study of Italian, photography, interior decorating. Personal E-mail: myrabrooksturner@aol.com.

BROOMAN, DAVID J., lawyer; b. Hackensack, NJ, Dec. 25, 1956; s. Bankston T. and Hildegard Brooman; m. Gardenia L. Brooman, July 26, 1958; children: David J., Richard W., Kyle M., Luke A. BA, Rutgers U., 1979; JD, Villanova U., 1982. Bar: Pa., 1982, NJ, 1983, U.S. Dist. Ct. (ea. and mid. dists.) Pa., N.J., U.S. Dist. Ct. N.J., U.S. Ct. Appeals (3d cir.). Ptnr. Cohen Shapiro Polisher Shiekman & Cohen, Phila., 1988-95; ptnr., environ. law group Drinker Biddle & Reath, Phila., 1995—, now mng. ptnr, mem. mgmt. com. Bd. dirs. Delaware Valley Child Care Coun., Phila., 1986-94; v.p., bd. dirs. Pa. Resources Coun., Media, 1990-98. Named Outstanding Child Adv., Support Ctr. Child Advs., Phila., 1995. Mem.: ABA, Phila. Bar Assn., Pa. Bar Assn. Office: Drinker Biddle & Reath One Logan Sq 18th & Cherry Sts Philadelphia PA 19103-6996 Office Phone: 215-993-2210. Office Fax: 215-993-8585. Business E-Mail: david.brooman@dbr.com.

BROOME, CLAIRE VERONICA, epidemiologist, researcher; b. Tunbridge Wells, Kent, England, Aug. 24, 1949; came to U.S., 1951; d. Kenneth R. and Heather C. (Platt) B.; m. John F. Head, Apr. 2, 1988; children: Gabriel K., Steven G. BA, Harvard U., 1970, MD, 1975. Diplomate Am. Bd. Internal Medicine. Dep. chief spl. pathogens br. Ctrs. for Disease Control, Atlanta, 1979-80, chief meningitis, spl. pathogens br., 1981-90, assoc. dir. sci., 1991-94, acting dir., nat. ctr. injury prevention and control, 1992-93, dep. dir., 1994-99, sr. advisor to dir. for health info. sys., 1999—2006. Steering com. on encapsulated bacterial vaccines, WHO, Geneva, 1989-91, chmn., 1992-96, sci. adv. group experts global program on vaccines and immunizations, 1996-2004; adv. com. on vaccines FDA, Washington, 1990-94; adj. prof. div. global health, sch. pub. health Emory U., 1992-; cons. in field. Contbr. numerous articles to profl. jours. M. C. Rockefeller fellow, 1970-71, Meritorious Svc. medal USPHS, 1986, Disting. Svc. medal USPHS, 1996, John Snow award Am. Pub. Health Assn., 2000; Rsch. grantee NIH, FDA, Dept. of State. Fellow Infectious Diseases Soc. Am. (Bristol-Myers Squibb award 1993); mem. ACP, Inst. of Medicine, Am. Epidemiologic Soc., Am. Soc. Microbiology, Phi Beta Kappa, Alpha Omega Alpha. Avocation: tennis. Office Phone: 510-248-4095. Personal E-mail: cvbroome@gmail.com.

BROOME, DAVID, federal official; BA in Liberal Arts, Am. U., Washington. Mem. Presdl. honor guard Dept. Air Force, US Dept. Def., 1989—91, legis. asst. Office of the Sec., 1991—93; rsch. asst. Am. Enterprise Inst. Pub. Policy Rsch., 1993—94; staff asst. to sergeant at arms US Senate, 1994—95, sr. legis. asst. to US Senator Bill Frist, 1995; dep. asst. adminstr. govt. and industry affairs, FAA US Dept. Transp.; dep. asst. sec. senate affairs US Dept. Def.; spl. asst. to pres. for legis. affairs The White House, Washington, 2006—. Dep. fin. dir. US Senate Campaign of Bill Brock from Md., 1994. Non-commissioned officer USAF, 1989—93, officer USMCR. Office: White House 1600 Pennsylvania Ave NW Washington DC 20500 Office Phone: 202-456-1806. Office Fax: 202-456-6468.*

BROOME, MARION, dean; BSN, Med. Coll. Georgia, 1973; MN in Family Health Nursing, U. S.C., 1977; PhD in Child and Family Devel., U. Georgia, 1984; post-doctoral studies, U. Ala., 1986—88. Nursing sci. study section NIH, 1997—2001; assoc. dean, prof. rsch. U. Ala., 1999—2004; cons. Ind. U. Sch. Nursing, 2004—, dean, 2004—. Pres. Soc. Pediatric Nurses; bd. dirs. Assn. Care of Children's Health, Midwest Nursing Rsch. Soc. Office: Ind U Sch Nursing Office Ednl Svcs 1111 Middle Dr NU 117 Indianapolis IN 46202-5107

BROOME, OSCAR WHITFIELD, JR., finance educator; b. Monroe, NC, Feb. 3, 1940; s. Oscar Whitfield and Irma (Hinson) B.; m. Julia Carol Renegar, June 14, 1964; children: Christine Irma, Michael Whitfield. AB, Duke U., 1962; MS, U. Ill., 1964, PhD, 1971. Prof. acctg. U. Va., Charlottesville, 1967-91, prof. law, 1998—. Frank S. Kaulback Jr. prof. commerce, 1991—, assoc. dean, 1992-98, interim dean, 1997, dir. grad. studies, 1986-92, dir. Ernst & Young master's program, 1998—2001; exec. dir. Inst. Chartered Fin. Analysts, Charlottesville, 1978-84. Faculty fellow Price Waterhouse & Co., NYC, 1964; vis. prof. U. Tex., Austin, 1975, Duke U., Durham, NC, 1977-78, Tulane U., New Orleans, 2002; vis. rsch. scholar, Lancaster (Eng.) U., 1994; adminstr. exams. Inst. CFAs, 1973-77; bd. regents Coll. Fin. Planning, 1984-89, chmn., 1987-89; mem. CPA Exam. Rev. Bd., 1984-87, chmn., 1986-87; mem. exams. com. Nat. Assn. State Bds. Accountancy, 1995-2000, 04-06; bd. dirs. Internat. Bd. Stds. and Practices for CFPs, 1989-91; mem. vis. adv. com. DePaul U. Sch. Accountancy, 1991-97; mem. Va. Bd. Accountancy, 2003—. Named Outstanding Educator Va. Soc. CPAs, 1979; recipient Outstanding Faculty award Z Soc., 1988, Commendation Career Contribution award, Va. Soc. CPAs, 2006 Mem. AICPA (bd. examiners 1977-82, 2006—), Assn. for Investment Mgmt. and Rsch. (investment analysis stds. bd. 1984-86), Nat. Assn. Accts. (pres. chpt. 1974), Phi Beta Kappa, Phi Kappa Phi, Beta Gamma Sigma, Beta Alpha Psi, Omicron Delta Kappa.

BROOMFIELD, ROBERT CAMERON, federal judge; b. Detroit, June 18, 1933; s. David Campbell and Mabel Margaret (Van Deventer) B.; m. Cuma Lorena Cecil, Aug. 3, 1958; children: Robert Cameron Jr., Alyson Paige, Scott McKinley. BS, Pa. State U., 1955; LLB, U. Ariz., 1961. Bar: Ariz. 1961, US Dist. Ct. Ariz. 1961. Assoc. Carson, Messinger, Elliot, Laughlin & Ragan, Phoenix, 1962-65, ptnr., 1966-71; judge Ariz. Superior Ct., Phoenix, 1971-85, presiding judge, 1974-85; judge US Dist. Ct. Ariz., Phoenix, 1985—, chief judge, 1994-99; judge Fgn. Intelligence Surveillance Ct., 2002—. Faculty Nat. Jud. Coll., Reno, 1975-82. Contbr. articles to profl. jours. Adv. bd. Boy Scouts Am., Phoenix, 1968-75; tng. com. Ariz. Acad., Phoenix, 1980—; pres. Paradise Valley Sch. Bd., Phoenix, 1969-70; bd. dirs. Phoenix Together, 1982—, Crisis Nursery, Phoenix, 1976-81; chmn. 9th Cir. Task Force on Ct. Reporting, 1988—; space and facilities com. U.S. Jud. Conf., 1987-93, chmn., 1989-93, chmn. security, space and facilities com., 1993-95, budget com., 1997—, chmn. economy subcom., 2003—; founding mem. Sandra Day O'Connor Inn of Ct., 1988-94. Recipient Faculty award Nat. Jud. Coll., 1979, Disting. Jurist award Miss. State U., 1986, Disting. Citizen award U. Ariz. Alumni Assn., 2006. Mem. ABA (chmn. Nat. Conf. State Trial Judges 1983-84, pres. Nat. Conf. Met. Cts. 1978-79, chmn. bd. dirs. 1980-82, Justice Tom Clark award 1980, bd. dirs. Nat. Ctr. for State Cts. 1980-85, Disting. Svc. award 1986), Ariz. Bar Assn., Maricopa County Bar Assn. (Disting. Pub. Svc. award 1980), Ariz. Judges Assn. (pres. 1981-82), Am. Judicature Soc. (spl. citation 1985), Maricopa County Med. Soc. (Disting. Svc. medal 1979), Rotary. Office: US

Dist Ct Sandra Day O'Connor Cthse 401 West Washington St #626 SPC 61 Phoenix AZ 85003-2158 Home Phone: 602-265-2068; Office Phone: 602-322-7540. Business E-Mail: robert_broomfield@azd.uscourts.gov.

BROOTEN, DOROTHY, retired dean, nursing educator; b. Hazleton, Pa. married; two children. BSN, U. Pa., 1966, MSN, 1970, PhD in Ednl. Adminstrn., 1980. Assoc. prof. nursing Thomas Jefferson U., 1972-77; from asst. to assoc. prof. nursing U. Pa., 1977-88, prof. nursing, chair Health Care of Women & Childbearing, 1980-93, dir. Ctr. for Low Birthweight, Sch. Nursing, 1990-96, Overseers prof. perinatal nursing, 1990-96; dean, prof. Frances Payne Bolton Sch. Nursing Case Western Res. U., Cleve., 1998—2000; prof. Florida International Univ., 2001—, assoc. dir. graduate program, School of Nursing, 2003—. Cons. Sch. Medicine, U. Utrecht, The Netherlands, 1989, Ministry of Health, Malawi, Africa, 1991. Recipient Contbrn. to Nursing Sci. award ANA, 1988. Mem. Inst. Medicine-NAS, Am. Acad. Nursing (mem. gov. coun. 1988-91). Achievements include research on low birthweight prevention, postdischarge care of low birthweight infants, health care delivery. Office: Fl Internat U Rm ACII230 11200 SW 8th St Miami FL 33199

BROOTEN, KENNETH EDWARD, JR., lawyer, writer, rancher; b. Kirkland, Wash., Oct. 17, 1942; s. Kenneth Edward Sr. and Sadie Josephine (Assad) B.; m. Patricia Anne Folsom, Aug. 29, 1965 (div. Apr. 1986); children: Michelle Catherine, Justin Kenneth; m. Judy Diane Robinette, July 14, 2001. Diploma, Lewis Sch. Hotel, Restaurant and Club Mgmt., Washington, 1963; student, U. Md., 1964-66; AA with honors, Santa Fe C.C., Gainesville, Fla., 1969; BS in Journalism with highest honors, U. Fla., 1971, MA in Journalism and Communications with highest honors, 1972, JD with honors, 1975; law student, U. Idaho, 1972-73; diploma in internat. law, Polish Acad. Scis., Warsaw, 1974; postgrad. in Internat. Law, Trinity Coll., Cambridge U., Eng., 1974. Bar: Fla., D.C., U.S. Dist. Ct. (no., mid. and so. dists.) Fla., U.S. Dist. Ct. D.C., U.S. Tax Ct., U.S. Ct. Appeals (5th, 9th, 11th and D.C. circs.), U.S. Supreme Ct., Trial Counsel Her Majesty's Govt. of United Kingdom in U.S. Asst. to several congressmen U.S. Ho. of Reps., Washington, 1962-67; adminstrv. asst. VA Cen. Office, Washington, 1967; adminstrv. officer VA Hosp., Gainesville, Fla., 1967-72; ptnr. Carter & Brooten, P.A., Gainesville, Fla., 1975-78, Brooten & Fleisher, Chartered, Washington and Gainesville, Fla., 1978-80; pvt. practice, Washington and Gainesville, 1980-86, Washington, 1987-88, Washington and Orlando, Fla., 1988-91, Washington and Winter Park, Fla., 1991-98; ret., 1998. Spl. counsel, acting chief counsel, dir. Chief Counsel Select Com. Assassinations U.S. Ho. of Reps., 1976-77; counsel Her Majesty's Govt. of U.K. (in U.S.). Author: Malpractice Guide to Avoidance and Treatment, 1987; episode writer TV series Simon and Simon; nat. columnist Pvt. Practice, 1988-90, Physicians Mgmt., 1991-93; commentator Med. News Network, 1993-94; contbr. more than 250 articles to profl. jours.; composer. Served with USCGR, 1960-68. Named one of Outstanding Young Men Am., U.S. Jaycees, 1977; Paul Harris fellow, 2002. Mem. Fla. Bar Assn., DC Bar Assn., Assn. Intelligence Officers, Sigma Delta Chi. Presbyterian. Avocations: writing, marksmanship, dangerous game hunting. Address: The Oxbow Ranch Bascom FL 32423-9361 Office Phone: 850-569-5881. Personal E-mail: kbrooten@aol.com.

BROPHY, GILBERT THOMAS, lawyer; b. Southampton, NY, July 15, 1926; s. Joseph Lester and Helen Veronica (Scholtz) B.; m. Canora Woodham Brophy, Sept. 3, 1957 (dec.); m. Isabel Blair Porter (dec.); children: Laure Porter Thompson, Erin Woodham Brophy. BS in Acctg. with high honors, U. Fla., Gainesville, 1949; LLB, George Washington U., DC, 1960; postgrad., U. Miami, 1970-73. Bar: Fla. 1960, US Supreme Ct. 1965, US Dist. Ct. DC 1970, DC 1974. Title examiner Jesse Phillips Klinge & Kendrick, Arlington, Va., 1959-60; ptnr. Beall, Beall & Brophy, Palm Beach, Fla., 1962-65; asst. city atty. West Palm Beach, Fla., 1965-67; ptnr. Brophy & Skrandel, Palm Beach, 1968-70, Brophy & Aksomitas, Tequesta, Fla., 1974-75, Brophy, Genovese & Sayler, Jupiter, Fla., 1977-78, Brophy & Genovese, 1978-83; town atty. Lantana, Fla., 1967-70; judge ad litem Village of Tequesta, 1970-72; town atty. Jupiter, 1974-75. Bd. dirs., disaster chmn. ARC, Palm Beach; past corr. sec. Palm Beach County Hist. Soc.; del. Fla. Caucus for Presidency, 1979, 87; mem. Rep. Com. Martin County, 1984-87. With AUS, 1944-46, ETO, USA, 1951-54, spl. agt. FECOM, Japan and Korea. Recipient Dedicated Svc. plaque Town of Jupiter, 1975. Mem. NRA (patron), Nat. CIC Assn., Assn. Former Intelligence Officers (life), Attys. Title Ins. Fund, Fla. Bar, Palm Beach County Bar Assn., Rotary Club (pres. 1977-78, dist. 6930 ethics chair-4 way test, Paul Harris fellow), Univ. Club (Washington), Elks, Everglades Rifle and Pistol Club (hon. life), Kappa Sigma Alumni. Home: 717 S US Highway 1-504 Jupiter FL 33477-5905 Office: 300 Prosperity Farms Rd Ste D North Palm Beach FL 33408-5212 Office Phone: 561-863-1605.

BROPHY, JAMES DAVID, JR., humanities educator; b. Mt. Vernon, NY, Oct. 5, 1926; s. James David and Mildred (Stall) B.; m. Elizabeth Bergen, Mar. 26, 1951; children: Sheila, David, Katharine, Elizabeth, James Mark. Student, MIT, 1944-45; BA, Amherst Coll., 1949; MA, Columbia U., 1950, PhD, 1965; postgrad., U. Dijon, 1950-51. Instr. English Iona Coll., New Rochelle, NY, 1951-58, asst. prof., 1958-64, asso. prof., 1964-68, prof., 1968—, chmn. dept., 1968-71, 80-82, emeritus prof., 1992—. Author: Edith Sitwell, 1968, W.H. Auden, 1970; Editor: The Achievement of Galileo, 1962, Modern Irish Literature, 1972, Contemporary Irish Writing, 1983, New Irish Writing, 1988. Served with USNR, 1945-46. Fulbright fellow France, 1950-51; N.Y. State scholar in internat. studies, 1965; recipient Pro Operis medal Iona Coll., 1971, Bene Merenti award, 1981, Pro Multis Annis award, 1991; Nat. Endowment for Humanities grantee, 1973; Wilton Park asso., 1979 Mem. Milton Soc. Am., English Inst., Columbia Club N.Y. Home: 39 Oceanview Dr Southampton NY 11968-4215 E-mail: j-ebrophy@worldnet.att.net.

BROPHY, JERE EDWARD, education educator, researcher; b. Chgo., June 11, 1940; m. Arlene Sept. 21, 1963; children: Cheryl, Joseph. BS in Psychology, Loyola U., Chgo., 1962; MA in Human Devel., U. Chgo., 1965, PhD in Human Devel., 1967; Doctorate (hon.), U. Liege, 2004. Rsch. assoc., asst. prof. U. Chgo., 1967-68; from asst. to assoc. prof. U. Tex., Austin, 1968-76; staff devel. coord. S.W. Ednl. Devel. Lab., Austin, 1970-72; prof. Mich. State U., East Lansing, 1976-92, co-dir. Inst. for Rsch. on Tchg., 1981-93, univ. disting. prof., 1993—. Co-author: Teacher-Student Relationships: Causes and Consequences, 1974; editor (book series) Advances in Research on Teaching, 1989—. Fellow Ctr. for Advanced Study in the Behavioral Scis., 1994. Fellow: APA, Internat. Acad. Edn., Am. Psychol. Soc.; mem.: Nat. Soc. for the Study of Edn., Nat. Coun. for the Social Studies, Nat. Acad. Edn., Am. Ednl. Rsch. Assn. (Palmer O. Johnson award 1983, Presdl. citation 1995). Office: Mich State U 213B Erickson Hall East Lansing MI 48824-1034

BROPHY, JERE HALL, manufacturing executive; b. Schenectady, Mar. 11, 1934; s. Gerald Robert and Helen Dorothy (Hall) B.; m. Joyce Elaine Wright, Aug. 18, 1956; children: Jennifer, Carolyn, Jere. BS in Chem. Engring, U. Mich., 1956, BS in Metall. Engring, 1956, MS, 1957, PhD, 1958. Asst. prof. Mass. Inst. Tech., 1958-63; sect. supr. nickel alloys sect. Paul D. Merica Research Lab., Inco, Inc., Suffern, NY, 1963-67, research mgr. non-ferrous group, 1967-72, asst. mgr., 1972-73, mgr., 1973-77; dir. research and devel. and dir. Paul D. Merica Research Lab., Inco, Inc. (Inco Research and Devel. Center), 1978-80; dir. advanced tech. initiation INCO Ltd., NYC, 1980-82; v.p., dir. Materials and Mfg. Tech. Ctr. TRW Inc., Cleve., 1982-86, v.p. mfg. and materials devel. automotive sect., 1986-88; v.p. technology Brush Wellman Inc., Cleve., 1988-96; cons., 1996—. Author: (with J. Wolff) Thermodynamics of Structure; Contbr. (with J. Wolff) tech. articles to profl. jours. Fellow Am. Soc. Metals, AAAS; mem. Am. Inst. Mining and Metall. Engrs. (dir. IMD div. 1973-76), Am. Mgmt. Assn. (research and devel. council 1975-87). Clubs: Edgewater Yacht. Episcopalian. Home and Office: 31905 Jackson Rd Chagrin Falls OH 44022-1707

BROPHY, JEREMIAH JOSEPH, retired finance company executive, military officer; b. NYC, Mar. 19, 1930; s. John Joseph and Mary Margaret (Moran) B.; m. Jane Guthrie, June 4, 1955; children: John, Sandy, Greg, Elizabeth, Diane, Stephen. *Son, John, a neurosurgeon and managing partner of Brophy & Lovell Neurosurgical Clinic in Memphis, is married to Claire Slade Brophy. Daughter, Sandy, President and CEO of Books-A-Millin, Inc, and her husband Donald Q. Cochran, live with their children Katerine and Quin in Brimingham, AL. Son, Greg, a private investor, and his wife Christina live with their sons, Mitchell and Nicholas in Knoxville. Daughter, Elizabeth, owner and operator of Viaticum Travel Consultants, is married to Fabian Unterzaucher and lives with their children, Julia and Alexander, in Greer, SC. Daughter, Diane, who works in computer support for continuing education for HealthStream Corp of Nashville, is married to Johyn McCamy. Son, Stephen is chief of staff for US Congresswoman Marsha Blackburn. He and his wife Deborah Barretto Brophy live in Alexandria with their daughter Hannah Jane.* Student, Manhattan Coll., 1947-48; BS, U.S. Mil. Acad., 1953; postgrad., Army Command and Gen. Staff Coll., 1963, Armed Forces Staff Coll., 1964, Army War Coll., 1969, Monmouth Coll., 1981. Commd. 2d lt. U.S. Army, 1953; advanced through grades to brig. gen., 1976; advisor 12th Vietnamese Inf. Rgt., Vietnam, 1963-64; comdr. 1st Bn., 327th Inf. 101st Airborne Divsn., Vietnam, 1969-70; comdr. U.S. garrison Aschaffenburg, Germany; comdr. 3d Brigade, 3d Inf. divsn., 1973-75; comdr. U.S. garrison Baumholder, Germany; asst. comdr. 8th Inf. div., 1976-78; dep. comdr. Combined Arms Tng. Devels. Agy., 1978-80; dep. comdr. U.S. Army Tng. Ctr. Ft. Dix, NJ, 1980-83; stockbroker Merrill, Lynch, Pierce, Fenner & Smith, Nashville; agt. Franklin Life Ins. Co.; exec. v.p. Gen. Trust Co.; divsn. mgr. Waddell & Reed Inc., Nashville, 1983-94; cert. fin. planner BMA Fin. Svcs. Inc., Nashville, 1995—2001. Decorated D.S.M., Bronze Star valor with oak leaf cluster, Purple Heart, Legion of Merit with oak leaf cluster, Vietnamese Cross of Gallantry (3 awards), Meritorious Svc. medal, Army Commendation medal with oak leaf cluster. Mem. Assn. Grad. U.S. Mil. Acad., West Point Soc. Mid. Tenn., Mil. Officers Assn. Am. (Mid Tenn. chpt. bd. dirs., pres. 1998, chmn. middle Tenn. chpt. scholarship com. 2003—). Roman Catholic. Home: 6071 Bethany Blvd Nashville TN 37221-4314 Personal E-mail: planner30@aol.com.

BROPHY, JOSEPH THOMAS, computer company executive; b. NYC, Oct. 25, 1933; s. Joseph R. and Mary (Mitchell) B.; m. Carole A. Johnson, June 8, 1957; children: Thomas J., David W., Patricia J., Maureen A., Kathleen M. BS cum laude, Fordham U., 1957; grad. sr. exec. program, MIT, 1987. Paramedic St. Clares Med. Ctr., NYC, 1955-57; mathematician Vitro Labs., West Orange, NJ, 1957; dir. mgmt. info. systems Prudential Ins. Co., Newark, 1957-67; v.p. Huggins & Co. (cons. actuaries and mgmt. cons.), Phila., 1967-68; v.p., chief actuary Bankers Nat. Life Ins. Co., 1968-72; pres. Travelers Ins. Co., Hartford, Conn., 1972-93; chmn. Workgroup on Elect Data Interchange, Washington, 1992-95; cons. Actuarial Scis. Assocs., Somerset, NJ, 1993—; owner, dir. Solution Point, 1996—. Bd. dirs. Engineered Bus. Sys., Travtech, Inc., Travelers TPA, Inc., Ctr. Corp. Health, U.S. Behavioral Health, Travelers Health Sys., Conservco, Accent Color Scis.; cons. in field; 1967—; enrolled actuary Employee Retirement Income Security Act (ERISA). Author: A User's Guide to Project Management. Tech. editor: Actuarial Digest. Pres. St. Patrick's Pipe Band, Inc.; bd. dirs. Cath. Family Svcs., Conn. Opera, Conn. Acad. for Edn. in Math., Sci. and Tech., Hartford Grad. Ctr.; corporator St. Francis Hosp.; chmn. adv. bd. info. scis. Grad. Bus. Sch., Fordham U., Bronx, N.Y.; advisor Actuarial Studies, Hartford U., Sch. Pub. Health, Harvard U.; trustee St. Joseph Coll., Conn. With USMCR, 1949-50, AUS, 1952-54. Recipient Disting. Info. Sci. award Data Processing Mgmt. Assn., 1986. Fellow Soc. Actuaries; mem. Am. Acad. Actuaries, Acoustical Soc. Am., Hartford Actuaries Club, N.Y. Actuaries Club, Am. Arbitration Soc. (arbitrator), Greater Hartford C. of C. (bd. dirs.), Hartford Club, Internat. Brotherhood of Magicians, Telemedicine 200, Lake Sunapee Yacht Club. Home: 154 Garnet Hill Rd PO Box 701 Sunapee NH 03782-0701 Office: Actuarial Scis Assocs 270 Davidson Ave Somerset NJ 08873-4140

BROPHY, PATRICK DAVID, pediatrician, researcher; b. Calgary, Alta., Can., Aug. 21, 1965; s. David John and Deirdre Brophy; m. Jodi Lynn Yeo, Nov. 17, 1990; children: Michael Cormac, Joseph Caelan. BA with honors, U. Sask., Saskatoon, Can., 1992, MD, 1994; BSc, U. Regina, Sask., Can., 1988. Lectr. dept. pediat. U. Mich., Ann Arbor, 2001—02, asst. prof., 2002—, co-dir. pediatric lupus program, 2001—, assoc. dir. pediatric dialysis, 2005—. Contbr. articles to profl. jours. Recipient Basic Sci. Fellows award, Soc. Pediatric Rsch., 2001; grantee, Polycystic Kidney Found., 2000—03, NIH, 2005—; Carl W Gottschalk grantee, Am. Soc. Nephrology, 2002—04. Fellow: Am. Acad. Pediat., Royal Coll. Physicians Can. (corr.), Am. Soc. Nephrology (assoc.); mem.: Internat. Pediat. Nephrology Assn. (corr.), Am. Soc. Pediat. Nephrology (corr.). Roman Catholic. Achievements include research in Renal development. Avocations: golf, scuba diving, hockey. Office: U Mich Dept Pediat 1505 Simpson Rd E F6865-0297 Mott Ann Arbor MI 48109-0297 Home Phone: 734-223-2135; Office Phone: 734-936-4210. Office Fax: 734-763-6997. Personal E-mail: pbrophy@umich.ed. Business E-Mail: pbrophy@umich.edu.

BRORBY, WADE, federal judge; b. Omaha, 1934; BS, U. Wyo., 1956, JD with honor, 1958. Bar: Wyo. County and prosecuting atty. Campbell County, Wyo., 1963—70; ptnr. Morgan Brorby Price and Arp, Gillette, Wyo., 1961—88; sr. judge, US Ct. Appeals (10th cir.), Cheyenne, Wyo., 1988—2001, sr. judge, 2001—. With USAF, 1958—61. Mem.: Wyo. Bar Assn. (commr. 1968—70), Campbell County Bar Assn. Office: US Ct Appeals 10th Cir PO Box 1028 Cheyenne WY 82003-1028 also: Byron White US Courthouse 1823 Stout St Denver CO 80257*

BROSCOE, PETER A., mortgage company executive, consultant; b. NYC, Sept. 6, 1963; s. Joseph Edward and Joan Broscoe; married, Aug. 24, 1984; children: Clark, Ashley, Prescott, McKenzie, Chase. BS in Music Bus. Adminstrn., St. Joseph's Coll., Rensselaer, Ind., 1985. Cert. direct endorsed underwriter Housing Urban Devel. Pres., CEO Mortgage Express, Inc., Greenwood, Ind., 1994—; mng. mem. Trinity Title Svcs., Greenwood, 1999—; mem. Broscoe Group Properties, Greenwood, 1999—, Express Mortgage LLC, Greenwood, 2003—. Bd. dirs. Premiere Credit of N.A., Indpls. Chmn. bd. Greenwood Christian Acad., 2002—; chmn. bd. Area Youth Ministry, Indpls., 2002—. Named one of Top 40 Most Influential People Under 40 in Ind., Indpls. Bus. Jour., 2003. Mem.: Ind. Assn. Mortgage Brokers, Nat. Assn. Mortgage Brokers. Republican. Office: Mortgage Express Inc Ste A 374 Meridian Parke Ln Greenwood IN 46142 Business E-Mail: peter@mortgageexp.com.

BROSDA VON KUPFERBERG, BARON ALEXANDER CHRISTIAN, investment banker; b. Huckeswagen, N. Rhine, Germany, Apr. 26, 1970; came to U.S., 1994; s. Christian-George and Emmi-Martina (Laugallies) B.; m. Katerina. Diploma, Humanistic-Classical and, Econ. Sch., Wuppertal, Germany, 1991. Investment banker various, Dusseldorf, Germany, 1991-92; exec. product mgr., sales trainer AWD, Hanover, Germany, 1992-93; chmn., CEO ABMK & Co. Internat. Ent., Inc., NYC, 1994; v.p., mktg. dir. Lyon Mountain Spring Water, Inc., Stamford, N.Y., 1994—; shareholder, 1994; bd. dirs. The Maui Inst., Hawaii, 1994—; pres. Stamford Inst. for Rsch., Consulting and Internat. Comm., 1995—; CEO and chmn. bd. Stamford Fin. Theatrical Fund, Inc., 1995—; pres. CEO Baby Solutions, 2000—. Exec. v.p., treas. European Mkt. Stamford Fin., Inc., N.Y., 1994-97; co-chmn. Taurus Internat. Investments, Inc., 1995; CEO B2B4 Solutions.com, 2000-. Chmn. ball com. Christmas Feeling Fund, Stamford, N.Y., vice chmn. of Fund. Recipient 20th Achievement award U.S. Libr. Congress, Degree of Merit for outstanding contribution to Finance and Industry, Melrose Press Ltd.; named Man of Yr., ABI, 1996, Hon. Dep. Gov., ABIRA, Hall of Fame of Internat. Bus. People. Mem. Club of Intellectuals, Cambridge, England, C. of C., Stamford, N.Y., Congressional Group, German-American C. of C., European-American C. of C., Rotary Internat., Police Benevolent Assn. (hon.), Comthur of Aragon Priory Order of St. John. Roman Catholic. Avocations: golf, reading, sailing, racing, diving. Personal E-mail: alexbrosda@prodigy.net.

BROSELOW, LINDA LATT, medical office technician, aviculturist; b. Harrisburg, Pa., July 9, 1940; d. Herman and Ricci (Buch) Latt; m. Robert Joel Broselow, Nov. 26, 1966; children: Andrew M., Katherine, Jordan. BS, Pa. State U., 1962; MA, Columbia U., 1965. Vol. Peace Corps, Ankara, Turkey, 1962-64; office mgr. Robert J. Broselow, M.D., Lubbock, Tex., 1984-88, med. office technician, 1990-98. Vol. South Park Hosp., Lubbock, 1986-87, Ronald McDonald House, Lubbock, 1990-92. Mem. ASPCA, MADD, Am. Diabetes Assn., Am. Assn. Ret. Persons, Audubon Soc., Arkadashlar, Assn. of Univ. Women, League of Women Voters. Avocation: reading. Home: 4609 9th St Lubbock TX 79416-4710 Fax: 806-795-2005. Personal E-mail: mamoollbb@sbcglobal.net.

BROSHAR, ROBERT CLARE, retired architect; b. Waterloo, Iowa, May 20, 1931; s. Clare McDanel and Stella Mae (Scott) B.; m. Joyce Elaine Lukes, June 27, 1953; children: Scott, Michael, Matthew, Patrick, Elizabeth. B.Arch., Iowa State U., 1954. With Thorson, Thorson and Madson, 1956—60; ptnr. Henry & Broshar, 1960-62, Thorson-Brom-Broshar-Architects, Waterloo, 1963-96; ret., 1996. Mem., chair Coll. Design Found., Iowa State U., 1984—87; founding chmn. Iowa Archtl. Found., 1988. Bd. dirs. First Federal Savings and Loan, Waterloo, 1972-86, Blackhawk County YMCA, 1972-75, pres., 1972-75; chmn. bd. dirs. Goodwill Industries, 1995-96; mem. Gov.'s Com. Employment of Handicapped, 1975-79; bd. dirs. Central Gardens North Iowa, 2003—, Wright on the Pk., 2005-; vice-chmn. Rivercity Soc. for Historic Preservation., 2003. 1st lt. engr. corps AUS, 1954—56. Recipient Disting. Svc. award Iowa Easter Seal Soc., 1976, Leon Chatelain award Nat. Easter Seal Soc., 1983, Iowa State U. Alumni Achievement award, 1982, Arch. Excellence award Master Builders of Iowa, 2001; named Iowa State U. Parent of Yr., 1980. Fellow: AIA (Iowa pres. 1972, nat. dir. 1975—78, nat. v.p. 1979—81, 1982, nat. pres. 1983, Iowa Medal of Honor 1992), Royal Archtl. Inst. Can. (hon.); mem.: Soc. Archs. Guatemala (hon.), Soc. Archs. Mex. (hon.), Rotary Internat. (Paul Harris fellow), Phi Kappa Phi, Tau Sigma Delta, Delta Upsilon, Tau Beta Pi, Knight of St. Patrick Engring. Soc., Iowa State U. Order of Knoll. Independent. Methodist. Home: 15340 Dodge Ave Clear Lake IA 50428-8773 Personal E-mail: rojobro@netins.net.

BROSILOW, COLEMAN BERNARD, chemical engineering educator; b. Phila., Nov. 14, 1934; s. Samuel and Ethel (Stein) B.; m. Rosalie Ziegleman, Feb. 18, 1962; children— Rachelle, Benjamin. BS, Drexel U., 1957; M.Ch.E., Poly. Inst. N.Y., 1959, PhD, 1962. Systems engr. Am. Cyanamid Co., Process Analysis Group, Wayne, NJ, 1962-63; asst. prof. chem. engring. Case Western Res. U., Cleve., 1963-67, assoc. prof., 1967-73, prof. chem. engring., 1973—2001, prof. emeritus, 2001—, chmn. dept. chem. engring., 1980-84. Chmn. bd. Control Soft Corp., 1985-2001, now bd. dirs.; vis. prof. chem. engring. The Technion, Haifa, Israel, 1971-72, Ben Gurion U., Israel, 2000; cons. in field. Contbr. articles to profl. jours.; editl. bd.: Am. Inst. Chem. Engrs. Jour, 1980-85, Techniques of Model-based Control, 2002; patentee in field. Founding mem. bd. trustees Solomon Schecter Day Sch. of Cleve., 1978— , pres., 1978-84; bd. dirs. Citizens Empowerment Ctr. in Israel, 2006—. Fellow AIChE (computing in chem. engring. award 1989); mem. Sigma Xi, Tau Beta Pi, Phi Lambda Upsilon. Jewish. Home: 25 Shoham St Rehovot 76227 Israel Office: Ben Gurion U of the Negev Dept Chem Engring PO Box 653 Be'er Sheva 84105 Israel E-mail: cbb@po.cwru.edu, cbb@case.edu.

BROSIO, RICHARD ANTHONY, social studies educator; b. Iron Mountain, Mich., Apr. 11, 1938; s. Henry and Flavia Domenica Brosio; m. Martha Josephine Risberg, Nov. 18, 1983. BA, U. Mich., Ann Arbor, 1960, M, 1962, PhD, 1972. Social studies tchr. Crawford HS, San Diego, 1962—68, Patrick Henry HS, San Diego, 1968—69; prof. Ball State U., Muncie, Ind., 1972—2000; prof., lectr. U. Wis., Milw., 2000—. Vis. prof. No. Mich. U., Marquette, 1972. Author: Philosophical Scaffolding For The Construction Of Critical Democratic Education, 2000 (Critics' Choice, Am. Ednl. Studies Assn., 2001), A Radical Democratic Critique Of Capitalist Education, 1994 (Critics' Choice, Am. Ednl. Studies Assn., 1994). Tchr. adj. prof. for Ind. U. Labor Studies - in reference to the UAW-CIO edn. project, Anderson, Ind., 1985—87. Recipient Outstanding Rsch. award in Tchrs. Coll., Ball State U., 1994, Outstanding Faculty Member award, 1994, The James and Helen Merritt Invited Speaker Award for Outstanding Contributions to the Philosophy of Education award. Mem.: Am. Ednl. Studies Assn. (assoc.), Am. Ednl. Rsch. Assn. (assoc.). Home: 1717 W Green Tree Rd Unit 302 Glendale WI 53209 Personal E-mail: rabrosio@yahoo.com.

BROSKY, JOHN G., retired judge; b. Scott Twp., Pa., Aug. 4, 1920; m. Rose F. Brosky, June 24, 1950; children: John C., Carol Ann, David J. BA, U. Pitts., 1942, LLB, 1949, JD, 1968; D in Pub. Svc. (hon.), La Roche Coll., Pa., 1996. Bar: Pa. 1950. Asst. county solicitor, Allegheny County, Pa., 1951-56; judge County Ct. Allegheny County, 1956-61; adminstrv. judge family divsn. Common Pleas Ct. Allegheny County, 1961-80; judge Superior Ct. Pa., 1980—. Mem. faculty Pa. Coll. Judiciary. Chmn. Operation Patrick Henry, Boy Scouts Am.; pres. Scott Twp. Sch. Bd., 1946-56; 1st pres. Chartiers Valley Joint Sch. Dist., Allegheny County; pres. Greater Pitts. Guild for Blind; v.p. Allegheny County World War II Veterans Meml., 2000, co-chair meml. com. Served with U.S. Army, 1942-46; maj. gen. (ret.) USAF-Pa. Air N.G. Recipient Disting. Jud. Svc. award Pa., Mason Juvenile Ct. Inst., Man of Yr. award in law Pitts. Jr. C. of C., 1960, Humanitarian award New Light Men's Club, 1960, Loyalty Day award VFW, 1960, Four Chaplains award, 1965, Man of Yr. award Cath. War Vets., 1960, 62, Svc. award Alliance Coll., Disting. citation Mil. Order World Wars, Humanitarian award Variety Club, 1974, Jimmy Doolittle fellow award Aerospace Edn. Found., 1975, Pa. Meritorious Svc. medal Pa. N.G., 1976, State Humanitarian award Domestic Rels. Assn. Pa., 1978, Man of Yr. award Am. Legion, 1978, Pa. Disting. Svc. medal, Disting. Svc. award Pa. N.G., 1980, Exceptional Svc. award USAF, 1982, Gen. Ira Eaker fellow, 1981, Brotherhood of Man award Fraternal Socs. Greater Pitts., 1987, Cmty. Svc. award Chartiers Valley Commn. on Human Rels., 1988, George Washington Honor medal Freedoms Found., 1990; named Pitts. Polonian of Yr., 1988; recipient St. Thomas More award Allegheny County Bar Assn., 1989, Man of Yr. award Kosciuszko Found., 1991, Vectors/Pitts., 1994, Gen. John G. Brosky Day Pride in Pa. award, 1995, Disting. Achievement award Sch. Law and Dept. Edn., U. Pitts., 2000, John Heinz Cmty. Advocate award, 2001, Dr. Samuel Francis Shc. of Law award, 2002, Vector Pitts. Richard S. Caliguiri award, 2002, Hall of Fame, Pa. Horseshoe Pitcher Assn., Hall of Fame, Pa. Air Nat. Guard, 2002, Patriot of Yr., Knights of Columbus, 2004. Mem. ABA, ATLA, Am. Judicature Soc., Pa. Bar Assn. (co-chmn. professionalism com. 1987-88), Inst. Jud. Adminstrn., Inc., Internat. Platform Assn., Air Force Assn. (nat. dir., nat. pres., chmn. bd., presdl. citation 1974, 80, 81), Am. Acad. Matrimonial Lawyers, N.G. Assn. Pa. (pres.), Pa. Conf. State Trial Judges (past pres.), Pa. Joint Family Law Coun., Mil. Affairs Coun. We. Pa. (pres. 2000), Press Club, Variety Club, Aero Club (past pres.). Office: Grogan Graffam PC Four Gateway Ctr 12th Fl Pittsburgh PA 15222 Office Phone: 412-553-6382. Business E-Mail: jbrosky@grogangraffam.com.

BROSNAHAN, GODELA, nephrologist, medical educator; d. Josef and Isolde Fick; m. David Brosnahan, May 28, 1994. MD, U. Wurzburg, 1983. Lic. Nephrologist State Bavaria, 1991, Am. Bd. Internal Medicine, 1997, Am. Bd. Internal Medicine, 2006. Tchr. U. Colo. Health Scis. Ctr., Denver, 1998—2001, U. Ark., Little Rock, 2006—. Scientific adv. com. Polycystic Kidney Rsch. Found. Grantee, NIH-NIDDK, 2001—06. Mem.: Nat. Inst. Diabetes and Digestive and Kidney Diseases, Nat. Kidney Found., Am. Soc. Nephrology. Office: U Ark 4301 W Markham Little Rock AR 72205 Office Phone: 501-661-7910.

BROSNAHAN, JAMES JEROME, lawyer; b. Boston, Jan. 12, 1934; s. James Jerome and Alice B. (Larkin) B.; m. Carol Simon, Nov. 8, 1958; children: Amy Rebecca, James Jerome III, Lisa Katherine. BBA, Boston Coll., 1956; LLB, Harvard U., 1959. Bar: Ariz. 1960, U.S. Ct. Appeals (9th cir.) 1961, Calif. 1963 (chmn. fed. courts commn. 1974-75), U.S. Dist. Ct. (no. dist.) Calif. 1964, U.S. Supreme Ct. 1970, U.S. Dist. Ct. (cen. dist.) Calif. 1974. Asst. U.S. atty. U.S. Dist. Ct. Ariz., Phoenix, 1961-63, U.S. Dist. Ct. (no. dist.) Calif., San Francisco, 1963-66; assoc. to ptnr. Cooper, White & Cooper, San Francisco, 1966-75; ptnr. Morrison & Foerster, San Francisco, 1975—. Spl. counsel Calif. Legislature Join Sub-Com. Crude Oil Pricing, 1973-74; chmn. Fed. Ctrs. com. State Bar Calif., 1974; chmn. del. U.S. Ct. Appeals (9th cir.) Jud. Conf., 1977-78, lawyer rep., 1977-79; mem. jud. coun. Calif. Adv. Com. on Gender Bias in the Cts., 1987-90; frequent lectr., panelist continuing legal edn. programs, various orgns., schs., and pub. interest groups. Author: Trial Handbook for California Trial Lawyers, 1974; contbr. articles to profl. jours. Treas. Mexican-Am. Legal Def. Fund, San Francisco, 1981-83, nat. bd. dirs. 1980-84; bd. dirs. ACLU, keynote speaker 1987; bd. dirs. Sierra Club Legal Def. Fund, 1974-77; bd. dirs. Legal Svcs. for Children, Inc., 1984—; civil adv. bd. Racketeer-Influenced and Corrupt Orgns., 1985—. With USAF, 1960. Named one of Five Best Attys. in San Francisco, San Francisco Examiner, 1980, one of 7200 Best Attys. in Am., 1987, one of 100 Powerful Lawyers, Nat. Law Jour., 1988, 1998, Legend of Law, Lawyers Club, San Francisco, 2002, one of the Top Ten Lawyers in Bay Area, San Francisco Chronicle, 1998, Best Lawyers in America, 2006, Top 10 Criminal Def. Lawyers, U.S. Lawyer Rankings, 2006, Top 100 Most Influential Lawyers in America, Nat. Law Jour., 2006, 500 Leading Litigators in America, The Law Dragon, 2006; recipient Am. Legal Def. and Edn. Legal Svcs award, 1985, MALDEF Legal Svcs. award, 1985, Polit. Parties and Dem. award, Meiklejohn award, 1986, Father Moriarty Cen. Am. Refugee Recognition award, 1987, Wm. O. Douglas award, 1988, Faculty award Nat. Inst. Trial Advocacy, Tree of Life award Jewish Nat. Fund, William J. Brennan Jr. award, U. Va., 2003, Champion of Justice award Loyola Law Sch. Marymount U., 2005. Fellow Am. Coll. Trial Lawyers (Samuel E. Gates Award, 2000), Internat. Acad. Trial Lawyers, Internat. Soc. Barristers, ABA Found.; mem. ABA (adv. com. to pres.-elect program on competency and contg. legal edn. 1979, active numerous panels, programs, convs., Pro Bono Publico award, 1987, sect. on individual rights and responsibilities), Calif. Bar Assn. (chmn. panel on cross-exam 1981), Am. Law Inst., Am. Bd. Trial Advs. (named Trial Lawyer of Yr., 2001), Nat. Inst. for Trial Advocacy (bd. trustees 1992), Bar Assn. San Francisco (past pres. 1977), Practicing Law Inst. (bd. dirs. 1975-77, chmn. com. on employment of minority 1988), Am. Judicature Soc. (bd. dirs.), Calif. Attys. for Criminal Justice (bd. dirs. 1981-83, San Francisco bail projects 1987—), Am. Bd. Criminal Lawyers, Com. on Minority Employment, Am. Lawyers Newspapers Group, Inc. (nat. bd. of contbrs. 1988—), Harvard Law Sch. Alumni Assn., U.S. Supreme Ct. Hist. Soc. Nat. Products Unit Lawyers Coop. (Am. jurists editorial adv. bd.). Clubs: Barristers (San Francisco) (pres. 1968). Office: Morrison & Foerster LLP 425 Market St San Francisco CA 94105-2482 Office Phone: 415-268-7000. Business E-Mail: jbrosnahan@mofo.com.

BROSNAHAN, ROGER PAUL, retired lawyer; b. Kansas City, Mo., Aug. 9, 1935; s. Earl and Helen (Mottin) Brosnahan; m. Jill Farley, Aug. 2, 1958; children: Paul, Connor, Helen, Farley, Tracy, Hugh, Lee. BS, St. Louis U., 1956; LLB, Mich. U., 1959. Bar: Mo. 1959, Minn. 1959, U.S. Supreme Ct. 1971, U.S. Dist. Ct. Appeals (8th cir.) 1975, U.S. Dist. Ct. Appeals (6th cir.) 1984, U.S. Dist. Ct. Appeals (10th cir.) 1999. Ptnr. Streater, Murphy, Brosnahan & Langford, Winona, Minn., 1959-78, Kutak, Rock & Huie, Mpls., 1979-82, Robins, Kaplan, Miller & Ciresi, Mpls., 1982-93, Brosnahan, Joseph & Suggs P.A., Mpls., 1993-99; prin. Law Offices of Roger P. Brosnahan, Winona, 1999—2005. Mem.: ABA (state del. 1976—88), Nat. Conf. Bar Pres. (pres. 1980—81), Minn. Bar Assn. (pres. 1974—75), Minn. Trial Lawyers Assn. Democrat. Roman Catholic. Office: Roger P Brosnahan Inc 116 Center St Winona MN 55987 Office Phone: 507-457-3000. Fax: 507-457-3001. E-mail: rpbros@mwt.net.

BROSNAN, CAROL RAPHAEL SARAH, retired art association administrator; b. Paterson, NJ, July 19, 1931; d. Basil Roger and Mary Ellen Carroll (McDonald) B. Piano student of, Iris Brussels, 1940—53; student, George Washington U., Washington, 1956—61, U. Va., 1975, U. Oxford, Eng., 1975; BA in History, George Washington U., 1981, MA in History, 1987. Adminstrv. clk. Dept. Army, Def., Pentagon, Office asst. chief staff intelligence, Washington, 1955-58; clk. fgn. sci. info. program NSF, Washington, 1958-60, adminstrv. clk., 1960-65, adminstrv. fellowship clk. grad. fellowship program, 1965-72; staff asst. to Jane Alexander, chmn. Nat. Endowment Arts, Washington, 1972-94; ret., 1994. Music tchr. (piano), Paterson, 1945—53; pianist at recitals U.S., Heidelberg, Germany. With WAC US Army, 1953—55. Recipient Young People's Concerts award, 1945. Hon. fellow Harry S. Truman Libr. Inst. Nat. Internat. Affairs, 1975. Mem. Am. Legion, Am. Hist. Assn., Nat. Assn. Uniformed Svcs., Acad. Polit. Sci. (contbg. 1978-81), Am. Classical League, Friends Bodleian Libr. (Oxford U.), Luther Rice Soc. George Washington U. (life), Heritage Soc. (life), Phi Alpha Theta. Home: 6030 Sunset Ridge Ct Centreville VA 20121-3051 Office: Nat Endowment for Arts 1100 Pennsylvania Ave NW Washington DC 20004-2501

BROSNAN, PIERCE, actor; b. Drogheda, County Louth, Ireland, May 16, 1953; m. Cassandra Harris, Dec. 27, 1980 (dec. Dec. 28, 1991); adopted children: Charlotte, Christopher children: Sean, Dylan Thomas; m. Keely Shay Smith, Aug. 4, 2001; 1 child, Paris Beckett. Owner prodn. co. Irish DreamTime. Stage appearances include Wait Until Dark, The Red Devil Battery Sign, Filumena, (London); film appearances include The Mirror Crack'd, The Long Good Friday, 1982, Nomads, 1986, The Fourth Protocol, 1987, The Deceivers, 1988, Mr. Johnson, 1989, The Lawnmower Man, 1991, Mrs. Doubtfire, 1993, Love Affair, 1994, Robinson Crusoe, 1995, GoldenEye, 1995, Mars Attacks!, 1996, The Mirror Has Two Faces, 1996, Dante's Peak, 1997, Tomorrow Never Dies, 1997, The Nephew, 1998, (voice) The Quest for Camelot, 1998, Grey Owl, 1999, The World is Not Enough, 1999, The Match, 1999, The Tailor of Panama, 2000, Die Another Day, 2002, After the Sunset, 2004, others; actor, prodr.: The Nephew, 1999, The Thomas Crown Affair, 1999, The Matador, 2005, actor, exec. prodr.: The Match, 1999, Laws of Attraction, 2004; TV appearances include Murphy's Stroke, The Manions of America, Nancy Astor, Remington Steele, 1982-87, Noble House, 1988, Around The World in 80 Days, 1989, Murder 101, 1991; TV guest appearances include The Professionals, 1977, Moonlighting, 1985, Muppets Tonight!, 1996.

BROSS, MATTHEW W., information technology executive; b. Mo. m. Janice Bross, 1981; children: Kristin, Rosie, Kennie, Keenan, Kaitlyn. Sr. positions ConTel, MasterCard; co-founder Critical Tech. (sold 1997); sr. v.p., chief tech. officer Williams Comm. Group; chief tech. officer Brit. Telecom. (now BT), NYC, 2002—. Commr. Global Info. Infrastructure Commn.; chmn. bd. adv. Global Innovation Rsch. Ctr. Named a Top 50 Agenda Setter, Silicon.com, 2006; named one of Top 25 Chief Tech. Officers, InfoWorld mag., 2006. Office: BT Americas Inc 350 Madison Ave New York NY 10017 also: BT 81 Newgate St London EC1A 7AJ England*

BROSZ, MARGARET HEADLEY, pediatrics nurse; b. Dover, NJ, Dec. 31, 1951; d. Charles E. and Carolyn (Cobb) H.; m. Walter J. Brosz, May 28, 1978. Student, Douglass Coll., New Brunswick, NJ, 1970-72; BS in Nursing, Cornell U., 1974; MS, Boston Coll., Chestnut Hill, Mass., 1978. Cert. trainer medication adminstrs. Nurse Vis. Nurse Assn. Boston, 1974-76; pediatric nurse practitioner Wrentham (Mass.) State Sch., Boston Children's Hosp., 1978-80; staff nurse pediatrics ICU Thomas Jefferson U. Hosp., Phila., 1980-81; employee health clinician Children's Hosp. Phila., 1981-83; nurse mgr. The Woods Svcs., Langhorne, Pa., 1983—. Vol. interpreter Pennsbury Manor, Morrisville, Pa.; former bd. dirs. Pennsbury Soc. Mem. Devel. Disabilities, 1996—2001. Mem.: Devel. Disabilities Nurses Assn.

BROTHERS, FLETCHER ARNOLD, minister, religious organization founder, director; b. Carthage, NY, Mar. 8, 1948; s. Rae L. and Hildred (Weaver) B.; m. Keri L. Ellis; children: Jeremy, Jamie Lynn. Student, Houghton Coll., 1965-66, Utica Coll., 1966-67; HHD (hon.), Freedom Bible Coll., Lakemont, NY, 1988. Ordained to ministry Ind. Bible Chs. Am., 1975. Pastor Gates Community Chapel, Rochester and Lakemont, NY, 1975—; founder Freedom Village U.S.A., Lakemont, 1981—. Chmn. Freedom Bible Coll., 1986—. Author several books; founder Victory Today Radio and TV Programs, 1977— Bd. dirs. Religious Round Table, Washington, 1979—; pres. Save Am.'s Youth, Washington, 1988—; bd. govs. Coun. for Nat. Policy, Washington, 1989-90; mem. Inner Circle, Rep. Party, 1990-91. Recipient Angels award, 1989. Mem. Ind. Bible Ch. Home and Office: Freedom Village USA RR 14 Lakemont NY 14857 *America and especially our children are in the state they are in today because we as a nation have forgotten God. We will not win the war on drugs, etc.—till we win the war declared against God!.*

BROTHERS, JOHN ALFRED, retired oil company executive, chemicals executive; b. Huntington, W.Va., Nov. 10, 1940; s. John Luther and Genevieve (Monti) B.; m. Paula Sprague Benson, June 21, 1975. BS, Va. Poly. Inst., 1962, MS, 1965, PhD, 1966; postgrad advanced mgmt. program, Harvard U., 1981. With Internat. Nickel Co., 1962-64; with Ashland Oil, Inc., Ky., 1966—, sr. v.p., 1983-87; sr. v.p., group operating officer Ashland Oil Inc., 1987-97; with Ashland Chem. Co., Columbus, Ohio, 1974-88, pres., 1983-88; exec. v.p. Ashland, Inc., 1997-99; ret., 1999. Adj. prof. engring. Ohio State U., 1978—; pres. bus. adv. coun., 1981—. Bd. dirs. Columbus Mus. Art, Columbus Children's Hosp., Ohio Dominican Coll., 1984—. NSF fellow, 1965-66; named Outstanding Young Man U.S. C. of C., 1972 Mem. Am. Petroleum Inst., Chem. Mfrs. Assn., Columbus C. of C. (bd. dirs.), Tau Beta Pi, Phi Kappa Phi. Clubs: Scioto Country, Rolling Rock, Double Eagle Golf, Hole-in-the-Wall Golf, Mill Reef, Columbus. Republican.

BROTHERS, JOYCE DIANE, television personality, psychologist; b. NYC; d. Morris K. and Estelle (Rapoport) Bauer; m. Milton Brothers, July 4, 1949; 1 child, Lisa Robin. BS, Cornell U., 1947; MA, Columbia U., 1950, PhD, 1953; LHD (hon.), Franklin Pierce Coll., Gettysburg Coll., Lehigh U., 1994, Mt. St. Mary Coll., 1998. Asst. in psychology Columbia U., NYC, 1948-52; instr. psychology Hunter Coll., NYC, 1948-52; ind. psychologist, writer, 1952—. Co-host: TV program Sports Showcase, 1956; appearances: TV program Dr. Joyce Brothers, 1958-63, Consult Dr. Brothers, 1960-66, Ask Dr. Brothers, 1965-75; hostess (TV syndication) Living Easy with Dr. Joyce Brothers, 1972-75; columnist TV syndication, N.Am. Newspaper Alliance, 1961-71, Bell-McClure Syndicate, 1963-71, King Features Syndicate, 1972— , Good Housekeeping mag., 1962—; appearances Sta. WNBC, 1966-70; radio program Emphasis, 1966-75, Monitor, 1967-75, Sta. WMCA, 1970-73, ABC Reports, 1966-67, NBC Radio Network Newsline, 1975—; news analyst radio program, Metro Media-TV, 1975-76, news corr., TVN, Inc., 1975-76, Sta. KABC-TV, 1977-82, Sta. WABC-TV, 1980-82, , 86-88, Sta. WLS-TV, 1980-82, NIWS Syndicated News Service, 1982-84, The Dr. Joyce Brothers Program, The Disney Channel, 1985, Sta. KCBS-TV News, 1987—; contbr. CBS News, 2003—, MSNBC, 2003—; spl. feature writer Hearst papers, UPI; current affairs spl. corr. Fox TV Syndication, 1990-97; featured on A&E's Biography, 1999; author: Ten Days to a Successful Memory, 1959, Woman, 1961, The Brothers System for Liberated Love and Marriage, 1975, How to Get Whatever You Want Out of Life, 1978, What Every Woman Should Know About Men, 1982, What Every Woman Ought to Know About Love and Marriage, 1988, The Successful Woman, 1989, Widowed, 1990, Positive Plus: The Practical Plan to Liking Yourself Better, 1994. Co-chmn. sports com. Lighthouse for Blind; door-to-door chmn. Fedn. Jewish Philanthropies, N.Y.C.; mem. fund raising com. Olympic Fund; mem. People-to-People Program. Winner $64,000 Question TV Program, 1956, $64,000 Challenge, 1957; recipient Mennen Baby Found. award, 1959, Newhouse Newspaper award, 1959, Am. Acad. Achievement award, Am. Parkinson Disease Assn. award, 1971, Deadline award Sigma Delta Chi, 1971, Pres.'s Cabinet award U. Detroit, 1975, Woman of Achievement award Women's City Club Cleve., 1981, award Calif. Home Econs. Assn., 1981, award Distrubutive Edn. Clubs Am., 1981, Golden Gavel Excellence in Comm. award Toastmasters, 1982, Pub. Svc. award Ridgewood Women's Club, 1987, Women Who Make a Difference award Sen. Bill Bradley, 1990, Gt. Am. award Bards of Bohemia, 1993, Diamond award, 1994, George M. and Mary Jane Leader Healthcare Achievement award, 1995, Nat. Cmty. Svc. award McQuade Children Svcs., 1998, Presdl. citation Am. Psychol. Assn., 2002. Mem. Sigma Xi. Office: NBC Westwood One Radio Network 1700 Broadway New York NY 10019-5905

BROTHERS, LYNDA LEE, lawyer; b. Palo Alto, Calif., Nov. 21, 1945; BS in genetics, U. Calif., Berkeley, 1968; MS in biochemical genetics, U. Va., 1971; JD, Golden Gate U., 1976. Bar: Calif. 1976, Wash. 1986. Counsel com. sci. and tech. subcom. environment and atmosphere US Ho. of Reps., Washington, 1977-79; dep. asst. sec. for environment US Dept. Energy, Washington, 1979-81; asst. dir. solid, hazardous and radioactive waste and air pollution Wash. Dept. Ecology, Olympia, 1984-86; with Heller, Ehrman, White & McAuliffe, Seattle, 1986-90; ptnr. Davis, Wright & Tremaine, Seattle, 1990—2000, Sonnenschein Nath & Rosenthal LLP, San Francisco, 2000—. Mem. Bd. on Radioactive Waste Mgmt. NRC, 1989—96. Mem. editorial bd. Golden Gate U. Law Rev., 1976; contbr. articles to sci. and legal jours. Mem. N.W. Citizens' Forum on High Level Nuclear Waste at Hanford, 1986-88; pres. Washington Environ. Found., 1983-90. Office: Sonnenschein Nath & Rosenthal LLP 685 Market St, 6th Fl San Francisco CA 94105 Office Phone: 415-882-0344. Office Fax: 415-543-5472. Business E-Mail: lbrothers@sonnenschein.com.

BROTHERTON, JOSEPH FALER, lawyer; b. Brevard, NC, July 10, 1954; s. Thomas Earl and Estelle Galloway Brotherton; m. Judy Ann Justice; children: Krystal Hardy, Paige, Ashley Allred, Katie. AB, U. NC, Chapel Hill, 1976, JD, 1979. Bar: NC 1979, US Dist. Ct. (mid. dist.) NC 1979. Assoc. Tuggle Duggins & Meschan, PA, Greensboro, NC, 1979—83, prin., 1983—86, ptnr., 1986—2004, Brotherton, Ford, Yeoman & Berry, PLLC, Greensboro, 2004—. Active Tabernacle United Meth. Ch., Greensboro, NC. Mem.: DRI, NC Assn. Def. Attys. Office: Brotherton Ford Yeoman & Berry PLLC 127 N Greene St Ste 400 Greensboro NC 27401

BROTMAN, DAVID JOEL, architectural firm executive, consultant; b. Balt., Jan. 21, 1945; BS in Architecture, U. Cin., 1968. Registered arch. Ariz., Calif., Colo., D.C., Fla., Ga., Hawaii, La., Md., N.J., N.Y., Nev., Ohio, Oreg., Tex., Utah. Arch. Locke & Jackson, Balt., 1968, The Archtl. Affiliation, Towson, Md., 1968-75; joined RTKL, Balt., 1975-79, arch. Dallas, 1979-90, v.p., 1984—2000, exec. v.p., mng. dir. LA, 1990-2000, vice chmn., 1994-2000; prin. Sunset Consultants, Malibu, Calif., 2000—. Tchr. U. Tex. Sch. Architecture, Arlington, Catonsville (Md.) C.C.; arbitrator Am. Stock Exch., N.Y. Stock Exch., Nat. Assn. Security Dealers. Prin. works include Galleria at South Bay, Redondo Beach, Calif., Eton Sq. (Design Tex. Soc. Archs., 1986), Computer Sci. Corp., Fairfax County, Va., AT&T Customer Tech. Ctr., Dallas (Honor award Dallas chpt. AIA 1988), Tysons Corner Ctr., McLean Va. (Design award Monitor Ctrs. and Stores of Excellence 1989, Design award Internat. Shopping Ctrs. 1989, Exceptional Design award Fairfax County, Va. 1990, Modernization Excellence award Bldgs., 1990, Excellence award Urban Land Inst. 1992), St. Andrews (Scotland) Old Course Hotel, Tower City Ctr., Cleve., Eastland Shopping Ctr., Melbourne, Australia, Morley City Shopping Ctr., Perth, Australia, Dong An Market, Beijing, Desert Passage at Alladin, Las Vegas, Sci. and Tech. Mus., Shanghi, 825 Market St., San Francisco, many others; contbr. articles to profl. jours. Mem.: AIA (pres. Calif. coun. 2004, Calif. regional dir.), Urban Land Inst., Nat. Coun. Archtl. Registration Bds., Internat. Coun. Shopping Ctrs. Home Phone: 310-457-0931; Office Phone: 310-457-6048. Personal E-mail: sunset100@verizon.net.

BROTMAN, JEFFREY H., wholesale distribution executive; b. 1942; married; 2 children. BA in polit. sci., U. Wash., JD, 1967. Ptnr. Lasher-Brotman & Sweet, 1967-74; with ENI Exploration Co., 1975-83; co-founder Costco Wholesale Corp., 1983, chmn. bd., chief exec. officer, 1983-88, chmn. bd., 1988—93, vice chmn., 1993—94, chmn., 1994—. Dir. Starbucks, 1988—99, Garden Botanika, 1989—98, Seattle-First Nat. Bank, 1990—99, The Sweet Factory, Inc., 1992—98. Trustee Seattle Art Mus., 1990—, Seattle Found., 1991—, U. Wash. Med. Ctr. Bd., 1991—, King County United Way Bd., 1996—; co-chair King County United Way Campaign Bd., 1997—, chair, 1997; regent U. Wash., 1998—2004, v.p. bd. regents, 2002—03, chair bd. regents, fin. and audit com., 2000—. Office: Costco Wholesale 999 Lake Dr Issaquah WA 98027*

BROTMAN, MARTIN, gastroenterologist; b. Winnipeg, MB, Canada, June 26, 1939; MD, U. Manitoba, 1962. Diplomate Am. Bd. Internal Medicine, Gastroenterology Am. Bd. Internal Medicine. Intern Winnipeg Gen. Hosp., 1962—63; resident internal medicine Mayo Grad. Med. Sch., Rochester, Minn., 1963—65, fellow gastroenterology, 1965—67; med. adminstr. San Francisco; pvt. practice; chmn. med. dept. Calif. Pacific Med. Ctr., San Francisco, 1992—95, pres., CEO, 1995—. Clin. prof. med. U. Calif. San Francisco, 1982—. Mem.: AMA, ASGE, AASLD, Am. Soc. Internal Medicine, Am. Coll. Physicians, Am. Gastroentrol. Assn. (pres.-elect 2001—02, pres. 2002—03). Home: 2333 Buchanan P-1200 San Francisco CA 94115 Office: California Pacific Med Ctr PO Box 7999 San Francisco CA 94120 Address: Pacific Internal Med Ctr 2100 Webster St #423 San Francisco CA 94115-2380

BROTMAN, PHYLLIS BLOCK, advertising and public relations executive; b. Balt., Mar. 23, 1934; d. Sol. George and Delma (Herman) Block; m. Don N. Brotman, Aug. 16, 1953; children: Solomon G., Barbara Brotman Kaylor. Student, Balt. Jr. Coll., U. Va., Mary Washington Coll.; LHD (hon.), Towson U., 2007. Assoc. Channel 13 TV, 1953-55; free-lance pub. rels., 1960-66; coord. pub. rels. Md. Coun. Ednl. TV, 1965-66; pres., CEO Image Dynamics, Inc., Balt., 1966—. Lectr., cons. Md. Gen. Assembly Legis. Info. Program, 1968-70; panelist TV and radio; bd. dirs., trustee Notre Dame Coll., Md.; bd. visitors Elon Coll., N.C.; vice chair bd. visitors Towson U., Md. Columnist Balt. Bus. Jour., 1965. State chair U.S. Olympics Com. Mid-Atlantic Region, 1989-92; chair, com. mem. Greater Balt. Com., 1985-87, econ. devel. coun., 1990-91; adv. bd. Nat. Aquarium Balt., 1988—; bd. dirs. Nat. Adv. Rev. Bd., 1988-89, Balt. Symphony Orch., 1989-2001, mktg. com. 75th ann. season, 1991; active Balt. Pub. Rels. Coun.; chair adv. bd. Children and Youth Trust Fund, 1989—; bd. dirs. Internat. Visitors Ctr., co-chair mktg. com., 1990—; founding mem. Chamber Symphony San Francisco, 1984, bd. dirs., 1984-91; pub. rels. com., pres. adv. coun. U. Md. Sys., 1988—; 20th ann. conf. com. Internat. Urban Fellows Program Johns Hopkins Inst. Policy Studies, 1989-90; cmty. resources bd. Jr. League Balt., 1982-87; bd. dirs. New Directions for Women, 1979, 87-90, Stella Maris Hospice Oper. Corp., 1985-87, Jewish Family and Childrens Soc., 1980-83, Nat. Coun. Jewish Women; mem. comm. United Way Ctrl. Md., 1981-83; mktg. and pub. rels. com. Balt. Mus. Art, 1982-84, hon. com. Joshua Johnson Coun. and Endowment Fund, 1988; active U. Md. Endowments Com., 1978-79; nat. commr. B'nai B'rith Youth Commn.; bd. electors Balt. Hebrew Congregation, pres. parents assn., religious sch. com., bd. congregation; past bd. dirs. Assoc. Placement and Guidance Bur., Levindale Home and Infirmary Ladies Aux., Sinai Hosp. Aux., Nat. Jewish Welfare Fund; chair Balt. County Econ. Devel. Commn., 1987-91; appointed commn., 1980; appointed Mayors Commn. Telecomm., 1987-90; appointed State of Md. Legis. Compensation Commn., 1979—, Mayor Balt. Bus. Delegation for Balt. Conv. Ctr., 1979; bd. trustees Loyola Coll. Balt., 1986-93, treas., 1981, 82-83; bd. adv. Towson State U., 1989-, bd. vice-chair, 2004-, bd. vis., adv. coun. Sch. Bus. & Econs., 1983-85; Found. bd. dirs. Mary Washington Coll., 1985-87, 88-92, speaker jr. class ring ceremony, 1981; exec. com. Inst. Politics and Govt. Coll. Continuing Edn. U. So. Calif.; commencement speaker U. Ky. Coll. Dentistry, 1982; chmn. panel State Dept. Edu., 2001-2002; mem. Bd. Edn. Visionary Panel, 2001—, chmn. support task force; bd. visitors Towson U.; chmn. Sch. Comms. Recipient Cert. Achievement, Young Womens Leadership Coun., Cert. Appreciation for svc. to Md. Gen. Assembly by Md. Senate, Cert. Achievement in profession Md. Ho. Dels., Legis. Info. Program Pub. Rels. Soc. Am. Md. Chpt., Cert. Appreciation pub. svc. Md. Area Residences Youth, Pub. Rels. award Great Chesapeake Balloon Race Pub. Rels. Soc. Am., Md. Chpt., Leadership award nat. svc. to profession Internat. Orgn. Women Execs., 1980, Dedicated Svc. award Jewish Family and Children, 1983, Pres. Citation pvt. sector initiatives, 1985, Guardian of Menorah Internat. award B'nai B'rith, 1986; named one of Balt. Most Powerful Women, Balt. Mag., Balt. Outstanding Women Mgts. WMAR-TV, U. Balt., 1983, Woman of Yr., Arlene Rosenbloom Wyman Guild-U. Md. Cancer Ctr., 1984, B'nai B'rith Internat., 1985, 94, Avon Products, Inc., 1990, Media Advocate of Yr. for Md. U.S. Small Bus. Adminstrn., 1985, Most Admired company Balt. Mag., 1987-89, Entrepreneur of Yr. Balt. County Econ. Devel., 1990, Save-A-Heart Humanitarian of Yr., 1991, Balt. County Woman of Yr., 2004. Mem. Am. Assn. Adv. Agencies (chair mid-Atlantic region 1981-82, gov. eastern region 1982-84, chair 1986-87, bd. dirs., gov. rels. com. 1982-87), Am. Assn. Polit. Cons. (pres. 1976-80, bd. dirs. 1974-76, 80—), Nat. Coun. Jewish Women (life, bd. dirs.), Pub. Rels. Soc. Am. (Md. chpt. chair rountable 1987-88, co-chair nat. conf. 1980, v.p. 1968, Silver Anvil award 1988, Lifetime Achievement award 1993), Am. Adv. Fedn. (co-chair pub. rels. com. 1986-88, nat. govt. rels. coun. 1982—, chair legis. com. 1981), Meeting Planners Internat. (co-chair pub. rels. 1978-80, task force election by-laws 1979), Adv. Assn. Balt. (bd. dirs. 1974-76), Md.-DC-Del. Press Assn. (co-chair assocs. sect. 1982-83), Am. Trauma Soc. (nat. bd. dirs. 1981-87, Md. bd. dirs. 1982-89), Balt. County C. of C. (co-chmn. pub. rels. 2003—, mem. legis. com., 2002—), Beta Gamma Sigma, Alpha Sigma Nu, Balt. Md. C. of C. (v.p. membership 1991—, v.p. leadership Md. bd. govs. 1992-93, v.p. ctrl. dist. 1985-91, legis. conf. chair 1990, exec. com. 1986—, bd. dirs. 1984—), Balt. County C. of C. (bd. dirs. 2004-, Woman of Yr. 2004), Ctr. Club Balt. (bd. dirs., comm. chair 1983—, pres. 2003—). Avocations: tennis, flying, wine tasting. Home: 8105 Mcdonogh Rd Baltimore MD 21208-1005 Office: Image Dynamics Inc 8105 Mcdonogh Rd Baltimore MD 21208-1005 Office Phone: 410-363-1565. Personal E-mail: pbbrotman@comcast.net.

BROTMAN, RICHARD DENNIS, counselor; b. Detroit, Nov. 2, 1952; s. Alfred David and Dorothy G. (Mansfield) B.; m. Debra Louise Hobold, Sept. 9, 1979. AA, East L.A. Jr. Coll., 1972; AB, U. So. Calif., 1974, MS, 1976. Lic. marriage, family and child counselor, Calif.; cert. counselor, Calif. Instructional media coord. Audiovisual divsn. Pub. Libr., City of Alhambra, Calif., 1971-78; clin. supr. Hollywood-Sunset Cmty. Clinic, LA, 1976—; client program coord. North Los Angles County Regional Ctr. for

Devel. Disabled, 1978-81; sr. counselor Eastern L.A. Regional Ctr. for Devel. Disabled, 1981-85; dir. cmty. svcs. Almansor Edn. Ctr., 1985-87; tng. and resource devel. Children's Home Soc. Calif., 1987-90; program supr. Pacific Clinics-East, 1990-94; assoc. dir. clin. svcs., dir. clin. svcs. Alma Family Svcs., 1994—2002; probable cause hearing officer Orange County (Calif.) Healthcare Agy., 1986—. Corp. dir. San Gabriel Mission Players, 1973-75. Mem. Am. Assn. for Marriage and Family Therapy (approved supr.), Calif. Pers. and Guidance Assn., Calif. Rehab. Counselors Assn. (officer), San Fernando Valley Consortium of Agys. Serving Devel. Disabled Citizens (chmn. recreation subcom), L.A. Aquarium Soc. Democrat. Home: 3515 Brandon St Pasadena CA 91107-4542 Office Phone: 626-577-9728. Personal E-mail: brieftherapy@sbcglobal.net.

BROTMAN, STANLEY SEYMOUR, federal judge; b. Vineland, NJ, July 27, 1924; s. Herman Nathaniel and Fanny (Melletz) B.; m. Suzanne M. Simon, Sept. 9, 1951; children: Richard A., Alison B. BA, Yale U., 1947; LLB, Harvard U., 1950. Bar: NJ 1950, DC 1951. Pvt. practice, Vineland, 1952-57; ptnr. Shapiro, Brotman, Eisenstat & Capizola, Vineland, 1957-75; judge U.S. Dist. Ct. N.J., Camden, 1975—; acting chief judge Dist. Ct. of V.I., 1989-92; judge U.S. Fgn. Intelligence Surveillance Ct., 1997—2004. Mem. NJ Bd. Bar Examiners, 1970-74. Chmn. editl. bd. NJ State Bar Jour, 1969-74; contbr. articles to profl. jours. Trustee Newcomb Hosp., Vineland, 1953-68. With US Army, 1943-45, 51-52. Recipient Medal of Honor, NJ State Bar Found., 1990, Person of Yr. award, Virgin Islands Bar Assn., 1991, Herbert Harley award, Am. Judicature Soc., 1994, William J. Brennan Jr. award, Assn. Fed. Bar NJ, 1995. Fellow Am. Bar Found., Jud. Conf. US (space and facilities com. 1987-93); mem. ABA (ho. of dels. 1975-80, state del. 1982-93, mem. judicial immigration edn. project, chmn. adv. com. 1996-2005), Nat. Conf. Fed. Trial Judges (exec. com. 1984-87, chmn.-elect 1986-87, chmn. 1987-88, chmn. standing com. jud. selection, tenure and compensation 1988-92, chmn. steering com. of nominating com. 1992-93, standing com. Fed. Jud. Improvements 1992-2003), Am. Judicature Soc. (dir. 1995-2000), NJ State Bar Assn. (pres. 1974-75), Cumberland County Bar Assn. (pres. 1969-70), Assn. of Fed. Bar of State of NJ, Harvard U. Law Sch. Assn. NJ (pres. 1974-75), Fed. Judges Assn. (v.p. 1993-97), Yale U. Alumni Assn., Am. Legion, Jewish War Vets., Yale Club, B'nai B'rith, Masons, Shriners. Avocations: photography, travel. Office: MH Cohen US Courthouse 6030 MH Cohen US Courthouse 4th and Cooper St Camden NJ 08102 Home Phone: 856-692-4863; Office Phone: 856-757-5062. E-mail: sbrotman@yahoo.com.

BROTMAN, STUART NEIL, management consultant, law educator, communications executive; b. Passaic, NJ, Dec. 5, 1952; s. William and Edith (Berkowitz) Brotman; m. Gloria Z. Greenfield, June 9, 1985; children: Daniel Greenfield, Rachel Greenfield, Gabriel Greenfield. BS, Northwestern U., 1974; MA, U. Wis., 1975; JD, U. Calif., Berkeley, 1978. Bar: Calif. 1978. Spl. asst. to the asst. sec. commerce comm. and info. Nat. Telecom. and Info. Adminstrn., Washington, 1978—81; pres. Comm. Strategies Inc., Cambridge, Mass., 1981—84, Stuart N. Brotman Comm., Lexington, Mass., 1984—; pres., CEO Mus. TV & Radio, NYC, LA, 2004—05; chmn., CEO Am. TV Experience Inc., Boston, 2006—. Adj. assoc. prof. Boston U. Sch. Law, 1990—97; adj. prof. internat. law Fletcher Sch. Law and Diplomacy Tufts U., 1990—97; lectr. Knight-Bagehot Program Grad. Sch. Journalism Columbia U., 1998—2005; lectr., rsch. fellow Harvard Law Sch., 1997—; counsel Winthrop, Stimson Putnam & Robert NY, 1993—95, Morrison & Foerster, San Francisco, 1996—97; chmn. adv. bd. Envivio Inc., 2000—02. Editor: The Telecom. Deregulation Sourcebook, 1987, Telephone Company and Cable Television Competition, 1990; author: Broadcasters Can Negotiate Anything, 1988, Communications Law and Practice, 1995; contbg. editor: Cable Comm. Mag., 1983—95; mem. editl. adv. com. Fed. Comm. Law Jour., 1986—94, Transnat. Data and Comm. Report, 1991—94, EuroWatch: Econs., Policy and Law in the New Europe, 1992—2004, mem. editl. adv. bd. Internat. Jour. Comm. Law and Policy, 1999—, Jour. Biolaw and Bus., 2004—, adv. bd. Jour. Sci. and Tech. Law, 1996—; contbr. articles to profl. jours. Mem. New Eng. steering com. Eisenhower Fellowships, 2003—; bd. dirs. US-Israel Sci. and Tech. Found., 2001—04, chmn., 2003—04; mem. nat. adv. com. Northwestern U. Sch. Comm., 1990—; mem. adv. com. UCLA Comm. Law Program, 1986—92; bd. dirs. Boalt Hall Alumni Assn. U. Calif., Berkeley, 2000—03; mem. comm. arts adv. bd. U. Wis., Madison, 2003—. Vis. scholar, MIT, 2005—; adj. fellow, Ctr. Strategic and Internat. Studies, 1999—2000, Eisenhower fellow, 2000—, Annenberg Washington Program Sr. fellow, 1988—94, Sr. fellow, Edward R. Murrow Ctr. Internat. Comm., 1994—97, Acad. fellow, Jaffee Ctr. Strategic Studies Tel Aviv U., 2003—04. Mem.: ABA (chmn. internat. comm. law com., internat. law and practice sect. 1992—95, internat. legal edn. 1995—96), Nat. Press Club, Fed. Comm. Bar Assn., Northwestern U. Alumni Assn. (Merit award 1996), Cosmos Club. Democrat. Jewish. Personal E-mail: sbrotman@brotman.com.

BROTT, WALTER HOWARD, retired cardiac surgeon, educator, military officer; b. Alamosa, Colo., Sept. 5, 1933; s. Walter Hugo and Viola Helen (Roscher) B.; m. Marie Helen Kuzniewski; children: Cheryl Marie, Michelle Marie, Kevin Walter. BA, Yale U., 1955; MD, U. Kans., 1959. Diplomate Am. Bd. Surgery, Am. Bd. Thoracic Surgery. Commd. 1st. lt. U.S. Army, 1959, advanced through grades to col., 1974; intern Walter Reed Army Med. Ctr., Washington, 1959; resident in gen. surgery William Beaumont Gen. Hosp., El Paso, Tex., 1960-64; resident in thoracic surgery Fitzsimmons Army Med. Ctr., Denver, 1967-69; comdr. 3d Surg. Hosp., Vietnam, 1969, 18th Surg. Hosp., 1970; asst. chief thoracic and cardiovascular surgery Walter Reed Army Med. Ctr., 1971-76, chief cardiothoracic surgery, 1977-84; ret. U.S. Army, 1982. Chief surg. cons. Surgeon Gen. Army, Washington, 1976-77; prof. surgery and subsequent clinical prof. surgery Uniformed Svcs. U. Health Scis., 1976—; assoc. clin. prof. surgery U. Tenn., Knoxville, 1984-94, hon. clinical prof., 1994—; mem. joint rev. com. Coun. for Perfusion Edn. and Accreditation, 1981-87. Contbr. articles to profl. jours.; chmn.: NATO editorial bd. Emergency War Surgery Handbook, 1977-82. Mem. physicians' panel Heritage Found., 1991—. Decorated Legion of Merit with oak leaf cluster; decorated Bronze Star (U.S.), Cross of Gallantry (Vietnam); recipient Cert. of Achievement Surgeon Gen. U.S., 1978 Fellow ACS (grad. edn. com. 1977-78); mem. AMA (cons. panel coun. allied health edn. accreditation 1981-87), Walter Reed Assn., Soc. Thoracic Surgeons, Washington Med. Soc., Thoracic and Cardiovascular Surgeons, Thoracic Surgery Program Dirs. Assn., Am. Assn. for Thoracic Surgery, Assn. Med. Cons. to Armed Forces, Assn. Mil. Surgeons, Heritage Found. (Physicians Coun.), Internat. Platform Assn., Alpha Omega Alpha. Clubs: Yale (Washington); Marine Meml., Univ. Faculty Club, Utah. Lutheran. *Using those opportunities to better the life of one's fellow man not only gives gratification in itself but enhances the person spiritually and occasionally materially by God's rewards.*

BROTTON, JOYCE DUPRAS, English language educator; m. Charles Michael Brotton, Oct. 26, 1968; children: Charles Michael, Ann. BA, George Mason U., 1992, MA, 1993, D in Arts, 2002. Intelligence processing US Dept. Def., Washington, 1963—68; prof. English, asst. dean No. Va. CC, Annandale, Va., 2007—. Exec. sec. Adv. Bd., Cert. in Profl. Writing, Annandale, Va., 1999—; coord., cert. in profl. writing No. Va. CC, Annandale, Va., 1999—; conf. chair Va. English Discipline Peer Group of C.C. English Tchrs., 2002, 06; bd. dirs. No. Va. Review, 2003—, George Mason World Project, 2006—. Prodr.(narrator): (televised video) The Theory of Editing, The Practice of Editing, Writing User Manuals; author: Revising Life Through Literature: Dialogical Change from the Reformation through Postmodernism, 2006; contbr. articles to profl. jours. Chair, scholarship awards Greenbriar Woman's Club, Fairfax, Va., 1995—; speaker-world lit. and profl. writing Speakers Bur., No. Va. C.C., Annandale, Va., 1998—. Mem.: Assn. Tchrs. of Tech. Writing (assoc.), Two-Year Coll. English (assoc.; presenter 1997—2001), Golden Key. Avocations: world travel, theater, book reviews. Office: Northern Va Cmty Coll 8333 Little River Turnpike Annandale VA 22003 Office Phone: 703-323-3430. Business E-Mail: jbrotton@nvcc.edu.

BROTZEN, FRANZ RICHARD, materials scientist, educator; b. Berlin, July 4, 1915; arrived in U.S., 1941; s. Georg and Lena (Paculły) Brotzen; m. Frances Burke Ridgway, Jan. 31, 1950; children: Franz Ridgway, Julie Ridgway. BSMetE, Case Inst. Tech., 1950, MS, 1953, PhD, 1954. Salesman a Quimica Bayer Ltda., Rio de Janeiro, 1934-41; mfrs. rep. R.G. Le Tourneau, Inc., Longview, Tex., 1947-48; sr. rsch. assoc. Case Inst. Tech., Cleve., 1951-54; mem. faculty Rice U., Houston, 1954—, prof. materials sci., 1959—88, prof. emeritus, 1988—, dean engring., 1962-66, master Brown Coll., 1977-82. Vis. prof. Max Planck Inst., Stuttgart, Germany, 1960—61, Stuttgart, 1973—74, Fed. Poly. Inst., Zurich, Switzerland, 1966—67, U. Lausanne, Switzerland, 1981. Contbr. scientific papers to profl. jours. Chmn. Houston Contemporary Arts Assn., 1964—65. Served to 1st lt. US Army, 1942—46. Recipient Sr. Scientist award, West German Govt., 1973—74; Guggenheim fellow, 1960—61. Fellow: Am. Soc. Metals (chmn. Houston chpt. 1980—81); mem.: AIME, Soc. Engring. Sci., Am. Phys. Soc., Sigma Xi, Tau Beta Pi. Home: 2701 Bellefontaine St # H Houston TX 77025 Office: Rice U Dept Materials Sci PO Box 1892 Houston TX 77251-1892 Home Phone: 713-668-4874; Office Phone: 713-348-3563.

BROUDE, RICHARD FREDERICK, lawyer, educator; b. LA, June 6, 1936; s. Leo Martin and Frances (Goldman) B.; m. Paula Louise Galnick, June 8, 1958; children: Julie Sue, James Matthew, Mark Allen. BS, Washington U., St. Louis, 1957; JD, U. Chgo., 1961. Bar: Ill. 1961, Calif. 1971, N.Y. 1989. Prof. law U. Nebr., Lincoln, 1966-69, Georgetown U., Washington, 1969-71; ptnr. Commons & Broude, LA, 1974-77, Irell & Manella, LA, 1977-80, Sidley & Austin, LA, 1980-87, White & Case, LA, 1987-90, Mayer, Brown & Platt, NYC, 1990-99. Adj. prof. law U. So. Calif., L.A., 1978-90, St. Johns U., 2000—; adv. panel World Bank Insolvency Initiative; cons. OECD Forum for Asian Insolvency Reform. Author: Reorganizations Under Chapter 11, 1986—, Cases and Materials on Land Financing, 3rd, 1985; editor: Insolvency and Finance in the Transportation Industry, 1993, Collier Internat. Bus. Guide; mem. editl. bd.: Collier on Bankruptcy, contbg. editor: Collier Bankruptcy Practice Guide. Fellow Am. Bar Found., Am. Coll. Bankruptcy; mem. ABA (com. on bus. bankruptcy), Am. Law Inst. (advisor Transnat. Insolvency Project), Internat. Bar Assn. (chair insolvency and credit rights com. 1996-2000), Bar Assn. of City of N.Y., Calif. Bar Assn., Nat. Bankruptcy Conf. (conferee, chair com. on internat. aspects, vice chair legis. com.). Office: Richard F Broude PC 400 E 84th St # 22A New York NY 10028-5611 Home Phone: 212-879-9810; Office Phone: 212-879-7042. E-mail: rfbroude@broudepc.com.

BROUDE, RONALD, music publisher; b. NYC, Oct. 15, 1941; s. Irving and Anne Broude; m. Janyce Ingalls, Aug. 19, 1982. AB, Columbia Coll., 1962; MA, Columbia U., 1962, PhD, 1967. Pres., exec. editor Broude Bros. Ltd., NYC and Williamstown, Mass., 1973—; trustee Broude Trust for the publ. musicological editions, NYC, 1981—. Mem. exec. bd. Early Music Am., 1994-98. Mem.: Soc. Textual Scholarship (mem. exec. bd. 1989—, exec. dir. 2004—05).

BROUGHTON, MARGARET MARTHA, mental health nurse; b. London, Ky., Feb. 1, 1926; d. Edward Broughton and Stella Alice Johnson; m. Louis Kurt Henkel, May 17, 1947 (div. Nov. 1957); children: Gretchen Maria Henkel Clark, Suzanne Henkel Guthrie, Elizabeth Henkel Stark, David Lawrence Henkel, John Arthur Henkel. RN, Christ Hosp. Sch. Nursing, Cin., 1947; BA in Religious Studies, U. Calif., Santa Barbara, 2003. Staff nurse, psychiatric nurse to asst. supt. psychiatric nurse and instr. Camarillo (Calif.) State Hosp., 1958—70; mental health nurse I and II, insvc. instr. Ventura County Mental Health, Calif., 1973—88; part-time spiritual group facilitator Hillmont Psychiatric Ctr., Ventura, Calif., 1995—. Democrat. Universalist Unitarian. Avocations: singing, reading, walking. Home: 980 Terracina Dr Santa Paula CA 93060 Personal E-mail: phoenixrise3@verizon.net.

BROUGHTON, PHILLIP CHARLES, lawyer, director; b. Findlay, Ohio, Sept. 21, 1930; s. Harold C. and Marian (Pierson) B.; children: Margaret Crockett, Phillip Charles, Anne Duvall, Elizabeth Cox. BA, Bowling Green U., 1953; JD, U. Mich., 1957; LLM, NYU, 1962. Bar: N.Y. 1957. Practiced in, NYC, 1957—; mem. firm Thacher, Proffitt and Wood, 1957-93, of counsel, 1993—. Pres., bd. dirs. Midgard Found., N.Y.C.; trustee Asheville (N.C.) Art Mus.; trustee United Way Asheville, N.C. Mus. Art, Achilles Meml. Fund. Mem. ABA.

BROUILLARD, JOHN CHARLES (JACK), automotive parts and former grocery company executive; b. Brockton, Mass., Apr. 7, 1948; s. Francis Arthur Brouillard and Marie Virginia Carroll; m. Elaine Ferguson, Oct. 12, 1974; children: John Jr., Carolyn, Michael, Diane, Jeffrey. BMechE, U. Mass., 1970; MBA, U. Pa., 1974. CPA, Mass. Sr. cons. Arthur Andersen & Co., Boston, 1974-77; with Hill Dept. Stores, Canton, Mass., 1977—91, pres., COO, 1990—91; CFO, chief adminstrv. officer H.E. Butt Grocery Co., San Antonio, 1991—2005; interim chmn., pres., CEO Advance Auto Parts Inc., Roanoke, Va., 2007—. Bd. dirs. HE Butt Grocery Co., 2003—, Advance Auto Parts Inc., 2004—, Eddie Bauer Holdings, 2005—. Served with U.S. Army, 1971-73. Office: Advance Auto Parts Inc 5008 Airport Rd Roanoke VA 24012*

BROUILLARD, ROBERT PAUL, maintenance planning manager; s. William Francis and Shirley Ann Brouillard; m. Kristine Anne Becker, Jan. 31, 1987; 1 child, Sarah Anne. Maintenance technician Orlando Sentinel, Fla., 1981—98, packaging maintenance mgr., 1998—2003, maintenance planning mgr., 2003—. Vol. Beta Ctr., Orlando, Fla., 2005—07. Recipient Employee Excellence award, Orlando Sentinel. Roman Catholic. Avocations: travel, family activities. Office: Orlando Sentinel 633 North Orange Ave Orlando FL 32801 Home Phone: 407-521-9254; Office Phone: 407-420-6285. Personal E-mail: brouill@hotmail.com. E-mail: bbrouillard@orlandosentinel.com.

BROUILLETTE, DAN R., former federal agency administrator; b. Paincourtville, La. m. Adrienne Brouillette; 2 children. Grad., U. Md. Legis. dir. to Congressman Billy Tallzin, 1989—97; sr. v.p. R. Duffy Wall & Assocs., 1997—2000; asst. sec. congl. and intergovtl. affairs U.S. Dept. Energy, Washington, 2001—03; ptnr. Alpine Group Inc., 2000—01, 2003; staff dir. U.S. Ho. Energy & Commerce com., Washington, 2003—. With US Army. Office: The Comm on Energy & Commerce 2125 Rayburn Ho Office Bldg Washington DC 20515

BROUMAND, STAFFORD R., Plastic Surgeon; b. 1959; m. Laura Tisch. BA Biology, Chemistry, Indianna U., 1981; MD, Yale U., 1985; grad. gen. surgery, Mount Sinai Medical Ctr., 1985—89. Cert. American Soc. of Plastic Surgeons. Clinical fellowship Mass. Gen. Hosp., Harvard Med. Sch.; intern College des Medicines de Paris, Paris, 1993; staff, burn victims Massachusetts Gen. Hosp. Shiners Burns Inst.; faculty, asst. prof. of plastic surgery Mount Sinai Hosp., 1993—; dir. Plastic and Cosmetic Surgery Ctr., New York City. Mem.: Plastic Surgery Edn. Foun., The New York Regional Soc. of Plastic Surgery. Office: 740 Park Ave New York NY 10021 Office Phone: 212-879-7900. Office Fax: 212-879-3387.*

BROUN, ELIZABETH, art historian, curator; b. Kansas City, Mo., Dec. 15, 1946; d. Augustine Hughes and Roberta Catherine (Hayden) Gibson. BA, U. Kans., 1968, PhD, 1976; cert. advanced study, U. Bordeaux, France, 1967. Curator prints and drawings Spencer Mus. Art, Lawrence, Kans., 1976-83; asst. prof. U. Kans., Lawrence, 1978-83; asst. dir. chief curator Nat. Mus. Am. Art, Washington, 1983-88, acting dir., 1988-89; dir. Smithsonian Am. Art Mus. (formerly Nat. Mus. Am. Art), Washington, 1989—. Author: exhbn. catalogues Prints of Zorn, 1979, Prints and Drawings of Pat Steir, 1983, Patrick Ireland; Drawings 1965-85, 1986, Albert Pinkham Ryder, 1989; co-author: Benton's Bentons, 1980, Engravings of Marcantonio Raimondi, 1981. Woodrow Wilson fellow, 1968-69; Ford. Found. fellow, 1970-72 Mem. Phi Beta Kappa Office: MRC 970 PO Box 37012 Washington DC 20013-7012 Office Phone: 202-633-8430.

BROUN, PAUL C., JR., congressman, physician; b. Athens, Ga., Dec. 7, 1946; s. Paul C. and Gertrude Margaret (Beasley) Broun; m. Niki Bronson; children: Carly, Lucy, Collins. Grad., U. Ga.; MD, Med. Coll. Ga., 1971. Mem. US Congress from 5th Ga. dist., 2007—. Founding pres. Ga. Rep. Assembly. Mem. Rotary Club, Athens-Clarke County C. of C. Mem.: NRA, Gun Owners Am., Ga. Sport Shooting Assn. Republican. Baptist. Office: US Congress 2104 Rayburn House Office Bldg Washington DC 20515 also: 1054 Claussen Rd Ste 316 Augusta GA 30907*

BROUS, THOMAS RICHARD, lawyer; b. Fulton, Mo., Jan. 7, 1943; s. Richard Pendleton and Augusta (Gilpin) B.; m. Patricia Catlin, Sept. 12, 1964; (dec. Sept. 1999); children: Anna Catlin Brous, Joel Pendleton Brous; m. Mary Lou McClelland Kroh, Sept. 8, 2001. BSBA, Northwestern U., 1965; JD cum laude, U. Mich., 1968. Bar: Mo. 1968, U.S. Dist. Ct. (we. dist.) Mo. 1968, U.S. Ct. Mil. Appeals 1968, U.S. Supreme Ct. 1971. Assoc. Watson & Marshall L.C., Kans. City, Mo., 1968-78, ptnr., 1978-96, mng. ptnr., 1992-94; shareholder Stinson, Mag & Fizzell, P.C., Kans. City, Mo., 1996—2002; ptnr. Stinson Morrison Hecker LLP, Kans. City, 2002—. Adj. faculty U. Kans. Sch. of Law, 2006—; mem. steering com. U. Mo. Kansas City Law Sch. Employee Benefits Inst., 1990—2001, chmn. 1992-93; with Ctrl. Mtn. Tax Exempt and Govtl. Entities Coun. IRS, 1997-2005. Author: Chapter 26, III Missouri Business Organizations, 1998, Chapter 10, Missouri Specialized Business Entities, 2006; asst. editor Mich. Law Rev., 1966-68. Mem. vestry St. Andrews Episcopal Ch., Kansas City, 1974-77, Grace & Holy Trinity Cathedral, 1994—, chancellor, 1998—; trustee Kansas City Repertory Theatre, Inc., 1990—, pres., 1995-98; v.p., treas. Barstow Sch., Kansas City, 1982-86; dir. Met. Orgn. to Counter Sexual Abuse, Kansas City, 1992-95; vis. com. Divinity Sch. U. Chgo., 2006-. Capt. US Army, 1968—72. Mem. ABA, Univ. Club (pres. 1988-89), Greater Kansas City Soc. Hosp. Attys., Kansas City Met. Bar Assn., Heart of Am. Employee Benefit Conf., The Mo. Bar Assn. (vice-chair employee benefits com. 1997-2000), Mo. Soc. Hosp. Attys., Delta Upsilon, Beta Gamma Sigma. Episcopalian. Avocations: reading, hiking, gardening. Office: Stinson Morrison Hecker LLP 1201 Walnut Ste 2800 Kansas City MO 64106 Office Phone: 816-691-3368. Personal E-mail: tbrous@stinson.com.

BROUSSARD, ALLISON M., secondary school educator, artist; b. Buffalo, Nov. 3, 1977; d. Robert E. and Joanne A. Sacilowski; m. Scott A. Broussard, June 17, 2000; children: Taylor Elyse, Camryn Grace, Jake Vernest, Ashlyn Rose. BFA, Rochester Inst. Tech., NY, 1999; postgrad., Walden U., 2006. Cert. tchr. N.Y. Tchr. Spencerport (N.Y.) H.S. Advisor Art Club Spencerport H.S., cheerleading coach. Avocations: drawing, painting, photography. Office: Spencerport HS 2707 Spencerport Rd Spencerport NY 14559

BROUSSARD, MALCOLM JOSEPH, pharmacist, consultant; b. Lake Charles, La., Mar. 14, 1953; s. Roy Joseph and Liller Leeova (Tubbs) B. BS in Biology, McNeese State U., Lake Charles, 1975; BS in Pharmacy, Xavier Coll. Pharmacy, 1978. Registered pharmacist. Staff pharmacist Hotel Dieu Hosp., New Orleans, 1978-80, JoEllen Smith Meml. Hosp., New Orleans, 1980-85; asst. dir. pharmacy St. Jude Med. Ctr., Kenner, La., 1985-91; dir. pharmacy MacKinnon Ctr., Metairie, La., 1991-93; pharmacist St. Jude Med. Ctr., Kenner, La., 1994—99; exec. dir. La. Bd. Pharmacy, 1999—. Founder, pres. Parenteral Therapy Svcs., Inc., Harvey, La., 1985—90; v.p. Lapalco Pharmacy, Inc., 1987—90, South La. Med. Supply Co., Inc., 1987—90; pharmacy cons. La. State Bd. Nursing, New Orleans, 1980—93; externship preceptor Xavier Coll. Pharmacy, 1980—99, vis. instr., 1982—83, asst. prof., 1991—99. Bd. dirs. New Orleans Pharmacy Mus., 1988—99; mem., advisor La. Pharmacists Polit. Action Com., 1984—99. Mem. Am. Pharm. Assn., Am. Soc. Hosp. Pharmacists (state del. 1991-93), Nat. Assn. Bds. Pharmacy (exec. com. 2006—), La. Pharmacists Assn. (pres. 1983-84, Pres.'s award 1984, Pharmacist of Yr. 1985, 2006), La. Soc. Hosp. Pharmacists (pres. 1988-89), S.E. La. Soc. Hosp. Pharmacists (pres. 1981-82, Pharmacist of Yr. 1984), Rho Chi, Phi Lambda Sigma. Republican. Roman Catholic. Home: PO Box 14914 Baton Rouge LA 70898 Office Phone: 225-925-6496. Business E-Mail: mbroussard@labp.com.

BROUSSARD, RICHARD C., lawyer; b. Lafayette, La., Apr. 1, 1949; s. Charles E. and Rose (Ashy) B.; m. Kathleen Alexis David, May 29, 1970; children; Rebecca, David, John. BS, U. Southwestern La., 1971; JD, La. State U., 1974. Bar: La. 1974, US Dist. Ct. (we., mid. & ea. dists.) La., US Dist. Ct. (ea. & no. dists.) Tex., US Ct. Appeals (5th cir.); cert. civil trial advocacy lawyer Nat. Bd. Trial Advocates. Law clk. to presiding judge La. Dist. Ct., Abbeville, 1974-75; from assoc. to ptnr. Domengeaux & Wright, Lafayette, La., 1975-92; ptnr. Anderson & Broussard, Lafayette, 1992—2002, Broussard & David, Lafayette, 2002—. Magistrate Youngsville Mcpl. Ct., La., 1982-02. Mem. La. Intrastate Air Carrier Bd., 1977—; chmn. Lafayette Regional Airport Commn., 1985; bd. dirs. St. Cecelia Sch. Bd., Broussard, 1980-83, Acadiana Med. Research Found., Lafayette, 1981-86. Served to 1st lt. USAFR, 1972-78. Named one of Top 50 Lawyers, La. Super Lawyers Mag., 2007. Mem. La. Bar Assn. (house of dels. 1980, bd. govs. 1993-96, Lifetime Achievement award 2005), Lafayette Parish Bar Assn. (v.p. 1985-86, pres. 1986-87), La. Trial Lawyers Assn. (bd. dirs. 1984-87, exec. coun. 1996-97), Am. Inns. of Ct. (sec.-treas. Aradiana Inn 1989-91, emeritus 1995—), Million Dollar Advs. Forum, Lions Club. Democrat. Roman Catholic. Avocations: aviation, hunting, sailing, scuba diving. Home: Sky Ranch Youngsville LA 70592 Office: Broussard & David PO Box 3524 Lafayette LA 70502-3524

BROWAR, LISA MURIEL, librarian; b. NYC, Jan. 22, 1951; d. Elliott Andrew and Shirley (Kahn) Browar. B in English Lit., Ind. U., 1973, MLS, 1977; M in English Lit., U. Kans., 1976; Exec. MA in Philanthropic Studies, Ind. U.-Purdue. U., Indpls., 2006. Cert. in fund raising mgmt. 2001. Asst. curator Beinecke Libr. Yale U., New Haven, 1979-81, archivist Sterling Meml. Libr., 1981-82; curator spl. collections Vassar Coll. Libr., Poughkeepsie, NY, 1982-87; asst. dir. rare books and manuscripts N.Y. Pub. Libr., NYC, 1987-96; dir. The Lilly Libr., Ind. U., Bloomington, 1996-2001; libr. for English and Am. lit., philosophy and film studies Main Libr., Ind. U., Bloomington, 2001—02; univ. libr. New Sch. U., NYC, 2002—. Editor RBM: A Jour. of Rare Books, Manuscripts, and Cultural Heritage, 1999-2003. Mem. ALA, Assn. Coll. and Rsch. Librs. (sec. rare books and manuscripts sect. 1987-89, chair, 1994-95, editor 1999—), Soc. Am. Archivists, Bibliog. Soc. Am., Grolier Club. Democrat. Avocations: opera, theater, photography. Office: Fogelman Libr 65 Fifth Ave New York NY 10011 Home Phone: 914-576-6077; Office Phone: 212-229-5598 ext. 3149. Business E-Mail: browarl@newschool.edu.

BROWDE, ANATOLE, electronics company executive, consultant; b. Berlin, June 10, 1925; arrived in US, 1940, naturalized, 1946; s. Alexander and Rebecca (Braude) Kutisker; m. Jacqueline Rousseau, Mar. 10, 1973;

children: David, Elizabeth, Richard. BEE, Cornell U., 1948; postgrad., Northwestern U., 1948, Columbia U., 1951-52; MLA, Washington U., St. Louis, 1994, MA, 1996, PhD in History, 1999. Engr. Capehart-Farnsworth Corp., Ft. Wayne, Ind., 1948-51, Arma Corp., Bklyn., 1951-53; project engr. BOMARC, Westinghouse Electric Co., Balt., 1953-55; assoc. dir. missile dept. Avco Corp., Cin., 1955-59; with McDonnell Douglas Corp., 1959-90, v.p. engring. and mktg., 1979-81; v.p., gen. mgr. info. systems div. McDonnell Douglas Electronics Co., St. Charles, Mo., 1981-82, v.p. Microelectronics Ctr., 1982-87; v.p. ops. McDonnell Douglas Electronics Systems Co., 1987-89, dir. ops. integration, 1989-90; pres. Browde Cons. Inc., St. Louis, 1990—97. Adj. prof. Maryville U., St Louis, 1992—. Chmn. secondary schs. com. Cornell U., 1968-1976, mem. univ. council, 1971-77, 79—; trustee First Unitarian Ch., St. Louis, 1977-80, chmn., 1979-80, chmn. fin. com., 1985-1989. Mem.: Cornell (St. Louis), Cornell U. Coun. Republican. Unitarian Universalist. Achievements include development of Mercury, Gemini Spacecraft electronics, 1961-68, airborne collision avoidance system, 1968-72. Home: 12031 Carberry Pl Saint Louis MO 63131-3124

BROWDER, FELIX EARL, mathematician, educator; b. Moscow, July 31, 1927; s. Earl and Raissa (Berkmann) Browder; m. Eva Tislowitz, Oct. 5, 1949; children: Thomas, William. SB, MIT, 1946; PhD, Princeton U., 1948; MA (hon.), Yale U., 1962; D (hon.), U. Paris, 1990. C.L.E. Moore instr. math. MIT, 1948—51, vis. assoc. prof., 1961—62, vis. prof., 1977—78; instr. Boston U., 1951—53; asst. prof. Brandeis U., 1955—56; from asst. prof. to prof. Yale U., 1956—63; prof. math. U. Chgo., 1963—72, Louis Block prof. math., 1972—82, Max Mason disting. svc. prof., 1982—87, chmn. dept., 1972—77, 1980—85; v.p. rsch. Rutgers, The State U. NJ, 1986—91; univ. prof. Rutgers U., New Brunswick, 1986—. Vis. mem. Inst. Advanced Study, Princeton U., NJ, 1953—54, 1963—64; vis. prof. Princeton U., 1968, Inst. Pure and Applied Math., Rio de Janeiro, 1960, U. Paris, 1973, 1975, 1978, 1981, 1983, 1985; sr. rsch. fellow U. Sussex, 1970, 1976, England; Fairchild Disting. visitor Calif. Inst. Tech., Pasadena, 1975—76; spkr. Internat. Congress of Math., 1970, Sci. Bd. Santa Fe Inst., 1986—98, U.S. Nat. Med. Sci., 1999. Contbr. theorems to books, including Nonlinear Problems, 1966, Functional Analysis and Related Fields, 1970, Nonlinear Operators and Nonlinear Equations of Evolution in Banach Spaces, 1976, Nonlinear Functional Analysis and Its Applications, 1986. With US Army, 1953—55. Fellow Guggenheim, 1953—54, 1966—67, Sloan Found., 1959—63, NSF sr. postdoctoral fellow, 1957—58. Fellow: AAAS (chmn. sect. A 1982—83); mem.: NAS (coun. mem. 1992—95), Math. Assn. Am., Am. Math. Soc. (editor bull. 1959—68, 1978—83, mem. coun. 1959—72, 1978—83, mng. editor 1964—68, 1980, exec. com. counl 1979—80, colloquium lectr. 1970, pres. 1999—2001), Am. Acad. Arts and Scis., Sigma Xi (pres. chpt. 1985—86). Achievements include development of linear and nonlinear partial differential equations; nonlinear functional analysis and fixed point and mapping theorems. E-mail: browder@math.rutgers.edu.

BROWDER, JOHN GLEN, former congressman, educator; b. Sumter, SC, Jan. 15, 1943; s. Archie Calvin and Ila (Frierson); m. Sara Rebecca Moore; 1 child, Jenny Rebecca. BA in History, Presbyn. Coll., 1965; MA in Polit. Sci., PhD in Polit. Sci., Emory U., 1971. Asst. in pub. relations Presbyn. Coll., Clinton, S.C., 1965; sportswriter The Atlanta Jour., 1966; investigator U.S. Civil Service Commn., Atlanta, 1966-68; prof. polit. sci. Jacksonville (Ala.) State U., 1971-87; mem. Ala. Ho. of Reps., Montgomery, 1982-86; sec. of state State of Ala., Montgomery, 1987-89; mem. 101st-104th Congresses from 3d Ala. dist., Washington, 1989-96; disting. vis. prof. nat. security affairs Naval Postgrad. Sch., Monterey, Calif., 1997—; eminent scholar in Am. democracy Jacksonville State Univ., Ala., 1999—. Contbr. articles to newspapers, profl. jours.; author: Study Guide for The Future of American Democracy, 2004. Mem. Am. Polit. Sci. Assn., So. Polit. Sci. Assn. Democrat. Methodist. Office: Naval Postgrad Sch NS/BG Nat Security Affairs Dept Monterey CA 93943 E-mail: igbrowder@nps.navy.mil.

BROWDY, JOSEPH EUGENE, lawyer; b. Bklyn., July 23, 1937; s. Philip and Fannie (Asherowitz) B.; m. Anita Sue Rubenstein, June 18, 1958; childrenF: Jennifer, Daniel. BA, Oberlin Coll., 1958; LLB, NYU, 1961. Bar: N.Y. 1962, D.C. 1982. Assoc. Paul, Weiss, Rifkind, Wharton & Garrison, NYC, 1962-71, ptnr., 1972-97, of counsel, 1998—. Adj. asst. prof. real estate NYU, 1976-86; lectr. in field. With U.S. Army Res., 1961-62. Mem. Assn. of Bar of City of N.Y. (com. real property law, chmn. subcom. on leasing 1989-92), Am. Coll. Real Estate Lawyers, Order of Coif, Phi Beta Kappa. Office: Paul Weiss Rifkind Wharton & Garrison 1285 Avenue of the Americas New York NY 10019-6065 Office Phone: 212-373-3039. Business E-Mail: jbrowdy@paulweiss.com.

BROWER, CHARLES NELSON, lawyer, judge; b. Plainfield, NJ, June 5, 1935; s. Charles Hendrickson and Mary Elizabeth (Nelson) B.; children: Michael Claudio Joseph Hutchings, Carmen Désirée Ponti, Frederica Anne Amity, Jasmin Maria Plekavich, Charles Hendrickson II. BA cum laude, Harvard U., 1957, JD, 1961; cert. Parker Sch. Comp. & Internat. Law, Columbia U., 1962. Bar: N.Y. 1962, D.C. 1970, U.S. Supreme Ct. 1967, U.S. Ct. Appeals (D.C. cir., 2d, 5th, 6th, 7th, 8th, 9th, 11th and fed. cirs.), U.S. Ct. Internat. Trade, U.S. Dist. Ct. (so. and ea. dists.) N.Y., U.S. Dist. Ct. D.C. Assoc., then ptnr. White & Case LLP, NYC, 1961-69; asst. legal adviser European affairs Dept. State, Washington, 1969-71, dep. legal adviser, 1971-73, acting legal adviser, 1973; ptnr. White & Case LLP, Washington, 1973-84, 88-00, spl. counsel, 2001—05; mem. 20 Essex St. Chambers, London, 2001—. Judge Iran-U.S. Claims Tribunal, The Hague, 1984—88, 2001—, substitute judge, 1983—84, 1988—2000; dep. spl. counselor to the Pres., Washington, 1987; counsel and advocate for U.S., 92, Costa Rica, 98, Internat. Ct. Justice, The Hague; mem. Register of Experts UN Compensation Commn., 1991—; mem. sec. of state adv. com. on internat. law, 1996—2006; mem. panels of arbitrators and conciliators Internat. Ctr. for Settlement of Investment Disputes, 1998—; judge ad hoc Inter-Am. Ct. of Human Rights, 1999—. Fulbright scholar, Rheinische Friedrich-Wilhelms-Universitaet, Bonn, and Hochschule fuer Politik, Berlin, 1957—78. Mem. ABA (chmn. sect. internat. law 1981-82, mem. ho. of dels. 1982, 84-98, bd. govs. 1985-88, nominating com. 1992-94), Internat. Law Assn. (hon. v.p. Am. br.), Internat. Bar Assn., Am. Soc. Internat. Law (v.p. 1994-96, pres. 1996-98, hon. v.p. 1998—2004, counsellor 2004—), Am. Law Inst., Assn. of Bar of City of NY, Coun. Fgn. Rels., Inst. Transnat. Arbitration (chmn. adv. bd. 1994-2000), Ctr. for Am. and Internat. Law (trustee 1996—), Met. Club, Chevy Chase Club. Episcopalian. Home and Office: Parkweg 13 2585 JH The Hague Netherlands Office: White & Case LLP 701 Thirteenth St NW Washington DC 20005 Office Phone: 31 70 3520064. E-mail: cbrower@20essexst.com.

BROWER, DAVID JOHN, lawyer, urban planner, educator; b. Holland, Mich., Sept. 11, 1930; s. John J. and Helen (Olson) B.; m. Lou Ann Brown, Nov. 26, 1960; children: Timothy Seth, David John, II, Ann Lacey. BA, U. Mich., 1956, JD, 1960. Bar: Ill. 1960, Mich. 1961, Ind. 1961, U.S. Supreme Ct. 1971. Asst. dir. div. community planning Ind. U., Bloomington, 1960-70; rsch. prof. dept. city and regional planning U. N.C., Chapel Hill, 1970—, assoc. dir. Ctr. for Urban and Regional Studies, 1970-94; pres. Coastal Resources Collaborative, Ltd., Chapel Hill and Manteo, NC, 1980—; counsel Robinson & Cole, Hartford, Conn., 1986—. Vis. prof., Vt. Law Sch., South Royalton, summers, 1994—. Author: (with others) Constitutional Issues of Growth Management, 1978; Growth Management, 1984, Managing Development in Small Towns, 1984, Special Area Management, 1985, Catastrophic Coastal Storms, 1989, Understanding Growth Management, 1989, Coastal Zone Management: An Evaluation, 1991, An Introduction to Coastal Zone Management, 1994, rev. edit. 2002, Natural Hazard Mitigation, 1999, Managing Coastal Hazards, 2006, Natural Hazard Prevention and Mitigation, 2006. Fellow Am. Inst. Cert. Planners (Coll. of Fellows); mem.Am. Planning Assn. (bd. dirs. 1982-85, chmn.-founder planning and law div.). Democrat. Episcopalian. Home: 612 Shady Lawn Rd Chapel Hill NC 27514-2009 Office: U NC CB # 3140 Chapel Hill NC 27599-0001 E-mail: brower@email.unc.edu.

BROWER, GREGORY A., lawyer; b. 1964; m. Loren Brower; children: Hayley, Kaitlin. Grad., U. Calif. Berkeley, 1986; JD, George Washington U., 1992. Litig. assoc. Ropers, Majeski, Kohn & Bently, San Francisco, 1992—94, Laxalt & Nomura, 1994—99; ptnr. Jones Vargas; with US Dept. Justice, 2003; inspector gen. US Govt. Printing Office, 2004—06, gen. counsel, 2006—. Rep. Nev. Legislature, 1998—2002. Svc. warfare officer USN. Office: US Govt Printing Office 732 N Capitol St NW Washington DC 20401*

BROWER, JAMES CALVIN, graphic artist, painter; b. Clarksburg, W.Va., Dec. 30, 1914; s. Leroy Cooper and Margaret Wood (Watkins) B.; m. Elsie Margaret Day, Sept. 19, 1936; children: James Lawrence, Sandra Joan, Margaret, Linda Ann, Beth. Grad. high sch., Charleston, W.Va., 1932. Pvt. practice, Huntington, W.Va., 1933-43, Toledo, 1952—; ptnr., art dir. Brower, Brownsberger and Burda, Toledo, 1944-51; dir. art and design Meeks Heit Pub. Co., 1992-99. Author, illustrator: Mood and Mode, 2003; illustrator: Education for Sexuality, 1970, Human Sexuality, 1982, Education for Sexuality and HIV/AIDS, 1993, Blowpipes, Northwest Ohio Glassmaking in the Gas Boom of the 1880s, 2002, Mood & Mode, A Selection of Transparent Watercolors, 2003; paintings featured in The Creative Artist, 1990, The Best of Watercolor 2, 1997, The Best of Watercolor Composition, 1997. Recipient Pres. award Okla. Watercolor Soc., 1987, Past Pres. award San Diego Watercolor Soc. Internat. Exhbn., 1989. Mem. Ohio Watercolor Soc. (hon.; bd. dirs. 1986-92, publicity chmn. 1986-92, Gold medal 1984, Charles Burchfield Meml. award 1991, Exhbn. award 1992, made hon. mem. 2001), Northwestern Ohio Watercolor Soc. (pres. 1983-84, Gold medal 2003), Nat. Water Color Soc. (Artist's Mag./Liquitex award 1990, Mem.'s Exhbn. awards 1996, 98, Holbein award, 2005), Ky. Watercolor Soc. (artist mem.), Ga. Watercolor Soc. (Gold award Nat. Exhbn. 1990, 1st Place Mem. Exhbn. 2006), Transparent Watercolor Soc. Am., Toledo Fedn. Art Soc. (pres. 1987-88), Tile Club Toledo, Toledo Artists Club (gold medal 1998). Republican. Presbyterian. Avocations: chess, bridge. Home and Office: 3433 Oak Valley Ct Apt 502 Toledo OH 43606-1380 Office Phone: 419-536-3984.

BROWER, JANICE KATHLEEN, library and information scientist; b. Chgo., July 29, 1952; d. Gerald B. (dec. Dec. 2000) and Emily (Kavicky) B. AA, Lincoln Coll., 1973; BS, Ill. State U., 1975; postgrad., U. Okla., 1984-86. Libr. assoc. Chgo. Pub. Libr., 1975-80, 81-83; libr. technician U. Okla. Biol. Sta., Norman, 1987; libr. technician III Jim E. Hamilton Correctional Ctr. Okla. Dept. of Corrections, Hodgen, 1987—. Lutheran. Avocations: reading, walking, visiting historical sites and museums, architecture. Office: Jim E Hamilton Correctional Ctr 53468 Mineral Springs Rd Hodgen OK 74939-3064 Office Phone: 918-653-7831 372. Business E-Mail: janice.brower@doc.state.ok.us. E-mail: jkbrower@alltel.net.

BROWER, ROBERT CHARLES, rehabilitation counselor, small business owner; b. Allendale, NJ; s. William P. and Adele B.; m. Hilja Kristiansen, Dec. 21, 1963; children: Robert K., Kristine D. BA in Psychology, Rutgers U., 1963; MDiv, Luth. Theol. Sem., Phila., 1966; postgrad. in counselign, Princeton Theol. Sem., 1970-71; postgrad. in Bus. Adminstrn., N.Y. Inst. Tech., 1993—. Cert. rehab. counselor, disability mgmt. specialist, case mgr., N.Y., U.S. Dept. Labor; ordained to ministry Lutheran Ch., 1966. Pastor St. Paul Luth. Ch., E. Windsor, NJ, 1966-71; psychiatric rehab. counselor N.Y. State Office of Vocations., Cen. Islip, 1971-73; coord. Rehab. Inst., Mineola, St. James, NY, 1973-74; program dir. and mental health clinic adminstr. Skills Unlimited, Oakdale, NY, 1974-78; dist. mgr. Intracorp subs. CIGNA, Woodbury, White Plains, NY, 1978-83; mgr. disability mgmt. svcs. Nat. Ctr. Disability Svcs. (formerly Human Resources Ctr.), Albertson, NY, 1984-90; pres. Brower Rehab. Svcs., Inc., Medford, NY, 1990—. Adj. prof. Sch. Counseling, Rsch., Spl. Edn. and Rehab., Hofstra U., Uniondale, N.Y., 1988-2001; speaker in field. Bd. dirs., treas. Cert. Disability Mgmt. Specialist Commn., 1993-94, vice-chmn., 1994-95; rep. to Found. for Rehab. Cert., Edn. and Rsch., 1993-94, 99-2003, chmn. govt. affairs and pub. rels. com., treas. found., treas., vice-chmn., 1994-95, chmn., 1995-96. Mem. AAUP, Internat. Assn. Rehab. Profls., Internat. Rehab. Assn. (chmn. commn. for certification of disability mgmt. specialists commn.), Internat. Assn. Rehab. Profls., Profl. Rehab. Assn. L.I. and NYC (Rehab. Profl. of Yr. in Ancillary Care 1994), Assn. Blauvelt Descendants (pres. 1998-2005), Delta Mu Delta Avocations: sailing, photography. Home: 37 Crooked Pine Dr Medford NY 11763-4329

BROWMAN, DAVID L(UDVIG), archaeologist; b. Dec. 9, 1941; s. Ludvig G. and Audra (Arnold) B.; m. M. Jane Fox, Apr. 24, 1965; children: Lisa, Tina, Becky. BA, U. Mont., 1963; MA, U. Wash., 1966; PhD, Harvard U., 1970. Hwy. archaeologist Wash. State Hwy. Dept., Olympia, 1964-66; field dir. Yale U., New Haven, 1968-69; tutor Harvard U., 1969-70; mem. faculty Washington U., St. Louis, 1970—, prof. archeology, 1984—, chmn., 1986—. Dir. Cons. Survey Archeology, St. Louis, 1976—, Inst. Study of Plants, Food and Man, Kirkwood, Mo. 1979-84: cons. St. Louis Dept. Parks and Recreation, 1978—. Editor/author: Advances in Andean Archaeology, 1978, Economic Organization of Prehispanic Peru, 1984, Risk Management and Arid Land Use Strategies in the Andes, 1986, New Perspectives on Americanist Archaeology, 2002; editor: Cultural Continuity in Mesoamerica, 1979, Early Native Americans, 1980. Charter mem. Confluence St. Louis, 1983; mem. Gov.'s Adv. Coun. Hist. Preservation, 1982-89, sec. 1989-91. NSF fellow, 1967, grantee, 1974-75, 85—. Fellow AAAS; mem. Soc. Profl. Archaeologists (sec.-treas. 1981-83, grievance coord. 1997-98), AAUP (chpt. pres. 1980-82), Registry Profl. Archaeologists (grievance coord. 1998-99), Mo. Assn. Profl. Archaeologists (v.p. 1981-82), Mo. Archaeology Soc. (trustee 1977—), Sigma Xi (chpt. pres. 1985-). Roman Catholic. Avocations: hiking, gardening. Office: Washington U Campus Box 1114 Saint Louis MO 63130-4899 Office Phone: 314-935-5231. Business E-Mail: dlbrowma@wustl.edu.

BROWN, ADRIANE M., aerospace transportation executive; b. Richmond, Va; BS in Environ. Health, Old Dominion Univ.; MBA, M.I.T. With Corning Inc., 1980—99, v.p., gen. mgr. environ. products divsn., 1994—99; v.p., gen. mgr. Aircraft Landing Systems Honeywell, Inc., South Bend, Ind., 1999—2001, v.p., gen. mgr. Honeywell Engine Systems & Accessories Tempe, Ariz., 2001—05, pres., CEO, Honeywell Transp. Systems Torrance, Calif., 2005—. Ariz. Gov. Coun. Innovation & Tech.; adv. coun. grad studies rsch. Univ. Notre Dame; bd. dir. Jobs for Am. Grads. Mem.: Ariz. Women's Forum. Office: HoneywellTransp Systems 2525 W 190th St Torrance CA 90504*

BROWN, ALAN CHARLTON, retired aeronautical engineer; b. Whitley Bay, Eng., Dec. 5, 1929; arrived in U.S., 1956; s. Stanley and Dorothy (Charlton) Brown; m. Gweneth Evelyn Bowler, July 26, 1952; children: Yvonne, Christine, Diane, Maureen. Diploma in aeronautics, Hull Tech. Coll., Eng., 1950; MS, Cranfield Inst Tech., Eng., 1952, Stanford U., 1965; DSc (hon.), Cranfield U., 2001. Apprentice Blackburn Aircraft Ltd., Brough, England, 1945-50; aerodynamicist BristolAeroplane Co., England, 1952—56; rsch. scientist U. So. Calif., LA, 1956-58, Wiancko Engring. Co., Pasadena, Calif., 1958-60, Lockheed Missiles & Space Co., Palo Alto, Calif., 1960-66; group leader Lockheed Aero. Sys. Co., Burbank, Calif., 1966-69, dept. mgr., 1969-78; chief engr. F-117A Lockheed Aerospace Sys. Co., Burbank, Calif., 1978-82, dir. stealth tech., 1982-89; dir. engring. Lockheed Corp., Calabasas, Calif., 1989-92; ret., 1992. Fellow: NAE, AIAA (Aircraft Design award 1990), Royal Aero. Soc. Democrat. Avocations: music, model aircraft. Home: 388 Aptos Ridge Cir Watsonville CA 95076-8518 Personal E-mail: alnbrown@cruzio.com.

BROWN, ALAN CRAWFORD, lawyer; b. Rockford, Ill., May 12, 1956; s. Gerald Crawford and Jane Ella (Herzberger) B.; m. Dawn Lestrud, Apr. 16, 1998; children: Parker Crawford, Sydney Danielle, Sarah Kate, Drew Kristen, Connor Austin. BA magna cum laude, Miami U., Oxford, Ohio, 1978; JD with honors, U. Chgo., 1981. Bar: Ill. 1981, U.S. Dist. Ct. (no. dist.) Ill. 1981, U.S. Tax Ct. 1986. Assoc. Kirkland & Ellis, Chgo., 1981-87; sr. assoc. Coffield Ungaretti Harris & Slavin, Chgo., 1987-89; ptnr. McDermott, Will & Emery, Chgo., 1989—2001, Neal, Gerber & Eisenberg, Chgo., 2001—. Deacon Northminster Presbyn. Ch., Evanston, Ill., 1989-92; apiarist Chgo. Botanic Garden, Glencoe, Ill., 1988-97. Mem. Order of Coif, Phi Beta Kappa. Office: Neal Gerber & Eisenberg Ste 2200 Two North LaSalle St Chicago IL 60602-3801 Office Phone: 312-269-8066. E-mail: acbrownesq@aol.com, abrown@ngelaw.com.

BROWN, ALICE ELSTE, artist; b. Balt., Nov. 5, 1922; d. Albert John and Anna Emily (Rosenbauer) Elste; m. Charles Hammond Brown, Nov. 30, 1946 (dec. Sept. 1994); children: Charles Hammond Jr., Barbara Brown Lander, Laurie Ellen. RN, U. Md., 1944; BS in Nursing Edn., Johns Hopkins U., 1949; BA in Art, Coll. Notre Dame, Balt., 1978; MA in Painting and Art Edn., Towson U., 1984. RN Md. Nurse, head nurse U.S. Army Nurse Corps, U.S., Europe, 1944-46; pub. health nurse Balt. Health Dept., 1950-52; artist Balt., 1960—; artist-in-residence Pyramid-Atlantic Studios, Balt., 1987-92. Adj. instr. drawing and design Coll. Notre Dame, 1980. One-woman shows include Roland Park Libr., 1965, Greater Balt. Med. Ctr., 1964, exhibited in group shows at Md. Fedn. Art, 1970—79, Jewish Cmty. Ctr., 1970, Towson YMCA, 1960, Easton (Md.) Acad. Arts, 1977, Coll. of Notre Dame, 1980, Western Md. Coll., Westminster, 1990, Pyramid Atlantic, Washington, 1990, Rehoboth (Del.)Art League, 1996—. Home nursing tchr. ARC, Balt., 1950s; asst. leader, leader Girl Scouts Am., Balt., 1960s; vol. docent Balt. Mus. Art, 1970s. 1st lt., U.S. Army Nurse Corps, 1944-46. Recipient Pi Lambda Theta award, Johns Hopkins U., 1949, Steinbugler award in art, Coll. Notre Dame, 1978. Mem. Nat. Mus. Women in the Arts (charter mem.), Md. Art Place, Rehoboth Art League (Thomas McFarland Skelly Meml. award 1998, Best in Show 2003), Johns Hopkins U. Alumni Club. Democrat. Avocations: walking, reading, archaeology, environmental concerns.

BROWN, ALTON C., television personality, chef; b. LA, July 30, 1962; m. DeAnna Brown; 1 child, Zoey. Degree in Drama, U. Ga.; degree in Culinary Arts, New England Culinary Inst., Montpelier, Vt., 1995. Cameraman; dir. commercials and corp. films. Author: I'm Just Here for the Food, 2002 (Best Cookbook in Reference category award, James Beard Found., 2003), Gear for Your Kitchen, 2003, I'm Just Here for the Food: Kitchen User's Manual, 2003, I'm Just Here for the Food: The Director's Cut, 2006; creator, dir., host (TV films) Feasting On Asphalt, 2006—; contbr. articles Bon Appetit mag., Men's Jour. mag.; writer, dir., host (TV series) Good Eats, Food Network, 1998— (Peabody award, 2006), commentator Iron Chef Am. Named 2004 Cooking Tchr. of Yr., Bon Appetit Am. Food & Entertaining awards. Avocations: bicycling, reading, cooking. Office: Food Network PO Box 9300 Central Islip NY 11722-9300*

BROWN, AMIRA KHALILA, neuropsychologist, researcher; d. Leonard Mason Brown and Aisha M. Robinson-Cobbs; 1 child, Turhan Taliaferro. BA in Psychology, U. D.C., 1998; MS in Neuropsychology, Howard U., 2000, PhD in Exptl. Neuropsychology, 2003. Behavior modification specialist St. Elizabeth's Hosp., Washington, 1997; clin. neuropsychology intern Ctr. for Mental Health, Washington, 1999—2000; neuropsychology intern Mt. Wash. Pediat. Hosp., Balt., 2001—02; rschr. Molecular Imaging Br. NIMH/NIH, Bethesda, Md., 2004—. Adj. prof. Howard U., Washington, 2001—02, Trinity U., Washington, 2003—04, Prince Georges C.C., Largo, Md., 2003—. Rape crisis hotline and companion counselor D.C. Rape Crisis Ctr., Washington, 1994—98. Recipient Ruth L. Kirschstein Nat. Rsch. Svc. award, Vanderbilt U. Neurosci. Dept. Sch. of Medicine, Nat. Intramural Rsch. Tng. award, NIMH/NIH. Fellow: Acad. Molecular Imaging (corr.); mem.: APA (assoc.), Women in Neurosci., Inc. (corr.), Internat. Neuropsychol. Soc. (assoc.), Beta Kappa Chi (life), Psi Chi (life), Alpha Kappa Alpha (life). Avocations: travel, reading. Home Phone: 301-847-1262; Office Phone: 301-435-1695.

BROWN, AMY CHRISTINE, art educator; d. Donald Brown and Lillian Vorbeck, Lowell Vorbeck (Stepfather). BA, Madonna U., 2001; MA (hon.), Nova Southeastern U., 2003. Cert. elem. tchr. Mich. Art educator Airport Cmty. Schs., Newport, Mich., 2001—. Exhibitions include sr. art exhibit, Madonna U., 1999, pvt. collection, plaster sculpture, 2000, Lucille Dedene. Mem.: PTO (sch. rep. 2001—05). Home Phone: 734-652-3838; Office Phone: 734-586-2676. Home Fax: 734-242-3416. Personal E-mail: amybrown@wwnet.net.

BROWN, ANDREAS LE, retail executive, art gallery owner; b. Coronado, Calif., Apr. 29, 1933; s. Harvey Clair and Helene Celeste (Kimball) B. AB, Calif. State U., San Diego, 1955; postgrad., Stanford U., 1955-57; DFA (hon.), Calif. State. U., 2005. Mem. faculty Calif. State U., 1960-63; staff rsch. fellow Humanities Rsch. Ctr., U. Tex., 1963-65; appraiser rare books, 1965-67; owner, pres. Gotham Book Mart & Gallery Inc., NYC, 1967—, Sorer Realty Corp., NYC, 1989—. Author: A Creative Century, 1970, (with Hal Morgan) Prairie Fires and Paper Moons, 1981; contbg. editor Antaeus; mem. adv. bd. Paris Rev. Trustee Edward Gorey Charitable Trust; adv. Anthony Found., Houston; With U.S. Army, 1958-59. Recipient Disting. Alumnus award, Calif. State U., San Diego, 2003. Mem. Manuscript Soc., Antiquarian Booksellers Assn. Am., Am. Booksellers Assn., Internat. League Antiquarian Booksellers, Sigma Chi, Grolier Club (N.Y.). Achievements include specializing in modern rare books and manuscripts. Home and Office: 16 E 46th St New York NY 10017

BROWN, ANGELIA, poet; b. Barnesville, Ga., Jan. 5, 1968; d. Charlie Fred and Elizabeth Brown; children: Demarius, Marcus, Jalessa Freeman, David Freeman. Poet: Nature, 1992, In Memory of Those We Love and Cherish, 1993, Love That Is Meant to Be, 1994, Love, 1997, Our Love, 1997, A Friendship, 1998 (Accomplishment of Merit award, 1998), Life, 1998 (Editors Choice award, 1998), All About Angelia and the Lord, 1998, Watch Them Dogs, 2003 (Editors Choice award, 2003). Mem.: Internat. Soc. Poets, Assn. Black Women Entrepreneurs Inc. Methodist. Avocations: gardening, art, baking, bookmaking. Home: 128 Roger Brown Dr Barnesville GA 30204 Personal E-mail: browna2365@aol.com.

BROWN, ANTHONY GREGORY, lieutenant governor, lawyer; b. Huntington, NY, Nov. 21, 1961; s. Roy Hershel and Lilly Ida B.; m. Patricia Arzuaga, Jan. 29, 1993; children: Rebecca, Anthony. AB cum laude (hon.), Harvard U., 1984, JD, 1992. Bar: NY 1993, Md. 1994, DC 1994. Law clk. US Ct. Appeals Armed Forces, Washington, 1992-94; del Md. Ho. Dels., Annapolis, 1999—2004; atty. Wilmer, Cutler & Pickering, Washington, 1994—98, Gibbs and Haller, Lanham, Md., 1998—; mem. Ho. of Dels., 1999—2004, majority whip, 2004; lt. gov. State of Md., 2007—. Lectr., Legal Asst. Prog. Georgetown U., 1996—97; mem. Legis. Black Caucus of Md., 1999—, law enforcement & state-appointed bd. com., 1999—2002, Econ. Matters Com., 1999—2003, Tech. & Bus.Divsn. Task Force, 2000, Joint Tech. Oversight Com., 2000—03, Joint Com. on Legis. Ethics, 2000—, Joint Com. on Adminstrv., Exec. and Legis. Review, 2003—04, Article 27 Revision Com., 2003—04, Judiciary Com., 2003—, co-chair, 2003—04; mem. Com. on Higher Edn. Affordability and Accessibility,

2003—04, Legis. Policy Com., 2005, Spl. Joint Com. on State Employee Rights and Protections, 2005, Gov. Task Force on Med. Malpractice and Health Care Access., 2004, Rules and Exec. Nominations Com., 2006—; chair Med. Malpractice Ins. Work Grp., 2004. Dir. Prince George's County Law Found., Hyattsville, Md., 2000; chmn. Prince George's C.C., Largo, Md., 1995-99; dir. Adoptions Together, Inc., 2001, Silver Spring, Md., 2001, mem bd of Trustees Prince George's Cmty. Coll., 1995-99 (chair 1998-99), pres. Lake Pointe Home Owners' Assn., 1996-98. Capt., Aviation US Army, 1984—89, served in USAR, 1989—, col. Judge Adc. General's Corps, sr. cons. to Iraqi Ministry of Displacement and Migration 353rd Civil Affairs Command, 2004—05. Decorated bronze star medal, meritorious svc. medal, army commendation, army reserve component achievement medal, nat. def. svc. medal, bronze star device, Iraq campaign medal, global war on terrorism svc. medal, mil. outstanding voluntary svc. medal, armed forces reserve medal, army svc. ribbon, army overseas svc. ribbon, army reserve component overseas tng. ribbon, aviator badge, airborne badge, air assault badge; recipient army achievement medal, pro bono award, Cutler & Pickering, 1998, Legis. award, Med. and Chirurgical Faculty of Md., 2003, Adoption Visionary award, Md. Soc. Services Adminstrn., 2003, Leadership award, Md. Justice Coalition, 2004, medal of Civic Hon., Nat. Conf. State Legislators, 2005, Medal of Civic Honor, Conference of State Legis., 2004, Distinguished Cmty. Svc. award, Prince George's County Educators' Assn., 2005. Mem.: Lake Pointe Home Owners' Assn. (pres. 1996—98), J. Franklyn Bourne Bar Assn., Md. State Bar Assn. (real property, planning & zoning sect.). Democrat. Roman Catholic. Avocations: golf, travel. Office: Office of Gov State of Md William Donald Schaefer Tower 6 St Paul St Ste 2000 Baltimore MD 21202 Office Phone: 410-767-3125.*

BROWN, ARNOLD LANEHART, JR., pathologist, educator, dean; b. Wooster, Ohio, Jan. 26, 1926; s. Arnold Lanehart and Wilda (Woods) B.; m. Betty Jane Simpson, Oct. 2, 1949; children— Arnold III, Anthony, Allen, Fletcher, Lisa. Student, U. Richmond, 1943—45; MD, Med. Coll. Va., 1949. Diplomate Am. Bd. Pathology. Intern Presbyn.-St. Luke's Hosp., Chgo., 1949-50, resident, 1950-51, 53-56, asst. attending pathologist, 1957-59; practice medicine specializing in pathology Rochester, Minn., 1959-78; cons. exptl. pathology, anatomy Mayo Clinic, Rochester, 1959-78, also prof., chmn. dept., 1968-78; prof. pathology U. Wis., Madison, 1978—, dean Med. Sch., 1978-91. Mem. nat. cancer adv. coun. NIH, 1971-74, HEW, 1972-74; chmn. clearing house on environ. carcinogens Nat. Cancer Inst., 1976-80, chmn. com. to study carcinogenicity of cyclamate, 1975-76; mem. Nat. Com. on Heart Disease, Cancer and Stroke, 1975-79; mem. com. on safe drinking water NRC, 1976-77; mem. award assembly Gen. Motors Cancer Rsch. Found., 1978-83, vice chmn., 1982-83; co-chmn. panel on geochemistry of fibrous materials related to health risks Nat. Acad. Scis.-NRC, 1978-80; chair working group Internat. Agy. for Rsch. on Cancer, Lyon, France, 1979, 83, 87. Contbr. articles to profl. jours. Bd. sci. counselors Nat. Inst. Environ. Health Scis., NIH Nat. Toxicology Program, 1992—. With USNR, 1943-45, 51-53. Nat. Heart Inst. postdoctoral fellow, 1956-59 Mem. Am. Soc. Exptl. Pathology, Internat. Acad. Pathology, Assn. Am. Med. Colls. (chmn. coun. deans 1984-85). Home: 211 2Nd St NW Apt 1503 Rochester MN 55901-2896 Home Phone: 507-529-8878. Personal E-mail: arnoldbro@msn.com.

BROWN, ARTHUR EDMON, JR., retired army officer; b. Manila, Nov. 21, 1929; s. Arthur Edmon and Grace E. M. (Montgomery) B.; m. Jerry Deane Cook, June 6, 1953; children: Marian Brown Shope, Nan Brown Irick, Arthur Edmon III. BS, U.S. Mil. Acad., 1953; M.Public and Internat. Affairs, U. Pitts., 1965. Commd. 2d lt. U.S. Army, advanced through grades to gen.; mem. faculty U.S. Army War Coll., 1970-73; comdr. 1st Brigade, 1st Infantry Div. Fort Riley, Kans., 1973-75; mem. gen. staff Dept. Army, Washington, 1975-78; asst. div. comdr. 25th Infantry Div. Hawaii, 1978-80; dep. supt. U.S. Mil. Acad., West Point, 1980-81; comdr. U.S. Army Readiness and Moblzn., Region IV, Fort Gillem, Ga., 1981-83; dir. army staff Dept. Army, Washington, 1983-87; vice chief of staff U.S. Army, 1987-89, retired. Decorated Def. D.S.M., Army D.S.M. with oak leaf cluster, Bronze Star with 3 oak leaf clusters, Silver Star, Legion of Merit with 3 oak leaf clusters. Episcopalian. Home: 35 Fairway Winds Pl Hilton Head Island SC 29928-5547 also: 3302 N St NW Washington DC 20007-2807 Personal E-mail: aebjr@roadrunner.com.

BROWN, ARTHUR EDWARD, physician; b. Trenton, NJ, June 7, 1945; s. Milton Charles and Jeanne Ruth (Swern) B.; m. Jo Frances Meltzer, Nov. 24, 1985. BS, Bucknell U., 1967; MD, Jefferson Med. Coll., 1971. Intern, resident Roosevelt Hosp., NYC, 1971-72, 74-76; trainee Nat. Cancer Inst., 1976-77; fellow infectious diseases Meml. Sloan-Kettering Cancer Ctr., NYC, 1976-78; clin. asst. physician Cornell U., Weill Med. Coll., NYC, 1978-82, asst. prof. medicine and pediat., 1979-85, assoc. prof. clin. medicine and pediat., 1985—94, prof. clin. medicine and pediat., 1994—; asst. attending physician Meml. Hosp. for Cancer and Allied Diseases, NYC, 1982—89, assoc. attending physician, 1989—93, attending physician, 1993—; asst. attending pediatrician NY Presbyn. Hosp., NYC, 1979—85, assoc. attending pediatrician, 1985-94, attending pediatrician, 1994—2004. Vis. assoc. physician The Rockefeller U. Hosp., NYC, 1995—96; cons. Anti-Infective Drugs adv. com FDA, USPHS, DHHS, 1997—; med. dir. Employee Health Svc. Meml. Sloan-Kettering Cancer Ctr., NYC, 2002—, chief, 2003—. Editor: Infectious Complications of Neoplastic Diseases Controversies in Management, 1985, Infections in Oncology, 1993-2000; consulting editor Am. Jour. Medicine, 1984-86; mem. editl. bd. Antimicrobial Agts. and Chemotherapy, 1985-87, European Jour. Clin. Microbiology and Infectious Diseases, 1993-2005, Infections in Medicine, 1995—, Microbial Drug Resistance, 1996—; contbr. numerous articles to profl. jours. Trustee The Peddie Sch., Hightstown, NJ, 1999—. Surgeon, USPHS, 1972-74. Recipient 2d pl. HeSCA Print Festival, 1985, Bronze Plaque award Film Coun. Columbus, 1985, Bronze medal Internat. Film & TV Festival, NYC, 1985, Semi-Finalist Am. Jour. Nursing Media Festival, 1986. Fellow ACP (councillor NY chpt. 2000-02, 05—, NY chpt. pub. health com. 2000—, NY chpt. nominating com. 2004), Soc. Healthcare Epidemiology Am., Infectious Diseases Soc. Am. (state and regional bd. dirs. 1995-98); mem. AAAS, Am. Fedn. for Med. Rsch., NY County Soc. Internal Medicine (pres. 1994-96), NY State Soc. Internal Medicine (dir. 1995-2000), NY Soc. Infectious Diseases (sec., treas. 1993-97; v.p. 1997-98, pres.-elect 1998-99, pres. 1999-2000), Am. Soc. Microbiology, NY Acad. Scis., Am. Soc. Clin. Oncology, Internat. Immunocompromised Host Soc., NY Soc. Tropical Medicine, Multinat. Assn. of Supportive Care in Cancer. Achievements include research on AIDS, management of infectious complications of neoplastic diseases. Office: Meml Sloan-Kettering Cancer Ctr 222 E 70th St New York NY 10021 Office Phone: 212-434-5103. Business E-Mail: brown2@mskcc.org.

BROWN, ASHLEY, actress; b. Gulf Breeze, Fla., Feb. 3, 1982; Ed., U. Cin. Conservatory of Music. Actress (plays) Candide, U. Cin., 2001, Sweeney Todd, 2002, Violet, 2002, The Mystery of Edwin Drood, 2004, Side by Side by Sondheim, The Muny, St. Louis, Mo., 2003, Crazy for You, 2003, Meet Me in St. Louis, 2004, Guys and Dolls, 2004, On the Record, 2005, (Broadway plays) Beauty and the Beast, 2005, Mary Poppins, 2006.*

BROWN, AUTRY, psychology professor, clergyman; b. Watson, Okla., May 1, 1924; s. Solon Lemley and Bessie Jane (Wilhelm) B.; m. Opal Irene Landers, Sept. 5, 1942 (dec.); children: Juanice, Rebecca, Steven, Deborah; m. Betty Parsons, Sept. 7, 2002. BA, Eastern N.M. U., 1950; M of Div., New Orleans Bapt. Theol. Sem., 1955, MRE, 1956, EdD, 1968; postgrad., Colo. State U., 1970, Southwest Mo. State U., 1985. Ordained to ministry Bapt. Ch., 1942. Pastor Bookcliff Bapt. Ch., Grand Junction, Colo., 1957-61, Carrollton Ave. Bapt. Ch., New Orleans, 1962-64, Immanuel Bapt. Ch., Ft. Collins, Colo., 1964-72; asst. prof. psychology Mo. Bapt. U., St. Louis, 1972-74, Southwest Bapt. U., Bolivar, Mo., 1974-76, prof. psychology, 1978-89, dir. counseling services, 1978-89; disting. prof. psychology, 1989—; cons. family ministry Colo. Bapt. Gen. Conv., Denver, 1976-78. Author: Church Family Life Conference Guidebook, 1973, Wire of the West, 2006; contbr. books, profl. jour. Recipient Spl. Services award Bd. Trustees New Orleans Bapt. Theol. Sem., 1972. Mem. Am. Assn. Marriage and Family Therapy, Mo. Assn. Marriage and Family Therapy (Spl. Service award 1984, treas. state exec. bd. 1979-83), Ozark Assn. Marriage and Family Therapy (pres. 1985-86), Mo. Assn. Counseling and Devel., Fellows Menniger Found. Avocation: collecting antique barbed wire. Home: 1526 W Laverne St Bolivar MO 65613 Office: Christian Tng Inst 1526 W Laverne St Bolivar MO 65613 Business E-Mail: sabrown@sbuniv.edu.

BROWN, AVERT HAYDEN, animal scientist, educator; s. A. Hayden and Imogene Wanda Brown; m. Helen Virginia Gann, Nov. 9, 1977; 1 child, Ashley. BSc, Tenn. Tech. U., 1968; MSc, U. Tenn., 1974, PhD, 1976. Cert. Am. Coll. Animal Genetics, 1995, registered Am. Registry Profl. Animal Scientist. Prof. U. Ark., Fayetteville, Ark., 1977—. Mem. editl. bd.: Jour. Animal Sci., 2001—03; contbr. articles to profl. jours. Named to American Cattle Breeders Hall Fame, 1982. Mem.: American Registry Profl. Animal Scientists (pres. 1999—2000), Sigma Xi. Office: University Arkansas AFLS B 106 Fayetteville AR 72701 Business E-Mail: hbrown@uark.edu.

BROWN, B. ANDREW, lawyer; b. Charleston, W.Va., Mar. 10, 1957; BA in History, Stanford U., 1979; MPA, Harvard U., 1981; JD, Duke U., 1986, MA in Philosophy, 1986. Bar: Minn. 1989. Legis. aide Sen. Gary Hart, Washington, 1981-82; atty. Donovan, Leisure, Newton & Irvine, Washington, 1986-88, Willkie, Farr & Gallagher, Washington, 1989, Dorsey & Whitney, Mpls., 1990—, ptnr., 1995—, head regulatory group, co-chmn. environ., natural resources, energy practice group. Office Phone: 612-340-5612. Office Fax: 612-340-8800. Business E-Mail: brown.andrew@dorsey.com.

BROWN, BACHMAN STORCH, JR., lawyer; b. Lexington, NC, Feb. 11, 1926; s. Bachman Storch and Beulah Louise (Isenhour) B.; m. Mabel Christine Patterson, June 12, 1953; children: Robert Bachman, Sarah Christine Brown Fishback. AB, Duke U., 1947, JD, 1950; LLD (hon.), Lenoir Rhyne Coll., 1970. Ptnr. Alexander & Brown, Attys., Kannapolis, N.C., 1950—. Judge Cabarrus County Domestic Rels. Ct., Concord, N.C., 1957-63; bd. dirs. Cabarrus Bank N.C., Concord. Chmn. Cabarrus County Bd. Elections, Concord, 1970-85; mayor City Kannapolis, 1984-93. Lt. USNR 1944-46. Named Young Man Yr., Jaycees, 1958, Citizen Yr., Jaycees, 1979, 85. Mem. Kannapolis C. of C. (v.p., dir. 1989—), Am. Legion (commdr. 1980), John R. Mott Men's Club (pres. 1966), Rotary (pres. 1970-71), 40 & 8 (chef du gare 1993—), Fellowship Lodge. Democrat. Lutheran. Avocations: gardening, hunting, fishing, reading. Office: Alexander & Brown Attys 121 S Main St Kannapolis NC 28081-3210

BROWN, BARBARA BERISH, lawyer; b. Washington, June 26, 1946; d. Alfred Edward and Sylvia (Kaufman) B.; m. Robert F. Berish, Mar. 26, 1988; 1 child, Jared. BA, Radcliffe-Harvard, 1968; JD, Yale U., 1971. Law clk. to Hon. J. Joseph Smith US Ct. Appeals (2d cir.), 1971—72; ptnr. Paul Hastings Janofsky & Walker, LLP, Washington, 1984—, chair DC office, 2000—. Co-author: Legal Guide to Human Resources, 1984, supplement, 2006. Fellow Coll. Labor and Employment Lawyers; mem. ABA (vice chair labor and employment law sect.). Office: Paul Hastings Janofsky & Walker 875 15th St NW Washington DC 20005 Office Phone: 202-551-1717. Office Fax: 202-551-0117. Business E-Mail: barbarabrown@paulhastings.com.

BROWN, BARBARA JUNE, hospital and nursing administrator; b. Milw., Aug. 17, 1933; d. Carl W. and Nora Anne (Damrow) Rydberg; children: Deborah, Robert, Andrea, Michael, Steven, Jeffrey. BSN, Marquette U., Milw., 1955, MSN, 1960, EdD, 1970. RN, Wis.; cert. nurse adminstr. advanced. Adminstr. patient care Family Hosp., Milw., 1973-78; assoc. clin. prof. U. Wash., Seattle, 1980-87; assoc. adminstr. nursing Virginia Mason Hosp., Seattle, 1980-87; assoc. exec. dir. King Faisal Specialist Hosp., Riyadh, Saudi Arabia, 1987-91; adj. prof. Univ. Ariz., 2001—. Project dir. NIH, Sexual Assault Treatment Ctr., Milw., 1975-78; lectr., cons., 1974—. Founder, editor-in-chief: Nursing Adminstrn. Quar., 1976—; editor-in-chief, regional v.p. Nurse Week, Mountain West, 2000—04; editor-in-chief: Modern Nurse, 2005—06. Vol. ski instr. for disabled, Winter Park, Colo. Fellow: Nat. Acad. Practice, Am. Acad. Nursing (governing coun.); mem.: ANA, Grand County Pub. Health and Emergency Svcs. (chmn. health adv. com. 1994—96), Nat. League Nursing (bd. govs. 2002—05, bd. dirs.), Am. Orgn. Nurse Execs., Sigma Theta Tau. Office Phone: 520-825-5629. Personal E-mail: naqbb@aol.com.

BROWN, BENJAMIN A., investment advisor; b. NYC, Feb. 13, 1943; s. Horace A. and Lillian A. (Hurwitz) B.; m. Elinore Carole Abravanel, Aug. 8, 1968; children— Adam Howard, Dina Lauren BBA in Acctg., Adelphi U., 1964; MBA in Fin. and Investments, Baruch Coll. CUNY, 1971. Registered investment advisor prin. Fin. Mgmt. Svcs. Acct. Samuel Greiff C.P.A., Atty., Forest Hills, NY, 1963-66; v.p. research dept. Walston & Co., NYC, 1967-73; treas. ENSERCH Corp., Dallas, 1974-78, v.p. fin., 1978-82, v.p. fin. relations, 1982-96. V.p. Enserch Exploration, Inc., 1995-96; v.p. fin. and investor rels. EEX Corp., Houston, 1997-98; chief investment officer, mng. dir. Fin. Mgmt. Svcs., Ltd., Dallas, 1999—. Mem. Am. Assn. Individual Investors, NY Soc. Security Analysts, DAC Country Club, Houston City Club. Avocations: walking, golf, coin collecting/numismatics, oenology. Home: 5200 Keller Springs Rd Apt 1225/1227 Dallas TX 75248-2744 Office: Candy & Schonwald Bldg 3116 Live Oak St Ste 201 Dallas TX 75204-6190 Office Phone: 214-826-6660. Business E-Mail: ben@financialmanagementservices.com. *I strive everyday to give more than I take and spend less than I make. My success and happiness are entirely attributable to a very loving and supportive family, including a perfect mate for more than 40 years, two children that reflect the best qualities parents could wish for, a mother and brother that are always there for me, in-laws that most can only dream about and four extraordinary grandchildren.*

BROWN, BENJAMIN ANDREW, retired journalist; b. Red House, W.Va., Apr. 30, 1933; s. Albert Miller and Mary Agnes (Donegan) B.; m. Joanne Gretchen Harder, May 22, 1956; children: Benjamin Andrew, Gretchen, Mark, Betsy Brown Larson. BA in Journalism, Fla. State U., 1955. Sportswriter Charleston (W.Va.) Daily Mail, 1955-57; with AP, 1957-93, gen. exec. NYC, 1976-78, 82-93, chief bur. Los Angeles, 1978-82; assoc. Am. Newspapers Cons., Ltd., Milw., 1993-95. Bd. dirs. Last Chance Press Club, Helena, Mont., 1969; v.p. Minn. Press Club, 1975. Office: PO Box 3012 Paso Robles CA 93447-3012 Personal E-mail: babrown@charter.net.

BROWN, BETTYE, librarian, educator; b. Ft. Valley, Ga., Mar. 14, 1945; d. Tom and Lucinda (Holt) B. BS in Secondary Edn., Ft. Valley State Coll., 1967; MSLS, Atlanta U., 1975. Cert. secondary tchr., Ga. Tchr. Pearl Stephens HS, Warner Robins, Ga., 1967-69, Perry (Ga.) HS, 1969-70; libr. Vienna (Ga.) Elem. Sch., 1971-72; libr. tech. asst. III State CC, East St. Louis, Ill., 1972-75, ref. libr., 1975—96, prof., 1983—; ref. libr. Southwestern Bell Libr. and Tech. Ctr. Harris-Stowe State U., St. Louis, 1997—. Historian, mem. pub. rels. com. Nat. Coun. Negro Women, East St. Louis, 1985, corr. sec., 1990—, newsletter editor, 1990—. Mem. AAUP (sec. 1983-85, v.p. 1988—), AAUW (fin. sec. 1987-90, sec. 1990—), NOW, Am. Fedn. Tchrs. (sec. 1980-82), Nat. Assn. U. Women, Ill. Libr. Assn., Bus. and Profl. Women East St. Louis (chmn. libr. com. 1987—), Women of Essence (treas. 1985-89), Women Organized for Community Survival (v.p. 1988—), Alpha Kappa Alpha. Democrat. Pentecostal. Avocations: reading, sewing, travel, aerobics, drama. Office: Harris-Stowe State U Southwestern Bell Libr and Tech Ctr 3026 Laclede Ave Saint Louis MO 63103 Office Phone: 314-340-3506. Business E-Mail: brownb@hssu.edu.

BROWN, BILLYE JEAN, retired nursing educator; b. Damascus, Ark., Oct. 29, 1925; d. William A. and Dora (Megee) B. BSNEd, U. Tex. Med. Br., Galveston, 1953; MSNEd, St. Louis U., 1958; EdD, Baylor U., 1975. Asst. prof. U. Tex. Med. Br. Sch. Nursing, 1958-60; assoc. prof. U. Tex. Nursing Sch., Austin, 1960-67, assoc. dean, prof., 1968-72, dean, prof., 1972-89; prof. emeritus Sch. Nursing U. Tex., 1989—; mem. Nat. Adv. Council Nurse Tng., 1982-87. Nat. League for Nursing fellow, 1957-58; recipient Alumni Merit award St. Louis U., 1981; Am. Acad. Nursing fellow, 1984. Mem. ANA, Am. Assn. Colls. Nursing (pres. 1982-84, Sister Bernadette Armiger award 1990), Tex. League Nursing, Tex. Nurses Assn. (Nurse of Yr. 1980), Sigma Theta Tau (pres. 1989-91, Internat. Mary T. Wright Founders award 1999), Phi Kappa Phi (life).

BROWN, BLANCHE Y., secondary school educator, genealogist, researcher; b. Saint Mary's, W.Va., Feb. 2, 1918; d. Lewis Frederick and Edna Clara (Walker) Yost; m. Vincent Robert Brown, June 1, 1946; children: Susan Elizabeth, Roberta Ann Brown Pugh. BA, Marietta Coll., 1939; postgrad., Columbia U., 1946-47. Cert. secondary tchr. in sci. and English. Pers. supr. Packard Electric divsn. Gen. Motors Corp., Warren, Ohio, 1940-44; tchr. bus. edn. New Matamoras (Ohio) H.S., 1945-49; fin. sec. St. Paul's United Meth. Ch., Houston, 1949-50; pers. dept. Olin Chem. Corp., Pasadena, Tex., 1951-53; tchr. biology Pasadena H.S., 1958-78. Co-editor: Grandview Township's First Trustees Journal--1803-1843, 1991; editor Matamoras Area Hist. Soc. Newsletter, 1987-99. Recipient First Families of Ohio award Ohio Geneal. Soc., 1989, Award of Achievement Ohio Hist. Soc. for Matamoras Area Hist. Soc. Newsletter, 1992. Mem. Tex. Ret. Tchrs. Assn. (life), Nat. Soc. DAR (Marietta, Ohio chpt. schs. chmn. 1988-94, corr. sec. 1995-99, nat. Photography award 1989), Matamoras Area Hist. Soc. (genealogy and local history coord. for Sesquicentennial Celebration 1846-1996, Bicentennial Celebration 1797-1997), VFW Aux. (life), AAUW. Republican. Methodist. Avocations: photography, artwork with shells, writing. Home: 733 Main St New Matamoras OH 45767-6013

BROWN, BOB (ROBERT JOSEPH BROWN), former state official; b. Missoula, Mont., Dec. 11, 1947; s. Clifford Andrew and Jeanne M (Knox) Brown; m. Susan Kay Stoeckig, Sept. 20, 1975; children: Robin Sue, Kelly Charlynn. BS in History, Mont. State U, 1970, BS in Polit. Sci., 1974; MEd, U. Mont., 1988. Cert. secondary tchr. State rep. Mont. Ho. Reps., Helena, 1971—74; senator 2d dist. Mont. State Sen., Helena, 1974—96; tchr. history Whitefish H.S., 1990—91; Tchr. govt., history Big Fork (Mont.) High Sch., 1979—86; tchr. history, econs. Flathead High Sch., Kalispell, Mont., 1986—89; instr. Flathead Valley C.C., 1990, 1994, dir. U. Mont. Ext., 1991—98; dir. govt. & pub. relations Columbia Falls Aluminum Co., 1998—2000; sec. state State of Mont., 2001—04; sr. fellow O'Connor Ctr. Rocky Mt. West U. Mont. With USN, 1972—73. Mem.: Mont. Edn. Assn. (Golden Gavel award 1979), Packyderm, Rotary, Am. Legion, Kiwanis, Moose, Phi Delta Kappa. Republican. Avocation: fishing. Office: Montant Univ Ctr Rocky Mt West 32 Campus Dr MS 3096 Missoula MT 59812 Office Phone: 406-243-7717.

BROWN, BOBBI, cosmetics executive; m. Steven Plofker; 3 children. Grad., Emerson Coll., Boston. Founder & CEO Bobbi Brown Cosmetics (div. Estee Lauder), 1992—. Beauty editor NBC's Today Show; frequent guest E! and Style channels; writer, nationally syndicated columns and advice features for Allure, Modern Bride, Working Mother, Prevention Mag.; involved with Dress for Success NY prog., Jane Addams Vocational Sch. Author: Bobbi Brown Beauty, 1998, Bobbi Brown Beauty Evolution: A Guide to a Lifetime of Beauty, 2002; co-author: Bobbi Brown Teenage Beauty, 2001. Bd. trustees Emerson Coll., 2006—. Office: Bobbi Brown Cosmetics, Inc 767 Fifth Ave New York NY 10153 Office Phone: 212-572-4200.*

BROWN, BONNIE MARYETTA, lawyer; b. North Plainfield, NJ, Oct. 31, 1953; d. Robert Jeffrey and Diana (Parket) B. AB, Washington U., St. Louis, 1975; JD, U. Louisville, 1978. Bar: Ky. 1978, U.S. Dist. Ct. (we. dist.) Ky. 1979, U.S. Dist. Ct. (ea. dist.) Ky. 1993. Pvt. practice, Louisville, 1978—; of counsel Morris, Garlove, Waterman and Johnson PLLC, 1998—2005, Pedley, Zielke, Gordinier & Pence, PLLC, 2005—. Lectr., seminar leader various profl., ednl., govtl. and civic groups; cons. marital rape; registered lobbyist 1994 Ky. Gen. Assembly for Ky. Assn. Marriage and Family Therapy. Editor Ky. Appellate Handbook, 1985; contbr. articles to profl. jours. Vol. legal panel Ky. Civil Liberties Union, Louisville, 1984-90; author, chief lobbyist Marital Rape Bill, Ky. Coalition Against Rape and Sexual Assault, 1984-90, Sexual Harassment bill, 1996; vol. advocate Louisville RAPE Relief Ctr., 1975—; treas. Family Support Group/Family Readiness Program. of USAR, 1994-96, 3d Bat., 2nd. bge, 87th divsn., 1996-2000, acting coord. 10th bat., 6th bge, 100th divsn.; chair City of Strathmoor Village Bd. Ethics, 2007. Recipient Cert. Spl. Recognition RAPE Relief Ctr., 1980, Cert. Outstanding Contbn., Louisville YWCA, 1983, Cert. of Appreciation, James Graham Brown Cancer Ctr., 1984, Decade of Svc. award YWCA/Rape Relief Ctr., Outstanding Victim Adv. award Fayette County Govt., 1990, cert. of Recognition Jefferson County Family Ct., 1995, other awards. Mem. ABA (family law sect.), Am. Acad. Matrimonial Lawyers (interdisciplinary com., treas. Ky. chpt. 1999-2001), Ky. Collaborative Family Law Network (treas. 2004-2006), Ky. Bar Assn. (family law sect., chair 1996-97, seminar spkr., task force solo practitioners and small law firms 1992, chair subcom. on law office automation and networking, solo practitioner and small Law Firm sect., chmn. 1999-2000, CLE award 1981, 1997-2006, Louisville Bar Assn. (liaison to mental health sect., organizer marital rape seminar, chmn. family law sect., mediation com. property divsn., seminar spkr., organizer joint custody child abuse seminars, solo practitioner and small law firm sect., chair 1995, pro bono consortium), Ky. Acad. Trial Attys. (spkr. seminar, editor The Advocate family law sect. 1995-2001), Bus. and Profl. Women (pres. River City chpt. 1983-84), Ky. Fedn. (legis. chair 1986-87, 90-92, legal counsel 1992, 1996-2001, lobby corps chair 1993-95), Louisville Internat. Cultural Ctr. Republican. Avocations: basketball fan, classic cars. Office: 2000 Meidinger Tower Louisville KY 40202 Office Phone: 502-589-4600.

BROWN, BOYD ALEX, physicist, researcher; b. Columbus, Ohio, Sept. 25, 1948; s. Frank L. and E. Catherine (Chenoweth) B.; m. Mary J. Hohenstein, July 21, 1984; children: Elizabeth Lorraine, Mark Alexander. BA in Physics, Ohio State U., 1970; MS in Physics, SUNY, Stony Brook, 1971, PhD in Physics, 1974. Research fellow Japan Soc. for the Promotion of Sci., Tokyo, 1974-75; research assoc. Mich. State U., East Lansing, 1975-78; research officer Oxford U., Eng., 1978-82; assoc. prof. physics Mich. State U., East Lansing, 1982-90, prof. physics, 1990—. Contbr. more than 400 articles to physics jours. Recipient Humboldt sr. rsch. fellow, 1991—, Dist. Faculty award, 2004 Fellow Am. Phys. Soc.; mem. The Am. Phys. Soc., Sigma Pi Sigma. Avocations: music, books. Office: Mich State U Cyclotron Lab East Lansing MI 48824

BROWN, BRENDA, library director; m. Mark Brown; 4 children. MLS, U. Ariz., 1989. Libr. clk. U. Ariz., 1986; reference and youth svcs. libr. Scottsdale Librs., Ariz.; with Peoria Pub. Libr., Ariz., 1996—98, dir., 1998—2004; mgr. Chandler Pub. Libr., Ariz., 2004—. Past pres. Ariz. Libr. Assn., co-chair legis. com. Office: Chandler Pub Libr 22 S Delaware St

Chandler AZ 85225 Office Phone: 480-782-2817. Office Fax: 480-782-2823. E-mail: brenda.brown@chandleraz.gov.

BROWN, BRIAN ELLIS, protective services official; b. Chatham, Ont., Can., Sept. 13, 1943; arrived in US, 1988; s. Dean Russel and Helen Ruth (Legate) Brown; m. Glenys Lorree Schwan, Apr. 20, 1968; children: Leslie Nadeane Archer, Jennifer Lee Bauer, Jeffrey Legate. BA in Psychology, Wayne State U., Detroit, 1965; cert., Chaptman U., San Diego, 1993. Law enforcement post cert.:. Mktg. rep. IBM, London, Ont., Canada, 1966—68; assoc. prof. Fanshawe Coll., London, 1968—73; mktg. mgr. Xerox Corp., Ont., Canada, 1973—83; v.p. Moduloc Concrete Products, Toronto, Ont., Canada, 1983—89; pres. Microman Cons., Burlington, Ont., Canada, 1985—92; tchr. County San Diego, 1992—96, peace officer, 1996—. Bus. mktg. advisor Internat. Inst. Martial Arts, San Marcos, Calif., 1997—2007. Patent moduloc interlocking system. Named Salesman of the Yr., Xerox Corp., 1974, Instnl. Employee of the Yr., San Diego County Probation Dept., 1998. Republican. Avocation: travel. Home: 31661 Rocking Horse Rd Escondido CA 92026

BROWN, BRITT, retired publishing company executive; b. Long Beach, Calif., Apr. 23, 1927; s. Harry Britton and Victoria (Eaton) B.; m. Anne Louise McCarthy, June 19, 1948; children— Cathy Lynn, Cynthia Ann, Britt Murdock, Bruce McCarthy. Student, U. So. Calif., 1944-46; BA, U. Kans., 1947. Classified advt. salesman Wichita (Kans.) Eagle (now Wichita Eagle & Beacon Pub. Co.), 1947-50, classified mgr., 1952-55, advt. dir., 1956-62, v.p., sec., 1963-71, pub., pres., 1971-73, chmn., 1973-79. Served with USMCR, 1944-46, 50-51. Mem. Sigma Delta Chi, Kappa Alpha.

BROWN, BRUCE BADEN, accountant; b. Seattle, Dec. 1, 1933; s. Charles Elric and Mabel Enid (Coleman) Brown; m. Lois Jean Bellemans-Brown, 1963 (div. 1979); 3 children; m. Teresita Grimarez Brown, 1981 (div. 1985); 1 child; m. Lois Jean Bellemans-Brown, 1991. BBA, U. Wash., 1960. Cert. enrolled agt. U.S. Treasury. Various to v.p. Weather Master of Wash., Lynnwood, 1975—77; sr. planning and programs analyst Saudi Aramco, Dhahran, Saudi Arabia, 1977—93; owner Lighthouse Tax Svc., Mukilteo, Wash., 1995—. Tax and bus. cons. Lighthouse Tax Svc., 1997—; property developer Puget Sound Hills No. 2, 1977—79. Author: Desert Duel, 1999. Officer Mukilteo Hist. Soc., 1995—2004; dir. Mukilted Lighthouse Festival Assn., 2004—05; design review com. City Hall, Mukilteo, 2007; coun. mem. City of Mukilteo, Wash., 1999—2003. Cpl. US Army, 1951—54, Germany. Named Mukilteo Citizen of Yr., 2002; appointed Commr., Mukilteo Civil Svc., 2004. Home: 312 Cornelia Ave Mukilteo WA 98275 Office: Lighthouse Tax Svc 312 Cornelia Ave Mukilteo WA 98275 Office Phone: 425-348-6448. E-mail: Bruceb33@aol.com.

BROWN, BRUCE MAITLAND, philanthropy consultant; b. Bryn Mawr, Pa., Sept. 2, 1947; s. Charles Stuart and Margaret (Houston) B.; m. Elaine Eldredge, Sept. 3, 1983; 1 child, Carter Houston Brown. BA, Lawrence U., 1969; MA, U. Ky., 1973. Program analyst FDA, Rockville, Md., 1973-75, exec. secretariat, 1975-78, spl. asst., 1978-82, dep. dir., press ofc., 1982-86; v.p. communications Council for Responsible Nutrition, Washington, 1986-87; v.p. for charitable trusts CoreStates Trust and Investment Group, 1987-93; cons. Inst. for Nonprofit Excellence, Radnor, Pa., 1993-95. Meteorologist Sta. WCAU Radio, Phila., 1965; news dir., sports broadcaster Sta. WLFM Radio, Appleton, Wis., 1965—69; aide U.S. Senator Hugh Scott, Washington, 1969; pub. rels. contbr. Fellowship of Reconciliation, Nyack, NY, 1982; speechwriter FDA commrs., Washington, 1979—82; cons. Sewell C. Biggs. Mus. Art, 1994; bd. advisors Wayne Art Ctr., 1994—2007, chmn., 2002—07; cons. Transworld Commerce Alliance, 1994—96; bd. dirs. PhilaPride, Inc., 1993—97; adv. bd. Resources for Human Devel., 1993—98; exec. bd, Am. Edn. Film and Video Ctr., 1995—, v.p., 1998—; lectr. in field. Officer Paint Br. Farms Civic Assn., Colesville, Md., 1978—83; rev. panelist cmty. devel. fund United Way Southeastern Pa., 1995—97; treas. 1702 Found., 2003—; adv. bd. Presbyn. Children's Village, 2006—, 1994—2003, mem. devel. com., 1994—2003, bd. dir., 2003—06; bd. trustees resources com. Episc. Acad., Merion, Pa., 1995—98, cmty. svc. adv. bd., 2006—; ch. found. bd. Episcopal Diocese Pa., 1998—2003, sec., audit com.; founder and trustee HBE Found., 1988—; co-pres. and mem. bd. dirs. Brooke Valley Conservancy Assn., 1988—95; non-profit MBA adv. coun. Ea. U., 1990—, bd. vis., 2000—, found. bd., 2005—, bd. trustees, 2006—; adv. bd. Ctr. Urban Resources, 1992—2000; bd. dir. Bermuda Artworks Found., 1992—96; trustee Lawrence U., 1994—97; bd. dir. Hoxie Harrison Smith Found., 1994—, sec.-treas., 1998—2005; bd. dir. Resources for Better Families, 1994—97; devel. adv. com. Fellowship of Reconciliation, 1996—2007; Phila. bd. World Vision's Love for Children, 1996—97; treas. bd. dir. Kearsley, 1996—2000; trustee Bryn Mawr Rehab. Found., 1997—98; beneficiary adv. bd. Trusts and Estates Group, 1998—; adv. coun. Esperanza Health Ctr., 1998; devel. com. Camphill Village, Kimberton Hills, 1998—2003; bd. dir. Chester Rural Cemetery Assn., 1998; adv. bd. Del. County Hist. Soc., 1999—; chmn., bd. advs. Delaware County Cmty. Found., 2007—, bd. dirs., 2007—, Friends of Libr., Ea. U., 2007—. With US Army, 1969—71. Mem.: Del. Valley Grantmakers (founding bd. dirs., v.p. 1989—91), The Assemblies, Bay Head Yacht Club, Merion Cricket Club, Skytop Club. Anglican. Avocations: reading, gardening, meteorology, soccer, swimming. Home Phone: 610-526-9440; Office Phone: 610-526-9069.

BROWN, BRUCE P., radiologist; b. Rochester, Minn., May 1, 1944; s. Henry Allen and Dorothy Allen Brown; m. Sara Ellen Brown, July 13, 1945; children: Gillian, Aaron. BS in Zoology, U. Mich., Ann Arbor, 1966; MD, Med. Coll. Va., Richmond, 1971. Intern U. Mich., Ann Arbor, 1971—72, resident in internal medicine, 1974—77; fellow in gastroenterology U. Iowa, Iowa City, 1977—79, from asst. to asst. prof. medicine, 1979—86, resident in radiology, 1986—90, from asst. prof. to assoc. prof. radiology, dir. body imaging sect., 1997—2007, dir. body imaging fellowship, 1997—. Contbr. articles to profl. jours. Lt. USN, 1972—74. Named Tchr. of Yr., U. Iowa Dept. Radiology, 1991, 1994. Achievements include research in imaging of the gastro intestinal tract. Avocation: writing.

BROWN, BUSTER See BROWN, J.

BROWN, BYRON W., JR., mayor, former state legislator; m. Michelle Austin; 1 child, Byron III. BA in polit. sci. and journalism, Buffalo State Coll. Mem. Buffalo City Council, 1995—99, N.Y. Senate from 57th Dist., Albany, 2001—05; mayor city of Buffalo, NY, 2006—. Democrat. Office: City Hall 65 Niagara Sq Buffalo NY 14202*

BROWN, C. HAROLD, lawyer; b. Mendenhall, Miss., July 28, 1931; children: Tracey Gwen, Terry Lynne, Allison Anne, Harold Allen. BA, Vanderbilt U., 1957; LLB, U. Tex., 1960. Bar: Tex. 1960. Sr. ptnr. Brown Pruitt Peterson & Wambsganss , P.C., Ft. Worth, 1960—. Pres. A.J. and Jessie Duncan Found.; past chmn. Ft. Worth Civil Svc. Commn.; past chmn. bd. dirs., past pres. Tarrant County Conv. Ctr., 1980; active Com. for Greater Tarrant County; past bd. dirs. Ft. Worth Camp Fire Girls, Nat. Com. for Adoption, Gladney Ctr. Hall of Fame, Adopt a Spl. Kid/Tex., Tex. Assn. Licensed Children's Svcs.; mgr. campaign R.M. Stovall for Mayor of Ft. Worth, 1969, 71, 73, Richard T. Andersen for Tarrant County Commr., 1972, 76, 80, 84, Senator Al Gore for Pres., Tarrant County, Tex., 1988; past deacon U. Christian Ch., Ft. Worth. Sgt. U.S. Army, 1953-55. Recipient cert. Carnegie Hero Fund Commn., 1972; named Outstanding Young Texan, 1976; named to Gladney Ctr. Hall of Fame. Fellow Tex. Bar Found. (life), Southwestern Legal Found., Tarrant County Bar Found. (life), Ft. Worth-Tarrant County Bar Assn. (charter, life, bd. dirs. family law sect. 1978-80); mem. ABA, Tex. Bar Assn., Tarrant County Probate Bar, Ft. Worth Jr. Bar Assn. (pres. 1963), Am. Acad. Adoption Attys., Am. Acad. Hosp. Attys., Nat. Health Lawyers Assn., Pro Bono Coll. of State Bar of Tex., Badge and Shield, Vanderbilt U. Alumni Assn. (pres. 1966-67), Am. Brittany Club (Hall of Fame), Ridotto Club (pres. 1974), Petroleum Club, River Crest Country Club, Steeplechase Club, Nat. Commodore Club (adm.), Rotary, Masons, Shriners, Jesters, Alpha Tau Omega, Phi Delta Phi. Office: Brown Pruitt Peterson & Wambsganss PC 201 Main St Ste 801 Fort Worth TX 76102-3817 Office Phone: 817-338-4888. E-mail: hbrown@brownpruittlaw.com.

BROWN, CAMPBELL, newscaster; b. Ferriday, La., June 14, 1968; d. James H. and Dale Campbell (Fairbanks) Brown; m. Daniel Samuel Senor, Apr. 2, 2006. BA in Polit. Sci., Regis Coll., 1991. Polit. reporter KSNT-TV, Topeka, WWBT-TV, Richmond, Va., WBAL-TV, Balt., WRC-TV, Wash.; corr. NBC News, 1996—98, White Ho. corr., 1998—2007; co-anchor NBC Weekend Today, 2003—07; newscaster CNN, 2007—. Recipient Alumni Achievement award, Regis Coll., 2006. Office: CNN 820 1st St NE Washington DC 20002

BROWN, CANDIA POST, psychologist; b. Amityville, NY; d. John E.H. and Marie (Calhoun) Post; m. David E. Brown; children: Steven, Heather, Danielle, Mitchell; stepchildren: Tim, Deborah, Sandra, Dina, Ben, Joshua, Aaron, Abigail, Jacob, Hannah. BA, Adelphi U., Garden City, NY, 1965; MA, UCLA, 1966, U. Mo., Columbia, 1989; PhD in Psychology, Ohio State U., Columbus, 1993; postgrad., U. Wash., Seattle. Intern Palo Alto VA Med. Ctr.; postdoctoral fellow U. Wash. Sch. Medicine; neuropsychologist Bus. Psychol. Transitions, Lynhurst, 2002—06, Beachwood, Ohio, 2007—. Contbr. articles to profl. jours. Fellow Am. Bd. Profl. Psychology Rehab., Am. Bd. Profl. Neuropsychology; mem. APA, Nat. Acad. Neuropsychology, Kappa Delta Pi, Phi Alpha Theta Office Phone: 216-591-0500. Personal E-mail: candiapost@aol.com.

BROWN, CAROL ANN, librarian, director; b. Denver, Mar. 7, 1948; d. Truman Veach and Mary Margaret Yowell; m. Robert Ray Brown, Sept. 15, 1974; 1 child, Nancy Ann. AA, Western Wyo. Coll., Rock Springs, 1969; BA, Western State Coll., Gunnison, Colo., 1971; MLS, Emporia State U., Kans., 1998. From libr. technician to assoc. libr. Western Wyo. Coll., 1972—2005, assoc. libr., interim libr. dir. Hay Libr., 2005—, libr. dir. Hay Libr., 2006—. Pres. Western Wyo. Coll. Para-Profl. Assn., 2003—04. Pres. Bus. and Profl. Women, Rock Springs, 2001—03. Recipient Performance Incentive award, Western Wyo. Coll., 2004—05; grantee, Wyo. State Libr., Cheyenne, 2003, 2005. Mem.: ALA, Wyo. Libr. Assn. (section chair 2003—04, exec. coun. 2003—04), Mountain Plains Libr. Assn. Avocations: reading, ATV riding, horseback riding, snow mobiling. Office Phone: 307-382-1701. Business E-Mail: cabrown@wwcc.wy.edu.

BROWN, CAROL LESLIE, gynecological oncologist; b. LA, Apr. 10, 1961; MD, Columbia Univ. Coll. Physicians & Surgeons, 1986. Cert. Obstetrics & Gynecology, Gynecologic Oncology. Intern, obstetrics & gynecology Hosp. Univ. Pa., Phila., 1986—87, resident, 1987—90; fellow Meml. Sloan-Kettering Cancer Ctr., NYC, 1990—94, asst. attending surgeon, 2000—; asst. prof. Cornell Univ. Med. Coll., NYC, 1994—. Chairperson adv. coun. NY State Dept. Health Ovarian Ctr. Info. Program; advisor, spl. populations Gynecologic Oncology Group. Named one of America's Leading Physician, Black Enterprise Mag., 2001. Mem.: AMA (alternate del., chair, cancer caucus), Soc. Gynecologic Oncologists (co-chair, govt. rels. com.), Alpha Omega Alpha. Office: Meml Sloan Kettering 1275 York Ave New York NY 10021 Office Phone: 212-639-7659.*

BROWN, CAROL ROSE, artist; BFA, Cornell U. Solo shows include The Witkin Gallery, N.Y.C., Charles Lucien Gallery, NYC, Farrell Fischoff Gallery, Santa Fe, Rettig Y Martinez, Santa Fe, Korn Gallery, Drew U., Madison, N.J., Farrell Fischoff Gallery, Santa Fe, N.Mex.; exhibited in group shows at Missoula Mus. Fine Arts, Mont., Parrish Mus., Southampton, NY, Provincetown Art Assn. and Mus., Mass., Whitney Mus. at Stamford, Conn., The Torrey Gallery, Utah; represented in collections U.S. Embassies, Athens, Greece, Rabat, Morrocco, Ashgabat, Turkmenistan. Individual fellow Nat. Endowment for the Arts, 1994. Personal E-mail: carolrosebrown@mac.com.

BROWN, CAROLE L., transportation executive; b. Baltimore, 1965; BA, Harvard U.; MBA, Kellogg Grad. Sch. of Mgmt., Northwestern U., 1989. Joined Lehman Brothers Inc., 1999, sr. v.p., mng. dir., 1999—; chmn. Chgo. Transit Authority Bd. (CTA), 2003—. Mem. bd. dirs. Chgo. Children's Mus., Mercy Found., Ill. Coun. Against Handgun Violence; mem. adv. bd. Chgo. Pub. Schools' Sch. Partner Program, Uhlich Children's Home. Named one of 25 Women to Watch, Crain's Chgo. Bus., 2007; fellow Fellow of Leadership Greater Chgo., 2001. Mem.: The Executives' Club of Chgo., The Econ. Club of Chgo., Women's Leadership Forum of the Dem. Nat. Com. Office: Chgo Transit Authority PO Box 7567 Chicago IL 60680 E-mail: ctaboard@transitchicago.com.*

BROWN, CARROLL, retired diplomat, association executive, consultant; b. Selma, Ala., Oct. 5, 1928; s. Jack Crisman and Bessie (Bedsole) B.; m. Elvira DiMiceli, Apr. 2, 1953; children: David, Suzanne. AB, Columbia U., 1951, MA, 1953; postgrad., Johns Hopkins U., 1964-65. Joined Fgn. Service, 1957; posts include Yugoslavia, Poland, Washington, Austria; dep. dir. for Eastern European affairs Dept. State, Washington, 1974-76; dep. chief mission Am. embassy, Warsaw, 1976-79; consul gen. Düsseldorf, Fed. Republic Germany, 1979-81, Munich, Fed. Republic Germany, 1981-84; dir. Office Can. Affairs Dept. State, Washington, 1984-86, acting dep. asst. sec., 1986; mem. U.S. delegations to 41st and 42nd UN Gen. Assemblies, NYC, 1986; pres., bd. dirs. Am. Council on Germany, 1988-99; owner ind. cons. firm, 1999—2002. Adv. bd. World Policy Inst. With USN, 1953-57. Decorated comdr.'s cross Order of Merit (Germany); recipient Meritorious Honor award and Superior Honor award U.S. Dept. State. Mem. Fgn. Svc. Assn., Diplomatic and Consular Officers, Ret., Coun. Fgn. Rels., Univ. Club. Home: 114 E 71st St # 3E New York NY 10021 E-mail: cbrown123@earthlink.net.

BROWN, CHARLES DODGSON, lawyer; b. NYC, Dec. 31, 1928; s. James Dodgson and Leonora Rose (Nichols) B.; m. Martha Lockhart Spindler, Apr. 5, 1963; children: Gregory Spindler, William Howard. BA, NYU, 1949, JD, 1952. Bar: N.Y. 1952, U.S. Dist. Ct. (so. and ea. dists.) N.Y. 1955, U.S. Supreme Ct. 1958, U.S. Ct. Appeals (2d cir.) 1968. Counsel, former ptnr. Thacher Proffitt & Wood, NYC, 1954—. Co-author: Equipment Leasing, 1995—. Chmn. zoning bd. Asharoken, N.Y., 1965, alt. chmn. environ. bd., 1967, trustee, 1967, village justice, 1980—; chmn. Boy Scout Am., Northport, N.Y., 1989—; elder 1st Presbyn. Ch., Northport; mem. admiralty law inst. faculty Tulane U. Sch. Law, 1999. With U.S. Army, 1952-54. Mem. ABA, N.Y. Bar Assn., Maritime Law Assn. U.S. (proctor in Admiralty 1956, former chair to marine fin. com. 1996-2000), N.Y. State Magistrate Assn., Suffolk County Magistrate Assn., Northport Tennis Club. Republican. Avocations: scuba diving, wind surfing, tennis. Office Phone: 212-912-7655. Personal E-mail: cbrown2@optonline.net. Business E-Mail: cbrown@tpw.com.

BROWN, CHARLES E., consumer products company executive; Grad. in Mgmt. Sci., Duke U., Durham, NC. CPA. Various positions KPMG; v.p., contr. Pizza Hut (subs. PepsiCo), 1989—94; v.p., CFO Aramark Corp., 1994—95; sr. v.p., CFO Denny's, Inc., 1996—98; sr. v.p. fin., contr. Office Depot, Inc., Delray Beach, Fla., 1998—2001, exec. v.p., CFO, 2001—05, pres. internat., 2005—. Office: Office Depot Inc 2200 Old Germantown Rd Delray Beach FL 33445*

BROWN, CHARLES EUGENE, retired electronics company executive; b. Duff, Ind., Oct. 31, 1921; s. Lemuel C. and Bertha (McCormack) B.; m. Elizabeth Sherman McAllister, Aug. 16, 1952; children— Deborah, Judith, Robert, Sarah. BS, Ind. U., 1948, MBA, 1950. Corp. staff Glidden Co., Cleve., 1949-59; dir. indsl. relations Cleve. Pneumatic Tool Co., 1959-62, Honeywell, Inc., Mpls., 1962—68; dir. employee relations Honeywell, 1968—73; v.p. employee relations Honeywell, Inc., Mpls., 1973—80, v.p. exec. human resources, 1980-85, sr. staff v.p., 1985-86. Bd. dirs. Family and Children's Services, Mpls., Honeywell Retiree Vol. Program. Served with U.S. Army, 1942-45, ETO Decorated Purple Heart Home: 5601 Dewey Hill Rd Unit 219 Edina MN 55439 E-mail: cebbrown@aol.com.

BROWN, CHARLES M., library director; MLS, Columbia U., NYC; postgraduate student, U. Va., Harvard U. Dir. Arlington County Libr., Va., Hennepin County Libr. Sys., Minn.; dir. libs. Pub. Libr. Charlotte & Mecklenburg County, NC, 2003—. Pres. Pub. Libr. Assn., 1990—91; exec. bd. mem. ALA, 1995—99; bd. mem. Coun. Libr. and Info. Resources, 2005—; pres. NC Pub. Libr. Dirs. Assn., 2006—; bd. dirs. Southeastern Libr. Network, 2006—07. Named Newcomer of Yr., Leadership Charlotte, 2005. Office: Pub Libr Charlotte & Mecklenburg County 310 N Tryon St Charlotte NC 28202 Office Phone: 704-336-4146. Office Fax: 704-336-2677. E-mail: cbrown@plcmc.org.

BROWN, CHARLES SAMUEL, singer, composer, educator; b. Marianna, Ark., Sept. 26, 1940; s. Carey Brown and Narcisse (Angel) Richards. Student, Morehouse Coll., 1963-66; MusB, U. Mich., 1974, MusM, 1975, postgrad., 1975-77. Asst. prof. music Lincoln U. Mo., Jefferson City, 1977-80; adj. prof. music Borough of Manhattan CC, NYC, 1980-81, 95-99; tchr. music NYC Bd. Edn., 1986—. Artist, mem. faculty Choral Festival, Sheffield, Mass., 1983-85; mus. dir. The Open Eye Inst., NYC, 1991-92; mem. adv. coun. sch. concert series NY Chamber Symphony, 1991-93; guest lectr., clinician, Berkshire Choral Festival, 1993; featured guest composer 15th Ann. Southeastern African-Am. Collegiate Choral Music Festival, So. U., Baton Rouge, 2006. Composer: The Barrier, 1974, A Song Without Words, 1977, Calvary, 1972, Pied Beauty, 1977, Black Sheep, Black Sheep, 1987, Leisure Cruise, 1986, 5 Spiritual Settings for Chorus, 1991; back-up vocalist Ray Charles, 1988, Cab Calloway, 1988; an arranger for Kathleen Battle and Jessye Norman Spirituals Concert, Carnegie Hall, NYC, 1990. Bd. dirs. Melodious Accord. With U.S. Army, 1966-69, Vietnam. Mem. Nat. Assn. Tchrs. Singing, Music Educators Nat. Conf., Am. Guild Mus. Artists, Am. Choral Dirs. Assn., Music Educators Assn. NYC, Pi Kappa Lambda. Avocations: cooking, photography, reading. Personal E-mail: cbrown26@schools.nyc.gov.

BROWN, CHRIS (CHRISTOPHER MAURICE BROWN), singer; b. Tappahannock, Va., May 5, 1989; s. Clinton Brown and Joyce Hawkins. Singer: (albums) Chris Brown, 2005, (songs) Run It!, 2005, Yo (Excuse Me Miss), 2005 (BET Viewer's Choice award, 2006); actor: (films) Stomp the Yard, 2007. Recipient Best New Artist award, Soul Train Music Awards, 2006, Image award for Outstanding New Artist, NAACP, 2006, Best New Artist award, Black Entertainment TV (BET), 2006, Music-Choice Breakout (Male), Teen Choice Awards, 2006, New Artist of Yr., Billboard Music Awards, 2006, Artist of Yr., 2006, Male Artist of Yr., 2006. Office: Jive Records 137 W 25th St New York NY 10001*

BROWN, CHRISTOPHER PATRICK, health care administrator, educator; b. Phoenix, June 7, 1951; s. Charles Francis and R. Patricia (Quinn) B.; m. Tracey Ann Wallenberg, May 23, 1987; 1 child, Ryan Matthew. AA in Biol. Scis., Shasta Coll., Redding, Calif., 1976; AS in Liberal Arts, SUNY, Albany, 1977; grad. Primary Care Assoc. Program, Stanford U., 1978; BA in Community Svcs. Adminstrn., Calif. State U., Chico, 1982; M. in Health Svcs., U. Calif., Davis, 1984. Gen. mgr. Pacific Ambulance Svc., El Cajon, Calif., 1974; primary care assoc. Family Practice, Oregon-Calif., 1978-82; cons. Calif. Health Profls., Chico, 1982-84; bus. ops. mgr. Nature's Arts, Inc., Seattle, 1985-86; instr. North Seattle C.C., 1984-89, program dir., 1986-89; asst. dir. Pacific Med. Clinic North, Seattle, 1990-92; dir. Pacific Med. Clinic Renton (Wash.), Pacific Med. Ctr., 1992-95; dir. ops./physician svcs. St. Luke's Regional Med. Ctr., Boise, Idaho, 1995-97, adminstr. ambulatory care, 1997-98; adminstr. St. Luke's Meridian (Idaho) Med. Ctr., 1997-98; COO, sr. v.p. Medford (Oreg.) Clinic, 1998-2000; pres./cons. Integra Healthcare Solutions, 2000—. Mem. Butte County Adult Day Care Health Coun., Chico, 1982-84; bd. dirs., pres. Innovative Health Care Svcs., Chico, 1982-84; bd. dirs. Highline W. Seattle Mental Health Ctr., 1985-90, v.p. 1988-90; tech. adv. com. North Seattle C.C., 1992-93; bd. dirs. ARC, 1997-98; commr. planning commn. City of Central Point, Oreg., 2004-05. Mem. Internat. Platform Assn., Soc. Ambulatory Care Profls., Med. Group Mgmt. Assn., Multispecialty Group Exec. Soc., Accreditation Assn. for Ambulatory Health Care (accreditation surveyor 1996-97), Am. Legion. Avocations: gardening, woodworking, church activities. Home: 345 Orth Dr Central Point OR 97502 E-mail: cratbrown@peoplepc.com.

BROWN, CLANCY, actor, publishing executive; b. Urbana, Ohio, Jan. 5, 1959; s. Clarence J. and Joyce (Eldridge) B.; m. Jeanne Ellen Johnson, June 26, 1993; 2 children. BS in Speech, Northwestern U., 1981. Bd. dirs. Brown Pub. Co., Cin.; mng. ptnr. The B's Nest Ohio Partnership, Urbana. Appeared in films including Bad Boys, 1983, Adventures of Buckaroo Bonzai, 1984, The Bride, 1985, Thunder Alley, 1985, The Highlander, 1986, Extreme Prejudice, 1987, Shoot to Kill, 1988, Season of Fear, 1989, Waiting for the Light, 1990, Blue Steel, 1990, Ambition, 1991, Pet Sematary II, 1992, The Shawshank Redemption, 1994, Gargoyles: The Heroes Awaken (voice), 1994, Donor Unknown, 1995, Dead Man Walking, 1995, Female Perversions, 1996, Fallout (voice), 1997, Annabelle's Wish, 1997, Starship Troopers, 1997, Flubber, 1997, Claire Makes It Big, 1999, The Hurricane, 1999, Chump Change, 2001, The Laramie Project, 2002, The Making of Daniel Boone, 2003, Finding Neo, 2004, Gambling, 2004, The SpongeBob Squarepants Movie, 2004, Dogg's Hamlet, Cahoot's MacBeth, 2005, A.T.O.M.: Alpha Teens on Machines (voice), 2005, The Guardian, 2006, Pathfinder, 2007; TV films include The Room Upstairs, 1987, The Man Who Broke 1,000 Chains, 1987, Johnny Ryan, 1990, Love, Lies and Murder, 1991, Cast a Deadly Spell, 1991, Past Midnight, 1992, Desperate Rescue: The Cathy Mahone Story, 1992, Bloodlines: Murder in the Family, 1993, Last Light, 1993, Earth 2, 1994, Radiant City, 1996, The Patron Saint of Liars, 1998, The Batman/Superman Movie, 1998, Vendetta, 1999, In the Company of Spies, 1999, The Night of the Headless Horseman (voice), 1999, Yesterday's Children, 2000, Boss of Bosses, 2001, Normal, 2003; TV series include Earth 2, 1994, Mortal Kombat: The Animated Series (voice) 1995, Might Ducks (voice), 1996, Superman (voice), 1996, ER, 1997, The New Batman/Superman Adventures (voice), 1997, The Legend of Calamity Jane (voice), 1997, Voltron: The Third Dimension (voice), 1998, Big Guy and Rusty the Boy Robot (voice), 1999-2001, Lloyd in Space, 2001, Breaking News, 2002, Battle Force: Andromeda (voice), 2003, Super Robot Monkey Team Hyperforce Go! (voice), 2004-06, Spawn: The Animation, 2007-. Mem. Northwestern Entertainment Alliance. Address: care The Gersh Agy 232 N Canon Dr Beverly Hills CA 90210-5302*

BROWN, COLIN, automotive executive; m. Cynthia Brown; 3 children. Grad., Williams Coll.; JD, Duke U. Gen. counsel Fuqua Industries, Atlanta, Cannon Mills, Kannapolis, NC; v.p., gen. counsel JM Family Enterprises, Deerfield Beach, Fla., 1992—97, COO, 1997—2000, pres., 2000—03, pres., CEO, 2003—. Office: JM Family Enterprises 100 Jim Moran Blvd Deerfield Beach FL 33442*

BROWN, COLLEEN, broadcast executive; BA bus admin and pol sci, U Dubuque, Iowa; MBA, U Colo. Gen. mgr. Sta. KPNX-TV, Phoenix, till

1998; v.p. broadcast Lee Enterprises, 1998-99, pres. Davenport, Iowa, 1999—2000; sr v.p. bus dev Belo Corp, Dallas, 2000—. Mem. March of Dimes. Mem. Young Press Assn. Office: AH Belo Corp 400 S Record St PO Box 655237 Dallas TX 75265-5237

BROWN, CONNELL JEAN, retired animal science educator; b. Everton, Ark., Mar. 6, 1924; s. Clarence Jackson and Winnie Dee (Trammell) B.; m. Erma Dexter (Taylor), May 19, 1946; children— Craig Jay, Mark Allen BSA., U. Ark., 1948; MS, Okla. State U., 1950, PhD, 1956. Asst. prof. dept. animal sci. U. Ark., Fayetteville, 1950-57, assoc. prof., 1957-62, livestock sect. leader, 1978-81, prof., 1962-86, Univ. prof., 1986-90, prof. emeritus, 1990—; lectr. Internat. Stockmans Short course, 1980. Contbr. articles to profl. jours. Served with USAAF, 1943-46; PTO. Recipient Rsch. award Performance Registry Internat., 1977, U. Ark. Coll. Agr. Rsch. award, 1981, Disting. Svc. award Ark. Cattlemans Assn., 1985; named to Am. Polled Hereford Assn. Hall of Merit, 1986, Ark. Agrl. Hall of Fame, 1994. Fellow AAAS, Am. Soc. Animal Sci. (pres. so. sect. 1975, leadership award so. sect. 1975); mem. Am. Genetics Assn., N.Y. Acad. Scis., So. Assn. Agrl. Scientists (bd. dirs.), Am. Registry Profl. Animal Scientists (pres. Ark. chpt. 1989), Kiwanis (dist. pres. 1984-85, lt. gov. 1992-93), Sigma Xi (pres. 1986-87), Gamma Sigma Delta (pres. 1967-68). Home: 188 Cydnee St Fayetteville AR 72703-3710 Personal E-mail: cjb36@cox.net.

BROWN, CORRINE, congresswoman; b. Jacksonville, Fla., Nov. 11, 1946; 1 child, Shantrel. BS, Fla. A&M U., 1969, MS, 1971; EdS, U. Fla., 1974. Prof. Fla. Community Coll., 1977—82, guidance counselor, 1982—92; mem. Fla. Ho. of Reps, 1982—92; del. Nat. Dem. Conv., 1988; mem. U.S. Congress from 3rd Fla. dist., 1993—, mem. transp. and infrastructure com., vet. affairs com. Named one of Most Influential Black Americans, Ebony mag., 2006. Mem. Sigma Gamma Rho. Democrat. Baptist. Home: 314 Palmetto St Jacksonville FL 32202-2619 Office: US Ho of Reps 2444 Rayburn Ho Office Bldg Washington DC 20515-0903 also: Dist Office Ste 202 101 E Union St Jacksonville FL 32202*

BROWN, DALE PATRICK, retired advertising executive; b. Richmond, Va., Aug. 11, 1947; d. Thomas Windom and Helen (Curtis) Patrick. BA in Journalism, U. Richmond, 1968, MA in English, 1978. Reporter city news sect. Richmond Times-Dispatch, 1968-71; free-lance writer, 1971-73; v.p., supr. pub. rels. account The Martin Agy., Richmond, 1973-77, account supr. advt., v.p., 1977-79, v.p., supr. advt. account, then group v.p. and sr. v.p., 1983-89; mgr. communications svcs. Mobil Chem. Co., Richmond, 1979-81; mgr. communications Whittaker Gen. Med., Richmond, 1981-83; exec. v.p. The Stenrich Group, Richmond, 1989-90; pres., chief exec. officer Sive/Young & Rubicam, Cin., 1990-98. Trustee U. Richmond, 1992-2004, hon. trustee, 2004—, mem. exec. com., 1999-2001, vice chair acad. program com., 2002-04; mem. devel. bd. Good Samaritan Hosp., 1992-95, Leadership Cin.; bd. dirs. Met. Growth Alliance, 1997-99, Downtown Cin. Inc., 1995-98, Midwest Strategic Trust, 1993-97, Ohio Nat. Life Ins. (exec. com.), bd. dirs. Frisch's Inc., 1998—, Mercantile Libr., 2000—, Cin. C. of C., 1995-98; chair Acad. Career Women of Achievement, 1996-2001; bd. govs. Cin. chpt. Am. Assn. Advt. Agys., 1990-98. Recipient 2 AAF Silver medals, 1988, 96, Richmond Advt. Person of Yr. award Advt. Club Richmond, 1988, Woman of Achievement award Cin. YWCA, 1993, Human Rels. award Am. Jewish Com., Cin. chpt., 1996, various others including Addy, Effie, Clio awards N.Y. Art Dirs. Club. Mem. Pub. Rels. Soc. Am., Advt. Club Cin., Queen City Club (bd. dirs.), Comml. Club of Cin. Avocations: reading, travel, arts. Home: 1231 Martin Dr Cincinnati OH 45202-1737

BROWN, DALE SUSAN, retired federal agency and academic administrator, consultant, writer, learning disabilities website manager; b. NYC, May 27, 1954; d. Bertram S. and Beatrice Joy (Gilman) Brown. BA, Antioch Coll., 1976. Rsch. asst. Am. Occupl. Therapy Assn., Rockville, Md., 1978—79; writer Pres.' Com. on Employment of People with Disabilities, Washington, 1979—82, program mgr. handicapped concerns com., 1982—85, program mgr. labor com., 1985, Washington, 1996—98, program mgr. work environment and tech. com., 1988—94, program mgr. com. on libr. and info. svcs., 1984—86, youth devel com., 1986—88, mem. team new products devel., 1987—90, agy. rep., 1991—93, with interagy. tech. assistance coordinating team, 1992—94; program mgr. Job Accomodation Network, 1997—99; mgr. Nat. Conf. of Youth with Disabilities, 2000; policy advisor Office Disability Employment Policy Dept. Labor, 2001—05, mem. youth team, 2002—05, ret., 2005; sr. mgr. LD Online, 2006—. Cons. in field, gen. assembly spkr. nat. conv. Gen. Fedn. Women's Clubs, 1981, mem. Rehab Svcs. Adminstrn. Task Force on Learning Disabilities, 1981-83. Author: Pathways to Employment for People with Learning Disabilities, 1991, Working Effectively with People Who Have Learning Disabilities and Attention Deficit Hyperactivity Disorder, 1995, I Know I Can Climb the Mountain, 1995, Learning Disabilities and Employment, 1997, Learning A Living Guide to Planning Your Career and Finding A Job for People with Learning Disabilities, Attention Deficit Disorder and Dyslexia, 2000, Job-Hunting Tips for the So-Called Handicapped, 2001, Steps to Independence for People with Learning Disabilities, 2005, (films) They Could Have Saved Their Homes, 1982; dir.: (videotape) Part of the Team People with Disabilities in the Workforce, 1990; co-editor: Learning Disabilities Quar. Americans with Disabilities Act and Learning Disabilities, 1992; mem. editl. bd. Perceptions, 1981—83, Learning Disabilities Focus, 1988—90, In the Mainstream, 1994—98; guest editor: Learning Disabilities Rsch. and Practice, 1990—96; guest editor Learning Disability and Career Development, 2002; guest editor: Career Planning and Adult Devel. Jour., 2002. Rep. interagy. com. Handicapped Employees, 1998—99; adv. com. Learning Disability Online web site, 2005—; bd. dirs. Closer Look Nat. Info. Ctr., Washington, 1980—83, Am. Coalition for Citizens with Disabilities, 1985—86; mem. Congl. Task Force Rights and Empowerment of Ams. with Disabilities, 1988—90; profl. adv. bd. Nat. Attention Deficit Disorder Assn., 1996—99; bd. dirs. Coun. on Quality and Leadership, 2001—05; adv. bd. Internat. Ctr. for Disability Resources on the Internet, 2003—; chair Conf. on Info. Tech. for User With Disabilities, 1989; spl. asst. for people with disabilities Federally Employed Women, 1991—92; mem. blue ribbon panel Nat. Telecomm. Access for People with Disabilities, 1989—94; pres. Assn. Learning Disabled Adults, Washington, 1979—80; del. Nat. Writer's Union, 1999; rep. com. on fed. govt. as model employer, com. on youth with disabilities Presdl. Task Force on Employment of Adults with Disabilities, 1999—2002; judge, Ten Outstanding Young Ams. U.S. Jr. C. of C. Jaycees, 2003. Named one of Ten Outstanding Young Ams., U.S. Jr. C. of C. Jaycees, 1994; recipient, Margaret Byrd Rawson award, 1989, Personal Achievement award Women's Program USDOL, 1989, Individual Achievement award, Nat. Coun. on Comm. Disorders, 1991, Spl. Achievement award, Pres.'s Com. on Employment of People with Disabilities, 1991, Gold Screen award, Nat. Assn. Gov. Communicators, 1991, Arthur S. Fleming award, 1992, Voices Campaign award, 2004, Honor award, Dept. Labor, 2004; grantee, Found. for Children with Learning Disabilities, 1982. Mem.: ALA, Inter Agency. Com. on Handicapped Employees (rep. 1989—91), Learning Disabilities Assn. Am. (bd. dirs. 1986—91), Nat. Assn. Govt. Communicators (Blue Pencil award 1986), Nat. Network of Learning Disabled Adults (founder, pres. 1980—81). Democrat.

BROWN, DALE WEAVER, clergyman, theology studies educator; b. Wichita, Kansas, Jan. 12, 1926; s. Harlow J. and Cora Elisa (Weaver) Brown; m. Lois D. Kauffman, Aug. 17, 1947; children: Deanna Gae, Dennis Dale, Kevin Ken. BA, McPherson Coll., 1946; BD, Bethany Theol. Sem., 1949; postgrad., Drake U., 1954-56, Northwestern U. and Garrett Bibl. Inst., 1956-58; PhD, Northwestern U., 1962. Ordained to ministry Ch. of Brethren, 1946; pastor Stover Meml. Ch. of Brethren, Des Moines, 1949-56; dir. religious life, asst. prof. philosophy and religion McPherson Coll., 1958-62; assoc. prof. Christian theology Bethany Theol. Sem., Oak Brook, Ill., 1962-70; prof. Christian theology Bethany Theol. Sem., 1970-94. Del. standing com. Ch. of Brethren, 1954; moderator Middle Iowa Dist., 1952-53, mem. dist. and regional bds., gen. bd., 1960-62, moderator-elect. ann. conf., 1970-71, moderator, 1971-72. Author: In Christ Jesus: The Significance of Jesus as the Christ, 1965, Four Words for World, 1968, So Send I You, 1969, Brethren and Pacifism, 1970, The Christian Revolutionary, 1971, Flamed by the Spirit, 1978, Understanding Pietism, 1978, rev. edit., 1996, Berea College: Spiritual and Intellectual Roots, 1982, What About the Russians, 1984, Biblical Pacifism, 1986, Bibical Pacifism, new edit., 2003, Another Way of Believing--A Brethren Theology, 2005. Mem. Am. Acad. Religion, Internat. Bonhoeffer Soc., Fellowship of Reconciliation, Am. Theol. Soc. Home: 1101 E College Ave Elizabethtown PA 17022-2236 E-mail: dbrown1101@comcast.net.

BROWN, DALLAS COVERDALE, JR., retired military officer, historian, educator; b. New Orleans, Aug. 21, 1932; s. Dallas Coverdale and Rita Sydney (Taylor) B.; m. Joyce Regina Bush, July 26, 1955, (div. Aug. 1985); children: Dallas Coverdale, III, Leonard, Jan, Karen, Barbara; m. Elizabeth Taylor Vance, Sept. 3, 1985 BA in History and Polit. Sci. (Disting. Mil. Grad. 1954), W.Va. State Coll., 1954; MA in Govt., Ind. U., 1967, postgrad. in Def. Lang. Inst., 1966; grad., Command and Gen. Staff Coll., 1968, USA Russian Inst., 1970; disting. grad., Naval War Coll., 1974. Commd. 2d lt. U.S. Army, 1954, advanced through grades to brig. gen., 1978; service in Korea, W. Ger., Vietnam; dep. chief staff intelligence U.S. Army Forces Command, 1978-79; dep. vice dir. fgn. intelligence Def. Intelligence Agy., 1979-80; dep. comdr. U.S. Army War Coll., Carlisle Barracks, Pa., 1980-84; ret., 1984; assoc. prof. history W.Va. State Coll., Institute, 1984-96. Mem. bd. advisors W.Va. State Coll., 1990-91; mem. W.Va. Gov.'s Higher Edn. Advocacy Team, 1992-93, Savannah (ga.) Coun. on World Affairs Inc., 2000-; World Affairs Coun. Hilton Head, 1999—; bd. dir. WPBY-TV (PBS), 1995-96. Constituent U.S. Army War Coll. Found.; mem. Mil. Adv. Coun., Ctr. for Def. Info. Decorated Def. Superior Service medal, Meritorious Service medal (2), Joint Service Commendation medal, Army Commendation medal, Meritorious Unit Commendations, Master Parachutist badge, Aircraft Crewman badge; named Alumnus of Yr. W.Va. State Coll., 1978; named to W.Va. State Coll. ROTC Hall of Fame, 1980; recipient Disting. West Virginian award, 1978, 1998. Mem. Assn. U.S. Army, Ret. Officers Assn., Nat. Eagle Scout Assn., Sun City Vets. Assn. (comdr. 1999-2000, trustee 2000—), W.Va. State U. Coll. Alumni Assn., Alpha Phi Alpha, Alpha Lambda Boule, Sigma Pi Phi, Pi Alpha Theta, Pi Sigma Alpha, Rocks Club. Unitarian Universalist. Achievements include first African American general officer in field of military intelligence. Home: Sun City Hilton Head 17 Devant Dr E Bluffton SC 29909-4537 Personal E-mail: dallas17@hargray.com.

BROWN, DAN, writer; b. NH, June 22, 1964; m. Blythe Brown. Grad., Phillips Exeter Acad., Amherst Coll., 1986. Former English teacher Phillips Exeter Academy. Author: Matter, 1996, Angels and Demons, 2000 (Publishers Weekly Bestseller paperback), Deception Point, 2001 (Publishers Weekly Bestseller paperback, 2005), The Da Vinci Code, 2003 (#1 NY Times Bestseller, #1 Publishers Weekly Bestseller), Digital Fortress, 2004 (Publishers Weekly Bestseller paperback list, 2005). Named one of Time Mag. 100 Most Influential People, 2005. Avocation: tennis. Office: c/o Random House Publicity 1745 Broadway New York NY 10019*

BROWN, DANA A., federal agency administrator; BA, Coll. William and Mary. Police officer, Fairfax County, Va.; with U.S. Secret Svc., 1978—2003; chief of staff Fed. Air Marshals Svc., U.S. Dept. Homeland Security, 2003—06, dir., 2006—; asst. adminstr. law enforcement, Transp. Security Adminstrn. U.S. Dept. Homeland Security, Washington, 2006—. Decorated Purple Heart. Office: US Dept Homeland Security Fed Air Marshals Svc 425 I St NW Washington DC 20536

BROWN, DANIEL, curator, executive secretary; b. Cin., Nov. 4, 1946; s. Sidney H. and Genevieve Florence (Elbaum) B. AB cum laude, Middlebury Coll., 1968; AM, U. Mich., 1970; postgrad., Princeton U., 1971-72. Dir. cultural events U. Cin., 1972, spl. asst. to pres., 1973; v.p., corp. sec. Brockton Shoe Trimming Co., Cin., 1974—2004, sec. treas., 1997—2004; curator Maple Knoll Villag Retirement Cmty. Curator KZF Gallery, Cin., 1987—94, 2003—06, Design Studio, 1998—99, Katz and Dawgs Gallery, 1989—90, Antiques Design Ctr., 1998—, U. Clubs Ann. Art Exhibit, Antique & Design Studios, 1999—, Christ Hosp., 1999—2003, Regional Women Mid-Career Artists, 2000, 537 Gallery, 2000—, Maple Knoll Retirement Cmty., 2000, U. Club Cin., 2004—, Univ. Club, 2005—, The Cin. Women's Club, 2005—, Universal Grille, Cin., 2006—, The Kidney Found Exhibit, The Healing Power of Beauty, 2006—, United Way Beauty Matters, 2006—, Children's Wellness Ctr., group show, 2007; instr. Art Acad. Cin., 1980, 1988—; prin. Daniel Brown, Inc., Cin. and Columbus, 1999—; panel leader Midwest Coll. Art Assn. Conv., 1995; curator, art adv. St. Joseph Orphanage, 2002—; art critic Cin. Mag., 1980—83, Cin. Herald, 1992—94, Cin. Art Acad. Newsletter, Provincetown Arts, 1988—90, USA Arts; editor, co-pub., co-owner The Blue Book of Cin., 1998—; commentator Sta. WKRC-TV, Cin.; art and music critic Sta. WCP-TV, Cin., 1986—88; arts editor, essayist Cin. City Beat, 1994—95; guest curator New Art from Academe: An Overview The Cen. Exch., Kansas City, Mo., 1988, Lyrical Abstractions, 1989, Design of the Future, 1989, Contemporary Landscape Kancabco Co., Cin., 1988, No. Ky. U., 1989, The Arts Consortium, 1991—94, Cuba Now Carnegie Arts Ctr., 1996; guest cocurator Tangeman Fine Arts Gallery, U. Cin., 1987, guest curator, 88, Art Without Boundaries, Cin., 2007—, Dilere Gallery, Cin., 2006—; permanent curator KZF Art Gallery, Cin., 1987—95; guest co-curator Artist at Mid-Career: A Dialogue Between Columbus and Cin., 1989—90; curator Liberties Restaurant, Cin., 1990—93, Fifth Third Bank, Cin., 1991—92, African-Am. Mus., 1992—93, African Am. Artists, 1994, United Way Art Program, 2006—; guest spkr. Arts Consortium, 1994; guest critic dept. painting and drawing U. Cin., 1993—, lectr. lit. Inst. for Learning in Retirement, 2004—; corr. editor Dialogue Mag., 1986—90, art reviewer, 1983—; lead editorialist The Arts Consortium Newsletter, 1992; monthly editorialist Antenna Newspaper, 1995—2001; lectr., curator art exhbns. The Christ Hosp. and the Maple Knoll Retirement Cmty., 1999—; lectr. fiction and art The Mercantile Libr., 2002—; Chinese painting tchr. Art Acad., 2004; exec. editor The Blue Chip Rev., 2004—06; adj. prof. contemporary fiction Union Inst., Cin., 2006—; lectr. 5th St. Gallery, Cin., 2006; solo juror Xavier U. 1st Annual Nat. Print Show, 2007; cons. in field. Author: David Bumbeck: The Romantic Classicist, 1989, Tom Bacher: High Tech American Impressionist, 1989, The Universe Watching: The Art of Nancy Fletcher Cassell, 1990, John Stewart: A Retrospective, 1991, Bukang Kim: Journey to the East, 1992, Hustlers, 1992-93, The Evolution of Form, Bukang Kim: A Retrospective, 1995, Robert Knipschid: Four Decades of Painting, 2002; contbg. writer: Weston Monthly, 2005-; columnist Art Acad. News, 1990-94, Cin. Post, 1991, Downtowner, 1991-95, Everybody's News, 1994; editor-in-chief Antenna Arts Mag., 1996-98, The Bluechipreview.com, 2004—; art critic, contbg. editor, critic Artist's Mag., 2006—. Mem. exhbns com. Contemporary Arts Ctr.; sec., bd. dirs. Mercantile Libr., 1985-91, treas., 1986, chmn. programs com., 1987—. Young Wing; trustee Contempory Arts Ctr., 1984-87, co-chmn. artists adv. bd., 1987, Vocal Arts Ensemble, 1984, Enjoy the Arts, 1985-88, v.p., 1986; mem. bd. advisors Cin. Artists Group Effort, 1986-88; guest curator Carnegie Arts Ctr., Covington, Ky., 1986—; juror art competitions, Cin. and Columbus, Ohio, 1986-87, Mansfield, Ohio, Kansas City, Mo., Over the Rhine, Cin., Plein Air Art Contest, 2007-; mem. citizens' adv. com. Art Acad. of Cin., 1989—, trustee, 1991—; trustee Art Acad. Cin. Coop. Gallery, 1990, Artists Without Boundries Gallery, 2007-; co-chmn. fine art com. The Arts Consortium, cin., 1990—, curator, 1991—; sole juror Art Acad. Alumni Juried Exhbn., 1992; trustee UMOJA Artists' Group, 1994; curator KZF Gallery, 2004—, Cin. Women's Club, lectr., 2005-. Recipient The Critic's Purse award Dialogue mag., 1985. Mem. Internat. Soc. Art Critics (N.Y. and Paris chpts.), Univ. Club (art com. 1990-91, guest curator 1992), Visiting Nurses Assn. of Cin. (bd. 2004-06). Home: 431 Collins Ave Cincinnati OH 45202-1803 Office Phone: 513-751-3134. Personal E-mail: daniellbrown@fuse.net.

BROWN, DARRELL JAMES, publishing executive; b. Abilene, Tex., Feb. 13, 1959; s. Don J. and Alma K. Brown; m. Patricia Lee Stevens, Apr. 2, 1983; children: Tova Lee, Devon Justice. BS in Psychology, U. Mo., 1981. Dir. retail dept. The May Cos., St. Louis, 1981; vice chmn., editor LEADERS Mag., NYC, 1981—; v.p. Dormann Pub., Inc., NYC, 1984—; v.p., sec. SIPA News Svc., NYC, 1984—, Internat. Bd. Indsl. Advisors, NYC, 1984—; pres. Global Change Inc., 1996—. Lectr., career guidance counselor in youth field. Founding exec. bd. mem., sec., treas. Acacia Frat., U. Mo., Columbia. Mem. The Young People's Leadership Found. (pres.), Scottish Rite Mason (33rd degree), Order of De Molay (Legion of Honor). Avocations: tennis, skiing. Office: Leaders Mag 59 E 54th St New York NY 10022-4211

BROWN, DAVE, professional sports team executive; b. Saskatoon, Sask., Can., Oct. 12, 1962; Left wing Phila. Flyers, 1982—89, 1991—95, Edmonton Oilers, 1989—91, San Jose Sharks, 1995—96; asst. coach Phila. Flyers, 1996—98, dir. player pers., 2006—; pro scout NY Rangers, 1998—2003, head profl. scout, 2003—06. Achievements include being a member of Stanley Cup Champion Edmonton Oilers, 1990. Office: c/o Phila Flyers First Union Ctr 3601 S Broad St Philadelphia PA 19148-5250

BROWN, DAVID, motion picture producer, writer; b. NYC, July 28, 1916; s. Edward Fisher and Lillian (Baren) B.; m. Liberty LeGacy, Apr. 15, 1940 (div. 1951); 1 son, Bruce LeGacy; m. Wayne Clark, May 25, 1951 (div. 1957); m. Helen Gurley, Sept. 25, 1959. AB, Stanford U., 1936; MS, Columbia U., 1937. Apprentice San Francisco News and Wall St. Jour., 1936; night editor, asst. drama critic Fairchild Publs., 1937-39; editorial dir. Milk Research Council, 1939-40; assoc. editor Street & Smith Publs., 1940-43; assoc. editor, exec. editor, editor-in-chief Liberty mag., 1943-49; editorial dir. Nat. Edn. Campaign, A.M.A., 1949; assoc. editor, mng. editor Cosmopolitan mag., 1949-52; mng. editor, story editor, head scenario dept. 20th Century-Fox Film Corp. Studios, Beverly Hills, Calif., 1952-56, mem. studio exec. com., 1956-60, producer, 1960-62; v.p., dir. story operation 20th Century Fox Film Corp., Beverly Hills, Calif., 1964-69, exec. v.p. creative operations, 1969-70, dir., 1968-70; exec. v.p. creative operations, dir. Warner Bros., 1971-72; ptnr. Zanuck/Brown Co., NYC, 1972-87; owner Manhattan Project Ltd., 1987—; pres. Island World, 1990-92; exec. story editor, head scenario dept., editorial v.p. New Am. Library World Lit., Inc., 1963-64. Final judge for best short story pub. in mags. Benjamin Franklin Mag. ann. awards, 1955-58. Author: Brown's Guide to Growing Gray, 1987, Let Me Entertain You, 1990, The Rest of Your Life is the Best of Your Life, 1991; Brown's Guide To The Good Life, 2006; contbr. Am. mag., Collier's, Harper's, Sat. Evening Post, Reader's Digest, Journalists in Action, 1963, others; editor: I Can Tell It Now, 1964, How I Got That Story, 1967; prodr.: (films) The Sugarland Express, 1974, The Eiger Sanction, 1975, Jaws, 1977, MacArthur, 1977, Jaws II, 1978, The Island, 1980, Neighbors, 1981, The Verdict, 1982, Target, 1985, Cocoon, 1985; exec. prodr.: Driving Miss Daisy, HBO Women and Men, 1 and 2, 1990, 1991, The Player, 1992, A Few Good Men, 1992, Watch It, 1993, The Cemetery Club, 1993, Canadian Bacon, 1994, Kiss The Girls, 1997, The Saint, 1997, Deep Impact, 1998, Angela's Ashes, 1999, Chocolat, 2000, Along Came a Spider, 2001; prodr.: (plays) A Few Good Men, TRU, The Cemetery Club, The Shawl, Mr. Goldwyn, Show Tune, Sweet Smell of Success, Vanilla, Dirty Rotten Scoundrels. Trustee com. on film Mus. Modern Art, N.Y.C. Served as 1st lt., M.I. AUS, World War II. Mem. Acad. Motion Picture Arts and Scis. (recipient Irving G. Thalberg Meml. award 1991), Producers Guild Am. (David O. Selznick Lifetime Achievement award 1993), Nat. Press Club (Washington), Coffee Ho. Club (N.Y.C.), Bd. of Visitors Columbia U. Grad Sch. of Journalism, Players Club (N.Y.C.), Dutch Treat (N.Y.C.), Century Assn. (N.Y.C.), N.Y. Friars Club. Office: Manhattan Project Ltd 1775 Broadway Ste 410 New York NY 10019-1903 Office Phone: 212-258-2541. Personal E-mail: dbrown1775@aol.com. *Success, after all, is no more and no less than doing well what one wants to do most-regardless of where such an endeavor places one in the hierarchy of society.*

BROWN, DAVID G., academic administrator; AB in Econs. with honors, Denison U., 1958; PhD, MA in Econs., Princeton U., 1961. From asst. to assoc. prof. econs. U. N.C., Chapel Hill, 1961-66; Am. Coun. on Edn. fellow U. Minn., 1966-67; provost, v.p. for acad. affairs Drake U., 1967-70; provost, exec. v.p. for acad. affairs Miami U., 1970-82; pres. Transylvania U., 1982-83; spl. cons. Assn. Governing Bds., 1983-84; chancellor U. N.C., Asheville, 1984-90; provost Wake Forest U., Winston-Salem, NC, 1990—98, v.p., dean Internat. Ctr. for Computer Enhanced Learning, 1998—2003, provost emeritus, 2004—; interim pres. Ga. Coll. and State U., 2003; coord., Inter-Instl. Collaborative Atlantic Coast Conf., 2002—. Chair Asheville's Econ. Devel. Summit, 1986, Nat. Small Pub. Ivys Conf., 1988, Asheville Hills Cabinet, 2006-; coord. Interinstl. Academic Collaborative, Atlantic Coast Conf. Univs., 2001—; interim exec. dir. Asheville-Alliance-HUB, 2007—; leader numerous workshops. Author: The Market for College Teachers, 1965, The Mobile Professors, 1967, Leadership Vitality, 1979, Leadership Roles of Chief Academic Officers, 1984, (monograph) Economic Development: 1987 and Beyond, 1986, Electronically Enhanced Education, 1999, Always in Touch, 1999, Interactive Learning, 2000, Teaching with Technology, 2000, Ubiquitous Computing, 2003, Developing Faculty to Use Technology, 2003, Univ Presidents As Moral Leaders, 2006; contbr. articles and papers to profl. bulls. and jours., also book chpts. Recipient Big A award Asheville Area C. of C., 1990; named one of 100 Young Leaders of the Acad., Change Mag., 1978; rsch. grantee Carnegie, 1979, U.S. Dept. Edn., 1965, NSF, 1965. Mem. Nat. Assn. State Univs. and Land Grant Colls. (chair coun. on acad. affairs 1975-76), Nat. Coun. Chief Acad. Officers (chair ACE 1978-80), Nat. Am. Assn. for Higher Edn. (chair 1981-82), Nat. Higher Edn. Colloquium (chair 1984-86), Phi Beta Kappa, Omicron Delta Kappa. Office: Wake Forest Univ 439 Vanderbilt Rd Asheville NC 28803 Office Phone: 828-274-0828. Business E-mail: brown@wfu.edu.

BROWN, DAVID M., surgeon, researcher; b. Amarillo, Tex., May 19, 1963; s. Lee Wayne and Norma Gaile Brown; m. Julie Jean Laflen, Nov. 30, 1985; children: Christopher David, Ashley Elizabeth, Christopher David, Ashley Elizabeth, Madeline Margaret, Caroline Mackenzie. MD, Baylor Coll., Houston, 1987. Retina attending surgeon Meth. Hosp., Houston, 1995—; dir. clin. rsch. Greater Houston Retina Rsch., 2000—. Internal adv. bd. Meth. Rsch. Inst., Houston, 2005—. Recipient Honor award, Am. Acad. Ophthalmology, 2000; Ron Michels fellowship, Ron Michels Soc., 1993, Heed- Knapp fellowship, Soc. Heed Fellows, 1993. Fellow: ACS; mem.: Iowa Eye Assn. (pres. 2002—03, Wolfe Lectr. award 2007), Harris County Ophthalmology Soc. (pres. 2000—01), Retina Soc. R-Conservative. Achievements include research in the first age related macular degeneration treatment demonstrating improvement in vision in a phase III FDA trial. Avocations: mountaineering, ranching. Office: Vitreoretinal Cons 6560 Fannin Ste 750 Houston TX 77030 Office Fax: 713-524-3220; Home Fax: 713-524-3220. Business E-mail: dmbmd@houstonretina.com.

BROWN, DAVID NELSON, lawyer; b. Harrodsburg, Ky, May 29, 1940; s. Irmel Nelson and Pauline (Harmon) Brown; m. Lois Aileen Everett, June 20, 1964; 1 child, Ian Richard. AB, Cornell U., 1963; JD, U. Chgo., 1966.

Bar: DC 1967. Assoc. Covington & Burling, Washington, 1966—74, ptnr., 1974—, mgmt. com., 1989—93. Comment editor: U. Chgo. Law Rev. Mem.: ABA, Cosmos Club, Order of Coif. Episcopalian. Office: Covington & Burling 1201 Pennsylvania Ave NW Washington DC 20004-2401 Office Phone: 202-662-5238.

BROWN, DAVID RANDOLPH, electrical engineer; b. LA, Oct. 31, 1923; s. Gilbert and Blanche Mabel (Phillips) B.; m. Sally England, Dec. 17, 1944; children: Philip, Ellen, Polly, Ann. BSEE, U. Wash., 1944; SMEE, MIT, 1947. Group leader MIT Lincoln Lab., Lexington, Mass., 1951-58; assoc. tech. dir. MITRE Corp., Bedford, Mass., 1958-63; lab. dir. SRI Internat., Menlo Park, Calif., 1963-85, staff scientist, 1985-93. Fellow IEEE. Avocation: genealogy. Home: 1470 Sand Hill Rd Apt 309 Palo Alto CA 94304-2031 Personal E-mail: drbrown@alum.mit.edu.

BROWN, DAVID RICHARD, school system administrator, minister; b. Manhattan, Kans., Oct. 22, 1929; s. Marion Arthur and Dorothy (Bailey) B.; m. Jeanette Christine Phoenix, July 28, 1962; children: David M., Mark, Thomas. BA, U. So. Calif., 1951; MDiv, U. Chgo., 1955; postgrad., U. So. Calif., 1956-57. Ordained minister, Presbyn. Ch. Assoc. pastor Federated Community Ch., Flagstaff, Ariz., 1957-59; minister of edn. Lakeside Presbyn. Ch., San Francisco, 1959-62; pastor of edn. 1st Presbyn. Ch., Medford, Oreg., 1962-69, pastor Newark, Calif., 1969-75; founder, pastor Community Presbyn. Ch., Union City, Calif., 1975-89; founder, supt. Christian Heritage Acad., Fremont, Calif., 1984—2000; organizing pastor New Life Presbyn. Ch., Fremont, 1989—99; asst. prof. Chabot Coll., Hayward, Calif., 1975-80; pastor New Life Presbyn. Ch., Castro Valley, Calif., 1999—. Moderator Presbytery of No. Ariz., 1959, Presbytery of No. Calif., 2001—02; religion editor The Valley Citizen, Danville, Calif., 2000—06. Dir.: various Shakespearian theatrical prodns., 1982—84 (Thesbian award, 1984); author: Shakespeare for Everyone to Enjoy, 2007. Pres. Boys Christian League, L.A., 1953-54, Coconino Assn. for Mental Health, Flagstaff, 1958-59; chaplain Mozumdar YMCA Camp, Crestline, Calif., 1952-56; chmn. Tri-City Citizens Action Com., 1986-90. Recipient plaque, KC, 1989. Mem. Rotary (chpt. pres. 1988-89, Paul Harris fellow 1989). Avocations: skiing, stamps, choir, drama. E-mail: revdavidbrown@sbcglobal.net.

BROWN, DAVID RONALD, lawyer; b. Turtle Creek, Pa., Jan. 25, 1939; s. James R. and Mary A.; m. Debra W. Brown; children: Michelle, Adrienne, Aaron, Eden, Jeremy. Student, Brown U., 1956-57; BS, U. Pitts., 1960; JD, Duquesne U., 1967. Bar: Penn. 1968, U.S. Dist. Ct. (we. dist.) Penn. 1967, U.S. Ct. Appeals (3d cir.) 1972, U.S. Tax Ct. 1986. Rschr. phys. chemistry Mellon Inst., Pitts., 1960-66; real estate lawyer Redevel. Authority of Allegheny County, Pitts., 1966-69; ptnr. Litman, Litman, Harris & Brown, Pitts., 1969-2000, Sherrard, German & Kelly, Pitts., 2000—. Lectr. Robert Morris Coll., 1978-84. Councilman Borough of Turtle Creek, Penn., 1963-67. Mem. ABA (real property and probate sect., bus. law sect.), Pa. Bar Assn., Allegheny County Bar Assn. (com. legal svcs. 1973-74, constrn. law sect., real property sect., probate and trust law sect.). Home: 1 Trimont Ln Apt 660 D Pittsburgh PA 15211-1157 Office: Sherrard German & Kelly 28th Fl 2 PNC Plaza Pittsburgh PA 15222 Office Phone: 412-355-0200. Business E-Mail: dbrown@sgkpc.com.

BROWN, DAVID RUPERT, engineering executive; b. Chgo., Sept. 11, 1934; s. Hugh Stewart and Sara (Daniels) B.; m. Mary Heaton Nicolaus, Sept. 6, 1958; children: David R. Jr., Robert N., Sara D. BSME, Purdue U., 1956; MBA, U. Akron, 1968. V.p. engring. Diamond Power Specialty Co., Lancaster, Ohio, 1974-77, v.p. ops., 1977-80, pres., 1980-82; sr. v.p., group exec. Babcock & Wilcox, Lancaster, 1982-85, Barberton, Ohio, 1985-87, v.p., gen. mgr., 1987; with Worldwide Procurement Inc., Akron, Ohio, 1987-90; v.p. mktg. Stock Equipment Co., Chagrin Falls, Ohio, 1990-95. With U.S. Army, 1957-58. Mem. ASME, Pi Tau Sigma, Tau Beta Pi. Home: 1717 Brookwood Dr Akron OH 44313-5072 E-mail: DBrown2020@aol.com.

BROWN, DAVID T., manufacturing executive; m. Nancy Brown; 2 children. B in Econs., Purdue U., 1970. Salesman Procter & Gamble, Shearson Hammill, Eli Lilly; with Owens Corning, 1978—, v.p. roofing and asphalt divsn., pres. roofing and asphalt divsn., 1994—96, pres. bldg. materials sales and distrbn., 1996—97, v.p. then pres. insulating sys. bus., 1997—2001, COO, 2001—02, CEO, pres., 2002—. Office: 1 Owens Corning Pkwy Toledo OH 43659*

BROWN, DAVID WARFIELD, management educator, lawyer, academic administrator; b. Evanston, Ill., Aug. 16, 1937; s. Lloyd Warfield and Nancy (Coleman) B.; m. Alice Bean, Feb. 29, 1964; children: Peter Bean, Sarah Alice. BA, Princeton U., 1959; JD, Harvard U., 1963. Bar: N.Y. 1966. Assoc. Patterson, Belknap & Webb, NYC, 1966-69; chief-of-staff Congressman Edward I. Koch, Washington and NYC, 1969-74; v.p. Rand Inst., NYC, 1974-75; chmn. N.Y. State Commn. Investigation, NYC, 1975-78; dep. mayor City of N.Y.C., 1978-79; commr. Met. Transp. Authority, NYC, 1979-85; ptnr. Hawkins, Delafield & Wood, NYC, 1980; pres. Blackburn Coll., Carlinville, Ill., 1989-91; prof. profl. practice (mgmt.) Milano Grad. Sch. Mgmt. and Urban Policy, New Sch. U., NYC, 1996—2004; cons. Kettering Found. Lectr., adj. prof. pub. mgmt. Sch. Mgmt., Yale U., New Haven, 1979-89. Author: When Strangers Cooperate: Using Social Conventions to Govern Ourselves, 1995, Organization Smarts, 2002; co-editor: Higher Edn. Exch.; contbr. articles to profl. jours. Capt. USAR, 1963-65. English Speaking Union scholar, London, 1959-60. Mem. Assn. of Bar of City of N.Y., Kettering Found. (assoc., vis. scholar 1991-92). Home and Office: PO Box 1266 Taos NM 87571-9998

BROWN, DAVID WILLIAM, economist, educator, consultant; b. Meriden, Conn., Nov. 10, 1931; s. William Horace and Elsie Miriam (Lovett) B.; m. Jean Margaret Young, Dec. 27, 1956; children: Cheryl Maurine, Kevin William. BS with distinction and honors, U. Conn., 1953; MS, Cornell U., 1954; PhD, Iowa State U., 1956. Asst., assoc. prof. U. Tenn., Knoxville, 1956-58, internat. prof., 1968-82; vis. prof. U. Malaya, Singapore, 1958-60; extension economist, asst. to dean Texas A&M U., College Station, 1961-63; team leader, tech. adv. Iowa Iowa-USAID program, Puno and Lima, Peru, 1963-66; vis. prof. Iowa State U., Ames, 1967-68; chief situation, outlook svc. UN Food and Agriculture Orgn., Rome, 1982-87; sr. economist food crops project, Acad. Ednl. Devel. USAID, Jakarta, Indonesia, 1988-90; social scis. specialist, adj. prof. U. Ill.-USAID project, Peshawar, Pakistan, 1990-94. Adj. prof. econs., tech. and humanities Salve Regina U., 1999-01; vol. career counselor Peace Corps, 1967-82; vol. economist RI Ctr. Comml. Agr., 1995-03, RI Conservation Dists., 1995—, RI Dept. Transp. Watch, 1995-05, mem. exec. bd. 2002-05; mem. Naval Installation Restoration Adv. Bd., Newport, 1996—. Mem., programmer, spkr. Coun. Internat. Visitors, Newport, RI, 1994-2006; planning bd. City of Newport, 1996-2000; mem. Aquidneck Island Planning Commn., 1996-2000; active RI Tree Coun., 1996—, Newport Tree Commn., 2002—, chmn., 2003-06; active EPA/TAG Aquidneck Island Citizen's Adv. Bd., 1996-03, Aquidneck Island Affordable Housing Planning Group, 2003-05; active Newport Scenic Roadways Com., 2005-; founding mem. RI People's Energy Coun., 2002—. Avocations: socio-economic history, folk music, urban forestry. Home: 421 Bellevue Ave Apt 4C Newport RI 02840-6944 Personal E-mail: djbrown2d@yahoo.com.

BROWN, DEANNA G., marketing executive; b. 1964; BA in Journalism, U. So. Calif., 1986. With Condé Nast; co-founder, acting CEO Powerful Media Inc.; v.p., gen. mgr. life mgmt. div. AOL; pub., CEO Breathe Media; gen. mgr. lifestyles bus. unit Yahoo Media Group, 2005; pres. interactive Scripps Networks, 2007—. Named a Woman to Watch, Advt. Age, 2007. Avocation: yoga. Office: Scripps Networks PO Box 51850 Knoxville TN 37950*

BROWN, DEL M. MAUHRINE, lawyer, educator; b. Ft. Meade, Md., May 26, 1965; BA, U. Md., College Park, 1987, JD, 1991. Bar: Va. 1993, U.S. Dist. Ct. (ea. dist.) Va. 1994, U.S. Ct. Appeals (4th cir.) 1994. Tchg. asst. Sch. Law U. Md., Balt., 1990, instr., 1991, assoc. dir. devel., mem. faculty College Park, 1991-92; Asper fellow, law clk. Md. Ct. Spl. Appeals, Balt., 1991; pvt. practice Virginia Beach, Va., 1993—; asst. prof., dir. recruitment Norfolk (Va.) State U., 1993-98; assoc. Poindexter and Brown, 1995-98; asst. pub. defender Office Pub. Defender Portsmouth, Va., 1998—2000. Vis. prof. U. Minn., Mpls., 1994. Editor: report N.J. Gov.'s Commn., 1991. Bd. dirs. Md. Women's Polit. Caucus, College Park, 1989—91; candidate Va. Ho. Dels., 1995, 1997. Mem.: ABA (mem. planning bd. young lawyers divsn. 1993—94), Va. Bar Assn. (6th cir. rep. young lawyers divsn.), Va. Trial Lawyers Assn., Hopewell Bar Assn., Golden Key, Delta Sigma Theta, Omicron Delta Kappa. Avocations: tennis, rollerblading. Office: PO Box 1506 Prince George VA 23876 Office Phone: 804-919-1777.

BROWN, DENISE MARIE, elementary school educator; b. Portsmouth, Va., Nov. 3, 1971; d. Dennis Mahlon Eberhart and Patsy Arlene Felty; m. Steven Russell Brown, Jan. 24, 2004. BA in Liberal Arts, Calif. Luth. U., Thousand Oaks, 1994. Cert. tchr. Calif., 1995. Libr. Pearson Libr., Thousand Oaks, Calif., 1990—96; tchr. elem. sch. Conejo Valley Unified Sch. Dist., Thousand Oaks, 1996—. Sound technician (plays) Cmty. Theatre Group. Small group leader Lighthouse Christian Fellowship, Newbury Park, Calif., costumer.

BROWN, DENISE SCOTT, architect, urban planner; b. Nkana, Zambia, Oct. 3, 1931; arrived in U.S., 1958, naturalized, 1971; d. Simon and Phyllis (Hepker) Lakofski; m. Robert Scott Brown, July 21, 1955 (dec. 1959); m. Robert Charles Venturi, July 23, 1967; 1 child, James C. Student, U. Witwatersrand, South Africa, 1948—51; diploma, Archtl. Assn., London, 1955; M of City Planning, U. Pa., 1960, MArch, 1965; DFA (hon.), Oberlin Coll., 1977, Phila. Coll. Art, 1985, Parsons Sch. Design, 1985; LHD (hon.), N.J. Inst. Tech., 1984, Phila. Coll. Textiles and Sci., 1992; DEng (hon.), Tech. U. N.S., 1991; HHD (hon.), Pratt Inst., 1992; DFA (hon.), U. Pa., 1994; LittD (hon.), U. Nev., 1998; D. Arch. (hon.), U. Miami, 1997; DFA (hon.), Lehigh U., 2002. Registered architect, U.K. Asst. prof. U. Pa., Phila., 1960—65; assoc. prof., head urban design program UCLA, 1965—68; with Venturi, Rauch and Scott Brown, Phila., 1967—, ptnr., 1969—89; prin. Venturi, Scott Brown and Assocs. Inc., Phila., 1989—. Asst. prof. U. Pa., 1960—65, vis. prof. Sch. Fine Arts, 1982, 83, mem. bd. overseers U. Librs., 1995—2004; vis. prof. arch. U. Calif., Berkeley, 1965, Yale U., 1967—70; mem. visitors com. MIT, 1973—83; mem. adv. com. dept. arch. Temple U., 1980—2001; Eliot Noyes design critic in arch. Harvard U., Cambridge, Mass., 1989—90, mem. jury Prince of Wales Prize in Urban Design, Grad. Sch. Design, 1993, mem. com. to rev. policies and practices Grad. Sch. Design, 2006, William E. Massey Sr. lectr history Am. civilization, 03; cons. to dean search com. Sch. Arch. Washington U., St. Louis, 1992; mem. adv. bd. dept. arch. Carnegie Mellon U., 1992—; master builder lectr. Carpenters' Co., 2005; Kassler lectr., Whitney J. Oates fellow in Humanities Coun. and Sch. Arch. Princeton U., NJ, 2006. Author: Urban Concepts, 1990; co-author: Learning from Las Vegas, 1972, (rev. edit.), 1977, A View from the Campidoglio: Selected Essays, 1953-84, 1985, Architecture as Signs and Systems for a Mannerist Time, 2004; contbr. numerous articles to profl. jours.; prin. works include campus plans U. Mich., Dartmouth Coll., Tsinghua U., Beijing, prin. works include city plans Miami Beach, Memphis, prin. works include plans U. Pa. Perelman Quadrangle, U. Mich., Palmer Dr. Life Sci. Complex Inst., Baker/Berry Libr. & Carson Hall, Dartmouth Coll., Nat. Gallery, London, Hotel du Dept. de la Haute Garonne, Toulouse, France. Policy panelist design arts program NEA, 1981—83; mem. bd. adv. Architects, Designers and Planners for Social Responsibility, 1982—; mem. capitol preservation com. Commonwealth of Pa., Harrisburg, 1983—87; trustee Chestnut Hill Acad., Phila., 1985—89; hon. vice patron The Royal Soc. for the Encouragement of Arts, Manufacture and Commerce in the U.S., 2004; active Civic Alliance Planning and Design Workshop for Lower Manhattan, 2002, Penn's Landing Pub. Forums, 2003; US patron The Friends of Benjamin Franklin House, London, 1996—; mem. curriculum com. Phila. Jewish Children's Folkshul, 1980—86; bd. dirs. Ctrl. Phila. Devel. Corp., 1985—95, Urban Affairs Partnership, Phila., 1987—91. Decorated commendatore Order of Merit Italy, chevalier de l'Ordre des Arts et des Lettres France; co-recipient The Phila. award, 1993, Luminary award, 2005, The Founder's award, Hist. Soc. Pa., 2006; named to Germantown Hall of Fame, Germantown Hist. Soc., Pa., 2002; recipient Chgo. Architecture award, 1987, U.S. Presdl. award, Nat. Medal of Arts, 1992, Hall of Fame award, Interior Design mag., 1992, The Benjamin Franklin medal, Royal Soc. for Encouragement of Arts., Mfg. and Commerce, 1993, Topaz medal, Am. Coll. Schs. of Architecture/AIA, 1996, Giants of Design award, House Beautiful Mag., 2000, Joseph Pennell medal, Phila. Sketch Club, 2000, Vincent J. Scully Prize, Nat. Bldg. Mus., 2002, Edith Wharton Women of Achievement award for Urban Planning, 2002, Soc. for Environ. Graphic Design Fellow award, 2003, Visionary Woman award, Moore Coll. Art and Design, 2003, The Franklin Founder Bowl, The Franklin Celebration, 2005, Harvard Radcliffe Inst. medal, 2005, Carpenters Co. Master Builder award, 2005, Phila. Artistic Legacy award, Woodmere Art Mus., 2006, Vilcek prize, 2007, Athena award, Congress New Urbanism, 2007, Nat. Design Mind award, Cooper-Hewitt Nat. Design Mus., 2007. Fellow: Internat. Royal Inst. Brit. Archs.; mem.: Am. Philos. Soc., Germantown Historical Soc. of Phila., Germantown Jewish Centre (Germantown Hall of Fame 2002), Royal Soc. Encouragement of Arts, Mfg. and Commerce (hon. vice patron 2004), Soc. Archtl. Historians (bd. dirs. 1981—84), Soc. Coll. and Univ. Planning, Archtl. Assn. London, Am. Planning Assn., Archs. Designers and Planners for Social Responsibility, Am. Acad. Arts and Scis., Royal Inst. Brit. Archs., Athenaeum of Phila., Carpenters Co. of City and County of Phila. Democrat. Jewish. Office: Venturi Scott Brown & Assocs Inc 4236 Main St Philadelphia PA 19127-1696

BROWN, DONALD DAVID, biology professor; b. Cin., Dec. 30, 1931; s. Albert Louis and Louise (Rauh) B.; m. Linda Jane Weil, July 2, 1957; children: Deborah Lin, Christopher Charles, Sharon Elizabeth. MS, MD, U. Chgo., 1956, D.Sc. (hon.), 1976, U. Md., 1983; DSc (hon.), U. Cin., 1992. Staff mem. dept. embryology Carnegie Instn. of Washington, Balt., 1963—, dir., 1976-94; prof. dept. biology Johns Hopkins U., 1968—. Pres. Life Scis. Research Found. Served with USPHS, 1957-59. Recipient U.S. Steel Found. award for molecular biology, 1973, V.D. Mattia award Roche Inst., 1975, Boris Pregel award for biology N.Y. Acad. Scis., 1976, Ross G. Harrison award Internat. Soc. Developmental Biology, 1981, Bertner Found. award, 1982, Rosenstiel award for biomed. sci., 1985, Louisa Gross Horwitz award, 1985, Feodor Lynen award U. Miami Winter Symposium, 1987. Fellow Am. Acad. Arts and Scis., AAAS; mem. Nat. Acad. Scis. (mem. coun. 1994-97), Soc. Devel. Biology (pres. 1975), Am. Soc. Biol. Chemists, Am. Soc. Cell Biology (pres. 1992, E.B. Wilson award 1996), Am. Philos. Soc. Home: 5721 Oakshire Rd Baltimore MD 21209-4217 Office: Carnegie Instn Washington 3250 San Martin Dr Baltimore MD 21218 E-mail: brown@ciwemb.edu.

BROWN, DONALD DOUGLAS, transportation executive, consultant, retired military officer; b. Montreal, Que., Can., Aug. 1, 1931; came to U.S., 1938; s. Donald Bannerman and Hilda Taylor (Noel) B.; m. Joan Teresa McAndrews, Aug. 7, 1954; children— Cathy J. Brown Peinhardt, James D., Nancy J. Brown May. BA, Columbia U., 1954; MBA, Syracuse U., 1965. Commd. officer U.S. Air Force, 1955, advanced through grades to maj. gen., 1979, ret., 1987, wing chief aircrew standardization Phan Rang Air Base, Vietnam, 1968-69, chief Weapon System Support div. in Directorate of Supply, then dir. logistics plans Scott AFB, Ill., 1973-75, asst. dep. chief of staff for logistics, 1975-76, from vice comdr. to comdr. McChord AFB, Wash., 1976-77, asst. dep. chief of staff for ops. Mil. Airlift Command Scott AFB, Ill., 1979-80, dep. chief of staff for plans, 1980-83, dep. chief of staff for ops. Mil. Airlift Command, 1983-84, comdr. 22d Air Force, Mil. Airlift Command Travis AFB, Calif., 1984-87, ret., 1987; chmn. bd. Evergreen Air Ctr. Inc. Cons. in aviation/logistics mgmt. Mem. bd. Tacoma Symphony Orch. Decorated Disting. Service medal with oak leaf cluster, Legion of Merit with oak leaf cluster, D.F.C. with oak leaf cluster, Bronze Star, Air medal with 4 oak leaf clusters, Republic of Vietnam Cross of Gallantry with palm Mem. Air Force Assn., Nat. Def. Transp. Assn. (appted. to bus. practices com.), Beta Gamma Sigma. Office Phone: 253-588-2149.

BROWN, DONALD JAMES, JR., lawyer; b. Chgo., Apr. 21, 1948; s. Donald James Sr. and Marian Constance (Scimeca) B.; m. Donna Bowen, Jan. 15, 1972; children: Megan, Maura. AB, John Carroll U., 1970; JD, Loyola U., Chgo., 1973. Bar: Ill. 1973, U.S. Dist. Ct. (no. dist.) Ill. 1973, U.S. Tax Ct. 1982. Asst. to state's atty. Cook County, Ill., 1973-75; assoc. Baker & McKenzie, Chgo., 1975-82, ptnr., 1982-95, Donohue, Brown, Mathewson & Smyth, Chgo., 1995—. Office: Donohue Brown et al 140 S Dearborn St Chicago IL 60603-5202 E-mail: donald.brown@dbmslaw.com.

BROWN, DONALD ROBERT, psychology professor; b. Albany, NY, Mar. 5, 1925; s. J. Edward and Natile (Rosenberg) B.; m. June Gole, Aug. 14, 1945; children: Peter Douglas, Thomas Matthew, Jacob Noah. AB, Harvard U., Cambridge, Mass., 1948; MA, PhD, U. Calif., Berkeley, 1951. Mem. faculty Bryn Mawr Coll., 1951-64, prof. psychology, 1963—. Sr. rsch. cons. Mellon Found., Vassar Coll., 1953-63; part-time vis. prof. Swarthmore Coll., U. Pa., also U. Calif.-Berkeley, 1953-61; fellow Ctr. Advanced Study Behavioral Scis., 1960-61; prof. psychology, sr. rsch. scientist, dir. Ctr. Rsch. Learning and Teaching, U. Mich., 1964—; cons. Peace Corps, 1965-71; hon. rsch. fellow Univ. Coll., London, 1970-71; Fulbright sr. rsch. fellow Max Planck Inst., Berlin, 1982; Netherlands Basic Sci. fellow, Leyden, 1983. Author: articles, chpts. in books; editor: Changing Role and Status of Soviet Women, 1967, Frontiers of Motivational Psychology, 1986; co-editor: Frontiers of Mathematical Psychology, 1990. Served with AUS, 1943-46, ETO. Fellow Am. Psychol. Assn., Chinese Acad. Sci.; mem. Soc. Psychol. Study of Social Issues, AAAS, AAUP, Sigma Xi, Psi Chi. Home: 2511 Hawthorne Rd Ann Arbor MI 48104-4031 Office Phone: 734-673-1097. Business E-Mail: donrobro@umich.edu.

BROWN, DONALD WESLEY, lawyer; b. Cleve., Jan. 2, 1953; s. Lloyd Elton Brown and Nancy Jeanne Hudson. AB summa cum laude, Ohio U., 1975; JD, Yale U., 1978. Bar: Calif. 1978, U.S. Dist. Ct. (no. dist.) Calif. 1978, U.S. Dist. Ct. (cen. dist.) Calif. 1990. Assoc. Brobeck, Phleger & Harrison, San Francisco, 1978-85, ptnr., 1985—2003, Covington & Burling, San Francisco, 2003—. Democrat. Home: 2419 Vallejo St San Francisco CA 94123-4638 Office: Covington & Burling One Front St San Francisco CA 94111 Home Phone: 415-776-8841; Office Phone: 415-591-7063. Business E-Mail: dwbrown@cov.com.

BROWN, DORIS JANE, medical technician; b. Mo., Dec. 6, 1934; d. Lowell Emmitt and Lottie Nancy (Downing) Heinrich; m. Thomas B. Brown, Aug. 12, 1958 (div. 1967); 1 child, Doris Ann. AA, Penn Valley Met. C.C., 1982. Cert. med. tech. Mo.; accredited nurse aide, Mo. Clk. Western Auto, Kansas City, Mo., 1952-55; acctg. sec. Allied Signal, Kansas City, 1955-58; various positions K.C. Paper Box Co., Kansas City, 1958-61, Winn-Senter Constrn. Co., Kansas City, 1961-90, exec. sec., 1990-92; adminstrv. asst. Miller & Assocs., Lee's Summit, Mo., 1992-93; nurse aide Nat. Health Care, West Plains, Mo., 1994-2001, Beverly Health Care, West Plains, 2001—03, Beautiful Savior Home, Belton, Mo., 2003, Jefferson Health Care, 2003—04, medications technician Lee's Summit, Mo., 2003—. Contbr. articles. Vol. Vista, Kansas City, Mo., 1961. Mem. nat. health care coms. Avocations: volunteer facilitator project literacy, sports. Home: 725 NE Tudor Rd #3 Lees Summit MO 64086-5789 Office: 615 SW Oldham Pkwy Lees Summit MO 64081 Office Phone: 816-524-3328.

BROWN, DUDLEY EARL, JR., psychiatrist, educator, health science association administrator, federal agency administrator, retired military officer; b. Berryville, Va., Apr. 10, 1928; s. Dudley Earl and Rosa Lee (Costello) B.; m. Lelia Adrienne Motley, June 22, 1953; children: Lelia Brown Farr, David, Kevin. BA, Washington and Lee U., 1949; MD, Med. Coll. Va., 1953. Diplomate Am. Bd. Psychiatry and Neurology. Commd. lt. (j.g.) M.C. USN, 1953, advanced through grades to rear adm., 1974; intern Naval Hosp., Portsmouth, Va., 1953-54, resident in neuropsychiatry Bethesda, Md., 1957-60; svc. in Vietnam; commdg. officer Nat. Naval Med. Ctr., Bethesda, 1975-76, Naval Regional Med. Ctr., San Diego, 1976-78; fleet surgeon U.S. Pacific Fleet and staff surgeon, comdr.-in-chief U.S. Forces, Pacific, Pearl Harbor, Hawaii, 1978-80; ret., 1980; dep. asst. chief med. dir. for profl. svcs. VA Ctrl. Office, Washington, 1980-82; assoc. dep. chief med. dir. VA, Washington, 1982-87; asst. prof. clin. psychiatry U. Pa. Med. Sch., 1967-70; prof. clin. psychiatry Uniformed Svcs. U. Health Scis., Bethesda, 1981—, Med. Coll. Va., Commonwealth U., Richmond, 1987—2004; dir. health policy studies, dir. Washington office Abt Assocs. Inc., 1987-93, v.p., 1992—, mng. v.p., 1993—2001. Sci. adv. bd. Ctr. Prisoner of War Studies, 1998-2003. Contbr. to med. jours. Decorated Legion of Merit; recipient Meritorious Svc. medal, Navy Commendation medal, VA Disting. Svc. medal, Disting. Alumnus Med. Coll. Va., 1993. Fellow ACP, Am. Psychiat. Assn., Am. Coll. Psychiatrists; mem. Washington Psychiat. Soc., Nat. Health Coun. (bd. dirs. 1989-94), Assn. Mil. Surgeons U.S., Soc. Med. Cons. to Armed Forces (v.p. 1988-89, pres. 1989-90), Phi Gamma Delta, Alpha Epsilon Delta. Presbyterian. Home: 2415 Black Cap Ln Reston VA 20191-3027 Office: Abt Assocs Inc 4800 Montgomery Ln Ste 600 Bethesda MD 20814-3460 Office Phone: 703-264-1953. Personal E-mail: dearlbown@aol.com.

BROWN, EARL KENT, historian, minister; b. Kent, Ohio, July 26, 1925; s. Earl Royal and Bernice Blanche (Howard) B. BA, Columbia U., 1948; S.T.B., Boston U., 1953, PhD (Howard fellow 1953-54, United Methodist Ch. Dempster fellow 1954-55), 1956. Ordained to ministry United Meth. Ch., 1957. Asst. prof. history Baldwin Wallace Coll., 1956-63, asso. prof., 1963; asso. prof. church history Boston U., 1963-70, prof., 1970-86, prof. emeritus, 1986—. Vis. prof. Case Western Res. U., 1961, Union Theol. Sem., Manila, 1970, United Theol. Coll., Bangalore, India, 1978, U. Manchester, Eng., 1979. Author: Women of Mr. Wesley's Methodism, 1983; Contbr. articles to acad. jours., religious periodicals. Fulbright fellow, 1962 Mem. Phi Beta Kappa. Home: Merrill Gardens #354 2261 Tuolumne Street Vallejo CA 94589 Office Phone: 707-643-6474.

BROWN, EDDIE C., investment company executive; married; 2 children. BSEE, Howard U., 1961; MSEE, NYU, 1968; MBA, Ind. U., 1970. Chartered fin. analyst; chartered investment counselor, Md. Engr. Titan missile project Martin Marietta Co., 1961; design engr. systems devel. div. (spl. cirs.) IBM Corp., 1963-68; mgr. investment systems, asst. to pres. Irwin Mgmt. Co., 1970-73; v.p., portfolio mgr. T. Rowe Price Assocs., 1973-83; v.p., mem. investment adv. com. T. Rowe Price Tax-Free Income Fund, 1973-83; pres. Brown Capital Mgmt. Inc., Balt., 1983—. Panelist Wall Street Week with Louis Rukeyser; bd. mem. Mercantile Bankshares Corp., Municipal Mortgage Equity. Bd. dirs. Community Found. of Greater

Balt. Area; mem. Greater Balt. Com.'s Pub. Policy Coun., Ind. U. Sch. of Bus. Dean's Adv. Coun., Pres.'s Round Table. 1st lt. Signal Corps U.S. Army, 1961-63. Consortium for Grad. Study in Mgmt. fellow; IBM study program resident. Mem. Md. Acad. Scis., C. of C. of U.S. (small bus. coun.), Inst. Chartered Fin. Analysts (chartered), Fin. Analysts Fedn., Balt. Soc. Security Analysts, Beta Gamma Sigma, Sigma Iota Epsilon. Office: Brown Capital Management 1201 North Calvert St Baltimore MD 21202

BROWN, EDEN ROSE, lawyer; 1 child, Natalie. BA, U. Calif., Berkeley; JD, Northwestern Sch. Law. Bar: Oreg., Hawaii, US Ct. Mil. Rev., US Ct. Mil. Appeals, US Dist. Ct. (we. dist. Wash.), US Supreme Ct. Spl. asst. US atty., 1989—93; prin. Law Office of Eden Rose Brown, Salem, Oreg. Appt. to JAG Air Nat. Guard Coun., 1999; lectr. in field. Co-author, editor: Giving - Philanthropy For Everyone, 2003; contbr. articles to profl. pubs. Translator various humanitarian missions; bd. dirs. Oreg. Jewish Cmty. Found., Marion-Polk County Med. Found., Cedar Sinai Pk., Portland, Oreg., Willamette Humane Soc., Salem's Riverfront Carousel. JAG USAF, 1989—93, state judge adv. Oreg. Air Nat. Guard, 1993—2001, lt. col. JAG USAFR. Named an Oreg. Super Lawyer, 2006; named one of Top 100 US Attys., Worth Mag., 2006; recipient Meritorious Svc. medal, Pres. George H.W. Bush. Mem.: Air Nat. Guard Assn. US, Mid-Valley Tax Coun., Willamette Valley Estate Planning Coun., Wealth Counsel (founding mem., mem. Nat. Study Group), Nat. Acad. Elder Law Attys., Nat. Network Estate Planning Attys. (charter mem.), Judge Adv. Assn., ABA (probate and trusts sect.), Hawaii Bar Assn., Oreg. Bar Assn. (probate and trusts sect.). Avocations: flying, kayaking, skiing, scuba diving, travel. Office: 1011 Liberty St S Salem OR 97302 Office Phone: 503-581-1800. Office Fax: 503-581-1818. Business E-Mail: eden@edenrosebrown.com.

BROWN, EDGAR HENRY, JR., mathematician, educator; b. Chgo., Dec. 27, 1926; s. Edgar Henry and Viola (Offen) B.; m. Gail Hamilton, June 13, 1954; children: Jessica, Nicholas. BS, U. Wis., 1949; MS, Wash. State U., 1951; PhD, MIT, 1954. Instr. Washington U., St. Louis, 1954-55, U. Chgo., 1955-57; Office Naval Res. fellow Brown U., 1957-58; from mem. faculty to prof. Brandeis U., Waltham, Mass., 1958—63, prof. math., 1963—, chmn. Dept. Math., 1960—62, 1978—80. Instr. math. Inst. Advanced Study, 1962—63, Math. Inst., Oxford, England, 1965—66, vis. prof., 1994; instr. math. U. Coll., London, 1973—74; vis. prof. Princeton U., 1971; vis. prof. New Coll. Oxford and Kings Coll. Cambridge (England) U., 1982—83; sr. rsch. fellow Jesus Coll., Oxford, 1986—87; vis. prof. Yale U., 1993. Served with USNR, 1944-46. Fellow, NSF, 1962—63, Guggenheim Found., 1965—66, Brit. SRC Rsch. Coun., 1973—74, 1982—83. Mem. Am. Math. Soc., Am. Acad. Arts and Sci. Home: 32 Fisher Ave Newton MA 02461-1117 Office: Brandeis U MS 050 Waltham MA 02454 Business E-Mail: brown@brandeis.edu.

BROWN, EDWARD J, III, bank executive; B in Indsl. Mgmt., Ga. Inst. Tech.; M in Fin., Harvard U., 1972. Credit analyst and various positions NationsBank, 1972—79, sr. v.p., dir. So. dept., 1979—80, sr. v.p. specialized industries divsn., 1980—82, Tampa Bay area exec., 1982—84, Tampa Bay region exec., 1984—85, mid. market group exec., 1985—88, pres. corp. banking, 1988, pres. global fin., 1997; pre. global capital raising and global capital markets Bank Am. Corp. (formerly NationsBank), 1998—2000; pres. global corp. and investment banking Bank Am. Corp., 2000—. Bd. dirs. Inst. Internat. Fin., Carolinas Health Care Sys., PGA TOUR Golf Course Properties. Commr. San Francisco Asian Art Mus. Office: Bank Am Corp 100 N Tryon St Charlotte NC 28255

BROWN, EDWARD JAMES, SR., utilities executive; b. Ft. Wayne, Ind., Sept. 30, 1937; s. William Theodore and Jane Elizabeth (Dix) Brown; m. Margaret Bessey, June 17, 1989; children: Edward James Jr., Elena Emily. BA, Yale U., New Haven, 1959; MA, Fordham U., NYC, 1962. CFA. Fin. writer E.F. Hutton & Co., NYC, 1970-71; economist N.Y. Power Authority, NYC, 1971-74, prin. economist, 1974-80, mgr., customer svcs., 1980-83, mgr. spl. projects, 1983-86, dir. strategic planning, 1986-93, dir. new bus., 1993-94. Mem. mgmt. com. Iroquois Gas Transmission Sys., 1989—94. Pres. Park Ave. Meth. Trust, NYC, 1981—; dir. Friends of Shakers, Inc., Sabathday Lake, Maine, 1980—95, pres., 1982—84, treas., 1995—2005; trustee United Soc. Shakers, Sabathday Lake, 1982—84, 1995—, John St. Meth. Episcopal Trust Soc., NYC, 1982—; bd. dirs. Meth. Ch. Home for Aged, Riverdale, NY, 1995—2001, 2003—, mem. investment com., 1983—, co-chmn., 1994—2003, treas., 1996—2001, pres., 2003—, Meth. Ch. Home Fund, 1996—99; bd. dirs., treas. John Wesley Towers, 1999—; bd. dirs. Yorkville Emergency Alliance, NYC, 1982—88; mem. internat. adv. coun. Mus. Am. Folk Art, NYC, 1988—2001; dir., chmn. investment com. United Meth. City Soc., NYC, 1999—, chartered fin. analyst. Mem.: Assn. Investment Mgmt. and Rsch., N.Y. Soc. Security Analysts. Home: 500 E 85th St New York NY 10028-7407

BROWN, EDWIN WILSON, JR., preventive medicine physician, educator; b. Youngstown, Ohio, Mar. 6, 1926; s. Edwin Wilson and Doris (McClellan) B.; m. Patricia Ann Currier, Aug. 9, 1952; children: Edwin Wilson, John Currier, Wende Patricia. Student, Carnegie Inst. Tech., 1943, Amherst Coll., 1943—44, Houghton Coll., 1946—47; MD, Harvard U., 1953, MPH (Nat. Found. fellow), 1957. Rsch. fellow U. Buffalo, 1953-54; intern E.J. Meyer Meml. Hosp., Buffalo, 1954-55; resident pub. health Va. Dept. Health, 1955-56; tchr. medicine specializing in preventive medicine Boston, 1958-61, Hyderabad, India, 1961-63; assoc. med. dir. People-to-People Health Found., Washington, 1965-66; assoc. prof. medicine Ind. U.-Purdue U., Indpls., 1966-85, dir. divsn. internat. affairs, 1966-74, assoc. dean student svcs., dir. internat. svcs., 1979-85; pres. Internat. Med. Assistance, Inc., Indpls., 1986—. Med. dir. Ind. Dept. Correction, 1974-76; sr. med. edn. advisor King Faisal U., Dammam, Saudi Arabia, 1977-78; field dir. Harvard Epidemiol. Project, Egedesminde, Greenland, 1956-57; asst. prof. preventive medicine Sch. Medicine Tufts U., 1958-61; dep. chief staff Boston Dispensary, 1961; vis. prof. preventive medicine Osmania Med. Coll., Hyderabad, India, 1961-63; asst. dir. divsn. internat. med. edn., dir. AAMC-AID project internat. med. edn. Assn. Am. Med. Colls., Evanston, 1963-65; exec. sec. Study Group on Childhood Accidents, Boston, 1959-61; rsch. assoc. Sch. Pub. Health, Harvard U., 1959-60; dir. Curtis Pub. Co., Inc.; cons. Boston City Health Dept., 1959-60, WHO, 1973-74; chmn. bd. dirs. Med. Assistance Programs, Inc. Contbr. articles to profl. jours. Bd. dirs. Paul Carlson Found., Campus Teams, Iran Found., CARE/MEDICO, Internat. Students Inc. Served with AUS, 1944-46, ETO. Recipient Pub. Svc. award Vets. Day Coun. Indpls., 1996, Patriarch of Antioch's award Knight Comdr. of Order of St. Mark, 1998. Fellow Am. Pub. Health Assn.; mem. Assn. Tchrs. Preventive Medicine, Indian Assn. Advancement Med. Edn., Mass. Med. Soc., Internat. Policy Forum (bd. govs.), Nat. Policy Coun., Rotary Internat., Sigma Xi. Home and Office: 8153 Oakland Rd Indianapolis IN 46240-2747 Home Phone: 317-257-7454; Office Phone: 317-257-7455. Personal E-mail: Ed@TheBrowns.com, ewhindy@aol.com.

BROWN, ELIZABETH ELEANOR, retired librarian; b. Charlotte, Mich., Aug. 29, 1921; d. Delbert Francis and Katherine Eleanor (Griffith) Brown. AB, Albion Coll., 1943; MLS, Pratt Inst., 1953. Info. specialist Enjay Co., NYC, 1943-50; reports indexer Bakelite Co., Bound Brook, NJ, 1950-52; reference libr. IBM, Poughkeepsie, NY, 1953—63, Yorktown Heights, NY, 1963—69, info. retrieval specialist, libr. White Plains, NY, 1969-82, ret., 1982. Vol. Nat. Archives Rocky Mountain Region, 1986—; mem. del. spl. librs. to Russia and Czech Republic Citizen Amb. program People to People Internat., 1995. Mem.: DAR, ALA, Spl. Librs. Assn. (sec.-treas. engring. divsn. 1968—70, chmn. tech. sci. group N.Y.C. chpt 1970—71, archivist 1970—72, founding mem. and past pres. Hudson Valley chpt.), Am. Chem. Soc., Remsen-Steuben Hist. Soc., Eaton County Geneal. Soc., Kalamazoo Valley Geneal. Soc., Wales, Ireland, Scotland and Eng. Family Hist. Soc., Internat. Soc. Brit. Genealogy and Family History, Gen. Soc. Mayflower Descs., Pilgrim John Howland Soc., New Eng. Hist. Geneal. Soc., Colo. Geneal. Soc., Colo. Mayflower Soc., Gwynedd Family History Soc., Columbine Geneal. and Hist. Soc., Welsh-Am. Geneal. Soc., Colo. Welsh Soc., Grand Traverse Area Geneal. Soc., Rowe Hist. Soc., Mortar Bd., Alpha Lambda Delta, Phi Beta Kappa, Delta Zeta. Personal E-mail: browneeb21@aol.com.

BROWN, ELIZABETH MCCARTHY, social services administrator; b. Omaha, Oct. 3, 1941; d. James John and Mary Theresa McCarthy; m. V.K. Brown, Aug. 3, 1974; children: V.K. III, Steven. BA, Ohio State U., 1963; MASW, U. Chgo., 1968. Cert. social worker Acad. Cert. Social Workers; lic. clin. social worker, Ill. Acting intake supr. Franklin County Welfare Dept., Columbus, Ohio; social worker Hull House Assn., Chgo.; unit dir. homebound programs Abraham Lincoln Centre, Chgo., dir. social work svc. dept.; exec. dir. coun. of internat. programs Loyola Univ. Chgo., 2004—05, pres. coun. internat. programs, 1989—91, 2005—06. Dir. program ops. Little Bros.-Friends of the Elderly; dir. social work svcs. Abraham Lincoln Ctr., 2001, cons. Recipient Svc. award Chgo. Osteo. Hosp. Pediatric and Adolescent Comprehensive Care and Prevention Program, Svc. award Coun. Internat. Programs, Loyola U., Chgo., 1987; named for Outstanding Field Work Supr., Valparaiso U., 1975-76. Fellow Am. Orthopsychiat. Assn.; mem. NASW. Home: Apt 2516N 4800 S Chicago Beach Dr Chicago IL 60615-2170 Office Phone: 773-415-2888. Business E-Mail: ag9803@ameritech.net.

BROWN, ELLYN L., lawyer, consultant; b. Detroit, Mar. 20, 1950; AB with honors, Vasser Coll., 1972; MS, John Hopkins U., 1975; JD, U. Md., 1980. Securities commr. State of Md., 1987—92; atty. in residence U. Md. Sch. Law, 1993—95; pres. Brown & Assocs., Balt., 1995—; visiting prof. Villanova U. Sch. Law, 2003—05. Dir., officer N. Am. Securities Administrators Assn., 1988—92; bd. mem. Nat. Assn. Securities Dealers Regulation, Inc., 1995—98; mem. Editorial Bd. Villanova Jour. Law and Investment Mgmt., 1998—; mem. CFP Bd. Standards, 2000—04; bd. dirs. NY Stock Exch., NYC, 2005—06, NYSE Group, Inc., 2006—. Mem. Balt. Symphony Orch., Planned Parenthood Md., U. Md. Law Sch. Alumni Assn. Mem.: ABA, Md. State Bar Assn. Office: Brown and Assocs 11055 Greenspring Ave Annex A Lutherville Timonium MD 21093 also: NYSE Group Inc c/o Corp Sec 11 Wall St New York NY 10005

BROWN, ERIC JOEL, biomedical researcher; b. Ann Arbor, Mich., Sept. 27, 1950; s. Bernard and Shirley (Mark) B.; m. Marion Glynn Peters, Apr. 2, 1983; 1 child, Abigail. AB, Harvard Coll., 1971; MD, Harvard Med. Sch., 1975. Intern, then resident Beth Israel Hosp., Boston, 1975-77; clin. assoc. LCI/NIAID/NIH, Bethesda, Md., 1977-79, expert, 1979-81, sr. investigator, 1981-85; assoc. prof. Washington U., St. Louis, 1985-90, co-dir. divsn. infectious diseases, 1989-99, prof., 1990-99; prof. medicine and immunology U. Calif., San Francisco, 1999—. With USPHS, 1981-85. Fellow Infectious Diseases Soc.; mem. Soc. for Clin. Investigation, Am. Assn. Physicians. Office: U Calif San Francisco PO Box 2140 San Francisco CA 94143-2140 E-mail: ebrown@medicine.ucsf.edu.

BROWN, ERNEST L., education educator; b. Pensacola, Fla., June 24, 1932; s. Annie B. (Brown) Pate. BS, Fla. A&M U., 1954, MEd, 1966; postgrad., U. Okla., 1970; PhD, Fla. State U., 1975. Cert. tchr. math. and sci., cert. vis. tchr., cert. in ednl. leadership, Fla. Tchr. math. and sci. Escambia County (Fla.) Sch. Bd., Pensacola, 1957-68, vis. tchr., 1968-70; prin. N.B. Cook Elem. Sch., Pensacola, 1970-74; grad. asst. Fla. State U., Tallahassee, 1973-74, interim prin. Developmental Rsch. Sch., 1974-75, prin., 1975-86; dir. Developmental Rsch. Sch. Fla. A&M U., Tallahassee, 1986-89, dir. student tchg., 1989-91, assoc. prof. of ednl. leadership, 1991—. Mem. adminstrv. coun., mem. adv. bd. Developmental Rsch. Sch. Fla. State U., 1974-86; mem. task force on lab. schs. Fla. State Dept. Edn., Tallahassee, 1980; mem. state adv. com. Fla. Statewide Com. on Program Assessment, Tallahassee, 1979-80; mem. rev. com. Fla. Ednl. Leadership Exam program U. South Fla., Tampa, 1993. Contbr. articles to edn. publs. NSF fellow Bklyn. Coll., 1959, Kellogg Found. fellow, 1965-66. Mem. Phi Delta Kappa, Kappa Alpha Psi (life, alumni), Sigma Pi Phi. Democrat. Baptist. Avocations: golf, sports, music, reading. Home and Office: 3049 Knotty Pine Dr Pensacola FL 32505-1853 Personal E-mail: ebro505@cox.net.

BROWN, EVA EVERLEAN, business executive; d. Robert Lee Creacy and Alzora Lee Bass; m. Royal Guy Brown, Apr. 14, 1963 (dec.); 1 child, Royal Guy Jr. BS, SUNY, Albany, 1979. Adminstrn. mgmt. IBM Corp., Albany, 1968—87; founder, pres. Get Smart, Inc., Sanford, NC, 1991—98, founder, COO, 1998—. Pres. NAACP, Sanford, 1989—93. Recipient IBM Master's award, IBM Corp., 1986, Vol. award, N.C. Govs. Office, 1991, Outstanding Citizen's award, Sanford Area C. of C., 1994, Razor Walker award, U. N.C., Wilmington, 1997, Image award, Lee County Chpt. NAACP, 1999, Sanford Rotary 4-Way Test award, Sanford Rotary Club, 1999, Lifetime Achievement award, The Sanford Herald, 2005. Mem.: Delta Kappa Gamma Theta (hon.; Delta Rho chpt.), Delta Sigma Theta. Democrat. Methodist. Avocations: writing, cooking, collecting cookbooks. Home: 2207 Spring Ln Sanford NC 27330 Office: Get Smart Inc 1309 Washington Ave Sanford NC 27330 Home Phone: 919-775-7405; Office Phone: 919-776-6119. Office Fax: 919-776-7905. Personal E-mail: eebrow@earthlink.net. Business E-Mail: getsmart@wave-net.net.

BROWN, FRANCES LOUISE (GRANDMA FRAN), artist, art gallery director; b. Indpls., Oct. 19, 1925; d. Harley and Lenore (Spencer) Netherland; m. C.G. Clarkson, July 24, 1943 (div. Aug. 1967); children: James E. Clarkson, John B. Clarkson, Deborah L. Cromis. Thomas L. Currey, June 9, 1972 (dec. May 1978); m. George L. Brown, Jr., Mar. 3, 1982; 1 stepchild, Nancy Snow. BS in Edn., Miami U., 1968; MA in Edn., Ball State U., 1970. Tchr. elem. sch. Liberty Elem. Sch., Ind., 1968—71; tchr. Ball State U., Muncie, Ind., 1971—72; instr. Colby C.C., Kans., 1972—75; gallery owner, primitive artist Grandma Fran Art Gallery (formerly Currey Studio Gallery), Berryville, Ark., 1975—. Author: Now Hear This, 1974; works exhibited at Nat. Mus. Am. Art, Washington, Wichita (Kans.) Art Assn. Gallery, Ark. Coll., Batesville, South Ark. Art Ctr., El Dorado, Harding Coll., Searcy, Ark., U. Ark., Fayetteville, Eureka Springs (Ark.) Hist. Mus., Western State Coll. Colo., Gunnison, MacMurray Coll., Jacksonville, Ill., Colby (Kans.) Coll., Claremore (Okla.) Coll., Warren Hall Coutts, III, Meml. Art Gallery, Inc., El Dorado, Kans., Masur Mus. Art, Monroe, La., Nebr. State Hist. Soc. Mus., Lincoln, Ind. State Mus., Indpls., Ozark Folk Ctr., Mountain View, Ark., Ft. Smith (Ark.) Art Ctr., Ctr. for So. Folklore, Memphis, Rogers (Ark.) Hist. Mus., Albrecht Art Mus., St. Joseph, Mo., Shiloh Mus., Springdale, Ark., Intenrat. Ctr. Contemporary Art, Paris, John Judkyn Meml. Mus., Eng., Mykonos (Greece) Folklore Mus., Musees Royaux des Beaux-Arts de Belgique, Brussels, Setagaya Art Mus., Tokyo, Fukuoka (Japan) Art Mus.; represented in permanent collections Smithsonian Instn., Washington, Mus. Am. Folk Art, N.Y.C., Nebr. State Hist. Soc. Mus., Lincoln, Ind. State Mus., Indpls., Ozark Mountain Folk Ctr., Mountain View, Ctr. for So. Folklore, Memphis, Setagaya Art Mus., others; paintings recognized in various books, newspapers and articles. Avocations: pilot, sewing, reading, fishing, cooking. Home and Office: Grandma Fran Art Gallery 3331 Highway 62 W Berryville AR 72616-8948 Office Phone: 870-423-2073. Business E-Mail: grandmafran@hbeark.com.

BROWN, FRANK, social sciences educator; b. Gallian, Ala., May 1, 1935; s. Tom and Ora L. (Lomax) B.; m. Joan Drake, July 6, 1963; children: Frank G., Monica J. BS, Ala. State U., 1957; MS, Oreg. State U., 1962; MA, U. Calif., Berkeley, 1969, PhD, 1970; grad. studies, Tenn. State U., U. Puget Sounds, San Francisco State U., Calif. State U., East Bay, SUNY, Buffalo. Chem., physics tchr. Oakland Pub. Schs. (Calif.), 1962-68; assoc. dir. N.Y. State Commn. on Higher Edn., NYC, 1970-72; dir. Urban Inst., prof. CCNY, 1971-72; prof., coll. master SUNY, Buffalo, 1972-77; dean U. N.C., Chapel Hill, 1983-90, Cary C. Boshamer prof. edn., dir. ednl. rsch. and policy project studies for rsch. in social sci., 1990—. Vis. scholar U. Calif., Berkeley; dir. sponsored rsch. Ford Found., N.Y.C., SUNY, Nat. Inst. Edn., Spencer Found., Buffalo, NSF, Washington, Rockefeller Found., US Dept. Edn., IBM Corp., Burroughs Corp.; speaker, presenter in field. Author: (with others) Fleischmann Commn. Report, Vols. I & II, 1973, Vol. III, 1974, Minority Enrollment in U.S. Institutions of Higher Education, Readings on the State of Education in Urban America, 1991, Challenges of Urban Education and Efficacy of School Reform, 2003; contbr. articles to Ednl. Forum, Ednl. Researcher, Jour. Negro Edn., Jour. Black Studies, Am. Sch. Bd. Jour., numerous others; book series editor: Educational Excellence, Equity; editor: Emergent Leadership; book review editor: Education and Urban Society; editorial bds. Afro-Am. History in NY State, Brigham Young U. Edn. & Law Jour., Jour. Black Students, Jour. Negro Edn., Jour. Ednl. Policy, Edn. and Urban Soc., Jour. Equity and Leadership, NABSE Jour., NOLPE Law, others. Bd. dirs. Buffalo Urban League, Langston Hughes Black Culture Ctr., Buffalo; trustee White Rock Bapt. Ch., Durham, N.C.; founder, first chair Black Faculty/Staff caucus CUNY, SUNY, U. N.C., Chapel Hill; established Inst. for AFrican Am. Rsch., U. N.C. With U.S. Army. Grad. fellow Tenn. State U., San Francisco State U., Washington U., Oreg. State U., U. Calif.-Berkeley, fellow Rockefeller Found., 1979. Mem. NAACP, Am. Assn. Colls. for Tchr. Edn. (bd. dirs.), Am. Ednl. Fin. Assn., Am. Ednl. Rsch. Assn. (sec. div. A, v.p., com. on minority affairs), Assn. Sch. Bus. Ofcls. Internat., Edn. Law Assn., Assn. Social and Behavioral Scientists, Nat. Alliance Black Sch. Ednl. Fin. Assn. of Sch. Bus. Assn., Educators, Nat. Assn. Multicultural Edn., Nat. Orgn. Legal Problems of Edn. (editorial bd. 1979-80, bd. dirs. 1990—), Politics of Edn. Assn., Phi Delta Kappa, Alpha Phi Alpha (chpt. pres.). Democrat. Baptist. Office: U NC 121B Peabody Hall CB 3500 Chapel Hill NC 27599-3500 Office Phone: 919-962-2522. Office Fax: 919-966-1533. Business E-Mail: fbrown@email.unc.edu.

BROWN, FRANK BEVERLY, IV, lawyer; b. Bryan, Tex., June 1, 1945; s. Frank B. III and Kathleen (Mangum) B.; m. Janice Parks, July 19, 1980; children: Frank Parks, Caroline Paige. BBA, U. Tex., 1967, JD, 1975. Bar: Tex. 1976; CPA, Tex. Assoc. Daugherty, Kuperman, Golden & Morehead, Austin, Tex., 1976-80, ptnr., 1980-84, Armburst & Brown, Austin, 1984-90, Strasburger & Price, Austin, 1990-97, Armbrust & Brown, Austin, 1997—. Capt. USAF, 1967-73. Mem. Tex. Bar Assn. (tax sect., bus. law sect.), Travis County Bar Assn. (corp. and real estate sects.). Presbyterian. Avocations: racquetball, skiing, flying. Office: Armbrust & Brown 100 Congress Ave Ste 1300 Austin TX 78701-2744 Office Phone: 512-435-2302. Business E-Mail: fbrown@abaustin.com.

BROWN, FRANK R., judge; b. Dec. 21, 1921; Attended, U. Okla., 1940, Okla. City U., 1941; JD, Southwestern U., LA, 1956. Bar: Calif. 1956. Owner Frank A. Brown Law Offices, Calif., 1958—94; judge US Dept. Health & Human Svc., Irvine, Calif., 2005—. Mem.: San Luis Obispo Bar Assn., San Fernando Valley Bar Assn., Calif. State Bar.

BROWN, FREDERIC JOSEPH, military officer; b. Fort Sill, Okla., July 18, 1934; s. Frederic Joseph and Kathryn (Richardson) B.; m. Harriette Anne Upham, July 7, 1956; children: Kathryn, Harriette, Judith. BS, U.S. Mil. Acad., 1956; MA, Grad. Inst. Internat. Studies, U. Geneva, 1963, PhD, 1967. Commd. officer U.S. Army, advanced through grades to lt. gen.; comdr. 1st squadron 4th cav. Vietnam, 1969-70; mem. staff NSC, 1972-73; comdr. 1st Tiger brigade 2d Armored Divsn., Ft. Hood, Tex., 1975-76; comdr. U.S. Army Tng. Ctr. Armor, Ft. Knox, Ky., 1977-78; asst. divsn. comdr. 8th Inf. Div. Baumholder, Germany, 1978-81; dep. chief of staff tng. U.S. Army Tng. and Doctrine Command, Ft. Monroe, Va., 1981-82; commdg. gen., chief armor U.S. Army Armor Ctr., Ft. Knox, Ky., 1983-86; comdr. 4th U.S. Army, Ft. Sheridan, Ill., 1986-89. Asst. prof. dept. polit. scis. US Mil. Acad., West Point, NY; mem. adj. rsch. staff Inst. Def. Analyses; cons. in tng. tech. and devel.; advisor, cons. advanced individual, team learning and knowledge mgmt. Dept. Def. Tng. fgn. armies, 1995—; advisor Dept. Army design advanced learning future Army, 1997—; sr. mentor army knowledge mgmt. Battle Command Knowledge Sys., 2003-06; sr. mentor info. and knowledge mgmt., US European Command, 2007-. Author: Chemical Warfare--A Study in Restraints, 1968 The United States Army in Transition II: Landpower in the Information Age, 1993; co-author: The United States Army in Transition, 1973; author numerous papers on info. age tng. for Inst. for Def. Analyses, 1989-2007; co-prodr. TV series on U.S. Army post-Vietnam All We Could Be, 1995-02; developer: advanced tng. policies and programs for U.S. Army Force XXI, 1996-98; designer: Army R & D of advanced learning and leader devel., 2000-, Army Knowledge Management, 2002-06, Knowledge Management for Joint, Interagency, Intergovernmental and Multinational Teams of Leaders in US European Command, 2007-. Decorated D.S.M. with oak leaf cluster, Silver Star, Legion of Merit; Olmsted scholar, 1961-63 Mem. Coun. Fgn. Rels., Internat. Inst. Strategic Studies, Army Battle Command Knowledge Sys. (sr. mentor). Home: 6317 Stoneham Ln Mc Lean VA 22101-2346 Office: Inst Def Analyses Joint Advanced Warfighting Program 1801 N Beauregard St Alexandria VA 22311-1701 Office Phone: 703-845-6800. Business E-Mail: fbrown@ida.org. *The essence of satisfaction is service to others. In my case, the opportunity to defend the values and strengths of our great nation.*

BROWN, FREDERICK CALVIN, retired physics professor; b. Seattle, July 6, 1924; s. Fred Charles and Rose (Mueller) B.; m. Joan Schauble, Aug. 9, 1952 (dec. Mar. 2003); children: Susan, Gail, Derek. BS, Harvard U., 1945, MS, 1947, PhD, 1950. Physicist Systems Research Lab., Harvard (NDRC), 1945-46; staff physicist Naval Research Lab., Washington, 1950; physicist Applied Physics Lab., U. Wash., 1950-51; asst. prof. Reed Coll., Portland, Oreg., 1951-55, U. Ill., Urbana, 1955-58, assoc. prof., 1958-61, prof., 1961-87, prof. emeritus, 1987—; assoc. Center for Advanced Study, 1969-70; prin. scientist, area mgr. Xerox Palo Alto (Calif.) Rsch. Ctr., 1973-74; prof. physics U. Wash., Seattle, 1987-99, prof. emeritus, 1999—; ret., 2000. Vis. mem. St. Johns Coll., Oxford, Eng., 1964-65; cons. prof., applied physics dept. Stanford U., 1973-74 Author: The Physics of Solids-Ionic Crystals, Lattice Vibrations and Imperfections, 1967; Contbr. articles profl. jours. Recipient Alexander von Humboldt sr. scientist award U. Kiel, 1978; NSF sr. postdoctoral fellow Clarendon Lab., Oxford, 1964-65 Fellow Am. Phys. Soc. Achievements include being innovator in use of synchrotron radiation for spectroscopy; first observation of polaron mobility and mass in ionic crystals, luminescence and lifetime of point defects such as F-centers, charge density waves in layered crystals, and early photoemission experiments on high temperature superconductors. Home: 5915 25th Ave W Everett WA 98203-1468

BROWN, FREDERICK LEE, health facility administrator; b. Clarksburg, W.Va., Oct. 22, 1940; s. Claude Raymond and Anne Elizabeth (Kiddy) B.; m. Shirley Fiille Brown; children: Gregory Lee, Michael Owen-Price, Kyle Stephen, Kathryn Alexis. BA in Psychology, Northwestern U., Evanston, Ill., 1962; MBA in Health Care Adminstrn., George Washington U., Washington, 1966; LHD (hon.), U. Mo., 1995. Vocat. counselor Cook County Dept. Pub. Aid, Chgo., 1962-64; adminstrv. resident to v.p. ops. Meth. Hosp. Ind., Inc., Indpls., 1965—72, v.p. ops., 1972-74; exec. v.p., COO Meml. Hosp. DuPage County, Elmhurst, Ill., 1974-82, Meml. Health Svcs., Elmhurst, 1980-82; pres., CEO CH Health Techs., Inc., St. Louis, 1983-93, Christian Health Svcs., St. Louis, 1986-93, CH Allied Svcs., Inc., St. Louis, 1988-93, BJC Health Sys., St. Louis, 1993—98, vice-chmn., 1999—2000; pres., CEO Christian Hosp. NE-NW, 1982—88, No. Ariz. Healthcare, Flagstaff, 2003—04. Adj. instr. Washington U. Sch. Medicine, St. Louis, 1982—2001; mem. chancellor's coun. U. Mo., 1990—94; mem. exec. com. HealthLink, Inc., 1986—92; pres., CEO Village North, Inc., 1986—93; chmn. shareholder comm. com. Am. Healthcare Systems, Inc., 1985—86, vice chmn., 1992; bd. dirs. Commerce Bank St. Louis, Am. Excess Inc. Ltd.; mem. corp. assembly Blue Cross Blue Shield Mo., 1991—95; vis. scholar, exec. in residence The George Washington U., 2001—02. Contbr. articles to profl. jours. Co-chmn. hosp. divsn. United Way Greater St. Louis, 1983, chmn., 1984, chmn. health svcs. divsn., 1985—86, vice chmn. region, 1988, bd. dirs., 1986—2001, exec. com., 1991—, chmn. audit com., 1992—2001; active Kammergild Chamber Orch., 1984—88, v.p., 1985—88, bd. dirs., 1987—91; active Mo. Heart Inst., 1988—92, Alton Meml. Hosp., 1987—91, bd. dirs., 1987—91; mem. exec. bd. St. Louis Area coun. Boy Scouts Am., 1989—2000, activities coun. chmn., 1993—95; chmn. Friends of Scouting Campaign, 1991—92; mem. medicaid budget task force Mo. Dept. Social Svcs., 1990; mem. emergency rm. svcs. task force St. Louis Regional Med. Ctr., 1985; mem. corp. assembly Blue Cross Blue Shield of Mo., 1991; bd. dirs. Sold on St. Louis, 1991—93, St. Louis Reg. Commerce & Growth Assn., 1993—98; bd. trustees Webster Hills Math. Ch., 1990—92, communion steward, 1987. Fellow Am. Coll. Healthcare Execs. (chmn. credentials com. 1978, chmn. task force governance and constituencies 1986-88; mem. Gold Medal award com. 1985, com. on ethics 1989-91, chmn. awards and testimonials com., 1992-93, bd. regents 1991-93, gov. dist. V, 1993-98); mem. Am. Acad. Med. Adminstrs. (life, state dir. 1988—, Health Care Exec. of Yr. 1990, Statesman in Healthcare, 1992), Hosp. Pres.'s Assn., Advt. Club Greater St. Louis, Am. Hosp. Assn. (coun. on mgmt. 1987, alt. del. for healthcare systems 1988-90, del. to ho. of dels. for health care systems 1991, fin. com. chair 1995, chair-elect 1998, chmn. 1999), APHA, George Washington U. Alumni Assn. for Health Svcs. Adminstrn. (preceptor 1975-93, Alumnus of Yr. award 1981, Frederick Gibbs award, 1993), Hosp. Assn. Met. St. Louis (bd. dirs. 1984-94, chmn. bd. 1988-89, sec. 1985-86, treas. 1987, chmn. coun. on pub. affairs and comm. 1985, vice chmn. 1987, various coms.), Greater St. Louis Health Care Alliance (co-chair 1992-96), Mo. Hosp. Assn. (mem. coun. on rsch. and policy devel. 1983-88, chmn. coun. on multi-instnl. hosps. 1986-88, mem. dist. coun. pres.'s 1986-89, bd. dirs. 1988-92, chmn. bd. trustees 1990), Ctrl. Ea. Profl. Rev. Orgn. (bd. dirs. 1982-85, various coms.), St. Louis Met. Med. Soc. (lay advisor 1990-92), Healthcare Execs. Study Soc., Internat. Health Policy and Mgmt. Inst. (bd. dirs. 1988—), Am. Protestant Health Assn. (bd. dirs. 1988-93, chmn. 1992-93), Pinnacle Peak Country Club, Forest Highlands Country Club. Republican. Home: 8409 E La Junta Rd Scottsdale AZ 85255-2859 Office Phone: 928-607-3069. Personal E-mail: fredlbrown@cox.net.

BROWN, GARY CHRISTIAN, ophthalmologist, director; b. Mineola, NY, May 14, 1949; m. Melissa M. Brown; children: Heather, Heidi, Kathryn. BS, Colgate U., 1971; MD, SUNY Upstate Med. Ctr., Syracuse, 1975. Intern Grady Hosp./Emory U., Atlanta, 1975-76; resident Wills Eye Hosp., Phila., 1976-79, fellow, 1979-81, dir., 2003—, chief, retina svc., 2003—; physician Retinovitreous Assocs., Wyndmoor, Pa., 1981—, practice, Bethlehem, Pa., Huntington Valley, Cherry Hill, NJ. Pres., chmn. bd. dirs. Pa. Physician Health Plan, Inc., Harrisburg, 1994-96; prof. Jefferson Med. Coll.; spkr. in field; co-dir. Center for Value Based Medicine Author or co-author 8 med. texts, 3 novels, more than 450 sci. papers in field; editor: Current Science in Ophthalmology, 1992-2006. Mem. AMA, Am. Acad. Ophthalmology (sr. honor award 1994), Pa. Med. Soc., Pa. Acad. Ophthalmology (pres.), Wills Eye Ex-Resident Soc. (pres. 1996), Wills Eye Hosp. Soc., Ophthalmologic Club of Phila. (pres. 1985), Phi Beta Kappa, Alpha Omega Alpha. Office: Retinovitreous Assocs 910 E Willow Grove Ave Wyndmoor PA 19038-7910 also: Wills Eye Hosp 840 Walnut St Philadelphia PA 19107 Office Phone: 215-233-4300.

BROWN, GARY SANDY, electrical engineering educator; b. Jackson, Miss., Apr. 13, 1940; s. John Leo and Welma (Kelley) B.; m. Mary Kathleen Connaughton, Mar. 16, 1970; children: Joshua John, Nathan Matthew. BSEE, U. Ill., 1963, MS, 1964, PhDEE, 1967. Grad. rsch. asst. Antenna Lab. U. Ill., Urbana, 1963-67; mem. tech. staff TRW Systems Group, Redondo Beach, Calif., 1969-70; sr. engr. Rsch. Triangle Inst., Durham, NC, 1970-73; sr. scientist Applied Sci. Assocs., Apex, NC, 1973-85; prof. elect. engring. Va. Poly. Inst. and State U., Blacksburg, 1985—, apptd. Bradley disting. prof. electromagnetics, 2002. With Wallops Flight Facility, NASA, Wallops Island, Va., 1974; cons. Naval Rsch. Lab., Washington, 1988-91, Decision Scis. Applications, Arlington, Va., 1988-91, DTI Inc., Torrance, Calif., 1987-91, Applied Physics Lab., Laurel, Md., 1987-88, Waste Policy Inst., Blacksburg, Va., 1991—, Motorola Corp., Chandler, Ariz., 1991-93; mem. NATO AGARD Electromagnetic Propogation Panel, 1993—; dir. Electromagnetic Interactions Lab. Contbr. chpts. to books, articles to profl. jours. Capt. U.S. Army, 1967-69. Recipient Best Paper awards R.W.P. King, 1978, Schelkunoff, 1999, Bradley Disting. Prof. Electromagnetics, 2002. Fellow IEEE (Third Millenium award 2000); mem. Antennas and Propagation Soc. of IEEE (pres. 1988), Am. Geophys. Union (editor's citation Radio Sci., Am. sects. 1986), Internat. Union of Radio Sci. (mem.-at-large 1987, sec. U.S. nat. com. 1997-99, chair U.S. nat. com. 2000-2002), NATO AGARD Sensors and Propagation Panel. Avocations: backpacking, jogging. Office: Va Poly Inst & State U Bradley Dept Elec & Computer Engr Blacksburg VA 24061 Office Phone: 540-231-4467. Business E-Mail: randem@vt.edu.

BROWN, GEORGE E., judge, educator; b. Hammond, Ind., July 27, 1947; s. George E. and Violet M. (Matlon) B.; m. Patricia A. Schneider, June 6, 1970; children: Janet M., Elizabeth A. BS, Ball State U., 1969; JD, DePaul U., 1974; cert., Ind. Jud. Coll., 1996, postgrad., 2002. Bar: Ind. 1974, Ill. 1974, U.S. Dist. Ct. (no. dist.) Ind. 1979, U.S. Supreme Ct. 1977, U.S. Tax Ct. 1977. Pvt. practice, LaGrange & Lake Counties, Ind., 1974-84; judge LaGrange County Ct., 1984-87, LaGrange Superior Ct., 1988—. Part-time chief dep. prosecutor LaGrange County, 1975—77; adj. faculty Tri-State U., Angola, Ind., 1991—2004, 2006—. Vol. Jr. Achievement, 1997—; vol. judge We The People Program. Mem.: ABA, Nat. Conf. State Trial Judges, Ind. Judges Assn. (com. criminal instrns.), LaGrange County Bar Assn. (pres. 1978), Ind. State Bar Assn. (ho. of dels., written publs. com.), Rotary (past dir., v.p. 1999—2000, pres. 2000—01, bd. dirs. 2002—). Office: Lagrange Superior Ct Courthouse Lagrange IN 46761 Home Phone: 260-463-3993; Office Phone: 260-499-6363.

BROWN, SIR GEORGE NOEL, judge; b. Gales Point Village, Belize, June 13, 1942; s. Noel Todd and Elma Priscilla (O'Brien) B.; m. Eleanor Marie Williams, June 5, 1962 (div. May 1972); children: Georgia Yvette Marie, Aubrey Noel David, Marsha Elizabeth, Roxanne Patricia; m. Magdalene Elizabeth Bucknor, Aug. 24, 1974. Cert. in pub. adminstrn., Carlton U., Ottawa, Ont., Can., 1970; LLB with 2d class honors, U. W.I., Barbados, 1976; cert. in legal edn., Norman Manley Law Sch., Kingston, Jamaica, 1978; cert. in legis. drafting, Commonwealth Secretariat Law Sch., Nairobi, Kenya, 1979. Customs examiner Belize Customs and Excise Dept., Belize City, 1960-67; clk. of cts. Belize Magistrates Cts., Belize City, 1967-69; adminstrv. asst. Belize Ministry Trade and Industry, Belize City, 1970-72; lay magistrate, various cities, Belize, 1972-73; crown counsel Atty. Gen.'s Ministry, Belmopan, Belize, 1978-81, solicitor gen., 1981-84; puisne judge Belize Supreme Ct., Belize City, 1984-90, chief justice, 1990-98; law revsion commr. Law Revision Office, Belize City, 1998-99; legal cons., 2000—. Dep. gov. gen. Gov. Gen's. Office, Belize, 1986—95; mem. Belize Adv. Coun., 1986—88, sr. mem., 1988—2002; mem. prison parole bd., 1998—2000; chmn. bd. dir. Tubal Trade and Vocat. Inst., 2003—; chmn. Nat. Rehab. Com., 2003—, mem., 2004—. Mgr., coach primary and secondary sch. soccer teams, Belize City, 1986-99, 1st divsn. and semi-pro soccer club, Belmopan and Belize City, 1981-2000; sec., chmn. Belize Harbour Regatta Com., Belize City, 1958-85. Decorated Knight Order of Brit. Empire, 1991. Mem. Belize Bar Assn. (sec. 1979-81). Seventh Day Adventist. Avocations: yachting, soccer, drama, cricket. Home: 6203 Cor Park Ave Seashore Dr PO Box 236 Belize City Belize Office: Welch House 76 Dean St PO Box 1117 Belize City Belize Home Phone: 501-223-3874; Office Phone: 501-227-7063.

BROWN, GEORGE STEPHEN, physics professor; b. Santa Monica, Calif., June 28, 1945; s. Paul Gordon and Frances Ruth (Moore) B.; m. Nohema Fernandez, Aug. 8, 1981 (div. 1992); 1 child, Sonya; m. Julie Claire Dryden, Mar. 22, 1997. BS, Calif. Inst. Tech., 1967; MS, Cornell U., 1968, PhD, 1973. Mem. tech. staff Bell Labs., Murray Hill, N.J., 1973-77; sr. research assoc. Stanford (Calif.) U., 1977-82, rsch. prof. applied physics, 1982-91; prof. physics U. Calif., Santa Cruz, 1991—, chair dept. physics, 1996-2000, vice provost, 2000—05. Assoc. dir. Stanford Synchrotron Radiation Lab., Stanford, 1980-91. Mem. editorial bd. Rev. Sci. Instruments, 1983-86; contbr. articles to profl. jours. Fellow Am. Phys. Soc. Avocation: music performance. Home: 115 Quarry Ct Santa Cruz CA 95060-2056 Office: U Calif Dept Physics Santa Cruz CA 95064

BROWN, GEORGE W., social psychiatrist; b. England; Grad., Univ. Coll. London. With Med. Rsch. Coun. Social Psychiatry Rsch. Unit, London; sr. hon. fellow, dept. social psychiatry St. Thomas' Hosp., London. Mem.: Inst. Medicine (assoc.).

BROWN, GERALD CURTIS, retired military officer, engineering executive; b. Worcester, Mass., Aug. 10, 1942; s. Victor Curtis and Ethel (Dean) B.; m. Alelaide M. Forshey, June 28, 1964 (div.); children: Deborah Ann, Suzanne Marie; m. Jean Jennings, Aug. 1, 1998. BS, U.S. Mil. Acad., West Point, NY, 1964; MS, U. Ill., 1970. Registered profl. engr., Tex., Md., D.C., Fla., Ill. Commd. 2d. lt. U.S. Army, 1964, advanced through grades to brig. gen., 1988; capt. 18th Engr. Brigade, Vietnam, 1966-67; maj. 1st Air Cavalry Div., Vietnam, 1970-71; assoc. prof. history U.S. Mil. Acad., West Point, 1974-77; bn. comdr. 82d Combat Engr. Bn., Bamberg, Fed. Republic Germany, 1978-80; dist. engr. Balt. Dist., Corps Engrs., 1982-84; staff engr. U.S. Army Tng. and Doctrine Command, Ft. Monroe, Va., 1984-86; mil. exec. Office Undersec. Army, Washington, 1986-88; fellow Harvard U., Cambridge, 1988-89; comdg. gen. U.S. Army Corps Engrs., North Atlantic Div., NYC, 1989-92; dir. Environ. programs Dept. of Army, The Pentagon, Washington, 1992-94; ret. U.S. Army, 1994; v.p. Sverdrup Civil, Inc., Falls Church, Va., 1994-95; v.p., mgr. Ea. Ops. Sverdrup Environ., Inc., Balt., 1995-98; v.p. Sverdrup Civil, Inc., Falls Church, 1998-99; program mgr. Parsons Brinckerhoff, London, 2000—01; assoc. dir. for ops. Fermi Nat. Accelerator Lab., Batavia, Ill., 2001—05; ret., 2005. Natl. Defense Exec. Reserve; Fed. Emerg. Mgmt. Agency, chmn. bd. of vis., fed. Emerg. Mgmt. Inst., Md., 1998-2000; founder, pres. Army Corps Engrs. Meml. Corp. Contbr. articles to mil. jours. Fellow Soc. Am. Mil. Engrs. (v.p. 1989-92, bd. dirs. 1993-96, founder, chmn. Acad. Fellows 1995-96); mem. ASCE, Army and Navy Club (Washington). Avocations: golf, opera, reading. Office: Fermi Natl Accelerator Lab PO Box 500 MS 200 Batavia IL 60510-0500 Home Phone: 630-208-7863; Office Phone: 630-840-8529. Business E-Mail: gcbrown@fnal.gov.

BROWN, GERALD EDWARD, physicist, researcher; b. Brookings, SD, July 22, 1926; BA, U. Wis., 1946; MS, Yale U., 1948, PhD, 1950; DSc, U. Birmingham, 1957; DSc (hon.), U. Helsinki, 1982, U. Birmingham, 1990, U. Copenhagen, 1998, Ohio State U., 2005. Prof. physics U. Birmingham, 1959-60, Nordic Inst. Theoretic Atomic Physics, 1960-85, Princeton U., 1964-68, SUNY, Stony Brook, 1968-74, leading prof., 1974-88, dist. prof. physics, 1988—. Lectr. math physics, 1955-58; reader U. Birmingham, 1958-59; dir. nuclear astrophysics Inst. Theoretical Physics NSF, U. Calif., 1960. Recipient Boris Pregel award N.Y. Acad. Sci., 1976, Tom W. Bonner prize Nuclear Physics, 1982, Sr. Dist. Sci. award Alexander von Humboldt Found., 1987, John Price Wetherill medal Franklin Inst., Phila., 1992, Max-Planck medaille German Phys. Soc., 1997, Hans A. Bethe prize nuclear physics and astrophysics Am. Physics Soc., 2001, Wilbur Lucius Cross medal Yale Grad. Sch. Arts and Scis., 2003. Office: SUNY Inst Theoretical Physics Stony Brook NY 11794-0001

BROWN, GERALDINE, nurse, freelance writer; b. Clemson, SC; d. Isaac and Gladys (Patterson) B. AS in Nursing, U. D.C., 1973; real estate cert., Long and Foster Inst., 1984; cert. in TV broadcasting, Columbia Sch., 1987; BSN, Bowie State U., Md., 1989, MA in Comm., 1991, MSN, 2000; PhD, Howard U., DC, 1994. RN, D.C., FCC Third Class License. Supr. staff nurse Walter Reed Hosp., Washington, 1970—76; supr. clin. nurse Dept. Human Svcs., Washington, 1976—78, cmty. health nurse, 1978—84; nursing instr. Phillips Bus. Sch., Alexandria, Va., 1984—85; pvt. nurse Washington, 1973—; faculty Howard U. Coll. Nursing, 1994—2001. Dir. pub. affairs Bible Way Chs. Worldwide, Inc., Washington, 1978-91; soc. columnist As It Happens, Charlotte (N.C.) Post, 1964-66; soc. editor Washington Cafe Soc. mag, 1971; contbr. feature stories Capital Spotlight newspaper, 1978—; mem. faculty Coll. Nursing, Howard U., 1994—. Asst. organizer DC Mayor's United Nations Day, 1980; vol. Met. Boys and Girls Clubs, Washington, 1980—; vol. Nursing Instr., The Washington Saturday Coll., 1982-84; Co. ARC, 1973—, Big Sisters of the Washington Met. Area, 1988—. Recipient certs. of excellence Govt. of D.C., 1978-84; cert. of appreciation Mayor of D.C., 1980, Meritorious Pub. Svc. award, 1980; svc. trophy Washington Saturday Coll., 1984. Mem. ANA, NAACP, Nat. Coun. Negro Women, Smithsonian Inst. (assoc.), Nat. Black Nurses Assn., Washington Urban League, Chi Eta Phi, Sigma Theta Tau. Democrat. Avocations: stamp collecting/philately, travel, poetry. Office Phone: 202-244-0313. Personal E-mail: G.Brown2@worldnet.att.net.

BROWN, GILES TYLER, history professor, lecturer; b. Marshall, Mich., Apr. 21, 1916; s. A. Watson and Ettroile (Kent) B.; m. Crysta Beth Cosner, Nov. 21, 1951 (dec. July 1992). AB, San Diego State Coll., 1937; MA, U. Calif., Berkeley, 1941; PhD, Claremont Grad. Sch., 1948. Tchr., counselor, Binet intelligence tester San Diego City Schs., 1937—46; chmn. social sci. divsn. Orange Coast Coll., Newport Beach, Calif., 1948—60; prof. history, chmn. social sci. divsn. Calif. State U., Fullerton, 1961—66, also chmn. history dept., dean grad. studies, 1967—83, assoc. v.p. acad. programs, 1979—83. Lectr. in field; cons. gerontology; participant Wilton Park Conf., Eng., 1976; mem. instl. rsch. bd. So. Calif. Coll. Optometry, 1980-97; past chmn. Hist. Landmarks Com. Orange County; mem. nat. task force Assessment Quality Masters' Degree, Coun. Grad. Schs., 1981-83. Author: Ships That Sail No More, 1966; Contbr. to: Help in Troubled Times, 1962; contbr. articles to profl. jours. Trustee, past pres., past chmn. bd. World Affairs Coun. Orange County; past pres. U. Calif.-Irvine Friends Libr.; nat. bd. dirs., past nat. pres. Travelers Century Club; emeritus bd. dirs. Pacific Symphony Orch. Named Citizen of Yr., Orange Coast Coll., 1993, Forum Bldg. in his name, 2006; recipient hon. medal, DAR, 1977, Nat. Soc. Daus. Colonial Wars, 1984, Golden Orange award, World Affair Coun. of Orange County, 2002. Mem. AAAS, SAR, Am. Hist. Assn. (Pacific History award 1950), We. Assn. Grad. Schs. (exec. com. 1981-83), Phi Beta Kappa, Phi Delta Kappa, Phi Alpha Theta, Phi Beta Delta (hon. internat. scholar), Kappa Delta Pi, Explorers, Masons. Baptist. Home: 413 Catalina Dr Newport Beach CA 92663-4105

BROWN, GLENDA ANN WALTERS, ballet director; b. Buna, Tex., July 22, 1937; d. Jesse Olaf and Kathryn Jeanette (Rogers) Walters; m. David Dann Brown, Dec. 13, 1958 (div. 1995); children: Kathryn, Jean, Vanessa Lea. Grad. h.s., Beaumont, Tex. Mem. Melody Maids, Beaumont, 1950-60; asst. tchr. Widman Sch., Beaumont, 1952-55; owner, tchr. Walters Sch. of Dance, Jasper, Tex., 1955-59; assoc. tchr. Emmamae Horn Sch., 1964-81, artistic dir., 1981—; assoc. dir. Allegro Ballet Houston, 1974-81, artistic dir., 1981—; owner, dir. Allegro Acad. Dance, Houston, 1981—. Dir. Regional Dance Am., Nat. Craft Choreography Conf., 1987—2001; mem. adv. bd. Dance Tchr. Mag., 1998—2003; founder, dir. Glenda Brown Choreography Project, 2002—. Dance panel Cultural Arts Coun., Houston, 1979, Tex. Commn. on the Arts, 1988-90; sec. Riedel Estates Civic Club, Houston, 1975-78; Rep. poll worker, Houston, 1970-81; bd. dirs. Austrian Alps Performing Arts Festival, 1996-98; coord. First Nat. Regional Dance Am. Festival, 1997, bd. dirs. Tanzsommer/Austria, 1998—; dir. Young Tanzsommer, 2006-. Mem. Dance Masters Am. (exam. chair chpt. 3 1980-86), Regional Dance Am. S.W. (exec. v.p. 1981-2001), Dance Am., Nat. Assn. Regional Ballet (bd. dirs. 1985-88), Regional Dance Am. (nat. bd. dirs., v.p. 1988-95, pres. 1995-2001, dir. emeritus 2002—). Methodist. Avocations: camping, singing, golf, travel. Office: Allegro Ballet and Dance Acad 1570 S Dairy Ashford St Ste 200 Houston TX 77077-3870 Home Phone: 713-465-7152; Office Phone: 281-496-4670. Personal E-mail: glendabrown@ev1.net.

BROWN, G(LENN) WILLIAM, JR., bank executive; b. Waynesville, NC, June 9, 1955; s. Glenn William and Evelyn Myralyn (Davis) B.; m. Amy Margaret Moss, Apr. 14, 1984; children: Elizabeth Quinn, Lauren Alexandra. BS in Biology, MIT, 1977, BS in Polit. Sci., 1977; JD, Duke U., 1980. Bar: N.Y., 1980. Assoc. Donovan Leisure Newton & Irvine, NYC, 1980-84, Sidley & Austin, NYC, 1984-87, ptnr., 1988-89; v.p. Goldman Sachs & Co., NYC, 1990-94; exec. dir. Goldman Sachs Internat. Fin., London, 1994-96; sr. v.p., global head sales AIG Internat. Inc., Greenwich, Conn., 1996-97; prin. Morgan Stanley & Co., Inc., NYC, 1997, mng. dir., head Am. sales for FX, 1997—2007, head Am. sales for emerging markets debt, 2003—05, global co-head listed derivatives, 2007—. Editl. bd.: jour. Duke Law Jour., 1978—80. Corp. adv. bd. Sch. of Am. Ballet, 2003—; mem. alumni assn. bd. Duke Law Sch., 2001—03, bd. visitors, 2003—; session mem. First Presbyn. Ch. of Greenwich, 2000—03. Mem.: ABA, NY Soc. Security Analysts, Am. Fin. Assn. Presbyterian. Home: Apt 39D One Central Park West New York NY 10023-7700 Office: Morgan Stanley Co 1585 Broadway Frnt 3 New York NY 10036-8200 Office Phone: 212-761-2754. Business E-Mail: bill.brown@morganstanley.com.

BROWN, GLORIA DIANE, elementary school educator; d. Earl and Joyce Taylor; m. Bobby Lee Brown, June 29, 1977 (dec. May 15, 2005); children: Danielle Marie Patterson, Bobby Lee Brown, II, Bradford Leverette. BA, Grambling State U., 1970; MA, Wayne State U., 1975, Edn. Specialist, 1997. Cert. Continuing Tchr. Wayne State. Remedial reading and reading lab Detroit (Mich.) Pub. Schs., 1972—73, tchr. social studies, 1973—74, tchr. homeroom, 1975—88, kindergarten and reading lab, 1988—89, tchr., 1989—94, tchr. sci., 1994—2000; tchr. in charge Vernor Elem. Sch., 2004—; tchr. grade 1 Detroit (Mich.) Pub. Schs., 2005—. Tutor; cons. Title I workshops. Mem. sci. edn. delegation to Russia People to People Ambassador Program, 2006; treas. St. Michael Ch., Detroit, 1977—2005, sec. Finalist Tchr. of Yr., State Mich. Dept. Edn., 1993-1994; named, Detroit Pub. Schs., 1993-1994; recipient Innovative Tchr. of Yr., Phi Delta Kappa Internat., 1988, Golden Apple Tchr. award, Wayne Intermediate Sch. Dist., 1994, Booker T. Wash. Bus. award, Booker T. Wash. Bus. Group, 1998, Air Force award, Selfridge AFB, 1998-1999; grantee Mich. Dept. Edn., State Mich., 1989-1990, Dwight D. Eisenhower Grant award, Detroit Pub. Schs., 1993; Title One Mini grant, 1991-1992. Mem.: Mich. Reading Assn., Nat. Sci. Tchr. Assn., Phi Delta Kappa Internat., Alpha Kappa Alpha Sorority (del. Boulefor Alpha Kappa 2006). Achievements include Master Tchr. for the Detroit Public Schs; Mich. Educator Exchange Opportunity Abroad Program. Avocations: reading, line dancing, travel, writing. Home: 20549 Bentler Ct Detroit MI 48219-1268 Office: Vernor Elem Sch 13726 Pembroke Detroit MI 48235 Home Phone: 313-538-3826; Office Phone: 313-494-7342. Personal E-mail: broglori@comcast.net.

BROWN, GREGORY K., lawyer; b. Warren, Ohio, Dec. 9, 1951; s. George K. and Dorothy H. (Gaynor) B.; m. Joy M. Feinberg, Apr. 10, 1976. BS in Bus. & Econs., U. Ky., 1973; JD, U. Ill., 1976. Bar: Ill. 1976. Assoc. atty. McDermott, Will & Emery, Chgo., 1976-80, Mayer, Brown & Platt, Chgo., 1980-84; ptnr. Keck, Mahin & Cate, Chgo., 1984-93, Oppenheimer Wolff & Donnelly, Chgo., 1994-97, Seyfarth, Shaw, Fairweather & Geraldson, Chgo., 1997-2000, Gardner, Carton & Douglas, Chgo., 2000—06, Katten Muchin Rosenman LLP, 2006—. Contbg. author: The Handbook of Employee Ownership Plans, 2005, Employee Stock Ownership Plans, 2005. Named One of the Top Benefits Lawyers Nat. Law Jour., 1998. Mem.: ABA (chair employee stock ownership plan com., tax law sect. Nat. Ctr. Employee Ownership, Employee Stock Ownership Plan Assn. chair legis. and regulatory adv. c 1997—99), Internat. Pension and Employee Benefit Lawyers Assn., Chgo. Bar Assn. (chmn. employee benefits com. 1988—89). Avocations: basketball, bicycling, golf, opera, theater. Office: Katten Muchin Rosenman 525 W Monroe St Chicago IL 60661-3693 Home Phone: 773-549-0559; Office Phone: 312-902-5404. Business E-Mail: gregory.brown@kattenlaw.com.

BROWN, GREGORY NEIL, academic administrator, forester, educator; b. Detroit, Feb. 10, 1938; s. Robert Octavus and Dorothy Etta May (Kingsbury) B.; m. Patricia Lee Talbott, Dec. 16, 1961 (div. 1974); children: Kathryn Duket, Julie Ann, Deborah Louise; m. Janeth Christine Hartman, May 24, 1974 (dec. 1997); children: Kimberly Suzanne, Kevin Scott; m. Laura Jean Dale, June 27, 1998. BS, Iowa State U., 1959; MF, Yale U., 1960; DF, Duke U., 1963. Cert. forester Soc. Am. Foresters, 2003. Plant physiologist Oak Ridge Nat. Lab., 1963—66; asst. prof. forestry to prof. U. Mo.-Columbia, 1966—77, dir. grad. studies Sch. Forestry, 1969—74; prof. Iowa State U., Ames, 1977—78; dept. head, prof. U. Minn.-St. Paul, 1978—83; dean, prof. U. Maine-Orono, 1983—86, acting v.p. acad. affairs, 1986-87, 91-92, v.p. rsch. and pub. svc., 1987—92; dean, prof. Coll. Natural Resources, Va. Poly. Inst. and State U., Blacksburg, 1992—2004, interim dean Coll. Agrl. and Life Scis., 2003; ret., 2004. Assoc. dir. Maine Agrl. Exptl. Sta., Orono, 1983-86, acting pres., 1992; assoc. dir. Va. Agrl. Exptl. Sta., Blacksburg, 1992-2004, interim provost, 1995; chair, bd. dirs. Powell River Project, 1996-2004; mem. sci. adv. bd. Nat. Ctr. Housing and the Environment, 2002-05; bd. dirs. Friends of Blue Ridge Pkwy., 2004—, adminstrv. v.p., 2006—. Author-editor: Seedling Physiology and Reforestation Success, 1984; editor International Directory of Woody Plant Physiologists, 1974-84, Jour. Forest Sci., 1979-82; editl. bd. Renewable Resources Jour., 2002—. Contbr. articles to profl. jours. Scoutmaster Boy Scouts Am., 1965-66; mem. Forestry Rsch. Adv. Coun., U.S. Sec. Agr., 2000-02. With USNR, 1955—63. Fellow Soc. Am. Foresters (chmn. physiology working group 1983-84, chmn. ednl. policies com. 2006—); mem. Nat. Assn. Profl. Forestry Schs. and Colls. (north Ctrl. rsch. chmn. 1981-82, nat. sec. treas. 1984-85, nat. pres. elect 1986-87, 94-95, pres. 1996-97), Internat. Union Forest Orgns. (chmn. working parties 1970-86), Nat. Assn. State Univs. and Land-Grant Colls. (chair bd. on natural resources 1997, chair U.S. geol. survey partnership com. 1997-2000), Soc. for Preservation and Encouragement of Barbershop Quartet Singing in Am. (pres. 1973-74), Sigma Xi, Xi Sigma Pi, Gamma Sigma Delta (jr. faculty award 1971), Rotary. Independent. Home: 1227 Old Fort Rd Fairview NC 28730 Personal E-mail: browngn@charter.net.

BROWN, GREGORY Q., communications executive; b. Aug. 14, 1960; BA in Econs., Rutgers U. Pres. Ameritech New Media Inc., 1994—96, Ameritech Custom Bus. Svcs.; chmn., CEO Micromuse Inc., San Francisco, 1999—2003; exec. v.p., pres., CEO comml., govt. & indsl. solutions sector Motorola, Inc., Schaumburg, Ill., 2003—05, exec. v.p., pres. networks & enterprise, 2005—07, pres., COO, 2007—. Bd. dirs. R.R. Donnelley & Sons Co., 2001—03, Micromuse, Inc., Nat. Merit Scholarship Corp., Chgo. Coun. Fgn. Rels.; mem. Pres. Nat. Security Telecom. Advisory Com., 2004; mem. Coll. Engring Advisory Coun. U. Notre Dame. Mem. bd. overseers Rutgers U. Office: Motorola Inc 1303 E Algonquin Rd Schaumburg IL 60196*

BROWN, HANK, academic administrator, former senator; b. Denver, Feb. 12, 1940; s. Harry W. and Anna M. (Hanks) B.; m. Nana Morrison, Aug. 27, 1967; children: Harry, Christy, Lori. BS, U. Colo., 1961, JD, 1969; LLM, George Washington U., 1986. Bar: Colo. 1969; CPA, 1988. Asst. pres. Monfort of Colo., Inc., Greeley, 1969—70, corp. counsel, 1970—71; v.p. Monfort Food Distbg., 1971—72, v.p. corp. devel., 1973—75, v.p. internat. ops., 1975—78, v.p. lamb div., 1978—80; mem. Colo. State Senate, 1972—76, asst. majority leader, 1974—76; mem. 97th-101st Congresses from Colo. 4th dist., 1981—90; US senator from Colo. Washington, 1991—96; pres. U. No. Colo., Greeley, 1998—2002, Daniels Fund, 2002—05; interim pres. U. Colo., 2005—06, pres. Denver, 2006—. Chmn. Fgn. Rel. subcom. Near Ea. and South Asian affairs, Judicorp subcom. on constl. law. Co-author: Lessons and Legacies. With USN, 1962—66. Decorated Air medal, Vietnam Svc. medal, Nat. Defense medal, Naval Unit citation. Republican. Congregationalist. Office: U Colo 1800 Grant St Ste 800 Denver CO 80203-1185 Office Phone: 303-860-5601. Office Fax: 303-860-5660, 303-860-5610. Business E-Mail: OfficeOfThePresident@cu.edu.*

BROWN, HARLEY PROCTER, JR., zoology educator, entomologist, researcher; b. Uniontown, Ala., Jan. 13, 1921; s. Harley Procter Brown and Martha Ida (McGinniss) Brown Coleman; m. Laura Clifford Williams, June 1, 1942 (dec. 1989); 1 child, Mary Hamilton Brown Catron; m. Marie Magdalen Jenkins, Dec. 20, 1989 (dec. 1997); m. Dorothy Ellis McGregor, Oct. 26, 1997. AB, AM, Miami U., Oxford, Ohio, 1942; PhD, Ohio State U., 1945. Grad. asst. in zoology Ohio State U., Columbus, 1942-45; instr. zoology U. Idaho, Moscow, 1945-47, Oreg. Inst. Marine Biology, Charleston, 1946; instr. biology Queens Coll., Flushing, N.Y., 1947-48; asst. prof., then assoc. prof. U. Okla., Norman, 1948-62, prof. zoology, 1962-84, prof. emeritus, 1984—; curator of invertebrates Stovall Mus. Sci. & History (now S.N. Okla. Mus. Natural History), Norman, 1962—. Rsch. prof. Franz Theodore Stone Inst., Put-In-Bay, Ohio, 1949. Author: Aquatic Dryopoid Beetles of the U.S.A., 1972; editor: Highlights and Lowlights, 1981; contbr. chpts. to Immature Insects, vol. 2, 1991; contbr. over 100 articles to biol. jours. Instl. rep., mem. dist. com., counselor Norman area Boy Scouts Am., 1949-70. NSF fellow, 1964, 70. Fellow AAAS (life); mem. Am. Inst. Biol. Scis. (governing bd.), Am. Microscopical Soc. (pres. 1975-76), N.Am. Benthological Soc., Sigma Xi, Phi Eta Sigma, Phi Sigma (nat. v.p. 1980—). Democrat. Presbyterian. Achievements include discovery of new genera and species of wasps (Pteromalidae, Eulophidae, Diapriidae) and water beetles (Elmidae, Dryopidae, Psephenidae, Lutrochidae, Limnichidae); research in life histories of various aquatic insects and their insect parasites (Sisyrids, Psephenids).

BROWN, HAROLD, former secretary of defense; b. NYC, Sept. 19, 1927; s. A.H. and Gertrude (Cohen) B.; m. Colene Dunning McDowell, Oct. 29, 1953; children: Deborah Ruth (Mrs. Eric Ploumis), Ellen Dunning (Mrs. Ray Merewether). AB, Columbia U., 1945, A.M., 1946, PhD in Physics (Lydig fellow 1948-49), 1949; 11 hon. degrees. Research scientist Columbia U., 1945-50, lectr. physics, 1947-48, Stevens Inst. Tech., 1949-50; divsn. leader E.O. Lawrence Radiation Lab. U. Calif., Berkeley, 1950-60, staff mem., group leader E.O. Lawrence Radiation Lab., 1952-60; dir. Lawrence Livermore (Calif.) Lab., 1960-61; dir. def. rsch. and engring. US Dept. Def., Washington, 1961-65; sec. USAF, Washington, 1965-69; pres. Calif. Inst. Tech., Pasadena, 1969-77; sec. US Dept. Def., Washington, 1977-81; disting. vis. prof. Sch. Advanced Internat. Studies Johns Hopkins U., Md., 1981-84, chmn. Fgn. Policy Inst., 1984-92, counselor Ctr. Strategic & Internat. Studies, 1992—; ptnr. Warburg, Pincus & Co., NYC, 1990—. Bd. dirs. Cummins Engine Co., Mattel, Inc., Evergreen Holdings, Inc.; mem. Polaris Steering Com., 1956-58; mem. Pres.'s Sci. Adv. Com., 1960-61; sr. sci. advisor Conf. Discontinuance Nuclear Tests, 1958-59; U.S. del. SALT, Helsinki, Vienna and Geneva, 1969-77; chmn. Tech. Assessment Adv. Coun. to U.S. Congress, 1974-77; chmn. Commn. on Roles and Capabilities of U.S. Intelligence Cmty., 1995-96; mem. exec. com. Trilateral Commn., 1973-76, trustee, 1992—; trustee Rand Corp., 1983-92, 93—; mem., ind. panel investigating abuses at Abu Ghraib prison, 2004. Author: Thinking About National Security: Defense and Foreign Policy in a Dangerous World, 1983. Trustee Beckman Found., 1982-95, chmn., 1993-95; trustee Rockefeller Found., 1983-93. Decorated Medal of Freedom; named One of 10 Outstanding Young Men U.S. Jaycees, 1961; recipient Medal of Excellence Columbia U., 1963; Joseph C. Wilson award in internat. affairs, 1976, Enrico Fermi award U.S. Dept. Energy, 1992. Mem. NAE, NAS, Am. Phys. Soc., Am. Acad. Arts and Scis., Bohemian Club, River Club, Met. Club, Phi Beta Kappa. Office: Ctr for Strategic & Intl Studies 1800 K St NW Ste 400 Washington DC 20006-2202

BROWN, HAROLD OGDEN JOSEPH, religious studies educator; b. Tampa, Fla., July 6, 1933; s. Harold Ogden Brown and Mary Anne Brown (nee Bakas); m. Grace Winifred Hancox, June 16, 1962; children: Cynthia Anne Erb, Peter Edward Harold. BA, Harvard Coll., 1953; PhD, Harvard U., Cambridge, Mass., 1968. Pastor Evangelische Kirchgemeinde, Klosters, Grisons, Switzerland, 1983—87; prof. Trinity Evang. Div. Sch., Deerfield, Ill., 1987—98, Reformed Theol. Sem., Charlotte, NC, 1998—. Editor: Christianity Today, Religion and Society Report, 1985—. Dir. Christian Action Coun./Care Net, Washington, 1975—92. Danforth Campus Ministry grant, Danforth Found., 1965-1966. Reformed Christian. Avocations: rowing, hiking, climbing. Home: 614 Nottingham Dr Charlotte NC 28211 Office: Reformed Theol Sem 2101 Carmel Rd Charlotte NC 28226 Office Phone: 704-366-5066. Personal E-mail: hbrown@rts.edu.

BROWN, HELEN DODSON, retired librarian; b. Englewood, Tenn., Jan. 6, 1925; d. Horace Calvin Dodson and Minnie Erie Womac; m. Buster Eldred Brown, Dec. 26, 1945 (dec.); children: Karla Jean, Lisa Leigh, Gregory Calvin. BS, Carson-Newman Coll., 1945; MS, U. Tenn., 1951. Libr., media specialist McMinn County Bd. Edn., Athens, Tenn., 1947—86; ret. Presenter in field; del. Am. Assn. State and Local History, Doylestown, Pa., 2002. Contbg. editor: Englewood, The Town and its People, 1985; co-editor: The History of Englewood First Baptist Church, 1872-1986, 1986, Then and Now, The Women of Englewood's Textile Mills, 1993, Women of World War II, 2002. Founding mem., project dir. Cmty. Action Group Englewood, 1986; mem. Fort Loudon Regional Libr. Bd., Athens, Tenn.; bd. dirs. Ret. Sr. Vol. Program, Decatur, Tenn., 2000—; mem. McMinn County Living Heritage Mus., Athens; project dir., grant writer Englewood Textile Mus.; organist, libr. First Bapt. Ch., Englewood, 1950—. Named Disting. Classroom Tchr., McMinn County Bd. Edn., 1986, McMinn County Mother of Yr., Athens Area C. of C., 1994; recipient Covenant Platinum award, Knoxville, Tenn., 2002, cert. of recognition, Nat. Fedn. Music Clubs, 2003, award for excellence in cmty. svcs., DAR, 2004. Mem.: AARP, McMinn County Ret. Edn. Assn., Tenn. Ret. Edn. Assn., Ret. NEA, Tenn. Edn. Assn. Libr. Sect. (vice chmn. 1972, del. to ALA 1972, chmn. 1973), Am. Assn. State and Local History, East Tenn. Hist. Assn., Tenn. Overhill Heritage Assn., Etowah Thursday Music Club, Phi Kappa Phi. Avocations: photography, travel, antiques. Home: 433 N Niota Rd Englewood TN 37329 Office: Englewood Textile Mus 101 S Niota Rd Englewood TN 37329

BROWN, HELEN GURLEY, editor-in-chief; b. Green Forest, Ark., Feb. 18, 1922; d. Ira M. and Cleo (Sisco) Gurley; m. David Brown, Sept. 25, 1959. Student, Tex. State Coll. for Women, 1940—41, Woodbury Coll., 1942; LLD, Woodbury U., 1987; DLitt, L.I. U., 1993. Exec. sec. Music Corp. Am., 1942—45; exec. sec. William Morris Agy., 1945—47; copywriter Foote, Cone & Belding (advt. agy.), Los Angeles, 1948—58; advt. writer, account exec. Kenyon & Eckhardt (advt. agy.), Hollywood, Calif., 1958—96; editor-in-chief Cosmopolitan mag., 1996—, Cosmopolitan Internat. Edits, 1997—. Author 8 books. Named 1 of 25 most influential women in U.S., World Almanac, 1976—81; recipient Francis Holmes Achievement award for outstanding work in advt., 1956—59, Disting. Achievement award, U. So. Calif. Sch. Journalism, 1971, Spl. award for editl. leadership Am. Newspaper, Woman's Club, Washington, 1972, Disting. Achievement award in journalism, Stanford U., 1977, Matrix award in mag. category, N.Y. Women in Comm., 1985, Henry Johnson Fisher award, Mag. Pubs. of Am., 1995, Helen Gurley Brown Rshc. Professorship established name, Northwestern U. Medill Sch. Journalism, 1986, inducted into Pubs.' Hall of Fame, 1988. Mem.: AFTRA, Am. Soc. Mag. Editors (Hall of Fame award 1996), Authors League Am., Eta Upsilon Gamma. Office: Cosmopolitan The Hearst Corp 300 W 57th St New York NY 10019 Office Phone: 212-649-3555.

BROWN, HENRY E., JR., congressman; b. Bishopville, SC, Dec. 20, 1935; m. Billye Beaver; 3 children. Student, Baptist Coll. (now Charleston So. U.), The Citadel, Charleston, SC; D in Bus. Adminstrn. (hon.), The Citadel, 1998; D (hon.), Coll. Charleston, SC, Med. U. SC, Charleston So. U., Coastal Carolina U. V.p. Piggly Wiggly Carolina Co.; mem. SC State Ho. Reps., 1985-2000, US Congress from 1st SC dist., 2001—, mem. transp. and infrastructure com., mem. vets.' affairs com., mem. natural resources com., ranking Rep. subcommittee on fisheries, wildlife and oceans. Apptd. to Ways and Means com., SC State Ho. Reps., 1989, chmn., 1995, chmn. Joint Tax Study Com., mem. Budget and Control bd., Legis. Audit Coun., Joint Bond Rev. com.; mem. Hanahan City Coun., 1996-2000, Hanahan Planning Com., 4 yrs. Mem. Cooper River Bapt. Ch. Served in SC N.G. Named Legislator of Yr., SC Assn. Sch. Librs., 1998-99, Natl. Rep. Legislators Assn., 1999, SC Vocat. Dirs. Assn., 1999, Ind. Colls. of SC, 1995, SC Coll. Legislators, 1995, Outstanding Legislator, SC Sch. Bd. Assn., 1997, SC Legislator of Yr., SC Assn. Realtors, 1997, Servant of Yr., SC Chamber, 1995, SC Taxpayers Watchdog, SC Treas. Office; recipient Dir. award, SC Dept. Revenue, Guardian of Small Bus. award, SC Chap. NFIB, 1996, Order of Palmetto, State of SC, 2000, Founder's medal, Coll. Charleston, 2005. Mem. Hammerton Lodge #332 A.F.M., North Charleston Rotary Club. Republican. Baptist. Office: US House Reps 1124 Longworth House Office Bldg Washington DC 20515 Office Phone: 202-225-3176. Office Fax: 202-225-3407.*

BROWN, HERBERT GRAHAM, entrepreneur; b. Opelousas, La., Nov. 22, 1923; s. T.G. and Mamie (Walker) B.; m. Diane Fontenot, Oct. 18, 1953; children: Deborah, Graham, Jared, Greg, Donna. Student, U. So. La., 1944, Eckerd Coll., St. Petersburg, Fla., 1985. Owner, prin. appliance and furniture stores, La., 1939-89, Fla., 1939—89, rice and cattle farm, La., 1948-89, Browns Thrift City, La., 1961-70; owner, developer shopping ctrs. and apts., various locations, 1955—2007; chmn. bd. Checker Drive-in Restaurants, 1989—95; pres. Am. Bank, La., 1954-63; sr. v.p. Jack Eckerd Corp., Fla., 1970-72; owner, ptnr., developer K-Marts, Mobile Home Parks, shopping ctrs., Fla., 1970—2007, La., 1970—89. Dist. gov., R.I., 1968-69;; vice chmn. ARC, United Way; pres. Fla. & La. vol. Boy Scouts Am.; trustee, vice chmn. Morton F. Plant Hosp., Clearwater, Fla.; world chmn. R.I. Health Hunger & Humanity Com., 1981-86; U.S. chmn. Polio Plus Campaign Com., 1986-88; chmn. bd. dirs. Checkers, 1989-95. Cpl. U.S. Army, 1943-45. Recipient Silver Medallion Brotherhood award NCCJ, Silver Beaver award Boy Scouts Am., Boy Scout Distinguished Citizen award, State of La., 2001, Humanitarian of Yr. award Fla. Mar. of Dimes, Goodwill Industries, Watson Clinic, Medulla Al Merito Rotario, Columbia, Meritorious Svc. award Rotary Internat., Svc. to Mankind award Sertoma; elected to Tampa Bay BUs. Hall of Fame; named Entrepreneur of Yr., State of Fla., named Mr. Clearwater, 2000-2001, Clearwater Chamber of Commerce. Mem. Heartbeat Internat. (bd. dirs.), La. C. of C. (bd. dirs., pres.), Rotary Internat. (bd. dirs. 1978-80, trustee Rotary Found., pres.-elect 1994-95, pres. 1995-96, chmn. Rotary Found. 2000-01, Disting. Svc. award 1986-87). Republican. Roman Catholic. Business E-Mail: hgb@herbertgbrown.com.

BROWN, HERBERT RUSSELL, lawyer, writer; b. Columbus, Ohio, Sept. 27, 1931; s. Thomas Newton and Irene (Hankinson) B.; m. Beverly Ann Jenkins, Dec. 2, 1967; children: David Herbert, Andrew Jenkins. BA, Denison U., 1953; JD, U. Mich., 1956. Assoc. Vorys, Sater, Seymour and Pease, Columbus, Ohio, 1956, 60-64, ptnr., 1965-82; treas. Sunday Creek Coal Co., Columbus, 1970-86; assoc. justice Ohio Supreme Ct., Columbus, 1987-93. Mem. Ohio Ethics Commn., 2002-04, Ohio Public Defender Commn., 2004-; examiner Ohio Bar, 1967-72, Multi-State Bar, 1971-76, Dist. Ct. Bar, 1968-71; commr. Fed. Lands, Columbus, 1967-68, Lake Lands, Columbus, 1981; bd. dirs. Thurber House, 1992-94, Sunday Creek Coal Co.; adj. prof. Ohio State U. Coll. Law, 1997-2000; panelist Am. Arbitration Assn., 1993—. Author: (novels) Presumption of Guilt, 1991, Shadows of Doubt, 1994, (plays) You're My Boy, 1999, Peace with Honor, 2000, Power of God, 2002, The Duchess, 2007; mem. editl. bd. U. Mich. Law Rev., 1955-56. Trustee Columbus Bar Found., 1993—2003, pres., 2001—02; candidate Ohio State Legis.; deacon, mem. governing bd. 1st Cmty. Ch., 1966—80; bd. dirs. Ctrl. Cmty. House Columbus, 1967—75. Capt. JAGC US Army, 1956—57. Recipient Disting. Alumni citation, Denison U., 2003. Fellow Am. Coll. Trial Lawyers; mem. Ohio Bar Assn., Columbus Bar Assn. Democrat.

BROWN, HILTON, artist, educator, writer; b. Momence, Ill., Sept. 22, 1938; s. Oswald E. and Maud M. (Shronts) B. Student, Goodman Theater/Art Inst. Chgo, 1956-58, U. Chgo., 1959-60, U. Ill., Chgo., 1961-62; cert. in fine arts, 1962; Diploma in Fine Arts, BFA in Painting, Sch. of Art Inst. Chgo., 1963, MFA in Painting, 1964. Instr. drawing/painting Sch. Art Inst. Chgo., 1962-65; asst. prof. fine art Sch. Fine Arts Washington U., St. Louis, 1965-68; asst. prof. fine arts Goucher Coll., Towson, Md., 1968-70, assoc. prof. fine arts, 1970-75, prof. and chair dept. visual arts, 1975-78; vis. assoc. prof. art history U. Del., 1974-78, prof. art conservation Newark, 1978-84, Mayer prof. artists techniques, 1984-88, prof. art, art history and art conservation, 1988-92, Harriet T. Baily prof. art, art conservation, art history and mus. studies, 1992—; dealer Gary Snyder Fine Art: Contemporary Am. Art, NYC. Cons., lectr. Nat. Tchr. Inst./Nat. Gallery of Art, Washington, 1990-2000, 06-. Author: (exhbn. catalog) The Art and Archives of Ralph Mayer, 1984; co-author (exhbn. catalog) Milk and Eggs: The American Revival of Tempera Painting, 1930-1950, 2002; co-curator (exhbn.) Brandywine River Mus., Akron Art Mus., Spencer Mus., U. Kans., 2002; one person show Susan Isaacs Gallery, Wilmington, Del., 1990; more than 140 invitational and juried shows, 1961—; work in mus. collections Balt. Mus. Art. Sec. bd. dirs. Gay and Lesbian Alliance of Del., Wilmington, 1991-93; co-chair Lesbian, Gay, Bisexual Caucus of Commn. to Promote Racial and Cultural Diversity, U. Del., 1992-99, chair faculty senate com. on diversity and affirmative action, 1993-95, 97-98. Democrat. Anglican Catholic. Avocations: reading, gardening. Office: Univ of Delaware Mus Studies 207 Mechanical Hall Newark DE 19716 Home Phone: 302-594-0724; Office Phone: 302-831-8237. Business E-Mail: hilton@udel.edu.

BROWN, HOLMES, public relations executive; b. Prescott, Kans., Oct. 2, 1914; s. Frank Emerson and May Holmes Brown; m. Mary Ellen Lynch, Oct. 17, 1938; children: Holmes Cheney, Hamilton Frank, James Emerson. BS, Iowa State U., 1936; postgrad., GE Inst., 1936-39. Mgmt. technician GE, various locations, 1936-43; with pub. rels. Am. Locomotive, NYC, 1945-50; pub. affairs exec. Colonial Williamsburg (Va.) Found., 1950; pub. rels. exec. Ford Motor Co., Dearborn, Mich., 1952-60; asst. to Sgt. Shriver War on Poverty, Washington, 1964-66; v.p. Am. Airlines, NYC, 1966-68; pub. affairs officer Continental Group, NYC, 1968-75; v.p. Continental Group Found., NYC, 1975-79; pres., chmn. The Inst. for Applied Econs., NYC, Va., 1979—. Prodr. nat. nutrition program GE Co., 1941-43; pres., chmn. N.Y. Bd. of Trade, 1979-85. Editor: How to Get the Most Our of the Food You Buy, 1942; prodr. Headstart Ednl. Guide Books, 1965; author: Can You Trust Network Evening News; author (newspaper article) Nixon's Enemy List, 1973. Pres. Fund for New Priorities, N.Y., 1977, bd. dirs., 1976-99. Recipient Outstanding Alumni award Iowa State U., 1957, Leadership award Fund for New Priorities, 1978, Silver Anvil award Am. Pub. Rels. Soc., 1959. Mem. Admirals Club (life), Nat. Press Club, Boars Head Sports Club, The Goodwin Soc. Colonial Williamsburg, The Nat. Hist. Soc., Va. Hist. Soc. Democrat. Episcopalian. Avocations: farming, tennis, sculpting, track, history. Office: Inst for Applied Econs 1 Ednam Village Charlottesville VA 22903-4636 Home: 1 Ednam Village Charlottesville VA 22903 Office Phone: 434-971-8333. Business E-Mail: holmesmbrown@earthlink.net.

BROWN, IFIGENIA THEODORE, retired lawyer; b. Syracuse, NY, Mar. 14, 1930; d. Gus and Christine Theodore; m. Paul Frederick Brown, Sept. 16, 1956; 1 child, Paul Darrow. BA, Syracuse U., 1951, LLB, JD, 1954. Bar: N.Y. 1956. Acting police justice Village of Ballston Spa, NY, 1960—62; sr. ptnr. Brown & Brown, Ballston Spa, 1958—95; ptnr. Brown Brown & Peterson Esqs, Ballston Spa, 1995—2000; of counsel Brown, Peterson, Craig and Thomas, Ballston Spa, 2000—06, ret., 2006. Chmn. N.Y. State Bd. Real Property Svcs., Albany, 1996—2006. Bd. dirs. Charlton Sch. for Girls, 1989-93, Ballston Spa Libr. Bd., 1991-94; founder, pres. Saratoga County Women's Rep. Club; vice-chmn. Saratoga County Rep. Com., 1958-72, treas. St. George Orthodox Ch., Schenectady, 2007—. Mem. N.Y. State Bar Assn., Saratoga County Bar Assn. (treas. 1983-84, pres. 1984-85), Zonta (pres. Saratoga County 1962, 90), Order Ea. Star. Republican. Greek Orthodox. Avocations: church choir, piano. Home: 42 Hyde Blvd Ballston Spa NY 12020-1608 Office: Brown Peterson Craig and Thomas One E High St Ballston Spa NY 12020 Office Phone: 518-885-9292, 518-885-7496.

BROWN, J. E. (BUSTER BROWN), lawyer, consultant; b. Dec. 10, 1940; BS, Tex. A&I U., 1963; JD, U. Tex., 1967. Mem. Tex. Senate, 1980—2002, chmn. natural resources com., chmn. sunset adv. com., chmn. natural resources interim com., chmn. water resources devel. com.; chmn. Gulf States Marine Fisheries Commn., Tex. Water Found. Mem. Criminal Justice Com., So. Legis. Conf. Energy Commn., Am. legis. Exch. Coun. Telecom. Commn., Nat. Conf. State Legis. Comm. and Info. Policy, Legis. and Congl. Redistricting Com., Fin. Com., Nominations Com., Vets. Affairs and Mil. Installations Com., alt. Environ. com., Legal Com. Interstate Oil and Gas Compact Commn.; past chmn. Energy Coun.; adj. prof. U. Tex. Sch. Law. Home Phone: 512-482-0404; Office Phone: 512-457-0600. E-mail: buster-brown@austin.rr.com.

BROWN, J. MARTIN, oncologist, educator; b. Doncaster, Eng., Oct. 15, 1941; married; 2 children. BSc, U. Birmingham, 1963; MSc, U. London, 1965; DPhil in Radiation Biology, Oxford U., 1968. NIH fellow radiation biology Stanford U. Med. Ctr., Calif., 1968-70, rsch. assoc. Calif., 1970-71, from asst. prof. to assoc. prof. Calif., 1971-84, prof., dir. divsn. radiation biology Calif., 1984—, dir. Cancer Biology Rsch. Lab. Calif., 1985—. Sr. fellow Am. Cancer Soc. Dernham, 1971-74; mem. adv. com. biol. effects of ionizing radiations NAS, 1971—. Recipient Bruce F. Cain Meml. award, Am. Assn. Cancer Rsch., 1999. Mem. AAAS, Am. Assn. Cancer Rsch., Am. Soc. Therapeutical Radiology & Oncology, Brit. Inst. Radiology, Brit. Assn. Cancer Rsch., Radiation Rsch. Soc. (9th Rsch. award 1980). Achievements include research in mammalian cellular radiobiology, tumor radiobiology, experimental chemotherapy, bioreductive cytotoxic agents, radiation carcinogenesis. Office: Stanford U Med Sch Cancer Biology Rsch Lab Dept of Radiation & Oncology GK103 Stanford CA 94305-5468

BROWN, J'AMY MARONEY, journalist, media consultant, investor; b. Oct. 30, 1945; d. Roland Francis and Jeanne (Wilbur) Maroney; m. James Raphael Brown, Jr., Nov. 5, 1967 (dec. July 1982); children: James Roland Francis, Jeanne Raphael. Student, U. So. Calif., 1963-67. Reporter LA Herald Examiner, 1966—67, Lewisville Leader, Dallas, 1980-81; editor First Person Mag., Dallas., 1981-82; journalism dir. Pacific Palisades Sch., LA, 1983—84; freelance writer, media cons., 1984-88; media dir., chief media strategist Tellem Inc., 1990-92, comm. cons., issues mgr., 1992—; editor Montecito/Montage@Independent.com. Press liaison US papal visit, LA, 1987; pres., CEO, owner PRformance Group Comm., 1995—. Contbr. columns to newspapers, jours. and websites. Auction chmn. Assn. Pub. Broadcasting, Houston, 1974, 1975; vice chmn. Dallas Arts Coun., 1976—80, Met. March of Dimes, Dallas, 1980—82; del. Dallas Coun. PTAs, 1976—80; pres. Montecito Assn.; bd. dirs. J.M. Brown Charitable Found., Women's Econ. Ventures, Santa Barbara Visual Arts Alliance, Counselors Cir.; hon. bd. Heal the Ocean; bd. dirs., pres. continuing edn. Santa Barbara City Coll.; coord. specialist World Cup Soccer Organizing com. Recipient UPI Editors award for investigative reporting, 1981. Mem. NAFE, Pub. Rels. Soc. Am. (accredited), Women Meeting Women, Women in Comm., Am. Bus. Women's Assn., Goleta Valley Art Assn., Santa Barbara C. of C. (media com.). Republican. Roman Catholic. Home: 1143 High Rd Santa Barbara CA 93108-2430 Office Phone: 805-969-5515.

BROWN, JACK A., state representative, rancher, real estate broker; b. St. Johns, Ariz., May 2, 1929; m. Beverly Van Camp Agr. and econs. degree, Brigham Young U., 1953. Mem. Ariz. Ho. Reps., 1963-74, 87-96, Dem. leader, 1969-72, asst. minority leader, 1989-92; mem. Ariz. Ho. Reps. 5th dist., 2004—; minority leader Ariz. Senate, 1997—2004. Former chair State Water Quality Control Coun. Mem. Apache City Bd. Realtors, Cattle Growers, Farm Bur., Ariz. Acad., State Chamber, Kiwanis. Democrat. also: PO Box 220 Saint Johns AZ 85936-0220 Office: Ariz Ho Reps 1700 W Washington St Ste H Phoenix AZ 85007-2844 Office Phone: 602-926-4129. Fax: 602-542-3429; Office Fax: 602-417-3010. Business E-Mail: jbrown@azleg.state.az.us.

BROWN, JACK H., supermarket company executive; b. LA, June 14, 1939; Student, San Jose State U, UCLA. V.p. Sages Complete Marktes, San Bernardino, Calif., 1960-67, Marsh Supermarkets, Yorktown, Ind., 1971-77; pres. Pantry Supermarkets, Pasadena, Calif., 1977-79; pres. mid-west divsn. Cullum Cos., Dallas, 1979-81; pres., CEO Stater Bros. Markets, Colton, Calif., 1981—; also chmn. Trustee U. Redlands, Calif.; bd. dirs. Goodwill Industries of inland Empire, San Bernardino; bd. councillors Calif. State U., San Bernardion. With USNR, 1956-62. Recipient Horatio Alger award Disting. Ams., 1992, Bus. Exec. of Yr. award U. so. Calif., 1993; Calif. State U., San Berardino Sch. Bus. named in his honor, 1992. Mem. Western Assn. Food Chains (v.p., bd. dirs., pres. 1987-88), Calif. Retailers Assn. (bd. dirs.), Food Mktg. Inst. (vice chmn.), So. Calif. Grocers Assn., Food Employers Coun. (bd. govs.), Life Savs. and Loan Assn. (dir.), Elks. Republican. Presbyterian. Office: Stater Bros Markets 21700 Barton Rd Colton CA 92324*

BROWN, JACQUELINE ELAINE, obstetrician, gynecologist; b. Houston, Sept. 20, 1948; d. Issac Cleve Brown and Hazel Eva (Mullen) Hill; m. Felton Watkins, Dec. 31, 1971 (div. Jan. 1974); 1 child, Alan Christopher Watkins; m. Ronald Hayes, Nov. 9, 1985. BA, North Tex. State U., 1970; postgrad., Tex. So. U., 1971-72; MD, U. Tex., Dallas, 1980; MPH, Johns Hopkins U., 1985. Intern in ob-gyn Pa. Hosp., Phila., 1980-84, resident in ob-gyn, 1980-84; ob-gyn physician Johns Hopkins Health Plan, Balt., 1984-85, Kaiser Permanente Health Plan, Washington, 1985-87; former asst. med. dir. ob-gyn Johns Hopkins Health Plan, Balt.; founder Total Women Health Care Ctr., 1991—. Advisor Black Women's Health Project, Phila., 1983-84; former cons. Women's Resource and Devel. Ctr., Balt., former Teen Parenting Prevention Program, Balt., Straight Talk, Washington, 1987. Mem. bd. trustees Bethel African Meth. Episcopal Ch., Balt., 1985. Southwestern Found. scholar, Dallas, 1976. Fellow Am. Coll. Ob-Gyn (jr.); mem. Am. Med. Women's Assn., Alpha Kappa Alpha. Avocations: bicycling, walking. Office: Total Woman Health Care Ctr

11821 East Freeway Ste 300 Houston TX 77029 Office Phone: 713-453-6773. E-mail: totalwomanhealth@yahoo.com.

BROWN, JAMES BENTON, lawyer, department chairman; b. Pitts., Jan. 18, 1945; s. Sidney J. and Marian R. (Bailiss) B.; m. Susan M. Brenner, Aug. 6, 1967; children: Jessica Lynn, Joshua David. BA, U. Louisville, 1967; JD, Duquesne U., 1971. Bar: Pa. 1971, U.S. Dist. Ct. (we. dist.) Pa. 1971, U.S. Ct. Appeals (3d cir.) 1974, U.S. Supreme Ct. 1982. Dir., ptnr. Cohen & Grigsby, P.C., chair labor and employment group, chair employment litig. group. Lectr. Pa. Bar Inst.; mediator Am. Arbitration Assn., US Dist. Ct. (we. dist.) Pa. Bd. dirs. Jewish Assn. Aging. Mem. ABA, Fed. Bar Assn., Pa. Bar Assn., Allegheny County Bar Assn., Internat. Assn. Def. Counsel. Democrat. Home: 100 Denniston St 1 Pittsburgh PA 15206 Office: Cohen & Grigsby PC 15th fl 11 Stanwix St Ste 15 Pittsburgh PA 15222-1312 Address: 675 Seaview Ct F-1 Marco Island FL 34145 Office Phone: 412-297-4900. Business E-Mail: jbrown@cohenlaw.com.

BROWN, JAMES CHANDLER, retired university administrator; b. Garden City, NY, Aug. 5, 1947; s. Harry Chandler and Lillian Marie (Cutter) B. BA, Susquehanna U., Selinsgrove, Pa., 1970; License es Lettres, Geneva U., 1978; postgrad., Stanford U., 1984. Rsch. asst. Geneva U., 1972—79; asst. Galerie Jan Krugier, Geneva, 1978—81; coord. pubs. So. Oreg. State Coll., Ashland, 1982-84; dir. pubs. So. Oreg. U., 1984—2001, emeritus faculty, 2003—; resident dir. Oreg. Ctr., Oreg. Univ. Sys., Lyon, France, 2001—03; owner J. Chandler Consulting. Cons. in field. Author: How to Sharpen Your Publications (brochure, Case award) 1985, College Viewbook (booklet), 1985. Sec. bd. dirs. Schneider Mus. Art, Ashland, 1985-94, Friends Polk County, 2006—. Mem. Omicron Delta Kappa Leadership Soc., Coun. of Mgrs. Methodist. Avocations: reading, hiking, travel, photography, kayaking. Home: 121 NW Howard Ln Dallas OR 97338 Business E-Mail: jimbrown@sou.edu.

BROWN, JAMES HEMPHILL, biology professor; AB in Zoology, with honors, Cornell U., 1963; PhD in Zoology, U. Mich., 1967. Rackham postdoctoral fellow UCLA, 1967—68, asst. prof. zoology, 1968—71; asst. prof. biology U. Utah, 1971—73, assoc. prof., 1973—75; assoc. prof. ecology and evolutionary biology U. Ariz., 1975—78, prof., 1978—87; prof. biology U. N.Mex, 1987—, ann. rsch. lectr., 1999, regents' prof., 1990—2001, disting. prof. biology, 2001—; external faculty mem. Santa Fe Inst., 1995—. John Simon Guggenheim Meml. Found. fellow, 1991—92. Fellow: AAAS, Am. Acad. Arts and Sciences; mem.: NAS, Soc. Conservation Biology, Am. Soc. Mammalogists (C. Hart Merriam award outstanding svc. mammalogy 1981), Soc. Study Evolution, Ecol. Soc. Am. (Eugene P. Odum award for edn. 2001, Robert H. MacArthur award rsch. 2002), Brit. Ecol. Soc. (Marsh award career achievement 2002), Am. Soc. Naturalists. Office: Dept Biology Univ New Mexico Castetter Hall 286 Albuquerque NM 87131 Office Phone: 505-277-9337. Office Fax: 505-277-0304. E-mail: jhbrown@unm.edu.

BROWN, JAMES KNIGHT, lawyer; b. Rainelle, W.Va., Sept. 25, 1929; s. Hugh Allen and Florence Catherine (Knight) B.; m. Sarah Elizabeth Droste, June 21, 1952; children: Carolyn, Patricia, Julia. BS, W.Va. U., 1951, LLB, 1956. Bar: W.Va. 1956, U.S. Ct. Appeals (4th and 6th cir.), U.S. Supreme Ct. Assoc. Jackson & Kelly, Charleston, W.Va., 1956-62, ptnr., 1962-98; mem. Jackson & Kelly PLLC, Charleston, 1999—2001, of counsel, 2001—. Former W.Va. adv. bd. dirs. BB&T Corp. 1st lt. USAF, 1951-53. Fellow Am. Bar Found., W.Va. Bar Found.; mem. ABA, W.Va. State Bar (pres. 1975-76), Order of Coif, Phi Beta Kappa. Democrat. Presbyterian. Avocations: woodworking, golf. Office: Jackson & Kelly PLLC 1600 Laidley Tower Charleston WV 25301-2189

BROWN, JAMES NELSON, JR., retired accountant; b. Bronx, Apr. 17, 1929; s. James Nelson and Agnes Mary (Cummins) B.; m. Lila Barbara Watt, Dec. 12, 1950; children: Constance Ellen Brown Buttacavole, Nelson Arthur, Richard John. BSBA, Drake U., 1956. CPA; cert. internal auditor, fraud examiner. Sr. acct. Arthur Andersen & Co., NYC, 1956-61; asst. v.p., dir. internal auditing Salomon Inc., NYC, 1961-86, asst. v.p., dir. projects mgmt. dept., 1986-91, asst. v.p. environ. litigation dept., 1991-93, v.p., mgr. environ. litig. dept., 1994-97; cons. environ. litig. dept Citigroup, Inc., 1998—2002; ret., 2002. Com. chmn. Cub Scouts, 1973-75; troop com. chmn. Boy Scouts Am., Carteret, N.J., 1976-77, 88-90, com. mem., 1978-87. Sgt. AUS, 1947-52. Mem. AICPA, VFW, Am. Mgmt. Assn., N.J. Soc. CPAs, Nat. Assn. Cert. Fraud Examiners, Inst. Internal Auditors, Am. Legion, Elks. Republican. Roman Catholic. Personal E-mail: jnbrownjr@aol.com.

BROWN, JAMES ROBERT, retired air force officer; b. Bozeman, Mont., June 17, 1930; s. Marley Robert and Ann Louise (Pace) B.; m. Sandra Shores, Dec. 19, 1964; children: James V., Brian R. BS, Mont. State U., 1953; grad., Squadron Officer Sch., 1962, Air Command and Staff Coll., 1964, Indsl. Coll. of Armed Forces, 1974. Commd. 2d lt. U.S. Air Force, 1953, advanced through grades to lt. gen., 1984, undergrad. pilot tng. program Williams AFB, Ariz., 1954-54, bomb comdr., intelligence officer 20th Fighter-Bomber Wing Royal Air Force Station Wethersfield, England, 1955—58, fighter gunnery, instr. pilot, acad. instr. Nellis AFB, Nev., 1958—60, fighter weapons sch., rsch. and devel. project officer, instr. pilot, 1960—62, flight evaluator Tactical Air Command Langley AFB, Va., 1962-63, flight comdr., instr. pilot Davis-Monthan AFB, Ariz., 1964-66, tour duty Vietnam, 1966—67, dir. tng. analysis and devel. Davis-Monthan AFB, Ariz., 1967-71, staff action officer tactics br. chief, acting chief tactical div. for Directorate of Plans and ops. Washington, 1971-75, dir. ops. 388th Tactical Fighter Wing Korat Royal Thai AFB, Thailand, 1975-76, vice comdr. 3d Tactical Fighter Wing Clark Air Base, Philippines, 1976, comdr. 3d Tactical Fighter Wing, 1976-78, comdr. 313th Air div. and 18th Tactical Fighter Wing Kadena Air Base, Japan, 1978-81, dep. chief of staff for ops. Ramstein Air Base, Germany, 1981, asst. chief staff ops. Supreme Hdqrs. Allied Powers, Europe Mons, Belgium, 1981-84, comdr. Allied Air Forces So. Europe, dep. comdr. in chief U.S. Air Forces in Europe Naples, Italy, 1984-86; vice comdr. Langley AFB Tactical Air Command, Va., 1986-88; ret., 1988; dir. aviation programs East Inc., Reston, Va., 1991—94, 1997—. Decorated D.D.S.M., D.S.S.M., Legion of Merit with oak leaf cluster, Bronze Star medal, Air Medal with four oak leaf clusters, Air Force Commendation medal with oak leaf cluster, Def. Superior Service medal Avocations: golf, bike riding, walking, fishing, horseback riding. Home: 18286 Buccaneer Terrace Leesburg VA 20176-8479 Office Phone: 703-263-0477. Business E-Mail: tfabyanic@eastinc.us.

BROWN, JAMES THOMPSON, JR., computer information scientist, logistics specialist; b. Orange, N.J., Jan. 3, 1935; s. James Thompson and Marjorie (Hale) B.; m. Alice Beasley, Oct. 3, 1959; children— Kathryn, James. B.M.E., Cornell U., 1957; M.S., Stanford U., 1964. Applied sci. rep. IBM Corp., Schenectady, N.Y., 1957-59, corp. staff mem., White Plains, N.Y., 1960-68; cons. Case & Co., Stamford, Conn., 1969-74, dir., 1975-83, pres., 1983-84; pres. Tom Brown & Co., Wilton, Conn., 1985—; developer optimum buying and inventory mgmt. sys. and svc. pricing techniques; designer warehouse and distbn. sys. Life mem. Rep. Inner Circle. Mem. Internat. Assn. Chain Stores (adviser, speaker 1971—), Nat. Grocers Assn. (adviser 1983—), Am. Inst. Indsl. Engrs. (sr. mem.), Inst. Ops. Rsch. and Mgmt. Scis., Landmark Club, Cornell Club (N.Y.), Capitol Hill Club. Republican. Home: 135 Middlebrook Farm Rd Wilton CT 06897-2019 Office: Tom Brown & Co PO Box 431 Wilton CT 06897-0431 *One of my guiding principles is not to try to solve a problem until I understand it. Understanding often means getting your hands dirty. And when I do understand, take the time to carefully think out the solution.*

BROWN, JAMES WARD, mathematician, educator, author; b. Phila., Jan. 15, 1934; s. George Harold and Julia Elizabeth (Ward) B.; m. Jacqueline Read, Sept. 3, 1957; children: Scott Cameron, Gordon Elliot. AB, Harvard U., 1955; AM, U. Mich., 1958, PhD (Inst. Sci and Tech. predoctoral fellow), 1964. Asst. prof. math. U. Mich., Dearborn, 1964-66, assoc. prof., 1968-71, prof., 1971—, acting chmn. dept., 1974, 85. Asst. prof. Oberlin Coll., 1966-68; editorial cons. Math. Rev., 1970-85; dir. NSF Grant, 1969 Author: (with R.V. Churchill) Complex Variables and Applications, 7th edit., 2004, Internat. Student edit., 1996, Japanese edit., 2004, Spanish edit., 2004, Chinese edit., 2005, Korean edit., 2004, Greek edit., 1993, Fourier Series and Boundary Value Problems, 6th edit., 2003, internat. student edit., 1993, Japanese edit., 1980; contbr. articles to U.S. and fgn. sci. jours. Recipient Disting. Faculty award U. Mich.-Dearborn, 1976, Disting. Faculty award Mich. Assn. Governing Bds. Colls. and Univs., 1983 Mem. Am. Math. Soc., Research Club of U. Mich., Sigma Xi. Home: 1710 Morton Ave Ann Arbor MI 48104-4522 Office: 4901 Evergreen Rd Dearborn MI 48128-1491

BROWN, JANICE ROGERS, federal judge, former state supreme court justice; b. Greenville, Ala., May 11, 1949; m. Allan Brown (dec.); 1 child, Nathan; m. Dewey Parker. BA, Calif. St. U., Sacramento, 1974; JD, UCLA, 1977; LLM, U. Va., 2004. Bar: Calif. 1977. Dep. legis. counsel Calif. Legis. Counsel Bur., 1977—79; dep. atty. gen. Calif. Dept. Justice, 1979—87; deputy sec., gen. counsel Calif. Business, Transportation & Housing Agy., 1987—90; sr. assoc. Nielsen, Merksamer, Parrinello, Mueller & Naylor, Sacramento, 1990—91; legal affairs sec. to Gov. Pete Wilson State of Calif., Sacramento, 1991—94; assoc. justice Calif. Ct. Appeals (3rd dist.), Sacramento, 1994—96, Calif. Supreme Ct., San Francisco, 1996—2005; judge US Ct. Appeals (DC cir.), 2005—. Adj. prof. law U. Pacific, 1998—99. Achievements include being the first African-American woman to serve on the California Supreme Court. Office: US Ct Appeals 333 Constitution Ave NW Washington DC 20001*

BROWN, JANINE, lawyer; b. Wheeling, W.Va., Oct. 5, 1961; BA with distinction, Univ. Mich., 1982; JD high honors, Duke Univ., 1986. Bar: Ga. 1986. Ptnr., chair, tech. group Alston & Bird LLP, Atlanta. Named a Ga. Super Lawyer, 2004; named one of the Top 50 Female Super Lawyers., 2004. Office: Alston & Bird LLP One Atlantic Ctr 1201 W Peachtree St NW Atlanta GA 30309-3424 Office Phone: 404-881-7834. Office Fax: 404-881-7777. Business E-Mail: jbrown@alston.com.

BROWN, JARED, theater director, educator, writer; BFA, Ithaca Coll., 1960; MA Theatre, San Francisco State Coll., 1962; PhD Theatre, U. Minn., 1967. Instr. creative writing St. Paul Pub. Sch. System, 1962-63; teaching asst. U. Minn., 1963-64, instr. Communication Dept., 1964-65; from asst. prof. to prof. dept. theatre Western Ill. U., 1965-89, acad. dir. Semester in London, 1979-80; dir. Sch. Theatre Arts, Prof. Theatre Arts Ill. Wesleyan U., 1989—2002; adj. prof. Ill. State U., 2003—. Aided devel. (policies, curriculum), Theatre Dept. Western Ill. U., 1971; panel discussant Western Ill. U., 1973, 1974; chmn. panel Ill. Theatre Assn. Convention, 1976; panel discussant Assn. Theatre in Higher Edn. Convention, 1987; disting. faculty lectr. Western Ill. U., 1986, dir. grad. program dept. theatre, 1975-89, chmn. directing, theatre history and playwriting programs, dept. theatre, 1972-89; mem. panel judges to award NEH Summer Stipends, Ill., 1990; mem. panel to award NEH Fellowship Grants, 2004; judge Am. Coll. Theatre Festival, 1973-74, 89-90; mem. various theatre coms. Ill. Wesleyan U.; mem. various coms. Univ., Coll. Fine Arts, Dept. Theatre Western Ill. U.; spkr., presenter in field. Author: The Fabulous Lunts, A Biography of Alfred Lunt and Lynn Fontanne, 1986, (Barnard Hewitt award 1987), Zero Mostel: A Biography, 1989, The Theatre in America During the Revolution, 1995, Alan J. Pakula: His Films and His Life, 2005 (Writers Notes Book award), Moss Hart, A Prince of the Theatre, 2006, also 15 plays; dir. 100 plays including The Merchant of Venice, Hedda Gabler, Henry IV, La Ronde, Death of a Salesman, Cat on a Hot Tin Roof, A Streetcar Named Desire, Who's Afraid of Virginia Woolf, You Can't Take It With You, Brighton Beach Memoirs, Inherit the Wind, Peter Pan, Bye Bye Birdie, Guys and Dolls, Kiss Me Kate, 110 In The Shade, Annie, Funny Girl, Broadway Bound, Tartuffe, Antigone, She Loves Me, Noises Off, Doubt, Sight Unseen, Bedroom Farce, Once in a Lifetime; appeared in My Fair Lady, Western Ill. U., 1978, On The Twentieth Century, 1986, Russian Dressing, 2005, Morning's at Seven, 2007, various radio and TV programs; contbr. chpts. to texts, 20 scholarly articles to profl. jours. Recipient stipend NEH, 1988, DuPont award for tchg. excellence, 1997; named Best Dir., The Pantagraph, 1991, 92, 94, 96; grantee Ill. Arts Coun., 1980, 81, 87, Western Ill. U., 1983-85, 86-87, 89, Cultural Arts Devel. Fund, 1980-89, Ill. Wesleyan U., 1990, Artistic/Scholarly Devel. grantee, 1999, 2002. Mem. Nat. Collegiate Players, Phi Kappa Phi, Theta Alpha Phi. Home: 18 Chatsford Ct Bloomington IL 61704-6220 Office: Sch Theatre Arts Ill Wesleyan U Bloomington IL 61702 Office Phone: 309-664-0708. E-mail: jbrown@iwu.edu.

BROWN, JASON ROBERT, composer, arranger; b. Ossining, NY, 1970; m. Georgia Stitt, 2003. Studied composition, Eastman Sch. Music, Rochester, NY. Tchr. musical theatre performance and composition U. Southern Calif. Composer, lyricist (Broadway plays) Parade, 1998 (Tony award best original score, 1999, Drama Desk award outstanding music, 1999), Urban Cowboy, 2003, (Off-Broadway) Songs for a New World, 1995, The Last Five Years, 2002 (Drama Desk award outstanding music, 2002, Drama Desk award outstanding lyrics, 2002), musical dir. NY Rock, The Petrified Prince, orchestrations John & Jen, orchestrations, arranger, music supr. Dinah Was, orchestrations, arranger Love's Fire: Fresh Numbers by Seven American Playwrights; composer: (Off-Broadway) Long Day's Journey Into Night, Fuddy Meers, The Waverly Gallery, Kimberly Akimbo, Last Dance, 13, 2006; arranger (musical theatre) A New Brain; musician (piano, co-orchestrations): (albums) Songs for a New World, 1997, Parade, 1999; musician: (piano, orchestrations) The Last Five Years, 2002; musician: (piano, baritone guitar, vocals, orchestrations) Lauren Kennedy: Songs of Jason Robert Brown, 2003; musician: (piano, vocals, orchestrations, arrangements) (solo album) Wearing Someone Else's Clothes, 2005; composer, lyricist (songs) Stars and the Moon, And I Will Follow, Letting You Go, You Don't Know This Man, All the Wasted Time, Kind of the World, Surabaya-Santa. Recipient Gilman and Gonzalez-Falla Mus. Theatre award, 1996. Mem.: Am. Fedn. Musicians Local 802, Dramatist's Guild. Office: Screen Composers of Am 2451 Nichols Canyon Rd Los Angeles CA 90046-1734 E-mail: askjrb@jasonrobertbrown.com.

BROWN, JASON WALTER, neurologist, educator, researcher; b. NYC, Apr. 14, 1938; s. Samuel Robert and Sylvia (Brown) B.; children: Jonathan Schilder, Jovana Millay; m. Carine Hoeusler; 1 child, Ilya. BA, U. Calif.-Berkeley, 1959; MD, U.S.C., 1963. Intern St. Elizabeth's Hosp., Washington, 1963-64; resident in neurology UCLA, 1964-67; practice medicine specializing in neurology NYC, 1970—; instr. Boston U. Med. Sch., 1969-70; asst. clin. prof. Columbia-Presbyn. Hosp., NYC, 1970-75; vis. asst. prof. neurology Albert Einstein Coll. Medicine, NYC, 1972-75; vis. assoc. prof. Rockefeller U., NYC, 1978-79; clin. assoc. prof. neurology NYU, 1975-79, clin. prof., 1979—; pres. Inst. Research in Behavioral Neurosci. Vis. scholar N.Y. Psychoanalytic Inst., 1993—. Author: Aphasia, Apraxia and Agnosia, 1972, Mind, Brain and Consciousness, 1977, Life of the Mind, 1988; editor: Jargonaphasia, 1982; English Translation of Aphasie by Arnold Pick (Aphasia), 1973, Neuropsychology of Visual Perception, 1989, Classics in Neuropsychology: Apraxia and Agnosia, Self and Process, 1991, Time, Will and Mental Process, 1996, Mind and Nature, 2000, The Self-Embodying Mind, 2002, Process and The Authentic Self, 2005; contbr. numerous articles on neurology to med. jours.; mem. edit. bd. Jour. Nervous and Mental Disease, Aphasiology, Advances in Neurolinguistics. Grantee NIH; fellow Alexander von Humboldt Found., 1979—, World Rehab. Fund, 1982, Founds. Fund for Research in Psychiatry, 1974-75. Jewish. Home and Office: 66 E 79th St New York NY 10021-0244 E-mail: drjbrown@hotmail.com.

BROWN, JAY MARSHALL, retired secondary school educator; b. Bklyn., July 26, 1933; s. Sidney and Bertha (Swirsky) Brown; m. Merle Thelma Kaminsky, Nov. 4, 1956; children: Sidney Matthew, Ellen Beth Factor. BS in Journalism, NYU, 1955, MA in Am. Civilization, 1960; postgrad., Yeshiva U., 1958-60, U. Conn., West Hartford, 1968-70; 6th yr. profl. diploma, So. Conn. State Coll., 1977. Pub. rels. dir, asst. credit mgr. Colonial Sand & Stone Co., NYC, 1955-60; employment counselor NYC Dept. Welfare, 1960-63; attendance tchr. Bd. Edn., NYC, 1963-65; youth dir. Jewish Cmty. Ctr., Rochester, NY, 1965-67; exec. dir. Conn. Valley Regional B'nai B'rith Youth, New Haven, 1967-70; resource tchr. Sheridan Mid. Sch., Bd. Edn., New Haven, 1970-72; learning ctr. tchr. Bd. Edn., New Haven, 1972-74; social studies tchr. Troup Mid. Sch., Bd. Edn., New Haven, 1974-80; history tchr. Hillhouse HS, Bd. Edn., New Haven, 1980-93; ret., 1993. Tchr. U.S. history New Eng. Acad. Jewish Studies, New Haven, 1984—85; specialist audio-visual and media Quinnipiac Coll., Hamden, Conn., 1982. Columnist: The Luna Spark, 1961—63; contbr. articles to profl. jours. Acting pres. Alliance Mentally Ill, 1993—94, pres., 1995—2007, facilitator, treas., 2007—; mem. Commn. on Disabilities Town of Hamden, 2001—04, chair Commn. on Disabilities, 2002—03; corr. sec. Jewish Hist. Soc., New Haven, 1980—81; v.p. Regency Hills Condo Assn., 1994—95; active Mental Health Month Com., 1995—99; family resource ctr. com. Consultation Ctr., 1994—98; coord. Mental Health Network Spkrs. Bur., 1996—98; facilitator Journey of Hope Ednl. Program, 2002—04; vice chmn. Catchment area 7 Regional Mental Health Bd., 1997—2004, chmn. Catchment area 7, 2004—06; rev. and evaluation team dist. 2 State Regional Mental Health Bd., 1996—2000, vice chmn. dist. 2, 1997—2000, chmn. dist. 2, 2004—06; bd. govs. Inst. Learning and Retirement, 1998—2000; coord. New Haven County's Mental Illness Awareness Week, 1998—2003, People Helping People Program, 1998—2003; active Hamden Commn. Disability Rights and Obligation, 2001—04; chmn. Hamden Commn. Disability Rights, 2002—03; active Hamden Dem. Town Com., 1974—76; pres. Brotherhood Mishkan Israel, 1976—78, 1983—89, 2001—02, sec., 1997—98, treas., 1998—2001, 2004—; asst. treas. Congregation Mishkan Israel, 1983—84, chmn. budget com., 1987—88, chmn. house and property com., 1979—84, trustee, 1978—84, 1986—92, 1994—2003, libr., archivist, 1981—84, pers. com., 1996—2002, abatement com., 1997—98, ops. com., 1999—2002. Recipient Man of Yr. award of Merit, Congregation Mishkan Israel's Brotherhood, 1978, People Helping People award, Sears and NAMI, 2001. Mem.: New Haven County Ret. Tchrs. Assn. (v.p. 1994—95, sec. 1997—2003), Phi Delta Kappa. Democrat. Jewish. Avocations: stamp collecting/philately, polit. items, sports items, cmty. svc. Home: 25 Wright Ln Hamden CT 06517-2126 Personal E-mail: jay_m_brown@sbcglobal.net, cac7@sbcglobal.net.

BROWN, JEAN WILLIAMS, former state supreme court justice; b. Birmingham, Ala. m. E. Terry Brown; 2 children. Grad. with honors, Samford U., 1974; JD, U. Ala., 1977. Bar: Ala. 1977, U.S. Ct. Appeals (11th cir.), U.S. Supreme Ct. Law clerk Tucker, Gray & Thigpen; asst. atty. gen. criminal appeals divsn., chief extradition officer Ala. Atty. Gen.'s Office; judge Ala. Ct. Criminal Appeals, 1997-99; justice Supreme Ct. Ala., 1999—2005. Mem.: Bench and Bar Legal Honor Soc. Office: Ala Supreme Ct 300 Dexter Ave Montgomery AL 36104-3741 Office Phone: 334-221-6488.

BROWN, JEANETTE GRASSELLI, retired director; b. Cleve., Aug. 4, 1928; d. Nicholas W. and Veronica Gecsy; m. Glenn R. Brown, Aug. 1, 1987. BS summa cum laude, Ohio U., 1950, DSc (hon.), 1978; MS, Western Res. U., 1958, DSc (hon.), 1995, Clarkson U., 1986; D Engring. (hon.), Mich. Tech. U., 1989; DSc (hon.), Wilson Coll., 1994, Notre Dame Coll., 1995, Kenyon Coll., 1995, Mt. Union Coll., 1996, Cleveland State U., 2000, Kent State U., 2000, Ursuline Coll., 2001; DSc, Youngstown State U., 2003; DSc (hon.), U. Pecs, Hungary, 2002. Project leader, assoc. Infrared Spectroscopist, Cleve., 1950-78; mgr. analytical sci. lab. Standard Oil (name changed to BP Am., Inc. 1985), Cleve., 1978-83, dir. technol. support dept., 1983-85, dir. corp. rsch. and analytical scis., 1985-88; disting. vis. prof., dir. rsch. enhancement Ohio U., Athens, 1989-95; ret., 1995. Bd. dirs. AGA Gas, Inc., USX Corp., McDonald Investments, BDM Internat., BF Goodrich Co., Nicolet Instrument Corp.; mem. bd. on chem. sci. and tech. NRC, 1986-91; chmn. U.S. Nat. Com. to Internat. Union of Pure and Applied Chemistry, 1992-94; mem. joint high level adv. panel U.S.-Japan Sci. and Tech., 1994-2001, Ohio Bd. Regents, 1995—, chmn., 2000-2002; vis. com. Nat. Inst. Stds. and Tech., 1988-91. Author, editor 8 books; editor: Vibrational Spectroscopy; contbr. numerous articles on molecular spectroscopy to profl. jours.; patentee naphthalene extraction process. Bd. dirs. N.E. Ohio Sci. and Engring. Fair, Cleve., Martha Holden Jennings Found., Cleve. Clinic Found., Sci. Svc. Inc.; chair bd. dirs. Cleve. Scholarship Programs, Inc., 1994-2000; trustee Holden Arboretum, Cleve., 1988—, Edison Biotech Ctr., Cleve., 1988-95, Cleve. Playhouse, 1990-96, Garden Ctr. Greater Cleve., 1990-93, Mus. Arts Assn., 1991—, Gt. Lakes Sci. Ctr., 1991—, Rainbow Babies and Children's Hosp., 1992-95, Nat. Inventors' Hall of Fame, 1993-2006, Ohio U., 1985-94, chmn. 1991-92; chair steering com. Mellen Ctr. Cleve. Clinic, 1996—, Cleve. Orchestra, 2000-; chair bd. dirs. ideastream, PBS, NPR, Ideastream Pub. TV and Radio, 2003-06; chair bd. dirs. Great Lakes Sci. Ctr., 2006. Recipient Disting. Svc. award Cleve. Tech. Soc. Coun., 1985, Great Am. award, 2004; named Woman of Yr. YWCA, 1980; named to Ohio Women's Hall of Fame State of Ohio, 1989, Ohio Sci. & Tech. Hall of Fame, 1991, Humanitarian award Nat. Conf. Cmty. Justice, 2000, Medal of Honor, Ellis Island, 2002. Mem. Am. Chem. Soc. (chair analytical divsn. 1990-91, Garvan medal 1986, Analytical Chem. award 1993, Encouraging Women into Careers in Sci. award 1999), Soc. for Applied Spectroscopy (pres. 1970, Disting. Svc. award 1983), Coblentz Soc. (bd. govs. 1968-71, William Wright award 1980), Royal Soc. Chemistry (Theophilus Redwood lectr. 1994), Phi Beta Kappa, Iota Sigma Pi (pres. fluorine chpt. 1957-60, nat. hon. mem. 1987). Republican. Roman Catholic. Avocations: swimming, dance, music. Home: 150 Greentree Rd Chagrin Falls OH 44022-2424

BROWN, JENNIFER KAY, lawyer; b. 1956; BA, Antioch Coll.; JD, Yale U., 1993. Bar: 1995. Pres., exec. dir. NOW; law clk. US Ct. Appeals (2nd cir.); asst. US atty. So. dist NY; dir. reproductive rights unit Office NY State Atty. Gen., NYC, 1999—; v.p., legal dir. Legal Momentum (formerly NOW Legal Defense & Education Fund), 2002—. Recipient Nova award, Planned Parenthood, 2002. Office: Legal Momentum 395 Hudson St New York NY 10014*

BROWN, JEREMY EARLE, advertising executive; b. Richmond, Va., Nov. 25, 1946; s. Earle Palmer and Barbara Brown; m. Sally McHugh, Feb. 2; children: Jeremy, Amy, Sarah, Tucker. BA in Drama and Fine Arts, Washington and Lee U., 1969; MBA, Harvard U., 1973. Account exec. Leo Burnett Cos., Chgo., 1973-74; former pres. Earle Palmer Brown, Bethesda, Md.; now chmn., CEO The Earle Palmer Brown Cos., Bethesda, 1974—. Mem. Washington Bd. Trade. Mem. Am. Assn. of Advt. Agys. (bd. dirs.), Young Pres.'s Orgn. (exec. com.), Am. Mgmt. Assn., Phi Gamma Delta. Clubs: Georgetown, The Advertising of Met. Washington (past pres., Silver Medal) (Washington); Columbia Country (Chevy Chase). Address: North Pier 401 E Illinois St # 500 Chicago IL 60611-4363

BROWN, JERRY, JR., (EDMUND GERALD BROWN JR.), state attorney general, former mayor, governor; b. San Francisco, Apr. 7, 1938; s. Edmund Gerald and Bernice (Layne) Brown; m. Anne B. Gust, June 18, 2005 BA in Latin/Greek, U. Calif., Berkeley, 1961; JD, Yale U., New Haven, 1964. Bar: Calif. 1965. Rsch. atty. Calif. Supreme Ct., 1964-65; atty. Tuttle & Taylor, LA, 1966-69; sec. state State of Calif., Sacramento, 1970-74, gov., 1975-83; chmn. Calif. Dem. Party, 1989-90; Dem. candidate for Pres. of US, 1992; mayor City of Oakland, Calif., 1999—2007; atty. gen. State of Calif., Sacramento, 2007—. Practiced law, LA. Author: (book) Dialogues, 1988. Trustee LA Cmty. Colls., 1969. Democrat. Office: Office of Atty Gen Calif Dept Justice PO Box 944255 Sacramento CA 94244-2550*

BROWN, JERRY A., federal bankruptcy judge; b. Detroit, Jan. 31, 1932; m. Florence Freedman; three children. BA, Murray State Univ., 1954; LLB, Tulane U., 1959. Bar: La. 1959, Ky. 1959, U.S. Ct. Appeals (5th cir.) 1960, U.S. Ct. Appeals (11th cir.) 1981, U.S. Dist. Ct. (ea. dist.) La. 1960, U.S. Dist. Ct. (we. dist.) La. 1961, U.S. Dist. Ct. (mid. dist. La.) 1973, U.S. Dist. Ct. (we. dist.) Ky. 1981. Law clk. to Hon. John Minor Wisdom US Ct. Appeals (5th cir.), 1959-60; assoc. Monroe & Lemann, New Orleans, 1960-63, ptnr., 1963-90; spl. counsel Bronfin & Heller, New Orleans, 1991-92; bankruptcy judge US Bankruptcy (ea. dist.) La., New Orleans, 1992—2006, 2006—. With US Army, 1954—56. Office: US Bankruptcy Ea Dist 500 Poydras St Rm B-741A New Orleans LA 70130-3319 Home Phone: 504-861-0900; Office Phone: 504-589-7886.

BROWN, JERRY MILFORD, health products executive; b. Anderson, SC, Apr. 30, 1938; s. James Milford and Jane Elizabeth (McCord) B.; m. Alice Alberta Thompson, July 30, 1960; children: John Milford, Allen Thompson, James Milford II. BS, Furman U., 1960; MA in Biology, Wake Forest U., 1963, Temple U., 1967; PhD in Physiology, Dental Sch., U. Md., 1972. Commd. lt. U.S. Army, 1960, advanced through grades to lt. col., 1980; rsch. instr. Hahanemann Med. Coll., Phila., 1967-68; sect. leader, exptl. medicine divsn. Biomed. Lab., Edgewood Arsenal, Md., 1967-68; instr. anatomy Med. Sch., U. Md., Balt., 1970-77; sect. leader exptl. medicine divsn. U.S. Army Rsch. Inst. Environ. Medicine, Natick, Mass., 1973-76; dep. dir. U.S. Army Med. Intelligence and Info. Agy., Ft. Detrick, Md., 1976-80; dir. internat. health affairs Dept. Def., Washington, 1980-84; chief plans ops. security 2d Gen. Hosp., Germany, 1984-87; med. coord. Fed. Emer. Mgmt. Agy., Washington, 1987-90; nat. disaster med. system staff, bd. govs. Nat. Coun. Internat. Health, 1980-90; cons. and spl. asst. to the pres. Bio Tech. Gen. Corp., Iselin, NJ, 1991-99; pres., chief oper. officer NeuroSurg. Internat., 1995—; v.p., chief oper. officer M/D Frontiers, Springfield, Va., 1990—; pres. Automated Med. Products, Inc., Springfield, Va., 1990—; CEO Automated Med. Products Corp., 1997—; mgr. Precision Med. Manufacturing L.L.C., Wheeling, Ill., 2002—. V.p. Automated Systems, 1991—; assoc. dir. rsch. nat. study ctr. trauma and emer. medicine U. Md.; U.S. mem. Internat. Com. Mil. Medicine and Pharmacy, 1981-87, U.S. mil. mem. Joint Civil/Mil. Med. Working Group U.S., NATO, 1981—; mem. program planning com. Internat. Assembly Emer. Med. Svcs., Balt., 1984; congress lobbyist; cons. in field. Contbr. articles to med. jours.; pub. books in field of philately. Commr. Explorer Scouts, Natick, Mass., 1975-76; trustee Cardinal Spellman Philatlic Mus., Weston, Mass., 1980-97. Decorated Meritorious Svc. medal with oak leaf clusters, Legion of Merit; recipient gold medal, Res. Officers Assn., 1960. Mem. Electron Microscopy Soc. Am., Am. Stamp Dealers Assn., Ctrl. Atlantic Stamp Dealers Assn. (pres. 1977-81), Rsch. and Engring. Soc. Am., Balt. Philatelic Soc., Sigma Alpha Epsilon, Sigma Xi. Republican. Baptist. Office Phone: 732-602-7717. Personal E-mail: btgc@mindspring.com. E-mail: jbrown@ironintern.com.

BROWN, JIM, investment company executive; BA, Whittier Coll.; MBA, Univ. So. Calif.; M taxation, Golden State Univ. CPA. Dir. taxes Ashton Tate Corp.; positions through sr. v.p., treas. Capital Group Companies, LA, 1991—; pres., treas. Capital Mgmt. Services; sr. v.p. Capital Internat. Home: Capital Group Cos 333 S Hope St Los Angeles CA 90071*

BROWN, JOBETH GOODE, food products executive, lawyer; b. Oakdale, La., Sept. 15, 1950; d. Samuel C. Goode and Elizabeth E. (Twiner) Baker; m. H. William Brown, Aug. 4, 1973; 1 child, Kevin William. BA, Newcomb Coll. Tulane U., 1972; JD, Wash. U., 1979. Assoc. Coburn, Croft & Putzell, St. Louis, 1979-80; staff atty. Anheuser-Busch Cos. Inc., St. Louis, 1980-81, exec. asst. to v.p. sec., 1982-83, asst. sec., 1983-89, sec., v.p., 1989—. Trustee Anheuser-Busch Found., St. Louis, 1989—, Girls, Inc., St. Louis; bd. dirs. Jr. Achievement Miss Valley, Inc., Met. Assn. Philanthropy. Mem.: ABA, Am. Soc. Corp. Secs. (pres. 1992), Bar Assn. Met. St. Louis, Mo. Bar Assn., Mo. Women's Forum, Algonquin Golf Club, Order of Coif. Republican. Office: Anheuser-Busch Cos Inc One Busch Pl 202-6 Saint Louis MO 63118-1852

BROWN, JOE BLACKBURN, judge; b. Louisville, Dec. 9, 1940; s. Knox and Miriam (Blackburn) B.; m. Marilyn McGowen, Aug. 10, 1963; children: Jennifer Knox, Michael McGowen. BA cum laude, Vanderbilt U., 1962, JD, 1965. Bar: Ky. 1965, Tenn. 1972, U.S. Supreme Ct. 1979. Asst. U.S. atty. Dept. Justice, Nashville, 1971-73, 1st asst. U.S. atty., 1974-81, U.S. atty., 1981-91, spl. asst. U.S. trustee, 1991-98; U.S. magistrate judge, U.S. Dist. Ct. (mid. dist.) Tenn., Nashville, 1998—. Lectr. law Atty. Gen.'s Advocacy Inst., 1982—; vice chmn. Atty. Gen.'s Adv. Com., 1986-87, chmn. subcom. on sentencing guidelines, mem. subcommittee on budget and office mgmt., 1982-91; instr. math. and bus. law Augusta Coll., Ga., 1966-69; instr. law Nashville Sch. Law, 1999—; adj. prof. law, Vanderbilt U., 2006-. Contbr. articles to legal jours. Bd. dirs. Mid-Cumberland Drug Abuse Coun., Nashville, 1977-86; asst. scoutmastr Boy Scouts Am.; vestryman St. David's Episcopal Ch., sr. warden, 1982, 90; ch. atty. Episcopal Diocese of Tenn., 1995-98; lt. col. CAP, 1996—. Maj. U.S. Army, 1965-71; col. JAGC, USAR ret. Decorated Legion of Merit, Meritorious Svc. medal with 3 oak leaf clusters; recipient Disting. Svc. award Atty. Gen.'s Adv. Com., 1988. Fellow Tenn. Bar Assn., Nashville Bar Found.; mem. FBA (treas. 1978), Nashville Bar Assn. (bd. dirs. 1995-97, exec. com. 1996-97, v.p. 1997, bd. dirs. 2004—, 1st v.p. 2007—), Radio Amateur Transmitting Soc. (pres. 1997-98), Nat. Assn. Flight Instrs., Profl. Assn. Div Instrs., Ky. Bar Assn., NRA (life, Disting. Rifleman award), Harry Phillip Inn of Ct. (master of bench and bar 1994—), Order of Coif, Phi Beta Kappa. Republican. Home: 3427 Woodmont Blvd Nashville TN 37215-1421 Office: US Courthouse Rm 745 801 Broadway Nashville TN 37203-3816

BROWN, JOEL S., evolutionary ecologist, educator; PhD, U Ariz. Head, Ctr. for Rsch. on Urban Ecology U. Ill. Chgo., prof. biology. Contbr. articles to profl. jours. Office: Univ Ill Chgo Dept Biol Sciences SES 3352 M/C 066 845 W TaylorSt Chicago IL 60607-7060 Office Phone: 312-996-4289. Office Fax: 312-413-2435. Business E-Mail: squirrel@uic.edu.

BROWN, JOHN LAWRENCE, JR., electrical engineering educator; b. Ellenville, NY, Mar. 6, 1925; s. John Lawrence and Grace Evelyn Brown; m. Marjorie Anne Schnelle, June 15, 1957 (div. Mar. 1969). BS, Ohio U., 1948; PhD, Brown U., 1953. Asst. prof. Pa. State U., State College, 1951-53, assoc. prof., 1953-60, prof. engring. rsch., 1960-69, prof. elec. engring., 1969-88, prof. emeritus, 1988—. Stocker vis. prof. Ohio U., Athens, Ohio, 1988-90. Author numerous papers in profl. jours. With U.S. Army, 1943-46, Prince vis. fellow Ariz. State U., Phoenix, 1982-83, Gen. Lew Allen Rsch. Chair Air Force Inst. Tech., Dayton, Ohio, 1984-85. Fellow IEEE (life); mem. Math. Assn. Am., Acoustical Soc. Am. Avocations: tennis, book collecting. Home: 1431 Curtin St State College PA 16803-3020 Business E-Mail: jlb6@psu.edu.

BROWN, JOHN LOTT, former university president, retired educator; b. Phila., Dec. 3, 1924; s. John Lott and Carolyn Emma (Francis) B.; m. Catharine Hertfelder, June 11, 1948; children: Patricia Carolyn, Judith Elliott, Anderson Graham, Barbara Smith. BSEE, Worcester Poly. Inst., Mass., 1945, DSc (hon.), 1984; MA, Temple U., 1949; PhD, Columbia U., 1952. Personnel tng. and personnel mgr. Olney foundry Link-Belt Co., Phila., 1948-50; tech. dir. air force contract, dept. psychology Columbia U., 1952-54; head psychology div., aviation med. lab. Naval Air Devel. Ctr., Johnsville, Pa., 1954-59; dir. grad. tng. program physiology, 1962-65; asst., then asso. prof. physiology U. Pa. Med. Sch., 1955-65; prof. physiology and psychology Kans. State U., 1965-69; dean Grad. Sch., 1965-66, v.p. acad. affairs, 1966-69; prof. optics and psychology, dir. center visual sci. U. Rochester, NY, 1969-78; pres. U. South Fla., Tampa, 1978-88, prof. psychology, physiology and opthalmology, 1978-92, prof. indsl. engring., 1988-92, interim dir. Ctr. for Microelectronic Rsch., 1993-94, pres. emeritus, 1988—; interim pres. Worcester Poly. Inst., 1994-95. Chmn. com. vision NRC-Nat. Acad. Scis., 1965-70; chmn. vision rsch. program com. Nat. Eye Inst., 1975-78; trustee Worcester Poly. Inst., 1970-83, mem. alumni coun., 1975-76; trustee Illuminating Engring. Rsch. Inst., 1974-79; mem. U.S. nat. com. Internat. Commn. Optics, 1977. Author chpts. in books, also monographs, articles, 1953—; cons. editor: Perception and Psychophysics, 1972-90; editorial adv. bd.: Vision Research, 1971-77. Bd. dirs. Pub. Broadcasting Svc., 1980-83, Mid-Am. Inst. Profl. Devel., 1980-82, Fla. Gulf Symphony, 1979-81, Tampa Gen. Hosp. Found., 1980-81, Smith-Kettlewell Eye Rsch. Inst., 1991-97; mem. Fla. Council 100, 1978-88; mem. corp. bd. Tampa Performing Arts Hall, 1980-88; chmn. Tampa Bay Area R&D Authority, 1979-86, Tampa Bay Area Fgn. Affairs Com., 1979-92; chmn. bd. dirs. H. Lee Moffitt Cancer Ctr. and Rsch. Inst., 1984-88, Exec. Svc. Corp. of Tampa Bay, 1989-97, pres., 1994. With USNR, 1943-46, comdr., 1947-69. Recipient Research Career Devel. award NIH, 1961-62, Robert Goddard award Worcester Poly. Inst., 1969; sr. research fellow USPHS, 1959-61; grantee NIH; grantee NSF; grantee Office Naval Research; grantee Nat. Eye Inst.; grantee NIMH; grantee NASA. Fellow Optical Soc. Am. (exec. coun. Rochester chpt. 1975-76, assoc. editor jour. 1972-77), Am. Psychol. Assn., AAAS; mem. Assn. Rsch. Vision and Ophthalmology (pres. 1978), Soc. Neurosci., Psychonomic Soc., Fla. Assn. Colls. and Univs. (pres. 1988-89), Sigma Xi, Tau Beta Pi, Psi Chi, Phi Eta Sigma, Phi Kappa Phi, Omicron Delta Kappa, Phi Gamma Delta. Mem. Soc. Of Friends. Home: 105 Kendal Dr Oberlin OH 44074-1905 Office Phone: 813-774-5049. Personal E-mail: jlottb@aol.com.

BROWN, JOHN PATRICK, publishing executive, financial consultant; b. NYC, Oct. 14, 1925; s. Patrick and Emma A (McCarrick) B.; m. Caroline T. Hopkins, Oct. 17, 1959 (dec. Nov. 2002); children: John Patrick, Anne B. Loftus. BBA, St. John's U., Jamaica, NY, 1949; MBA, N.Y.U., 1960. C.P.A., N.Y. Accountant Arthur Young & Co., C.P.A.s, NYC, 1950-58; asst. treas. Paramount Pictures Corp., 1962-65; controller, treas. Washington Star, 1966-76; v.p. fin., treas. Bergen Evening Record Corp., N.J., 1976-82; dir. fin. and adminstrn. Washington Times, 1982-88. Adj. prof. acctg. Am. U., U. Va., Va. Tech. Served with AUS, 1944-46. Mem. AICPA, Fin. Execs. Inst., Internat. Newspaper Fin. Execs. Clubs: Metropolitan (Washington). Roman Catholic. Home and Office: 4230 Embassy Park Dr NW Washington DC 20016-3619

BROWN, JOHN ROBERT, lawyer, priest; b. Muskogee, Okla., Apr. 22, 1948; s. John Robert and Betty Jane (Singleterry) B. BA, MA, Cambridge U., 1972; STB, Gen. Theol. Sem., 1973; STM, Union Theol. Sem., 1978, Harvard U., 1982; MA, STL, U. Louvain, Belgium, 1979; JD, Howard U., 1991. Bar: Ga. 1991, D.C. 1991, U.S. Supreme Ct. 1997; admitted Middle Temple, London, 2000; ordained priest Episcopal Ch., 1972, received into Roman Cath. Ch., 2001. Tchr., headmaster St. John's Sch., Oklahoma City, 1973-77; novice Soc. St. John the Evangelist, Cambridge, Mass., 1979-81; minor canon Pro-Cathedral of Holy Trinity, Brussels, 1981-83; assoc. rector St. James Ch., LA, 1983-87; hon. assisting priest Ch. of the Ascension and St. Agnes, Washington, 1987-91; legis. aide U.S. Ho. of Reps., Washington, 1987-91; hon. asst. priest Ch. of Our Savior, Atlanta, 1991—2001; staff atty. Ga. Legal Svcs., Atlanta, 1991-1995; asst. gen. counsel State Bar Ga., Atlanta, 1996—2003; novice Quarr Abbey, Isle of Wight, 2003—05; chaplain St. Elizabeths Hosp., Washington, 2005—06. Reader Ecumenical Inst. World Coun. Ch., Geneva, 1978, Huntington Libr., San Marino, Calif., 1985-86, Coll. of Preachers, Nat. Cathedral, Washington, 1987, fellow, Center for Ethics in Public Policy and the Professions, Emory U., 1996-98. Contbr. articles to profl. jours. Vol. NIH, 1987—88, Fed. Charitable Campaign, Washington, 1988—89, Atlanta Project, 1991—96; spiritual adv. com. AIDS Project, LA, 1984—86; mem. Mayor's Task Force on Family Diversity, 1984—86, Mcpl. Elections Com. L.A., 1984—86; governing bd. Robert Wood Johnson Homeless Health Care Project, LA, 1985—87; trustees com. Opera Am., 1994—2001; co-trustee Freeman Found., 1994—97; adv. bd. Caring Hands Programs, 1983—87; mem. adv. bd. United Way of Metro Atlanta, 1993—97; adv. bd. Metro Atlanta Cmty. Found., 1994—97; chmn. social justice grants com. Threshold Found., 1994—96; capt. The Old Guard of The Gate City Guard, Atlanta, 1998—; bd. dirs. S.W. Assn. Episcopal Schs., 1974—77, Anglican Roman Cath. Commn. of Belgium, 1981—83; chaplain Most Venerable Order of St. John of Jerusalem, 1996—; bd. dirs. Cmty. Counseling Svc., LA, 1983—86, Acad. Performing Arts, LA, 1984—85, Right to Life League So. Calif., 1984—86, Cape Coast Outreach Found., 1984—86, Coun. Battered Women, Atlanta, 1991—94, AID Atlanta, 1993—2002, Atlanta Opera, 1993—2003, ACLU of Ga., 1994—2002, Fund for So. Cmtys., 1995—98, Funding Exch., 1997—99, Cathedral of St. Philip Bookstore, 1998—2003. Named one of Outstanding Young Men of Am., 1974; Yale U. rsch. fellow, 1983; recipient Mayor's Phoenix award, Atlanta, 1997. Fellow: Ga. Bar Found. (life); mem.: ABA (vice-chmn. fed. legis. com. gen. practice sect. 1989—91), Nat. Assn. Cath. Chaplains, Soc. Colonial Wars, Patrons of the Vatican Mus., Commerce Club (Atlanta), City Tavern Club (Washington), United Oxford and Cambridge U. Club (London), Knights of Malta.

BROWN, JOHN WALTER, vocational education supervisor; b. Waverly, Va., Dec. 13, 1937; s. Wilburt Herman and Martha Ann (Holmes) B. BS in Vocat. Indsl. Edn., Va. State U., 1968; MEd in Vocat. Indsl. Edn., Pa. State U., 1970; cert. advanced study in edn., Johns Hopkins U., 1973; PhD in Vocat. Indsl. Edn., Pa. State U., 1976. Cert. tchr., advanced profl., prin., supr., supt., vocat. edn., Md. and Pa. Drafting instr. Peabody Sr. High Sch., Petersburg, Va., 1962-63; electronics instr. Hampstead Hill Jr. High Sch., Balt., 1965-66, Calverton Jr. High Sch., Balt., 1966-73, dep. prin., 1975-80; vice prin. Carver Vocat. Tech. Sr. High Sch., Balt., 1975; ednl. specialist Balt. City Pub. Schs., 1974, coord., 1980-84, div. specialist, 1984-89, curriculum specialist, 1989-93; prin. House One Rowland Intermediate Sch., Harrisburg, Pa., 1993-94; coord. profl. pers. devel. Pa. State Dept. of Edn., Harrisburg, 1994—, acting mgr. divsn. product quality, 2001—02. Instr. Va. State U., Petersburg, 1962-63, Coppin State Coll., Balt., 1972-73; mem. Balt. City Adv. Coun. on Vocat. Edn. and trade adv. subcoms. With U.S. Army, 1963-65. Named to Va. State U. Sports Hall of Fame. Mem. Am. Vocat. Edn. Assn., Nat. Assn. Indsl. and Tech. Edn., Pub. Schs. Adminstrs. and Suprs. Assn., Johns Hopkins Alumni Assn., Pa. State U. Alumni Assn., Va. State U. Alumni Assn., Iota Lambda Sigma, Phi Delta Kappa. Methodist. Avocations: sports, reading, travel, writing, gardening. Home: 5914 Charnwood Rd Baltimore MD 21228-1205 Office: Pa State Dept Edn Bur of Career and Tech Edn 333 Market St Harrisburg PA 17101-2210 E-mail: jobrown@state.pa.us.

BROWN, JOHN WILFORD, health products executive; b. Paris, Tenn., Sept. 15, 1934; s. Albert T. and Treva (Moody) Brown; m. Rosemary Kopel, June 7, 1957; children: Sarah Beth, Janine. BSChemE, Auburn U., 1957. Process engr. Ormet Corp., Hannibal, Ohio, 1958-62; sr. engr. Thiokol Chem. Corp., Marshall, Tex., 1962-65; with Squibb Corp., Princeton, NJ, 1965-72, asst. to pres., 1970-72; pres. Edward Weck & Co. divsn. Squibb Corp., NYC, 1972-77; chmn. bd. dirs. Stryker Corp., Kalamazoo, 1979—, pres., CEO, 1979—2003. Named one of 400 Richest Ams., Forbes mag., 2006. Mem. Am. Chem. Soc., Health Industries Mfg. Assn. (bd. dirs.). Democrat. Mem. Ch. of Christ. Mailing: Stryker Corp 2725 Fairfield Rd Portage MI 49002*

BROWN, JONATHAN, art historian, educator; b. Springfield, Mass., July 15, 1939; s. Leonard Melvin and Jeanette (Levy) B.; m. Sandra Backer, July 22, 1966; children: Claire, Michael, Daniel. AB, Dartmouth Coll., 1960; M.F.A., Princeton U., 1963, PhD, 1964; MA (hon.), Oxford U., 1981. Mem. faculty Princeton, 1965-73, asso. prof. art and archaeology, 1971-73; asso. prof. art NYU, 1973-75, prof., 1976-84, Carroll and Milton Petrie prof., 1984—; dir. Inst. Fine Arts, 1973-78; Slade prof. fine arts Oxford (Eng.) U., 1981-82. Vis. mem. Inst. Advanced Study, Princeton, N.J., 1978-79; adv. com. dept. European paintings Met. Mus. Art, 1974-79; adv. bd. Master Drawings jour.; bd. dirs. Fundacion Duques de Soria, 1990—; curator Am. Philos. Soc., 1992-98, Velazquez in New York Museums, 1999, Los siglos de oro en los virreinatos de America, 1550-1700, 1999, Velazquez, Rubens, Van Dyck: Pintores Cortesanos del Siglo XVII, 1999, El Greco: Themes and Variations, 2001, (with Sir John Elliott) La almoneda del siglo, 2002, Princeton U. Art Mus., The Frick Collection; Andrew W. Mellon lectr. in fine arts Nat. Gallery of Art, 1994; mem. adv. com. Mus. del Prado. Author: Prints and Drawings by Jusepe de Ribera, 1973, Zurbaran, 1973, Murillo and His Drawings, 1976, Images and Ideas in Seventeenth Century Spanish Painting, 1978, A Palace for a King: The Buen Retiro and the Court of Philip IV, 1980; (with J.H. Elliott) also articles on Spanish art, (with others) El Greco of Toledo, 1982, Velazquez, Painter and Courtier, 1986, (with R.G. Mann) Spanish Paintings of the Fifteenth through Nineteenth Centuries, National Gallery of Art, 1990, The Golden Age of Painting in Spain, 1991, Kings and Connoisseurs: Collecting Art in 17th Century Europe, 1995, (with C. Garrido) Velázquez. The Technique of Genius, 1998, Painting in Spain, 1500-1700, 1998; editor: Picasso and the Spanish Tradition, 1996, Franklin and Condorcet: Two Portraits from the American Philosophical Society, 1997, Velázquez, Rubens y Van Dyck, 1999; co-editor: Sources and Documents in the History of Art: Italy and Spain 1600-1750, 1970, Los siglos de oro en los virreinatos de América, The Sale of the Century, 2002, (with S.G. Galassi) Goya's Last Works, 2006. Recipient Medalla de Oro de Bellas Artes, Gov. of Spain, 1986; Fulbright fellow, 1964-65; Am. Council Learned Socs. fellow, 1968-69; Nat. Endowment Humanities fellow, 1978-79; Guggenheim fellow, 1980-81; Order of Isabel la Catolica, 1986, Gran Cruz de Alfonso X el Sabio, 1996, Premio Elio Antonio Nebrija U. de Salamanca, 1997. Mem. AAAS, Coll. Art Assn. Am. (Arthur Kingsley Porter prize 1971), Hispanic Soc. Am. (corr.), Am. Philos. Soc., Real Academia de Bellas Artes (Madrid, corr., Valencia, corr.). Home: 71 Battle Rd Princeton NJ 08540-4945 Office: 1 E 78th St New York NY 10021-0119

BROWN, JOSEPH W., JR., (JAY BROWN), insurance company executive; Grad. in Probability and Stats., Northern Ill. U., 1974. Pres., CEO Fireman's Fund Ins. Co., 1975-92; chmn., pres., CEO Talegen Holdings, Inc., 1992-98; chmn., CEO MBIA Inc., 1998—2004, dir., 1986—, chmn., 2004—. Bd. dir. Safeco Corp., 2001—, non-exec. chmn., 2006—; bd. dir. Oxford Health Plan, 2000—04. Fellow: Property Casualty Acturial Soc.; mem.: Soc. of Chartered Property and Casualty Underwriters, Am. Acad. of Actuaries. Office: MBIA Ins Inc 113 King St Ste 1 Armonk NY 10504-1610*

BROWN, JOYCE F., academic administrator; b. NYC, July 7, 1946; d. Robert E. and Joyce Cappie Brown; m. H. Carl McCall, Aug. 13, 1983. BA, Marymount Coll., Tarrytown, NY, 1968; MA in Counseling Psychology, NYU, 1971, PhD, 1980. Cert. for ednl. mgmt. Harvard U. From vice chancellor to prof. emeritus CUNY, 1983—98, prof. emeritus, 1998—. Dep. mayor pub. and cmty. affairs, NYC, 1990; pres. Fashion Inst. Tech. SUNY, 1998—; bd. dirs. Polo Ralph Lauren, Paxar Corp. Dir. Ctrl. Pk. Conservancy, women's com.; dir. US Enrichment Corp., Linens'n'Things, Inc., Warm Up Am. Found. Office: Fashion Institute Technology Seventh Ave at 27th St New York NY 10001-5992

BROWN, JUDITH OLANS, retired lawyer, educator; b. Boston, May 29, 1941; d. Sidney and Evelyn R. (Lefkowitz) Olans; m. James K. Brown, Oct. 5, 1969. AB magna cum laude with distinction, Mt. Holyoke Coll., 1962; LL.B. cum laude, Boston Coll., 1965. Bar: Mass. 1965. Law clk. Supreme Jud. Ct., 1965-66; assoc. Foley, Hoag and Eliot, Boston, 1966-69; chief counsel Mass. Dept. Cmty. Affairs, Boston, 1969-70; atty. adv. Office Regional Counsel, HUD, Boston, 1970, asst. regional counsel, 1971, assoc. regional counsel, 1971-72; instr. Boston U. Law Sch., 1971, Northeastern U. Sch. Law, Boston, 1972, assoc. prof., 1972-75, prof., 1975-98; prof. emeritus Faculty Inst. Lifelong Edn. Dartmouth, 1998—. Vis. prof. Law Sch., Boston Coll., 1992. Contbr. articles to legal jours.; article and book rev. editor: Boston Coll. Indsl. and Comml. Law Rev., 1964-65. Mem. steering com. Lawyers Com. for Civil Rights under Law (emeritus); trustee Kimball Union Acad.1993-2003. Loeb fellow, 1972—73. Mem.: Order of Coif, Phi Beta Kappa. Home: PO Box 82 Plainfield NH 03781-0082 Personal E-mail: jkbjob@verizon.net.

BROWN, JUNE GIBBS, retired government official; b. Cleve., Oct. 5, 1933; d. Thomas D. and Lorna M. Gibbs; children: Ellen Rosenthal, Linda Windsor, Victor Janezic, Carol Janezic. BBA summa cum laude, Cleve. State U., 1971, MBA, 1972; postgrad., Cleve. Marshall Law Sch., 1973-74; JD, U. Denver, 1978; postgrad. Advanced Mgmt. Program, Harvard U., 1983. Cert. govt. fin. mgr., 1995; CPA, Ohio. Real estate broker, officer mgr. N.E. Realty, Cleve., 1963-68; staff acct. Frank T. Cicirelli, C.P.A., Cleve., 1970-71; asst. to comptr. S.M. Hexter Co., Cleve., 1971; grad. tchg. fellow Cleve. State U., 1971-72; dir. internal audit Navy Fin. Ctr., Cleve., 1972-75; dir. fin. sys. design Bur. of Land Mgmt., Denver, 1975-76; project mgr. Bur. of Reclamation, 1976-79; insp. gen. Dept. Interior, Washington, 1979-81, NASA, Washington, 1981-85; v.p. fin. and adminstrn. Sys. Devel. Corp., a Burroughs Co., 1985-86; assoc. adminstr. for mgmt. NASA, 1986-87; insp. gen. U.S. Dept. Def., Arlington, Va., 1987-90; dep. insp. gen. USN-CINCPACFLT, 1990; insp. gen. USN Pacific Fleet, Pearl Harbor, Hawaii, 1991-93, HHS, Washington, 1993-2001; inspector gen. HHS, SSA, Washington, 1995-96; ret., 2001. Bd. dirs. Fed. Law Enforcement Tng. Ctr., 1984-85, Interagy. Auditor Tng. program Dept. Agr. Grad. Sch., 1983-85; chmn. interagy. com. on Info. Resource Mgmt., 1984-85; mem. bd. advisors Nat. Contract Mgmt. Assn., 1987-89, NSF, 2002-05; mem. Pres.'s Coun. on Integrity and Efficiency, 1993-2001, vice chair, 1994-97, 1998-2001, rep. Nat. Intergovtl. Audit Forum, 1994-98; bd. dirs. Insps. Gen. Auditor Tng. Inst. Mem. bd. advisors Howard U. Sch. Bus., 1987-89. Recipient award Am. Soc. Women Accts., 1969, 70, 71, Raulston award Cleve. State U., 1971, Pres.'s award Cleve. State U., 1971, Outstanding Achievement award U.S. Navy, 1973, Career Svc. award Chgo. region Fed. Exec. Bd., 1974, Outstanding Contbn. to Fin. Mgmt. award Denver region Fed. Exec. Bd., 1977, Donald L. Scantlebury award Joint Fin. Mgmt. Improvement Program, 1980, Outstanding Svc. award Nat. Assn. Minority CPA Firms, 1980, NASA Exceptional Svc. medal, 1985, Outstanding Achievement in Aerospace award, 1987, Woman of Yr. award, YWCA 1988, Bur. Land Mgmt., Dept. Interior, 1975, Disting. Pub. Svc. award Dept. Def., 1989, Meritorious Civilian Svc. award U.S. Navy, 1993, Nat. Capital Area chpt./Govt. Exec. Mag. award for leadership, 1994, George Washington U. Pi Alpha Alpha Pub. Svc. award, 1996; named Disting. Alumni Cleve. State U., 1990, named Outstanding Fellow of Coun. for Ethical Org. for Creating the Standards for Healthcare Compliance, 2001 Fellow Nat. Acad. Pub. Adminstrn. (standing panel exec. orgn.

and mgmt., pub. svc. panel); mem. AICPA (mem. govt. auditing stds. 1996-99), Assn. Govt. Accts. (nat. pres. 1985-86, nat. exec. com. 1977-87, vice chmn. nat. ethics com. 1978-80, 90, chmn. fin. mgmt. standards bd. 1981-82, service award 1973, 76, 93, outstanding achievement award 1979, Robert W. King Meml. award 1988, dir. Hawaii chpt. 1991-93, Nat. Pres.'s award 1999, Disting. Fed. Leadership award 1998), Hawaii Soc. CPAs (bd. dirs. 1991-93), Am. Accts. Assn., Nat. Contract Mgmt. Assn. (bd. advisors 1988-90), NASA Alumni Assn., Women in Aerospace, ASPA (at-large mem. nat. coun. 1994-98, Profl. Responsibility Exemplary Practice award 1990, pres.-nat. capital area chpt. 1989), Exec. Women in Govt., Nat. Sci. Found. (adv. panel 2003-05), Beta Alpha Psi. Personal E-mail: igjgb@yahoo.com.

BROWN, KATHERINE YVONNE, occupational therapist, educator; b. Chgo., Nov. 8, 1974; d. Keith Rouse and Roberta B. (Baines) Wheeler; m. Irving Brown, II, Jan. 18, 2000; children: Sydney, Irving III, Anthony Rodgers. BS, Chgo. State U., 1996; MEd, Purdue U., 1999; EdD, Nat. Louis U., 2005. Lic. occupl. therapist Ill., Ind., Tenn., cert. devel. therapist Ill.; lic. tchr. and sch. counselor K-12 Ind., cert. Tenn., phys. agt. Tenn., fund devel. Ctr. Non-profit Mgmt., early intervention specialist Ill., thermal phys. agt. modalities Tenn. Occupl. therapist level I Therapeutic Work Ctr., Chgo., 1996; occupl. therapist level II Provider's Therapeutic Svcs., Chgo., 1996, St. Joseph Hosp. & Medical Ctr., Joliet, Ill., 1996; occupl. therapist Jackson Park Hosp. & Medical Ctr., Chgo., 1997; activity therapy supr. Advocate Christ Hosp. & Medical Ctr., Oak Lawn, Ill., 1997—98; ind. contractor mental health, 1998—2001; counselor Alexian Brothers Behavioral Health Ctr., Hoffman Estates, Ill., 1998—2001; graduate asst. Purdue U., Hammond, Ind., 1998—2000, tchg. asst.-supr., 1999, practicum supr., 1999; home health occupl. therapist St. Catherine Hosp., East Chgo., 2000—01; mental health counselor The Children's Connection Therapeutic Sch., Chgo., 2000—01; occupational therapist Baptist Ch., Nashville, 2001—05; occupl. therapist Baptist Hosp., 2001—05, temp. occupl. therapist, 2002; assoc. prof. Tenn. State U., 2006—. Adj. prof. Nashville State CC, 2002—; acad. coord. clinical & FW edn., asst. prof. Belmont U., Nashville, 2002—04, mktg. info. group mem., 2002—04, search com. mem. Coll. health Scis. for assoc. dean & chair, 2002—05, advisor honor society, 2002—05, curriculum com. mem., 2002—05, recruitment rep., 2002—05, judge debate competition, 2002, mktg. task force, 2002—04, social events task force, 2002, adj. prof., 03, faculty senate rep., 2003—04, mktg. com. Coll. Health Scis., 2002—04, search com. mem. Coll. Health Scis. for asst./assoc. prof., 2003—05, Dr. Martin Luther King Jr. com. mem., 2003—05, Dr. Martin Luther King Jr. sub-com. chair, 2003—05, asst. prof. Coll. Health Scis., Sch. Occupl. Therapy, 2004—, accreditation review com. mem., 2004—05, graduation com. mem., 2005; alumni career specialist Purdue U., 2004—05; vis. assoc. prof. So. Ill. U., Carbondale, 2005—. Contbr. articles to profl. jours. Advocate Luth. Gen. Hosp. Good Times Classic, 1996, Food/Clothes Drive & Toys for Tots Program, 1997, Christ Hosp. & Medical Ctr. Psychiatry & Substance Abuse Performance Improvement Com., 1997—98, Christ Hosp. & Medical Ctr. Annual Assoc. Picnic Com., 1997—98, Chase Corp. Challenge, Health Care Team, 1998; vol. Aids Walk, Chgo., 1998; advocate Good Samaritan Hosp. Autumn Classic, 1998; delta com. 18th Ave Enrichment Ctr., 2003—04; governance facilitator Nat.-Louis U., 2004—05; co-chair 18th Ave Enrichment Ctr., 2004—05; mem. W.A. Bass Mid. Sch. Adopt a Family Program, 2004, Nat. Coalition of 100 Black Women, 2006, Flirt Found.; mem. housing and acquisition of property com. Minerva Found., 2005—06; grad. Top Sales Minority Leadership Program, Young Leader Coun.; bd. dirs. Minerva Found., 2005—, Jr. Achievement. Nominee Galloway Empowerment award, Nat. Coalition 100 Black Women, Inc., 2005; named one of Mid. Tennesseeans Top African Am. Leaders, Nashville Bus. Quar. Mag., 2005; recipient Advisor Appreciation award, Delta Sigma Theta Sorority, Inc., 2004, Excellence for Exemplary Tchg. Higher Edn. award, Tenn. Occupl. Therapy Assn., 2003. Mem.: Tenn. Caucus of Black Occupl. Therapists (pres., nat. sec.), Kellogg Elec. Rsch. Acad. (3d v.p. 1999—2000, 1st v.p. 2000—01, pres. 2001), Tenn. Occupl. Therapy Assn. (exec. bd. mem. 2002—04, treas. 2002—04, R.H. Boyd steering com. 2005—), R.H. Boyd African Am. Leadership Soc. (steering com. 2005, mem. steering com. 2005—), R.H. Boyd Leadership Soc., Frist Ctr. Visual Arts, Lakeview PTO (1st pres. 2002—03), Kellogg Sch. PTA (fin. com. mem. 1997—2001), Nat. Coalition 100 Black Women, Top Stars Minority Leadership Program Alumni, Young Leaders Coun. Grad. Alumni, Lakeview YMCA, Psi Configuration Psychology Club (pres. 1999). Avocations: reading, flute. Home: 3044 Summercrest Trail Antioch TN 37013

BROWN, KATHLEEN, diversified financial services company executive; b. 1946; d. Edmund G. and Bernice Brown; m. George Rice (div. 1979); children: Hilary, Alexandra, Zebediah; m. Van Gordon Sauter, 1980; 2 stepsons. BA in History, Stanford U., 1969; JD, Fordham U., 1985. Mem. L.A. Bd. Edn., 1975-80; atty. O'Melveny & Myers, NYC, LA; commr. L.A. Bd. Pub. Works, 1987-89; treas. State of Calif., 1990-94; exec. v.p. Bank of Am., LA, 1994-99, pres. Pvt. Bank for Investment Mgmt. Group, 1999—2001; sr. pvt. wealth adv. investment mgmt. divsn. Goldman, Sachs & Co., LA, 2001—03, sr. adv., head of pub. fin. We. region, 2003—. Co-chmn. Capital Budget Commn., Washington, 1997—. Mem. Pacific Coun. on Internat. Policy, Stanford Inst. for Internat. Studies; dir. Children's Hosp. L.A., San Francisco Ballet, Calif. Endowment, L.A. C. of C. Democrat. Office: Goldman Sachs & Co Fox Plz Ste 2600 2121 Ave Stars Los Angeles CA 90067

BROWN, KATHLEEN, education educator; PhD, State U., Blacksburg. Prof. Niagara U., Coll. Edn., NY, 2004—. Mem.: Coun. Exceptional Children. Office: Niagara U Coll Edn Niagara University NY 14109 Office Phone: 716-286-8623. Business E-Mail: kbrown@niagara.edu.

BROWN, KATIE, columnist; b. Petosky, MI, 1963; m. William Corbin, Nov. 25, 2003; 1 child. BA art history, Cornell U. Propr. GOAT antique stores, LA, Mackinac Island, Mich. Host (TV series) Next Door with Katie Brown, Lifetime, 1998, All Yr. Round with Katie Brown, A&E, 2003, Simple Solutions with Katie Brown, PBS, 2006, frequent contbr. Oprah!, Good Morning America, Live with Regis & Kelly; author: Katie Brown Entertains, 2000, Katie Brown Decorates, 2002, Katie Brown's Weekends, 2005, (syndicated column) Domestic Dilemmas, 2005—. Office: NY Times Syndication Sales Corp 14th Fl 122 E 42nd St New York NY 10168 Office Phone: 212-499-3411. Office Fax: 212-499-3382.

BROWN, KAY (MARY KATHRYN BROWN), retired state official, consultant, political organization worker; b. Ft. Worth, Dec. 19, 1950; d. H. C., Jr. and Dorothy Ruth (Ware) Brown; m. William P. Dougherty, Dec. 15, 1978 (div. 1984); m. Mark A. Foster, Aug. 24, 1991; 1 adopted child, Kathryn Yucui. BA, Baylor U., 1973. Reporter UPI, Atlanta, 1973-76; reporter, feature writer Anchorage Daily Times, 1976-77; reporter, co-owner Alaska Adv., Anchorage, 1977; aide, rschr. Alaska State Legislature, Juneau, 1979-80; dep. dir. divsn. of oil and gas (formerly divsn. minerals and energy mgmt.) Alaska Dept. Natural Resources, Anchorage, 1980-82, dir., 1982-86; elected Alaska Ho. of Reps., 1986-96; exec. dir. Alaska Conservation Alliance and Voters, 1997-2000; prin., owner Kay Brown Comms., 2000—05; Alaska comms. dir. Dem. Nat. Com., 2005—. Del. White Ho. Conf. Libr. and Info. Svcs., 1991. Co-author: (book) Geographic Information Systems: A Guide to the Technology, 1991; talk radio host, 1996—2000. E-mail: kaybrown@alaska.net.

BROWN, KEITH, musician, educator; b. Colorado Springs, Colo., Oct. 21, 1933; s. Kenneth Vernon and Audrey Lucille (Nelson) B.; m. Leslee Joanne Scullin, June 13, 1954 (div. Jan. 1991); children: Robert Vernon, Lise Joanne, Kristin Patricia; m. Joann Alexander, May 14, 1994 (div. Feb. 2007). MusB cum laude, U. So. Calif., 1957; MusM, Manhattan Sch. Music, 1964. Trombonist Indpls. Symphony Orch., 1957-58; mem. faculty, solo trombonist Aspen Festival, 1957-69; trombonist N.Y. Brass Quintet, 1958-59; prin. trombonist Casals Festival, San Juan, 1958-80; assoc. prin. trombonist Phila. Orch., 1959-62; prin. trombonist Met. Opera Orch., 1962-65; performed with Chamber Music Soc. of Lincoln Ctr., 1969-88; participant Marlboro Festival, 1970-73; dir. instrumental activities, prof. music, condr. univ. orch. Temple U., Phila., 1965-71; prof. emeritus, condr. Ind. U., Bloomington, 1971-97; condr., music dir. Bloomington Symphony Orch., 1975-80; chmn. brass dept., condr. Music Acad. of West, 1978-82, 85-87; co-founder Ensemble Mediation, 1998—. Artistic dir., condr. Camerata Orch., Bloomington, 1989-96; artistic/mus. dir. InterAm. Youth Orch. of the Festival Casals, San Juan, P.R., 1989-91. Regular guest condr. Orquesta Sinfonica Venezuela, coach, adv., guest condr, Orquesta Nacional Juvenil and Orquesta Sinfonica Simon Bolivar, Caracas, 1979—; coach, adviser Joven Orquesta Nacional de Espana, 1984-94; bd. advisers N.Y. Cornet and Sacbut Ensemble, 1984—; tchr. master classes, lectr., recitalist (1st western trombonist), conservatories in, Beijing and Shanghai, China, 1982, Beijing, 1988; guest condr. Sapporo (Japan) Symphony Orch., 1990, Orquesta del Principado de Asturias, Spain, 1991 Served with U.S. Army, 1953-56. Recipient spl. award Asociacion Musical, Caracas, Venezuela, 1979, Alumni award U. So. Calif. Sch. Music, 1957; Nat. Arts assoc. Sigma Alpha Iota, 1995. Mem. Internat. Trombone Assn., Phi Mu Alpha Sinfonia, Pi Kappa Lambda, Kappa Kappa Psi (hon.) Clubs: Rotary. Methodist. Avocations: tennis, sailing. Home: 2925 Olcott Blvd Bloomington IN 47401-2403 Personal E-mail: keithbrown@alumni.usc.edu.

BROWN, KEITH E., lawyer; b. 1943; BS, Oreg. State Univ.; JD, Stanford Univ. Bar: Alaska 1969. Atty Brown Waller & Gibbs, Anchorage. Mem.: ABA (bd. gov. 2004—). Office: Brown Waller & Gibbs Suite 202 821 North St Anchorage AK 99501 Office Phone: 907-276-2050. Office Fax: 907-276-2051.

BROWN, KEITH LAPHAM, retired ambassador; b. Sterling, Ill., June 18, 1925; s. Lloyd Heman and Marguerite (Briggs) B.; m. Carol Louise Liebmann, Oct. 1, 1949; children: Susan, Briggs (dec.), Linda, Benjamin. Student, U. Ill., 1943-44, Northwestern U., 1946-47; LLB, U. Tex., 1949. Bar: Tex., Okla., Colo. Assoc. Lang, Byrd, Cross & Ladon, San Antonio, 1949-55; v.p., gen. counsel Caulkins Oil Co., Oklahoma City, 1955-70, Denver, 1955-70; founder, developer Vail Assocs., Colo., 1962; pres. Brown Investment Corp., Denver, 1970-87; developer Colo. State Bank Bldg., Denver, 1971; amb. to Lesotho Dept. State, 1982-84, amb. to Denmark Copenhagen, 1988-92; ret., 1992; chmn. Brown Investment Corp., Denver, 1993—. Mem. adv. bd. Ctr. for Strategic and Internat. Studies. Chmn. Rep. Nat. Fin. Com., 1985-88; hon. trustee, past pres. bd. Colo. Acad.; mem. Am. Acad. Diplomacy. Ensign USN, 1943-46. Mem. Coun. Am. Ambs. (pres.), San Antonio Country Club, Bohemian Club. Republican. Presbyterian. also: 11 Auburn Pl San Antonio TX 78209-4739 Office: 1490 Colo State Bank Bldg 1600 Broadway Denver CO 80202-4927 Home Phone: 210-804-0556; Office Phone: 303-830-7379.

BROWN, KENNETH LLOYD, lawyer; b. NYC, Sept. 28, 1927; s. Edythe Schneider; m. Freya Dorothy Finkelstein, July 10, 1954; children: Ivy Hope Brown Hill, Patrice Shari Brown. BS, NYU, 1951; LLB, St. John's U., Bklyn., 1954. Bar: NY 1955. Pvt. practice, Forest Hills, NY, 1955-61; asst. corp. counsel City of N.Y., 1962-78; ptnr. Rivkin, Radler & Kremer and predecessor firms, Uniondale, NY, 1978—98; pvt. practice Jamaica, NY, 1998—. Dem. dist. leader Queens County Dem. Orgn., Forest Hills, until 1982; mem. Forest Hills Jewish Ctr. With U.S. Army, 1945-47. Mem. Queens County Bar Assn. (various coms.), Am. Legion, Jewish War Vet. Post, Continental Regular Dem. Club (founder), Robert F. Kennedy, Jr. Dem. Club, B'nai B'rith, Masons, Knights of Pythias. Avocation: politics. Home: PO Box 457 Flushing NY 11375-0457 Office: 15049 Hillside Ave Jamaica NY 11432-3319 Home Phone: 718-897-6946; Office Phone: 718-297-7711. Personal E-mail: litax.ny@verizon.net.

BROWN, KENT NEWVILLE, ambassador; b. Oakland, Calif., May 7, 1944; s. Victor B. and Mary E. (Shaver) B.; m. Norma Giorno, Dec. 29, 1995; children from previous marriage: Steven D., Karen E. BA, U. Calif., Davis, 1964, MA, 1966. 3rd sec. U.S. Embassy, Panama, 1967-69, 2nd sec. Prague, Czechoslovakia, 1970-73; watch officer to exec. secretariat U.S. Dept. of State, Washington, 1973-74; fellow Hoover Instn., Stanford, Calif., 1974-75; officer Soviet desk U.S. Dept. of State, Washington, 1976-80; 1st sec. U.S. Embassy, Moscow, 1980-83; sr. advisor U.S. Arms Control Del., Vienna, Austria, 1984-88; office dir. Strategic Nuc. Policy U.S. Dept. of State, Washington, 1989-90; polit. advisor Supreme Allied Comdr. Europe, Belgium, 1990-92; amb. U.S. Embassy, Tbilisi, Georgia, 1992-95; dir. pers. U.S. Dept. of State, Washington, 1995-96; v.p. govt. rels. Ea. Europe J.T. Internat., Geneva, 1996—. Bd. dirs. NATO workshop, Menlo Park, Calif. Bd. dirs. U.S.-Russia Bus. Coun. Mem. Internat. Inst. for Strategic Studies. Office: 12 Ch de Rieu Geneva 17 Switzerland Office Phone: 011-381-11-20-50-300.

BROWN, KEVIN PAUL, secondary school educator; s. Vern Andrew Brown and Maxine Irene Scherzberg-Brown. BS in Edn., U. Nebr., Lincoln, 1977, MEd, 1981. Tchr. Stanton Cmty. Schs., Nebr., 1977—80, Loup County Pub. Sch., Taylor, Nebr., 1982—. Contbr. articles to local history publs. Sec.-treas. Harrop Sandhills Park, Taylor, 1994—. Recipient Disting. Alumni award, Coll. Edn. and Human Svcs. Alumni Assn., U. Nebr., Lincoln, 2005. Mem.: Nebr. Speech Comm./Theatre Arts Assn., Nebr. State Edn. Assn. (v.p. Sandhills dist. 2005—), Willow Springs Cemetery Assn. (pres. 1990—), Loup County Hist. Soc. (pres. 1986—). Lutheran. Avocations: history, genealogy. Office: Loup County Pub Sch 608 Williams St Taylor NE 68879

BROWN, KIMLEIGH CLAYTON, special education educator, biologist; b. Lima, Ohio, July 31, 1943; s. Joy Alice and Clayton Henry Brown; m. Marsha Jean Miller, Sept. 13, 1965; children: Bernard Morgan, Conrad Merrion, Marco Clayton. BA, U. No. Colo., Greeley, 1971; MEd, U. Alaska, Anchorage, 1998. Cert. spl. edn., sci. tchr. N.Mex., 1997. Fishery biologist, hatchery mgr. Prince William Aquaculture Assn., Cordova, Alaska, 1977—78, Alaska Dept. Fish and Game, Cold Bay, 1978—90; prin. biologist Alaska Fisheries Cons., Anchorage, 1990—97; tchr. sci., spl. edn. Aztec Mcpl. Schs., N.Mex., 1997—2001, Farmington Mcpl. Schs., N.Mex., 2001—06, tchr. gifted students, 2006—. Author: Learning Disabilities In The Secondary Setting, 2007. Pres. SW Alaska Regional Assn. Sch. Bds., Cold Bay, 1986—89; mayor City of Cold Bay, 1985—88; pres. Aleutian Region Sch. Dist., Anchorage, 1979—89. Named All-Star Bd. Mem., Alaska State Bd. Edn., 1989, Tchr. of Yr., Hondo, N.Mex Sch. Dist., 1971; recipient Meritorious Svc. award, Alaska Dept. Fish and Game, 1985. Mem.: Am. Fisheries Soc. (assoc.), Coun. Exceptional Children (assoc.), Mensa, Kappa Delta Pi (pres Rho Zeta chpt. 1993—94). Conservative. Mem. Lds Ch. Achievements include development of unique, high-efficiency salmon incubation system involving oxygen supersaturation and re-use; research in effect of column length and substrate on the efficiency of oxygen contractors. Avocations: photography, trap shooting, fishing. Home: 1909 Brenwood Dr Farmington NM 87401 Office: Farmington Mcpl Schs 5700 College Blvd Farmington NM 87401 Home Phone: 505-327-6173; Office Phone: 505-599-8880. Home Fax: 505-327-6178. Personal E-mail: chumfish2005@msn.com. Business E-Mail: cbrown@fms.k12.nm.us.

BROWN, KWAME, professional basketball player; b. Mar. 10, 1982; Basketball player Wash. Wizards, 2001—05, LA Lakers, 2005—. Achievements include becoming first high-school student ever drafted first overall in NBA Draft, 2001. Office: LA Lakers Staples Center 1111 S Figueroa St Los Angeles CA 90015

BROWN, LAIMA ADOMAITIS, art therapist, artist, writer; b. Balt., June 6, 1960; d. Vytautas Albin and Ona Miliauskas Adomaitis; m. Thomas William Brown, Aug. 3, 1985. BA in Journalism magna cum laude, U. ND, 1982; MA in Art Therapy, George Washington U., 1995. Graphic artist The Viguerie Co., Falls Church, Va., 1983—85; art dir. Absolutely Art, Inc., Herndon, Va., 1986—90; clin. art therapist Graydon Manor, Psychiat. Residential Treatment Ctr., Leesburg, Va., 1994—96, supr. expressive therapy program, 1996—99; supr. clin. program, clin. art therapist Safe Haven Youth Shelter, Pensacola, Fla., 2000—02; dir. therapeutic activity, clin. art therapist BayPointe Hosp./Mobile Mental Health Ctr., Ala., 2003—06; program coord., art therapist Girl's Residential Wilderness Program, Dept. Youth Svcs., Baldwin County, Ala., 2006—. Participant Nat. Hon. Student Exchange Humboldt State U., Arcata, Calif., 1981; field supr. MA art therapy interns George Washington U., 1996—98; art therapy cons., Orange Beach, Ala., 2000—03; presenter in field. Exhibitions include Art with a Southern Drawl, Mobile, 2001, 621 Gallery, Tallahassee, 2000; artist, writer: essay and acrylic painting H20 Project (included in juried collection promoting clean water and conservation, U.S. tour), contbg. writer, poet, art therapist: Word Pictures: The Poetry and Art of Art Therapists; author: Essay: Creativity is Supernatural, 2004; Sunrise and Sunset Murals Project, 2006; project designer, coord. Girls Residential Wilderness Program, Baldwin County TV RE: Art Therapy, 2007. Mem. Nat. Coun. of Cath. Woman, Arlington, Va., 2003, Nat. Mus. of Women in Arts, Washington, 1996; supporter Lithuanian Heritage, Lemont, Ill., Parabola Soc., NYC, 1996. Mem.: Assn. Humanistic Psychology, Am. Art Therapy Assn. (registered art therapist). Roman Catholic. Avocations: painting, folkcrafts, creative writing.

BROWN, LAMAR BEVAN, lawyer; b. Tooele, Utah, Apr. 26, 1951; s. John B. and Reva M. B.; children: Sean La Mar, Kyle Ross, Ian Lawrence. BA, Utah State U., 1974; JD, We. State U., 1980. Bar: Calif. 1980, U.S. Dist. Ct. (so. dist.) Calif. 1980, U.S. Ct. Appeals (9th cir.) 1986, U.S. Dist. Ct. (no. and ctrl. dist.) 1992. Assoc. Law Offices George Andrews, San Diego, 1980-82, Higgs, Fletcher & Mack, San Diego, 1982-90, Law Offices Craig McClellan, San Diego, 1990-95; mem. McClellan & Brown, San Diego, 1995—. Mem. Consumer Attys. Calif., Consumer Attys. San Diego, Western Trial Lawyers Assn., San Diego County Bar Assn. Democrat. Office: McClellan & Brown 1144 State St San Diego CA 92101-3529 E-mail: lamarbrown@aol.com.

BROWN, LARRY (LAWRENCE HARVEY BROWN), professional sports team executive, former professional basketball coach; b. Bklyn., Sept. 14, 1940; Student, U. NC, Chapel Hill, 1959—63. Amateur basketball player Akron Goodyears, Ohio, 1963-65; asst. coach U. NC, Chapel Hill, 1965-67; player New Orleans (ABA), 1967-68, Oakland (ABA), 1968-69, Washington (ABA), 1969-70, Va. Squires (ABA) - Denver Nuggets (ABA), 1970-71, Denver Nuggets (ABA), 1971-73; head coach Carolina Cougars (ABA), 1972-74, Denver Nuggets (ABA), 1974-76, Denver Nuggets (NBA), 1976-79, UCLA, 1979-81, NJ Nets, Newark, 1981-83, U. Kans., Lawrence, 1983-88, San Antonio Spurs, 1988-92, LA Clippers, 1992-93, Ind. Pacers, 1993-97, Phila. 76ers, 1997—2003, exec. v.p., 2007—; head coach Detroit Pistons, 2003—05, NY Knicks, 2005—06. Mem. Am. Basketball Assn. All-Star Team, 1968—70, US Olympic Team, 1964, Am. Basketball Assn. Championship Team, 1969; asst. coach US Olympic Team, 2000, head coach, 04. Named MVP, ABA All-Star Game, 1968, ABA Coach of Yr., 1973, 1975, 1976, IBM Coach of Yr., NBA, 2001; recipient Espy Award for Best Coach/Mgr., ESPN, 2004. Achievements include coaching NBA Championship Team, 2004; being the only coach in history to win NCAA and NBA Titles. Office: Phila 76ers Wachovia Ctr 3601 S Broad St Philadelphia PA 19148*

BROWN, LARRY DOUGLASS, research consultant, writer; b. Greenville, Miss., July 10, 1955; s. Bobby Jene and Jo Ann B.; m. Rebecca Askew, Aug. 7, 1985; children: January Sullivan, Benjamin, Nicholas, Caroline. PhD, MPhil, DeMontfort U., 1998; advanced diploma, Oxford U., 2003. Cons. Bus. and Polit. Cons., London, 1996-2000; rsch. cons. art and hist. rsch. PRI, Little Rock, Ark., also London, 1996—. White collar crime investigator Ark. State Police, 1980-96. Author: Crossfire: Witness in the Clinton Investigation, 1999, (novels) The Memphis Kingmaker, 2006, Madame President, 2007. Ark. dir. criminal justice issues George Bush presdl. campaign, 1988, Little Rock, 1988; mem. Drug and Alcohol Abuse Coun., 1984 Recipient Scholastic Achievement award US Dept. Justice, 1978, Cert. of Recognition Gov. Bill Clinton, 1984. Fellow Acad. of Polit. Sci., Nat. Troopers Coalition (vice-chmn. 1988-90, Spl. Svc. award 1990), Ark. State Police Assn. (pres. 1986-90), Am. Polit. Sci. Assn. Baptist. Home: 5217 Country Club Blvd Little Rock AR 72207 Office Phone: 501-960-4052. Personal E-mail: prillc@earthlink.net.

BROWN, LARRY K., psychiatrist, researcher; MD, Columbia U., NY, 1976. Cert. gen. psychiatrist Amer Bd. Psychiatry and Neurology, 1981, child and adolescent psychiatry Amer Bd. Psychiatry and Neurology, 1986. Dir. rsch. in child and adolescent psychiatry Rhode Island Hosp., Providence, 2004—; prof. psychiatry and human behavior Brown U., Providence, 2004—. Prin. investigator NIMH funded projects. Recipient Outstanding Faculty Mentor award, Brown U. Dept Psychiatry, 2006; grantee HIV Prevention with Adolescent Projects award, NIMH, 1993—. Fellow: Amer. Acad. Child and Adolescent Psychiatry. Office: Rhode Island Hos Brown Univ 1 Hoppin St Ste 204 Coro West Providence RI 02903 Office Phone: 401-444-8539. Business E-Mail: lkbrown@lifespan.org.

BROWN, LAUREN EVANS, zoologist, researcher, educator; b. Waukesha, Wis., Sept. 4, 1939; s. Winston Dever and Julianne Evelyn Brown; m. Jill Rae Hollingshead, Feb. 21, 1968; children: Lara Nell, Kara Anne Nash, Evan Saxon. BS in Biology, Carroll Coll., 1961; MS in Zoology, So. Ill. U., Carbondale, 1963; PhD in Zoology, U. Tex., Austin, 1967; postgrad. in Zoology, U. Melbourne, Australia, 1968. Lab asst., zoology Carroll Coll., Waukesha, Wis., 1957—61; rsch. asst. biochem. Dairyland Food Lab., Waukesha, 1960; tchg. asst. genetics Mark Twain Inst., St. Louis, 1961; tchg. and rsch. asst. So. Ill. U., Carbondale, 1961—63, rsch. asst. plant ecology Pine Hills Field Sta. Pine Hills Swamp, Ill., 1963; tchg. and rsch. asst. U. Tex., Austin, 1963—67; asst. prof. vertebrate zoology Ill. State U., Normal, 1967—71, assoc. prof., 1971—77, prof., 1977—2002, prof. emeritus, 2002—, curator amphibians and reptiles, 1990—, chair sect. ecology, evolution, ethology and systematic biology, maj. prof. for numerous MS and PhD students, 1978—79, interdisciplinary studies, 1996—, adj. prof., 2002—. Endangered species and environ. cons., 1966—; mem. athletic coun. Ill. State U., 1992—95, mem. faculty svcs. com. Libr., 1999—2000, hon. libr., 2002—, grad. degree program maj. prof.; mem. Houston Toad Recovery Team US Fish and Wildlife Svc., 1978—84, 1998—; affiliate profl. scientist Ill. Natural History Survey, Champaign, Ill., 1997—; reviewer profl. jours.; presenter in field. Co-author: Recovery Plan for the Houston Toad, 1984; editor: Herpetologica, 1978—81, Alytes, 2000—; mem. editl. bd.: Ill. Natural History Survey, 1999—; contbr. chapters to books, numerous articles to profl. jours. Grantee in field, 1962—. Mem.: Mo. Herpetological Assn., Chgo. Herpetological Soc., Md. Herpetological Soc., Internat. Soc. for the History and Bibliography of Herpetology, N.Am. Native Fishes Assn., Ill. Ornithol. Soc., Coleopterists Soc., Coun. Biology Editors, Internat. Soc. Study and Conservation Amphibians (mem. editl. bd. 2000—, mem. bd. councillors 2003—), Am. Soc. Ichthyologists and Herpetologists, Declining Amphibian Populations Task Force, Soc. Study Amphibians and Reptiles (conservation com.), Herpetologists' League (bd. trustees 1979—80), Am. Rabbit Breeders Assn. (chair libr. com. 2001—02), SAR, Soc. Colonial Wars, Soc. War of 1812. Achievements include rediscovery of the near extinct Houston Toad in Lost Pines. Avocations: hiking, breeding and rearing animals, genealogy, swimming. Home: 15958 E 2550 North Rd Hudson IL 61748-9391 Office: Ill State Univ Dept Biological Sci Campus Box 4120 Normal IL 61790-4120 Office Phone: 309-438-5990.

BROWN, LAURENCE DAVID, retired bishop; b. Fargo, ND, Feb. 16, 1926; s. John Nicolai and Ada Amelia (Johnson) B.; m. Virginia Ann Allen, Sept. 6, 1950; children: Patricia Ann, Julia Louise, Claudia Ruth. BS, U. Minn., 1946; BA, Concordia Coll., 1948; M of Theology, Luther Theol. Sem., 1951. Ordained to ministry Evang. Luth. Ch., 1951. Pastor Our Savior's Luth. Ch., New Ulm, Minn., 1951-55; nat. assoc. youth dir. Evang. Luth. Ch., Mpls., 1955-60; nat. youth dir. Am. Luth. Ch., Mpls., 1960-68; instn. dir. Tchr. Tng., U. Minn., Mpls., 1968-69; exec. dir. Freedom from Hunger Found., Washington, 1969-73; sr. pastor St. Paul Luth. Ch., Waverly, Iowa, 1973-79; bishop Iowa Dist. Am. Luth. Ch., Des Moines, 1979-89, N.E. Iowa Synod, Evang. Luth. Ch. in Am., Waverly, 1989-92; prof. religion Wartburg Coll., Waverly, Iowa, 1992-93; interim sr. pastor Ctrl. Luth. Ch., Mpls., 1994-95, Calvary Luth. Ch., Mpls., 1996-97; ret. Bd. regents Luther Coll., Decorah, Iowa, 1989-92, Wartburg Coll., 1988-92, Wartburg Theol. Sem., Dubuque, Iowa, 1988-91, Self-Help, Inc., 1989-94. Author: Take Care: A Guide for Responsible Living, 1983; contbr. articles to profl. jours. Lt. USN, 1943-46. Lutheran. Avocation: reading. Home: 7500 York Ave S 916 Edina MN 55435

BROWN, LAURIE MARK, physicist, researcher; b. Bklyn., Apr. 10, 1923; s. William and Elvira (Fleischman) B.; m. Judith Kobrin, Dec. 27, 1942 (dec. May 1963); children: Joanna Lisa, Julie Elena; m. Brigitte Dziumbla-Winzeler, June 6, 1969; children: Judith, Jean. AB, Cornell U., 1943, PhD, 1951. Mem. faculty physics Northwestern U., Evanston, Ill., 1950—, prof., 1961-93, prof. emeritus, 1993—. Mem. Inst. for Advanced Study (NSF fellow), Princeton, 1952-53; cons. Argonne Nat. Lab., 1960-70; vis. prof., Vienna, 1966, Rome, 1967, São Paulo, 1972-73 Editor and author profl. books; contbr. articles to profl. jours. Fulbright research scholar Italy, 1958-60 Fellow Am. Phys. Soc. (chmn. div. history of physics 1983-84, 2001-2002). Home: 724 Noyes St Evanston IL 60201-2847 Business E-Mail: lbrown@northwestern.edu.

BROWN, LAWRENCE CHARLES, lawyer; b. Johnson City, NY, Apr. 5, 1951; s. Charles Hugh and Cora Rose (O'Connor) Brown; m. Constance Angela Grimes, July 28, 1973; children: Jason P., Christina M. BS, Cornell U., 1973; MA, SUNY, Albany, 1974; JD, Syracuse U., 1977. Bar: NY 1978, US Dist. Ct. (we. dist.) NY 1978, US Dist. Ct. (so. dist.) NY 1986, US Tax Ct. 1987, US Ct. Appeals (2d cir.) 1998, US Supreme Ct. 1998. Assoc. Phillips, Lytle, Hitchcock, Blaine & Huber, Buffalo, N.Y., 1977-78, Hodgson, Russ, Andrews, Woods & Goodyear, Buffalo, 1978-82; ptnr. Lipsitz, Green, Fahringer, Roll, Salisbury & Cambria, Buffalo, 1982-94, Kavinoky & Cook, LLP, 1994-96; prin. Law Offices of Lawrence C. Brown, Buffalo, 1996—. Bd. dirs. Fund Pub. Edn./Comml. Law Found., treas., 2002—04, sec., 2004—; advisor HS moot ct. teams for state bar program; presenter in field. Rsch. editor: Syracuse U. Law Rev., 1976—77; mem. editl. bd. Comml. Law Jour., 1998—2002, Comml. Law Bull., 1998—2004, bd. editors DePaul Bus. and Comml. Law Jour., 2002—; contbr. articles to profl. jours. Mem.: ABA, Comml. Law League Am. (nat. vice chmn. practice and procedure com. 1989—91, nat. vice chmn. uniform laws com. 1990—, nat. chmn. uniform laws com. 1992—95, advisor 1995—2002, nat. chmn. profl. responsibility com. 2006—, exec. coun. barkruptcy sect. 2006—), Erie County Bar Assn., NY State Bar Assn., Pi Kappa Alpha. Methodist. Avocation: public speaking. Office: 385 Cleveland Dr Buffalo NY 14215 Office Phone: 716-831-1994. Personal E-mail: brownl724@aol.com.

BROWN, LAWRENCE GEORGE, medical director; b. Ohio, 1948; BA, Earlham Coll., 1970; MD, Ohio State U., 1973. Cert. family medicine. Med. resident, Lansing, Mich., 1973—76; family physician Albany, Oreg., 1976—82; regional med. officer US Fgn. Svc., 1982—89; mem. Washington mgmt. team Office of Med. Svcs., US Dept. of State, Washington, 1989—95, chief med. clearances, chief fgn. programs, dep. med. dir., med. dir., 2003—. Fellow Am. Acad. Family Physicians. Office: US Dept State 2401 E St NW Washington DC 20522

BROWN, LAWRENCE HAAS, retired banker; b. Evanston, Ill., July 29, 1934; s. Robert C. and Alice (Haas) Brown; m. Ann Ferguson, June 23, 1956 (dec. May 23, 2006); children: Michael, Kenneth, Russell; m. Ann Hartman, May 28, 2007. Student, Cornell U., Ithaca, NY, 1952-54; BBA, U. Mich., 1956. Sr. v.p. No. Trust Co., Chgo., 1958-89, ret., 1989. Chmn. Pub. Securities Assn., N.Y.C., 1980; vice chmn. Mcpl. Securities Rulemaking Bd., Washington, 1982; bd. dirs. Nuveen Funds, 1993-2007. Pres. Highwood (Ill.) Pub. Libr., 1993—97; bd. dirs. United Way of Highland Park/Highwood, Michael Rolfe Pancreatic Cancer Found. Lt. USN, 1956—58. Mem.: Mcpl. Bond Club (pres. 1997), Exmoor Country Club (Highland Park, Ill.) (pres. 1984—85). Republican. Presbyterian. Avocations: tennis, curling, golf. Home: 201 Michigan Ave Highwood IL 60040-1808 Personal E-mail: ablbcurler@aol.com.

BROWN, LEE KELVIN, pulmonary, critical care and sleep medicine physician, researcher; b. Bklyn., Apr. 25, 1950; s. Bernard and Rosalind Schneider Brown; m. Carol Jean Yormack, Aug. 27, 1972; children: Matthew Ian, Douglas Elliot. BEE, MIT, 1972; MD, Mt. Sinai Sch. Medicine, 1976. Diplomate in internal medicine, pulmonary disease and critical care medicine Am. Bd. Internal Medicine, sleep medicine Am. Bd. Sleep Medicine. Resident medicine Mt. Sinai Hosp., NYC, 1976—79; fellow pulmonary disease Mt. Sinai Med. Ctr., Miami, Fla., 1979—81; assoc. prof. medicine Mt. Sinai Sch. Medicine, NYC, 1981—93; assoc. program dir. St. Joseph's Hosp. Med. Ctr., Phoenix, 1993—97; prof. clin. medicine U. Ariz., Tucson, 1994—97; chair divsn. sleep medicine Lovelace Health Sys., Albuquerque, 1997—2003; exec. dir. program sleep medicine Health Sci. Ctr. U. N.Mex., Albuquerque, 2003—, assoc. chief outpatient svcs., divsn. pulmonary, critical care medicine Sch. Medicine, 2003—, prof. medicine and pediats., 2003—, vice chair dept. internal medicine, 2004—. Mem. editl. bd. CHEST, —; contbr. chapters to books, articles to profl. jours. Asst. scoutmaster Boy Scout Troop 40, 1994—97; physician vol. Phoenix Open Golf Tournament, 1995—96; v.p. Rosalee Ranch Homeowners Assoc., Scottsdale, Ariz., 1996—97. Grantee, Grumman Aerospace Inc., 1968—72; Pulmonary Winter Course fellow, Fla. Lung Assn., 1980—81. Fellow: ACP, Am. Coll. Chest Physicians (chmn. sleep network 2004—06, Alfred Soffer Award for Editorial Excellence 2003), NY Acad. Medicine, Am. Acad. Sleep Medicine (bd. dirs. 2006—, assoc. editor jour.), Am. Coll. Critical Care Medicine; mem.: Greater Albuquerque Med. Assn. (pres.-elect 2007—), Eta Kappa Nu, Tau Beta Pi. Achievements include research in respiration and neurological disease; pulmonary physiology; sleep disorders. Avocations: hiking, amateur radio, computer science. Office: Univ NMex Bldg #2 1101 Medical Arts Ave NE Albuquerque NM 87102 Office Phone: 505-272-6110. E-mail: lkbrown@alum.mit.edu, lkbrown@salud.unm.edu.

BROWN, LEE PATRICK, retired mayor, federal official, protective services official, educator; b. Wewoka, Okla., Oct. 4, 1937; s. Andrew and Zelma (Edwards) B.; m. Yvonne Carolyn Streets, July 14, 1958 (dec.); children: Patrick, Torri, Robyn, Jenna; m. Frances M. Young, Dec. 29, 1995. BA, Fresno State U., 1960; MA, San Jose State U., 1964; MS, U. Calif., 1968; PhD in Criminology, U. Calif., Berkeley, 1970; D of Pub. Affairs (hon.), Fla. Internat. U., 1982; LLD (hon.), John Jay Coll., 1985; HHD (hon.), Portland State U., 1990; LHD (hon.), Fresno State U., 1994; LLD (hon.), SUNY Brockport, 1995; doctorate (hon.), Howard U., Wiley Coll.; Doctorate (hon.), Paul Quinn Coll., 2002. Officer San Jose (Calif.) Police Dept., 1960-68; prof. Portland (Oreg.) State U., 1968-72; assoc. dir. Urban Affairs Inst. Howard Inst., Washington, 1972-75; sheriff Sheriff's Dept., Mulnomah County, Oreg., 1975-76; dir. Dept. Justice Services, Mulnomah County, 1976-78; commr. Dept. Pub. Safety, Atlanta, 1978-82; chief of police Houston Police Dept., 1982-90; police commr. NYC, 1990-92; prof. Tex. So. Univ., 1992-93; dir. Nat. Drug Control Policy, Washington, 1993-96; mem. Pres. Cabinet, 1993-96; prof. Rice Univ., Houston, 1996-98; mayor City of Houston, 1998—2004; vis. scholar Rice U., 2004—05; chmn., CEO Brown Group Internat. Adj. prof. U. Houston, U. Tex. Health Sci. Ctr., Houston, Tex. So. U., Houston; vis. prof. Dalian Sch. Tech., China; hon. prof. Beijing Normal Sch., Tongji U.; guest prof. Tianjin U., China; cons. U.S. Dept. Justice, Washington, Police Found., Washington, various state and local govts., Houston; chmn. Nat. Minority Adv. Council on Criminal Justice; mem. Nat. Adv. Commn. on Criminal Justice Standards and Goals, Washington, Nat. Commn. on Higher Edn. for Police, Washington, Commn. on Accreditation for Law Enforcement Agencies, Washington, Presdl. Task Force, 1993—; mem. adv. bd. Stanford Fin. Group; chmn. bd. Unity Nat. Bank, Houston, CAMA Internat., Scicom Infrastructure; mem. adv. bd. Stanford Fin. Group. Co-author: Attitudes of Black Police Officers, 1976, Police and Society, 1981; editor: Neighborhood Team Policing, 1976, Violent Crime, 1981; author of numerous articles and book chpts. Bd. dirs. Boy Scouts Am., United Way, Urban League, Blue Bonnet Bowl, "Just Say No", Peoples Workshop for Visual and Performing Arts, Houston, 1987—, Nat. Black Child Devel. Inst., Washington, 1987—, Nat. Alliance Against Violence, N.Y., 1986—, Sheltering Arms, Houston, 1985—; task force mem. Nat. Ctr. for Missing and Exploited Children, Washington, 1986—; mem. adv. bd. Nat. Inst. Against Prejudice and Violence, Balt., 1987—; mem. Police Activities League, Houston, 1987—; mem. adv. policy bd. Nat. Incident Based Reporting System, 1988—; mem. adv. com. Fannie Mae, Washington, 1999; bd. dirs. Police Found., 2000; mem. U.S. Conf. of Mayors, Mayors and CEOs. Recipient Peace and Justice award Martin Luther King Jr., 1981, Nat. Law Enforcement award Nat. Black Police Assn., 1982, Disting. Alumnus award Fresno State U., 1983, Police Leadership award, Police Exec. Research Forum, 1987, Liberty Bell award Houston Young Lawyers Assn., 1987, August Vollmer award Am. Soc. Criminology, 1988, Cartier Pasha award Cartier Internat., 1992, Exemplary Leader award Am. Leadership Forum, 1994, Mikey Leland Lifetime Achievement award Mickey Leland Ctr. for World Hunger; named to Gallup Hall of Fame by Gallup, Inc., 1993; named Mgr. of Yr., Nat. Mgmt. Assn., Practitioner of Yr., Nat. Assn. of Blacks Criminal Justice, 1984, Communicator of Yr. Washington News Service, 1986, Father of Yr. Nat. Father's Day com., 1991, Politician of Yr. Libr. Jour., Technologist of Yr., Pub. Tech., Inc., 2002, Alumnus of Yr., U. Calif., Berkeley, 2004; named one of 100 Most Influential Black Ams., Ebony Mag., 2003; rsch. fellow Harvard U., 1988; Berkeley fellow, 2002. Mem. Internat. Assn. Chiefs of Police (past pres.), Nat. Orgn. of Black Law Enforcement Execs. (v.p. 1985, Robert Lamb Jr. Humanitarian award 1987), Police Exec. Research Forum, Internat. Narcotic Enforcement Officers Assn., Nat. Forum for Black Pub. Adminstrs., N.Y. Police Chiefs Assn., Tex. Police Assn., Tex. Criminal Justice Task Force, Nat. Police Athletic League, Mich. State U. (adv. council nat. neighborhood foot patrol ctr.), Nat. Research Council (com. on research on law enforcement and the adminstrn. of justice, com. on status of Black Ams.), Harvard U. (com. exec. session on community policing), Nat. Council on Crime and Delinquency (bd. dirs.), Nat. Acad. Pub. Adminstrn. (Nat. Pub. Svc. award 1988), Am. Soc. Pub. Adminstrn. (Nat. Pub. Svc. award 1988), Am. Leadership Forum, Forum Club of Houston (bd. dirs. 1987—), Calif. Alumni Club of Tex., Houston Bus. and Profl. Men's Club, Alpha Phi Alpha (Award of Merit 2000), Sigma Pi Phi. Democrat. Avocations: travel, reading, writing. Office Phone: 832-366-1584. Personal E-mail: leepbrown1@aol.com. Business E-Mail: lbrown@bgi-intl.com.

BROWN, LEON CARL, historian, educator; b. Mayfield, Ky., Apr. 22, 1928; s. Leon Carl and Gwendolyn (Travis) B.; m. Anne Winchester Stokes, Aug. 29, 1953; children: Elizabeth Boone, Joseph Winchester, Jefferson Travis. BA, Vanderbilt U., 1950; postgrad., U. Va., 1950-51, London Sch. Econs., 1951-52; PhD, Harvard, 1962. Fgn. Svc. officer., Beirut, 1954-55, Khartoum, Sudan, 1956-58; asst. prof. Mid. Ea. studies Harvard U., Cambridge, Mass., 1962-66; assoc. prof. Nr. Ea. history and civilization Princeton (N.J.) U., 1966-70, Garrett prof. fgn. affairs, 1970-93, Garrett prof. emeritus, 1993—, chmn. dept. Nr. Ea. studies, 1969-73, dir. program Nr. Ea. studies, 1969-73, 80-93. Author: (with C.A. Micaud and C.H. Moore) Tunisia: The Politics of Modernization, 1964, The Tunisia of Ahmad Bey, 1974, International Politics and the Middle East, 1984, Religion and State: The Muslim Approach to Politics, 2000; editor: State and Society in Independent North Africa, 1966, From Madina to Metropolis: Heritage and Change in the Near Eastern City, 1973; (with Norman Itzkowitz) Psychological Dimensions of Near Eastern Studies, 1977, Centerstage: American Diplomacy Since World War II, 1990; (with Cyril E. Black) Modernization in the Middle East, 1992, Imperial Legacy: The Ottoman Impact On The Balkans & The Middle East; (with Matthew Gordon) Franco-Arab Encounters, 1996, Diplomacy in the Middle East, 2001; translator with commentary: The Surest Path; The Political Treatise of a 19th Century Muslim Statesman, 1967. Served with USAAF, 1945-46. Mem. Middle East Studies Assn. (pres. 1975-76) Home and Office: 191 Hartley Ave Princeton NJ 08540-5613 Personal E-mail: lcbrown@princeton.edu.

BROWN, LES (LESTER LOUIS), journalist; b. Indiana Harbor, Ind., Dec. 20, 1928; s. Irving H. and Helen (Feigenbaum) B.; m. Jean Rosalie Slaymaker, June 12, 1959; children: Jessica, Joshua, Rebecca. BA in English, Roosevelt U., Chgo., 1950. Entertainment industry reporter, reviewer theatrical events Chgo. bur. Variety, 1953-55; asso. editor Downbeat mag., 1955; co-founder, operator folk music cabaret The Gate of Horn, Chgo., 1956; Chgo. bur. mgr. Variety, 1957-65; editor radio-TV dept. NYC, 1965-73; asst. mng. editor, 1973; radio-TV corr. N.Y. Times, 1973-80; editor in chief Channels mag., 1980-87; sr. v.p. editorial devel. C.C. Pub., NYC, 1987-91; pub. TV Bus. Internat. mag., 1988-91, editor in chief, 1990-91; columnist, 1992—; pub. World Guide, 1990. Cons. Revson Found., 1978, Ctr. for Comm., NYC, 1991-2003, World Alliance TV for Children, 1993-2001, Golden Rose Montreux TV Festival, 1994-2001, Monte Carlo TV Festival, 1994-2001; lectr. creative writing and entertainment industries Columbia Coll., Chgo., 1959-62, scholar-in-residence, 1985; lectr. comm. Hunter Coll., NYC, 1973-75, New Sch., NYC, 1977-80, Columbia U., 1994-96; lectr. Fordham U., 1995-2002, dir. TV Pantheon Oral History Project, 1996; Poynter fellow in modern journalism Yale U., 1977, lectr., 1978-80; assoc. fellow Morse Coll., 1978-86; Presdl. fellow Aspen Inst., 1978; bd. dirs. Dore Schary Awards, World TV and Radio Coun. UNESCO; sr. fellow Freedom Forum Media Studies Ctr. Columbia U., 1992-93. Author: lyrics Abilene, 1963, Television: The Business Behind The Box, 1971, Electric Media, 1973, New York Times Encyclopedia of Television, 1977, Keeping Your Eye on Television, 1979; Les Brown's Encyclopedia of Television, 1982, Fast Forward: The New Television and American Society, 1983, Les Brown's Encyclopedia of Television, 1992; also articles. Mem. Film-TV adv. bd. N.Y. State Coun. on Arts, 1975; pres. Media Commentary Coun. Inc. With AUS, 1951-53. Recipient Silver Cir. award N.Y. Chpt. Nat. Acad. TV Arts and Scis., 1996.

BROWN, LESTER B., social worker, educator; b. Whitmire, SC, Jan. 11, 1943; s. William Barney and Minnie Eugenia (Vaughn) Brown. AB in Psychology, U. Chgo., 1969, AM in Social Work, 1971, PhD in Social Treatment, 1980. Sr. child care counselor, therapist Nicholas J. Pritzker Ctr. and Hosp., Chgo., 1964-68, 69; social worker I Ill. Dept. Children and Family Svcs., Chgo., 1967-70, social worker II, 1971; group homes social worker Jewish Children's Bur., Chgo., 1971-73; social worker, field instr. Jackson Park Hosp., Chgo., 1973, clin. dir., 1973-74, cons., 1975-77, SUNY, Albany, 1981, asst. prof. social work, chmn. undergrad. social welfare, 1981-86; prof. social worker Wayne State U., 1986-89; assoc. prof. social work Calif. State U., Long Beach, 1989-95, prof. social work, 1995—. Lectr. U. Wis., Milw., 1977—78, instr., 1978—80; lectr. U. Chgo., 1977—78; guest lectr. Boston Coll., 1981; cons., presenter in field. Author: (book) Two Spirit People: American Indian Lesbian Women and Gay Men, 1997, Gay Men and Aging, 1997, Brief Treatment and a New Look at the Task Centered Approach, 2003; contbr. articles to profl. jours., chapters to books; mem. editl. bd. Health Care Mgmt. Rev., 1981—84. Bd. dirs. Capital Dist. Travelers Aid Soc., 1983—86; condr. workshops ethnic sensitive work Pittsfield Sch. Dist., Mass., 1984; participant workshops mental health and child welfare; mem. com. Urban League. Grantee, SUNY, 1981, U.S. HHS, 1981, Sch. Social Welfare, 1982. Mem.: NASW, Coun. Social Work Edn., Acad. Cert. Social Workers. Democrat. Avocations: cooking, aerobics. Home: 726 Obispo Ave Long Beach CA 90804-5069 Office: Calif State U Long Beach Social Work 1250 N Bellflower Blvd Long Beach CA 90840-0006 Office Phone: 562-985-4984. Business E-Mail: lbrown2@csulb.edu.

BROWN, LESTER RUSSELL, research and development company executive; b. Bridgeton, NJ, Mar. 28, 1934; s. Calvin C. and Delia (Smith) B.; m. Shirley Ann Woolington, June 12, 1960 (div.); children: Brian, Brenda. BS in Agrl. Sci., Rutgers U., 1955; MA in Agrl. Econs., U. Md., 1959; MPA, Harvard U., 1962; LHD (hon.), Dickinson Coll.; LLD (hon.), U. Md.; LHD (hon.), Franklin Coll.; LLD (hon.), Williams Coll., Rutgers U.; LHD (hon.), Glassboro State Coll., Tufts U.; LLD (hon.), Coll. of Wooster; LHD (hon.), Clark U., Ripon Coll., Otterbein Coll.; DSc (hon.), U. Pisa, McGill U.; LLD (hon.), U. Notre Dame; D of Pub. Svc. (hon.), Northland Coll.; LHD (hon.), St. Lawrence U.; DSc (hon.), Claremont Coll.; D of Social Sci. (hon.), Villanova U.; DSc (hon.), Westminster Coll., Utah, Westminster Coll., Pa., U. Conn., Ohio State U., Hitotsubashi U., Mich. State U. With Dept. of Agr., 1958—69, adminstr. internat. agr. devel. service, 1966-69; adv. to sec. U.S. Dept. Agr., Washington, 1965—69; sr. fellow Overseas Devel. Council, 1969-74; pres., founder Worldwatch Inst., Washington, 1974-2000, Earth Policy Inst., Washington, 2001—. Faculty Salzburg Seminar in Am. Studies, 1971, 1974; guest scholar Aspen Inst., summers 1972-74; sr. adv. Japanese Ministry Agr., Forestry, & Fishery; vice chmn. Adv. Com. of the U.S. China Assoc. Environ. Edn.; hon. prof. U. Shanghai, China, 2003; hon. prof. U. Shanghai, 2003, Chinese Acad. Scis., 2005. Author: Man, Land and Food, 1963, Increasing World Food Output, 1965, Seeds of Change, 1970, World Without Borders, 1972, In the Human Interest, 1974, (with Gail Finsterbusch) Man and his Environment: Food, 1974, (with Erik Eckholm) By Bread Alone, 1974 (Christopher award), The Twenty-Ninth Day, 1978 (Ecologia Firenze award), (with Colin Norman and Christopher Flavin) Running on Empty, 1979, Building a Sustainable Society, 1981, State of the World, 1984-2001, (with others) Vital Signs, 1992-2001, (with Hal Kane) Full House, 1994, Who Will Feed China?, 1995, Tough Choices: Facing the Challenge of Global Food Scarcity, 1996; editor: (with Ed Ayres) World Watch Reader, 1998, (with Flavin and Sandra Postel) Saving the Planet, 1991, (with Gardner and Halweil) Beyond Malthus, 1999, Eco-Economy: Building an Economy for the Earth, 2001 (Peka award 2004), (with Larsen and Fischlowitz-Roberts) The Earth Policy Reader, 2002, Plan B: Rescuing a Planet Under Stress and a Civilization in Trouble, 2003, Worldwatch Issue Alert, 2000-01, Eco-Economy Updates, 2001-, Outgrowing the Earth: The Food Security Challenge in an Age of Falling Water Tables & Rising Temperatures, 2005, Plan B2.0: Rescuing a Planet Under Stress & A Civilization in Trouble, 2006; (permanent exhibit) The Works of Lester R. Brown, Cook Coll., Rutgers U., 2005; contbr. articles to profl jours. Mem. adv. com. Inst. Internat. Econs.,UN Found., Eco-Policy Ctr./Rutgers U.; mem. bd. advisors Internat. Fund for China's Environment; bd. dirs. Inst. for Sustainable Devel., Poland; treas. and bd. mem. Farview Found.; mem. adv. coun. Internat. Fund for Agrl. Rsch.; advisor Clean Up the World Project, Australia, Internat. Coun. Earth Day 2000; mem. adv. bd. Ctr. for a New Am. Dream; mem. nat. adv. bd. Population Connection (formerly Zero Population Growth); mem. adv. com. Internews; mem. adv. bd. Green House Network; bd. patrons Internat. Network Green Planners; mem. steering com. Ecol. Cities Project, U. Mass.; dir. Japan for Sustainability; mem. adv. coun. Ecology channel. Recipient Superior Svc. award Dept. Agr., 1965, Arthur S. Flemming award, 1965, A.H. Boerma award UN Food and Agrl. Orgn., 1981, UNEP Environ. Leadership medal, 1982, Lorax award Global Tomorrow Coalition, 1985, award World Wildlife Fund for Nature Internat., 1989, UN Environment prize, 1987, A Bizzozero award U. Parma, 1991, Humanist of Yr. award, 1991, Pro Mundo Habitabili award King Carl XVI Gustaf, Sweden, 1991, Delphi Internat. Cooperation award, 1991, Cervia Ambiente prize, Italy, 1992, Robert Rodale Lectr. award, 1992, Environmentalist of Yr. award Japan Jaycees, 1992, Cert. Spl. Recognition Assn. Am. Geographers, 1993, Blue Planet prize Asahi Glass Found., 1994, J. Sterling Morton Arbor Day award, 1995, Pub. Svc. award Fedn. Am. Scientists, 1995, Disting. Achievement award Heylar House Alumni Assn. Rutgers U., 1995, Rachel Carson Environ. Achievement award Nat. Nutritional Foods Assn., 2000, Bruno H. Schubert Found. environment award, 2001, Natural Bus. Leadership award, 2002, Excellence Adv. award Internat. Fund for China's Environment, 2002, Italian Presdl. medal, 2003, Georg and Greta Borgström prize Royal Swedish Acad. Agriculture & Forestry, 2005, Claire Matzger Lilienthal Disting. Lectr. award Calif. Acad. Scis., 2005; selected as 100 Who Made A Difference The Earth Times, 1995, 100 Champions of Conservation, Audubon Soc., 1998; named one of People of the Century The Daily Jour., NJ, 2000, One of 500 Most Influential People in US in Fgn. Policy World Affairs Coun. Am., 2003, One of 30 Global Visionaries Planet Mag., 2005; named to Bridgeton HS Disting. Alumni Hall of Fame, 2005. Fellow World Bus. Acad.; mem. Coun. Fgn. Rels., World Future Soc., Cosmos Club, Sierra Club (adv. coun. for excellence in environ. engring.). Office: Earth Policy Inst Ste 403 1350 Connecticut Ave NW Washington DC 20036-1995 Office Phone: 202-496-9290. Business E-Mail: epi@earth-policy.org.

BROWN, LINDA HARPER, bookkeeping company executive; b. Dallas, Mar. 20, 1948; d. Harold Eugene and Opal Lee Gooch; m. Charles Michael Harper (div.); children: Timothy Drake Harper, Terry Christopher Harper; m. William E. Brown III; 1 child, William Craig. Cyma cert. computer cons. Acct. W.E. Brown III CPA, Duncanville, Tex., Brown & Hildebrand CPA, DeSoto, Tex.; comptr. Prism Graphics, Inc., Dallas; pres. H & H Bookkeeping, Inc., Irving, Tex., 1990—. Trustee Duncanville Sch. Bd., 1985-91, v.p., 1989-90; mem. Irving City Coun., 1997-2002, mayor pro tem, 1998-99; treas., bd. dirs. Dallas Regional Mobility Coalition, 1997—; bd. dirs. North Ctrl. Tex. Coun. of Govts., 1998—, Irving Heritage Soc.; founding mem. Irving Lyric Stage, treas., 1995-95; bd. dirs. Irving Schs. Found., pres., 1997-98; mem. steering com. Nat. League of Cities Crime Prevention and Pub. Safety, 1998-2002; mem. Tex. Ho. of Reps., 2002, 2004, vice chair select com. on state healthcare expenditures, 2004, mem. transp. com. and elections com., interim com. for child welfare and adoption, 2005, vice chmn. land and resource mgmt. com.; mem. Tex. Higher Edn. Coordinating Bd., 2006Y—; mem. Tex. Legis. Coun., 2006. Named Entrepreneur of Yr., Las Colinas Bus. and Profl. Women, 1993, Irving Women of the Yr., Irving Cancer Soc., 1995, Outstanding Woman in Govt., YWCA, 1998, Nat. Rep. Freshman Legislator, Nat. Rep. Legislators Assn., 2003; recipient Irving High Spirited Citizen award, 1994, Leader of Excellence award Rep. Caucus, 2003, Fighter of Free Enterprise award Tex. Assn. Bus., 2003, 06. Avocations: reading, research, travel, hunting, walking. Office: H & H Bookkeeping Inc Ste 250 125 E John Carpenter Fwy Irving TX 75062 Home Phone: 972-650-1244.

BROWN, LORA ALICE, entertainment company executive, educator; b. Nashville, Oct. 23, 1975; d. Barry Lee and Susan James Brown. BA in Music cum laude, U. Tenn., 1997; MusM, Belmont U., 2003. Dir. string methods and music edn. The Renaissance Ctr., Dickson, Tenn., 2000—03;

pres., founder Amadeus Entertainment, Inc., Dickson, Tenn., 2003—. Musical dir. Amadeus Cmty. Orch., Dickson, 2004—. Prodr.: (annual musical benefit) A Home Town Christmas. Tchr. Poplar Grove Ch. of Christ, McEwen, Tenn., 1998—. Mem.: Suzuki Assn. Am., Music Educators Nat. Conf., Conductor's Guild, Am. String Tchrs. Assn., Dickson Area Women in Bus. (founding 50 mem.), Phi Kappa Lamda, Golden Key Honor Soc., Sigma Alpha Iota (life; pres. 1994—95). Home Phone: 931-582-8911; Office Phone: 615-446-4340. E-mail: amadeusentertainment@yahoo.com.

BROWN, LOREN H., lawyer; b. 1966; BS, U. Md., 1988; JD, Hofstra U., 1992. Admitted: US Ct. of Appeals, Second Cir., US Dist. Ct., Southern Dist. NY, US Dist. Ct., Eastern Dist. NY, US Dist. Ct., Northern Dist. NY, US Dist. Ct., Western Dist. NY, US Dist. Ct., Dist. Conn. Ptnr. DLA Piper, NYC. Named one of Litigation's Rising Stars, The Am. Lawyer, 2007. Mem.: NY State Bar Assn., NYC Bar Assn., Def. Rsch. Inst., ABA. Office: DLA Piper 1251 Ave of Americas New York NY 10020-1104 Office Phone: 212-335-4846. Office Fax: 212-335-4501.*

BROWN, LORENE B(YRON), retired library educator; b. Plant City, Fla., Nov. 9, 1933; d. Benjamin and Sallie (Barton) Byron; m. Paul L. Brown, Aug. 1, 1974. BS, Fort Valley State Coll., 1955; MSL.S., Atlanta U., 1956; PhD, U. Wis., Madison, 1974. Cataloguer N.C. Central U., Durham, 1956-58, Gibbs Jr. Coll., St. Petersburg, Fla., 1958-60, Fort Valley State Coll., Ga., 1960-65, Norfolk State U., Va., 1965-70; assoc. prof., dean Atlanta U., 1970-89, prof., 1989—2003; dir. Info. Retrieval Workshops, Atlanta, 1976-78; evaluator Coop. Coll. Library Ctr., Atlanta, 1979-82; cons. United Bd. Coll. Devel., Atlanta, 1976-79. Mem. southeastern/Atlantic regional adv. coun. Nat. Network Librs. Medicine, 2001—03. Author: Subject Access for African American Material, 1995. Mem. Friends of Library, Atlanta, 1982. Recipient Rachel Schenk award Library Sch. U. Wis., Madison, 1971; So. Fellowship Found. fellow Atlanta, 1972-74; Libr. and Info. Studies Centennial Celebration Alumnus of Yr. award in Libr. Edn., U. Wis. Libr. and Info. Studies, Madison, 2006. Mem. ALA, Am. Soc. for Info. Sci., Assn. Library and Info. Sci. Edn., Ga. Library Assn., Met Atlanta Library Assn., Beta Phi Mu. Democrat. Baptist. Home: 855 Flamingo Dr SW Atlanta GA 30311-2402

BROWN, LOWELL SEVERT, physicist, researcher; b. Visalia, Calif., Feb. 15, 1934; s. Volney Clifford and Anna Marie Evelyn (Jacobson) B.; m. Shirley Isabel Mitchell, June 23, 1956; 1 son, Stephen Clifford. AB, U. Calif., Berkeley, 1956; PhD (NSF predoctoral fellow 1956-61), Harvard U., 1961; postgrad., U. Rome, 1961-62, Imperial Coll., London, 1962-63. From rsch. assoc. to assoc. prof. physics Yale U., 1963-68; mem. faculty U. Wash., Seattle, 1968—, prof. physics, 1970-2001, prof. emeritus, 2001—; mem. staff Los Alamos Nat. Lab., N.Mex., 2001—. Vis. prof. Imperial Coll., London, 1971-72, Columbia U., N.Y.C., 1990; vis. scientist Brookhaven Nat. Lab., summer, 1965-68, Lawrence Berkeley Lab., summer 1966, Stanford Accelerator Ctr., summer, 1967, CERN, Geneva, summer, 1979, Inst. for Theoretical Physics, U. Calif., Santa Barbara, winter 1999; mem. Inst. Advanced Study, Princeton, N.J., 1979-80; cons. Los Alamos Nat. Lab., spring 1999, vis. scientist, 1991; vis. physicist Deutches Elektronen-Synchrontron, Hamburg, 1986 Author: Quantum Field Theory, 1992; mem. editl. bd. Phys. Rev., 1978-81; editor Phys. Rev. D, 1987-95; contbr. articles to profl. publs. Trustee Seattle Youth Symphony Orch., 1986—95. Postdoctoral fellow NSF, 1961-63; sr. postdoctoral fellow, 1971-72; Guggenheim fellow, 1979-80 Mem. Ferrari Club of Am. (dir. Northwest region 1999-2003). Office: X-3 MS F644 PO Box 1668 Los Alamos NM 87545 Personal E-mail: gt330@comcast.net.

BROWN, LYNETTE RALYA, journalist, publicist; b. Beloit, Wis., Dec. 15, 1926; d. Lynn Louis and Ethel Clara (Meeker) Ralya; m. Donald Adair Brown, Jr., Dec. 20, 1947; children: Donald Adair III, Alison Laura, Julia Carol. BA in Journalism, Mich. State U., 1948, MA in Journalism, 1985; MA in Mass Comm., Wayne State U., 1983. Actress, publicist Grand Traverse Playhouse, Traverse City, Mich., 1946 (summer), N.Y. Summer Playhouse, Mackinac Island, Mich., 1947 (summer); writer WILS Radio, Lansing, Mich., 1947-48; writer, performer WJBK Radio, TV, Detroit, 1948-49; editor Denby Ctr. News, Detroit, 1949-51; freelance writer Oakland County, Mich., 1952-78; editor Henry Ford Mus., Dearborn, Mich., 1979-81; writer, reporter Legal Advertiser Newspaper, Detroit, 1983-85; publicist Bloomfield (Mich.) and Birmingham (Mich.) Pub. Librs., 1986-89; freelance writer, publicist Lynette Brown Comm., Birmingham, Mich., 1989—. Columnist: (newspaper) At the Libraries, 1986-89; solo performer Elizabeth Cady Stanton, 1995—. Probation sponsor Dist. Ct. Mich., 1960-70; publicist Oakland County Vol. Bur., 1979-82; leader sr. high/jr. high youth group Drayton Ave. Presbyn. Ch., Oakland County, 1952-54, 62-66, Pine Hill Congl. Ch., Oakland County, 1968-71, Northbrook Presbyn. Ch., Oakland County, 1976-77; polit. campaign worker Rep. candidates and non-partisan jud. candidates, 1952—; Cub Scout leader Royal Oak Emerson Sch., Oakland County, 1961-64; Girl Scout troop leader Bloomfield Twp. Meadow Lake Sch., Oakland County, 1966-71; dir. Martha Griffiths Project, 1989-. Grantee N.Y. State's Thanks Be To Grandmother Winifred Found., 1996, Elizabeth Kummer Award AAUW Mich., 2002. Mem. AAUW (chair women's issues, pub. info. dir. 1995-2000, state projects dir. 2000—), Oakland County C. of C. (Athena award 1995), Mich. Women's Studies Assn. (bd. dirs. 1999—). Home and Office: 6120 Westmoor Rd Bloomfield Township MI 48301 Home Phone: 248-626-5414; Office Phone: 248-626-5414.

BROWN, MACK, college football coach; b. Cookeville, Tenn., Aug. 27, 1951; m. Sally Brown; children: Matt, Katherine, Barbara, Chris. Bachelor's degree in Education, Fla. State Univ., 1974; MEd, Univ. So. Miss., 1976. Receivers coach Univ. So. Miss., 1975—78, Memphis St., 1978, Iowa St., 1979, offensive coord., 1980—82; quarterbacks coach LSU, 1982; head football coach Appalachian St., 1983; offensive coord. U. Okla., 1984; head football coach, athletic dir. Tulane U., 1985—88; head football coach UNC, 1988—97, U. Tex., Austin, 1997—. Mem. NCAA Coll. Football Rules Com., NCAA Football Issues Com. Hon. co-chmn. Capital Campaign Helping Hands, Austin, Tex.; mem. bd. dir. The Rise Sch., Austin, Tex. Recipient Paul "Bear" Bryant award, Nat. Sportscasters & Sportswriters Assn., 2005. Mem.: Am. Football Coaches Assn. (past mem. ethics com.), Coll. Football Assn. (past mem. bd. dir.), Football Coaches Com. (past chmn.). Achievements include coaching U. Tex. to the 2005 BCS Nat. Championship. Office: U Tex PO Box 7399 Austin TX 78713-7399*

BROWN, MADELINE MORGAN, internist; b. Marlton, NJ, Dec. 4, 1976; d. Wallace Francis and Dianne Edythe Brown; m. Donald John Bitto, Jr., Oct. 10, 2004. BA in Molecular Biology, Rosemont Coll., 1998; MD, MCP Hahnemann (Drexel) Med., Phila., 2002. Internal med. internship Med. U. S.C., Charleston, 2002—03, internal medicine resident, 2003—04, Temple U. Hosp., Phila., 2004—05; gen. internist/physician Fountainville Med. Specialists, Doylestown, Pa., 2005—. Resident rep., infection ctrl. com. Med. U. S.C., 2003—04. Author: (invention) Patient Data Cards, 2002, (book) The Intern Survival Guide, 2003. Trainer for standardized patients Nat. Bd. Med. Examiners, Phila., 2005. Mem.: ACP, AMA. Democrat. Avocations: piano, drums, ice skating, reading, bicycling. Office: Fountainville Med Specialists 1456 Ferry Rd Ste 600 Fountainville PA 18923 Office Phone: 215-230-8390.

BROWN, MALCOLM CHARLES, conservator; b. Wheaton, Ill., July 30, 1963; Degree in constrn. mgmt., SIU Carbondale, Ill., 1984—87. Pvt. conservator, Springfield, 1991—; conservator Ill. Hist. Preservation Agy., Springfield, 1994—; exhibits specialist Abraham Lincoln Presdl. Mus., Springfield, 2006—. Pvt. conservator, Springfield, 1991—. Achievements include conservatin of wooden artifact; gilded conservation for the state of Illinois. Office: Ill Historic Preservation Agy 313 S 6th St Springfield IL 62701 Office Fax: 217-785-8117. Business E-Mail: malcolm.brown@illinois.gov.

BROWN, MARGARET ANN, lawyer; b. Mobile, Ala., 1952; BA, Univ. Va., 1974, JD, 1977. Bar: La. 1977, Va. 1986. Ptnr., practice group leader, real estate fin. Troutman Sanders LLP, McLean, Va. Mem.: ABA, Fairfax Bar Assn., La. State Bar Assn. Office: Troutman Sanders LLP Ste 500 1660 Industrial Dr Mc Lean VA 22102 Office Phone: 703-734-4336. Office Fax: 703-448-6506. Business E-Mail: ann.brown@troutmansanders.com.

BROWN, MARGARET CATHERINE, artist; d. Joseph Brown Pearson and Helen Minnie Dusenberry; m. Tyler T. Brown (div.). BS, W. Va. U., 1961. Tchr. Fairfax Pub. Schs., Va., 1961—65; program analyst Fed. Govt./Dept. Navy/NOAA, Washington, 1974—99. One-woman shows include Rachael M. Schlesinger Concert Hall and Arts Ctr., 2003, Willowcroft Winery, 2005, Cosi Restaurant, 2005, exhibited in group shows at Nat. Exhbn. River Rd., Baton Rouge, 2003—04, Nat. Exhbn. NC, Southport, 2003, Nat. Exhbn. Barnsite Gallery, Kewannee, Wis., 2003, Internat. Exhbn. Fine Art Miniatures, Bethesda, Md., 2003—06, Cobblestone Gallery, 2004, 2005, 2006, 2007, Internat. Miniature Show, NC, 2005, Nat. Exhbn. Calif. Watercolor Assn., 2006, Nat. Pitts. Watercolor Soc., 2006, Frame Decor Gallery, 2006, Nat. Exhbn. Boca Grande Art Show, 2007, Balt. Waltercolor Exhbn., 2007, Nat. Assn. Woman Artists, 2007, Art Ctr. Manassas, 2007, Art League of Alexandria, Springfield Art Guild, E.C. May Gallery, Art at the Mill, Millwood, Va., Four Seasons of Oatlands, Reston Art League, Gallery 222, Potomac Gallery, numerous pvt. collections. Recipient Equal award, Art League of Alexandria, Famous Artisans of the 21st Century Show, Peoples Choice award, Old Town Hall Gallery, numerous 2d place awards various art shows, Grand Prize award, Art Supply Warehouse Catalog Contest, 2003—04. Mem.: Loudoun Arts Coun., Miniature Painters Soc. (juried instr. 2006), Vienna Art Soc., Nat. Assn. Women Artists, Potomac Valley Watercolorists, Art League of Alexandria, Nat. League of Am. Pen Women, Washington Watercolor Assn. (bd. dirs.), Springfield Art Guild (v.p.), Fairfax Art League (v.p.), Va. Watercolor Soc. (assoc.), So. Watercolor Soc. (assoc.), Nat. Watercolor Soc. (assoc.), Am. Watercolor Soc. (assoc.). Methodist. Avocations: piano, reading, aerobics, travel. Home and Office: 7765 Shooting Star Dr Springfield VA 22152-3105 Personal E-mail: peggy-brown@msn.com.

BROWN, MARILYN BRANCH, retired educational administrator; b. Richmond, Va., Apr. 11, 1944; d. Elbert LeRoy and Edna Harriett (Eley) Branch; m. Winfred Wayland Brown, Jr., June 19, 1982; 1 dau., Lesli Antoinette; 1 dau. by previous marriage, Kara Rachelle Lancaster-Gay. B.S., Va. State U., 1966; M.S., U. Nebr., 1968; postgrad. U. Ala., Va. Commonwealth U. Nat. Tchr. Corps intern U. Nebr. at Omaha and Omaha Pub. Schs., 1966-68; tchr. McKlenburg County Pub. Schs., Boydton, Va., 1968-71; cmty. organizer model cities health planning Capital Area Comprehensive Health Planning Coun., Richmond, Va., 1971-72; asst. dir. com. mental health mental retardation svcs. bd. Va. Dept. Mental Health and Mental Retardation, Richmond, 1972-75, spl. edn. dir., 1975-76; civil rights coord. Va. Dept. Social Svcs., Richmond, 1976-88, chmn. EEO adv. com., 1984-88; supr. spl edn. compliance Va. Dept. Edn., 1988-92; ret., 1992. Chmn. adv. com. on Black adoption Va. Dept. Social Svcs., 1983-86; program coord. Swansboro Bapt. Ch., Richmond, 1979-07; mem. Swansboro Ensemble, 1973-04, Swansboro Mass Choir, 2002—, Sanctuary Choir, 2006-; coord. One Ch. One Child; pres. Swansboro Deaconess Ministry, 2004—. Recipient Youth Motivation Commendation, Nat. Alliance of Bus., 1983. Fellow Am. Orthopsychiat. Assn.; mem. Am. Assn. Affirmative Action (fed. program grant reviewer 1994-02), Black Adminstrs. in Child Welfare, Alliance for Black Social Welfare, Regional Youth Coord. National Tots & Teens, Inc., Ea. Star (Elizabeth Harris chpt.), Alpha Kappa Alpha, Psi Chi. Home: 5500 Larrymore Rd Richmond VA 23225-6020

BROWN, MARK E., manufacturing executive; b. Peosta, Iowa; BA, U. Iowa. Acct. Whirlpool Corp., Marion, Ohio, 1973, mgr. Columbia plant SC, 1988, contr. North Am. Appliance Group, 1991—93, v.p., procurement North Am. Appliance Group, 1993—95, gen. mgr. mktg. North Am. Appliance Group, 1995—96, contr. Whirlpool Asia, 1996—97, corp. v.p, contr., 1997—99, exec. v.p., CFO, 1999—2002, sr. v.p. global strategic sourcing, 2002—. Office: Whirlpool Corp 2000 N M-63 Benton Harbor MI 49022*

BROWN, MARY ELLEN, former state legislator, accountant; b. Hartland, Maine, July 26, 1952; d. Justin O. and Ernestine (Garnett) Humphrey; m. Gary R. Brown, June 6, 1971; children: John A., Jessica I. AA, Franklin Pierce C.C., Concord, NH, 1978. Pvt. practice Automated Bookkeeping Svcs., Pittsfield, NH, 1976—; realtor historic properties and distinctive homes Pembroke. Author: Out of Season, 1997, Messages From Mothers to Daughters, 2001, The Impeachment Trial of the New Hampshire Surpreme Court Justuce, 2002, Promoting Your Book in New Hampshire, 2004, others; contbr. articles to newspapers, mags. State legislator, N.H., 1995-96; pres. Chichester (N.H.) PTO, 1979, Tax Payers Assn., 1996. Mem. Internat. Women's Writers Guild, Nat. Soc. Pub. Accts., N.H. Wildlife Fedn., Go N.H. (polit. group), N.H. Writers Project. Avocations: writing, fishing, gardening.

BROWN, MARY ROSE, energy executive; B in Comm., S.W. Tex. State U. VP pub. rels. Atkins Agy., 1983—97, Valero Corp., San Antonio, 1997, sr. v.p. corp. comm., 1997—. Trustee Our Lady of The Lake U. Recipient Women's Leadership award, San Antonio Bus. Jour., Silver Anvil award, Pub. Rels. Soc. Am. Mem.: Pub. Rels. Soc. Am., Tex. Pub. Rels. Assn. (nearly 20 Silver Spur and Best of Texas awards). Office: Valero PO Box 696000 San Antonio TX 78269-6000

BROWN, MARY WILKES, secondary school educator; d. Jackson Wilkes Jr. and Thelma McDonald Wilkes; m. James H. Brown Jr., Oct. 12, 1974; children: Raena Antoinette, James Henry III, Ryan Jackson. BA in Spanish, Norfolk State U., Va., 1974, endorsement in adminstrn. and supervision, 2005; MA in Edn., Old Dominion U., Norfolk, 1998. Endorsement in English. Spanish tchr. Smithfield HS, Va., 1974—80, Lake Taylor HS, Norfolk, 1980—87, 1996—, Chesterfield Heights Elem. Sch., Norfolk, 1987—96. Named Tchr. of Yr., Lake Taylor HS, 1986, Chesterfield Heights Elem. Sch., 1990; scholar, Valencia, Spain, 1989. Mem.: NEA (assoc.), Fgn. Lang. Assn. Va., Edn. Assn. Norfolk (assoc.), Am. Assn. Tchrs. of Spanish and Portuguese (assoc.). Avocation: exercise. Home: 4782 Christopher Arch Virginia Beach VA 23464 Office: Lake Taylor HS 1384 Kempsville Rd Norfolk VA 23502 Home Phone: 757-467-0897; Office Phone: 757-892-3200. Office Fax: 757-892-3210. Business E-Mail: mwbrown@nps.k12.va.us.

BROWN, MATTHEW S., lawyer; b. Chgo., Jan. 29, 1955; BA magna cum laude, Conn. Coll.; JD, Georgetown U., 1978. Bar: Ill. 1978. Ptnr. Katten Muchin Rosenman, Chgo. Mem.: ABA, Chgo. Bar Assn. Office: Katten Muchin Rosenman Ste 1600 525 W Monroe St Chicago IL 60661 Office Phone: 312-909-5207. Office Fax: 312-577-8726. E-mail: matthew.brown@kattenlaw.com.

BROWN, MEREDITH M., lawyer; b. NYC, Oct. 18, 1940; s. John Mason Brown and Catherine (Screven) Meredith; m. Sylvia Lawrence Barnard, July 17, 1965; 1 child, Mason Barnard. AB, Harvard U., 1961, JD, 1965. Bar: N.Y. 1965, U.S. Ct. Appeals (2d cir.) 1966, U.S. Dist. Ct. (so. dist.) N.Y. 1976. Law clk. to Hon. Leonard P. Moore U.S. Ct. Appeals (2d cir.), NYC, 1965-66; assoc. Debevoise & Plimpton, NYC, 1966—72, ptnr., 1973—2004, co-chair corp. dept., 1993—2002, chair or co-chair mergers and acquisitions group, 1985—2004, of counsel, 2005—. Author: (with others) Takeovers: A Strategic Guide to Mergers & Acquisitions, 2d edit., 2004, Global Offerings, 1994, Privatisations, 1994, Mechanics of Global Equity Offerings, 1995, International Mergers and Acquisitions: An Introduction, 1999; contbr. articles to profl. publs. Mem. ABA (bus. law sect.), Assn. of Bar of City of N.Y. (chmn. profl. responsibility com. 1987-90), Internat. Bar Assn. (co-chmn. com. on issues and trading of securities, sect. on bus. law 1994-98, co-chmn. capital markets forum, sec. bus. law 1998-2002). Home: 79 Tipping Rock Rd Stonington CT 06378 E-mail: mmbrown@debevoise.com.

BROWN, MICHAEL D., shadow senator; m. Patricia E. Brown; children: Tricia, Nick, Mary. BA, U. Md., MA in Pub. Policy. Founder, pres. Horizon Comms., 1989—; dir. donor devel. Dem. Nat. Com.; DC shadow senator to US Congress, 2007—. Mem. Adv. Neighborhood Commn. Mem.: Western Ave. Citizens Assn. (pres.). Democrat. Office: 4501 Western Ave NW Washington DC 20016 also: John A Wilson Bldg 1350 Pennsylvania Ave, NW Washington DC 20004 Office Phone: 202-727-1000. E-mail: hrzcom@aol.com.*

BROWN, MICHAEL DEWAYNE, former federal agency administrator, lawyer; b. Guymon, Okla., Nov. 11, 1954; s. Wayne E. and R. Eloise B.; m. Tamara Ann Oxley, July 19, 1973; children: Jared Michael, Amy Aryann. Student, Southeastern State Coll., 1973-75; BA in Pub. Adminstrn./Polit. Sci., Cen. State U., Edmond, Okla., 1978; JD, Oklahoma City U. Sch. Law, 1981. Bar: Okla. 1982, Colo. 1992, U.S. Dist. Ct. (no. and we. dists.) Okla. 1982, U.S. Ct. Appeals (10th cir.) 1982, U.S. Ct. Appeals (D.C. cir.) 1987. Asst. to city mgr., Edmond, Okla., 1975—78; assoc. Long, Ford, Lester & Brown, Enid, Okla., 1982-87; pvt. practice Enid, Okla., 1987—88; gen. counsel & dep. dir. Fed. Emergency Mgmt. Agy. (FEMA), Washington, 2001—02; under sec. for preparedness & response (FEMA dir.) US Dept. Homeland Security, Washington, 2003—05; founder Michael D. Brown LLC, Boulder, Colo., 2005—; dir., emergency mgmt. programs Resilient Corp., 2006—. Adj. prof. state and local govt. law legis. Oklahoma City U.; cons. No. Okla. Devel. Assn., Enid, 1983-91; gen. counsel Alpha Oil Co., Duncan, Okla., 1985, Physicians Mgmt. Svc. Corps., 1985-90, Physicians of Okla., Inc., Physicians Med. Plan Okla., Inc., City Nat. Bank & Trust Co., 1987-88, Stanfield Printing Co., 1987—, Hammell Newspapers, Inc., 1987-90, Dillingham Ins., 1989-91, Suits Rig Corp., Suits Drilling Co., 1989-91; chmn. bd. dirs. Okla. Mcpl. Power Authority, Edmond, 1982-88, judges & stewards commr. Internat. Arabian Horse Assn., 1991—2001. Councilman City of Edmond, 1981; cons. Okla. Reps., Oklahoma City, 1983; bd. dirs. Okla. Christian Home, Edmond, 1985; Rep. nominee 6th Dist. U.S. Congress, 1988; co-chmn. Nat. Challengers Polit. Coalition, 1989-91; trustee, co-chair fin. com. Theodore Roosevelt Assn., 1994—. Michael D. Brown Hydroelectric Power Plant and Dam named in his honor, Kaw Reservoir, Okla., 1987. Mem. Okla. Bar Assn. (assoc. bar examiner 1984—), MD Physicians Okla., Ariz. and La., MD Physicians of Tulsa. Mem. Christian Ch. (Disciples Of Christ). Avocations: travel, photography, reading, wilderness adventures, swimming.*

BROWN, MICHAEL E., astronomer, astronomy educator; b. Huntsville, Ala. m. Diane Binney, Mar. 1, 2003; 1 child. AB with high honors in Physics, Princeton U., NJ, 1987; MA in Astronomy, U. Calif., Berkeley, 1990, PhD in Astronomy, 1994. Assoc. systems engr. SPARTA, Inc., Huntsville, Ala., 1987—88; grad. rsch. asst. U. Calif., Berkeley, 1988—94; Hubble postdoctoral fellow U. Ariz., Tucson, 1995, Calif. Inst. Tech., Pasadena, 1996, asst. prof., 1997—2002, assoc. prof., 2002—03, prof. planetary astronomy, 2003—. Vis. grad. fellow Lunar and Planetary Inst., Houston, 1992. Contbr. articles to sci. jours. Named one of 100 Most Influential People, Time Mag., 2006; recipient Presdl. Early Career award, 2000, Urey prize, Am. Aston. Soc. divsn. of planetary scis., 2001; grantee fellowship, NSF, 1988, NASA, 1992, rsch. fellowship, Alfred P. Sloan Found., 1998. Achievements include discovery of an object that may be the tenth planet in the solar system. Office: Divsn of Geol and Planetary Scis Calif Inst Tech Pasadena CA 91125

BROWN, MICHAEL JAY, lawyer; b. 1955; AB cum laude, Harvard Coll., 1976; JD, Boston Univ., 1979. Bar: Wash. 1979. Atty., corp. fin., securities practice group Bogle & Gates PLLC, 1997—99; ptnr., corp. dept. Dorsey & Whitney LLP, Seattle, 1999—, co-chair venture capital and emerging companies group. Mem.: Wash. State Bar Assn. (exec. com., editor, bus. law sect. 1989—96). Office: Dorsey & Whitney LLP Ste 3400 US Bank Ctr 1420 Fifth Ave Seattle WA 98101 Office Phone: 206-903-8811. Office Fax: 206-903-8820. Business E-Mail: brown.michael@dorsey.com.

BROWN, MICHAEL K., retail executive; Various pos., including store mgr., mgr. and dir. re-merchandising, retrofits and splty. sales Lowe's Cos., Inc., 1984—96, merchandising v.p., lawn and garden, bag goods/chems. and outdoor power equipment, 1996—98, regional v.p., northeast divsn., 1998—99, v.p., splty. sales, 1999—2001, sr. v.p., store ops., we. & so. ctrl. divisions, 2001—06, exec. v.p., store ops., 2006—. Office: Lowes Cos Inc 1605 Curtis Bridge Rd Wilkesboro NC 28697*

BROWN, MICHAEL K., lawyer; b. Woodside, NY, Aug. 13, 1956; m. Martha Brown; 3 children. AB, Georgetown U., 1978; JD, U. San Francisco, 1982. Bar: Calif. 1982. With Crosby, Heafey, Roach & May (combined with Reed Smith LLP, 2003), LA, 1982—2002, mng. ptnr., LA office, 1991—94, mem. exec. com., 1991—2002, chair, LA Product Liability Group, 1996—2000, chair, LA Comml. Litig. Group, 2000—01, chair, Complex Litig. Practice Group, 2002; ptnr., mem. exec. com. Reed Smith LLP, LA, 2003—. Mem. Product Liability Adv. Coun., Inc. Bd. governors U. San Francisco Law Soc., 1989—91; bd. counselors U. San Francisco Sch. Law, 1991—; legal policy adv. bd. Wash. Legal Found. Mem.: Food and Drug Law Inst., Def. Rsch. Inst. (mem. drug and med. device com.), Assn. So. Calif. Def. Counsel, LA County Bar Assn., Internat. Assn. Def. Counsel (mem. legis. jud. and govtl. affairs com. 2000—, vice chair drug, device and biotech com. 2000—02, 2004—), Internat. Trademark Assn., Assn. Bus. Trial Lawyers (bd. governors LA chpt. 2000—04), ABA. Office: Reed Smith LLP 355 S Grand Ave Ste 2900 Los Angeles CA 90071-1514 Office Phone: 213-457-8018. Office Fax: 213-457-8080. Business E-Mail: mkbrown@reedsmith.com.

BROWN, MICHAEL ROBERT, lawyer; b. Worcester, Mass., Apr. 5, 1938; s. Walter David and Ethel Fay (Berman) B.; m. Susan Fay Lappin, July 8, 1962; children: Laura, Pamela. BA, Bowdoin Coll., 1959; JD, Columbia U., 1962. Bar: Mass. 1963, N.Y. 1968. Staff atty. NLRB, Washington, 1963-66; assoc. Simpson, Thacher & Bartlett, NYC, 1966-70; ptnr. Herrick & Smith, Boston, 1970-84, Goldstein & Manello, Boston, 1984-90, Palmer & Dodge, Boston, 1990—2002, Seyfarth Shaw, Boston, 2002—. Adj. prof. employment law Sch. Law Suffolk U., Boston, Selectman, Wellesley, Mass., 1992-95. Fellow Coll. Labor and Employment Lawyers; mem. ABA, Mass. Bar Assn., Boston Bar Assn. Office: Seyfarth Shaw Two Seaport Ln Boston MA 02210-2028 Home Phone: 781-237-9047; Office Phone: 617-946-4907. Business E-Mail: mrbrown@seyfarth.com.

BROWN, MICHAEL ROBERT, healthcare corporation executive; b. Joliet, Ill., Aug. 9, 1960; s. Robert Raymond and Virginia A. (Bianchi) B. AAS, Joliet Jr. Coll., 1980; BS, No. Ill. U., 1983, MBA, 1996. Acctg. supr. northern region DeKalb (Ill.) Genetics, 1982-85; fin. analyst Baxter Healthcare Corp., Deerfield, Ill., 1985, sr. fin. analyst, 1985-87, sr. consols.

analyst, 1987-88, mgr. acctg. svcs., 1988-89, mgr. corp. acctg., 1989-93, dir. fin. planning McGaw Park, Ill., 1993-95, asst. contr. renal divsn., 1995-99, v.p. fin. renal divsn., 1999—2003, dir. fin., medication delivery, 2003—05, dir. fin. compliance, 2005—. Vol. Jr. Achievement, United Way; bd. exec. advisors No. Ill. U. Recipient Accounting Alumni of Yr., No. Ill. U., 2006. Mem. Inst. Mgmt. Accts., Chgo. Coun. Fgn. Rels., No. Ill. U. Alumni Assn., No. Ill. U. Exec. Club, Beta Gamma Sigma Honor Soc. Avocations: music, tennis. Personal E-mail: mrbrown9@aol.com.

BROWN, MICHAEL STUART, geneticist, educator, science administrator; b. Bklyn., Apr. 13, 1941; s. Harvey and Evelyn (Katz) Brown; m. Alice Lapin, June 21, 1964; children: Jane Elizabeth, Ellen Sara. BA, U. Pa., 1962, MD, 1966; DSc (hon.), Rensselaer Poly. Inst., 1982, U. Chgo., 1982, U. Pa., 1986, U. Buenos Aires, 1988, U. Paris, 1988, So. Meth. U., 1993, U. Miami, 1996; DSc (hon.), Rockefeller U., 2001. Intern, then resident in medicine Mass. Gen. Hosp., Boston, 1966-68; served with USPHS, 1968-70; clin. assoc. NIH, 1968-71; asst. prof. U. Tex. Southwestern Med. Sch., Dallas, 1971-74; Paul J. Thomas chair in med. Jonsson Ctr. Molecular Genetics, 1977—; W. A. (Monty) Moncrief Disting. Chair in Cholesterol and Arteriosclerosis Rsch. Southwestern Med. Sch. of biomed. scis., 1989—. Mem. med. adv. bd. Scripps Inst.; bd. dirs. Pfizer Inc., 1996—, Regeneron, Inc., 1991—. Co-editor: The Metabolic Basis of Inherited Disease, 1983. Recipient Pfizer award, Am. Chemical Soc., 1976, Passano award, Passano Found., 1978, Lena Annenberg Hazen award, 1982, Albert Lasker Med. Rsch. award, 1985, Horwitz prize, 1985, Nobel prize in physiology or medicine, 1985, Nat. Med. Sci., U.S. Govt., 1988, Albany Med. Ctr. prize in medicine, 2003. Mem.: Royal Acad. Scis. (fgn.), Harvey Soc., Assn. Am. Physicians, Am. Soc. Clin. Investigation, Nat. Acad. Scis. (Lounsbery award 1979). Office: UT Southwestern Med Ctr Dept Molecular Genetics 5323 Harry Hines Blvd Dallas TX 75390-9046 E-mail: mike.brown@utsouthwestern.edu.

BROWN, MIKE, professional basketball coach; b. Mar. 5, 1970; s. Paul and Katie Brown; m. Carolyn Brown; children: Elijah, Cameron. Student, Mesa CC; grad. in Bus., U. San Diego, 1992. Video coord. to scout Denver Nuggets, 1992—97; asst. coach Washington Wizards, 1997—99, scout, 1999—2000; asst. coach San Antonio Spurs, 2000—03; assoc. head coach Ind. Pacers, 2003—05; head coach Cleve. Cavaliers, 2005—. Office: Cleve Cavaliers Quicken Loans One Center Ct Cleveland OH 44115-4001*

BROWN, MORGAN, federal agency administrator; m. Susan Brown; 3 children. BA, Carleton Coll., 1991. Rsch. asst. Nat. Rep. Congl. Com.; legis. asst. to legis. dir. for Rep. Jim Ramstad; legis. asst. foreign affairs issues for Senator Rod Grams; dir. pub. policy and comms. Minn. Family Coun., Mpls., 1997; sr. cmty. affairs officer Twin Cities Fin. Found., 1998; dir. Partnership for Choice in Edn., 1999—2000, Minn. Edn. League, 2001—02; sr. fellow edn. policy Ctr. of Am. Experiment, Mpls.; dir. Div. Sch. Choice and Innovation Minn. Dept. Edn., 2003—06; asst. dep. sec. Office of Innovation and Improvement US Dept. Edn., Washington, 2006—. Fellow Hubert H. Humphrey Inst. Pub. Affairs, U. Minn., 1997. Office: US Dept Edn 400 Maryland Ave. SW Washington DC 20202 Office Phone: 202-205-4500. Office Fax: 202-401-4123.*

BROWN, MORRIS, lawyer; b. Rahway, NJ, Mar. 16, 1928; s. Frank and Celia (Roth) B.; m. Sylvia Cohen, Aug. 2, 1953; children: David H., Alan S. BA, George Washington U., 1951; LLB, Harvard U., 1955. Bar: N.J. 1956, U.S. Dist. Ct. N.J. 1956. Law clk. to Judge Thomas F. Meaney U.S. Dist. Ct. for N.J., 1955-56; assoc. Wilentz, Goldman & Spitzer, Woodbridge, NJ, 1956-67, ptnr., 1967—. Mem. adv. commn. on profl. ethics N.J. Supreme Ct., 1983-95. Assoc. editor N.J. Law Jour., 1985-91. V.p. Temple Neve Shalom, Metuchen, N.J., 1971-73, bd. dirs. 1973, 75; co-chmn. United Jewish Appeal, 1971; v.p. No. Middlesex County YMHA, 1972-73; interim pres. Jewish Fedn. No. Middlesex County, 1975; trustee John F. Kennedy Med. Ctr. Edison, N.J., 1975—. with USN, 1946-48. Mem. ATLA-N.J. (pres. 1976-77), N.J. State Bar Assn., N.J. Trial Lawyers Assn., Middlesex County Bar Assn., Middlesex County Trial Lawyers Assn. (pres. 1970-72), Am. Bd. Trial Attys., Am. Coll. Trial Lawyers. Democrat. Home: 9 Fairway Ln Ocean NJ 07712-3634 Office: Wilentz Goldman & Spitzer PA PO Box 10 90 Woodbridge Ctr Woodbridge NJ 07095-1304 Office Phone: 732-855-6060. Business E-Mail: brownm@wilentz.com.

BROWN, MYRA SUZANNE, university librarian; b. Gainesville, Fla., Jan. 6, 1949; d. Samuel Jackson and Myra Frances (Whiddon) B.; m. Roman Jonas Yoder, Jan. 5, 1973 (dec.); m. Jeremy Gallaudet Hole, May 3, 1986. Student European divsn., U. Md., West Berlin, 1967-69; BA, U. South Fla., 1971; MSLS, Fla. State U., 1972; postgrad., U. Cin., 1974. Libr. asst. Strozier Libr., Fla. State U., Tallahassee, 1973, libr. serials dept., 1973; libr. sci. and tech. dept. Pub. Libr. of Cin. and Hamilton County, 1973-74; libr. assoc. II Coll. Design, Architecture and Art Libr. U. Cin., 1975-77; assoc. univ. libr. State U. Sys. of Fla. Extension Libr., St. Petersburg, Fla., 1979-81, Edn. Libr. U. Fla. Librs., Gainesville, 1982-84, head and edn. bibliographer, 1984-90; asst. dept. chair humanities and social scis. svcs. dept. Smathers Librs. U. Fla., Gainesville, 1990—92, head and edn. bibliographer Edn. Libr., 1992—2002, asst. edn. libr., 2002—, univ. libr., 2002—. Reference liaisons discussion group Rsch. Librs. Group, Inc., 1990-92; reviewer Gale Rsch. Co., Inc., 1988—Ednl. Librs., 1995—; rsch. panel Univ. Microfilms Internat., 1992, Libr. Supplies, 1999; nat. user group Libr. of Congress Cataloging Distbn. Svc., 1992-96; cons. Mus. Fine Arts Libr., St. Petersburg, Fla., 1981-82, Design, Architecture and Art Libr., U. Cin., 1975-77; focus group ISI, 1998-99; cons. New Bus. Devel. Edn. titles Gale Rsch., 1998-2004; presenter in field. Mem. editl. bd. Edn. Librs., 1999—; contbr. World Architecture Index: A Guide to Illustrations, 1991; contbr. chpts. to books, articles to profl. jours. Aux. mem., vol. Shands Hops. of U. Fla., Gainesville, 1993-96, nominating com., 1995-96, sustaining mem., 1997-2002; advocate for homeless; outreach com., evangelism com., implementation team VIA media program Holy Trinity Episcopal Ch.; advocate for animal rights; vol. Interfaith Hospitality Network, 2003—; co-chair Holiday Bazaar-Jewelry Room, 2004-06; exec. bd. Cedar Creek Homeowners Assn., 2004-07, v.p., 2004-07. Mem. ALA (chmn., planner, moderator preconf. and conf. program, mem. divsns., reference svcs. in medium-sized rsch. librs. discussion group 1992—2001, presenter), ALA/Assn. Coll. and Rsch. Librs. (edn., behavioral and social scis. sect., ERIC users forum 2005—, ERIC users forum steering com. 2005—), Reference and User Svcs. Assn., Fla. Ednl. Rsch. Assn., U. Fla. Librs. Assn. (v.p. 1983-84), U. Faculty Fla. (U. Fla. chpt. sec. 2004-05, v.p. 2005—). Democrat. Episcopalian. Avocation: art. Office: Smathers Librs of U Fla Edn Libr 1500 Norman Hall PO Box 117016 Gainesville FL 32611-7016 Office Phone: 352-273-2780. Business E-Mail: msbrown@ufl.edu.

BROWN, NADINE, sommelier; B in Soc. Work, Wheelock Coll., Boston. Host Bistro Bis, Washington, server, banquet captain, office mgr., floor mgr.; worked at Signatures, Butterfield 9, 701, Ten Penh; head sommelier Charlie Palmer Steakhouse, Washington. Named one of Washington DC's Rising Stars, StarChefs.com, 2006; recipient Rammy award. Office: Charlie Palmer Steakhouse 101 Constitution Ave NW Washington DC 20001 Office Phone: 202-547-8100.*

BROWN, NANCY FIELD, editor; b. Troy, NY, Feb. 20, 1951; d. Robert Grant and Barbara Katherine (Field) B. BS in Journalism, Mich. State U., East Lansing, 1974. Asst. editor Mich. Am. Legion, Lansing, 1974-76, State Bar of Mich., Lansing, 1976-78, editor, 1976—, sr. dir. pubs., 1995-98, asst. exec. dir. publs., 1998—. Mem. Nat. Assn. Bar Execs. (cons. pubs. com. Chgo. chpt. 1989—), Mich. State U. Alumni Assn., Nat. Assn. Desktop Pubs., Am. Soc. Assn. Execs. Presbyterian. Avocations: reading, writing, photography, travel. Office: State Bar of Mich 306 Townsend St Lansing MI 48933-2012

BROWN, NANCY J., literature educator; b. Oakland, Calif., Feb. 26, 1945; d. Kathaleen Brown-Renn and Frank Gregory Brown, Charles Francis Renn (Stepfather). AB, Defiance Coll., Ohio, 1967; MA, U. Toledo, 1992; postgrad., Wayne State U., Detroit, 2001. Exec. dir. NW Ohio Crisis Line for Domestic Violence, Defiance, 1981—83; non-credit programming coord. Defiance Coll., 1986—89, instr. ESL, 1984—89; assoc. prof. Lourdes Coll., Sylvania, Ohio, 1989—. Pres. Bus. and Profl. Women, Defiance, 1987—88; publicity chair Wemmer Scholarship Trustees, Toledo, 2004—07; mem. Defiance Coll. Alumni Assn., 2002—06. Recipient Tchg. Excellence award, Lourdes Coll., 1993, Alumni Achievement award, Defiance Coll., 2002, Spirit of Detroit award, Detroit City Coun., 2005. Mem.: AAUW (pres. Toledo br. 2006—), MLA, Conf. on Coll. Composition and Comm., Nat. Conf. Tchrs. English, Thoreau Soc., Emily Dickinson Soc. Episcopalian. Home: 2333 Royce Rd Toledo OH 43615 Office: Lourdes College 6832 Convent Blvd Toledo OH 43560 Home Phone: 419-841-0262; Office Phone: 419-824-3756. Business E-Mail: nbrown@lourdes.edu.

BROWN, NEIL W., bank executive; Audit ptnr. KPMG LLP; exec. v.p., treas., CFO TCF Fin. Corp., 1998—2005, pres., CFO, 2005—. Chmn. bd. dirs. Vail Place. Office: TCF Financial 200 Lake Street East Wayzata MN 55391-1693

BROWN, NORMAN DONALD, history professor; b. Pitts., June 28, 1935; s. Donald Madden and Regina Deborah (Koehler) B.; m. Betty Jane Aldrich, Apr. 2, 1966; children: David, Tracy. BA summa cum laude, Ind. U., 1957; MA, U. N.C., 1959, PhD, 1963. Instr. history U. Tex., Austin, 1962-65, asst. prof., 1965-69, assoc. prof., 1969-83, prof., 1983-84, Barbara White Stuart Centennial prof. Tex. history, 1984—. Author: Daniel Webster and the Politics of Availability, 1969, Edward Stanly, 1974, Hood, Bonnet, and Little Brown Jug, 1984; editor: One of Cleburne's Command, 1980, Journey to Pleasant Hill, 1982. Woodrow Wilson fellow, 1957. Fellow: Tex. State Hist. Assn. (coun. 1989—93, 2d v.p. 1997—98, 1st v.p. 1998—99, pres. 1999—2000, coun. 2000—02); mem.: Civil War Preservation Trust, Civil War Round Table Assocs., Soc. Civil War Historians (adv. bd. 1986—), Soc. Historians Early Am. Republic, So. Hist. Assn., Orgn. Am. Historians, Sons of Union Vets. of the Civil War, Phi Kappa Phi, Phi Alpha Theta, Phi Beta Kappa. Democrat. United Methodist. Avocation: book collecting. Home: 2607 Barton Skyway Austin TX 78704-4602 Office: Univ Tex Dept History Austin TX 78712 Office Phone: 512-475-7216.

BROWN, OLEN RAY, microbiologist, biomedical researcher, educator; b. Hastings, Okla., Aug. 18, 1935; s. Willis Edward and Rosa Nell (Fulton) B.; m. Pollyana June King, Aug. 30, 1958; children: Barbara Kathryn, Diana Carol, David Gregory. BS in Lab. Tech., Okla. U., 1958, MS in Bacteriology, 1960, PhD in Microbiology, 1964. Diplomate Am. Bd. Toxicology. Instr. Sch. Medicine, U. Mo., Columbia, 1964-65, asst. prof., 1965-70, assoc. prof., 1970-77, prof. dept. molecular microbiology and immunology, 1981-96, rsch. prof., 1996—2001; joint appointments, prof. depts. microbiology and biomed. scis. Coll. Vet. Medicine, U. Mo., 1977-96, prof. biomed. scis., 1987-96. Guest lectr. Ross U., St. Kitts, W.I., 1984, 88; asst. dir. Dalton Rsch. Ctr., U. Mo., 1974-78, Dalton rsch. investigator grad. sch., 1968—; grant peer reviewer for program projects SCOR and Superfund grants NIH, 1979, Nat. Inst. Environ. Health Scis., Dept. Commerce, EPA, 1986, 90-99, Am. Inst. Biol. Scis. for Dept. Def., USAMRMC, Fund for Improvement of Secondary Edn., 2002; cons. drug abuse policy office White House, 1982, Immunol. Vaccines, Inc., Columbia, 1984—, Lab. Support, Inc., Chgo., 1988-89, Ea. Rsch. Group, Lexington, Mass., 1991—, Teltech, Mpls., 1992—, Scis. Internat., Inc., Alexandria, Va.; judge top 100 products for 1996, 99, Rsch. and Devel. Mag. Author: Laboratory Manual for Veterinary Microbiology, 1973, The Art and Science of Expert Witnessing, 2002; co-author: elem. and advanced lab. manuals for med. microbiology, 2 vols., 1978, 79; contbr. Progress in Clinical Research, Vol. 21, 1978, 79, Oxygen, 5th Internat. Hyperbaric Conf., Vols. I, II, 1974, 79, numerous articles to profl. jours.; book and film critic AAAS, Washington, 1986—; item preparer Am. Coll. Test, Med. Coll. Admissions Test, 1981—; mem. editorial staff Biomed. Letters, 1981—; responder Sci. and Math. Helpline for Mus. Sci. Discovery, Harrisburg, Pa., 1996—, reviewer profl. jours. Track and field ofcl. U. Mo. and Big Eight Conf., Columbia, 1979-86. Investigative rsch. grantee Office Naval Rsch., Dept. Def., 1968-81, NIH, 1976-88, NIEHS, 1981-94, 95—, USAID, 1983-86, Nat. Inst. Dental Health Scis., 1989-92. Fellow Am. Inst. Chemists (cert. chemistry and chem engring., profl. program bd. 1989-90, sd com. chemistry and environ. concerns); mem. Top One Percent Soc., Soc. Toxicology, Internat. Soc. Study Xenobiotics, Am. Chem. Soc., Am. Heart Assn., Internat. Soc. Exposure Analysts, Nat. Space Soc., Oxygen Soc., Columbia Track Club (sec.-treas. 1979-82). Avocations: long-distance running, painting. Office: U Mo Dalton Rsch Ctr Columbia MO 65211-0001 Office Phone: 573-449-7444. E-mail: browno@missouri.edu.

BROWN, OMER FORREST, II, lawyer; b. Somerville, NJ, Mar. 4, 1947; s. George Alvin and Frances (Schnitzler) B.; m. Sandra J. Cannon, Apr. 3, 1982. AB, Rutgers U., 1969; JD, Cornell U., 1972. Bar: NJ 1972, DC 1974, U.S. Supreme Ct. 1976. Dept. atty. gen. dept. law and pub. safety State of NJ, Trenton, 1972-75; sr. trial atty. US Dept. Energy, Washington, 1979-83; ptnr. Davis Wright Tremaine, Washington, 1987-96, Harmon, Wilmot, Brown & Bagwell, LLP, Washington, 1997—. Bd. dirs., sec. VideoTakes, Inc., Arlington, Va., 1986—; vis. lectr. Cornell U. Law Sch., 1993-95, 2002; mem. OECD Contact Group on Nuc. Safety Assistance for Eastern Europe, 1994—; mem. G-7 Joint Task Force on Ukrainian Nuc. Legis., 1996—. Contbr. numerous articles on energy, environ. and ins. law to legal jours.; mem. editl. bds. Atoms for Peace, Internat. Jour. Nuc. Law, 2004-. Capt. USAR, 1969—75. Recipient Class of 1931 award Rutgers U. Alumni Assn., 1979, Loyal Son of Rutgers award, 1980. Mem. ABA (various offices tort and ins. practice sect. 1981-96, coord. group on energy law 1995-99), Fed. Bar Assn., The Counsellors, DOE Contractor Atty. Assn., Univ. Club (Washington), Miles River Yacht Club. Democrat. Roman Catholic. Address: PO Box 419 Saint Michaels MD 21663-0419 Office Phone: 202-842-4711. Personal E-mail: omerb@aol.com.

BROWN, PAMELA S., former attorney general; BA in Cultural Anthropology, U. Wash., 1982, JD with honors, 1988. Tech. dir, news dir., news ed. KOMO TV, ABC, Seattle, 1981—85; Rule 9 atty., King County prosecutors and Wash. State, atty. gen., consumer protection div., 1986—87; criminial def. atty. Seattle, 1987—89; criminal prosecutor, off. of atty. gen. No. Mariana Islands, 1989—90, chief sen. legal counsel, 1990—94; ptnr. Long & Brown, attys. at law, 1994—98; pvt. practice, 1998—99; fed. ombudsman, off. of ombudsman, off. of insular affairs US Dept. Interior, Saipan, 1999—2001; of counsel Teker Civille Torres and Tang attys. at law and MP mng. atty. for Saipan Off., Labor, Immigration and Civil Litig., Saipan, 2001—02; legal counsel to gov. No. Mariana Islands, Saipan, 2002—03, atty. gen., 2003—06. Mem. Am. Bar Assn., Commonwealth Bar Assn.

BROWN, PAMELA WEDD, artist; b. Cauderan, Gironde, France, Nov. 21, 1928; came to U.S., 1953; d. William Basil and Nora Marsh (van Nostrand) Wedd; m. Charles Freeman Brown, Nov. 29, 1952; children: Penelope Susan, Nicholas Wedd. Student, Ecole des Beaux Arts, Paris, 1947-48, Academie Julian, 1946-51. Freelance fashion illustrator, Paris, 1947-48; dir. arts and crafts YWCA, Toronto, Ont., Canada, 1951; dir. Washington Womens Arts Ctr., 1987-88; dir., pres., founding mem. Washington Printmakers Gallery, 1990-91; co-pres. Studio Gallery, 1992-94. Artist in residence The Art Barn, Washington, 1986. Designer book plate Nat. Mus. Women in Arts Libr., 1985; represented in permanent collections Libr. of Congress, NIH, Nat. Mus. Am. History, Nat. Mus. Women in Arts. Precinct capt. Bd. of Elections and Ethics, Washington, 1970-80. Recipient First prize drawing, Academie Julian, Paris, 1947, Purchase award, Jr. League, Newport News, Va., 1971. Mem. Studio Gallery D.C. (assoc.), Art League (Equal award 1980, 82, 85, 88, 2000, 02), Woman's Nat. Dem. Club. Avocations: music, tennis, sailing, dance. Home: 3050 Military Rd NW # 636 Washington DC 20015 E-mail: cfbrown@his.com.

BROWN, PAT CRAWFORD, actress; b. NYC, June 29, 1929; d. Thomas J. and Charlotte (Huber) Crawford; m. Calvin B. Brown, Jan. 3, 1961 (dec. Dec. 1976); 1 child, Charlotte Brown Swanson. BA in Speech and Lit., Coll. of New Rochelle, 1951; MFA in Theatre, Fordham U., 1958. Cert. secondary tchr., Calif. Tchr. L.A. City Schs., Carson, Calif., 1964-84. Entertainment dir. U.S. Army Spl. Svcs., Kaiserslautern, Fed. Republic Germany, 1959-61; bd. dirs. Theatre West, Hollywood, Calif., 1988-90; producer, bd. dirs. Torrance (Calif.) Community Theatre, 1980-84. Actor: (films) Elvira, Mistress of the Dark, 1988, 18 Again, 1988, Upworld, 1990, The Rocketeer, 1991, Sister Act, 1992, Sister Act 2: Back in the Habit, 1993, Reality Bites, 1994, Romy and Michele's Hight School Reunion, 1997, Johnny Skidmarks, 1998, The Godson, 1998, Jack Frost, 1998, Forces of Nature, 1999, Playing Mona Lisa, 2000, The Woman Every Man Wants, 2001, The Medicine Show, 2001, Daredevil, 2003, Stuck on You, 2003, Crazylove, 2005, You, Me and Dupree, 2006, Norbit, 2007, others, (TV series) Desperate Housewives, 2004-; guest appearances (TV series) Moonlighting, Chicken Soup, Mama's Family, Teddy Z, Knots Landing, Dear John, Who's the Boss?, Coach, Designing Women, Murphy Brown, L.A. Law, Carol Burnett Show, ER, Home Improvement, Murder She Wrote, Ellen, Fresh Prince, Profiler, Pretender, Dark Skies, Beverly Hills, 90210, Coach, Caroline in the City, Two Guys, a Girl and a Pizza Place, The Norm Show, Malcom & Eddie, The Drew Carey Show, Suddenly Susan, 3rd Rock from the Sun, NYPD Blue, State of Grace, The Steve Harvey Show, Lizzie McGuire, Buffy the Vampire Slayer, Judging Amy, The Bernie Mac Show, Life with Bonnie, Monk, Jack & Bobby, Arrested Development, Gilmore Girls, CSI: Las Vegas, others; also numerous other theatrical prodns. Chair recycling com. Burchett Gardens Home Owners Assn., Glendale, Calif., 1990. Recipient Best Actress award Dramalogue Mag., 1988. Mem. Actors Equity Assn., AFTRA, SAG, Theatre West (St. Seema award 1989) Avocations: piano, tennis, swimming, guitar, marionettes. Office: Lovell and Assocs 7905 Hollywood Blvd # 1006 Los Angeles CA 90046-2611*

BROWN, PATRICIA ANN, child health nurse; b. Kokomo, Ind., Apr. 4, 1938; d. John Conrad and Marie L. (Landseadel) B. BSN, Ind. U., 1959, MSN, 1969; Pediatric Nurse Assoc., U. Tenn., 1976. Staff nurse, asst. head nurse Ind. U. Children's Hosp., Indpls., 1960-66; chief nurse Child Devel. Ctr., Memphis, 1966-67; instr., asst. prof. child health nursing Ctr. for Health Scis., U. Tenn., Memphis, 1969-73; asst. prof. child health nursing U. Tenn., Knoxville, 1973-75, U. Tenn. Ctr. for Health Scis., Memphis, 1975-84; child health nursing faculty Holmes Jr. Coll., Grenada, Miss., 1985-89; dir. nursing East Ark. C.C., Forrest City, Ark., 1989-96. Chairperson Nursing Faculty Coun., Memphis. Hospice vol. Hospice of Memphis, 1981-84. Mem. Nat. League for Nursing, Tenn. Nurses Assn. (chairperson Maternal Child Health), Ark. State Bd. Nursing, Coun. Nursing Adminstrs. of Nursing Edn. Programs in Ark. (chairperson assoc. degree nursing coun. 1992-94), Ind. U. Alumni, Sigma Theta Tau, Pi Lambda Theta. Methodist. Avocations: needlecrafts, baking, travel, family, yard work. Home: 7625 Saddlebrooke Dr Knoxville TN 37938-4044

BROWN, PATRICIA IRENE, retired law librarian, lawyer; b. Boston; d. Joseph Raymond and Harriet A. (Taylor) Brown. BA, Suffolk U., 1955, JD, 1965, MBA, 1970; MST, Gordon Conwell Theol. Sem., 1977. Bar: Mass. 1965. Libr. asst. Suffolk U., Boston, 1951-60, asst. libr., 1960-65, asst. law libr., 1965-85, assoc. law libr., 1985-92, ret., 1992. Author: A League of My Own: Memoir of a Pitcher for the All-American Girls Professional Baseball League, 2003; author: (with Ralph E. Sirianni, Patricia I. Brown) POW #3959: Memoir of a World War II Airman Shot Down Over Germany, 2006. Vol. health benefits counselor Mass. Dept. Elder Affairs, 1994—99; human resources counselor Winthrop (Mass.) Sr. Ctr., 1993—, counselor, 2000—; mem. All-Am. Girls Profl. Baseball League, 1950—51; dir. Referral/Resource Ctr. Union Congl. Ch., Winthrop. Named to Nat. Baseball Hall of Fame, 1988. Mem.: Mass. Bar Assn., Assn. Am. Law Librs., Am. Congl. Assn. (former bd. dirs.). Avocations: movies, walking, computers. Home: 1100 Governors Dr Apt 26 Winthrop MA 02152-3254 Personal E-mail: pbrown@suffolk.edu.

BROWN, PATRICK ALAN, systems analyst; b. Wash., DC, Jan. 17, 1964; s. Donald Everett and Juanita Louise Brown; m. Nubia Edith Bravo-Villareal, May 20, 1994; children: Erin Michelle, Genesis Edith, Tia Marie, Caitlin Sinead. BS, SUNY, Albany, 1998; postgrad. diploma, Royal Holloway Sch. Mgmt., London, 2002; MBA, Benedictine U., Lisle, Ill., 2005. NERC Certified System Operator, Reliablity NERC, 2000, cert. project. mgmt. Stanford U., Calif., 2005. Shift mgr. PJM Interconnection, Norristown, Pa., 1999—; treas., bd. dirs. Berks Counseling Ctr., Reading, Pa., 2003—. Mem., counsel energy advisors Gerson-Lehrman Grp., NYC, 2005—. Treas. Berks Counseling Ctr., Reading, Pa., 2003—07; mem. St. Catharine's Parish Sch. Bd., Reading, 2003—07. Sgt. 1st class US Army, 1998, Ft. Drum, NY. Mem.: Inf. Assn., VFW. Home: 25 Golfview Ln Reading PA 19606 Office: PJM Interconnection 955 Jefferson Norristown PA 19403 Personal E-mail: patrickbrown@att.net. Business E-Mail: brownp@pjm.com.

BROWN, PATRICK JOSEPH, corporate financial executive, consultant; b. Spooner, Wis., Apr. 28, 1966; s. John Leslie and Kathleen Anne Brown; m. Sheryl Lynn Wilkinson, Oct. 7, 1989; children: Ashley Cassandra, Chelsea Alicia. BBA in Acctg., U. Wis., Eau Claire, 1989. Plant contr. trainee Johnson Controls Inc., Milw., 1989—93; supr. cost acctg. Rocco Quality Foods, Harrisonburg, Va., 1993—95; cost acct. SPX, Owatonna, Minn., 1995—99; dir. plant acctg. Oshkosh Truck Corp., Dodge Center, Minn., 1999—2001; CFO Michel Sales Co., St. Paul, 2001—03; contr. Ready Mix Concrete Co. LLC, Rochester, Minn., 2003—05; pres. Pat Brown Aviation LLC, Kasson, Minn., 2006—. Bd. mem. Dodge Ctr. Airport Bd., 1997; mem. Holy Family Cath. Ch., Kasson, Minn., 1995. With Army Nat. Guard, 1988—96. Decorated Desert Storm Svc. award US Army; recipient Eagle Scout, Boy Scouts Am., 1984. Mem.: Exptl. Aircraft Assn. (assoc.), South Ea. Minn. Flying Club (assoc.), Am. Legion (assoc.). Office: Pat Brown Aviation LLC PO Box 221 Kasson MN 55944 Office Phone: 507-319-6762.

BROWN, PATRICK O., molecular biologist, educator; b. Washington, Sept. 23, 1954; m. Sue Klapholz; children: Zach, Ariel, Isaac. BA with honors, U. Chgo., 1976, PhD, 1980, MD, 1982. Pediat. resident Children's Meml. Hosp., Chgo., 1982—85; post-doctoral fellowship U. Calif., San Francisco, 1985—88; asst. prof. biochemistry and pediatrics Stanford U. Sch. Medicine, Calif., 1988—95, assoc. prof. biochemistry Calif., 1995—2000, prof. biochemistry Calif., 2000—. Investigator Howard Hughes Med. Inst., 1988—; bd. dir., co-founder Pub. Libr. Sci. (PLoS), 2003—. Contbr. scientific papers articles to profl. jours. Named one of America's Best in Science and Medicine, Time mag.; recipient Millennium Pharma. award for Genomics Rsch. in Clin. Immunology, 2001, BioTech Helsinki Prize, 2003. Fellow: World Tech. Network (World Tech. Network award (Media and Journalism) 2005), AAAS; mem.: NAS (NAS award in molecular biology 2000). Office: Stanford Sch Medicine B439 300 Pasteur Dr Stanford CA 94305 Address: Pub Libr Sci 185 Berry Street Ste 3100 San Francisco CA 94107 Business E-Mail: pbrown@cmgm.stanford.edu.*

BROWN, PAUL A., medical services executive; b. Boston, Apr. 1, 1938; s. Morton G. and Helen C. (Appleton) B.; m. Cynthia R. Shrier, June 4, 1961; children: Richard, Mark. AB, Harvard U., 1960; MD, Tufts U., 1964. Intern Tufts New Eng. Med. Ctr., Boston, 1964-65; resident in pathology Columbia Presbyn. Hosp., NYC, 1965-69; chmn., chief exec. officer Metpath Inc., Teterboro, NJ, 1970-83, chmn., 1983-84, Sci/Med Advances Corp., Teaneck, NJ, 1983-88, HearUSA, West Palm Beach, Fla., 1986—. Chmn., chief exec. officer Permark Corp., Hacksensack, N.J., 1985-89; lectr. pathology Columbia U., 1981—. Trustee Tufts U., 1978—88; mem. vis. com. Boston U. Sch. Medicine, 1987—2000; trustee, chmn. bd. overseers Tufts U. Sch. Medicine, 1978—82. Home: 223 Grand Pointe Dr Palm Beach Gardens FL 33418 Office: HearUSA Inc 1250 Northpoint Pkwy West Palm Beach FL 33407 Office Phone: 561-478-8770 x 123. Personal E-mail: pbrown@hearusa.com.

BROWN, PAUL M., lawyer; b. Jan. 10, 1938; s. I. Harry and Rose L. (Kresge) B.; m. Helga J. Fischer, Aug. 4, 1962 (div. 1977); children: Stephanie J., William A.; m. Ruth Reiter, June 28, 1986. Student, Williams Coll., 1955-57; BS in Econs., U. Pa., 1959; LLB, Columbia U., 1962. Bar: N.Y. 1963, U.S. Ct. Appeals (2d cir.) 1963, U.S. Dist. Ct. (so. and ea. dists.) N.Y. 1964, U.S. Dist. Ct. Mass. 1981, U.S. Ct. Appeals (3d cir.), U.S. Ct. Appeals (1st cir.) 1982, U.S. Dist. Ct. (we. dist.) N.Y. 1983, U.S. Ct. Appeals (6th cir.) 1983, U.S. Dist. Ct. R.I. 1985, U.S. Dist. Ct. (ea. dist.) Mich. 1986. Assoc. Berman & Frost, NYC, 1963-66; ptnr. Havens, Wandless, Slitt and Tighe, NYC, 1966-74, Whitman and Ransom, NYC, 1975-94, Parson & Brown, NYC, 1994-99, Satterlee Stephens Burke & Burke, NYC, 1999—. Councilman Closter, N.J., 1970-74; police commr. Closter, 1970-73; trustee No. Valley Regional H.S., Demarest, N.J., 1972. With USAR, 1962-68. Mem. Assn. of Bar of City of N.Y., N.Y. State Bar Assn., Fed. Bar Coun., Am. Arbitration Assn. (panel of arbitrators), Univ. Club, Columbia Golf & Country Club, Las Campanas (N.Mex.) Club. Democrat. Office: Satterlee Stephens Burke & Burke 230 Park Ave New York NY 10169-0079 Home Phone: 212-472-3354; Office Phone: 212-404-8786. Business E-Mail: pbrown@ssbb.com.

BROWN, PAUL NEELEY, federal judge; b. Denison, Tex., Oct. 4, 1926; s. Arthur Chester and Nora Frances (Hunter) B.; m. Frances Morehead, May 8, 1955; children: Paul Gregory, David H. II. JD, U. Tex., 1950. Assoc. Keith & Brown, Sherman, Tex., 1951-53, Brown & Brown, Sherman, 1953; asst. U.S. atty. for Ea. Dist. Tex. Texarkana and Tyler, Tex., 1953-59; U.S. atty. Ea. Dist. Tex., Tyler, 1959-61; ptnr. Brown & Brown and Brown Brothers & Perkins, Sherman, 1961-65, Brown and Perkins, Sherman, 1965; sole practice, Sherman, 1965-67; ptnr. Brown & Hill, Sherman, 1967, Brown Kennedy Hill & Minshew, Sherman, 1967-71, Brown & Hill, Sherman, 1971-76, Brown Hill Ellis & Brown, Sherman, 1976-85; U.S. dist. judge U.S. Dist. Ct. (ea. dist.) Tex., Sherman, 1985—, sr. US dist. judge, 2001. Served with USN, 1944-46, 50-51. Fellow Tex. Bar Found.; mem. Rotary. Presbyterian. Office: US Dist Ct Fed Bldg 101 E Pecan St Sherman TX 75090-5989 Office Phone: 903-892-9405.

BROWN, PEARLIE MURRAY, retired school librarian; b. Kings Mountain, NC, Mar. 24, 1940; d. Sloan George and Mary Lee Murray; m. Marvin Brown, June 27, 1964; children: Vincent Allen, Adrienne Brown Lee. BS, N.C. Ctrl. U., 1961, MLS, 1971; EdD, Nova Southeastern U., 1982; post grad., U N.C.-Charlotte, 1975. Libr. Carver HS, Spindale, NC, 1961—64; tchr. Pleasant Ridge Elem., Gastonia, 1964—65; libr. Gaston Coll., Dallas, NC, 1966—2007, ret., 2007. Mem. Gaston Coll. Assn. Educators, 1970—, Gaston Coll. Personal Assn., 1985—; bd. mem. Gaston County's Children Coun., 1990—91. Trustee bd. Vestibule AME Zion Ch., young adult ministries; mem. United Arts Coun., Gastonia, 1998—. Mem.: NEA, Black Caucus of Am. Libr. Assn., NCCC Learning Resources Assn., Zeta Phi Beta Sorority (Humanitarian award 2007). Methodist. Avocations: reading, bowling.

BROWN, PEGGY LEE, academic administrator, consultant, singer; b. Trenton, NJ; d. Fitzhugh and Mary Susan Brown. BS cum laude, The Coll. N.J., 1987. Pres. PLB Tng. Consultants, Trenton, 1991—2002; asst. dir. ednl. talent search Mercer County CC, Trenton, 2003—. Singer: (recital) Carnegie Hall, Hotel Fiuggi Terme, Italy, N.J. State Mus., (concert) Trenton War Meml., Opera Internat.-Princeton U., Teatro Della Fonti, Italy, (opera performance) Rider U., Fine Arts Series throughout N.J. and Pa., (CD) Simply Peggy, Good News. Mem. Mercer County Youth Svcs. Commn., Trenton, 1994—96; mem. bd. Trenton YWCA Bd., 1986. Recipient alt. semi-finalist, Queens Opera Ninth Ann. Vocal Competition, 1994, semi-finalist, N.Y. Vocal Artists Competition, 1997. Mem.: ASTD. Christian-Church Of Christ. Avocation: travel. Office: Mercer County Community Coll North Broad & Academy Sts Trenton NJ 08608 Home Phone: 609-671-0016; Office Phone: 609-586-4800 6677. Personal E-mail: plbrown@surfree.com. E-mail: brownpl@mccc.edu.

BROWN, PERRY JOE, dean; Student, Foothill Coll., Los Altos, Calif., 1962-63; BS in Forestry, Utah State U., 1967, MS in Forest Recreation, 1968, PhD in Outdoor Recreation & Social Psych, 1971; postgrad., U. Mich., 1968, 69-70. Lectr. forest sci. Utah State U., Logan, 1968-71, asst. prof. forest sci., 1971-73; from asst. prof. recreation resources to asst. dean Colo. State U., 1973—82; assoc. dean instrn., continuing edn. and internat. programs Oreg. State U., 1988-94; dean Coll. Forestry and Conservation U. Mont., Missoula, 1994—, prof. forest resources, 1994—, dir. Mont. Forest and Conservation Expt. Sta., 1994—. Social sci. project leader Oreg. State U.-Nat. Park Svc. Coop. Park Studies Unit, 1990-93; interim dir. Oreg. Tourism Inst., Oreg. State Sys. Higher Edn., 1987-89; mem. adv. bd. Va. Poly. Inst. and State U. Coll. Forestry and Wildlife; mem. numerous panels and task forces NAS, regional planning commns., fed. and state agys. and domestic and internat. profl. orgns.; profl. cons. to numerous fed., state and internat. land mgmt. agys., univs., cos. and the Forest Ecosystem Mgmt. Assessment Team social sci. team; leader Rocky Mountain Coop. Ecosys. Studies Unit; mem. nat. adv. bd. Nat. Forest Found., 2002—. Editor Utah Tourism and Recreation Rev., 1972-73; assoc. editor Jour. Leisure Rsch., 1977-79, Jour. Leisure Scis., 1982-85; mem. editl. bd. Jour. Forest and Landscape Rsch., 1993-99; author over 110 books, articles, papers and reports including 2 books and 16 book chpts. Recipient Cert. of Appreciation, USDA Forest Svc., 1988. Fellow Acad. Leisure Scis.; mem. Soc. Am. Foresters, Human Dimensions in Wildlife Study Group, Internat. Union Forestry Rsch. Orgns. (leader forest recreation, landscape planning and nature conservation sect. 1986-96, dep. coord. divsn. 6 1996—), Nat. Assn. Profl. Forestry Schs. and Colls. (western region chair, exec. bd. 1996-97, pres.-elect 1998-00, pres. 2000-02, past pres. 2002—). Office: U Mont Coll Forestry and Conservation Missoula MT 59812-0001

BROWN, PETER C., movie theater company executive; b. 1959; Founder, chmn. Entertainment Properties Trust, 1997—2003; CFO AMC Entertainment Inc., Kansas City, Mo., co-chmn., 1998—99, chmn., CEO, pres. Mo., 1999—. Bd. dir. Nat. Assn. Theatre Owners, Nat. CineMedia, Midway Games Inc. Office: AMC Entertainment Inc 920 Main St Kansas City MO 64105 Office Phone: 816-221-4000.*

BROWN, PETER DAVID GILSON, German language educator; b. Alton, Ill., Oct. 18, 1943; s. Weir Messick and Vivian Virginia (Bauer) B.; m. Elaine Greenblatt, Sept. 10, 1966 (div. Aug. 1970); 1 child, Stephanie; m. Susan Roberta Jensen, Sept. 11, 1970 (div. Mar. 1992); 1 child, Andrew J.B. BA summa cum laude, Columbia Coll., 1964; MA, Columbia U., 1965, PhD, 1971. Instr. of German Columbia U., NYC, 1967-71, Barnard Coll., NYC, 1968-71; asst. prof. German SUNY, New Paltz, 1971-74, assoc. prof. German, 1974-86, prof. German, 1986—99, disting. svc. prof. German, 1999—. Dir. SUNY Acad. Summer Program, Hamburg/Stade, Fed. Republic Germany, 1974-98; mem. editl. adv. bd. Peter Lang Pub., NYC, 1986—; mem. United Univ. Professions, v.p. academics, New Paltz chpt., 2005-. Author: Oskar Panizza: His Life and Works, 1983; editor: (series of 100 vols.) Studies in Modern German Literature, 1985—, Studies in German Jewish History, 1995—, Women in German Literature, 1997—, The Love Council: A Heavenly Tragedy in Five Acts, 2005; contbr. articles to profl. jours. Chmn. Mid-Hudson Nuclear Opponents, New Paltz, N.Y., 1974-80; legis. coord. Safe Energy Coalition of N.Y. State, Albany, 1974-75; bd. dirs. Environ. Planning Lobby, Albany, 1976-77, Hudson River Sloop Clearwater, Poughkeepsie, N.Y., 1981-83. Recipient Advanced German Studies Prize German Consulate, 1963, Experienced Faculty Travel award NYS/UUP, 1987; Woodrow Wilson fellowship Woodrow Wilson Found., 1964; Tech. Assistance Study grant US Dept. Energy, 1980, SUNY Chancellor's Award for Excellence in Teaching, 1993, Bundesverdienstkreuz German Pres. Roman Herzog, 1999, Tchr. of Yr. award SUNY New Paltz, 2000. Mem. MLA, Am. Assn. Tchrs. German. Avocations: poetry, piano playing, photography. Office: SUNY Dept Fgn Langs 414 Jacobson Faculty Tower New Paltz NY 12561-2499 Office Phone: 845-257-3492. E-mail: brownp@newpaltz.edu.

BROWN, PETER MEGARGEE, lawyer, educator, writer; b. Cleve., Mar. 15, 1922; s. George Estabrook and Miriam (Megargee) B.; m. Alexandra Johns Stoddard, May 18, 1974; children: Peter, Blair Tillyer, Andree de Rapalyee, Nathaniel Holmes; stepchildren: Alexandra, Brooke Stoddard, Wallace Davis. Student, U. Calif., Berkeley, 1943-44; BA, Yale U., 1945, JD, 1948. Bar: N.Y. 1949. Spl. asst. atty. gen. State N.Y. and asst. counsel N.Y. State Crime Commn., 1951-53; asst. U.S. atty. So. Dist. N.Y., 1953-55, spl. asst., 1956; ptnr. firm Cadwalader, Wickersham & Taft, NYC, 1959-82, head litigation and ethics coms.; ptnr. Brown & Seymour, NYC, 1983-96; counsellor-at-law Peter Megargee Brown, NYC, 1996—2004. Mem. Mayor's Com. on Judiciary, 1965-72, vice chmn., 1972-74 Author: The Art of Questioning: Thirty Maxims of Cross-Examination, 1987, Flights of Memory-Days Before Yesterday, 1989, Rascals: The Selling of the Legal Profession, 1989, One World at a Time: Tales of Murder, Joy and Love, 1991, Village: Where to Live and How to Live, 1997; editor: Riot of the Century (Civil War Draft Riot 1863), 1999; author essays, articles on law profession, life and humor, pub. nationally. Mem. N.Y. County Rep. Com., 1958—; counsel on crime to Nelson Rockefeller, Campaign for Gov. N.Y.S., 1968; bd. dirs. Yale Alumni Fund, 1979-84; bd. dirs., pres. Episcopal Ch. Found., 1989-93; master of ceremonies Yale Class of 1944 50th Reunion, 1994, 55th reunion, 1999; chmn., co-founder Design and Art Soc., Ltd., N.Y.C.; pres. Trustees Riot Relief Fund; mem. Presdl. Libr. George H.W. Bush, 2004; founding mem. Henry Morrison Flagler Mus., Palm Beach, Fla.; mediator, East Side N.Y. gang warfare, 1956-57; counsel Grand Jury Assn. N.Y. County, 1956-79; orientation specialist U.S. Army WWII, 1943-46; editor in ch. Camp Bowie Blade (commendation), Brownwood, Tex., 1945. Decorated knight Order St. John of Hosp. of Jerusalem, Soc. of Anchor Cross; recipient award for svc. to profession Fed. Bar Assn., N.Y., N.J. and Conn., 1962; recipient Trustees Gold medal Fed. Bar Coun., 1971, Chmn.'s award Yale Alumni Fund, 1979, Disting. Svc. award Class of 1944, Yale U., 1983, Henry Knox Sherrill medal Episcopal Ch. Found., 1993, Speakers prize Browning Sch., Headmaster's medal St. Andrew's Sch.; Named record scorer U.S. Army Phys. Efficiency Test 1943 (697 out of possible 700 a score still unbroken). Fellow Am. Bar Found., NY State Bar Found.; mem. ABA, World Assn. Lawyers (founding), Soc. Colonial Wars, New England Soc., Sons of the Revolution, N.Y. State Bar Assn., Assn. of Bar of City of N.Y., Fed. Bar Coun. Found. (trustee, pres. 1961-62, chmn. bd. 1962-64, chmn. judiciary com. 1960-85), chmn. planning and program com. 2d cir. judicial conf. 1976-80), St. Nicholas Soc. (past pres.), Coral Beach Club (Bermuda), Delta Kappa Epsilon (Phi chpt. Yale), Phi Delta Phi (magister Waite Inn 1947, pres. province I 1950-55). Episcopalian (vestryman, sr. warden 1961-77). Home Phone: 212-289-5509; Office Phone: 212-427-6434.

BROWN, PETER STEWART, lawyer, electronics executive; b. Jersey City, Jan. 8, 1951; s. George John and Marie Therese (Coyne) B.; m. Charlotte Anne Tileston, Mar. 31, 1978; children: Christopher, Olivia, Emma. BA summa cum laude, Drew U., Madison, NJ, 1974; JD, Harvard U., 1977. Bar: NY 1977, US Dist. Ct. (so. dist. NY) 1978. Assoc. Winthrop, Stimson, Putnam & Roberts, NYC, 1977-84; ptnr. Winthrop, Stimson, Putnam & Roberts (later Pillsbury, Winthrop, Shaw, Pittman, LLP), London, 1985—2001; sr. v.p., gen. counsel, sec. Arrow Electronics, Inc., Melville, NY, 2001—. Office: Arrow Electronics Inc 50 Marcus Dr Melville NY 11747-4210 Office Phone: 631-847-2000.*

BROWN, PETER W., lawyer; b. St. Louis, June 28, 1944; s. Willis Andrew and Alice Louise (Heckel) B.; m. Lynne K. Lochmoeller, Nov.27, 1970; children: Jeff, Emily. BA, Westminster Coll., 1966; JD, Washington U., 1969; LLM in Taxation, U. Mo., Kansas City, 1977. Bar: Mo. 1969, Kans. 1982, US Dist Ct. (we. dist. Mo.) 1990, US Tax Ct. 1979. Estate tax atty. IRS, St. Louis, 1969-72, mgr. estate tax and gift tax grp. Kansas City, 1973-75; ptnr. Brown, Koralchik & Fingersh, Overland Park, Kans., 1975-85, Husch & Eppenberger, Kansas City, Mo., 1986—2006, Lathrop & Gage, Kansas City, 2006—. Bd. dirs. Briarcliff Devel. Co., Inc., Garney Cos., Inc. Dir. Estate Planning Symposium, Kansas City; mem. tax. and legal com. Jewish Cmty. Found., Kansas City; mem. steering and project oversight coms. Met. Kansas City Performing Arts Ctr. Named one of Top 100 Attys., Worth mag., 2006. Fellow Am. Coll. Trust and Estate Coun. (mem. bus. planning and charitable gift coms.); mem. ABA, Kans. Bar Assn., Mo. Bar Assn., Estate Planning Soc. Kansas City, Lawyers Assn. Greater Kansas City. Presbyterian. Avocations: tennis, golf, water activities, reading. Office: Lathrop & Gage 2345 Grand Blvd Ste 2800 Kansas City MO 64108 Office Phone: 816-460-5403. Office Fax: 816-292-2001. E-mail: pbrown@lathropgage.com.*

BROWN, PHILIP ALBERT, lawyer; b. Gettysburg, Pa., June 12, 1949; s. Clyde Raynor and Jean (McCullough) B.; m. Donna Leslie Lohr, May 25, 1985; 1 child, Andrew Raynor. BA in History, George Washington U., 1971; JD, U. Mich., 1974. Bar: Ohio 1974. Assoc. Vorys, Sater, Seymour & Pease, Columbus, Ohio, 1974-81, ptnr., 1981—. Arbitrator Nat. Assn. Security Dealers: mem. Ohio civil legal needs assessment implementation com. Ohio Supreme Ct., 1991-94. Trustee Legal Aid Soc. Columbus, 1985-91, pres. 1989-90; trustee Ohio State Legal Svcs. Assn., 1994—; mem. Nat. Coun. for Arts and Scis. of George Washington U. Fellow Columbus Bar Found.; mem. Phi Beta Kappa. Avocation: fishing. Office: Vorys Sater Seymour & Pease 52 E Gay St Columbus OH 43215-3161

BROWN, PRESTON, lawyer; b. NYC, Oct. 6, 1936; s. John Mason and Catherine (Meredith) B.; m. Betsey G. Pinckney, Oct. 9, 1965 (div. Mar. 1982); children: Catherine St. George, John Preston; m. Eva N. Kasten, June 10, 2000. AB, Harvard U., 1958, LLB, 1961. Bar: NY. 1962, D.C. 1969, U.S. Supreme Ct. 1974. Assoc. Davis, Polk & Wardwell, NYC, 1961-67; adminstrv. asst., del N.Y. State Constl. Conv., Albany, 1967; spl. asst. to under sec. HUD, Washington, 1967-69; resident counsel Curtis, Mallet-Prevost, Colt & Mosle, Washington, 1969-75, ptnr., 1975—. Contbr. articles to profl. jours. Bd. dirs. Goodwill Industries Am., Washington, 1969-75, Young Audiences of DC, 1985-92, 93-99, 2000-2004, pres., 1989-92; tutor DC Preparatory Acad., 2003-. Mem.: Met. Club (Washington), Knickerbocker Club (N.Y.C.). Episcopalian. Home: 2231 48th St NW Washington DC 20007-1036 Office: Curtis Mallet-Prevost Colt & Mosle 1200 New Hampshire Ave NW Ste 430 Washington DC 20036 Office Phone: 202-452-7373. Personal E-mail: presbrown3@msn.com. Business E-Mail: pbrown@cm-p.com.

BROWN, R. LARRY, human resources specialist, transportation executive; b. Jackson, Tenn. BA, Lane Coll.; JD, U. Memphis. Supervisory trial atty. EEOC, 1980—82; asst. U.S. atty. we. dist., Tenn., 1982—87; mng. dir. litigation FedEx Express Corp., Memphis, v.p. legal, sr. v.p., chief human resources officer, 1999—. Bd. dirs. Yes Found., Ptnrs. in Pub. Edn. Office: FedEx Express Corp 3610 Hacks Cross Rd Memphis TN 38125 Office Phone: 901-369-3600. Office Fax: 301-395-2000.

BROWN, RALPH BROWNING, sociologist, educator; b. Twin Falls, Utah, Jan. 25, 1960; s. Boyd Hayes and Charilla Browning Brown; m. Jerilyn M. Muhlestein, June 5, 1984; children: Nicole M., Aisha M., Jessica M. BA, Utah State U., 1986, MS, 1988; PhD, U. Mo., 1992. Asst. prof. sociology Miss. State U., Starkville, Miss., 1992—97, assoc. prof. sociology, 1997—98, Brigham Young U., Provo, Utah, 1998—2005, prof. sociology, 2005—. Grad. coord. Miss. State U., 1997—98; grad. coord. sociology Brigham Young U., 1999—2005, faculty dir. southeast Asian internship, 2003—, assoc. dept. chair sociology, 2005, coord. internat. devel. minor, 2007—; mem. scientific com., minerals mgmt. US Dept. Interior Outer Continental Self, 2006—. Translator: Examining Islam in the West: Addressing Accusations, Correcting Misunderstandings; contbr. chapters to books, articles to profl. jours. Adv. Charles Redd Ctr. for Western Studies, Provo, 2004. Alcuin Tchg. fellowship, Brigham Young U. Gen. Edn., 2005. Mem.: Rural Sociol. Soc. (mem. coun., chmn. program, chmn. devel. com., Excellence in Instrn. award 2004). Democrat. Lds Ch. Office: Brigham Young University 2034 JFSB Provo UT 84602 Home Phone: 801-422-3242; Office Phone: 801-422-3242. Office Fax: 801-422-0625. Business E-Mail: ralph_brown@byu.edu.

BROWN, RALPH SAWYER, JR., retired lawyer; b. Cohasset, Mass., July 21, 1931; s. Ralph Sawyer and Rosemary (Wyman) B.; m. Elizabeth Atkinson Rash, June 12, 1953; children— Lucy Victoria Phillips, Alexander Sawyer Batson. BA, Swarthmore Coll., Pa., 1954; LLB, Harvard U., Cambridge, Mass., 1957. Bar: Mass. bar 1957, NY State 1963. Assoc. Hutchins & Wheeler, Boston, 1957-62, Carter, Ledyard & Milburn, NYC, 1962-68; ptnr. Janklow & Traum, NYC, 1968-71; sec., asst. gen. counsel Indian Head, Inc., NYC, 1971-76, v.p., treas., 1976-79; v.p., gen. counsel, sec. Esquire, Inc., NYC, 1979-83, sr. v.p., gen. counsel, sec., 1983-84; assoc. counsel Paramount Communications Inc., NYC, 1984-93, sr. counsel, 1993-94. Bd. mem. Correctional Assn. NY, NY Soc. Libr., Osborne Assn. Mem. Phi Beta Kappa. Home: 160 W 86th St Ph 4 New York NY 10024-4074 E-mail: rsbrown160@aol.com.

BROWN, RANDY, human resources specialist, health insurance company executive; BA summa cum laude in Econs., Lycoming Coll., Williamsport, Pa. With RCA, 1982—87, GE, 1987—91, Thomson Multimedia, 1991—2001; exec. v.p., chief human resources officer Wellpoint, Inc., 2001—. Mem.: World at Work, Soc. Human Resource Mgmt. Office: Wellpoint Inc 120 Monument Cir Indianapolis IN 46204*

BROWN, RAY KENT, biochemist, physician, educator; b. Columbus, Ohio, Apr. 7, 1924; s. Ray Stemen and Grace (Nunemaker) B.; m. Gertrude Lydia Harris, Jan. 25, 1947 (dec. Feb. 1998); children— Kimberly Brown, Kitene Kading, Kevin; m. Dorothy Skinner, Mar. 19, 1998. BA, Ohio State U., 1944, MD, 1947, MS, 1948; PhD, Harvard U., 1951. Intern Boston City Hosp., 1947-48; sr. asst. surgeon USPHS, Bethesda, Md., 1951-53; asst. dir. div. labs. and research N.Y. State Dept. Health, Albany, 1953-59, assoc. dir. div., 1959-63; asst. prof. biochemistry Albany Med. Coll., 1954-56, assoc. prof., 1956-61, prof., 1961-63, Wayne State U. Sch. Medicine, 1963-96, chmn. dept. biochemistry, 1963-87, prof. emeritus, 1996—. Mem. Highland Twp. (Mich.) Planning Commn., 1968-96. Served with U.S. Army, 1943-45, with USPHS, 1951-53. Mem. Am. Soc. Biol. Chemistry (Travel award 1958, 61, 64), Am. Assn. Immunologists, Biochem. Soc. Gt. Britain, Am. Chem. Soc. Home: 3820 Middle Rd Highland MI 48357-3044

BROWN, RAYMOND M., lawyer, television personality; b. Jersey City; BA, Columbia U., 1968; JD, U. Calif. Boalt Hall Sch. Law, 1974. Bar: NJ 1974, NY 1983. Ptnr. litig. dept., chair white collar def. & corp. compliance practice grp. Greenbaum, Rowe, Smith & Davis, LLP, Woodbridge, NJ. Cons. prof., rsch. fellow Seton Hall U. Sch. Law, NJ, 2001—; adj. prof. Seton Hall U. Sch. Diplomacy. Host (TV series) Due Process (Emmy award, Best Host of a Talk Prog., 2005). Counsel Union County Vocat. Tech. Bd. Edn., 1988—. Fellow: Am. Bar Found., Am. Coll. Trial Lawyers; mem.: Nat. Conf. Black Lawyers, Garden State Bar Assn. (v.p. 1979—), ABA, NJ State Bar Assn., Nat. Assn. Criminal Def. Lawyers (bd. mem. 1991—97, parliamentarian 1997—2000, v.p. 1985—88, pres. 1989—90).*

BROWN, RENEE M., sports association executive; b. Henderson, Nev. B, UNLV, 1978. Asst. coach women's basketball U. Kans., Stanford U., Calif., San Jose State U., Calif.; asst. coach USA Women's Nat. Basketball Team, Colorado Springs, Colo., 1995—96; dir. player pers. WNBA, NYC, 1996—99, sr. dir. player pers., 1999—2000, v.p. player pers., 2000, chief basketball ops. and player pers. Mem. exec. com., v.p. sr. women USA Basketball, 2000—. Named one of 25 Influential Black Women in Bus., The Network Jour., 2007. Office: WNBA Olympic Tower 645 Fifth Ave Fl 10 New York NY 10022-5986*

BROWN, RHONDA JEAN, special education educator; b. Montgomery, Ala., May 25, 1947; d. R.C. and Essie Belcher Brown. AB magna cum laude, Benedict Coll., 1969; MEd, Ga. State U., 1977, EdS, 2001. Cert. tchr. English Ga. Dept. Edn., 1969, tchr. learning disabilities Ga., 1983, tchr. interrelated spl. edn. Ga., 1984, data collection Ga., 1989, behavior disorders Ga., 1990, dir. spl. edn. Ga., 1992. Tchr. H.S. English Atlanta Pub. Sch. Sys., 1970—77; tchr. learning disabled Dekalb County Sch. Sys., Decatur, Ga., 1978—82, tchr. interrelated spl. edn., 1986—89, lead tchr. spl. edn. and ednl. diagnostician, 1990—, exceptional edn. instructional specialist; tchr. interrelated spl. edn. Fulton County Sch. Sys., Coll. Park, Ga., 1983—85. Specialist spl. edn. support and diagnostics Dekalb County Sch. Sys., 1990—, instr. staff devel. courses, 1999—, collector behavior analysis data, 2001—. Named Woman of Yr., Am. Bus. Women's Assn. Northlake chpt., 1982, Founding Sponsor, Martin Luther King Jr. Meml.; named to Civil Rights Meml. Wall of Tolerance, Montgomery, Ala., 2005. Mem.: Coun. Exceptional Children, Pi Lambda Theta, Alpha Kappa Mu, Zeta Phi Beta. Democrat. Baptist. Home: 3447 Cobbs Ferry Dr Decatur GA 30032 Office: Dekalb County School Dept Exceptional Edn 5839 Memorial Dr Stone Mountain GA 30083 Office Phone: 678-676-2041. Personal E-mail: rjbrown5@bellsouth.net.

BROWN, RICHARD ALEXANDER, chemist; b. Waterbury, Conn., Aug. 16, 1949; s. Spenser Allen and Helen (Pendo) B.; m. Susan Eileen Haringa, June 26, 1976; children: Jeffrey, Michele, Robert. AB, Harvard Coll., 1971; MS, Cornell U., 1974, PhD, 1977. Rsch. chemist FMC Corp., Princeton, NJ, 1976-81, group leader, 1981-84, tech. mgr. aquifer remediation, 1984—86; dir. bus. devel. Cambridge Analytical Assocs., Princeton, 1987; regional mgr. bioremediation Groundwater Tech., Inc., Trenton, NJ, 1988-89, dir. chem. treatment, 1990-91, v.p. remediation tech., 1992-98; sr. tech. cons. IT Corp., 1998-99; dir. tech. devel. ERM Inc., 1999—. Author: Handbook of Bioremediation, 1994; contbr. chpts.: Bioremediation: Field Experience, 1994, Air Sparging for Site Remediation, 1994. Chmn. local com. Intervarsity Christian Fellowship, NJ, 1988-92; deacon Lawrenceville Presbyn. Ch., 2006-, mem. peacemaking com., 2006-; mgr. Lawrence Flames Bantam B Hockey Team, 1998-2002, Recipient award for editl. excellence Pollution Engring., 1992. Mem. Am. Chem. Soc., Water Environment Fedn., Assn. Groundwater Scientists and Engrs. Democrat. Presbyterian. Achievements include patents for method for decontamination of subterranean formations, stimulation of bioxidation in subterranean formation, composition and method for treating a subterranean formation, oxidation of sulfides. Home: 42 W Long Dr Lawrenceville NJ 08648-2714 Office: ERM Inc 250 Phillips Blvd Ste 280 Ewing NJ 08618-1433 Office Phone: 609-895-0050. Business E-Mail: dick.brown@erm.com.

BROWN, RICHARD HOLBROOK, library director, historian, researcher; b. Boston, Sept. 25, 1927; s. Joseph Richard and Sylvia (Cook) Brown. BA, Yale U., 1949, MA, 1952, PhD, 1955. Instr. history U. Mass., Amherst, 1955—59, asst. prof., 1959—62; assoc. prof. No. Ill. U., De Kalb, 1962—64; dir. Amherst Project, Amherst and Chgo., 1964—72; dir. rsch. and edn. Newberry Libr., Chgo., 1972—83, acad. v.p., 1983—94, sr. rsch. fellow, 1994—. Vis. prof. history and edn. Northwestern U., Evanston, Ill., 1971—84; cons. NEH, 1977—; bd. dirs. Chgo. Metro History Fair, 1977—, pres., 1984—91; cons. Ctr. Study So. Culture, U. Miss., 1979—; mem. Ill. Humanities Coun., 1980—86, chmn., 1982—83. Author: The Hero and the People, 1964, The Missouri Compromise: Political Statesmanship or Unwise Evasion?, 1964; gen. editor: Amherst Project Units in American History, 25 vols., 1964—75. Recipient George Washington Eggleston prize, Yale U., 1955; Andrew Mellon Postdoctoral fellow, U. Pitts., 1960—61. Mem.: Orgn. Am. Historians, Social Sci. Edn. Consortium (pres. 1975—77), Am. Antiquarian Soc. Democrat. Roman Catholic. Office: The Newberry Libr 60 W Walton St Chicago IL 60610-3380 Home Phone: 313-787-1113; Office Phone: 312-255-3594. Business E-Mail: brownr@newberry.org.

BROWN, RICHARD LEE, lawyer; b. Ft. Worth, Dec. 7, 1925; s. Marvin H. and Janie (McIntosh) B.; m. Elizabeth McPherson, Nov. 19, 1949; children: Beverly Elizabeth, Leigh Ann (dec.). Student, Rice U., 1942-43; LLB, U. Tex., 1949; LLM, George Washington U., 1954. Bar: Tex. 1949. Asst. dist. atty., Tarrant County, 1949- 50; spl. atty. Chief Counsel's Office, IRS, Washington, 1953-56; partner Friedman & Brown, 1956-60, Stone, Parker, Snakard & Brown, 1961-66, Law, Snakard, Brown & Gambill, 1967-81, 83-84; of counsel Bishop Payne Harvard & Kaitcer, Ft. Worth, 1984-89, 91—; judge Ct. Appeals Tex. 2d Dist., 1981-83; chief civil div. Tarrant County Dist. Atty's Office, 1989-91. Former mem. bd. commrs. Pub. Housing Authority Ft. Worth, chmn., 1976-77; Chmn. bd., chmn. competition Van Cliburn Internat. Piano Competition, 1966-69. Served with AUS, 1944-46; Served with U.S. Army, 1950-53. Decorated Bronze Star medal, Combat Infantry badge and 3 battle stars. Fellow Tex. Bar Found. (life); mem. Tex. Bar Assn., Tarrant County Bar Assn. (pres. 1977-78) Office: 1800 Bank of Am Bldg 500 W 7th St Fort Worth TX 76102-4700 Home Phone: 817-732-2547; Office Phone: 817-297-9297.

BROWN, RITA MAE, writer; b. Hanover, Pa., Nov. 28, 1944; d. Ralph and Julia Ellen B. AA, Broward Jr. Coll., 1965; BA, NYU, 1968; cinematography degree, Sch. Visual Arts, NYC, 1968; PhD, Inst. Policy Studies, 1976; DLitt, Wilson Coll., 1992; LLD (hon.), William Woods U., Fulton, Mo., 2000; LLD (hon.), York Coll., Pa., 2003; LHD (hon.), Franklin Pierce Coll., 2002. Photo editor Sterling Pub., NYC, 1969-70; lectr. Fed. City Coll., Washington, 1970-71; rsch. fellow Inst. Policy Studies, Washington, 1971-73; pres. Am. Artists Inc., Charlottesville, Va., 1980—. Vis. mem. faculty in feminist studies Goddard Coll., Plainfield, Vt., 1973—; mem. lit. panel NEA, 1978-81; Hemingway judge for 1st fiction PEN Internat., 1983; blue ribbon panelist Prime Time Emmy Awards, 1984, 86; tchr. Nebr. Summer Writers Conf., U. Nebr., Lincoln, 2003, 04. Author: (translator) Hrotsvitra: Six Medieval Plays, 1971, (novels) The Plain Brown Rapper, 1972, The Hand That Cradles the Rock, 1971, Songs to a Handsome Woman, 1973, Rubyfruit Jungle, 1974, In Her Day, 1976, Six of One, 1977, Southern Discomfort, 1982, Sudden Death, 1983, High Hearts, 1986, Starting from Scratch, 1987, Bingo, 1988, Wish You Were Here, 1989, Rest in Pieces, 1991, Murder at Monticello, 1993, Venus Envy, 1993, Dolley, 1994, Paydirt, 1995, Riding Shotgun, 1996, Murder, She Meowed, 1996, Loose Lips, 1998, Outfoxed, 2000, Mrs. Murphy Mysteries, 2001, Outfoxed, 2000, Alma Mater, 2001, Hotspur, 2002, Full Cry, 2003, Whisker of Evil, 2004, Cat's Eyewitness, 2005, The Hunt Ball, 2005; (poetry) The Poems of Rita Mae Brown, 1987; TV series include I Love Liberty, 1982, Long Hot Summer, 1985, My Two Loves, 1986, The Alice Marble Story, 1986, Southern Exposure, 1990, Cat on the Scent, 1999, Loose Lips, 1999, Outfoxed, 2000, Pawing Through The Past, 2000; TV films include The Girls of Summer, 1989, Selma, Lord, Selma, 1989, Passing Through, 1993, A Family Again, 1994, others; (cable TV) The Mists of Avalon, 1986, The Nat Turner Story-African American Anthology, 1993, The Wall, K-9, 1993; (films) Slumber Party Massacre, 1982, Sweet Surrender, 20th Century Fox, 1986, Table Dancing, 1987, Mary Pickford, 1998. Former exec. officer NOW; bd. dirs. Human Rights Campaign Fund, N.Y.C., 1986; co-founder Radical Lesbians; founder Redstockings Radical Feminist Group, Nat. Gay Task Force, Nat. Women's Polit. Caucus. Recipient Award for Best Variety Show on TV Writers Guild Am., 1982, Outstanding Alumni, Am. Assn. Cmty. Colls., 1999, Outstanding Alumna, Broward Cmty. Coll., 1999, Literary Lion award N.Y. Pub. Library, 1986, Emmy award nomination for The Long Hot Summer, ABC mini-series, 1985; Emmy nomination for best variety show I Love Liberty, 1982; named Charlottesville favorite author The Observer, 1990, Athlete of the Week, The Observer, 1990. Mem. PEN Internat., Oak Ridge Foxhunt Club (Master of Foxhounds). Office: care of The Wendy Weil Agy 232 Madison Ave Ste 1300 New York NY 10016-2901 E-mail: waywardwomen@aol.com.

BROWN, ROBERT ALAN, geophysicist, educator; b. LA, June 11, 1934; s. Carl Clayton and Olive (Hirst) B.; m. Marcia Louise Jobe, Dec. 12, 1957; children: Vanessa, Morgan, Tristin. BS, U. Calif., Berkeley, 1957, MS, 1963; PhD, U. Wash., 1969. Fellow U. Wash., Seattle, 1969-70, Nat. Ctr. Atmospheric Sci., Boulder, Colo., 1970-71; rsch. prin. investigator U. Wash. Polar Sci. Ctr., Seattle, 1971—83; prof. atmospheric sci. U. Wash., Seattle, 1983—. Adj. prof.: Naval Postgrad. Sch., 1983, Fraunhofer Inst., Garmish, Germany, 1991, U. Concepcíon, Chile, 1996, 2003, Ecole Poly., Paris, 1997. Author: Analytic Methods in Planetary Boundary Layer Models, 1973, Fluid Mechanics of the Atmosphere, 1991, The Tree or the Panzaic Plea, 2005; co-author: The Panzaic Principle, 1971, Microwave Remote Sensing for Ocean and Marine Weather Forecast Models, Ency. of Earth System Science, Surface Waves and Fluxes: Current Theory, Polar Oceanography, 1990; editor Pacific Ocean Remote Sensing Congress book series, 1992—. Remote Sensing of the Pacific Ocean with Satellites, 1998; contbr. over 80 articles to profl. jours. 1st lt. U.S. Army, 1957-59. Recipient Disting. Sci. award, Pan Ocean Remote Sensing Confs., 2000. Fellow Am. Meteorol. Soc.; mem. Am. Geophys. Union, Am. Oceanographic Soc., Sigma Xi, Phi Kappa Psi. Democrat. Office: U Wash Dept Atmospheric Sci PO Box 351640 Seattle WA 98195-0001 Business E-Mail: rabrown@atmos.washington.edu.

BROWN, ROBERT ARTHUR, academic administrator, chemical engineering professor; b. San Antonio, July 22, 1951; s. Ralph and Lillian (Rilling) B.; m. Beverly Ann Lamb, June 22, 1972; children: Ryan Arthur, Keith Andrew. BS, U. Tex., 1973, MS, 1975; PhD, U. Minn., 1979. Instr. U. Minn., Mpls., 1978; from asst. prof. chem. engring. to provost MIT, Cambridge, 1979—88, provost, 1988—2005, dean Sch. of Engring., 1996-98, co-dir. supercomputer facility, 1989-94; pres. Boston U., 2005—. Cons. Lincoln Labs., Lexington, Mass., 1985-87, Mobil Solar Energy, Waltham, Mass., 1982-93. Contbr. over 160 articles to profl. jours. Recipient Outstanding Jr. Faculty award Amoco Oil Co., 1981, Camille and Henry Dreyfus Tchr.-Scholar award 1983; named one of Outstanding Young Texans-Execs. U. Tex., 1991; named hon. citizen Rep. of Singapore, 2006. Mem. AAAS, NAE, NAS, AIChE (Allen P. Colburn award 1986, Profl. Progress award 1996), Soc. Indsl. and Applied Math., Am. Assn. Crystal Growth (Young Author award 1985, Crystal Growth award 2005), Am. Phys. Soc., Am. Acad. Arts and Scis. Office: Boston U Office of Pres One Sherborn St Boston MA 02215 Office Phone: 617-353-2200. Business E-Mail: rabrown@bu.edu.

BROWN, ROBERT BALDWIN, III, lawyer; b. Atlanta, Sept. 17, 1961; m. Cara Ryskamp Brown; children: Leigh, Dana. BA, Cornell U., Ithaca, NY, 1983; JD, U. Fla., Gainesville, 1986. Bar: Fla. 1986, US Dist. Ct. (so., no. and mid. dists.) Fla., US Cir. Ct. (11th dist.). Atty., equity ptnr. Kubicki Draper, 1986—2001; founding equity ptnr. Alters, Boldt, Brown, Rash & Culmo, PA. Bd. dirs. Miami-Dade Justice Assn.; sec. Miami chpt. Am. Bd. Trial Advocates. Mem.: AAJ (mem. Leaders Forum, mem. nat. fin. com.), Acad. Fla. Trial Lawyers (eagle level). Achievements include being the youngest equity partner in the history of Kubicki Draper law firm; in over 17 years, tried more than 50 medical and legal malpractice, product liability, wrongful death, intellectual property and commercial litigation cases to verdict. Avocations: surfing, running, boating, diving, fishing.

BROWN, ROBERT C., engineering educator; BA in Math., U. Mo., Columbia, 1976, BS in Physics, 1976; MS in Mech. Engring., Mich. State U., 1977, PhD in Mech. Engring., 1980. Tchg. asst. Mich. State U., 1976—78, rsch. asst., 1978—80; sr. engr. thermodynamics grp. Gen. Dynamics Corp., Ft. Worth, 1980—83; asst. prof. Iowa State U., 1983—87, assoc. prof., 1987—93, prof. chem. engring., 1993—, prof. mech. engring., 1993—, Bergles prof. thermal sci. dept. mech. engring., 2002—, prof. agrl. and biosystems engring., 2004—. Dir. Ctr. Coal and the Environment Iowa State U. Inst. Phys. Rsch. and Tech., 1996—; lead sustainable energy tech. initiative Ames Nat. Lab., 1997—98. Contbr. articles to profl. jours. Recipient R & D 100 award, R & D Mag., 1997; grantee Kodak fellowship, 1976. Fellow: ASME; mem.: AIChE. Achievements include patents in field. Office: Mech Engring Dept Iowa State U 2025 HM Black Engring Bldg Ames IA 50011-2161 E-mail: rcbrown@iastate.edu.

BROWN, ROBERT CARROLL, JR., lawyer; b. Ridley Park, Pa., June 24, 1948; s. Robert Carroll Sr. and Marjorie Elizabeth (Nowell) B.; m. Charlene M. Lipp, Oct. 4, 1986; children: Robert Charles, Gregory Scott, Michael Joseph. AB in Polit. Sci., Pa. State U., 1970; JD, Temple U., 1973. Bar: Pa.; US Dist. Ct. (ea. dist.) Pa. 1977, Pa. Supreme Ct. 1973, US Ct. Appeals (3d cir.) 1980. Judicial law clk. Ct. Common Pleas/Northampton County, Easton, Pa., 1973-74; assoc. Fox & Oldt, Easton, 1974-82; ptnr. Fox, Oldt & Brown, Easton, 1982—. Sec. Greater Easton Corp., 1977-82, Two Rivers Area Commerce Coun., Easton, 1983-85; officer Lehigh Valley Flying Club, Allentown, Pa., 1979-99. Mem.: Nat. Acad. Elder Law Attys., Pa. Bar Assn., Northampton County Bar Assn. (sec. 1983—84). Republican. Presbyterian. Avocations: private pilot, sports cars, golf, spectator sports. Home: 420 Wedgewood Dr Easton PA 18045-5753 Office: Fox Oldt & Brown 940 W Lafayette St Ste100 Easton PA 18042 Home Phone: 610-252-5617; Office Phone: 610-258-6111. Personal E-mail: foanob@cs.com.

BROWN, ROBERT DALE, wildlife science educator, dean; b. Red Bluff, Calif., July 31, 1945; s. Charles Arthur and Carol Joyce (Dale) Brown; m. Regan Mensch, June 30, 1981; children: Alex, Jason, Adam. Student, U. Calif., Davis, 1963—65; BS, Colo. State U., Ft. Collins, 1968; PhD, Pa. State U., 1975. From asst. prof. to assoc. prof. Tex. A&I U., Kingsville, 1975-81; from assoc. rsch. scientist to rsch. scientist C. Kleberg Wildlife Rsch. Inst., Kingsville, 1981-87; dept. head Miss. State U., Starkville, 1987-93, Tex. A&M U., College Station, 1993—2006, coord. Gulf Coast Coop. Ecosys. Studies Unit, 2002—06; dean Coll. Natural Resources N.C. State U., Raleigh, 2006—. Editor: Antler Development in Cervidae, 1983, Translocation of Wild Animals, The Biology of Deer, 1991. Lt. col. USMCR, 1968—93. Mem. Am. Inst. Nutrition, Wildlife Soc. (past pres.), NC Forestry Coun., Nat. Assn. Univ. Fish and Wildlife Programs (past pres.). Episcopalian. Avocations: scouting, hunting, fishing, kayaking. Office: Dean Coll Natural Resources NC State Univ 2028 Biltmore Hall Campus Box 8001 Raleigh NC 27695-8001 Office Phone: 919-515-2883. Business E-Mail: bob_brown@ncsu.edu.

BROWN, ROBERT DONALD, lawyer; b. Orange, NJ, Sept. 23, 1952; s. Francis Robert and Elizabeth Brown; children: William Robert, Daniel Thomas. BA, Clemson U., 1974; JD, Am. U., 1982. Bar: Fla. 1982, U.S. Dist. Ct. (so. and mid. dists.) Fla. 1982. Mktg. cons. New Eng. Tel. Co., Boston, 1977—79; econometrician Chesapeake & Potomac Tel. Co., Washington, 1979—81; atty. Blackwell Walker , P.A., Miami, Fla., 1982—94, Akerman Senterfitt & Eidson, Miami, 1994—96, Freidin & Brown, P.A., Miami, 1996—2005, Robert D. Brown, P.A., Miami, 2005—. Named one of Legal Elite, Fla. Trend Mag., 2004, 2005. Mem.: Dade County Trial Lawyers Assn. (bd. dirs. 1999—2004, editor newsletter 1999—2004). Office: Robert D Brown PA 9350 South Dixie Highway 10th Floor Miami FL 33156 Home Phone: 305-234-1423; Office Phone: 305-670-2010. Office Fax: 305-670-9009. E-mail: bbrownesq@bellsouth.net.

BROWN, ROBERT E., transportation executive; b. Croydon, Eng., 1945; BS, Royal Mil. Coll., Kingston, Can.; postgrad., Harvard U., 1983. With Can. Armed Forces, Atomic Energy Can., Pub. Svc. Commn., Treasury Bd., Coun. Maritime Premiers, 1976-78; assoc. dep. mininster Dept. Regional Indsl. Expansion; v.p. corp. devel. Bombardier, Inc., Montreal, Canada, 1987-89, sr. v.p. corp. devel. and strategic planning, 1989-90; pres. Canadair, 1990-92, Bombardier Aerospace Group-N.Am., 1992-96, pres., COO, 1996-99; pres., CEO Bombardier, Inc., Montreal, Canada, 1999—2002; chmn. Air Can., 2003—. Bd. dirs. Nortel Networks Corp.; pres., CEO CAE, Inc., Montreal.

BROWN, ROBERT GROVER, engineering educator; b. Shenandoah, Iowa, Apr. 25, 1926; s. Grover Whitney and Irene (Frink) B. BS, Iowa State Coll., 1948, MS, 1951, PhD, 1956. Instr. Iowa State Coll., Ames, 1948-51, 53-55, asst. prof., 1955-56, assoc. prof., 1956-59, prof., 1959-76, Disting. prof., 1976-88, Disting. prof. emeritus, 1988—; research engr. N. Am. Aviation, Downey, Calif., 1951-53. Cons. various aerospace engring. firms., 1956— Author: (with R.A. Sharpe, W.L. Hughes) Lines, Waves and Antennas, 1961, (with J.W. Nilsson) Linear Systems Analysis, 1962, (with Patrick Y.C. Hwang) Introduction to Random Signals and Applied Kalman Filtering with MATLAB Exercises and Solutions, 3d edit., 1997. Fellow IEEE, Inst. Navigation (Burka award 1978, 84, Weems award 1994). Home: 16E Venetian Dr Clear Lake IA 50428-1005

BROWN, ROBERT JOHN, social sciences educator, consultant; b. Stillwater, Minn., June 15, 1935; s. Lindsay and Bertha Brown; m. Janet Rae Johnson, Aug. 22, 1959 (div.); m. Jacquelyn Marie Heidtke, Apr. 24, 1992; children: Anthony, Daniel, Linda Richie, Michael, Andrew. BS, Winona State U., Minn., 1957; MA, U. Minn., 1958, PhD, 1964. Cert. tchr. Minn., sch. counselor Minn. Tchr.-counselor, coach Farmington (Minn.) Pub. Schs., 1958—60; guidance dir. Sch. Dist. 192, Inver Grove Heights, Minn., 1960—63; instr. U. Minn., Mpls., 1963—64; prof. leadership and policy U. St. Thomas, Mpls., 1964—; spl. asst. to the sec. U.S. Dept. Edn., Washington, 1981—85. Scholar in residence Nat. Assn. Secondary Sch. Prins., Reston, Va., 1990—91; editl. adv. com. Rowman and Littlefield Edn. Press, Lanham, Md., 2000—05; charter sch. adv. bd. State Dept. Edn., St. Paul, 2003—05; mem. Minn. Bd. Med. Practice, 2006—. Author: (monograph) Reflections on the Education Activities of the Business Roundatable, 1991, The Entrepreneurial Education, 2000; editor: (book series) Innovations in Education, 2001—; creator and co-exec. prodr. (TV series) Critical Issues in Education. State senator Minn. Legislature, St. Paul, 1967—77; mem. State Bd. Edn., St. Paul; Minn. nat. committeeman Rep. Party, Washington, 1979—81; organizer, co-chmn. Nat. Educators for Reagan-Bush, Washington, 1984; state chmn. Minn. Rep. Party, St. Paul, 1973—75; bd. dirs. DeLaSalle H.S., Mpls., Minn. Assn. Charter Schs., 2006—. Fellow Tozer Found., 1957—58; grantee Nat. Conf. on Rural Edn., Control Data Corp., C.C. Cooperation in Human Svc. Delivery, Comprehensive Employment and Tng. Act; scholar Tozer Found., 1953—57. Mem.: Nat. Assn. Secondary Sch. Prins. (state bd. dirs.), Am. Edn. Rsch. Assn. Republican. Roman Catholic. Home: 405 W County Rd C Roseville MN 55113 Office: U St Thomas 1000 Lasalle Ave Minneapolis MN 55403-2009 Home Phone: 651-330-1170; Office Phone: 651-962-4992. Office Fax: 651-962-4169. Personal E-mail: bobjbrown@comcast.net. E-mail: rjbrown@stthomas.edu.

BROWN, ROBERT LAIDLAW, state supreme court justice; b. Houston, June 30, 1941; s. Robert Raymond and Warwick (Rust) B.; m. Charlotte Banks, June 18, 1966; 1 child, Stuart Laidlaw. BA, U. of the South, 1963; MA in English and Comparative Lit., Columbia U., 1965; JD, U. Va., 1968. Bar: Ark. 1968, U.S. Dist. Ct. (ea. and we. divs.) Ark. 1968. Assoc. Chowning, Mitchell, Hamilton & Burrow, Little Rock, 1968-71; dep. prosecuting atty. 6th Jud. Dist., Prosecuting Atty. Office, Little Rock, 1971-72; legal aide Office Gov. Dale Bumpers, Little Rock, 1972-74; legis. asst. U.S. Senator Dale Bumpers, Washington, 1975-76; adminstrv. asst. Congressman Jim Guy Tucker, Washington, 1977-78; ptnr. Harrison & Brown, P.A., Little Rock, 1978-85; pvt. practice law, 1985-90; assoc. justice Ark. Supreme Ct., Little Rock, 1991—. Contbr. articles to profl. jours. Trustee U. of the South, Sewanee, Tenn., 1983-89, bd. regents, 1989-95. Fellow ABA, Ark. Bar Found (cert. of recognition 1981); mem. Ark. Bar Assn. Episcopalian. Office Phone: 501-682-6864. Business E-Mail: Robert.Brown@arkansas.gov.

BROWN, ROBERT MUNRO, museum director; b. Riverside, NJ, Mar. 4, 1952; s. James Wendell and Janet Elizabeth (Munro) B.; m. Mary Ann Noel, June, 1973 (div. 1977); m. Claudia Leslie Haskell, Jan. 14, 1978. BA in Polit. Sci. cum laude, Ursinus Coll., 1973; MA in Social Scis., Rivier Coll., 1978; PhD in Early Am. History, U. N.H., 1983. Grad. asst. dept. history U. N.H., Durham, 1979-83, instr., 1983-84; site curator T.C. Steele State Hist. Site Ind. State Mus. System, Nashville, Ind., 1984-91; exec. dir. Hist. Mus. at Ft. Missoula, Mont., 1991—. Hist. interpreter Strawberry Banke, Portsmouth, N.H., 1980-83; instr. Rivier Coll., Nashua, N.H., 1986-91, N.H. Coll., Nashua and Salem, 1986-91; supr. pub. programs Mus. Am. Textile History, North Andover, Mass., 1985-91; sec.-treas. Western Mont. Heritage Ctr./No. Rockies Heritage Ctr., 1992-93; mem. grad. com. U. Mont., 1993; mem. steering com. Ft. Missoula, 1993; reviewer Inst. Mus. and Libr. Svcs., 1993--; reviewer Am. Assn. Mus.-Mus. Asessment Programs, 1997—; mem. Mont. Com. of the Humanities Spkrs. Bur., 1995—; lectr., presenter, chair panels in field. Contbr. articles to profl. jours. Trustee Historic Harrisville, N.H., 1989-91; bd. dirs. United Peoples Found., 1991-93, v.p., 1993; mem. planning com. Western Mont. Heritage Ctr., 1991, U. Mont. Centennial Celebration, 1992, Leadership Missoula, 1992; active open space, parks and resource planning and mgmt. project team City of Missoula, 1993; mem. blue ribbon task force Five Valleys Luth. Retirement Cmty. Planning Com., 1994, Western Mont. Vol. Ctr. Coun., 2004-05. Fellow, Kellogg Found., 1987; grantee, Mass. Coun. on Arts and Humanities, 1986—88, Int. Mus. Svcs., 1988—91, 1993, 1995, 1997, 1999, AT&T, 1988, Am. Wool Coun., 1988, BayBank, 1989, Am. Yarn Assn., 1989, Insured Titan, 1990—2005, North Andover Arts Lottery Coun., 1989—90, Mass. Cultural Coun., 1990, Greater Lawrence Cmty. Found., 1991, Mass. Arts Lottery Coun., 1991, Gallery Assn. for Greater Art, 1991, 1992, 1994—98, Mont. Comm. for Humanities, 1991—2005, Sinclair Oil Co., 1991, Mont. Rail Link, 1992, 1998, 1999, 2001—03, U. Mont. Found., 1992, Pepsi-Cola Co., 1992—97, 2001—07, Coca-Cola Bottling Co., 1998, Cmty. Med. Ctr., 1999, St. Patrick Hosp., 1999, U.S. WEST Found., 1992, 1995, The Missoulian, 1992, 1995, 2005, 2006, Champion Internat., 1992, Mont. Cultural Trust, 1993, 1995, 1997, Missoula Rotary, 1993, Tex. Mus. Austin, 1993, Inst. Mus. Svcs., 1993, 1995, 1997, 1999, 2002, Zip Beverage Co., 1994, 2000—07, Bitterroot Motors, 1994—2007, Grizzly Hackle, 1994, University Motors, 1995, 1996, Earl's Distbg., 1996, Norwest Bank, 1996—98, ALPS, 2001, 2002, Southgate Mall, 1997—2007, NEH, 2003; scholar, U. N.H., 1979—83; rsch. grantee, 1982. Mem.: Greater Boston Mus. Educator's Roundtable (steering com. 1988—90), Mtn. Plains Mus. Assn. (Mont. state rep. 1995—97, ann. meeting local arrangements chair 1997, chmn. scholarship com. 1998, sec. 1998—2000, chmn. scholarship com. 1999—2004, ann. meeting program co-chair 2000, treas. 2001—04), Western Mont. Fundraisers Assn. (charter 1991, v.p. 1993—95, pres. 1995—97), Mus. Assn. Mont. (panelist 1994, conf. host 2007), Mont. Hist. Soc., Assn. Records Mgrs. and Adminstrs. (charter Big Sky chpt. 1992—94), Am. Hist. Assn., Am. Assn. State and Local History (state membership rep. 1996—98, state awards chair 2001—, program com. 2003, mem. coun. 2005—, Leadership History award 2007), Am. Assn. Mus. (small mus. adminstrs. com., Mountain-Plains regional rep. 2000—03), Kiwanis (Sentinel chpt.), Masons (Missoula chpt.), Phi Alpha Theta. Democrat. Avocations: canoeing, cross country skiing, snowshoeing. Home: 216 Woodworth Ave Missoula MT 59801-6050 Office: Hist Mus at Ft Missoula Ft Missoula Bldg 322 Missoula MT 59804 Office Phone: 406-728-3476. Business E-Mail: ftmslamuseum@montana.com.

BROWN, ROBERT WALLACE, mathematics professor, educator; b. Portland, Oreg., May 20, 1925; s. Bert and Stella (Conway) B.; m. Doris Arrilda Burroughs, Sept. 4, 1948; children: Robert Wallace, Janice Dianne. BS, Pacific U., 1950; MS, Oreg. State U., 1952, PhD, 1958. Mathematician, Nat. Bur. Standards, Corona, Calif., 1952-54; Mathematician Boeing Co., Seattle, 1958-66; vis. asso. prof. Oreg. State U., Corvallis, 1966-67; prof. math. U. Alaska, Fairbanks, 1967-82, head dept., 1967-77, 79-82; vis. prof. math. Lewis and Clark Coll., Portland, Oreg., 1982-85; ret., 1985. Contbg. author: Error in Digital Computation, 1965. With USNR, 1942—45. Mem. Math. Assn. Am., Am. Math Soc., AAAS, Sigma Xi, Pi Mu Epsilon, Sigma Pi Sigma. Home: 20755 SW Prindle Rd Tualatin OR 97062-9701

BROWN, ROBERT WAYNE, lawyer; b. Allentown, Pa., July 6, 1942; s. P.P. and Rose (Ferrara) B.; m. Rochelle Kaplan, Oct. 23, 1977; m. Shelley Sherman, Mar. 3, 1973; children: Courtney Sherman, Robin Thea, Ryan Palmer; m. Lupe Pearce, Nov. 22, 1996. AB, Franklin and Marshall Coll., 1964; JD, Cornell U., 1967. Bar: Ill. 1969, Pa. 1971. VISTA atty. Cmty. Legal Svcs., Detroit, 1967-68; asst. prof. law U. Ill., 1968-70; ct. adminstr., law clk. Lehigh County Ct. Common Pleas, 1971-72; ptnr. Gross & Brown, Allentown, 1972-76; pvt. practice law Allentown, 1976-77; sr. ptnr. Brown & Brown, Allentown, 1977-82, Brown, Brown & Solt, Allentown, 1982-85, Brown, Brown, Solt & Krouse, Allentown, 1985-89, Brown, Brown, Solt & Ferretti, Allentown, 1989—; city solicitor Allentown, 2002—06. Instr. bus. law Muhlenburg Coll., 1973-76; pub. defender Lehigh County, 1973-74; adv. bd. PNC Bank. Active Rape Crisis Coun. Lehigh Valley, 1978-84, Lehigh County Pre-trial Svcs., 1975-82; bd. dirs. Hispanic Am. Orgn., 1982-90, treas., 1983-86; bd. dirs. Lehigh County Sr. Citizens, 1980-88, pres., 1984-86; bd. dirs. Lehigh County Legal Svcs., 1973-77, Boys and Girls Club Allentown, 1994-2002, pres., 1998-2000; founding trustee Robert Clemente Charter Sch., 1998—. Recipient Cmty. Svc. award Hispanic Am. Orgn., 1985, Human Rels. Commn. award, Allentown, 1986; Lindback scholar Franklin and Marshall Coll., 1963-64. Mem. ABA, Pa. Bar Assn., Lehigh County Bar Assn., Order of Coif, Rotary (bd. dirs.

Allentown 1998—, pres. 2004-05), Club of Allentown. Democrat. Home: 225 Parkview Ave Allentown PA 18104-5323 Office: 1425 W Hamilton St Allentown PA 18102-4224 Office Phone: 610-433-6771. Personal E-mail: rwbrown2@verizon.net.

BROWN, ROBERT WILLIAM, elementary school educator; b. Pinckneyville, Ill., Jan. 1, 1965; s. Kenneth Robert Brown and Martha Elenor Berry; m. Susan Jean Berry, Jan. 15, 1993; 1 child, Courtney Rochelle. BS in Elem. Edn., McKendree, Lebanon, Ill., 1985—88; M in Ednl. Adminstrn., So. Ill. U., Edwardsville, 2007. Cert. elem. edn. tchr. Ill., 1988. Funeral home worker Rogers-Atkins Funeral Home, Salem, Ill., 1983—; sci. & social studies tchr. Irvington Grade Sch., Ill., 1988—. Youth pastor Orchardville Cmty. Ch., Xenia, Ill., 2000—06; commitee mem. Sch. Improvement Planning Com., Irvington, Ill., 2005—06. Mem.: Phi Kappa Phi, Kappa Gamma Epsilon, Mensa (assoc.). R-Consevative. Assembly God. Avocations: reading, martial arts, exercise. Home: 325 Country Club Estates Salem IL 62881 Office: Ivington Grade Sch 500 Superior Irvington IL 62848 Home Phone: 618-548-9135.

BROWN, ROGER H., academic administrator; m. Linda Mason. BS in Physics, Davidson Coll., 1978; MBA, Yale U. Pres. Berklee Coll. Music, Boston, 2004—. With CARE and UNICEF, Thailand, Cambodia; co-dir. Save the Children, Sudan, 1985—86; co-founder Bright Horizons Family Solutions, 1986, CEO, 1986—2002; co-founder Horizons Initiative, Boston, bd. mem. Stand for Children; mgmt. cons. Bain and Co. Co-author: Rice, Rivalry, and Politics. Mem. gov. bd. Nat. Assn. for Edn. of Young Children; chairperson NAEYC Commn. on Accreditation. Named Nat. Entrepreneur of Yr., Ernst and Young/USA Today, 1996, Best Entrepreneur, BusinessWeek, 1997; named one of the 25 Friends of the Family, Working Mother mag., 1997; recipient Caring Corporation Award, Child Care Action Campaign, 1999. Office: Office of President Berklee College Music 1140 Boylston St Boston MA 02215 Office Phone: 617-747-2000.*

BROWN, RONALD, retired stockbroker; b. Aug. 30, 1930; s. Arthur S. and Eleanor (Smith) B.; m. Patricia Joan Milner, Aug. 2, 1952; children: Mitchell Ronald, Valerie Patricia. BS, Purdue U., 1953; MBA, NYU, 1957. Security analyst E.W. Axe & Co., Tarrytown, N.Y., 1955-56, Stillman, Maynard, NYC, 1956-61; instl. salesman Clark Dodge & Co., NYC, 1961-67; gen. ptnr. Buttonwood Assocs., Jersey City, 1967-71; pres. Personal Investment Mgmt. Co., Mahwah, N.J., 1971-72; asst. v.p., account exec. E.F. Hutton N.Y.C., 1972-77; sr. v.p. Dean Witter Reynolds, Inc., 1979-97; ret., 1997. Contbr. articles to profl. jours. Rockland County Rep. committeeman, 1958-60. With U.S. Army, 1953-55. Mem. N.Y. Soc. Security Analysts Inst., Chartered Fin. Analysts, N.Y. Athletic Club, Assn. Investment Mgmt. and Rsch., Kappa Sigma, Scarsdale Golf Club. Home: 100 W 57th St New York NY 10019-3302 E-mail: dufferon@nyc.rr.

BROWN, RONALD C., hotel executive; LLB, Osgoode Hall Law Sch., Toronto, Can.; LLM, London Sch. Econs. Exec. v.p., CFO Can. Pacific Hotels and Resorts; exec. v.p. fin. and planning, chmn. Doubletree Hotels Corp., 1990; pres. Doubletree Corp., 1994; sr. v.p., CFO Starwood Lodging Trust, Phoenix, 1995-98; exec. v.p., CFO Starwood Hotels and Resorts Worldwide, Inc., White Plains, NY, 1998—2003, exec. v.p., strategy, 2003—. Pres. Sonoran Hotel Advisors. Office: Starwood Hotels and Resorts 1111 Westchester Ave White Plains NY 10604

BROWN, RONALD DELANO, endocrinologist; b. Grosse Pointe, Mich., Dec. 28, 1936; s. Carroll Bradley and Alice Ruth (Chapper) B.; m. Marylee Ethel Lucas, July 27, 1957; children: Linda Diane, Kent William, Mark Steven. BS with distinction, U. Mich., 1959, MD with distinction, 1963. Diplomate Am. Bd. Internal Medicine, subspecialty in endocrinology and metabolism; lic. physician Mich. Intern Detroit Gen. Hosp., 1963-64; asst. resident in medicine U. Calif. Med. Ctr., San Francisco, 1966-68; chief resident in medicine San Francisco Gen. Hosp., 1968-69; fellow in endocrinology Vanderbilt U., Nashville, 1969-71, instr. medicine, 1969-71, asst. prof. medicine, 1971-73; assoc. prof. medicine Baylor Coll. Medicine, Houston, 1973-74, Mayo Med. Sch., Rochester, Minn., 1975-80; prof. medicine Health Scis. Ctr., U. Okla., Oklahoma city, 1980-93; clin. staff St. Joseph's Mercy Hosp., Clintown Twp., Mich., 1993—. Dir. U. Okla. Hypertension Ctr., 1986-93; chief clin. hypertension Health Scis. Ctr., U. Okla., 1980-93; chief hypertension VA Hosp., Oklahoma City, 1980-86; dir. multidisciplinary hypertension rsch. tng. program (NIH), Mayo Clinic, Rochester, 1977-80; chief endocrinology Ben Taub Hosp., Houston, 1973-74, assoc. dir. clin. rsch. ctr., 1973-74; coord. Tenn. Mid-South Regional Hyper-Control Program, Vanderbilt U., 1971-73; lectr. in field. Editl. bd. Jour. Clin. Endocrinology and Metabolism, 1987-91; reviewer for Life Scis., Annals of Internal Medicine, Jour. Lab. Clin. Medicine, Am. Jour. Medicine, Endocrinology, Mayo Clinic Proceedings, Steroids; contbr. 58 articles to profl. jours. Capt. USAF, 1964-66. Fellow ACP. Am. Coll. Endocrinologists; mem. Am. Soc. Hypertension, Am. Assn. Clin. Endocrinologists, Phi Kappa Phi, Phi Lambda Upsilon, Alpha Omega Alpha. Office: Ronald D Brown MD 7237 1st St Marine City MI 48039-2801

BROWN, RONALD JOSEPH, religious studies educator; b. Johnstown, Pa., Mar. 3, 1949; s. Irvan A. and Helen Brown. BA, Gannon U., Erie, Pa., 1971; MA, Hebrew U. Jerusalem, 1976; D in Internat. Rels., U. Geneva, 1986; M in Theol. Studies, Harvard U., Boston, 1987. Prof. Godollo U., Budapest, Hungary, 1991—92; assoc. prof. Touro Coll., NYC, 1994—; prof. Unification Theol. Sem., NYC, 2002—. Adj. faculty Mercy Coll., NYC, 1993—97; guide AARP, NYC, 1995—; lic. tour guide NY Dept. Consumer Affairs, 1999—; presenter and lectr. in field. Docent NY Hist. Soc., 1992—; featured spkr. NY Coun. for the Humanities, 2003—. Named Tchr. of Yr., Touro Coll., 2002. Mem.: Assn. Isidro Fabela, Am. Hist. Assn., Am. Acad. Religion. Democrat. Roman Catholic. Avocations: travel, photography, research, languages. Home: 86-29 56 Ave 2F Elmhurst NY 11373

BROWN, RONALD MALCOLM, engineering corporation executive; b. Hot Springs, SD, Feb. 21, 1938; s. George Malcolm and Cleo Lavonne (Plumb) B.; m. Sharon Ida Brown, Nov. 14, 1964 (div. Apr. 1974); children: Michael, Troy, George, Curtis, Lisa, Brittney. AA, Southwestern Coll., 1970; BA, Chapman U., Orange, Calif., 1978. Commd. USN, 1956, advanced through grades to master chief, 1973, ret., 1978; engring. mgr. Beckman Inst., Fullerton, Calif., 1978-82; mfg. engring. br. mgr. Northrop Corp., Hawthorne, Calif., 1982-83; dir. of ops. Transco, Marina Del Rey, Calif., 1983-85; v.p. engring. and design Decor Concepts, Arcadia, Calif., 1985-87; design dir. Lockheed Aircraft Corp., Ontario, Calif., 1987-97; v.p. engring. and program mgmt. Ducommon Inc., Carson, Calif., 1997—2003; pres. Basic Cons., Inc., Brea, Calif., 2003—. Mem. Rep. Nat. Com. and Pres.'s Club. Mem. Soc. Mfg. Engrs., Inst. Indsl. Engrs., Nat. Trust for Hist. Preservation, Fleet Res. Assn., Am. Film Inst., Nat. Mgmt. Assn. Avocations: golf, running, racquetball. Office: 101 W Central Brea CA 92821

BROWN, RONALD OSBORNE, telecommunications and computer systems consultant; b. Winchester, Mass., Apr. 9, 1941; s. Herbert Walcott and Madeleine Louise (Osborne) B.; children: Melinda E., Jeffrey J. BS with distinction, U. Maine, 1963; MS, Tufts U., 1965; PhD, Queens U., Kingston, Ont., 1972. Mem. tech. staff Bell Telephone Labs., 1964; Mem. tech. staff RCA Corp., Burlington, Mass., 1965-66; rsch. assoc. Queen's U., Kingston, Ont., 1966-71; mem. sci. staff BNR, Ottawa, Ont., 1971-72; sr. systems engr. GTE Corp., Needham, Mass., 1973-83; mgr. Coopers & Lybrand, Boston, 1983-87, nat. dir, 1987-88; pres. R.O. Brown Cons., Caslo, Maine, 1988—; COO Locatum LLC, 2001—03, bd. dirs. Bd. dirs. Coop. Comms., PRG Group. Contbg. editor: Networking Mgmt. Mag., 1988—93. Mem. IEEE (life), Assn. Profl. Engrs. Ont., Tau Beta Pi, Phi Kappa Phi, Eta Kappa Nu. Home and Office: 864 Quaker Ridge Rd Casco ME 04015 Office Phone: 207-655-7685. Personal E-mail: brownro@aol.com.

BROWN, ROWLAND CHAUNCEY WIDRIG, library and information scientist, consultant; b. Detroit, Oct. 11, 1923; s. Rowland Chauncey and Rhea (Widrig) B.; m. Kathleen Heather Sayre, May 18, 1946; children: Stephanie Anne Kugelman, Geoffrey Rowland Sayre (dec.), Kathleen Heather. BA cum laude, Harvard U., 1947, JD, 1950; sr. in mgmt. Sloan Sch., MIT, 1969; D. Humane Letters (hon.), Ohio Dominican Coll., 1999; D. in cmty. devel., Franklin U., 2005. Bar: D.C. 1951. Counsel Econ. Sablzn. Agy., 1950-52; staff counsel SBA, 1954; counsel Machinery and Allied Products Inst., Washington, 1955-59; with Dorr Oliver, Stamford, Conn., 1959-70, pres., 1968-70; pres., chief exec. officer Buckeye Internat., Inc., Columbus, Ohio, 1970-80; chief exec. officer Online Computer Libr. Ctr., Columbus, 1980-89; with R. Brown & Assocs., Columbus. Adv. bd. tchg. and learning Ohio State U. sr. internat. cons. Coun. for Ethics Econs. inter-profl. panel on tech. and ethics; hon. trustee Columbus Cmty. Cable Access; bd. dirs., visitor's bd. Ohio Dominican Coll.; trustee Coun. for Pub. Deliberation, Civic Life Inst. Decorated Air medal (3), Purple Heart, Korean Republic citation. Mem. Am. Soc. Info. Sci., Am. Assn. for Higher Edn., N.Y. Harvard Club, Columbus Club, Torch Club, Columbus Rotary. Home: 2565 Charing Rd Apt 2 Columbus OH 43221-3668 E-mail: rcwbrow@columbus.rr.com.

BROWN, ROXANNE (JERENE ROXANNE BROWN), sales executive; b. LA, July 5, 1947; d. John Phillip and Margaret Leona (Dalrymple) Ortiz; m. Terry Lee Wood, May 7, 1966 (div. Sept. 1969); 1 child, Tiffany Christine Wood Suraco; m. Christopher Corey Brown, July 17, 1984 (dec. Sept. 1984); children: Jason Michael and John Charles (twins); m. Richard L. Gibbs, Apr. 18, 1996 (dec. Feb. 2000). Student, Casper Coll., 1977. Info. operator Gen. Telephone, Baldwin Park, Calif., 1965-67, long distance operator Santa Maria, Calif., 1967-69; office mgr. Monroe Calculator, Las Vegas, Nev., 1972-74; mgr. Exch. Club, Salt Lake City, 1977-81, Pouches Inc., Salt Lake City, 1981-82; asst. producer KSTU TV 20, Salt Lake City, 1982-84; sec. ADVO - Sys., Inc., Orange, Calif., 1984-85, terr. sales rep., 1985-88, major account exec. Garden Grove, Calif., 1988-95; v.p. JRB & Assocs., Long Beach, Calif., 1995—; ptnr. LA Choprods, Torrance, Calif., 2005—; office mgr. West Coast Lending Corp., Lake Forest, Calif., 2006—. Cons. Rice - Urmana Advt., Huntington Beach, Calif., 1989-91. Actor: (TV series) Andy Richter Controls the Universe, 2001—02. Bd. dirs. ACLU, Salt Lake City, 1977; precinct worker Voter Registrar, Huntington Beach, 1988, Long Beach, Calif., 1990; bd. dirs., sec. Alamitos Bay Beach Peninsula Preservation Group, 1996-98. Mem.: ACLU, SAG, Platform Speakers Assn., Alamitos Bay Garden Club (v.p., ways and means com. 1996—98). Avocations: sculpting, photography, sailing. Home: 77 Ximeno Ave Long Beach CA 90803-3056 Personal E-mail: rocknsand@yahoo.com.

BROWN, RUTH GEISLER, retired electronics engineer; b. Beaver Falls, Pa., Mar. 17, 1924; d. Carl Charles and Emily (Pletz) Geisler; m. Stuart Fife Brown, Apr. 13, 1944. Student, Johns Hopkins U., Balt., 1960—70. Svc. rep. Bell. Tel. of Pa., Pitts., 1942—43; draftsman to group engr. Martin Marietta Co., Middle River, Md., 1944—49, 1950—63; design draftsman Bendix Radio, Balt., 1949—50; engring. staff assoc. missile programs and microelectronics Johns Hopkins U./Applied Physics Lab., Laurel, Md., 1963—75, sr. engring. staff, supr. hybrid ops., 1975—79, divsn. staff, 1979—81, electronic design supr., 1981—83, engring. design supr., 1983—90; ret., 1990. Mem.: NAFE, Internat. Electronic Packaging Soc., Internat. Soc. Hybrid Microelectronics. Republican. Home: 12628 W Parkwood Dr Sun City West AZ 85375-4626

BROWN, SAMUEL PAUL, biologist; b. Bolton, England, Oct. 10, 1972; BA, U. Cambridge, England, 1994; MSc, U. Oxford, England, 1996; PhD, U. Cambridge, England, 2000. Fellow U. Montpellier II, France, 2001—03, U. Tex., Austin, 2004—. Contbr. over 30 articles to profl. jours. Fellow, Marie Curie Found., 2001—03, CNRS, 2001—, Human Frontier Sci. Program, 2004—. Office: Univ Texas Austin 1 Univ Sta C0930 Austin TX 78712 Office Phone: 512-297-4013. Business E-Mail: sam.brown@cantab.net.

BROWN, SANDRA, writer; b. Waco, Tex., Mar. 12, 1948; m. Michael Brown; children: Ryan, Rachel. Mgr. Merle Norman Cosmetics Studios, Tyler, Tex., 1971-73; weather reporter KLTV-TV, Tyler, 1972-75, WFAA-TV, Dallas, 1976-79; model Dallas Apparel Mart, 1976-87. Author: (romance novels) Breakfast in Bead, 1983, Heaven's Price, 1983, Relentless Desire, 1983, Tempest in Eden, 1983, Temptation's Kiss, 1983, Tomorrow's Promise, 1983, In a Class by Itself, 1984, Send No Flowers, 1984, Bittersweet Rain, 1984, Sunset Embrace, 1984, Words of Silk, 1984, Riley in the Morning, 1985, Thursday's Child, 1985, Another Dawn, 1985, 22 Indigo Place, 1986, The Rana Look, 1986, Demon Rumm, 1987, Fanta C, 1987, Sunny Chandler's Return, 1987, Adam's Fall, 1988, Hawk's O'Toole's Hostage, 1988, Slow Heat in Heaven, 1988, Tidings of Great Joy, 1988, Long Time Coming, 1989, Temperatures Rising, 1989, Best Kept Secrets, 1989, A Whole New Light, 1989, Another Dawn, 1991, Breath of Scandal, 1991, Mirror Image, 1991, French Silk, 1992, The Silken Web, 1992, Honor Bound, 1992, A Secret Splendor, 1992, Shadows of Yesterday (also published as Relentless Desire), 1992, Three Complete Novels, 1992, Charade, 1994, The Witness, 1995, "TEXAS!" series: Texas! Lucky, 1990, Texas! Sage, 1991, Texas! Chase, 1991, Texas! Trilogy, 1992, (as Laura Jordan) Hidden Fires, 1982, The Silken Web, 1982, (as Rachel Ryan) Love Beyond Reason, 1981, Love's Encore, 1981, Eloquent Silence, 1982, A Treasure Worth Seeking, 1982, Prime Time, 1983, (as Erin St. Claire) Not Even for Love, 1982, A Kiss Remembered, 1983, A Secret Splendor, 1983, Seduction By Design, 1983, Led Astray, 1985, A Sweet Anger, 1985, Tiger Prince, 1985, Above and Beyond, 1986, Honor Bound, 1986, The Devil's Own, 1987, Two Alone, 1987, Thrill of Victory, 1989, Exclusive, 1996, Fat Tuesday, 1997, Unspeakable, 1998, The Alibi, 1999, Stand Off, 2000, The Switch, 2000, The Crush, 2002 (NY Times Bestseller), Hello Darkness, 2003, White Hot, 2004 (Publishers Weekly Bestseller, 2005), Chill Factor, 2005, Ricochet, 2005. Recipient Am. Bus. Women's Assn's Disting. Circle of Success award, B'nai B'rith's Disting. Literary Achievement award, A. C. Greene award, Romance Writers Am. Lifetime Achievement award. Mem.: Literacy Partners, Novelists, Inc, Internat. Assn. Crime Writers, Mystery Writers Am., Author's Guild.

BROWN, SANFORD DONALD, lawyer; b. Neptune, NJ, May 16, 1952; s. Richard B. and Janet (Flint) B.; m. Joan Miller, Sept. 5, 1978; children: Jennifer, Sanford Flint, Edward. BA, Brown U., Providence, 1974; JD, Seton Hall U., Newark, 1978. Bar: NJ 1978, US Dist. Ct. NJ 1978, US Ct. Appeals (3d cir.) 1998, US Supreme Ct. 1999. Law clk. to Hon. Patrick J. McGann, Freehold, NJ, 1978-79; assoc. Dawes & Youssouf, Freehold, 1979-81; ptnr. Dawes & Brown, Freehold, 1981-86, Cerrato, O'Connor, Dawes, Collins et al, Freehold, 1986-89, Cerrato, Dawes, Collins et al, Freehold, 1989—2002; mem. Brown & Connelly, LLC, 2002—. Counsel Manalapan-Englishtown Regional Bd. Edn., NJ, 1979-85, 87—; gen. counsel Monmouth Vocat. Bd. Edn., Freehold, NJ, 1979—, Allenhurst Bd. Edn., 1990-98, Interlaken Bd. Adjustment Planning Bd., 1990-, Interlaken Bd. Edn., 1990-2004, Manasquan River Regional Sewer Authority, Howell, 1979-91, Pioneer Farm Credit, 1990-2003, United Meth. Homes NJ, 1992—, Freehold Borough BOE, 2003-, Neptune City BOE, 2003-07, Deal BOE, 2003-, Ocean Twp. Planning, 2005-; fee arbitrator NJ Supreme Ct., 1995-99, panel chair, 1998-99. Chancellor, So. NJ Ann. Conf., United Meth. Ch., 1995-2000, co-chancellor Greater NJ Ann. Conf., 2000—; coach Ocean Twp. Recreation League, NJ, 1986-97, Ocean Twp. Little League, 1992-95; chmn. bd. trustees United Meth. Ch., 1986-91, mem., 2002-2005; chmn. county advancement com. Boy Scouts Am., 1989-92, atty., county exec. bd., 1992—, gen. counsel, 1995—2005, dist. chmn., 1996-99, at. rep., 1997-99, 2001—, v.p. 2000-05, pres. 2005-07, exec. v.p. 2007-. Recipient Monmouth Legal Sec. assn. Employer of the Year award, 1993, Monmouth Coun. Boy Scouts Disting. Adult Eagle Scout award, 1997, Silver Beaver award, 1998, Dist. Award of Merit, 1999. Mem.: NJ Sch. Bd. Attys. Assn. (regional v.p. 1991, trustee 2007), NJ Bar Assn., Monmouth Bar Assn. (chmn. com. 2004—05, com. chair 2005), Rotary (exec. bd. 2004—, v.p. 2006, pres.-elect 2007), Wemrock Profl. Condo Assn. (pres. 1988—96, v.p. 1996—2001), Brown U. Alumni Assn. (chpt. pres. 1986—89, 1995—2007), Nat. Eagle Scout Assn. (life). Methodist. Avocation: swimming. Office: Brown & Connelly LLC 1127 Hwy 35 Ocean Twp Ocean NJ 07712 Office Phone: 732-517-0720. Business E-Mail: sbrown@brownconnelly.law.com.

BROWN, SETH M., otolaryngologist; b. NY, Mar. 6, 1974; s. David Lewis and Barbara Ellen Brown; m. Betsy Kaye Brown, Oct. 29, 2000; children: Ella Kaye, Tessa Pearl. BA magna cum laude, Union Coll., Schenectady, NY, 1996; MBA, Union U., Schenectady, NY, 1997; MD, U. Conn., Farmington, 2001. Surg. intern Albert Einstein Coll. Medicine, NY, NY, 2001—02, resident, 2002—06; instr. Weill med. coll. Cornell U., NY, 2006—, fellow rhinology, endoscopic sinus and skull base surgery Weill med. coll., 2006—07. Recipient Calvin G. Schmidt award, Union Coll., 1995, Chief Resident of the Yr. award, Albert Einstein Coll. Medicine, 2006, Leo M. Davidoff Soc. Tchg. award, 2006. Mem.: North Am. Skull Base Soc., Am. Acad. Otolaryngology Head and Neck Surgery, Am. Rhinologic Soc. Achievements include research in real-time image-guided endoscopic sinus surgery; 3D endoscopic skull base surgery; endoscopic pituitary and skull base surgery. Home Phone: 914-771-7402; Office Phone: 212-452-3005.

BROWN, SEYMOUR R., retired lawyer; b. Cleve., Oct. 24, 1924; s. Leonard and Ella (Rubinstein) B.; m. Madeline Kusevich, July 8, 1956; children: Frederic M., Thomas R., Barbara L. N. Rybicki. BA, Case-Western Res. U., 1948; JD, Cleve. State U., 1953. Bar: Ohio 1953. Prin. Seymour R. Brown & Assocs., Cleve.; ptnr. Brown-McCallister Real Estate, Residential & Comml. Constrn., Melbourne, Fla., 1973-81. Spl. counsel to atty. gen. State of Ohio, 1963-70. Editor, pub.: Gt. Lakes Architecture, 1955-59. Chmn. CSC, University Heights, Ohio, 1978-82, 84-86, mem., 1976-2003; mem. exec. com. Cuyahoga County Rep. Orgn., 1966-2003; pres. Nat. Permanent Endowment Fund, Inc., 1988-92. With AUS, 1943-45. Decorated Purple Heart, Bronze Star; named to Ohio Mil. Hall of Fame, 2003. Mem. Ohio Bar Assn., Cleve. Bar Assn., Am. Arbitration Assn. (comml. arbitration panel), Zeta Beta Tau (nat. dir., nat. pres. 1978-80), Masons. Home: 1344 Continental Ave Melbourne FL 32940-6702 Office Phone: 321-751-7124. Business E-Mail: srb2@peoplepc.com.

BROWN, SHEBA ANN, elementary school educator; b. Miss., 1951; married; 1 child, Joshua. BS in Elem. Edn., U. So. Miss., 1973. Tchr. 4th grade Biloxi (Miss.) Pub. Schs., 1973-74; tchr. 3d grade Ferncrest Acad., New Orleans, 1974-75, Cifton Ganus Pvt. Sch., New Orleans, 1975-78; tchr. 4th grade Putnam County Schs., Palatka, Fla., 1986-87; tchr. multi-age primary class Biloxi Pub. Schs., 1987—. Condr. workshops; presenter in field. Recipient Beverly Briscoe award Biloxi Schs., 1990, Enhancement award City of Biloxi, 1995, Leo Seal Tchr. Recognition award, 1999; named Miss. Tchr. of Yr., 1995, Women at the Top Coast Mag., 1996. Mem. Internat. Reading Assn., Nat. Coun. Tchrs. English, Jeff Davis PTA (treas.), Delta Kappa Gamma. Home: 135 Travia Ave Biloxi MS 39531-5328

BROWN, SHERROD CAMPBELL, senator, former congressman, former state official; b. Mansfield, Ohio, Nov. 9, 1952; s. Charles G. and Emily (Campbell) Brown; m. Connie Schultz; children: Emily, Elizabeth; 2 stepchildren. BA in Russian Studies, Yale U., 1974; MEd, Ohio State U., 1979, MPA, 1981. Mem. Ohio State Ho. Reps., Columbus, 1975-82; sec. state State of Ohio, Columbus, 1983-91; mem. US Congress from 13th Ohio dist., 1993—2007, mem. energy and commerce com., ranking minority mem. health subcommittee, mem. internat. rels. com., founding mem. India Caucus, founding mem. Taiwan Caucus; US Senator from Ohio, 2007—; mem. agrl., nutrition, & forestry com., banking, housing & urban affairs com., health, edn., labor, & pensions com., vets affairs com. Instr. polit. sci. Ohio State U., Mansfield, 1979-80, faculty assoc. Mershon Ctr., 1991-93. Author: Congress from the Inside: Observations from the Majority and the Minority, 1999, Myths of Free Trade, 2004. Recipient Eagle Scout Am. 1966, Friend of Edn. award, 1978, Disting. Pub. Health Legislator of Yr. award, APHA, 2002. Mem. Nat. Assn. Secs. State Democrat. Lutheran. Office: US Senate 2332 Rayburn House Office Bldg Washington DC 20515*

BROWN, SHIRLEY MARGARET KERN (PEGGY BROWN), interior designer; b. Ellensburg, Wash., Mar. 30, 1948; d. Philip Brooke and Shirley (Dickson) Kern; m. Ellery Kliess Brown, Jr., Aug. 7, 1970; children; Heather Nicole Coco, Rebecca Cherise, Andrea Shirley Serene, Ellery Philip. BA in Interior Design, Wash. State U., Pullman, 1973. Apprentice then interior designer L.S. Higgins & Assocs., Bellevue, Wash., 1969-72; interior designer ColorsPlus Interiors, Inc., Bellevue, Wash., 1972, Strawns Office Furniture & Interiors, Inc., Boise, 1973-75, Empire Furniture, Inc., Tulsa; owner Inside-Out Design Co., Ltd., Boise, 1973-82; interior designer Architekton, Inc., Tulsa, 1984-86, Johnson Brand Design Group, Inc., 1986-87, Ellery Brown & Assocs. Arch., 1987—, Seattle Design Ctr.-Visions & Studio Programs, Scottsdale, Ariz., 1998—, Mehagian's Fine Furniture, Scottsdale, Am. Soc. Interior Designers Showhouse, 2000, Ladlows Fine Furniture, 2003—05; with Dept. Design Robb & Stucky Interiors, Scottsdale, 2006—. Lectr. in field. Featured designer Ariz. Lifestyle mag., 2002, 06, AZ. Mag., 07; contbr. articles to profl. jours. Pres. PTA, co-chair capital bond prin. sel. com., enrollment rev. com., 1989-95; bd. dirs. Paradise Valley Young Life; designer West Valley Child Crises Ctr., Inc.; contributing designer West Valley Child Crisis Ctr. Recipient Seattle Design Ctr. Marjorie Siegel award, 1997, Phoenix Home and Garden Mag. ASID Showhouse, 2000. Mem.: AAUW, Interior Design Soc. (profl.) (Gold award 2007, Bronze award 2007), Nat. Soc. Interior Designers, Am. Soc. Interior Designers (dir. chpt. 1976—77, presdl. citation Oreg. chpt. 1977, chmn. Boise subchpt. 1977—79, sec. 1980—81, chmn. Wash. chpt. step workshop chmn. 1993—97, NCIDQ chmn. 1993—97, Wash. state presdl. citation 1995, presdl. citation Oreg. chpt. 1995—96, Wash. state presdl. citation 1996, 1997, bd. dirs. North Ariz. chpt. 2003—, pres.-elect 2006—, chmn. awards banquet 2006, Showhouse Mehagian's Designer award Phoenix Home and Garden Mag. 2000, bd. dirs. Ariz. chpt. 2003—), Jr. League Phoenix, Idaho Hist. Co., Wash. State U. Alumni Assn., Jr. League Seattle, Zonta, Alpha Gamma Delta. Republican. Presbyterian. Office: Robb & Stucky Interiors 15440 N Scottsdale Rd Scottsdale AZ 85254 Office Phone: 480-321-8108. Personal E-mail: az_browns@hotmail.com, ekbrownjr@cox.net. Business E-Mail: shirley.kernbrown@robbstucky.net.

BROWN, SHONA L., information technology executive; b. 1966; BS in computer systems engring., Carleton U.; MA in econ. and philosophy, Oxford U.; PhD in indsl. engring. and engring. mgmt., post-doctorate in indsl. engring. and engring. mgmt., Stanford U. Prof. dept. indsl. engring. and grad. sch. bus. Stanford U.; former ptnr. Global Strategy Practice McKinsey and Co.; sr. v.p. bus. ops. Google Inc., 2003—. Author: Competing on the Edge: Strategy as Structured Chaos. Office: Google Inc 1600 Amphitheatre Pky Mountain View CA 94043 Office Phone: 650-623-4000. Office Fax: 650-618-1499.

BROWN, SIDNEY DEVERE, history professor; b. Douglass, Kans., Jan. 29, 1925; s. Leonard Reeves and Jessie Maybelle (Berger) B.; m. Ruth Esther Murray, Jan. 24, 1948; children: Margaret, Nancy, Russell, Frederick. AB, Southwestern Coll., Winfield, Kans., 1947; MA, U. Wis., 1950, PhD, 1952. Cert. in Japanese, U.S. Naval Oriental Langs. Sch. Tchr. history Protection (Kans.) High Sch., 1947-48; prof. history Okla. State U., Stillwater, 1952-71, U. Okla., Norman, 1971-95, dir. Asian studies, 1971-95, prof. emeritus history, 1995—; regents prof. history U. Sci. and Arts, Chickaska, Okla., 1996-2001. Vis. prof. U. Kans., Lawrence, summer 1958, U. Wis., Madison, summer 1960, U. Colo., Boulder, summer 1964, U. Nebr., Lincoln, summer 1965, U. Ill., Champaign, 1968-69, U. Mich., Ann Arbor, 2001-02. Author, translator: The Diary of Kido Takayoshi, 1986 (Japan Culture Translation prize 1986); contbr. chpts. to books. Dir. Okla. Symposium on East Asia, Norman, 1975-95; curator Okla. Mus. Natural History, Norman, 1974-95; Dem. precinct chmn., Cleveland County, Okla., 1984-86; adv. bd. Okla. Jazz Hall of Fame, Tulsa, 1989-90. Lt. (j.g.) USNR, 1943-46. Decorated Order of Sacred Treasure with gold rays with neck ribbon (Japan); Japan Found. fellow, 1977-78, 84-85; Ford Found. fellow, 1956-57; inductee Okla. Higher Edn. Hall of Fame, 2000. Mem. AAUP (state sec.-treas. 1982-84), Assn. for Asian Studies (exec. com. 1983-84), Midwest Conf. on Asian Affairs, (pres. 1959-60), S.W. Conf. on Asian Studies (pres. 1977-78), Am. Hist. Assn. (exec. sec. conf. on Asian history 1970-75), Okla. Assn. Prof. Historians, Japan-Am. Soc. Okla. (life, pres. 1983), Asia Soc. Okla. (adv. bd. 1988—). Methodist. Avocations: jazz music, college basketball, foreign travel, political biographies. Home: 700 Nancy Lynn Ter Norman OK 73069-4222 Personal E-mail: sdbrown4@juno.com. Business E-Mail: sidnay.v.brown-1@ou.edu.

BROWN, STEPHEN D., lawyer; b. Boston, 1949; BA, Williams Coll., 1971; JD, Villanova U., 1976. Bar: Mass. 1976, Pa. 1978. Law clk. to Hon. Daniel H. Huyett, 3d U.S. Dist. Ct. (ea. dist.) Pa., 1976-78; ptnr. Dechert LLP, Phila. Editor-in-chief Villanova U. Law Rev., 1976. Office: Dechert LLP 2929 Arch St Philadelphia PA 19104 Office Phone: 215-994-2240. E-mail: stephen.brown@dechert.com.

BROWN, STEPHEN F., health facility administrator; BS, U. Ala. Joined Am. Med. Internat., 1976; CIO Am. Med. Internat. (now Tenet Healthcare Corp.), 1990—95; sr. exec. v.p., CIO Tenet Healthcare Corp., Dallas, 1995—99, exec. v.p., CIO, 1999—. Active The Wharton Sch., Info. Week mag., CEO mag., The Healthcare Collaboration Group, Sheldon I. Dorenfest and Assocs. Consulting; mem. adv. bd. Nat. Health Founds. Ctr. for Health Info. Tech. Contbg. author: Financial Information Systems Manual, 1992. Office: Tenet Healthcare Corp 13737 Noel Rd Ste 100 Dallas TX 75240*

BROWN, STEPHEN IRA, philosophy professor; b. Bklyn., July 14, 1938; s. Milton Frank and Ruth (Mittman) B.; m. Eileen Thaler, June 12, 1960; children: Jordan David, Sharon Jean. AB, Columbia Coll., 1960; MA in Teaching (Sloan fellow 1960-61), Harvard U., 1961, Ed.D., 1967. Instr. math. and edn. Simmons Coll., Boston, 1962-65; asst. prof. edn. Harvard U., 1966-72; vis. prof. Hebrew U., Jerusalem, 1970-71; asso. prof. Syracuse (N.Y.) U., 1972-73; mem. faculty SUNY, Buffalo, 1973-98, prof. math. edn., 1979-98, prof. philosophy of edn., 1982-98, prof. emeritus, 1998—. Vis. prof. U. Ga., Athens, 1979-80; vis. scholar Harvard U., Cambridge, Mass., 1993-94; participant ethics workshops Coll. Jewish Studies, Buffalo, 1974-76. Author: Some Prime Comparisions, 1978, Student Generations, 1987, Posing Mathematically, 1996, Reconstructing School Mathematics: Problems with Problems and the Real World, 2001, Essays in Honor of Retirement: Educational Transformations: The Influences of Stephen I. Brown, 2006; co-author: The Art of Problem Posing, 1983, rev. edit., 2005; co-author: Mathematics, Pedagogy and Secondary Teacher Education, 1996; co-editor: Progresssive Education: A Movement and Its Professional Journal, 1988, Problem Posing: Reflections and Applications, 1993; editor: Creative Problem Solving, 1989; mem. rev. bd. Ednl. Theory, 1983-87; mem. editl. bd. Math. Tchr., 1977-80, For Learning of Math., 1980-97; mem. adv. bd. Humanistic Math. Network Jour., 1995-2003; contbr. articles to profl. jours. Mem. adv. council Inst. Jewish Life, 1973-75. Grantee Dewey Found., 1979-80, NSF, 1983-86, 90-97; John Dewey sr. fellow, 1986-87. Fellow Philosophy Edn. Soc.; mem. John Dewey Soc. (bd. dirs. 1976-78), Math. Assn. Am., Nat. Council Tchrs. Math., Phi Beta Kappa, Phi Delta Kappa. Home: 4721 Chandlers Forde Sarasota FL 34235 *I attribute a large part of my success to lack of clarity and specificity with regard to goals, to ambiguity and vagueness with regard to principles, to a sense of humor which provides distance between a taken for granted reality and my personal world, and to a general disinclination to analyze what accounts for my success.*

BROWN, STEPHEN LEE, retired insurance company executive; b. Providence, July 6, 1937; AB, Middlebury Coll., 1958. CLU. With John Hancock Fin. Svcs. Inc. and John Hancock Life Ins. Co., Boston, 1958-2001, pres., chief ops. officer, vice chmn. bd., 1987-92, chmn., CEO, 1992-2000, chmn., 2000-2001. Trustee emeritus Wang Ctr. for Performing Arts; bd. dirs. Alfred P. Sloan Found., Palm Beach (Fla.) Civic Assn. 1st lt. US Army, 1956—59. Fellow: Soc. Actuaries; mem.: Comml. Club Boston. Office: John Hancock Fin Svcs Inc John Hancock Place PO Box 111 Boston MA 02117-0111

BROWN, STEPHEN PAT, artist; b. Greeley, Colo., Aug. 26, 1950; s. Carl Adrian Brown and Mildred Louise (Van Beber) Ballard; m. Gretchen Anna Treitz, June 12, 1982; children: Rushton Jeremiah Treitz. Student, Inst. of European Studies, Vienna, Austria, 1969; postgrad., Skowhegan Sch. Painting and Sculp, Maine, 1972; BFA, Colo. State U., 1972; MFA, Bklyn. Coll., 1978. Asst. prof. Hartford U., 1988—. Guest artist La. State U., 1979; guest artist, lectr. Cortland (N.Y.) U., 1982; bd. dirs. painting Nat. Dance Inst. Mural, N.Y.C., 1984-85; insr. Pratt Inst., N.Y.; instr. aesthetic edn. program Cooper-Union, N.Y.C., 1984; artist in residence Parsons Sch. of Design, N.Y.C., instr., 1987; artist in residence Arts Ptnrs., N.Y.C. Bd. of Edn., 1985-87; guest lectr. Pa. State U., State College, 1988—; instr. Sch. of Art Chautauqua (N.Y.) Inst., 1988; guest lectr. Grad. Art Dept. Bklyn. Coll., N.Y., 1989, Am. U., 1989. One-man shows include Bowery Gallery, N.Y.C, 1978, Alex Rosenberg Gallery, N.Y.C., 1981, 82, Cortland U., 1982, Artists Choice Mus., N.Y.C., 1983, 84, N.Y. Studio Sch., 1984, One Penn Pla., N.Y.C., 1985, Sherry French Gallery, N.Y.C., 1986, Nat. Acad. of Design, N.Y.C, 1986, Allan Stone Gallery, N.Y.C., 1987, Prince St. Gallery, Rockefeller Gallery, SUNY at Fredonia, 1988; group show Allan Stone Gallery, 1989; collections appear at Hosta Museum, New Bntain Museum of American Art, The Speed Museum, The Albany Museum, Mattatuck Museum. Bd. Govs. Painting scholar Art Students League, N.Y.C., 1973, Charles B. Shaw Painting scholar Bklyn. Coll., 1978; Yaddo fellow Saratoga Spring, N.Y., 1981, fellow Millay Colony for the Arts, 1981; recipient, Academy Award in Art, American Academy of Arts and Letters, 1994, Academy Award for Painting, American Academy of Arts and Letters; elected, National Academy of Design, 1999 Democrat. Mem. Pilgram Covenant Ch. Office: 47 Barnard Rd Granville MA 01034-9514 also: Hartford U 200 Bloomfield Ave Hartford CT 06117-1545

BROWN, STEPHEN PHILLIP, judge; b. Birmingham, Ala., June 29, 1941; s. William P. and Milledge (Anderson) B.; m. Dorothy Louise Ogden, Aug. 6, 1967; children: Katherine, Phillip, Stephen. Student, Auburn U., 1963; LLB, Walter F. George Sch. Law, 1967. Bar: Ga. 1967, U.S. Dist. Ct. (mid. dist.) Ga. 1967, U.S. Ct. Appeals (11th cir.) Ga. 1967, U.S. Supreme Ct. 1967. Atty., regional counsel IRS, NYC, 1967-69; ptnr. Brown, Katz, Flatau & Hasty, Macon, Ga., 1969-95; judge Superior Ct. Macon Jud. Cir., 1996—. Rep. Ga. House of Reps., Atlanta, 1971-74. Democrat. Methodist. Avocations: organic gardening, woodworking. Home: 2434 Wesleyan Dr N Macon GA 31210-6043 Office: Superior Ct Bibb City 310 Bibb County Courthouse Macon GA 31201 Home Phone: 478-477-3807; Office Phone: 478-621-6328. E-mail: pbrown@co.bibb.ga.us, fpbrown@cox.net.

BROWN, STEPHEN S., telecommunications industry executive; B in Bus. Mktg., Tex. Tech. U.; M in Mgmt. Info. Sys., Naval Post Grad. Sch. Dir. sys. integration GE Aerospace; dir. enterprise integration and telecom. Pillsbury; CIO Imation; v.p., CIO Micron Electronics; sr. v.p., CIO Carlson Cos., Minnetonka, Minn., 2000—. With USMC. Office Phone: 763-212-1330.

BROWN, STEVEN BRIEN, radiologist; b. Ft. Collins, Colo., Jan. 18, 1952; s. Allen Jenkins and Shirley Irene (O'Brien) B.; m. Susan Jane DiTomaso, Sept. 10, 1983; children: Allison Grace, Laura Anne. BS, Colo. State U., Fort Collins, 1974; MD, U. Calif., San Diego, 1978. Diplomate Am. Bd. Radiology with cert. of added qualifications in Neuroradiology. Surg. intern U. Wash., Seattle, 1978-79; resident in radiology Stanford U., Calif., 1979-82, chief resident Calif., 1981—82; fellow in interventional and neuro-radiology Wilford Hall, USAF Med Ctr., San Antonio, 1982-83, staff radiologist, 1983-86, Luth. Med. Ctr., Wheat Ridge, Colo., 1986—, chief angiography and interventional radiology, 1987-96, v.p. pres. med. staff, 2002—03, pres. med. staff, 2004—07; credentials com. Exempla Luth. Med. Ctr., Wheat Ridge, 2007—. Pres. Luth. Med. Ctr. Joint Venture, 1992-95; bd. mgrs. Primera HealthCare LLC, 1995-97; pres. HealthCare Select Inc., 1995—; chmn. dept. med. imaging Exempla Luth. Med. Ctr., 1994-97, 2007—. Contbr. articles to profl. jours. Mem. Rep. Nat. Com., Washington, 1984—, Nat. Rep. Senatorial Com., 1985—, Rep. Presdl. Task Force, 1986—; grad. Rep. Leadership Program, 2000; bd. dirs. The Health Care Initiative. Maj. USAF, 1982-86. Fellow: Am. Coll. Radiology (exec. com. intersoc. commn. 1996—2000, counselor 2000—06, managed care com. 2001—04, state legis. com. 2003—06), Radiol. Soc. N.Am.; mem.: Colo. Preferred Physicians Orgn. (bd. dirs. 1987—, treas. 1998—2007, v.p. 2007—), Soc. Cardiovasc. and Interventional Radiology, Western Neuroradiol. Soc. (sr.), Am. Soc. Neuroradiology (sr.), Rocky Mt. Radiol. Soc. (pres. 1994—95), Colo. Radiol. Soc. (pres. 1995—96), World Wildlife Orgn., Colo. Angio Club. Republican. Roman Catholic. Avocations: skiing, sailing, hiking, gardening. Office: Luth Med Ctr 8300 W 38th Ave Wheat Ridge CO 80033-6005

BROWN, STEVEN HARRY, engineering executive; b. Phila., Sept. 16, 1948; ABS, Temple U., 1970, BS, 1971; MA, West Chester U., Pa., 1974. Diplomate Am. Acad. Health Physics (panel examiner 1988-91, appeals com. 1999-2001). Health physicist Temple U., Phila., 1969-71; tchr. phys. sci. Phila. Sch. Dist., 1971-76; mgr. radiation protection Westinghouse Electric Corp., Lakewood, Colo., 1976-80; mgr. western regional office Radiation Mgmt. Corp., Phila., 1980-82; prin. safety analysis engr. Rockwell Internat., Golden, Colo., 1982-83, program mgr. waste isolation pilot project, 1983-85; sr. project mgr. West Valley Demonstration Project Dames and Moore, West Valley, NY, 1985-87; dir. Radiol. Svcs., 1987-92; v.p. govt. svcs. Internat. Tech. Corp., Englewood, Colo., 1992—2006; v.p. radiol. ops. Shaw Group, Centennial, Colo., 2003—07; pres. SHB, Inc., Centennial, 2007—. U.S. rep. Internat. Conf. on Radiation Hazards in Mining, Beijing, 1986. Mem. Nat. Health Physics Soc. (pres. Rocky Mountain chpt. 1982-83), Am. Nuc. Soc. Office Phone: 303-941-1506. Personal E-mail: shb12@msn.com.

BROWN, STEVEN RAY, language professional; b. Hayward, Calif., July 5, 1952; s. Curtis Ray and Clara Belle Brown. BA, U. Calif., 1974; MA, San Diego State U., 1979; PhD, U. Pitts., 1996. Cert. tchr. adult edn., Calif. Tchr. Castro Valley (Calif.) Sch. Dist., 1979-81; instr. Tohoku Fgn. Lang. Sch., Sendai, Japan, 1981-82, Tohoku Gakuin U., Sendai, Japan, 1984-86, James English Sch., Sendai, Japan, 1982-84, head tchr., 1984-86; instr. Japan program U. Pitts. English Lang. Inst., Tokyo, 1986-87, asst. dir., 1987-88, dir., 1988-91; instr. MA TESOL program Columbia U. Tchrs. Coll., Tokyo, 1988-91, summer 1996; staff adminstr. English Lang. Inst. U. Pitts., 1991-95; instr. English Youngstown State U., Ohio, 1995—96, asst. prof., 1996—2000, assoc. prof., 2000—04, prof., 2004—. Series editor: Journeys, 1997-99; co-author: English Firsthand, 1998, 2d edit., 2004, Active Listening, 3 vols. 1994-96, 2d edit., 2006; co-author: Topics in Language and Culture for Teachers, 2004, Understanding Language Structure, Interaction and Variation, 2005, Practical English Teaching: Listening, 2006. Mem. Am. Assn. for Applied Linguistics, Nat. Coun. Tchrs. English, Tchrs. English to Speakers of Other Langs. Democrat. Unitarian Universalist. Avocations: walking, reading, travel. Home: 228 Upland Ave Youngstown OH 44504-1849 Office: Youngstown State U English Dept Youngstown OH 44555-0001 Home Phone: 330-744-8455; Office Phone: 330-941-1654. Business E-Mail: srbrown02@ysu.edu.

BROWN, STEVEN SPENCER, lawyer; b. Manhattan, Kans., Feb. 26, 1948; s. Gerald James and Buelah Marie (Spencer) B. BBA, U. Mo., 1970, JD, 1973. Bar: Mo. 1973, U.S. Tax Ct. 1974, Ill. 1977, U.S. Dist. (no. dist.) Ill. 1979, U.S. Ct. Appeals (7th cir.) 1980, U.S. Ct. Claims 1986, Calif. 1989, U.S. Ct. Appeals (11th cir.) 1989, U.S. Ct. Appeals (5th cir.) 2000., U.S. Supreme Ct., 2003. Trial atty. IRS Regional Counsel, Chgo., 1973-78; sr. trial atty. IRS Dist. Counsel, Chgo., 1978-79; assoc. Silets & Martin Ltd., Chgo., 1979-85, ptnr., 1985-92, Martin, Brown & Sullivan Ltd., Chgo., 1992—. Adj. prof. John Marshall, Chgo., 1985—. Republican. Presbyterian. Avocations: golf, tennis. Home: 1030 N State St Apt 10H Chicago IL 60610-5485 Office: Martin Brown & Sullivan Ltd 10th Fl 321 S Plymouth Ct Chicago IL 60604-3912 Office Phone: 312-360-5000. Business E-Mail: brown@mbslaw.com.

BROWN, STUART F., writer; BA, Bard Coll. Tech. journalism fellow Univ. Mich., 1989—90; writer, editor Popular Sci. mag., 1983—95; contbr. Fortune mag., 1995—97, sr. writer, 1997—. Recipient James T. Grady - James H. Stack Award for Interpreting Chemistry for the Public, Am. Chem. Soc., 2007. Office: Sr Writer Fortune Mag Time Warner Publ 1271 Ave of Americas New York NY 10020

BROWN, SUSAN LOUISE, philosopher, educator; b. Quantico, Va., Jan. 1, 1955; d. John Bomar and Margaret G. Brown; 1 child, Codi E. AA, St. Petersburg Jr. Coll., Fla., 1995; BA, U. West Fla., Pensacola, 1998, MA, 2000, ABD, 2006. Assoc. prof. Kaplan U., Boca Raton, Fla., 2002—; instr. philosophy U. West Fla., Pensacola, 2001—. Vol. Santa Rosa Sch. Dist., Milton, Fla., 1995—2001; chair Title I Parent Adv. Bd., Santa Rosa County, Fla., 2001—02, mem., 2003—04. Fellow, Coll. Profl. Studies, U. West Fla., 2001. Office: Univ West Florida 11000 University Parkway Pensacola FL 32514 Home Phone: 850-626-7865; Office Phone: 850-474-2671. Business E-Mail: sbrown1@uwf.edu.

BROWN, TERRENCE CHARLES, art association executive, researcher, lecturer; b. NYC, Oct. 2, 1949; s. Robert Carl and Ruth Carothers Johnson; m. Catherine Simms Citarella, Apr. 24, 1982; children: Peter Huston, Christopher Simms. BA, Vanderbilt U., Nashville, 1971. Curator Soc. Illustrators Mus. Am. Illustration, NYC, 1972-83; dir. Soc. Illustrators, NYC, 1983—. Instr. Sch. Visual Arts, NYC, 1995—2000. Contbr.: 200 Years of American Illustration, 1976, The Illustrator in America: 1880-1980, 1984 Served to capt. USAR, 1971-79 Office: Soc of Illustrators 128 E 63rd St New York NY 10021-7303 Business E-Mail: dir@societyillustrators.org.

BROWN, THADDEUS B., professional sports team executive; m. Janice Brown; children: Kennedy, Addison, Nicolette, Chloe. Grad., Colgate U. Founder, pres. Streetball Ptnrs. Internat.; v.p. corp. devel. Houston Rockets/Clutch City Sports & Entertainment, 2001, sr. v.p. sales, mktg. and broadcasting, 2004—06, CEO, 2006—. Office: Houston Rockets Toyota Ctr 110 Polk St Houston TX 77002*

BROWN, THEODORE LAWRENCE, chemistry professor; b. Green Bay, Wis., Oct. 15, 1928; s. Lawrence A. and Martha E. (Kedinger) B.; m. Audrey Catherine Brockman, Jan. 6, 1951; children: Mary Margaret, Karen Anne, Jennifer Gerarda, Philip Matthew (dec.), Andrew Lawrence. BS in Chemistry, Ill. Inst. Tech., 1950; PhD, Mich. State U., 1956. Mem. faculty U. Ill., Urbana, 1956—, prof. chemistry, 1965-93, prof. chemistry emeritus, 1993—, vice chancellor for rsch., dean Grad. Coll., 1980-86, dir. Beckman Inst. for Advanced Sci. and Tech., 1987-93. Vis. scientist Internat. Meteorol. Inst., Stockholm, 1972; Boomer lectr. U. Alta., Edmonton, Can., 1975; Firth vis. prof. U. Sheffield, Eng., 1977; mem. bd. govs. Argonne Nat. Lab., 1982-88, Mercy Hosp., Urbana, 1985-89, Chem. Abstracts Svc., 1991-96, Arnold and Mabel Beckman Found., 1994—, Am. Chem. Soc. Pub., 1996-2001; adv. bd. Spatial Learning and Intelligence Ctr., 2006-. Author: (with R.S. Drago) Experiments in General Chemistry, 3d edit., 1970, General Chemistry, 2d edit., 1968, Energy and the Environment, 1971, (with H.E. LeMay and B.E. Bursten) Chemistry: The Central Science, 1977, 10th edit., 2006, Making Truth: Metaphor in Science, 2003; assoc. editor Inorganic Chemistry, 1969-78; contbr. articles to profl. publs. Mem. Govt.-Univ.-Industry Roundtable Coun., 1989-94; bd. dirs. Champaign County Opportunities Industrialization Ctr., 1970-79, chmn. bd. dirs., 1975-78. With USN, 1950-53. Sloan rsch. fellow, 1962-66, NSF sr. postdoctoral fellow, 1964-65, Guggenheim fellow, 1979. Fellow AAAS, Am. Acad. Arts and Scis.; mem. Am. Chem. Soc. (award in inorganic chemistry 1972, award for disting. svc. in advancement of inorganic chemistry 1993), Philosophy of Sci. Assn., Cognitive Sci. Soc., Soc. for Social Studies of Sci., Sigma Xi, Alpha Chi Sigma. Avocations: films, literature, running. Home: Apt 203 10751 Crooked River Rd Bonita Springs FL 34135-1727 E-mail: tlbrown1@earthlink.net.

BROWN, THOMAS ANDREW, retired aircraft/weaponry manufacturing executive; b. Iowa City, Iowa, July 24, 1932; s. Charles Valentine and Mary Clementine (Proestler) B.; m. Louise Grafton Baggott, Aug. 31, 1957; children: James, Mary, Catherine. BA, State U. Iowa, 1953; BA with honors, Oxford U., 1955; MA, Harvard U., 1958, PhD, 1962. With Rand Corp., 1962-74, assoc. head info. sci., 1966-74, dir. strategic studies Washington, 1983-85; asst. v.p. Sci. Applications, Inc., Los Angeles, 1974-77; dep. asst. sec. of def. program analysis and evaluation Dept. Def., Washington, 1977-81; ptnr. Booz, Allen & Hamilton, Bethesda, Md., 1981-83; mgr. strategic studies Northrop Corp., 1985-94. Served with USAF, 1955-57. Recipient Disting. Pub. Svc. medal Dept. Def., 1981; Rhodes scholar, 1953-55; NSF fellow, 1957-61 Home: 21912 234th Ave SE Maple Valley WA 98038-8423 Personal E-mail: LittleTom@aol.com.

BROWN, THOMAS CARTMEL, JR., lawyer; b. Marion, Va., June 20, 1945; m. Sally Guy Lynch; children: Sarah Preston, Taylor Cardwell. AB, Davidson Coll., 1967; JD, U. Va., 1970. Bar: Va 1971. Assoc. Boothe, Prichard & Dudley, Alexandria, Va., 1971-76, ptnr., 1976-86, McGuire-Woods LLP and predecessors, McLean, Va., 1986—. Lawyers com. Nat. Ctr. State Cts., 1993—2003, Warren E. Burger Soc.; sec., gen counsel Potomac KnowledgeWay, 1995—99; chmn. bd. dir. No. Va. Health Found., 2006—. Mem. Va. Child-Day Coun., Richmond, 1987—91, No. Va. Roundtable, 1995—2001; pres. Alexandria Libr. Co., 2002—04; bd. visitors Davidson Coll., 2006—; mem. exec. bd. Nat. Capital Area Coun. Boy Scouts Am., 2002—07. Fellow: Va. Law Found. (bd. dirs. 1997—2005, pres. 2003), Am. Bar Found.; mem.: Va. State Bar (chmn. bus. law sect. 1987—88, chmn. health law sect. 2002—03), Va. Bar Assn. (pres. 1992), Omicron Delta Kappa. Office: McGuireWoods LLP 1750 Tysons Blvd Ste 1800 Mc Lean VA 22102-4231 Home Phone: 703-370-1963; Office Phone: 703-712-5393. Business E-Mail: tbrown@mcguirewoods.com.

BROWN, THOMAS HUNTINGTON, neuroscientist; b. NYC, June 13, 1945; s. Thomas Huntington and Elvira R. (Crandall) B. BA in Molecular Biology, Calif. State U.-San Jose, 1972, MA in Psychology, 1972; PhD in Neurosci., Stanford U., 1977. Postdoctoral fellow Stanford U., Calif., 1977-79; asst. rsch. scientist Beckman Rsch. Inst., Duarte, Calif., 1979-82, assoc. rsch. scientist, 1982-86, rsch. scientist, 1986-88; prof. dept. psychology Yale U., New Haven, 1988—. Mem. joint appt. dept. cellular molecular physiology Yale U., 1992—, dir. Ctr. for Theoretical and Applied Neurosci., 1992-96; adviser NIH, NIMH study sects., 1982-83, 89-94, 94-98, mem. NIH-IFCN5 study sect., IFCN1 study sect., 1998—. Mem. editl. bd. Behavioral Neurosci. Jour., 1983-89, Network: Computation in Neural Systems, 1990-92, Synapse, 1990-2002, Hippocampus, 1990-93, Psychobiology, 1997-2000; contbr. articles to sci. jours., 1976—. Recipient Epilepsy Found. Am. award, 1980, McKnight Found. Scholar's award, 1981, McKnight Found. Career Devel. award 1984, Muscular Dystrophy Found. fellow, 1977, NIH fellow, 1978; grantee in field, 1980—. Mem. AAAS, Am. Psychol. Assn., Am. Psychol. Soc., Am. Physiol. Soc., N.Y. Acad. Sci., Conn. Acad. Sci. Engring., Soc. Neurosci., Internat. Neurol. Network Soc. Office: Yale U Dept Psychology PO Box 208205 New Haven CT 06520-8205 Office Phone: 203-432-7008.

BROWN, THOMAS PHILIP, III, lawyer; b. Washington, Dec. 18, 1931; s. Raymond T. and Beatrice (Cullen) B.; m. Alicia A. Sexton, July 28, 1955; children: Thomas, Mark, Alicia, Maria, Beatrice. BS, Georgetown U., 1953, LL.B., 1956. Bar: D.C., Md. Pvt. practice law, 1958—. Author monograph and articles on legal malpractice. Pres. Cath. Youth Orgn. of Washington, 1972. Served to 1st lt. USMCR, 1955-58. Mem. Bar Assn. D.C. (pres. 1986, bd. dirs. 1987), Barristers Club, Columbia Country Club. Home: 5610 Wisconsin Ave Apt 208 Chevy Chase MD 20815 Office: Unit 2 5247 Wisconsin Ave NW Washington DC 20015

BROWN, TOD DAVID, bishop; b. San Francisco, Nov. 15, 1936; s. George Wilson and Edna Anne (Dunn) B. BA, St. John's Coll., 1958; STB, Gregorian U., Rome, 1960; MA in Theology, U. San Francisco, 1970, MAT in Edn., 1976. Dir. edn. Diocese of Monterey, Calif., 1980—82, chancellor Calif., 1982—89, vicar gen., chancellor Calif., 1983—89; pastor St. Francis Xavier, Seaside, Calif., 1977—82; bishop Roman Catholic Diocese of Boise, Idaho, 1989—98; appointed and installed bishop Roman Cath. Diocese of Orange, Calif., 1998. Past mem. 3rd millenium com. U.S. Conf. Cath. Bishops, past chmn. com. on ecumenical and interreligious affairs, past mem. com. on mission, pastoral practices, past chair laity com.; chmn. subcom. interreligious affairs U.S. Conf. Cath. Bishop; mem. Episcopal bd. govs. N.Am. Coll. Named Papal Chaplain Pope Paul VI, 1975. Mem.: The Sovereign Mil. Hospitaller Order of St. John of Jerusalem of Rhodes and of Malta, The Equestrian Order of the Holy Sepulchre of Jerusalem, Canon Law Soc. Am. (past mem. Bishop's com. on liturgy, econ. concerns of the Holy See, Ea. Chs.), Cath. Biblical Assn., Cath. Theol. Soc. Am. Roman Catholic. Avocations: films, travel, reading, exercise. Office: Diocese of Orange Marywood Ctr 2811 E Villa Real Dr Orange CA 92867-1932 Office Phone: 714-282-3000.

BROWN, TOM CHRISTIAN, newspaper publishing executive; b. Nampa, Idaho, July 24, 1947; s. Frank Thomas and Esther (Ulrich) B.; m. Carol Burroughs, May 31, 1969; children: Brian J., Maree C. BA in History with honors, Oreg. State U., 1969; MS in Journalism, Northwestern U., 1970. Reporter Corvallis (Oreg.) Gazette-Times, 1969; reporter, asst. city editor Billings (Mont.) Gazette, 1970-74; ops. mgr. Mont. Std., Butte, 1974-76; gen. mgr. Missoulian, Missoula, Mont., 1976-80, pub., 1980-86, Concord (N.H.) Monitor, 1987—2005; CEO, pres. Newspaper of New. Eng., 2005—. Bd. dir. Newspapers of New Eng., Concord; pres. Page Buying Coop, Phila., 1994-96, chmn. bd., 1996-2001; bd. dir. East

Oregonian Pub. Co. Bd. dir. United Way, Concord, 1989-96, 1998-2000, Capital Ctr. for Arts, 1998—2004, Missoula YMCA, 1984-86; pres. Missoula Symphony, 1985, Mont. Press Assn., Helena, 1985; v.p. N.H. BBB, Concord, 1995-99; 2d v.p. Pacific N.W. Newspaper Assn., Portland, 1986; mem. Concord Task Force on Racism. Mem. Newspaper Assn. Am., New England Newspaper Assn. (com. chair 1994-2004, bd. dir. 2004—), Merrimack C. of C. (bd. dir. 1993-98, 99—), Missoula C. of C. (bd. dir. 1977-84, v.p. 1983), Rotary (bd. dir. Missoula chpt. 1976-79), Sigma Delta Chi. Avocations: running marathons, skiing, hiking, climbing, reading. Home: 15 Dwinell Dr Concord NH 03301-2542

BROWN, TOMMIE FLORENCE, social work educator; b. Rome, Ga., June 25, 1934; d. Phillip and Mary Louise (Murden) B. BA, Dillard U., 1957; MSW, Washington U., St. Louis, 1964; DSW, Columbia U., 1984. Social svc. supr. Tenn. Dept. Pub. Welfare, Chattanooga, 1964-67, dir. tng., 1967-71; asst. prof. sociology U. Tenn., Chattanooga, 1971-73, head social work dept., 1973-82, UC Found. assoc. prof. social work, 1982—; mem. Tenn. Ho. of Reps., Nashville, 1992—, mem. commerce, conservation and environ. coms., 1992-94, mem. edn. com., 1995—, sec. fin. ways and means com., 1995—. Named Nat. Social Worker of Yr., NASW, 1971. Democrat. Baptist. Home: PO Box 3258 Chattanooga TN 37404-0258 Office: Tenn Gen Assembly Legislative Plz Ste 36 Nashville TN 37243-0128

BROWN, TRISHA, dancer; b. Aberdeen, Wash., Nov. 25, 1936; BA in Dance, Mills Coll., Calif.; D (hon.), Mills Coll., 1997; PhD in Fine Arts (hon.), Oberlin Coll. Founder, artistic dir. Trisha Brown Dance Co., NYC, 1970—; founding mem. Judson Dance Theater; choreographer Grand Union Improvisation Group, 1970-76. Lectr. Mills. Coll., Calif., Reed Coll., Oreg., NYU, NYC, Goucher Coll., Md., Carnegie Mellon U., Pa.; condr. workshops and seminars throughout world. Choreographer Untitled, 1961, Trillium, 1961, Lightfall, 1963, Untitled Duet, 1963, Part of a Tango, 1963, Target, 1964, Rulegame Five, 1964, Motor, 1965, Homemade, 1965, Inside, 1966, Skunk Cabbage, 1967, Saltgrass and Waders, 1967, Medicine Dance, 1967, Snapshots, 1968, Ballet, 1968, Falling Duet, 1968, Sky Map, 1969, Dance with Duck's Head, 1968, Yellow Belly, 1969, Leaning Duets, 1970, The Stream, 1970, Man Walking Down the Side of a Building, 1970, Accumulation 4 1/2, 1971, Walking on the Wall, 1971, Leaning Duets II, 1971, Falling Duet II, 1971, Rummage Sale and the Floor of the Forest, 1971, Planes, 1968, Roof Piece, 1971, Primary Accumulation, 1972, Accumulating Pieces, 1973, Group Accumulation, 1973, Roof and Fire Piece, 1973, Spanish Dance, 1973, Structured Pieces, 1973, Figure 8, 1974, Drift, 1974, Spiral, 1974, Pamplona Stones, 1974, Locus, 1975, Line Up, 1976, Water Motor and Splang, 1978, Glacial Decoy, 1979, Opal Loop, 1980, Son of Gone Fishin', 1981, Set and Reset, 1983 (N.Y. Dance and Performance award, 1984), Lateral Pass, 1985 (N.Y. Dance and Performance award, 1986), Carmen, 1986, Newark, 1987, Astral Convertible, 1989, For M.G.: The Movie, 1991, Astral Converted, 1991, Another Story as in Falling, 1993, If you couldn't see me, 1994, Foray Forêt, 1990, You Can See Us, 1995, M.O., 1995, Twelve Ton Rose, 1996; featured (TV series) M.O., Sta. WNET-TV, N.Y.C., Dance in America, Sta. WGBH-TV, Boston, Dancing on the Edge, Making Dances; exhibitions include Venice Biennale, Toulon Mus., exhibited in group shows at Musée de Marseille, Numerals: Math. Concepts in Contemporary Art, The Pluralist Decade, New Notes for New Dance, Art and Dance: Images From the Modern Dialogue. Mem. Nat. Coun. on Arts, 1994. Decorated chevalier Ordre des Arts et des Lettres; recipient Creative Arts award, Brandeis U., 1982, Dance Mag. award, 1987, Samuel H. Scripps Am. Dance Festival award, 1994, Prix de la Danse la Société des Auteurs et Compositeurs Dramatiques award, 1996, Nat. medal of Art, 2003; fellow, Guggenheim Found., 1975, 1984, NEA Creative Artists Svc. Program, 1977, 1981—84; grantee, NEA, N.Y. State Coun. on Arts; MacArthur fellow, 1991. Mem.: Am. Acad. Arts and Letters (Nat. medal of Art 2003). Office: Trisha Brown Co care Rebecca Davis 625 W 55th St New York NY 10019-3560

BROWN, TROY ANDERSON, JR., retired electric power industry executive; b. Tampa, Fla., July 7, 1934; s. Troy Anderson and Valerie Aldona (Mohler) B.; m. Jean Thompson, Aug. 22, 1962; children: Troy Anderson, III, George Albert, Douglas Alan. AB, Harvard U., 1956; JD, U. N.C., 1959. Bar: Fla. bar 1959. With Raybro Electric Supplies Inc., Tampa, 1960-99, exec. v.p., 1964-74, pres., 1974-99. Bd. dirs. Bay Cities Bank; dir. Exchange Nat. Bank, 1978—83, 1st Fla. Bank, 1983—90, 1st Fla. Holding, 1989—91. Mem. exec. com. Tampa Com. 100, 1975, U. South Fla. Found., 1974-75; chmn. bd. fellows U. Tampa, 1978; bd. dirs., vice chmn. Tampa Mus., 1977-79; bd. dirs. Tampa YMCA, 1977-79, Tampa Marine Inst., 1976-77. With USAFR, 1959. Mem.: Tampa Mchts. Assn. (bd. dirs. 1980), Pres. Round Table Tampa (pres. 1971), Exch. Club Tampa (pres. 1970), Greater Tampa C. of C. (gov. 1968—74), Nat. Assn. Elec. Distbrs. (bd. dirs. 1989—91), Harvard Club N.Y.C., Harvard Club of Fla. (pres. 1984), Tampa Yacht and Country Club (bd. dirs. 1982—83), Ye Mystic Krewe Gasparilla, Jesters, Shriners. Episcopalian. Home: 1013 S Skokie St Tampa FL 33629-5237

BROWN, VALERIE ANNE, psychotherapist, social worker, educator; b. Elizabeth, NJ, Feb. 28, 1951; d. William John and Adelaide Elizabeth (Krasa) B. BA summa cum laude (fellow), C.W. Post Coll., 1972; MSW (Silberman scholar), Hunter Coll., NYC, 1975; PhD, Am. Internat. U., 1996. Diplomate Am. Bd. Examiners, Am. Bd. Clin. Social Work, Nat. Assn. Social Work; cert. addictions specialist; cert. master hypnotherapist; cert. psychophilogic integration therapist. Social work intern Greenwich House Counseling Ctr., NYC, 1973-74, Metro Cons. Ctr., NYC, 1974-75; sr. psychiat. social worker, co-adminstr. Essex County Guidance Ctr., East Orange, NJ, 1975-80; pvt. practice psychiat. social work, psychotherapy, 1979—. Sr. psychiat. social worker John E. Runnells Hosp., Berkeley Heights, NJ, 1980-86; dir. social work Northfield Manor, West Orange, NJ, 1987; clin. coord. Project Portals East Orange Gen. Hosp., 1987-88; asst. dir. ARS/Century House Riverview Med. Ctr., Red Bank, NJ, 1988-93; sr. clin. case mgmt. specialist Prudential Ins. Co., Woodbridge, NJ, 1993; clin. dir. Greenhouse-KMC, Lakewood, NJ, 1994-2000, Shoreline-KBH, Toms River, NJ, 1996-2000; tech. advisor Nat. Comm. Network, 1988—; mental health clinician III UMDNJ-UBHC, Edison, NJ, 2000—; instr. Brookdale Coll., 1991—; co-founder Women's Growth Ctr., Cedar Grove, NJ, 1979; counselor Passaic Drug Clinic, 1978-80; field instr. Fairleigh Dickinson U., Madison, NJ, 1981-86, Brookdale Coll., 1989-92; field supr. Union Coll., Cranford, NJ, 1986; instr. Sch. Social Work, NYU, NYC, 1980-83, asst. prof., 1983-85; evaluator Intoxicated Driver Resource Ctr., Essex County, NJ, 1987-88. Alt. Monmouth County profl. adv. bd.; founding mem. Nat. Campaign Tolerance of So. Poverty Law Project, 2004. Recipient Congl. Order of Merit, Nat. Rep. Congl. Com., 2005; named Dist. Alumnae Mother Seton Regional H.S., Clark, N.J., 1997. Mem. NASW (Whittman Lifetime Achievement nominee 1997-98), Psi Chi, Pi Gamma Mu, Sigma Tau Delta. Avocations: reading, swimming, travel. Office: 20 Ellsworth Ct Red Bank NJ 07701-5403

BROWN, WALTER FRANCIS, JR., lawyer; AB, U. Calif., Berkeley, 1982; JD, U. Notre Dame, 1985. Bar: Ariz. 1986, Calif. 1987, US Ct. Appeals (9th cir.), US Dist. Ct. (no., ea. and ctrl. dists. Calif.), US Dist. Ct. (ea. dist. Wis.), US Dist. Ct. (dist. Ariz.). Asst. US atty. (ctrl. dist. Calif.) US Dept. Justice, LA, 1989—94; with Thelen Reid & Priest; ptnr. Gray Cary, San Francisco, Orrick, Herrington & Sutcliffe LLP, 2003—. Named one of Top 10 Trial Lawyers in Am., Nat. Law Jour., 2006, Am.'s Leading Lawyers, Chambers USA, 2006. Mem.: ABA, State Bar Calif., State Bar Ariz. Office: Orrick Herrington & Sutcliffe LLP The Orrick Bldg 405 Howard St San Francisco CA 94105 Office Phone: 415-773-5995. Office Fax: 415-773-5759. E-mail: wbrown@orrick.com.*

BROWN, WARREN, chef; BA in Hist., Brown U., 1993; M in Pub. Health, George Washington U., 1998, JD, 1998. Bar: NY 1998. Health educator, Providence, 1993, LA; litig. lawyer office of Insp. Gen., US Dept. Health and Human Svc., 1998—2000; founder, exec. pastry chef CakeLove bakery, Washington, 2002—; founder Love Cafe, Washington, 2003—. Host Sugar Rush, Food Network, apperanaces on The Oprah Winfrey Show, The Today Show, Dateline, Fox News Sunday, featured in GQ mag., 2005, Inc Mag. 26 Entrepreneurs We Love, 2005, People mag., Reader's Digest, Southern Living, Black Enterprise, The Am. Lawyer, Kiplinger's Personal Fin., The Washington Post, The Washington Times, Washington mag., The Plain Dealer, Brown Alumni Monthly, George Washington U. alumni mag. Office: CakeLove 1506 U St NW Washington DC 20009 Office Phone: 866-708-7100. Office Fax: 202-588-7100.

BROWN, WENDY WEINSTOCK, nephrologist, educator; b. NYC, Dec. 9, 1944; d. Irving and Pearl (Levack) Weinstock; m. Barry David Brown, May 2, 1971 (div. Sept. 1995); children: Jennifer Faye, Joshua Reuben, Julie Aviva, Rachel Ann. BA, U. Mass., 1966; MD, Med. Coll. of Pa., 1970; MPH, St. Louis U., 1999. Diplomate Am. Bd. Internal Medicine. Intern U. Ill. Affiliated Hosps., Chgo., 1970-71; resident in internal medicine The Med. Coll. Wis. Affiliated Hosps., Milw., 1971-74; gen. practitioner Vogelweh (W. Germany) Health Clinics, 1975-76; fellow in nephrology Med. Coll. of Wis. Milw. County Med. Complex, Milw., 1976-78; staff physician St. Louis VA Med Ctr., 1978—2003, acting chief, hemodialysis sect., 1983-85, chief dialysis/renal sect., 1985-90, dir. clin. nephrology, 1990—2003; staff physician St. Louis U. Hosps., 1978—2003, St. Louis City Hosp., 1982-85, St Mary's Health Ctr., St. Louis, 1994—2003; chief of staff VA Tenn. Valley Healthcare Sys., Nashville, 2003—06, Jesse Brown VA Med. Ctr., 2006—. Assoc. prof. internal medicine St. Louis U. Health Sci. Ctr., 1985—98, prof. internal medicine, 1998—2003; prof. medicine Meharry Med. Coll. Vanderbult Univ., 2003—. Reviewer Clin. Nephrology, Nephrology, Dialysis and Transplantation, Am. Jour. Nephrology, Am. Jour. Kidney Disease, Jour Am. Geriatric Soc., Jour. Am. Soc. Nephrology, Geriatric Nephrology and Urology, Kidney Internat.; med. editor NKF Family Focus; mem. editl. bd. Clin. Nephrology, Geriatric Nephrology, Internat. Urology and Nephrology, Advances in Renal Replacement Therapy; editor-in-chief: Advances in Chronic Kidney Disease, 2004-; contbr. articles to profl. jours. Mem. adv. coun. Mo. Kidney Program, 1985-91, chmn., 1988-89; numerous positions Nat. Kidney Found., 1984—, nat. chmn., 1995-97; bd. dirs. United Way, St. Louis, 1994-2003, Nat. Kidney Found. Ea. Mo. and Metro East, Inc., 1980-94; bd. dirs. Combined Health Appeal Greater St. Louis, Inc., 1988, pres., 1989-92; bd. dirs. Combined Health Appeal Am., 1991-98, sec., 1992-96, vice chmn., 1996-98. Named Casual Corner Career Woman of Yr., 1986, Combine Health Appeal of Am. Vol. of Yr., 1991, Olympic Torch Bearer, 1996, St. Louis Health Profl. of Yr., 1997; recipient Upjohn Achievement award, Med. Coll. Wis. Affiliated Hosps., 1972, Cert. of Leadership, St. Louis YWCA, 1989, Chmn.'s award, Nat. Kidney Found. of Ea. Mo. and Metro East, 1990, award of excellence, 2002, Chmn.'s award, Nat. Kidney Found., Washington, 1990, Martin Wagner award, Nat. Kidney Found., 1999, award of excellence, Nat. Kidney Found. Ea. Mo. and Metro East, 2002. Fellow ACP, AHA; mem. Am. Soc. Nephrology, Internat. Soc. Nephrology, Coun. on Kidney in Cardiovascular Disease, Am. Heart Assn., St. Louis Soc. Am. Med. Women's Assn., St. Louis Internists (v.p. 1983-84, pres. 1984-85), Women in Nephrology (pres. 2000-02), Internat. Soc. for Peritoneal Dialysis, Am. Geriatrics Soc., Soc. for Exec. Leadership in Acad. Medicine (bd. dirs., program chair 1999—), Alpha Omega Alpha. Jewish. Home: 1728 Glen Echo Rd Nashville TN 37215-2910 Office: VA Tenn Valley Healthcare Sys 1310 24th Ave S Nashville TN 37212-2637 Home Phone: 615-279-0388; Office Phone: 615-327-5330. Business E-Mail: wendy.brown@va.gov.

BROWN, WESLEY ERNEST, federal judge; b. Hutchinson, Kans., June 22, 1907; s. Morrison H. H. and Julia (Wesley) B.; m. Mary A. Miller, Nov. 30, 1934 (dec.); children: Wesley Miller, Loy B. Wiley; m. Thadene N. Moore (dec.) Student, Kans. U., 1925-28; LLB, Kansas City Law Sch., 1933. Bar: Kans. 1933, Mo. 1933. Pvt. practice, Hutchinson, 1933-58; county atty. Reno County, Kans., 1935-39; referee in bankruptcy U.S. Dist. Ct. Kans., 1958-62, judge, 1962-79, sr. judge, 1979—. Apptd. Temporary Emergency Ct. of Appeals of U.S., 1980-93; dir. Nat. Assn. Referees in Bankruptcy, 1959-62; mem. bankruptcy divsn. Jud. Conf., 1963-70; mem. Jud. Conf., U.S., 1976-79. With USN, 1944-46. Mem. ABA, Kans. Bar Assn. (exec. council 1950-62, pres. 1964-65), Reno County Bar Assn. (pres. 1947), Wichita Bar Assn., S.W. Bar Kan., Delta Theta Phi. Office: US Dist Ct 414 US Courthouse 401 N Market St Wichita KS 67202-2089

BROWN, WILLIAM A., lawyer, mediator, arbitrator; b. Memphis, Nov. 6, 1957; s. Winn D. Sr. and Annie Ruth (Hurt) B.; m. Mary Lee Walker, Dec. 27, 1980. BBA, U. Miss., 1978, JD, 1981. Bar: Miss. 1981, U.S. Dist. Ct. (no. and so. dists.) Miss. 1981, U.S. Dist. Ct. (we. dist.) Tenn. 1987. Ptnr., pres. Walker, Brown & Brown, P.A., Hernando, Miss., 1981—. Bd. dir. The Baddour Ctr. Pres. DeSoto Literacy Coun., Hernando, 1988, Am. Cancer Soc., Hernando, 1988, DeSoto County Econ. Devel. Coun., 1995—96; active Leadership 2000, 1990—91; dir. Hist. DeSoto Found., 2005—; chmn. Ch. Coun. Hernando United Meth. Ch., 2002—04, chmn. bd. dirs., 2006; vice-chmn. Hernando Preservation Commn., 1997—2000, chmn., 2001—06; chmn. design com. Main St. Project, 2001—06; allocations chmn. United Way of Mid-South DeSoto County; dir. DeSoto Health and Wellness Ctr., Baddour Meml. Ctr. James O. Eastland scholar, 1978-81; Paul Harris fellow Rotary Internat., 1997. Mem. Miss. Bar Assn. (bd. dirs. young lawyers sect. 1988-89, Bd. Bar Commrs. 2002-05), DeSoto County Bar Assn. (v.p. 1988-89, pres. 1996-98), Rotary (pres. Hernando chpt. 1989-90), Boy Scouts Am., N.W. Miss. (membership chmn. 1990, activities chmn. 1991). Methodist. Avocations: gardening, design and construction projects. Home and Office: Walker Brown & Brown PA PO Box 276 Hernando MS 38632-0276 Office Phone: 662-429-5277.

BROWN, W(ILLIAM) DOUGLAS, lawyer; b. 1946; BA, Lafayette College, 1968; JD, U. Va., 1971. Atty.-legal dept. Air Product & Chemicals Inc., Allentown, Pa., 1975—80; gen. counsel, sec. Catalytic Inc. (subsidiary of Air Products), 1980—83; v.p., sec. Stearns-Catalytic World Corp. (subsidiary of Air Products), 1983—87, Am. Ref-Fuel (jointly owned by Air Products and Browning-Ferris Industry), 1987—96, sr. v.p., sec., 1996—97; v.p., gen. counsel, sec. Air Products & Chemicals Inc., 1990—99, v.p. adminstrn. Gases and Equipment Group, 1997—99, v.p., gen. counsel, sec., 1999—. Office: Air Products & Chemicals Inc 7201 Hamilton Blvd Allentown PA 18195-1501 Office Phone: 610-481-7350.

BROWN, WILLIAM ERNEST, dentist; b. Benton Harbor, Mich., Aug. 29, 1922; s. William Ernest and Gertrude (Eliot) B.; m. T.N. McDonald, Oct. 21, 1944 (dec. July 1969); children: Judith M. Brown Smith, Wendy E. Brown Kerschbaum, Terrence N.; m. E.M. Tyree, Sept. 11, 1970 (dec. Jan. 2000). DDS, U. Mich., 1945, MS, 1947. Practice pediatric dentistry, Ann Arbor, Mich., 1947-62; part-time tchr. U. Mich., 1947-62; from asst. prof. to prof. dentistry, assoc. dir. W.K. Kellogg Found. Inst. Grad. and Postgrad. Dentistry, 1962-69; dean Coll. Dentistry, U. Okla., Oklahoma City, 1969-87; acting provost Health Scis. Ctr. U. Okla., 1973-75. Author: Oral Health, Dentistry and the American Public, 1974, Dental Education in the United States, 1976. Mem. City of Ann Arbor Human Rels. Commn., 1960-66, chmn., 1965-66; chmn. bd. dirs. ARC, Oklahoma County chpt., 1991-93; pres. Cmty. Coun. Ctrl. Okla., 1998-2000; bd. dirs. United Way of Metro Oklahoma City, 1998-2000; mem. Hall of Honor com. U. Mich. Dental Sch., 2003—. Recipient Gies Editorial award, 1965, 67 Mem. ADA, Am. Assn. Dental Schs. (pres. 1984-85), Am. Acad. Pediatric Dentistry, Am. Soc. Dentistry for Children. Home: 1666 Coburn Dr Ann Arbor MI 48108-9626 E-mail: driffil22@aol.com.

BROWN, WILLIAM HARRIS, editor; b. Winston-Salem, NC, Apr. 19, 1962; s. Reuben William and Ella Brown; m. Catherine Welborn Brown, May 19, 1989; children: Cora Elizabeth, Jessica Pearl. BA, High Point Coll., NC, 1984; MA, U. N.C., Greensboro, 1987. Ref. archivist N.C. State Archives, Raleigh, 1991—97, gov.'s records archivist, 1997—2001; editor Hist. Pubs. Sect., Raleigh, 2001—. Author: Encyclopedia of the American Civil War, 2000, Encyclopedia of the American Revolution, 2006, Encyclopedia of War and American Society, 2006. Mem.: So. Hist. Assn., Soc. Mil. History. Baptist. Avocations: reading, writing, hiking. Home: 1542 Indian Camp Rd Clayton NC 27520 Office: Historical Publications Section 4672 Mail Service Ctr Raleigh NC 27699

BROWN, WILLIAM HILL, III, lawyer; b. Phila., Jan. 19, 1928; s. William H. Jr. and Ethel L. (Washington) B.; m. Sonya Morgan Brown, Aug. 29, 1952 (div. 1975); 1 child, Michele D.; m. D. June Hairston, July 29, 1975; 1 child, Jeanne-Marie. BS, Temple U., 1952; JD, U. Pa., 1955. Bar: Pa. 1955, D.C. 1972, U.S. Ct. Appeals (3d cir.) 1959, U.S. Ct. Appeals (4th cir.) 1978, U.S. Dist. Ct. (ea. dist.) Pa. 1957, U.S. Ct. Appeals (10th cir.) 1986, U.S. Ct. Appeals (5th cir.) 1988, U.S. Dist. Ct. D.C. 1994, U.S. Ct. Appeals (D.C. cir.) 1994, U.S. Ct. Appeals (fed. cir.) 1997, U.S. Ct. Appeals (8th cir.) 2002. Assoc. Norris, Schmidt, Phila., 1955-62; ptnr. Norris, Brown, Hall, Phila., 1962-68, Schnader, Harrison, Segal & Lewis, Phila., 1974—, mem. exec. com., 1983-87; chief of frauds Dist. Atty.'s Office, 1968, dep. dist. atty., 1968; commr. EEOC, Washington, 1968-69, chmn., 1969-73. Lectr. S.W. Legal Found., Practising Law Inst., Nat. Inst. Trial Advocacy; bd. dirs. United Parcel Svc., Inc., 1983-2003, mem. audit com., 1988-2003, chair, 1996-2003, Lawyers Com. Civil Rights Under Law; chmn. Phila. Spl. Investigation Commn. MOVE; pres. Nat. Black Child Devel., Inc., 1986-90; bd. dirs. Cmty. Legal Svcs., 1986—; mem. exec. com. Schnader, Harrison, Segal & Lewis, 1983-87; bd. dirs., mem. exec. com. Lawyers Com. Civil Rights Under law, 1977—, co-chair, 1991-93; mem. Commn. on Comml. Operation of U.S. Customs Svc., 1994-98. Contbr. articles to profl. jours. Bd. dirs. Mid. States Colls. and Secondary Schs., 1983-89, Main Line Acad., 1982—, Nat. Sr. Citizens Law Ctr., 1988-94; mem. nat. bd. govs. Am. Heart Assn., 1994-96, mem. audit com., mem. pub. affairs policy com., bd. dirs., 1986-94, mem. audit com., mem. pub. affairs policy com.; mem. adv. com. on appellate ct. rules Supreme Ct. Pa., 1989-95. With USAF, 1946-48. Recipient award of merit Fed. Bar Assn., Columbus, 1971, NAACP award, 1971, Dr. Edward S. Cooper award Am. Heart Assn., 1995, Whitney M. Young Jr. Leadership award Urban League, 1996, Whitney North Seymor award Lawyers Com. for Civil Rights Under Law, 1996, Champions for Social Justice and Equality award Black Law Students Assn. Rutgers-Camden, 1997, Fidelty award, 1998, Earl G. Harrison Pro Bono award, U. Pa. Disting. Law Alumni award, 2000, Earl G. Harrison Pro Bono award, 2001, Equal Employment Opportunity Commn. Spirit of Partnership award 2003, Lawyers' Com. for Civil Rights Under Law Lifetime Achievement award, 2004. Fellow Internat. Acad. Trial Lawyers, Am. Law Inst.; mem. ABA, Phila. Bar Assn. (Fidelity award 1990), D.C. Bar Assn., Pa. Bar Assn., Fed. Bar Assn., Nat. Bar Assn., Inter-Am. Bar Assn., World Assn. Lawyers (founding mem.), Am. Arbitration Assn. (past bd. dirs.), Barrister's Assn. Phila., Inc. (J. Austin Norris award 1987), Citizens Commn. on Civil Rights, NAACP (bd. dirs. legal def. and ednl. fund), Alpha Phi Alpha (Recognition award 1969); hon. mem., United Parcel Svc. Legal Dept., 2003. Republican. Episcopalian. Office: Schnader Harrison Segal & Lewis 1600 Market St Suite 3600 Philadelphia PA 19103-7286 Home Phone: 610-896-0684; Office Phone: 215-751-2434. Business E-Mail: wbrown@schnader.com.

BROWN, WILLIAM L., retired banker; b. Hendersonville, NC, Feb. 1, 1922; s. William W. and Sarah (Maxwell) B.; m. Helen Presbrey, August, 1947; children: Kathryn H., Richard P., Steven J., Melissa M. Student, Mars Hill Coll., Newbury Coll.; MBA, Harvard, 1947. With First Nat. Bank Boston/Bank of Boston Corp., 1949-89, asst. v.p., 1949-59, v.p., 1959-66, sr. v.p., 1966-69, exec. v.p., 1969-71, bd. dirs., 1969-92, dir. of corp., 1970-92, pres., COO, 1971-83, chmn., CEO, 1983-87, ret., 1989. Bd. dirs. Gen. Cinema Corp., Chestnut Hill, Mass., Ionics, Inc., Watertown, Mass., N.Am. Mortgage Co., Santa Rosa, Calif.; trustee Bradley Real Estate Trust, Boston. Hon. life overseer Children's Hosp. Med. Ctr., Boston; trustee assoc. Boston Coll., Marine Biol. Lab., Woods Hole, Mass.; trustee, mem. corp. Mus. Sci.; bd. dirs. Jobs for Mass., Inc., John F. Kennedy Libr. Found., Ret. Artery Bus. Com., Ret. Friends of Post Office Sq.; mem. corp. Northeastern U. Lt. USNR, World War II. Office: Bank of Boston MS/01-28-02 100 Federal St Fl 8 Boston MA 02110-1898

BROWN, WILLIAM ROBERT, trade association administrator, consultant; b. Delaware, Ohio, Jan. 19, 1926; s. Omar Lloyd and Olive Ida (Johnson) B.; m. Dorothy Judd Curtis, Dec. 30, 1950; children: Darmae Judd, Ann Bartlett Brown Nutt. BA, Ohio Wesleyan U., 1948; MA; rsch. scholar, Ohio State U., 1949. Asst. Inst. Practical Politics, Ohio Wesleyan U., 1947-48; research dir. Mo. State C. of C., 1950-64; govtl. research dir. Del. State C. of C., 1964-65; assoc. research dir. Council of State Chambers of Commerce, Washington, 1965-78, pres., 1979-90, Commerce Service Ctr., Inc., 1986-90; cons., 1991—. Editor: State Tax Report, 1969-81, Jud. Report, 1969-81, Property Tax Report, 1979, State UC Report, 1984-90, State Chamber News, 1988-90. Trustee Nat. Found. for Unemployment Compensation and Workers Compensation; precinct chmn. Rep. Party, 1968-70; pres. Friends of the Railroad, 1980-89. Recipient BNA Tax Mgmt. award for disting. svc. in state and local tax law. Mem. Nat. Tax Assn., Estero (Fla.) C. of C. (exec. dir. 1998-2000), Bonita-Estero Rep. Club (pres. 1999-2001), Phi Beta Kappa, Pi Sigma Alpha, Kappa Delta Pi, Sigma Chi. Methodist. Home: 4160 Gunnison Ct # 821 Estero FL 33928 E-mail: aquilla@ix.netcom.com.

BROWN, WILLIAM SAMUEL, JR., communication sciences and disorders educator; b. Pottstown, Penn., Apr. 25, 1940; s. William Samuel and Elizabeth (Gallager) B.; m. Elaine Kay Whitehouse, Aug. 18, 1962; children: William Samuel III, Allen Reed. MA, SUNY, Buffalo, 1967, PhD, 1969. Speech therapist Crawford Cty. Schools, Meadville, Pa., 1962-65; rsch. asst. SUNY, Buffalo, 1965-68; prof. U. Fla., Gainesville, Fla., 1970—. Contrib. numerous articles to sci. jours. Postdoctoral fellow U. Fla, Gainsville, 1968-70. Fellow Internat. Soc. Phonetic Sci. (coun. rep. 1980—), Am. Speech-Lang.-Hearing Assn., Acoustical Soc. Am.; mem. Am. Assn. Phonetic Sci. (exec. sec. 1980—). Republican. Presbyterian. Office: U Fla IASCP Dauer 63 Gainesville FL 32611 Business E-Mail: wsbrown@csd.ufl.edu.

BROWN, WILLIAM TERREL, psychology professor, educational consultant; b. Orlando, Fla., July 21, 1970; s. William Jerome and Annette Hinson Brown; m. Yulonda Candelario, July 3, 2000; 1 child, Zion T. BS, U. Fla., 1991; MA in Psychology, U. Del., 1995, PhD in Clin. Psychology, 2001. Lic. psychologist Conn. Sch. counselor Brookside Elem. Sch., Newark, Del., 1995—97; postdoctoral fellow Yale Child Study Ctr., New Haven, 2000—01, NIMH rsch. fellow, 2001—03; program analyst Yale Sch. Devel. Program, New Haven, 2003—04; instr. psychology Norwalk (Conn.) C.C., 2004—05, asst. prof. psychology, 2005—. Cons. Impact Analysis & Strategies Group, New Haven, 2001—; reviewer Contemporary Psychology: APA Rev. of Books, 2003, Jour. Am. Acad. Chil and Adolescent Psychiatry, 2005. Contbr. articles to profl. jours., chapters to books. Bd. dirs. Conn. Acad. for Edn. in Math., Sci. and Tech., Middletown, 2003—, Boys & Girls Village, Milford, Conn., 2004—. Recipient Ann A. Lynch Svc. award, U. Fla., 1991, Svc. and Ministry award, Bethel AME Ch., Wilmington, 1996, Rev. John Jasper Christian Edn. Svc. award, Immanuel Bapt. Ch., New Haven, 2003. Mem.: APA, Soc. for Tchg. of Psychology, Phi Kappa Phi, Beta Eta Sigma. Baptist. Avocations: scuba diving, video editing, cooking, travel. Office: Norwalk CC 188 Richards Ave Norwalk CT 06854 Office Phone: 203-857-3356. Office Fax: 203-857-7297. E-mail: wbrown@ncc.commnet.edu.

BROWN, WILLIAM VIRGIL, internal medicine educator; b. Royston, Ga., Sept. 25, 1938; m. Alice Brown; 2 children. BA in Physics and Chemistry, Emory U., 1960; MD, Yale U., 1964. Diplomate Am. Bd. Internal Medicine, Am. Bd. Endocrinology. Intern, asst. resident Osler Med. Svc. Johns Hopkins Hosp., Balt., 1964—66; clin. assoc. Nat. Heart and Lung Inst., Bethesda, Md., 1966—69; fellow in endocrinology and metabolism Yale-New Haven Hosp., 1969—70; asst. prof. medicine U. Calif. Dept. Medicine, San Diego, 1970—74, assoc. prof. medicine, 1974—78; dir. lipid rsch. clinic U. Calif., San Diego, 1972—78; prof. medicine Mt. Sinai Sch. Medicine, NYC, 1978—87, dir. divsn. arteriosclerosis and metabolism, 1978—87; pres., CEO Medlantic Rsch. Found., Washington, 1987—91; Charles Howard Candler prof. internal medicine, dir. divsn. arteriosclerosis and lipid metabolism Emory U., Atlanta, 1991—, pres. faculty coun. and univ. senate, 1998—99; chief of medicine Atlanta VA Hosp., 1998—. Chmn. Gordon Conf. on Lipid Metabolism, 1984; metabolism study sect. NIH, 1985; pres. Am. Bd. Clin. Lipidology, 2004—. Editor: Jour. Clinical Lipidology, 2007—. Fellow, Alexander von Humboldt. Master: ACP; mem.: Internat. Atherosclerosis Soc. (pres.-elect 2006—), Nat. Lipid Assn. (pres. 2002—03), Am. Bd. Bioanalysis (high-complexity clin. lab. dir.), Am. Soc. Exptl. Biology, Am. Soc. Clin. Investigation, Am. Fedn. Clin. Rsch., Am. Heart Assn. (mem. physiology study sect. 1978—80, mem. credentials com. atherosclerosis coun. 1978—80, chmn. credentials com. arteriosclerosis coun. 1979—82, mem. nutrition com. 1981—86, mem. several rsch. con., chmn. nutrition com. 1982—86, bd. dirs. 1983, vice chmn. edn. and cmty. program com., nat. pres. 1991—92, gold heart award 1996, R. Bruce Logue award 2000, fellow arteriosclerosis coun., fellow epidemiology and preventive cardiology coun., numerous others), Alpha Omega Alpha, Phi Beta Kappa. Achievements include research in structure and metabolism of lipoproteins; lipolytic enzymes, including their molecular and kinetic characteristics, diagnosis and treatment of the hyperlipoproteinemias; the relationship of lipoprotein metabolism to atheromatous vascular disorders. Office: Atlanta VA Hosp 1670 Clairmont Rd Decatur GA 30033-4004 Home Phone: 404-266-9006; Office Phone: 404-235-3001. Office Fax: 404-235-3005. Business E-Mail: w.virgil.brown@va.gov.

BROWN, YVONNE NARDIN, secondary school educator; b. Silver Spring, Md., Apr. 18, 1977; d. Nusrat O. Rahimi and adopted d. Sheila Theresa Jacobs. B with honors, U. Md., College Park, 2003. English tchr. Prince George's County Pub. Schs., Riverdale, Md., 2003—. Co-dir. Lyrikal Storm, Riverdale, Md., 2003—. Nominee Tchr. of Yr. award, Prince George's County Pub. Schs., 2004. Mem.: Toni Morrison Soc. (assoc.). Office: Parkdale HS 6001 Goodluck Rd Riverdale MD 20735 Personal E-mail: yvoniks@aol.com. Business E-Mail: yvonne2.brown@pgcps.org.

BROWNA, JO MCINTYRE, nurse; d. Cornelius Daniel McIntyre and Josephine Rafferty McIntyre; children: Marc L., Patrick J. Diploma in Nursing, Albert Einstein Med. Ctr., Phila., 1972. Cert. oper. rm. nurse, Assn. of Oper. Rm. Nurses, 1992, RN 1st asst., Assn. of Oper. Rm. Nurses, 1998. Mgr., staff Virtua Health Sys., Voorhees, NJ, 1993—2003; tech. support rep. Medtronic Neurol., Phila., 2000—03. Nurse 1st asst. various hosp. affiliations, NJ, 2001—. Recipient Excellence Leadership award, Dale Carnegie, 1997. Mem.: Assn. of Oper. Rm. Nurses, Am. Assn. of Neurol. Surgeons (assoc.). Achievements include working with other RNFAs to change N.J. laws prohibiting RNFAs to work in N.J; having N.J. ins. cos. value our roles and have mandatory reimbursement from all ins. cos; support of legislature to vote for Medicare reimbursement. Home and Office: Jo Browna PC 13 Dori Court Sicklerville NJ 08081

BROWNBACK, SAM DALE, senator, lawyer; b. Parker, Kans., June 12, 1956; m. Mary S. Stauffer; children: Abby, Andy, Liz, Mark, Jenna. BS in Agrl. Economics, with honors, Kan. State U., 1979; JD, U. Kans., 1982. Bar: Kans. 1982. Farm broadcaster KKSU; instr. law Kans. State U.; city atty. Ogden & Leonardville, Kans.; sec. agr. State of Kans., Topeka, 1986—93; mem. US Congress from 2nd Kans. dist., Washington, 1994-96; US Senator from Kans., 1996—. Mem. commn. security and coop. in Europe US Senate, com. appropriations, com. judiciary, congressional-exec. commn. China. Co-author: (with Jim Nelson Black) From Power to Purpose: A Remarkable Journey of Faith and Compassion, 2007 Pres. Kans. Prayer Breakfast; developer Family Impact Statement; vice chmn. Riley County Rep. Com. Recipient Hon. Am. Farmer degree, FFA; named Outstanding Young Person, Osaka, Japan Jaycees, Kansan of Distinction, 1988, Award for Manufacturing Excellence Nat. Assn. Manufacturers, 2001, Oncology Nursing Soc. Honor award, 2002, US Oncology Medal of Honor, 2002, William Wilberforce award Prison Fellowship, 2003, Pro Deo et Patria medal Christendom Coll., Va., 2005. Mem.: Nat. Future Farmers Am. (v.p. 1977), Am. Judicature Soc., Am. Agrl. Law Assn., Riely County Bar Assn., Kans. Bar Assn., ABA. Republican. Roman Catholic. Office: US Senate 303 Hart Senate Office Bldg Washington DC 20510-0001 also: District Office 612 S Kansas Ave Topeka KS 66603 Office Phone: 202-224-6521, 785-233-2503. Office Fax: 785-233-2616, 202-228-1265.*

BROWN-BARTON, GRACE OLIVE, music educator; b. Kingston, Jamaica, Apr. 15, 1942; arrived in U.S., 1968; d. Wilfred Owen and Lucille May Brown; children: Babafemi Barton, Nayo Barton. BS, NYU, 1979, MA, 1980. Music coord. Jamaica Cult. Devel. Corp., Kingston, 1983—85; tchr. Bd. Edn., NYC, 1985—87; music tchr. Yonkers Bd. Edn., NY, 1987—. Founder, dir. The Bronx Chorale, NY. Recipient Spl. Mother Award, UN, 2004. Baptist. Avocations: stamp collecting/philately, coin collecting/numismatics. Personal E-mail: grabro@msn.com.

BROWNE, ARTHUR, newspaper editor; BA, Boston Coll.; JD, St. John's U. Various editl. positions The Daily News, NYC, 1973—2000, editl. page editor, 2003—; founding editor Petplace.com, 2000—00; enterprise editor Bloomberg News, 2002—03. Adj. faculty Columbia U. Sch. Journalism, 2004. Co-author: I Koch. Co-recipient Pulitzer Prize for Editl. Writing, 2007. Mem.: Am. Soc. Newspaper Editors. Office: NY Daily News Inc 450 W 33rd St New York NY 10001-2603 E-mail: abrowne@edit.nydailynews.com.*

BROWNE, AUTUMN LEE, theater educator, actress, theater director; b. North Hollywood, Calif., Sept. 21, 1957; d. Harry Browne and Gloria Maxwell; m. Michael C. Buss, July 22, 1999; m. Barry Fasman; m. William Wilson. BA in Comms., Calif. State U., Fullerton, 1978; tchg. credential, Chapman U., Orange, Calif., 1995; MA in Theater Prodn., Ctrl. Wash. U., Ellensburg, 2005. Drama tchr. Brookhurst Jr. HS, Anaheim, Calif., 1996—; actress TV commls., theatrical prodns. Bd. dirs. New Voices Playwrights Theatre. Dir.: (plays) Pure as the Driven Show, 1998, Brighton Beach Memoirs, 1999, Toyer, 2004, Social Security, 2006, numerous others. Mem. edn. com. South Coast Repertory Theatre, 2003—; Libertarian Party candidate Calif. State Assembly, 1998, 2000. Recipient Theatre Educator of Yr. award, 2001. Mem.: Toastmasters Internat. (area gov. 1994—96). Address: 601 N Brookhurst St Anaheim CA 92801-3832

BROWNE, DALLAS, anthropologist, educator; b. Chgo., Oct. 9, 1944; s. William Eldridge and Ann (Sherman) Browne; m. Imelda M. Siedentopf, Apr. 8, 1972; children: Eldridge, La Salle, Hubert, William. BA, Northeastern U., 1966; MA, U. Ill., 1971, PhD in Anthropology, 1983. Asst. prof. Wabash Coll., Crawfordsville, Ind., 1980—82, Colby Coll., Waterville, Maine, 1983—85, York Coll. CUNY, 1985—91; assoc. prof. anthropology So. Ill. U., Edwardsville, 1991—. Cons. evaluation Kenya Govt., 1976; with UNICEF; hon. consul, Tanzania. Author: Current Discourse on Dilemmas Facing Developing Nations, 2005; editor: Dilemmas in Higher Education in Developing Nations, 2005, Current Discourse on Education in Developing Nations, 2006. Fellow, Ford Found., 1971, Inst. Study Racism, 1980, Ctr. Polit. Studies and Inst. Social Rsch., 1984. Mem.: St. Louis Consular Corps (pres., 2004—05), Midwest Latin Am. Assn., Midwest African Studies Assn. (pres.-elect), World Affairs Coun., Am. Com. Fgn. Rels., Eugene Redman Writers Assn. (pres. 2005—06), Midwest Assn. Latin Am. Studies, New Eng. Black Studies, Assn. Black Anthropologists, Soc. Urban Anthropology, Am. Anthropol. Assn. Avocation: model building. Office: Dept Anthropology Box 1451 S Ill U Edwardsville Edwardsville IL 62026-0001

BROWNE, DONALD VICTOR, broadcast executive; b. Passaic, NJ, May 16, 1943; s. Donald James and Roseanna (Hopp) B.; m. Maria Junquera, May 9, 1981; children: Christopher Barret, Ryan Alexander. BS in Mktg., Fairleigh Dickinson U., 1971. Traffic expediter CBS News, NYC, 1967-70, prodr., 1970-71, reporter, assignment editor, 1971-75, prodr., dep. bur. chief Atlanta, 1975-79; bur. chief, Fla., L.Am. NBC News, Miami, Fla., 1979-88, bur. chief, L.Am., S.E. US, 1988-89, exec. news dir. NYC, 1989-90, exec. v.p., 1990-93; pres., gen. mgr. Sta. WTVJ-TV, NBC, Miami, 1993—2003; COO Telemundo Network, Hialeah, Fla., 2003—05, pres., CEO, 2005—. With USCG, 1967-73. Office: Telemundo Network 2290 W 8th Ave Hialeah FL 33010 Office Phone: 305-889-7979. Business E-Mail: dbrowne@telemundo.com.

BROWNE, FREDERICK DOUGLAS, physiologist, educator; b. Springfield, Ohio, June 3, 1929; s. Charles David and Ruth Noami Browne; m. Joyce Louise Burton, June 11, 1955; children: Fred, Sharon, Michael, Regina, Stephan, Monica. BS, U. Dayton, Ohio, 1956; MS, Miami U., Oxford, Ohio, 1958; postgrad., Case Western Res. U., Cleve., 1963-66; EdD, Nova U., Fort Lauderdale, Fla., 1981. Ordained permanent deacon Maronite Cath. Ch., 1992. Rschr. artificial organs and exptl. heart surgery Cleve. Clinic, 1958-63; predoctoral fellow Coll. Medicine Case Western Res. U., Cleve., 1963-66; instr. sci. Cleve. Bd. Edn., 1966-69; asst. prof. St. John's Coll., Cleve., 1969-73; instr. Sch. Anesthesia Cleve. Clinic, 1973-74; prof. anatomy and physiology Cuyahoga C.C., Warrensville, Ohio, 1973-92; chair/CEO Rameso, Inc., Copley, Ohio, 1993—. Contbr. articles to profl. jours. Pres., Bd. Cath. Edn., Diocese of Cleve., 1972-73; chmn. Civil Svc. Commn. Warrensville Heights, Ohio, 1970-72; councilman Warrensville Heights, 1982-85; bd. dirs. Summit County Cath. Social Svc.; parish rep. Boy Scouts Am., Cuyahoga County, 1958-63; mem. precinct com., AMA minority affairs com., Rep. Nat. Conv., 2004; pres. Holy Name Soc., St. Cecilia Cath. Ch., 1958-63. 2d lt. U.S. Army, 1952-54. NIH fellow, 1963-66. Mem. AAUP, AMA, NRC, Nat. Assn. Advancement Sci., N.Y. Acad. Scis., Ohio Coll. Biology Tchrs. Assn., Secular Franciscan, Am. Legion, Knights of Columbus, Alpha Phi Alpha. Republican. Personal E-mail: hrtdr02@adelphia.net.

BROWNE, G.M. WALTER SHAWN, journalist, publisher; b. Sydney, Jan. 10, 1949; s. Walter Francis and Hilda Louise (Leahy) B.; m. Raquel Emilse Facal, Mar. 9, 1973; 1 stepson, Marcello Garcia. Grad. high sch. Chess player, 1957—; U.S. jr. champion, 1966; Australian champion, 1968-69; U.S. Open champion, 1971-73; Nat. Open champion, 1971-73, 75, 84, 86-87, 91, 94-95, 2002; U.S. champion, 1974-78, 80-83; Pan-Am. champion, 1974; Internat. German champion, 1975; mem. U.S. Olympic Team, 1974, 78, 82, 84; Nat. and U.S. Open Blitz chess champion, 1989; Pan-Pacific Blitz chess champion, 1991. Columnist Chess Life & Rev., Berkeley, Calif., 1973—; lectr. in field; lead commentator at 1999 Fide World Championship, Las Vegas, Nev. Publisher: Strongest International Chess Tourneys, 1978-85. Named Internat. Master Fedn. Internat. des Eshecs, 1969, Internat. Grandmaster, 1969; winner German Open Championship, Mannheim, 1975; 1st pl. Venice, 1971; 1st pl. Rejkavik, Iceland, 1978; 1st pl. Wijk Am. Zee, Holland, 1974, 80; 1st pl. Santiago, 1981; 1st pl. Indonesia, 1982, Gjovik, 1983, Naestved, 1985, 2d-3d World Open, Phila., 1988; only 11 time winner Nat. Open, Can. Open champion, 1991, U.S. class champion, 1991, 7 time Am. Open champion, US Sr. Champ, Las Vegas, 2005; winner N.Am. Open 1991, 93, 94, 96; inducted into U.S. Hall of Fame, 2003. Mem. World Blitz Chess Assn. (pres., founder, pub., editor quar. mag. Blitz Chess 1988-2003). Address: 8 Parnassus Rd Berkeley CA 94708-2041 Personal E-mail: wbkingchess@sbcglobal.net.

BROWNE, JACKSON, singer, songwriter; b. Heidelberg, West Germany; s. Clyde Browne. Joined Nitty Gritty Dirt Band, 1966. Musician, songwriter: albums Jackson Browne (Saturate Before Using), 1972, For Everyman, 1973, Late for the Sky, 1974, The Pretender, 1976, Running on Empty, 1977, Hold Out, 1980, Lawyers in Love, 1983, Lives in the Balance, 1986, World in Motion, 1989, I'm Alive, 1993, Everywhere I Go, 1994, Looking East, 1996, The Naked Ride Home, 2002, co-wrote: Take it Easy (with Glen Frey for the Eagles). Recipient Founders award, ASCAP, 2004. songs "These Days" and "Shadow Dream Song", were recorded by Tom Rush, Nico, Gregg Allman and others; inducted Rock and Roll Hall of Fame, 2004.

BROWNE, JEFFREY FRANCIS, lawyer; b. Clare, South Australia, Australia, Mar. 1, 1944; came to U.S., 1975; s. Patrick Joseph and Irene Kathleen (Cormack) B.; m. Deborah Mary Christine West, Aug. 28, 1971; children: Veronique Namur Irene, Jeffrey James, Nicholas Patrick, Sophie Christina, Amy Elizabeth. LLB, Adelaide U., South Australia, 1966; LLM, Sydney U., Australia, 1968, Harvard U., 1976. Bar: South Australia 1969, Australian Capital Territory 1973, N.Y. 1978, Victoria 1982, New South Wales 1983, Western Australia 1983. Assoc. High Ct. Australia, Canberra, Australian Capital Territory, 1967-68; diplomat Dept. Fgn. Affairs, Canberra, 1969; 2d sec. Australian High Commn., London and Malaysia, 1970-71, acting high commr. Ghana, 1972; counsel nuclear tests case Internat. Ct. Justice, 1973-74; assoc. Sullivan & Cromwell, NYC, 1976-81, ptnr., 1983—2005, of counsel, 2006—; gen. counsel Alcoa of Australia, Melbourne, 1981-82. Mem. bd. guardians Australian Govt. Future Fund; mem. adv. bd. Australian Govt. Solicitor. Mem. Law Inst. Victoria, Australian Mining and Petroleum Law Assn., Law Coun. Australia (chmn. fin. and securities subcom., internat. trade and bus. law com.), Inst. Dirs. of Australia, Internat. Bar Assn. (sect. on energy and natural resources), Am. C. of C. in Australia (bd. dirs.), Am. Soc. Internat. Law, Melbourne Club. Office: 101 Collins St Melbourne Victoria 3000 Australia Home Phone: 61-3-9822-1562; Office Phone: 61-3-9635-1501. Personal E-mail: brownej@bigpond.net.au. Business E-Mail: brownej@sullcrom.com.

BROWNE, JOHN CHARLES, physicist, researcher, lab administrator; b. Pottstown, Pa., July 29, 1942; s. Charles Ignatius and Mary Agnes (Titzer) B.; m. Susan Mary Mazzarella, Dec. 30, 1972 (div. Dec. 1984); children—Christopher Ryan, Adam Charles; m. Marti Moore, May 4, 1985; 1 child, Courtney Keese. BS, Drexel U., 1965; PhD, Duke U., 1969; DSc (hon.), Drexel U., 1998. Instr. Duke U., Durham, NC, 1969-70; staff scientist Lawrence Livermore Lab., Calif., 1970-79; group leader Los Alamos Nat. Lab., 1979-81, div. leader, 1981-84, assoc. dir., 1984-93; dir. Los Alamos Neutron Sci. Ctr., Los Alamos, 1993—97; lab. dir. Los Alamos Nat. Lab., 1997—2003, sr. scientist, 2003, ret, 2003; owner JCB Sci. Cons., LLC, 2005—. Contbr. articles to profl. jours. Bd. mem. Hertz Found., 2000—, Nev. Test Site Historical Found., 2004—. NASA fellow, 1965-67 Fellow AAAS, Am. Phys. Soc. Avocations: golf, hiking, skiing, tennis. Office Phone: 435-668-7265. E-mail: jcbrowne729@msn.com.

BROWNE, JOSEPH PETER, retired librarian; b. June 12, 1929; s. George and Mary Bridget (Fahy) B. AB, U. Notre Dame, 1951; STL, Pontificium Athenaeum Angelicum, Rome, 1957, STD, 1960; MLS, Cath. U. Am., 1965. Joined Congregation of Holy Cross, Roman Cath. Ch., 1947, ordained priest, 1955. Asst. pastor Holy Cross Ch., South Bend, Ind., 1955-56, libr., prof. moral theology Washington, 1959-64; mem. faculty U. Portland, Oreg., 1964-73, 75—, dir. libr., 1966-70, 76-94, dean Coll. Arts and Scis., 1970-73, assoc. prof. libr. sci., 1967-95, prof. emeritus, 1995—, regent, 1969-70, 77-81, chmn. acad. senate, 1968-70. Prof., head dept. libr. sci. Our Lady of Lake Coll., San Antonio, 1973-75; chmn. Interstate Libr. Planning Coun., 1977-79. Mem. Columbia River chpt. Huntington's Disease Soc. Am., 1975-90, pres., 1979-82; pastor St. Birgitta Ch., Portland, 1993-2005; chmn. Archdiocesan Presbyteral Coun., 1994-98, 2000-02; mem. Coll. of Cons. Archdiocese of Portland, 1995-2005. Recipient Culligan award U. Portland, 1979. Mem. ALA, Cath. Libr. Assn. (life, pres. 1971-73), Cath. Theol. Soc. Am., Pacific N.W. Libr. Assn. (pres. 1985-86), Oreg. Libr. Assn. (life, pres. 1967-68), Nat. Assn. Parliamentarians, Oreg. Assn. Parliamentarians (pres. 1985-87), Mensa Internat., All-Ireland Cultural Soc. Oreg. (pres. 1984-85), Ancient Order of Hibernians, KC. Democrat. Home: 5410 N Strong St Apt 3 Portland OR 97203-5731 Office Phone: 503-943-4663. Business E-Mail: browne@up.edu.

BROWNE, JOY, psychologist, radio personality; b. New Orleans, Oct. 24, 1950; d. Nelson and Ruth (Strauss) B.; Carter Thweatt, June 9, 1966 (div. 1979); 1 child, Patience. BA, Rice U.; PhD, Northeastern U.; postgrad., Tufts U. Registered psychologist, Mass. With rsch./optics dept. Sperry Rand, Boston, 1966-68; engr. space program Itek, Boston, 1968-70; head social svcs. dept. Boston Redevel. Authority, 1970-71; staff psychologist South Shore Counselling Assocs., Boston, 1971-82; on-the-air psychologist Sta. WITS, Boston, 1978-82, Sta. KGO, San Francisco, 1982-84; host, news Sta. KCBS, San Francisco, 1984-85; on-air psychologist Sta. WABC, NYC, 1985-87, ABC Talkradio, NYC, 1987-92, WOR Radio Network, NYC, 1992—, Sta. WABC-TV, 1995-97, Dr. Joy Browne Show, Syndicated Eyemark Entertainment, 1999—. On-air psychologist WCBS-TV Five O'Clock News, 1999; dir. Town of Hull Adolescent Outreach Program; cons. human sexuality PBS, 1994—. Author: The Used Car Game, 1971, The Research Experience, 1976, Nobody's Perfect, 1988, Why They Don't Call When They Say They Will and Other Mixed Signals, 1989, Dating for Dummies, 1998, 2d edit., 2006, 9 Fantasies That Will Ruin Your Life, 1998, It's a Jungle out There Jane! Understanding the Male Animal, 1999, Getting Unstuck: 8 Simple Steps To Solving Any Problem, 2002, Dating Disasters and How to Avoid Them, 2005, The Dr. Joy Browne Show Live on Discovery Health Network, 2006. Named One of 25 Outstanding Broadcasters USA Today, 1995-96, 100 Most Influential Talkers, Legend La., 1996, Best Female Talk Show Host, Nartash, 1996, 97, Female Talk Show Host of Yr., Vanity Fair Hall of Fame, 1996. Mem. APA (bd. dirs. 1994-97), Phi Kappa Phi (Communicator of Yr. award 1992). Office: care WOR Radio 111 Broadway 3d Fl New York NY 10006 E-mail: drjoybrowne@compuserve.net.

BROWNE, MALCOLM WILDE, journalist; b. NYC, Apr. 17, 1931; s. Douglas Granzow and Dorothy Rutledge (Wilde) B.; m. Huynh thi Le Lieu, July 18, 1966. Student, Swarthmore Coll., 1948-50, N.Y.U., 1950-52. Cons. chemist, tech. writer, 1952-56; newsman, copy editor Middletown (N.Y.) Daily Record, 1958-60; with Balt. bur. A.P., 1960-61; chief Indochina corr., 1961-65; Saigon corr. ABC, 1965-66; freelance writer and corr. NYC, 1966-68; corr. NY Times, Buenos Aires, 1968-71, S. Asia, 1971-73, Eastern Europe, 1973-77, sci. corr., 1977-81, sci writer, 1985-00, retired, 2000; sr. editor Discover mag., 1981-84; McGraw prof. writing Princeton U., NJ, 1995-96. Author: The New Face of War, 1965, Muddy Boots and Red Socks, 1993. Served with AUS, 1956-58. Recipient First prize World Press Photo award The Hague, 1963, Pulitzer prize fgn. corr., 1964, Overseas Press Club award, 1964, Sigma Delta Chi award, 1964, Louis M. Lyons award, 1964, Nat. Headliners Club award, 1964; A.P. Mng. Editors award, 1964, Grady-Stack medal Am. Chem. Soc., 1992, George Polk Meml. award; Edward R. Murrow Meml. fellow Coun. on Fgn. Rels., 1966-67. Mem.: Sigma Xi (hon.). Address: 36 E 36th St New York NY 10016-3463

BROWNE, MICHAEL L., insurance company executive; Bachelor's degree, Princeton U.; JD, U. Pa. Sch. Law. Ins. commr. State Pa., 1980—83; ptnr. Reed Smith, LLP, Phila., 1983—93, mng. ptnr. Delaware Valley, 1993—2000, head, internat. insurance practice group Phila., 2001—04; pres., CEO Harleysville Mutual, 2004—; dir. Harleysville Group, Inc., 1986—, CEO, 2004—; non-exec. chmn. Harleysville Companies, 2003—. Office: Harleysville Group Inc 355 Maple Ave Harleysville PA 19438-2297 Office Phone: 800-523-6344.

BROWNE, MICHAEL LEON, lawyer; b. Beaumont, Tex., Sept. 2, 1946; s. Ernest Jewell and Marjorie Jane (Heisig) B.; m. Elizabeth Oswald, Feb. 22, 1969; children: Sarah Skelton, Patrick Michael; m. Anne Farrell, Dec. 28, 2000. AB, Princeton U., 1968; JD, U. Pa., 1974. Bar: Pa. 1974. Law clk. to presiding justice U.S. Dist. Ct. (ea. dist.) Pa., 1974; assoc. Dilworth, Paxson, Kalish, Levy & Coleman, Phila., 1974-75; spl. asst. to U.S. Sec. of Transp., 1975-77, dep. under sec. transp., 1976-77; assoc. Dilworth, Paxson, Kalish, Levy & Kauffman, Phila., 1977-78, ptnr., 1979-80; ins. commr. Commonwealth of Pa., 1980-83, chmn. Gov.'s task force on health care cost containment, 1981-83; ptnr. Reed Smith LLP, Phila., Pitts., Washington, 1983—2004, mem. exec. com., 1987—2000, mng. ptnr. Delaware Valley Region, 1993—2000, chair internat. ins. practice group, 2001—04; CEO, pres. Harleysville Mutual Ins. Co., 2004—; CEO Harleysville Group, 2004—. Bd. dirs. Harleysville Ins. Co. Del. Rep. Nat. Conv., 1984, 88, 92, 96; mem. nat. fin. com. Rep. Party; co-chmn. Pa. fin. com. for George Bush for Pres., 1987-88; trustee Temple U. Decorated Bronze Star with Combat V. Mem. ABA, Pa. Bar Assn., Phila. Bar Assn. Office: Harleysville Group 355 Maple Ave Harleysville PA 19438

BROWNE, RAY, insurance agent, retired congressman; b. Washington, Dec. 8, 1938; s. Woodrow Lee and Mary Isabelle (Manning) B.; m. Barbara Lee Andrus, May 17, 1979; children: Ray II, Molly Lee. Student, U. Md., 1959-62. CLU; ChFC. Life ins. agt., gen. agt. Aetna Life & Casualty, Washington, Cleve., Charleston, W.Va., 1964-82; ins. broker The Browne Co., Washington, 1982—; shadow rep. from D.C. U.S. Ho. of Reps., Washington, 2001—07. Vis. lectr. John Carroll U., Cleve., 1972-77; speaker in field. Featured in documentary: Washington A Tale of Two Cities; contbr. polit. and bus. commentary to newspapers, articles to profl. jours. Adv. neighborhood commr. Washington Govt., 1989-90; mem. drug strategy team Washington Govt., 1989-90; vice chair Hurt Home Bd., Washington, 1987-89; candidate for City Coun., Washington, 1990; del Dem. Nat. Com., 2004; mediator Washington Superior Ct., 1985-88; mem. parish coun. Holy Trinity Cath. Ch., Washington, 2001-2004. With USN, 1956-58. Recipient Big Bros. and Big Sisters Merit award, 1990. Mem. Nat. Assn. Life Underwriters (dir. No. Va. 1964-66), Greater Washington Chpt. CLU (bd. dirs., sec., treas., v.p., pres. 1982-91), Million Dollar Roundtable (life), Mensa, U. Md. M Club, Alpha Tau Omega (Silver Circle award 1984). Democrat. Roman Catholic.

BROWNE, RAY BROADUS, popular culture educator; b. Millport, Ala., Jan. 15, 1922; s. Garfield and Annie Nola (Trull) Browne; m. Olwyn Orde, Aug. 21, 1952 (dec.); children: Glenn, Kevin; m. Alice Pat Matthews, Aug. 25, 1965; 1 child, Alicia. AB, U. Ala., 1943; A.M., Columbia U., 1947; PhD, UCLA, 1956. Instr. U. Nebr., Lincoln, 1947-50; instr. U. Md., College Park, 1956-60; asst. prof., assoc. prof. Purdue U., Lafayette, Ind., 1960-67; prof. popular culture Bowling Green (Ohio) State U., 1967—, Univ. disting. prof., 1975—. Author, editor: Melville's Drive to Humanism, 1971, Popular Culture and the Expanding Consciousness, 1973, The Constitution and Popular Culture, 1975, Dominant Symbols in Popular Culture, 1990, The Many Tongues of Literacy, 1992, Continuities in

Popular Cultures, 1993, The Cultures of Celebrations, 1994, Popular Culture Studies in the Future, 1996, Lincoln-Lore: Lincoln in Contemporary Popular Culture, 1996, Pioneers in Popular Culture Studies, 1998, The Defining Guide to United States Popular Culture, 2000, The Detective as Historian, 2000, vol. II, 2007, Preview, 2001, Mission Underway: The History of the Popular Culture Association/American Culture Association and Popular Culture Movement, 2002, Popular Culture of the Civil War and Reconstruction, 2003, Murder on the Reservation: American Indian Crime Fiction, 2004, Popular Culture Studies Across the Curriculum, 2005, Profiles of Popular Culture, 2005, The Detective as Historian: History and Art in Historical Crime Fiction, vol. II, 2007, creator, editor: Jour. Popular Culture, 1967—82, Jour. Am. Culture, 1977—82. With US Army, 1942—46. Mem.: Am. Culture Assn. (sec.-treas. 1977—), Popular Culture Assn. (treas. 1970—, founder, sec. 1970—2002). Democrat. Avocation: scholarly research. Home: 210 N Grove St Bowling Green OH 43402-2335 Office: Bowling Green U Bowling Green OH 43403-0001 Office Phone: 419-372-7861. Business E-Mail: rbrowne@bgnet.bgsu.edu.

BROWNE, RICHARD CULLEN, lawyer; b. Akron, Ohio, Nov. 21, 1938; s. Francis Cedric and Elizabeth Ann (Cullen) Browne; m. Patricia Anne Winkler, Apr. 23, 1962; children: Richard Cullen, Catherine Anne, Paulette Elizabeth, Maureen Frances, Colleen Marie. BS in Econs., Holy Cross Coll., 1960; JD, Cath. U. Am., 1963. Bar: Va. 1963, U.S. Ct. Claims 1963, U.S. Ct. Customs and Patent Appeals 1963, D.C. 1964, U.S. Ct. Mil. Appeals 1963, U.S. Ct. Appeals (D.C. cir.) 1964, U.S. Supreme Ct. 1966, U.S. Ct. Appeals (fed. cir.) 1982, U.S. Ct. Appeals (9th cir.) 1983, U.S. Ct. Appeals (6th cir.) 1991, U.S. Ct. Appeals (7th cir.) 1998. Assoc. Browne, Beveridge, DeGrandi & Kline, Washington, 1963-68, ptnr., 1968-72, Shaffert, Miller & Browne, Washington, 1972-74; sr. counsel Office of Enforcement EPA, Washington, 1974-76; asst. chief hearing counsel U.S. Nuclear Regulatory Commn., Washington, 1976-78; sole practice Washington, 1978-79; ptnr. Winston & Strawn, Washington, 1980-2001, of counsel, 2001—. Lectr. U. R.I., 1975, Washburn U., 1978, Legal Ins., CSC, 1975—78, Hofstra U., 1987—, Nat. Inst. for Trial Advocacy, 1986—. Del. Montgomery County Civic Fedn., 1970—74; chmn. Citizens Adv. Com. on Rockville Corridor, 1972—77; mem. Montgomery County Potomac River Basin Adv. Com., 1972—74; chmn. Cath. U. Am. Fund, 1996—2001. Capt. JAGC USAF, 1963—66, capt. USAFR, 1966—69. Named Disting. Mil. Grad., Holy Cross Coll., 1960; recipient In Hoc Signo award, 2004. Mem.: Centesimus Annus Pro Pontifice Found. (bd. dirs. 2002—06, v.p. D.C. chpt. 2004—06), Cath. U. Gen. Alumni Assn. (bd. govs. 1992—2005, chmn. Gibbons medal com., exec. com. 1995—2001), Cath. U. Law Sch. Alumni Soc. (bd. dirs. 1991—98, pres. 1992—93, bd. visitors 1998—2006), Coll. Holy Cross General Alumni Assn. (bd. dirs. 1971—78, alumni senate 1978—97, nominations and elections com. 1995—, bd. dirs. 1997—, pres. 2002—03, exec. com. 2006—07). Republican. Home: 7203 Old Stage Rd Rockville MD 20852-4438 Office: Winston & Strawn 1700 K St NW Washington DC 20006 E-mail: rbrowne@alumni.holycross.edu.

BROWNE, STANHOPE STRYKER, lawyer; b. Colorado Springs, Colo., July 22, 1931; s. Samuel Stanhope Stryker and Florence Jeanette (Reynolds) B.; m. Elizabeth Whitney Sturges, Sept. 12, 1964; children: Katrina C., Whitney R. AB, Princeton U., 1953; LL.B., Harvard U., 1956. Bar: Pa. 1957. Assoc. Dechert LLP, Phila., 1956-65, ptnr., 1965-97, of counsel, 1998—, resident ptnr. Brussels, 1972—76. Lectr. internat. law. Contbr. articles to profl. jours. Chmn. Penn's Landing Corp., Phila., 1981-97, Com. to Preserve Am.'s Birthplace, 1965-72; vice chmn. World Affairs Council, 1978-90; bd. dirs. Phila. 1976 Bicentennial Corp., 1971-72, Greater Phila. Movement, 1970-71, Phila. Port Corp., 1984-90, Ecole Française Internationale de Philadelphie, 1991-99, The Ch. Found., 1998-01, French Heritage Soc., Inc., 1999-05; mem. exec. com. Cen. Phila. Devel. Corp., 1968-72, 77-99; mem. Phila. Dist. Export Council US Dept. Commerce, 1983-96; vice pres. Pa. Prison Soc., 1962-69; pres. Greater Phila. Council of Chs., 1966-67; mem. Diocesan Coun. Episcopal Diocese of Pa., 1967-71; rector's warden St. Peter's Ch., 1983-90, mem. bd. fgn. parishes Episcopal Ch., 2005-; chmn. Democrats Abroad, Belgium, 1975-76, Pa. Internat. Trade Conf., 1977-79; mem. adv. commn. Independence Nat. Hist. Park, Phila., 1969-72; hon. consul of France in Phila., 1986-96; mem. vestry Am. Cathedral in Paris, 2001-02. Recipient Pub. Service and Polit. Courage award Southeastern Pa. chpt. Ams. for Democratic Action, 1965; decorated Nat. Order of Merit, France, 1998. Mem. Phila. Bar Assn., Phila. Com. on Fgn. Rels., Brook Club (N.Y.C.), Phila. Club (bd. dirs. 1988-92), Phi Beta Kappa Democrat. Episcopalian. Office: Cira Ctr 2929 Arch St Philadelphia PA 19104 Office Phone: 215-994-2804. Personal E-mail: stanlibby@verizon.net.

BROWNE, THOM, apparel designer; b. Allentown, Pa., 1966; Grad., Notre Dame U. Former designer Club Monaco; launched collection Thom Browne Ltd., 2001—. Recipient Swarovski's Perry Ellis award nomination, Menswear Designer of Yr. award, Coun. of Fashion Designers of Am., 2006. Office: Thom Browne 17 Little W 12th St New York NY 10012

BROWNE, THOMAS JEFFREY, healthcare executive; b. Highland Park, Mich., May 16, 1955; s. Thomas Patrick Browne and Nina Louise Warrick; m. Colleen Anne Burhoe, Dec. 14, 1984; children: Amy C., Erin E. BS in Bus. Adminstrn., Kent State U., Ohio, 1981. Cert. mgmt. acct., Inst. Mgmt. Acct., 1998. Dir. fin. & info. sys. Sulliar Corp., Mich. City, 1992—96; CFO Wingspan Care Grp., Shaker Heights, Ohio, 1996—. Bd. mem. Monarch Tchg. Tech., Shaker Heights, 2005—. Treas. Women's Svcs. Orgn., Cleve. Heights, 2006. Specialist 4 US Army, 1974—77, Ft. Sill, Okla. Mem.: Inst. Mgmt. Accts.

BROWNELL, BLAINE ALLISON, educational association and academic administrator, history professor; b. Birmingham, Ala., Nov. 12, 1942; s. Blaine Jr. and Annette (Holmes) B.; m. Mardi Ann Taylor, Aug. 21, 1964; children— Blaine, Allison. BA, Washington and Lee U., 1965; MA, U. N.C., 1967, PhD, 1969. Asst. prof. Purdue U., West Lafayette, Ind., 1969-74; assoc. prof., chmn. dept. U. Ala., Birmingham, 1974-78, prof., 1980-90, dean grad. sch., 1978-84, dean social and behavioral scis., 1984-90; provost, v.p. for acad. affairs U. North Tex., Denton, 1990-98; exec. dir. Ctr. Internat. Programs and Svcs. U. Memphis, 1998-2000; pres. Ball State U., Muncie, Ind., 2000—04; CEO U21pedagogica Ltd., Charlottesville, Va., 2004—05; sr. univ. advisor U. South Fla., St. Petersburg, 2006—. Sr. fellow Johns Hopkins U., Balt., 1971-72; Fulbright lectr. Hiroshima U., Japan, 1977-78; dir. U. Ala. Ctr. Internat. Programs, 1980-90; chair Internat. Student Exch. Program Bd., 2007—. Author: The Urban Ethos., 1975, City in Southern History, 1977, Urban America, 1979, 2d edit., 1990, The Urban Nation 1920-80, 1981; editor Jour. Urban History, 1976-90, assoc. editor, 1990-95. Mem. Birmingham City Planning Commn., 1975-77, Jefferson County Planning Commn., 1975-77, Dallas Com. Fgn. Rels., 1990-98; chmn. Birmingham Coun. on Fgn. Rels., 1988-90, Charlottesville Com. Fgn. Rels., 2004—. Mem. Am. Hist. Assn., Orgn. Am. Historians, So. Hist. Assn., Philos. Soc. Tex. Home: 4640 Mockernut Ln Earlysville VA 22936

BROWNELL, BLANCHE PARISI, retired secondary school educator; b. Waterbury, Conn., Oct. 27, 1934; d. Gustavo Mario and Philomena Marie (Santoro) Parisi; m. Edwin Rowland Brownell; children: Elizabeth R., Elaine B. Dorrans, Evelyn B. Mika. BBA, U. Miami, Coral Gables, 1956. Cert. tchr. U. Miami, 1962. Sec. Radio and Electronic Equipment Co., Miami, Fla., 1952; classified, display ad rep. Miami Herald Pub. Co., 1953—56, 1962; sec. advt. dept. Burdines Dept. Store, Miami, 1961; tchr. bus. edn. Miami Jackson Sr. HS, 1962—68; corp. sec. E.R. Brownell & Assoc. Inc., Miami, 1968—92; ret., 1992. Founder ladies aux. Fla. Soc. Surveying and Mapping, Tallahassee, 1973, Dade County Soc. Surveying and Mapping, Tallahassee, 1973. Named Sponsor of Yr., Future Bus. Leaders Am., Tallahassee, 1965—66; recipient Outstanding Svcs. award, Am. Congress Surveying and Mapping, Washington, 1973. Mem.: U. Miami Woman's Gulid, Garden Club Coral Gables (corr. sec. 2005—), Woman's Club City of Coral Gables, Elkettes. Roman Catholic. Avocations: crafts, ballroom dancing, gardening, travel, computers. Personal E-mail: blanchepb@aol.com.

BROWNELL, EDWIN ROWLAND, banker, civil engineer, land surveyor; b. Tampa, Fla., Sept. 19, 1924; s. Clarence DeWolf and Helen Lucy (Hill) B.; m. Helen Marie Kegel, Jan. 22, 1948 (dec. Apr. 1967); 1 child, Nancy; m. Blanche Rosina Parisi, Dec. 26, 1967; children: Elizabeth, Elaine, Evelyn. BCE, U. Fla., 1947. Registered profl. surveyor, Fla., Ark., Ga., Miss., Nev., N.D., S.D., S.C., Tenn., W.Va. Cadastral engr. City of Miami, Fla., 1948-53; pres., CEO, chmn. E.R. Brownell & Assocs., Inc., Miami, 1953-93, real estate salesman, 1975—; founding dir. Total Bank, 1983—85, Am.'s Bank, 1980—83; pres., chief exec. officer, chmn. Brickellbanc Savs. Assn., Miami, 1985-89, also bd. dirs.; pres. Tri-County Engring. Co., 1983-89, Naples (Fla.) Title and Abstract Co., 1st Title and Abstract Co. Chmn. surveying com. U. Fla., Gainesville, 1974—, mem. pres.'s coun.; mem. nat. engring. degree accreditation team Nat. Coun. Engring. Examiners, Md., 1985-95, mem. team evaluating engring. readiness U.S. Armed Forces, 1980-81; chmn. engring. adv. com. Fla. Bd. Regents, Tallahassee, 1982-85; vice-chmn. legal grievance com. Fla. Bar, 1992-94. Elected county surveyor State of Fla., Dade County, 1956-60; chmn. Zoning Bd. Adjustment, Coral Gables, Fla., 1978-87; chmn. Coral Gables Planning and Zoning Bd., 1987-95; mem. Coral Gables Code Enforcement Bd., 1995-97, City of Coral Gables Historic Preservation Com., 1997, City of Coral Gables Constrn. Regulation Bd., 1997-05, 07—; emergency preparation com. City of Coral Gables, 1995—; bd. dirs. Boys Club of Miami, 1980-83, Salvation Army South Fla., dir., 1990-94. Named Man of Yr., Dade County, Fla., 1989. Master Am. Contract Bridge Assn. (nat.); fellow Am. Congress Surveying and Mapping (hon. life, pres. 1980-81, Surveying Excellence award 1977, Miami Man Yr. 1990, Presdl. award 1994), NSPE, Nat. Soc. Profl. Surveyors (pres. 1978-79), Fla. Surveying and Mapping Soc. (hon., life), Profl. Surveyors and Mappers (pres. 1981), Fla. Soc. Profl. Land Surveyors (hon. life mem., Fla. Land Surveyor of Yr. 1973, pres. 1972, pres. Dade County chpt. 1965-69, hon., life mem. Dade County chpt. 1993); mem. AIA, NSF, Profl. Surveyors of Fla. (bd. dirs., chmn. 1993-94), Am. Soc. Photogrammetry and Remote Sensing (Presdl. citation 1982, 91, Merit award 1992), Am. Soc. Photogrammetry Found. (vice chmn. 1985-91), Am. Mil. Engrs., Am. Planning Assn., Internat. Geog. Info. Found. (vice-chmn.), Miami Bd. Realtors, Fla. Engring. Soc. (bd. dirs. 1992-94), Fla. Planning and Zoning Assn. (S. Fla. chpt.), Fla. Assn. Cadastral Mappers, Bus. Inc., Sierra Club (pres. 1977), Com. of 100, Bus. Inc., Granada Golf Assn., 10th Holers Golf Assn. (treas. 1995-96, pres. 1996-97, pres. 2003-04, bd. dirs.), Coral Gables Country Club Fleet, Coral Gables 30 Yr. Club, Coral Gables Fin. Club (pres. 1998-01), U. Miami Yacht Club, Century Club Coral Gables (exec. sec., treas. 1993-96), Coral Gables Country Club (dir., pres. 1991-97, chmn., vice chmn. found. 1992-94, pres. fin. club 1998-02), Riviera Country Club 9 (fin. com.), Holly Hills Country Club (NC), Computer Club Coral Gables (bd. dirs.), U. Miami Sailing Club, Kiwanis (pres. Southwest Miami chpt. 1979-81), Elks, Duplicate Bridge Nat. Master, Lambda Alpha Internat., Kappa Alpha Republican. Roman Catholic. Avocations: golf, bridge, travel. Home: 1207 Sorolla Ave Coral Gables FL 33134-3515 Personal E-mail: ebrow40862@aol.com.

BROWNELL, F. WILLIAM, lawyer; b. Ashland, Wis., July 18, 1952; BS, Georgetown Univ., 1974, MS, JD, Georgetown Univ., 1978. Bar: DC 1978, lic.: US Ct. Appeals, DC 1979, US Supreme Ct. 1983, US Ct. Appeals, 11th Cir. 1987, US Ct. Appeals, 2nd, 7th Cir. 1988. Ptnr., resources, regulatory, environ. law Hunton & Williams LLP, Washington. Mem.: ABA, Phi Beta Kappa. Office: Hunton & Williams 1900 K St NW Washington DC 20006-1109 Office Phone: 202-955-1555. Office Fax: 202-778-2201. Business E-Mail: bbrownell@hunton.com.

BROWNELL, KELLY DAVID, psychologist, educator; b. Evansville, Ind., Oct. 31, 1951; s. Arnold Buffum and Margaret Elizabeth (Egly) Brownell; m. Mary Jo Gabriele, Aug. 20, 1977; children: Matthew Joseph, Kevin David, Kristy Elizabeth. BA, Purdue U., 1973; PhD, Rutgers U., 1977. Lic. clin. psychologist Conn. Postdoctoral fellow Brown U., Providence, 1977; from asst. prof. to assoc. prof. U. Pa., Phila., 1977—87, prof., 1987-90; prof. psychology Yale U., New Haven, 1991—, prof. epidemiology and pub. health, 2003—06, chair dept. psychology, 2003—06, dir. Rudd Ctr. for Food Policy and Obesity, 2005—, dir. Yale Ctr. Eating and Weight Disorders, 1994-2000, master of Silliman Coll. Dir. Rudd Ctr. Food Policy and Obesity. Author: (books) Handbook of Eating Disorders, 1986, Handbook of Behavioral Medicine, 1988, Eating Disorders in Athletes, 1991, Eating Disorders and Obesity, 1995, vol. 2, 2002, Behavioral Medicine and Women, 1998, Food Fight, 2004; contbr. articles to profl. jours. Named one of World's 100 Most Influential People, Time Mag., 2006; recipient Cattell award, N.Y. Acad. Scis., 1978, Choice award, ALA, 1989, Disting. Alumni award, Purdue U., 2001. Fellow: APA (pres. divsn. health psychology 1989—90), Acad. Behavioral Medicine Rsch., Soc. Behavioral Medicine (pres. 1988—89); mem.: Inst. of Medicine, Assn. Advancement Behavior Therapy (pres. 1988—89). Office: Yale Univ Rudd Ctr 309 Edwards St Box 208369 New Haven CT 06520-8369 Office Phone: 203-432-7790. E-mail: kelly.brownell@yale.edu.

BROWNELL, NORA MEAD, former commissioner; b. Erie, Pa., May 18, 1947; d. George J. and Mary E. (Burke) Mead; m. Frederic M. Brownell, Sept. 9, 1972 (div.); children: Samantha, Peter, Alexa. Student, Manhattanville Coll., 1965-66, U. Syracuse, NYC, 1966-69. Auction dir. channel 12 Stas. WHYY, Phila., 1980-81; inaugural dir., campaign cons. Re-election Campaign for Gov. Thornburgh, Harrisburg, 1981-82; dep. exec. asst. Gov. Richard Thornburgh, Harrisburg, Pa., 1982-87; v.p. corp. community rels. Meridian Bancorp, Inc., Phila., 1987-92; sr. v.p. corp. affairs Meridian Bancorp, Inc., Corestates Bancorp., 1992-96; acting exec. dir. Regional Performing Arts Ctr. Inc., 1997; commr. Pa. Pub. Utility Commission, 1997—2001, Fed Energy Regulatory Commn., US Dept. Energy, Washington, 2001—06. Bd. dirs. NARUC, Times Pub. Co., Pa. Free Libr., Need Indeed, Please Touch Mus., Pa. Humanities Council, Susquehanna Art Mus., NRRI, Millennium Bank. Mem. Greater Phila. Cultural Alliance, Harmony House, Bus. Vols. for the Arts.

BROWNER, CAROL M., management consultant, former federal agency administrator; b. Fla., Dec. 16, 1955; d. Michael Browner and Isabella Harty Hugues; m. Michael Podhorzer; 1 child, Zachary. Grad., U. Fla., 1977, JD, 1979. Gen. counsel govt. ops. com. Fla. Ho. of Reps., 1980; with Citizen Action, Washington; chief legis. aide environ. issues to Sen. Lawton Chiles US Senate, 1986—88, legis. dir. to Sen. Al Gore, Jr., 1988-91; sec.Dept. Environ. Regulation State of Fla., 1991-93; administr. EPA, Washington, 1993—2000; prin. The Albright Group L.L.C., Washington, 2001—. Mem. adv. coun. Harvard Med. Sch., Ctr. for Health and the Global Environment. Recipient Mother of the Yr. award, Nat. Mother's Day Com., 1997, Lifetime Achievement award, NY State Bar Assn., Woman of the Yr. award, Glamour mag., Guy M. Bradley Lifetime Achievement award, Audubon Soc. (S. Fla. chapter). Democrat. Office: The Albright Group 901 15th St NW Ste 1000 Washington DC 20005

BROWNFIELD, WILLIAM R., former ambassador; b. Fort Bragg, NC, May 1952; m. Kristie A. Kenney. BA, Cornell U., 1974; Student, U. Tex. Sch. of Law, 1976—78; grad., Nat. War Coll., 1993. Entered fgn. svc. US Dept. State, 1979, polit. adv. to comdr.-in-chief U.S. So. Command Panama, 1989—90, counselor for humanitarian affairs Geneva, 1995—98, prin. dep. asst. sec. for internat. narcotics & law enforcement Washington, 1998—99, dep. asst. sec. for We. Hemisphere, 1999—2002, US amb. to Chile Santiago, 2002—04, US amb. to Venezuela Caracas, 2004—07.*

BROWN-HRUSKA, SHARON, economist, former commissioner; m. Donald Hruska; 1 child, Jacob. PhD in Econ., Va. Tech., 1994. Asst. prof. fin. AB Freeman Sch. Business, Tulane Univ., 1995—98, George Mason U., 1998—2002; commr. Commodity Futures Trading Commn., Washington, 2002—06, acting chmn., 2004—05; v.p. securities & fin. practice NERA Econ. Consulting, Washington, 2006—. Contbr. articles to numerous profl. jours. Recipient Key Women in Energy's Global Leadership award, 2004. Office: NERA Econ Consulting 1255 23rd St NW Ste 600 Washington DC 20037*

BROWNING, CANDACE, investment company executive; b. Jan. 24, 1956; BA in Hist., Brandeis U., 1977; MBA in Mktg., Columbia U., 1979. Rsch. analyst airline industry Merrill Lynch and Co., NYC, 1990—2000; dep. dir. global rsch. product Pan-Europe Merrill Lynch EMEA Rsch. Mgmt., London, 2000—01; dir. equity rsch. for Ams. region Merrill Lynch and Co., NYC, 2001—03, sr. v.p., head global securities rsch. and econs. group, 2003—07, pres. Merrill Lynch Global Rsch., 2007—. Named to all-star analyst survey for 17 years, Institutional Investor. Mem.: Soc. Airline Analysts (past. pres.), Wings Club (past bd. dir.). Office: Merrill Lynch & Co Inc 4 World Fin Ctr 250 Vesey St New York NY 10080*

BROWNING, CHRISTOPHER R., historian, educator; b. Durham, NC, May 22, 1944; s. Robert Willard and Eleanor (Oechsli) B.; m. Jennifer Jane Horn; children: Kathryn, Anne. BA, Oberlin Coll., 1967; MA, U. Wis., 1968, PhD, 1975. Instr. history Allegheny Coll., Meadville, Pa., 1969-71; asst. prof. history Pacific Luth. U., Tacoma, 1974-79, assoc. prof., 1979-84, prof., 1984-97, disting. univ. prof., 1997-99; Frank Porter Graham prof. history U. NC, Chapel Hill, 1999—. J.B. and Maurice C. Shapiro sr. scholar in residence U.S. Holocaust Mus., 1996, Ina Levine scholar, 2002-03; George Macaulay Trevelyan lectr. Cambridge U., 1999; George L. Mosse lectr. U. Wis., Madison, 2002. Author: The Final Solution and the German Foreign Office, 1978, Fateful Months, 1985, Ordinary Men, 1992 (Nat. Jewish Book award 1993), The Path to Genocide, 1992, Nazi Policy, Jewish Workers, German Killers, 2000, Collected Memories: Holocaust History and Post-War Testimony, 2003, The Origins of the Final Solution, 2004 (Nat. Jewish Book award 2004). Woodrow Wilson fellow, 1967-68, Alexander von Humboldt fellow, Germany, 1980-81, Fulbright rsch. fellow, Israel, 1989, Inst. for Advanced Studies fellow, Princeton, NJ, 1995. Fellow: Am. Acad. Arts and Scis. Office: U NC Dept History Chapel Hill NC 27599-0001

BROWNING, JAMES ROBERT, federal judge; b. Great Falls, Mont., Oct. 1, 1918; s. Nicholas Henry and Minnie Sally (Foley) Browning; m. Marie Rose Chapell. BA, Mont. State U., Missoula, 1938; LLB with honors, U. Mont., 1941, LLD (hon.), 1978, Santa Clara U., 1989. Bar: Mont. 1941, D.C. 1953, U.S. Supreme Ct. 1952. Spl. atty. antitrust divsn. US Dept. Justice, 1941—43, spl. atty. gen. litigation sect. antitrust divsn., 1946—48, chief antitrust dept. N.W. regional office, 1948—49, asst. chief gen. litigation sect. antitrust divsn., 1949—51, 1st asst. civil divsn., 1951—52, exec. asst. to atty. gen., 1952—53, chief, Exec. Office for US Attys., 1953; pvt. practice Washington, 1953—58; lectr. NYU Sch. Law, 1953, Georgetown U. Law Center, 1957—58; law clk. US Supreme Ct., Washington, 1958—61; judge US Ct. Appeals (9th cir.), 1961—76, 1988—2000, chief judge, 1976—88, sr. judge, 2000—. Reed justice com. on continuing edn., tng. and adminstrn. Jud. Conf. of US, 1967—68, com. on ct. adminstrn., 1969—71, chmn. subcom. on jud. stats., 1969—71, com. to study the illustrative rules of jud. misconduct, 1969, com. on the budget, 1971—77, adminstrn. office, subcom. on budget, 1974—76, mem., 1976—88, exec. com. of conf., 1978—87, com. to study the illustrative rules of jud. misconduct, 1985—87, com. to study U.S. jud. conf., 1986—88, com. on internat. conf. of appellate judges, 1987—90; David T. Lewis disting. judge-in-residence U. Utah, 1987; Blankenbaker lectr. U. Mont., 1987; Sibley lectr. U. Ga., 1987; lectr. Human Rights Inst., Santa Clara U. Sch. Law, Strasbourg. Editor-in-chief: Mont. Law Rev. Dir. Western Justice Found.; chmn. 9th Cir. Hist. Soc. 1st lt. US Army, 1943—46. Decorated Bronze Star; named to, Order of the Grizzly, U. Mont., 1973; recipient Devitt Disting. Svc. to Justice award, 1990; scholar in residence, Santa Clara U., 1989, U. Mont., 1991. Mem.: FBA (bd. dirs. 1945—61, nat. coun. 1958—62), ABA (judge adv. com. to standing com. on Ethics and Profl. Responsibility 1973—75), Am. Soc. Legal History (adv. bd. jour.), Am. Judicature Soc. (chmn. com. on fed. judiciary 1973—74, bd. dirs. 1972—75, Herbert Harley award 1984), Inst. Jud. Adminstrn., Am. Law Inst., Mont. Bar Assn. (Jameson award 2001), D.C. Bar Assn., Nat. Lawyers Club (bd. govs. 1959—63). Office: US Ct Appeals 9th Cir 95 7th St San Francisco CA 94103 *Notable cases include: pro bono case Bell vs. U.S., 349 U.S. 81, 1955.**

BROWNING, JAY D., energy executive; BBA in Fin., Tex. Tech. U., MBA, JD, Tex. Tech. U. Atty. corp./transactional divsn. Baker & Botts, LLP, Austin, Tex.; assoc. corp. and securities divsn. Akin, Gump, Strauss, Hauer & Feld, LLP, San Antonio; various legal positions Valero Energy Corp., San Antonio, 1993, corp. sec., mng. atty. corp. law, v.p., 2002, sr. v.p. corp. law, sec. Office: Valero Energy Corpn PO Box 696000 San Antonio TX 78269-6000

BROWNING, KEITH D., automotive executive; Contr. we. coast div. Circuit City, 1984—87, asst. corp. contr., 1987—90, corp. contr., 1990—96; exec. v.p., CFO, sec. CarMax Inc., Richmond, Va., 1996—. Office: CarMax Inc 12800 Tuckahoe Creek Pkwy Richmond VA 23238-1115*

BROWNING, KURT S., state official; b. Fla., 1958; BA in Polit. Sci., U. South Fla. Supr. elections Pasco County, 1980—2006; sec. state State of Fla., Tallahassee, 2006—. Pres. Downtown Dade City Main St., Inc. Mem.: Pasco County United Way, Boy Scouts Am. Republican. Office: Office Sec State R A Gray Bldg 500 S Bronough St Tallahassee FL 32399*

BROWNING, PETER CRANE, manufacturing executive; b. Boston, Sept. 2, 1941; s. Ralph Leslie and Nancy (Crane) Browning; m. Carole Ann Shegog, Dec. 14, 1963 (div. 1974); children: Christina, Jennifer; m. Kathryn Anne Klucharich, July 27, 1974; children: Kimberley, Peter. AB in History, Colgate U., Hamilton, NY, 1963; MBA, U. Chgo., 1976. Salesman, mktg. mgr. White Cap divsn. Continental Can, Northbrook, Ill., 1964-75; mgr. mktg. Conally Venture divsn. Continental Can, 1975-79; gen. mktg. and sales mgr. Bondware divsn. Continental Can, 1979-81, v.p., gen. mgr., 1981-84; v.p. gen. mgr. White Cap. divsn. Continental Can, 1984-86, exec. v.p., oper. officer, 1987-89; pres. Gold Bond Bldg. Products divsn. Nat. Gypsum Co., Charlotte, NC, 1989-90; pres., chmn., CEO Nat. Gypsum Co., Charlotte, 1990-93; exec. v.p. Sonoco Products Co., Hartsville, SC, 1993-96, pres., COO, 1996-98, pres., CEO, 1998-2000; chmn. bd. dirs. Nucor Corp., 2000—06, lead dir., 2006—. Bd. dirs. Wachovia Corp., Lowe's Cos., Inc., Phoenix Cos., Inc., Acuity Brands, Inc., ENPRO Industries; dean McColl Grad. Sch. Bus. Queens U., Charlotte, 2002—06. Life mem. coun. U. Chgo. Grad. Sch. Mem.: DeBordieu Country Club, Quail Hollow Country Club. Republican. Episcopalian. Avocations: mountain climbing, running, reading. Office: Nucor Corp 1915 Rexford Rd Charlotte NC 28211 Office Phone: 704-366-7000. Office Fax: 704-362-4208.

BROWNING, STEVEN ALAN, ambassador; Consular officer Office U.S. Amb., Dominican Republic, gen. svcs. officer Kenya, administrv. officer Alexandria br. Egypt, adminstrv. and gen. svcs. officer Sri Lanka, Tanzania, 1993—96; spl. asst. to under sec. mgmt. US Dept. State, exec. dir. Bur. African Affairs, 1996—98; dean sch. profl. and area studies Nat. Fgn. Affairs Training Ctr., 1998—2000; diplomat in residence Ctr. Internat. Studies U. So. Calif., 2000—03; U.S. amb. to Malawi US Dept. State, 2003—04; mgmt. officer Office U.S. Amb., Iraq, 2004—05; US amb. to Uganda US Dept. State, 2006—. Office: DOS Amb 2190 Kampala Pl Washington DC 20521-2190

BROWNING, WILLIAM J., child protective service director; b. Scranton, Pa., May 1, 1965; s. William Ralph Browning and Jeannette Elizabeth Engelhart; m. Celia Jane Nigro; children: Kaitlin Makenzie, Rhiannon Alexandra. BS, Pa. State U., University Park, 1988. Coord. NY County Dist. Attys. Office, Child Abuse Bur., NYC, 1991—95; milieu supr. Jewish Bd. Family & Children's Svcs., Geller Ho. Diagnostic, SI, NY, 1991—2005; child fatality rev. coord. NY County Med. Examiners Office, NYC, 1995—97; asst. adminstr. Monroe County Children & Youth Svcs., Stroudsburg, Pa., 1996—2005; exec. dir. Lackawanna County Children & Youth Svcs., Scranton, Pa., 2005—. Trainer U. Pitts., Mechanicsburg, Pa., 1999—. Bd. mem. NE Pa. Child Advocacy Ctr., Scranton, 2006. R-Conservative. Achievements include development of government child welfare as a research and clinically based institution. Office: Lackawanna County Children & Youth 200 Adams Ave Scranton PA 18503 Business E-Mail: browningw@lackawannacounty.org.

BROWN LEATHERBERRY, THOMAS HENRY, performing company executive, clergyman; b. Wilmington, Del., June 24, 1930; s. Glenn Ford and Rita (Leatherberry) Brown; m. Grace L. Wilson, Mar. 1, 1950 (div. 1978), m. Wendolyn M. King, Oct. 8, 2002; children: Linda Henry, Patricia Williams, Lucinda Brown, Martha Baccus, Tommy Jr. (dec.), Jason James. Student, Carnegie Hall Sr. Drama Sch., NYC, 1961; A. in Engring. Comms., NY Sch. Announcing, NYC, 1968; BA in Behavioral Sci. and Bibl. Edn., U. Del.; M Bibl. Theology, Ea. Bapt. U.; DD (hon.), Trinity Coll., Knoxville, Tenn., 1970. Artist, comedian Mantan Moreland, NYC, 1959-62; road mgr., negotiator Langston Hughes Prodns., NYC, 1963-66; dir. music Chs. of God in Christ, Bklyn., 1968-78; dir. arts Gospel Arts Coalition, Inc., Wilmington, 1978—; pastor Bible Way House of Prayer Worldwide Inc., Wilmington, 1989—; minister of music Bibleway Mid-Atlantic Diocese, Balt., 1990—. Dir. asst. Alvin Ailey Dancers, NYC, 1963; disk jockey Sta. WWRL, NYC, 1969, tchr. Christina Cultural Arts, Wilmington, 1983-89; music dir. World Christian Fellowship, 1989—. Dir. recs.: Rite Enterprise Rec. Co., 1954; actor: Prodigal Son, 1963, Black Nativity, 1964; asst. to producer: (TV) MD, 1967; stage dir., program mgr.: Gospel Music shows, CBS-TV, 1967; author: (radio) America Calls, 1967, Israel Radio Calls, 1967; dir., engr. RCA Inst. TV, Sta. ABC-TV, 1968; pianist: (with Mahelia Jackson); songwriter: (with Sally Martin Singers), (with Wilson & Watson Singers), (plays) Langston Hughes, James Baldwin and Marion Willliams, (songs) God Specializes, God is Still on the Throne, Come on in the Room, Hold the Light, Tiney Crumbles of Happiness, The Only Hope We Have is in Christ Jesus and others. Program dir. YMCA, Wilmington, 1978-81; entertainer for Gov. Dupont, State of Del., 1980; dir. gospel music coun. 6602, City of Wilmington, 1983. With US Army, 1950-53. Named State Leader, African Am. Proclamation Inc., Phila., 1983; recipient Attestation Pilgrimage award, Minister of Courison, Jerusalem, 1983, award of Grand Performance, Jewish Community Rels. Com., Wilmington, 1988. Mem. BMI, Am. Guild Authors and Composers, Trinity Coll. Alumni Assn., Am. Legion (chaplain Brandywine, Del.), VFW (life), Masons (grand music dir. 1989—, past worshipful master, illustrious master, imperial dep. chaplain 1997—, past grand high priest, 33 degree, hon. past emperial potentate, 2002, royal select master thrice, Ill. master), Order Ea. Star (past worthy patron), Shriners, Elks (Appreciation award Paul Lawrence Dunbar lodge #106 1981), Heroines of Jericho (grand Joshua), Honor Guard Assn. (lt. col.), Del. Phylaxis Soc. (pres.), Epsilon Delta Psi (life). Democrat. Avocations: football, basketball, movies, playing organ and piano.

BROWNLEE, DAVID A., lawyer; BA, Yale Univ., 1962; MA, Oxford Univ., England, 1964; LLB, Yale Univ., 1968. Bar: Pa. 1969, Supreme Ct. Pa., US Dist. Ct. (no. NY & we. Pa.), US Ct. Fed. Claims, US Tax Ct., US Ct. Appeals (2d, 3d & 6th cir.). Law clk. Justice Thomas W. Pomeroy, Jr., Pa. Supreme Ct.; ptnr. & gen. counsel Kirkpatrick & Lockhart Nicholson Graham LLP, Pitts. Mem. Pitts. Bd. Edn.; past chmn. Gov. merit selection com. for state ct. judges, Allegheny County, Pa. Rhodes scholar. Fellow: Am. Bar Found.; mem.: ABA, Am. Law Inst., Pa. Bar Assn., Allegheny County Bar Assn. Office: Kirkpatrick & Lockhart Nicholson Graham LLP Henry W Oliver Bldg 535 Smithfield St Pittsburgh PA 15222-2312 Office Phone: 412-355-6446. Office Fax: 412-355-6501. Business E-Mail: dbrownlee@klng.com.

BROWNLEE, DONALD EUGENE, II, astronomer, educator; b. Las Vegas, Nev., Dec. 21, 1943; s. Donald Eugene and Geraldine Florence (Stephen) B.; m. Paula Szkody. BS in Elec. Engring, U. Calif., Berkeley, 1965; PhD in Astronomy, U. Wash., 1970. Research assoc. U. Wash., 1970-77, asso. prof. astronomy, 1977-89; asso. geochemistry Calif. Inst. Tech., Pasadena, 1977-82; prof. astronomy U. Wash., 1989—. Cons. NASA, 1976— Author papers in field, chpts. in books. Grantee NASA, 1975; recipient J. Lawrence Smith medal Nat. Acad. of Sciences, 1994. Fellow Am. Acad. Arts & Scis.; mem. Internat. Astron. Union, Am. Astron. Assn., Meteoritical Soc. (Leonard medal 1996), Com. Space Rsch. Dust, NAS (NASA PI stardust mission). Office: U Wash Dept Astronomy Seattle WA 98195-0001*

BROWNLEE, JOHN L., prosecutor; BA, Washington and Lee U., 1987; MBA, Golden Gate U.; JD, Coll. William and Mary, 1994. Law clk. US Dist. Ct. (we. dist.) Va., 1994—96; asst. US atty. DC, 1997—2001; assoc. Woods, Rogers and Hazlegrove, Richmond, Va., 2001; US atty. (we. dist.) Va. US Dept. Justice, Roanoke, Va., 2001—. Lt. US Army, 1987—91, capt. JAG USAR, 1991—. Office: US Attys Office 310 First St SW Rm 906 Roanoke VA 24011*

BROWNLEE, LES (ROMIE LESLIE BROWNLEE), former civilian military employee; Degree, U. Wyo.; MBA, U. Ala.; grad. U.S. Army War Coll. Commd. 2d lt. US Army, advanced through grades to col.; mem. Rep. staf Senate Armed Svcs. Com., 1987—2001; prin. profl. staff mem. for Army and M.C. Corps program Spl. Ops. Forces and Drug Interdiction Policy and Support, 1987—96; nat. security adv. to Sen. John Warner US Senate, 1993—96; staff dir. Spl. Ops. Forces and Drug Interdiction Policy and Support, 1996—2001; under sec. Dept. of Army, US Dept. Def., Washington, 2001—04, acting sec., 2003—04. Decorated Silver Star, Bronze Star, Purple Heart.

BROWNLEE, PAULA PIMLOTT, higher education consultant; b. London, June 23, 1934; came to US, 1959; d. John Richard and Alice A. (Ajamian) Pimlott; m. Thomas H. Brownlee, Feb. 10, 1961; children: Kenneth Gainsford, Elizabeth Ann, Clare Louise. BA with honors, Somerville Coll., Oxford U., Eng., 1957, PhD in Organic Chemistry, 1959. Postdoctoral fellow U. Rochester, NY, 1959-61; rsch. chemist Am. Cyanamid Co., Stamford, Conn., 1961-62; lectr. U. Bridgeport, Conn., 1968-70; asst. prof., then assoc. prof. Rutgers U., NJ, 1970-76, assoc. dean, then acting dean Douglass Coll. NJ, 1972-76; dean faculty, prof. chemistry Union Coll., Schenectady, NY, 1976-81; pres., prof. chemistry Hollins U., Va., 1981-90; pres. Assn. Am. Colls. and Univs., Washington, 1990-98; prin. Pres.' Group, LLC, 1997—2003; founding prin. Nat. Acad. for Acad. Leadership. Vice chmn. bd. dirs. Am. Academic Leadership Inst., 2007—. Contbr. articles to profl. jours., chapters to books. Sr. trustee U. Rochester; trustee Wilson Coll., Pa. Hon. fellow Somerville Coll., Oxford, Eng., 1996—. Mem. Am. Chem. Soc., Sigma Xi. Office Phone: 540-869-7066. Business E-Mail: pbrownlee@hughes.net.

BROWNLEE, ROBERT CALVIN, pediatrician, educator; b. Due West, S.C., Mar. 13, 1922; s. Robert Calvin and Eleanor Louise (Pressly) B.; m. Judith Frances Irby; children: Eleanor Koets, Susan, Katherine Chambers, Jonathan, Robert Calvin. AB, Erskine Coll., 1943; MD, Vanderbilt U., 1945. Diplomate Am. Bd. Pediat. (pres. 1975), Am. Bd. Family Practice. Intern Vanderbilt U. Hosp., Nashville, 1945-46, resident, 1948-49, U. Va., Charlottesville, 1949-50; chief resident Vanderbilt U., Nashville, 1950-51; practice medicine, specializing in pediat. Christie Pediatric Group, Greenville, SC, 1951-70; dir. pediat. Greenville Hosp. Sys., 1970-75; assoc. exec. sec. Am. Bd. Pediat., Chapel Hill, NC, 1976, exec. sec., 1977-87, pres., 1987-92. Clin. prof. pediat. U. Pa., 1976-78; prof. pediat. U. S.C., 1971-75; clin. prof. U. N.C., 1978-96. Contbr. articles to med. jours. With AUS, 1943-45; with M.C. USAF, 1946-48, 53. Mem. Am. Acad. Pediat., Ambulatory Pediat. Assn. Presbyterian.

BROWNLEE, ROBERT HAMMEL, lawyer; b. Chester, Ill., Dec. 15, 1951; s. Robert Mathis and Geneva (Hammel) B.; m. Sue F., June 17, 1978. BS, So. Ill. U., Carbondale, 1973; JD, Vanderbilt U., Nashville, 1976. Bar: Mo. 1976, Ill. 1977, U.S. Dist. Ct. (ea. and we. dists.) Mo. 1976, U.S. Dist. Ct. (so. and cen. dists.) Ill. 1977, U.S. Ct. Appeals (8th cir.) 1979, Ky. 1999, U.S. Supreme Ct. 1999. Assoc. Thompson & Mitchell, St. Louis, 1976-82; ptnr. Thompson Coburn, St. Louis, 1982—. Mng. editor Vanderbilt Law Review, Nashville, 1975-76; mem. Bar Assn. of Met. St. Louis, 1976—, Ill. State Bar Assn., Springfield, Ill., 1977—, Am. Bankruptcy Inst., 1988—, Ky. Bar, 1999—. Co-author: Rights of Secured Creditors in Bankruptcy, 1987, Lender Liability in Missouri, 1988, Protection of Secured Interests in Bankruptcy, 1989, Litigation in Bankruptcy Proceedings, 1994, Interlocutory Appeal Issues Before the Bankruptcy Reform Commission, 1996; Author: Bankruptcy Impact on Commercial Leases, Advanced Missouri Real Estate Law, 1997, updated, 1999, 2001, Impact of the Bankruptcy Review Commission's Report on Creditor Issues, 1997, Vendor Protection in Maritime Bankruptcy Reorganizations, 2003, The Sarbanes-Oxley Act of 2002: Potential Impacts on Future Administration of Large Chapter II Cases, 2003, rev. edit., 2006. Mem. Friends of the St. Louis Zoo., 1986—, St. Louis Bot. Garden Sponsors, 1987—; builder of the community United Way of Greater St. Louis, 1988—. Fellow Am. Coll. Bankruptcy Lawyers (8th cir. coun. 2005—); mem. ABA (litigation sec. 1976—, co-chair jury instrn. subcom. of bankruptcy and insolvency com. 1994-99, bus. sec. 1976—, vice-chair claims trading subcom. bus. bankruptcy com. 1998-2001, chmn. subcom. adminstrn., U.S. trustee and jurisdiction and venue 2002-05, co-chmn. planning subcom. 2006—), Mo. Athletic Club, Mo. Bankers Assn. (chmn. legal adv. bd. 1997-98). Avocations: fishing, american art pottery, antiques, gardening. Office: Thompson Coburn LLP 1 US Bank Plz Ste 2600 Saint Louis MO 63101-1643 Office Phone: 314-552-6017. Business E-Mail: rbrownlee@thompsoncoburn.com.

BROWNLEE, THOMAS MARSHALL, manufacturing executive; b. Omaha, Nebr., Oct. 11, 1926; s. John Templeton and Reed (Marshall) B.; children: Linda Sue, Thomas John, Curtis Marshall, Reed Ann; m. Lenora A. Hollingsworth, Mar. 31, 1994. BSBA, U. Nebr., 1950. Asst. mgr. Daytona Beach (Fla.) C. of C., 1950, Tampa (Fla.) C. of C., 1952-53; exec. mgr. Tallahassee C. of C., 1953- 58; exec. v.p. Greater Columbia (S.C.) C. of C., 1959-63, Winston-Salem (N.C.) C. of C., 1963-64, Orlando Area (Fla.) C. of C., 1964-78; chmn. Brownlee Lighting Co., Orlando, 1978—. Mem. energy policy com. Orange County (Fla.) Schs.; mem. Fla. Energy Action Com.; mem. energy com. Nat. League Cities Contbr. articles to profl. jours. Bd. dirs. Loch Haven Art Mus.; bd. dirs. Chamber Inst., U. Ga.; mem. Orlando City Council.; pres. Christian Service Ctrs. Daily Bread. Served with USNR, 1944-46; as 1st lt. AUS, 1951-52. Mem. Fla. Energy Mgmt. Assn. (pres.), Illuminating Engring. Soc. (pres. Ctrl. Fla. chpt., bd. dirs., pres. internat. soc. 1996), Am. C. of C. Execs. Assn. (hon., pres. 1966), S.C. C. of C. Execs. Assn., Fla. C. of C. Execs. Assn. (pres. 1971), Better Bus. Bur. Ctrl. Fla. (chmn.), Knights Temple, Scottish-Am. Soc. Ctrl. Fla. (bd. dirs.), Orlando Scottish Games (exec. coun.), St. Andrews Soc. Ctrl. Fla. (pres.), Coun. Scottish Clans and Assn., Scottish Coalition (chmn.), Caledonian Found., Country Club Orlando, Univ. Club, Tiger Bay Club (pres.), Clan Hamilton Soc. (Fla. commr.), Rotary, Phi Delta Theta. Episcopalian. Office: Brownlee Lighting 4600 Dardanelle Dr Orlando FL 32808-3832 Office Phone: 407-297-3677.

BROWNLIE, ROBERT WILLIAM, lawyer; b. Sasebo, Japan, Mar. 5, 1962; s. Robert Philip and Sachiko (Sugita) B.; m. Perla Esteban, Jan. 7, 1989. BA in Economics, U. Calif. San Diego, 1985; JD, U. Calif. Davis, 1988. Bar: Calif. 1988, U.S. Dist. Ct. (so., ea. ctrl. & no. dist. Calif.), U.S. Ct. Appeals (5th, 9th cir.), U.S. Ct. Fed. Claims, US Supreme Ct. Rsch. asst. U. Calif. Davis Sch. of Law, 1986-87, teaching asst., 1987-88; summer assoc. Gray, Cary, Ames & Frye, San Diego, 1987, assoc., 1988-90, Milberg, Weiss, Bershad, Specthrie & Lerach, San Diego, 1990-92, Gray, Cary, Ware & Freidenrich, San Diego, 1992-95, mem., 1995—2004; ptnr., co-chmn. Securities Litigation practice group DLA Piper Rudnick Gray Cary, San Diego, 2005—. Contbr. articles to profl. jours. Pres., v.p., bd. dirs. Asian Bus. Assn., San Diego, 1994-98; bd. dirs. San Diego Mediation Ctr., 1994-95; fin. com. mem. San Diego Automotive Mus., 1993-95. Mem. ABA (mem. class action and derivative litigation com.), Nat. Asian Pacific Am. Bar Assn. (bd. dirs. 1997-99), Calif. Bar Assn., San Diego County Bar Assn. (legis. com. mem. 1988-95), Pan Asian Lawyers Assn. of San Diego (v.p., pres., bd. dirs. 1995-99), Order of Coif, Phi Kappa Phi. Democrat. Avocations: automobile enthusiast, golf, travel, sailing, boating. Home: 1450 Woodglen Ter Bonita CA 91902-4283 Office: DLA Piper US LLP 401 B St Ste 1700 San Diego CA 92101-4297 Office Phone: 619-699-3665. Office Fax: 858-699-2701. Business E-Mail: robert.brownlie@dlapiper.com.

BROWNLOW, FRANK WALSH, literature and language professor; b. Dundonald, Northern Ireland, Sept. 2, 1934; came to U.S., 1959; s. Frank and Katherine Georgina (Darroch) B. BA, Liverpool U., Eng., 1956; PhD, U. Birmingham, Eng., 1963. From instr. to assoc. prof. English U. Mich., Ann Arbor, 1959-61, 63-69; lectr. U. Western Ont., London, Can., 1961-63; from assoc. prof. to prof. Mt. Holyoke Coll., South Hadley, Mass., 1969—. Vis. assoc. prof. Dartmouth Coll., Hanover, Mass., 1968-69. Author: Two Shakespearean Sequences, 1977, Shakespeare, Harsnett and the Devils of Denham, 1993, Robert Southwell, 1996; editor: John Skelton: The Book of the Laurel, 1991; contbr. articles on Shakespeare, Skelton, Byron, Herbert, Chesterton, also others, to profl. jours. Mem.: Renaissance English Text Soc., Byron Soc. Avocation: music. Office: Mt Holyoke Coll Dept English South Hadley MA 01075 Office Phone: 413-538-2126. Business E-Mail: fbrownlo@mtholyoke.edu.

BROWN-OLMSTEAD, AMANDA, public relations executive; b. Oct. 7, 1943; Founder ABOA (formerly a divsn. Shandwick PLC), 1972; pres., CEO A Brown Olmstead Assocs., Atlanta. Mem. Atlanta Pub. Rels. Seminar Group. Bd. dirs. Ctrl. Atlanta Progress, Councilors for The Carter Ctr., Atlanta Bot. Garden; mem. adv. bd. Sheperd Spinal Ctr., U. Miss. Bus. Sch.; mem. adv. guild Clark U.; pres. Ga. chpt. Internat. Women's Forum; mem. exec. com. Regional Bus. Coalition, bd. dirs., Atlanta Regional Health Forum; mem. exec. com. Robinson Coll. Bus., chair Hall of Fame program. Named a Recognized Woman of Achievement, Internat. Women's Forum; named one of The Ten Outstanding Atlantans; named to Georgia Pub. Rels. Hall of Fame; recipient Gold medal, N.Y. Film and TV Festival; YWCA honoree, Salute to Women of Achievement. Fellow: Pub. Rels. Soc. Am. (mem. Counselors Acad., mem. eligibility bd., Silver Anvil award); mem.: Order of the Phoenix, Leadership Atlanta. Achievements include being featured in Mademoiselle magazine, Business Week, Savvy, Atlanta Weekly, Atlanta magazine, and Movers and Shakers in Georgia. Office: A Brown Olmstead Assocs 274 W Paces Ferry Rd NW Atlanta GA 30305-1167

BROWNRIGG, JOHN CLINTON, lawyer; b. Detroit, Aug. 7, 1948; s. John Arthur and Sheila Pauline (Taffe) B.; m. Rosemary F. Brownrigg; children: Brian M., Jennifer A., Katharine T. BA, Rockhurst Coll., 1970; JD cum laude, Creighton U., 1974. Bar: Nebr. 1974, U.S. Dist. Ct. Nebr. 1974, U.S. Tax Ct. 1977, U.S. Ct. Appeals (8th cir.) 1990. Ptnr. Eisenstatt, Higgins, Kinnamon, Okun & Brownrigg, P.C., Omaha, 1974-80, Erickson & Sederstrom, P.C., Omaha, 1980—. Lectr. law trial practice Creighton U. Sch. Law, Omaha, 1978-83; dir. Legal Aid Soc., Inc., Omaha, 1982-88, pres., 1987-88, devel. coun., 1989—; dir. Nebr. Continuing Legal Edn., Inc., 1991-93. Chmn. law sect. Archbishop's Capital Campaign, Omaha, 1991; dir. Combined Health Agys. Drive, 2001-03. Sgt. USAR, 1970-76. Fellow Nebr. State Bar Found. (dir. 1991-93); mem. Nebr. State Bar Assn. (pres. 1992-93), Nebr. Assn. Trial Attys., Omaha Bar Assn. (pres. 1990-91). Avocations: golf, bicycling, hiking. Office: Erickson & Sederstrom PC Ste 100 10330 Regency Parkway Dr Omaha NE 68114-3761

BROWNRIGG, WALTER GRANT, cartoonist; b. Boston, Oct. 26, 1940; children by previous marriage: Elizabeth Grant, Christopher Hertel; m. Judith Courtney Hamilton, Apr. 28, 1984; children: Carter Grant, Taylor Hamilton, Kelsey Anderson. AB in History cum laude, Princeton U., 1962; MBA, Columbia U., 1964. Asst. plant mgr. Berwick Weaving, Inc., Pa., 1964-72; asst. to v.p. Frank & Stessel, Inc., NYC, 1972-73; sr. assoc. Drake Sheahan/Stewart Dougall, Inc., NYC, 1973-76; exec. dir. Greater Hartford (Conn.) Arts Council, 1976-79; dir. Am. Council Arts, NYC, 1979-83; cartoonist, creator Grantland, 1984—. Mem. Charlottesville Rotary Club, Beta Gamma Sigma.

BROWNSON, JACQUES CALMON, architect; b. Aurora, Ill., Aug. 3, 1923; s. Clyde Arthur and Iva Kline (Felter) B.; m. Doris L. Curry, 1946; children: Joel C., Lorre J., Daniel J. (dec. Jan 2005). BS in Architecture, Ill. Inst. Tech., 1948, MS, 1954. Instr., asst. prof. architecture Ill. Inst. Tech., 1949-59; prof. architecture, chmn. dept. U. Mich., 1966-68; chief design C.F. Murphy Assocs., Chgo., 1959—61; project arch., chief designer Chgo. Civic Ctr. Archs., 1961—68; dir. state bldg. divsn. State of Colo., Denver, 1986—88; pvt. practice Denver, 1988—. Former mng. arch. Chgo. Pub. Bldg. Commn.; past dir. planning and devel. Auraria Ctr. for Higher Edn., Denver; bd. dirs. Capital Constrn., Denver; guest lectr. architecture in U.S. and Europe. Prin. works include Chgo. Civic Ctr., Lake Denver, Colo., 1985, Chgo. Tribune/Cabrini Green Housing, 1993; author: History of Chicago Architects, 1996, Oral History of Jacuqes Calmon Brownson, 1996. Recipient award for Geneva House Archtl. Record mag., 1956; Design award for steel framed factory Progressive Architecture mag., 1957. Home and Office: 659 Josephine St Denver CO 80206-3722

BROWNSON, KENNETH C., dean; b. Hazleton, Pa., Apr. 16, 1945; s. Kenneth George and Mary Louise (Dennion) B. AAS in Nursing, Del. Tech. and C.C., 1978; BS in Profl. Arts, St. Joseph's Coll., Standish, Maine, 1984; MS in Mgmt., The Am. Coll., 1986; MS in Psychology, Calif. Coast U., 1989; EdD in Adult and Nontraditional Edn., Newport U., 1991; Cert. in Cmty. Health Edn., Calif. Coll. Health Sci., 1999. RN, Del., Pa.; cert. psychiat. and mental health nurse; cert. allied health instr. Evening supr., asst. head nurse intensive/critical care unit Riverside Hosp., Wilmington, Del., 1980-83; staff RN, nurse, counselor crisis svc. unit Crozer-Chester Med. Ctr., Chester, Pa., 1983-94; pres. Adult Edn. Resource, New Castle, Del., 1987—; dean undergrad. studies Greenwich U., Australia, 1989—2001; prof. social studies, assoc. prof. health Am. Pub. U. Sys., 2001—. Mem. adv. bd. Insvc. Tng. Inst., 1991—99; v.p., bd. dirs. Brandywine Counseling, Inc., Wilmington, 2001—04. Mem. editl. bd. Health Care Mgr.; author: College at Home for Nurses and All Healthcare Professionals, 2002; contbr. articles to profl. jours. With USN, 1965-69, Vietnam. Recipient First Place, Feature Writing, Am. Med. Technologists, 2003, 2004. Home and Office: 33 W 4th St New Castle DE 19720-5092 E-mail: kbrownson@comcast.net.

BROWNSON, MARY LOUISE, counselor, educator, artist; b. Detroit, Dec. 8, 1927; d. Max Curt Poppe and Hilda Caroline Larson; m. Elwyn James Brownson, Dec. 30, 1950 (div. Sept. 1979); children: Elwyn James, Richard, Matthew, Mary. B of Design, U. Mich., Ann Arbor, 1950; MS, No. Mont. Coll., Havre, 1976. Cert. secondary sch. tchr. Mont., 1972. Instr. Wittenburg U., Springfield, Ohio, 1950—53, No. Mont. Coll., Havre, 1963—71; drug and alcohol counselor Alcohol Svcs. Ctr., Boise, Idaho, 1979—80; migrant career placement counselor Boise State U., Idaho, 1981—85; mgr. Ctr. Use, Boise Sr. Ctr., Idaho, 1985—88; employment counselor Fed. Cmty. Treatment Ctr., Boise, Idaho, 1988—90; mgr. activities Hillcrest Retirement Ctr., Boise, Idaho, 1990—94. Represented in permanent collections, Kent State U. Collection. Pres. PTA, Havre, Mont.; Dem. candidate for state legislature Havre, Mont. Mem.: AAUW (pres.), LWV (pres. 1999—2003). Democrat. Unitarian-Universalist. Avocations: gourmet cooking, swimming, reading, painting. Home: 3820 Sheringham Dr Boise ID 83704 Personal E-mail: mlbrownson@hotmail.com.

BROWNSON, SUE MCPHERSON, music educator; b. Burlington, NC, Apr. 7, 1958; d. William Steadman and Versa (Price) McPherson; children: Patrick Michael, Jessica Sue. BM, N.C. Sch. of the Arts, Winston-Salem, 1980; AS Sci., Coll., Burlington, NC, 1985. Private music tchr., Winston-Salem, NC, 1980—81; actress The Lost Colony, Mantec, NC, 1981; music tchr. Happy Acres Ranch, Jacksonville, 1982—85; lab. technician Roche Labs., Burlington, NC, 1985—87; sheet music dept. head Flesher Higher Music, Aurora, Colo., 1987—93; minister of music Aurora First Presbyn. Ch., Colo., 1987—93; music tchr. Elbert County Charter Sch., Elizabeth, Colo., 1997—2002; music tchr. voice and piano Brownson Music Studio, Elizabeth, Colo., 2000—. Mem.: Douglas Elbert Music Tchrs. Assn. (chair nominations com. 2000), Am. Coll. Musicians. Republican. Presbyn. Achievements include Students in voice and piano are divsn. winners and hon. mentions in local music competitions. Avocation: gardening. Home: 35711 Darting Bird Ride Elizabeth CO 80107 Office: Brownson Music Studio 35711 Darting Bird Ride Elizabeth CO 80107

BROWN SPITZMUELLER, JANIECE MARIE, lawyer; d. Shirle Lee and Jean Florence (Ferguson) Brown; m. Thomas Joseph Spitzmueller, July 31, 1998. BA, Calif. State U., San Bernardino, 1979; JD, Boston U., 1987. Bar: N.Y. 1993. Ct. atty. N.Y. State Unified Ct. Sys., NYC, 1993—95; assoc. Law Office of Julie A. Clark, Bklyn., 1996—96; hearing officer N.Y.C. Dept. Edn., NYC, 1997—2001; litigator N.Y.C Dept. Housing, NYC, 2001—. Contbr. articles to profl. jours. Mem. exec. com. Cmty. Bd. 1-Manhattan, NYC, 2000—; vol. missionary Mosaic Manhattan Ch., NYC, 2004—04. Fellow: N.Y. Bar Found.; mem.: NYC Civil Ct. Small Claims Arbitration Assn. (small claims arbitrator 2006—), Assn. of Bar of City of NY, Met. Black Bar Assn. (life), N.Y. State Bar Assn. (ho. of dels.), N.Y. County Lawyers' Assn. (com. sec. 2002—03, subcommittee chair 2002—, co-chair annual auction 2002—, com. chair 2004—07, Justice Ctr. adv. bd., comm. com., bd. dirs.). Roman Catholic. Avocations: reading, piano, writing, yoga, travel. Home Phone: 212-349-0821.

BROWNSTEIN, ALAN P., health foundation executive, consultant; b. NYC, Sept. 20, 1944; s. Charles S. and Thelma S. (Blauweiss) B.; m. Patricia Marie Rosenberg, June 15, 1968; children— Joshua B., Jeremy S. BS, SUNY-Buffalo, 1967, MSW, 1969; MPH, U. Mich., 1973. Dir. health policy and legisl. research Local 1199, Drug and Hosp. Union/Nat. Union

Hosp. and Nursing Home Employees, RWDSU, AFL-CIO, NYC, 1970-72; dep. dir. Office Comprehensive Health Planning, Exec. Office Human Services Mass., Boston, 1973-75; dir. office grants mgmt. and devel. NYC Health and Hosps. Corp., 1975-77; asst. dir. dept. for the community Community Service Soc. NY, NYC, 1977-80; dir. Council of Home Health Agys. and Community Health Services, Nat. League for Nursing, NYC, 1980-81; exec. dir. Nat. Hemophilia Found., NYC, 1981-94; pres., CEO Am. Liver Found., Cedar Grove, NJ, 1994—2004; pres. Nat. Down Syndrome Soc., NYC, 2005—. Expert witness U.S. Congress, 1971-95; cons. Citizens' Com. for Children, N.Y.C., 1979-81, Blue Cross Mass., Boston, 1981, Office Maternal and Child Health, USPHS, Rockville, Md., 1983; mem. adj. faculty in health econs., hosp. and healthcare mgmt. program Sch. Bus. Adminstrn., Adelphi U., Garden City, N.Y., 1979-81, mem. profl. adv. bd., 1977-81; mem. adj. faculty in health svcs. mgmt. New Sch. for Social Rsch., N.Y.C., 1979; mem. nat. adv. com. Nat. Pediatric HIV Resource Ctr. Co-author monographs: Consumers Guide to Health Insurance, 1974; Consumers Guide to Nursing Homes, 1975. Contbr. chpts. to books, articles to profl. jours. Vice pres. Health Systems Agy. Bd. G., Queens, N.Y., 1979-81; v.p. Jamaica Estates Assn., N.Y., 1980-92, Friends of Cunningham Park, Queens, 1983-85; bd. dirs. Cmty. Health Charities, 2002—. Recipient Faculty Fund for Social Work Students award SUNY-Buffalo Sch. Social Welfare, 1969, Disting. Alumni award SUNY Buffalo, 1993; fellow NIMH, 1967-69, USPHS, 1972-73 Mem. APHA, Pub. Health Assn. N.Y.C. (bd. dirs. 1979-82), World Fedn. Hemophilia, Nat. Health Coun. (bd. dirs. 1988—), Digestive Disease Nat. Coalition (bd. dirs. 1994—), Am. Soc. of Assn. Execs., Nat. Ctr. for Non-Profit Bds., Health Care Quality Alliance (bd. dirs. 1996-2001). Office: Nat Down Syndrome Soc 666 Broadway New York NY 10012 Office Phone: 212-460-9330. Office Fax: 212-979-2873.

BROWNSTEIN, ANDREW RICHARD, lawyer; b. Waterbury, Conn., Oct. 22, 1953; s. Jack and Edith (Wortman) B.; m. Elise Jaffe; children: Alexander, Julia. BA, BS in Econs., U. Pa., 1975, MBA, 1976; JD, Harvard U., 1979. Bar: N.Y. 1980, U.S. Ct. Appeals (3rd cir.) 1980. Law clk. to Hon. Leonard I. Garth U.S. Ct. Appeals (3d cir.), 1979-80; assoc. Wachtell, Lipton, Rosen & Katz, NYC, 1980-85, ptnr., corp. dept., 1985—, chmn. diversity com. Adj. prof. securities law Rutgers U. Sch. Law,1983; chmn. Ray Garrett Jr. Corp. & Securities Law Inst., Northwestern Univ. Sch. Law, 1998-99. Articles editor, Harvard Law Rev.; contbr. articles to profl. jours. Mem. ABA (securities regulation and bus. law divsn.), N.Y.C. Bar Assn., Phi Beta Kappa, Beta Gamma Sigma. Office: Wachtell Lipton Rosen & Katz 51 W 52nd St Fl 29 New York NY 10019-6150 Office Phone: 212-403-1233. Office Fax: 212-403-2233. Business E-Mail: arbrownstein@wlrk.com.

BROWNSTEIN, BARBARA LAVIN, geneticist, educator, director; b. Phila., Sept. 8, 1931; d. Edward A. and Rose (Silverstein) Lavin; m. Melvin Brownstein, June 1949 (div. 1955); children: Judith Brownstein Kaufmann, Dena. Asst. editor Biol. Abstracts, Phila., 1957-58; research fellow dept. microbial genetics Karolinska Inst., Stockholm, 1962-64; assoc. Wistar Inst., Phila., 1964-68; assoc. prof. molecular biology, dept. biology Temple U., Phila., 1968-74, prof., 1974-96, prof. emeritus, 1996—, chmn. dept., 1978-81, provost, 1983-90; sr. assoc. Ctr. Ednl. Rsch. U. Wash., Seattle, 1994—. Vis. scientist dept. tumor cell biology Imperial Cancer Rsch. Fund Labs., London, 1973-74; bd. dirs. Univ. City Sci. Ctr., Greater Phila. Econ. Devel. Coun., Forum Exec. Women; program officer NSF, 1992-93; sr. assoc. Inst. Ednl. Inquiry, Seattle, 1994—. Bd. dirs. Lopez Island Sch., 2001—. Recipient Liberal Arts Alumni award for excellence in teaching Temple U., 1980; recipient Outstanding Faculty Woman award Temple U., 1980 Fellow AAAS; mem. Am. Soc. Cell Biology, N.Y. Acad. Sci., Assn. Women in Sci., NSF (program officer 1992-93). Home: PO Box 835 Lopez Island WA 98261 Personal E-mail: bbrownst@msn.com.

BROWN-WAITE, VIRGINIA (GINNY BROWN-WAITE), congresswoman; b. Albany, NY, Oct. 5, 1943; m. Harvey Waite; children: Jeannine Bradford, Danene Mitchell, Lorie Sue Busiere. BS, SUNY, 1976; MS, Russell Sage Coll., 1984. Legis. dir. NY State Senate, 1970—87; commr. Hernando County Bd. of Commr., 1991—93; mem. Fla. State Senate, 1992—2002, US Congress from 5th Fla. dist., 2003—; mem. fin. svcs. com., govt. reform com., vet. affairs com. Adj. prof. Springfield Coll.; owner Mr. Donut franchise. Active W Hernando GOP, United Way; bd. dirs. Hernando County Spouse Abuse Ctr. Mem. Bus. and Profl. Women's Club, Suncoast MG Club. Republican. Roman Catholic. Office: Dist Office 38008 Meridian Ave Dade City FL 33526 Office Phone: 202-225-1000.*

BROWNWOOD, DAVID OWEN, lawyer; b. LA, May 24, 1935; s. Robert Scott Osgood and Ruth Elizabeth (Bellamy) B.; m. Sigrid Carlson, Mar. 3, 1956 (div. 1972); children: Jeffrey Owen, Kirsten, Scott David, Daniel Stuart; m. Susan Sloane Jannicky, July 4, 1975; 1 child, Mary Ruth Bellamy; stepchildren: Bradbury, Stephanie Ellington. AB with distinction, Stanford U., 1956; LLB magna cum laude, Harvard U., 1964. Bar: Calif. 1965, NY 1969. Law clk. Ropes & Gray, Boston, 1963; assoc. McCutchen, Doyle, Brown & Enersen, San Francisco, 1964-66; lectr. law U. Khartoum, Sudan, 1966-67, Kenya Inst. Adminstrn., Lower Kabete, 1967-68; assoc. Cravath, Swaine & Moore, NYC, 1968-72, ptnr., 1973—2003, sr. counsel, 2003—, recruiting ptnr., 1978-82, mng. ptnr. for legal staff, 1983-86; ptnr. in charge London office, 1995—2001. Treas. NY Law Inst., 1978-83, chmn. exec. com., 1983-88, pres., 1988-93. Mem. editorial bd. Harvard U. Law Rev., 1963-64. Nat. chair Harvard U. Law Sch. Fund, 1991—93; bd. dirs. Royal Oak Found., 2003—, treas., 2004—; pres. Benjamin Franklin House Found., 2002—07; trustee Greenwich Country Day Sch., Conn., 1985—92, v.p., 1986—88, pres., chmn. bd. trustees, 1988—92; co-chmn. Harvard U. Law Sch. 25th Reunion Gift, 1988—89, 40th Reunion Gift, 2003—05; co-chmn Stanford U. 50th Reunion Gift, 2005—06; NY regional com. campaign Harvard Law Sch., 1991—95; com. on univ. resources Harvard U., 1991—2006, mem. Harvard law sch. vis. com., 1995—2001; keystone regional vice chair centennial campaign Stanford U., 1986—92; exec. com. Stanford U. NY Coun., 1992—95; vice chmn. Stanford U. NY Major Gifts Com., 1993—95; co-chair Stanford U. Ea. Coun., 1993; bd. govs. Stanford Assocs., 1993—95, pres., chmn. bd. govs., 1994—95; bd. advisors Stanford U. Trust (UK), 1995—2002; mem. nat. bd. Outward Bound USA, 1993—96; trustee Greenwich Libr., 2003—, chair, planning com., 2007—; bd. dirs. Literacy Assistance Ctr., NYC, 1983—94, Collegiate Chorale, NYC, 2005—; co-chmn. bd. dirs. Literacy Assistance Ctr., NYC, 1987—94. 1st lt. USAF, 1956—61, fighter pilot Air Def. Command, capt. USAFR, Mass. Air N.G., 1961—66. Recipient Centennial medallion Stanford U., Stanford Assocs. award. Fellow Am. Bar Found., NY State Bar Found.; mem. ABA, NY State Bar Assn., Assn. Bar City NY, Stanford U. Alumni Assn. (bd.dirs. 2004—, chmn. fin. com. 2006—), The Pilgrims, Round Hill Club, Field Club of Greenwich, Sankaty Head Golf Club, Siasconset Casino Assn., Harvard Club NYC. Home: 296 Old Church Rd Greenwich CT 06830 also: 61 Orange St Nantucket MA 02554 Office: Cravath Swaine & Moore 825 8th Ave Fl 46 New York NY 10019-7416 Home Phone: 203-869-3982; Office Phone: 212-474-1218. Business E-Mail: dbrownwood@cravath.com.

BROXMEYER, HAL EDWARD, medical educator; b. Bklyn., Nov. 27, 1944; s. David and Anna (Gurman) B.; m. C. Beth Biller, 1969; children: Eric Jay, Jeffrey Daniel. BS, Bklyn. Coll., 1966; MS, L.I. U., 1969; PhD, NYU, 1973. Postdoctoral student Queens U., Kingston, Ont., Canada, 1973-75; assoc. rschr., rsch. assoc. Meml. Sloan Kettering Cancer Ctr., NYC, 1975-78, assoc., 1978-83, assoc. mem., 1983; asst. prof. Cornell U. Grad. Sch., NYC, 1980-83; assoc. prof. Ind. U. Sch. Medicine, Indpls., 1983-86, prof. medicine, microbiology and immunology, 1986—; sci. dir. Walther Oncology Ctr., Indpls., 1988—, chmn. microbiology and immunology, 1997—, Disting. prof., 2004—. Mem. hematology II study sect. NIH, Bethesda, Md., 1981—86, 1995—2000, chair, 1997—2000; adv. com. NHLBI, NIH, Bethesda, 1991—94; chmn. bd. sci. counselors Nat. Space Biomed. Rsch. Inst., 1997—2006, mem. coun., 1999—2006; bd. dirs. Nat. Disease Rsch. Interchange, 1998—, chmn., 2007—; co-chmn. sec. hematopoiesis Faculty of 1000 Medicine. Assoc. editor Exptl. Hematology, 1981—90, Jour. Immunology, 1987—92, Stem Cells, 1996—97, Brit. Jour. Haematology, 1998—, editor Jour. Leukocyte Biology, 1995—, sr. editor Stem Cells and Devel. (formerly Jour. Hematotherapy and Stem Cell Rsch.), 2000—, mem. editl. bd. Blood, 1983—87, Biotech. Therapeutics, 1988—95, Internat. Jour. Hematology, 1991—, Jour. Lab. Clin. Medicine, 1992—2006, Jour. Exptl. Medicine, 1992—, Annals Hematology, 1993—, Cell Transplantation, 1994—, Critical Rev. Oncology/Hematology, 1995—, Stem Cells, 1998—, Jour. Blood and Marrow Transplantations, 1998—, Cytokines, Cellular and Molecular Therapy, 1998—, Current Trends Immunology, 2004—, Internat. Jour. Biol. Scis., 2006—; contbr. over 620 articles to profl. jours. Ednl. com. Leukemia Soc. Am., Indpls., 1983—86; nat. career devel. study sect. Leukemia and Lymphoma Soc., NY, 1991—95, 2000—04. Recipient Founder's Day award NYU, 1973, Merit award Nat. Cancer Inst.; Leukemia Soc. Am. award, 1987-95, Spl. Fellow award, 1976-78, Scholar award, 1978-83, Gold medal City of Paris, 1993, World of Difference award Ind. Health Industry Forum, 1997, Landsteiner award Am. Assn. Blood Banks, 2002, Health Care Heroes award Indpls. Bus. Jour., 2002, Prestigious External Recognition award Ind. U. Purdue U. Indpls., 2003, Disting. Alumni award L.I. U., Bklyn. Ctr., 2005, Dr. Joseph T. Taylor Excellence in Diversity award Ind. U. Purdue U. Indpls., 2006, Dirk van Bekkum award Autologous Blood and Bone Marrow Soc., 2006, E. Donnall Thomas prize Am. Soc. Neonatal, 2007. Mem.: AAAS, Am. Soc. Blood and Marrow Transplantation, Am. Fedn. Clin. Rsch., Am. Soc. Hematology (coun. 2000—05, E. Donnall Thomas prize 2007), Internat. Soc. Stem Cell Rsch., Internat. Soc. Exptl. Hematology (pres. 1990—91), Am. Assn. Immunologists, Am. Assn. Cancer Rsch., Soc. Leukocyte Biology, NY Acad. Scis. Achievements include 13 patents in field. Avocation: competitive Olympic-style weightlifting. Home: 1210 Chessington Rd Indianapolis IN 46260-1630 Office: Ind U Sch Medicine 950 W Walnut St Rm 302 Indianapolis IN 46202-5181 Office Phone: 317-274-7510. Office Fax: 317-274-7592. Business E-Mail: hbroxmey@iupui.edu.

BROYLES, DEBORAH J., lawyer; b. Worcester, Mass., July 8, 1963; BA, Mt. Holyoke Coll., 1985; JD, Harvard U., 1993. Bar: Calif. 1993, US Ct. Appeals (9th Cir.), US Dist. Ct. (No. Dist.) Calif., US Dist. Ct. (Ea. Dist.) Calif., US Dist. (Ctrl. Dist.) Calif., US Dist. Ct. (So. Dist.) Calif. Ptnr., Diversity Com. Thelen Reid & Priest LLP, San Francisco. Mem.: Charles Houston Bar Assn., Nat. Bar Assn., Nat. Employment Law Coun., Calif. Minority Counsel Program (steering com. 2004—05), Calif. Assn. of Black Lawyers (ann. convention co-chmn. 1996, v.p.-north 1998—99, jud. appointments com. 1999—2002), Bar Assn. San Francisco, ABA. Office: Thelen Reid & Priest LLP 101 Second St Ste 1800 San Francisco CA 94105-3601 Office Phone: 415-369-7203. Office Fax: 415-371-1211. Business E-Mail: djbroyles@thelenreid.com.

BROYLES, FRANK (JOHN FRANKLIN BROYLES), athletic director, retired college football coach; b. Decatur, Ga., Dec. 26, 1924; m. Barbara Broyles; children: Jack, Hank, Dan, Tommy. BS in Indsl. Mgmt., Ga. Tech U., 1947. Asst. football coach Baylor U., Waco, Tex., 1947-50, Fla. U., 1950-51; offensive backfield coach Ga. Tech. U., 1951-57; head football coach Mo. U. Tigers, 1957-58, Ark. U. Razorbacks, Fayetteville, 1958-76, athletic dir., 1973—. Named Coach of Yr. Am. Football Coaches Assn., 1964; named to the Ark. Sports Hall of Honor, Ark. Hall of Fame, Ga. Tech Hall of Fame, Coll. Football Hall of Fame, 1983, Cotton Ball Hall of Fame, 1999; recipient Bob Woodruff award, John L. Toner award, 1997, Lifetime Achievement award Nat. Sportscasters & Sportwriters Assn., 2003 coached U. Arkansas to 7 Southwest Conf. championship and led them to 10 Bowl appearances. Office: Broyles Athletic Ctr U Ark Fayetteville AR 72701

BROYLES, WILLIAM DODSON, JR., author, editor, scriptwriter; b. Houston, Oct. 8, 1944; s. William Dodson and Elizabeth (Bills) B.; m. Linda Purl (div.); m. Sylvia Ann Newman (div.), 1 child; Andrea Bettina Berndt, 5 children. BA in History, Rice U., 1966; BA in Politics, Philosophy and Econs, Oxford U., 1968, MA, 1971. Tchr. philosophy U.S. Naval Acad., 1970-71; asst. supt. Houston Public Schs., 1971-72; editor Tex. Monthly, Austin, 1972-80, New West and Calif. mags., 1980-82, Newsweek mag., 1982-84; columnist U.S. News and World Report, 1986. Author: Brothers in Arms, 1986; co-creator, exec. cons. TV program China Beach, 1988; screenwriter: Apollo 13, 1995 (Acad. award nominee for best adapted screenplay with Al Reinert 1996), Entrapment, 1999, Cast Away, 2000, Planet of the Apes, 2001, Unfaithful, 2002, The Polar Express, 2004, Jarhead, 2005, Flags of Our Fathers, 2006. Served with USMCR, 1969-71, Vietnam. Decorated Bronze Star.*

BROZAK, EDITH See MCMANN, EDITH

BROZENA, SUSAN C., cardiologist; d. Vincent and Blanche Kaporch. RN, Wilkes-Barre Gen. Hosp. Sch. Nursing, 1972; BSN, Wilkes Coll., 1976; MD, Temple U., 1981. Diplomate in internal medicine and cardiovasc. medicine Am. Bd. Internal Medicine. Assoc. prof. medicine Hahnemann U., Phila., 1992—98; assoc. prof. medicine, Heart Failure and Transplant Ambulatory Care Program U. Pa., 1998—. Contbr. articles to profl. jours. Recipient Tchg. award, Temple U., 1990, U Pa., 2000. Fellow: Am. Coll. Cardiology, Am. Heart Assn.; mem.: Heart Failure Soc. Am., Internat. Soc. Heart and Lung Transplantation. Office: Cardiovascular Medicine Divsn Univ Pa Hosp-- 6 Penn Tower 3400 Spruce St Philadelphia PA 19104-4385 also: Penn Medicine at Radnor 250 King of Prussia Rd Wayne PA 19087 Office Phone: 215-615-0812.*

BROZOWSKI, LAURA ADRIENNE, mechanical engineer; b. Yokohama, Japan, May 12, 1960; arrived in U.S., 1961; d. John and Muriel Sydney (Jackson) Brozowski. BSME, U. Calif., 1982; MSME, Calif. State U., 1987; MBA, Pepperdine U., Calif., 1988. Registered profl. engr., Calif.; cert. profl. mgr. Inst. Cert. Profl. Mgrs. Engring. scientist Pratt & Whitney Rocketdyne, Inc., Canoga Park, Calif., 1982—. Author: in field. Recipient Space Achievement Mid Career award, Rotary Nat., Rotary Nat. award for Space Achievement, 2003, Stellar award, 2003. Fellow: Inst. Advancement Engring.; mem.: NSPE, ASME, Nat. Mgmt. Assn. Avocations: music, continuing education, dance.

BRU, ABELARDO E., retired food products executive; BS in Mech. Engring., CCNY; AMP in Fin. Adminstrn., Mex. Inst. Banking and Fin.; AMP, Kellogg's Bus. Sch. With Ford Motor Co., Avon Products; various positions Pepsico, Inc., 1976—2005, pres., gen. mgr. Sabritas Mexico, 1992—99, pres., CEO, 1999—2003, chmn., CEO, Frito-Lay N.Am., 2003—04, vice-chmn., 2005, ret., 2005. Mem. global leadership coun. Frito-Lay Co.; bd. dir. Kimberly-Clark Corp., 2005—.

BRUBAKER, CRAWFORD FRANCIS, JR., federal agency administrator, aerospace scientist, consultant; b. Fruitland, Idaho, Apr. 23, 1924; s. Crawford Francis and Cora Susan (Flora) B.; m. Lucile May Christensen, May 5, 1945; children: Eric Stephen, Alan Kenneth, Craig Martin, Paul David. BA, Pomona Coll., 1946; MBA, U. Pa., 1948. Office mgr. Lockheed Calif. Co., Burbank, 1948-54, sales adminstr., 1954-57, with fighter contracts divsn., field office rep., 1959-65, asst. dir. fighter sales, 1965-69, dep. mgr. bid and proposals, 1969-74, mgr. govt. sales, 1974-76; dir. internat. mktg. devel. and policy Lockheed Corp., Burbank, 1976-83; dep. asst. sec. for aerospace U.S. Dept. Commerce, Washington, 1983-87; internat. aerospace cons., 1987—. Vice chmn. Industry Sector Adv. Com., Washington, 1979-83; mem. Aero. Policy Rev. Com., Washington, 1983-87. Vice chmn. So. Calif. Dist. Export Coun., L.A., 1980-83, 88-91, chmn., 1992-93. Lt. (j.g.) USN, 1943-45, PTO. Mem. AIAA, Am. Def. Preparedness Assn., Sigma Alpha Epsilon. Republican. Presbyterian. Avocations: coin collecting/numismatics, golf, fishing, photography. E-mail: bru102@roadrunners.com.

BRUBAKER, JAMES EDWARD, mechanical engineer; b. Chgo., Feb. 24, 1935; s. Samuel James and Mary Louise (Alward) B.; m. Phyllis Ann Evans, Aug. 18, 1956; children: David, Richard, Lisa, Mark. BS in Gen. Engring., U. Ill., Champaign-Urbana, 1956. Instr. engring. U. Ill., Champaign, 1956—57; mgr. mechanism and core barrel devel. advanced submarine project Bettis Atomic Power Lab., Pitts., 1959-75; cog. engr. head access area and refueling equipment Clinch River Breeder Reactor, Pitts., 1975-83; project engr. Peacekeeper (MX) Missile Project, Advanced Reactor Divsn., 1983—85; prin. engr. West Valley Nuc. Demonstration Project. Advanced Reactor Divsn., 1985-87; prin. engr. Tomahawk missile sys., naval environ. equipment, 1987-95; sr. project engr. advanced submarine reactor pumps Machinery Tech. Divsn. Westinghouse Elec. Corp., Pitts., 1996—2000. Cons. in field. Patentee in field; editor Mechanism Design Manual and Mil. Specification for Naval Reactor CRDMs. Recipient Environ. Protection commendation U.S. Navy, 1995. Mem. Pleasant Hills Athletic Assn. (pres. 1976-77), Lions Club Internat. (14-B dist. gov. 2005-06, Internat. Pres.'s Leadership medal, Melvin Jones fellow), Phi Kappa Tau. Republican. Avocations: tennis, golf, reading, travel.

BRUBAKER, LAUREN EDGAR, minister; b. Birmingham, Ala., Oct. 8, 1914; s. Lauren Edgar and Nora (Drake) B.; m. Leonte Saye, June 6, 1944; children: Lauren Eugene, Edward Saye; m. Patricia Barnett, July 23, 1994. AB, Birmingham So. Coll., 1935; MDiv, Princeton Theol. Sem., 1938, postdoctoral, 1946-47; STM, Union Theol. Sem., NYC, 1942, ThD, 1944. Ordained to ministry Presbyn. Ch., 1938. Asst. pastor in, Parkersburg, W.Va., 1938-41; grad. asst. Union Theol. Sem., 1941-43; chaplain U.S. Army, 1943-46; grad. instr. Princeton Theol. Sem., 1946-47; prof. philosophy and religion, chaplain Parsons Coll., Fairfield, Iowa, 1947-49. Assoc. prof. U. S.C., Columbia, 1949-58, prof., 1958-79, Disting. prof., 1979-80, Disting. prof. emeritus, 1980—, univ. chaplain, 1949-94, chmn. dept. religious studies, 1949-80; adj. prof. Luth. Theol. So. Sem.; moderator Univ. Forum on S.C. Ednl. TV, 1965-73. Contbr. articles to profl. jours. Dir. S.C. Coun. Human Rels., 1966-69; exec. committeman Columbia and Richland County Dem. party, 1950-60. Served to maj. AUS, 1943-46. Mem. AAUP (past officer), Inst. Religion (dir. 1960-63), S.C. Acad. Religion (founder 1968, pres. 1968), Am. Acad. Religion (pres. 1959), Presbyn. Edn. Assn. South, Columbia Ministers Assn. (pres. 1972), Assn. Coll. and Univ. Religious Affairs (bd. dirs. 1985-86), Columbia Forum Internat. Affairs (pres. 1971), Columbia Coun. for Internat. (bd. dirs., pres. 1986, 87), Nat. Assn. Coll. and Univ. Chaplains, Soc. Bibl. Lit. (past officer), Christian Jewish Congress S.C. (sec. 1982-90), Columbia CROP WALK (treas. 1983-98), Common Cause of S.C. (dir. 1988-2000, sec. 1989-96), Exec. Club Columbia (pres. 1960-61), Kiwanis (pres. 1986-87), Omicron Delta Kappa (faculty adviser 1968-71), Pi Gamma Mu, Phi Kappa Phi, Tau Kappa Alpha. Achievements include research on the teaching of religion in accredited colleges and universities. Home: 10450 Lottsford Rd Apt 4207 Mitchellville MD 20721-2752 E-mail: laubru2003@msn.com.

BRUBAKER, ROBERT LORING, lawyer; b. Louisville, May 22, 1947; s. Robert Lee and Betty (Brock) B.; m Jeannette Marie Montgomery, Dec. 21, 1968; children: Benjamin Brock, Anne Montgomery. BA, Earlham Coll., 1969; JD, U. Chgo., 1972. Bar: Ohio 1972, U.S. Dist. Ct. (so. dist.) Ohio 1973, U.S. Ct. Appeals (6th cir.) 1975, U.S. Supreme Ct. 1978, U.S. Ct. Appeals (D.C. cir.) 1979, U.S. Ct. Appeals (3d, 4th and 7th cirs.) 1995. Asst. atty. gen. Atty. Gen.'s Office State of Ohio, Columbus, 1972-76; assoc. Porter Wright Morris & Arthur, Columbus, 1976-78, ptnr., 1979—. Editor: Ohio Environmental Law Handbook, 1990, 5th edit., 2004, Deposition Strategy, Law and Forms: Environmental Law. Fellow Am. Bar Found.; mem. ABA (natural resources, energy and environ. law sect., pub. utility sect., chmn. environ. law com., standing com. on environ. law), Ohio Bar Assn. (environ. law com.), Air and Waste Mgmt. Assn. (chmn. S.W. Ohio chpt. 1990-91, chmn. East Ctrl. sect. 1991-92), Columbus Bar Assn. (environ. law com.), Nat. Coal Coun., The Breathing Assn. (bd. dirs.) Home: 2661 Wexford Rd Columbus OH 43221-3217 Office: Porter Wright Morris & Arthur 41 S High St Ste 2800 Columbus OH 43215-6194 Home Phone: 614-488-5530; Office Phone: 614-227-2033. Business E-Mail: rbrubaker@porterwright.com.

BRUBAKER, WILLIAM W., JR., federal agency administrator, civil engineer; b. May 13, 1949; m. Sandra Ann Squaglia; children: Taralyn, William W. III. BS in Civil Engring., U. Va., 1972; MS in Civil Engring., Ga. Inst. Tech., 1975; MS in Bus. Adminstrn., Boston U., 1978. Registered profl. engr., Minn., Fla. Gen. engr. South Railroad, Atlanta, 1972-75; civil engr. U.S. Army Corps Engrs., 1976-92; gen. engr., mem. fed. sr. exec. svc. NASA, Washington, 1992—, dir. facilities engring., 1995—. Mem. exec. com. Constrn. Industry Inst.; adv. com. mem. civil engring. dept. U. Va. Decorated Meritorious Civilian Svc. medal U.S. Army, 1992; recipient Fed. Engr. of the Year award NSPE, 1997. Fellow ASCE; mem. Soc. Am. Mil. Engrs.

BRUBECK, DAVID WARREN, musician; b. Concord, Calif., Dec. 6, 1920; s. Howard and Elizabeth (Ivey) Brubeck; m. Iola Whitlock, Sept. 21, 1942; children: David Darius, Michael, Christopher, Catherine, Daniel, Matthew. MusB, U. Pacific, 1942; postgrad. study with Darius Milhaud, Mills Coll., 1946-49; PhD (hon.), U. Pacific, Fairfield U., U. Bridgeport, Mills Coll., Niagara U., Kalamazoo Coll., U. Duisburg, Germany, U. Nottingham, England, Cleve. Inst. Music. Leader Dave Brubeck Octet, Trio and Quartet, 1946—, formed Dave Brubeck Quartet, played colleges, festivals, clubs, symphony orchestras, 1951, 3 month tour Europe and Middle East for U.S. Dept. State, followed by tours Australia, Japan, and USSR, recordings with Atlantic Record Co., Columbia Record Co., Decca, Horizon, Concord Jazz, Fantasy Records, Music Masters, GRP, Telarc Records, Time Out (1st jazz LP to receive Gold Record); composer: (ballets) Points on Jazz, Glances, (orchestral) Elementals, They All Sang Yankee Doodle, (flute and guitar) Tritonis, (piano) Reminiscences of the Cattle Country, Four by Four, Chromatic Fantasy Sonata, (oratorios) Beloved Son, The Light in the Wilderness, Voice of the Holy Spirit, (cantatas) Gates of Justice, Truth Is Fallen, La Fiesta de la Posada, (chorus and orchestra) Pange Lingua, Mass: To Hope, I See, Satie, Four New England Pieces, Lenten Triptych, In Praise of Mary, Joy in the Morning, (choral) Earth Is Our Mother, and over 100 jazz compositions including Blue Rondo a la Turk, In Your Own Sweet Way, The Duke. Decorated John Gense award NYC; named to Nat. Medal of the Arts, 1994, Hollywood Walk of Fame, 1994, Am. Jazz Hall of Fame, 1995; recipient NEA Jazz Master award, jazz polls conducted by Downbeat, Melody Maker, Cashbox, Billboard and Playboy mags., 1952—55, first jazz musician on cover of Time Mag., 1954, B.M.I. Jazz Pioneer award, 1985, Compostela Humanitarian award, 1986, Conn. Arts award, 1987, Am. Eagle award Nat. Music Coun., 1988, Officier de L'Ordre des Arts et Lettres, Govt. France, 1988, Ct. Bar Assn. award, 1992, Simon's Rock Disting. Achievement, 1992, Lifetime Achievement award NARAS, 1996, Lugano award, Switzerland, 1996, Cyril Magnin award, San Francisco, 1997, Spirit of the City award, NYC, 1999, James Smithson award, Smithsonian Inst., 2000, Calif. Golden State award, 2000, Bocconi Univ. medal, Milan, 2000, Honor Cross for Sci. and Art, 1st Class, Austrian Govt., 2002; Duke Ellington fellow Yale U., 1992. Mem.: Phi Mu Alpha. also: care Sutton Artists Corp 20 W Park Ave Ste 305 Long Beach NY 11561-2019 Office: Derry Music Co PO Box 150270 San Rafael CA 94915

BRUCE, CAROL ELDER, lawyer; b. East Orange, NJ, June 7, 1949; BA, George Washington U., 1971, JD, 1974. Bar: DC 1975. Law clk. to Hon. Harold H. Greene, Chief Judge DC Superior Ct.; asst. atty. U.S. Dist. Atty. Office, Washington, 1975—85; ptnr. comml. litig. and white collar criminal def. Venable LLP, Washington; dep. ind. counsel in field. Mem., Lawyer Counseling Panel US Dist. Ct. (Dist. DC); faculty Georgetown U., Washington. Bd. adv. George Washington U. Law Ctr., Washington. Named a Top Washington Lawyer, criminal def., Washingtonian Mag., 2004, Leading Lawyer, litig., Legal Times, 2003. Master: Edward Bennett Williams Am. Inn of Ct. (charter mem.); fellow: Am. Coll. Trial Lawyers (internat. affairs com.); mem.: DC Bar Assn. (bd. gov.). Office: Venable LLP 575 7th St NW Washington DC 20004 Office Phone: 202-344-4717. Office Fax: 202-344-8300. Business E-Mail: cebruce@venable.com.

BRUCE, DAVID LIONEL, retired anesthesiologist, educator; b. Champaign, Ill., Oct. 27, 1933; s. Lionel Harry and Freda Eleanor (Tipsword) B.; m. Geraldine Zawasky, Nov. 24, 1956 (div. 1967); children: Ellen Marie, Brian David; m. Sharon Jean Wells, Jan. 18, 1985 (div. 2004). Student, U. Ill., 1951-54, MD, 1960. Diplomate Am. Bd. Anesthesiology. Intern Ill. Rsch. and Ednl. Hosp., Chgo., 1960-61; resident U. Pa., Phila., 1961-64; asst. prof. anesthesiology U. Ky. Med. Ctr., Lexington, 1964-66; from asst. prof. to prof. Northwestern U. Med. Sch., Chgo., 1966-77; prof. U. Calif., Irvine, 1977-81; prof. anesthesiology NYU Med. Sch., 1981-84; prof. U. Miss. Med. Ctr., Jackson, 1984-90, chmn. dept., 1985-90; dir. outpatient surgery Athens (Ga.) Regional Med. Cr., 1990-92; prof. anesthesiology U. South Fla., Tampa Gen. Hosp., 1992-93; med. dir. surg. svcs. Tampa Gen. Hosp., 1993; med. dir. outpatient surgery ctr. Athens (Ga.) Regional Med. Ctr., 1993-95. Cons. FDA, Rockville, Md., 1972-75, mem. adv. com., Bethesda, Md., 1973-77. Author: Klaus and Max: Their Friendship Defied Hitler, 2000; contbr. numerous articles to profl. jours. Cpl. U.S. Army, 1954-56. Recipient Rsch. Career Devel. award USPHS, 1967-72 Fellow Royal Soc. Medicine (Eng.) (travelling fellow 1975); mem. Am. Soc. Anesthesiologists. Avocations: music, writing.

BRUCE, DEREK ANDREW, neurosurgeon, educator; b. Falkirk, Scotland, Mar. 25, 1943; arrived in US, 1967; s. Alfred and Isobel Dobbie Bruce; m. Frances Marion Robertson, Aug. 6, 1965; children: Simon, Ashley. MB, U. Edinburgh, Scotland, 1966; MA, U. Pa., Phila., 1985. Diplomate Am. Bd. Pediat. Resident U. Pa., Phila, 1969—74, assoc. prof. to prof. Phila., 1974—86; clin. prof. U. Tex., Dallas, 1986—2001, George Wash. U., Washington, 2003—; pediatrician Children's Nat. Med. Ctr., Washington, 2003—. Contbr. chapters to books, articles to profl. jours. Grantee, NIH, 1976—85, 1989—99. Fellow: Acad. Pediat., Am. Coll. Surgeons, Am. Bd. Neurol. Surgery. Home: 2577 Township Rd Quakertown PA 18951 Office: Children's Nat Med Ctr 111 Michigan Ave NW Washington DC 20010

BRUCE, DUNCAN ARCHIBALD, investor, writer; b. Pitts., Feb. 19, 1932; s. Archibald Duncan Bruce and Marian Colley; m. Tamara Bruce, Dec. 4, 1965 (dec. Apr. 2005); children: Jennifer, Elizabeth. BS in Econs., U. Pa., 1954. Pres. Edgewood Holdings, Inc., NYC, 1989—2002, Normandie Holdings, Ltd., NYC, 1996—. Author: (book) The Mark of the Scots, 1996, The Scottish 100, 2000, King Arthur Revisited, 2001, The Great Scot, 2004. Hon. chieftan Bonnie Brae Scottish Games, Millington, NJ, 1990. Recipient Ellis Island medal of honor, Nat. Ethnic Coalition Orgns., 1998, Odom Heritage award, Scottish Weekend, 2002, Nat. Tartan Day award, Scottish Coalition, 2003. Fellow: Soc. Antiquaries Scotland; mem.: Britannia Lodge, Royal Order Scotland, Caledonian Found., Burns Soc. City of NY (past trustee), St. Andrew's Soc. NY (historian, bd. mgrs., pres., chmn. 250th ann. com., mem. exec. com.), Am. Scottish Found. (bd. dir., treas., v.p., past hon. sponsoring com.), Scottish Heritage USA (bd. dirs.), Mask and Wig Club, An Ceud Fear. Home: 185 E 85th St Apt 35D New York NY 10028-2150 Personal E-mail: dbruce@nyc.rr.com.

BRUCE, ESTEL EDWARD, lawyer; b. Hutchinson, Kans., Nov. 23, 1938; s. Kenneth Dean and Josephine (Vigna) Bruce; m. Marnell Elaine Higley, Aug. 9, 1960; children: Anthony Dean, Caroline Bruce Macauley. BA summa cum laude, Yale U., 1960, LLB magna cum laude, 1966. Bar: DC 1967, US Ct. Appeals (1st, 2d, 3d, 4th, 5th, 6th, 8th, 9th, 10th, DC and Fed. cirs.), US Supreme Ct. 1969. Law clk. for Justice Potter Stewart of U.S. Supreme Ct., 1966—67; assoc. Covington & Burling, Washington, 1967-73, ptnr., 1973—; adj. prof. constitutional law Georgetown U. Law Center, 1970-75. Mem. Appellate Judges Conf., Com. Appellate Practice, 1993—2000; mem. faculty ABA Appellate Inst., 1992—2000. Bd. dirs. Audobon Nat. Soc., 1986—92, Yale Law Sch. Fund, 1992—98, Washington Area Lawyers for the Arts, 1993—99, Young Concert Artists Washington, 2003—; mem. adminstrv. bd. Cornell Lab. Ornithology, 1998—2004. Lt. (j.g.) USN, 1960—63. Mem.: ABA, Edward Coke Appellate Inn of Ct. (v.p. 2000—02, pres. 2002—03), D.C. Bar Assn., Am. Acad. Appellate Lawyers, Am. Law Inst., Chevy Chase Club, Met. Club, Phi Beta Kappa, Order of Coif. Home: 2701 Foxhall Rd NW Washington DC 20007-1128 Office: Covington & Burling 1201 Pennsylvania Ave NW Washington DC 20004-2401 Office Phone: 202-662-5284. Business E-Mail: ebruce@cov.com.

BRUCE, HARRY, dean, library and information science educator; BA, Macquarie U., 1982; MLS, U. NSW, 1993, PhD, 1996. Lectr. Sch. Info. Studies, Sydney, 1989—95, sr. lectr., 1995—98, dir. MA in info., 1995—98, acting dept. head Dept. Info. Studies, 1998; assoc. dir. rsch. and program devel., assoc. prof. Grad. Sch. Libr. and Info. Sci., U. Wash., Seattle, 1999—2001; program chair PhD in info. sci. Info. Sch., U. Wash., Seattle, 2001—04, assoc. dean, assoc. prof., 2001—05, dean, prof., 2006—. Spkr. in field. Editl. bd. mem. Jour. of Am. Soc. for Info. Sci., 1997—; contbr. articles to profl. jours. Office: U Wash Info Sch Box 352840 Mary Gates Hall, Ste 370M Seattle WA 98195-2840 Office Phone: 206-616-0985. E-mail: harryb@u.washington.edu.*

BRUCE, JACKSON MARTIN, JR., lawyer; b. Milw., Apr. 10, 1931; s. Jackson Martin and Harriet (Edgell) B.; m. Lilias M. Morehouse, June 30, 1954; children: Lilias Stephanie, Andrew Edgell. AB magna cum laude, Harvard U., 1953, JD cum laude, 1957; MA with 1st class honors in Law, Cambridge U., 1955. Bar: Wis. 1957, Fla. 1973. Assoc. Quarles & Brady, Milw., 1957-64, ptnr., 1964-96; shareholder Dunwody, White & Landon, Naples, Fla., 1996—; counsel Michael Best & Friedrich, Milw., 1996—. Mem. joint editl. bd. Uniform Trusts and Estates Acts; contbr. articles to profl. jours. Bd. dirs. Living Ch. Found., Inc., 1965-98; trustee Univ. Sch. Milw., 1973-79. Fellow Am. Coll. Trust and Estate Counsel (bd. regents 1976-82, treas. 1990-91, sec. 1991-92, v.p. 1992-93, pres. 1994-95); mem. ABA (bd. govs. 1994-97, chmn. sect. real property, probate and trust law 1984-85, ho. dels. 1988-97, ethics com. 1998-2001), State Bar Wis. (chmn. bd. govs. 1979-80), Am. Bar Found., Am. Law Inst., Internat. Acad. Estate and Trust Law (mem. exec. coun. 1980-86), Nat. Conf. Bar Pres., Town Club, Milw. Club (bd. dirs. 1985-2001), The Club Pelican Bay. Home: 6101 Pelican Bay Blvd Apt 1201 Naples FL 34108-8183 also: 9008 N Bayside Dr Milwaukee WI 53217-1913 Office: Dunwody White & Landon 4001 Tamiami Trl N Ste 200 Naples FL 34103-3591 also: Michael Best & Friedrich 100 E Wisconsin Ave Ste 3300 Milwaukee WI 53202-4107 Office Phone: 239-263-5885, 414-225-4963. Business E-Mail: jbruce@dwl-law.com, jmbruce@michaelbest.com.

BRUCE, JAMES EDMUND, retired utilities executive; b. Boise, Idaho, June 23, 1920; s. James E. and Bessie (Barcus) B.; m. Lois I. Stevens, Aug. 24, 1946; children: James E., IV, Steven, Robert, David. Student, Coll. Idaho, 1937-39; BA, Portland U., 1941; postgrad., Georgetown U., 1941-42; LLB, U. Idaho, 1949. Bar: Idaho 1948. Asst. atty. gen. State of Idaho, 1948-49; dep. pros. atty. Ada County, Idaho, 1949-51; with Idaho Power Co., Boise, 1951-87, v.p., 1968-74, pres., chief operating officer, 1974-76, pres., chief exec. officer, 1976-85, chmn., 1985-87, ret., 1987. Dir. Albertson's Inc., First Security Corp., 1981-93; chmn. Blue Cross of Idaho, 1988-90. Bd. dirs. Mountain States Legal Found., 1977-88; mem. St. Alphonsus Found., Boise State U. Found., Bishop Kelly Found., Boise Park Bd., 1958-78; chmn. Idaho State Lottery; Idaho chmn. U.S. Savs. Bonds, 1976-85; chmn. bd. trustees St. Alphonsus, 1985-2002; trustee Coll. Idaho, YMCA, Idaho Nature Conservancy; pres. Ada County Hwy. Dist. Commn. With U.S. Army, 1942-46. Mem. ABA, Boise Execs. Assn., Edison Electric Assn. (dir. 1978-85), N.W. Electric Light and Power Assn. (pres. 1982), Boise C. of C., Arid Club, Crane Creek Country Club, Rotary, Elks, K.C. Roman Catholic.

BRUCE, JOHN ALLEN, retired foundation executive, educator; b. Kansas City, Mo., Sept. 17, 1934; BA, Wesleyan U., Middletown, Conn., 1956; MDiv., Gen. Theol. Sem., NYC, 1959; PhD, U. Minn., 1972. Ordained to ministry Episcopal Ch., 1959. Clergyman, 1959-68; prof. U. Ala., Tuscaloosa, 1972-74; exec. dir. E.C. Brown Found., Portland, Oreg., 1974-98. Cons. to philanthropies and corp. programs; clin. prof. community medicine Sch. Medicine, Oreg. Health Scis. U., Portland, 1976-01. Author, editor various scholarly publs.; exec. prodr. ednl. films on family life, health and values. Bd. dirs., officer various cmty. orgns. Served to lt. USN, 1964-67. Recipient awards from med. orgns. and related groups. Mem. Cosmos Club. Republica. Home: 4909 Mulholland Dr Lake Oswego OR 97035-4393

BRUCE, JOHN ANTHONY, artist; b. LA, Apr. 8, 1931; s. Merle VanDyke and Katherine Mary (Butler) B.; children: Marsha Lee, Margaret Lorren, James Cole, Glenn Allen, Mark Corwin, Leslie Ann. BA in Psychology and Art, Calif. State U., LA, 1965. Design engr. N.Am. Aviation Corp., Downey, Calif., 1952-57; comml. artist Aerojet Gen. Corp., Sacramento, 1957-59; advt. mgr. Flow Equipment Co., Santa Fe Springs, Calif., 1959-63; art dir. Barnes-Champ Advt., Santa Ana, Calif., 1963-66, Long Beach (Calif.) Ind. Press Telegram News, 1970-73. Freelance art cons. Epcot project Walt E. Disney Enterprises, Glendale, Calif., 1976-77. Permanent collections Smithsonian Inst., Washington, D.C.; one man shows Ghormley Gallery, L.A., 1966, Les Li Art Gallery, L.A., 1970, Upstairs Gallery, Long Beach, Calif., 1973, El Prado Gallery, Sedona, Ariz., 1987; group shows Newport Beach Invitational, Newport Beach, Calif., 1964, Laguna Beach Art Festival, Laguna Beach, Calif., 1962, 63, 64, 65, Butler Inst. Am. Art, Youngstown, Ohio, 1970, Allied Artists, N.Y.C., 1988; currently exhibiting with Bartfield Gallery, N.Y.C., New Masters Gallery, Carmel, Calif. With U.S. Army, l949-52, Korea. Recipient John B. Grayback award Am. Profl. Artists League, 1988, Best of Show award Gene Autry Mus. AICA Show, 1996, San Dimas Festival of Western Art, 1996, Best of Show Chgo. Windy City Artists, 1999, numerous others. Republican. Studio: 5394 Tip Top Rd Mariposa CA 95338-9609

BRUCE, PETER WAYNE, lawyer, insurance company executive; b. Rome, NY, July 12, 1945; s. G. Wayne and Helen A. (Hibbling) B.; m. Joan M. McCabe, Sept. 20, 1969; children: Allison, Steven. BA, U. Wis., 1967; JD, U. Chgo., 1970; postgrad., Harvard Bus. Sch., 1986. Bar: Wis. 1970. Atty. Northwestern Mut. Life Ins. Co., Milw., 1970-74, asst. gen. counsel, 1974-80, gen. counsel, sec., 1980—, v.p., 1983-87, sr. v.p., gen. counsel, sec., 1987-90, sr. v.p. ins. ops., 1990-95, exec. v.p. ins. ops. & adminstrn., chief compliance officer, 1995-98, exec. v.p. accumulation products and long term care, 1998-2000, sr. exec. v.p. ins. ops. and long term care, 2000, sr. exec. v.p., 2000—. Bd. dirs. Northwestern Mut. Life Ins. Co., Milw., Northwestern Long-Term Care Ins. Co., Alverno Coll. Badger Meter Found., Growth Design Corp. Former chmn. Alverno Coll., Curative Rehab. Ctr., former mem. Shorewood Civic Improvement Found.; chair Milw. Archdiocese Resource Devel. Coun.; bd. dirs., chair Curative Found.; mem. Milw. Archdiocese Cath. Cmty. Found.; mem. Village of Shorewood (Wis.); mem. Village Shorewood Cmty. Devel. Assn., Wis. Equal Justice Fund; former mem. Planning and Devel. Commn. Mem. Wis. Bar Assn., Milw. Bar Assn., Am. Law Inst. Office: Northwestern Mut Life Ins Co 720 E Wisconsin Ave Milwaukee WI 53202-4703

BRUCE, ROBERT VANCE, historian, educator; b. Malden, Mass., Dec. 19, 1923; s. Robert Gilbert and Bernice Irene (May) B. Student, MIT, 1941-43; BS, U. N.H., 1945; MA, Boston U., 1947, PhD, 1953. Instr. U. Bridgeport, Conn., 1947-48; master Lawrence Acad., Groton, Mass., 1948-51; rsch. asst. to Benjamin P. Thomas, Washington, 1953-54; mem. faculty Boston U., 1955—, assoc. prof. history, 1960-66, prof., 1966-84, prof. emeritus, 1984—. Vis. prof. U. Wis., Madison, 1962-63. Author: Lincoln and the Tools of War, 3d edit., 1989, 1877, Year of Violence, 3d edit., 1989, Bell: Alexander Graham Bell and the Conquest of Solitude, 3d edit., 1995, Brit. edit., 1973, Japanese edit., 1991, Lincoln and the Riddle of Death, 1982, The Launching of Modern Am. Sci., 2d edit., 1988 (Pulitzer prize 1988); contbg. author: Lincoln the War President, 1992, Feeding Mars, 1993, War Comes Again, 1995, The Lincoln Enigma, 2001; contbr. articles to profl. jour. With AUS, 1943-46. Guggenheim fellow, 1957-58; Henry E. Huntington fellow, 1966; recipient Pulitzer Prize in history, 1988. Fellow AAAS, Soc. Am. Historians; mem. Orgn. Am. Historians (life mem.), AAAS, Lincoln Group of Boston (pres. 1969-74), Phi Beta Kappa. Democrat. Home: 3923 Westpark Ct NW Olympia WA 98502 E-mail: yov1877@wbtv.net.

BRUCE, THOMAS ALLEN, physician, educator; b. Mountain Home, Ark., 1930; s. Rex Floyd and Dora Madeline (Fee) B.; m. Dolores Fay Montgomery; children: T.K. Montgomery, Dana Fee Thomas. BSM, MD, U. Ark., 1955, DSc (hon.), 1995. Intern Duke Hosp., 1956-57; resident medicine Bellevue Hosp., NYC, 1957, Meml. Ctr. Cancer and Allied Diseases, NYC, 1958, Parkland Meml. Hosp., Dallas, 1958—59; cardiopulmonary trainee Southwestern Med. Sch. of U. Tex., 1959—60; cardiac rsch. fellow Hammersmith Hosp. and U. London Postgrad. Med. Sch., London, 1960—61, Harvard Bus. Sch., 1974. From instr. to prof. medicine Wayne State U., 1961—68, also asst. dean Sch. Medicine; prof. medicine, head cardiovascular sect. U. Okla. Med. Ctr., 1968—74; prof. medicine, dean Coll. Medicine U. Ark. Med. Scis., 1974—85, emeritus prof., 1997—, dean pro tem Coll. Pub. Health, 2001—02, prof. health policy and mgmt., 2001—; dean pro tem U. Ark. Clinton Sch. Pub. Svc., 2003—04, assoc. dean, 2004—07; med. dir. Barton Rsch. Inst., 1974—85; coord. Sino-am. Med. Exch. Program, 1979—85; rsch. support rev. com. NIH, 1983—85; program dir. W.K. Kellogg Found., 1985—97; co-chair session 312 Salzburg Seminar, Austria; mem. History of Medicine Assocs.; chair nat. adv. bd. cmty. health leadership program Robert Wood Johnson Found., 2004—06; policy adv. bd. Ark. Ctr. for Health Improvement; chmn. bd. trustees Watershed Found.; adj. staff Ark. Cmty. Found.; bd. dirs. Heifer Project Internat., 1996—2006, chair, 2003—04; mem. Nat. Assn. Schs. of Pub. Affairs and Adminstrn.; bd. dirs. Nat. Polit. Sci. Assn. Master gardener, chmn. garden docents Wildwood Park Performing Arts; exec. bd. Ark. Com. on Fgn. Rels.; bd. dirs. Garvan Woodland Gardens, 2000—06. Named Profl. of Yr., U. Ark. at Little Rock, 2003; named to U. Ark. Med. Scis. Coll. Medicine Hall of Fame, 2004; recipient Ark. Gov. Meritorious Achievement award, 1974, Lugene Chilcote award, 1999, Double Helix award U. Ark. Med. Sci., 2001, Lucy Lockett Cabe award Wildwood Park for the Performing Arts, 2001, Giving Tree Soc. award, 2003, Ctrl. High Mus. Appreciation award, 2001, Ark. Ctr. Health Improvement award, 2002, Sen. David Pryor Carelink award, 2004, Bruce Commons Dedication award U. Ark. Med. Scis. Coll. Publ Health, 2004, Martin Luther King Salute to Greatness award, 2005, Humanitarian of Yr. award Just Communities Ctrl. Ark., 2007. Fellow: ACP, Am. Coll. Cardiology; mem.: AMA, APHA, Leila Arboretum Soc. (pres. 1989—92), Am. Rhododendron Soc., Ark. Caduceus Club, Alpha Omega Alpha, Sigma Xi. Rsch. and publs. on cardiovascular disease including left ventricular function in cardiac denervation, coronary heart disease, myocardial metabolism relating to phospholipids in graded cardiac ischmia, med. edn. with particular reference to rural health care, health promotion and disease prevention, primary health care, community-based pub. health. Home: 6 Spy Glass Ln Little Rock AR 72212-4418

BRUCE, THOMAS EDWARD, thanatologist, psychology professor; b. Vinton, Iowa, Dec. 3, 1937; s. George Robert and Lucille Etta (Aurner) B.; children: Scott Thomas and Suzanne Laura. BA, U. No. Iowa, 1961, MA, 1964; postgrad., U. Colo., 1968-71; MA, U. San Francisco, 1985. Lic. psychology educator, counselor, Calif. Tchr. various Iowa high schs., 1961-65; sociologist, counselor Office Econ. Opportunity, Denver, 1965-66; social sci. educator Arapahoe Coll., Littleton, Colo., 1966-69; lectr. U. Colo., Boulder, 1968-71; psychology educator Sacramento City Coll., Calif., 1972—. Thanatology cons. for hospices, survivor support groups, No. Calif., 1984—. Author: Grief Management: The Pain and the Promise, 1986, Thanatology: Through the Veil, 1992; contbr. articles to profl. publs. Co-founder, bd. dirs. Bereavement Resources Network, Sacramento, 1983-87; profl. dir. Children's Respite Ctr., Sacramento, 1985-88; pres.-elect., bd. dirs. Hospice Care of Sacramento, 1979-85. With U.S. Army, 1955-58. Recipient Pres.'s award Nat. Hospice Orgn., 1985. Mem. Sacramento Mental Health Assn. (Vol. Svc. award 1985, 87), Assn. for Death Edn. and Counseling, Thanatology Found., Am. Fedn. Tchrs., Faculty Assn. Calif. C.C.'s, Pi Gamma Mu, Phi Delta Kappa. Avocations: music, visual arts, travel, reading. Office: Sacramento City Coll 3835 Freeport Blvd Sacramento CA 95822-1318 Home Phone: 916-421-8941; Office Phone: 916-558-2294. Personal E-mail: brucete@yahoo.com.

BRUCE, WILLIAM A., airport executive; BS in Polit. Sci., UCLA, 1967; MPA, Calif. State U., LA, 1971. Budget analyst, chief negotiator employee rels. City of L.A., 1969-80, various other positions, 1980-99; dir. airports adminstrn. L.A. World Airports, 1999—. Office: Los Angeles Dept Airports 1 World Way Los Angeles CA 90045-5803

BRUCE-NOVOA, JUAN DAVID, literature and language professor, writer; b. San Jose, Costa Rica, June 20, 1944; s. James Heinzmann Bruce and Dolores Novoa-Bruce; m. Mary Ann Giroux, June 13, 1969; 1 child, Juan Carlos Bruce. PhD, U. Colo., Boulder, 1974. Dir. Mex. Am. edn. program U. Colo., Denver, 1972—74; prof. Yale U., New Haven, 1974, U. Calif., Santa Barbara, 1983—85, Trinity U., San Antonio, 1985—89, U. Calif., Irvine, 1989—. Fulbright prof. U. Mainz, Germersheim, Germany, 1983—84, Erlangen-Nürnberg U., Germany, 1990, 98; vis. prof. Harvard U., Cambridge, Mass., 1990, 99, Frei U., Berlin, 2002, U. Düssedorf, Germany, 2007. Author: (novels) Only the Good Times, short stories, od poems. Recipient José Fuentes Mares Nat. Lit. prize, Universidad Autonoma de juarez, 1989, Critica Nueva Disting. Lit. Theory award, U. N.Mex, 1997; fellow, Nat. Chicano Coun. Higher Edn., 1977, Rockefeller Found., 1979—80, Tinker Found., 1981, Fulbright Found., 1983—84, 1998. Mem.: U. Calif. Mexicanistas (assoc.; exec. dir. 2005—07). Roman Catholic. Avocation: art collecting. Office: U Calif 332 Humanities Hall Irvine CA 92697-5275 Home Phone: 949-854-4233; Office Phone: 949-824-6901. Office Fax: 949-824-2803. Business E-Mail: jbruceno@uci.edu.

BRUCH, CAROL SOPHIE, law educator; b. Rockford, Ill., June 11, 1941; d. Ernest and Margarete (Willstätter) B.; m. Jack E. Myers, 1960 (div. 1973); children: Margarete Louise Myers Feinstein, Kurt Randall Myers. AB, Shimer Coll., 1960; JD, U. Calif.-Berkeley, 1972; Dr. honoris causa, U. Basel, 2000. Bar: Calif. 1973, U.S. Supreme Ct. 1980. Law clk. to Justice William O. Douglas U.S. Supreme Ct., 1972-73; acting prof. law U. Calif., Davis, 1973—78, prof., 1978—2001, rsch. prof., prof. emeritus, 2001—05, chair doctoral program in human devel., 1996—2001, disting. rsch. prof., disting. prof. emeritus, 2005—. Acad. vis. law dept. U. Munich, 1978-79, 92, U. Cologne, 1990, U. Cambridge, 1990, London Sch. Econs. and Polit. Sci., 1991, Kings Coll., London, 1991; vis. prof. U. Calif., Berkeley, 1983, Columbia U., 1986, U. Basel, 1994, vis. Fulbright prof. Hebrew U., Jerusalem, 1996-97; vis. fellow Fitzwilliam Coll., Cambridge, Eng., 1990, U. Calif. Humanities Rsch. Inst., Irvine, 1999, vis. scholar Inst. for Advanced Legal Studies (Univ. London), 1991, UCLA Ctr. Study of Women, 2004-05; cons. to Ctr. for Family in Transition, 1981, Calif. Law Revision Commn., 1979-82, NOW Legal Def. and Edn. Fund, 1980-81; lectr., legis. drafting and testimony, 1976—; mem. U.S. del. 4th Inter-Am. Specialized Conf. on Pvt. Internat. Law, OAS, 1989. Contbr. articles to legal jours. Editor Calif. Law Rev., 1971; editorial Bd. Family Law Quar., 1980-87; Representing Children, 1995—, Am. Jour. of Comparative Law, 2001—; lectr. in field. Mem. adv. com. child support and child custody Calif. Commn. on Status of Women, 1981-83, child support adv. com. Calif. Jud. Coun., 1991-94, adv. com. on private internat. law U.S. Dept. State, 1989—, internat. child abduction steering com. Internat. Ctr. for Missing and Exploited Children (London), 1999-2001; host parent Am. Field Service, Davis, 1977-78. Max Rheinstein sr. rsch. fellow Alexander von Humboldt Found., Fed. Republic Germany, 1978-79, 92, Fulbright fellow, Western Europe, 1990, Fulbright Sr. Scholar, Israel, 1997, Disting. Pub. Svc. award U. Calif. Davis Acad. Senate, 1990. Mem. ABA, Calif. State Bar Assn., Am. Law Inst., Internat. Soc. Family Law (exec. coun. 1994-2000, 2002—), Internat. Acad. Comparative Law, Order of Coif. Democrat. Jewish. Office: U Calif Sch Law 400 Mrak Hall Dr Davis CA 95616-5201

BRUCH, LUDWIG W., physicist, researcher; b. Rockford, Ill., Jan. 23, 1940; s. Ernest and Margarete Bruch; m. Nancy Bernice Schlaefer, July 31, 1966; children: Carl Edward, Andrew Richard. BA, U. Wis., Madison, 1959; MA, Oxford U., England, 1961; PhD, U. Calif. San Diego, La Jolla, 1964. Asst. prof. physics U. Wis., Madison, Wis., 1966—69, assoc. prof. physics, 1969—75, prof. physics, 1975—. Vis. prof. Tokyo U. Edn., 1972—73; vis. scientist U. Utrecht, Netherlands, 1977—78; sr. vis. fellow U. Sussex, England, 1983—84; assoc. prof. U. Marseille, France, 1984; Foster fellow US Arms Control and Disaramament Agy., Washington, 1988; vis. prof. Tech. U. Denmark, Lyngby, 1991—2006; vis. scientist Max Planck Inst. Strommungsforschung, Gottingen, Germany, 1994—2000. Lt. Signal Corps US Army, 1964—65. Grantee, U.S. NSF - Japan Program, 1972—73; Rhodes Scholar, 1959—61. Fellow: Am. Phys. Soc. Achievements include research in theory of physically adsorbed layers. Office: Dept Physics U Wis 1150 University Ave Madison WI 53706 Home Phone: 608-849-5352; Office Phone: 608-262-8968. E-mail: lwbruch@wisc.edu.

BRUCH, RUTH E., information technology executive; BA in fin., U. Iowa. Contr. Davenport Bank and Trust Co., Iowa; with ctr. bus. innovation Ernst & Young; v.p. and dir. IT planning First Bank Sys. (now US Bank), St. Paul; v.p. and mng. dir. info. sys. Continental Bank (now Bank Am.), Chgo.; prin. JGA Consulting, Barrington, Ill., 1991—93; from dir. info. tech. strategic planning to v.p. and CIO Union Carbide Corp., Danbury, Conn., 1993—99; pres. and COO Zonetrader.com, Chgo., 1999—2000; v.p. and CIO Visteon Corp., Dearborn, Mich., 2000—02; sr. v.p. and CIO Lucent Tech., Murray Hill, NJ, 2002—. Bd. dir. Mellon Fin. Corp., 2003—; tech. adv. bd. Blue Star Solutions. Office: Lucent Tech Inc 600 Mountain Ave New Providence NJ 07974

BRUCHAC, JOSEPH, writer, storyteller; m. Carol Bruchac; children: James, Jesse. BA, Cornell U.; MA in Lit. & Creative Writing, Syracuse U.; PhD in Comparative Lit., Union Inst. Ohio. Founder & co-dir. Greenfield

(NY) Rev. Lit. Ctr., Greenfield (NY) Rev. Press. Editor: Songs from this Earth on Turtle's Back, 1983, Breaking Silence (Am. Book award); co-author: The First Strawberries, 1993; author: Dawn Land, 1995, The Waters Between, 1998, The Heart of a Chief, 1998, Pushing up the Sky: Seven Native Am. Plays for Children, 2000, Hidden Roots, 2004 (AILA Am. Indian Youth Lit. award, 2006), Code Talker, 2005, Wabi, 2006, Jim Thorpe, Original All-American, 2006, Geroninmo, 2006 (Spur award, Best Western Juvenille Fiction), The Way, 2007; performer (and songwriter): contemporary and traditional Abenaki Indian music. Recipient Cherokee Nation Prose award, Knickerbocker award, Hope S. Dean award for Notable Achievement in Children's Lit., Writer of Yr. award & Storyteller of Yr. award, Wordcraft Cir. Native Writers & Storytellers, 1998, Lifetime Achievement award, Native Writers Cir. of the Americas, 1999, Conservation Achievement award, Nat. Wildlife Fedn., 2004, Indian of Yr. award, Thunderbird Dancers, 2006; Rockefeller Humanities fellow, NEA Writing Fellow for Poetry. Avocations: martial arts, gardening. Address: PO Box 308 Greenfield Center NY 12833 Office Phone: 518-584-1728. Office Fax: 518-583-9741. E-mail: nudatlog@earthlink.net.*

BRUCK, BILL, educational association administrator; b. Dayton, Ohio, Aug. 1, 1951; s. Emil J. and Lucy A. (Lombardi) B.; m. Jacqueline Youden, June 6, 1984 (div. Dec. 1987); m. Anita M. Brack, June 15, 1996; 1 child, Abby Elizabeth. AB, Brown U., 1973; MA, Duquesne U., 1974; PhD, U. Fla., 1977. Lic. clin. psychologist, Va. Asst. prof. psychology Seattle U., 1978-79, West Ga. Coll., Carrollton, 1979-81; prin. Leadership Resources, Inc., Fairfax, Va., 1981-83; assoc. prof. psychology Marymount U., Arlington, Va., 1983-91, dir. instnl. rsch., 1986-91, prof. psychology, 1991-99; owner/operator Bill Bruck & Assocs., Falls Church, Va., 1986—2003; prin. Caucus Systems, Inc., Arlington, Va., 1999-2001; ptnr. Q2Learning LLC, 2001—. Author: Special Edition Using WordPerfect Office, 1994, Special Edition Using PerfectOffice 3, 1995, Special Edition Using Novell GroupWise 4, 1995, Using Corel WordPerfect Suite 7, 1996, Using Corel WordPerfect Suite 8, 1997, The Essential Book for Microsoft Office 95, 1996, The Essential Book for Microsoft Office 97, 1997, The Essential Book for Microsoft Office 2000, 1999, Make Your Mouse Roar, 2001, Taming the Information Tsunami, 2002. Avocations: martial arts, racquetball, gardening, folk music. Office: 2686 Hillsman St Falls Church VA 22043 Office Phone: 877-751-2200. Personal E-mail: billbruck@yahoo.com. Business E-Mail: bill@bruck.com.

BRUCKEN, ROBERT MATTHEW, lawyer; b. Akron, Ohio, Sept. 15, 1934; s. Harold M. and Eunice B. (Boesel) B.; m. Lois R. Gilbert, June 30, 1960; children: Nancy, Elizabeth, Rowland, Gilbert. AB, Marietta Coll., 1956; JD, U. Mich., 1959. Bar: Ohio 1960. Assoc. Baker & Hostetler, Cleve., 1960-69, ptnr., 1970—2004. Trustee Lakeside Assn., 1979-97, Marietta Coll., 1983—; treas. Leader Shape, Inc., 1990—. Served with AUS, 1959-60. Mem. Ohio State Bar Assn. (chmn. probate and trust law sect. 1981-83), Cleve. Bar Assn. (chmn. probate ct. com. 1973-75), Am. Coll. Trust and Estate Counsel, Phi Beta Kappa. United Ch. Of Christ. Office: 3200 National City Ctr 1900 E Ninth St Cleveland OH 44114 Home Phone: 216-751-1401; Office Phone: 216-861-7552. Business E-Mail: rbrucken@bakerlaw.com.

BRUCKER, PAUL C., academic administrator, physician; BSc, Muhlenberg Coll., 1953; MD, U. Pa., 1957. Pres. emeritus Thomas Jefferson U., Phila., 1990—2004. Office: Thomas Jefferson U Rm 303 Curtis Bldg 1015 Walnut St Philadelphia PA 19107-5567 Office Phone: 215-955-3790. Business E-Mail: paul.brucker@jefferson.edu.

BRUCKHEIMER, JERRY LEON, producer; b. Detroit, Sept. 21, 1945; m. Linda Bruckheimer. Grad., U. Ariz., DFA (hon.), 2006. Former prodr., art dir. advt. agy.; co-founder Don Simpson/Jerry Bruckheimer Films, 1983. Assoc. prodr. (films) Culpepper Cattle Company, 1972, Rafferty and the Gold Dust Twins, 1975; prodr. (films) American Gigolo, 1980, Young Doctors in Love, 1982,(with George Pappas) Farewell My Lovely, 1975, (with Dick Richards) March or Die, 1977, (with William S. Gillmore) Defiance, 1980, (with Ronnie Caan) Thief, 1981, Cat People, 1982, (with Don Simpson) Flashdance, 1983, Beverly Hills Cop, 1984, Thief of Hearts, 1984, Top Gun, 1986, Beverly Hills Cop II, 1987, Days of Thunder, 1990, Bad Boys, 1995, Crimson Tide, 1995, Dangerous Minds, 1995, The Rock, 1996, Con Air, 1997, Enemy of the State, 1998, Armageddon, 1998, Gone in 60 Seconds, 2000, Coyote Ugly, 2000, Remember the Titans, 2000, Pearl Harbor, 2001, Black Hawk Down, 2001, Bad Company, 2002, Kangaroo Jack, 2003, Pirates of the Caribbean: The Curse of the Black Pearl, 2003, Bad Boys II, 2003, Veronica Guerin, 2003, King Arthur, 2004, National Treasure, 2004, Glory Road, 2006, Pirates of the Caribbean: Dead Man's Chest, 2006, Deja Vu, 2006; exec. prodr. (films): (with Don Simpson) The Ref, 1994, Soldier of Fortune, 1997, Dangerous Minds, 1995, (TV films) Max Q, 1998, Swing Vote, 1999; exec. prodr. (TV series): CSI: Crime Scene Investigation, 2000, The Amazing Race, 2001— (Emmy award for Outstanding Reality/Competition Program 2003, 04, 05, 06), CSI: Miami, 2002, Without a Trace, 2002-06, Profiles From the Front Line, 2003, Skin, 2003, Cold Case, 2004-06, Close to Home, 2005, CSI: NY, 2006. Recipient ShoWest award Prodr. of Yr., 1999, David O. Selznick Lifetime Achievement award Prodrs. Guild of Am., 2000, Salute to Excellence award Mus. TV and Radio, 2006, Norman Lear Achievement award in TV, 2007; named Variety Showman of Yr., 2006; named one of 50 Most Powerful People in Hollywood Premiere mag., 2003-05, 100 Most Powerful Celebrities, Forbes.com, 2006-07; named to LA Times Power Issue, 2006, Premiere Mag. Power Players List, 2006. Office: Jerry Bruckheimer Films 1631 10th St Santa Monica CA 90404-3705

BRUCKNER, DANIEL RAYMOND, history educator; b. Waynesburg, Pa., July 30, 1947; s. Raymond Oscar and Aldene Grooms Bruckner; m. Sandra Gesko Bruckner, Aug. 3, 1973. BA, Waynesburg Coll., Pa., 1969; MA, W.Va. U., 1973. Social studies tchr. Thomas Stone H.S., Waldorf, Md., 1973—2001; substitute tchr. High Point H.S., Beltsville, Md., 2001—. Mem. history adv. bd. Harper Collins Pub., NYC, 1988—92; mem. world history adv. bd. Prentice-Hall, Inc., NYC, 1994—2000. Mem. Greenpeace, Inc., Washington, 1976—, Clean Water Action, Washington, 1984—, Children's Wish Found., Atlanta, 1992—. Sgt. US Army, 1970—71, Vietnam. Recipient Outstanding award, McDonald's, Inc., 1970; bus. fellow, Washington Bd. of Trade, 1985. Mem.: Md. Humanities Coun., Md. Hist. Soc., Am. Hist. Assn. Democrat. Roman Catholic. Avocations: reading, collecting small flags, collecting classic films, genealogy. Home: 5022 Geronimo St College Park MD 20740 Office: High Point HS 3601 Powdermill Rd Beltsville MD 20705 Office Phone: 301-572-6400. Personal E-mail: brucknerdan05@comcast.net.

BRUCKNER, MARTHA, academic administrator; B, M, U. Nebr., Omaha; Doctorate, U. Nebr., Lincoln. Assoc. supt. for ednl. svcs. Millard (Nebr.) Pub. Schs.; tchr. h.s., asst. prin., prin. pub. schs.; assoc. prof., chairperson ednl. adminstrn. U. Nebr., Omaha. Contbr. articles to profl. jours. Recipient award, Nebr. Coun. Sch. Adminstrs., Nebr. Schoolmasters Orgn. Mem.: ASCD (pres. 2005—06, bd. dirs., budget liaison, organizer student chpt. U. Nebr., Omaha). Office: Don Stroh Adminstrn Ctr 5606 S 147th St Omaha NE 68137 Home Phone: 402-339-1823; Office Phone: 402-895-8301. E-mail: mmbruckner@mpsomaha.org.

BRUCKNER, WILLIAM J., lawyer; b. Atlanta, Mar. 28, 1944; s. William Paul and Ruth (Seibert) B.; m. Lucy Clark, June 27, 1970; children: Heather, Christina. BS, The Citadel, 1966; JD, U. Ga., 1969. Bar: Ga. 1970, S.C. 1982, U.S. Dist. Ct. (no. and mid. dists.) Ga., U.S. Ct. Appeals (5th cir.), U.S. Supreme Ct. Asst. solicitor Solicitor's Office County of Fulton, Atlanta, 1971-73; labor solicitor So. Bell, Atlanta, 1973-82, gen. atty. Columbia, S.C., 1982-83, Atlanta, 1983-86; ops. and litigation counsel BellSouth Enterprises, Atlanta, 1986; assoc. gen. counsel Bell South Enterprises, Atlanta, 1990—; gen. atty. human resources divsn. Bell South Corp., Atlanta, 1986-90, assoc. gen. counsel, 1993—. Mem. Atlanta Soc., 1990—; bd. dirs. Ashford-Dunwoody YMCA, Atlanta, 1986-87, Horizon Theater, Atlanta, 1990—. Capt. U.S. Army, 1970-71. Mem. Atlanta Lawyers Club, Greater Atlanta U. Ga. Club (pres. 1990, trustee Ga. Student Ednl. Fund, chmn. ACCA legal office mgmt. com.), Buckhead Club. Roman Catholic. Avocations: photography, sports. Home: 11315 Bowen Rd Roswell GA 30075-2238

BRUCKSTEIN, ALEX HARRY, internist, gastroenterologist, geriatrician; b. Germany, Dec. 2, 1949; came to U.S., 1950; s. Jacob and Rose B., m. Dorothy Krausman, Mar. 23, 1973; children: Tammy, Sharon, Sarah, Michael. BS in Chemistry, CCNY, 1971; MD, Albert Einstein Coll. Medicine, 1975. Diplomate Am. Bd. Internal Medicine, Am. Bd. Gastroenterology, Am. Bd. Internal Medicine- Geriatrics. Intern in internal medicine Roosevelt Hosp., NYC; resident in internal medicine St. Luke's Hosp., NYC; resident in gastroenterology VA Hosp., N.Y.U., NYC; pvt. practice internal medicine, gastroenterology Staten Island, NY. Hosp. affiliations: Doctors' Hosp. Staten Island, N.Y., Staten Island U. Hosp. N., Staten Island U. Hosp. S., St. Vincent's Hosp., Staten Island; vis. clin. fellow Columbia U. Dept. Medicine, 1975-78, NYU Dept. Medicine, 1978-80; clin. asst. prof. medicine N.Y. Med. Coll., 1983-90, SUNY Health Sci. Ctr. at Bklyn., 1990—. Fellow ACP, Am. Coll. Gastroenterology; mem. AMA, Med. Soc. State N.Y., Richmond County Med. Soc., Am. Gastroent. Assn., N.Y. Soc. Gastrointestinal Endoscopy, N.Y. Acad. Gastroenterology, Am. Geriatrics Assn. Office: 2627 Hylan Blvd Staten Island NY 10306-4339 Home Phone: 516-239-9780; Office Phone: 718-667-3200. Personal E-mail: sevenbr@aol.com.

BRUDER, GEORGE FREDERICK, retired lawyer; b. Ann Arbor, Mich., June 4, 1938; s. George G. and Mary Louise (Pfisterer) Bruder; m. Jean Riley, July 10, 1965; children: Roxanne, Stephanie. AB, Dartmouth Coll., 1960; JD, U. Chgo., 1963. Bar: D.C. 1964. Counsel FPC, Washington, 1964—67; counsel Long Lines Dept. AT&T, Washington, 1967—68; assoc. Debevoise & Liberman, Washington, 1968—70, ptnr., 1971—75, Bruder, Gentile & Marcoux, Washington, 1976—97. Democrat. Episcopalian. Home: 8 E Lenox St Chevy Chase MD 20815-4211 E-mail: gfbruder@erols.com.

BRUDER, HAROLD JACOB, artist, educator; b. NYC, Aug. 31, 1930; s. Julius and Della (Wlodinger) B.; m. Anet Sirna, July 15, 1979; 1 child, Dellan; children from previous marriage: David, Shari. Cert., Cooper Union, 1951. Mem. faculty Kansas City Art Inst., 1963-65, Pratt Inst., 1965-66; prof. art Queens Coll., Flushing, NY, 1965-95, chmn. art dept., 1982-85, prof. emeritus, 1995—. Artist-in-residence, Aspen, Colo., 1967; one-man shows include, Robert Isaacson Gallery, N.Y.C., 1962, Forum Gallery, N.Y.C., 1968, 69, 72, 76, 79, Durlacher Bros., N.Y.C., 1964, 1967, William and Mary Coll., 1979, Queens Coll., N.Y.C., 1974, Queens Mus., N.Y.C., 1982, Armstrong Gallery, N.Y.C, 1984, 86, Contemporary Realist Gallery, San Francisco, 1988, Mitchell Algus Gallery, N.Y.C., 2004, Queens Coll. Art Ctr., 2005; group exhbns. include, Whitney Mus., 1970, Balt. Mus., 1970, Butler Inst., 1972, Cleve. Mus., 1974, Phila. Mus., 1976, represented in permanent collections, Hirshhorn Mus., Washington, Sheldon Meml. Gallery, Lincoln, Nebr., N.J. State Mus., Trenton; contbr. articles to profl. jours. NEA grantee, 1985 Studio: 1123 Broadway #811 New York NY 10010 Home: 500 W 56th St Apt 2506 New York NY 10019 E-mail: dellan580257058@aol.com.

BRUDNER, HARVEY JEROME, physicist; b. NYC, May 29, 1931; s. Joseph and Anna (Fiddelman) B.; children: Mae Ann, Terry Joseph, Jay Scott. BS in Engring. and Physics, NYU, 1952, MS, 1954, PhD, 1959; postgrad., U. Md., 1954-56, CCNY, 1958, Columbia U., 1959-61. Electronics engr. Bendix Corp., Teterboro, NJ, 1952; physicist U.S. Naval Ordnance Lab., White Oak, Md., 1953-54; sr. physicist Emerson Rsch. Labs., Washington, 1954-57; prin. physicist Emerson Radio, Jersey City, 1957-61; rsch. assoc. N.Y. U. Inst. Math. Scis., NYU, 1957-60; guest scientist Rockefeller Inst. for Med. Rsch., NYC, 1960-61; sr. rsch. assoc. Am. Can Co., Princeton (N.J.) Lab., 1964-67; v.p. R & D Westinghouse Learning Corp., NYC, 1967-71, pres., 1971-76; also dir.; mem. adminstrv. com. Westinghouse Electric Corp., Pitts., 1971-76; pres. Westinghouse Electric Corp. (Westinghouse Learning Group), 1971-76, H.J.B. Enterprises, NYC, 1961—, Med. Devel., Inc., NYC, 1962; dir. Ideal Sch. Supply Corp., Ednl. Products, Inc., Document Reading Svcs., Ltd., Linguaphone Inst. Ltd., Info. Synergy, Inc., Cambridge Learning Connection, Inc.; chmn. new devels. com. Project ARISTOTLE (Annual Rev. & Info. Symposium on Tech. of Tchg., Learning, Edn.) Nat. Security Indsl. Assn., 1966—72; acting dir. Gottscho Info. Center, Coll. Engring., Rutgers U.; prof. math., physics, dean sci. and tech. N.Y. Inst. Tech., 1962-64; instr. atomic physics N.Y. U., NYC, 1953-54. Cons. Nat. Inst. Edn., Mass. Inst. Tech., Rutgers U., Worcester Poly. Inst., Poly. Inst. N.Y., Nat. Inst. Community Devel., U.S. Ho. of Reps. Com. on Sci. and Tech.; with amateur radio K2EXN, 1953-57; mem. adv. com. Middlesex County Coll., 1966—, Paterson State Coll., 1975; mem. exec. planning com. tng. adv. sect. Nat. Security Indsl. Assn., 1966; nat. adv. bd. Am. Coll. in Jerusalem; dir. computers in edn. study Nat. Inst. Edn., 1979; bd. dirs. World Learning and Comms.; mem. Raritan Millstone Heritage Alliance, Inc., Somerset, N.J., 1998—, bd. dirs., 2006—. Editl. commentator Another Opinion, Sta. WCBS, N.Y.C., N.Y. Power Authority; author: Semiconductor Physics, 1954, College Technical Mathematics, 1967, Algebra and Trigonometry-A Programmed Course with Applications, 1971, On Fermat's Last Theorem, 1979, Fermat and The Missing Numbers, 1994, How the Babylonians Solved Numbered Triangle Problems 3600 Years Ago, 1998; columnist Light-On Series: Ednl. Tech. Mag., Source Data: Datamation Mag., Home News Tribune, 2006; chmn. editl. adv. bd. Tech. Horizons in Edn. Jour.; participated Borough Highland Park March, 2005; commentator Rockefeller Ctr. Christmas Tree chosen from Suffern, N.Y., Sta. WOBM, 2004; centennial logo design stamp cacellation U.S. Postal Svc., 2005; centennial logo-design USPS Stamp Collection, 2005; contbr. articles to mags., jours., and newspapers. Mem. steering com. Project PROCEED, NSF, Mcpl. Alliance Com., Highland Park, 1990—; capt. long-range planning com. Highland Park Sch. Bd.; trustee Ross Hall Heights Assn., 1966; chmn., pres. Joyce Kilmer Authority, New Brunswick, NJ, 1986—, Joyce Kilmer Centennial Commn., New Brunswick, 1986—2007; coord. WABC-TV News, NYC, Joyce Kilmer Trees, 1994; coord. program Fermat and Babylonian Rectangles, Sta. WCTC, 1994; apprd. to Mcppl. Alliance Against Drugs and Alcohol, 1990—99; apptd. to Middlesex County Mcpl. Alliance Network, 1995—; coord. Project DATE (Drugs, Alcohol, Tobacco, Education), Rutgers U. N.J. Forum, 1995—, New Brunswick Cmty. Bridge Project, 2001, Vets. Day Project, 2001; pres. Highland Park Centennial Commn., 2002—06; dir. cir. George Street Playhouse, New Brunswick, 2002—. Recipient cert. Americanism Vets. Alliance of Raritan Valley, 1992, award Kiwanis Internat., 1993, 2 Nobel Laureate speeches Sta. WCTC, 2003, speeches on Mayor Robert Wood Johnson, Highland Park, Triangles from Rectangles article, The Daily Targum, 2004; named Knight, Order of the Swan, 1996, New Brunswick Hist. Assn., 2003, Grand Marshall, Vets. Alliance Meml. Day Parade, 2004, Joyce Kilmer Magna Carta Day, Centennial Day 789 Yrs., 2004. Fellow IEEE (life, ednl. adminstrn. com., solar standards com., photovoltaic subcom.), mem., Am. Phys. Soc., Soc. Motion Picture and TV Engrs., Internat. Fedn. Med. Electronics, AAAS, Electronic Industries Assn. (edn. com.), Am. Ednl. Research Assn., Adult Edn. Assn. U.S.A., N.Y. Acad. Scis., Am. Mgmt. Assn. (ednl. adv. com.), Math. Assn. Am., Am. Soc. Tng. and Devel., Council Ams., Am. Judicature Soc., Am. Math. Soc., Am. Soc. Curriculum Devel., Knight, Order of the Swan, Sigma Xi, Sigma Pi Sigma, Tau Beta Pi. Clubs: Chemists (N.Y.C.); N.Y. Univ., The Midtown Exec. and Chemists' Club, N.Y.C., Toastmasters, Westinghouse SURE Home: 812 Abbott St Highland Park NJ 08904-2909 Office Fax: 732-572-0524. Personal E-mail: hjbe@aol.com. *I have tried: to play a constructive part in permitting others to make a positive contribution to society; to achieve a proper mix of idealism, reason, and faith in my decision making; to apply science and technology for the betterment of humanity.*

BRUDNER, HELEN GROSS, social sciences educator; b. NYC; d. Nathan and Mae (Grichtman) Gross; children: Mae Ann, Terry Joseph, Jay Scott. BS, NYU, 1959, MA, 1960, PhD, 1973. Tchr. NYC Bd. Edn., 1959-60; instr. Pratt Inst., Bklyn., 1959-61; asst. prof. history NY Inst. Tech., NYC, 1961-63, dir. guidance, 1962-63; assoc. prof. Fairleigh Dickinson U., Rutherford, NJ, 1963-73, prof. history, polit. sci. Teaneck, NJ, 1974—, dir. Honors Coll. Rutherford, NJ, 1972-84, chmn. dept. social sci., 1980-88, pres. univ. senate, 1975-78, asst. provost, 1983—, dean, 1984, dir. grad. programs, assoc. dir. Sch. History, Polit., Internat. Studies, 1995—, dir. lang. grad. studies, pres. acad. senate, 1996—; v.p. HJB Enterprises, Highland Park, NJ, 1970—. Vice-chmn. bd. dirs. WLC Inc., Highland Park, 1990-, Casitas De Monte Corp., Calif., treas., 2005; vice-chmn. Casitas De Monte Assoc., Palm Springs, Calif., 2000-04, treas., 2005; cons. auto ednl. systems, 1971-; participant bd. trustees F.D.U.; spkr. NJ Com. Humanities. Contbr. articles to profl. jours. constl. law, transfer tech., futurism. Active women politics project NSF, 1981; active consortium project women Am. history NEH Woodrow Wilson Found., 1980, Consortium Global Interdependence, Princeton, 1984; bd. dirs. Options Spkrs. Bur., NJ Credit Union League, NJ Credit Union Shared Network, WLC Inc.; mem. Mcpl. Alliance Highland Park, Hist. Preservation Commn., Highland Park; chmn. bd. dirs. Fairleigh Dickinson U. Fed. Credit Union, 1987—; vice chmn. NJ Adv. Com. on Women Vets., 1993-; design selection com. NJ Korean Vets. Meml.; mem. N.J. VA Women's Health Com., 2005—. Recipient Woman Yr. award Am. Businesswomen's Assn., 1980, Meritorious Svc. award NJ Credit Union League, 1997, Cert. Spl. Congrl. Recognition, 2000, NJ Divsn. Mil. and Vet. Affairs award, 2004. Mem. Am. Judicature Soc., Am. Hist. Soc., Acad. Polit. Sci., Phi Alpha Theta, Phi Sigma Alpha. Office: Fairleigh Dickinson U Sch History, Polit Internat Studies Teaneck NJ 07666 Address: PO Box 1407 Highland Park NJ 08904 Office Phone: 201-692-2272.

BRUDVIG, GARY W., chemistry professor; b. Grand Forks, ND, May 10, 1954; s. Glenn L. and Myrna W. Brudvig; m. Colleen M. Brudvig, July 31, 1976; children: Lars, Erik, Karin. BS, U. Minn., 1976; PhD, Calif. Inst. Tech., 1981. NIH predoctoral trainee Calif. Inst. Tech., Pasadena, 1976-80; Miller postdoctoral fellow U. Calif., Berkeley, 1980-82; asst. prof. Yale U., New Haven, 1982-87, assoc. prof., 1987-91, prof., 1991—, chmn. dept. chemistry, 2003—. Chmn. Eastern Regional Photosynthesis Conf., Woods Hole, Mass., 1985; review panelist Dept. Energy, Washington, 1985, 93, Dept. Agrl., Washington, 1987, NIH, Washington, 1992, 93, 95, 96, 97, 98; external examiner Oberlin (Ohio) Col., 1996; mem. phys. biochemistry study section NIH, Washington, 2000-2004. Contbr. numerous articles to profl. jours.; editor: (with others) Photosynthesis Rsch., Am. Scientist, Biospectroscopy; asoc. editor Biochemistry, 2000—. Recipient Scholar award Searle Found., 1983-86, rsch. fellowship Alfred P. Sloan Found. 1986-88, teacher-scholar award Camille and Henry Dreyfus Found., 1985-90. Fellow: AAAS; mem.: Internat. Carotenoid Soc., Internat. Soc. Bio-Inorganic Chemistry, Internat. Electron Paramagnetic Resonance Soc., Biophys. Soc. (exec. com. bioenergetics subgroup 1994—97), Am. Chem. Soc. Avocations: canoeing, soccer, guitar. Office: Yale Univ Dept Chemistry PO Box 208107 New Haven CT 06520-8107 Business E-Mail: gary.brudvig@yale.edu.

BRUEMMER, FRED, writer, photographer; b. Riga, Latvia, June 26, 1929; emigrated to Can., 1951, naturalized, 1956; s. Arist and Dorothea (Wahl) B.; m. Maud van den Berg, Mar. 31, 1962; children: Aurel, Rene. Student Fed. Republic Germany schs.; DLitt (hon.), U. N.B., Can., 1989. Self-employed writer-photographer specializing in arctic and antarctic regions, 1961—; books include The Long Hunt, 1969, Seasons of the Eskimo, 1971, Encounters with Arctic Animals, 1972, The Arctic, 1974, The Life of the Harp Seal, 1977, Children of the North, 1979, Summer at Bear River, 1980, The Arctic of the World, 1985, Arctic Animals, 1986, Seasons of the Seal, 1988, World of the Polar Bear, 1989, (with Eric S. Grace) Seals, 1991, The Narwhal, 1993, (with Angèle Delaunois), Les Animaux du Grand Nord, 1993, (with Karen Pandell) Land of Dark, Land of Light, 1993, Arctic Memoires: Living with the Inuit, 1993, (with Angèle Delaunois) Nanook and Naoya: The Polar Bear Cubs, 1995, Kotik: The Baby Seal, 1995, (with Thomas D. Mangelsen) Polar Dance, 1996, Seals in the Wild, 1998, Glimpses of Paradise: The Marvel of Massed Animals, 2002, Survival: A Refugee Life, 2005, Islands of Fate, 2006. Decorated Order of Can.; Recipient Queen Elizabeth II Silver Jubilee medal, 1978, Canadian Anniversary Commemorative medal, 1993. Fellow Arctic Inst. N.Am., Royal Can. Acad. Art, Travel Journalists Guild, N.Am. Nature Photography Assn. (Lifetime Achievement award 2003). Address: 2 Strathearn South Montreal West Montreal PQ Canada H4X 1X4 Office Phone: 514-482-5098. E-mail: fredbruemmer@yahoo.ca.

BRUEMMER, RUSSELL JOHN, lawyer; b. Decorah, Iowa, Apr. 23, 1952; s. John William and Marion Jean (Wartinbee) B. BA, Luther Coll., 1974; JD, U. Mich., 1977. Bar: Minn. 1978, D.C. 1980, U.S. Dist. Ct. D.C. 1981, U.S. Supreme Ct. 1990, N.Y. 2001. Law clk. Judge William H. Webster, U.S. Ct. Appeals (8th cir.), 1977-78; spl. asst. to the dir. FBI, Washington, 1978-80, chief counsel congl. affairs, 1980-81; assoc. Wilmer, Cutler & Pickering, Washington, 1981-84, ptnr., 1985—87; counsel to Dir. of Ctrl. Intelligence CIA, Washington, 1987-88, gen. counsel, 1988-90; ptnr. Wilmer, Cutler & Pickering, Washington, 1990—; ptnr., chmn. Fin. Inst. dept. Wilmer Cutler Pickering Hale & Dorr, Washington, 2004—. Mem. bd. regents Luther Coll., 2007—; spkr. in field. Editor-in-chief U. Mich. Jour. Law Reform; mem. editl. bd. Electronic Banking Law and Commerce Report; contbr. articles to profl. jours. Recipient Meritorious Intelligence Officer award, 1988, Disting. Intelligence medal, 1990, CIA, Disting. Svc. award Luther Coll., 2004. Mem. ABA (banking law com. 1982—, subcom. on bank holding cos. and nonbanking activities, chmn. 1985-87, chmn. subcom. on securities activities 1994-96, 98-99, standing com. on law and nat. security 1995-98, corp. compliance com., vice-chmn. subcom. on developing codes of conduct 2003-05), Am. Law Inst., Order of the Coif. Republican. Lutheran. Home: 4024 40th St N Arlington VA 22207-4608 Office: Wilmer Cutler Pickering Hale & Dorr LLP 1875 Pennsylvania Ave NW Washington DC 20006 Home Phone: 703-241-5489; Office Phone: 202-663-6804. Office Fax: 202-663-6363. Business E-Mail: russell.bruemmer@wilmerhale.com.

BRUEN, JAMES A., lawyer; b. South Hampton, NY, Nov. 29, 1943; s. John Francis and Kathryn Jewell (Arthur) B.; m. Carol Lynn Heller, June 13, 1968; children: Jennifer Lynn, Garrett John. BA cum laude, Claremont Men's Coll., 1965; JD, Stanford U., 1968. Bar: Calif. 1968, US Dist. Ct. (no., ea., so. and ctrl. dists.) Calif. 1970, US Ct. Claims 1972, US Tax Ct. 1972, US Ct. Appeals (9th cir.) 1972, US Ct. Appeals (10th cir.) 2006, US Supreme Ct. 1973, US Dist. Ct. Ariz. 1993, N.Mex. 1999. Atty. FCC, Washington, 1968—70; asst. U.S. atty. criminal div. Office of U.S. Atty., San Francisco, 1970—73, asst. U.S. atty. civil divsn., 1973—75, chief of civil divsn., 1975—77; ptnr. Landels, Ripley & Diamond, San Francisco, 1977—2000, Farella Braun & Martel LLP, San Francisco, 2000—. Faculty Practising Law Inst. Def. Rsch. Inst., ABA/Am. Law Inst. Co-author: Pharmaceutical Products Liability, 1989; contbg. editor: Hazardous Waste and Toxic Torts Law and Strategy, 1987-92; contbr. numerous articles to profl. jours. Fellow Am. Bar Found.; mem. ABA (vice chmn. environ. quality com. nat. resources sect. 1989-93, co-chmn. enforment litig. subcom. environ. litig. com. litig. sect. 1990-92), Am. Inn of Ct. (master-at-large), Internat., Soc. for Environ. Epidemiology. Avocations: scuba diving, travel. Office: Farella Braun & Martel Russ Bldg 17th Fl 235 Montgomery St San Francisco CA 94104 Office Phone: 415-954-4430. Business E-Mail: jbruen@fbm.com.

BRUEN, JOHN DERMOT, management consultant; b. Glen Cove, NY, Oct. 19, 1930; s. John D. and Kathleen M. (Halferty) B.; m. Ann Theone Lee, June 22, 1957; children: Michael J., Kathleen A., Thomas L., Lisa M. BS, U. Md., 1959; MBA, U. Pitts., 1963; grad., Naval War Coll. Command and Staff Course, 1966, Army War Coll., 1972. Enlisted in U.S. Army, 1948, commd. 2d lt., 1953, advanced through grades to lt. gen., 1983; service in Korea, Germany, Azores, Thailand and Vietnam; dir. resources and mgmt. Office Dep. Chief Staff Logistics Hqrs., DA, 1977—79; comdr. Mil. Traffic Mgmt. Command Washington, 1979-83; comdr. 21st Support Command Europe, 1983-86; ret., 1986; pres. Bruen & Assocs., Springfield, Va., 1986—; vice chmn. internat. U.S. Computer-Aided Acquisition and Life-Cycle Support Industry Steering Group, 1991—95; hon. col. U.S. Army Transp. Corps Regt., 1997—2001. Contbr. articles on leadership, mgmt. to profl. jours. Decorated Def. D.S.M., Army D.S.M., Legion of Merit with two oak leaf clusters, Bronze Star with one oak leaf cluster, Meritorious Svc. medal with one oak leaf cluster, Army Commendation medal with one oak leaf cluster; decorated grand officer Order of the Crown (Belgium); named to U.S. Inf. Officer Candidate Sch. Hall of Fame, 1979, U.S. Army Transp. Corps Hall of Fame, 2000; recipient Computer-Aided Acquisition and Life-Cycle Support Meritorious Svc. award, 1996. Mem. U.S. Army Transp. Corps Regiment Assn. (pres. 1997-2001), Nat. Def. Transp. Assn., Assn. U.S. Army, Mil. Officers Assn. Am. (bd. dirs. 1986-94). Roman Catholic. Office: 6104 Greenlawn Ct Springfield VA 22152-1314 Home Phone: 703-644-7072; Office Phone: 703-644-7072. Personal E-mail: jdbruen@aol.com.

BRUER, SCOTT VINCENT, music educator; b. Madison, Wis., Jan. 19, 1969; s. Lloyd H. and Mary Lou Bruer; m. Nicole Marie Schnese, July 1, 2000; 1 child, Benjamin Timothy. MusB, U. Wis., Stevens Point, 1993. Instrumental music instr. Mukwonago Sch. Dist., Wis., 1993—98; dir. bands Reedsburg Area HS, Wis., 1998—. Mem.: Music Educators Nat. Conf. Home: 700 E Main St Reedsburg WI 53959 Office: Reedsburg Area HS 1100 S Albert Ave Reedsburg WI 53959 Home Phone: 1-608-524-6709; Office Phone: 1-608-524-4327 ext 1116. Office Fax: 1-608-524-1373. Personal E-mail: sbruer1964@yahoo.com. Business E-Mail: sbruer@rsd.k12.wi.us.

BRUESCHKE, ERICH EDWARD, physician, researcher, educator; b. nr. Eagle Butte, SD, July 17, 1933; s. Erich Herman and Eva Johanna (Joens) B.; m. Frances Marie Bryan, Mar. 25, 1967; children: Erich Raymond, Jason Douglas, Tina Marie, Patricia Frances, Susan Eva. BS in Elec. Engring, S.D. Sch. Mines and Tech., 1956; postgrad., U. So. Calif., 1960-61; MD, Temple U., 1965. Diplomate Am. Bd. Family Practice, also cert. in geriatrics. Intern Germantown Dispensary and Hosp., Phila., 1965-66; mem. tech. staff Hughes Research and Devel. Labs., Culver City, Calif., 1956-61; practiced gen. medicine Fullerton, Calif., 1968-69; dir. research Ill. Inst. Tech. Research Inst., Chgo., 1970-76; research asst. prof. Temple U. Sch. Medicine, 1965-69; mem. staff Mercy Hosp. and Med. Center, Chgo., 1970-76; vis. prof. Rush Med. Coll., Chgo., 1974-76, prof., chmn. dept. family practice, 1976—95, program dir. Rush. Christ family practice residency, 1978-93, vice dean, 1992—93, acting dean, 1993-94, dean, 1994-2000, v.p. univ. affairs, 2000—02; trustee Anchor HMO, 1976-81, v.p. med. and acad. affairs, 1981—2000; trustee Synergon Health Systems, 1993-98; vice chmn., bd. dirs. Rush Presbyn. St. Lukes Health Assocs., disting. prof. medicine, 2002—, Rush Med. Coll. of Rush U., 2002—. Bd. dirs. Comprehensive Health Planning Met. Chgo., 1971—74, Fedn. of Ind. Ill. Colls. and Univs., West Suburban Higher Edn. Consortium; adv. com. Edn. to Careers, Health and Medicine/Chg. Bd. Edn.; med. dir. Chgo. Bd. of Health West Side Hypertension Ctr., 1974—78; sr. attending Presbyn.-St. Luke's Hosp., Chgo., 1976—2003; vis. attending Rush U. Hosp., Chgo., 2003—. Editor-in-chief Disease-a-Month, 1998-2003; assoc. editor Primary Cardiology, 1979-85; cons. editor for family practice Hosp. Medicine, 1986-2003; med. editor World Book/Rush Presbyn. St. Lukes/Med. Ency., 1987-2003; contbr. articles to profl. jours. Served with M.C., USAF, 1966-68. Named Physician Tchr. of Yr. Ill. Acad. Family Physicians, 1988, alumni of yr. Temple U. Sch. Medicine, 1996. Master Mason; fellow Am. Acad. Family Physicians, Inst. of Medicine of Chgo.; mem. IEEE (chmn. Chgo. sect. Engring. in Medicine and Biology group 1974-75), Internat. Soc. for Artificial Internal Organs, Am. Fertility Soc., Am. Occupational Med. Assn. (recipient Physician's recognition award 1969, 72, 75), Am. Wireless Assn., Chgo. Med. Soc., Am. Heart Assn., Am. Wireless Assn., Assn. for Advancement Med. Instrumentation, N.Y. Acad. Scis., Sigma Xi, Phi Rho Sigma, Eta Kappa Nu, Alpha Omega Alpha. Home: 319 N Lincoln St Hinsdale IL 60521-3442 *It is important to be courageous and do what you really want to do rather than what is expected or what seems to be currently popular. If life is approached with a spirit of goodwill and one is strong enough to follow one's own desires, then the contribution made and the success achieved can be a credit to humanity and also a source of endless enjoyment. The real secret of life is self-discipline; this allows the tempering of short-term needs with the necessary long-term planning to achieve a stable life and a meaningful contribution to humankind.*

BRUESEKE, HAROLD EDWARD, judge; b. Sandusky, Ohio, Mar. 19, 1943; s. Edward W. and Jolanda (Sommer) B.; m. Bonnie A. Beaver, Aug. 12, 1967; children: Matthew E., Michael A. BA with honors, Elmhurst Coll., 1965; JD, Ind. U., 1968; grad., Ind. Judicial Coll., 2000. Bar: Ind., 1968, U.S. Dist. Ct. (no. and so. dists.) 1968, U.S. Supreme Ct. 1978; lic. real estate broker, Ind. Staff atty. Legal Svcs./Legal Edn., South Bend, Ind., 1968-70; pvt. practice South Bend, 1971-92; dep. pros. atty. St. Joseph County, South Bend, 1971-73; juvenile referee St. Joseph Probate Ct., South Bend, 1973-92, judge pro tem, 1993, magistrate, 1993—. Instr. Ivy Tech. State Coll., South Bend, Ind., 2003—04. Contbg. author: Juvenile Benchbook, 1980-92. Bd. dirs. Eden Theol. Sem., St. Louis, 1989-2001, various other civic orgns., South Bend, 1968—; bd. dirs., elder Zion United Ch. of Christ, South Bend, 1994-96, 2004-06. Mem. ABA, Ind. State Bar Assn., St. Joseph County Bar Assn., Nat. Coun. Juvenile and Family Ct. Judges, Ind. Coun. Juvenile and Family Ct. Judges (bd. dirs., sec., v.p. pres. 1980-2000), Jud. Conf. Ind. (dir. 1998-2000). Avocations: amateur radio, computers. Home: 52741 Arbor Dr South Bend IN 46635-1205 Office: Juvenile Justice Ctr 1000 S Michigan St South Bend IN 46601-3426 E-mail: bhbruese@comcast.net, hbrueseke@jjconline.org.

BRUESS, CHARLES EDWARD, lawyer; b. St. Paul, Oct. 15, 1938; s. Edward Charles and Eleanor Mabel (Hammersten) B.; m. Jean Ellen Gustafson, Aug. 26, 1962; children: Steven Charles, Karen Jean. BA, U. Minn., 1959; student, Ohio U., 1959-60; JD, Ind. U., 1963. Bar: Ind. 1963, U.S. Dist. Ct. (so. dist.) Ind. 1968, U.S. Supreme Ct. 1966. Assoc. Barnes, Hickam, Pantzer & Boyd, Indpls., 1967-71; ptnr. Barnes & Thornburg (formerly Barnes, Hickam, Pantzer & Boyd), Indpls., 1972-94, of counsel, 1995-96, ret., 1996; dep. clk. U.S. Dist. Ct. (so. dist.) Ind., 1999—. Trustee Eagle-Union Community Sch. Corp., Zionsville, Ind., 1978-90; dir. Tri-County Ctr. Inc., 1991-94, Zionsville Pub. Libr., Leasing Corp., 1992—; bd. dirs. Hussey-Mayfield Meml. Pub. Libr. Found., 1999—. Fellow Ind. Bar Found.; Lawyers Club (Indpls.). Republican. Methodist.

BRUFF, HAROLD HASTINGS, law educator, former dean; b. 1944; BA in Am. History and Lit., Williams Coll.; JD magna cum laude, Harvard U. Law faculty Ariz. State U., Tempe, 1971-79; sr. atty.-advisor Office of Legal Counsel, U.S. Dept. Justice, 1979-81; cons. to chmn. Pres.'s Commn. on the Accident at Three Mile Island, 1981; law faculty U. Tex., Austin, 1983-85, John S. Redditt prof. law, 1985-92; Donald Rothschild rsch. prof. George Washington U. Law Sch., Washington, 1992-96; dean U. Colo. Sch. Law, Boulder, 1996—2003, Charles Inglis Thomson prof. law, 2003—. Contbr. articles to profl. jours. Mem. ABA, Phi Beta Kappa. Office: U Colo Boulder Sch Law 208 Fleming Law Bldg Campus Box 401 Boulder CO 80309-0001 E-mail: Harold.Bruff@colorado.edu.

BRUGAM, RICHARD BLAIR, biology educator; b. Phila., Dec. 23, 1946; s. Richard Jerrom and Margaret Suzanne (Blair) B.; m. Ella Suzanne Oren, Aug. 1, 1970; children: Amy Susann, Matthew Richard. BA in Biology, Lehigh U., 1968; M Philosophy, Yale U., 1974, PhD in Biology, 1975. Rsch. assoc. Limnol. Rsch. Ctr. U. Minn., Mpls., 1975-78; asst. prof. So. Ill. U., Edwardsville, 1978-84, assoc. prof., 1984-90, prof., 1990—; vis. scholar U. Wash., Seattle, 1984-85. Chair dept. biol. scis. So. Ill. U., Edwardsville, 1996-2002. Mem. editl. bd.: Jour. of Paleolimnology, 1998—; contbr. articles to Ecology, Archiv fur Hydrobiologie, Jour. of Paleolimnology, Holocene. Sgt. U.S. Army, 1969-72. Recipient J. Willard Gibbs prize Yale U., 1968; grad. fellowship NSF, 1968. Mem. AAAS, Ecol. Soc. Am., Am. Quaternary Assn., Ill. Acad. Scis., Phi Beta Kappa, Sigma Xi (grant 1973). Achievements include discovery that recently deposited sediment of lakes can be used to reconstruct pollution histories of the lakes, that acid lakes on coal mine sites eventually neutralize, that land clearance and watershed development in Pacific Northwest caused lakes to become more alkaline, that the addition of organic matter to acid coal mine lakes causes them to neutralize, that water levels in lakes and bogs in the Upper Peninsula of Michigan have risen in the last 4,000 years due to increase in available moisture. Home: 1400 Lantz Ct Edwardsville IL 62025-3901 Office: So Ill U PO Box 1651 Edwardsville IL 62026-1651 Home Phone: 618-656-9190; Office Phone: 618-650-2377. Business E-Mail: rbrugam@siue.edu.

BRUGGEMAN, TERRANCE JOHN, corporate financial executive; b. Mandan, ND, Oct. 20, 1946; s. George Edward and Marcella Merle (Gray) B.; m. Nancy Ellen Hohman, June 28, 1969 (div. 1997); children: Todd M., Megan P; m. Dianne Dyer, 2003. BA, U. Notre Dame, 1968; postgrad. bus. adminstrn., U. Chgo., 1968-70. Div. mgr., v.p. Continental Ill. Nat. Bank, Chgo., 1968-77; asst. treas. Gould Inc., Rolling Meadows, Ill., 1977-78, treas., 1978-80, v.p., treas., 1980-81; chmn. Gould Fin. Inc., Rolling Meadows, 1978-81; v.p. fin. and adminstrn. AM Internat., Inc., Chgo., 1981-85; mng. dir. Dean Witter Reynolds, Inc., 1985-86; sr. mng. dir. Bear, Stearns and Co., Inc., NYC, 1986-89; sr. v.p., bd. mem., chief ops. officer Lear Siegler Inc., Livingston, NJ, 1989-90; sr. v.p., bd. dirs., chief fin. officer chief ops. officer Grimes Aerospace and FL Industries, Livingston, 1989-90; mng. ptnr. Three Cities Rsch., Inc., NYC, 1990-93; chmn., pres. and CEO Network Mgmt. Inc., Fairfax, Va., 1993-97; chmn., CEO Piatl Holdings Inc., Mt. Laurel, NJ, 1993-99; chmn., pres., CEO Syscon Corp., Falls Church, Va., 1995-96; chmn., CEO Norcross Safety Products, Oak Brook, Ill., 1996, Red Ball Inc., Louisville, 1996, So. Cross O'Fallon Bldg. Products, St. Louis, 1996, Red Giraffe, Louisville, 1996; chmn., CEO, pres. Diversa Corp., San Diego, 1996-99; chmn., pres., CEO Provasis Therapeutics, Inc., San Diego, 1999—2002; pres., dir., CEO Sure Beam Corp., San Diego, 2003—04; exec. chmn. Somanta Pharms. Inc., 2004—. Bd. dirs. Yulex Corp., Harnifschfeger Industries, Inc. SGI, Inc., Silver Eagle Transport, Inc., Stationers Distbg., Inc., Alpha Wire Inc., Miss Erika Inc., Garden Ridge Pottery Corp., Pameco Holding Inc., Curtis Industries Inc., Gulf Coast Lubrication, Advanced Cardiovascular Devices, Bridge Products, Leas Sieglar Holdings, SureBeam, Somanta Pharms., Inc., Provasis Therapeutics, Diversa Corp., SYSCON Corp., PIATL Holdings, Network Mgmt., Regent Lighting, Curtis Industries, Pameco Inc. Bd. dirs. Lincoln Park Zool. Soc., 1972—, pres., CEO, 1984-87; bd. dirs. North Shore Youth Health Svc., 1979-80, N.Y. Zool. Soc./The Wildlife Conservation Soc., 1987-96, Biocom, 1999—, Chmn.'s Roundtable, 1999—, Burnham Inst. for Med. Rsch., 2002- , Calif. State U. San Marcos, 2003- , Amen Clinics, Inc., 2005-. Mem. Fin. Execs. Inst., Am. Assn. Zool. Parks and Aquariums, Forum for Corp. Dirs., Nat. Assn. Corp. Dirs., Chgo. Club, Notre Dame Club. Home: 10 Old Course Drive Newport Beach CA 92660-9025 Home Phone: 949-706-3697.

BRUGGER, DAVID JOHN, media consultant; b. Bethlehem, Pa., Feb. 5, 1943; s. Vincent Francis and Frances Stephanie (Miller) Brugger; m. Joanne Kay Strouf, Oct. 26, 1973. BA in Journalism, Duquesne U., 1965; MS in Theater, CUNY, 1968; postgrad., Drake U., 1973-74, Harvard U., 1980. Exec. prodr. Sta. KDIN-TV, Des Moines, 1968-70; prodn., ops. mgr. Iowa Pub. Broadcasting Network, Des Moines, 1970-71, network ops. mgr., 1971-73, dir. adminstrn., 1973-77; gen. mgr. Sta. WUFT-TV-FM, Gainesville, Fla., 1977-81; dir. Broadcast Svc. Corp. Pub. Broadcasting, Washington, 1981-83; v.p. Telecomm Corp. Pub. Broadcasting, Washington, 1983-87; sr. v.p. Corp. Pub. Broadcasting, Washington, 1987; pres., bd. dirs. Assn. Am.'s Pub. TV Stas., Washington, 1988-2000; pres. Global Media Consulting, Washington, 2000—. Lectr. Fundacion Agnel Ramos, Hato Rey, PR, 1990; mem. consumer adv. com. FCC, 2003—; cons. in field. Prodr.: (TV program) Interracial Dating and Marriage, 1967 (N.E.T. award, 1968); exec. prodr. (TV program) The Bicycle, 1968 (Ohio State award, 1968). Mem. coun. Salvation Army; chair Taipei Internat. Summit on Multi-culturalism. Named to Hall of Fame, Boys and Girls Clubs Am., 1992; recipient Disting. Svc. award, Ea. Pub. Radio Network, 1984, Disting. Grad. award, Ctrl. Cath. H.S., 1998, Lowell award, Pub. Broadcasting, 2000; Bklyn. Coll. TV Ctr. scholar, 1965. Mem.: Soc. Profl. Journalists, Greater Washington Soc. Assn. Execs., Am. Soc. Assn. Execs. (Excellence in Govt. Rels. award 1992), US-Indonesia Soc. (mem. world affairs coun.), USIA Pvt. Sector Ctr., Nat. Boys Club Alumni Assn. (award 1988), Asia Soc., Nat. Friends Pub. Broadcasting, Cosmos Club. Roman Catholic. Avocation: international cultures.

BRUGGINK, ERIC G., federal judge; b. Kalidjati, Indonesia, Sept. 11, 1949; naturalized citizen US, 1961; m. Melinda Harris; children: John, David. BA cum laude in Sociology, Auburn U., 1971, MA in Speech, 1972; JD, U. Ala., 1975. Bar: Ala., DC. Law clk. to chief judge US Dist. Ct. (no. dist. Ala.), 1975-76; assoc. Hardwick, Hause & Segrest, Dothan, Ala., 1976-77; asst. dir. Ala. Law Inst., 1977-79; assoc. Steiner, Crum & Baker, Montgomery, Ala., 1979-82; dir. Office of Appeals Counsel Merit Systems Protection Bd., 1982-86; judge US Ct. Fed. Claims, Washington, 1986—2001, sr. judge, 2001—. Office: US Ct Fed Claims 717 Madison Pl NW Washington DC 20439-0002*

BRUHN, JOANN MARIE, radiologic technologist, writer, speaker; b. Perham, Minn., Oct. 3, 1952; d. Raymond Ellsworth and Donna Jeanne (Peterson) Bruhn; children: Mark Schermerhorn, Justin, Craig Schermerhorn(dec.). Student, Bernice Robe Studio, Detroit Lake, Minn., 1981; cert., Meritcare Sch. Radiologic Tech., Fargo, ND, 1987. Registered technologist Am. Registry Radiologic Technologists; cert. grief recovery specialist. Piano tchr., Vergas and Moorhead, Minn., 1978—86; music coord. Moorhead Healthcare Ctr., Moorhead, 1985—86; registered radiologic technologist Healtheast/St. John's Hosp., St. Paul, 1987—. Songwriter and presenter; nat. spkr. HPSS Global, Inc. Author: Sundance, The Story of Craig, 2002, composer; psychic. Vol. pianist Leukemia and Lymphoma Soc., Wayzata, Minn., 2003; vol. spkr. Am. Cancer Soc., Minn., 2004; vol. pianist, spkr. White Bear Lake (Minn.) United Meth., 1987—; vol. pianist, organist Vergas United Meth. Ch., 1968—81. Mem.: Am. Registry Radiol. Technologists, Am. Soc. Radiologic Technologists. Avocations: songwriting, piano and vocal performance, kayaking, swimming, bicycling. Home and Office: Sundance Project 5296 Portland Ave White Bear Lake MN 55110 Office Phone: 651-762-1412. Personal E-mail: joannbruhn@hotmail.com. Business E-Mail: joann@sundanceproject.com.

BRUICE, THOMAS C., chemist, educator; b. LA, 1925; BS, U. So. Calif., 1950, PhD, 1954. Postdoctoral fellowship UCLA; asst. prof. biochemistry Yale Med. Sch., 1955—58; assoc. prof. biochemistry Johns Hopkins Med. School, 1958—60; prof. chemistry Cornell U., 1960—64, U. Calif., Santa Barbara, 1964—95, rsch. prof. chemistry and biochemistry, 1995—. Contbr. articles to profl. journals. Served USN, 1943—46. Recipient Richard C. Tolman Medal of So. Calif. Sect., Am. Chem. Soc., 1979, Repligen Medal, 1987, Arthur C. Cope Scholar Award, 1987, Alfred Bader Medal, 1988, Renaud Award of Mich. State Sect., 1988, James Flack Norris Award, 1996, Career Devel. Award, NIH, 1956, Lifetime Investigator Award, 1962, MERIT Award, 1990, 1997; Guggenheim Fellow, 1979—80. Fellow AAAS, Royal Soc. Chemistry; mem. NAS (Award in Chem. Sciences, 2005), Am. Acad. Arts and Sciences. Office: U Calif Santa Barbara Dept Chemistry and Biochemistry 9510 Santa Barbara CA 93106-9510 Office Phone: 805-893-2044. Office Fax: 805-893-4120. Business E-Mail: tcbruice@chem.ucsb.edu.

BRUININKS, ROBERT H., academic administrator, psychologist, educator; b. Mich. m. Susan Andrea Hagstrum; children: Robert, Brian, Brett. BS in Spl. Edn., Music and Social Sci., Western Mich. U., 1964; MA, Vanderbilt U., 1965, PhD in Edn., 1968. Joined as asst. prof. ednl. psychology U. Minn., 1968, Emma M. Birkmaier prof. ednl. leadership Mpls., 1991—94, dean Coll. Edn. and Human Devel., 1991—97, exec. v.p., provost, 1997—2002, pres., 2002—, prof. ednl. psychology. Dir. Devel. Disabilities Office Govs. Coun. on Developmental Disabilities, State Planning Agy., Minn., 1974—76; mem. J. William Fulbright Fgn. Scholarship Bd., 2003—. Contbr. chapters to books, articles to profl. jours. Trustee Com. for Econ. Devel. Named Minnesotan of Yr., Minn. Monthly Mag., 2004; recipient Disting. Alumni award, Mich. U. Alumni Assn., 2004; nat. leadership fellow, Kellogg Found., 1981—84. Fellow: APA, Am. Psychol. Soc., Am. Assn. on Mental Retardation (pres. 1990—91, Edn. award 1996); mem.: Nat. Assn. State Univs. and Land-Grant Colls. (bd. dirs.). Office: Univ Minn 202 Morrill Hall 100 Church St SE Minneapolis MN 55455 Office Phone: 612-626-1616. Business E-Mail: upres@umn.edu.*

BRUKARDT, GARY A., health facility administrator; Undergrad., Univ. Wisc.; grad., Am. Grad. Sch. Internat. Mgmt. With St. Luke's Med. Ctr., Phoenix, Presbyterian St. Luke's Med. Ctr., Denver; found., sr. officer Partners Nat. Health Plans; with VHA; chmn., pres. Healthnet, 1991—96; exec. vice-pres. Baptist Healthcare Affiliates, Nashville, 1991—96; pres., COO Renal Care Group, Nashville, 1996—2003, pres., CEO, 2003—. Office: Renal Care Group Ste 600 2525 West End Ave Nashville TN 37203 Office Phone: 615-345-5500, 615-345-5505.

BRULAND, GREGORY LEE, agricultural studies educator; b. Soquel, Calif., Feb. 5, 1975; s. Kenneth Wayne and Anne Muente Bruland; m. Holly Huff Bruland, May 27, 2001. PhD, Duke U., Durham, NC, 2004. Post doctoral rsch. assoc. U. Fla. Soil and Water Sci. Dept., Gainesville, 2004—05; asst. prof. U. Hawaii, Honolulu, 2006—. Contbr. articles profl. jours. Supr. Alachua County Soil and Water Conservation Dist. Bd., Gainesville, 2004—05; first reader The First Ch. Christ, Scientist, Durham, NC, 1998—2003; pres. bd. dirs. The C.S. Soc., Gainesville, 2005. Recipient Hon. Mention Student Presentation, Soc. Wetland Scientists Ann. Meeting, 2002, Best Paper award, 3d Internat. Conf. on Edn. and Info. Sys. Technologies and Applications, 2005, Faculty Travel award, U. Rsch. Coun., 2006; fellow Grad. Fellowship, NC Ctr. for Transp. & the Environment, 2001—02; grantee Wetland Program Devel. Grant, EPA Region IX, 2006—, Hatch Program, Coll. Tropical Agr. and Human Resources Hatch Program, 2006—. Mem.: Soil Sci. Soc. Am. (assoc.), Soc. Wetlands Scientists (assoc.), Ecol. Soc. Am. (assoc.). Office Phone: 808-956-8901.

BRULEY, DUANE FREDERICK, academic administrator, consultant, engineer; b. Chippewa Falls, Wis., Aug. 3, 1933; s. Casper Sepharald and Hazel Ella (Kuehn) B.; m. Suzanne Bigler, June 14, 1959; children: Scott, Randall, Mark. Student, Eau Clare State U., Wis., 1951-53; BSChemE, U. Wis., 1956; grad., Oak Ridge Sch. of Reactor Tech., Tenn., 1957; M in Mech. Engring., Stanford U., 1959; PhD in Chem. Engring., U. Tenn., 1962. Registered profl. engr., S.C. Nuclear engr. Union Carbide Nuclear Co., Oak Ridge, Tenn., 1956-59; head tennis coach U. Tenn., 1961; prof. chem. engring., head tennis coach Clemson U., SC, 1962-73; head chem. engring., head tennis coach Tulane U., New Orleans, 1973-77; head tennis profl. Timberlane Country Club, Gretna, La., 1973-76; v.p. acad. affairs, asst. tennis coach Rose Hulman Inst. Tech., Terre Haute, Ind., 1977-81; head biomed. engring., dir. rehab. engring. ctr. La. Tech. U., Ruston, 1981-84; dean sch. of engring., prof. engring. sci. Calif. Poly U., San Luis Obispo, 1984-91; program dir. biochem. and biomass engring. NSF, Washington, 1987-90, sect. head bioengring. and environ. systems, 1989-90; pres. Synthesizer, Inc., 1988—; dean engring. U. Md., Baltimore County, 1991-94, dir. bioengring., rsch. prof., 1994—2005, prof. emeritus, 2005—. Vis. prof. Princeton U., NJ, 1970, U. Yamagata, Japan, U. Hokkido, 1975, U. Minn., 1997; adj. prof. dept. chem. engring. U. Louisville, 2002—; cons. Westvaco, Charleston, SC, 1964-67, DuPont, Ponchartrain, La., 1974-79, Am. Enka Corp., 1970-71, Milliken and Co., 1978-79, Exxon, Baton Rouge, La., 1978-79, El Paso Products Co., 1980-82, Electronics Assocs., Inc., Long Branch, NJ, 1984-88, CRAY Rsch., 1986, EDS, 1995; varsity football and tennis U. Wis., Eau Claire, football adv. coun., 2003—; semi profl. football Chippewa Marines, 1952-53; co-program dir. Nat. Heat Transfer Conf., Balt., 1997, chmn. conf. coord. com., 1998, 99. Editor: Oxygen Supply, 1973, Oxygen Transport to Tissue, 1973, 83, 88, 91, 92, 94, 98, 2005, 06, Hyperthermia, 1988, Protein C and Related Anticoagulants, 1990; rsch. editl. bd.: Biomedical Instrumentation and Technology, 1993-97; contbr. chpt. to book, articles to profl. jours.; co-developer BWK Technique for high speed numerical integration. Cons. ARC; narrator five part TV series on biomed. engring., 1982, TV Biomed. Engring. Sta. WEAU, Eau Clare, Wis., 1982; keynote spkr. First Cray Acd., Rsch. Louisville, 2001; recorded for Wis. Pub. TV Network Biotechnology/Bioengring.; head tennis profl. Montebello Tennis Club, 1989-90; referee Sunshine Cup Internat. Jr. Tennis Tournament, Miami, 1966-69. Recipient Ann. Rsch. award La. Tech. U., 1983, Gold medal downhill skiing Nat. Standard Race, 1987, Alumni Disting. Svc. award U. Wis., Eau Claire, 1992, Spl. Opportunity award in Bioengring. The Whitaker Found., 1994—, Disting. Alumni award Chippewa Falls HS, Wis., 2004, C. William Hall award So. Biomed. Engring. Conf., Washington, 2007; named 2d Winningest Tennis Coach in Atlantic Coast Conf. history, 1990, one of Outstanding Educators of Am., 1972; NSF GOALIE grantee with ARC-Protein C, 2001-2004. Fellow AIChE (chmn. heat transfer energy conversion divsn., chmn. nat. heat transfer coord. com. 1998, dir. ann. biodownstream processing symposium 2003-07, chmn. com. Donald Q. Kern award 1997, chmn. com. Max Jakob Meml. award 1997, disting. spkr.), ASME (exec. bd., bioprocess engring. program, chmn. bioprocess engring. subdivsn., chmn. nat. heat transfer coord. com. 1998, dir. ann. biodownstream processing symposium 2003-07, disting. spkr.), Am. Inst. Med. and Biol. Engring. (founding fellow acad. coun.), Biomed. Engring. Soc. (hon., emeritus fellow); mem. Internat. Soc. Oxygen Transport Tissue (co-founder 1973, pres. 1983, exec. com., founder, chmn. com. Melvin H. Knisely award 1983—, keynote spkr. 25th anniversary Milw., 1997, 26th ann. meeting, Budapest, Hungary 1998, keynote spkr. Bari, Italy 2004, editor-in-chief Springer/Plenum, Oxygen Transport to Tissue, Advances and Exptl. Medicine and Biology 1999—, named Duane F. Bruley award in his honor, C. William Hall award 2007), NY Acad. Scis., Calif. Soc. Profl. Engrs. (hon.), Soc. Automotive Engrs. (Ralph R. Teetor Ednl. award 1986), Nat. Soc. Profl. Engrs., Am. Soc. Engring. Edn. (1st Pl. Rsch. award 1967, Biomed. Instrumentation and Tech. Outstanding Rsch. Paper award 1966, 97), La. Engring. Soc. (Charles

M. Kerr Pub. Rels. award 1983), US Profl. Tennis Assn. (Disting. Svc. award), US Tennis Assn. (hon. life), Sigma Xi, Tau Beta Pi. Avocation: tennis (#1 mens 35 doubles and #3 mens 35 singles in SC). Home: 2773 Westminster Rd Ellicott City MD 21043 Office Phone: 410-455-3693. Business E-Mail: bruley@umbc.edu.

BRUMBACK, CHARLES TIEDTKE, retired newspaper executive; b. Toledo, Sept. 27, 1928; s. John Sanford and Frances Henrietta (Tiedtke) B.; m. Mary Louise Howe, July 7, 1951; children: Charles Tiedtke Jr., Anne Meyer, Wesley W., Ellen Allen. BA in Econs., Princeton U., 1950; postgrad., U. Toledo, 1953-54. CPA, Ohio, Fla. With Arthur Young & Co., CPAs, 1950—57; bus. mgr., v.p., treas., pres., CEO Sentinel Star Co. subs. Tribune Co., Orlando, Fla., 1957-81; pres., CEO Chgo. Tribune subs. Tribune Co., 1981-88, pres., COO, 1988-90, CEO, 1990-95; chmn. Tribune Co., 1993-95. Trustee Culver Ednl. Found. 1st lt. U.S. Army, 1951-53. Decorated Bronze star. Mem. Fla. Press Assn. (treas. 1969-76, pres. 1980, bd. dirs.), Am. Newspaper Pubs. Assn. (bd. dirs., treas. 1991-92), Newspaper Assn. Am. (bd. dirs., sec., 1992-93, vice chmn. 1993-94, chmn. 1994-95), Comml. Club Chgo., Chgo. Club.

BRUMBACK, CLARENCE LANDEN, physician; b. Denver, Apr. 19, 1914; s. Carl Alvin and Hildur Athelia (Landen) B.; m. Lucile Leslie Gillie, June 17, 1943; children— Richard, Carl. AB, U. Kans., 1936, MD, 1943; MPH, U. Mich., 1948. Diplomate Am. Bd. Preventive Medicine. Intern U.S. Marine Hosp., San Francisco, 1943-44; dir. pub. health Laclede County, Mo., 1947, AEC, Oak Ridge, 1948-50; dir. Palm Beach County (Fla.) Health Dept., 1950-86; coord. grad. edn. Palm Beach County Health Dept., 1986-2000. Clin. prof. U. Miami; adj. prof. Fla. Atlantic U., Boca Raton, Fla.; trustee Am. Bd. Preventive Medicine, 1969-78. Mem. editl. bd. Jour. Public Health Policy, 1981-88; contbr. articles to profl. jours. Bd. dirs. Palm Beach County chpt. A.R.C., Am. Lung Assn. S.E. Fla., Heart Assn. Palm Beach County, Community Mental Health Center Palm Beach County, Palm Beach County unit Am. Cancer Soc., Palm Beach County Mental Health Assn., Palm Beach County Health Dept., 1950-86; pres. YMCA of Palm Beaches, 1970. With AUS, 1944-47. Recipient Meritorious Svc. award Fla. Public Health Assn., 1968; Merit award State of Fla., 1972; Physician of Yr. award Am. Assn. Public Health Physicians, 1975, Lifetime Achievement award, 2000. Fellow APHA (Sedgwick Meml. medal 1989, mem. exec. bd. 1964-70), Am. Coll. Preventive Medicine, Royal Soc. Health; mem. AMA (Dr. Nathan Davis award 1993), Fla. Med. Assn. (cert. of Merit award 1995), Palm Beach County Med. Soc., Rotary, Elks. Democrat. Lutheran. Home: 1242 Devonshire Way Palm Beach Gardens FL 33418-6864 Office: 826 Evernia St West Palm Beach FL 33401-5708

BRUMBAUGH, HARLEY AARON, retired music educator, conductor, composer, poet; b. Renton, Wash., Oct. 23, 1934; s. Aaron Emery and Alice Jane Brumbaugh; m. Catherine Terry Aldridge, June 14, 1958; children: Blaine Harley, Heidi Lynn Magstadt. B of Edn., Ctrl. Wash. U., 1957, M of Music Edn., 1962. Cert. tchr. Wash., 1957. Supr. music Ketchikan Sch. Dist., Ketchikan, Alaska, 1959—62; dir. instrumental music Port Angeles Sch. Dist., 1962—63; dir. choral music Renton Sch. Dist., 1963—72; prof. music Bellevue C.C., 1972—92. Trumpeter Seattle Opera Orch., 1966—67; festival condr. Tacoma All-City Honor Choir, 1982—86, All Southeastern Alaska Massed Choir, Ketchikan/Skagway, 1974—78, All-Bellevue Massed Choir, 1975, Olympic Penninsula Massed Choir, Chimacum, 1979; condr. Celebration Singers Australian Youth Music Festival, Melbourne, 1983; condr. Celebration Singers, Nandi, Fiji, 1985, U. Mex. Concert Series, Mexico City, 1981, Tahiti Typhoon Benefit Radio Broadcast, Papeete, French Polynesia, 1983; lead trumpet/vocalist Kings of Swing jazz band White Nights Festival, St. Petersburg, Russia, 1992; v.p. Wash. Jazz Educator's Assn., Yakima, 1970—72; trumpeter Seattle Symphony, Seahawks Band, Sonic Six, Seattle World's Fair Band, Mel Torme, Nelson Riddle, Lawrence Welk, Tex Beneke, Tenn. Ernie Ford; trumpet player Marion Hutton, Eartha Kitt, Morey Amsterdam, Kay Starr, Frankie Laine, Vick Schoen; lead trumpet in Seattle bands Jackie Souders Orch., Max Pillar, Norm Hougy, Archie Kyle, Hank Ohstus, Ted Carper, Red Shepherd, Ben Blakeman, Reg Hudman, Terry King, The Many Sounds of Nine Orch.; leader Harley's Horns-A-Plenty!; v.p. Puget Sound Choral Director's Assn., Seattle, 1973—75, East Side Musician's Assn., 1995—97; co-founder Wash. Assn. of Cmty. Bands, Bellevue, 1986; nat. chmn. for cmty. and two yr. colleges Music Educator's Nat. Conf., Chgo., 1977—78; chmn., clinician NW Music Educator's Conf., Portland, 1972—73; clinician Wash. Music Educator's Conf., Yakima, 1970; singer Seattle Opera Chorus, 1964—65; guest appearances on Saturday with Saldonia, The Don Lane Show, The Daryl Somers Show, 1982—83. Composer: Drums of God, No Greater Love, Tattered Sandals, Four Riverside Reflections, Molly Malone (arrangement), 1970-1974; author: (poems) Riverside Reflections; composer (performer): (musical score for documentary video) Snoqualmie Falls Mill Town Images; dir.(producer): (television bicentennial musical) Sounds of Freedom!. Dir., founder The Valley Cmty. Players, Renton, Wash., 1965; co-founder Wash. Assn. of Cmty. Bands, Bellevue, 1986; condr. Renton City Concert Band, 1985—2003; founding mem. entertainment bd. Renton River Days Ann. Festival, 1985—2001; co-founder/prodr. Snoqualmie Valley Arts Live, 1992—96; founder Celebration Singers; founding mem. Bellevue Jazz Festival, 1974. With US Army, 1957—59. Named Honored Citizen of Yr., Greater Renton C. of C., 2003; named to State of Wash. Music Educator's Hall of Fame, 1998; recipient Golden Acorn award, Renton PTA, 1964—65, Exemplary Status, Wash. C.C. Humanities Assn., 1965, Man of the Yr. Arts, Bellevue Mcpl. Arts Commn., 1985, Musical Expression award, Evergreen Safety Coun., 1987, Life Achievement award, Bellevue Lion's Club, 1992, BRAVO award, Renton Mcpl. Arts Commn., 2002. Mem.: Internat. Trumpet Guild, Poets West, Wash. State Hist. Soc., Snoqualmie Valley Hist. Soc. (life; bd. 2003). Avocations: history, reading, walking. Home: 524 Orchard Avenue NE North Bend WA 98045 Personal E-mail: hcbrum@earthlink.net.

BRUMBY, ANDREW M., lawyer; b. Feb. 4, 1954; BA with high distinction, U. Va., Charlottesville, 1976, JD, 1979. Bar: Ga. 1979, Fla. 1987. Assoc. Kilpatrick & Stockton LLP, Atlanta, 1979—86; shareholder Swann & Haddock, P.A., Orlando, Fla., 1987—90; ptnr. Shutts & Bowen LLP, Orlando, 1990—. Named one of Best Lawyers in Am., 2006, 2007, Best Lawyers in Orlando, 2006, 2007, Fla. Super Lawyers, 2006, 2007, Fla.'s Legal Elite, Florida Trend, 2007. Mem.: Am. Bankruptcy Inst., Ctrl. Fla. Bankruptcy Law Assn. (bd. mem. 1991—, pres. 1991—95). Office: Shutts and Bowen Ste 1000 300 S Orange Ave Orlando FL 32801-5403 Office Phone: 407-835-6901.

BRUMBY, JAMES REMLEY, III, (KNOX BRUMBY), retired priest; b. Marietta, Ga., Apr. 24, 1921; s. James Remley and Martha Louise Brumby; m. Vesta Frances Palmer, Aug. 20, 1971; m. Ferrell Louise West, Dec. 24, 1944; children: Ferrell Lynora, Martha Suzanne; stepchildren: Dana, Christine, Liana, Erik, Jenny. At, U. Fla., 1940—42; BA, U. of the South, Sewanee, Tenn., 1948, MDiv, 1951. Priest-in-charge St. Johns Episcopal Ch., Brooksville, Fla., 1951—53, St. Margarets Episcopal Ch., Inverness, Fla., 1951—53; asst. Holy Trinity Episcopal Ch., West Palm Beach, Fla., 1953—54; vicar Holy Spirit Ch., West Palm Beach, 1953—55, rector, 1955—60, St. Mary's Ch., Daytona Beach, Fla., 1960—66; canon missioner Diocese S. Fla., Ft. Lauderdale, 1966—70; chmn. dept. of missions Diocese Fla., Ft. Lauderdale, 1966—70; founder, priest Ch. Atonement, Ft. Lauderdale, 1966—70; supply priest Diocese Fla., Tallahassee, 1970—88; priest-in-charge Ch. Ascension, Carrabelle, Fla., 1988—2003. Dept. Christian edn. Diocese S. Fla., Orlando, 1952—58, dept. promotions, 1954—56, chair dept. young people, 1954—56, chair dept. mission and ch. ext., 1957, chair dept. camps and conf., 1958—66, mem. exec. bd., 1960—66; mem. Youth Bd. Provence IV, 1956—59; pres. Palm Beach Ministerial Assn., 1957—58, Volusia County Ministerial Assn., Daytona Beach, 1962—63; trustee Univ. South, Sewanee, Tenn., 1963—69, chair trustees com. to make student body co-ed, 1969, acting dir. ch. rels., 1984—90; founder, chmn. bd. Louttit Manor for Elderly, Daytona Beach, 1964—66; hon. canon St. Lukes Cathedral, Orlando, 1966; dep. to Gen. Conv., 69; mem. diocesan coun. Diocese Fla., 1996—2000, canon Apalachee regional coun. ministry, mem. exec. bd., 1996—2000. Author: (book) I Am a Part of All I Have Met, 1999. Lt. col. USAAF, 1942—45 USAR, 1946—58. Democrat. Avocations: painting, sailing, flying. Home: Village of Shell Point 67 Connie Dr Crawfordville FL 32327

BRUMFIELD, WILLIAM CRAFT, Slavic studies educator, photographer, writer; b. Charlotte, NC, June 28, 1944; s. Lewis F. and Pauline Elizabeth (Craft) Brumfield. BA, Tulane U., New Orleans, 1966; PhD in Slavic langs., U. Calif., Berkeley, 1973. Vis. lectr. U. Wis., Madison, 1973-74; asst. prof. Harvard U., Cambridge, Mass., 1974-80; lassoc. prof. Tulane U., New Orleans, 1984-91, prof. Slavic langs., 1992—. Resident dir. Am. Coun. Tchrs. Russian Pushkin Inst. Program, Moscow, 1979—80; co-dir. Summer INst. Coll. Faculty, NEH, 1994; adv. dir. Russian Children's Welfare Soc.; lectr. architecture, photography and lit. mus. and univs. throughout US and Europe. Author: Gold in Azure: One Thousand Years of Russian Architecture, 1983, The Origins of Modernism in Russian Architecture, 1991, A History of Russian Architecture, 1993, 2004 (Notable Book of Yr. NY Times Book Rev., 1993), An Architectural Survey of St. Petersburg: 1840-1916, 1994, Lost Russia: Photographing the Ruins of Russian Architecture, 1995, Landmarks of Russian Architecture: A Photographic Survey, 1997, Vologda Album: Photographing Architectural Monuments in the Volodga Region, 2005, Totma: Architectural Heritage in Photographs, 2005, Irkutsk: Architectural Heritage in Photographs, 2006, Tobolsk: Architectural Heritage in Photographs, 2006, Solikamsk: Architectural Heritage in Photographs, 2007; editor, contbr.: Reshaping Russian Architecture: Western Technology, Utopian Dreams, 1990, Christianity and the Arts in Russia, 1991, Russian Housing in the Modern Age: Design and Social History, 1993, Commerce in Russian Urban Culture: 1861-1914, 2001, Zhilischche V Rossil: vek XX, 2001, Predprinimatelstvo i gorodskaia kultura V Rossii, 2002, Vologda Album, 2005; contbr. articles to profl. jours.; exhibitions include Duke U. Mus. Art, 1996, New Orleans Mus. Art, 1996, U. Mich. Mus. Art, 1997, Arkhangelsk Mus. Art, 1999, Shchusev Mus. Architecture, Moscow, 2001, Represented in permanent collections Photog. Archives, Nat. Art Gallery, Washington, Libr. Congress, New Orleans Mus. Art. Fellow, Harvard Russian Rsch. Ctr., 1980—81; grantee, Samuel H. Kress Found., 1996—97, Nat. Coun. Eurasian and E. European Rsch., 1999—2000; Woodrow Wilson fellow, 1966, NEH fellow, Nat. Humanities Ctr., 1992—93, John Simon Guggenheim fellow, 2000—01, NEH Collaborative fellow, Am. Coun. Internat. Edn., 2001—02, Sr. Exch. scholar, Internat. Rsch. Exchs. Bd./Am. coun. Learned Socs. US-USSR Exch., 1983—84, Rsch. scholar, Kennan Inst., 1989. Fellow: Russian Acad. Art; mem.: Soc. Historians E. European and Russian Art and Architecture, Am. Coun. Tchrs. Russian, Inst. Modern Russian Culture (head photography sect.), Soc. Archtl. Historians, Am. Assn. Advancement Slavic Studies, Phi Beta Kappa. Office: Tulane U Slavic Dept 305 Newcomb Hall New Orleans LA 70118 Office Phone: 504-865-5276. Business E-Mail: brumfiel@tulane.edu.

BRUMIT, LAWRENCE EDWARD, III, oil field service company executive; b. Brunswick, Ga., Feb. 5, 1950; s. Lawrence Edward Jr. and Felicite (Smith) B.; m. Leila Ann Parker, Feb. 21, 1976; children: Mary Louise, Lawrence Edward IV. BS in Petroleum Engring., Mont. Tech., 1974. Field engr. Dowell, Farmington, N. Mex., 1974; service engr. Dowell Schlumberger, Warri, Nigeria, 1975, mgr., Cork, Ireland, 1976, tech. engr., Galeota, Trinidad, 1977, mgr., San Fernando, Trinidad, 1978-79, tng. ctr. mgr., Pau, France, 1980, div. mgr. S.W. Africa, Luanda, Angola, 1981-82, tech. mktg. mgr., Paris, 1983-84, v.p., region mgr., Paris, 1984-86, pres. compagnie de services, 1985—, mgr., v.p. Europe Africa, 1986-88; dir. personnel Schlumberger Ltd. Drilling and Pumping Svcs., Paris, 1988-90; v.p., gen. mgr. Dowell Schumberger North Am., Houston, 1991-95, rancher Flying "B" Ranch, 1995—; bd. dirs. Mont. Tech. Found., 1993-96. Recipient All Conf. Baseball Outstanding Coll. Athlete of Am. award Frontier Conf., 1969-71, 72, No. 1 Player and Capt. award, 1971. Mem. Soc. Petroleum Engrs. Romann Catholic. Avocations: flying; golf. Home: 4425 Sundown Rd Missoula MT 59804-7109

BRUMLEY, JON S., oil industry executive; b. 1971; BBA, Univ. Tex. Mgr. commodity risk & comml. projects Pioneer Nat. Resources Co., 1997—98; exec. v.p. Encore Acquisition Co., Fort Worth, Tex., 1998—2002, pres., 2002—, CEO, 2005—. Named Entrepreneur of the Yr., Forbes Mag., 2005. Office: Encore Acquisition Co Ste 1400 777 Main St Fort Worth TX 76102

BRUMM, JAMES EARL, lawyer, import/export company executive; b. San Antonio, Dec. 19, 1942; s. John Edward and Marie Oletha (Gault) B.; m. Alicia Joan Pine, Aug. 17, 1968 (div. Mar. 1991); children: Christopher Kenji, Jennifer Kimiko, Laurie Kiyoko; m. Yuko Tsuchida, Apr. 17, 1991. AB, Calif. State U., Fresno, 1965; LLB, Columbia U., 1968. Bar: N.Y. 1969. Assoc. Reid & Priest, NYC, 1968—72, Logan, Takashima & Nemoto, Tokyo, 1973—76; exec. v.p., gen. counsel, dir. Mitsubishi Internat. Corp., NYC, 1977—; pres. Mitsubishi Internat. Corp. Found., NYC, 1992—. Bd. dirs. Brunei LNG, 1987—, Mitsubishi Corp., Japan, 1995—2002, Tembec Inc., 1999—. Trustee Spuyten Duyvil Nursery Sch., Bronx, NY, 1991—95; bd. dirs. Sanctuary for Families, 2000—06; bd. visitors Columbia Law Sch., 1998—; mem. nat. bd. visitors Calif. State U., Fresno, 2005—; bd. dirs. Jr. Achievement Internat., 1997—2000, Internat. Sch. Svcs., 1997—99, Forest Trends, 2003—, Am. Bird Conservancy, 2003—. Mem. ABA, Internat. Bar Assn. (co-chair corp. counsel forum 2007—), Assn. Bar City N.Y. (chmn. com. on internat. trade 1990-93, chmn. task force on internat. legal svcs. 1998-2001, rep. to Internat. Bar Assn. 2001—), Univ. Club, Nippon Club. Home: 255 W 84th St Apt 6C New York NY 10024-4327 Office: Mitsubishi Internat Corp 655 3d Ave New York NY 10017 Home Phone: 212-501-7374; Office Phone: 212-605-2565. Business E-Mail: james.brumm@mitsubishicorp.com.

BRUMMEL, MARK JOSEPH, religious organization administrator; b. Chgo., Oct. 28, 1933; s. Anthony William and Mary (Helmreich) B. BA, Cath. U. Am., 1956, STL, 1961, MSLS, 1964. Joined Order of Claretians, Roman Cath. Ch., 1952; ordained priest Order of Caretians, Roman Cath. Ch., 1960; librarian, tchr. St. Jude Sem., Momence, Ill., 1961-70; asso. editor U.S. Cath. mag., Chgo., 1971-72; editor U.S. Cath. Mag., 1970—2002; dir. St. Jude League, Chgo., 1970—2002, 2005—. Treas. Eastern Province Claretians, 1998—, also bd. dirs.; bd. dirs. Chgo. Family Health Ctr.; adminstr. Our Lady of Guadalupe Ch., 2006-07. Editor Today mag., 1970-71; contbr. article to publ. Chmn. bd. Eighth Day Ctr. for Justice, Chgo., 1988-92; bd. dirs. Assn. of Chgo. Priests, 1994-96; mem. Ill. Cath. Conf., 1993-96. Mem. Cath. Press Assn. (St. Francis De Sales award 1996), Associated Ch. Press (v.p. 1985-87). Avocation: photography. Home: 3200 E 91st St Chicago IL 60617 Office: Claretian Missionaries 205 W Monroe St Fl 7 Chicago IL 60606-5033 Home Phone: 773-768-0793; Office Phone: 312-236-7782. Business E-Mail: brummelm@claretians.org.

BRUN, HENRY, publishing executive; b. NYC, Feb. 11, 1940; BA, Bklyn. Coll., 1958-62; MS, Pace U., 1975. Supr. N.Y.C. Sch. Sys., 1962-90; prin. John Jay H.S., Bklyn., 1990-94; COO Amsco Sch. Pubs. Inc., NYC, 1994-95, pres., 1995—. Author: Women of the Ancient World, The Retreat from Imperialism, Global Studies: Civilizations of the Past and Present, The World Today, America Today, Global History: The Growth of Civilizations, Essential World History. Mem. Am. Archeol. Assn., Soc. Antiquaries Newcastle upon Tyne, Soc. Promotion Roman Studies. Office: Amsco Sch Pubs Inc 315 Hudson St New York NY 10013-1009

BRUNALE, VITO JOHN, aerospace engineer; b. Mt. Vernon, NY, July 2, 1925; s. Donato and Antoinette (Wool) B.; m. Joan Florence Montuori, Apr. 23, 1949; 1 child, Stephen. AAS, Stewart Aero. Inst., 1948; BSAE, Tri-State U., 1958; MSME, U. Bridgeport, 1966; DSc, Nev. Inst. Tech., 1973; PhD (hon.), Internat. U., Spain, 1987; DSc, Pacific Western U., 1984. Rsch. engr. Norden Labs., White Plains, NY, 1948-55; instr. Tri-State U., Angola, Ind., 1955-58; engring. cons. Norden Div. United Aircraft, Norwalk, Conn., 1958-67; chief engring. cons. Singer-Kearfott Corp., Pleasantville, NY, 1967-73; chief engr. Diagnostic/Retrieval Systems, Mt. Vernon, NY, 1973-76; tech. problem mgr. Fairchild Republic Co., Farmingdale, NY, 1977-87; sr. tech. expert Sikorsky Aircraft, 1987—. Cons. in field; engring. tutor to coll. students; v.p. Lithoway, Inc., 1969-73; lectr. in field; tech. guest speaker numerous tech. soc. meetings.; participant engring. exchange program, USSR, People's Republic China. Contbr. articles to profl. jours. including Product Engring., Aviation Week, Environ. Scis. Participant U.S.A. Citizen Amb. Program. Served with USAAF, 1943-45. Decorated Purple Heart (3), Air medals, D.F.C. Tri-State U. tcht. fellow, 1955-58; NSF grantee; recipient Aircraft Design award, 1948, Inst. Aero. Sci. Lecture award, 1948, Norden Rsch. award, 1963, Cost Reduction award, 1965, Singer Engring. award, 1970, 72, Fairchild outstanding achievement award, 1985, 86, 87, Fairchild award of excellence, 1984, Am. Biographical Inst. and Research Assn. Outstanding Performance award, 1989, Aircraft Recognition award, 1986, citation N.Y. State Assembly, 1988, Conspicuous Service Cross N.Y. State, 1988, Prisoner of War medal, 1988, others; honoree Nat. Air and Space Mus.; named to Wisdom Hall of Fame, 1998. Mem. AIAA (award 1973, Aviation award 1994, Sr. Mem. award 1994, Merit award 1998, membership award 1998, award 1998), VFW, DAV, K.C., U.S. Naval Inst., Air Force Assn., Am. Ordnance Asssn., Inst. Environ. Sci., Nat Space Inst., Newman Club, Internat. Students Assn., Internat. Platform Assn., World Inst. of Achievement. Roman Catholic. Achievements include patent (with others) for Bearing Spin Rail Test; development of method of discriminate displacement for equilibrium of structures, of the position point vibration isolation technique, of the vapress vibration system, of advanced techniques for structural and vibration analyses, of the Doppler-Inertial-Loran system, of state of the art mathematical and structural analyses techniques, of Mars Doppler Lander system, computer time studies, anti-corrosion methods; resolution of 140 technical problems on the Fairchild A-10 aircraft, of more than 30 technical problems with the Saab-Fairchild 340; solution of Grumman A-6A radar tracking problem in Vietnam; elimination of technical problems on LEM inertial guidance; rsch. in mfg. productivity, co-planer structural analyses. Office: Main St Bronxville NY 10708-1102

BRUNDA, DANIEL DONALD, retired aerospace engineer, consultant, inventor, writer; b. Lansford, Pa., Oct. 22, 1930; s. Michael Theodore and Ella (Jurba) B. BSME, Lehigh U., 1952, MSME, 1953; postgrad., Johns Hopkins U., 1955, Princeton U., 1958—65, Drexel U., 1983. Registered profl. engr., N.J.; cert. expert witness and cons. Engr. Bell Aircraft aerodynamicist Glenn L. Martin, Balt.; devel., test, evaluation and performance propulsion engr. Bell Aircraft Glenn L. Martin & Curtiss Wright, Princeton, NJ, 1953—57; aerospace engr. rsch. U.S. Naval Air Propulsion Ctr., Ewing, NJ, 1957—72, local mgr. ind. R&D, 1972—83; electro magnetic engring. cons. Ewing, 1978—. Dep. dir. gen. Internat. Biog. Inst. in the Americas, 2000, sci. adv. to dir. gen., 2003; founder Electromagnetic Powerline Radiation Engrs., Am. Biog. Inst., 2000. Author: Powerline Radiation, Your Genes, Hereditary Diseases, The Unified Nature of Electromagnetic Radiation Energy and Control, and the Radiation Limits of Human Beings, 2003, Design of Safe Electric Transmission and Distribution Lines, 2003; contbr. over 20 articles to profl. jours. Internat. amb. of goodwill World Peace and Diplomacy Forum, 2003. Fellow Bioelectromagnetic Soc. (assoc.); mem. ASME (life), AIAA. Achievements include research and patents on powerline radiation, which determined the molecular weight, radiation limits and inductive impedance of average adult human beings; proved that powerline radiation is a cause of cancer and many other diseases; explained mathematically Volta's electrophonic effect 1800 A.D.; discovered Brunda's Absorbance Law and the Absorbance of DNA; research exploring causes of cancer, autism, birth defects, mental illness, heart disease, neuropathy and other illnesses scientifically. Home and Office: 106 W Upper Ferry Rd Ewing NJ 08628-2724 Office Phone: 609-882-2598.

BRUNDAGE, GERTRUDE BARNES, pediatrician; b. Neptune, NJ, May 13, 1941; d. John Holt and Mary Downey (Chatham) B. BS in Chemistry, Marietta Coll., 1964; MD, Jefferson Med. Coll., 1971. Diplomate Am. Bd. Pediatrics. Chemist Lederle Labs., Pearl River, NY, 1964-67; intern pediatrics Harrisburg Polyclinic Hosp., Pa., 1971-72; resident pediatrics Wilmington Med. Ctr., Del., 1972-74; pediatrician St. Barnabas Med. Ctr., Livingston, NJ, 1974—. Chief dept. pediat. Hosp. Ctr. At Orange, 1990—98. Moderator Presbytery of Newark, 1996; active 1st Presbyn. Ch., elder, trustee, 1982—87, 1989—92, 2004—. Mem. AMA, N.J. Med. Women's Assn., Am. Med. Women's Assn., Essex County Med. Soc., Med. Soc. N.J., Alpha Gamma Delta. Republican. Presbyterian. Avocations: choral singing, needlecrafts, gardening. Home: 18 Farrington St West Caldwell NJ 07006-7716 Home Phone: 973-226-5982. Personal E-mail: trudyb18@comcast.net.

BRUNDAGE, JEFFREY J., human resources specialist, air transportation executive; m. Diane Brundage; 3 children. Attended, Johnson and Wales Coll. Pilot Pocono Airlines, Atlantic Coast Airlines; sr. collective bargaining coord. Airline Pilots Assn. Internat.; mng. dir. employee rels. for flight function Am. Airlines, 1999—2001, v.p. employee rels., 2001—04, sr. v.p. human resources, 2004—. Office: AMR Corp 4333 Amon Carter Blvd Fort Worth TX 76155 Office Phone: 817-963-1234. Office Fax: 817-967-9641.

BRUNDAGE, MAUREEN A., lawyer, insurance company executive; b. 1957; m. Terence Brundage; children: Katie, Brian. BA, Fordham U., NY, 1978; JD, NYU, 1981. Assoc. White & Case LLP, ptnr., 1988—2006, co-head worldwide securities practice group, chief corp. securities practice; exec. v.p., gen. counsel The Chubb Corp., 2006—. Office: The Chubb Corp 15 Mountain Valley Rd Warren NJ 07059 Office Phone: 908-903-2000. Office Fax: 908-903-2027.*

BRUNDAGE, RUSSELL ARCHIBALD, retired data processing executive; b. NYC, Feb. 16, 1929; s. Eugene Columbus and Sophia Catherine (Gillies) B.; m. Barbara Jane Nelson, May 18, 1958; children: Russell Archibald, Nelson David, Beth Ellen, Paul Winston. BA, Washington Sq. Coll., NYU, 1957. With U.S. Fgn. Service, State Dept., 1950-55; applied sci. writer IBM Corp., NYC and White Plains, NY, 1957-60; with Colonial Penn Group, Phila., 1960-81, v.p., 1972-81; pres. Colonial Penn Group Data Corp., 1970-77; v.p. Nat. Assn. Plans, Inc., 1971-81; v.p. data processing SAI Group, Inc., 1982; pres. SAI Data Services Div., 1983-86; v.p. MIS Mut. Assurance Co., Phila., 1989-94; v.p. Green Tree Ins. Co., Phila., 1989-94; v.p., bd. dirs. Valley Ins. Co., Phila., 1990-92, Green Tree Ins. Co., Phila., 1992-94. V.p. Am. Loyalty Ins. Co., Gahanna, Ohio, 1989-94, also bd. dirs.; v.p., sec. Mut. Assurance Co., Green Tree Ins. Co., Am. Loyalty Ins. Co., 1991-94. Chmn. Lee Magisterial Dist. Republican Com., Fairfax County, Va., 1966; bd. dirs. S.E. Pa. chpt. Am. Heart Assn., 1993-96; ret. elder; ret. deacon. Served with USAF, 1947-50. Mem.: Vets. 7th Regt. NY, St. Andrews Soc. Phila. Republican. Presbyterian. Home: 23 Wincrest Dr Phoenixville PA 19460-5735

BRUNDIGE, ROBERT WILLIAM, JR., lawyer; b. Dayton, Ohio, Feb. 4, 1944; s. Robert W. and Elizabeth (Marquardt) B.; m. Katherine D. Muller, Dec. 18, 1971; children: Elizabeth, Allyson. BA, Yale U., 1966; JD, Vanderbilt U., 1969. Bar: NY 1970, US Dist. Ct. (so. & ea. dists.) NY 1972, US Tax Ct. 1973, US Ct. Appeals (2d cir.) 1975, US Ct. Appeals (11th cir.) 1983, US Ct. Appeals (5th cir.) 1985, US Supreme Ct. 1996, NJ 1997, US Dist. Ct. NJ 1997, US Ct. Appeals (3rd cir.) 2000. Assoc. Sage, Gray, Todd & Sims, NYC, 1969-75, ptnr., 1976-86, Hughes, Hubbard & Reed, LLP, NYC, 1987—. Mem. Vanderbilt Law Sch. Nat. Alumni Bd., Nashville, 1993-98; del. Yale U. Assn. of Yale Alumni, 1994-98; class co-chair Yale Alumni Fund, 1971-, bd. dirs. 2004-; mem. Yale Club of Bergen County and Vicinity, 1977—; presenter in field. Author: (with others) The McGraw-Hill Construction Business Handbook, 2d edit., 1985; mem. adv. bd. Vanderbilt Jour. Transnational Law, 2000—; contbr. articles to profl. jours. Trustee Ridgewood Pub. Edn. Found., 1990-97, pres., 1990-93; pres. dean's coun. Vanderbilt U. Law Sch., Nashville, 1996—. Recipient Disting. Svc. award Vanderbilt Law Sch., 1995. Mem. ABA (sect. litigation, chmn. subcom. on commodities 1984-86). Episcopalian. Avocations: tennis, fly fishing, gardening. Home: 251 Palmer Ct Ridgewood NJ 07450-2316 Office: Hughes Hubbard & Reed 1 Battery Park Plz Fl 17 New York NY 10004-1405

BRUNE, CATHERINE S., insurance company executive; BS, Univ. SC, 1974. Mgmt. positions through v.p. tech. shared services Allstate Ins. Co., Northbrook, Ill., 1976—2002, sr. v.p., chief info. officer, 2002—. Bd. mem. Chgo. & worldwide Junior Achievement. Named one of Premier 100 IT Leaders, Computerworld mag.; named to Academy of Women Achievers, YWCA; recipient Excellence in Corp. IT Leadership award, Women in Tech. Internat. Office: Allstate Ins Co 2775 Sanders Rd Northbrook IL 60062*

BRUNELLO-MCCAY, ROSANNE, sales executive; b. Cleve., Aug. 26, 1960; d. Carl Carmello and Vivan Lucille (Caranna) B.; m. Walter B. McCay, Feb. 26, 1994; children: Angela Breanna, Mikala Bell. Student, U. Cin., 1978—81, Cleve. State U., 1981—82. Indsl. sales engr. Alta Machine Tool, Denver, 1982; mem. sales./purchases Ford Tool & Machine, Denver, 1982-84; sales/ptnr. Mountain Rep. Enterprises, Denver, 1984-86; pres., owner Mountain Rep. Ariz., Phoenix, 1986—; pres. Mountain Rep. Oreg., Portland, 1990—, Mountain Rep. Wash., 1991—, Mountain Rep. Calif., Sunnyvale, 1997—, San Clemente, 1998—, Port Clinton, Ohio, 1999—; we. regional sales mgr. Offshore Internat., Inc., Tucson, 2002—. Sec. Computer & Automated Systems Assoc., 1987, vice chmn., 88, chmn., 89. Active mem. Rep. Party, 1985—; mem. Phoenix Art Mus., Grand Canyon Minority Coun., 1994; vol. fundraiser Make-A-Wish Found., 1995—, Leukemia Soc., 2006; founder Ariz. Sonora Corridor Network. Named Mrs. Chandler Internat., Mrs. Ariz. Internat. Orgn., 1996, Mrs. East Valley U.S., 1997; finalist Mrs. Ariz. Internat., 1996, Ms. Ariz. 2000, Ms. U.S. Continental Pageant; nominated The 19th Ann. Athena award Greater Phoenix C. of C., 2006. Mem. NAFE, Soc. Mfg. Engrs. (pres. award 1988), Computer Automated Assn. (sec. 1987, vice chmn. 1988 chmn. 1989), Manufacturers and Agents Nat. Assn. (chair-elect 2002), Nat. Hist. Soc., Italian Cultural Soc., Tempe C. of C., Vocat. Ednl. Club Am. (mem. exec. bd., pres. 1987—). Roman Catholic. Avocations: sports, aerobics, dance, skiing, golf, tennis. Office: Mountain Rep 254 S Lakeview Blvd Chandler AZ 85225-5792 Office Phone: 480-899-1900. Business E-Mail: rosanne@mtnrep.com.

BRUNER, JEROME S., law educator; BA, Duke U., 1937; PhD, Harvard U., 1941. Prof. NYU, Sch. of Law, NYC, 1998—; prof. Psychology Harvard U.; watts prof. Oxford U.; Meyer vis. prof. NYU Sch. of Law, NYC, 1991, Univ. prof., 1998—. Founder Head Start. Author: The Process of Education, 1961, Acts of Meaning, 1991, Minding the Law, 2000, Making Stories, 2003. Recipient Internat. Balzan prize, CIBA Gold medal for Dist. Rsch., Dist. Scientific award, Am. Psychological Assn. Mem.: Pres. Sci. Adv. Com., Nat. Acad. Edn. Office: NYU Sch of Law Vanderbilt Hall 40 Washington Sq S New York NY 10012 Home: 200 Mercer St New York NY 10012 Business E-Mail: jerome.bruner@nyu.edu.

BRUNER, NANCY J., publishing executive; B, N.Mex. State U.; MFA, U. So. Calif. With US West Media Group, Denver; cons. dir. bus. devel. Spring Multimedia, Kansas City; dir. new media Seattle Times, now v.p. new media. Office: Seattle Times PO Box 70 Seattle WA 98111-0070

BRUNER, PHILIP LANE, lawyer; b. Chgo., Sept. 26, 1939; s. Henry Pfeiffer and Mary Marjorie (Williamson) B.; m. Ellen Carole Germann, Mar. 21, 1964; children: Philip Richard, Stephen Reed, Carolyn Anne. AB, Princeton U., 1961; JD, U. Mich., 1964; MBA, Syracuse U., 1967. Bar: Wis. 1964, Minn. 1968. Mem. Briggs and Morgan P.A., Mpls., St. Paul, 1967-83; founding shareholder Hart and Bruner P.A., Mpls., 1983-90; ptnr. Faegre & Benson, Mpls., 1991—2007, head constrn. law group, 1991—2001. Adj. prof. William Mitchell Coll. Law, St. Paul, 1970—76, 2006—07, U. Minn. Law Sch., Mpls., 2003—07; chmn. Supreme Ct. Minn. Bd. CLE, Mpls., 1994—98. Co-author: Bruner and O'Conner on Construction Law, 7 vols., 2002; contbr. articles to profl. jours. Mem. Bd. Edn., Mahtomedi Ind. Sch. Dist. 832, 1978-86; bd. dirs. Mahtomedi Area Ednl. Found., 1988-94, 2002—, pres., 1988-91, 2002—07; bd. dirs. Minn. Ch. Found., 1975—, pres., 1989-97; chmn. constrn. industry adv. bd. West Group, 1991—. Served to capt. USAF, 1964-67. Decorated Air Force Commendation Medal; recipient Disting. Service award St. Paul Jaycees, 1974; named One of Ten Outstanding Young Minnesotans, Minn. Jaycees, 1975. Fellow Am. Coll. Constrn. Lawyers (founding mem., bd. govs. 1999-2002, sec. 2003-2005, pres.-elect 2005-06, pres. 2006—07), Nat. Contract Mgmt. Assn., Am. Bar Found.; mem. ABA (chmn. internat. constrn. divsn. forum com. on constrn. industry 1989-91, chmn. fidelity and surety law com. 1994-95, regional chmn. pub. contract law sect. 1990-96, recipient Forum com Cornerstone award, 2005), Internat. Bar Assn., Inter-Pacific Bar Assn. (vice chmn. internat. constrn. com. 1995-97), Minn. Bar Assn. (vice chmn. litigation sect. 1979-81), Wis. Bar Assn., Hennepin Bar Assn., Am. Arbitration Assn. (nat. panel arbitrators), Mpls. Club. Presbyterian. Home: 8432 80th St N Stillwater MN 55082-9331 Office: Faegre & Benson 2200 Wells Fargo Ctr 90 S 7th St Minneapolis MN 55402-3901 Office Phone: 612-766-7412. E-mail: pbruner@faegre.com, Philipbruner@hotmail.com.

BRUNER, WILLIAM EVANS, II, ophthalmologist, educator, researcher; b. Cleve., Oct. 10, 1949; s. Clark Evans and Pauline (Schrenk) B.; m. Susan Lee Fraser, June 7, 1975; children: Amanda Lee, Andrew Evans. BA, Wesleyan U., 1971; MD, Case Western Res. U., 1975. Diplomate Am. Bd. Ophthalmology. Intern in surgery Univ. Hosps., Cleve., 1975-76, resident in ophthalmology, 1976-79; fellow in cornea and anterior segment surgery Johns Hopkins Hosp., Balt., 1979-81; asst. prof. ophthalmology Case Western Res. U., Cleve., 1981-89, assoc., 1989-93, assoc. clin. prof., 1993-96, clin. prof., 1996—. Sr. editor; manual of Corneal Surgery, 1987; contbr. chpts. to med. textbooks and articles to profl. jours. Trustee Case Western Res. U, Cleve., Hawken Sch., Gates Mills, Ohio. Recipient Alfred S. Maschke award Case Western Res. U. Sch. Medicine, 1975, Clinical Tchg. award, Case Western Reserve U., 2003, 2006. Fellow Am. Acad. Ophthalmology; mem. Wilmer Residents Assn., cleve. Acad. Medicine, Alpha Omega Alpha, Tavern Club, Cleve. Skating club, The Kirtland Club. Avocations: skiing, boating, sailing, golf, music. Office: 1611 S Green Rd Cleveland OH 44121-4128 Home: 13515 Shaker Blvd #8A Cleveland OH 44120 Personal E-mail: bruner2020@aol.com.

BRUNETT, ALEXANDER J., archbishop; b. Detroit, Jan. 17, 1934; s. Raymond and Cecilia Gill Brunett. BA, Sacred Heart Seminary; STL in Sacred Theology, Pontifical Gregorian U., STB. ordained priest July 13, 1958. Assoc. pastor St. Rose of Lima Parish, Detroit, 1959—61, St. Alphonsus Parish, Dearborn, 1961—62; chaplain U. Mich., Ann Arbor, 1962—64, Ea. Mich. U., Ypsilanti, 1968; academic dean St. John's Provincial Seminary, Plymouth, 1969—73; dir. Div. of Ecumenical and Interreligious Affairs Archdiocese of Detroit, 1973—91; pastor St. Aidan Parish, Livonia, Shrine of Little Flower Parish, Royal Oak, 1991—94; ordained bishop Diocese of Helena, 1994; archbishop Diocese of Seattle, 1997—. Mem. Internat. Roman Cath.-World Meth. Dialogue; co-chair Anglican-Roman Cath. Internat. Commn.; chmn. Archdiocesan Theol. Commn.; vicar N.W. Wayne Vicariate, Archdiocese of Detroit; nat. chmn. Third Jewish-Christian Dialogue, Detroit. Editl. writer Mich. Cath. newspaper. Bd. trustees Cath. Near East Welfare Assn.; mem. bd. dirs. St. Patrick Seminary, Menlo Park, Calif., Mundelein Seminary, Ill. Recipient DOVE Award, Ecumenical Inst. for Jewish-Christian Studies, 1996. Mem.: Nat. Assn. of Diocesan Ecumenical Officers (pres. 1974—81), US Conf. of Cath. Bishops Com. on Ecumenical and Interreligious Affairs (chmn. 1996). Office: Archdiocese of Seattle 910 Marion St Seattle WA 98104-1274

BRUNETTI, MELVIN T., federal judge; b. Reno, 1933; m. Gail Dian Buchanan; children: Nancy, Bradley, Melvin Jr. Attended, U. Nev., 1951-53, 1956-57, 1960; JD, U. Calif., San Francisco, 1964. Mem. firm Vargas, Bartlett & Dixon, 1964-69, Laxalt, Bell, Allison & Lebaron, 1970-78, Allison, Brunetti, MacKenzie, Hartman, Soumbeniotis & Russell, 1978-85; judge US Ct. Appeals (9th cir.), Reno, 1985-99, sr. judge, 1999—. Mem. Council of Legal Advisors, Rep. Nat. Com., 1982-85. Served with US Army N.G., 1954-56. Mem. ABA, State Bar of Nev. (pres. 1984-85, bd. govs. 1975-84). Office: US Ct Appeals Ste 506 US Courthouse 400 S Virginia St Reno NV 89501-2194*

BRUNGER, AXEL THOMAS, biophysicist, researcher, educator; b. Leipzig, Germany, Nov. 25, 1956; came to U.S., 1982; s. Hans and Hildegard (Müller) B. Diploma, Hamburg U., Germany, 1980; PhD, Tech. U. Munich, 1982. Postdoctoral fellow Max-Planck Inst., Martinsried, Germany, 1984; rsch. assoc. Harvard U., Cambridge, Mass., 1982-83, 85-87; asst. investigator Howard Hughes Med. Inst., New Haven, 1987-92, assoc. investigator, 1992-95, investigator, 1995—; asst. prof. Yale U., New Haven, 1987-91, assoc. prof., 1991-93, prof., 1993-2000, Stanford U., Calif., 2000—. Recipient Röntgen prize for bioscis. Würzburg U., 1995, Gregori Aminoff prize Royal Swedish Acad. Scis., 2003, Nat. Acad. of Sci., 2005; NATO postdoctoral fellow Deutscher Akademischer Austauschdienst, Bonn, Germany, 1982-83 Mem. AAAS, NAS, Am. Crystallographic Assn., Am. Chem. Soc., Protein Soc. Achievements include studies of protein structure and function, developments in macromolecular x-ray crystallography and solution NMR spectroscopy. Office: Stanford U J H Clark Ctr Rm E300-C 318 Campus Dr Stanford CA 94305-5432 Business E-Mail: brunger@stanford.edu.

BRUNGER, ERIC GEOFFREY, social studies educator, coach; b. Syracuse, NY, Aug. 21, 1948; s. Eric and Una Kenny Brunger; m. Carol Lee Senne, June 19, 1971; children: Alison Elizabeth, Eric Andrew. BA, Alfred U., NYC, 1970; attended, SUNY Albany, 1970—71, Canisius Coll., Buffalo, 1971—73, MS, 1993. Cert. tchr. social studies N.Y. Tchr. social studies grades 7-8 Kenmore Jr. HS, 1971—81, freshman football asst., 1973—74, 1974—75, head freshman football, girls outdoor track and field, 1975—76, 1975—76, head freshman football, girls outdoor track and field, boys jr. varsity basketball, 1976—77, head girls outdoor track and field, boys jr. varsity basketball, 1977—78, head cross country, girls outdoor track, boys jr. varsity basketball, 1978—79, 1978—80, head girls outdoor track, boys jr. varsity basketball, 1980—81; tchr. social studies grade 8, head girls outdoor track and field and boys jr. varsity basketball Kenmore Mid. Sch., 1981—85, head girls outdoor track and field, 1989—90, dist. dept. chair, girls outdoor track and field, 1990—92; tchr. social studies grade 8, head girls outdoor track and field, 1989—90; tchr. social studies, head girls outdoor track and boys jr. varsity basketball Kenmore East, 1985—87, tchr. work study, girls outdoor track and field, 1987—88, pupil svcs. adminstrn. bldg. girls outdoor track and field, 1988—89, dept. chair, tchr. social studies, dist. dept. chair, head girls outdoor track and field, 1992—93, mentor, dist. dept. chair, head girls outdoor track and field, 1993—94, mentor, dist. dept. chair, head girls jr. varsity basketball, 1994—95, mentor, K-12 curriculum learning specialist, girls jr. varsity basketball, 1995—96, tchr. social studies, K-12 curriculum learning specialist, head girls jr. varsity basketball and girls outdoor track and field, 1996—2000, tchr. social studies, K-12 curriculum learning specialist, asst. boys & girls cross country, head boys & girls indoor track, head girls outdoor track, 2000—06; attendance counselor/home instrn. coord., 1988—89; tchr. mentor & curriculum learning specialist, 1993—96; curriculum learning specialist social studies, tchr. Kenmore East HS, 1996—. Asst. and head coach boys' and girls' baseball football, cross-country, 1975—; treas. Niagara Frontier Coun. for the Social Studies, Buffalo, 1993—95. Editor: (workbook) New York: A Study of Your State, 1995. Named Kenmore East Coach of Yr., 1998, Supr. of Yr., N.Y. State Social Studies Suprs. Assn., 2006. Mem.: Nat. Coun. of the Social Studies, N.Y. State Coun. for the Social Studies. Avocations: running, reading, painting. Office: Kenmore-Town of Tonawanda Pub Schs 350 Fries Rd Tonawanda NY 14150 E-mail: au70@aol.com.

BRUNGRABER, ROBERT J., civil engineer, educator; b. Dec. 20, 1929; s. Louis Rudolph and Beatrice Emogene B.; m. Ruth Ann Rupp, June 13, 1951; children: Robert Lyman, Margaret Ruth. BSCE, U. Mich., 1951; MS, Cornell U., 1956; PhD, Carnegie Inst. Tech., 1963. Field engr. Porter-Urquhart-Skidmore, Owings & Merrill, cons. engrs., Casablanca, Morocco, 1951—53; instr. Cornell U., Ithaca, NY, 1953—56; rsch. engr. Alcoa Rsch. Labs., New Kensington, Pa., 1956—60; asst. prof. civil engring. Princeton U., 1962—66; assoc. prof. civil engring. Union Coll., Schenectady, NY, 1966—68; prof. civil engring. Bucknell U., Lewisburg, Pa., 1968—, presdl. prof., 1979—92, prof. emeritus, 1992—. Founder, pres. Slip-Test, Inc., 1976; structural cons. Borough Hall, Princeton, NJ, 1966; Intergovtl. Pers. Act appointee Nat. Bur. Stds., 1974—76; dir., treas., mem. nat. exec. com. Nat. Inst. Bldg. Scis., 1976—81. Contbr. articles to profl. publs. Mem.: ASTM (Charles H. Irvine award, Merit award), ASCE (chmn. com. lightweight alloys of metals structural divsn. 1969—73), Moles, Cosmos Club, Nassau Club, Phi Kappa Phi, Sigma Xi, Phi Gamma Delta, Chi Epsilon, Tau Beta Pi. Achievements include patents in field; research in structural applications of aluminum, particularly welded applications, pile foundations, and slip resistance of footwear and/or walkway surfaces; supr. design and constrn. of Stephen J. Potter Meml. Lab., Union Coll., 1967; structural test facility at Bucknell U., 1985 (now named R.J. Brungraber Structural Test Facility); design of original system for reinforcing obsolete steel truss bridges; invention of NBS-Brungraber device for measuring the slip-resistance of footwear and/or walkway surfaces. Personal E-mail: slip-testinc@verizon.net.

BRUNI, FRANK, restaurant critic; b. White Plains, NY, Oct. 31, 1964; BA, U. NC, Chapel Hill, 1986; MS, Columbia U., 1988. Writer Detroit Free Press, 1990—95; met. reporter NY Times, 1995—98, nat. corr. San Francisco bur., 1998, corr. Washington, DC bur., 1998—2002, Rome bur. chief, 2002—04, restaurant critic, 2004—. Contbr. (articles) Sunday mag., NY Times, 1995—98; co-author: A Gospel of Shame: Children, Sexual Abuse, & the Catholic Church, 1993, Consumer Terrorism, 1997; author: In the Eye of a Storm Over Gay Clergy, 1996, Ambling Into History: The Unlikely Odyssey of George W. Bush, 2002. Co-recipient George Polk award, 1996; finalist Pulitzer Prize, 1992. Office: NY Times 229 W 43rd St New York NY 10036 Office Phone: 212-556-1435. Office Fax: 212-556-1481.*

BRUNI, STEPHEN THOMAS, museum director; b. Phila., Feb. 3, 1949; s. Eugene Thomas and Frances Isabel (McMorran) B.; m. Barbara Natalie Plunket, May 13, 1949; children: Christopher Stephen, Katherine Elizabeth. BA, George Washington U., 1971. Curatorial asst. Del. Art Mus., Wilmington, 1972-74, program asst., 1974-77, adminstrv. asst., 1977-79, mgr. support svcs., 1979-82, asst. dir. adminstrn., 1982-84, dep. dir. adminstrn., 1984-85, acting dir. adminstrn., 1985-86, exec. dir., 1986—. Mem. arts selection com. Del State Arts Coun., 1985-86, State Divsn. Librs., 1984-86; mem. Gov.'s Arts Adv. Com., 1983-85; mem. adv. bd. Siena Hall and Seton Villa, Creative Artists Network; bd. dirs. Studio Group, Inc. Mem. bd. Literacy Vols. Am. (affiliate Wilmington Libr.). Mem. Am. Assn. Mus., Assn. Art Mus. Dirs., Bd. Greater Wilmington Conv. and Visitors Bur. Avocations: skiing, racquet sports, golf, bicycling. Office: Del Art Mus 2301 Kentmere Pky Wilmington DE 19806-2019

BRUNIE, CHARLES HENRY, investment manager; b. NYC, July 17, 1930; s. Charles Henry and Olivia (Swanston) B.; m. Jean Isbell Corley, June 23, 1965; stepchildren: William Corley, Jean Corley Yankus, Ellen Corley. BA, Amherst Coll., 1952; MBA, Columbia, 1956. Analyst N.Y. Life Ins. Co., NYC, 1956-60, Faulkner, Dawkins & Sullivan, 1960-63, Oppenheimer & Co., NYC, 1963-65, gen. ptnr., 1965-82, mem. exec. com., 1969-82; chmn. Oppenheimer Capital, 1969-96, chmn. emeritus, 1996-2000; trustee Manhattan Inst., 1978—, chmn. bd., 1980-1990, chmn. emeritus, 1990—; chmn. Brunie Assocs., NYC, 2001—. Served with AUS, 1952-54. Mem. N.Y. Soc. Security Analysts, Chartered Financial Analysts, Mont Pelerin Soc., Delta Upsilon. Clubs: Knickerbocker (N.Y.C.), Doubles (N.Y.C.), Annabell's (London), Bronxville Field, Siwanoy Country (Bronxville). Office: Brunie Assocs 320 Park Ave Fl 10 New York NY 10022-6815

BRUNING, EARL H., music educator; s. Earl H. Bruning, Sr. and Frances E. Bruning; m. Merribeth D. Davis, June 13, 1971; 1 child, Brandon Earl. B in Music Edn., Ind. U., 1966; MA, Ball State U., 1970, ArtsD, 1980. Lic. profl. tchr. Ind., 1981. Asst. dir. bands Goshen Cmty. Schs., Goshen, Ind., 1966—68; dir. instrumental music Wa-Nee Cmty. Schs., Nappanee, Ind., 1968—69; assoc. dir. bands and instr. of trumpet Ark. State U., Jonesboro, 1970—71; part-time instr. trumpet and summer festival orch. condr. Ball State U., Muncie, 1971—75; dir. brass studies, trumpet specialist, asst. dir. bands So. Utah U., Cedar City, 1975—76; adj. instr. U. Indpls., 1980—83; dir. of instrumental music U. Ozarks, Clarksville, Ark., 1983—88; marching band dir., 8th grade band dir., band and choir substitute NW Hendricks Sch. Corp., Lizton, Ind., 1976—81; vis. prof. dir. bands and high brass Gonzaga U., Spokane, Wash., 1988—89; music edn. instr. and asst. prof. secondary edn., contract music instr. Ball State U. and Muncie Cmty. Schs., 1989—93; adj. prof. music, condr. and music dir. U. Tenn. Martin; Ken-Tenn Youth Orch., Martin, Tenn., 1993—97; assoc. faculty, asst. prof. music and edn. Ind. U. South Bend, South Bend, 1998—2002; conductor IUSB Philharm. Orch., 1998—2002; half-time music faculty Ea. Ill. U., Charleston, 2004; adj. faculty McKendree Coll., Lebanon, Ill., 2003—. Condr. summer music festival orchs. Ball State U. and St. Mary's Ch., Muncie, 1973—74; condr. and music dir. Ken-Tenn Youth Orch. and Cmty. Choir, and Chamber Music Program, Martin, 1993—97; guest condr. Elkhart County Symphony Assn. Youth Honors Orch., Elkhart, 1998; guest condr. and clinician Murray State U., Ky., 1994; asst. condr. Masterworks Chorale and America's Hometown Band, Muncie, 1990—92. Author: (doctoral dissertation) A Survey and Handbook of Analysis for the Conducting and Interpretation of Seven Selected Works in the Standard Repertoire for Wind Band (Ball State University); co-author (jour. article) Optimizing Learning: Integrating the Fine Arts and the Language Arts, 2005. Condr. and music dir. Michiana Concert Band, South Bend, Ind., 2001; assisting min. Christ the King Luth. Ch., Granger, Ind., 1999—2002; bd. mem., rehearsal condr., coach South Bend Youth Symphony, 1998—2000. Recipient Arts Educator of Yr., Obion County Arts Coun., Tenn., 1995, hon. membership, Zoltan Kodaly Acad. and Inst., Kecskemet, Hungary, Collegiate Membership Chpt. Growth award, Ind. Music Educators Assn., 2000, 2002. Mem.: Coun. Music Tchr. Edn., Music Educators Nat. Conf. (coun. for music tchr. edn., apptd. mem. 1983—84), NEA (life), Phi Mu Alpha Sinfonia, Phi Delta Kappa (pres. and seated coun. del., NW Tenn. chpt. 1995—97), Kappa Kappa Psi (life; nat. conv. orgn. com. and host 1963—64). Achievements include design of the Arts Education curriculum for the State of Arkansas, which served as a prototype for the National Standards for Music Education. Home Phone: 870-245-3027. Personal E-mail: ebruning@sbcglobal.net.

BRUNING, JAMES LEON, academic administrator, educator; b. Bruning, Nebr., Apr. 1, 1938; s. Leon G. and Delma Dorothy (Middendorf) Bruning; m. E. Marlene Schaff, Aug. 24, 1958; children: Michael, Stephen, Kathleen. BA, Doane Coll., 1959; MA, U. Iowa, 1961, PhD, 1962. Chmn. dept psychology Ohio U., Athens, 1972-76, acting dean arts and scis., 1976-77, assoc. dean, 1977-78, vice provost, 1978-81, provost, 1981-93, acting pres., 1991, trustee prof., 1993—, v.p. regional higher edn., 1998—99, dir. Enterprise project, 2002—03. Planning cons. NCHEMS, Boulder, Colo., 1979—80; provost Shawnee (Ohio) State U., 1996. Author: (book) Computational Handbook of Statistics, 1997, Research in Psychology, 1970; contbr. articles to profl. jours. Chair task force Ohio Bd. Regents, 1994—95. Grantee, Esso, 1963—64, NIMH, 1963—66, EPDA, 1974—75, OBOR, 1989—91. Mem.: APA (vis. scientist), AAAS, Midwestern Psychol. Assn., Sigma Xi. Democrat. Lutheran. Home: 6148 Melnor Dr Athens OH 45701-3577 Office: Ohio U Psychology Dept Athens OH 45701 Business E-Mail: bruningj@ohio.edu.

BRUNING, JON CUMBERLAND, state attorney general; b. Lincoln, Nebr., Apr. 30, 1969; s. Roger Howard and Mary Genevieve (Cumberland) Bruning; m. Deonne Leigh Niemack, July 8, 1995, two children, Lauren Caroline, Jon Cumberland Jr. BA with high distinction, U. Nebr., 1990, JD with distinction, 1994. Bar: Nebr. 1994, US Dist. Ct. Nebr. 1994, US Ct. Appeals (8th cir.) 1994. Pvt. practice, Papillion, Nebr., 1993-97; mem. Nebr. Legislature from 3rd dist., Lincoln, 1997—2002; atty. gen. State of Nebr., 2003—. Mem., Gretna United Methodist Ch., Nebr. State Bar Assn., Phi Beta Kappa. Republican. Methodist. Home: 17501 Riviera Dr Omaha NE 68136-1951 Office: Office of Atty Gen State Capitol PO Box 98920 Lincoln NE 68509-8920 Office Phone: 402-471-2682.*

BRUNK, SAMUEL FREDERICK, oncologist; b. Harrisonburg, Va., Dec. 21, 1932; s. Harry Anthony and Lena Gertrude (Burkholder) B.; m. Mary Priscilla Bauman, June 24, 1976; children: Samuel, Jill, Geoffrey, Heather, Kirsten, Peter, Christopher, Andrew, Paul, Barbara BS, Ea. Mennonite Coll., 1955; MD, U. Va., 1959; MS in Pharmacology, U. Iowa, 1967. Diplomate Am. Bd. Internal Medicine, Am. Bd. Internal Medicine in Med. Oncology. Straight med. intern U. Va., Charlottesville, 1959-60; resident in chest diseases Blue Ridge Sanatorium, Charlottesville, 1960-61; resident in internal medicine U. Iowa, Iowa City, 1962-64, fellow in clin. pharmacology (oncology), 1964-65, 66-67, asst. prof. internal medicine, 1967-72; assoc. prof. internal medicine, 1972-76; fellow in medicine (oncology) Johns Hopkins U., Balt., 1965-66; clin. assoc. prof. med. Okla. State U. Coll. Osteo; vis. physician bone marrow transplantation unit Fred Hutchinson Cancer Treatment Ctr., U. Wash., Seattle, 1975; practice medicine specializing in med. oncology Des Moines, 1976-94; attending physician Iowa Luth. Hosp., 1976-94, Iowa Meth. Med. Ctr., 1976-94, Charter Hosp., 1976-94, Mercy Hosp. Med. Ctr., 1976-94; dir. med. oncology Hahne Regional Cancer Ctr., DuBois, Pa., 1994; attending physician DuBois Regional Med. Ctr., 1994; dir. Pa. Cmty. Cancer Care, 1995; attending physician St. Mary's Regional Med. Ctr., 1994; med. oncologist Cancer Treatment Ctrs. Am., Southwestern Regional Med. Ctr., Tulsa, Okla., 1995—2001, chief med. oncology Cancer Treatment Ctrs. Am., 2002—06; attending physician Meml. Med. Ctr., Tulsa, Okla.,

1995—2005; med. oncologist Cancer Treatment Ctrs. Am., Eastern Regional Med. Ctr., Phila., 2006—. Chief of staff Iowa Luth. Hosp., 1990, chmn. dept. internal medicine, 1988; cons. physician Des Moines Gen. Osteo. Hosp., 1976-94; prin. investigator Iowa Oncology Rsch. Assn. in assn. with N. Cen. Cancer Treatment Group and Ea. Coop. Oncology Group, 1978-83; prin. investigator Iowa Oncology Rsch. Assn. Comty. Clin. Oncology Program, 1983-84; mem. cancer care com. St. Mary's, Pa., 1995. Contbr. articles to profl. jours. Bd. dirs. Iowa div. Am. Cancer Soc., 1971-89, Johnson County chpt., 1968-72. Mosby scholar, U. Va., 1959 Fellow ACP, Am. Coll. Clin. Pharmacology; mem. AMA, Okla. Medical Soc., Tulsa County Medical Soc., Am. Soc. Clin. Oncology, Raven Soc., Alpha Omega Alpha. Roman Catholic. Home: 2401 Pennsylvania Ave Unit 12 b 24 Philadelphia PA 19130-3043

BRUNK, THOMAS WALTER, art historian; b. Romeo, Mich., Nov. 25, 1949; s. Norman Brunk and Margie Velma Smith. MA in Art and Archtl. History, Norwich U., 1992; PhD in Art History, Union Inst., 1997. Clk. coord. Sever Stal N.Am., Dearborn, Mich., 1971—, UAW Local 600, 1971—; founder, pres. Indian Village Hist. Collections, Inc., Detroit, 1973—92; pres. Stapleton Found. for Health Edn., Wayne State U., Detroit, 1980—95, Detroit Masonic Temple Libr. and Mus., Detroit, 2001—, Friends of Freer House, 2003—; instr. archtl. history Coll. for Creative Studies, Detroit, 2001—, Merrill-Palmer Inst. Wayne State U., Detroit, 2003—. Guest curator Mich. State U., Detroit, 1976, Detroit Inst. Arts, 1976, Detroit Hist. Mus., 1978, 79, 81, 84, mem. adv. bd., 2006—; guest curator U. Mich. Mus. Art, Ann Arbor, 1995—96, Kresge Art Mus., Mich. State U., 2004—05, Marshall M. Fredericks Sculpture Mus. Saginaw Valley State U., 2006—; pres. The Pewabic Soc., Inc., Detroit, 1988—89; instr. art history Coll. Creative Studies, Detroit, 2001—; adv. bd. Detroit Hist. Mus., 2004—. Author: Arts and Craft in Detroit 1906-1976: The Movement, The Society, The School, 1976, Pewabic Pottery: Marks and Labels, 1978, Pewabic in Architecture, 1979, Dichotomy, 1980, 1981, 1999, Bulletin of the Detroit Institute of Arts, 1981, The Acanthus Club, 1981, Leonard B. Willeke: Excellence in Architecture and Design, 1986, A Tribute to Edgar Louis Yaeger, 1988, American Craft, 1989, Selected Works By Contemporary Hispanic Artists in Michigan, 1989, The Grosse Pointe Artists Association, 1992, The Grand American Avenue 1850-1920, 1994, Tonnancour, 1994, 1997, Painting with Fire, 1995, Pewabic Pottery and the MSU Connection, 2005. Mem.: Romeo Hist. Soc., Detroit Hist. Soc. (adv. coun. 2006—), Mich. Archival Assn., Detroit Inst. Arts Founders Soc., Alliance Francaise Detroit, Soc. Archtl. Historians (pres. The Saarinen (Mich.) chpt. 1989—93, 1998—), The Players, Wawentonong Club, Acanthus Club, Witenagemote Club, The Scarab Club (pres. 1990—92), Algonquin Club Detroit and Windsor, Prismatic Club, Masons, Scottish Rite. Avocations: historic preservation, ceramics, photography, genealogy, travel. Home: 1479 Seminole Ave Detroit MI 48214-2708 Office: Detroit Masonic Temple Libr and Mus 500 Temple Ave Detroit MI 48201-2659 Office Phone: 313-331-4930. Personal E-mail: brunk@spamcop.net.

BRUNK, WILLIAM EDWARD, astronomer; b. Cleve., Nov. 24, 1928; s. Edgar Rea and Mabel Mowbray (Pearson) B.; 1 dau., Anna Kathryn. BS, Case Inst. Tech., 1952, MS, 1954, PhD, 1963. Aero. research scientist Lewis Flight Propulsion Lab., NACA, Cleve., 1954-58; aerospace engr. Lewis Research Center, NASA, Cleve., 1958-64; staff scientist for planetary astronomy NASA Hdqrs., Washington, 1964-65, program chief planetary astronomy, 1965-77, discipline scientist planetary astronomy, 1977-82, chief planetary sci. br., 1982-85; mgr. solar system sci. Univ. Space Rsch. Assn., Washington, 1985-94; ret., 1994. Recipient Exceptional Service medal NASA, 1985. Fellow AAAS; mem. Am. Astron. Soc. (Harold Mazursky Meritorious Svc. award 1995), Internat. Astron. Union; Mem. Sigma Xi. Home: 4802 51st St W Apt 710 Bradenton FL 34210-5107 Home Phone: 941-794-6142. E-mail: webrunk@earthlink.net.

BRUNKHORST, ROBERT JOHN, computer programmer, analyst; b. Waverly, Iowa, Dec. 5, 1965; s. John Blaine and Edna C. (Atkins) B.; m. Kris Nielsen, Sept. 12, 1992; 1 child, Karalynn Kristine. BS in Computer Sci., Loras Coll., 1989. Computer programmer Century Cos. Am., Waverly, 1990—, computer analyst. Press intern Sen. Charles Grassley, Washington, fall 1986. State rep. State of Iowa, 1992—; organizer Solid Waste Adv. Com., Waverly, 1990—; active Boy Scouts Am., N.E. Iowa, 1982—. Mem. Jaycees, Farm Bur. Home: 413 10th St NE Waverly IA 50677-2739

BRUNNER, GEORGE MATTHEW, management consultant, former business executive; b. Newark, Jan. 17, 1925; s. Mathias J. and Mary E. (Fuith) B.; m. Ruth E. Owens, Nov. 16, 1953. AB in Chemistry, Columbia U., 1949, MChemE, 1950. Devel. engr. J.T. Baker Chem. Co., Phillipsburg, N.J., 1950-53; plant mgr. Internat. Minerals & Chem. Corp., Niagara Falls, N.Y. and Houston, 1953-62; mfg. engring. mgr. Gen. Foods Corp., Hoboken, N.J., Houston and Lafayette, Ind., 1962-71; v.p. mfg. W.R. Grace & Co., St. Simons Islands, Ga., 1971-73; pres., chief exec. officer S.A. Schonbrunn & Co., Inc., Palisades Park, N.J., 1973-82; v.p. ops. Am. Maize Products Co., Stamford, Conn., 1982-84; mgmt. cons., 1984—. Served with AUS, 1943-45. Decorated Purple Heart. Mem. Nat. Coffee Assn. (dir.), Pres.'s Assn., Am. Chem. Soc., Am. Inst. Chem. Engrs., Electrochem. Soc., 5th Armored Div. Assn. (pres. 1980-81). Patentee in field. Home and Office: 1221 Clays Trl Oldsmar FL 34677-4866

BRUNNER, JAMES EDWIN, lawyer; b. Kalamazoo, June 11, 1952; m. Rosemary C. Brunner; children: Matthew, Jacob, Seth. BS magna cum laude in Engring., U. Mich., 1974, JD cum laude, 1977. Assoc. Consumers Energy Co., Jackson, Mich., 1977-93, asst. gen. counsel litig., 1993, v.p., gen. counsel, 2004—06; sr. v.p., gen. counsel CMS Energy and Consumers Energy Co., 2006—. Mem. Summit Twp. Zoning Bd. Appeals, United Way Investment Cabinet, Jackson, Mich. Mem.: ABA, Jackson County Bar Assn. Office: CMS Energy One Energy Plz Jackson MI 49201-2276 Office Phone: 517-788-1237.*

BRUNNER, JENNIFER LEE, state official, lawyer; b. Springfield, Ohio, Feb. 5, 1957; d. Samuel Lawrence and Barbara Lee (Swan) Junk; m. Rick Louis Brunner, May 27, 1978; children: J. Katherine, Laura J., Johnathon P. BA cum laude in Sociology, Miami U., Oxford, Ohio, 1978; JD, Capital U., Columbus, Ohio, 1983. Bar: Ohio 1983, US Dist. Ct. (so. and no. dists. Ohio) 1983, US Ct. Appeals (6th cir.) 1983. Com. sec., legis. aide Ohio State Senate, Columbus, 1979-81; legis. counsel, dep. dir. Staff of Sec. State Sherrod Brown, Columbus, Ohio, 1983-87; assoc. Walter, Haverfield, Buescher and Chockley, Columbus, 1987-89; of counsel J. Richard Lumpe, 1989; prin. The Brunner Firm Co., L.P.A., Columbus; judge Ct. Common Pleas Franklin County, 2000—05; sec. state State of Ohio, Columbus, 2007—. Legal, past bd. dirs. Downtown Playschool, Columbus, 1985-87. Contbr. articles to profl. jours.; pub., editor: Polit. Action Quar., 1990—91. Active statewide campaign re-election Sherrod Brown Sec. State, Columbus, 1985; mem. Federated Dem. Women of Ohio, 1985; treas. Westerville City Schs. Levy campaign; treas. Judge Jon Marshall campaign; mem. Ohio Student Loan Commn.; mem. Franklin County Bd. Elections, 1997; bd. mem. Mental Health Assn. Franklin County A.R. McMicken scholar Miami U., 1977; recipient Extra Mile award Nat. Alliance for the Mentally Ill, 2002. Mem. ABA, Ohio Bar Assn., Columbus Bar Assn., Columbus Area Women's Polit. Caucus, Bus. and Profl. Women's Club (Young Career Woman of Yr. 1985), YWCA, Univ. Club, Order of Curia, Omicron Delta Kappa. Avocations: interior design, art, music. Office: Office Sec State Borden Bldg 180 E Broad St Columbus OH 43215*

BRUNNER, KATHLEEN MARIE, humanities educator; b. Torrance, Calif., Nov. 5, 1953; d. Earl Allen and Patricia Nellie Brunner. MA in Comparative Lit., U. Wash., Seattle, 1990—92, PhD in Comparative Lit., 1990—97, MA in Romance Langs. & Lit., 1993—94. Reader U. Wash., Seattle, 1991—94, tchg. asst., 1994—96; lectr. Alliance Francaise de Seattle, 1999—2004; instr. Highline C.C., Des Moines, Wash., 2001—02. Bd. dirs., past pres., past v.p., past sec. Alliance Francaise, 1998—2004; bd. dirs., sec. French-American C. of C. Pacific-Northwest, Seattle, 1999—; bd. dirs., v.p., admin. Nat. French Contest Washington, Alaska, B.C. and Alberta chpt. Am. Assn. Tchrs. French, 1999—; adv. bd. dept. French studies U. Wash., Seattle, 2003—. Contbr. articles to profl. jours. Recipient Vignernon d'honneur du Beaujolais, Union Interprofessionel des vins du Beaujolais, 2002; Study Grant, French Govt., 2000. Mem.: MLA, Wash. Assn. Lang. Tchng., Soc. Prof. Français and Francophone Am., Groupe D'Etudes Sartriennes. Avocations: swimming, travel, photography. Business E-Mail: brunnerk@lanepowell.com.

BRUNNER, KIM M., insurance company executive, lawyer; b. 1949; BA, Augustana Coll.; JD, Univ. Ariz. Chief counsel Ill. Ins. Dept.; atty. Nationwide Ins. Co.; with State Farm Ins. Cos., Bloomington, Ill., 1987—, assoc. gen. counsel, 1991-93, v.p.-counsel, 1993-97, sr. v.p., then exec. v.p., sec., gen. counsel, 1997—. Co-chmn. Civil Justice Reform Group; mem. bd. overseers RAND Inst. for Civil Justice. Office: State Farm Ins Cos 1 State Farm Plz Bloomington IL 61710-0001 Office Phone: 309-766-2311.*

BRUNNER, LILLIAN SHOLTIS, nurse, writer; b. Freeland, Pa. d. Andrew J. and Anna (Tomasko) Sholtis; m. Mathias J. Brunner, Sept. 8, 1951; children: Janet Brunner Cramer, Carol Ann Brunner Burns, Douglas Mathias. RN, diploma, U. Pa., 1940, BS, 1945, LittD (hon.), 1985; MS in Nursing, Case-Western Res. U., 1947; ScD (hon.), Cedar Crest Coll., 1978. RN, Pa. Head nurse U. Pa. Hosp., Phila., 1940-42, operating room supr., 1942-44, head, fundamentals of nursing dept., 1944-46; asst. prof. surgical nursing Yale U. Sch. Nursing, New Haven, Conn., 1947-51; surgical supr. Yale-New Haven Hosp., 1947-51; Lillian Sholtis Brunner chair med.-surg. nursing U. Pa., 2001. Rsch. project dir. Sch. Nursing Bryn Mawr (Pa.) Hosp., 1973-77; co-founder History of Nursing Mus., Pa. Hosp., Phila., 1974; mem. bd. overseers Sch. Nursing U. Pa., 1982-88; bd. overseers emeritus, 1988—; chmn. nursing adv. Presbyn.-U. Pa. Med. Ctr., Phila., 1970-88, 90-93, trustee, 1976-88, 90-95, vice chmn. bd. trustees, 1985-88; mem. com. profl. advisory Vis. Nurse Assn., Lancaster, Pa., 1996-99; sec. Glen Coun., Willow Valley Manor North, 1997-2000. Author: Manual of Operating Room Technology, 1966, (with others) Lippincott Manual of Nursing Practice, 1974, 4th edit., 1986, Textbook of Medical and Surgical Nursing, 1964, 6th edit., 1988; mem. editl. bd. Jour. Nursing and Health Care, Nursing 1978-1999, Nursing Photobook Series, 1978-90. Bd. dirs. Presbyn. Found. for Phila., 1995-99. Recipient Disting. Alumnus award Frances Payne Bolton Sch. Nursing, Case Western Res. U., 1980, Alumni award for merit Soc. Alumni Assns., U. Pa., and Am. Dream Achievement award Class of '45, U. Pa., 1995, Mentor award, Millersville U. Sch. Nursing, 2004. Fellow: Am. Acad. Nursing (Living Legend award 2002); mem.: Nurses Alumni Assn. U. Pa. Hosp., Philanthropic Ednl. Orgn., Nat. League for Nursing (judge nat. writing contest 1982—84, Disting. Svc. award 1979), ANA, Acad. U. Pa., Ben Franklin Soc., Internat. Old Lacers Soc., Nat. League Am. Pen Women (sec. Phila. chpt. 1972—76, nat. sec. 1984—88), Pi Lambda Theta, Pi Gamma Mu, Sigma Theta Tau. Home and Office: Apt J-411 645 Willow Valley Sq Lancaster PA 17602-4871 Office Phone: 717-464-6247.

BRUNNER, ROBERT E., engineering executive; BS in Fin., U. Ill., grad. student in Econs.; MBA, Baldwin-Wallace Coll., Berea, Ohio. With Ill. Tool Works (ITW), 1980—, various sales and mktg. positions, v.p./gen. mgr. Shakeproof Automotive divsn., pres. North Am. Automotive Fasteners, 2002—05, pres. Global Automotive Fasteners divsn., 2005—06, exec. v.p., 2006—. Office: Ill Tool Works 3600 W Lake Ave Glenview IL 60026-1215 Office Phone: 847-724-7500. Office Fax: 847-657-4572.*

BRUNNER, THOMAS WILLIAM, lawyer; b. NYC, Sept. 9, 1945; s. Robert G. and Louise (Koblitz) B.; m. Rochelle Leifer, Jan. 19, 1967; children: Robert, Emily, David. AB cum laude, Columbia U., 1966; JD, Yale U., 1970. Bar: Conn. 1970, D.C. 1973, U.S. Ct. Appeals (D.C. cir.) 1973, U.S. Dist. Ct. D.C. 1976, U.S. Supreme Ct. 1978, U.S. Ct. Appeals (1st, 2nd, 3rd, 4th, 5th, 6th, 7th, 8th, 9th and D.C. cirs.) 1988. Asst. to chief New Haven Dept. Police Svc., 1969-71; gen. counsel, sec., treas. Ins. Crime Prevention Inst., Westport, Conn., 1971-72; assoc. Wald, Harkrader & Ross, Washington, 1973-76, ptnr., 1976-85, Piper & Marbury, Washington, 1985-87, Wiley, Rein & Fielding, Washington, 1988—. Counsel Ins. Environ. Litigation Assn., 1986—; gen. counsel Ins. Crime Prevention Inst., Westport, 1982-91, Nat. Health Care Anti-fraud Assn., Washington, 1986-94. Author (with others) Mergers in New Antitrust Era 1985, contbr. articles to profl. journs. Bd. dirs. Temple Sinai Assisted Housing, Inc., 1992—; v.p. Homeless Children Tutorial Project, Inc., 1994-96, pres., 1996—, bd. dirs., 1994—. Recipient America's Leading Bus. Lawyers., Chambers USA, Internat. Who's Who of Business Lawyers for Ins., Leading Lawyers in Am., Lawdragon 3000, Best Lawyers in Am., Corp. Counsel. Mem. Columbia Coll. Alumni Assn. (regional v.p. 1995—), mem. Ctr. Pub. Resources (CPR) Disting. Panel Ins. Neutrals., co-chair, bd. of dir. Wash. Lawyers' Com. Civil Rights & Urban Affairs, mem. Mealey Publs. (ins. Adv. coun.)2003-. Office: Wiley Rein & Fielding 1776 K St NW Washington DC 20006-2304 Office Phone: 202-719-7225. Office Fax: 202-719-7049. Business E-Mail: tbrunner@wrf.com.

BRUNNGRABER, ERIC HENRY, banker; b. Madison, Wis., Feb. 12, 1957; s. Eric G. and Lois M. (Ihde) B.; m. Ann M. Roberson, May 30, 1987. BSBA in Fin., U. Mo., 1979; MBA in Fin., St. Louis U., 1982; diploma, U. Del., 1991. Asst. to chmn. Cass Bank & Trust Co., St. Louis, 1979-82, mgr. spl. projects, 1982-84, asst. v.p. comml. lending, 1986-88, v.p., treas., 1989-92, exec. v.p., 1993—; mgmt. cons. Cass Bus. Cons., St. Louis, 1984-86; v.p., sec. & CFO Cass Comml. Corp., Bridgeton, Mo. Mem. Robert Morris Assocs. Office: Cass Comml Corp 13001 Hollenberg Dr Bridgeton MO 63044

BRUNO, ANTOINETTE, food service executive; married; 2 children. MBA, Harvard Bus. Sch.; post-grad. degree, London Sch. Econ. Founder, mgr. retail store chain; securities negotiator Salomon Brothers; CEO, editor-in-chief StarChefs, 1999—. Organizer, moderator, celebrity chef panels Wine & Cuisine Soc. Harvard Bus. Sch. Featured in Bus. Week, Venture Wire, Nation's Restaurant News. Office: StarChefs 9 East 19th St Fl 9 New York NY 10003 Office Phone: 212-966-3775. Office Fax: 212-477-6644.*

BRUNO, AUDREI ANN, nurse educator, administrator; b. Pitts., Oct. 31, 1946; d. Vincent Joseph and Julia Elizabeth (Karaffa) Mataya; m. Edward Orlando Bruno, Apr. 30, 1966; children: Brent Edward, Bradley Edward. AA, Community Coll. Alleghany County, 1976; BSN, Pa. State U., 1984; MSN, U. Pitts., 1988. Cert. nurse adminstr. Psychiat. nursing supr. Western Psychiat. Clinic and Inst., Pitts., 1976-81; staff charge nurse Magee Women's Hosp., Pitts., 1981-82; charge team leader Central Med. Pavillion, Pitts., 1982-84; clin. specialist Vis. Nurse Assn. of Allleghany County, Pitts., 1984-92. Rschr. U. Pitts.; speakers bur. C.C. Allegheny County; project developer WPIC Adolescent Module, 1980-81; CEO Psycho-Ednl. Cons., 1996; coord. grant Putting Cmty. Health into AD Curriculum, 1993-96; bd. dirs. Theos Internat.; mem. Nurses' Health Study II, Harvard Sch. Pub. Health, 1989-99. Chmn. North Huntington (Pa.) Suicide Awareness and Prevention Com., 1986-88; fieldworker Project Star, Pitts., 1986-88; mem. Pa. Task Force on Elder Abuse, Nurses Interest in Care of Elderly; mem. adv. com. Nat. Project DART; bd. dirs. Am. Found. Suicide Prevention. Mem. Nursing Quality Assurance (cons.), Sigma Theta Tau. Home: 707 Duncan Ave Apt 401 Pittsburgh PA 15237-5025

BRUNO, CATHY EILEEN, management consultant, former state official, social sciences educator; b. Binghamton, NY; d. Martin Frank and Beverly Carolyn (Hamlin) Piza; m. Frank L. Delaney (div.); m. Paul R. Bruno, May 5, 1990. BA, SUNY, Binghamton; MSW, Syracuse U. Psychiat. social worker Broome Devel. Ctr., Binghamton, 1973-74, 76, congl. legis. aide, 1975; asst. dir. Bur. Program and Fiscal audits N.Y. State Office Mental Retardation and Devel. Disabilities, Albany, 1976-80; statewide coord. Intermediate Care Facilities for Developmentally Disabled, 1980; cert. coord. Western County Svc. Group, 1980-83. Upstate unit dir. Bur. Cert. Control, 1983-85; dir. ICF/DD Survey and Rev., 1985-89; area dir. Bur. Program Cert., 1989-95; dir. Bur. Transitional Svcs., 1995-97, mgmt. cons., 1997—. Adj. instr. SUNY Sch. Social Welfare, Albany, 1982-83; adj. faculty C.C. of Southern Nev., Las Vegas, 1998. Vol. U. Nev. Coop. Ext. Master Gardener program, 1997—; bd. dirs. Worldwide AIDS Movement, 2000—01. Mem. Am. Mgmt. Assn. Home and Office: 293 Canyon Spirit Dr Henderson NV 89012-3472

BRUNO, GRACE ANGELIA, accountant, retired educator; b. St. Louis, Oct. 11, 1935; d. John E. and Rose (Goodwin) B. BA, Notre Dame Coll., 1966; MEd, So. Ill. U., 1972; MAS, Johns Hopkins U., 1983; PhD, Walden U., 1985. CPA, Mo., Md., N.J. Tchr. Sch. Sisters of Notre Dame (SSND) of St. Louis, 1962-80; pres. Bruno-Potter, Inc., Avon By The Sea, NJ, 1981—2007, Grace A. Bruno, CPA. Asst. treas., instr. acctg. Coll. of Notre Dame of Md., Balt., 1978-80, treas., 1979-80; asst. prof. acctg. Georgian Ct. Coll., Lakewood, N.J., 1985-91; fin. advisor James Harry Potter gold medal award ASME, N.Y.C., 1980—. Elected to Internat. Platform Assn., 1987. Mem. AICPA, N.J. Soc. CPAs, St. Louis Bus. Educators (treas. 1972-73), Johns Hopkins Univ. Faculty Club. Democrat. Roman Catholic. Home and Office: 419 3rd Ave Avon By The Sea NJ 07717-1244 Office Phone: 732-776-7334. E-mail: gbruno4u@optonline.net.

BRUNO, HAROLD ROBINSON, JR., retired journalist, writer; b. Chgo., Oct. 25, 1928; s. Harold R. and Tallulah H. (Kandel) B.; m. Margaret E. Christian, Nov. 12, 1959; children: Harold, Daniel. BS in Journalism, U. Ill., 1950. Reporter Advt. Age, Chgo., 1950; sports editor DeKalb (Ill.) Chronicle, 1950-51; reporter City News Bur., Chgo., 1953-54, Chgo. American, 1954-60, Newsweek mag., 1960-63, bur. chief Chgo., 1963-66, news editor NYC, 1966-71, chief polit. corr. Washington, 1971-78; polit. dir. ABC News, Washington, 1978-97, polit. analyst, 1997-98; ret., 1998; sr. polit. analyst Politics.com, 1999-2000. Adv. bd. Internat. Programs and Studies, pres.'s coun., U. Ill.; adv. bd. Washington Ctr. for Politics and Journalism; moderator Vice Presdl., 1992. Columnist Firehouse mag; Contbr. articles to various publs. Bd. dirs. Chevy Chase Fire Dept.; adv. bd. Presdl. Classroom for Young Ams.; mem. Port Chester (N.Y.) Vol. Fire Dept.; dir., chmn. Fallen Firefighters Found., Nat. Fire Acad. With U.S. Army, 1951-53. Recipient Lowell Thomas award Internat. Platform Assn., 1984, Pres. award Internat. Assn. Fire Chiefs, 1999; Fulbright scholar, 1956-57; named Fire Svc. Person of Yr. Cong. Fire Svc. Inst., 1995. Mem. Nat. Fire Protection Assn., Nat. Vol. Fire Coun., AFTRA, Chgo. Newspaper Reporters Assn., Friendship Fire Assn., U. Ill. Alumni Assn. (bd. dirs., Illini achievement award 1984), Bethesda-Chevy Chase Rescue Squad Alumni, Soc. Profl. Journalists, Chgo. Press Vets. Assn. (Press Vet. of Yr. award 1999), Internat. Assn. Fire Fighters (hon.), Tau Delta Phi. Jewish. Home: 3414 Cummings Ln Chevy Chase MD 20815-3238

BRUNO, IRENE EVELYN, mathematician, educator; b. Pitts., Pa., Mar. 6, 1962; d. Joe Steven and Ann Laurene (Lally) Hitt; m. Mark J. Bruno; children: Joseph Michael, Anna Michelle, Maria Elizabeth. BS in Math., U. Pitts., 1984; MEd in Math., The Pa. State U., U. Pk., Pa., 1991; PhD in Orgnl. Mgmt., Capella U., Mpls., 2003. Secondary cert. in math. and computer sci. Pa., 1985, Va., 2002. Tchr. State Coll. Area Sch. Dist., Pa., 1985—91; prof., assoc. dean, chmn. dept. Strayer U., Manassas, Va., 1995—2002; asst. prof. George Mason U., Fairfax, Va., 2002—. Trainer, lead software devel. team Am. Online, Dulles, Va., 1996—98. Recipient Prof. of Yr. award, Strayer U., 1997. Mem.: Assn. Computing Machinery, Spl. Interest Group Info. Tech. Edn. Office: George Mason University 10900 University Boulevard MS4F5 Manassas VA 20169 Home Phone: 703-754-8612; Office Phone: 703-993-8541. Office Fax: 703-995-8450. Business E-Mail: ibruno@gmu.edu.

BRUNO, JOSEPH L., state legislator; BS, Skidmore Coll. Mem. N.Y. State Senate, Albany, 1976—, chmn. senate elections com., 1989-93, chmn. senate ins. com., 1985-89, vice chmn. legis. commn. on solid waste mgmt., 1985-89, chmn. senate com. on consumer protection, 1979-84, pres., 1995—. State senate majority leader, 1995—; asst. majority leader for conf. ops., 1989-95; chmn. senate commerce, econ. devel. and small bus. com., 1993-95; chmn. legis. com on pub.-pvt. cooperation, 1989-95 Mem., chmn. Rensselaer County Rep. Com., 1974-77; past pres. N.Y. State Assn. Young Reps.; mem. Italian Cmty. Ctr., Troy, N.Y., Troy Boy's Club, Troy Music Hall Assn. Mem. N.Y. State Sheriffs Assn. (hon.), St. Mary's Acad. Alumni Assn. (past pres), N.Y. State Jaycees (past v.p.), Soc. ofthe Friends of St. Patrick (bd. dirs.), VFW (Brunswick Post 831), Elks. Office: NY State Senate State Capitol 909 Legislative Office Bldg Albany NY 12247

BRUNO, LOUIS VINCENT, principal; b. Allegheny County, Pa., Feb. 10, 1959; s. Thomas E. and Anna Marie (Lavra) B. BS in Elem. Edn., U. Pitts., 1981, MEd in Mentally/Physically Handicapped, 1982, Cert. Secondary Prin., 1990; EdD, Sch. Leadership, U. Pitts., 2004; Supt.'s Letter of Eligibility, U. Pitts., 2003. Cert. tchr. expectations and student achievement/gender/ethnic expectations and student achievement coord., learning potential assessment device instr., instrumental enrichment trainer; cert. supt. Tchr. Steel Valley Sch. Dist., Munhall, Pa., 1981-82; adult living program instr. United Cerebral Palsy Assn., Pitts., 1982; from learning disabilities tchr. to asst. prin. Wilkinsburg (Pa.) Sch. Dist., 1982—98, asst. prin. Wilkinsburg (Pa.) Mid. Sch., 1998—; prin. 8th Linton Mid. Sch., Pitts., 1999—. Recipient Supt.'s letter, U. Pitts., 2004. Home: 301 Mcgregor Dr Verona PA 15147-3433 Office Phone: 412-793-7000 201. Personal E-mail: loubruno@aol.com. Business E-Mail: lbruno@phsd.k12.pa.us.

BRUNO, PHILIPPE M., lawyer; b. 1955; JD in Civil Law, Univ. Grenoble Law Sch., 1977, LLM in European Integration, 1978, PhD in European and Internat. Law cum laude, 1989; LLM in Internat. and Comparative Law, Georgetown Univ., 1984. Bar: France 1980, Va. 1987, DC 1998. Assoc., litig. Criffo & Olivier, Grenoble, France, 1980—82; European cons. Busby, Rehm and Leonard PC, 1982—84, assoc., 1984—88, Dorsey & Whitney LLP, Washington, 1988—94, ptnr., internat. dept., 1995—2004; ptnr., global trade practice group Greenberg Traurig LLP, Washington, 2005—. Lectr., European and civil law Univ. Grenoble, France, 1980—82. Office: Greenberg Traurig LLP Ste 500 800 Connecticut Ave NW Washington DC 20006 Office Phone: 202-331-3193. Office Fax: 212-331-3101.

BRUNS, DAVID EUGENE, medical educator, researcher; b. St. Louis, Dec. 12, 1941; s. Eugene H. and Ellen E. (Johnson) B.; m. M. Elizabeth Hirst; children: Elizabeth, David. BSChemE, Washington U., 1963, AB, 1965; MD, St. Louis U., 1973. Diplomate Nat. Bd. Med. Examiners, lic. Va. State Bd. Medicine. Instr. pathology Sch. Medicine Washington U., St. Louis, 1973—77, vis. prof. pathology, 1985—86; asst. prof. U. Va., Charlottesville, 1977—81, assoc. prof. dept. pathology, 1981—90, prof. pathology Sch. Medicine, 1990—, assoc. dir. clin. chem. and toxicology, 1977—2003, assoc. dir. molecular diagnostics, 1986—, dir. clin. chemistry, 2003—. Lectr. in field. Author, editor, with Lo and Wittwer: Molecular Testing in Laboratory Medicine, 2002; editor: Clin. Chemistry, 1990—;

co-editor: Yearbook of Pathology and Laboratory Medicine, 1995—97; contbr. articles to profl. jours.; author, editor (with Burtis and Ashwood): Tietz Textbook of Clinical Chemistry and Molecular Diagnostics, 4th edit., 2005. Bd. dirs. Little League Baseball, Charlottesville. Recipient St. Louis-San Francisco RR Scholarship, Washington U., 1959—63; Rsch. Grant award, NIH, Am. Cancer Soc., Am. Dairy Coun. Mem.: Am. Assn. Clin. Chemistry (Outstanding Contbns. to Rsch. award 1987, Outstanding Contbns. to Clin. Chemistry award 1998, Norman Kubasik award 2001, Presdl. Citation 2001, Bernard Gerulat award 2001, Miriam Reiner award 2003, Speaker Award 2003, Presdl. Citation 2005), Acad. Clin. Lab. Physicians and Scientists (mem. exec. coun. 1990—93, pres. 2003—04), Assn. Clin. Scientists (pres. 1985—86, Sunderman award 1987). Achievements include patents for immunochemical assays for human amylase isoenzymes and related monoclonal antibodies, 1993; identification of toxicity of polyethylene glycol. Avocations: travel, reading, theater. Business E-Mail: dbruns@virginia.edu.

BRUNS, NICOLAUS, JR., retired agricultural products executive, lawyer, educator; b. NYC, Sept. 27, 1926; s. Nicolaus and Emily Marie (Hawkins) B.; m. Joan-Carol Littleton, Aug. 29, 1959; children: Nicolaus III, Gregory. BS, U. Miami, Fla., 1947; JD, Georgetown U., 1949, LL.M., 1952. Bar: D.C. 1950, Ill. 1965, U.S. Supreme Ct. 1965, N.Y. 1980. Spl. asst. U.S. Navy Dept., Washington, 1950-57; sr. trial atty. U.S. Dept. Justice, Washington, 1957-65; sr. atty. Internat. Minerals and Chem. Corp., Skokie, Ill., 1965-70, asst. gen. counsel, 1970-74, gen. counsel ops., 1974-79, v.p., sec., assoc. gen. counsel Northbrook, Ill., 1979-87; sr. v.p., sec., gen. counsel IMC Fertilizer Group Inc., Northbrook, Ill., 1987-90; antitrust policy coun. U.S. C. of C., Washington, 1981-90. Adj. prof. Loyola U., Chgo., 1980-81, Lake Forest Grad. Sch. Mgmt., Ill., 1981—2003; cert. arbitrator Am. Arbitration Assn., Nat. Assn. Securities Dealers, 1990—. Adminstrv. asst. to v.p. Boy Scouts Am., N.E. Ill. area, 1967, 80; pres. Fund for Perceptually Handicapped, Skokie, Ill., 1976, Concerned Help in Learning Devel., Highland Park, Ill., 1974-75. With U.S. Army, 1945-46. Mem. ABA (antitrust and securities com.), Chgo. Bar Assn., Fed. Bar Assn., Am. Soc. Corp. Secs. (bd. dirs. 1985-87, pres. Midwest region 1984), K.C. (past grand knight Washington coun.), Mich. Shore Club (Wilmette, Ill.), Harbour Ridge Club (Stuart, Fla.). Republican. Roman Catholic. Home: 2500 Indigo Ln Apt 348 Glenview IL 60026

BRUNS, WILLIAM JOHN, JR., business administration educator; b. Pasadena, Calif., July 13, 1935; s. William John and Carol Jane (Stalder) B.; m. Barbara Jean Dodge, Apr. 12, 1957 (div. 1980); children: Robert William, John Richard, David James, Michael Alan.; m. Sharon Merle McKinnon, July 16, 1982; 1 child, Anastasia Catherine. BA, U. Redlands, Calif., 1957, DBA (hon.), 1976; MBA, Harvard U., 1959; PhD, U. Calif., Berkeley, 1963. Asst. prof. econs., then asst. prof. econs. and indsl. adminstrn. Yale U., 1962-66; asso. prof., then prof. accounting U. Wash., 1966-72; prof. bus. adminstrn. Harvard U., 1972-93, Henry R. Byers prof. bus. adminstrn., 1993—2001, emeritus, 2001—; vis. prof. bus. adminstrn. Northeastern U., 2001—. Cons. to industry. Author: Accounting for Decisions: A Business Game, 1966, Accounting and Its Behavioral Implications, 1969, Introduction to Accounting: Economic Measurement for Decisions, 1971, A Primer on Replacement Cost Accounting, 1976, Cases in Management Accounting, 1981, 85, Accounting and Management: Field Study Perspectives, 1987, Performance Measurement, Evaluation, and Incentives, 1992, The Information Mosaic, 1992, Accounting for Managers: Text and Cases, 1994, 3d edit., 2005; book rev. editor: Accounting Rev, 1967-69; mem. editorial bd., 1969-72, 76-78; advisory editor: Addison-Wesley Pub. Co; mem. editorial bd.: Accounting, Orgns., and Soc, 1975-79, Jour. of Managerial Issues, 1993—. Mem. Quinnipiac council Boy Scouts Am., 1964-66; Chief Seattle council, 1966-72, Algonquin council, 1972-81. Danforth grad. fellow, 1957-62; Danforth assoc., 1967-89. Mem. Am. Acctg. Assn., Inst. Mgmt. Accts. Home: 46 Garden Rd Wellesley MA 02481-3015 Office: Harvard Bus Sch Soldiers Fld Boston MA 02163-1317 E-mail: wbruns@hbs.edu.

BRUNSON, CURTIS, communications systems company executive; BS in Computer Sci., NY Inst. Tech.; MS in Computer Sci., Poly. Inst., Bklyn. With Sperry Systems Mgmt. Divsn., 1972; various mgmt. positions Unisys Govt. Svcs.; divsn. pres. Unisys Communication Systems, Salt Lake City; sr. v.p. corp. strategy and devel. L-3 Comm. Holdings, Inc. Office: L-3 Comm Holdings Inc 600 Third Ave New York NY 10016 Office Phone: 212-697-1111. Office Fax: 212-805-5477.*

BRUNSON, JOHN SOLES, lawyer, investor; b. Houston, Jan. 8, 1934; s. Nathan Bryant and Jonnie E. (McMillian) B.; m. Joan Erwin, Dec. 26, 1953; children: W. Mark, Dana Ruth BBA, Baylor U., 1956, LLB, 1958, JD, 1965. Bar: Tex., 1958, U.S. Supreme Ct., 1961. Assoc. Dillingham, Schleider & Lewis, Houston, 1958-64; ptnr. Brunson & Brill, Houston, 1964-70, Baker, Heard & Brunson, Houston, 1970—72, Brunson & Erwin, Houston, 1972-84. Chmn. Clavis Group, Inc., 1984- Active Harris County Dem. Exec. Com., Tex., 1959-65, Tex. Dem. Exec. Com., 1963-74; exec. bd. Bapt. Gen. Conv. Tex., 1988-94; trustee First Bapt. Acad., 1996-2002, chmn., 2000-2002; trustee Houston Christian HS, 1997—, Macedonian Call Found., 1991—; exec. bd. So. Bapt. Tex. Conv., 2003— Mem. ABA, State Bar Tex Office: 7555 Katy Fwy Apt 70 Houston TX 77024-2119 Business E-Mail: onejsb@swbell.net.

BRUNSVOLD, BRIAN GARRETT, lawyer, educator; b. Mason City, Iowa, Apr. 10, 1938; s. P.O. and Arlene J. (Garrett) B.; m. Mary Sue Willey, Nov. 28, 1963; 1 child, Laura Ann. BSChemE, Iowa State U., 1960; JD, George Washington U., 1967. Bar: Va. 1967, D.C. 1967. Law clk. U.S. Ct. Claims, Washington, 1966-67; atty. firm Finnegan, Henderson, Farabow, Garrett & Dunner, Washington, 1967—. Professorial lectr. in law George Washington U., Washington, 1975-96. Co-author: Drafting Patent License Agreements, 1984, 91, 98, 2004. 1st lt. C.E., U.S. Army, 1961-63, Korea. Mem. Licensing Execs. Soc. (trustee 1987-89, counsel 2000-03, Cert. of Merit 1988). Avocations: tennis, hunting, fishing. Office: Finnegan Henderson Farabow Garrett & Dunner 901 New York Ave NW Washington DC 20001 Office Phone: 202-408-4000. Business E-Mail: brunsvob@finnegan.com.

BRUNT, MANLY YATES, JR., psychiatrist; b. Winston-Salem, N.C., Nov. 7, 1926; s. Manly Yates and Jessie Corina (Evans) B.; M.D., Wake Forest U., 1948; m. Jacklyn Beatrice Bray, Dec. 2, 1961; children— Diane Strachan, William Bray, Douglas Evans, Kenneth Sherman. Intern, Grad. Hosp. U. Pa., 1949-50; exec. med. officer Inst. of Pa. Hosp., Phila., 1952-62, mem. sr. attending staff, 1968—, prin. investigator Behavior Research Lab., 1957-61; mem. faculty U. Pa., 1953-68; dir. emeritus dept. psychiatry Bryn Mawr (Pa.) Hosp., past pres. staff and chmn. exec. com. Pres. Community Nursing Bur. Met. Phila., 1961-64; bd. dirs. Main Line Health Care Group, Inc. Served with M.C., AUS, 1950-52. Diplomate Am. Bd. Psychiatry and Neurology. Mem. AMA, Am. Psychiat. Assn., Am. Psychoanalytic Assn., Phila. Coll. Physicians and Surgeons, Wake Forest U. Med. Alumni Assn. (pres. 1985), Alpha Omega Alpha. Republican. Presbyterian. Clubs: Merion Cricket, Phila. Skating and Humane Soc., Little Egg Harbor Yacht. Mailing: 1084 E Lancaster Ave Bryn Mawr PA 19010

BRUNTON, DANIEL WILLIAM, mechanical engineer; b. Ft. Wayne, Ind., Sept. 25, 1956; s. Paul Edward and Margaret Alice (Rice) B.; m. Carol Marie Pryor, Feb. 19, 1994; children: Edward Daniel, Ann Marie. BS, UCLA, 1978, MS in Engring., 1980, M of Engring., 1986. Mem. tech. staff Hughes Missiles Group, Canoga Park, Calif., 1978-89, dept. mgr., 1989-93; mech. engr. dept. mgr. Litton Itek, Lexington, Mass., 1993-94; sr. engr. Raytheon Missile Sys., Tucson, 1994-97, engring. fellow, 1997—. Mem. Soc. Photonic Instrumentation Engrs., Tau Beta Pi. Achievements include 3 patents on optical design, optical material testing, and mechanisms. Office: Raytheon Missile Sys PO Box 11337 Tucson AZ 85734-1337

BRUS, LOUIS EUGENE, physical chemist; b. Cleve., Aug. 10, 1943; s. Victor John and Mary Alicia (Megede) B.; m. Marilyn Drennan, Apr. 10, 1970; children: Michael, Christina, Elizabeth. BS in Chem. Physics, Rice U., Houston, 1965; PhD in Chem. Physics, Columbia U., 1969. Disting. mem. tech. staff AT&T Bell Labs., Murray Hill, NJ, 1973—96; assoc. dir., Thomas A. Edison prof. Columbia U., 1996—. Chmn. bd. trustees Gordon Rsch. Conferences, 2001. Mem. editorial bd. Jour. Phys. Chemistry, Chem. Phys. Letters; contbr. articles to profl. jours. Lt. Naval Rsch. Lab. USN, 1969—73. Hutchinson lectureship, Rochester U., 1991, Welsh lectureship, 1988; Kistiakowsky lectureship, Harvard U., 1993, Irving Langmuir prize, Am. Physical Soc., 2001, Chemicals Materials prize, Am. Chemical Soc. & Dupont, 2005. Fellow Am. Phys. Soc. (Irving Langmuir Prize in Chem. physics 2001); mem. NAS, Am. Chem. Soc. (Chemistry of Materials Prize 2005). Achievements include research in quantum effects in semiconductor crystallites, resonance raman investigations of transient chemical species, carbon nanotubes and organic electronics, local electromagnetic field enhancement, transition metal oxide nanocrystals and electric force microscopy. Office: Columbia Radiation Lab 1001 Schapiro Ctr Columbia Univ 530 W 120th St Mail Code 8903 New York NY 10027 also: Columbia U Dept Chemistry Havermeyer Hall MC 3125 3000 Broadway New York NY 10027 Business E-Mail: brus@chem.columbia.edu.

BRUSA, AMILCAR, boxing trainer; b. Santa Fe, Argentina, Oct. 28, 1922; Trainer S.Am. and US, 1950—, La Brea Boxing Acad., LA; head trainer, tech. advisor Golden Boy Promotions, LA, 2003. Named Trainer of Yr., World Boxing Assn., 1989, Latin Trainer of Yr., 1995; named to World Boxing Assn. Hall of Fame, Internat. Boxing Hall of Fame, 2007. Achievements include training 14 world champions. Office: c/o Golden Boy Promotions 626 Wilshire Blvd Ste 350 Los Angeles CA 90017

BRUSCA, RICHARD CHARLES, biologist, researcher, educator, science administrator; b. LA, Jan. 25, 1945; s. Finny John and Ellenora C. (McDonald) B.; m. Caren Irene Spencer, 1964 (div. 1971); children: Alec Matthew, Carlene Anne; m. Anna Mary Mackey, 1980 (div. 1987); m. Wendy Moore, 1998. BS, Calif. Poly. State U., 1967; MS, Calif. State U., LA, 1969; PhD, U. Ariz., 1975. Curator, rschr. Aquatic Insects Lab., Calif. State U., LA, 1969—70; resident dir. U. Ariz. and U. Sonora (Mex.) Coop. Marine Lab., Sonora, 1970—71; prof. biology U. So. Calif., LA, 1975—86; head Invertebrate Zoology sect. Los Angeles County Mus. Natural Hist., 1984—87; Joshua L. Baily curator, chmn. dept. invertebrate zoology San Diego Natural History Mus., 1987—93; prof., dir. grad. program in marine biology U. Charleston, SC, 1993—98, assoc. dir. Grice Marine Lab. SC, 1993—98; rsch. prof. Columbia U., 1998—2000; rsch. prof. dept. ecology and evolutionary biology U. Ariz., 1998—; exec. dir. Ariz.-Sonora Desert Mus., Tucson, 2001—. Dir. acad. programs Catalina Marine Sci. Ctr., U. So. Calif., 1978—82; field rschr. No., Ctrl. and So. Ams., Galapagos Island, Polynesia, Australia, New Zealand, Antarctica, Saharan and Sub-Saharan Africa, Europe, Caribbean; bd. dirs. Orgn. for Tropical Studies, Slocum-Lunz Found., Intercultural Ctr. for the Study of Deserts and Oceans, Sonoran Sea Aquarium, Tucson, Discover Life in Am.; mem. panels NAS/NSF; chairperson adv. com. Smithsonian Instn.; adv. com. Systematics Agenda 2000; chairperson adv. com., inland waters crustacea specialist Internat. Union for Conservation of Nature Species Survival Commn.; mem. adv. bd. All Species Found., 2001; mem. adv. bd. Sch. Natural Resources U. Ariz., 2003—; mem. sci. and tech. adv. team Sonoran Desert Conservation Plan, Pima County, Ariz. Author: Common Intertidal Invertebrates of the Gulf of California, 1980; co-author: A Naturalist's Seashore Guide, 1978, Invertebrates, 1990, 2d edit., 2003, English, Spanish, Portuguese, Italian transls., Isopod Systematics and Evolution, 2001, Seashore Guide to Northern Gulf of California, 2004, Conserving Migratory Pollinators and Nectar Corridors in Western North America, 2004, Distributional Checklist of the Macrofauna of the Gulf of California, 2005; contbr. over 150 articles to sci. jours. Recipient U.S. Antarctic Svc. medal, 1965, numerous rsch. awards; grantee NSF, Nat. Geog. Soc., Charles Lindberg Found, David & Lucile Packard Found., NOAA, Nat. Park Svc., Dept. Def., Am. Philos. Assn., others. Fellow: AAAS, Linnean Soc. London; mem.: Soc. for Systematic Biology, Assn. Sea Cortez Rschrs. (hon.; life), Crustacean Soc. (pres.), Sigma Xi. Avocations: Mexican and Mesoamerican indigenous art and culture, Latin American politics. Office: Ariz-Sonora Desert Mus 2021 N Kinney Rd Tucson AZ 85743 Home Phone: 520-615-3069; Office Phone: 520-883-3007. Business E-Mail: rbrusca@desertmuseum.org.

BRUSCA, ROBERT ANDREW, economist; b. Detroit, Mar. 14, 1950; s. Andrew Adam and Doris Rita (Lozon) B.; m. Kathleen Hays. BA, U. Mich., 1973; MA, Mich. State U., 1976, PhD, 1977. Chief economist Fed. Res. Bank NY, 1977-82; economist, fedwatcher Irving Trust Co., NYC, 1982-85; chief economist, exec. v.p. Nikko Securities Co Internat., Inc., NYC, 1986-99; chief economist Ecobest Cons., NYC, Fact and Opinion Econs. Adj. prof. Columbia U., 1978—; appeared frequently on TV, radio as fin. specialist, 1983—. Author (column) Money Current, Fin. World mag., 1987-88, Econ. Currents, 1988—; columnist for CNBC.com.; contbr. articles in field. Mem. Money Marketeers NYU (bd. dirs. 1966—, pres.). Avocations: golf, basketball, reading, travel. Home: 357 West End Ave Apt One New York NY 10024-6815 Office Phone: 212-875-8637.

BRUSCH, JOHN LYNCH, physician, educator, hospital administrator; b. Boston, Nov. 3, 1943; s. Charles and Margaret Agnes (Lynch) Brusch; m. Patricia Gahan, May 12, 1973; children: Amy Claire, Meaghan, Patrick. BS, Tufts U., 1965, MD, 1969. Diplomate Am. Bd. Internal Medicine, Am. Bd. Infectious Disease, Am. Bd. Geriatrics. Intern New Eng. Med. Ctr., Boston, 1969-70, resident in medicine, 1970-71, resident in infectious disease, 1971-74; asst. chief medicine Brighton Pub. Health Svc. Hosp., Boston, 1974-76; pvt. practice physician Cambridge, Mass., 1976—; chief medicine Youville Hosp., Cambridge, 1991—2007, dir. cmty. medicine, 1995—2007, sr. cons., 2007—; clin. assoc. medicine Mass. Gen. Hosp., Boston, 1996—; med. dir. transitional care unit, chief medicine Somerville Hosp., 1999—, med. dir., 2001—. Assoc. chief medicine Cambridge Health Alliance, 1999—, dir. hosp. bd., 2003—; asst. prof. medicine Harvard Med. Sch., 2001—; bd. dirs. North Cambridge Coop Bank. Co-author, editor: Infective Endocarditis: Management in the Era of Intravascular Devices, 2007, assoc. editor: Infectious Disease Practice, 1984—, mng. editor: Emedicine, 2001—; contbr. articles to profl. jours. Bd. dirs. Coun. on Aging, Belmont, 2000—. With USPHS, 1974—76. Fellow: ACP; mem.: Equestrian Order of Holy Sepulchre, Am. Soc. Microbiology, Longwood Cricket Club. Home: 52 Radcliffe Rd Belmont MA 02478-3340 Office: Cambridge Hosp 1493 Cambridge St Cambridge MA 02139-1099 Home Phone: 617-489-1424; Office Phone: 617-661-1800. Personal E-mail: jbruschmd@aol.com.

BRUSCHI, TEDY, professional football player; b. San Francisco, Ca, June 9, 1973; s. Anthony Jr. and Juanita; m. Heidi; 3 children. BA communication, U. of Az. Linebacker New England Patriots, 1996—. Named NFL Comeback Player of the Yr., AP, 2005, Best Comeback, Espy award, 2006; named to NFL Pro Bowl Team, 2004. Achievements include being the only player in NFL history to return four consecutive interceptions for touchdowns. Office: c/o New England Patriots 1 Patriot Place Foxboro MA 02035

BRUSH, FLORENCE CLAPHAM, kinesiologist, exercise physiologist, physical education educator; b. Little Rock, May 16, 1928; d. Thomas Wilson and Clara Sumpter Clapham; children: Robert Charles, Elizabeth Wrenne. BS, BA, Tex. Women's U., 1950, MA, 1951; PhD, U. Md., 1966. Instr. U. Ark., Fayetteville, 1950—53; assoc. prof., aquatics dr. Northwestern State Coll., Natchitoches, La., 1953—54; asst. prof. U. Md., 1954—59, Temple U., 1963—64; rsch. assoc. divsn. rsch. Lankenau Hosp., Phila., 1962, 1963; assoc. prof. Direct Execise Physiology Lab. Portland State U., Oreg., 1965—69; assoc. prof. SUNY Coll. Cortland, 1971—92, assoc. prof. emeritus. Vis. scholar dept. growth and devel. Inst. Child Health U. London, 1970—71; vis. scholar Emory U., 1976; tutor math. Editor: Jour. Phys. Edn., Oreg. Assn. Health Phys. Edn. Recreation, 1969—70; contbr. articles to profl. jours. Tchr. swimming YWCA; vol. ARC Aquatics and Blood Drives. Recipient several grants. Mem.: ACLU, Nat. Strength and Conditioning Assn. Am. Assn. Health Phys. Edn. Recreation and Dance, Internat. Soc. Electrophysiological Kinesiology, United U. Professions (alt. del. to NY State assembly, mem. State relay submcom.), Environ. Orgn., Am. Coll. Sports Medicine. Democrat. Presbyterian. Achievements include research in anthropometric, physiological, neurological and electromyographic correlates of motor performance. Avocations: piano, kayaking, birdwatching. Home: 773 Blue Creek Rd Cortland NY 13045 Personal E-mail: brushf@cortland.edu.

BRUSH, JULIANNA R., marine biologist; married. MS in Marine Sci. for Coral Pathology, U. SC, 2003. West Nile virus technician; marine mammal and sea turtle stranding coord. Md. Dept. Natural Resources; fellow Office Protected Resources Nat. Marine Fisheries Svc.; with Nat. Ocean Svc. NOAA. Contbr. articles to profl. jours. Recipient W.P. Carey Field Rsch. award, Wings WorldQuest Women of Discovery Awards, 2006; grantee Sea Grant fellowship. Office: NOAA Nat Ocean Svc SSMC Bldg 4 1305 East-West Hwy Silver Spring MD 20910 E-mail: julianna.brush@noaa.gov.

BRUSH, STEPHEN GEORGE, historian, educator; b. Bangor, Maine; s. Edward Newcomb and Lillian Maynard (Hatfield) B.; m. Phyllis Egbert; children: Denise, Nicholas. AB in Physics, Harvard U., Cambridge, Mass., 1955; DPhil in Physics, Oxford U., Eng., 1958. Postdoctoral fellow Imperial Coll., London, 1958-59; physicist Lawrence Radiation Lab., Livermore, Calif., 1959-65; rsch. assoc. Harvard Project Physics, Cambridge, Mass., 1965-68; lectr. Harvard U., Cambridge, Mass., 1966-68; assoc. prof. U. Md., College Park, 1968-71, prof., 1971—, Disting. univ. prof. history of sci., 1995—2006, prof. emeritus, 2006—. Author: The Kind of Motion We Call Heat, 1976, Statistical Physics and the Atomic Theory of Matter, 1983, History of Modern Science, 1988, History of Modern Planetary Physics, 1996; co-author: Physics, The Human Adventure: From Copernicus to Einstein and Beyond, 2001; co-author: Introduction to Concepts and Theories in Physical Science, 1973, 2d rev. edit.; author, editor: Kinetic Theory, 1965, vol. II, 1966, Vol. III, 1972, The Kinetic Theory of Gases: An Anthology of Classic Papers with Historical Commentary, 2003; editor: Resources for the History of Physics, 1972; co-editor: History in the Teaching of Physics, 1972, Maxwell on Saturn's Rings, 1983, Maxwell on Molecules and Gases, 1986, Maxwell on Heat and Statistical Mechanics, 1995. Recipient History of Geology award Geol. Soc. Am., 2004; Rhodes scholar, Oxford U., 1955-58; NSF grantee, 1965—; Guggenheim fellow, 1999-2000. Fellow AAAS, Am. Phys. Soc. (councillor 1987-90); mem. Internat. Acad. History Sci., History Sci. Soc. (pres. 1990-91, Pfizer award 1977, Hazen Edn. prize 2001). Achievements include theoretical research calculation showing that a system of charged particles (plasma) will condense from gas to solid under conditions of high pressure and low temperature. Office: U Md Inst Phys Sci and Tech College Park MD 20742-0001 Office Phone: 301-405-4846.

BRUSHABER, GEORGE KARL, academic administrator, minister; b. Milw., Dec. 15, 1938; s. Ralph E. and Marie C. (Meister) B.; m. N. Darleen Dugar, Jan. 27, 1962; children: Deanna Lyn Dalberg, Donald Paul. BA, Wheaton Coll., 1959, MA, 1962; MDiv, Gordon-Conwell Theol. Sem., 1963; PhD, Boston U., 1967. Ordained to ministry Bapt. Gen. Conf., 1966. Prof. philosophy, chair dept. Gordon Coll., Wenham, Mass., 1963-72; dir. admissions and registration Gordon-Conwell Theol. Sem., 1970-72; v.p., acad. dean Westmont Coll., Santa Barbara, Calif., 1972-75; v.p., dean of coll. Bethel. Coll., St. Paul, 1975-82; pres. Bethel U., St. Paul and San Diego, 1982—. Staley Found. lectr. Anderson U., Sioux Falls Coll.; sec. for higher edn. Bapt. Gen. Conf., Arlington Heights, Ill., 1982—; cons., evaluator Minn. Humanities Commn., St. Paul. Editor Gordon Rev., 1965-70; pub., founding editor Christian Scholar's Rev., 1970-79; exec. editor Christianity Today, 1985-90, chmn. sr. editors, 1990-2000; contbr. articles to religious jours. Bd. dirs. Youth Leadership, Mpls., 1982—, Fairview Elders' Enterprises Found., 1989—, Scripture Press Ministries Found., 1994—; adv. bd. Mpls./St. Paul Salvation Army, 1992--; chair bd. Scripture Press Ministries, 1994—; adv. coun. Evang. Environ. Network, 1994—; mem. Commn. on Minorities in Higher Edn. Am. Coun. Edn., 1995-99. Mem. Nat. Assn. Evangs. (trustee 1982—), Minn. Pvt. Coll. Coun. (bd. dirs. 1982—), Minn. Consortium Theol. Sems. (bd. dirs. 1982—), Cook Comm. Internat. (bd. dirs. 1998—), Coun. Ind. Colls. (bd. dirs. 1984-89), Am. Philos. Assn., Evang. Theol. Soc., Am. Assn. Higher Edn., Swedish Coun. Am. (bd. dirs. 2000—), Am. Assn. of Pres. of Indenp. Coll. and Univ. (bd. dirs.), Soc. Christian Philosophers, Christian Environ. Assn. (bd. dirs.), Christian Coll. Consortium (bd. dirs.), Fellowship Evang. Sem. Pres., Cook Comm. Ministries (vice chmn. bd. dirs. 1999—), North Oaks Country Club. Home and Office: Bethel Univ 3900 Bethel Dr Saint Paul MN 55112-6902

BRUSIC, KEN, editor-in-chief; m. Pam Brusic; 1 child, Mike. BA in English, U. Denver; MA, U. Colo., 1972. With Boulder Daily Camera; journalism fellow U. Mich.; city editor Wichita Eagle and Wichita Beacon, 1978—79; assoc. prof. U. Mont., Missoula; spl. projects editor The Patriot Ledger, Quincy, Mass.; mng. editor The Sun of San Bernardino, Balt. News Am.; projects editor Orange County Register, Santa Ana, Calif., 1989—90, asst. mng. editor, 1990—92, mng. editor, 1992—97, exec. editor, 1997—2002, editor, 2002—; sr. v.p. Freedom Comm., Inc. Head of content Freedom Orange County Info., 2002; mem. adv. bd. Asian Am. Journalists Assn., LA. Avocations: motorcycling, reading, running. Office: Orange County Register PO Box 11626 625 N Grand Ave Santa Ana CA 92701 Office Phone: 714-796-2226. Office Fax: 714-565-3681. E-mail: kbrusic@ocregister.com.*

BRUSKEWITZ, FABIAN W., bishop; b. Milw., Sept. 6, 1935; STD, Gregorian Univ., Rome, 1969. Ordained priest Roman Catholic Ch. 1960. Bishop Diocese of Lincoln, Nebr., 1992—. Office: Chancery Office PO Box 80328 Lincoln NE 68501-0328

BRUST, DAVID, physicist; b. Chgo., Aug. 24, 1935; s. Clifford and Ruth (Klapman) B. BS, Calif. Inst. Tech., 1957; MS, U. Chgo., 1958, PhD, 1964. Rsch. assoc. Purdue U., Lafayette, Ind., 1963—64, Northwestern U., Evanston, Ill., 1964—65, asst. prof. physics, 1965—68; theoretical rsch. physicist U. Calif. Lawrence Radiation Lab., Livermore, 1968—73. Cons. Bell Telephone Lab., Murray Hill, N.J., 1966. Campaign coord. No. Calif. Scientists and Engrs. for McGovern, 1972. NSF travel grantee, 1964; NSF rsch. grantee, 1966-68. Mem. Am. Phys. Soc., Am. Assn. Coll. Profs., Internat. Solar Energy Soc., Astron. Soc. of Pacific, Nature Conservancy, Calif. Acad. Sci., Commonwealth Club. of Calif., World Affairs Coun. No. Calif., Commonwealth Club Anza Borrego Desert, Natural History Assn., Planetary Soc., Sierra Club, Sigma Xi. Office: PO Box 13130 Oakland CA 94661-0130

BRUST, FREDERICK WILLIAM, JR., structural and mechanical engineer; b. Pitts., Apr. 3, 1955; s. Frederick William and Theresa Joan (Halligan) B.; m. Milica Matejic, June 4, 1983; children: Nenad, Zachary Matthew, Alexander Frederick. BSCE, U. Dayton, 1977; MS in Structural

Engring., Purdue U., 1978; PhD in Computational Mechanics, Ga. Tech. U., 1984. Rschr. Battelle Meml. Inst., Columbus, Ohio, 1978-81; rsch. assoc. Ga. Tech. U., Atlanta, 1981-84; prin. rsch. scientist Battelle Meml. Inst., Columbus, 1985-89, sr. rsch. scientist, 1990-95, rsch. leader, 1996—, sr. rsch. leader computational engring. and sci., 2004—. Student advisor U. Mich., Ann Arbor, 1989-92, U. Rome, Italy, 1992, 94; sabbatical yr. at Ga. Tech. U., 1995. Co-editor books on fatigue and fracture; contbr. chpts. to books, numerous articles to profl. jours.; mem. editl. bd. Computer Modeling in Engring. and Scis. Coach youth basketball North Columbus Intramural League, 1985—, bd. dirs., dir. travel teams; coach youth basketball Immaculate Conception Grade Sch., 1998—; coach youth soccer COSA, Westerville, Ohio, 1994-96; spkr. Columbus Schs. Youth Sci. Mentors Program, Columbus, 1992, 94, Immaculate Conception Grade Sch., 1998—. Recipient Team Achievement award for tech. transfer NASA, 1997; grantee Dept. Energy, 1989—. Mem.: Internat. Soc. for Computational Engring. and Scis., Am. Soc. Naval Engrs., Am. Soc. Composites, Am. Soc. Testing and Materials, Am. Welding Soc., Am. Soc. Mech. Engrs. (materials and fabrication com., applied mechanics divsn.). Roman Catholic. Achievements include development of fracture methodologies; directing development of two commercial software products. Office: Battelle Meml Inst 505 King Ave Columbus OH 43201-2681 Home: 2434 Wimbledon Rd Upper Arlington OH 43220 Office Phone: 614-424-5034. Business E-Mail: brust@battelle.org.

BRUST, JOHN CALVIN MORRISON, neurologist, educator; b. Syracuse, NY, Aug. 20, 1936; s. John C. M. and Constance (Cook) Brust; m. Mary Duncan, Oct. 23, 1965; children: Mary Duncan, Frederick Eliot Noyes, James Charles Morrison. AB, Harvard U., 1958; MD, Columbia U., 1962. Diplomate Am. Bd. Psychiatry and Neurology. Intern Presbyn. Hosp., NYC, 1962-63, resident in neurology, 1966-69, attending neurologist, 1969—, Harlem Hosp. Ctr., NYC, 1969-75, dir. dept. neurology, 1975—; prof. clin. neurology Columbia U., NYC, 1975—. Author: Neurological Aspects of Substance Science, 1999, 2d edit., 2004, The Practice of Neural Science, 2000; contbr. articles to profl. jours. Lt. USNR, 1962—65. Fellow: Am. Acad. Neurology; mem.: N.Y. Practitioners Soc., Century Assn., Am. Clin. and Climatological Assn., Am. Neurol. Assn., Alpha Omega Alpha. Office: Harlem Hosp Ctr Dept Neurology 506 Lenox Ave Dept New York NY 10037-1802 Business E-Mail: jcb2@columbia.edu.

BRUSTAD, ORIN DANIEL, lawyer; b. Chgo., Nov. 11, 1941; s. Marvin D. and Sylvia Evelyn (Peterson) B.; m. Ilona M. Fox, July 16, 1966; children: Caroline E., Katherine L., Mark D. BA in History, Yale U., 1963, MA, 1964; JD, Harvard U., 1968. Bar: Mich. 1968, U.S. Dist. Ct. (so. dist.) Mich. 1968. Assoc. Miller, Canfield, Paddock and Stone, Detroit, 1968-74, sr. ptnr., 1975—, chmn. employee benefits practice group, 1989-96, dep. chmn. tax dept., 1989-93. Bd. dirs. Electrocon Internat., Inc., Ann Arbor, Mich. Mem. editl. adv. bd. Benefits Law Jour.; contbr. articles to profl. jours. Fellow Am. Coun. Employee Benefits Counsel (charter); mem. ABA, Mich. Bar Assn., Detroit Bar Assn., Mich. Employee Benefits Conf. Avocations: sailing, skiing, reading, piano. Home: 1422 Macgregor Ln Ann Arbor MI 48105-2836 Office: Miller Canfield Paddock & Stone 150 W Jefferson Ave Fl 25th Detroit MI 48226-4432 Home Phone: 734-994-4406; Office Phone: 313-496-7605. E-mail: odbrusta@aol.com, brustad@millercanfield.com.

BRUSTEIN, ABRAM ISAAC, sales executive, insurance company executive; b. Bridgeport, Conn., Jan. 14, 1946; s. Louis and Flora (Forman) B.; m. Barbara Bederick Rudman, July 3, 1969; children: Asher Jeremey, Darrah Bethany, Garrett Michael. BA, U. Conn., 1968; MS in Mgmt., Am. Coll., 1985. CLU, CLF, chartered fin. cons. Agt. NY Life Ins. Co., Stamford, Conn., 1968-70, sales mgr., 1970-75, gen. mgr. Amherst, NY, 1975-79, Bala Cynwyd, Pa., 1979-87; gen. agt. Penn Mut. Life Ins. Co., Phila., 1987-94; exec. dir. Prudential Ins. Co. Am., Lutherville, Md., 1994-95; v.p. Phoenix Home Life Ins. Co., Hartford, Conn., 1995-98; mng. dir. Mut. NY, Towson, Md., 1998—; mng. dir. nat. recruiting MONY Group, NYC, 1999—2006; regional sales dir. Woodbury Fin. Svcs., 2006—, regional v.p., 2007. Mem. rev. panel Am. Coll., Bryn Mawr, Pa., 1984—, focus group mem. Masters Degree com., 1986; lectr. local univs., 1985—. With USAR, 1969—75. Named to, NAIFA-G.P. Hall of Fame, 2002. Mem. Gen. Agts. and Mgrs. Assn. (pres. 1986-87, Nat. Mgmt. award 1978-91), Am. Soc. CLUs and Chartered Fin. Cons., Phila. Assn. Life Underwriters (pres. 1988-89), Penn Mut. Agy. Assn. (pres. 1990-91), Germantown Cricket Club (Phila.), Chestnut Ridge Country Club (Lutherville, Md.). Jewish. Avocations: tennis, golf, aerobics, skiing, bicycling. Home: 313 W Timonium Rd Lutherville Timonium MD 21093-2930 Office Phone: 410-916-5744. Business E-Mail: abram.brustein@woodburyfinancial.com.

BRUSTEIN, LAWRENCE, finance company executive; b. Liberty, NY, Oct. 11, 1936; s. Leo and Rae (Smoller) B.; m. Ellen Gloria Sheppard, June 20, 1965; children: Jacqueline, Michael. BS, U. Buffalo, 1958. CPA, N.Y. With Irving Handel & Co., CPAs, NYC, 1959-62, Robert Simons & Co., CPAs, NYC, 1962-64, E&L Distbrs., Inc., 1964-66, Barney's, NYC, 1966-68; controller Holly Stores div. K-Mart, North Bergen, NJ, 1968-70; v.p., treas. Marcade, Jersey City, 1970-86; exec. v.p. Modells, NYC, 1987—. Editl. adv. bd. Retail Tech mag. Exec. v.p. Reform Temple of East Brunswick, 1977—. Mem. AICPA, N.Y. State Soc. CPAs, Internat. Mass Retail Assn. (chmn. fin.). Home: 15 Rolling Meadows Blvd S Ocean NJ 07712 Office: Modells 498 7th Ave Fl 20 New York NY 10018-6704 Office Phone: 212-822-1011. Personal E-mail: brustein@aol.com.

BRUSTEIN, ROBERT SANFORD, literature and language professor, theater director, writer; b. NYC, Apr. 21, 1927; s. Max and Blanche (Haft) B.; m. Norma Ofstrock, Mar. 25, 1962 (dec.); children: Daniel Anton; m. Doreen Beinart, Dec. 20, 1996; stepchildren: Jean Beinart, Peter Beinart. BA, Amherst Coll., 1948, LittD; postgrad., Yale Drama Sch., 1948-49, U. Nottingham, Eng., 1953-55; MA, Columbia U., 1950, PhD, 1957; LittD, Lawrence U.; LLD, Beloit Coll., 1975; ArtsD, Bard Coll., 1981; LHD, Emory U., 1983; Arts D, Marlboro Coll., 1995, Middlebury Coll., 1996, Hebrew Coll., 1997. Instr. English Cornell U., 1955-56; instr. drama Vassar Coll., 1956-57; faculty Columbia, 1957-66, prof. English and comparative lit., 1965-66; prof. English Yale U., New Haven; dean Yale U. (Sch. Drama); founder, artistic dir. Yale Repertory Theatre, 1966-79; dir. Loeb Drama Centre; also founder, artistic dir. Am. Repertory Theatre Co.; prof. English Harvard U., 1979—2002, sr. rsch. fellow, 2002—. Co-founder, actor Studio 7, 1948; actor Group 20 Theater on Green, 1949-57; contbr. Commentary Mag., 1953-57; drama critic Harper's Mag., 1958-59, New Republic, 1959-67, 78—, contbg. editor, 1959-79; guest theatre critic London Observer, 1972-73; contbr. to NY Times, 1972—; directed and adapted plays including: Ghosts, 1982, Six Characters in Search of an Author, 1984, The Changeling, 1985, Tonight We Improvise, 1986, Right You Are, 1987, The Father, 1990, When We Dead Awaken, 1992, The Seagull, 1994, The Cherry Orchard, 1995, The Wild Duck, 1996, The Master Builder, 1999, Enrico IV, 2001, Lysistrata, 2002; panel mem. Nat. Endowment for Arts, 1969-72, 81-84; created, adapted Shlemiel the First, 1994; disting. scholar in residence Suffolk U., 2007-. Author: The Theatre of Revolt: Studies in the Modern Drama, 1964, Seasons of Discontent: Dramatic Opinions 1959-1965, 1965, The Third Theatre, 1969, Revolution as Theatre: Notes on the New Radical Style, 1971, The Culture Watch, 1975, Critical Moments, 1980, Making Scenes, 1981, Who Needs Theatre, 1987, Reimagining American Theatre, 1991, Dumbocracy in America, 1994, Cultural Calisthenics, 1998, The Siege of the Arts, 2001, Letters to a Young Actor, 2005, Millennial Stages, 2006, (plays) Demons, 1995, Nobody Dies on Friday, 1996, Poker Face, 1999, The Face Lift, 1999, Chekhov on Ice, 2000, Three Farces and A Funeral, 2000, Divestiture, 2001, Spring Forward, Fall Back, 2004, The English Channel, 2006; editor: The Plays and Prose of Strindberg, 1964; contbr. articles to profl. jours. Trustee Sarah Lawrence Coll., 1973-77. Served with U.S. Mcht. Marine, 1945-47. Recipient George Jean Nathan award dramatic criticism, 1962, 87, George Polk Meml. award outstanding criticism, 1965, Eliot Norton award, 1984, award in criticism Jersey City Jour., 1967, award Outstanding Achievement in Am. Theater, New Eng. Theater Coun., 1985, Tiffany award for excellence in theatre Internat. Soc. Performing Arts Adminstrs., 1987, Thomas De Gaetano award UITT, 1991, Disting. Svc. to Arts award Am. Acad. Arts and Letters, 1995, ATHE award for lifetime achievement in the theatre, 2000, named to Theater Hall of Fame, 2002; Fulbright fellow, 1953-55; Guggenheim fellow, 1961-62; Ford Found. fellow, 1964-65, Nat. Arts Journalism Program sr. fellow Columbia U., 2003, Nat. Arts Program in Criticism U. SC, 2005-06. Mem. Am. Acad. Arts and Scis., Am. Acad. Arts and Letters. Avocations: tennis, kayaking, travel. Office: Harvard U Loeb Drama Center Cambridge MA 02138 Office Phone: 617-429-1021. E-mail: brustein@fas.harvard.edu.

BRUSTEIN, WILLIAM IRVING, sociology educator; b. Fairfield, Conn., July 13, 1947; s. Louis I. and Flora Eva Brustein; m. Yvonne Christine Ramey, Feb. 14, 1981; children: Arielle Lauren, Maximilian Samuel. BA, U. Conn., 1969; MA, John Hopkins U., 1971; PhD, U. Wash., 1981. Asst. prof., then assoc. prof. sociology U. Utah, Salt Lake City, 1981—88; assoc. prof. sociology U. Minn., Mpls., 1989—94, prof., Morse alumni disting. tchg. prof. sociology, 1994—2000, adj. prof. polit. sci., 1994—2000, dir. Ctr. for European studies, 1992—95, chair dept. sociology, 1995—98, disting. McKnight univ. prof., 2000—01; prof. sociology, history and polit. sci. U. Pitts., 2001—, UCIS prof. internat. studies, 2001—, dir. Ctr. Internat. Studies, 2001—06; prof. sociology, history and polit. sci. U. Ill., Champaign, 2007—, alumni prof. internat. studies, 2007—, assoc. provost internat. affairs, 2007—. Panelist sociology program NSF, Washington, 1998-2000; vis. scholar London Sch. Econs. and Polit. Sci., 1999. Author: The Social Origins of Political Regionalism: France, 1849 to 1981, 1988, The Logic of Evil: The Social Origins of the Nazi Party, 1925-1933, 1996 (James S. Coleman Disting. Contbn. to Rational-Choice scholarship 1997), Roots of Hate: Anti-Semitism in Europe before the Holocaust, 2003; editor: Nazism as a Social Phenomenon, 1998; cons. editor Am. Jour. Sociology, 1998-2000. Bd. dirs. Jewish Family Svc., St. Paul, 1991-95, Hillel, Mpls., 1998-2000; exec. bd. Student Project for Amity Among Nations, Mpls., 1998-2000. Grantee NSF, Washington, 1999. Mem. Am. Sociol. Assn. (coun. mem. polit. sociology and comparative hist. sociology 1987-90, 88-91, chair rational choice sect. 2004-05, chair PhD granting depts. 1996-98), Am. Polit. Sci. Assn., Assn. Internat. Edn. Adminstrs. (exec. com. 2003—, pres.-elect 2006-2007, pres.2007—), Nat. Assn. State Univs. Land-Grant Colls. (task force internat. edn. 2003—, chair acad. affairs com., exec. com. 2005—), Phi Beta Kappa, Assn. for Studies in Internat. Edn. (bd. dirs., 2004—). Democrat. Avocations: coaching boys soccer, reading, international travel, skiing. Home: 5 Old Timber Trail Pittsburgh PA 15238 Office: Univ Ill Dept Internat Affairs 303 Internat Studies Bldg 910 S Fifth St Champaign IL 61820 Office Phone: 217-333-6104. Business E-Mail: brustein@uiuc.edu.

BRUSTER, ANTHONY K., lawyer; b. Knoxville, Tenn., Oct. 17, 1976; m. Amy Bruster; 2 children. BBA, Baylor U., 1999, JD summa cum laude, 2002. Bar: Tex. 2002, Ark. 2003, La. 2003, N.Mex. 2004, US Dist. Ct. (ea., we. and no. dist. Tex.), US Dist. Ct. (we. dist. Ark.). Assoc. Nix, Patterson & Roach, L.L.P., Texarkana, Tex. Contbr. articles to profl. publs.; exec. editor: Baylor Law Rev., 2001. Named a Rising Star, Tex. Super Lawyers mag., 2006. Mem.: N.Mex. Trial Lawyers Assn., Ea. Dist. Tex. Bar Assn., Texarkana Bar Assn., Ark. Trial Lawyers Assn., Assn. Trial Lawyers of Am., La. Bar Assn., Ark. Bar Assn. Office: Nix Patterson & Roach LLP 205 Linda Dr PO Box 679 Daingerfield TX 75638 Office Phone: 903-645-7333. E-mail: akbruster@nixlawfirm.com.*

BRUTON, JOHN MACAULAY, trade association executive, consultant; b. Mexico City, Nov. 13, 1937; s. Edmund Macaulay and Byrd (Grant) B.; m. Frances McMillan Marks, Nov. 25, 1960; children: Alexander, Macaulay, Brinley. BA, Duke U., 1959. Pres., gen. mgr. Grant Advt. Panama, Panama City, 1970-72, Mexico City, 1972; comm. dir. Am. C. of C. Mex., Mexico City, 1972-74, gen. mgr., 1974-77, exec. v.p., CEO, 1977—2002, councillor, 2002—, v.p., mem. bd. dirs., 2005—; sr. mng. dir. Manatt Jones Global Strategies, Mexico City, 2003—. V.p. exec. mgmt. Assn. Am. C. of C. in Latin Am., L.A., Washington, 1985-88, v.p. membership svc., 1988—. Bd. dirs. Am. Benevolent Soc., Mex., 1964-68, Am. Soc. Mex., 1975-78, 80-84; adv. bd. Jr. League Mexico City, 1978—; bd. trustees Fomento Educacional A.C., 1988—, treas., 1993—, pres. 2005-. Decorated Order of Aztec Eagle Gov. Mex., 2005. Mem. Univ. Mex. (bd. dirs. 1979-83, pres. 1981-82). Episcopalian. Home: Ameyalcalli Ocotepec 80 10200 Mexico City Mexico Office: Manatt Jones Global Stratagies Edificio Omega Campos Eliseos 345-5 11560 Mexico City Mexico Business E-Mail: jbruton@manattjones.com.

BRUZELIUS, NILS JOHAN AXEL, journalist; b. Stockholm, Feb. 27, 1947; (parents Am. citizens); s. Axel Sture and Constance (Brickett) B.; m. Lynne A. Weil, Aug. 10, 2002. BA in History, Amherst Coll., 1968. Reporter, bur. chief Middlesex News, Framingham, Mass., 1968-70; reporter, state house corr. AP, Boston, 1970-73; med./mental health writer Boston Globe, 1973-79, investigative reporter, 1979-81, asst. met. editor, 1981-86, health and sci. editor, 1986-99, fgn. editor, 1999—2001; sr. editor sci. desk Nat. Pub. Radio, Washington, 2002—03; dep. nat. editor sci. Washington Post, 2003—. Mem. Boston Globe investigative team receiving Disting. Investigative Reporting award Investigative Reporters and Editors Assn., 1979, Disting. Journalism citation Scripps-Howard Found., 1979, Pulitzer prize for spl. local reporting, 1980; Knight Sci. Journalism fellow MIT, 1992-93. Mem.: DC Sci. Writers Assn., Investigative Reporters and Editors, Nat. Assn. Sci. Writers, Capitol Hill Restoration Soc., Ocean Cruising Club. Avocations: sailing, tennis, bicycling, guitar, photography. Home: 133 D Street SE Washington DC 20003 Office Phone: 202-334-7204. Business E-Mail: bruzeliusn@washpost.com.

BRYAN, A(LONZO) J(AY), retired service club official; b. Washington, NJ, Sept. 17, 1917; s. Alonzo J. and Anna Belle (Babcock) B.; m. Elizabeth Elfreida Koehler, June 25, 1941 (div. 1961); children: Donna Elizabeth, Alonzo Jay, Nadine; m. Janet Dorothy Onstad, Mar. 15, 1962 (div. 1977); children: Brenda Joyce, Marlowe Francis, Marilyn Janet. Student. Retail florist, Washington, NJ, 1941-64; with WalMart Corp., 1989—. Fund drive chmn. ARC, 1952; bd. dirs. Washington YMCA, 1945-55, N.J. Taxpayers Assn., 1947-52; mem. Washington Bd. Edn., 1948-55. Mem. Washington Grange, Sons and Daus. of Liberty, Soc. Am. Florists, Nat. Fedn. Ind. Businessmen, Florists Telegraph Delivery Assn., C. of C., Masons, Tall Cedars of Lebanon Club, Jr. Order United Am. Mechanics, Kiwanis (pres. Washington N.J. 1952, lt. gov. internat. 1953-54, gov. N.J. dist. 1955, sec. 1957-64, sec. S.E. area Chgo. 1965-74, editor The Jersey Kiwanian 1958-64, internat. staff 1964-85, sec.-treas. Rocky Mountain dist. 1989, pres. South Denver 1990-91, editor Rocky Mountain Kiwanian 1990-96), Breakfast Club (Chgo., pres. 1981-82). Methodist. Home: 8115 S Poplar Way B 203 Centennial CO 80112-3174

BRYAN, BARBARA DAY, retired librarian; b. Livermore Falls, Maine, May 20, 1927; d. Lorey Clifford and Olga Elvira (Bergquist) Day; m. Robert S. Bryan, June 24, 1950. BA in Psychology, U. Maine, 1948; MS in Library Sci., So. Conn. State U., 1964. Catalog dept. asst. Yale U. Library, New Haven, 1948-49; departmental library cataloger Harvard U., Cambridge, Mass., 1949-51; descriptive cataloger Yale U. Library, New Haven, 1951-52; cataloger Fairfield (Conn.) Pub. Library, 1952-54, reference librarian, 1954-57, asst. librarian, order librarian, 1957-65; asst. dir. libraries Fairfield U., 1965-74, university librarian, 1974-96, u. libr. emerita, 1996—. Mem. Conn. State Libr. Bd., Hartford, 1978—92, chair, 1987—92; bd. dirs. Bibliomation, Inc., Stratford, Conn., 1987—91. Pres. Friends Nyselius Libr., Fairfield U., 1998-2000, exec. bd., 2001-06; commr. Fairfield Hist. Dist. Commn., 2003-06. Named Conn. Libr. Assn. Libr. of Yr., 1988; recipient Disting. Alumnus award, So. Conn. State U. Sch. of Libr. Sci., 1979. Mem. ALA (life, Conn. chpt. councilor 1977-80), Assn. Coll. and Rsch. Librs. (constn. and by-laws com. 1986-90, mem. coll. libr. sect. stds. com. 1991-95), New Eng. Libr. Assn. (mem. com. 1981-85, coun. mem. 1975-77), Conn. Libr Assn. (legis. com. 1996—), Fairfield Hist. Soc. (libr. vol.), Conn. Audubon Soc., Oak Lawn Cemetery Assn. (bd. dirs. 1994—), Assn. Conn. Libr. Bds. (bd. dirs., chair legis. com. 1996—), Inst. Ret. Profl. (adv. bd. 1998-2001, 05-), Fairfield U. Retirees Assn. (pres. 2003-04), Phi Beta Kappa, Phi Kappa Phi. Democrat. Avocations: reading, walking. Home: 999 Merwins Ln Fairfield CT 06824-1919

BRYAN, BARRY RICHARD, lawyer; b. Orange, NJ, Sept. 5, 1930; s. Lloyd Thomas and Amy Rufe (Swank) B.; m. Margaret Susannah Elliot, July 24, 1953; children— Elliot Christopher, Peter George (dec.), Susannah Margaret, Sallie Catharine. BA, Yale U., 1952, JD cum laude, 1955; diploma in comparative legal studies, Cambridge U., Eng., 1956. Bar: N.Y. 1959. Legal advisor to gen. counsel Sec. of U.S. Air Force, Washington, 1956-58; assoc. Debevoise & Plimpton, NYC, 1958-62, ptnr., 1963-93, presiding ptnr., 1993-98, of counsel, 1999—2002. Served to 1st lt. USAF, 1956-58. Fulbright scholar Trinity Coll., Cambridge U., 1956. Mem. ABA, Assn. of Bar of City of N.Y., Union Internationale des Avocats, Country Club of New Canaan, Fishers Island Club, Order of Coif, Phi Beta Kappa. Episcopalian. Home: PO Box 197 Isabella Beach Rd Fishers Island NY 06390 Office: Debevoise & Plimpton 919 3rd Ave Fl 43 New York NY 10022

BRYAN, BILLIE MARIE (MRS. JAMES A. MACKEY), retired biologist; b. Norfolk, Va., Dec. 30, 1932; d. William B. and Marie (Fortescue) Bryan; m. James A. Mackey. BA in Biology, U. Richmond, 1954; MEd, Am. U., 1966. Bacteriologist Arlington County Health Dept., Arlington, Va., 1954-58; med. bacteriologist Walter Reed Army Inst. Rsch. Walter Reed Army Med. Ctr., Washington, 1959-62; tchr. Fairfax HS, Va., 1962-66; biologist NIH, Bethesda, 1966—2004; ret. Contbr. articles to profl. jours. Mem. AAAS, DAR, Internat. Soc. for Polit. Psychology.

BRYAN, BOB CHARLES, professional tennis player; b. Camarillo, Calif., Apr. 29, 1978; s. Wayne and Kathy. Attended, Stanford U., 1996—98. Profl. tennis player ATP, 1998—. Mem. Bryan Bros. Band. Mem. WECAAN, Andrea Jaeger's Silver Lining Found., Elton John's AIDS Found., Tennis For Africa. Named Doubles Team of Yr. (with brother Mike Bryan), 2006 ATP Awards, ATPTennis.com Fans' Favorite Doubles Team; named to ATP Player Coun., 2006. Mem.: Sigma Alpha Epsilon. Achievements include winning over 100 jr. doubles titles with brother Mike; winning 41 career doubles titles, ATP. Avocations: music, keyboards, basketball. Office: Bryan Brothers 1774 Ramona Dr Camarillo CA 93010*

BRYAN, CHARLES STONE, internist, educator; b. Columbia, SC, Jan. 15, 1942; s. Leon Stone and Mary Morrill (Leadbeater) Bryan; m. Donna Hennesee, Oct. 30, 1982; children: Eleanor Chandlee, Emily Singleton. Student, Harvard U., Cambridge, Mass., 1960-62; BA, Johns Hopkins U., Balt., 1964, MD, 1967. Diplomate Am. Bd. Internal Medicine, Am. Bd. Infectious Diseases. Intern in pathology Johns Hopkins Hosp., Balt., 1967-68; intern in medicine Vanderbilt U. Hosp., Nashville, 1968-69, resident, fellow, 1971-74; pvt. practice Columbia, SC, 1974-77; dir. infectious diseases U. SC Sch. Medicine, Columbia, 1977-93, Heyward Gibbes disting. prof. medicine, chmn. dept., 1992-2000; dir. Ctr. Bioethics and Med. Humanities, 2000—. Author: A Most Satisfactory Man, 1996, Osler: Inspirations from a Great Physician, 1997, Infectious Diseases in Primary Care, 2002; editor: Jour. S.C. Med. Assn., 1977—; contbr. articles to profl. jours. Chmn. Midlands Care Consortium, Columbia, 1993—2006. Surgeon USPHS, 1969—71. Master: ACP (Laureate award 1993, Nicholas E. Davies award 2007); fellow: Infectious Diseases Soc. Am., Royal Coll. Physicians (Edinburgh); mem.: Columbia Med. Soc. (pres. 1992), S.C. Infectious Diseases Soc. (pres. 1994), Am. Osler Soc. (sec.-treas. 2000—), Am. Assn. History Medicine (William Osler medal 1967), Am. Clin. and Climatological Assn., Waring Libr. Soc. (pres. 1988). Avocations: medical history, golf. Office: U SC Sch Medicine 2 Richland Medical Park Dr Columbia SC 29203-6864 Office Phone: 803-540-1000. Business E-Mail: cbryan@gw.mp.sc.edu.

BRYAN, GREYSON, lawyer; b. LA, 1949; BA with distinction and honors, Stanford U., 1971; JD cum laude, Harvard U., 1976. Bar: Calif. 1976, NY 1978, DC 1985, Japan (Gaikokuho-Jimu-Bengoshi, withdrew in 1990) 1987. Dir. tng. Harvard Law Sch. Internat. Tax Program, 1979—81, rsch. assoc., 1981—82; adj. prof. law, regulation internat. bus. UCLA Sch. Law, 1994—97; adj. prof. internat. bus. law UCLA Anderson Grad. Sch. Mgmt., 1995—98; established, partner-in-charge O'Melveny & Myers LLP, Tokyo, 1987—90, co-chair global practice group, 1990—94, ptnr. litig. Los Angeles, Calif., coordinates internat. practice, head litig. dept. internat. practice group. Cons., Office of Tax Analysis US Dept. Treasury; mem. litig. dept. of yr. American Lawyer; founding mem. Pacific Coun. on Internat. Policy. Articles editor Harvard Internat. Law Jour.; contbr. articles to profl. jours. Assoc. and acting dir. Volunteers in Asia, Inc., 1971—73; mem. bd. student advisors Harvard U.; chmn. Asia Soc. So. Calif. Ctr., 1992—2001; bd. visitors Stanford U. Inst. Internat. Studies, 1995—2004. Sheldon Traveling Fellow, 1976—77, sr. fellow, UCLA Sch. Pub. Policy and Social Rsch., 1998—99. Mem.: Am. Law Inst. (mem. tax advisory group, fed. income tax project 1982—84), DC Bar. Office: O'Melveny & Myers LLP 1999 Avenue of the Stars 7th Fl Los Angeles CA 90067-6035 Office Phone: 310-246-8444. Office Fax: 310-246-6779. Business E-Mail: gbryan@omm.com.

BRYAN, HENRY C(LARK), JR., retired lawyer; b. St. Louis, Dec. 8, 1930; s. Henry Clark and Faith (Young) B.; m. Sarah Ann McCarthy, July 28, 1956; children— Mark Pendleton, Thomas Clark, Sarah Christy Nussbaum. AB, Washington U., St. Louis, 1952, LL.B., 1956. Bar: Mo. 1956. Law clk. to fed. judge, 1956; assoc. McDonald & Wright, St. Louis, 1956-60; ptnr. McDonald, Bernard, Wright & Timm, St. Louis, 1961-64, McDonald, Wright & Bryan, St. Louis, 1964-81, Wright, Bryan & Walsh, St. Louis, 1981-84; pvt. practice law, 1984-96; ret., 1996. V.p., dir. Harbor Point Boat & Dock Co., St. Charles, Mo., 1966-80, Merrell Ins. Agy., 1966-80. Served to 1st lt. AUS, 1952-54 Mem. ABA, Mo. Bar Assn., St. Louis Bar Assn. (past chmn. probate and trust sect., marriage and div. law com.), Kappa Sigma, Phi Delta Phi Lodges: Elks. Republican. Episcopalian. Home: 41 Ladue Ter Saint Louis MO 63124-2047

BRYAN, J(AMES) P(ERRY), JR., energy executive; b. Houston, Jan. 17, 1940; s. James Perry Bryan Sr. and Gretchen (Smith) Josey; m. Mary Jon Lewis, Jan. 24, 1964; children: Alicia and John Bracken. BA, U. Tex., 1962, LLB, 1965; BFT, Am. Inst. Foreign Trade, 1966. V.p. Morgan Guaranty Trust Co., NYC, 1966-69; v.p. dir. investment banking Dominick & Dominick, NYC, Houston, 1969-74; pres., CEO The MortgageBanque, Inc., Houston, 1974-78; v.p, regional dir. corp. fin. dept. E.F. Hutton & Co., Inc., Houston, 1978-81; chmn., CEO Torch Energy Advisors, Inc., Houston, 1981—; Neuvo Energy Energy Assets Internat. Corp., Houston, 1987—95; chmn. & CEO Bellwether Exploration Co., Houston. Bd. dirs. Torch Energy Advisors, Inc., Bellwether Exploration Co., Neuvo Energy Co., Park Nat. Bank, Torchmark Corp., Republic Waste Inds. Founder, editor Internat. Law Jour.; contbr. reviews and articles on Tex. history to mags. and jours. Chmn. endowment fund, other offices Tex. State Hist. Assn.; chmn. fund raising com., past. chmn., pres. Tex. Hist. Found.; chmn. devel., adv. bd. Inst. Texan Cultures; trustee Nita Stewart Haley Meml. Libr.; past trustee, chmn. nominating com. Harris County Heritage Soc; mem. adv. bd. Bazoria County Hist. Mus.; founding chmn., past bd. dirs. South Main Ctr. Assn.; founder, bd. dirs. Collector's Inst.; bd. dirs. The Book Club of Tex.; chmn., dir. fund raising River Oaks Bapt. Sch., others. Mem. ABA, Tex. Bar Assn., Houston Bar Assn., Univ. Tex. Ex-Students Assn. (life), Philos. Soc. Tex., Houston Country Club, Tex. Breakfast Club (treas. Houston), Tejas Club, Argyle Club, Nat. golf Links Am., Phi Delta, Delta Phi Epsilon.

BRYAN, JOHN HENRY, food and consumer products company executive; b. West Point, Miss., 1936; BA in Econs. and Bus. Adminstrn., Rhodes Coll., Memphis, 1958. Joined Bryan Foods, 1960; with Sara Lee Corp. (formerly known as Consol. Food Corp.), Chgo., 1960—; from exec. v.p. to pres. Sara Lee Corp. (formerly known as Consol Food Corp.), Chgo., 1974, CEO, 1975—2000, chmn. bd., 1976—2000, also bd. dirs.; consultant Sara Lee Corp., Chgo., 2001—. Bd. dirs. GM Corp., 1993—, BP p.l.c., Goldman Sachs Group, Inc. Chmn. bus. adv. coun. Chgo. Urban League; bd. govs. Nat. Women's Econ. Alliance, Chgo.; trustee, vice chmn., exec. com. U. Chgo., Rush-Presbyn.-St. Luke's Med. Ctr.; trustee Com. Econ. Devel.; trustee, treas. Art Inst., Chgo.; chmn. Catalyst, Chgo. com. Chgo. Coun. on Fgn. Rels.; mem. trustee's coun. Nat. Gallery Art, Washington; mem. Pres.'s com. on the arts and humanities; bd. dirs. Bus. Com. for Arts. Decorated Legion of Honor France, Order of Orange Nassau The Netherlands, Order of Lincoln medallion; named Man of Yr., Harvard Bus. Sch. Club Chgo., Exec. Yr., Crain's Chgo. Bus., 1992; named to Jr. Achievement Chgo. Bus. Hall of Fame, 1992, Miss. Hall of Fame, 1992; recipient Nat. Humanitarian award, NCCJ, William H. Albers award, Food Mktg. Inst. Mem.: Bus. Roundtable, Bus. Coun., Grocery Mfrs. Assn. (sr.; past chmn. bd.). Office: Sara Lee Corp 3 1st Nat Plz 70 W Madison St Ste 4500 Chicago IL 60602-4260

BRYAN, JOHN RODNEY, management consultant; b. Berkeley, Calif., Dec. 29, 1953; s. Robert Richard and Eloise (Anderson) Putz; m. Karen Nelson, Jan. 20, 1990. BA in Chemistry, U. Calif., San Diego, 1975; MBA, Rutgers U., 1985. Cert. Inst. Mgmt. Cons. Agt. Prudential, San Diego, 1975-79; sales mgr. Herman Schlorman Showrooms, LA, 1980-83; pvt. practice mgmt. cons. Basking Ridge, N.J., 1983-85; mgmt. cons. The Brooks Group, Hollywood, Fla., 1985-99; pvt. practice San Diego, 1988—. With Western Productivity Group, 1990-95; pres. eProcesses Consulting, Inc., 1999—, with Kaufman Global, 2005—. Elder La Jolla Presbyn. Ch., 1991—; chmn. bd. Allicance for African Assistance, 2004—. Mem. Inst. Indsl. Engring., Inst. Mgmt. Consultants, Rutgers Club So. Calif., Beta Gamma Sigma. Avocations: singing, golf. Address: 6265 Hurd Ct San Diego CA 92122-2917 Home Phone: 858-452-1621. Personal E-mail: jbryan@eprocessesinc.com.

BRYAN, JOHN STEWART, III, newspaper publisher; b. Richmond, Va., May 4, 1938; s. David Tennant and Mary Davidson Bryan; m. Alice Pyle Zimmer, 1963 (div. 1985); children: Elizabeth Talbott, Anna Saulsbury; m. Lisa-Margaret Stevenson, 1993. BA, U. Va., 1960; LHD (hon.), Hampden-Sydney Coll., 1997, Emory and Henry Coll., 1999, Coll. of William and Mary, 2001, Randolph Macon Coll., 2004. Former advt. salesman Burlington (Vt.) Free Press; former reporter The Tampa (Fla.) Times; pub. The Tampa Tribune and Times, 1976—77, Richmond Times-Dispatch, Richmond News Leader, 1978—2004. Bd. dirs. Media Gen., Inc., Richmond, vice-chmn., exec. v.p., 1985—90, chmn., pres., CEO, 1990—2005, chmn., 2005—; bd. dirs. Mut. Ins. Co., Bermuda. Past pres. or chmn. Tampa Bay Art Ctr., Tampa Citizens Safety Coun., Tampa United Way, Gulf Coast Symphony, Jr. Achievement Richmond, Goodwill Industries Richmond, United Way Greater Richmond; trustee Va. Found. Ind. Coll., chmn., 1993—95; trustee Va. Performing Arts Found., Thomas Jefferson Found., George C. Marshall Found., Va. Hist. Soc.; former dir., trustee Episc. H.S., U. Tampa, St. Catharine's Sch., Hoover Instn. at Stanford, Tampa Bay Buccaneers, Tampa Rowdies, Richmond C. of C., Maymont Found., Valentine Mus., Richmond World Affairs Coun., Tampa Bay Coun. on Fgn. Rels., Va. Coalition for Open Govt., U. Va. Coll. Found.; mem. Va. Adv. Coun. Freedom of Info. With USMC, 1960—62. Mem.: Va. Bus. Coun., World Bus. Coun., Soc. Profl. Journalists, Newspaper Assn. Am. (dir. 1990—93, 1997—2005), Newspaper Advt. Bur. (chmn. 1991—92), Va. Press Assn. (bd. dirs. 1980—86), So. Newspapers Pub. Assn. (found. chmn. 1978—79, pres. 1981—82), Fla. Press Assn. (life; pres. 1971—72, Disting. Svc. award 1975), Fla. Soc. Newspapers Editors (life), Soc. Colonial Wars, Soc. Cin., Fla. Coun. of 100, Farmington Country Club, Tampa Yacht and Country Club, Commonwealth Club, Country Club Va., Bohemian Club. Home: 4608 Sulgrave Rd Richmond VA 23221-3119 Office: Media Gen Inc PO Box 85333C Richmond VA 23293-5333

BRYAN, KAREN SMITH, lawyer; BA in Psychology, Bryn Mawr Coll., 1972; MA, UCLA, 1973; JD, U. So. Calif., 1979. Bar: Calif. 1979. With Latham & Watkins LLP, LA, 1979—, ptnr., 1987—. Mem. planning com. U. So. Calif. Tax Inst. Named So. Calif. Super Lawyer, 2003—07; named one of Am.'s Leading Bus. Lawyers, Chambers & Ptnrs., 2003—07. Mem.: ABA (corp. tax com. and ind. income tax com.). Office: Latham & Watkins LLP 633 W Fifth St Ste 4000 Los Angeles CA 90071 Office Phone: 213-485-1234. Business E-Mail: karen.bryan@lw.com.

BRYAN, KIRK, JR., meteorologist, oceanographer, researcher; b. Albuquerque, July 21, 1929; married, 1956; 2 children. BS, Yale U., 1951; PhD in Meteorology, MIT, 1957. Rsch. assoc. meteorologist Woods Hole Oceanography Inst., 1958-61; rsch. meteorologist Gen. Circulation Rsch. Lab. U.S. Weather Bureau, 1961-68; oceanographer Geophys. Fluid Dynamics Lab., NOAA and Princeton (N.J.) U., 1968-94; vis. lectr. Princeton U., 1968-94, rsch. scientist, 1994-96, sr. rsch. scholar, 1996—. Mem. panel climatic variation global atmosphere rsch. program NAS, 1972-74; chmn. working group numerical models Sci. Com. Ocean Rsch., 1975-77. Fellow Am. Meteorol. Soc., Am. Geophys. Soc., Am. Geophys. Union (pres. oceanography sect., Maurice Ewing award 1993); mem. Russian Acad. Sci. (fgn.). Achievements include research in dynamic meteorology, physical oceanography, and general circulation of the atmosphere and oceans. Home: 700 Hollinshead Spring Rd Apt C205 Skillman NJ 08558-2037 Office: Princeton Univ Program Atmos and Ocean Sci Sayre Hall Princeton NJ 08544-1003 Office Phone: 609-258-3688. Business E-Mail: kbryan@splash.princeton.edu.

BRYAN, LAWRENCE DOW, college president; b. Barberton, Ohio, Jan. 30, 1945; s. W. Richard and Celia A. (Evans) B.; m. Marjorie Napier, June 15, 1968; children: Mark Evans, Alexa Marie. BA, Muskingum Coll., 1967; MDiv., Garrett Theol. Sem., 1970; PhD, Northwestern U., 1973. Tchg. asst. Nat. Coll. Edn., Evanston, Ill., 1969-71; biog. rsch. fellow Garrett Theol. Sem., Evanston, 1972-73; asst. prof. religious studies, chaplain McKendree Coll., Lebanon, Ill., 1973-77, asst. v.p. acad. affairs, 1977-78, dean, 1978-79, assoc. prof., 1978-79; prof. philosophy and religion, v.p., dean Franklin (Ind.) Coll., 1979-90; pres. Kalamazoo Coll., 1990-96, MacMurray Coll., Jacksonville, Ill., 1997—. Trustee Parkstone Group of Funds, 1994-98. Mem. Forum for Kalamazoo County, 1990-94, Kalamazoo Symphony Orch. Bd., 1990-96; pres. Heyl Found., Kalamazoo, 1990-96; bd. dirs. Bronson Hosp., 1991-96; trustee Interlochen Ctr. for Arts, 1994-97; pres. Jacksonville Main St. Bd. Dirs. Mem. Internat. Bonhoeffer Soc., Fed. Ind. Ill. Colls. and Univs., Rotary, Phi Sigma Tau, Delta Sigma Rho-Tau Kappa Alpha, Alpha Psi Omega, Theta Alpha Phi. Methodist. Business E-Mail: president@mac.edu.

BRYAN, MIKE CARL, professional tennis player; b. Camarillo, Calif., Apr. 29, 1978; s. Bob and Kathy. Attended, Stanford U., 1996—98. Profl. tennis player ATP, 1998—. Mem. Bryan Brothers Band. Mem. WECAAN, Andrea Jaeger's Silver Lining Found., Elton John's AIDS Found., Tennis For Africa. Named Doubles Team of Yr. (with brother Bob Bryan), 2006 ATP Awards, ATPTennis.com Fans' Favorite Doubles Team. Mem.: Sigma Alpha Epsilon. Achievements include winning over 100 jr. doubles titles with brother Bob; winning 43 career doubles titles, ATP. Avocations: drums, basketball. Office: Bryan Bros 1774 Ramona Dr Camarillo CA 93010*

BRYAN, RICHARD H., lawyer, educator, former senator; b. Washington, July 16, 1937; m. Bonnie Fairchild; 3 children. BA, U. Nev., 1959; LLB, U. Calif., San Francisco, 1963. Bar: Nev. 1963, DC 2002. Dep. dist. atty., Clark County, Nev., 1964—66; pub. defender, 1966—68; counsel Clark County Juvenile Ct., 1968—69; mem. Nev. Assembly, 1969—73, Nev. Senate, 1973—79; atty. gen. State Nev., 1979—83, gov., 1983—89; senator from Nev. U.S. Senate, 1989—2001; ptnr., mem. exec. com. Lionel, Sawyer & Collins, 2001—. Former mem. U.S. Senate coms. on commerce, sci. and transp., Dem. Policy Com., Fin. Com., Banking, Housing and Urban Affairs Com., Senate Nominating Steering and Coord. Com., Select Com. on Intelligence; adj. prof. polit. sci. U. Nev., Las Vegas, 2001—. Former pres. Clark County Legal Aid Soc.; bd. dirs. Las Vegas C. of C.; bd. trustees Nev. Devel. Authority, 2001—. 2d lt. US Army, 1959—60. Recipient Disting. Svc. award, Vegas Valley Jaycees. Mem.: ABA, Coun. of State Govts. (past pres.), Am. Judicature Soc., Clark County Bar Assn., Elks, Masons, Lions, Phi Alpha Theta, Phi Alpha Delta. Democrat. Office: Lionel Sawyer & Collins 1700 Bank Am Plaza 300 S 4th St Las Vegas NV 89101

BRYAN, ROBERT ARMISTEAD, academic administrator, educator; b. Lebanon, Pa., Apr. 26, 1926; s. Morris Armistead and Katherine (Maulfair) B.; m. Kathryn Elizabeth Williams, Feb. 3, 1953; children: Lyla, Matthew. BA, U. Miami, 1950; MA, U. Ky., Lexington, 1951, PhD, 1956. Tchg. asst. U. Ky., Lexington, 1950-54, instr., 1956-57; lectr. extension div. U. Calif., Tokyo, 1955-56; dean advanced studies, dir. sponsored rsch. Fla. Atlantic U., 1969-70; mem. faculty, adminstrn. U. Fla., Gainsville, 1957-90, prof. English, 1968-90, dean faculties, 1970-71, assoc. v.p. acad. affairs, 1971-75, v.p. acad. affairs, 1975-85, provost, 1985-89, interim pres., 1989-90, ret., 1990; interim pres. U. Cen. Fla., 1991-92, U. South Fla., 1993-94. Reader Coll. Bd. Exams., Ednl. Testing Svc., 1958-61; cons. So. Assn. Schs. and Colls., 1965-73, also chmn. visitation com., 1966-67; cons. HEW, Nat. Assn. of State Univs. and Land Grant Colls., 1990-91; cons. Fla. Bd. Regents, 1994-95; trustee Bethune-Cookman Coll., 1994-2001; mem. Fla. Postsecondary Edn. Planning Commn., 1996-2000. Bibliographer: Twentieth Century Literature, 1958-61. Served with U.S. Mcht. Marine, 1944-47, with AUS, 1954-56. Decorated Royal Order North Star (Sweden) Mem. MLA, Southeastern Renaissance Conf., S. Atlantic Mod. Lang. Assn., Sigma Chi. Episcopalian. Home: 5000 SW 25th Blvd Apt 4122 Gainesville FL 32608 Personal E-mail: rbryan@gator.net.

BRYAN, ROBERT E., editor; b. 1946; Fashion editor Men's Wear, M, The Civilized Man, 1983—93; men's fashion dir. W mag., 1993—95; sr. fashion designers features editor Daily News Record, 1993—95; men's style editor NY Times, 1995—; head style dept. T: The NY Times style mag., 2004—. Contbr. When I Knew, 2005.

BRYAN, ROBERT J., federal judge; b. Bremerton, Wash., Oct. 29, 1934; s. James W. and Vena Gladys (Jensen) B.; m. Cathy Ann Welander, June 14, 1958; children: Robert James, Ted Lorin, Ronald Terence. BA, U. Wash., 1956, JD, 1958. Bar: Wash. 1959, U.S. Dist. Ct. (we. dist.) Wash. 1959, U.S. Tax Ct. 1965, U.S. Ct. Appeals (9th cir.) 1985. Assoc., then ptnr. Bryan & Bryan, Bremerton, 1959-67; judge Superior Ct., Port Orchard, Wash., 1967-84; ptnr. Riddell, Williams, Bullitt & Walkinshaw, Seattle, 1984-86; judge U.S. Dist. Ct. (we. dist.) Wash., Tacoma, 1986—. Mem. State Jail Commn., Olympia, Wash., 1974-76, Criminal Justice Tng. Com., Olympia, 1978-81, State Bd. on Continuing Legal Edn., Seattle, 1984-86; mem., sec. Jud. Qualifications Commn., Olympia, 1982-83; chair Wash. Fed.-State Jud. Coun., 1997-98; mem. 9th Cir. Jud. Coun., 2001-03. Author: (with others) Washington Pattern Jury Instructions (civil and criminal vols. and supplements), 1970-85, Manual of Model Criminal Jury Instructions for the Ninth Circuit, 1992, Manual of Model Civil Jury Instruction for the Ninth Circuit, 1993. Chmn. 9th Ct. Jury Com., 1991-92; bd. dirs. Fed. Jud. Ctr., 2000-04. Served to maj. USAR. Mem.: 9th Cir. Dist. Judges Assn. (sec.-treas. 1997—99, v.p. 1999—2001, pres. 2001—03). Office: US Dist Ct 1717 Pacific Ave Rm 4427 Tacoma WA 98402-3234

BRYAN, SHARON ANN, lawyer; b. Kansas City, Mo., Dec. 18; d. George William and Dorothy Joan (Henn) Goll; children: Lisa Ann, Holly Renee. BJ, U. Mo., 1963; diploma, Stanford Radio and TV Inst., 1961; postgrad., NYU Sch. Arts and Sci., 1963—64; cert. personal fin. planning profl., UCLA, 1986; JD, U. So. Calif., 1989. Cert. specialist in family law. Proofreader, copy editor Cadwalader, Wickersham and Taft, NYC, 1963—64; manuscript editor, writer nonsci. sects. N.Y. State Jour. Medicine, Med. Soc. State N.Y., NYC, mng. editor Staffoscope, 1965—66; manuscript editor Transactions, editor Perceiver Am. Acad. Ophthalmology and Otolaryngology, Rochester, Minn., 1963—72, hist. writer, 1972—82; atty. Burkley, Moore, Greenberg & Lyman, Torrance, Calif., 1989—91; with Christopher M. Moore & Assocs., 1991—99, Moore, Bryan & Schroff, 1999—. Writer publicity articles Ft. Lee (Va.) Cmty. Theatre; mediator Dept. 2 Superior Ct. of Calif., Ctrl. Dist. and Dept SWJ, S.W. Dist. Author: Pioneering Specialists: History of the American Academy of Ophthalmology and Otolaryngology, 1982. Vol. honor roll soc. Meml. Sloan-Kettering Cancer Ctr.; active N.Y. Hosp. Women's League, 1965-67; docent L.A. County Mus. Natural History, 1982-86; vol. Harriet Buhai Ctr., 1990-97; pres. Malaga Cove Homeowners Assn., 1999-2000. Mem.: NOW, ATLA, ABA, Assn. Cert. Family Law Specialists (bd. dir. 2003—, editor newsletter 2004—06, pres.-elect 2007, chair spring seminar 2007), South Bay Women Lawyers Assn. (rec. sec. 1994—, pres. 1996—97), Los Angeles County Bar Assn. (exec. com. L.A. delegation 1996—98, family law sect. exec. com. 2001—04, L.A. del. to State Bar Calif. 2004), Women's Lawyers Assn. L.A (bd. govs. 1991—97, chmn. family law sect. 1993—97), N.Y. Acad. Scis., Am. Med. Writers Assn. (editor conv. bull. 1966), Kappa Alpha Theta (chmn. membership com. N.Y. chpt. 1966), Kappa Tau Alpha. Home: 533 Via Del Monte Palos Verdes Estates CA 90274-1205 Office: 21515 Hawthorne Blvd Ste 490 Torrance CA 90503 Office Phone: 310-540-8855. Business E-Mail: sharon@mbslawcorp.com.

BRYAN, THOMAS LYNN, lawyer, educator; b. Wichita, Kans., June 10, 1935; s. Herbert Thomas and Ruth Marjorie (Williams) B.; m. Virginia Alice Cooper, June 13, 1981; children from previous marriage: Victoria Lynne Hague, Douglas Edward BA, U. Kans., 1957; LLB, Columbia U., 1960. Bar: N.Y. Assoc. Willkie Farr & Gallagher, NYC, 1960-66, ptnr., 1967-92; adj. prof. Stetson U. Coll. Law, 1993-97. Co-author: Business Acquisitions, 1971, 2d edit. 1981 Mem. Longboat Key Club, Phi Beta Kappa Republican. Avocations: sports, golf, theater. Address: 3448 Mistletoe Ln Longboat Key FL 34228-4146

BRYANS, HENRY S., lawyer; b. Bryn Mawr, Pa., 1946; BA, Yale Univ., 1968; JD, Univ. Pa., 1971. Bar: Pa. 1972, Del. 2004. Law clerk, Hon. Henry J. Friendly, chief judge US Ct. Appeals (2d cir.); joined Drinker Biddle & Reath LLP, Phila., 1972, ptnr., bus., fin. dept., firm gen. counsel. Lectr. in field. Mem.: Am. Law Inst. Office: Drinker Biddle & Reath LLP One Logan Sq 18th & Cherry Sts Philadelphia PA 19103-6996 Office Phone: 215-988-2823. Office Fax: 215-988-2757. Business E-Mail: henry.bryans@dbr.com.

BRYANT, ANDY D., computer company executive; BA in Econs., U. Mo.; MBA in Fin., U. Kans. With Chrysler Corp., Ford Motor Co.; contr. comml. memory sys. operation Intel Corp., Santa Clara, Calif., 1981-83, sys. group contr., 1983-87, dir. fin. for corp., 1987-90, v.p., dir. fin. Intel products group, 1990-94, corp. v.p., CFO, 1994—99, sr. v.p., CFO, chief enterprise services officer, 1999—2001, exec. v.p., CFO, chief enterprise services officer, 2001—. Office: Intel 2200 Mission College Blvd Santa Clara CA 95054-1537*

BRYANT, ANNE LINCOLN, educational association administrator; b. Jamaica Plain, Mass., Nov. 26, 1949; d. John Winslow and Anne (Phillips) B.; m. Peter Harned Ross, June 15, 1986; stepchildren: Charlotte Ross, George Ross. BA in English and Secondary Edn., Simmons Coll., 1971; EdD in Higher Edn., U. Mass., 1978. Intern U. Mass., Amherst, 1972; asst. to dean Springfield Tech. CC, 1972—74; dir. Nat. Assn. Bank Women Ednl. Found., Chgo., 1974—86; v.p. P.M. Haeger, Chgo., 1978—86; exec. dir. AAUW, Washington, 1986—96, exec. dir. Ednl. Found., Legal Advocacy Fund; exec. dir. Nat. Sch. Bds. Assn., Washington, 1996—. Contbr. articles to profl. jours. Mem. exec. com. Simmons Coll., Boston, 1971—; adv. commr. Edn. Commn. States, 1986—; mem. bd. govs. UNA of U.S.A., 1991—97, Ind. Sector, 1988-94, Hosp. Corp. Am., 1993-94. Recipient William H. Cosby Jr. award U. Mass., 1983; named Woman of Yr. for Edn., YWCA, 1976. Fellow Am. Soc. Assn. Execs. (bd. dirs. 1985-88, Key award 1992); mem. Am. Assn. Higher Edn. (bd. dirs. 1980-87). Episcopalian. Avocations: tennis, skiing, reading, walking. Office: NSBA 1680 Duke St Alexandria VA 22314 Office Phone: 703-838-6700. E-mail: abryant@nsba.org.*

BRYANT, ARTHUR H., lawyer; b. Harrisburg, Pa., Aug. 11, 1954; s. Albert Irwin and Marjorie (Weinrib) B.; m. Nancy Kaye Johnson, Aug. 17, 1991; 1 stepchild, Vinnie Johnson; 1 child, Wallace Johnson Bryant. AB with hons., Swarthmore Coll., 1976; JD, Harvard U., 1979; D (hon.), Ripon Coll., 1998. Bar: Pa. 1981, U.S. Dist. Ct. (ea. dist.) Pa. 1981, U.S. Ct. Appeals (3d cir.) Pa. 1981, U.S. Ct. Appeals (11th cir.) Ga. 1985, U.S. Ct. Appeals (6th cir.) Ohio 1986, U.S. Ct. appeals (D.C. cir.) 1986, U.S. Ct. Appeals (9th cir.) Calif. 1987, U.S. Ct. Appeals (7th cir.) Ill. 1988, U.S. Ct. Appeals (5th cir.) Tex. 1988, D.C., 1989, U.S. Supreme Ct. 1989, U.S. Ct. Appeals (1st cir.) 1996. Intern Rosenman, Colin & Freund, NYC, 1978, N.Y. Civil Liberties Union, NYC, 1978, Cambridge & Somerville Legal Svcs., Cambridge, Pa., 1979; law clk. U.S. Dist. Ct. (so. dist.), Tex., 1979-80; atty. Kohn, Savett, Marion & Graf., Phila., 1980-84; staff atty. Trial Lawyers for Pub. Justice, Washington, 1984-87; exec. cir. Pub. Justice, Washington, 1987—. Recipient George Moscone Meml. award Consumer Atty. Assn. L.A., 2003; named one of 20 young lawyers making a difference in the world ABA Barrister mag., 1991, one of 50 most influential people in coll. sports Coll. Sports Mag., 1994, one of 45 lawyers whose vision and commitment are changing lives The Am. Lawyer, 1997, one of 100 most influential lawyers in Am. Nat. Law Jour., 2000, 2006; recipient Wasserstein Pub. Interest law fellowship, 1996; Honored by Oreg. Trial Lawyers Asn., renamed pub. svc. award to Arthur H. Bryant Pub. Justice Award, 2003. Mem. ABA (Pursuit of Justice award 2003), Am. Assn. for Justice. Office: Pub Justice 555 Twelfth St Ste 1620 Oakland CA 94607 Office Phone: 510-622-8150. Business E-Mail: abryant@publicjustice.net.

BRYANT, BARBARA EVERITT, academic administrator, researcher, retired marketing professional, federal agency administrator; b. Ann Arbor, Mich., Apr. 5, 1926; d. William Littell and Dorothy (Wallace) Everitt; m. John H. Bryant, Aug. 14, 1948; children: Linda Bryant Valentine, Randal E., Lois. AB, Cornell U., 1947; MA, Mich. State U., 1967, PhD, 1970; HonD, U. Ill., 1993. Editor art Chem. Engring. mag. McGraw-Hill Pub. Co., NYC, 1947-48; editl. rsch. asst. U. Ill., Urbana, 1948-49, free-lance editor, writer, 1950-61; with continuing edn. adminstrn. dept. Oakland Univ., Rochester, Mich., 1961-66; grad. rsch. asst. Mich. State U., East Lansing, 1966-70; sr. analyst to v.p. Market Opinion Rsch., Detroit, 1970-77, sr. v.p., 1977-89; dir. Bur. of the Census, U.S. Dept. Commerce, 1989-93; rsch. scientist Ross Sch Bus., U. Mich., 1993—. Author: High School Students Look at Their World, 1970, American Women Today & Tomorrow, 1977, Moving Power and Money: The Politics of Census Taking, 1995; contbr. articles to profl. jours. Mem. U.S. Census Adv. Com., Washington, 1980—86, Mich. Job Devel. Authority, Lansing, 1980—85; state editor LWV of Mich., 1959—61; bd. dirs. Roper Ctr. for Pub. Opinion Rsch., 1993—2007; mem. nat. adv. com. Inst. for Social Rsch., U. Mich., 1993—. Fellow: Am. Statis. Assn.; mem.: Am. Assn. Pub. Opinion Rsch., Am. Mktg. Assn. (pres. Detroit 1976—77, midwestern v.p. 1978—80, v.p. mktg. rsch. 1982—84, found. trustee 1993—2001), Rotary, Cosmos Club. Republican. Presbyterian. Avocation: swimming. Home: 1505 Sheridan Dr Ann Arbor MI 48104-4051 Office: Ross Sch of Business U Mich Ann Arbor MI 48109-1234 Office Phone: 734-763-9062. Business E-Mail: bryantb@umich.edu.

BRYANT, BERTHA ESTELLE, retired medical/surgical nurse; b. Va., Jan. 11, 1927; d. E.F. and Julia B. Diploma, Sibley Meml. Hosp., Washington, 1947; BS, Am. U., 1948; MA, Tchrs. Coll., Columbia U., 1962. Staff nurse, head nurse NIH, Bethesda, Md., 1954-59; asst. dir. nursing USPHS Alaska Native Hosp., Mt. Edgecumbe, 1959-61; instr. Sch. Nursing, U. Mich., 1962-64; chief div. clin. nursing Bur. Nursing, D.C. Dept. Public Health, Washington, 1964-65; commd. Nurse Corps, USPHS, 1965, nurse dir., capt., 1974—. Nurse cons., hosp. facilities services br., div. hosps. and med. facilities Bur. Health Services, HEW, Silver Spring; nurse cons., social analysis br., div. health services research and analysis Nat. Center Health Services Research, Health Resources Adminstrn., HEW, Rockville, Md.; nurse cons. div. extramural research Nat. Center Health Services Research, Office Asst. Sec. Health, HHS, Hyattsville, Md., 1977-81 Contbr. articles to profl. jours. Mem. AAUW, Assn. Mil. Surgeons U.S., Commd. Officers Assn. USPHS

BRYANT, BRENDA K., psychologist, educator; b. Waukegan, Ill., May 4, 1945; d. Donald Loyd and Eileen Galloway Bryant; 1 child, Matthew Bristol. AB, Cornell U., Ithaca, NY, 1967; PhD, U. Minn., 1971. Lic. psychologist Calif. Asst. full prof. U. Calif., Davis, 1971—. Author: Child Development; contbr. articles to profl. jours. Cook Free meal program, Davis, Calif., 1994—96; treas. Friends of Davis, Davis, Calif., 1995—96. Fogarty Sr. Internat. fellow, NIH, 1990—91. Mem.: Am. Ednl. Rsch. Assn., Am. Psychology Assn., Nat. Assn. Sch. Psychologists, Soc. for Rsch. in Child Devel. Protestant. Avocations: piano, swimming, interior decorating, cooking. Office: Univ of Calif Davis 1 Shields Ave Dept of HCD Davis CA 95616 Home Phone: 530-756-5092. Business E-Mail: bkbryant@ucdavis.edu.

BRYANT, CLIFTON DOW, sociologist, educator; b. Jackson, Miss., Dec. 25, 1932; s. Clifton Edward and Helen (Dow) B.; m. Nancy Ann Arrington, Sept. 13, 1953; m. Patty Maurine Watts, Feb. 1, 1957; children: Melinda Dow, Deborah Carol, Karen Diane, Clifton Dow II. Student, U. Miss., 1950-53, BA, 1956, MA, 1957; postgrad., U. N.C., Chapel Hill, 1957-58, La. State U., 1958-60, PhD, 1964. Vis. instr. dept. sociology and anthropology Pa. State U., summer, 1958; instr., rsch. assoc. dept. sociology and anthropology U. Ga., 1960-63; asst. prof., assoc. prof., chmn. dept. sociology and anthropology Millsaps Coll., Jackson, Miss., 1963-67; summer research participant, tng. and tech. project Oak Ridge Asso. Univs., summer 1967; prof., head dept. sociology and anthropology

Western Ky. U., Bowling Green, Ky., 1967-72; prof. sociology Va. Poly. Inst. and State U., Blacksburg, 1972—; head dept. Va Poly. Inst. and State U., Blacksburg, 1972-82. Vis. prof. Xavier U., Philippines, 1984-85; vis. prof., vis. rsch. scholar Miss. Alcohol Safety Edn. Program, Miss. State U., (summer), 1985; vis. Fulbright prof. dept. grad. inst. sociology Nat. Taiwan U., Taipei, Republic of China, 1987-88; vis. scientist U.S. Army summer faculty rsch. and engring. program, 1993; participant Fulbright-Hays Seminar Abroad program, Hungary, 1993, China, 1998. Author: Khaki-Collar Crime: Deviant Behavior in Military Context, 1979, Sexual Deviancy and Social Proscription, 1982; editor and contbr.: Deviant Behavior: Occupational and Organizational Bases, 1974, The Social Dimensions of Work, 1972, Sexual Deviancy in Social Context, 1977, Deviant Behavior: Readings in the Sociology of Norm Violations, 1990; editor-in-chief: The Encyclopedia of Criminology and deviant Behavior, 4 vols., 2001, Death and Dying: A Reference Handbook, 2 vols., 2003; co-editor, contbr.: Deviancy and the Family, 1973, The Rural Work Force: Nonagricultural Occupations in America, 1985; compiler: Handbook of Audio-Visual Resources to Accompany Social Problems Today, 1971; editor: Social Problems Today: Dilemmas and Dissensus, 1971; co-editor: Introductory Sociology: Selected Readings for the College Scene, 1970; editor in chief Deviant Behavior: An Interdisciplinary Jour., 1978-91; editor So. Sociologist, 1970-74; mem. editorial bd. Criminology: An Interdisciplinary Jour, 1978-91; chmn. editorial policy bd., founding editor-in-Chief Deviant Behavior: An Interdisciplinary Journal, 1992—; chmn. editorial bd. Sociol. Symposium, 1968-80; assoc. editor Sociol. Forum, 1979-80, Sociol. Spectrum, 1981-85; mem. bd. adv. editors Sociol. Inquiry, 1981-85, assoc. editor, 1997—; bd. editors Society and Animals, 1997—; assoc. editor spl. issue Marriage and Family Relations, fall 1982, Sociological Inquiry, 1997—; contbr. chpts. to books, articles, book reviews to profl. publs. Served to 1st lt., M.P. U.S. Army, 1953-55. Recipient E. Gordon Ericksen Outstanding Grad. Faculty award sociology dept. Va. Poly. Inst. and State U., 1992, 93, spl. award for continuing contbn. to undergrad. tchg. enterprise, 1992, Undergraduate Tchg. Excellence award, 1995-96, 2001. Mem. Am. Sociol. Assn., Am. Soc. Criminology, So. Sociol. Soc. (pres. 1978-79, Disting. Book award 2001), Mid-South Sociol. Assn. (pres. 1981-82, Disting. Career award 1991), Rural Sociol. Soc., Soc. Anthropology of Work, Internat. Sociol. Assn., Inter-Univ. Seminar on Armed Forces and Society, So. Assn. Agr. Scientists, Omicron Delta Kappa, Phi Kappa Phi, Alpha Phi Omega, Alpha Kappa Delta, Pi Kappa Alpha, Phi Beta Delta. Presbyterian. Home: 1724 E Ridge Dr Blacksburg VA 24060-8568 Office: Va Poly Inst State U Dept Sociology Blacksburg VA 24061 E-mail: cbryant@vt.edu.

BRYANT, DANIEL JAMES, food and beverage company executive, former federal agency administrator; b. 1965; married; 2 children. BA, Am. U., JD, 1992; MA, Oxford U., Eng. Law clk., spl. asst. U.S. Dept. Justice, 1987—92; speech writer former Atty. Gen. William Barr; policy dir. First Freedom Coalition, 1994—95; majority counsel Crime Subcom., 1995—99; majority chief counsel House Judicary Com. Crime Subcom., 1999—2001; asst. atty. gen. legis. affairs U.S. Dept. Justice, Washington, 2001—03, counselor, sr. adv. to atty gen. legal and policy matters, 2003, asst. atty. gen. Office Legal Policy, 2003—05; v.p. pub. policy & fed. govt. affairs Pepsi Co., Inc., Purchase, NY, 2005—. Mem. gov. affairs com. permanent subcom. investigations U.S. Senate. Office: PepsiCo Inc 700 Anderson Hill Rd Purchase NY 10577

BRYANT, DAVID J., lawyer; b. Fostoria, Ohio, Dec. 17, 1961; BS, U. Ill., 1984; JD, Northwestern U., 1987. Bar: Ill. 1987. Ptnr. comml. real estate law Katten Muchin Zavis Rosenman, Chgo. Mem.: ABA, Pension Real Estate Assn., Nat. Assn. Real Estate Investment Trusts, Chgo. Bar Assn. Office: Katten Muchin Zavis Rosenman 525 W Monroe St, Ste 1600 Chicago IL 60661 Office Phone: 312-902-5380. Office Fax: 312-577-8665. E-mail: david.bryant@kmzr.com.

BRYANT, DONALD L., JR., insurance and benefits company executive; b. Mt. Vernon, Ill., June 30, 1942; s. Donald Loyd and Eileen (Gallaway) B.; m. Barbara Frances Murphy, July 9, 1981; children: Derek Lawrence, Christina Murphy, Justin Donald. BA, Denison U., Granville, Ohio, 1964; JD, Washington U., St. Louis, 1967. CLU, Chartered fin. cons. Chmn., chief exec. officer Donald L. Bryant Assocs., St. Louis, 1968-75, Bryant Group, Inc., St. Louis, 1975—. Owner family vineyard, Napa Valley, Calif. Pres. Herbert Hoover Boys Club, St. Louis, 1987—; active Arts and Edn. Coun. Greater St. Louis, 1983—, Dance St. Louis, 1988—, Opera Theatre St. Louis, 1985—, Boy Scouts Am., 1972—, St. Louis Art Mus., 1990; bd. trustees Mus. Modern Art. Named Outstanding Alumni, Sch. of Law Washington U., 1990; named one of Top 200 Collectors, ARTnews Mag., 2004. Mem. Million Dollar Round Table (life), The Internat. Forum, Assn. Advanced Life Underwriters, St. Louis Assn. Life Underwriters, Estate Planning Coun. St. Louis, Mo. Bar Assn., ABA, Bellerive Country Club (St. Louis) (golf champ 1976), Vintage Club (Indian Wells, Calif.), Winged Foot (Mamaroneck, N.Y.), Castle Pines (Castlerock, Calif.), Meadowood (Napa Valley, Calif.), Sunningdale Golf. Republican. Presbyterian. Avocations: wine, golf, collecting abstract expressionism, especially de Kooning, contemporary art. Office: Bryant Group Inc 701 Market St Ste 1200 Saint Louis MO 63101-1884 Office Fax: 314-231-4859.

BRYANT, DONALD LOYD, insurance company executive; b. Orchard, Iowa, Jan. 30, 1919; s. Lester E. and Bessie (Farless) B.; m. Eileen Galloway, May 11, 1941; children: Donald Loyd, Hedy E. Bryant Garlock, Brenda K., Becky Bryant Hubert. B.Ed., So. Ill. U., 1940. With War Manpower Commn., Mt. Vernon, Ill., 1940; agt., dist. mgr. Equitable Life Assurance Soc. U.S., Elgin and Carbondale, Ill., 1946-54, agy. mgr. St. Louis, 1954-69, v.p., chief agy. staff ops. NYC, 1969-71, v.p. corp. relations, 1971-72, sr. v.p. corp. relations, 1972-74, exec. v.p., spl. asst. to pres., 1974-78, exec. v.p., 1978-81. Bus exec.-in-residence Tex. Christian U., Ft. Worth, 1980—; cons. Nat. Exec. Services Corp.; bus. exec.-in-residence So. Ill. U. Served to lt. USN, 1942-46. Recipient Alumni Achievement award So. Ill. U., 1964, 88. Mem.: Quail Ridge Golf and Tennis (Boynton Beach, Fla.). Presbyterian. Home and Office: 1489 Partridge Pl N Boynton Beach FL 33436-5409 Personal E-mail: donaldl.bryantsr@mac.com. *On each job, behave as though you will be on that job for the remainder of your working life. In this way you avoid mistakes because you'd have to live with those mistakes. You are careful to pick good associates because you will have to live with them forever. You give security to your subordinates, command their loyalty, because they sense you'll be there forever. Ironically you'll then do such a superior job that you'll be promoted over and over while behaving as though you'll be on your job forever.*

BRYANT, FRED BOYD, psychology professor; b. Princeton, NJ, Nov. 26, 1952; s. George Macon and Merrilee B.; m. Linda Sue Perloff, July 12, 1980; children: Hilary Jacyln, Erica Lindsay. BA, Duke U., 1974; MA, Northwestern U., Evanston, 1977, PhD, 1980. Postdoctoral fellow Inst. for Social Rsch., U. Mich., Ann Arbor, 1979-82; asst. prof. Loyola U., Chgo., 1982-85, assoc. prof., 1985-90, prof., 1990—. Rsch. cons. in field, 1982—; legal cons., N.Y., Ill., 1985—. Author (with Joseph Veroff) Savoring: A New Model of Positive Experience, 2006; editor Methodological Issues in Applied Social Psychology, 1992; contbr. numerous articles to profl. jours. Mem. APA, Am. Evaluation Rsch. Assn., Midwestern Psychol. Assn. Office: Loyola U Dept Psychology 6525 N Sheridan Rd Chicago IL 60626-5344 Office Phone: 312-508-3033. E-mail: fbryant@luc.edu.

BRYANT, GREGORY ALEXANDER, bishop; b. Atlanta, Ga., Dec. 9, 1953; s. Silas Johnson and Mildred Bryant; m. Yvonne De Bryant, Oct. 26, 1996 (div.); children: Antwoine, Gregory Jr., Titus, Sheranda, Shawana, Tiffany. BA in religious arts, Jacksonville Theological Seminary, 2001, MA in religious studies; ThD in religious studies, Christ is the Answer U., 1995. Founder, pastor The Fountain of Praise, Atlanta, 1976—; founder, pres., CEO The More Than Conquerors Fellowship, Inc., Atlanta, 1985—; founder, pastor The Trumpet In Zion, Douglasville, Ga., 1985—, Shield of Faith Ministries, Carrollton, Ga., 2004—; founder, bishop Fountain of Life Ministries, McDonough, Ga., 2004—; founder Healing Streams Ministries, Newnan, Ga., 2005. Counselor Am. Assn. of Christian Counselors; founder New Directions with a Positive Change, Atlanta, 2004—, Camp Praise for Inner City Children, Atlanta. Author: Stongholds, 2003, My Warfare is Not With You, 2003, Let Your Haters Be Your Motivators, 2003. Serving and counseling Hosea Williams Feed the Hungry, Atlanta, 1994—. Recipient various proclamations and congratulatory letters of acknowledgement, 1983—2004. Mem.: SCLC, NAACP, Urban League, Rainbow Push. Achievements include 1st African Am. preacher on regular TV, Atlanta Ga., 1980. Avocations: football, fishing, travel, reading, boating. Office: The More Than Conquerors Fellowship Internat Inc 770 N Elizabeth Pl Atlanta GA 30318 Office Phone: 404-794-9514. Business E-Mail: fountainofpraise2006@yahoo.com.

BRYANT, HUBERT HALE, lawyer; b. Tulsa, Jan. 4, 1931; s. Roscoe Conkling and Curlie Beatrice (Marshall) B.; m. Elnora Geraldine Roberson, Oct. 25, 1952; children: Cheryl Denise, Tara Kay. BA, Fisk U., 1952; LLB, Howard U., 1956. Bar: Okla. 1956, U.S. Dist. Ct. (no. dist.) Okla 1956, U.S. Ct. Appeals (10th cir.) 1967, U.S. Supreme Ct. 1980. Individual practice law, Tulsa, 1956—67, 1981—84, 1986—. Asst. city prosecutor, City of Tulsa, 1961-63, chief city prosecutor, 1963-67, asst. U.S. atty., No. Dist. Okla., 1967-77, U.S. atty., 1977-81; mcpl. ct. judge City of Tulsa, 1984-86. Trustee 1st Bapt. Ch., Tulsa, 1970-75, 96-2002; bd. dirs. Tulsa Urban League, 1962-64. Recipient Outstanding Alumni award Howard U. Sch. Law, 1981, 30 Yr. Outstanding African Am. Lawyer award Met. Tulsa Urban League, 1997. Mem. NAACP, Nat. Bar Assn. (Named to Hall of Fame), Okla. Bar Assn. (50 Yr. Membership award 2006), Tulsa County Bar Assn., Okla. Trial Lawyers Assn., Nat. Set, Masons (named Mason of Yr. local chpt. 1963, Outstanding Citizen award 1978), Sigma Pi Phi, Alpha Theta Boule, Alpha Phi Alpha. Democrat. Home: 1818 N Boston St Tulsa OK 74106 Office: 2623 N Peoria Ave Tulsa OK 74106-2512 Office Phone: 918-428-6665.

BRYANT, IRENE MELBA, retired elementary school educator, artist; d. Leon Lawrence and Dorothea Irene Spottswood; m. S.L. Bryant (div.). BFA, U. Cin., 1973, MFA, 1975, MA, 1993; MEd, Xavier U., 1992. Permanent tchg. cert. Ohio. Classroom art specialist Cin. Pub. Schs., 1984—91, 1992—2005; Montessori art specialist Lackland Elem. Sch., Ohio, 1992—93; ret., 2005. Represented in permanent collections U. Cin., numerous pvt. collections. Mem. adv. coun. Pub. Rels. Commn., Cin., 1980—88; trustee Comm. of the Arts, Cin., 1997—98; vol. Cin. Art Mus., 1994—; bd. dirs. Crayons to Computers, Cin., 1997—99. Fellow U. Cin., 1983; scholar, 1973, 1977. Avocations: painting, swimming. Home: 17 Merzen Ct Cincinnati OH 45217-2002

BRYANT, J(AMES) BRUCE, lawyer; b. Dettlebach, Fed. Republic Germany, Jan. 23, 1961; came to U.S., 1964; s. John Thomas and Doris Jean (Hazenbuahler) B.; 1 child, James Bruce II. BA, Northwestern State U., Natchitoches, La., 1984; MJ, La. State, 1986; cert. supervisory tech., La. State U., 2003, cert. mgmt. of people, 2006; JD, Miss. Coll., 1989. Bar: Miss., Tex. 1995, US Dist. Ct. (no. and so. dists.) Miss., US Ct. Appeals (5th cir.) La. 1991, US Dist. Ct. (we. dist.) La. 1994; cert. supervisory techniques La. State U., 2003, cert. in mgmt. of people, 2007. With residential life La. State U., Baton Rouge, 1985-86; law libr. worker Miss. Coll. Sch. Law, Jackson, 1986-87; clk. Brunini Law Firm, Jackson, 1987-88; ptnr. Cook & Bryant, Bay St. Louis, Miss., 1989-90; assoc. Cook, Yancey, King & Galloway, Shreveport, La., 1990-93; prof. bus. law La. State U., 1991-92, prof. paralegal sci., 1994-96; staff atty. State of La. Office of Support Enforcement, Shreveport, 1993-95; atty. Storm Operating Co. Inc. of La., 1994-98; sr. regional atty. State of La. Dept. Health and Hosps., Shreveport-Bossier City, 1995—, liaison on gov.'s healthcare consortium, 2005—; prof. comms. law, pub. rels and advt. Northwestern State U., 1996—; spl. asst. dist. atty. 1st Jud. Dist., Caddo Parish, La., 1998—. Bd. dirs. Extra Mile; cons. Wyman Fed. Credit Union, Geismar, La., 1989-90, Comml. Nat. Bank, Shreveport, 1990-93; owner, pres. Showbiz Entertainment Agys., Shreveport, 1992—; v.p. Godfather Prodns., Inc., Shreveport-Bossier City, La., 1994—; owner La. Ctr. Law and Justice, 1995—; spl. asst. dist. atty. Caddo Parish, 1998—; owner, pres. Dreamworks Internat., 1999—. Author: Development of Defamation Law in Louisiana, 2007; editor, author: (with others) Art & Bylaws for Moot Court, 1989, Advanced Topic in Communication Law, 2007; contbr.: The Silence Within, 2000. Del. Rep. Dist. IV, 1994—; bd. dirs. Shreveport Little Theatre, 1995-2000, Extra Mile, 1996—; vol. N.W. La. Coalition for Mentally Ill, 1995—, pres., 2002-05; vol. Shreveport/Bossier Svc. Connection, 2001—; liaison officer Gov.'s Health Consortia, 2004-; mem. LA Pro Bono Project, Tex. Bar Assn. Pro Bono Project (Outstanding Svc. award 2002); rewrite subcom. La. Legislation MR/DD, 2004-05, mem. legis. subcom. on involuntary commitment; capt. Shreveport Police Neighborhood Watch., 2007. Recipient Outstanding Svc. award, Tex. State Bar Pro Bono Project, 2002. Mem. ABA, La. Bar Assn. (mem. health law sect.), Miss. Pro Bono Project, Miss. Bar Assn., Assn. Trial Lawyers Am., La. Trial Lawyers Assn., Hancock County Bar Assn. (social chmn.), Shreveport Bar Assn. (comml. litigation sect., editor newsletter), TKE Alumni Assn. (pres.), Univ. Club (mem. com. 1994—). Roman Catholic. Avocations: martial arts, weightlifting, skiing, shooting. Home: PO Box 444 Shreveport LA 71162-0444 Personal E-mail: brucebeeee@yahoo.com.

BRYANT, JENNIFER CAMPBELL, mathematics educator; B, Ea. Ky. U., Richmond; M, Morehead State U. Instr. adult edn. Ky. Valley Ednl. Coop., Hazard; tchr. math. Owsley County H.S., Booneville, Ky. Coach acad. team Owsley County H.S., Booneville, coach mathcounts. Coord. Save the Children, Booneville, Ky. Scholar Burrier award, Ea. Ky. U., 1996. Mem.: NEA, Ky. Assn. Adult and Continuing Edn., Ky. Edn. Assn., Nat. Coun. Tchrs. Math. Office Phone: 606-593-5185.

BRYANT, JOHN A., food products executive; b. Brisbane, QLD, Australia, Nov. 6, 1965; m. Alison Bryant; 5 children. B Commerce, Australian Nat. U.; MBA, U. Pa. Various leadership positions Deloitte & Touche, Marakon and A.T. Kearney; with Kellogg Australia and Kellogg Europe, 1998; v.p. strategy devel./bus. understanding Kellogg N.Am.; v.p. fin. planning cereal Kellogg Co., 1998—2000, v.p. trade mktg., mem. sales leadership team Kellogg USA, 2000; sr. v.p., CFO Kellogg USA, 2000—02, mgr., natural & frozen foods divsn., 2003—; sr. v.p. Kellogg Co., 2002, exec. v.p., 2002—, CFO, 2002—04, 2006—; pres. Kellogg Internat., 2004—. Recipient Palmer Grad. scholarship, Wharton Sch., U. Pa. Mem.: Securities Inst. Australia (assoc.), Inst. Chartered Accts. Australia (assoc.). Office: Kellogg Co PO Box 3599 1 Kellogg Sq Battle Creek MI 49016-3599

BRYANT, JOHN BRADBURY, economics professor, consultant; b. July 7, 1947; s. Royal Calvin and Martha Preble (Jones) B.; m. Evelyn Sandra Seltzer, June 24, 1973; 1 child, Aryn Royale. BA, Oberlin Coll., 1969; MS, Carnegie-Mellon U., 1973, PhD, 1975. Economist, bd. govs. FRS, Washington, 1974-77; sr. economist Fed. Res. Bank, Mpls., 1977-81; assoc. prof. U. Fla., Gainesville, 1980-81; cons. Fed. Res. Bank, Dallas, 1983-86, 91-92; Fox assoc. prof. Rice U., Houston, 1981-84, Fox prof. econs., 1984—, prof. mgmt., 1987—. Vis. scholar Hoover Inst., Stanford U., 1988-89; vis. fellow Center, Tilburg U., Netherlands, 1998-99. Contbr. articles to profl. jours., chapters to books. Office: Rice U Dept Econs MS22 6100 Main St Houston TX 77005-1892 Business E-Mail: jbb@rice.edu.

BRYANT, JOSEPHINE HARRIET, library executive; b. Oshawa, Ont., Can., Dec. 3, 1947; d. Donald Joseph and Margaret Mary (Quilty) B.; children: David Joseph, Michael Andrew. BA, U. Toronto, Ont., 1969, BLS, 1970, MLS, 1974; diploma in Pub. Adminstrn., U. Western Ont., London, 1988. Libr. Ont. Hydro, Toronto, 1970-74; libr. supr. Brampton Pub. Libr. and Art Gallery, Ont., 1974-77, br. head Ont., 1977-79; regional dir. Fairview North York Pub. Libr., Ont., 1983-85, mgr. century libr. Ont., 1986, dep. dir. Ont., 1986-88, CEO Ont., 1988-98; city libr. Toronto Pub. Libr., Ont., 1998—. Jon Dellandrea scholarship com. U. Toronto; adv. com. Ctr. Fin. Svcs. Seneca Coll.; mem. Thomson Gale Strategic Adv. Bd. Mem. Toronto Bd. Trade. Mem. ALA, Can. Libr. Assn., Ont. Libr. Assn., Inst. Pub. Adminstrn., Urban Libr. Coun., Can. Urban Libr. Coun., Can. Urban Inst., Fedn. Ont. Pub. Librs., Public Libraries Internat. Network. Avocation: golf. Office: Toronto Pub Libr 789 Yonge St Toronto ON Canada M4W 2G8 Office Phone: 416-393-7032. Business E-Mail: jbryant@torontopubliclibrary.ca.

BRYANT, KAREN WORSTELL, financial advisor, investment company executive; b. Cadillac, Mich., Sept. 7, 1942; d. Harley Orville and Rose Edith (Bell) Worstell; children: Lynda Jean Bashoor, Tracey Jo Taylor, Cynthia Jill Bryant, Troy Thomas; m. Robert Melvin Bryant, Nov. 29, 1968. Student, Ctrl. Mich. U., 1963—67, Mich. State U., 1966, Johns Hopkins U., 1982—83, Loyola U., 1983. Registered fin. gerontologist U. NC, 2007. Sales rep. Xerox Corp., Southfield, Mich., 1972—74; cons. and employment contracts IBM World Trade Asia, The Policy Study Group, Johnson & Johnson Internat., Tokyo, 1974—79; mgr. area sales Universal Plastics, McLean, Va., 1979—81; exec. mgr. product Western Union Telegraph Co., Upper Saddle River, NJ, 1981—86; dir. mktg. and sales support Nat. Guardian Corp., Greenwich, Conn., 1986—88; v.p., fin. cons. Smith Barney, Paramus, NJ, 1988—97; sr. v.p., fin. advisor, retirement planning specialist Morgan Stanley, Pearl River, NY, 1997—. Guest lectr. for orgns.; guest on TV documentaries. Mem.: Nature Conservancy, World Wildlife Fedn., N.Y. State Horse Coun. Avocations: horseback riding, power boating, decorating, horticulture. Office: Morgan Stanley Box 1726 One Blue Hill Plz 1st Fl Pearl River NY 10965-2535 Home: PO Box 651 Pomona NY 10970-0651 Office Phone: 845-731-2535. E-mail: karen.bryant@morganstanley.com.

BRYANT, KEITH LYNN, JR., history professor; b. Oklahoma City, Nov. 6, 1937; s. Keith Lynn and Elsie L. (Furman) B.; m. Margaret A. Burum, Aug. 14, 1962; children: Jennifer Lynne, Craig Warne. BS, U. Okla., 1959, MEd, 1961; PhD, U. Mo., 1965. From asst. prof. to prof., assoc. dean U. Wis., Milw., 1965-76; prof. Coll. Liberal Arts Tex. A&M U., College Station, 1976-88, head dept. history Coll. Liberal Arts, 1976-80, dean, 1980-84; prof. history U. Akron, Ohio, 1988-2000, head dept. Ohio, 1988-95, prof. emeritus Ohio, 2000—. Cons. So. Ry., NEH. Author: Alfalfa Bill Murray, 1968, Arthur E. Stilwell, Promoter with a Hunch, 1971, History of the Atchison, Topeka and Santa Fe Railway, 1974, William Merritt Chase: A Genteel Bohemian, 1991, Culture in the American Southwest, 2001; co-author: A History of American Business, 1983; bd. editors Western Hist. Quar., 1984-87, Southwestern Hist. Quar., 1980-87; editor Railroads in the Age of Regulation, 1900-1980, 1988. Various offices local Rep. Party, Okla., Tex.; chmn. Bush for Pres., Brazos County, 1979-80. Served to 1st lt. U.S. Army, 1959-60. Recipient William H. Kiekhofer award U. Wis., 1968, George W. and Constance M. Hilton book award Ry. and Locomotive Hist. Soc., 1990, David P. Morgan Article award Ry. and Locomotive Hist. Soc., 1998; grantee Am. Philos. Soc., 1968, NEH, 1984. Mem. So. Hist. Assn. (chmn. Frank Owsley book award com. 1988), Western History Assn., Tex. Hist. Assn., Lexington Group, S.W. Conf. Humanities Consortium (pres. 1982-83). Home: PO Box 5366 Bryan TX 77805-5366

BRYANT, KIMBERLY ZIEGLER, dental hygienist, educator; b. Springfield, Mass., Nov. 20, 1955; d. John Taggart and Madge Merkley Ziegler; m. Jeffrey Charles Bryant, Sept. 8, 1979; children: Conor Jeffrey, Ashley Ziegler, Allison Shay. Cert. in dental hygiene, U. Pa., BS in Dental Hygiene; MS in Curriculum Devel. and Evaluation, SUNY, Albany, NY, 1989. Registered dental hygienist ADA, 1978. Assoc. prof. Hudson Valley C.C., Troy, NY, 1981—. Recipient President's Excellence in Tchg. award, Hudson Valley C.C., 1999. Mem.: NY State Dental Hygiene Educators Assn., Capital Dist. Dental Hygienists' Assn., Dental Hygienists' Assn. State of NY, Am. Dental Hygienists Assn. Office: Hudson Valley Cmty Coll 80 Vandenburgh Ave Troy NY 12180 Home Phone: 518-861-5243; Office Phone: 518-629-7450.

BRYANT, KOBE, professional basketball player; b. Phila., Aug. 23, 1978; s. Joe "Jellybean" and Pam Bryant; m. Vanessa Laine, Apr. 18, 2001; 1 child, Natalia. Player LA Lakers, 1996—. Mem. NBA Championship team, 2000, 01, 02. Named National HS Player of Yr. (Lower Merion HS), 1996, NBA All-Star Game MVP, 2002, 2007; named to All-NBA 1st Team, 2002—04, 2006—07, Western Conf. All-Star Team, NBA, 1998, 2000—07, NBA All-Defensive First Team, 2000, 2003, 2004, 2006; recipient Under Armour Undeniable Performance award (81 Points), ESPY award, 2006. Achievements include entering the NBA right out of high school; being the youngest player ever (19 yrs. of age) in NBA All-star game, 1998; scoring a career high 81 points in a single game (second-highest total in NBA history), 2006; winner of NBA scoring title, 2005-2006. Office: LA Lakers 555 N Nash St El Segundo CA 90245-2818*

BRYANT, LA KESHA JOY, physical education educator; b. Pa., June 27, 1980; d. Percy J. Bryant III and Darlene Smith Bryant. BA, Rowan U., Glassboro, NJ, 2004. EMT Nat. Registry of EMTs; std. cert. tchr. of health and phys. edn. State Bd. of Edn., basic mil. tng. course USAF. Cashier Dollar Store, Washington, NJ, 1996—98; dispatcher C.O.P.S. Monitoring, Williamstown, NJ, 1998—2005; asst. sec. Inst. of Bus. Mgmt., Rowan U., Glassboro, 1998—2000; mem. phys. and recreation asst. staff Equal Opportunity Fund/Minority Achievement Program Pre-Coll. Inst., Rowan U., Glassboro, 2001, 177th Figther Wing, Air N.G., Egg Harbor Township, NJ, 2002—; substitute tchr. Wash. Twp. Bd. of Edn., NJ, 2004—05; tchr. of health and phys. edn. Gloucester County Inst. of Tech., Sewell, NJ, 2005—. Coach jr. varsity cheerleading Gloucester County Inst. of Tech., Sewell, NJ, 2005—; adviser Christian Fellowship of Athletes, Gloucester County Inst. of Tech., Sewell, 2005—; mem. Airmen's Coun., Egg Habor Township, NJ, 2002—. Mem., treas. NAACP, Glassboro, 1999—2004; mem., corr. sec., parliamentarian Black Cultural League, Rowan U., Glassboro, 1999—2002; vol. coach Glassboro Midget Football / Cheerleading Assn., 2002—03; mem., historian, treas. Nat. Panhellenic Coun., Rowan U., Glassboro, 2000—04; mem., historian 3-D Dance (Dangerously Diverse Dancers), Rowan U., Glassboro, 1998—2004; mem., sr. yr. capt. Clayton H.S. Field Hockey, 1994—98; mgr. Clayton H.S. Girls Basketball, 1995—96; v.p., mem. Students United for Racial Equality Club, Clayton, 1993—98. Named Student of the Month, Clayton Pub. Sch., 1994—96, Airman of the Quar., 177th Figther Wing Air N.G., 2005; recipient Honors Acad. awards, Clayton Pub. Schs., 1994—97, Student Excellent awards, 1994—97, USAF Cert. of Appreciation Sheppard AFB Chapel Squadron Program, Sheppard AFB Chapel Rope Program Dir., 2004. Mem.: AAHPERD (assoc.), Alpha Kappa Alpha (assoc.). Home Phone: 856-881-6807; Office Phone: 856-468-1446.

BRYANT, LELAND MARSHAL, business and nonprofit executive; b. Gainesville, Ga., Apr. 28, 1950; s. William Marcus and Pierre Lou (Milner) B.; children: Shauna, Natalie, Marcus, Jacob. Student, Vanderbilt U., 1968-70; BBA with hons., U. Tex., 1972; MBA, U. Pa., 1978. CPA, Tex. Acct. Arthur Andersen and Co., Dallas, 1978-81; exec. v.p. Walter Bennet Comms., Dallas, 1981-89; pres. Grand Canyon Railway, Flagstaff, Ariz., 1989-97; v.p., CFO, Grand Canyon (Ariz.) Assn., 1997—. Pres. Fray

Marcos Hotel, Flagstaff, 1995-97. Bd. dirs. Grand Canyon Nat. Park Found., 1995—; nat. adv. bd. No. Ariz. U., Flagstaff, 1994-97. Mem. AICPA, Grand Canyon Assn. (bd. dirs. 1995-97), Nat. Parks Conservation Assn. (nat. adv. coun. 1995-98). Republican. Office: Grand Canyon Assn PO Box 399 Grand Canyon AZ 86023-0399

BRYANT, MELISSA LEE, elementary school educator; d. Jerry Lee and Joyce June Wells; m. Rusty Bryant, Sept. 30, 1988; children: Kyle, Marshall. BS in Elem. Edn., North Tex. State U., Denton, 1985. Tchr. Long Elem. Sch., Garland, Tex., 1985—2003; curriculum specialist math. Garland Ind. Sch. Dist., 2003—.

BRYANT, MOLLIE ANNETTE, rehabilitation services professional, director; b. Columbus, Ga., Apr. 5, 1949; d. Nathan and Lula Pearl Bryant; children: Reginald Dennard Bush, Erica Denise Bush. MEd, Ga. State U., 1978. Lic. counselor, mental health profl., substance abuse profl. Ga. Rehab. counselor Ga. Divsn. Rehab. Svcs., Decatur, 1980—95; dir. Comprehensive Vocat. Svcs., Atlanta, 1994—95; counselor New Horizons Cmty. Svc. Bd., Columbus, Ga., 2000—02; clin. dir. Ga. Therapy Assoc., Columbus, 2002—. Social resources cons. L.I.F.E., Inc., Stone Mountain, Ga., 1992—2006. Sponsoring founder Martin Luther King, Jr. Nat. Meml., Washington, 2006; mem. So. Poverty Law Ctr., Montgomery, Ala., 2005; sponsoring founder Civil Rights / Wall of Tolerance, Montgomery, 2005. Mem.: ASPCA, Nat. Assn. Negro Bus. and Profl. Women's Club, Inc., Humane Soc., Alpha Kappa Alpha. Home: 5280 Kingsberry St Columbus GA 31907-4233 Office: Georgia Therapy Assoc 1301 Wynnton Ct Columbus GA 31906 Home Phone: 706-565-6313; Office Phone: 706-576-4033. Office Fax: 706-576-4230; Home Fax: 706-576-4230. Personal E-mail: bryantmollie@bellsouth.net. Business E-Mail: mbryantgtacol@bellsouth.net.

BRYANT, MYNORA JOYCE, not-for-profit fundraiser; EdD, U. Md. Coord. counseling svcs. and student activities No. Va. CC; internat. grand basileus Sigma Gamma Rho. Named one of 100 Most Influential Black Americans, Ebony mag., 2006. Office: Ste 200 1000 Southhill Dr Cary NC 27513 Office Phone: 919-678-9721. E-mail: Mbryant@nvcc.edu.

BRYANT, RICHARD TODD, lawyer; b. Kansas City, Mo., Sept. 3, 1952; s. Francis Todd and Marion Audrey (Weum) Bryant; m. Carol H. Olsen, Mar. 24, 1979. AA, AAS, Longview C.C., 1972; BBA, U. Mo., Kansas City, 1974, MPA, 1975, JD, 1978. Bar: Mo. 1978, U.S. Dist. Ct. (we. dist.) Mo. 1978, DC 1995, U.S. Dist. Ct. (ea. dist.) Mo. 1995, Kans. 1996, Superior Ct. V.I. 1999, Iowa 2002. Assoc. Harding & Copilevitz P.C., Kansas City, Mo., 1978—85; ptnr. Copilevitz, Bryant, Gray & Jennings, P.C., Kansas City, 1985-95; bailiff ct. Overland Park, Kans., 1974-84; ptnr. Richard T. Bryant & Assocs. PC, Kansas City, 1995-98, mng. shareholder, 1998—. Cons. Westwood & Lenexa (Kans.) Police Dept., 1977—78. Contbr. articles to profl. jours. Adminstrv. hearing officer Housing Authority Kansas City, 1988—; chmn. ad hoc com. Kansas City City Coun., 1992. Mem.: ABA (mem. com. adminstrn. cirminal justice 1977—78, mem. liaison standing com. assn. stds. criminal justice 1978), First Amendment Lawyers, Kansas City Bar Assn. (mem. mcpl. ct. com., vice chmn. 1991—94, chmn. 1994—95), Am. Arbitration Assn. (bd. arbitrators, bd. mediators), Phi Theta Kappa, Omicron Delta Kappa, Phi Delta Phi. Office: 804 Bryant Bldg 1102 Grand Blvd Kansas City MO 64106-2316 Office Phone: 816-221-9000. Personal E-mail: dick2479@aol.com.

BRYANT, ROBERT LEAMON, mathematics educator; b. Harnett County, NC, Aug. 30, 1953; s. James Ray and Josephine (Strickland) B. BS, NC State U., Raleigh, 1974; PhD in Math., U. NC, Chapel Hill, 1979. Asst. prof. Rice U., Houston, 1979-81, assoc. prof., 1981-82, prof., 1982-85, Noah Harding prof., 1986—88; prof. Duke U., Durham, ND, 1984, arts and sciences prof., 1987-88, Juanita M. Kreps prof., 1988—. Assoc. prof. Harvard U., 1982; mem. Max Planck Inst., 1985, Institue des Hautes Etudes Scientifiques, 1985, Instituto Nacional de Matematica Pura e Applicada, 1986, 90, visitor, 96; W.R. Reynolds prof. U. NC, Chapel Hill, 1987; visitor U. Adelaide, 1993, Nankai Inst. Math., 1995; director's visitor Inst. for Advanced Study, 1993; Andre Aisenstadt prof. Centre de Recherches Mathematique, 1984; prof. Inst. Elie Cartan, 1998; Samuel Eilenberg prof. Columbia U., 2004; Nachdiplom lectr. Eidgenössische Technische Hochschule Zürich, 2006; mem. Math. Sciences Rsch. Inst., Berkeley, Calif., 1983, Berkeley, 94, trustee, 1999—2004, chmn. bd., 2001—04, sr. visitor, 2001, Clay rsch. prof., 2001—02, Simons Rsch. prof., 2003, co-organizer, rsch. program in differential geometry, 03, dir.-elect, 07, dir., 2007—; dir. undergrad. program Inst. for Advanced Study (IAS)/Park City Math. Inst. (PCMI), 1993—2000, mem. steering com., 2006—07, dir., 2007—; invited lectr. in field. Mem. editl. bd. Duke Mathematical Journal, 1997, Differential Geometry and Its Applications, 1999, Communications in Analysis and Geometry, 2002; contbr. articles to profl. jours. Academic mem. bd. dir. Vietnam Edn. Found., 2002—05; bd. visitor Harvard U., 2001—04. Mem., NSF Postdoctoral Fellow, Inst. for Advanced Study, 1979-80, Alfred P. Sloan fellow, 1982-84; recipient Presdl. Young Investigator award NSF, 1984-89, Trinity Coll. Disting. Tchg., 1992, Disting. Alumni award, Coll. Phys. and Math. Sciences, NC State U. Alumni Assn., 2005 Fellow: NAS; mem.: Math. Assn. Am. (southeastern sect. lectr. 2001—03, Southeastern Region Disting. Tchg. 1993), Am. Math. Soc. (past chair, com. on publications 1998—2004, exec. coun. 2000—04, assoc. editor 2005—08, mem. editl. bd. com. 2006—, v.p. 2007, mem. editl. bd. com. and on von Neumann Symposium Com., coun. mem.-at-large, Coun. Am. Math. Soc., mem. task force on membership 1998—2000, editor, Transactions 1992—97), Am. Acad. Arts & Sciences, Chamber Arts Soc. Durham, NC (dir., dir. emeritus), Phi Beta Kappa. Democrat. Home: 6310 Turkey Farm Rd Chapel Hill NC 27514-9590 Office: Duke U 128A Physics Building Durham NC 27706 Office Phone: 919-660-2805. Office Fax: 919-660-2821. Business E-Mail: bryant@math.duke.edu.*

BRYANT, RUTH ALYNE, banker; b. Memphis, Jan. 12, 1924; d. James Walter and Leola (Edgar) B. Student, Rhodes Coll. (formerly Southwestern Coll.), Memphis, 1941-43; LHD (hon.), U. Mo., St. Louis, 1990. Clk. Fed. Res. Bank of St. Louis (Memphis Br.), 1943-47, exec. sec., 1947-68, asst. cashier, 1968-69, asst. v.p., 1969-73, v.p., 1973-90. Trustee chancellor's coun. U. Mo., St. Louis, 1979—, chmn., 1985-88; pres. Premiere Performances, 1990-96, vice chmn., 1996-98, bd. dirs., 1998; mem. adv. bd. Salvation Army, St. Louis, 1983-91, DePaul Health Ctr., St. Louis, 1984-87; adv. coun. Hope Ctr., St. Louis, 1987, chmn., 1990-91; chmn. adv. coun. Riverway Sch., 1989-95; bd. dirs. Assocs. of St. Louis U. Librs., 1977—, pres., 1983-85; bd. dirs. The Vanderschmidt's Sch., 1980-86, Internat. Edn. Consortium, 1988-92; bd. dirs. St. Louis Merc. Libr., 1989—, sec., 1990-92, v.p., 1992-94, pres., 1994-2000; trustee Mo. Coun. on Econ. Edn., 1989-93; bd. dirs. Dance St. Louis, 1992—2003, v.p., 1993-94, English Lang. Sch., 1993-97; mem. devel. bd. U. Mo. Press, 2002—; bd. dirs. Ctr. French Colonial Studies, 1994-, pres. 2003-. Fellow: Winston Churchill Meml.; mem.: Bank Mktg. Assn. (dir. Mo.-Ill. chpt. 1976—79), English Speaking Union (bd. dirs. 1989—, 1989—, v.p. 1992—96, nat. bd. dirs. 1995—96, pres. 1997—, nat. bd. dirs. 1998—2004), Nat. Assn. Bank Women (editor Woman Banker 1959—62, v.p. so. region 1967—68, pres. 1970—71, trustee ednl. found. 1974—75), Mo. Bankers Assn. (mktg. and pub. rels. com. 1974—76), Am. Inst. Banking (nat. women's com. 1962—63, pres. Memphis chpt. 1968—69), Alliance Francaise of St. Louis (exec. v.p. 2001—03, pres. 2003—), Nat. Soc. Arts and Letters, Rhodes Coll. Internat. Alumni Assn. (exec. bd. 1999—2000), Univ. Club (St. Louis), The Venerable Order of St. John in Jerusalem (comdr.). Home: 625 S Skinker Blvd Apt 202 Saint Louis MO 63105-2301

BRYANT, SUSAN V., academic administrator; m. David Gardiner. BSc, King's Coll. London U., 1964; PhD in Developmental Biology, St. Mary's Hosp. Med. Sch. U. London, 1967. Postdoctoral fellow Case Western Reserve U., Cleve.; with U. Calif. Irvine, 1969—, asst. vice chancellor for plans and programs, 1973—75, acting dean, sch. biol. sciences, 1979—80, chair, developmental & cell biology, 1995—97, prof., developmental & cell biology, sch. biol. sciences, dean, sch. biol. sciences, 2000—06, vice chancellor for rsch., 2006—. Mem. Calif. Independent Citizen's Oversight Com., Calif. Regenerative Medicine; mem. adv. bd. VA office Regeneration Programs; program dir., developmental biology program NSF, 1981—82; spkr. in field. Contbr. scientific papers; mem. editl. bd.. Developmental Biology, Regenerative Medicine, Journal Experimental Zoology. Mem. Ind. U. Axolotl Colony. Fellow: Assn. Women in Sci.; mem.: Am. Soc. for Cell Biology, Soc. for Developmental Biology, AAAS. Office: U Calif Sch Biol Sciences 100 BSA Mail Code 1450 Irvine CA 92697 Office Phone: 949-824-5316. Office Fax: 949-824-3035. Business E-Mail: svbryant@uci.edu.

BRYANT, TAIMIE L., law educator; b. 1953; BA, Bryn Mawr Coll., 1975; MA Anthropology, UCLA, 1978, PhD, 1984; JD, Harvard U., 1987, Acting prof. law UCLA, LA, 1987—, prof. law (property, nonprofit organs.,animals law), 1995—. Lead drafter Calif. state (legis. shift animal sheltering from killing to saving lives), 1998. Writing articles that concern issues of theory in animal law; contbr. Office: UCLA Sch Law Box 951476 Los Angeles CA 90095-1476 Office Phone: 310-825-4841. Business E-Mail: bryant@law.ucla.edu.

BRYANT, TAMMI D., history professor; BS in History, U. Mo., Kansas City, 1998, BS in Edn., 1998; M, Baker U., Baldwin City, 2001. Tchr. Belton High Sch., Mo., 1998—. Sponsor SADD; sophomore class sponsor; text mentor Avila Coll. Mem.: Mo. State Tchrs. Assn., Nat. Coun. Social Studies. Office: Belton High Sch 107 Pirate Pkwy Belton MO 64012 Office Phone: 816-348-2768. Business E-Mail: tbryant@bsd124.org.

BRYANT, THOMAS LEE, magazine editor; b. Daytona Beach, Fla., June 15, 1943; s. Stanley Elson and G. Bernice (Burgess) B.; m. Patricia Jean Bryant, June 30, 1979. BA in Polit. Sci., U. Calif., Santa Barbara, 1965, MA in Polit. Sci., 1966. Fgn. svc. officer U.S. Dept. State, Washington, Buenos Aires, 1967-69; radio broadcaster KDB Sta., Santa Barbara, Calif., 1969-72; magazine editor, now editor-in-chief Road & Track, Newport Beach, Calif., 1972—. Mem. Internat. Motor Press Assn., Motor Press Guild, Sports Car Club of Am. Avocations: golf, skeet shooting. Office: c/o Hachette Filipacchi Mags Inc 1499 Monrovia Ave Newport Beach CA 92663-2752*

BRYANT, TIMOTHY CLARK, investment brokerage executive; b. Akron, Ohio, Apr. 11, 1943; s. Alan Willard and Clara Sherman (Clark) B.; m. Mary Esther Snell, Jan. 17, 1981. AB, Dartmouth Coll., 1967; MBA, U. Chgo., 1971; MS in Taxation, DePaul U., 1975. CPA, Ill. Dir. fin. and adminstrn. Fibre Box Assn., Chgo., 1975-77, Akers Packaging Co., Middletown, Ohio, 1977-78; dir., sec., treas. CompuShop, Inc., Dallas, 1978-80, dir., 1980-85; v.p. fin., dir. Rubicon Corp., Richardson, Tex., 1980-82, Automated Mgmt. Inc., Dallas, 1982-83, Avian Corp., Clearwater, Fla., 1983-85, pres., bd. dirs., 1985-87; v.p. investments A.G. Edwards and Sons, 1990—. Chmn. bd. dirs. Adventures Away, Inc., Chgo., 1983-87; pres., treas., bd. dirs. Talk2 Corp., Clearwater, 1987-90; cons. Nevada Brake Corp., 1985-91, So. Conf. Bur., Inc., 1987-90, Innovative Products Group, Inc., 1987-90. With U.S. Army, 1965-66, Korea. Mem. AICPA, Chgo. Yacht Club, Vinoy Club. Home: 307 Brightwaters Blvd NE Saint Petersburg FL 33704-3709 Office: A G Edwards & Sons 700 Central Ave Saint Petersburg FL 33701 Office Phone: 727-550-2222.

BRYANT, VANESSA LYNNE, federal judge, lawyer; b. Queens, NY, Jan. 27, 1954; d. George Dewey and Muriel Louise (Black) B.; m. Tracy L. Rich, Apr. 11, 1981; children: Bryant Rich, Dana Rich. BA, Howard U., 1975; JD, U. Conn., Hartford, 1978. Assoc. Day, Berry & Howard, Hartford, 1978-81; counsel Aetna Life & Casualty Co., Hartford, 1981-88, Shawmut Bank, Hartford, 1989—90; v.p., gen. counsel Conn. Housing Fin. Authority, Rocky Hill, 1990-92; ptnr. Hawkins, Delafield & Wood, Hartford, 1992—98; judge Conn. Superior Ct., Hartford, 1998—2007, US Dist. Ct. Conn., Hartford, 2007—. Bd. dirs. Greater Hartford Rehab. Ctr., 1992, U. Conn. Found., Storrs, 1992, Greater Hartford Arts Coun., 1992; alt. del. Rep. Nat. Conv., 1980, 92; mem. Avon (Conn.) Rep. Town Com. Mem. Conn. Bar Assn. (exec. com. comml. law sect.), George W. Crawford Law Assn. (bd. dirs. 1991—). Republican. Baptist. Avocations: cooking, jogging, theater. Office: US Dist Ct 450 Main St Hartford CT 06103*

BRYANT, WARREN F., retail executive; BA, Calif. State U., LA; MBA, Azusa Pacific U. Sr. v.p. supermarket divsn. Dillon Co. Inc., pres., CEO, 1995—99; sr. v.p. Kroger Co., 1999—2002; CEO, pres. Long Drug Stores Corp., 2002—, chmn., 2003—, acting COO, 2003, 2005—. Bd. dirs. Pathmark Stores Inc., Boise Cascade Corp. Office: 141 N Civic Dr Walnut Creek CA 94596*

BRYCE, TERESA AUDREY, lawyer; b. Norfolk, Va., July 31, 1959; d. Burie O'Neal and Dorothy Mae (Hicks) Bryce. BA, U. Va., 1981; JD, Columbia U., NYC, 1984. Bar: Md. 1985, DC 1985. Rsch. asst., legis. drafting rsch. fund Columbia U. Sch. Law, NYC, 1983-84; law clk. to Chief Justice Robert N. Wilentz NJ Supreme Ct., Perth Amboy, 1984-85; assoc. Piper & Marbury, Balt., 1985-90; v.p., assoc. gen. counsel Prudential Ins. Co. of Am., Frederick, Md., 1990-94; v.p., gen. counsel PNC Mortgage Corp. of Am., Vernon Hills, Ill., 1994-97; assoc. gen. counsel Bank of Am. Corp., Charlotte, NC, 1997; gen. counsel Bank of Am. Mortgage, Charlotte, NC, 1997; gen. counsel, sr. v.p., sec. Nexstar Fin. Corp.; exec. v.p., gen. counsel, sec. Radian Grp. Inc., Phila., 2006—. Mem. Chesapeake Bay Outward Bound Prog. adv. bd., Balt., 1988-93; bd. dirs. Total Health Care, Balt., 1988-90, Parks and People Found., Balt., 1993-94, Cmtys. in Schs., Charlotte, 1998—; mem. Coalition of 100 Black Women of Greater Charlotte; bd. mem. Shakespeare Festival, 2004; mem. bd. mgrs. U. Va. Alumni Assn. Named one of Most Influential Bus. Women, St. Louis Bus. Jour., 2004; recipient Distng. Svc. award, Mortgage Bankers Assn. Am., 2005. Mem. ABA (forum on affordable housing and cmty. devel. law, fair housing practice divsn. 1989—, sect. real property, probate and trust law 1986—, com. secondary market financing of affordable housing 1995—, mortgages and financing of home ownership com. 1993—), Md. Bar Assn., DC Bar Assn., Am. Corp. Counsel Assn., Leary Bar Assn. (treas. 1998-99), Alliance of Black Women Attys. (treas. 1987-88), Mortgage Bankers Assn. (resdl. bd. govs., legis. com., state legis. and regulatory com. chair 1996-97, chair legal issues com. 1998-99, state issues pub. policy liaison 1996—, mem. RESPA/TILA task force, Am. State and Local Svc. award 1999, Disting. Svc. award 2005), Rsch. Inst. Housing Am. (exec. com.), Delta Sigma Theta. Presbyterian. Avocations: golf, reading, tennis, theater. Office: Radian Grp Inc 1601 Market St Philadelphia PA 19103*

BRYCE, WILLIAM DELF, lawyer; b. Georgetown, Tex., Aug. 7, 1932; s. D.A. Bryce and Frances Maxine (Wilson) Bryce Bakke; m. Sarah Alice Riley, Dec. 20, 1954; children: Douglas Delf, David Dickson. BA, U. Tex., 1955; LLB, Yale U., 1960. Bar: Tex. 1960. Briefing atty. Tex. Supreme Ct., Austin, 1960-61; sole practice, 1961—. Lectr. U. Tex., 1965—66. Served to 1st lt. USAF, 1955—57. Fellow Tex. Bar Found. (sustaining; life); mem. ABA, State Bar Tex., Austin Bar Assn., Williamson County Bar Assn., Rotary Internat. (dist. 5870 gov. 1999-2000). Office: 511 S Main St Georgetown TX 78626-5609 Home: 119 Blue Quail Dr Georgetown TX 78628

BRYCHTOVA, JAROSLAVA, sculptor; b. Semily, Czechoslovakia, 1924; m. Stanislav Libensky (dec. Feb. 2002). Student, Acad. Applied Arts, Prague, Czechoslovakia, 1945—51, Acad. Fine Arts, Prague, 1947—50. Designer Zeleznobrodské sklo, Zelezny Brod, Czech Republic, 1950—84. Guest lectr. Pilchuck Summer Sch., Stanwood, Wash., Ctr. Creative Studies, Detroit, others; presenter in field. also: Heller Gallery 420 W 14th St New York NY 10014-1064 Office Phone: 212-414-4014.

BRYDGES, THOMAS EUGENE, lawyer; b. Niagara Falls, NY, June 1, 1942; s. Earl W. and Eleanor M. (Mahoney) B.; m. Melissa May, May 26, 1990; children: Andrew MacLeod, Elizabeth Hendricks. BA in History, Syracuse U., 1971, JD, 1973. Bar: N.Y. 1974, U.S. Dist. (we. dist.) N.Y. 1974, U.S. Ct. Appeals (2d cir.) 1978. Assoc. Jaeckle, Fleischmann & Mugel, Buffalo, 1973-78, ptnr., 1979—. Bd. dirs., sec. Theodore Roosevelt Inagural site, 1999—. Author: (with others) Employment Discrimination Law, 1980—. Trustee Daemen Coll., Amherst, N.Y., 1988—; bd. dirs., v.p. Art Park & Co., Lewiston, N.Y., 1976—. Capt. U.S. Army, 1962-68, Vietnam. Decorated Bronze Star, Air medal, Army Commendation (2). Mem. ABA (labor sect.), Erie County Bar Assn. (bd. dirs. 2002--), N.Y. Bar Assn. (labor law com.). Office: Jaeckle Fleischmann & Mugel 12 Fountain Plaza Buffalo NY 14202 Office Phone: 716-843-3812. E-mail: tbrydges@jaeckle.com.

BRYFONSKI, DEDRIA ANNE, publishing executive; b. Utica, NY, Aug. 21, 1947; d. Lewis Francis and Catherine Marie (Stevens) B.; m. Alexander Burgess Cruden, May 24, 1975 BA, Nazareth Coll., Rochester, NY, 1969; MA, Fordham U., 1970. Editorial asst. Dial Press, NYC, 1970-71; editor Walker & Co., NYC, 1971-73; from editor to v.p., assoc. editl. dir. Gale Rsch. Co., Detroit, 1974—84, from sr. v.p., editl. dir. to pres., CEO, 1984—98; pres. Gale Pub. Gale Group, Farmington Hills, Mich., 1999—2002; exec. v.p. Thomson Gale, Farmington Hills, 2003—06; pres. Rethorica, Grosse Pointe, Mich., 2007—. Author: The New England Beach Book, 1974; editor: Contemporary Literary Criticism, Vols. 7-14, 1977-80, Twentieth Century Literary Criticism, vols. 1-2, 1977-78, Contemporary Issues Criticism, vol. 1, 1982, Contemporary Authors Autobiography Series, vol. 1, 1984 Bd. dirs. Friends of Detroit Pub. Libr., 1980-89, pres., 1984-86; bd. dirs. Friends of Librs. U.S.A., 1995-2003. Mem. ALA, Assn. Am. Pubs. (chmn. libraries com. 1983-85, exec. council gen. pub. div. 1985-87, co-chmn. joint com. resources and tech. services div. 1983-85), Am. Friends of Vatican Libr. (bd. dirs. 2005—). Home and Office: 546 Lincoln Rd Grosse Pointe MI 48230-1218 E-mail: rethorica@comcast.net.

BRYMER, CHARLES EDWARD (CHUCK BRYMER), advertising executive; b. Chgo., July 30, 1959; s. Robert Lewis and Natalie (Snell) B.; m. Virginia Tate, June 12, 1982; children: Lindsay Rae, Hope Carlyle. BS, U. Ky., 1981. Gen. mgr./acct. mgmt. BBDO, Inc., Houston, 1982-84; acct. mgr., 1984-85; vice chmn. Interbrand Corp., NYC, 1985—94, chmn., CEO, 1994—2006; pres., CEO DDB Worldwide Comm. Group Inc., NYC, 2006—. Bd. dirs. Interbrand Group PLC, London. Fellow: Am. Mktg. Assn. Republican. Presbyterian. Avocations: golf, speaking. Office: DDB Worldwide Communications Group Inc 437 Madison Ave New York NY 10022 Office Phone: 212-415-2000.*

BRYNER, ALEXANDER O., state supreme court justice; b. Tientsin, China, 1943; m. Carol Crump; 2 children. BA, Stanford U., 1966, JD, 1969. Law clk. to Chief Justice George Boney Alaska Supreme Ct., 1969-71; legal editor Bancroft Whitney Co., San Francisco, 1971; with Pub. Defender Agy., Anchorage, 1972-74; ptnr. Bookman, Bryner & Shortell, 1974; Alaska dist. ct. judge Anchorage, 1975-77; U.S. atty. Alaska, 1977-80; chief judge Alaska Ct. Appeals, 1980-97; state supreme ct. justice Alaska Supreme Ct., Anchorage, 1997—, state supreme ct. chief justice, 2003—06. Office: Alaska Supreme Ct 303 K St Anchorage AK 99501-2013

BRYNJOLFSSON, ARI, nuclear physicist; b. Akureyri, Iceland, Dec. 7, 1926; arrived in U.S., 1965, naturalized, 1970; s. Brynjolfur and Gudrun (Rosinkarsdottir) Sigtryggsson; m. Marguerite Reman, Dec. 22, 1950; children: Ariane, Olaf, Erik, John, Alan Cand. Phil., U. Copenhagen, 1949, Cand. Mag., 1954, Mag. Scien., 1954; Dr.Phil., Niels Bohr Inst., U. Copenhagen, 1973; post grad., Advanced Mgmt. Program, Harvard U., 1971. Dir. radiation rsch. Danish Atomic Energy Rsch. Establishment, Roskilde, Denmark, 1957-65; chief radiation rsch. U.S. Army Natick (Mass.) Lab., 1965—72, dir. U.S. food irradiation program, 1972—80, spl. asst. for physics, 1980—88; project dir. Facility for Food Irradiation Tech. UN Joint FAO/IAEA Divsn., Wageningen, Netherlands, 1988-90; project dir. internat. tng. ctr. joint FAO/IAEA divsn. Internat. Atomic Energy Agy., Vienna, 1990-92; pres. Applied Radiation Industries, Wayland, Mass., 1992—. Contbr. articles to profl. jours. Subspecialties: Nuclear physics; radiation biology. Current work: Astrophysics, theoretical physics, general theory of relativity. Biological effects of radiation. Spl. scholar NRC and U. Iceland, 1954-55, Alexander von Humboldt scholar U. Göttingen, Fed. Republic Germany, 1955-57; recipient Mollers Found. award for exceptional svc. to Danish industry, 1965, Tech. award Am. Nuc. Soc. Radiation Sci., 1988. Mem.: Am. Phys. Soc. Home and Office: Applied Radiation Industries 7 Bridle Path Wayland MA 01778-3206 E-mail: aribrynjolfsson@comcast.net.

BRYNJOLFSSON, ERIK, finance educator, researcher; b. Roskilde, Denmark, Apr. 14, 1962; m. Martha Pavlakis. AB, SM, Harvard U., 1984; PhD, MIT, 1991. Ptnr., co. founder Foundation Technologies, Cambridge, Mass., 1986-90; instr. Harvard U.; asst. prof. MIT Sloan Sch., Cambridge, Mass., 1990-95, assoc. prof., Douglas Drane chair, 1995-2000, Schussel chair, prof., 2001—; dir. Ctr. for Digital Bus. MIT, 1999—. Vis. prof. Stanford (Calif.) U., 1996-98, Marvin Bower fellow Harvard Bus. Sch., Boston, 2004-05. Contbr. numerous articles to profl. jours. Office: MIT Sloan Sch 50 Memorial Dr Rm E53-313 Cambridge MA 02142-1347

BRYNN, EDWARD PAUL, former ambassador; b. Pitts., Aug. 1, 1942; s. Walter Bruggeman and Mary Margaret (Callahan) B.; m. Jane Cooke , Apr. 1, 1967; children: Sarah, Edward, Kiernan, Anne-Elizabeth, Justin-Oliver. BS in Fgn. Svc., Georgetown U., 1964; MA in History, Stanford U., 1965, Phd in History, 1968; MLitt, Trinity Coll., Dublin, Ireland, 1968, PhD in Politics, 1977. Prof. history USAF Acad., Colorado Springs, Colo., 1968-72, 76-78; polit. officer Am. Embassy, Colombo, Sri Lanka, 1973-75, Bamako, Mali, 1978-80, dep. chief of mission Nouakchott, Mauritania, 1982-85, Moroni, Comoros, 1985-87, charge d'affaires Yaounde, Cameroon, 1987-89, amb. Ouagadougou, Burkina Faso, 1990-93, Accra, Ghana, 1995—98; staff mem. Senate Select Com. on Intelligence, Washington, 1981-82; prin. dep. asst. sec. Bur. of African Affairs, 1993-95; internat. affairs advisor Nat. War Coll., Washington, 1998-99; assoc. provost internat. programs U. N.C., Charlotte, 1999—2005. Chmn. Charlotte World Affairs Coun., 2002—04; tng prof. history U. N.C., Charlotte, 2005—. Author: Crown and Castle, 1979, Church of Ireland, 1980. Lt. col. USAFR, 1990. Mem. Am. Fgn. Svc. Assn. Home: 3306 Lakewood Edge Dr Charlotte NC 28269 Office Phone: 704-687-2414. E-mail: ebrynn@email.uncc.edu.

BRYNTESON, SUSAN, library director; May Morris dir. librs. U. Del., Newark, 1980—. Bd. dirs. Ctr. for Rsch. Librs., Chgo.; bd. mem. Chesapeake Info. and Rsch. Libr. Alliance. Mem.: Assn. Rsch. Librs., Am. Libr. Assn. Coun., Assn. Libr. Collections and Tech. Svcs. (past pres.), Yaddo (life; libr., spl. advisor, mem. bd. dirs. 1998—), Grolier Club. Office: U Del Libr 181 S College Ave Newark DE 19716-5267 Office Phone: 302-831-2231. E-mail: susanb@udel.edu.*

BRYSON, JOHN E., utilities executive; b. NYC, July 24, 1943; m. Louise Henry BA with distinction, Stanford U., 1965; student, Freie U. Berlin, Federal Republic Germany, 1965-66; JD, Yale U., 1969. Bar: Calif., Oreg., D.C. Asst. in instrn. Law Sch., Yale U., New Haven, 1968-69; law clk. U.S. Dist. Ct., San Francisco, 1969-70; co-founder, atty. Natural Resources Def. Council, 1970-74; vice chmn. Oreg. Energy Facility Siting Council, 1975-76; assoc. Davies, Biggs, Strayer, Stoel & Boley, Portland, Oreg., 1975-76; chmn. Calif. State Water Resources Control Bd., 1976-79; vis. faculty Stanford U. Law Sch., Calif., 1977-79; pres. Calif. Pub. Utilities Commn., 1979-82; ptnr. Morrison & Foerster, San Francisco, 1983-84; sr. v.p. law and fin. So. Calif. Edison Co., Rosemead, 1984; exec. v.p., chief fin. officer Edison Internat. and So. Calif. Edison Co., 1985-90, chmn. of bd., CEO Rosemead, 1990-99; chmn., pres., CEO Edison Internat., 2000—. Lectr. on pub. utility, energy, communications law.; former mem. exec. com. Nat. Assn. Regulatory Utility Commrs., Calif. Water Rights Law Rev. Commn., Calif. Pollution Control Financing Authority; former mem. adv. bd. Solar Energy Research Inst., Electric Power Research Inst., Stanford Law Sch.; bd. dirs. Pacific Am. Income Shares Inc., The Boeing Co., Walt Disney Co. Mem. bd. editors, assoc. editor: Yale U. Law Jour. Past bd. dirs. World Resources Inst., Washington, Calif. Environ. Trust, Claremont U. Ctr., Grad. Sch., Stanford U. Alumni Assn.; bd. dirs. The Keck Found., Calif. Endowment, 2003-; former trustee Stanford U., 1991. Woodrow Wilson fellow Mem. Calif. Bar Assn., Oreg. Bar Assn., D.C. Bar Assn., Nat. Assn. Regulatory Utility Commrs. (exec. com. 1980-82), Stanford U. Alumni Assn. (bd. dirs. 1983-86), Phi Beta Kappa. Office: Edison Internat 2244 Walnut Grove Ave Rosemead CA 91770-3714*

BRYSON, LOUISE HENRY, broadcast executive; m. John E. Bryson; 4 children. BA, Univ. Wash.; MAT, MBA, Stanford Univ. V.p. Nat. Broadcasting Co.; sr. v.p. FX Networks; exec. v.p., distbn. & bus. devel. Lifetime Television, 1999—2005; exec. v.p. gen. mgr. Lifetime Movie Network, 2005—; pres. distbn. & bus. develop. Lifetime Television, 2005—. Past dir. & chmn. KCET TV, LA; past dir. So. Calif. Public Radio; dir. Investment Co. of Am.; past. mem. PBS Nat. Bd. Mem. bd. councilors Annenberg Sch. for Comm., Univ. So. Calif.; trustee J. Paul Getty Trust, 1998—, chmn., 2006—. Recipient Excellence in Public TV Leadership award, 1998. Office: Lifetime Television 309 W 49th St New York NY 10019

BRYSON, NANCY SOUTHARD, lawyer, former federal agency administrator; b. 1951; BA in History, Boston U.; JD, Georgetown U. Bar: DC. Staff atty., asst. counsel for appellate litig. US Dept. of Labor, Occupl. Safety and Health Divsn. Solicitor's Office, 1975—79; trial atty., asst. chief land and natural resources divsn. environ. def. sect. US Dept. of Justice, 1979—84; ptnr., natural resources and environment group Crowell & Moring LLP, Washington, 1998—2002, co-chair, biotechnologies practice; gen. counsel USDA, Washington, 2002—05. Vol. mediator US Dist. Ct., DC; lectr. in the field of environ. law. Contbr. articles in environ. law.

BRYSON, VALRICA, high school music educator; Grad., Coll. of V.I. (now Univ. of V.I.). Music tchr. St. Croix Ednl. Complex, Kingshill, V.I. Named St. Croix Dist. Tchr. of Yr., 2006, V.I. Tchr. of Yr., 2007. Office: St Croix Ednl Complex RR 1 Box 10360 Kingshill VI 00850-9701 E-mail: valricab@yahoo.com.*

BRYSON, WILLIAM CURTIS, federal judge; b. Houston, Aug. 19, 1945; m. Julia Penny Clark; 2 children. AB magna cum laude, Harvard Coll., 1969; JD, U. of Tex. Sch. of Law, 1973. Law clk. to Justice Henry Friendly US Ct. of Appeals, 2d Cir., 1973—74; law clk. to Justice Thurgood Marshall US Supreme Ct., 1974—75; atty. Miller, Cassidy, Larroca & Lewin, 1975—78; asst. to the Solicitor Gen. US Dept. of Justice, 1978—79; chief Appellate Sect., Criminal Divsn., 1979—82; spl. counsel Organized Crime & Racketeering Sect., Criminal Divsn., 1982—86; dep. solicitor gen., 1986—94; dep. assoc. atty. & acting assoc. atty. gen., 1994; judge US Ct. Appeals (Fed. cir), Washington, 1994—. Office: US Ct of Appeals for the Fed Cir 717 Madison Pl NW Washington DC 20439*

BRYSON, WILLIAM HAMILTON, law educator; b. Richmond, Va., July 29, 1941; s. William Alexander and Lillian Sutton (Wilkinson) B. BA, Hampden-Sydney Coll., 1963; LLB, Harvard U., 1967; LLM, U. Va., 1968; PhD, Cambridge U., Eng., 1972. Bar: Va. 1967. Asst. prof. U. Richmond Sch. Law, 1973-76, assoc. prof., 1976-80, prof., 1980—; Blackstone prof. law U. Richmond Sch. Law, 2001. Mem. adv. com. on rules of ct. Jud. Coun. Va. Author: Equity Side of the Exchequer, 1975, Legal Education in Virginia 1779-1979: A Biographical Approach, 1982, Virginia Civil Procedure, 1997, 4th edit., 2005, Virginia Circuit Court Opinions, 1985—, Virginia Law Books, 2000, Samuel Dodd's Reports, 2000, Cases Concerning Equity, 2001; mem. editl. bd., asst. editor Am. Jour. Legal History, 1999—. William Senior scholar, 1970-72; Max Planck Inst. fellow, Frankfurt, Germany, 1972-73; Fulbright grant, 1963, Am. Coun. Learned Socs. grant, 1980; recipient Yorke prize Cambridge U., 1973 Fellow Royal Hist. Soc.; mem. Selden Soc. (Va. corr.), Va. Hist. Soc., Va. Bar Assn., Am. Soc. Legal History (bd. dirs. 1981-84), Supreme Ct. Va. Hist. Commn., John Marshall Inn of Ct. (exec. com.), Phi Beta Kappa. Episcopalian. Office: U Richmond Sch Law Richmond VA 23173

BRZEZINSKI, ZBIGNIEW, political science professor, former national security advisor; b. Warsaw, Mar. 28, 1928; came to U.S., 1953, naturalized, 1958; s. Tadeusz and Leonia (Roman) B.; m. Emilie Anna Benes, June 11, 1955; children: Ian, Mark, Mika. BA with 1st class honors in Econs. and Polit. Sci., McGill U., 1949, MA in Polit. Sci., 1950; PhD, Harvard U., 1953. Inst. govt. and research fellow Russian Research Center, Harvard U., 1953-56; asst. prof. govt., research assoc. Russian Research Center and Center Internat. Affairs, Harvard U., 1956-60; assoc. prof. public law and govt. Columbia U., 1960-62, prof., 1981-89. Dir. Rsch. Inst. Internat. Change, 1962-77; mem. faculty Russian Inst., 1960-77; dir. Trilateral Commn., 1973-76; asst. to the Pres.for nat security affairs, NSC, 1977-81; counselor Ctr. Strategic and Internat. Studies, 1981—; prof. Nitze Sch. Advanced Internat. Studies, Johns Hopkins U., 1989—; mem. policy planning coun. U.S. Dept. State, 1966-68, Pres.'s Fgn. Intelligence Adv. Bd., 1987-91; mem. Joint Com. Contemporary China, Social Sci. Rsch. Coun., 1961-62; guest lectr. numerous pvt. and govt. instns. 1953—, participant internat. confs., 1955—. Author: The Permanent Purge-Politics in Soviet Totalitarianism, 1956, The Soviet Bloc— Unity and Conflict, 1960, Ideology and Power in Soviet Politics, 1962, Alternative to Partition, 1965, Between Two Ages: America's Role in the Technetronic Era, 1970, The Fragile Blossom, 1971, Power and Principle, 1983, Game Plan, 1986, The Grand Failure: The Birth and Death of Communism in the Twentieth Century, 1989, Out of Control: Global Turmoil on the Eve of the 21st Century, 1993, The Grand Chessboard: American Primacy and Its Geostrategic Imperatives, 1997, The Choice: Global Domination or Global Leadership, 2004, Second Chance: Three Presidents and the Crisis of American Superpower, 2007; co-author: Totalitarian Dictatorship and Autocracy, 1957, Political Power: USA/USSR, 1964 (German edit. 1966), also numerous articles.; editor, co-author, contbr.: Political Controls in the Soviet Army, 1954; Editor, co-author, contbr.: Africa and the Communist World, 1963, Dilemmas Of Change In Soviet Politics, 1969, Dilemmi Internationazionali In Un-epoca. Teconetronica, 1969; columnist: Newsweek, 1970-72; co-editor: Russia and the Commonwealth of Independent States: Documents, Data and Analysis, 1997. Mem. hon. steering com. Young Citizens for Johnson, 1964. Recipient Presdl. Medal of Freedom, 1981, U Thant award, 1995, Order of White Eagle, Poland, 1995. Fellow AAAS; mem. Coun. Fgn. Relations. Clubs: Metropolitan (Washington). Office: Ctr Strategic & Internat Studies 1800 K St NW Washington DC 20006-2202

BRZUSTOWICZ, JOHN CINQ-MARS, lawyer; b. Rochester, NY, Feb. 1, 1957; s. Richard J. and Alice (Cinq-Mars) B.; m. Diane Day, Aug. 22, 1981; children: Richard Reed, Megan Day, Emily Day-Hanson. BA, Coll. Wooster, 1979; JD, Case Western Res. U., 1985; cert., Cornell Inst. Labor Rels., 1982. Bar: Pa. 1985, U.S. Dist. Ct. (we. dist.) Pa. 1985, U.S. Ct. Appeals (3d cir.) 1986, U.S. Supreme Ct. 1990. Asst. to dir. Inst. Am. Music U. Rochester, Rochester, 1979-82; assoc. Peacock, Keller, Yohe, Day & Ecker, Washington, Pa., 1985-88, Sable, Makoroff & Libenson, Pitts., 1988-90; pvt. practice Brzustowicz Law Offices, McMurray, Washington, Pa., 1990-94; pres., shareholder Day, Brzustowicz & Malkin, P.C., McMurray, Pa., 1995—. Chmn. bd. dirs. Inst. for Am. Music of Eastman Sch. Music, 1997-2000; chmn. law libr. Washington County (Pa.) Bar, 1992; mem. com. Jud. Inquiry Bd., Pa., 1991-94. Co-author: Pennsylvania School Law, 1992, Pennsylvania Adminstrative Law, 1987; editor: So You Want to Be A Lawyer, 1990; advisor on PBC documentary: Life of Howard Hanson, An American Masterpiece, 1987. Pres. Newman Club, Coll. Wooster, 1976-79, pres., alumni chair of 1979, 80-94; v.p. Young Reps., Wooster, Ohio, 1977-79; co-founder, officer Wooster Polo and Hunt Club, 1976-79; bd. dirs. Hanson Inst. Am. Music Eastman Sch. Music, 1996, Washington County Fund, 1998-00, Pyramid Gallery, Rochester, NY, 1997-06; mem. fin. com. JFK Sch., 1998-05. Recipient Merit award Inst. Am. Music, 1981, Outstanding Scholar award Rotary, Albert H. Robbins award for Meritorious Svc. in Advancement of Am. Art, 2000. Mem.: KC, ATLA, ABA, Pa. Young Lawyers for Washington County (state rep. 1988), Washington County Bar Assn. (legis. com. 2001—04), Allegheny County Bar Assn., Pa. Bar Assn. (del. 1992), Wash. C. of C., Peters Twp. C. of C. Roman Catholic. Avocations: reading, woodworking, biology. Home: 56 Mckennan Ave Washington PA 15301-3531 Office: 3821 Washington Rd Mc Murray PA 15317-2964 Office Phone: 724-942-3789. Personal E-mail: dexterdawg@aol.com, dandblaw@comcast.net.

BU, RULEI, artist, educator; b. Shanghai, July 23, 1970; arrived in U.S., 1998; s. Xinnong Bu and Grace Gao. BFA, Shanghai U., 1993. Tchr. Shanghai U., 1993—98; artist Rockville, Md., 1998—2000; pres. A A Studio, Inc., Boyds, Md., 2001—. One-man shows include Rockville City Hall, 1999, Gaithersburg (Md.) City Hall Gallery, 2000, Strathmore Hall Arts Ctr., Md., 2000, NIH, 2000, Dumbarton Concerts Gallery, Washington, 2000, Rockville (Md.) Arts Pl., 2000, Glenview Mansion Art Gallery, Md., 2001, Kensington Art Gallery, 2002, Framer's Choice Gallery, 2001, 2002, 2003, 2004, 2005, 2006, Weinberg Ctr. Arts, 2002, Gaithersburg Arts Barn, 2003, 2005, Alvear Studio, Washington, 2004, 2006, 2007, The Art League Gallery, Alexandria, Va., 2005, Blackrock Ctr. Arts, Germantown, Md., 2006, Arts Club Washington, 2006. Named one of Top Ten Finalist, The Kirkland's Home Next Great Am. Artist Contest, Tenn., 2006; recipient Clemente Family award, The Art League, Alexandria, Va., 2000, Marshall award, 2002, JoAnn Rose award, League of Reston (Va.) Artists, 2001, 1st pl. award, The Delaplaine Visual Arts Edn. Ctr., Frederick, Md., 2001. Mem.: Montgomery County Art Assn. (1st pl. 1999, 2001, 2004, 2005), Rockville Art League (1st pl. 1999, 2000, 2002, 2003, Best-in-Show award 2006, 1st pl. 2007), Gaithersburg Fine Arts Assn. (1st pl. 1999, 2000, 2001, Sharon Sage award 2003, 1st pl. 2004, 2005, 2006). Office: A A Studio Inc 13915 Schaeffer Rd Boyds MD 20841 Home Phone: 301-916-5991; Office Phone: 301-916-5991. E-mail: ruleibu@hotmail.com.

BUATTA, MARIO, interior designer; b. N.Y.C., Oct. 20, 1935; s. Felix and Olive B.; student Wagner Coll., 1953-54, Cooper Union, 1958-59, Parsons Sch. Design, Europe, 1961; Ph.D. (hon.), Wagner Coll. Asst. decorator B. Altman & Co., N.Y.C., 1959-61, Elisabeth Draper Inc., N.Y.C., 1961, Keith Irvine and Co., N.Y.C., 1962; pvt. practice interior decorating, N.Y.C., 1963—, works include: Protocol Offices of 1964 World's Fair, exec. offices Met. Opera House at Lincoln Center, N.Y.C.; dean of design Chgo. Merchandise Mart Design Community. Bd. dir. East Side House Settlement, N.Y.C.; past bd. dir. Kips Bay Boys Club, N.Y.C., Fashion Inst. Tech., N.Y.C.; work in process includes: redecoration of Blair House, the White House Guest House. Bd. dir. Royal Oak, Nat. Trust Gt. Britain, The Hist. House Trust, N.Y.C.; chmn. Winter Antiques Show, East Side House Settlement benefit; hon. chmn. Cooper Hewitt Mus., Decorative Arts Soc. Mem. Am. Soc. Interior Designers. Designs included in numerous publs. Inducted into Interior Design Hall of Fame; recipient Giant of Design award Ho. Beautiful Mag., 2002, Pratt Legend award Pratt Inst., 2003, Design award Parson's NY, 2007, Criteria award Parson's Sch. Design, NY, 2007; named Royal Oak Designer of Distinction, 2006. Office: 120 E 80th St New York NY 10021-0306 Office Phone: 212-988-6811.

BUBE, RICHARD HOWARD, retired materials scientist, educator; b. Providence, Aug. 10, 1927; s. Edward Neser and Ella Elvira (Baltteim) B.; m. Betty Jane Meeker, Oct. 9, 1948 (dec. Apr. 2, 1997); children: Mark Timothy, Kenneth Paul, Sharon Elizabeth, Meryl Lee; m. Mary Anne Harman, Sept. 9, 2000. Sc.B., Brown U., 1946; MA, Princeton U., 1948, PhD, 1950. Mem. sr. research staff RCA Labs., Princeton, N.J., 1948-62; prof. materials sci. and elec. engring. Stanford U., 1962-92, chmn. dept., 1975-86, assoc. chmn. dept., 1990-91, ret., 1997, prof. emeritus, 1992—. Cons. to industry and govt. Author: A Textbook of Christian Doctrine, 1955, Photoconductivity of Solids, 1960, The Encounter between Christianity and Science, 1968, The Human Quest: A New Look at Science and Christian Faith, 1971, Electronic Properties of Crystalline Solids, 1974, Electrons in Solids, 1981, 3d edit., 1992, Fundamentals of Solar Cells, 1983, Science and the Whole Person, 1985, Photoelectronic Properties of Semiconductors, 1992, Putting It All Together: Seven Patterns for Relating Science and Christian Faith, 1995, One Whole Life: Personal Memoirs of Richard H. Bube, 1995, Photoinduced Defects in Semiconductors, 1996, Photovoltaic Materials, 1998; also articles; editor Jour. Am. Sci. Affiliation, 1969-83; mem. editl. bd. Solid State Electronics, 1975-94, Christians in Sci.; assoc. editor Ann. Rev. Materials Sci., 1969-83. Fellow Am. Phys. Soc., AAAS, Am. Sci. Affiliation; mem. Am. Soc. Engring. Edn. (life), Internat. Solar Energy Soc., Sigma Xi. Evangelical. Home: 753 Mayfield Ave Stanford CA 94305-1043 Personal E-mail: rhbube@comcast.net. *I find no contradiction or conflict between science and Christian faith, but rather a marvelous compatibility that touches all aspects of life.*

BUBEN, JEFFREY ALAN, restaurant owner, chef; b. Detroit, Oct. 8, 1958; s. Alvin Alexander and Helen (Thomas) B.; m. Sarah Warren Woollen, May 19, 1984; children: Sarah MacPhail, John Alexander, Thomas McLean. Assoc. in Occupl. Sci., Culinary Inst. Am., 1978. Chef de partie Sign of the Dove, NYC, 1978-79, Four Seasons Hotel Corp., Washington and NYC, 1980-82, Le Cygne, NYC, 1982-83, Le Chantilly, NYC, 1983-84; chef de cuisine La Bagatelle, Washington, 1984, Nicholas, The Mayflower Hotel, Washington, 1984-86; exec. chef Occidental, Washington, 1986-93; chef, owner Vidalia Restaurant, Washington, 1993—. Bd. dirs. Christmas for Homeless, Washington, 1992-95; active Share Our Strenght, Washington, 1986—; mem. mentor program Culinary Inst. Am., Hyde Park, N.Y., 1993—; mem. chef coalition Pub. Voice, Washington, 1992—. Vidalia named one of nation's best new restaurants Bon Appetit, 1984; named Restaurateur of Yr., Washingtonian, 1994, Chef of Yr., Nat. Restaurant Assn. of Met. Washington, 1996; recipient DiRona award, 1996; nominated Best Chef Mid-Atlantic, James Beard Found. Perrier-Joliet award, 1994-96. Mem. Culinary Inst. Alumni Assn., Assn. Wine and Food, Nat. Restaurant Assn. Roman Catholic. Avocations: hunting, fishing. Office: Vidalia 1990 M St NW Washington DC 20036-3404

BUBENCIK, JOHN WILLIAM, II, civil engineer, consultant, transportation engineer; b. Little Falls, NY, Apr. 24, 1958; s. William John Bubencik and Dorothy Hayes-Bubencik; life ptnr. Regina Marie Zamblauskas; 1 child, Stephanie Lynn Santoro. AS, Herkimer County CC, NY, 1979; BS, State U. at Albany, 1981. Engineering Level IV, Nat. Inst. Cert. in Engring. Tech., 2001, NETTCP-Concrete Technician, North East Tech., 2002, NETTCP-Hot Mix Asphalt Paving Inspector, North East Tech., 2001, NETTCP-Siols and Aggregate Inspector, North East Tech., 2001, cert. Nuclear Density Gauge, Field Safety Corp., 2000, Concrete, Am. Concrete Inst., 2001, Federal Railroad Adminstrn., Fed. RR Adminstrn., 1998, Railroad Crossing, Tex. A&M U., 1992. Laborer, driver I.L. Richer Co., Richfield Springs, NY, 1976—79; apprentice, elec., mech., archtl. Shadow Brook Farms, Schuyler Lake, NY, 1976—83; spl. projects coord. NY Susquehanna and We. RR, NY, NJ, Pa., 1982—87; ctrl. divsn. engr. Guilford Transp., NH, Maine, Mass., Conn., 1998—99; constrn. engr. Daniel, Mann, Johnson, Mendenhall and Harris, Milford, Conn., 1999—; Consulting engr. II Arch. Engrs. Conglomerate, Milford, Conn., 1999—. Fellow: St. Labre Indian Sch. (hon.), Disabled Am. Vets. (assoc.); mem.: Paralyzed Vets. Am. (hon.), Law Enforcement Officers Legal Defence Fund (assoc.), Help Hospitalized Vets. (assoc.), Nat. Police & Trooper Assn. (assoc.), Law Enforcement Alliance of Am. (assoc.), Am. Fedn. of Police & Concerned Citizens (assoc.), Concerns of Police Survivors (assoc.). Avocation: travel. Office: DMJM and Harris Harborwalk 22 Broad Stt 2nd Floor Milford CT 06460 Home: 1546 County Highway 22 Richfield Springs NY 13439-4510 Home Phone: 203-217-5259; Office Phone: 203-874-2288. Office Fax: 203-874-2868; Home Fax: 203-874-2868. E-mail: exavierII@37.com, john.bubencik@dmjmarris.com.

BUBLÉ, MICHAEL, singer; b. 1975; Signed to 143 Records (Reprise), 2001. Singer: (albums) Michael Bublé, 2003 (double platinum, #1 in Canada), Down With Love Soundtrack, 2003, Let It Snow, 2003, Spider-Man 2 Original Motion Picture Soundtrack, 2004, It's Time, 2005, Caught in the Act, 2005, Chistmas, 2006, Call Me Irresponsible, 2007, (CD/DVD) Come Fly With Me, 2004; guest appearance Dancing with the Stars, 2006. Office: Reprise Records Warner Brothers Records Inc 3300 Warner Blvd Burbank CA 91505*

BUBLITZ, DEBORAH KEIRSTEAD, pediatrician; b. Boston, Feb. 28, 1933; d. George and Dorothy (Kingsbury) Keirstead; m. Clark Bublitz, June 1, 1958; children: Nancy B. Dyer, Susan B. Schooleman, Philip K. Bublitz, Caroline D. Bublitz, Elizabeth E. Bublitz. BS, Bates Coll., 1955; MD, Johns Hopkins U., 1959. Resident St. Louis Children's Hosp., 1959-60, U. Colo. Health Sci. Ctr. and Dept. Health and Hosps., Denver, 1968-74; pvt. practice Littleton, Colo., 1974—; asst. clin. prof. pediatrics U. Colo. Health Sci. Ctr. and Children's Hosp., 1975-87, assoc. clin. prof. pediatrics, 1987—. Creditials com. Swedish/Porter Hosp., Englewood, Colo., 1985-87, chief dept. pediatrics, 1985-87; med. assoc., advisor LaLeche League, 1975—. Author: (with others) Clinical Pediatric Otolaryngology, 1986. Fellow Am. Acad. Pediatrics; mem. AMA, Colo. Med. Soc. (women's governing coun. 1990-96, asst. chair women's governing coun. 1993-94, chair, 1994-95), Arapahoe Med. Soc., Am. Women's Med. Assn. Episcopalian. Avocations: painting, gardening, bird watching. Home: 5621 Blue Sage Dr Littleton CO 80123-2713 Office: Littleton Pediatric Med Ctr 206 W County Line Rd Ste 110 Highlands Ranch CO 80129-2319 E-mail: littletonpeds@uswest.net.

BUBRICK, MELVIN PHILLIP, surgeon; b. Chgo., June 2, 1944; m. Barbara Lynn Jacobs, Jan. 26, 1969; children: Jerome Bradley, Ellen Jeanne, Dena Beth. BA with honors, U. Ill., 1964, MD, 1968. Diplomate Am. Bd. Surgery, Am. Bd. Colon and Rectal Surgery; lic. Minn. Intern in surgery Univ. Hosps., Madison, Wis., 1968-69; resident in gen. surgery Hennepin County Gen. Hosp., Mpls., 1969-74; postdoctoral fellow colon and rectal surgery U. Minn. Health Scis. Ctr., Mpls., 1974-75; clin. instr. div. colon and rectal surgery U. Minn., Mpls., 1975-77, clin. asst. prof., 1977-78, clin. asst. prof. dept. surgery, 1978-80, asst. prof., 1980-87, assoc. prof., 1987—; chief surgery, program dir. surg. residency Hennepin County Med. Ctr., 1988-94; pres. Hennepin Facility Assocs., 1995—2000, chmn. bd. dirs., 1991—2001. V.p. Mpls. Med. Rsch. Found., 1991-2000; chmn. bd. dirs. Hennepin Faculty Assocs., 1991-2000, CEO, 1991-2001. Author: (with others) Conn's Therapy, 1985, The Pancreas. Principles of Medical and Surgical Practice, 1985, Applied Therapeutics: The clinical use of drugs, 4th rev. edit., 1988; contbr. over 90 articles to Minn. Med. jour., Am. Surg. jour., Diseases of Colon and Rectum, Surgery, others. Bd. dirs. Mpls. Med. Rsch. Found., Inc., 1981-89. Mem. AMA, ACS, Am. Assn. Surgery of Trauma, Am. Soc. Colon and Rectal Surgeons (co-chair Self Assessment Exam. Com. 1984-85), Am. Soc. Microbiology, Assn. Program Dirs. of Surgery, Cen. Surg. Assn., Collegium Internat. Chirurgiae Digestivae, Soc. Surgery of Alimentary Tract, Minn. Assn. Pub. Teaching Hosps., Minn. Surg. Soc., Minn. Med. Assn., Mpls. Surg. Soc., Hennepin County Med. Soc. (mem. and chair various coms. 1975—, Hennepin faculty assoc. 1983—). Achievements include research in assessment of bursting strength and healing of intestinal anastomoses, predictive value of surface oximetry in assessing healing in irradiated bowel, use of antibiotic microspheres for infected vascular grafts and peritonitis, clinical and anatomic assessment of first rib-clavicular decompression on subclavian catheters and pacemaker leads, influence of nutritional deficits in intestinal anastomotic strength, iron chelation with a Deferoxamine (DFO) conjugate in hemorrhagic shock. Personal E-mail: mbubrick@comcast.net.

BUC, NANCY LILLIAN, lawyer; b. Orange, NJ, July 27, 1944; d. George L. and Ethel Buc. AB, Brown U., 1965, LLD (hon.), 1994; LLB, U. Va., 1969. Bar: Va. 1969, N.Y. 1977, D.C. 1978. Atty. Fed. Trade Commn., Washington, 1969-72; assoc. Weil, Gotshal & Manges, NYC, 1972-77, ptnr., 1977-78, Washington, 1978-80, 81-94, Buc & Beardsley, Washington, 1994—; chief counsel FDA, Rockville, Md., 1980-81. Mem. recombinant DNA adv. com. NIH, 1990-94, reduced risk tobacco products core com. Life Scis. Rsch. Office, 2005-; consensus panelist NIH Consensus Devel. Conf. on Effective Med. Treatment of Heroin Addiction, 1997; adj. prof. law Georgetown U. Law Ctr., 2000-02; bd. dirs. Dynavax Techs. Corp., Food and Drug Law Inst. Mem. editl. bd. Food Drug and Cosmetic Law Jour., 1981-87, 94-97, Jour. of Products Liability, 1981-92, Health Span: The Jour. of Health, Bus. & Law, 1984-95. Mem. adv. com. on new devels. in biotech. 1986-89, mem. adv. com. on govt. policies and pharm. R & D, 1989-93, Office of Tech. Assessment, Washington, mem. com. to study drug abuse medications devel. and rsch., 1993-95; mem. com. on contraceptive R&D, Inst. Medicine, Washington, 1994-96; trustee Brown U., 1973-78, 1998-2004, fellow, 1980-92. Recipient Disting. Svc. award Fed. Trade Commn., Washington, 1972, Award of Merit FDA, Rockville, 1981, Sec.'s Spl. citation HHS, Washington, 1981, Ind. award Associated. Alumni of Brown U., 1991. Mem. ABA (mem. spl. com. to study FTC 1988-89), Nat. Partnership for Women and Families (bd. dirs.). Office: Buc & Beardsley 919 18th St NW Ste 600 Washington DC 20006-5507 Home Phone: 202-244-3015; Office Phone: 202-736-3610. Business E-Mail: nlb@bucbeardsley.com.

BUCCINO, DANIEL L., psychotherapist, consultant; BA, MA, Johns Hopkins U., 1987; MSW, Smith Coll., 1989. Diplomate NASW, Am. Bd. Examiners in Clin. Social Work, lic. Clinical Social Worker. Clin. supr./student coord. cmty. psychiatry, psychotherapist Johns Hopkins Bayview Med. Ctr., Balt., 1989—; pvt. practice psychotherapy Balt., 1992—; founder, dir. Balt. Psychotherapy Inst., 1994—. Asst. prof. psychiatry Johns Hopkins U. Sch. Medicine, Balt., 2000—; clin. asst. prof. U. Md. Sch. Social Work, Balt., 1996—; clin. assoc. prof., faculty field instr. Smith Coll. Sch. Social Work, Northampton, Mass., 1998—; mem. Md. Bd. Social Work Examiners, 2005—; presenter and cons. in field. Editor: Maryland Social Work Legal Handbook, Vol. 1, 1994, Vol. 2, 1996; contbr. articles to profl. jours., books, and newspapers. Mem. Internat. Fed. Psychoanalytic Edn., Johns Hopkins Civility Initiative, Md. Soc. Clin. Social Work, Assn. Psychoanalysis of Culture and Soc Avocations: books, music, films, running. Office: 711 W 40th St Ste 456 Baltimore MD 21211-2199

BUCCINO, ERNEST JOHN, JR., lawyer; b. Oct. 29, 1945; s. Ernest J. and Rachel (Talarico) B.; m. Martha Mollinedo, Dec. 27, 1968; 1 child, Anastasia. BS, Temple U., 1967, MEd, 1969, JD, 1973. Bar: Pa. 1973, N.J. 1974, U.S. Dist. Ct. (ea. dist.) Pa. 1973, U.S. Ct. Appeals (3d cir.) 1973, U.S. Supreme Ct. 1978. Officer, counsel Blue Cross Greater Phila., 1973-74; law clk. Supreme Ct. Pa., Phila., 1974; mem. Gross & Buccino, P.A., Phila., 1975-96; pvt. practice Phila., 1996-97; prin. Buccino Law Office, Phila., 1997—. Lectr. Roscoe Pound, 1986, Trial Advocacy Found. Pa., Phila., 1984; mem. civil procedure rules com. Supreme Ct. Pa., 1994—. Author: The Barrister Vol. XVI, #3, 1985. Chmn. eastern dist. LAWPAC, Harrisburg, Pa., 1983—. Mem. ABA, ATLA, Pa. Bar Assn., Pa. Trial Lawyers Assn. (bd. dirs. 1982—), Phila. Trial Lawyers Assn. (bd. dirs. 1982—, lectr. luncheon series 1986), Justinian Soc. (bd. dirs. 1982—), Phila. Bar Assn. (chmn. econs. of law practice 1983, nominating com. 1982-83), Sons of Italy. Office: 2112 Walnut St Philadelphia PA 19103-4808 Office Phone: 215-568-3010. Business E-Mail: EJB@buccino.com.

BUCH, JAN, medical research administrator, director; b. Copenhagen, Feb. 2, 1943; s. Holger and Inger Buch; m. Jette Simonsen, Apr. 30, 1988. MD, Copenhagen U., 1969. With dept. cardiology and aviation medicine Rigs Hosp., 1969—75, with dept. cardiology invasive lab., 1977—83; med. and surg. resident Diakonissestiftelsen, 1975—77; with med. and cardiology dept. Amtsygehuset Glostrup, 1983—86; specialist internal medicine Copenhagen U., 1984, specialist cardiology, 1984; physician, cardiologist Copenhagen U. Hosp., Copenhagen, 1969—87; med. dir. Pfizer, Copenhagen, 1987—91, med. dir., world wide team leader, global team leader, cardiovas. metabolic endocrine obesity, 1992—. Contbr. articles to profl. jours. Mem.: Danish Soc. History, Lit. and Arts, Danish Soc. Internal Medicine, Danish Cadiol. Soc. (Numerous grants 1969—87), Danish Bibliophile Club. Avocations: history, art, classical music. Office: Pfizer Inc 235 E 42nd St New York NY 10017-5755

BUCHAN, DOUGLAS CHARLES, gas industry executive, government agency administrator; b. Bklyn., Aug. 4, 1936; s. Charles J. and Amelia P. (Petraca) B.; 1 son, Paul Douglas. Student, U. Fla., 1954—56. Pres. Buchan Gas Co., St.Petersburg, Fla., 1955-86, Buchan Oil Co., St.Petersburg, 1966-89, Grill Parts Distbrs., 1982-86, Site Mgmt., 1983—; dep. asst. sec. energy U.S. Dept. Energy, Washington, 1989—. Mem. U.S. Senate Bus. Adv. Com., 1984—, Petr Equipment Inst., Common Ground Alliance, Pinellas County Gas Bd., Pinellas County Plumbing and Mech. Bd., So. Bldg. Code Congress. Pres. Pinellas County Rep. Ivory Club; chmn. Pinellas campaign Reagan-Bush, Fla. campaign George Bus for Pres. 1st lt. U.S. Army, 1958-65. Mem. Nat. Oil Jobbers Coun., Nat. Liquified Petroleum Gas Assn., Nat. Assn. Fire Investigators (mem. Internat. Code Coun., Energy Tng. Network), Nat. Fire Protection Assn., Fla. Petroleum Marketers Assn. (v.p.), Oil Fuel Inst. Fla (pres., chmn. bd.), St. Petersburg Yacht. Episcopalian. Home: 1067 42nd Ave NE Saint Petersburg FL 33703-5235 Office: US Dept Energy 1000 Independence Ave SW Washington DC 20585-0001 Personal E-mail: buchandoug@msn.com.

BUCHAN, JONATHAN EDWARD, JR., lawyer; b. Mullins, SC, Sept. 1, 1950; s. Jonathan Edward and Margaret Alice (Liles) B.; m. Suzette Rogers Phillips, Nov. 22, 1986; 1 stepchild, Geoffrey Eliot Eloge; 1 child, Caroline Phillips. AB magna cum laude, Princeton U., 1972; JD, Duke U., 1978. Bar: N.C. 1978. Co-founder, sr. editor, Osceola News Weekly, Columbia, SC, 1973—74; govt. reporter Charlotte Observer, Columbia, SC, 1974—75, govt. editor, 1983—84; ptnr. Helms Mulliss & Wicker and predecessor firms, Charlotte, 1984—. Mem. adj. faculty dept. mass media law Wake Forest Law Sch., 1992-2002; bd. dirs. Legal Svcs. for So. Piedmont, Inc., 1993-98. Co-author: 50-State Survey of Libel Law, NC Sect., 1981—; contbg. author: North Carolina Media Law Handbook, 1992, rev. edit., 2007. Pres., bd. dirs. Hospice at Charlotte, Inc., 1982-88; adv. bd. Trust for Pub. Land, Carolinas. 2001—. Mem.: Mecklenburg County Bar Assn. (pres. 2004—05). Avocations: fly fishing, tennis, reading. Home: 2342 Thetford Ct Charlotte NC 28211-3268 Office: Helms Mulliss & Wicker PO Box 31247 201 N Tryon St Ste 3000 Charlotte NC 28202-1157 Office Phone: 704-343-2063. Personal E-mail: Buchan247@aol.com. Business E-Mail: jon.buchan@hmw.com.

BUCHANAN, BRUCE, publishing executive; Editor, pub. Olanthe Daily News, Kans., 1990—95, Hutchinson News, Kans., 1996—; mem. mgmt. staff Harris Enterprises Inc., Hutchinson, Kans., 1995—, v.p., COO, 1997—2006, pres., CEO, 2006—. Office: Harris Enterprises Corp 1 N Main St Hutchinson KS 67501 Office Phone: 620-694-5830.

BUCHANAN, BRUCE, II, political science professor; b. Shelby, Mont., July 28, 1945; s. Neil and Dorothy Jean (Gallup) B.; m. Susan Safford Bright, June 10, 1964 (div. June 1976); m. Stephanie Ann Sokolewicz, Jan. 3, 1981; children: Kathryn Elaine, Douglas Neil, Jacqueline May. BA, Stanford U., 1967; MA, Yale U., 1969; MPhil, 1970, PhD, 1972. Prof. U. Ga., Athens, 1973-74, U. Tex., Austin, 1974—. Author: The Presidential Experience, 1978, The Citizens Presidency, 1987,Electing A President, 1991, Renewing Presidential Politics, 1996, Presidential Campaign Quality, 2004, The Policy Partnership, 2004. Exec. dir. Markle Commn. on Media and Electorate, 1988-90; rsch. dir. Markle Found. Presdl. Election Study, 1992, dir. Markle Presdl. Watch, 1996. Mem. Am. Polit. Sci. Assn. (award for best paper on presidency 1997), Presidency Rsch. Group. Avocations: cello, sports, gardening. Home: 1304 Wilshire Blvd Austin TX 78722-1127 Office: U Tex Dept Govt Austin TX 78712-1087 Office Phone: 512-232-7212. Business E-Mail: bruceb@mail.la.utexas.edu.

BUCHANAN, BRUCE G., computer scientist, educator; b. St. Louis, July 7, 1940; AB, Ohio Wesleyan U., 1961; MA, Mich. State U., PhD in Philosophy, 1966. Rsch. assoc. computer sci. Stanford U., Palo Alto, Calif., 1966-71, rsch. computer scientist, 1972-76, adj. prof. computer sci., 1976—; univ. prof. computer sci., prof. philosophy, intelligent systems and medicine U. Pitts. Mem.: AAAI, AAAS, Am. Assn. Artificial Intelligence (pres. 2000—01), NAS Inst. Medicine. Office: U Pitts Dept Computer Sci 205 Mineral Industries Bldg Pittsburgh PA 15260-3803

BUCHANAN, CAROLEE HORSTMAN, special education educator, consultant; b. Sheridan, Wyo., Oct. 16, 1944; d. Carl Edgar and Marjorie Rowell Horstman; divorced; children: Carl Jeffries, P. Kent Jeffries, Jennie L. Anderson. BE, Black Hills State Univ., Spearfish, SD, 1983; cert. in resource specialist, U. Calif., 1994. Cert. Special Edn. Black Hills State Univ., 1988, tchg. endorsement Wyo., 2001. Special edn. profl. Spearfish S.D. Pub. Sch., 1986—88; special edn. tchr. Albuquerque Pub. Sch., Albuquerque, 1988—90, Alvord Pub. Sch., Riverside, Calif., 1990—94, Bedford Pub. Sch., Mass., 1994—95, Turqoise Trail Charter Sch., Santa Fe, 1995—96, Ayer Pub. Sch., Mass., 1996—98; special edn. cons. Wyo. Dept. Edn., Cheyenne, Riverton, 1998—2006; special edn. case mgr. Fremont Ctrl. Sch. Dist., 2006—. State coord. McKinney Veto Homeless Edn., Wyo., 2000—06. Mem.: P.E.O. Ednl. Orgn. Methodist.

BUCHANAN, EDWARD A., education educator; b. Newark, Aug. 28, 1937; s. Osborne B. and Edna Dorothy (Weber) B.; m. Gladys J. Buchanan, Aug. 28, 1965; children Roger, Becky. AB, Rutgers U., 1959; MRE, N.Y. Theol. Sem., 1962; PhD, So. Bapt. Theol. Sem., 1970. Tchr. Ctrl. Sch., Middlesex, NJ; assoc. prof. psychology and edn. Grand Rapids Bapt. Coll., Mich.; dean acad. affairs, prof. Lancaster Bible Coll., Pa.; prof. edn., dir. continuing edn. Bethel Theol. Sem., St. Paul; sr. prof. edn. Southeastern Bapt. Theol. Sem., Wake Forest, NC, assoc. dean ministry studies. Author (handbook) The Bible, 2004, Christian Heritage, 2004, The Bible II, 2005, Christian Heritage II, 2006; contbr. articles to profl. jours. Mem. APA, ASCD, Am. Ednl. Rsch. Assn., Nat. Soc. Study of Edn. Home: 1113 Silent Brook Rd Wake Forest NC 27587-7145 Office: Southeastern Bapt Theol Seminary 122 N Wingate Wake Forest NC 27587 Office Phone: 919-761-2457. Business E-Mail: ebuchanan@sebts.edu.

BUCHANAN, GALE ARLON, federal agency administrator, former dean; b. Madison County, Fla. BS, U. Fla., 1959, MS, 1962; PhD, Iowa State U., 1965. Prof. dept. agronomy and soils Auburn U., dean, dir. agrl. experiment station, 1980—85; assoc. dir. Ga. agrl. experiment stations U. Ga., 1986—94, resident dir. coastal plain experiment station, 1986—94, interim dir. Ga. agrl. experiment stations, 1994—95, dean, dir. coll. agrl. and environmental scis., 1995—2006; under sec. rsch. edn. & economics USDA, 2006—. Office: Jamie L Whitten Fed Bldg 14th and Independence Ave SW Rm 216-W Washington DC 20250 Office Phone: 202-720-5923. Office Fax: 202-690-2482.

BUCHANAN, JAMES MCGILL, economist, educator; b. Murfreesboro, Tenn., Oct. 2, 1919; s. James McGill and Lila (Scott) Buchanan; m. Anne Bakke, Oct. 5, 1945. BS, Middle Tenn. State Coll., 1940; MA, U. Tenn., 1941; PhD, U. Chgo., 1948; D honoris causa (hon.), U. Giessen, 1982, U. Zurich, 1984, George Mason U., U. Valencia, New U. Lisbon, 1987, Ball State U., 1988, City U., London, 1988, Lycoming Coll., 1992, Free U., Rome, 1993, U. Bucharest, 1994, Acad. Econ. Studies, Romania, 1994, U. Catania, 1994, U. Porto, 1995, U. Valladolid, Spain, 1996, Fuanceso Marroquin U., Guatemala, 2001. Assoc. prof. U. Tenn., 1948—50, prof. econs., 1950—51; prof. Fla. State U., 1951—56, U. Va., 1956—62, Paul G. McIntyre prof. econs., 1962—68, chmn. dept., 1956—62; prof. UCLA, 1968—69; Univ. Disting. prof. Va. Poly. Inst., 1969—83, prof. emeritus, 2000—; Univ. Disting. prof. George Mason U., 1983—99, prof. emeritus, 1999—; adv. dir. Ctr. for Pub. Choice, 1969—; assoc. prof. Francesco Marroquin U., Guatemala, 2001. Fulbright rsch. scholar, Italy, 1955—56; Ford Faculty rsch. fellow, 1959—60; Fulbright vis. prof. Cambridge U., 1961—62. Author (with C.L. Allen and M.R. Colberg): Prices, Income and Public Policy, 1954; author: Public Principles of Public Debt, 1958, The Public Finances, 1960, Fiscal Theory and Political Economy, 1960; author: (with G. Tullock) The Calculus of Consent, 1962; author: Public Finance in Democratic Process, 1966, The Demand and Supply of Public Goods, 1968, Cost and Choice, 1969; author: (with N. Devletoglou) Academia in Anarchy, 1970; editor (with R. Tollison): Theory of Public Choice, 1972; editor: (with G.F. Thirlby) LSE Essays on Cost, 1973; author: The Limits of Liberty, 1975; author: (with R. Wagner) Democracy in Deficit, 1977; author: Freedom in Constitutional Contract, 1978, What Should Economists Do?, 1979; author: (with G. Brennan) The Power to Tax, 1980, The Reason of Rules, 1985; author: Liberty Market and State, 1985, Economics: Between Predictive Science and Moral Philosophy, 1987, Explorations in Constitutional Economics, 1989, Economics and Ethics of Constitutional Order, 1991; editor: Better than Plowing, 1992, Ethics and Economic Progress, 1994; editor: (with Yong Yoon) Return to Increasing Returns, 1994; author: Post-Socialist Political Economy, 1997; author: (with R. Congleton) Politics By Principle, Not Interest, 1998; author: Collected Works of James Buchanan, Vols. I-XIII, 2000, Collected Works of James Buchanan, Vols. XIV-XIX, 2001, Collected Works of James Buchanan, Vol. XX, 2002, Why I, Too, Am Not a Conservative, 2006. Lt. USNR, 1941—46. Decorated Bronze Star; recipient Seidman award, 1984, Nobel Prize in Econs., 1986, Nat. Humanities Medal, NEH, 2006. Fellow: Am. Acad. Arts and Scis.; mem.: Mt. Pelerin Soc. (pres. 1984—86), Western Econ. Assn. (pres. 1983), So. Econ. Assn. (pres. 1963), Am. Econ. Assn. (exec. com. 1966—69, v.p. 1971, dist. fellow 1983—). Achievements include development of the contractual and constitutional bases for the theory of economic and political desision-making. Home: PO Box G Blacksburg VA 24063-1021 Office: George Mason U Buchanan House Mail Stop 1 E6 Fairfax VA 22030-4443

BUCHANAN, JOHN DONALD, retired nuclear scientist; b. Mesa, Ariz., Oct. 1, 1927; s. John Freeborn and Marguerite (Brimhall) B.; m. Donna Marie Smith, Aug. 27, 1955; children— Margaret MacNeil, John Michael, Andrew Tierney, David Brimhall. BS in Chemistry, U. Ariz., 1949. Diplomate Am. Bd. Health Physics. Sr. chemist Tracerlab, Inc., Richmond, Calif., 1950-59; staff assoc. Gen. Atomic divsn. Gen. Dynamics Corp., San Diego, 1959-62; mgr. nuc. applications and measurements Teledyne-Isotopes Inc., Palo Alto, Calif., 1962-71; mgr. applied rsch. Internat. Nutronics Inc., Palo Alto, 1971-73; supr. radiol. monitoring programs NUS Corp., Rockville, Md., 1973-75; sr. health physicist, radiochemist U.S. Nuc. Regulatory Commn., Washington, 1975-94. Author papers on radiation protection, radioanalytical chemistry, radioactivity measurements, radioisotope applications. Served with USNR, 1945-46. Fellow AAAS, Am. Inst. Chemists, Health Physics Soc.; mem. Am. Nuc. Soc., Am. Chem. Soc., Am. Acad. Health Physics, Phi Lambda Upsilon, Phi Delta Theta. Home: 7508 Dew Wood Dr Rockville MD 20855-1007

BUCHANAN, JOHN EDWARD, JR., museum director; b. Nashville, July 24, 1953; m. Lucy Buchanan. BA in English Lit. with honors, U. of the South, 1975; MA in Art History, Vanderbilt U., 1979. Exec. dir. Lakeview Mus. of Arts and Scis., Peoria, Ill., 1982-86; dir. The Dixon Gallery and Gardens, Memphis, 1986—94; exec. dir. Portland Art Mus., Portland, Oreg., 1994—2006; dir. mus. Fine Arts Mus. San Francisco, 2006—. Presdl. appointee nat. mus. svcs. bd. Inst. Mus. & Libr. Svcs. Recipient Chevalier dans l'Ordre des Arts et des Lettres, French Govt., Chevalier, Legion of Honor. Mem.: Am. Ceramics Cir., Assn. Art Mus. Dirs. Office: de Young Mus Golden Gate Park 50 Hagiwara Tea Garden Dr San Francisco CA 94118

BUCHANAN, JOHN LYNN, retired broadcast executive; b. Garland, Tex., Aug. 19, 1920; s. William Irl and Kathryn Raney Buchanan; m. Stella West, Oct. 31, 1947; children: John Lynn II, Elizabeth Ann Ashurst. Grad., Ryan Sch. Aeronautics, San Diego, 1941; student in engring., North Tex. State U.; student, U. Minn., NYU. Autopilot, radio-compass test engr. C5 Bombsight Sperry Gyroscope Co., NYC; B-29 aircraft field engr. Honeywell, 1943—46; assigned Pacific Air Svc. Command, Manila; B-29 tr. command 2d A.F. Hdqrs., Colorado Springs, 1944—46; instr. 313th, 314th, 315th, 73d, 58th & 509th wings in high level precision bombing technique using Honeywell autopilot and Norden bombsights B-29 XX A.F. Hdqrs., Guam, Tinian; indsl. sales engr. Honeywell, NYC and Phila., 1947—50; sta. mgr. KTLN, Denver, 1950—55; founder, owner Sta. KWBY, Colorado Springs, 1954; founder Sta. KSSS, Colo. Springs, 1955, Sta. KDAB, Denver, 1959, Sta. KKSN, Dallas-Ft. Worth, 1960; pres. Ameco Cable-TV, Inc., Phoenix, 1959—65; v.p. acquisitions Am. Cable TV (subs. Ameco, Inc.); founder Diversified Media Brokers, Dallas, 1966; ret., 1985. Contbr. poems to anthologies including Anthologies Internat. Libr. Poetry, Famous Poets (Bards of Burbank) and Noble Ho. London. Founding mem. U.S. Air Mus., Duxford, England, Smithsonian Udvar-Hazy Air & Space Ctr. Wall of Honor; docent Pima Air and Space Mus., Tucson; mem. Rep. Nat. Com., presdl. task force, 2004. Instr. pilots, bombardiers, flight engrs. USAF, 1941—46. Mem.: Ariz. Air and Space Assn., USAF Assn., Nat. Cable TV Assn., Nat. Assn. Broadcasters, Sigma Chi (life).

BUCHANAN, JOHN MACLENNAN, Canadian provincial official; b. Sydney, NS, Can., Apr. 22, 1931; s. Murdoch William and Flora Isabel (Campbell) B.; m. Mavis Forsyth, Sept. 1, 1954; children: Murdoch, Travis, Nichola, Natalie, Natasha. BSc, Mt. Allison U., cert. engring., 1954; LLB, Dalhousie U., Halifax, NS, 1958; DEng (hon.), N.S. Tech. Coll., 1979; LLD (hon.), St. Mary's U., 1982; DCL, Mt. Allison U., 1981; LLD (hon.), St. Francis Xavier U., 1986; D Polit. Sci. (hon.), U. de St. Anne, 1989. Bar: Called to bar, created queen's counsel 1972. Pvt. practice, Halifax, 1958-71; mem. N.S. Legislative Assembly, Halifax, from 1967; min. public works, then fisheries; premier of N.S., 1978-90. Created Queen's Counsel, 1972; leader Progressive Conservative Party in N.S., from 1971; elected mem. legis. assembly for Halifax-Atlantic provinces gen. election, 1967, 70, 74, 78, 81, 84, 88, apptd. Privy Coun., 1972; apptd. to Senate of Can., 1990, bd. dirs. Legal Aid for N.S. Barristers Assn. Active Boy Scouts Am., pres. exec. oun., chmn. policy bd., 1978-90. Mem. Can. Bar Assn., N.S. Barristers Assn., Can.-U.S. Parliamentary Assn. (bd. dirs.), Royal Can. Legion, Buchanan Soc. of Glasgow, Scotland (bd. dirs.), Halifax Club, City Club, Lions, Masons, Shriners, Odd Fellows. Progressive Conservative. Mem. Progressive Ch. Can. Office: The Senate Ottawa ON K1A OA4 Canada

BUCHANAN, J(OHN) ROBERT, physician, educator; b. Newark, Mar. 8, 1928; s. John Hamilton and Elsie (Castles) Buchanan; m. Susan Townsend Carver, Oct. 27, 1962; children: Ross, Allyn. AB cum laude, Amherst Coll., 1950; MD, Cornell U., 1954; postgrad., Inst. Arthritis and Metabolic Diseases, USPHS, 1956—57, postgrad., 1960—61. Diplomate Am. Bd. Internal Medicine, Nat. Bd. Med. Examiners. Intern N.Y. Hosp., NYC, 1954—55, resident physician, 1955—58, physician to outpatients, 1960—62, from asst. to assoc. attending physician, 1962—71, attending physician, 1971—76, assoc. dir. welfare med. care project, 1961—64; capt. U.S. Army Med. Corps, 1958—60; vis. asst. physician Rockefeller Inst. Hosp., NYC, 1960—61; assoc. vis. physician Bellevue Hosp., NYC, 1965—68; fellow Cornell U., 1956—57, instr. medicine, 1961—63, asst. prof. medicine, 1963—67, asst. dir. comprehensive care and teaching program, 1961—64, asst. to chmn. dept. medicine, 1964—65; assoc. dean Cornell U. (Med. Coll.), 1965—69, dean, 1969—76, clin. assoc. prof. medicine, 1967—69, assoc. prof., 1969—71, prof., 1971—76; pres. Michael Reese Hosp. and Med. Center, Chgo., 1977—82; prof. medicine Pritzker Sch. Medicine, U. Chgo., 1977—82, assoc. dean, 1978—82; gen. dir. Mass. Gen. Hosp., Boston, 1982—94, gen. dir. emeritus, 1994—; prof. medicine Harvard Med. Sch., Boston, 1982—. Mem. com. on sci. policy Sloan-Kettering Inst., 1969—76, State of Ill. Med. Determination Bd., 1980—82; adminstrv. bd. Coun. Tchg. Hosps., 1984—89; mem. composite com. U.S. Med. Licensing Exam sponsored by Nat. Bd. Med. Examiners, Fedn. of State Bd. Med. Examiners, and Ednl. Coun. Fgn. Med. Grads.; sr. program cons. prepaid managed health care program Robert Wood Johnson Found., 1982—85; bd. dirs. Charles River Labs., i-STAT, chmn., 1999—2003; trustee Ednl. Commn. Fgn. Med. Grads., 1989—96, vice chmn., 1992—93, chmn., 1994—96; bd. dirs. MetCare. Chmn. nat. adv. coun. Children's TV Workshop, 1974—75; trustee Cornell U., 1970—76, China Med. Bd. of N.Y., Inc., 1970—99, vice-chmn., chmn., 1989—99; bd. mgrs. Meml. Hosp., 1969—76; mem. adv. com. Edwin L. Crosby and W.K. Kellogg Found. Fellowships, 1979—80; trustee Ctr. for Effective Philanthropy, 1981—85, Aga Khan U., Karachi, Pakistan, 1985—; mem. coordinating com. Boston Bus. Roundtable, 1994; bd. dirs. Pub. Health Rsch. Inst. of N.Y.C., 1969—76, Winnifred Masterson Burke Relief Found., 1972—80, 1982—88; trustee Goodspeed Musicals, 2002—. Fellow: APHA, ACP; mem.: NAS (Inst. Medicine 1984—), Vol. Hosps. Am. (bd. dirs. 1990), Pvt. Industry Coun. Boston, Mass. Hosp. Assn. (chmn.-elect 1989—90, chmn. 1990—91), N.Y. Acad. Medicine, Ill. Hosp. Assn. (chmn. 1979—80), Inst. Medicine NAS, Assn. Med. Schs. N.Y. N.J. (trustee 1970—76, pres. 1972—76), Assn. Am. Med. Colls. (coun. deans 1969—77, chair elect 1975—76, mem. assembly 1976—77, liaison cmty. med. edn. 1982—88, chmn. 1983—91, exec. coun. 1985—89, chmn. 1988—90, coun. tchg. hosps. 1988—94, chmn. 1991—92), N.Y. Acad-.Medicine, N.Y. County Med. Soc., N.J. State Med. Soc., Harvey Soc. Personal E-mail: jrobertbuchanan@aol.com.

BUCHANAN, LOUISE, political organization worker, consultant; d. James Ellis and May (Hall) Buchanan. BA, Blue Mountain Coll., 1958; MA, Carver Sch. Missions and Social Work, 1960. Exec. dir. Bapt. Good Will Ctr., Charleston, SC, 1960—65; comty. organizer Inner City Meth. Coun., Louisville, 1965—66; neighborhood coord. Comty. Action Commn., Louisville, 1966—71; supr. comty. resources Ky. Dept. Child Welfare, Louisville and Frankfort, Ky., 1971—74; exec. asst. to Rep. Jack Kemp U.S. Ho. Reps., Washington, 1974—76, exec. asst. to Rep. Joe Early, 1976—93; cons. child advocacy Washington, 1993—; mem. adv. bd. Efforts from Ex-Convicts, Washington, 1978—96; exec. bd. pres. Life Pieces to Masterpieces, Washington, 1997—; mem. adv. bd. Congl. Chorus, Washington, 1989—. Organizer Capitol Hill Staffers for Hungry and Homeless, Washington, 1976—93; trainer benefit walks For Love of Children, Washington, 1988; active Arlingtonians for Better County, 1997; mem. Common Cause, 1989—; coord. Capitol Hill Women's Polit. Caucus, Washington, 1976—83; mem., v.p. Park Spring Bd. Park Spring Condo Assn., 1999—. Recipient Keys to City of Worcester, Mass., Worcester City Coun., 1986, 1988, outstanding Svc. award, Efforts from Ex-Convicts, 1992, Leadership award, Life Pieces to Masterpieces, 2002. Democrat. Presbyterian. Avocations: music, writing, travel, tennis, being a loyal friend. Home: # 201 5075 7th Rd S Arlington VA 22204 Office: Consulting for Creative Change # 201 5075 7th Rd S Arlington VA 22204 Office Phone: 703-820-7293. Personal E-mail: lbuch44@msn.com.

BUCHANAN, MARGARET E., publishing executive; m. Greg Buchanan; 2 children. BA, MBA, U. Cin. Various mgmt. positions Rockford Register Star, Ill.; pres. & pub. Elmira Star-Gazette, NY, 1996—99, Idaho Statesman, Boise, 1999—2003, Cin. Enquirer, 2003—. Bd. trustees U. Cin., 2006—. Mem. Cin. Bus. Com., Comml. Club., Cin., Women's Leadership Collaborative, Cin., Northern Ky. Vision 2015 Leadership Team; bd. dirs. Marvin Lewis Cmty. Fund, Fine Arts Fund, Cin. Ctr. City Devel. Corp. Named one of Career Women of Achievement, Cin. YMCA, 2006. Office: Cin Enquirer 312 Elm St Cincinnati OH 45202*

BUCHANAN, MARY BETH, prosecutor; BA, Calif. U. Pa., 1984; JD, U. Pittsburgh Sch. Law, 1987. Assoc. Strassburger, McKenne, Gutnick and Potter, Pittsburgh, 1987—88; asst. US atty. civil divsn. (we. dist.) Pa. US Dept. Justice, 1988—92, asst. US atty. criminal divsn. (we. dist.) Pa., 1992—2001, US atty. (we. dist) Pa., 2001—, dir. exec. office US Attorneys Washington, 2004. Mem. adv. com. U.S. Sentencing Commn., 2002—03; chair adv. com. U.S. Attys., 2003—04. Pres. bd. dir. Am. Heart Assn.; chairperson Crimes Against Children Task Force; v.p. Parental Stress Ctr.; sec. Found. Calif. U. of Pa. Recipient Susan B. Anthony award, Women's Bar Assn., 2002, Vectors Pitts. Person of Yr. award, law and govt., 2003, Athena award, Pitts. C. of C., 2004. Mem.: Internat. Women's Forum, Pa. Commn. on Women in the Profession, Women's Bar Assn. of Western Pa. (pres.), Am. Inns of Court (pres., U. Pitts. Chapt.), Allegheny County Bar Assn. (chair, judiciary com., chair, criminal practice com., Fed. Ct. Sect.). Office: US Attys Office 633 US Post Office & Courthouse Pittsburgh PA 15219*

BUCHANAN, NANCY PAGE, artist, educator; b. Boston, Aug. 30, 1946; d. Louis Nicot Ridenour, Jr. and Gretchen K. Ridenour; m. John M. Buchanan, Nov. 1964 (div.); 1 child, Page Myles; m. Ransom W. Rideout Jr., Dec. 19, 1974 (div.); m. Douglas J. Wichert, Mar. 22, 1987. BFA, U. Calif., Irvine, 1969, MFA, 1971. Lectr. U. Calif., LA & San Diego, 1982; asst. prof. U. Wis., Madison, 1982—84; vis. artist U. Ariz., Tucson, 1985—86; faculty, film & video Calif. Inst. Arts, Valencia, 1988—. Curator social works exhbn. LA Inst. Contemporary Art, 1979; curator Umetnostna Galerija, Maribor, Slovenia, 2000—00. Exhibitions include Ctr. Pompidou Exhibit: LA, 1955-1985, Paris, CD-ROM, Developing: The Idea of Home, 1999, video screening, Talking Back: Video Viewpoints-Nancy Buchanan, Mus. Modern Art, one-woman shows include San Francisco McBean Gallery, 1988. Co-prodr. artist's program Close Radio, LA, 1977; founding mem., artist F Space Gallery, Santa Ana, Calif., 1971—73, Grandview I & II Galleries, The Woman's Bldg., LA, 1974—75; founding mem. Double X Feminist Art Collective, LA, 1975—78; exhibitions com. Arroyo Arts Collective, LA, 1998—2001. Grantee Artists in Cmtys. grant, Calif. Arts Coun., 1986—88, City of LA Artist's grant, Cultural Affairs Dept., City

LA, 1999; Individual Artist's fellowship, Nat. Endowment for the Arts, 1978, 1980, 1983, 1989, Rockefeller New Media fellowship, Rockefeller Found., 1996. Office: Calif Inst Arts 24700 McBean Pky Valencia CA 91355 Office Phone: 661-255-1050. Business E-Mail: buchanan@calarts.edu.

BUCHANAN, PAT (PATRICK JOSEPH BUCHANAN), journalist, political commentator; b. Washington, Nov. 2, 1938; s. William Baldwin and Catherine E. (Crum) B.; m. Shelley Ann Scarney, May 8, 1971. AB in English cum laude, Georgetown U., 1961; MS in Journalism, Columbia U., 1962. Editorial writer St. Louis Globe-Dem., 1962-64, asst. editorial editor, 1964—65; exec. asst. to Richard M. Nixon, 1966-69; spl. asst. to Pres. Richard NIxon The White House, 1969-73; cons. to Presidents Nixon and Ford, 1973-74; commentator NBC Radio Network, 1978-82; columnist TV Guide, 1975—77; syndicated columnist NY Times Spl. Features, 1975-78, Chgo. Tribune-NY News Syndicate, 1978-85; dir. comm. The White House, Washington, 1985-87; syndicated columnist Tribune Media Svcs., 1987-91, 93-95, Creators Syndicate, 1997—99, 2001—. Co-host Buchanan-Braden Show, Sta. WRC, 1978-83, columnist; co-host Crossfire (TV show) Cable News Network, 1982-85, 87-91, 93-95, 97-99; panelist The McLaughlin Group, NBC/PBS, 1982-85, 88-92, 97-99, 2001—, After Hours WTOP-TV, 1979-1982; moderator Capital Gang (TV Show) Cable News Network, 1988-91; co-host Buchanan and Press, MSNBC, 2002-2003; editor-in-chief newsletter PJB-From the Right, 1990-91; co-founder, editor The Am. Conservative, 2002—; candidate for Rep. Nomination for Pres., 1992, 96, Reform Party candidate for Pres., 2000; founder, chmn. The Am. Cause, 1993-95, 97-99, 2001—, Pat Buchanan & Co., Mut. Broadcasting System, 1993-95; polit. analyst MSNBC, 2003-. Author: The New Majority: President Nixon at Mid-Passage, 1973, Conservative Votes, Liberal Victories: Why the Right Has Failed, 1975, Right from the Beginning, 1988, America Asleep, 1991, The Great Betrayal: How American Sovereignty and Social Justice Are Being Sacrificed to the Gods of the Global Economy, 1998, A Republic, Not an Empire: Reclaiming America's Destiny, 1999, Death of the West: How Dying Populations and Immigrant Invasions Imperil Our Country and Civilization, 2002, Where the Right Went Wrong: How Neoconservatives Subverted the Reagan Revolution and Hijacked the Bush Presidency, 2004, State of Emergency: The Third World Invasion and Conquest of America, 2006. Mem. Pres.'s Commn. White House Fellowships, 1969-73; v.p. Am. Coun. of Young Polit. Leaders, 1974-75, 76-79. Named Knight of Malta, 1987. Independent. Roman Catholic.*

BUCHANAN, RICHARD KENT, electronics company executive; b. Schenectady, Sept. 10, 1951; s. Richard Linton and Jeanette (Dunn) B.; m. Diane Carolyn Laffler, Oct. 14, 1984; 1 child, Lindsay Sarah. BSEE, USAF Acad., 1973; MBA, Harvard U., 1980. Commd. 2d lt. USAF, 1973, advanced through grades to capt., 1976; resigned, 1978; mgmt. cons. Bain and Co., Boston, 1979-82; corp. dir. strategy Gen. Instrument Corp., NYC, 1982-84; mgr. strategic planning GE Med. Systems Group, Milw., 1984-86, mgr. mktg. magnetic resonance, 1986-87, product gen. mgr. magnetic resonance bus. unit, 1987-89; dir. strategic mktg. Motorola Communications Sector, Schaumburg, Ill., 1989-91; dir. internat. networks svcs. Motorola Land Mobile Sector, Schaumburg, Ill., 1991-94; v.p., gen. mgr. Am. Parts Divsn., Motorola, Schaumburg, Ill., 1994-97, Radio Products Group, N.Am. Divsn., Motorola, Rolling Meadows, Ill., 1997-2000; v.p., gen. mgr. Global eBusiness, Motorola, Deer Park, Ill., 2000—05; v.p. corp. tech. and devel, chief growth officer Harris Corp., Melbourne, Fla., 2005—. Contbr. numerous articles on time div. multiple access comm. systems to profl. jours. Scholar, NSF, 1968. Mem. IEEE, N.Y. Acad. Scis. Republican. Avocations: skiing, travel, art, swimming. Home: 1085 Hwy A1A Ste 1302 Satellite Beach FL 32937 Office: Harris Corp 1245 NASA Blvd Melbourne FL 32919 Office Phone: 321-724-3760. Personal E-mail: rkentb333@aol.com. Business E-Mail: kent.buchanan@harris.com.

BUCHANAN, RICHARD N., dean, dental educator; m. Patricia Buchanan; children: Jennifer, Brian. Grad., U. Tex., Austin; DMD, U. Pa. Sch. Dental Medicine, 1969. Dental officer US Mil. Acad.; pvt. dental practice; instr. Georgetown U. Sch. Dentistry, 1972—73; mem. faculty U. Tex. Health Sci. Ctr., San Antonio, 1973—89, chair dept. gen. practice, assoc. dean academic affairs, interim dean, spl. cons. strategic planing Grad. Sch. Biomedical Sciences; exec. assoc. dean NJ Dental Sch., U. Medicine & Dentistry NJ, Newark, 1989—91, acting dean, 1990—91, dean, 1991—96, Baylor Coll. Dentistry, Tex. A&M Sys. Health Sci. Ctr., Dallas, 1996—2000, dir. advanced clin. edn., 2001—02; sr. fellow Ctr. for Ednl. Policy & Rsch. Am. Dental Edn. Assn., Washington, DC, 2000—01; dean SUNY Buffalo Sch. Dental Medicine, 2002—, prof. restorative dentistry, 2002—. Reviewer Jour. Dental Edn.; bd. mem. Friends of the Nat. Inst. of Dental and Craniofacial Rsch., 2005—. Fellow: Internat. Coll. Dentists, Am. Coll. Dentists; mem.: Am. Dental Edn. Assn. (Member-at-Large 2005—), ADA, S.W. Acad. Restorative Dentistry, Omicron Kappa Upsilon. Office: SUNY Sch Dental Medicine 3435 Main St 325 Squire Hall Buffalo NY 14214 Office Fax: 716-833-3517.

BUCHANAN, RICHARD W., sports association executive, lawyer; Grad., Amherst Coll., Mass., 1985, Harvard Law Sch., 1988. Clk. to Judge Kenneth W. Starr US Ct. Appeals (DC cir.); atty. Covington & Burling, Washington; asst. gen. counsel NBA, NYC, 1993—95. dep. gen. counsel, 1995—99, v.p., gen. counsel, 1999—2001, sr. v.p., gen. counsel, 2001, exec. v.p., gen. counsel. Mem. faculty Practicing Law Inst. Editor: Harvard Law Rev. Office: NBA Olympic Tower 645 5th Ave Fl 10 New York NY 10022-5986*

BUCHANAN, ROBERT MCLEOD, lawyer; b. NYC, Oct. 4, 1932; s. Albert William and Elizabeth (McLeod) B.; m. Jane Vidaud Britton, July 6, 1957; children: Robert M. Jr., Jamy B. Buchanan Madeja, Stephen S., Genevra V. Buchanan Casais. BA, Dartmouth Coll., 1954; JD, Harvard U., 1959. Bar: N.Y. 1960, Mass. 1969, U.S. Supreme Ct. 1973. Assoc. Debevoise & Plimpton, NYC, 1959-68; ptnr. Sullivan & Worcester LLP, Boston, 1968-2000, of counsel, 2000—. Contbr. articles on antitrust law to profl. jours. Moderator Town of Weston, Mass., 1980—, mem., chmn. fin. com., 1975-80; chmn. weston Hist. Dist. Study Com., 1973. With U.S. Army, 1954-56. Mem. Mass. Bar Assn. (ethics com. 1986—), Boston Bar Assn. (chmn. antitrust com. 1980-86). Avocations: reading, guitar playing, bicycling, kayaking. Office: Sullivan & Worcester LLP 1 Post Office Sq Ste 2100 Boston MA 02109-2129 Office Phone: 617-338-2861. Business E-Mail: rbuchanan@sandw.com.

BUCHANAN, ROBIN BYINGTON, school system adminifstrator; b. Columbus, Ohio, Jan. 20, 1953; d. Eugene Clare (Stepfather) and Patricia Clark Battels, Robert Clifford and Betty Byington (Stepmother); m. Brooks Wayne Buchanan, June 28, 1980; children: Nathan Brooks, Daniel Clark. AA, Wingate Coll., 1972; BA, Meredith Coll., Raleigh, NC, 1974; Masters, Appalachian State U., Boone, NC, 1978; Ednl. Specialist, Western Carolina U., Cullowhee, NC, 2003, EdD, 2006. Cert. early childhood edn. tchr. N.C. Dept. of Pub. Instrn., 1974, prin. N.C. Dept. of Pub. Instrn., 1981, supt. N.C. Dept. of Pub. Instrn., 2003. Tchr. Montgomery County Schs., Troy, NC, 1974—75, Mitchell County Schs., Bakersville, NC, 1975—86, asst. prin., 1986—96, prin., 1997—2000, asst. supt., 2000—04, assoc. supt., 2004—. Ext. adv. coun. Mitchell County Agrl. Ext., Bakersville, NC, 2000—; bd. dirs. Mitchell County 4-H, Bakersville, NC, Mitchell County Communities in Schs., Spruce Pine, NC. Mem. Mitchell County Juvenile Crime Prevention Coun., Bakersville, NC, 1990; vol. leader Mitchell County 4-H, Spruce Pine, NC, 1994—2005; sanctuary choir mem. First Bapt. Ch., Spruce Pine, NC, 1988, children's Bible drill dir., 1993—2001, Sunday sch. dept. dir., 1994—, Sunday sch. dir., 1996—2000, youth Bible drill dir., 2002—. Mem.: ASCD, N.C. Prins. and Asst. Prins. Assn., N.C. ASCD, N.C. Assn. of Sch. Administrs., Delta Kappa Gamma, Phi Kappa Phi, Pi Lambda Theta. Avocations: reading, walking. Office: Mitchell County Schs 72 Ledger School Rd Bakersville NC 28705 Home Phone: 828-688-4432.

BUCHANAN, TOM, academic administrator; m. Jacque Buchanan; 1 child, Eric. BS, SUNY; MS, Univ. Wyo.; PhD, Univ. Ill., Urbana-Champaign. Instr. Pa. State Univ., Univ. Ill.; asst. prof. Univ. Wyo., Laramie, 1979—85, assoc. prof., 1988—91, prof. geog., 1991, assoc dean, Coll. Arts & Sci., 1991—97, assoc. provost, 1997—98, v.p. acad. affairs, 1998—2005, pres., 2005—. Past. pres. NW Acad. Forum. Office: Univ of Wyoming Dept 3434 1000 E University Ave Laramie WY 82071*

BUCHANAN, VERN (VERNON G. BUCHANAN), congressman; b. Detroit, May 8, 1951; m. Sandy Buchanan; children: James, Matt. BBA, Cleary U., 1975; MBA, U. Denver, 1986. Founder, chmn. Am. Speedy Printing, 1976—91; chmn. Buchanan Enterprises, 1994—; mem. US Congress from 13th Fla. dist., 2007—; mem. transp. & infrastructure com., vets com., small bus. com. State fin. chair Mel Martinez's Election Campaign, 2004; co-chair Rep. Nat. Fin. Com. Chmn. Fla. C.of C., Sarasota C. of C. Served in Mich. Air Nat. Guard, 1970—76. Republican. Baptist. Office: 1516 Longworth House Office Bldg Washington DC 20515 also: 235 N Orange St Ste 201 Sarasota FL 34236

BUCHANAN, WALTER WOOLWINE, electrical engineer, educator, academic administrator; b. Lebanon, Ind., Oct. 6, 1941; s. Eugene Neptune and Amy Malvina (Woolwine) B.; m. Carol Ann Saunders, Dec. 28, 1968 (div. 1978); children: William Saunders, John Douglas; m. Charlotte Jane Drake, 1985. BA, Ind. U., 1963, JD, 1973, PhD, 1993; BS in Engring., Purdue U., 1982, MS in Elec. Engring., 1984. Bar: Ind.; registered profl. engr., Ind., Fla., Tenn., Oreg., Mass., Tex. Aerospace engr. Martin Co., Denver, 1963-64, Boeing Co., New Orleans, 1964-65; audit coord. Ind. Tax Bd., Indpls., 1970-73; atty. VA, Indpls., 1973-79; electronics engr. Naval Avionics, Indpls., 1979-86; asst. prof. Ind. U.-Purdue U., Indpls., 1986-93, U. Ctrl. Fla., Orlando, 1993-95; assoc. prof., chair Mid. Tenn. State U., Murfreesboro, 1995-96; prof., dean Oreg. Inst. Tech., Klamath Falls, 1996-99; prof., dir. Northeastern U., Boston, 1999—2005; prof. and J.R. Thompson chair Tex. A&M U., College Station, 2005—. Evaluator Accreditation Bd. for Engring. and Tech., Balt., 1987—, mem. tech. accreditation commn., 1998—2003, mem. exec. com., 2004—07; past chair Nat. Engring. Tech. Ednl. Clearinghouse; grants reviewer NSF, Washington; cons. in field. Mem. editl. bd. Jour. Engring. Tech.; mem. editl. bd.: Nat. Engring. Tech. Ednl. Clearinghouse, Internat. Jour. of Modern Engring.; contbr. over 100 articles to profl. publs. Faculty coun. Ind. U.-Purdue U., Indpls., 1989-92, exec. com., 1991-92; fundraiser Ind. U. Found., Indpls.; tech. com. Ind. Bus. Modernization Corp., Indpls., 1990-93; vestry St. Paul's Ch., Klamath Falls, Oreg., 1998-99; vestry King's Chapel, Boston, 2004-05. Lt. comdr. USN, 1965-69, Vietnam. Recipient Glenn W. Irwin award, Peter Marbaugh award Ind. U.-Purdue U. Indpls., 1988; Wright scholar Ind. U., 1961; Rsch. grantee Ctr. on Philanthropy, 1992, Fla. Engring. and Indsl. Experimentation Sta., 1993, NSF, 2004. Fellow: NSPE (chair 2007—, educator, exec. bd., past sec., Profl. Engr. in Edn. award 1993, 1997), Am. Soc. for Engring. Edn. (exec. bd. ednl. rsch. and methods divsn. 1986—92, exec. com. engring. tech. divsn. 1994—, bd. dirs. 2003—, past chmn. engring. tech. divsn., internat. enrgring. tech. Listserv adminstr., Centennial award 1993, Frederick J. Berger award 2000, James H. McGraw award 2003, rsch. grantee); mem.: IEEE (sr.; com. tech. accreditation activities, past chair, press electronics tech. editl. bd.), Mass. Soc. Profl. Engrs. (past pres.), Engring. Tech. Coun. (exec. com. 2002—, chair 2006—), Indpls. Sci. and Engring. Found. (bd. dirs. 1988—92), Profl. Engrs. in Oreg. (chair engring. edn. 1997—99, pres. elect 1999), Soc. Mfg. Engrs. (sr.), Tenn. Soc. Profl. Engrs. (chair engring. edn. 1996), Fla. Engring. Soc. (chair engring. edn. 1993—95), Ind. Soc. Profl. Engrs. (chair engring. edn. 1988—92), Engring Tech. Leadership Inst. (past chair), Ancient and Honorable Arty. Co. Mass., Univ. Faculty Club (bd. dirs. 1988—93), Scientech Club (bd. dirs. 1990—92), Sigma Epsilon Rho, Epsilon Pi Tau, Alpha Phi Omega, Phi Beta Delta, Delta Phi Alpha, Tau Alpha Pi (past pres.), Order of Engr., Engring. and Sci. Hall of Fame. Republican. Episcopalian. Achievements include systems test evaluation on the Apollo booster rocket. Home: 2240 Rockingham Loop College Station TX 77845-4854 Office: Tex A&M Univ Dept Engring Tech and Indsl Distbrn 3367 TAMU College Station TX 77843-3367 Business E-Mail: buchanan@entc.tamu.edu.

BUCHANAN, WILLIAM H., JR., retired lawyer, venture capitalist; b. Summit, NJ, July 2, 1937; s. William Hobart and Margaret R. B.; m. Eleanor A. Lincoln, June 18, 1966; children: Diana A., Jessica R. AB, Princeton U., 1959; LL.B., Harvard U., 1963. Bar: N.Y. 1964. Assoc. firm Shearman & Sterling, NYC, 1963-70; v.p., sec., gen. counsel Reuben H. Donnelley Corp., NYC, 1970-91, sr. v.p., chief legal counsel, 1991-97; asst. sec., assoc. gen. counsel Dun & Bradstreet Corp., NYC, 1976-79, v.p., sec., assoc. gen. counsel, 1979-91, v.p. law, 1991-96, v.p. law, sec., 1996-97; pres. Spencer Trask Spin-Off Group LLC, 1998—2001; exec. v.p. Spencer Trask Intellectual Capital Co. LLC, 1999—2001; ret., 2001. Served with USMCR, 1959-60. Mem. Am. Soc. Corp. Secs. (pres. N.Y. regional group 1979-80, nat. treas. 1979-83, bd. dirs. 1983-86). Clubs: Princeton (N.Y.C.); New Canaan Field, Port Royal Club, Naples, Fl., Grey Oaks County Club, Naples, Fl. Republican. Presbyterian.

BUCHBINDER, DARRELL BRUCE, lawyer; b. NYC, Oct. 17, 1946; s. Julian and Bernice (Levy) Buchbinder; m. Janet Grey McLean, Jan. 22, 1977; children: Julian Bradford, Andrew Grey, Ian Jeffress. BA in Politics with honors, NYU, 1968, JD, 1971. Bar: N.Y. 1972, U.S. Dist. Ct. (so. and ea. dists.) N.Y. 1973. Sole practice, NYC, 1972-79; atty. Port Authority of N.Y. and N.J., NYC, 1979-83, prin. atty., 1983-86, dep. chief fin. divsn. law dept., 1986-92, chief pub. securities law divsn. law dept., 1992-2001, asst. gen. counsel, 2001—02, dep. gen. counsel, 2002—03, 1st dep. gen. counsel, 2003—04, gen. counsel, 2004—. With USNR, 1968—70. Mem.: Govt. Fin. Officers Assn., Fed. Bar Coun., Nat. Assn. Bond Lawyers, Pi Sigma Alpha. Republican. Home Phone: 914-834-6041; Office Phone: 212-435-3515. Business E-Mail: dbuchbin@panynj.gov.

BUCHBINDER, ELLEN MAUD, allergist; b. NYC, 1950; MD, Tulane U., 1978. Diplomate Am. Bd. Allergy and Immunology. Intern New England Deaconess Hosp., Boston, 1978-79, resident Bsoton, 1979-81; with Mt. Sinai Hosp., NYC. Asst. clin. prof. Mt. Sinai Sch. Medicine. Allergy & Immunology fellow Mass. Gen. Hosp., Boston, 1981-83. Fellow ACP, Am. Acad. Allergy and Immunology, Am. Coll. Allergy and Immunology; mem. AMA. Office: 111 E 88th St Ph B New York NY 10128-1173

BUCHBINDER, LIGAYA H., dermatologist; b. Iliolo, Philippines, May 2, 1953; d. Fernando and Consejo Hubero; children: Aaron, Lana. BS in Biology, U. Philippines, Manila, 1973; MD, U. East, Philippines. Diplomate Am. Bd. Dermatology. Intern Good Samaritan Hosp., Cin.; resident U. Cin., chief resident dept. dermatology; pvt. practice dermatology Boca Raton, Fla. Author: Young at 45 and Forever, Skin Care: Clear and Simple. Scholar, Philippine Govt., 1966—71. Fellow: Am. Acad. Dermatology; mem.: Palm Beach Dermatology Soc. (pres. 1988—89). Achievements include invention of eyebrow shaver. Office: 2499 Glades Rd Ste 310 Boca Raton FL 33436

BUCHELE, WESLEY FISHER, retired agricultural engineering educator; b. Cedar Vale, Kans., Mar. 18, 1920; s. Charles John and Bessie (Fisher) B.; m. Mary Jagger, June 12, 1945 (dec. 2000); children: Rod, Marybeth, Sheron, Steven BS, Kans. State U., 1943; MS, U. Ark., 1951; PhD, Iowa State U., 1954. Registered profl. engr., Iowa, Calif. Jr. engr. John Deere Tractor Works, Waterloo, Iowa, 1946—48; asst. prof. U. Ark., Fayetteville, 1948—51; agrl. engr. USDA, Ames, Iowa, 1954—56; assoc. prof. Mich. State U., East Lansing, 1956—63; prof. Iowa State U., Ames, 1963—89, prof. emeritus, 1989—; ret., 1989. Vis. prof. U. Ghana, Legon, 1968-69, Beijing Agrl. Engring. U., 1983-84; vis. scientist Commonwealth Sci. and Indsl. Rsch. Orgn., Australia, Internat. Inst., Tropical Agr., Ibadan, Nigeria, 1979-80, Internat. Rice Rsch. Inst., Manila, 1991-92; cons. engr. Detroit Arsenal, Ordnance Corps, Waterways Exptl. Sta., Corps of Engrs., US Steel Corp., GM, Detroit, 1974-76; bd. dirs. Farm Safety 4 Just Kids, Earlham, Iowa, Self-Help, Inc., Waverly, Iowa, JAC Tractor Co Author 18 books; inventor 23 patents Mem. Ames Energy Com., 1974-75; advisor Living History Farm, Urbandale, Iowa, 1965—, bd. govs., 1984—. Maj. U.S. Army, 1943-46, PTO; maj. Ordnance Corps, USAR, 1946-69, ret Named Eminent Engr., Iowa Engring. Soc., 1989; recipient Outstanding Engring. award, U. Ark., 2005, Disting. Alumni 7th Coll. Engring., 2005. Fellow Am. Soc. Agrl. Engrs. (bd. dirs. 1978-80, McCormick-Case award 1988, Henry A. Wallace award for significant contbn. to agr. 2003, Outstanding Engring. Alumni award 2005), Nat. Inst. Agrl. Engrs.; mem. AAAS, Soc. Automotive Engrs., Am. Soc. Agronomy (com. 1961-65), Steel Ring, Internat. Assn. Mechanization of Field Experiments (v.p. 1964-93), Internat. Platform Assn., Osborne Club, Toastmasters Avocations: photography, travel, golf, inventing, writing. Home and Office: 239 Parkridge Cir Ames IA 50014-3645 Personal E-mail: wbuchele@msn.com.

BUCHENROTH, STEPHEN RICHARD, lawyer; b. Bellefontaine, Ohio, Feb. 8, 1948; s. Richard G. and Patricia (Muller) B.; m. Vicki Anderson, June 6, 1974; children: Matthew Brian, Sarah Elizabeth. BA, Wittenburg U., Springfield, Ohio, 1970; JD, U. Chgo., 1974. Bar: Ohio 1974, U.S. Dist. Ct. (so. and no. dists.) Ohio 1974, U.S. Ct. Appeals (6th cir.) 1974. Ptnr. Vorys, Sater, Seymour & Pease, Columbus, Ohio, 1974—. Author: Ohio Mortgage Foreclosures, 1986, Ohio Franchising Law, 1990, also chpts. in books. Trustee, v.p. Godman Guild Assn., Columbus, 1977-83; trustee, sec. Neighborhood Homes, Inc., Columbus, 1977-85; bd. rev. Worthington Pers., 1981—; pres. Worthington Alliance for Quality Edn., 1989-91; bd. adv. paralegal program Capitol U. Law Sch., 1991-2004; pres. chmn. bd. trustees Worthington Edn. Found., 1997-98; mem. Ohio Supreme Ct. Commn. on CLE, 1994-2000, chmn., 1999; bd. advisors C.H.A.D.D. of Ctrl. Ohio, 1993-97; trustee Wittenberg U., 2000—, vice chmn 2005—; bd. trustees Ohio Legal Assistance Found., 2006—. Recipient Cmty. Svc. award, Legal Assts. Ctrl. Ohio, 1987. Mem.: ABA (forum com. franchising), Am. Coll. Real Estate Lawyers, Columbus Bar Assn. (pres. 1992—93, bd. govs., Bar Svc. medal 2000), Ohio State Bar Assn. (bd. govs. real property sect. 1994—, chmn. real property sect. 2003—05, real property splty. bd. 2003—, coun. dels., chmn. legal assts. com., chmn.). Republican. Lutheran. Home: 2342 Collins Dr Columbus OH 43085-2810 Office: Vorys Sater Seymore & Pease 52 E Gay St PO Box 1008 Columbus OH 43215-3161 Home Phone: 614-436-0098; Office Phone: 614-464-6366. Business E-Mail: srbuchenroth@vssp.com.

BUCHHOLZ, CARL M., lawyer; b. Phila., Mar. 12, 1965; BA, U. Va., 1987; JD, U. Penn., 1992. Bar: Pa. 1992, NJ 1992, U.S. Dist. Ct., Eas. Dist., Pa. 1992, US Dist. Ct., NJ 1992, US Ct. of Appeals, Third Circuit 1994, US Supreme Ct. 1997. Spl. asst. to US Senator John Heinz US Senate, Washington, 1987—89; law clk. to Hon. Anita B. Brody US Dist Ct., (ea. dist.) Pa., 1992—93; assoc., litigation dept. Blank Rome LLP, Phila., 1993—99, ptnr., litigation dept., 1999—2001, exec. ptnr., commercial litigation group & sr. principal, govt. relations, 2003—06, mng. ptnr., CEO, 2006—; spl. asst. to Pres. & exec. sec. Office of Homeland Security, Washington, 2001—02. Gen. counsel for Pa. Bush-Cheney 2000 Campaign; gen. counsel Ridge Inaugural Com., 1998—99, Ridge Leadership Fund, 1994—2001; exec. com. Sam Katz for Mayor, 2003; gen. counsel for Pa. Bush-Cheney 2004 Campaign; transition team co-chair Atty. Gen. Tom Corbett, 2004—05. Named one of Best Lawyers in Am., 2005. Mem.: ABA, Temple Am. Inn of Ct. (exec. com. 1994—99), Pa. Bar Assn., Phila. Bar Assn. (young lawyers div. exec. com. 1994—97). Office: Blank Rome LLP One Logan Sq Philadelphia PA 19103-6998 Office Fax: 215-832-5726. Business E-Mail: buchholz@blankrome.com.

BUCHHOLZ, DEBBY, lawyer; B, U. Calif, San Diego; JD, Harvard Law Sch. Gen. counsel John F. Kennedy Ctr. Performing Arts, Washington; gen mgr La Jolla Playhouse, La Jolla, Calif., 2003—. Office: La Jolla Playhouse 2910 La Jolla Village Dr PO Box 12039 La Jolla CA 92039

BUCHHOLZ, DONALD ALDEN, stock brokerage company executive; b. LaPorte, Tex., Mar. 10, 1929; s. Fred T. and Chrystine (McCombs) B.; m. Ruth Vernon, May 17, 1958; children: Robert, Chrystine Louise. BBA, North Tex. U., 1952. C.P.A., Tex. Acct., staff auditor Peat, Marwick & Mitchell, Dallas, 1952-54; asst. sec.-treas., chief acct. ICT Discount Corp., 1954-56; comptr. Eppler-Guerin & Turner, Inc., 1956-59; ptnr. Cheshier-Buchholz, pub. accts., 1959-60; comptroller, sec. Parker Ford, Inc., stock brokers, Dallas, 1960-63, also dir., 1962-63; v.p., chief adminstrv. officer, sec. Weber, Hall, Cobb & Caudle, Inc., Dallas, 1963-72, also bd. dirs.; ptnr., chmn. bd. S.W. Securities Group, 1972—; chmn. bd. Buckley Oil Co., Dallas, 1994-99, 1st Savs. Bank, Arlington, Tex., 1994—. Bd. govs. N.Y. Stock Exch., 1969-71; assoc. mem. Am. Stock Exch.; mem. Chgo. Bd. Trade, Midwest Stock Exch.; bd. dirs. Security Bank N.A., Garland, Tex., 1987-2003; mem. found. bd. U. North Tex., 1998—; dir. Nat. Ctr. for Policy Advisors, 2003—, U.S. Home Systems, 2003--. Trustee Garland Ind. Sch. Bd., 1971-74, pres., 1973-74; trustee Dallas County C.C. Dist., 1978-97, pres., 1982-84, 90-92; bd. dirs. Garland Meml. Hosp., 1981-85, Garland Meml. Hosp. Found., 1981, Alliance of Higher Edn., 1994-96, Coun. for Higher Edn. Accreditation, 1996-97, Dallas Citizens Coun., Old Red Found. 1997-2002, Nat. Ctr. Policy Analysis, 2003—.; dir. Dallas County C.C. Dist. Found., 2003--; mem. bus. adv. bd. Baylor U., 1991-94, pres. adv. bd. Hankamer Sch. Bus., 1995-97; bd. North Tex. U. Found, 2004—, Mannatech Corp., 2004-2005; mem. blue ribbon com. Parkland Hosp., 2005-2006. Recipient U. North Tex. Outstanding Alumnus Svc. award, 1999, U. North Tex. Disting. Alumnus award, 2001; named Disting. Alumni, GHS, 2006. Mem. Nat. Security Dealers Assn. (chmn. bus. conduct com. dist. 6 1985-87, bd. govs. 1988-91), Securities Industry Assn. (exec. com. south ctrl. dist. 1986—, exec. bd. 1990-93), Dallas Security Dealers Assn. (sec. 1961), Tex. Stock and Bond Dealers Assn. (treas. 1982, v.p. 1986-87, pres. 1987-88), Chief Execs. Round Table, Alto Lakes Golf and Country Club, Dallas Country Club, City Club Dallas, Kiwanis (pres. 1957-58). Baptist. Home: 7712 Glenshannon Cir Dallas TX 75225- Office: SWS Group Inc 1201 Elm St Ste 3500 Dallas TX 75270-2180

BUCHHOLZ, TODD, journalist, social sciences educator, consultant; Degree econ., JD, Cambridge, Harvard. Pres. G7 Group, Inc.; assoc. dir. econ. policy The White House, Washington, 1989—92; mng. dir. Tiger Mgmt., NYC; econ. commentator (TV), contbg. editor Worth mag. Worth Capital Pub., L.P., NYC; tchr. econs. Harvard; journalist Wall Street Jour., Forbes, Reader's Digest. Advisor Soros Fund, Goldman Sachs, Tiger Mgmt., Pres.; lectr. in field; spkr. IBM, U.S. C. of C. Author: From Here to Economy, 1996, New Ideas From Dead Economists, 1999, Market Shock, 9 Economic and Social Upheavals that Will Shake the Financial Future, 1999; author Global Markets column Worth mag.; commentator PBS Nightly Bus. Report, ABC News, CNN; appeared on CNN, CNBC, CBS, PBS's Newshour, Firing Line with William F. Buckley, Jr.; contbg. editor: Worth mag. Named one of 21 Top Speakers of the 21st Century, Successful Meetings mag.; recipient Allyn Young Teaching prize, Harvard U.*

BUCHHOLZ, WILLIAM JAMES, communications executive, educator; b. Ladysmith, Wis., July 17, 1945; s. James Fossegard and Hazel Winnefred (Crandell) B.; m. Dorothy Ann Kostka, June 17, 1967; children:

Christopher, Jeffrey. BA, U. Wis., Eau Claire, 1967; MA, Ohio U., 1968; PhD, U. Ill., 1976. Grad. asst. U. Ill., Urbana, 1972-76; asst. prof. English, bus. communication, info. design Bentley Coll., Waltham, Mass., 1976-83, assoc. prof., 1983-91, prof., 1991—, dir. undergrad./grad. bus. communication programs, 1988-95, co-chmn. dept. English, 1993; chmn. dept. English, 1995-2000; cons. in corp. comm. and internet Waltham, Mass., 1978—; chmn. dept. info. design and corp. comm., 2001—. Mgr. pubs. Scholastech Inc., Cambridge, Mass., 1983-9; cons. in field. Author: Writing in Business and Manufacturing, 1998, Truth and Taste: Revisiting High Ethical Standards, 1994, Ontology, Encyclopedia of Knowledge Management, 2006; editor, author: Communication Training and Consulting in Business, Industry and Government, 1983; co-editor, contbr.: The Challenge of Change, Managing Communications and Building Corporate Image in the 1990s, 1989, Global Communications: Applying Resources Strategically, 1990; co-editor: New Corporate Relationships, 1991; contbr. articles to profl. jours., chpts. to books. With USN, 1968-72. Grantee FIPSE, 1986, 87; fellow NDEA-IV, 1967-68, inst. fellow Bentley Coll., 1991-92. Mem.: Boston IA, Phi Sigma Epsilon. Roman Catholic. Avocations: personal computing, swimming, cross country skiing, reading, travel. Home: 44 Raffaele Dr Waltham MA 02452-0313 Office: Bentley Coll Grad Ctr 175 Forest St Waltham MA 02452-4713 Office Phone: 781-891-2216. E-mail: wbuchholz@bentley.edu.

BUCHIN, JACQUELINE CHASE, psychologist; b. Providence, Nov. 27, 1935; d. Leslie Thurber and Mary Hillyer (Lyon) Chase; m. Stanley Ira Buchin, Sept. 14, 1957; children: Linda Chase Sullivan, David Lyon, Gordon Tomlinson. BA, Wellesley Coll., 1957; MEd in Counseling Psychology, Antioch U., 1979; PsyD, Mass. Sch. Profl. Psychology, Boston, 1990. Lic. clin. psychologist Mass. Dir., coord. emergency housing program Multi-Svc. Ctr., Newton, Mass., 1978-81; family therapy intern Newtom Guidance Clinic, 1981-82, Framingham (Mass.) Youth Guidance, 1982-84; psychology intern The Arbour Hosp., Boston, 1984-85, Solomon Carter Fuller Hosp., Boston, 1985-86, Behavior Assocs., Boston, 1986-90; staff psychologist Biobehavioral Treatment Ctr., Brookline, Mass., 1990—; fellow in clin. cognitive therapy program Mass. Gen. Hosp., Boston, 1993-95, clin. assoc., 1995—, rsch. clinician, 1995—; clin. assoc. dept. psychology Ctr. for Anxiety and Related Disorders, Boston U., 2005—. Clin. instr. Psychology Dept. Harvard Med. Sch., Boston, 1995—; faculty mem. Inst. Cognitive Therapy Mass. Gen. Hosp., Boston, 1996—99; founding mem. Acad. Cognitive Therapy, 2000. Pres. Wellesley Jr. Svc. League, 1972—73; mem., bd. dirs. Jr. League of Boston, 1975—77; bd. dirs. Wellesley Cmty. Chest and Coun., 1972—73, Wellesley Friendly Assoc., 1972—73, Family Counseling Region W, 1969; bd. dirs. Wellesley chpt. ARC; bd. dirs. Wellesley Cmty. Child Care, 1976, Human Rels. Svc.; trustee Mass. Sch. Profl. Psychology, 1991—. Mem.: Assn. Advancement Cognitive Behavior Therapy. Episcopalian. Home: Union Wharf Boston MA 02109-1206 Office: Biobehavioral Treatment Ctr 1051 Beacon St Brookline MA 02446-3282 Office Phone: 617-738-4814. Personal E-mail: jbuchin@att.net.

BUCHIN, JEAN, psychologist, educator; b. NYC, Aug. 15; d. Mac and Celia Jacobs; children: Peter J., John D. BA, CUNY; MA, Columbia U., NYC; PhD, NYU. Tchr. NYC Pub. Schs.; counselor, asst. prof. CUNY; mgmt. tng. cons. Met Life Ins. Co., NYC; cons. assessment programs N.Y.C. Divsn. Pers., Sci. and Tech. Adv. Bd., NYC. Mem. Nat. Bd. Cert. Counselors, Nat. Bd. Cert. Career Counselors; asst. prof. school. Which Way With Women program Baruch Coll.; vis. asst. prof. NYU; cons. NYC Tchrs. Consortium; mem. Spkrs. Bur., Child Abuse Ctr.; cons. N.J. Human Resources Divsn.; career cons. AARP; lectr., leader workshops 53d St. Y., NYU, Queens Coll., A.W.E.D., leader workshops Marymount Coll.; mediator ABA; cons. Child Abuse Ctr. Author: Singular Parent, Noah's Ark Minus One. Washington Sq. Coll. fellow. Mem. AAUP, ACA, APA (pres. Tri State chpt. divsn. 35), Ea. Psychol. Assn., Met. NY Assn. for Applied Psychology, Bus. and Profl. Women, Career Devel. Specialists Network.

BUCHIN, STANLEY IRA, management consultant, finance educator; b. NYC, Sept. 7, 1931; s. K. and Bertha (Handman) B.; m. Jacqueline Thurber Chase, Sept. 14, 1957; children: Linda C., David L., Gordon T. SB, MIT, 1952; MBA, Harvard U., 1956, DBA, 1962. Asst. to treas. Bay State Abrasives, 1956-58; rsch. asst. Harvard Bus. Sch., 1958-59, rsch. assoc., 1959-60, instr., 1960-61, lectr., 1961-62, asst. prof., 1962-66, assoc. prof., 1966-69; pres. Applied Decision Sys., Wellesley, Mass., 1969-78; v.p. Temple, Barker & Sloane, Inc., Lexington, Mass., 1975-80, sr. v.p., 1980-90; prin. Arthur D. Little, 1991-99. Pres. Boston-Bermuda Cruising Ltd., 1992-97, Gen. Ship Cruising Corp., 1994-97; bd. dirs. Electrolyzer Corp.; vis. lectr. Templeton Coll. Oxford (Eng.), 1991-93; prof. Arthur D. Little Sch. Mgmt., 1992—; assoc. prof. Boston U., 1997—; chmn. acad. policy com. Met. Coll.; chmn. long-range planning com. Mass. Sch. Profl. Psychology. Author: E-Book about Business Strategy, 2000, E-Book about Marketing, 2001. Trustee, Mass. Sch. Profl. Psychology. With Chem. Corps, U.S. Army, 1952-54. IBM fellow, 1962-63; George F. Baker scholar, 1956. Mem. Am. Mktg. Assn., Inst. Mgmt. Sci., Fin. Mgmt. Assn., Harvard Club Boston, Tau Beta Pi. Republican. Congregationalist. Home: Union Wharf # 304 Boston MA 02109-1206 Office: 928 Commonwealth Ave Boston MA 02215-1206 Office Phone: 617-353-0932. Business E-Mail: sbuchin@bu.edu.

BUCHMAN, KENNETH WILLIAM, lawyer; b. Plant City, Fla., Nov. 20, 1956; s. Paul Sidney and Beryle (Solomon) B.; m. MarDee H. Buchman, May 9, 1985; 1 child, Katherine Elizabeth. AA, U. Fla., 1976, BBA, 1978, JD, 1981. Bar: Fla. 1981; U.S. Dist. Ct. (Mid. dist.) Fla. 1981; U.S. Ct. Appeals (11th cir.) 1986; U.S. Supreme Ct. 1988; bd. cert. city, county, local govt. law., 1996. Ptnr. Buchman and Buchman, Plant City, 1981-85, Buchman and Buchman, PA, Plant City, 1985-91; pvt. practice Plant City, 1991-2000; asst. city atty. City of Plant City, 1982-91, city atty., 1991—. City atty. San Antonio, Fla., 1995-2000; mem. exec. coun. city, county and local govt. law sect. Fla. Bar., 1997—2005, chair, 2003-04. Mem.: Plant City Bar Assn., Fla. Mcpl. Attys. Assn. (steering com. 1999—2002, exec. bd. 2002—04, treas. 2004—05, pres. 2005—06), Kiwanis Club of Plant City (pres. 1986—87), Masons. Jewish. Office: 302 W Reynolds St Plant City FL 33566-3314

BUCHMANN, MOLLY O'BANION, choreographer, educator; b. Baton Rouge, Nov. 22, 1949; d. James Dennis and Annie Laurie (Joffrion) O'Banion; m. Fred J. Buchmann, Aug. 23, 1969; children: F. Jason (dec.), Dennis Andrew. BS in Secondary Edn., La. State U., 1971, MS in Dance, 1973. Artistic dir. Baton Rouge Ballet Theatre, 1976—; choreographer Baton Rouge Little Theatre, 1983—; tchr. dance Baton Rouge Magnet H.S., 1979-85; owner, mgr. The Dancers' Workshop, Baton Rouge, 1973—; dir. dance Scotlandville Magnet H.S., 1986-98; dance dir., profl.-in-residence dept. theatre La. State U., Baton Rouge, 1999—. Vis. artist Arts and Humanities Council of Greater Baton Rouge, 1976; choreographer Aubin Lane Dinner Theatre, Baton Rouge, 1980-82; mem. cultural caucus steering com. La. State Div. of Arts, cons., 1986. Editor La. Dance News, 1976-77. Choreographer numerous ballets. Mem. cmty. fund for the arts com. and campaign cabinets, 2004-07; vol. La. Public Broadcasting, Baton Rouge Symphony, La. Arts and Sci. Ctr., Magnolia Mound, others. Outstanding Undergraduate Tchg. award, La. State U. Tiger Athletic Found., 2002; recipient Mayor-Pres. award for Excellence in the Arts, 1999; State of La. Div. Arts Choreographic grantee, 1982; Baton Rouge Alumni Fedn. scholar, 1967. Mem. Southwest Regional Ballet Assn. (bd. dirs., sec. 1984-88, parliamentarian 1993). Democrat. Roman Catholic. Office: Baton Rouge Ballet Theatre PO Box 82288 Baton Rouge LA 70884-2288 Home Phone: 225-926-6248. Business E-Mail: mbuchm1@lsu.edu.

BUCHOLZ, ROBERT ORLAND, history professor, writer; b. LA, Mar. 17, 1958; s. Robert Edward and Lillian (Aguirre) Bucholz; m. Laurie Lee Noel; children: Katherine Hope, Jeffrey Nicholas. AB, Cornell U., Ithaca, NY, 1980; DPhil, Oxford U., Eng., 1988. Prof. history Loyola U., Chgo., 1988—. Adj. faculty Calif. State U., Long Beach, 1985—88; vis. prof. history Cornell U., Ithaca, 1988; presenter in field. Author: The Augustan Court: Queen Anne and the Decline of Court Culture; co-author (with Newton Key): Early Modern England 1485-1714: a Narrative History; co-editor: Sources and Debates in English History 1485-1714; co-editor: (with Sir John Sainty) Officeholders of the Royal Household 1660-1837 2 vols. Recipient Sujack award, Coll. Arts and Sciences, Loyola U., 1994, Cir. of Excellence Gold medal, Coun. for Advancement and Support Edn., 1998; scholar, English-Speaking Union, Chgo., 1994, Prince of Wales Found. for Architecture in Am., 1997. Mem.: Soc. for Ct. Studies (North Am. com. 1998), Midwest Conf. on Brit. Studies (pres. 2000—02), English-Speaking Union (scholarship chmn. 2002—06). Roman Catholic.

BUCHSBAUM, KAREN FUSON, public relations executive, consultant; b. New Bern, NC, Dec. 26, 1953; d. Robert Henderson and Amelia Carmen Fuson; m. Frederick Joel Buchsbaum, Nov. 23, 1979; 1 child, Ashley. BS in Comms., U. Tenn., Knoxville, 1975. Asst. dir., pub. info. dir. Greater Tampa (Fla.) Bicentennial Coun., 1975-76; dir. pub. rels. St. Francis Hosp., Miami Beach, Fla., 1977-79; dir. advt., comms. and pub. rels. Cedars Med. Ctr., Miami, Fla., 1979-84; prin., co-owner Comms. Strategies, Inc., Coral Gables, Fla., 1984—2002; comm. cons., 2002—. Bd. visitors U. Tenn. Coll. Comms., Knoxville, 1987—; mem. pub. rels. adv. coun. U. Miami, Coral Gables, 1997-2002. Advisor Crime Watch Am., 1994-95; pres. Epilepsy Found. South Fla., Miami, 2000-2002; pres. Carver Elem. Sch. PTA, Coral Gables, 1992-93; participant Leadership Miami, 1984; pub. rels. chair spl. events Gulliver Schs. Parents Assn., 2001-03; pub. rels. chair charity golf tournament Kidney Found. South Fla., 2002. Recipient award Nat. Health Info. Coun., 1999,2000, Pub. Rels. award, 1988-94, 98—, Fla. Hosp. Assn., 1978, 80, 81, 82, 83, 84, 86, 88, 89, 91, 92, 93, 96, 97, 98, 99, 2000, touchstone award Am. Soc. Hosp. Mktg. and Pub. Rels., 1986, 2000, Health and Medicine award for direct mktg. videos Telly Awards, 2000, Cardiovascular Comms. award Am. Heart Assn., 1998, 99, Healthcare Mktg. Report awards 1988, 89, 90, 91, 92, 93, 94, 98, 99, 2000, 2001. Fellow Pub. Rels. Soc. Am. (accredited, chmn. Sunshine dist. 1989, pres. Miami chpt. 1983, MacEachern award 1986), South Fla. Hosp. Pub. Rels. and Mktg. Assn. (pres. 1979), Fla. Soc. for Healthcare Pub. Rels. and Mktg. (bd. dirs. 1979-84). Avocations: travel, reading, antiques, golf, dance. Home: 13627 Deering Bay Dr # 804 Coral Gables FL 33158

BUCHSBAUM, PETER A., judge; b. Bklyn., Dec. 27, 1945; s. Arnold and Rose (Chanes) B.; m. Elaine Frey, Dec. 24, 1967; children: Matthew, Andrew, Aaron. AB, Cornell U., 1967; JD, Harvard U., 1970. Law sec. to Chief Justice Hon. Joseph Weintraub, Trenton, 1970-71; lawyer N.J. State Tax Policy Commn., Trenton, 1971-72; staff counsel ACLU, Newark, 1972-74; asst. dep. pub. adv. N.J. Dept. Pub. Adv., Trenton, 1974-79; lawyer Warren, Goldberg, & Berman, Princeton, NJ, 1979-84; atty., ptnr. Sterns Herbert and Weinroth and Hannoch Weisman, Princeton, 1984-91; ptnr. Greenbaum, Rowe, Smith, Ravin & Davis, Woodbridge, NJ, 1991—2004; judge Superior Court of N.J., 2004—. Spl. counsel N.J. State League Mcpl., Trenton, 1988—94; counsel Boroughs of High Bridge and Flemington, NJ, 1986—2004; commr. N.J. Law Rev. Commn., Newark, 1994—2004; adj. faculty Rutgers-Camden (N.J.) Law Sch.; former cons. APA Growing Smart Project. Columnist: N.J. Reporter Mag., Princeton, 1982—2000, State and Local Law News ABA, 1996—2004; co-editor: State and Regional Comprehensive Planning, 1993; reporter: Land Use Law and Zoning Digest Mag.; contbr. articles to profl. jours. Bd. dirs. Hunterdon County United Way, 1999-2004, Hunterdon County Housing Corp., Flemington, N.J., 1992-2004; mem. twp. com. West Amwell Twp., N.J., 2001-04, mayor, 2003; mem. N.J. State Dem. Com., 1997-2004 Mem. ABA (coun. sect. on state and local govt. law), Am. Coll. Real Estate Lawyers, N.J. State Bar Assn. (chmn. land use law sect. 1986-87, sect. trustee 1983-96, Media award, 1987). Jewish. Avocations: gardening, writing. Home: 126 Bowne Station Rd Stockton NJ 08559-1907 Office: Superior Ct of NJ Hunterdon County Justice Ctr 65 Park Ave Flemington NJ Business E-Mail: pbuchsbaum@aol.com.

BUCHWALD, DON DAVID, lawyer; b. Bklyn., May 10, 1944; BA, Cornell U., Ithaca, NY, 1965, JD, 1968. Assoc. Marshall, Bratter, Greene, Allison & Tucker, NYC, 1970-73; asst. US atty. So. Dist. of NY, NYC, 1973-80, dep. chief criminal, 1977-80; ptnr. Buchwald & Kaufman, NYC, 1980-99; pvt. practice NYC, 1999—2007; ptnr. Kelley Drye & Warren LLP, 2007—. Served to sgt. US Army, 1968-70. Mem. ABA, Fed. Bar Coun., Fed. Bar Found.(pres., 2004-), NYC Bar Assn., NY State Bar Assn. Office: 100 Park Ave New York NY 10017-5516 Personal E-mail: donbuch12@aol.com. Business E-Mail: dbuchwald@kelleydrye.com.

BUCHWALD, EPHRAIM, rabbi; Studied, Yeshiva U. Ordained Rabbi Yeshiva U. Former dir. edn. Modern Orthodox Lincoln Square Synagogue, NYC; founder Nat. Jewish Outreach Program, 1987; founding pres. Assn. Jewish Outreach Programs. Lectr. in field of Religion and Theology. Named one of The Top 50 Rabbis in America, Newsweek Mag., 2007. Office: Nat Jewish Outreach Program 10th Fl 989 Sixth Ave New York NY 10018 Office Phone: 646-871-4444. Office Fax: 646-871-0100.*

BUCHWALD, HENRY, surgeon, educator, researcher; b. Vienna, June 21, 1932; arrived in U.S., 1939, naturalized; s. Andor and Renee (Franzos) B.; m. Emilie D. Bix, June 6, 1954; children: Jane Nicole, Amy Elizabeth, Claire Gretchen, Dana Alexandra. BA summa cum laude, Columbia U., 1954, MD, 1957; MS in Biochemistry, PhD in Surgery, U. Minn., 1967. Diplomate Am. Bd. Surgery. Intern Columbia/Presbyn. Med. Ctr., NYC, 1957-58; resident fellow in surgery U. Minn., Mpls., 1960-67; asst. prof. surgery U. Minn. Med. Sch., Mpls., 1967-70, assoc. prof., 1970-77, prof. surgery, prof. biomed. engring., 1977—, dir. grad. surg. tng., resident tng. program, in-tng. exam., chmn. credentials com.; chair Owen and Sarah Davision Wangensteen Chair in Express Surgery, 2001—. Pres. Minn. Inventors Hall of Fame, 1989-92, chmn. bd. dirs. 1992-94; vis. prof., lectr. McLaren Gen. Hosp., Flint., Mich., 1979, Buffalo Surg. Soc., Mpls., 1980, G.P. Wratten Surg. Symposium, Washington, 1980, Frontiers of Medicine Series, Chgo., 1980, Minn. Endocrine Club, Mpls., 1980, Symposium on Surgery, Tokyo, 1980, Northwestern Med. Assn., Sun Valley, Idaho, 1981, Mayo Clinic, Rochester, Minn., 1981, BSG/Glaxo Internat. Tchg. Day, Norwich, Eng., 1982, Mass. Gen. Hosp., Boston, 1983, SUNY, Stony Brook, 1984, DC Gen. Hosp., Washington, 1984, LA Surg. Soc., 1987, Sch. Dentistry, Dept. Continuing Edn., U. Minn., 1988, others; Alfred Strauss vis. lectr., Chgo., 1989; dir. postgrad. course Bariatric Surgery Primer, ACS; spkr., presenter, cons. in field. Author: (with others) Hepatic, Biliary and Pancreatic Surgery, 1980, Lipoproteins and Coronary Atherosclerosis, 1982, Atherosclerosis: Clinical Evaluation and Therapy, 1982, Nutrition and Heart Disease, 1982, Advances in Vascular Surgery, 1983, Advances in Surgery, 1984, others; contbr. Gibbon's Surgery of the Chest, 4th edit., 1983, Hardy's Textbook of Surgery, 1983, Implantable Pumps: ASAIO Primers in Artificial Organs, 1987, editor, author (textbook) Surgical Management of Obesity, 2006, (book) Pioneer of Gastrointestional Surgery, 2006; contbr. over 300 articles to profl. jours., trans.; mem. editorial bd. Chirurgia Generale, Jour. Clin. Surgery, Infu-Systems Internat., Diabetes, Nutrition and Metabolism, Obesity Surgery Jour. Am. Soc. Artificial Int. Orgn., Jour. Bacteriol. Surgery, Online Jour. Current Clin. Trials, also guest editor other jours. Capt. SAC, USAF, 1958-60. Recipient Inventor of Yr. award Minn. Inventors Hall of Fame, 1988, 90, Clin. Scholar award U. Minn., 1991, Diehl award U. Minn.; recipient numerous rsch. grants univs., Nat. Heart and Lung Inst., Nat. Cancer Inst., Nat. Inst. Arthritis, Metabolism and Digestive Diseases, NIH, med. founds., pharm. cos., corps., 1956—. Fellow ACS (gov. 1999—, Samuel D. Gross award 1969), Am. Surg. Assn., Soc. Univ. Surgeons, Ctrl. Surg. Assn. (program com. 1982-85, chmn. 1984-85, treas. 1992-94, pres. 1997-98), Assn. Acad. Surgery (Disting. Svc. award 1976), Epidemiology Coun. and Cardiovasc. Coun. Am. Heart Assn. (established investigator), Am. Coll. Cardiology, Soc. Surgery Alimentary Tract, Soc. Clin. Trials (program com. 1984-85); mem. AAAS, Minn. Surg. Assn. (First Clin. Rsch. award 1965), Mpls. Surg. Assn., Minn. Heart Assn., Am. Assn. History Medicine, Am. Soc. Artificial Internal Organs (program com. 1984-87, sect. editor Trans.), Internat. Study Group Diabetes Treatment with Implantable Insulin Delivery Devices (sec.-gen. 1984-88, chmn. 1989-94), St. Paul Surg. Soc. (hon.), Am. Coll. Nutrition (mem. editorial bd.), Am. Soc. Bariatric Soc. (pres. 1998-99), Internat. Soc. Obesity Surgery (pres. 2003-04), Owen H. Wangeensteen Soc. (pres. 2007), Paleopathology Club, Alpha Omega Alpha. Avocations: running, riding, tennis, reading, chess. Office: 420 Delaware St SE Minneapolis MN 55455 Office Phone: 612-625-8413. Business E-Mail: buchw001@umn.edu.

BUCHWALD, JED ZACHARY, environmental health researcher, science history educator; b. NYC, June 25, 1949; BA, Princeton U., 1971; MA, Harvard, 1973, PhD, 1974. Instr., dir. Inst. History Philosophy Sci. and Tech. U. Toronto, 1974—92; prof., dir. Dibner Inst. for History of Sci. and Tech. MIT, 1992—2001; Doris & Henry Dreyfuss prof. of history Calif. Inst. Tech., Pasadena, 2001—. Author: (book) The Creation of Scientific Effects, 1994; co-editor: Isaac Newton's Natural Philosophy, 2000, Histories of the Electron, 2001; contbr. articles to profl. jours. Named MacArthur fellow, John D. and Katherine T. MacArthur Found., 1995; recipient award for excellence in environ. health rsch., Lovelance Inst., Albuquerque, 1995. Office: Calif Inst tech Div Humanities & Soc Sci MC 101-40 Pasadena CA 91125

BUCHWALD, NAOMI REICE, federal judge; b. Kingston, NY, Feb. 14, 1944; BA cum laude, Brandeis U., 1965; LLB cum laude, Columbia U., 1968. Bar: N.Y. 1968, U.S. Ct. Appeals (2d cir.) 1969, U.S. Dist. Ct. (so. and ea. dists.) N.Y. 1970, U.S. Supreme Ct. 1978. Litigation assoc. Marshall, Bratter, Greene, Allison & Tucker, NYC, 1968-73; asst. U.S. atty. So. Dist. N.Y., NYC, 1973-80, dep. chief civil divsn., 1976-79, chief civil divsn., 1979-80; U.S. magistrate judge U.S. Dist. Ct. (so. dist.) N.Y., NYC, 1980-99, chief magistrate judge, 1994-96, U.S. dist. judge, 1999—. Editor Columbia Jour. Law and Social Problems, 1967-68. Recipient spl. citation FDA Commrs., 1978, Robert B. Fiske Jr. Assn. William B. Tendy award, Outstanding Pub. Svc. award Seymour Assn., Columbia Law Sch. Class of 1968 Excellence in Pub. Svc. award, 1998. Mem. Fed. Bar Coun. (trustee 1976-82, 97-00, v.p. 1982-84), Assn. of the Bar of the City of NY (trademarks and unfair competition com. 1988-89, mem. long range planning com. 1993-95, litig. com. 1994-96, ad hoc com. on jud. conduct 1996-99, prof., jud. ethics com. 2002-04), Phi Beta Kappa, Omicron Delta Epsilon.

BUCHWALD, PETER SANDOR, science association director; b. Kolozsvar, Transylvania, Romania, Feb. 27, 1963; arrived in U.S., 1992; s. Péter Szilard and Margit (Török) Buchwald; m. Amy Formanek, May 16, 1986; children: Zoltan, Zsuzsa. BS, U. Babes-Bolyai, Kolozsvar, Romania, 1986; PhD, U. Fla., 1997. Tchr. Petru Maior Lyceum, Gherla, Romania, 1986—90, Brassai Samuel Lyceum, Cluj, Romania, 1990; computerized info. mgr. RMDSz, Cluj, 1990—92; rsch. assoc. U. Fla., Gainesville, 1992—97, post doctoral rsch. assoc., 1998—2000; sr. rsch. scientist IVAX Rsch., Inc., Miami, 2000—03, assoc. dir. drug discovery, 2003—. Contbr. over 60 articles to profl. jours., chapters to books; author: (software program) LinBiExp, QLOGP, Soft Drug Design, 1999. Mem.: AAAS, Am. Assn. Pharm. Sci., Am. Chem. Soc., Phi Kappa Phi. Achievements include development of simple molecular size-based model for organic liquids and water. Office: IVAX Rsch Inc 4400 Biscayne Blvd Miami FL 33137

BUCICCHIA, CAROLANNE STEPHANIE, elementary school educator; b. Rockville Centre, NY, Dec. 25, 1982; d. Vincent James and Carol Bucicchia Jr. BS in Music Edn., Hartwick Coll., Oneonta, NY, 2004; postgrad., Five Towns Coll., Dix Hills, NY, 2005—. Cert. music tchr. NY. Music educator Hampton Bays (NY) Union Free Sch. Dist., 2004—. Fellow: Hampton Music Educators Assn.; mem.: NY State United Tchrs., Music Educators Nat. Conf., NY State Sch. Music Assn., Suffolk County Music Educators, Hampton Bay Tchrs. Assn. Office: Hampton Bays Elem Sch 72 Ponquogue Ave Hampton Bays NY 11946 Home Phone: 631-669-3219.

BUCK, EARL WAYNE, private investigator, motel owner; b. La Porte City, Iowa, Jan. 15, 1939; s. Edwin Earl and Uleta Pearl (Purdy) B.; m. Maxine E. Parker, Oct. 19, 1969; children: Brian, Douglas, Stuart, Teresa. LLB, La Salle U., 1969. Asst. mgr. Chgo. br. Atwell, Vogel & Sterling, Scarsdale, NY, 1965-70; pvt. detective, Sioux City, Iowa, 1968-74; mgr. Milw. br. Atwell, Vogel & Sterling, Scarsdale, NY, 1970; sr. auditor Comml. Union Ins. Co., Chgo., 1970-74; police chief McHenry Shores (Ill.) Police Dept., 1973-79; self-employed ins. investigator McHenry, Ill., 1980-88, Rapid City, SD, 1988—; owner Corral Motel, Rapid City, 1988—. Liquor liability investigator for various ins. cos., 1980-88; farm owner, 1986-96; owner High Plaines Detective Agy., 1990-. Chmn. McHenry Shores (Ill.) Zoning Commn., 1972, Police Support Subcom., C. of C. Pub. Safety Com.; key contact Help Abolish Legal Tyranny; active Rapid City Police Res., 1989-90, North Rapid Civic Assn., 1991—, pres., chmn. bd., 1993-94; active Pennington County Air Quality Bd., 1990-93, chmn., 1992-93. With U.S. Army, 1957-61. Recipient Police Meritorius Service award Vill. of McHenry Shores, 1979. Mem. Midwest Ins. Auditors Assn., McHenry County Police Chief's Assn., Rapid City Police Officers Assn., Rapid City Area Hospitality Assn. (bd. dirs.), Rapid City Area C. of C. (safety com. 1989-91), Am. Legion, Fed. Weed and Seed Program Rapid City (steering com.), NRA, Moose, Black Hills Sr. Games. Republican. Lutheran. Avocations: flying, amateur archaeology, photography, fishing, hunting. Office Phone: 605-342-7511. Personal E-mail: buckwayne9@wmconnect.com.

BUCK, GURDON HALL, lawyer, urban planner, mediator; b. Hartford, Conn., Apr. 10, 1936; s. Richard Saltonstall and Aloha Frances (Hall) Buck; m. Martha Finder, 1996; children from previous marriage: Keith Saltonstall, Frances Josephine, Daniel Winthrop. BA in English, Lehigh U., 1958; JD, U. Pa., 1965. Bar: Conn. 1965, US Dist. Ct. 1966, US Ct. Appeals (2d cir.) 1966. Assoc. Shipman & Goodwin, Hartford, 1965-67; v.p., counsel R. F. Broderick & Assocs., Hartford, 1968-69; ptnr. Pelgrift, Byrne, Buck & Connolly, Hartford and Farmington, Conn., 1969—78, Byrne, Buck & Steiner and predecessor Byrne & Buck, Farmington, 1975-78; ptnr. real estate and land use sects., chmn. common interest group Robinson & Cole, Farmington and Hartford, 1979—2002, sr. counsel, 2002—04, of counsel, 2004—. Author: Condominium Development, Forms with Commentary, 1990, 2d edit., 1992; prin. co-author: The Connecticut Condominium Manual, 1972, Real Estate Brokers Community Associations Handbook, rev. edit., 1982, Connecticut Common Interest Ownership Manual, 1984, 2d edit., 2007, The Alaska Common Interest Ownership Manual, 1985, Attorney's and Lenders Guide to Common Interest Communities, 1989, 2d edit., 1999; contbr. articles to profl. jours.; columnist: various newspapers. Lt. USCGR, 1958—62. Recipient Disting. Svc. award, Glastonbury Jaycees, 1968, Pro Bono award, Conn. Law Tribune, 2001. Fellow: Conn. Bar Found. (bd. dirs. 2006—); mem.: ABA (mem. common interest com. law com., real property and probate, joint editl. bd. real property laws, advisor Uniform Planned Cmty. Act, Model Real Estate Coop. Act, Uniform Common Interest Ownership Act), Conn. Assn. Homebuilders Orgn. (mem. developer's coun.), Hartford County Bar Assn., Statewide Legal Svcs. (bd. dirs., pres. 1998—2006, Susan B.

Wolfson award 2006), Conn. Bar Assn. (chmn. com. opinions, chmn. real estate sect., editor Conn. Bar Jour., mem. ethics com., mem. pro bono com., chair pub. svc. recognition com., Pro Bono award 2004, Charles Parker Pub. Svc. award 2006), Internat. Bar Assn. (panelist common ownership consumer protection 1987), Am. Inst. Cert. Planners, Am. Planning Assn., Cmty. Assns. Inst. (pres. Conn. chpt. 1980—83, pres. rsch. found. 1980—83, nat. trustee 1982—88, sec. 1986—89, bd. dirs. 1992—98, Acad. of Authors, Century Club, Byron Hanke Disting. Svc. award), Anglo-Am. Real Property Inst. (bd. govs. 1994—), Am. Coll. Cmty. Assn. Lawyers, Am. Coll. Real Estate Lawyers (bd. dirs. 1986—92, mem. common ownership com.), Am. Law Inst. (advisor Restatement Property 3d Servitudes). Office: 280 Trumbull St Hartford CT 06103-3507 Home Phone: 860-633-5375; Office Phone: 860-275-8222. *The common interest community is the mutual sharing of resources and lives through the land. It is as old as civilization itself and as modern as the latest marketing techniques.*

BUCK, HENRY WILLIAM, JR., obstetrician, gynecologist; b. Kansas City, June 4, 1934; s. Henry William Sr. and Nina Irene (Krebs) B.; m. Barbara Laviece Mallory, Sept. 6, 1963; children: Mallory Renee, Andrew William. BA, U. Kans., 1956, MD, 1960. Cert. Am. Bd. Ob.-Gyn. Gynecologist emeritus Student Health Svc. U. Kans., Lawrence, head gynecology dept. Student Health Svc., 1987—2005; pvt. practice Lawrence, 1967—87. Pres. bd. dirs. Douglas County Citizens' Com. on Alcoholism, Lawrence, 1983-2005; chmn. task force HPV disease Am. Coll. Health Assn. Capt. USAF, 1965—67. Fellow ACS, Am. Coll. Ob-Gyns.; mem. AMA, Kans. Med. Soc., Kans. Ob-Gyn. Soc. (pres. 1980-81), Kappa Sigma, Omicron Delta Kappa. Republican. Lutheran. Avocations: photography, music, writing, travel. Home and Office: 306 Homestead Dr Lawrence KS 66049-2000 Office Phone: 785-843-5610. E-mail: hbuck@ku.edu.

BUCK, JAMES MAHLON, JR., venture capitalist; b. Bryn Mawr, Pa., Apr. 27, 1925; s. J. Mahlon and Grace Irene (Knapp) B.; m. Elia Garrett Durr, Sept. 15, 1953; children: Caroline Buck Rogers, James M. III. AB in Econs., Princeton U., 1946. Ops. mgr. Smith, Kline and French, Inc., Phila., 1948-56, v.p. ops., 1956-65; chmn., chief exec. officer The Drug House, Inc., Phila., 1965-77; chmn. Alco Health Services Group, Valley Forge, Pa., 1977-83; pres., CEO TDH Capital Ptnrs., Radnor, Pa., 1977—. Mem. adv. bd. Phila. Phillies, 1981—. With U.S. Army, 1943-45, ETO. Mem.: Merion Golf (Ardmore, Pa.); Merion Cricket (Haverford, Pa.). Republican. Presbyterian. Avocations: tennis, golf, music, spectator sports. Home: 121 Rose Ln Haverford PA 19041-1724 Office: TDH Capital Corp PO Box 8234/Radnor Ct 259 N Radnor Chester Rd Ste 210 Radnor PA 19087-5259 also: Phila Phillies PO Box 7575 Philadelphia PA 19101-7575

BUCK, JOE (JOSEPH FRANCIS BUCK), sportscaster; b. St. Petersburg, Fla., Apr. 25, 1969; s. Joseph Buck; m. Ann Buck; children: Natalie, Trudy. BA in English, Ind. U., 1991. Announcer St. Louis Cardinals, 1991—; lead play-by-play announcer MLB on Fox, 1996—; play-by-play announcer NFL on Fox, 1994—97, lead play-by-play announcer, 2002—. Recipient Emmy award, Outstanding Sports Personality for play-by-play, 1999, 2001—03, 2005—06. Achievements include became the youngest play-by-play announcer to call a World Series, 1996; has announced World Series, 1996, 98, 2000, 01, 02, 03, MLB All-Star Game, 1997, 99, 2001, 02, 03, 04, Mark McGwire's record breaking 62nd home run, 1998; son of Jack Buck, Hall of Fame broadcaster, and former voice of the St. Louis Cardinals. Office: c/o William Morris Agy 1325 Avenue of the Americas New York NY 10019*

BUCK, LAWRENCE PAUL, history professor, former academic administrator; b. Pittsburg, Kans., Oct. 6, 1944; m. Judy L.; children: David L., Laura T. BA, Wichita State U., 1966; MA, Ohio State U., 1967, PhD in History, 1971. Asst. prof. Widener U., Chester, Pa., 1971-77, assoc. prof. history, 1977-85, prof. history, 1985—, dean Coll. Arts and Scis., 1981-84, acad. v.p., provost, 1984—2004, acting pres., 1994, 2001—02. Author: Die Haltung der Nurnberger Bauernschaft im Bauernkrieg, 1970, Opposition to Tithes in the Peasants' Revolt, 1973, Civil Insurrection in a Reformation City, 1976, Demands for Reform by Urban Dissidents During the German Peasants' Revolt, 1977, The Reformation, Purgatory, and Perpetual Rents in the Revolt of 1525 at Frankfurt am Main, 1985; translator: Monemvasia: The Town and Its History, 1981; co-editor: The Social History of the Reformation; contbr. articles to profl. jours., book chpts. Rsch. grantee Am. Philos. Soc., 1973, NEH, 1974. Mem. Am. Soc. Reformation Rsch., 16th Century Study Conf. Office: Widener U Humanities Divsn One University Pl Chester PA 19013 Business E-Mail: lpbuck@widener.edu.

BUCK, LINDA B., medical educator; b. Seattle, Jan. 29, 1947; BS in Psychology, U. Wash., Seattle, 1975, BS in Microbiology, 1975; PhD in Immunology, U. Texas Southwestern Med. Ctr., Dallas, 1980. Postdoctoral fellow Columbia U., 1980—84; assoc. Howard Hughes Medical Inst., Columbia U., NY, 1984—91; asst. investigator Howard Hughes Medical Inst., 1994—97, assoc. investigator, 1997—2000, full investigator, 2001—; asst. prof. neurobiology Harvard U., Boston, 1991—96, assoc. prof. neurobiology, 1996—2001, prof. neurobiology, 2001—02; full mem., divsn. basic sciences, dir. Buck Lab Fred Hutchinson Cancer Rsch. Ctr., Seattle, 2002—; affiliate prof. physiology & biophysics U. Wash. Sch. of Medicine, Seattle, 2003—. Director's Lecture NIH, 1999; Ulf von Euler Lecture Karolinska Inst., Sweden, 1999; bd. dirs. Internat. Flavors & Fragrances Inc., 2007—. Contbr. articles to profl. jours. Recipient McKnight Scholar award, McKnight Endowment Fund for Neuroscience, 1992, Takasago award for Rsch. in Olfaction, Takasago Corp., 1992, Disting. Alumnus, Grad. Sch., U. Tex. Southwestern Med. Ctr., 1995, Louis Vuitton-Moet Hennessy Sci. for Art prize, R. H. Wright award in Olfactory Rsch, 1996, Unilever Sci. award, 1996, Lewis S. Rosentiel award for Disting. Work in Basic Med. Rsch., 1997, Kenji Nakanishi award for Rsch. in Olfaction, Gairdner Found. Internat. award, Toronto, 2003, Perl/U. NC Neuroscience Prize, 2003, Golden Plate award, Acad. Achievement, 2005; co-recipient of Nobel Prize in Medicine, 2004; named one of Leading Women and Minority Scientists, NY Acad. Sciences, 2005. Fellow: Am. Assn. for the Advancement of Sci.; mem.: NAS. Achievements include discovery of odorant receptors and the organization of the olfactory system. Office: Basic Scis Divsn Fred Hutchinson Cancer Rsch Ctr A3-020 1100 Fairview Ave N PO Box 19024 Seattle WA 98109-1024 Office Phone: 206-667-6316. Office Fax: 206-667-1031. E-mail: lbuck@fhcrc.org.*

BUCK, LOUISE ZIERDT, psychologist; b. Edgewood, Pa., Nov. 21, 1919; d. Conrad Henry and Nancy Leora (Harshberger) Zierdt; div. 1954; children: David Randall, Susan Buck Sutton. BS, Pa. State U., 1940; MEd, U. Pitts., 1954; EdD, Columbia U., 1978; advanced cert., Bklyn. Coll., 1984. Lic. sch. psychologist, clin. psychologist, N.Y. Tchr., dir. Chatham Village Nursery Sch., Pitts., 1953-55, Yellow Springs (Ohio) Community Nursery Sch., 1955-58; tchr. Oak Lane Country Day Sch., Phila., 1958-59, Walden Sch., NYC, 1959-60, Bank St. Sch. for Children, NYC, 1960-61; early childhood tchr., coord. sch. psychology Bd. Edn., City of N.Y., 1961-87; asst. prof. Bklyn. Coll., 1978-80; rsch. fellow Albert Einstein Coll. Medicine, Bronx, N.Y., 1988-89; psychotherapist Fifth Ave Ctr. for Psychotherapy, NYC, 1989, Met. Ctr. for Mental Health, NYC, 1990—2006. Psychologist cons. Bd. Edn. City of N.Y., 1987-88; pvt. practice, N.Y.C. Contbr. articles to profl. jours. Mem. APA, N.Y. State Psychol. Assn., Soc. for Psychoanalytic Psychotherapy. Democrat. Avocations: travel, swimming, the arts. Home: 444 E 86th St Apt 34C New York NY 10028-6459 Office: 27 W 96th St Ste 1A New York NY 10025-6515 Office Phone: 212-749-3867. Personal E-mail: louisebuck@rcn.com.

BUCK, MICHELE, food products executive; BA, Shippensburg Univ.; MBA, Univ. NC. Mktg. Frito Lay, Kraft Gen. Foods.; v.p., mktg.-confections Kraft Foods, sr. v.p., gen. mgr.-confections; sr. v.p. Hershey Corp., 2005—, and pres. US Snacks divsn., 2005—. Named one of Next 20 Female CEOs, Pink Mag. & Forté Found., 2006. Office: Hershey US Snacks Divsn 100 Crystal A Dr PO Box 810 Hershey PA 17033 Office Phone: 800-468-1714.*

BUCK, PETER, musician, guitarist; b. Oakland, Calif., Dec. 6, 1956; m. Stephanie Dorgan, 1995; children: Zoe, Zelda. Student, U. Ga. Guitarist R.E.M., 1980—. Albums include Chronic Town, 1982, Murmur, 1983 (Rolling Stone Critics Poll Best Album of Yr. 1983), Reckoning, 1984, Fables of the Revolution, 1985, Life's Rich Pageant, Dead Letter Office, Document, 1987, Eponymous, 1988, Green, 1988, Out of Time, 1991 (7 Grammy nominations, 3 Grammy awards for Best Pop Vocal Performance, Best Alternative Music Performance, and Best Music Video, 1992), Automatic for the People, 1992 (4 Grammy nominations), Monster, 1994, New Adventures in Hi-Fi, 1996, Up, 1998, Reveal, 2001, Around the Sun, 2004; songs include The One I Love, Losing My Religion, Everybody Hurts (4 MTV Video Music awards, 1994), The Great Beyond, Imitation of Life, It's the End of the World As We Know It. Recipient 2 Billboard Music awards for Top Modern Rock Artist & Top World Album, 1991, MTV Video Music Best Video of Yr. award, 1992, Brit award for Best Internat. Group, 1993, 1995, Patrick Lippert award, Rock the Vote, 1994, Video Vanguard award, MTV Video Music Awards, 1995; named Rolling Stone Critics Poll Best New Group, 1983, Best Band, 1995, 1996, Rolling Stone Group Artist of Yr., 1992; named to Rock & Roll Hall of Fame, 2007. Office: Warner Bros Records 3300 Warner Blvd Burbank CA 91505-4694*

BUCK, REBECCA A., museum administrator, registrar; MS, Boston U., 1972; BA, Oberlin Coll., Ohio, 1968. Curator of collections Eastern Wash. State Hist. Soc., Spokane, Wash., 1975; registrar Hood Mus. Art, Dartmouth Coll., Hanover, NH, 1982—90, U. Pa. Mus. Archeology and Anthropology, 1990—95; chief registrar Newark Mus., NJ, 1995—; adj. prof. mus. professions grad. prog. Seton Hall U., South Orange, NJ. Chair Nat. Registrars' Com., 2000—02. Co-editor: New Museum Registration Methods, 1998; co-author: On the Road Again: Developing and Managing Traveling Exhibitions, 2003, Collection Conundrums, 2007. Mem.: Am. Assn. Museums (Dudley Wilkinson award of Distinction 2001, named to Centennial Hon. Roll 2006). Office: c/o The Newark Mus 49 Washington St Newark NJ 07102 Office Phone: 973-596-6667.

BUCK, THOMAS RANDOLPH, retired lawyer, diversified financial services company executive; b. Washington, Feb. 5, 1930; s. James Charles Francis and Mary Elizabeth (Marshall) B.; m. Alice Armistead James, June 20, 1953; children: Kathryn James, Thomas Randolph, Douglas Marshall, David Andrew; m. Sunny Clark, Sept. 15, 1971; 1 child, Carey Virginia; me. Yvonne Brackett, Nov. 27, 1981. BA summa cum laude, Am. U., 1951; JD, U. Va., 1954. Bar: Va. 1954, Ky. 1964, Fla. 1974. Asst. gen. atty. Seaboard Air Line R.R. Co., 1958-63; sec., gen. counsel Am. Comml. Lines. Inc., Houston, 1963-68; asst. gen. counsel Tex. Gas Transmission Corp., 1968-72; sec., gen. counsel Leadership Housing Inc., 1972-77; pres. law firm Buck and Golden, P.A., 1975-92; exec. v.p., gen. counsel Buck Fin. Svcs., Inc., Ft. Lauderdale, Fla., 1992-99; ret., 1999. Chmn. Hanover Bank Fla.; adj. prof. bus. law Broward C.C., Fla. Bd. dirs. Sheridan House for Youth; trustee Fla. Bapt. Found. Served to capt. USMCR, 1954-58. Mem. Assn. ICC Practitioners (nat. v.p., mem. exec. com.), Maritime Law Assn. U.S., Am. Judicature Soc., Omicron Delta Kappa, Alpha Sigma Phi, Delta Theta Phi. Clubs: Kiwanian, Propeller of U.S. Home: 2222 Woodbine Dr Tallahassee FL 32309 Personal E-mail: trbuck@comcast.net.

BUCKAWAY, WILLIAM ALLEN, JR., lawyer; b. Bowling Green, Ky., Dec. 3, 1934; s. William Allen and Kathryn Anne (Scoggin) B.; m. Bette Joan Cross, July 27, 1963; 1 child, William Allen III. AB, Centre Coll., Danville, Ky., 1956; JD, U. Louisville, 1961. Bar: Ky. 1961, US Dist Ct. (we. dist.) Ky. 1961, US Dist. Ct. (ea. dist.) Ky. 1986, US Ct. Appeals 2004, US Supreme Ct. 1975. Assoc. Tilford, Dobbins, Caye & Alexander, Louisville, 1961-78; ptnr. Tilford, Dobbins, Alexander, Buckaway & Black LLP, 1978—; gen. counsel Clean Coal Power Resources Inc., 2003—. Atty. Masonic Homes of Ky., Louisville, 1985—; gen. counsel Kosair Charities. Elder 2d Presbyn. Ch., Louisville, 1975; emeritus mem. bd. govs. Lexington unit Shriners Hosp. for Crippled Children, 1986, sec., 1989-94; mem. children's oper. bd. Kosair Children's Hosp., 1986-99; mem. bd. govs. Norton Health Care, Louisville, 1999—. With USNR, 1956-58. Named Disting. Alumnus, U. Louisville Sch. Law, 1986, Centre Coll., 1986. Mem. SAR (pres. Ky. soc. 1999-2000, pres. Louisville-Thruston chpt. 2002-03), Nat. Eagle Scout Assn., Soc. of the Cin. in State of Va., Sons Confederate Vets. (adj. John Hunt Morgan Camp 1993-96), Masons (33 deg., past master Crescent Hill lodge 1967, chmn. jurisprudence and law com. imperial coun. Shrine of N.Am. 1989-91), Kosair Shrine Temple (potentate 1986), Rotary, Soc. Colonial Wars (Ky. coun.), Soc. War of 1812 (pres. Ky. soc. 1998-2000, judge adv. gen., gen. soc. 2003—), Sigma Chi, Phi Alpha Delta, First Families Kentucky (chancellor gen. 2006-). Home: 1761 Sulgrave Rd Louisville KY 40205-1643 Office: Tilford Dobbins Alexander Buckaway & Black LLP 401 W Main St Ste 1400 Louisville KY 40202 Office Phone: 502-584-1000. Business E-Mail: wbuckaway@tilfordlaw.com.

BUCKELS, MARVIN WAYNE, savings and loan association executive; b. Sterling, Colo., Feb. 11, 1929; s. Harvey and Myrl (Tarr) B.; m. Doris Torrance, Aug. 1, 1959; children: Lisa K., Devon Carol. BA, U. Denver, 1951; MS, U. Wis., 1952. With Beatrice Foods, Denver, 1952-55; loan counselor Midland Fed. Savs. and Loan Assn., Denver, 1955-56, treas., 1956-62, exec. v.p., 1962-85, Western Capital Investment Corp., Denver, 1985-91. Vice-chmn. Colo. State Bd. C.C.s, 1967-79, chmn., 1974-79; pres. Adult Edn. Coun. Met. Denver, 1970; bd. dirs. Auraria Higher Edn. Ctr., 1975-79, vice chmn. bd., 1977-78; bd. dirs. Auraria Found., 1992—, treas., 1997—; bd. dirs. Rocky Mountain Hosp., 1979, pres., 1980; chmn. Colo. Postsecondary Edn. Facilities Authority, 1981-2005; bd. dirs. Denver Civic Ventures, Inc., 1986, chmn., 1987-90; legis. policy com. Colo. Assn. Commerce and Industry, 1986-89; treas. Colo. Pub. Affairs Coun., 1987-89; bd. dirs. Colo. Symphony Orch., 1990-2000, treas., 1990-96; chmn. The Downtown Denver Partnership, 1991-92. With U.S. Army, 1946-48. Mem. U.S. Savs. and Loan League, Colo. Savs. and Loan League (legis com.), Am. Savs. and Loan Inst. (past pres. Denver chpt.), Contrs. Soc. (past pres. Denver chpt., nat. bd. govs.), Sys. and Procedures Assn. (past pres. Denver chpt.), Adminstrv. Mgmt. Soc. (past pres. Denver chpt.), Denver Metro C. of C. (past chmn. spl. task force studying sch. bond issue, mem. pub. affairs coun. 1991-2005, loaned exec. Nat. Alliance Business-men's program), Phi Beta Kappa. Democrat.

BUCKENMAIER, CHESTER, III, military officer, anesthesiologist; BA, Catawba Coll., 1986; MS, East Carolina U., 1988; MD, Uniformed Svcs. U., 1992. Commd. lt. US Army, advanced through grades to chief; resident WRAMC, 2001. Dir. Army Regional Anesthesia Fellowship. Lt. Col. US Army. Nominee Rave award in Medicine, WIRED, 2005; fellow Duke U., 2002. Office: Walter Reed Army Med Ctr Regional Anesthesia Section Anesthesia & Operative Svc 6900 Georgia Ave NW Washington DC 20307 Office Phone: 202-782-0039. Business E-Mail: chester.buckenmaier@na.amedd.army.mil.

BUCKHOLZ, ROBERT E., JR., lawyer; b. New Haven, 1955; AB, Dartmouth Coll., 1976; JD, Columbia U., 1979. Bar: NY 1980. Assoc. Sullivan & Cromwell, NYC, 1980—87, ptnr., 1987—, now mng. ptnr., corp. and fin. practice area. Mem.: ABA. Office: Sullivan & Cromwell 125 Broad St Fl 28 New York NY 10004-2489 Office Phone: 212-558-4000. Business E-Mail: buckholzr@sullcrom.com.

BUCKI, CARL LEO, judge; b. Buffalo, July 11, 1953; s. John Ferdinand and Adeline (Graczyk) B.; m. Deborah Colleen Bruch, July 22, 1978; 1 child, Craig R. BA magna cum laude, Cornell U., 1974, JD cum laude, 1976. Bar: NY 1977, US Dist. Ct. (we. dist.) NY 1978. Confidential clk. NY Ct. Appeals, Buffalo, 1976-77; assoc. Moot & Sprague, Buffalo, 1977-83, ptnr., 1983-90, Cohen, Swados, Wright, Hanifin, Bradford & Brett, 1990-93; judge US Bankruptcy Ct. we. dist. NY, 1993—, chief judge, 2007—. Editor: The American Constitution From a Polish Ethnic Perspective, 1990, Am. Bankruptcy Law Jour., 2007—; contbr. articles to profl. jours.; assoc. editor: The Am. Bankruptcy Law Jour., 2006—. Pres. Polish Cmty. Ctr., Buffalo, 1978—80, St. Gregory the Great Sch. Bd., Amherst, NY, 1991—96, chair, 1992—95; v.p. Parents Anonymous of Buffalo, 1981; bd. mgrs. Buffalo and Erie Hist. Soc., 1993—, vice-chair, 1995—96, chair, 1996—2001; nat. bd. dirs. Polish Union Am., Buffalo, 1982—86, nat. atty., 1986—93; bd. dirs. Polish Arts Club, 1997—99. Named citizen of yr. Ampol Eagle Newspaper, Buffalo, 1977, 98. Mem. ABA (exec. com. young lawyers divsn. 1987-89), NY State Bar Assn. (mem. exec. com. young lawyers sect. 1984-91, chmn. 1988-89, mem. Ho. Dels. 1989-91, nominations com. 1990-94), Erie County Bar Assn. (chmn. comml. bankruptcy law com. 1987-90), Nat. Conf. Bankruptcy Judges (cir. rep. bd. govs. 2001-04), Profl. Businessmen's Assn. (pres. 1981), Chopin Singing Soc. Home: 225 Halston Pky East Amherst NY 14051-1856 Office: U S Bankruptcy Ct 300 Pearl St Buffalo NY 14202-2510 Home Phone: 716-688-0697. Personal E-mail: carlbucki@aol.com.

BUCKINGHAM, AMYAND DAVID, chemistry professor; b. Sydney, NSW, Australia, Jan. 28, 1930; s. Reginald Joslin and Florence Grace (Elliot) B.; m. Jillian Bowles, July 24, 1965; children: Lucy Elliot, Mark Vincent, Alice Susan. BSc with honors, Sydney U., 1951, MSc, 1953; PhD, Cambridge U., Eng., 1956, ScD, 1985. Cert. chemist; cert. physicist. Lectr., tutor Christ Ch., Oxford, Eng., 1955-65; lectr. Oxford U., 1958-65; prof. theoretical chemistry Bristol (Eng.) U., 1965-69; prof. chemistry Cambridge (Eng.) U., 1969-97, prof. emeritus, 1997—; fellow Pembroke Coll., Cambridge, 1970-97, emeritus fellow, 1997—2005, hon. fellow, 2005—. Author: Laws and Applications of Thermodynamics, 1964; editor: Organic Liquids, 1978, Principles of Molecular Recognition, 1993; editor Molecular Physics, 1968-72, Internat. Revs. in Phys. Chemistry, 1981-89, Chem. Physics Letters, 1978-99. Trustee Henry Fund, 1976—2006. Decorated comdr. Brit. Empire; recipient Ahmed Zewail prize, 2007. Fellow Royal Soc. (coun. 2000-01, Hughes medal 1996), Royal Soc. Chemistry (Faraday medal, 1998), Inst. of Physics (Harrie Massey medal, 1995), Optical Soc. Am. (Townes Award 2001), Am. Phys. Soc., Royal Australian Chem. Inst. (Rennie medal 1958); mem. AAAS (hon.), NAS (fgn. assoc.), Am. Chem. Soc., Internat. Acad. Quantum Molecular Sci., Internat. Union Pure and Applied Chemistry (com. phys. chemistry and biophys. chemistry divsn., v.p. 2001-03), Royal Swedish Acad. Scis. (fgn.). Avocations: cricket, travel. Office: Univ Chem Lab Lensfield Rd Cambridge CB2 1EW England E-mail: adb1000@cam.ac.uk.

BUCKINGHAM, DAVID COWAN, judge; b. Murray, Ky., Oct. 29, 1951; s. Robert Ray and Betty Sue (Hutson) B.; m. Dianne Lee Armstrong, July 10, 1982; 1 child, Tyler Daniel. BA, Murray State U., 1974; JD, U. Louisville, 1977. Bar: Ky. 1977. Asst. county atty. Calloway County, Murray, 1978-81; sole practice Murray, 1978-81; dist. judge 42d Jud. Dist., Murray, 1982-86, circuit judge, 1987-96; judge Ct. of Appeals, Murray, 1997—2006, sr. judge, 2006—. Mem. Ky. Bar Assn., Calloway County Bar Assn. Democrat. Mem. Ch. of Christ. Avocations: golf, baseball card collecting. Home Phone: 270-753-8458; Office Phone: 270-753-8458. Business E-Mail: dbuck01@murray-ky.net.

BUCKINGHAM, EDWIN JOHN, III, lawyer; b. Grand Forks, ND, Sept. 15, 1947; s. Edwin John Jr. and Kathryn Ruth (Aird) B.; m. Cheryl Ann Pantalone, 1971; 1 child, Emma Nicole. AB, Yale U., 1969, JD, 1972. Bar: N.Y. 1973, Tex. 1978. Assoc. Shea Gould Climenko & Kramer, NYC, 1972-74; assoc. gen. counsel Celanese Corp., NYC, 1974-77; mgr. legal affairs Solvay Polymers, Inc., Houston, 1977-79, dir. legal affairs, 1979-81, gen. counsel, v.p., 1981—, Solvay Am., Inc., Houston, 1984—. Sec. Wessex Civic Assn., Houston, 1986-88. Named Chevalier de l'Ordre de Leopold, Belgium. Mem. ABA, Am. Corp. Counsel Assn., Tex. Bar Assn., Tex.-Mex. Bar Assn. Avocations: fencing, birding. Office: Solvay NAm 3333 Richmond Ave Houston TX 77098-3007 Office Phone: 713-525-6080.

BUCKINGHAM, ELIZABETH C., lawyer; b. 1964; AB magna cum laude, Smith Coll., 1985; JD, Harvard Univ., 1988. Bar: DC 1988, Minn. 1994. Ptnr., co-head, trademark and litig. group Dorsey & Whitney LLP, Mpls. Articles editor Harvard Jour. on Legis., 1987—88, lectr., writer in field. Mem.: Minn. Intellectual Property Lawyers Assn., Internat. Trademark Assn., Midwest Intellectual Property Inst., WomenVenture (bd. dir. 2000—), Phi Beta Kappa. Office: Dorsey & Whitney LLP Ste 1500 50 S Sixth St Minneapolis MN 55402-1498 Office Phone: 612-343-2178. Office Fax: 612-340-8856. Business E-Mail: buckingham.elizabeth@dorsey.com.

BUCKIUS, RICHARD O., mechanical engineer, educator; b. Sacramento, July 17, 1950; s. Orland Edwin and Holley (Lynip) B.; m. Kathleen Marie Mariani Buckius, Aug. 21, 1972; children: Sarah Jane, Emily Ann. BS in Mech. Engring., U. Calif., Berkeley, 1972, MS in Mech. Engring., 1973, PhD in Mech. Engring., 1975. Asst. prof. dept. mech. and indsl. engring. U. Ill. Urbana-Champaign, 1975-80, assoc. prof., 1980-84, prof., 1984—, Richard W. Kritzer prof., 1992—97. Assoc. head dept. mech. and indsl. engring. U. Ill. Urbana-Champaign, 1985—87, assoc. vice chancellor rsch., 1988—91, faculty affiliate dept. nuc. engring., 1993—98, head dept. mech. and indsl. engring., 1998—2004; prog. dir. thermal systems and engring. NSF, 1987—88, dir. divsn. chem. and transport systems, 2004—05, acting asst. dir. engring., 2005—06, asst. dir. engring., 2006—. Contbr. articles to profl. jours.; assoc. tech. editor: ASME Jour. Heat Transfer, 1987—93; co-author: Fundamentals of Engring. Thermodynamics, SI version, 1987; mem. editl. bd.: Microscale Thermophysical Engring., Heat Transfer Rsch., Heat Transfer-Japanese Rsch. Fellow: ASME (mem. heat transfer in energy systems 1982—2000, mem. basic engring. tech. operating bd. 1999—, v.p. 2004—05, James Harry Potter Gold medal 2006), AIAA (assoc.); mem.: Am. Soc. Engring. Edn. (Dow Outstanding Young Faculty from Ill.-Ind. sect. 1978, Western Electric Fund award 1981, Ralph Coats Roe award 2003), Pi Tau Sigma. Office: U Ill Dept Mech Sci and Engring 3003 Mech Engring Lab 1206 W Green St MC-244 Urbana IL 61801-2906 E-mail: buckius@uiuc.edu.

BUCKLAND, BARRY CHRISTOPHER, chemical engineer; b. London, Jan. 6, 1948; BSc, Manchester U., Eng., 1970; MSc, U. Coll. London, 1971, PhD in Biochem. Engring., 1974. Biochem. engr. Abbott Lab., Chgo., 1974-77; sr. engr. Lederle Lab., Pearl River, N.Y., 1977-80; dir. Fermentation Pilot Plant, Merck & Co. Inc., Rahway, N.J., 1980-86, biochem. process R&D, 1986-90, sr. dir., 1990-93, exec. dir., 1993-96; v.p. Bio Process R&D, Merck & Co. Inc., 1996—. Vis. prof. Univ. Coll., London, 1989—, Rutgers U., 1990—. Fellow Am. Inst. Med. & Biol. Engring., Internat. Inst. Biotechnology (lectr. 1995); mem. AICE (dir. Food, Pharm. & Bioentring. Divsn. 1993-95), Am. Chem. Soc. (lectr. 1994), Nat. Acad. Engring. Office: PO Box 4 West Point PA 19486-0900 E-mail: barry_buckland@merck.com.

BUCKLAND, JON, musician; b. London, Nov. 11, 1977; Student, U. Coll. London. Lead guitarist Coldplay, 1998—. Musician: (albums) Parachutes, 2000 (Grammy award: Best Alternative Music Album, 2001), A Rush of Blood to the Head, 2002 (Grammy awards: Best Alternative Music Album, 2002, Best Rock Performance By A Duo Or Group With Vocal for song "In My Place", 2002, Record Of The Yr. for song "Clocks", 2003),

Live 2003, 2003, X&Y, 2005, Love, Actually, 2006. Recipient Favorite Alternative Artist (Coldplay), Am. Music Awards, 2005. Office: Capital Records 1750 North Vine St 10th Floor Hollywood CA 90028

BUCKLAND, MARC, television director; Dir.: (TV series) NYPD Blue, 1993—2005, Murder One, 1995—97, Maximum Bob, 1998, Buddy Faro, 1998, Sports Night (episodes: How are Things in Gloca Morra?, Louise Revisited), 1999, Felicity (episode: Cheating), 1998, Providence (episode: Tying the Knot), 1999, Popular, 1999—2001, The West Wing (episode: A Proportional Response), 1999, News from the Edge, 2000, Brutally Normal, 2000, Ed, 2000—04, Couples, 2002, Scrubs (6 episodes), 2001—03, Partners, 2003, Cracking Up, 2004, My Name is Earl (11episodes), 2005—06 (DGA Award fo Outstanding Directorial Achievement in Comedy Series, 2005, Emmy award for Outstanding Directing for a Comedy Series, 2006); exec. prodr.: Medical Investigation, 2004, My Name is Earl, 2005—; dir., prodr. (TV series) Murder One, 1995—97, (TV miniseries) Murder One: Diary of a Serial Killer, 1997, dir., exec. prodr. (TV series) Medical Investigation, 2004, The Jake Effect, 2006, dir., supervising prodr. Brooklyn South, 1997—98; actor: LA Law (episode: Rohner vs. Gradinger), 1987, Tour of Duty (episode: Lonesome Cowboy Blues), 1989, Star Trek: The Next Generation (episode: The High Ground), 1990. Office: c/o Paul Alan Smith Broder/Webb/Chervin/Silbermann 9242 Beverly Blvd Ste 200 Beverly Hills CA 90210

BUCKLAND, MICHAEL KEEBLE, librarian, educator; b. Wantage, Eng., Nov. 23, 1941; came to U.S., 1972; s. Walter Basil and Norah Elaine (Rudd) B.; m. Waltraud Leeb, July 11, 1964; children: Anne Margaret, Anthony Francis. BA, Oxford U., 1963; postgrad. diploma in librarianship, Sheffield U., 1965, PhD, 1972. Grad. trainee Bodleian Library, Oxford, Eng., 1963-64; asst. librarian U. Lancaster (Eng.) Library, 1965-72; asst. dir. for tech. svcs. Purdue U. Libraries, West Lafayette, Ind., 1972-75; assoc. prof. Sch. of Info. U. Calif., Berkeley, 1976-79, dean, 1976-84, prof., 1979—2003, prof. emeritus Sch. Info., 2004—, asst. v.p. library plans and policies, 1983-87; v.p. Ind. Coop. Library Svcs. Auth., 1974-75. Co-dir. Electronic Cultural Atlas Initiative, 2000—; vis. scholar Western Mich. U., 1979; vis. prof. U. Klagenfurt, Austria, 1980, U. New South Wales, Australia, 1988. Author: Book Availability and the Library User, 1975, (with others) The Use of Gaming in Education for Library Management, 1976, Reader in Operations Research for Libraries, 1976, Library Services in Theory and Context, 1983, 2d edit., 1988, Information and Information Systems, 1991, Redesigning Library Services, 1992, Emanuel Goldberg and his Knowledge Machine, 2006; editor: Historical Studies in Information Science, 1998, Robert Gitler and the Japan Library School, 1999. Fulbright Rsch. scholar U. Tech., Graz, Austria, 1989. Mem. ALA, Am. Soc. Info. Sci. (pres. 1998), Calif. Libr. Assn. Office: U Calif Sch Info Berkeley CA 94720-4600

BUCKLAND, WENDY, medical products executive; b. Johannesburg, June 5, 1967; d. Isabel Joan and Hugh William Kincaid Smith; m. Charles Reginald Lytton Buckland, May 8, 1992. B in Pharmacy, U. Witwatersrand, Johannesburg, 1988; diploma in bus. mgmt., Damelin Mgmt. Sch., South Africa, 1995. Registered pharmacist South African Pharmacy Coun. Regulatory pharmacist Ciba Geigy (Pty) Ltd., Johannesburg, 1990—92; clin. rsch. assoc. Novartis, Johannesburg, 1992—94, clin. rsch. mgr., 1995—98; clin. ops. mgr. PPD Devel., 1998—99, dir. clin. ops. mgmt. Europe Cambridge, England, 1999—2002, exec. dir. clin. ops., 2002—04, sr. exec. dir. Latin Am., Asia Wilmington, NC, 2005—. Bd. govs. Treverton Schs., Mooi River, South Africa, 1995—99. Mem.: Assn. Clin. Rsch. Profls., Inst. Clin. Rsch. Address: PO Box 976 Wrightsville Beach NC 28480 Office: PPD Inc 929 North Front St Wilmington NC 28401 Office Phone: 910-558-7122. Business E-Mail: wendy.buckland@wilm.ppdi.com.

BUCKLER, MARILYN LEBOW, school psychologist, educational consultant; b. NYC, Mar. 18, 1933; d. Herman and Gertrude (Abolitz) Lebow; m. Sheldon A. Buckler, June 1, 1952 (div. 1978); children: Julie, Eve, Sarah Buckler Welcome. BS cum laude, NYU, 1954; MEd in Counseling, Northeastern U., 1970. Cert. ednl. psychologist, Mass.; sch. guidance counselor, Mass., sch. psychologist, Mass. Kindergarten tchr. Washington Pub. Schs., 1955-56; Stamford (Conn.) Pub. Schs., 1956-58; guidance counselor Framingham (Mass.) Pub. Schs., 1969-70; sch. psychologist, guidance counselor Carlisle (Mass.) Pub. Schs., 1970-95; parent program cons. Reach out to Schs. program Wellesley Coll.-Stone Ctr., 1993—. Tchr. parenting course Middlesex C.C., Bedford, Mass., 1990—, cons. LEAP program, 1992-93; workshop leader, creator parenting courses, various pvt. schs. and orgns., Mass., 1990—; spl. project cons., workshop specialist "Families First" Wheelock Coll., 1995—. Mem. ACA, Mass. Sch. Counselor Assn., Mass. Sch. Psychologists Assn., Pi Lambda Theta. Avocations: films, cooking, travel, reading.

BUCKLER, SHELDON A., technology company executive; b. NYC, May 18, 1931; s. Morris H. and Mollie M. (Smith) B.; m. Dorothea J. Chandler, June 30, 1978; children: Julie, Eve, Sarah. BA, NYU, 1951; PhD, Columbia U., 1954. Rsch. assoc. U. Md., 1954-56; rsch. group leader Am. Cyanamid Co., Stamford, Conn., 1956-62; mgr. organic unit AMF, Springdale, Conn., 1962-64; with Polaroid Corp., Cambridge, Mass., 1964-94, vice-chmn. bd., 1990-94; chmn. bd. Commonwealth Energy Sys., Cambridge, 1995-99. Chmn. bd. Lord Corp., 2000—. Contbr. articles to profl. jours. Trustee Va. Union U., 1973-75; chmn. bd. Mass. Eye and Ear Infirmary, 1996-02. With U.S. Army, 1954-56. Recipient Maurice Holland award Indsl. Rsch. Inst., 1998. Mem. Am. Chem. Soc., Phi Beta Kappa. Achievements include patents in field. Office: Lord Corp 111 Lord Dr Cary NC 27511-7923 Office Phone: 800-524-2885 ext. 6228. Personal E-mail: sheldonbuckler@comcast.net.

BUCKLES, ROBERT HOWARD, retired investment company executive; b. Champaign, Ill., June 30, 1932; s. Renick Hull and Ethel Maxine Buckles; m. Linda Carol Porter, Dec. 27, 1958; children: Meredith Ann, Christopher John. BA, Stanford U., 1953; MBA, Harvard U., 1957. Security analyst Lehman Corp., NYC, 1957-65, v.p., 1965-69, exec. v.p., 1969-73, pres., 1973-84, also bd. dirs.; pres. Gas Properties, Inc., 1973-84; exec. v.p., dir. Lehman Mgmt. Co., 1973-84; pres., chief investment officer Rothschild Asset Mgmt. Inc., 1984-87; mng. dir. Rothschild, Inc., 1984-87; chief investment officer, sr. mng. dir. Furman Selz Capital Mgmt., 1987-97. Dir. One William St. Fund.; bd. dirs. Assn. Publicly Traded Investment Funds. Contbr. articles to profl. publs. With security agy. AUS, 1954-56. Mem. N.Y. Soc. Securities Analysts. Home: 425 E 58th St Apt 35C New York NY 10022-2300

BUCKLES, STEPHEN GARY, economist, educator; b. Kansas City, Mo., June 11, 1943; s. Orland and Leighfern (Emry) B.; m. Mary Parker Harmon, Nov. 28, 1970. AB, Grinnell Coll., 1965; PhD, Vanderbilt U., 1976. Economist Joint Coun. Econ. Edn., NYC, 1970-74; prof. U. Mo., Columbia, 1976-88; pres. Nat Coun. Econ. Edn., NYC, 1989-94; prof. econs., sr. lectr. Vanderbilt U., Nashville, 1994—. Vis. prof. Vanderbilt U., 1983; tchr. NYU, 1972-74; past chair individual investors adv. com. N.Y. Stock Exch.; mem. mgmt. team, standing com. 2006 Econs. Nat. Assessment. Recipient tchg. awards U. Mo., 1986-87, John Schramm Leadership award Nat. Assn. Econ. Educators, 1989, Student's Choice award Vanderbilt, 1996, William Forbes award for Pub. Awareness, 1998, Marvin Bower award in econ. edn., 2002, Egxinga Disting. Tchg. award So. Econs. Assn., 2006. Office: Vanderbilt U Dept Econs Nashville TN 37235 Office Phone: 615-322-0199. E-mail: stephen.buckles@vanderbilt.edu.

BUCKLEW, NEIL S., former academic administrator, educator; b. Morgantown, W.Va., Oct. 23, 1940; s. Douglas Earl and Lanah L. (Martin) B.; children— Elizabeth, Jennifer, Jeffrey. AB, U. Mo.; MS, U. N.C.; PhD (grad. fellow), U. Wis. Dir. personnel Duke U., 1964-66; dir. employee relations U. Wis., 1966-70; prof., v.p. Central Mich. U., Mt. Pleasant, 1970-76; prof., provost Ohio U., Athens, 1976-80; pres. U. Mont., Missoula, 1981-86, W.Va. U., 1986-95, prof. Morgantown, 1995—. Vis. rsch. fellow Pa. State U.; arbitrator in field. Author: Public Sector Collective Bargaining, Planning in Higher Education. Mem. Nat. Assn. State Univs. and Land Grant Colls. Office: West Va U PO Box 6025 Morgantown WV 26506-6025 Business E-Mail: nbucklew@wvu.edu.

BUCKLEY, CHARLES E., retired museum director, curator; b. Apr. 1919; Curator Corcoran Gallery of Art, Wadsworth Atheneum; mus. dir. Currier Gallery of Art, Manchester, NH, St. Louis Art Mus., 1964—75; ret., 1975. Mem.: Am. Assn. Museums (pres. 1972—74, named to Centennial Honor Roll 2006). Mailing: PO Box 416 Mont Vernon NH 03057-0416*

BUCKLEY, CHARLES ROBINSON, III, lawyer; b. Richmond, Va., Oct. 9, 1942; s. Charles Robinson and Eleanor (Small) B.; m. Virginia Lee, Apr. 17, 1971; children: Richard, Rebecca. BS, U. N.C., 1965, JD, 1969. Bar: N.C. 1969, U.S. Supreme Ct. 1979. Asst. city atty. City of Charlotte, NC, 1969-78; ptnr. Constagny, Goines, Buckley & Boyd, 1978-81, Taylor & Buckley, Charlotte, 1981-85, Buckley McMullen & Buie, P.A., Charlotte, 1994—. Town atty. Town of Matthews, N.C., 1978—; faculty Ctrl. Piedmont C.C., 1970. Bd. dirs. Charlotte City Employees Credit Union, 1974-78; pre. PTA, 1980-82; bd. visitors Luth. Theol. So. Sem., 1989-93. Recipient Cert. of Merit, City of Charlotte, 1982. Mem.: Internat. Mcpl. Lawyers Assn., N.C. Assn. Mcpl. Attys. (bd. dirs. 1979—81, v.p. 1995—96, 1st v.p. 1996—97, pres. 1997—98), N.C. State Bar, Optimist Club (pres. 1982—83), Rotary Club (pres. Charlotte South Rotary Found. 2003—), Phi Alpha Delta. Democrat. Lutheran. Home: 6813 Linda Lake Dr Charlotte NC 28215-4019 Office: 4421 Sharon Rd # 200 Charlotte NC 28211-3520 Home Phone: 704-536-5398; Office Phone: 704-362-1056. E-mail: CRB3@bellsouth.net.

BUCKLEY, CHRISTOPHER TAYLOR, editor, author; b. NYC, Sept. 28, 1952; s. William F. Jr. and Patricia (Taylor) B.; m. Dec. 8, 1984; children: Caitlin, Conor. BA, Yale U., 1975. Mng. editor Esquire Mag., NYC, 1977; chief speech writer V.P. of U.S., Washington, 1981-83; editor-in-chief Forbes Life Mag., NYC, 1990—. Author, fiction: Steaming to Bamboola, 1982, The White House Mess, 1986, Campion, 1988, Wet Work, 1991, Thank You For Smoking, 1994 (film version, 2006), Wry Martinis, 1997, God is My Broker, 1998, Little Green Men, 1999, No Way to Treat a First Lady, 2002, Florence of Arabia, 2004; author, non-fiction: Washington Schlepped Here, 2003, Boomsday, 2007; contbr. articles to numerous profl. jours. Mem. The Century Assn., Kollegewidgwok Yacht Club, Bohemian Club. Republican. Avocations: sailing, scuba diving, bicycling, the outdoors. Office: Forbes FYI 60 5th Ave New York NY 10011-8802 Office Phone: 202-244-2024. E-mail: cbuckley@forbes.com.

BUCKLEY, ELEANOR JANE, retired elementary school educator; b. Pitts., Pa., Jan. 23, 1936; d. Jesse Anderson and Virginia (Gillespie) Hiller; m. Richard Dale Buckley, June 19, 1965 (dec.). BSc, Ind. State Tchrs. Coll., Ind., Pa., 1958; MEd, U. Pitts., Pitts., Pa., 1960. Cert. Elem. Edn. K-8. 1st elem. tchr. Dept. Instruction Evaluation Team, Wis., 1972—77; ret. Blood drive coord. Am. Red Cross, 2000—06; citizens adv. ARC, 2000—06; pres. Delta Kappa Gamma hon. Educators Assn., 1974—75, Oshkash Educators Assn., 1984—85; bd. Oshkosh Symphony, Oshkosh, 2001—03; pres. Oshkosh Symphony League, 2002—03. Recipient Expectional Vol. Svc., Am. Red Cross, 2002, Outstanding Vol., United Meth. Women, 2002. Mem.: Oshkosh Educators Assn., Nat. Edn. Assn., Wis. Edn. Assn. Avocations: travel, painting, reading.

BUCKLEY, FRANCIS H., economist, lawyer, educator; b. Saskatoon, Can., Aug. 4, 1948; s. F.J. and H.B. Buckley; m. Esther Goldberg; 1 child, Sarah. BA, McGill U., Montreal, Canada, 1969, LLB, 1974; LLM, Harvard U., 1975. Bar: Ont. 1982. Asst. prof. McGill U., 1977—82, assoc. prof., 1984—89; assoc. Osler Hoskin & Harcourt, Toronto, 1982—84; prof. George Mason U. Sch. Law, Arlington, Va., 1989—, assoc. dean, found. prof. law, exec. dir. Law & Econ. Ctr. Vis. Olin fellow Univ. Chgo. Law Sch., 1988—89; vis. prof. Sorbonne, Paris, 1999—2001, Fondation Nationale des Sciences Politiques, Paris, 2006. Author: The Morality of Laughter, 2003, Just Exchange: A Theory of Contract, 2005; editor: The Fall and Rise of Freedom of Contract, 1999; contbr. articles to prof. jour. Office: George Mason Law and Econs Ctr 3301 N Fairfax Dr Arlington VA 22201 Office Phone: 703-993-8028. E-mail: fbuckley@gmu.edu.*

BUCKLEY, FRANCIS J., JR., librarian; b. Aug. 1942; m. Victoria D. Buckley. BA, U. Mich., MLS, 1965. Libr. Detroit Pub. Libr., 1968—94, reference libr., documents specialist, asst. dir. pub. services; dir. Shaker Heights Pub. Libr., Shaker Heights, Ohio, 1994—97; supr. documents US Govt. Printing Office, 1997—2001; interim dir. DC Pub. Libr., Washington, 2003—04. Chmn. Inter-Assn. Working Group on Govt. Info. Policy; bd. trustees Online Computer Libr. Ctr., Cleve. Area Met. Libr. Sys.; mem. literacy adv. com. Detroit Head Start Prog.; bd. dirs. Detroit Literacy Coalition; rsch. com. United Cmty. Services of Met. Detroit; mem., pres. Govt. Documents Roundtable of Mich. Served with US Army. Mem.: DC Libr. Assn., ALA (mem. coordinating com. on acces to info., mem. spl. com. on freedom and equality access to info., mem. legis. com., chmn. govt. info. subcom., coun. mem., chmn. Govt. Documents Roundtable, chmn. ad hoc com. to forma a coalition on govt. info., chmn. Lippincott award jury, mem. exec. bd. 2005—08), Spl. Libraries Assn., Mich. Libr. Assn., Mich. Libr. Consortium, Southeast Mich. League of Libraries, Ohio Libr. Coun., Beta Phi Mu. Avocations: reading, travel, gardening. Home: 3767 Santa Fe Trail Ann Arbor MI 48108 Home Phone: 734-369-6348. E-mail: francisjbuckley@aol.com.

BUCKLEY, FREDERICK JEAN, lawyer; b. Wilmington, Ohio, Nov. 5, 1923; s. William Millard and Martha (Bright) B.; m. Josephine K. Buckley, Dec. 4, 1945; children: Daniel J., Fredrica Buckley Elder, Matthew J. Student, Wilmington Coll., 1941-42, Ohio State U., 1942-43; AB, U. Mich., 1948, LLB, 1949; LLD (hon.), Wilmington Coll., 2004. Bar: Ohio 1950, U.S. Dist. Ct. (so. dist.) Ohio 1952, U.S. Supreme Ct. 1978, U.S. Ct. Appeals (6th cir.) 1981, Fla. 1982, U.S. Dist. Ct. (mid. dist.) Fla. 1991; cert. cir. ct. mediator, Fla. Assoc. G.L. Schilling, Sr., Wilmington, 1951-52; ptnr. Schilling & Buckley, Wilmington, 1953-56; sole practice Wilmington, 1956-62; sr. ptnr. Buckley, Miller & Wright, Wilmington, 1962—2002. Chmn. The Wilmington Savs. Bank, 1971—2003; solicitor City of Wilmington, 1954-63. Contbr. articles in field. With AUS, 1943-46, ETO. Joint program Mich. Inst. Pub. Adminstrn. fellow, 1948. Fellow Am. Coll. Trial Lawyers; mem. ABA, Am. Arbitration Assn. (comml. panel), Ohio State Bar Assn., Clinton County Bar Assn., Fla. Bar, Fla. Acad. Profl. Mediators, Collier County Bar Assn., Ohio State Bar Found. Republican. Methodist.

BUCKLEY, GEORGE W., manufacturing executive; b. Sheffield, Eng., Feb. 23, 1947; divorced; 5 children; m. Carol Buckley; 2 children. BSc in elec. and electronic engring., Univ. Huddersfield, Eng., 1972, PhD, 1975, U. Southhampton, 1975; DSc (hon.), Univ. Huddersfield, Eng. Rsch. officer UK Ctrl. Electricity Generating Bd., 1975; gen. mgr. dist. heating Detroit Edison Co., 1976—86; pres. generator div. GEC Turbine Generators Ltd., Stafford, England, 1986—88; dir., pres. ctrl. services unit Brit. Railways, 1988—93; pres. elec. motors divsn. Emerson Elec. Co., 1993—97; pres. Mercury Marine unit Brunswick Corp., Fond du Lac, Wis., 1997, corp. sr. v.p., 1999, corp. exec. v.p., 2000, pres., COO, 2000, chmn., CEO Lake Forest, Ill., 2000—05; chmn., CEO, pres. 3M Corp., 2005—. Bd. dir. Tyco Internat. Ltd, 2002—, Ingersoll-Rand Co., Thule AB. Office: 3M Co 3M Ctr Saint Paul MN 55144-1000*

BUCKLEY, JEREMIAH STEPHEN, lawyer; b. San Francisco, Oct. 12, 1944; s. Jeremiah Stephen and Flora (Saur) Buckley; m. Deborah Stanley, Nov. 5, 1983. AB, Fairfield U., 1966; JD, U. Va., 1969. Bar: Conn. 1969, D.C. 1972, U.S. Supreme Ct 1980. VISTA vol. Wayne County Legal Svcs., Detroit, 1969-70; asst. counsel govt. ops. com. U.S. Ho. of Reps., Washington, 1971-73; minority counsel housing subcom. U.S. Senate, Washington, 1973-77, minority staff dir. banking com., 1977-79; ptnr. Leighton, Lemov, Jacobs & Buckley, Washington, 1979-84, Thacher Proffitt & Wood, Washington, 1984-93, Goodwin Procter LLP, Washington, 1994—2003, Buckley Kolar LLP, Washington, 2003—. Co-author: The Law of Electronic Signatures and Records, 2004, Introduction to Mortgage Lending, 2006. Mem.: ABA, Fed. Bar Assn., Electronic Fin. Svcs. Coun., Exchequer Club, Millwood Golf Club, Kenwood Golf Club. Office: 1250 24th St NW Washington DC 20037 Office Phone: 202-349-8000. Business E-Mail: jbuckley@buckleykolar.com.

BUCKLEY, JOAN N., retired literature and language professor; b. Mpls., Jan. 27; d. Carl J. and Helene (Groth) Naglestad; m. Wendell D. Buckley, June 7, 1957; children: David, Julie. BA, St. Olaf Coll., Northfield, Minn., 1952; MA, U. Chgo., 1956; PhD, U. Iowa, 1976. Instr. English Concordia Coll., Moorhead, Minn., 1956-63, asst. prof., 1963-69, assoc. prof., 1969-76, prof. English, 1976—2005, ret., 2005. Vis. lectr. Martin-Luther-Schule, Rimbach, Germany, 1952—53. Named Flaat Disting. Prof., Concordia Coll., Glydenvand Prof.; NEH grantee 1977, 1980, 1983. Mem.: Norwegian-Am. Hist. Assn. (bd. dirs.), Delta Kappa Gamma (Tau State 1st v.p., US forum chair, Woman of Achievement 2001). Home: 2317 Rivershore Dr Moorhead MN 56560 E-mail: buckley@cord.edu.

BUCKLEY, JOHN JOSEPH, JR., healthcare executive; b. Evanston, Ill., Oct. 5, 1944; s. John Joseph and Mary Ruth (Smith) B.; m. Sarah Amelia Puceloski, May 16, 1970; children: Ruth Mary, Patricia Kimberly, John Joseph III. AB, Kenyon Coll., 1966; MBA, George Washington U., 1969. Asst. adminstr. Maricopa County Gen. Hosp., Phoenix, 1969-71, St. Joseph's Hosp. and Med. Ctr., Phoenix, 1971-74, assoc. adminstr., 1974-76, v.p., 1976-79, pres., 1984-88, St. Anthony's Hosp., Amarillo, Tex., 1979-84, St. Anthony's Devel. Corp., Amarillo, 1982-84; chief operating officer Harrington Cancer Ctr., Amarillo, 1982-84; sr. v.p. Mercy Health System, Cin., 1988-91; pres. So. Ill. Healthcare Enterprises, Carbondale, Ill., 1992—2001, Jack Buckley & Assocs., College Station, Tex., 2001—; interim pres., CEO St. Mary's Hosp. of East St. Louis, Ill., 2002; interim COO, St. Joseph Campus of Via Christi Med. Ctr., Wichita, Kans., 2003; interim CEO St. Joseph Regional Health Ctr., Bryan, Tex., 2003—04, CEO, 2004—; pres., CEO, St. Joseph Health Sys., Bryan, Tex., 2005—. Pres. So. Ill. Hosp. Svcs., Health Svcs. So. Ill., Regional Health Plan, 1992-2001; chmn. external adv. bd. Tex. A&M U. Health Sci. Ctr. Sch. Rural Pub. Health, 2003—; mem. external adv. bd. Coll. Bus. and Adminstrn., So. Ill. U., 2000—. Active Amarillo Alliance of Cmty. Svc. Execs., Amarillo Area Acad. Health Ctr. Corp., Amarillo Area Hosp. Home Care, Amarillo Found. Health and Sci., Panhandle chpt. Tex. Soc. to Prevent Blindness, Amarillo Jr. League, Children's Oncology Svcs. Tex. Panhandle; Amarillo diocesan coord. health affairs; adminstrv. com. Amarillo; pres. Mercy Svcs. Corp., 1984-88; bd. dirs. Greater Phoenix Affordable Health Care Found., 1984-88; trustee Kenyon Coll., Gambier, Ohio, 1991-95, alumni coun., 1998-2003, pres., 2001-02; active SI Edge, 1995-2003. Fellow: Am. Coll. Healthcare Execs. (regent Ariz. 1984—88, regent So. Ill. 1998—2002); mem.: Ariz. Hosp. Assn., Ariz. Kidney Found., Cath. Health Assn. U.S., Ill. Hosp. Assn. (trustee 1995—2001, chmn. 2000), Tex. Hosp. Assn. (trustee 1983—84), Alumni Assn. of George Washington U. Health Svcs. Mgmt. and Policy (pres. 1995—97), Delta Phi (pres. alumni assn. 1988—2000). Republican. Roman Catholic. Office: St Joseph Health System 2801 Franciscan Dr Bryan TX 77802-2544 Home Phone: 979-731-8235; Office Phone: 979-776-2446. Personal E-mail: jackbuckleyjr@earthlink.net. Business E-Mail: jbuckley@st-joseph.org.

BUCKLEY, JOSEPH PAUL, III, computer technician; b. Chgo., July 6, 1949; s. Joseph Paul and Helen (Lavelle) B.; m. Patricia Nemeth, June 17, 1972; children: Megan, Michael, Patrick, Thomas. BA, Loyola U., Chgo., 1971; MS in Detection of Deception, Reid Coll. Detection of Deception, Chgo., 1973. Lic., Ill. Detection of deception examiner John E. Reid & Assocs., Inc., Chgo., 1971—, chief polygraph examiner, 1978-80, dir. Chgo. office, 1980-82, pres. corp. Chgo., Milw., 1982—. Chmn. Ill. Detection of Deception Examiner Com., 1978-82; mem. adv. com. Office of Tech. Assessment, 1983 Co-author: Criminal Interrogation and Confessions, 1st edit., 1962, 4th edit., 2001, The Investigator Anthology, 1999, Essentials of the Reid Technique, 2004; contbr. articles to profl. jours. Mem. Am. Polygraph Assn. (v.p. 1979-80, chmn. pub. rels. com. 1979-80, 84-95, awards), Ill. Polygraph Soc. (v.p. 1981, pres. 1982-83), Am. Acad. Forensic Scis., Am. Mgmt. Assn., Am. Soc. Indsl. Security (investigations com. 1983-89), Spl. Agts. Assn., Internat. Pers. Mgmt. Assn., Internat. Assn. Chiefs Policy, Chgo. Crime Commn. Home Phone: 815-455-3261; Office Phone: 312-876-1600. E-mail: jbuckley@reid.com.

BUCKLEY, KEVIN JOSEPH, lawyer; b. Stamford, Conn., Apr. 16, 1957; s. Ernest William and Mary Teresa (Conroy) B.; m. Amanda Lee Bernheim, June 13, 1981; children: Austin Bernheim, Erin Arceneaux, Emmett Conroy, Isaac Kevin. BS in Civil Engring., U. Notre Dame, 1979; JD, Washington and Lee U., 1985. Bar: Va. 1985, NY 1999. Project engr. Corning Inc., 1980-82; assoc. Hunton & Williams, Richmond, Va., 1985-94, ptnr., 1994—, co-head asset securitization group. Spkr., panelist for continuing legal edn. seminars. Contbg. author & editor Washington & Lee Law Rev., 1984-85; contbr. articles to profl. jours. Chmn. Diocesan Sch. Bd., Richmond, 1986-92; chmn. steering com. Richmond Cath. HS, 1994-98; dir. Concilium for Edn., 1992-94; dir. Haitian Edn. Fund, 2002-04; leadership coun. Mid-Atlantic Cath. Schs. Consortium. Recipient Nat. Cath. Edn. Assn. award, 1992; named Sch. Bd. Mem. of Yr., Concilium for Edn., 1992; nominee Chambers USA award for excellence, 2006. Mem. ABA (com. on fed. regulation securities, subcom. on securitization assets and structured fin.), Va. State Bar Assn., Richmond Bar Assn., N.Y. Bar Assn. Roman Catholic. Avocations: basketball, woodworking. Office: Hunton & Williams Riverfront Plz East Tower 951 East Byrd St Richmond VA 23219-4074 also: Hunton & Williams 200 Park Ave New York NY 10166-0136 Office Phone: 804-788-8616, 212-309-1370. Office Fax: 804-344-7999, 212-309-1100. Business E-Mail: kbuckley@hunton.com.

BUCKLEY, KEVIN WILLIAM, lawyer; b. Wausau, Wis., Aug. 23, 1968; s. Kent William Santelman and Maureen Lansdale Buckley; m. Celine Buckley, June 3, 2000. BS in Biochemistry, Chemistry, U. Calif. San Diego, La Jolla, 1996; JD, U. Pitts., 2000. Bar: Mo. 2001, US Patent and Trademark Office 2000. Assoc. Thompson Coburn LLP, St. Louis, 2000—02, Sonnenschein Nath & Rosenthal LLP, St. Louis, 2002—06; pres. Biotactica, LLC, 2006—. Editor-in-chief Pitts. Jour. Tech. Law & Policy, 1999—2000. Named to Who's Who in Tech., St. Louis Bus. Jour., 2007; recipient Forty Under 40 award, 2005—06. Mem.: Ill. Biotech. Industry Orgn., Mo. Biotechnology Assn. (legis. coun. 2001—05), Internat. Soc. Stem Cell Rsch. Avocations: gardening, surfing, rock climbing. Home: 9 Nolan Dr Saint Louis MO 63122 Office: Biotactica LLC 10733 Sunset Office Dr Ste 261 Saint Louis MO 63127 Home Phone: 314-965-7572; Office Phone: 314-966-8111, 877-438-8228. Office Fax: 314-966-8112. Business E-Mail: kevin@biotactica.com.

BUCKLEY, KRISTY LORAINE, lawyer, accountant; d. Richard Orville and Kim Woo Cha Brewer; m. James Russell Buckley, Aug. 20, 2005. BS in Bus., Mont. State U., 2001, BS in Sociology, 2001, MS in Profl. Accountancy, 2002; JD, U. Miami, Coral Gables, 2005, LLM in Taxation, 2006. Bar: Fla. 2006, Mont. 2006. Acct.'s asst. Jim Runyan, CPA, Bozeman, Mont., 1999—2002; auditing cons. Clark Nuber, Seattle, 2002; summer assoc. Akerman Senterfitt, Orlando, Fla., 2004; assoc. Shubin & Bass, Miami, Fla., 2003—06, Crowley, Haughey, Hanson, Toole & Dietrich, PLLP, Bozeman, 2006—. Educator Ctr. Ethics and Pub. Svc. U. Miami, Coral Gables, Fla., 2003—04, NYC, 2003—04. Acct. Vol. Income Tax Assistance Program, Bozeman, Mont., 2000—02. Recipient Nat. Residence Hall hon., Residence Hall Assn., 1999—2001, Bus. Assocs. Book award, Ctr. Computer Legal Instrn. Excellence for Future, 2003, Ctr. Ethics Workshop II Book award, CALI Excellence for Future, 2004; David & Dorothy Patterson Acctg. scholar, Mont. State U., 2001—02, Judge Balaban scholar, U. Miami Sch. Law, 2004—05, Paul R. Gordon scholar, 2004—05, Mary T. Hennessey scholar, 2005. Mem.: Tax Law Soc. (pres. 2003—04), U. Miami Bus. Law Rev. (sr. ace comments editor 2004—05), Tax Law Chronicle (exec. editor 2003—04), Bar and Gavel (chmn. race judicata 2004—04), Beta Alpha Psi. Avocations: hunting, crocheting, fishing, violin, knitting. Personal E-mail: kristyb222@hotmail.com. Business E-Mail: kbuckley@crowleylaw.com.

BUCKLEY, MICHAEL EDWARD, lawyer; b. LA, June 13, 1950; s. Robert and Barbara Ann (Johansing) B.; m. Catherine Delores Busch, Oct. 14, 1978; children: Robert Timothy, Mara Busch, Jeffrey Johansing, Thomas Elliot. BA, UCLA, 1972; JD, Santa Clara U., Calif., 1975. Bar: Nev. 1975, Calif. 1976, DC 1982, US Dist. Ct. Nev. 1975. Shareholder Jones Vargas, Las Vegas, Nev., 1975—. Instr. dept. fin. U. Nev. Las Vegas, spring 1987, fall 1989; mem. Block Grant Com., State of Nev. Dept. Human Resources, 1996-2003, chair, 1998-99; mem. dept. bus. and industry real estate divsn. Common Interest Cmty. Commn., Nev., 2003—, chair, 2004-. Author: (with others) Nevada Real Estate Transactions, 1988. Bd. trustees HELP of So. Nev., Las Vegas, 1985-91, adv. bd., 1991-2005, pres. 1987-89; mem. City of Las Vegas Planning Commn., 1994-2002, chmn., 1999-2000. Mem. ABA, Cmty. Assn. Inst. (legis. action com. 1993-2003), State Bar Nev. (bus. law com.), Am. Coll. Real Estate Lawyers, State Bar Calif., DC Bar. Democrat. Roman Catholic. Avocations: reading, writing, travel. Office: Jones Vargas 3rd Fl S 3773 Howard Hughes Pkwy Las Vegas NV 89169 Office Phone: 702-862-3397. Business E-Mail: meb@jonesvargas.com.

BUCKLEY, MICHAEL FRANCIS, lawyer; b. Saranac Lake, NY, Nov. 1, 1943; s. Francis Edward and Marjorie (Mooney) B.; m. Mary Thornton, June 26, 1965; children: Sean, Kathleen. BA, Dartmouth Coll., 1965; JD, Cornell U., 1968. Bar: N.Y. 1969, Fla. 1982, U.S. Dist. Ct. (we. dist.) N.Y. 1970. Assoc. Harter, Secrest & Emery, Rochester, NY, 1968-75, ptnr., 1976—. Contbg. author: Estate Planning and Probate in New York, 1985; co-editor: Administration of New York Estates, 1990. Bd. dirs. Highland Hosp. Found., Rochester, 1981-95, pres., 1984-87; bd. dirs. Highland Hosp., 1987—, pres., 1992-94; bd. dirs. Highland Health Sys., Inc., 1995-97, Strong Ptnrs. Health System, Inc., 1997—, YMCA of Greater Rochester, 1997-05, Highland Cmty. Devel. Corp., 1998-02, Highland Living Ctr., Inc., 1998-02, Rochester Area Cmty. Found., 1999—, James P. Wilmot Found., Inc., 2000—, U. Rochester Med. Ctr., 2000—, James P. Wilmot Cancer Ctr., 2005-. Fellow Am. Coll. Trusts and Estates Counsel; mem. N.Y. State Bar Assn. (exec. com. trusts and estates law sect. 1988-92), Monroe County Bar Assn. (chmn. trusts and estates sect. 1984-85, banking liaison com. 1985-86), Fla. Bar Assn., Estate Planing Coun. Rochester, Internat. Assn. Fin. Planners. Roman Catholic. Avocations: basketball, platform tennis. Home: 571 Thomas Ave Rochester NY 14617-1432 Office: Harter Secrest & Emery 1600 Bausch & Lomb Pl Rochester NY 14604-2711 Office Phone: 585-231-1173. Business E-Mail: mbuckley@hselaw.com.

BUCKLEY, PAMELA KAY, educational association administrator; BA in English, U. Evansville, 1964; MAT, U. Louisville, 1970; EdD in Curriculum and Instrn., U. Houston, 1977. Various ednl. positions, 1964—78; prog. staff devel. coord. U. Houston Tchr. Corps Project, 1978—80, assoc. project dir., 1981; assoc. rsch. scientist Far West Lab. Ednl. R & D, San Francisco, 1980; tng. mgr. tng. divsn. City of Houston Civil Svc. Dept., 1981—83; sr. instr. manpower devel. divsn. The Gulf Bank, Kuwait, 1984—85; faculty developer staff instructional devel. dept. Houston Cmty. Coll. Sys., 1985—88; co-dir. Commonwealth Ctr. Edn. Tchrs. James Madison U., Harrisonburg, 1988—92, assoc. prof. Coll. Edn. and Psych., 1988—92; sr. tng. specialist tng. divsn. Kuwait Inst. Sci. Rsch.; dir. Eisenhower Math/Sci. Consortium, 1992; positions up to v.p. tech. assistance and tng. Appalachia Ednl. Lab.; exec. dir., CEO Hands On Sci. Outreach; dir. mktg. govt. divsn. Gallup Orgn.; prog. dir. RTI Internat.; exec. dir. Kappa Delta Pi, Indpls., 2006—. Contbr. articles and revs. to profl. jours. Mem. ASTD, ASCD, Am. Ednl. Rsch. Assn., Assn. Tchr. Educators, Phi Delta Kappa. Office: Kappa Delta Pi Internat Honor Soc Edn 3707 Woodview Trace Indianapolis IN 46268-1158 Office Phone: 317-871-4900 ext. 222. E-mail: buckley@kdp.org.*

BUCKLEY, PAUL RICHARD, SR., insurance executive; b. Brownfield, Maine, Jan. 8, 1935; s. John Joseph and Ruth Ann B.; m. Anita Lucia Lebel, Oct. 11, 1958; children: Lisa, Paul Jr., Scott, Julie. BA, U. Maine, 1957; LLB, U. Maine, Portland, 1961. Bar: Maine 1961. Ptnr. Longley Assocs., Lewiston, Maine, 1958-80; prin. The Buckley Group, Lewiston, 1980—. Contbr. articles to profl. jours. Pres., bd. dirs. St. Mary Hosp., Lewiston, Maine, 1970-77; bd. dirs. Maine Dental Svcs., Portland, 1975-80. Recipient J. Putnham Stephens award, Maine Life Assn., 1987. Mem. ABA, Maine Bar Assn. (bd. dirs. ins. trust 1975-80), Androscoggin Bar Assn., New Eng. Life Leaders Assn. (pres. 1974-75), Am. Coll. Life Ins. Underwriters, Advanced Underwriters, Million Dollar Round Table (pres. 1984-85). Avocations: hunting, fishing, tennis, reading. Home: 10 Amy Ln Cumberland Foreside ME 04110 Office: The Buckley Group Ste 401 75 Market St Portland ME 04101 Office Phone: 207-772-4311.

BUCKLEY, REBECCA HATCHER, allergist, immunologist, pediatrician, educator; b. Hamlet, NC, Apr. 1, 1933; d. Martin Armstead and Nora (Langston) Hatcher; m. Charles Edward Buckley, III, July 9, 1955; children: Charles Edward IV, Elizabeth Ann, Rebecca Kathryn, Sarah Margaret. BA, Duke U., 1954; MD, U. NC, 1958. Intern Duke U. Med. Ctr., Durham, NC, 1958-59, resident, 1959-61, pediat. allergist and immunologist, 1961—. Dir., chair exam. com. Am. Bd. Allergy and Immunology, Phila., 1971—73, co-chair bd. dirs., 1982—84; chair Diagnostic Lab. Immunology, 1984—88; mem. staff Duke U. Med. Ctr., asst. prof. pediat. and immunology, 1968—72, assoc. prof. pediat., 1972—79, prof. pediat., 1976—79, prof. immunology, J. Buren Sidbury prof. pediat., 1979—. Contbr. articles to profl. jours. Fellow: AAAS (chair med. scis. sect. 2001—03); mem.: NAS, Inst. Medicine of NAS, Am. Pediat. Soc. (coun. mem. 1991—, pres. 1999—2000, chmn. immune deficiency found. med. adv. com. 2003—), Southeastern Allergy Assn. (pres. 1978—79), Am. Acad. Pediat. (Bret Ratner award 1992), Soc. Pediat. Rsch., Am. Assn. Immunologists, Am. Acad. Allergy and Immunology (exec. com. 1975—82, pres. 1979—80, hon. fellow award 1999). Republican. Episcopalian. Home: 3621 Westover Rd Durham NC 27707-5032 Office: Duke U Med Ctr PO Box 2898 Durham NC 27710 Office Phone: 919-684-2922. Business E-Mail: buckl003@mc.duke.edu.

BUCKLEY, ROBERT MATTHEW, electrical engineer; b. Bklyn., Nov. 14, 1947; s. Matthew Louis and Catherine Sienna Buckley; m. Linda Susan Montagne, May 16, 1971; children: Christopher, Kevin, Michael. BSc, N.Y. Inst. Tech., 1972; MAS, Embry Riddle U., 2004; MSc, Nova Southeastern U., Ft. Lauderdale, Fla., 2006. Engring. asst. N.Y. Telephone, Bklyn., 1972-74; project engr. PRD, Syosset, N.Y., 1974-77; engr. Citibank, Melville, N.Y., 1977-81; engring. specialist ILS Divsn. Grumman Aerospace, Bethpage, N.Y., 1981-84; engring. mgr. AIL, Deer Park, N.Y., 1984-85; v.p. engring. TTI, Ronkonkama, N.Y., 1985-90; v.p. ATTI, Hauppague, N.Y., 1990—. Contbr. articles to profl. jours. Leader Boy Scouts Am., Medford, N.Y., 1985; pres. NYPMAC, Medford, 1987-89. With USMCR, 1969-71. Mem. IEEE, SPIE, AOPA, UPE. Roman Catholic. Achievements include patent for video display and analyzer, new phase noise measurement technique, new use for phase noise measurement, and patent for generating programmable spectrally pure doppler signals. Office: ATTI 110 Ricefield Ln Hauppauge NY 11788-2008 Home Phone: 631-654-2599; Office Phone: 631-231-8777. E-mail: rbuckley@nova.edu, buckleyr@erau.edu.

BUCKLEY, SUSAN, lawyer; b. Rockville Center, NY, Dec. 24, 1951; BA, Mt. Holyoke Coll., 1973; JD, Fordham U., 1977. Bar: N.Y. 1978, D.C. 1980. Ptnr. Cahill Gordon & Reindel LLP, NYC, 1985—. Mem. ABA, N.Y. State Bar Assn. (com. on media law 1992-95), Bar Assn. N.Y.C. (com. comm. law 1986-89). Office: Cahill Gordon & Reindel LLP 80 Pine St Fl 17 New York NY 10005-1790 Office Phone: 212-701-3000.

BUCKLEY, TERRENCE PATRICK, lawyer; b. NYC, May 7, 1945; s. Cornelius and Catherine (Sheehan) B.; children: Shannondoah, Heather. BA, Iona Coll., 1967; JD, Bklyn. Law Sch., 1972. Bar: N.Y. 1972, U.S. Dist. Ct. (so. and ea. dists.) N.Y. 1977, U.S. Supreme Ct. 1993. Asst. dist. atty. Dist. Atty.'s Office, NYC, 1972-74; law instr. Western State U., Fullerton, Calif., 1975; assoc. McDonald, Pulaski & Harlan, San Diego, 1975-77; atty.-in-charge Nassau-Suffolk Law Svcs., Riverhead, N.Y., 1977-78; spl. asst. atty. gen. N.Y. State Atty. Gen. Office, NYC, 1978-86; trial counsel Pelletreau & Pelletreau, Patchogue, N.Y., 1986-87; pvt. practice Islandia, N.Y., 1988—. Instr. health law SUNY, Stony Brook, 1988, 90; adminstrv. law judge Divsn. Parole, L.I. City, N.Y., 1987-88. With U.S. Army, 1969-71. Recipient Excellence award Am. Jurisprudence, 1972. Mem. ATLA, NACDL, Suffolk County Bar Assn., Am. Inns of Ct. (Alexander Hamilton Inn), Brehon Law Soc., Frank Hogan Assocs. Roman Catholic. Avocations: skiing, running, sailing, hiking, kayaking. Office: 1 Suffolk Sq Ste 520 Islandia NY 11749-1528 Office Phone: 631-234-5311. E-mail: terrencepbuckley@aol.com.

BUCKLEY, THOMAS HUGH, historian, educator; b. Elkhart, Ind., Sept. 11, 1932; s. Bernard Leroy and Martha B. (Swoveland) B.; m. Julie Griffith; children: Christopher, Kathryn, Elizabeth, Thomas, Barbara. Student, Northwestern U., 1950-53; AB, Ind. U., 1955, MA, 1956, PhD (grad. fellow), 1961. From instr. to prof. U. S.D., 1960-69; vis. prof. Ind. U., 1969-71; prof., chmn. dept. U. Tulsa, 1971-81, chmn. humanistic studies, 1975-81, Jay Walker research chair Am. History, 1981—, assoc. dean Grad. Sch., 1995-2000; cons. on overseas edn. to Nat. Edn. Corp. Author: The United States and the Washington Conference, 1921-1922, 1970 (award as best first book by an historian 1971); co-author: American Foreign and National Security Policies, 1914-1945, 1987; editor: Research and Roster Guide of Soc. Historians of Am. Fgn. Relations, 1980-86; contbr. chpts. in books. Postdoctoral fellow Stanford U., 1968, U. Wis., 1983, Brown U., 1986, U. Tex., 1991; Fulbright fellow, U. Western Australia, 1986. Mem. Orgn. Am. Historians, Soc. Historians of Am. Fgn. Relations, Tulsa Com. Fgn. Relations, Phi Alpha Theta, Lambda Chi Alpha. Republican. Methodist. Home: 1301 Terrace Dr Tulsa OK 74104-4409 Office: Univ Tulsa Dept History Tulsa OK 74104 Office Phone: 918-631-2824. Business E-Mail: thomas-buckley@utulsa.edu. *Success comes in the race of life not always to the swiftest but to those who keep on running.*

BUCKLEY, VINCENT H., lawyer; BA, Rice U., 1947; LLB, U. Tex., 1950. Various legal and mgmt. positions Dow Chemical, asst. gen. counsel, gen. counsel Pacific region, pres., gen. mgr. oil and gas divsn.; with Lock, Liddell, and Sapp, 1990—2002; exec. v.p., gen. counsel, bd. dirs. Adams Resources & Energy, Inc., Houston, 2002—05, exec. v.p., gen. counsel, 2005—. Office: Adams Resources & Energy Inc 4400 Post Oak Pky Ste 2700 Houston TX 77027 Office Phone: 713-881-3600. Office Fax: 713-881-3491.*

BUCKLEY, WILLIAM FRANK, JR., magazine editor, writer; b. NYC, Nov. 24, 1925; s. Willliam Frank and Aloise (Steiner) Buckley; m. Patricia Taylor, July 6, 1950 (dec. Apr. 15, 2007); 1 child, Christopher Taylor. Student, U. Mexico, 1943; BA, Yale U., 1950; LHD (hon.), Seton Hall U., 1966, Niagara U., 1967, Mt. St. Mary's Coll., 1969, U. SC, 1985, Converse Coll., 1988, U. South Fla., 1992, Adelphi U., 1995, Yale U., 2000, Hillsdale Coll., 2005; LLD (hon.), St. Peter's Coll., 1969, Syracuse U., 1969, Ursinus Coll., 1969, Lehigh U., 1970, Lafayette Coll., 1972, St. Anselm's Coll., 1973, St. Bonaventure U., 1974, U. Notre Dame, 1978, NY Law Sch., 1981, Colby Coll., 1985; DScO (hon.), Curry Coll., 1970; LittD (hon.), St. Vincent Coll., 1971, Fairleigh Dickinson U., 1973, Alfred U., 1974, Coll. William and Mary, 1981, William Jewell Coll., 1982, Albertus Magnus Coll., 1987, Coll. St. Thomas, 1987, Bowling Green State U., 1987, Coe Coll., 1989, St. John's U., Minn., 1989, Grove City Coll., 1991. Instr. Spanish lang. Yale U., New Haven, 1947-51; assoc. editor Am. Mercury, NYC, 1952; founder, pres., editor-in-chief Nat. Rev., NYC, 1955-90, editor-at-large, 1991—2004; syndicated columnist, 1962—; host weekly TV show Firing Line, 1966-99; Froman disting. prof. Russell Sage Coll., 1973. Lectr. New Sch. Social Rsch., 1967—68; vis. lectr. Yale U., 1996—97. Author: God and Man at Yale, 1951; author: (with L. Brent Bozell) McCarthy and His Enemies, 1954; author: Up from Liberalism, 1959, Rumbles Left and Right, 1963, The Unmaking of a Mayor, 1966, The Jeweler's Eye, 1968, The Governor Listeth, 1970, Cruising Speed, 1971, Inveighing We Will Go, 1972, Four Reforms, 1973, United Nations Journal, 1974, Execution Eve, 1975, Saving the Queen, 1976, Airborne, 1976, Stained Glass, 1978 (Am. Book award for Best Mystery, 1980), A Hymnal, 1978, Who's On First, 1980, Marco Polo, If You Can, 1982, Atlantic High, 1982, Overdrive, 1983, The Story of Henri Tod, 1984, The Temptation of Wilfred Malachey, 1985, See You Later Alligator, 1985, Right Reason, 1985, High Jinx, 1986, Racing Through Paradise, 1987, Mongoose, R.I.P., 1988, On the Firing Line, 1989, Gratitude, 1990, Tucker's Last Stand, 1991, Windfall, 1992, In Search of Anti-Semitism, 1992, Happy Days Were Here Again, 1993, A Very Private Plot, 1994, The Blackford Oakes Reader, 1995, Brothers No More, 1995, Buckely: The Right Word, 1996, Nearer, My God, 1997, The Lexicon, 1998, The Redhunter, 1998, Let Us Talk of Many Things, 2000, Spytime, 2000, Elvis in the Morning, 2001, Nuremberg, 2002, Getting It Right, 2003, The Fall of the Berlin Wall, 2004, Miles Gone By: A Literary Autobiography, 2004 (Benjamin Franklin award for autobiography/biography/memoirs, 2005), Last Call for Blackford Oakes, 2005, The Rake, 2007; editor: The Committee and Its Critics, 1962, Odyseey of a Friend: Whittaker Chambers' Letters to William F. Buckley, Jr., 1954-1961, 1970, Did You Ever See a Dream Walking: American Conservative Thought in the Twentieth Century, 1970; editor: (with Charles Kesler) Keeping the Tablets, 1988; co-author: Racing at Sea, 1959, The Intellectuals, 1960, What is Conservatism?, 1964, Dialogues in Americanism, 1964, Violence in the Streets, 1968, The Beatles Book, 1968, Spectrum of Catholic Attitudes, 1969, Great Ideas Today Annual, 1970, Essays on Hayek, 1976; contbr. articles to periodicals. Mem. USIA Adv. Commn., 1969—72; pub. mem. US del. 28th Gen. Assembly UN, 1973; Conservative Party candidate for mayor NYC, 1965. Served to 2d lt. Inf. US Army, 1944—46. Recipient Best Columnist of the Yr. award, 1967, Disting. Achievement award in journalism, U. So. Calif., 1968, Emmy award for Outstanding Program Achievement, NATAS, 1969, Cleveland Amory award for Best Interviewer/Interviewee, TV Guide, 1974, Bellarime medal, 1977, Americanism award, Young Rep. Nat. Fedn., 1979, Carmel award, Am. Friends of Haifa U., 1980, Creative Leadership award, NYU, 1981, Lincoln Lit. award, Union League, 1985, Shelby Cullom Davis award, 1986, Lowell Thomas Travel Journalism award, 1989, Julius award for Outstanding Pub. Svc., U. So. Calif. Sch. Pub. Adminstrn., 1990, Gold medal award, Nat. Inst. Social Scis., 1992, Presdl. Medal of Freedom, 1991, Adam Smith award, Hillsdale Coll., 1996, Clare Boothe Luce award, Heritage Found., 1999, Henry Salvation award, Claremont Inst., 2000, Phillips Found. lifetime Achievement award, 2002, Alexander Hamilton award, Manhattan Inst., 2004, Mightier Pen award, Ctr. Security Policy, 2004, Am. History award, Union League Club, 2005, Lifetime Achievement award, Am. Soc. Mag. Editors, 2006, Truman-Reagan medal of Freedom, Victims of Communism Meml. Found., 2007. Fellow: Soc. Profl. Journalists, Sigma Delta Chi; mem.: Mont Pelerin Soc., Phila. Soc., NY Yacht Club. Republican. Roman Catholic. Office: Nat Rev 215 Lexington Ave New York NY 10016-6023

BUCKLIN, DONALD THOMAS, lawyer; b. Providence, July 11, 1938; s. Elmer F. and Anne (Scott) B.; m. Kathryn L. Alfera, Nov. 30, 1963; children: Donald R., Heather Anne. BS in Acctg., Providence Coll., 1960; JD cum laude, Am. U., 1967. Bar: Va. 1968, D.C. 1968. Supervisory acct. GAO, 1960-67; law clk. to judge U.S. Dist. Ct. D.C., 1967-68; asst. U.S. atty. for D.C. Dept. Justice, Washington, 1968-71; ptnr. Rowley & Scott, Washington, 1971-74, Truitt, Fabrikant, Bucklin & Lenzner, Washington, 1974-76, Wald, Harkrader & Ross, Washington, 1977-85; sr. counsel Squire, Sanders & Dempsey LLP, Washington, 1986—. Contbg. author: Antitrust Counseling and Litigation Techniques, 1984. Served to 1st lt. USAR, 1960-68. Fellow Am. Coll. Trial Lawyers, Internat. Acad. Trial Lawyers; mem. ABA (criminal law sect. white collar crimes and offenders 1976-77, litigation sect. com. on liaison with state and local bar assns.), D.C. Bar Assn. (treas. Criminal Practice Inst. 1972-73, exec. coun. young lawyers sect. 1973-75, Young Lawyer of Yr.), D.C. Bar (litigation sect. steering com., treas. 1985, bd. govs. 1986-89, bd. dirs., exec. com. 1989—, pres. 1995-96), Am. Coll.Trial Lawyers. Office: Squire, Sanders & Dempsey LLP 1201 Pennsylvania Ave NW PO Box 407 Washington DC 20044-0407 Office Phone: 202-626-6816. Office Fax: 202-626-6780. E-mail: dbucklin@ssd.com.

BUCKLIN, LOUIS PIERRE, business educator, consultant; b. NYC, Sept. 20, 1928; s. Louis Lapham and Elja (Barricklow) B.; m. Weylene Edwards, June 11, 1956; children: Randolph E., Rhonda W. Student, Dartmouth Coll., 1950; MBA, Harvard U., 1954; PhD, Northwestern U., 1960; PhD (hon.), Stockholm Sch. Econs., 2001. Asst. prof. bus. U. Colo., Boulder, 1954-56; instr. in bus. Northwestern U., Evanston, 1958-59, assoc. dean Grad. Sch. Bus. Adminstrn., 1981-83; prof. bus. adminstrn. U. Calif., Berkeley, 1960-93, prof. emeritus, 1993—. Mem. ASUC Aux. Enterprise Bd., 1999-2004, chmn., 2000-2001; vis. prof. Stockholm Sch. Econs., 1983, INSEAD, Fontainebleau, France, 1984, Erasmus U., Rotterdam, Netherlands, 1993-94, Cath. U. Leuven, Belgium, 1994; prin. Bucklin Assocs., Lafayette, Calif., 1975—; adv. bd. Gemini Cons., San Francisco, 1987-94. Author: A Theory of Distribution Channel Structure, 1966, Competition Evolution in the Distrubutive Trades, 1972, Productivity in Marketing, 1979; editor: Vertical Marketing Systems, 1971, Channels and Channel Institutions, 1986, Jour. Retailing, 1996—2001. Mem. City of Lafayette Planning Commn., 1990-93. Capt. USMC, 1951-53, Korea. Recipient Alpha Kappa Psi Found. award for best paper in Jour. Mktg., 1993, Lifetime Recognition for scholarly contbns. to retailing Soc. for Mktg. Advances, 2001. Mem. Am. Mktg. Assn. (Paul D. Converse award 1986). Democrat. Avocations: travel, microcomputers, photography. Office: U Calif Haas Sch Bus Berkeley CA 94720-0001 Personal E-mail: lpbucklin@comcast.net.

BUCKLO, ELAINE EDWARDS, United States district court judge; b. Boston, Oct. 1, 1944; married. AB, St. Louis U., 1966; JD, Northwestern U., 1972. Bar: Calif. 1973, U.S. Dist. Ct. (no. dist.) Calif. 1973, Ill. 1974, U.S. Dist. ct. (no. dist.) Ill. 1974, U.S. Ct. Appeals (7th cir.) 1983. Law clk. U.S. Ct. Appeals (7th cir.), Chgo.; pvt. practice, 1973-85; U.S. magistrate judge U.S. Dist. Ct. (no. dist.) Ill., Chgo., 1985-94, judge, 1994—. Spkr. in field. Contbr. articles to profl. jours. Mem. jud. conf. com. on adminstrn. Magistrate Judge Sys., 1998-2004; mem. vis. com. No. Ill. U. Sch. Law, 1994—; mem. Northwestern U. Law Bd., 1996-99. Mem. ABA (standing com. law and literacy 1995-98, assoc. editor Litigation), FBA (v.p. 1990-92, pres. Chgo. chpt. 1992-93), Women's Bar Assn. Ill. (bd. dirs. 1994-96), Chgo. Coun. Lawyers (pres. 1977-78). Office: US Dist Ct No Dist Everett McKinley Dirksen Bldg 219 S Dearborn St Ste 1446 Chicago IL 60604-1794

BUCKMAN, DEBRA ANN, science educator; b. Williamsport, Pa., Sept. 9, 1950; d. Dorsey Eugene and MaryJane Ringler; m. James Watson Buckman; children: Nicholas, Sean. BA, Mansfield U., Pa., 1972; M in Edn., Arcadia U., Glenside, Pa., 1977. Hazardous Waste Operator Pa. Coll. of Tech., 2005, cert. tchr. Pa. Tchr. physics and biol. scis. Sch. Dist. Phila., 1974—79; chemist Avco Lycoming, Williamsport, Pa., 1979—83; sr. chemist Litton Electron Devices, Williamsport, 1984—91; environ. engr. Textron Lycoming, 1991—95; asst. prof. environ. tech. Pa. Coll. of Tech., Williamsport, 1995—; tchr. of phys. and biol. sciences Sch. Dist. of Phila. Mem. Lycoming County Local Emergency Planning Com., Williamsport, Pa., 1985—; regional dir. Pa. Assn. of Environ. Educators. Pres. local chpt. NGA, Inc., Warminster, Pa., 1991—2006; pres., treas. Williamsport Civic Chorus, 1975—2006; author emergency response plan Litton. Environ. Edn. grant, Pa. Dept. of Environ. Protection, 2002. Mem.: Water Environment Fedn. Achievements include development of curriculum for the environmental technology program at Pennsylvania College of Technology. Avocations: music, theater. Office: Pa Coll of Tech One College Ave Williamsport PA 17701 Home Phone: 570-323-1707; Office Phone: 570-320-2400 ext. 3526. Business E-Mail: dbuckman@pct.edu.

BUCKMAN, JAMES EDWARD, lawyer; b. NYC, Oct. 2, 1944; s. John Burr and Mary Dolores (Ullery) B.; m. Nancy Lee McLaughlin, Aug. 23, 1969; children: Elizabeth Ahern, Anne Tracy, Julia Walsh. AB, Fordham U., 1966; JD, Yale U., 1969. Bar: N.Y. 1969, Ga. 1974, U.S. Dist. Ct. (no. dist.) Ga. 1974. Assoc. Dewey, Ballantine, Bushby, Palmer & Wood, NYC, 1969-72; asst. gen. counsel Gable Industries, Inc., Atlanta, 1972-74; assoc. to ptnr. Troutman, Sanders, Lockerman & Ashmore, Atlanta, 1974-85, ptnr., 1990-92; exec. v.p., gen. counsel Days Inns of Am., Inc., Atlanta, 1985-89, HFS Inc., Parsippany, NJ, 1992-96; vice chmn., gen. counsel Cendant Corp, Parsippany, 1996—; bd. dirs. Wyndham Worldwide, 2006—. 1st lt. USAFR, 1969-75. Mem. ABA, Atlanta Bar Assn., State Bar Ga. Roman Catholic. Avocation: running. Office: Wyndham Worldwide Corp c/o Corp Sec 7 Sylvan Way Parsippany NJ 07054*

BUCKMAN, RAYMOND WILLIAM, JR., engineering educator; s. Raymond William Buckman and Rose Wihebrink; m. Norma Caldwell, June 5, 1954; children: Raymond William, III, Cynthia Roseann Roberts, Gregory Clayton, Michael Robert. BS in Metall. Engring., U. Cin., 1954. Cert. profl. engr., Ohio, 1968. Engr. Bell Aerospace Co., Buffalo, 1956—60; prin. investigator, refractory metal alloy devel. Westinghouse Electric, Astronuclear Lab., Large, Pa., 1960—66; mgr., materials tech. Westignhouse Electric, Large, 1967—90; pres., owner Refractory Metals Tech., Pitts., 1991—. Recipient H. R. Ogden award, ASTM-B-10 Com., 2003. Mem.: Am. Vacuum Soc. (Disting. Svc. award 1975), Minerals, Metals and Materials Soc. (life), Am. Inst. Mining, Metallurgical and Petroleum Engrs. (life). Achievements include 10 patents granted in field. Avocations: exercise, history. Home Phone: 412-653-0940; Office Phone: 412-653-0940.

BUCKMAN, THOMAS RICHARD, foundation executive, educator; b. Reno, May 3, 1923; s. Thomas Eli and Georgia Christina (Damm) B.; m. Gunhild Margareta Malmkjell, May 1, 1948; children: Anne Christina, Carol Erica. BA, U. Pacific, 1947; MA, U. Minn., 1951, B.L.S. (H.W. Wilson scholar), 1953. Clk., Permit Office for Germany, Allied High Commn., Stockholm, 1949-50; sr. clk. U. Minn. Libr., 1952-53; asst. reference libr. Oreg. State U. Libr., 1953-54; King Gustav V fellow in Sweden, Am. Scandinavia Found., 1954-55; asst. libr. Modesto (Calif.) Jr. Coll. Libr., 1955-56; head acquisitions dept. U. Kans. Libr., 1956-60, assoc. dir., 1960-61, dir. libraries, 1961-68, lectr. in Scandinavian, 1958-61; prof. bibliography, univ. libr. Northwestern U., Evanston, Ill., 1968-71; pres. Found. Ctr., NYC, 1971-91, sr. advisor, 1991-93; pres., chmn. Engring. Info. Found., 1995—. Past chairperson bd. dirs. Telecom. Coop. Network, E.S.T.C., N.A., Engring. Info., Inc. Editor, translator: Modern Theatre: Seven Plays and an Essay (by Pär Lagerkvist), 1966; editor: Bibliography and Natural History, 1966, University and Research Libraries in Japan and the United States, 1972; contbr. articles to profl. jours. With USNR, 1943-46. Guggenheim fellow, 1964-65, Scandinavian studies fellow U. Minn., 1952, H.W. Wilson scholar, 1953. Mem. ALA (chmn. internat. rels. adv. com. for liaison with Japanese librs. 1967-71, dir. internat. rels. office 1966-67), Soc. for Advancement of Scandinavian Study (sec.-treas. 1959-69), Am. Scandinavian Found. (bd. dirs. 1978-82). Home: 30 Lincoln Plz Apt 30S New York NY 10023-7126 Office: Engring Info Found 180 W 80th St Ste 207 New York NY 10024-6301

BUCKMAN, WILLIAM H., lawyer; b. 1953; married. BS, Stockton State Coll.; JD, Rutgers U. Bar: NJ 1978, cert.: NJ Supreme Ct. (Criminal Def. Atty.) 1989. With pub. defender's office, Gloucester County, NJ; pub. defender Rutland, Vt., 1995—97; prin. William H. Buckman Law Firm, Moorestown, NJ. Mem. Nat. Orgn. Reform Marijuana Laws. Contbr. articles to profl. jours. Named to Ten Leaders of Criminal Def. Law of So. NJ, 2004—. Mem.: NACDL, NY Assn. Criminal Def. Lawyers, Pa. Assn. Criminal Def. Lawyers, Burlington County Bar Assn., Assn. Criminal Def. Lawyers NJ. Office: William H Buckman Law Firm 714 E Main St Ste 1B Moorestown NJ 08057 Office Phone: 856-608-9797. Office Fax: 856-608-6244. E-mail: wbuckman@whbuckman.com.*

BUCKMASTER, DENNIS RENE, agricultural engineer, educator; b. Angola, Ind., Jan. 16, 1962; s.Ivan E. and Ruby B. (Horner) B.; m. Corinne L. Thayer, Sept. 14, 1985; children: Stacey R., Stephanie J., Nathan A. BS in Agrl. Engring., Purdue U., West Lafayette, Ind., 1984; MS in Agrl. Engring., Mich. State U., 1986, PhD in Agrl. Engring., 1989. Registered profl. engr., Pa.; fluid power specialist. Rsch. asst. Mich. State U., East Lansing, 1984-88; asst. prof. agrl. engring. Pa. State U., University Park, 1989-95, assoc. prof. agrl. engring., 1995—2006; assoc. prof. biol. engring. Purdue U., West Lafayette, Ind., 2006—. Mem. Am. Soc. Agrl. Engrs. (Blue Ribbon for software 1992), Fluid Power Soc., Am. Forage and Grassland Soc. (2d pl. Young Scientist 1987, Merit award 2001). Avocations: farming, woodworking. Office: Purdue Univ Dept Agrl and Biol Engring 225 S University St West Lafayette IN 47907 Business E-Mail: dbuckmas@purdue.edu.

BUCKMASTER, JIM, online community bulletin board company executive; B in BioChemistry summa cum laude, Va. Tech; studied medicine and classics, U. Mich. Lead web developer Inter-University Consortium for Polit. and Soc. Rsch., U. Mich.; dir. web develop. dotcom Creditland, Quantum Corp.; chief tech. officer, CFO, lead programmer Craigslist, San Francisco, pres., CEO, 2000—. Bd. transportation, San Francisco. Built the world's first multi-terabyte database-driven public website at the University Michigan; Craigslist is a network of local community bulletion boards, where millions of people research subjects such as: jobs, housing, goods & services, events, friendships, and advice. Office: Craigslist 1319 9th Ave San Francisco CA 94122-2308 Office Phone: 415-566-6394. Office Fax: 415-504-6394. Business E-Mail: jim@craigslist.org.

BUCKMASTER, MATTHEW TOBE, musician, educator; b. Naples, Fla., July 25, 1978; s. Harvey Elba and Barbara Munson Buckmaster; m. Ana Parris, Aug. 13, 2000. MusB, Fla. So. Coll., 2000; M in Music Performance, U. South Fla., 2001, PhD in Music Edn., 2006. Cert. tchr. Fla., 2002, NC, 2006. Musician Walt Disney World, Lake Buena Vista, Fla., 1998—; tchg. asst. U. South Fla., Tampa, 2000—01; musician Busch Gardens, Tampa, 2000—02; adj. prof. Southeastern Coll., Lakeland, 2001—05; band dir. Kathleen H.S., 2002—03; co-owner B and B Pub., 2004—; asst. dir. athletic bands U. South Fla., 2005—; asst. prof. music edn. and low brass Elon U., 2006—. Treas. Ctrl. Fla. Trombone Soc., 2004—. Composer: (musical arrangement) Londonderry Air, The Rite of Spring. Va. Bridges Doctoral fellow, U. South Fla., 2003-2005. Mem.: NC Music Educator's Assn., Coll. Music Soc., Music Educator's Nat. Conf., Internat. Trombone Assn. (Jour. News Editor 2007—), Phi Kappa Lambda, Phi Mu Alpha Sinfonia (chpt. pres. 1998—99, Sinfonia Found. scholar 1999). Independent. Avocations: travel, basketball, gardening. Office: Elon U Campus Box 2800 Elon NC 27244 Personal E-mail: mattbuckmaster@hotmail.com.

BUCKMORE, ALVAH CLARENCE, JR., computer scientist, ballistician; b. Lewiston, Maine, Sept. 11, 1944; s. Alvah Clarence and Mary (Begin) Buckmore; m. Lolita F. Laurina. Student, Holyoke C.C., Nat. Radio Inst., Famous Writers Sch., U. Mass. Cert. firearms instr.; lic. amateur radio operator. CEO, chief scientist Buckmore Enterprises, Westfield, Mass., 1974—; developer math./engring. software database for microcomputer Calculated Solutions (formerly SC Applied Tech. Inc.), Columbia, SC. Mgmt. cons. firearms industry; instr. Mass. Mil. NCO Acad., 1976; mem. Mass. State Rifle and Pistol Team, 1976. Contbr. Collier's Ency., articles to profl. jours. Mem. Mass. Rep. Party, Rep. Presdl. Task Force, Mass. Rep. Senate Com., at-large del., 1992—; comm. officer, dir. RACES for Mass. Emergency Mgmt. Agy., Area III, 1996-98. Recipient Internat. Recognition award, 1979; NSF fellow, 1978—. Mem. AAAS, Computer Soc. of IEEE, NRA (life), DAV (life), Am. Def. Preparedness Assn., Nat. Assn. Federally Lic. Firearms Dealers (mem. sr. coalition), Assn. for Computer Tng. and Support, Math. Assn. Am., Am. Radio Relay League, Soc. Amateur Radio Astronomers, Amateur Radio Satellite Corp., Vietnam Vets. Am. (mem. vets. coun. Liberty chpt. 219 1988), Am. Fedn. Police, Am. Legion, N.Y. Acad. Scis., Mount Tom Amateur Repeater Assn. Achievements include development of amateur radio satellite communications, of parallel processing techniques, algorithms, and code for ballistic applications; over 38 major discoveries made in ballistics, including the discovery of 3 new sciences: time physics, the study of the physical properties of time; force-fields, the study of the absorption, displacement, projection, or reflection of kinetic energy; and ballistic signatures, the study of the physical characteristics of a bullet in terminal flight. Address: 18 Tannery Rd Westfield MA 01085-4822 Personal E-mail: k1tma@hotmail.com. *Since the age of 15 years it has been my consistent objective in life to develop a genuine ability to think, talk and use information properly and, over these years—which include the experience of my serving as an illegal POW with only partial official recognition—I have wavered very little, if at all.*

BUCKNALL, WILLIAM L., JR., human resources professional; BS, U. New Haven, 1965; MS in Mgmt., MIT. Various positions including corp. dir. salaried employee relations United Technologies Corp., Hartford, Conn., 1966-92, v.p. human resources and orgn., 1991—92, sr. v.p. human resources and orgn., 1992—. Mem. dean's adv. coun. MIT Sloan Sch. Mgmt.; mem. adv. bd. Ctr. Advanced Human Resource Studies Cornell U.; bd. dirs. Labor Policy Assn. Mem. nat. corp. com., United Negro Coll. Fund. Mem.: Nat. Acad. Human Resources. Office: United Technologies Corp United Technologies Bldg 1 Financial Plz Hartford CT 06101 Office Phone: 860-728-7000.*

BUCKNER, ELMER LA MAR, retired insurance company executive; b. Provo, Utah, Apr. 27, 1922; s. Elmer R. and Altis LaVern (Maxfield) B.; m. Melba Hale, Oct. 3, 1945; children: Lynda, Brent, Terry, Kathy, David. BS, Brigham Young U., 1946; HHD (hon.), Weber State U., 1994. CLU. Ptnr. Buckner-Radmall Ins. Counselors, Ogden, Utah, 1947-62, co. inc. pres., 1962-85. Mem. Utah Ho. of Reps., 1965-67, Utah Senate, 1967-75, asst. majority leader, 1971-75. Bd. govs. ARC, 1956-62, mem. exec. com., 1961-62; mem. gen. bd. Young Men's Mut. Improvement Assn., LDS Ch., 1957-58, young men's gen. bd., 1980, regional rep., 1981-87; bishop Ogden 55th Ward, 1958-63, pres. Ogden LDS Temple, 1987-90; 2d counselor Weber Heights Stake presidency, 1963-68; pres. Weber State Coll. Stake, 1968-73, Sacramento mission, 1975-78; former dir. Citizens Com. for Hoover Report; mem. Com. on Religion in Am. Life Inc.; former mem. adv. com. FOA; v.p. Lake Bonneville coun. Boy Scouts Am., 1968-69, pres., 1970, program chmn. Western region, 1973-75; mem. alumni bd. Brigham Young U., 1959-63, pres., 1961-62; v.p. Ogden Area United Fund, 1962, pres. No. Utah, 1963; chmn. Utah Cancer Crusade, 1970; v.p. Utah Cancer Soc., 1971, Utah div. Am. Cancer Soc.; del. Rep. Nat. Conv., Chgo., 1960, chmn. Weber County Reps., 1960-64; elector Utah State Reps., 1964; mem. Utah Bd. Regents Higher Edn., 1981-85; bd. dirs. western region bd. Boy Scouts Am., 1986-2002, pres. area II coun., 1985-87. 1st lt. USAAF, World War II; 23 missions. Recipient Silver Beaver award Boy Scouts Am., 1967, Silver Antelope award, 1983; Disting. Alumni award Weber State Coll., 1983, Alexis de Tocqueville award United Way Am., 1987, Alumni Disting. Svc. award Brigham Young U., 1991; named Utah Ins. Agt. of Yr., 1973. Mem. U.S. C. of C. (bd. dirs. 1955-56), U.S. Jaycees (pres. 1954-55), Utah Jaycees (pres. 1952-53), Ogden C. of C. (bd. dirs. 1980, pres. 1982, Utah Hall of Fame award 1989), Ogden Jaycees (pres. 1950), Jr. Chamber Internat. (treas. 1956), Weber Coll. Alumni Assn. (pres. 1958-59), Kiwanis (pres. Ogden club 1967), Sigma Gamma Chi (internat. pres. 1967-69). Home: 1550 Country Hills Dr Ogden UT 84403-2512 E-mail: elbuckner@comcast.net.

BUCKNER, JAN CRAIG, oncologist, educator; b. NC, Apr. 24, 1954; MD, U. NC, Chapel Hill, 1980. Cert. Am. Bd. Internal Medicine, Am. Bd. Internal Medicine, Med. Oncology. Intern, internal medicine Butterworth Hosp., Grand Rapids, Mich., 1980—81, resident, med. oncology, 1981—83; fellow, med. oncology Mayo Clinic, 1983—85, cons.; prof. oncology Mayo Med. Sch., Rochester, Minn.; vice-chair, practice integration facility subcommittee Mayo Clinic Cancer Ctr., Minn., chair, clin. practice com., divsn. med. oncology Minn. Group chair N. Ctrl. Cancer Treatment Group; cons. FDZ Ctr. for Drug Evaulation and Rsch. in Divsn. Oncology Drug Products and Oncologic Drug Adv. Com.; lectr., presenter in field. Contbr. articles to profl. jours.; mem. editl. bd. Neuro-Oncology Jour., manuscript reviewer for various scientific jours. Recipient Soc. for Neuro-Oncology award for Excellence in Clin. Rsch, 2001. Mem.: Am. Brain Tumor Assn. (mem. scientific adv. coun.). Office: Mayo Clinic 4500 San Pablo Rd Jacksonville FL 32224*

BUCKNER, JOHN KNOWLES, investor; b. Springfield, Mo., Sept. 8, 1936; s. Ernest Godfrey and Mary Helen (Knowles) B.; m. Lorraine Catherine Anderson, Sept. 22, 1962; children: John Knowles, Allison. BA, Williams Coll., 1958; MS, Mass. Inst. Tech., 1960; PhD, nuclear engring., Stanford U., 1965; grad., Advanced Mgmt. Program, Harvard, 1974. Mgr. analysis dept. EG&G Inc., Bedford, Mass., 1966-70; dir. electronic data processing, controller, v.p. financial ops. Eastern Gas & Fuel Assos., Boston, 1970-77; exec. v.p., chief operating officer, dir. Waters Assos., Inc., Milford, Mass., 1977-80; v.p., chief fin. officer Prime Computer, Inc., Natick, Mass., 1980-83; sr. v.p., chief fin. officer EG & G, Inc., Wellesley, Mass., 1983-86; vice chmn., chief fin. officer Control Data Corp., Mpls., 1986-89; chmn. Pensco Pension Svcs. Inc., San Francisco, 1989-98, Bohdan Automation, Inc., Mundelein, Ill., 1994-98. Contbr. articles on engring., data analysis and systems to profl. jours. AEC spl. fellow nuclear sci. and engring., 1959, 62-65 Mem.: Assn. Univs. for Rsch. in Astronomy (bd.d ir. 2003—), Sigma Xi, Phi Beta Kappa, Chi Psi. Office: Pensco Pension Svcs Inc 450 Sansome St 14th Fl San Francisco CA 94111-3306 *My present success, such as it is, has resulted from a willingness and ability to work hard, motivate others, and apply my own training and ideas to the particular task at hand, irrespective of the nature of the field of endeavor. My approach has always been to attain a level of technical and managerial competence necessary to bring about change. Generally, my goal is to make a contribution in as many areas of human conduct as my diligence and native ability will allow.*

BUCKNER, JOYCE, psychologist, educator; b. Benton, Ark., Sept. 25, 1937; d. Waymond Floyd Pannell and Willie Evelyn (Wright) Whitley; m. John W. Buckner, Aug. 29, 1958 (div. 1970); children: Cheryl, John, Chris. BA, Ouachita Bapt. Coll., 1959; MS in Edn., Henderson State U., 1964; PhD, North Tex. State U., 1970. Lic. psychologist, Tex., marriage and family therapist; cert. Nat. Registry Health Svc. Providers in Psychology; master trainer in imago relationship therapy. Assoc. prof. U. Tex., Arlington, 1970-80, chmn. dept. edn., 1976-78; pvt. practice Arlington, 1974—. Dir., chief profl. officer Southwest Inst. Relationship Devel.; appeard on tv shows including Oprah; spkr. in field. Author: Making Real Love Happen: The New Era of Intimacy. Mem. APA, Nat. Assn. for Imago Relationship Therapy (pres.), Nat. Speakers Assn., Am. Assn. Marital and Family Therapy. Avocations: dance, travel, art. Home: 4118 Bishop Creek Court Arlington TX 76016 Home Phone: 817-478-5037; Office Phone: 817-478-5257. Personal E-mail: joybuckner@aol.com.

BUCKNER, PHILIP FRANKLIN, newspaper publisher; b. Worcester, Mass., Aug. 25, 1930; s. Orello Simmons and Emily Virginia (Siler) B.; m. Ann Haswell Smith, Dec. 21, 1956 (div. Nov. 1993); children: John C., Frederick S., Catherine A.; m. Mary Emily Aird, Dec. 15, 1995 (div. Sept. 1997). AB, Harvard U., 1952; MA, Columbia U., 1954. With Bay State Abrasive Products Co., 1954-59; Reporter Lowell (Mass.) Sun, 1959-60; pub. East Providence (R.I.) Post, 1960-62; asst. to treas. Scripps League Newspapers, Seattle, 1964-66, divsn. mgr., 1966-71; pres. Buckner News Alliance, Seattle, 1971—. Pub. daily newspaper group including Carlsbad (N.Mex.) Current-Argus, 1971-90, Pecos (Tex.) Enterprise, 1971—, Fontana (Calif.) Herald-News, 1971-89, Banning and Beaumont (Calif.) Gazette, 1971-74, Lewistown (Pa.) Sentinel, 1971-93, Tiffin (Ohio) Advertiser-Tribune, 1973-93, York (Pa.) Daily Record, 1978-2004, Winsted (Conn.) Citizen, 1978, Excelsior Springs (Mo.) Standard, 1978, Oroville (Calif.) Mercury-Register, 1983-89, Corona (Calif.) Independent, 1984-89, Minot (N.D.) News, 1989-93, York (Pa.) Dispatch, 2004—. Avocation: mountain climbing. Office: Buckner News Alliance 2101 4th Ave Ste 1870 Seattle WA 98121-2345

BUCKNER, RANDY L., psychology professor, neuroscientist; BA in Psychology, Washington U., St. Louis, 1991, MA in Psychology and Neuroscience, 1993, PhD in Psychology and Neuroscience, 1995. Postdoctoral fellowships Harvard Med. Sch., Washington U., St. Louis, asst. prof. psychology and neurobiology, 1997—2001, asst. prof. radiology, 1998—2001, assoc. prof., psychology, neurobiology & radiology, 2001—05; prof., psychology, faculty of arts and sciences Harvard U., Cambridge, Mass., 2005—; neuroscientist, dept. radiology Mass. Gen. Hosp.; mem. faculty Athinoula A. Martinos Ctr. for Biomedical Imaging, Charlestown, Mass.; asst. investigator Howard Hughes Med. Inst., 2000—04, investigator, 2005—. Affiliated with Ctr. for Brain Sci., Harvard U. Mem. of several editl. boards including Neuron, Nature Reviews, Neuroscience and Journal of Cognitive Neuroscience; contbr. articles to profl. jours. Co-recipient Troland Rsch. award, NAS, 2007; recipient Wiley Young Investigator award for Human Brain Mapping, Orgn. of Human Brain Mapping, 1999, Young Investigator award, Cognitive Neuroscience Soc., 2002. Fellow: Am. Psychological Assn. Office: Athinoula A Martinos Ctr for Biomedical Imaging Bldg 149 Rm 2301 13th St Charlestown MA 02129 Office Phone: 617-726-5464. Business E-Mail: buckner@nmr.mgh.harvard.edu.*

BUCKNER, THOMAS RANDOLPH, lawyer; b. Goldsboro, NC, Aug. 23, 1947; s. Samuel Lee and Helen Faris Buckner; m. Karen Renée Wagner; children: Kelly Buckner Dallas, Susan Elizabeth, Samuel Randolph. BA, Va. Mil. Inst., 1969; JD, Vanderbilt U., 1972. Bar: Tenn. 1972. Sole practitioner, Memphis, 1972—81; assoc. Wildman Harrold Allen, Dixon, McDonnell, Memphis, 1981—84, ptnr., 1985—87; mem. Apperson, Crump & Maxwell, PLC, Memphis, 1987—. Bd. editors Vanderbilt Jour. Transnat. Law, 1970—71. Chmn. planned giving com. Boys & Girls Club, Memphis, 2003—. Capt. USAF, 1972. Named one of Best Lawyers in Am., Woodward, Best 101 Lawyers in Tenn., Bus. Tenn. Mag., 2004, Best 150 Lawyers in Tenn., 2005—07. Mem.: Planned Giving Coun. of Greater Memphis, Estate Planning Coun. of Memphis, Tenn. Bar Assn. (vice chair tax, probate and trust sect. 1999), Memphis Bar Assn. (chmn. wills and probate sect. 2000—03, chmn. CLE com. 2005), Am. Coll. Trust and Estate Counsel. Methodist. Avocations: tennis, golf, running, reading. Home: 6589 May Hollow Cove Memphis TN 38119 Office: Apperson Crump & Maxwell PLC 6000 Poplar Ave Ste 400 Memphis TN 38119 Office Phone: 901-756-6300. Office Fax: 901-756-9782. E-mail: tbuckner@appersoncrump.com.

BUCKNUM, MICHAEL JOHN, chemist, crystallographer, educator; b. Trenton, NJ, Apr. 23, 1963; s. Walter Frederick and Barbara Dockter B.; m. Hsi-cheng (Kathy) Shen, July 7, 1995. BA, Indiana U. Pa., 1985; MS, U. Ky., 1988, Cornell U., 1992, PhD, 1996. Staff editor Chem. Abstracts Svc., Columbus, Ohio, 1988-89; patent examiner US Patent and Trademark Office, Crystal City, Va., 1996-97; rschr. Hard Materials Corp., Ithaca, NY, 1997-2000; instr., rschr. Ill. East CC, Olney, 2000-2001, Ga. Coll. and State U., Milledgeville, 2001—03, Fullerton Coll., Calif., 2003—04, Ky., 2003—04; rschr. El Instituto Investigacíones Fisicoquímicas Teóricas and Aplicadas, U. La Plata, Buenos Aires, 2004—07; corr. investigator NRC, Argentina, 2007—. Mem. adv. bd. Chemistry Ctrl. Current Sci. Ltd., London, 2007—; corr. investigator Nat. Rsch. Coun., Argentina, 2007—; mem. internat. com. World Sci. and Engring. Acad. and Soc., Cairo, 2007. Contbr. more than 30 articles to profl. jours. Grad. fellow U. Ky., 1985-86, NIH fellow Cornell U., 1994-96. Mem. AAAS, Am. Chem. Soc., Joseph Campbell Found., Sigma Xi. Democrat. Roman Catholic. Achievements include contributions to the theory of light, theory of elasticity, theory of spiroconjugation, theory of carbon allotropy, crystallography, chemical topology, inorganic chemistry, organic chemistry and biological chemistry; examined more than 25 patents. Avocations: reading, films, art, gemology, hiking. Office Phone: 626-203-9514. Business E-Mail: mjbucknum@gmail.com.

BUCKSBAUM, JOHN, real estate company executive; BA in Econs., U. Denver. Pres. Gen. Growth Calif.; CEO, bd. dir. Gen. Growth Properties, Inc., 1999—. Chmn., mem. exec. com. Internat. Council Shopping Centers; trustee Nat. Assn. REITs, Urban Land Inst.; mem. Nat. Realty Roundtable; mem. adv. bd. Univ. Calif. Real Estate Ctr.; chmn. Zell/Lurie Real Estate Ctr., Wharton Sch. Bd. mem. U.S. Ski & Snowboard Team Found., USA Cycling Found., World T.E.A.M. Sports; trustee Univ. Chgo. Hospitals. Mem.: Young Presidents Org. Office: Gen Growth Properties inc 110 N Wacker Dr Chicago IL 60606-1511*

BUCKSBAUM, MATTHEW, real estate investment trust company executive; b. Marshalltown, Iowa, Feb. 20, 1926; s. Louis and Ida (Gerwin) B.; m. Carolyn Swartz, Aug. 3, 1952; children: Ann B. Friedman, John. BA in Econ. cum laude, U. Iowa, 1949. Owner, operator Regional Supermarket Chain, Marshalltown, 1949-54; owner, developer Pvt. Real Estate, Iowa, 1954-64; chmn. Gen. Growth Properties, Chgo., 1964—. Trustee, past chmn. Aspen (Colo.) Music Festival and Sch.; bd. dirs. Chgo. Symphony Orch., Lyric Opera Chgo. Sgt. USAF, 1944-46, PTO. Named one of Forbes' Richest Americans, 2005—, World's Richest People, Forbes mag., 2006—. Mem.: Nat. Assn. Real Estate Investment Trusts, Urban Land Inst., Internat. Coun. Shopping Ctrs. (past chmn.), Order of Artus, Phi Beta Kappa. Jewish. Office: General Growth Properties Inc 110 N Wacker Dr Chicago IL 60606-1511 Office Phone: 312-960-5123. Office Fax: 312-960-5463.

BUCKSBAUM, MELVA, foundation administrator; m. Martin Bucksbaum (dec.); 1 child, Mary; m. Raymond J. Learsy. Mgr. Martin Bucksbaum Family Found., 1995—; dir. Robert I. Goldman Found., 1996—; bd. mem. Am. Friends of Israel Mus., NY, The Jewish Mus., NY, Hirshhorn Mus. & Sculpture Garden, Washington, Save Venice, New York & Venice; visiting com. Grad. Sch. Design, Harvard U. Named one of top 200 collectors (with Raymond Learsy), ARTnews Mag., 2004; recipient Gertrude Vanderbilt Whitney Award for outstanding arts patronage & philanthropy, 2004. Mem.: Whitney Mus. Am. Art (trustee 1996—, vice chmn. 2004—), Tate Gallery (Internat. Com.). Avocation: collector of contemporary art. Mailing: 646 Willoughby Way Aspen CO 81611 also: c/o Whitney Mus Am Art 945 Madison Ave New York NY 10021

BUCKSBAUM, PHILIP HOWARD, physicist; b. Grinnell, Iowa, Jan. 14, 1953; s. Arnold M. and Corinne P. (Schlass) B.; m. Roberta J. Morris, June 15, 1985. AB in Physics, magna cum laude, Harvard Coll., 1975; MA in Physics, U. Calif., Berkeley, 1978, PhD, 1980. Postdoctoralfellow Lawrence Berkeley Lab., Berkeley, Calif., 1980-81, Bell Labs., Holmdel, N.J., 1981-82; mem. tech. staff AT&T Bell Labs., Murray Hill, N.J., 1982-90; prof. physics U. Mich., Ann Arbor, 1990—98, Otto Laporte prof. physics, 1998—. Editor: VJUltrafast, APS Virtual Jour. Ultrafast Sci. Recipient Disting. Traveling Lectr., APS Divsn. Laser Sci., 1996—97, Mich. Sokal award for rsch., 2001; John Simon Guggenheim Meml. Found. fellow, 1996—97. Fellow Am. Phys. Soc., Optical Soc. Am.; mem. NAS.

BUCKSPAN, RANDY JAY, plastic surgeon; b. Nurnberg, Germany, Oct. 9, 1954; (parents Am. citizens); s. Harold and Betty Jane (Marker) B.; m. Amy Denise Boynton, May 2, 1981; children: Elizabeth Anne, Caitlin Elaine, Andrew David. BS in Chemistry, U. Tex., Austin, 1976; MD, U. Tex., Galveston, 1980. Diplomate Am. Bd. Plastic Surgery. Resident in gen. surgery Vanderbilt U. Hosp., Nashville, 1980-85; fellow in plastic surgery U. Ky., Lexington, 1985-87. Contbr. articles to med. jours. Mem. ACS, Am. Soc. Plastic Surgeons, Southeastern Soc. Plastic and Reconstructive Surgeons, Tampa Bay Soc. Plastic Surgeons. Avocations: bicycling, running, fishing. Office: 1607 Dr Martin Luther King Jr St N Ste B Saint Petersburg FL 33704 Office Phone: 727-822-6531. Business E-Mail: drbuckspan@tampabayplasticsurgery.net.

BUCKSTEIN, CARYL SUE, writer; b. Denver, Aug. 10, 1954; d. Henry Martin and Hedvig (Neulander) B. BS in Journalism, U. Colo., 1976. Editor Rifle (Colo.) Telegram, 1976; corr. So. Colo. Pueblo (Colo.) Star-Jour. and Chieftain, 1977-84; corr. The Denver Post, 1985; staff editor Nat. Over-the-Counter Stock Jour., Denver, 1985-89; writer Rocky Mountain News, Denver, 1990-92; editor Urban Spectrum, Denver, 1993; contbg. writer Boulder (Colo.) County Bus. Report, 1992—. Bd. mem. Holiday Project, Denver, 1996; mem. exec. bd. Denver Newspaper Guild, 1998. Recipient 1st Place Gen. Assignment Bus. Articles, Colo. Press Women, Denver, 1985, 90, 91. Mem. Colo. Soc. Profl. Journalists (sec.-treas. 1988), Denver Newspaper Guild (bd. dirs. 1998). Avocations: inventing, writing. Home: 9995 E Harvard Ave Apt 0215 Denver CO 80231-3906 Personal E-mail: doewrite1701@comcast.net.

BUCKSTEIN, MARK AARON, lawyer, educator, mediator; b. NYC, July 1, 1939; s. Henry Al and Minnie Sarah (Russ) B.; children: Robin Beth, Michael Alan. BS in Math., CCNY, 1960; JD, NYU, 1963. Bar: N.Y. 1963, U.S. Dist. Ct. (so. and ea. dists.) N.Y. 1965, U.S. Supreme Ct. 1981. Assoc. Russ & Weyl, Massapequa, NY, 1963-64; assoc. counsel Mut. Life Ins. Co. N.Y., NYC, 1964-65; assoc. Moses & Singer, NYC, 1965-67, Leinwand, Maron & Hendler, NYC, 1967-68; sr. ptnr. Baer Marks & Upham, NYC, 1968-86; sr. v.p. external affairs, gen. counsel TWA, Inc., NYC, 1986-92; exec. v.p. Am. Arbitration Assn., NYC, NJ, 1992-93; exec. v.p., gen. counsel GAF Corp. and Internat. Specialty Products, Wayne, NJ, 1993-96; counsel Greenberg Traurig, Ft. Lauderdale, Fla., 1996-99, Profl. Dispute Resolution, Inc., Boca Raton, Fla., 1999—. Spl. prof. law Hofstra U. Law Sch., Hempstead, N.Y., 1981-93; adj. prof. law Rutgers U. Law Sch., Newark, 1994-96; adj. prof. Fla. Atlantic U., Grad. Sch. Bus., 2004—; bd. dirs. Bayswater Realty & Capital Corp., N.Y.C., Travel Channel Inc., N.Y.C., TWA, GAF Corp., Internat. Specialty Products, Consultis; mem. exec. com. Herzfeld & Stern, N.Y.C., 1981-84; mem. nat. arbitration and mediation com. NASD, 1998-2001. Trustee Bronx H.S. Found., 1984-96. Mem. ABA, N.Y. Bar Assn., Assn. of Bar of City of N.Y., KP (past dep. grand chancellor 1978). Jewish. Avocations: tennis, music, theater, puzzles. Office: Profl Dispute Resolution 2424 N Federal Hwy Boca Raton FL 33431 Home: 8654 Valhalla dr Delray Beach FL 33446 Office Phone: 561-417-6602. Personal E-mail: mabresolve@aol.com.

BUCKWALTER, JOSEPH ADDISON, orthopedic surgeon, educator; b. Ottumwa, Iowa, June 21, 1947; s. Joseph Addison and Carole Ann (Kelly) B.; m. Kathleen Coen, May 31, 1975; children: Jody, Andrea, Abigail. BS with high distinction, U. Iowa, 1969, MS, 1972, MD, 1974. Diplomate Am. Bd. Orthopaedic Surgery (recert., oral examiner 1988—, dir. 1990—, mem. examinations com. 1992—, chmn. examinations com. 1992-93, chmn. cert. renewal com. 1992—); lic. surgeon Iowa. Intern in internal medicine U. Iowa, Iowa City, 1974-75, resident in orthopaedics, 1975-77, 78-79, Nat. Rsch. Svc. Award rsch. fellow, 1977-78, from asst. prof. to assoc. prof. orthopaedic surgery, 1979-85, prof. orthopaedic surgery, 1985—. Mem. R&D devel. com. VA Med. Ctr. Com., 1985-88; mem. orthopaedic tumor therapy group U. Iowa Cancer Ctr., 1981—, cancer edn. subcom., 1982-90; mem. grants and fellowships adv. com. Iowa City Vets. Med. Ctr., 1983-86, chief orthopaedic surgery, 1987-91; mem. Arthritis Found. Rsch. Com., 1985-86; mem. panel NIH Consensus Devel. Confs., Bethesda, Md., 1984, 88; mem. rheumatology rsch. adv. bd. Syntex Corp., 1987-94; mem. adv. bd. WHO Multinational Collaborative Study on Predictors of Osteoarthritis, 1992; mem. sci. adv. com. Specialised Ctr. Rsch. on Osteoarthritis Rush-Presbyn.-St. Luke's Med. Ctr., Chgo., 1993—; mem. Nat. Arthritis and Musculoskeletal and Skin Diseases Adv. Coun., NIH, 1993—; disting. lectr. Hosp. Spl. Surgery, N.Y.C., 1982, Coll. Physicians and Surgeons-N.Y. Orthopaedic Hosp., 1988, U. N.Mex., 1989; guest lectr. Wilford Hall Med. Ctr., San Antonio, 1983, vis. prof., 1984; vis. prof. U. Miami, Fla., 1986, Cath. Med. Colls., Seoul, Republic of Korea, 1989, U. Pitts., 1993, Ohio State U., Columbus, 1994; vis. orthopaedic prof. U. So. Calif., L.A., 1990; Am. Orthopaedic Assn. 1991 Internat. vis. prof. Nuffield Orthopaedic Ctr., Oxford (Eng.) U., 1991, vis. prof. orthopaedics, 1991; vis. prof. orthopaedics, U. N.C., 1991; OREF Hark lectr. and vis. prof. U. Wash., Seattle, 1992; Watson Jones lectr. Royal Coll. Surgeons (Gt. Britain), 1992; A.M. Rechtman lectr. Phila. Orthopaedic Soc., 1993; Predl. guest spkr. 1993 Japanese Orthopaedic Assn. Rsch. Meeting, Matsumoto, Japan, 1993; Kelly Rsch. Award vis. prof. Mayo Clinic, Rochester, Minn., 1993; participant numerous workshops and confs. Cons. reviewer: Jour. Bone and Joint Surgery, 1979—, cons. editor for rsch., 1989—; bd. assoc. editors: Jour. Orthopaedic Rsch., 1982-85, mem. editl. adv. bd., 1985-88, co-editor-in-chief, 1993—; mem. editl. adv. bd. Orthopaedics, 1986-90; reviewer: The Lancet, 1993—; contbr. articles to profl. jours. Student rsch. fellow U. Iowa Coll. Medicine, 1970. Fellow Am. Inst. Med. and Biol. Engring. (founding), Am. Acad. Orthopaedic Surgeons (mem. com. basic scis. 1983-85, chmn. com. evaulation 1985-90, mem. at large, bd. dirs. 1988-89, mem. steering com. for devel. Musculoskeletal Conditions in U.S. 1990-92, chmn. coun. for rsch. and sci. affairs 1990-93, 94—, sec. 1993-94); mem. AAAS, Inst. Medicine, Internat. Soc. Limb Salvage, Brit. Orthopaedic Assn. (companion mem.), Orthopaedic Rsch. Soc. (sec.-treas. 1985-88, bd. dirs. 1985-91, pres. 1989-90), Am. Orthopaedic Assn. (exch. fellowship com. 1989-90, chmn. internat. vis. prof. com. 1993—), Am. Orthopaedic Soc. for Sports Medicine (chmn. rsch. awards com. 1988-90, rsch. com. 1989-91), Internat. Skeletal Soc., Iowa Orthopaedic Soc., Johnson County Med. Soc., Musculoskeletal Tumor Soc., 20th Century Orthopaedic Assn., Girdlestone Orthopaedic Soc., Phi Beta Kappa, Alpha Omega Alpha. Office: U Iowa Hosps Dept Orthopaedics 200 Hawkins Dr Iowa City IA 52242-1009 Office Phone: 319-356-2595.

BUCKWALTER, KATHLEEN C., academic administrator, educator; BSN, U. Iowa; MA in Psychiatric/Mental Health Nursing, U. Ill., Chgo., PhD in Nursing. Assoc. dir. Gerontological Nursing Interventions Rsch. Ctr., dir. Ctr. on Aging U. Iowa, Found. disting. Prof., assoc. provost health scis., 1997—. Contbr. over 200 articles to profl. jours., 75 chpts. to books; editor: Nursing Diagnosis and Intervention for the Elderly (Maas, M., Buckwalter, K.C., Hardy, M.A.), 1991, Geriatric Mental Health: Current and Future Challenges, 1994, others. Mem.: IOM. Office: U Iowa Coll Nursing 101 Nursing Bldg 234 CMAB Iowa City IA 52242

BUCKWALTER, ROGER JEROME, editor, columnist; b. New Britain, Conn., Aug. 14, 1946; s. Benjamin Irving and Harriet (Hoskins) Buckwalter; m. Karen Ruth Adelson, June 8, 1974. BS in Broadcasting, U. Fla., 1968, MA in Journalism, Comm., 1969. Columnist Jupiter (Fla.) Courier, 1978—, editl. page editor, 1982-2001, sr. writer, 2000-01. Guest lectr. Palm Beach CC, Lake Worth, Fla., 1992, Lake Worth, 98, Fla. Atlantic U., Jupiter, 2000; guest interviewer Sta. WPTV, Channel 5, West Palm Beach, Fla., 1994—99; polit. forum moderator Jupiter-Tequesta-Juno Beach C. of C., 1995—; mem. adv. bd. Honors Coll. Fla. Atlantic U., 1999—, com. chair, 2001—; mem. Wal-Mart Scholarship Selection Bd., 2000—01; mem. adv. bd. Palm Beach Atlantic Nat. Vocal Competition, 2001—06, Smoke Free Workplaces Campaign, Fla., 2002, Keep Kids Smoke Free campaign, Fla., 2006. Vice chmn. Charter Rev. Com., Juno Beach, Fla., 1973—74; bd. dirs. Jupiter-Tequesta (Fla.) Unit Am. Cancer Soc., 1996—, pres., 1997—2000, chmn. com., 2000—; v.p. Loxahatchee River Hist. Soc., 2005—06, bd. dirs., v.p. strategic planning, 2003—05, chmn. bd. dirs., 2006—; bd. dirs. Cancer Alliance Help and Hope, 2003—, chmn. mktg., bd. dirs., 2003—, v.p., 2007—; chmn. bd. dirs. No. Palm Beaches Cultural Alliance, 2004—; chmn. Cmty. Cancer Coun., 2006—. 1st lt. US Army, 1969—71, Vietnam. Recipient 37 journalism awards including Best News Story award, Suburban Newspapers Am., 1976. Mem.: Fla. Press Assn. (Best Serious Column award 1987, 1996, Best Editl. award 1989, 1990, 1993, 1996), Nat. Conf. Editl. Writers, Fla. Press Club (Opinion and Feature Writing awards 1997). Avocations: painting, theater, writing. Personal E-mail: rogekar@aol.com.

BUCKWALTER, RONALD LAWRENCE, federal judge; b. Lancaster, Pa., Dec. 11, 1936; s. Noah Denlinger and Carolyn Marie (Lawrence) B.; m. Dollie May Fitting, May 9, 1963; children: Stephen Matthew, Wendy Susan. AB, Franklin and Marshall Coll., 1958; JD, Coll. William and Mary, 1962. Prin. Ronald L. Buckwalter, Esquire, Lancaster, 1963-71; ptnr. Shirk, Reist and Buckwalter, Lancaster, 1971-80; dist. atty. Lancaster County, Lancaster, 1978-80; judge 2nd Jud. Dist. Commonwealth Pa., 1980-90, U.S. Dist. Ct., Phila., 1990—. Sec. City Lancaster Authority, 1970; bd. dirs. Am. Cancer Soc., Lancaster, 1982, Boy Scouts Am., Lancaster, 1984, YMCA, Lancaster, 1990. 1st lt. U.S. Army NG, 1962-68. Recipient Pub. Life and Letter award Phi Sigma Alpha, 1990. Mem. Am. Judicature Soc., Fed. Bar Assn., Fed. Judges Assn., Pa. Bar Assn., Lancaster Bar Assn. (pres. 1988). Office: US Dist Ct 14614 US Courthouse 601 Market St Philadelphia PA 19106-1713 Office Phone: 215-597-3084.

BUCOVE, ARNOLD DAVID, psychiatrist; b. Toronto, Sept. 22, 1934; BA, Columbia U., NYC, 1956; MD, NYU, 1961. Diplomate Am. Bd. Psychiatry and Neurology. Intern Lenox Hill Hosp., NYC, 1961-62; resident in psychiatry Bellevue Hosp., NYC, 1962-63, St. Luke's Hosp., NYC, 1963-65; chief psychiatry 36th Tactical Hosp., Bitburg, Germany, 1965-67; pvt. practice psychiatry Pleasant Valley, NY, 1967—92, Poughkeepsie, NY, 1992-93; pvt. practice Oneonta, NY, 1993-99, Millbrook, NY, 1967—; attending staff Craig House, Beacon, NY, 1977-93; asst. dir. Dutchess County Mental Health Clinic, Poughkeepsie, NY, 1967-68; chief psychiatry Fox Meml. Hosp., Oneonta, 1993-99, sec.-treas. med. staff, 1997-98, pres.-elect, 1998-99, pres., 1999; med. dir. Lexington Ctr. Recovery, Poughkeepsie, 1999—. Cons. psychiatrist Greer Children's Cmty., Millbrook, NY, 1968-77; mem. courtesy staff Sharon Hosp., Conn., 1967-90; cons. IBM, Poughkeepsie, 1968; mem. med. staff St. Francis Hosp., Poughkeepsie, 1999—. Contbr. articles to profl. jours. Bd. dirs. Town of Washing Civic Assn., Millbrook, 1986-93, Millbrook Music Assn., 1986-92; mem. vestry Grace Ch., Millbrook, 1971-74, mem. vestry St. Peter's Ch., Millbrook, 1989-92. Capt. USAF, 1965-67. Fellow Am. Psychiat. Assn. (disting. life; pres. Mid-Hudson chpt. 1977-79); mem. Millbrook Hunt (bd. govs. 1968-71), Millbrook Golf and Tennis Club, Tamarack Preserve. Avocations: skiing, golf.

BUCY, J. FRED, JR., retired electronics company executive; b. Tahoka, Tex., July 29, 1928; s. J. Fred and Ethel (Montgomery) Bucy; m. Odetta Greer, Jan. 25, 1947 (dec. Dec. 2000); children: J. Fred III, Roxanne, Diane. B.Physics, Tex. Tech. U., 1951; M.Physics, U. Tex., 1953; DSc (hon.), Tex. Tech U., 1994. With Tex. Instruments, Inc., Dallas, 1953-85, engr. 53-63, corp. v.p. mil. sys., 1963-67, corp. group v.p. microchips, 1967-72, exec. v.p., 1972-75, exec. v.p., chief operating officer, dir., 1974-76, pres., chief operating officer, dir., 1976-84, pres., chief exec. officer, dir., 1984-85, cons., 1985-97. Bd. dirs. Thomas Group, Inc., Optical Data Sys., Inc., Hypres, Inc., S.W. Rsch. Inst., Rectractable Tech. Inc., Intrusion Inc., Sanders Assocs., Inc., Alliant Techsystems, Inc.; cons., chmn. Tex. Nat. Rsch. Lab. Com. Patentee in field. Mem. Tech. Assessment of U.S. Congress; mem. Comptroller Gen's Panel, Pres.'s Commn. for Nat. Agenda for 80's,; comm. chmn. Nat. Rsch. Coun., Washington, Def. Sci. Bd. Dept. Def.; mem. bd. regents Tex. Tech U., Health Sci. Ctr. Tex. Tech U., 1973-91; chmn. bd. regents Tex. Tech U. and Health Sci. Ctr., 1980-82, 89-90; mem. adv. com. rsch. Tex.Higher Edn. Coordinating Bd.; external adv com. Arnold O. and Mabel M. Beckman Inst. Advanced Sci. Tech., U. Ill.; adv. coun. Woodrow Wilson Internat. Ctr. for Scholars, Washington; chmn. Tex. Sci. Adv. Coun.; nat. chmn. Enterprise Campaign Tex. Tech U.; mem. vis. com. Russian Rsch. Ctr., Harvard U.; mem. physics vis. com. MIT; mem. exec. com. marine sci. adv. coun. U. Tex., 2005 Recipient Disting. Engr. award Tex. Tech U., 1972, Disting. Alumnus award, 1991. Fellow IEEE; mem. NAE, Am. Inst. Physics, Soc. Exploration Geophysicists, Conf. Bd., Cosmos Club (Washington), Dallas Petroleum Club, Tau Beta Pi, Sigma Pi Sigma, Eta Kappa Nu (Eminent Mem.). Office Phone: 214-363-8650. Personal E-mail: jfbuce@aol.com.

BUDA, JAMES B., lawyer, manufacturing executive; b. South Bend, Ind., Mar. 9, 1947; BA, Ball State U., 1969; JD, U. Notre Dame, 1973. Bar: Ind. 1973, Ill. 1987, U.S. Ct. Appeals (7th cir.) 1987, U.S. Supreme Ct. 1987. Atty., legal dept. and other positions Caterpillar, Inc., 1987—96, assoc. gen. counsel, 1996—99, assoc. gen. counsel, legal services divsn. UK, 1999—2001, v.p., legal services divsn., gen. counsel, sec. Peoria, Ill., 2001—. Mem. Civil Justice Reform Group. Mem.: ATLA, ABA, Gen. Counsel Roundtable, Corp. Exec. Bd., CLO Roundtable, Assn. Gen. Counsels, Am. Soc. Corp. Secs., Internat. Assn. Def. Counsel, Fedn. Corp. and Ins. Counsel, Def. Rsch. Inst., Am. Corp. Counsel Assn., Ind. State Bar Assn., Ill. State Bar Assn. Office: Caterpillar Inc Legal Dept 100 NE Adams St Peoria IL 61629-7310 Office Phone: 309-675-4428. Business E-Mail: budajb@cat.com.*

BUDA, THADDEUS J., JR., retired lawyer; b. Wyandotte, Mich., Apr. 9, 1943; m. Maureen A. Buda; children: Susan M., Julie A. BS, Wayne State U., 1965, JD, 1972. Bar: Mich. 1972. Sr. v.p., gen. counsel, sec. Auto-Owners Ins. Co., Lansing, Mich., 1st v.p., gen. counsel, sec., 2003—05, ret., 2005. Mem.: Mich. State Bar Assn.*

BUDALUR, THYAGARAJAN SUBBANARAYAN, chemistry professor; b. India, July 14, 1929; came to U.S., 1969, naturalized, 1977; s. Subbanarayan Subbuswamy and Parvatham (Gopalakrishnan) B.; children: Chitra, Poorna, Kartik. MA, U. Madras, 1951, M.Sc., 1954, PhD, 1956. Reader organic chemistry U. Madras, 1960-68; prof. chemistry U. Idaho, Moscow, 1968-74; prof. chemistry, dir. div. earth phys. sci. U. Tex., San Antonio, 1974-2000, emeritus prof., 2000—. Lectr. in field. Author: Mechanisms of Molecular Migrations; Selective Organic Transformations; Editorial bd. chem. jours.; contbr. articles to profl. jours.; 3 patents in field. Recipient Intra Sci. Research award, 1966 Fellow Am. Chem. Soc.; mem. Chem. Soc. London, Soc. Cosmetic Chemistry N.Y. Acad. Sci., Am. Inst. Chemists, Sigma Xi, Phi Kappa Phi. Clubs: Lions. Home: 6119 Amble Trl San Antonio TX 78249-2108 Personal E-mail: sulphone@aol.com.

BUDD, DAVID GLENN, lawyer; b. Dayton, Ohio, May 19, 1934; s. Glenn E. and Anna Elizabeth (Purdy) B.; m. Barbarann Dumbaugh, Apr. 4, 1964; children: Anne Elizabeth, David Glenn II. AB with honors, Ohio U., 1959; JD with honors, U. Cin., 1962. Bar: Ohio 1962, U.S. Dist. Ct. (so. dist.) Ohio 1963, U.S. Dist. Ct. (no. dist.) Ohio 1967, U.S. Supreme Ct. 1967, Fla. 1980, U.S. Dist. Ct. (mid. dist.) Fla. 1981, U.S. Tax Ct. 1989. Assoc. Young, Pryor, Lynn, Strickland & Falke, Dayton, 1962-65; trial atty. U.S. Dept. Justice, Cleve., 1965-67; chief antitrust sect. Atty. Gen. Ohio, Columbus, Ohio, 1967-69; ptnr., sr. corp. atty. Cox & Brandabur Attys., Xenia, Ohio, 1969-74; asst. v.p., asst. sec. law Jim Walter Corp., Tampa, Fla., 1974-76; sec., gen. counsel, asst. treas. Gardinier Big River, Inc., Gardinier, Inc., Tampa, 1976-80; assoc. Young, Van Assenderp, Varnadoe & Benton, P.A., Naples, Fla., 1981-84; ptnr. Van Koughnet & Budd, Naples, 1984-85; sr. ptnr. Budd, Hines & Thompson, Naples, 1985-88, Budd & Thompson, Naples, 1989-92, Budd, Thompson & Zuccaro, Naples, 1993-95, Budd & Zuccaro, Naples, 1996-97, Budd and Bennett, Naples, 1998—2003, Budd, Bennett & Macia, Naples, 2004—06, Budd & Macia, Naples, 2006—07; sr. counsel Grant Fridkin Pearson Athan & Crown, PA, Naples, 2007—. Legal counsel to bd. dirs. of numerous corps. Vol. Legal Aid Soc., Xenia, 1972. With USN, 1952-54. Mem. ABA (bus. law sect.), Fla. Bar Assn., Collier County Bar Assn., Blue Key Club, Omicron Delta Kappa, Pi Gamma Mu, Phi Kappa Tau. Republican. Presbyterian. Avocations: health fitness club, tennis, golf, boating. Home: 3757 Fountainhead Ln Naples FL 34103-2734 Office: Grant Fridkin Pearson Athan & Crown PA 5551 Ridgewood Dr Ste 501 Naples FL 34108 Home Phone: 239-262-7061; Office Phone: 239-514-1000. Business E-Mail: dbudd@gfpac.com.

BUDD, JIM, communications manager; b. Austin, Minn. s. Stanley James and Margaret (Deutschman) B. Student, Austin State Jr. Coll. Head of CCTV dept. Northwest Camera Svc., Mpls., 1971-72; head of video svc. dept., engring., TV studio and video svc. dept. ops. Internat. Communications Svcs., Mpls., 1972-73; talent scout coord. and video cons. Wag Arts Prodns.-Talent Agy., Mpls., 1972-75; electronics dept. svc. mgr. Gordon Electric Co., Austin, 1975-78; operational ptnr. in design and mfr. of projection TV consoles with McAllister Trading Co. and ABC Electronics, Austin, 1979-84; video systems specialist The Electronics Warehouse, Inc., Rochester, Minn., 1984-85; engr., video dir., mgr. ABC Electronics & Video, Austin, 1985—; producer, dir. N.W. TV-Prodns., Austin, 1986—; mem. broadcast video staff KAAL-TV, Austin, 1997-98. Video sys. design cons. Script author, narrator of documentary videofilm: "Celebration of Hmong New Year"--Laos, 1991; producer: (video) Big Isl. Rendezvous, 1995, (video film) Olympic Torch Relay Festival, 1996. Videographer Summerset Theatre of Austin, 1987; prodn. fund vol. PBS Sta. KSMQ-TV, Austin, 1988-2005. Mem. Am. Film Inst. Roman Catholic. Office: ABC Electronics Svcs & Video Prodns 1008 5th Ave NW Austin MN 55912-2114 Office Phone: 507-433-4316.

BUDD, LOUIS JOHN, language educator; b. St. Louis, Aug. 26, 1921; s. Vincent and Sophia (Kajszo) Budrewicz; m. Isabelle Amelia Marx, Mar. 3, 1945; children: Catherine Lou, David Harry. BA, U. Mo., 1941, MA, 1942; PhD, U. Wis., 1949; DLitt, U. Mo., 1988, Elmira Coll., 1995. Instr. U. Mo., Columbia, 1942, 46, U. Ky., Lexington, 1949-52; asst. prof. Duke U., Durham, N.C., 1952-60, assoc. prof., 1960-66, prof., 1966-83, James B. Duke prof., 1983-91, chmn. dept. English, 1973-79. Mem. vis. faculty Washington U., St. Louis, summer 1954, Northwestern U., Evanston, Ill., summer 1961; lectr. seminar Kraft div. Internat. Paper Co., summer 1959; Fulbright lectr., India, 1967, 72; vis. lectr. U. Damascus, Syria, 1978; chmn. Jay B. Hubbell Ctr. for Am. Lit. Historiography, 1976-87. Author: Mark Twain: Social Philosopher, 1962, Robert Herrick, 1971, Newspaper and Magazine Interviews with Samuel L. Clemens, 1874-1910, 1977, Our Mark Twain: The Making of His Public Personality, 1983; editor: Robert Herrick's The Web of Life and Clark's Field, 1970; editor: (with others) Toward a New American Literary History, 1989, Critical Essays on Mark Twain, 1867-1910, 1982, 1910-1980, 1983, New Essays on Adventures of Huckleberry Finn, 1985, On Mark Twain: The Best from American Literature, 1987, Mark Twain's Collected Tales, Sketches, Speeches and Essays (2 vols.), 1992, Mark Twain: The Contemporary Reviews, 1999, A Companion to Mark Twain, 2005; mem. editl. bd. A Selected Edition of W.D. Howells, South Atlantic Rev., 1978—81, U. Miss. Studies in English, 1979—95, South Atlantic Quar., 1980—87, mng. editor Am. Lit., 1979—86, chmn. editl. bd., 1986—91, Am. Lit. Realism 1870-1910, 1986—, Studies in Am. Humor, 1974—; contbr. numerous articles to profl. jours. Hon. trustee Mark Twain Meml., 1992—. 2d lt. USAAF, 1942-45. Guggenheim fellow, 1965-66; Am. Philos. Soc. grant, 1956, 70, 73; Nat. Endowment for Humanities sr. fellow, 1979-80; recipient J.H. Fisher award South Atlantic Depts. of English, 1997. Mem. MLA (Hubbell medal 1998), Am. Humor Studies Assn. (pres. 1979, 93), AAUP (pres. Duke chpt. 1971-72), Internat. Humor Studies Assn., Mark Twain Circle of Am. (founding pres. 1986-87, hon. life mem.), Phi Beta Kappa (pres. Duke Chpt. 1963-64). Home: 2753 Mcdowell Rd Durham NC 27705-5715 Office: Duke U Dept English Durham NC 27708-0015 Home Phone: 919-489-2953; Office Phone: 919-684-2741. Business E-Mail: budd@duke.edu.

BUDD, RICHARD WADE, academic administrator, dean, priest; b. Henderson, Md., Aug. 24, 1934; s. Bryan William and Dorothea Marie (Fouvy) B.; m. Claudia L. Wolff; children: Kimberly, Richard Wade, Janna, Eric, Gary, Stephanie. BA, Bowling Green U., 1956; MA, U. Iowa, 1962, PhD, 1964. Ordained priest Episcopal Ch., 2001. Reporter, staff writer Dayton (Ohio) Daily News, 1956-57; rsch. assoc., instr., asst. prof., dir. Inst. Comm. Studies, U. Iowa, Iowa City, 1960-71; prof., disting. prof., assoc. dean Rutgers Coll. Rutgers U., New Brunswick, NJ, chmn. dept. human comm., 1971-80, dir. Sch. Comm. Studies, 1980-83, founding dean Sch. Comm., Info. and Libr. Studies, 1983-97; v.p. for info. and technology Regent U., Virginia Beach, Va., 1997—2000, disting. scholar, 2000—; chmn. bd. Newstatements Comm. Cons., 1973-80; cons. in field.; rector Ch. of the Good Shepherd, Richmond, Va., 2002—06, Christ the King Episcopal Ch., Tabb, Va., 2006—. Author: Introduction to Content Analysis, 1964, Content Analysis of Communication, 1967, Approaches to Human Communication, 1972, Human Communication Handbook Simulations and Games, 1975, Mass Communication: Dialogue and Alternatives, 1976, Interdisciplinary Approaches to Communication, 1979, Beyond Media, 1988; assoc. editor Human Communication Research, 1974-83, Communication Quar, 1975-83; mem. editorial bd. Jour. Communication, 1976-82, Communication Yearbook, 1977-86, Mass Communications Yearbook, 1979—95. Mem. Cmty. Arts Coun. East Brunswick, 1973—80; exec. coun. East Brunswick Youth Baseball Program, 1974; active Boy Scouts Am.; priest Episcopal Diocese of So. Va., 2001; chmn. bd. dirs. Anglican Ctr. for Theology and Spirituality, Diocese of So. Va., 2003—; dean Sch. of Ministry Formation, Diocese of So. Va. Lt. USNR, 1957—60. Mem. Internat. Comm. Assn. (pres. 1976-77), AAAS, Nat. Comm. Assn., Am. Assn. Public Opinion Rsch., Assn. Edn. in Journalism, ALA (com. on accrediting 1995-99), Assn. Libr. Info. Edn. Episcopalian. Avocations: golf, harmonica, painting. Home: 120 Cypress Crk Williamsburg VA 23188-7804 Office: Christ the King 4109 Big Bethel Rd Tabb VA 23693 Office Phone: 757-865-7227. Business E-Mail: rwbudd@regent.edu. E-mail: rwbudd@msn.com.

BUDD, ROSE ANTOINETTE, language educator; d. Cyprian Alexander and Zerish May Leslie; m. Theophilus N. Budd, Dec. 22, 2001. BA in English, So. Meth. U., Dallas, 1973, MA in English, 1977; MLS, U. North Tex., Denton, 1980. Tchr. Ministry Edn., Jamaica, West Indies, 1956—70; libr. assoc. Dallas Pub. Libr., 1972—80; adminstrv. asst. So. Meth. U., Fondren Libr., 1980—84; libr. Ft. Worth Pub. Libr., 1984—86, Dallas Pub. Libr., 1986, Greiner Mid. Sch., Dallas, 1986—89; prof. English, devel. writing Eastfield C.C., Mesquite, Tex., 1983—. Cons. in field. Author: Yes, You Can Write!, 2003. Co-founder, presenter Am. read-in Eastfield Coll., Dallas, 1990; vol. Heritage Pl. Nursing Home, Mesquite, 2005—06; mem. Polit. Congress African Am. Women, Dallas, 1998—; pianist First United Meth. Ch., Seagoville, Tex., 2004—. Recipient award, Eastfield Coll. Bapt. Student Assn., 1995, Image award, Eastfield Coll. African Am. Support Group, 1995, Excellence in Tchg. award, Eastfield Coll., 1999, Vol. award, Dallas Ind. Sch. Dist., 1995. Mem.: Eastfield Coll. Faculty Assn., Tex. C.C. Tchrs. Assn., Conf. Coll. Composition and Comm., Nat. Coun. Tchrs. English. Methodist. Avocations: travel, reading, piano, movies, music. Office: Eastfield Coll 3737 Motley Dr Mesquite TX 75150 Office Phone: 972-860-8351.

BUDD, THOMAS WITBECK, lawyer; b. Phila., Nov. 1, 1939; s. Reginald Masten and Elizabeth (Charlton) B.; divorced; children: Kelly Budd Tinsley, Paige Budd Glickman; m. Bernadette Smith Budd, July 4, 1988; stepchildren: Amanda Gregerich, Karen Campisi BA, Washington and Lee U., 1961, LLB, 1964. Bar: Va. 1964, N.Y. 1965, U.S. Supreme Ct. 1982. Assoc. Buell Clifton & Turner, NYC, 1964-69, ptnr., 1969-70, Clifton Budd & Burke, NYC, 1970-76, Clifton Budd Burke & Demaria, NYC, 1976-88, Clifton, Budd & Demaria, NYC, 1988—. Contbr. Labor and Employment Law; editor (newsletter): Labor and Employment Law; co-author: (Labor and Employment Aspects of Bankruptcy Reorganization) Jour. of Bankruptcy Law and Practice, 2002. Mem. law coun. Washington and Lee U., 1978-81, 84-85. Mem. ABA (labor and employment law sect.), NY Bar Assn. (labor law sect.), NYC Bar Assn. (labor law sect.), Suffolk County Bar Assn., Washington Soc. Washington and Lee U., St. George's Golf and Country Club (Stony Brook, NY). Home: 3 Colgate Ct Shoreham NY 11786-1221 Office: Clifton Budd & Demaria 420 Lexington Ave New York NY 10170-0002 E-mail: twbudd@cbdm.com.

BUDIANSKY, STEPHEN PHILIP, writer; b. Boston, Mar. 3, 1957; s. Bernard and Nancy (Cromer) B.; m. Martha Polkey, Sept. 10, 1982; children: Rachael Elizabeth, Andrew Aaron. BS in Chemistry, Yale Coll., 1978; MS in Applied Math., Harvard U., 1979. From asst. editor to assoc. editor ES&T Mag. Am. Chem. Soc., Washington, 1979-81; science writer

Am. Chem. Soc., Washington, 1981-82; corr., Washington editor Nature Mag., Washington, 1982-85; congrl. fellow Office of Tech. Assessment, Washington, 1985-86; writer, asst. mng. editor U.S. News & World Report, Washington, 1986-97, dep. editor, 1997-98. Corr. Atlantic Monthly, Boston, 1998—. Author: The Covenant of the Wild, 1992 (short-listed for Rhone-Poulenc prize sci. books 1995), Nature's Keepers, 1995 (short-listed for Rhone-Poulenc prize sci. books 1996), The Nature of Horses, 1997, If a Lion Could Talk: Animal Intelligence and the Evolution of Consciousness, 1998, Battle of Wits: The Complete Story of Codebreaking in World War II, 2000, The Truth About Dogs, 2000, Air Power, 2004, Her Majesty's Spymaster: Elizabeth I, Sir Francis Walsingham, and the Birth of Modern Espionage, 2005; contbr. articles to profl. jours. including Nature, Jour. AVMA, Cryptologia, Intelligence and Nat. Security. Grad. fellow NSF, 1978; recipient Disting. Writing award Army Hist. Found., 2004. Mem. Loudoun Hunt, Sigma Xi. Office: Black Sheep Farm 14605 Chapel Ln Leesburg VA 20176-5277

BUDIMIROVIC, DEJAN B., academic child psychiatrist; b. Sabac, Serbia-Monteneg, July 19, 1962; arrived in US, 1994, permanent resident; s. Borisav and Milijana Budimirovic; m. Tatjana Bojanic, May 23, 1992; children: Miliana, Andrei Budimirovich, Nicholas Budimirovich. MD, Belgrade Sch. Medicine, 1982—87; BS in Nursing, 1981. Diplomate Am. Bd. Psychiatry & Neurology, 1999, in child & adolescent psychiatry Am. Bd. Psychiatry & Neurology, 2000. Intern Belgrade Sch. Medicine, Serbia and Montenegro, 1987—89; family practitioner Zagreb, Croatia, 1990, Belgrade Sch. Medicine, Serbia and Montenegro, 1991—93; adult psychiatry residentcy tng. Harvard Med. Sch., Boston, 1984—97; child and adolescent psychiatry resident NYU, Bellevue Hosp, NYC, 1997—99; asst. prof. psychiatry Yale U. Sch. Medicine, New Haven, 1999—2003, Johns Hopkins Sch. Medicine, Balt., 2004—. Co-dir. adolescent svc. Yale-New Haven Psychiat. Hosp. Yale U. Sch. Medicine, 2000—01; med. dir. Children's Psychiat. Inpatient Unit Stony Brook U. Hosp., NY, 2004. Recipient Clin. Excellence award, Faculty & Dir. Child & Adolescent Psychiatry, NYU Child Study Ctr., 1999. Mem.: AMA, Am. Psychiat. Assn., Am. Acad. Child & Adolescent Psychiatry. Office: Kennedy Krieger Inst Dept Psychiatry 3901 Greenspring Ave Baltimore MD 21211 Home Phone: 410-461-3484. Office Fax: 443-923-7628. Business E-Mail: budimirovic@kennedykrieger.org.

BUDIN, BEVERLY R., lawyer; b. Phila., Jan. 20, 1945; d. Max and Evelyn Rutman; m. Michael A. Budin, Aug. 23, 1964; children: Eric, Katherine. BA cum laude, U. Pa., 1965; JD, Stanford U., 1969. Bar: Mass. 1970, Pa. 1975, Fla. 1983. With Ctr. Law and Edn. Harvard U., Cambridge, Mass., 1970; assoc. Maloney, Williams & Baer, Boston, 1972-75, Wolf, Block, Schorr & Solis-Cohen, Phila., 1975-78, Spector, Gadon & Rosen, Phila., 1978-94; with Ledgewood Law Firm, Phila., 1994-99; ptnr. Ballard, Spahr, Andrews & Ingersoll, LLP, Phila., 1999—. Speaker, panelist in field Estate Planning Coun. Southeastern Pa., Dickinson Coll. Law Sch., Inst. Paralegal Tng., Phila., U. Pa. Wharton Sch., Pa. Bar Inst., Profl. Edn. Sys., Inc., Notre Dame Tax and Estate Planning Inst., NYU Tax Inst., So. Fed. Tax Inst., UCLA-CEB Ann. Estate Planning Inst., Heckerling Estate Planning Inst., Ann. Phila. Tax Conf., Am. Law Inst., ABA, Am. Coll. Trust and Estate Counsel, also others; adj. prof. Villanova U. Sch. Law, 1987, 88; mem. tax mgmt. adv. bd. Estates, Gifts and Trusts Jour. Columnist in Estates, Gifts and Trusts Jour.; author Bur. Nat. Affairs, Life Ins., 1987, 94, 2006; contbr. articles to legal publs. Named one of Top 100 Attys., Worth mag., 2006. Fellow Am. Coll. Trust and Estate Counsel (jour. editor 2001, bd. regents 2003—); mem. ABA (chair estate and gift tax com. sect. taxation), Phila. Bar Assn. (exec. com. orphans' ct. sect. 1986-87, taxation com.) Pa. Bar Assn. Office: Ballard Spahr Andrews & Ingersoll LLP 1735 Market St Fl 51 Philadelphia PA 19103-7599 Office Phone: 215-864-8303. Office Fax: 215-864-9816. E-mail: budin@ballardspahr.com.*

BUDIN, WENDY C., nursing educator, researcher; m. Arnold I. Budin, June 13, 1973; children: Barri, Sarah, Jill. BSN, Adelphi U., Garden City, NY, 1973; MSN, Seton Hall U., South Orange, NJ, 1986; PhD, NYU, NYC, 1996. Cert. perinatal nurse, ANCC, 2002; Lamaze childbirth educator Lamaze Internat., 1998. Assoc. prof. nursing Seton Hall U. Coll. Nursing, South Orange, NJ, 1986—2002, program dir.-Lamaze childbirth educator program, 1994—, assoc. dean grad. nursing programs and rsch., 2002—; acad. dir. online MSN program SetonWorldWide-Seton Hall U., South Orange, NJ, 2001—. Co-chair nursing/ psychosocial adv. group N.J. State Commn. on Cancer Rsch., Trenton, 1994—; cons. rsch. in nursing Excelsior Coll., Albany, NY, 1996—; med. adv. bd. North Jersey Affiliate of Susan G. Komen Breast Cancer Found., Summit, NJ, 1999—; collateral reviewer Sigma Theta Tau Internat., Indpls., 2001—. Author (co-author with j. hott): (book) Notter's Essentials of Nursing Research (Brandon/Hill Selected List of Nursing Books for Rsch., 2000); author: (co-author with c. hoskins and j. haber) Breast Cancer: Journey to Recovery; editor (contributing editor): Journal of Perinatal Education; contbr. articles to profl. jours. Recipient Rudin Family award doctoral student achievement, NYU, 1994, Arch award, NYU Sch. Edn., 1996, Sigma Theta Tau Internat. Regional Rsch. Dissertation Award, Sigma Theta Tau Internat., 1997, NJ Gov.'s Nursing Merit award nurse rschr., NJ Dept. of Health and Sr. Svcs., 1999, N.J. Nurse of Yr. award, AWHONN, 2004, CARE award for nursing rsch., NJ State Nurses Assn., 2004, Disting. Alumnae award, NYU divsn. nursing, 2004; grantee Co-Investigator & Project Dir. Stress and Coping in Caregivers of AIDS Children, NIH - NINR, 1991, Am. Nurses Found., 1994, Co-Investigator and Nurse Interventionist for Breast Cancer: Edn., Counseling and Adjustment, AREA Grant - NINR, 1998, Fed. Nurse Traineeship, Divsn. of Nursing -Dept. of Health and Human Svcs., 2002-03; Doctoral scholarship, Sigma Theta Tau Internat., 1992, Erline P. McGriff Doctoral scholarship, NYU - Divsn. of Nursing, 1995, N.J. Breast Cancer Rsch. Vis. Scholar fellowship, N.J. Commn. on Cancer Rsch., 1996. Mem.: Oncology Nursing Soc., Assn. for Woman's Health, Obstet. & Neonatal Nursing-AWHONN, Ea. Nursing Rsch. Soc., Lamaze Internat. (certification coun.), Sigma Theta Tau (past president-gamma nu chpt.). Achievements include research in breast cancer. Office: Seton Hall Univ College of Nursing South Orange NJ 07079 Business E-Mail: budinwen@shu.edu.

BUDINGTON, WILLIAM STONE, retired librarian; b. Oberlin, Ohio, July 3, 1919; s. Robert Allyn and Mabel (Stone) B.; m. Irma Johnson BA, Williams Coll., 1940, L.H.D., 1975; BS in L.S, Columbia U., 1941, MS, 1951; BS in Elec. Engring, Va. Poly. Inst., 1946. Reference librarian Norwich U., 1941-42; librarian, engring. and phys. scis. Columbia, 1947-52; asso. librarian John Crerar Library, Chgo., 1952-65, librarian, 1965-69, exec. dir., librarian, 1969-84. Mem. U.S.-USSR Spl. Libraries Exchange, 1966; bd, dirs. Center for Research Libraries, 1970-72, chmn., 1972; mem. vis. com. on libraries Mass. Inst. Tech., 1972-77 Served with AUS, 1942-46. Fellow AAAS, Med Library Assn.; mem. ALA, Am. Soc. Info. Sci., Spl. Libraries Assn. (pres. 1964-65, Hall of Fame 1984), Am. Soc. Engring. Edn., Assn. Research Libraries (dir. 1970-74, pres. 1973), Assn. Coll. and Research Libraries (Acad. Research Librarian of Year 1982), Phi Beta Kappa, Tau Beta Pi, Eta Kappa Nu. Clubs: Caxton, Arts. Home: 211 Wood Terrace Dr Colorado Springs CO 80903-2337

BUDISH, ARMOND DAVID, state legislator, lawyer, journalist; b. Cleve., June 2, 1953; s. Irving I. and Janice (Ziev) B.; m. Amy Jacoby, Aug. 26, 1979; 1 child, Ryan. BA, Swarthmore Coll., 1974; JD, NYU, 1977. Bar: Ohio, Md., D.C., U.S. Dist. (no. dist.) Ohio, U.S. Dist. Ct. D.C., U.S. Ct. Appeals (6th and D.C. cirs.), U.S. Supreme Ct. Law clk. US Dist. Ct., DC, 1977-79; with Hahn, Loeser & Parks, Cleve.; mem. Budish Solomon Steiner & Peck Ltd. (formerly Budish & Solomon), Cleve., Ohio Ho. Reps. from Dist. 8, 2007—. Columnist:(syndicated newspaper column) You and the Law, 1982— (OSBA Media award 1985, Communicator award 1986), 1982—; (weekly real estate column) Law of the Land, Cleve. Plain Dealer, 1985—; author: Why Wills Won't Work (If You Want to Protect Your Assets), 2007; host: (TV series) Golden Opportunities Campaign chmn. numerous polit. candidates, 1979—; mem. exec. com. Cuyahoga County Dem. Party, 1980—; pres. Hillel Found. N.E. Ohio, Cleve., 1988; mem. allocations com. Cleve. area United Way, 1986. Mem. ABA (exec. council young lawyers div. 1985-87), Ohio Bar Assn. (exec council young lawyers sect. 1985-87), Cleve. Bar Assn. (trustee 1983-84, chmn. young lawyers sect. 1983-84), Order of Coif. Democrat. Office: Budish & Solomon Ltd Commerce Pk IV Ste 450 23240 Chagrin Blvd Beachwood OH 44122 also: 77 High St 11th Fl Columbus OH 43215 E-mail: abudish@budsolo.com, district08@ohr.state.oh.us.*

BUDLER, JOANNE, library director; MFA, MLS, U. Iowa. Curator spl. collections Lincoln City Libraries, Nebr.; legis. reference libr. Nebr. Legis. Rsch. Divsn.; dir. network svcs. Nebr. Libr. Commn., 1994—2000; dep. state libr. State Libr. Mich., Lansing, 2000—04; state libr. State Libr. Ohio, Columbus, 2004—. Office: State Libr Ohio Ste 100 274 E 1st Ave Columbus OH 43201 Office Phone: 614-644-7061. Office Fax: 614-644-3584. E-mail: jbudler@sloma.state.oh.us.*

BUDMAN, CATHY LINDA, psychiatrist, physician; b. Bklyn., Mar. 15, 1957; ScB, Brown U., 1979; MD, SUNY, Buffalo, 1984. Diplomate Australian Med. Coun., Am. Bd. Neurology and Psychiatry. Intern, then resident in psychiatry U. Calif.-San Francisco Sch. Medicine, 1984-86; sr. resident in family medicine Royal Australian Coll. Family Medicine, St. Leonards, NSW, 1987-88; med. registrar drug and alcohol unit Royal Prince Alfred Hosp., Sydney, NSW, 1987-88; resident in psychiatry North Shore Hosp., Manhasset, N.Y., 1988-90, rsch. fellow neuropsychiatry, 1990-91, dir. med. student clerkship in psychiatry, 1994—; pvt. practice Manhasset, 1990—; dir. med. student edn. in psychiatry North Shore U. Hosp., Manhasset, 1994—; asst. prof. psychiatry and neurology Cornell U. Med. Coll., NYC, 1993-98, NYU Sch. Medicine, NYC, 1998—2001, assoc. prof. psychiatry, 2002—. Dir. Movement Disorder Clinic, 1990—; rsch. cons. dept. drug and alcohol Royal Prince Alfred Hosp., Westmead Hosp., 1986-88. Mem. APA, Nassau County Psychiat. Soc., Tourette Assn., Royal Australian Coll. Family Practitioners (assoc.). Office: North Shore Hosp Dept Psychiatry 400 Community Dr Manhasset NY 11030-3815 Office Phone: 516-562-3223. Office Fax: 516-562-3108.

BUDNER, CRAIG W., lawyer; b. Dallas, Dec. 2, 1964; AB cum laude, Dartmouth Coll., 1987; JD, U. Tex., 1990. Bar: Tex. 1990, US Dist. Ct. (all dists. Tex.), US Ct. Appeals (2nd, 4th, 5th, 7th and 9th cirs.), US Supreme Ct. Ptnr. Hughes & Luce, LLP, Dallas. Mem. Lamplighter New Families Com., Dallas; pres. Vogel Alcove Childcare Ctr. for Homeless, Dallas; bd. mem. Dallas Furniture Bank. Named one of Best Lawyers in Dallas, D Mag., 2005. Mem.: Dallas Bar Assn., ABA. Office: Hughes & Luce LLP 1717 Main St Ste 2800 Dallas TX 75201 Office Phone: 214-939-5806. Office Fax: 214-939-5849. E-mail: craig.budner@hughesluce.com.*

BUDNICK, ERNEST JOSEPH, recording industry executive; Cert. Data Processing, Comml. Programming Unltd., NYC, 1968; grad., Dale Carnegie Inst., 1988; cert. in pub. rels., NYU, 1991, cert. in real estate sales, 1998. Lic. real estate sales, N.Y. IBM computer operator Seamen's Bank for Savs., 1966-68; programmer/analyst W.T. Grant and Co., 1969-73; owner Underground Records, NYC, 1970; systems analyst Ins. Svcs., NYC, 1973-77; pres., owner Bernard Friedman Video Prodns., NYC, 1973-85, Nat. Digital Diagnostics, NYC, 1973-75; systems analyst Mfrs. Hanover, NYC, 1977-80; mgr. corp. video/media Salomon Bros., Inc., NYC, 1980-92; pres., CEO Consol. Mgmt., Tech. & Comm., NYC, 1993-99; pres. UMO.com Music, NYC, 1995—; owner, record prodr. UMO Underground Records, NYC, 2003—. Songwriter, 1980—; pres. UMO Music, 1995—, UMO Film/TV, 2007—; host UMO Music Showcase of Greenwich Village, NYC, 1995—. Author: Effectively Leveraging Business Technology, 1993; creator, writer: (TV series) The Observers, 1986; composer, singer, engr. (single) Keep on Playing, 1980; record producer, engr. The 14 Best Singer/Songwriters of Greenwich Village, vol. 1, 2003, The 14 Best Singer/Songwriters of Greenwich Village, vol. 2, 2004, vol. 3, 2005. Conservator N.Y. Pub. Libr., 1990—; mem. Am. Mus. of Moving Image, 1990—. Fellow Mus. of Broadcasting; mem. Am. Film Inst. (mem. coun. 1984—), Nat. Assn. Rec. Arts and Scis., Pub. Rels. Soc. Am., Internat. Assn. Bus. Communicators, Nat. Assn. TV Arts and Scis., Am. Mgmt. Assn., Toastmasters. Avocations: chess, video effects, computer engineering, music engineering. Business E-Mail: umo@umo.com.

BUDNICK, THOMAS PETER, social worker; b. Ludlow, Mass., Feb. 16, 1947; s. Henry F. and Mildred Mary (Killian) B. BS, Am. Internat. Coll., 1972, MA, 1975. Lic. cert. profl. social worker. Mailhandler U.S. Postal Svc., Springfield, Mass., 1970-72; substitute tchr. Pub. Schs. Dept., Ludlow, Mass., 1973-74; social worker Mass. Dept. Pub. Welfare, Springfield, 1975—. Pres. Am.'s Manifest Destiny Soc., Inc., West Harwich, Mass., 1979—; bd. dirs. Mass. Astronomy Club, Boston, 1988—. Contbr. numerous articles to jours. V.p. Local 509, Boston, 1989. Democrat. Home: 19 Harding Ave Ludlow MA 01056-2327

BUDNICKI, MICHAEL J., nurse; b. Perth Amboy, NJ, Aug. 1, 1957; s. Xavier and Ingrid Budnicki. Student in computer sci., 1999. LPN Jersey Shore Med. Ctr., Neptune, 1992—2002. Author: (poetry) Our Special Place, 2001, At Home on the Sea, 2005. Personal E-mail: michaelbudnicki@hotmail.com.

BUDOFF, MATTHEW JAY, cardiologist; m. Victoria Billit, Oct. 3, 1998; children: Daniel Oliver, Garrett Clark. BS in Biochemistry, U. Calif., Riverside, 1986; MD, George Wash. U., DC, 1990. Lic. physician DC, 1990, bd. cert. Internal Medicine 1994, bd. cert. Cardiology 1997. Internal medicine internship and residency Harbor UCLA Med. Ctr., Torrance, Calif., 1990—93, cardiology fellow, 1994—97; rschr. physician LA Biomedical Rsch., Torrance, 1997—; asst. prof. UCLA Sch. Medicine, 1997—2003, assoc. prof., 2003—. Editor (author): Enhancing Heart Health, 2003, Cardiac CT Imaging, 2006, Atlas of Cardiac CT, 2007; contbr. Named one of Am. Top Doctors for Men, 2007; named to LA Superdoctors, 2007. Fellow: Am. Coll. Cardiology, Am. Heart Assn., Am. Heart Assn. (life; bd. dirs. 2000—06); mem.: Soc. Atherosclerosis and Prevention (founder, pres. 2006—), Soc. Cardiovascular CT (founding mem., exec. bd. mem. 2004—). Achievements include patents for imaging. Office: Los Angeles Biomedical Research Institut 1124 West Carson Street Torrance CA 90502 Office Phone: 310-222-4107. Business E-Mail: mbudoff@labiomed.org.

BUDREVICS, ALEXANDER, landscape architect; b. Riga, Latvia, Jan. 3, 1925; arrived in Can., 1952; m. Milija Vite, Apr. 8, 1948; children: Valdis, Dace, Arnis. Grad. hort. sch., Latvia, 1944; grad. landscape architect, St. Albans Coll., Eng., 1949, London Coll. Art, 1951. Registered landscape architect, Ont., Can. Practice landscape architecture, 1960; staff various firms, Canada, 1960; pres. Alexander Budrevics & Assocs. Ltd., Don Mills, Ont., 1965—. Ptnr. Golf Course Devel. Assn., 1969—. Designer over 3000 projects including Nat. Home Show, 1958—, CNE hort. shows, Century Sq.; contbr. articles to profl. jours. Trustee Helen M. Kippax Meml. Scholarship Fund.; chmn. exec. bd. Latvian Boy Scouts Assn.; pres. gen. assembly Latvian Nat. Fedn. Can., 1992—2000, hon. mem., 2000—; pres. Kristus Darz Home for the Aged, 1989—92, Ont. Swimming Pool Assn., Toronto, 1964; pres. cultural and edn. fund Latvian Nat. Fedn. Can., 2002—04. Fellow Can. Soc. Landscape Architects (life), Am. Landscape Architects Soc., Am. Inst. Landscape Architects (internat. pres. 1969-71), Ont. Assn. Landscape Architects (emeritus, pres. 1977-79, Disting. Achievement award 1987), Can. Latvian Bus. and Profl. Assn. (pres. 1971—), Latvian Nat. Fedn. Can. (pres. 2003), Latvian Credit Union Assn. (pres. 2007-), Bd. of Trade Club, Empire Club of Can. Lutheran. Avocations: gardening, travel. Office: Alexander Budrevics & Assoc Ltd 895 Don Mills Rd Ste 212 Toronto ON Canada M3C 1W3 Office Phone: 416-444-5201 ext. 4. Office Fax: 416-444-5208. Business E-Mail: alex@budrevics.com.

BUDZAK, STEPHEN HOWARD, tax specialist, consultant; b. NYC, July 15, 1938; s. Steve and Elizabeth Katherine Budzak; m. Maria Teresa Silva, Mar. 30, 1974; children: Douglas Alan, Mike A., Jennifer E., Christopher A. AA, Glendale Coll., Glendale, Calif., 1973. Cert. Calif. Soc. Tax. Cons., Nat. Soc. Tax Profls. Revenue protection clk. U.S. Postal Svc., LA, 1975—92, revenue protection coord., 1992—2003; tax profl. Tax Masters, Diamond Bar, Calif., 1976—. Training instr. U.S. Postal Svc., LA, 1987—2003. Contbr. articles to profl. jours. Career day rep. YMCA, Los Angeles, 1996—97, L.A. City Sch. Dist., 2003. Mem.: Lions Club. Independent. Roman Catholic. Avocations: reading, photography, travel. Office: Tax Masters 21022 Golden Springs Dr Walnut CA 91789 Office Phone: 909-594-9926.

BUDZINSKI, RONALD J., architect; With Phillips Swager Assocs.; pres. PSA-Dewberry, Peoria, Ill., sr. prin., 2007—. Prin. works include Peoria Civic Ctr. expansion, Jack Evans Police Hdqs., Dallas, US Courthouse, Rockford, Ill., Gilbert Mcpl. Cts. and Pub. Safety Complex, Ariz., Police Sta. and Pub. Libr., Naperville, Ill. Chair definition com. GSA and Adminstrv. Office the US Cts.; Justice Team Leader Fed. Emergency Mgmt. Agy., 2005; ombudsman Pub. Assistance Justice Team, La. Fellow: AIA (chmn. adv. group 2004, mem. Acad. Architecture for Justice); mem.: Nat. Sheriff's Assn., Am. Jail Assn., Nat. Inst. Corrections, Am. Correctional Assn. (mem. commn. on accreditation for corrections 2006—). Office: PSA Newberry 401 SW Water St Ste 701 Peoria IL 61602-1530 Office Phone: 309-282-8000.*

BUDZINSKY, ARMIN ALEXANDER, investment banker; b. Steyr, Austria, Nov. 25, 1942; arrived in US, 1951, naturalized, 1957; s. Alexander Wladimir and Maria Gisella B.; m. Pamela Plimmer, 1978 (div. 1992); children: Andrea, Natalie; m. Laura Martin, 2000 (div. 2003). AB, John Carroll U., 1964; MA. (NDEA fellow) Fulbright fellow, Rutgers U., 1969. Instr. in English Cleve. State U., 1969-72; corp. fin. cons. Citibank NA, NYC, 1974-76, Dean Witter & Co., NYC, 1976-77, Merrill Lynch Pierce Fenner & Smith, NYC, 1977-83; v.p. corp. fin. Dunoco Corp., Houston, 1983; pres. Porcari Fearnow Capital Markets Group, Inc., Houston, 1985-86, Itec Securities Corp., Houston, 1985-86; v.p., dir. project fin., prin. Eppler, Guerin & Turner, Inc., Dallas, 1987—92; ptnr. Garland Group, 1992-93; sr. v.p., CFO Heard Energy Corp., 1993-98; pres. Archangel Diamond Corp., Vancouver, B.C., 1996-97, pres, CEO, 1997-98, chmn., 1997-98; exec. v.p., dir. United Am. eHealth Techs. Inc., Cambridge, Mass., 1998-2001; exec. v.p., CFO Decorize Inc., Springfield, Mo., 2002—04. Home: 1413 S St Marys Ave Springfield MO 65804 Personal E-mail: aab@albud.com.

BUE, CARL OLAF, JR., retired federal judge; b. Chgo., Mar. 27, 1922; s. Carl Olaf and Mabel Port (Shollar) B.; m. Mary Kathryn Waring, Dec. 27, 1948; children: Kathryn Anne, Richard Charles. AA, U. Chgo., 1942; student, U. Rome, Italy, 1945; PhB, Northwestern U., 1951; D of Jurisprudence, U. Tex., 1954. Bar: Tex. 1954. Assoc. firm Royston, Rayzor & Cook, Houston, 1954-58, mem. firm, 1958-70; U.S. dist. judge So. Dist. Tex. (Houston div.), 1970-87. Lectr. various law schs. and admiralty seminars in Tex. and other states. Contbr. articles to profl. jours. Served to capt., Adj. Gen. Corps AUS, 1942-46, MTO. Recipient Good Citizenship medal Houston chpt. SAR, 1975, Tex. Supreme Ct. Justice Joe R. Greenhill award as outstanding jurist Mcpl. Cts. Assn., 1977, Northwestern U. Alumni Merit award for disting. profl. svc. in law, 1997; establishment at U. Tex. Sch. of Law of the Judge Carl. O. Bue Jr. Endowed Presdl. scholarship in law, 1988. Mem. Am., Fed., Tex., Houston Bar Assns., Maritime Law Assn. of U.S., Houston Philos. Soc. at Rice U., Alpha Delta Phi, Phi Alpha Delta. Republican. Lutheran. Home: 338 Knipp Rd Houston TX 77024-5044

BUECHLEIN, DANIEL MARK, archbishop; b. Jasper, Ind., Apr. 20, 1938; s. Carl and Rose (Blessinger) Buechlein. BA, St. Meinrad Coll., 1961; student, St. Meinrad Sch. Theology, 1961—64; Lic. Sacred Theology, Benedictine U. Sant' Anselmo, Rome, 1966. Ordained priest Roman Cath. Ch., 1964, consecrated bishop 1987, archbishop 1992. Asst. dean students St. Meinrad Coll., 1966—68, dir. spiritual formation, 1968—71; pres., rector St. Meinrad Sch. Theology, 1971—82, St. Meinrad Sch. Theology and St. Meinrad Coll., 1982—87; bishop Diocese of Memphis, 1987—92; archbishop Indpls., 1992—. Chmn. divsn. religion St. Meinrad Coll., 1967—71; mem. Archabbey Coun., 1967—87; formation com. Conf. of Major Superiors of Men USA, 1971—78; nat. steering com. for follow-up of Nat. Assembly Sem. Rectors and Ordinaries, 1983; com. on priestly formation Nat. Conf. Cath. Bishops, 1987—89, chmn., 1990—93, com. on marriage and family life, 1987—89, advisor doctrine com., com. on doctrine, 1989—93, adminstrv. com., 1990—93, budget com., bishop's emergency relief com., 1990—92, chmn. ad hoc com. to oversee use of Catechism of Cath. Ch., subcom. on pastoral message in abortion, 1994—, bd. dirs.; peritus Internat. Synod on Priestly Formation, Rome, 1990; bd. dirs. S.E. Regional Office for Hispanics Affairs, S.E. Pastoral Inst.; co-pres. Disciples of Christ-Roman Cath. Internat. Dialogue, 1995—. Co-author (with Bleichner and Leavitt): Preparing a Diocesan Priest: The Holistic Experience, 1987, Celibacy for the Kingdom, 1990, Commentary on a Survey of Priests Ordained Five to Nine Years, 1991; contbr. articles to profl. jours. Named Hon. chaplain, KC, Tenn., 1987. Mem.: Nat. Cath. Edn. Assn. (chmn. exec. com. sem. divsn. 1984—86), Theol. Edn. Assn. Mid-Am. (sec. 1972—74, 1980—82, v.p. 1974—76, pres. 1976—78, 1982—84), Midwest Assn. Theol. Schs. (sec.-treas. 1972—74, ptrd. 1974—75), Midwest Assn. Sem. Spiritual Dirs. (founding coord. 1971), Nat. Assn. Sem. Spiritual Dirs. (founding coord. 1972). Office: Archdiocese Indpls PO Box 1410 Indianapolis IN 46206

BUECHNER, CARL FREDERICK, minister, author; b. NYC, July 11, 1926; s. Carl Frederick and Katherine (Kuhn) B.; m. Judith Friedrike Merck, Apr. 7, 1956; children: Katherine, Dinah, Sharman. Grad., Lawrenceville Sch., 1943; AB, Princeton U., 1947; BD, Union Theol. Sem., 1958; DD, Va. Episc. Sem., 1982, Lafayette U., 1984; LittD, Lehigh U., 1987, Cornell Coll., 1989; DD, Yale U., 1990, Sewanee U., 1993; LittD, Susquehanna U., 1997, Wake Forest U., 1998, Wake Forest U., 2000. Ordained minister United Presbyn. Ch. U.S.A., 1958. Tchr. English Lawrenceville Sch., 1948-53; tchr. creative writing, summer sessions N.Y.U., 1954-55; chmn. dept. religion Phillips Exeter Acad., 1958-67, sch. minister, 1960-67; William Belden Noble lectr. Harvard, 1969; Russell lectr. Tufts, 1971; Lyman Beecher lectr. Yale U., 1977; Harris lector Bangor Sem., 1979; Smyth lectr. Columbia Sem., 1981. Lectr. Trinity Inst., 1990. Author: A Long Day's Dying, 1950, The Seasons' Difference, 1952, The Return of Ansel Gibbs, 1958, The Final Beast, 1965, The Magnificent Defeat, 1966, The Hungering Dark, 1969, The Entrance to Porlock, 1970, The Alphabet of Grace, 1970, Lion Country, 1971, Open Heart, 1972, Wishful Thinking, 1973, Love Feast, 1974, The Faces of Jesus, 1974, Treasure Hunt, 1977, Telling the Truth, 1977, Peculiar Treasures, 1979, The Book of Bebb, 1979, Godric, 1980 (Pulitzer Prize finalist), The Sacred Journey, 1982, Now and Then, 1983, A Room Called Remember, 1984, Brendan, 1987, Whistling in the Dark, 1988, The Wizard's Tide, 1990, Telling Secrets, 1991, The Clown in the Belfry, 1992, Listening to Your Life, 1992, The Son of Laughter, 1993, The Longing for Home, 1996, On the Road with the Archangel, 1997, The Storm, 1998, The Eyes of the Heart, 1999, Speak What We Feel,

2001, Beyond Words, 2004, The Christmas Tide, 2005, Secrets in the Dark, 2006. Trustee Barlow Sch., 1965-71. With AUS, 1944-46. Recipient Irene Glascock Meml. intercollegiate poetry award, 1947; O'Henry prize for story The Tiger, 1955; Richard and Hinda Rosenthal award for the Return of Ansel Gibbs, 1958 Mem. Nat. Coun. Churches (com. on lit. 1954-57), Coun. Religion in Ind. Schs. (regional chmn. 1958-63), Presbytery No. New Eng., Century Assn., Univ. Club (N.Y.C.). Presbyterian. Home and Office: 3572 State Rte 315 Pawlet VT 05761-9753

BUECHNER, JACK W(ILLIAM), lawyer, consultant, educational association administrator; b. St. Louis, June 4, 1940; s. John Edward and Gertrude Emily (Richardson) B.; children from previous marriage: Patrick John, Terrence J.; m. Nancy Chanitz (dec. Jan. 2006); 1 child, Charles Chanitz. BA, Benedictine Coll., 1962; JD, St. Louis U., 1965. Bar: Mo. 1965, US Dist. Ct. (ea. dist.) Mo. 1965, DC, 1998, US Ct. Appeals (8th cir.) 1965, US Ct. Appeals (DC cir.) 1998. Ptnr. Buechner, McCarthy, Leonard, Kaemmerer, Owen & Laderman, Chesterfield, Mo., 1965-93; mem. 100th-102d U.S. Congresses from 2d Mo. dist., 1987-91; dep. minority whip, 1989-90; vice-chmn. Rep. study group, pres. Internat. Rep. Inst., Washington, 1991-93; prin., dir. internat. svcs. The Hawthorn Group, Arlington, Va., 1993-95; ptnr. Manatt Phelps & Phillips, Washington, 1995—2001; pres., CEO A Presdl. Classroom for Young Americans, 2002—06, ret., 2006; of counsel Schmeltzer, Aptaker and Shepard, 2003—06; atty. Anderson, Kill & Olick, Washington, 2006—. State rep. 94th dist. Mo. Gen. Assembly, 1972-82, minority leader, 1974-78; mem. state adv. com. US Commn. on Civil Rights, 1975-82; bd. dirs. Coun. Cmty. Democracies; cons. to McElligott & Assocs.; counselor SoapBox Consulting, Washington; sr. counsel Hawthorn Group, Alexandria, Va., 2007—. Lay advisor St. Louis Med. Soc., 1989-92; Mo. Tourism Commn., 1976, 82-85; prin. Coun. for Excellence in Govt.; bd. dirs. Presdl. Classroom, 2000—; bd. dirs. Goodwin House, 2005—. Recipient Meritorious Svc. award St. Louis Globe-Democrat, 1973, Legis. Achievement award St. Louis Police Officers, 1982, Pub. Svc. award Women's Polit. Caucus, Mo., Disting. Svc. award Cardinal Glennon Hosp., Mo., 1982, Nat. Security Leadership award Am. Security Coun. Found., 1988, 89, Family and Freedom award, Golden Bulldog award, 1987, 88, Guardian of Small Bus. award Nat. Fedn. Ind. Bus., 1987, 88, 90, 91, Enterprise award U.S. C. of C., 1988, 89, 90, Sound Dollar award, 1988, Eagle of Freedom award Am. Security Coun. Foun., 1990, Missourian award Mo. Heart Assn., 2003. Mem. Mo. Bar Assn., DC Bar Assn., Mo. Soc. Washington (pres.), Nat. Conf. State Socs. (1st v.p.), Ctr. Nat. Policy (bd. dirs. 1997-, bd. dirs. Alliance for responsible Cuba policy), The Pericles Inst. (pres. 2001-), US Assn. Former Mems. Congress (pres. 2004-), The Zorig Found. (v.p.), John Marshall Club (Outstanding Atty. award 1986), Lions, Phi Delta Phi. Republican. Episcopalian. Avocations: golf, reading, travel. Home: 1303 Altamira Ct Mc Lean VA 22102-2201 Office: Anderson Kill & Olick 2100 M St NW Ste 650 Washington DC 20037 Office Phone: 202-218-0042. Personal E-mail: xmo2rep@aol.com. Business E-Mail: jbuechner@andersonkill.com.

BUECHNER, THOMAS SCHARMAN, artist, museum director, retired glass manufacturing company executive; b. Sept. 25, 1926; s. Thomas Scharman and Anne Evans (Lines) B.; m. Mary C. Hawkins, Sept. 15, 1949; children: Barbara Lines, Thomas Scharman, Matthew. Student, Princeton U., 1945, Ecole des Beaux Arts, Fontainebleau, 1946, Paris, 1947, Arts Students League, NYC, 1946-48, Institut voor Pictologie, Amsterdam, 1947; LittD, Elmira Coll., 2003. Designer Compañía de Fomento, San Juan, 1946; asst. display mgr. Met. Mus. Art, NYC, 1949-51, tchr., 1949-51; dir. Corning Mus. Glass, NY, 1951-60, 75-80, pres. NY, 1971-87; v.p., dir. cultural affairs Corning Glass Works, 1985-87, ret., 1987, cons., 1987—; faculty art sch. Bild-Werk, Fravenau, Germany, 1988—. Head dept. art Corning Community Coll., 1958-60; bd. dir. Bklyn. Mus.; chmn. Corning Glass Works Found., 1971-87; v.p. Steuben Glass, Corning, 1971-73, pres., 1973-82, chmn., 1982-85. Author: Glass Vessels in Dutch Painting of the 17th Century, 1952, Life and Work of Frederick Carder, 1952, Guide to the Collections of the Corning Museum of Glass, 1955, Guide to the Collections of the Brooklyn Museum, 1967, Norman Rockwell, Artist Illustrator, 1970, Arts of David Levine, 1979, Ogden Pleissner, 1984, How I Paint, 2000, Seeing A Life, 2007; portrait and landscape painter; one-man shows: Adler Gallery, N.Y.C., 1982, 84, Arnot Art Mus., 1985, 95, Heller Gallery, N.Y.c., 1989, Gallery M, Lindau, Germany, 1989, Gallery Nakama, Tokyo, 1990, 93, 96, O.K. Harris Gallery, N.Y.C., Schloss Weissenstein, Regen, Germany, 1996, Melberg Gallery, Charlotte, N.C., 2002, Principle Gallery, Alexandria, Va., 2002, West End Gallery, Corning, N.Y., 2005; represented in permanent collections Met. Mus. Art, Nat. Mus. Am. Art, Smithsonian Inst., Bklyn. Mus., Lincoln Ctr., Herbert F. Johnson Mus. Cornell U., Musée des Arts Decoratifs, Lausanne, Switzerland, Renwick Mus., Smithsonian, Washington, Corning Mus. of Glass, Corning, N.Y., Elmira Coll. Trustee Tiffany Found., Pilchuck Sch., Corning Mus. Glass, Corning Glass Works Found., Rockwell Mus., Arnot Art Mus. Arts of the Southern Finger Lakes; pres. Rockwell Mus. 1982-87, trustee 1987—. Recipient Forsythia award Bklyn. Bot. Garden, 1971, Gari Melchers medal Am. Artist fellows, 1971, Lifetime Achievement Glass Art Soc., 2000. Mem. Bklyn. Inst. Arts and Sci. (trustee 1971-72, pres. 1971-72), Nat. Collection Fine Arts. (commr. 1972-91). Century Assn. Club, Knickerbocker Club, Elmira City Club. Episcopalian. Studio: 10503 North Rd Corning NY 14830-3264 Personal E-mail: bvechner@lightlink.com.

BUEHLER, THOMAS, psychotherapist, expressive therapist, artist; b. Zurich, Switzerland, Aug. 9, 1943; came to U.S 1989. s. Adolf and Margrit (Gredig) B.; m. Rosemarie Schiller, Apr. 19, 1995. MS, Med. Sch. U. Zurich, 1970. Cert. psychotherapist, Switzerland. Intern Accredited Swiss Hosp., 1969-75; multimedia artist Switzerland, 1973—. Psychotherapist and expressive therapist, 1979—; co-founding, training therapist Internat. Sch. of Interdisciplinary Studies, 1982-85, advisory bd. Swiss Assocs. of Psychotherapists, 1984-85; founding chmn. Cardon Found., 1991—, Cirio Found., N.Y., 1993—Author: Der Vulkan ist aufgebrochen, 1976; one man performance Roter Stadtkriecher, 1985, Red Broadway Crawler, 1985, one-man shows, New World Art Ctr., N.Y.C., 1999, The Depot Gallery, Montauk, N.Y., 1999, The Office Gallery, N.Y.C., 2001, 02, 03, 04, The Broome Street Gallery, N.Y.C., 2005, 06, 07, Gallery Gora, Montreal, 2006. Mem. Internat. Assoc. of Artist Therapists, Nat. Expressive Therapy Assn., Swiss Assoc. of Psychotherapists. Avocations: piano, guitar, travel, wilderness, foreign cultures. Home: 380 Riverside Dr 6 T/U New York NY 10025 Office: Cirio Found Ste 1004 80 8th Ave New York NY 10011

BUEHLMEIER, HARRY SCOTT See GORDON, SCOTT

BUEHRER, STEPHEN, state senator; b. Toledo, Ohio, Jan. 1, 1967; married; 3 children. BS in Edn., Bowling Green State U., 1989; JD, Capital U., 1997. Atty.; mem. Ohio Ho. of Reps., Columbus, 1998—2006, mem. criminal justice com., chair state govt. com., asst. majority fl. leader, 2001—04; mem. Ohio Senate, Columbus, 2007—. Mem.: United Conservatives of Ohio, Coun. State Govt. (chmn. midwest-Can. rels. com.), Am. Legis. Exch. (state co-chair, Nat. Legislator of Yr. 2002), Ohio Twp. Assn., Fulton County Bar Assn., Ohio Bar Assn., Bowhay Legis. Leadership Inst., Ohio Right to Life, C. of C., Nat. Assn. Sports Legislators, Ohio Farm Bur., Fulton County Hist. Soc., Ducks Unlimited, Pheasants Forever. Republican. Office: First Flr Statehouse Rm #125 Columbus OH 43215 Business E-Mail: sd01@mailr.sen.state.oh.us.

BUEHRLE, MARK, professional baseball player; b. St. Charles, Mo., Mar. 23, 1979; Pitcher Chgo. White Sox, 2000—. Achievements include Starting pitcher, MLB All-Star Game, 2005; throwing no-hitter, 2007. Office: Chgo White Sox 333 W 35th St Chicago IL 60616*

BUEL, RICHARD VAN WYCK, JR., retired history professor, editor, writer; b. Morristown, NJ, July 22, 1933; s. Richard Van Wyck Sr. and Frances Worthington (Thompson) B.; m. Joy Evelyn Margaret Day, June 5, 1964 (dec. Apr. 1987); m. Marilyn Ellman Frankel, July 18, 1992; 1 child, Margaret Alexandra. AB, Amherst Coll., 1955; A.M., Harvard U., 1957, PhD in Am. History, 1962. Tchg. fellow in history Harvard U., Cambridge, Mass., 1958-62; asst. prof. history Wesleyan U., Middletown, Conn., 1962-69, assoc. prof., 1969-75, prof., 1975—2002, emeritus prof., 2002—, chmn. history dept., 1978-81; ret., 2002. Ray A. Billington vis. prof. U.S. history Occidental Coll., 1999—2000. Author: Securing the Revolution, 1972, Dear Liberty, 1980 (Round Table of Am. Revolution award, 1981); author: (with Joy D. Buel) The Way of Duty, 1984 (Colonial Dame of Am. Book award, 1985); author: In Irons, 1998 (Fraunces Tavern Mus. Book award, 1999), America on the Brink, 2005; assoc. editor History and Theory, 1970—91; contbr. articles to profl. jours., chapters to books. Mem. Bd. Fin., Haddam, Conn., 1972—74; mem. Conn. Hist. Commn., 1996—2003, Conn. Humanities Coun., 1997—2003, Conn. Hist. Coun., 2003—; bd. dirs. No. Middlesex United Fund, Middletown, Conn., 1965—68. Fellow Charles Warren Ctr., Harvard U., 1966—67, Am. Coun. Learned Socs., 1966—67, 1974—75, NEH, 1985, Guggenheim Found., 1988; Jr. Humanist fellow, NEH, 1971—72, John Carter Brown fellow, 1986, Andrew W. Mellon emeritus faculty fellow, 2005—07. Mem. Conn. Acad. Arts and Scis. (v.p. 1975-81), Am. Hist. Assn., Inst. Early Am. History and Culture, Soc. History Early Republic, Orgn. Am. Historians, Am. Antiquarian Soc., New Eng. Hist. Assn. (v.p. 1991, pres. 1992), Assn. Study Conn. History, Conn. Coord. Com. for Promotion History (pres. 2001—03), Pettipaug Yacht Club (rear commodore 1984-86, vice-commodore 1986-88, commodore 1988-90), Acorn Club, Phi Beta Kappa. Avocation: dinghy racing. Home: 55 N Main St Essex CT 06426-1073 Office: Wesleyan Univ Dept History Middletown CT 06459-0002 Office Phone: 860-685-2372. Business E-Mail: rbuel@wesleyan.edu.

BUELL, DUNCAN ALAN, computer scientist; b. Detroit, Oct. 17, 1950; s. David Newcomb and Verna May (Lusk) B.; m. Mary Ann Grandjean, Oct. 31, 1986. BS, U. Ariz., 1971; MA, U. Mich., 1972; PhD, U. Ill., Chgo., 1976. Rsch. assoc. Carleton U., Ottawa, Ontario, Can., 1976-77; asst. prof. Bowling Green State U., Bowling Green, Ohio, 1977-79, La. State U., Baton Rouge, 1979-82, assoc. prof., 1982-86; rsch. staff mem. Ctr. for Computing Scis., Bowie, Md., 1986-87, dir. algorithms rsch., 1987-90, sr. rsch. scientist, 1990—. Author: Binary Quadratic Forms, 1989; co-author: Splash 2: FPGAs in Custom Computing Machine, 1996; contbr. articles to profl. jours.; co-inventor, patentee in field. Mem. state bd. ACLU, La., 1983-85. Mem. Am. Math. Soc., Assn. for Computing Machinery, IEEE, AAAS, Phi Beta Kappa, Phi Kappa Phi. Office: Ctr for Computing Scis 17100 Science Dr Bowie MD 20715-4300

BUELL, EVANGELINE CANONIZADO, advocate; b. San Pedro, Calif., Aug. 28, 1932; d. Estanislao (C.) and Felicia (Stokes) Canonizado; m. Ralph D. Vilas, 1952 (dec.); m. Robert Alexander Elkins, July 1, 1961 (dec.); children: Nikki Vilas, Stacey Vilas, Danni Vilas Plump; m. William David Buell, Feb. 21, 1987. Student, San Jose State Coll., 1952—53; grad., U. San Francisco, 1978. With Consumers Coop. Berkeley Inc., Calif., 1958—64, edn. asst. for cmty. rels., 1964—73, supr. edn. dept., 1973—76, asst. to edn. dir., 1976—78, program coord. edn. dept, 1980—81, pers. tng. coord., 1981—92; ret., 1992. Events coord. Internat. House, U. Calif., Berkeley, 1984; pvt. guitar tchr., 1958—75. Author: (memoir) Twenty Five Chickens and a Pig for a Bride: Growing Up in a Filipino Immigrant Family, 2006—; author, co-editor: anthology Seven Card Stud with Seven Manangs Wild, 2002, 2d edit., 2003; columnist Coop. News, 1964—; contbr. articles to profl. jours. and mags. Dir. various activities YMCA, YWCA, Oakland City Recreation Dept., 1959—73; pres. Berkeley Cmty. Chorus and Orch.; co-chair Berkeley Art Commn., 1992—94; mem. Asian Pacific adv. coun. Oakland Mus., Calif., 2003—07; bd. dirs. Philippine Ethnic Arts and Cultural Exch., 1994—96; mem. cmty. adv. com. Bonita House, Berkeley, 1974; mem. steering com. for cultural and ethnic affairs Guild of Oakland Mus., 1973—74; bd. dirs. Berkeley Art Ctr., pres., 1998, v.p., 2007. Recipient Outstanding Staff award, U. Calif. Berkeley Chancellor, 1992, Outstanding Instrn. Program Support award, Cole Sch. Visual & Performing Arts, 1992, Disting. Vol. award, Nat. Philanthropy Day, San Francisco, 1993, Outstanding Berkeley Woman award, Berkeley Commn. on Status of Women, 1996, Congl. Recognition, Barbara Lee & Pete Stark, 2004, Leadership award, Filipino Affirmative Action, 2004, others. Mem.: Coop. Educators Network Calif., Filipino Am. Nat. Hist. Soc. (pres. East Bay chpt. 1996, trustee, pres. emeritus East Bay chpt., Silver Arts & Music award 1994). Democrat. Unitarian Universalist. Home: 516 Santa Barbara Rd Berkeley CA 94707-1746 Personal E-mail: vangiec@berkeley.edu.

BUELL, LAWRENCE INGALLS, language educator; b. Bryn Mawr, Pa., June 11, 1939; s. Clarence Addison and Marjorie (Henderson) B.; m. Phyllis Kimber; children: Denise, Deirdre. AB, Princeton U., NJ, 1961; MA, Cornell U., Ithaca, NY, 1962, PhD, 1966. From asst. prof. to prof. English Oberlin Coll., Ohio, 1966-90; prof. dept. English Harvard U., Cambridge, 1990—, dean undergrad. edn, 1992-96. Dir. Summer Inst. for High Sch. Tchrs., NEH, Oberlin, 1984-85; vis. prof. English U. Chgo., 1986; mem. faculty Bread Loaf Sch. English, 1987-88. Author: Literary Transcendentalism, 1973, New England Literary Culture, 1986, The Environmental Imagination, 1995, Writing for an Endangered World, 2001, Emerson, 2003, The Future of Environmental Criticism, 2005; mem. editl. bd. Am. Quar., Phila., 1979-82, Am. Lit., Durham, NC, 1983-86, PMLA, 1994-96. Trustee, officer Oberlin Shansi Meml. Assn., 1972-87. Recipient Christian Gauss award, 2004; Woodrow Wilson Found. fellow, 1961-62; Howard Found. fellow, 1969-70; NEH Rsch. fellow, 1979-80, 2002; Guggenheim Found. fellow, 1987-88. Mem. MLA, Am. Studies Assn. Democrat. Mem. United Ch. of Christ. Avocation: sports. Business E-Mail: lbuell@fas.harvard.edu.

BUELL, SAMUEL W., law educator, lawyer; AB magna cum laude, Brown U., 1987; JD summa cum laude, NYU, 1992. Bar: NY, Mass., U.S. Supreme Ct., U.S. Ct. Appeals (1st, 2d and 5th cir.). Law clk. to Hon. Jack B. Weinstein U.S. Dist. Ct. (ea. dist.) NY, 1992—93; assoc. Covington & Burling, Washington, 1993—94; asst. U.S. atty. (ea. dist.) NY U.S. Dept. Justice, 1994—98, asst. U.S. atty. Mass., 1998—2004, spl. atty. Enron task force, 2002—04; vis. asst. prof. U. Tex., Austin, 2004—06; assoc. prof. Washington U., St. Louis, 2006—. Spkr. in field. Contbr. articles to profl. jours. Recipient Dir. award for Superior Performance, US Dept. Justice, 1998, Atty. Gen's award for Exceptional Svc., 2004. Office: U Tex Sch Law 727 E Dean Keeton St Austin TX 78705 Office Phone: 512-232-1353. E-mail: sbuell@law.utexas.edu.

BUENTE, STEPHEN M., manufacturing executive; BS in Engring., Valparaiso U., Ind., 1972; MBA, Western Mich. U., Kalamazoo; grad. Exec. Program, Williams Coll., Williamstown, Mass. With Bendix Corp.; engring. program mgr. Assembled Products Divsn. Eaton Corp., 1976, product engring. mgr. valvetrain products, 1985, worldwide mktg. and product planning mgr., gen. mgr. engine components/Europe Turin, Italy, 1991, v.p. engine components ops./worldwide, 1995—99, v.p. automotive controls ops./worldwide, 1999—2000, sr. v.p., pres. automotive bus., 2000—. Bd. dirs. Shanghai Eaton Engine Components Co.; past chmn., bd. mem. US Engine Valve Co.; mem. Pres.'s Coun. Motor and Equipment Mfr.'s Assn. Campaign chmn. NE Ohio United Way, 2002; bd. trustees YMCA Greater Cleve. Mem.: Soc. Automotive Engrs. Office: Eaton Corp Eaton Ctr 1111 Superior Ave Cleveland OH 44114-2584 Office Phone: 216-523-5000.*

BUENTE, WAYNE GERALD, information scientist, researcher; b. Kankakee, Ill., Mar. 21, 1971; s. Orlin Wayne and Sue Lynn Buente. BS in Econ. (hon.), Purdue U., 1993; MS in Info., U. Mich., 2003; postgrad., Ind. U., 2003—. Merchandising mgr. PetsMart, Indpls., 1996—2001; info. tech. analyst City of Ann Arbor, Mich., 2002—03; rschr. Ind. U., Bloomington, 2003—. Info. tech. disaster recover planner AmeriCorps, City of Detroit, 2002. Geog. info. systems vol. City of Ann Arbor Planning Dept., Mich., 2003; rsch. cons. HoosierNet, Bloomington, Ind., 2005—06; youth mentor Big Brother Big Sisters South Ctrl. Ind., Bloomington, Ind., 2005—06, Big Brother Big Sisters Will and Grundy County, Joliet, Ill., 1996—97. Fellow, U. Mich., 2002, U.S. Dept. Edn., 2003—; grantee, U. Mich., 2002. Mem.: Am. Soc. Info. Sci. and Tech., Assn. Internet Rschr.s, Am. Polit. Sci. Assn., Assn. Computing Machinery, Computer Profls. for Social Responsiblity. Avocation: basketball. Home: 702 S Clarizz Blvd Bloomington IN 47401 Office: Sch of Lib and Info Sci 1320 E 10th St LI 011 Bloomington IN 47405-3907 Home Phone: 812-336-4364; Office Phone: 812-855-2018. Personal E-mail: wbuente@indiana.edu.

BUERGENTHAL, THOMAS, judge; b. Lubochna, Slovakia, May 11, 1934; came to U.S., 1951, naturalized, 1957; children: Robert, John, Alan; m. Marjorie J. Bell, 1983; stepchildren: Sebastian, Cristina. BA, Bethany Coll., 1957, LLD, 1981; JD, NYU, 1960; LLM, Harvard U., 1961, SJD, 1968; dr.jur. (hon.), U. Heidelberg, 1986; dr. jur. (hon.), Free U. of Brussels, 1997; LLD, SUNY, Buffalo, 2000, Am. U., 2002, U. Minn., 2003, George Washington U., 2004. Bar: NY 1961, DC 1983, U.S. Supreme Ct. 1982. Instr. law U. Pa., 1961-62; from asst. prof. to prof. SUNY, Buffalo, 1962-75; vis. prof. U. Tex., Austin, 1975-76, prof., 1976-77, Fulbright and Jaworski prof., 1977-80; judge Inter-Am. Ct. Human Rights, 1979-91, pres., 1985-87; dean, prof. law Am. U., Washington, 1980-85; disting. prof. law and human rights Emory U. Sch. Law, 1985-86, I.T. Cohen prof. of human rights, 1987-89; Lobingier prof. comparative law and jurisprudence George Washington U., Washington, 1989-2000, Lobingier prof. emeritus, 2000—; judge Adminstrv. Tribunal, Inter-Am. Devel. Bank, 1989-94, pres., 1993-94; judge Internat. Ct. of Justice, The Hague, Netherlands, 2000—. Mem. UN Truth Commn. for El Salvador, 1992—93, UN Human Rights Commn., 1995—99, U.S. Holocaust Meml. Coun., 1996—2001, Claims Resolution Tribunal for Dormant Accounts in Switzerland, 1998—2002, Ethics Commn. Internat. Olympic Com., 2005—; vice-chmn. Claims Resolution Tribunal for Dormant Accounts in Switzerland, 1999—2000; adv. com. Restatement (3d) of the Fgn. Rels. Law of U.S.; chmn. human rights com. U.S. Nat. Commn. for UNESCO, 1976—79; U.S. rep. UNESCO Human Rights Working Group, 1977—78; U.S. expert UN Interregional Expert Meeting on Crime Prevention and Control, 1978; mem. adv. bd. Pres. Holocaust Commn., 1978—80; v.p. UNESCO Congress on Tchg. of Human Rights, 1978; chmn. com. on conscience U.S. Holocaust Meml. Coun., 1997—2000; mem. ethics commn. Internat. Olympic Com., 2005. Author: Law-Making in the International Civil Aviation Organization, 1969; (with L.B. Sohn) International Protection of Human Rights, 1973; (with J.V. Torney) International Human Rights and International Education, 1976, International Law and the Helsinki Accord, 1977; (with R.E. Norris) Human Rights: The Inter-Am. System, 1982; (with D. Shelton) Protecting Human Rights in the Americas, 1982, 4th edit., 1995; (with S. Murphy) Public International Law in a Nutshell, 4th edit., 2007, (with D. Shelton and D. Stewart) International Human Rights in a Nutshell, 3d edit., 2002; (with Grossman and Nikken) Manual Internacional de Derechos Humanos, 1990; (with Kiss) La Protection Internationale des Droits de l'Homme, 1991; contbr. articles to profl. jours. Recipient Pro-Humanitas Ring, West-Ost Kulturwerk, Fed. Republic of Germany, 1978, Disting. Svc. in Legal Edn. award NYU Law Sch. Assn., 1987, Wolfgang Friedmann Meml. award Columbia U. Law Sch., 1989. Mem. Am. Law Inst., Am. Soc. Internat. Law (v.p. 1980-82, hon. pres. 2001—, Goler T. Butcher medal for excellence in internat. human rights 1997, Manley Hudson medal 2002), Coun. Fgn. Rels., Inter-Am. Inst. Human Rights (pres. 1980-92, hon. pres. 1992—). Office: Internat Ct Justice Peace Palace 2517 KJ The Hague Netherlands Office Phone: (31-70) 302-2408. Fax: (31-70) 302-2464. Business E-Mail: t.buergenthal@icj-cij.org.*

BUERHAUS, PETER I., nursing administrator; BSN, Mankato State U., Minn.; MS in Nursing Health Svcs. Adminstrn., U. Mich.; PhD in Econs. of Health Care and Nursing, Wayne State U., Detroit. Staff nurse cmty. hosp., Ohio; asst. to CEO U. Mich. Med. Ctr., Ann Arbor, 1983—86, asst. to vice provost for med. affairs, 1987—90, chief adminstr. med. ctr.; faculty Coll. Nursing U. Iowa, 1990—91; Robert Wood Johnson Found. faculty fellow in health care fin. Johns Hopkins U., Balt., 1991—92; asst. prof. health policy mgmt. Harvard Sch. Pub. Health, Boston, 1992—2000; dir. Harvard Nursing Rsch. Inst., Boston; sr. assoc. dean for rsch., Valere Potter prof. nursing Vanderbilt U., Nashville, 2000—. Mem. NIH nat. adv. coun. nursing rsch. Contbr. articles to profl. jours., chpts. to books. Mem.: Am. Acad. Nursing, Inst. of Medicine (life), Sigma Theta Tau Internat. (bd. dirs.). Office: Vanderbilt Univ Sch Nursing 415 Godchaux Hall 461 21st Ave Nashville TN 37240 Office Phone: 615-343-7618.

BUESCHEN, ANTON JOSLYN, physician, educator; b. Toledo, June 7, 1940; s. Robert F. and Mary J. (Joslyn) B.; m. Norma Jean McClanahan, Sept. 5, 1964; children— Anton, Elaine. Student, Va. Mil. Inst., 1958-61; MD, U. Va., 1965. Diplomate Am. Bd. Urology. Intern in surgery Vanderbilt U., 1965-66, asst. resident in surgery, 1966-67; resident in urology Ind. U., Indpls., 1969-72; practice medicine specializing in urology Birmingham, Ala., 1973—; instr. urology Tulane U. Sch. Medicine, 1972-73; asst. prof. div. urology dept. surgery U. Ala., Birmingham, 1973-75, assoc. prof., 1975-79, prof., 1979—, dir. div. urology, 1975—95, dir. divsn. urology, 1999—2005; chief urology sect. Children's Hosp., Birmingham, 1978-86. Pres. U. Ala. Health Svcs. Found., 2001—05. Contbr. numerous articles on urology to profl. jours. Served with M.C. U.S. Army, 1967-69. Mem. ACS, AMA (Billings Gold medal 1978), AAUP, Am. Urol. Assn. (bd. dirs., 2003—), Am. Urol. Assn. Southeastern Sect. (sec. 1997-2000, pres.-elect 2000-01, pres. 2001-02, bd. dirs. 1994-2003), Am. Found. Urologic Disease (bd. dirs. 2000-05), Am. Assn. Clin. Urologists, Soc. Univ. Urologists, Birmingham Urology Club, Jefferson County Med. Soc., Soc. for Pediatric Urology, Soc. Urologic Oncology, So. Med. Assn. (chmn. urology sect. 1987), Med. Assn. Ala. Office: U Ala Div Urology University Sta Birmingham AL 35294-0001 Office Phone: 205-996-8765.

BUESING, KAREN MEYER, lawyer; b. San Jose, Calif., Oct. 27, 1953; d. George Clifton and Marjorie Helen (Woodruff) Meyer; m. Robert Henry Buesing, Apr. 26, 1986; children: Robert Henry Jr., Juliet Kristen. BS, U. Fla., Gainesville, 1975, JD, 1982. Bar: Fla. 1982, US Dist. Ct. (mid. dist.) Fla. 1982, US Ct. Appeals (11th cir.) 1982. News reporter, editor Fla. Today, Cocoa, 1975-79; assoc. Trenam, Simmons et al, Tampa, Fla., 1982-86; ptnr. Rudnick & Wolfe, Tampa, 1986—98, Zinober & McCrea, Tampa, 1998—2007, Akerman Senterfitt, Tampa, 2007—. Adj. lectr. U. Fla., Gainesville, 1979-81; founder, dir. Fed. Trial Vols. Project, Tampa, 1985-88. Mem. Hillsborough County Bar Assn. (chmn. availibility of legal svcs. com. 1985-87, pro bono svc. award 1985). Democrat. Methodist. Office: Akerman Senterfitt 401 E Jackson Ste 1700 Tampa FL 33602 Office Phone: 813-223-7333.

BUESSER, ANTHONY CARPENTER, lawyer; b. Detroit, Oct. 15, 1929; s. Frederick Gustavis and Lela (Carpenter) B.; m. Carolyn Sue Pickle, Mar. 13, 1954; children: Kent Anderson, Anthony Carpenter, Andrew Clayton; m. Bettina Rieveschl, Dec. 14, 1973. BA in English with honors, U. Mich., 1952, MA, 1953, JD, 1960. Bar: Mich. 1961. Assoc. Chase, Goodenough & Buesser, Detroit, 1961-66; ptnr. Buesser, Buesser, Snyder & Blank, Detroit and Bloomfield Hills, Mich., 1966-81; sole practice Birmingham, Mich., 1981—. Trustee Detroit Country Day Sch., Beverly Hills, Mich., 1970-94, chmn. bd., 1977-82, 84-87, bd. chmn. emeritus, 1987—, chmn. nominating com., 1987-94. Served with AUS, 1953-55. Recipient Avery Hopwood award major fiction U. Mich., 1953, Outstanding Alumnus award Detroit Country Day Sch., 1988. Mem. ABA, State Bar Mich., Detroit Bar Assn. (pres. 1976-77), Oakland County Bar Assn., Am. Judicature Soc., Thomas M. Cooley Club (pres. 1974-76), Alpha Delta Phi, Phi Delta Phi. Home: 756 Honey Creek Dr Ann Arbor MI 48103-1638

BUETOW, DENNIS EDWARD, physiologist, educator; b. Chgo., June 20, 1932; s. Earl Frank and Helen Anna (Roeske) Buetow; m. Mary Kathleen Carney, Oct. 29, 1960; children: Katherine, Thomas(dec.), Michael, Ellen. BA, UCLA, 1954, MS, 1957, PhD, 1959. Biologist NIH, Bethesda, Md., 1959-65; biochemist Balt. City Hosps., 1959-65; assoc. prof. physiology U. Ill., Urbana, 1965-70, prof., 1970—2000, head dept. physiology and biophysics, 1983-88, prof. emeritus, 2000—. Cons. in field. Contbr. articles to profl. jours. Grantee, NIH, NSF, Life Ins. Med. Rsch. Fund, Am. Heart Assn., USDA. Fellow: AAAS, Gerontol. Soc.; mem.: Am. Soc. Plant Biology, Am. Fedn. Aging Rsch., Soc. Protozoologists, Am. Physiol. Soc., Am. Soc. Cell Biology. Home: 2 Eton Ct Champaign IL 61820-7602 Office: Univ Ill 524 Burrill Hall Urbana IL 61801 Business E-Mail: d-buetow@uiuc.edu.

BUETOW, KENNETH H., federal agency administrator; BA in biology, Indiana U., 1980; PhD in human genetics, U. Pitts., 1985. With Fox Chase Cancer Ctr., Phila., 1986—98; now chief Lab. Population Genetics Nat. Cancer Inst., NIH, dir. Ctr. Bioinformatics. Office: Nat Cancer Inst Lab Population Genetics Bldg 41 Rm D702 41 Center Dr Bethesda MD 20892 Office Phone: 301-435-8954. Office Fax: 301-435-8963. E-mail: buetowke@mail.nih.gov.

BUFALINO, VINCENT JOHN, cardiologist, medical administrator; b. 1952; m. Joan Bufalino; 2 children. Grad. magna cum laude, Loyola U.; MD, Loyola U. Stritch Sch. Medicine, 1977. Cert. internal medicine, cardiovasc. disease. Intern to resident, internal medicine Loyola U. Foster McGaw Hosp., fellowship to chief fellow, cardiovasc. disease; pres., CEO Midwest Heart Specialists, chmn. bd., Midwest Heart Found.; med. dir., cardiologist Edward Heart Hosp., Naperville, Ill. Mem. practicing physicians adv. coun. HHS, 2006—. Named Man of Yr., Italo-Am. Nat. Union; recipient Michelangelo award, 1998, Leonardo DiVinci award in medicine, 2004. Mem.: Am. Heart Assn. (past pres. greater midwest affiliate, nat. bd. dirs., chmn. advocacy coord. com., Physician of Yr. award 1997, Chmn.'s award for Excellence in Vol Svc. 2005). Office: Edward Heart Hosp 4th Fl 801 S Washington St Naperville IL 60566

BUFANO, RALPH A., retired museum executive; BS in Fine Arts, U. Minn. Dir. Exptl. Aircraft Aviation Found., Oshkosh, Wis.; pres. Kansas City (Mo.) Mus.; exec. dir. Ward Found. Mus., Salisbury, Md.; pres., CEO The Mus. of Flight, Seattle, 1991—2005. Fellow: Fedn. Aeronautica Internat. (Paul Tissadier award for svcs. to aeros. and airsports), Royal Aero. Soc. Office: The Mus of Flight 9404 E Marginal Way S Seattle WA 98108-4097 Personal E-mail: ralph.bufano@comcast.net.

BUFE, CHARLES GLENN, geophysicist, researcher; s. Bancroft Washington and Margaret Elizabeth Bufe; life ptnr. Jacquelyn Claire Abbott, Nov. 18, 1967; children: Sierra Noel, Nathaniel Renfield children: Glennica Joy Magee. BS in Geophys. Engring., Mich. Technol. Univ., 1960, MS in Geophysics, 1962; PhD in Geology, U. Mich., 1969. Rsch. geophysicist U. Mich., Ann Arbor, 1967—69, NOAA, San Francisco, 1969—73; vis. prof. U. Wis., Milw., 1973; geophysicist U.S. Geol. Survey, Menlo Park, Calif., 1973—80, liaison to DOE and FEMA Washington, 1980—85, rsch. geophysicist Denver, 1986—2006, scientist emeritus, 2006—; sci. advisor to U.S. govt. Joint Commn. on Econ. Cooperation, Riyadh, Saudi Arabia, 1985—86. Lt. NOAA Officer Corps, 1964—66. Fellow, NSF, 1960—62, Grove Karl Gilbert Fellowship, U.S. Geol. Survey, 1993; scholar, Nat. Merit Scholarship Corp., 1956—60. Mem.: Soc. Exploration Geophysicists, Seismol. Soc. Am., Am. Geophys. Union. Liberal. Achievements include research in plate tectonics,earthquake recurrence and prediction and time-varying earthquake hazard mapping; discovery of a precise, time-predictable earthquake recurrence model; development of time-to-failure analysis in nonlinear, predictive earthquake models. Avocations: photography, sailing, scuba diving, high country hiking, fly fishing. Home: 901 Miami Way Boulder CO 80305 Office: U S Geological Survey MS 966 Box 25046 DFC Denver CO 80225 Office Phone: 303-273-8413. Personal E-mail: geoling@gmail.com. E-mail: cbufe@usgs.gov.

BUFF, FRANK PAUL, chemist, educator; b. Munich, Feb. 13, 1924; came to U.S., 1937, naturalized, 1944; s. Heinrich and Johanna Helene (Guggenheimer) B.; m. Iva Mary Moore, Dec. 21, 1956; children— Susan Kathleen, Marjorie Anne. AB, U. Calif., Berkeley, 1944; PhD, Calif. Inst. Tech., 1949. Jr. chemist Shell Devel. Co., Emeryville, Calif., 1946; research fellow Calif. Inst. Tech., Pasadena, 1949-50; from instr. to emeritus prof. chemistry U. Rochester, NY, 1950—; vis. prof. Inst. Theoretical Physics, Utrecht, Netherlands, 1959-60; cons. Mobil Research Corp.; summer visitor Bell Telephone Labs., 1962. Contbr.: chpt. to Handbook of Physics, 1960; mem. bd. editors Jour. Statis. Physics; contbr. articles profl. jours. Served with AUS, 1944-46. Recipient research grants NSF, Office Saline Water; AEC postdoctoral fellow, 1949-50; NSF sr. postdoctoral fellow, 1959-60 Fellow Am. Phys. Soc., Am. Inst. Chemists, A.A.A.S.; mem. Am. Chem. Soc., Phi Beta Kappa, Sigma Xi. Home: 90 Roby Dr Rochester NY 14618-2112 Personal E-mail: imbfpb@aol.com.

BUFF, IVA MOORE, librarian, musicologist; b. Port Arthur, Tex., Aug. 28, 1932; d. Thomas Richard and Iva Catherine (Smith) Moore; m. Frank P. Buff, Dec. 21, 1956; children: Susan Kathleen, Marjorie Anne. BA, MusB, U. Rochester, 1953, PhD, 1973; MA, Smith Coll., Northampton, Mass., 1954. Tchr. math. Brearley Sch., NYC, 1954-55; research assoc. in musicology U. Rochester (N.Y.), 1973-75, head dept. acquisition and collection devel., 1979-91. Reader-cons. AAUW, 1989—. Author: The Chamber Duets & Trios of Carissimi, 1973, A Thematic Catalog of the Sacred Works of Giacomo Carissimi, 1979; articles Modern Music Librarianship, 1989, reviewer; asst. music rev. editor NOTES, 1986-87; assoc. editor: Am. Choral Rev., 1990-91. Fellow AAUW, 1973-75. Mem. Am. Musicol. Soc., Music Libr. Assn., Internat. Assn. Music Librs., Genesee Early Music Soc. (bd. dirs. 1990—), Mu Phi Epsilon. Avocation: photography. Home: 90 Roby Dr Rochester NY 14618-2112 Personal E-mail: imbfpb@aol.com.

BUFFENBARGER, (ROBERT) THOMAS, labor union administrator; b. 1950; s. Bob and Betty Buffenbarger; m. Linda Buffenbarger; children: Amy, Andrew. Former journeyman tool and die maker General Electric, Evendale, Ohio; with Internat. Assn. Machinists and Aerospace Workers, 1986-87, bus. rep. IAM Dist. 34 Cin., 1977, spl. rep. for Great Lakes Ter., 1980, adminstrv. asst. to gen. v.p. for Great Lakes Ter., 1983, exec. asst. to internat. pres., 1987-91, gen. v.p. Upper Marlboro, Md., 1991-97, internat. pres., 1997—. Co-chair. Machinists Non-Partisan Political League; mem. exec. council AFL-CIO, chmn. Com. on St. and Local Central Bodies; mem. exec. com. Internat. Metalworkers Fed.; mem. U.S. Treasury Dept. Adv. Com. to the Internat. Monetary Fund. Bd. mem. Guide Dogs of America. Office: Internat Assn Machinists and Aerospace Workers 9000 Machinists Pl Upper Marlboro MD 20772-2675 Office Phone: 301-967-4500.

BUFFENSTEIN, DARYL R., lawyer; b. Harare, Zimbabwe, June 12, 1951; BA in Econs. and Comparative African Govt. and Law, U. Cape Town, South Africa, 1972; BL with honors, U. Rhodesia, 1974, LLB, 1975; LLM, U. Exeter, Eng., 1977. Bar: Ga. 1978; advocate High Ct. Zimbabwe. Ptnr. Paul, Hastings, Janofsky & Walker, Atlanta, chmn. immigration practice group. Commonwealth scholar, 1975-76. Mem. Am. Immigration Lawyers Assn. (pres. 1995-1996, chair Atlanta chpt. 1982-84, nat. dir. 1984-, gen. counsel 1999-2003), State Bar of Ga. (chmn. internat. sect. 1984-85, global personnel alliance gen. counsel 2003—). Office: 600 Peachtree St NE Ste 2400 Atlanta GA 30308-2265 Office Phone: 404-815-2232. Office Fax: 404-685-5232. Business E-Mail: darylbuffenstein@paulhastings.com.

BUFFETT, JIMMY (JAMES WILLIAM BUFFETT), vocalist, songwriter, writer; b. Pascagoula, Miss., Dec. 25, 1946; s. James Delaney and Lorraine (Peets) B.; m. Margie Washichek, 1969 (div.), m. Jane Slagsvol, Aug. 27, 1977; children: Savannah Jane, Sarah Delaney and Cameron Marley. BS in History and Journalism, U. So. Miss., 1969. Free-lance journalist Inside Sports, Outside mag. Albums include Down to Earth, 1970, High Cumberland Jubilee, 1971, White Sport Coat and a Pink Crustacean, 1973, Living and Dying in 3/4 Time, 1974, A1A, 1974, Rancho Deluxe (film soundtrack), 1975, Havana Daydreamin', 1976, Changes in Latitudes (featuring the song "Margaritaville"), 1977, Son of a Son of a Sailor, 1978, You Had To Be There, 1978, Volcano, 1979, Coconut Telegraph, 1981, Somewhere Over China, 1981, One Particular Harbor, 1983, Riddles in the Sand, 1984, Last Mango in Paris, 1985, Songs You Know By Heart, 1985, Floridays, 1986, Hot Water, 1988, Off To See The Lizard, 1989, Feeding Frenzy, 1990, Boats, Beaches, Bars & Ballads, 1992, Before the Beach, 1993, Fruit Cakes, 1994, Barometer Soup, 1995, Banana Wind, 1996, Christmas Island, 1996, Don't Stop the Carnival, 1998, Beach House on the Moon, 1999, Buffett Live-Tuesdays, Thursdays, Saturdays, 1999, Captain America, 2002, Far Side of the World, 2002, License to Chill, 2004, Live at Texas Stadium, 2007; author: Tales from Margaritaville, 1988, Where is Joe Merchant?, 1992, A Novel Tale, 1992, Daybreak on the Equator, 1997, Sea Level: Adventures of a Saltwater Angler, 2002, A Salty Piece of Land, 2004 (Publishers Weekly bestseller), (with Savannah Jane Buffett) The Jolly Mon, 1988, Trouble Dolls, 1990, (memoir) A Pirate Looks at Fifty, 1998; performed benefit concert for anti-nuclear legislation; film appearances include Rancho Deluxe, 1975, FM, 1978, Repo Man, 1984, Dr Duck's Super Secret All-Purpose Sauce, 1985, Hook, 1991, Cobb, 1994, Congo, 1995; actor, prodr.: Hoot, 2006; TV appearances include SCTV Network 90, 1981, From the Earth to the Moon, 1998. Chmn. Save the Manatee Commn., Fla.; hon. dir. Greenpeace Found. Mem. Cousteau Soc. Democrat. Roman Catholic. Office: Margaritaville Inc Cindy Thompson 424A Fleming St Key West FL 33040 also: Mailboat Records 9200 Sunset Blvd Ste 550 Los Angeles CA 90069

BUFFETT, WARREN EDWARD, entrepreneur, investment company executive; b. Omaha, Aug. 30, 1930; s. Howard Homan and Leila (Stahl) B.; m. Susan Thompson, Apr. 19, 1952 (dec. July 29, 2004); children: Susan A., Howard, Peter; m. Astrid Manks, Aug. 30, 2006. Student, U. Pa., 1947-49; BS, U. Nebr., 1950; MS, Columbia, 1951. Investment salesman Buffett-Falk & Co., Omaha, 1951-54; security analyst Graham-Newman Corp., NYC, 1954-56; gen. partner Buffett Partnership, Ltd., Omaha, 1956-69; chmn. & CEO Berkshire Hathaway Inc., Omaha, 1970—. Chmn. bd. Berkshire Hathaway, Inc., Nat. Indemnity Co.; bd. dirs. The Coca-Cola Co., 1989-, The Washington Post Co., 1974-86, 96-. Life trustee Grinnell Coll., 1968—, Urban Institute. Named one of Forbes Richest Americans, 2006, Forbes World's Richest People, 2007, The World's Most Influential People, TIME mag., 2007 Mem.: Am Acad Arts & Scis. Ranked number two on the World's Richest People list by Forbes magazine in 2001, 2002, 2003, 2004, 2005. Office: Berkshire Hathaway Inc 1440 Kiewit Plz Omaha NE 68131*

BUFFINGTON, GARY LEE ROY, safety engineer, construction executive; b. Custer, SD, Dec. 6, 1946; s. Donald L. B. and Madge Irene (Selby) Lampert; m. Kathleen R. Treloar, Aug. 3, 1965; children: Katherine, Lowell, Gary Jr. BS in Bus. Edn., Black Hill State Coll., 1971; AA in Criminal Justice, U. S.D., 1972, MS, 1974. Cert. safety profl., EMT, law enforcement officer, mine safety and health adminstrn. instr., OSHA instr., safety exec., safety mgr., safety specialist; Canadian registered safety profl.; lic. pvt. investigator; cert. safety and health mgr. Contract miner Homestake Mining Co., Lead, SD, 1966—72; dep. sheriff, criminal investigator Pennington County Sheriff's Dept., Rapid City, SD, 1972—77; fed. mine inspector U.S. Dept. of Labor, Mine Safety and Health Adminstrn., Birmingham, Ala., 1977—79, supr., spl. investigator, 1979—81, supr., mine inspector Grand Junction, Colo., 1981—83; mgr. safety and security Black & Veatch Engrs. Stanton Energy Ctr., Orlando, Fla., 1983—87; mgr. loss control Black & Veatch Engrs. AES Thames Cogeneration Plant, Uncasville, Conn., 1987—90; mgr. loss control Trans-Mo. River Tunnel project Black & Veatch, Engrs.-Architects, Kansas City, Mo., 1990—92; mgr. safety and security, mgr. metro rail constrn. Parsons-Dillingham, LA, 1992—95; asst. dir. constrn. safety L.A. Metro Rail Project Met. Transp. Authority, 1995—99; owner Safety Expert Witness Am. Safety Cons., LA, 1990—; mgr. constrn. safety Parsons Constructors Inc., Pasadena, Calif., 1999—2002. Mem. ANSI A-10 Accredited Standards Com., Washington, 1984—, Mine Safety and Health Adminstrn. Standards Com., Arlington, Va., 1981-83. Named Police Officer of the Year, Sundown Optimist Club, Rapid City, 1975; recipient Meritorious Achievement award, U.S. Dept. of Labor, Arlington, 1979, Monetary Spl. Achievement award, U.S. Dept. Labor, Arlington, 1980. Mem. Am. Soc. Safety Engrs. (adminstr. mining divsn. 1998—, Safety Profl. of Yr. constrn. splty. 2000-01, Safety Profl. of Yr. mining practice splty. 2002-03), World Safety Orgn., Am. Indsl. Hygiene Assn., Am. Soc. for Indsl. Security, Nat. Safety Coun., Inst. for Safety and Health Mgmt., Nat. Fire Protection Assn., Assn. for Can. Registered Safety Profls., Moose Lodge. Republican. Lutheran. Avocations: photography, sports. Home: 26035 Bouquet Canyon # 301 Santa Clarita CA 91350 Office: PO Box 71017 Los Angeles CA 90071-0017 Home Phone: 661-298-0006; Office Phone: 213-952-1308. Personal E-mail: gbuff46@yahoo.com.

BUFFKINS, LERACHEL HAROMBE, small business owner; b. Portland, Maine, Dec. 8, 1970; d. Archie Lee Buffkins and Carol Jane Christian, Lewis Kim Christian (Stepfather); m. Tal Ricardo Valentin, Aug. 18, 1999 (div.); 1 child, Jakob Taylor. BA in Sociology, St. Mary's Coll. Md., 1992; MSW, Howard U., Washington, 1996. Cert. profl. resume writer Pa. for Resume Writers and Career Coaches, 2003, fed. job search trainer Md. Inst. for Employment and Tng. Profls., 2003. Asst. men's dept. mgr. Nordstrom Rack, Silver Spring, Md., 1992—96; tech. asst. Governor's Office for Children, Youth & Families, Baltimore, Md., 1996—97; career resource coord. Morgan State U. - Ctr. for Career Devel., Balt., 1996—97, internship/co-op coord., 1997—2003; resume writer/owner Writing For You, Inc., Laurel, Md., 2002—. Mem.: Md. Assn. for Counseling and Devel. (sec. 2004—), Nat. Resume Writers Assn., Md. Career Devel. Assn., Career Masters Inst., Nat. Assn. of Workforce Devel. Profls. (life), Nat. Career Devel. Assn. (life). R-Consevative. Avocation: flute. Office: Writing For You Inc 14518 Cambridge Cir Laurel MD 20707 Home Phone: 301-604-2082; Office Phone: 301-604-2048. Office Fax: 301-604-2100. E-mail: lbuffkins@writingforyouinc.com.

BUFFLER, PATRICIA ANN, epidemiologist, educator, dean; b. Doylestown, Pa., Aug. 1, 1938; d. Edward M. and Evelyn G. (Axenroth) Happ; m. Richard T. Buffler, Jan. 20, 1962; children: Martyn R., Monique L. BSN, Cath. U. Am., 1960; MPH, U. Calif., Berkeley, 1965, PhD in Epidemiology, 1973. Prof. epidemiology sch. pub. health U. Tex. Health Sci. Ctr., Houston, 1979—91; prof. U. Calif., Berkeley, 1991—, dean sch. pub. health, 1991—98, dean emerita, 1998—. Mem. expert adv. panel on occupl. health WHO, 1985—2002; mem. environment, safety and health adv. com. U.S. DOE, 1992—95; mem. bd. on water sci. and tech. NRC, 1992—94; chair, bd. dirs. Mickey Leland Nat. Urban Air Toxics Rsch. Ctr., 1994—97, Societal Inst. of Math. Scis.; mem. Nat. Commn. on Superfund, Keystone Ctr., 1992—94; mem. adv. panel on mng. nuc. materials from warheads U.S. Congress Office Tech. Assessment, 1992—93; bd. sci. counselors Nat. Inst. for Occupl. Safety and Health, 1991—93; mem. sci. adv. bd. radiation adv. com. subcom. on cancer risks associated with electric and magnetic fields U.S. EPA, 1990—93, mem. sci. adv. bd., 1996—98; mem. Nat. Adv. Coun. on Environ. Health Scis., 1995—98, NAS, Nat. Coun. Radiation Protection. Contbr. articles to profl. jours. Fellow: AAAS, Inst. Medicine of NAS, Am. Coll. Epidemiology (pres.-elect 1990—91, pres. 1991—92); mem.: APHA (epidemiology sect. 1964—), Internat. Soc. for Environ. Epidemiology (pres.-elect 1989—91, pres. 1992—94), Soc. of Toxicology, Internat. Commn. on Occupl. Health, Internat. Soc. for Exposure Assessment (charter, bd. internat. councillors 1993—98), Internat. Epidemiol. Assn., Soc. for Occupl. and Environ. Health, Am. Epidemiol. Soc., Soc. for Epidemiol. Rsch. (pres.-elect, pres., past pres. 1984—88), Collegium Ramazzini. Office: U Calif Sch Pub Health 714-F Univ Hall 140 Earl Warren Hl Berkeley CA 94720-0001

BUFFON, CHARLES EDWARD, lawyer; b. Topeka, Sept. 8, 1939; s. Merritt Woodbridge and Clare Marie (Waterfall) B.; m. Kathleen Craig Vreeland, June 6, 1964; children: Alexandra, Nathaniel Edward. AB in Internat. Rels. magna cum laude, Dartmouth Coll., 1961; LLB cum laude, Harvard U., 1964. Bar: D.C. 1965, U.S. Ct. Appeals (D.C. cir.) 1965, U.S. Ct. Appeals (6th cir.) 1966, U.S. Supreme Ct. 1971, U.S. Ct. Appeals (9th cir.) 1975, U.S. Ct. Appeals (2d cir.) 1980, U.S. Ct. Appeals (4th cir.) 1980, U.S. Ct. Appeals (3d cir.) 1981, U.S. Ct. Appeals (fed. cir.) 1982, U.S. Dist. Ct. Md. 1992, U.S. Ct. Appeals (11th cir.) 2000. Assoc. Covington & Burling, Washington, 1964-73, ptnr., 1973—, gen. counsel, 2005—. Adj. faculty U. Va. Law Sch., 1968-86, Am. U. 1988-92; lectr. in field. Contbr. articles to profl. jours. Fellow Am. Bar Found.; mem. ABA (litigation and antitrust sects.), D.C. Bar Assn. (past chmn. legal ethics com., spl. com. legal specialization, mem. steering com. sect. cts., lawyers and adminstrn. justice, D.C. rules profl. com., com. on interdisciplinary practice, Cert. Appreciation 1987, 2002), Phi Beta Kappa. Office: Covington & Burling 1201 Pennsylvania Ave NW Washington DC 20004-2401 Home Phone: 301-654-1516; Office Phone: 202-662-5542. Office Fax: 202-778-5542. Business E-Mail: cbuffon@cov.com.

BUFFONE, SAMUEL J., lawyer; b. New Kensington, Pa., Oct. 3, 1946; BA, Univ. Pitts., 1968; JD, Georgetown Univ., 1971. Bar: Pa. 1971, D.C. 1973, US Ct. Appeals (1st, 2d, 3d, 4th, 5th, 9th, 11th & D.C. cir.), US Supreme Ct. 1978. Law clk. Judge Francis L. Van Dusen, US Ct. Appeals 3d cir., 1971—72; ptnr. litigation dept. Ropes & Gray, Washington, 1992—, co-chmn. govt. enforcement practice group. Chmn. Practicioners Adv. Group U.S. Sentencing Commn., 1989—92. Mem.: ABA (chmn. Com. on U.S. Sentencing Commn., vice chmn. RICO Com. 1986—88, mem. White Collar Crime Com. 1984—). Office: Ropes & Gray One Metro Ctr Suite 900 700 12th St NW Washington DC 20005-3948 Office Phone: 202-508-4657. Office Fax: 202-508-4650. Business E-Mail: samuel.buffone@ropesgray.com.

BUFFORD, SAMUEL LAWRENCE, federal judge; b. Phoenix, Nov. 19, 1943; s. John Samuel and Evelyn Amelia (Rude) B.; m. Julia Marie Metzger, May 13, 1978. BA in Philosophy, Wheaton Coll., 1964; PhD, U. Tex., 1969; JD magna cum laude, U. Mich., 1973. Bar: Calif., N.Y., Ohio. Instr. philosophy La. State U., Baton Rouge, 1967-68; asst. prof. Ea. Mich. U., Ypsilanti, 1968-74; asst. prof. law Ohio State U., Columbus, 1975-77; assoc. Gendel, Raskoff, Shapiro & Quittner, LA, 1982-85; atty. Paul, Weiss, Rifkind, Wharton & Garrison, NYC, 1974-75, Sullivan Jones & Archer, San Francisco, 1977-79, Musick, Peeler & Garrett, LA, 1979-81, Rifkind & Sterling, Beverly Hills, Calif., 1981-82, Gendel, Raskoff, Shapiro & Quittner, LA, 1982-85; U.S. bankruptcy judge Ctrl. Dist. Calif., 1985—. Cons. in field; lectr. in field. Sr. author: International Insolvency, 2001, editor-in-chief: Am. Bankruptcy Law Jour., 1990—94; contbr. articles to profl. jours. Younger Humanist fellowship NEH. Mem. ABA, L.A. County Bar Assn. (mem. profl. responsibility and ethics com. 1979—, chair profl. responsibility and ethics com. 1985-86, chair ethics 2000 liaison com. 1997-2002), Order of Coif. Office: US Bankruptcy Ct 255 E Temple St Ste 1582 Los Angeles CA 90012-3332

BUFIS, MATTHEW PETER, music educator; b. Ridgewood, NJ, June 16, 1980; s. Philip Anthony and Sophia Cynthia Bufis. MusB, Ithaca Coll., 2002. Cert. tchg. NY, Md. Pvt. instrument tchr. Misically Yours Music Store, Calif., 2002—, Md., 2002—; dir. of bands Great Mills HS, Great Mills, Md., 2002—; asst. coach Misericordia Swim Team, Dallas, Pa., 2005. Band conductor St. Mary's County Pub. Schs., Great Mills, Md., 2004; guest clinician Leonardtown Mid. Sch., Leonardtown, Md., 2004. Mem.: NEA, World Assn. of Syphonic BOE, So. Md. Music Conf. Avocations: running, swimming, composing, arranging. Home: 65 Marcla Rd Ringwood NJ 07456 Office: Great Mills HS 21130 Great Mills Rd Great Mills MD 20634 Office Phone: 301-863-4001 x116. Office Fax: 301-863-4006. E-mail: bufonium2002@yahoo.com.

BUFORD, R.C., professional sports team executive; m. Beth Buford; 1 adopted child, Alexis Wangmene children: Chase, C.C. Student, Tex. A&M U., Okla. State U.; grad., Friends U. Coach U. Kans., 1983—88; asst. coach San Antonio Spurs, 1988—92, head scout, 1994—97, dir. scouting, 1997—99, v.p., asst. gen. mgr., 1999, gen. mgr., 2002—, sr. v.p., 2004—; asst. coach LA Clippers, 1992—93, U. Fla., 1993—94. Bd. mem. Roy Maas' Youth Alternatives; bd. dirs. Playing for Peace; hon. bd. mem. Juvenile Diabetes Found. Office: San Antonio Spurs One AT&T Ctr San Antonio TX 78219*

BUFORD, ROBERT PEGRAM, lawyer; b. Roanoke Rapids, NC, Sept. 7, 1925; s. Robert Pegram and Edith (Rawlings) Buford; m. Anne Bliss Whitehead, June 26, 1948; children: Robert, Bliss, Peyton. LLB, U. Va., 1950. Bar: Va. 1949. Sr. counsel Hunton & Williams, Richmond, Va. Bd. visitors U. Va., Charlottesville, 1972—80; chmn. Met. Richmond C. of C., 1973; bd. trustees St. Paul's Coll., Lawrenceville, Va., 1977—85. Recipient Disting. Svc. award, Jr. C. of C., 1961, Va. Profl. Assn., 1965, Good Govt. award, Richmond First Club, 1967. Fellow: Va. Law Found., Am. Bar Found.; mem.: Va. Bar (assoc.), Commonwealth Club, Country Club of Va. Home: 506 Kilmarnock Dr Richmond VA 23229-8102 Office: Hunton & Williams Riverfront Pla E Tower PO Box 1535 Richmond VA 23218-1535 Business E-Mail: rbuford@hunton.com.

BUGBEE-JACKSON, JOAN, sculptor, educator; b. Oakland, Calif., Dec. 17, 1941; d. Henry Greenwood and Jeanie Lawler (Abbot) B.; m. John Michael Jackson, June 21, 1973; 1 child, Brook Bond. BA in Art, U. Calif., San Jose, 1964, MA in Art and Ceramics, 1966; student, Nat. Acad. Sch. Fine Arts, NYC, 1968-72. Instr. pottery Greenwich House Pottery, NYC, 1969-71, Craft Inst. Am., NYC, 1970-72, Cordova Ext. Ctr., U. AK, 1972-79, Prince William Sound Cmty. Coll., 1979—. One-woman exhbn. in Maine, NYC, Alaska, Calif.; group exhbns. include Allied Artists Am., 1970-72, Nat. Acad. Design, 1971, 74, Nat. Sculpture Soc. Ann., 1971, 72, 73, Alaska Woman Art Show, 1987, 88, Cordova Visual Artists, 1991-96, Alaska Artists Guild Show, 1994, Am. Medallic Sculpture Nat. Travelling Exhbn., 1994-95, pres. Cordova Arts and Pageants Ltd., 1975-76; commns. include Merle K. Smith Commemorative plaque, 1973, Eyak Native Monument, 1978, Anchorage Pioneer's Home Ceramic Mural, 1979, Alaska Wildlife Series Bronze Medal, 1980, Armin F. Koernig Hatchery Plaque, 1985, Cordova Fishermen's Meml. Sculpture, 1985, Alaska's Five

Gov., bronze relief, Anchorage, 1986, Reluctant Fishermen's Mermaid, bronze, 1987, Charles E. Bunnell, bronze portrait statue, Fairbanks, 1988, Alexander Baranof Monument, Sitka, Alaska, 1989, Wally Noerenberg Hatchery Plaque, Prince William Sound, Alaska, 1989, Russian-Alaskan Friendship Plaque (edit. of 4), Kayak Island, Cordova, Alaska and Vladivostok & Petropavlovsk-Kamchatskiy, Russia, 1991, Sophie-Last Among Eyak Native People, 1992, Alaska Airlines Medal Commn., 1993, Hosp. Aux. plaque, 1995, La Cirena, Mex., 1998, Alaska Vets. Monument lifesize bronze, Anchorage, 2001, Alaska R.R.: Sheffield Plaque, 2002, Joe Redington Sr., Father of the Iditarod, statue, Wasilla, Alaska, 2003, Pioneer Aviator Monument, Anchorage, 2005; also other portraits. Bd. dir. Alaska State Coun. Arts, 1991-95. Scholar, Nat. Acad. Sch. Fine Arts, 1969-72; recipient J.A. Suydam Bronze medal, 1969, Dr. Ralph Weiler prize, 1971, Helen Foster Barnet award, 1971, Daniel Chester French award, 1972, Frishmuth award, 1971, Allied Artists Am. award, 1972, C. Percival Dietsch prize, 1973, citation Alaska Legis., 1981, 82; named Alaskan Artist of Yr., 1991; Alaska Gov. Award, 2002. Fellow Nat. Sculpture Soc. Address: PO Box 374 Cordova AK 99574-0374 E-mail: artworks@ctcak.net.

BUGEJA, MICHAEL JOSEPH, director, educator, writer; b. Hackensack, NJ, May 24, 1952; s. Michael Carl and Josephine (Apap) B.; m. Diane Faye Sears, Sept. 16, 1979; children: Mikayle Joseph, Shane Michael, Erin Marie BA in German, St. Peter's Coll., 1974; MS in Comms., S.D. State U., 1976; PhD in English, Okla. State U., 1985. State editor UPI, Sioux Falls, SD, 1976—79; prof. Okla. State U., Stillwater, 1979—86, Ohio U., Athens, 1986—2003, spl. asst. to pres., 1996—2003; dir. Greeniee Sch. Journalism and Comm. Iowa State U., Ames, 2003—. Hon. chancellor Nat. Fed. of State Poetry Soc. Author: Art and Craft of Poetry, 1994, Living Ethics, 1996, Guide to Writing Magazine Nonfiction, 1997, Millennium's End, 1999, Living Without Fear, 2001, Interpersonal Divide: The Search for Community in a Technological Age, 2005, Living Ethics Across Media Platforms, 2007. Fellow Nat. Endowment for Arts, 1990, Ohio Arts Coun., 1997; NEH grantee, 1984; recipient Outstanding Tchr. award Amoco, 1985. Lutheran. Office: Iowa State U Hamilton Hall Ames IA 50010 Business E-Mail: bugeja@iastate.edu.

BUGGE, LAWRENCE JOHN, lawyer, educator; b. Milw., June 1, 1936; s. Lawrence Anthony and Anita (Westenberg) B.; m. Mary Daly, Nov. 28, 1959 (div.); m. Elaine Andersen, Jan. 29, 1977; children: Kristin, Laura, Jill, David, Carol. AB, Marquette U., 1958; JD, Harvard U., 1963. Bar: Wis. 1963. Assoc. Foley and Lardner, Milw., Madison, Wis., 1963-70, ptnr., 1970-96, of counsel, 1996—. Pres. Nat. Conf. Commrs. on Uniform State Laws, 1989-91; adj. prof. law U. Wis. Law Sch., Madison, 1997—. Mem. Wis. Bar Assn. (pres. 1980-81), Mil. Bar Assn. (pres. 1974-75), Milw. Young Lawyers Assn. (pres. 1969-70). Home: 313 Walnut Grove Dr Madison WI 53717-1228 Office: Foley & Lardner PO Box 1497 150 E Gilman St Madison WI 53701-1497 Personal E-mail: lbugge@charter.net.

BUGGIE, FREDERICK DENMAN, management consultant; b. Toledo, Mar. 27, 1929; s. Horace and Loraine (Denman) B.; m. Betty Jo Chilcote, Sept. 7, 1951 (div. 1988); children: Martha Louise Buggie Kenney, John Chilcote Buggie; m. Debra Hingley, July 15, 1997. BA, Yale U., New Haven, Conn., 1956; MBA, George Washington U., Washington, DC, 1961. Sales engr. Alcoa, Balt. and Phila., 1956-66; pres. Gt. Lakes Rsch. Inst., Erie, Pa., 1967-69; mktg. mgr. Technicon Instruments, Tarrytown, NY, 1969-71; program mgr. Innotech, Norwalk, Conn., 1971-74; pres. Inomation divsn. Van Dyck Corp., Westport, Conn., 1974-76; founder, CEO Strategic Innovations Internat., Inc., Lake Wylie, SC, 1976—. Pres. SII Strategic Innovations A.G., Zurich, Switzerland; founder, chmn. Strategic Innovations Internat. Ltd., Keele, Staffordshire, Eng., Strategic Innovations B.V., Rijswijk, The Netherlands; conf. leader, lectr.; adj. prof. various univs. Author: New Product Development Strategies, 1981; contbr. over 50 articles to profl. jours. With USAF Security Svc., 1950-54. Fellow Inst. Dirs.; mem. Assn. Corp. Growth, Strategic Leadership Forum, Comml. Devel. Mktg. Assn., Soc. Plastics Engrs., Product Devel. and Mgmt. Assn., Yale Club (London, NYC). Office: Strategic Innovations Internat Inc 12 Executive Ct Lake Wylie SC 29710 E-mail: frederick.buggie.sy.51@aya.yale.edu.

BUGGS, DWAYNE ANDRE, fine arts coordinator, music educator; b. Springhill, La., Sept. 24, 1954; s. Faye Evelyn (Thomas) and Overton Joe Buggs; married. BA, La. Tech U., Ruston, 1975; MusM, So. Ill. U., Edwardsville, 1977. Cert. Lifetime K-12 Vocal Music Mo. Dept. Elem. and Secondary Edn., 1977, La. State Bd. Edn., 1975. Vocal music educator Normandy Sch. Dist., St. Louis, 1977—, k-12 coord. fine arts, 1995—. Music dir. St. James AME Ch., St. Louis, 1977—2002; choral dir. Normandy Sr. HS, St. Louis, 1985—95; organist Cote Brilliante Presbyn. Ch., St. Louis, 2003—; adj. prof. music U. Missouri-St. Louis, St. Louis, 2005—. Dir.: (mshsaa choral, solo and ensemble festiva) Choral and Vocal Competitions (Honor I - Superior Rating, 1995). Vice-chair St. Louis Legend Singers Bd. of Directors, St. Louis, Mo., 2003—05; artist-in-training co-chair Opera Theatre St. Louis Guild Bd., St. Louis, Mo., 2000—05; adv. bd. mem. E. Desmond Lee Fine Arts Collaborative, St. Louis, Mo., 1999—2005; program com. mem. Young Audiences, Inc., St. Louis, Mo., 2003—05. Recipient Outstanding Employee of Yr., Normandy Sr. HS, 1995, Outstanding Svc. award, St. James A.M.E. Ch., 1995, Eminent Educator award, Phi Delta Kappa Sorority, 1999, Apple for the Tchr., Iota Phi Lambda Sorority, 2001; fellow Grad. Minority Fellowship, So. Ill. U., Edwardsville, Ill., 1976, Summer Music Fellow, Northwestern U., Evanston, Ill., 1995. Mem.: Nat. Educators Assn., Urban Music Leadership Conf., Nat. Assn. Negro Musicians, Nat. Art Educators Assn., Assn. Theatre Arts Edn., Am. Choral Directors Assn., Music Educators Nat. Conf. (assoc.), Phi Mu Alpha Sinfonia (life). Home: 5615 Bermuda Dr Saint Louis MO 63121 Office: Normandy Sch Dist 6701 St Charles Rock Rd Saint Louis MO 63133 Home Phone: 314-524-4403; Office Phone: 314-493-0693. Office Fax: 314-493-0696. Personal E-mail: dwaynebuggs@sbcglobal.net. E-mail: dbuggs@normandy.k12.mo.us.

BUGHER, ROBERT DEAN, professional society administrator; b. Lafayette, Ind., Oct. 17, 1925; s. Walter Earl and Lillie Victoria (Feldner) B.; m. Patricia Jean McConnell, Sept. 7, 1945; children: Vickie Leigh, Robert James. Student, Millsaps Coll., 1943, Miami U., Oxford, Ohio, 1944; BS in Civil Engring, Purdue U., 1948; MPA, U. Mich., 1951. Staff engr. Mich. Mcpl. League, 1948-53; mgr. Mcpl. Purchasing Svc., 1951-53; sec.-treas. Mich. Mcpl. Utilities Assn., 1951-53; asst. dir. Am. Pub. Works Assn., 1953-58, exec. dir., 1958-89, exec. dir. emeritus, 1990—. Lectr. Internat. Seminar on Ekistics, Athens, Greece, 1970; chmn. nat. adv. coun. Keep Am. Beautiful, Inc., 1974-75; chmn. Nat. Conf. on Solid Waste Disposal Sites, Washington, 1971; advisor pub. mgmt. program Northwestern U., 1977-82; bd. dirs. Pub. Adminstrn. Svc., Chgo., 1958-73; trustee Nat. Acad. Code Adminstrs.; chmn. Coun. Internat. Urban Liaison, 1982-84; trustee Nat. Tng. and Devel. Svc., Am. Consortium for Internat. Pub. Adminstrn.; adv. com. internat. divsn. GAO, 1979-80. Editor: pub. works sect. Municipal Yearbook Internat. City Mgmt. Assn., 1953-58, People Making Public Works History-A Century of Progress 1894-1994, 1998; cons. editor pub. works sect., Mcpl. Pub. Works Adminstrn., 1957; chmn. adv. bd. Internat. Ctr. Acad. State and Local Govts., 1985-87. Served to 1st lt. USMCR, 1943-45. Mem. ASCE (life), Am. Pub. Works Assn. (hon.), Internat. Pub. Works Fedn. (treas. 1985-89, sec.-gen. 1990), Am. Soc. Assn. Execs., Am. Soc. Pub. Adminstrn., Internat. Union Local Authorities (pres. U.S. sect. 1977-79, v.p. 1968-70, 75-77), Internat. Solid Wastes and Pub. Cleansing Assn. (v.p. 1968-70), Internat. Fedn. Mcpl. Engrs. (treas. 1976-79), Pub. Works Hist. Soc. (hon., treas. 1975-89), Sigma Alpha Epsilon. Baptist. Home: 7501 E Thompson Peak Pkwy Unit 124 Scottsdale AZ 85255 Office: 2345 Grand Blvd Ste 700 Kansas City MO 64108-2625 Business E-Mail: rdbugher@cox.net.

BUGLIARELLO, GEORGE, academic administrator, educator; b. Trieste, Italy, May 20, 1927; arrived in U.S., 1951, naturalized, 1964; s. Federico and Spera (Gefter-Wondrich) Bugliarello; m. Virginia Upton Harding, 1960; children: Federico David, Nicholas Luigi. DEng summa cum laude, U. Padua, Italy, 1951; MSCE, U. Minn., 1954; DSc, MIT, 1959; LLD (hon.), Carnegie-Mellon U., 1986, Trinity Coll., 1997; MD (hon.), U. Trieste, 1989; EngD (hon.), Milw. Sch. Engring., 1991; LLD (hon.), Ill. Inst. Tech., 1993, EngD (hon.); LLD (hon.), Pace U., 1994, LHD (hon.); D in Arts and Humane Letters (hon.), Rensselaer Poly. Inst., 2004; DSc (hon.), U. Minn. Rsch. engr. U. Padua, 1951; from rsch. asst. to rsch. assoc. MIT, 1956-59; mem. faculty Carnegie-Mellon U., 1959-69, prof. biotech. and civil engring., 1956-69, chmn. biotechnology program, 1964-69; dean engring. U. Ill. Chgo. Cir., 1969-73; pres. Poly. U., Bklyn., 1973-94, chancellor, 1994—2003, pres. emeritus, Univ. prof., 2003—. Bd. hydraulic cons. U.S. Waterways Exptl. Sta., 1968—74; mem. sci. adv. panel Armed Forces Explosive Safety Bd., 1968—69; mem. biomed tng. engring. com. NIH, 1966—70; mem. commn. edn. Nat. Acad. Engring., 1970—73, chmn. com. ednl. sys., 1970—73, mem. tech. edn. stds. com.; chmn. bd. sci. and tech. for internat. devel. NAS, 1979—83; sci. policy reviewer Portugal OECD, 1982—83, others; U.S. rep. steering com. on sci. for stability program NATO, 1984—97, mem. steering com. on sci. for peace, 1997—2000; chair engring. adv.com. Lawrence Livermore Nat. Lab.; mem. U. Chgo. rev. com. for the decision and info. scis. divsn. Argonne Nat. Lab.; trustee William R. Kenan Jr. Inst. Engring. Tech. and Sci., Paul and Daisy Soros Fellowship for New Ams.; mem. Found. Future Bd. Advisors; bd. dirs. Lord Corp., Comtech. Corp., Keyspan Energy, Symbol Techs., Inc., Jura Corp. Author: The Biosoma-Reflections on the Syntesis of Biology, Society and Machines, 2003; co-author: (book) Computer Systems and Water Resources, 1974, The Impact of Noise Pollution, 1976, Technology, The Community and the University, 1976; editor: Bioengineering--An Engineering View, 1967, Women in Engineering, 1972, The History and Philosophy of Technology, 1979; co-editor: East-West Technology Transfer, 1996, Technology in Society; interim editor-in-chief: The Bridge; contbr. articles to profl. jours. Trustee ANSER, 1974-2000, Teagle Found., Greenwall Found., 1984-2000, Lord Found. N.C., Commn. Ind. Colls. and Universities, 1993-96; bd. visitors Duke U. Sch. Engring., 1975-2000; mem. N.Y. Partnership, 1980—, High Tech. Task Force, 1985-90, chmn., 1988-90, Mayor's Commn. Sci. and Tech., 1984-90, chmn., 1987-90; exec. com. Bd. Trustees Commn. Ind. Colls. and Univs., N.Y., 1986-89; alumni rep. MIT vis. com. for Civil Engring., 1985-91; chair, N.Y.C. Mayor's Task Force on Gramercy Park Steam Pipe Explosion, 1989-90, N.Y.C. Mayor's Adv. Coun. on Devel. of Recycling Markets and Businesses; active Nat. Medal Tech. Nomination Evaluation Com., 1987-92, chmn. 1991-92; chair Nat. Acads. Megacities Project Habitat II Conf.; mem. Nat. Acad. Sci. Com. Human Rights; mem. U.S. Nat. Acads.-Russian Acad. Sci. Com. on Terrorism Confronting the U.S. and Russia. Recipient Alza prize Biomed. Engring. Soc.; NATO sr. fellow Tech. U. Berlin, 1968; N.Y. Mayor's Awd. Excellence Sci. and Tech., 1994, N.Y. Acad. of Scis. Fellow AAAS (chair com. sci., engring. and pub. policy, 1986-89, chair panel on phys. scis. and engring. 1987-89, project 2061 1985-89), Am. Soc. Engring. Edn., ASCE (chmn. exec. com. engring. mechanics divsn. 1971-72, chmn. interdivisional task com. civil engring. in medicine and health care delivery 1969-73, Huber rsch. prize 1967), Am. Inst. Med. and Biol. Engring. (founding fellow), Biomed. Engring. Soc.; mem. NAE (coun. 1989-93, adv. com. tech. and the environ. 1989-92, internat. affairs adv. com. 1988-92, fgn. sect. 2007-), Internat. Assn. Hydraulic Rsch. (chmn. task com. computer langs. 1969-72), N.Y. Acad. Medicine, Nat. Assn. for Sci., Tech. and Soc. (trustee 1988—, pres. 1989-90, hon. lifetime mem.), Nat. Rsch. Coun. (bd. engring. edn. 1991-96, chair bd. on infrastructure and constructed environ. 1994-97, chair com. on alt. techs. to replace anti-pers. landmines 1999-2000, vice chair com. on army sci. and tech. for homeland def. 2002—, others), N.Y. Acad. Scis. (pres'. coun. 1990—, mem. com. human rights 1996—), Italian Soc. Advancement Sci. (hon. mem.), Sigma Xi (disting. lectr. 1996—, past pres., bd. dirs., chair ethics com.), Nat. Acad. Engring. (chair steering com. on megacities 1999-, Russian prize com. 2000, fgn. sec. 2003—, chair com. on internat. affairs), Marco Polo Soc. (pres. U.S. br.), Italian Nat. Acad. Science. Home: 5 Terrace Dr Port Washington NY 11050-3419 Office: Polytechnic U 6 Metrotech Ctr Brooklyn NY 11201-3840*

BUGLIOSI, VINCENT T., lawyer; b. Hibbing, Minn., Aug. 18, 1934; s. Vincent and Ida (Valerie) B.; m. Gail Margaret Talluto, July 21, 1956; children: Wendy Suzanna, Vincent John. BBA, U. Miami, Fla., 1956; LL.B., UCLA, 1964. Bar: Calif. 1964. Dep. dist. atty., Los Angeles County, 1964-72; pvt. practice law Beverly Hills, Calif., 1972—. Prof. criminal law Beverly Sch. Law, Los Angeles, 1968-74 Author: Drugs in America, The Case For Victory, 1991, Outrage: The Five Reasons O.J. Simpson Got Away with Murder, 1996, No Island of Sanity: Paula Jones v. Bill Clinton-The Supreme Court on Trial, 1998, The Betrayal of America: How the Supreme Court Undermined the Constitution and Chose Our President, 2001, Reclaiming History: The Assassination of President John F. Kennedy, 2007; co-author: (with Curt Gentry) Helter-Skelter: The True Story of the Manson Murders, 1974, (with Ken Hurwitz) Till Death Us Do Part: A True Murder Mystery, 1978, (with Bruce B. Henderson) And the Sea Will Tell, 1991 Candidate for dist. atty., Los Angeles County, 1972, Dem. candidate Calif. atty. gen., 1974. Served to capt. AUS, 1957. Office: 3699 Wilshire Blvd #850 Los Angeles CA 90010*

BUGNI JUHN, GLORIA See MCMASTER, GLORIA

BUHAGIAR, MARION, editor, writer; b. NYC, Oct. 27, 1932; d. George and Mae (Pietrzak) B.; 1 child, Alexa Ragozin. BA cum laude, Hunter Coll., 1953; postgrad., Mt. Holyoke Coll., 1954. Economist U.S. Dept. Commerce, 1954-57; bus. reporter Time mag., 1957-59; assoc. editor Fortune mag., 1960-73, story devel. editor, 1970-73; text editor Time-Life Books, NYC, 1973-76; v.p. Boardroom Inc., 1977-84; editor Boardroom Reports, 1977-84; exec. editor Bottom Line/Personal, 1980-84; pres. Expert Connections, NYC, 1994—2002; editor Street Smart Investing, 1987-89; ret., 2003. Author: How to Build a College Fund for Your Child, 1989, Battle Plan for American Business, 1992, I-Power, 1992; editor: The Book of Secrets, 1989. Trustee, Save Chelsea Hist. Dist., NYC E-mail: buhmarion@yahoo.com.

BUHAIN, WILFRIDO JAVIER, medical educator; b. Bacoor, Cavite, Philippines, Oct. 12, 1940; m. Carlota Torres; children: Ronald, Edgar. AA, BS, U. Philippines, 1959, MD, 1964. Diplomate Am. Bd. Internal Medicine, Am. Bd. Pulmonary Diseases. Rsch. fellow in cardiology U. Philippines, Philippine Gen. Hosp., 1964-65; rotating intern Queens Hosp. Ctr., NYC, 1965-66, resident in internal medicine, 1965-68; clin. fellow in pulmonary diseases Hosp. of U. Pa., 1968-69, chief pulmonary function lab. dept. medicine, 1971-72; rsch. fellow in pulmonary diseases Hosp. of U. Pa., VA Hosp., Phila., 1969-71; assoc. in medicine, cardiovascular-pulmonary div. med. dept. U. Pa. Sch. Medicine, 1971-72; assoc. in medicine, dept. medicine Mt. Sinai Sch. Medicine, CUNY, 1972-74; clin. instr. medicine Georgetown U., 1976-95; ret. Chief pulmonary function lab. dept. medicine Mt. Sinai Hosp. Svcs./City Hosp. Ctr. at Elmhurst, 1973-74; med. dir. respiratory therapy dept. Mt. Vernon Hosp., 1978—2003, chmn. dept. medicine, 1987-88, pres. med. staff, 1996-98; mem. exec. com. Alexandria Hosp., 1983; trustee, chmn. med. affairs coun. Inova Health Sys., 1998-99. Contbr. articles to profl. jours. Grantee, Queensborough Soc., Pa. Thoracic Soc. Fellow ACP, Am. Coll. Chest Physicians; mem. Am. Soc. Internal Medicine, Alexandria Med. Soc., Va. Med. Soc., Philippine Med. Assn. (exec. dir., past pres. Metro-Washington), Assn. Philippine Physicians in Am. (v.p.). Avocations: tennis, golf, ballroom dancing. Personal E-mail: wbs1997@cox.net.

BUHKS, EPHRAIM, college administrator, technology educator; b. Kishinev, U.S.S.R., Apr. 30, 1949; came to U.S., 1980; BS in Physics, Kishinev U., 1971; PhD in Chemistry, Tel Aviv U., 1980. Rsch. fellow U. Del., Newark, 1980-81; project leader Solavolt Internat. (Shell), Newark, 1981-83; mgr. R&D B.F. Goodrich R&D Ctr., Brecksville, Ohio, 1983-87; tech. dir. Sunstone Inc., Dayton, N.J., 1987-89; asst. dir. ORT Ops. U.S.A., NYC, 1990-97, dep. dir., 1996-97, dir., 1997—; acting dir. Bramson ORT Tech. Inst., NYC, 1994—97; dir. Bramson ORT Coll., 2003—. Exec. vice chmn. bd. trustees Bramson ORT Coll., 2002—; cons. Johnson Rsch. Found., U. Pa., Phila., 1981—83, Kingston Tech., Inc., Dayton, 1989, Energia, Inc., Princeton, NJ, 1989—90. Editor: Protein Structure & Electronic Reactivity, 1987; contbr. over 42 articles to profl. jours. Recipient Outstanding Svc. award, Real Estate and Constrn. chpt. Am. ORT, 2002, Disting. Svc. award, Temple Israel of Jamaica, N.Y., 2003, Corning Inc. 10-Yr. Leadership award, Commn. on Ind. Colls. and Univs., 2004; fellow Von Humboldt Found., 1980; Solar Energy Rsch. Inst. fellow, 1980. Mem. Am. Chem. Soc., Am. Phys. Soc., Optical Soc. Am., Soc. Photo-Electric Engrs. Achievements include patent for Electrodeless Heterogeneous Polypyrrole Composites; inventor of Method and Device for Optical Storage of Information, Fiber-Optic Viewer, Application of IR Stimulation Phosphors in IR Detectors, IR Imaging System, X-Ray Imaging with Fluorescence Dyes and Memory Phosphors, PVC/Copper Sulfide Electrical Composites, Electrochromic Displays, Solar Cells, Sensors, Optical Disc Replication Process, Resistance Heating Device Bond on Polypyrrole, Electronic and Optical Ice Sensors, administration of higher education/degree programs in computer programming, computer networks, computer aided design, computerized accounting, business management, electronics and office technology, med. asst. programs, tchr. tng. in computer technology and internet, internet based distance learning. Home: 26 Indian Run Rd Princeton Junction NJ 08550-1406 Office: ORT Ops USA 6930 Austin St Forest Hills NY 11375 Home Phone: 609-275-7184; Office Phone: 718-268-7110. E-mail: ebuhks@ortopsusa.org.

BUHL, CYNTHIA MAUREEN, advocate, educator; b. LA, Apr. 14, 1952; d. Albert Buhl and Dorothy Jane (Loth) Henry. BA, Lewis & Clark Coll., 1974. Dir. Resource and Counseling Ctr., Portland Youth Advs., Oreg., 1971-72; resource coordinator S.E. Youth Service Ctr., Portland Action Coms. Together, 1975-77; sec., asst. Human Rights Office Nat. Council Chs. Christ, NYC, 1977-78; human rights coordinator Coalition for a New Fgn. and Mil. Policy, Washington, 1978-85; cons. Fgn. Policy Edn. Fund, Washington, 1986; nat. adv. bd. Caribbean Basin Info. Project, 1983-85; bd. dirs., legis. dir. Pax Am.'s/Priorities-PAC, 1986-90; legis. dir. Ctrl. Am. Working Group, 1990-93; dir. Indigenous Peoples Program, Bank Info. Ctr., 1994-96; legis. dir. U.S. Rep. James A. McGovern, 1997—. Author: Citizen's Guide to the Multilateral Development Banks and Indigenous Peoples: The World Bank, 1994, Spanish transl., 1995, Bahasa transl., 1996, Russian transl., 1996; co-editor: Central America 1985: Basic Information and Legislative History on U.S.-Central American Relations, 1985. Contbr. articles to various jours., mags. Co-chmn. Human Rights Working Group, Washington, 1978-81, chmn., 1982-85; chmn. Central Am. Lobby Group, 1983-85. Office Phone: 202-225-6101.

BUHLER, JILL LORIE, editor, writer; b. Seattle, Dec. 7, 1945; d. Oscar John and Marcella Jane (Hearing) Younce; 1 child, Lori Jill Moody; m. John Buhler, 1990; stepchildren: Christie Reynolds, Cathie Zatarian, Mike. AA in Gen. Edn., Am. River Coll., Sacramento, 1969; BA in Journalism with honors, Sacramento State U., Calif., 1973. Reporter Carmichael (Calif.) Courier, 1968-70; mng. editor Quarter Horse of the Pacific Coast, Sacramento, 1970-75, editor, 1975-84, Golden State Program Jour., 1978, Nat. Reined Cow Horse Assn. News, Sacramento, 1983-88, Pacific Coast Jour., Sacramento, 1984-88, Nat. Snaffle Bit Assn. News, Sacramento, 1988; pres., CEO Comm. Plus, Port Townsend, Wash., 1988—; bd. sec. N.W. Maritime Ctr., 2001—; editor-in-chief Peninsula Lifestyle mag., 2006—. Mag. cons., 1975—. Interviewer Pres. Ronald Regan, Washington, 1983; mng. editor Wash. Thoroughbred, 1989-90; editor-in-chief Peninsula Lifestyle Mag., 2005-. Mem. 1st profl. communicators mission to USSR, 1988; bd. dirs. Carmichael Winding Way, Pasadena Homeowners Assn., 1985-87; mem. scholarship com. Thoroughbred Horse Racing's United Scholarship Trust; mem. governing bd. Wash. State Hosp. Assn., 1996-2000, mem. legis. policy com., 1999—, hosp. commr. Jefferson Healthcare, 1995—, chair bd. dirs. 1997-2000, 2006-, sec., 2004; mem. Jefferson County Bd. Health, 1997—, vice chmn., 1998, chmn. 2001; mem. Wash. State Health Care Leadership Com., 2003-. Recipient 1st pl. feature award, 1970, 1st pl. editl. award Jour. Assn. Jr. Colls., 1971, 1st pl. design award WCHB Yuba-Sutter Counties, Marysville, Calif., 1985, Photography awards, 1994, 95, 96. Mem. Am. River Jaycees (Speaking award 1982), Am. Horse Publs. (1st Pl. Editl. award 1983, 86), Port Townsend C. of C. (trustee, v.p. 1993, pres. 1994, officer 1996, 97, 98), Mensa (bd. dirs., asst. local sec., activities dir. 1987-88, membership chair 1988-90), Kiwanis Internat. (chair maj. emphasis program com., treas. 1992—), 5th Wheel Touring Soc. (v.p. 1970). Republican. Roman Catholic. Avocations: sailing, photography. Home Phone: 360-385-1375; Office Phone: 360-379-1385. Personal E-mail: jillb@olypen.com.

BUHLER, LESLIE LYNN, museum director; BA in History and Art History with honors, Syracuse U., 1969; postgrad., New Sch. for Social Rsch., 1971, Am. U., 1980. Asst. for cmty. programs Met. Mus. Art, NYC, 1970-72; resident assoc. program Smithsonian Instn., Washington, 1972-75; instl. devel. officer Nat. Archives and Records Svc., Washington, 1975-78; cons. Alban Inst., Inc., Bethesda, Md., 1978—95; exec. dir. Tudor Place Hist. House and Garden, Washington, 2000—. Grant reviewer Office of Mus. Programs, NEH, Washington, 1973-74. Bd. dirs. Mus. of City of Washington, 1980-84; vol. advisor Nat. Mus. for Bldg. Arts, Washington, 1977-79. Recipient cert. of appreciation Am. Revolution Bicentennial Adminstrn., 1976. Office: Tudor Place Found 1644 31st St NW Washington DC 20007

BUHNER, BYRON BEVIS, health science facility administrator; b. Hammond, Ind., Feb. 19, 1950; s. John Colin and Betty (Bevis) B.; children: Zachery Aaron, Rebecca Bevis. AB in Comm., Ind. U., 1976, MS in Human Resource Devel., 1981. Adminstr. Ind. U., Indpls., 1976-77, instr. evaluator sch. nursing, 1981-82; tng. specialist Ayr-Way, Target Stores, Indpls., 1977-81; assoc. exec. dir. Cen. Ind. Regional Blood Ctr., Indpls., 1984-88, pres., chief exec. officer, 1988—; founding mem. Blood Ctrs. Ins. Exch., Risk Retention Group, 1993, chmn. bd. dirs., 1993-96, dir., 1996—2006; adminstr. Blood Rsch. and Edn. Foundn. of Ind., Inc., Indpls., 1985-89, bd. mem., 1989-94. Dean's adv. coun. Ind. U. Sch. Liberal Arts, 1999—; bd. dirs. Irwin Union Bank & Trust, Hamilton County. Producer: Multi-Image film, Focus on Transition, 1981, A Manager's Perspective, 1981; photographer: Sound, Slide program, Wearable - Arts '81. Trustee Coun. Cmty. Blood Ctrs., 1986-97, chmn. purchasing com., 1988-92, chmn. fin. com., treas., 1992-94, v.p., 1994-96, pres., 1997-99, chmn. exec. com., chmn. group svcs. com., chmn. long-range planning com. Mem. Am. Acad. Healthcare Execs. (diplomate), Ind. U. Alumni Assn. (bd. dirs. 1983-88), Am. Assn. Blood Banks, Ind. Assn. Blood Banks (bd. dirs. 1988-91). Avocations: sailing, jogging, hockey, photography, coaching youth sports. Home: 13002 Fairfax Ct Mc Cordsville IN 46055 Office: Indiana Blood Ctr 3450 N Meridian St Indianapolis IN 46208-4437 Office Phone: 317-916-5001. Business E-Mail: bbuhner@indianablood.org.

BUHNER, STEPHEN HARROD, research scientist; b. Louisville, July 15, 1952; s. John Harrod Buhner and Sue Morrow Cox; m. Trishuwa Buhner, Dec. 17, 1982; 1 child, Benjamin Bailey-Buhner. BA, Loretto Heights, Denver, 1981. Furniture maker The Skilled Hand, Denver, 1975—84; psychotherapist Boulder, 1985—96; sr. rschr. Found. for Gaian Studies, Silver City, N.Mex., 1990—; clin. herbalist Boulder, 1990—2000; instr. Rocky Mountain Ctr. for Botanic Studies, Boulder, 1992—97. Lectr., workshop leader Found. for Gaian Studies, Silver City, N.Mex., 1996—. Author: (book) Sacred Plant Medicine, 1996 (Finalist Colo. and Small Press Book awards, 1996), One Spirit Many Peoples, 1997, Sacred and Herbal Healing Beers: The Secrets of Ancient Fermentation, 1998 (Foreword Mag. book Yr., 1999, Benjamin Franklin award, 1999, Quill and Tankard award, 1999), Herbal Antibiotics, 1999, Herbs for Hepatitis C and the Liver, 2000, The Lost Language of Plants: The Ecological Importance of Plant Medicines to Life on Earth, 2002 (Nautilus award, 2003, ForeWord Mag. award, 2003), Vital Man, 2002, The Fasting Path, 2003 (Spirituality and Health Book Yr., 2004), Secret Teachings of Plants, 2004, Healing Lyme, 2005, Natural Testosterone Plan, 2007, The Taste of Wild Water: Poems and Stories Found While Walking in Woods. Pres., lobbyist, mng. editor Colo. Assn. Holistic Healing Profls., Boulder, 1990—95. Mem.: PEN, Acad. Am. Poets, Western Writers Am., Authors Guild, Intertel, Mensa. Independent. Mem. Earth-Centered Ch. Home: 8 Pioneer Rd Silver City NM 88061 Office: Found for Gaian Studies 8 Pioneer Rd Silver City NM 88061 Home Phone: 505-538-5498. Personal E-mail: stephen@gaianstudies.org.

BUHRMASTER, ROBERT C., manufacturing executive; b. 1947; B in Mech. Engring., Rensselaer Poly. Inst.; MBA, Dartmouth Coll. With Corning Inc., Corning, N.Y.; exec. v.p. Jostens, Inc., Mpls., 1992-93, pres., COO, 1993, CEO, 1994, chmn. bd. dirs., 1998—. Bd. dirs. Toro Corp., Nat. Alliance of Bus. Pres. Viking coun. Boy Scouts. Am.; past bd. dirs. Exec. Coun. Fgn. Diplomats, Marietta Corp. Mem. U.S. Advanced Ceramics Assn. (founding mem.). Office: 5501 Norman Center Dr Minneapolis MN 55437-1040 Office Fax: 952-897-4116.

BUHROW, WILLIAM CARL, religious organization administrator; b. Cleve., Jan. 18, 1934; s. Philip John and Edith Rose (Leutz) B.; m. Carole Corinne Craven, Feb. 14, 1959; children: William Carl Jr., David Paul, Peter John, Carole Lynn. Diploma, Phila. Coll. Bible, 1954; BA, Wheaton Coll., Ill., 1956, MA, 1959. Ordained to ministry Gen. Assn. Regular Bapt. Chs., 1958. Asst. pastor (Hydewood Park Bapt. Ch.), N. Plainfield, NJ, 1959-63; with Continental Fed. Savs. & Loan Assn., Cleve., 1963-81, sr. v.p., 1971-75, pres., chief exec. officer, dir., 1975-81; chmn. bd. Security Savs. Mortgage Corp., Citizens Service Corp., New Market Corp., CFS Service Corp., 1975-81; trustee Credit Bur. Cleve., 1975-81, Bldg. Expositions, Inc., 1974-84; registered rep. IDS/Am. Express, Cleve., 1982-83; gen. credit mgr. Forest City Enterprises, Inc., Cleve., 1983-85; pres. Forest City Ins. Agy., Inc., Cleve., 1983-85; asst. v.p. Mellon Fin. Services Corp., Cleve., 1985-87; exec. adminstr. The Gospel Ho. Ch. and Evangelistic Ctr., Walton Hills, Ohio, 1988—. Trustee Bapt. Bible Coll. and Theol. Sem., Clarks Summit, Pa., 1977-90; vice chmn. bd. deacons Cedar Hill Bapt. Ch., Cleveland Heights, Ohio, 1981-87; trustee, sec. and treas. Gospel House Prison Ministry Found., 1992—. Mem. Christian Bus. Men's Com. Internat., Nat. Assn. Ch. Bus. Adminstrn. Baptist. Home: 1044 Linden Ln Lyndhurst OH 44124-1051 Office: 14707 Alexander Rd Cleveland OH 44146-4924 *The supreme goal of my life is to please and honor the Lord Jesus Christ in all that I say and do. The standards, goals, and ideals outlined in the Bible, God's Holy Word, are the ones which I have adopted for my life. True happiness for me lies in the accomplishment of God's perfect will in my life and that of my family and in introducing others to Christ so they may know Him as their own personal Saviour, too. Herein lies the key to my success as a Christian administrator.*

BUI, MAI HA, molecular biologist, researcher; b. Da-Lat, Viet Nam, Apr. 28, 1972; d. Thanh Duong and Hong Lam; m. Tuan Le Bui, July 4, 1996; children: Kimberly Thanh, Anthony Le, Phillippe Le, Alan Le. BS, Rush U., Chgo., 1995. Med. technologist Rush Med. Ctr., Chgo., 1996—96; assoc. microbiologist, infectious disease rsch. Abbott Labs., Abbott Park, Ill., 1996—2003, assoc. microbiologist, anti-cancer rsch., 2003—06, cell/molecular biologist, cancer rsch., 2006—. Group leader Vietnamese Buddhist Truc Lam Youth Assn., Chgo., 1995—2007. Recipient Discovery Microbiology award, Abbott Labs., 1997, Star award, 2000. Home: 1033 S Sienna Ct Round Lake IL 60073 Business E-Mail: mai.bui@abbott.com.

BUI, PHONG, painter; b. Hue, Vietnam, 1964; arrived in US, 1980; BFA, Phila. Coll. Art, 1985; student, NY Studio Sch. Painting, 1985—87. Lectr. Parsons Sch. Design; tchr. Internat. Sch. Art. One-man shows include Galleria ISA, Montecastello, 1994, Sussex County Cmty. Coll. Gallery, NJ, 1995, Homage to Meyer Schapiro: An Architectonic Installation, Holland Tunnel Art Projects, 2000, For Meyer and Lillian, U. of the Arts, Phila., 2002, Hybrid Carnival for St. Exupery #2 and #3, Sarah Bowen Gallery, 2005, exhibited in group shows at Am. Acad. Arts & Letters, NY, 2005, Segments & Connections, Wooster Arts Space, NY, 2005, Continuous Mark: 40 Yrs. of NY Studio Sch., 2005. Grantee Arcadia Traveling fellowship, Hobenberg Traveling fellowship, Charles Revson Found. grant, Pollock-Krasner Found. fellowship, 1994. Mailing: c/o Sarah Bowen Gallery 210 N 6th St Williamsburg Brooklyn NY 11211

BUIA, CALIN IOAN, neuroscientist; b. Blaj, Alba, Romania, May 1, 1973; s. Ioan and Eva Buia. PhD, U. NC, Chapel Hill, 2003. Assoc. U. NC, Chapel Hill, 2003—. Mem.: Soc. Neurosci. (assoc.).

BUISHAS, KRISTIN MAUREEN, elementary school educator; b. Harvey, Ill., Jan. 1, 1980; d. John Martin and Mary Louise Buishas. BA, Ea. Ill. U., 2002. Cert. elem. educator Ill., 2003. Tchr. St. Kieran, Chicago Heights, Ill., 2003—. Recipient Spl. Edn. Achievement award, Ea. Ill. U., 1999. Mem.: ASCD (assoc.). Office: St Kieran School 700 W 195th St Chicago Heights IL 60411 Home Phone: 708-606-3280; Office Phone: 708-754-8999. Personal E-mail: kbuishas@hotmail.com.

BUISSONNIÈRE, MARINE, international organization administrator; physician; Korea rep. Doctors Without Borders/Médecins Sans Frontières, now sec. gen. Office: Doctors Without Borders 2nd Floor 333 7th Ave New York NY 10001-5004

BUIST, KATHY, artist; b. Allendale, Mich., Nov. 12, 1959; d. Robert and Nina Buist; BFA, Kendall Sch. of Design, Mich., 1981; MFA (hon.), NY Acad. Art, 1996. Fellowship Va. Ctr. for Creative Arts, Vt. Studio Ctr., 1993—97. Exhibitions include Nabi Gallery, Frederick Gallery, Allenhurst, NJ, Water St. Gallery, Boston Art, Mass., Sotheby's, Parrish Art Mus. Mem.: Audubon Artists Art Soc. (assoc.), Guild Shrewsbury (assoc.), Nat. Plein Air Painters (assoc.), Jersey Shore Plein Art Painters (assoc.), Salmagundi Art Club (assoc.). Home: 16E 201 E 21st St New York NY 10010 Home Phone: 786-390-3338. Personal E-mail: artist@kathybuist.com.

BUIST, NEIL ROBERTSON MACKENZIE, pediatric educator, medical association administrator; b. Karachi, India, July 11, 1932; m. Sonia Chapman; children: Catriona, Alison, Diana. Degree with commendation, U. St. Andrews, Scotland, MB, ChB, 1956; Diploma of Child Health, London U., England, 1960. Diplomate Am. Bd. Med. Genetics, Am. Bd. Clinical Genetics. House physician internal medicine Arbroath Infirmary, 1956-57; house physician externe cardiopulmonary dept. Hosp. Marie Lannelongue, Paris, 1957; house surgeon Royal Hosp. Sick Children, Edinburgh, Scotland, 1957; commd. far east med. officer Regimental Military Svc., 1957-60; house physician Royal Infirmary, Dundee, Scotland, 1960; registrar internal medicine Maryfield Hosp., Dundee, Scotland, 1960-62; lectr. child health U. St. Andrews, Dundee, Scotland, 1962-64; rsch. fellow pediatric micro-chemistry, Sch. Health Sci. U. Colo., Denver, 1964-66; asst. prof. pediatrics, Sch. Medicine U. Oreg., Portland, 1966-70; dir. Pediatrics Metabolic Lab, Oreg. Health Sci. U., Portland, 1966-93, Metabolic Birth Defects Ctr., Oreg. Health Sci. U., Portland, 1966-98; assoc. prof. pediat. and med. genetics Oreg. Health Sci. U., Portland, 1970—76, prof. pediat. and med. genetics, 1976—98, prof. emeritus. Med. cons. Northwest Regional Newborn Screening Program, Portland, 1970—; vis. prof. WHO, China, 1988, U. Colo., 1990, Wesley Med. Ctr., Kans., 1991, Phoenix Children's Hosp., Ariz., 1991, Tucson Med. Ctr., Ariz., 1991, U. Ill., Chgo., 1991, Kapoiolani Med. Ctr., Hawaii, 1992, Shriners Hosp. for Crippled Children., Hawaii, 1992, Ark. Children's Hosp., 1993, Australasian Soc. for Human Genetics, New Zealand, 1994, LBJ Med. Ctr., Americas Samoa, 1994, Mahidol U., Bangkok, 1996, U. P.R., 1996, U. Auckland (New Zealand), 1997, Ctrl. Valley Children's Hosp., 1996-, U. Rochester, 2004, emergency disaster response physician, N.W. Med. Teams Internat., Afghanistan, 2002, Ethiopia, 2004, Sri Lanka, 2005. Author: (with others) Textbook of Pediatrics, 1973, Inherited Disorders of Amino Acid Metabolism, 1974, 1985, Clinics in Endocrinolog and Metabolism: Aspects of Neonatal Metabolism, 1976, Textbook of Pediatrics, 1978, Practice of Pediatrics, 1980, Management of High-Risk Pregnancy, 1980, Current Occular Therapy, 1980, Practice of Pediatrics, 1981, Clinics in Endocrinology and Metabolism: Aspects of Neonatal Metabolism, 1981, Textbook of Pediatrics, 1984, Disorders of Fatty Acid Metabolism in the Pediatric Practice, 1990, Birth Defects Encyclopedia, 1990, 1991, Treatment of Genetic Disease, 1991, Pediatric Clinics of North Americs Medical Genetics II, 1992, Forfar & Arneil's Textbook of Paediatrics, 1992, 97, Galactosemia New Frontiers in Research, 1993, New Horizons in Neonatal Screening, 1994, New Trends in Neonatal Screening, 1994, Alpha-1-Antitrypsin Deficiency, 1994, Diseases of the Fetus and Newborn, 1995, Inborn Metabolic Diseases: Diagnosis and Treatment, 1995; cons. editor: Inborn Metabolic Disease Text, 1995; editorial bd. mem.: Jour. of Inherited Metabolic Diseases, 1977—, Kelley Practice of Pediatrics, 1980-87, Screening, 1991-96; jour. reviewer: Am. Jour. of Human Genetics, Jour. of Pediatrics, Pediatric Rsch., Screening. Adv. com. Tri County March of Dimes, Portland, 1977—; physician Diabetic Children's Camp, 1967—, Muscle Biopsy Clinic Shriners Hosp., 1989—; bd. dirs. Mize Info. Enterprises, Dallas, 1987—. Fellow Royal Coll. Physicians Edinburgh, Fogarty Internat. Vis. Scientist, Royal Coll. Physicians Edinburgh; mem. Brit. Med. Assn., Western Soc. Pediatric Rsch. (coun. mem. 1966—), Pacific North West Pediatric Soc., Am. Pediatric Soc., Soc. for the Study of Inborn Errors of Metabolism, Soc. for Inherited Metabolic Disorders (treas. 1977-2000, pres. 2000-02), Oreg. Pediatric Soc., Oreg. Diabetes Assn., Portland Acad. Pediatrics, Internat. Newborn Screening Soc. Coun. (founding mem. 1988—). Avocations: fishing, gardening, travel. Personal E-mail: buistnrm@aol.com.

BUIST, RICHARDSON, retired corporate executive, retired banker; b. Bklyn., Aug. 8, 1921; s. George Lamb and Adelaide (Richardson) Buist; m. Jean Mackerley, Oct. 2, 1948; children: Peter Richardson, Jean Morford Buist Earle, M. Betsi Bixby. Student, Yale U. Advt. copywriter Ecloss Co., Sparta, NJ, 1946-48; advt. mgr. Sussex County Ind., Newton, NJ, 1948-50, Dover Advance, 1950-53; bus. mgr. N.J. Herald, Inc., Newton, 1953-70, dir., v.p., 1958-70, pub., 1967-70; dir. N.J. Press Assn., 1966-70; asst. sec., asst. treas. Morford Conservation Co., Hamburg, 1965-72, pres., 1986-95, v.p., 1995-2000, dir. emeritus, 2000—. Trust officer Midlantic Nat. Bank/Susex & Mchts., Newton, 1971—88, Midlantic Nat. Bank, Edison, NJ, 1972—86, cons., 1986—90; dir. Newton Cemetery Co., 1989—2000, v.p., 1998—2000. Chmn. pub. rels. Morris-Sussex area coun. Boys Scouts Am., 1955—75; trustee Sussex County Music Found., 1955—75, pres., 1959—61; pres. Sussex County chpt. Am. Cancer Soc., 1956—58; mem. Morris-Sussex Area Health Facilities Planning Coun., 1965—68; v.p. Sussex County Coun. Arts, 1971—73; v.p., chmn. fin. devel. com. Newton Meml. Hosp., 1966—68, bd. govs., 1993—95, pres. bd. govs., 1968—71, chmn., 1971—73, emeritus, 1995—; founding incorporator, trustee NW Jersey Health Care, 1971—76; trustee, mem. exec. com. regional health planning coun. Health Sys. Agy., 1976—83, 1984—87, v.p., 1978—79; trustee United Way Sussex County, 1984—90, spl. gifts chmn., 1984—88, mem. allocations com., 1990—93; mem. Sussex County Arts and Heritage Coun., chmn. hist. house tour, 1993—95; mem. steering com. N.J. Highlands Coalition, 1993—; dir. N. Jersey Health Care Corp., 1988—95, asst. treas., 1991—93, dir. emeritus, 1995—; dir. Prime Care, Inc., 1989—95, chmn. bd. trustees, 1989—92. Mem.: Am. Vet. Med. Soc. Aux. (nat. chmn. legis. com. 1986—88, mem. long-range planning com. 1990—95, chmn. 1992, mem. constn. by-laws com. 1993—95), N.J. Vet. Med. Soc. Aux. (del. 1979—82, 1988—91, 2d v.p. 1990—91), Vernon Civic Assn. (dir. 1996—2000, v.p. 1997—98), Rotary (pres. 1967—68, Paul Harris fellow 1988, Above Self award 1993, Meritorious Svc. award 1998). Home: 4123 Fellowship Rd Basking Ridge NJ 07920 E-mail: rbuist@verizon.net.

BUJA, L. MAXIMILIAN, pathologist, academic administrator, educator; b. New Orleans, Dec. 30, 1942; s. Louis Marcus and Fay Maxine (Kofler) B.; m. Donna Steele Kinney, Apr. 7, 1966; children: Maximilian Kinney, Evan Louis, Gregory James. BS in Biology magna cum laude, Loyola U., New Orleans, 1964; MD with honors, Tulane U., 1967, MS in Anatomy, 1968. Diplomate Am. Bd. Pathology. Resident in pathology Nat. Cancer Inst./NIH, Bethesda, Md., 1970—72; sr. investigator pathology Nat. Heart and Lung Inst./NIH, Bethesda, Md., 1972—74; asst. prof. pathology U. Tex. Health Sci. Ctr. at Dallas, 1974—77, assoc. prof. pathology, 1977—81; prof. pathology U. Tex. Southwestern Med. Ctr. at Dallas, 1981—89, acting chmn. dept. pathology, 1988—89; prof. pathology and lab. medicine U. Tex. Health Sci. Ctr. at Houston, 1989—, chmn. dept. pathology and lab. medicine, 1989—96; chmn. dept. clin. lab. scis. U. Tex.-Houston Health Sci. Ctr., 1993—96, disting. chair pathology and lab. med., 1995—, dean, 1996—2003, exec. v.p. acad. affairs, 2003—, H. Wayne Hightower disting. prof. in med. scis., 2000—03; chief of svc. clin. pathology lab. Hermann Hosp., Houston, 1989—96; pathologist-in-chief clin. pathology lab. Lyndon Baines Johnson Gen. Hosp., Houston, 1990—96; prof. lab. medicine U. Tex. Anderson Cancer Ctr., Houston, 1990—. Lectr. pathology; mem. autopsy svc.; mem. Tex. Heart Inst. St. Luke's Episcopal Hosp., Houston, 1989—, dir. Cardiovascular Pathology Rsch., 1989—95, chief cardiovasc. pathology, 2000—; 1st Chancellor's Health fellow in edn. U. Tex. System; cons. in field. Author (with Hillis and Willerson): Ischemic Heart Disease-Clinical and Pathophysiological Aspects, 1982; author: (with others) Calcium Antagonists and Cardiovascular Disease, 1984; author: Physiology and Pathophysiology of the Heart, 1984, Cardiovascular Imaging, 1991, Cardiovascular Medicine, 1995; co-author: Netter's Illustrated Human Pathology, 2005; contbg. editor: Clin. Nuc. Cardiology, 1979; mem. editl. bd. Am. Jour. Cardiovascular Pathology, 1985—95, Am. Jour. Cardiology, 1982—88, 1999—, Am. Jour. Pathology, 1980—92, Archives of Pathology and Lab. Medicine, 1985—96, assoc. editor, 2006—, mem. editl. bd. Cardiovascular Pathology, 1991—, Circulation, 1983—88, Circulation Rsch., 1990—99, Lab. Investigation, 1984—2005, Tex. Medicine, 1984—87, Exptl. Molecular Pathology, 1999—, Jour. Am. Coll. Cardiology, 2000—04, Jour. Burns, 2001; assoc. editor: Circulation, 1993—2004; contbr. articles to profl. jours. Surgeon with USPHS, 1968-74. Recipient Joseph Diaz award Loyola U., Order of the Gold-Tipped Stethoscope award Tulane U., John Herr Musser Meml. prize; Sabbatical fellow German Sci. Found., U. Cologne, West Germany, 1988; grantee NIH, 1979, 80, 81, 84, 86-87, 89-90, 93-98, U. Tex., 1993—. Fellow: AAAS, Internat. Soc. for Heart Rsch., Am. Heart Assn. (fellow coun. on basic sci. on clin. cardiology, on atherosclerosis, on circulation, inaugural fellow basic cardiovasc. scis.), Am. Coll. Cardiology; mem.: AMA, U.S. and Can. Acad. Pathology, Tex. Soc. Microscopy, So. Soc. for Clin. Investigation, Soc. Exec. Leadership in Acad. Medicine, Histochem. Soc., Assn. Am. Med. Colls. (coun. deans 1996—2003), Am. Soc. Clin. Pathologists, Am. Soc. Clin. Investigation, Tex. Soc. Pathologists (pres. 1998, George T. Caldwell, M.D. Disting. Svc. award 2005), Tex. Med. Assn., Soc. Cardiovasc. Pathology (Merit award 1998), Internat. Acad. Pathology, Houston Soc. Clin. Pathologists (pres. 1995—96, Harlan J. Spjut award 1997), Harris County Med. Soc. (bd. dirs. 1997—), Coll. Am. Pathologists, Am. Soc. Cell Biology, Am. Fedn. Med. Rsch., Am. Coll. Healthcare Execs. (assoc.), ACP Execs., Am. Soc. Investigative Pathology, Houston Philos. Soc., Sigma Xi Sci., Beta Beta Beta, Alpha Omega Alpha. Achievements include rsch. on cardiovascular pathology; on mechanisms of cell injury, with emphasis on cell membrane integrity and intracellular electrolyte balance; on measurement of intracellular electrolytes, electron probe x-ray microanalysis and fluorescent probes; on the devel. and regenerative potential of cardiac muscle. Office: U Tex Health Sci Ctr 7000 Fannin St Ste 1715 Houston TX 77030-1501 Office Phone: 713-500-3062.

BUJESE, ARLENE, artist, art dealer, curator; d. Alfred L. Bujese and Catherine E. Carroll. Grad. in graphics, Corcoran Sch. Art, Washington, 1970; AB, Hood Coll., Frederick, Md., 1975, MA, 1998. Tchr. St. John's Literary Inst., Frederick, 1975—82; dir., pres. Phoenix II Gallery, 1980—82; dir. Benton Gallery, Southampton, NY, 1983—93; dir., owner Arlene Bujese Gallery, East Hampton, NY, 1994—2006; curator Ossorio Found., Southampton, 2006—. Instr. part-time Hood Coll., Frederick, 1980—84; ind. curator Spanierman Gallery, East Hampton, 2006—; curator Springs Invitational, East Hampton, 2007; spkr. in field at numerous art events. Editor: (book) 25 Artists, 1981; one-woman shows include Hood Coll., Frederick, 1974, Weinberg Ctr. Arts, DC, 1983, Represented in permanent collections Arbusto and Assocs., NY, Chelsey and Co., Chgo., Parrish Mus., Southampton, Shell Oil, San Juan, PR, Reinauer Transp. Co., Washington Post, DC, World Bank, exhibitions include Margaret Dickey Gallery, 1969, Corcoran Dupont Ctr., 1969, Arts Club Washington, 1970, Washington Theatre Club, 1970, Charles Mann Gallery, NYC, 1970—75, No. Va. CC, 1971, Shady Grove Theatre, Md., 1971, Parrish Mus., Southampton, 1971, 1974, Okla. Art Ctr., 1972, Internat. Monetar Fund, 1972, Hood Coll., Frederick, 1974, Guild Hall Mus., East Hampton, 1975, Ann. Artist Springs Invitationals, 1979—, Hunterdon Art Ctr., NJ, 1984, Millenium Galley, East Hampton, 1995. Chair Ann. East End Hospice Box Art Benefit, West Hampton, 2001—; art donor orgns. including: East Hampton Childcare Ctr., NY, The Retreat, Guild Hall Mus. Mem.: Garden Conservatory, Parrish Mus. Democrat. Avocation: landscaping. Office: Ossorio Found 164 Mariner Dr Southampton NY 11968

BUJOLD, LOIS MCMASTER, writer; b. Columbus, Ohio, Nov. 2, 1949; d. Robert Charles and Laura Elizabeth (Gerould) McMaster; m. John Fredric Bujold, Oct. 9, 1971 (div. Dec. 1992); children: Anne Elizabeth, Paul André. Author: (novels) Shards of Honor, 1986, The Warrior's Apprentice, 1986, Ethan of Athos, 1986, Falling Free, 1988 (Nebula award, 1989), Brothers in Arms, 1989, Borders of Infinity, 1989, The Vor Game, 1990 (Hugo award, 1991), Barrayar, 1991 (Hugo award, 1992, 1st place Locus poll, 1992), Mirror Dance, 1994 (Hugo & Locus awards, 1995), Cetaganda, 1996, Memory, 1996, Komarr, 1998 (Minn. book award, 1999), A Civil Campaign, 1999, The Curse of Chalion, 2001 (Mythopoeic award, 2002), Diplomatic Immunity, 2002, Paladin of Souls, 2003 (Hugo award, 2004, Locus award, 2004, Nebula award, 2005), The Hallowed Hunt, 2005, The Sharing Knife, 2006, Beguilement, 2006, Legacy, 2007, (novellas) The Borders of Infinity, 1987, The Mountains of Mourning, 1989 (Nebula and Hugo awards, 1990), Labyrinth, 1989 (Best Novella/Novelette Analytical Lab., 1990), Weatherman, 1990 (Best Novella Analytical Lab., 1991), Winterfair Gifts, 2004; contbr. short stories to sci. fiction mags., articles to profl. jours. Mem.: Sci. Fiction and Fantasy Writers Am. Office: Spectrum Literary Agency 320 Central Park W Ste 1D New York NY 10025-7659 Personal E-mail: lois@dendarii.com.

BUKATY, RAYMOND M., lawyer; b. NYC, Aug. 19, 1957; BA, Stanford U., 1979; MBA, JD, U. Southern Calif., 1983. Bar: Calif. 1983. Atty. Riordan & McKinzie, Los Angeles, Calif.; asst. gen. counsel Fluor Corp., Aliso Viejo, Calif., 1995—97, sr. counsel, 1998; v.p. corp. law Western Digital, Lake Forest, Calif., 1999—2002, v.p., gen. counsel, sec., 2002—04, sr. v.p., gen. counsel, sec., 2004—. Bd. mem. Mercy House, Orange County, Calif., Orange County ARC. Mem.: ABA, Orange County Bar Assn., Calif. State Bar Assn. Office: Western Digital 20511 Lake Forest Dr Lake Forest CA 92630-7741

BUKER, EDWIN L., manufacturing executive; BSME, Tri-State Univ.; MBA, Ohio Univ. Mgmt. positions Honda Motor Co., East Liberty, Ohio, BMW, Spartanburg, SC, v.p. new model develop. Munich; pres. elec. systems, Americas United Technologies Automotive; v.p., gen. mgr. chassis systems Visteon Automotive; pres., CEO Citation Corp., Birmingham, Ala., 2002—07; CEO Tecumseh Products Co., Tecumseh, Mich., 2007—. Office: Tecumseh Products Co 100 E Patterson St Tecumseh MI 49286*

BUKER, ROBERT HUTCHINSON, SR., army officer, thoracic surgeon; b. Loi Mwe, Kengtung, Burma, Dec. 6, 1928; came to U.S., 1940; s. Richard S. and Minola (Hutchinson) B.; m. Ethel Hunt, Sept. 25, 1949; children: Robert Hutchinson, Traci, Nina Ruth. AB, Boston U., 1949; MS, U. Maine, 1952; MD, Columbia U., 1956; postgrad., Indsl. Coll. of Armed Forces, 1978-79. Diplomate: Am. Bd. Surgery, Am. Bd. Thoracic Surgeons. Intern Gorgas Hosp, C.Z., 1956-57; gen. surg. residency Gorgas Hosp., C.Z., 1957-60; resident in thoracic surgery Kennedy V.A. Hosp., 1962-64, Tenn. Med. Ctr., 1962-64; capt. U.S. Army, 1964, advanced through grades to maj. gen.; chief surg. cons. Pentagon, Washington, 1973-76; comdr. U.S. Army Hosp., Wuerzburg, Germany, 1976-78; dep. chief staff opns. Health Services Command, Fort Sam Houston, Tex., 1979-80; comdr. Gen. Leonard Wood Army Hosp., Ft. Leonard Wood, Mo., 1980-81; commdr. Acad. Health Scis., Ft. Sam Houston, 1981-83; comdg. gen. Brooke Army Med. Center, Ft. Sam Houston, 1983-85; dep. Surgeon Gen. U.S. Army, Washington, 1985-89; chief surg. svcs. S.E. Kaiser-Permanente Med. Group, Atlanta, 1989-91. Chief legal medicine and risk mgmt. Kaiser-Permanente Med. Group, Atlanta, 1991-94; clin. prof. surgery Uniform U. Health Scis., Bethesda, Md., 1981—. Fellow ACS (bd. govs. 1987-89), Am. Coll. Chest Physicians, Am. Coll. Physician Execs.; mem. AMA, Soc. Thoracic Surgeons, So. Thoracic Surg. Assn., Am. Acad. Med. Dirs. Baptist. Home Phone: 239-389-1159. Personal E-mail: mgrbuker@att.net.

BUKH, JENS, medical researcher; b. Flade, Mors, Denmark, Apr. 10, 1960; s. Niels and Inger Marie Bukh; m. Abelone Marup Bukh, July 3, 1994; children: Clara, Niels Johan. MD, U. Copenhagen, 1989. Attending physician U. Hosp. of Copenhagen, Copenhagen, Denmark, 1989—90; rsch. investigator NIH, Bethesda, Md., 1990—. Mem. editl. bd.: Hepatology, Jour. Clinical Microbiology; contbr. chapters to books, articles to profl. jours. Pvt. Danish Army, 1979—80. Recipient Achievement award, NIAID, 2004. Mem.: Am. Assn. Study of Liver Disease. Achievements include research in field of hepatitis C virus and related viruses. Office: NIH Bldg 50 Rm 6529 S Dr Bethesda MD 20892-8009 Office Phone: 301-594-2311. E-mail: jbukh@niaid.nih.gov.

BUKOSKY, RICHARD J., allergist; b. Elizabeth, NJ, 1934; BA, Rutgers U., 1956; MD, Med. Coll. Wis., 1960. Intern Martin Army Hosp., Ft. Benning, Ga., 1960-61; resident Wood VA Hosp., 1963-66; with St. Elizabeth (N.J.) Hosp., Rahway (N.J.) Hosp., Union (N.J.) Hosp., Elizabeth Gen. Med. Ctr.; assoc. clin. prof. medicine Seton Hall U. Sch. Grad. Med. Edn. Asst. clin. prof. medicine U. Med., Dent. N.J. Allergy & Immunology fellow Milw. County Gen. Hosp., 1966-68. Mem. AMA, Am. Acad.

Allergy & Immunology, Am. Assn. Cert. Allergists, Am. Coll. Allergy & Immunology, N.J. Allergy Soc. Office: 926 N Wood Ave Linden NJ 07036-4040 Office Phone: 908-925-3318. Personal E-mail: rjbukosky@yahoo.com.

BUKOVAC, MARTIN JOHN, horticulturist, educator; b. Johnston City, Ill., Nov. 12, 1929; s. John and Sadie (Fak) B.; m. Judith Ann Kelley, Sept. 5, 1956; 1 dau., Janice Louise. BS with honors, Mich. State U., 1951, MS, 1954, PhD, 1957; D honoris causa, U. Bonn, Germany, 1995. Asst. prof. horticulture Mich. State U., East Lansing, 1957-61, assoc. prof., 1961-63, prof., 1963; NSF sr. postdoctoral fellow Oxford U., U. Bristol, Eng., 1965-66; univ. disting. prof., 1992—. Vis. lectr. Japan Atomic Energy Rsch. Inst., 1958; adviser IAEA, Vienna, 1961; NAS exch. lectr. Coun. Acads., Yugoslavia, 1971; vis. scholar Va. Poly. Inst., Blacksburg, 1973; guest lectr. Polish Acad. Scis., 1974; disting. vis. prof. N.Mex. State U., 1976; vis. prof. Japan Soc. Promotion Sci., Osaka Prefecture U., 1977; guest lectr. Serbian Sci. Coun., Fruit Rsch. Inst., Cacak, Yugoslavia, 1979; John A. Hannah Disting. lectr. Mich. State Hort. Soc., 1980; vis. prof. U. Guelph, Ont., Can., 1982, Ohio State U., 1982, U. Zagreb, Yugoslavia, 1983, Ohio State U., 1990; collaborator Agrl. Rsch. Svc. USDA, 1982-2003; guest rschr. Hort. Rsch. Inst., Budapest, Hungary, 1983, Inst. Obstbau und Gemusebau U. Bonn, Fed. Republic Germany, 1986; Batjer Meml. lectr. Wash. State Hort. Soc., 1985; mem. agrl. rsch. adv. com. Eli Lilly Co., Indpls., 1971-88; cons. Dept. Agr.; disting. lectr. Dept. Sci. and Tech. Peoples Republic China, 1984; commencement spkr. Mich. State U., 1986; mem. internat. adv. bd. divsn. life scis. Ctr. for Nuclear Studies, Atomic Energy Commn., Grenoble, France, 1993-2000; Monselise Meml. lectr. Hebrew U., 1994; Agrl. Rsch. Svc. B.Y. Morrison Meml. lectr., 1994, Kermit Olson Meml. lectr. Univ. Minn., 1997; pres. Martin J. Bukovac Inc., 1996-2001; Donald L. Reichard Meml. lectr., Ohio State U., 1999; sci. exch. lectr. Nara (Japan) Inst. Sci. and Tech., 2000. Mem. exec. adv. bd. Ency. of Agrl. Scis., 1991-96; mem. editl. adv. bd. Ctr. for Agr. and Bioscis. Internat., 1989-2003; internat. editl. bd. Horticultural Sci., Budapest; mem. editl. bd. Ency. of Agrl. Sci., 1991-96. Pres. Okemos Music Patrons, Mich., 1973-74; bd. dirs. Mich. State U. Press, 1983-92. 1st lt. U.S. Army, 1951-53. Recipient citation meritorious rsch. Am. Hort. Soc., 1970, Disting. Faculty award Mich. State U., 1971, Disting. Svc. award Mich. Hort. Soc., 1974, Disting. Faculty award Mich. Assn. Governing Bds., 1986, Hatch Meml. Medallion award USDA, 1987, Industry Man of Yr. award Nat. Cherry Festival, 1987, Alexander von Humboldt Rsch. prize, 1995, Am. Soc. Agrl. Engrng. Outstanding Paper award, 1995, Gold Veitch Meml. medal Royal Hort. Soc., 2003, Spiridon Brusina medal Croatian Soc. for Natural Scis., 2004; Bukovac Disting. Lectr. established in his honor Mich. State Hort. Soc., 1995. Fellow AAAS, Am. Soc. Hort. Sci. (hon. life, pres. 1974-75, Joseph Harvey Gourley award 1969, 76, Marion Meadows award 1975, citation of appreciation 1975, Carroll R. Miller award 1980, Outstanding Rschr. award 1988, M.A. Blake award for disting. grad. tchg. 1975, Hall of Fame inductee 2001); mem. NAS, Am. Chem. Soc., Am. Soc. Plant Biologists (Dennis R. Hoagland award 1988), Bot. Soc. Am., Scandinavian Soc. Plant Physiologists, Japanese Soc. Plant Physiologists, Internat. Soc. Hort. Sci., Soc. Exptl. Biology, Croatian Soc. Plant Physiologists (hon.), Mich. State U. Faculty Club, Sigma Xi (pres. 1978-79 rsch. award Kedzie chpt.), Phi Kappa Phi, Gamma Sigma Delta. Home: 4428 Seneca Dr Okemos MI 48864-2946 Office: Mich State U Dept Horticulture East Lansing MI 48824 Business E-Mail: bukovacm@msu.edu.

BUKRY, JOHN DAVID, geologist; b. Balt., May 17, 1941; s. Howard Leroy and Irene Evelyn (Davis) Snyder. Student, Colo. Sch. Mines, 1959—60; BA, Johns Hopkins U., 1963; MA, Princeton U., 1965, PhD, 1967; postgrad., U. Ill., 1965—66, De Anza Coll., 1995—96. Geologist U.S. Army Corps Engrs., Balt., 1963; rsch. asst. Mobil Oil Co., Dallas, 1965; geologist U.S. Geol. Survey, La Jolla, Calif., 1967-84, scientist emeritus, 1996-98; geologist U.S. Minerals Mgmt. Svc., La Jolla, 1984-86, U.S. Geol. Survey, Menlo Park, Calif., 1986-96, scientist emeritus, 1998—; rsch. assoc. Geol. Rsch. Divsn. Scripps Instn. Oceanography-U. Calif., San Diego, 1970—2003. Cons. Deep Sea Drilling Project, La Jolla, 1967-87; lectr. Vetlesen Symposium, Columbia U., NYC, 1968, 3d Internat. Planktonic Conf., Kiel, Germany, 1974, Brit. Petroleum Exploration Seminar on nannoplankton biostratigraphy, Houston, 1989; shipboard micropaleontologist on D/V Glomar Challenger, 5 Deep Sea Drilling Project cruises, 1968-78; mem. stratigraphic correlations bd. NSF/Joint Oceanog. Instns. for Deep Earth Sampling, 1976-79; vis. scholar U. Calif., 2003-. Author: Leg I of the Cruises of the Drilling Vessel Glomar Challenger, 1969, Coccoliths from Texas and Europe, 1969, Leg LXIII of the Cruises of the Drilling Vessel Glomar Challenger, 1981; editor: Marine Micropaleontology, 1976-83, mem. editl. bd. Micropaleontology, 1985-90. Mobil Oil, Princeton U. fellow, 1965-67; Am. Chem. Soc., Princeton U. fellow, 1966-67. Fellow AAAS, Geol. Soc. Am., Explorers Club; mem. NSTA, Hawaiian Malacological Soc., Paleontol. Rsch. Inst., Am. Assn. Petroleum Geologists, Mars Soc., Planetary Soc., Soc. Econ. Paleontologists and Mineralogists, Internat. Nannoplankton Assn., Ecol. Soc. Am., European Union Geoscis., Oceanography Soc., Mus. Contemporary Art San Diego, San Diego Mus. Art, San Diego Natural History Mus., U. Calif.-San Diego Ida and Cecil Green Faculty Club, San Diego Shell Club, Princeton Club No. Calif., Sigma Xi. Achievements include research in stratigraphy, paleoecology and taxonomy for 300 new species of marine nannoplankton used in ocean history studies; new study of Holocene global climate change showing Medieval Warm and Little Ice Age in nannoplankton cored in the Gulf of California. Avocations: basketball, photography, shell and mineral collecting. Office: US Geol Survey MS-910 345 Middlefield Rd Menlo Park CA 94025-3591 E-mail: dbukry@usgs.gov.

BUKSZÁR, JÓZSEF, mathematics professor; b. Miskolc, Hungary, Dec. 30, 1969; s. József Bukszár and Lujza Irén Tóth; m. Zsuzsa Diána Kozma, May 26, 2004; 1 child, Loránd Richárd. Degree in math., Eötvös Loránd U., Budapest, Hungary, 1994; PhD in Applied Math., Eötvös Loránd U., 1998. Asst. prof. U. Miskolc, Hungary, 1999—2002; postdoctoral scientist U. Del., Newark, 2002—04, Va. Inst. Psychiat. & Behavioral Genetics, Richmond, 2004—06; assoc. prof. Ctr. Biomarker Rsch. & Personalized Medicine, Richmond, 2006—. Recipient Gyula Farkas prize, Bolyai Math. Soc., 1999, Spl. Young Scientists prize, Hungarian Acad. Scis., 2000; grantee Rsch. grant, OTKA, 1998—2002. Office: Va Commonwealth Univ 410 N 12th St Richmond VA 23298-0533 Office Fax: 804-828-8359. Business E-Mail: jbukszar@vcu.edu.

BULAN, LIANA, dentist; b. Bucharest, Romania, Mar. 7, 1971; arrived in U.S., 1998; d. Sergiu and Stephanie Bulan; m. Petru Groza, Apr. 5, 1997. DDS, U. Toronto, Can., 1995. Postgrad. intern Toronto Hosp., Canada, 1995—96; gen. practice dentistry Toronto, Canada, 1996—98, Walterboro, SC, 1998—2004, Macon, Ga., 2005—06, Spokane, Wash., 2006—. Founder, exec. editor: Jour. Non-Locality and Remote Mental Interactions; contbr. articles to profl. jours. Mem.: Soc. for Sci. Exploration, Omicron Kappa Upsilon. Home: 3524 S Woodlawn Drive Spokane WA 99206

BULAONG, GRACE F., library director; d. Gabriel F. and Maura Padlan Fabella; m. Renato A. Bulaong (dec.); children: Rowena McIntosh, Rosanne Bergin. BS in Libr. Sci. cum laude, U. Philippines, 1959; MA, U. of the Philippines, 1967; MA in Libr. Sci., U. Mich., 1963. Instr. Inst. Libr. Sci., U. of the Philippines, 1963—67; cataloger SE Asia Ctr. No. Ill. U., DeKalb, 1967; work-study scholar U. Mich., Ann Arbor, 1962—63; sr. cataloger, libr. III Queens U. Douglas Libr., Kingston, Ont., Canada, 1968—70; head cataloging dept. Metro Toronto Reference Libr., 1970—85; chief libr. Ont. Inst. for Studies in Edn., Toronto, 1985—94; libr. dir. New Jersey City U., 1994—. Author: Satire in Philippine Society, 1969; co-author: Nang Mauring: Humanitarian, 2005. Past pres. Toronto chpt. U. Philippines Alumni, 1984—85; past pres. Ladies Knights of Rizal, 1993—94. Grantee, Philippines Bd. of Scholarships for SE Asia, 1960—62. Mem.: ALA, Ont. Coll. and Univ. Libr. Assn. (past pres., chair profl. coms., conf. organizer, spkr.), Can. Libr. Assn. Home: 10 Saddlewood Ct Jersey City NJ 07302 Office: NJ City U Congressman Frank J Guarini Libr 2039 Kennedy Blvd Jersey City NJ 07305 Office Fax: 201-200-2330. E-mail: gbulaong@njcu.edu.

BULGER, BRIAN WEGG, lawyer; b. Chgo., May 27, 1951; s. John Burton and Mary Jane (Wegg) B.; m. Laura Ellen McErlean, Sept. 12, 1981; children: Burton, Kevin. AB cum laude, Georgetown U., 1972, JD, 1977. Bar: Ill. 1977, U.S. Dist. Ct. (no. dist.) Ill. 1977, U.S. Ct. Appeals (4th, 7th and 8th cirs.) 1977, U.S. Supreme Ct. 1980. From assoc. to ptnr. Pope Ballard Shepard & Fowle, Chgo., 1977-87; ptnr., dept. head Katten Muchin & Zavis, Chgo., 1987-94; founding ptnr. Meckler, Bulger & Tilson, Chgo., 1994—. Adj. prof. U. Wis. Mgmt. Inst., Milw., 1980-2000, U. Chgo. Grad. Sch. Bus., 2000— Contbr. articles to profl. jours. Mem. ABA (former chair pub. employer labor rels. com. sect. on urban state and govt. law), Ill. State Bar Assn., Georgetown Law Alumni (bd. dirs. 1984-93). Roman Catholic. Avocations: baseball, reading, boating, skeet shooting. Office: Meckler Bulger Tilson Ste 1800 123 N Wacker Dr Chicago IL 60606

BULGER, ROGER JAMES, academic administrator; b. Bklyn., May 18, 1933; s. William Joseph and Florence Dorothy (Poggi) B.; m. Ruth Ellen Grouse, June 8, 1960; children: Faith Anne, Grace Ellen. AB, Harvard U., 1955, MD, 1960; postgrad., Cambridge U., Eng., 1955—56; degree (hon.), Thomas Jefferson U., 1995, U. Md., Western U. Health Scis., 1998, Kirkesville U. Osteo. Medicine, 1999, Rush U., 2001. Intern, then resident in internal medicine U. Wash. Hosps., 1960—62; trainee in infectious disease and microbiology U. Wash., 1962—63; renal and metabolic diseases Boston U., 1963—64; from asst. prof. to assoc. prof. medicine U. Wash. Med. Sch., Seattle, 1966—70; med. dir. Univ. Hosp., Seattle, 1967—70; prof. cmty. health scis., dean allied health Duke U. Med. Ctr., 1970—72; exec. officer Inst. Medicine, Nat. Acad. Scis., 1972—76; prof. internal medicine George Washington U. Sch. Medicine, 1972—76; prof. internal medicine, family and community medicine, dean Med. Sch., chancellor Worcester campus U. Mass., 1976—78; pres. U. Tex. Health Sci. Ctr., Houston, 1978—88; pres., CEO Assn. Acad. Health Ctrs., 1988—2005; sr. advisor to Nat. Ctr. for Minority Health and Disparities, NIH, 2006—07. Author: Hippocrates Revisited, 1973, In Search of Modern Hippocrates, 1987, Technology, Bureaucracy and Healing, 1988, Mission Management, 1998, The Quest for Mercy, 1998, Edmund Pellegrino, Philosopher and Physician, 2001, The Honorable Paul G. Rogers, A Portrait of Leadership, 2005; also articles, chpts. in books; mem. editl. bd. various jours. Bd. dirs. Georgetown U., Rsch. Am., Am. Internat. Health Alliance, Medicine/Pub. Health Initiative. Lionel de Jersey Harvard fellow, 1955-56. Fellow ACP, Royal Soc. Medicine, Acad. for Health Svcs. Rsch. (disting.); mem. Inst. Medicine, Infectious Disease Soc. Am., Nat. Acad. Social Ins. Home: 12505 Grey Fox Ln Potomac MD 20854 Personal E-mail: rbulger@comcast.net.

BULKLEY, GREGORY BARTLETT, fisheries biologist, retired research scientist, academic surgeon, educator, cattle rancher; b. Spokane, Wash., Apr. 28, 1943; s. George J. and Patricia (Bartlett) B.; m. Bernardine P. Healy, Aug. 13, 1967 (div. Aug. 1982); 1 child, Bartlett Anne; m. Jacqueline Ransford Graham, Oct. 9, 1993. BA with high honors, Princeton U., 1965; MD with honors, Harvard U., 1970; MD (hon.), Uppsala U., Sweden, 1997. Diplomate Am. Bd. Med. Examiners, Am. Bd. Surgery. Rsch. fellow Harvard Med. Sch., Boston, 1967—68, Nat. Cancer Inst., 1972—74; intern Johns Hopkins Hosp., Balt., 1970—71, resident in surgery, 1971—72, 1974—77, Halsted Resident in surgery, 1977—78, asst. chief of svc. dept. surgery, 1977—78; faculty cellular and molecular medicine tng. program Johns Hopkins U., 1995—2005, dir. NIH tng. program for gastrointestinal surgeon-scientists, 1996—2005; mem. staff Johns Hopkins Hosp., Balt., 1970—2005; from instr. to assoc. prof. Johns Hopkins U. Sch. Medicine, 1977—88, dir. surg. rsch., 1985—2003, prof., 1988—2005, Mark M. Ravitch prof., endowed chair, 1989—2005; mem. faculty Johns Hopkins U. Sch. Hygiene and Pub. Health, Balt., 1991—95; prof. emeritus surgery Johns Hopkins U. Sch. Medicine, 2005—; ret., 2005. Vis. prof., cons. in field; GMA II study sect. NIH, Bethesda, Md., 1988-91, chmn., 1990-91, grant reviewer NIH, Med. Rsch. Coun. Can., VA US, mem. panel, 1989, chmn. subcom. NIH Consensus Panel, 1992; grant reviewer Med. Rsch. Coun., Australia; reviewer Med. Rsch. Coun., New Zealand; mem. multiple consensus confs. NIH; dean's lectr. Johns Hopkins U. Sch. Medicine, 1988, professorial promotion com., 1993-99; Sigma Xi lectr. U. Kans., 1991; founder, chair SSAT, AGA, ASLD, ASGE Consensus Confs., 1996-2000; chair multiple spl. grant rev. groups NIH, 1990—; cattle rancher, fisheries biologist, 2005-; found. bd. Oreg. Inst. Tech., 2007—; review com. Klamath Basin Ecosystem Found., Klamath Falls, Oreg., 2007; lectr. in field. Author, editor: book Measurement of Blood Flow, 1980, Splanchnic Ischemia and Multiple Organ Failure, 1990, former mem. editl. bd.: med. jours. Gastroenterology, Surgery, Free Radical Biology and Medicine, Shock, Ann. Chirugae et Gynecologie, Archives of Gerontology and Geriat., former reviewer: New Eng. Jour. Medicine, Am. Jour. Physiology, Jour. Clin. Investigation, Jour. Sci., others; contbr. articles to profl. jours. Vice chmn. FASEB Conf., 1994, chmn., 1996; nominator physiology or medicine Nobel Prize, 1990-05. Lt. comdr. USPHS, 1972—74. NIH grantee, 1983-05; named in his honor Bulkley lectr. Johns Hopkins U. Sch. Medicine, 2004-; recipient Shipley award Southern Surg. Assn., 1987, Royal Coll. medal Royal Coll. Surgeons Ireland, 1989. Fellow: ACS; mem.: Soc. Surgery Alimentary Tract (nominating com. 1995, trustee, chmn.rsch. com. 1997—2000), Soc. Internat. Digestive Surgery (trustee), Am. Gastroenterol. Assn. (chmn. subcom. program com. 1993, nominating com. 1994, chmn. subcom. program com. 1997), Am. Surg. Assn. (program com. 1995—99, chmn. 1999), Am. Physiol. Soc., Halsted Soc. (program com. 1997—99, chmn. 1999), Cosmos Club, Alpha Omega Alpha, Sigma Xi. Avocation: fly fishing. Office Phone: 541-353-2566. Business E-Mail: greg@blackdrakeranch.com.

BULL, BERGEN IRA, retired equipment manufacturing company executive; b. Lansing, Mich., Feb. 28, 1940; s. W. Ira and Thelma (Roof) B.; m. Janet Mary Blachford, Sept. 22, 1961; children: Damon, Lauren. BA, Mich. State U., 1962; MA, Middle Tenn. State U., 1965; JD, Lewis and Clark Coll., 1969. Bar: Oreg. 1969. Acct. Hyster Co., Portland, Oreg., 1965-66, mem. credit dept., 1966-67, asst. to sec., 1967-71, asst. sec., 1971-72, sec., 1972-78, v.p., legal officer, sec., 1978-86, v.p., gen. counsel sec., 1986-87, v.p. corp. adminstrn., gen. counsel, sec., 1987-89; v.p., gen. counsel, sec. NACCO Materials Handling Group, Inc., 1989-95, ret., 1995. Instr. bus. law Portland State U., 1971-72 Loaned exec. United Fund, 1968; vice chancellor Episcopal Diocese Ea. Oreg., 2000—, mem. diocesan coun., 2000—06; bd. dirs. Assoc. Oreg. Industries, 1981—96, Jr. Achievement, 1980—2001, vice-chmn., 1993, chmn., 1994; bd. dirs. Modern Group, Ltd., 1995—, Sunriver Music Festival, 1997—, treas., 1997—99, pres., 2000—03, 2006; bd. dirs. Sunriver Nature Ctr., 1998—2004, v.p., 2000, pres., 1999—2000. Adminstrv. officer USAF, 1963—65. Mem. Oreg. Bar Assn. (inactive), Multnomah Athletic Club, Sage Springs Club & Spa, Crosswater Club. Episcopalian. Personal E-mail: bergenjan747@cmc.com.

BULL, BRIAN STANLEY, pathologist, educator; b. Watford, Hertfordshire, Sept. 14, 1937; arrived in U.S., 1954, naturalized, 1960; s. Stanley and Agnes Mary (Murdoch) B.; m. Maureen Hannah Huse, June 3, 1963; children: Beverly Velda, Beryl Heather. BS in Zoology, Walla Walla Coll., 1957; MD, Loma Linda U., Calif., 1961. Diplomate Am. Bd. Pathology. Intern Yale U., 1961-62, resident in anat. pathology New Haven, 1962-63; resident in clin. pathology NIH, Bethesda, Md., 1963-65, fellow in hematology and electron microscopy, 1965-66, staff hematologist, 1966-67; rsch. asst. dept. anatomy Loma Linda U., 1958, dept. microbiology, 1959, asst. prof. pathology, 1968-71, assoc. prof., 1971-73, prof., 1973—, chmn. dept. pathology, 1973—, chmn. dept. pathology and human anatomy, 1993—, assoc. dean for acad. affairs Sch. Medicine, 1993-94, dean Sch. Medicine, 1994—2003. Cons. mfrs. of med. testing devices; mem. Internat. Commn. Standardization in Hematology, pres., 1997-99, inaugural lectr. Houwen Meml. Lectures, Internat. Soc. Lab. Hematology, 2005; founding dir. Centrify Health, bd. dirs. Mem. bd. editors Blood Cells, Molecules and Diseases, 1995-, editor-in-chief, 1995-95; contbr. chpts. to books, articles to med. jours.; patentee in field; editor-in-chief Blood Cells NY Heidelberg, 1985-94. Editor Understanding Genesis: Contemporary Adventist Perspectives, 2006. Served with USPHS, 1963-67. Nat. Inst. Arthritis and Metabolic Diseases fellow, 1967-68; recipient Merck Manual award, 1961, Mosby Scholarship Book award, 1961; Ernest B. Cotlove Meml. lectr. Acad. Clin. Lab. Physicians and Scientists, 1972; named Alumnus of Yr., Walla Walla Coll., 1984, Honored Alumnus, Loma Linda U. Sch. Medicine, 1987, Humanitarian award, 1991; named Citizen of Yr., Loma Linda C. of C., 1997, President's award, Loma Linda U. Adventist Health Scis. Ctr., 2003, Disting. U. Svc. award Sch. Medicine Loma Linda U., 2003, Inaugural lectr. Houwen Meml. lectr. Internat. Soc. for Lab. Hematology, 2005. Fellow Am. Soc. Clin. Pathologists, Am. Soc. Hematology, Coll. Am. Pathologists, FDA Panel on Hematology and Pathology Devices, Nat. Com. on Clin. Lab. Stds., NY Acad. Scis.; mem. AMA, Calif. Soc. Pathologists, San Bernadino County Med. Soc. (William C. Cover Outstanding Contbn. to Medicine award 1994), Acad. Clin. Lab. Physicians and Scientists, Am. Assn. Pathologists, Sigma Xi, Alpha Omega Alpha. Adventist. Achievements include patents in field of blood analysis instrumentation; development of quality control algorithms for blood analyzer calibration; origination of techniques and instrumentation for the measurement of thrombosis risk and for regulation of anti-coagulation during cardiopulmonary bypass and solid organ transplantation. Office: LLUMC Rm 2516 11234 Anderson St Loma Linda CA 92354-2871 Office Phone: 909-558-4094. Business E-Mail: bbull@llu.edu.

BULL, DAVID, fine art conservator; b. Bristol, Eng., Mar. 5, 1934; came to U.S., 1978; s. Andrew John Michael and Betty (Horler) B.; m. Janette Christine Brewer, July 26, 1955 (div. Nov. 1986); children: Victoria, Stephen, Matthew, Nicholas, Sebastian; m. Teresa Jarvis Longyear, June 3, 1989; 1 child, David Douglas John. Nat. diploma, city and guilds diploma, West of Eng. Coll. Art, 1955. Restorer of paintings City Art Gallery, Bristol, 1957-60; restorer Nat. Gallery, London, 1960-65; ptnr. David Bull and Robert Shepherd (art restorers), London, 1965-78; head painting conservation J. Paul Getty Mus., Malibu, Calif., 1978-80; dir. Norton Simon Mus., Pasadena, Calif., 1980-81; pres. Fine Art Conservation and Restoration Inc., 1981—; head of painting conservation Nat. Gallery Art, Washington, 1984-89, chmn. of painting conservation, 1990-99, sr. cons., 1999—. Bd. dirs. Save Venice, Inc. Fellow Internat. Inst. Conservation. Home and Office: 173 E 80th St New York NY 10021-0438 Office Phone: 212-439-1659. E-mail: david@fineartconservation.net.

BULL, FRANK JAMES, retired architect; b. Chattanooga, June 25, 1922; s. Louis H. and Augusta (Clausius) B.; m. Betty Frances Graham, May 7, 1949; 1 child, Birney O'Brian. BS in Architecture, Ga. Inst. Tech., Atlanta, 1948, BArch, 1949. Registered architect, Ga., 1951; cert. Nat. Coun. Archtl. Registration Bds. Pilot Pan Am. World Airways, NY, Fla., 1942—46; arch. Aeck Assocs. Architects, Atlanta, 1948-57; ptnr. Bull & Kenney Architects, Atlanta, 1957-88, Bull, Brown & Kilgo, Architects, Atlanta, 1988—2003; ret., 2006. Cons. Fed. Republic of Germany Embassy, Washington, 1986-93; archtl. cons. for golf clubhouse Quinta do Peru, Sesimbra, Portugal and Palheiro Golfe, Funchal, Madeira Island, Portugal, 1991; lectr. in field. Co-author: Asbestos Abatement: Vol. 5 The Sourcebook on Asbestos Diseases, 1991; contbr. articles to profl. jours.; prin. works include Sanctuary for Holy Innocents Episc. Ch., Atlanta, Atlanta Speech Sch. and Clin., Hummel Hall Episc. H.S., Alexandria, Va., Jekyll Island Golf Clubhouse, McLarty Hall, Tull Hall, Turner Gymnasium, Westminster Schs., Atlanta, Dunwoody Country Club, Atlanta, East Lake Golf Clubhouse Restoration, Atlanta, others. Charter trustee Holy Innocents Episcopal Sch., Atlanta, 1962-68, chmn., 1966; founder Galloway Schs., Atlanta, 1969-75. Recipient Rambusch prize, Ecole de Beaux Arts, 1940. Mem. AIA (mem. emeritus, treas. Atlanta chpt. 1976-78, bd. dirs. Ga. assn. 1971-74), Am. Arbitration Assn. (mem. nat. panel constrn. industry arbitrators 1977-2002), Nat. Asbestos Coun. (founder, charter v.p., bd. dirs. 1983-86, 89-90, treas. 1987, exec. com. 1983-87), Cherokee Town and Country Club (charter, bd. govs. 1976-79, chmn. capital appropriations com., chmn. green com.), Omicron Delta Kappa, Tau Beta Pi, Phi Kappa Phi, Phi Eta Sigma, ANAK, Beta Theta Pi. Republican. Episcopalian. Avocations: golf, writing. Home: 34 Willow Gln NE Atlanta GA 30342-1341 Personal E-mail: frank@addressabull.com.

BULL, GEORGE ALBERT, retired banker; b. Red Lion, Pa., May 28, 1927; s. Mervin E. and Edna May (Gohn) B.; m. Grace Kathryn Rudolph, Nov. 13, 1949; children: Donna Carol, Diana Sue, David Alan. Student, Rutgers U., 1961. From teller to cashier Citizens Nat. Bank, Front Royal, Va., 1947-64; asst. vp., cashier Monticello Nat. Bank, Charlottesville, Va., 1964; asst. cashier Nat. Bank & Trust Co., Charlottesville, 1964-80, asst. to pres., 1985-88, sr. exec. v.p., asst. to pres., 1988-89; exec. v.p., treas. Jefferson Bankshares Inc., Charlottesville, 1979-89. With U.S. Army, 1945-46. Mem. Masons. Home: 2315 Wakefield Rd Charlottesville VA 22901-1843

BULL, HENRIK HELKAND, architect; b. NYC, July 13, 1929; s. Johan and Sonja (Geelmuyden) B.; m. Barbara Alpaugh, June 9, 1956; children: Peter, Nina. BArch, MIT, 1952. With Mario Corbett, San Francisco, 1954-55; pvt. practice, 1956-68; ptnr. Bull, Field, Volkmann, Stockwell, Calif., 1968-82, Bull, Volkmann, Stockwell, Calif., 1982-90, Bull Stockwell and Allen, Calif., 1990-93, Bull, Stockwell, Allen & Ripley, San Francisco, 1993-96, BSA Archs., San Francisco, 1996—. Vis. lectr. Syracuse U., 1963; mem. adv. com. San Francisco Urban Design Study, 1970-71. Works include Sunset mag. Discovery House, Tahoe Tavern Condominiums, Lake Tahoe, Calif., Snowmass Villas Condominiums, Aspen, Colo., Northstar Master Plan Village and Condominiums, Moraga Valley Presbyn. Ch., Calif., Spruce Saddle Restaurant and Poste-Montane Hotel, Beaver Creek, Colo., Bear Valley visitor ctr., Point Reyes, Calif., The Inn at Spanish Bay, Pebble Beach, Calif., Taluswood Cmty., Whistler, B.C., Jackson Gore Inn, Okemo, Vt. 1st lt. USAF, 1952—54. Fellow AIA (pres. N. Calif. chpt. 1968, Firm award Calif. chpt. 1989). Democrat. Office: BSA Architects 501 Folsom St 4th Fl San Francisco CA 94105 Office Phone: 415-281-4720. Business E-Mail: hbull@bsaarchitects.com.

BULL, INEZ STEWART, retired curator, director, singer, writer, musician, educator; b. Newark, Apr. 13, 1920; d. Johan Randulf and Aurora (Stewart) B. Artist diploma in piano, Juilliard Sch., NYC, 1946; cert., Chautauqua Inst. Sch. Music, 1940-46; diploma, U. Oslo Grad. Sch., Norway, 1955; MusB, N.Y. Coll. Music, 1965; MA, NYU, 1972, EdD, 1979. Piano tchr. Juilliard Inst. Musical Art, NY, NY, 1942-43; chmn. music dept. Casement's Coll., Ormond Beach, Fla., 1949-50; dir. music Essex County Girls Vocat. & Tech. HS, Newark, 1953-57; dir. music, organist State of NJ Institution for Retarded Girls North Jersey Tng. Sch., Totowa, NJ, 1953-68; spl. edn. gifted coord. Jefferson Magnet Sch. Pub. Sch. Sys., Union City, NJ, 1956-95; dir. Upper Montclair Music Sch., Montclair, NJ, 1945—, Ole Bull Music Sch., Potter County, Pa., 1952-68. Pres. NJ Music Educators Assn. Aux. 1935-48; adjudicator Lycoming Coll., Williamsport, Pa., 1948—; conductor Whippany Symphony Orch., 1951-52; curator, builder Ole Bull Mus., Galeton, Pa., 1968—; dir. youth chorus Jefferson Sch., Union City, NJ, 1956-95; dir. Hudson County Elem.

Choral Festival, 1971—; artist-in-residence, Union City; guest lectr. Columbia U., NYC, Yale U. Grad. Sch. Music, Hartford, Conn., NYU, Lycoming Coll., Williamsport, Pa., Mansfield U., Pa., Princeton U., NJ, U. Scranton, Pa., Jersey City State Coll. Author: 35 books; editor: various newsletters and mag.; author: (song) Evening Prayer, 1934, I Will Bow and Be Humble, 1954, Voice of Am., 1952; recording artist Educo Records, soloist WFMB radio sta., Daytona Beach, Fla., 1949—50, NBC, Hartford, Conn., WNJR, Union, N.J., 1952—68, WNBT-ABC, Wellsboro, Pa., 1997—2007, Norsk Rikskringkasting, Oslo, Radio and TV Francaise, Paris, recitals, France, Norway, Eng., Switzerland, S. Am., US. Choir dir. First Congl. Ch., 1940-43, Holy Trinity Luth. Ch., Nutley Luth. Ch., 1953-55; organist, choir dir. North Jersey Tng. Sch. Chapel, 1952-68; founder, dir. Ole Bull Music Festival, Galeton, Pa, 1952—; dep. gov. and mem. rsch. bd. advisors Am. Biog. Inst., Raleigh; US State Dept amb. of goodwill to Norway by order of Pres. Dwight D. Eisenhower, 1953, Norwegian Goodwill amb. to US by order of King Haakon VII, 1953. Recipient Freedom medal-Eisenhower medal, 1953, Sterling Silver plaque King Olav V of Norway, 1966, NJEA award, 1970, Performing Arts Prestige award in Edn., 1976, Olympic Gold medal Norwegian Govt., 1992, Silver medal of Honor, 1991, Gold medal of Honor, 1992, Pa. Senate Legis. citation, 1992, Outstanding Tchr. of the Handicapped in the U.S. Nat. Rsch. Coun., 1970, Woman of Distinction honorable mention award Girl Scout Coun. of Greater Essex County, 1996, Artisan award Oakeside Bloomfield Cultural Ctr., 1996, 50 Women You Should Know award Internat. YWCA, 1996, St. Olav medal King Harald V (Norway), 1999, Outstanding Woman in Arts award World History Project/Twp. of Montclair, 2000, Key to City of Renovo award, Pa., 2000, 2002, Am. Medal of Honor award Pres. of U.S., 2001, Nobel Peace prize, 2002, Congl. Medal of Merit, 2003, Congl. Medal of Excellence, 2003, Amb. of Grand Eminence, 2004, Legion of Honor medal United Cultural Conv., 2005, Spl. Alumni Svc. award NYU, 2005; Fulbright scholar U. Oslo (Norway) Grad. Sch., 1955; film made in her honor A Child is Waiting, 1963. Mem. Ole Bull Hist. Soc. (pres. 1972—), Phi Delta Kappa (pres. 1984-86, newsletter editor 1984-92), Kappa Delta Pi (pres. 1984—, newsletter editor 1984—, counselor NYU Beta Pi chpt. 1996), Pen & Brush Club, Internat. Percy Grainger Soc. (v.p.), NYU Alumnae Club Inc. (bd. dirs., rec. sec., newsletter editor, 1979—), Swedish Cultural Soc. (hon.), Sons of Norway (hon.), Edvard Grieg Soc. (hon.), Alliance Francaise de Montclair, Victorian Soc., Montclair Women's Club, Montclair Cosmopolitan Club. Republican. Avocations: piano, singing, writing. Home (Summer): 79 S Cherry Springs Rd Galeton PA 16922

BULL, JAMES C., poet; b. Blaine, Tenn., Mar. 20, 1945; s. James Conley and Esther F. (Hensley) Bull; m. Maret Delavallade, June 15, 1965 (div. Dec. 1967); 1 child, Maarja Esther. Spkr. in field. Author: (poetry) Spirit of Earth, 1999, Voices of Quiet, 2001, Braids of Fire, 2001, Western the Big Red, 2002, Land of the Yellowstone, 2004, Stars Over the Yellow Stone River, 2005, (short story) To Walk with the Bear, 2006, A Photographic History of Fort Ringgold Texas and the Men Who Patroled the Military Trail, Circa 1900, 2002, (short stories) Year of the Comet, 2004. Supporter St. Joseph Sch. for Am. Indian Children. Served with US Army, 1962—65. Mem.: Am. Legion. Home: 2455 Indian Ridge Rd Blaine TN 37709-5927

BULL, SANDY (ALEXANDER BENJAMIN BULL), musician, composer; b. NYC, Feb. 25, 1941; s. Harry and Daphne (Bayne) B.; m. Candice Ann Marks, June 20, 1979; children: Cassandra, Jesse, Jackson. Studied banjo with Eric Darling, 1955-57; student in music, Boston U., 1959-61; studied percussion with Billy Higgins, 1961-64, studied oud with Hamza El Din, 1963-68, studied sarod with Ali Akbar Khan, 1976-77. Multi-instrumentalist on guitar, keyboards, bass, banjo, pedal steel, percussion, oud and sarod, also engr., composer, arranger, prodr.; host/prodr. The Music of Man/WNCN-FM, N.Y.C., 1963; compositions include Blend, Gospel Tune, No Deposit No Return Blues, Carnival Jump, Moodswing Salsa, Serious City, Alligator Wrestler, Rain Forest, Sanctified Steel, Love is Forever; recordings include The Samplers in Person, 1960, The Folksingers of Washington Square, 1962, Fantasias, 1963, Inventions, 1965, E. Pluribus Unum, 1969, Demolition Derby, 1972, Jukebox Sch. of Music, 1988 (Best Liner Notes award Nat. Assn. Ind. Record distbr. 1989, 20 Best Albums of 1988 Nat. Pub. Radio), Vehicles, 1991, Steel Tears, 1996 (nominated best folk album Nashville Music Awards 1997), Sandy Bull: Re-inventions: The Best of the Vanguard Yrs., 1999; arrangements include L. Bonfa's Manha de Carnival for oud, two movements of Carl Orff's Carmina Burana for 5 string banjo, excerpt from J.S. Bach's Brandenburg Concerto # 5 for Fender guitar, strings and Fender Rhodes; instrumental arrangement of C. Berry's Memphis. Mem. NARAS, ASCAP, Audio Engring. Soc. Avocations: learning bach chorales on keyboard, skiing. Office: Timeless Rec Soc PO Box 1177 Franklin TN 37065-1177

BULL, VIVIAN ANN, retired academic administrator, educator; b. Ironwood, Mich., Dec. 11, 1934; d. Edwin Russell and Lydia (West) Johnson; m. Robert J. Bull, Jan. 31, 1959; children: R. Camper, W. Carlson. BA, Albion Coll., Mich., 1956, DEcons (hon.), 1999; postgrad., London Sch. Econs., 1957; PhD, NYU, 1974; DHL (hon.), Drew U., 2003, Albion Coll., U. Portland. Economist Nat. Bank Detroit, 1955-59; with Bell Telephone Labs., Murray Hill, NJ, 1960-62; dept. econs. Drew U., Madison, NJ, 1960-92, assoc. dean, 1978-86; pres. Linfield Coll., McMinnville, Oreg., 1992—2005, ret., 2005, emeritus. Bd. dirs. Chem. Bank N.J., Morristown; trustee Africa U., Zimbabwe; treas. Joint Expedition to Caesareu Maritima Archaeology, 1971-96. Author: Economic Study The West Bank: Is It Viable?, 1975. Trustee, assoc. Am. Schs. Oriental Rsch., 1982-90; trustee Colonial Symphony Soc., 1984-92, The Albright Inst. of Archaeol. Record; commr. Downtown Devel. Commn., Madison, 1986-92; mem. Univ. Sen. United Meth. Ch., 1989-96, 2000-, gen. bd. higher edn., 1988-92; mem. planning bd. Coll. Bus. Adminstrn., Africa U., Zimbabwe, 1990-91; exec. com. Nat. Assn. Commns. on Salaries, United Meth. Ch., 1986-92. Fulbright scholar, 1956, Paul Harris fellow Rotary Internat., 1988; named Disting. Alumna Albion Coll., 1979; recipient Salute to Policy Makers award Exec. Women in N.J., 1986, John Woolman Peace-making award George Fox Coll., 1994, Equal Opportunity award Urban League of Portland, 1995. Mem. Nat. Assn. Bank Women, N.W. Assn. Colls. and Univs. (exec. com. 2000-05), Phi Beta Kappa. Avocations: archaeology, travel, music. Home: 54 Prospect St Madison NJ 07940 Personal E-mail: vbull@armigerint.com.

BULLARD, EDGAR JOHN, III, museum director; b. LA, Sept. 15, 1942; s. Edgar John and Katherine Elizabeth (Dreisbach) B. BA, UCLA, 1965, MA, 1968; LHD (hon.), Loyola U., New Orleans, 1987. Asst. to dir., curator spl. projects Nat. Gallery Art, Washington, 1968-73; Montine McDaniel Freeman dir. New Orleans Mus. Art, 1973—. Alternate mem. Citizens Stamp Adv. Com., 1969-71; mus. adv. panel Nat. Endowment for Arts, 1974-77; bd. vis. Xavier U., La., 2006—. Author: Edgar Degas, 1971, John Sloan 1871-1951, 1971, Mary Cassatt: Oils and Pastels, 1972, A Panorama of American Painting, 1975. Nerdrum: The Drawings, 1994, Henry Casselli: Master of the American Watercolor, 2000, In Celebration of Light: Photographs from the Pierce Collection, 2004. Bd. dirs. La. Cultural Alliance, 1988-91, New Orleans Jazz and Heritage Found., 1974-78; trustee New Orleans Opera Assn., 2001-06, Ga. Mus. Art, U. Ga., Athens, 1975-80, Kneisel Hall Chamber Music Sch., Blue Hill, Maine, 1986-02, La. Soc. for Prevention Cruelty to Animals, 1986-93, New Orleans Jazz Orch., 2003-06, Haystack Mountain Sch. of Crafts, Deer Isle, Maine, 2003—; mem. adv. bd. Tulane Univ. Coll., 1999-2001; trustee Amistad Rsch. Ctr., Tulane U., 2001—; bd. visitors Xavier U. La., 2007—. Decorated Order of Republic of Egypt, officer Am. Soc. Venerable Order St. John Jerusalem, Order of Arts and Lettres of France; Samuel H. Kress Found. fellow, 1967-68; recipient New Orleans Mayor's Art award, 1993. Mem.: Am. Assn. Mus. (bd. dirs. 1996—98), Assn. Art Mus. Dirs. Democrat. Episcopalian. Home: 1805 Milan St New Orleans LA 70115-5443 also: Greenlea Reach Rd Deer Isle ME 04627 Home Phone: 504-897-2655; Office Phone: 504-658-4102. Business E-Mail: jbullard@noma.org.

BULLARD, ERVIN TROWBRIDGE, horticulturist; b. NYC, May 25, 1920; s. Frank Marcus and Elizabeth Trowbridge Bullard; m. Marie Jump Groo Bullard, Apr. 20, 1995; m. Madonna Jean Bullard, Sept. 4, 1948 (dec. Dec. 1, 1993); children: John Marcus, Carol Ann Rice, Ellen Sue Schedin. PhD, Purdue U., West Lafayette, IN, 1950; MS, Cornell U., Ithica, NY, 1946; BS, NC State, Raleigh, NC, 1943. Pres. Bullard Consulting, 1986—; chief of party Ohio State U. in Burma, 1984—86; agr. advisor US AID, Washington, 1954—79; assoc. educator U. of Idaho, Parma, Idaho, 1950—54; ret., 1990. Contbr. to various books on tropical horticulture. Pfc Marine Corps, 1942—44, United States. Recipient Fulbright Award, US Govt., 1951. Mem.: Interamerican Soc. for Tropical Horticulture. Presbyterian. Avocations: fishing, stamp collecting/philately. Personal E-mail: ervinbullard@aol.com.

BULLARD, JOHN KILBURN, educational association administrator; b. New Bedford, Mass., Aug. 21, 1947; s. John Crapo and Katharine (Kilburn) B.; m. Anne Dunbar, June 27, 1981; children: Elizabeth, Anthony, Matthew. BA magna cum laude, Harvard U., 1969; MArch, M in City Planning, MIT, 1974. Agt. Waterfront Hist. Area League (WHALE), New Bedford, 1974-85; mayor City of New Bedford, 1986-92; dir. fisheries representation New Bedford (Mass.) Seafood Co-op, 1992-93; dir. Office of Sustainable Devel. NOAA, Dept. Commerce, Washington, 1993-98; fellow Harvard Inst. Politics, 1998; dir. Family Bus. Ctr. U. Mass., Dartmouth, 1998—2002; pres. Sea Edn. Assn., 2002—. Chmn. urban econ. policy com. U.S. Conf. of Mayors, 1988-92. Photographer 3 covers for Sail mag., 1970-71. Recipient Honor Award Nat. Trust for Hist. Preservation, 1981, Preservation award Mass. Hist. Commn., 1983, Design award Mass. Gov. Michael Dukakis, 1987. Democrat. Unitarian Universalist. Avocations: sailing, tennis. Home: 19 Irving St New Bedford MA 02740-3426 Personal E-mail: jbullard@sea.edu.

BULLARD, JOHN MOORE, religious studies educator, church musician; b. Winston-Salem, NC, May 6, 1932; s. Hoke Vogler and May Evangeline (Moore) B. AB, U. N.C., 1953; AM, 1955; MDiv, Yale U., 1957; PhD, 1962. Ordained to ministry United Meth. Ch., 1955. Asst. in instrn. Yale U., New Haven, 1957-61; asst. prof. religion Wofford Coll., Spartanburg, SC, 1961-65, assoc. prof., 1965-70, Albert C. Outler prof. religion, 1970—, chmn. dept., 1962—, faculty sec., 1988—. Minister music, organist-choirmaster Central United Meth. Ch., Spartanburg, 1961-72, Bethel United Meth. Ch., 1972-88, Second Presbyn. Ch., Spartanburg, 1994, Palmetto Moravian Fellowship, 1994—; lectr. Eureka Coll., 1967, Furman U., 1982, Barton Coll., 1992; vis. prof. Biblical Lit. U. NC, Chapel Hill, 1966-67, U. NC, Charlotte, 1974; vis. prof. comparative religion Converse Coll., Spartanburg, 1984. Author: History of the Spartanburg Chapter, American Guild of Organists, 1954-2004, 2004; editor: Wofford Lectures in Religion, Ethics, and Society, 2004; co-author (with Hugh Sanborn): The Prophetic Call: Celebrating Community, Earth, Justice and Peace, 2004; contbr. articles to profl. jours. With Naval ROTC, 1950-52. Grantee NEH summer seminar Harvard U., 1982, U. Pa., 1986, Yale U., 1987; Fulbright-Hays grantee, Pakistan 1973, Fund for the Study of Gt. Religions in Asia, 1970-71; James fellow Yale U.; NEH/Wofford rsch. grantee U. London, 1975; named to Ky. Cols.; Dana Fellow Emory Univ's. Grad. Inst. Liberal Arts, 1989-90. Mem. Soc. Bibl. Lit. (pres. so. sect. 1968-69), Am. Acad. Religion, Am. Guild Organists (dean chpt. 1965-67), Organ Hist. Soc., S.C. Acad. Religion (pres. 1974-75), Southeastern Hist. Keyboard Soc., New Bach Soc. (Leipzig), Moravian Music Found. (bd. trustees), Phi Mu Alpha Sinfonia. Avocation: early keyboard music. Home: 104 Hickman Ct Hillbrook Forest Spartanburg SC 29307 Office: Wofford Coll Dept Religion 429 N Church St Spartanburg SC 29303-3612 Office Phone: 864-582-8589. Business E-Mail: bullardjm@wofford.edu.

BULLARD, JUDITH EVE, psychologist, systems engineer; b. Oneonta, NY, Oct. 5, 1945; d. Kurt and Herta (Deutsch) Leeds; divorced; children: Nicholas A., Elizabeth A. BA in Polit. Sci., Spanish U., Oreg., 1966, MA in Psychology, 1973; MBA, George Washington U., 1994. Cert. Project Mgr. 1993, lic. realtor N.J. Supr. residential program Skipworth Juvenile Home, Eugene, Oreg., 1966-68; research asst. Oreg. Research Inst., Eugene, 1968-69, 83-85; supr. residential program Ky. Correctional Facility, Lexington, 1969-70; research asst. U. Oreg., Eugene, 1970-73; asst. dir. Regional Mental Health Clinic, Frankfort, Ind., 1974-76; dir. mental health Lane County Mental Health, Eugene, 1977-80; cons. Managerial Communications, Eugene, 1980-83; sys. engr. AT&T Bell Labs., Holmdel, N.J., 1985-91, mgr. strategic/tech. planning, 1992-95, mgr. reliability, customer satisfaction, process engring., 1996—; dir Lucent/Bus. Comm. Sys., 1998—2000; tech. mgr. Sys. Test Quality Configuration Processes, Alameda, Calif., 1999—2001; ret., 2001; art tchr. St. Agnes Cath. Sch., 2002—03; cons., 2002—05; nat. svcs. mgr. Avaya, Inc., 2005—. Mem. strategic bus. planning task force Globa Bus. Comm. Sys., chairperson customer focus groups-new products edn. forum, 1991-95, mgr. forward looking work/tech. coord. tech. bus.-customer partnership program, 1994—, chairperson 2-day software symposium, tech. chmn. strategy conf., 1995, chmn. Breakthru Tech. project, 1996, software design project, 1999-2000, coord. planned and executed Rsch. Tech. Exch. Symposium, mem. leadership team Cultural Change project; exec. prodr. 13TV Broadcast Solutions, 1996. Prodr. (video) The World is Our Work Place, 1991. Bd. dir. Asbury Park 10K, Jersey Shore 1/2 Marathon, 1985—, Women's Resource and Survival Ctr., Keyport, N.J., 1986—; chairperson Area Affirmative Action Com., 1990—; pres. Affirmative Action Diversity Coun.; active Alliance Neighbors 9/11 Support Group, 2002—. Mem. Women's Profl. Network (trustee Holmdel br. 1987—), N.J. Bd. Realtors, Nat. Bd. Realtors, Nat. Art Collectors Assn., Partnership in Edn. & Bus., Corrections in Mental Health, Human Factors Soc. Avocations: running, biking, swimming, tennis, cooking. Office Phone: 408-456-5178. Business E-Mail: jbullard@avaya.com.

BULLARD, WILLIS CLARE, JR., lawyer; b. Detroit, July 12, 1943; s. Willis C. and Virginia Katherine (Gilmore) B.; children: Willis C. III, Melissa Ann, Kaila Michelle. AB, U. Mich., 1965; JD, Detroit Coll. Law, 1971. Bar: Mich. 1971. Practice of law, Detroit, 1971-77, Troy, Mich., 1977-80, Milford, Mich., 1983—; supr. Highland Twp., Mich., 1980-82; mem. Mich. Ho. of Reps., 1983-96, Mich. Senate from 15th dist., Lansing, 1996—2002; mem. from 2d dist. County Commn., 2003—, chmn. bd., 2005—. Asst. Rep. caucus chmn., 1983-84, asst. Rep. floor leader, 1985-88, chmn. House Rep. campaign, 1987-90; chmn. House taxation com., 1993-96; chmn. task force Midwestern Legis. Conf. Coun. State Govts., 1985-86; mediator cir. and dist. cts., 1988—. Bd. dirs. Dunham Lake Property Owners Assn., 1975-78, treas., 1975-76, pres., 1976-78; mem. Dunham Lake Civic Com., 1982-87; trustee Highland Twp., 1978-80, mem. zoning bd. appeals, 1979. Named Legislator of Yr. Mich. Twp. Assn., 1984, Nat. Rep. Legislator of Yr., 2000. Mem. Oakland County Bar Assn., State Bar Mich., Oakland County Assn. Twp. Suprs. (sec.-treas. 1981), Michigamua. Clubs: U. Mich. of Greater Detroit, Highland Republican, Highland Men's (sec. 1979, pres. 1980). Republican. Home: 1849 Lakeview Dr Highland MI 48357-4817 Office Phone: 248-684-1444.

BULLARD-BATES, PATRICIA CAROL, psychologist, neuropsychologist; b. Purcell, Okla., Dec. 19, 1949; d. Howard Benjamin and Patricia Gilpin Bullard; m. Harvey Bullard-Bates (dec.); 1 child, Daniel Martin; m. Kent Robert Beduhn, Sept. 22, 2001. BA in Psychology, Wellesley Coll., Mass., 1971; PhD in Clin. Psychology, Washington U., St. Louis, 1976. Lic. psychologist Washington, Md. Postdoctoral fellow U. Fla., Gainesville, 1976—79; coord. neuropsychology Med. Ctr. Rehab. Hosp., Grand Forks, ND, 1979—81; staff psychologist Royal Ottawa Rehab. Ctr., Ont., Canada, 1981—84, Nat. Rehab. Hosp., Washington, 1987—; cons., staff psychologist St. Vincent Hosp., Ottawa, 1984—87. Pres. Bethany, Inc., Washington, 1993—; activist Ch. of Saviour, Washington, 2005—. Grantee, NIH, 1977—79; scholar, Wellesley Coll., 1967—71. Mem.: APA, Nat. Register Health Svc. Providers in Psychology, Nat. Acad. Neuropsychology, Internat. Neuropsychol. Soc. Democrat. Avocation: jewelry making. Home: 10702 Lombardy Rd Silver Spring MD 20901-1631 Office: Nat Rehab Hosp 102 Irving St NW Washington DC 20010

BULLARO, GRACE RUSSO, literature, film and foreign language educator, critic; b. Salerno, Italy, July 11, 1949; arrived in U.S., 1958; d. Salvatore and Carmela (Paciello) Russo; m. Frank John Bullaro, Sept. 19, 1971; children: Christian, Adrian Alexander. BA magna cum laude, CCNY, 1971; MA, SUNY, Stony Brook, 1989, PhD in Comparative Lit., 1993. Grad. tchg. asst. SUNY, Stony Brook, 1988-92; adj. asst. prof. SUNY-Nassau C.C., Garden City, 1990—, CUNY-Lehman Coll., Bronx, 1991-2000, adj. assoc. prof., 2000—02, asst. prof., 2002—06, assoc. prof., 2006—, dir. grad. English program, 2007—. Mem. acad. senate CUNY, 1997—, mem. libr. com., 1998, mem. exec. com. of the faculty, acad. senate, 1998—, liaison English Dept. Libr. Acquistions, 2000—, sec. Faculty Exec. Com., 2004—, chair English dept. honors com., 2004—06, faculty advisor English honors program, 2004—06; with Lincoln Ctr., NYC, 1998; mem. Exec. Com. Faculty Lehman Coll., Bronx, NY, 1999—; English dept. libr. acquisitions liaison Lehman Coll., 2000—, mem. tchr. of yr. selection com.; acad. senate Lehman Coll. CUNY, 1997—99, 2001—; mem. Exec. Com. Faculty CUNY, 1999—, elected sec., 2004—; cons. Pub. Libr. Fgn. Lang. Acquisitions, Syosset, NY, 2002—; book reviewer in field. Author: Beyond Life is Beautiful: Comedy and Tragedy in the Cinema of Roberto Benigni, 2005, Man in Disorder: The Cinema of Lina Wertmiller in the 1970's, 2006; contbr. chapters to books, articles to profl. jours. Recipient Excellence in Tchg. award, Excellence in Tchg. Selection Com., SUNY, Stony Brook, 1992, Adj. Tchr. Yr. award, conferred by Tchr. Yr. Selection Com., CUNY, Lehman Coll., 2001. Mem. MLA, Popular Culture Assn./Am. Culture Assn., N.E. MLA, Nat. Coun. Tchrs. English, Assn. Italian-Am. Educators, Inst. Français, Soc. Profs. Français, Phi Beta Kappa (sec. 2005—, bd. dirs. Lehman Coll. chpt. 2006-, mem. student election rev. com. 2007-). Avocations: fitness trainer, tennis, travel, swimming, horseback riding. Office: CUNY Lehman Coll English Dept Bedford Park Blvd W Bronx NY 10468 Office Phone: 718-960-8362. Business E-Mail: grace.bullaro@lehman.cuny.edu.

BULLEIT, THOMAS NELSON, JR., lawyer; b. Washington, Feb. 11, 1957; s. Thomas Nelson and Jeanne Marie (Parsley) Bulleit; m. Kristy Ann Niehaus, May 25, 1991; children: Emma Madeleine, James Vaughan. AB cum laude, Yale U., 1979; JD, U. Mich., 1985. Bar: Md. 1987, DC 1988, U.S. Supreme Ct. 1991. Law clk. to Hon. Bailey Brown U.S. Ct. Appeals (6th cir.), Memphis, 1985—86; assoc. Pierson, Ball & Dowd, Washington, 1986—89, Reed Smith Shaw & McClay, Washington, 1989—90, Hogan & Hartson, LLP, Washington, 1990—93, ptnr., 1994—. Mem. steering com. health law sect. DC Bar, 1991—94, chmn., 1994—97, chmn. coun. on sects., 1997—98. Bd. dirs. Children's Law Ctr., Washington, 1999—, chmn. bd. dirs., 2003—05. Recipient Louis Honigman award, U. Mich. Jour. Law Reform, 1985, Masters in Fraud and Abuse Law award, Nat. Health Lawyers Assn., 1996. Mem.: ABA, Am. Health Lawyers Assn. Avocations: vocal music, hiking, running. Office: Hogan & Hartson LLP 555 13th St NW Washington DC 20004 Office Phone: 202-637-8276. Business E-Mail: tnbulleit@hhlaw.com.

BULLEN, DANIEL BERNARD, mechanical engineering educator; b. Iowa City, July 20, 1956; s. John Bernard and Helen May (Ferguson) B.; m. Elizabeth Ann Clark, Aug. 17, 1979; children: Katherine Andrea, Mark Bernard, Sarah Elizabeth, Rachel Suzanne. BS in Engring. Sci., Iowa State U., 1978; MS in Nuclear Engring., U. Wis., 1979, MS in Material Sci., 1981, PhD in Nuclear Engring., 1984. Registered profl. engr., Calif., N.C., Ga., Iowa. Engr. Lawrence Livermore (Calif.) Nat. Lab., 1984-86; sr. engr. Sci. and Engring. Assocs., Inc., Pleasanton, Calif., 1986-88; pres. DG Engring., Inc., Livermore, 1988-89; asst. prof. nuclear engr. N.C. State U., Raleigh, 1989-90, Ga. Inst. Tech., Atlanta, 1990-92; assoc. prof. mech. engring. Iowa State U., Ames, 1992—2004, dir. nuclear reactor lab., 1993-2000, coord. nuclear engring. program, 1993-96; mng. engr. Exponent, Wood Dale, Ill., 2004—. Cons. Lawrence Livermore Nat. Lab., 1988-91, Electric Power Rsch. Inst., Palo Alto, Calif., 1989-96, Internat. Lead Zinc Rsch. Orgn., Research Triangle Park, N.C., 1990-98, HDR Engring., Inc., Omaha, 1991-2003, APA, Inc., Omaha, 1996-97; mem. U.S. Nuclear Waste Tech. Rev. Bd., 1997-2004. Contbr. articles 60 to profl. jours. Mem. NSPE, ASME, ASM Internat., Materials Soc., Am. Nuclear Soc., Am. Ceramic Soc. (tech. reviewer 1986—), Materials Rsch. Soc., Am. Soc. Engring. Edn. Roman Catholic. Home: PO Box 167 Itasca IL 60143-0167 Office: Exponent 185 Hansen Ct Ste 100 Wood Dale IL 60191 Office Phone: 630-274-3223. E-mail: dbullen@exponent.com.

BULLER, STEVEN E., diversified financial services company executive; b. July 16, 1951; B., Northwestern U., 1973, M., 1975. CPA. Ptnr. Arthur Young, Chgo., 1986, Ernst & Young LLP, 1992—2005, nat. dir. investment co. group, SEC liaison, co-dir. Global Asset Mgmt. Services; head global fin. policy & controls BlackRock Inc., NYC, 2005—, CFO, 2005—07. Mem.: Am. Inst. CPAs (chmn. investment co. com. 1993—96). Office: BlackRock Inc 40 E 52nd St New York NY 10022*

BULLERDICK, KIM H., lawyer, petroleum executive; b. Richmond, Ind., 1953; BA, Wittenberg U., 1975; JD, U. Va., 1978. Legal dept. dir. Giant Industries, Inc., Scottsdale, Ariz., 1998—2000, v.p., corp. sec., subs. officer, 1998—, gen. counsel, 2000—. Office: Giant Industries Inc 23733 N Scottsdale Rd Scottsdale AZ 85255-3466 Office Phone: 480-585-8888. Fax: 480-585-8893.*

BULLIET, RICHARD WILLIAMS, historian, educator, writer; b. Rockford, Ill., Oct. 30, 1940; s. Leander Jackson and Mildred Idell (Williams) B.; m. Lucianne Cherry, June 24, 1962; 1 child, Mark Paul BA, Harvard U., 1962, MA, 1964, PhD, 1967. Instr. Harvard U., Cambridge, Mass., 1967-70, asst. prof., 1970-73; lectr. U. Calif.-Berkeley, 1973-75; assoc. prof. history Columbia U., NYC, 1976-79, prof., 1979—. Author: The Patricians of Nishapur, 1972, The Camel and the Wheel, 1977 (Dexter prize), Conversion to Islam in the Medieval Period, 1979, Islam: The View from the Edge, 1993, The Case for Islam-Christian Civilization, 2004, Hunters, Herders, and Hamburgers, 2005; (novels) Kicked to Death by a Camel, 1973; The Tomb of the Twelfth Imam, 1979, The Gulf Scenario, 1984, The Sufi Fiddle, 1991; co-author: The Earth and Its Peoples, 1997; co-editor: The Encyclopedia of the Modern Middle East, 1996; editor: The Columbia History of the Twentieth Century, 1998; host-narrator: (documentary TV series) The Middle East, 1985; editor Jour. Iranian Studies, 1987-90. Guggenheim fellow, 1975-76 Mem. Mid. East Studies Assn. (exec. sec. 1977-81), Phi Beta Kappa. Avocation: painting. Home: 90 Morningside Dr New York NY 10027-7124 Office: Columbia U Mid East Inst New York NY 10027 Home Phone: 212-666-6034.

BULLINGTON, GAYLE ROGERS, writer, researcher; b. Watsonville, Calif., May 17, 1923; d. Manley Duane and Gladyce Thelma (Horton) Rogers; m. Keith Charles Brown, Nov. 26, 1944 (div. Feb.4, 1963); children: Kendall Keith, Kevin Doran; m. Jack William Bullington, Dec. 23, 1978. BA, UCLA, 1947; postgrad., Northridge U., 1962; MA, Calif. Luth. U., 1974. Cert. tchr., secondary tchr. Calif. Tchr. Southgate (Calif.) Jr. H.S., 1947-48, Virgil Jr. H.S., LA, 1948-50, North Hollywood (Calif.) H.S., 1950-52, Van Nuys (Calif.) H.S., 1953-54, Thousand Oaks (Calif.) H.S.,

1963-79. Author: The Second Kiss, 1972, NAKOA's Woman, 1975—81, Gladyce With a C, 2000, Dark Corners, 2002, My Name Was Mary, 2003, Mary's Little Lamb, 2004, For Love's Sake Only, 2005, Castle of Dreams the Divinity Within: How Jesus Christ Survives Christianity, 2007. Mem. ACLU, Pub. Citizen, Common Cause, Nation Assocs. Home: 23119 19th Ave NE Arlington WA 98223-7631 Office Phone: 360-435-4622. Personal E-mail: gaylerogers@verizon.net.

BULLOCK, ANNA MAE See TURNER, TINA

BULLOCK, CHARLES SPENCER, III, political science educator, author, consultant; b. Nashville, July 22, 1942; s. Charles Spencer and Elenor Alice (Davis) B.; m. Frances Lee Mann, Sept. 10, 1965; children—Georgia Beth, Judith Rebecca Lee. AB, William Jewell Coll., 1964; MA, Washington U., St. Louis, 1967, PhD, 1968; postgrad., Emory U., 1964-65. Asst. prof. U. Ga., Athens, 1968-72, assoc. prof., 1972-75; prof. U. Houston, 1975—77; prof. polit. sci. U. Ga., Athens, 1977—, Richard B. Russell chair polit. sci., 1980—, research fellow Inst. Behavioral Research, 1977—84, Josiah Meigs Disting. tchg. prof., 2005—. Adj. prof. U. Okla., 1987—; sr. fellow Rothermere Am. Inst., Oxford U., 2005. Co-author or co-editor: Black Political Attitudes, 1972, The New Politics, 1970, Law and Social Change, 1972, Racial Equality in America, 1975, Coercion to Compliance, 1977, Public Policy in the Eighties, 1983, PublicPolicy and Politics in America, 1978, 84, Implementation of Civil Rights Policy, 1984, Governing a Changing America, 1984, Georgia Political Almanac, 1991, Runoff Elections in the United States, 1992, Forest Resource Policy, 1993, Georgia Political Almanac, 1993-94, 1993, Georgia Political Almanac, 1995-96, 1995, David Duke and the Politics of Race in the South, 1995, New Politics of the Old South, 1998, rev. 2d edit. 2003, 3d edit., 2007, Open Seat Elections to the U.S. House, 2000. Mem. Ga. adv. com. to U.S. Commn. on Civil Rights; mem. Leadership Athens, 1992-93. Recipient citation for achievement William Jewell Coll., 1983, William A. Owens award for creativity in social sci. rsch., 1991, V.O. Key award for best book on so. politics, 1993, Outstanding Tchg. award, 1970, 87, 93, 95, 99, 2003, 05, 06; grantee NSF, 1973-75, Nat. Inst. Edn., 1973-76. Mem. Am. Polit. Sci. Assn. (exec. coun. 1989-91), Southwestern Polit. Sci. Assn. (Pi Sigma Alpha Outstanding Paper award 1975, 2007, Jewell Prestage Best Paper award 2003), Midwest Polit. Sci. Assn., So. Polit. Sci. Assn. (exec. coun. 1979-87, pres. 1985-86, Scott-Foresman award 1984, award for best paper on women and politics 1988-89), Ga. Polit. Sci. Assn. (pres. 2001-02), Legis. Study Group (chmn. 1983-85), Rotary. Episcopalian. Home: 1011 River Run Bishop GA 30621-1663 Office: U Ga Dept Polit Sci Athens GA 30602

BULLOCK, ELLIS WAY, JR., architect; b. Birmingham, Ala., Sept. 11, 1928; s. Ellis Way Sr. Bullock and Martha (Foute) Alexander; m. Ann Ardelia Pope, Nov. 28, 1950; children: Ellis Way III, Elbert Pope, John Howard Keith, William Frank. BArch, Auburn U., 1954. Registered architect, Fla., Ala., Ga., Miss., S.C., N.C. Apprentice architect Yonge, Look & Morrison, Pensacola, Fla., 1954-58; owner Ellis Bullock Architect, Pensacola, 1958-73; pres., CEO Bullock-Tice and Assocs. Arch., Inc., Pensacola, 1973—96. Pres. Fla. AIA, 1977, treas. AIA Rsch. Corp., Washington, 1980-81; chmn. Energy in Arch., Washington, 1980-82; mem. faculty adv. com. Auburn U. Sch. Architecture, 1980—, chmn., 1988-89; mem. Nat. Architecture Accrediting Bd., Washington, 1982-86; mem. adv. coun. U. Fla. Coll. Architecture, 1986—. Contbr. articles to profl. jours. Chmn. Pensacola Hist. Commn., 1967; chmn. City of Pensacola Archtl. Review Bd., 1968, Pensacola Bldg. Bd. of Appeals, 1970—; bd. dirs. Pensacola Symphony, 1998-2000, Fla. Bd. Architecture and Interior Design, 2002-06, chair, 2005; exec. bd. Auburn U. Coll. Architecture, Design and Constrn., 2000—; mem. Blue Ribbon Task Force on Edn., Escambia County, Fla., 1985-86; mem. adv. coun. U. Fla., 1986—; mem. sesquicentennial commn. State of Fla. 1st lt. U.S. Army, 1950-54. Recipient 1st Honor AIA-Navy, 1977, 78, Award of Merit, 1976; recipient Outstanding Design award for Air Force Systems Command Hdqrs., 1980, Gov.'s Design award, 1982, 84, Merit award for U.S. Air Force Design, 1983, Design Excellence award Air Force Regional Civil Engrs., 1984, award of merit Navy Youth Ctr., 1990, award of merit Navy Bowling Ctr. Complex, 1990; named Profl. of Yr., Pensacola News Jour., 1977. Fellow AIA (bd. dirs. 1979-82, v.p. 1981-82, jury coll. of fellows 1988-91, exec. com. coll. of fellows 1993—, bursar 1993—, vice chancellor 1994-95, chancellor 1995-96, regional rep. Fla. Caribbean 1990—, numerous awards N.W. chpt. 1974—, award of excellence Fla. N.W. chpt. 1980, 82, 86, 89, 90, Gold medal Fla. chpt. 1988, Millennium award of honor Fla. chpt. 2000), Am. Archtl. Found. (regent 1995-96, EXCOM 1995-96, task force account and reason 1988, program chmn. nat. conv. com. 1986); mem. Fla. Assn. AIA (pres. 1977, govtl. liaison com. 1984—, Gold medal 1988, gold medal nominating com. 1990-91, balanced curriculum task force 1990, chmn. design awards jur. Ctrl. Fla. chpt. 1980, speaker ann. conf. 1997-98), Fla. Archtl. Found. (trustee 1988—, chmn. 1993), Inst. Bus. Designers (award for contractual interiors 1977), NRA, St. Andrews Soc., Rotary (Paul Harris fellow 1994). Office: Bullock Tice Assocs 909 E Cervantes St Ste B Pensacola FL 32501-3281 Home: 608 Bayshore Dr Pensacola FL 32507 Office Phone: 850-434-5444. E-mail: ewbjr@ewbullock.com.

BULLOCK, FRANK WILLIAM, JR., lawyer, retired federal judge; b. Oxford, NC, Nov. 3, 1938; s. Frank William and Wilma Jackson (Long) B.; m. Frances Dockery Haywood, May 5, 1984; 1 child, Frank William III BSBA, U. N.C., 1961, LLB, 1963. Bar: N.C. 1963. Law clk. to Hon. Algernon L. Butler US Dist. Ct. (ea. dist.) NC, 1963—64; assoc. Maupin, Taylor & Ellis, Raleigh, NC, 1964-68; asst. dir. Adminstrv. Office of Cts. of N.C., Raleigh, NC, 1968-73; ptnr. Douglas, Ravenel, Hardy, Crihfield & Bullock, Greensboro, NC, 1973-82; judge US Dist. Ct. (mid. dist.) N.C., Greensboro, NC, 1982—2006, chief judge, 1992-99; ptnr. Womble Carlyle Sandridge & Rice LLP, Greensboro, NC, 2006—. Mem. bd. editors N.C. Law Rev., 1962-63; contbr. articles to profl. jours. Mem. N.C. Bar Assn., Greensboro Bar Assn., N.C. Soc. of Cin., Fla. Soc. Colonial Wars, Greensboro Country Club. Republican. Presbyterian. Avocations: golf, tennis, running, history. Office: Womble Carlyle Sandridge & Rice LLP PO Box 21104 Greensboro NC 27402

BULLOCK, JAMES JEFFERSON, II, literature and language professor, director; b. El Dorado, Ark., Dec. 15, 1952; s. Joe Harville and Pauline Eunice (White) Bullock; m. Susie Jane Richburg, June 16, 1984; children: James Jefferson III, Sarah Elizabeth. BA, La. Tech U., Ruston, 1975, MA, 1977; PhD, Tex. Tech U., Lubbock, 1997. Instr. La. Tech U., Ruston, 1975—77; min. North 5th Ch. of Christ, West Monroe, La., 1977—83; tchr. West Monroe HS, La., 1981—83; min. Fairview Ch. of Christ, Austin, Tex., 1983—90; owner, operator Double Rainbow Enterprises, Austin, Tex., 1990—92; owner, editor, pub. Gospel Tidings, Austin, Tex., 1983—87; regional v.p. Primerica Corp., Austin, Tex., 1987—92; tchg. asst. Tex. Tech U., Lubbock, Tex., 1992—93; prof. English Lubbock Christian U., Tex., 1993—, dir. honors program, 2000—, pres. faculty senate, 2002—03, co-chair scholars colloquium, 2005—, faculty rep. steering com. 50th anniversary campaign. Faculty cons. Coll. Board's AP English Lit Reading, Daytona Beach, Fla., 2002—; faculty leader Washington Ctr. for Internships and Academic Seminars, 2005—; tour leader EF Edn. Tours, Boston, 2002—; co-host Gt. Plains Honors Coun. Conf., Lubbock, Tex., 2005—06. Author numerous poems, short stories. Steering com. Stblzn., Revitalization Master Plan for Ctrl. Lubbock, 2004—; asst. scoutmaster Boy Scouts of Am., Lubbock, 2000—04; honors acad. adv. com. Washington Ctr. for Internships and Acad. Seminars, 2005—; bd. dirs. Smithlawn Maternity Home and Adoption Agy., Lubbock, 1996—97. Recipient L.R., Sr., and Ruth Wilson Tchg. award, Lubbock Christian U., 2004—05. Mem.: Tex. Coll. English Assn., Nat. Conf. for Tchrs. English, Conf. for Coll. Tchrs. English (Rhetoric or Tech. Communication Best Paper award 2002), Nat. Collegiate Honors Coun., Gt. Plains Honors Coun., Sigma Tau Delta (hon.; pres. Rho Gamma chpt. 1974—75). Republican. Mem. Ch. Of Christ. Avocations: travel, gardening, antiques, tennis. Office: Lubbock Christian Univ 5601 19th St Lubbock TX 79407-2099

BULLOCK, JOSEPH DANIEL, pediatrician, educator; b. Cin., Jan. 23, 1942; s. Joseph Craven and Emilie (Woide) B.; m. Martha Foss, June 20, 1964; children: Jennifer Zane, Sarah Harrison. BA, Wittenberg U., 1963; MD, Ohio State U., 1967, degree in pediatrics, 1969; degree in immunology, allergy, U. Calif., San Francisco, 1971. Diplomate Am. Bd. Pediat., Am. Bd. Allergy and Immunology. Clin. prof. pediatrics Ohio State U., Columbus, 1971—; pres. Midwest Allergy Assocs., Inc., Worthington, Ohio, 1971—. Contbr. articles to profl. jours. Active fund raising Wittenberg U., Springfield, Ohio, 1980-83, Columbus Sch. for Girls, 1977-86. Served to capt. USAF, 1967-71. Recipient Mead Johnson award, 1965. Fellow Am. Acad. Pediatrics, Am. Acad. Allergy, Am. Coll. Allergists (Bd. Regents 1979-82, Clemens von Pirquet award 1968, 69, 70, 71), Am. Thoracic Soc., Interasma, Ohio Soc. Allergy and Immunology (pres. 1985-87). Clubs: Columbus Country; The Golf (New Albany, Ohio); Indian Creek Country (Miami Beach, Fla.), The Surf (Surfside, Fla.). Republican. Lutheran. Home: 189 N Parkview Ave Columbus OH 43209-1435 Office: 8080 Ravines Edge Ct Columbus OH 43235-5424 Office Phone: 614-846-5944.

BULLOCK, MARY BROWN, adult education educator; m. George Bullock; children: Ashley, Graham. BA, Agnes Scott Coll., Atlanta, 1966; MA in Chinese history, Stanford U., 1968, PhD in Chinese history, 1973. Profl. assoc. Com. on Scholarly Comm. with People's Republic of China, 1973—77, dir., 1977—88; dir. Asia program Woodrow Wilson Internat. Ctr. Scholars, Washington, 1988—95; pres. Agnes Scott Coll., Decatur, Ga., 1995—2006; disting. prof. China studies Emory U. Chair, bd. trustees China Med. Bd. of N.Y.; dir. Nat. Com. on U.S.-China Rels.; mem. adv. coun. on U.S.-China cooperation in sci., policy, rsch. and edn. NSF; chair Nat. Assn. Ind. Colls. and Univs., 2002—04, Women's Coll. Coalition, 2004—06; bd. dirs. Sun Trust Bank, Atlanta, Genuine Parts Co.; trustee Asia Found., Luce Found. Recipient Elizabeth Luce Moore Visionary Leadership award, Dist. Svc. award, NAS; fellow, Woodrow Wilson Internat. Ctr. Scholars, Rockefeller Conf. Ctr., Bellagio, Italy; grantee, Ford Found., Henry Luce Found., Rockefeller Found., NSF. Mem.: Coun. on Fgn. Rels., Carter Ctr. Bd. of Councilors.

BULLOCK, MOLLY, retired elementary school educator; d. Wiley and Annie M. Jordan; m. George Bullock; children: Myra A. Bauman, Dawn M. Law. BS in Edn., No. Ariz. U., 1955, postgrad., 1958, LaVerne U., 1962, Claremont Grad. Sch., 1963, Calif. State U. L.A., 1966. Tchr. Bur. Indian Affairs, Kaibeto, Ariz., 1955-56, Crystal, N.Mex., 1956-59, Covina Valley Unified Sch. Dist., Calif., 1961-95, supervising master tchr. trainees LaVerne U., Calif. State U.-LA, 1961-71, mem. curriculum devel. adv. bd., 1977-79; ret., 1995. Cons. Bauman Curry Co., PR; mem. voting com. Excellence in Edn. awards Lawry's Foods; attendee reading conf. Claremont Grad. Sch., Calif. Author: (poems) A Tree (Golden Poet, 1991), What is Love (Golden medal of honor), The Change of Seasons (Dimond Homer trophy, 1999, Poet of the Yr. medallion). Vol. visitor area convalescent hosps.; mentor to former students. Mini grantee, Hughes/Rotary Club/Foothill Ind. Bank, 1986—90. Mem.: NAFE, Covina Unified Edn. Assn., Internat. Platform Assn., Internat. Soc. Poets (hon.). Avocations: poetry, collecting jewelry, dolls, paintings.

BULLOCK, PETER BRADLEY, company director, consultant; b. Tipton, Eng., June 9, 1934; s. William Horace Bradley and Catherine (Garner) Bullock; m. Joyce Rea, Nov. 1, 1958; children: Claire Elizabeth Bradley Locke, Penelope Jane Bradley Hembrow. BSc, U. London. Chartered engr. and marketer, UK. With Nat. Coal Bd., 1959-65, Thomas Potterton Ltd., 1966-67, Fibreglass Ltd., 1965-66, 67-69; pres., mng. dir. Flymo Ltd.; dir. Electrolux Ltd.; joint mng. dir. Electrolux Group UK, 1976-83; group chief exec. James Neill Holdings PLC, 1983-89, Spear & Jackson Internat. PLC, 1986-90; chmn. Neill Tools Ltd., 1983-90; pres, dir., gen. AMV (France), 1986-90; chmn. London & Geneva Securities Ltd., 1990—, James Dickie Pub. Ltd. Co., 1995-98, Scala Collections Ltd., 1997—2006. Bd. dirs. 600 Group Pub. Ltd. Co., 1998-2004, Syltone Pub. Ltd. Co., 1990-99. With Brit. Army, 1956-58. Mem. Inst. Energy, Inst. Mktg., Leander Club, Henley-on-Thames Club, Phyllis Court. Mem. Ch. Of Eng. Home: 5 Old Brewery Lane Henley on Thames RG9 2DE England Personal E-mail: genelond1@aol.com.

BULLOCK, SANDRA (SANDRA ANNETTE BULLOCK), actress; b. Arlington, Va., July 26, 1964; d. John and Helga Bullock; m. Jesse James, July 16, 2005; stepchildren: Chandler, Jesse Jr., Sunny. Attended, East Carolina U. Actor (films) Hangmen, 1987, Fire on the Amazon, 1991, Religion Inc., 1989, Love Potion #9, 1992, When the Party's Over, 1992, Who Do I Gotta Kill, 1992, The Vanishing, 1993, Demolition Man, 1993, The Thing Called Love, 1993 (also composer for Song Heaven Knocking On My Door), Wrestling Ernest Hemingway, 1993, Speed, 1994 (Best Female Performance, Most Desirable Female MTV Movie awards), While You Were Sleeping, 1995 (Favorite Actress in a Motion Picture award People Choice Awards 1996), The Net, 1995, Two if by Sea, 1996, A Time to Kill, 1996, In Love and War, 1996, Speed 2: Cruise Control, 1997, Practical Magic, 1998, Forces of Nature, 1999, Exactly 3:30, 1999, 28 Days, 2000, Divine Secrets of the Ya-Ya Sisterhood, 2002, Crash, 2004, Loverboy, 2005, Infamous (Hollywood award for Best Supporting Actress Hollywood awards, 2006) 2006, Premonition, 2007; actor, dir., writer Making Sandwiches, 1998; actor, prodr. Gun Shy, 1999, Miss Congeniality, 2000, Two Weeks Notice, 2002, Miss Congeniality 2: Armed and Fabulous, 2005, The Lake House, 2006 (with Keanu Reeves Movie-Choice Liplock, Teen Choice Awards, 2006); actor, exec. prodr. Hope Floats, 1998, Murder By Numbers, 2002; actor (TV movies) Bionic Showdown: The Six-Million Dollar Man and the Bionic Woman, 1989, Who Shot Patakango, 1989, The Preppie Murder, 1989; (TV series) Working Girl, 1990; (TV mini-series) Lucky/Chances, 1990; prodr. (films) Our Father, 1996, Trespasses, 1999; exec. prodr. (TV series) George Lopez, 2002- Recipient Best Actress MTV's Big Picture, 1994 and 1995, Best Actress US Mag., 1995, Favorite Actress in a Comedy/Drama Theatrical and Favorite Actress-Comedy Video awards BlockBuster Entertainment Awards, 1996, Favorite Actress People's Choice award, 1997, 1999, ShoWest Female Star of the Year, 2001, Am. Comedy Award for Funniest Female Performer in a Motion Picture, 2001, Favorite Female Movie Star, People's Choice Award, 2006, Outstanding Performance by a Cast in a Motion Picture, SAG awards, 2006; named Woman of the Yr. Glamour mag, 2006; named one of 50 Most Beautiful People, People Mag., 1996, 1999, 100 Most Powerful Celebrities, Forbes.com, 2007.*

BULLOCK, STEVEN CARL, lawyer; b. Anderson, Ind., Jan. 19, 1949; s. Carl Pearson and Dorothy Mae (Colle) B.; m. Debra Bullock; children: Bradford, Christine, Justin, Evan. BA, Purdue U., 1971; JD, Detroit Coll., 1985. Bar: Mich. 1985, U.S. Dist. Ct. (ea. dist.) 1985, Ct. of Appeals (6th cir.) 1993, U.S. Supreme Ct. 1993. Pvt. pracitce, Inkster, Mich., 1985—. With USAF, 1971-75. Mem. Mich. Bar Assn. (criminal law sect.), Detroit Bar Assn., Detroit Founders Soc., Recorder's Ct. Bar Assn., Suburban Bar Assn., Nat. Assn. Criminal Def. Attys., Criminal Def. Lawyers of Mich., Wayne County Criminal Def. Bar Assn. Avocations: golf, travel. Office: 2228 Inkster Rd Inkster MI 48141-1811 Office Phone: 313-562-6500. E-mail: lawone123@aol.com.

BULLOUGH, JOHN DONOVAN, information scientist, educator; b. Holyoke, Mass., Nov. 15, 1969; s. Jeanne Marie and John Bullough; m. Sloane Donovan Bullough; 1 child, Honorah Donovan. BS, Rensselaer Poly. Inst., Troy, NY, 1991, MS, 1992, PhD, 2004. Technologist Bell Comm. Rsch., Piscataway, NJ, 1990; scientist Rensselaer Poly. Inst., 1992—. Contbr. chapters to books. Vol. Hudson Mohawk Indsl. Gateway, Troy, 1996—2005; committeeman Rensselaer County Dem. Com., Troy, 1998—2006; vol. Interfaith Alliance NY State, Latham, NY, 1996—2006. Recipient Gov's. award for Energy Excellence, NY State Gov. Mario Cuomo, 1994, Excellence award, Soc. for Tech. Communication-Mohawk Chpt., 1999, 2004, Walsh-Weston award, Chartered Instn. Bldg. Svcs. Engrs., 2004, 2005. Fellow: Illuminating Engring. Soc. N.Am. (chmn. spcl. effects 2003—06, Cert. Appreciation 1999); mem.: Coun. for Optical Radiation Measurements (bd. dirs. 2004—), Internat. Mcpl. Signaling Assn., Soc. Automotive Engrs. (Cert. Appreciation 2002, 2003, 2004, 2005, 2006). Democrat. Roman Catholic. Achievements include patents pending for retinal flux density meter. Office Phone: 518-276-6000.

BULLOUGH, JOHN FRANK, musician, educator; b. Washington, Oct. 15, 1928; s. John and Mabel Jean (McCalip) B.; m. Dorothy Baines, Apr. 10, 1950; children: John Frank, Lynn Diane Lazar, Patricia Ann Gibbs. BA, George Washington U., 1954; ChM choirmaster cert., Am. Guild Organists, 1956; SMM, Union Theol. Sem., 1958. Organist, asst. prof. music Hartford Theol. Sem. Found., Conn., 1958-64; from asst. prof. music to assoc. prof. to prof. Fairleigh Dickinson U., Teaneck, NJ, 1964-93, chmn. dept. fine arts, 1974-79. Music dir. Hartford Ctr. Ch., 1960-64; organist, choirmaster St. Paul's Episcopal Ch., Englewood, NJ, 1973-95; music dir., conductor The Bergen Chorale, Tenafly, NJ, 1987-91. Contbr. articles to profl. jour. V.p. bd. trustees Bergen Philharm. Orch., NJ, 1973—80; pres., bd. dirs., mem. auditions com. Rodland Found., 2002—. Mem. AAUP, Am. Guild Organists (dean Hartford chpt. 1963-64, No. Valley NJ chpt. 1975-77, chmn. region II 1984-88, convener No. NJ dist. 1991-92, dean No. NJ cpth. 1995-97), Coll. Music Soc. Episcopalian. Home: 488 Fairidge Ter Teaneck NJ 07666-2617 Personal E-mail: jbmadrigal@aol.com.

BULLOUGH, ROBERT VERNON, JR., educational studies professor; b. Salt Lake City, Feb. 12, 1949; s. Robert Vernon and Dolores Elaine (Clarke) B.; m. Dawn Ann Mortensen, June 18, 1976; children: Joshua Benjamin, Seth Thomas, Adam Neve, Rachel Elizabeth. BS in History, U. Utah, 1971, MEd, 1973; PhD, Ohio State U., 1976. Tchr. East High Sch., Salt Lake City, 1971-73; teaching assoc., then fellow Ohio State U., Columbus, 1973-76; asst. prof., then assoc. prof. U. Utah, Salt Lake City, 1976-89, prof. ednl. studies, 1989—99, emeritus prof., 1999—; dir. rsch. Ctr. Improvement Tchr. Edn. and Schooling and prof. tchr. edn. Brigham Young U., 1999—. Mem. Holmes Group Writing Com., 1984-86. Author: Democracy in Education: Boyd H. Bode, 1981, Human Interests in the Curriculum: Teaching and Learning in a Technological Society, 1984, The Forgotten Dream of American Education, 1988, First Year Teacher: A Case Study, 1989, Emerging as a Teacher, 1992, First Year Teacher--Eight Years Later, 1997, Becoming a Student of Teaching, 1995, 2d edit., 2001, Uncertain Lives: Children of Promise, Teachers of Hope, 2001, Stories of the Eight Year Study and Reexamining Secondary Education in America, 2007; mem. editl. bds.; contbr. articles to profl. jours. Recipient Outstanding Writing award, AACTE, 1997. Mem. Am. Ednl. Rsch. Assn. (Outstanding Book award divsn. B 2003), Profs. of Curriculum, Phi Beta Kappa, Phi Kappa Phi, Phi Delta Kappa. Mem. Lds Ch. Avocations: book collecting, house restoration, furniture restoration. Office: Brigham Young U 149 McKay Bldg Provo UT 84602 Business E-Mail: bob_bullough@byu.edu.

BULLY-CUMMINGS, ELLA M., police chief; b. Japan; d. Daniel Lee Bully; m. William Cummings. BA with hons. in Pub. Adminstrn., Madonna State U., 1993; JD cum laude, Mich. State U., 1998. Bar: Mich. 1998. From police officer to chief police Detroit (Mich.) Police Dept., 1977—2003, chief police, 2003—; assoc. Miller, Canfield, Paddockand Stone, PLC, 1999—2000, Foley & Lardner, 2000—02. Mem.: Mich. Assn. Chiefs Police, Nat. Orgn. Black Law Enforcement Execs., Internat. Assn. Chiefs Police, Wolverine Bar Assn., Nat. Bar Assn. Office: Detroit Police Dept 1300 Beaubien Detroit MI 48226

BULMAN, JOHN, lawyer; b. Washington, July 13, 1958; s. John Shea and Louise Bronson Bulman; m. Kathryn Marlow, June 7, 1980; children: Kimberly, Alison, Evan. BA, Hobart Coll., 1980; JD cum laude, Georgetown U., 1984. Bar: RI 1984, U.S. Dist. Ct. RI 1985, U.S. Ct. Appeals (1st cir.) 1987, Mass. 1990, U.S. Dist. Ct. Mass. 1990, U.S. Ct. Appeals (11th cir.) 1996. Assoc. Tillinghast, Collins & Graham, Providence, 1984—90, ptnr., 1990—95; prin. Little, Bulman & Reardon, Providence, 1995—99, Little, Bulman Medeiros and Whitney, Providence, 1999—2003, Little Medeiros Kinder Bulman & Whitney, Providence, 2003—, Am. Coll. Constrn. Lawyrs, 2006—. Hon. dir. Barrington Land Trust, Barrington, 1987—; mem. adv. bd. Cmty. Mediation Ctr., 2000—. Fellow: Am. Coll. Construction Lawyers; mem.: ABA (chmn. subcom. litigation sect. 1998—), Am. Arbitration Assn. (bd. dirs. 2002—, panel mem. comml., mediation and complex case panels 1991—). Avocations: woodworking, golf, fishing. Office: Little Medeiros Kinder Bulman & Whitney 72 Pine St Providence RI 02903 Office Phone: 401-272-8080. Business E-Mail: jbulman@lmkbw.com.

BULOVIC, VLADIMIR, engineering educator; BS in Engring., Princeton U., 1991; MS in Elec. Engring., Coulmbia U., 1993; MA in Elec. Engring., Princeton U., 1995, PhD in Elec. Engring., 1998. Grad. research, Eectrical Engineering dept. Columbia Radiation Lab, Columbia U., 1991—93, Optoelectronic Components and Materials Lab, Princeton U, 1993—98, post-doctoral research, Electrical Engineering dept., 1998—99; sr. scientist Universal Display Corp., Ewing, NJ, 1999—2000; asst. prof., dept. of Electrical Engineering and Computer Science M.I.T., 2000—. Office: c/o MIT Dept of Electrical Engineering 77 Massachusetts Ave Cambridge MA 02139

BULOW, JACK FAYE, retired library director; b. Elmira, NY, June 7, 1942; m. June Burwell, May 22, 1971. Associates degree, Corning CC, NY, 1968; BA, U. Ala., Birmingham, 1971; MLS, U. Ala., Tuscaloosa, 1973. Community svcs. libr. Birmingham Pub. Libr., 1973-77, assoc. dir., 1977-93, dir., 1993—2002, ret., 2002. Developer Books-by-Mail program, Birmingham and Jefferson County, 1976; participant exec. in residence program Birmingham-So. Coll., 1987, Leadership Birmingham, 1992; elected as del. White House Conf. on Libr. and Info. Svc., Washington, 1991; elected as regional rep. White House Conf. on Libr. and Info. Svcs. Task Force, Washington, 1992; bd. dirs. Literacy Coun. Ctrl. Ala., Birmingham, 1993-2000; mem. Nat. League Cities, Washington, 1993—; mem. long range planning com. Birmingham Mus. Art, 1993-99; mem. cultural affairs com. Operation New Birmingham, 1988—; sec. Birmingham Pub. Libr. Found.; patron Cahaba River Soc. Birmingham, 1992—. With USCG, 1960-64. Recipient Forestry Recognition award Ala. Forestry Commn., 1977. Mem. ALA (chair fundraising and fin. devel. sect. 1997), Am. Hist. Print Collectors Soc., Am. Mgmt. Assn., Nat. Soc. Fund Raising Execs., Southeastern Libr. Assn., Ala. Libr. Assn. (pres. 1995, Eminent Libr. award 2000), Birmingham-So. Coll. Fine Arts Soc. Avocations: reading, golf, travel, fishing. Personal E-mail: JaBu12@aol.com.

BULOW, JEREMY ISRAEL, economist; b. NYC, Jan. 30, 1954; s. Norman W. and Tova H. Bulow; m. Rhona Mahony; children: Talia, Maya, Zoe. BA, MA, Yale U., 1975; PhD, MIT, 1979. Prof. econs. Stanford (Calif.) Bus. Sch., 1979—; dir. Bur. Econs, Fed. Trade Commn., Washington, 1998—. Fellow Econometric Soc., Am. Acad. Arts & Scis. 2004; mem. ABA (vice chair antitrust sect. 1999—). Office: Stanford Bus Sch 450 Memorial Dr Stanford CA 94305-5015

BULTAN, AYKUT, communications systems engineer; came to U.S., 1997; BSEE, Middle East Tech. U., Ankara, Turkey, 1986, MSEE, 1989, PhD in Elec. Engring., 1995. Rsch. and design engr. Comm. Lab. ASELSAN Corp., Ankara, 1986-89; rsch./tchg. asst. dept. elec. engring. Middle East Tech. U., Ankara, 1990—95; asst. prof. computer engring. dept. Ea. Mediterranean U., Famagusta, Cyprus, 1996-97; vis. scholar elec. and computer engring. dept. N.J. Ctr. for Multimedia Rsch., N.J. Inst. Tech., Newark, 1997-99; comms. sys. engr. Interdigital Comm. Corp., Melville, NY, 2000—. Contbr. articles to profl. jours. Undergrad. student fellow Turkish Sci. and Tech. Rsch. Assn., 1982-86. Achievements include design of algorithms for third generation wireless systems; OFDM-MIMO systems; patents in field; research in time-frequency signal analysis and its applications in wireless communication. Avocations: skiing, scuba and skin diving, reading. Office: Interdigital Comm Corp 2 Huntington Quadrangle Melville NY 11747-4508 Office Phone: 631-622-4196. Office Fax: 631-622-0100. E-mail: aykutbultan@yahoo.com.

BULTAS, WILLIAM FITZGERALD, Internet company executive; s. William Anthony Bultas and Janice Helen Fitzgerald; m. Kameeka Denise Gerald, July 5, 1997; 1 child, William Rasheed. BS, SW Mo. State U. (now Mo. State U.), Springfield, 1995. Pres. Puzz.com, LLC, Webster Groves, Mo., 1998—. Author, prodr., editor: online publishing Puzz.com, AllIQTests.com, FreeDungeons.com. Specialist Mo. Army N.G., 1990—92, Springfield. Walter O. Cralle scholar, SW Mo. State U., 1993—95, 1995. Mem.: Am. Mensa (life). Avocations: reading, writing, Brazilian Ju Jitsu, movies, puzzles. Home and Office: PO Box 260015 Saint Louis MO 63126

BULTHUIS, SIDNEY AARON, secondary school educator; b. Cherokee, Iowa, Apr. 20, 1977; s. Byron Duane and Lynda Marie Bulthuis; m. Christie Carol Veen, July 11, 1999; children: Trygve Arthur, Miles Jonathan. B in Math Edn., Northwestern Coll., Orange City, Iowa, 2000. Cert. tchr. Iowa. Sci. tchr. Remsen (Iowa) Union HS, 2001; math/physics tchr. Rock Valley (Iowa) Pub., 2001—. Sponsor Rock Valley chpt. Nat. Honor Soc., 2005—. Home: 1801 13th St Rock Valley IA 51247 Office: Rock Valley Pub 1712 20th Ave Rock Valley IA 51247

BUMB, RENEE MARIE, federal judge; b. Bellevue, Ohio, 1960; BA, Ohio State U., 1981; MA, U. Chgo., 1983; JD, Rutgers U., 1987. Law clk. Judge Garrett E. Brown, Jr., US Dist. Ct. NJ, 1987—88; assoc. Riker, Danzig, Scherer, Hyland & Peretti, 1988—91; asst. US atty. US Atty's Office, NJ dist., 1991—2006; judge US Dist. Ct. NJ, 2006—. Office: Martin Luther King Jr Fed Bldg & US Courthouse 50 Walnut St Newark NJ 07102 Office Phone: 973-645-3730.*

BUMBECK, DAVID, artist, retired educator; BFA, RISD; MFA, Syracuse U. Prof. Middlebury Coll., 1968—2002, prof. emeritus, 2005—, dir. Christian A. Johnson Meml. Gallery, 1973—85. Exhibitions include Dartmouth Coll., Everson Mus., U. No. Ariz., The Mary Ryan Gallery, Represented in permanent collections Bklyn. Mus. Art, Libr. of Congress, NY Pub. Libr., Met. Mus. Art, Carnegie Mus. Art, Boston Pub. Libr. Mem.: Nat. Acad. Design. Home: 63 Drew Ln Middlebury VT 05753

BUMBRY-BRONSON, VENETTA, music educator; b. Washington, July 12, 1957; d. Lillian Holmes Myrick and Ventura Bumbry; m. Kevinll Willard Bronson, Feb. 3, 1990; children: Venetta Lucille Bronson, Katrina Jean Bronson. MusB Edn., U. D.C., 1982; MS, McDaniel Coll., Westminister, Md., 2004. Cert. Adminstr. McDaniel Coll., 2005, Advance Profl. Prince George's County Pub. Schs., 2005. Tchr. gen. music D.C. Pub. Schs., 1983—95, Prince George's County Pub. Schs., Suitland, Md., 1996—. Instr. piano Charles Houston Magnet Sch., Washington, 1988—95. Mem.: Music Educators Nat. Conf. Home Phone: 301-808-1270. Personal E-mail: vbumbry@msn.com.

BUMGARNER, JAMES MCNABB, judge; b. Peru, Ill., Sept. 13, 1919; s. Joshua Mills and Ethel (McNabb) Bumgarner; m. Helen D Welker, Feb. 7, 1942 (dec. May 1981); children: Barbara Malany, Sally Guth; m. Elizabeth L Miller, Feb. 12, 1983; stepchildren: Tad Miller, Brian Miller, Mathew Miller. BS in Psychology with honors, U. Ill., 1941, JD, 1946. Commd. 2nd lt. USAAF, 1942; advanced through grades to col. USAF, 1967, ret., 1974; pvt. practice Rantoul, Ill., 1947, Hannah, Mattoon, Ill.; cir. judge 10th Jud. Cir. of Ill., 1979—. Mem. pres. coun. U. Ill. Named Disting. Grad. of, U. Ill. Coll. Law; named to, Sr. Illinoisians Hall of Fame. Mem.: VFW, Air War Col Alumni Asn, Judge Advs Asn, Timber Growers Asn, Putnam County Hist Soc, Putnam County Bar Asn, Univ Ill Alumni Asn, Ill Bar Asn, Vietnam Vets Bar Asn, Ret Judge Advs Asn, Ret Officers Asn, Vietnam Vets Ill, Am Legion, Ill Col Law Deans Club, Rotary, Phi Alpha Delta. Home: 1010 Market St PO Box 225 Hennepin IL 61327-0225 Home Phone: 561-301-1333; Office Phone: 772-878-3578. Business E-Mail: jimbum@bumgarner.org.

BUMP, BEVIN B., lawyer; b. Chadron, Nebr., Sept. 7, 1926; Attended, Chadron State Coll.; BS, JD, Univ. Nebr., 1952. Bar: Nebr. 1952, US Dist. Ct. Nebr. Dist. 1952. City atty., Chadron, Nebr., 1953—2006; dep. county atty. Dawes County, Nebr., 1955—59, county atty. Nebr., 1959—70; atty. Bump & Bump, Chadron, Nebr., 1952—. Fellow: Am. Coll. Trust & Estate Counsel; mem.: Am. Bar Found., Nebr. Bar Found., Am. Judicature Soc., Nebr. Assn. Trail Attys., Nebr. County Atty. Assn. (pres. 1966), Nebr. State Bar Assn. (pres. 1990—91), W Nebr. Bar Assn. (pres. 1978—79), ABA (bd. gov. 2004—). Office: Bump & Bump PO Box 1140 Chadron NE 69337-1140 Office Phone: 308-432-4411.

BUMPAS, STUART MARYMAN, lawyer; b. Little Rock, Oct. 7, 1944; s. Hubert Wayne Bumpas and Martha Conway (Maryman) Gaylord; m. Diane Ellen DeWare, Oct. 1, 1977. BA, Brown U., 1966; JD, U. Tex., 1969; LLM, George Washington U., 1973. Bar: Tex. 1969, D.C. 1972. Atty.-advisor Office of Chief Counsel, Washington, 1969-72; asst. to commr. IRS, Washington, 1973-74; ptnr. Locke, Purnell, Rain, Harrell, Dallas, 1974-98, Locke, Liddell & Sapp, Dallas, 1999—. Adj. prof. employee benefits So. Meth. U., Dallas, 1975; lectr. Washington Non-Profit Tax Conf., Am. Law Inst., Ann. Non-Profit Orgns. Inst. Contbr. articles to profl. jours. Exec. com. Meadows Sch. of Arts, So. Meth. U., Dallas; bd. dirs. Callier Ctr. for Comm. Disorders, Dallas, 1984—, Friends of Alzheimer's Dis. Ctr., Southwestern Med. Sch., Goodwill Industries, Dallas; bd. dirs., v.p. Dallas Grand Opera Assn., 1984; mem. Mayor's Commn. on Internat. Devel. Task Force on Arts and Culture, Dallas, 1988; nat. counsel Am. Heart Assn., Dallas, 1979—; trustee The Lamplighter Sch.; gen. counsel The Hockaday Sch.; gen. counsel, trustee, mem. exec. com. Dallas Mus. Art; trustee Southwestern Med. Found.; mem. chancellor's coun. U. Tex. Sys. Mem. ABA (mem. exempt orgns. com.), Tex. Bar Assn. (former chmn. legal aspects of arts com.), Dallas Bar Assn., Bus. Adv. Com., Am. Coun. on Germany, Coun. on Fgn. Rels. Clubs: Dallas Petroleum, Brook Hollow Golf, Idlewild (Dallas); Soc. Cin. (Washington), Coral Beach and Tennis (Bermuda). Episcopalian. Home: 5306 Surrey Cir Dallas TX 75209-2427 Office: Locke Liddell & Sapp 2200 Ross Ave Ste 2200 Dallas TX 75201-6776 Office Phone: 214-740-8000. E-mail: sbumpas@lockeliddell.com.

BUMPUS, FLOYD DAVID, JR., microcomputer analyst; b. Little Rock, Aug. 18, 1952; s. Floyd David and Wilma Ruth (Bishop) B.; m. Bonnie Suzanne Buckner, June 22, 1991; 1 child, Jamie Suzanne Jay. BS in Computer Sci., Math., U. Mary Hardin Baylor, 1993. Enlisted U.S. Army, 1970, advanced through grades to staff sgt., 1980, resigned, 1984; mechanic's helper Otis Elevator, Little Rock, 1984-87; microcomputer analyst Bell County, Belton, Tex., 1987-98; network adminstr. Artco Bell Corp., Temple, Tex., 1997—. Vol. firefighter Belton Fire Dept. Mem. Temple Amateur Radio Club (vol. examiner coord.), Am. Radio Relay League (vol. FCC examiner, ofcl. observer North Tex. sect.). Republican. Mem. Ch. of Christ. Avocations: amateur radio, computers, organized sports. Home: 3608 North Dr Belton TX 76513-5136 Office: Artco Bell Corp Info Sys 1302 Industrial Blvd Temple TX 76504-1127 E-mail: dbumpus@artcobell.com, dbumpus@vtm.com.

BUMPUS, JEANNE, lawyer; JD, Univ. Calif., Berkeley, 1993. Legislative counsel U.S. Senator Slade Gorton, 1995—2000; counsel Comm. Subcommittee, U.S. Senate; staff dir. & gen. counsel Com. Commerce, Sci. & Tech., U.S. Senate; staff dir. Com. Indian Affairs, US Senate; dir., Office of Congl. Relations Fed. Trade Commn., 2006—. Office: Office Congressional Relations Federal Trade Commn 600 Pennsylvania Ave NW Washington DC 20580

BUNCH, C. ROBERT, oil industry executive, lawyer; BA, Rice Univ., 1976; JD, Univ. Houston, 1994; M Admin. in acctg., Rice Univ., 1997. Staff acct. Deloitte & Touche, 1977—81; asst. contr. Hughes Tool Co., 1981—85; sr. v.p., CFO Tescorp Inc., 1985—89, pres., COO, 1989—92; CFO Siberian Am. Oil Co., 1992—94; assoc. Scott Douglass & McConnico LLP, 1994—95; exec. v.p., CFO, COO OYO Geospace Corp., 1995—96; assoc. King & Pennington LLP, 1996—97, ptnr., 1997—99; v.p., chief adminstrv. officer Input/Output Inc., 1999—2002, pres., COO, 2002—03; oil svc. cons., 2003—04; bd. dir. Maverick Tube Corp., Chesterfield, Mo., 1991—, pres., 2004—05, chmn., CEO, 2005—. Bd. dir. Olin Corp., Pioneer Drilling Co. Office: Maverick Tube Corp Ste 700 16401 Swingley Ridge Rd Chesterfield MO 63017

BUNCH, CHARLES E., manufacturing executive; b. 1950; BA, Internat. Affairs, Georgetown U.; MBA, Harvard U. With PPG Industries, Inc., Pitts., 1980—, mgr., European fin. and planning Paris, 1982—85, mgr. European flat glass and comml. products, 1985, mng. dir., Italian glass subs. Italy, 1986—88, corp. dir., purchasing and distbn. Pitts., 1988—92, gen. mgr., archtl. coatings, 1992—94, v.p., archtl. coatings, 1994, v.p., fiber glass, 1995—97, sr. v.p. strategic planning and corp. svcs., 1997—2000, exec. v.p., 2000—02, pres., COO, dir., 2002—05, chmn., CEO, 2005—. Bd. dirs. H.J. Heinz Co., Nat. Paint and Coatings Assoc., Nat. Assoc. Manufacturers, chmn., 2007; dir., deputy chmn. Fed. Reserve Bank of Cleveland. Bd. dirs. U. Pitts. Office: PPG Industries 1 PPG Pl Pittsburgh PA 15272*

BUNCH, CHARLOTTE, advocate; b. Ashe County, NC, Oct. 13, 1944; d. Pardue and Marjorie Bunch. BA in History magna cum laude, Duke U., 1966; postgrad., Inst. Policy Studies, Washington, 1967-68. Founder Ctr. Women's Global Leadership Rutgers U., New Brunswick, NJ, 1989—, dir., disting. prof. women's and gender studies. Spkr. in field. Creator, editor: Quest: A Feminist Quar., 1974, 1980. Office: Ctr Womens Global Leadership Douglass Coll Rutgers U 160 Ryders Ln New Brunswick NJ 08901-8555 Office Phone: 732-932-8782. Business E-Mail: cwgl@igc.org.

BUNCH, JENNINGS BRYAN, JR., retired electrical engineer; b. Richmond, Va., Feb. 9, 1929; s. Jennings Bryan and Cora Irving (Wilson) B.; m. Dale Metcalf, Feb. 2, 1952 (dec. Nov. 1996); children: Jennifer, Pamela; m. Harriet Walton, Jan. 2, 1999. BSEE with distinction, Va. Mil. Inst., 1950; MSEE, U. Pitts., 1969. Lic. profl. engr., NY. Engr. in tng. Va. Electric & Power Co., Alexandria, Richmond, 1950, 53; test engr. and mktg. assignments GE, Schenectady, NY, 1956-63, application engr., 1956-63, regional application engr. Pitts., Phila., 1963-73, sr. application engr., project mgr. Phila. and Schenectady, 1973-82, Malvern, Pa., 1982-91; cons. Star Design, Moorestown, NJ, 1992-96. Contbr. articles on electric utility distbn. automation systems to profl. publs. Exec. dir. Sending Experienced Ret. Vols. Everywhere (SERVE), 1993-2003; bd. chair Am. Internat. Cultural Exchange Inst., 2005—. 1st lt. U.S. Army, 1950-52. Fellow: IEEE; mem.: Tau Beta Pi. Republican. Presbyterian. Avocations: hiking, astronomy.

BUNCH, LONNIE, III, museum director; b. Newark; m. Maria Marable Bunch; children: Sarah, Katie. B, Am. U., Washington, DC, 1974, M, 1976. Adj. lectr. Am. U., Washington, 1978—79; edn. specialist Smithsonian's Nat. Air and Space Mus., 1978—79; asst. prof. Am. and Afro-Am. hist. U. Mass., Dartmouth, 1979—81; historian, tchr. Packer Collegiate Inst., Bklyn., 1981—83; curator hist., prog, mgr. Calif. Afro-Am. Mus., LA, 1983—89; adj. prof. mus. studies George Washington U., Washington, 1989—2000; supervising curator Nat. Mus. Am. Hist., Washington, 1989—92, asst. dir. curatorial affairs, 1992—94, assoc. dir., 1994—2000; founding dir. Nat. Mus. African Am. Hist. and Culture, Washington, 2005—. Appointed by Pres. George W. Bush to Commn. for Preservation of the White House, 2002. Mem.: Am. Assn. State and Local Hist. (adv. bd. mem.), Am. Assn. Museums (adv. bd. mem., named to Centennial Honor Roll 2006), Chgo. Hist. Soc. (pres. 2001—05). Office: Nat Mus of African Am Hist and Culture Capital Gallery Ste 7001 MRC 509 PO Box 37012 Washington DC 20013-7012*

BUNCH, RICHARD ALAN, writer, educator, poet, philosopher; b. Honolulu, June 1, 1945; s. Thornton Carlisle and DeLores B.; m. Rita Anne Glazar, Aug. 11, 1990; children: Katharine, Richard Jr. AA in Liberal Arts, Napa Coll., 1965; student, Stanford -in-Britain, Grantham, Lincolnshire, Eng., 1966; BA in Comms., Stanford U., 1967; MA in History, U. Ariz., 1969, MDiv, 1970, DD in Religion and Theology, 1971; student in Philosophy, Vanderbilt U., 1972—75; postgrad., Temple U., 1975—76; JD, U. Memphis, 1980. Tchg. asst. philosophy Vanderbilt U., Nashville, 1973-74; instr. philosophy Belmont U., 1973-74; law clk. Cir. Ct. Shelby County, Tenn., 1979-81; atty. Horne and Peppel, Memphis, 1981-83; law clk. Tenn. Ct. Appeals, 1983; instr. philosophy Chapman U., 1986-87; instr. law Sonoma State U., 1986-87, instr. philosophy, 1990-91; lectr. religion U. Calif., Berkeley, 1995; instr. history and humanities Diablo Valley Coll., 1991—94, 1997. Adj. humanities and philosophy faculty Napa Valley Coll., 1985—; adj. history and philosophy faculty Solano Coll., 1988—; poetry reviews Hawaii Rev., Poetry New Zealand, Oregon Rev., Poetry Cornwall. Author: Summer Hawk, 1991, Night Blooms, 1992, Wading the Russian River, 1993, Santa Rosa Plums, 1996, A Foggy Morning, 1996, South By Southwest, 1997, Sacred Space, 1998, Rivers of the Sea, 1998, Greatest Hits: 1970-2000, 2001, Running for Daybreak, 2004; (play) The Russian River Returns, 1999, Hawking Moves: Plays, Poems and Stories, 2007. Staff Nashville Human Rights Forum, 1974-75; chmn. Housing Authority-Bldg. Authority Bd. City of Napa, Calif., 1985-89. Recipient Grand prize Ina Coolbrith Nat. Poetry Day Contest, 1989, Jessamyn West prize in creative writing, 1990. Mem.: Ina Coolbrith Cir. Home: 248 Sandpiper Dr Davis CA 95616-7546

BUNCH, ROBERT CRAIG, librarian; b. Houston, Mar. 31, 1954; s. Robert Kern and Gretchen Ann (Schopps) B.; m. Delana Ann Roberts, Oct. 30, 1986. BA in Philosophy, U. Houston, 1979, MA in Philosophy, BS in Psychology, 1982, MEd, 1986; MLS, Sam Houston State U., Huntsville, 1992; MLIS, U. Tex., 1994. Cert. tchr., Tex. Psychiat. technician Meth. Hosp., Houston, 1979-83, 84-89; tchg. asst. U. Houston, 1981-82; acad. asst. U. Tex., Austin, 1983-84; tchr. Houston Ind. Sch. Dist., 1986-89, Coldspring-Oakhurst (Tex.) pub. schs., 1989-90; student libr. asst. Sam Houston State U., Huntsville, 1991; dist. libr. Coldspring-Oakhurst Consolidated Ind. Sch. Dist., 1991—. Editl. bd. Ref. Books Bull., Chgo., 1994-98; rev. editor Popular Culture in Librs., 1991-96. Mem. adv. bd. Humanities Exhibits Interactive, Tex. Com. for Humanities, Austin, 1996-99; libr. adv. bd., Helicon Pub., Oxford, Eng., 1997-2001. NEH fellow, 1992, 95, 97, Coun. for Basic Edn. fellow, 1996; Fulbright Meml. Fund scholar, 2000. Mem. ALA, Am. Assn. Sch. Librs. (Frances Henne award 1994), Tex. Libr. Assn., Tex. Assn. Sch. Librs. Home: PO Box 117 Oakhurst TX 77359-0117 Office: Coldspring-Oakhurst H S Libr PO Box 39 Coldspring TX 77331-0039 Business E-Mail: cbunch@cocisd.org.

BUNCHER, CHARLES RALPH, epidemiologist, educator, biostatistician; b. Dover, NJ, Jan. 18, 1938; BS, MIT, 1960; MS, Harvard U., 1964, ScD, 1967. Statistician Atomic Bomb Casualty Comsn., NAS, 1967-70; chief biostatistician Merrell-Nat. Labs., 1970-73, asst. prof. stats., 1970-73; prof. and dir. divsn. epidemiology and biostats. Med. Coll., U. Cin., 1973-96, prof. biostats. and epidemiology, 1973—, dir. grad. edn., 2001—. Editor: Pharmaceutical Industry, 2006. Fellow Am. Stats. Assn., Am. Coll. Epidemiology; mem. APHA, Soc. Epidemiol. Rsch., Soc. Med. Decision Making, Soc. Clin. Trials, Tau Beta Pi, Delta Omega. Achievements include design of experiments; clinical trials; screening; risk analysis; statistical research; pharmaceutical research; biostatistical analysis; pharmaceutical statistics; diagnosis; treatment; research in ALS epidemiology; cancer epidemiology; environmental epidemiology; occupational epidemiology. Office: U Cincinnati Div of Epidemiology & Biostatistics PO Box 670183 Cincinnati OH 45267-0183 Office Phone: 513-558-1410. Business E-Mail: charles.buncher@uc.edu.

BUNDA, STEPHEN MYRON, political advisor, counselor, lawyer, classical philosopher; b. Jersey City, Oct. 5, 1949; s. Stephen and Anna (Yaschak) B. BA summa cum laude, St. Peter's Coll., Jersey City, 1971; MA with honors, New Sch. Grad. Faculty, NYC, 1976; JD, Rutgers U., 1987. Bar: N.J. Pol. cons. Democratic Party, NJ, 1977-92; pol. adv. Govt. of Ukraine, 1991—; counsellor-at-law Bunda & Co., Lyndhurst, NJ, 1994—. Advisor on Ukraine to U.S. Congress, Office of the Pres., Nat. Security Coun., Washington, 1991—. Mem. Nat. Honor Soc., Am. Hist. Assn., Am. Philos. Assn., Ukrainian-Am. Bar Assn., N.J. Bar Assn., Soc. for Ukrainian-Jewish Rels., Ukrainian Nat. Assn., Lawyers Com. for Human Rights. Democrat. Mem. Ukrainian Catholic Ch. Avocations: reading, travel, music, art, literature, theater. Home: 691 Union Ave Lyndhurst NJ 07071-2815 Office: Stephen Myron Bunda Esquire PO Box 461 Lyndhurst NJ 07071

BUNDCHEN, GISELLE, model; b. Horizontina, Rio Grande do Sul, Brazil, July 20, 1980; d. Valdir and Vania Bundchen. Model appearing on covers of various magazines including Vogue USA, Vogue Italia GQ, Harper's Bazaar, W, Rolling Stone, marie claire, ELLE, i-D, Allure, Big, Arena, The Face; model Christian Dior, Missoni, Ralph Lauren, Celine, Victoria's Secret, ZARA, Dolce & Gabbana, Strenesse, Versace, Valentino, Gianfranco Ferre, Chloe, Forum, Alphorria, Daslu, Hering, Lycra, Cori, Stella McCartney, BelStaff; featured in Pirelli Calendar, 1997; launched a clothing line at British fashion retailer Topshop, 2007. Actor: (films) Taxi, 2004. Named one of World's Richest Model (#1), Forbes, 2007. Achievements include highest paid model in the world. Office: IMG Models Penthouse North 12th Fl 304 Park Ave South New York NY 10010*

BUNDRUM, KENNETH OWEN, lawyer, writer; b. Anniston, Ala., Feb. 6, 1955; s. Cecil David Bundrum and Jessie Mae Stevenson. LLB, Roosevelt U., Zurich, 1974—78. Lawyer Nat. Bar Assn., NYC, 1982—86, Nat. Lawyers Guild, NYC, 2002—. Author: (book) The Fighting Stevensons: Honor and War, 1998. Candidate Ala. State Ho. Reps., Dist. 5, 1982; candidate for Ala. Atty. Gen., 2002. Recipient Legion of South Award, League of the South, 1999. Mem.: Sons of Confederate Veterans (hon. col. 1988). Republican. Roman Catholic. Home: 555 Cottaquilla Rd Jacksonville AL 36265 Office Phone: 256-473-6043. Personal E-mail: p.bundrum@bellsouth.net.

BUNDY, ANNALEE MARSHALL, library director; b. Chgo., Feb. 11, 1938; d. Warren Elmer and Marie Thresa (Madden) Marshall; m. John Willard Bundy, Mar. 11, 1961. BA, U. N.H., 1960; MLS, Simmons Coll., 1961. Assoc. head libr. Coll. Guam Libr., Agana, 1961-62, head libr., 1962-63; tech. libr. E.I. duPont de Nemours & Co., Maydown Works, Londonderry, No. Ireland, 1963-65; head libr. children's rm. Schenectady County (N.Y.) Libr., 1965-66; documents and periodicals libr. Grad. Sch. Pub. Affairs, SUNY, Albany, 1966-67; asst. dir. Medford (Mass.) Pub. Libr., 1967-73; dir. librs. Somerville (Mass.) Pub. Libr., 1973-78; dir. Providence Pub. Libr., 1978-88; program dir. EPA Librs. and Records Ctrs., 1990-91; exec. dir. Ames Free Libr., Easton, Mass., 1992—. Adj. faculty U. RI Grad. Libr. Sch.; cons. libr. bldgs., automation, govt. rels.; mem. adv. com. R.I. Sch. Design; mem. accreditation vis. team New Eng. Bd. Higher Edn.; challenge grant panelist NEH; mem. bd. Sails Inc., 2005-07, treas., 2005-06. Compiler: Alternatives in Print, II, 1972; mem. editl. bd. The Bottom Line: A Fin. Mag. for Librs.; contbr. articles to profl. jours. Mem. Mass. Cable TV Commn., 1975-79; bd. corporators Butler Hosp., 1983-2004; bd. dirs. Leadership R.I., 1984-88, R.I. Film and Video Competition. Recipient David E. Sweet award Leadership R.I., 1987, Disting. Leadership Alumni award Nat. Assn. Cmty. Leadership Orgns., 1987; Brown Humanities Inst. fellow, 1985-87. Mem. ALA (PLA/MLS sect. pres. 1981-82, chmn. Allie Beth Martin award com. 1986), Agawam Hunt Club, Providence Art Club, Am. Libr. Assn., Pub. Libr. Assn. Office: 53 Main St North Easton MA 02356-1496

BUNDY, BLAKELY FETRIDGE, advocate; b. Chgo., Aug. 31, 1944; d. William Harrison and Bonnie Jean (Clark) Fetridge; m. Harvey Hollister Bundy III, Aug. 20, 1966; children: Harvey Hollister Bundy IV, Clark Harrison, Elizabeth Lowell, Reed Fetridge. BA cum laude, Wheaton Coll., Mass., 1966; MEd, Nat.-Louis U., 1985. Tchr. Norwich (Vt.) Kindergarten, 1966-67, Willow Wood Pre-Sch., Winnetka, Ill., 1983-93, bd. dirs., 1972-81, adv. bd., 1981-83, 93—. Bd. dirs. North Ave. Day Nursery, Chgo., 1970-76; exec. dir. Winnetka Alliance for Early Childhood, 1989—; accreditation system validator, mentor Nat. Acad. Early Childhood Programs, Washington, 1986-2004; mem. pres.'s commn. Wheaton Coll., Norton, Mass., 1987-99, 2006—; trustee Brooks Sch., North Andover, Mass., 1993-2004; mem. adv. bd. Ctr. for Early Childhood Leadership, 2002—, Filene Ctr. for Work and Learning, Wheaton Coll., 1999—; cons. editor Nat. Assn. Edn. Young Children, 1991-94. Editor Early Childhood, 1990—; contbr. articles to Chgo. Tribune, Redbook, Glamour mags., Early Childhood News, Child Care Ctr. Mag., Chgo. Sun-Times, Day Care and Early Education, Young Children, other publs. Mem. Ill. Shore Coun. Girl Scouts U.S., 1981-89, World Found. for Girls Guides and Girl Scouts Friends of Our Cabana Com., Cuernavaca, Mexico, 1986-94. Mem.: Olive Baden-Powell Soc. (London), Chgo. Metro Assn. Edn. Young Children (steering com. Near North Suburban chpt. 1986—2001, commn. on salaries and working conditions 1988—92, co-chair pub. rels. com. 1992—2000, photography editor Connections 1992—2000, bd. dirs. 1992—2007, chair accreditation project mgmt. com. 1994—98, co-editor News & Views: The Accreditation Project Newsletter 1996—98, pres. 2003—05), Ill. Soc. Early Childhood Profls. (bd. dirs. 1993—96, editor newsletter), World Assn. Girl Guides and Girl Scouts, Nat. Assn. for the Edn. Young Children, Ocean Reef Club (Key Largo, Fla.), Yacht Club, Stevensville Club (Mich.), Indian Hill Club (Winnetka). Episcopalian. Avocations: golf, boating. Office: Winnetka Alliance for Early Childhood 1235 Oak St Winnetka IL 60093-2168 Office Phone: 847-441-9001. E-mail: blakelybundy@yahoo.com, director@winnetkaalliance.org.

BUNDY, CHARLES ALAN, retired foundation executive; b. Cheraw, SC, Jan. 5, 1930; s. Jackson Corbett and Ruby Jones (Hughes) B.; m. Margaret Ellen Jackson, Feb. 27, 1954; children: Charles Alan, Robert Jackson, Dan Hughes. AB, Wofford Coll., 1951; DH (hon.), Charleston So. U. Mgr. prodn. planning J.P. Stevens & Co., Inc., Rockingham, NC, 1951-54; mgr. Jesup (Ga.) C. of C., 1954-56, Lancaster (S.C.) C. of C., 1956-61; dist. mgr. U.S. C. of C., Birmingham, Ala., 1961-65; exec. v.p. Macon (Ga.) C. of C., 1965-71, Greg Enterprises, Lancaster, 1971-72; pres. Springs Found., Inc.

and Close Found., Inc., Lancaster, 1972-97, ret., 1997; pvt. practice cons., 1997—; ret., 2004. Chmn. SC Parks, Recreation and Tourism Commn., 1983—89; mem. SC Coordinating Coun. for Econ. Devel., 1986—89; mem., past chmn. S. E. Coun. on Founds.; trustee Columbia Coll., 1976—88, SC Found. Ind. Colls., 1982—93; chmn. Gov.'s Freshwater Wetlands Forum, 1989, Lancaster County Strategic Plan, 1990; past pres. U. SC Ednl. Found., Lancaster; mem. State Govt. Reorgn. Commn., 1991; chmn. bd. 1st Meth. Ch., 1978—79; chmn. bd. dirs. Springs Meml. Hosp. Mem. Lancaster County Higher Edn. Commn., Lancaster County C. of C. (past pres.), Rotary (past pres.). Home: 518 Briarwood Rd Lancaster SC 29720-1802

BUNDY, JAMES ABBOTT, performing company executive; b. Boston, Mass., May 8, 1959; s. McGeorge and Mary L. Bundy; m. Anne Marie Tofflemire, Jan. 2, 1988; children: Eleanor Tofflemire, Mary Peyton. AB, Harvard U., Cambridge, Mass., 1981; MFA, Yale Sch. of Drama, New Haven, Conn., 1995. Mng. dir. Cornerstone Theater Co., NYC, 1989—91; assoc. producing dir. The Acting Co., NYC, 1996—98; artistic dir. Gt. Lakes Theater Festival, Cleve., 1998—2002; dean, artistic dir. Yale Sch. of Drama, Repertory Theatre, New Haven, 2002—; dir. Theatre Comm. Group, NYC, 2007—. Trustee Groton Sch., Groton, 2003—. Office: Yale Sch Drama/Yale Repertory Theatre 222 York St New Haven CT 06520 Office Phone: 203-432-1505.

BUNDY-DESOTO, TERESA MARI, language educator, vocalist; d. Jose Jesus Avila-Carrillo and Maria del Pilar Lozano Avila; m. Glendon B. Bundy, Oct. 15, 1972 (div. May 20, 1987); children: Pete Hernandez Bundy, Angelita Dianne Bundy, Crystal Lorraine Bundy-Schwabenland, Ivan Glen Bundy; m. John B. Soto, Mar. 31, 1996. AA magna cum laude, Fresno City Coll., 1976; BA summa cum laude, Calif. State U., Fresno, 1978; Spanish and bilingual tchg. credential, Calif. State U. Fresno, 1979. Master tchr., trainer Proteus Adult Edn., Visalia, Calif., 1967—73; tchr. trainer Fresno City-County Manpower Commn., Calif., 1973—76; tchr. Spanish, mentor tchr. Ctrl. Unified Sch. Dist., Fresno, 1979—86; dept. chairperson Madera Unified Sch. Dist., Calif., 1986—89; tchr. Spanish, English Hoover H.S./Fresno Unified Sch. Dist., 1989—; dept. chairperson Hoover H.S. Rschr., trainer Office of Edn., Washington, 1968—74; adult edn. tchr. Chavez Adult Edn. Ctr.; alt. chief examiner ofcl. GED testing ctr. Gen. Ednl. Devel. Testing Svc., 1999—; world lang. dept. chair. Hoover H.S., 2007—; spkr. in field. Singer: recorded 2 CDs and mus. videos under stage name Luz De Luna. Profl. radio announcer Spanish Radio Stas., Fresno, 1978—96; TV model Spanish TV Univision, Fresno, 1980; judge Miss Laverkin, Utah, 1982. Named Miss El Futuro C.U., 1967, 1972. Mem.: Am. Coun. on Edn., Calif. Tchr. Assn. Democrat. Mem. Lds Ch. Home: 1149 E San Bruno Ave Fresno CA 93710 Office Phone: 559-225-4880. Business E-Mail: tadesot@fresno.k12.ca.us.

BUNE, KAREN LOUISE, state agency administrator, legal assistant; b. Washington, Mar. 6, 1954; d. Harry and Eleanor Mary (White) B. BA in Am. Studies cum laude, Am. U., Washington, DC, 1976, MS in Adminstrn. of Justice with distinction, 1978. Diplomate in traumatic stress, bd. cert. in domestic violence. Case mgr. Arlington Alcohol Safety Action Program, Va., 1979-94; victim specialist Office of Commonwealth's Atty., Arlington, 1994—2004; cons. victim issues Dept. Justice, Office for Victims, 2001—; victim specialist, legal asst. States Attys. Office for Prince George's County, Md., 2004—. Case mgr. regional rep. of case mgmt. com. of Dirs. Assn. Commn. on Va. Alcohol Safety Action Program, Richmond, 1980-81, 84-85, 88-89, mem. subcom. studying treatment issues, 1988-94; chair career guidance subcom. alumni adv. com. Sch. Pub. Affairs Am. U., Washington, 1991-94; participant IACP Summit on Victims of Crime, 1999, nat. forum on terrorism, NCJA, 2002; adj. prof. George Mason U., Fairfax, Va., Marymount U., Arlington; lectr. Am. U., Washington; mem. George Mason U. Spkr.'s Bur.; victim contbr./specialist www.officer.com Author: nycop.com Online Mag.; contbg. author (online mags.) Office-.com, Am. Police Beat, NYcop.com. Bd. vis. Marymount U. Named Woman of Yr., Am. Biog. Inst., 1990; named to Outstanding Achievement in Case Mgmt. Hall of Fame; recipient Spl. Achievement award, Dept. Navy, 1973, Merit award, Arlington County, 1986, 1997, cert. Recognition Svc. to Crime Victims, 3d Ann. Neighborhood Day, 1999, cert. Appreciation, US Dept. Justice, 2000, 2004, Carl T. Earles Meml. Cmty. Svc. award, No. Va. Crime Prevention Assn., 1999, 2001, cert. Appreciation, Peddlers for Peace, 2004, Stacie award for dedicated svc. to homicide victims, 2006, Outstanding Alumni award, Sch. Pub. Affairs, Am. U., 2007. Fellow: Am. Acad. Experts in Traumatic Stress (cert. in domestic violence); mem.: APHA, NAFE, Am. Soc. Pub. Adminstrn. (pres. No. Va. chpt. 2003—04, Kathy Hensley Disting. Svc. award No. Va. chpt. 2005, exec. coun. bd. mem. 2005—), DC Sociol. Soc., Am. Soc. Victimology, Va. Network for Victims and Witnesses of Crime, Md. Coalition Against Sexual Assault, Justice Studies Assn., Am. Criminal Justice Assn., Nat. Dist. Atty.'s Assn., Internat. Assn. Forensic Mental Health Svcs., Am. Acad. Experts in Traumatic Stress, Am. Sociol. Assn., Am. Pub. Human Svcs. Assn., Am. Profl. Soc. on Abuse of Children, Nat. Ctr. Women in Policing, Am. Probation and Parole Assn., Soc. for Study of Social Problems, Va. Assn. Female Execs., No. Va. Fraternal Order Police, No. Va. Crime Prevention Assn., Soc. Profl. Journalists, Va. Crime Prevention Assn., Internat. Narcotic Enforcement Officers Assn., Va. Sheriffs Inst., Am. Soc. Criminology, So. Criminal Justice Assn., Acad. Criminal Justice Scis., Am. Police Hall of Fame (cert. of appreciation 1985), Nat. Assn. Women Law Enforcement Execs., Nat. Ctr. Victims of Crime, Nat. Orgn. Victim Assistance, Nat. Criminal Justice Assn., Nat. Assn. Chiefs Police (award of merit 1986), Internat. Assn. Chiefs of Police (nat. adv. bd. on police-based victim response 2000—), MD Network Against Domestic Violence, Am. U. Alumni Assn. (immediate past pres. sch. pub. affairs chpt. 1994—96), World Affairs Coun., Nat. Air Disaster Alliance Found., Lambda Alpha Epsilon, Phi Delta Gamma (1st v.p. 1981—82), Phi Alpha Alpha, Phi Kappa Phi. Avocations: concerts, dance, travel, theater, writing. Home: 926 16th St S Arlington VA 22202-2606 Office: 14735 Main St Ste M3406 Upper Marlboro MD 20772 Office Phone: 703-472-5811. Business E-Mail: kbune@gmu.edu.

BUNGAARD, ERNEST See GRAY, ALLEN

BUNGE, CHARLES ALBERT, library science educator; b. Kimball, Nebr., Mar. 18, 1936; s. Louis Herman and Leona Hazel (Cromwell) B.; m. Joanne C. VonStoeser, Aug. 20, 1960; children: Lorraine A., Jeffrey C. Stephen L. AB, U. Mo., 1959; MSLS, U. Ill., 1960, PhD, 1967. Reference libr. Daniel Boone Regional Libr., Columbia, Mo., 1960-62; Ball State Tchrs. Coll., Muncie, Ind., 1962-64; rsch. assoc. Libr. Rsch. Ctr., U. Ill., 1964-67; mem. faculty Sch. Libr. and Info. Studies U. Wis., Madison, 1967—97, prof. emeritus, 1997—. Author: Professional Education and Reference Efficiency, 1967; columnist: Wilson Library Bull, 1972-81. Mem. ALA (pres. ref. and adult svcs. divsn. 1987-88, chair com. on accreditation 1990-92, Mudge award 1983, mem. coun. 1993-96, Beta Phi Mu award 1997), Assn. Libr. and Info. Sci. Edn. (pres. 1980-81, Prof. Contribution award 1997), Wis. Libr. Assn. (pres. 1972-73, Libr. of Yr. 1983), Phi Beta Kappa, Beta Phi Mu. Home: 509 Orchard Dr Madison WI 53711-1316

BUNGE, JONATHAN GUNN, lawyer; b. La Crosse, Wis., Oct. 20, 1936; s. Jonathan Clement and Anne Liddell (Gunn) Bunge; m. Gertrude Shoemaker, June 18, 1961; children: Jonathan C., William H., Katherine E. BA cum laude, Princeton U., 1958; JD, Harvard U., 1961. Bar: Ill. 1961, US Supreme Ct. 1968. Assoc. Lees & Bunge, Chgo., 1961—62, Keck, Mahin & Cate, Chgo., 1964—71; ptnr., 1971—95, Ross & Hardies, Chgo., 1995—2000; atty. Law Offices Jonathan G. Bunge, PC, Chgo., 2000—; of counsel Davis & Campbell, LLC, Peoria, Ill., 2004—; pres. DePaul Mgmt. Co., 1985—; instr. John Marshall Law Sch., 1968—73; mem. adv. pane. Ea.-we. Trade US Dept. Commerce, 1977—78. Served US Army, 1962—64. Mem.: ABA, Maritime Law Assn., Bar Assn. 7th Cir., Chgo. Bar Assn., ARC (bd. dir. Mid-Am. chpt. 1975—87, vice chmn. 1981—82, Chgo. region 1981—95, vice chmn. 1982—85, chmn. 1983—86), St. Gregory's Episcopal Sch. (mem. 1990—), Holy Comforter Ch. (vestryman Kenilworth, Ill. 1979—84, 1998—2001), Chgo. Work Ethic Corp. (bd. dir. 1988—94), Mich. Shores Club (Chgo.), Lawyers Club, Sheridan Shores Yacht Club, Econ. Club. Episcopalian. Home: 821 Sheridan Rd Wilmette IL 60091 Office Phone: 773-404-5900. Business E-Mail: jbunge@bungelaw.com.

BUNGE, RUSSELL KENNETH, writer, poet, educator; b. Long Beach, Calif., Apr. 28, 1947; s. Kenneth Duncan Bunge and Mona Irene (Deleree) Coker; ptnr. Mr. Kelly A. Quiros. BA in Creative Writing, Calif. State U., Long Beach, 1972; MA in Humanities, Calif. State U., Dominguez Hills, 1985. Cert. C.C. tchr., Calif. Spl. svcs. cons. AT&T Comms., San Luis Obispo, Calif., 1973-90; info. cons. Obispo Info. Group, San Luis Obispo, 1990-95; pub. deleree com, San Luis Obispo, Calif., 1996—. Mem. adv. bd. Calif. Online Resources for Edn., Long Beach, 1993-94; edn. coord. SLONET Info. Network, 1993-95, dir., 1997-98. Author: Double Lives: Poems 1984-1985, 1985, Junction, 2001; editor: Obispo Web Digest: on the World Wide Web, 1994-96; contbr. poems to profl. publs. Founding mem. AIDS Support Network, San Luis Obispo, 1984. Mem. MLA, Assn. Study Lit. & Environ. Office: Wirewove Web Solutions PO Box 771 San Luis Obispo CA 93406-0771

BUNGER, ROLF, physiology educator; b. Hamburg, Germany, Oct. 19, 1941; came to U.S., 1979; s. Heinz Johannes Albert and Helga (Franz) B.; m. Margriet Akkerman, Dec. 14, 1973; children: Nils, Frank. MD, U. Hamburg, 1969, U. Heidelberg, Germany, 1970; MD habil., U. Munich, 1979. Intern Heidberg Infirmary, Hamburg, 1970; asst. of physiology U. Aachen, Germany, 1970-75, U. Munich, 1975-79; asst. prof. dept. physiology F. E. Hebert Med. Sch., USUHS, Bethesda, Md., 1979-82, assoc. prof., 1983-92; prof. USUHS, Bethesda, Md., 1992—; prof. of molecular and cellular biology US Univ. Health Svc., Bethesda, Md., 1994—, prof. anesthesiology, 2000—. Cons. U. Buffalo, 1983, U. Ala., 1986-89, U. Tex., Ft. Worth, 1990-96, AAALAC, 1997-2001; referee, editl. reviewer domestic and fgn. sci. med. rsch. jours. and instns., including NIH, VA, NSF, HFSP, Dutch Heart Found., 1974—; referee MRC, 1974-2004; vis. prof. Erasmus U., Rotterdam, 1992; lectr. in field. Mem. editl. bd. Internat. Jour. Purine and Pyrimidine Rsch., 1989-93, Internat. Jour. Angiology, 1991-95, Am. Jour. Physiology, 1999—, Heart and Circulation; guest referee editor Jour. Applied Physiology, 1998-2004. Webelo leader Boy Scouts Am., McLean, Va., 1986-87, packmaster, 1987-89. Capt., German Air Force Med. Corp. Grantee, Uniformed Svcs. U. Health Scis., 1979—, NIH, 1982—2000, 2005—, Dept. Def., 1995—99. Fellow Am. Physiol. Soc., Am. Heart Assn.; mem. Deutsche Physiol. Gesellschaft. Achievements include clarification of adenylate compartments in myocardium; demonstration of energy-linked (ATP potential) and work dependence (demand) of myocardial pyruvate dehydrogenase flux, of intracellular free AMP in myocardium; research in metabolic enhancement of isolated and in-situ preischemic and postischemic heart preparations; metabolic protection of cytosolic ATP phosphorylation potential by pyruvate and adenosine during myocardial reperfusion and stunning; adenylate-related theory of metabolic coronary control, energy linked control of sarcoplasmic reticulum Ca 2+ - ATPase; pyruvate protection against apoptosis, infarct size and hemorrhagic shock, Redox control of NADH oxidase and survival signaling; complement-related pseudoanaphylaxis mediated in part by adenosine. Home: 1922 Kenbar Ct Mc Lean VA 22101-5321 Office: USUHS Dept Anatomy Physiology and Genetics 4301 Jones Bridge Rd Bethesda MD 20814-4799 Home Phone: 703-241-1254; Office Phone: 301-295-3523. Business E-Mail: rbunger@usuhs.edu.

BUNGO, MICHAEL WILLIAM, cardiologist, educator, science administrator; b. Passaic, NJ, July 18, 1950; s. John C. and Mary Bungo; children: Elise Nicole, Jonathan Michael. BS in Chemistry, Rensselaer Poly. Inst., 1971; MD, N.J. Med. Sch., 1975. Diplomate Am. Bd. Internal Medicine, Subsplty. Bd. Cardiovasc. Diseases, Am. Coll. Physician Execs. Intern in internal medicine New England Deaconess Hosp., Boston, 1975-76, resident, 1976—78; asst. in medicine Peter Bent Brigham Hosp., 1976—77; cardiology fellow New England Deaconess Hosp., Harvard Med. Sch., 1978—80; head cardiovascular lab. NASA Johnson Space Ctr., Houston, 1980—85; mem. Aerospace Medicine Bd., 1980—91; dir. Space Biomed. Rsch. Inst. NASA Johnson Space Ctr., 1986—90; chief scientist med. scis. divsn. NASA, 1990—91; prof. medicine U. Tex., Galveston, med. dir. heart sta. divsn. cardiology, 1995—2002, vice chmn. dept. internal medicine, 1999—2002; assoc. dean U. Tex. Med. Sch., Houston, 2002—05, vice dean, 2005—07; chief of staff LBJ Gen. Hosp., 2002—06; pres. and CEO UT Physicians, 2005—07. Chmn. dept. medicine St. John Hosp., Houston, 1987—89; fellowship advisor NRC, Washington, 1984—89. Editor: Results of Life Sciences Aboard the Space Shuttle, 1987; contbr. abstracts and articles to jours., chpts. to books; tech. reviewer Circulation, Aviation, Space and environ. Medicine, 1989—; mem. editl. bd. Aviation, Space and Environ. Medicine, 1997-2000. Recipient medal NASA, 1986. Fellow ACP, Am. Coll. Cardiology; mem. Am. Heart Assn., Aerospace Med. Assn. (Louis H. Bauer Founders award 1987), Tex. Med. Assn., Am. Coll. of Physician Exec., Phi Lambda Upsilon. Office: U Tex Houston Med Sch MSB Ste G 150 6431 Fannin St Houston TX 77030 Office Phone: 713-500-5010.

BUNIAK, RAYMOND, educational professional; b. Sao Paulo, Mar. 21, 1955; came to U.S., 1959; s. Wasyl and Katarina (Kurpita) B.; m. Karen Sue Harbecke, Apr. 28, 1957; children Kirsten, Karl. BA in Edn., Northeastern Ill. U., Chgo., 1977; MMus, DePaul U., 1981; EdD in Curriculum and Instrn., Loyola U., 2006. Cert. Cert. tchr. K-12, 6-12 music Ill., adminstr. K-12 Ill. Profl. musician/trombone and euphonium player, condr., Chgo. metro area, 1973—; studio tchr. of brass instruments various, Chgo. metro area, 1979—; band dir. New Trier West High, Northfield, Ill., 1981-82, O.L.P.H. Sch., Glenview, Ill., 1986-94; instrnl. devel. and grants officer/tchr. Kelly HS, Chgo., 1994—. Grant writer for sch. improvement and devel., fine and performance arts chmn., coord. Internat. Baccaleureate Program, Kelly H.S., 1997—, coord. AP program, ILCA program; presenter, cons. in field. Author: A 20th Century Treatise on the Trombone, 4 vols., 1984. Bible tchr. Recipient Univ. Talent scholarship Northeastern Ill. U., 1974-77. Mem. ACSCD, AERA, Francis Galpin Soc., Internat. Trombone Assn., Nat. Cath. Bandmaster's Assn., Music Educators Nat. Conf., Chgo. Fedn. of Musicians. Avocations: household renovation, photography, technology, auto restoration. Home: 105 N Western Ave Bartlett IL 60103-4030 Office: Thomas Kelly High Sch 4136 S California Ave Chicago IL 60632-1817 Home Phone: 630-289-1065; Office Phone: 773-535-4900. Personal E-mail: buniakraymond@sbcglobal.net. Business E-Mail: rbuniak@cps.k12.il.us.

BUNKER, BERYL H., retired insurance company executive, volunteer; b. Chelsea, Mass., Aug. 18, 1919; d. Albert Crocker and Eva Agnes Hardacker; m. John Wadsworth Bunker, Oct. 31, 1942 (dec. Apr. 2006). Student, Simmons Coll., Boston, 1936—38, D (hon.) of Humane Svc., 2001; student, Boston Coll. Law, 1948—49; grad., Bentley Sch. Acctg., 1958; BBA with highest honors, Northeastern U., Boston, 1962, MBA, 1967. CFA, CFA Inst. Legal rsch. clk. Frank Shepard Co., NYC, 1938—43; cost acct. Johns Manville Corp., Pittsburg, Calif., 1943—46; studio mgr. Wheelan Studios, Boston, 1946; clerical supr. Columbian Purchasing Group, Boston, 1946—48; office mgr. Wellesley Coll., Mass., 1948—51; statistician Eastman Kodak Co., Rochester, NY, 1951—53; investment officer John Hancock Mut. Life, Boston, 1953—74; sr. v.p. John Hancock Advisers, Boston, 1974—84; ret., 1984. Mem. Ct. Women in Politics and Public Policy, Assocs. of Boston Pub. Libr. Bd., Cambridge YWCA, Neighborhood Assn. of Back Bay; mem. world svc. coun. YWCA USA, 1992—, nat. bd. dir., 1988—94, hon. bd. dir., 1998—; pres. bd. dir. YWCA, Boston, 1985—87, active, 1977—96; bd. dirs. Old South Meeting House Mus., 1989—92; coun. Pine St. Inn, 1992—; trustee Simmons Coll., 1994—2000, chair centennial com., 1999—2000, corporator, 2000—05, hon. trustee, 2005—; chair bd. Vis. Nurses Assn. Cape Cod Found., South Dennis, 1995; mem. adv. com. On the Rise, 1997—, Boston Women's Fund, 2001—; mem. adv. com; Inst. Leadership & Change Simmons Coll., 2004—. Recipient Philanthropy award Women in Devel., 1990, Disting. Alumni award Bentley Coll., 1994; named Woman of Achievement, Cambridge YWCA, 1991, Lifetime Service to Women award, On The Rise, 1998, Lifetime Achievement award, College Club of Boston, 1998, Outstanding Alumna Northeastern U., 2000, Cmty. Cornerstone award, Woman in Devel., 2005; honoree Pine St. Inn Women's Coun., 2000. Mem. AARP, LWV, NOW, AAUW, CFA Inst., Mass. Action for Women, Mass. Women Polit. Caucus, Boston Security Analysts Soc. (treas. 1973-76), Simmons Coll. Alumnae Assn. (pres. 1989-91, Alumnae Svc. award 1984, Planned Giving award 1993), Older Women's League, Harwich Hist. Soc., Project Vote Smart, Crittenton Women's Union, Friday Forum, Eire Soc., Wellesley Ctrs. for Women, Coll. Club Boston. Avocations: fundraising, theater, reading. Home: 790 Boylston St Apt 22F Boston MA 02199-7921 Personal E-mail: berylb@mailstation.com.

BUNKER, KIMBERLY LEANN, critical care nurse, emergency nurse practitioner; b. New Albany, Ind., Nov. 16, 1969; d. William Albert and Sherry Lee Taylor; m. Donald Edward Bunker, Sept. 23, 1995; children: Sara Ann, Taylor Matthew. AS in Nursing, Livingston C.C., 1991; BSN, Rutgers U., 2001. Staff nurse Scott County Hosp., Georgetown, Ky., 1991, Naples Cmty. Hosp., Fla., 1991—93; patient care coord. Naples Collier Home Health, 1993—94; staff nurse NY Downtown Hosp., NYC, 1995, Robert Wood Johnson Hosp., New Brunswick, NJ, 1995—2000; clin. rsch. coord. dept. surgery U. Medicine and Dentistry J, 2000—02. Owner, oper. Critical RN Cons. Svcs., Alpharetta, 2005. Head nurse Hunterdon County Red Cross, NJ, 2003, bd. mem., 2003. Mem.: Air and Surface Transport Nursing Assn., Emer. Nurses Assn., Alpharetta's Am. Legal Nurse Cons. Avocations: tennis, gardening. Home: 310 Galloway Ave Alpharetta GA 30004 Home Phone: 770-521-1063; Office Phone: 770-317-8244. Business E-Mail: info@criticalrnconsulting.com.

BUNKER, NANCY A(NN), librarian, researcher; b. Spokane, Wash., 1960; d. Robert and E. Etta Tederman; m. Richard Bunker; children: Raymond, Megan. BA in Edn./Social Studies, Wash. State U., Pullman, 1983; MA in Librarianship, U. Denver, 1984; MA in History, Ea. Wash. U., Cheney, 1999. Children's libr. Englewood Pub. Libr., Colo., 1985—86, local history specialist, 1987—92; reference libr. Spokane County Libr. Dist., 1992—93; children's & young adult libr. Spokane Pub. Libr., 1993—94; assoc. prof./coord. reference svcs. Whitworth U., Spokane, 1994—. Hist. rschr. Bunker Rsch., Spokane, 1992—; cons. Colo. State Libr., Denver, 1985. Author: (reference book) Primary Source Collections in the Pacific Northwest: An Historical Researcher's Guide; prodr.(editor): (video) Englewood: A History in the Oral Tradition; author: Tuileries Amusement Park: A Short History; contbr. reference work. Grantee Oral History Project Grant - Englewood Colo., Colo. Endowment for the Humanities, 1990, History Trunks Project Grant, Libr. Svcs. and Constrn. Act, 1991. Mem.: Pacific NW Historian's Guild, Am. Assn. for State and Local History, ALA, Western History Assn., Assn. Coll. and Rsch. Librs. Office: Whitworth Univ 300 W Hawthorne Rd Spokane WA 99251 Office Phone: 509-777-4481. Business E-Mail: nbunker@whitworth.edu.

BUNKER-SOLER, ANTONIO LUIS, physician; b. Caguas, PR, Oct. 2, 1948; BS, U. P.R., Mayaguez, 1970; MD, U. P.R., San Juan, 1974. Diplomate Am. Bd. Allergy and Immunology, Am. Bd. Pediatrics. Commd. 2d lt. U.S. Army, 1973, advanced through grades to lt. col.; resident in pediatrics Brooke AMC, San Antonio, 1977; with pediatric svc. SHAPE, Belgium, 1977-79; various positions U.S. Army, Ft. Campbell, Ky., 1981-83, chief allergy-immunology svc. Frankfurt, Germany, 1989-92, various positions Ft. Hood, Tex., 1988-89, chief allergy-immunology svc. Frankfurt, Germany, 1989-92, asst. chief allergy-immunology svc. El Paso, Tex., 1992-94; various positions EAMC, Ga., 1983-88; pediatric pulmonary fellow Tex. Children's Hosp., Houston, 1994-95; pvt. practice Houston, 1995-96, Tampa, 1996—. Asst. clin. prof. MCG, Augusta, Ga., 1983-88; allergy cons. southeastern region CONUS, 1984-88, 7th MEDCOM, Europe, 1989-92, allergy cons.; presenter in field. Contbr. articles to profl. jours. Active Asthma and Allergy Support Group, Augusta, 1985-87. Decorated Army Commendation medal with oak leaf cluster, Order of Mil. Med. Merit; Allergy fellow Fitzsimons AMC, 1981. Fellow Am. Coll. Asthma, Allergy and Immunology, Tex. Med. Assn., Mil. Allergists (Dura Pharm. award 1987); mem. AMA, Am. Acad. Pediatrics, Am. Acad. Allergy and Immunology, Am. Thoracic Soc. Office: 3645 Madacahane Tampa FL 33618-2059

BUNKIS, JURIS, plastic surgeon; b. Lubeck, Germany, Aug. 27, 1949; came to the U.S., 1974; s. Janis and Jadviga (Buzinskis) B.; Tina Stensland Haworth, Oct. 8, 2005; children: Justin, Jessica. Degree, U. Toronto, 1970, MD, 1974. Intern gen. surgery Mary Imogene Bassett Hosp., Columbia U., Cooperstown, NY, 1974-75, jr. resident gen. surgery, 1975-76, Beth Israel Hosp., Mass. Gen. Hosp. & Shriner's Burn Inst., Harvard U., Boston, 1976-77; sr. resident gen. surgery Mary Imogene Bassett Hosp., Columbia U., Cooperstown, 1977-78, chief resident gen. surgery, 1978-79; sr. resident, chief resident plastic surgery Peter Bent Brigham & Children's Hosps., Harvard U., Boston, 1979-81; clin. instr. in surgery Harvard U., 1979-81; asst. prof. surgery divsn. plastic surgery U. Calif., San Francisco, 1981-83, asst. clin. prof. surgery, 1983-85; chmn., founder Orange County Plastic Surgery Medical Associations, Inc., 2002—. Asst. chief plastic surgery San Francisco Gen. Hosp. U. Calif., 1981-82, chief plastic surgery, 1983; chmn. bd. dirs., pres. Juris Bunkis M.D., Inc., Danville, Calif., 1983-95; chmn. bd. dirs., pres., med. dirs. Blackhawk Surgery Ctr., Inc., Danville, 1989-96, asst. med. dir., 1996-2001; chmn. bd. dirs., pres., sec. United Bridges, Inc., 1994-98; COO, bd. dirs., co-founder, OnlySports.com (now Captivision), Pleasonton, Calif., 1999-2001, sec., bd. dirs. 2001-02; chmn., co-founder Orange County Plastic Surgery Medical Associations, Inc., 2002—; invited lectr. numerous confs. Film F-Stops (silver medal, Houston Film Festival 2001); contbr. chpts. to books and articles to med. jours. Vol. deputy San Bernardino County Sheriff's Dept. Recipient Angels Wings award, Angels Wings Found., Concord, Calif., 2000, Man of CharaAngel Winds award, Concord Actor award, Orange County Coun., Boy Scouts of Am.; Knight, Cavalieri di San Marco (Knights of San Marco), Venice, 1995. Mem. Am. Assn. Hand Surgery (mem. program com. 1983-84, socioecons. com. 84-85), Am. Soc. Plastic and Reconstructive Surgery (mem. Tel Med subcom. 1986-87), Am. Soc. Aesthetic Surgery, Calif. Med. Soc., Calif. Soc. Plastic Surgeons (mem. program com. 1984-85, mem. ethics com. 86-87, mem. newsletter com. 87-89, mem. B.M.Q.A. liaison com. 87-89), Alameda-Contra Costa Med. Assn., Lipoplasty Soc. N.Am., Internat. Soc. Aesthetic Plastic Surgery, Pan Pacific Surg. Assn., Latvian Med. and Dental Assn., Plastic Surgery Rsch. Coun., Assn. Medicorum Bohemoslovacorum J.E. Purkyne (hon.), Soc. Bohemoslovaca Chirurgiae Plasticae (hon., Prague). Avocations: flying, fly fishing, travel. Office: Orange County Plastic Surgery 30212 Tomas Rancho Santa Margarita CA 92688

BUNKOWSKE, EUGENE WALTER, religious studies educator; b. Wecota, SD, July 3, 1935; s. Walter Adolph and Ottille Sophie (Richter) B.; m. Bernice Bock; children: Barbara, Nancy, Walter, Joel. AA, Concordia Acad. and Jr. Coll., St. Paul, 1955; BA, Concordia Seminary, 1958, BD,

MDiv, 1960; MA in Linguistics, UCLA, 1964, C Phil in Linguistics, 1968, PhD in Linguistics, 1976; LittD, Concordia Coll., 1983; DD, Christ Coll., 1991; DLitt, Concordia U., St. Paul, 1997. Missionary Luth. Ch.-Mo. Synod, Africa, 1960-82, congl. pastor, pioneer ch. planter, 1960-74, chmn. Nung Udoe dist., 1960-61, builder chs., schs., hosp., 1960-67, medical worker Ogoja Province, 1961-66, justice of peace Ogoja Province, 1962-74, chmn. Ogoja dist., 1964-69, chmn. Evang. Luth. Mission in Nigeria, 1965-67, analyzer Yala lang., orthography devel. & Bible translator, 1967-71, counselor to Yala Paramount Chief, 1969-74, fourth v.p., 1989-92, 95-98, third v.p., 1992-95; dir. mission Concordia Theol. Seminary, Ft. Wayne, Ind., 1982-88, mission prof., 1982—2002, mission chair prof., 1986—2002, grad. prof. mission, 1990—2002, chmn. dept. pastoral ministries, 1985-88, chmn. mission dept., 1988—90, supr. D Missiology program, chmn. Mission and Comm. Congress, 1984—; Fiechtner chair prof. Oswald Hoffmann Sch. Christian Outreach Concordia U., St. Paul, 2002—. Ling. cons. and adminstr. Luth. Bible Translators, Liberia, Sierra Leone, 1970-74; dir. Vacation Inst. for Tng. in Applied Linguistics and Bible Translation, U. Liberia, Monrovia, 1971-74; cons. United Bible Soc., 1974-80, regional translations coord., 1980-82; cons. Near West Side Cleve. Cluster, St. Paul Internat. Mission Bd. Author: Orede, 1973, Woka yi Ijona, 1974, Topics in Yala Grammar, 1976, God's Mission in Action, 1986, The Body of Christ in Mission, 1987, God's Communicators in Mission, 1988, Receptor Oriented Gospel Communication, 1989, The State of Gospel Communication Today, 1990, Church Growth: A Biblical Perspective, 1991, The Role of the Laity in Gospel Communications, 1992, The Christian Family: Nurture and Outreach, 1993, Multicultural Outreach: Bridging Cultures - Theirs and Ours, 1995, Struggling with Change: Reaching the Lost in Changing Times, 1999, The Lutherans in Mission, 2000; translator Yala Bible, 1967-74; contbr. articles to religious and profl. publs., chpts. to books. Mem. God's Word to Nations Bible Soc. (bd. dirs., trans. and tech. cons.), World Mission Prayer League (bd. dirs.), All Nations Mission (bd. dirs., cons.), Luth. Soc. for Missiology (founding organizer). Republican. Lutheran. Avocations: travel, reading, hiking. Office Phone: 651-603-6252. Business E-Mail: bunkowske@csp.edu.

BUNN, MATTHEW G., political scientist, writer; m. Jennifer Weeks; 2 children. B in Polit. Sci., M in Polit. Sci., MIT, 1985. Adv. Office Sci. and Tech. Policy; sr. rsch. assoc. project on mng. the atom Belfer Ctr. Sci. and Internat. Affairs Harvard U. John F. Kennedy Sch. Govt., Cambridge, Mass., 1997—. Bd. dirs. Arms Control Assn., Partnership for Global Security; mem. Com. on the Internationalization of the Nuc. Fuel Cycle. Contbr. articles to profl. and popular publs. Recipient Joseph A. Burton Forum award, Am. Phys. Soc., 2007. Fellow: AAAS. Office: Belfer Ctr Sci and Internat Affairs Littauer 339C 79 John F Kennedy St Mailbox 53 Cambridge MA 02138 Office Phone: 617-495-9916. Office Fax: 617-495-8963. E-mail: matthew_bunn@harvard.edu.*

BUNN, PAUL A., JR., oncologist, educator; b. NYC, Mar. 16, 1945; s. Paul A. Bunn; m. Camille Ruoff, Aug. 17, 1968; children: Rebecca, Kristen, Paul H. BA cum laude, Amherst Coll., 1967; MD, Cornell U., 1971. Diplomate Nat. Bd. Med. Examiners, Am. Bd. Internal Medicine, Am. Bd. Med. Oncology. Intern U. Calif., H.C. Moffitt Hosp., San Francisco, 1971-72, resident, 1972-73; clin. assoc. medicine br. Nat. Cancer Inst., NIH, Bethesda, Md., 1973-76; sr. investigator med. oncology br. Nat. Cancer Inst., Washington VA Hosp., 1976-81; asst. prof. medicine med. sch. Georgetown U., 1978-81; head cell kinetic sect., Navy med. oncology br. Nat. Cancer Inst., Bethesda, 1981-84; assoc. prof. medicine uniformed svcs. Univ. Health Scis., Bethesda, 1981-84; prof. medicine health scis. ctr. U. Colo., Denver, 1984—, head divsn. med. oncology, 1984-94, dir. cancer ctr., 1987—. Instl. rev. bd. NIH, Nat. Cancer Inst., 1982-84; intramural support contract rev. com. Nat. Cancer Inst., 1982-84; cancer com. U. Colo., 1984—, faculty senate health scis. ctr., 1985—, exec. com. sch. medicine, 1987—; med. bd. Univ. Hosp., 1987—; external sci. advisor cancer ctr. U. Miami, 1988-92, U. Ark., 1989-94, U. Va., 1991-94, others; oncology drug adv. com. FDA, 1992-96; sci. secretariat 7th World Conf. Lung Cancer, 1994; bd. dirs. Univ. Hosp. Resource Coun.; oncology drug adv. com. FDA, 1992-96. Author: Carboplatin (JM-8) Current Perspectives and Future Directions, 1990, Clinical Experiences With Platinum and Etoposide Therapy in Lung Cancer, 1992, (with M.E. Wood) Hematology/Oncology Secrets, 1994; assoc. editor Med. and Pediatric Oncology, 1984—, Jour. Clin. Oncology, 1991—, Cancer Rsch., 1992—, others; contbr. chpts. to books and articles to profl. jours. Bd. dirs. Colo. divsn. Am. Cancer Soc., 1989—, Leukemia Soc. Am., 1991—; bd. dirs. The Cancer Venture, 1993-94, Fair Share Colo., 1993-94; chmn. Solid Tumor Oncology Edn. Found., 1996—. With USPHS, 1973-84. Decorated Medal of Commendation; recipient Sci. of Yr. award Denver chpt. ARCS, 1992; named one of 400 Best Drs. in Am., Good Housekeeping Mag., 1991, 92; grantee Schering Plough, 1988-89, Burroughs Wellcome, 1991—, Bristol-Myers Squibb, 1993—, others. Fellow ACP; mem. AAAS, Am. Soc. Hematology (mem. sci. subcom. neoplasia 1989-92), Am. Assn. Cancer Rsch., Am. Soc. Clin. Oncology (chair program subcom. 1985-86, 90, pres.-elect 2001—), Am. Fedn. Clin. Rsch., Am. Assn. Cancer Insts. (bd. dirs. 1992—), Internat. Assn. Study Lung Cancer (bd. dirs. 1988—, pres. 1994-97, exec. dir.), Western Assn. Physicians, S.W. Oncology Group, Lung Cancer Study Group, Alpha Omega Alpha. Office: U Colo Cancer Ctr PO Box 6511 MS 8111 Aurora CO 80045 E-mail: paul.bunn@uchsc.edu.

BUNN, RONALD FREEZE, retired lawyer, academic administrator, political scientist; b. Jonesboro, Ark., Aug. 11, 1929; s. S. Neal and Velma (Freeze) B.; m. Rita E. Hess, Mar. 29, 1955; children: Robin Gail, Katharine Sue, Lisabeth Joann. BA, Rhodes Coll., 1951, LLD (hon.), 1973; MA, Duke U., 1953, PhD, 1956; postgrad., U. Cologne, Fed. Republic Germany, 1954-55; JD, U. Mo., 1989. Bar: Mo. 1990. Instr. U. Tex., Austin, 1956-59, asst. prof., 1960-64; asso. prof. La. State U., Baton Rouge, 1964-67, U Houston, 1967-69; prof., dean U Houston (Grad. Sch.), 1969-74, interim dean arts and scis., 1972-74, asso. dean faculties, 1974-75, acting v.p., dean faculties, 1975-76; v.p. acad. affairs State U. N.Y. at Buffalo, 1976-80; provost U. Mo., Columbia, 1980-86, prof. polit. sci., 1986—2000, prof. emeritus, 2000—; ptnr. Shurtleff, Froeschner and Bunn, Columbia, 1992—2007; adj. prof. law, 2001. Vis. lectr. Ind. U., 1962; cons. Coun. Grad. Schs., 1970-77. Author: (with others) Politics and Civil Liberties in Europe, 1967, German Politics and the Spiegel Affair: A Case Study of the Bonn System, 1968; contbr.: Employers Association and Industrial Relations, 1984; News and Notes editor: Jour. Politics, 1968-70; contbr. articles profl. jours. Bd. dirs. S.W. Center for Urban Research, Houston, chmn. bd., 1975-76. Fulbright predoctoral scholar, 1954-55, Fulbright rsch. scholar, 1963; NATO sr. fellow in sci., 1973. Mem. Mo. Bar Assn. (labor law com.), So. Polit. Sci. Assn. (past mem. exec. coun.), Nat. Employment Lawyers Assn., Southwestern Polit. Sci. Assn. (past v.p.), Am. Coun. on Germany, Phi Beta Kappa (pres. Mo. Alpha chpt. 1986-88), Omicron Delta Kappa. also: 25 N 9th St Columbia MO 65201-4845

BUNN, TIMOTHY DAVID, newspaper editor; b. Syracuse, NY, Sept. 29, 1946; s. John Stewart and Katherine (Smolnycki) B.; m. Nancy Grady, May 27, 1968 BS in Journalism, Syracuse U., 1972. Pub. info. officer Central N.Y. Regional Planning Bd., Syracuse, 1972-74; met. editor Rochester Democrat & Chronicle, NY, 1974-79; asst. city editor Miami Herald, Fla., 1979-81; mng. editor Syracuse Post-Standard, 1981-82; exec. editor Syracuse Herald Jour., 1982-95; dep. exec. editor Syracuse Post-Std., 1995—. Served to capt. U.S. Army, 1967-71. Recipient Cmty. Svc. award NAACP, 1984, Cmty. Appreciation award Am.-Arab Anti-Discrimination Com. Mem. ACLU. Office: The Post-Standard Clinton Sq PO Box 4915 Syracuse NY 13221-4915

BUNN, WM. JEFFREY, secondary school educator, director; b. Havre de Grace, Md., June 25, 1974; s. Fred Lewis Bunn, II and Ramona Bunn. BA, BS, King Coll., 1996; MusM in Edn., Westminster Choir Coll., 2004; MusM, Newcastle U., 2004. Cert. tchr. Md., 2004. Asst. coodinator music minsitries Mountain Christian Ch., Joppa, Md., 1998—2001; dir. music, organist The Luth. Ch. of the Holy Comforter, Balt., 2002—04; chair music dept., organist-in-residence Mt. Carmel H.S., Essex, 2002—. Adj. instr. music Mountain Christian Ch., Joppa, Md., 1996—2001. Musician: Organ and Voice Recitals (Am. Choral Director's Assn. Nat. Student award, 1996). Recipient Eagle Scout, Boy Scouts Am., 1992, Govs. citation, State of Md., 1992. Mem.: Am. Choral Dirs. Assn. (Nat. Student award 1996), Nat. Assn. Pastoral Musicians, Gospel Music Assn., Nat. Rec. Acad. Arts and Scis., Music Educator's Nat. Conf., Am. Guild Organists, Toastmaster' Internat., Am. Numistmatist Assn. Conservative. Avocation: coin collecting/numismatics. Home: 671 Bourbon Street Havre De Grace MD 21078-3134 Office: Mt Carmel High School 1704 Old Eastern Avenue Essex MD 21221 Personal E-mail: wmjbunn@aol.com. E-mail: jbunn@olmcmd.org.

BUNNELL, BEN, information technology manager; BA in English, Va. Commonwealth U.; M Library Sci. & Bus., U. Mich., 1998. Rsch. libr. Avalon Investments; digital info. assoc. Internet Pub. Libr.; libr. partnerships mgr. Google book search Google, Inc., 2002—. Named Outstanding Recent Graduate, U. Mich. Sch. Info., 2006. Office: Google Inc 1600 Amphitheatre Pkwy Mountain View CA 94043

BUNNELL, GEORGE ELI, lawyer, director; b. Miami, Fla., Apr. 28, 1938; s. George A. and Lillian E. (Hurley) B.; Dianne Railton, Dec. 1, 1990; children: Kelley, Courtney. BA, U. Fla., 1960, LLB, 1962. Bar: Fla. 1963, U.S. Dist. Ct. (so. dist.) Fla. 1963, U.S. Supreme Ct. 1970, U.S. Ct. Appeals (11th cir.) 1982. Assoc. Nicholson, Howard & Brawner, Miami, 1963-64, Dean, Adams, George & Wood, Miami, 1964-67, ptnr., 1968-71; officer, dir. Huebner, Shaw & Bunnell, P.A., Ft. Lauderdale, Fla., 1972—77; pres., dir. Bunnell, Woulfe, Kirschbeum, Keller, McIntyre Gregoire & Klein, Ft. Lauderdale, 1977—2004, of counsel, 2007—. Mem. advance staff White House, 1974-76; mem. City of Ft. Lauderdale Marine Adv. Bd., 1974-76, City of Ft. Lauderdale Civil Svc. Bd., 1977-79; bd. dirs., sec. Ft. Lauderdale Mus. Art, 1990-05. Fellow Am. Coll. Trial Lawyers; mem. Internat. Assn. of Def. Counsel, Am. Bd. Trial Advs. (pres. Ft. Lauderdale chpt. 1992, nat. bd. rep. 2003—), Def. Rsch. inst., Fla. Def. Lawyers Assn., Broward County Bar Assn., Fla. Acad. of Hosp. Attys., Am. Health Lawyers Assn., Lauderdale Yacht Club. Republican. Office: Bunnell Woulfe Kirschbaum Keller McIntyre Gregoire & Klein One Financial Plz 100 SE Third Ave Ste 900 Fort Lauderdale FL 33394 Home Phone: 954-522-6568; Office Phone: 954-761-8600. Business E-Mail: geb@bunnellwoulfe.com.

BUNNELL, PETER CURTIS, retired art educator, curator; b. Poughkeepsie, NY, Oct. 25, 1937; s. Harold Curtis and Ruth (Buckhout) B. BFA, Rochester Inst. Tech., 1959; MFA, Ohio U., 1961; MA, Yale U., 1965. Curator of photography Mus. Modern Art, NYC, 1966-72; prof. history of photography and modern art Princeton (N.J.) U., 1972—2002, prof. emeritus, 2002—. Curator of photography Art Mus. Princeton U., 1972-02, dir., 1973-78, 98-2000. Author; Clarence H. White, 1987, Minor White: The Eye That Shapes, 1989, Degrees of Guidance, 1993, Thomas Joshua Cooper, 1995, Ruth Bernhard: Photographs, 1996, Aaron Siskind: The Bond and The Free, 1997, Walter Chappell: Time Lived, 2000, Remembering Limelight, 2001, Edward Ranney: The Character of the Place, 2003, La Photographie Pictorialiste, 2004, Inside the Photograph, 2006; editor: A Photographic Vision, 1980, The Art of Pictorial Photography, 1992, Photography at Princeton, 1998. Guggenheim fellow, 1979, Asian Cultural Coun. Rsch. fellow, 1984. Fellow Royal Photographic Soc. (hon.); mem. Soc. for Photog. Edn. (chmn. 1973-76), The Friends of Photography (pres. 1978-87, chmn. 1987-92), Century Assocs. Club. Office: Princeton U Dept Art And Archaelogy Princeton NJ 08544-1018

BUNNER, WILLIAM KECK, lawyer; b. Fairmont, W.Va., Sept. 2, 1949; s. Scott Randolph and Virginia Lenore (Keck) B. BS in Secondary Edn. magna cum laude, W.Va. U., 1970, MA in History, 1973, ABD in History, 1975, JD, 1978, postgrad., 1998—. Bar: W.Va. 1978, U.S. Dist. Ct. (so. dist.) W.Va. 1978, U.S. Dist. Ct. (no. dist.) W.Va. 1985. Tchr. Monongalia County Bd. Edn., Morgantown, W.Va., 1970-78; contract lawyer dept. fin. and adminstrn. State of W.Va., Charleston, 1978-79; pvt. practice law Fairview, W.Va., 1979-84; pres. Farm Home Svc., Inc., 1983—; ptnr. Bunner & Bunner, Morgantown and Fairview, 1984-92. Pres. Climates, 1988—; presenter Rush D. Holt History Conf., W. Va. U., 1999, ann. meeting Lawand Soc. Amm., 2003, Rocky Mountain Interdisciplinary History Conf., U. Colo., 2003. Author: Planting Churches: A Case Study of Western Monongaliu County, West Virginia, 2000, Anxiety, Alienation and Adjustment: Filmnoir and the Returning Warriorfrom WWII, 2000. Pres. Monongalia County Young Dems., 1974; parliamentarian Monongalia County Dem. Exec. Com., 1982-94; counsel, parliamentarian Young Dem. Clubs W.Va., 1974-77; bd. dirs., supr. Monongahela Soil Conservation Dist., 1982—; advisor West Run Watershed Improvement Dist., 1983—; mem. W.Va. Commn. on Rural Abandoned Mines, Rural Alliance, Monongalia County Solid Waste Auth., 1989—, also chmn., 1990-92. Mem. ABA, Monongalia County Bar Assn., Assn. Rural Conservation, Soil Conservation Soc. Am., United Taxpayers' Assn. (counsel), Monongalia County Hist. Soc., Marion County Hist. Soc., Marion County Bar Assn., W.Va. Trial Lawyers Assn, Phi Alpha Delta, Phi Alpha Theta. Democrat. Avocations: music, politics, farming, videos, regional history and genealogy. Home and Office: 15 Devine Rd Fairview WV 26570-8711 Office Phone: 304-798-3542. E-mail: Keck50@mail.westco.net.

BUNNETT, JOSEPH FREDERICK, chemist, educator; b. Portland, Oreg., Nov. 26, 1921; s. Joseph and Louise Helen (Boulan) B.; m. Sara Anne Telfer, Aug. 22, 1942 (dec. Oct. 2006); children: Alfred Boulan, David Telfer, Peter Sylvester (dec. Sept. 1972). BA, Reed Coll., 1942; PhD, U. Rochester, 1945. Mem. faculty Reed Coll., 1946-52, U. N.C., 1952-58; mem. faculty Brown U., 1958-66, prof. chemistry, 1959-66, chmn. dept., 1961-64; prof. chemistry U. Calif., Santa Cruz, 1966-91, prof. emeritus, 1991—. Erskine vis. fellow U. Canterbury, N.Z., 1967; vis. prof. U. Wash., 1956, U. Wurzburg, Germany, 1974, U. Bologna, Italy, 1988; rsch. fellow Japan Soc. for Promotion of Sci., 1979; Lady Davis vis. prof. Hebrew U., Jerusalem, Israel, 1981; mem. adv. coun. dept. chemistry Princeton (N.J.) U., 1985-89; mem. NRC com. on alternative chem. demilitarization techs., 1992-93; mem. Dept. Def. panel on Gulf War Health Effects, 1993-94; co-chmn. peer rev. com. Russian-Am. Joint Evaluation Program, 1995-96; co-chmn. NATO Advanced Rsch. Workshop on Chem. Problems Associated with Old Arsenical and Mustard Munitions, Lodz, Poland, 1996; working group chem. weapons destruction, scientific adv. bd. Orgn. Prohibition Chem. Weapons, 1999—. Co-editor: Arsenic and Old Mustard: Chemical Problems in the Destruction of Old Arsenical and Mustard Munitions, 1998; contbr. articles to profl. jours. Trustee Reed Coll., 1970-97, trustee emeritus, 1997—. Fulbright scholar, U. Coll., London, 1949—50, U. Munich, 1960—61, Guggenheim fellow, 1960—61. Fellow AAAS, Internat. Union Pure and Applied Chemistry (chmn. commn. phys. organic chemistry 1978-83, sec. organic chemistry divsn. 1981-83, v.p. 1983-85, pres. 1985-87, chmn. task force on sci. aspects of destruction of chem. warfare agts. 1991-95, chmn. com. on chem. weapon destruction 1995-2001, fellow, 2002); mem. Am. Acad. Arts and Scis., Am. Chem. Soc. (editor jour. Accounts of Chem. Rsch. 1966-86, James Flack Norris award 1992), Royal Soc. Chemistry, Pharm. Soc. Japan (hon.), Acad. Gioenia (U. Catania, hon.), Soc. Argentina de Investigaciones en Quimica Organica (hon.), Soc. Chimica Italiana (hon.). Home: 608 Arroyo Seco Santa Cruz CA 95060-3148 Office: U Calif Dept Chemistry Santa Cruz CA 95064 Office Phone: 831-459-2261. Office Fax: 831-459-2935. Personal E-mail: bunnett@cruzio.com. Business E-Mail: bunnett@chemistry.ucsc.edu.

BUNNING, JIM (JAMES PAUL DAVID BUNNING), senator, former professional baseball player; b. Southgate, Ky., Oct. 23, 1931; m. Mary Catherine Theis; 9 children. BS in Economics, Xavier U., 1953. Profl. baseball player, 1955-71; with Detroit Tigers, 1955-63, Phila. Phillies, 1964-67, Pitts. Pirates, 1968-69, LA Dodgers, 1969, Phila. Phillies, 1970-71; ret. profl. baseball, 1971; congressman Ky. State Senate, Frankfort, 1979-83; mem. 100th-104th Congresses from 4th Ky. dist., 1987-98; mem. budget com.; mem. ways and means com.; US Senator from Ky., 1999—. Mem. com. banking, housing and urban affairs US Senate, com. budget, com. energy and natural resources, com. fin. Author: Grand Slam: The Secrets of Power Baseball, 1965. Mem. Brighton St. Ctr. Cmty. Action Group; bd. dirs. Ky. Spl. Olympics. Played in eight All-Star Baseball games during career; inducted into Nat. Baseball Hall Fame, Cooperstown, NY, 1996; recipient Taxpayer Friend award Nat. Taxpayers Union, 2001, Gerald Solomon Legis. of Yr. award Independent Ins. Agents and Brokers Am., 2003, Walter R. Dunlevy-Frontiersman award Northern Ky. C. of C., 2003, Lawmaker of Month award 60 Plus Assn., 2004. Republican. Roman Catholic. Office: US Senate 316 Hart Senate Office Bldg Washington DC 20510-0001 also: District Office Ste 220 1717 Dixie Highway Fort Wright KY 41011 Office Phone: 202-224-4343, 859-341-2602. Office Fax: 859-331-7445, 202-228-1373.*

BUNSHAFT, CHARLES EDWARD, elementary school educator, consultant; s. Warren Owen and Marilyn Bunshaft; m. Patricia McDonagh Bunshaft, Aug. 10, 1997; children: Owen, Quinn. BA in Sociology, SUNY, Albany, 1991; MS in Elem. Edn., LI U. C.W. Post, Greenvale, NY, 1993. Cert. sch. dist. adminstr. NY, 2003, sch. adminstr. and supervisory NY, 2003. Tchr. grades 5-6 Island Trees Sch. Dist., Levittown, NY, 1994—96; v.p. Internat. Mortgage Ctr., Jamaica, 1996—99; tchr. Pub. Sch. 131Q NYC Pub. Schs., 1999—. Nominating fellow Nat. Young Scholars Program, 2004—, Nat. Ctr. Early Academic Excellence, 2004—; author sch. sci. websites. Recipient Excellence in Tchg. awards (2), NY Coun. Excellence in Tchg., Space Explorers grant, NASA, Rose award, NY Restoration Project, 2005, Team Up Clean Up award, NYC Sanitation Dept., 2005; grantee, Beaumont Found., 2005—06; Fulbright scholar, 2004—05. Mem.: NAESP, Nat. Sci. Tchrs. Assn., NY Sci. Tchrs. Assn. Avocations: soccer, hiking, botany, hockey. Office: PS 131 Q 172 84th Ave Jamaica NY 11432 Home: 50 Syosset Cir Syosset NY 11791 Office Phone: 718-739-4229.

BUNTEN, WILLIAM DANIEL, retired banker; b. Goodland, Kans., Sept. 18, 1931; s. William Livingston and Nelle Elizabeth (Boyle) B.; m. Charlene Sue Riemen, May 23, 1954; children: Jane Denise Bunten-Hanisch, Barbara Sue Bunten Shuck, Patricia Joann Bunten-Buckner. AB, Baker U., 1953; LLB, Washburn U., 1956; MBA, U. Pa., 1958. Bar: Kans. 1956, Mich. 1959. From asst. cashier to v.p. Nat. Bank Detroit, 1957-67; from v.p. to pres. Mchts. Nat. Bank, Topeka, 1967-79; sr. exec. v.p. United Cen. Bank, Des Moines, 1979-81; from sr. v.p. to exec. v.p. United Cen. Bancshares, Des Moines, 1979-82; pres. INTRUST Bank and predecessor firm 1st Nat. Bank, Wichita, Kans., 1982-96, also bd. dirs. Vice chmn. bd. dir. INTRUST Fin. Corp. and predecessor firm 1st Fin. Corp., Wichita, Kans., 1982—96; bd. dir. Lakeway Airpark, Inc., pres., 2000—01; bd. dirs. Am. Home Life Insl. Corp., Topeka, 1974—99. Bd. dirs., v.p. Jayhawk coun. Boy. Scouts Am., Topeka, 1968-78, Mid-Iowa coun., 1980-2; bd. dirs. United Way, Topeka, 1969-77, pres. 1977; bd. dirs. United Way, Des Moines, 1980-82, United Way Wichita, 1983-88, pres. 1987; bd. dirs. Topeka C. of C., 1969-74, pres. 1973; bd. dirs. Wichita C. of C., 1986-88, Greater Downtown Wichita, 1986-88, pres. 1987; bd. dirs. Downtown Action Corp., Wichita, 1988-91; bd. dirs. YMCA, Wichita, 1988-96, pres. 1992-94; sec. bd. dirs. Boys/Girls Clubs S. Cen. Kans., 1990-96; trustee Quivira coun. Boy Scouts Am., 1983-96; trustee Stormont Vail Hosp., Topeka, 1974-79, treas. 1978-79; trustee Baker U., Baldwin City, Kans., 1987-90; bd. dirs. Hospice, Wichita, 1983-84, Wichita State U. Endowment Assn., Wichita, 1984-95, dir. Health Affiliates Inc., Wichita, 1992-96; dir., treas. Washburn Law Sch. Found., 2006—; mem. SCORE, 2002—. Mem.: Washburn U. Law Sch. Alumni Assn. (trustee 2002—), Washburn U. Endowment Assn. (trustee 1990—, dir. 2006—), Washburn U. Alumni Assn. (bd. dirs. 1989—92, pres. 1991—92), Shriners, Blue Lodge, Masons, Rotary (bd. dirs. Topeka club 1977—78, treas. Wichita club 1988—89, trustee Lakeway Rotary Found. 1999, Topeka Rotary Found. 2003—04). Republican. Methodist. Avocations: flying, golf, reading, running. Home: 4000 SW Clarion Place Topeka KS 66610 Personal E-mail: bbunten@3r9.org.

BUNTING, JOHN CHARLES, pastoral associate, youth minister; b. Mt. Holly, NJ, Aug. 6, 1959; s. Shreve Wilbur Bunting and Virginia Bunting Haas. BA, Thomas Edison State Coll., Trenton, NJ, 1993; MA in Pastoral Theology, St. Joseph Coll. Maine, Standish, 2005. Cert. Youth Ministry Studies Ctr. for Ministry Devel., 2004. Dir. music & liturgy/elem. tchr. St. Joseph Ch., Beverly, NJ, 1986—92; pastoral intern Diocese of Raleigh, NC, 1992—95; youth min./pastoral assoc. St. Egbert Ch., Morehead City, NC, 1995—2003; pastoral assoc. St. Elizabeth Ann Seton Ch., Fayetteville, NC, 2003—. Coord. liturgy for youth events Diocese of Raleigh, 2000—. Dist. commr. Ea. N.C. Babe Ruth Softball, 2005—06. Mem.: Am. Guild Organists, Nat. Assn. Cath. Youth Ministry Leaders, Nat. Assn. Pastoral Musicians, Southeastern Athletic Officials Assn., Cardinal Gibbons Assy., 4th Degree KC, Sons of Mother Seton Coun., KC. Conservative. Roman Catholic. Avocations: music, sports. Office: St Elizabeth Ann Seton Catholic Church 700 Carnegie Dr Fayetteville NC 28311 Home Phone: 910-488-1797; Office Phone: 910-488-1797. Office Fax: 910-488-7116.

BUNTING, KENNETH FREEMAN, newspaper editor; b. Houston, Dec. 9, 1948; s. Willie Freeman and Sarah Lee (Peterson) B.; m. Juliana Amy Jafvert, July 13, 1989; 1 child, Maxwell Freeman. Student, U. Mo., 1966-67; AA in Journalism, Lee Coll., 1968; BA in Journalism and History, Tex. Christian U., 1970; advanced exec. program, Northwestern U., 1996. Mgmt. trainee, reporter Harte-Hanks Newspapers Inc., Corpus Christi, Tex., 1970-71; reporter, then copy editor San Antonio Express-News, 1971-73; exec. asst. to Hon. G.J. Sutton Tex. Ho. of Reps., San Antonio, 1973-74; reporter Cin. Post, 1974-78, Sacramento Bee, 1978; reporter, asst. city editor, state capitol corr. L.A. Times, 1978-87; capitol bur. chief, city editor, dep. mng. editor, sr. editor Ft. Worth Star-Telegram, 1987-93; mng. editor Seattle Post-Intelligencer, 1993-99; exec. editor Seattle Post-Intelligence, 2000—. Journalism instr. Orange Coast Coll., Costa Mesa, Calif., 1981-82; mem. adv. bd. Maynard Inst., Oakland, Calif., 1994—. Bd. dirs. Seattle Symphony, 1995-97; mem. commn. Woodland Park Zoo, Seattle, 1995-96, 98; mem. Leadership Ft. Worth; former mem. journalism adv. bd. Tex. Christian U.; former mem. minorities task force Assn. for Edn. in Journalism and Mass Comms.; past pres. Press Club, Orange County, Calif.; past bd. dirs. Covington (Ky.) Cmty. Ctr.; past 1st v.p. Young Dems. of Tex.; past treas., mem. exec. bd. Freedom of Info. Found. of Tex.; leadership coun. ARC; bd. dirs. Alfred Friendly Press Fellowships. Mem. Nat. Assn. Black Journalists, AP Mng. Editors Assn. (mem. ethics com. 1995-96, bd. dirs. 1996-99), Am. Soc. Newspaper Editors (mem. diversity, leadership coms., chair edn. com., bd. dirs. 1999—), Soc. Profl. Journalists (bd. dirs. western Wash. chpt. 1995-96), Seattle C. of C. (mem. cmty. devel. roundtable 1994—), Alliance for Edn. (bd. dirs.), Tex. Christian U. Alumni Assn. (bd. dirs.), Freedom of Info. Found. Tex., Rainier Club, Washington Athletic Club. Unitarian Universalist. Avocations: tennis, bridge, reading. Office: Seattle-Post Intelligencer PO Box 1909 101 Elliott Ave W Seattle WA 98111

BUNTS, FRANK EMORY, artist; b. Cleve., Mar. 2, 1932; s. Alexander Taylor and Mary (Corbin) B.; m. Norah Jean Grassle, Aug. 1, 1964. Student, Yale U., Cleve. Inst. Art; MA, Case Western Res. U., 1964. Instr. Cleve. Inst. Art, 1963-64, Ark. State U., 1965-67; mem. faculty U. Md., 1967-77, prof., 1973-77, dir. grad. art studio program, 1972-77; pres. VIA Art. One-person shows include Comara Gallery, L.A., 1967, 68, Franz Bader Gallery, Washington, 1969, 73, 75, St. John's Coll., Annapolis, Md., 1972, Deson Zaks Gallery, Chgo., 1972, Gallery 118, Mpls., 1974, NAS, Washington, 1976, Cath. U. Am., Washington, 1978, Plum Gallery, Washington, 1979, Flatiron Studio, NYC, 1987, Maryanne McCarthy Fine Art, NYC, 1988-89, Limelight Club, NYC, 1988, Loft Lawyers, NYC, 1990, 91, Roberta Wood Gallery, Syracuse, NY, 1993, Effect/Cause Mail Project, 1993-95, others; group shows: San Francisco Mus. Art, 1965, Cleve. Mus. Art, 1961, 62, 63, 65, 66 (2), 67, 68, Cleve. Inst. Art, 1964, Purdue U., Lafayette, Ind., 1964-69, El Paso Mus. Art, 1965, Nat. Arts Club, NYC, 1965, Wittenberg U., Springfield, Ohio, 1966, Pacific Luth. U., Tacoma, 1966, Scripps Coll., Clairmont, Calif., 1967, U. Detroit, 1967, U. Calif., Long Beach, 1967, Palm Springs Desert Mus., Calif., 1967, Loyola U., L.A., 1968, Salt Lake City Art Ctr., 1968, U. NH, 1968, Brigham Young U., Provo, Utah, 1968, Ind. State U., Terre Haute, 1968, Brooks Meml. Art Gallery, Memphis, 1968, 73, Cath. U., Washington, 1969, U. Md., 1969, 70, 72, Traveling Show, 1975-76, Fine Arts Gallery San Diego, 1971, Henri Gallery, Washington, 1971, Reicher Gallery, Barat Coll., Lake Forest, Ill., 1972, Corcoran Gallery Art, 1972, Va. Poly. Inst., Blacksburg, 1973, Birmingham Mus. Art, Ala., 1973, Indpls. Mus. Art, 1976, Gallery K, Washington, 1978, Studio Gallery, Washington, 1976-77, Modern Mus. Art, Rijeka, Yugoslavia, 1978, Baak Gallery, Cambridge, Mass., 1978, 79, Maryanne McCarthy Fine Art, NYC, 1987, 88, 89, and Southampton, NY, 1989, Christie's NYC Preview and Auction, 1990, Univ. Sch., Cleve., 1990, Guild Hall, East Hampton, NY, 1991, 92, Lillian Heidenberg Gallery, NYC, 1991-92, Roberta Wood Gallery, Syracuse, 1993-96, Angel Art Pacific Design Ctr., LA, 1993, Divine Design 95, LA, Black and Herron Gallery, NYC, 1996; Intercomm. Ctr., Tokyo Opera City, Tokyo, Japan, 1998, VIA Art Found., New York (one person exhbn.), 1999—, Roberta Wood Gallery, Chapel Hill, NC, 2001, Sterling Meml. Libr. Yale U., New Haven, 2005, represented in collections Mus. Art, Cleve. Mus. Art, Fine Arts Gallery, San Diego, Libr. of Congress, Corcoran Gallery Art, Washington, Cooperstown Art Assn., NY, Chinese Artists Assn., Beijing; artwork in the following videos: The Man from U.N.C.L.E., episode The Pop Art Affair, 1966, Callanetics, M.C.A., 1986, Portrait of an Artist by Konrad Gylfason, 1986, music video Always and Forever, Whistle CC Prodns., 1990, documentary video San Francisco Ctr. for Visual Studies, 1990, A Man Flies in Manhattan, 2003, Breaking Some Eggs-A Wisconsin Breakfast, 2003; work reproduced in Cleve. Mus. Art. Bull., May 1962, May 1968, Md. Art Gallery Catalog, 1969, 72, Indpl. Mus. Art catalog Painting and Sculpture Today, June 1976, Internat. Exhbn. catalog Modern Mus. Art, Rijeka, Yugoslavia, 1978, The Catalog of Am. Drawings, Watercolors, Pastels and Collages Corcoran Gallery Art, Washington, 1983, NY Art Rev., 1988, Millenium Art Collection, 2002, Awakened Pyramids, 2005. Office: VIA Art Found 15 W 24th St 7th Fl New York NY 10010-3214 E-mail: bunts@earthlink.net.

BUNT SMITH, HELEN MARGUERITE, lawyer; b. LA, Oct. 8, 1942; d. Alan Verbanks and Nettie Virginia (Crandall) Bunt; m. Charles Robert Smith, Jan. 12, 1974; children: John, Sharon. BS, U. Calif., LA, 1964; JD, Southwestern U., 1972. Bar: Calif. 1972; cert. secondary tchr., Calif. Tchr. L.A. City Schs., 1965-72; pvt. practice Pasadena, Calif., 1973—. Law Day chmn. Pasadena Bar Assn., 1980, sec., 1981. Editor (newsletter) Lawyer's Club, 1984-85. Mem. Pasadena Sister Cities Com., 1990—96; Sunday sch. tchr. Lake Ave. Ch., Pasadena, 1977—98, mem. choir, 1999—. Mem. San Gabriel Bar Assn. (bd. dirs., sec. 1999-2005, pres. 2004-05). Avocations: jogging, singing, stained glass. Office: 465 E Union St Ste 102 Pasadena CA 91101-1783

BUNYAN, ELLEN LACKEY SPOTZ, retired chemist; b. Clark Mills, Pa., Aug. 14, 1921; d. Scott Richard and Mary Ellen (Beal) Lackey; m. Robert J. Spotz, 1944 (div. 1976); m. Arthur H. Bunyan, 1978 (dec. 1996); children: Mark Stephen Spotz, Leslie Claire Spotz, Elizabeth Grace O'Rourke Xavier. BS, U. Pitts., 1942; PhD, U. Wis., 1950. Sr. technologist Eastman Kodak Co., Kingsport, Tenn., 1942-44; instr. chemistry U. Wis., Milw., 1946-47, rsch. assoc. dept. chemistry Madison, 1950-52; instr. physics St. Agnes Acad., Houston, 1965; Welch fellow chemistry Rice U., Houston, 1968-69; lectr. Montgomery Coll., Rockville, Md., 1970-72; asst. prof. chem. tech. Univ. D.C., Washington, 1972-78, assoc. prof., 1978-91; ret., 1991. Guest worker Nat. Bur. Stds., 1976; adj. prof. continuing edn. Walter Reed Army Med. Ctr. U. D.C., Washington, 1991—94, adj. prof., 1995—2000, mem. adv. coun. mortuary sci. program, 2002; curriculum developer Allied Health Chemistry. Contbr. articles to profl. jours. Bd. dirs. Takoma Pk. Symphony, 1988—2001; mem. adv. bd. Cambodian Children's Assn., Inc., 1991—2000. Fellow, Nat. Urban League Eastman Kodak Co., 1976. Mem.: Am. Chem. Soc., Sigma Delta Epsilon, Sigma Xi. Methodist.

BUNZA, LINDA HATHAWAY, editor, writer, composer, director; b. Hartford, Conn., Feb. 23, 1946; m. Geoffrey J. Bunza; children: Stephen, Matthew. BA, Bates Coll., 1968; MA, The Hartford Sem. Found., 1971; PhD, Syracuse U., 1974. Editl. asst. The Harvard Ednl. Rev., Cambridge, Mass., 1974—76; mng. editor The Andover Rev., Andover, Mass., 1976—79; dir. Columbia Rsch. Inst. Arts and Humanities, Portland, Oreg., 1998—2002. Editor Renaissance Mag., Hartford, 1963—64; editl. asst. Symposium Mag., Syracuse, NY, 1973—74; editor Soc. Arts, Religion, and Contemporary Culture, NYC, 1974—78; lectr. in field. Composer: (Classical Music Composition) There is Something Still Floating, 1999, Report From A Spiral, 1998, Snow Mountain, 2000, RiverMusic, 1995, Mythology of Clouds, 1993, Sphere, 1992, Cascadia, 1989, Widmanstatten Lines, 1987, View from a Mobius Strip, 1986, Sounds from the Olympic Peninsula, 1998, Electric Night, 1984, Odalisque, 1982, Awakening Night, 1981; editor: (Book) Adventures and Misadventures of Dr. Sonjee by Dr. Prasanna Pati, Snehalata Press, 2001, (Novel) Against Parched Winds by Kanta Luthra, (Book) Art of Literary Criticism, 2000; author: Theories of Modern Art-I, 1972, Theories of Modern Art-II, 1973, Theories of Modern Art-III, 1973; author: (catalog) Blue Note: The Art of Bruce Warner, 2000, Air, 2001, Where Art Reveals Itself in Symbols, Words are Hard to Find, 2001; mem. editl. bd. Anima Mag., 1973—95. Bd. dirs. Fear No Music 20th Century Ensemble, 2000—02, Third Angle New Music Ensemble, Portland, 2000—04, Contemporary Art Coun., Portland Art Mus., 2001—04, Portland Baroque Orch., 2000—04; arts and culture com. City Club of Portland, 2000—04, arch. com., 1999—2002. Recipient Pres.'s award, Beaverton Arts Commn., 2000. Mem.: Portland Inst. Contemporary Art, European and Am. Art Coun., Portland Art Mus., Northwest Bookfest (program com.), Ancient Egypt Studies Assn., The Coll. Music Soc., Soc. Composers Internat., Friends William Stafford Assn. (life). Office: Columbia Rsch Inst Arts and Humanities PO Box 25316 Portland OR 97298 Personal E-mail: bunza@teleport.com. Business E-Mail: columbiaarts@aol.com.

BUNZEL, JOHN HARVEY, political science professor; b. NYC, Apr. 15, 1924; s. Ernest Everett and Harriett (Harvey) B.; m. Barbara Bovyer, May 11, 1963; children: Cameron, Reed. AB, Princeton U., 1948; MA, Columbia U., 1949; PhD, U. Calif.-Berkeley, 1954; LL.D., U. Santa Clara, 1976. Mem. faculty San Francisco State U., 1953-56, 63-70, vis. scholar Ctr. Advanced Study in Behavioral Scis., 1969-70; mem. faculty Mich. State U., East Lansing, 1956-57, Stanford U., Calif., 1957-63; pres. San Jose State U., Calif., 1970-78; sr. research fellow Hoover Inst. Stanford U., Calif., 1978—. Mem. U.S. Commn. on Civil Rights, 1983-86. Author: The American Small Businessman, 1962; Anti-Politics in America, 1967; Issues of American Public Policy, 1968; New Force on the Left, 1983, Challenge to American Schools: The Case For Standards and Values, 1985, Political Passages: Journeys of Change Through Two Decades 1968-1988, 1988, Race Relations on Campus: Stanford Students Speak, 1992; contbr. articles to profl. jours., popular mags., newspapers. Weekly columnist San Jose Mercury-News. Bd. dirs. No. Calif. Citizenship Clearing House, 1959-61; mem. Calif. Atty. Gen.'s Adv. Com., 1960-61; del. Calif. Democratic Conv., 1968; del. Dem. Nat. Conv., 1968 Recipient Presdl. award No. Calif. Polit. Sci. Assn., 1969, cert. of Honor San Francisco Bd. Suprs., 1974, Hubert Humprey Pub. Policy award Policy Studies Orgn., 1990; grantee Ford Found., Rockefeller Found., Rabinowitz Found. Mem. Am. Polit. Sci. Assn. Home: 1519 Escondido Way Belmont CA 94002-3634 Office: Stanford U Hoover Inst Stanford CA 94305

BUNZL, RUDOLPH HANS, retired manufacturing executive; b. Vienna, July 20, 1922; arrived in U.S., 1940, naturalized, 1944; s. Robert Max and Nellie Margaret (Burian) Bunzl; m. Rema R. Templeton, Apr. 6, 1947 (div.); children: Ann Mary Bunzl Kamoe, Carol Elizabeth Bunzl Showker; m. Esther R. Mendelsohn, Nov. 14, 1970. BSChemE, Ga. Inst. Tech., 1943; MA in History, U. Richmond, 1994. With Shell Chem. Co., Calif., 1943-54; v.p. Am. Filtrona Corp., Richmond, Va., 1954-59, pres., 1959-83, CEO, 1983-87, chmn. bd., 1987-95. Pres. R.E.B. Found.; trustee Richmond Symphony Found. With US Army, 1944—46. Mem.: AICE. Office: 5516 Falmouth St Ste 205 Richmond VA 23230-1819

BUONAMICI, APRIL GRAHAM, elementary school and music educator; b. Maumee, Ohio, Apr. 16, 1950; d. John and Claudine Graham; m. James Buonamici, May 31, 1975; children: Domenick, Brett, Byron. MusB, Bowling Green State U., Ohio, 1972, MEd, 1973. Cert. music and elem. tchr. Ohio. Tchr. Toledo City Schs., 1972—73, Euclid City Schs., Ohio, 1973—74, Lyndhurst City Schs., Ohio, 1974—76, Colegio Internacional, Caracas, Venezuela, 1976—78, Solon City Schs., Ohio, 1978—2005. Composer: (percussion ensemble) Boredom, 1969. Pres. 1st Ch. of Christ, Scientist, Painesville, Ohio, 1983, 1986, bd. dirs. Chagrin Falls, Ohio, 2003—05. Mem.: Solon Edn. Assn. (pres., v.p., grievance chmn., trustee 1979—2005). Christian Scientist. Avocations: skiing, piano. Home: 110 Bennett Dr Bozeman MT 59715 Personal E-mail: abuonamici@aol.com.

BUONEMANI, JAMES PAUL, church musician, director, composer; b. Rochester, NY, June 1, 1956; s. Raymond A. and Lena Buonemani. MusB with Highest Distinction, Eastman Sch. Music, Rochester, 1978; MusM summa cum laud, Westminster Choir Coll., Princeton, NJ, 1980. Performer's cert. Eastman Sch. Music, 1978. Dir. music, organist Ch. of the Good Shepherd, Corpus Christi, Tex., 1980—87, Ch. of the Epiphany, Washington, 1987—94, St. James Ch., LA, 1995—; organist Corpus Christi Symphony Orch., 1981—87, Temple Emanuel, Kensington, Md., 1989—94. Adjudicator San Marino Organ Competition, Calif., 1996—98, Music Teachers Nat. Assn. Conv., LA, 1999; condr. St. James choir residency Westminster Abbey, London, 1999, 2006, organ recitalist; organ accompanist LA Master Chorale, 2001—03; organ demonstrator Am. Inst. Organ Builders Nat. Conv., 2002; guest condr. William Ferris Chorale, Chgo., 2003—04, Chgo. Choral Artists; organ recitalist Grace Cathedral, San Francisco, 2003; organ accompanist Am. Choral Dirs. Assn. Regional Conv., Honolulu. Composer: Missa Miamiensis, 1994, Preces and Responses, 1999, Magnificat, 2006; editor (organ version): Lux Aeterna by Morten Lauridsen; dir.: (recordings) Rejoice in the Lamb, Choir of St. James, 2002, Evensong, Choir of St. James, 2005. Founder, dir. Musicians Against AIDS, Washington, 1992. Recipient First prize, Baylor U. Nat. Young Composer Competition, 1974. Mem.: Am. Guild Organists (chair scholarship com. 1988—90), Guild Carolloneurs in N.Am. (assoc.), Pi Kappa Lambda (life). Office: St James Ch 3903 Wilshire Blvd Los Angeles CA 90010 Home Phone: 323-656-3441; Office Phone: 213-388-3015. Office Fax: 213-388-3339. E-mail: greatmus@earthlink.net.

BUOTE, ROSEMARIE BOSCHEN, retired special education educator; b. Jamaica, NY, Nov. 13, 1939; d. George Frederick and Mary (Bernadick) Boschen; m. Victor Roy Buote, June 27, 1964; children: Kristine Enos, Alissa Cassidy. BA, Barrington Coll., RI, 1962; MEd, RI Coll., Providence, 1985, Fitchburg U., Mass., 1991. Cert. spl. edn. and elem. tchr. Elem. tchr. Town of Barrington, 1962-68, 69-70; resource rm. instructional aide Town of Rehoboth, Mass., 1983-84; spl. edn. tchr., behavior mgmt. specialist Dept. of Edn. Tri-County Dist., Ednl. Svcs. in Instnl. Schs., Taunton, Mass., 1985—2002; ret., 2002. Sec. Conservation Commn., Town of Dighton, 1971—74, Friends Taunton Libr. Bd., pres., 2004—; vol. usher Providence Performing Arts Ctr.; lay eucharistic minister Pastoral Outreach Commn., Episcopal Diocese Mass.; mem. mission and stewardship com. Ch. of Our Saviour; bd. dir. Gordon Coll. Alumni Bd., Wenham, Mass., 1989—92. Recipient Winfield Curry award, Gordon Coll., 2004. Mem.: AAUW (Mass. state v.p. membership 2003—06, sec., Taunton area br. past pres. 1996—98, bd. dirs.), Ret. Educators Assn. Mass., Mass. Computer Using Educators, Coun. Children with Learning Disabilities, Coun. Children with Behavioral Disorders, Coun. Exceptional Children, Southeastern New Eng. Marine Educators, Nat. Marine Educators Assn., Bristol County Ret. Tchrs. Assn., S.E. Mass. Ladies Tea Guild, Red Hat Soc., Dighton Garden Club (pres. 1979—82), Delta Kappa Gamma (pres. 2002—04). Avocations: reading, writing, gardening, theater. Home: 1690 Wellington St Dighton MA 02715-1000 Home Fax: 508-669-5894. Personal E-mail: rosemariebuote@aol.com.

BURACK, MICHAEL LEONARD, lawyer; b. Willimantic, Conn., Oct. 10, 1942; s. Meyer and Rose Ann (Kravitz) B.; m. Maria Gallego, Oct. 20, 1978; children: Victoria Luisa, Cristina Maria. BA in physics summa cum laude, Wesleyan U., Middletown, Conn., 1964; postgrad. in physics, Calif. Inst. Tech., 1965; MS in Applied Physics, Stanford U., 1967, JD, 1970. Bar: Calif. 1971, DC 1972. Law clk. to judge US Ct. Appeals for 9th Cir., San Francisco, 1970-71; assoc. Wilmer, Cutler & Pickering, Washington, 1971-77, ptnr., 1978-2000. Mem. staff DC Jud. conf. Com. on Adminstrn. of Justice under Emergency Condition, 1972-73; mem. adv. com. govt. applications of ADR of Ctr. for Pub. Resources, 1988; mem. jud. evaluation com. DC Bar, 1991-94. Assoc. editor Jour. Pub. Contract Law, 1988-94. Mem. bd. Glen Echo Pk. Partnership for Arts & Culture, 2007. Mem. ABA, Order of the Coif, Phi Beta Kappa, Sigma Xi.

BURAK, H(OWARD) PAUL, lawyer; s. Harry and Bette (Hauer) B.; m. Edna K. Goodman, Oct. 18, 1970; children: Hally Ann., Jason Lewis. BS, Cornell U., 1954; LLB, Columbia U., 1957. Bar: N.Y. 1958, D.C. 1967, U.S. Dist. Ct. (so. and ea. dists.) N.Y. 1967, U.S. Ct. Appeals (2d cir.) 1960, U.S. Supreme Ct. 1964. Assoc. Cadwalader, Wickersham & Taft, NYC, 1957-63; dep. asst., asst. gen. counsel Agy. for Internat. Devel. U.S. State Dept., Washington, 1963-67; assoc. Rosenman Colin Kay Petschek & Freund, NYC, 1967-69; ptnr. Rosenman & Colin, NYC, 1969—2002, Katten Muchin Zavis Rosenman, NYC, 2002—05; of counsel Katten Muchin Rosenman, NYC, 2005—. Bd. dirs. Sony USA Found., NYC. Rev. editor Columbia Law Rev., 1956-57; author pamphlets. Mem. adv. bd. N.Y.C. Ballet, 2001-04. Mem.: ABA, Assn. Bar City NY, NY Bar Assn., Internat. Bar Assn., Univ. Club, Birchwood Country Club. Office: Katten Muchin Rosenman LLP 575 Madison Ave New York NY 10022-2585 Office Phone: 212-940-8870. Business E-Mail: hpburak@kattenlaw.com.

BURAKOVSKY, LEONID, physicist, researcher; b. Kiev, Ukraine, Jan. 14, 1964; s. Nahum and Polina Burakovsky; m. Maya Derechin, Nov. 19, 1989; children: Arik, Naftali. MS, Kiev State U., Kiev, Ukraine, 1990; PhD, Tel Aviv U., Israel, 1995. Rsch. fellow theoretical divsn. Los Alamos Nat. Lab., N.Mex., 1995—99, tech. staff mem. theoretical divsn., 1999—. Achievements include development of new unified analytic model for the Grüneisen parameter, melting temperature, and shear modulus. Office: T-1 MS B221 Los Alamos Nat Lab Los Alamos NM 87545 Home: 886 Estates Dr Los Alamos NM 87544-2781 Home Phone: 505-662-5301; Office Phone: 505-667-5222. Office Fax: 505-665-4055. Business E-Mail: burakov@lanl.gov.

BURANELLO, RAYMOND TERRENCE, quality assurance executive, chemist; b. Wilmington, Del., Nov. 26, 1950; s. Raymond and Dorothy (Reed) B.; m. Helen Grace O'Brien, Sept. 13, 1979. BS in Chemistry, U. Del., 1972, MBA, 1977. Cert. quality engr., Del. Rsch. chemist Wilmington Chemical Co., 1972-75; chief chemist Phila. Coke Co., 1977-80; sr. chemist Congoleum Corp., Marcus Hook, Pa., 1980-89; quality assurance mgr. Speciality Composites, Newark, Del., 1989-91; quality assurance specialist PQ Corp., 1992-99; sr. quality control rep. Eli Lilly and Co., 2003—. Inventor chem. compound, 1973. Libertarian cand. U.S. Senate, Del., 2002. Mem. Am. Soc. for Quality Control, Del. Assn. of Profl. Engrs. (assoc.). Libertarian. Office: 1555 S Harding St Indianapolis IN 46221 Office Phone: 317-276-4739. E-mail: buranellora@lilly.com.

BURATTI, DENNIS P., lawyer; b. Madison, Wis., 1949; JD, U. Wis., 1973. Bar: Wis. 1973, Minn. 1973. Gen. counsel Ryan Cos., Mpls. Office: Ryan Companies Ste 300 50 S 10th St Minneapolis MN 55403

BURATYNSKI, THERESA JOAN, physician; b. Steubenville, Ohio, Apr. 21, 1964; d. Raymond Stanley and Anna Sue Buratynski; m. Peter Randall Daspit, Apr. 1, 2000. BSc, U. Akron, 1986; MPH, Johns Hopkins U., 1999; MD, Case We. Res. U., 1995. Student fellow pathology U. Hosps. Cleve., 1992—93; gen. med. officer Naval Hosp., Yokosuka, Japan, 1996—98; resident Navy Aerospace Medicine Inst., Pensacola, Fla., 1999—2000; head dept. aviation medicine Med. Clinic Kaneohe Bay, 2000—01; flight surgeon Marine Heavy Helicopter 363, Kaneohe, 2001—04; sr. med. officer Marine Aircraft Group 24, Kaneohe, 2004—05; med. officer Navy Health Clinic, Kaneohe, 2006—. Contbr. articles to profl. jours. Activist Kailua Neighborhood, Hawaii, 2004—; med. support and aid USN, 2000. Lt. comdr. USN, 1996—. Decorated Navy Achievement medal, Navy Commendation medal; recipient Dr. Roger Keller, Jr. award for Genetics and Biotech., U. Akron, 1986, Daniel Lewis Raven, MD award, Case We. Res. U. Sch. Medicine, 1995, Physician Recognition award, AMA, 2003—06; Rsch. grantee, Am. Heart Assn., 1986, Armed Forces Health Scis. Edn. and Tng. scholar, USN, 1990—95, Betty Ford Ctr. Resident in Tng. scholar, 1991, March of Dimes rsch. scholar, 1991, fellow in pathology, U. Hosp. Cleve., 1992—93, Chattanooga Corp. grantee, 1985, Ohio Bd. Regents scholar, 1982—86. Mem.: APHA, Am. Coll. Occupl. and Environ. Medicine, Aerospace Med. Assn., Soroptomists Internat., Phi Sigma Alpha. Avocations: running, gardening, community service, reading. Home: 1286 Aulepe St Kailua HI 96734 Home Phone: 808-230-2342; Office Phone: 808-778-4541. Personal E-mail: doctjb@hotmail.com.

BURBACH, MIKE, editor; BA in Journalism and German, U. ND, 1982. With Grand Forks Herald, ND; news editor AgWeek Mag., Grand Forks; mng. editor Aberdeen Am. News, SD, 1990—92; editor Minot Daily News, ND, 1992—95; asst. bus. editor Detroit Free Press, 1995—97; v.p., exec. editor Columbus Ledger-Enquirer, Ga., 1997—2004; mng. editor Akron Beacon Jour., Ohio, 2004—. Office: Akron Beacon Journal 44 E Exchange St PO Box 640 Akron OH 44309-0640

BURBANK, DANIEL C., astronaut; b. Manchester, Conn., July 27, 1961; s. Dan and Joan Burbank; married; 2 children. BSEE, USCG Acad., 1985; MSc in Aero. Sci., Embry-Riddle Aero. U., 1990. Commd. 2nd lt. USCG, 1985, advanced through grades to comdr., various assignments, 1985—88; assigned to Coast Guard Air Sta., Elizabeth City, NC, 1988—92, Cape Cod, Mass., 1992—95, Sitka, Alaska, 1995—96; astronaut NASA, Houston, 1996—. Mission specialist Space Shuttle Atlantis, 2000; flight engr. Space Shuttle Atlantis (STS-115), 2006. Decorated Defense Superior Svc. meda USCG, Nat. Def. Svc. medal, Humanitarian Svc. medal, Commendation medal (2), Achievement medal, Commandant's Letter of Commendation Ribbons (2), Meritorious Team Commendations (3); recipient Achievement award, Tex. Soc. Daughters of Am. Revolution, 1988, NASA Space Flight medal, Air medal. Mem.: Nat. Space Soc., USCG Acad. Alumni Assn., USCG Pterodactyls, Order of Daedalians (Orville Wright Achievement award 1988). Avocations: running, skiing, hiking, sailing, amateur astronomy, guitar. Office: Astronaut office CB NASA Johnson Space Ctr Houston TX 77058

BURBANK, NELSON STONE, investment banker; b. Winchester, Mass., Sept. 16, 1920; s. Willis H. and Vivian (Caxson) B.; m. Rita B. Healey, Feb. 12, 1950; children: Peter N., Nelson Stone, Jane Vivian. Student, Boston U., 1946-47. Registered rep. Vance, Sanders & Co., Inc., Boston, 1946-53; pres. Burbank & Co., Inc., Boston, 1953-83; dir., registered rep. A.G. Edwards and Sons, Inc., 1982-83; pres., bd. dirs. Colonial Investment Services, Inc., 1983-85. Bd. dirs. MassBank for Savs., Reading, ret., 1994; bd. govs. Boston Stock Exch., 1965-73, vice chmn., 1968-71, chmn., 1971-73; bd. dirs. Ag Edwards & Sons, Inc. Vice chmn. ARC, 1963-82. With AUS, 1942-45. Decorated D.F.C., Air medals. Mem. Nat. Assn. Securities Dealers (mem. bus. conduct com. 1971-73, gov. 1974-77, cons 1985-88) Home and Office: 24 Juniper Cir Reading MA 01867-1836

BURBANK, STEPHEN BRADNER, law educator; b. NYC, Jan. 8, 1947; s. John Howard and Jean (Gedney) B.; m. Ellen Randolph Coolidge, June 13, 1970; 1 child, Peter Jefferson. AB, Harvard U., 1968, JD, 1973. Bar: Mass. 1973, Pa. 1976, U.S. Supreme Ct. 1977. Law clk. Supreme Jud. Ct. of Mass., Boston, 1973-74, Chief Justice Warren Burger, Washington, 1974-75; gen. counsel U. Pa., Phila., 1975-80, asst. prof. law, 1979-83, assoc. prof. law, 1983-86, prof. law, 1986—, Fuller prof. law, 1991-95, Berger prof. law, 1995—. Reporter 3rd Cir. Jud. Discipline Rules, Phila., 1981-82, 84, 3rd Cir. Task Force on Rule 11, Phila., 1987-89; mem. Nat. Commn. on Jud. Discipline and Removal, 1991-93; mediator, arbitrator Ctr. for Pub. Resources, NY, 1986—; cons. Dechert LLP, Phila., 1986—; mem. CPR Arbitration Commn., 1997-2000; spl. master NFL, 2002—. Mem. Com. to Visit Harvard and Radcliffe Coll., Cambridge, Mass., 1979-85; mem. adv. bd. Inst. Contemporary Art, Phila., 1982-99; charter trustee Phillips Acad., Andover, Mass., 1980-97. Mem. Am. Law Inst. (life, adviser transnat. rules of civil procedure 1997-04, adviser internat. jurisdiction and judgments 1999-05), Am. Arbitration Assn. (mem. panel of arbitrators 1985—), Am. Acad. Polit. and Social Sci. (bd. dirs. 2002-07, chair 2004-07), Am. Judicature Soc. (mem. exec. com. 1997-02, v.p. 1997-99), Century Assn., Phi Beta Kappa. Avocations: swimming, travel, tennis. Office: U Pa Sch Law 3400 Chestnut St Philadelphia PA 19104-6204 Office Phone: 215-898-7072. E-mail: sburbank@law.upenn.edu.

BURBIDGE, E. MARGARET, astronomer, educator; b. Davenport, Eng. d. Stanley John and Marjorie (Stott) Peachey; m. Geoffrey Burbidge, Apr. 2, 1948; 1 child, Sarah. BS, PhD, U. London; Sc.D. hon., Smith Coll., 1963, U. Sussex, 1970, U. Bristol, 1972, U. Leicester, 1972, City U., 1973, U. Mich., 1978, U. Mass., 1978, Williams Coll., 1979, SUNY, Stony Brook, 1985, Rensselaer Poly. Inst., 1986, U. Notre Dame, 1986, U. Chgo., 1991. Mem. staff U. London Obs., 1948-51; rsch. fellow Yerkes Obs. U. Chgo., 1951-53, Shirley Farr fellow Yerkes obs., 1957-59, assoc. prof. Yerkes Obs., 1959-62; rsch. fellow Calif. Inst. Tech., Pasadena, 1955-57; mem. Enrico Fermi Inst. for Nuclear Studies, 1957-62; prof. astronomy dept. physics U. Calif. San Diego, 1964—89; dir. Royal Greenwich Obs. (Herstmonceux Castle), Hailsham, Eng., 1971-73; univ. prof. U. Calif., San Diego, 1984-91, prof. emeritus, 1991—, rsch. prof. dept. physics, 1990—. Lindsay Meml. lectr. Goddard Space Flight Ctr., NASA; Abby Rockefeller

Mauze prof. MIT, 1968; David Elder lectr. U. Strathclyde, 1972; V. Gildersleeve lectr. Barnard Coll., 1974; Jansky lectr. Nat. Radio Astronomy Observatory, 1977; Brode lectr. Whitman Coll., 1986; Hitchcock lectr. U. Calif., Berkeley, 2001. Author (with G. Burbidge): Quasi-Stellar Objects, 1967; editor: Observatory mag., 1948—51; mem. editl. bd.: Astronomy and Astrophysics, 1969—85. Co-recipient Warner prize in Astronomy, 1959; recipient Bruce Gold medal, Astronomy Soc. Pacific, 1982, U.S. Nat. medal of Sci., 1984, Sesquicentennial medal, Mt. Holyoke Coll., 1987, Einstein medal, World Cultural Coun., 1988; fellow hon. fellow, Univ. Coll., London, Girton Coll., Lucy Cavendish Coll., Cambridge. Fellow: Royal Astron. Soc. (Gold medal 2005), Am. Acad. Arts and Scis., Nat. Acad. Scis. (chmn. sect.12 astronomy 1986), Royal Soc.; mem.: Internat. Astron. Union (pres. commn. 28 1970—73), Am. Astron. Soc. (v.p. 1972—74, pres. 1976—78, Henry Norris Russell lectr. 1984), Grad. Women Sci. (hon.). Office: U Calif-San Diego Ctr Astrophysics Space Scis Mail Code # 0424 La Jolla CA 92093 Home Phone: 858-459-4968; Office Phone: 858-534-4477. Business E-Mail: mburbidge@ucsd.edu.

BURBIDGE, GEOFFREY, astrophysicist, educator; b. Chipping Norton, Oxon, Eng., Sept. 24, 1925; s. Leslie and Eveline Burbidge; m. Margaret Peachey, 1948; 1 dau. B.Sc. with spl. honors in Physics, Bristol U., 1946; PhD, U. Coll., London, 1951. Asst. lectr. U. Coll., London, 1950-51; Agassiz fellow Harvard, 1951-52; research fellow U. Chgo., 1952-53, Cavendish Lab., Cambridge, Eng., 1953-55; Carnegie fellow Mt. Wilson and Palomar Obs., Calif. Inst. Tech., 1955-57; asst. prof. dept. astronomy U. Chgo., 1957-58, assoc. prof., 1958-62, U. Calif. San Diego, La Jolla, 1962-63, prof. physics, 1963-83, 88—; dir. Kitt Peak Nat. Obs., Tucson, 1978-84. Phillips vis. prof. Harvard U., 1968; bd. dirs. Associated Univs. Research in Astronomy, 1971-74; trustee Associated Univs., Inc., 1973-82 Author: (with Margaret Burbidge) Quasi-Stellar Objects, 1967, (with F. Hoyle and J. Narlikar) A Different Approach to Cosmology, 2000; editor Ann. Rev. Astronomy and Astrophysics, 1973-2004; sci. editor Astrophys. Jour., 1996-02; contbr. articles to sci. jours. Recipient Jansky prize, Nat. Radio Astronomy Observatory, 1985, Vainu Bappu Meml award, Indian Nat. Acad. Sci., 1989, NAS award for Scientific Reviewing, 2007. Fellow Royal Soc. London, Am. Acad. Arts and Scis., Royal Astron. Soc. (co-recipient Gold medal 2005), Am. Phys. Soc., AAAS; mem. Am. Astron. Soc.(co-recipient Helen Warner prize, 1959), Internat. Astron. Union, Astron. Soc. Pacific (pres. 1974-76, Bruce medal 1999). Office: U Calif-San Diego 0424 Ctr Astrophysics Space Scis La Jolla CA 92093 Office Phone: 858-534-6626. Business E-Mail: gburbidge@ucsd.edu.

BURBINE, THOMAS HEWEY, science educator, researcher; b. Schenectady, NY, Aug. 11, 1966; s. Thomas and Mary Lou Burbine. PhD, MIT, Cambridge, 1993—2000. Contbr. articles to profl. jours. Home: 21 Woodbridge St 2R South Hadley MA 01075 Office: Mount Holyoke Coll 50 College St South Hadley MA 01075 Home Phone: 413-303-9209. Business E-Mail: tburbine@mtholyoke.edu.

BURCAT, JOEL ROBIN, lawyer; b. Phila., Oct. 28, 1954; s. David Sidney and Jessie (Goldberg) B.; m. Gail Rene Hartman, May 30, 1982; children: Dina Michelle, Shira Elizabeth. Student, Temple U., 1972—73; BS, Pa. State U., 1976; JD, Vt. Law Sch., 1980. Bar: Pa. 1980, U.S. Dist. Ct. (mid. dist.) Pa. 1980, U.S. Ct. Appeals (3d cir.) 1981, U.S. Supreme Ct. 1984, U.S. Dist. Ct. (we. dist.) Pa. 1988, U.S. Dist. Ct. (ea. dist.) Pa. 1993, U.S. Ct. Appeals (fed. cir.) 2001, U.S. Ct. Fed. Claims 2001. Asst. atty. gen. Pa. Dept. Environ. Resources, Harrisburg, 1980—83; assoc. Rhoads & Sinon, Harrisburg, 1983—88, Kirkpatrick & Lockhart, Harrisburg, 1988—91, ptnr., 1992—2002, Saul Ewing LLP, Harrisburg, 2002—, vice chair environ. dept., 2003, chair environ. dept., 2004—. Spl. counsel Pa. Senate Com. on Environ. Resources and Energy, Harrisburg, 1986—87; gen. counsel Nat. Wilderness Inst., Washington, 1991—93; mem. rules com. Pa. Environ. Hearing Bd., 1984—88. Author, editor: Pennsylvania Environmental Law and Practice, 1994, 4th edit., 2006. Trustee United Jewish Cmty., Harrisburg, 1991—94, v.p., 1996—97, Yeshiva Acad., Harrisburg, 1986—, pres., 1996—97; dir. Friends State of Pa. Mus., 1999—2003, Concertante, 2004—. Recipient Best Publ. award Assn. Continuing Legal Edn., 1999. Mem. ABA (standing com. environ. law 1979-80, law student liaison), Pa. Bar Assn. (sec. environ. mineral and natural resource law sect. 1990-91, vice-chmn. 1991-92, chmn. 1992-93, ethics com. 1984-97, chmn. pro bono com. 1999-03, Spl. Achievement award 1993, Cert. of Recognition 1994, Disting. Svc. award 2007). Republican. Jewish. Avocations: guitar playing, classical music, jogging, hiking, gardening. Office: Saul Ewing LLP Two N Second St 7th Flr Harrisburg PA 17101 Home Phone: 717-234-8105; Office Phone: 717-257-7506. Business E-Mail: jburcat@saul.com.

BURCH, ANNETTA JANE, writer; b. Valdosta, Ga., Feb. 10, 1947; d. James Louie and Ethel Lucille (Padgett) B. Student, N. Fla. C.C., Madison, Ctrl. Fla. C.C., Lecanto. Activity dir. Concordia Manor, Inc., St. Petersburg, Fla., 1983-84; rsch. clk. St. Petersburg Times, 1987; columnist Tampa Tribune, Citrus County, Fla., 1994-96; activity dir. Sugarmill Manor, Inc., Homosassa, Fla., 1990-92; activity dir. resident svcs. Barrington Place, Lecanto, Fla., 1992-94; office mgr. Boys and Girls Club, Crystal River, Fla., 1995-96; dir. pub. rels. Nature Coast Tourism Devel., Inc., Crystal River, 1999—2001; activity dir. Taylor Sr. Citizens Ctr., 2005—06. Former mem. Citrus County Code Enforcment Bd., vice chmn., 1998, chmn., 1999; corr. The Newscaster. Published in Fla. Living Mag., 1999, 00. Former amb. Citrus County C. of C.; former bd. dirs. Homosassa Springs Area C. of C.; former officer Friends of Beverly Hills Libr., 1994; former mem. com. Ctrl. Fla. Symphony, 1994; vol. writer for various clubs and orgns. for local newspapers, correspondent, The Newscaster weekly newspaper; sec. Nature Coast Rep. Club, 1996, pres. 1997, 99; chmn. Citrus County Ad Hoc Fla. WWII Meml. Com.; mem. Citrus County Federated Rep. Women; mem. Rep. Nat. Com., Fla. State Rep. Party; vice chair Taylor County Rep. exec. Com.; founder, pres. Taylor County Rep. Women Network; numerous other activities. Recipient Disting. Svc. award Fla. Rep. Party, 1998, Appreciation cert. Taylor County Sch. Dist. Job Prep Students, 2006, Recognition cert. City Perry, Fla., 2006; named Taylor County Sr. Citizens Ctr. Vol. of Yr., Fla. Area Agy. Aging North Fla., 2006. Mem.: Fla. State Assn. Pen Women (historian), Nature Coast Br. Nat. Orgn. Am. Pen Women (pres.), Citrus County Rep. Women, Humane Soc. Citrus County (life), Old Courthouse Restoration Hist. Soc., Phi Theta Kappa. Avocations: travel, writing, reading. Personal E-mail: gritsrus@hotmail.com.

BURCH, BARBARA G., academic administrator; BA in English, Western Ky. U.; MA in Edn., PhD in Edn., U. Ind. Dir. curriculum devel. and rsch. Shelby County Schs., Memphis; asst. v.p. U. Memphis, acad. affairs, interim dean, assoc. dean, dir. grad. studies; dean Sch. Edn. and Human Svcs. Calif. State U., Fresno; v.p. for acad. affairs Western Ky. U., Bowling Green, 1996—, provost, 1998—. Mem.: Am. Assn. for Colls. Tchr. Edn. (pres.). Office: Provost & VP for Acad Affairs Western Ky Univ 1 Big Red Way Bowling Green KY 42101-3576*

BURCH, BOBBY JOE, secondary school educator; b. Monticello, Ark., Nov. 7, 1948; s. Ira Joe and Violet McCourt Burch; m. Diane Joan Brewer, Aug. 16, 1987; 1 child, Morgan Aaron; m. Brenda Kay Morgan (div.). BS in Earth Sci. Comprehensive, U. Ark., Monticello, 1972; MS in Edn., U. So. Miss., Hattiesburg, 1973; student, Henderson State U., Arkadelphia, Ark., 1995—96. Tchr. Pass Christian H.S., Miss., 1973—74, U. Ark., Monticello, 1974—75, 1979—80, Selma Sch., Ark., 1975—79, Drew Ctrl. HS, Monticello, 1979—84, Livadais Jr. HS, New Orleans, 1984, Lake Hamilton HS, Pearcy, Ark., 1985—. Mem. adv. bd. Pro Program So. Ark. U. Medicine, 1997—99. Recipient Outstanding Tchr. award, Tandy Corp., 1991—92. Mem.: NEA, Ark. Edn. Assn. (del. 1979—), Nat. Soc. HS Scholars (del. 1979—). Avocations: reading, films, music. Home: 160 Elice Cir Hot Springs AR 71913 Office: Lake Hamilton Sch Dist 280 Wolf Street Pearcy AR 71964

BURCH, FRANCIS BOUCHER, JR., lawyer; b. Balt., Feb. 27, 1948; s. Francis Boucher and Mary Patricia (Howe) B.; children: Sara E., Francis B. III, Michael F.; m. Elisabeth J. Harper, Sept. 29, 2002. Student, U. Fribourg, 1968—69; BA, Georgetown U., 1970; JD with honors, U. Md., 1974. Bar: Md. 1974, U.S. Ct. Appeals (4th cir.) 1975, U.S. Supreme Ct. 1994. Assoc. litig. dept. Piper & Marbury LLP, Balt., 1974—81, ptnr. litig. dept., 1981—91, chmn. litig. dept., 1991—94, chmn., 1994—99; co-chmn. Piper Rudnick LLP, 1999—2004; ptnr., joint CEO DLA Piper (formerly Piper Rudnick LLP), Balt., 2005—. Contbr. articles to profl. jours. Bd. dirs. Greater Balt. Com., 1996—2006, vice-chmn., 1998—2001, chmn., 2001—03; mem. Leadership Program, 1990—, bd. dirs., 1993—98, vice-chmn., 1994—96, chmn., 1996—98, chmn. selection com., 1994—95; trustee Calvert Sch., 1989—2000, exec. com., 1991—2000, chmn., 1991—95, sec., 1991—95; trustee We. Md. Coll., 1996—2001, Johns Hopkins Health Sys. Corp., 1994—96, Johns Hopkins Hosp., 1994—96, Johns Hopkins Medicine, 1996—, Johns Hopkins U., 2005—, Balt. Mus. Art., 1990—96, 1998—2000, mem. exec. com., 1991—96, chmn. ann. giving com., 1991—93, treas., 1992—94, v.p., 1994—96, co-chmn. devel., 1994—96; bd. visitors U. Md. Sch. Law, Balt., 1993—, U. Md., 1995—; campaign cabinet, chmn. emerging markets United Way Ctrl., Md., 1994; chmn. Leadership Giving, 1999. With U.S. Army N.G., 1970—76. Fellow Am. Bar Found., Am. Coll. Trial Lawyers, Md. Bar Found.; mem. ABA, Am. Law Inst., Md. Bar Assn. (Disting. Svc. award litig. sect. 1981), Balt. City Bar Assn. (chmn. jud. appts. com. 1990-91, exec. coun. 1990-91), 4th Cir. Jud. Conf., Rule Day Club, Lawyers' Round Table Balt., Ctr. Club, River Bend Club. Democrat. Roman Catholic. Avocations: skiing, surfing. Office: DLA Piper 6225 Smith Ave Baltimore MD 21209-3600 Office Phone: 410-580-4040. Office Fax: 410-580-3001. Business E-Mail: frank.burch@dlapiper.com.

BURCH, FRANCIS FLOYD, clergyman; b. Balt., May 15, 1932; s. Thaddeus Joseph and Frances Fidelis (Greenwell) Burch. BA, Fordham U., 1956, MA, 1958; PhL, Woodstock Coll., 1957, STL, 1964; postgrad., Tronchinnes, Belgium, 1964-65; Docteur, U. Paris, Sorbonne, 1967. Joined Soc. of Jesus, 1950, ordained priest Roman Cath. Ch., 1963. Tchr. Gonzaga HS, Washington, 1957-60; from asst. prof. to assoc. prof. English St. Joseph's U., Phila., 1967—76, prof., 1976—, asst. acad. dean, 1972-74, bd. dirs., 1971-76, sec. bd. dirs., 1971-75. Artist-scholar-in-residence Millersville U., Pa., 1978. Author: Tristan Corbiere: l'orginalite des "Amours janues" et leur influence sur T. S. Eliot, 1970; editor (with P. O. Walzer): Tristan Corbiere: Ouevres completes, 1970, Sur Tristan Corbiere: lettres inedites adressees au poete et premieres critiques le concernant, 1975; translator: The Path to Transcendence: From Philosophy to Mysticism in Saint Augustine (Paul Henry), 1981, 2d edit., 2002, The Personalist Challenge: Intersubjectivity and Ontology (Maurice Nedoncelle), 1984; contbr. articles to profl. jours. Recipient Merit award, St. Joseph's U., 1980, 1983. Mem.: MLA, Alpha Sigma Nu, Alpha Epsilon Delta. Home and Office: 5600 City Ave Philadelphia PA 19131-1308 E-mail: fburch@sju.edu.

BURCH, JAMES LEO, science research institute executive; b. San Antonio, Nov. 28, 1942; s. Joseph Leo Jr. and Doris Babette (Hagy) B.; m. Kathleen Marie Dowdy, Dec. 30, 1965; children: Angela Marie, Charles Joseph, Kenneth James. BS in Physics, St. Mary's U., San Antonio, 1964; PhD, Rice U., 1968; MS in Adminstrn., George Washington U., 1973. Space physicist Goddard Space Flight Ctr. NASA, Greenbelt, Md., 1971-74, space physicist Marshall Space Flight Ctr. Huntsville, Ala., 1974-77; sr. rsch. physicist S.W. Rsch. Inst., San Antonio, 1977-78, sect. mgr., 1978-80, dept. dir., 1980-85, v.p., 1985—. Prin. investigator NASA Dynamics Explorer Mission, 1978-92, Nasa Atlas Shuttle Mission, 1989-93, ESA Rosetta Comet orbiter, 1996—, NASA Image Midex mission, 1996—. NASA Magnetosphere Multiscale Mission, 2005—; mem. space sci. and applications adv. com. NASA, 1990-93; mem. NAS Space Studies Bd., 2000-04; chair NAS com. Solar and Space Physics, 2000-04. Assoc. editor Jour. Geophys. Rsch., 1977-79, 94-96, Geophys. Rsch. Letters, 1978-82, editor, 1989-90, editor-in-chief, 1990-93; contbr. numerous articles to profl. jours. Capt. U.S. Army, 1968-71. Recipient Disting. Alumnus award St. Mary's U., 1987, Van Allen Lectureship Am. Geophys. Union, 2001 Fellow Am. Geophys. Union (pres. space physics and aeronomy sect. 1996-98), Internat. Acad. Astronautics. Roman Catholic. Avocation: golf. Office: SW Rsch Inst 6220 Culebra Rd San Antonio TX 78238-5100 Business E-Mail: jburch@swri.edu.

BURCH, JOHN CHRISTOPHER, JR., investment banker; b. Nashville, Jan. 18, 1940; s. John Christopher and Frances Vivian (Harris) B.; m. Susan Marie Klein, Sept. 13, 1969; children: Frances Marie, Christina Polk, John Christopher III. BA, Vanderbilt U., 1966. Credit analyst Bank N.Y., NYC, 1966-70; v.p. instl. sales Loeb Rhoades & Co., NYC, 1970-75, J.C. Bradford & Co., Nashville, 1976-82; mng. dir. SunTrust Equitable Securities Corp., Nashville, 1982-2001; pres. Capital Markets Advisors LLC, Nashville, 2001—. Co-author: Capital Markets Handbook, 1999, 6th edit., 2007. With U.S. Army, 1962-65. Mem.: CFA Soc. Nashville (bd. dirs. 2006—), Nat. Assn. Security Dealers (arbitrator), Securities Industry Assn. (chmn. syndicate com. 1998—2000, bd. dirs. chair so. dist. 2001), CFA Inst., Soc. of the Cincinnati, Belle Meade Country Club (Nashville). Episcopalian. Home: 705 Hillwood Blvd Nashville TN 37205-1315 Office: Capital Markets Advisors LLC Ste 228 2200 Twenty First Ave S Nashville TN 37212 Office Phone: 615-292-6323. Fax: 615-292-6757. E-mail: jburch@capitalmarketsadvisors.com.

BURCH, JOHN RUSSELL, retired military officer; b. Lexington, Ky., Aug. 6, 1945; s. Oakley Burch and Frances Lyle Ramsey; m. Idalia Amparo Murgas (div.); children: John Russell Jr., Eustacia Frances Burch O'Malley; m. Elizabeth Allen Murphy, June 20, 1999. AA, South Puget Sound CC, Olympia, Wash., 1992; BA cum laude, St. Martin's Coll., Lacey, Wash., 1993; MA, Pacific Luth. U., Tacoma, 1999. From pvt. to sgt. US Army Airborne Infantry, 1964—67; commd. 2nd lt. US Army, 1967, advanced through grades to capt., 1969, with Spl. Forces (Green Berets) Vietnam, 1967—70, from sgt. to 1st sgt. Spl. Forces, 1971—90, ret., 1990. Cubmaster, scoutmaster, dist. commr., Order of the Arrow advisor Boy Scouts Am., 1965—; mem. neighborhood and coun. com. Girl Scouts USA, 1972—80. Decorated Bronze Star, Purple Heart, Meritorious Svc. medal with Oak Leaf Cluster, Air medal, Combat Infantryman badge, Master Parachutist badge, Spl. Forces tab, Pathfinder badge. Mem.: MOAA, VFW, DAV, Sons Am. Revolution, Spl. Forces Assn., Mil. Order Purple Heart (chpt. comdr. 2004—, Dept. Ky. sr. vice comdr. 2007—), Mensa, Nat. Eagle Scout Assn., Sons Union Vets Civil War (camp comdr. 2006—07, Dept. Ky. sr. vice comdr. 2007—), Spl. Ops. Assn., Am. Legion, Phi Theta Kappa. Roman Catholic. Avocations: history, genealogy, archaeology, Civil War reenactment, heraldry. Home: 200 Norwood Dr Richmond KY 40475

BURCH, JOHN RUSSELL, JR., library director; b. Peoria, Ill., Mar. 22, 1968; s. John Russell and Idalia Amparo (Murgas) B.; m. Samantha Jo Bailey, July 1, 1989; children: Morgan Lourrae, Alexandra Christine, Christopher Simpson, Kayleigh Jo. BA in History, Berea Coll., Ky., 1990; MS in Libr. Sci., U. Ky., 1992, MA in History, 2003, PhD in History, 2005. Grad. asst. U. Ky. Agrl. Libr., Lexington, 1991-92; govt. documents libr. So. Ark. U., Magnolia, 1992-93; reference libr. Cumberland Coll., Williamsburg, Ky., 1993-95, pub. svcs. libr., 1995, tech. svcs. libr., 1995-2000; dir. libr. svcs. Campbellsville (Ky.) U., 2000—. Book reviewer Libr. Jour., Am. Ref. Books Ann., Choice Mag. Author 2 books. Mem.: Phi Alpha Theta. Republican. Office: Campbellsville U Montgomery Libr 1 University Dr Campbellsville KY 42718-2799 Office Phone: 270-789-5015. E-mail: jrburch@campbellsville.edu.

BURCH, JOHN THOMAS, JR., lawyer; b. Balt., Feb. 22, 1942; s. John T and Katheryn Estella (Peregoy) Burch; m. Linda Anne Shearer, Nov. 1, 1969; children: John Thomas, Richard James. BA, U. Richmond, Va., 1964, JD, 1966; LLM, George Washington U., 1971. Bar: Va. 1966, U.S. Supreme Ct. 1969, DC 1974, Md. 1993. Pvt. practice, Richmond, 1966, Washington, 1974-77; pres. Burch, Kerns and Klimek, 1977-82, Burch & Assocs., Washington, 1982-95, Burch & Bennett, P.C., Washington, 1983-85; ptnr. Alagia, Day, Marshall, Mintmire & Chauvin, Washington, 1985-90, Maloney & Burch, Washington, 1990-96; pres. Burch & Cronauer, P.C., Washington, 1995—2001, Burch & Assocs., Washington, 1982-95; with office of gen. counsel Dept. of Vets. Affairs, 2001—. Rep. committeeman City of Alexandria, Va., 1975—92; aide-de-camp brigadier gen to gov State of Va., 1976—; alt. del. Rep. Nat. Conv., 1988, 1994. Decorated Bronze Star, Meritorious Svc. medal. Mem.: VFW (dep. comdr. 1986—87), ABA (sec. pub. contract law sect. 1976—77), Va. War Meml. Found. (trustee), Nat. Vietnam and Gulf War Vets. Coalition (nat. chmn. 1983—2001), Spl. Forces Assn., Fed. Bar Assn. (nat. coun., dep. sec. 1982—83), Mil. Order of Carabou, Soc. War of 1812, Va. Soc. SAR (pres. 1975—76, Good Citizenship award 1970, Patriots medal 1978), Am. Legion, SCV, Order St. Constantine Magna, Scabbard and Blade, Phi Sigma Alpha, Phi Alpha Delta. Republican. Episcopalian. Home: 1015 N Pelham St Alexandria VA 22304

BURCH, JOHN WALTER, mining equipment company executive; b. Balt., July 14, 1925; s. Louis Claude and Constance (Boucher) B. m. Robin Neely Sinkler, Apr. 19, 1952; children: John C., Robert L., Charles C., Anne N. BS in Commerce, U. Va., 1951; postgrad., U.S. Coast Guard Acad., 1951. With Procter & Gamble Co., Phila., 1953-65, sales mgr., 1960-65; v.p. Warner Co., Phila., 1965-73; chmn. bd., CEO S.S. Keely Co., Phila., 1973-75; pres., chmn. bd., CEO Burch Materials Co., Inc., Berwyn, Pa., 1975—; ptnr., mgr. Integrated MRO, LLC, 1998—2004. Dir. Eagle's Eye, Inc., Wayne; bd. dirs. Pa. Sports Hall of Fame, 1974-79, v.p., exec. com., 1974-79; chmn. Am. Legion Tennis Tournaments for State of Pa., 1975-82; mem. U.S. Congl. Adv. Bd., 1982, bd. dirs. Eagle's Eye Lacrosse Club, 1982-87; mem. Bus. Adv. Coun., 2003, Presdl. Bus. Commn., 2004; bd. dirs. juvenile justice divsn. Cath. Social Svcs., Archdiocese Phila., 2004. Bd. dirs. Nat. Multiple Sclerosis Soc., 1970-81, v.p., exec. com., 1974-77. With USN, 1943-46, USCG, 1951-53. Named All-Am. in lacrosse, 1949; named to Pa. Sports Hall of Fame, 2006; gymnasium named in honor of John Burch family, Archdiocese of Phila., 2003. Mem. Merion Cricket Club, Merion Golf Club, Willoughby Golf Club. Republican. Roman Catholic. Office: Burch Materials Co Inc 685 Kromer Ave Berwyn PA 19312-1317 Office Phone: 610-640-4877.

BURCH, KELLY JOAN, pharmacist, consultant; b. Fredericksburg, Va., Oct. 8, 1958; d. James E. and Janice Zug Burch; m. Paul Edward Molaskey; children: Katherine Jane Molaskey, Margaret Ann Molaskey. PharmD, U. Nebr., Omaha, 1981. Clin. specialist St. John's Mercy Med. Ctr., Creve Coeur, Mo., 1995—; pres. Your Child's Pharmacist, St. Louis, 1995—. Cons. Ranken Jordan Children's Rehab. Hosp., Maryland Heights, Mo., 1997—. Contbr. articles to profl. jours. Mem.: Am. Soc. Parenteral and Enteral Nutrition, Am. Soc. Health Sys. Pharmacist, Am. Coll. Clin. Pharmacy, PTO (pres. Pky. South mid. sch. chpt. 2003—05). Democrat. Roman Catholic. Avocations: reading, travel, cooking. Home: 2336 East Royal Ct Des Peres MO 63131 Office: St John's Mercy Med Ctr 621 South New Ballas Rd Creve Coeur MO 63131 Home Phone: 314-965-5862; Office Phone: 314-251-6933 29133. Personal E-mail: kjburch@aol.com. Business E-Mail: burckj@stlo.mercy.net.

BURCH, MARY SEELYE QUINN, law librarian, consultant; b. Worcester, Mass., Oct. 16, 1925; d. James Henry and Mary Seelye (O'Donnell) Quinn; m. Walter Douglas Burch, Aug. 18, 1972; children: Cathi, Andrew, David, John, Joan. BS, Suny, 1976; MLS, Pratt Inst., 1979. Law libr. N.Y. Supreme Ct., Troy, 1969-82; chief law libr. Office Ct. Adminstrn., Albany, N.Y., 1982-86; libr. N.Y. State Libr., 1986-89, ret., 1989; owner Mary S. Burch Law Libr. Svc., 1983—2003. Instr. legal rsch. SUNY, 1981; selected to meet with deans of law schs. in China for improvement of legal reference materials in China. Mem. N.Y. State Bar Assn. (lectr. 1980), Ulster County Bar Assn. (cons. 1980), Am. Assn. Law Librs., Assn. Law Librs. Upstate N.Y. (pres. 1971, v.p. 1981). Roman Catholic. Avocations: pilot, swimming, sewing. Home: 312 Diamond Rock Cir Troy NY 12182

BURCH, MICHAEL IRA, public relations executive, retired federal agency administrator; b. St. Louis, June 20, 1941; s. Horatio and Iona (Anderson) B.; m. Sherilynn J. Hummel, Dec. 26, 1987; children: Paige Anne Engelson, Michelle Hummel. BA, U. Mo., 1963; postgrad., Boston U., 1965, Am. U., 1972-75. Commd. 2d lt. U.S. Air Force, 1963, advanced through grades to lt. col., 1979, served in tactical air command units, 1963-72, served at Pentagon in offices Air Force and Def. secs., 1972-83, ret., 1983; pres. Washington Communications Corp., 1983; asst. sec. for pub. affairs U.S. Dept. Def., Washington, 1983-85; v.p. communications Aerospace group McDonnell Douglas Corp., Washington, 1985-88, v.p. pub. relations St. Louis, 1988-92; sr. v.p. Burson-Marsteller, Washington, 1992-95; pres. Civitas Comm. Group, Alexandria, Va., 1995—, Nature Works, Inc., 1997—. Recipient Disting. Service medal Dept. Def., 1983, Disting. Pub. Service medal Dept. Def., 1985 Mem. Air Commando Assn., Am. Legion. Republican. Episcopalian. Avocation: sailing. Office: Nature WOrks Inc PO Box 639 Burgess VA 22432-0639

BURCH, ROBERT DALE, lawyer; b. Washington, Jan. 30, 1928; s. Dallas Stockwell and Hepsy (Berry) B.; m. Joann D. Hansen, Dec. 9, 1966; children: Berkeley, Robert Brett, Barrett Bradley. Student, Va. Mil. Inst., 1945—46; BS, U. Calif. Berkeley, 1950, JD, 1953. Bar: Calif. bar 1954. Since practiced in, L.A. and Beverly Hills; ptnr. Gibson, Dunn & Crutcher, 1961—93. Lectr. U. So. Calif. Inst. Fed. Taxation, 1960, 62, 65, 75; guest lectr. U. Calif.-L.A. Law Sch., 1959; lectr. C.E.B. seminars U. Calif.; founder Robert D. Burch Ctr. for Tax Policy and Pub. Fin., U. Calif., Berkeley. Author: Federal Tax Procedures for General Practitioners; Contbr. profl. jours., textbooks. Bd. dirs. charitable founds. With AUS, 1945-47. Mem. Beverly Hills Bar Assn. (bd. govs., chmn. probate and trust com.), Law Trust, Tax and Ins. Council (past czar), Los Angeles World Affairs Council. Home: 1301 Delresto Dr Beverly Hills CA 90210-2100 Office: Gibson Dunn & Crutcher 2029 Century Park E Ste 4000 Los Angeles CA 90067-3032 also: 333 S Grand Ave Los Angeles CA 90071-1504

BURCH, THADDEUS JOSEPH, JR., physics professor, priest; b. Balt., June 4, 1930; s. Thaddeus and Francis Fidelis (Greenwell) B. AB, Bellarmine Coll., 1954; MA, Fordham U., 1956, MS, 1966, PhD, 1968; STB, Woodstock Coll., 1960, STL, 1962. Ordained priest Roman Cath. Ch., 1961. Joined S.J. Roman Cath. Ch., 1948; asst. prof. St. Joseph's Coll., Phila., 1969-72, Fordham U., NYC, 1972-74; vis. assoc. prof. U. Conn., Storrs, 1974-76; assoc. prof. Marquette U., Milw., 1976-80, prof., 1980—, chmn. dept. physics, 1977-86, acting dean grad. sch., 1985-87, dean grad. sch., 1987—2003, dir. spl. projects, 2003—, acting vice provost rsch. and dean Grad. Sch., 2005, dir. spl. projects, 2005—. Univ. del. Argonne (Ill.) Univs. Assn., 1977-82; instl. rev. bd. Med. Coll. Wis., 2000— Contbr. articles on physics to profl. jours. Mem. Am. Phys. Soc., Am. Assn. Physics Tchrs., Sigma Xi Home: 230 Jefferson St Leonardtown MD 20650-4800 Office: 1404 W Wisconsin Milwaukee WI 53233 Business E-Mail: thaddeus.burch@marquette.edu.

BURCH, TORY, apparel designer; b. Valley Forge, Pa. m. Christopher Burch, 1997 (div.); 3 children. BA in Art History, U. Pa., 1988. Fashion asst. Zoran, NYC; sittings asst. Harper's Bazaar; PR positions Ralph Lauren, Vera Wang, Loewe; launched fashion line Tory Burch, 2004—; opened boutiques NYC, LA, Atlanta, Dallas, Costa Mesa, Calif., Greenwich, Conn., East Hampton, Chgo., Ball Harbour; collection available Bergdorf Goodman, select Saks Fifth Ave, Neiman Marcus, Nordstrom, Bloomingdales, Holt Renfrew, Canada, Harvey Nichols, London, Dubai. Recipient Rising Star award, Fashion Group Internat., 2005. Office: Corp Office 99 Madison Ave 12th Fl New York NY 10016

BURCH, VORIS REAGAN, mediator, arbitrator, retired lawyer; b. Liberty, Tex., Feb. 10, 1930; s. Voris Reagan and Jessamae (Coffey) B.; m. Claudia Ramsland, Dec. 30, 1978; children: Melissa Burch Lively, Voris Reagan III. BBA, Tex. A&M U., 1952; JD, U. Tex., 1957. Bar: Tex. 1957. Assoc. Baker & Botts, Houston, 1957-69, ptnr., 1969-95, ret., 1995. Served to 1st lt. USAF, 1952-54. Mem. State Bar Tex. (chmn. labor law sect. 1970-71), Houston Bar Assn., Phi Delta Phi. Home and Office: 5761 Indian Cir Houston TX 77057-1302 Office Phone: 713-780-0196. E-mail: reaganburch@houston.rr.com.

BURCHAM, DAVID W., law educator; BA, Occidental Coll.; JD, Loyola Law Sch. Law clerk to Hon. Ruggero J. Aldisert Chief Judge, U.S. Ct. Appeals Third Cir.; Justice Byron R. White U.S. Supreme Ct.; atty. Dunn & Crutcher, Los Angeles; joined faculty Loyola Law Sch., 1991, assoc. dean Academic Affairs, 1999—2000, Fritz B. Burns Dean & prof law, 2000—. Lawyer rep. Ctrl. Dist. Calif.; cons. Long Beach Unified Sch. Dist. Contbr. articles to law jours. Office: Loyola Law Sch 919 Albany St Los Angeles CA 90015-1211 Office Phone: 213-736-1028. E-mail: david.burcham@lls.edu.*

BURCHARD, ELLEN WILLIAMS, actress, film producer, artist, writer; b. Newport, RI; d. Clarence Raymond and Mary Christine (Stewart) Williams; m. John Church Burchard; 1 child, John Church. Student, U. Wis., Stella Adler Studio, Herbert Berghof Studio, Harold Clurman's Profl. Acting Classes, NYC. Founder Carriage House Theatre, Little Compton, R.I. Actress on Broadway, films and TV, also in Rome and London; prodr., artistic dir., actress Pro Summer Repertory Co.; off-Broadway prodr., N.Y.C., 1959-2001; prodr., artistic dir. Actors Repertory Co., Little Compton, 1959-2001; actress R.I. Playwrights Theatre; lyricist Morning Song; playwright Marguerite, Scenes from the Past; off-Broadway plays include Journey to Endor, Ashen Victors, Love Letters; films include Mr. North, The Buccaneers, The Fitzgeralds and the Kennedys, True Lies, Ashen Victors, Amistad. Founder, pres. Young Women's Rep. Club, Newport, Little Compton Rep. Club, Newport Players Guild; founder New Eng. Coun. Young Reps.; young Rep. nat. committeewoman from R.I. Mem. AFTRA, SAG, Actors Equity Assn., R.I. Short Story Club (pres.), R.I. Water Color Soc., Newport Art Mus., Mosaic Club (charter mem.) (Newport). Congregationalist.

BURCHARD, JOHN KENNETH, retired chemical engineer; b. St. Louis, May 12, 1936; s. Kenneth Reginald and Vernora Emma (Angell) B.; m. Elizabeth Lee Suesserott, Aug. 23, 1958; children— John Christopher, Gregory Charles. BS, Carnegie Mellon U., 1957, MS, 1959, PhD, 1962. Head systems analysis group United Tech. Ctr., Sunnyvale, Calif., 1961-68; chief scientist Combustion Power Co., Menlo Park, Calif., 1968-70; lab. dir. EPA, Research Triangle Park, N.C., 1970-80; dir. chem. engring. div. Research Triangle Inst., Research Triangle Park, 1980-83; pres. Search Assocs., Inc., Chapel Hill, N.C., 1983-85; dir. Office of Research Adminstrn. U. Cen. Ark., Conway, 1985-87; asst. dir. Office Research Devel. Ariz. State U., Tempe, 1987-90; mgr. spl. projects Ariz. Dept. Environ. Quality, Phoenix, 1990-98, sr. sci. advisor, 1998-2001; vol. Tempe (Ariz.) Police Dept., 2001—. Mem. bd. sci. advisors N.C. Energy Inst. Contbr. articles to profl. jours. Served with AUS, 1963-64. Shell Oil fellow, 1958-59; NSF fellow, 1960-61 Mem. Am. Inst. Chem. Engrs., Soc. Rsch. Adminstrs., Sigma Xi, Tau Beta Pi.

BURCHELL, HOWARD BERTRAM, retired internist; b. Athens, Ont., Can., Nov. 28, 1907; s. James Edward and Edith (Milligan) B.; m. Margaret Helmholz, Aug. 14, 1942; children: Susan Burchell Profeta, Judith Burchell Bush, Cynthia Burchell Patterson, Rebecca Burchell Wilbur. MD, U. Toronto, Can., 1932; PhD., U. Minn., 1939. Intern Toronto Gen. Hosp., 1932-34; rsch. fellow U. Pitts., 1934-36; fellow in medicine Mayo Clinic, Rochester, Minn., 1936-39, cons. in medicine, 1946-68; spl. student London Hosp., 1939-40; prof. medicine U. Minn., Mpls., 1968-85, prof. emeritus, 1985—. Mem. adv. com. USAAF, 1947-40, Nat. Heart Coun., NIH, 1955-60; lectr. U.S., Can., The Netherlands, Israel. Contbr. more than 350 articles to profl. jours. Maj. USAAF, 1941-46. Fellow Am. Coll. Cardiology (master tchr. 1969, 74); mem. Am. Heart Assn. (Herrick award 1972), Assn. Am. Physicians, Am. Physiol. Soc. Mem. Unitarian-Universalist Ch. Avocation: history. Home: 3701 Bryant Ave S #412 Minneapolis MN 55409

BURCHELL, KENNETH WAYNE, historian, appraiser; s. Robert Francis Burchell and Rosemary Ellen Braun; children: Xochitl Maria Garcia, Jesse Dylan. BA in Am. History, U. Idaho, 2001, MA in Am. History, 2003. Historian Thomas Paine Nat. Hist. Assn., New Rochelle, NY; pres. Thomas Paine Inst., Coeur d'Alene, Idaho, 2003—. Contbr. articles to profl. publs. Pres. bd. dirs. Coeur d'Alene/Hayden Lake Sch. Dist., 1991—92. Recipient Academic Excellence award, U. Idaho, 2007. Mem.: NRA (life), Gemmological Inst. Am. (grad.), Am. Hist. Assn., Orgn. Am. Historians, Masons (32nd degree 1993), Phi Alpha Theta. Achievements include design of jewelry.

BURCHFIELD, BOBBY ROY, lawyer; b. Middlesboro, Ky., Oct. 23, 1954; s. Roy and Anna Lee (McCreary) B.; m. Teresa J. Miller, Apr. 6, 1996; 1 child, Taylor Nicole. BA, Wake Forest U., 1976; JD, George Washington U., 1979. Bar: D.C. 1980, U.S. Ct. Appeals (3rd cir.) 1981, U.S. Dist. Ct. D.C. 1982, U.S. Dist. Ct. Md. 1982, U.S. Ct. Appeals (D.C. cir.) 1982, U.S. Ct. Appeals (9th cir.) 1985, U.S. Supreme Ct. 1986, U.S. Ct. Appeals (5th cir.) 1989, U.S. Ct. Appeals (6th cir.) 1993. Law clk. to Judge Ruggero J. Aldisert U.S. Ct. Appeals (3rd cir.), Pitts., 1979-81; assoc. Covington & Burling, Washington, 1981-87, ptnr., 1987—; co-ptnr.-in-charge D.C. Office McDermott Will & Emery LLP, Washington. Gen. counsel Bush-Quayle '92, 1992; dean's adv. bd. George Washington U.; bd. trustees Wake Forest U., 2004— Editor-in-chief George Washington U. Law Rev., 1978-79. Gen. counsel Rep. Nat. Lawyers Assn., 1991—92; nat. chmn. George Washington U. Nat. Law Ctr. Ann. Fund, 1990—91, Wake Forest U. Coll. Fund, 1999—2000; coun. mem. Wake Forest U. Alumni, 1990—93, 1997—2001, pres., 2000—01; vol. George Bush for Pres., Washington, 1986—88; presdl. appointee Antitrust Modernization Commn., 2004—. Mem.: ABA. Republican. Office: McDermott Will & Emery LLp 600 13th St NW 12th Fl Washington DC 20005-3096 Home: 623 Potomac Ave NW Mc Lean VA 22102 Office Phone: 202-756-8003. Office Fax: 202-756-8087. Business E-Mail: bburchfield@mwe.com.

BURCHINOW, NARAN U., lawyer; b. Newark, 1953; m. Eileen Conlon; children: Alexandra, Emily, Stephanie, Victoria. Grad., Princeton U., 1975, Boston U., 1978. Pvt. practice Csaplar & Bok, Boston, Fine & Ambrogne, Chgo.; sr. atty. Continental Bank N.A., Chgo., 1987—91; ops. counsel, gen. counsel Deutsche Fin. Svcs. (formerly ITT Comml. Fin. Corp.), St. Louis, 1991—2004; gen. counsel The Andersons, Inc., 2004—. Office: The Andersons Inc 480 W Dussel Dr Maumee OH 43537 Office Phone: 419-893-5050. Office Fax: 419-891-6670.

BURCHMAN, LEONARD, federal official, journalist; b. NYC, Jan. 30, 1925; s. Hyman John-Hood and Edith (Speedely-Cohen) B.; m. Marilyn F. Burchman, June 11, 1950; children— Marc Harris, Corey Andrew BA, U. Denver, 1949; MA, Columbia U., 1950. Dir. press affairs N.Y. State Eisenhower presdl. campaign, 1951-52; info. officer-advance sec. labor Dept. Labor, Washington and NYC, 1953-60; pres. Medigard Chem. Corp., NYC, 1961; dir. integovtl. rels. Dept. Labor, Washington, 1971-78; acting asst. sec., gen. sr. asst. sect. pub. affairs HUD, Washington, 1981—. Dir. labor rels. to U.S. Senator Kenneth Keating, N.Y., 1964; pub. affairs cons. to Gov. John Lodge of Conn., 1952; sr. advisor to Coretta Scott King; chmn. Martin Luther King Jr. Fed. Holiday Commn., 1985—, commr., 1989—, treas., 1989-92. Producer Office Mgmt. Budget/NSF film: Strengthening Intergovernmental Relations between Federal and State and Local Governments, 1976; journalist, creator (newspaper column) Scam Alert. Chmn. bd. Am. Heart Assn., Washington, 1981-83; pres. Found. for Study U.S. Cabinet, 1985-89; pres. J.R.L.W., Leisure World, Md., 1994-96; chmn. Found. to Interrupt Illegal Narcotics and Drugs To Children, 1989—; founding pres. Voice of the Elderly, 1997—; founder nat. Consumer Watch-Out, to protect sr. citizens against Scams and Frauds, 1988—; mem. Montgomery County (Md.) Commn. on Aging, 1997-2004, States Attys. Task Force on Elder Abuse, Md., 1997—. Recipient Disting. Svc. award Sec. HUD. Mem.: DAV (life), Am. Legion (comdr. U.S. Dept. Labor Post).

BURCH-MARTINEZ, BERKELEY ALISON, primary school educator; b. Santa Monica, Calif., Nov. 20, 1967; d. Robert Dale and Joann Hansen B.; m. Gilbert Jesse Martinez, June 24, 1998; children, Sterling Alexander, Carsen Aren. BA, U. Calif., Irvine, 1992; MA, Pepperdine U., 1993. Tchr. spl. edn. King City (Calif.) Union Sch. Dist., 1997-98; tchr. kindergarten, 1st grade Ocean View Sch. Dist., Oxnard, Calif., 1998—. Mem. NEA, Calif. Tchrs. Assn., Internat. Reading Assn., Calif. Kindergarten Assn., So. Calif. Kindergarten Assn Avocations: writing, education.

BURCK, JOSEPH RUSSELL, medical educator, consultant, minister; b. Roswell, N.Mex., Dec. 28, 1937; s. William Joseph and Leta Gladys (Menefee) Burck; m. Dorothy Antoinette Pilc, Aug. 6, 1960; children: Peter Warren, Elisabeth Varner. AB, Princeton U., 1959; BD, Princeton Theol. Sem., 1964, PhD, 1976. Ordained Presbytery of Phila., 1970, cert. pastoral counselor Am. Assn. Pastoral Counseling, 1977, chaplain supr. Assn. Clin. Pastoral Edn., 1981, bd. cert. chaplain Assn. Profl. Chaplains, 1998. Assoc. editor bibliography in polit. sci. Princeton Info. Tech., 1967—69; educator in pastoral care in Germany, seminaries in Lueckendorff near Zittau, Herborn, Stuttgart, Tuebingen U., Innere Mission, Berlin, 1972—74; dir. chaplaincy svcs. Larned (Kans.) State Hosp., 1976—78; asst. prof of religion and health Rush-Presbyn.-St. Luke's Med. Ctr., Chgo., 1978—85, assoc. prof. religion, health, and human values, 1985—, dir. program in ethics and ethics consultation svc., 1988—2005. Peer reviewer of articles Critical Care Medicine, Des Plaines, Ill., 1999—; chairperson ethics adv. com. Inst. of Medicine of Chgo., 1990—91; project dir. Clergy Ethics Study Group, 1988—90; interpreter Internat. Congress on Pastoral Care and Counseling, Arnoldshain, Germany, 1973, mem., U.S. del., Edinburgh, 79, San Francisco, 83; outside mem. animal care and use com. U. of Ill. at Chgo., 1988—93; mem. nat. task force to prepare a brief course in ethics Assn. of Profl. Chaplains, 1993—95; chairperson com. on sr. faculty appointments and promotions, Coll. Health Scis. Rush U., 1988—92; editor, Rush ethics reporter Rush-Presbyn. St. Luke's Med. Ctr., 1991—94; bd. of dirs. representing Rush Coll. of Health Scis. Rush Geriatric Interdisciplinary Team Tng. Program, Chgo., 1997—; co-course dir. ethics in medicine Rush Med. Coll., Chgo., 1998—2005, course dir., clerkship, med. ethics, 1993—; vice-chair work group on governance and adminstrn. NCA accreditation rev. Rush U., Chgo., 1997; chair ethics grand rounds Rush-Presbyn.-St. Luke's, 1980—99; cons. to author of book, ethical issues, and patient rights Joint Commn. on the Accreditation of Health Care Orgns., Chgo., 1997—98; course dir. spiritual dimensions of health care Teleconference Network of Tex., Austin, 1992—97; pres. Chgo. Clin. Ethics Programs, 1994—95; lay mem., nat. ethics and peer rev. com. Am. Assn. of Electrodiagnostic Medicine, 1993—2000; marshal Rush U. graduation, representing Coll. Health Scis., 2004; chair faculty coun. Coll. Health Scis., Rush U. Med. Ctr., 2005—; mem. Ill. Task Force on Preparedness for Avian Flu Pandemic, 2006—. Co-editor: Clergy Ethics in a Changing Society: Mapping the Terrain (10 Best Books in Ministry of the &r., 1991); author: (e-book) Is it OK to have money and still go to church?; contbr. articles, columns, essays to profl. jours., chapters to books. Adult Christian educator, instr. courses in adult Christian edn., faith and illness, theology of genetics, med. ethics, faith and money, various chs., Chgo., 1980—. Recipient Profl. Svc. award, Teleconf. Network of Tex., 1993, Rsch. award, Joint Coun. on Rsch. in Pastoral Counseling, 1988, World Coun. of Chs. fellowship, 1971—72, doctoral fellowship in theology and personality, Princeton Theol. Sem., 1964—67; grantee, Greenwall Found., 1999—2000. Mem.: Presbytery of Chgo., Assn. for Clin. Pastoral Edn., Assn. of Profl. Chaplains (nominated to White Ho. bioethics adv. commn. 1999), Inst. of Medicine of Chgo. (bd. of govs. 1990—91), Assn. for Bioethics and the Humanities. Presbyterian. Achievements include One of the first Americans teaching pastoral care in Germany, when pastoral care paradigm changed from communicating messages to listening to people; development of one of the early professionalized ethics consultation services in U.S. hospitals; Only American involved in founding of German Society for Pastoral Psychology; First online certificate of graduate study in bioethics in the U.S; development of Innovative Language For Education In Health Care Ethics; Intensive use of clinical working rounds for teaching clinical ethics; teaching about ethics in research and ethical responsibilities of scientific medicine to diagnose and treat on the basis of knowledge. Avocations: travel, photography, hiking, opera, films. Home: 1138 Clinton Ave Oak Park IL 60304-1826 Office: Rush-Presbyn-St Luke's Med Ctr 1653 W Congress Pkwy Chicago IL 60612 Office Phone: 312-942-8933. Business E-Mail: russell_burck@rush.edu.

BURCKHARDT, TOM, artist; b. 1964; BFA, SUNY, Purchase, 1986; student, Skowhegan Sch. Painting and Sculpture, Maine, 1986. Exhibitions include PMW Gallery, Stamford, Conn., 1991, Painting, Self Evident: Abstraction, Spoleto Festival, Charleston, SC, 1992, Salon, Art in Gen., NYC, 1992, Fever, Exit Art, NYC, 1992, Frankel Nathanson Gallery, Maplewood, NJ, 1993, Point Now, Black and Greenberg Gallery, NYC, 1995, Urban Tantra, Esso Gallery, NYC, 1996, 25 Yrs. of Visual Arts at Purchase, Neuberger Mus., NY, 1996, Summer Salon, Frick Gallery, 1997, Bernard Toale Gallery, Boston, 1998, Summer Slam, Anna Kustera Gallery, NYC, 1999, Works on Paper, Bridgewater, Lustberg & Bloomfield, NYC, 2000, Self-Made Men, DC Moore Gallery, NYC, 2001, Totems, Tibor de Nagy Gallery, NYC, 2002, New York, New York, Now!, Currier Gallery of Art, Manchester, NH, 2002—03, In the Land of Nod, McDonough Mus. Art, Youngstown, Ohio, 2004, one-man shows include Work on Paper, Hunterdon Mus. Art, Clinton, NJ, 2005, FULL STOP, Caren Golden Fine Art, NYC, 2005—06, Tom Burckhardt, Tibor de Nagy Gallery, NYC, 2006. Recipient Richard & Hinda Rosenthal Found. award, Am. Acad. Arts and Letters, 2002, George Hitchcock award, Nat. Acad. Arts, 2002, Best Emerging Artist award, Internat. Assn. Art Critics (AICA), 2003; grantee Marie Walsh Sharpe Art Found. Studio grant, 1992—93, NY Found. for the Arts Painting grant, 1996, Pollock-Krasner Found. grant, 1997, 2005. Mailing: c/o Tibor de Nagy Gallery 724 Fifth Ave New York NY 10019

BURCKLE, LLOYD HENRY, geologist, researcher; b. Green Bay, Wis., Apr. 18, 1931; s. George August Burckle and Hildegarde Beth; m. Evelyn Greta Kost, July 23, 1953 (div.); children: Colleen Robin, William Felix Soeltz, Michele Ann Duest. BS, MS, Brigham Young U., Provo, Utah, 1964; PhD, NYU, NYC, 1971. Rsch. scientist Columbia U., NYC, 1965—71, sr. rsch. scientist, 1972—98, adj. sr. rsch. scientist, 1998—. Asst. prof. Hunter Coll., NYC, 1971—75; rsch. scientist Columbia U., NYC, 1965—72. Pvt. first class US Army, 1956—57, Panama. Scholar, Gen. Petroleum Corp., 1956, NY State, 1965—69; Rsch. grants, NSF, 1964—2006. Mem.: Am. Geophys. Union (assoc.). Achievements include research in plate tectonics; paleoclimate; stradivarius and climate; diatom biostratigraphy. Avocation: travel. Home: 150 Forest Ave Pearl River NY 10965 Office: Lamont-Doherty Earth Obs 61 Route 9W Palisades NY 10964 Home Phone: 845-735-6773; Office Phone: 845-965-8406. Business E-Mail: burckle@ldeo.columbia.edu.

BURD, JOHN STEPHEN, retired academic administrator, music educator; b. Lock Haven, Pa., Apr. 6, 1939; s. John Wilson and Lily (Fye) Burd; m. Patricia Ayers, June 3, 1961; children: Catherine Elizabeth, Emily Susanne. B in Music Edn., Greenville Coll., 1961; MS in Sacred Music, Butler U./Christian Theo. Sem., 1964; PhD, Ind. State U., 1971. Adj. music instr. Rose Hulman Inst. Tech., Terre Haute, Ind., 1969-71; assoc. prof. Greenville (Ill.) Coll., 1971-76; prof. edn. Lindenwood Coll., St. Charles, Mo., 1976-80; v.p. acad. affairs Maryville U., St. Louis, 1980-85; pres. Brenau U., Gainesville, Ga., 1985—2004, ret., 2004; pres. emeritus, 2004—. Team evaluator Nat. Coun. Accreditation Tchr. Edn., 1979—84, 1985—; mem. exec. coun. Women's Coll. Coalition, 1989—92, NAICU Commn. State Rels. Bd., 1991—93; adv. bd. Wachovia Bank, Gainesville, 1991—. Editor: New Voices in Education, 1969—71; contbr. articles to profl. jours. V.p. Christian Arts, Inc., NJ, 1965—, pres.; choir dir. Maryville U., St. Louis, 1983—85; bd. dirs. Gainesville Symphony, 1991—94, W. Crawford Long Mus.; chair Gainesville Redevelopment Authority, Chicopee Pk. Commn.; choir dir. Ctr. Presbyn. Ch., St. Louis, 1984—85; adv. bd. N.E. Ga. Med. Ctr.; bd. dirs. Met. Atlanta Arts Fund, bd. mem., 2004—. Recipient Outstanding Young Alumnus award, Greenville Coll., 1982, Disting. Alumnus award, 1991. Mem.: Ga. Assn. Colls. (pres. 1989—90, 2003—04), Ga. Found. Ind. Colls. (exec. bd. 1986—, vice chmn. 1993, 2002), So. Assn. Women's Colls. (pres. 1988—89), Am. Assn. Higher Edn., Am. Assn. Tchr. Edn., Gainesville C. of C. (bd. dirs.). Methodist. Avocations: tennis, travel, art. Office: Brenau Univ 500 Washington St Gainesville GA 30501-3697 Home Phone: 770-535-7673; Office Phone: 770-297-5952. Business E-Mail: jburd@brenau.edu.

BURD, JOYCE ANN, librarian; d. James Edgar and Azile Danehower Odom; m. Robert Banks Burd, Mar. 29, 1983 (dec. Nov. 15, 2001); 1 child, Sarah Azile Fratta. MLS, U. Tenn., 1976. Cert. elem. and secondary edn. Va., 1981. Audio visual cataloger Norfolk Pub. Schs., Va., 1978—81; media specialist, resource tchr. Houston Ind. Sch. Dist., 1982—87; original materials/govt. docs. cataloger Chesapeake Pub. Libr., Va., 1988—2000; cataloger Suffolk Pub. Libr., Va., 2000—02, tech. svcs mgr., network adminstr., 2002—. Libr. rep. Suffolk Civil War Days, Va., 2004—05; girl scout liason/com. mem. Chesapeake Civil War Days, 1994—2000; coord. Native Am. Gathering / Chesapeake Pub. Libr., 1996—98. Mem.: NAFE, ALA, Va. Libr. Assn. Independent. Church Of Christ. Avocations: travel, computers, knitting. Office: Suffolk Public Library 443 W Washington St Suffolk VA 23434 Home Phone: 757-523-4244. Business E-Mail: jburd@city.suffolk.va.us.

BURD, ROBERT MEYER, hematologist, oncologist, educator; b. NYC, Aug. 25, 1937; s. David and Anne (Popkin) B.; m. Alice Stoller, May 30, 1964; children: Russell J., Stephen J. AB, Columbia U., 1959, MD, 1963. Diplomate Am. Bd. Internal Medicine, Am. Bd. Hematology and Oncology. Intern Albert Einstein Med. Sch., NYC, 1963-64, resident in internal medicine, 1964-66; hematology fellow Montefiore Hosp., NYC, 1966-67; specializing in hematology and oncology pvt. practice medicne, Fairfield, Conn., 1969—; assoc. prof. medicine Yale U., New Haven, 1975, assoc. clin. prof. of medicine, 1975—; chief of hematology/oncology St. Vincent's Med. Ctr., 1980—; asst. prof. clin. medicine Columbia U. Coll. Physicians & Surgeons, 1998—. Chmn. hosp. com. on cancer, mng. ptnr. Med. Specialists of Fairfield, LLC, 1995—; attending physician Yale Hosp., New Haven; mem. staff Bridgeport (Conn.) Hosp.; adj. prof. medicine N.Y. Med. Coll.; med. cons. U.S. News and World Report, 1990; dir. oncology fellowship Yale-St. Vincent Hosp., 1991—96, N.Y. Med. Coll., St. Vincent's Med. Ctr., Bridgeport; adv. bd. rituxan Genentech; adv. bd. taxotere Aventis. Mem. editl. bd. (exhibitions), 1974—78. Active Leukemia Soc. Am., Hemophilia Found.; chmn. profl. edn. com. Am. Cancer Soc. Lt. comdr. USN, 1967-69. Ettinger Meml. fellow Am. Cancer Soc., 1982. Fellow ACP; mem. AMA, AAAS, Am. Soc. Hematology, Am. Soc. Internat. Medicine, Am. Soc. Clin. Oncology, N.Y. Acad. of Scis., Internat. Soc. Thrombosis and Hemostasis, Conn. Oncology Assn., Soc. Columbia Grads., Columbia U. Alumni Fedn. Coun., Columbia U. Alumni Club (pres. Fairfield Co. 1983-85, editor newsletter 1982-91), Bridgeport Med. Soc. (Physician of Yr. 1993). Office: 425 Post Rd Fairfield CT 06430-6232 Office Phone: 203-255-4545.

BURD, STEVEN A., food service executive; b. 1949; m. Chris Burd; 2 children. BS, Carroll Coll., 1971; MA in Econs., U. Wis., 1973. With fin. and mktg. So. Pacific Transp. Co., San Francisco; with Arthur D. Little, NYC, 1982-87; mgmt. cons., Safeway Stores Kohlberg Kravis Roberts & Co., 1986—91; cons. Stop & Shop Cos., Boston, 1988-89; cons., interim CEO Fred Meyer Inc., Portland, Oreg., 1991—92; pres. Safeway Inc., 1992—, CEO, 1993—, chmn., 1998—. Dir. Kohl's Corp. Office: Safeway Inc 5918 Stoneridge Mall Rd Pleasanton CA 94588-3229*

BURDA, STEVEN, financial analyst and manager; b. Kiev, Ukraine, May 6, 1981; s. Zoya and Lev Burda. MBA, St. Joseph's U., Phila., 2006; Post MBA in Internat. Bus. Mgmt. Cert. Engr., Pa., 2005. Sr. fin. analyst Lockheed Martin Co., King of Prussia, Pa., 2003—. Recipient President's award, George W. Bush, 1999, 2002. Citizens. Office: Lockheed Martin Co 230 Mall Blvd King Of Prussia PA 19406

BURDEKIN, RICHARD CHARLES KEIGHLEY, economics professor; b. Poole, Dorset, Eng., Dec. 16, 1958; arrived in US, 1982; s. Charles Walter and Dorothy Agnes Burdekin; m. Yanjie Feng, Mar. 24, 1991; children: Eileen Frances, Emma Dorothy, Josephine Ellen. BA, U. Warwick, Coventry, Eng., 1981; MSc, U. Bristol, Eng., 1982; PhD, U. Houston, 1985. Vis. scholar Fed. Res. Bank Dallas, 1985—86; asst. prof. econs. U. Miami, Coral Gables, Fla., 1986—89; Jonathan B. Lovelace prof. econs. Claremont McKenna Coll., Calif., 1989—. Vis. sr. fellow East-West Ctr., Honolulu, 2005. Author: (books) Budget Deficits and Economic Performance, 1992, Establishing Monetary Stability in Emerging Market Economics, 1995, Confidence, Credibility and Macroeconomic Policy: Past, Present, Future, 1995, Distributional Conflict and Inflation: Theoretical and Historical Perspectives, 1996, Deflation: Current and Historical Perspectives, 2004; contbr. articles to profl. jours. Chiang Ching-kuo Scholar grantee, 2005—06. Mem.: Am. Econ. Assn., Western Econ. Assn., Chinese Economist Soc., Chinese Econ. Assn. (UK). Avocations: travel, swimming, water sports. Office: Claremont McKenna College 500 E Ninth St Claremont CA 91711 Office Phone: 909-607-2884. Office Fax: 909-621-8249. Business E-Mail: richard.burdekin@claremontmckenna.edu.

BURDEN, AMANDA M., urban planner; PhD in Public Administration (hon.), Pratt Inst., 2005. Planner & designer Battery Park City, NYC, 1983—90; mem. NYC Planning Commn., 1990—2002, chair, 2002—; dir. NYC Dept. of City Planning, 2002—. Bd. chair Creative Time, Inc.; bd. mem. Ctr. for Arts Ed., Nature Conservancy, Arch. League, Fund for NYC; trustee Louis Comfort Tiffany Found. Recipient Design Patron award, Cooper Hewitt Nat. Design Mus., 2004. Mem.: Am. Inst. Cert. Planners, NY Soc. Arch. (Sidney Strauss award 1987), Am. Inst. Architects, NY Chapter (Ctr. Archtl. award 2005). Office: NYC Planning Commn 22 Reade St New York NY 10007*

BURDEN, CEDRIC JEROME, SR., language professor; b. Mobile, Ala., Nov. 6, 1969; s. Andrew O'Neal and Juanita (Coleman) B.; m. Teresa Ballard, Mar. 26, 1995; children: Jasmine Renee, Cedric Jerome Jr. AS, S.D. Bishop State Coll., 1989; BA, Univ. Montevallo, 1991, M, 1992. English prof. Lawson State Cmty. Coll., Birmingham, Ala., 1993—. Editing cons. Writing Voyage, 1996, Fictions, 1997, 98; author companion website Progressions, 5th edit. Sec. Alabaster Parks and Recreation Adv. Bd., 1997-98; mem. Alabaster Planning and Zoning Bd.; grad. Ala. C.C. Leadership Acad.; mem. young adv. bd. Big Bros Big Sisters Birmingham. Mem. Ala. Assn. for Developmental Edn., Nat. Assn. for Devel. Edn., Nat. Coun. of Tchrs. of Eng., Alabaster Lions Club (sec.-treas. 1997-98), Alpha Phi Alpha. Avocations: model car building, pets, playing saxophone. Home: 620 Park Forest Ln Alabaster AL 35007 Office: Lawson State Cmty Coll 3060 Wilson Rd SW Birmingham AL 35221-1717 Office Phone: 205-929-2079. Personal E-mail: cburdensr@aol.com. Business E-Mail: cburden@lawsonstate.edu.

BURDEN, JAMES EWERS, lawyer; b. Sacramento, Oct. 24, 1939; s. Herbert Spencer and Ida Elizabeth (Brosemer) B.; m. Kathryn Lee Gardner, Aug. 21, 1965; children: Kara Elizabeth Crabtree, Justin Gardner. BS, U. Calif., Berkeley, 1961; JD, U. Calif., Hastings, 1964; postgrad., U. So. Calif., 1964-65. Bar: Calif. 1965, Tax Ct. U.S. 1969, U.S. Supreme Ct. 1970. Assoc. Elliott and Aune, Santa Ana, Calif., 1965, White, Harbor, Fort & Schei, Sacramento, 1965-67, Miller, Starr & Regalia, Oakland, Calif., 1967-69, ptnr., 1969-73, Burden, Aiken, Mansuy & Stein, San Francisco, 1973-82, James E. Burden, Inc., San Francisco, 1982—; co-founder, COO, sec. KineMed, Inc., Emeryville, Calif., 2001—05, also bd. dirs.; co-founder, dir. Tekton Software Corp., San Francisco, 2003—06; co-founder, dir., CBO Emiliem, Inc., Emeryville, 2006—. Bd. dirs. IP Floor Products, Inc., San Leandro, Calif., Denver; co-founder Gloucestershire Innovation Centre, Gloucester, Eng., EuroGen Pharmas. Ltd., Gloucester, Info4cars, Inc., Asheville, NC; underwriting mem. Lloyds of London, 1986-93; instr. U. Calif., Berkeley, Merritt Coll. 1968-74; pres., prin. Dorset Capital LLC. Contbr. articles to profl. jours. Mem.: Inst. of Dirs. (London), St. Andrews Golf Club (Fife, Scotland), Faculty Club U. Calif. Berkeley, Univ. Club, Commonwealth Club of Calif., Claremont Country Club. Office: One Maritime Plz 4th Fl San Francisco CA 94111-3407 Office Phone: 415-421-0404. Personal E-mail: jimburden@dorsetcapllc.com.

BURDEN, JEAN PRUSSING, retired poet, editor; b. Waukegan, Ill., Sept. 01; d. Harry Frederick and Miriam (Biddlecom) Prussing; m. David Charles Burden, 1940 (div. 1949). BA, U. Chgo., 1936. Sec. John Hancock Mutual Life Ins. Co., Chgo., 1937-39, Young & Rubicam, Inc., Chgo., 1939-41; editor, copywriter Domestic Industries, Inc., Chgo., 1941-45; office mgr. O'Brion Russell & Co., Los Angeles, 1948-55; adminstr. pub. relations Meals for Millions Found., Los Angeles, 1955-65; editor Stanford Research Inst., South Pasadena, Calif., 1965-66; propr. Jean Burden & Assocs., Altadena, Calif., 1966-82; ret. Lectr. poetry to numerous colls. and univs., U.S., 1963—; supr. poetry workshop Pasadena City Coll., Calif., 1960-62, 66, U. Calif. at Irvine, 1975; also pvt. poetry workshops. Author: Naked as the Glass, 1963, Journey Toward Poetry, 1966, The Cat You Care For, 1968, The Dog You Care For, 1968, The Bird You Care For, 1970, The Fish You Care For, 1971, A Celebration of Cats, 1974, The Classic Cats, 1975, The Woman's Day Book of Hints for Cat Owners, 1980, 84, Taking Light from Each Other, 1992; poetry editor: Yankee Mag, 1955—2002; pet editor: Woman's Day Mag. 1973-82; contbr. numerous articles to various jours. and mags. MacDowell Colony fellow; 1973, 74, 76; Recipient Silver Anvil award Pub. Relations Soc. of Am., 1969, 1st prize Borestone Mountain Poetry award, 1963, Gold Crown award for lit. achievement, 1989. Mem. Poetry Soc. Am., Acad. Am. Poets, Authors Guild. Address: 1129 Beverly Way Altadena CA 91001-2517 *I think that man is constantly trying to bring down into the world of time the essences of what he dimly but intuitively feels is timeless. One of the ways in which he tries is through poetry. Without poetry, a certain kind of Reality is speechless. Or to put it a slightly different way, I believe that we inhabit two worlds at once, the world of time and the world of timelessness, and that poetry is a bridge that lets us cross over.*

BURDEN, ORDWAY PARTRIDGE, investment banker; b. NYC, Nov. 20, 1944; s. William A. M. and Margaret L. (Partridge) B.; m. Jean Poor Lynch, October 5, 1991. AB magna cum laude, Harvard U., 1966, MBA, 1968; postgrad., Harvard Law Sch., 1969-71. Gen. ptnr. William A.M. Burden Co., NYC, 1968-86, dir., 1986—. Cons. on police functions Nat. Commn. for Rev. Fed. and State Laws Relating to Wiretapping and Electronic Surveillance; cons. Commn. on Rev. Nat. Policy Toward Gambling. Former mem. adv. bd. Bur. Justice Stats., Dept. of Justice; mem. nat. sponsoring com. Nat. Law Enforcement Officers Meml. Fund; v.p. Florence V. Burden Found., N.Y.C., 1990—. Mem. Internat. Assn. Chiefs Police (past mem. 5 coms.), Nat. Sheriffs Assn. (former mem. standards-ethics-edn.-devel. com.), Nat. Crime Prevention Coun. (bd. dirs.), Law Enforcement Assistance Found. (founder, pres. 1977—), Nat. Law Enforcement Coun. (founder, chmn. 1979—), Capitol Hill Club, Metropolitan Club.

BURDEN, W. EUGENE, oil industry executive; BBA, MBA, U. Tex., Arlington; JD, St. Mary's U., San Antonio. Sr. v.p. govt. rels. Tesoro Corp., 1999—2001, pres. Tesoro Alaska Co., 2001—02, sr. v.p., pres. NW Region Tesoro Refining and Mktg. Co., 2001—02, sr. v.p. human resources and govt. rels., sr. v.p. external affairs. Mem.: Tex. Bar Assn., Alaska Bar Assn. Office: Tesoro Corp 300 Concord Plz San Antonio TX 78216-6999 Office Phone: 210-283-2000.

BURDESHAW, WILLIAM BROOKSBANK, engineering executive; b. East Orange, NJ, Nov. 20, 1930; s. Thomas Anderson and Margaret (Villecco) B.; m. Monica Dorr, Sept. 27, 1957; children: Leath, Thomas, Anne, Alison. BS, U.S. Mil. Acad., 1953; MSEE, Ga. Inst. of Tech., 1961. Commd. 2d lt. U.S. Army, 1953, advanced through grades to brig. gen., 1975, ret., 1979; prin., owner Burdeshaw Assocs., Ltd., 1979—. Cons. Def. Sci. Bd., 1985-87. Engring. mgmt. cons. co. named by INC. mag. as 121st of 500 fastest growing pvt. cos., 1985. Mem. Burning Tree Club, Congl. Country Club, George Town Club (Washington), Cripple Creek Club (Bethany Beach, Del.). Republican. Episcopalian. Office: Burdeshaw Assoc Ltd 4701 Sangamore Rd Bethesda MD 20816-2500

BURDETT, JAMES R., lawyer; b. Taylor, Pa., Sept. 29, 1951; BS, US Naval Acad., 1973; MS, George Washington U., 1981; JD, Widener U. Sch. Law, 1984. Bar: Pa. 1984, NJ 1985, Tex. 1991, DC 1998, admitted to practice: US Dist. Ct. (Dist. NJ) 1985, US Patent and Trademark Office. Ptnr., Intellectual Property Dept. and Patent Prosecution Dept. Venable LLP, Washington. LCDR USN, 1969—79. Master: Giles S. Rich Am. Inn of Ct.; mem.: Am. Intellectual Property Law Assn., ABA (Patent, Trademark and Copyright Law Sect.). Fluent in French. Office: Venable LLP 575 7th St NW Washington DC 20004 Office Phone: 202-344-4893. Office Fax: 202-344-8300. Business E-Mail: jrburdett@venable.com.

BURDETTE, BROOKS R., lawyer; b. Ga., Oct. 6, 1961; BA summa cum laude, Wofford Coll., SC, 1983; JD cum laude, Harvard Law Sch., 1986. Bar: NY 1987, registered: US Dist. Ct. (So. Dist.) NY 1987. Atty. Cravath, Swaine & Moore LLP, NYC; ptnr., pro bono dept. Schulte Roth & Zabel LLP, NYC. Dir. Harvard Legis. Rsch. Bur., 1985—86. Contbr. articles to profl. jour. Pres. Truman Scholars Assn.; v.p. Brainstorm Afterschool Inc.; trustee Harvard Law Sch. Alumni Assn., NYC. Harry Truman Scholar, Presdl. Scholar. Mem.: Fed. Bar Coun. (second cir. courts com.), NY County Lawyers Assn. (judiciary com.), ABA (co-chmn. trial evidence com.). Office: Schulte Roth & Zabel LLP 919 Third Ave New York NY 10022 Office Phone: 212-756-2272. Office Fax: 212-593-5955. Business E-Mail: brooks.burdette@srz.com.

BURDETTE, ROBERT BRUCE, retired lawyer; b. Cin., Oct. 8, 1945; s. Lumas Carter and Myrtle Margaret (Diesel) B. AB, Columbia Coll., 1967; JD, U. Cin., 1973. Bar: Ohio 1973, U.S. Supreme Ct. 1978. Legis. atty. Libr. Congress, Washington, 1973—2003; ret. Author: A Step Beyond The Graetz Prepayment Analysis, 1992. Mem. Mensa, St. Andrew Club, W.A.R. Goodwin Soc. Colonial Williamsburg. Methodist. Avocation: gilding. Home: 3672 Willowlea Ct Apt A Cincinnati OH 45208 E-mail: rburdette@fuse.net.

BURDGE, RABEL JAMES, sociology educator; b. Columbus, Ohio, Dec. 14, 1937; s. Alonzo Marshall and Mariam Francis (Prentice) B.; m. Sharon Sue Payne, June 30, 1962 (dec. June 1975); children: Stephanie, Amy, Jill; m. Joyce Loretta Piggush, Aug. 2, 1977. BS, Ohio State U., 1959, MS, 1961; PhD, Pa. State U., 1965. Asst. prof. sociology U.S. Air Force Acad., Colo., 1966-68; lectr. U. Colo., Colorado Springs, 1966-68; asst. prof. sociology U. Ky., Lexington, 1968-72, assoc. prof., 1972-76; assoc. prof. environ. sociology, rural sociology, urban and regional planning and leisure studies; dept. agrl. econs. and leisure studies U. Ill. Inst. Environ. Studies, Urbana, 1976-80, prof., 1980—96; prof. emeritus U. Ill., 1996—; prof. sociology and environ. studies Western Wash. U., Bellingham, 1996—. Vis. scholar Sch. of Australian Environ. Studies, Griffith U., Brisbane, 1982, 86, hon. prof., 1991—; vis. prof. Sch. Planning and Landscape, U. Manchester, Eng., 2002. Author: (with N. Cheek and D. Field) Leisure and Recreation Places, 1976, (with Paul Opryszek) Coping with Change: An Interdisciplinary Assessment of the Lake Shelbyville Reservoir, 1981, (with E.M. Rogers) Social Change in Rural Societies, A Rural Sociology Textbook, 3d edit., 1988, A Community Guide to Social Impact Assessment, 1998, 3d edit., 2004, A Conceptual Approach to Social Impact Assessment, 1994, 2d edit., 1998, The Concepts, Process and Methods of Social Impact Assessment, 2004; editor Jour. Leisure Rsch., 1971-74; co-editor, founder: Leisure Scis., an Interdisciplinary Jour., 1977-82, Society and Nat. Resources: An Internat. Jour., 1988-98; co-editor Longman-Cheshire Internat. Environ. Studies Series, 1990—; contbr. articles to profl. publs. Mem. Whatcan County Planning Commn., 2003—04. Capt. arty. USMC, 1965—68. Recipient George B. Hartzog Jr. award for environ. rsch. Clemson U., 1995. Lifetime Achievement award Internat. Assn. Society and Natural Resources, 2004. Mem. AAAS, Am. Sociol. Assn., Rural Sociol. Soc. (v.p. 1982-83, treas. 1994-2000, editor The Rural Sociologist, 1994-2000, named Disting. Rural Sociologist, 1996), Nat. Recreation and Park Assn. (Theodore/Franklin D. Roosevelt award for outstanding rsch. 1982), Internat. Assn. for Impact Assessment (pres. 1990-91, treas. 1993-96, Rose-Hulman Inst. Tech. award for contbns. to impact assessment), Acad. Leisure Scis., Sigma Xi, Phi Kappa Phi, Gamma Sigma Delta, Alpha Kappa Delta. Democrat. Methodist. Home: PO Box 4056 Bellingham WA 98227-4056 E-mail: burdge@comcast.net.

BURDI, ALPHONSE ROCCO, anatomist; b. Chgo., Aug. 28, 1935; s. Alphonse Rocco and Anna (Basilo) B.; m. Sandra Shaw, Mar. 22, 1968; children— Elizabeth Anne, Sarah Lynne. BS, No. Ill. U., DeKalb, 1957; MS, U. Ill., 1959, U. Mich., 1961, PhD, 1963; Doctorate (hon.), U. Athens, Greece, 2000. Predoctoral fellow physiology U. Ill., 1957-59; NSF summer fellow U. Mich., 1960, NIH trainee, 1960-61, NIH predoctoral research fellow, 1962, mem. faculty, 1962—, prof. emeritus cell and devel. biology, 2003—. Rsch. scientist emeritus Ctr. Human Growth and Devel., 2003; dir. integrated pre-med.-med. program U. Mich. Mem. editorial bd.: Cleft Palate Jour. 1972-88 , Am. Jour. Phys. Anthropology, 1971-75, C.C. Thomas Am. Lectr. Series in Anatomy, 1971-88 , Jour. Dental Research, 1977-87. Grantee NIH. Mem. Internat. Assn. Dental Research, Am. Assn. Dental Research, Am. Cleft Palate Assn., Teratology Soc., Am. Assn. Anatomists, Am. Assn. Phys. Anthropology, Sigma Xi. Home: 2600 Page Ct Ann Arbor MI 48104-6249 Office: U Mich Dept Cell & Devel Biology Basic Science Research Bldg Ann Arbor MI 48109-0616 Office Phone: 734-764-4358. Business E-Mail: alburdi@umich.edu.

BURDICK, GINNY MARIE, state senator; b. Portland, Oreg., Dec. 3, 1947; BA, U. Puget Sound, 1969; M in Journalism, Oreg. U., 1973. Reporter, editor Port Angeles Daily News, Wash., 1969—79, Daily News, Eugene, Oreg., Register-Guard, AP, Bur. Nat. Affairs, Legal Times of Washington; environ. issues mgr. Atlantic Richfield Co., 1981—84; self-employed crisis mgmt. specialist, 1989—2004; v.p., sr. counsel Gard & Gerber Advt. and Pub. Rels., 2004—06. Mem. Oreg. State Senate, Eugene, 1996—, mem., chair senate judiciary comm., 1996—. Democrat. Home: 4641 SW Dosch Rd Portland OR 97239-1244 Office: S 317 State Capitol Salem OR 97301 E-mail: sen.ginnyburdick@state.or.us.

BURDICK, GLENN ARTHUR, physicist, engineering educator; b. Pavilion, Wyo., Sept. 9, 1932; s. Stephen Arthur and Mary Elizabeth (McClurg) Burdick; m. Joyce Mae Huggett, July 14, 1951; children: Stephen Arthur, Randy Glenn. BS, Ga. Inst. Tech., 1958, MS, 1959; PhD, MIT, 1961. Registered profl. engr., Fla. Office mgr. Statewide Contractors, Las Vegas, Nev., 1955—56; spl. tool designer Ga. Inst. Tech., Atlanta, 1954—55, instr., 1956—59; sr. mem. rsch. staff Sperry Microwave, Oldsmar, Fla., 1961—65; prof. elec. engring. U. So. Fla., Tampa, 1965—, dean Coll. Engring., 1979—86, disting. prof. engring., 1986—, dean emeritus, 1986—; pres. Burdick Engring. and Sci., Inc., 1983—. Mem. Tampa Bay Fgn. Affairs. Com., 1981—88, Pinellas County (Fla.) High Speed Rail Task Force, 1982—91, Gov. of State of Fla. Energy Task Force, 1980—85; vice chmn. Fla. Task Force for Sci. Energy and Tech. Svc. to Industry, 1981—82. Named Engring. Faculty Mem. of Yr., State of Fla., 1986; Tex. Gulf scholar, 1957—58, Woodrow Wilson fellow, 1958—59, NSF fellow, 1958—61. Fellow: Nat. Acad. Forensic Engrs., Am. Bd. Forensic Examiners, Nat. Fire Protection Agy., Am. Assn. Forensic Sci.; mem.: IEEE (sr. Engr. of Yr. award 1980), U.S. Profl. Engrs. Edn. (vice-chmn. SE region 1986—88), N.Y. Acad. Scis., Nat. Acad. Forensic Engring., Internat. Soc. Hybrid Microelectronics (nat. pre. 1974), Fla. Engring. Soc. (Engr. of Yr. award 1981), Downtown Club, Clearwater Tennis Club (pres. Fla. chpt. 1965, 1969). Achievements include invention of underground pipeline leak detector; sail boat mast insulation. Home: 18728 Lake Iola Rd Dade City FL 33523-6117 Office: Burdick Engring and Sci Inc 18530 Lake Iola Rd Dade City FL 33523-6149

BURDICK, LOU BRUM, public relations executive; b. Bloomer, Wis., Nov. 4, 1943; s. Francis Albert and Lucille May (Gorton) Peil; m. Robert P. Brum, Dec. 26, 1971 (div. 1977); m. Allan L. Burdick, Feb. 12, 1981; 1 child, Matthew Francis. Adminstr. Bozell & Jacobs, Mpls., 1965-67; pub. rels. mgr. Apache Corp., Mpls., 1967-76; v.p., dir. fin. rels. Edwin Neuger & Assocs., Mpls., 1976-78; chmn. bd., chief exec. officer Brum & Anderson Pub. Relations, Inc., Mpls., 1978-86; pres. Padilla, Speer, Burdick & Beardsley, Inc., Mpls., 1987, Lou Burdick and Assocs., Mpls., 1988—; dir. communications Office of Gov., St. Paul, 1989-91. Bd. dirs. Hennepin County Libr. Found., 1991-97, Minn. Coun. on Founds., 1998-2000, Courage Found., 2002-05, Nami-MN, 2002—; campaign mgr. Printy for Gov., 1990. Recipient Outstanding Achievement award for entrepreneurship Mpls. YWCA, 1985. Mem. Pub. Rels. Soc. Am. (pub. rels. recognition award 1985), Minn. Women's Econ. Roundtable (bd. dirs.), Minikahda Country Club. Home: 45 Univ Ave SE #405 Minneapolis MN 55414

BURDICK, MARGARET SEALE (MARGE BURDICK), interior designer; b. Ft. Worth, Tex., July 24, 1919; d. Walter Braton and Ivy (McCleskey) Seale; m. Donald K. Bennett (dec. May 1943); 1 child, Donald Jr.; m. William J. Walsh, Dec. 1, 1945 (div. June 1959); children: Susan S. Lynch, William J. Jr., Margaret J. Tannery; m. Lorence Connable Burdick, Oct. 21, 1961 (div. Aug. 1979); children: Michael, John, Timothy (dec.). Student, So. Meth. U., 1937-38. Interior redesigner Kalamazoo (Mich.) Country Club, 1948; interior desiger Child Guidance Ctr. Jr. League (formerly Service Club), Kalamazoo, 1956, designer nearly new shop, 1955; co-owner, interior designer Red Lion Inn, Vail, Colo., 1962-80; owner MSB Designs, 1980-2001; interior designer Outstanding Homes in Vail, 1981-99. Co-organizer 1st Sch. Bd. Vail, 1963; charter bd. dirs. Vail Inst Performing Arts, 1973-84; pres. Vail Inst., 1979-84, also hon. bd. dirs. 1984-87; mem. Art Selection Com. Vail, 1981-84; bd. dirs. Gerald R. Ford Commemorative Com., Vail, 1980-85; charter mem. bd. dirs. Bravo! Colo. Music Festival, Vail and Beaver Creek, 1987-95, adv. bd., 1995-2005; bd. dirs. Betty Ford Alpine Carden Found., 1986-97, nat. adv. bd., 1997-2001; bd. dirs. Vail Religious Found. Endowment Com., 1995-2004, Bravo! Music Festival Endowment Com., 1991-98, Ctr. for the Arts Com. (now Vilar Ctr.), Beaver Creek, Vail Valley Arts Coun., 1991—, pres., 1993-97. Honoree Bravo! Colo. Music Festival, 1997. Mem.: Racquet Club (charter), Homestead Ct. Club, Vail Athletic Club (charter). Republican. Episcopalian. Home and Office: 2833 Newport Cir Grand Junction CO 81503-3108 E-mail: msb@vail.net.

BURDICK, ROBERT W., newspaper editor; b. Feb. 11, 1948; m. Patty Burnett; 1 child, David. B in Polit. Sci., Fla. Atl. U., 1969. Reporter Miami Herald, Fla. Today; night city editor Palm Beach (Fla.) Post; mng. editor Palm Beach Daily News; asst. mng. editor Wichita (Kans.) Eagle; city editor/metro editor/asst. to exec. editor San Jose (Calif.) Mercury News, 1978-82; asst. mng. editor Denver Post, 1982-84; asst. mng. editor/mng. editor/editor L.A. Daily News, 1984-94; mng. editor, editor Rocky Mountain News, Denver, 1994-98, pres., 1998—2000; exec. v.p., gen. mgr. Naples (Fla.) Daily News, 2000—02, pres., pub., 2002—. Mem. Am. Soc. Newspaper Editors, Soc. Profl. Journalists, AP News Execs. Coun. (past bd. mem., past pres. Calif., Nev. chpt., past editor AP Mng. Editors News), Metro Denver C. of C. (bd. dirs.), NCCJ (bd. dirs. Denver chpt.). Avocations: skiing, hiking. Office: Naples Daily News 1075 Central Ave Naples FL 34102

BURDICK, ROGER S., state supreme court justice; BS, U. Colorado; JD, U. Idaho Sch. of Law, 1974. Bank examiner Dept. Finance, Boise, Idaho, 1970—71; atty. Webb, Pike, Burton & Carlson, Twin Falls, 1974—80; dep. prosecuting atty. Ada County; prtnr. Hart and Burdick, Jerome, 1976—80; prosecuting atty. Jerome County, 1980—81, magistrate judge, 1981—93; dist. judge Twin Falls County, 1993—2001; administrative judge Fifth Jud. Dist., 2001—03; justice Idaho Supreme Ct., 2003—. Former chmn. Juvenile Rules Com.; mem. Idaho Jud. Coun., 1990—2001; dist. judge Snake River Basin Water Adjudication, 2001—03. Mem.: Magistrate Judges Assn. (pres. 1989—91), Idaho State Bar Assn., Dist. Judges Assn. (pres. 2001—03). Office: Idaho Supreme Ct PO Box 83720 Boise ID 83720-0101*

BURDICK, WILLIAM MACDONALD, biomedical engineer; b. Providence, Apr. 24, 1952; s. Franklin Pierce and Lola Alice (Cook) B. BS, Ind. U. Pa., 1975; M of Engring., Tex. A&M U., 1981; postgrad., U. Tex., 1982-86. Engring. analyst FDA, Winchester, Mass., 1988-90, reviewer neurological devices Rockville, Md., 1990-94, reviewer, gen. hosp. and personal use devices, 1994—. Inventor in field; contbr. articles to profl. jours.; contbr. poem to: Dance on the Horizon (Editor's Choice award Nat. Libr. Poetry), America at the Millennium. With USAF, 1976-78. Mem. Biomed. Engring. Soc., Humane Soc. U.S., Am. Assn. Med. Instrumentation, Nat. Multiple Sclerosis Soc. Congregationalist. Avocations: reading, writing (poetry, songs, fiction), gardening, sports. Office: 9200 Corporate Blvd Rockville MD 20850-3229 Office Phone: 240-276-3719. Business E-Mail: william.burdick@fda.hhs.gov.

BURDO, AMY, elementary school educator; b. Toledo, Ohio, Oct. 25, 1967; BS in Edn., No. Ariz. U., Flagstaff, 1985—90, MusM, 1997—99. Elem. Edn. Tchr. Colo. Bd. Edn., 2005. Pvt. piano tchr., Flagstaff, 1992—97; pvt. voice tchr., 1999—2005; pvt. academic tutor, 1994—2005; adult educator Native Americans for Cmty. Action, Flagstaff, 1994—97; academic advisor, grad asst No. Ariz. U., 1997—99, transcript evaluator, 1999—2001, career counselor, 2001—05; vocal music tchr. Carmel Mid. Sch., Colorado Springs, Colo., 2005—06; 6th grade tchr. Colo. Springs. Charter Acad., 2006—. Cons. Flagstaff Montessori Sch., 1998—2000. Actor: (musical) Oliver, The Robber Bridegroom, 1997, My Fair Lady, 2004, (play) Five Tellers Dancing in the Rain, 1997, (opera) Evita, 2003; singer: (oratorio) Messiah, 1987, (political event) National Anthem Soloist, 2002. Bd. mem. Children's Chorale of Flagstaff, 2004—05; climb the mountain to conquer cancer Am. Cancer Soc., Flagstaff, 2000—05. Grantee Choral Dinner scholarship, No. Ariz. U. Music Dept., 1986—88; scholar Gen. Academic scholarship, No. Ariz. U., 1985—89, Dougherty Found., 1990, 1997—99. Mem.: Colo. Springs Chorale. Office: 2577 N Chelton Rd Colorado Springs CO 80909 Home Phone: 719-473-4847; Office Phone: 719-636-2722. Personal E-mail: singingdove92@hotmail.com.

BURDUMY, STEPHEN T., lawyer; b. Phila., 1957; BSFS cum laude, Georgetown Univ., 1979; JD, Univ. San Francisco, 1982. Bar: Pa. 1982, NJ 1982. Ptnr. Klehr, Harrison, Harvey, Branzburg & Ellers LLP; ptnr., corp. and securities practice group Drinker Biddle & Reath LLP, Phila. Mem.: ABA, NJ Bar Assn., Pa. Bar Assn. Office: Drinker Biddle & Reath LLP One Logan Sq 18th & Cherry Sts Philadelphia PA 19103-6996 Office Phone: 215-988-2880. Office Fax: 215-988-2757. Business E-Mail: stephen.burdumy@dbr.com.

BURFEIND, BETTY RUTH, retired secondary school educator, coach; b. Chgo., Feb. 10, 1947; d. William Frederick Burfeind and Ruth Pauline Amanda Batzer; m. Joseph Andres Ibanez, June 8, 1992. BS in Phys. Edn., Ea. Ill. U., Charleston, 1969, MS in Phys. Edn., 1977; paralegal cert., Roosevelt U., Chgo., 1982; type 75 adminstrv. cert., Govs. State U., 1994. Tchr. health and phys. edn. James Hart Jr. HS, Homewood, Ill., 1969—80; tchr. sci. and phys. edn. Carl Sandburg HS, Orland Park, Ill., 1980—83, Victor J. Andrew HS, Tinley Park, Ill., 1983—2004; ret., 2004. Swimming coach Victor J. Andrew HS, 1983—2005, water polo coach, 1998—; swimming coach Carl Sandburg HS, 2005—; mem. governing bd,. Dist. 230 NEA, Orland Park, 1980—2004. Instr. ARC, Chgo., 1969—. Mem.: Nat. Sr. Games Assn., U.S. Water Polo Assn., Am. Swim Coaches Assn., Nat. Intercollegiate Swimming Coaches Assn. Lutheran. Avocations: golf, bicycling, travel, writing, swimming. Home: 10601 Brookridge Dr Frankfort IL 60423 Office: Consol Sch Dist 230 15100 W 94th Ave Orland Park IL 60462

BURG, BRENT LAWRENCE, lawyer, judge; b. Houston, Mar. 2, 1940; s. Abner Danford and Bess (Levin) B.; m. Patricia S. Petitt, 1980; 1 child, Brook Lawrence. BA, U. Tex., 1962; JD, 1966. Bar: Tex. 1966, U.S. Dist. Ct. (so. dist.) Tex. 1966, U.S. Ct. Appeals (5th cir.) 1966, U.S. Supreme Ct. 1970, U.S. Ct. Appeals (4th cir.) 1976, U.S. Dist. Ct. Md. 1976, U.S. Ct. Appeals (11th cir.) 1981. Dist. judge 309th Dist. Ct., Harris County, Tex., 1981-82; assoc. mcpl. judge City of Piney Point Village, 1990-98, City of Bunker Hill Village, 1991-98; ptnr. Rentz, Burg and Assocs., Houston, 1983-95; pvt. practice Brent Burg, Houston, 1995-98; assoc. judge 312th Dist. Ct., Houston, 1999—; of counsel Fouts & Moore, L.L.P., 1996-98. Chairperson Houston Vol. Lawyers Program, Inc., 1988-89, 89-90. Fellow Tex. Bar Found.; mem. Houston Bar Found., State Bar Tex. (grievance com.), Houston Bar Assn. (family law sect. treas. 1978-79, chairperson elect 1980-81, dir. 1982-83, chairperson 1984-85; mem. Supreme Ct. of Tex. child support and visitation guidelines adv. com. 1986-87, 96-97), Phi Alpha Delta. Office: 312th District Ct 1115 Congress St Houston TX 77002-1927

BURG, JOHN PARKER, electric power industry executive; b. Great Bend, Kans., Dec. 17, 1931; s. Kenneth Edwin and Viola Mae (Parker) B.; m. Ida Elizabeth Groome; children Ida Elizabeth, Clarence Oscar Edwin; m. Shirley Joan Steele, Apr. 10, 1976; children: Nathan Parker, Emily Diane, Paul Andrew. BS in Physics, BA in Math., U. Tex., 1953; MS in Physics, MIT, 1960; PhD in Geophysics, Stanford U., 1975. Asst. engr. Tex. Instruments, Inc., 1956-57, engr. Dallas, 1960; sr. rsch. geophysicist Geophys. Svc., Inc., Dallas, 1960-73; chmn. bd. dirs. Time and Space Processing, Inc., Santa Clara, Calif., 1973-83; pres. Entropic Processing, Inc., Cupertino, Calif., 1983—, also chmn. bd. dirs. Cons. oil cos., ESL, Inc., Naval Undersea Ctr., 1969-75; cons. Digicon, Inc., Houston, 1982-83; chmn. bd. dirs. Entropic Rsch. Lab., Washington, 1984-98, Entropic Geophysical, Inc., 1984-91, Entropic Speech Inc., 1984-02, Affordable Bldg. Sys., 2000—. Inventor patent predictive seismic deconvolution, multi-channel filtering. Recipient Rsch. Publication award Naval Rsch. Lab., 1984; named Life Master Am. Contract Bridge League. Fellow IEEE (contbr. to jour.). Avocation: bridge theory. Office: Durra Bldg Systems LLC 2747 State Hwy 160 PO Box 10 Whitewright TX 75491 Home: 2301 W White Ave Apt 214 Mc Kinney TX 75071 Business E-Mail: john.burg@durra.com.

BURG, RALPH, art association executive; b. Malden, Mass., Jan. 2, 1914; s. Joseph and Bessie (Meyer) B.; m. Fay E. Pristaw, Jan. 10, 1937; children: Stephen, Harvey. BA, Boston U., 1936. V.p. Beacon Musical Inst. Co., Boston, 1939-70; pres., owner Quisisana Lodge, Center Lovell, Maine, 1946-76; chmn. Edna Hibel Soc., Coral Springs, Fla., 1979-99. Mem. Friends for Life, B'Nai B'rith. Recipient Cultural award Minister of Culture, Flanders, Belgium, 1983. Mem. Kiwanis (various coms. Boston chpt. 1946-70), Synergistic Assn. (pres. Boston chpt. 1962-70), Edna Hibel Soc. (pres., chmn. 1979-2002, editor Hibeletter newsletter 1979-2002), Woodlands Country Club. Avocations: golf, tennis, writing, bridge, saxophone. Home: 4604 King Palm Dr Tamarac FL 33319-6121 Office: Edna Hibel Soc PO Box 9721 Coral Springs FL 33075-9721 Personal E-mail: maestroralph@cs.com.

BURGARD, TIMOTHY ANGLIN, curator; BA in Art History, Dartmouth Coll., Hanover, NH, 1981; MA in Art History, Columbia U., NYC, 1985, MPhil in Art History, 1988. Asst. curator paintings, drawings and sculpture NY Hist. Soc., NYC, 1989—93; Henry Luce Found. assoc. curator Am. art Harvard U. Art Museums, Cambridge, Mass., 1993—95; Ednah Root curator Am. art, curator-in-charge Am. art dept. Fine Arts Museums San Francisco. Lectr. in field. Contbr. articles, essays to profl. publs. Fellow, Samuel H. Kress Found., 1987; grantee, Henry Luce Found., 1989—90; scholar, Reynolda Ho., 1983; Pres.' fellow, Columbia U., 1982—85. Office: Fine Arts Museums San Francisco de Young Mus 50 Tea Garden Dr San Francisco CA 94118

BURGDOERFER, JERRY, lawyer; b. Jeffersonville, Ind., May 3, 1958; s. Jerry Jack and Barbara Jean Burgdoerfer. BS, Ind. U., 1980, MBA, 1983, JD cum laude, 1983. Bar: Ill. 1984, U.S. Dist. Ct. (no. dist.) Ill. 1984, U.S. Tax Ct. 1984. Assoc. Adams, Fox, Adelstein, Rosen & Bell, Chgo., 1983-88, ptnr., 1988-89; assoc. Jenner & Block, Chgo., 1989-90, ptnr., 1991—; with Mori Hamada Matsumoto, Tokyo, 1991—93; co-chair corp. dept. Jenner & Block, Chgo., 1999—2002, co-chair securities practice group, 2000—, mem. mgmt. com., 2002—05; mem. State of Ill. Sec. of State Bus. Orgn. Acts Com., 2004—. Author: (book) Director and Officers Liability: Prevention, Insurance and Indemnification, 2000, Securities Law, 2003; contbr. articles to profl. jours. Vol. United Cerebral Palsy Assn., 1995—, dir., 1999—; mem. bus. orgn. acts adv. com. State of Ill. Sec. of State, 2004—; mem. exec. com. Northwestern U. Sch. Law Ann. Garrett Corp. and Securities Law Inst. Named 2d Benton, Nat. Moot Ct. Competition, 1982. Mem.: ABA, Cleve. Clin. Heart Ctr. Internat. Leadership Comm., Chgo. Coun. Fgn. Rels., Chgo. Bar Assn. (chairperson '34 Act Com. 1996—98, reporter securities com. 1997—98, vice chair 1998—99, chair 1999—2000), Ill. Bar Assn., Inter Pacific Bar Assn., Internat. Bar Assn., Japan Am. Soc. Chgo., Exec. Club Chgo., Econ. Club Chgo., Ind. U. Alumni Club Chgo. (vol. 1988—89), Phi Delta Theta (sec. chpt. 1977—78, co-founder, mem. steering com. Chgo. alumni club 1988—89), Phi Delta Phi, Phi Eta Sigma. Avocations: bicycling, water-skiing, Japanese language. Office: Jenner & Block 1 E Ibm Plz Fl 4000 Chicago IL 60611-7603

BURGDOERFER, JERRY J., marketing and distribution executive; b. Connersville, Ind., Nov. 20, 1935; s. Louis M. and Edna (Seele) B.; m. Barbara Jean Hofherr, Aug. 15, 1954; children: Steven, Jerry, Jeffrey, Stuart. BS, Ind. U., 1957. Indsl. engr. Colgate Palmolive Co., Jeffersonville, Ind., 1958-59, mktg. mgr. NYC, 1959-63, Am. Can Co., Green Bay, Wis., 1963-65, dir. sales, 1966-67, v.p. Greenwich, Conn., 1968-70; pres., dir. Am. Garden Products, Inc., Boston, 1970-71; exec. v.p. Facelle Co. div. Internat. Paper Co., NYC, 1971-73; v.p. worldwide mktg. Hertz Corp., NYC, 1973-77, exec. v.p., dir., from 1977; pres., chief exec. officer Berkey Inc., NYC, 1979-86, Carysfort Enterprises Inc., Key Largo, Fla., 1987—; v.p. corp. mktg. AT Cross Co., Lincoln, RI, 1991—, also bd. dirs.; prin. JJB Assocs., Bracey, Va., 1996—. Bd. dirs. Avis Inc. Served with arty. U.S. Army, 1957-58. Recipient Torch of Liberty-Man of Yr. award. Mem. Acad. Alumni Fellows (Ind. U.), Phi Delta Theta, Barrington Yacht Club (bd. govs.). Office Phone: 434-636-6666.

BURGDOERFER, STUART, retail executive; m. Laney Burgdoerfer; 2 children. BS, Ind. U.; MBA Mgmt. Strategy, Northwestern U. Mgr. CSC Index, Deloitte and Touche; sr. dir. fin., dir. strategic and fin. planning Pizza Hut/Tricon Global Restaurants, 1992—98; v.p. fin. planning Limited Brands, Inc., Columbus, Ohio, 1998; CFO White Barn Candle Co., Ltd. Brands, 1999—2000; v.p. to sr. v.p. fin., controller Limited Brands., Inc., Columbus, Ohio, 2000—04; sr. v.p. fin. Home Depot, 2004—06; exec. v.p. fin. Limited Brands, Inc., Columbus, Ohio, 2006—07; exec. v.p., CFO Limited Brands., Inc., Columbus, Ohio, 2007—. Office: Limited Brands Inc 3 Limited Pkwy Columbus OH 43230*

BURGE, CONSTANCE M., television producer; d. Phil. MFA in Playwriting, UCLA. Cons. prodr.: (TV series) Ally McBeal, 1997—2002; Ed, 2000—04; prodr.: Savannah, 1996—97, Charmed, 1998—2000, Boston Public, 2003; author: The Power of Three: A Novelization, 1999, The Crimson Spell, 2000, Haunted By Desire, 2000, Kiss of Darkness: An Original Novel, 2000, Voodoo Moon, 2000, Whispers from the Past, 2000, Beware What You Wish, 2001, The Gypsy Enchantment, 2001, The Legacy of Merlin, 2001, Soul of the Bride, 2001, Charmed Again, 2002, Spirit of the Wolf, 2002.

BURGE, DAVID ALAN, lawyer, writer; b. Anderson, Ind., July 22, 1943; s. James Swisher and Esther M. (Sheppard) B.; m. Carolyn J. Alter, Nov. 24, 1966; children: Benjamin, Thomas. BS in Gen. Engring. with highest honors, U. Ill., 1966; JD, U. Louisville, 1970. Registered patent atty. Pvt. practice, Cleve., 1975—. Author: Patent and Trademark Tactics and Practice, 1980, 3rd edition, 1999; contbr. chpts. to John Wiley & Sons Engineering Handbooks, 1986-2006. Pres. Gen. Engring. Constituent Alumni Assn., 1984, 85. Mem.: ABA, Cleve. Intellectual Property Law Assn., Sigma Delta Kappa, Gamma Epsilon, Associated Locksmiths of Am., Am. Intellectual Property Law Assn., Cleve. Bar Assn., Phi Eta Sigma, Sigma Tau, Phi Kappa Phi. Avocations: antique tools, woodworking. Office: 2901 S Park Blvd Cleveland OH 44120-1842

BURGE, DAVID RUSSELL, concert pianist, composer, educator; b. Evanston, Ill., Mar. 25, 1930; s. Russell David and Sylvia (Swensen) B.; m. Liliane Choney, 1993; 1 child, Russell David. MusB, Northwestern U., 1951, MusM, 1952; DMus Arts, Eastman Sch. Music, 1956; postgrad., Cherubini Conservatory, Florence, Italy, 1956-57; DFA, Bucknell U., 1980. Instr. piano Northwestern U., 1949-52; assoc. prof. music, composer-pianist in resident Whitman Coll., 1957-62; dir. MacDowell Hall Concert Series at coll., 1959-62; organist Ch. of Christ Scientist, Walla Walla, 1958-62; from asst. prof. music to prof. U. Colo., 1962-75; chmn. piano dept. Eastman Sch. Music, U. Rochester, NY, 1975-87, prof. NY, 1975-93, Kilbourn prof. NY, 1978-79; artist-in-residence U. Calif., Davis, 1975; guest prof. piano U. Stockholm, Sweden, 1981, 92, Banff Ctr., Canada, 1983-84, 86, U. Auckland, New Zealand, 1988; composer-in-residence San Diego Ballet Co., 1997—2005. Guest prof. Odense, Denmark, 1997; guest prof. composition U. Pa., 1977; guest prof. music history U. Gothenberg, Sweden, 1980, 92; feature writer San Diego Reader; guest prof. composition San Diego State U., 2000. Rec. artist, Mercury, Advance, Candide, Nonesuch (grammy nomination 1974), CRI Records, Mus. Heritage Soc. Records, Vox Records, Proviva Records, Wergo, Albany, Capstone Records, Classico Records, Fleur de Son Classics; composer: opera Intervals, 1961; trio for violin, cello, piano, 1962; work for piano Eclipse, 1963; for flute-piano Sources I, 1964; for violin-celeste-piano Sources II, 1965; for piano Eclipse II, 1966, Sources IV, 1969; for clarinet-percussion Sources III, 1967; for soprano-piano A Song of Sixpence, 1967, Life Begins at 40, 1998; for flute-clarinet-violin-cello-piano-tape Aeolian Music, 1968; String Quartet, 1969, Twone in Sunshine, an Entertainment for Theater, 1969; for violin-orch. that no one knew, 1969, Songs of Love and Sorrow, 1989, for solo piano Go-Hyang, 1994, Sonata for Violin and Piano, 1994, Liana's Song: A Ballet in Six Parts, 1995, The Dark Journey, 12 Pieces for Dance, 1995, 24 Preludes for Piano, 1996, Luna Lunera, a Ballet in 12 Parts, 1996, Moku (Island) for three percussionists, 1998; La Loteria Ballet, 1998, The Thousand Paper Cranes, 2001, Kaleidoscope (ballet), 2001; for piano and orch. Dances of Love and Laughter, 1998, When Love Prevails for solo vibraphone, 2002, Dibujos (sketches) for violin and piano, 2003, Rainbows: A Ragtime Ballet, 2003, La Noche del Huerto, 2004 Reminiscence, 2004, Emma's Day, 2005, Azaleas: A Sonata for Viola and Piano, 2005, also songs, anthems.; contbr. over 200 articles to periodicals; columnist: Keyboard Mag., Clavier Mag., Piano Quar.; music reviewer: Music Library Assn. Notes; first major postarmistice concert, Seoul, Korea, 1953, New York debut playing all-modern program, 1961; toured, Korea, 1953-54, Europe, 1956-57, U.S.A., annually, 1960— , Eastern Europe, 1974, Far East, Australia, N.Z., 1984, 88; author: Twentieth-Century Piano Music, 1990; Vanishing Spring, 1998, Bricks and Other Stories, 2004. Served with AUS, 1952-54, Korea. Decorated by U.S. Army for cultural relations work in Korea, 1954; recipient Alumni Merit award Northwestern U., 1974, Colo. Gov.'s award, 1975, Distinguished Alumni award Eastman Sch. Music, 1975, Deems Taylor award for mus. journalism ASCAP, 1978-79; Fulbright fellow in Italy, 1956-57; Faculty Research lectr. U. Colo., 1972 Mem. ASCAP, Internat. Webern Soc. (charter), Am. Soc. Univ. Composers (founder, nat. chmn. 1970-74), Pi Kappa Lambda. Address: 52 Urquhart St Cranston RI 02920 Personal E-mail: drbleb@cox.net.

BURGE, JOHN WESLEY, JR., management consultant; b. Mobile, Ala., Sept. 11, 1932; s. John Wesley and Mary Jo (Guest) Burge; m. Shirley Paulette Roberts, Mar. 29, 1958; children: John, Delene, Eric, Kurt, Karen. Student, Centenary Coll., San Antonio Coll.; PhD in Aerospace Program Mgmt., UCLA, 1967. Engring. and mgmt. staff ITT Gilfillan, 1954-69; pres., gen. mgr. Rantec, Calabasas, Calif., 1969-71, chmn. bd. dirs.; pres., gen. mgr. electronics and space divsn. Emerson Electric Co., St. Louis, 1971-80, corp. group v.p. govt., def., 1977-89; ret., 1989; pvt. practice Pensacola, Fla., 1975—. With USAF, 1950—54. Decorated Grand Cordon Order Al-Istiqlal (Jordan). Baptist. Office Phone: 850-457-7160.

BURGE, MICAH BENJAMIN, school psychologist; b. Pequannock, NJ, Aug. 6, 1978; s. Marc and Jacqueline Burge; m. Corrie Goldblat, Aug. 16, 2005. BA in Psychology with distinction, Richard Stockton Coll. N.J., 2000; MA in Ednl. Psychology, Kean U., 2003. Cert. sch. psychologist N.J., 2004. Sch. psychologist intern North Plainfield (N.J.) Pub. Schs., 2003—04; sch. psychologist North Brunswick (N.J.) Twp. Schs., 2004—. Contbr. articles to profl. jours. Mem.: NEA, NJ Edn. Assn., NJ Assn. Sch. Psychologists, Psi Chi (life). Avocations: puzzle books, guitar, music, basketball. Home: 109 Cromwell Dr Robbinsville NJ 08691-3072 Office: North Brunswick Township Schools Old Georges Rd North Brunswick NJ 08902 Home Phone: 609-443-6496; Office Phone: 732-289-3300 3320. Business E-Mail: mburge@mail.nbtschools.org.

BURGE, STEVEN DONALD, city administrator; b. Omaha, Mar. 14, 1950; s. Melvin Lloyd and Mary Ann Burge. Cert. EMT, We. Iowa Tech. Coll., 1985; BS in Polit. Sci., Sociology, Wayne State Coll., Detroit, 1992; MPA, U. Nebr., 1997; postgrad., SD State U., Brookings, 1999. Cert. emergency med. technician. Mgr. housing devel., Norfolk, Nebr., 1994; city adminstr. City of Creighton, Nebr., 1995, City of Dakota City, Nebr., 1998—2000; adj. instr. intro. to sociology/sociology of deviance Wayne State Coll., Nebr., 2004—. Bd. dirs. Cardinal Devel.; pres. Northeast Nebr. Devel. Network, 1997; pres. retail Ccom. Nebr. Public Power Dist., 1997; active Overall Econ. Devel. Plan, 1998. Active Knox County 911 Sys., 1995—98, Creighton Devel. Corp., 1995—98, Temporary Housing Action Team, 1994—95, Sgt Bluff Planning and Zoning, 1985—86; Sunday sch. tchr. Dakota City United Meth. Ch., 1998—2000; bd. dirs. N.E. Loess Hills Resource and Conservation and Devel., West Point, Nebr., 1998—2000; pres. Hwy. 35 Expy. Com., 1998—2000; active Pioneer Valley Days Com., 1986—87. Mem.: Nebr. Econ. Devel. Assn., Nebr. Planning and Zoning Assn,., Midwest Sociol. Soc., Great Plains Sociol. Soc., Am. Sociol. Assn., Assn. Humanist Sociology, Jaycees (bd. dirs. Kimball County 1977—78, v.p. Kimball County 1979, v.p. Lyons 1980, regional dir. Nebr. 1981, pres. Council Bluffs 1982, pres. Sgt. Bluff 1985—87, regional dir. Iowa 1988, chmn. bd. Sgt. Bluff 1988, Iowa Hawkeye Corps 1989—2003), Alpha Kappa Delta (pres. 2000). Avocation: motorcycles/motorcycle riding. Home: 29338 US Highway 212 Lot 733 Gettysburg SD 57442-8625 Personal E-mail: grizza@hotmail.com.

BURGE, WILLARD, JR., software company executive; b. Johnson City, NY, Oct. 2, 1938; s. Willard Sr. and Catherine Bernice (Matthews) B.; m. Carol Crockenberg, June 16, 1961; children: Willard III, Pennie Lynn. Registered profl. engr., Ohio. Indsl. engr. Harnischfeger Corp., Escanaba, Mich., 1966-67; sr. indsl. engr. Gen. Electric, Ladson, S.C., 1968-74, advanced mfg. engr. Mentor, Ohio, 1971-74; corp. staff engr. Eaton Corp., Willoughby Hills, Ohio, 1974-79, supr. N/C programming, 1979-80, supr. mfg. engring., 1980-82, mgr. mfg. systems engring., 1982-87; bus. unit mgr. MSC Products, Eaton Corp., Costa Mesa, Calif., 1987-91; pres., CEO CAM Software, Inc., Provo, Utah, 1991-93; chief exec. officer Key Svcs., Cypress, Calif., 1993—. Bd. dirs. CAM Software, Inc.; presenter in field. With U.S. Army, 1957. Mem. Soc. Mfg. Engrs. Republican. Avocations: photography, computers, start-up businesses. Home and Office: 1260 Oakmont Rd 53H Seal Beach CA 90740 E-mail: wburgejr@verizon.net.

BURGE, WILLIAM LEE, retired credit manager; b. Atlanta, June 27, 1918; s. William Frederick and Leona (Payne) B.; m. Willette Richey, Feb. 27, 1937; children: Judith, William Roger. Student, Ga. State U. Bus. Adminstrn., 1937—42; LLD (hon.), Mercer U., 1978, Ga. State U., 2005. With Equifax Inc. (formerly Retail Credit Co.), 1936-88, br. mgr. Greensboro, NC, 1949-51, div. mgr. Pitts., 1951-58, v.p. Atlanta, 1959-65, exec. v.p., 1964-65, pres., 1965—, CEO, 1967-83, chmn. bd., 1976-88; chmn. Equifax Inc. (Equifax Inc. affiliates), 1988, ret., 1988; chmn. emeritus Equifax Inc. (Equifax Services Ltd.), Canada. Ret. dir. First Nat. Bank Atlanta Nat. Svc. Industries, Informes de Centrales de Mex.; chmn. Fernbank, Inc., 1951-57. Gen. chmn. United Way, Atlanta, 1961; chmn. United Negro Coll. Fund, 1974-75; regional chmn. Nat. Alliance of Businessmen, 1969-70; chmn. bd. regents Univ. System Ga., 1972-73; mem. coll. accreditation commn. So. Assn. Colls. and Schs.; mem. Commn. Postsecondary Edn.; trustee Atlanta Arts Alliance, YMCA; mem. bd. Central Atlanta Progress; mem. Gov.'s Adv. Council on Job Tng. Coordination, 1985-88; bd. dirs. Atlanta chpt. ARC; pres. Mus. Nat. History, 1995-96, Fernbank Mus.; chair Ga. Consortium for Fin. Literacy. Served with AUS, World War II. Named Atlanta's Young Man of Year, 1948, one of Atlanta's Leaders of Tomorrow Time mag., 1952, Alumnus of Yr. Ga. award State U., 1968, 87. Mem. Conf. Bd., Atlanta C. of C. (pres. 1966), Nat. C. of C. (panel on privacy), Jr. C. of C. (pres. 1947-48) Clubs: Kiwanis (pres. 1965). Office: Equifax Inc Ste 240 3060 Peachtree Rd Atlanta GA 30305 Office Phone: 404-760-3772. Business E-Mail: lee.burge@equifax.com.

BURGEE, JOHN HENRY, architect; b. Chgo., Aug. 28, 1933; s. Joseph Zeno and Helen (Dooley) B.; m. Gwendolyn Mary Henson, June 30, 1956; 1 son, John Gerard. BArch, U. Notre Dame, 1956, DEngr (hon.), 1983. Supt. constrn. Holabird & Root & Burgee, Chgo., 1955-56; project mgr. Naess & Murphy, Chgo., 1958-61; adminstr. design, project architect C. F. Murphy Assos., Chgo., 1961-65; assoc. ptnr. C. F. Murphy Assocs., 1965-67, ptnr., 1967; assoc. Philip Johnson (Architects), NYC, 1967-68; ptnr. Johnson/Burgee, NYC, 1968-82, John Burgee Architects, NYC, 1982-98, Santa Barbara, Calif., 1998—. Chmn. Archtl. Rev. Bd., Bronxville, N.Y., 1974-75; chmn. Bronxville Planning Commn., 1975-77 Works include, I.D.S. Center, Mpls., Niagara Falls Conv. Center, Pennzoil Place, Houston, Crystal Cathedral, Los Angeles, AT&T Hdqrs., N.Y.C., PPG Hdqrs., Pitts., Transco Tower, Houston, Republic Bank, Houston, Nat. Center for Performing Arts, Bombay, 101 California Street, San Francisco, International Place, Boston, 190 South LaSalle Street, Chicago, IBM Headquarters, Atlanta, Mus. of Broadcasting, New York Canadian Broadcast Ctr., Toronto, Takashamya Dept. Store, N.Y., Capital Holding Ctr., Louisville, Puerto de Europa, Madrid, One Detroit Ctr., Marina Hotel and Shopping Ctr., Singapore, Ch. St. Mary, Lakeville, Conn. Pres. German-Am. Club, Bad Kreuznach, Germany, 1957-58; chmn. bldg. material sect. Met. Crusade of Mercy, Chgo., 1966-67; pres. Chgo. Br. North Montessori Sch. Bd., 1962-63, Lawrence Park Hilltop Assn., 1974-75; chmn. architecture com. Statue of Liberty/Ellis Island Centennial Commn.; mem. adv. coun. Coll. Engring. U. Notre Dame, 1982-88; bd. dirs. Lenox Hill Hosp., 1982-91, Parsons Sch. of Design, 1985-92, U. Notre Dame, 1988—, Chgo. Athenaeum, 1989-92, Music Acad. of the West, 2002-, 1st vice chmn., 2003, chmn., 2005. With US Army, 1956—58. Recipient Reynolds Aluminum prize, 1978, honor award U. Notre Dame, 1981, Chgo. Architecture award. Fellow AIA, Urban Design Inst.; mem. Archtl. League N.Y. (dir.), Inst. Architecture and Urban Studies (dir. 1983, chmn., pres. 1984) Clubs: Saddle Cycle (Chgo.), Arts (Chgo.), University (Chgo.), Shenarock Shore (Rye, N.Y), Am. Yacht, Century Assn. Home: 639 Hot Springs Rd Santa Barbara CA 93108-2030 E-mail: burgeearchitect@cox.net.

BURGER, EDMUND GANES, architect; b. Yerington, Nev., Mar. 28, 1930; s. Edmund Ganes and Rose Catherine (Kobe) B.; m. Shirley May Pratini, Jan. 21, 1968; 1 dau., Jane Lee. B.M.E., U. Santa Clara, 1951; B.Arch., U. Pa., 1959. Engr. Gen. Electric Co., 1951-52; design engr. U. Calif. Radiation Lab., 1952-57; John Stewardson fellow in architecture, 1959; architect Wurster, Bernardi & Emmons, San Francisco, 1960-63; founder Burger & Coplans, Inc. (Architects), San Francisco, 1964, pres., 1964-79; owner Edmund Burger (Architect), 1979—. Guest lectr. U. Calif., Berkeley. Important works include Acorn Housing Project, Oakland, Calif., Crescent Village Housing Project, Suisun City, Calif., Coplans residence, San Francisco, Betel Housing Project, San Francisco, Grand View Housing Project, San Francisco, Albany (Calif.) Oaks Housing, Grow Homes, San Pablo, Calif., Mariposa Housing, Dunleavy Plaza Housing, Potrero Ct. Housing, San Francisco, Lee residence, Kentfield, Calif., Burger residences, Lafayette, Calif., Oceanside, Oreg., and El Cerrito, Calif., Yamhill Valley Vineyards Winery, McMinneville, Oreg., Portico De Mar, shop and restaurant complex, Barcelona, Spain, Hendrickson residence, Newport Beach, Calif., Hamilton residence, Winters, Calif., Sanders residence, Yuba City, Calif., Strack/Villars residence, Kentfield, Calif., Breton residence, Oakland, Visitors Facilities Yosemite Nat. Park, Calif., Rogers Residence, El Cerrito, Calif, Stern Grove Outdoor Theater, San Francisco, Petersen Residence, El Cerrito, Blum Residence, Beverly Hills, Calif., Pride and Joy Presch.-Day Care Ctr., El Cerrito, Calif.; author: Geomorphic Architecture, 1986. Recipient citation for excellence in community architecture AIA, 1969, award of merit AIA, award of merit Homes for Better Living, 1970, 79, 1st Honor award, 1973, 81, Holiday award for a beautiful Am., 1970, Honor award 4th Biennial HUD awards for design excellence, 1970, Bay Area awards for design excellence, 1969, 74, 78, Apts. of Year award Archtl. Record, 1972, Houses of Year award, 1973, Calif. Affordable Housing Competition award, 1981, HUD Building Value into Housing award, 1981, Community Design award Calif. Council AIA, 1986; design grant Nat. Endowment for Arts, 1980, HUD, 1980; constrn. grant HUD, 1981. Office: 8445 Wildcat Dr El Cerrito CA 94530 Office Phone: 510-237-8336.

BURGER, HENRY G., linguist, anthropologist, writer; b. NYC, June 27, 1923; s. B. William and Terese R. (Felleman) Burger; m. Barbara G. Smith, Nov. 29, 1991. BA with honors (Pulitzer scholar), Columbia Coll., 1947; MA, Columbia U., 1965, PhD in Cultural Anthropology (State Doctoral fellow), 1967. Indsl. engr. various orgns., 1947-51; Midwest mfrs. rep., 1952-55; social sci. cons. Chgo. and NYC, 1956-67; anthropologist Southwestern Coop. Ednl. Lab., Albuquerque, 1967-69; assoc. prof. anthropology and edn. U. Mo., Kansas City, 1969-73, prof., 1973-93, prof. emeritus, 1993—, founding mem. univ. wide doctoral faculty, 1974-93; founder, pub. The Wordtree, Overland Park, Kans., 1984—. Lectr. CUNY; adj. prof. ednl. anthropology U. N.Mex., 1969; anthrop. cons. US VA Hosp., Kansas City, 1971—72; spkr. in field; columnist linguistic column New Times, New Verbs, 1988—. Author: Ethno-Pedagogy, 1968, 2nd edit., 1968; editor, compiler: The Wordtree, a Branching Dictionary for Solving Phys. and Social Problems, 1984, selected for exhibit at 3 insts., selected as topic Cambridge Ency. of the English Lang., 1995—, 7 time citee Oxford English Dictionary, mem. editl. bd. Coun. Anthropology and Edn., 1975—80; contbr. to anthologies, articles to profl. jours.; globally interviewed by Voice of America, 2002. Capt. US Army, 1943—46. NSF Instl. grantee, 1970. Fellow: World Acad. Art and Sci., Royal Anthrop. Inst. Gt. Britain (life), Am. Anthrop. Assn. (life); mem.: Academie Europeenne des Scis., English-Speaking Union (v.p. Kansas City chpt. 1995—96), Am. Soc. Semiotics, Kans. Acad. Sci. (life), Dictionary Soc. N.Am. (life; mem. terminology com.), Arts et Lettres (corr.), Internat. Assn. Semiotic Studies, European Assn. Lexicography, Columbia U. Club, Phi Beta Kappa. Achievements include discovery of branchability of processes (corresponding, for materials, to the periodic table of elements); research in computerized causality and reasoning. Office: The Wordtree 10876 Bradshaw St Overland Park KS 66210-1148 Office Phone: 913-469-1010. Business E-Mail: burger@cctr.umkc.edu. *The computer analyzes prose information into tabulation, whence it can be re-formed diversely. Therefore computerization has revolutionized my authorship from textbooks to reference books.*

BURGER, HERBERT FRANCIS, retired advertising agency executive; b. Ligonier, Pa., Mar. 5, 1930; s. Adolph G. and Elizabeth (Johannsen) Burger; m. Jane Coulter, Oct. 1, 1966; children: Matthew F., Jennifer. BS in Econs, Thiel Coll., Greenville, Pa., 1952; MA in Journalism, Syracuse U., NY, 1955. C. Mgmt. trainee Joy Mfg. Co., 1955-56; account exec. Ketchum, MacLeod & Grove, Pitts., 1956-58, Marsteller Inc., Pitts.,

1958-65; with Creamer Inc., Pitts., 1965-76; pres. Creamer Inc. (Pitts. divsn.), 1976-86; chmn., ptnr. St. George Group, Inc., Pitts., 1986-98; ret., 1998. Bd. dirs. Overly Mft. Co., Pitts., Offices of Promotion; chmn. Pitts. Media Group, Pitts. Downtown Partnership; pres. Speedwell Enterprises, 1986—. Chmn. Pitts. Downtown Plan, Pitts. Task Force. With US Army, 1953—55. Mem.: Pitts. Press Club, Pitts. Advt. Club (dir.), Grove City Country Club, Longue Vue Country Club, Duquesne Club. Republican. Lutheran. Home: 301 Wildberry Rd Pittsburgh PA 15238

BURGER, LESLIE B., library director, library association executive; m. Alan Burger; children: Benjamin, Sarah, Jessica. BS, Southern Conn. State Coll., 1973; MLS, U. Md. Coll. Park, 1974; MS in Orgnl. Behavior, U. Hartford, 1988. Cmty. info. specialist Bridgeport Pub. Libr., Conn., 1974—76; libr. specialist Conn. State Libr., Hartford, 1976—77, planning dir., 1977—85, network dir., 1985—87; project specialist, head libr. devel. NJ State Libr., Trenton, 1988—91; prin. Libr. Devel. Solutions, Princeton Juntion, NJ, 1991—; dir. Princeton Pub. Libr., NJ, 1999—. Named Alumna of Yr., Coll. Info. Studies, U. Md., 2005; recipient Tribute to Women award, Princeton YWCA, 2003, Libr. award, NY Times, 2004. Mem.: NJ Libr. Assn. (pres. 2001—02), Ind. Librarians Exchange Round Table (chair 1998—2000), ALA (Conn. Chpt. Councilor 1984—87, coun. mem. 2002—, pres.-elect 2005—06, pres. 2006—07, immediate past pres. 2007—), Conn. Libr. Assn. (pres. 1982—83), New England Libr. Assn. (Conn. Chpt. Rep. 1979—81), Assn. Specialized and Coop. Libr. Agencies (chair State Libr. Agy. Sect. 1981—82, pres. 1995—96). Avocations: reading, gardening, travel, cooking. Office: Princeton Pub Libr 65 Witherspoon St Princeton NJ 08542 Office Phone: 609-924-8822. Office Fax: 609-924-7937. Business E-Mail: lburger@princetonlibrary.org.*

BURGER, MAX MARCEL, biochemist; b. Zurich, Switzerland, July 8, 1933; came to U.S., 1960, naturalized, 1966; s. Joseph and Olga (Humbel) B.; m. Monique Sautter, July 22, 1961 (div. 1984); children: Christina, Maya, Catherine, Elizabeth MD, U. Zurich, 1959; PhD in Biochemistry, Washington U., St. Louis, 1964. Intern hosps., Paris and Zurich, 1957-59; instr. biochemistry Washington U., 1964-65; mem. faculty Princeton U., 1965-72, prof. biochem. scis., 1971-72, mem. adv. coun., 1972—2003; prof. biochemistry U. Basel, Switzerland, 1972—2004; chmn. Biocenter U. Basel, Switzerland, 1973-78; dir. Friedrich Miescher Inst., Basel, 1987—2000; chmn. Novartis Sci. Bd., Basel, 1999—. Investigator, corp. mem. Marine Biol. Lab., Woods Hole, Mass., 1966—; mem. study sects. NIH, 1968—72; mem. fellwship panels NSF, 1968—72; mem. Roche Rsch. Found., 1975—2001; mem., v.p. Swiss NRC, 1975—91; adv. Ger. Ministry Tech. and Israeli Nat. Coun. R&D, 1978—; dir. CIBA-GEIGY, Inc., 1980—96; chmn. Nat. Med. and Nat. Biol. Rsch. Coun., 1981—84; mem. Gen Motors Cancer Rsch. Found., 1982—84; mem. sci. adv. bd. Inst. Pasteur, 1991—99; v.p. bd. dirs. Oxford Glyco Scis. (U.K.) Ltd., 1995—2003; chmn. bd. dirs. Novartis Agr. Discovery Inst., Inc., La Jolla, Calif., 1998—2000; bd. dirs. Genomics Inst. of Novartis Found., Inc., La Jolla, 1998—. Editor: BBA Cancer Revs., 1974—81; mng. editor: Cellular Biochemistry, 1981—; author: numerous books; contbr. articles to profl. jours. Hon. fgn. mem. Am. Acad. of Arts and Scis., 1988; founding mem. Senate Hermann von Helmholtz-Gemeinschaft Deutscher Forschungszentren, Bonn, 1995—; mem. sci. com. DKFZ, Heidelberg, 1993—2002. With Swiss Army, 1952—60. Decorated Order of Merit 1st Class, Fed. Republic Germany, 2005; recipient Waksman medal, 1971, Otto Naegeli prize, 1975, Cancer prize Swiss Cancer League, 1999; Helen Hay Whitney fellow, 1964-66 Mem.: Academia Europaea, Swiss Med. Assn., Soc. Biol. Chemists, Internat. Cancer Found. (chmn. 1998—), Internat. Union Against Cancer (coun. 1978—82, exec. coun. 1982—98), Internat. Union Biophysics (chmn. commn. membrane and cell biophysics 1975—80), Precolumbian Collectors Club, Swiss Acad. Ski Club. Home: 66 Hinckley Rd Woods Hole MA 02543-1009 Address: 5 Pfaffenrainstrasse CH4103 Bottmingen Switzerland E-mail: max.burger@group.Novartis.com.

BURGERT, DAVID LEE, lawyer; b. Kansas City, Kans., Jan. 30, 1959; s. Marion Lawrence and Barbara Jean (Marmont) B.; m. Amy Marlyse Wilson; children: Melissa Christine, Grace Josephine. BS summa cum laude, Ohio U., 1980; JD, U. Mich., 1983. Bar: Tex. 1983, U.S. Dist. Ct. (so. dist.) Tex. 1984, U.S. Dist. Ct. (we. dist.) (no. dist., 2002) Tex. 1999, U.S. Ct. Appeals (5th cir.) 1984, U.S. Tax Ct. 1993, U.S. Ct. Appeals (fed. and 8th cirs.) 1996, U.S. Dist. Ct. (ea. dist.) Tex. 2006; bd. cert. civil trial lawyer, 1990, Tex. Bd. Legal Spec. Assoc. Vinson & Elkins, Houston, 1983-86, Porter & Clements, Houston, 1986-90, ptnr., 1991-93, Porter & Hedges, Houston, 1993—. Named Tex. Superlawyer in Intellectual Property Litigation, Tex. Monthly mag., 2003—, One of Houston's Top Lawyers, Tex. Mag., 2005. Office: Porter & Hedges 1000 Main St 36th Fl Houston TX 77002-6336 Home Phone: 713-856-6992. Business E-Mail: dlburgert@porterhedges.com.

BURGESS, ANN WOLBERT, nursing educator; Van Ameringen prof. nursing U. Pa., Phila.; prof. of psychiat. and mental health nursing Boston Coll. Author: Advanced Practice Psychiatric Nursing, 1998, Psychiatric Nursing: Promoting Mental Health, 1997, Child Trauma I: Issues & Research, 1992, Community Mental Health: Target Populations, 1976, Rape: Victims of Crisis, 1974; co-editor: (with Robert K. Kessler and John E. Douglas) Sexual Homicide: Patterns and Movies, 1988, Rape and Sexual Assault II, 1985; co-author: (with Robert R. Hazelwood) Practical Aspects of Rape Investigation: A Multidisciplinary Approach, 3d edit., 1993, (with Robert Ann Prentsky) Forensic Management of Sexual Offenders, 2000, (with Robert R. Hazelwood and Park Elliott Dietz) Autoerotic Fatalities, 1983, (with Bruce A. Baldwin) Crisis Intervention Theory and Practice: A Clinical Handbook, 1981, (with Nicholas Groth and Suzanne M. Sgroi) Sexual Assault of Children and Adolescents, 1978. Mem.: Inst. Medicine, NAS. Office: Boston Coll Sch Nursing Cushing Hall 414 140 Commonwealth Ave Chestnut Hill MA 02467

BURGESS, BRIAN LOUIS, state supreme court justice; b. Washington, Jan. 14, 1951; s. Louis Arthur and Barbara Ann (Babcock) B.; m. Maureeen Elizabeth O'Connor, Oct. 24, 1975; children— Brian Thomas, Devin Louis. BA, Coll. of Holy Cross, Worcester, 1973; JD, Villanova U. Sch. of Law, 1976. Bar: Vt. 1976, Mass. 1977, U.S. Dist. Ct. Vt. 1979, U.S. Ct. Appeals (2d cir.) 1979, U.S. Supreme Ct. 1980. Asst. atty. gen. Office Vt. Atty. Gen., Montpelier, 1978-81, chief prosecutor medicaid fraud control unit, 1981-83, dep. atty. gen., 1985-92, judge Vt. Dist. Ct., 1992-2004, administrative trial judge, 2004, assoc. justice Vt. Supreme Ct., 2005-. Dep. commr. Vt. Dept. Labor and Industry, 1983-84, commr., 1984; chmn. Vt. Elec. Licensing Bd., 1984; chmn. Vt. Ski Tramway Safety Bd., 1984. Nat. Assn. Attys. Gen., Nat. Dist. Attys. Assn. Office: Vt Supreme Ct 109 State St Montpelier VT 05609*

BURGESS, CHARLES ORVILLE, history professor; b. Portland, Oreg., Jan. 18, 1932; s. Rex Orville and Glendora Almanda (Sundrud) B.; m. Cora Cloepfil, June 22, 1952; children: Donna Claire Majer, Jo Dell Nicholls, Robert Charles; m. Patricia Stewart Anderson, Apr. 22, 1976; children: Marc Richard Anderson, Brian Stewart Anderson, Tricia Louise Crozier, Kristen Anne Klein. BA, U. Oreg., 1957; MS (Danforth fellow), U. Wis., 1958, PhD, 1962; Nat. Postdoctoral fellow, Harvard U., 1967-68. Asst. prof. U. Calif., Riverside, 1962-64; asst. prof. history edn. U. Wash., Seattle, 1964-66, assoc. prof., 1966-70, prof., 1970—, chmn. area ednl. policy studies, 1970-92; prof. emeritus, 1992. V.p. divsn. F Am. Ednl. Rsch. Assn., 1977-79; fgn. expert Peoples Republic of China, 1984-85. Author: The Origins of American Thought (published in China as Meiguo Sixiang Yuanyuan); 1988, (with M.L. Borrowman) What Doctrines to Embrace, 1969, Profile of an American Philanthropist (Nettie Fowler McCormick), 1962; co-editor: (with Charles Strickland) G. Stanley Hall on Natural Education, 1965; co-author: (with Y. Yang and G. Zhu) Cultivating the World of Selfhood (published in China as Kaituo Zi Wode Shijie), 1997. Wash. com. civil rights ACLU, 1965-67; bd. dirs. Seattle Folklore Soc., 1966—. With USAF, 1950-54. Mem.: History of Edn. Soc. (pres. 1971—72), Phi Beta Kappa. Home: 14350 22nd Ave SW Burien WA 98166

BURGESS, CLARA SKIPWITH, retired principal; b. Newburgh, NY, Nov. 3, 1930; d. Luther Kerman and Clara Bell (Pickens) Skipwith; m. Joseph Edward Burgess, May 14, 1966 (dec. Sept. 1968). BA, Hunter Coll., 1953, MA, 1954; Profl. Diploma Adminstrv. Supervision, Fordham U., 1970, PhD, 1975. Early childhood instr. N.Y. Inst. Blind, Bronx, 1953—54; tchr. kindergarten, early childhood tchr. trainer, exceptional edn. Pub. Sch. 43, Bronx, 1954—69; supr. Headstart Dist. 7, Bronx, 1970; evaluator Headstart and Pre-Kindergarten Funding, 1970—71; dir. Morrisania Early Childhood Learning Ctr. 3 Dist. 9, Bronx, 1971—72; prin. Cmty. Elem. Sch. 236, Dist. 9, Bronx, 1972—91, ret., 1991. Recreational counselor Pub. Sch. 43, Bronx, 1955—61; tchr. piano Pub. Sch. 18, Bronx, 1960—61, dir. ctr., 1961, tchr. dance, 1961—63; adj. instr. early childhood curriculum devel. CCNY, 1972—; rep. Non-Govtl. Orgn. at UN, 1980—; presenter in field. Women's editor Cmty. Jour. of Air, Radio Sta. WLIB, 1964—69. N.Atlantic rep. Ednl. Advancement Found.; workshop presenter Women's Conf., Nairobi, Kenya, 1985, Beijing Plus Ten, UN, 2005; bd. dirs. Wiltwyck Sch. Boys, 1967—. Named Tchr. of Yr., Bronx Boro Pres.; grantee, Ford Found., 1970. Mem.: Fordham Assn. Sch. Suprs. and Adminstrs., Coalition Assns. Black and Puerto Rican Educators and Suprs., Urban Educators Comparative Studies (founder), Bronx Reading Coun., N.Y. Assn. Black Educators, Nat. Soc. Edn. Young Children, Nat. Soc. Study Edn., Alpha Kappa Alpha. Home: 609 W 147th St New York NY 10031

BURGESS, DAVID, lawyer; b. Detroit, Nov. 30, 1948; s. Roger Edward and Claire Theresa (Sullivan) B.; m. Rebecca Culbertson Stuart, 1985 (dec. 1988); m. Catherine Mounteer, 1993; children: Jalil Riahi, Leila Riahi, Bryan Valentine, Grace Catherine. BS in Fgn. Svc., Georgetown U., 1970, MS in Fgn. Svc., 1978, JD, 1978. Bar: D.C. 1978, U.S. Dist. Ct. D.C. 1979, U.S. Ct. Appeals (D.C. cir.) 1979, U.S. Ct. Appeals (fed. cir.) 1988, U.S. Ct. Internat. Trade 1988. Rsch. asst. Georgetown U. Sch. Bus. Adminstrn., Washington, 1975, asst. to dean, 1975-76; rsch. assoc., prof. Acad. in the Pub. Svc., Washington, 1976-79; asst. editor Securities Regulation Law Report, Washington; legal editor Internat. Trade Reporter Bur. Nat. Affairs, Washington, 1978-79; atty. Cadwalader, Wickersham & Taft, Washington, 1979-81; mng. editor Bur. Nat. Affairs, Washington, 1981-82; dir. U.S. Peace Corps, Niamey, Niger, 1982-84, Rabat, Morocco, 1984-85; dir. policy planning, mgmt. Peace Corps, Washington, 1985-87; dir. Bur. Human Rights and Humanitarian Affairs U.S. Dept. State, Washington, 1987-92; regional dir. Lawyers for Bush-Quayle Re-Election Campaign, 1992; chief party Rwanda Dem. and Governance Project, 1994, Russia NGO Sector Project, Moscow, 1994. Dir. democracy and civil soc. program, sr. advisor World Learning, Washington, 1995, dir. U.S. Democracy Fellows program, Washington, 1995-2002, dir. bus. devel., 2002-03; exec. v.p. Am.'s Devel. Found., Alexandria, Va., 2003-04; democracy cons., 2004—; adj. prof., Inst. World Politics, Washington, 2002—. Author: Financing Local Government, 1977, 2d edit., 1978, Preparation of the Local Budget, 2 vols., 1976, 2d edit., 1978, Local Government Accounting Fundamentals, 2d edit., 1977, Understanding Federal Assistance Programs, 2d edit., 1978, The POW/MIA Issue: Perspectives on the National League of Families, 1978; contbr. articles to publs. Mem. adv. com. Arlington County Fiscal Affairs, 1993-94; mem. pres. coun. Mary Washington Coll.; bd. mem. U.S. Selective Svc. Sys., Region II Va., 2002-. Mem. D.C. Bar Assn., Hoyas Unltd. (pres. 1992-94), Federalist Soc., Georgetown U. Alumni Assn. (bd. govs. 1975-00, class rep. 1971-91, mem. alumni senate 2000—). Republican. Roman Catholic. Home and Office: 3115 1st Pl N Arlington VA 22201-1037 E-mail: burgessdavid4@aol.com.

BURGESS, DAVID LOWRY, artist; b. Phila., Apr. 27, 1940; s. Eric Turner and Ruth Elizabeth (McNees) Burgess; m. Janet Levengood, Mar. 25, 1960; children: Kirsten Deidre, Audrey Veronica, Vashti Gabrielle. Grad., Pa. Acad. of Fine Art, U. Pa., 1961. Lectr. Phila. Coll. Art, 1964-66; arts advisor Edn. Devel. Center, 1966-68; mem. faculty Harvard U. Sch. Edn., Cambridge, Mass., 1967-68; instr. Boston U., 1969; prof. Mass. Coll. Art, 1969-89; fellow Ctr. Advanced Visual Studies M.I.T., 1971-89; dean Carnegie-Mellon U. Coll. Fine Arts, Pitts., 1989-92, A.W. Mellon prof. art, 1992—; dir. SIMLAB, 1995-97; Koopman disting. chair in art Hartford (Conn.) U. Sch. Art, 2000. Mem. Nat. Humanities faculty, 1968—80; disting. artist ECHO-UQAM, Montreal, Canada; disting. fellow Studio Creative Inquiry, Carnegie Mellon U.; mem. Ctr. for the Arts and Soc. Carnegie Mellon U.; advisor EXPO 2000, Hannover, Germany. Author: Fragments, 1967, Looking and Listening, 1969, Memory, Environment, Utopia, 1973, Burgess: The Quiet Axis Trècarrè, Montreal, Canada, 1987; one-man shows include Inst. Contemporary Art, Boston, 1971, Carpetner Ctr., Harvard U., 1975, MIT, 1978, U. Que., Montreal, 1984, De Cordova Mus., Mass., 1985, 1988, Pa. Acad. Fin Arts Mus., 1987—88, exhibited in group shows at Boston Mus. Fine Arts Elements Exhbn., 1971, Multiple Interaction Team, 1972—74, CAYAC, Spain and Latin Am., 1972—74, Documenta 6, Kassel, Germany, 1977, Vienna Biennal, 1979, Sky Arts Conf. MIT, 1981—83, 1986, Ars Electronica, Austria, 1982, 1986, Kunst Acad., Germany, 1982, Artists Earthwatch, N.Mex., 1984, Monocle, Hamburg, Kunsthalle, Germany, 1985, De Cordova Mus., 1985, Pa. Acad. Fine Arts, 1987—88, Herning Kunst Mus., Denmark, 1989, Kunstverein, Karlsrahe, Germany, 1989, Contemporary Mus., Helsinki, Finland, 1989, Art Transition, 1991, Differentiel, Aix en Provence, France, 1992, Mu Gallery, Boston, 1993, MIT Mus., Cambridge, 1994, Tufts U., Mass., 1995, Pitts. Biennal, 1996, Nagoya City Mus., 1997, Fed. Res. Bank, Boston, 1998, Common Light, Cambridge, 2000, Joselott Mus. Hartford Sch. Art, 2000, Pitts. Ctr. for the Arts, 2003, Represented in permanent collections Boston Mus. Fine Arts, Houghton Libr., Harvard U., Nat. Collection Fine Arts, Washington, Smithsonian Collection, Pa. Acad. Fine Arts, Herning Kunstmuseum, Denmark, De Cordova Mus., Lincoln, Mass., SkyArt, Delphi, Greece, Mandala Pitts. Ctr. Arts, Lincoln Ctr. Archives, NYC; appearances: (TV series) Nova, Artists in the Lab, 1982; Artists Earthwatch, KNME, 1985; Smithsonian World, 1987; New VR Techs. MSNBC, 1997; Seed of the Infinite Absolute, 2001; appearances (TV series) KQED, San Francisco, 2005, Hartford Museum of Political Life, Hartford, Conn., 2002, Pitts. Ctr. for the Arts, 2002. Founding mem. exec. bd. Cambridge Arts Coun.; mem. adv. bd. Art, Edn. and Ams. Recipient Am. Acad. Arts and Letters, Nat. Inst. Arts and Letters award, 1972, Gold award, Le Devoir, Montreal, 1989, Leonardo DeVinci Space Art award, Nat. Space Soc., 2006; grantee Nat. Endowment Arts, 1977—78, 1984, 1986, Rockefeller Found., 1979—80, 1985—87, Mass. Coun. Arts and Humanities, 1982, 1987—88, Mass. Artists Found., 1983, Cambridge Arts Coun., 2000, Kellogg Found., 2001, Berkman Fund, 2004; Guggenheim fellow, 1973—74. Address: 1375 Cordova Rd Pittsburgh PA 15206-1430 Office Phone: 412-268-7294. Business E-Mail: lb30@andrew.cmu.edu.

BURGESS, DONNA ANGELE, researcher; d. Jim Burgess. BSc, U. Houston, 2003. Rsch. asst. Vet. Affairs, Houston, U. Tex., Houston; rsch.coord. MD Anderson Cancer Ctr., Houston. Vol. Big Bros. Big Sisters; para counselor Houston Area Women's Ctr. Mem.: APS, APA, Neuropsychological Soc., Sigma Xi, Psi Chi. Avocations: art, photography, nature, reading.

BURGESS, HAYDEN FERN (POKA LAENUI), lawyer; b. Honolulu, May 5, 1946; s. Ned E. and Nora (Lee) B.; m. Puanani Sonoda, Aug. 28, 1968. B in Polit. Sci., U. Hawaii, JD, 1976. Bar: Hawaii 1976, U.S. Tax Ct., U.S. Ct. Appeals (9th cir.). Pvt. practice, Waianae, Hawaii, 1976—; pres. Hawaii Coun. 1993 and Beyond, Honolulu, 1991—; exec. dir. Waianae Coast Cmty. Mental Health Ctr., 1997—. V.p. World Coun. Indigenous Peoples before UN, 1984-90; human rights adv., writer, speaker in field; pres. Pacific and Asia Coun. Indigenous Peoples; cons. on indigenous affairs, 1984; indigenous expert to ILO Conv.; expert UN seminar on effects of racism and racial discriminations on social and econ. rels. between indigenous peoples and states, 1989—; del. Native Hawaiian Convention, chmn.; lead atty. Legal Svcs. Children, 2004-; radio , TV host Hawaiian Nat. Broadcast Corp., 1991-. Trustee Office Hawaiian Affairs, Honolulu, 1982-86; mem. Swedish Nat. Commn. on Mus., 1986; leader Hawaiian Independence Movement; mem. Hawaiian Sovereignty Elections Coun. Named Outstanding Exec. Dir., Mental Health Assn. Hawaii, 2007.

BURGESS, JAMES EDWARD, publishing executive; b. LaCrosse, Wis., Apr. 5, 1936; s. William Thomas and Margaret (Forseth) B.; m. Catherine Eleanor, Dec. 20, 1958; children: Karen E. Burgess Hardy, J. Peter, Sydney Ann, R. Curtis Student, Wayland Acad.; BS, U. Wis. Pub. Ind. Record, Helena, Mont., 1969-71, Tribune, LaCrosse, Wis., 1971-74; v.p. newspapers Lee Enterprises, Davenport, Iowa, 1974-81, exec. v.p., 1981-84, dir., 1974-85, Madison (Wis.) Newspapers, Inc., 1975-93, pres., 1984-93; pub. Wis. State Jour., Madison, 1984-94. Chmn. Edgewood Coll., Madison, 1984—; founder Future Madison, Inc.; chmn. SAVE Commn.; chair bd. dirs. Madison Cmty. Found., U. Wis. Med. Found.; v.p. Madison Mus. Modern Art. Mem. Wis. Newspaper Assn. (past pres.), Inland Daily Press Assn. (pres., chmn. 1982-84), Wis. Assn. Lakes (bd. dirs., pres., chair). Home: 125 N Hamilton St Madison WI 53703

BURGESS, JAMES HARLAND, physics professor, researcher; b. Portland, Oreg., May 11, 1929; s. Harland F. B. and Marion U. (Burgess); m. Dorothy R. Crosby, June 10, 1951; children: Karen, Donald, Joanne. BS, Wash. State U., 1949, MS, 1951; PhD, Washington U., St. Louis, 1955. Sr. engr. Sylvania Electric Products, Mountain View, Calif., 1955-56; research assoc. Stanford U., Palo Alto, Calif., 1956-57, asst. prof. physics, 1958-62; assoc. prof. Washington U., St. Louis, 1962-73, prof., 1973-98, prof. emeritus, 1998—. Cons. in field, 1956-66. Mem. Am. Phys. Soc., Am. Assn. Physics Tchrs., Phi Beta Kappa, Sigma Xi Office: Washington U Physics Dept 1 Brookings Dr Saint Louis MO 63130-4899 Business E-Mail: jhb@wuphys.wustl.edu.

BURGESS, JOHN ALLEN, lawyer; b. Waltham, Mass., Feb. 6, 1951; s. William A. and Joyce E. (Finkle) B.; m. Nancy S. Adams; children: Rachel, Eleanor. BA summa cum laude, Yale U., 1973; JD cum laude, Harvard U., 1976. Bar: Mass. Former co-chair Hale and Dorr, Boston, 1976—; ptnr. Wilmer Hale, Boston. Adj. prof. Fletcher Sch. Law and Diplomacy Tufts U. Spkrs. in field. Trustee Roxbury Latin Sch.; mem. bd. Mass. Found. Humanities. Coun. fellow U.S. State Dept., 1987. Best Lawyers in Am. 2006, Listed as leading lawyer in IT by Legal Media Grp., Top 100 Mass. Super Lawyers 2004, named as one of top 5 IPO lawyers by IPO Jour. Mem. Coun. on Fgn. Rels., ABA, Mass. Bar Assn., Boston Bar Assn., life mem. US Naval Inst. Office: Wilmer Hale 60 State St Boston MA 02109 Office Fax: 617-526-5000. Business E-Mail: john.burgess@wilmerhale.com.

BURGESS, JOHN FRANK, retired utilities executive; b. Lanett, Ala., Nov. 18, 1917; s. John Frank and Mary Catherine (Heard) B.; m. Helen Hamby, Aug. 26, 1939; children: Beverly, Barbara, Frank. BS, Auburn U.; MA, George Washington U. Commd. 2d lt. U.S. Army, 1941, advanced through grades to col., ret., 1969; regional v.p. Consol. Edison Co. of N.Y., Inc., NYC, 1969-83; cons. mgmt. Melville, NY, 1983-85; assoc. cons. Power Mgmt. Assocs., Inc., Groton, Conn., 1985-87; Columbia, Md., 1985-89. Active bds. various civic and profl. orgns., Queens, N.Y., 1969-83. Decorated Legion of Merit with 2 oak leaf clusters; named Man of Yr. Queens County Bldg and Contractors Assn., 1977 Episcopalian. Home: Roswell, Ga. Died 2007.

BURGESS, JOHN HERBERT, cardiologist, educator; b. Montreal, Que., Can., May 24, 1933; s. John Frederick and Willa Reta (McGinness) B.; m. Andrea Clouston Rutherford, May 30, 1958; children: Willa, Cynthia, Lynn, John. BSc, McGill U., Montreal, 1954, MD, CM, 1958. Med. resident Montreal Gen. Hosp., 1958-60, 62-64, dir. div. cardiology, 1973-94; Nuffield rsch. fellow U. Birmingham, Eng., 1960-62; McLaughlin rsch. fellow Cardiovascular Rsch. Inst., San Francisco, 1964-66; asst. prof. medicine McGill U., 1966-69, assoc. prof., 1969-75, prof., 1975—. Emeritus cardiologist McGill U. Health Ctr. Contbr. articles to profl. jours. Decorated Order of Can.; hon. fellow Coll. Medicine, South Africa. Master ACP; fellow Am. Coll. Cardiology, Royal Coll. Physicians and Surgeons Can. (pres. 1990-92), Royal Coll. Physicians (Edinburgh), Royal Australasian Coll. Physicians (hon.), Royal Coll. Physicians (London); mem. Can. Soc. Clin. Investigation. Avocations: cross country skiing, photography. Home: 639 Murray Hill Westmount PQ Canada H3Y 2W8 Office: Montreal Gen Hospital 1650 Cedar Ave Montreal PQ Canada H3G 1A4 Office Phone: 514-934-1934. Business E-Mail: john.burgess@muhc.mcgill.ca.

BURGESS, JOHN THOMAS, physical education educator, consultant; b. Bklyn., Apr. 23, 1950; s. John Edward and Margaret Mary Burgess; m. Barbara Ann Ernst, Jan. 20, 1972; children: Brian Christopher, Kimberly Ann. AA, Suffolk County CC, Selden, NY, 1970; BS, SUNY, Brockport, 1972; MA in Liberal Studies, SUNY, Stony Brook, 1976; MS in Edn., CUNY, Flushing, 1993. Cert. pool/spa operator Nat. Swimming Pool Found., spinning instr. Mad Dogg Athletics, phys. edn. tchr. K-12 N.Y., lifeguard ARC, water safety instr. ARC, lic. corporate wellness coach Wellcoaches, Inc., cert. strength-conditioning specialist with distinction. Prof. phys. edn. Suffolk County CC, Brentwood, NY, 1974—. Head coach-men's & women's cross country, indoor & outdoor track Suffolk County CC, Selden, 1976—82, athletic trainer, 1981—92, coord. athletics, Brentwood, 1993—99; sport/fitness mgmt. cons., NY, 1992—; circuit Reebok profls and specialists program Reebok Internat. Ltd., Staunton, Mass.; nat. instr. edn. bd. Nat. Health Club Assn.; legal cons. - sport/fitness law, NY. Staff mem. track & field tng. site coord. Atlanta Com. Olympic Games, Atlanta, 1996; mem. Suffolk CC Found., Inc., Selden, 1999—2001. Mem.: AAHPERD, Nat. Athletic Trainers Assn. (cert. athletic trainer), U.S. Weightlifting (cert. club coach), U.S. Track and Field (cert. level 1 coach), Nat. Strength and Conditioning Assn. (cert. strength and conditioning specialist), Am. Coll. Sports Medicine (cert. health/fitness instr.). Avocations: running, swimming, strength training, bicycling, travel. Home: 64 Furman Ave East Patchogue NY 11772-5522 Office: Suffolk County CC Crooked Hill Rd Brentwood NY 11717 Home Phone: 631-289-9036; Office Phone: 631-851-6758. Home Fax: 631-289-9036. Personal E-mail: jtbironman@aol.com. Business E-Mail: burgesj@sunysuffolk.edu.

BURGESS, KEVIN L., lawyer; b. Elyria, Ohio, June 8, 1968; BSEE, Ohio State U., 1990, MSEE, 1992, PhD in Elec. Engring., 1995, JD summa cum laude, 1998. Bar: Tex. 1998, US Ct. Appeals (Fed. cir.) 1999, US Dist. Ct. (no., ea. and we. dists. Tex.). Law clk. to Hon. William C. Bryson Fed. Cir. Ct. Appeals, 1998—99; assoc. Brobeck, Phleger & Harrison; atty. McKool Smith, P.C., Austin, Tex. Named a Rising Star, Tex. Super Lawyers mag., 2006. Mem.: Travis County Bar Assn., Tex. State Bar Assn., Fed. Cir. Bar Assn., ABA, Am. Intellectual Property Law Assn. Office: McKool Smith PC 300 W 6th St Ste 1700 Austin TX 78701 Office Phone: 512-692-8704. E-mail: kburgess@mckoolsmith.com.*

BURGESS, LARRY EUGENE, library director, historian, educator; b. Montrose, Colorado, July 18, 1945; s. Eugene Floyd and Edyth Eleanor (Faussone) B.; m. Charlotte Reid (Gaylord), Oct. 7, 1973. BA, U. Redlands, Calif., 1967; MA, Claremont Grad. Sch., 1969, PhD, 1972. Archivist A.K. Smiley Pub. Libr., Redlands, Calif., 1972-85, libr. dir., 1986—. Adj. prof. history, U. Redlands, 1972—, U. Calif., Riverside,

1979—; book reviewer Lincoln Herald, 1988—. Author: Mohonk: Its People and Spirit, 1980; (with others) A Day with Mr. Lincoln, (with others), 1994; co-author: The Hunt for Willie Boy, 1994. Vice-chmn. Calif. Heritage Preservation Commn., 1977-84; Hist. Soc. So. Calif., L.A., pres., 2003—06; bd. dirs. U. Redlands, 1987—. Recipient Archival Award of Excellence Calif. Heritage Preservation Commn., 1991; Preservation Merit Award Calif. Hist. Soc., 1992, Cmty. Enrichment Award Hist. Soc. So. Calif., 1994. Mem. Soc. Am. Archivists, So. Calif. Archivists (past pres.), Zamorano Club (bd. dir. 1994—, pres. 1999-2002), Rotary Club Relands (pres. 1999-2000). Avocations: travel, gardening, book collecting. Home: 923 W Fern Ave Redlands CA 92373-5877 Office: A K Smiley Pub Libr 125 W Vine St Redlands CA 92373-4728 Home Phone: 909-793-1529; Office Phone: 909-798-7565. E-mail: admin@aksmiley.org, admin@akspl.org.

BURGESS, LYNNE A., lawyer; BA, William Smith Coll.; JD, Fordham U. Asst. gen. counsel Am. Nat. Can Co.; of counsel Colier, Shannon, Rill & Scott, Washington, 1992—94; sr. v.p., gen. counsel Entex Info. Svcs., 1994—2000; gen. counsel, sec. Oliver, Wyman & Co., LLC, 2001—02; v.p., gen. counsel Asbury Automotive Grp., 2002—. Office: Asbury Automotive Group 622 Third Ave 37th Fl New York NY 10017*

BURGESS, MICHAEL (ROBERT REGINALD BURGESS), librarian, writer; b. Fukuoka, Kyushu, Japan, Feb. 11, 1948; came to U.S., 1949; s. Roy Walter and Betty Jane (Kapel) B.; m. Mary Alice Wickizer, Oct. 15, 1976; stepchildren: Richard Albert Rogers, Mary Louise Reynnells AB with honors, Gonzaga U., 1969; MLS, U. So. Calif., 1970. Periodicals librarian Calif. State U., San Bernardino, 1970-81, chief cataloger, 1981-94, prof., 1984—2005, head tech. svcs. and collection devel., 1994—2005, emeritus, 2005—. Editor Newcastle Pub. Co., North Hollywood, Calif., 1971—92; pub. Borgo Press, San Bernardino, 1975—99, Brownstone Books, San Bernardino, 1991—99, Sidewinder Press, San Bernardino, 1991—99, Unicorn & Son, San Bernardino, 1991—99, Burgess & Wickizer, San Bernardino, 1991—99, Emeritus Enterprises, 1993—99, Starmont House, 1993—99; assoc. editor SFRA Rev., 1993—94, Millefleurs Info. Svcs., San Bernardino, 2000—; editor Wildside Press/Borgo Press Imprint, 2005—. Author 113 books under pen names Michael Burgess, R(obert) Reginald, Boden Clarke, and others, with occasional co-authors, including: Stella Nova, 1970, Cumulative Paperback Index, 1939-1959, 1973, Contemporary Science Fiction Authors, 1975, The Attempted Assassination of John F. Kennedy, 1976, Things to Come, 1977, Up Your Asteroid!, 1977, Science Fiction and Fantasy Literature, a Checklist, 1700-1974, 1979, The Paperback Price Guide, 1980, 2nd edit., 1983, Science Fiction & Fantasy Awards, 1981, If J.F.K. Had Lived, 1982, The House of Burgesses, 1983, 2nd edit., 1994, The Wickizer Annals, 1983, Tempest in a Teapot, 1983, A Guide to Science Fiction & Fantasy in the Library of Congress Classification Scheme, 1984, 2nd edit., 1988, The Work of Jeffrey M. Elliot, 1984, Futurevisions, 1985, Lords Temperal & Lords Spiritual, 1985, 2nd edit., 1995, The Work of Julian May, 1985, The Work of R. Reginald, 1985, The Work of George Zebrowski, 1986, 2nd edit., 1990, 3rd edit., 1996, Mystery and Detective Fiction in the Library of Congress Classification Scheme, 1988, The Work of William F. Nolan, 1988, 2nd edit., 1998, The Arms Control, Disarmament, and Military Security Dictionary, 1989, Hancer's Price Guide to Paperback Books, 3d edit., 1990, Reginald's Science Fiction and Fantasy Awards, 2nd edit., 1991, 3d edit., 1993, Reference Guide to Science Fiction, Fantasy, and Horror, 1992, Science Fiction and Fantasy Literature, 1975-1991, 1992, The Work of Robert Reginald, 2nd edit., 1992, The State and Province Vital Records Guide, 1993, The Work of Katherine Kurtz, 1993, St. James Guide to Science Fiction Writers, 1996, CSUSB Faculty Authors, Composers and Playwrights, 1996, 2d. edit., 2006, BP 250, 1996, Xenograffiti, 1996, 2nd edit., 2005, Codex Derynianus, 1998, Katydid and other Critters, 2001, The Dark-Haired Man, 2004, The Exiled Prince, 2004, Quaestiones, 2004, Murder in Retrospect, 2005, Codex Derynianus II, 2005, Classics of Fantastic Literature, 2005, The Eastern Orthodox Churches, 2005, Quaestiones, 2005, Trilobite Dreams, 2006, BP 300, 2007, The Phantom's Phantom, 2007, Invasion! Or, Earth vs. the Aliens, 2007; editor: Ancestral Voices, 1975, Alistair MacLean, 1976, Ancient Hauntings, 1976, Phantasmagoria, 1976, R.I.P., 1976, The Spectre Bridegroom and Other Horrors, 1976, John D. MacDonald and the Colorful World of Travis McGee, 1977, Dreamers of Dreams, 1978, King Solomon's Children, 1978, They, 1978, Worlds of Never, 1978, Science Fiction & Fantasy Book Review, 1980, 2d edit., 2007, Candle for Poland, 1982, The Holy Grail Revealed, 1982, The Work of Bruce McAllister, 1985, rev. edit., 1986, George Orwell's Guide Through Hell, 1986, 2nd edit., 1994, The Work of Charles Beaumont, 1986, 2nd edit., 1990, California Ranchos, 1988, 2d edit., 2007, The Work of Chad Oliver, 1989, The Work of Colin Wilson, 1989, The Work of Ian Watson, The Work of Reginald Bretnor, 1989, The Work of Ross Rocklynne, 1989, To Kill or Not To Kill, 1990, The Work of Dean Ing, 1990, The Work of Jack Dann, 1990, The Work of Pamela Sargent, 1990, 2nd edit., 1996, The Trilemma of World Oil Politics, 1991, The Work of Louis L'Amour, 1991, The Work of Brian W. Aldiss, 1992, Geo. Alec Effinger, 1993, Polemical Pulps, 1993, Sermons in Science Fiction, 1994, The Work of Elizabeth Chater, 1994, The Work of Jack Vance, 1994, The Work of William Eastlake, 1994, The Work of William F. Temple, 1994, The Work of Gary Brandner, 1995, The Work of Stephen King, 1996, Running From The Hunter, 1996, San Quentin, 2005, Cal State Comes, 1965-2006, 2006, Viva California!, 2007, Across the Wide Missouri, 2007, First-century Palestinian Judaism, 2007; author of 13,000 essays, 30 short stories; editor 1,500 books for Wild Side Press St. Alia. Recipient MPPP award, 1987, Lifetime Collectors award for Contbn. to Bibliography, 1993, Pilgrim award, 1993; named title II fellow U. So. Calif., 1969-70. Mem. NEA, ACLU, Sci. Fiction and Fantasy Writers Am., Mystery Writers Am., Calif. Tchrs. Assn., Calif. Faculty Assn. (statewide librs. task force 1986-89, 93-2005, editor newsletter 1987-89), Internat. PEN, U.S.A. Ctr. West, Sci. Fiction Rsch. Assn., Horror Writers Am. Democrat. Avocations: genealogical and historical research, films, travel. Office: Millefleurs PO Box 2845 San Bernardino CA 92406-2845 also: Calif State U Libr 5500 University Pkwy San Bernardino CA 92407-2318 E-mail: robert@millefleurs.tv.

BURGESS, MICHAEL C., congressman; b. Denton, Tex., Dec. 23, 1950; s. Tim Burgess; m. Laura Burgess; 3 children. BS, North Tex. State U., 1972, MS, 1976; MD, U. Tex. Med. Ctr., Houston, 1977; M in Med. Mgmt., U. Tex., Dallas, 2000. Resident Parkland Hosp., Dallas; physician pvt. practice Ob-Gyn. Assocs., Lewisville, Tex.; chief of staff Lewisville Med. Ctr., chief obstetrics; mem. US Congress from 26th Tex. dist., 2003—, mem. energy and commerce com., chmn. Rep. Ho. Policy Com. subcommittee on medicare and medicaid svcs. Mem.: Denton County Med. Soc. (pres.). Republican. Office: US Ho Reps 1721 Longworth Ho Office Bldg Washington DC 20515 Office Phone: 202-225-7772.*

BURGESS, RICHARD RAY, oncologist, molecular biologist, biotechnologist, educator, researcher, consultant; b. Mt. Vernon, Wash., Sept. 8, 1942; s. Robert Carl and Irene Marjorie (Wegner) B.; m. Ann Baker, June 17, 1967; children— Kristin, Andreas BS in Chemistry, Calif. Inst. Tech., 1964; PhD in Biochemistry and Molecular Biology, Harvard U., 1969. Helen Hay Whitney fellow Inst. Molecular Biology, Geneva, 1969-71; asst. prof. oncology McArdle Lab. Cancer Research U. Wis., Madison, 1971-77, assoc. prof., 1977-82, prof., 1982—, dir. Biotech. Ctr., 1984-96, James D. Watson Prof. Oncology, 2001—. Cons. in field; mem. NSF study sect. in biochemistry, 1979-84; chmn. bd. Consortium for Plant Biotech. Rsch., Inc., 1992-96. Series editor U. Wis. Biotech. Ctr. Resource Manuals; editor-in chief Jour. Protein Expression and Purification, 1990—; contbr. articles to profl. jours. Bd. dirs. Coun. Biotech. Ctrs., 1991-93; mem. Gov.'s Coun. on Biotech. Grantee NSF, 1978-80, 85-90, NIH, 1980—, Nat. Cancer Inst., 1971—; Guggenheim fellow, 1983-84; recipient medal Waksman Inst., 1999. Fellow Am. Acad. Microbiology; mem. Am. Soc. Biochemistry and Molecular Biology, Am. Chem. Soc. (Pfizer award 1982), Am. Assn. Cancer Research, Am. Soc. Microbiology, Protein Soc. Home: 10 Knollwood Ct Madison WI 53713-3479 Office: U Wis McArdle Lab Cancer Rsch 1400 University Ave Madison WI 53706-1526 Office Phone: 608-263-2635. Business E-Mail: burgess@oncology.wisc.edu.

BURGESS, ROBERT KYLE, lawyer; b. Fairfield, Iowa, Sept. 5, 1948; s. Charles and Eleanor Pearl (Morris) B.; children: Alyssa, Kristen, Ryan; m. Michelle Wenz. BS, Northwestern U., 1970, JD, 1973. Bar: Calif. 1973, US Dist. Ct. (cen. dist.) Calif. 1974, US Tax Ct. 1975, US Ct. Appeals (9th cir.) 1976, US Ct. Appeals (5th cir.) 1977, US Supreme Ct. 1977, DC 1980, US Dist. Ct. Md. 1980, US Ct. Appeals (DC cir.) 1981, Ill. 1982. Assoc. Latham & Watkins, Los Angeles, 1973-78, Washington, 1978-81, ptnr., 1981-82, Chgo., 1982-95; sr. v.p., gen. counsel, sec. Munich Re Am. (Am. Reinsurance Co.), Princeton, NJ, 1995-97, exec. v.p., gen. counsel, sec., 1997—. Mem. Calif. Bar Assn., Ill. Bar Assn., DC Bar Assn. Office: Munich Re America PO Box 5241 555 College Rd E Princeton NJ 08543

BURGESS, RONALD L., JR., federal agency administrator, career military officer; b. 1952; m. Marta Jordan; children: Lee, Regina, Julia, Mary, John. Grad., Auburn U., 1974; MS in Edn., U. So. Calif., 1980; M in Mil. Arts & Sci., US Army Command & Gen. Staff Coll., 1986. Advanced through grades to lt. gen. US Army, 2005; armor platoon leader, S-2 2d battalion 69th armor, 179th military intelligence detachment exec. officer 197th Infantry Brigade, Ft. Benning, Ga., 1974—78; strategic intelligence staff officer, aide-de-camp to U.S. comdr. Berlin, 1978—81; asst. S-3, co. comdr. S-3 124th military intelligence battalion 24th Infantry Divsn. (Mechanized), Ft. Stewart, Ga., 1982—85; dep. G-2, exec. officer 106th military intelligence battalion 6th Infantry Divsn. (Light), Ft. Richardson, Ala., 1987—90; asst. exec. officer to dep. chief of staff intelligence US Army, Washington, 1990; comdr. 125th military intelligence battalion, 1991—93; G-2 25th Infantry Divsn. Schofield Barracks, Hawaii, 1993—94; comdr. 470th Military Intelligence Brigade, Panama, 1995—97; dir. intelligence (J-2) Joint Spl. Ops. Command, Fort Bragg, NC, 1997—99, US So. Command, Miami, Fla., 1999—2003, The Joint Staff, Washington, 2003—05; dep. dir. customer outcomes (requirements) Office Nat. Intelligence, Washington, 2005—07, acting prin. dep. dir., 2006—07, dir. intelligence, 2007—. Decorated Def. Superior Svc. award with two oak leaf clusters, Legion of Merit, Meritorious Svc. medal with four oak leaf clusters, Joint Svc. Commendation medal, Army Commendation medal, Army Achievement medal, NATO medal for Yugoslavia, Army Gen. Staff Badge, Joint Staff Identification Badge, Parachutist Badge; recipient Disting. Vet. award, City of Auburn, 2006. Office: Office Nat Intelligence Office of Dir of Nat Intelligence Washington DC 20511*

BURGESS, R(OY) BRANDON, communications executive; m. Saira Burgess. Graduate European Bus. Sch., MBA Wharton Sch. Bus. Investment banker Goldman Sachs, London; CFO NBC TV Network, dir. bus. devel.; exec. v.p. devel. NBC Universal, 2002—04, exec. v.p., internat. channels, bus. devel., 2004—05; corp. planner PesiCo, Purchase, NY; CEO Paxson Comm., 2005—. Mem. bd. NBC Univ., A&E Networks, MSNBC, Miss Universe. Office: Paxson Communications 601 Clearwater Rd West Palm Beach FL 33401 Office Phone: 561-569-4122. Office Fax: 561-659-4252.

BURGESS, RUTH LENORA VASSAR, speech and language educator; b. Pune, India, Aug. 6, 1939; arrived in US, 1952; d. Theodore R. and F. Estelle (Barnett) Vassar; m. Stanley Milton Burgess, Feb. 26, 1960; children: John Bradley, Stanley Matthew, Scott Vassar, Heidi Amanda Elizabeth, Justin David. BS in Edn., Tex. Tech. U., 1960; MA, U. Mo., 1968, PhD, 1979. Speech therapist Inkster (Mich.) Pub. Schs., 1961-62; mid. sch. tchr. Strafford (Mo.) Pub. Schs., 1962-63; speech therapist Fulton (Mo.) Pub. Schs., 1967-68; speech-lang. clinician Springfield (Mo.) Pub. Schs., 1963-66; asst. prof. Evangel Coll., Springfield, 1968-76; prof. Sch. Tchr. Edn. S.W. Mo. State U., Springfield, 1976—2005, dir. Ctr. Rsch. and Svc., 1990-97; adj. prof. Regent U., Va., 2005—. Mem. sci. adv. bd. Internat. Ctr. Enhancement of Jerusalem, Israel, 1993—; field reviewer Dept. Edn., Washington, 1993-96, U.S. Vocat. Rehab., Washington, 1993, 94, 96,99; mem. evaluation team Title I Springfield Schs., 1994. Author: The Status of the Educational Resource Teacher, 1981, Shantistan: A Peace Building Curriculum, 2005; editor The Learner in the Process, 1978-80; contbr. articles to profl. jours. Ex-officio bd. dirs. Orphanage Assn., Pune, 1968—; mem. Kodaikanal-Woodstock Alumni Assn., Atlanta, 1956—; mem. Women Issues Network, Springfield, 1993-2005. Grantee Dept. Edn., 1978-83, 90-92, Dept. Elem. and Secondary Edn., 96, Mellon Found., 1988-90. Mem. AAUW, ASCD, Am. Speech, Lang. and Hearing Assn. (cert.), Internat. Assn. for Cognitive Edn. (field editor 1990-94). Avocations: hiking, creative writing, travel. Office: SW Mo State U 901 S National Ave Springfield MO 65804-0088 Personal E-mail: rvburgess@earthlink.net.

BURGESS, TIMOTHY M., federal judge, former prosecutor; b. San Francisco, 1956; BA, U. Alaska, 1978, MBA, 1982; JD, Northeastern U., 1987. Legis. asst. to Frank H. Murkowski US Senate; assoc. Gilmore and Feldman, Anchorage, 1987—89; asst. US atty Dist. AK US Dept. Justice, Anchorage, 1989—2001, US atty., 2001—06; judge US Dist. Ct. AK, Anchorage, 2006—. Mem.: AK Bar Assn. Office: US Dist Ct 222 W 7th St #33 Anchorage AK 99513*

BURGESS, WILLIAM PATRICK, management consultant; b. St. Louis, Oct. 18, 1955; s. Richard William and Esther M. B.; m. Leah Kathleen Vie. BA, St. Louis U., 1987. Computer programmer St. Louis Stag Beer Sales, 1976-80, Wis. Barge Inc., St. Louis, 1980-81; data processing mgr. Switzer Candies, St. Louis, 1981-85; dir. info systems Switzer Clark, St. Louis, 1985-87; mgmt. cons. Coopers & Lybrand, St. Louis, 1987—94; prin. MB Consulting Group, St. Louis, 1994—. Mem. internat. adv. com. spl. interest group for software quality Brit. Computer Soc. Mem. Am. Assn. Artificial Intelligence, Spl. Interest Group for Artificial Intelligence, Info. Systems Security Assn., Assn. Systems Mgmt., Sigma Chi Alumni Assn. Roman Catholic. Office: MB Consulting Group 225 S Maramec Ave Saint Louis MO 63105

BURGET, DEAN EDWIN, JR., plastic surgeon; b. Toledo, June 29, 1936; s. Dean E. Sr. and Marie E. (Alwine) B.; m. A. Undine Ehrman, Mar. 16, 1957 (div. Mar. 1993); children: Mark A.E., Kevin Phillips, Undine Peeples; m. Gabriella Morocz, May 14, 1993. BS, U. Toledo, 1958; MD, Yale U., 1962. Diplomate Am. Bd. Plastic Surgery. Intern surgery U. Hosps., Cleve., 1962, resident in anesthesiology, 1963; resident in gen. surgery Hahnemann Med. Coll. and Hosp., Phila., 1966-68, asst. prof., dir. divsn. plastic surgery, 1972-75; resident in plastic surgery Temple U. Hosp., Phila., 1968-70, U.S. Govt. fellow in rehab. surgery, 1970-71, instr. plastic surgery, 1970-71, Med. Coll. Pa., Phila., 1970-71, assoc. clin. prof., 1979-81; staff surgeon, cons. surgeon various cmty. hosps., 1975—; pvt. practice Paoli, Pa., 1985—. Fellow ACS; mem. Am. Soc. Plastic and Reconstructive Surgeons, Pickering Hunt Club (Phila.), Ausable Club/Adirondack Mountain Res. (St. Huberts, NY), Yale Club (NYC), Rittenhouse Club (Phila.), Penn Club, St. Nicholas Soc. City of NY, Pa. Soc. Sons Revolution, Colonial Soc. Pa., Soc. Colonial Wars Pa., Nat. Huguenot Soc., Soc. War 1812, Phila. Soc. Promoting Agr. Office: 1410 Russell Rd Ste 205 Paoli PA 19301 Office Phone: 610-644-8225.

BURGGRAF, FRANK BERNARD, JR., landscape architect, retired educator; b. NYC, Nov. 13, 1932; s. Frank Bernard and Johanna (Verbaan) B.; m. Jane Martin Rannenberg, June 25, 1955 (div. 1997); children: Helen Marguerite, Frank Bernard, John Christian; m. Margaret Goff, Oct. 31, 1998. BS, SUNY-Syracuse, 1954; MLA, U. Pa., 1958. Registered landscape architect, NY. Asst. prof. U. Ga., Athens, 1958-63; assoc. prof., dir. regional planning grad. program Pa. State U., University Park, 1963-70; chief planning analyst NY State Pub. Svc. Commn., Albany, 1970-80; cons. landscape architect, planner Delmar, NY, 1980-84; prof. landscape architecture U. Ark., Fayetteville, 1984-97, dir. program in landscape architecture, 1984-87, emeritus prof. landscape architecture, 1997—. Mem. NY State Bd. Landscape Architecture, 1977-84, chmn., 1979-81 Contbr. articles to profl. jours. Pres. Winslow Cmty. Devel. Coun., 2002—; bd. dirs. Fayetteville Mcpl. Airport, 1997—2002. Served to lt. col. USAF, 1954—81. Fellow Am. Soc. Landscape Architects; mem. Am. Planning Assn., Elks (exalted ruler local lodge, 1990). Home: 18665 Brentwood Mountain Rd Winslow AR 72959-9755 Personal E-mail: fburggraf@hotmail.com.

BURGHART, JAMES HENRY, electrical engineer, educator; b. Erie, Pa., July 18, 1938; s. Chester Albert and Mary Virginia (Burke) B.; m. Judith Ann Hoff, July 8, 1961; children— Jill Kathryn, Mark Alan. BS in Elec. Engring, Case Inst. Tech., 1960, MS (U.S. Steel Found. fellow 1961-63), 1962, PhD, 1965. Asst. prof., then assoc. prof. elec. engring. SUNY, Buffalo, 1969-75; prof. elec. engring. Cleve. State U., 1975—2005, chmn. dept., 1975-85, 89-97; ret. Served as officer USAF, 1965-68. Mem. IEEE (chmn. Cleve. sect. 1980-81, sec. region 2 1989-96, profl. activities coord. region 2 1997-2000, Ohio area chair region 2 2001—2002, awards and recognition chair, 2003, admission and advancement com. 2006-07), Sigma Xi, Eta Kappa Nu. Home: 5501 Strathaven Dr Cleveland OH 44143-1970 Office: 1983 E 24th St Cleveland OH 44115-2403 Address: 2121 Euclid Ave Cleveland OH 44115 E-mail: j.burghart@ieee.org.

BURGHEIM, RICHARD, magazine editor; b. St. Louis, July 5, 1933; s. Nathaniel H. and Mary (Rudman) B. BA, Harvard U., 1955. Writer Time Mag., NYC, 1960-71; dir. cable TV programming Time Inc., NYC, 1972-73; editor People Mag., NYC, 1974-81, 89-92; mng. editor TV-Cable Week, White Plains, NY, 1982-83; editor Life Mag., NYC, 1984—85, Money Mag., NYC, 1986-89; cons. editor Time Inc., NYC, 1993—, N.Y. Times Upfront, 1999—2005. Cons. cable programming Ford Found., N.Y.C., 1972; lectr. Harvard Inst. Telecomm. and Pub. Policy, Cambridge, 1972. Bd. dirs. Children's Express, NYC, 1994-97, Doe Fund, NYC, 1999—2007, Goddard Riverside Comty. Ctr., NYC, 1999—. With USCG, 1955—59. Home: 230 Central Park W Apt 16D New York NY 10024-6041 Office: Time Inc Time And Life Bldg New York NY 10020

BURGHER, LOUIS WILLIAM, physician, educator, academic administrator; b. Centerville, Iowa, Oct. 31, 1944; s. Wendell and Dorothy (Probasco) B.; m. Susan Stephens, May 20, 1979; children: Tanya Jo, Tara Lynn, Lucas William, Rachel Elizabeth. BS, U. Nebr., 1966, MD with honors, 1970, M in Med. Sci., 1972, PhD in Med. Sci., 1978. Diplomate Am. Bd. Internal Medicine, Am. Bd. Pulmonary Medicine. Intern U. Nebr. Coll. Medicine, 1970-71, resident in internal medicine, 1971-72; practice medicine specializing in pulmonary medicine Omaha, 1974-93; NIH fellow in pulmonary diseases Mayo Grad. Sch. of Medicine, Rochester, Minn., 1972-74, assoc. prof., 1981-97, chief sec. pulmonary medicine, 1980-84, prof., 1997—, vice chancellor, 1999—2001. Clin. rsch. assoc. in pulmonary disease U. Nebr. Coll. of Medicine, 1969-72; med. dir. pulmonary medicine Bishop Clarkson Meml. Hosp., Omaha, 1974-93, pres., CEO, 1993-97; pres., CEO Nebr. Health Sys., 1997-2001; mem. pulmonary-allergy drugs adv. FDA, 1984-86; Tb cons. to Nebr. Dept. Health, 1972-96; med. dir. Nebr. Opportunity for Vols. in ACTION, 1971-72; trustee Nebr. Found., 1982-94. Contbr. articles on pulmonary disease to profl. jours. Recipient Upjohn award Nebr. Coll. Medicine, 1970. Fellow Am. Coll. Chest Physicians; mem. AMA (coun. on med. edn. 1973-78, mem. liaison com. on med. edn. 1974-79), Nebr. Med. Assn., Zumbro Valley Med. Soc. (exec. com. 1973-74), Univ. Med. Ctr. Ho. Officers Assn. (pres. 1971-72), Nat. Assn. Med. Dirs. Respiratory Care (pres. 1985-87), Mayo Fellows Assn. (pres 1973-74), Nat. Acad. Scis. (mem. task force study Inst. Medicine), Nebr. Thoracic Soc. (pres. 1980-81), U. Nebr. Med. Ctr. Alumni Assn. (pres. 1986-88), Alpha Omega Alpha. Home: 12229 N 179th Cir Bennington NE 68007 Office Phone: 402-689-2000. Personal E-mail: lburgher@goeframe.net.

BURGIN, CHARLES EDWARD, lawyer; b. Marion, NC, Dec. 16, 1938; m. Ellen Salsbury Burgin; children: Ellen, Lucy. BA, U. N.C., 1961; LLB, Duke U., 1964. Bar: N.C.; U.S. Supreme Ct. Law clk. to Hon. J. Braxton Craven Jr. U.S. Dist. Ct., U.S. Ct. Appeals, 1964—66; pros. atty. McDowell County Criminal Ct., 1966—68; sr. ptnr. Dameron, Burgin & Parker, P.A., Marion, 1968—. Bd. dirs. Shadowline, Inc.; lectr. in field. Contbr. articles to profl. jours. Bd. dirs. McDowell County Recreation Commn. 1977-87, First Union Nat. Bank; McDowell County Mountain Rescue Team, McDowell Arts and Crafts Assn. Named Legal Elite in N.C., Bus. N.C., 2004; named one of N.C.'s Super Lawyers, 2006. Fellow Am. Coll. Trial Lawyers (state chmn. 1996-98, named Best Lawyers in Am. 1993—, N.C. Super Lawyer 2006), Internat. Soc. Barristers, Am. Bar Found.; mem. ABA, N.C. Bar Assn. (pres. 1993-94), Def. Rsch. Inst., Am. Soc. Hosp. Attys., N.C. Assn. Def. Lawyers, U.S. Supreme Ct. Bar Assn. Office: Dameron Burgin & Parker PA PO Drawer 1049 26 W Court St Marion NC 28752-3906 Office Phone: 828-652-2441. E-mail: cburgin@dameronburginlaw.com.

BURGIN, GEORGE HANS, computer scientist, educator; b. Liestal, Switzerland, Feb. 13, 1930; s. Jakob and Fanny B.; m. Ulrike Franziska, July 8, 1960; children: Bernard, Claudia, Paul. Diploma in engring., Swiss Fed. Inst. Tech., Zurich, 1953, PhD, 1961. Cert. profl. engr., Calif. Design specialist Gen. Dynamics Corp., San Diego, 1962-64; sr. scientist Decision Sci., 1964-82; chief scientist Titan Systems, 1982-94; prin. staff engr. Titan Info. Systems, 1994-96, chief engr., 1996-98; staff engr. CommQuest Techs., 1998-99, IBM/Encinitas, 1999-2000, Triton Newtork Systems, 2000—01; sr. staff scientist Natural Selection, Inc., La Jolla, Calif., 2002—. Lectr. San Diego State U., 1979—89. Contbg. author: book Simulation, 2d edit., 1989; author: (program) Adaptive Maneuvering Logic; contbr. articles profl. jours. 1st lt. Swiss Army. Mem.: IEEE (life). Achievements include invention of adaptive maneuvering logic air combat simulation program; patents for algorithm for a quadrature modulator precompensation. Home: 6284 Avenida Cresta La Jolla CA 92037-6505 Office: Natural Selection Inc 9330 Scranton Rd San Diego CA 92121 Office Phone: 858-455-6449. Business E-Mail: gburgin@natural-selection.com.

BURGIN, RICHARD WESTON, writer, educator, editor; b. Brookline, Mass., June 30, 1947; s. Richard and Ruth (Posselt) B.; m. Linda Kinnard Harris, Sept. 7, 1991 (div.); 1 child, Richard Daniel. BA with honors, Brandeis U., Waltham, Mass., 1968; MA with highest honors, Columbia U., NYC, 1969, MPhil in Modern Am. Lit., 1980. Instr. English Tufts U., Medford, Mass., 1970-74; editor N.Y. Arts Jour., NYC, 1975-80; assoc. prof. Drexel U., Phila., 1984-96, St. Louis U., 1996—2003, prof. comm. and English, 2003—. Vis. lectr. U. Calif., Santa Barbara, 1981-83 Author: (novel) Ghost Quartet, 1999; (short stories) The Spirit Returns: Stories, 2000, The Identity Club: New and Selected Stories, 2005, The Conference on Beautiful Moments, 2006; Man Without Memory, 1989, Private Fame, 1991, Fear of Blue Skies, 1998, Conversations with Jorge Luis Borges, 1969, Conversations with Isaac Bashevis Singer, 1985, Stories and Dream Boxes, 2002; editor: Jorge Luis Borges: Conversations, 1998; editor Boulevard Mag., 1985—; composer: (CD) In All of the World, 2000,

House of Sun, 2001, Doll of Dreams, 2002, Cold Ocean, 2005, Don't Go There, 2005; contbr. articles to mags. Recipient Pushcart Press prize, 1982, 86, 98, 2002, 06. Mem. Nat. Book Critics Cir., St. Louis Writers Guild. Achievements include story included in Best Am. Mystery Stories, 2005, other anthologies. Avocations: travel, sports. Home: Apt 2N 7545 Cromwell Dr Saint Louis MO 63105-2966 Office: PO Box 325 6614 Clayton Rd PMB325 Saint Louis MO 63117 Office Phone: 314-977-3510. Personal E-mail: richardburgin@netzero.com.

BURGIN, WALTER HOTCHKISS, JR., retired academic administrator; b. Harrisburg, Pa., Apr. 14, 1935; s. Walter Hotchkiss and Wilhelmina (Buntin) B.; m. Barbara Isabelle Waddell, June 15, 1957; children: Christine, Jennifer. AB, Dartmouth Coll., 1957; postgrad., Princeton U., 1957-59; EdM, Harvard U., 1964. Tchr. math. Phillips Exeter (N.H.) Acad., 1964-72, Mercersburg (Pa.) Acad., 1959-64, chmn. dept., 1961-64, headmaster, 1972-97; tchr. math. Sidwell Friends Sch., Washington, 1997-98; exec. dir. Edward E. Ford Found., Washington, 1998—2002; tchr. math. Maret Sch., Washington, 2002—04; ret., 2004. Mem. Pa. Bd. for Pvt. Acad. Schs., 1973—94; bd. dirs. Assist. Bd. trustees Maret Sch., Washington; hon. regent Mercersburg Acad.; bd. adv., chair Edward E. Ford Found. NSF fellow, 1957-59, Shell fellow, 1964. Mem. Math. Assn. Am., Nat. Assn. Prins. Sch. for Girls, Headmasters Assn. (treas. 1993-96, v.p. 1996-97), Nat. Coun. Tchrs. Math., Nat. Assn. Ind. Schs. (bd. dirs. 1989-96, sec. 1992-96), Pa. Assn. Ind. Schs. (exec. com. 1980-90), Calif. Ct. Assn. (bd. pres. 2001-06). Democrat. Mem. United Ch. of Christ. Home: 2153 California St NW Apt 402 Washington DC 20008-1845 Personal E-mail: whburgin@aol.com.

BURGIN, WILLIAM LYLE, architect; b. Colorado Springs, Colo., Apr. 30, 1946; m. Virginia Margaret Wojtul, Sept. 23, 1967; 1 child, Desdemona. BA, R.I. Sch. Design, 1972, BArch, 1973. Ptnr. Estes/Burgin Partnership, Providence, 1980-89; pres. William L. Burgin Architects, Newport, RI, 1989—. Recipient Preservation award Nat. Trust for Hist. Preservation, 1986, Custom Housing Selection award Builder mag., Nat. Assn. Home Builders, 1989, Design and Planning Merit award Builder's Choice, 1993, Mayor's award City of Newport, 1988-90, People's Choice award for affordable housing design R.I. Housing and Fin. Corp., 1990, AIA honor award, 1995-96, Gold medal for best new house, 1995, Housing award Fine Homebuilding mag., 1997; Rhode Island AIA Honor award Capt. Roger Wheeler Stage Beach Pavilion, 1998, Custom Home Mag. merit award Black Point House, 1999, New England AIA Honor award, 1999. Mem. AIA (citation 1993, Spl. citation for care 1987, honor award 1988, 93, RI Merit award 2005), Conanicut Yacht Club (commodore 1996-98), Nat. Tennis Club (pres. Newport, R.I.), Jamestown Hist. Soc. (v.p. 1994, pres. 2003-05), U.S. Court Tennis Assn. (bd. govs. 2006). Avocations: court tennis, skiing, yachting, astronomy. Office: William L Burgin Architects Inc 150 Bellevue Ave Newport RI 02840-3230 Personal E-mail: wburgin@williamburgin.com.

BURGIO, MICHAEL, medical researcher; b. Bklyn., Sept. 20, 1942; s. John Duffy and Diega Burgio; m. Roberta Somersetin, Aug. 28, 1966 (div. July 31, 1990); children: Todd, Andera Lyn. BS, CCNY, 1963; MS in Physics, NYU, 1971. Med. rschr. Siemens Cardiac Pacemaker, Yardley, Pa., 1985—94, Home Infusion Therapy, Bklyn., 1994—97, Burgio Enterprises, Ltd., Bronx, 1995—. Lectr. in field; bd. dirs. United Medscan Corp., NJ; lectr. in field. Author: (book) Manual for Rehabilitation of Chronic Pulmonary Disease, 1989, Manual for Rehabilitation of Chronic Cardiac Disease, 1989, Training Manual for Cardiac and Pulmonary Rehabilitation, 1989, Nursing Manual of Policies and Procedures, (chpt.) Surgical Implant of A/V Pacemaker and It's Functions; co-author: (pilot study) Disc Dessication in Low Impact Injury in Young Trauma Victims; author: Burgio's Consultation Agreement, Burgio's License Agreement. Roman Catholic. Achievements include development of new method to restart heart after surgery; 11 federal copyrights in field. Home: 2440 Pearsall Ave Bronx NY 10469 Personal E-mail: miburg7@aol.com.

BURGMAN, DIERDRE ANN, lawyer; b. Logansport, Ind., Mar. 25, 1948; d. Ferdinand William Jr. and Doreen Walsh Burgman. BA, Valparaiso U., 1970, JD, 1979; LLM, Yale U., 1985. Bar: Ind. 1979, U.S. Dist. Ct. (so. dist.) Ind. 1979, N.Y. 1982, U.S. Dist. Ct. (so. dist.) N.Y. 1982, U.S. Ct. Appeals (7th cir.) 1982, U.S. Ct. Appeals (D.C. and 2d cirs.) 1984, U.S. Supreme Ct. 1985, D.C. 1988, U.S. Dist. Ct. (ea. dist.) N.Y. 1992. Law clk. to chief judge Ind. Ct. Appeals, Indpls., 1979-80; prof. law Valparaiso U., Ind., 1980-81; assoc. Dewey, Ballantine, Bushby, Palmer & Wood, NYC, 1981-84, Cahill Gordon & Reindel, 1985-92; sr. v.p., gen. counsel NY State Urban Devel. Corp., 1992-95; dep. insp. gen. State NY, 1992-95; of counsel Vandenberg & Feliu, NYC, 1995-99; cons. Salans, 1999—2000, counsel, 2000—04, Sullivan & Worcester, 2004—06. Note editor Valparaiso U. law rev., 1978-79; contbr. articles to law jours. Mem. bd. visitors Valparaiso U. Sch. Law, 1986—95, chmn., 1989—92, mem. nat. coun., 2001—. Ind. Bar Found. scholar, 1978. Mem. ABA (trial evidence com. 1983-86, profl. liability com. 1986-89, ins. coverage litigation com. 1990-92), Assn. Bar City N.Y. (com. profl. responsibility 1988-91, com. profl. and jud. ethics 1991-95, mem. coun. jud. adminstrn. 1997-99), New York County Lawyers Assn. (com. Supreme Ct. 1987-94, chmn. 1990-93, bd. dirs. 1991-97, 2002-03, exec. com. bd. dirs. 1992-95, fin. and pers. com. 2003, mem. found., 2003-), N.Y. State Bar Assn. (mem. Ho. Dels. 1994-98, mem. com. on profl. stds. of atty. conduct 2002-). Home: 345 E 56th St Apt 5C New York NY 10022-3744

BURGOMASTER, FREDERICK, music director; m. Mary Ellen Roggero, July 21, 1968; children: Kenneth Michael, Kathryn Marie Nazarian. MusB, Drury Coll., 1962; M in Sacred Music, Union Theol. Sem., 1966; D in Musical Arts, U. So. Calif., 1968. Cert. assoc. Am. Guild Organists. Music dir. St. Paul's Cathedral, Buffalo, 1968—77, Christ Ch. Cathedral, Indpls., 1977—. Chmn. Episc. Diocesan Music Commn., Buffalo, 1973—77; condr. and music dir. Indpls. Festival Chorus and Orch., Indps., 1980—. Composer: (anthem) As the Deer Longs for the Water-Brooks, My Heart is Glad. Mem. Episc. Standing Com., NYC, 1985—91. Fulbright scholarship, Germany, 1962-64, Winston Churchill fellowship, English-Speaking Union, 1984. Mem.: Royal Sch. Ch. Music, Am. Guild Organists, Assn. Anglican Musicians (pres. 1980—81), Omicron Delta Kappa, Sigma Alpha Iota (hon.). Office: Christ Ch Cathedral 55 Monument Cir Indianapolis IN 46204 Office Phone: 317-636-4577.

BURGOS-SASSCER, RUTH, chancellor emeritus; b. NYC, Sept. 5, 1931; m. Donald Sasscer, June 14, 1958; children: Timothy, James, Julie, David. BA, Maryville Coll., Tenn., 1953; MA, Columbia U., 1956; PhD, Fla. State U., 1987. Mem. faculty Inter-Am. U., P.R., 1968-71; dept. chair U. P.R., Aguadilla, 1972-76, dir. non-traditional programs Cen. Adminstrn. Regional Coll., 1976-81, dir., dean, chief exec. officer Aguadilla, 1981-85; v.p. faculty and instrn. Harry S. Truman Coll., Chgo., 1988-93; pres. San Antonio Coll., 1993-96; chancellor Houston C.C. Sys., 1996-2000; sr. fellow U. Houston Law Ctr. Inst. of Higher Edn Law and Goverance, 2001—03. Bd. dirs. Nat. Postsecondary Edn. Coop., Maryville Coll. Nat. Adv. Coun., Montgomery County Coalition for Adult Literacy and ESOL. Mem. Am. Assn. C.C. Presbyterian. Home: 15115 Interlachen Dr Apt 403 Silver Spring MD 20908 Office Phone: 301-598-2288. E-mail: ruthburgossas@hotmail.com.

BURGOYNE, SUZANNE, theater educator, writer; b. St. Joseph, Mich., Oct. 25, 1946; d. Leon Edward and Betty Louise Burgoyne. Cert., Belgian Nat. Theatre Inst. (L'INSAS), Brussels, 1969; BA, Mich. State U., 1968; MA, Ohio State U., 1970; PhD, U. Mich., 1975. Vis. asst. prof. theatre N.E. Mo. State U., Kirksville, 1973—74; head dept. dramatic art So. Sem. Jr. Coll., Buena Vista, Va., 1975—77; from asst. to assoc. prof. fine and performing arts Creighton U., Omaha, 1977—89; vis. prof. directing and dramaturgy L'INSAS, Brussels, 1986—87; assoc. prof. theatre U. Mo., Columbia, 1989—97, prof. theatre, 1997—, Catherine Paine Middlebush chair fine and performing arts, 2005—. Dir.: (student-authored play) Survival Dance (show selected for performance at regional Kennedy Ctr. Am. Coll. Theatre Festival (KCACTF), 2003), (play) Oleanna (show selected for regional KCACTF-meritorious achievement award for directing (regional); Hon. Mention Award for Directing (Nat.), 1999), (and translator) La Vita Breve (by Paul Willems) (show selected for performance at regional KCACTF; Meritorious Achievement Award for Directing (regional), 1996), The Fool's Journey, 2005 (Meritorious Achievement award for directing KCACTF, 2005); co-author: Teaching and Performing: Ideas for Energizing Your Classes, revised edit.; translator: (play) Paul Willems' The Drowned Land and La Vita Breve.; translator: (of 2 of 4 plays, vol. editor) Four Plays of Paul Willems: Dreams and Reflections; contbr. articles to profl. jours., chapters to books. Recipient Author of the Month awrd, Highlights for Children Mag., 1986; Kellogg Nat. fellow, W.K. Kellogg Found., 1981—84, Summer Rsch. fellow, U. Mo. Rsch. Coun., 1992, Summer salary and travel grantee, 1994, Carnegie scholar, Carnegie Acad. for the Scholarship of Tchg. and Learning, 2000—01, NEH Summer Seminar fellow, 1979, 1985, U. Mo. Kemper fellow, 2004. Mem.: Pedagogy and Theatre of the Oppressed, Kennedy Ctr. Am. Coll. Theatre Festival (regional playwriting awards chair 1978—80), Mid-America Theatre Conf. (v.p., pres. 1991—95), Assn. for Theatre in Higher Edn. (editor, theatre topics 1993—95, v.p. for profl. devel. 1999—2003, pres. 2007, award as editor of Theatre Topics 1995, Outstanding Tchr. award 2003). Avocations: water aerobics, reading, gardening, swimming. Home: 103 Tracy Dr Columbia MO 65203 Office: Dept Theatre U Missouri 129 Fine Arts Columbia MO 65211 Office Phone: 573-882-0528. Personal E-mail: burgoynes@missouri.edu.

BURGUJIAN, RICHARD V., lawyer; b. NYC, Aug. 11, 1949; BS, Stevens Inst. Tech., 1971; MS, Rensselaer Polytech. Inst., 1972, Farleigh Dickinson U., 1975; JD, Rutgers U., 1984. Lic. profl. engr., NJ; bar: NJ 1985, NY 1987, DC 1989, US Dist. Ct. NJ, US Patent & Trademark Office. Ptnr. Finnegan, Henderson, Farabow, Farrett & Dunner LLP, Reston, Va., resident ptnr. Tokyo Office Japan, 1992—96, leader, Elec. Practice Group Reston, Va. Mem.: Am. Intellectual Property Law Assn., Inst. Elec. & Electronic Engrs., ABA, DC Bar Assn. Office: Finnegan Henderson Farabow Garrett & Dunner LLP Two Freedom Sq 11955 Freedom Dr Reston VA 20190-5675 Office Phone: 571-203-2700. Office Fax: 202-408-4400. Business E-Mail: rich.burgujian@finnegan.com.

BURGWEGER, FRANCIS JOSEPH DEWES, JR., lawyer; b. Evanston, Ill., July 5, 1942; s. Francis Dewes and Helen Theodosia (Chancellor) B.; m. Kathleen Marie Wessel, Sept. 3, 1978; children: Lauren Elizabeth, Francis Joseph Dewes III, Sherman Ward Chancellor. BA, Yale U., 1964; JD, U. Pa., 1970. Bar: Calif. 1971, N.Y. 1988, U.S. Ct. Appeals (9th cir.) 1971, U.S. Dist. Ct. (cen. dist.) Calif. 1971. Law clk. to Hon. Shirley M. Hufstedler U.S. Ct. Appeals 9th Cir., LA, 1970-71; assoc. O'Melveny & Myers, LA, 1971-78, ptnr., 1978-85, O'Melveny & Myers LLP, NYC, 1985-97, sr. counsel, 1997—2003. Contbr. articles on environ. law. Capt. U.S. Army, 1964-67, Vietnam. Mem. Assn. of Bar of City of N.Y., N.Y. State Bar Assn., L.A. County Bar Assn. (exec. com. R.P. sect.). Avocations: books, wine, agriculture. Office: O'Melveny & Myers LLP Seven Times Sq 34th Fl New York NY 10036

BURHOE, BRIAN WALTER, automotive executive; b. Worcester, Mass., Apr. 9, 1941; s. Walter De Forest and Dorothy Merrium Burhoe; m. Lynda Clayton, May 28, 1960 (div. May 1972); children: Mark S., Ty C., Scott M.; m. Joan Elaine Bredenberg, Oct. 21, 1989. Arts Baccalaureate, Clark U., Worcester, 1963, MA in History, Internat. Rels., 1971; cert. advanced mgmt. program, Northwestern U., 1985. Tchr. Orleans Sch. Sys., Mass., 1965-67; mgr. labor rels. Ill. Ctrl. RR, Chgo., 1967-74, exec. asst., 1974-77; dir. human resources Midas Internat. Corp., Chgo., 1977-79, v.p. human resources, 1979-89, sr. v.p. human resources, 1989—97; pres. The Old Bookseller, Inc., 1997—. Mem.: Ill. Safety Coun. (chmn. 1992—94). Avocation: collecting out of print books. Home and Office: 325 Nebraska St Frankfort IL 60423

BURI, CHARLES EDWARD, lawyer; b. Lancaster, Pa., Jan. 20, 1950; s. Karl Emerson and Verna Irene (Linville) B.; m. Susan Louise Camou, May 8, 1971; 1 child, Charles David. BS, U. Ariz., Tucson, 1971; JD, U. Ariz., 1973. Bar: Ariz. 1974, U.S. Dist. Ct. Ariz., 1974, U.S. Ct. Appeals (9th cir.) 1977, U.S. Supreme Ct. 1980. Asst. atty Gen. Office Atty. Gen., Phoenix, 1974—83; exec. dir. Ariz. State Lottery, Phoenix, 1983—87; ptnr. Friedl, Richter & Buri, Phoenix, 1987—. Life mem. Fiesta Bowd com., Phoenix, 1984—, Luke's Men, Phoenix, 1985-98, Gov.'s Cabinet, Phoenix, 1983-87; trustee St. Luke's Hosp., Phoenix, 1990-91. Mem. ABA, Nat. Trial Lawyers Assn., Ariz. Trial Lawyers Assn., Ariz. Bar Assn., Maricopa County Bar Assn. Democrat. Avocations: tennis, skiing, jogging. Home: 6002 E Lafayette Blvd Scottsdale AZ 85251-3040 Office: Friedl Richter & Buri 6909 E Greenway Pkwy Ste 200 Scottsdale AZ 85254-2172 Home Phone: 480-947-8660; Office Phone: 480-315-8050. E-mail: cburi@frblaw.com.

BURIAN, PETER, ambassador; b. Mar. 21, 1959; m. Nina Burianova. M in Oriental Studies, St. Petersburg U., Russia, 1983; PhD, Diplomatic Acad. Moscow, 1991. Diplomat Mid. East Dept. Czechoslovak Fed. Ministry Fgn. Affairs, 1983-87, 1991, dep. chief of mission Mid. East Dept. Beirut, 1987-89, 2nd sec. Washington, 1992; chargé d'affaires a.i Slovak Republic Ministry Fgn. Affairs, Washington, 1993, min. counselor dep. chief of mission, 1994, dir. gen. human dimension affairs, 1997, amb. to NATO and World European Union Brussels, 1999, amb.-at-large spl. coord. for UN security coun. membership Policy Planning and Analysis Dept., 2003, amb., permanent rep. to UN NYC, 2004—. Office: Permanent Mission of Slovak Republic to UN 801 Second Ave New York NY 10017 Office Phone: 212-286-8880. Office Fax: 212-286-8419. E-mail: mission@newyork.mfa.sk.

BURICK, LAWRENCE T., lawyer; b. Dayton, Ohio, May 15, 1943; s. Lee and Doris (Brenner) B.; m. Cynthia Joy Rosen, Aug. 31, 1969; children: Carrie R., Samuel J. BA, Miami U., 1965; JD, Northwestern U., 1968. Bar: Ohio 1968. Assoc. Smith & Schnacke, Dayton, 1969-78, ptnr., 1978-89, Thompson Hine LLP, Dayton, 1989—. Chmn. Dayton Jewish Ctr., Ohio, 1982—83, Jewish Cmty. Rels. Coun., 1980—81; pres. Jewish Fedn. Greater Dayton, Ohio, 1989—93, bd. dirs., 1977—2003; chmn. United Jewish Campaign, 1997—99; bd. dirs. Jewish Edn. in Svc. to N.Am., 1994—99, v.p., 1997—99; mem. Dayton region Nat. Conf. Cmty. and Justice, 1997—, v.p., 1999—2002, chair, 2002—04; bd. dirs. Beth Abraham Synagogue, 1997—2003. Recipient Wasserman Leadership award, Jewish Fedn. Greater Dayton, 1978. Mem. Ohio State Bar Assn., Dayton Bar Assn., Am. Bankruptcy Law Forum, Am. Bankruptcy Inst. Office: Thompson Hine LLP PO Box 8801 2000 Courthouse Plz NE Dayton OH 45401-8801 E-mail: larry.burick@thompsonhine.com.

BURINI, SONIA MONTES DE OCA, apparel manufacturing executive, public relations executive; b. Havana, Cuba, Apr. 28, 1935; d. Francisco and Nilda (Diaz) Montes de Oca; m. Franco Burini, Apr. 5, 1959. Student, U. Havana, 1954-57, Georgetown U., 1958; BA in History cum laude, U. Miami, Coral Gables, Fla., 1971. Adminstr. Roma Fashions, Inc. D/B/A Franco B., Coral Gables, 1976-95; entrepreneur, pub. rels. exec., 1995—; dir. promotions and special events Social Mag., 2004—. Founder Nat. Parkinson Found., 1986—; v.p. Vizcayans Fund Raising Orgn., 1990—, chmn. fine arts events, 1993-95; co-chmn. 1st annual fund raising event Am. Cancer Soc. Winn-Dixie Hope Lodge Ctr.; mem. women with heart group Heart Assn. Greater Miami, Fla., 1981—; founder, bd. dirs. Cancer Link program U. Miami Comprehensive Cancer Ctr., 1987; chmn. spring fantasy luncheon Am. Cancer Soc., 1988; founding chmn. Rose Group, Am. Lung Assn., chmn. Rose Ball, 1989; amb. Mercy Hosp. Found., 1987-95; bd. dirs. Newborn program U. Miami, 1978, bd. dirs., 1982-87, amb. category years; vol. guide Viscaya Mus., Dade County, Fla., 1972-79, chmn. various coms., 1979—, found. bd. dirs., steering com., mem. com. of 100; bd. dir., Young Patroness of the Opera, 1979-87; grand patron Greater Miami Opera, 1986-95, bd. dirs., 1978—, chmn. opera gala, 1987, mem. opera guild, 1988; founding bd. mem. Ears Dears U. Miami, 1986—, chmn. 1990 gala; mem. Dade County Performing Art Ctr. Trust, 1993—; spl. chmn. fine arts events Vizcayans, 1993—; mem. sister cities com. Cities of Miami, Fla. and Nice, France, 1994—, Nat. Trust Hist. Preservation, 1997—. Named Oustanding Woman of Yr. Mayor of Dade County, 1986, Woman of Yr. Heart Assn. Greater Miami, 1986, named to Miss Charity Biscayne Bay Marriott Hotel and Marina, 1987, One of the Leading Ladies for the March of Dimes, 1998. Mem. Nat. Trust Historic Preservation, Ballet Soc. Miami (bd. dirs. 1979-80, named one of Miami's Oustanding Women 1986), Confrerie de la Chaine des Rotisseurs, NAFE, Am. Children's Orch. for Peace (bd. adv. 2001—), Opera Guild Fla. Grand Opera (bd. dirs. 2003—). Home: 5401 Collins Ave Apt 1016 Miami Beach FL 33140 Office: Roma Fashions Inc 3311 Ponce De Leon Blvd Coral Gables FL 33134-7210 Address: 4730 SW 67th Ave Miami FL 33155 Office Phone: 305-663-0473. Fax: 305-864-2047; Office Fax: 305-663-4644. E-mail: strokespokes@aol.com.

BURISH, ANDREW D., investment advisor; B in mktg., Univ. Wis., Eau Claire, 1981, MBA, 1982. CIMA. Sr. v.p. investments UBS Fin. Services, Madison, Wis., 1984—. Named one of Top 100 Fin. Advisers, Barron's Mag. & Winners Circle, 2006—07. Office: UBS 8020 Excelsior Dr Madison WI 53717 Office Phone: 608-831-4282. Business E-Mail: andrew.burish@ubs.com.*

BURISH, THOMAS GERARD, academic administrator, psychology professor; b. Peshtigo, Wis., May 4, 1950; s. Bennie Charles and Donna Mae (Willkom) B.; m. Pamela Jean Zebrasky, June 19, 1976; children: Mark Joseph, Brent Christopher. AB summa cum laude, U. Notre Dame, 1972; MA, U. Kans., 1975, PhD, 1976. Lic. psychologist, Tenn. Asst. prof. psychology Vanderbilt U., Nashville, 1976-80, assoc. prof., 1980-86, prof., 1986—2002, dir. clin. tng., 1980-84, chair dept. psychology, 1984-86, assoc. provost, 1986—92, provost, 1992—2002; pres. Washington and Lee U., Lexington, Va., 2002—05; provost U. Notre Dame, 2005—, prof. psychology, 2005—. Mem. cancer rsch. manpower rev. com. Nat. Cancer Inst., 1991-96; co-chair Bridge task force com. Am. Cancer Soc., 1994-96; mem. breast cancer rsch. panel US Army Med. Rsch., 1995-2001. Co-editor: Coping with Chronic Disease, 1983, Cancer, Nutrition and Eating Behavior, 1985; co-author: Behavior Therapy, 1987, Health Psychology, 1991. Chmn. St. Mary's Sch. Bd., Nashville, 1982-83; participant Leadership Nashville, 1989-90; chair, bd. dir. Am. Cancer Soc., 2004-05. Fellow Am. Psychol. Assn., Am. Psychol. Soc.; mem. Acad. Behavioral Medicine Rsch., Phi Beta Kappa. Roman Catholic. Office: U Notre Dame 300 Main Bldg Notre Dame IN 46556 Office Phone: 574-631-6631.

BURITZ, ROBERT SAMSON, retired electrical engineer; b. Detroit, Feb. 6, 1919; s. Joseph Frederick Buritz and Hazel de Guise; m. Shirley Elaine Nelson, Jan. 8, 1945; children: Bhagavan, Deborah Taylor, Pamela Buritz-Dew, Kimberley. BSEE, U. Mich., Ann Arbor, 1941. Divsn. engr. Westinghouse Electric Corp., Bloomfield, NJ, 1941—46; rsch. engr. U. Mich. Inst. Engring. Rsch., Ann Arbor, 1946—48; physicist Westinghouse Rsch. Lab., Turtle Creek, Pa., 1949—55; chief project engr. Thomas A. Edison Industries, East Orange, NJ, 1955—57; mgr. beam tube engring. Nat. Co., Malden, Mass., 1957—60; project mgr. High Voltage Engring. Corp., Burlington, Mass., 1960—65; sr. scientist Hughes Aircraft Co., Culver City, Calif., 1965—89; ret. Contbr. articles to profl. jours. Achievements include design of system to measure the temperature and pressure of the upper atmosphere using V-2 rockets as a test vehicle; research to determine the linearity of the Bayard-Alpert ion gauge, vapor pressure of tungsten, diffusion of helium and argon through glass, measurement of partial gas pressures at ultrahigh vacuum; developed an oil pressure transducer and indicator for jet engines, aircraft inverter change-over control and sub-miniature thermostat; developed cesium beam tubes for atomic clocks; built a large isotope separator consisting of means for accelerating positive ions, electrostatic focusing lenses, analyzing magnet, collector, vacuum system, power supplies & remote control console; high voltage technology and advanced development of high voltage capacitors, transformers and impregnation processes for airborne radar and space systems; developed technology to manufacture the first 3cm and 10 cm radar magnetrons and T-R switches; patents for cathode assembly for magnetrons; cesium oven. Avocations: photography, travel.

BURK, BRYAN, television producer; b. Dec. 30, 1968; Prodr.: (TV series) Alias, 2001; exec. prodr.: (TV series) Lost, 2004 (best TV series, drama, Producers Guild Am., 2006), What About Brian, 2006; exec. prodr.: (TV series) Six Degrees, 2006. Mailing: c/o Lost ABC Inc 500 South Buena Vista St Burbank CA 91521-4562

BURK, MARTHA GERTRUDE, political psychologist; b. Tyler, Tex., Oct. 18, 1941; d. Ivan Lee Burk and Dorothy May (White) Dean; m. Eddie C. Talley, Sept. 2, 1960 (div. Sept. 1985); children: Edward, Mark; m. Ralph Estes, July 3, 1986. BS, U. Houston, 1962; MS, U. Tex., Arlington, 1968, PhD, 1974. Lic. psychologist, Tex. Asst. prof. mgmt. U. Tex., Arlington, 1976-79, rsch. dir. Grad. Sch. Social Work, 1974-76, ptnr. Sch. Psychology Cons., 1979-80; pres. A.U. Software, Inc., Wichita, Kans., 1981-90, Ctr. for Advancement of Pub. Policy, Washington, 1990—; now chair Nat. Coun. of Women's Organizations, Washington. Syndicated columnist. Author (software) Talley Spl. Edn. Mgmt. System, 1984, Testlab 2000, 1988, (books) Cult of Power: Sex Discrimination in Corporate America and What Can Be Done About It, 2005. Mem. Commn. Responsive Democracy, Washington, 1990, Nat. Task Force on Pay Equity, 1993—. Rsch. grantee U.S. Dept. Edn., 1989-94, named Woman of Yr., Ms Mag., 2003. Mem. NOW (nat. bd. dirs. 1988-90). Democrat. Office: Nat Coun Women's Orgns Ste 250 1050 17th St NW Washington DC 20036 Office Phone: 202-293-4505.

BURK, RAYMOND FRANKLIN, JR., internist, educator, medical researcher; b. Kosciusko, Miss., Dec. 9, 1942; s. Raymond Franklin and Florence Annie (Davis) B.; m. Enikoe Vikor, June 17, 1967; children: Teresa Marie, Stephen Morrison. BA, U. Miss., 1963; MD, Vanderbilt U., 1968. Diplomate Am. Bd. Internal Medicine. Intern Vanderbilt Hosp. , Nashville, 1968—69; resident in medicine Vanderbilt Hosp., Nashville, 1969—70; asst. prof. medicine and biochemistry U. Tex. S.W. Med. Sch., Dallas, 1975—78; assoc. prof. medicine and biochemistry La. State U. Sch. Medicine, Shreveport, 1978—80; assoc. prof. medicine U. Tex. Health Sci. Ctr., San Antonio, 1980—82, prof., 1982—87; prof. medicine Vanderbilt U., 1987—. Rschr. in field; mem. staff Vanderbilt U. Hosp., Nashville. Contbr. articles to med. jours. Maj. M.C., U.S. Army, 1970-73. Grantee NIH, 1974—. Mem. Am. Soc. Biol. Chemists, Am. Soc. Clin. Investigation, Am. Inst. Nutrition.

BURK, ROBERT S., lawyer; b. Mpls., Jan. 13, 1937; s. Harvey and Mayme (Cottle) B.; m. Eunice L. Silverman, Mar. 22, 1959; children: Bryan, Pam, Matt. BBA in Indsl. Rels., U. Minn., 1959; LLB, William Mitchell Coll. Law, 1965. Bar: Minn. 1966; qualified neutral under Rule 114 of the Minn. Gen. Rules of Practice, 1995—. Labor rels. cons. St. Paul Employers Assn., 1959-66; labor rels. mgr. Koch Refining Co., St. Paul, 1966-72, mgr. indsl. rels., 1972-75, mgr. indsl. rels., environ. affairs,

1975-77; sr. atty. Popham, Haik, Schnobrich & Kaufman, Ltd., Mpls., 1977-95, pres., CEO, 1986-90; ptnr. Burk & Seaton, P.A., Edina, Minn., 1995-2001, Burk & Landrum, P.A., Edina, 2001—07. Chair bd. trustees William Mitchell Coll. Law, St. Paul, 1994-96, sec. 1991, trustee emeritus, 2006—. Recipient Hon. Ronald E. Hachey Outstanding Alumnus award William Mitchell Coll. Law Alumni Assn., 1993, Disting. Svc. award William Mitchell Coll. Law, 2004. E-mail: rburk@burklandrum.com. *Credibility is the only trait that marks your existence.*

BURKA, ROBERT ALAN, lawyer; b. Washington, Dec. 25, 1944; s. Fred and Louise S. (Lehmann) B.; m. Maria Eva Karpati, Dec. 22, 1968; children: Jacqueline A., Michael S., Jennifer L. AB, Dartmouth Coll., 1966; MSc in Econs., U. London, 1967; JD, Harvard U., 1970. Bar: N.Y. 1971, D.C. 1975, U.S. Supreme Ct. 1978. Law clk. to Hon. Judge Milton Pollack US Dist. Ct. (so. dist.) NY, NYC, 1971; assoc. Kaye Scholer Fierman Hays & Handler, NYC, 1971-74, Bergson, Borkland, Morgolis & Adler, Washington, 1974-79; dep., then acting asst. dir. Bur. of Competition FTC, Washington, 1979-82; ptnr. LaRoe Winn & Moerman, Washington, 1982-84; pvt. practice Washington, 1984-87; ptnr. Knopf & Burka, Washington, 1987-92, Foley & Lardner L.L.P., Washington, 1992—. Fulbright and Reynolds scholars, 1966-67. Mem. Phi Beta Kappa. Office: Foley & Lardner LLP 3000 K St NW Ste 500 Washington DC 20007-5143 Home Phone: 202-363-5951; Office Phone: 202-672-5345. Business E-Mail: rburka@foley.com.

BURKARD, HEATHER C., prosecutorial investigator; AA, St Leo U., Fla., 1994; BA in Criminology and Biology, St. Leo U., Fla., 1999; M in Forensic Scis., Nat. U., La Jolla, Calif., 2006; postgrad., Capella U., Mpls., 2006—. Cert. family safety mentor Fla. Dept. Children and Families, 2001, child protection profl. Fla. Dept. Children and Families, 2001; crime scene technician Internat. Assn. for Identification, 2004. Child protection investigator Fla. Dept. Children and Families, Bartow, 2000—02; forensic investigator Hillsborough County Med. Examiner's Office, Tampa, Fla., 2002—03; crime scene investigator Charlotte-Mecklenburg Police Dept., NC, 2003—06; dist. atty. investigator Cabarrus County Dist. Attys. Office - Dist. 19A, Concord, NC, 2006—. Mem.: NC Divsn. Internat. Assn. for Identification, Internat. Crime Scene Investigators Assn., Internat. Assn. Bloodstain Pattern Analysts, Internat. Assn. for Identification, Am. Acad. Forensic Sci., Theta Phi Alpha (asst. pledge mistress). Avocations: softball, hiking, camping. Office: District Attorneys Office-Cabarrus Cty 77 Union St South Room # 303 Concord NC 28025 Office Phone: 704-786-6171. Personal E-mail: forensicclues@yahoo.com. Business E-Mail: heather.c.hogan@nccourts.org.

BURKART, WALTER MARK, retired manufacturing company executive; b. Ferndale, Mich., Sept. 29, 1921; s. Michael A. and Beatrice (Pominville) B.; m. Mary Jane Hilts, Apr. 22, 1942; children: Michael Robert, Michele Sue. Student, Lawrence Inst. Tech., 1941-43. Supr. Ex-Cello Corp., Detroit, 1940-51, v.p. machine tool div., 1965-69; chief process engr. Wright Aero Co., Detroit, 1951-55; mgr. Machine Tool div. Sheffield Corp. div. Bendix, Dayton, Ohio, 1956-65; chmn. bd. Kingsbury Machine Tool Corp., Keene, N.H., 1969-98; pres. Am. Machine Tool Consortum, Tehran, 1976-77. Mem. industry sector adv. com. on capital goods for U.S.A. trade policy matters, Dept. Commerce. Active Boy Scouts Am., 1958—; mem. N.H. Gov.'s Mgmt. Rev. Bd., 1981-82. Served with USNR, 1944-46. Mem. Keene C. of C. (dir. 1971), Bus. and Industry Assn. N.H. (dir. 1980-81), Am. Mgmt. Assn., Soc. Mfg. Engrs., Nat. Machine Tool Builders Assn. Clubs: Orchard Lake (Mich.); Keene Country (N.H.); Piper's Landing Country (Fla.). Republican. Presbyterian. *It has been my managerial philosophy to give people a goal and let them choose which road to take in reaching that goal. This allows people to utilize their strengths while becoming more committed and involved. Through this participation the individual can get a greater sense of personal accomplishment. Rarely will two people go about solving a problem in the same way. While some problems do require a group solution, most simply require a solution and I believe the method is not as important as the result.*

BURKE, ALEXANDER JAMES, JR., publishing executive; b. NYC, Apr. 24, 1931; s. Alexander James and Josephine Eleanor (McGrath) B.; m. Suzanne Jeanne Gatti, June 25, 1955; children: James, Brian, Christopher, Nancy, Thomas, Matthew, Alexander John. BA cum laude, Holy Cross Coll., 1953; MA, Fordham U., 1956; MA in Scripture, Immaculate Conception Sem., 1997; PhD in Scripture, Fordham U., 2002. Prof. English Fordham U., 1953-56, 59-60; editor W.H. Sadlier Co., NYC, 1959-60; mgr. Doubleday Bookstore, Manhasset, NY, 1952; with McGraw-Hill Book Co., NYC, 1960—87, gen. mgr., 1969-70, v.p., 1970-73, exec. v.p., 1973-74, pres., 1974-82, McGraw-Hill Internat. Book Co., NYC, 1983-85, exec. v.p., 1985-87; pres. Phoenix Learning Resources, 1987—; prof. English, prof. N.T., dir. pub. studies program Hofstra U., NYC, 1994—. Author: The Raising of Lazarus and The Passion of Jesus in John 11 and 12, 2003, John The Baptist: Prophet and Disciple, 2006. Bd. dirs. Adult Edn. Council St. Louis, 1965, Commn. on Radio and TV, Cath. Archdiocese St. Louis, 1968-72. With USAF, 1956—59. Mem. Assn. Am. Pubs. (exec. com., dir., chmn. 1978-85), Book Industry Study Group (exec. com., dir. 1976—), Am. Soc. Curriculum Devel., Nat. Coun. Tchrs. English, Cath. Bibl. Assn., Alpha Sigma Nu Roman Catholic. Home: 455 Ryder Rd Manhasset NY 11030-2761 Personal E-mail: ajburkejr@optonline.net.

BURKE, ANNE M., state supreme court justice; b. Chgo., Feb. 3, 1944; m. Edward M. Burke; children: Jennifer, Edward, Emmett, Sarah; 1 foster child. BA in Edn., DePaul U., 1976; JD, IIT/Chgo.-Kent Coll. Law, 1983. Bar: Fed. Ct. No. Dist. Ill. 1983, U.S. Ct. Appeals (7th cir.) 1985, cert.: Trial Bar Fed. Dist. Ct. 1987. Phys. edn. tchr. Chgo. Park Dist.; pvt. practice, 1983—94; judge Ill. Ct. Claims, 1987—94; spl. counsel to Gov. Child Welfare Services State of Ill., 1994—95; judge Ill. Appellate Ct. (1st dist.), Chgo., 1995—96, 1996—2006; justice Ill. Supreme Ct., Chgo., 2006—. Founder of the first Special Olympics. Grantee, Kennedy Found. Avocations: dance, antiques. Office: Ill Supreme Ct 160 N LaSalle St Chicago IL 60601 Office Phone: 312-793-5470.

BURKE, BERNARD FLOOD, physicist, researcher; b. Boston, June 7, 1928; s. Vincent Paul and Clare (Brine) B.; m. Jane Chapin Pann, May 30, 1953 (dec. Aug. 1993); children: Geoffrey Damian, Elizabeth Chapin, Mark Vincent, Matthew Brine; m. Elizabeth King Platt, Oct. 28, 1998. SB, MIT, 1950, PhD, 1953. Staff mem. terrestrial magnetism Carnegie Instn. of Washington, 1953-65, chmn. radio astronomy sect., 1962-65; prof. physics, Burden prof. astrophysics MIT, 1965-2001, prof. physics, Burden prof. emeritus, 2001—. Vis. prof. U. Leiden, Netherlands, 1971-72, U. Manchester, Eng., 1992-93; trustee N.E. Radio Obs. Corp., 1973-95, vice chmn., 1975-82, chmn., 1982-95; cons. NSF, NASA, Dept. Transp.; Oort lectr. U. Leiden, 1993; Karl Jansky lectr. NAt. Radio Astronomy Obs., 1998. Trustee Associated Univs., Inc., 1972-90; mem. Nat. Sci. Bd., 1990-96; commr. Marsh Conservation Dist., Cambridge, 2001—. Recipient Helen Warner prize Am. Astron. Soc., 1963; Rumford prize Am. Acad. Arts and Scis., 1971; Sherman Fairchild scholar Calif. Inst. Tech., 1984, Smithsonian Regents fellow, 1985; sr. fellow Carnegie Instn. of Washington, 1997. Fellow AAAS; mem. NAS, Am. Acad. Arts and Scis., Am. Phys. Soc., Am. Astron. Soc., Royal Astron. Soc., Internat. Astron. Union, Internat. Astron. Fedn. (Pecek lectr. 1993), Internat. Sci. Radio Union, Merle Tuve Sr. fellow Carnegie Instn. of Washington. Achievements include research on microwave spectroscopy, radio astronomy, galactic structure, antenna design, cosmology. Office: MIT Rm 37-691 Cambridge MA 02139 Personal E-mail: bfburke@comcast.net.

BURKE, BRIAN, professional sports team executive; m. Jennifer Burke; children: Katie, Patrick, Brendan, Molly, Mairin, Fiona Grace. BA, Providence Coll., 1977; JD, Harvard U., 1981. V.p., dir. hockey ops. Vancouver Canucks, 1987—92, gen. mgr., 1998—2004, Hartford Whalers, Conn., 1992—93; sr. v.p., dir. hockey ops. NHL, 1993—98, chief disciplinarian; exec. v.p., gen. mgr. Anaheim Ducks (formerly Mighty Ducks of Anaheim), 2005—. Adj. prof. BC U. Sch. Law. Named NHL Exec. of Yr., The Sporting News, 2001. Mem.: Sports Lawyers Assn., Nat. Sports Law Inst. Achievements include being the general manager of Stanley Cup Champion Anaheim Ducks, 2007. Office: Anaheim Ducks 2695 E Katella Ave Anaheim CA 92806*

BURKE, BROOKE, actress, model; b. Hartford, Conn., Sept. 8, 1971; d. George and Donna; m. Garth Fisher, 2001 (div. 2005); children: Neriah Fisher, Sierra Sky Fisher; 1 child, Heaven Rain Charvet. Studied bus. advertising and broadcast journalism, Santa Monica Coll. and UCLA. Has calendar and swin-wear line. Host Wild On, 1999—2002, co-host (infomercial) Peterson's Core Secrets workouts, 2005, 2006, Rock Star: INXS, 2005, Rock Star: Supernova, 2006—, guest appearances That's Life, 2002, Rock Me Baby, 2003, Monk, 2004, Less Than Perfect, 2004, The Hazing, 2004, It's All Relative, 2004, Knuckle Sandwich, 2004, Eve, 2005, Las Vegas, 2006, The Bernie Mac Show, (off-broadway) Pieces, (video game) Need For Speed: Underground 2 (Spike TV Video Game award, Best Performance by a Human-Female), (commercials) Burger King, voice-celebrity host, People and Places category (video game) Trivial Pursuit Unhinged (Atari), judge Pet Star, 2005. Photographed for charity book project, PRECIOUS Starlight Children's Found. Avocations: yoga, pilates, walking, cooking, watching movies and plays.

BURKE, CARLA MICHELLE, lawyer; b. Slaton, Tex., Aug. 17, 1969; BA, So. Meth. U., 1991, MA, 1994, JD, 1999. Bar: Tex. 1999, US Ct. Appeals (5th cir.) 2000, NY. Atty. water contamination litig. sect. Baron & Budd, P.C., Dallas, 2000—. Adj. clin. instr. law So. Meth. U. Legal Clinic, 2001. Contbr. articles to profl. publs. Recipient Rising Star, Tex. Super Lawyers mag., 2006. Fellow: Dallas Bar Found.; mem.: Dallas Bar Assn., Dallas Trial Lawyers Assn., Tex. Trial Lawyers Assn., Bar Assn. of 5th Fed. Ct., Trial Lawyers for Pub. Justice, Assn. Trial Lawyers of Am. Office: Baron & Budd PC 3102 Oak Lawn Ave Ste 1100 Dallas TX 75219 Office Phone: 214-521-3605.*

BURKE, CLEM, musician; b. NYC, Nov. 24, 1955; Drummer with Blondie, 1975—82, 1998—, with The Romantics, 1990—2004, with Nancy Sinatra, 2004—05. Musician (with Blondie): (albums) Blondie, 1976, Plastic Letters, 1977, Parallel Lines, 1978, Eat to the Beat, 1979, Autoamerican, 1980, The Hunter, 1982, No Exit, 1999, Live in New York, 1999, Livid, 2000, The Curse of Blondie, 2004, Best Live, 2005. Named to Rock and Roll Hall of Fame, 2006. Office: care 10th St Entertainment Ste G410 700 San Vincente Blvd West Hollywood CA 90069 E-mail: clemburke@dhbis.com.

BURKE, CONRAD, energy executive; b. 1967; BS in Physics, U. Coll., Dublin; MS in Physics, Trinity Coll., Dublin; attended, The London Sch. of Bus. Rsch. engr. NEC Corp., Ctr. Rsch. Labs, Japan, 1989—92; mgmt. positions in engring., mktg. and product mgmt. AT&T, 1992—99; mgmt. responsibilities Lucent Technologies', 1999—2000; sr. v.p. for mktg., sales, & bus. devel. OMM, 2000—03; venture ptnr. Sevin Rosen Funds, 2003; sr. v.p. worldwide sales & mktg. Bookham Inc.; pres., CEO Innovalight. Bd. dirs. Capella Photonics, Inc., San Jose, Calif., 2005—. Office: Innovalight Inc 3303 Octavius Dr Ste 104 Santa Clara CA 95054 Office Phone: 408-987-9400. Office Fax: 408-987-9494. E-mail: info@innovalight.com.

BURKE, BROTHER DANIEL, museum director, educator; PhD in Lit. Criticism, La Salle U. Tchr. English West Phila. Cath. HS; v.p. academic affairs La Salle U., Phila., pres., 1969—77; founding dir. La Salle U. Art Mus., Phila., 1976—. Office: La Salle U Art Mus 1900 W Olney Ave Philadelphia PA 19141

BURKE, E. JAMES, lawyer, state supreme court justice; b. Wilmington, Del., June 26, 1949; s. Earl J. Burke and Elizabeth M. (Glenn) Jones; m. Michele C. Haney, Aug. 16, 1975 (div. May 1981); 1 child, Erick; m. Linda G. Matthew, Apr. 15, 1982; children: Matthew, Leanna. BS in Psychology, St. Joseph's U., Phila., 1971; JD, U. Wyo., 1977. Bar: Wyo. 1977, U.S. Dist. Ct. Wyo. 1977, U.S. Ct. Appeals (10th cir.) 1981. Ptnr. Burke, Woodard and O'Donnell, Hanes & Burke P.C., Cheyenne, Wyo., 1977—2001; judge Dist. Ct. Laramie County, 2001—04; justice Wyo. Supreme Ct., 2005—. Mem. Cheyenne-Laramie County Economic Joint Powers Bd.; founder, dean People's Law School prog. Served to 1st lt. USAF, 1971-74. Mem. Wyo. Bar Assn., Laramie County Bar Assn., Assn. Trial Lawyers Am. (state del. 1985—), Wyo. Trial Lawyers Assn. (bd. dirs. 1977—, pres. 1980), Western Trial Lawyers Assn. (bd. dirs. 1979—, pres. 1986—), Cheyenne C. of C. (leadership award 1986). Office: Wyo Supreme Ct 2301 Capitol Ave Cheyenne WY 82001*

BURKE, EDMUND W., lawyer; BA in History with honors, Georgetown U., 1970, JD, 1973. Bar: DC 1973, Tex. 1985, US State Supreme Ct. V.p., Law & Govt. Affairs Burlington No. R.R., Mass.; assoc. to ptnr., litig. & transp. depts. Steptoe & Johnson lLP, Washington, 1974—, co-chmn. hiring com. Editor: Georgetown Law Jour. Mem.: Phi Beta Kappa. Office: Steptoe & Johnson LLP 1330 Connecticut Ave NW Washington DC 20036 Office Phone: 202-429-3008. Office Fax: 202-429-3902. Business E-Mail: eburke@steptoe.com.

BURKE, FORREST G., lawyer; JD magna cum laude, U. Pa. Atty., chair Bus. Services Group Dorsey & Whitney LLP; prin. Dorsey Health Strategies; joined UnitedHealth Group, Mpls., 2005, acting gen. counsel, 2006—. Office: UnitedHealth Group PO Box 1459 Minneapolis MN 55440-1459*

BURKE, HENRY PATRICK, lawyer; b. Scranton, Pa., May 12, 1942; s. Thomas and Dorothy Maria (McCloskey) B.; m. Alyce Louise McCrone, July 5, 1975; children: Henry Patrick, Daniel. BS, U. Scranton, 1964; JD, Villanova U., 1967. Bar: Pa. 1968, U.S. Dist. Ct. (mid. dist.) Pa. 1968, U.S. Ct. Appeals (3d cir.) 1994, U.S. Ct. Appeals (fed. cir.) 2001, U.S. Ct. Internat. Trade 2001; lic. real estate broker, Pa. Law clk. Ct. Common Pleas, Lackawanna County, Pa., 1968-69; lectr. bus. law U. Scranton, 1968-69; assoc. Haggerty & McDonnell, Scranton, 1969-75; assoc. counsel Scranton Redevel. Authority, 1969-70; spl. atty. gen. and legal opinion writer Pa. State Workers' Compensation Bd., 1972-97, legal opinion writer, 1972-97; sec., gen. counsel Opportunity Products Today, Inc., 1998; assoc. Burke and Douglass, Scranton, Pa., 1975-80; co-owner Directel Inc. Wireless, 1999-2000; pvt. practice law Scranton, 1969—. Mem. exec. com. Pa. unit Am. Heart Assn., 1973-74, asst. treas. Keystone chpt., 1972; del. Dem. Nat. Conv., 1972, chmn. econ. com. Dem. Nat. Platform Com., 1972; trustee Lackawanna Jr. Coll., 1977-79, solicitor, 1979-83; mem. alumni bd. govs. U. Scranton, 1969-75, pres. Nat. Alumni Soc., 1983-85; solicitor Cath. Social Svcs., 1978-95, bd. dirs., 1978-97; pres., owner Scranton-Wilkes Barre Twins, Inc., 1993-94; pres. Atlantic Collegiate Baseball League, 1995-97. Bd. dirs. Pennsylvanians for Human Life, 2001—04, Secular Franciscan Order, 2002—; bd. dirs. Lackawanna br. Pa. Assn. for Blind, 1988—, chmn., 2003—05, pres., 2003—05. Mem. ABA, Pa. Bar Assn., Lackawanna Bar Assn., Greater Scranton Bd. Realtors, Pa. Assn. Realtors, Nat. Assn. Realtors, Intertel, Internat. Soc. Philos. Enquiry, Mensa, Alpha Sigma Nu. Democrat. Roman Catholic. Home: 319 Church St Dunmore PA 18512-1911 Office: Scranton Bank Bldg 12th Fl 108 N Washington Ave Scranton PA 18503 Home Phone: 570-347-3896; Office Phone: 570-344-0200. Business E-Mail: burkehp@verizon.net.

BURKE, JAMES JOSEPH, JR., investment banker; b. Wilmington, Del., Dec. 19, 1951; s. James Joseph and Kathleen Gertrude (Nauss) B.; m. Jeanne Elizabeth Burke, Aug. 6, 1977 (div. Oct. 2002); children: James III, Jennifer, Brian. AB in Psychology, Brown U., 1973; MBA with distinction, Harvard U., 1979. 2d v.p. program JPMorgan Chase Bank, NYC, 1973-77; assoc. Merrill Lynch, NYC, 1979-83, v.p., 1983-85, mng. dir., 1985-94; pres., CEO Merrill Lynch Capital Ptnrs., NYC, 1987-94; mng. ptnr. First Capital Ptnrs., NYC, 1994—, Stonington Ptnrs., Inc. (formerly First Capital Ptnrs.), NYC, 1995—. Bd. dirs. Ann Taylor Stores Corp., NYC, Lincoln Ednl. Svcs. Corp., West Orange, NJ., Roundabout Theatre Co., NYC. Trustee Seton Hall Prep. Sch., West Orange, Brown U., Providence, Devel. Sch. Youth, NYC, Roundabout Theatre Co., NYC; bd. overseers Seton Hall U. Sch. Diplomacy and Internat. Rels., Brown U. Sports Found.; mem. exec. com. Boy Scouts Am., NY. Mem.: Econ. Club N.Y. Office: Stonington Ptnrs 540 Madison Ave 25th Flr New York NY 10022 Business E-Mail: JBurke@stonington.com.

BURKE, JANE, software company executive; b. Aurora, Ill., June 17, 1947; d. Joseph Martin and Leona Pearl (Ory) B.; m. Joseph Kulinski, Aug. 24, 1968 (div. Apr. 1975); m. James Michael O'Brien, Nov. 23, 1977. BA, St. Dominic Coll., St. Charles, 1969; MLS, Rosary Coll., River Forest, 1970; M in Mgmt, Northwestern U., Evanston, 1986. Librarian Cook Memorial Library, Libertyville, Ill., 1970-74; various pos. CL Systems, Inc., Newton, Ma., 1974-83; dir. Northwestern U., Evanston, Ill., 1983-87; pres. NOTIS Systems, Inc., Evanston; co-founder, pres. & CEO Endeavor Info. Systems, 1994—2003; dir. new bus. devel. Cadmus Profl. Comm., 2003—05; v.p. ProQuest Info. & Learning, Ann Arbor, Mich., 2005—; gen. mgr. Serials Solutions, Seattle, 2005—. Bd dirs. ITAL editl. board, Dominican U. Grad. Sch. Libr. Info. Sci.; bd. govs. Northwestern U. Libr. Named to Chgo. Area Entrepreneurship Hall of Fame. Mem. ALA, Am. Mgmt. Assn. Office: Serials Solutions #400 501 N 34th St Seattle WA 98103-8645 also: ProQuest Info & Learning PO Box 1346 Ann Arbor MI 48106-1346*

BURKE, JOHN, priest; b. Washington, Sept. 15, 1928; s. William Francis and Grace Allison (Logan) B. AB, Cath. U. Am., 1950, MA, 1965, STD, 1969. Joined Order Preachers, ordained priest Roman Cath. Ch., 1960. Prof. homiletics St. Stephen's Coll., Dover, Mass., 1961-64, Immaculate Conception faculty, 1964-67, 90, asst. prof., summers 1964-69, asst. prof. drama, 1968-72, dir. Preaching Workshop, 1965-67, dir. Preachers Inst., 1967-72; mem. faculty Washington Theol. Coalition, 1968-69; coord. Nat. Congress for the Word of God, 1972; founder, exec. dir. Nat. Inst. for the Word of God, Washington, 1972—; prof. Dominican House of Studies, Washington, 1990—. Author: Bible Sharing Youth Retreat Manual, 1983, Beginners' Guide to Bible Sharing, Vol. I, II, 1984, The Homilist's Guide to Scripture, Theology and Canon Law, 1987, Dominican Preaching in the Province of St. Joseph: 1832-1960, 2005; editor: Gospel Power: Toward the Revitalization of Preaching, 1978, Bible Sharing: How to Grow in the Mystery of Christ, 1979, A New Look at Preaching, 1983,A Good News Spirituality, 2000; contbr. articles to profl. jours.; producer TV film Chimbote, 1964. Mem. Radio-TV Dirs. Guild of AFTRA, Phi Beta Kappa. Roman Catholic. Address: 487 Michigan Ave NE Washington DC 20017-1584 E-mail: burkeop@aol.com. *For lasting happiness in life, one needs to experience the active presence of God.*

BURKE, JOHN EDWARD, communications editor; b. Huntington, W.Va., Aug. 10, 1942; s. Charles Joseph and Eloise Marie (Sang) B.; m. Mary Catherine Enright; children: John Lindsey, Elizabeth Ann, Caroline Catherine. BA, Marshall U., Huntington, W.Va., 1965; MFA, Ohio U., 1966; PhD, Ohio State U., 1971. Intern U.S. Ho. Reps., 1960-61; news writer, editor Sta. WSAZ-TV, Huntington, 1962-65; instr. Kent State U., 1966-69; dir. TV Arts dept. Cleve. Summer Sch. for Arts, 1967-68; asst. to dir. Ohio State U. Telecomms. Ctr., 1969-71; project dir. Ohio Valley Med. Microwave TV System, Columbus, 1971-73; dir., assoc. prof. biomed. comms. Ohio State U. Coll. Medicine; assoc. prof. comms. Coll. Social and Behavioral Scis., 1972-84; assoc. dean acad. affairs, prof. U. Ill. Coll. Associated Health Professions, Chgo., 1984-87; sr. mgr. sci. rels. Pharm. Products divsn. Abbott Labs., 1987-97; exec. dir., CEO Accreditation Assn. Ambulatory Health Care Inc. Adj. prof. Ohio State U., Columbus, 1989—; cons. univs., bus., industry, including U. Tenn., Nat. Med. Audio-Visual Ctr., Upjohn Co., N. Ctrl. Assn. Colls. and Univs., WHO, AMA. Author: History of Public Broadcasting Act of 1967, 1979; contbr. articles to profl. jours.; editor Jour. Allied Health, 1978-87; editor emeritus Jour. Allied Health, 1987—. USPHS grantee, 1972-77. Fellow Am. Soc. Allied Health Professions; mem. Health Scis. Comms. Assn., Coun. of Biology Editors, Am. Med. Writers Assn., Am. Soc. Assn. Execs., Alpha Psi Omega, Alpha Epsilon Rho. Democrat. Roman Catholic. Home: 567 Maple St Winnetka IL 60093-2335

BURKE, JOHN K(IRKLAND), JR., lawyer; b. Richmond, Va., Jan. 26, 1952; s. John Kirkland and Archer (Christian) B.; m. Miriam Smith, July 23, 1977; children: John K. III, Ruth H., B. Smith. BA in History with distinction, U. Va., Charlottesville, 1974, JD, 1977. Bar: Va. 1977, US Dist. Ct. (ea. and we. dists.) Va. 1977, US Ct. Appeals (4th cir.) 1977. Law clk. to Justice George M. Cochran Supreme Ct. Va., Staunton, 1977-78; assoc. Mays and Valentine, L.L.P., Richmond, Va., 1978-84; ptnr. Mays and Valentine, Richmond, Va., 1984-2000, chmn. bus. and comml. litigation practice group; ptnr. Troutman Sanders LLP, Richmond, 2001—. Mem. City of Richmond's Human Rels. Comm., 1991-97; bd. dirs. St. Andrews Sch., Richmond, Va., 2005—. Mem. Va. Bar Assn., Bar Assn. of City of Richmond (bd. dirs. 1994-98, 2007-), Soc. of Cin. for State of Va. (sec.), Va. State Bar, Country Club Va. (bd. dirs. 1999-2001). Avocations: sports, reading, music. Office: Troutman Sanders LLP PO Box 1122 Richmond VA 23218-1122 Office Phone: 804-697-1210. Business E-Mail: john.burke@troutmansanders.com.

BURKE, JOHN MICHAEL, lawyer; b. Chgo., Oct. 9, 1941; s. John and Catherine Mary (Barrett) B.; m. Maureen Kay Fox, Oct. 5, 1968; children: Brian, Timothy, Michael. BBA, Loyola U., 1964, JD, 1965. Bar: Ill. 1965, U.S. Dist. Ct. (no. dist.) Ill. 1965, U.S. Ct. Appeals (7th cir.) 1968, U.S. Dist. Ct. (no.dist.) Ind. 1986. Assoc. Pretzel & Stouffer, Chgo., 1965—69, Shaheen, Lundberg & Callahan, Chgo., 1969—70; ptnr. Burke & Burke, Ltd., Chgo., 1970—. Sgt. U.S. Army, 1965-68. Mem. ATLA, Chgo. Bar Assn., Ill. State Bar Assn. (chmn. tort coun., svc. award 1984, civil practice com. 1997-2003, jud. evaluation com. 2002—), Ill. Trial Lawyers (bd. mgrs. 1988—), Appellate Lawyers Ill., Westmoreland Country Club (Wilmette, Ill.) Home: 2241 Kenilworth Ave Wilmette IL 60091-1523 Office: Burke & Burke Ltd 30 N LaSalle St Ste 2800 Chicago IL 60602 Office Phone: 312-726-6630. Business E-Mail: jburke@burke-burke.com.

BURKE, JOHN PATRICK, internist, educator; b. Marshalltown, Iowa, Jan. 19, 1940; s. Raphael Eggleston and Marjorie N. (Busch) B.; m. Andrea Marie Keane, May 9, 1970; children: Paul, Matthew, Edward, Erin. BA, summa cum laude, U. Iowa, 1961, MD, 1964. Diplomate Am. Bd. Internal Medicine, Am. Bd. Infectious Disease. Intern Yale-New Haven Hosp., 1964-65, resident in medicine, 1965-67; rsch. fellow Harvard med. unit Boston City Hosp., 1968-70; chief infectious disease sect. LDS Hosp., Salt Lake City, 1970—; epidemic intelligence svc. officer Ctr. for Disease Control and Prevention, 1967—70. Asst. prof. medicine U. Utah, Salt Lake City, 1970-75, assoc. prof., 1975-83, prof., 1983—, Mark Presdl. endowed chair in medicine, 1999—; spl. reviewer NIH, Bethesda, Md., 1978, 80; mem. tech. panel on infections within hosps. Am. Hosp. Assn., 1996; cons. Inst. Medicine, NAS, 1998—, Ctrs. for Disease Control and Prevention, 1994, 99, 2005, Nat. Patient Safety Found., 1999, Lewin Group, 1999-2000; mem. sci. adv. coun. Heart and Lung Inst. LDS Hosp. Found., 1990—; co-founder TheraDoc, Inc., 1999. Mem. editl. bd. Am. Jour.

Infection Control, 1981-97, Infection Control and Hosp. Epidemiology, 1979-88, 2003-; contbr. numerous articles to med. jours., chpts. to books. Surgeon USPHS, 1967-70. NIH-Nat. Inst. Allergy and Infectious Disease grantee, 1974-79, 79-82, 83-85, 86-89, FDA, 1999. Fellow Infectious Disease Soc. Am., ACP, Soc. for Healthcare Epidemiology Am. (councillor 1981-82, treas. 1985-88, v.p. 1991, mem. bd. dirs. 1991-93, pres. 1992); mem. Utah Med. Assn. (del. 1975-77), Am. Epidemiol. Soc., Alpha Omega Alpha, Phi Beta Kappa. Mem. Christian Ch. Home: 1966 Yale Ave Salt Lake City UT 84108-1827 Office: LDS Hosp Med Office Bldg Ste 204 370 9th Ave Salt Lake City UT 84103 Home Phone: 801-582-2897; Office Phone: 801-408-1006. Business E-Mail: john.burke@hsc.utah.edu.

BURKE, JOSEPH C., former university official; b. New Albany, Ind., Mar. 20, 1932; s. Dennis F. and Beatrice V. (McDevitt) B.; m. Joan Thompson, Sept. 1, 1956; children: Maura, Colleen. BA, Bellarmine Coll., Louisville, 1954; MA, Ind. U., 1958, PhD, 1965. Instr. Ohio Wesleyan U., Del., 1960-62; asst. prof. to prof. history Duquesne U., Pitts., 1962-70; prof. history Loyola of Montreal, 1970-73, acad. v.p., 1970-73, SUNY Coll., Plattsburgh, 1973-74, pres., 1974-85; provost, vice chancellor for acad. affairs SUNY Sys., Albany, 1985-95; pres. Rsch. Found. SUNY, Albany, 1990-95, interim chancellor, 1994; sr. fellow, dir. higher edn. prog. Nelson A. Rockefeller Inst. Govt., Albany, 1956. Cons. leadership adn planning for colls. and univs. Contbr. books and articles on accountability in higher edn. and performance funding and reporting. Trustee Miner Found. Rsch.; chmn. bd. Miner Agrl. Inst. Grantee Pew Charitable Trusts Luce Found., 1996—, Ford Found., 1996—. Home Phone: 518-465-1833; Office Phone: 518-443-5835. Business E-Mail: burkejo@rockinst.org.

BURKE, KAREN A., medical/surgical nurse; b. Ariz., Jan. 23, 1945; d. Halder John and Virgie Lee (Harris) Rex; children from previous marriage: Virgie Ann, Lori Jan. AS, Cen. Ariz. Coll., 1974. RN, Ariz.; CPR; ACLS; cert. crisis intervention and trauma nurse, Ariz. Charge nurse med. surg., emergency rm., ob. Miami Inspiration Hosp., Ariz., 1974-84; med./surg. nurse Gila Gen. Hosp., Globe, Ariz., 1980-81; relief charge nurse ob. Yavapai Regional Med. Ctr., Prescott, Ariz., 1984—2006, interim unit dir., 1988-89, charge nurse, emergency rm., med./surg., others, 1990—, clin. nurse I, 2004—. Med. mission, Papalote, Mexico, 1993; mem. Med. Res. Corps. Homeland Security Yavapai County, 2004—.

BURKE, KATHLEEN B., lawyer; b. Bklyn., Sept. 2, 1948; BA, St. John's U., 1969, JD, 1973. Bar: Ohio 1973. Ptnr. Jones Day, Cleve. Chair Notre Dame Coll. of Ohio, 2002-06. Pres. Cleve. Skating Club, 2000-02. Named a Woman of Achievement, Cleve. YWCA, 2004; recipient Ohio Bar medal, 2002. Fellow Ohio State Bar Found. (pres. 2000); mem. Ohio State Bar Assn. (pres. 1993-94). Office: Jones Day North Point 901 Lakeside Ave E Cleveland OH 44114-1190 Office Phone: 216-586-3939. Business E-Mail: kbburke@jonesday.com.

BURKE, KELLY HOWARD, retired military officer, entrepreneur, philanthropist; b. Mobile, Ala., June 7, 1929; s. Kelly Howard and Vesta (Trussell) B.; m. Denny Ray Hosey, Dec. 30, 1951; children: Bethany, Patricia, Kelly Howard, III. BS in History, Auburn U., 1952; MS in Internat. Rels., George Washington U., 1968; postgrad., Naval War Coll., 1967-68, RAF Staff Coll., 1969-71, Indsl. Coll. Armed Forces, 1964-65. Commd. 2d lt. U.S. Air Force, 1953, advanced through grades to lt. gen.; 1979; comdr. 379th Bomb Wing Wurtsmith AFB, Mich., 1973-74; comdr. 2d Bomb Wing Barksdale AFB, La., 1974-75; dep. chief of staff/plans SAC, 1975-78; dir. operational requirements Hdqrs. U.S. Air Force, Washington, 1978-79, dep. chief of staff/research, devel. and acquisition, 1979-82; ret., 1982; chmn. bd. Stafford, Burke and Hecker, Inc., Alexandria, Va., 1982. Bd. dirs. Singer Co., Tiger Internat. Inc., Flying Tigers Line Inc., Orbital Scis. Corp., OWC Found., Children's Advocacy Ctr.; cons. White House Sci. Office, NRC, Def. Sci. Bd., Sci. Adv. Bd., others; frequent lectr. Chmn. editl. bd. Aerospace Am.; contbg. editor Armed Forces Jour.; contbr. numerous articles on nat. security issues to publd. Decorated D.S.M. with oak leaf cluster, Legion of Merit, D.F.C., Meritorious Svc. medal, Air medal with oak leaf clusters; established Burke Scholarship Endowment for 15 4-yr. coll. scholarships annually to needy students, established Burke Scholarship for outstanding AFROTC cadet, Auburn U.; named Fla. Benefactor of Yr. for this and other charitable activities, 1995. Mem. Nat. Space Club, Nat. Aviation Club Episcopalian. Home: 803 Choctaw Ln Shalimar FL 32579-2248 Office: Stafford Burke and Hecker 1006 Cameron St Alexandria VA 22314-2427 Personal E-mail: kbxel@aol.com.

BURKE, KENNETH ANDREW, advertising executive; b. Sept. 9, 1941; s. Frank Flory and Margret Anne (Tomè) B.; m. Karen Lee Burley, July 1, 1968; children: Allison Leigh Hart, Aric Jason. BSBA in Mktg., Bowling Green State U., Ohio, 1965. Mem. Green Bay Packers Nat. Football League, Sask. Roughriders, Can. Football League; acct. exec. lang, Fisher, Stashower, Cleve., 1967-69; v.p., acct. supr. Tracy-Locke, Dallas, 1969-72; v.p. Grey Advt., NYC, 1972-76, Griswold Eshleman, Cleve., 1976-79; sr. v.p., gen. mgr. Simpson Mktg., Columbus, Ohio, 1979-81; pres., CEO, chmn. Martcom Inc., Columbus, Ohio, 1981-91; chmn. ret. Ad Factory, Inc., Advt. and Mktg., Ad Factory Outlets, Columbus, Ohio, 1991-98; exec. v.p. Berkshire Product Inc., Tampa, Fla., 1983-89. Bd. dirs. Ad Factory, Newport Mktg. Svcs. Author: (children's stories) Bordini and the Black Knight, 1975. Mem. adv. bd. columbus chpt. Am. Cancer Soc., 1980-88. Recipient USN Achievement award Am. Legion USN Meml. Found., 1975. Mem. NRA, Am. Mktg. Assn., Columbus Advt. Fedn., NFL Alumni Assn., Columbus Numis. Soc., Am. Numis. Assn, Columbus NFL Alumni, Cleve. Advt. Club (Merit award 1968), Columbus C. of C., Upper Arlington C. of C., Theta Chi. Republican. Roman Catholic. Home: 1753 Bedford Rd Columbus OH 43212-2004 Office: Ad Factory Corp Offices 22 Gay Street Columbus OH 43215

BURKE, KEVIN, utilities executive; m. Patricia Burke; 2 children. BE, Cooper Union; ME, Rensselaer Polytechnic Inst.; MS, Columbia Univ.; JD, Fordham Univ.; student Advanced Mgmt. Program, Harvard U., Cambridge, Mass. Engr. Consolidated Edison Inc., NYC, 1973—77, atty., 1977—81, dir. regulatory affairs, 1981—82, gen. mgr. nuclear adminstrv. svc., 1982—85, gen. mgr. bldg. & plant projects, 1985—87, v.p. constrn., 1987—90, v.p. Bklyn. customer svc., 1990—93, v.p. corp. planning, 1993—98, sr. v.p. customer svc., 1998—99; pres. Orange & Rockland Utilities, 1999—2000; pres., COO Consolidated Edison Co. of NY, NYC, 2000—05; pres., CEO Consolidated Edison Inc., NYC, 2005—, chmn., 2006—. Bd. dir. Am. Gas Assn., Energy Assn. NY. Bd. dir. Edison Elec. Inst. Partnership of NYC, NY State Bus. Council, NY Botanical Garden, United Way NYC, YMCA Greater NY. Office: Consolidated Edison Inc 4 Irving Pl Rm 1610 New York NY 10003

BURKE, KEVIN, finance company executive; Co-founder Tonic 360; pres. JWT, San Francisco; sr. v.p. brand mgmt., advt. and web mktg. Visa USA, Foster City, Calif., 2005—07, head US mktg., 2007—. Office: Visa USA 900 Metro Center Blvd Foster City CA 94404

BURKE, KEVIN CHARLES ANTONY, geologist; b. London, Nov. 13, 1929; came to U.S., 1973; s. Charles Henry and Kathleen B.; m. Angela Marion Phipps, Jan. 23, 1960; children: Nicholas, Matthew, Jane. BSc, Univ. Coll., London, 1951, PhD, 1953. Lectr. U. Ghana, 1953-56; geologist Brit. Geol. Survey, 1956-61; head geology dept. U. West Indies, Kingston, Jamaica, 1961-65; prof. geology U. Ibadan, Nigeria, 1963-71, SUNY-Albany, 1973-83; prof. U. Houston, 1983—; dir. Lunar and Planetary Inst., 1983-88; scholar in residence NRC, Washington, 1989-92. Vis. prof. U. Toronto, 1971-73, Calif. Inst. Tech., 1976, U. Minn., 1977, U. Calgary, 1979; cons. in field. NSF grantee, 1976— Fellow: Geol. Soc. Am. (Penrose medal 2007); mem.: AAAS, Nigerian Mining, Geol. and Metall. Soc. (pres. internat. com. on the lithosphere 1992—95, Du Toit Meml. lectr. 1995), Am. Geophys. Union. Achievements include research in plate tectonics. Office: Univ Houston Dept Geoscis Houston TX 77204-5007 Home Phone: 978-282-3493; Office Phone: 713-743-3397. *There is much luck in a scientific career. I could not have known when I chose to become a geologist in 1948 that understanding of the problems I studied would be revolutionized by Plate Tectonics in 1965. To make the most of such an opportunity in geology a breadth of experience, both geographically and in different branches of geology, has proved vital.*

BURKE, KIM DONALD, science educator; b. Manchester, Iowa, Sept. 13, 1952; s. Donald Elwin and Evelyn L. Burke; m. Nancy Kay Burford, Aug. 24, 1974; children: Erin Liane Loving, Landon Tyler. BA in Bus. and Pre-Med., Graceland U., Lamoni, Iowa, 1975, MA in Collaborative Edn., 2002; MA in Healthcare Adminstrn., U. Wis., Madison, 1977. Cert. tchr. unified sci.-chemistry. Adminstrv. intern United Hosp., Inc., St. Paul, 1977—78; asst. adminstr. Independence Regional Hosp., Mo., 1978—81, The Groves Nursing Facility, Independence, 1981—95; sci. tchr. Hogan H.S., Kansas City, Mo., 1997—98, Raytown H.S., Mo., 1998—2007, Paseo Acad. of Arts, Kansas City, 2004—. Sch. planning com. Paseo Acad. of Arts, Kansas City, 2003—04, sch. tech. com., 2003—04, coach Robotics Club, 2003—07. Pres. Independence West Rotary Club, 1993—94; priesthood mem. Cmty. of Christ Beacon Heights Congregation, 1969—. Recipient Judges award 1st Robotics, St. Louis Regional, 2006. Mem.: Kansas City Fedn. Tchrs. Avocations: building, fishing, gardening. Home: 19109 E 27th St Ct 5 Independence MO 64057

BURKE, LILLIAN WALKER, retired judge; b. Thomaston, Ga., Aug. 2, 1917; d. George P. and Ozella (Daviston) Walker; m. Ralph Livingston Burke, July 8, 1948 (dec.); 1 son, R. Bruce. BS, Ohio State U., 1947; LLB, Cleve. State U., 1951, postgrad., 1963-64; grad., Nat. Coll. State Judiciary, U. Nev., 1974. Bar: Ohio 1951. Gen. practice law, Cleve., 1952-62; asst. atty. gen. Ohio, 1962-66; mem., vice chmn. Ohio Indsl. Commn., 1966-69; judge Cleve. Mcpl. Ct., 1969-87, chief judge, 1981, 85, vis. judge, 1988-97; ret., 1997. Guest lectr. Heidelburg Coll., Tiffin, Ohio, 1971; cons. Bur. Higher Edn., HEW, 1972. Pres. Cleve. chpt. Nat. Coun. Negro Women, 1955-57; sec. East dist. Family Service Assn., 1959-60; mem. coun. human rels. Cleve. Citizens League, 1959-79; mem. Gov.'s Com. on Status of Women, 1966-67; pres. Cleve. chpt. Jack and Jill of Am., Inc., 1960-61; v.p.-at-large Greater Cleve. Safety Coun., 1969-79; mem. Cleve. Landmarks Commn., 1990-97; woman ward leader 24th Ward Republican Club, 1957-67; mem. Cuyahoga County Ctrl. Com., 1958-68; sec. Cuyahoga County Exec. Com., 1962-63; alt. del. Rep. Nat. Conv., Chgo., 1960; bd. dirs., chmn. minority div. Nat. Fedn. Rep. Women, 1966-68; life mem., past bd. dirs. Cleve. chpt. NAACP; bd. dirs. Greater Cleve. Neighborhood Ctrs. Assn., Cath. Youth Counselling Svcs.; trustee Ohio Commn. on Status of Women, 1966-70, Consumers League Ohio, 1969-75, Cleve. Music Sch. Settlement; bd. mgmt. Glenville YWCA, 1960-70; mem. project com. Cleve. Orch.; apptd. mem. City Planning Comm. Cleve., 1997-2002. Recipient achievement award Parkwood Christian Meth. Episcopal Ch., 1968, Martin Luther King Citizen's award, 1969, outstanding achievement award Ta-Wa-Si Scholarship Club, 1969, Outstanding Svc. award Morning Star Grand chpt., Cleve., 1970, award of honor Cleve. Bus. League, 1970, svc. award St. Paul AME Ch., Lima, Ohio, 1972, Woman of Achievement award Inner Club Coun., Cleve., 1973, cert. of award Nat. Coun. Negro Women, 1969, Cleve. Found. Golf Philanthropic Leadership award, 1997; named Career Woman of Yr., Cleve. Women's Career Clubs, 1969, Jewel of Yr., Women's City Club, 2002, award for hist. preservation So. African Hist. Soc., 2002, Woman of Achievement award YWCA, 2003. Mem. ABA, Nat. Assn. Investment Clubs (pres. Dynasty Investors Club 1992-96, bd. dirs. N.E. Ohio Coun. 1993-2003), Nat. Bar Assn., Ohio Bar Assn., Cuyahoga County Bar Assn., Cleve. Bar Assn., Am. Judicature Soc., Am. Judges Assn. (bd. govs. 1982-86, chmn. conv. agenda com. 1981-83), Phillis Wheatley Assn., Women Lawyers Assn. (hon. adviser), Ohio State U. Alumni Assn. (life), Cleve. Marshall Law Sch. (life), Am. Bridge Assn. (life), Women's City Club of Cleve. (life), Altrusa, Alpha Kappa Alpha. Anglican. Home and Office: 1357 East Blvd Cleveland OH 44106-4018

BURKE, LINDA BEERBOWER, lawyer, mining executive, metal products executive; b. Huntington, W.Va., June 19, 1948; d. William Bert and Betty Jane (Weddle) Beerbower; m. Timothy F. Burke, Jr., Aug. 26, 1972; children: Ryan Timothy, Hannah Elizabeth. BA in Govt., Coll. of William and Mary, 1970; JD, U. Pitts., 1973. Bar: Pa. 1973. Tax atty. legal dept. Aluminum Co. Am., Pitts., 1973-77, gen. tax atty. tax dept., 1977-80, mgr. legal and planning taxes, 1980-86, tax counsel, 1987-2000, asst. officer, 1992-2000, dir. taxes, 1993-2000; now v.p. Suriname Aluminum Co., Pitts., Alcoa Minerals of Jamaica, Inc., Pitts., Alcoa Steamship Co., Inc., Pitts.; with Alcoa Svc. Corp., Pitts., to 2000; v.p. Northwest Alloys, Inc., Pitts.; oper. divsn. counsel large and mid-size bus. IRS, Washington, 2000—03; cons., sole practitioner, 2004—. V.p. various Alcoa subs.; presenter on fields internat. and employee benefits taxation, IRS audit procedures, atty.-client privilege. Note editor U. Pitts. Law Rev., 1972-73. Bd. dirs. YWCA Greater Pitts., 1987-95, 97-2000, v.p., 1989-92, pres., 1993-94; Alcoa co-chmn. Taylor Allderdice-Alcoa Partnership in Edn., 1982-84, chmn., 1985-88; mem. law fellows com. U. Pitts. Law Sch., 1988—, chmn. class ann. giving fund for law sch. class, 1982-94, chmn. law fellows, 1998—; bd. dirs. Soc. Alumni Coll. William and Mary, 2000—06; mem. rev. com. United Way, 1987-94; bd. dirs. Vol. Action Ctr., 1982-85, Chattering Children, 2004—; mem. bd. visitors U. Pitts. Sch. Law, 2006; mem. pers. com. Woman's Ctr. and Shelter Greater Pitts., 1986-94; trustee St. Edmund's Acad., 1986-94, sec., 1989-90, treas., 1990-92, mem. fin. com., 1986-93, chmn. enrollment com., 1988-90, co-chmn. ann. giving, 1986-87; mem. Leadership Pitts., 1990-91, bd. dirs., 1997-2000, sec., 1999-2000; trustee Am. Tax Policy Inst., 1996-2000; mem. program com. Tax Found., 1996-2000; mem. adv. group to commr. Internal Revenue, 1996-98. Recipient tribute in corp. tax Triangle Corner, 1982, Asst. Commr.'s award IRS, 1992 Mem. ABA, Allegheny County Bar Assn., Am. Corp. Counsel Assn., Pitts. Internat. Tax Soc. (program com. 1988-94), Tax Execs. Inst. (bd. dirs. Pitts. chpt. 1981-86, pres. 1985-86, nat. bd. dirs., nat. exec. com. 1988-89, 90-91, 92-95, nat. chmn. IRS adminstrv. affairs com. 1989-90, 91-92, nat. sec. 1992-93, nat. sr. v.p. 1993-94, v.p. region VI 1990-91, internat. pres. 1994-95), Pitts. Tax Club (bd. dirs. 1989-95, pres. 1993-94), Duquesne Club. Democrat. Avocations: skiing, bridge, cooking, golf.

BURKE, MARGARET ANN, computer company and communications executive; b. NYC, Feb. 25, 1961; d. David Joseph and Eileen Theresa (Falvey) B. BS in Computer Sci., St. John's U., Jamaica, NY, 1982; MBA, U. Md., 1994. Cert. data processor. Software specialist Bell Atlantic Corp., Washington, 1983—. Active Friends of Hillwood Mus., Washington. Mem. NAFE, Alliance Francaise, Nat. Fedn. Rep. Women, Am. Film Inst. Roman Catholic. Home: 6652 Hillandale Rd Unit A Bethesda MD 20815-6406 Office: Bell Atlantic 13100 Columbia Pike Silver Spring MD 20904-5296

BURKE, MARGUERITE JODI LARCOMBE, application developer, consultant; b. Pasadena, Calif. d. Richard Albert and Marguerite (Colella) L.; m. M. Theodore Jockers; children: Richard Larcombe, Sir Blair; m. Roger Eugene Burke. PhD, Columbia U. Photographers model Ford Agy., NYC; freelance writer Savannah, Ga.; pres. Jodi Larcombe Assocs., Murfreesboro, N.C., 1970—; freelance computer programmer Murfreesboro, 1981—. Exec. asst. Resinall Corp., Severn, N.C., 1981—, computer programmer, 1981-89. Author: Sailing Cookbook, 1979, others; contbr. numerous articles to mags.; dir. Shotgun Theater Prodns., 1995. Chmn. bd. dirs. Shotgun Theater Prodns., N.Y., 1996—; patron Avery Fischer Hall, N.Y.C., 1979—; mem. Mus. Art N.Y.C., 1979—. Mem. Met. Opera Oncore Soc., Am. Film Soc., Met Opera Patron Assn. (2d century cir.), Met. Opera Nat. Coun., N.Y.C. Opera, Murfreesboro Hist. Soc. Avocations: sailing, reading, sewing, travel, classical music. Home and Office: Jodi Larcombe Assocs 12 Gale Ln Ormond Beach FL 32174 Office Phone: 386-437-3351. Personal E-mail: thejodil@cs.com.

BURKE, MARIANNE KING, state agency administrator, finance company executive, consultant; b. Douglasville, Ga., May 30, 1938; d. William Horace and Evora (Morris) King; divorced; 1 child, Kelly Page. Student, Ga. Inst. Tech., 1956-59, Anchorage C.C., 1964-66, Portland State U., 1968-69; BBA, U. Alaska, 1976. CPA, Alaska. Sr. audit mgr. Price Waterhouse, 1982-90; v.p. fin., asst. sec. NANA Regional Corp., Inc., Anchorage, 1990-95; v.p. fin. NANA Devel. Corp., Inc., Anchorage, 1990-95; sec.-treas. Vanguard Industries, J.V., Anchorage, 1990-95, Alaska United Drilling, Inc., Anchorage, 1990-95; treas. NANA/Marriott Joint Venture, Anchorage, 1990-95; v.p. fin. Arctic Utilities, Inc., Anchorage, 1990-95, Tour Arctic, Inc., Anchorage, 1990-95, Purcell Svcs., Ltd., Anchorage, 1990-95, Arctic Caribou Inn, Anchorage, 1990-95, NANA Oilfield Svcs., Inc., Anchorage, 1990-95, NANA Corp. Svcs., Inc., Anchorage, 1992-95; dir. divsn. ins. State of Alaska, 1995-99; pres. Marianne K. Burke Cons., 1999—. Cons. Ins. Regulatory and Devel. Authority of India, 2002—, Superintendencia de Banca y Seguros de Peru, 2004, Ins. Supervisory Commn. Republic of Albania, 2004, Saudi Arabian Monetary Authority, 2006—; cons. Bosnia and Herzegovina ins. sector Fin. Svcs. Vol. Corps, 2003, cons. assessment mission in Kosovo, 05, cons. assessment of ins. cos. supervision, Croatia, 05; mem. State of Alaska Medicaid Rate Commn., 1985—88, State of Alaska Bd. Accountancy, 1984—87; bd. dirs. Nat. Assn. Ins. Commrs. Edn. and Rsch. Found.; chair Bd. Equalization Municipality of Anchorage, 2004—; instr. IAIS Core Ins. Principles, Croatia, 2006. Bd. dirs. Alaska Treatment Ctr., Anchorage, 1978, Alaska Hwy. Cruises; treas. Alaska Feminist Credit Union, Anchorage, 1979-80; mem. fund raising com. Anchorage Symphony, 1981. Mem. AICPA, Internat. Assn. Ins. Suprs. (funded mem.), Alaska Soc. CPAs, Govtl. Fin. Officers U.S. and Can., Fin. Execs. Inst. (bd. dirs.), Nat. Assn. Ins. Commrs. (bd. dirs.). Avocations: travel, reading. Home: 3818 Helvetia Dr Anchorage AK 99508-5016 Office Phone: 907-563-9790. Personal E-mail: mkburke@gci.net.

BURKE, MARY GRIGGS (MRS. JACKSON BURKE), art collector; b. St. Paul; m. Jackson Burke (dec.). BA, Sarah Lawrence Coll.; MA in Clin. Psychology, Columbia U.; postgrad., New Sch. for Social Rsch. Pvt. collector Japanese art, St. Paul, 1966—; founder The Mary & Jackson Burke Found., NYC, 1972—. Mem. vis. com. Freer Gallery Art, Smithsonian Instn.; mem. Met. Mus. Art; pres. The Mary and Jackson Burke Found. Mem. nominating com., mem. membership com., mem. exec. com., mem. activities com. The Japan Soc., 1959-77, chmn. student and visitors com., 1957-63, chmn. art gallery adv. com., 1970-73, bd. dirs., 1968-77, also hon. life trustee; chmn. friend mem. Japan House Gallery, 1969-75, 87—; bd. dirs. The Cable (Wis.) Natural History Mus., 1968-92, also hon. life trustee, Sarah Lawrence Coll., Bronxville, N.Y., 1968-78, also hon. life trustee, The Internat. Crane Found., Baraboo, Wis., 1978-90, The Hobe Sound (Fla.) Nature Ctr., 1987—; mem. adv. coun. dept. art history and archeology Columbia U., N.Y.C., 1970—; mem. internat. coun. Mus. Modern Art, N.Y.C., 1970—; mem. vis. com. Freer Gallery of Art, Smithsonian Instn., Washington, 1971—, vice chmn., 1989-92; mem. vis. com. dept. Asiatic art Mus. Fine Arts, Boston, 1972-90, also friend, 1972-90; mem. vis. com. dept. Islamic art, mem. vis. com. dept. Asian art, mem. edn. com., mem. acquisitions com., bd. dirs. Met. Mus. Art, N.Y.C., 1976—, also friend Far Ea. dept., 1984—; mem. Smithsonian Assocs. nat. bd. Smithsonian Instn., Washington, 1977-83; mem. art gallery adv. com., mem. exec. com., mem. devel. com., bd. dirs. The Asia Soc., 1978-88, also hon. life trustee; friend Bklyn. Mus. Art, 1982—, Friends of Asian Art, Freer and Sackler Galleries, 1991—; William Beene fellows N.Y. Zool. Soc., 1986—. Decorated Order of The Sacred Treasure (Japan), Second Leve Gold and Silver Star (Japan), named one of top 200 collectors, ARTnews Mag., 2004. Achievements include The Mary Griggs Burke Collection of Japanese Art at Met. Mus. of Art in NY is the largest ptv. collection of Japanese art outside Japan. Avocation: collector of Japanese art. Mailing: Mary Livingston Griggs & Mary Griggs Burke Foundation 1400 Fifth Street Ctr Saint Paul MN 55101

BURKE, MATTHEW M., lawyer; b. St. Louis, Sept. 30, 1964; BA cum laude, Holy Cross Coll., 1987; JD cum laude, Harvard Univ., 1990. Bar: Mass. 1990, US Dist. Ct. (Mass.) 1991, US Ct. Appeals 3d cir. 2001. Assoc. to ptnr. litigation dept. Ropes & Gray, Boston, 1990—, head insurance practice group. Mem.: ABA, Mass. Bar Assn., Boston Bar Assn. Office: Ropes & Gray 1 International Pl Boston MA 02110-2624 Office Phone: 617-951-7589. Office Fax: 617-951-7050. Business E-Mail: matthew.burke@ropesgray.com.

BURKE, MICHAEL, apparel executive; V.p. ops. Christian Dior, 1980; gen. mgr. Louis Vuitton N.Am., pres., 1993—97; CEO LVMH Moet Hennessy Louis Vuitton; COO Christian Dior Couture, 1997—2003, CEO; pres., CEO Fendi, 2003—. Office: LVMH Moet Hennessy Louis Vuitton 22 avenue Montaigne 75008 Paris France

BURKE, MICHAEL DESMOND, pathologist, educator; b. Galway, Ireland, May 25, 1935; arrived in US, 1959; s. James and Margaret (McKee) B.; m. Joan Long, June, 1960 (div. Apr. 1966); children: James Niall, Richard Joseph; m. Maria Sperazi, June 19, 1966: children: Marina, Claudia. MB, BCh., BAO, Nat. U. of Ireland, Galway, 1959. Diplomate in clin., anat. and chem. pathology Am. Bd. Pathology. Assoc. pathologist Mt. Sinai Hosp., Mpls., 1969-81; from asst. prof. to prof. pathology U. Minn., Mpls., 1971-81; prof. pathology and dir. clin. pathology U. Hosp. SUNY, Stony Brook, NY, 1981-95; prof. pathology NY Presbyn. Hosp./Weill Cornell Med. Ctr., NYC, 1996—2005, prof. emeritus, 2005—. Faculty of Pathology fellow Royal Coll. Physicians of Ireland, 1993; trustee Am. Bd. Pathology, Tampa, Fla., 1997, v.p., 2004, pres. 2005; editl. cons. clin. pathology Stedman's Med. Dictionary 25th edit., 1990. Editor Clinical Decisions and Laboratory Use, U. Minn. Press, 1982; adv. editor Lab. Medicine, 1985; assoc. editor Am. Jour. of Clin. Pathology, 1990-2000. Capt. USAR, 1961-63. Fellow Am. Soc. Clin. Pathologists (pres. 1995-96, Disting. Svc. award 1984, Ward Burdick award 1998), Coll. Am. Pathologists; mem. AMA, Am. Assn. for Clin. Chemistry (Outstanding Speaker award 1991), Acad. Clin. Lab. Physicians and Scientists (pres. 1993-94, Gerald T. Evans award 1997, Cotlove Lectureship award 1998). Business E-Mail: dburke@med.cornell.edu.

BURKE, MICHAEL HENRY, lawyer; b. Washington, Oct. 28, 1952; s. John Joseph and Mary Catherine (Gaul) B.; m. Ann McFarland, Jan. 31, 1981; children: Allison M., Andrew M. BA magna cum laude, Tufts U., 1974; JD, Georgetown U., 1977. Bar: Mass. 1977, U.S. Dist. Ct. Mass. 1979. Assoc. Bulkley, Richardson and Gelinas L.L.P., Springfield, Mass., 1977-83, ptnr., 1983—. Pub. adminstr. Commonwealth of Mass., 1980-90. Mem. ABA, Mass. Bar Assn., Hampden County Bar Assn. Roman Catholic. Home: 50 Meadowbrook Rd Longmeadow MA 01106-1341 Office: Bulkley Richardson and Gelinas LLP 1500 Main St Springfield MA 01115-0001 Office Phone: 413-272-6231. Business E-Mail: mburke@bulkley.com.

BURKE, MICHELLE C., lawyer; b. Cleve., Oct. 2, 1952; d. Andrew L. and Catherine L. (Sedlak) Matlak; m. Michael E. Burke, Dec. 29, 1971. BA with honors, Lake Forest Coll., 1980; JD cum laude, Harvard, 1983. Bar: Ill., 1983; U.S. Dist. Ct. (no. dist.) Ill., 1984; U.S. Ct. Appeals (3rd. cir.), 1994. Assoc. Sidley & Austin, Chgo., 1983-86, McDermott, Will & Emery,

Chgo., 1986-88, ptnr., 1989—, counsel. Contbr. Mem. Phi Beta Kappa. Office: McDermott Will & Emery 227 W Monroe St Chicago IL 60606-5096 Office Fax: 312-984-7700. Business E-Mail: mburke@mwe.com.

BURKE, PAUL NORMAN, publishing executive, automotive executive; b. Detroit, Apr. 22, 1955; s. Carl Andrew and Elaine Rita (Giguere) B.; m. Gretchen Maureen Schneider, Oct. 14, 1982; children: Janelle, Jason. Pres., founder Stabur East Music/Western Stabur Music, Redford, Mich., 1981—; pres. Stabur Graphics, Inc., Redford, 1982—96, Stabur Corp., Livonia, Mich., 1983—96, Stabur Press, Redford, 1983—96, Can-Am. Music Corp., Toronto, Canada, 1983—, Whiffart Co., Prescott, Ariz., 1989—94, Creative Boxers, Inc., Malibu, Calif., 1989—91, Stabur/RHPS, Inc., Livonia, 1989—95, Stadium Svcs., Inc., Livonia, 1993—95, TMP Internat., Inc. and McFarlane Toys, Inc., Plymouth, 1993—99, TMP Asia, Ltd., Hong Kong, 1994—99, TMP-Irwin Licensing Corp., Carson City, Nev., 1994—98, McFarlane Design Group, Inc., Cedar Grove, NJ, 1994—99, McFarlane Toys Can., Calgary, 1996—99, McFarlane Worldwide BV, Rotterdam, Netherlands, Blue Dot Design LLC, Livonia, 1999—2002, Clarke Hudson Tech., Inc., Vancouver, British Columbia, Canada, 1999—2002, Virsal Oil Co., Bakersfield, Calif., 2002—, TCS, LLC, Bakersfield, Calif., 2002—, BTR, Inc., Walled Lake, Mich., 2003—. Ptnr. Edmonton Oiler Hockey Team, Canada, 1998—99. Mem. ASCAP, Soc. Can. Music Pubs., Broadcast Music, Inc. Avocation: art collector.

BURKE, RACHEL E., lawyer; b. Newcastle Upon Tyne, Eng., Aug. 31, 1971; BS, Miami U., 1993; JD, Coll. of William & Mary, 1996. Bar: Ohio 1996, US Dist. Ct. Southern Dist. Ohio 1997, US Dist. Ct. Northern Dist. Ohio 2006. Of counsel Porter Wright Morris & Arthur LLP, Cin. Trustee Cin. Fire Mus. Named one of Ohio's Rising Stars, Super Lawyers, 2006. Mem.: Order of Coif, ABA, Ohio State Bar Assn., Cin. Bar Assn. Office: Porter Wright Morris & Arthur LLP 250 E Fifth St Ste 2200 Cincinnati OH 45202-5118 Office Phone: 513-369-4236. Office Fax: 513-421-0991.

BURKE, RAYMOND LEO, archbishop; b. Richland Center, Wis., June 30, 1948; s. Thomas F. and Marie Burke. Attended, Holy Cross Seminary, La Crosse, Wis., 1966—68, Catholic U. of Am., 1968—71, Pontifical Gregorian U., Rome, 1971—75. ordained June 29, 1975. Ordained a priest, 1975; assoc. rector Cathedral of St. Joseph the Workman, La Crosse, Wis., 1975—84; instructor of religion Aquinas High Sch., La Crosse, Wis., 1977—84; moderator of Curia and vice-chancellor Diocese of La Crosse, La Crosse, Wis., 1984, adjunct judicial vicar, 1985; visiting prof. of Canonical Jurisprudence Pontifical Gregorian U., Rome, 1985—94; bishop Diocese of La Crosse, 1994—2003; archbishop Archdiocese of St. Louis, 2004—. Bd. dirs. Nat. Catholic Rural Life Conference, 1995, bd. pres., 1996—2001; mem. Canonical Affairs Com. Nat. Conference of Catholic Bishops, 1997—99; mem. Commn. on Religious Life and Mission US Conference of Catholic Bishops, 2001—03; nat. dir. Marian Catechist Apostolate, 2000—; spiritual dir. Real Presence Assn., 2002—; mem. Vatican's Congregation for Clergy, 2003—. Office: Archdiocese of St Louis 4445 Lindell Blvd Saint Louis MO 63108

BURKE, REDMOND PAUL, pediatric cardiologist, surgeon; b. Honolulu, Hawaii, Nov. 4, 1958; married; 1 child. BA, Stanford U., Palo Alto, CA, 1980; MD, Harvard Med. Sch., Boston, MA, 1984. Lic. Mass., 1989, Fla., 1995, cert. Nat. Bd. Med. Examiners Diplomate, 1985, Advanced Trama and Life Support, 1986, Advanced CPR and Emergency Cardiac Care, 1989, Am. Bd. Surgery Diplomate, 1990, Am. Bd. Thoracic Surgery Diplomate, 1993, Am. Bd. Surgery Recertification, 2002. Rsch. asst., dept. immunology Stanford U. Children's Hosp., Palo Alto, Calif., 1977; rsch. asst., statistician, dept. radiology Palo Alto Veteran's Adminstrn. Hosp., Palo Alto, Calif., 1978; rsch. fellow, surgery Harvard Med. Sch., Boston, 1989—90, instructor, surgery, 1992—95; intern, surgery Brigham and Women's Hosp., Boston, 1984—85, resident, surgery, 1985—89, chief resident, cardiothoracic surgery, 1990—91, assoc., cardiac surgery, 1991—95, attending surgeon, 1992—95; clin. fellow, surgery Children's Hosp., Boston, 1984—89, assoc., cardiac surgery, 1991—95, attending surgeon, 1992—95, chief resident, cardiovascular surgery, 1992; chief, divsn. cardiovascular surgery Miami Children's Hosp., Fla., 1995—2002, mem. mortality review com. Fla., 1995—, divsn. chief, daily adminstrn. pediatric cardiovascular surgery program Fla., 1995—; apptd. cardiac surgeon, cardiac surgeon program Arnold Palmer Hosp., Orlando, Fla., 2002—. Vis. scientist MIT, Cambridge, Mass., 1989—92, mem. adv. com., spectroscopy lab., 1994—; vis. instr., dept. biomedical engring. U. Miami, Fla., 1995—; attending surgeon Boston Adult Congenital Heart Svc., Mass., 1992—95; mem. adv. com. Premier Cardiac Surgery Physician, 1999—; co-dir. Congenital Heart Inst., Miami, Fla., 2002—; lectr. in field. Contbr. articles to profl. jours., chapters to books; reviewer Jour. Thoracic and Cardiovascular Surgery, 1995—, Annals of Thoracic Surgery, 1995—, mem. editl. bd. Heart Surgery Forum, 1999—, Jour. Laparoendoscopic & Advanced Surgical Techniques, 1999—, mem. med. team Miracle Workers, ABC, 2006—, guest appearance The View, 2006. Vice-chmn. American Heart Walk, Miami, Fla., 2000; mem. med. adv. bd. Children's Heart Found., 2004—; bd. dir. Island Dolphin Cove, Key Largo, Fla., 2000—. Named Best Doctors in South Fla., Miami Metro Mag., 1998—2000, Most Wired Physician, State Fla., 2002; recipient Best Doctor in Am. award, 2001—02, Fla. Med. Bus. Healthcare award, 2002, Valor award, Am. Diabetes Assn., 2004. Fellow: Am. Coll. Surgeons, Coun. on Cardiothoracic and Vascular Surgery, Am. Heart Assn.; mem.: Internat. Soc. for Heart and Lung Transplantation, Candidate Soc. Thoracic Surgeons, Mass. Med. Soc., Southern Thoracic Surgical Assn., Soc. Thoracic Surgeons (active mem. 1998—), Internat. Soc. for Minimally Invasive Cardiothoracic Surgery, Cardiothoracic Surgery Network, Harvard Med. Sch. Alumni Assn. (class rep. 1985—), Phi Beta Kappa. Achievements include performing the first pediatric heart lung transplant in New England in 1992; developing and refining of minimally invasive surgical techniques in pediatric cardiothoracic surgery; patents in field. Office: Miami Children's Hosp Dept Cardiovascular Surgery 3200 SW 60th Ct Ste 102 Miami FL 33155 Office Phone: 305-663-8401. Office Fax: 305-669-6574. Business E-Mail: redmond111@aol.com.*

BURKE, RHONDA WILLIAMS, counselor; d. Charles O. and Rebekah Sue Williams; m. William H. Burke, Apr. 21, 1984; children: Ashley Elizabeth, Courtney Celeste. BS in Edn. cum laude with hons., Winthrop Coll., 1984; MEd, The Citadel, 1989. Lic. profl. counselor, nat. cert. counselor. Tchr. Berkeley County Schs., SC, 1984—87, Dorchester County Schs., 1987—90; counseling assoc. Summerville, 1989—, Charter Hosp., Charleston, 1994—95, Summerville Behavioral Health, 1999—. Troop leader Summerville Girl Scouts, 1991, 1996; bd. mem. Robert Ivey Young Profls., Summerville, 2003—04; state dir. for SC/NC Am.'s Nat. Teenager Scholarship Orgn.; Sunday sch. leader Bethany Meth. Ch., Summerville, 1995—2001; mem. bd. YMCA, 1996; bd. dirs. Create-a-Smile-Team Program, 2004—. Named Tchr. of Yr, Berkeley Country Schs., 1988. Mem.: Phi Kappa Phi. Methodist. Avocations: reading, scuba diving, photography, travel. Office: Summerville Behavioral Health 709 Trolley Rd Summerville SC 29485 Office Phone: 843-821-2480. Personal E-mail: id28532673@aol.com.

BURKE, RICHARD T., SR., professional sports team executive; b. Raleigh, NC; m. Jude; children: Taylor, Ryan, Brendan, Ian, Shannon. Grad., Ga. State U., U. Va. Founder, chmn., CEO United HealthCare Corp., 1974—88; owner, CEO, gov. Phoenix Coyotes (formerly Winnipeg Jets) hockey club, 1995—2001; non-exec. chmn. UnitedHealth Group, Mpls., 2006—. Bd. dir. UnitedHealth Group, 1977—, First Cash Fin. Services, 1993—, Meritage Homes Corp., 2004—. Office: UnitedHealth Group PO Box 1459 Minneapolis MN 55440-5979*

BURKE, ROBERT BERTRAM, lawyer, political scientist, lobbyist; b. Cleve., July 9, 1942; s. Max and Eve (Miller) B.; m. Helen Choate Hall, May 5, 1979 (div. Oct. 1983). BA, UCLA, 1963, JD, 1966; LLM, London Sch. Econs., 1967. Bar: D.C. 1972, U.S. Supreme Ct. 1977, Calif. 1978. Exec. dir. Lawyer's Com. Civil Rights Under Law, Washington, 1968-69; ptnr. Fisk, Wolfe & Burke, Paris, 1969-71; assoc. O'Connor & Hannan, Washington, 1972-74; pvt. practice Washington, 1974-79, LA, 1978-93; contract lobbyist GCG Rose & Kindel, L.A., Sacramento, Washington, 1993—. Cons. Commonwealth Pa., Harrisburg, 1973. Chmn. So. Calif. Hollings for Pres., 1984; pres. Bldg. and Appeals Bd. City of L.A.; bd. dirs. Vols. of Am.; mem. exec. com. State Bar of Calif. pub. law sect. Mem. ABA UCLA Law Alumni Assn. (pres.). Jewish. Home: 277 S Irving Blvd Los Angeles CA 90004-3809 Office Phone: 213-896-8920. Personal E-mail: bob@bobburkela.com.

BURKE, ROBERT HARRY, surgeon, educator; b. Cambridge, Mass., Dec. 22, 1945; s. Harry Clearfield and Joan Rosalyn (Spire) B.; m. Margaret Cauldwell Fisher, May 4, 1968; children: Christopher David, Catherine Cauldwell. Student, U. Mich. Coll. Pharmacy, 1964—67; DDS, U. Mich., 1971, MS, 1976; MD, Mich. State U., 1980. Diplomate Am. Bd. Oral and Maxillofacial Surgery, Am. Bd. Cosmetic Surgery. Pvt. practice cosmetic and reconstructive surgery, Ann Arbor, Mich. House officer oral and maxillofacial surgery U. Mich. Sch. Dentistry, U. Mich. Hosp., Ann Arbor, 1973-76; clin. asst. prof. dept. oral surgery U. Detroit Sch. Dentistry, 1976-77; adj. asst. rsch. scientist Ctr. Human Growth and Devel. U. Mich., 1976-77, adj. rsch. investigator, 1982-85; clin. asst. prof. Mich. State U., East Lansing, 1978-80, 1987-2007, clin. assoc. prof., 2007-; house officer surg. emphasis St. Joseph Mercy Hosp., Ann Arbor, 1980-81, sec. Dept. Plastic Surgery, 1981-82; adj. rsch. investigator dept. anatomy U. Mich. Med. Sch., 1982-85; adj. clin. asst. prof. oral and maxillofacial surgery U. Mich., 1984-86, 2002-2003, adj. clin. assoc. prof. maxillofacial surgery, 2003—; lectr. U. Detroit Sch. Dentistry, 1986, assoc. clin. prof. oral and maxillofacial surgery, 1987-90; cons., lectr. dept. occlusion U. Mich. Sch. Dentistry, 1986, asst. clin. prof. dept. maxillofacial sugery, 2002, assoc. adj. clin. prof., 2002—; head sect. dentistry and oral surgery dept. gen. surgery St. Joseph Mercy Hosp., 1982-87, mem. exec. com. dept. gen. surgery, 1984-87; chmn. com. emergency care rev. Beyer Meml. Hosp., Ypsilanti, Mich., 1986, also active, 1987, 1990-2000; active staff St. Joseph Meml. Hosp.; courtesy staff Saline Cmty. Hosp., Mich., 1978-88; Chelsea Med. Ctr., Mich., 1978-88, 90-92, McPherson Cmty. Hosp., Howell, Mich., 1984-87, Herrick Meml. Hosp., 1998—, Bixby Hosp., 1998—, Annapolis Hosp., 2000-2002, Oakwood Hosp., 2000-2002; dir. Mich. Ctr. Cosmetic Surgery. Mem. editl. bd. Topics in Pain Mgmt., 1985—; contbg. editor: Am. Jours. Cosmetic surgery, 1990-91; sect. editor: Internat. Jour. Aesthetic and Restorative Surgery, 1992-95, 96-2000, Breast Surgery sect. Internat. Jour. Cosmetic Surgery, 2000-, Am. Jour. Cosmetic Surgery, 2007-. Campaign chmn. med. and dental sects. United Way Washtenaw County, Ann Arbor, 1982, dental sect. 1983; profl. adv. com. March of Dimes Genesee County Valley Chpt., Flint, 1979; pres. Huron Pkwy. Pla. Condominium, 1984—. Fellow: Am. Acad. Cosmetic Surgery, Am. Acad. Aesthetic and Restorative Surgery, Internat. Coll. Surgeons, Am. Coll. Oral and Maxillofacial Surgeons, ACS; mem.: Am. Soc. Cosmetic Breast Surgery, Inst. Study Profl. Risk, Washtenaw County Med. Soc., European Assn. for Cranio-Maxillofacial Surgery, Chalmers Lyons Acad. oral Surgery, European Soc. Aesthetic Surgery and Liposuction, Internat. Soc. Cosmetic Laser Surgeons, Am. Assn. Craniomaxillofacial Surgeons, Am. Assn. Cosmetic Maxillofacial Surgeons, AMA, Pres.'s Club, Victor's Club, Omicron Kappa Upsilon. Congregationalist. Office: 2260 S Huron Pky Ann Arbor MI 48104-5151 Home Phone: 734-971-0325. Business E-Mail: info@robertburke.com.

BURKE, SANDRA E., information technology executive; b. Libertyville; AB, Boston U.; M in Physiology, Fairleigh Dickinson U.; PhD in Physiology, Thomas Jefferson U. Postdoctoral rschr. Robert Woods Johnson Cardiovascular Rsch. Inst., NJ; dir. cardiovascular systems rsch. Abbot Laboratories, Volwiler assoc. rsch. fellow. Founding mem. Black Bus. Network, exec. coun. mem. Named a Woman of Achievement, YWCA of Lake County, 2004; named to Hall of Fame, Women in Tech. Internat., 2005. Mem.: Volwiler Soc. Office: Abbott Laboratories 100 Abbott Park Rd Abbott Park IL 60064-6400

BURKE, SHEILA P., federal agency administrator; b. San Francisco, Jan. 10, 1951; d. George Abbott and Mary Joan (Winfield) B.; m. David Chew, Jan. 1983; children: Daniel, Kathleen, Sarah. BSN, U. San Francisco, 1973; MA in Pub. Adminstrn., Harvard U., 1982. Staff nurse Alta Bates Hosp., Berkeley, Calif., 1973-74; dir. student affairs Nat. Student Nurses Assn., NY, 1974-75, dir. program and field svcs., 1975-77; legis. asst. Senator Bob Dole, 1977-78; profl. staff mem. Senate Com. Fin., U.S. Senate, 1979-82, dep. staff dir., 1982-85; dep. chief of staff Senate Majority Leader Bob Dole, U.S. Senate, 1985-86; chief of staff Senator Bob Dole, 1986-96; sec. U.S. Senate, Washington, 1995; undersec. Am. Mus. and nat. programs Smithsonian Instn., Washington, 2000—03, dep. sec., COO, 2004—07. Adj. nursing faculty Georgetown U.; rsch. asst. J.F. Kennedy Sch. Govt., Harvard U., 1980-81, advisor to dean, 1996, exec. dean, lectr. pub. policy, 1996-2000, adj. lectr., 2000—. Mem.: Inst. Medicine. Republican. Address: 1323 Merrie Ridge Rd Mc Lean VA 22101-1826

BURKE, STEPHEN B. (STEVE BURKE), communications company executive; s. Dan Burke; married; 5 children. BA with hons., Colgate U., 1980; MBA, Harvard U., 1982. Joined The Walt Disney Corp., 1985, from developer to exec. v.p., Disney Stores, 1985—92, exec. v.p. operations, Euro Disney S.A. France, 1992—95, pres., COO Euro Disney S.A., 1995—96, pres. ABC Broadcasting, 1996—98; from sr. v.p. to exec. v.p. Comcast Corp., 1998—2002; pres. Comcast Cable, Phila., 2000—, Comcast Cable Comm. Holdings, Phila., 2002—; COO Comcast Corp., 2004—. Bd. dirs. JP Morgan Chase & Co., 2003—; chmn. exec. com. C-SPAN; mem. adv. bd. Cable in the Classroom. Bd. dir. Children's Hosp. Phila. Recipient Vanguard award for cable ops. mgmt., Nat. Cable & Telecom. Assn., 2001. Mem.: Phi Beta Kappa. Office: Comcast Corp 1500 Market St Philadelphia PA 19102*

BURKE, THOMAS JOSEPH, civil engineer; b. Grosse Pointe Park, Mich., Sept. 1, 1927; s. Cyril Joseph and Marie Estelle (Sullivan) Burke; m. Elaine Kiefer, Nov. 10, 1951; children: Judy Lee Burke Brooks, Kathleen Marie Harness, Maureen Elaine Beck, Thomas P. BCE, Villanova U., Pa., 1949. Chmn. Burke Rental Svc., Sterling Heights, Mich., 1949—, Cyril J. Burke, Inc., Sterling Heights, Mich., 1949—. Trustee Villanova U., 1980—. Served to lt. USAF, Korea. Mem.: ASCE (life), Detroit Builders Exchange (v.p. 1976—78, dir. 1975—78), Associated Equipment Distbrs. (dir. 1955—58, 1975—78), Associated Underground Contractors (dir. 1965—68), Mich. Ready Mix Concrete Assn. (dir. 1960—65), Detroit Engring. Soc., Villanova U. Alumni Assn. (nat. v.p. 1978—79, nat. pres. 1980), Grosse Pointe Yacht Club, Otsego Ski Club, Ocean Reef Club, Detroit Athletic Club, Huron Shores Golf Club, Villanova U. of Detroit Club (pres. 1955—65). Roman Catholic. Home: 578 Shelden Rd Grosse Pointe Shores MI 48236-2640 also: 688 N Lakeshore Rd Port Sanilac MI 48469-9713

BURKE, THOMAS JOSEPH, JR., lawyer; b. Oct. 23, 1941; s. Thomas Joseph and Violet (Green) B.; m. Sharon Lynne Forke, Aug. 29, 1964; children: Lisa Lynne, Heather Ann. BA, Elmhurst Coll., 1963; JD, Chgo.-Kent Coll. Law, 1966. Bar: Ill. 1966, U.S. Dist. Ct. (no. dist.) Ill. 1967, U.S. Ct. Appeals (7th cir.) 1972, U.S. Supreme Ct. 1972, U.S. Ct. Appeals (11th cir.) 1994, U.S. Ct. Appeals (6th cir.) 1995. Assoc. Lord, Bissell & Brook, Chgo., 1966-74, ptnr., 1974—2003; of counsel Hall, Prangle & Schoonveld, LLC, 2004—. Fellow: Am. Coll. Trial Lawyers; mem.: Assn. Advancement Automotive Medicine, Soc. Automotive Engrs., Product Liability Adv. Coun., Ill. Assn. Def. Trial Counsel, Def. Rsch. Inst., Soc. Trial Lawyers, Chgo. Bar Assn., Mid-Day Club, Phi Delta Phi, Pi Kappa Delta. Republican. Roman Catholic. Office: Hall Prangle & Schoonveld LLC 200 S Wacker Dr Ste 3300 Chicago IL 60606 Office Phone: 312-267-6229. Business E-Mail: tburke@hpslaw.com.

BURKE, THOMAS MICHAEL, lawyer; b. Summit, NJ, Feb. 10, 1956; s. Robert William and Eleanor Mary (Kelley) B.; m. Nancy Robin Mogab, Sept. 24, 1983; children: Colleen Margaret, Michael Thomas, Brendan Robert. BA, Notre Dame U., 1978; JD, St. Louis U., 1981. Bar: Mo. 1981, Ill. 1982, U.S. Dist. Ct. (ea. dist.) 1981. Assoc. Moser, Marsalek, Carpenter, Cleary & Jaeckel, St. Louis, 1981—86; ptnr. Noonan & Burke, St. Louis, 1986—92; prin. Thomas M. Burke, PC, St. Louis, 1992—2006; mem. The Hullverson Law Firm, St. Louis, 2006—. Bd. dirs. Legal Svcs. Ea. Mo., 1995-97. Active Vol. Lawyers program, St. Louis, St. Louis Hills Home-owner's Assn., 1984-94. Mem. Mo. Bar Assn. (bd. govs., 1998—, chair fin. com. 2002—, exec. com. 2004-05, v.p. 2006-07, pres.-elect 2007—), Ill. Bar Assn., Interest On Lawyers' Trust Accounts (bd. dirs. 1997-2002, pres. 2000-01), Bar Assn. Met. St. Louis (treas. 1992-93, sec. 1993-94, v.p. 1994-95, pres.-elect 1995-96, pres. 1996-97), St. Louis Bar Found. (sec. 1993-94, treas. 1995-96), Lawyers Assn. St. Louis (exec. com. 1987-92, sec. 1992-93, treas. 1992-93, v.p. 1993-94). Office: 1010 Market St Ste 1480 Saint Louis MO 63101 Office Phone: 314-421-2313. Business E-Mail: tburke@hullverson.com.

BURKE, THOMAS RICHARD, community college administrator; b. St. Louis, Oct. 2, 1944; s. Lloyd Richard and Frances Elizabeth (Yelton) B.; m. Sara Lou Janes, July 3, 1969; 1 child, Kimberly Ayre. BA, U. Miss., 1970, MA, 1972, PhD, 1981. Instr. Mountain Empire C.C., Big Stone Gap, Va., 1972-74, asst. prof., 1974-77, assoc. prof. history, 1977-80, acting pres., 1977, dean instrn., 1976-80; v.p. Three Rivers C.C., Poplar Bluff, Mo., 1980-86; pres. Independence C.C., 1986—, Kansas City (Kans.) C.C. Chmn. City of Poplar Bluff Hist. Commn. Served with USAF, 1965-69. Edn. Professions Devel. Act fellow, 1970-72. Mem. Am. Assn. Cmty. and Jr. Colls. (chmn. 1984-85), Kans. Assn. C.C. (chmn.), S.E. Kans. Consortium Colls. and Univs., Mo. Hist. Assn., Phi Delta Kappa, Masons, Shriners. Methodist. Office: Kansas City CC Office of Pres 7250 State Ave Kansas City KS 66112-3003

BURKE, THOMAS WILLIAM, benefits compensation analyst; b. Harmon, Ill., Aug. 1, 1947; s. John William and Mary Eileen (Long) B.; m. Mary Ellen Bosau, Nov. 27, 1970; children: Kelly, Colleen, Shannon, Tommy, Michael. BS, St. Joseph's Coll., Rensselaer, Ind., 1969. CLU; ChFC; CFP; lic. ins. counselor. Asst. mgr. Conn. Gen., Chgo., 1970-77; v.p. Fin. Industries, Austin, Tex., 1977; pres. T.W. Burke Assocs., Austin, 1978-87; dir. advanced underwriting SunLife, Dallas, 1988-92; pres. Hefner Assocs., Richardson, Tex., 1992—. Tchr. continuing edn. ABA, Tex. Soc. for CPA's and Atty. CPA's, U. Tex., 1986—. Coach Little League, 1991—; bd. advisor St. Joseph's Coll. Mem. Nat. Assn. Life Underwriters, Nat. Assn. Securities Dealers, Assn. Advanced Life Underwriters, Soc. CLU's, Dallas C. of C. (govt. affairs com. 1993-94), Million Dollar Round Table (life mem. Ct. of Table). Roman Catholic. Avocations: golf, coaching baseball. Office: Hefner & Assocs 600 W Campbell Rd Ste 7 Richardson TX 75080-3388 Office Phone: 972-994-0800. Business E-Mail: tburke@hefnerandassociates.com.

BURKE, TIMOTHY JOHN, lawyer; b. Syracuse, NY, June 5, 1946; s. Francis Joseph and Alice Marie Burke; m. Denise Kay Blied, Mar. 18, 1978; 1 child, Aimee Noel; 1 child from a previous marriage, Ryan Alexander. BA with distinction, Ariz. State U., 1967, JD cum laude, 1970. Bar: Ariz. 1970, U.S. Dist. Ct. Ariz. 1970, U.S. Ct. Appeals (9th cir.) 1974. Trial atty. Antitrust divsn. U.S. Dept. Justice, Washington, 1970-72, asst. to dir. ops., 1972-74; assoc. Fennemore Craig, Phoenix, 1974—, dir., 1978—. Part-time instr. legal writing Ariz. State U., 1974-75, adj. faculty assoc. profl. responsibility Coll. of Law, 2001-03. Mem. panel rev. bd. Phoenix United Way, 1975-76; bd. dirs. Florence Crittenton Svcs., Phoenix, 1980-88, pres., 1985-87; bd. dirs. Law Soc. Ariz. State U. Coll. Law, 1991-97, 99—, pres., 2000-05; bd. dirs. Valley of Sun Cmtys. in Schs., 1995-2001. Recipient spl. commendation U.s. Dept. Justice, 1973 Fellow Am. Bar Found., Ariz. Bar Found.; mem. ABA (antitrust and litigation sects., vice chmn. bus. torts and unfair competition com. 1996-98, chair 1998-2001, vice chmn. state enforcement com., 2001-04, editor Bus. Torts and Unfair Competition Newsletter 1996-98), FBA, Assn. Profl. Responsibility Lawyers (bd. dirs. 1993-98, pres. 1996-97), State Bar Ariz. (coun. antitrust sect., chmn. 1985-88, chmn. advt. com. 1992-94, ethics com. 1994-2001, chmn. 1995-2001, mem. task force on future of profession 2000, mem. case conflicts com. 2001-, mem. unauthorized practice of law adv. com., 2003-, chmn. 2006—), Maricopa County Bar Assn. Office: Fennemore Craig 3003 N Central Ave Ste 2600 Phoenix AZ 85012-2913 Home Phone: 602-266-2217; Office Phone: 602-916-5334. Business E-Mail: tburke@fclaw.com.

BURKE, WILLIAM, neurologist; b. Milw. s. Luke Wencil and Margaret Glenview (Mineau) Burke; m. Mary Frances Roe, Oct. 15, 1977; children: Catherine Margaret, Christine Elizabeth, Erin Rose, Joseph Vincent. BS in Biology, Marquette U., 1962; PhD in Biochemistry, St. Louis U., 1972, MD, 1972. Cert. neurology. Asst. prof. neurology St. Louis U., 1976—83, assoc. prof. neurology, 1983—93, prof. neurology, 1993—, assoc. prof. anatomy, 1989—, assoc. prof. medicine, 1992—. Vis. scientist Cornell Med. Ctr., NYC, 1971, 77, Burke Rehab. Ctr., White Plains, 1988; chmn. Mo. State Adv. Bd. for Grants in Alzheimer's and Related Disorders, 1995—97. Editor: Central Nervous System Didorder of Aging, 1987; contbr. articles to profl. jours. Expert witness Mo. Pub. Health and Safety Subcom., Jefferson City, 1992. Grantee, VA, 1978—2000, NIH, 1991—94. Fellow: Am. Acad. Neurology; mem.: AAAS, Soc. Neurosci. Roman Catholic. Avocation: golf. Home: 5517 Pinewood Forest Saint Louis MO 63118 Office: St Louis U Health Sci Ctr 3635 Vista at Grand Saint Louis MO 63110 Home Phone: 314-849-3893; Office Phone: 314-577-8026. Business E-Mail: burkewj@slu.edu.

BURKE, WILLIAM ROMNEY, urologist; b. Safford, Ariz., May 31, 1943; s. Ernest William and Hannah (Romney) B.; m. Mary Susan Wilkinson, June 11, 1969; children: Caroline, Kimberly, Suzanne, Brendan, Juliana, Kevin, Christopher, Kathleen, Brynn, David. AB, Stanford U., 1964; MD, Yale U., 1970. Diplomate Am. Bd. Urology. Surg. intern U. UT Med. Ctr., Salt Lake City, 1970-71, resident in surgery, 1971-72; resident in urology Yale-New Haven (Conn.) Hosp., 1972-76; instr. surgery Yale Med. Sch., New Haven, 1975—76; urologist Denver Clinic, 1976-78, Clackamas Urol. Clinic, Oreg. City, Oreg., 1978-95, The Urology Clinic, Portland, 1995-99; pvt. practice Oreg. City, Oreg., 1999—. Asst. clin. prof. urology U. Colo. Med. Ctr., Denver, 1978; chmn. dept. of surgery Willamette Falls Hosp., Oregon City, 1987-89. Contbr. articles to profl. jours. Mem. City of West Linn (Oreg.) Planning Commn., 1985-86; chmn. long range com. West Linn Sch. Dist., 1984, 89, mem. budget com. 1987-93. Mem.: Am. Urol. Assn. (We. sect.), N.W. Urol. Soc., Oreg. Urol. Soc., Oreg. Med. Assoc. (del. 1986—2002, trustee 2002—), Clackamas County Med. Soc. (pres. 1989, bd. dirs. 1992—), Democrat. Mem. Ch. LDS. Office: 1510 Division St Ste 10 Oregon City OR 97045-1527 Home Phone: 503-656-8462. Personal E-mail: romneyburke@hotmail.com.

BURKE, WILLIAM TEMPLE, JR., lawyer; b. San Antonio, Oct. 30, 1935; s. William Temple and Adelaide H. (Raba) B.; m. Mary Sue Johnson, June 8, 1957; children: William Patrick, Michael Edmond, Karen Elizabeth. BBA, St. Mary's U., San Antonio, JD, 1961. Bar: Tex. 1961. Practice law, Dallas; founder, pres. Burke Wright & Keiffer, PC, 1985-98; of counsel Hance/Scarborough/Wright, Dallas, 1998-2000, Hance, Scarborough, Wright, Ginsberg and Brusilow, Dallas, 2000—. Co-founder, v.p., dir. Tex. Cath. Cmty. Credit Union, 1966—69, vice-chmn. bd. dirs., 1990—91; v.p. Dallas County Hist. Survey Com., 1966; pres. Dallas Mil. Govt. Assn., 1962—63; trustee Montserrat Jesuit Retreat House, 1999—2000, treas., 1997; pres. Dallas County Small Bus. Devel. Corp., 1981—82; trustee Dallas Ecol. Found., 2004—; chmn. scout troop com. St. Patrick's Parish Roman Cath. Ch., 1976—78, chmn. fin. com., 1984—87, bldg. com., 1978—87, chmn. bd. consultors, 1978—81; vice-chmn. Cath. Commn. Appeal Diocese of Dallas, 1993—97; pres. men's club St. Patrick's Parish Roman Cath. Ch., 1963, prin. jr. H.S. Christian devel. program, 1970; bd. dirs. Dallas County War on Poverty, 1965—66; trustee Montserrat Found., 1999—2000. 1st lt. US Army, 1958—60, capt. USAR, ret. Fellow Tex. Bar Found. (life), Dallas Bar Found. (sr., life); mem. ABA, Tex. Bar Assn., Dallas Bar Assn. (co-founder, chmn. bankruptcy and comml. law sect. 1976-77, 86-87, courthouse liaison com. 1985—, lectr. 1985—, chmn. spkrs. com. 2001-02), John C. Ford Am. Inn Ct. (co-founder, pres. 2000-04, emeritus and mem. exec. com. 2000—, hon. sgt. of the Inn 2003), Dallas Safari Club (life), Serra Internat. Met. Club (pres. Met. Dallas 1997-98, dist. gov. 2004-05, Outstanding Mem. award 1995), Internat. Order Alhambra (exemplar 1978-95), KC (co-founder Greater Dallas chpt., coun. 799 grand knight, trustee 1964-69, dist. exemplar 4th degree 1968-69, Man of Yr. award 1970), Optimists (v.p., bd. dirs. Dallas 1965-66, Man of Yr. award 1966, Pres.'s award 1968), Phi Delta Phi (life, magister 1960-61, mem. of yr. 1961), Tau Delta Sigma (pres. 1957). Home: 9751 Larchcrest Dr Dallas TX 75238-2112 Office: 1401 Elm St Ste 4750 Dallas TX 75202 Home Phone: 214-348-3406; Office Phone: 214-651-6500. Business E-Mail: wburke@hswgb.com.

BURKE, WILLIAM THOMAS, lawyer, educator; b. Brazil, Ind., Aug. 17, 1926; JD, U. Ind., 1953; JSD, Yale U., New Haven, Conn., 1959. Bar: Ind. 1953. Rsch. assoc. and lectr. Yale U., 1956-62; assoc. prof. Ohio State U., 1962-64, prof., 1964-68, U. Wash. Sch. Law, Seattle, 1968-99, prof. emeritus, 1999—. Mem. adv. com. Law of Sea Task Force, Dept. State; mem. A217 Ocean Policy Com., NAS. Author: (with M. S. McDougal) The Public Order of the Oceans, 1962, Contemporary Legal Problems in Ocean Development, 1969, (with Legatski and Woodhead) National and International Law Enforcement in the Ocean, 1975, The New International Law of Fisheries, 1994, International Law of the Sea-Documents and Notes, 1997, 99. Office: U Wash Sch Law Gates Hall Seattle WA 98195 Office Phone: 206-543-2275. Personal E-mail: sealaw1@comcast.net. Business E-Mail: burke@u.washington.edu.

BURKE, YVONNE WATSON BRATHWAITE (MRS. WILLIAM A. BURKE), lawyer; b. LA, Oct. 5, 1932; d. James A. and Lola (Moore) Watson; m. William A. Burke, June 14, 1972; 1 child, Autumn Roxanne; 1 stepchild, Christine. AA, U. Calif., 1951; BA, UCLA, 1953; JD, U. So. Calif., 1956; Doctorate (hon.), Pepperdine U. Bar: Calif. 1956. Mem. Calif. Assembly, 1966-72, chmn. urban devel. and housing com., 1971, 72; mem. 93d-95th Congresses, 1973—79, House Appropriations Com.; chmn. Congl. Black Caucus, 1976; Los Angeles county supervisor 4th dist., 1979—80; ptnr. Jones, Day, Reagis & Pogue, 1987—92. Dep. corp. commr., hearing officer Police Commn., 1964-66; atty., staff McCone Commn. (investigation Watts riot), 1965; past chmn. L.A. Fed. Res. Bank; U.S. adv. bd. Nestle. Vice chmn. 1984 U.S. Olympics Organizing Com.; bd. dirs. or bd. advisers numerous orgns.; former regent U. Calif., Bd. Ednl. Testing Svc.; Amateur Athletic Found.; former bd. dirs. Ford Found., Brookings Inst.; mem. bd. supr's. 2d Dist., L.A. County Bd. of Supr's., 1992—, chair, 1993-94, 97-98, 2002-03; bd. govs. L.A. Met. Transp. Authority; pres. So. Calif. Assn. Govts., 2006, LA Coliseum Commn., 2006. Recipient Profl. Achievement award UCLA, 1974, 84; named one of 200 Future Leaders Time mag., 1974, Alumni of Yr., UCLA, 1996; recipient Achievement awards C.M.E. Chs.; numerous other awards, citations.; fellow Inst. Politics John F. Kennedy Sch. Govt. Harvard, 1971-72; Chubb fellow Yale, 1972 Office: 500 W Temple St Rm 866 Los Angeles CA 90012 Office Phone: 213-972-2222. Business E-Mail: yburke@bos.lacounty.gov.

BURKE-ABLES, KIM S., biology educator; Biology tchr. Benjamin Banneker Academic H.S., Washington. Ednl. cons. NAS, 2004. Named DC Tchr. of Yr., 2006; recipient Milken Found. Nat. Educator award, 2003; grantee TEACH Fellowship (Teaching Educators Agriculture and Conservation Holistically), US Dept. Agr., Ghana W. Africa, 2004. Office: Benjamin Banneker Academic HS 800 Euclid St NW Washington DC 20001 Business E-Mail: kim.ables@k12.dc.us.*

BURKET, ROBERT RANDALL, artist; b. Racine, Wis., Aug. 20, 1930; s. Clarence George and Margaret Ann (Sorenson) B.; m. Nancy Ekholm, Aug. 29, 1953; children: Claire, Rand. BS, U. Wis., 1952, MS, 1955. Instr. art Denison U., 1955-56; prof. drawing, printmaking, painting U. Wis., Milw., 1956-92, prof. emeritus, 1993—. One-man shows include Bradley Galleries, Milw. (8 shows), 1972-86, Rubiner Galleries, Detroit (6 shows), 1973-85, Posner Galler, Milw., 1990, 93, Retrospective, U. of Wis., Milw., 1994, Myhelan Cultural Ctr., Long Valley, Pa., 2001, others; group shows include Pratt Graphic Ctr., 1972, U.S. Cultural Ctr., Tel Aviv, 1973, Milw. Art Mus., 1975, 30 Yr. Retrospective, Wustum Mus., Racine, Wis., 1985; represented in permanent collections Tate Gallery, London, Boston Mus. Fine Arts, Met. Mus. Art, Phila. Mus., numerous others; wall mural Road to Country, 1972, wall mural Butterflies, 1986; work reproduced in Artist Proof, 1971, Compleat Printmaker, 1973, Art of the Print, 1976, 100 Years of American Printmaking, 1983, 150 Years of Wis. Printmaking, 1998; directed and produces "Colors of Change" documentary video, 1994. Former trustee Milw. Art Mus. Recipient numerous awards for prints, drawings and paintings; U. Wis. research grantee, 1969, 71, 73, 75, 77; Knapp grantee for ednl. research, 1973, Wis. Arts grantee, 1977; Fromkin grantee, 1980; recipient Gov.'s Print Commn., 1985. Home: PO Box 858 East Orleans MA 02643-0858

BURKES, LIONEL SEATON, science educator, writer, researcher; b. Hindsville, Ark., Mar. 25, 1933; s. Elmo C. and Bernie Ethel (Cook) B.; m. Pansy Lenora Hobbs Burkes, Dec. 24, 1961; children: Geoffrey Dion (dec.), Eric Kevin, Cynthia Michele, Aaron Shane, Mark Alan. BSE, U. Ark., Fayetteville, 1960; MA in Biol. Sci., U. Mont., Missoula, 1964. Cert. adminstrn. and sci., Ark., Iowa; sci. N. Mex. Instr. sci. and sociology Corona Mcpl. Schs., N.Mex., 1960-62; rsch. biological technician Vets. Adminstrn. Hosp., Albuquerque, 1963—64; instr. sci. Albuquerque Pub. Schs., 1964-66; instr. biology and zoology U. Wis., Whitewater, 1966-69; asst. prof. edn. Mo. We. State Coll., St. Joseph, 1970-71; asst. campus dir. Southeastern Cmty. Coll., West Burlington, Iowa, 1971-75; dir. Inst. Mgmt. and Continuing Edn. Iowa Wesleyan Coll., Mt. Pleasant, 1977-78, 83-84; staff devel. specialist and tng. cert. officer La. Dept. Health and Human Resources, Office Mental Retardation, Ruston (La.) State Sch., 1982—83; instr. scis. Ft. Smith Pub. Schs., Ark., 1985-94; ret., 1995; rschr., writer, 1995—. Spl. rschr. Sandia Nat. Labs., Albuquerque, summers 1985-87. Contbr. articles to profl. jours. Leader U.S. delegation People to People Youth Sci. Exchange, Russia, Ukraine, 1990, China, Hong Kong, 1991, New Zealand, Australia, 1992; judge sci. fair pub. schs. N. Mex. and Ark., 1984-95; spkr. Career Days Westark C. C., Fort Smith, Ark., 1991-93. Nat. Sci. Found. Fellow U. Mont., 1961-64; recipient Nat. Security Clearance U.S. Dept. Energy, 1986, Outstanding Tchr. Proclamation Mayor of Fort Smith, Ark., 1995. Avocations: writing, reading, travel, hiking.

BURKET, GEORGE EDWARD, JR., retired family physician; b. Kingman, Kans., Dec. 10, 1912; s. George Edward and Jessie May (Talbert) Burket; m. Mary Elizabeth (Sue) Wallace, Nov. 12, 1938; children: George Edward III, Carol Sue, Elizabeth Christine. Student, Wichita State U., 1930—33; MD, U. Kans., 1937. Diplomate Am. Bd. Family Practice (pres. 1975-1977). Intern Santa Barbara (Calif.) Gen. Hosp., 1937—38, resident, 1938—39; grad. asst. in surgery Mass. Gen. Hosp., Boston, 1955—56; practice medicine Kingman, 1939—73; preceptor in medicine U. Kans. Med. Sch., 1950—73, assoc. prof., 1973—78, clin. prof., 1978—84; ret. Bd. dirs. Kingman Savings and Loan Assn. Contbr. articles to profl. jours. Mem. Kingman Bd. Edn., 1946—58, Kans. State Bd. Health, 1960—66. Mem.: AMA, Soc. Tchrs. Family Medicine, Assn. Am. Med. Colls., Am. Acad. Family Physicians (pres. 1967—68, John Walsh Founders award 1979), Kans. Med. Soc. (pres. 1966—67), Inst. Medicine NAS (sr.), Wichita Country Club, Garden of Gods Club (Colorado Springs, Colo.), Shriners, Masons, Alpha Omega Alpha. Republican. Episcopalian. Home: Larksfield Pl W318 7373 E 29th St N Wichita KS 67226-3405

BURKET, JOHN MCVEY, retired dermatologist; b. Des Moines, Oct. 4, 1935; s. George Austin and Elma (McVey) B.; m. Janice Lee Feilmeyer, Dec. 29, 1956; children: Denise, Bradley, Brent, Diana, Dawn, Brian. BA, U. Iowa, 1957, MD, 1960. Diplomate Am. Bd. Dermatology, Am. Bd. Dermopathology. Resident in dermatology U. Iowa Hosp., Iowa City, 1964; chief dermatology USAF, March AFB, 1964-66; pvt. practice dermatology Medford, Oreg., 1966—. Contbr. articles to profl. jours., chpts. to books. Avocations: hunting, fishing. Personal E-mail: jburket10435@charter.net.

BURKETT, BRADFORD CHARLES, lawyer; b. Phila., Aug. 29, 1960; s. Frederick R. and Barbara E. Burkett; m. Marcia P. Borggaard, Aug. 17, 1985; children: Gillian, Brady, Kate. BA, Rutgers U., New Brunswick, NJ, 1982; JD, Rutgers U., Camden, NJ, 1985. Bar: N.Y. 1985, N.J. 1985. Assoc. Kaye Scholer Fierman Hays & Handler, NYC, 1985-94; sr. v.p., gen. counsel The Multicare Cos., Inc., Hackensack, NJ, 1994-97; sr. v.p., gen. counsel, bus. devel. Telesis Med. Mgmt., Inc., White Plains, NY, 1997-2000; CEO Physician Weblink, Inc., Englewood Cliffs, NJ, 2000—02; CEO, bd. dirs. deNovis, Inc., Lexington, Mass., 2002—05; mng. dir. Scott Malon Ltd., NYC, 2005—06, Navigant Capital Advisors, NYC, 2006—. Co-CEO CareMatrix, Inc., Newton, Mass., 2003—06; bd. dirs. N.Am. Health Plans, Buffalo, 2004—07, Health Edge, NYC, 2005—07. Mem. ABA, Nat. Health Lawyers Assn., Assn. Bar City N.Y., Turnaround Mgmt. Soc. Office: 17 Mayhew Ave Larchmont NY 10538 E-mail: b.burkett@att.net, burkett@gbkadvisors.com.

BURKETT, GERALD ARTHUR, lawyer, musician; b. Oklahoma City, Apr. 23, 1939; s. Francis Gerald and Leta Carey (Weaver) B.; m. Carolyn Ruth Hicks, Aug. 7, 1960; 1 child, Debora Lynne Burkett Nutt. BA, David Lipscomb U., 1962; MA, Peabody Coll., 1967; JD, Nashville Sch. of Law, 1974. Bar: Tenn. 1975, U.S. Dist. Ct. (mid. dist.) Tenn., 1976, U.S. Ct. Appeals (6th cir.), 1977, U.S. Tax Ct., 1981, U.S. Supreme Ct. 1993. Leader Fritz's German Band, Nashville, 1972-97; pvt. practice law office Nashville, 1975—; jud. commr. Met. Nashville/Davidson County, Tenn., 1999—. Adj. prof. Vol. State C.C., Gallatin, Tenn., 1979-93, 2001—, Nashville State Tech. Inst., 1984-89; band leader Strohaus, 1982 World's Fair, Knoxville, 1982; appears on Metro Night Ct., Channel 50, Nashville. Condr.German band for commls. and concerts including Monday Night Football, 1994-2000, Super Bowl, 1995, Oktoberfest Concert, Soldier Field, Chgo., 1995; appeared on weekly TV show Metro Night Ct., Channel 50, Nashville, 2000. Accordionist Charlie Rich's Bi-Centennial Album, 1976, film soundtrack Sweet Dreams, 1983. Mem. Nashville Assn. Musicians, Alliance Francaise (treas. 1985-86), Nashville Bar Assn., Tenn. Assn. of Spanish Spkg. Attys., Phi Delta Kappa (treas. 1967-68). Mem. Ch. of Christ. Avocations: travel, foreign languages. Office: PO Box 8566 Hermitage TN 37076-8566 E-mail: geraldburkett@hotmail.com.

BURKETT, HELEN, artist; b. Washington, Feb. 15, 1942; d. Harding Theodore and Helen Louise (Torris) B.; m. J.D. Collins, Sept. 1, 1961 (Apr. 16, 1975); children: Mark W. Collins, Donna L. Collins; m. Charles Talbot Marshall, Dec. 24, 1975; 1 child, Gabrielle T. Marshall. Student, Strayer Sch. of Bus., 1960-61, Corcoran Sch. of Art, 1968-69, Md. U., 1970-73, Hilton Leech Studio-Gallery, 1976-80, Ringling Sch. Art, 1980-81. Asst. to dir. Hilton Leech Studio, Sarasota, Fla., 1975-80, workshop organizer, figure study coord., 1978-80; demonstrator, tchr., artist, owner/operator Helen Burkett Studios, Sarasota, Fla., 1975—. Juror Ann Arbor St. Art Fair, 1998; art tchr. Brevard County Watercolor Soc., Melbourne, Fla., Longboat Key Ctr. Arts, Sarasota,Fla, 2000, Art League Ft. Myers, 2006. One person shows at Manatee Jr. Coll., 1984, Ctrl. Fla. C.C., Ocala, 1987, Springfield Art Mus., Mo., State Capitol, Tallahassee, Fla., Divsn. Cultural Affairs, Sec. State Offices, 1997, Chesterton Art Ctr. 2001-07, Watercolor USA, 2003, Miami Watercolor Soc., 2007; exhibited in group show at Nat. Watercolor Soc. Show, Thousand Oaks, Calif., 1999, WB Tattr Studio Gallery, 2006; permanent exhibits include Ctrl. Fla. C.C., Ocala, Epsom Clinic, Orlando, Fla., Orlando Sentinel, Winter Park (Fla.) Meml. Hosp., Polk Mus., Lakeland, Fla., The Disney Corp., The Ford Motor Co., The Amoco Corp., Fla. Dept. State, Hayfield Mansion, Louisville, The Former Duchess of Winsor; exhibitor numerous art festivals, 1987—; subject of periodical The Artist Mag., 1992, The Am. Artist Mag., 1996, also newspaper article Ann Arbor News, 1998. Tchr. Vis. Artist Program, Coconut Grove, Fla., 1990—. Recipient 2d prize in watercolor U. Tampa, 1991, 93, 1st prize in watercolor Lowe Art Mus./U. Miami, 1992, 2d prize in watercolor, 2001, 05, Purchase award Festival of the Masters-Disney Corp., 1995, Purchase award Wayne State U.-Ford Motor Co., 1995, 2d prize Hope Ho., Norfolk, Va., 2006. Mem. ACLU, Am. Watercolor Soc. (assoc.), Nat. Watercolor Soc. (assoc.), Nat. Assn. Ind. Artists, Sarasota Art Assn. (bd. dirs. 1980-82), Fla. Watercolor Soc. (life, Award of Distinction 1985, 92), So. Watercolor Soc., Mich. Guild Artists. Avocations: photography, reading, hiking, bicycling. Home: Helen Burkett Studio 2988 Oak St Sarasota FL 34237-7346

BURKETT, LAWRENCE V., retired insurance company executive, lawyer; BA, U. Va., 1967, JD, 1973. Bar: Mass. 1974. V.p., assoc. gen. counsel Mass. Mut. Life Ins. Co., Springfield, 1984-88, sr. v.p., assoc. gen. counsel, 1988-92, exec. v.p., gen. counsel, 1993.*

BURKETT, MARVIN D., electronics executive; b. 1943; BS, MBA, U. Ariz. With semicondr. divsn. Raytheon Co., to 1972; v.p., contr., chief planning officer Advanced Micro Devices, Inc., 1972-88, sr. v.p., chief adminstrv. officer, CFO, 1989-98; exec. v.p. worldwide fin., CFO, Packard Bell NEC Inc., Sacramento, 1998—; CFO, chief adminstrv. officer Arcot Sys., Inc., Santa Clara, Calif., 2000—. Office: Arcot Systems Inc 455 W Maude Ave # 210 Sunnyvale CA 94085-3517

BURKETT, ROBERT E., JR., lawyer, insurance company executive; b. Kansas City, Mo., Aug. 20, 1954; m. Molly Boso, 1981. BA, Purdue U., 1977; JD, Ind. U., 1980. Bar: Ind. 1981, Fla. 1986. Sr. v.p., legal Conseco Inc., Carmel, Ind. Office: Conseco Inc 11825 N Pennsylvania St Carmel IN 46032 Office Phone: 317-817-6100. Office Fax: 317-817-3578.*

BURKEY, LEE MELVILLE, lawyer; b. Beach, ND, Mar. 21, 1914; s. Levi Melville and Mina Lou (Horner) B.; m. Lorraine Lillian Burghardt, June 11, 1938; 1 child, Lee Melville, III BA, U. Ill., 1936, MA, 1938; JD with honor, John Marshall Law Sch., 1943. Bar: Ill., 1944, U.S. Dist. Ct., 1947, U.S. Ct. Appeals, 1954, U.S. Supreme Ct.; 1983; cert. secondary tchr., Ill. Tchr. Princeton Twp. High Sch., Princeton, Ill., 1937-38, Thornton Twp. High Sch., Harvey, Ill., 1938-43; atty. Office of Solicitor, U.S. Dept. Labor, Chgo., 1944-51; ptnr. Asher, Gubbins & Segall and successor firms, Chgo., 1951-94; of counsel, 1995—. Lectr. bus. law Roosvelt Coll., Chgo., 1949—52. Contbr. numerous articles on lie detector evidence. Trustee, Village of La Grange, Ill., 1962-68, mayor, 1968-73, village atty., 1973-87; commr., pres. Northeastern Ill. Planning Commn., Chgo., 1969-73; mem. bd. dirs. United Ch. Christ, Bd. of Homeland Ministries, 1981-87; mem. exec. com. Cook County Coun. Govts., 1968-70; life mem. La Grange Area Hist. Soc.; bd. dirs. Better Bus. Bur. Met. Chgo., Inc., 1975-82, Plymouth Place, Inc., 1973-82; mem. exec. bd., S.W. Suburban Ctr. on Aging, 1993—04. Brevet 2nd Lt. Ill. Nat. Guard, 1932. Recipient Disting. Alumnus award John Marshall Law Sch., 1973, Meritorious Svc. award Am. Legion Post 1941, 1974, Honor award LaGrange Area Hist. Soc., 1987, Cmty. Svc. award S.W. Suburban Ctr. on Aging, 2000. Fellow: Coll. Labor and Employment Lawyers. (charter); mem.: SAR (state pres. 1977, Good citizenship medal 1973, Patriot medal 1977), ABA (coun. sect. labor and employment law 1982—86, governance officer 1986—96), Chgo. Bar Assn., Ill. Bar Assn. (sr. counsellor 1994), United Empire Loyalists Assn. Can., La Grange Country Club, Masons, Theta Delta Chi, Order John Marshall. Mem. First Congl. Ch.

BURKHALTER, SUSAN SHIVELY, music educator, organist; b. Washington, Apr. 16, 1946; d. William Mays and Thelma Louise (Kanatzer) B.; m. Curtis Allen Shively, Feb. 5, 1977; children: Rachel Mirabel, Stuart William MusB, Coll. Wooster, 1970. Organist, choir dir. Olivet Episcopal Ch., Springfield, Va., 1976-77, Grace Reformed United Ch. of Christ, Washington, 2001; children's choir dir. Our Savior Lutheran Ch. and Sch., Arlington, Va., 1997-1998; piano tchr., organist, 1976—2006; interim organist Kirkwood Presbyn. Ch., Springfield, 2001—02; organist Luth. Ch. of Abiding Presence, Burke, Va., 2004—05; assoc. organist First Ch. of Christ Scientist, Mt. Vernon, Va., 2006—. Advisor music majs. Coll. Wooster, Ohio, 1995—. Contbr. mags. and newspapers including Washington Post, American Organist, Psychology Today, and more; performer in various concerts. Vol. Carderock Springs Elem. Sch., Bethesda, Md., 1988-95, Pyle Middle Sch., 1994-2000, Walt Whitman High Sch., 1997-2005; mem. Sierra Club, ASPCA, World Wildlife Fund, African Wildlife Fund; mem. Gen. Fedn. Women's Clubs, Suburban Women's Club of Montgomery County, Md., 1999—. Mem. Music Tchrs. Nat. Assn., Am. Guild Organists. Democrat. Avocations: sewing, gardening, art, poetry. Home: 7504 Hamilton Spring Rd Bethesda MD 20817-4542 Personal E-mail: scastlekep@aol.com.

BURKHARD, FRED (BUD), academic administrator; b. Jersey City, Feb. 17, 1956; s. Kenneth William and Eileen Clare Cobleigh; m. Jeannine (Nina) May Lafiner, Oct. 9, 1999; children: Rose Francis, Amanda Eileen. PhD, U. Wis., 1986. Assoc. prof. history Morgan State U., Balt., 1992—99; acad. dir., collegiate prof. history U. Md. U. Coll., Adelphi, Md., 1999—2006; assoc. dean continuing edn. Mt. St. Mary's U., Emmittsburg, Md., 2006—. Participant wingspread conf. history curriculum Johnson Found., Am. Hist. Assn., 2005. Author: (scholarly monograph) French Marxism Between the Wars; contbr. scholarly article, and revs. Fellow Curriculum Transformation Project/Women's Studies Summer Inst., Ford Found., 1997, Summer Seminar participant, Nat. Endowment for the Humanities, 1991; grantee Rsch., Am. Coun. of Learned Societies, 1994, Schmitt Rsch. Grant, Am. Hist. Assn., 1992, rsch., Ministre des Affaires Etrangeres, France, 1987. Mem.: Nat. Women's Studies Assn., Western Soc. French History, Soc. French Hist. Studies, Am. Assn. History and Computing (pres. 2003—04), Am. Hist. Assn., Phi Alpha Theta. Office: Mt St Marys Univ 5305 Spectrum Dr Ste A Frederick MD 21703 Office Phone: 301-682-4806. Business E-Mail: burkhard@msmary.edu.

BURKHARDT, EDWARD ARNOLD, rail transportation executive; b. NYC, July 23, 1938; s. Edward Arnold Burkhardt Sr. and Kathryn C. Dow; m. Sandra Kay Schwaegel, June 9, 1967; 1 child, Cynthia Kay. BS Indsl. Adminstrn., Yale U., 1960. Various operating positions Wabash R.R., St. Louis, 1960-64, Norfolk and Western Rlwy., St. Louis, 1964-67; asst. to gen. mgr. Chgo. Northwestern Railway Co., 1967-68, gen. supt. transp., 1968-70, asst. v.p. transp., 1970-76, v.p. mktg., 1976-79, v.p. transp., 1979-87; bd. dirs., chmn., pres., CEO Wis. Ctrl. Transp. Corp., Chgo., 1987-99; chmn. Tranz Rail Ltd., 1993-99; bd. dirs., pres. Algoma Ctrl. Rlwy. Inc., 1995-99; bd. dirs., chmn., CEO English, Welsh and Scottish Ry. Ltd., 1995-99; bd. dirs., chmn. Australian Transport Network, 1997-99; pres./CEO Rail World, Inc., 1999—; pres. RailPolska, 1999—. Chmn. Baltic Rail Svc., 2000—, Estonian Ry. Ltd., 2001—, Montreal, Maine & Atlantic Ry. Ltd., 2003—; bd. dirs. Valeant Pharms. Internat., Aliso Viejo, Calif., Poly Medica Corp., Wakefield, Mass. Trustee Village of Kenilworth, Ill., 1984—93; bd. dirs. John W. Barringer R.R. Libr., St. Louis, Wheeling & Lake Erie Rlwy. Co., Lake Superior Mus. Transp., Duluth, Minn. Named Hon. consul New Zealand, Chgo. Mem.: Am. Assn. R.R. Supts., Union League Club, Western Ry. Club. Republican. Episcopalian. Office: Rail World Inc Ste 500N 8600 W Bryn Mawr Ave Chicago IL 60631-3579 Business E-Mail: eaburkhardt@railworld-inc.com.

BURKHARDT, FREDERICK HENRY, editor; b. Bklyn., Sept. 13, 1912; BA, Columbia U., 1933; LittB, Oxford U., 1935; PhD, Columbia U., 1940, LLD (hon.), 1974, Mich. U., 1968, Ball State U., 1976. Instr., asst. prof. philosophy U. Wis., Madison, 1937—43, assoc. prof. philosophy, 1946—47; pres. Bennington Coll., Vt., 1947—57, Am. Coun. Learned Socs., NYC, 1957—74; gen. editor The Works of William James, 19 vols. Harvard Press, 1975—88; founder, editor The Correspondence of Charles Darwin, 15 vols. sponsored by ACLS and Cambridge U. Libr., 1985—. Rsch. analyst Office of Strategic Svcs., 1943-45; acting chief Divsn. Rsch. for Europe, Dept. State, 1945-46; dep. dir. Office Pub. Affairs, U.S. High Commr. for Germany, 1950-51; mem. N.Y.C. Bd. Higher Edn., 1966-73, chmn., 1969-71; trustee N.Y. Pub. Libr., 1970-71; chmn., 1974; chmn. Nat. Commn. on Librs. and Info. Sci., 1971-78. Editor, translator: J.G. Herder: God, Some Conversations On Spinoza's System, 1940, 62; editor: Cleavage in Our Culture, 1952; contbr. The Comparative Reception of Darwinism, 1975. Lt. USNR, 1944-46. Recipient Alumni award for excellence Columbia U., 1987, Morton N. Cohen award for disting. edition of letters MLA, 1991; Queen's Univ. prize Cambridge U., 2002, citation fo disting. contbn. History of Sci. Soc., 2005. Mem. Am. Philos. Soc. (Thomas Jefferson gold medal, 2003), Am. Acad. Arts and Scis., Century Assn. Home and Office: PO Box 1067 Bennington VT 05201-1067 E-mail: fhb@sover.net.

BURKHARDT, ROGER, information technology executive; B in Physics, Oxford U., M in Physics, 1982; MBA, NYU. With IBM Corp., 1982—97, mgr. advanced exch. sys.; v.p. Strategic Alliances Optimark Techs. Inc., Jersey City, 1997—2000, pres. Listed Equities, 1997—2000; CTO N.Y. Stock Exch., Inc., NYC, 2000—06, exec. v.p., 2005—06; pres., COO Ingres Corp., 2006—. Bd. advisors IBM, 2004—06. Office: Ingres Corp 500 Arguello St Suite 200 Redwood City CA 94063 Office Phone: 917-338-7313. E-mail: roger.burkhardt@ingres.com.

BURKHARDT, RONALD ROBERT, advertising executive, writer, artist, filmmaker; b. Jackson, Mich., July 25; s. Robert Edward and Lois Jeane (Ordway) B. AA, Jackson C.C., 1968; BBA in Advt., We. Mich. U., 1970. Copywriter, prodr. Campbell-Ewald Co., Detroit, 1973—75; sr. writer Cargill-Wilson & Acree/DDB, Atlanta, 1976—78; sr. v.p., creative dir. Flemister & Burkhardt, Atlanta, 1978—80; sr. writer Bozell & Jacobs, NYC, 1980—81; creative supr. Young & Rubicam, NYC, 1981—84; v.p., creative group head Lowe-Marschalk, NYC, 1984—86; chmn., CEO, exec. creative dir., founder Burkhardt & Christy Advt. Inc., NYC, 1986—95; CEO, creative dir., and founder Burkhardt & Ptnrs. Ltd., NYC, 1996—; co-founder, CEO Pillow Vision, Inc., 2001—; chief creative officer e-Fusion Consortium, 2006—; founder, CEO, exec. creative dir. Cowboy West LLC, Calif., 2007—. Pro bono cons. mayor's office, NYC, Save Am. Forests, Washington; judge Clios, Internat. TV and Film Festival N.Y., CEBA Awards, Andy Awards, Stephen Kelly Awards, Addy Awards,

Mercury Radio Awards, N.Y. Festivals. Exec. prodr.: (short feature film) Red, 2001; exec. prodr., creative cons. (feature film) The Mark, 2005; one-man shows include Soho Star-T Gallery, 2001, Forbes Gallery, N.Y.C., 2002, Trump Towers Art Release Galleries, NYC, 2003, Grand Havana Rm. Gallery, 2003, Think Art Gallery, 2003, Gallery Asto, L.A., 2004, Laguna Colony Art Gallery, Calif., 2004, One Fine Art Gallery, Chgo., 2005, Muhammad Ali Mus., Louisville, 2006, Biennnale Internat. Dell 'Arte Contemporanea, Florence, Italy, 2005 (won Medici medal), B.J. Spoke Gallery, 2005, Paperworks, 2005 (Internat. Winner Juror Art in Am. mag.), 7 Degrees Gallery, Laguna Beach, Calif., 2006, Austria Biennale of Internat. Contemporary Art, 2006, Art Basel, Miami, Fla., 2006; contbr. articles to profl. jours. including Adweek, AdAge; WNBC-TV, 2006. Exec. com. NY Korean Vets. Meml. Commn.; pro-bono Riverkeeper, Ft. Worth Symphony, 2007; mem. benefit com. Edwin Gould ARTrageous Children's Svcs., Sheltering Arms Children's Svcs.; bd. dirs., branding chmn. Miss America Pageant, Las Vegas, 2003-. Recipient over 200 creative and mktg. awards including Andy awards, Advt. Club, Clio awards, Art Dirs. Club, NY Internat. Festivals awards, Gold Addy award, Creativity awards, Graphics Ann. award, Mobius Gold, Black Book award, Telly Gold statues, Internat. Broadcast award, Hollywood TV and Film Festival, Comm. Arts Advt. Ann. award, Effie Silver award, Effie Gold award, Cannes Internat. Film Festival, France. Mem.: MOMA, NY, Guggenheim Mus., NY, Whitney Mus., NY, One Club for Art and Copy. Republican. Avocations: skiing, tennis, motorcycling, baseball, Karate. Office: Burkhardt Ltd PO Box 1070 Quogue NY 11959-1070 Home Phone: 917-328-2614. Personal E-mail: ronreach@aol.com. *Intensity of purpose fuels energy, and makes life a relentless series of powerful achievements.*

BURKHARDT, SUSANNE M., elementary school educator; BA, Wittenberg Univ., Ohio; MA, John Carroll Univ., Ohio. Cert. early childhood generalist Nat. Bd. Profl. Tchg. Tchr. Simpsonville (Ky.) Elem. Sch., 2003—. Named Ky. Tchr. of Yr., 2007; recipient Mayfield Excellence award, Innovative Tchg. Grant. Office: Simpsonville Elem Sch 6725 Shelbyville Rd Simpsonville KY 40067 Business E-Mail: s.burkhardt@insightbb.com.*

BURKHART, CATHERINE RAY, retired secondary school educator; b. Tucson, Mar. 2, 1939; m. Bruce Burkhart; children: Lee, Katy, Dottie. BA, U. Ariz., Tucson, 1961, MEd, 1966. Tchr. Tucson Sch. Dist., 1961—66, Whittier HS Dist., 1966—99; ret., 2006. Mentor tchr.; cons. ETS, instr., Rio Hondo Coll., 1974-04, Nogales HS, Rowland, 2003-05; guest spkr. at various confs. Editor Southland Coun. Tchrs. English newsletter. Personal E-mail: bwburkhart@aol.com, crburkhart@aol.com.

BURKHART, CRAIG GARRETT, dermatologist, researcher; b. Toledo, Apr. 15, 1951; s. Garrett Giles and Mary Katherine (Egarius) Burkhart; m. Anna Kristina Jutila, Apr. 12, 1975; children: Kristina Maria, Craig Nathaniel, Heidi Rebecca. BA, U. Pa., 1972; MD, Med. Coll. Ohio, 1975; MPH, U. Toledo, Ohio, 1983. Diplomate Am. Bd. Dermatology. Intern, resident, fellow U. Mich. Hosps., 1976-79; pvt. practice dermatologist, 1979—; pres. Gar-Nat Lab., Inc., 1997—. Clin. prof. medicine Med. U. Ohio; clin. asst. prof. dermatology Ohio U. Coll. Osteo. Medicine. Editor: Jour. Dermatology and Allergy, 1980—; mem. editl. bd. Jour. Current Adolescent Medicine, 1980—, mem. editl. adv. bd. Ohio State Med. Jour., 1982—, Cortlandt Forum, 1999—; contbr. chapters to books, articles to profl. jours. Mem. Toledo Zoo, Toledo Mus. Art. F. M. Douglass Found. Rsch. grantee, 1998, 2000, 2001. Mem.: AMA, Ohio Dermatologic Found. (bd. dirs. 2005—, v.p. 2006—), Toledo Acad. Medicine (bd. dirs. 2002—, v.p. 2005—), Mich. Dermatologic Assn., Ohio State Med. Assn., Ohio Dermatologic Assn. (bd. dirs. 2002—, pres. 2005—), Acad. Dermatology, U. Toledo Alumni Assn. (bd. dirs. 2006—), Med. U. Ohio Alumni Assn. (bd. dirs. 2000—03), Phi Beta Kappa (pres. N.W. Ohio 1984—86). Achievements include patents in field. Home: 4556 Crossfields Rd Toledo OH 43623-2628 Office: 5600 Monroe St Ste 106B Sylvania OH 43560-2728 Office Phone: 419-885-3403. Personal E-mail: cgbakb@aol.com.

BURKHART, HAROLD EUGENE, forester, educator; b. Wellington, Kans., Feb. 29, 1944; s. Walter F. and Zelma (Lutz) B.; m. Katherine West, June 12, 1971; 1 child, Anna Katherine. BS, Okla. State U., 1965; MS, U. Ga., 1967, PhD, 1969. From asst. prof. to profl. Va. Poly. Inst. and State U., Blacksburg, 1969—81, Thomas M. Brooks prof., 1981-99, univ. disting. prof., 1999—. Author: Forest Measurements, 1983, 94, 2002; contbr. sci. articles to profl. jours. Sr. Rsch. fellow NRC, 1976-77; recipient Sci. Achievement award Internat. Union Forestry Rsch. Orgns., 1981, J. Shelton Horsley Rsch. award Va. Acad. Sci., 1983, Outstanding Faculty award State Coun. for Higher Edn. in Va., 1988, Disting. Agr. Alumnus award Okla. State U., 1993. Fellow AAAS, Soc. Am. Foresters (Barrington Moore Meml. award 1991); mem. Biometric Soc., Am. Forestry Assn., Sigma Xi, Phi Kappa Phi, Xi Sigma Pi. Presbyterian. Avocations: gardening, running. Office: Va Poly Inst and State U Dept Forestry Blacksburg VA 24061 Home Phone: 540-951-0605; Office Phone: 540-231-6952. Business E-Mail: burkhart@vt.edu.

BURKHART, JOHN ERNEST, minister, theology studies educator; b. Riverside, Calif., Oct. 25, 1927; s. Joseph Ernest and Lockie Louisa (Dryden) B.; m. Virginia Bell French, Sept. 16, 1951; children: David Aaron, Audrey Elizabeth, Deborah Ann. BA, Occidental Coll., 1949; BD, Union Theol. Sem., 1952; PhD, U. So. Calif., 1959; DD, Occidental Coll., 1964. Ordained to ministry United Presbyn. Ch., 1952. Pastor Presbyn. U. U. So. Calif., LA, 1953-59, from instr. to prof. of Theology, 1959-1990; prof. Systematic Theology McCormick Theol. Sem., Chgo., 1990-93, prof. emeritus, 1993—. Vis. prof. Garrett Theol. Sem. Evanston, Ill., 1966, DePaul U., Chgo., 1970. Author: Kingdom, Church, and Baptism, 1959, Understanding the Word of God, 1964, Worship, 1982; contbr. articles to profl. jours. 1st lt., chaplain USAF, 1952—53. Fellow Royal Anthrop. Inst., Soc. for Values in Higher Edn.; mem. Am. Acad. Religion, Cath. Theol. Soc. of Am., N.Am. Acad. Liturgy, Am. Theol. Soc. (pres. 1969-70), Midwest Alumni Club (v.p. 1985-90), Quadrangle Club, Blue Key, Rotary, Phi Beta Kappa. Democrat. Presbyterian. Home: 569 Woodland Ridge Dubuque IA 52003 Personal E-mail: burkhart@mchsi.com.

BURKHART, WILLIAM R., lawyer; b. May 30, 1965; m. Theresa A. Burkhart. B in polit. sci., U. Fla.; JD, Harvard U., 1990. Bar: Pa. 1990. Atty. Reed Smith Shaw & McClay LLP, Pitts.; joined The Timken Co., Canton, Ohio, 1994, atty., corp. atty., legal counsel for Europe, Africa, and West Asia Colmar, France, dir. affiliations and acquistions Canton, Ohio, 1998—2000, sr. v.p., gen. counsel, 2000—. Mem. law coun. Manufacturers Alliance. Bd. dirs. Ohio C. of C.; mem. Vision Coun. Program Adv. Subcom. Ctrl. Stark County United Way, Ohio. Office: The Timken Co 1835 Dueber Ave SW Canton OH 44706-2798*

BURKHOLDER, DONALD LYMAN, mathematician, educator; b. Octavia, Nebr., Jan. 19, 1927; s. Elmer and Susie (Rothrock) B.; m. Jean Annette Fox, June 17, 1950; children: Kathleen, Peter, William. BA, Earlham Coll., 1950; MS, U. Wis., 1953; PhD, U. N.C., 1955. Asst. prof. math. U. Ill., Urbana, 1955-60, assoc. prof., 1960-64, prof., 1964-98, prof. Ctr. for Advanced Study, 1978-98, prof. emeritus, 1998—. Sabbatical leaves U. Calif., Berkeley, 1961-62, Westfield Coll., U. London, 1969-70; vis. prof. Rutgers U., 1972-73; researcher Stanford U., 1961, Hebrew U., 1969, Mittag-Leffler Inst., Sweden, 1971, 82, U. Paris, 1975, Institut des Hautes Études Scientifiques, 1986, U. Edinburgh, 1986, Tel Aviv U., 1989, U. New South Wales, 1991; Mordell lectr. Cambridge U., 1986; Zygmund lectr. U. Chgo., 1988; trustee Math. Scis. Rsch. Inst., 1981-84; bd. govs. Inst. Math. and Its Applications, 1983-85, chmn., 1985. Editor: Annals Math. Statistics, 1964-67. Fellow Inst. Math. Statistics (Wald lectr. 1971, pres. 1975-76); mem. NAS, Am. Math. Soc. (mem. editorial bd. Trans. 1983-85), London Math. Soc., Am. Acad. Arts and Scis. Achievements include research in probability theory and its applications to other branches of analysis. Home: 506 W Oregon St Urbana IL 61801-4044 Business E-Mail: donburk@math.uiuc.edu.

BURKHOLDER, JOANN M., botany educator; BS in Zoology, Iowa State U., 1975; MS in Botany, U. R.I., 1981; PhD in Botany, Mich. State U., 1986. Asst. prof. dept. botany N.C. State U., Raleigh, 1986-91, assoc. prof. dept. botany, 1992—. Apptd. N.C. Marine Fisheries Commn., 1992—, Coastal Futures com., 1993-94; speaker Harvard, AAAS, Nat. Acad. Scis., NATO, Internat. Conf. on Modern and Fossil Dinoflagellates, others. Pew fellow in Conservation and Environment, 1997—; recipient Scientific Freedom and Responsibility award AAAS, 1998, Environ. Guardian award Charlotte Observer, 1996. Mem. Am. Soc. Limnology and Oceanography (chair sessions at annual meetings, bd. dirs. 1994-97), Internat. Soc. Study of Harmful Algae, Estuarine Rsch. Fedn., Phycological Soc. Am. (mem. editl. bd. 1995-97), Soc. Protozoologists, Sigma Xi. Achievements include research emphasizing in nutritional ecology of algae, hetortrophic dinoflagellates, and aquatic angiosperms, especially the effects of cultural eutorphication on both freshwater and estuarine/coastl blooms, and on seagrass disappearance; involved in discovery of a group of mixotrophic dinoflagellates resembling clay particles, which can dominate the plankton of turbid reservoirs, a severe inhibitory impact of water-column nitrite engrichment on Zostera marina, the dominant seagrass habitat species on the Atlantic Coast, a toxic dino-flagellate, Pfiesteri piscicida implicated as a major causative agent fo fish deeath and disease, with potential linkages to serious human health effects as well. Office: NC State U Dept Botany 4214 Gardner Hl Raleigh NC 27695-0001 Fax: (919) 515-3436. E-mail: burkholder@ncsu.edu.

BURKHOLDER, PETER MILLER, retired physician, educator; b. Cambridge, Mass., May 7, 1933; s. Paul Rufus and Lillian Maud (Miller) B.; m. Barbara Beers, June 3, 1956; children: Kristen Ryner, Lisanne Ryner. BS, Yale U., New Haven, Conn., 1955; MD, Cornell U., NYC, 1959; degree in naturopathy (hon.), S.W. Coll. Naturopathic Medicine, 2001. Intern pathology NY Hosp.-Cornell Med. Ctr., 1959-60; NIH trainee in pathology Cornell U., Ithaca, NY, 1960-63, instr., 1963-64, asst. prof., 1964-65, Duke U., Durham, NC, 1965-69, asso. prof., 1969-70, U. Wis.-Madison, 1970-72, acting chmn. dept. pathology, 1971-72, prof., 1972-79, chmn. dept. pathology, 1972-74; dir. Kidney Disease Inst., NY State Dept. Health, 1979-80; dep. dir. div. labs. and research NY State Dept. Health, 1980-81, dir. Ctr. Lab. Scis., 1981-82; chief of staff VA Med. Ctr., Ann Arbor, Mich., 1982-84, staff pathologist, 1984-89; prof. pathology U. Mich., Ann Arbor, 1982-89; chmn. dept. pathology Maricopa Med. Ctr., Phoenix, 1989-95, asst. med. dir., 1995; clin. prof. dept. pathology U. Ariz., Tucson, 1989—. Prof. pathology Southwest Coll. Naturopathic Medicine, 1996-2000, chief acad. officer, 2000. Author: Atlas of Human Glomerular Pathology, 1974; contbg. author: Structural Basis of Renal Diseases, 1968, Pathobiology Annual, 1971, Tissue Typing and Transplantation, 1973, Glomerulonephritis Morphology Natural History and Treatment, 1973, Cornell Seminars in Nephrology, 1975; mem. editorial bd. Kidney Internat, 1970-76, Lab. Investigation, 1972-83, Exptl. Pathology, 1984-86, Clin. Nephrology, 1989-92; contbr. numerous articles to profl. jours. NIH grantee, 1961-78 Mem. AMA, Am. Soc. Exptl. Pathology, Am. Assn. Pathology, Am. Soc. Immunology, Am. Soc. Nephrology, Internat. Acad. Pathology, Internat. Soc. Nephrology, Coll. Am. Pathology, Am. Soc. Clin. Pathologist, Am. Coll. Physician Execs., Renal Path. Soc., Pluto Soc. Home: 7248 N Red Ledge Dr Paradise Valley AZ 85253-2849 Personal E-mail: pmburk7@msn.com.

BURKI, ARDE A., retired military officer; b. St. Albans, NY, May 7, 1924; s. Oscar and Freda Christen Burki; m. Barbara Thacher Burki, Oct. 26, 1948; children: Deborah Christen, PEter Gerrit, JEffrey Alan, Christopher Saltoustall. Commd. 2d lt. USN, 1945, advanced through grades to comdr., ret., 1965. Republican. Episcopalian. Home: 85 E MEadow Rd Wilton CT 06897

BURKI, FRED ALBERT, labor union official; b. Chgo., Apr. 8, 1926; s. John and Helen (Kramer) B.; children— Bill, Ken, Scott. Student, Northwestern U., U.Ill. Started as grocery clk., 1947; pres. local 470 United Retail Workers Union, Westchester, Ill., 1951-53, rep., 1953-62, field supr., 1963-65, nat. v.p., 1966-71, nat. exec. dir., 1971-81; internat. v.p. United Food and Comml. Workers Union, AFL-CIO, 1981—; pres. local 881, 1981—. Guest lectr. labor edn., advisor U. Ill. Circle Campus, Chgo.; labor edn. adv. U. Ind., 1967—, Loyola U., 1978—; mem. Midwest Com. Labor Study in Europe; labor adv. com. Senator Charles Percy, 1977—; chmn. Westchester Bldg. Corp., 1971-83. Bd. dirs. Chgo. Regional Blood Bank/Blood Services, Blood Ctr. of No. Ill., 1983— , Midwest Assn. for Sickle Cell Anemia, 1986—; trustee United Retail Workers Union-Super-Valu Trust Fund.; mem. Ill. Detection of Deception Com., 1982—; pres. Human Services Ltd., 1984—. Served with AUS, 1943-47; battalion exec. officer, maj. Res., 1947-67, ret. Decorated Bronze Star medal; named Man of Year Combined Counties Police Assn., 1977 Mem. V.F.W. (past officer), Mil. Police Assn., Res. Officers Assn. Home Phone: 918-296-3513; Office Phone: 918-296-3513. Personal E-mail: FBurki@aol.com.

BURKLE, RONALD W., entrepreneur, retired food service executive; b. 1953; Pvt. practice, 1975-88; pres. Jurgensen's, Pasadena, Calif., 1986-88; prin. Yucaipa Mgmt. Co., Claremont, Calif., 1986—; chmn. Food 4 Less Supermarkets, La Habra, Calif., 1989—, Dominick's Finer Foods, Northlake, Ill., until 1998; chmn., mem. exec. com. Kroger's Foods, Inc.; CEO Smith's Food & Drug Ctrs., Inc., Salt Lake City; chmn. Fred Meyer. Majority owner (with Mario Lemieux) Nat. Hockey League, Pitts. Penguins; bd. mem. Yahoo!, Yucaipa Equity Ptnrs., L.P., Occidental Petroleum Corp., Kaufman & Broad Home Corp.; bd. mem., chmn., mem. exec. com. The Kroger Co. Mem. bd. and exec. com. Campaign Against Youth Violence; trustee J. Paul Getty Trust, 2001—, John F. Kennedy Ctr. for the Performing Arts, Nat. Urban League, L.A. County Mus. Art; chmn. bd. D.A.R.E. Am.; mem. exec. bd. for med. scis. UCLA; co-chmn. Burkle Ctr. for Internat. Rels., UCLA; mem. edn. adv. bd. RAND; founder, chmn. bd. trustees Ralphs/Food4Less Found., The Fred Meyer, Inc. Found.; bd. mem. Children's Scholarship Fund, Carter Ctr., AIDS Project L.A.; mem. e-bd. Claremont Grad. U. Named Humanitarian of Yr., AFL-CIO, Man of Yr., L.A. County Fedn. Labor; named one of Forbes' Richest Americans, 2006; recipient Whitney M. Young award, L.A. Urban League.*

BURKMAN, ERNEST, JR., education educator; b. Detroit, Oct. 4, 1929; s. Ernest and Rose (Emmehizer) B.; m. Nancy Barron, Mar. 11, 1953; children: Laura, Linda, Jan, Patricia. BS, Ea. Mich U., 1952; MS, U. Mich., 1955, MA, 1958, EdD, 1961. Sci. tchr. Edsel Ford High Sch., Dearborn, Mich., 1955-60; from asst. prof. to prof. Fla. State U., Tallahassee, 1960—. Co-dir. Turkish Nat. Sci. Lise Project, Ankara, 1961-66; dir. Intermediate Sci. Curriculum Study, 1966-72, U.S. and nationwide, Individualized Sci. Instruction System Project, U.S. and nationwide, 1972-81; cons. over 35 agys., U.S. and 15 countries, 1961—. Author: Current Trends in Science Education, 1966, The Natural World, 1975-88; co-author, editor: Individualized Science Instructional System, (25 vol. book series), 1981-88; contbr. articles to profl. jours. Fellow AAAS; mem. Nat. Sci. Tchr. Assn., Am. Ednl. Rsch. Assn. Office: Fla State U Coll Edn Tallahassee FL 32306

BURKO, LIOR M., physicist, educator; b. Haifa, Israel, July 18, 1968; s. Moshe and Ruth (Stamboli) Burko; 1 child, Eylon Mendel. BA, Technion-Israel Inst. Tech., Haifa, 1992, MSc, 1995, PhD, 1999. Rsch. scholar Calif. Inst. Tech., Pasadena, 1999—2001; rsch. assoc. U. Utah, 2001—03, rsch. asst. prof., 2003—04; asst. prof. Bates Coll., Lewiston, Maine, 2004—05, U. Ala., Huntsville, 2005—. Co-editor: Internal Structure of Black Holes and Spacetime Singularities, 1997; contbr. over 50 sci. papers to profl. jours. Achievements include research in black holes and space time singularities; black hole interiors and radiation reaction in general relativity; co-discoverer of the Beetle-Burko scalar. Office: U Ala Dept Physics 301 Sparkman Dr Huntsville AL 35899 Office Phone: 256-824-2934. Office Fax: 256-824-6873. Business E-Mail: burko@uah.edu.

BURKOFF, JOHN MICHAEL, law educator; b. Louisville, Nov. 16, 1948; s. Stanley Thomas and Joyce Ann (Switow) B.; m. Nancy Mammen, Aug. 17, 1969; children: Amy Nicole, David Michael. AB, U. Mich., 1970, JD, 1973; LLM, Harvard U., 1976. Bar: Mich. 1974, Pa. 1979. Law clk. to justice Mich. Supreme Ct., Detroit, 1973-75; adj. prof. law Wayne State U., Detroit, 1974-75; instr. law Boston U., 1975-76; asst. prof. U. Pitts., 1976-79, assoc. prof., 1979-82, prof., 1982—, assoc. dean, 2000—04. Of counsel Marcus & Shapira, Pitts., 1976-2000; mem. Pa. Com. Judicial Independence, 2006-; mem. faculty Pa. Coll. of Judiciary, 1983—; reporter Prosecution Function and Def. Function Stds. Task Force, ABA, 1988-93; mem. commn. jud. ind. Pa., 2006—. Author: Criminal Offenses and Defenses in Pennsylvania, 1984, 5th edit., 2004, Criminal Defense Ethics: Law and Liability, 1986, 2d edit., 2002, Search Warrant Law Desk Book, 1987, Ineffective Assistance of Counsel, 1993, Readings in Criminal Law, 1998, Criminal Procedure: Cases, Problems and Exercises, 2000, 3d edit, 2007, Criminal Law: Cases, Problems and Exercises, 2002, 2d edit., 2005, Principles of Criminal Procedure, 2004, 2d edit., 2007, Inside Criminal Law, 2007; editor: Search and Seizure Law Report. Del. Dem. Nat. Conv., N.Y.C., 1980; chair Pitts. Citizens Police Rev. Bd., 1997-99. Named Hon. Chief Police City of Louisville, 1980; Ford Found. fellow, 1976. Mem. ABA (chair trial judge standards task force 1997-2000), ACLU, Pa. Bar Assn., Assn. Am. Law Schs. (chair criminal justice sect. 1980, exec. coun. 1977-82), U.S. Supreme Ct. Hist. Soc. Democrat. Jewish. Home: 6104 Kentucky Ave Pittsburgh PA 15206-4213 Office: U Pitts Sch Law Pittsburgh PA 15260 Business E-Mail: burkoff@pitt.edu.

BURKS, A. WESLEY, pediatrics educator; b. Marshall, Ark., Apr. 21, 1954; m. Jan Getty; children: Chris, Sarah, Collin. BS in Gen. Sci., U. Cen. Ark., 1976; MD, U. Ark., 1980. Diplomate Am. Bd. Pediatrics, Am. Bd. Allergy and Immunology. Fellow in allergy/immunology/pulmonary diseases dept. pediatrics Duke U. Med. Ctr., Durham, N.C., 1983-85; intern in pediatrics Ark. Children's Hosp./U. Ark. for Med. Scis., Little Rock, 1980-81, resident in pediatrics, 1981-83, chief resident, 1983; prof. pediatrics U. Ark. for Med. Scis., 1996—2003; prof. pediatrics Med. Sch. Duke U., Chapell Hill, SC, 2003—. Mem. rsch. coun. U. Ark. for Med. Scis., 1989-2003; co-dir. pediatric clin. rsch. unit Ark. Children's Hosp., 1990-2003, dir. HLA tissue typing lab., 1991-2003. Mem. editorial bd., ad hoc reviewer Jour. Allergy and Clin. Immunology; ad hoc reviewer Pediatrics, Jour. Pediatrics, Pediatric Allergy and Immunology; contbr. numerous articles to sci. jours. Bd. dirs. Food Allergy Network, 1992, Ark. Regional Organ Recovery Agy., 1992. Named one of Outstanding Young Men of Am., 1981. Mem. AMA, Am. Acad. Allergy and Immunology (chmn. adverse reactions fo foods com. 1992), Am. Acad. Pediatrics, Ark. Acad. Pediatrics, Soc. for Pediatric Rsch., So. Soc. Pediatric Rsch. (rsch. councilor 1990-91), Clin. Immunology Soc., Southeastern Allergy Soc., Alan Cazort Allergy Soc., Alpha Chi (chpt. pres. 1975-76). Presbyterian. Avocations: soccer, baseball, basketball, youth coaching. Home: 306 Faison Rd Chapel Hill NC 27517-5667 Office: Duke Univ Med Sch Box 3530 DUMC Durham NC 27710 Office Phone: 919-681-2949. Business E-Mail: wesley.burks@duke.edu.

BURKS, DAVID BASIL, academic administrator, educator; b. Ava, Mo., May 13, 1943; m. Leah Ann Gentry; children: Bryan, Stephen, Marleah. BA, Harding Coll., 1965; MBA, U. Tex., 1966; PhD, Fla. State U., 1974. CPA, Tex. Mem. internal audit staff Exxon Inc., Houston, 1966-67; dir. placement, bus. instr. Harding Coll., Searcy, Ark., 1967-71, dean sch. bus., 1974-87, dir. Am. Studies program, 1982, pres., 1987—. Deacon Coll. Ch. of Christ, Searcy, 1985, elder, 1996, chmn. bd. dirs. Camp Wildwood, Searcy, 1975-79. Author: The Christian Alternative for Business, 1978; creator computerized bus. game Strategic Management Simulation, 1974. Mem. Kiwanis, Searcy Club. Republican. Office: Harding U Office of Pres 900 E Center Ave Stop 12256 Searcy AR 72149-0002

BURKS, ROCKY ALAN, disability access manager and consultant; b. San Bernardino, Calif., June 12, 1952; s. Lloyd Jackson and Vivian Elnora B.; m. Nikki Ann Stone (div. 1974); 1 child, Gannon Leroy; m. Lydia Ann Deatherage, Aug. 20, 1983. BA in Social Welfare, Calif. State U., Chico, 1979, BA in Sociology, 1979. Instrument flight instr. USAF, Del Rio, Tex., 1971—75; dir. outreach and recruitment, Office of Vets. Affairs Calif. State U., Chico, 1976—81; exec. dir. Easter Seal Soc. of Butte County, Chico, 1981—82, No. Calif. Ind. Living Program, Chico, 1982—85; soc. worker Butte County (Calif.) Welfare Dept., 1985—87; exec. dir. Ind. Living Svcs. of No. Calif., Inc., Chico, 1988—2004; disability access coord. supr. County of Marin, 2003—06; disability access mgr. dept. transp. City of Sacramento, 2006—. Mem. disability access adv. bd. Divsn. of the State Arch., Sacramento, 1995-99, Disabled Access Bd. of Appeals, Butte County Building Divsn., Oroville, 1994-2003; disability access code adv. com. Calif. Bldg. Stds. Commn., 1999-06, bldg., fire and other codes adv. com., 2002-06; mem. DRA fund, adv. and distbn. com. The San Francisco Found., 1999—; universal design adv. bd., Divsn. State Architect, 2002-03; mem. ADA adv. com. Butte County Bd. Suprs. 2002-03; mem. accessibility com. adv. bd. Divsn. State Arch., 2006—. Editor: (newsletter) Independent Life, 1988—2004, Voice, 1976—81. Transp. adv. commn. Butte County Assn. Govts., Oroville, 1992-04; mem. Californians Disability Rights, Coalition Disability Access Profls.; bd. dirs. Marin Ctr. Ind. Living, 2004-07. Recipient Cert. of Congl. Recognition, Congressman Wally Herger, Chico, 1993, 96, Disability Advocate award Calif. Assn. Persons with Handicaps, 1994, Region IX Disability Advocate award Nat. Coun. Ind. Living, 1998, Master Instr. award Air Tng. Command, USAF, 1975; named citizen Chickasaw Indian Nation. Mem. Am. Legion, Vietnam Vets. Am., Masons, Shriners, Scottish Rite, Chico Breakfast Lions (pres. 1991-92, Lion of Yr. award 1990, Melvin Jones fellow), Lions Eye Found. Calif. and Nev. (life). Avocations: scuba diving, boating, reading, art. Home: 7476 Maximillian Pl Rohnert Park CA 94928 Office: City of Sacramento Dept Trans 915 I St Rm 2000 Sacramento CA 95814 Office Phone: 916-808-5521. Personal E-mail: rockyaburks@comcast.net. Business E-Mail: rburks@cityofsacramento.org.

BURLAGE, DOROTHY DAWSON, clinical psychologist; b. San Antonio, Sept. 13, 1937; d. Joseph M. and Virginia (Hendrix) Dawson. BA, U. Tex., 1959; EdM, Harvard U., 1972, PhD, 1978. Lic. psychologist, Mass. Horace Lentz lectr. Harvard Coll., 1972-73; rsch. assoc. in psychiatry Harvard Med. Sch., Cambridge, Mass., 1976-78; rsch. assoc. Children's Hosp. Med. Ctr., Boston, 1978-79; clin. fellow psychology Harvard Med. Sch., 1978-80; staff psychologist Eliot Community Mental Health Ctr., Concord, Mass., 1980-85; instr. dept. psychiatry Harvard Med. Sch., 1984-88; mem. staff dept. psychiatry Newton Wellesley Hosp., 1986-92; cons. psychologist Harvard U. Health Svcs., 1991—2000; pvt. practice clin. psychologist Boston; clin. supr. Children's Hosp., Boston, 1994-96. Cons. in field. Co-author: Deep in Our Hearts, 2000; contbr. articles to profl. jours. Bd. dirs. Children's Mus., Boston, 1988-94, Families First, 1992-96, Profls. for Parents and Families, 1994; mem. scientist adv. bd. Mind Sci. Found., 1994. Grantee HEW, Bus. and Profl. Women's Found., 1976; fellow NIMH, 1972-73, 73-74, Zeta Tau Alpha, 1972-73; Woodrow Wilson fellow in Women's Studies, 1976-77. Mem. Am. Psychol. Assn., Mass. Psychol. Assn., AOA. Home: 166 Oakleigh Rd Newton MA 02458-2224 Personal E-mail: burlaged@aol.com.

BURLEIGH, A. PETER, ambassador; b. LA, Mar. 7, 1942; s. Ralph Wendell and Margaret (McKenney) B. AB, Colgate U., 1963; postgrad., U. Pa., 1965-66. Vol. Peace Corps, Nepal, 1963-65; joined Fgn. Svc., 1967; various positions Dept. State, Washington, 1967-85, dir. No. Gulf Affairs, 1985-87, dep. asst. sec. for Near Eastern and South Asian Affairs, 1987-89, dep. asst. sec. for intelligence and rsch., 1989-91, coord. for counter-terrorism, amb., 1991-92, dep. asst. sec. for pers., 1992-95; amb. Dem. Socialist Republic Sri Lanka, Republic Maldives, 1995-97; dep. U.S. rep. to UN, 1997-99; ret. Vis. disting. prof., amb.-in-residence U. Miami, 2004—. Bd. dirs. Kathmandu Valley Preservation Trust, 2007—. Recipient Presdl. Svc. award U.S. Govt., 1990, 93, Disting. Svc. award Sec. of State, Washington, 2000, Presdl. Disting. Svc. award, 2000. Office: 2300 Riverlane Ter Fort Lauderdale FL 33312-4762 Personal E-mail: apburl@bellsouth.net.

BURLEIGH, LEWIS ALBERT, lawyer; b. Augusta, Maine, May 15, 1940; s. Lewis A. and Ursula (Maher) B.; m. Rinda H. Burleigh, June 22, 1963; children: Lewis A. IV, Jennifer, Erica. AB cum laude, Harvard U., 1962, JD, 1965. Bar: N.Y. 1966, Mass. 1973,Calif. 1982, Pa. 1985. Assoc. Dewey Ballantine Bushby Palmer & Wood, NYC, 1965-72; ptnr. Csaplar & Bok (name changed to Gaston & Snow), Boston and San Francisco, 1973-91, Day Berry & Howard, Boston, 1991—2001, Dechert LLP, Boston, 2001—. Fellow Am. Coll. Investment Counsel; mem. ABA, N.Y. State Bar Assn., Calif. Bar Assn., Am. Soc. Internat. Law, Harvard Club. Avocation: flying. Office: Dechert LLP 200 Clarendon St Fl 27 Boston MA 02116 Office Phone: 617-654-8601. Business E-Mail: lewis.burleigh@dechert.com.

BURLEIGH, WILLIAM ROBERT, media executive; b. Evansville, Ind., Sept. 6, 1935; s. Joseph Charles and Emma Bertha (Wittgen) B.; m. Catherine Anne Husted, Nov. 28, 1964; children: David William, Catherine Anne, Margaret Walden. BS, Marquette U., Milw., 1957; LLD (hon.), U. So. Ind., 1979. From reporter to editor, pres. Evansville Press, 1951-77; editor Cin. Post, 1977-83; v.p., gen. editl. mgr. Scripps-Howard Newspapers, Cin., 1984-86, sr. v.p. newspapers and publs., 1986-90, exec. v.p., 1990-94, pres., COO, 1994-96, pres., CEO, 1996-99; chmn., CEO E.W. Scripps Co., Cin., 1999-2000, chmn., 2000—. With AUS, 1957-58. Mem. Queen City Club, Cin. Lit. Club, Cin. Country Club, Cin. Comml. Club, Alpha Sigma Nu. Roman Catholic. Office: E W Scripps 312 Walnut St Cincinnati OH 45202-4024

BURLESKI, JOSEPH ANTHONY, JR., information technology executive; b. Poughkeepsie, NY, June 30, 1960; s. Joseph Anthony, Sr. and Fredeline (Cyr) Burleski; m. Judith Ann Lezon, June 10, 1989; children: Joseph Anthony III, Jessica Ann. BSBA, Marist Coll., 1982; MBA Mktg., U. Phoenix, 1992; grad. in human rels. and effective speaking, Dale Carnegie, 1990. Cert. project mgmt. profl. Project Mgmt. Inst., exec. project mgr. IBM. Computer operator IBM, Poughkeepsie, 1982-83, lead/sr. computer operator, 1983-84, systems programmer, 1984-85, assoc. systems programmer, 1985-86, mgr. offshift computer ops., 1986-87, mgr. info. processing Boulder, Colo., 1987-88, mgr. MVS systems programming, 1988-91; mgr. location and field svcs. devel. Integrated Systems Solutions Corp. subs. IBM, Boulder, 1991-93, mgr. location and field svc. devel. ind. test, 1992-93; mgr. VM/VSE svcs. Integrated Sys. Solutions Corp. subs. IBM, Boulder, 1993-94, account mgr., 1994-96; delivery project exec. IBM Global Svcs., Boulder, 1997-98, delivery exec. St. Louis, 1998—2000, sr. delivery project exec., 2001—07, global networking competency leader, 2007—. Mem. IBM Data Processing Ops. Coun., Poughkeepsie, 1983—92, Project Mgmt. Inst., 1995—; bd. dirs. IBM Cert. Bd. Coach Spl. Olympics, 1987—98; asst. cubmaster Boy Scouts Am., 2002—03, cubmaster, 2003—05, cub scout roundtable chmn., 2004—, asst.scoutmaster, 2005—, scout tng. com., 2005—; staff Boy Scout World Jamboree, England, 2007. Mem.: Am. Assn. Individual Investors, Marist Coll. Alumni Assn. (contbr.), Nat. Eagle Scout Assn., KC (Ascension Coun. # 11139), Order of Arrow (lodge sec., editor 1976—77, lodge pres. 1977—78, lodge treas. 1980—81), Vigil Nat. Honor Soc. Roman Catholic. Avocations: running, reading, camping, hiking. Office: Bld 306 Mailcode 306-627 325 JS McDonnell Blvd Hazelwood MO 63042 Office Phone: 314-252-6069. Business E-Mail: burleski@us.ibm.com.

BURLING, JAMES C., lawyer; b. 1950; AB, Grinnell Coll., 1972; JD, Harvard Univ., 1976. Bar: Mass. 1977, US Supreme Ct. Atty. FTC, 1976—78, Hale & Dorr, 1978—2004, past chmn. exec. com.; ptnr., co-chmn. Antitrust & Competition dept., mem. Litigation dept. Wilmer Cutler Pickering Hale & Dorr, Boston, 2004—. Contbr. articles to profl. jours. Bd. dir. Ctr. for Pub. Representation, New Eng. Ctr. for Children. Named a Mass. Super Lawyer, Boston Mag., 2004. Fellow: Mass. Bar Assn.; mem.: ABA (past vice chmn., Intellectual Property com.), Boston Bar Assn., Phi Beta Kappa. Office: Wilmer Cutler Pickering Hale & Dorr 60 State St Boston MA 02109 Office Phone: 617-526-6416. Office Fax: 617-526-5000. Business E-Mail: james.burling@wilmerhale.com.

BURLING, STACY, reporter; m. Jeff Bredenberg; 2 children. Reporter, mental health writer Phila. Inquirer. Recipient AAAS Sci. Journalism award (large newspaper), 2006. Office: Phila Inquirer--News Dept 400 N Broad St Philadelphia PA 19130 Office Phone: 215-854-4944. Business E-Mail: sburling@phillynews.com.

BURLINGAME, ALMA LYMAN, chemist, educator; b. Cranston, RI, Apr. 29, 1937; s. Herman Follett Jr. and Rose Irene (Kohler) B.; children: Mark, Walter; m. Marilyn F. Schwartz, Feb. 14, 1993 (dec. Aug. 24, 2004); 1 stepchild, Corey Schwartz. BS, U. R.I., 1959; PhD, MIT, 1962. Asst. prof. U. Calif., Berkeley, 1963-68, assoc. chemist, 1968-72, rsch. chemist, 1972-78, prof. San Francisco, 1978—, Univ. Coll., London, 1996—2002. Vis. prof. Ludwig Inst. for Cancer Rsch., London, 1993-94. Editor: Topics in Organic Mass Spectrometry, 1970, Mass Spectrometry in Health and Life Science, 1985, Biological Mass Spectrometry, 1990, Mass Spectrometry in the Biological Sciences, 1995, Mass Spectrometry in Biology and Medicine, 2000, Biological Mass Spectrometry, Methods in Enzymology, 2005, Mass Spectrometry: Modified Proteins and Glycoconjugates, Methods in Enzymology, 2005; co-editor: Molecular and Cellular Proteonics, 2006—; dep. editor Molecular and Cellular Proteomics, 2002—06; contbr. articles to profl. jours. With USAR, 1954-62. Guggenheim Found. fellow, 1970. Fellow AAAS. Office: U Calif Dept Pharm Chemistry San Francisco CA 94143-0446 Office Phone: 415-476-5641. Business E-Mail: alb@cgl.ucsf.edu.

BURLINGAME, MARK WAYNE, cardiothoracic surgeon; b. St. Paul, Oct. 8, 1950; s. Charles Frank and Patricia Ann (Meyer) B.; m. Anine Marie Davidson, May 18, 1975; children: Patrick, Kathleen, Julia, Ross. BA in Biology, Northwestern U., 1971; MD cum laude, Creighton U., 1975. Diplomate Am. Bd. Surgery, Am. Bd. Thoracic Surgery; lic. surgeon, Ala., Wis., Mich., Pa. Quality control microbiologist Allergan Pharms., 1971; extern Tex. Heart Inst. Baylor U., 1974; intern U. Ala. Hosps., Birmingham, 1975-80; resident in cardiothoracic surgery Med. Coll. Wis. Hosps., Milw., 1980-82; pvt. practice Pontiac, Mich., 1982-83, Lancaster, Pa., 1983—; active staff Lancaster Gen. Hosp., 1983—. Dir. critical care Lancaster Gen. Hosp., 1993—, chmn. dept. surgery, 1997-2000, chief divsn. of cardiothoracic surgery, 2000—; courtesy staff Lancaster Regional Med. Ctr., 1983—2001, Cmty. Hosp. Lancaster, 1983—2001. Contbr. articles to profl. jours. Rsch. fellow NSF, 1969, 70, Argonne Nat. Lab./U.S. Atomic Energy Commn., 1970; Summer fellow Creighton U., 1972. Fellow ACS, Am. Coll. Cardiology, Am. Coll. Chest Physicians, Soc. Thoracic Surgeons; mem. Pa. Med. Soc., Pa. Assn. Thoracic Surgery, Lancaster City and County Med. Soc., Beta Beta Beta, Alpha Omega Alpha. Avocations: piano, golf, gourmet food, wine. Office: Cardiothoracic Surgeons Lancaster 555 N Duke St Lancaster PA 17604-3555 Home: 39 Deer Ford Dr Lancaster PA 17601-5642 Home Phone: 717-295-9334; Office Phone: 717-544-4995. E-mail: CTSL@cardiacsurgeons.com.

BURMAN, DARRYL MICHAEL, lawyer; b. 1958; B, U. South Fla., 1980; JD, South Tex. Coll. Law, 1983. Bar: Tex. 1984. Head corp. and securities sect. Fant & Burman, LLP, Houston; ptnr., head corp. and securities practice Epstein, Becker & Green, Houston; v.p., gen. counsel, corp. sec. Grp. 1 Automotive, Houston, 2006—. Office: Grp 1 Automotive Inc Ste 100 950 Echo Ln Houston TX 77024*

BURMAN, KENNETH DALE, physician; b. St. Louis, Aug. 9, 1944; s. Philip and Henrietta Burman; m. Mary Eileen Schmidt, Sept. 23, 1973; children: Ed, Steve, Andrew, David, Emily. AB, Washington U., St. Louis, 1966; MD, Mo. U., 1970. House officer med. dept. Barnes Hosp., St. Louis, 1970—72; fellow in endocrinology Walter Reed Army Med. Ctr., Washington, 1972—74, asst. chief endocrinology dept., 1974—91, chief endocrinology, 1991—94; dir. sect. endocrinology Washington Hosp. Ctr., 1994—; prof. dept. medicine Georgetown U., 1995—. Mem. editorial bd. Jour. Clin. Endocrinology, Thyroid Jour. Col. U.S. Army, 1972-94. Master: ACP. Office Phone: 202-877-6563.

BURMASTER, ELIZABETH, school system administrator; b. Balt., July 26, 1954; m. John Burmaster; 3 children. B in Music Edn., U. Wis., Madison, 1976, M in Ednl. Adminstrn., 1984. Vocal music and creative dramatics dir. Longfellow Elem. and Sennett Middle Sch., Madison, Wis., 1976—78; choral and drama dir. East HS, Madison, 1978—85; asst. prin. Marquette Middle Sch., Madison, 1985—88; fine arts coord. Madison Sch. Dist., 1988—90; prin. Hawthorne Elem., Madison, 1990—92, Madison West HS, 1992—2001; state supt. pub. instrn. State of Wis., Madison, 2001—. Mem. Govs. Econ. Growth Coun., Coun. Chief State Sch. Officers, chair task force on early childhood learning, bd. dirs.; bd. mem., past chair Nat. Ctr. for Learning and Citizenship. Nat. bd. advisor Pre-K Now; mem. bd. regents U. Wis.; mem. Edn. Commn. of the States, Wis. Tech. Coll. Sys. Bd., Ednl. Comms. Bd., Very Spl. Arts Wis., Gov.'s Work-Based Learning Bd.; bd. dirs. TEACH Wis. Mem.: Coun. of Chief State Sch. Officers (pres.), SAI-Music Assn., Tempo Internat., Assn. Wis. Sch. Adminstrs. Mailing: Dept Pub Instruction 125 S Webster St PO Box 7841 Madison WI 53707-7841*

BURMEISTER, JOHN LUTHER, chemistry professor, consultant; b. Fountain Springs, Pa., Feb. 20, 1938; s. Luther John and Frieda May (Tielmann) B.; m. Doris Aileen Crawford, June 25, 1960; children: Lisa Anne, Jeffrey Scott. BS in Chemistry, Franklin and Marshall Coll., 1959; PhD in Chemistry, Northwestern U., 1964. Instr. chemistry U. Ill., Urbana, 1963-64; asst. prof. chemistry U. Del., Newark, 1964-69, assoc. prof., 1969-73, prof., 1973-93, alumni disting. prof., 1993—, assoc. chmn. dept., 1974—, NCAA faculty athletic rep., 1982—. Pres. Covered Bridge Farms Maintenance Corp., Newark, 1977-79; chmn. chemistry editl. rev. bd. Control Data Corp., Mpls., 1981-85. Mem. editl. bd. Inorganica Chimica Acta, Padua, Italy, 1967-88, Synthesis and Reactivity Inorganic Metal-Organic Chemistry, NYC, 1970-98; contbr. numerous articles to profl. jours. Ruling elder Head Christiana Presbyn. Ch., Newark, 1969—. Recipient Excellence Tchg. award Lindback Found. Del. Alumni Assn., 1968, 79, award Excellence chemistry Tchr., Chem. Mfrs. Assn., Washington, 1981, faculty recognition award Mortar Bd., 1984, Prof. Yr. award Coll. Arts Sci., 1985, Del. Prof. Yr. award Carnegie Found., 1994, Advancement Tchr. Cun. Advancement Support Edn., 1994, Disting. Del. Scientist award, 1994, Excellence Tchg. award Alpha Lambda Delta, 1997, Coll. Arts Sci. Disting. Alumni Prof. award, 1997. Mem. Am. Chem. Soc. (sec.-treas. inorganic divsn. 1975-77, alt. councillor, 1977-79, assoc. nat. com. chem. edn. 1983-84, councillor Del. sect. 1987-89), Sigma Xi, Phi Lambda Upsilon, Phi Kappa Phi (v.p. Del. chpt. 1979-80, pres. 1980-81), Omicron Delta Kappa. Republican. Office: U Del Dept Chemistry-Biochemistry Newark DE 19716 Home Phone: 302-731-4336; Office Phone: 302-831-1130. Business E-Mail: jlburm@udel.edu.

BURMEISTER, PAUL FREDERICK, farmer; b. Great Bend, Kans., June 11, 1938; s. Ferdinand Frederick Adam and Gertrude Nellie (Hanson) B. BA in Chemistry and Agr., Ft. Hays State U., 1960; postgrad., U. Kans., 1961. Farmer, Claflin, Kans., 1952-61, 64—. Farmer coop. Kans. Agrl. Experiment Sta., Ft. Hays Br. Sta., Hays, Kans., 1970, Kans. Rural Ctr., Whiting, 1991-92; panel mem. Kans. Sustainable Agr. Conf., Great Bend and Salina, 1991-92; mem. Kans. Natural Resource Coun., Topeka, 1975—, Nat. Resources Def. Coun., NYC, 1975—; participant U. Akron Nat. Energy Forum, 1976, Nat. Low-Level Radioactive Waste Mgmt. Strategy Rev. Workshop, Washington, 1981, Office Radiation Programs, EPA, Denver, 1978; guest spkr., Rapid City, S.D., 1993; mem. farmer adv. com. Sunshine Farm Project, The Land Inst., Salina, 1995-2001. Contbr. articles to environ. and agrl. jours. Vol. Am. Peace Corps, Ludhiana, India, 1961-63; local organizer campaign Union of Concerned Scientists, Cambridge, Mass.; lobbyist on environ. protection and conservation issues, Topeka, 1976-80; mem. Renew Am., Washington, 1980—; mem. The Menninger Found., Topeka, 1989—, Environ. Action, 1982—; lay mem. ad hoc task force on ecology Christian lifestyle United Ch. of Christ, 1977-78, commn. on outreach Kans.-Okla. conf., 1988-96, 98-99, network environ. and econ. responsibility; del. to 23rd Gen. Synod meeting of United Ch. of Christ, Kansas City, Mo., 2001; mem. Kans.-Okla. Conf. Coun. United Ch. Christ, 1999-2003; participant Kans. Citizens Forum Com. for Humanities, Topeka, 1987; bd. trustees Clara Barton Hosp. Found., Hoisington, Kans., 2005-. With USNG, 1963—69. Recipient Bankers award Banks of Barton County, Kans. and U.S. Soil Conservation Svc., 1990. Mem. Nat. Wildlife Fedn. (life), Nat. Coun. Returned Peace Corps Vols., Nat. Arbor Day Found., World Wildlife Fund (charter), Am. Wind Energy Assn., Am. Solar Energy Soc. (life), Heartland Renewable Energy Soc., Midwest Renewable Energy Assn., 1998—, Kans. Assn. Wheat Growers, Kans. Farmers Union (life), Kans. Organic Prodrs., Inc., Friends of the Earth, Cousteau Soc. (founding yr. mem.), Kans. State Hist. Soc. (life), Kans. Wildlife Fedn., Sierra Club (life), Native Forest Coun., Ducks Unltd. Inc., Environ. Def., Wilderness Soc., Friends of India, Rainforest Alliance, Nat. Parks Conservation Assn., Nature Conservancy, Tau Kappa Epsilon (sec. 1958-59, scholar 1959), Phi Eta Sigma (historian 1958-59), Phi Kappa Phi, Delta Epsilon. Avocations: photography, hiking, exploring. Address: 1332 NE 180th Rd Claflin KS 67525-9219 Home Phone: 620-587-3919; Office Phone: 620-587-3919.

BURN, BARBARA LOUISE, literature and language educator; d. Edgar George Nuss and Jeanette Pauline Nuss Mennenga; m. Doyle Dohn Burn, June 4, 1965; children: Twila, John, David. BA, Wartburg Coll., Iowa, 1965; MA, Viterbo U., Wis., 2002. Girls' phys. edn. educator Saydel HS, Des Moines, 1965—66; phys. edn., English educator Des Moines Christian Sch., 1967—68, 1971—73, phys. edn. and English educator, girls' dean, girls' basketball coach, yearbook adviser, 1980—97; phys. edn. educator Des Moines Pub. Schs., 1974—77; English educator, yearbook Nat. Honor Soc., Grandview Park Bapt. Sch., Des Moines, 1997—. Adv. bd. Des Moines Pub. Schs., 1975—77; adj. grammar instr. AIB Coll. Bus., Des Moines, 2000—03. Libr. bd. mem. City Libr., Carlisle, Iowa, 1980—82; bd. mem. Alpha Women's Ctr., Des Moines, 1992—93; vol. Right to Life Iowa, Rep. Party, Iowa, 2004; mem. Grandview Park Bapt. Ch., 1996—; mem. adv. panel, Christian edn. dept. Faith Bapt. Bible Coll., Ankeny, Iowa. Mem.: Assn. Christian Schs. Internat. (conv. workshop facilitator 1985—95), Kappa Delta Pi. Republican. Baptist. Avocations: sports, dramas, concerts. Office: Grandview Park Bapt Sch 1701 E 33d Des Moines IA 50317

BURNES, KENNETT FARRAR, chemicals executive; b. Washington, Feb. 23, 1943; s. Richard M. and Ruth (Carney) B.; m. Barbara Jackson; children: Jennifer, Nathaniel, Lisa, Alison. AB, Harvard U., 1965, LLB, 1968. Ptnr. Choate, Hall & Stewart, Boston, 1968-87; v.p., gen. counsel Cabot Corp., Waltham, Mass., 1987-88, exec. v.p. Boston, 1988-95, pres., COO, 1995—2001, chmn., pres., CEO, 2001—. Bd. dirs. Neozyme Corp., Renaissance Properties Inc., Boston, White Flower Farm, Inc., Litchfield, Conn., Cabot Corp. Chmn. bd. Park Sch., Brookline, Mass., 1971-82. Office: Cabot Corp 2 Seaport Ln Boston MA 02210*

BURNETT, ARTHUR LOUIS, SR., judge; b. Spotsylvania County, Va., Mar. 15, 1935; s. Robert Louis and Lena Victoria (Bumbry) B.; m. Ann Lloyd, May 14, 1960; children: Darnellena, Arthur Louis II, Darryl, Darlisa, Dionne. BA summa cum laude, Howard U., 1957; LLB, NYU, 1958; grad., Fed. Exec. Inst., 1978. Bar: D.C. 1958, U.S. Dist. Ct. Md. 1963, U.S. Supreme Ct. 1964. Atty. Gen.'s Honor Program atty. fraud sect. criminal divsn. U.S. Dept. Justice, Washington, 1958, atty. to acting dep. chief gen. crimes sect., 1960-65; spl. asst. U.S. atty., Balt. and East St. Louis, Ill., 1961-63; asst. U.S. atty. D.C., 1965-68; legal adviser, gen. counsel D.C. Dept. Met. Police, 1968-69; U.S. magistrate U.S. Dist. Ct., Washington, 1969-75; asst. gen. counsel legal adv. divsn. U.S. CSC, 1975-78; assoc. gen. counsel Office of Personnel Mgmt., 1979-80; U.S. magistrate U.S. Dist. Ct. D.C., 1980-87; judge Superior Ct. D.C., 1987-98, sr. judge, 1998—; faculty Fed. Jud. Center, 1970—, Nat. Jud. Coll., 1974—; nat. exec. dir. Nat. African Am. Drug Policy Coalition, 2004—. Judge-in-residence Children's Def. Fund, 1998—; program chmn. ann. meeting Nat. Conf. Spl. Ct. Judges, Washington, 1973, chmn. elect, acting chmn., 1974-75, chmn., 1975; program chmn. ann. meeting Nat. Council U.S. Magistrates, Williamsburg, Va., 1974, pres., 1983-84; program participant D.C. Circuit Jud. Conf., 1974, U.S. Ct. Claims Jud. Conf., 1979; adj. prof. Columbus Sch. Law, Cath. U. Am., 1997—, Cath. U., 1997—, Sch. Law Howard U., 1998—. Mem. NYU Law Rev., 1957-58; editor Directory of Minority Judges of U.S., 1997—. Bd. dirs. Fellowship of Christian Athletes, Washington, 2000—03, Nat. Assn. for Children of Alcoholics, 2000—. Recipient Founders Day award NYU, 1958, Sustained Superior Performance award U.S. Atty. Gen., 1963, Disting. Service award CSC, 1978, Meritorious Service award U.S. Office of Personnel Mgmt., 1980, Jud. award of excellence Washington Met. Trial Lawyers Assn., 1999, award of excellence Nat. Conf. State Trial Judges, 1999, Outstanding Disting. Service award Fed. Bar Assn., 1983, Spirit of Excellence award, 2005. Mem. ABA (Franklin N. Flaschner jud. award as outstanding judge on ct. of spl. jurisdiction 1985, coun. adminstrv. law and regulatory practice sect. 1987-90, liaison rep. of adminstrv. law and regulatory practice sect. to adminstrv. conf. of U.S. 1990-94, JAD task force on improving opportunities for minorities (now called standing com. on minorities in judiciary) 1988-04, 05-, judge Edward R. Finch Law Day USA Speech award 1991, asst. sec. 1991-93, chair civil right and employment discrimination com. 1992-95, sec. adminstrv. law and regulatory practice 1993-95, chmn. CJS com. on criminal rules and evidence 1993-97, standing com. on substance abuse 1995-99, adv. com. substance abuse 2005—, standing com. unmet legal needs of children 2003-06, co-chmn. editl. bd. Criminal Justice Mag. 1997-2000, State Justice Initiatives award 2002, Spirit Excellence award 2005), Fed. Bar Assn. (sect. coord. 1987-88, chmn. fed. litigation sect. 1984-85, chmn. standing com. on U.S. magistrates, dep. chmn. sect. adminstrn. of justice 1983-84, chmn. standing com. on U.S. magistrate, chmn. sect. adminstrn. of justice 1983-84, 95-97, pres. DC chpt. 1984-85, chmn. profl. ethics com. 1991-93, chmn. audit com. 1999-2006, Disting. Svc. award 1978, Pres.'s award 1994, Earl Kintner award 2002), Washington Bar Assn. (chmn. jud. coun. 2000-01, Ollie Mae Cooper award 1997), Nat. Bar Assn. (chmn. cmty. and youth action com. jud. coun. 1995-2006, chmn. profl. ethics com., jud. coun. asst. sec., The Pres.'s award 1996, Raymond Pace Alexander award, 2004, E. Francis Stradford award, 2004, Pres.'s award, 2005, 06, Internat. Cmty. Corrections Assn. Jud. award 2006), Bar Assn. DC, DC Unified Bar, Am. Judicature Soc., Am. Judges Assn. (sec-treas. Prettyman-Leventhal Inn of Ct. Washington 1991-94, pres. 1994-95), Phi Beta Kappa, Omega Psi Phi. Avocations: farming, writing. Office: Howard U Sch Law Holy Cross Hall Rm 412-414 2900 Van Ness St NW Washington DC 20008 Home Phone: 202-362-6210; Office Phone: 202-806-8622, 202-806-8623. Personal E-mail: albsr2alb@aol.com, aburnettsr@aol.com.

BURNETT, CAROL, actress, comedienne, singer; b. San Antonio, Apr. 26, 1933; d. Jody and Louise (Creighton) B.; m. Joseph Hamilton, 1963 (div.); children: Carrie Louise, Jody Ann, Erin Kate; m. Brian Miller, 2001. Student, UCLA, 1952-54. Introduced comedy song I Made a Fool of Myself Over John Foster Dulles, 1957; Broadway debut in Once Upon a Mattress, 1959; regular performer in Garry Moore TV show, 1959-62; appeared several CBS-TV spls., 1962-63; star Carol Burnett Show, CBS-TV, 1966-77, Carol & Co., 1990-91; appeared on Broadway, Once Upon a Mattress, 1960, Plaza Suite, 1970, I Do, I Do, (musical) 1973, Same Time Next Year, 1977, Moon Over Buffalo, 1995 (Tony nomination), co-wrote play (with Carrie Hamilton), Hollywood Arms, 2001; films include Who's Been Sleeping in My Bed, 1963, Pete 'n' Tillie, 1972, Front Page, 1974, A Wedding, 1977, Health, 1979, Four Seasons, 1981, Chu Chu and the Philly Flash, 1981, Annie, 1982, Noises Off, 1992, Moon Over Broadway, 1997, Get Bruce, 1999, The Trumpet of the Swan (voice), 2001; TV movies Friendly Fire, 1978, The Grass is Always Greener Over the Septic Tank, 1979, The Tenth Month, 1979, Life of the Party, 1982, Between Friends, 1983, Hostage, 1988, Men, Movies, and Carol, 1994, Seasons of the Heart, 1994, The Marriage Fool, 1998 (American Comedy award, 1998), Grace, 1998, Once Upon a Mattress, 2005; club engagements, Harrah's Club, The Sands, Caesar's Palace, MGM Grand; TV specials Julie and Carol: Together Again, 1989, Happy Birthday Elizabeth: A Celebration of Life, 1997, Putting it Together, 2000, Carol Burnett: Show Stoppers, 2001; TV series Mad About You, 1996-1998; TV miniseries Fresno, 1986, A Century of Women, 1994; dir., writer The Universal Story, 1995, also prodr. Southern Star: Portrait of Atlanta, 1996; prodr. Fred Astaire: Puttin' On His Top Hat, 1980, Fred Astaire: Change Partners and Dance, 1980, Bacall on Bogart, 1988, Fred Astaire Songbook, 1991, Southern Star: A Portrait of Atlanta, 1996, others. Recipient outstanding comedienne award Am. Guild Variety Artists, 5 times, Emmy award for outstanding variety performance Acad. TV Arts and Scis., 5 times, Emmy award for best supporting actress in a comedy series for Mad About You, 1997, TV Guide award for outstanding female performer, 1961, 62, 63, Peabody award, 1963, Golden Globe award for outstanding comedienne of year Fgn. Press Assn., 8 times, 12 People's Choice awards, 1st ann. Nat. TV Critics Circle award for outstanding performance, 1977, San Sebastian Film Festival award for best actress for A Wedding, 1978, 1st Ace award Best Actress Between Friends, 1983, Horatio Alger award Horatio Alger Assn. Disting. Ams., 1988, Presdl. Medal of Freedom, The White House, 2005, Career Achievement award, TV Critics Assn., 2006; named One of 20 Most Admired Women Gallup Poll, 1977; named Woman of Year award Acad. TV Arts and Scis. Address: ICM 8942 Wilshire Blvd Fl 2 Beverly Hills CA 90211-1934

BURNETT, CRYSTAL BLYTHE, marketing professional; b. Moundridge, Kans., Nov. 12, 1965; d. John Milford and Judy Carlene (Stucky) S.; married, 1993. Student, Wichita State U., Kans., 1984-87; BS in Journalism, U. Kans., Lawrence, 1989. Dispatcher, sec. Digital Computing Ctr., Wichita, Kans., 1985-86; production asst. Stephan Advt. Agy., Wichita, 1986-87; asst. to exec. sec. Kans. Scholastic Press Assn., Lawrence, 1987-89; recreation leader Boston Recreation Ctr., Wichita, 1987; profl. intern The Clay Ctr. Dispatch, Clay Center, Kans., 1988; photography stringer AP, 1988; profl. intern Stephan Advt. Agy., Wichita, 1989; retail exec. trainee Dillard Dept. Stores, Inc., Wichita, 1989-90, area sales mgr., 1990-91; asst. mktg. dir. West Ridge Mall, Topeka, 1991-92, The Forum

Shops at Caesers, Las Vegas, Nev., 1992; mktg. dir. Machesney Park Mall, Ill., 1992-94, West Ridge Mall, Topeka, 1994-98; regional mktg. dir. Simon Property Group, Little Rock, 1998-99, Independence, Mo., 1999—. Steering com. Topeka Breast Cancer Coalition; bd. dirs. Honor A Student Incentive Program, 1995-98. Recipient US Nat. Leadership Merit award, 1984; Frances E. Taylor scholar, U. Kans., 1988. Mem. Am. Mktg. Assn. (Nat. and Kansas City chpts.), Internat. Coun. Shopping Ctrs. (cert. mktg. dir.), Topeka C. of C. (Honor A bd. dirs.), Order of Omega, Alpha Phi (promotions chmn. and philanthropy chmn. Gamma Xi chpt. 1984—). Office: Kansas City Regional Office 18600 E 37th Terr Ste 102 Independence MO 64055 Office Phone: 816-350-1665. Business E-Mail: cburnett@simon.com.

BURNETT, E. C., III, state supreme court justice; b. Spartanburg County, SC, Jan. 26, 1942; s. E. C., Jr. and Lucy (Byers) Burnett; m. Jami Grant, 1963; children: Curry, Sharon, Jeffrey. AB, Wofford Coll., 1964; JD, U. S.C., 1969. Bar: S.C. 1969, US Dist. Ct. , SC, Fourth Circuit Ct. of Appeals, US Supreme Ct. Pvt. practice atty., Spartanburg; mem. SC Ho. of Reps., 1973-74; probate judge Spartanburg County, 1976-80; judge family ct., 1980-81, Seventh Jud. Cir., 1981-95; assoc. justice SC Supreme Ct., 1995—. Elder Mt. Calvary Presbyn. Ch. Maj. USAR, 1964—66. Mem.: ABA, Spartanburg County Bar Assn., S.C. Bar Assn. Home: 200 Burnett Rd Pauline SC 29374-2610 Office: State Supreme Court PO Box 11330 Columbia SC 29211*

BURNETT, ELIZABETH B., lawyer; b. 1955; married; 2 children. BA, Brown U., 1976; JD cum laude, U. Mich., 1979. Bar: Mass. 1979, US Dist. Ct. (Dist. Mass.), US Ct. Appeals (1st Cir.). Ptnr., chair, Litig. Sect. Mintz Levin Cohn Ferris Glovsky & Popeo PC, Boston. Founding bd. mem. Jane Doe Safety Fund.; bd. dir. NewFund, Greater Boston YMCA; active Brown U. Sports Found. Named a Super Lawyer, Boston Mag. Office: Mintz Levin Cohn Ferris Glovsky & Popeo PC One Financial Ctr Boston MA 02111 Home Phone: 617-965-7546; Office Phone: 617-348-1613. Office Fax: 617-542-2241. Business E-Mail: eburnett@mintz.com.

BURNETT, ELLA M. GLENN, education educator; b. Girard, Kans., Nov. 06; d. Louis W. and Minnie Watkins Glenn; children: Allen Glenn, Ashley Dawn. BS, Pitts. State U., 1968, MS, 1969; EdD, U. Calif., LA, 1977. Cert. tchr. Kans., Calif. Elem. tchr. ABC Unified Sch. Dist., Artesia, Calif., 1969—77; evaluation cons. Springfield Pub. Schs., Mass., 1977—82; dir. institutional rsch. Springfield Tech. C.C., Mass., 1982—84; asst. prof. Framingham State Coll., Mass., 1985—89, Wheelock Coll., Boston, 1987—92; assoc. prof. Lesley U., Cambridge, Mass., 1992—97; prof. edn. Calif. State U., Long Beach, 1997—. Cons. Math. Engring. Sci. Achievement, Long Beach, Calif. Author: Surviving to Thriving, 2003. Com. chair Coalition of 100 Black Women, Boston, 1992; founder Black Women's Lit. Guild, Boston, 1995. Recipient Meritorious Achievement award, Pitts. State U., 2005. Mem.: Nat. Assn. Multicultural Edn. (presenter), Nat. Coun. Tchrs. of Math. (presenter), Am. Ednl. Rsch. Assn. (reviewer). Avocations: choral singing, piano, tai chi. Office: Calif State Univ 1250 Bellflower Blvd Long Beach CA 90840-2201 Office Phone: 562-985-7045. Office Fax: 562-985-5733. E-mail: eburnett@csulb.edu.

BURNETT, ERIN, finance newscaster; b. 1976; BA Polit. Econ., Williams Coll. Analyst Goldman Sachs, 1998; writer, booker CNN, Moneyline; v.p., fin. anchor Citigroup/CitiMedia; anchor Bloomberg on the Markets, Bloomberg TV, 2003—05; co-anchor CNBC, Squawk on the St., 2005—; anchor CNBC, Street Signs, 2005—. Named one of 40 Under 40, Advt. Age, 2007; recipient Deadline Club Award for Bus. Reporting, 2006. Office: CNBC Hdqs 900 Sylvan Ave Englewood Cliffs NJ 07632 Office Phone: 201-735-2622.*

BURNETT, HENRY, lawyer; b. NYC, Feb. 24, 1927; s. Lucien Dallam and Ruth (Hinkle) B.; m. Florence Stewart, July 19, 1952; children: Marian Starr, Betsy Callaway, Henry Stewart. BA, U. Va., 1947, LLB, 1950. Bar: Va. 1950, Fla. 1951. Ptnr. Fowler, White, Burnett, Miami, Fla., 1957—93, pres., 1957—93, ptnr., 1993—. Bd. dirs. Dade County Citizens Safety Council, Travelers Aid, United Family and Children's Services. Served with USNR, 1945-46. Fellow Am. Coll. Trial Lawyers; mem. Am., Fla., Dade County bar assns., Fla. Def. Lawyers Assn. (pres. 1967-68), Dade County Def. Bar Assn. (pres. 1966-67), Internat. Assn. Def. Counsel (exec. com. 1972-74, pres. 1976-77), Riviera Country Club. Episcopalian. Home: 8871 SW 68th Ave Miami FL 33156 Office: Espirito Santo Bldg 1395 Brickall Ave 14th Fl Miami FL 33131 Home Phone: 305-666-6363; Office Phone: 305-789-9206. E-mail: hburnett@fowler-white.com.

BURNETT, IRIS JACOBSON, corporate communications specialist; b. Bklyn., Nov. 14, 1946; d. Milton and Rose (Dubroff) Groman; m. Allan Jacobson; 1 child, Seth Jacobson; m. David Burnett, Jan. 29, 1984; 1 child, Jordan Burnett. BS, Emerson Coll., 1968, MS in Commn. Theory, 1971. Instr. Boston U., 1971-73; dir. press and pub. rels. Dept. Parks and Recreation, Boston, 1975-77; dir. internat. visitors U.S. Dept. State, Washington, 1977-80; dir. security Dem. Nat. Conv., NYC, 1980; sr. v.p. Arrive Unltd., Washington, 1980-84; pres. In Advance, Arlington, 1984-87; asst. prof. Am. U., Washington, 1987-90; pres. Sound Remarks, Arlington, 1990-92; exec. dir. Debates '92, Washington, 1992; chief staff USIA, Washington, 1993-96; sr. v.p. corp. comm. USA Network, NYC, 1997—99; prof. Am. U. Sch. Comm., Washington, 1999—2001; exec. v.p. pub. affairs, comms. Life Medical Technologies, Cedar Knolls, NJ. Co-founder, co-chair, pres. Count Me In for Women's Econ. Ind., 2002; pres. Kai Prodns. Author: Hart for Pres., 1984, Nat. Surrogate Schedule, 1984, Inauguration, Transition: Clinton Gore Campaign, 1992, Schlepper: A Mostly True Tale of Presidential Politics, 2003, So You Think You Can Be President!, 2007; prodr.: (documentary) The Gefilte Fish Chronicles, 2006. Active McGovern presdl. campaign, Boston, 1972; mem. nat. staff Udall for Pres., Washington, 1974-76, Carter-Mondale '76, 1976-77; bd. dirs. Tap Am. Project, 1994—; official del. 4th World Conf. on Women; bd. gov.'s USO.; founder Broad Confidence in Chair Women; bd. dirs. Erase the Hate Found.; mem. Bretton Woods Com. Named Presdl. appt. to Bd. Govs. USO. Mem. Women's Fgn. Policy Group, Emily's List, Nat. Jewish Dem. Coalition.

BURNETT, JEAN B., biochemist; b. Flint, Mich., Feb. 19, 1924; d. Chester M. and Katheryn (Krasser) Bullard; B.S., Mich. State U., 1944, M.S., 1945, Ph.D. (Council fellow), 1952; m. James R. Burnett, June 8, 1947. Research assoc. dept. zoology Mich. State U., East Lansing, 1954-59, dept. biochemistry, 1959-61, acting dir. research biochem. genetics, dept. biochemistry, 1961-62, assoc. prof., asst. chmn. dept. biomechanics, 1973-82, prof. dept. anatomy, 1982-84, prof. dept. zoology, Coll. Natural Sci. and Coll. Osteo. Medicine, 1984—; assoc. biochemist Mass. Gen. Hosp., Boston, 1964-73; prin. research assoc. dermatology Harvard, 1962-73, faculty medicine, 1964-73, also spl. lectr., cons., tutor Med. Sch.; vis. prof. dept. biology U. Ariz., 1979-80. USPHS, NIH grantee, 1965-68; Gen. Research Support grantee Mass. Gen. Hosp., 1968-72; Ford Found. travel grantee, 1973; Am. Cancer Soc. grantee, 1971-73; Internat. Pigment Cell Conf. travel grantee, 1980; recipient Med. Found. award, 1970. Mem. AAAS, Am. Chem. Soc., Am. Inst. Biol. Sci., Genetics Soc. Am., Soc. Investigative Dermatology, N.Y. Acad. Scis., Sigma Xi (Research award 1971), Pi Kappa Delta, Kappa Delta Pi, Pi Mu Epsilon, Sigma Delta Epsilon. Home: PO Box 805 Okemos MI 48805-0805

BURNETT, JOHN HUSZAGH, physicist; b. Chgo., May 6, 1955; s. Joseph Geddes Burnett and Dianne Huszagh Damico. BS, Stanford U., Calif., 1978; PhD in Physics, Harvard U., Cambridge, Mass., 1990. Postdoctoral rsch. fellow physics dept. Harvard U., Cambridge, 1990—; physicist Nat. Inst. Stds. and Tech., Gaithersburg, Md., 1994—. Recipient Silver medal for Sci. Achievement, U.S. Dept. Commerce, 2000, 2002, Arthur S. Flemming Sci. award, Arthur S. Flemming Found., 2002. Mem.: Chesapeake Bay Seaplane Pilots Assn. (co-founder 1996—2006, Seaplane Pilot of Yr. 2002). Achievements include research in symmetry-breaking effect in crystalline UV optical materials which results optical anisotropy and an intrinsic birefringence that spoils their use for precision UV optics; patents for minimizing spatial-dispersion-induced birefringence which provides exact solution to intrinsic birefringence problem. Home: 1068 Thomas Jefferson St NW Washington DC 20007 Office: NIST 100 Bureau Dr Stop 8423 Gaithersburg MD 20899 Home Phone: 202-337-6842; Office Phone: 301-975-2679. Business E-Mail: john.burnett@nist.gov.

BURNETT, JUDITH JANE, public relations executive; b. Muncie, Ind., Aug. 21, 1947; d. Albert Ward and Jane M. (Collins) Burnett. Grad., Ind. U. Svc. dir., ops. mgr. Indiana Homemakers, Inc., Indpls., 1975-80, exec. v.p., 1980-83, dir.; corp. sec. Mgmt. Alternatives, Inc., Indpls., 1984-85; exec. v.p., dir. Three-I Homemakers, Inc., Illini Homemakers, Inc., 1980-83; dir. Home Care Med. Products Co., 1980-82; adminstrv. Extended Svcs., 1988-92; owner Lab Plus, Inc., 1989-93, Projects & Promotions, 1990—2002; exec. dir. Ryan White Found., 1994-97; assoc. pub. and dir. Weiss Comm., Indpls., 2002—06; owner Solutions, Indpls., 2006—. Pres. Marion County Step Ahead, 1999—2003. Named One of Indpls.'s Influential Woman, 1999. Mem. US Tennis Writers Assn., Soc. Profl. Journalists. Home: 9992 Estep Dr Indianapolis IN 46280-1588 Home Phone: 317-580-1555; Office Phone: 317-443-9943. Personal E-mail: judyburnett@iquest.net. Business E-Mail: solutions@iquest.net.

BURNETT, LEN, publishing executive; Mem. founding staff, assoc. publisher Vibe/Spin Ventures, 1993—99; co-founder, publisher Vanguarde Publications, 2000—03; co-founder, chmn. Uptown Media Ventures (formerly Harlemwood Publishing), 2004—; group publisher Vibe and Vibe Vixen Vibe/Spin Ventures, NYC, 2005—. Office: VIBE 215 Lexington Ave New York NY 10016 Office Phone: 212-448-7300. Office Fax: 212-448-7400.

BURNETT, LONNIE SHELDON, obstetrics and gynecology educator; b. Saratoga, Tex., Aug. 2, 1927; s. Lonnie and Lois (Swift) B.; m. Betty Pearle Scruggs, Dec. 22, 1950; children: Anne Julian, Michael Julian. BS, U. Tex., 1948; MD, U. Tex., Galveston, 1953. Diplomate Am. Coll. Ob-Gyn. (chmn. Tenn. sect. 1988-91, mem. com. on sci. program 1988-91). Intern Henry Ford Hosp., Detroit, 1953-54; resident in internal medicine Mayo Clinic, Rochester, Minn., 1954-55; resident in ob-gyn. Johns Hopkins Hosp., Balt., 1957-62, fellow in microbiology, 1962-64; asst. prof. microbiology Johns Hopkins U., Balt., 1964-67, asst. prof. ob-gyn., 1964-70, assoc. prof., 1970-76; chmn. dept. ob-gyn. Vanderbilt U., Nashville, 1976-95, prof. ob-gyn., 1976—, Frances and John C. Burch prof. ob-gyn., 1995—. Mem. ob-gyn. text com. Nat. Bd. Med. Examiners, 1988-91. Co-author: Novak's Textbook of Gynecology, 11th edit., 1988; contbr. articles to profl. jours. Capt. USAF, 1955-57. Macy scholar Josiah Macy Jr. Found., 1965-70. Mem.: Canby Robinson Soc. of Vanderbilt U. Med. Ctr. (pres. 2006), Nashville Acad. Medicine (pres. 1999—2000), Tenn. Ob-Gyn. Soc. (pres. 1988—90). Republican. Episcopalian. Avocation: photography. Home: 78 Concord Park W Nashville TN 37205-4707 Office: Vanderbilt Med Ctr N Dept Ob-Gyn 1611 21st Ave S Nashville TN 37212-3103 Home Phone: 615-385-3048; Office Phone: 615-322-0093. Personal E-mail: lsburnett@comcast.net. Business E-Mail: lonnie.burnett@vanderbilt.edu.

BURNETT, LYNN BARKLEY, health science educator; b. Reedley, Calif., Oct. 20, 1948; s. Charles Erbin and Ruth Clarice (Erickson) B. BS, MSc, Columbia Pacific U.; diploma in nat. security mgmt., Nat. Def. U. of U.S.; EdD in Higher Edn., Nova Southeastern U.; Faculty of Laws, U. Lond. Cert. C.C. tchr., Calif.; cert. health edn. specialist Nat. Commn. for Health Edn. Credentialing; instr. in emergency care, basic CPR, ACLS, Pediatric ALS; instr./Heartsaver Automated Ext. Defibrillation for the Lay Rescuer and First Responder, AHA; trainer EMS and Hosp. Mgmt. of Nuclear, Biol. and Chem. Casualities, U.S. Nat. Domestic Preparedness Program for Terrorism. Med. advisor Fresno County Sheriff's Dept., 1972—; assoc. dir. Cen. Valley Emergency Med. Svcs. System, Fresno, Calif., 1974-75; faculty Fresno City Coll., 1978—; prof. health sci., 1981-87; dir. continuing edn. in health Calif. State U., Fresno, 1981-91; mem. nat. faculty Core Content Rev. of Family Medicine, 2001—. Vis. prof. VA Med. Ctr., Fresno, 1988; vis. prof. dept. family and community medicine U. Calif.-Davis, 2000; vis. prof. Calif. State U., Fresno, 2000—02; adj. faculty West Coast Christian Coll., 1989—92; lectr., cons. emergency med. svcs., 1975—; lectr., cons. bioethics, 1992—; clin. and path. forensic scis., 1992—; co-dir. cojoint rsch. program Stanford U. Sch. Medicine and Dept Health Sci. Calif. State U., Fresno, 1986; est. pilot paramedic program Fresno County, 1974—75; dir. Cen. Valley's Inaugural Paramedic Tng. Program, 1975; est. CPR tng. programs Fresno Fire Dept., 1968, Fresno Police Dept., 1972, Fresno County Sheriff's Dept., 1973, est. Law Enforcement Automated Ext. Defibrillation Program, 99; chmn. eMedicine Ethics Com., Boston Med. Pub. Co.; adj. instr. emer. med. svcs. ops. and planning for weapons mass destruction program Tex. A&M U., 2003—; adj. prof. forensic medicine and forensic pathology Nat. U., 2003—; trainer Edn. Physician Palliative and End of Life Care Project, 2003—; mem. end of life care com. Cmty. Med. Ctrs., 2006—. Editor: Textbook of Medicine, Ob/Gyn, Psychiatry, and Surgery; co-author: manuscript for motion picture "Quarantine"; author: (textbooks) Domestic Violence, 1998, Sudden Infant Death Syndrome, 1998, Cocaine Toxicity, 1998; editor: The role of ethics in criminal profiling, 2000, Grief and Bereavement, 2001; contbr. articles to profl. publs. Chmn. Fresno County steering com. The Chem. People, 1983-86, Generation at Risk, 1987; mem. Emergency Med. Care Com. Fresno County, 1979-85, vice-chmn., 1984-85; mem. Calif. State Commn. Emergency Med. Svcs., 1974-75; mem. Fresno County Adv. Bd. on Drug Abuse, 1984-92, chmn. drug adv. bd., 1985-88;bd. mgrs. First Bapt. Ch. Fresno, 1994-96, 99-2001, vice chmn. 1995, chmn. 1996, pres. copr., 1996; chmn. pub. edn. Fresno County unit Am. Cancer Soc., 1984-87, 90-92, bd. dirs. 1984-96, v.p., 1985-87, pres. elect 1987-88, pres. 1988-90, past pres., 1990-92, chmn. nominations and leadership devel. Fresno County unit, 1990-92, task force cancer and underserved populations Fresno County unit, 1990-92, task force cancer and underserved populations Fresno County unit, 1992-94, youth and cancer, Calif. Divsn. Am. Cancer Soc., 1992-94; com. mem. Early Detection and Treatment, Prevention and Risk Reduction, Fresno County Unit Am. Cancer Soc., 1992-94; chmn. Alcohol, Drug adv. bd. Fresno County, 1985-88, 92-98; pres. Fresno County Safety Coun., 1985—; mem. steering com. Fresno Health Promotion Coalition, 1987-92; attending cons. clin. ethics Cmty. Med. Ctr., 1992—, vice chmn., 1997-2005, chmn. 2005—, interim chmn.; chmn. com. on crime, violence and safety, 1987-89; chmn. bd. Fresno County Drug and Alcohol Prevention Coalition, Inc., 1987-92, 96-98; mem. med. staff, All-Star Football Game, 1965-98; emergency med. cons. Dept. Intercollegiate Athletics Calif. State U., Fresno, 1982—; mem. Cmty. Collaborative of Fresno Tomorrow, Inc., com. Juv. Crime Benchmarks, 1990-91; mem. core com. Student Assistance Program for Substance Abuse and Related Problems Fresno City Coll., 1989-93; numerous others. Recipient State Svc. medal Calif. Mil. Dept., 1980; Bronze medal AHA, 1974, Appreciation award Am. Cancer So., 1985, Outstanding Svc. award Fresno County Drug & Alcohol Prevention Coalition, Inc. Fellow Royal Soc. Medicine; mem. AAAS, ABA (assoc.), Am. Assn. Suicidology, Am. Profl. Soc. Abuse Children, Am. Acad. Forensic Scis. (alt. del. People's Rep. of China, citizen amb. program People to People Internat. 1986), Am. Acad. Hospice and Palliative Medicine, Am. Acad. Med. Ethics, Am. Cancer Soc., Am. Coll. Sports Medicine, Am. Heart Assn., Am. Pub. Health Assn., Am. Soc. Bioethics and Humanities, Am. Soc. of Law, Medicine and Ethics, Am. Stroke Assn., Assn. Mil. Surgeons of U.S., Christian Med. and Dental Soc., Faculty Conflict and Catastrophe Medicine, Faculty Prehospital Care, Royal Coll. Surgeons Edinburgh, Soc. Acad. Emergency Medicine, Soc. Critical Care Medicine, N.Y. Acad. Scis., Applied Rsch. Ethics Nat. Assn., Pub. Responsibility Medicine and Rsch., Christian Legal Soc., Health Physics Soc., Internat. Homicide Investigators Assn. Republican. Baptist. Avocations: musical conducting, writing screenplays. Home: PO Box 4512 Fresno CA 93744-4512 Personal E-mail: drlbburnett@sbcglobal.net.

BURNETT, MARK, television producer; b. London, July 17, 1960; m. Diane Burnett (div.); children: James, Cameron; m. Roma Downey, Apr. 28, 2007. Founder Mark Burnett Productions, also pres. Creator: (televised annual adventure race) Eco-Challenge, 1995— (Sports Emmy award for Outstanding Program Achievement for Eco-Challenge: Morocco, 2000, Banff Rockie award in the Sports Program Category, Banff Rockie Awards Festival, 2000); creator, exec. prodr.: (TV series) Survivor, 2000— (Favorite Reality Based Television Program, People's Choice Award, 2001, 2002, 2003, 2004, Special Recognition award, Gay & Lesbian Alliance Against Defamation, Emmy award for Outstanding Non-Fiction Program, 2001); exec. prodr.: (TV series) Combat Missions, Boarding House: North Shore, 2003; creator, exec. prodr.: (TV series) The Apprentice, 2003—; exec. prodr.: The Restaurant, 2003—04, The Casino, 2004, The Contender, 2005—, Rock Star: INXS, 2005—; exec. prodr.: (TV series) Apprentice: Martha Stewart, 2005, On the Lot, 2007—; author: Dare to Succeed: How to Survive and Thrive in the Game of Life, 2002, Jump In! Even if You Don't Know How to Swim, 2005. Bd. dirs. Elizabeth Glaser Pediatric Aids Found. Served with British Army Paratroop Regiment, N. Ireland and Falkland Islands. Named to 100 Most Influential People list, Time mag., 2004; recipient Philanthropist of the Year award, Reality Cares Found. Mem.: Nat. Academy of Television Arts and Sciences, British Academy of Film and Television Arts, LA (two elected terms, bd. dirs.). Avocations: scuba diving, skydiving. Office: CBS Corp 51 W 52nd St New York NY 10019*

BURNETT, MICHAEL BRUCE, benefits compensation analyst; b. Arlington, Va., Jan. 5, 1950; s. Arden Louis and June Elizabeth Burnett; m. Julie Ann Ophaug, Apr. 18, 1953; children: Kylie Marie, Lindsey Arden. BS in Bus. Edn. and Secondary Edn., U. N.D., 1976. Cert. phlebotimist Nat. Bd. of Lab. Profl. Technicans, 2000; Stephens' min. Holy Trinity Luth. Ch., Va., 1988; counselors Cert. Rehab. Provider of Va., 2004, vocational case mgr. Workers' Compensation Commn., Md., 2004. Sr. vocat. case mgr. CorVel Corp., Fairfax, Va., 1997—. Cons. mgmt. tng. Intelligent Solutions, Inc., Fairfax, Va., 1994—96. Editor sales manual-vocational counselors, author return to work program for fed. govt. Bd. dirs. Holy Spirit Luth. Ch., Centreville, Va., 2000—01. Recipient Achievement award, Travelers Ins. Co.-Conservco, Student Tchr. of the Yr. award, Lake Area Vocat. Tech. Ctr., 1975-1976. Mem.: Nat. Assn. of Rehab. Profls. in Pvt. Sector, Nat. Rehab. Assn., Toastmasters (cert.). Baptist. Avocation: counselor for men's anger. Home: 5806 Waterdale Ct Centreville VA 20121 Office: Eckman Freeman PO Box 140347 Nashville TN 37214 Office Phone: 703-470-5279. Personal E-mail: mburnett3@cox.net.

BURNETT, PATRICIA HILL, artist, educator; b. Bklyn. d. William Burr and Mimi (Uline) Hill; m. William Anding Lange, 1944 (div. 1947); 1 child, William Hill; m. Harry Albert Burnett Jr., , Oct. 9, 1948 (dec. 1979); children: Harry Burnett III, Terrill Hill, Hillary Hill; m. Robert L. Siler, 1989. Student, U. Toledo, 1937-38, Goucher Coll., 1939-41, MA program Inst. D'Allende, Mex., 1967, Wayne State U., 1972; pvt. studies with, John Carroll, Detroit, 1941-44, Sarkis Sarkisian, 1956-60, Wallace Bassford, Provincetown, Mass., 1968-72, Walter Midener, Detroit, 1960-63. Actress Long Ranger and Green Hornet prgrams, Radio Blue Network, 1941-46; tchr. painting and sculpture U. Mich. Extension, Ann Arbor, 1965—. Lectr. N.Y. Speakers Bur., 1971—; propr. Burnett Studios, Detroit, 1962-88, mgr., 1962—; appt. to Mich. Quarter Commn. by gov. Engler, 2002; pres. Burnett Enterprises Inc., 1950—. Numerous one-woman shows of paintings and sculptures include Scarab Club, Detroit, 1971, Midland (Mich.) Art Ctr., Wayne State U., Detroit, The Gallery, Ft. Lauderdale, Fla., Agra Gallery, Washington, Salon des Artes, Paris; numerous group shows include: Palazzo Pruili Gallery, Venice, 1971, Detroit Inst. of Arts, 1967, Butler Mus., Cleveland, 1972, Windsor (Ont., Can.) Art Ctr., 1973, Weisbaden (Germany) Gallery, 1976, Retrospective Show: Birmingham Bloomfield Art Assn., 1997; represented in permanent collections: Detroit Inst. Arts, Wayne State U., Wooster (Ohio) Coll., Ford Motor Co., Detroit, Bloomfield Art Assn., Bloomfield Hills, Mich., Henry Ford Hosp. Collection, Fed. Ct. Appeals in Washington, City-County Bldg., Detroit, Mich. State Capitol Bldg., Royal Acad. of Art, London, Moscow Mus., Moscow, Russia, Mich. State Capital, Lansing. Mich., Royal Palace of India, New Delhi, Palace of The Philippines, Manila, Mansion of Prime Minister, Greece; also pvt. collections: numerous portrait paintings including Indira Ghandi, Benson Ford, Joyce Carol Oates, Mrs. Edsel Ford, Betty Ford, Mayor Roman Gribbs, Princess Olga Mrivani, Lord John Mackintosh, Marlo Thomas, Viveca Lindfois, Betty Freidan, Gloria Steinem, Congresswoman Martha Griffiths, Margaret Papandreou, Valentina Tereshkova, Barbara Walters, Margaret Thatcher, Corazon Aquino, Violetta Chamarra, Jackie Joyner Kersee, Mayor Dennis Archer, Wayne U. pres. David Adamany, author Kate Millett, Michele Engler and triplets, Patricia Ireland, Rosa Parks, others; mem. editl. bd. Am. Portrait Soc.; author: True Colors: An Artist's Journey from Beauty Queen to Feminist. Chairwoman of Mich. Women's Commn., 1972—; pres. Detroit House of Correction Commn., 1975—; treas. Rep. Dist. 1 of Mich., 1973—; mem. Issues com., Rep. State Ctrl. Com., 1975-76; sec. Rep. State Ways and Means com., 1975—, Detroit Libr. Commn., 1980-85, Detroit Human Rights Comn., 1976-80, Detroit City Planning Commn., 1985-90; mem. Mich. State Adv. Coun. vocat. Edn.; mem. Mich. Arts in Edn. Coun., 1978—; mem. New Detroit Arts Com., 1979—; chmn. World Feminist Commn., 1974—; life mem. NAACP. Recipient Silver Salute award Mich. State U., 1976, Most Popular award San Diego Sculpture Show, 1971, First prize award Cape Cod Artists Show, 1968, State of Mich. award for creativity Gov. John Engler, 1999, Life Accomplishment award Mich. Women's Found., 2001; named Disting. Woman of Mich., Bus. and Profl. Women's Orgn., 1974, Disting. Woman Northwood Inst., 1977, Artist of Yr., Mich. Art Train, 1989, Disting. Woman award Mich. Bus. and Profl. Women Internat.; named to Ohio Hall of Fame, 1987, Mich. Women's Hall of Fame, 1988, one of Most Outstanding Women in Mich., Women in Advt., 1998, one of 10 People with Most Clout Outside of County, Detroit Free Press, 1998, one of 95 Most Powerful Women in Mich., Corp. Mag., 2002; elected to Internat. Hall of Fame, 2002. Mem. Mich. Women's Forum (founder 1989, bd. dirs. 1989-99, Internat. Women's Forum, bd. dirs. 1989-99), Detroit Inst. Arts (dir. membership com. 1958—), Nat. Assn. Commns. for Women (pres. 1976-78), Mich. Acad. of Arts, Detroit Soc. Women Painters and Sculptprs, Women in the Arts, Scarab Club (dir. 1962-63), Ibex Club (pres. 1951), NOW (nat. bd. 1971-75, del. UN conf. Mex., 1975, Feminist of Yr.), Coun. Leading portrait Painters (elect), Women's Econ. Club, N.Y. Portrait Club (nat. adv. bd. 1977—), French-Am. C.of C. (v.p.), Alpha Phi, Zonta, Detroit Econ. Club (bd. dirs.) Episcopalian. Home: 13 Oaks Ct Bloomfield Hills MI 48304-2120

BURNETT, RALPH GEORGE, lawyer; b. Milw., Apr. 13, 1956; s. Ralph G. and Joan T. Burnett; m. Eileen M. Gallagher, May 31, 1980; children: Christopher, Jessica, Thomas, Sarah, Andrew. BA, Marquette U., 1978; JD, U. Wis., 1981. Bar: Wis. 1981, U.S. Dist. Ct. (ea. and we. dists.) Wis. 1981, U.S. Ct. Appeals (7th cir.) 1981, U.S. Dist. Ct. (we. dist.) Mich. 1997, U.S. Ct. Appeals (6th cir.) 1997. Law clk. to Hon. Judge Harlington Wood U.S. Ct. Appeals 7th Cir., Chgo., 1981-82; lawyer Smith & O'Neil, Milw., 1983-84, Trowbridge, Planert & Schaefer, Green Bay, Wis.,

1985-86, Liebmann, Conway, Olejniczak & Jerry, S.C., Green Bay, Wis., 1986—. Officer Robert J. Parins Inn of Ct., Green Bay, 1997—. Co-author: Wisconsin Trial Practice, 1999. Mem. allocations com. United Way N.E. Wis., Green Bay, 1988-91; bd. mem. paralegal program N.E. Wis. Tech. Coll., Green Bay, 1993-2000; bd. mem. parish coun. St. Mary's Ch., De Pere, 1997-2003; bd. mem. Cerebral Palsy, Green Bay, 1989-92; bd. mem. steering com. Notre Dame Sch., De Pere, 1998. Fellow Am. Coll. Trial Advocates, Am. Coll. Trial Lawyers, Am. Bar Found., Wisc. Bar Found.; mem. ABA, State Bar Wis. (bd. dirs., chmn. litigation sect. 1996-99, pres-elect 2003, pres. 2003-04), Wis. Acad. Trial Lawyers (bd. dirs. 1995-2000; amicus commuter, constitutional challenge com., exec. com., regional dir. N.E. Wis. chpt., pres.-elect 2002-03). Avocations: woodworking, athletics. Office: Liebmann Conway Olejniczak & Jerry SC 231 S Adams St PO Box 23200 Green Bay WI 54305 Business E-Mail: RGB@lcojlaw.law.

BURNETT, SUSAN WALK, personnel service company owner; b. Galveston, Tex., Aug. 21, 1946; d. Joe Decker and Ruth Corinne (Lowe) Walk; m. Rusty Burnett, Dec. 27, 1973; stepchildren: Barbara, Sara. BA in Journalism, U. Ark., Fayetteville, 1968. Asst. pub. rels. mgr. Sta. KATV, Little Rock, 1968-69; speech writer Assoc. Milk Producers, Inc., Little Rock, 1969-70; mgr. Allied Personnel, Houston, 1970-74; owner, pres. Burnett Pers. Svcs., Houston, 1974—. Exec. bd. dirs. Arthritis Found.; bd. dirs. Goodwill, Better Bus. Bur. Recipient Appreciation awards Lyndon Johnson Space Ctr., NASA, 1983, State of Tex., 1984, Top Houston Woman Bus. Owner award Nat. Assn. Women Bus. Owners, 1996, Blue Chip award U.S. C. of C., Philanthrophy award Houston Bus. Jour., Better Bus. Bur. Pinnacle award, 2006; named one of 10 Women on the Move in Houston, Houston Chronicle, 1996, Most Outstanding Woman in Bus. YWCA, 1997, Entrepreneur of Yr., Ernst & Young, 1998; named 2001 Woman Bus. Entrepreneur, Women's Bus. Enterprise Alliance; named to 2000 Women of Excellence, Women's Enterprise. Mem.: Am. Staffing Assn. (bd. dirs.), Houston Assn. Pers. Cons. (v.p. 1985, pres. 1986, Outstanding Contbn. to Placement Industry and Cmty. award 1995), Tex. Assn. Pers. Cons. (v.p. 1985), Nat. Assn. Pers. Cons., Chi Omega Alumnae. Avocations: reading, golf, travel. Office: Burnett Staffing Specialists Inc 9800 Richmond Ave Ste 800 Houston TX 77042-4548

BURNETT, T-BONE (HENRY JOHN BURNETT), music producer, musician; b. St. Louis, Jan. 14, 1948; m. Sam Phillips, 1989 (div.); 1 child, Simone. Rec. artist: (with Alpha Band) The Alpha Band, 1976, Spark in the Dark, 1977, The Statue Makers of Hollywood, 1978, (with Elvis Costello as the Coward Brothers) The People's Limousine, 1985, (solo recs. as J. Henry Burnett) The B-52 Band & the Fabulous Skylarks, 1972, (solo recs.) Truth Decay, 1980, Trap Door, 1983, Proof Through the Night, 1983, Behind the Trap Door, 1984, T Bone Burnett, 1986, The Talking Animals, 1988, The Criminal Under My Own Hat, 1992, The True False Identity, 2006, Twenty Twenty, 2006; prodr.: Sunday Kind of Love for The Van Dykes, 1966, Paralyzed for The Legendary Stardust Cowboy, 1968, Delbert and Glen for Delbert and Glen, 1971, Live at the New Bluebird Nightclub for Robert Ealey and His Five Careless Lovers, 1972, There Is a Love for Maria Muldaur, 1982, Time Step for Leo Kottke, 1983, ...And a Time to Dance for Los Lobos, 1985, Downtown for Marshall Crenshaw, 1985, Peter Case for Peter Case, 1986, King of America for Elvis Costello, 1986, Love and Hope and Sex and Dreams for BoDeans, 1986, The Turning for Leslie (Sam) Phillips, 1987, By the Light of the Moon for Los Lobos, 1987, In Dreams: His Greatest Hits for Roy Orbison, 1987, Spike for Elvis Costello, 1988, Shuffletown for Joe Henry, 1990, Cruel Inventions for Sam Phillips, 1991, Nothing but a Burning Light for Bruce Cockburn, 1991, Go Slow Down for BoDeans, 1993, August and Everything After for Counting Crows, 1993, Martinis and Bikinis for Sam Philips, 1994, Dart to the Hart for Bruce Cockburn, 1994, Bringing Down the Horse for The Wallflowers, 1996, Electro-Shok Blues for Eels, 1998, Five Easy Pieces, 1998, Hell Among the Yearlings for Gillian Welch, 1998, Evan & Jaron, 2000, Down from the Mountain, 2001 (Grammy award for Best Traditional Folk Album), A Wonderful World, 2003 (Grammy award for Best Traditional Pop Album); prodr. (film & TV soundtracks) Stealing Beauty, 1996, The Big Lebowski, 1998, Clay Pigeons, 1998, Hope Floats, 1998, The Horse Whisperer, 1998, Down to You, 2000, Keeping the Faith, 2000, O Brother, Where Art Thou?, 2000 (2 Grammy awards for Album of Yr. and Best Soundtrack Album), Jay & Silent Bob Strike Back, 2001, Divine Secrets of the Ya-Ya Sisterhood, 2002, Our Little Corner of the World, 2002, Cold Mountain, 2003 (Anthony Asquith award for Film Music, BAFTA, 2004), Crossing Jordan, 2003, A Mighty Wind, 2003, The L Word, 2004, The Ladykillers, 2004, Walk the Line, 2005 (Grammy award for Best Compilation Soundtrack Album, 2007). Named Songwriter of Yr., Rolling Stone Critics Poll, 1983; recipient Grammy award for Best Non-Classical Prodr. of Yr., 2001. Office: Addis Wechsler 955 Carrillo Dr Fl 3 Los Angeles CA 90048-5400

BURNETTE, ADA M. PURYEAR, program coordinator; b. Darlington, SC; d. Theodore and Floia (King) Peoples; m. Paul Lionel Puryear, March 27, 1954 (div. 1975); children: Paul Lionel, Jr., Paula Lynn. BA in Math., Talladega Coll., 1953; postgrad., Chgo. State U., 1954-56; MA in Reading, U. Chgo., 1958; PhD, Fla. State U., 1986; postgrad., Fla. A&M U., 1994, Oxford U., 2005. High sch. math tchr., Winston-Salem, NC, 1953-54; elem. tchr. Chgo. Pub. Schs., 1954-58; reading clinician U. Chgo., 1958; dir. reading clinic, asst. prof. Norfolk State U., 1958-61, Tuskegee Inst., 1961-66; coord. freshman math., asst. prof. math. Fisk U., 1966-70; adminstr. early childhood basic skills and elem. edn. State of Fla. Dept. Edn., Tallahassee, 1973-88; assoc. prof., program dir., grad. studies dir. Bethune-Cookman Coll., Daytona Beach, Fla., 1988-90; dir., supt. Fla. A&M U. Devel. Rsch. Pub. Sch. Dist., Tallahassee, 1990-93; coord., prof., dept. chmn., dir. PhD program devel. Fla. A&M U., 1993-98, coord., prof., 1998—2003, prof., dir. Robert H. Anderson Ednl. Leadership Libr., 1998—2003, prof. emerita, 2003—; assoc. prof., coord. off campus programs Valdosta State U., 2005—. Hostess radio talk show, 1977—79; sec.-treas. Afro-Am. Rsch. Assocs., 1968—74; tutor, diagnostician, lectr., cons., planner, 1958—; cons. Job Corps, N.C. Advancement Sch., pub. co.; lectr. univ. classes; trustee Fla. A&M U., 2003, pres. faculty senate, 1999—2003, adj. prof., 2003—05. Regular columnist profl. jours., 1974—; writer grants proposals; weekly columnist Capitol Outlook, 1991-97; contbr. articles to profl. publs. Pres. PTA, 1975—76, v.p., 1983—84; edn. commentator Sta. WFSU, 1993—94; mem. United Fund com., Leon County 4C Bd.; pres. Norfolk Women's Interracial Coun., 1960; mem. Dem. Exec. Com. Leon County, 1981—88, 1991—93; deacon Presbyn. Ch., 1981—2004, AME ch. grief chmn., 2004—; bd. dirs. Tallahassee Coalition for the Homeless, 2002—, sec., 2004—. Mem.: AAUW (regional dir. 2003—, pres. Tallahassee chpt. 2005—, dir. Fla. 2005—), Am. Acad. Cert. Pub. Mgmt., Fla. Assn. Cert. Pub. Mng. NF (bd. dirs. 2004—), Nat. Assn. African Am. Studies (coord. 1999—), Fla. Soc. Cert. Pub. Mgrs. (newsletter bd., pres. North Fla. chpt. 2004, pres. North Fla. chpt. 2004—, state bd. 2004—), Am. Assn. Sch. Adminstrs., Socs. Docta Inc. (co-founder, sec. 1987—93), So. Assn. Colls. and Schs. (elem. and mid. sch. commn.), Assn. Childhood Edn. Internat., Leon Assn. Children Under Six (pres. 1977), So. Assn. Children Under Six, Fla. Assn. Children Under Six, Nat. Assn. Edn. Young Children, Nat. Assn. Elem. Sch. Prins., Internat. Reading Assn. (pres. Concerned Educators Black Students 1983—86, nat. early childhood com., nat. textbook com., libr./media com., nat. med. com., nat. awards com., nat. media com.), Fla. ASCD (regional dir. policy rev. jour. editl. bd. 1995—), Alliance of Black Sch. Educators, Assn. State Cons. on Early Childhood Edn., Fla. State Reading Assn., Fla. Coun. Elem. Edn., Fla. Assn. Suprs. and Adminstrs., The Holidays (nat. sec. fin. 1993—97, nat. v.p. 1997—2001, nat. pres. 2001—, chpt. pres.), Drifters (nat. membership chmn. 1977—79, Nat. Now Black Woman 1984, historian, reporter 1992—94, pres. 1994—99, cluster coord. 2000—), FAMU Ladies Art and Social Club (pres.), Alpha Kappa Alpha (treas., summer sch. dir., undergrad. adv., parliamentarian, sec.), Pi Lambda Theta, Phi Kappa Phi (pres. 1985—86, v.p. pub. rels. chair), Phi Delta Kappa (advisor 2004—). Home: PO Box 1513 Valdosta GA 31603 Office: Valdosta State U 1800 N Patterson St Valdosta GA 31698 Home Phone: 229-671-9670; Office Phone: 229-333-5622. Personal E-mail: draburnette@wmconnect.com. Business E-Mail: amburnette@valdosta.edu. *Never do anything illegal or immoral as you strive for excellence and do your best in all you do in your journey to make this world a better place.*

BURNETTE, OLLEN LAWRENCE, JR., historian; b. Bethel, NC, Sept. 30, 1927; s. Ollen Lawrence and Eva E. (Highsmith) Burnette; m. M. Elizabeth Tull, Aug. 25, 1951 (div. 1995); children: Ollen L. III, Elizabeth B. Newsome-Cousins, Graham T., John H., William N.; m. Jeanne A. MacRitchie, June 10, 2000. BA in History, U. Richmond, 1945; MA in History, U. Va., Charlottesville, 1948, PhD in History, 1952; LLD, Southwestern Adventist Coll., Keene, Tex., 1989. Instr. history Petersburg H.S., Va., 1948-49, VMI, Lexington, 1951-53, asst. to supt., 1981—86; editor Charles Scribner's Sons, NYC, 1953-57; dir. publs. State Hist. Soc. Wis., Madison, 1957-63; rsch. prof. history, dept. chmn. Birmingham So. Coll., Ala., 1963-72; dean of faculty, rsch. prof. history Stratford Coll., Danville, Va., 1972-74; vis. prof. history N.C. State A&T U., Greensboro, 1974-75; exec. dir. West Piedmont Planning Commn., Martinsville, Va., 1975-80; pres. Timber Ridge Enterprises, Ltd., Lynchburg, 1980—, Around Again, LLC, Cons., Lillian, 1996—. Author: Beneath the Footnote: A Guide to the Use of American Historical Documentation, 1970, A Syllabus of American History, 1959, Wisconsin Witness to F. J. Turner, 1958; editor: Life in America, 1972, A Soviet View of the American Past, 1962, Coastal Kingdom: A History of Baldwin County, Alabama, 2001, Readings on the Development of the American Constitution, 2005, From the Heart: Poems, 2005—. Elder Timber Ridge Presbyn. Ch., Lexington, 1980—; moderator Shenandoah Presbytery, 1988; bd. dirs. Stonewall Jackson Hosp., Lexington, 1980—83. Mem.: Orgn. Am. Historians, Am. Hist. Assn., Am. Inst. Cert. Planners, Nat. Assn. Rev. Appraisers (sr.), Va. Highlands Scottish Soc. (bd. dirs. 1989—), Phi Beta Kappa, Omicron Delta Kappa. Avocations: photography, hiking, travel. Home and Office: 34231 Kathryn Dr Lillian AL 36549-5105

BURNETTE, RALPH EDWIN, JR., judge; b. Lynchburg, Va., Sept. 25, 1953; s. Ralph Edwin and Carlease (Samuels) B. BA, Coll. William & Mary, 1975, JD, 1978. Bar: Va. 1978. Assoc. Edmunds & Williams, Lynchburg, 1978-83, ptnr., 1983-2001; gen. dist. ct. judge 24th Jud. Dist. Ct. Va., 2001—. Adj. prof. law Coll. William and Mary, 1996-2002, Washington & Lee U., 2003—. Deacon Peakland Bapt. Ch., Lynchburg, 1983-86; pres. Kaleidoscope Festival, Lynchburg, 1985, Lynchburg Symphony Orch., 1989-91; bd. dirs. Centra Health, Inc., 1987-97, United Way Cen. Va., 1989-90, Amazement Sq. Children's Mus. Mem. Va. Bar Assn., Va. State Bar (pres. 1993-94, pres. young lawyers conf. 1985, chmn. com. on alternative dispute resolution 1985-89, mem. bar coun., 1986-95, vice chmn. standing com. on legal ethics 1986-88, chmn. com. on long range planning 1988-91, mem. exec. com. 1990-95), Lynchburg Bar Assn. (pres. 1991-92), Avocations: golf, music, boating. Office: Lynchburg Gen Dist Ct 905 Court St Lynchburg VA 24504 Office Phone: 434-455-2630. Business E-Mail: reburnette@courts.state.va.us.

BURNETTE, SUSAN LYNN, lawyer; b. Sylva, NC, Nov. 20, 1955; d. William M. and Mary (McGrady) B.; m. Mark Howard Morey, June 2, 1984; children: Barbara Elizabeth Morey, Marianne McGrady Morey. Student, Institut d'Etudes Politiques, Paris, 1974-75; BA, U. S.C., 1975, BS, 1976; JD, U. Va., 1979. Bar: Va. 1979, S.C. 1979, Tex. 1980, U.S. Dist. Ct. (no. dist.) Tex. 1980, U.S. Ct. Appeals (5th cir.) 1984, U.S. Tax Ct. 1985; bd. cert. estate planning and probate law Tex. Bd. of Legal Specialization. Ptnr. Whittenburg, Whittenburg & Schachter, P.C., Amarillo, Tex., 1983-90, shareholder, 1999—2002, Conant Whittenburg Whittenburg & Schachter, P.C., Amarillo, 1991-95, Conant Whittenburg French & Schachter, P.S.C., Amarillo, 1995-99, pvt. practice, Amarillo, 2002—. Lectr. in field. Fellow: Tex. Bar Found. (life); mem.: ABA, Amarillo Area Estate Planning Coun., Amarillo Bar Assn. (pres. 2003—04), Tex. Acad. Probate and Trust Counsel, Va. Bar Assn., SC Bar Assn., Tex. Bar Assn. (dist. 13A grievance com. pres. 1994—95, course dir. Advanced Tax Law Course 1999, coun. tax sect. 1999—2002). Home: 2709 Sunlite St Amarillo TX 79106-6113 Office: Burnette Law Firm Lobby Box 206 500 S Taylor Ste 504 Amarillo TX 79101-2445 Office Phone: 806-372-4900. Business E-Mail: susan@burnettelawfirm.com.

BURNHAM, BRYSON PAINE, retired lawyer; b. Chgo., Oct. 11, 1917; s. Raymond and Patti (Paine) Burnham; m. Frances Katherine Burns, Feb. 8, 1941; children: Janice Young, Stephanie Paine. BA, U. Chgo., 1938, JD, 1940. Bar: Ill. 1940, Colo. 1983. From assoc. to ptnr. Mayer, Brown & Platt, Chgo., 1940-83; of counsel Shand, McLachlan and Newbold, Durango, Colo., 1985-93; ret., 1993. Bd. dirs. Ft. Lewis Coll. Found., 1986—2002. Home: 315 Highland Hill Dr Timberline View Estates Durango CO 81301

BURNHAM, CHRISTOPHER BANCROFT, former international organization official, former federal agency administrator; b. NYC, Sept. 28, 1956; s. Alexander O. and Joan B.; m. Courtney Burnham; 1 child, George Emerson. BA, Washington & Lee, 1980; MPA, Harvard U., 1992. Mem. N.Y. Futures Exch., NYC, 1983-85; rep. Conn. Gen. Assembly, Hartford, 1987-92; banker First Boston, NYC, 1990-93, Advest Corp. Fin., Hartford, 1993-95; state treas. State of Conn., Hartford, 1995—97; chmn, CEO InviteUSA.com, 2000—02; CFO, asst. sec. for resource mgmt., Bur. Resource Mgmt. US Dept. State, Washington, 2002—05, acting under sec. for mgmt., 2005; under-sec. gen. for mgmt. UN, NYC, 2005—06. Maj. USMCR, Persian Gulf War. Republican. Episcopalian.

BURNHAM, DAVID BRIGHT, writer, educator; b. Boston, Jan. 24, 1933; s. Addison Center and Dorothy (Moore) B.; m. Sophy Tayloe Doub, Mar. 12, 1960 (div. 1984); children: Sarah Tayloe, Molly Bright; m. Joanne Omang, 1985. BA, Harvard, 1955; DHL (hon.), John Jay Coll., CUNY, 2003. Reporter UPI, Washington, 1959-61, Newsweek mag., Washington, 1961-63; writer CBS, NYC, 1963-65; asst. dir. Pres.'s Commn. Law Enforcement and Adminstrn. of Justice, Washington, 1965-67; reporter NY Times, 1967-86; journalist/writer Aspen Inst. Humanistic Studies, 1980-82. Co-dir., co-founder Transactional Records Access Clearinghouse, 1989—; assoc. rsch. prof. S.I. Newhouse Sch. Pub. Communications, Syracuse U.; mem. adv. bd. EPIC. Author: The Rise of the Computer State, 1988, A Law Unto Itself: Power, Politics and the IRS, 1989 (Best Investigative Book Investigative Editors and Reporters 1990), Above The Law: Secret Deals, Political Fixes, and other Misadventures of the U.S. Dept. of Justice, 1996. Recipient George K. Polk award, 1968, Silurians award, 1968; NY Newspaper Guild award, 1968; Gold Typewriter award for investigative reporting NY Reporters Assn., 1972; named fellow Alicia Patterson Found., 1987, Rockefeller Found. scholar, Bellagio, Italy, 1992; inducted into Nat. Freedom of Info. Hall of Fame, 2006. Home: 3016 Tilden St NW Washington DC 20008 Office: Transactional Records Access Clearinghouse 666 11th St 900 Washington DC 20001 Home Phone: 202-244-4377; Office Phone: 202-518-9000. Business E-Mail: dburnham@syr.edu.

BURNHAM, DAVID HENDERSON, management consultant; b. Quincy, Mass., Mar. 4, 1942; s. Roger Appleton and Phyllis Katherine (Kline) B.; m. Frances Margarita Parry, Feb. 15, 1964; children: Amery Appleton, Hugh Tebault Ramseyer. BA, Northeastern U., 1964; MBA, Harvard U., 1969. With U.S. Peace Corps, Ethiopia, 1964—66; assoc. Sterling Inst., Boston, 1969; v.p., treas. McBer & Co., Boston, 1970-72, pres., 1972-77, David H. Burnham and Assocs., orgn. devel. cons., Boston, Singapore, Sydney, London, 1977-91; dir. strategic planning Interaction Assocs., Cambridge, Mass., 1992-94; ptnr. Burnham Rosen Group, Boston, 1994—. Proprietor Boston Athaeneum, 2000—. Producer film Motives Moving Business (Am. Film Festival award 1975); contbr. articles to profl. jours. Treas., v.p. Children's Mus., Boston, 1972-81, pres., CEO, 1981-83, chmn., 1984-86, hon. trustee, 1988—; pres. Cavalier King Charles Spaniel Club, Louisville, 1972-78; bd. dirs. Children's Mus., London, 1984-86, Mental Health Found., U.K., 1987-88, Drive for Youth Programme, U.K., 1986-91; mem. com. Derby Acad. Coun., Hingham, Mass., 1974-81; mem. vestry St. Stephen's Episcopal Ch., Cohasset, 2001-05, vice chmn. profile com., 2006. Honoree Boston Coun. for Arts for svc. to Boston Pub. Libr., 2000; recipient McKinsey award Harvard Bus. Rev., 1976. Mem.: ASTD, OD Network, Greater Boston Assn. Tng. and Devel. (dir. 1997—2000), New England Hist. and Genealogical Soc. (dir. 1999—2005, coun. 2005—), Assn. Mgmt. Edn. and Devel., Harvard Bus. Sch. Assn., Colonial Soc. Mass. (life; bd. dirs. 2003—05), Bostonian Soc. (life), Harvard Clubs Boston and NYC, Harvard Faculty Club, Lansdowne Club, Cohasset Yacht Club, Cohasset Golf Club, Somerset Club. Home: 30 Atlantic Ave Cohasset MA 02025-1803 Office: Burnham Rosen Group 88 Broad St Boston MA 02110 Home Phone: 781-383-1339; Office Phone: 617-350-6100. Business E-Mail: david.burnham@burnrose.com.

BURNHAM, HAROLD ARTHUR, pharmaceutical executive, physician; b. Boston, Nov. 6, 1929; s. Howard Rowland and Edna Adelaide (Teachout) B.; m. Lucienne Jeanne Seas, June 28, 1952; children: Philippe Henri, Isabelle Jeanne BS, Union Coll., 1951; MA, Middlebury Coll., 1952; postgrad., Albany State Tchrs. Coll., 1953-54, Adelphi U., 1958-59, Nassau Community Coll., 1961-62; MD, U. Md., 1966. Diplomate Am. Bd. Med. Examiners, Am. Bd. Family Practice (charter). Tchr. sci., French and track team coach South Glens Falls Cen. High Sch., NY, 1952-54; med. rep., hosp. salesman Upjohn Co., Bklyn., 1956-62; intern South Baltimore Gen. Hosp., 1966-67; resident in family practice Glen Cove Community Hosp., NY, 1967-69; practice family medicine Glen Cove, 1969-75; assoc. med. dir. Winthrop Labs. div. Sterling Drug Inc., NYC, 1975-76, med. dir. Glenbrook Labs. div., 1977, v.p. med. affairs, sr. v.p. Winthrop Product Inc., 1977-80, NJ, 1977-80, Sydney Ross Co. and Sterling Products Internat., NYC, 1977-80; v.p., med. dir. Glenbrook Labs. div. Sterling Drugs, Inc., NYC, 1980; med. dir. Choay Labs. Inc., NYC, 1980-82; asst. med. dir. L.I. State Vets. Home, Stony Brook, 1993-94; primary care physician ambulatory care clinics Nassau County Dept. Health, Mineola, NY, 1995-96; physician, English transl. cons. hematology dept. Hotel Dieu Hosp., Paris, 2001—. Spl. cons. Labs. Choay, S.A., Paris, 1982—; asst. med dir. United Presbyn. Residence, Woodbury, N.Y., 1983-93; instr. Sch. Practical Nursing, Glen Cove Community Hosp., 1970-75; instr. geriatrics in coop. with Glen Cove Community Hosp. Family Practice Residency Program, 1983-93; cons., clinician in medicine Nassau County Pub. Health Dept., 1975-76, mem. long term health care com., 1989-96; med. cons. Webb Inst. Naval Architecture and Marine Design, Glen Cove, N.Y., 1970-96; clin. asst. prof., SUNY, 1993-94; attending physician infectious diseases HIV Clinic, Nassau County Med. Ctr., East Meadow, N.Y., 1995-96; preceptor family practice program North Shore U. Hosp. at Glen Cove, 1999—, hon. staff dept. family practice, 2003—, named chmn. ethics com., 2005. N.Am. corr. weekly Internet French med. publ. Expression Médicale, 1998—. Scoutmaster Boy Scouts Am., Glens Falls, N.Y., 1953-54, com. mem., 1968—, merit badge counsellor for first aid, pub. health emergency care, chemistry and mammals for Sagamore dist., 1968—; mem. Clan Gordon, 1983—, bagpiper Highlanders Pipes and Drums Band, Locust Valley, N.Y., 1982—, chmn., 1986—; lay reader St. John's of Lattingtown Episcopal Ch., N.Y., 1968—, vestryman, 1983—, clk. of vestry, 1986—, 7-8th gr. Sunday Sch. tchr., 1967—; mem. search com. for new rector, 1993, 2004, jr. high Sunday sch. tchr., 1967-, mem. outreach com., 2005—; trustee Hawley Found., 1984—, v.p. bd., 1991-99, v.p. emeritus, 1999—; Rep. election site inspector Nassau County, 1997—; del. to 120th conf. Episcopal Diocese of L.I.; vol. primary care physician Project U.S.A., Rural Indian Health Svc. Ctrs., Oneida (N.Y.) Iroquois Reservation and Owyhee (Nev.) Indian Hosp., 1995—; bd. edn. election inspector, Glen Cove, 2001-. Named hon. chieftain, Annual Scottish Games, Old Westbury Gardens, 2004; recipient Alvin H. Toffler award, North Shore U. Hosp. Class of 2002. Fellow Am. Acad. Family Physicians (charter); mem. AMA (life; 14 continuing edn. awards), Pan Am. Med. Soc., N.Y. State Med. Soc. (life), Nassau County Med. Soc. (life), L.I. Scottish Clans Assn. (trustee 1984—, piper to chief 1986—), Nu Sigma Nu. Episcopalian. Office: 18 Purdue Rd Glen Cove NY 11542-2009 Personal E-mail: haburnham@earthlink.net.

BURNHAM, J. V., retired sales executive; b. Pascagoula, Miss., May 23, 1923; s. George Luther and Eli Vashti (Hough) B.; m. Patti Lauri Latham, May 18, 1946 (dec. Aug. 6, 2006); children: James Steven, Jon Douglas, Richard Scott, Bruce Edward, Vernon Alan. AA, Jones County Jr. Coll., Miss., 1946; AS, Rochester Inst. Tech., 1948; BS, U. Houston, 1951, MEd, 1963. Mgr. The Progress-Item, Ellisville, Miss., 1948-50; asst. prof., asst. mgr. U. Houston Journalism and Printing Plant, 1950-57; estimator, product supt. purchasing Chas. P. Young Co., Houston, 1957-67, asst. sec.-treas., 1967-69, v.p. sales, 1969-91, sr. v.p., 1991—2001, ret., 2001. Assoc. editor Am. Oceanography, 1968-71; southwest corr. Inland Printer and Nat. Lithographer, 1952-60. Founding mem. Am. Air Mus. in Britain; pres. Printing Industries of Gulf Coast, Houston, 1971—73; chmn. emeritus, bd. dirs. Tex. Printing Edn. Found., Houston; active The Heritage Found., The Concord Coalition, Adm. Nimitz Found., St. Joseph Found., Hist. Mt. Vernon, Young America's Found., Rep. Presdl. Task Force, Nat. Rep. Senatorial Com. Order of Merit, Nat. Rep. Congl. Com.; life, chmns. adv. bd. Rep. Nat. Com.; active Rep. Party of Tex., Rep. Nat. Candidate Trust, George Bush Pres. Libr. & Mus., Reagan Pres. Found., Young Am. Found., Judicial Watch. Lt. USNR, 1943—46. Named Man of Yr., Houston Graphics Soc., 1968, Printing Industry of Gulf Coast, 1970. Mem.: BAMPAC, Rochester Inst. tech. Alumni Assn., Tex. Police Officers Assn., Pres's. Club of Chas. P. Young Co. (charter, Outstanding Sales Achivement award), Mt. Vernon Ladies Assn., Juvenile Diabetes Found., Am. Diabetes Assn., Am. Kidney Found., High Frontier, Hummel Collectors Club (Houston), Crime Stoppers of Houston (gold cir. member), Ducks Unltd., U.S. Navy Meml. Found., Naval Aviation Mus. Found., Houston Public TV, United Srs. Assn., WWII Meml. Found., Claremont Inst., U.S. Hist. Soc. (life), Nat. Eagle Scout Assn. (life), Tex. State Rifle Assn. (life), Naval Airship Assn. (life), Am. Legion (life), U. Houston Alumni (life), Jones County Jr. Coll. Alumni (life), U.S. Navy Pub. Affairs Alumni Assn. (life), VFW (life), NRA (life), PGA Ptnrs. Club (life; charter), Am. Fedn. Police, Gun Owners Am., Second Amendment Found. (charter), USS Constitution Mus. Found., Houston Lithographic Club, Rep.-Presdl. Legion of Merit, U.S. Golf Assn., Houston Golf Assn., Citizens Against Govt. Waste, NRA Whittington Ctr. Founders Club, Braeburn Country Club, 100 Club Houston, Houston Craftsmens Club (hon.; life, past pres., Ben Franklin award 1971), Nat. Home Gardening Club (life), Santa Fe Trail Gun Club (life). Republican. Episcopalian.

BURNHAM, JOHN LUDWIG, agent; b. LA, Mar. 1, 1953; s. Jerome Ludwig and Linda (Benjamin) B.; m. Andrea Buckland Feldstein, Aug. 12, 1989; 1 child, Daisy. BA, UCLA, 1976, JD, 1980. Agt. Kohnner Levy, LA, 1979-81, ICM, LA, 1981-84, William Morris Agy., Beverly Hills, Calif., 1984—, co-head, sr. v.p. movie dept., 1991—. Office: William Morris Agy Inc 1 William Morris Pl Beverly Hills CA 90212 Office Phone: 310-859-4000. Office Fax: 310-859-4462.

BURNHAM, LEM, psychologist, think-tank executive; b. Winter Haven, Fla., Aug. 30, 1947; s. John L. and Lillie Belle B.; m. Barbara J. Mackin, Sept. 8, 1981; children: Shannon LeeAnne, Lewis, Kara, Bryan. Diploma,

N.Am. Sch. Conservation, Irvine, Calif., 1969; BA in Psychology, U.S. Internat. U., 1974; MS in Counseling Psychology, Minn. State U., 1978; PhD in Psychoednl. Processes, Temple U., 1984. Diplomate Am. Bd. Forensic Examiners, Am. Bd. Psychol. Specialties, Am. Psychotherapy Assn.; cert. forensic clin. psychology, psychol. assessment, evaluation and testing, substance abuse psychology. Profl. football player World Football League, Honolulu, 1974-75, Can. Football League, Winnipeg, Can., 1976, NFL Phila. Eagles, 1977-80; cross-cultural community planner City and County of Honolulu, 1975; sr. counselor Pa. Prison Soc., Phila., 1982; pres. bd. Career Transition Inst., Inc., Phila., 1981-83; psychologist, health care adminstr. West Jersey Health System, 1984-87; pvt. practice cons., 1988—92; pres. and CEO ANTIS Mgmt., LLC, 2003—. Vice chmn. Digital Champions, LLC, 2003—; pres., chief exec. officer Athletic Motivation, Inc., 1989-92; team psychologist for Balt. Orioles, 1989-94, Phila. Eagles, 1988-92, Phila. 76ers, 1986-92; lectr. in field; dir. and v.p. player devel. NFL, 1992-2002; bd. dirs. YMCA of Greater N.Y., 1991-2001. Mem. Nat. Adv. Coun. on Violence Against Women, chmn. sports subcom., 1995—; bd. dirs. Corp. Alliance to End Ptnr. Violence, 1995-2002. Served with USMC, 1965-69, Vietnam. Decorated Vietnamese Service award, Vietnamese Commendation award; recipient cert. of appreciation Kiwanis Club, Ramon, Calif., 1979, Del. Valley Med. Ctr., Phila., 1980, Community Service award Com. on Alcohol and Drug Abuse Crozer Chester Hosp., 1981. Mem. Am. Psychotherapy Assn., Am. Psychol. Soc., Am. Coll. Forensic Examiners, NFL Alumni Assn. (bd. dirs. Phila. Eagles chpt. 1986-98), Maxwell Football Club (life, v.p. community rels. 1990—, bd. govs.). Office: ANTIS Mgmt LLC 109 Muirfield Moorestown NJ 08057-9754 Home Phone: 856-608-0243; Office Phone: 856-608-9753. E-mail: drlemburnham@antiscorp.com.

BURNHAM, PATRICIA WHITE, consultant, advocate, writer, business executive; b. Omaha, July 30, 1933; d. William Max and Berniece Irene (Shockey) Orr; m. William L. White, June 18, 1955 (div. Nov. 1979); children: Lucinda, Christopher, Duncan; m. Robert A. Burnham, Feb. 23, 1980. BA in English, DePauw U., Greencastle, Ind., 1955; MA in English, Ill. State U., 1966, PhD in Adminstrn., 1977. Tchr. Morton Grove (Ill.) and Evansville (Ind.) pub. schs., 1955-60; instr. Ill. State U., Normal, 1963-71, dir. Nat. Student Exchange, 1971-74, acad. advisor and continuing edn. coord., 1974-76, asst. dean, 1976-79; assoc. dir. Ill. Bd. Higher Edn., Springfield, 1979-80; assoc. vice provost Ohio State U., Columbus, 1980-81; specialist bus. ins. Nationwide Ins. Co., Columbus, 1981-83; v.p. pvt. banking Chase Manhattan Bank, N.A., NYC, 1983-88; pres. Transitions Group, Inc., East Burke, Vt., 1986—. Adj. prof. U. Vt., 1997—; presenter in field. Author: Life's Third Act, 1994; contbr. articles to publs. Pres. Cmty. Vt. Elders, 1994—99; active Vt. Health Resource Allocation Adv., 2004—05; bd. dirs. Northeastern Vt. Hosp., St. Johnsbury, 1997—2006, bd. chair, 2000—04; bd. dirs. Vt. Cmty. Loan Fund, 1998—2006, Vt. Assn. Non-Profit Orgns., 1998—2000, Dartmouth Hitchcock Alliance, 2004—07; mem. palliative care advisory coun. Dartmouth Med. Ctr. Mem. Phi Beta Kappa, Phi Delta Kappa. Congregationalist. Avocations: hiking, literature, writing. Home: 80 Lyme Rd Apt 1023 Hanover NH 03755-1237 Home Phone: 603-643-2658. E-mail: pat.burnham@together.net.

BURNHAM, REBECCA LYNNE, lawyer; b. West Monroe, La., Feb. 26, 1953; d. Ralph Norris and Rose Marie Mahoney; children: James, Clare. BS magna cum laude, Ariz. State U., Tempe, 1977; JD, UCLA, 1980. Bar: Ariz. 1980. Ptnr. Gammage & Burnham, Phoenix, Fennemore Craig, Phoenix, Storey & Burnham, PLC, Phoenix; shareholder, practice group mgr. Greenberg Traureg, LLP, Phoenix. Bd. dirs. Crisis Nursery Found., Teach for Am.; mem. adv. bd. Ariz. State U. Found., chmn. women and philanthropy program com. Mem.: Coronado Yacht Club, Lambda Alpha Epsilon. Republican. Avocations: boating, hiking, bicycling, reading, travel. Office: Greenberg Traurig LLP 2375 E Camelback Rd # 700 Phoenix AZ 85018

BURNHAM, WALTER DEAN, political science professor; b. Columbus, Ohio, June 15, 1930; s. Alfred Huntington Jr. and Gertrude Elinor (Hamburger) B.; m. Patricia Ann Mullan, June 7, 1958; children: John Patrick, Anne More. BA, Johns Hopkins U., 1951; AM, Harvard U., 1958, PhD, 1962; LittD (hon.), Rutgers U., 1982. Instr. polit. sci. Boston Coll., 1958-61; asst. prof. Kenyon Coll., Gambier, Ohio, 1961-64, Haverford (Pa.) Coll., 1964-66; from assoc. to full prof. Washington U., St. Louis, 1966-71; prof. MIT, Cambridge, Mass., 1971-88, Ruth and Arthur Sloan prof. polit. sci., 1984-88; Frank C. Erwin Jr. Centennial prof. govt. U. Tex., Austin, 1988—94, prof. emeritus, 1994—. Vis. scholar Phi Beta Kappa, 1995—. Author: Presidential Ballots, 1955, 2d. edit., 1976, Critical Elections, 1970, The Current Crisis in Am. Politics, 1982, Democracy in the Making, 1983, 2d edit., 1986. With U.S. Army, 1953-56. Fellow Social Sci. Rsch. Coun., 1963, Guggenheim Found., 1974, Ctr. Advanced Study in Behavioral Sci., 1979. Fellow Am. Acad. Arts and Scis.; mem. Am. Polit. Sci. Assn. (mem. coun. 1984-86, pres. organized sect. on politics and history 1993-94), Phi Beta Kappa (vis. scholar 1995-96). Avocation: opera. Office: U Tex Dept Govt Burdine Hall # 536 Austin TX 78712 Home: 4203 Greenridge Pl Austin TX 78759 Personal E-mail: tishmb@sbcglobal.net.

BURNINGHAM, KIM RICHARD, educational association administrator, former state legislator; b. Salt Lake City, Sept. 14, 1936; s. Rulon and Margie (Stringham) Burningham; m. Susan Ball Clarke, Dec. 19, 1968; children: Christian, Tyler David. BS, U. Utah, 1960; MA, U. Ariz., 1967; MFA, U. So. Calif., 1977. Cert. secondary tchr., Utah. Tchr. Bountiful (Utah) High Sch., 1960-88; mem. Utah Ho. of Reps., Salt Lake City, 1979-94; cons. Shipley Assocs., Bountiful, 1989-94, Franklin Covey, 1994—. Gubernatorial appointee as exec. dir. Utah Statehood Centennial Commn., 1994-96; mem. Utah State Bd. Edn., 1999-2000, vice chmn., 2000-01, chmn., 2001-; bd. dirs. Nat. Assn. State Bds. Edn., 2000-01, pres.-elect, 2004, pres. 2005-06, past pres., 2006. Author dramas for stage and film, also articles; columnist, Davis County Clipper, 2000—. Mem. state strategic planning com. Utah Tomorrow, 1989-2003 Recipient Carl Perkins Humanitarian of Yr. award, ACTE, 2002. Mem. NEA, PTA (life), Utah Edn. Assn., Davis Edn. Assn., Nat. Forensic League. Mem. Lds Ch. Avocations: gardening, history. Home: 932 Canyon Crest Dr Bountiful UT 84010-2002 E-mail: krb84010@aol.com.

BURNISON, BOYD EDWARD, lawyer; b. Arnolds Park, Iowa, Dec. 12, 1934; s. Boyd WIlliam and Lucile (Harnden) B.; m. Mari Amaral; children: Erica Lafore, Alison Katherine. BS, Iowa State U., 1957; JD, U. Calif., Berkeley, 1961. Bar: Calif. 1962, U.S. Supreme Ct. 1971, U.S. Dist. Ct. (no. dist.) Calif. 1962, U.S. Ct. Appeals (9th cir.) 1962, U.S. Dist. Ct. (ea. dist.) Calif. 1970, U.S. Dist. Ct. (ctrl. dist.) Calif. 1992. Dep. counsel Yolo County, Calif., 1962-65; assoc. Steel & Arostegui, Marysville, Calif., 1965-66, St. Sure, Moore & Hoyt, Oakland, Calif., 1966-70; ptnr. St. Sure, Moore, Hoyt & Sizoo, Oakland and San Francisco, 1970-75; v.p. Crosby, Heafey, Roach & May, P.C., Oakland, 1975-2000, also bd. dirs.; pres. Boyd E Burnison A Profl. Law Corp., Walnut Creek, Calif., 2001—05, Diablo, 2005—. Advisor Berkeley YMCA, 1971—, Yolo County YMCA, 1962—65, bd. dir., 1965; trustee, sec., legal counsel Easter Seal Found., Alameda County, 1974—79, hon. trustee, 1979—; trustee Alameda County Law Libr., 2001—, v.p., 2003—05, pres., 2005—07; mem. adv. coun. Diablo Mcpl., 2007—; bd. dir. Easter Seal Soc. Crippled Children and Adults of Alameda County Calif., 1972—75, Moot Ct. Bd., U. Calif., 1960—61, East Bay Conservation Corps, 1997—2000, treas., 2000. Named Vol. of Yr., Berkeley YMCA, 1999. Fellow: ABA Found. (life); mem.: ABA (equal employment law com., labor rels., employment law sect. 1972—2004), Sproul Assoc. Boalt Hall Law Sch. U. Calif. Berkeley, Indsl. Rels. Rsch. Assn., Contra Costa County Bar Assn. (labor law sect.), Bar Assn. San Francisco (labor law sect.), Yuba Sutter Bar Assn., Yolo County Bar Assn. (sec. 1965), Alameda County Bar Found. (bd. dirs. 1993—95), Alameda County Bar Assn. (chmn. memberships and directory com. 1973—74, chmn. law office econs. com. 1975—77, chmn. memberships and directory com. 1980, assn. dir. 1981—85, vice chmn. bench bar liaison com. 1983, pres. 1984, chmn. 1984, Disting. Svc. award 1987), State Bar Calif. (spl. labor counsel 1981—84, labor and employment law sect. 1982—), Nat. Conf. Bar Pres.'s, Rotary (Paul Harris fellow), Round Hill Country Club, Iowa State Alumni Assn., Order Knoll, Phi Delta Phi, Pi Kappa Alpha. Democrat. Home: PO Box 743 2704 Caballo Ranchero Dr Diablo CA 94528-0743 Office: Boyd E Burnison A Profl Law Corp PO Box 743 Diablo CA 94528 Home Phone: 925-820-3019; Office Phone: 925-855-9032. Office Fax: 925-855-9332. Personal E-mail: bburnison@sbcglobal.net.

BURNLEY, JAMES HORACE, IV, lawyer; b. High Point, NC, July 30, 1948; s. James Horace and Dorothy Mary (Rockwell) B. BA magna cum laude, Yale U., 1970; JD, Harvard U., 1973. Bar: NC 1973, DC 1989. Assoc. Brooks, Pierce, McLendon, Humphrey & Leonard, 1973-75; ptnr. Turner, Enochs, Foster, Sparrow & Burnley, P.A., 1975-81; dir. VISTA, 1981-82; assoc. dep. atty. gen. Dept. Justice, Washington, 1982-83; gen. counsel Dept. Transp., Washington, 1983, dep. sec., 1983-87, sec., 1987-89; ptnr. Shaw, Pittman, Potts & Trowbridge, Washington, 1989-92, Winston & Strawn, Washington, 1993—2002; ptnr., legis. & govt. affairs dept. Venable LLP, Washington, 2002—. Trustee Jamestown Found., Intercollegiate Studies Inst.; bd. dirs. Reagan Alumni Assn., Freedom Works; chmn., Roe Inst. Adv. Com. Heritage Found. Republican. Office: Venable LLP 575 7th St NW Washington DC 20004 Office Phone: 202-344-4054. Office Fax: 202-344-8300. Business E-Mail: jhburnley@venable.com.

BURNLEY, JUNE WILLIAMS, secondary school educator; b. St. Augustine, Fla., Mar. 13, 1936; d. Marcellus Henry Gilford and Ella (Broadus) Williams. BS, N.C. Agrl. and Tech. State U., 1958; MA, Villanova U., 1975, St. John's Coll., Annapolis, Md., 1993; student, Oxford U., London, 1995. Cert. English tchr., counseling psychologist. Grade sch. tchr., 1958-59; lang. arts supr. Wharton Ctr., Phila., 1967-68; English/French lang. tchr. Hatch. Jr. H.S., Camden, NJ, 1962-68; English tchr. George Washington H.S., Phila., 1968-93, secondary counseling intern, 1975. Mem. Pa. State Coun. English Tchrs., 1968-93, Educators to Africa, Phila., 1993-97; tutor Temple-New Career Ladders, 1975-76. Mem. Germantown Civic League, Phila., 1993, West Mt. Airy Neighbors, Phila., 1968—, Social Action Com., Phila., 1993-95, Germantown Hist. Soc., Unitarian Soc. Germantown; vol. guide in tng. Phila. Mus. Art, 1996—. Pa. State Bd. Edn. fellow, 1985, Arco & Exxon fellow, 1991, St. John's Coll. fellow, 1992-93. Fellow Commonwealth Partnership; mem. Nat. Coun. English Tchrs. (Svc. award 1972), Eleanor Trailor Readers (co-founder), Literary Group (founder), Literati (founder), Amnesty Internat., Phi Delta Kappa, Delta Sigma Theta. Avocations: reading, knitting, sewing, word games, travel. Home: 700 Elkins Ave Apt E3 Elkins Park PA 19027-2315 Personal E-mail: alithaevol@aol.com.

BURNS, ALTON JAY, plastic surgeon; b. Garland, Tex., Apr. 16, 1955; BS magna cum laude, Baylor U., Waco, Tex., 1977; MD, U. Tex. Southwestern Med. Sch., Dallas, 1981. Cert. Tex. State Bd. Med. Examiners, 1981, Am. Bd. Surgery, 1987, Am. Bd. Plastic Surgeons, 1990. Intern, gen. surgery U. Utah Sch. Medicine, Salt Lake City, 1981—82, resident, gen. surgery, 1982—86; resident, plastic surgery U. Tex. Southwestern Med. Sch., Dallas, 1986—88; fellow, vascular anomalies Boston Children's Hosp., 1988; asst. prof., plastic surgery U. Tex. Southwestern Med. Ctr., Dallas, 1988—. Contbr. articles to profl. journals. Fellow: ACS; mem.: AMA, Dallas County Medical Soc., Am. Soc. for Aesthetic Plastic Surgeons (chair, facial surgery com.), Am. Soc. for Laser Medicine and Surgery, Plastic and Cosmetic Surgeons of Dallas, Am. Soc. Plastic Surgeons, Tex. Soc. Plastic Surgeons, Dallas County Med. Soc., Tex. Med. Assn. Office: Univ Texas Southwestern Med Ctr Dept Plastic Surgery Bldg G8239 5323 Harry Hines Blvd Dallas TX 75390-9132

BURNS, AMY MARGARET, music educator; d. Robert W. and Ruth H. Willis; m. Christopher R. Burns, June 26, 1999. B in Music Edn./Performance, Ithaca Coll., Ithaca, NY, 1995; MS in Music Edn., Ctrl. Conn. State U., New Britain, Conn., 2006. Technology Institute for Music Educators (TI:ME) Level 1 Tech. Inst. for Music Educators (TI:ME), 2001, Technology Institute for Music Educators (TI:ME) Level 2 Tech. Inst. for Music Educators (TI:ME), 2004, Orff-Schulwerk Level 1 Am. Orff-Schulwerk Assn. (AOSA), 2001. Music educator Musically Yours, Millburn, NJ, 1996—97; pvt. flute and clarinet instr. Mendham, NJ, 1996—; music educator for grades prekindergarten through three Far Hills Country Day Sch., Far Hills, NJ, 1997—, founder, dir. philharm., 1998—2006, founder, dir. conservatory, 2002—04. Com. mem. NJ Assn. Ind. Schs., Edison, NJ, 2002—04; presenter in field. Author: (lesson plans) Nine Lesson Plans that Integrate Technology into the Elementary Music Classroom; contbr. articles pub. tro profl. jour. Recipient Tchr. of the Yr., Tech. Inst. for Music Educators (TI:ME), 2005. Mem.: NJ. Music Educators Assn., Music Educators Nat. Coun., Tech. Inst. Music Educators. Home: PO Box 612 Far Hills NJ 07931 Office: Far Hills Country Day Sch Rt 202/ Box 8 Far Hills NJ 07931 Home Phone: 908-719-2672; Office Phone: 908-766-0622 484. Personal E-mail: awillis2@aol.com.

BURNS, ANDREW E., chemistry professor, researcher; s. Gerald and Carole Burns; m. Elizabeth Burns, Nov. 20, 1993; children: Nathan, Emma, Adam. PhD, Brown U., Providence, 1989. Asst. prof. Kent State U., North Canton, Ohio, 1994—2000, assoc. prof., 2000—. Contbr. scientific papers. Office: Kent State Univ 6000 Frank Ave North Canton OH 44720 Office Phone: 330-244-3444. Business E-Mail: aburns@kent.edu.

BURNS, ARNOLD IRWIN, lawyer; b. NYC, Apr. 14, 1930; s. Herman Leon and Rose (Lauterstein) B.; m. Felice Bernstein, June 17, 1951; children: Linda Susan, Douglas Todd. AB, Union Coll., Schenectady, 1950; LL.B., Cornell U., 1953; postgrad., Parker Sch. Internat. Law, 1960; JD, Hofstra U., 1986. Bar: NY 1953, DC 1977. Ptnr. Burns Summit Rovins & Feldesman (and predecessors), NYC, 1960-86; assoc. atty. gen. US Govt., Washington, 1986; dep. atty. gen. U.S. Dept. Justice, Washington, 1986-88; mem. Proskauer Rose LLP, NYC, 1988-99; mng. dir. Natexis Bleichroeder Inc., NYC, 1999—2003; chmn. The QuanStar Group, LLC, 2004—. Bd. dirs. Blastgard Internat. Inc.; bd. dirs., mem. exec. com. New Valley Corp. Note editor: Cornell Law Quar, 1952-53. Former chmn., life trustee Union Coll., Schenectady; former chmn., now chmn. emeritus bd. dirs. Freedom Found., Valley Forge, Pa.; emeritus chmn. nat. bd. govs. Boys and Girls Clubs Am.; co-chmn. nat. capital campaign Cornell Law Sch., Ithaca, NY; bd. dirs., exec. com. Econ. Devel. Corp, City of NY; former chmn. NYC Commn. on Youth Empowerment Svcs.; former chmn. NYC Commn. to Monitor Police Corruption; former chmn. Nat. Ctr. for Victims of Crime; chmn. Internat. Ctr. for Missing and Exploited Children; vice chmn. Nat. Ctr. for Missing and Exploited Children; bd. dirs. Vis. Nurse Svc., NY; dir. YES Network; chmn. emeritus Coun. for Unity; active Nat. Prison Indsl. Task Force Capt. US Army, 1953—57. Mem. Anti-Defamation League (life; nat. com.), Fed. Bar Coun., Cornell Law Assn., Met. Club, Army Navy Club, NY Athletic Club, Friars Club, Rockefeller Club, Terrace Club, Order of Coif, Phi Kappa Phi, Kappa Nu, Alpha Phi Omega. Republican. Jewish. Home: 25 Sutton Pl S Apt 11F New York NY 10022-2462 Office Phone: 212-956-3037. Business E-Mail: aburns@quanstar.com.

BURNS, ARTHUR LEE, architect; b. Indpls., July 5, 1924; s. Charles Raymond and Dorothy Frances (Young) B.; m. Dorothy Maxine Kingsland, Oct. 26, 1946 (dec.); children— Stephen Robert (dec.), Melody Lee; m. Frances C. Mathers, Jan. 12, 1988. BS in Architecture, U. Cin., 1949. Archtl. draftsman Foster Engring. Co., Ltd., Indpls., 1941-42; archtl. draftsman Albert V. Walters (Architect), Cin., 1946-48; chief draftsman Arend & Arend (Architects), Cin., 1948-49; architect The McGuire & Shook Corp., Indpls., 1949-84, v.p., 1964-71, sec.-treas., 1972-73, pres., 1974-75, exec. v.p., 1976-77, v.p., 1978-79, sec.-treas., 1980-84; archtl. cons., 1984—. Bd. dirs. Friends of Winter Haven Pub. Libr., 1995—2001, 2002—, pres., 1997—98. With USAF, 1943—46. Fellow AIA (sec.-treas. Indpls. chpt. 1965-66, v.p. 1967, pres. 1968, mem. documents bd. 1973-85, chmn. 1978-79); mem. Ind. Soc. Architects (bd. dirs. 1968-69, v.p. 1971, pres. 1972, Edward D. Pierre medal 1972), Constrn. Specifications Inst. (v.p. Indpls. chpt. 1966-67, pres. 1967-68), Broad Ripple Sertoma Club Indpls. (v.p. 1973-74, pres. 1974-75, Gold Honor Club), Cypress Gardens Sertoma Club Winter Haven (bd. dirs. 1991-99, 2000-02). Republican. Methodist. Home: 2987 Plantation Rd Winter Haven FL 33884-1235

BURNS, BERNARD JOHN, III, public defender; b. Alexandria, Va., Apr. 28, 1956; s. Bernard John and Mary Theresa (O'Malley) B.; m. Pamela Sue Endres, June 9, 1990; 1 child, Kristie Keener. BA in Journalism, U. Iowa, 1982, JD with distinction, 1984. Bar: Iowa 1985, U.S. Dist. Ct. (so. dist.) Iowa 1987, U.S. Supreme Ct. 1989, U.S. Ct. Appeals (8th cir.) 1992. Asst. appellate defender Iowa Appellate Defender, Des Moines, 1985-94; asst. pub. defender Des Moines Adult Pub. Defender, 1994-99; asst. fed. defender Office of Fed. Defender, Des Moines, 1999—. Author: 4A Iowa Practice: Criminal Procedure. Bd. dirs. Met. Arts Alliance Greater Des Moines, 1996-2003, pres., 2000; bd. dirs. Drama Workshop, 2004-05; mem. Iowa Criminal and Juvenile Justice Planning Commn., 1993-99; chmn. Jazz in July Planning Com., Des Moines, 1997-2003; keyboard player Goodnight Dallas. Named Outstanding Sr., Iowa Sch. Journalism, 1982. Mem. Nat. Assn. Fed. Defenders, Iowa Pub. Defenders Assn. (pres. 1991-99), Chopin Soc. (v.p. 1982), Blackstone Inn of Ct., Am. Mock Trial Assn., Judges Hall of Fame, Friends of Iowa Civil Rights, Inc. (Spl. Recognition award), Phi Beta Kappa. Avocations: musician, acting, writing, producing, martial arts. Office: Fed Defender 400 Locust St Ste 340 Des Moines IA 50309-2258 Home Phone: 515-334-7205. Business E-Mail: bjohnb@mchsi.com.

BURNS, BRIAN PATRICK, lawyer; b. Cambridge, Mass., July 12, 1936; s. John Joseph and Alice (Blake) B.; m. Sheila Ann O'Connor, June 23, 1962; children: Sheila Ann, Brian Patrick, Sean Richard, Roderick O'Connor. BA, Holy Cross Coll., 1957; LLB, Harvard U., 1960. Bar: Mass. 1960, N.Y. 1961, Calif. 1965. Law clk., spl. asst. to regional adminstr. New York Regional Office, SEC, 1958-59; asso. Webster, Sheffield, Fleischmann, Hitchcock & Brookfield, NYC, 1960-64; ptnr. Cullinan, Hancock, Rothert & Burns, San Francisco, 1965-74; sr. ptnr. Cullinan, Burns & Helmer, San Francisco, 1975-78; firm Burns & Whitehead, San Francisco, 1978-86; chmn., chief exec. officer, chmn. exec. com. Boothe Fin. Corp., San Francisco, 1981-87, also bd. dirs.; chmn. Robert Half Internat. Inc., 1987-88; chmn., CEO BF Enterprises Inc., 1987—. Dir. U.S. Banknote Corp., N.Y.C., from 1967, chmn. exec. and fin. coms., 1973-76; dir. Coca Cola Bottling Co., N.Y., 1974-86, chmn. exec. com., 1979-86; dir. Kellogg Co., 1979-89, chmn. fin. com. 1984-89; dir. Calif. Jockey, 1980-89; dir., chmn. audit com. Flexi-Van Corp., N.Y.C., 1984-85; dir., chmn. exec. com. Pinnacle Petroleum Corp., The Woodlands, Tex., 1983-85; dir., chmn. ops. review com. Brink's Inc., Chgo., 1976-78; dir., chmn. acquisition com. Pacific Holding Corp., Los Angeles, 1972-78; dir., mem. exec. com. Beverly Wilshire Hotel, Beverly Hills, Calif., Calif., 1967-86; dir., chmn. exec. com. USR Industries, The Woodlands, 1980-83; dir., chmn. audit com. ROCOR Internat., Palo Alto, Calif., 1976-82; underwriting mem. Lloyds of London, 1978-89; lectr. continuing edn. of bar U. Calif., 1969, 74, 76, advanced bus. seminar, 1971; seminar on investment opportunities in wine industry McGraw Hill Coll., N.Y., 1973, Legal Edn. Inst., 1976. Bd. dirs. Boys Club of San Francisco, 1971-80, Am. Irish Found., 1978-87, Am. Ireland Fund, 1987—; trustee Holy Cross Coll., 1978-89. Mem. ABA (mem. small bus. com. corp. bus. and banking sect. 1972-76), State Bar Cal. (vice chmn. com. on corps. 1971-75), Bar Assn. San Francisco (chmn. com. on corp. banking and bus. law 1968-69), Calif. Jockey Club (dir. San Mateo, Calif. 1988-89). Clubs: Royal Dublin Soc.; Bohemian, Burlingame Country, Family, Olympic, Sky, N.Y. Athletic, Les Ambassadeurs, Mil. and Hospitaller Order St. Lazarus of Jerusalem (comdr. companion). Roman Catholic. Office: BF Enterprises Inc 100 Bush St Ste 1250 San Francisco CA 94104-3914

BURNS, CASSANDRA STROUD, prosecutor; b. Lynchburg, Va., May 22, 1960; d. James Wesley and Jeanette Lou (Garner) Stroud; m. Stephen Burns; children: Leila Jeanette, India Veronica. BA, U. Va., 1982; JD, N.C. Cen. U., 1985; MBA candidate, Regis U., 2005. Bar: Va. 1986, N.J. 1986, U.S. Dist. Ct. (ea. dist.) Va. 1987, U.S. Ct. Appeals (4th cir.) 1987, U.S. Bankruptcy Ct. (ea. dist.) Va. 1987; cert. in criminal law. Law clk. Office Atty. Gen. State of Va., Richmond, summer 1984; law intern Office Dist. Atty. State of N.C., Durham, 1985; staff atty. Tidewater Legal Aid Soc., Chesapeake, Va., 1987-89; asst. atty. Commonwealth of Va., Petersburg, 1989-90; assoc. atty. Bland and Stroud, Petersburg, 1990; asst. pub. defender City of Petersburg, 1990-91, Commonwealth's atty. Va., 1991—; adj. prof. Va. Commonwealth U., 2003, Va. State U., 2004—. Founder BED Task Force on Babies Exposed to Drugs, 1991, Buddies of Petersburg Program, 1997—. Sec. Chesapeake Task Force Coun. on Youth Svcs., 1987-89; ch. directress and organist; mem. NAACP; chair Petersburg-Dinwiddie Cmty. Criminal Justice Bd.; bd. dirs. Mary Carter Beacon House, 2004—; mem. leadership coun. United Way, 2004—. Mem. Va. Bar Assn. (mem. coun. 1993-99), Old Dominion Bar Assn., Va. Assn. Commonwealth Attys. (bd. dirs., mem. coun. 1993-2000), Legal Svcs. Corp. Va. (bd. dirs.), Nat. Bd. Trial Advocacy (cert.), Nat. Dist. Attys. Assn., Southside Va. Legal Aid Soc. (bd. dirs.), Petersburg Bar Assn., Nat. Black Prosecutors Assn. (regional dir.), Petersburg Jaycees, Order Eastern Star, Peterburg C. of C., Kiwanis, Internat., Buddies Club, Phi Alpha Delta, Alpha Kappa Alpha. Democrat. Baptist. Avocations: piano, organ, volleyball, needlework, pets. Home: 326 N Park Dr Petersburg VA 23805-2442 Office: Commonwealth's Atty 150 N Sycamore St Petersburg VA 23803 Office Phone: 804-861-8899. E-mail: bossyda@aol.com.

BURNS, C(HARLES) PATRICK, hematologist, oncologist; b. Kansas City, Mo., Oct. 8, 1937; s. Charles Edgar and Ruth (Eastham) B.; m. Janet Sue Walsh, June 15, 1968; children: Charles Geoffrey, Scott Patrick. BA, U. Kans., 1959, MD, 1963. Diplomate Am. Bd. Internal Medicine, subsplty. bds. hematology, med. oncology. Intern Cleve. Met. Gen. Hosp., 1963-64; asst. resident in internal medicine Univ. Hosps., Cleve., 1966-68, sr. resident in hematology, 1968-69; instr. medicine Case Western Res. U., Cleve., 1970-71; asst. chief hematology Cleve. VA Hosp., 1970-71; asst. prof. medicine U. Iowa Hosps., Iowa City, 1971-75, assoc. prof. medicine, 1975-80, prof., 1980—2006, prof. emeritus, 2006—, dir. sect. med. oncology, co-dir. divsn. hematatol./oncology, 1980-85, dir. div. hematology, oncology, blood marrow transplantation, 1985-99. Vis. scientist Imperial Cancer Rsch. Fund Labs., London, 1982-83; cons. U.S. VA Hosp.; mem. study sect. on exptl. therapeutics NIH, Cancer Ctr. Support Rev. Commn. Nat. Cancer Inst., NIH, NIH Cancer Clin. Investigation Rev. Com., Com. H Nat. Cancer Inst., VA Med. Rsch. Svc. Career Devel. Com.; mem. external adv. com. U. Oreg. Cancer Ctr., 1994-2000; mem. oncology group external adv. com., ACS, 2004-; cons. Irish Rsch. Bd., Dublin, 2000— Mem. bd. assoc. editors Cancer Rsch., 1988-2000, rsch. and publs. on hematologic malignancies, tumor lipid biochemistry, leukemia and oncology, role of oxidation in cancer treatment. Vol. Medicine Clinic, Hilton Head, SC. Served to capt. USMC, 1964—66. Am. Cancer Soc. fellow in hematology-oncology, 1968-69, USPHS fellow in medicine, 1969-70; USPHS career awardee, 1978; Outstanding Paper Presentation, Am. Oil Chemists Soc., 1992. Fellow ACP; mem. AAAS, Am. Bd. Internal Medicine (subsplty. bd. hematology test writing com. 1992-98, com. on recent advances in hematology, 2002—, chair 2006—), Am. Soc. Hematology, Am. Assn. Cancer Rsch., Internat. Soc. Hematology, Ctrl. Soc. Clin. Rsch., Am. Soc. Clin. Oncology, Soc. Exptl. Biology and Medicine, Oxygen Soc., Royal Soc. Medicine, Am. Fedn. Clin. Rsch., Internat. Soc. for the Study of Fatty Acids and Lipids, Phi Beta Pi, Lambda Chi Alpha, Alpha Omega Alpha. Home: 2046 Rochester Ct Iowa City IA 52245-3246 Office: U Iowa Univ Hosps Dept Medicine Iowa City IA 52242 Office Phone: 319-356-2038. Business E-Mail: c-burns@uiowa.edu.

BURNS, CHESTER RAY, retired medical educator; b. Nashville, Dec. 5, 1937; s. Leslie Andrew and Margaret (Drake) B.; m. Ann Christine Griffey, Aug. 31, 1962; children: Christine, Derek. BA, Vanderbilt U., 1959, MD, 1963; PhD, Johns Hopkins U., 1969. Asst. prof. history medicine U. Tex. Med. Br., Galveston, 1969-71, James Wade Rockwell asst. prof. history medicine, 1971-75, James Wade Rockwell assoc. prof., 1975-79, James Wade Rockwell prof., 1979—; ret., 2006—. Cons. Nat. Ctr. for Health Svcs. Rsch., Washington, 1976-78; mem. nat. bd. cons. NEH, Washington, 1978-83. Editor: Humanism in Medicine, 1973, Legacies in Ethics and Medicine, 1977, Legacies in Law and Medicine, 1977; co-editor: Philosophy of Medicine and Bioethics: A Twenty Year Retrospective and Critical Appraisal, 1997; co-editor: Proceedings of the 37th International Congress on the History of Medicine, 2002, Saving Lives, Training Caregivers, Making Discoveries A Centennial History of the University of Texas Medical Branch at Galveston, 2003, Practicing the Medical Humanities, 2003; author numerous essays. Bd. dirs. The Grand 1894 Opera House, Galveston, 1986—88. Mem. Am. Assn. for History of Medicine (exec. coun. 1972-75), Soc. for Health and Human Values (pres. 1975-76), Am. Osler Soc. (bd. govs. 1984-87, 2002—, pres. 2004—05), Internat. Soc. for History of Medicine (treas. 1991—2003), Tex. State Hist. Assn. (exec. coun. 1993-97), Tex. Oral History Assn. (bd. dirs. 2005—), Rotary (pres. Galveston club 1980-81, gov. Dist. 5910, 1993-94). Democrat. Methodist. Avocations: swimming, photography. Home and Office: 33 LeBrun Ct E Galveston TX 77551-5185 Personal E-mail: chetbaby@earthlink.net.

BURNS, CLARE MARIE, retired elementary school educator; b. Providence, Aug. 31, 1953; d. Eugene Joseph and Virginia Louise Trainor; m. Thomas Joseph Burns, Apr. 26, 1980. AA, C.C. R.I., Warwick, 1974; BA, R.I. Coll., Providence, 1976, M, 1999. Cert. reading specialist - cons. RI, 1999. First grade tchr. St. James Sch., West Warwick, RI, 1982—90, Blessed Sacrament Sch., Providence, 1990—99; reading specialist Globe Pk. Elem. Sch., Woonsocket, 1999—2002; first grade tchr. Woonsocket Sch. Dept., 2002—04; ret., 2004. Vol. Dysart Unified Sch. Dist., Surprise, Ariz., 2006—. Named Wal-Mart Tchr. of Yr., 1999. Home: 17109 W Ironwood St Surprise AZ 85388-1246 Home Phone: 623-256-6259.

BURNS, CONRAD RAY, former senator; b. Gallatin, Mo., Jan. 25, 1935; s. Russell and Mary Frances (Knight) B.; m. Phyllis Jean Kuhlmann; children: Keely Lynn, Garrett Russell. Student in Agr., U. Mo., Columbia, 1952—54. Field rep. Polled Hereford World Mag., Kansas City, Mo., 1963-69; pub. rels. Billings Livestock Com., Mont., 1969-73; mgr. No. Internat. Livestock Exposition and Rodeo, Riverton Livestock Auction, Wyo.; farm dir. KULR TV, Billings, 1974; pres., founder No. Ag-Network, Billings, 1975-86; Mont. commr. Yellowstone County, Billings, 1987-89; US Senator from Mont., 1989—2007; sr. adv. GAGE, Washington, 2007—. Mem. spl. com. on aging US Senate, com. small bus. and entrepreneurship, com. energy and natural resources, com. commerce, sci. and transp., com. appropriations. Served to cpl. USMC, 1955—57. Recipient Congressional Leadership award, Nat. Telephone Cooperative Assn., 1998, Rural Telecommunications Leadership award, Orgn. Advancement and Promotion Small Telecommunication Companies, 2001, Legis. of Yr., Agrl. Retailers Assn., 2004, Wheat Leader of Yr. award, Nat. Assn. Wheat Growers, 2004. Mem. Nat. Assn. Farm Broadcasters, Am. Assn. Farm Broadcasters, Am. Legion, Rotary, Masons, Shriners. Republican. Lutheran. Avocation: football. Office: GAGE 122 C St NW Ste 380 Washington DC 20001*

BURNS, DAN W., manufacturing executive; b. Auburn, Calif., Sept. 10, 1925; s. William and Edith Lynn (Johnston) B.; 1 child, Dan Jr. Dir. materials Menasco Mfg. Co., 1951-56; v.p., gen. mgr. Hufford Corp., 1956-58; pres. Hufford div. Siegler Corp., 1958-61; v.p. Siegler Corp., 1961-62, Lear Siegler, Inc., 1962-64; pres., dir. Electrada Corp., Culver City, Calif., 1964; pres., chief exec. officer Sargent Industries, Inc., LA, 1964-85, chmn. bd. dirs., 1985-88. Now chmn. bd. dirs., CEO Arlington Industries, Inc.; bd. dirs. Gen. Automotive Corp., Dover Tech. Internat., Inc., Kistler Aerospace Corp. Bd. dirs. San Diego Aerospace Mus., Smithsonian Inst., The Pres.'s Cir., Nat. Acad. Scis., Atlantic Coun. of U.S., George C. Marshall Found.; bd. overseers Hoover Instn., Stanford U. Capt. U.S. Army, 1941-47; prisoner of war Japan; asst. mil. attache 1946, China; adc to Gen. George C. Marshall 1946-47. Mem. OAS Sports Com. (dir.), L.A. Country Club, St. Francis Yacht Club, Calif. Club, Conquistador del Cielo, Cosmos Club Washington, Pacific-Union Club (San Francisco). Home: 7400 Bryan Canyon Rd Carson City NV 89704-9588

BURNS, DANIEL HOBART, management consultant; b. Atlanta, Jan. 26, 1928; s. Hobart H. and Florence (Kuhn) B.; B.A., U. Ala., 1949; grad. Armed Forces Staff Coll., 1966, Air Command and Staff Coll., 1969, Air War Coll., 1972; postgrad. U. S.C., 1975, Regent Coll., U. B.C., 1978-79, Trinity Episcopal Sch. for Ministry, 1979-80; m. Barbara Ann Grimsley, Jan. 15, 1949 (div. July 1974); children: Eric Grimsley, Daniel Hobart, Barbara Bennett, Arlene Chester; m. Ann Lyn Horrell, Sept. 28, 1979 (div. Mar. 1997); children: Jessica Florence, Stephen John. Account exec. Sta. WCOS, Columbia, S.C., 1949-51; sales mgr. sta. WIS, Columbia, 1951-57; ins. agt. Aetna Life Ins. Co., Columbia, 1957-60; propr. Daniel H. Burns Co., mgmt. cons., broker, Columbia, 1960—; pres., dir. Nat. Search, Inc., 1966—, Indsl. Surveys, Inc., 1968—; Alliance Bldg. Industries, 1971-84; cons., Ednl. TV Network, govts. of Israel, Greece, W. Ger., Fed. Grants Projects, S.C. Ednl. TV Network; guest lectr. U. S.C.; cons. sales mgmt. and market analysis, analytical and conceptual problem solving; owner Western Rare Books-Fine Art, 1983—, Internat. Galleries, Empire Gallery, Empire Pub. Co.; bd. dir. Boulder Sch. of Massage Therapy. Pres., Schneider Sch. PTA, 1963-66; supr. registration City of Columbia, 1962-69; asst. project dir., statewide law enforcement edn. through TV, 1966-69; cons. Pitts. Leadership Found., 1980-81; dist. commr. Boy Scouts Am.; pres., committeeperson Boulder County Rep. Party; pres., bd. dirs. Internat. Communications Resources Found.; bd. dirs. Travelers Aid Assn. Am., Nat. Council USO; Columbia Sch. Theology for Laity; bd. dirs., exec. com. Consol. Agys. of United Funds; Richland County chpt. Nat. Found. Served with USAAF, 1943-46; lt. col. USAF ret. Mem. S.C. Football Ofcls. Assn., Columbia Real Estate Bd., Air Force Assn., Am. Y-Flyer Yacht Racing Assn., AAUP, Am. Mgmt. Assn., Nat. Assn. Ednl. Broadcasters, Soc. for Advancement Mgmt., Am. Soc. Real Estate Appraisers, Interprofl. Cons. Council, Nat. Assn. Security Dealers, Soc. Am. Archivists, Nat. Hist. Soc., Internat. Platform Assn., Hist. Columbia Found., S.C. Press Assn., Columbia C. of C., Am. Soc. Personal Adminstrn., Sierra Club, Columbia Lyric Opera, Internat. Christian Leaders, Fellowship Christian Athletes, English Speaking Union, N. Am. Yacht Racing Union, Sigma Phi Epsilon. Episcopalian/Anglican. Clubs: Charleston (S.C.) Yacht; Yachting of Am., Workshop Theatre, First Nighters, Columbia Squash Racquets, Town Theatre, Masons (Shriner), Rotary. Author publs. in field. Home: 7425 Empire Dr Boulder CO 80303-5007 E-mail: empgal@earthlink.net.

BURNS, DAVID ALAN, lawyer; b. Independence, Kans., Nov. 26, 1945; AB summa cum laude (hon.), U. Okla., 1968; JD, Harvard U., 1971. Bar: Tex. 1971. Sr. ptnr. Baker & Botts L.L.P., Houston; mem. Dewey Ballantine LLP, Houston. Mem. ABA, Am. Bankruptcy Inst., Am. Coll. Investment Counsel, Houston Bar Assn., Phi Beta Kappa. Office: Dewey Ballantine LLP 700 Louisiana Ste 2050 Houston TX 77002 Office Phone: 713-445-1500. Office Fax: 713-445-1533.

BURNS, DAVID MITCHELL, writer, retired diplomat; b. Pineville, Ky., Dec. 1, 1928; s. Judge and Louise (Cooke) B.; m. Sandra Dunlop, June 8, 1955; children: David A., Patrick C. BA, Princeton U., 1953; student, Sch. Advanced Internat. Studies, Johns Hopkins U., 1957-60, Howard U., 1957-60, Fgn. Service Inst., Tangier, Morocco, 1967-69. Advt. trainee Gen. Electric Co., 1953; instr. English, U. Kans., 1954-55; asst. cultural affairs officer Am. embassy, Damascus, Syria, 1955-56, Beirut, 1956; dir. Iran-Am. Soc., Isfahan, 1957; information officer Am. consulate general Salisbury, Fedn. Rhodesia and Nyasaland, 1957-59; pub. affairs officer Am. embassy, Bamako, Mali, 1960-62, cultural affairs officer Tunis, Tunisia, 1962-63; cultural policy officer Africa, USIA, 1963-67; pub. affairs officer Am. interests sect. embassy of Switzerland, Algiers, Algeria, 1969-72; dir. sci. and tech. programs USIA, 1972-77; dir. climate project AAAS, Washington, 1978-90. Author: Gateway: Dr. Thomas Walker and the Opening of Kentucky, Quests; CD's as leader of Hot Mustard Quintet include Swing Song, Don't Postpone Joy, Nothing Loved Is Ever Lost, Rainbow Room, 1975—; contbr. articles to newspapers and mags., 1953—. Fulbright grantee U. Lille and Salzburg Seminar in Am. Studies, 1953-54; recipient award of merit Ky. Hist. Soc., 2001. Mem. Cosmos Club, Dacor Club (Washington). Office: 1712 19th St NW Washington DC 20009-1606 E-mail: davesand@comcast.net.

BURNS, DRUSILLA LORENE, microbiologist; b. Manhattan, Kans., Feb. 14, 1953; BS in Chemistry, Tulane U., 1975; PhD, U. Calif., Berkeley, 1980. Fellow lab cellular metabolism NIH, 1980-84; from sr. fellow to rsch. chemist FDA Ctr. for Biologics Evaluation and Rsch., Bethesda, 1984-94, chief lab. pertussis, 1994-99, chief lab. respiratory and spl. pathogens, 1999—. Ad hoc reviewer in field. Mem. editl. bd. Infection and Immunity, 1989-98, Jour. Biol. Chemistry, 1995-2000; editor Infection and Immunity, 1998-2007; contbr. articles to profl. jours. Recipient Am. Inst. Chemists award, 1975, FDA Commrs. Spl. Citation, 1989. Mem. AAAS, Am. Acad. Microbiology, Am. Soc. Microbiology (internat. activities com., pub. and sci. affairs bd. 1989-92, councilor divsn. B 1999), Phi Beta Kappa. Achievements include patents for process for isolation of the B oligomer of pertussis toxin; process for the purification of a 69,000 da outer membrane protein of Bordetella pertussis. Office: Ctr for Biologics Eval 8800 Rockville Pike Bldg 29 Bethesda MD 20892-0001 Business E-Mail: drusilla.burns@fda.hhs.gov.

BURNS, EDWARD J., JR., actor, film director; b. Valley Stream, NY, Jan. 29, 1968; s. Edward Sr. and Molly Burns; m. Christy Turlington, June 7, 2003; children: Grace, Finn. BA, Hunter Coll. Entrepreneur Irish Twin Prodn. Co. Co-owner Irish Twins Prodn. Co.; owner Marlboro Road Gang Films. Actor, dir., writer (films) The Brothers McMullen, 1995 (Jury Spl. prize Deauville Film Festival, 1995, Ind. Spirit award, 1995, Nova award, 1995, Grand Jury prize Sundance Film Festival, 1995), She's the One, 1996, No Looking Back, 1998, Sidewalks of New York, 2001; actor: (films) Saving Private Ryan, 1998, Any Given Sunday, 1999, 15 Minutes, 2001, Life or Something Like It, 2002, Confidence, 2003, The River King, 2005, A Sound of Thunder, 2005, The Holiday, 2006; actor, dir. (films) Looking for Kitty, 2004, writer, actor, prodr., dir. Ash Wednesday, 2002, writer, prodr. (TV series) The Fighting Fitzgeralds, 2001, writer (films) Flight of the Phoenix, 2004. Recipient ShoWest award for Screenwriter of Yr., 1996.*

BURNS, ELIZABETH MURPHY, media executive; b. Superior, Wis., Dec. 4, 1945; d. Morgan and Elizabeth (Beck) Murphy; m. Richard Ramsey Burns, June 24, 1984. Student, U. Ariz., 1963-67. Promotion and programming sec. Sta. KGUN-TV, Tucson, 1967-68; programming and traffic sec. Sta. KFMB-TV, San Diego, 1968-69; owner, operator Sta. KKAR, Pomona, Calif., 1970-73; co-owner, pres. Evening Telegram Co. (parent co. Murphy Stas.); pres. Morgan Murphy Stas., Madison, Wis., 1976—. Bd. dirs. Nat. Guardian Life Ins. Co., Republic Bank, Nat. Assn. Broadcasters, various media stas. and corps. Mem. Wis. Broadcasters Assn., Madison Club, Northland Country Club (Duluth), Boulders Country Club (Carefree, Ariz.), Bishop's Bay Country Club, Silverleaf Golf Club (Scottsdale, Ariz.). Roman Catholic. Avocations: golf, travel. Home: 180 Paine Farm Rd Duluth MN 55804-2609 Office: Sta WISC-TV 7025 Raymond Rd Madison WI 53719-5053 Personal E-mail: emb@embtv.com.

BURNS, GEORGE FRANKLIN, archivist, retired English language educator; b. Milan, Aug. 17, 1921; s. George Franklin Burns and Pearle Barbee Katherine; m. Mary John Wade, Aug. 24, 1968 (dec. 1999); 1 stepchild, Scott Lockwood II. BA, Cumberland U., 1942, JD, 1944; MA, George Peabody Coll., 1967; PhD, Vanderbilt U., 1973. Reporter Wilson County News, Lebanon, Tenn., 1942—43; assoc. editor Lebanon Dem., 1943—66; staff corr. Nashville Banner, 1948—65; reviewer lit. page The Tennessean, Nashville, 1962—77, columnist, 1980—81; prof. English and pub. rels. dir. Cumberland U., Lebanon, 1959—63, 1966—74; faculty Tenn. Technol. U., Cookeville, 1974—90; emeritus prof. Cumberland U., Lebanon, 1989—, English archivist, 1991—. Historian, editor Tenn. Commn. for Commemoration of 50th Anniversary of 2d Army Tenn. Maneuvers, 1993—95; founder Vol. State Athletic Conf., 1947. Author: (critical book) Mr. Faulkner in Tennessee, 1986, 5 books on Tenn. history; contbr. Tennessee Encyclopedia, 1998. Cir. Dem. Nat. Com., 1999—; chair Wilson County Libr. Bd., 1956; sec. Regional Planning Commn., 1950—60. Recipient Disting. Svc. award, Jaycees, 1952, C. of C., 1958. Mem.: MLA (life), History Assocs. (past pres.), Rotary (Paul Harris award), Sigma Alpha Epsilon. Democrat. Presbyterian. Avocations: photography, travel. Home: 1809 Andover Dr Garland TX 75041 Office: Cumberland U Archives PO Box 1415 Lebanon TN 37088

BURNS, IVAN ALFRED, grocery products and industrial company executive; b. Leamington Spa, Eng., Jan. 18, 1935; s. Cecil Ivan and Dorothy Constance (Mote) B.; m. Angela Loeffel, May 16, 1959; children: Pauline Cecile, Charla Cheyney, Claudine. BS, Coventry Coll., 1958. Various positions Deere & Co., Moline, Ill., 1969-73; dir. internat. ACF Industries Inc., NYC, 1973-75, v.p., 1975-81, pres., COO, 1981-84, chmn., CEO, 1983-90; dir. CPC Internat. Inc., Englewood Cliffs, NJ, 1985-87, pres. corn refining divsn., 1987-90, exec. v.p. adminstrn., 1987—; pres., dir. Picca Enterprises, Inc., New Canaan, Conn., 1984-96. Bd. dirs. Continental Corp., N.Y.C. Patentee valve, 1980. Bd. dirs. United Way, New York, 1984-85; mem. bus. adv. bd. Northwestern U., 1983-92. Mem. Conf. Bd. Republican. Mem. Ch. of England. Avocations: horse breeding, collecting netsukes, martial arts. Home and Office: 57 Deer Park Rd New Canaan CT 06840

BURNS, JAMES W., education educator; b. New Haven, Jan. 24, 1937; s. James W. and Helen M. (Wieliesz) B.; children: Amy, Kristin, Katherine. BS, Ctrl. Conn. State U., 1958; MEd, Pa. State U., 1964, EdD, 1969. Tchr. Greenwich (Conn.) Pub. Schs., 1958-64; dir. Curriculum Ctr. Pa. State U., University Park, 1964-68; prof. edn., reading recovery tchr. and leader trainer Western Mich. U., Kalamazoo, 1968—. Mem. Internat. Reading Assn., Nat. Coun. of Tchrs. of English, Mich. Reading Assn., NGA. Home: 1023 Par 4 Cir Kalamazoo MI 49008-2915 Office: 3414 Sangren Hall Kalamazoo MI 49007

BURNS, JAMES WESLEY, academic administrator, researcher, consultant; s. Wesley and Zelda Burns; m. Suzanne M. Barnell. Masters, No. Ariz. U., 1985, Doctorate, 1990. Dir. grad. studies MNU, Olathe, Kans., 1995—2001; dir. grad. sch. Calif. State U., Turlock, 2002—04, dean grad. sch., 2004—. Tchr. edn. reform task force US Dept. Edn., Nat. Assn. Colls. Tchr. Edn., Topeka; moderator Olathe Unified Sch. Bd. Candidate Debates, 1996; mem. Policy and Procedures com. Kans. State Bd. Edn., Topeka, 1998—2001, mem. Tchr. of Yr. Selection com., 1998—2001; exec. com. Kans. Assn. Colls. Tchr. Edn., Topeka, 1998—2001. Named Alumnus of Yr., MidAm. Nazarene U., 1996; Internat. Program Devel. grantee, Henry Luce Found., 2000, Program Planning and Implementation grantee, Ford Found., 2003—05, Devel. grantee, Alfred P. Sloan Found., 2003—05. Mem.: Coun. Grad. Schs. (Program Devel. grants 2003—05), Western Assn. Grad. Schs., Phi Kappa Phi (life; sec., treas. 2004). Avocations: music, art, travel, photography. Office: Calif State U 801 W Monte Vista Ave Turlock CA 95382 Home Phone: 209-552-0655. Personal E-mail: burns.jim@comcast.net.

BURNS, JAMES WILLIAM, financial executive; b. Winnipeg, Man., Can., Dec. 27, 1929; s. Charles William and Helen Gladys (Mackay) B.; children: James F.C., Martha J., Alan W. B in Commerce, U. Man., 1951; MBA, Harvard U., 1953, LLD (hon.), 1988. With Great-West Life Assurance Co., 1953—, dir., 1970, pres., CEO, 1971-79, chmn., 1979—92; pres. Power Corp. Can., 1979-86, dep. chmn., 1986—2002; chmn., CEO Power Fin. Corp., 1986-90. Bd. dirs. Investors Group Gt.-West Life Assurance Co., Gt.-West Lifeco, Inc., Gt.-West Life and Annuity Ins. Co., London Life Ins. Co., London Ins. Group, Inc.; dir. emeritus Power Corp. Can., Power Fin. Corp. Founding dir. Man. Mus. Man and Nature, Coun. Bus. & Arts; past chmn. Conf. Bd. Can.; mem. Gov.'s Coun., Shaw Festival. Named Officer of the Order of Can.; Hon. col. Queen's Own Cameron Highlanders of Can. Mem. St. Charles Country Club, Man. Club, Toronto Club, Mount-Royal Club.

BURNS, JOHN F., reporter; b. Nottingham, Eng., Oct. 4, 1944; With Globe and Mail, Toronto; fgn. corr. NY Times, 1975—, bur. chief Beijing, 1986, fgn. corr., New Delhi bur. chief, 1994-98, spl. corr. Islamic affairs, 1999—, bur. chief Johannesburg, Moscow, Peking, Toronto, Sarajevo, New Delhi, Baghdad, 2003—07, London, 2007—. Recipient Pulitzer Prize for internat. reporting, 1993, 97, George Polk award for Fgn. Corr., 1979, 97. Office: NY Times 229 W 43rd St New York NY 10036-3959*

BURNS, JOHN JOSEPH, JR., financial and insurance holding company executive; b. Cambridge, Mass., June 27, 1931; s. John Joseph and Alice (Blake) Burns; m. Barbara Ann Miller, Oct. 18, 1958; children: John J. Burns III, Christine, Gregory, Timothy, Jennifer. BS in Fin., Boston Coll., 1953; MBA, Harvard U., 1955. Asso. buying dept. and arbitrage dept. Goldman Sachs & Co., 1957-63; assoc. N.Y. Securities, 1963-67, gen. ptnr., 1968; v.p. fin., dir. Alleghany Corp., NYC, 1968-77, pres., dir., 1977—, mem. exec. com., 1977—, CEO, 1992—, vice chmn., 2005—, dir., 2007—. With USN, 1955—57. Mem.: Links Club. Roman Catholic. Office: Alleghany Corp 161 Cherry St New Canaan CT 06840 Business E-Mail: jburns@alleghany.com.

BURNS, JOHN MACDOUGAL, III, lawyer; b. Ft. Worth, Aug. 23, 1933; s. John MacDougal and Mary Tabitha (Kenney) B.; m. Lorraine Lovell, Aug. 31, 1957; 1 son (dec.). A.B., Columbia U., 1955, M.A., 1960, LL.B., 1961. Bar: N.Y. 1961, U.S. Dist. Ct. (so., ea. and no. dists.) N.Y. 1962, U.S. Ct. Appeals (2d cir.) 1963, U.S. Ct. Appeals (3d cir.) 1980, U.S. Ct. Appeals (6th cir.) 1989, U.S. Ct. Appeals (fed. cir.) 2004. Assoc. Hughes, Hubbard, Blair & Reed, N.Y.C., 1961-68; legis. counsel to State Senator Whitney North Seymour, Jr., N.Y.C., 1965-68; ptnr. Spear & Hill, N.Y.C., 1969-70, 71-74; exec. asst. U.S. atty. So. Dist. N.Y., 1970-71; ptnr. Alexander, Katz & Rosenberg, N.Y.C., 1974-76; sole practice, N.Y.C., 1976-81; ptnr. Burns & Fox, N.Y.C., 1981-86; sole practice, 1986-87, 94—; ptnr. Burns, Beck & Stumpp, 1988, Burns & Beck, 1989-93. Mem. ABA, Assn. of Bar of City of N.Y., Gipsy Tr. Club (Carmel, N.Y.) Democrat. Home: 33 Greenwich Ave Apt 7H New York NY 10014-2788 Office Phone: 212-360-1990. Personal E-mail: jayburnsiii@nyc.rr.com.

BURNS, JOSEPH ARTHUR, planetary science educator; b. NYC, Mar. 22, 1941; s. John Driscoll and Genevieve Mary (McCarthy) B.; m. Judith Ann Klein, July 1, 1967; children: Patrick M., Caitlin M. BS, Webb Inst., Glen Cove, NY, 1962; PhD, Cornell U., 1966. Asst. prof. Cornell U., Ithaca, NY, 1966-67, 68-74, assoc. prof., 1974-81, prof., 1981-94; Irving Porter Church prof. engring. and astronomy, 1994—; chmn. theoretical and applied mechs. Cornell U., Ithaca, NY, 1987-93, vice provost phys. scis. and engring., 2003—; NRC rsch. assoc. NASA Goddard Space Ctr., Greenbelt, Md., 1967-68; NAS exch. fellow Inst. Geophysics, Moscow, 1973; sr. scientist NASA Ames Rsch. Ctr., Mountain View, Calif., 1975-76, 82-83. Astronome titulaire Observatoire de Paris, France, 1979, 84; vis. prof. astronomy U. Calif., Berkeley, 1982-83; vis. prof. planetary sci. U. Ariz., Tucson, 1989-90; mem. space and earth scis. adv. com. NASA, 1983-87, solar sys. exploration com., 1988-92, NAS space studies bd., 1989-95, chair NAS com. planet exploration, 1992-95, mem. solar sys. decadal panel NRC, 2001-02. Author 160 rsch. articles, 1966—; editor: Planetary Satellites, 1977, Satellites, 1986; editor Icarus-Internat. Jour. of Solar Sys. Studies, 1979-97, assoc. editor, 1998-; bd. rev. editors Sci., 2000—; assoc. editor Celestial Mechanics and Dynamical Astronomy, 2005—. Recipient various rsch. awards and grants NSF, 1976-86, 97, NASA, 1976—, NATO, 1998-2000, N.Y. Coun. Arts, 1972, NASA Sci. Achievement awards, 1997, 98, 2000. Fellow AAAS, Am. Geophys. Union; mem. Internat. Acad. Astronautics, Russian Acad. Sci., Am. Astron. Soc. (chmn. planetary scis. 1983-84, chmn. dynamical astronomy 2000-01, v.p. 2001-04, Masursky Prize 1994), Internat. Astron. Union (mem. solar sys. com. 1986-89, v.p. solar system 1996-99, v.p. celestial mechanics 2003-06, pres. 2006—). Office: Cornell U Kimball Hall Dept Astronomy Ithaca NY 14853 E-mail: jab16@cornell.edu.

BURNS, JOSEPH M., economist; b. NYC, Aug. 2, 1938; s. Arthur F. and Helen (Bernstein) B.; m. Ellen N. Herbst, Sept. 3, 1992; children: Stephen Juran, Rebecca Anne. AB, Swarthmore Coll., 1960; MA, U. Chgo., 1961, PhD, 1967. Economist rsch. dept. Fed. Reserve Bank N.Y., NYC, 1961-62; asst. prof. dept. econs. UCLA, 1966-71; assoc. prof. dept. econs. Rice U., Houston, 1971-74; sr. economist, dep. dir. monetary rsch. office asst. sec. for internat. affairs U.S. Dept. Treasury, Washington, 1974-76; sr. economist, assoc. dir. rsch. div. econs. and edn. Commodity Futures Trading Commn., Washington, 1976-79; sr. economist antitrust div. U.S. Dept. Justice, Washington, 1979-2000. Vis. assoc. prof. dept. econ. Stanford U., Calif., 1973—74; professorial lectr. fin. dept. Georgetown U. Sch. Bus., Washington, 1979, 84. Author: Acctg. Standards and Internat. Fin., 1976, A Treatise on Markets, 1979; contbr. articles to profl. jours. Fellow, Earhart Found, 1960—61, 1963—65, Ford Found., 1965—66, Hoover Instn., 1973—74. Mem.: Am. Econ. Assn. (census adv. com. 1972—75). Personal E-mail: jmburns88@msn.com.

BURNS, JUDITH O'DELL, library assistant, educator; b. Lenoir, NC, May 28, 1941; d. James Horace and Mary Douglas O'Dell; m. David Capps Creech, Apr. 2, 1989 (div.); children: Laurel Anne, Mary Carolynn. MusB, Greensboro Coll., 1963; certificate in Edn., Sacred Heart Coll., 1976; student, Appalachian State U., 1988—94. Cert. Educator K-6 NC, 1976. Tchr. Gaston County Schs., Gastonia, NC, 1976—87; presch. coord. Watauga County Schs., 1990—94; tchr. Gaston County Schs., 1994—2000; libr. asst. Gaston County Pub. Libr., 2001—. Piano & voice instr., Gastonia, 1964—; parent counselor, Gastonia, 1994—; cons. Watauga County Children's Coun., 1990—, pres., Boone, NC, 1988—94; mem. Watauga County Interagy. Bd., Boone, 1990—94. Singer; author: various parent handbooks, 1990—94, poetry and short stories. Sec. Gastonia Dist. United Meth. Women, 2002—06; nat. del. Pioneer Girl Scout Coun., Gastonia, 2002; pres. Nat. Assn. Edn. of Young Children, Boone, 1990—91, Christ Ch. United Meth. Women, Gastonia, 2002—04;

choir dir. various chs., Gastonia, 1965—82; founder, dir. Christ United Meth. Ch. After Sch. Care, Gastonia, 2000. Mem.: AAUW, Gaston County Friends of Libr. (v.p. 2000—01, com. chmn. 2000—01), Sharps & Flats Music Club (former pres., com. chmn.). Methodist. Avocations: writing, reading, needlecrafts, music, walking. Home: 855 Nottingham Dr #65 Gastonia NC 28054

BURNS, JURATE, library director; b. Schwabisch Gmund, Bavaria, Mar. 21, 1948; arrived in U.S., 1949; d. Leonardas and Emilija Montvidas Kutkus; m. Matthew Wallace Burns, Dec. 21, 1968; children: Matthew Jr., Jeffrey. BA theatre, Mich. State U., 1969; MLS, U. Ala., 1975. Tchr. English and reading Anne Arundel County, Md., 1970—72; tchr. speech, English Tuscaloosa, Ala., 1972—75; real estate broker Destin, Fla., 1981—99; dir. libr., 1999—. Bd. pres. Panhandle Libr. Access Network, Panama City Beach, 2005. Mem. Choctawhatchee Basin Alliance, 2000—05. Mem.: ALA, Pub. Libr. Assn., Fla. Libr. Assn., Beta Phi Mu. Roman Catholic. Office: Destin Libr Destin FL 32541 Office Phone: 850-837-8572. Office Fax: 850-837-5248. E-mail: jburns@cityofdestin.com.

BURNS, KATHLEEN ADLEY, educational consultant; b. Boston, Mass., Apr. 17, 1947; d. Edward Myles and Marguerite Frances (Garten) Adley; m. Thomas Michael Burns, June 30, 1973; 1 child, Bridget Michaela. BEd, Framingham State Coll., 1970; MEd, Univ. Mass., Boston, Mass., 1975; MEd summa cum laude, Salem State Coll., Salem, Mass., 1999. Cert. tchr., guidance counselor, guidance dir., prin. Tchr. Burlington Pub. sch., Burlington, Mass., 1970—85, guidance counselor, 1985—90, asst. prin., 1993—2002, prin., 2002—. Exec. bd. mem. Burlington Educators Assn., Burlington, Mass., 1975—82; sec. Burlington Sch. Adminstrn. Assn., Burlington, Mass., 1995—2000. Recipient Svc. award. Democrat. Roman Cath. Avocations: golf, photography, travel, sports, theater. Business E-Mail: burns@burlington.mec.edu.

BURNS, KEN, documentary filmmaker; b. Bklyn., July 29, 1953; s. Robert Kyle and Lyla Smith (Tupper) B.; children: Sarah, Lilly. BA, Hampshire Coll., 1975; LHD (hon.), Bowdoin Coll., 1991; LittD (hon.), Amherst Coll., 1991; LHD (hon.), U. N.H.; DFA, Franklin Pierce Coll.; LittD (hon.), Notre Dame Coll., Manchester, NH; HHD (hon.), Coll. of St. Joseph, Rutland, Vt.; LHD (hon.), Springfield Coll. Ill., Pace U.; PhD (hon.), CUNY. Pres., owner Florentine Films, Walpole, N.H., 1975—. Dir., prodr.: (documentaries) Brooklyn Bridge, 1981 Christopher award 1963, Erik Barnouw prize Hist. Films), Remembering Chicago and World War 2, 1982, The Shakers: Hands to Work, Hearts to God, 1984 (CINE Golden Eagle award 1984), Huey Long, 1985 (Silver Baton award Dupont-Columbia Journalism 1988), The Statue of Liberty, 1985 (Christopher award 1987, CINE Golden Eagle award, Acad. award nomination 1986), Thomas Hart Benton, 1988 (CINE Golden Eagle award 1988, Golden Apple award Nat. Ednl. Film Festival 1989), The Congress, 1988 (CINE Golden Eagle award 1989, Red Ribbon Am. Film Festival 1989), The Civil War, 1990 (Emmy award for outstanding information series 1991, for outstanding individual achievement, writing 1991, CINE Gold Eagle award, Lincoln prize Gettysburg Coll. 1991, Dartmouth Film award 1990, Bell I. Wiley award Civil War Round Table, N.Y., 1991, D.W. Griffiths award, Christopher award, Peabody award 1990, Gabriel award 1991, People's Choice award 1991, Humanitas award 1991, Charles Frankel prize NEH 1991, Grammy award (2) 1992, numerous others), Radio Pioneers, 1981, Baseball (Outstanding Informational Series Emmy award), The West, 1996 (Erik Barnouw prize 1997), Thomas Jefferson, 1997, Lewis and Clark: The Journey of the Corps of Discovery, 1997, Frank Lloyd Wright, 1998, Not for Ourselves Alone: The Story of Elizabeth Cady Stanton & Susan B. Anthony, 1999, Jazz, 2000, Mark Twain, 2001, Horatio's Drive: America's First Road Trip, 2003; Unforgivable Blackness: The Rise and Fall of Jack Johnson, 2004 (Emmy nom., outstanding directing for nonfiction programming, 2005), The War, 2007; author: (with others) Centennial, 1986, (with Amy Stechler Burns) The Shakers: Hands to Work, Hearts to God, 1987, (with Geoffrey Ward and Ric Burns) The Civil War: An Illustrated History, 1990, Empire of the Air, 1992: retrospectives Smithsonian Instn., 1991, Walker Arts Ctr., Mpls., 1991, Pub. Broadcasting Svc., 1991-92, (with Geoffrey C. Ward) Baseball, 1994, (with Dayton Funcan) Lewis & Clark: The Journey of the Corps of Discovery, 1998. Trustee Hampshire Coll., Amherst, Mass., 1992—, N.H. Humanities Coun.; bd. dirs. MacDowell Colony, Peterborough, N.H. Mem. Acad. Motion Picture, Arts and Scis., Soc. Am. Historians, N.H. Humanities Coun. (trustee), Mass. Hist. Soc. (corr.). Home and Office: Maple Grove Rd P O Box 613 Walpole NH 03608*

BURNS, LAWRENCE D., automotive executive; B in Mech. Engring., GM Inst.; M in Engring, Pub. Policy, U. Mich.; PhD in Civil Engring., U. Calif., Berkeley. Rsch. devel. staff GM Corp., 1969—, v.p. rsch., devel. and strategic planning, 1998—. Mem. GM Automotive Strategy Bd., Automotive Strategy Bd. Mem.: U. Mich. Ctr. Hearing Problems (bd. mem.), Deafness Rsch. Found. (bd. mem.). Office: GM Corp 300 Renaissance Ctr PO Box 300 Detroit MI 48265-3000

BURNS, LINDA D., elementary school educator; b. Tulsa, Okla., Oct. 1, 1948; d. Leonard Leo and Frances Jordan Dyer; m. John Thomas Burns; 1 child, Malinda. BA, McNeese State U., 1972, M, 1974, postgrad., 1976. Cert. in elem. edn., grades 1-8, for supervision of student tchrs. Bd. dirs. Sch. Employees of Allen Parish Credit Union, 1988—94. Relay for Life chair Am. Cancer Soc., Oakdale, La., 2005; mem. Friends of Glenmora Libr., 2004—. Recipient Award of Merit for Regional Publs., Antique Automobile Club Am., 2002, 2003, 2004, 2005, 2006, Nike award, LA Bus. Profl. Women Club, 2005. Mem.: ASCD, La. Fedn. Bus. and Profl. Women (exec. bd. mem. 2000—, pres. 2003—04), Oakdale Bus. Profl. Women Club (Woman of Yr. award 1985), Cenla Old Car Club, Bus. Profl. Women Club USA (bd. dirs. 2003—04). Baptist. Home: 1424 Evangeline Rd Glenmora LA 71433

BURNS, M. MICHELE, human resources company executive; b. Rincon, Ga. B in bus. adminstrn. summa cum laude, U. Ga., M. Accountancy. Mgmt. Arthur Anderson, 1981-84, mgr., 1984-91, ptnr., 1991-99; v.p. corp. taxes, treas. Delta Airlines, 1999, sr. v.p. fin., treas., 2000, exec. v.p., CFO, 2000—04; exec. v.p., CFO, chief restructuring officer Mirant Corp., Atlanta, 2004—06; exec. v.p., CFO Marsh & McLennan Companies, Inc., NYC, 2006, chmn., Mercer Human Resource Consulting, 2006—. Bd. dirs. Wal-Mart Stores Inc., 2003—, Cisco Systems, Inc., Ivan Allen Co., Atlanta Symphony Orch. Recipient Distinguished Alumna award, U. of Ga. Terry Coll. of Bus., 1993. Office: Marsh & McLennan Companies Inc 1166 Avenue of the Americas New York NY 10036-2774

BURNS, MARCELLINE, retired psychologist, researcher; BA in Psychology, San Diego State U., 1955; MA, Calif. State U., LA, 1969; PhD, U. Calif., Irvine, 1972. Co-founder So. Calif. Rsch. Inst., LA, 1973—2003, ret., 2003. Cons., expert witness alcohol and drug effects on performance, FSTs, HGN, and drug recognition; lectr. in field. Contbr. articles to profl. jours. Recipient Public Svc. award U.S. Dept. Trans., 1993. Achievements include research on alcohol and drug effects, field sobriety tests and drug recognition. Office Phone: 805-382-4696. Personal E-mail: mburns4430@roadrunner.com.

BURNS, MARVIN GERALD, lawyer; b. LA, July 3, 1930; s. Milton and Belle (Cytron) B.; m. Barbara Irene Fisher, Aug. 23, 1953; children: Scott Douglas, Jody Lynn, Bradley Frederick. BA, U. Ariz., 1951; JD, Harvard U., 1954. Bar: Calif. 1955. With US Army, 1955—56. Mem.: Beverly Hills Tennis, Sycamore Park Tennis. Home: 10350 Wilshire Blvd Ph 4 Los Angeles CA 90024-4734 Office: 9107 Wilshire Blvd Ste 800 Beverly Hills CA 90210-5533 Home Phone: 310-275-4045; Office Phone: 310-278-6500. Business E-Mail: mburns@lurie-zepeda.com. E-mail: burns5401@aol.com. *I believe that hard work in its time and place, play in its time and place, love, understanding and practice of the golden rule at all times, in all places, a firm belief in truth and honesty and that there is no better land, no better system, no better life than our imperfect, necessary to improve, America, leads to personal fulfillment and a better life for all.*

BURNS, MATTHEW KEVIN, psychology professor; b. Flint, Mich., Sept. 20, 1968; s. Robert Joseph and Ethel Maureen Burns; m. Mary Elizabeth Baldwin, Sept. 1, 1991. BA, Mich. State U., 1991; MA, Andrews U., Mich., 1992, EdS, 1997, PhD, 1999. Cert. sch. psychologist Mich. Sch. psychologist South Bend Schs., Ind., 1993—94, Bay Arenac Ind. Sch. Dist., Bay City, Mich., 1994—96, Midland Pub. Schs., Mich., 1996—99; assoc. prof. Ctrl. Mich. U., Mt. Pleasant, 1999—2004, U. Minn., Mpls., 2004—. Co-author, co-editor: Handbook of Response to Intervention, 2006. Recipient Provost award, Ctrl. Much. U., 2004. Mem.: Mich. Assn. Sch. Psychologists (pres. 2000—01), Nat. Assn. Sch. Psychologists. Office: 346 Elliott Hall 75 E River Rd Minneapolis MN 55455

BURNS, MAX, former congressman; b. Millen, Ga., Nov. 8, 1948; m. Lora Dean Black, 1972; children: Andrew, Nathan. B in Indsl. Engring., Ga. Tech. U., 1973; M in Bus. Info. Sys., Ga. State U., 1977, PhD in Bus. Adminstrn., 1987. Mgr. Oxford Industries, N.Am. Mission Bd. So. Bapt. Conv.; prof. info. sys. Ga. So. U. Coll. Bus. Adminstrn., Statesboro; congressman 12 Dist. Ga. U.S. Ho. Reps., 2003—05. Instr., Australia, New Zealand, Republic of Korea; cons. Gulfstream Aerospace and Grinnell Corp. Mem. CSRA Regional Devel. Ctr.; former chmn. regional 1 adv. coun. Ga. Dept. Industry, Trade, and Tourism; mem. Screven County Commn., 1993—98, chmn., 1997—98; deacon Jackson Bapt. Ch.; bd. dirs. Screven County Livestock Assn., Cmty. Christian Sch. Bd., Ga. Limousin Assn. 1st lt. USAR. Republican.

BURNS, MICHAEL J., automotive executive; b. Monticello, Ind., Mar. 1, 1952; B of Mech. Engring., Kettering U., 1975; MBA, U. Pa., 1979. Ops. mgr. Delco electronics GM Corp., Singapore, 1981—85, from treas. office staff to dir. overseas fin. analysis NY, 1985—87, from head hybrid electronics ops. to v.p. vehicle sys. bus. unit Delco electronics Singapore, 1988—93, v.p. Delphi Harrison thermal sys. Lockport, NY, 1994—95, v.p., gen. mgr. Delphi Delco electronics sys., 1996—98, group v.p., pres. Europe divsn. Zurich, Switzerland, 1998—2004; chmn. pres. & CEO Dana Corp., Toledo, 2004—. Supervisory bd. Adam Opel AG; bd. dirs. Saab Automobile AB; key exec. Wharton Sch.-U. Pa. Mem.: European Automobile Mfrs. Assn. (bd. dirs.), Soc. Automotive Engrs., Swiss-Am. C. of C. (bd. dirs.). Office: Dana Corp PO Box 1000 Toledo OH 43697-1000*

BURNS, MICHAEL JOSEPH, operations and sales-marketing executive; b. Passaic, NJ, Feb. 18, 1943; s. Michael Joseph and Ellen Kathryn B.; m. Emma Anne, Dec. 19, 1964; children: Michael, Jeffrey, Tricia, Stephen. BA in English, William Paterson Univ., Wayne, NJ, 1964; JD, Seton Hall U., Newark, 1975. Bar: NJ 1975. Purchasing analyst Am. Brands Co., 1972-75; div. purchasing mgr. Dutch Boy Paints, NL Industries, 1975-76; v.p. purchasing Dutch Boy, Inc., 1977-78; pres., gen. mgr. Dutch Boy, Inc. (Dutch Boy coatings div.), 1978-80; pres., CEO Kroehler Mfg. Co., Naperville, Ill., 1980-88; pres., COO Rymer Co., Rolling Meadows, Ill., 1983-88; pres. Emerald Group, Lake Forest, Ill., 1989-90; pres., CEO Designer Foods, Inc., Wilmington, Del., 1990-91; chmn., pres., CEO SeaWatch Internat., Ltd., Easton, Md., 1991-99; pres., CEO Pioneer Human Svcs., Seattle, 1999—2007; ret. Bd. dirs. Second Chance, 1999-07, Eastside Acad., 2001-07. Served to capt. USMCR, 1964-67, Vietnam. NJ State scholar; recipient Disting. Alumni award Wm. Paterson Univ. Mem. ABA, Am. Arbitration Assn. Presbyterian. Office Phone: 206-768-1990. Personal E-mail: mike.burns@p-h-s.com.

BURNS, MICHAEL KENT, retired educator, chemical dependency counselor; b. Sarasota, Fla., Jan. 4, 1945; s. Richard Andrew and Lilian Ida (Kent) B. BA (Univ. scholar), Capital U., 1967; MA, Ohio State U., 1969; ednl. staff personnel adminstrv. specialist cert., Cleve. State U., 1978; cert. sch. counselor Cleve. State U., 1982, chem. dependency counselor, nat. counselor. Grad. tchg. fellow Ohio State U., 1967-69; instr. Wright State U., 1969-70; tchr. Spanish Euclid HS, Ohio, 1970—76, tchr. social studies, 1977-81, psychology, 1982-89; at-risk counselor Euclid Cen. Middle Sch., 1990-99; ret.; summer intern Euclid Fisher Body Plant, Gen. Motors Corp., 1978; fellow Taft Inst. Govt., 1978, 79; career guidance inst. intern Cleve. Met. Jobs Coun., 1980; group facilitator insight and aftercare chem. dependency programs, peer counseling co-facilitator, 1981-89; chem. dependency counselor Glenbeigh Adolescent Hosp., Cleve., 1983-86; coordinator summer youth employment and tng. program City of Euclid, Ohio, 1987-88; mental health therapist Lorain County Coun. on Alcoholism and Drug Abuse, Inc., 1988—; detoxication counselor addictive disease program Laurelwood Hosp., Willoughby, Ohio, 1989-91; internat. presenter in field. Golden Apple Achiever award Ashland Oil Co., 1990; counselor Lorain County Ct., 1999-2000, Homeless Men's Program Recovery Resources, 2003; clin. supr. North Coast Correctional Treatment Facility, 2001, Acad. Inc. Driver Intervention Program, 2006-; case mgr. St. Vincent Charity Hosp., 2004; resource mgr. Luth. Met. Ministries, 2005. Mem. Euclid Tchrs. Assn. (v.p. 1974-76, pres. 1977-78), Ohio Retired Tchrs. Assn., Greater Cleve. Retired Tchrs. Assn., Nat. Retired Tchrs. Assn., Nat. Assn. Forensic Counselors. Democrat. Unitarian. Home: 21215 Detroit Rd #213C Cleveland OH 44116-2221 Office Phone: 216-272-0012. Personal E-mail: mburns34@cox.net.

BURNS, NED HAMILTON, civil engineering educator; b. Magnolia, Ark., Nov. 25, 1932; s. Andrew Louis and Ila Mae (Martin) B.; m. Martha Ann Fontaine, June 11, 1955; children: Kathryn Jane, Stephanie Ann, Michael Everett. BS, U. Tex., 1954, MS, 1958; PhD, U. Ill., 1962. Registered profl. engr., Tex. Instr. U. Tex., Austin, 1957-59, asst. prof., 1962-65, assoc. prof., 1965-70, prof. civil engring., 1970-83, Zarrow Centennial prof. engring., 1983—; assoc. dean engring. for acad. affairs, 1989-93; dir. Ferguson Structural Engring. Lab., 1994-97. Rsch. asst. U. Ill., Urbana, 1959-62. Author: (with T. Y. Lin) Design of Prestressed Concrete Structures, 1981 (McGraw Hill Book of Month 1982), S.I. Version-Design of Prestressed Concrete Structures, 1982, Legend of Post-Tensioning, 2005; contbr. articles to profl. jours. With US Army, 1955—57. Recipient Gen. Dynamics Tchg. award U. Tex. Coll. Engring., 1965, AMOCO Tchg. award, 1983, Martin P. Korn award, 1993, Blunk Meml. Professorship Tchg. award U. Tex., 1996-97; named Disting. Grad. U. Tex., 2005. Fellow: Post-Tensioning Inst. (bd. dirs. 1975—, Legends award, 2005), Am. Soc. Civil Engrs.(com. chmn. 1975—, T. Y. Lin award 1994), Prestressed Concrete Inst. (com. mem. 1968-, Martin Korn award for best paper 1993, Disting. Educator award 2000); mem. NAE, NSPE (chpt. pres. 1970), Am. Concrete Inst. (bd. dirs. 1983-87, Joe Kelley award 1990, Structural Rsch. award 2005, Arthur Anderson award 2006), Tex. Soc. Profl. Engring. (Young Engr. of Yr. award 1970, Travis chpt. Engr. of Yr. award 1987). Democrat. Baptist. Home: 3917 Rockledge Dr Austin TX 78731-2921 Office: U Tex Dept Civil Engring Austin TX 78712

BURNS, PATRICK OWEN, venture capital company executive; b. Yonkers, NY, Aug. 6, 1937; s. Edward Dermott and Anne L. (Gallagher) B.; m. Barbara Hope Van Riper, Nov. 4, 1967; children: Patrick Owen, Elizabeth Willett. AB, Dartmouth Coll., 1959; LLB cum laude, Harvard U., 1962. Bar: N.Y. 1964, U.S. Dist. Ct. (so. dist.) N.Y. 1965. Legal advisor Dept. Coops., Lesotho, 1962-63; assoc. Milbank, Tweed, Hadley & McCloy, NYC, 1963-69; nat. dep. dir. Interracial Coun. Bus. Opportunity, NYC, 1969-75, acting nat. exec. dir., 1972-74; exec. v.p. Minority Equity Capital Co., Inc., NYC, 1971-78, dir., 1974-85, pres., 1978-85; ptnr. Consumer Venture Group, 1985; v.p. R&D Funding Corp., 1986-97; v.p., 1st v.p., sr. v.p. Prudential Securities, 1986-97; sr. advisor Early Stage Enterprises, 1997—2002, AcrossFrontiers Internat., Inc., 1999—2002, Pharmalab, Sydney, 2004—. Bd. dirs., vice chmn. Euclid Sys. Corp.; bd. dirs. Progen Inds., Ltd., Brisbane, Australia, FirmView, Inc., ChemGenex Pharms., Melbourne, Australia; chmn. StablEyes, Inc.; cons. Warren Commn., 1964; mem. exec. com. SEC Govt. Bus. Forum on Small Bus. Capital Formation, 1983—85; chmn. Task Force State Capital Formation, 1984. Contbr. articles to profl. jours. Regent L.I. Coll. Hosp., 1976—, vice chmn. bd., 1981—97; trustee Continuum Health Ptnrs., Inc., 2001—, St. Luke's-Roosevelt Hosp. Ctr., 2001—, Beth Israel Med. Ctr., 2001—, Beth Israel Found., 2001—, New Cmty. Found., 1998—; pres. Friends of Bushnell-Sage Libr., Sheffield, Mass., 2002—; trustee Continuum Hospice Care, 2003—, chmn. fin. com., 2004—; candidate NYC City Coun., 1969; bd. dirs. Resources for Children with Spl. Needs., Inc., 1990—, pres., 1994—, acting chmn., 2006—; bd. dirs. Cobble Hill Health Ctr., 1976—, Nat. Ctr. Social Entrepreneurs, 1985—2002, Heights & Hill Cmty. Coun., Inc., 1992—, pres., 1999—2002; dir. New Cmty. Devel. Loan Corp., 2002—. Class of '26 fellow Dartmouth Coll. Mem. Am. Assn. Minority Enterprise Small Bus. Investment Cos. (dir. 1979-85, chmn. bd. 1983-85), Coun. Fgn. Rels., N.Y. Venture Capital Forum, Nat. Assn. Small Bus. Investment Cos. (gov. 1983-85), Sheffield (Mass.) Hist. Soc. (fin. com. 1999—). Democrat. Home: 22 Sidney Pl Brooklyn NY 11201-4607 Office: 2776 Towerview Rd Herndon VA 20171 Office Phone: 718-246-7007. Office Fax: 718-246-5964. Personal E-mail: pburns64@aol.com.

BURNS, PAUL YODER, forester, educator; b. Tulsa, Okla., July 4, 1920; s. Paul Patchin and Mary Emily (Knowles) B.; m. Kathleen Iola Chase, Dec. 4, 1942; children: Virginia B. Belland, Margaret B. Feierabend, Nancy B. McNeill. BS, U. Tulsa, 1941; M in Forestry, Yale U., 1946, PhD, 1949. Asst., assoc. prof. U. Mo., Columbia, 1948-55; prof. forestry La. State U., Baton Rouge, 1955-86, prof. emeritus of forestry, 1986—. Dir. sch. forestry La. State U., Baton Rouge, 1955-76; commr. La. Forestry Commn., Baton Rouge, 1955-76. Editor: Forest Management in Plan & Practice, 1956, Southern Forest Soils, 1959; co-editor: Southern Forestry in Practice, 1977, Christmas Tree Production & Marketing, 1983. Pres. bd. dirs. La. State U. YMCA-YWCA, Baton Rouge, 1957-59; mem. La. Conf. Ch. Bd., Baton Rouge, 1967-73; pres. La. Coun. Human Rels., Baton Rouge, 1987-89; chair bd. dirs. The FISH Good Samaritans, Baton Rouge, 1996. Recipient Disting. Alumnus award U. Tulsa, 1974, Humanitarian award Baton Rouge Coun. Human Rels., 1984, Peacemaking award, Bienville House Ctr. for Peace, Baton Rouge, 1991, Vol. Activist award Baton Rouge, La., 1992, Brotherhood award Baton Rouge chpt. NCCJ, 1995. Fellow Soc. Am. Foresters, La. Soc. Am. Foresters (chmn. 1990, Disting Svc. to Forestry 1989), Phi Kappa Phi, Sigma Xi, Xi Sigma Pi. Presbyterian. Avocations: tennis, piano. Home: 2137 Cedardale Ave Baton Rouge LA 70808-2810 Office: La State Univ Sch Renewable Natural Resources Baton Rouge LA 70803-0001 Office Phone: 225-578-4204. Personal E-mail: pburns@lsu.edu.

BURNS, PETER C., science and engineering educator; b. Fredericton, New Brunswick, Can., Oct. 17, 1966; came to U.S., 1995; s. Carman George Burns and Ruth Joyce Linden; m. Tammy E. Chesley, 1992; children: Kelson O., Sarah V. BSc with honors, U. New Brunswick, Can., 1988; MSc in Geology, U. Western Ont., Can., 1990; PhD in Geology, U. Man., Can., 1994. Rsch. fellow U. Cambridge, England, 1994-95; post doctoral fellow U. N.Mex., 1995-96; vis. asst. prof. U. Ill., Urbana-Champaign, 1996-97; from asst. prof. to assoc. prof., dir. grad. studies U. Notre Dame, 1997-99, assoc. prof., 1999—2002, prof., 2002—, Massman chair dept. civil engring. and geol. sci., 2002—. Contbr. articles to profl. jours. Recipient Donath medal Geol. Soc. Am., 1999, award Mineral. Soc. Am., 2001. Fellow: Mineral. Soc. Am. (life MSA award 2001); mem.: Am. Chem. Soc., Mineral. Assn. Can. (councillor 1997—2005, Young Scientist medal 1998, Hawley medal 1997). Achievements include research in mineralogy and crystallography, mineralogy of nuclear waste disposal, environmental mineralogy, mineral crystal structures and crystal chemistry, mineral structure energetics, mineral paragenesis. Office: U Notre Dame 160 Fitzpatrick Engring Notre Dame IN 46556 E-mail: pburns@nd.edu.

BURNS, REBECCA ANN, elementary school educator, librarian; b. Waynesboro, Pa., Dec. 28, 1946; d. John Albert and Betty Jane (Mason) Castelluccio; m. Terry Lee Burns, 1966; children: Todd Darin, Derick Jason. BS, Shippensburg U., 1968, postgrad., 1969, 70, 75, Pa. State U., 1973-74, 87, 89, U. Wyo., 1989. Cert. elem. tchr., libr. sci. tchr. Pa. Migrant educator Waynesboro (Pa.) Sch. Dist., 1971-72, elem. tchr., 1968-71, 74-79, Mifflin County Sch. Dist., Lewistown, Pa., 1972-74; test examiner Office Personnel Mgmt. U.S. Govt., State College, Pa., 1982-83; instr. Adult Basic Edn.- Gen. Edn. Devel. and Career Tng. Mifflin County Job Tng. Partnership Act, Lewistown, 1985-86; libr. State Correctional Inst.-Rockview, Bellefonte, Pa., 1983-85, Midd-West Sch. Dist., Middleburg, Pa., 1986-89; edn. adminstrn. assoc., pupil transp. specialist Pa. Dept. Edn., Harrisburg, 1989-90, edn. adminstrn. specialist, coord. non pub. sch. svcs., 1990-93, basic edn. assoc., youth edn. and employment coord., 1993-97, basic edn. assoc., work-based learning coord., 1997—2005; pvt. practice Harrisburg, 2005—. Lobbyist for stamp commemorating adult edn.; educator for women's rights devel. and implementation of regis. apprenticeships for youth in Pa.; vol. advocate for ethics and state govt. reform. Mem.: AARP, Fedn. State Cultural and Ednl. Profl. (founding mem. retirees local chpt. 2005), Apprenticeship Assn., Pa. Fedn. Tchrs., Eastern Seaboard Apprenticeship Conf., Nat. Assn. State and Territorial Apprenticeship Dirs., Alliance Ret. Ams. (charter, charter Pa. chpt.), Aux. to Pa. Ret. State Police. Roman Catholic. Avocations: reading, collecting antique prints, travel. Home and Office: 2412 Abbey Ln Harrisburg PA 17112 Personal E-mail: racb1228@aol.com.

BURNS, RED, academic administrator; 4 children. Joined, co-founder, interactive telecomms. program Tisch Sch. Arts NYU, 1979—, chair, interactive telecomms. program Tisch Sch. Arts, 1981—, Tokyo Broadcasting System Prof. Communications, 1997—. Bd. dirs. Media Lab Europe, The Visual Media Task Force, The Convergent Media Group; mem. adv. bd. The N.Y. Times Digital Company; juror On-Line Journalism Awards, Nat. Mag. Awards, Webby Awards; prin. investigator three on-going rsch. programs funded by Interval Rsch., Intel and Microsoft. Creator CD-ROM on chaos theory, Electronic Neighborhood. Bd. dirs. The Charles H. Revson Found.; ProBono.net; Ivrae Inst.; mentor The Ross Sch. Named one of 100 top leaders of N.Y.'s economy, Crain's N.Y., top 100 most influential women in bus., Top 25 Influential People on the Net, Newsweek's 50 for the Future, N.Y. Cyber Sixty, N.Y. Mag.; named to Silicon Alley's 100; recipient Matrix award, 1997, All-Star Educator award, Crain's, Award of Excellence in Sci. and Tech., Mayor of N.Y.C., Spl. Educator award, Art Dir. Club, Chrysler Design Award, 2002. Mem.: N.Y. New Media Assn. (founding mem.). Office: NYU Tisch Sch Arts 721 Broadway 4th Fl New York NY 10003-6807

BURNS, RICHARD DEAN, historian, educator, writer; b. Des Moines, June 16, 1929; s. Richard B. and Luella (Everling) B.; m. Frances R. Sullivan, Jan. 14, 1950 (dec. July 1993); 1 son, Richard Dean; m. Glenda F. Burns, Sept. 21, 1996; stepchildren: Scott E. Burns, Kent C. Burns, Dana Burns Mayadag. BS with honors, U. Ill., 1957, MA, 1958, PhD, 1960. Prof. emeritus Calif. State U., LA, 1960-92, prof., 1970-92, chmn. dept., 1969-72, 86-92. Pubr./pres. Regina Books, 1980—; vis. lectr. L.A. City Coll., Whittier Coll., U. Minn., Mpls., 1964-65, UCLA, U. So. Calif.; program cons., lectr. Western Ctr., NEH, 1973-75. Author: (with W. Fisher) Armament and Disarmament, 1964, (with D. Urquidi) Disarmament in Historical Perspective, 4 vols, 1969, (with E. Bennett) Diplomats in Crisis,

1975; (with L. Brune) The Quest for Missile Defenses: 1944-2003, 2004; editor: Chronology of the Cold War, 2005, An Arms Control and Disarmament Bibliography, 1977, Guide to American Foreign Relations Since 1770, 1982, (with M. Leitenberg) The Wars in Vietnam, Cambodia, and Laos, 1945-82, 1984, Harry S. Truman: A Bibliography of His Times and Presidency, 1984, Herbert Hoover: A Bibliography of His Times and Presidency, 1991, Encyclopedia of Arms Control and Disarmament, 3 vols., 1993, (with A. DeConde, F. Logevall) Encyclopedia of American Foreign Policy, 3 vols., 2002, (with Lester Brune) Chronological History of U.S. Foreign Relations, 3 vols., 2002, Chronology of the Cold War, 2005; bibliographer, series editor: War/Peace Bibliographies, 1973—; contbr. articles to profl. jours. Served with USAF, 1947-56. Named Univ. Outstanding Prof., 1978-79; Social Sci. Rsch. Coun. fellow, 1959-60; grantee NEH, 1978-79, U.S. Inst. Peace, 1991-92. Mem. Conf. on Peace Rsch. (nat. coun. 1970-72), Soc. Historians Am. Fgn. Rels. (nat. coun. 1986-89), Phi Kappa Phi, Phi Alpha Theta. Office: Regina Books PO Box 280 Claremont CA 91711-0280

BURNS, RICHARD GORDON, retired lawyer, writer, consultant; b. Stockton, Calif., May 15, 1925; s. Earl Gordon and Alberta Viola (Whale) Burns; m. Eloise Estelle Beil, June 23, 1951 (div. May 25, 1985); children: Kenneth Charles, Donald Gordon. AA with honors, U. Calif., Berkeley, 1948; AB, Stanford U., 1949, JD, 1951. Atty. Clausen & Burns, San Francisco, 1951—61; cons. Wyo. Pacific Oil Co., LA, 1956—; pvt. practice Corte Madera, Calif., 1961—86; pub. Good Book Pub., Kihei, Hawaii, 1991—. Advisor God's Way Ministry, Inc., 1997—; exec. dir. Freedom Ranch Maui, Inc., 2003; cons. United Info. Tech. Inst., 2003—. Editor: Stanford Law Rev., 1950; co-author (with Bill Pittman): Courage To Change, 1998; author (as Dick B.): New Light on Alcoholism: God, Sam Shoemaker and A.A., 1999; author: The Akron Genesis of Alcoholics Anonymous, 1998, Anne Smith's Journal, 1998, Dr. Bob and His Library, 1998, The Good Book and The Big Book: A.A.'s Roots in the Bible, 1998, The Oxford Group and Alcoholics Anonymous, 1998, That Amazing Grace, 1996, Turning Point: A History of Early A.A.'s Spiritual Roots and Successes, 1997, Good Morning!Quiet Time, Morning Watch, Meditation, and Early A.A., 1998, The Books Early AAs Read for Spiritual Growth, 1999, Utilizing A.A.'s Spiritual Roots for Recovery Today, 1999, The Golden Text of A.A., 1999, By the Power of God, 2000, Why Early A.A. Succeeded: The Good Book in Alcoholics Anonymous Yesterday and today, 2001, God and Alcoholism: A Growing Opportunity in the 21st Century, 2002, Hope!: The Story of Geraldine Owen Delaney, Alina Lodge and Recovery, 2002, Cured! A Proven Solution for Alcoholics and Addicts, 2005, When Early AAs Were Cured and Why, 2005, The James Club and the Original A.A. Program's Absolute Essentials, 2005, Making Known the Biblical Roots of A.A., 2006;: Twelve Steps for You, 2006, The First Nationwide AA Hist. Conf., 2006, Henrietta B. Seiberling: Ohio's Lady With A Cause, 2006, The Good Book- Big Book Guidebook, 2006, The Conversion of Bill W., 2006, A New Way Out, 2006, A New Way In, 2006, Real Twelve Step Fellowship History, 2006, Introduction to the Sources and Founding of A.A., 2007. Pres. Almonte Improvement Club, Mill Valley, Calif., 1960; dir. Almonte Dist. Sanitary Bd., Marin County, Calif., 1962—64; pres. C. of C., Corte Madera, 1972, Corte Madera Ctr. Merchant Co., 1975, Redwoods Retirement Ctr., Mill Valley, 1980, Cmty. Ch., Mill Valley, 1971. Sgt. US Army, 1943—46. Mem.: Orgn. Am. Historians, Rsch. Soc. Alcoholism, Internat. Substance Abuse and Addiction Coalition, Assn. Med. Edn. and Rsch. Substance Abuse, Christian Assn. Psychol. Studies, Maui Writers Guild, Am. Hist. Assn., Coalition Prison Evangelists, Stanford Alumni Assn., Alcohol and Drugs History Soc., Phi Beta Kappa, Phi Delta Phi, Delta Tau Delta. Avocations: travel, Bible study, swimming, walking. Office: PO Box 837 Kihei HI 96753-0837 Office Phone: 808-874-4876. Personal E-mail: dickb@dickb.com.

BURNS, RICHARD OWEN, lawyer; b. Bklyn., Nov. 16, 1942; s. James I. and Ida (Shore) B.; m. Lynda Gail Birnbaum, Dec. 24, 1967; children: Marc Adam, Lisa Ann, Susan Danielle. BS, Wilkes Coll., 1964; JD, Bklyn. Law Sch., 1967. Bar: N.Y. 1967, U.S. Dist. Ct. (so. dist.) N.Y. 1969, U.S. Dist. Ct. (ea. dist.) N.Y. 1979. Assoc. Clune & O'Brien, Mineola, N.Y., 1967-73, Clune, Burns, White & Nelson, Harrison, N.Y., 1973-78; ptnr. Schurr & Burns, P.C., Spring Valley, N.Y., 1978-98; pvt. practice, Chestnut Ridge, N.Y., 1998—. Bd. dirs. Rockland County unit Am. Cancer Soc., West Nyack, NY, 1979-92, pres., 1981-83; Vets. Meml. Assn., Congers, NY, 1980-86; coun. mem. Wilkes U., Wilkes-Barre, Pa., 1995-2004. Recipient Reese D. Jones award Wilkes Coll. Jr. C. of C., 1964. Mem.: ATLA, NY State Trial Lawyers Assn., NY State Bar Assn., Rockland County Bar Assn. Democrat. Jewish. Home: 140 Waters Edge Congers NY 10920-2622 Office: 500 Chestnut Ridge Rd Chestnut Ridge NY 10977-5646 Office Phone: 845-356-0300.

BURNS, RICHARD RAMSEY, lawyer; b. Duluth, Minn., May 3, 1946; s. Herbert Morgan and Janet (Strobel) B.; children: Jennifer, Brian; m. Elizabeth Murphy, June 15, 1984 BA distinction, U. Mich., 1968, JD magna cum laude, 1971. Bar: Calif. 1972, U.S. Dist. Ct. (no. dist.) Calif. 1972, U.S. Ct. Appeals (9th cir.) 1972, Minn. 1976, U.S. Dist. Ct. Minn. 1976, Wis. 1983, U.S. Tax. Ct. 1983. Assoc. Orrick, Herrington, Rowley & Sutcliffe, San Francisco, 1971—76; ptnr. Hanft, Fride, P.A., Duluth, 1976—. V.p. bus. devel. and gen. counsel Morgan Murphy Stas., Madison, Wis., 1982—. Chmn. Duluth-Superior Area Cmty. Found., 1988-90; chair United Way Greater Duluth, Inc., 1998-99; bd. dirs. Northland Coll., Ashland, Wis. Fellow Am. Coll. Trust and Estate Counsel (state chair); mem. Calif. Bar Assn., Wis. Bar Assn., Minn. Bar Assn. (past. exec. com., past chmn. probate and trust coun.), 11th Dist. Bar Assn. (past pres., past chmn. ethics com.), Arrowhead Estate Planning Coun. (pres. 1980), Northland Country Club (pres. 1982), Boulders Club, Silverleaf Golf Club and Spa, Kitchi Gammi Club (bd. dirs.) Republican. Avocations: travel, golf, reading, fishing. Home: 180 Paine Farm Rd Duluth MN 55804-2609 Office: Hanft Fride PA 1000 First Bank Pl 130 W Superior St Ste 1000 Duluth MN 55802-2056 Home Phone: 218-525-3995; Office Phone: 218-722-4766. Business E-Mail: rrb@hanftlaw.com.

BURNS, ROBERT, JR., retired architect, painter; b. Jackson, Miss., Jan. 29, 1936; s. Robert Sr. and Grace Hortense (Inmon) B. BS in Architecture, Ga. Inst. Tech., 1959, BArch, 1960. Registered architect emeritus, Miss. Architect Overstreet, Ware, Ware & Lewis, Jackson, 1961-70, Ware, Lewis & Eaton, Jackson, 1970-71, Jones & Haas, Jackson, 1971-74, Leon Burton & Assocs., Jackson, 1974-75, Glenn Albritton Designer, Jackson, 1975-83, Breland & Farmer, Jackson, 1983-84, The Plan House, Jackson, 1984-86; part-time tchr. art dept. Miss. Coll., 1987; architect Johnny Wynne & Assocs., Ltd., Jackson, 1995-96; ret., 1996. Author: numerous poems, (short stories) My Antique, It Isn't Nice, Marie and Me, Rich Folk Have Roaches, Too, The Snake and Mr. D.; Represented in permanent collections Miss. Mus. Art (Mrs. Horace Hammond award, 1965), Miss. Coll., Hinds Jr. Coll., others, one-man shows include, Miss., Ga., Fla. Tenor soloist 1st Bapt. Ch., Jackson, 1967-68, 1st Christian Ch., Jackson, 1968-71, Covenant Presbyn. Ch., Jackson, 1971-74, Galloway Meml. United Meth. Ch., 1989-91, Northminster Bapt. Ch., Jackson, 1995-97, St. Luke's United Meth. Ch., Jackson, 1991-94, song leader, 1991-94; tenor soloist Woodland Hills Bapt. Ch., Jackson, 98-00; mem. Friends of the Gallery, Mcpl. Art Gallery, Jackson, 1981-93; mem. rev. panel Arts Alliance of Miss., 1989. Sgt. USAR, 1961-67. Mem. Am. Hemerocallis Soc., Inc. Republican. Baptist. Avocations: art, writing, music, gardening. Home: 609 Broadway Ave Jackson MS 39216-3206

BURNS, ROBERT EDWARD, dean, retired history professor; b. Newark, Nov. 3, 1927; s. Joseph Raymond Burns and Vera Wilna Blaisdell; m. Phyllis K. Burns, Sept. 11, 1955. BA, Northeastern U., Boston, 1951; MA, Harvard U., Cambridge, 1957, PhD, 1961. Instr. Northeastern U., 1952; prof. U. Notre Dame, Ind., 1957—95, assoc. dean Ind., 1971—81, dean Ind., 1981—83, ret., 1994. Cons. HS Office Edn., Washington, 1968—70; mem. adv. coun. Ind. Higher Edn. Telecommunication Sys., 1972—77; cons. Nat. Endowment for Humanities, Washington, 1974. Author: (book) Irish Parliamentary Politics 1713-1730, 1989, Irish Parliamentary Politics 1731-1760, 1990, Being Catholic, Being American, The Notre Dame Story 1842-1934, 1999, Being Catholic, Being American, The Notre Dame Story 1934-1952, 2000. Mem. Ind. Com. for Humanities, 1971—72; legis. asst., speech writer for senator Abraham A. Ribicoff US Senate, Washington, 1965. With USCG, 1945—48. Rsch. Grant, ACLS, 1961, SSRC, 1963, APS, 1963. Mem.: Am. Philos. Soc., Social Scis. Rsch. Coun., Am. Coun. Socs. Learned, Am. Hist. Assn. Home: 9615-1 Estuary Way Sebastian FL 32958

BURNS, R(OBERT) NICHOLAS, federal agency administrator, former ambassador; b. Buffalo, Jan. 28, 1956; m. Elizabeth Baylies; 3 children. BA summa cum laude in European Hist., Boston Coll., 1978; MA with distinction in Internat. Econs. and Am. Fgn. Policy, Johns Hopkins Sch. Advanced Internat. Studies, 1980. Intern US Embassy Nouakchott, Mauritania, 1980-81; prog. officer A.T. Internat., 1981-82; vice consul and staff asst. to the Amb. in Cairo, Egypt, 1983-85; polit. officer Am. Consulate Gen., Jerusalem, 1985-87; staff officer dept. ops. ctr. and secretariat US Dept. State, 1987-88, spl. asst. to the counselor of the dept. Soviet & Ea. European Affairs, 1989-90, White House dir. Soviet affairs, 1990-93, sr. dir. for Russian, Ukraine & Eurasia affairs & spl. asst. to the Pres., 1993-95, sr. fgn. svc. officer, nat. security coun. staff at the White House, 1991—93, spokesman for Sec. of State, acting asst. sec. pub. affairs, 1995-97, US amb. to Greece Athens, 1997-2001; US permanent rep. NATO, Brussels, 2001—05; under sec. for polit. affairs US Dept. State, Washington, 2005—. Mem. Phi Beta Kappa. Office: US Dept State 2201 C St NW Rm 7240 Washington DC 20520

BURNS, ROBERT PATRICK, law educator; b. NYC, Mar. 23, 1947; s. Frances William and Helen (Moskol) B.; m. Mary Elizabeth Griffin, June 7, 1975; children: Matthew, Elizabeth. AB, Fordham U., 1969; JD, U. Chgo., 1974, PhD, 1982. Bar: Ill. 1974, U.S. Dist. Ct. (no. dist.) Ill. 1974, U.S. Ct. Appeals (7th cir.) 1977, U.S. Supreme Ct. 1978. Litigation atty. Legal Assistance Found., Chgo., 1974-79, dir. atty. training, 1979; gen. counsel Ill. Legis. Commn., Springfield, 1979-80; prof. law Northwestern U., Chgo., 1980—. Tchr. Nat. Inst. Trial Advocacy, South Bend, Ind., 1981—. Author: A Theory of the Trial, 1999, Problems and Materials in Evidence and Trial Advocacy, 2001, exercises and Problems in Professional Responsibility, 2001, Evidence in Context, 2001; contbr. articles to profl. jours. Bd. dirs. Evanston Dems., Ill., 1984. Kent fellow Danforth Found., 1974, NSF fellow, 1970. Mem. ABA, Soc. for Values in Higher Edn. Roman Catholic. Office: Northwestern U Sch Law 357 E Chicago Ave Chicago IL 60611-3059 E-mail: r-burns@law.northwestern.edu.

BURNS, SANDRA, lawyer, educator; b. Bryan, Tex., Aug. 9, 1949; d. Clyde W. and Bert (Rychlik) B.; 1 son, Scott. BS, U. Houston, 1970; MA, U. Tex., 1972, PhD, 1975; JD, St. Mary's U., 1978. Bar: Tex. 1978; cert. tchr., adminstr., supr. instrn., Tex. Tchr. Austin Ind. Sch. Dist., Tex., 1970—71; prof. child devel./family life and home econs. edn. Coll. Nutrition, Textiles and Human Devel. Tex. Women's U., Denton, 1974—75; instrnl. devel. asst. Office of Ednl. Resources divsn. instr U. Tex. Health Sci., San Antonio, 1976—77; legis. aide William T. Moore Tex. Senate, Austin, 1978, com. clk.-counsel, 1979; legal cons. Colombotti & Assocs., Aberdeen, Scotland, 1980; corp. counsel 1st Internat. Oil and Gas, Inc., 1983; contracted atty. Humble Exploration Co., Inc., Dallas, 1984; assoc. Smith, Underwood, Dallas, 1986—88; pvt. practice Dallas, 1988—; mem. grad. faculty Tex. A&M U., Commerce, 2003—04. Atty. contracted to Republic Energy Inc., Bryan, Tex., 1981-82, ARCO, Dallas, 1985; vis. lectr. Tex. A&M U., fall 1981, summer, 1981; lectr. home econs. Our Lady of the Lake Coll., San Antonio, fall, 1975; legal advisor Tex. Old Missions & Forts Restoration Assn.; chair First Internat. Oil & Gas Conf. Contbr. articles to profl. jours. Mem.: Dallas Bar Assn. (chair ADR sect.), Coll. of the State Bar of Tex., Learning Disabilities Assn. Tex. (bd. mem. 2005—06). Achievements include development of a special needs church program that provides care for all ages. Office: Preston Commons West 300 8117 Preston Rd Dallas TX 75225 Office Phone: 972-601-2176.

BURNS, SCOTT, columnist; b. Cambridge, Mass., Nov. 9, 1940; s. Robert Milton Clark Burns and Joanne (Mahoney) Blasius; m. Allegra Wendy Eames, Dec. 11, 1965 (div. Sept. 1990); children: Jasper Bayard (dec.), Oliver Byron; m. Carolyn Jo Schroeder, Jan. 2, 1995. BS, MIT, 1962. Columnist, editor Boston (Mass.) Herald Am., 1977-83; columnist Dallas (Tex.) Morning News, 1985—; syndicated columnist, 1980—. Author: Squeeze It Til The Eagle Grins, 1972, Home, Inc., 1975; co-author: The Coming Generational Storm, 2004. Office: Dallas Morning News Communications Ctr PO Box 655237 Dallas TX 75265-5237 Home: 50 Calle Sin Sonte Santa Fe NM 87507 Personal E-mail: sburnscolumn@yahoo.com. Business E-Mail: sburns@dallasnews.com.

BURNS, SCOTT PATRICK, lawyer; b. Balt., 1964; BA with honors, Johns Hopkins U., 1986; JD, U. Pa., 1989. Bar: Md. 1989, US Ct. Appeals (Md.), US Ct. Appeals (4th cir.), US Dist. Ct. (dist. Md.). Ptnr. Tydings & Rosenberg, LLP, Balt. Editor: The Defense Line, 1995—99. Named one of Top 20 Lawyers in the next Generation, Balt. Mag., 2003. Mem.: Def. Rsch. Inst., Md. Def. Counsel (mem. exec. com. 1995—2003, pres. 2001—02). Office: Tydings & Rosenberg LLP 100 E Pratt St 26th Fl Baltimore MD 21202 Office Phone: 410-752-9743. Office Fax: 410-727-5460. E-mail: sburns@tydingslaw.com.

BURNS, STEPHANIE A., chemicals executive; PhD in Organic Chemistry, Iowa State U.; post-doctoral student, U. Languedoc-Rousillon, France. Rschr. Dow Corning, Midland, Mich., 1983—87, prod. devel. mgr., electronics industry, 1987—94, dir. women's health, 1994—97, sci., tech. dir., Europe Brussels, 1997—99, industry dir. life scis., Europe to European elec. industry dir., 1999—2000, exec. v.p. Midland, Mich., 2000—03, pres., 2003—, COO, 2003—04, CEO, 2004—, chmn., 2006—. Bd. dirs. Dow Corning, 2000—, Manpower Inc., Chem. Bank Midland area, Mich. Molecular Inst. Adv. bd. Chem. & Engring. News. Bd. trustees Midland Cmty. Ctr. Named Mich. Woman Exec. of Yr., 2003; named one of 100 Most Powerful Women, Forbes Mag., 2005, 2006; recipient Vanguard award, Chem. Edn. Found., 2006. Mem.: Soc. Chem. Industry (mem. exec. com.), Am. Chem. Coun. (bd. dirs.), Am. Chem. Soc. Office: Dow Corning PO Box 994 Midland MI 48686-0994 Office Phone: 989-496-7881. Office Fax: 989-496-6731.

BURNS, STEPHEN GILBERT, lawyer; b. NYC, Apr. 29, 1953; s. Gilbert Leo and Ellen (Scully) B.; m. Joan Louise Wallace, Aug. 6, 1977; children: Christopher, Allison. Student, U. Vienna, Austria, 1974; BA, Colgate U., 1975; JD, George Washington U., 1978. Bar: D.C. 1978, U.S. Ct. Appeals (D.C. cir.) 1980. Atty. Nuclear Regulatory Commn., Washington, 1978-83, dep. chief counsel regional ops. and enforcement, 1983-86, legal asst. to commr., 1986-89, exec. asst. to chmn., 1989-91, dir. Office of Commn. Appellate Adjudication, 1991-94, assoc. gen. counsel, 1994-98, dep. gen. counsel, 1998—. Recipient DSM, Nuclear Regulatory Commn., 2001. Mem. ABA. Presbyterian. Office: US Nuclear Regulatory Commn Office Of Gen Counsel Ms 15B21 Washington DC 20555-0001 Office Phone: 301-415-1740.

BURNS, STEPHEN L., lawyer; b. Tulsa, Okla., Mar. 3, 1965; BBA, Univ. Okla., 1987; JD, Univ. Tex., Austin, 1990. Bar: NY 1991. Assoc. Cravath Swaine & Moore LLP, NYC, 1990—98, ptnr., corp., 1998—. Office: Cravath Swaine & Moore LLP Worldwide Tower 825 Eighth Ave New York NY 10019-7475 Office Phone: 212-474-1146. Office Fax: 212-474-3700. Business E-Mail: sburns@cravath.com.

BURNS, THEODORE WEBER, gastroenterologist; b. New Iberia, La., Apr. 15, 1944; s. James Patout and Mary T. (Weber) B.; m. Linda Ann Cox, Aug. 29, 1970 (dec.); children: Theodore W. Jr., David D., William J., Jennifer L. DDS, Loyola U., New Orleans, 1968; MD, La. State U., 1972. Diplomate Am. Bd. Internal Medicine, Am. Bd. Gastroenterology. Intern, then resident U. Fla., Gainesville, 1972-75, fellow in gastroenterology, 1975-77; asst. prof. medicine Uniformed Svcs. Sch. Medicine, Bethesda, Md., 1977-79; staff physician, ptnr., dir. gastrointestinal rsch. Ochsner Clinic, New Orleans, 1979-86; ptnr., physician Digestive Disease Assocs., Gainesville, 1986—. Contbr. articles to profl. jours. Vol. United Way, Gainesville, 1990. Lt. comdr. USN, 1977-79. NIH rsch. svc. grantee U. Fla., 1976-77. Fellow ACP, Am. Coll. Gastroenterology; mem. Am. Soc. for Gastrointestinal Endoscopy, Alpha Omega Alpha. Roman Catholic. Avocation: water sports. Office: Digestive Disease Assocs 6400 W Newberry Rd Ste 302 Gainesville FL 32605-6604

BURNS, THOMAS DAVID, lawyer; b. Andover, Mass., Apr. 4, 1921; s. Joseph Lawrence and Catherine (Horne) Burns; m. Sylvia Lansing, Sept. 14, 1946 (div. 1982); children: Wendy Conquest, Lansing, Diane Longley, Lisa; m. Marjorie Andrew Brown, Mar. 12, 1983. Student, Brown U., 1938—41; LLB, Boston U., 1943. Bar: Mass. 1944, US Dist. Ct. 1948, US Ct. Appeals 1951, US Supreme Ct. 1957. Assoc. Friedman, Atherton, King & Turner, Boston, 1946—50, ptnr., 1950—60; sr. and founding ptnr. Burns & Levinson, Boston, 1960—. Chmn. com. jud. selection Joint Com. Boston and Mass. Bar, 1970—75; mem. jud. coun. Com. of Mass., 1973—77; mem. Mass. Spl. Legis. Commn. Malpractice, 1975—, Mass. Jud. Nominating Commn., 1979—83; spl. counsel Boston City Coun., 1981. Co-editor: Recollections of World War II Phillips Andover, 1938; contbr. articles to profl. jours. Chmn. Planning Bd. Appeals, Andover, 1956—57; trustee Stratton Mountain Vt. Civic Assn., Mus. Am. Textile History, 1992—2004; bd. dir. Birch Hill Corp., Stratton, Vt.; trustee, clk. Pike Sch., Andover; mem. Mass. Hist. Soc., Western Front Assn.; mem. adv. bd. PBS channel II WGBH, Boston; chmn. Andover Rep. Fin. Com., 1953—57; mem. alumni coun. and devel. com. Phillips Andover Acad. Lt. USNR, 1943—46, PTO, ETO. Fellow: ABA, Mass. Def. Lawyers Assn. (dir.), Nat. Assn. R.R. Trial Counsel, Internat. Assn. Def. Counsel, Boston Bar Found., Boston Bar Assn. (mem. exec. coun.), Mass. Bar Assn. (mem. exec. com.), Am. Coll. Trial Lawyers (state chmn. 1968, bd. regents 1970—76, treas. 1974—77), Mass. Bar Found. (trustee), Am. Bar Found., Boston Vis. Nurses Assn., Fed. Ins. and Corp. Counsel, Boston U. Law Sch. (mem. alumni coun. and devel. com., alumni award, Disting. Profl. Svc. award 1996), Boston City Club, Coral Beach Club (Bermuda), North Adnover Country Club, The Country Club (Brookline), Duxbury Yacht Club, Delta Kappa Epsilon; mem.: Am. Coll. Trial Lawyers Found. (dir.). Office: Burns & Levinson 125 Summer St Ste 602 Boston MA 02110-1616 Office Phone: 617-345-3000. Business E-Mail: tburns@burnslev.com.

BURNS, THOMAS PATRICK, orthopedic surgeon; b. Columbus, Ohio, Mar. 23, 1959; s. Paul Allan and Dorothy Ann (Eberly) B.; m. Phoebe Orr, July 14, 1984; children: Kendall Catherine, Peyton Thomas. BA in Biology, U. Tex., 1981; MD, Southwestern Med. Sch., Dallas, 1985. Lic. physician; diplomate Am. Bd. Orthopedic Surgeons. Resident in orthopedics U. Cin. Med. Ctr., 1985-90; fellow in sports medicine Steadman Hawkins Clin., Vail, Colo., 1990-91; orthopedic surgeon U. Cin. Med. Ctr., 1985-90; sports medicine fellow Steadman Hawkins Clinic, Vail, Colo., 1990-91; orthopedic surgeon Tex. Bone & Joint Inst., Austin, 1991—; pvt. practice Austin. Team physician U.S. Olympic Ski Team, 1991—, vol. physician, 1991—; team physician St. Edwards U., Austin, 1992—. Contbr. articles to profl. jours., chpt. to book. Com. mem. Am. Cancer Soc., Austin, 1994. Named. Gold Club Mem. YMCA of Austin, 1993, Hon. Letterman St. Edward's U., Austin, 1994. Fellow Am. Acad. Orthopedic Surgeons; mem. Hawkins Shoulder Soc., Tex. Sports Medicine Soc. Roman Catholic. Avocations: skiing, hunting, golf, tennis. Office: 5656 Bee Caves Rd West Lake Hills TX 78746-5280 Office Phone: 512-329-6644.*

BURNS, THOMAS SAMUEL, history professor; b. Michigan City, Ind., June 7, 1945; m. Carol Ann Morris, June 29, 1968; 1 child, Catherine Elizabeth. AB, Wabash Coll., 1967; postgrad., Am. Sch. Classical Studies, Athens, summer 1967; MA, U. Mich., 1968, PhD, 1974. Asst. prof. history Emory U., Atlanta, 1974-80, assoc. prof., 1980-85, Samuel Candler Dobbs prof. history, 1985—, chmn. dept. history, 1989-92, 2006—07. Dir. summer seminar for sch. tchrs. NEH, 1985, 88; adj. prof. U. Windsor, Ont., 1978, 79; vis. rsch. prof. Kommission für alte Geschichte und Epigraphik des deutschen archäologischen Inst. in München, 1982; vis. rsch. prof. Römisch-Germanische Kommission des deut. arch. Inst., Frankfurt, 1982; Gastprof. U. Augsburg, 1986; co-dir. of Archaeological excavations in Passau, Germany, 1978-79, Manching, Germany, 1985, Pecs, Hungary, 1998. Author: The Ostrogoths: Kingship and Society, 1980, A History of the Ostrogoths, 1984, (with B.H. Overbeck) Rome and the Germans as Seen in Coinage, 1987, Barbarians within the Gates of Rome, 1994; (with J.W. Eadie) Urban Centers and Rural Realities, 2000, Rome and the Barbarians 100 B.C.-A.D. 400, 2003; (with H. Bender, F. Fazekas, Z. Visy) The Roman Settlement near Barbac, Komitat Baranya, Hungary, 2007; contbr. articles to profl. jours. With U.S. Army, 1969-71. Recipient Emory Williams Disting. Teaching award Emory U., 1982, Thomas Jefferson award Emory U., 2004, Student Govt. Disting. Tchg. award Emory U., 2007; Fulbright fellow Fed. Republic Germany, 1986, Boak fellow in ancient history U. Mich., 1971-74; Disting. Vis. scholar-in-residence U. Adelaide, Australia. Mem. Medieval Acad. Am. (nominating com. 1987-88), Ga. Classical Assn., AAUP (pres. Emory U. chpt. 1983-84), Phi Beta Kappa, Omicron Delta Kappa. Avocations: camping, fishing, wilderness canoeing, kayaking. Office: Emory U Dept History Atlanta GA 30322-0001 Office Phone: 404-727-6555. Business E-Mail: histsb@emory.edu.

BURNS, TONI ANTHONY, artist; b. LA, Sept. 6, 1937; d. Earle Francis and LaVerne Myrtle (Holmberg) Anthony; m. George Orin Burns, May 14, 1965; children: Robert Anthony, James Randolph. BFA, Calif. State U. Long Beach, 1959, postgrad., 1960. Cert. secondary tchr. Calif. Interior decorator Ruth Connor Interiors, Downey, Calif., 1960—62; tech. illustrator N.Am. Rockwell Corp., Downey, 1962—64, McDonnell-Douglas Aircraft, Long Beach, 1964—65; graphic layout artist Beckman Instruments, Fullerton, Calif., 1968—70; owner, creator Original Art Rock Owls, San Juan Capistrano, Calif., 1970—78; custom jewelry designer Jewelry by Toni Burns, San Juan Capistrano, 1979—98; jewelry designer, ptnr. SuperNatural Art, San Juan Capistrano, 1999—. Wholesale exhibitor L.A. Gift Show, 1971-78, Beckman Handcrafts, L.A., 1982. Juried shows include Village West Gallery, Laguna Beach, Calif., summers 1971-75, Art-A-Fair Festival, Laguna Beach, 1984-86, Downey Art Mus., 1992, Fine Arts Pavillion, 1993. Recipient 1st pl. San Clemente Art Gallery, 1984, 99. Mem. Am. Craft Coun., Metal Arts Soc. So. Calif., Bowers Mus. Avocations: family genealogy, travel, photography. Office Phone: 949-388-4309. Business E-Mail: sales@supernaturalart.com.

BURNS, URSULA M., printing company executive; b. NYC, Sept. 20, 1958; m. Lloyd Bean; children: Malcolm, Melissa. BS, Poly. Inst., 1980; MS in Mech. Engring., Columbia U., NYC, 1981. Mech. engr., held several positions in engring., including product devel. and planning Xerox Corp., Stamford, Conn., 1980, exec. asst. to chmn. & CEO Paul A. Allaire, 1991, lead several bus. teams, 1992—2000, sr. v.p. corp. strategic svc., 2000—02, pres. bus. group ops., 2002—07, pres., 2007—. Bd. dirs. Hunt Corp., Banta Corp., U. Rochester Med. Sch., Am. Express, Boston Sci. Corp., FIRST, PQ Corp., Rochester Bus. Alliance, Xerox Corp., 2007—.

Named one of 50 Most Powerful Women in Bus., Fortune mag., 2006, 50 Women to Watch, Wall St. Jour., 2006, Next 20 Female CEOs, Pink Mag. & Forté Found., 2006. Mem.: NAM (bd. dirs.), Indsl. Mgmt. Coun. Rochester (bd. dirs.). Office: Xerox Corp 800 Long Ridge Rd Stamford CT 06904 Office Phone: 203-968-3000.*

BURNS, WILLIAM EARL, historian; b. Chgo., Nov. 17, 1959; s. William Burns and Mary Sargent. BA, Shimer Coll., 1980; MA, San Francisco State U., 1986; PhD, U. Calif., Davis, 1994. Lectr. Howard U., Washington, 2005—06, George Wash. U., 2006—. Author: (non-fiction book) Science and Technology in Colonial America, 2005, An Age of Wonders, 2002, (reference book) Witch Hunts in Europe and America, 2003, Science in the Enlightenment, 2003, The Scientific Revolution, 2003. Vol. Friends SE Libr., Washington, 2002—. Home Phone: 202-547-2012. Personal E-mail: williamburns@verizon.net.

BURNS, WILLIAM GLENN, lawyer; b. Shreveport, La., Jan. 13, 1949; s. Carrol and Doris Yvonne (Broadway) B.; m. Linda Roach, Aug. 14, 1971 (div. 1981); m. Marilyn Waites, Oct. 28, 1982 (div. 1992); 1 child, Brandon Nicholas; m. Marianne Everard, Aug. 15, 1992. BS, La. State U., 1971, JD, 1973. Bar: La. 1973, US Ct. Appeals (5th cir.) 1974, US Dist. Ct. (ea. dist.) La. 1976, US Ct. Appeals (11th cir.) 1981, US Dist. Ct. (mid. dist.) La. 1985, US Supreme Ct. 1986. Asst. atty. gen. La. Dept. Justice, New Orleans, 1973-76; assoc. Murray & Murray, New Orleans, 1976-80; asst. U.S. atty. US Dept. Justice, New Orleans, 1980-85; ptnr. Monroe & Lemann, New Orleans, 1985-91; spl. counsel Hoffman, Sutterfield, New Orleans, 1992; ptnr. Hailey, McNamara, New Orleans, 1993—. Fellow Inst. of Politics Loyola U., 1978; adj. faculty Tulane U. Law Sch., 1997—. Editor: Consumer Relations and Bank Holding Companies, 1972. Del. Nat. Dem. Mid-Term Conf., La., 1978; mem. bd. devel. Mercy Hosp., New Orleans, 1979, mem. met. area com., 1988-91, curriculum com. 1988, 89. Mem. ABA, La. Bar Assn. Republican. Baptist. Avocations: sports, Am. history, La. polit. history. Office: Hailey McNamara Hall Larmann Papale 1 Galleria Blvd Metairie LA 70001-2082 Business E-Mail: gburns@hmhlp.com.

BURNS, WILLIAM JOSEPH, ambassador, former federal agency administrator; b. Ft. Bragg, NC, Apr. 4, 1956; m. Lisa Carty, 2 children. BA in Hist., LaSalle U., 1978; M Internat. Rels., Oxford U., PhD, 1981. With US Fgn. Svc., 1982—, polit. officer Amman, Jordan, 1982—84, staff mem. Bur. Near East Affairs, staff mem. Office of Dep. Sec. State; spl. asst. to Pres., sr. dir. Near East, South Asian Affairs NSC; acting dir., prin. dep. dir. policy planning staff US Dept. State; min.-counselor for polit. affairs US Fgn. Svc., Moscow; exec. sec. and spl. asst. to sec. US Dept. State, US amb. to Kingdom of Jordan Amman, 1998—2001, asst. sec. Bur. Near Eastern Affairs Washington, 2001—05, interim under sec. for polit. affairs, 2005, US amb. to Russian Fedn. Moscow, 2005—. Author: Economic Aid and American Policy Toward Egypt, 1955-1981, 1985. Recipient Disting. Honor award State Dept., James Clement Dunn award, Presdl. Disting. Svc. awards, Disting. Svc. awards State Dept., 2005, Robert C. Frasure Meml. award, 2006, Charles E. Cobb Jr. award Initiative and Success Trade Develop., 2006, others; Marshall scholar, 1978-81. Office: DOS Amb 5430 Moscow Pl Washington DC 20521-5430

BURNS-BOWIE, MAUREEN ELIZABETH, sculptor; b. Wilmington, Del., Sept. 14, 1949; d. William John and Jean (Ribsam) Burns; m. Norman Ernest Bowie, Sept. 19, 1987; children: Brian Paul Bowie, Peter Mark Bowie. Student, U. Sorbonne, Paris, 1966, U. Del., 1968—73, studied under numerous ceramic masters, 1970—76. Exhibitions include UN 4th World Congress on Women, Beijing, China, 1995, Radcliffe Coll./Harvard U., 1997, Ceres Gallery, NY, 1997, World Artists for Tibet, Mpls., 1998, St. Louis Artists Guild, 2000, Indpls. Mus. Art, Columbus, 2001, WPA Corcoran, Washington, 2002, Bienniale Internazionale Dell'Arte Contemporanea, Florence, Italy, 2003, Md. State Arts Coun., Balt., 2004, NH Inst. Art, Manchester, 2004, Acad. Mus., Easton, Md., 2005, A.I.R. Vallauris, France, numerous others. Active Dalai Lama Found.; co-founder, dir. Internat. Alliance Women in the Arts, 1993—98; v.p. Women's Art Registry of Minn., 1993—95. Grantee, Nat. Endowment Arts/Pa. Coun. Arts, 1983. Mem.: Tibet House, Rubin Mus., Coll. Art Assn., Am. Crafts Coun. Women's Caucus for Art, Bioneers, Art and Healing Network, Am. Ceramic Soc., Bklyn. Potters, Balt. Clayworks, Internat. Scupture Ctr., Nat. Coun. Edn. in Ceramic Arts, Urban Glass. Green Party. Buddhist. Home: Innisfree PO Box 508 Trappe MD 21673

BURNSIDE, WANDA JACQUELINE, elementary school educator; b. Highland Park, Mich., Mar. 9, 1950; d. Minor and Willie Lee (McCann) Palm; m. Simmie Lee Burnside, Jr., Nov. 4, 1972. BA in Humanities and Social Scis., U. Detroit. Clk. pers. dept. Blue Cross Blue Shield, Detroit, Mich., 1968-69; student asst. dir. libr. U. Detroit Edn. Libr., 1969-72; head clk NARO Fed. Project U.S. Atty.'s Office, Detroit, 1970; editor, office mgr. Detroit Ch. World, 1974-78; SDIP and IIE, ASIP Marygrove Coll., Detroit, 1979-81; elem. tchr. Martin L. King Jr. Ednl. Ctr., Detroit, 1981-88; sales rep. Five Stars Heating, Detroit, 1990-91; exec. sec. Second Ecclesiastical Ch. of God in Christ, Detroit, 1990—, office mgr., 1991—. Tchr. Head Start, Detroit, 1967; drama coach Martin L. King Jr. Ednl. Ctr., Detroit, 1980-88; monitor State of Mich. Nurse Lic. Dept., Detroit, 1980-81; tutor private home, Detroit, 1983-87; founder/pres. The Mother Willie Lee Palm Found., Write the Vision Min., 1995. Author: In My Neighborhood, 1972, Rejections-12 Steps To Recovery (Browning Internat. award), The Poetry Guide for Christian Writers. Mem. Joy of Jesus Ministries, 1975-76, So. Christian Leadership Coun., Detroit chpt., 1993. Recipe contest winner, Fayco Beverage Co., 1979, 2d, Thornapple Valley, 1988, 2d, Progresso Soups, 1989, 1st; cited for laity leadership Congress of Nat. Black Chs., Washington, 1990; Recipient Persistent Christian Writer of Yr., 1999, Am. Christian Writer Assn. Mem. Black Writers Guild, Christian Edn. for Handicapped, Christian Writers Inst., Am. Family Jour., The Called and Ready Writers (v.p.) Democrat. Avocations: writing devotional and poetry, cooking, crafts, reading, travel. Home: 8245 Mendota St Detroit MI 48204-3028 Office: Ch of God in Christ Hdqtrs SW Michigan 4439 E Nine MIle Rd Detroit MI 48091-2631 Personal E-mail: wtvision@hotmail.com.

BURNS-RIVIELLO, MICHAELA AILEEN, social studies educator; b. West Islip, NY, Dec. 23, 1974; d. Arthur Abercrombie and Maryanne Elizabeth Burns; m. Thomas Joseph Riviello, Dec. 3, 2005. BA in Social Sci. and Tchg. with honors, SUNY, Stony Brook, 1999, MA with honors, 2001. Cert. profl. development SUNY, 2001. Girls field hockey, volleyball & lacrosse athletic coach Babylon Sch., NY, 1994—2001; history tchr., chairperson Acad. St. Joseph's Sch., Brentwood, NY, 1999—2000; girls field hockey & lacrosse athletic coach Smithtown Schs., NY, 2000—05, social studies tchr., 2000—, instrnl. specialist. Mentor for new tchrs. Smithtown Schs., Smithtown, 2001—03. Organizer, coord. Nat. Geog. Geography Bee, 2003—, Tsunami Fundraiser, 2004—05, Hurricane Katrina Relief & Aid; creator, organizer, coord. Letters to Soldiers Campaign, Washington, 2004—05; co-creator, co-organizer Salvation Army Food Dr., Smithtown, 1999—; creator, organizer, coord. Salvation Army Charity Dinner, 2002—04. Recipient Cmty. Svc. award, Salvation Army, 2004. Mem.: PTA, ASCD, Tchr. Web, LI Coun. Social Studies. Roman Catholic. Avocations: gardening, crafts, stained glass artwork. Office: Smithtown Schs Great Hollow MS 150 Southern Blvd Nesconset NY 11767 Home Phone: 631-369-7635; Office Phone: 631-382-2805. Office Fax: 631-382-2807. Business E-Mail: mriviello@smithtown.k12.ny.us.

BURNSTEIN, DANIEL, lawyer; b. Hartford, Conn., Oct. 12, 1946; AB, U. Calif., Berkeley, 1968; JD cum laude, New Eng. Sch. Law, 1975; student, Harvard Law Sch., Cambridge, Mass., 1989—90. Bar: Mass. 1975, U.S. Dist. Ct. Mass. 1976, U.S. Ct. Appeals (1st cir.) 1976. Pres. Negotiation Pro Co., Boston, 1990—. Dir. Interactive Video Project Harvard Law Sch., Cambridge, 1985-89; pres. Ctr. for Atomic Radiation Studies, Acton, Mass., 1982—; advisor Am. Mgmt. Assn. for Negotiation Curriculum to Mgrs., 1993; adj. prof. Gibbs Coll., Boston, Pine Manor Coll. Editor: The Digital MBA, 1995. Mem. Mass. Adv. Coun. on Radiation Protection, 1990—2002, Brookline Town Meetings, 1993—96.

BURPEE, LYLE FREDERICK, retired industrial engineer; b. Royal Oak, Mich., May 6, 1927; s. Clarence Everett Burpee and Ruth Priscilla Ball-Burpee; m. Shirley Jean Lange; 1 child, Gloria Jean Burpee-Brom. BA in Indsl. Engr., Lawrence Inst. Tech., Southfield, Mich., 1959. Tool & die maker Pontiac Motor divsn. GM, Mich., 1947—51, indsl. engr., 1951—85; ret., 1985. Commr. Eaton Twp. Planning Commn., Mich., 2004—; co-founder Mid-Mich. Woodworker's Guild, 1992, various offices. With USN, 1945—46, PTO. Mem.: Am. Mensa. Avocations: woodworking, genealogy. Home: 2915 Twelve Oaks Dr Charlotte MI 48813

BURR, BROOKS MILO, zoology educator; b. Toledo, Aug. 15, 1949; s. Lawrence E. and Beverly Joy (Herald) B.; m. Patti Ann Grubb, Mar. 5, 1977 (div. July 1987); 1 child, Jordan Brooks; m. Ingrid M. Hansen, May 25, 1999. BA, Greenville Coll., 1971; MS, U. Ill., 1974, PhD, 1977. Cert. scuba diver Nat. Assn. Underwater Instrs. Lab. instr. dept. biology Greenville (Ill.) Coll., 1971-72; rsch. asst. Ill. Natural History Survey, Champaign, 1972-77, affiliate scientist Ctr. for Biodiversity Urbana, 1989—; from asst. prof. to prof. dept. zoology So. Ill. U., Carbondale, 1977—. Adv. panel US Fish and Wildlife Svc., 1990—; adj. prof. dept. biology U. N.Mex., Albuquerque, 1991—; adj. prof. dept. ecology, ethology and evolution U. Ill., 1993—. Co-author: A Distributional Atlas of Kentucky Fishes, 1986, A Field Guide to Fishes, North America North of Mexico, 1991 (selected as one of Outstanding Acad. Books of 1992, Choice Mag.); contbr. articles to profl. jours. Recipient Paper of Yr. award Ohio Jour. Sci., 1986, Coll. Sci. Rsch. award, So. Ill. Univ., 2001; Phi Kappa Phi Outstanding scholar So. Ill. U., 2002. Mem. AAAS, Am. Soc. Ichthyologists and Herpetologists (sec., mem. exec. com. 1990-94, pres.-elect 2000, pres. 2001—), Soc. Systematic Zoology, Biol. Soc. Washington, Assn. Systematic Collections, Sigma Xi (Leo M. Kaplan award 1990), Phi Kappa Phi (Scholar of Yr. 2002). Achievements include the discovery and description of 10 species of fish new to science from North American fresh waters. Home: 203 S Wedgewood Ln Carbondale IL 62901-2147 Office: So Ill Univ Dept Zoology Carbondale IL 62901-6501 Home Phone: 618-559-0243; Office Phone: 618-453-4112. Business E-Mail: burr@zoology.siu.edu.

BURR, DAVID BENTLEY, anatomy educator; b. Findlay, Ohio, June 28, 1951; s. Willard Bentley and Dorothy Eleanor (Beiler) B.; m. Lisa Marie Pedigo; children: Kathryn Lise, Michael David, Erik Johan. BA, Beloit Coll., Wis., 1973; MA, U. Colo., 1974, PhD, 1977. Instr. anatomy U. Kans. Med. Ctr., Kansas City, 1977-78, asst. prof. anatomy, 1978-80; asst. prof. anatomy and orthop. surgery W.Va. U., Morgantown, 1980-83, assoc. prof., 1983-86, prof., 1986-90; chmn. dept. anatomy and cell biology, prof. anatomy, bioengring. and orthopedic surgery Ind. U., Indpls., 1990—. Mem. adv. bd. dirs. Primate Found. Am., Tempe, Ariz., 1978—; cons. County Med. Examiner, Morgantown, 1983-89; mem. Adv. Group for the Treatment Human Remains, USDA, Monongahela Nat. Forest Svc., 1989; cons. NASA, 1990-91, Am. Inst. Biol. Sci., NAS, 1990—, U.S. Congress Office Tech. Assessment, 1990; mem. biochemistry study sect. Arthritis found., 1992-95; spl. grants rev. com. NIH, 1996-2000. Author: Structure, Function & Adaptation of Compact Bone, 1989, Skeletal Tissue Mechanics, 1998, Musculoskeletal Fatigue and Stress Fracture, 2001, Bridging the Gap Between Dental and Orthopaedic Implants, 2002; mem. edit. bd. Bone, 1993-2003, Jour. Bone and Mineral Metabolism, 1994-, Jour. Biomech., 1999-, Calcif. Tiss. Int., 2000-; assoc. editor Bone, 2004—, Jour. Musculoskeletal Neuronal Interactions, 2004—, Exptl. Biol. Medicine, 2006—; contbr. articles to profl. jours. Pres. First Ward Sch. PTA, Morgantown, 1987—88; sec. Cub Scout Pack Com., 1989; chmn. troop com. Boy Scouts Am., 1993—95; linesman Morgantown Soccer League, 1988; sec. Classic Ragtime Soc., 1997—98; clk. witness and svc. First Friends Meeting, 1999—2001; mem. adminstrv. bd. Epworth United Meth. Ch., Indpls., 1992—93. Rsch. grantee NIH, 1988—, Orthopedic Rsch. and Edn. Found., 1985-86. Mem.: Internat. Soc. for Musculoskeletal and Neuronal Interactions (bd. dirs. 1999—2000, 2002—), Assn. Anatomy, Cell Biology and Neurobiology Chairpersons (pres. 2001—02), Am. Anatomy Assn. (exec. com. 1998—2001, chmn. jour. trust fund com. 2002—04, sec.-treas. 2004—05, pres. 2007—), Orthop. Rsch. Soc. (chmn. membership com. 2002—03, program chair 2005—06, pres.-elect 2007—), Internat. Soc. Bone Mineral Rsch., Am. Soc. Bone Mineral Rsch. Avocations: piano, softball, racquetball, stamps, reading. Office: Ind U Sch Medicine Dept Anat & Cell Biology 635 Barnhill Dr Indianapolis IN 46202-5126 Office Phone: 317-274-7496. Business E-Mail: dburr@iupui.edu.

BURR, RICHARD M., senator, former congressman; b. Charlottesville, Va., Nov. 30, 1955; m. Brooke Fauth; children: Tyler, William. BA in Comm., Wake Forest U., 1978. Nat. sales mgr. Carswell Distributing, Winston-Salem, NC, 1978-94; state co-chmn. NC Taxpayers United, 1993-98; mem. US Ho. of Reps. from 5th N.C. dist., 1995—2005; US Senator from NC, 2005—. Mem. com. veterans affairs US Senate, mem. com. Indian affairs, com. health, edn. labor, and pensions, com. energy and natural resources, commn. security and coop. in Europe. Co-chmn. Partnership for Drug Free NC; bd. dirs. Brenner Children's Hosp., Winston-Salem, NC; mem. Forsyth County Earning by Learning. Recipient Award for Mfg. Legis. Excellence, Nat. Assn. Mfrs., 1999, Ground Water Protector award, Nat. Ground Water Assn., 2000, Jefferson award, Citizens for a Sound Econ., 2001, Legis. of Yr., Biotechnology Industry Orgn., 2002. Mem.: Optimist Soccer League, Rotary. Republican. Office: US Senate 217 Dirksen Senate Office Bldg Washington DC 20510 also: District Office Ste 508 2000 West First St Winston Salem NC 27104 Office Phone: 202-224-3154, 336-631-5125. Office Fax: 202-228-2981, 336-725-4493.*

BURR, RONALD EDWIN, publisher; b. Chgo., Oct. 5, 1949; m. My Hanh Duong-Tran. AB in Polit. Sci., Ind. U., 1972, MBA in Fin., 1976. Circulation mgr. The Am. Spectator, Bloomington, Ind., 1970—75, bus. mgr., 1975—79, sr. pub., 1979—80, gen. mgr., 1980—81, pub. Arlington, Va., 1981—97; pres. Red Line Mktg. LLC, Vienna, Va., 1979—; COO CHQ website, 1999—2001; pres. Burr Media Group LLC, Vienna, Va., 2003—. Mng. ptnr. Lemley Yarling & Co., Chgo., 1976—; bd. dirs., Launchspace Publs. Mem. Ind. Hist. Soc., Cath. Press Assn. Roman Catholic. Office: Red Line Mktg LLC PO Box 156 Vienna VA 22183-0156 E-mail: Ronaldeburr@hotmail.com.

BURR, SCOTT ALLEN, lawyer; s. Walter B. III and Patricia (Lord) Rothenberger. BA, Albright Coll., 1985; JD, The Dickinson Sch. Law, 1988; LLM in Internat. Law, Georgetown U., 1994; LLM in Trial Advocacy, Temple U. Law Sch., 1999. Bar: Pa. 1988, U.S. Dist. Ct. (ea. dist.) Pa. 1988, N.J. 1988, U.S. Dist. Ct. N.J. 1988. Sr. assoc. Spector, Gadon & Rosen, Phila., 1994—2000; sr. counsel Astigarraga Davis, Miami, 2002—. V.p. Nite & Day Mag., Ltd., Phila., 1990—. Author: (published law review article) 15 U. Pa. J. Int'l. Bus. L. 221 (1994), 6 Dick. J. Int.'l L. Active 237, 1987, ACLU, Phila., 1989—. Scholar, Albright Coll., 1985. Mem. ABA (internat. law sect., litigation and ins. and torts sect.), Fla. Bar Assn. (vice chair corp. and banking litigation), Dade County Bar Assn. Democrat. Lutheran. Avocations: sailing, equestrian riding, body building, water-skiing. Office: Astigarra Davis 701 Brickell Ave Ste 1650 Miami FL 33131 E-mail: sburr@astidavis.com.

BURR, TRACY L., food products executive; BS, U. Utah; M in Accountancy, Utah State U. CPA Tex., Calif., Utah. N.Am. corp. contr. Albert Fisher N.Am.; ptnr. Ernst & Young LLP, Deloitte & Touche; exec. v.p., CFO Schwan Food, Marshall, Minn., 2002—. Office: Schwan Food 115 W College Dr Marshall MN 56258

BURRELL, GARY, retired manufacturing executive; BS, Wichita State U.; MS, Rensselaer Polytechnic Inst. Dir., v.p. engring Lowrance Electronics, King Radio Corp., Allied Signal; co-founder Garmin Corp., 1989, co-chmn., 1989—2004, chmn. emeritus, 2004—. Named one of Forbes' Richest Americans, 2006. Office: Garmin Internat Inc 1200 E 151st St Olathe KS 66062

BURRELL, LIZABETH LORIE, lawyer; b. Bklyn., Feb. 1, 1952; d. George A. and Ione E. (Smith) B.; m. Michael F. Cataldo, Dec. 31, 1977 (div.); 1 child, Alexis C. B. Cataldo; m. Geoffrey J. Ginos, Sept. 6, 1996. BA cum laude, Swarthmore Coll., 1973; MA with honors, Columbia U., 1974, postgrad. degree in English Lit. with distinction, 1976; JD, NYU, 1980. Bar: NY 1981, US Dist. Ct. (so. dist.) NY 1981, US Supreme Ct. 1988, US Dist. Ct. (ea. dist.) NY 1990. Assoc. Burlingham, Underwood, NYC, 1980-88, ptnr., 1989—2002; counsel, maritime law Levy Phillips and Konigsberg, LLP, NYC, 2002—06, Curtis, Mallet-Prevost, Colt & Mosle LLP, 2006—. Lectr. in field. Editor (assoc.): Am. Maritime Cases, 1999-, Benedict's Maritime Bulletin, 2003-; contbr. articles to profl. jours. and pubs. Alumni rep. Swarthmore Coll., 1980—; bd. advisors U. San Francisco Maritime Law Jour., 1994-; mem. nat. adv. bd. Tulane U. Admiralty Law Inst., 2000-; mem. adv. com. Seamen's Ch. Inst. Ctr. for Seafarers' Rights, 1997-2005. Fellow: NY Bar Found., Am. Bar Found.; mem.: ABA (litigation, internat., torts and ins. practice sect., admiralty com. vice chair), Maritime Law Assn. of US (sec., com. on uniformity of US Maritime Law 1985—88, chmn. com. on uniformity of US Maritime Law 1988—94, del. to Com. Maritime Internat. 1990, steering com., com. on carriage of goods 1991—96, bd. dir. 1992—, membership sec. 1994—96, sec. 1996—2002, 2nd v.p. 2002—04, del. to Com. Maritime Internat. 2003, 2004, 1st v.p. 2004—06, pres. 2006—, titulary mem., Com. Maritime Internat. 2000—), NY Women's Bar Assn., Assn. of Bar City of NY (admiralty com. 1986—89, arbitration com. 1991—94), NY State Bar Assn. Avocations: sailing, skiing. Office: Curtis Mallet-Prevost, Colt and Mosle LLP 101 Park Ave New York NY 10178-0061 Office Phone: 212-696-6995. Business E-Mail: lburrell@cm-p.com.

BURRELL, ORVILLE RICHARD (SHAGGY), popular musician; b. Kingston, Jamaica, Oct. 22, 1968; arrived in Bklyn., 1986; 2 children. Albums Pure Pleasure, 1993, Boombastic, 1995 (Grammy award, best reggae album, 1996), Midnite Lover, 1997, Hot Shot, 2000, Mr. Lover Lover: The Best of Shaggy Part 1, 2002, Hot Shot Ultramix, 2002, Lucky Day, 2003, Boombastic Hits, 2004, Essential Shaggy, 2004, Clothes Drop, 2005. With USMC, 1988—92, Operation Desert Storm, Persian Gulf War.

BURRELL, STANLEY KIRK See HAMMER

BURRI, BETTY JANE, research chemist; b. San Francisco, Jan. 23, 1955; d. Paul Gene and Carleen Georgette (Meyers) B.; m. Kurt Randall Annweiler, Dec. 1, 1984. BA, San Francisco State U., 1976; MS, Calif. State U., Long Beach, 1978; PhD, U. Calif. San Diego, La Jolla, 1982. Research asst. Scripps Clinic, La Jolla, 1982-83, research assoc., 1983-85; research chemist Western Human Nutrition Rsch. Ctr., USDA, San Francisco, 1985-99, Davis, Calif., 1999—; adj. prof. nutrition dept. U. Nev., 1993-98, U. Calif., 2000—; leader cris rsch. Davis, Calif., 2003—. Mem. steering com. Carotenoid Rsch. Interaction Group, 1994-97. Co-editor Carotenoid News, 1995-99; contbr. articles to profl. jours. Grantee NIH, 1982, 85, USDA, 1986-2002, Spinal Cord Rsch. Found., 1998, Am. Chem. Soc., 1998-2002; affiliate fellow Am. Heart Assn., 1983, 84. Mem. Assn. Women in Sci. (founding dir. San Diego chpt.), N.Y. Acad. Sci., Carotenoid Rsch. Interaction Group, Internat. Carotenoid Soc., Am. Chem. Soc. Office: Western Human Nutrition Rsch Ctr 208 WHNRC 430 W Health Sciences Dr Davis CA 95616 Business E-Mail: bburri@whnrc.usda.gov.

BURRIDGE, MICHAEL JOHN, veterinarian, educator, research director; b. St. Albans, Eng., Apr. 27, 1942; came to U.S., 1973; s. Arthur Wilfred Bailey and Georgina Augusta (Davis) Burridge; m. Desree Margaret Wiggins, Aug. 13, 1973 (div. Sept. 1981); m. Karen Maureen Bengtsson, Jan. 1, 1983; 1 child, Christina Michelle. BVM&S, U. Edinburgh, Scotland, 1966; MPVM, U. Calif., Davis, 1974, PhD, 1976. Rsch. asst. East African Trypanosomiasis Rsch. Orgn., Tororo, Uganda, 1966; vet. practitioner Grant and Arnold, Woking, Eng., 1967-68; animal health officer Food & Agr. Orgn., Kabete, Kenya, 1968-73; grad. rsch. asst. U. Calif., Davis, 1973-76; assoc. prof. U. Fla., Gainesville, 1976-82, prof., 1982—, chmn. dept., 1984-93. Mem. com. on animal health NAS, Washington, 1980-83; cons. World Bank, Zaire, 1982, USAID, India, 1987, 91; cons. vet. medicine Williams & Wilkins, Balt., 1982-99; bd. dirs. Internat. Laveran Found., Annecy, France, 1991-94. Editor: Impact of Diseases on Livestock Production in the Tropics, 1984. Grantee US AID, 1985-2005 Achievements include co-invention of attractant decoy for tick control, self-medicating applicators for parasite control, and diagnostic tests and vaccines for rickettsial diseases. Home: 10021 SW 67th Dr Gainesville FL 32608-6304 Office: U Fla Dept Infectious Diseases and Pathology PO Box 110880 Gainesville FL 32611-0880 Home Phone: 352-371-3236; Office Phone: 352-392-4700 x3131. Business E-Mail: burridgem@mail.vetmed.ufl.edu.

BURRIDGE, ROBERT, former mathematics educator, scientific consultant; b. Essex, Eng., Dec. 6, 1937; came to U.S., 1971; s. Sydney Stanmore and Phebe Mercy (Raven) B.; BA (Major scholar King's Coll.), U. Cambridge, 1959, MA, 1962, PhD, 1963, ScD, 1980; m. Elizabeth Nelson Bingham, Sept. 22, 1962 (dec.); children: Rosalind, Lucinda, Robert; m. Marylyn Louise Sexton, Aug. 29, 1987. Research fellow Calif. Inst. Tech., Pasadena, 1963-64; rsch. geophysicist UCLA, 1964-65; asst. lectr. U. Cambridge, 1965-67; research fellow U.K. Atomic Energy Authority, 1967-71; fellow King's Coll., Cambridge, 1965-71; assoc. prof. math. NYU, N.Y.C., 1971-75, prof., 1975-86; sci. advisor Schlumberger-Doll Rsch., Ridgefield, Conn., 1986—. Recipient Adams prize in math. U. Cambridge, 1971; NSF research contract in earthquake mechanism studies, 1971—. Mem. Soc. Exploration Geophysicists, Soc. Indsl. and Applied Math., Am. Math. Soc., Inst. Math. Applications (bd. govs.). Mem. editorial bd. Wave Motion (Internat.); contbr. papers on applied math., theoretical seismology and wave propagation to tech. jours. Home: 142 Warren Ave Boston MA 02116-5914 Office: Schlumberger-Doll Rsch Old Quarry Rd Ridgefield CT 06877

BURRIS, BOYD LEE, psychiatrist, psychoanalyst, physician, educator; b. Knoxville, Tenn., Jan. 28, 1930; s. Fred Roosevelt and Mildred Blanche Burris. BS, U. Tenn., Knoxville, 1951; MD, U. Tenn., Memphis, 1952. Diplomate in psychiatry Am. Bd. Psychiatry and Neurology; cert. in psychoanalysis. Tng. and supervising analyst Balt.-Washington Inst. for Psychoanalysis, Washington, 1974—, co-dir., 1980-86; clin. prof. psychiatry and behavioral scis. George Washington U. Sch. Medicine, Washington, 1983—; clin. prof. psychiatry Georgetown U. Sch. Medicine, Washington, 1990—; mem. bd. trustees Ctr. for Advanced Psychoanalytic Studies, Princeton, N.J., Aspen, Colo., 1982—, pres. bd. trustees and dir., 1994—2003; pvt. practice psychiatry and psychoanalysis Washington, 1960—. Active staff George Washington U. Hosp., 1963-96; cons. Potomac Found. for Mental Health, Bethesda, Md., 1969-78, St. Elizabeth's Hosp., Washington, 1969-88. Contbr. chpt. to book, articles to profl. jours. Lt.

comdr. M.C., USN, 1954-56. Mem. Am. Psychiat. Assn. (chair tellers com. 1987-88), Am. Psychoanalytic Assn. (bd. on profl. standards 1982-86, 2000-2002), Balt./Washington Soc. for Psychoanalysis (pres. 1978-79). Home: 3100 Rolling Rd Chevy Chase MD 20815-4038 Office: 4545 42nd St NW Ste 310 Washington DC 20016-4623 Home Phone: 301-656-2564.

BURRIS, CRAVEN ALLEN, retired college administrator, educator; b. Wingate, NC, Sept. 11, 1929; s. Craven Cullom and Virginia Neulin (Currie) B.; m. Jane Russell Burris, June 19, 1955; children: Christa Cullom, David Allen. AA, Wingate Coll., 1949; BS, Wake Forest U., 1951; BDiv, Southeastern Bapt. Sem., Wake Forest, NC, 1958; MA, Duke U., 1959, PhD, 1964. Prof. history and govt. Gardner-Webb U., Boiling Springs, NC, 1958-66; prof. history, govt. and interdisciplinary studies St. Andrews Presbyn. Coll., Laurinburg, NC, 1966-69; v.p., dean of coll., prof. history and politics Meredith Coll., Raleigh, NC, 1969-98, ret., 1998, acting pres., 1971. Vis. lectr. in politics N.C. State U., Raleigh, 2003, tchr. ENCORE Program, 2000—07. Contbr. articles to profl. jours. Precinct officer State Conv. del., N.C. Dem. Party, 1969, 71; pres., dir. Tammy Lynn Found./Retarded Children, Raleigh, 1980—; chmn. Raleigh Hist. Dists. Commn., 2000-01; ch. sch. tchr. Lt. USNR, 1951-55, Italy and Atlantic Fleet. Recipient Disting. Alumni award Wingate U., 1983, Fulbright Study Trip, U.S. Govt., Pakistan, 1973, Study Trip USSR, 1988, Rsch. Brit. Mus. and Libr., 1963, 97. Mem. Civitan Internat. (v.p. bd. dirs. 1970—), Lions Club (editor 1965), Masons. Baptist. Avocations: choral singing, tennis, racquetball, golf, sailing, gardening. Home: 1322 Duplin Rd Raleigh NC 27607-3721 Office: Meredith Coll 3800 Hillsborough St Raleigh NC 27607-5237

BURRIS, HOWARD L., investment company executive; BA, Princeton U.; MBA, U. Tex. Pvt. real estate investor, developer; bd. dirs. AMT Tech., Inc., 1992—98; CEO Sci. Mgmt. Systems, Inc., Austin, Tex., 1995—2000; asset mgr. Long Point Ptnrs., LLP, Houston, 2002—03; dep. CFO Coalition Provisional Authority, Baghdad, 2004; dir. def. reconstruction support Office Sec. of Def., 2004—06; v.p., CFO Overseas Pvt. Investment Corp. (OPIC), 2006—. Office: Overseas Pvt Investment Corp 1100 New York Ave NW Washington DC 20527

BURRIS, JAMES FREDERICK, federal healthcare administrator, educator; b. Mauston, Wis., Apr. 15, 1947; s. James Duane and Margaret Katherine (Jones) B.; m. Christine Tuve, July 3, 1971; 1 child, Cameron William Tuve. AB, ScB, Brown U., 1970; MD, Columbia U., 1974. Diplomate Am. Bd. Internal Medicine, Subspecialty Bd. Geriatrics, Am. Bd. Clin. Pharmacology. Intern Roosevelt Hosp., NYC, 1974-75; resident in internal medicine Georgetown U. Med. Ctr., Washington, 1977-79; fellow in hypertension VA Med. Ctr., Washington, 1979-81; asst. prof. Sch. Medicine, Georgetown U., Washington, 1981-86, assoc. prof., 1986-91, coord. MD/PhD program, 1988-94, prof., 1991-97; clin. prof., 1997—; asst. dean Sch. Medicine, Georgetown U., Washington, 1987-90; assoc. dean Sch. Medicine Georgetown U., 1990-97, dir. continuing profl. edn., 1994-97; dep. chief R&D officer Vets. Health Adminstrn., U.S. Dept. Vets Affairs, Washington, 1997—2003; chief cons. Geriatrics and Extended Care, Vets. Health Adminstrn, US Dept. Vets Affairs, Washington, 2003—. Bd. dirs. Inst. for Clin. Rsch., Washington, 1989-92; bd. regents Am. Bd. Clin. Pharmacology, 1992-98, 2002—; rsch. adminstr. cert. coun.; rsch. assoc. hypertension unit VA Med. Ctr., Washington, 1981-92; vis. investigator Centre Hospitalier, U. Vaudois, Lausanne, Switzerland, 1982-83; dir. clin. rsch. Cardiovasc. Ctr. No. Va., Falls Church, 1988-92; delegate White House Conf. Aging, 2005 Mem. editl. bd. Jour. Clin. Pharmacology, Jour. Am. Geriat. Soc., Clin. Pharmacology and Therapeutics; contbr. over 250 articles to profl. jours. Cubmaster Boy Scouts Am., 1995-98, asst. scoutmaster, 1998—. Lt. comdr. USPHS, 1975-77, reserves 1977—. Recipient svc. award ARC, 1970, outstanding svc. citation DAV, 1987, meritorious svc. award Am. Heart Assn., 1994, Cubmasters award Boy Scouts Am., 1998, James E. West award, 1997, Scouter's Tng. Key award, 2000, Vicennial medal Georgetown U., 2000; commd. officer student tng. and extern program scholar USPHS, 1973-74; rsch. fellow Found. for Rsch. of Cardiovascular Diseases, Lausanne, 1983; under-sec. health's exec. performance award U.S. Dept. of Vet. Affairs, 1999, 2000, commendation award, 2003 Fellow: ACP, Am. Coll. Cardiology, Am. Coll. Clin. Pharmacology (bd. regents 1990—95, 1998—2003, hon. regent 2003, sec. 2004—, Disting. Svc. award 1992), Am. Coll. Preventive Medicine, Am. Geriatrics Soc.; mem.: AMA (physician's recognition award 1982, 1985, 1988, 1991, 1994, 1997, 2001), Am. Heart Assn. (chmn. rsch. peer rev. com. 1992—94, rsch. com. 1994—96, bd. dirs. Nation's Capital affiliate 1994—97, v.p. 1995—96, fellow couns. on high blood pressure rsch., circulation, epidemiology, coun. clin. cardiology), Sigma Xi. Achievements include education and research in hypertension, hyperlipidemia, preventive cardiology and clinical pharmacology; grants and contracts management and regulatory affairs and technology transfer administration; direction of continuing professional education programs; federal research and healthcare policy development and program implementation. Office: Vets Health Adminstrn (114) Dept VA 810 Vermont Ave NW Washington DC 20420-0001 E-mail: james.burris@va.gov.

BURRIS, JOHN EDWARD, academic administrator, biologist, educator; b. Feb. 1, 1949; s. Robert Harza and Katherine (Brusse) Burris; m. Sally Ann Sandermann, Dec. 21, 1974; children: Jennifer, Margaret, Mary. AB, Harvard U., 1971; postgrad., U. Wis., 1971—72; PhD, U. Calif., San Diego, 1976. Asst. prof. biology Pa. State U., University Park, 1976—83, assoc. prof. biology, 1983—85; dir. bd. biology NRC/NAS, Washington, 1984—89; exec. dir. Commn. Life Scis., 1988—92; dir., CEO Marine Biology Lab, Woods Hole, Mass., 1992—2000; pres. Beloit College, Beloit, Wis., 2000—. Adj. assoc. prof. biology Pa. State U., University Park, 1985—89, adj. prof., 1989—2001; chmn. adv. com. student sci. enrichment program Burroughs Wellcome Fund, 1995—2002; life and microgravity scis. and applications adv. com. NASA, 1997—2001; trustee Krasnow Inst., 1999—2002. Bd. dirs. Radiation Effects Rsch. Found., Grass Found., 2001—07, Naples Stazione Zoological, Consiglio Sci. Mem.: AAAS (bd. dirs. 2002—06), Naples Stazione Zoologica, Consiglio Sci., Phi Beta Kappa. Office: 700 College St Beloit WI 53511 Home Phone: 608-363-2299; Office Phone: 608-363-2201. Business E-Mail: burrisj@beloit.edu.

BURRIS, KELLY L., lawyer; b. Mpls., Sept. 22, 1974; BA, U. Tex., Austin, 1997; JD, Tex. Tech U., 2000. Bar: Tex. 2000. Assoc. Godwin, Pappas, Langley & Ronquillo, L.L.P., Dallas. Assoc. editor: Tex. Tech Law Rev., 1998—99, articles editor:, 1999—2000. Mem. bd. barristers Tex. Tech U., 1998—2000. Named a Rising Star, Tex. Super Lawyers mag., 2006. Mem.: Dallas Assn. Young Lawyers (co-chair poker for playgrounds com. 2005, co-chair host com. Acad. Am. and Internat. Law 2004—), Tex. Young Lawyers Assn. (dist. 4 dir., state bd. 2002—03), ABA (mem. young lawyers divsn., mem. family lawyers divsn.), Dallas Bar Assn. (mem. family law sect.).*

BURRIS, ROBERT HARZA, biochemist, educator; b. Brookings, SD, Apr. 13, 1914; s. Edward T. and Mabel T. (Harza) Burris; m. Katherine Irene Brusse, Sept. 12, 1945; children: Jean Carol, John Edward, Ellen Louise. BS, S.D. State Coll., 1936, D.Sc., 1966; MS, U. Wis., 1938, PhD, 1940. NRC fellow Columbia U., 1940—41; faculty U. Wis., Madison, 1941—, prof., 1951—84; chmn. biochemistry Coll. Agr., 1958—70, W.H. Peterson prof. biochemistry, 1976—84, prof. emeritus, 1984—. Recipient Charles Thom award, Soc. Indsl. Microbiology, 1977, Nat. Medal of Sci., 1980, Carty award, NAS, 1984, Wolf award in agr., Wolf Found., Israel, 1985; fellow Guggenheim Found., Cambridge U., 1954. Mem.: NAS, AAAS, Am. Soc. Plant Physiologists (pres. 1960, Stephen Hales award 1968, Charles Reid Barnes award 1977), Indian Nat. Sci. Acad. (fgn. assoc.), Am. Soc. Microbiology, Biochem. Soc., Am. Philos. Soc., Am. Soc. Biochemistry and Molecular Biology, Am. Chem. Soc. (Spencer award 1990). Home: 6225 Mineral Point Rd Madison WI 53705 Business E-Mail: burris@biochem.wisc.edu.

BURRIS, STEVEN MICHAEL, lawyer; b. LA, Dec. 30, 1952; s. Michael Victor and Patricia (McNeer) Burris; m. Melanie Schultz, Oct. 29, 1983; 1 child from previous marriage, Michael Steven. AB with distinction, Stanford U., 1975; JD with honors, U. So. Calif., 1978. Bar: Nev. 1978, Calif. 1978, U.S. Dist. Ct. Nev. 1978, U.S. Ct. Appeals (9th cir.) 1982. Assoc. Rogers, Monsey, Woodbury et al, Las Vegas, Nev., 1978—81; ptnr. Sacco & Burris, Las Vegas, 1981—84; pres. Burris & Thomas, Las Vegas, 1984—. Tchr. Clark County CC, Las Vegas, 1979—80. Author: (booklet) Your Personal Injury Case, 1982; co-author: (manual) Trial Advocacy in Nevada, 1991, Trying the Auto Injury Case in Nevada, 1992; editor-in-chief: The Advocate, 2000—. Bd. dirs. Sr. Citizens Mobile Home Pk. Found., Las Vegas, 1981—84; adminstrv. coun. Green Valley Bapt. Ch., Henderson, 1988. Recipient Am. Jurisprudence award, Bancroft Whitney's Pubs., 1977, Pres.'s award, U.S. Jaycees, 1981. Mem.: ATLA, Am. Bd. Trial Advocates, Clark County Bar Assn. (cert. of Merit 1987—88), Nev. Bar Assn., Nev. Trial Lawyers Assn. (bd. govs. 1992—, pres. 1997), Gideons (pres.). Democrat. Office Phone: 702-731-9222.

BURRITT, DAVID B., manufacturing executive; BS in Acctg., Bradley Univ., 1977; MBA, Univ. Ill., 1990; completed Exec. Program, Stanford Univ., 1998, Aspen Inst., 2005. CPA, Cert. Mgmt. Acct. Inventory, budget acct., foundry ops. to gen. office fin. reporting Caterpillar, Peoria, Ill., 1978—90, mgr., bus. measurements, 1990—94; bus., mgr. Cat Belgium SA; gen. mgr., strategic, bus. svcs. Europe, Africa, Middle East, Switzerland; corp. controller Caterpillar Inc., Peoria, Ill., 2002—04, v.p., CFO, 2004—. Mem.: Fin. Execs. Internat., Inst. Mgmt. Acct., AICPA, Phi Kappa Phi (life). Office: Caterpillar Inc 100 NE Adams St Peoria IL 61629 Office Fax: 309-675-1000.*

BURROS, MARIAN FOX, writer; b. Waterbury, Conn. children: Michael, Ann. BA English lit., Wellesley. Food editor Washington Post, 1974—81; food reporter NY Times, 1981—83; food columnist NY Times Dining Sect., 1983—; syndicated columnist NY Times Syndicated Sales Corp. Consumer reporter WRC-TV, Washington DC (Emmy award, 1973), contbr. NBC Radio Network News, United Features, Washington Daily News, Washington Star; author: (cookbooks) Elegant but Easy, 1967, Freeze with Ease, 1968, Come for Cocktails, Stay for Supper, 1970, The Summertime Cookbook, 1972 (Tastemaker award), Pure & Simple, 1978 (Tastemaker award), Keep It Simple, 1981, You've Got It Made, 1984, The Best of De Gustibus, 1988, 20 Minute Menus, 1989, Eating Well is the Best Revenge, 1995, The Elegant but Easy Cookbook, 1995, The New Elegant but Easy Cookbook, 2003, Cooking for Comfort, 2003. Recipient Nat. Press Club award, 1988, Matrix Award, NY Women in Comm., 1990, Betty Furness Consumer Media Svc. award, Consumer Fedn. Am., 2000, Mass Media award (3-time winner), AAUW, Vesta award (3-time winner), Hearth & Home, Penney-Mo. award, James Beard award. Office: NY Times Dining Sect 229 W 43rd St New York NY 10036

BURROUGHS, AUGUSTEN XON, advertising executive; b. Pitts., Oct. 23, 1965; s. John Gordon and Margaret (Richter) Robison. Student, pub. schs. Copywriter Ketchum Advt., San Francisco, 1985—. Author: (novels) Sellevision, 2000, Running With Scissors, 2002, Dry (A Memoir), 2003, Magical Thinking, 2004, Possible Side Effects, 2006.*

BURROUGHS, BENTON, JR., lawyer; b. Washington, Aug. 24, 1943; s. Charles Benton and Pauline Massey Burroughs; m. Dorinda Walker Burroughs; children: Dawn B. Pilleteri, Todd B. BS in Pre-Law and Acctg., U. Ala., 1967; JD, Emory U., 1971; LLM in Tax, Georgetown U., 1975. Bar: Va. 1971, Ala. 1977, D.C. 1972. Acct. Ernst & Ernst, Houston, 1967—68; tax mgr. Uniroyal, Inc., Houston, 1968—69; atty. tax divsn., atty. gen. honor program U.S. Dept. Justice, Washington, 1971—79; ptnr. Bainbridge & Mims, Birmingham, Ala., 1977—79; shareholder, officer, dir. Metrocall of Del., Inc., Alexandria, Va., 1985—89; shareholder, mng. ptnr. Hazel & Thomas P.C., Falls Church, Va., 1989—99; ptnr. Reed Smith LLP, Falls Church, 1999—. Gen. counsel Alexandria C. of C., 1979—86; vice chmn. Cellular One Washington D.C., Greenbelt, Md., 1986—88; mem. fin. com. Madeira Sch., McLean, Va., 2004—; mem. bd. govs. tax Va. State Bar, Richmond, 1998—2004. Coach McLean Youth, 1992—98; coach, bd. dirs. Mt. Vernon Youth, Alexandria, 1979—87; co-chmn. capital campaign Ronald McDonald House, Falls Church, 2005—; co-chmn. Good Shephard Cath. Ch., Alexandria, 1981—84. Mem.: Washington Golf Country Club. Avocations: sports, tennis, bridge. Office: Reed Smith LLP Ste 1400 3110 Fairview Pk Falls Church VA 22042

BURROUGHS, HAROLD R., lawyer; BA cum laude, Middlebury Coll., 1982; JD cum laude, U. Mich., 1990. Bar: Mo 1990. Ptnr., group dep. Banking, Bus. and Pub. Fin. Bryan Cave LLP, St. Louis. Office: Bryan Cave LLP One Metropolitan Square 211 N Broadway, Ste 3600 Saint Louis MO 63102 Office Phone: 314-259-2706. E-mail: hrburroughs@bryancave.com.

BURROUGHS, JEANNETTE, elementary school educator; d. Harry and Mary Manning; m. Gary Burroughs; children: April, Mary Albert, Lavada Eggart, Tommy. BA, Fla. Atlantic U., 1977. Cert. Elem. Edn. grades 1-6 Fla., 1977, Middle grades English 5-9 Fla., 1989. 4th grade tchr. Ctrl. Elem. Sch., Clewiston, Fla., 2003—. Leadership team Ctrl. Elem. Sch., Clewiston, Fla., 2004—. Cmty. advisor Pahokee Fire Rescue Explorer Program, Fla., 2000—04; Sunday sch. tchr. Lakeside Bapt. Ch., Pahokee, Fla., 1992—2006; sec. Lakeside Condominium Assn., Pahokee, Fla., 2004—06. Recipient Tchr. of Month, Edn. Found. of Palm Beach County, 1988, 1998; grantee Edn. Grant, Citicorp, 2006. Mem.: Hendry County Edn. Assn. (assoc.; pres. 2006—). Baptist. Avocations: reading, travel, crocheting. Office: Ctrl Elem Sch 1000 Deane Duff Ave Clewiston FL 33440 Home Phone: 561-924-6176; Office Phone: 863-983-1550. Office Fax: 863-983-1558. Business E-Mail: burroughsj@hendry.k12.fl.us.

BURROUGHS, MARGARET TAYLOR GOSS, artist, former museum director; b. St. Rose, La., Nov. 1, 1917; d. Alexander and Octavia (Pierre) Taylor; m. Bernard Goss, 1937; 1 child, Gayle; m. Charles Burroughs, 1949; 1 adopted child, Paul. BA in Edn, Art Inst. Chgo., 1946, MA, 1948; LHD (hon.), Lewis U., 1972; DHL (hon.), Chgo. State U., 1983. Tchr. art Chgo. Public Schs., 1944-68; prof. humanities Kennedy King Coll., Chgo., 1969-79; exec. dir., founder DuSable Mus. African Am. History, Chgo., 1961-84, dir. emeritus, 1984—; group shows include: LA County Mus., 1976, Corcoran Gallery, 1980; mem. Chgo. Council Fine Arts, 1976-80, Nat. Commn. Negro History and Culture, 1981—; founder Nat. Conf. Artists, 1959. Fellow NEH, 1968. Office: DuSable Museum 740 E 56th Pl Chicago IL 60637-1495 Office Phone: 312-374-4737.

BURROW, GERARD NOEL, internist, educator; b. Boston, Jan. 9, 1933; s. William and Noelle Elvira (Money) Burrow; m. Ann Huntington Rademacher, June 22, 1956; children: Peter Noel, Elisabeth Huntington, Sarah Rogers. BA, Brown U., 1954; MD, Yale U., 1958. From asst. prof. to prof. Yale U. Sch. Medicine, New Haven, 1966-76; prof. dept. medicine U. Toronto, Ont., Canada, 1976-81, Sir John and Lady Eaton prof. medicine, 1981-88, chmn. dept., 1981-88; vice-chancellor for health scis., dean U. Calif. Sch. Medicine, San Diego, 1988-92; dean Yale U. Sch. Medicine, New Haven, 1992-97; David Paige Smith prof. medicine Yale U., New Haven, 1997—2002; dean emeritus Yale U. Sch. Medicine, 2002—; CEO Sea Rsch. Found., Mystic, Conn., 2002—. Chmn. Internat. Coun. Control Iodine Deficiency, 2006—. Author: The Thyroid Gland in Pregnancy, 1972, A History of Yale's School of Medicine: Passing Torches to Others, 2002; editor (with Ferris): Medical Complications During Pregnancy, 1975, 1982, 1988, 1994, 1999; editor: (with Duffy), 2004. Chmn., bd. dirs. U. Conn. Health Ctr.; trustee U. Conn. Fellow: ACP, Royal Coll. Physicians (Can.). Office: Sea Rsch Found 55 Coogan Blvd Mystic CT 06355-3289 Office Phone: 860-572-5955.

BURROW, HAROLD, retired gas industry executive; b. Navasota, Tex., Dec. 1, 1914; s. Benjamin Donald and Minnie (Weaver) B.; m. Vassa Woodley; children: Larry W., Harry W., Janice K. With Tenneco, Inc., Houston, 1943-66, pres., mem. exec. com., 1960-66; chmn. bd., mem. exec. com. Colo. Interstate Gas Co., Colorado Springs, 1974—, also bd. dirs.; vice chmn. bd., mem. exec. com. Coastal Corp. (formerly Coastal States Gas Corp.), Houston, 1974—2001; chmn. bd., CEO Coastal Natural Gas Co., 1995-2001. Mem. exec. bd., bd. dirs., mem. exec. com. Am. Nat. Resources, Detroit. Mem. Petroleum Club (Houston), Ramada-Tajas Club (Houston). Methodist.

BURROW, PAUL IRVING, secondary school educator; b. Iowa City, Iowa, Aug. 16, 1955; s. George Irving and Elizabeth Zane (Miller) B.; m. Nancy Kay Rader, Sept. 8, 1979; children: Rachel, Timothy. BA, Drake U., 1976, MA, 1981. Tchr. Spanish, social studies Adair (Iowa) -Casey Schs., 1977-78, Oskaloosa (Iowa) Sr. H.S., 1978—. Bd. dirs. Iowa State Employee's Benefits Assn., chmn. 2002-2005; exec. bd. Crisis Intervention Svcs., Oskaloosa, 1996-2000; mem. coun. Boy Scouts Am., Oskaloosa, 1988-95; pastor Kirkville United Meth. Ch., 1999—, Hispanic Ministries, Central United Meth. Ch., Oskaloosa, 2001—. Mem. Am. Coun. Tchrs. Fgn. Langs., Iowa Fgn. Lang. Assn. (pres. 1985-87, Secondary Tchr. of Yr. 2004), Iowa Edn. Assn. (exec. bd. 1997-2007), Oksaloosa Edn. Assn. (spokesperson 1985-2000, 2005—, grievance chair 1998—, Tchr of Yr. 1992). Democrat. Methodist. Avocations: computers, genealogy, camping, travel. Home: 2212 Lynndale Rd Oskaloosa IA 52577-9129 Office: 1816 N 3rd St Oskaloosa IA 52577

BURROWS, BERTHA JEAN, retired academic administrator; b. Brush, Colo., June 15, 1930; d. John and Marie Pabst; m. Leslie R. Burrows, Sept. 2, 1951; children: Paul Eric, Amy Susan, Julie Diane, David Arthur. BA in Bus., U. Colo., 1952. Sec. Dental Found. Colo., Denver, 1969—70, John Boswick, MD, Denver, 1970—72; adminstrv. cons. dept. contg. edn. U. Colo. Sch. Dentistry, Denver, 1975—76; asst. dir. vol. svcs. U. Colo. Health Sci. Ctr., 1977—80; sec. Denver Neurosurg. Assn., Denver, 1981—83; ret., 1983. Bookkeeper Clark & Co., Denver, 1981—83; com. mem. U. Colo. Hosp., Denver, 1999—. Vol. U. Colo. Hosp., Denver, 1970—; treas., asst. mgr. U. Colo. Hosp. Gift Shop, 1997—, bd. mgrs., 1987—. Recipient Who Care award, Channel 9 TV Denver, 2005. Mem.: Colo. Assn. Healthcare Auxilians and Vols. (treas. 2000—01, chmn. gift shop 2002—03, pres.-elect 2003—04, pres. 2004—05), U. Colo. Srs. Assn. (pres. 2002—). Home: 6911 E Iliff Place Denver CO 80224

BURROWS, BRIAN WILLIAM, retired research and development company executive; b. Burnie, TAS, Australia, Nov. 15, 1939; came to US, 1966; s. William Henry and Jean Elizabeth (Ling) B.; 1 child, Karin; m. Penny Nathan Kahan, 1998. BSc, U. Tasmania, 1960, BSc with honors, 1962; PhD, Southampton U., 1966. Staff scientist Tyco Labs., Inc., Waltham, Mass., 1966-68; lectr. Macquarie U., Sydney, Australia, 1969-71; chef de sect. Battelle-Geneva, Switzerland, 1971-75; group leader Inco, Ltd., Mississauga, Ont., Canada, 1976-77; program mgr., lab. dir. Gould, Inc., Rolling Meadows, Ill., 1977-86; v.p. rsch. and tech. USG Corp., Chgo., 1986—2005, ret., 2005. Contbr. articles to tech. jours.; patentee in field. Fellow: AAAS; mem.: Union League Club. Home: 927 Longmeadow Ct Barrington IL 60010-9391

BURROWS, DONALD ALBERT, artist, painter, photographer, dean; b. Chgo., June 26, 1937; s. Charles Fredrick and Bertha Lillian (Olesen) B.; m. Philomena Durkin, Mar. 3, 1962 (div. 1983); children: Jennifer Maria, Charles Fredrick, Quentin Connor; m. Charlyn Butterfield, Apr. 2, 1995. BFA, Sch. of the Art Inst. of Chgo., 1961, MFA, 1963. Dir. Mobile (Ala.) Art Mus., 1964-66, Ft. Worth Art Mus., 1966-67, Ctr. for Creative Studies, Detroit, 1967-68; prof. humanities City Colls. of Chgo., 1968-83; assoc. dean Harrington Inst., Chgo., 1974-84; acad. dean Ray Coll. of Design, Chgo., 1986-93; prin. artist, designer Misaine/Chaleur, Inc., Gardena, Calif., 1990—, Modern Classic Artworks, Lexington, Ky., art dir.; pres., CEO ChyCogo and Co., Ltd., Willowbrook, Ill., 1987—. One-man shows include Hansen Gallery, Chgo., 1986, Elmhurst (Ill.) Coll., 1986, Galleria Renata, Chgo., 1988, Vin Gallery, Jerome, Ariz., 2006. Mem. Am. Soc. Interior Designers, Alumni Assn. Sch. of Art Inst. Chgo., Alumni Assn. U. Chgo., Art Inst. Chgo. (Ryerson Fgn. Traveling fellow, 1961-63). Personal E-mail: dburrows100@yahoo.com.

BURROWS, EDWIN GLADDING, retired broadcaster, writer, poet; b. Dallas, July 23, 1917; s. Millar Burrows, Irene B. (Gladding); m. Gwenyth Lemon, 1940 (div. 1971); children: Edwin Gwynne, Daniel William, David John; m. Beth Elpern, Dec. 7, 1973. BA, Yale U., 1938; MA, U. Mich., 1940. Program dir. Sta. WWJ-FM, Detroit, 1940-43, Sta. WPAG, Ann Arbor, Mich., 1946-48; program dir., mgr. Stas. WUOM-WVGR, U. Mich., Ann Arbor, 1948-70, exec. prodr., 1973-82; dir. Nat. Ctr. for Audio Experimentation, U. Wis., Madison, 1970-73; ret., 1982. Condr. poetry readings through Mich., 1965—82; poetry readings State of Wash., 1986—; helped charter radio divsn. Nat. Ednl. Radio of Nat. Assn. Ednl. Broadcasters, former region III dir., chmn. bd., 1965; chmn./mem. bd. network adv. com. Nat. Assn. Ednl. Broadcasters; lobbyist for inclusion of radio in Pub. Broadcasting Act of 1967. Author: (poetry) The Arctic Tern and Other Poems, 1957, Man Fishing, 1970, Kiva, 1976, Properties: A Play for Voices, 1979, The House of August, 1985, (chapbooks) The Crossings, 1976, On the Road to Bailey's, 1979, Handsigns for Rain, 1989, The Birds Under the Earth, 1997, Sailing As Before, 2001; contbr. poetry to anthologies including Anthology of Magazine Verse, 1984, A Centennial Sampler of Edmonds Writing, 1989, ORL 50th Anniversary Anthology, 1993, The Age of Koestler: Practices of the Wind, 1994, The Sumac Reader, poems to over 150 jours. including Atlantic Monthly, Ascent, Am. Poetry, Black Warrior, Blue Mesa, Chariton, Cream City, Gettysburg, Hawaii, Iowa, Mass., Mich. Quar., Paris, Seattle, and Va. Quar. revs., Confluence, Epoc. Lt. USN, 1943—46. Recipient Ohio State awards, 1953, 1954, 1955, 1956, 1971, 1974, Borestone Mountain poetry award, 1964, 1st ann. poetry award Ascent, 1987, donated his papers to U. Md. at College Park Librs., 1991; fellow Yaddo Found., 1963, 1966.

BURROWS, ELIZABETH MACDONALD, religious organization executive, educator; b. Portland, Oreg., Jan. 30, 1930; d. Leland R. and Ruth M. (Frew) MacDonald. Certificate, Chinmaya Trust Sandeepany, Bombay; PhD (hon.), Internat. U. Philosophy and Sci., 1975; ThD, Christian Coll. Universal Peace, 1992. Ordained to ministry First Christian Ch., 1976. Mgr. credit Home Utilities, Seattle, 1958, Montgomery Ward, Crescent City, Calif., 1963; supr. Oreg. dist. tng. West Coast Tele., Beaverton, 1965; pres. Christ Ch. of Universal Peace, Seattle, 1971—, prof. religion, also bd. dirs.; pres. Archives Internat., Seattle, 1971—; v.p. James Tyler Kent Inst. Homeopathy, 1984-95; sec. Louis Braille Inst. for the Blind, 1995—. Author: Crystal Planet, 1979, Pathway of the Immortal, 1980, Odyssey of the Apocalypse, 1981, Harp of Destiny, 1984, Commentary for Gospel of Peace of Jesus Christ According to John, 1986, Seasons of the Soul, 1995, Voyagers of the Sand, 1996, The Song of God, 1998, Hold the Anchovies, 1996, Pilgrim of the Shadow, 1998, The Secret Jesus Scroll, 2002, Poetry Chapbook, 2002, Visions, 2002, Eat to Heal, 2002, Mystic Voyage, 2004, Htrae, 2005, Psalms Solemnis, 2005. Recipient Pres. award for literary excellence CADER, 1994, 95, 97, Diamond Homer award Famous Poets

Soc., 1998, Pub.'s Choice award Poets of the New Era, 2002. Mem. Internat. Speakers Platform, Internat. New Thought Alliance, Cousteau Soc., Internat. Order of Chivalry, The Planetary Soc. Home: 10529 Ashworth Ave N Seattle WA 98133-8937 Home Phone: 206-375-6948; Office Phone: 206-362-4134. Personal E-mail: starbase2001@earthlink.net. *Oneness with God is mankind's ultimate vision. This results in a profound journey which covers strange and wonderful worlds beyond mortal boundaries. To reach oneness is to achieve more than anyone can imagine, or more than anyone has ever dreamed.*

BURROWS, JAMES, television and motion picture director, producer; b. LA, Dec. 30, 1940; s. Abe Burrows. BA, Oberlin Coll.; MFA, Yale U. Co-founder Charles Burrows Charles Productions. Off-Broadway prodns.: dir. (motion picture) Partners, 1982, (TV films) Butterflies, 1978, More Than Friends, 1978, Every Stray Dog and Kid, 1981, Dexter Prep Pilot, 2002, (TV pilots) Lou Grant, Dear John, Night Court, Wings, Roc, Stark Raving Mad, The Weber Show/ Cursed, The Boys Are Bak, 1994, Veronica's Closet, 1997, Good Morning, Miami, 2002, Bram and Alice, 2002, Two and a Half Men, 2003,(TV series episodes) The Mary Tyler Moore Show, The Bob Newhart Show, Frasier, Friends, Newsradio, Third Rock from the Sun, (TV series) Rhoda, 1974-78, Laverne & Shirley, 1976-83, Busting Loose, 1977, The Betty White Show, 1977-78, Husbands, Wives & Lovers, 1978, Taxi, 1978-82, A New Kind of Family, 1979, The Associates, 1979-80, Good Time Harry, 1980, Night Court, 1984-92, Valerie, 1986-88, The Tortellis, 1987, Wings, 1990-97, The Fanelli Boys, 1990-91, Flying Blind, 1992-93, Cafe American, 1993-94, The Preston Episodes, 1995, Partners, 1995-96, Hudson Street, 1995, Caroline in the City, 1995-99, Men Behaving Badly, 1996-97, George & Leo, 1997-98, Dharma & Greg, 1997-2002, Union Square, 1997-98, Conrad Boom, 1998, Jessie, 1998-2000, Stark Raving Mad, 1999-2000, Ladies Man, 1999-2001, Madigan Men, 2000, Cursed, 2000-01, The Stones, 2004, Beverly Hills S.U.V., 2006, Four Kings, 2006, Courting Alex, 2006, Teachers, 2006; co-creator, co-exec. producer, dir. Cheers, 1982-93, exec. producer, dir. The Secret Lives of Men, 1998, All is Forgiven, 1986, Will & Grace, 1998-2006. Recipient Dirs. Guild Am. award for comedy direction, 1984, 91, 94, 99, Emmy awards NATAS for dir. in comedy series Taxi, 1979-80, 81-82 seasons, Cheers, 1982-83, 90-91 seasons; Emmy award as co-producer Cheers, 1982-83, 83-84, 89-90, 90-91 seasons; Emmy award as director of a Comedy Series for Fraiser, 1994, American Comedy award for Lifetime Achievement, 1996, US Comedy Festival Career Tribute award, 2006; named to Acad. TV Arts & Sciences Hall of Fame, 2006

BURROWS, JOHN EDWARD, communications company executive, writer; b. Englewood, NJ, Aug. 6, 1950; s. Laurence McCallum and Pauline Hannah (McClave) B. BA in Journalism, Rutgers U., 1972. From staff asst. to account exec. Ogilvy & Mather Inc., NYC, 1977-80; mgr. sales devel. CBS Radio Spot Sales, NYC, 1980-81; dist. dir. affiliate relations CBS Radio Network, NYC, 1981-84, dir. affiliate relations, 1984-86, v.p. affiliate relations, 1986-87; v.p. news and sports affiliate relations CBS Radio Networks, NYC, 1987-89; classical piano instr. Norfolk, Conn., 1991—2003; freelance writer, 2004—. Author: A Country Heart, 1983. Treas. Town of Colebrook, 2005—. Episcopalian. Avocations: cross country skiing, hiking, genealogy. Mailing: PO Box 113 Colebrook CT 06021 Home Phone: 860-738-8421. Personal E-mail: jeburrows@aol.com.

BURROWS, KENNETH DAVID, lawyer; b. Bklyn., Mar. 26, 1941; s. Selig S. and Gladys (Spatt) B.; m. Erica Jong, Aug. 5, 1989. BA, Brown U., Providence, 1962; JD, Fordham U., NYC, 1970. Bar: NY 1971, Conn. 1993, U.S. Dist. Ct. (so. dist.) N.Y. 1972, U.S. Dist. Ct. Conn. 1993, U.S. Supreme Ct. 1973. Spl. asst. controller of currency US Treasurer, 1965—67; assoc. Phillips, Nizer, Benjamin, Krim & Ballon, NYC, 1970-77; ptnr. Kleinberg, Kaplan, Wolff, Cohen & Burrows, NYC, 1977-79, Burrows & Poster, NYC, 1980-89, Burrows & Franzblau, NYC, 1990-91; arbitrator small claims ct. City of N.Y., 1975-95; lectr. Practising Law Inst., 1996—; spl. master Supreme Ct. State of N.Y., NY County, 1980-89; arbitrator U.S. Dist. Ct. (ea. dist.) N.Y., 1994—; mediator U.S. Dist. Ct. (so. dist.) N.Y., 1994—; ptnr. Bender Burrows & Rosenthal LLC, NYC, 2003—. Mem. Appellate Divsn. 1st Dept. Com. on Law Guardians. Served with USCGR, 1960-69. Named one of the Best Lawyers in Am., 2006-, Superlawyers, 2006-. Mem. ABA, NY State Bar Assn., Assn. Bar City NY, Am. Acad. Matrimonial Lawyers, NY County Lawyers Assn., Am. Arbitration Assn. (mem. nat. arbitrators panel 1973-97), Internat. Acad. Matrimonial Lawyers, NY Yacht Club. Office: Bender Burrows and Rosenthal 451 Park Ave S Fl 8 New York NY 10016 Office Phone: 212-725-7111. Business E-Mail: kburrows@pipeline.com.

BURROWS, MICHAEL DONALD, lawyer; b. Oak Park, Ill., May 23, 1944; s. Milford Denton and Helen Jean (Spitali) B.; m. Sandi Miller, Feb. 6, 1982; 1 child, Matthew Denton. BA, Williams Coll., 1967; JD, N.Y. Law Sch., 1973. Bar: N.Y. 1974, U.S. Dist. Ct. (ea. and so. dists.) N.Y. 1974, U.S. Ct. Appeals (2d cir.) 1978, U.S. Supreme Ct. 1981. Assoc. Baker & McKenzie, NYC, 1973-80, ptnr., 1980-95, of counsel, 1995-99, mem. internat. exec. com., 1986-88; ptnr. Winston & Strawn, NYC, 1999—2004, exec. com., chmn. N.Y. Litigation dept., 2004; shareholder Greenberg Traurig, 2004—. Co-author: The Practice of International Litigation, 1992. With USMC, 1968-70. Mem. ABA, Assn.of Bar of City of N.Y. Office: 160 E 89th St New York NY 10128 Business E-Mail: burrowsm@gtlaw.com.

BURROWS, ROBERT PAUL, optometrist; b. Chehalis, Wash. s. Fremont O. and Pauline A. (Kostick) B.; m. Marilyn Burrows. BS in Visual Sci., Pacific U., 1979, OD, 1981. Assoc. optometric physician L.E. Hedgen, O.D. & Assocs., Chehalis, 1981—86; ptnr. Lewis County Eye & Vision Assocs., Chehalis, 1986—. Active United Way, 1981—. Rsch. grant PTU, 1980. Mem.: Wash. Assn. Optometric Physicians, Am. Optometric Assn. (charter contact lens sect., recognition awards 1984—2007), Twin City C. of C., Kiwanis (dir. 1984—85, 1989—90, 2000—03), Omega Epsilon Phi. Methodist. Office: 1179 S Market Blvd Chehalis WA 98532-3427 Home Phone: 360-866-0973; Office Phone: 360-748-9228. E-mail: l.c.eye@localaccess.com.

BURROWS, SHANIA KAY, civilian military employee; b. Russellville, Ala., Mar. 21, 1967; d. J. W. Saint and Dorothea Patricia Melton; m. Kim Stewart Burrows, Mar. 31, 1999; children: Conor Stewart, Shandi Nicole. Student, John C. Calhoun State C.C., Decatur, Ala., 1996—98; BA in Psychology summa cum laude, Athens State U., Ala., 2000; MS in Mgmt. and Logistics Mgmt, Fla. Inst. Tech., Melbourne, 2004; grad. with honors, U.S. Army Logistics Leadership Ctr., 2001; grad. with distinction, US Army Logistics Mgmt. Coll., 2001. AMCOM Lean Six Sigma Green Belt US Army Aviation and Missile Command, Ala., 2005, cert. acquisition profl. level III Life Cycle Logistics Def. Acquisition U., 2004. Logistics mgmt. specialist and data analyst US Army Logistics Support Activity, Redstone Arsenal, Ala., 2001—04; logistics mgmt. specialist and item mgr. US AMCOM Utility Helicopter Directorate, 2004; assoc. dir. aviation staff US AMCOM Integrated Materiel Mgmt. Ctr., 2004—05; asset acquisition mgr. US Army AMCOM Utility Helicopter Directorate, 2005; continuous improvement facilitator US Army AMCOM Office Continuous Improvement, 2005—06; program integrator demilitarization US Army AMCOM G-3 Ops., 2006—. Retrograde distbn. managment integration product team US AMC LOGSA, Redstone Arsenal, Ala., 2003—04; mem. enterprise bd. AMCOM G-3 Ops., 2006—; designer demil integration product team PM Demilitarization, Picatinny Arsenal, NJ, 2006—, demilitarization R&D integration product team, 2006—, strategic planning integration product team, 2006—. Named Outstanding Psychology Grad., Athens State U., 2000—01; named to, Nat. Dean's List, 1997—98; scholar, Athens State U., 1996—98. Mem.: Nat. Def. Indsl. Assn., Mensa. Avocations: reading, puzzles, swimming, contining education, internet research. Home: 124 Greenwood Dr Madison AL 35758 Office: US Army Aviation and Missile Command G-3 Bldg 5308 Sparkman Cir Huntsville AL 35898 Home Phone: 256-655-0912; Office Phone: 256-876-6156. E-mail: shania.burrows@us.army.mil.

BURRUS, DANIEL ALLEN, research and development company executive, consultant; b. Portland, Oreg., Aug. 22, 1947; s. Joe Howard and Mary Kathleen B. BS, U. Wis., Oshkosh. Founder, pres. Burrus Media Prodns., Brookfield, Wis., 1978-80, Burrus Powered Gliders, Waukesha, Wis., 1980-82, Midwest Skynasaurs, Waukesha, 1982-84, Ultrasports Inc., Waukesha, 1982-84, Burrus Research Assocs., Inc., Milw., 1983—, Burrus Consumer Rsch., Inc., Milw., 2005—. Cons. various corps., assns. and univs.; speaker in field. Author (editor): Tech. Futures Newsletter, 1985—93, Technotrends Newsletter, 1993—; author: (audio tape learning sys.) The Future of Education, 1985, Beyond Megatrends, 1985, Teaching Creativity, 1986, Futureview: A Look Ahead, 1986, 1988, Maximimizing your Creativity, 1989, Reengineering Yourself, 1995, The New Tools of Technology, 1990, Technotrends, 1993, Desining Thriving Schools, 2001; co-author: Medical Advances, 1990, Environmental Solutions, 1990, Advances in Agriculture, 1990, Insights into Excellence, 1992; editor: Applied Sci. Rev., 1985, 1988; writer, dir., prodr.: films Deja Vu, 1972, Phantasmagoria, 1972, The New Adventures of Superman, 1972; author: Designing Thriving Schools, 2000, The Advantage Business Strategy Game, 2000, The Marketing Advantage Strategy Game, 2005; contbr. articles to profl. publs. Mem. AAAS, Internat. Personal Robot Assn. (founding), Internat. Ctr. Profl. Speaking (founding, bd. dirs.), Nat. Speakers Assn. (bd. dirs. 1991-96, cert. speaking profl., Profl. Speakers Hall of Fame 1992). Avocations: film making, photography, mountain climbing, flying, scuba diving. Office: Burrus Rsch Assocs 557 Cottonwood Ave Ste 106 Hartland WI 53029-2347 Office Phone: 262-367-0949. Business E-Mail: office@burrus.com.

BURRUS, ROBERT LEWIS, JR., lawyer; b. Richmond, Va., Sept. 16, 1934; s. Robert Lewis and Bessie (Hart) Burrus; m. Ann Williams, Aug. 1, 1964; children: David Curran, Peter Tandy, Lewis Graves BA, U. Richmond, 1955, LLD (hon.), 2005; LLB, Duke U., 1958. Bar: Va. 1958. Assoc. McGuireWoods LLP, Richmond, Va., 1959-63, ptnr., 1963—, chmn., 1990—2006, chair emeritus, 2007—. Bd. dirs. Smithfield Foods, Smithfield, Va., S&K Famous Brands, Richmond, Amvest Corp., Charlottesville, Va.; former dir. CSX Corp., Jacksonville, Fla. Trustee U. Richmond, chmn. presdl. search com., 1997-98 and 2005-06, rector, 1998-2002; bd. visitors Duke U. Law Sch., Durham, NC; dir. R.E.B. Found., Richmond, Va.; dir. Va. Mus. Fine Arts Found.; past trustee Va. Mus. Fine Arts, Va. Hist. Soc., Richmond Children's Mus.; past chmn. State Coun. Higher Edn. for Va.; past dir., chmn. exec. com. Richmond Renaissance; past bd. dirs. Circuit City Found.; past mem. Gov.'s Commn. Intercollegiate Athletics, 1991-92; past pres. St. Christopher's Sch. Found., Richmond. Capt. USAR. Recipient Charles S. Rhyne Award Duke U., 1998, Alumni of Yr. Award U. Richmond, 1998, Trustees Disting. Svc. Award, 2002, Silver Hope Award Nat. Multiple Sclerosis Soc., 2000, Humanitarian Award Nat. Conf. for Cmty. and Justice, 2001; scholarship established in his name, U. Richmond, 2002. Fellow Am. Bar Found., Va. Law Found.; mem. ABA, Va. Bar Assn. (chmn. corp. law com. 1975-77, chmn. bus. sect. 1976-77), Richmond Bar Assn., Commonwealth Club, Chgo. Club, Country Club Va., Bull and Bear Club, Kinloch Golf Club, Forum Club, Omicron Delta Kappa. Episcopalian. Office: McGuireWoods LLP One James Ctr 901 E Cary St Richmond VA 23219-4030 Office Phone: 804-775-4306. Office Fax: 804-698-2023. Business E-Mail: rburrus@mcguirewoods.com.

BURRUS, (CHARLES) SIDNEY, electrical engineering educator; b. Abilene, Tex., Oct. 9, 1934; s. Charles Hooker B. and Aleta (Hunter) Hoffman; m. Mary Lee Powell, June 7, 1958; children: Mary Virginia, Charles Stephen. BA, Rice U., 1957, BSEE, 1958, MS, 1960; PhD, Stanford U., 1965. Registered profl. engr., Tex. Lectr. Stanford U., Calif., 1964-65; asst. prof. elec. engring. Rice U., Houston, 1965-70, assoc. prof., 1970-74, prof., 1974—, chmn. dept. elec. engring., 1984—92, dir. Computer and Info. Tech. Inst., 1992—, Maxfield and Oshman Prof. Elec. and Computer Engring., dean George R. Brown Sch. Engring., 1998—2005. Vis. prof. Universitaet Erlangen-Nürnberg, Germany, 1975, 79, MIT, 1989-90; vis. fellow Trinity Coll., Cambridge, Eng., 1984.cons. IBM, Tex. Instruments, VA Hos., 1975— Author: Algorithms for DSP, 1984, Digital Filter Design, 1987; contbr. articles to profl. jours. Served to lt. USN, 1958-62. Recipient Humboldt Award, 1975, Signal Processing Soc. Award, 1995; Sr. Fulbright Fellowship, 1985. Fellow IEEE (Sr. Paper award 1974, Tech. Achievement award 1985); mem. Am. Soc. Elec. Engring., Sigma Xi, Tau Beta Pi Democrat. Baptist. Office: Rice U Dept Elec Engring PO Box 1892 Houston TX 77251-1892 Office Phone: 713-348-5484. Business E-Mail: csb@rice.edu.

BURRUS, WILLIAM HENRY, labor union administrator; b. Wheeling, W.Va. s. William and Gertrude Burrus; m. Ethelda Burrus; 4 children. Attended, W.Va. State Coll. Distbn. clk. Cleve. Post Office, 1958; mem., nat. human rels. com. Am. Postal Workers Union, 1972, pres. Cleveland Local Chpt., 1974—80, exec. v.p. Washington, 1980—2001, nat. pres., 2001—. Bd. mem. Fed. Adv. Coun. Occupl. Safety and Health; dir. rsch. edn. Ohio State Postal Workers, 1971. Bd. mem. A. Philip Randolph Inst., 1984, Nat. Black Coll. Alumni Hall Fame, Nat. Coalition Black Voter Participation, Ohio Adv. Bd. US Civil Rights Commn., 1979—81; v.p. A. Philip Randolph Inst., 1982—, Black Trade Labor Union, 1977; Ohio adv. bd. US Civil Rights Commn., 1980. Served with 101st Airborne Divsn. US Army, served with 4th Armored Tank Divsn. US Army. Named one of 100 Most Influential Black Americans, Ebony mag., 2004, 2006; recipient Frederick O'Neal award, 1981, Philip Randolph Achievement award, 1982, Disting. Svc. award, Martin Luther King Ctr., 1989. Office: Am Postal Workers Union 1300 L St NW Washington DC 20005 Office Phone: 202-842-4200, 202-842-8500.*

BURSCH, JOHN JOSEPH, lawyer; s. Robert Joseph and Marlyce Elizabeth Bursch; m. Angela Lynn Maxwell, Aug. 19, 1994; 5 children. BA, BM summa cum laude, We. Mich. U., Kalamazoo, 1994; JD magna cum laude, U. Minn., Mpls., 1997. Bar: Mich. 1997, US Dist. Ct. (we. dist.) Mich. 1998, US Ct. Appeals (8th cir.) 1998, US Ct. Appeals (6th cir.) 1999, US Ct. Appeals (4th cir.) 2003, US Dist. Ct. (ea. dist.) Mich. 2004, US Ct. Appeals (3d, 10th, 11th, D.C., and Fed. cir.) 2004, US Ct. Appeals (2d cir.) 2005, US Ct. Appeals (7th cir.) 2006, US Supreme Ct. 2001. Law clk. to James B. Loken U.S. Ct. Appeals, 8th cir., Mpls., 1997—98; atty. Warner Norcross & Judd LLP, Grand Rapids, Mich., 1998—, chair appellate practice group. Presenter in field. Contbr. articles to profl. jours. Bd. trustees Hugh Michael Beahan Found., Grand Rapids, 2003—05; bd. dirs. Hispanic Ctr. We. Mich., Grand Rapids, 2006—; chair St. John Vienney Worship Commn., Wyoming, Mich., 2000—01. Medallion scholar, We. Mich. U., 1990. Mem.: DRI, ABA (mem. coun. appellate lawyers, exec. com, pub. com. chair, litig. sect., chair supreme ct. cases subcom.), Nat. Assn. Diocesan Attys., Grand Rapids Bar Assn. (litig. sect.), Mich. Bar Assn. (treas. appellate practice sect., litig. sect.), US Supreme Ct. Hist. Soc. Avocations: chess, music. Office: Warner Norcross & Judd LLP 111 Lyon St NW Ste 900 Grand Rapids MI 49503 Office Phone: 616-752-2474. Office Fax: 616-222-2474. Business E-Mail: jbursch@wnj.com.

BURSEY, MAURICE M., retired chemistry professor; b. Balt., July 27, 1939; s. Reginald Price and Edna Frances (Moyer) B.; m. Joan Marie Tesarek, Dec. 28, 1970; children— John Thomas Kieran, Sara Helen Moyer. BA, Johns Hopkins U., 1959, MA, 1960, PhD, 1963. Lectr. Johns Hopkins U., Balt., 1963-64; asst. prof. Purdue U., Lafayette, Ind., 1964-66; asst. prof. chemistry U. N.C., Chapel Hill, 1966-69, assoc. prof., 1969-74, prof., 1974-96, prof. emeritus, 1996—. Editor Mass Spectrometry Revs., 1990-93; contbr. articles to profl. jours. Recipient various research grants. Fellow Am. Inst. Chemists, Royal Soc. Chemistry; mem. Am. Chem. Soc. (council, 1976-2001, bd. dirs. 1993-2001), Am. Soc. Mass Spectrometry, Alpha Chi Sigma (Grand Master Alchemist nat. pres. 1986-88). Democrat. Roman Catholic. Home: 101 Longwood Pl Chapel Hill NC 27514-9584 Home Phone: 919-493-3025. Personal E-mail: mauricebursey@aol.com.

BURSKY, HERMAN AARON, lawyer; b. Bklyn., Jan. 16, 1938; s. Abraham S. and Anna R. (Polstein) B.; m. Dolores Kelner, Sept. 3, 1961; children: Daniel Jay, Jennifer Dina. BA, B in Hebrew Lit., Yeshiva U., NYC, 1959; LLB, Cornell U., Ithaca, NY, 1962. Bar: NY 1963. Assoc. Levin & Weintraub, NYC, 1963-69; atty. CIT Fin. Corp., NYC, 1969-70; assoc. Otterbourg, Steindler, Houston & Rosen, P.C., NYC, 1970-71; ptnr. Shea & Gould, NYC, 1971-91, Rosenman & Colin, NYC, 1991-98; counsel Fischbein, Badillo, Wagner and Harding, 2000—. Contbg. author: Practical Guide to Bankruptcy and Debtor Relief, 1964. Served as pvt. US Army, 1962-63. Mem. ABA, NY State Bar Assn., Fed. Bar Council, Assn. Comml. Fin. Attys., NY County Lawyers Assn. (bankruptcy com. 1973-80), Inwood Country Club (NY). Jewish. Home: 25 Muriel Ave Lawrence NY 11559-1810 Personal E-mail: hbursky@optonline.net.

BURSLEY, KATHLEEN A., lawyer; b. Washington, Mar. 20, 1954; d. G.H. Patrick and Claire (Mulvany) B. BA, Pomona Coll., 1976; JD, Cornell U., 1979. Bar: N.Y. 1980, U.S. Dist. Ct. (ea. and so. dists.) N.Y. 1980, U.S. Ct. Appeals (5th and 11th cirs.) 1981, Fla. 1984, U.S. Dist. Ct. (mid. dist.) Fla. 1984, Tex. 1985, Mass. 1995. Assoc. Haight, Gardner, Poor & Havens, NYC, 1979-81; counsel Harcourt Brace Jovanovich, Inc., NYC and Orlando, Fla., 1981-85, v.p. and counsel San Antonio and Orlando, 1985-92; gen. counsel Harcourt Gen., Inc., Chestnut Hill, Mass., 1992—; gen. counsel Harcourt, Inc., Chestnut Hill, Mass., 1992—; v.p. Harcourt Gen., Inc., 1998—. Mem. Maritime Law Assn. (proctor). Home: 351 Termino Ave Long Beach CA 90814-2838 E-mail: kbursley@harcourtgeneral.com.

BURSON, BETSY LEE, librarian; b. Olney, Tex., Dec. 16, 1942; d. James Hollis and Lora Elizabeth (Talbott) B.; m. Winston Rabb Henderson, June 26, 1976. BS in Edn., Kans. State Tchrs. Coll., 1964; MLS, Tex. Woman's U., 1967, PhD in Libr. Info. Studies, 1987. With Phoenix Pub. Libr., 1967-74; libr. dir. Glendale (Ariz.) Pub. Libr., 1974-75; project archivist Phoenix History Project, 1975-77; adj. faculty U. Ariz., Tucson, 1979, Tex. Woman's U., Denton, 1980; libr. cons. La. State Libr., Baton Rouge, 1982-85; libr. dir. El Paso Pub. Libr., Tex., 1987-90, Arlington Pub. Libr., Tex., 1990—2001. Named Librarian of the Yr. Tex. Library Assn., 1995. Office Phone: 817-795-2194.

BURSON, CHARLES W., retired agricultural products executive, former federal official, state attorney general; b. Memphis; m. Marion 1971; children: Clare, Kate. BA, U. Mich., 1966; MA, Cambridge U., England, 1968; JD, Harvard U., 1970. Assoc. Burson & Burson and Burson & Walkup, Memphis; ptnr. Wildman, Harrold, Allen, Dixon, & McDonnell, Memphis, 1981-88; atty. gen. State of Tenn., Nashville, 1988—96; legal counsel to v.p. The White House, Washington, 1993-99, asst. to pres., chief of staff & counselor to v.p., 1999—2001; exec. v.p., sec., gen. counsel Monsanto Co., St. Louis, 2001—06, spl. asst. & counsel to the CEO, 2006. Del. Tenn. Constl. Conv., 1977, (chmn. State Spending Limitation Com.). Mem. Nat. Assn. Attys. Gen. 1988-97 (pres. 1994-95, chair FTC working group, mem. exec. com. securities group, chair consumer protection com. 1990-91, vice chair securities working group, Wyman award 1994), Tenn. Bd. Law Examiners, 1982-88 (pres. 1987-88).*

BURSON, HAROLD, public relations executive, director; b. Memphis, Feb. 15, 1921; s. Maurice and Esther (Bach) Burson; m. Betty Ann Foster, Oct. 30, 1947; children: Scott, Mark. BA, U. Miss., 1940; DHL (hon.), Boston U., 1988. Corr., reporter Memphis Comml. Appeal, 1938—40; dir. Ole Miss News Bur., Oxford, Miss., 1939—40; dir. pub. rels. H.K. Ferguson Co., NYC, 1941—43; chmn. Burson-Marsteller, NYC, 1953—; bd. dirs., mem. exec. com. Young & Rubicam, NYC; pub. affairs adviser to Pres. Ronald Reagan, 1989—94; mem. adv. coun. Emory U. Bus. Sch., Medill Sch. Journalism Northwestern U., U. So. Calif. Sch. Journalism; trustee Ab. Fortas Meml. Fund, Kennedy Ctr.; hon. prof. Fudan U., Shanghai, 1999; vis. prof. Leeds Met. U., Yorkshire, 2001; exec.-in-residence U. Ky. Coll. Commn., 2000. Harold Burson chair pub. relations Boston U., 2002. Chmn. bd., mem. exec. com. Nat. Coun. on Econ. Edn.; bd. dirs., exec. com., v.p. pub. info. Nat. Safety Coun., 1968—76; bd. dirs. Kennedy Ctr. Prodns., Washington, Catalyst Inc., 1978—89; former trustee World Wildlife Fund, 1979—81, Found. for Pub. Rels. Rsch. and Edn.; trustee Hackley Sch., Tarrytown, NY, 1968—76; chmn. pvt. sector pub. rels. com. USIA; mem. Fine Arts Commn., 1981—85; exec. com. Young Astronauts Coun., 1984—88; adv. bd. Bus. Coun. for Internat. Understanding; pres. coun. N.Y. Acad. Sci.; trustee World Environ. Ctr. Named Pub. Rels. Profl. of Yr., Pub. Rels. News, 1977, 1989, Most Influential Person in Pub. Rels. in 20th Century, PR Week, 1999, to U. Miss. Hall of Fame, 1980; named to Hall of Fame, Internat. Coun. Consulting Orgs., 2003; recipient Gold Anvil award, Pub. Rels. Soc. Am., 1980, Horatio Alger award, 1986, Arthur Page award, 1990, Lifetime Achievement award, Inside PR, 1993, Alexander Hamilton award for lifetime achievement in pub. rels., Inst. Pub. Rels. Mem.: Horatio Alger Assn., N.Y. Acad. Med. (trustee 2003), Am. Philatelic Soc., N.Y. Soc. Security Analysts, Internat. Pub. Rels. Assn., Am. Pub. Rels. Assn., Blue Key Club, Econ. Club N.Y. (exec. com.), Scarsdale Golf Club, Overseas Press Club, Mid-Am. Club, Omicron Delta Kappa. Office: Burson-Marsteller 230 Park Ave S New York NY 10003-1513 Office Phone: 212-614-4444. Business E-Mail: harold_burson@nyc.bm.com.

BURSON, THOMAS DANIEL, retired aerospace executive; b. Hartselle, Ala., Jan. 7, 1936; s. Daniel Webster and Ardia Burson; m. Mary Frances Wilson, June 7, 1958; children: Kelly Frances, Robyn Elizabeth, Thomas Scott. BME with high honor, Auburn U., Ala., 1958; MBA, U. So. Calif., 1969. Asst. mgr. contract adminstrn. Hycon Co., Monrovia, Calif., 1961-63, mgr. customer contracts, 1963-66, asst. to pres., 1966-67, dir. mktg., 1967-71, v.p., 1969-71; dir. contracts and pricing Actron Divsn. McDonnell Douglas Corp., Monrovia, 1971-76, v.p. fiscal mgmt., 1976-79, v.p., gen. mgr., 1979-83; v.p. ops. McDonnell Douglas Astronautics Co., Huntington Beach, Calif., 1983-84, v.p. fiscal mgmt., 1984-87, v.p., dep. gen. mgr., 1987-88, v.p., gen. mgr. Space Transp. Divsn., 1989-96; ret., 1996. Chmn. comml. space transp. adv. com. to Sec. Transp., 1996. With USN, 1958—61. Mem. AIAA (George M. Low Space Transp. award 1996), ASME, Nat. Contract Mgmt. Assn., Phi Kappa Phi, Tau Beta Pi, Pi Tau Sigma, Beta Gamma Sigma, Kappa Alpha. Home: 19731 Seashore Cir Huntington Beach CA 92648-3037

BURSON-DYER, LORRAINE, library executive; b. Omaha, Dec. 20, 1925; d. Elmer Ivan and Marie Eleanor (Benedict) Eastman; m. Francis Mark Burson, Apr. 25, 1948 (wid.); children: Melanie Burson Daniel, Brent Donald, Brian Lee; m. Eldon A. Dyer, July 11, 2004. BA with honors, Portland State U., 1975. Cons. Congregational Libr., Portland, 1975—; libr. Peace Ch. of Brethren, Portland, 1948—55, Burlingame Bapt. Ch., Portland, 1961—88, Village Bapt. Ch., Beaverton, Oreg., 1987—93; exec. dir. Ch. and Synagogue Libr. Assn., Portland, 1987—2006; ret. Author: Recruiting and Training Volunteers for Church/Synagogue Libraries, 1986; contbr. articles to numerous mags. Named Outstanding Scholar, Portland State U., 1974. Mem. Pacific N.W. Assn. Ch. Librs. (pres. 1988-89), N.W.

Assn. Christian Librs., Assn. Christian Librs., Nat. Ch. Libr. Coun., Congregational Librs. Assn. of B.C., Luth. Ch. Libr. Assn., Evangel. Ch. Libr. Assn. Baptist. Home: 10880 SW Davies Rd Apt 1014 Beaverton OR 97008-8007

BURSTEIN, ELIAS, physicist, researcher; b. NYC, Sept. 30, 1917; s. Samuel and Sarah (Plotkin) B.; m. Rena Ruth Benson, Sept. 19, 1943; children— Joanna Bliss, Sandra Joy, Miriam Stephanie. AB, Bklyn. Coll., 1938; A.M., U. Kans., 1941; postgrad., MIT, 1941—43, Cath. U., 1946—48; DTech (hon.), Chalmers U. Tech., Göteborg, Sweden, 1982; DSc (hon.), Bklyn. Coll., 1985, Emory U., 1994, Ohio State U., 1999. Physicist Crystal br. U.S. Naval Research Lab., 1945-58, head semiconductor br., 1958; prof. physics U. Pa., Phila., 1958-82, Mary Amanda Wood prof. physics, 1982-88, emeritus, 1988—. Vis. scientist Japanese Soc. for Promotion of Sci., 1977; Jubilee vis. prof. physics Chalmers U. Tech., Goteborg, 1981; solid state scis. adv. panel NRC-NAS, 1971-80, chmn., 1977-79, condensed matter physics adv. com. Internat. Ctr. for Theoretical Physics, 1990-96, Trieste; com. on sci. and the arts, Franklin Inst., 1994—; Miller Inst. vis. rsch. prof. physics U. Calif., Berkeley, 1996. Founding editor Solid State Comms., 1963, sec. bd. editors, 1963-69, editor-in-chief, 1969-1992; co-editor Comments on Solid State Physics, 1971-93, co-editor Contemporary Concepts of Condensed Matter Science series, Elsevier, 2004-. Recipient Navy Civilian Meritorious Svc. award, 1957; John Price Wetherill medal Franklin Inst., 1979; Guggenheim fellow, 1980; Alexander Von Humboldt Sr. U.S. Scientist award, 1988-90, 92-93. Fellow AAAS, Am. Phys. Soc. (sec.-treas. div. solid state physics 1956-61, Isakson prize 1986), Optical Soc. Am.; mem. Nat. Acad. Scis., Phi Beta Kappa, Sigma Xi. Democrat. Jewish. Office: U Pa Dept Physics and Astronomy Philadelphia PA 19104 Office Phone: 215-898-8160. Business E-Mail: burstein@physics.upenn.edu.

BURSTEIN, HAROLD JOHN, oncologist; s. Stuart and Catherine B.; m. Mary Mullen, Nov. 17, 1996; children: Ellen, Katherine. AB magna cum laude, Harvard U., 1986; MD, PhD, Harvard U., Boston, 1994. Diplomate Am. Bd. Internal Medicine, Am. Bd. Oncology. Intern, resident Mass. Gen. Hosp., Boston, 1994—96; oncology fellow Dana-Farber Cancer Inst., Boston, 1996—99, oncologist, 1999—. Asst. prof. medicine Harvard Med. Sch., 2002—. Recipient George P. Canellos award for Excellence in Clin. Investigation & Patient Care, 2001. Office: Dana-Farber Cancer Inst 44 Binney St Boston MA 02115 Office Phone: 617-632-3800. Business E-Mail: hburstein@partners.org.*

BURSTEIN, HARVEY, lawyer, educator; b. St. Louis, Jan. 3, 1923; m. Morris and Rachel (Johannes) B.; m. Ina Bebchick, Sept. 25, 1947. LLB, Creighton U., 1948. Bar: Nebr. 1948, U.S. Supreme Ct. 1953, Mass. 1954, N.Y. 1963. Spl. agt. FBI, 1948-53; chief fgn. and domestic investigations, surveys and phys. security U.S. Dept. State, 1953-54; pvt. practice, 1954—61, 1978—79; security officer M.I.T., Cambridge, 1956-61; v.p. and gen. counsel Norman Co., Inc., Valley Stream, NY, 1961-73; pres. Harvey Cons. Corp., Valley Stream, 1961-73; corp. security dir. Sheraton Corp., Boston, 1973-74; dir. security and safety New Eng. Mut. Life Ins. Co., Boston, 1975-78; corp. dir. safety and security, staff atty. Data Gen. Corp., Westboro, Mass., 1979-90. Guest lectr. Ind. U., Mich. State U., Wellesley Coll., Babson Coll.; adj. asst. prof. Coll. Liberal Arts Fordham U.; adj. prof. Grad. Sch. Bus. Adminstrn., Fordham U.; vis. prof. Sch. Hotel Adminstrn. Cornell U.; adj. assoc. prof. Coll. Criminal Justice, Northeastern U., vis. prof., 1990-95, David B. Schulman prof. security, 1995-2005, prof. emeritus, 2005-07; arbitrator Civil Ct. NYC, 1971-73. Author: 11 books on security mgmt.; contbr. articles on security mgmt. and investigations to profl. jours. Liaison with aux. police for Chief of Police, Brookline, Mass., 1955—61; mem. bd. overseers Spaulding Rehab. Hosp., Boston, 2003—; mem. Citizens Com. Better Law Enforcement, Town of Mamaroneck, NY, 1971—73. With AUS, 1942—46. Recipient Big Pi award Pi Lambda Phi, 1981. Mem.: Boston Bar Assn., Am. Soc. for Indsl. Security, Soc. of Ex-FBI Agts., Am. Judicature Soc., Masons, Pi Lambda Phi. Democrat. Jewish. Home: 19 Linden Sq Wellesley MA 02482-4717 Office Phone: 617-373-3057. Personal E-mail: barrybchs@verizon.net.

BURSTEIN, JUDD, lawyer; b. N.Y.C., Nov. 23, 1953; s. Herbert and Beatrice Florence (Sobel) B.; m. Janet Clarke, June 3, 1978 (div. 1984); m. Martha Wachtel, Dec. 7, 1986. B.A. summa cum laude, Brandeis U., 1975; M.A., McGill U., Can., 1977; J.D., NYU, 1981. Bar: N.Y. 1981. Teaching asst. McGill U., Montreal, Can., 1975-78; assoc. Gerald L. Shargel, Esq., N.Y.C., 1981-83; ptnr. Shargel & Burstein, N.Y.C., 1984; ptnr., Judd Burstein, P.C. N.Y.C., 1984—; of counsel Summit, Rovins & Feldesman, N.Y.C., 1984-86. Contbr. articles to profl. jours. Recipient Merit scholarship McGill U., Research and Travel grantee. Mem. N.Y. State Bar Assn., Assn. Bar City N.Y., ABA, N.Y. Council of Def. Lawyers, Assn. Trial Lawyers Am., Nat. Assn. Criminal Def. Lawyers (N.Y. council). Office: Judd Burstein PC 1790 Broadway Ste 1501 New York NY 10019

BURSTEIN, MICHAEL CLIFFORD, enterprise integration consultant; s. Edward Marion and Ethel Kaplan Burstein; 1 child, Adam; m. Eileen Reed Burstein, July 29, 2007. BA in Math. (Concentration), Johns Hopkins U., 1964; MS in Ops. Rsch., George Wash. U. Sch. Engring. and Applied Scis., 1969; PhD in Managerial Econ. & Decision Scis., Northwestern U., 1977. Cert. enterprise integrator Soc. Mfg. Engrs., 2000, cert. engring. mgr. Soc. Mfg. Engrs., 2004, registered rep. Nat. Assn. Securities Dealers, 2002. Asst. prof. indsl. engring. and ops. rsch. Sch. Engring. U. Mass., Amherst, 1980—85; prin. scientist Indsl. Tech. Inst., Ann Arbor, Mich., 1985—88; vis. assoc. prof. ops. mgmt. U. Mich., Sch. Mgmt., Ann Arbor, 1989—90; adj. assoc. prof. ops. mgmt. Yale U., Sch. Mgmt., New Haven, 1991—92; assoc. prof. ops. mgmt., dir. Ctr. Bus. Competitiveness U. Wis., Milw., 1992—96, dir. Ctr. Bus. Competitiveness, 1992—95; cons. Milw., 1996—97; CEO, pres. T.I.P.E., Inc., Belchertown, Mass., 1998—. Fellow Yale U., Jonathan Edwards Coll., New Haven, 1991—92. Co-editor and contbr. (book) Manufacturing Strategy: The Research Agenda for the Next Decade, 1990; assoc. editor: Mgmt. Sci., 1985—90, Internat. Jour. Flexible Mfg. Sys., 1986—2000, IIE Transactions, 1986—90; editl. bd. Engring. Economist, 1986—89; contbr. articles and chapters to books and jour. Mem. Planning Bd., Pelham, Mass., 1982—85; chair Cub Scout Pack Com., Dexter, Mich., 1986—87, asst. scout master, 1989—91; mem. Zoning Bd. Appeals, Westhampton, Mass., 2001—04. With US Army, 1965—70. Mem.: Soc. Concurrent Product Devel. (Boston chpt. bd.), Soc. Mfg. Engrs. (chair product and process design and mgmt. tech. cmty. 2001—, mem. cert. oversight and appeals com. 2003—, chair tech. cmty. network 2007), Soc. Concurrent Product Devel. (Boston chpt. bd. mem. 2000—, Outstanding Contributor 2002), CAMI Consortium (academic rev. panelist, cost mgmt. sys. program 1986—88), Zeta Beta Tau, Omicron Delta Epsilon (hon.; econs. bd.), Alpha Pi Mu (hon.; indsl. engr.), Tau Beta Pi (hon.; engr.). Jewish. Achievements include development of methodology for integrating multi-generational technology planning with replacement and capacity decision-making (first applied at Harley Davidson, 1993); strategy-based approach for the identification of technology opportunities and threats (first applied through the Michigan Modernization Service, 1986); coordinated the development of the Video-instructional MS in Engineering Management Program at the University of MA (Amherst) and then worldwide via the National Technological University (1984). Avocations: hiking, cross country skiing, snowshoeing, bicycling, swimming. Home and Office: TIPE Inc 632 Warrenwright Rd Belchertown MA 01007 Office Phone: 413-237-3359. Personal E-mail: mcb.tipe@charter.net.

BURSTEIN, RICHARD JOEL, lawyer; b. Detroit, Feb. 9, 1945; s. Harry Seymour and Florence (Rosen) B.; m. Gayle Lee Handmaker, Dec. 21, 1969; children: Stephanie Faith, Melissa Amy. Grad., U. Mich., 1966; JD, Wayne State U., 1969. Bar: Mich. 1969, U.S. Ct. Appeals (ea. dist.) Mich. 1969. Ptnr. Smith Miro Hirsch & Brody, Detroit, 1969-81, Honigman Miller Schwartz & Cohn, Detroit, 1981—. Bd. dirs. Sandy Corp., Troy, Mich.; bd. dirs. Met. Affairs Corp., Detroit; co-chmn. Artrain. Mem. Am. Coll. Real Estate Lawyers. Office: Honigman Miller Schwartz & Cohn Ste 100 38500 Woodward Ave Bloomfield Hills MI 48304-5048

BURSTEIN, SHARON ANN, corporate communications specialist, apparel designer; b. Schenectady, NY, July 18, 1952; d. Harold Edward and Lois Ida (Hesner) Rieck; m. Richard Lyle Burstein, Sept. 8, 1985; 1 child, Alexandra Blaire. BA, Nat. Lewis U., 1974; postgrad., Russell Sage Coll., 1974-78, Union Coll., 1980. Cert. tchr., N.Y. Elem. tchr. Saratoga Springs (N.Y.) Schs., 1974-80; ednl. cons. Whitcomb Assocs., Boston, 1980-81; ednl. mktg. specialist Monroe Sys. for Bus., Newington, Conn., 1981-83; nat. mktg. mgr. Victor Techs., Hartford, Conn., 1983, Exclusives, Boston, 1984-85; dir. pub. rels. Lawrence Group, Albany, NY, 1985-87, dir. corp. comm., 1987-88, v.p., 1988-89, v.p investors rels. NYC, 1987-89; pres. S.A. Burstein & Assocs., Albany, 1989—; pres., designer women's tennis, golf and sports apparel Neswick Court, 1994-99. Adj. prof. Russell Sage Coll., Troy, N.Y., 1994-99; exec. prodr. Carmine's TV Show-NBC; cons. N.Y. Assn. Bus. Ofcls., 1982-83; trustee Nat. Lewis U., 2005—. Editor: Helpline newspaper, 1985, 87; co-prodr. Playing It Safe, 1986 (Nori award 1987), To Be As Independent As You Can be (Nori award 1989), Cookbook Capital Connoisseur (Nori award 1989), Camp Ever Young (Nori award 1993); acted in TV comml., 1981 (Addy award 1982); prodr. Carmine's Table TV Show (NBC); exec. prodr. A Place With a Heart, 2004 (Comm. award). Bd. dirs. Multiple Sclerosis Soc., Albany, 1986, Mohawk Pathways Girl Scouts U.S.; active N.Y. Spl. Olympics, 1987; v.p. bd. dirs. Capital Repertory Theater Guild, 1999—. Recipient Disting. Alumni award, Nat. Lewis U., 2004. Mem. Nat. Investor Rels. Inst., Am. Mgmt. Assn., Assn. Profl. Communicators, Nat. Assn. Investment Clubs, Tennis Industry Assn., Albany C. of C. (women's bus. coun.), Women's Press Club, Kappa Delta Pi. Democrat. Avocations: writing, tennis, golf, skiing, reading. Home: 4 Birch Hill Rd Loudonville NY 12211-2004

BURSTEN, STUART LOWELL, physician, biochemist; b. LA, Jan. 19, 1953; s. Leo and Goldie (Zeff) B.; m. Colleen Sue Thompson, May 4, 1980; children: Elisa Michelle, Shawna Mariel, Tiana Marie; m. Lesley Domino, Mar. 26, 2000. BS in Biology, Stanford U., 1975, AB Psychology, 1975; MD, Yale U., 1980. Diplomate Am. Bd. Internal Medicine, Am. Bd. Nephrology. Intern Boston City Hosp., 1980-81; resident internal medicine U. Wash., Seattle, 1981-83, fellow nephrology, 1983-85, postdoctoral rsch. fellow, nephrology, 1985-86; acting instr. U. Wash. Sch. Medicine, 1986-88, asst. prof. medicine, 1988-92, clin. asst. prof. medicine, 1992-94, clin. assoc. prof. medicine, 1994-2001; co-dir., second messenger protein chemistry divsn. Cell Therapeutic, Inc., Seattle, 1992-95, prin. scientist, lipid biology and biochemistry, 1995-2000; prin. cons., rsch. dir. Inst. Lipid Studies, 2000—. Contbr. articles to profl. jours.; patentee. Rsch. dir. Friends of Snoqualmie Valley, Wash., 1986-89. Nat. Merit Found. scholar 1971, Nat. Grocers Assn. scholar, 1971, S&H Green Stamps Assn. scholar 1971; grantee NIH, 1975-78; recipient Northwest Kidney Found. Rsch. award, 1988-89, Nat. Inst. Arthritis, Diabetes, Digestive, and Kidney Diseases fellowship, 1985-86, others. Fellow: ACP; mem.: AAAS, Am. Stats. Assn., Am. Chem. Soc., Am. Soc. Nephrology, N.Y. Acad. Scis., Am. Fedn. Med. Rsch., Am. Heart Assn. Achievements include discovering that theobromine-based alkyl chains with patentable substitutions result in modulation of fatty acid and lipid peroxidative metabolism in mammalian cells, which in turn results in profound protection against acute inflammation and oxidant injury - this has introduced or is introducing an entire new class of compounds for treatment of a broad range of human diseases, incuding renal and liver disease, and protection against acute immune damage and the side effects of radiation; in addition, related compounds have been found to have potent anti-tumor activity based on interaction with lipid-directed enzymes. Home Phone: 707-255-0503; Office Phone: 707-252-8407. Business E-Mail: lpaatbaby@msn.com.

BURSTON, RICHARD MERVIN, marketing executive; b. Brookline, Mass., Oct. 31, 1924; s. Mark and Anita (Andrews) B.; m. Phoebe Harvey Hopkins, Aug. 29, 1958; children: Abby Lyn, Seth Hopkins, Joshua Craig, Mark Andrews, Amanda Lee. BA, Bowdoin Coll., 1949; MBA, Harvard U., 1952. Mgr. beauty dept. Kendall Co., Boston, 1953-58; regional sales mgr. M. Pier Co., Ft. Lauderdale, Fla., 1958-59; nat. sales mgr. Ozon Products, Inc., Bklyn., 1959-63; v.p., co-founder Burston/Larkin Assocs., Stamford, Conn., 1964-88; pres., CEO Excalibur, Inc., Stamford, 1981-88; founder, pres. Burston Inc., Stamford, 1987-98, cons., 1999—. Dir. Nat. Beauty and Barber Reps. Assn., N.Y.C., 1973-74, Louv Yacht Yard, Norwalk, Conn., 1969-73; cons. Ruckel Mfg., Inc., N.Y.C., 1969-87. Dir. Roxbury-Riverbank Little League, Stamford, 1971-82; fundraiser Bowdoin Coll., Brunswick, Maine, 1983-90, mem. alumni coun., 1994-98, pres., 1997-98. Lt. USNR, 1943-46, PTO. Recipient Man of Yr. award United Beauty Supply Corp., Bridgeport, Conn., 1983. Mem. Beauty and Barber Supply Inst., Am. Beauty Assn., Kents Hill Sch. Alumni Assn. (bd. dirs. 1994-2000, trustee 1994-2004, hon. trustee for life 2004), Miramichi Rod and Gun Club Inc. (pres. 2002), High Head Yacht Club (dir. 1997-2000). Republican. Jewish. Avocation: fly fishing. Home: 408 High Head Rd Harpswell ME 04079-2917 Office: Burston Inc 45 Church St Stamford CT 06906-1711 Business E-Mail: dpburst@suscom-maine.net.

BURSTYN, ELLEN (EDNA RAE GILLOOLY), actress; b. Detroit, Dec. 7, 1932; m. William Anderson, 1950 (div. 1955); m. Paul Roberts, 1957 (div. 1959); m. Neil Burstyn, 1960 (div. 1971); 1 child, Jefferson. LHD (hon.), Dowling Coll.; DFA (hon.), Sch. Visual Arts. Artistic dir. The Actor's Studio, NYC, 1982-88. Actress (films) Gunfight in Black Horse Canyon, 1961, Alex in Wonderland, 1970, Tropic of Cancer, 1970, The Last Picture Show, 1971, The King of Marvin Gardens, 1972, The Exorcist, 1973, Harry and Tonto, 1974, Alice Dosen't Live Here Anymore (Acad. award for Best Actress), 1974, Same Time, Next Year, 1978, Resurrection, 1980, Silence of the North, 1981, In Our Hands, 1984, The Ambassador, 1984, Twice in a Lifetime, 1985, Hanna's War, 1988, Grand Isle, 1991, Dying Young, 1991, The Cemetery Club, 1993, The Color of Evening, 1994, Choosing One's Way: Resistance in Auschwitz/Birkenau (narrator, presenter), 1994, When a Man Loves a Woman, 1994, Roommates, 1995, The Baby-Sitters Club, 1995, How to Make an American Quilt, 1995, The Spitfire Grill, 1996, Deceiver, 1997, You Can Thank Me Later, 1998, Playing by Heart, 1998, Walking Across Egypt, 1999, Requiem for a Dream, 1999, The Yards, 1999, Divine Secrets of the Ya-Ya Sisterhood, 2002, Distance, 2002, (voice only) Red Dragon, 2002, Down in the Valley, 2005, The Elephant King, 2006, The Wicker Man, 2006, 30 Days, 2006, The Fountain, 2006; (TV films) Thursday's Game, 1974, The People vs. Jean Harris, 1981, Acting: Lee Strasberg and the Actos Studio, 1981, Surviving, 1985, Into Thin Air, 1985, Something in Common, 1986, Act of Vengeance, 1986, Hellow Actors Studio, 1987, (voice only) Dear America: Letters Home from Vietnam, 1987, Pack of Lies, 1987, When You Remember Me, 1990, Mrs. Lambers Remembers Love, 1991, Taking Back My Life: The Nacy Ziegenmeyer Story, 1992, Shattered Trust: The Shary Karney Story, 1993, Getting Out, 1994, Getting Gotti, 1994, Trick of the Eye, 1994, My Brother's Keeper, 1995, Follow the River, 1995, Timepiece, 1995, Our Son, The Matchmaker, 1996, Murder in the Mind, 1996, A Deadly Vision, 1997, Flash, 1998, The Patron Saint of Liars, 1998, Night Ride Home, 1999, Mermaid, 2000, Within These Walls, 2001, Dodson's Journey, 2001, Brush with Fate, 2003, The Madam's Family: The Truth About the Canal Street Brothel, 2004, The Five People You Meet in Heaven, 2004, Our Fathers, 2005, Mrs. Harris, 2005; (TV series) The Ellen Burstyn Show, 1986-87; (mini-series) A Will of Their Own, 1998; (TV appearances) Cheyenne, 1955, Gunsmoke, 1955, Maverick, 1957, The Big Valley, 1965, The Time Tunnel, 1966, The Bold Ones: The Lawyers, 1969; Author:(autobiography) Lessons in Becoming Myself, 2006 Mem. individual artists grants and policy overview panels Nat. Endowment for the Arts, Theater Adv. Council City of New York. Named to, The Mich. Women's Hall of Fame, 1997. Mem. Actors Equity Assn. (pres. 1982-85) Office: Creative Artists Agy care Steve Tellez 9830 Wilshire Blvd Beverly Hills CA 90212-1804

BURT, ALVIN MILLER, III, anatomist, educator, cell biologist, writer; b. Bridgeport, Conn., Aug. 14, 1935; s. Alvin Miller and Esther Louise (Carey) B.; m. Dorothy Hanlin, July 15, 1961 (div.); children: Constance Walker, Carolyn Marie; m. Judith Nath, July 13, 1991; 1 stepchild, Stephen Jacob Nath. BA, Amherst Coll., 1957; PhD (USPHS fellow 1960-61), U. Kans., 1962. Asst. prof. anatomy Med. Coll. Va., Richmond, 1962-63; instr. Yale U. Med. Sch., 1963-66; mem. faculty Vanderbilt U. Med. Sch., 1966—, prof. anatomy, 1974-85, prof. cell biology, 1985-2000, prof. cell biology emeritus, 2000—; prof. cell biology Nursing Sch. Vanderbilt U., Nashville, 1994-2000, prof. cell biology in nursing emeritus, 2000—; sole proprietor Creative Manuscripts and CM Web Graphics, Hendersonville. Vis. scientist Agrl. Rsch. Coun., Inst. Animal Physiology, Babraham, Cambridge, Eng., 1972-73; bd. dirs. Trinity Health Svcs., LLC Author: Textbook of Neuroanatomy, 1993; contbr. articles to profl. jours. Vestryman Episcopal Ch. of Advent, Brentwood, Tenn., 1977-81, sr. warden, 1979-81, lay reader, chalice bearer, 1975-87, tchr. adult classes, mem. diocesan lay ministry com., 1981-85; lay reader, chalice bearer St. Philips Episcopal Ch., Donelson, Tenn., 1989-92, vestryman, 1991-92, mem. diocesan total ministry com., 1990-93; mem. Stephen Ministry Diocese of Tenn., 1991—; dir. pastoral care St. Ann's Episcopal Ch., Nashville, 1993-96, lay reader, 1994—, chalice bearer, 1996—, vestryman, 2002-05; mem. steering com. Interfaith AIDS Ministry, 1994-96; vol. ombudsman rep. Mid Cumberland Human Resources Ctr., 2001—. Recipient Research Career Devel. award USPHS, 1968-73 Mem. Am. Assn. Anatomists, Am. Soc. Neurochemistry, Human Anatomy & Physiology Soc., Internat. Soc. Neurochemistry, Internat. Brain Rsch. Orgn., Soc. Neurosci., Tenn. Outdoor Writers Assn. (v.p. 1985-86, pres.-elect 1986-87, pres. 1987-88, chmn. bd. dirs. 1988-89), Southeastern Outdoor Press Assn. (Webmaster 2002-2005), Bass Anglers Sportsmens Soc., Tenn. Spoonplugging Club (bd. dirs. 1980-88, editor newsletter 1980-85), Sigma Xi. Home and Office: 149 Bay Dr Hendersonville TN 37075-4040

BURT, ALVIN VICTOR, JR., journalist; b. Oglethorpe County, Ga., Sept. 11, 1927; s. Alvin Victor and Mabel (Sorrow) B.; m. Gloria White. BA in Edn, U. Fla., 1949. With U.P., 1949-50, Atlanta Jour., 1950-51, Jacksonville (Fla.) Jour., 1951-55; with Miami (Fla.) Herald, 1955-66, Latin Am. editor, 1962-66, assigned Washington, 1962, editorial writer, 1967-73, columnist, 1973-96; editor Hartwell (Ga.) Sun, 1966-67. Co-author: Papa Doc, 1969; author: Florida A Place in the Sun, 1974, Becalmed in the Mullet Latitudes, 1983, Al Burt's Florida, 1997, The Tropic of Cracker, 1999. Recipient Ernie Pyle award for newspaper writing, 1961, State award A.P. for feature writing, 1964, citation Fla. Legislature, 1965, Scripps-Howard award for best interviews in nation, 1966, Editorial Writing award Fla. Soc. Newspaper Editors-Fla. Press Assn., 1973, Overseas Press award, 1974, J.C. Penney spl. award U. Mo., 1980, Outstanding Journalist award Fla. Audubon Soc., 1984, First Ann. AL Burt award for extraordinary lifelong commitment 1000 Friends of Fla., 1989, Commentator of Yr. award Fla. Wildlife Fedn., 1990, Patrick Smith Lit. award Fla. Hist. Soc., 1998, LeRoy Collins Lifetime Chievement award Leadership Fla., 2004, Ichetucknee Springs bronze plaque, State of Fla., 2006; inducted into Ind. Alligator Hall of Fame, 1998; named Alumnus of Distinction U. Fla. Coll. of Journalism and Comms., 1999, Conservation Steward 2006, Alaska Conservation Trust. Office: PO Box 17 Melrose FL 32666-0017

BURT, FRANK DAVIES, lawyer, real estate company executive; b. Washington, Sept. 19, 1958; s. William Charles and Margery (Davies) B.; m. Carol Hackett, Sept. 3, 1988. BA, Brown U., 1980; JD, U. Pa., 1983. Bar: Mass. 1983. Assoc. Nutter, McClennan, Fish, Boston, 1983-86; sr. v.p., gen. counsel Boston Properties, Inc., 1986—. Mem. Moot Ct. Bd. U. Pa., Phila., 1982. Mem. Boston Bar Assn., Assn. Corp. Coun., New Eng. Corp. Counsel Assn., Phi Beta Kappa. Democrat. Avocation: skiing. Office: Boston Properties Inc 111 Huntington Ave Boston MA 02199

BURT, GWYNNE ELAYNE, minister, theology studies educator; b. Hackensack, NJ, June 28, 1962; s. Eugene Marshall Sr. and Hortense Marshall. BS in adminstr. and Mgmt., LaRoche Coll., 1984. Personnel asst. Kmart Apparel, North Bergen, NJ, 1984—87; recruiter JJT, Tab Richards, Anython Ryan Assoc., NJ, 1988—92; tchr. Hackensack Pub. Schs., Hackensack, NJ, 1992—2007, Plaza Sch. of Tech., Paramus, NJ, 1994—99; sr. rsch. editor Lexis-Nexis, New Providence, NJ, 1999—2001; min. Mt. Calvary Bapt. Ch., Englewood, NJ, 2000—05; tchr. St. James Preparatory Sch., Newark, 2002—04; pastor Arms Christ Christian Fellowship, East Orange, NJ, 2006—. Contbr. articles various profl. jours. Bapt. Avocations: writing, singing, dance. Home: 119 Poplar Ave Hackensack NJ 07601 E-mail: prophetGB@aol.com.

BURT, JEFFREY AMSTERDAM, lawyer; b. Phila., Apr. 27, 1944; s. Samuel Matthew and Esther (Amsterdam) B.; m. Sandra Cass, Dec. 17, 1967; children: Stephen, Daniel, Jonathan, Andrew. BA, Princeton, 1966; LLB, Yale U., 1970; MA in Econs., 1970. Bar: Md. 1971, DC 1971. Law clk. to judge U.S. Ct. Appeals (4th cir.), Balt., 1970-71; assoc. Arnold & Porter, Washington, 1971-77; ptnr., 1978—. Adj. prof. law Georgetown U., 1987-95; frequent lectr. Pres., Green Acres, Inc. Ind. Sch., Rockville, Md., 1984-86. Author: (with others) International Joint Ventures, 1986, 2nd edit., 1992; co-editor: Joint Ventures with Internat. Ptnrs., 1997. Mem. ABA (co-chairperson NIS Law Com. Sect. Internat. Law and Practice 1992-98), Russian Am. C. of C. (dir., sec.), Nat. Synagogue (dir.). Office: Arnold & Porter 555 12th St NW Washington DC 20004-1206

BURT, MARVIN ROGER, financial advisor, investment manager; b. LA, Mar. 5, 1937; s. Henry Howard Burt and Iris Faith (Green) Welton; m. Joy Lee Rougk, July 20, 1958; children: Sandra Marie, Scott Marvin. BA, UCLA, 1958; MPA, George Washington U., 1965, D in Pub. Adminstrn., 1969. CFP. Mgmt. trainee Bank Am., LA, 1961—62; program analyst Dept. Def., Washington, 1962—65, Exec. Office Pres., Washington, 1965—66; mem. sr. rsch. staff Resource Mgmt. Corp., Bethesda, Md., 1966—67; sr. cons. Peat Marwick Mitchell, Washington, 1967—68; cons. Potomac, Md., 1968—69; mem. sr. staff Urban Inst., Washington, 1969—72; pres. Burt Assocs., Inc., Bethesda, 1972—2002, Inst. Human Resources Rsch., Bethesda, 1973—82; asst. v.p. Sci. Applications Internat., McLean, Va., 1982—85; chmn. bd. Burt Assocs., Inc., Bethesda, 1972—. Cons. Govt. Agys., Washington, 1965—82. Author: Options for Improving the Care of Neglected and Dependent Children, 1971, Policy Analysis, 1974, A Comprehensive Emergency Services System for Neglected and Abused Children, 1977, Drug Abuse, 1979, Children of Heroin Addicts, 1980; contbr. articles to profl. jours. Mem. Cmty. Coordinated Child Care, Bethesda, 1976—77; mem. drug abuse adv. com. Montgomery County, 1990—92, bd. dirs. cmty. ministry, 2006—; chmn. coun. on ministries North Bethesda United Meth. Ch., Md., 1975—76, 1981—82, chmn. bd. dirs., 1977—78, bd. dirs., 1986—92, lay del. to ann. conf., 1989, chmn. staff-parish rels. com., 1990—92, chmn. fin. com., 2001—06; bd. dirs., Mental Health Assn. Montgomery County, 2002—03. Grantee, USPHS, 1977—82. Mem.: Inst. Cert. Fin. Planners (dean mid-atlantic conf. 1995), Fin. Planning Assn. (v.p. nat. capital chpt. 1987—89), Ops. Rsch. Soc. Am. (chmn. tech. sect. 1979—80), Avenel Commn. Assn. (pres. 1998—2000, bd. dirs. 1996—2001), Bethesda/Chevy Chase C. of C. (chmn. small bus. com. 1990—91, v.p. small bus., bd. dirs. 1991—93), Potomac Rotary (pres. 1991—92, bd. dirs. 1987—93, pres. Potomac Rotary Charities, Inc. 1992).

Avocations: hiking, golf. Home: 5 Willow Gate Ct Bethesda MD 20817-4110 Office: Burt Assocs Inc 6010 Executive Blvd Ste 900 Rockville MD 20852 Home Phone: 301-299-3402; Office Phone: 301-770-9880. Personal E-mail: mburt@comcast.net. Business E-Mail: mburt@burtassociates.com.

BURT, RICHARD, lawyer; V.p. fin. and devel. Sandoz Corp., 1978—89, v.p., gen. counsel, sec., 1978—89; v.p. legal affairs ABB subs. Asea Brown Boveri Ltd., NY, 1989; sr. v.p., gen. counsel, sec. ABB Inc. N.Am. subs. ABB Group, Zurich, Switzerland; sr. v.p., gen. counsel Bechtel, San Francisco, 2002—. Mem.: Am. Corp. Counsel Assn. (Westchester/So. Conn. chpt.).

BURT, RICHARD K., physician, educator; b. Billings, Mont., Oct. 20, 1956; m. Shalina Gupta; children: Michael, Rajan, Reena, Shantha. BS in Chemistry, U. Mo., 1976—80; MD cum laude, St. Louis U. Sch. Medicine, 1984. Cert. Am. Bd. Internal Medicine, 1987, Hematology Bd., 1992, Med. Oncology Bd., 1992. Resident Baylor Coll. Medicine, Houston, 1984—87, chief resident, medicine, 1987; biotechnology tng. fellow, lab. of exptl. carcinogenesis Nat. Cancer Inst., NIH, Bethesda, Md., 1987—90, clin. assoc., med. oncology br., 1990—91; vis. fellow, bone marrow transplantation Fred Hutchinson Cancer Ctr., Seattle, 1992, Johns Hopkins Hosp., Balt., 1992; clin. assoc., bone transplantation unit Nat. Heart, Lung and Blood Inst., NIH, Bethesda, Md., 1993—94; dir., allogeneic bone marrow transplantation, asst. prof. Northwestern U., Chgo., 1994—2000; chief, divsn. of immunotherapy, assoc. prof. Northwestern U. Med. Sch., Chgo., 2000—. Contbr. articles to profl. jours., chapters to books; mem. editl. bd. Bone Marrow Transplantation, 1998—, Jour. of Biotechnology in Healthcare, 1998—, Graft, 1998—. Lt. cmdr. USPHS, 1991—94. Recipient Compassionate Care Physician Award, Robert J. Lurie Cancer Ctr., 1999, Fidelitas Award, Lupus Found. of Am., 2000; grantee, Roderick Duncan Rsch. Fund, 1988, Nat. Multiple Sclerosis Soc., 1995, Am. Cancer Soc., 1996, Leukemia Soc. Am., 1997—99, NIH, Nat. Inst. Allergy & Infectious Disease, 1999—, Cumming Found. for Med. Rsch., 2002, Broad Found., 2002; scholar, Leukemia Soc. Am., 1998—2003. Mem.: AAAS, AMA, Am. Soc. for Blood and Marrow Transplantation. Avocations: flying, weightlifting, jogging. Office: Northwestern Univ Med Sch Divsn Immunotherapy 750 N Lakeshore Dr Ste 649 Chicago IL 60611 Office Phone: 312-908-0059. Fax: 312-908-0064. Business E-Mail: rburt@northwestern.edu.*

BURT, ROBERT AMSTERDAM, lawyer, educator; b. Phila., Feb. 3, 1939; s. Samuel Matthew and Esther (Amsterdam) B.; m. Linda Gordon Rose, June 14, 1964; children: Anne Elizabeth, Jessica Ellen. AB, Princeton U., 1960; BA in Jurisprudence, Oxford U., 1962, MA, 1968; JD, Yale U., 1964, MA (hon.), 1976. Bar: D.C. 1966, Mich. 1973, U.S. Supreme Ct. 1971. Law clk. to chief judge U.S. Ct. Appeals D.C., 1964—65; asst. gen. counsel Office Pres.'s Spl. Rep. Trade Negotiations, 1965—66; senatorial legis. asst., 1966—68; assoc. prof. law U. Chgo. Law Sch., 1968—70; assoc. prof., then prof. law U. Mich. Law Sch., 1970—76; prof. law in psychiatry U. Mich. Med. Sch., 1973—76; Southmayd prof. Yale U. Law Sch., 1976—93, Alexander M. Bickel prof., 1993—. Spl. master U.S. Dist. Ct. Conn., 1987-92, 95. Author: Taking Care of Strangers, 1979, Two Jewish Justices: Outcasts in the Promised Land, 1988, Constitution in Conflict, 1992, Death Is That Man Taking Names: Intersections of American Medicine, Law and Culture, 2002. Bd. dirs. Benhaven Sch. Autistic Persons, New Haven, 1977—, chmn., 1983-96; bd. dirs. Judge David L. Bazelon Ctr. Mental Health Law, 1985—, chmn., 1990-00; bd. dirs. Slifka Ctr. Jewish Life at Yale, 1996—; mem. adv. bd. Project on Death in Am., Open Soc. Inst., 1994-04; mem. adv. bd. bioethics faculty scholars program Greenwall Found., 2003-. Rockefeller fellow, 1976, John Simon Guggenheim fellow, 1997—98. Mem.: NAS, Inst. Medicine. Democrat. Jewish. Home: 66 Dogwood Cir Woodbridge CT 06525-1254 Office: Yale U Sch Law PO Box 208215 127 Wall St New Haven CT 06511-6636 Office Phone: 203-432-4960. Business E-Mail: robert.burt@yale.edu.

BURT, THOMAS WILLIAM, lawyer; b. Spokane, Wash., Jan. 24, 1955; s. Jack Wallace and Peggy (Windes) B.; m. Ann Darling, Apr. 2, 1989; children; Trevor D. Welling, Griffin D., Caroline D. AB in Human Biology, Stanford U., 1976; JD, U. Wash., 1979. Bar: Wash. 1979, U.S. Ct. Appeals (9th cir.) 1979, U.S. Dist. Ct. (we. dist.) Wash. 1980. Law clk. to judge Ozell Trask U.S. Ct. Appeals (9th cir.), Phoenix, 1979-80; ptnr., atty. Riddell, Williams, Bullitt & Walkinshaw, Seattle, 1980-95; corp. v.p., dep. gen. counsel litig. Microsoft Corp., Redmond, Wash., 2003—. Bd. dirs. Bainbridge Island (Wash.) Land Trust, 1990-91. Mem. ABA, Wash. Bar Assn., Seattle-King County Bar. Avocations: sports car racing, skiing, sailing. Office: Microsoft Corp One Microsoft Way Redmond WA 98052 Office Phone: 425-703-6323. Business E-Mail: tburt@microsoft.com.

BURT, WALLACE JOSEPH, JR., insurance company executive; b. Burlington, Iowa, Apr. 1, 1924; s. Wallace Joseph and Lel (Catlow) Burt; m. Alice Olmsted, June 22, 1946; children: Lockwood, David, Virginia. Student, Iowa State Coll., 1942, U. Wis., 1945. V.p., dir. 1st Ins. Fin. Co., Des Moines, 1946—50, Northea. Ins. Co., Hartford, Conn., 1950—59; pres., owner Hail Reins. Mgmt., Inc., Ormond Beach, Fla., 1960—89; chmn. Burt & Scheld, Inc., Ormond Beach, 1961—89; chmn. U.S. br. Hamburg Internat. Reins. Co., 1976—81; chmn. 1st N.Y. Syndicate Corp., 1979—89, W.J. Burt Mgmt., Inc., NYC, 1979—89; pres. Ormond Reins. Co., 1976—92, Oceanside RE Group, Inc., 1989. Dir., v.p. Barnett Bank, Ormond Beach; underwriting mem. Lloyd's of London; dir. N.Y. Ins. Exch., 1983—84. Trustee, pres. Ormond Beach Meml. Hosp. Served to 1st lt. USAAF, WWII. Decorated D.F.C., Purple Heart, Air medal with 5 oak leaf clusters. Home: 222 Riverside Dr Ormond Beach FL 32176-6504 Office: 140 S Atlantic Ave Ormond Beach FL 32176-6689 Office Phone: 386-677-5217.

BURTEN, BARRY LEE, lawyer; b. NYC, Aug. 3, 1948; s. Nathan and Shirley (Mayer) B.; m. Cindy Gae Gorin, Aug. 2, 1980; children: Courtney Nicole, Andrew Allen. BA magna cum laude, Colgate U., 1970; JD, Harvard U., 1973. Bar: NY 1974, Calif. 1984, US Dist. Ct. (ctrl. dist.) Calif., US Dist. Ct. (so. and ea. dists.) NY. Assoc. Dewey Ballantine (formerly Dewey Ballantine Bushby Palmer & Wood), NYC, 1973-76, Sage Gray Todd & Simms, NYC, 1976-77; v.p., corp. counsel Orion Pictures Corp. (formerly Filmways, Inc.), LA, 1978-84; ptnr. Shea & Gould (formerly Pacht Ross Warne Bernhard & Sears, Inc.), LA, 1984-89, Myerson & Kuhn, LA, 1989, Varet Marcus & Fink (formerly Milgrin Thomajan & Lee), LA, 1989-93, Marcus Montgomery Wolfson & Burten, LA, 1993, Jeffer, Mangels, Butler & Marmaro LLP, LA. Mem.: ABA (bus law sect.), LA County Bar Assn., Beverly Hills Bar Assn. Office: Jeffer Mangels Butler & Marmaro LLP 1900 Ave of Stars 7th Fl Los Angeles CA 90067 Office Phone: 310-785-5359. Office Fax: 310-712-3359. Business E-Mail: blb@jmbm.com.

BURTLESS, GARY THOMAS, economist, consultant; b. Cayuga County, NY, Apr. 11, 1950; s. Charles Bernie and Patricia Ann (MacCone) B.; m. Elise Kathe Bruml, Nov. 27, 1976; children: Andrew B., Matthew B. BA, Yale U., 1972; PhD, MIT, 1977. Economist Office Sc., HEW, Washington, 1977-79, U.S. Dept. Labor, Washington, 1979-81; John D. and Nancy C. Whitehead chair in econ. studies Brookings Instn., Washington, 1981—. Vis. prof. pub. affairs U. Md., College Park, 1993; cons. various orgns., 1981—, U.S. Dept. Lab., 1985—, World Bank, Washington, 1990-97. Author: Can America Afford To Grow Old, 1989, Growth With Equity: Economic Policymaking for the Next Century, 1993, Globaphobia: Confronting Fears about Open Trade, 1998; co-editor Jour. Human Resources, 1988-96, Brookings-Wharton Papers on Urban Affairs, 2003—, A Future of Lousy Jobs?, 1990, Five Years After: Long Term Effects of Welfare-to-Work Programs, 1995, Does Money Matter? Effect of School Resources, 1996, Work, Health and Income Among the Elderly, 1997, Aging Societies: The Global Dimension, 1998; mem. editl. bd. Jour. Policy Analysis and Mgmt., 1999-, Australian Econ. Rev., 2006-; contbr. articles to profl. jours. Commn. mem. panel on fin. adequacy Trustees Social Security, 1989; mem.tech. panel Adv. Coun. on Social Security, 1994—95; mem. com. on health and safety needs of older workers NAS, 2001—04. Recipient Leontief prize Ea. Econ. Assn., 1978. Mem.: Assn. Pub. Policy Analysis & Mgmt., Nat. Acad. Social Ins. (commn. mem. panel on Social Security notch 1988, panel on privatizing Social Security 1997—98), Am. Econ. Assn. Avocations: history, hiking. Office: Brookings Instn 1775 Massachusetts Ave NW Washington DC 20036-2103 Office Phone: 202-797-6000, 202-797-6130. Business E-Mail: communications@brookings.edu.

BURTLEY, CALVIN, art director; b. Cairo, Ill., Feb. 28, 1945; s. Brooks Jr. and Gustava (Robinson) B. Cert., Famous Artist Sch., Conn., 1973; AA, L.A. Trade Tech. Coll., 1982; BFA, U. So. Calif., 1992. Ordained elder, Presbyn. of Pacific. Graphic artist U. So. Calif., LA, 1982-92; art cons. LA, 1992-95; pub. rels. adminstr. Cultural Affairs, LA, 1995-96; pres. Burtley Fine Arts, LA, 1997—; tchr. Jr. Art Ctr., LA, 1999. Exhbns. include Palms Westminster Presbyn. Ch., L.A., 1995, L.A. Mcpl. Art Gallery, 1996, St. Andrews Abbey, Valyermo, Calif., 1997, The Presbytery of the Pacific, L.A., 1997, Hollywood Digital, L.A., 1998, City of Brea Gallery, 1998, Palos Verdes Art Ctr., 1999, Nat. Art Program City of L.A., 1999. V.p. Palms Westminster Presbyn. Ch., L.A., 1996—; mem. Cmty. Coalition, L.A., 1999; vol. Cir. of Friends, Easter Seals, After Sch. Programs, L.A., 1999. With USN, 1965-69. Named Person of Yr., Palms Westminster Woman's Assn., 1996. Mem. Am. Legion. Democrat. Avocations: painting, reading, languages, classical music. E-mail: artbrush@email.com.

BURTON, AL, television producer, television director, writer; b. Chgo. s. D. Chester and Isabelle (Olenick) G.; m. Sally Lou Lewis, Jan. 8, 1956; 1 dau., Jennifer. BS cum laude, Northwestern U. Exec. v.p. creative affairs Norman Lear-Embassy Communications, Inc., 1973-83; exec. producer-cons. Universal TV, 1983-92; exec. prodr., v.p. syndication Castle Rock Entertainment, 1992-95; pres. Al Burton Prodns., Beverly Hills, Calif., 1995—. Bd. dirs. Pilgrim Group Funds; adv. bd. Samantha Smith Found. Producer Johnny Mercer's Mus. Chairs, 1952-55, Oscar Levant Show, 1955-61; creative producer Teen-Age Fair, 1962-72; exec. producer Charles in Charge, CBS-TV, 1984-85, Tribune Entertainment, 1986-91, Together We Stand, CBS-TV, 1986-87, Nothing Is Easy, 1987-88, The New Lassie, The Family Channel, 1989-92 (Outstanding Family Classic award Youth in Film 1994), Out of the Blue, Tribune Entertainment, 1995-96, Win Ben Stein's Money, Disney, Comedy Ctrl., 1997— (Cable Ace nomination, Emmy nomination 1998, 99, 2001, shared 2 Emmys, 1998, Emmy award for Outstanding Game Show 1999); creative supr. Mary Hartman, Mary Hartman, Fernwood 2Night, America 2Night; prodn. supr. One Day At a Time, Facts of Life, Silver Spoons, The Jeffersons, Square Pegs, Different Strokes; composer-lyricist theme songs for Facts of Life, Different Strokes, Charles in Charge, The New Lassie (Genesis award, 1992), Together We Stand, Nothing Is Easy; cons. Domestic Life CBS-TV, 1983-84, Alan King Show, 1986. Shared Emmy honors for outstanding comedy series All in the Family, 1978-89, Producers award Nat. Coun. for Families and TV, 1984, Jackie Coogan award for Oustanding Contbn. to Youth through Entertainment, 1991; honored for Different Strokes, NCCH, 1979-80; honored by Calif. Gov.'s Com. for employment of the handicapped for Facts of Life, 1981-82, for Charles in Charge, 1988; recipient Youth in Film award Charles in Charge, 1990, The New Lassie, 1994, Genesis award for portrayal animal issues The New Lassie, 1992; spl. commendation Entertainment Industries Coun. for The New Lassie and Charles in Charge, 1990. Mem. AFTRA, Chmn.'s Coun. of Caucus for Producers, Writers and Dirs., Dirs. Guild Am., Writers Guild Am., Acad. TV Arts and Scis., Acad. Magical Arts. Home: 555 Laurel Ave San Mateo CA 94401 Office Phone: 650-348-3463. Personal E-mail: alburton22@aol.com. *I believe that, in order to achieve success, one should make an occupation of his or her hobby.*

BURTON, BETSY (MARY ELIZABETH), retail executive; b. Richmond, Va., Dec. 18, 1951; d. Samuel Bayard and Dottie (Brown) Jeter. BA in Sociology, Coll. William and Mary, 1973; MBA, U. Chgo., 1975. Corp. trainee Jewel Cos., Chgo., 1975—82, mdse. mgr. Osco Drug div., 1980—82; pres. Bee Discount, Hillside, Ill., 1982—83, Victory Beauty Systems (parent of Bee Discount), Hillside, Ill., 1983—87; CEO Supercuts Inc., 1987—91, PIP Printing, 1991—92, BB Capital Inc., 1992; chmn., CEO The Cosmetic Centre, 1998—99; acting CEO Zale Corp., 2006, pres., CEO, 2006—. Bd. dirs. Zale Corp., Staples Inc., Rent-A-Center, Aeropostale Inc; past bd. dirs. Sports Authority. Mem. mental health task force United Methodist Ch., Naperville, Ill., 1982. Grantee, NSF, 1972, George Hay Brown Found., U. Chgo. Grad. Sch. Bus., 1975. Mem.: Com. of 200, U. Chgo. Women's Bus. Group. Republican. Avocations: aerobics, jogging. Office: Zale Corp 901 W Walnut Hill Ln Irving TX 75038*

BURTON, BRIAN JOSEPH (DANGER MOUSE), sound recording engineer, musician; b. White Plains, NY; Mem. Danger Mouse (DM) & Jemini, Dangerdoom, Gnarls Barkley, 2004—. Prodr.: (albums) The Chilling Effect, as Pelican City, 1999, Rhode Island, as Pelican City, 2000, Ghetto Pop Life, for DM & Jemini, 2003, Lexoleum, 2003, Genocide in Sudan, 2004, Slickness, for Prince Po, 2004, Twenty Six Inch EP, for Danger Mouse & Jemini, 2004, The Grey Album, 2004 (Best Record of Yr., Entertainment Weekly, 2004), Demon Days, for Gorillaz, 2005, Fear of a Black Tangent, for Busdriver, 2005, Healthy Distrust, for Sage Francis, 2005, The Mouse and the Mask, for DangerDoom, 2005, Pieces of the People We Love, for The Rapture, 2006, St. Elsewhere, for Gnarls Barkley, 2006 (Grammy award for Best Alternative Music Album, 2007), Dramt for Light Years in the Belly of a Mountain, for Sparklehorse, 2006, The Good, the Bad, & the Queen, 2007; prodr.: (songs) Crazy, 2006 (2 MTV Video Music awards for Best Direction & Best Editing, MTV Europe Music award for Best Song, 2006, Grammy award for Best Alternative Performance, 2007, Soul Train award for Best Soul Single, 2007). Named one of Men of Yr., GQ mag., 2004; recipient Rave award, Wired mag., 2005, Left Field Woodie award, mtvU, 2006, Best Group award (as Gnarls Barkley), Black Entertainment TV (BET) Awards, 2007. Office: Waxploitation Inc 11601 Wilshire Blvd Los Angeles CA 90025

BURTON, BRUCE ARTHUR, education educator; b. Newark; s. Donald Lawrence and Alice Beatrice Burton; m. Jamie Ann Crowl, June 24, 1967; children: Bruce Harold, William Trahern. BA, Bowdoin Coll., Brunswick, Maine, 1967; MLitt, Univ. Edinburgh, Edinburgh, Scotland, 1969. Tchr. Scarborough Sch., Briarcliff Manor, NY, 1969—70; prof. Castleton State Coll., Castleton, Vt., 1970—96. Editor Turtle Quarertly, Niagara Falls, NY, 1988—. Author: Hail! Nene Karenna The Hymn, 1981, Japanese translation, 1988, (novels) In the Valley of the Shadow: The Story of David Jones and Jane McCrea, September Morning, 2006; contbr. articles to profl. jour. Past chair Zoning Bd. of Adj., Castleton, Vt., 1972, Planning Commn., Castleton, Vt., 1972. Mem.: Writers Guild of Am. Achievements include patents for inlaid brick walkway bed leveler; heating, ventilating, air conditioning for workers' servicing cart. Avocations: anthropology, camping, gardening, nature study. Personal E-mail: bruceburton1@aol.com.

BURTON, CHARLES VICTOR, neurosurgeon; b. NYC, Jan. 2, 1935; s. Norman Howard and Ruth Esther (Putziger) B.; m. Joy Burton; children—Matthew, Timothy, Andrew, Dawn, Stacy, Chad. Student, Johns Hopkins U., Balt., 1952-56; MD, N.Y. Med. Coll., 1960. Diplomate Am. Bd. Neurol. Surgery, Nat. Bd. Med. Examiners, Am. Bd. Forensic Medicine, Am. Bd. Spinal Surgery. Intern surgery Yale U. Med. Ctr., 1961—62; asst. resident neurol. surgery Johns Hopkins Hosp., Balt., 1962—66, chief resident, 1966—67; assoc. chief surgery, chief neurosurgery USPHS Hosp., Seattle, 1967—69; vis. research affiliate Primate Ctr., U. Wash., 1967—69; asst. prof. neurosurgery Temple U. Health Scis. Ctr., Phila., 1970—73, assoc. prof., 1973—74, neurol. research coordinator, 1970—74; dir. dept. neuroaugmentive surgery Sister Kenny Inst., Mpls., 1974—81, med. dir. Low Back Clinic, 1978—81; med. dir. Inst. Low Back & Neck Care, Mpls., 1981—2004, Ctr. Restorative Spine Surgery, St. Paul, 2004—, Pouncefort Techs. Ltd., 2006—. Biomed. Instrumentations Internat., Ltd., 1988-92; co-chmn. Joint Neurosurg. Com. on Devices and Drugs, 1973-77; chmn. adv. panel on neurologic devices FDA, 1974-77, Internat. Standards Orgn., 1974-76; mem. U.S. Biomed. Instrumentation Del. to Soviet Union, 1974; co-chmn. Am. Bd. Spine Surgery. Editor Neuroorthopedics jour., 1987-1998, editor The Burton Report; editor-in-chief www.burtonreport.com, 2000, 04, 06. Rsch. fellow, Nat. Polio Found., 1956, HEW, 1958, neurosurg. fellow, Johns Hopkins Hosp., 1960—61, 1962—67, 1969—70. Fellow ACS (exec. com. Minn. chpt. 1989-92); mem. Congress Neurol. Surgeons (chmn. com. materials and devices 1972-79), Am. Assn. Neurol. Surgeons, Minn. Neurosurg. Soc., AAAS, ASTM (chmn. com. materials 1973-78), Internat. Soc. Study of Lumbar Spine (exec. com. 1986-89), N.Am. Spine Soc. (exec. com. 1987-91, chmn. com. on profl. conduct 1991-92, dir. coun. mem. affairs 1992-94, bd. dirs. 1990-94), Am. Nat. Standards Inst. (med. device tech. adv. bd. 1973-78), Am. Bd. Spine Surgery (bd. dirs. 1997—, vice chair 2002—, chair ethics com. 1998—), Philadelphia County Med. Soc. (med.-legal com. 1970-74), Minn. Med. Assn. (Gold medal award, subcom. on med. testimony 1978—), Hennepin County Med. Soc. (med.-legal com. 1975—), Mpls. Acad. Medicine, Cor et Manus Soc., Profl. Assn. Diving Instrs. (underwater photography splty. diver), Am. Back Soc., Twin Cities Spine Soc. (pres. 1994-95), Back Pain Assn. Am. (hon. chmn. 1995—), Am. Bd. Spine Surgery (bd. dirs. 1997, chmn. ethics com., v.p. 2002—, chmn. med.-legal com., co-chmn. 2002—), Assn. Ethics Spine Surgery (bd. dirs. 2007—), Johns Hopkins U. Alumni Assn. (pres. Minn. chpt. 1988-92), Yale Surg. Soc., Alpha Epsilon Delta. Achievements include patents for surgical devices, operating room fiberoptic headlights, clinical therapy systems and techniques. Home: The Lowry 901 350 St Peter St Ste 901 Saint Paul MN 55102 Office: Ctr Restorative Spine Surgery Ste 220 Gallery Tower Office Bldg 514 St Peter St Saint Paul MN 55102 Office Phone: 651-287-8781. Business E-Mail: cburton@restorativespinesurgery.com. E-mail: burtrep@eus.net.

BURTON, CHERYL, newscaster; b. Chgo. BS in Psychology and Biology, U. Ill., Champaign. Host Minority Bus. Report WGN-TV, Chgo., 1989; reporter WMBD-TV, Peoria, Ill., 1990; weekend anchor KWCH-TV, Wichita, Kans., 1990—92, host Viewpoint, 1990—92; weekend co-anchor and reporter WLS-TV, Chgo., 1992—2003, co-anchor and contbg. anchor 5 pm news, 2003—. Vol. Boys and Girls Club of Am., Rush-Presbyn./St. Luke's Fashion Show; motivational spkr. Chgo. Pub. Sch.; bd. mem. City Yr., Chgo. Recipient Kizzy Image and Achievement award, 1998, Phenomenal Woman award, Expo Today's Black Woman, 1997, Emmy award, 2002. Mem.: Nat. Assn. of Black Journalists, Chgo. Assn. of Black Journalists (now named Russ Ewing award 1996, 2003), Life with Lupus Guild, Delta Sigma Theta. Office: WLS-TV 190 N State St Chicago IL 60601*

BURTON, DALE EDWARD, aerospace engineering exectuve; BS in Physics, U. Ark., Monticello; DSc in Applied Math., Fla. State U., 1981. With Raytheon, Hughes Radar Systems Grp., United Technologies Rsch. Ctr., Sikorsky Aircraft; lead engr. Northrup Grumman Corp., Melbourne, Fla., 1987—88; chief systems engr. Northrop Grumman Corp., 1988, dir. Advanced Systems, dep. prog. mgr. Joint Surveillance Target Attack Radar Sys. prog., 1996, chief engr., dep. dept. mgr. Engring., Tech. and Integrated Logistics Support, 1998—99, v.p. engring., logistics and tech., 1999, v.p. Advanced Architectures for Integrated Systems' Advanced Capabilities Devel. orgn., 2003, sector v.p. tech., chief tech. officer Integrated Systems. Mem. Air Force Sci. Adv. Bd., 1994—98. Mem.: NAE. Office: Integrated Systems Northrup Grumman Corp 2000 NASA Blvd Melbourne FL 32904 Office Phone: 321-951-5000.*

BURTON, DAN L., congressman; b. Indpls., June 21, 1938; m. Barbara Jean Logan, 1959; children: Kelly, Danielle Lee, Danny Lee II. Mem. Ind. Ho. Reps., Indpls., 1967-68, 77-80, Ind. State Senate, 1969-70, 81-82; owner ins. and real estate firm, 1968—; mem. U.S. Congress from 5th Ind. dist. (formerly 6th), 1983—. Mem. internat. rels. com.; chmn. govt. reform and oversight com. Pres. Vols. of Am.; pres. Ind. Christian Benevolent Assn., Com. for Constl. Govt., Family Support Ctr. Served with U.S. Army, 1957-58. Republican. Office: US Ho Reps 2185 Rayburn Ho Office Bldg Washington DC 20515-1405*

BURTON, DAVID K., lawyer; b. Phila., July 11, 1970; s. Kenneth Burton and Georgia May Peters; m. Tyler Katherine Bradford, Dec. 28, 1993; children: Joshua David, Alexander Bradford. BA, Ithaca Coll., NY, 1993; JD, Georgetown U., Washington, DC, 1996. Bar: Pa. 1997, NJ 1996, US Tax Ct. 1997. Atty. Morgan, Lewis & Bockius LLP, Phila., 1996—2000; tax counsel leasing and M&A GE Comml. Fin., Stamford, Conn., 2000—. Mem. Equiment Leasing and Fin. Assn. Fed. Tax Com. Author: Leasing Outside the United States; contbr. articles to profl. jours. Dailey scholar, Georgetown U. Law Ctr., 1994. Mem.: ABA (tax sect.), Phi Kappa Phi. Office: GE Comml Fin 901 Main Ave Norwalk CT 06851 Office Phone: 203-840-6303.

BURTON, DONALD JOSEPH, chemistry professor; b. Balt., July 16, 1934; s. Lawrence Andrew and Dorothy Wilhelmina (Koehler) B.; m. Margaret Anna Billing, June 21, 1958; children— Andrew, Jennifer, David, Julie, Elizabeth. BS, Loyola Coll., Balt., 1956; PhD, Cornell U., 1961; postgrad., Purdue U., 1961-62. Asst. prof. chemistry dept. U. Iowa, Iowa City, 1962-67, assoc. prof., 1967-70, prof., 1970—, Roy Carver/Ralph Shriner prof. chemistry, 1989—. Recipient Gov.'s Sci. Medal for Sci. Achievement, 1988; Japanese Soc. for Promotion Sci. fellow, 1979 Mem. Am. Chem. Soc. (chmn. fluorine divsn. 1978, award for creative work in fluorine chemistry 1984, Midwest Chemistry award 1990, ACS divsn. Fluorine Chemistry Disting. Svc. award 2003), Chem. Soc. London, Sigma Xi, Alpha Chi Sigma. Home: 105 Notting Hill Ln Iowa City IA 52245-9217 Office: U Iowa Dept Chemistry Iowa City IA 52242 Office Phone: 319-335-1363. Business E-Mail: donald-burton@uiowa.edu.

BURTON, EVE BRADLEY, lawyer; b. NYC, Oct. 16, 1958; d. John C. Burton; m. John Arnold Finck, Aug. 22, 1987. BA, Hampshire Coll., 1982; JD, Columbia U., 1989. Bar: NY 1990, U.S. Dist. Ct. NY (ea. and so. dist.) 1993, U.S. Ct. Appeals (2nd cir.) 1996, U.S. Supreme Ct. 1997. Law clk. to Judge Shirley Wohl Kram US Dist. Ct. (So. Dist. NY), 1985—86; internat. corp. fin. assoc. Milbank, Tweed, Hadley & McCloy, NY and Hong Kong, 1989—90; v.p., dep. gen. counsel Daily News, NYC, 1990—91; sr. litigation assoc. Weil, Gotshal & Manges, 1991—95; v.p., chief legal counsel CNN, NYC, 2000—01; v.p., gen. counsel Hearst Corp., NYC, 2002—. Mem. ethics com. CNN, 1995—2000; adj. prof. Columbia U., 1999—. Contbr. articles to profl. jours. Recipient First Amendment award, Nat. Press Club, 1998, NY Press Club, 1998, Soc. Profl. Journalists, 1999; Fulbright Rsch. Scholar, Thmmasat U., Thailand. Mem.: ABA, Assn. Bar. City of NY (mem. comm. com.). Office: Hearst 250 W 55th St New York NY 10019-5201 Office Phone: 212-649-2000. E-mail: eburton@hearst.com.

BURTON, GEORGE AUBREY, JR., accountant; b. Texarkana, Ark., June 21, 1926; s. George Aubrey Burton and Theo Marvis Simmons-Burton; m. Joan Cunningham, July 31, 1947 (dec. Oct. 2002); m. Gloria Brantley, June 18, 2005; children: George Aubrey Burton, III, Sandra

Burton-Batten. BS, Centenary Coll., 1947—50. CPA, State Bd. Of Acctg./La., 1953. Reporter Dun & Bradstreet, Shreveport, La., 1947—49; acct. Opferkuch, Mc Guirt, Watts & West CPA's, Shreveport, La., 1949—53. Ptnr. Opferkuch, McGuirt, Watts & West CPA's, Shreveport, 1953, Burton & Penn CPA'S, Shreveport, 1964—74; CPA George A. Burton, Jr., Shreveport, 1953—64, George A. Burton, Jr. CPA, Shreveport, 1978—; commr. fin. City Of Shreveport, 1971—78. Treas. Jaycees, Shreveport, 1953—54, exec. v.p., 1955—56, pres., 1956—57; regional v.p. La. Jaycees, 1958—59, exec. v.p., 1959—60; mem. Shreveport Airport Authority; chmn. Caddo Parish Exec. Com., La.; pres. Caddo Parish Bd. Election Suprs., 1978—; exec. com. La. State Fair, Shreveport, 1971—78; dir. Shreveport C. of C., 1956—57. Seaman 1/c Navy Seabees, 1943—46, Central Pacific. Recipient JCI Life Mem., Jr. C. of C., 1973. Mem.: La. CPA Soc. (state committe), Jr. ROTC Parents Club (life). Home: 300 Pieremont Rd #3 Shreveport LA 71106 Office: George A Burton Jr CPA 1300 Grimmett Dr Shreveport LA 71107 Office Phone: 318-222-7555. Personal E-mail: gburton@worldnet.att.net.

BURTON, JAKE (JAKE BURTON CARPENTER), sports apparel executive; b. NYC, Apr. 29, 1954; m. Donna Gafton; children: George, Taylor, Timmy. Studied, U. Colo.; BA, NYU, 1977. Founder, CEO Burton Snow Boards, 1977—. Founder Chill Program, Burlington, Vt., 1995—. Office: Burton Snowboards 80 Industrial Pkwy Burlington VT 05401

BURTON, JANET RUTH WISNER, music educator; b. Ft. Payne, Ala., Nov. 25, 1955; d. Robert Thurston and Mary Lou (Garrett) Wisner; m. David Lee Malone (div.); 1 child, Mara Ruth Malone; m. O.E. "Buddy" Burton, Oct. 18, 1991. AA in Music, Nat. Sch. Music, Roanoke, Ala., 1979; Assoc., N.E. State Jr. Coll., Rainsville, Ala., 1990; BSE, Athens State Coll., 1992; MusMA, Jacksonville State U., Ala., 2004. Cert. tchr. Ala., Tenn. Substitute tchr. Catawba County Schs., Maiden, NC, 1992—94; music dir. Cornerstone Ch., Maiden, NC, 1992—95; tchr. Lincolnton (NC) H.S., 1994—95; music dir. Gault Ave. Bapt. Ch., Ft. Payne, Ala., 1995—96; substitute tchr. Lake Travis Schs., Austin, Tex., 1995—99; tchr. Hilltop Acad., Cedar Park, Tex., 1997—99; program dir. Hilltop Bapt. Ch., Cedar Park, Tex., 1997—99; band interium Geraldine (Ala.) H.S., 1999—2000; music tchr. K-6 Plainview H.S., Rainsville, Ala., 2000—01, Huntland (Tenn.) H.S., 2004—05. Owner, prodr. (TV show) Gospel Music Time with Buddy & Janet Burton, 2002—05; composer: numerous songs, 1980—2000; author, instr. Do Re Mi's of Music. Named Miss Congeniality, DeKalb County Jr. Miss, Ft. Payne, 1974; recipient Ballroom Dance award, Fred Astaire Studios, 1985, Leadership award, Omicron Delta Kappa, 2003; grantee, Ala. Arts Coun., 1995. Mem.: Tenn. Tchrs. Edn. Assn., Nat. Assn. Music Educators, C.C. Rainsville. Avocations: painting, reading, nature walks, movies, musical instruments. Home: PO Box 8 Rainsville AL 35986 Office: Huntland HS 300 Gore St Huntland TN 37345 Office Phone: 256-638-6591. Personal E-mail: buddy@fumcscottsboro.org.

BURTON, JAY H., sports management executive; b. Fernandina Beach, Fla., Nov. 27, 1954; s. Jay H. and Caroline E. Burton; m. Brenda Ann Zielinski, Apr. 6, 1991; children: Christine Boote Work, Rebecca Caroline Sulzer, Kate Mae, Charles Davis. AB, Heidelberg Coll., Tiffin, Ohio, 1976; BS, Lake Erie Coll., Painesville, Ohio, 1977. CPA Ohio, 1979. V.p. IMG, Cleve., 1992—2005, sr. v.p., 2005—. Office: IMG 1360 E 9th St Cleveland OH 44114

BURTON, JOHN BRYAN, music educator; b. Lubbock, Tex., Nov. 10, 1948; s. John Clark and Geraldine (Wolf) B. B in Music Edn., West Tex. State U., 1970; MA, Western State Coll. Colo., 1973; D in Music Edn., U. So. Miss., 1986. Dir. bands, humanities Jal (N.Mex.) Schs., 1978-79; dir. bands, gen. music Bronte (Tex.) Schs., 1979-80; dir. bands Comfort (Tex.) Schs., 1980-82; dir. high sch. band, music coord. Kirbyville (Tex.) Ind. Schs., 1982-84; grad. asst. U. So. Miss., Hattiesburg, 1984-86; asst. prof. music, dir. bands, music theatre dir. Frostburg (Md.) State U., 1986-91; prof. music edn. West Chester (Pa.) Univ., 1991—, coord. grad. studies, 1997—, dir. post baccalaureate tchr. cert. program, 2001—. Panelist Symposium on Native Am. Musics, Coll. Music Soc. 33d Nat. Meeting, Washington, 1990; curriculum cons. Prince Georges County Schs., Upper Marlboro, Md., 1991, other Mid-Atlantic schs.; guest condr. Allegany County Honor Band, Tri-State Honor Band, 1986-87, Allegany County Band, Bedford County Band, Mineral County Band, 1987-88, Allegany Solo and Ensemble Festival Harford County Intermediate Bands Festival, 1990-91; cons. Native Am. music, 1993, 94, nat. chair, editor Social Scis. Rsch. Group Soc. for Rsch. in Music Edn., 1994-96; edit. adv. bd. mem. Tchg. Music, 1996-98; vis. prof. U. Washington, 1995, Ga. State U., 1995, Trenton State Coll., 1996, U. Okla., 1996, U. Nebr., 1997, U. Sioux Falls, 1997, Rider U., 1998; presenter, lectr. in field. Assoc. editor: Scholars, 1994-2003; author: moving Within the Circle: Contemporary Native American Music and Dance, 1993, 2d edit., 2007, Music of the Minority Nationalities of the People's Republic of China, 1989, When the Earth Was Like New: Songs and Stories of the Western Apache, 1994, Songs of A Living Apache Tradition: The Musical Life of Chesley Goseyun Wilson, 1994, (with Maria P. Kreiter) Voices of the Wind: Native American Flute Music, 1997; co-author: Welcome to Mussomeli: Italian Children's Songs, 1999; contbg. author: Multicultural Perspectives in Music Education, 2d edit., 1996, Getting Started with Teaching Multicultural Music, 1996, Making Connections: Multicultural Traditions and the National Standards in Music Education, 1996, Strategies for Teaching: General Music K-4, 1996, Strategies for Teaching: General Music 5-8, 1996, Strategies for Teaching: General Music 9-12, 1996, Strategies for Teaching: Beginning and Middle Level Band Grades 5-8, 1996, Strategies for Teaching: High School Band, 1996, Strategies for Teaching: College Methods Class, 1996, Strategies for Teaching: High School Chorus, 1996, Many Seeds, Different Flowers--The Music Education Legacy of Carl Orff, 1997, On the Sociology of Music Education, 1997; mem. editl. bd. Music Edn. Internat., 2001--; contbg. editor, mem. editl. bd. New Grove Dictionary of American Music, 2006-; contbr. songs to World of Children's Song, 1993, lessons and photographs to The Music Connection, 1995, songs and lessons to Share the Music, 1995, World Music and Music Education: Facing the Issue, 2002, Making Music (classroom music texttbook series), song transcriptions to OAKE Multicultural Songs, Dances and Games, 1995, online instrl. manual, Music in South India, 2003, Music of West Africa, 2004, Music in East Africa, 2004, Music in Brazil, 2006, Music in Central Java, 2007, World Music and Traditional Transformations, 2007; contbr. articles to profl. jours. Mem. Internat. Soc. Music Edn.(commn. cmty. music activity, Durban, South Africa, 1998, mem. exec. bd.), Nat. Band Assn., Music Educators Nat. Conf. (presenter nat. meetings), Australia Soc. Music Educators, Pa. Music Educators Assn., Coll. Band Dirs. Nat. Assn., Coll. Music Soc., Soc. for Ethnomusicology (chair edn. com. 1999—), Soc. Music Tchr. Edn. (ea. rep. 1998-2004), Associated Photographers Internat., Audubon Soc., Amnesty Internat., Phi Mu Alpha, Alpha Chi, Kappa Delta Pi, Kappa Kappa Psi. Avocations: photography, travel, gardening. Home: 441 Webb Rd Chadds Ford PA 19317-9125 Office: West Chester U Sch Music West Chester PA 19383-0001 E-mail: jburton3@wcupa.edu.

BURTON, JOHN CAMPBELL, accounting educator, former dean; b. NYC, Sept. 17, 1932; s. James Campbell and Barbara (French) B.; m. Jane Garnjost, Apr. 6, 1957; children: Eve Bradley, Bruce Campbell. BA, Haverford Coll., 1954; MBA, Columbia U., 1956, PhD, 1962. C.P.A., N.Y. Staff acct. Arthur Young & Co., NYC, 1956-60; prof. acctg. and fin. Grad. Sch. Bus. Columbia U., NYC, 1962-72, Ernst & Young prof. acctg. and fin., 1978—, dean Grad. Sch. Bus., 1982-88. Chief acct. SEC, Washington, 1972-76; dep. mayor fin., NYC, 1976-77; bd. dirs. Scholastic Inc.; dir., chmn. audit com. Commerce Clearing House Inc., 1979-95, First Pa. Corp.-First Pa. Bank, 1982-85; mem. adv. and valuation com. Warburg-Pincus Venture Capital Funds; mem. U.S. Comptroller Gen. Cons. Panel, 1978-95; bd. dirs. Accts. for Pub. Interest, 1978-85. Editor: Corporate Financial Reporting: Conflicts and Challenges, 1969, Corporate Financial Reporting: Ethical and Other Problems, 1972, (with Russell Palmer and Robert Kay) Handbook of Accounting and Auditing, 1981, The International World of Accounting: Challenges and Opportunities, 1981; co-mng. editor Acctg. Horizons, 1989-91; author: Accounting for Business Combinations, 1970, (with W.T. Porter) Auditing: A Conceptual Approach, 1971, and others; contbr. articles to profl. jours. Pres., trustee Millbrook Sch. (N.Y.), 1958-88; trustee ex officio Am. Assembly, 1982-88. Recipient Disting. Scholar award Hofstra U., 1975; Ford Found. fellow, 1961-62; Named to Acctg. Hall of Fame, 1997 Mem. AICPA (coun. 1980-83), Am. Acctg. Assn. (acad. v.p. 1980-82), Am. Fin. Assn., Am. Econ. Assn., Fin. Execs. Inst., Assn. Govtl. Accts., Nat. Assn. Securities Dealers (pub. gov. 1990-94), Met. Club (N.Y.C.), Lake Sunapee Yacht Club (N.H.). Clubs: Metropolitan (N.Y.C.); Lake Sunapee Yacht (N.H.). E-mail: jcb5@columbia.edu.

BURTON, JOHN PAUL (JACK BURTON), lawyer; b. New Orleans, Feb. 26, 1943; s. John Paul and Nancy (Key) Burton; m. Anne Ward; children: Jennifer, Michele Kfouri, Marcos Maiken, Susanna, Derek, Catherine. BBA magna cum laude, La. Tech. U., 1965; LLB, Harvard U., 1968. Bar: N.Mex. 1968, U.S. Dist. Ct. N.Mex. 1968, U.S. Ct. Appeals (10th cir.) 1973, U.S. Supreme Ct. 1979. Assoc. Rodey, Dickason, Sloan, Akin & Robb, Albuquerque, 1968-74, dir., 1974—, chmn. comml. dept., 1980-81, mng. dir. Santa Fe, 1986-90. Settlement facilitator N.Mex. 1st Jud. Dist., 1997—. Co-author: Boundary Disputes in New Mexico, 1992, Unofficial Update on the Uniform Ltd. Liability Co. Act, 1994, Effective Boundary Dispute Resolution in New Mexico, 2004. Pres. Brunn Sch., 1987—89, divsn. chmn., 1993—95, 1999—2001, exec. com., 1997—99; chmn. drafting com. on uniform durable powers of atty. Nat. Coun. Commrs. on Uniform State Laws, 2003—06; vice chair St. Simeon's Found., 1986—87. Named one of Best Lawyers in Am., 1986—, Southwest Super Lawyers, 2007—. Fellow: Am. Coll. Real Estate Lawyers; mem.: ABA, Chartered Inst. Arbitrators, N.Mex. State Bar Assn. (chmn. comml. litig. sect. 1985—86, Bus. Lawyer of Yr. 2004), Am. Arbitration Assn. (comml. panel arbitrators, large, complex case panel arbitrators, panel mediators), Am. Coll. Mortgage Attys., Am. Law Inst. Office: Rodey Dickason Sloan Akin & Robb PA PO Box 1357 Santa Fe NM 87504-1357 Office Phone: 505-954-3900. Business E-Mail: jburton@rodey.com.

BURTON, JOSEPH RANDOLPH, lawyer; b. Houston, Sept. 10, 1951; s. Joseph Milburn and Lee (Hillegeist) B.; m. Regina Helen O'Brien, Mar. 13, 1982; children: Cara Eileen, Ross Andrew. BS, Yale U., 1974; JD, South Tex. Coll., Houston, 1982. Bar: Tex. 1983, U.S. Dist. Ct. (so. and ea. dists.) Tex. 1983, U.S. Supreme Ct. 1996. Asst. dist. atty. Harris County Dist. Atty's Office, Houston, 1984-87; litigation assoc. Kennedy, Sanford, Kuhl & Hackney, Houston, 1987-90; ptnr. Moerer & Burton, Houston, 1990—. Contbr. articles to profl. jours.; featured on TV shows, including ABC News Prime Time Live, 20/20, HBO, Discovery Channel, Donahue, Good Morning Am. Founder, spokesperson Justice for Children, Houston, 1987—, Citizens Response Group; bd. dirs. Houston Area Women's Ctr., 1987-89, Aid to Victims of Domestic Abuse, 1987, Children's Trust Fund of Tex. Coun., 1994-98; child advocate mem. Tex. Child Fatality Rev. Com. Recipient AIA Pres.'s award, 1998, Victims' Resource Inst. with U. Houston Kim Houston award, 1999; named Outstanding Young Lawyer of Houston, Houston Young Lawyers' Assn., 1987-88, Mayor's award Outstanding Vol. Svc., 1998, e-town Achievement award, 2002. Fellow Tex. Bar Found.; mem. ABA, Houston Bar Assn., South Tex. Coll. of Law Alumni Assn., Garland Walker Inns of Ct. Democrat. Avocation: bicycling. Home: 18418 Snowwood Dr Spring TX 77388-5100 Office: The Burton Law Firm 440 Louisiana St Ste 1300 Houston TX 77002-1634 Home Phone: 281-353-9410; Office Phone: 713-222-6262.

BURTON, KATE, actress; b. Geneva, Sept. 10, 1957; arrived in NYC, 1961; d. Richard Burton and Sybil Christopher; m. Michael Ritchie, 1984; children: Morgan, Charlotte. BA in Russian Studies and European History, Brown U., 1979; grad., Yale Drama Sch., 1983. Actress (Broadway plays) Present Laughter, 1982 (Theatre World award, 1983), Alice in Wonderland, 1982 (Theatre World award, 1983), Doonesbury, 1983, Wild Honey, 1986, Some Americans Abroad, 1990, Jake's Women, 1992, Company, 1995, An American Daughter, 1997, The Beauty Queen of Leenane, 1998, Hedda Gabler, 2001 (Callaway award, 2002), The Elephant Man, 2002, The Constant Wife, 2005, (plays) Boston Marriage, (Off-Broadway) The Water's Edge, 2006, (plays) Three Sisters, Give Me Your Answer, Do!, Company, The Playboy of the Western World, Winners (Theatre World award, 1983), The Cherry Orchard, 2007, (films) Anne of the Thousand Days, 1969, Big Trouble in Little China, 1986, Life With Mikey, 1993, August, 1996, The First Wives Club, 1996, The Ice Storm, 1997, Celebrity, 1998, The Opportunists, 2000, Unfaithful, 2002, Swimfan, 2002, The Paper Mache Chase, 2003, Stay, 2005, Some Kind of Heaven, 2005, (TV miniseries) Ellis Island, 1984, Evergreen, 1985, Empire Falls, 2005, (TV series) Home Fires, 1992, Monty, 1994, (TV films) Uncle Tom's Cabin, 1987, Journey Into Genius, 1988, Notes for My Daughter, 1995, Mistrial, 1996, Ellen Foster, 1997, Obsessed, 2002, The Diary of Ellen Rimbauer, 2003, (guest appearance TV series) The West Wing, 2004, The Practice, Law & Order, 2004, Judging Amy, 2005, Grey's Anatomy, 2005. Bd. trustees Broadway Cares/Equity Fights AIDS. Mem.: Actor's Equity Assn.*

BURTON, LAWRENCE DEVERE, agriculturist, educator; b. Afton, Wyo., May 27, 1943; s. Lawrence VanOrden and Maybell (Hoopes) B.; m. Arva Merrill, Nov. 20, 1967; children: LauraLee, Paul, Shawn, Renee, Kaylyn, Kelly, Brett. BS, Utah State U., 1968; MS, Brigham Young U., 1972; PhD, Iowa State U., 1987. Tchr. agr. Box Elder County Sch. Dist., Brigham City, Utah, 1967—68, Morgan County Sch. Dist., Morgan, Utah, 1968—70, Minidoka County Sch. Dist., Rupert, Idaho, 1972—79, Cassia County Sch. Dist., Declo, Idaho, 1979—84; instr. Iowa State U., Ames, 1984—87; coord. area vocat. edn. Idaho State Divsn. Vocat. Edn., Pocatello, 1987—88, state supr. agrl. sci. and tech. Boise, 1988—97, dir. rsch., 1997—99; mem. telecomm. coun. Idaho State Bd. Edn., 1997—98, mem. coun. acad. affairs and programs, 1997—; instrnl. dean Coll. So. Idaho, Twin Falls, 2000—05. Biochem. cons. rep. Ctr. for Occupational Rsch. and Devel., Waco, Tex., 1989-94; chmn. Nat. Task Force, Agrl. Edn. Ind. Study Honors program, 1993, mem. tech. commn.; mem. Nat. Task Force, Environ. Edn., 1996. Author: Agriscience and Technology, 1991, 97, Ecology of Fish and Wildlife, 1995, 2d edit., 2003, Introduction to Forestry Science, 1998, Agriscience, Fundamentals and Applications, 2000, 4th edit., 2007; contbr. articles to profl. jours. Vice-chmn. Minidoka County Fair Bd., Rupert, Idaho, 1977-80. Mem. Am. Vocat. Assn., Am. Vocat. Info. Assn., Nat. Vocat. Agrl. Tchrs. Assn., Idaho Vocat. Agrl. Tchrs. Assn. (pres. 1981-82, Adminstr. of Yr. 1989), Nat. Assn. Suprs. Agrl. Edn. (we. v.p. 1990-91, nat. pres. 1993-94), Gamma Sigma Delta, Alpha Zeta. Mem. Lds Ch. Home Phone: 208-732-8123; Office Phone: 208-420-9423. Business E-Mail: ldevereb@yahoo.com.

BURTON, MARY LOUISE HIMES, information technology executive; b. Altoona, Pa., Oct. 4, 1948; d. Paul Silas and Clara Marie (Bettwy) Himes; m. Carl Hansel Burton, Aug. 28, 1983; children: Michael, Edward, Carla. AA, Mt. Aloysius Jr. Coll., 1968; BS in Edn., Slippery Rock U., 1970; MLS magna cum laude, U. Pitts., 1982. Microsoft office specialist, cert. security profl. Cataloguer Slippery Rock (Pa.) U., 1968-70; cataloguer, children's librn. Altoona Area Pub. Libr., 1970-71; dir. libr. svcs. Altoona Hosp., 1971-83; project coord. Coll. of Physician of Phila., 1983-84; med. libr. VAMC, Coatesville, Pa., 1984-85, acting chief libr. svc., 1985-86, chief libr. svc., 1986-94; asst. chief IRM, 1994-96, computer specialist, 1996—. Mem. Nat. Adv. Group for Info. Security, 1991-2001, vice chmn., 1996-98; security officer Automated Info. Sys., 1988—; local resource libr. Mideastern Regional Med. Libr. Program, Phila., 1976-82, Greater Northeastern Regional Med. Libr. Program, N.Y.C., 1983-93; master instr. MS office, 2000. Mem. United Ch. of Christ. Mem. Spl. Librs. Assn., Pa. Libr. Assn. (chmn. spl. librs. divsn. and bd. dirs. 1980-82, 85-86, 89-90), Med. Libr. Assn., Acad. Health Info. Profls. (sec. DV-MUG 1996), VFW Aux., Assn. Health Info. Profls., Consortium Health Info. (pres. 1990-93). Avocations: vocalist, organist, pianist. Home: 5495 Highview Dr Gap PA 17527-9553 Home Phone: 717-442-4176. Personal E-mail: chmlburton@aol.com.

BURTON, MICHAEL LADD, anthropology educator; b. Long Beach, Calif., June 6, 1942; s. Warren Nathan Burton and Dorothy Brent (Braden) Asquith; children: Melissa, Christopher; m. Ellen Greenberger, Aug. 26, 1979. BS in Econs., MIT, 1964; PhD in Anthropology, Stanford U., 1968. Rsch. fellow Harvard U., 1968-69; asst. prof. U. Calif., Irvine, 1969-76; rsch. fellow U. Nairobi, Kenya, 1973-74; assoc. prof. U. Calif., Irvine, 1976-83, prof., 1983—, chmn., dept. anthropology, 1986-91, 2003—05. Contbr. articles to profl. jours. NSF grantee, 1981-89, 91-93. Mem. Am. Anthropol. Assn., Soc. for Cross-Cultural Rsch., Soc. Econ. Anthropology, Soc. Applied Anthropology, Assn. Social Anthropology of Oceania. Home: 10 Morning Sun Irvine CA 92603-3715 Office: U Calif Dept Anthropology Irvine CA 92697-5100 Office Phone: 949-824-7208. Business E-Mail: mlburton@uci.edu.

BURTON, PEGGY, advertising and marketing executive; b. NYC; BSBA, NYU, 1960. Freelance TV producer, NYC, 1964-67; TV producer Young & Rubicam, NYC, 1967-69; sr. acct. exec. Daniel & Charles, NYC, 1969-74; ptnr., v.p. Bruderer Hartnett Advt. Agy., NYC, 1974-76; dir. Comm. Am. Express Co., NYC, 1976-83; pres. advt. Dreyfus Corp., NYC, 1983-95; pres. Burton Commns. Multi Media, NYC, 1995—. Vol. Met. Mus. Art; bd. dirs. Nat. Sch. Com. Econ. Edn., Mallon Fund. Mem. Internat. Advt. Assn., N.Y. New Media Assn., Fin. Women's Assn., Fgn. Policy Assn., Bus. Execs. for Nat. Security, NYU Gallatin Arts Com., N.Y. Athletic Club, Nat. Arts Club. Address: 220 Central Park S New York NY 10019-1417 Office Phone: 212-581-4592. E-mail: pegbur@aol.com.

BURTON, RANDALL JAMES, lawyer; b. Sacramento, Feb. 4, 1950; s. Edward J. and Bernice Mae (Overton) B.; m. Kimberly D. Rogers, Apr. 29, 1989; children: Kelly Jacquelyn, Andrew Jameson. BA, Rutgers U., 1972; JD, Southwestern U., 1975. Bar: Calif. 1976, U.S. Dist. Ct. (ea. dist.) Calif. 1976, U.S. Dist. Ct. (no. dist.) Calif. 1990, Supreme Ct. 1991. Assoc. Brekke & Mathews, Citrus Heights, Calif., 1976; pvt. practice Sacramento, 1976—93; ptnr. Burton & White, Sacramento, 1993—; judge pro tem Sacramento Small Claims Ct., 1982—, Sacramento Traffic Ct., 2004—. Bd. dirs. North Highlands Recreation and Park Dist., 1978—86, Family Svc. Agy. Sacramento, 1991—96; active local bd. 22 Selective Svc., 1982—2001; active 20-30 Club Sacramento, 1979—90, pres., 1987. Recipient Disting. Citizen award Golden Empire Coun., Boy Scouts Am. Mem.: Sacramento Young Lawyers Assn., Sacramento Bar Assn., Rotary (pres. Foothill-Highlands club 1980—81). Presbyterian. Office: 1325 Howe Ave Ste 214 Sacramento CA 95825 Office Phone: 916-923-2030.

BURTON, RICHARD IRVING, orthopedist, educator; b. Providence, Sept. 18, 1936; s. Kenneth Gould and Edith Irving (Vayro) B.; m. Margaret Ann Leaman, Apr. 5, 1961; children: Thomas Kenneth, Douglas Leaman. BA, Amherst Coll., Mass., 1958; MD, Harvard U., Cambridge, Mass., 1962. Diplomate Am. Bd. Orthopaedic Surgery (examiner 1980—, bd. dirs. 1989-98). Intern U. Rochester, NY, 1962-63, resident in surgery NY, 1963-64; resident in orthopedic surgery Harvard U., 1966-70; fellow in hand surgery Roosevelt Hosp., NYC, 1970-71; asst. prof. Cleve. Clinic Found., 1971-72, head sect. surgery of hand, 1971-74, assoc. prof., 1973-74; mem. faculty U. Rochester Med. Sch., 1974—, head sect. surgery of hand, 1974—2003, prof. orthopedics, 1979—, Marjorie Strong Wehle prof. orthopedics, 1995-2000, dean's prof., 2000—02, assoc. chmn. dept. orthopedics, 1981-88, chmn., 1988—2000, acting chmn. dept. neurol. surgery, 2000—02, sr. assoc. dean for acad. affairs, 2002—; sr. assoc. orthopedist Strong Meml. Hosp., Rochester, 1974-79, orthopedist, 1979—; sr. assoc. dean for acad. affairs U. Rochester Med. Sch., 2002—. Chmn. cert. of added qualifications com. Am. Bd. Orthopaedic Surgery, 1994-98. Assoc. editor Jour. Hand Surgery, 1980-84; contbr. articles to profl. jours., chpts. to books. Mem. exec. com. Monroe County chpt. Am. Arthritis Found., 1983-86; elder Presbyn. Ch. Buswell Disting. Svc. fellow, U. Rochester, 1980-81. Recipient Exec. of Yr. award, Profl. Secs. Internat., Flower City chpt., 1981. Mem. ACS, AAAS, Am. Acad. Orthopedic Surgeons (chmn. hand and wrist com. 1986-89, orthopedic resources com. 1989-91), Am. Bd. Orthop. Surgery (dir. 1988-98), Am. Bd. Med. Specialties (voting rep. 1995-98), Am. Soc. Surgery of the Hand (coord. divsn. edn. 1982-85, coun. 1985-89, chmn. membership com. 1991, v.p. 1990, pres.-elect 1991, pres. 1992), Am. Orthopedic Assn. (exec. com. 1986, resident rsch. conf. com. 1987-89, chair 1989, membership com. 1989-92, chmn. 1992, exec. com. 1992, forward planning com. 1996-99), Interurban Orthopedic Soc., Eastern Orthopedic Assn., Monroe County Med. Soc., NY State Med. Soc., Rochester Acad. Medicine, Rochester Orthopedic Soc., Soc. NY State Orthopedic Surgeons, Littler-Eaton Soc., Amherst Alumni Assn Office: U Rochester Med Ctr Deans Office Box 706 601 Elmwood Ave Rochester NY 14642-0001 Office Phone: 585-275-2747.

BURTON, RICHARD JAY, lawyer; b. NYC, May 4, 1949; s. Melvin F. Burton and Shirley (Burton) Silber; m. Truly Demetra Dourdis, June 11, 1972; 1 child, Marc Aaron. BA, George Washington U., 1971; JD, U. Miami, 1974. Bar: Fla. 1974, DC 1976, US Supreme Ct. 1979. Founder Med. Commn. on Human Rights, Washington, 1969-71; adminstrv. aide Fla. Legis., 1973-74; gov. affairs liaison Dade County Fla. Legis., 1974; assoc. Richard H.W. Maloy and Assocs., Coral Gables, Fla., 1974-76; atty., advisor FAA, Washington, 1976-77; assoc. Pompan, Rumizen & Reynolds, Washington, 1978-79, Donald M. Murtha and Assocs., Washington, 1978-79; ptnr. Schoninger, Siegfried, Kipnis, Burton & Sussman PA, Miami, Fla., 1979-82; sole practice Miami, 1982—; gen. counsel Rexall Sundown Inc., 1982-90. Guest lectr. U. Miami Sch. of Law, Coral Gables, 1982. Mem. constrn. law panel Am. Arbitration Assn., 1974—; mem. legis. com. Builders Assn. South Fla., 1980—; mem. Builder Industry Polit. Action Com.; fire commr. Met. Dade County, 1988, 92, vice chmn. fire commn., 1989-90. Mem. ABA, DC Bar Assn., Fed. Bar Assn., Fla. Bar Assn. (constr. law com.), Phi Alpha Delta. Democrat. Jewish. Avocations: skiing, scuba diving, tennis. Office Phone: 305-705-0888. E-mail: RB@Burtons.net.

BURTON, ROBERT GENE, printing company executive; b. Pontiac, Mich., Apr. 4, 1939; s. Earl R. and Verna L. Burton; m. Paula M. Suwanski, May 26, 1972; children: Robert Gene Jr., Michael, Joseph. BS, Murray State U., Ky., 1962; MA, U. Tenn., 1964; postgrad., U. Chgo., 1964, U. Ala., 1965—67; D (hon.), Murray State U., 1968, U. Conn., 2000. From salesman to nat. sales dir. SRA/IBM Corp., Dallas and Chgo., 1967—76; from midwest dir. to mktg. dir. CBS, Chgo. and NYC, 1976—78, v.p. mktg., 1978—79, v.p. ops. NYC, 1978—79; v.p. pub. ABC, NYC, 1980, pres. leisure mags., 1980—81, group v.p. spl. interest pub. through pres. ABC Publishing, 1981—91; chmn. bd., pres., CEO World Color Press Inc., 1991—99; chmn., pres., CEO Walter Industries Inc., 1999—2000, Moore Corp., 2000—02; chmn., CEO Burton Mgmt. Group., LLC, 2003—, Cenveo Inc., Stamford, Conn., 2005—. Mem. adv. bd. NYU Bus. Press. Trustee Eagle Hill Sch., Greenwich, Conn.; mem. bd. overseers U. Conn. Sch. Bus. Adminstrn.; past trustee Murray State U., Boy Scouts Am. Nat. Mus., Murray; former chmn. Nat. Bible Week/Laymen's Nat. Bible Assn.; former pub. industry chmn. Juvenile Diabetes Found.; bd. dirs. Cancer Care of Conn.; bd. advisors Breast Cancer Alliance; bd. dirs. Kentuckians of N.Y., Burton Charitable Found., NYU, past pres. adv. bd.; bd. dirs. Murray State U. Coll. Bus. and Pub. Affairs, past dean's adv. coun. Named to Murray State Football Hall of Fame, Printing Industry Hall of Fame; recipient award, Spl. Achievement Soc. and Athletic Hall of Fame, West Frankfort, Ill., Oak award, Ky. Advocates for Higher Edn. Mem.: Assn. Bus. Pubs. (past chmn.), Greenwich (Conn.) Country Club, Washington Nat. Press Club. Republican. Baptist. Office: Cenveo Inc 1 Canterbury Green Stamford CT 06901 E-mail: info@burtonmg.com.

BURTON, ROBERT LYLE, accounting firm executive; m. Lee Sanders; 2 children. Diploma, Kinman Bus. U. CPA. With LeMaster & Daniels, Spokane, Wash., 1963-86, mng. ptnr., 1986-97, sr. advisor, 1997—. Adv. bd. acctg. dept. U. Wash.; chmn. The Am. Group of CPA Firms. Trustee Econ. Devel. Coun.; past chmn. Samaritan Hosp. Found., Moses Lake, Wash. Mem. AICPA (agri-bus. com., adv. group B), Washington Soc. CPAs (former dir., v.p., com. chmn., legis. com.), Spokane Club, Inland Empire Fly Fishermen, Moses Lake Golf and Country Club, Rotary. Office: LeMaster and Daniels PLLC 601 W Riverside Ave Ste 700 Spokane WA 99201-0622

BURTON, THOMAS RUSSELL, lawyer; b. Vernon, Conn., July 14, 1971; s. Thomas Russell and Kathleen Anne Burton; m. Leslie Faye Everingham, Aug. 6, 1994; children: Elise, Lauren. BA cum laude, Boston Coll., 1993, JD magna cum laude, 1996. Bar: Mass. 1996. Assoc. Mintz, Levin, Boston, 1996—2005, mem., 2005—. Mem. life scis. task force Commonwealth Workforce Devel. Bd.; mem. 10-250 com. MIT Enterprise Forum, mem. energy tech. spl. interest group; lectr. in field. Mem. adv. bd. Youthcare Cmty. Svcs., Boston, 1998—; mem. marathon com. Children's Hosp. Boston, 2005—; former chmn. Fulton Bus. Group, Boston Coll.; bd. dirs. Doug Flutie, Jr. Found., Framingham, Mass., 2006—. Named a Mass. Super Lawyer, Boston mag., 2004; named one of Boston's Future Leaders, Boston C. of C., 2004; recipient Saucony 26 award, Boston Marathon, 2005. Mem.: ABA, Mass. Bar Assn., Boston Bar Assn., Order of Coif, Ipswich Country Club. Avocations: marathons, golf, fishing, cooking. Office: Mintz Levin Cohn Ferris Glovsky and Popeo 1 Financial Ctr Boston MA 02111 Office Phone: 617-542-6000. Business E-Mail: tburton@mintz.com.

BURTON, TIM (TIMOTHY WILLIAM BURTON), film director, film producer; b. Burbank, Calif., Aug. 25, 1958; m. Lena Gieseke, Feb. 24, 1989 (div. Dec. 31, 1991); engaged Lisa Marie, 1992-2001; engaged Helena Bonham Carter, 2001-; 1 child: Billy Ray. Student Calif. Inst. Arts (Disney Fellowship), 1979—80. Cartoon artist Disney Prodn., apprentice animator. Animator: The Fox and the Hound, 1981; Dir.: (films) Vincent, 1982, Frankenweenie, 1984, Pee-Wee's Big Adventure, 1984, Beetlejuice, 1988, Batman, 1989, Sleepy Hollow, 1999, Planet of the Apes, 2001, Big Fish, 2003, Charlie and the Chocolate Factory, 2005, Corpse Bride, 2005; prodr. The Nightmare Before Christmas, (also production designer) 1993, Cabin Boy, 1994, Batman Forever, 1995, James and the Giant Peach, 1996; dir., prodr.: (films) Stalk of the Celery, 1979, Edward Scissorhands, 1990, Batman Returns, 1992, Ed Wood, 1994, Mars Attacks!, 1996, The World of Stainboy, 2000; dir.: (TV films) Hansel and Gretel, 1982; exec prodr.: (TV films) Lost in Oz, 2000; exec. prodr.: (TV series) Beetlejuice, 1989-91, Family Dog, 1992; author: My Art & Films, 1993, The Melancholy Death of Oyster Boy and Other Stories, 1997. Named one of 50 Greatest Directors of All Time, Entertainment Weekly, Tropopkin's Top 25 Most Intriguing People; recipient Lifetime Achievement award, Venice Internat. Film Festival, 2007. Office: Chapman Bird & Grey 1990 S Bundy Dr Ste 200 Los Angeles CA 90025-5240*

BURTON, TIMOTHY ALAN, biologist; b. Salt Lake City, Apr. 27, 1949; s. David Earl and Ora Burton; m. Suzanne Bay Gibbons, Feb. 23, 1972; children: Joseph Timothy, Emily Richards, Amy Lorette Boyer, Spencer David, Jacob Timothy. BS in Geology, U. Utah, Salt Lake City, 1974; MS in Watershed Sci., Utah State U., Logan, 1976. Hydrologist USDI Bur. Land Mgmt., Lewistown, Mont., 1976—80, fishery biologist Boise, Idaho, 2000—; hydrologist USDA Forest Svc., Vernal, Utah, 1980—83, fishery biologist, hydrologist Pocatello, Idaho, 1983—88, fishery biologist Boise, 1991—2000. Spl. interagency assignment USDA Forest Svc. - USEPA - Idaho Water Quality Bur., Boise, 1988—91. Bishop LDS Ch., Boise, 2004—07. Recipient Merit award, USDA Forest Svc., 1986, Commendation, Idaho Dept. Environ. Quality, 1999, award for visionary leadership and commitment to advance fisheries sci. comm., Am. Fisheries Soc., 2000, Award of Excellence, Project WET Idaho, 2005, Merit - Superior Performance award, USDI Bur. Land Mgmt., 2006. Independent. Avocations: fishing, backpacking, golf. Office: USDI Bureau Land Management 1387 S Vinnell Way Boise ID 83709 Home Phone: 208-362-4742; Office Phone: 208-373-3819. Office Fax: 208-373-3805. Business E-Mail: tburton@blm.gov.

BURTON, WARD, professional race car driver; b. South Boston, Va., Oct. 25, 1961; married; m. Tabitha Burton; children: Sarah, Jeb. Student, Elon Coll. Race car driver NASCAR Busch Series Grand Nat. Divsn., 1990, Bill Davis Racing, High Point, NC. Achievements include winner Winston Cup, 1995; 23 top 5 career starts; 37 top 10 stars in 148 races; career finishes include 5 top 5 finishes and 24 top 10 finishes in 146 races; winner N.C. Motor Speedway, 1995; AC Delco 400, 1995; Mall.com 400, 2000. Avocations: wildlife conservation, hunting. Office: c/o Bill Davis Racing 301 Old Thomasville Rd High Point NC 27260-8190 Mailing: Ward Burton Enterprises PO Box 519 Halifax VA 24558

BURTON, WILLIAM JOSEPH, engineering executive; b. Gaffney, SC, Mar. 22, 1931; s. Emory Goss and Olivia (Copeland) B.; m. Joan Holland Burton, Sept. 26, 1987. BSME, U. S.C., 1957, MSME, 1964; PhDME, Tex. A&M U., 1970. Registered profl. engr., Tenn., Fla. Sr. dynamics engr. Lockheed-Ga. Co., Marietta, 1957-62; sr. project engr. Allison div. GM Corp., Indpls., 1964-67; asst. prof., researcher Tex. A&M U., College Station, 1968-70; asst. prof. U. Tenn., Knoxville, 1970-74; projects mgr. Tenn. Valley Authority, Chattanooga, 1974-79; program mgr. Dept. Navy, Washington, 1979-94; chair equal employment opportunity com. Chesapeake divsn. Naval Facilities Engring. Command, Washington, 1982—83; cons. engr. Ocean and Power Applications, Lakeland, Fla., 1993—. Lectr. in field nat. and internat. audiences; adj. prof. mech. and aerospace engring., energy conversion tech. U. Tenn., Knoxville, 1974—75; spkr. and presenter, various venues and topics. Author: On the Heating Surface Effects of Nucleate Boiling Data Correlation, 1964, The Effects of Surface Roughness on the Wave Forces on a Circular Cylindrical Pile, 1970; author more than 50 articles on ocean engring., power and propulsion, aircraft structures, planning and economics, ethics. Sec., mem. hospitality com. Exch. Club, Knoxville, 1975, bd. dirs., 1976; coord. charitable campaign Naval Facilities Engring. Com., Washington, 1982; mem. Heritage Found., Rep. Nat. Com., Fla. With U.S. Army, 1951-53. Recipient Occupation medal, 1952, Nat. Def. Svc. medal U.S. Army, 1953, Antarctic Svc. medal U.S. Dept. of Navy, 1962, Wisdom award of honor, 2000; Eminent Wisdom fellow Scroll of Wisdom Hall of Fame, 2000. Fellow ASME (organizer, chmn. tech. sessions for internat. confs. 1982-87, chmn. exec. com. ocean engring. divsn. 1985, mem.-at-large energy resources bd. 1986-92, chmn. com. honors and awards energy resources bd. 1992-98, com. on tech. planning coun. on engring. 1992-94, fellow peer rev. bd. 1992-97, tech. and editl. reviewer Jour. Energy Resources Tech., 1995, rep. energy resources bd. to nat. nominating com. 1998—, Golden Cert. ocean engring. divsn. 1989), Va. Soc. Profl. Engrs. (no. Va. regional coun. 1988); mem. AAAS, NSPE (pres.-elect Fairfax chpt. 1988), Soc. Mfg. Engrs., Soc. Naval Archs. and Marine Engrs., Am. Concrete Inst., U.S. Naval Inst., S.C. Hist. Soc., Nat. Trust for Hist. Preservation, Polk County (Fla.) Hist. Assn., VFW, Marine Tech. Soc., U. S.C. Alumni Assn. (life), U. South Caroliniana Soc.(life), Heritage Found., Tau Beta Pi Hon. Engring. Soc. (life, SC Beta 1958), Sigma Xi, Texas A&M U. Assn. Former Students Bronze Level. Baptist. Avocations: travel, bicycling, classic guitar, golf, tennis. Home: 307 Miramar Dr Lakeland FL 33803-2633 Office: Naval Facilities Engring Svc Ctr East Coast Detachment 901 E M St SE 218 Wash Navy Yard Washington DC 20374-0001 Personal E-mail: wmburton@hotmail.com.

BURTSON, JAMES E., multimedia company executive; BA in Hist., Columbia U., 1991; MBA in Fin., Columbia U. Grad. Sch. Bus., 1994. Fin. analyst corp. fin. and mergers and acquisitions Time Warner; investment banking mergers and acquistions J.P. Morgan, 1996—98; v.p. strategic devel. Clear Channel Comm.; positions to sr. v.p. investor rels. Time Warner, Inc., NYC, 2002—. Office: Time Warner Inc 1 Time Warner Ctr New York NY 10019-8016

BURTT, LARICE ANNADEL ROSEMAN, artist; b. Phila., June 22, 1928; d. Milo A.J. Roseman and Anna Sterling; m. James C. Burtt, June 25, 1960; childen, James M., Kyleann S. BS in Biology, Bucknell U., 1950; MS in Nursing, Yale U., 1955; studied art with Dr. Selma Burke, studied with William A. Smith; cert., Katherine Gibbs Sec. Sch., 1951. Med. clinical instr. Jefferson Hosp., Phila., 1956-57; med. surgical instr. Rowan Meml. Hosp., Salisbury, NC, 1958-59. Workshop leader Yale, New Haven Hosp. Pain Mgmt. Ctrs., New Haven, Ct., 1996, Attleboro Nursing Home, Langhorne, Pa., Chandler Hall, Newtown, Pa.; demo instr. Delaware Valley Schs., Pa., 1979—; profl. demonstrator in field, 1977—. Painter (3 dimensional stone painting), many locations, 1976-99; one person shows include Phila. Art Mus. Gallery, 1985, Arnot Art Mus., Elmira, N.Y., 1987, Cannon Bldg., Washington, DC 1995, Yale Univ. Sch. Nursing, New Haven, Conn., 1996, Abington Art Ctr., Pa., Upstairs Gallery, Buckingham, Pa.; exhibited in group shows at Immaculata Coll., Accent and Images Gallery, Lahaska, Pa., Nova, 1990-2004, Jane Anthony Gallery, Newtown, Pa., 2000, Abington (Pa.) Art Ctr., Wilson Sch. Mt. Lakes Gallery Show, 2001-04, Galleria Veronese, New Orleans 2005, 07, many area group exhbns., 1977—; represented in permanent collection Grand Canyon Nat. Pk. Mus. Mem. AAUW, Northhampton Hist. Soc., Middletown Grange, Bucks County Guild Craftsman (exhbn. at Franklin and Marshall Coll. 1979-96), James Michener Art Mus., Doylestown (Pa.), Doylestown Art League, Pa. Guild, Bucks County Arts and Culture Coun., Charchville Nature Ctr. Avocations: tennis, piano, visual/performing arts, community affairs, service art shows. Home: 31 Beth Dr Richboro PA 18954-1901 Personal E-mail: laricebutt@aol.com.

BURWICK, DAVID, beverage company executive; m. Carey Burwick; 4 children. BA in History, Middlebury Coll.; MBA, Harvard U., 1989. Dir. Mountain Dew Pepsi N. Am., 1989—97, v.p. flavors, 1997—98, v.p. marketplace initiative develop., 1998—2000, sr. v.p. mktg. carbonated soft drinks, 2000—02, sr. v.p., CMO, 2002—05; pres. Pepsi-QTG Canada, 2005—. Bd. dirs. The Boston Beer Co., Inc., 2005—. Bd. dirs. Do Something. Mem.: Assn. Nat. Advertisers (bd. dirs.). Office: Pepsi QTG Canada Quaker Park 14 Hunter St Peterborough ON K9J 7B2 Canada

BURYK, ALEXIS, advertising executive; b. 1953; Attended, Wagner Coll., Fordham U. With NY Times, NYC, 1977—, retail advt. dir., advt. sales mgr. retail, advt. sales mgr. spl. projects and direct response, sales mgr. free standing inserts, v.p. advt. dept., 1993—2000, group v.p. advt. sales, 2001—06, sr. v.p. advt., 2006—. Office: The NY Times Co 229 W 43rd St New York NY 10036

BURZIK, CATHERINE M., health products executive; b. Nov. 11, 1950; m. Frank Burzik. BS in Math., Canisius Coll., 1972; MS in Math., U. Buffalo. Software engr. to various mgmt. positions Eastman Kodak; mgmt. positions Critikon, Inc.; pres. Ortho-Clinical Diagnostics, Inc.; COO, exec. v.p. Applied Biosystems, Foster City, Calif., pres., 2004—06; and sr. v.p. Applera Corp., Foster City, Calif., 2004—06; CEO Kinetic Concepts Inc., San Antonio, 2006—. Bd. dirs. Bausch & Lomb, 2007—. Bd. trustees Canisius Coll. Office: Kinetic Concepts Inc 8023 Vantage Dr San Antonio TX 78230 Office Phone: 650-638-5800. Office Fax: 650-638-5884.*

BURZYNSKI, JAMES BRADLEY, state legislator; b. Christopher, Ill., July 13, 1955; m. Judy Burzynski; 2 children. AA, Rend Lake CC; BA, Ill. Wesleyan Coll. Tchr. Pinckneyville Mid. Schs.; farm bur. mgr. Clark, Clinton counties; govtl. affairs dir. DeKalb County Farm Bur.; chmn. DeKalb County Rep. Com.; mem. Ill. State Ho. Reps., 1990—93, Ill. State Senate Dist. 35, 1993—. Chair licenced activities com.; mem. state govt. ops. com.; mem. exec. edn. and higher edn. appropriations com.; senate rep. caucus chmn., 2003—. Adv. bd. DeKalb Salvation Army. Mem.: C. of C. Rockford, C. of C. Belvidere, C. of C. Rochelle, C. of C. Dekalb, Midwest Higher Edn. Commn., C. of C. Sycamore, Sycamore Kiwanis. Address: 505 Dekalb Ave Sycamore IL 60178-1719 Office Phone: 815-895-6318. E-mail: info@senatorbrad.com.

BURZYNSKI, STANISLAW RAJMUND, internist; b. Lublin, Poland, Jan. 23, 1943; came to U.S., 1970; s. Grzegorz and Zofia Miroslawa (Radzikowski) B. MD with distinction, Med. Acad., Lublin, 1967, PhD, 1968. Tchg. asst. Med. Acad., 1962-67, intern, resident, 1967-70; rsch. assoc. Baylor U., 1970-72, asst. prof., 1972-77; pvt. practice specializing in internal medicine Houston, 1977—; pres. Burzynski Clinic, 1979—. Dir. Burzynski Rsch. Lab., 1977-83; pres. Burzynski Rsch. Inst., Inc., 1983-2002. Contbr. articles to profl. jours. Nat. Cancer Inst. grantee, 1974, West Found. grantee, 1975. Mem. AMA, AAAS, Am. Assn. Cancer Rsch., Harris County Med. Soc., Polish Nat. Alliance (pres. Houston chpt. 1974-75), Soc. Neurosci., Soc. Neuro-oncology, Tex. Med. Assn., Sigma Xi. Roman Catholic. Achievements include discovery of antineoplastons components of biochem. def. system against cancer; described structure of Ameletin, 1st substance known to be responsible for remembering sound in animal's brain; invented new treatment for cancer, AIDS, viral infections, autoimmune diseases, neurofibromatosis, and Parkinson's disease; gene silencing theory of aging. Home: 20 W Rivercrest Dr Houston TX 77042-2127 Office: 9432 Old Katy Rd Ste 200 Houston TX 77055-6330 Home Phone: 713-781-4782; Office Phone: 713-335-5697. Business E-Mail: info@burzynskiclinic.com.

BURZYNSKI, SUSAN MARIE, newspaper editor; b. Jackson, Mich., Jan. 1, 1953; d. Leon Walter and Claudia (Kulpinski) B.; m. James W. Bush, May 22, 1976 (div. 1989); children: Lisa M., Kevin J.; m. George K. Bullard, Jr., Mar. 21, 1992. AA, Jackson C.C., 1972; BA, Mich. State, 1974. Reporter Saratogian, Saratoga Springs, N.Y., 1974, Gongwer News Svc., Lansing, Mich., 1975, The State Jour., Lansing, 1975-79; Metro editor Port Huron (Mich.) Times Herald, 1979-82, mng. editor, 1982-86; asst. city editor Detroit News, 1986-87, Sunday news editor, 1987, news editor, 1988-91, asst. mng. editor/news, 1991-96, asst. mng. editor, recruiting and tng., 1996-98, asst. mng. editor, adminstr., 1998-2000, assoc. editor, 2000—04, mng. editor, 2004—. Roman Catholic. Avocations: swimming, tennis, bicycling, knitting. Office: Detroit News 615 W Lafayette Blvd Detroit MI 48226-3197 Office Phone: 313-222-2772. Business E-Mail: sburzynski@detnews.com.

BUS, JAMES STANLEY, toxicologist; b. Kalamazoo, June 27, 1949; s. Charles J. and Sena (Wolthuis) B.; m. Gerda W. Hekman, Apr. 20, 1974; children: Sara E., Timothy J., Brian M. BS in Medicinal Chemistry, U. Mich., 1971; PhD in Pharmacology, Mich. State U., 1975. Diplomate Am. Bd. Toxicology (v.p., pres. 1985-87). NIH predoctoral trainee Dept. Pharmacology, Mich. State U., East Lansing, 1971-75; asst. prof. environ. health U. Cin., 1975-76; scientist I (biochem. toxicologist) Chem. Industry Inst. Toxicology, Research Triangle Park, NC, 1977-84, scientist II (biochem. toxicologist), 1984-86; assoc. dir. pathology/toxicology, dir. drug metabolism rsch. The Upjohn Co., Kalamazoo, 1986-89; toxicology rsch. lab. Dow Chem. Co., Midland, Mich., 1989-91, project mgr., 1992-93, rsch. mgr., tech. dir., 1994—2001, dir. external tech., 2001—. Adj. assoc. prof. curriculum in toxicology U. N.C., Chapel Hill, 1984-88; adj. prof. pharmacology/toxicology Mich. State U., East Lansing, 1987—; toxicology expert Am. Conf. for Govtl. Indsl. Hygienists, Cin., 1993-2002; safety assessment bd. advisors Merck, Sharp & Dohme Lab., West Point, Pa., 1985-86; mem. bd. sci. counselors EPA, 1996-2003, mem. sci. adv. bd., 2003; mem. sci. adv. bd. NTP, 1997-2001, NCTR (FDA), 2006-. Co-editor: Patty's Industrial Hygiene and Toxicology, Vol. 3B, 1995; assoc. editor Toxicology and Applied Pharmacology, 1989-92, speciality editor, 2003—; editl. bd. Reproductive Toxicology, 1986-96; contbr. articles to profl. jours. Trustee Covenant Coll., Lookout Mountain,. Ga., 1984-87. Recipient Robert A. Scala award, Environ. Occupl. Health Sci. Inst., Rutgers U., 1999, Disting. Alumni award, Mich. State U. Dept. Pharmacol. Toxicology, 2001. Fellow Acad. Toxicology Scis.; mem. Soc. Toxicology (pres. 1996-97, Achievement award 1987), Am. Soc. for Pharmacology and Exptl. Therapeutics, Teratology Soc., Am. Conf. Govt. Indsl. Hygiene (mem. chem. substances threshold limit value com. 1993-2002), Nat. Acad. Scis. (emerging issues and data on environ. contaminants com. 2002—2007, bd. on environ. scis. and toxicology 2005-). Republican. Achievements include research dealing with mechanisms of chemical toxicity, including oxidant and glutathione mediated toxicities. Office: Dow Chemical Co Toxicology Rsch Lab 1803 Bldg Midland MI 48674-0001 Office Phone: 989-636-4557. Business E-Mail: jbus@dow.com.

BUSBY, DAVID, lawyer; b. Ada, Okla., Jan. 29, 1926; s. Orel and Hope B.; m. Ann Sears, Sept. 10, 1948 (div. 1959); m. Mary Beth Baker, June 9, 1962; children: Helen Hope Busby Burleigh, Alison Sears Busby Vareika, Robert David, John Orel. BA, Yale U., New Haven, Conn., 1948; LLB, Okla. U., Norman, 1951. Bar: Okla. 1950, DC 1959, NY 1959, US Supreme Ct. 1959. Assoc. Busby, Harrell & Trice, Ada, 1951-55; counsel Subcom. on Automobile Mktg. Practices, Com. on Interstate and Fgn. Commerce, U.S. Senate, Washington, 1955-58, Subcom. Fgn. Commerce, 1958; ptnr. Hays, Busby & Rivkin, NYC, 1958-77, Busby, Rehm & Leonard, 1977-87, Dorsey & Whitney, Washington, 1988—2004. Trade advisor Ministry of Fin., Republic of Latvia, 1996; lectr., Moscow, Kiev, Chisinev, Kampala, 1995-98; mem. accountability rev. bd. terrorist attack on U.S. Embassy, Dar Es Salaam, 1998-99. Mem. Nat. Motor Vehicle Safety Adv. Coun., 1966-68; pres. League Young Dems. of Okla., 1951; city judge, Ada, 1952-53; bd. dirs. Legal Aid Soc. D.C.; mem. Washington Nat. Cathedral chpt., 1984-91. With USN, 1944—46. Mem. ABA (chmn. standing com. on customs law 1973-76), Fed. Cir. Bar Assn. (bd. dirs.), Customs and Internat. Trade Bar Assn. (bd. dirs.), Nat. Cathedral Assn. (bd. trustees 1992-96), Met. Club. Episcopalian. Office: Dorsey & Whitney 1050 Connecticut Ave NW Ste 1250 Washington DC 20036 Office Phone: 202-442-3512. Business E-Mail: busby.david@dorseylaw.com.

BUSBY, EDWARD OLIVER, retired dean; b. Macomb, Ill., June 22, 1926; s. Lynn John and Pauline (Hoebel) B.; m. Lois E. Tehan, June 17, 1950; children: Thomas L., John E., Paula L. BS, U. Wis., 1950, MS, 1962, PhD, 1971. Resident engr. Wis. Hwy. Commn., 1950-51; asst. city engr. City of LaCrosse, Wis., 1951-53; sales engr. Wis. Culvert Co., 1953-59; lectr. civil engring. U. Wis., Madison, 1959-66; dean Coll. Engring. U. Wis.-Platteville, 1966-84, dean emeritus, 1985—. Mem. Wis. Examining Bd. for Profl. Engrs., 1981-84; v.p. Platteville Area Indsl. Devel. Corp., 1977-80; vis. prof. U. Tenn., 1984-85; treas. U. Wis.-Platteville Found., 1989-95. Contbr. articles in field to profl. jours. Served with U.S. Navy, 1944-46 NSF fellow, 1970-71 Fellow ASCE (chmn. profl. registration com. 1985-86); mem. Wis. Soc. Profl. Engrs (pres. 1972-73), Nat. Soc. Profl. Engrs. (nat. dir. 1976-81, vice chmn. engrs. edn. 1971-73) Republican. Home: 7628 Widgeon Way Madison WI 53717-1805

BUSBY, MARJEAN (MARJORIE JEAN BUSBY), retired journalist; b. Kansas City, Mo., Jan. 31, 1931; d. Vivian Eric and Stella Mae (Lindley) Phillips; m. Robert Jackson Busby, Apr. 11, 1969 (dec. Feb. 1989). B.J., U. Mo., 1952. With Kansas City Star Co., 1952-2000, editor women's news, 1969-73, assoc. Sunday editor, People Sect. editor, 1973-77, fashion editor, 1978-81, feature and home writer, 1981-2000; ret., 2000. Mem. Fashion Group (1st recipient Kansas City appreciation award 1978), LSV, Mortar Board, Soc. Profl. Journalists, Friends of Art, Belle of Am. Royal Orgn., Kappa Alpha Theta (pres. Alpha Mu chpt. 1951-52) Presbyterian. Home: 9804 Mercier St Kansas City MO 64114-3860

BUSBY, NITA JUNE, small business owner; b. Pitts., Aug. 28, 1932; d. William Frederich and Monica (Vinciunes) Guidotti; m. Michael Petrunio (div.); children: Michele, Donna, David, Elizabeth, William; m. Harry Leslie Busby BA in English, Calif. State U., Fullerton, 1973, MLS, 1976; cert. in Career Transition Coaching, Chapman U., 2005, cert. in Job Career Transition Coaching, 2004. Health sci. libr. Whittier Hosp., Calif., 1978-82; owner, gen. mgr. Resumés, Etc., Orange, 1982—. Sec. Orange County chpt. Calif. Staffing Profls., 2000—04. Founder So. Calif. Porphyria Support Group, 2001—. Mem. Nat. Assn. Women Bus. Owners (pres. Orange county chpt. 1991-92), Women in Mgmt. (pres. Orange County chpt. 1984-85), Profl. Assn. Resumé Writers (author monthly book revs. 1992-93), Assn. Profl. Cons., Calif. State U. Libr. Sci. Alumni Assn. (pres. 1976-77, 89-90, 90-91) Republican. Roman Catholic. Avocations: reading, walking, vegetable gardening. Office: Resumés Etc 438 E Katella Ave Ste G Orange CA 92867-4857 Home Phone: 714-792-0140; Office Phone: 714-633-2783. Personal E-mail: resumes100@aol.com. Business E-Mail: nbusby@resumesetc.net.

BUSCAGLIA, ROBERT M., financial analyst; b. Buffalo, Mar. 6, 1966; s. Sandra McGuire and George Buscaglia, John McGuire (Stepfather); m. Rita Chandler, July 15, 2000. BA, Canisius Coll., 1988; MBA, Syracuse U., 1990. Bus. analyst Adam, Meldrum & Anderson, Buffalo, 1990—94; mdse. planning adminstrv. supr. Pamida, Omaha, 1994—. Mem.: Mensa. Libertarian. Roman Catholic. Avocations: running, reading. Home Phone: 402-551-6706. Personal E-mail: rbuscag@yahoo.com.

BUSCEMI, PETER, lawyer; b. Bklyn., Sept. 25, 1950; s. Vincent and Ilse (Griesser) Buscemi; m. Judith Ann Miller, June 27, 1981. BA, Columbia U., 1969, JD, 1976; MA, Princeton U., 1971. Bar: N.Y. 1977, D.C. 1979, U.S. Supreme Ct. 1980, U.S. Dist. Ct. (D.C. dist.) 1981, U.S. Ct. Appeals (D.C. cir.) 1981, U.S. Dist. Ct. (so. dist.) N.Y. 1982, U.S. Ct. Appeals (5th and 11th cirs.) 1982, U.S. Ct. Appeals (2d cir.) 1985, U.S. Ct. Appeals (fed. cir.) 1986, U.S. Ct. Appeals (3d and 4th cirs.) 1990, U.S. Ct. Appeals (6th cir.) 1993, U.S. Ct. Appeals (1st cir.) 1994, U.S. Ct. Appeals (7th cir.) 1995, U.S. Ct. Appeals (10th cir.) 1998. Law clk. to Hon. Carl McGowan U.S. Ct. Appeals (D.C. cir.), Washington, 1976—77; asst. to solicitor gen. U.S. Dept. Justice, Washington, 1977—81; spl. asst. U.S. atty. U.S. Atty.'s Office, Alexandria, Va., 1980; assoc. Paul, Weiss, Rifkind, Wharton & Garrison, Washington, 1981—86, Morgan, Lewis & Bockius, LLP, Washington, 1986—87, ptnr., 1987—, mem. litig. practice group. Mem.: D.C. Prisoner's Legal Svcs. Project (bd. dirs.), D.C. Bar Assn.-litig. sect., criminal law sect., cts. lawyers & adminstrn. justice sects., ABA-antitrust& criminal law sects., ABA-litig. adminstrv. sect., Lifeline (bd. dirs.). Office: Morgan Lewis & Bockius LLP 1111 Pennsylvania Ave NW Washington DC 20004 Office Phone: 202-739-5190. Office Fax: 202-739-3001. Business E-mail: pbuscemi@morganlewis.com.

BUSCEMI, STEVE, actor; b. Bklyn., Dec. 13, 1957; m. Jo Andres, 1987; 1 child, Lucian. Student, Lee Strasberg Inst., NYC. Fireman; stand-up comedian NYC. Appeared in films Parting Glances, 1986, Sleepwalk, 1986, Kiss Daddy Good Night, 1987, Vibes, 1988, Heart of Midnight,

1989, Slaves of New York, 1989, Mystery Train, 1989, The Grifters, 1990, Miller's Crossing, 1990, King of New York, 1990, Zandalee, 1991, Barton Fink, 1991, Billy Bathgate, 1991, Criscross, 1992, In the Soup, 1992, Reservoir Dogs, 1992, Me and the Mob, 1992, Twenty Bucks, 1993, The Hudsucker Proxy, 1994, Airheads, 1994, Pulp Fiction, 1994, Floundering, 1994, Desperado, 1995, Things to Do in Denver When You're Dead, 1995, Fargo, 1996, Black Kites, 1996, Kansas City, 1996, Search for One-Eye Kimmy, 1996, Escape from LA., 1996, The Real Blonde, 1997, Divine Trash, 1997, Con Air, 1997, The Big Lebowski, 1998, The Wedding Singer, 1998, Louis et Frank, 1998, Armageddon, 1998, The Impostors, 1998, Big Daddy, 1999, 28 Days, 2000, Ghost World, 2000, Monsters Inc. (voice), 2001, Domestic Distrubance, 2001, The Laramie Project, 2002, Mr. Deeds, 2002, Spy Kids 2: Island of Lost Dreams, 2002, Deadrockstar, 2002, Spy Kids 3-D: Game Over, 2003, Big Fish, 2003, Home on the Range (voice), 2000-2004, Who's the Top?, 2005, The Island, 2005, Romance and Cigarettes, 2005, Art School Confidential, 2006, Paris, je t'aime, 2006, Monster House (voice), 2006, Delirious, 2006, Charlotte's Web (voice), 2006, I Think I Love My Wife, 2007, Interview, 2007, (TV films) Borders, 1989, The Last Outlaw, 1994; prodr., dir. (films) What Happened to Pete?, 1993; dir. (films) Trees Lounge, 1996; actor, dir. writer Interview, 2007; TV appearances include Tales from the Crypt, 1993, Miami Vice, L.A. Law, The Sopranos, others.*

BUSCH, ANNIE, library director; b. Joplin, Mo., Jan. 6, 1947; d. George Lee and Margaret Eleanor (Williams) Chancellor; 1 child, William Andrew Keller. BA, Mo. U., 1969, MA, 1976; D in Pub. Affairs (hon.), Mo. State U., 2007. Br. mgr. St. Charles City Coun. Libr., Mo., 1977-84, Springfield/Greene County Libr., Mo., 1985-89, exec. dir., 1989—. Exec. bd. Mo. Libr. Network Corp., St. Louis, 1991-96; bd. dirs. Jordan Valley Innovation Ctr. Adv. bd. Springfield Pub. Sch. Found., 1992—94, St. John's Health Sys., Boys and Girls Town, Good Cmty. Task Force, 1999—2002; pres. Ozarks Regional Info. On-Line Network, Springfield, 1993—98; mem. Gov.'s Commn. on Informational Tech., Cmty. Task Force, Springfield, 1993—98, Cmty. Partnership of the Ozarks, 1998; exec. bd. Mo. Rsch. and Edn. Network, pres., 1996—97; task force Mo. Goals 2000, Mo. Census 2000 Complete Count Com., 1999—2000; coord. com. Springfield Vision 20/20; chair Sec. of State Adv. Coun., 2001—05; adv. com. S.W. Mo. State U. Coll. Humanities and Pub. Affairs; bd. dirs. Ozarks Pub. TV, 1994—2000, Every Kid Counts, Wilson's Creek Nat. Battlefield Found., Mayors Commn. for Children, 2005—; bd. trustees Forest Inst. Profl. Psychology. Mem.: Mo. Libr. Assn. (exec. bd. 1990—94, pres. 1993—94), Springfield Area C. of C. (bd. dirs.), Springfield Rotary (pres. 1998—99). Office: Springfield-Greene Cty Libr PO Box 760 Springfield MO 65801-0760 Home Phone: 417-887-8485; Office Phone: 417-847-8120 ext 5. E-mail: annie@mail.sgcl.org.

BUSCH, AUGUST ADOLPHUS, III, retired brewery company executive; b. St. Louis, June 16, 1937; s. August Anheuser and Elizabeth (Overton) Busch; m. Susan Marie Hornibrook, Aug. 17, 1963 (div. 1969); children: August Adolphus IV, Susan Marie II; m. Virginia L. Wiley, Dec. 28, 1974; children: Steven August, Virginia Marie. Student, U. Ariz., 1957—58, Siebel Inst. Tech., 1960—61. With Anheuser-Busch, Inc., St. Louis, 1957—2002, pres., 1974—75, CEO, 1975—2002, chmn., 1977—2006. Bd. dirs. Southwestern Bell Tel. Co., 1980—83, AT&T Inc. (formerly SBC Comm. Inc.), 1983—, Emerson Electric Co., Grupo Modelo SA de CV; chmn., Corporate Governance and Nominating Com. AT&T Inc., San Antonio, mem., Corp. Devel. Com., mem., Exec. Com. Exec. bd. St. Louis Boy Scouts Am.; bd. dirs. United Way Greater St. Louis. Mem.: Log Cabin Club, St. Louis Country Club.*

BUSCH, AUGUST ADOLPHUS, IV, brewery company executive; b. June 15, 1964; s. August Adolphus Busch III and Susan Marie (Hornibrook). BS in Fin., St. Louis U., MS in Bus. Adminstrn.; Brewmaster's degree, Internat. Brewing Inst., Berlin; Ph.D in Bus. Adminstrn. (hon.), Webster U., 2006. Line foreman Anheuser-Busch, Inc., St. Louis, exec. asst. to brewing v.p., with mktg. dept., 1989, brand dir., 1991, v.p. brand mgmt., 1994, v.p. mktg., 1996—2000, v.p. mktg. and wholesale ops., 2000—02, pres., 2002—, CEO, 2006—, mgmt. com., bd. dirs.; group v.p. mktg. and wholesale ops. Anheuser-Busch Cos., Inc., St. Louis, 2000—06, strategy com. mem., pres., CEO, 2006—. Chmn. Beer Inst.; bd. mem. FedEx Corp., Memphis, 2003—. Bd. mem. Muscular Dystrophy Assn., Loyola Inst., St. Louis, The BackStoppers; mem. adv. bd. Am. Paralysis Assn., Gen. Henry Hugh Shelton Leadership Initiative, NC State U.; bd. fellows Claremont U. Ctr. and Grad. Sch.; bd. govs. Cardinal Glennon Hosp., St. Louis; gen. co-chmn. St. Louis Am. Found. Awards program. Named Corp. Mktg. Exec. of Yr., Delaney Report, 1999, Lew Wasserman Spirit of Democracy Man of Yr., 2003, Advertiser of Yr., 48th Cannes Internat. Advt. Festival, 2001; named to Am. Advt. Fedn. Hall of Achievement, 2000; recipient Intrepid Salute award, Gerald S. Snyder Heart award, Larry King Cardiac Found. Office: Anheuser Busch Cos Inc One Busch Pl Saint Louis MO 63118*

BUSCH, BEVERLY GAIL, English language educator, literature educator, instructional resource center administrator; b. Boston, Oct. 27, 1948; d. Andrew Earl Thompson and Martha Bartlett; m. Peter Raymond Busch, Apr. 15, 1972; children: Cheyenne J., Carin S., Luke W. BA, U. Mass., 1970; MA, Middlebury Coll., 1978; MPhil, Drew U., 1981, PhD, 1986. Cert. English tchr. Mass., NJ. Adj. faculty mem. Coll. St. Elizabeth, Madison, NJ, 1981-83, Centenary Coll., Hackettstown, NJ, 1981-83; coord. ministries program Phillipsburg (N.J.) Alliance Ch., 1995-99; adj. prof. English Warren County Cmty. Coll., Washington, NJ, 1995-99; prof. English Somerset Christian Coll., Zarephath, NJ, 1999—, dir. Instructional Resource Ctr., chmn. Dept. Gen. Edn., 1999—. Author poetry and inspirational articles; mem. editl. adv. bd.: Collegiate Press, 2002—04, Rowman & Littlefield Pubs., Inc., 2004—05; editor: (poetry) Broken, Vol. 1. Mem. Greenwich Twp. Bd. Edn., Stewartsville, N.J., 1995-99; pres. Greenwich Twp. Parent Tchr. Orgn., 1989-92, Parents On Site, 1994-96. Mem.: MLA, Acad. Am. Poets, NJ Coun. Tchrs. English, Nat. Coun. Tchrs. English, Evangel. Theol. Soc., Drew U. Alumni Assn., Middlebury Coll. Alumni Assn., U. Mass. Alumni Assn. Republican. Avocations: walking, biking, crafts. Home: 113 Kennedy Mill Rd Stewartsville NJ 08886 Office Phone: 732-356-1595 ext. 1126. Business E-Mail: bbusch@somerset.edu.

BUSCH, DANIEL ADOLPH, geologist, educator; b. St. Paul, May 31, 1912; s. Karl George Adolph and Lulu Elizabeth Busch; m. Emilie Louise Finch; children: Daniel Andrew(dec.) , David Arthur. BSc, Capital U., Columbus, Ohio, 1934, DSc (hon.), 1960; MA, Ohio State U., Columbus, 1936, PhD, 1939. Instr. U. Pitts., 1938—42; with Pa. Geol. Survey, Pitts., 1943—44, Huntley & Huntley Petroleum Cons., Pitts., 1944—46; sr. rsch. geologist Carter Rsch. Lab., Tulsa, 1946—51; chief geologist Zephyr Petroleum Co., Tulsa, 1951—54; petroleum geology cons. Tulsa, 1955—89; ret., 1989. Vis. prof. geology U. Okla., Norman, 1964—74; lectr. Oil & Gas Cons., Internat., Tulsa, 1967—89; lectr. in field; cons. in field. Author: Stratigraphic Traps in Sandstones - Exploration Techniques, 1974 (Robert Dott Best Publ. award, 1975), Exploration Methods for Sandstone Reservoirs, 1985. Fellow: Geol. Soc. Am. (sr.); mem.: Am. Assn. Petroleum Geologists (hon.; v.p. 1966—67, pres. 1973—74, Matson award 1959, Leverson award 1971, Sidney Powers medal 1982, Monroe Cheney award 2003, Am. Registry of Outstanding Profls. 2003—), Sigma Xi. Avocations: travel, gardening, investments. Home: 3757 S Wheeling Ave Tulsa OK 74105

BUSCH, DAVID DENNIS, writer, photographer; b. Ravenna, Ohio, Dec. 3, 1947; s. George William Busch and Norma Jean Tobias, Ralph Walter Tetzel (Stepfather); m. Catherine Veronica Miazga, July 19, 1969; children: David Dennis Jr., Michael Christopher, Jonathan Ralph, Teryn Nicole. BA in Journalism, Kent State U., Ohio, 1970. Account exec. Rumrill-Hoyt Pub. Rels. Inc., Rochester, NY, 1970—74; sr. ptnr. CCS/PR Inc., Carlsbad, Calif., 1974—92. Author: more than 100 non-fiction books (Computer Press awards, 1985). Mem.: Am. Mensa (pres. East Ctrl. Ohio 1992—94). Office Phone: 330-296-8410.

BUSCH, J. HERBERT, electrical contractor, writer; b. Cleve., Mar. 16, 1920; s. Edward A. and Anna Busch; m. Ruth Singer Busch, June 14, 1942; children: Pamela Friedman, Sheryl Pariser(dec.). Contractor Discount Electric of Va., Inc., Fairfax. Tchr. Elec. Trade Sch., Parma, Ohio. Author: 9 books, more than 1,700 poems, stories, and songs. Capt. signal corps US Army, 1942—46. Jewish.

BUSCH, JOHN ARTHUR, lawyer, business executive; b. Indpls., Mar. 23, 1951; s. John L. and Betty (Thomas) B.; m. Barbara Ann Holt, June 23, 1973; children: Abigail, Elizabeth, Amanda, Rachel. BA, Wabash Coll., 1973; JD, Duke U., 1976. Bar: Wis. 1976, U.S. Dist. Ct. (ea. we. dists.) Wis., U.S. Ct. Appeals (5th and 7th cirs.) 1976. Assoc. Michael, Best & Friedrich, Milw., 1976-83, ptnr., 1983—; chmn. litigation dept. Michael Best & Friedrich, 1990—95, mgmt. com., 1995—2001, mng. ptnr. Milw. office, 2003—04; CEO Lorman Edn. Svcs., Eau Claire, 2006—. Mem. ad hoc com. on alternative dispute resolution Milw. Cir. Ct., ad hoc com. on multidisciplinary practices State Bar, mem. bd. govs., 2001-03. Treas. North Shore Rep. Club, Milw., 1984-85, vice chmn., 1985-86, chmn., 1987-89; del. Rep. State Conv., Milw., 1986; mem. local rules adv. com. Ea. dist., Wis.; mem. com. Fed. Bench Bar; bd. dir. New Am. Policy Inst., 2005—; bd. trustees Mich. Maritime Mus., bd. dir., 2005—. Master: Am. Inns of Ct.; mem.: ABA, Wis. Bar Assn., Milw. Bar Assn. Home: 1025 E Lyon St Milwaukee WI 53202 Office: Michael Best & Friedrich 100 E Wisconsin Ave Ste 3300 Milwaukee WI 53202-4108 Office Phone: 414-225-4977. Business E-Mail: jabusch@michaelbest.com.

BUSCH, JOYCE IDA, small business owner; b. Madera, Calif., Jan. 24, 1934; d. Bruno Harry and Ella Fae (Absher) Toschi; m. Fred O. Busch, Dec. 14, 1956; children: Karen, Kathryn, Kurt. BA in Indsl. Arts and Interior Design, Calif. State U., Fresno, 1991. Cert. interior designer, Calif. Stewardess United Air Lines, San Francisco, 1955-57; prin. Art Coordinates, Fresno, 1982—, Busch Interior Design, Fresno, 1982—. Art cons. Fresno Cmty. Hosp., 1981-83; docent Fresno Met. Mus., 1981-84. Treas. Valley Children's Hosp. Guidance Clinic, 1975-79, Lone Star PTA, 1965-84,; mem. Mothers Guild San Joaquin Mem. H.S., 1984-88. Mem. Am. Soc. Interior Designers. Republican. Roman Catholic. Avocations: gardening, art history. Office Phone: 559-260-3202. Personal E-mail: joyce.busch@sbcglobal.net.

BUSCH, KURT, race car driver; b. Las Vegas, Nev., Aug. 4, 1978; s. Tom and Gaye Busch. Race car driver Roush Racing, Concord, NC. Named NASCAR Hobby Stock Rookie of Yr., Champion, 1996, Featherlite S.W. Series Rookie of the Yr., 1998, Featherlite S.W. Series Champion, 1999, Craftsman Truck Series Rookie of the Yr., 2d in points, 2000. Achievements include finished first, NEXTEL Cup Racing, 2004; winner, Subway 500, 2005; Pocono Raceway 500, 2005; Chevy Rock and Roll 400, 2005, Food City 500, 2006; winner, Pa. 500, 2007, 3M Performance 400, 2007. Office: Kurt Busch Inc 151 Lugnut Ln Mooresville NC 28117 Office Phone: 704-799-2428. Office Fax: 704-799-2326.*

BUSCH, KYLE, race car driver; b. Las Vegas, Nev., May 2, 1985; Driver, Craftsman Truck Series Billy Ballew Motorsports, 1985—; driver, Nexfel Cup Series and Busch Series Hendrick Motorsports, 2003—. Named Busch Series Rookie of Yr., 2004; finished runner-up in Busch Series; 5 Busch Series victories. Winner of NASCAR Nextel Cup Series events including the 2005 Sony HD 500, Fontana, California, 2005 Checker Auto Parts 500, Phoenix, 2006 Lenox Industrial Tools 300, Loudon, New Hampshire; winner of Craftsman Truck Series events including the Quaker Steak and Lube 200, Charlotte, North Carolina, 2005, 06, MBNA RacePoints 200, Dover, Delaware, 2005, EasyCare Vehicle Service Contracts 200, Hampton, Georgia; winner of Busch Series events including the Funai 250, Richmond, Virginia, 2004, Carquest Auto Parts 300, Charlotte, North Carolina, 2004, 05, Meijer 300, Sparta, Kentucky, 2004, Kroger 200, Indiana, Cabela's 250, Michigan, Sharpie Mini 300, Bristol, Tennessee, 2006; youngest driver ever to win a race in the Nextel Cup history.

BUSCH, MICHAEL, state legislator; b. Balt., Jan. 4, 1947; BS, Temple U., 1970. Tchr., coach St. Mary's H.S., 1973-79; adminstr. youth athletics Anne Arundel County, Md., 1979—; del. dist. 30 Md. State Delegation, 1987—, spkr. ho., 2003—. Mem. numerous coms. including most recently Md. State Delegation, chmn. econ. matters com., 1994—, mem. legis. policy com., 1994—, mem. rules and exec. nominations com., 1994—. Chmn. Anne Arundel County Delegation, 1992-93; mem. St. Mary's Sch. Bd., 1992—; bd. trustees The Md. Hist. Trust, 1995. Named Coach of the Yr., 1978, Man of Yr., Anne arundel County Lacrosse Assn., 1982, Legislator of Yr., Anne Arundel County Nurses Assn., 1989; recipient Presdl. Citation, Md. Recreation and Parks Assn., 1989; named to Sports Hall Fame, Anne Arundel County, 2003, Legis. of Yr., Annapolis and Anne Arundel County C. of C., 2005. Office: State House H 101 Annapolis MD 21401

BUSCH, ROBERT HENRY, geneticist, researcher; b. Jefferson, Iowa, Oct. 22, 1937; s. Henry and Lena Margaret (Osterman) B.; m. Mavis Ann Bushman, Nov. 23, 1958; children: Shari Lynne, Todd William. BSc, Iowa State U., 1959, MSc, 1963; PhD, Purdue U., 1967. Asst. prof. N.D. State U., Fargo, 1967-72, assoc. prof., 1973-77, prof., 1977-78; rsch. geneticist USDA-ARS/U. Minn., St. Paul, 1978—. Cons. Nat. Hail Ins. Coun., Ill. and Colo., 1969-75, Internat. Atomic Energy Agy., UN. Developer 9 wheat varieties; contbr. chpts. to books, articles to profl. jours. Recipient Dedicated Svc. award Polk County Crop Improvement Assn., East Grand Forks, Minn., 1984; named Premier Seedsman Minn. Crop Improvement Assn., St. Paul, 1985. Fellow Crop Sci. Soc. Am. (editor 1976-78, com. chair 1988-90, bd. dirs. 1989-90), Am. Soc. Agronomy (Achievement award, Midwest Sr. Sci. 1998). Methodist. Avocations: sailing, fishing. Home: 2485 Galtier Cir Saint Paul MN 55113-3609 Office: U Minn Dept Agronomy Saint Paul MN 55108

BUSCHBACH, THOMAS CHARLES, geologist, consultant; b. Cicero, Ill., May 12, 1923; s. Thomas Dominick and Vivian (Smiley) B.; m. Mildred Merle Fletcher, Nov. 26, 1947; children— Thomas Richard, Susan Kay, Deborah Lynn BS, U. Ill., 1950, MS, 1951, PhD, 1959. Geologist, structural geology, stratigraphy, underground storage of natural gas Ill. Geol. Survey, 1951-78; coordinator New Madrid Seismotectonic Study, U.S. Nuclear Regulatory Commn., 1976-85; research prof. geology St. Louis U., 1978-85; geologic cons. Champaign, Ill., 1985—. Served to lt. comdr. USNR, 1942-47 Fellow Geol. Soc. Am. Home: 604 Park Lane Dr Champaign IL 61820-7631 Office: PO Box 1608 Champaign IL 61824-1608 Office Phone: 217-356-3667. E-mail: tcbusch@aol.com.

BUSCHKE, HERMAN, neurologist; b. Berlin, Oct. 15, 1932; came to U.S., 1934, naturalized, 1945; s. Franz Julius and Ruth Helen (Minkowski) B.; children: Thomas, Katherine; m. Bertelle Selig, 1993. BA, Reed Coll., 1954; MD, Western Res. U., 1958. Diplomate: Am. Bd. Psychiatry and Neurology. Intern Bronx (N.Y.) Mcpl. Hosp. Center, 1958-59, resident in neurology, 1959-62; asst. instr. neurology Albert Einstein Coll. Medicine, Bronx, NY, 1961-62, asso. prof., 1969-74, prof., 1974—, prof. neurosci., 1974—; practice medicine specializing in neurology Bronx, NY, 1969—. Staff mem., attending neurologist Hosp. of Albert Einstein Coll. of Medicine; instr. medicine Stanford U., 1962-63, asst. prof., 1963-69 Named Lena and Joseph Gluck Disting. Scholar in Neurology, 1973. Office: Albert Einstein Coll Medicine Saul R Korey Dept Neurology 50 E 89th St New York NY 10128 Home Phone: 212-996-4848; Office Phone: 718-430-2432. Business E-Mail: buschke@aecom.yu.edu.

BUSCHMANN, SIEGFRIED, retired manufacturing executive; b. Essen, Germany, July 12, 1937; s. Walter and Frieda Maria (von. Stamm) B.; m. Rita Renate Moch, May 7, 1965; children: Verena, Mark. Diploma, Wilhelms U. Various exec. positions Thyssen AG, Duesseldorf, Germany, 1964-82; pres. Thyssen Holding Corp., Troy, Mich., 1982-99; chmn. ThyssenKrupp USA, Inc., 1999—2006; ret., 2006; sr. v.p. The Budd Co., Troy, 1982-83, sr. v.p., CFO, 1983-86, vice chmn., CFO, 1986-89, chmn., CEO, 1989—2001, chmn. bd., 2001—02. Chmn. exec. bd. Thyssen Budd Automotive GmbH, Essen, Germany, 1997—99; v.chmn., exec. bd. Thyssen Krupp Automotive AG, Bochum, Germany, 1999—2001, mem. supervisory bd., 2001—05. Avocation: golf. Office: Thyssenkrupp USA Inc PO Box 5084 3155 W Big Beaver Rd Troy MI 48007-5084

BUSDICKER, GORDON GENE, retired lawyer; b. Winona, Minn., Oct. 12, 1933; s. Harry John and Edna Mae (Rogers) B.; m. Noreen Decker; children— Karla E., Pamela J., Alison G., Neal A. BA, Hamline U., St. Paul, 1955; JD, Harvard U., 1958. Bar: Minn. Atty. Aluminum Co. of Am., Pitts., 1958-61; assoc. Faegre & Benson, Mpls., 1961-67, ptnr., 1967-99, ret., 1999. Trustee Hamline U., St. Paul, 1973—. Mem. ABA, Minn. Bar Assn., Interlachen Golf Club. Republican. Congregationalist. Avocations: boating, genealogy. Home: 3833 Abbott Ave S Minneapolis MN 55410-1036 Office Phone: 612-925-2091. Personal E-mail: busdick1@gmail.com.

BUSE, ELIZABETH L., finance company executive; BA, UCLA; grad. fellow, Univ. Complutense, Spain; MBA, Univ. Calif., Berkeley. Sr. mgr. Windermere Associates; v.p. strategic initiatives First Data Corp.; exec. v.p. product devel. & mgmt. Visa USA, San Francisco, 1998—. Mailing: Visa USA PO Box 194607 San Francisco CA 94119-4607*

BUSELMEIER, BERNARD JOSEPH, insurance company executive; b. Detroit, Feb. 10, 1956; s. Bernard August and Rita Mathilda (Cook) Buselmier; m. Carolyn Diane Karamon, Mar. 22, 2003; 1 child, Andrew Joseph. BBA in Acctg., U. Detroit, 1980, MBA, 1990. Various fin. positions ins. group Auto Club Mich., Dearborn, Mich., 1974-81; various fin. positions Motors Ins. Corp., Detroit, 1981-89, treas., 1989-98, v.p., treas., 1993-98; exec. v.p., CFO, Integon Corp., Winston-Salem, N.C., 1998-99; CFO GMAC Ins. Personal Lines, St. Louis, 1999—. Office: GMAC Ins Personal Lines 13736 Riverfort Dr Ste 700 Maryland Heights MO 63043

BUSER, CAROLYN ELIZABETH, adult education educator; b. St. Paul, June 14, 1946; d. Jerome Alfred and Ella Caroline (Anderson) B.; m. Richard John Ward, Sept. 17, 1977; children: John Jerome Buser Ward, Carl Alfred Buser Ward. BA in English, Carleton Coll., 1968; MS in Spl. Edn., U. Md., 1985, PhD in Ednl. Policy and Adminstrn., 1996. Correctional tchr. Md. Div. Correction, Hughesville, 1970-74, Balt., 1974-76; correctional edn. supr. Md. Dept. Edn. Md. Penitentiary, Balt., 1976-80, Md. Correctional Instn., Jessup, 1980-88; correctional edn. supr. Md. Dept. Edn., Md. correctional pre-release program Md. Correctional Instn. for Women, Jessup, 1988-94; field coord. correctional edn. Md. Dept. Edn., 1994-2001, dir. correctional edn., 2001—06; edn. program specialist adult edn. U.S. Dept. Edn., Washington, 2006—. Cons. Am. Correctional Assn., Laurel, Md., 1980; Md. state dir. Region II Correctional Edn. Assn., Laurel, 1972-74, 88-90; exemplary program supr. Prison Literacy, Nat. Inst. Corrections, Washington, 1986; mem. Md. State Use Indus. Coun., 2001-06; Md. State Adv. Coun. on Adult Edn., 2004-05. Fellow Edn. Behaviorally Disordered Students, U. Md., 1985. Mem.: Am. Correctional Assn., Md. Assn. Adult Cmty. and Continuing Edn., Correctional Edn. Assn. (region II sec. 1986, editl. bd. Jour. Correctional Edn. 2002—), Phi Kappa Phi. Office: US Dept Edn 550 12th St SW Washington DC 20202

BUSEY, PHIL GORDON, lawyer; b. Oklahoma City, Okla., Jan. 22, 1952; s. C.L. and Hazel (Brown) B.; m. Catherine Jean Callaway, Sept. 17, 1977; children: Phil G. Jr., Brian Marshall, Emily C. BA in Polit. Sci. and History, Oklahoma City U., 1974; JD, Okla. U., 1977. Bar: Okla. 1978, U.S. Dist. Ct. (we. dist.) Okla., U.S. Ct. Appeals (10th cir.) 1987. Aircraft and ins. examiner Insured Aircraft Title Service, Inc., Oklahoma City, 1975-77; asst. v.p., trust officer Am.-First Title and Trust Co., Oklahoma City, 1977-79; asst. gen. counsel First Nat. Bank and Trust Co. and First Oklahoma Bancorp., Inc., Oklahoma City, 1979-81; atty. Linn, Helms, Kirk & Burkett, Oklahoma City, 1981-82; v.p., atty. Penn Sq. Bank, Oklahoma City, 1982; atty. Kornfeld Franklin & Phillips, Oklahoma City, 1982-84, Robinson, Boese & Davidson, Tulsa, 1984-85; of counsel Kirk & Chaney, Tulsa, 1985-91; shareholder Pats & Payne, P.C., 1987-91, Hall, Estill, Attys. at Law, 1991-95; of counsel Phillips McFadden, 1995-97; sr. v.p., global counsel Advanica Corp., 1997-99; pres., CEO ProForma Group Inc., 1999-2000; pres., founder Busey Resource Group Inc., 2000—; pvt. practice, 2000—; founder, chmn, CEO Del. Resource Gap, Inc., 2002—. Adj. prof. South Oklahoma City Jr. Coll. and Inst. of Banking, 1979-82, Oklahoma City U., 1983-95; mem. Okla. Regents Coun. for Career and Tech., 1999—. Contbr. articles to profl. jours. Baseball coach YMCA Youth Baseball team, Oklahoma City, 1977-93; bd. dirs. Ch. of the Servant, Oklahoma City, 1983; pres. Classen Awards Alumni Assn., Oklahoma City, 1983-95; mem. adminstrv. bd. St. Lukes United Meth. Ch., 1998—; mem. alumni bd. Oklahoma City U., 1997-99. Mem. ABA, Okla. Bar Assn., Oklahoma County Bar Assn., Nat. Assn. Bond Lawyers, Del. Chamber Indian Nations, Okla. State C. of C., So. Oklahoma City C. of C. (bd. dirs. 2000—), Phi Alpha Delta, Oklahoma City Young Men's Dinner Club. Democrat. Office: 2800 NW 36 Ste 202 Oklahoma City OK 73112 E-mail: pbuseylaw@aol.com.

BUSEY, ROXANE C., lawyer; b. Chgo., June 15, 1949; BA cum laude, Miami U., 1970; MAT, Northwestern U., 1971, JD, 1975. Bar: Ill. 1975. Ptnr. Baker & McKenzie LLP, Chgo. Mem. ABA (chair antitrust sect. 2001-02, chmn. task force antitrust modernization 2004-07; chair health com., antitrust sect. 1989-92, antitrust sect. coun. 1992-95, officer 1995-03), Ill. State Bar Assn. (chair antitrust coun. 1984-85), Chgo. Bar Assn. (chair antitrust sect. 1990-91). Office: Baker & McKenzie LLP 1 Prudential Plz 130 E Randolph Dr Ste 3500 Chicago IL 60601 Office Phone: 312-861-8281. Business E-Mail: roxane.c.busey@bakernet.com.

BUSFIELD, ROGER MELVIL, JR., retired trade association executive, educator; b. Ft. Worth, Feb. 4, 1926; s. Roger Melvil and Julia Mabel (Clark) B.; m. Jean Wilson, Mar. 26, 1948 (div. Oct. 1960); children: Terry Jean, Roger Melvil III, Timothy Clark; m. Virginia Bailey, Dec. 1, 1962 (dec. July 1991); 1 child, Julia Lucille; m. Addie Howard Davis, June 17, 1995. Student, U. Tex., 1943-46; BA, Southwestern U., 1947, MA, 1948; PhD, Fla. State U., 1954. Instr. U. Tex., 1943, 1946; asst. prof. Southwestern U., 1947-49; instr. U. Ala., 1949-50, Fla. State U., 1950-54; asst. prof. speech Mich. State U., 1954-60; editl. svcs. specialist Oldsmobile divsn. Gen. Motors Corp., Lansing, Mich., 1960; gen. publs. supr. Consumers Power Co., Jackson, Mich., 1960-61; assoc. dir. Mich. Hosp. Assn., Lansing, 1961-73; exec. dir. Ark. Hosp. Assn., Little Rock, 1973-81, pres., 1981-94, pres. emeritus, 1994—. Adj. prof. health svcs. mgmt. Webster U., 1979-97. Author: The Playwright's Art, 1958, Arabic transl., 1964, (with others) The Children's Theatre, 1960; editor Theatre Arts Bibliography, 1964; contbr. articles to profl. jours.; author profl. motion picture scenarios. Trustee Ctrl. Mich. U., 1967-73, chmn., 1970; mem. Mich. Gov.'s Commn. on Higher Edn., 1972-74; mem. Ark. Gov.'s Emergency Med. Svcs. Adv. Coun., 1975-94, chmn., 1978-84; mem. Ark. Gov.'s Task Force on Rural

Hosps., 1988-89, Ark. Dept. of Health Long Range Planning Com., 1988-89; chmn. AIDS adv. com. Ark. Dept. Health, 1990-97; mem. Ark. Gov.'s Task Force Health Care Reform, 1993-96; chmn. Health Data Task Force, Ark. Resources Comm., 1994-95; mem. adv. bd. Ark. Pediat. Facility, 1995-96. Served with USMC, 1943-46. Named Tex. Outstanding Author, Theta Sigma Phi, 1958; recipient Disting. Alumnus award Southwestern U., 1971, Senate-House Concurrent Resolution of Tribute, Mich. Legis., 1973, Bd. Trustees award Am. Hosp. Assn., 1994, Merit award Ark. Hosp. Assn., 1994. Mem. Am. Soc. Assn. Execs., Ark. Soc. Assn. Execs. (pres. 1981-82), Pub. Rels. Assn. Mich. (pres. 1966), Speech Comm. Assn., Am. Coll. Health Care Execs., State Hosp. Assn. Exec. Forum (sec., treas. 1989, pres. 1991), Am. Hosp. Assn. (coun. legis. 1975-77, coun. allied and govtl. rels. 1983-86), San Gabriel Writers League (pres. 2000-01), Rotary (Little Rock). Methodist. Home: PO Box 2267 Georgetown TX 78627-2267 Office Phone: 512-930-1396. Personal E-mail: busfield@suddenlink.net.

BUSH, BARBARA PIERCE, former First Lady of the United States, volunteer; b. Rye, NY, June 8, 1925; d. Marvin and Pauline (Robinson) Pierce; m. George Herbert Walker Bush, Jan. 6, 1945; children: George Walker, Pauline Robin (dec.), John Ellis, Neil Mallon, Marvin Pierce, Dorothy Walker. Student, Smith Coll., 1943-44; degree (hon.), Stritch Coll., Milw., 1981, Mt. Vernon Coll., Washington, 1981, Hood Coll., Frederick, Md., 1983, Howard U., Washington, 1987, Judson Coll., Marion, Ala., 1988, Bennett Coll., Greensboro, NC, 1989, Smith Coll., 1989, Morehouse Sch. Medicine, 1989. First Lady of the U.S., Washington, 1989—93; oper. & facilities div. Dept. Administration, Washington, 1992. Author: C. Fred Story, 1984, Millie's Book, 1990, Barbara Bush: A Memoir, 1994, Reflections: Life After the White House, 2003. Hon. chair adv. bd. Reading is Fundamental; hon. mem. Bus. Coun. for Effective Literacy; mem. adv. coun. Soc. of Meml. Sloan-Kettering Cancer Ctr.; hon. mem. bd. dirs. Children's Oncology Svcs. of Met. Washington, The Washington Home, The Kingsbury Ctr.; hon. chmn. nat. adv. coun. Literacy Vols. of Am., Nat. Sch. Vols. Program; sponsor Laubach Literacy Internat.; nat. hon. chmn. Leukemia Soc. of Am.; hon. mem. bd. trustees Morehouse Sch. of Medicine; hon. nat. chmn. Nat. Organ Donor Awareness Week, 1982-86; pres. Ladies of the Senate, 1981-88; mem. women's com. Smithsonian Assocs., Tex. Fedn. of Rep. Women, life mem., hon. mem.; hon. chairperson for the Nat. Com. on Literacy and Edn. United Way, Barbara Bush Found. for Family Literacy, 1989-, Washington Parent Group Fund, Girls Clubs of Am., 10th anniversary Harvest Nat. Food Bank Network; hon. chmn. Nat. Com. for the Prevention of Child Abuse and Childhelp U.S.A.; hon. pres. Girl Scouts U.S; hon. chair Nat. Com. for Adoption; mem. bd. trustees Mayo Clinic Found.; hon. chair Read Am., Boarder Baby Project; mem. bd. visitors M. D. Anderson Cancer Ctr.; hon. chair Leukemia Soc. Am., Children's Literacy Initiative; hon. mem. Reading is Fundamental; ambassador at large Americares; honorary mem. Barbara Bush Found. for Family Literacy. Recipient Nat. Outstanding Mother of Yr. award, 1984, Woman of Yr. award USO, 1986, Disting. Leadership award United Negro Coll. Fund 1986, Disting. Am. Woman award Mt. St. Joseph Coll., 1987, Free Spirit award Freedom Forum, 1995. Mem. Tex. Fedn. Rep. Women (life), Internat. II Club (Washington), Magic Circle Rep. Women's Club (Houston), YWCA. Episcopalian. Avocations: reading, gardening, needlepoint.*

BUSH, BILLY, television personality; s. Jonathan and Jodi Bush; m. Sydney Bush; children: Josephine, Mary Bradley. B in internat. studies and govt., Colby Coll., 1994. Host afternoon show WLKZ-FM, NH; host midday show WARW-FM, Washington; host "Billy Busy and the Bush League Morning Show" WWZZ-FM, Washington, 1997—2001; East coast corr. Access Hollywood, 2001—04, co-anchor, 2004—; host Let's Make a Deal, NBC, 2003. Contbr. The Today Show, NBC; co-host Miss USA, 2003, 04, Miss Universe, 2003. Office: Access Hollywood NBC Studios 3000 W Alamea Ave Burbank CA 91523 Office Phone: 818-526-7000.

BUSH, CARLETTA ANN, historian, educator; b. Morgantown, W.Va., Sept. 2, 1957; d. Truman Duane Harvey and Alicia Ann King; m. Robert G. Bush, Nov. 1, 2003; children from previous marriage: Mark Savage Jr., Mary Ann Savage. BS in Elem. Edn., W.Va. U., Morgantown, 1980, MA in History, 1999, PhD in History, 2006. Substitute tchr. Monongalia County Schs., Morgantown, 1980—86; tchr. Alliance Christian Sch., Morgantown, 1986—97; grad. instr. W.Va. U., 1999—2002, Stuart Joyce Robbins chmn. rsch. asst., 2002, Appalachian historian, lectr., 2005—06, sr. faculty lectr., 2006—. Curriculum cons. Pocahontas Comms. Coop., Dunmore, W.Va., 1999—2004. Recipient William D. Barnes award in history, W.Va. U., 2001. Mem.: Labor and Working Class History Assn., Oral History Assn., Appalachia Studies Assn. Avocations: gardening, fishing. Office: WVa U Dept History PO Box 6303 Morgantown WV 26506-6303

BUSH, DEBRA W., occupational health nurse; b. Salem, Ill., Dec. 22, 1952; d. Merle D. and Georgia Lee (Johnson) Anderson; m. Thomas E. Howarth, June 16, 1973 (div. Sept. 1979; 1 child, Michael T.; m. Gene Bush, Feb. 14, 2004. Diploma in Practical Nursing, Vo-Tech Teche Area, New Iberia, La., 1972; ADN, Miss. Delta Jr. Coll., Moorhead, 1975. LPN, La.; cert. occupl. health nurse. LPN in ICU Iberia Gen. Hosp., New Iberia, 1972-73, head nurse ICU, 1979-81; charge nurse infection control Bolivar County Hosp., Cleveland, Miss., 1973-79, dir. long-term care, 1981-89; sr. indsl. nurse Baxter Healthcare Corp., Cleveland, 1989-96, Tampa, Fla., 1996—. Mem.: Fla. Assn. Occupl. Health Nurses, Am. Assn. Occupl. Health Nurses. Republican. Baptist. Avocations: reading, singing, cross-stitch, exercise. Office: Baxter Healthcare Corp 7511 114th Ave Largo FL 33773-5129 Office Phone: 727-548-2770. Business E-Mail: debbie_bush@baxter.com.

BUSH, EILEEN SHANIN, voice educator; b. Kansas City, Mo. d. Benjamin Shanin and Celia Cohen; 1 child, Cynthia. MusB, New Eng. Conservatory, 1952. Opera singer NE Opera Theater, Boston, 1951—53, Capitol Artists Opera Co., Albany, NY, 1971—77, Cin. Opera co., Saratoga, NY, 1975; voice tchr. Schenectady (NY) C.C., 1976—96; pvt. voice studio Schenectady, 1980—. Dir. sch. programs Capitol Artists Opera Co., 1975; bd. dirs. Schenectady Light Opera Co., 1965—70. Mem.: Nat. Assn. Tchrs. of Singing. Avocations: tennis, ballet.

BUSH, ELIZABETH OLNEY, marine lab technician; d. Robert Olney and Marcia Allen Bush. BS, Coll. William and Mary, 1977. Libr. asst. Coll. William and Mary, Williamsburg, Va., 1975—77; lab. technician Va. Rsch. Ctr. for Archaeology, Williamsburg, Va., 1978—81; lab. asst. Colonial Williamsburg Found., 1982, lead excavator, lab. analyst, 1982—84, lab. technician, 1984—86, conservation technician, 1986—88; lab. technician Va. Inst. Marine Sci., Gloucester Point, Va., 1988—89, lab. specialist, 1989—. Interpretive asst. War Meml. Mus. Va., Newport News, 1981, clk., mus. asst., 1981—82. Mem.: Am. Chem. Soc. Office: Va Inst Marine Sci 1208 Greate Rd Gloucester Point VA 23062 Home Phone: 804-642-0176; Office Phone: 804-684-7697. E-mail: ebush@vims.edu.

BUSH, ELLEN D., music educator; b. Orange County, Calif., Aug. 8, 1942; d. David Moy Bush and Mary Ellen Morgan; m. Lewis Dale Norwood, July 27, 1960 (div. Dec. 1990); children: N. Jayne Klossner, Angela Ellen Norwood. D of Naturopathy, Trinity Coll. Natural Health, Warsaw, Ind., 1999. Instr. piano pvt. practice. Mem.: Tex. Music Tchrs. Assn., Cypress Tchrs. Assn., Music Tchrs. Nat. Assn. (founder campaign tolerance, mediator world peace 1987—). Home Phone: 281-989-0442; Office Phone: 281-374-9303.

BUSH, EUGENE NYLE, retired pharmacologist, pharmacist; b. McKeesport, Pa., Apr. 14, 1952; s. Nyle E. and Rosalia M. (Merlino) B.; m. Janet Rosemary Ruscitto, May 7, 1977; children: Stephen Michael, Rebecca Renee, Timothy George. BS in Pharmacy, U. Pitts., 1977, PhD in Pharmacology, 1981. Registered pharmacist, Pa., Ill. Tchg. asst. U. Pitts., 1978—81; staff pharmacist We. Pa. Hosp., Pitts., 1977—81; pharmacologist Abbott Labs., 1981—87, sr. rsch. scientist Abbott Park, Ill., 1986—88, rsch. investigator, 1988—89, group leader, endocrine pharmacol., 1989—91, sr. group leader endocrine pharmacol., 1991—97, assoc. Volwiler rsch. fellow, 1996—2007; pharmacist Vista Med. Ctr., Waukegan, Ill., 2007—. Co-author numerous publs.; contbr. articles to profl. jours. Mem.: Am. Coll. Clin. Pharmacy, Am. Diabetes Assn., Am. Pharm. Assn., Endocrine Soc., Nat. Eagle Scout Assn., Sigma Xi. Republican. Roman Catholic. Avocations: gardening, photography, computers, bicycling. Home: 816 Bedford Ln Libertyville IL 60048-3002 Office Phone: 847-309-4135. Personal E-mail: genenbush@ameritech.net.

BUSH, FREDERICK MORRIS, former federal agency administrator; b. Newport News, Va., Feb. 6, 1949; s. Morris and Dorothy Montony B.; m. Catherine Marie Murphy, Sept. 10, 1977; children— Alexander Murphy Morris, Taylor McGrath, Channing Barbara and Margaret Montony (twins). BA, U. Colo., 1971; MA in Internat. Studies, Am. U., 1974. Clk. Republican policy com. U.S. Senate, 1971-73; legis. asst. US Ho. of Reps., 1973; asst. to fin. chmn. Rep. Nat. Com., 1973-74; dep. fin. dir. Pres. Ford Com., 1975-77; nat. fin. dir. George Bush for Pres., 1979-80; asst. sec. for tourism US Dept. Commerce; dep. chief of staff to v.p. The White House; pres. Bush & Co.; commr. gen. U.S.A. Universal Expn., Seville, Spain, 1991-92; U.S. amb., commr. gen. Expo 92, Seville, 1992—; assoc. dir. for devel. & constituent rels. Woodrow Wilson Internat. Ctr. for Scholars, Washington. Founder Rep. Assocs. Chgo.; trustee Am. Ctr. Internat. Leadership; dep. fin. chmn. for George Bush for Pres.; fin. chmn. San Diego host com. Rep. Nat. Conv.; fin. chmn. Reps. Abroad; fin. chmn. Washington bdi. com. 2012 Olympic Games, 1998—; assoc. dir. Woodrow Wilson Internat. Ctr. for Scholars, 1998—. Republican. Office Phone: 202-691-4000. E-mail: fred.bush@wilsoncenter.org.

BUSH, GAIL, librarian, educator, director, writer; b. Chgo., May 2, 1952; d. George William and Norma T. Fish; m. Robert K. Bush, Sept. 7, 1978; children: Matthew Thomas, Claire Anne. BA in Anthropology (magna cum laude), U. Ill., Urbana-Champaign, 1973; MLS, U. Ill., 1977; PhD in Ednl. Psychology, Loyola U., Chgo., 2001. Cert. libr. media, Ill. Head libr. Nat. Coll. Edn. (now Nat.-Louis U.), Chgo., 1977—79; mgr. corp. libr. Heidrick & Struggles, Chgo., 1979—82; instr. grad. rsch., reference libr. Nat. Coll. Edn., Wilmette, Ill., 1982—92; curriculum libr. Maine Twp. H.S. West, Des Plaines, Ill., 1992—2002; dir. sch. libr. media program Dominican U., River Forest, Ill., 2002—06, assoc. prof., 2002—06; prof., dir. sch. libr. program Ctr. Tchg. Through Children's Books Nat.-Louis U., Skokie, Ill., 2006—. Adv. com. Ill. State Libr., 2003—; edits. adv. bd., ALA, 2002—, Tchr. Libr. Adv. Bd., 2002—; goals 2000 cons. Loyola U. Chgo., 1997-00, lectr., 1998—; pub. cons. Greenwood Press, Westport, Conn., 2000-02; info. lit. cons. Great Plains Network, Lincoln, Nebr., 1999-2000; mem. adv. bd. MindU., 1998-, Knowledge Quest, 2003-; spkr. in field. Author: The School Buddy System: the Practice of Collaboration, 2003, Every Student Reads: Collaboration and Reading to Learn, 2006-; mem. editl. bd. Am. Assn. Sch. Librs., 1997-; contbr. articles to profl. jours. Named Sch. Libr. of Yr. North Suburban Libr. Sys., 1999; named among Top 100 Sch. Librarians in Whole Sch. Libr. Catalog, 2005; Shoah Visual History Found. fellow, 2001—02. Mem. ALA, ASCD, Am. Assn. Sch. Librs. (Nat. Sch. Libr. Media Program of Yr. 1996), Internat. Reading Assn., Am. Ednl. Rsch. Assn., Freedom to Read Found., Beta Phi Mu, Phi Delta Kappa Mailing: National Louis Univ 5202 Old Orchard Rd Ste 300 Skokie IL 60077 Office Phone: 224-233-2522. Personal E-mail: gailbush@gmail.com. Business E-Mail: gail.bush@nl.edu.

BUSH, GEORGE HERBERT WALKER, 41st President of the United States; b. Milton, Mass., June 12, 1924; s. Prescott Sheldon and Dorothy (Walker) B.; m. Barbara Pierce, Jan. 6, 1945; children: George W., Robin (dec.), John E. (Jeb), Neil M., Marvin P., Dorothy W. Koch. BA in Econs., Yale U., 1948; numerous hon. degrees; LHD (hon.), U. NH, 2007. Co-founder Bush-Overbey Oil Devel. Co., 1951; co-founder, dir. Zapata Petroleum Corp., Midland, 1953-59; pres. Zapata Off Shore Co., Houston, 1956-64, chmn. bd., 1964-66; mem. US Congress from 7th Dist. Tex., 1967-71, ways and means com.; US amb. to UN US Dept. State, NYC, 1971-73; chmn. Rep. Nat. Com., Washington, 1973-74; chief US Liaison Office, People's Rep. of China US Dept. State, Peking, 1974—76; dir. CIA, Washington, 1976-77; chmn. First Internat. Bank, Houston, 1977—80; v.p. US, 1981-89, pres., 1989-93; sr. adv. Carlyle Group, 1998—2003. Adj. prof. adminstrv. sci., Jones Sch. Bus. Rice U., Houston, 1978; bd. visitors M.D. Anderson Cancer Ctr., Houston. Co-author (with Brent Scowcroft): A World Transformed, 1998; author: All The Best, George Bush: My Life and Other Writings, 1999. Co-founder (with Bill Clinton), fundraiser Bush-Clinton Tsunami partnership, 2005—, Bush-Clinton Katrina Fund, 2005—; del. Rep. Nat. Conv., San Francisco, 1964, Miami Beach, Fla., 1968; Rep. candidate US Senate, Tex., 1964, 1970. Pilot USN, WWII, Lt. (j.g.) USN, WWII. Decorated DFC, 3 Air medals; co-recipient Liberty medal, Nat. Constitution Ctr., 2006; named Man of Yr., TIME mag., 1990, Hon. Knight of the British Empire, 1993; named one of 100 Most Influential People, TIME mag., 2006; recipient Internat. Security Leadership award, 1993, Albert Schweitzer Gold Medal for Humanitarianism, 1997, George C. Marshall award, 2002, Dwight D. Eisenhower medal, 2003, Ronald Reagan Freedom award, 2007. Fellow: Am. Acad. Arts & Sciences. Republican. Office: 10000 Memorial Dr Ste 900 Houston TX 77024-3422*

BUSH, GEORGE WALKER, 43rd President of the United States; b. New Haven, Conn., July 6, 1946; s. George Herbert Walker and Barbara (Pierce) Bush; m. Laura Lane Welsh, Nov. 5, 1977; children: Barbara, Jenna. BA in History, Yale U., 1968; MBA, Harvard U., 1975. Founder, CEO Arbusto Energy Inc., Midland, Tex., 1977—82, Bush Exploration (formerly Arbusto Energy Inc.), Midland, Tex., 1982—84; chmn. Spectrum 7 Energy Corp. (formerly Bush Exploration), Midland, Tex., 1984—86; bd. dirs. Harken Energy Corp. (formerly Spectrum 7 Energy Corp.), Midland, Tex., 1986—99; sr. adv. George Herbert Walker Bush Presidential campaign, 1988; mng. gen. ptnr. Tex. Rangers (baseball franchise), 1989—94; gov. State of Tex., Austin, 1994—2000; pres. US, Washington, 2001—. Bd. dirs. Caterair Internat., Inc., 1990—94. Co-author (with Karen Hughes): A Charge to Keep, 1999. Pilot Texas Air Nat. Guard, 1968—70. Named Person of the Year, Time mag., 2004; named one of Most Influential people, 2005, 100 Most Influential People, 2006; recipient Big D award, Dallas All Sports Assn., 1989. Mem.: Delta Kappa Epsilon (pres. 1965—68). Republican. Achievements include first Governor in Texas history to be elected to two consecutive four-year terms; won re-election as Pres. in 2004; first American President to visit Mongolia, Nov. 2005. Office: The White House 1600 Pennsylvania Ave NW Washington DC 20500*

BUSH, JEB (JOHN ELLIS BUSH), former governor; b. Midland, Tex., Feb. 11, 1953; s. George Herbert Walker and Barbara Pierce Bush; m. Columba Garnica Gallo, Feb. 23, 1974; children: George, Noelle, John Jr. BA in Latin Am. Affairs, U. Tex., 1974. V.p. Tex. Commerce Bank, Caracas, Venezuela, 1974—79; co-founder Codina Bush Group, Miami, Fla., 1981—93; pres., COO Codina Group, Miami, Fla., 1995—98; sec. commerce State of Fla., Tallahassee, 1987—88, gov., 1999—2007. Chmn., Dade County Rep. Party, 1984-86; bd. dirs. Safecard Services, 1995-96, Tenet Healthcare Corp., 2007- Co-author (with Brian Yablonski): Profiles in Character, 1996. Chmn. Miami-Dade County Beacon Coun., 1990-91, vol. Miami Children's Hosp., United Way of Dade County, Dade County Homeless Trust; founder Found. for Fla.'s Future, 1995; co-founder Liberty City Charter Sch., 1995, trustee, Heritage Found., 1995 Republican. Roman Catholic.*

BUSH, JEFFREY E., music educator, art association administrator; b. Moose Jaw, Saskatchewan, Canada, Mar. 24, 1955; s. Earl A. and June E. Bush; m. Candace Wilson, Dec. 4, 1982. B in Music Edn., No. Ill. U., 1978, MusM in Performance, 1979; PhD, U. Ariz., Tucson, 1996. Cert. tchr. Sask., Can., 1979. Music tchr. Regina Pub. Sch. Divsn., Canada, 1979—90; arts edn. specialist Sask. Edn., Regina, 1990—92; percussionist Regina Symphony Orch., Regina, 1979—92; percussion instr. U. Regina, 1979—92, music edn. prof., 1994—97; asst. prof. Ariz. State U., Tempe, 1997—2001, assoc. prof., assoc. dir. Sch. Music, 2001—. Author: more than 50 articles in profl. jours. Western divsn. rep. Soc. for Music Tchr. Edn., Reston, Va., 2000—06; sec. Ariz. Alliance for Arts Edn., 2006—. Recipient Dirs. award, Ariz. State U. Coll. Edn., 2001; grantee, US Dept. of Edn., 2005—. Mem.: Ariz. Alliance for Arts Edn. (sec. 2006—, former bd. dirs.), Nat. Assn. for Music Edn. (various offices 2000—, chair adult and cmty. music 2004—06), Ariz. Music Educators Assn. (pres. 2005—07, former v.p. for profl. devel., past pres. 2007—, George C. Wilson Leadership award 2004). Office: Ariz State Univ PO Box 870405 Tempe AZ 85287-0405 Home Phone: 480-202-6986; Office Phone: 480-965-3372.

BUSH, KAREN LEE, lawyer; b. Denville, NJ, May 29, 1958; BA with honors in English, cum laude, Bucknell U., 1980; JD with honors, George Washington U., 1984. Bar: Calif. 1984, DC 1988, Md. 1996. Assoc. Rutan & Tucker, 1985—86; dep. city atty. Signal Hill & Laguna Beach, Calif., 1985—86; ptnr. Anderson Kill Orlick & Oshinsky LLP, Washington, 1986—, co-chmn. diversity com./quality of life com. Mem.: Md. State Bar Assn., DC Bar. Office: Dickstein Shapiro Morin & Oshinsky 1201 L St NW Washington DC 20037-1526 Office Phone: 202-955-6601. Office Fax: 202-887-0689. Business E-Mail: BushK@dsmo.com.

BUSH, KRISTIAN, musician; Mem. Billy Pilgrim, 1994—, Sugarland, 2002—. Musician (with Billy Pilgrim): (albums) Billy Pilgrim, 1994, St. Christopher's Crossin', 1995, Bloom, 1995; musician: (with Sugarland) Twice the Speed of Life, 2004, Enjoy the Ride, 2006; musician: (songs) Want To, 2006 (Duo Video of Yr., Country Music TV, 2007). Recipient New Duo/Group award, Acad. Country Music, 2006. Office: Gail Gellman Mgmt 23852 PCH 920 Malibu CA 90265 Office Phone: 310-456-2620. Office Fax: 310-456-1415. E-mail: gellmanmgmt@aol.com, sugarlandmail@aol.com.

BUSH, LAURA WELCH, First Lady of United States; b. Midland, Tex., Nov. 4, 1946; d. Harold Bruch and Jenna Louise (Hawkins) Welch; m. George Walker Bush, Nov. 5, 1977; children: Jenna, Barbara. BS in Edn., So. Meth. U., 1968; MLS, U. Tex., Austin, 1973. Tchr. Longfellow Elem. Sch., Dallas, 1968—69, John F. Kennedy Elem. Sch., Houston, 1969—72; libr. Houston Pub. Lib., 1973—74, Dawson Elem. Sch., Austin, 1974—77; First Lady State of Tex., 1995—2001; First Lady of the U.S., 2001—. Established Adopt-A-Caseworker programs, Tex., Rainbow Rooms, Tex.; launched National Book Festival, 2001; speaker Republican Nat. Convention, NYC, 2004. Vol. Hurricane Help for Schools. Named one of Most Powerful Women, Forbes mag., 2004, 2005; recipient President's Crystal Apple award, Am. Assn. Sch. Librarians, 2006. Republican. Address: The White House 1600 Pennsylvania Ave NW Washington DC 20500

BUSH, LYNN JEANNE, federal judge; b. Little Rock, Dec. 30, 1948; d. John E. Bush III and Alice Saville B.; 1 child, Brian Bush Ferguson. BA, Antioch Coll., 1970; JD, Georgetown U., 1976. Assoc. Steptoe and Johnson, Washington, summer 1975; part-time law clk. Nat. Labor Rels. Bd., Washington, 1976; trial atty. comml. litig. br. US Dept. Justice, Washington, 1976-87; sr. trial atty. Naval Facilities Engring. Command, Dept. Navy, Alexandria, Va., 1987-89, counsel engring. field activity, 1989-96; adminstr. judge Bd. Contract Appeals US Dept. Housing & Urban Devel., Washington, 1996-98; judge US Ct. Fed. Claims, Washington, 1998—. Mem. Nat. Bar Assn., Nat. Assn. Women Judges, Bd. Contract Appeals Judges Assn., Bd. Contract Appeals Bar Assn., Sr. Exec. Assn. Office: US Ct Fed Claims 717 Madison Pl NW Washington DC 20439-0002*

BUSH, MARGARET EILEEN, elementary school educator; b. Columbus, Ohio, Jan. 22, 1951; d. Frederick Lawrence and Margaret Eileen (Doyle) Eyerman; m. George E. Bush, Sept. 13, 1975; children: Kate, Benjamin, Rachael. BS in Elem. Edn., Ohio State U., Columbus, 1974, M Early and Mid. Childhood Edn., 1998, postgrad., 2000—02. Cert. K-8 tchr., TESOL Ohio. ESL tchr., coord. Office Migration and Refugee Resettlement, Cambodian Mut. Asst. Assn., Columbus, 1979—83; ESL tchr. Whitehall City Schs., Ohio, 1985—88, 2d-4th grade tchr., 1988—2002, tchr., literacy coord., 2002—. Named Tchr. of Yr., Beechwood/Whitehall Edn. Assn. Mem.: ASCID, OCTELA, Nat. Coun. Tchrs. English. Democrat. Roman Catholic. Avocations: gardening, choral singing. Office: Whitehall City Schs 625 S Yearling Rd Columbus OH 43213

BUSH, MICHAEL KEVIN, lawyer; b. Davenport, Iowa, May 23, 1952; s. Roy Alvin and A. Camella (Gilroy) B.; m. Kathleen M. Grace, Nov. 26, 1977; children: Kelly Anne, Daniel Stephen, Brendan Michael. BA, U. Notre Dame, South Bend, Ind., 1974; JD, Valparaiso U., Ind., 1977. Bar: Iowa 1977, U.S. Dist. Ct. (no. dist.) Iowa 1980, U.S. Ct. Appeals (7th cir.) 1980, U.S. Dist. Ct. (ctrl. dist.) Ill. 1983, U.S. Ct. Appeals (8th cir.) 1996, U.S. Supreme Ct. 1990, Ill. 1999. Mem. Wells, McNally & Bowman, Davenport, 1977-80; prosecutor Scott County Atty.'s Office, Davenport, 1980-82; mem. Henninger & Henninger, Davenport, 1979-82; founding ptnr. Walton, Creen & Bush, Davenport, 1982-86; ptnr. Carlin, Hellstrom & Bittner, Davenport, 1987—2000; sr. ptnr. Bush, Motto, Creen and Koury, Davenport, 2000—. Recipient Iowa Trial Lawyer's Public Justice award, 2001. Mem. ATLA (sustaining mem.), Am. Bd. Trial Advocates (assoc.), Iowa Assn. Trial Lawyers (Pub. Justice award 2000), Million Dollar Advocates Forum, Iowa Bar Assn., Scott County Bar Assn., Am. Coll. Barristers (sr. counsel). Roman Catholic. Avocation: tennis. Home: 2806 E 42nd Ct Davenport IA 52807-1576 Office: Bush Motto et al 5505 Victoria Ave Ste 100 Davenport IA 52807 Home Phone: 563-355-7432; Office Phone: 563-344-4900. Personal E-mail: bushlaws@yahoo.com.

BUSH, NORMAN, research and development company executive; b. NYC, Dec. 10, 1929; s. Louis and Ida (Trembola) B.; m. Audrey Faith Blumberg, Dec. 28, 1952; children: Stewart Alan, I. Jeffrey, Ellen Gail Dash. BBA, CUNY, 1951, MBA, 1952; PhD, N.C. State U., 1962. Statistician Army Chem. Ctr., Edgewood, Md., 1952-56, RCA Svc. Co., Patrick AFB, Fla., 1956-58, DBA and ICF, Melbourne, Fla., 1962-64, Pan Am Airlines, Patrick AFB, Fla., 1964-72; div. mgr. ENSCO Inc., Melbourne, Fla., 1972-83, pres., chief oper. officer Springfield, Va., 1983-94, chmn. bd., 1989-95. Contbr. articles to statis. jours. With U.S. Army, 1952-54. Mem. Am. Statis. Assn. Republican. Avocation: travel.

BUSH, RAYMOND T., accountant, architectural firm executive; b. Providence, Sept. 7, 1939; s. Raymond F. and Regina C. (Pearl) B.; m. Barbara Ann Cormier, May 31, 1962; children: Laura Jean, Raymond F., Matthew T., James J., Michael. BS in Acctg. and Fin., Bryant Coll., 1960. CPA, R.I. Auditor USDA, Providence, 1960-66; audit supr. KPMG Peat Marwick LLP, Providence, 1966-69; mgr. system and audit Ludlow Corp., Needham Heights, Mass., 1969-71, asst. treas., 1971-73, v.p., gen. mgr., 1973-80; pres. Recticel Foam Corp., Needham Heights, 1980-83; sr. v.p.

fin. and adminstrn. Maguire Group Inc., Providence, 1983—. Dir. Ocean State Bus. Devel.; pres. East Atlantic Casualty Co. Ltd.; cons. Bryant Coll. Small Bus. Devel. Ctr. Mem. R.I. Indsl. Recreational Bldg. Authority; trustee Providence Pub. Libr. Fellow R.I. Soc. CPA's; mem. Am. Inst. CPA's. Roman Catholic. Home: 3 Hayfield Ln Cumberland RI 02864-4114 Office: Maguire Group Inc 33 Commercial St Foxboro MA 02035-2885 Office Phone: 508-543-1700.

BUSH, REGGIE, professional football player; b. Spring Valley, Calif., Mar. 2, 1985; s. Denise and Lamar Griffin (Stepfather). BA in Polit. Sci., U. So. Calif., 2006. Running back New Orleans Saints, 2006—. Named Coll. Player of the Year, Touchdown Club, 2004, Pac-10 Co-Offensive Player of the Year, 2004, Player of the Yr., AP, 2005, Offensive Player Yr., Pigskin Club of DC, 2005; named to All-American first team, 2004, 2005; recipient Doak Walker award, 2005, Walter Camp award, 2005, Heisman Meml. Trophy, Heisman Trophy Trust, 2005. Achievements include setting a Pac-10 single game record of 513 all-purpose yards, Nov.19, 2005; the second overall selection in the 2006 NFL Draft. Office: c/o New Orleans Saints 5800 Airline Dr Metairie LA 70003

BUSH, SARAH LILLIAN, historian; b. Kansas City, Mo., Sept. 17, 1920; d. William Adam and Lettie Evelyn (Burrill) Lewis; m. Walter Nelson Bush, June 7, 1946 (dec.); children: William Read, Robert Nelson. AB, U. Kans., Lawrence, 1941; BS, U. Ill., Champaign-Urbana, 1943. Clk. circulation dept. Kansas City Pub. Library, 1941-42, asst. librarian Paseo br., 1943-44; librarian Kansas City Jr. Coll., 1944-46; substitute librarian San Mateo County Library, Woodside and Portola Valley, Calif., 1975-77; various temporary positions, 1979-87; owner Metriguide, Palo Alto, Calif., 1975-78. Author: Atherton Lands, 1979, rev. edition 1987. Editor: Atherton Recollections, 1973. Pres., v.p. Jr. Librarians, Kansas City, 1944-46; courtesy, yearbook & historian AAUW, Menlo- Atherton branch (Calif.) Br.; asst. Sunday sch. tchr., vol. Holy Trinity Ch., Menlo Park, 1955-78; v.p., membership com., libr. chairperson, English reading program, parent edn. chairperson Menlo Atherton High Sch. PTA, 1964-73; founder, bd. dirs. Friends of Atherton Community Library, 1967-2002, oral historian, 1968-2002, chair Bicentennial event, 1976; bd. dirs. Menlo Park Hist. Assn., 1979-82, oral historian, 1973-2002; bd. dirs. Civic Interest League, Atherton, 1978-81; mem. hist. county commn. Town of Atherton, 1980-87; vol. Allied Arts Lucile Packard Children's Hosp. at Stanford, 1967—, oral historian, 1978—, historian, 1980—; vol. United Crusade, Garfield Sch., Redwood City, 1957-61, 74-88, Encinal Sch., Menlo Park, Calif., 1961-73, program dir., chmn. summer recreation, historian, sec.; vol. Stanford Mothers Club, 1977-81, others; historian, awards chairperson Cub Scouts Boy Scouts Am.; founder Atherton Heritage Assn. 1989, bd. dirs., 1989-2004, dir., 1989-94; mem. Guild Gourmet, 1971—, Mid Peninsula History Consortium, 1993-95; oral historian St. Andrew's Ch., Saratoga, Calif., 2003—; vol. Los Gatos Meadows, Calif.; family hist. rschr. for writer. Recipient Good Neighbor award Atherton Civic Interest League, 1992. Mem. PTA (life). Episcopalian. Avocations: gourmet cooking, entertaining, reading.

BUSH, SOPHIA, actress; b. LA, July 8, 1982; d. Charles William and Maureen Bush; m. Chad Michael Murray, Apr. 16, 2005 (div. Dec. 29, 2006). Actor: (films) Van Wilder, 2002, Learning Curves, 2003, Supercross, 2005, Stay Alive, 2006, John Tucker Must Die, 2006 (Choice Movie Actress: Comedy, Teen Choice Awards, 2007, Choice Movie: Breakout Female, Teen Choice Awards, 2007), The Hitcher, 2007 (Choice Movie Actress: Horror/Thriller, Teen Choice Awards, 2007); (TV films) Point of Origin, 2002; (TV series) One Tree Hill, 2003—; guest star Sabrina, the Teenage Witch, 2003, Nip/Tuck, 2003. Office: c/o United Talent Agency 9560 Wilshire Blvd, 5th Fl Beverly Hills CA 90212*

BUSH, WESLEY G., aerospace transportation executive; B in Elect. Engring., MIT, MSEE; grad., UCLA. With engring. staff Serospace Corp.; corp. v.p., pres. space tech. Comsat Labs; from. sys. engr. to v.p., gen. mgr. telecomm. programs divsn. TRW Aero. Sys., 1987—99, pres., CEO, 2001—03; v.p., gen. mgr. TRW Ventures, 2000—01; pres., CEO, global aeronautical sys. TRW-United Kingdom, 2001—03; corp. v.p., pres. space tech. Northrop Grumman Corp. (acquired TRW), LA, 2003—05; corp. v.p., CFO Northrop Grumman Corp., LA, 2005—06, pres., CFO, 2006—07, pres., COO, 2007—. Office: Northrop Grumman Corp 1840 Century Park E Los Angeles CA 90067-2199*

BUSH, WILLIAM MERRITT, lawyer; b. Long Beach, Calif., June 23, 1941; s. Lloyd Merritt and Barbara Ann (Bufkin) B.; m. Dorothy Irene Vasvary, June 25, 1966; children: Steven Merritt, Amy Elizabeth. BA, Stanford U., 1963; JD, U. Calif., Hastings, 1966. Bar: Calif. 1967, U.S. Dist. Ct. (ctrl. dist.) Calif. 1967, U.S. Dist. Ct. (so. dist.) Calif. 1976. Assoc. Dannemeyer & Tuohey, Fullerton, Calif., 1967, Miller, Bush & Minnott, Fullerton, Calif., 1967-69, ptnr., 1970-88; pvt. practice Fullerton, Calif., 1989—. Human rels. commr., City of Fullerton, 1971-77; mem. site coun., Fullerton H.S., 1986-88. Fellow Am. Acad. Matrimonial Lawyers; mem. Orange County Bar Assn. (dir. 1982-85), Calif. State Bar (mem. family law cons. group, family law sect. 1979, mem. family law adv. commn. 1979-85, chmn. commn. 1982-85, bd. legal specialization 1982-89, chmn. 1987-88). Republican. Methodist. Avocations: computers, walking. Office: 1235 N Harbor Blvd Ste 200 Fullerton CA 92832-1349 Office Phone: 714-992-0800. Business E-Mail: wmbushesq@lawbush.com.

BUSHEE, WARD, III, newspaper editor; b. Redding, Calif., 1949; m. Claudia Bushee; children: Ward Gardiner, Mary Standish. BS in History, San Diego State U., 1971. Sports editor Gilroy (Calif.) Dispatch, 1973—75; asst. city editor/sports editor/reporter/copy editor The Californian, Salinas, Calif., 1975—79; sports editor Marin County (Calif.) Ind. Jour., 1979—82; asst. content editor sports USA Today, Arlington, Va., 1982—85; asst. mng. editor sports Westchester (N.Y.) Suburban Newspapers, 1985—86; exec. editor Argus Leader, Sioux Falls, SD, 1986—90; editor Reno (Nev.) Gazette-Jour., 1990—99, Cin. (Ohio) Enquirer, 1999—2002, Ariz. Republic, Phoenix, 2002—, v.p. news, 2002—. Named Editor of Yr., 1992, 97, 2005, Gannett Co., Inc., Pres.'s Ring winner 1992-97, 99-2001, 04, 05. Mem. Nev. Press Assn. (pres. 1993, 94, API discussion leader 1996). Office: The Arizona Republic 200 E Van Buren St Phoenix AZ 85004 Business E-Mail: ward.bushee@arizonarepublic.com.*

BUSHEY, ALAN SCOTT, retired insurance holding company executive; b. Peoria, Ill., Apr. 16, 1930; s. Leo James and Luella Frederica (Brunnenmeyer) B. BA, Augustana Coll., Rock Island, Ill., 1952; MBA, Stanford U., 1954. Asst. prof. mktg. and stats. San Jose State Coll., Calif., 1958-59; dir. econ. and mktg. rsch. Continental Casualty Co., Chgo., 1959-68; asst. v.p. CNA/Ins., Chgo., 1968-72; v.p. CNA Fin. Corp., Chgo., 1972-74, USLIFE Corp., NYC, 1974-84, sr. v.p., 1984-88, exec. v.p., 1988-97. Bd. dirs. Ecumenical Inst., Chgo., 1963-74. Served to lt. (j.g.) USNR, 1954-57 Mem. Nat. Assn. Bus. Economists (coun. 1973-76), Life Ins. Mktg. Rsch. Assn. (chmn. mkt. rsch. com. 1985-87, vice chmn. rsch. coun. 1994, chmn. adv. svcs. coun. 1995), Am. Statis. Assn. (bd. dirs. Chgo. chpt. 1965-67), LOMA (strategic mgmt. com. 1987-93), Brit. Schs. and Univs. Found. (bd. dirs. 1993—, hon. sec. 1995-97, pres. 1997-2001, chmn. 2001-06), Caledonian Found. USA (trustee 2000—), Sarasota Yacht Club. Republican. Lutheran. Home: 340 S Palm Ave # 122 Sarasota FL 34236-6741 E-mail: a.scottbushey@verizon.net.

BUSHINSKY, JAY (JOSEPH MASON), journalist, news correspondent; b. Buffalo, Dec. 8, 1932; s. Joshua M. and Malka (Coralnik) B.; m. Dvora Apte, Dec. 30, 1952; children: Shay, Aviv, Dahlia. BA, Queens Coll., 1955; MS in Edn., Yeshiva U., NYC, 1959; MS in Journalism, Columbia U., 1963. Mcpl. reporter Times Herald/Record, Middletown, NY, 1963-64; copy editor Miami (Fla.) Herald, 1964-66; spl. corr. Chgo. Daily News Fgn. Svc., 1966—78; corr. Westinghouse Broadcasting Co., 1967—; Tel Aviv bur. chief Westinghouse Broadcasting Co. (now CBS Radio, Inc.), 1969—; corr. Chgo. Sun-Times, Tel Aviv, 1978-85, Middle East bur. chief, columnist, 1986-96; Jerusalem bur. chief Cable News Network, 1980-85; corr. Independent News Network, 1985-87, WWOR-TV, NYC, 1987—89, WPIX-TV, NYC, 1991-94, Global TV Network (Can.), 1993—95, Toronto Sun, 1994—, Fox TV Network, 1995—98, Boston Herald, 1998-99; diplomatic corr. The Jerusalem Post, 1997-98. Tchr. social studies L.I. City HS, NY, 1958-59, William C. Bryant HS, NYC, 1959-62; lectr. journalism Tel Aviv U., 1966-70, 1970-92, Bar Ilan U., 1993-2004; asst. prof. journalism coll. mgmt. U. Mo., 1976-1981; columnist Jewish Chronicle, Pitts., 1990—, Daily Herald, 1996-2000, correspondant, 2002-05, Intermountain Jewish News, 2005-. Served with AUS, 1955-57. Chgo. Newspaper Guild award for investigative reporting for expose of Nazi war criminals in U.S., 1978; co-recipient Media award for econ. understanding Amos Tuck Sch. Bus. Adminstrn., Dartmouth Coll., 1979; named to Chgo. Journalism Hall of Fame, 2002. Mem. Fgn. Press Assn. in Israel (chmn. 1968-71), Overseas Press Club Am. (award for Best Radio Spot News Reporting from Abroad to Group W Foreign News Service for coverage of Yom Kippur War in Mideast, Joint citation 1974). Home and Office: PO Box 2257 Rehov Hatsafon 5 Savyon 56530 Israel E-mail: jay@actcom.co.il.

BUSHKIN, MERLE JEROME, investment banker; b. Dayton, Ohio, Mar. 21, 1935; s. Charles D. and Eva (Flegel) B.; m. Leone Edricks, Aug. 6, 1961; children: Elizabeth Bushkin Schnitzer, Nancy Louise. AB, Harvard U., 1956, MBA, 1960. Mgmt. cons. Cresap, McCormick & Paget, NYC, 1960—64; planning and mktg. positions Mobil Oil Corp., NYC, 1964-70; fin. v.p., treas., corp. sec. Wollensak, Inc., Rochester, NY, 1970-71; v.p., mgr. mergers and acquisitions CBWL-Hayden Stone Inc. (predecessor of today's Smith Barney), NYC, 1971—72; pres. Bushkin Assocs., Inc., NY, 1972—, Health Record Corp., White Plains, 2006—. Lectr. in field. Mem.: Harvard Club NY, Woodstock Country Club. Home: 86 Caterson Ter Hartsdale NY 10530-2605 also: PO Box 639 Brownsville VT 05037 Office: Bushkin Assocs Inc PO Box 111 White Plains NY 10602-0111 Office Phone: 914-761-3024. Business E-Mail: mbushkin@bushkin.com, mbushkin@medkaz.com.

BUSHNELL, CANDACE, columnist, writer; b. Glastonbury, Conn., 1959; d. Calvin Camille Bushnell; m. Charles Askegard, July 4, 2002. Attended, Rice U., NYU. Writer Ladies' Home Journal, Good Housekeeping, Self, Mademoiselle, Cosmo Beauty and Fitness, Family Circle, GQ, Vogue; Sex and the City columnist New York Observer, 1994—96; host Candace Bushnell's Sex, Success, and Sensibility talk show, Sirius Stars Channel 102, 2006—. Author: (short stories) Four Blondes, 2000, (novels) Sex and the City, 1996, Trading Up, 2003, Lipstick Jungle, 2005. Recipient Matrix award for books, NY Women in Comm. Inc., 2006. Achievements include collection of columns for New York Observer, Sex and the City, was made into HBO series of same name, 1998-2004. Office: c/o Atlantic Monthly Press 841 Broadway New York NY 10003 Mailing: c/o Heather Schroder ICM 40 West 57th St New York NY 10019

BUSHNELL, DAVID SHERMAN, social psychologist, consultant; b. Whittier, Calif., Jan. 7, 1927; s. David Sherman and Lillian Dudley Bushnell; m. Susan Ratner, Jan. 1, 1984; children: Beckie Lynn Krantz, Kimberlie Anne Laderriere, Karen Jo McCarthy, Douglas Scott. PhB, U. Chgo., Chgo., 1947, MA, 1950. Asst. study dir., survey rsch. ctr. U. Mich., Ann Arbor, Mich., 1953—55; pres. Bushnell and Assoc., Potomac, Md., 1995—; mgmt. comm. cons. I.B.M., NYC, 1955—61; rsch. social psychologist Stanford Rsch. Inst., Menlo Pk., Calif., 1961—64; rsch. dir. U.S. Office of Edn., Washington, 1964—69; v.p. devel. Human Resources Rsch. Orgn., Alexandria, Va., 1971—74; rsch. dir. Am. Assn. of Cmty. and Jr. Colleges, Washington, 1974—78; rsch. prof., ctr. dir. Am. U., Washington, 1979—83, George Mason U., Fairfax, Va., 1983—90; ctr. dir. Human Resources Rsch. Orgn., Alexandria, Va., 1990—95. External evaluator Bowie State U., Bowie, Md., 1995—; bd. mem. Meridian Pub. Charter Sch., Washington, 2001—; fellow Battelle Meml. Inst., Columbus, Ohio, 1969—70; chmn. Network of Quality and Productivity Ctrs., Gary, Ind., 1990—91; editl. bd. mem. Jour. of Human Resources, Madison, Wis., 1966—70; bd. mem. DC Chpt. Am. Sociol. Assn., Washington; assoc. editor Jour. of Tech. Transfer, Indpls., 1988—95. Co-author: (text book) Planned Change in Education; author: Organizing for Change: New Priorities for Community Colleges, (a model for evaluating tng.) Training and Development Journal (Cited one of best articles, 1991); co-author: (millennium review of productivity trends) National Productivity Review (Millennium Edit. of NPR, 2000); contbr. articles to profl. jours. 3rd class petty officer USN, 1945—46, San Francisco. Recipient Disting. Svc. Award, Bowie State U., 2001, Gold Medal Educator of the 70's, Edn. Mag., 1971, Phi Kappa Delta Sociology Hon., Am. Sociol. Assn., 1952; scholar Honor Entrance Scholarship, U. Chgo., 1943-1947; grad. fellow, Batelle Meml. Inst. Mem.: Luxberry Ct. Assn. (bd. mem.), Am. Edn. Rsch. Assn. (hon.; bd. mem. 1972—74), Rochester Pers. Assn. (assoc.; pres. 1959), Ea. Evaluation Rsch. Soc. (assoc.), Am. Assn. of Higher Edn. (assoc.). Avocations: tennis, fishing. Office: Bowie State Univ 14000 Jerico Pk Rd Bowie MD 20715 Office Phone: 301-860-3885. Business E-Mail: dbushnell@bowiestate.edu.

BUSHNELL, GEORGE EDWARD, III, lawyer; b. Detroit, Feb. 18, 1952; s. George Edward Jr. and Elizabeth (Whelden) B.; m. Eileen Mary Heppler, Sept. 16, 1989; children: Ann-Elizabeth, Emily Spears, George Edward. BA, Bucknell U., 1974; JD, Emory U., 1981. Bar: Ga. 1981, D.C. 1983, N.Y. 1986. Vol. U.S. Peace Corps, Burkina Faso, 1974-76, tng. dir., 1976-77; staff asst. to hon. Lucien Nedzi U.S. Ho. of Reps., Washington, 1977-78; assoc. Duncan, Allen and Mitchell, Washington, Ivory Coast, Congo, 1981-85, Shearman & Sterling, NYC, 1985-91; corp. counsel Joseph E. Seagram & Sons, Inc., 1991-2001; sr. v.p., dep. gen. counsel Vivendi S.A., 2001—. Mem.: ABA, N.Y. State Bar Assn. Home: 1075 Park Ave Apt 2A New York NY 10128-1003 Office: Vivendi SA 5th Fl 800 3rd Ave New York NY 10022-7604 Office Phone: 212-572-7855.

BUSHNELL, RODERICK PAUL, lawyer; b. Buffalo, Mar. 6, 1944; s. Paul Hazen and Martha Atlee Bushnell; m. Suzann Yvonne Kaiser, Aug. 27, 1966; 1 child, Arlo Phillip. BA, Rutgers U., 1966; JD, Georgetown U., 1969. Bar: Calif. 1970, U.S. Supreme Ct. 1980.; cert. Civil Trial Advocate, Nat. Bd. Trial Advocates. Atty. dept. water resources, Sacramento, 1969-71; ptnr. Bushnell, Caplan Fielding & Maier, San Francisco, 1971—. Adv. bd. dirs. Bread & Roses, Inc., Mill Valley, Calif. Named a No. Calif. Super Lawyer, Law and Politics, 2006. Mem. ATLA, ABA (labor and employment sects.), San Francisco Bar Assn. (labor and employment sects.; arbitrator), San Francisco Superior Ct. (arbitrator), Fed. Ct. Early Neutral Evaluator, Calif. Bar Assn. (labor and employement sects.), Consumer Attys. Calif., San Francisco Trial Lawyers Assn., Nat. Employment Lawyers Assn., Calif. Employment Lawyers Assn. Office: Bushnell Caplan Fielding & Maier 900 Kearny St Ste 299 San Francisco CA 94133 Home Phone: 415-454-2870; Office Phone: 415-217-3800.

BUSHWAY, DEBORAH, psychologist, educator; d. Margaret Bushway; children: Isabel, Paco. PhD, Iowa State U., Ames, 1985. Lic. psychologist Minn. Prof., chmn. psychology dept. Met. State U., St. Paul, 1992—. Pvt. practice psychology, St. Louis Park, Minn. Vol. Mano a Mano, St. Paul. Named Outstanding Tchr., Met. State U., 1998, Outstanding Advisor, 2007. Office: Met State U 1450 Energy Park Dr Saint Paul MN 55108 Office Phone: 651-999-5823.

BUSICK, SEAN R., history professor, writer; b. Sept. 24, 1969; s. Russell and Sharon Busick; m. Jennifer Boone, Aug. 11, 1990; children: Ashley Rose, Cora Lily. BA in History and Polit. Sci., Purdue U., West Lafayette, Ind., 1992; MA in History, U. SC., Columbia, 1995, PhD in History, 2001. Vis. asst. prof. history Brevard Coll., NC, 2000—02; asst. prof. history Ky. Wesleyan Coll., Owensboro, 2002—06, Athens State U., Ala., 2006—. Author: (history book) A Sober Desire for History; editor: (novel) The Cassique of Kiawah, (biography) The Life of Francis Marion; book rev. editor (in Am. polit. history). Bible class tchr. Marion St. Ch of Christ, Athens, Ala. Recipient Hon. Order Ky. Cols. award, State Ky., 2004; fellow, Earhart Found.; William Gilmore Simms Rsch. fellow, Caroliniana Soc., William Gilmore Simms Rsch. scholar. Mem.: Hist. Soc., So. Hist. Assn., Phi Alpha Theta. Office: Athens State Univ 300 North Beaty St Athens AL 35613 Home Phone: 256-230-1272; Office Phone: 256-216-3652. Business E-Mail: sean.busick@athens.edu.

BUSKA, SHEILA MARY, chief financial officer, columnist, writer; b. Brewer, Maine, May 9, 1941; d. George William Sanderlin and Margaret Owenita Harrah; m. Roland Michael Buska, Nov. 28, 1959; children: Bryan Michael, Craig William, Christine Mary, Paul Kevin. AA, U. San Diego, 1959; BS in Acct. magna cum laude with distinction, San Diego State U., 1984. Cert. mgmt. acct., CPA Calif. Sr. acct. Peak Health Plan, San Diego, 1984-86; legal entity acct. M/A-COM Govt. Sys., San Diego, 1986-87; sr. acct. Lois A. Brozey, CPA, San Diego, 1987-89; CFO Soco-Lynch Corp. dba Crown Chem. Corp., Chula Vista, Calif., 1989—98; fin. mgr. Dermagraft Joint Venture, 1998—99; controller Monarch Sch. Project, San Diego, 2003—; sec., treas. Monarch Café, Inc., 2005—. Author: (poems) Young America Sings, 1957, Sermons in Poetry, 1957, (non-fiction) Time Outs for Grown-Ups: 5 Minute Smile Breaks, 2003; columnist: newspapers, 1997—, www.smile-breaks.com, interim editor: The Columnist, 2005, web editor: Nat. Soc. Newspaper Columnists, 2005—. Mem.: Inst. Mgmt. Accts. (v.p. membership and mktg. 1985—86, dir. cert. mgmt. accts. 1989—90, dir. corp. devel. 1992—93, treas. 1993—94, dir. membership acquisition 1995—96, Most Valuable Mem. 1990—91), Hardhats Toastmasters (v.p. pub. rels., editor Hardhats Herald 1998, pres. 2000). Democrat. Roman Catholic. Avocations: travel, music, poetry, tennis, theater. Home: 509 Burgasia Path El Cajon CA 92019-2640 Office: Monarch School Project 808 W Cedar St San Diego CA 92101 Office Phone: 619-685-8242. Personal E-mail: sbuska@cox.net.

BUSKIRK, ELSWORTH ROBERT, physiologist, educator; b. Beloit, Wis., Aug. 11, 1925; s. Ellsworth Fred and Laura Ellen (Parman) B.; m. Mable Heen, Aug. 28, 1948; children: Laurel Ann Buskirk Wiegand, Kristine Janet Buskirk Hallett. Student, U. Wis., Madison, 1943; BA, St. Olaf Coll., Northfield, Minn., 1950; MA, U. Minn., Mpls., 1951, PhD, 1954. Lab. and tchg. asst. Lab. Physiol. Hygiene, U. Minn., 1951-53; rsch. fellow Life Inst. Med. Rsch. Fund, 1953-54; physiologist Environ. Rsch. Ctr., Natick, Mass., 1954-57, Nat. Inst. for Arthritis, Metabolic and Digestive Diseases, NIH, Bethesda, Md., 1957-63; prof. applied physiology Pa. State U., University Park, 1963-92, dir. Lab. Human Performance Rsch., 1963-92, Marie Underhill Noll prof. Human Performance, 1988-92, emeritus, 1992—. Mem. sci. adv. com. Pres.' Coun. on Phys. Fitness, 1959-61; mem. applied physiology study sect. divsn. rsch. grants NIH, 1964-68, 76-80; mem. com. on interplay of engring. with biology and medicine NAS-NAE, 1968-74, 82-88; mem. rsch. com. Pa. Heart Assn., 1970-73, 82-86, 87-89, 90-95; mem. Pa. Gov.'s Coun. on Phys. Fitness and Sports, 1978-82; mem. com. on mil. nutrition rsch. NAS/NRC, 1982-90; mem. clin. scis. study sect. divsn. rsch. grants NIH, 1989-92, spl. reviewer, 1992-99; mem. Def. Women's Rsch. Com. IOM, NAS-NRC, 1995. Sect. editor Jour. Applied Physiology, 1974-78, assoc. editor, 1978-84; co-editor Sci. and Medicine in Sports and Exercise, 1974, editor, 1973-75; editor-in-chief, 1984-88, cons., editor, 1989-94; mem. editl. bd. Physician and Sports Medicine, 1974-85, Jour. Cardiopulmonary Rehab., 1980-2000, Underseas and Hyperbaric Medicine, 1988-95, Am. Jour. Clin. Nutrition, 1982-92, Jour. Gerontology, 1982-92, Exptl. Gerontology, 1989-98; also over 250 articles on physiology, revs. to sci. jours. Bd. visitors Sargent Coll., Boston U., 1976-92; bd. dirs. Ctr. Cmty. Hosp., Pa., 1966-70, sec., 1971-72, v.p., 1973, pres., 1974-75. With US Army, 1943—46, with ETO, 1943—46, mem. 3rd Army commd. 2d lt. infantry, France, Germany. Recipient Disting. Alumni award St. Olaf Coll., 1969, U. Minn., 2006, Daggs Svc. award Am. Physiol. Soc., 2000; rsch. grantee NIH, 1963-92, U.S. Olympic Com., 1965-68, USAF, 1965-69, Pa. Dept. Health, 1966-67, Pa. Heart Assn., 1966, 76-80, NSF, 1968-70, Nat. Inst. Occupl. Safety and Health, 1969-74; NATO sr. fellow in sci., 1977; named to Athletic Hall of Fame, St. Olaf Coll., 2000. Mem. AAAS, AAPHERD, ASHRAE, Aerospace Med. Assn., Am. Acad. Phys. Edn., Am. Coll. Sports Medicine (citations 1973, 75, Honor award 1984, editl. award 1989, 93, Mid-Atlantic regional chpt. Svc. award 1991), Am. Inst. Nutrition, Am. Physiol. Soc. (pres. environ. and exercise sect. 1987-91, com. on coms. 1988-92, Honor award environ. exercise physiology sect. 1993, Daggs award 2002), Am. Heart Assn. (coun. on epidemiology), N.Y. Acad. Scis., NIH Alumni Assn., Pa. Heart Assn. (rsch. com. 1988-94), Am. Diabetes Assn., Coun. Biology Editors (Healthy Am. Fitness Leaders award 1992), Centre Hills Country Club; fellow Am. Soc. Nutrition. Lutheran. Home: 216 Hunter Ave State College PA 16801-6947 Office: Pa State U 119 Noll Lab University Park PA 16802-6900

BUSNER, PHILIP H., retired lawyer, judge; b. Bklyn., Mar. 26, 1927; s. Joseph and Ray (Grajewer) B.; m. Naomi Marcia Greenfield, June 24, 1951; children: Joan Alexandra, Carey Elizabeth. BA cum laude, NYU, 1949; LLB, Harvard U., 1952. Bar: N.Y. 1953, U.S. Dist. Ct. (so. dist.) N.Y. 1956, U.S. Dist. Ct. (ea. dist.) N.Y. 1958, U.S. Ct. Appeals (2d cir.) 1956, U.S. Supreme Ct. 1974. Assoc. Rein, Mound & Cotton, NYC, 1953, Hess, Mela, Segall, Popkin & Guterman, NYC, 1954-55, Carroad & Carroad, NYC, 1955-72; ptnr. Young, Sonnenfeld & Busner, NYC, 1972-75, Sonnenfeld & Busner, NYC, 1976-78, Sonnenfeld, Busner & Weinstein, NYC, 1978-85, Sonnenfeld, Busner & Richman, NYC, 1986-88; pvt. practice Great Neck, N.Y., 1989-97; ret., 1998. Trustee Asthmatic Children's Found. N.Y., 1978-87; adminstrv. judge N.Y.C. Dept. Transp., 1989-93; arbitrator N.Y.C. Civil Ct., 1990-92, Nassau County Dist. Ct., 1990-95, Suffolk County Dist. Ct., 1990-93. With USAAF, 1945-47. Mem. Am. Arbitration Assn. (arbitrator 1990-92), Phi Beta Kappa. Home: 600 Pine Hollow Rd #18-3B East Norwich NY 11732

BUSQUET, ANNE M., Internet company executive; b. 1950; BS in Hotel Adminstrn., Cornell U., 1973; MBA, Columbia U. Mktg. mgr. Am. Express, 1978, sr. v.p., gen. mgr. Optima card divsn., 1988—92, sr.-vp., gen. mgr. mdse. svcs. bus., 1992—93, exec. v.p. consumer card group, 1993—95, pres. relationship svcs. divsn., 1995—2000, pres. interactive svcs. and new bus. divsn., 2000—01; sr. adv. InterActiveCorp, 2003—04, CEO local svcs., 2004—06; prin. AMB Advisors, LLC. Bd. dirs. Blyth, Inc., 2007—.*

BUSS, DANIEL FRANK, environmental scientist; b. Milw., Jan. 13, 1943; s. Lynn Charles and Pearl Elizabeth (Ward) B.; m. Ann Makal, Jan. 22, 1977; children: Jessica, Jonathan. BS, Carroll Coll., 1965; MS in Biology, U. Wis., 1972, MS in Environ. Engring., 1977, P.D.D. in Environ. Engring., 1985. Registered profl. engr., Wis. Dir. limnological studies Aqua-Tech, Inc., Waukesha, Wis., 1969-72; project mgr. environ. studies Point Beach Nuclear Plant, Two Creeks, Wis., 1972-76; assoc., dir. aquatic studies environ. sci. div. Camp Dresser & McKee, Inc., Milw., 1977—, dir. indsl. service, 1978-90, office mgr., coord. for environ. assesments Milw., 1990—; mgr. Buss Environ. Cons. LLC, Milw. Lectr. noc. power and environ., environ. auditing; mgr. hazardous waste superfund projects, dredge disposal planning projects; asbestos insp., mgmt. planner EPA, 1988, nat. accounts mgr. performance environ. site assessments property trans.; instr. environ. site assessments according to domestic and internat. stds. with consideration of bus. environ. risk for real property; crew leader, project task mgr. Hurricane Katrina Asbestos Bldg. Inspections, St. Bernard Parish, La., 2006. Author: An Environmental Study of the Ecological Effects on Lake Michigan of the Thermal Discharge from the Point Beach Nuclear Plant, 1976, Environmental Auditing-- A Systematic Approach, 1984; contbr. articles to profl. jours, chpts. to books Mem. ASCE (chmn. site constrn. and remediation implementation manual task com.),Am. Nuclear Soc. (sec.-treas. Wis. sect., program mgr. waste disposal studies, program mgr. for remedial programs involving jet fuel and deicer contamination at Gen. Mitchell Internat. Airport), Midwest Soc. Electron Microscopists, Internat. Soc. Theoretical and Applied Limnology and Oceanography, Internat. Assn. Gt. Lakes Rsch., Am. Indsl. Hygiene Soc., Nat. Assn. Environ. Profls., Fed. Water Pollution Control Adminstrn., Cons. Engrs. Coun. (chmn. liaison com. Ill. and Chgo. Bar Assn., mem. com. for devel. site investigation manual ASCE, sec. ASCE com. to develop remedial design, feasibility study manual), Am. Assn. Environ. Engrs. (diplomate 1990, cert. hazardous materials mgr. 1988, hazard control mgr. 1988), Program mgr. design, construction mgmt., oper. UV/Oxidation system (used for treating herbicide contaminated ground water in Wisconsin), Am. Acad. Environ. Engrs. (Wis. state rep.), Glendale Wis. Econ. Devel. Com. and Bus. Coun., Sigma Xi. Achievements include research in environmental baseline studies and permitting of a public bulk terminal port in New Orleans. Home: 5543 N Shasta Dr Milwaukee WI 53209-4924 Office Phone: 414-559-8808. E-mail: danbuss@wi.rr.com.

BUSS, GEORGE EDWARD, JR., museum program director; b. Edison, NJ, Sept. 1, 1977; s. George Edward and Patricia Buss; m. Holly Jean Tobey, June 28, 2003; 1 child, Elia Tierney. BA in Theater Arts, Messiah Coll., Grantham, Pa., 1999. Pub. programs mgr. Whitaker Ctr. Sci. and Arts, Harrisburg, Pa., 2001—; actor educator Saltworks Theater Co. Children's entertainment cons. Inch Enterprises, Gettysburg, Pa., 2000—04; pub. speaking cons. Am. Assn. Museums Conf., Washington, 2003—, Leigh Yowkey Woodson, Wausau, Wis., 2006. Author: (plays) Apollo's Eve, 2003, The Good, the Bad and the Ugly, 2005, Nutrition Expedition, 2007. Mem.: Assn. Am. Museums, Am. Assn. Theater and Edn., Internat. Mus. Theater Alliance (treas., pres. 2002—06, 2006—). Avocations: backpacking, reading, theater, board games, geocoaching. Home: 42 Campground Rd Dillsburg PA 17019 Office: Whitaker Ctr Sci and the Arts 222 Marker St Harrisburg PA 17101 Office Phone: 717-221-8201 ext 1232. Personal E-mail: fedora_21@hotmail.com.

BUSS, JERRY (GERALD HATTEN BUSS), professional sports team owner; b. Salt Lake City, 1934; children: John, Jim, Jeanie, Jane. BS in Chemistry, U. Wyo.; MS, PhD in Chemistry, U. So. Calif., 1957. Chemist Bur. Mines; mem. faculty dept. chemistry U. So. Calif.; mem. missile divsn. McDonnell Douglas, LA; ptnr. Mariani-Buss Assocs.; former owner LA Strings; chmn. bd., owner NBA LA Lakers, 1979—; owner NHL LA Kings, 1979—88. Office: LA Lakers 555 N Nash St El Segundo CA 90245*

BUSSABARGER, MARY LOUISE, mental health services professional; b. Chgo., Sept. 16, 1923; d. Joseph and Nellie Wheelen Sterling; m. Robert Franklin Bussabarger, May 11, 1946; children: Wendi Newell, David. BA, U. Mo., 1960, MA English Lit., 1963. Instr. English U. Mo., Columbia, 1960—82; mental health commr. State of Mo., Jefferson City, 2001—07. Instr. English as a fgn. lang. Indo-Am. Soc., Calcutta, India, 1961—62, 1968—69, Seoul, South Korea, 1995—96; tchr. Yoga, 1969—2002; co-dir. Women's Place Agy., 1974—77; liaison officer Danforth Found., 1976—80. Mem. Nat. Alliance for the Mentally Ill, 1985—; commr. parks and recreation City of Columbia, 1975—77; mem. spkrs. bur. Internat. Women's Year, 1975—; mem. Planning Coun. for Devel. Disabilities, 1990—97, State Adv. Coun. for Psychiat. Svcs., 1985—90; mem. nat. steering com. Nat. Women's Polit. Caucus, 1974—75; pres. Columbia Women's Polit. Caucus, 1975—76; del. State Dem. Convs., 1968, 1972, alt., 1976; mem. state steering com. Mo. Women's Polit. Caucus, 1972—76. Mem.: MLA, AAUW, Delta Tau Kappa. Achievements include invitation and attendance to the John F. Kennedy School of Government at Harvard University for "Leadership for the 21st century", Oct. 2004. Office: Dept Mental Health 1706 E Elm St PO Box 677 Jefferson City MO

BUSSAN, JAMES A., tax specialist; s. Allen J. and Kathleen T. Bussan; m. Kathryn E. Summers, Sept. 4, 1971; children: James A., Christina M. BA, U. Wis., Madison, 1971; MBA, Drake U., Des Moines, 1979. Computer programmer John Deere, Dubuque, Iowa, 1971—80, computer sys. analyst, 1980—88, db2 adminstr., 1988—96, y2k project mgr., 1996—2000, computer sys. supr., 2000—01; tax preparer Bussan Tax & Acctg. Svc., LLC, Dickeyville, Wis., 1993—. Computer cons. Database Assocs., Dubuque, 1985—2003. Troop advancement chmn. Boy Scouts Am., Cuba City, 1994—2006, scoutmaster, 1994—2000, arrowhead dist. eagle rep. Dickeyville, Wis., 1998, arrowhead dist. roundtable commr. Darlington, Wis., 2001—06, arrowhead dist. v.p., mem., 2006; adv. coun. Cuba City Sch. Bd., 2002; dickeyville planning commn. Dickeyville Village Bd., Dickeyville, Wis., 2006. Avocations: reading, fishing. Home Phone: 608-568-3177.

BUSSE, EILEEN ELAINE, special education educator; b. Green Bay, Wis., Oct. 16, 1957; d. Ervin F. Dohl and Elaine I. (Behnke) Richmond; m. John F. Busse, July 5, 1980; children: Jessica Lynn, Jeremy John. BS in Elem. and Spl. Edn., U. Wis., Eau Claire, 1979; MS in Spl. Edn., U. Wis., Whitewater, 1985. Cert. tchr. elem. and spl. edn. Tchr. spl. edn.-mentally retarded Ithaca Pub. Schs., Wis., 1979-80; spl. edn. tchr. various schs. Walworth County CDEB, Whitewater, Wis., 1980—2000; spl. edn. tchr. Whitewater HS, 2000—, transition specialist, 2004—. Coop. tchr. U. Wis., Whitewater, 1988—; summer sch. tchr. St. Thomas U., St. Paul, Minn., 2003-2005. Author: Student Owned Spelling, 1991, II, 1992, III, 1994. Mem. First English Luth. Ch. edn. com., Whitewater, 1990-95, 98-2005, chmn. edn. com., 1993-95, mem. ch. coun., 1993-94, 97-2005; active Girl Scouts U.S.A., 1992-2000; advisor sr. high youth 1st English Luth. Ch., 1998-2005. Recipient Excellence in Edn. award U.S. Dept. Edn., 1984-85, Recognized spl. educator, 1998. Mem. Coun. for Exceptional Children (divsn. on career devel. and transition), Delta Kappa Gamma. Avocations: reading, travel, gardening. Home: 455 Ventura Ln Whitewater WI 53190-1548 Office: Whitewater HS 534 S Elizabeth St Whitewater WI 53190 Personal E-mail: bussee@charter.net. Business E-Mail: ebusse@wwusd.org.

BUSSE, KEITH E., manufacturing executive; BA in Bus., U. Saint Francis; MBA, In. U, 1978. Division controller to v.p. Nucor Corp., 1972—93; founder Steel Dynamics, Fort Wayne, Ind., 1993, pres., CEO, 1993—2007, chmn., CEO, 2007—. Named Entrepreneur of the Yr., Ernst & Young, 1997; named one of the top 10 entrepreneurs in the U.S., Business Week, 1997, the best 5 Undiscovered CEO's, Investor Magazine, 1999; recipient Distinguished Alumnus Award, Indiana University, 1991. Office: c/o Steel Dynamics 6714 Pointe Inverness Way Fort Wayne IN 46804*

BUSSE, LEONARD WAYNE, banker, financial consultant; b. Chgo., June 29, 1938; s. Edwald William and Elsie Helen (Weidner) B.; m. Gretchen Guam Beal, Sept. 7, 1963; children: Whitney Lee, Carter Douglas. BS, Purdue U., Lafayette, Ind., 1960; postgrad., Northwestern U., Evanston, Ill., 1964—67. CPA, Ill. With Continental Ill. Corp., Chgo., 1963-88, v.p., 1973-81, sr. v.p., 1981-85, head internat. banking dept., 1985; exec. v.p. Continental Bank, Chgo., 1985-88; cons. The Busse Group, Vail, Colo., 1989-93; pres., CEO, bd. dirs. The Pacific Bank, San Francisco, 1993-94; CEO, bd. dirs. First Citizen Bank Ltd., Port of Spain, Trinidad, 1994-96; CFO, bd. dirs. Worldbridge Broadband Svcs., Denver, 1998-2000; v.p. fin. Open Access Broadland Network, Denver, 1999-2001; sr. advisor Headwaters MB, Denver, 2001—06. Bd. dirs. Exabyte Corp., Boulder, Colo., 2002—06. Bd. dirs. McGraw Wildlife Found., Elgin, Ill., 1982-92, Vectra Banking Corp., Denver, 1993-94. Mem. AICPA. Republican. Lutheran. Avocations: skiing, hunting, biking, fishing.

BUSSE, PAUL LAWRENCE, science educator; b. Evanston, Ill., Sept. 3, 1949; children: Christopher, Matthew. BS in Biology, Coll. William & Mary, Williamsburg, Va., 1967—71; MEd, Va. Commonowealth U., Richmond, 1974—76. Cert. postgrad. profl. Dept. Edn., Va., 1976. Pers. specialist US Army Res., Richmond, 1971—77; tchr., dept. head, adminstrv. aide, summer sch. adminstr. Byrd Mid. Sch., Richmond, 1971—86; coord. Math. & Sci. Ctr., Richmond, 1986—2001; sci. tchr. Steward Sch., Richmond, 2001—. Contbr. articles to profl. jours. Mem.: Mensa, Greater Richmond Coun. Sci. Tchrs. (pres. 1988—89), Va. Sci. Tchrs. Assn., Nat. Sci. Tchrs. Assn. Independent. Avocations: photography, travel. Home Phone: 804-914-5868. Business E-Mail: paul.busse@stewardschool.org.

BUSSEL, JAMES, pediatrician, obstetrician, gynecologist, educator; s. John David and Lili Renata Bussel; m. Charlotte Anne Cunningham-Rundles, Nov. 13, 1982; 1 child, Amy Christine Cunningham-Bussel. BS cum laude, Yale U., New Haven, Conn., 1971; MD, Columbia Coll. Physicians and Surgeons, NY, 1975. Diplomate in pediat. Am. Acad. Pediat., 1979, on pediat. hematology oncology Am. Acad. Pediat., 1981. Prof. pediat., medicine, and ob-gyn. Weill Cornell Med., NY, 1999—. Lectr. in field. Mem.: Am. Soc. Hematology. Achievements include development of diagnosis and treatment of immune thrombocytopenias. Office: Weill Cornell Med NY Presbyn Hosp 525 East 68th St P609 New York NY 10021 Home Phone: 212-734-4346; Office Phone: 212-746-3474.

BUSSGANG, JULIAN JAKUB, electronics engineer, consultant; b. Lwow, Poland, Mar. 26, 1925; came to U.S., 1949, naturalized, 1954; s. Joseph and Stephanie (Philipp) B.; m. Fay Rita Vogel, Aug. 14, 1960; children: Jessica Edith, Julia Claire, Jeffrey Joseph. BSc in Engring., U. London, 1949; SM in Elec. Engring., MIT, Cambridge, 1951; PhD in Applied Physics, Harvard U., Cambridge, 1955. Mem. tech. staff Lincoln Lab., MIT, Lexington, 1951-55; mgr. applied rsch. RCA, Burlington, Mass., 1955-62; pres. Signatron, Inc., Lexington, 1962-87; pvt. practice cons. Lexington, 1988—. Vis. lectr. Harvard U., 1964; lectr. Northeastern U., Boston, 1962-65; mem. Mass. del. White House Conf. on Small Bus., 1980. Assoc. editor: Radio Sci., 1976-78; translator: The Last Eyewitnesses: Children of the Holocaust Speak, Vol. 1, 1998, Vol. 2, 2005; contbr. chpts. to books, also articles; patentee in field. Mem. Town Mtg., Lexington, 1975-93; mem. alumni coun. MIT, 1965-72; bd. overseers Mus. of Sci., Boston, 1989-95; vol. exec. Internat. Exec. Svc. Corps., 1993, 94, 95. With Free Polish Forces, 1942-46. Fellow IEEE (life fellow, chmn. Boston sect. 1994-95, vice chmn. life members com. 2005). Home and Office: 2 Forest St Lexington MA 02421-4911 *I was a child-refugee, an adolescent-soldier, a student-immigrant, a young engineer and an adult entrepreneur. In every phase of my life I was blessed with the friendship and support of many wonderful people from various walks of life. Even in the darkest moments I had faith that each of us could improve the world a little.*

BUSTAMANTE, CARLOS J., biophysicist, educator; b. Lima, Peru, May 8, 1951; BS in Biology, Cayelano Heredia U., Lima, Peru, 1973; MSc in Biochemistry, San Carlos U., Lima, 1978; DSc in Biophysics, U. Calif, Berkeley, 1981. Asst. prof. Dept. Chemistry U. N.Mex, 1982—86, assoc. prof., 1986—89, presidential lectr. in chemistry, 1986, prof., 1989—90, U. Oregon, 1991—98, Howard Hughes Med. Inst. Investigator, 1994—98, U. Calif., Berkeley, 2000—, prof. of Molecular and Cell Biology, Physics, and Chemistry, 1998—. Mem. Sci. Adv. Bd. Searle Scholars Prog., 1997—2000; Head advanced microscopics dept. Lawrence Berkeley Nat. Lab. Phys. Bioscis. Divsn.; served on Interfaces Adv. Com. Burroughs Wellcome Fund, 2001—03, bd. dir., 2004—. Contbr. articles to profl. jours. Fellow Alfred P. Sloan, 1985; scholar Fulbright, 1975—80, Searle, 1984, (eminent) New Mexico, 1989. Fellow: Am. Phys. Soc.; mem.: NAS (Alexander Hollaender award in Biophysics 2004). Office: Univ Calif Berkeley Dept Physics 231 Birge Hall Berkeley CA 94720 E-mail: carlos@alice.berkeley.edu.*

BUSTAMANTE, CRUZ M., former lieutenant governor; b. Dinuba, Calif., Jan. 4, 1953; s. Cruz and Dominga Bustamante Jr.; m. Arcelia De La Pena; children: Leticia, Sonia, Marisa. BA, Fresno State U. Past intern for Congressman B.F. Sisk, Washington; formerly with Fresno employment and tng. commn. City of Fresno, past program dir. summer youth employment tng. program, 1977—83; past dist. rep. Congressman Rick Lehman and Assemblyman Bruce Bronzan State of Calif.; mem. Calif. State Assembly, 1993, spkr. of assembly, 1996-98; lt. gov. State of Calif., 1998—2007. Mem. US Census Monitoring Bd. Trustee Calif. State U.; regent U. Calif.; chair State Lands Commn.; vice chair Aerospace States Assn. Named Legislator of Yr. Assn. Mexican Am. Educators, U. Calif. Alumni Assn.; recipient True Am. Role Model award Mexican Am. Polit. Assn., Calif. Coastal Hero award, Pres.'s award NAACP, Friend of Labor award Mexican Am. Polit. Assn. Democrat. also: 300 S Spring St Ste 12702 Los Angeles CA 90013 Address: 2550 Mariposa Mall Rm 5006 Fresno CA 93721*

BUSTAMANTE, NESTOR, lawyer; b. Havana, Cuba, Apr. 20, 1960; came to the U.S., 1961; s. Nestor and Clara Rosa (Sanchez) B.; m. Marilyn Gonzalez, Sept. 20, 1986; children: Tiffany Alexandra, Nestor C. AA, U. Fla., 1980, BS in Journalism, 1982, JD, 1985. Bar: Fla. 1986, U.S. Dist. Ct. (so. dist.) Fla. 1989, U.S. Supreme Ct. 1991. Asst. state atty. State Atty.'s Office 11th Cir., Miami, 1986-88; juvenile serious offender prosecutor State Atty.'s Office, Miami, 1987-88, spl. prosecutor, gang prosecutor, 1987-88; asst. divsn. chief State Atty.'s Office-11th Jud. Cir., Miami, 1987-88; of counsel Fernandez-Caubi, Fernandez & Aguilar et al., Miami, 1988-89; atty. Ferencik, Libanoff, Brandt, Bustamante and Williams PA, Ft. Lauderdale, Fla., 1989—, ptnr., 1996—. Mem. code and rules of evidence com. The Fla. Bar, 1989—90, jud. evaluation com., 2000; chmn. Dade County Constrn. Trades Qualifying Bd.; adj. faculty dept. constrn. mgmt. Fla. Internat. U. Contbr. articles to newsletters. Chmn. Miami-Dade Constrn. Trades Qualifying Bd. Named Hon. mem. Quien es Quien Publs., Inc., N.Y.C., 1990. Mem. ATLA (scoring judge nat. finals student trial advocacy competition 1994, 95), Fed. Bar Assn., Dade County Bar Assn. (mem. juvenile divsn. com. 1988-92, mem. media and pub. rels. com. 1989-91, mem. constrn. law com. 1990—), Phi Delta Phi, U. Fla. Alumni Assn. Office: Ferencik Libanoff Brandt Bustamante & Williams PA 150 S Pine Island Rd Ste 400 Fort Lauderdale FL 33324-2667 Office Phone: 305-949-8003. Business E-Mail: nbustamante@flbbwlaw.com.

BUSTER, JOHN EDMOND, obstetrician, medical researcher; b. Oxnard, Calif., July 18, 1941; s. Edmound B. and Beatrice (Keller) B. Student, Stanford U., 1959-62; MD, UCLA, 1966. Diplomate Am. Bd. Obstetrics and Gynecology. Intern Harbor UCLA Med. Ctr., Torrance, Calif., 1966-67; resident, 1967-71, rsch. fellow, 1971-73, faculty, 1975—; prof. ob-gyn. UCLA Sch. Medicine, 1983, U. Tenn., Memphis, 1987-94; prof. ob-gyn., dir. divsn. reproductive endocrinology Baylor Coll. Medicine, Houston, 1994—; div. divsn. reproductive endocrinology UCLA Sch. Medicine. Examiner Am. Bd. Ob-Gyn. Contbr. articles to profl. jours. Served to lt. col. U.S. Army, 1973-75. Fellow: Am. Coll. Obstetricians and Gynecologists; mem.: Soc. Reproductive Endocrinologists, Am. Gynecol. and Obstet. Soc., Am. Soc. Reproductive Medicine, Soc. Gynecologic Investigation, Endocrine Soc. Presbyterian. Home: 1709 Dryden Rd Ste 1100 Houston TX 77030-2414 also: 3030 Post Oak Blvd Houston TX 77030

BUSTILLOS, TIMOTHY D., management consultant; s. Guadalupe and Daniel Bustillos; m. Vanessa M. Velasco, Nov. 11, 2000; 1 child, Makai Alexander. BS in Bus. Mgmt., Calif. Luth. U., Thousand Oaks, 2006; cert. in applied project mgmt., Villanova U., Pa., 2006. Project mgr. Somers Bldg., Sacramento, 2004—06; project mgr. for contract mfg. Baxter Biosci., Thousand Oaks, 2006—. Mem.: Project. Mgmt. Inst. (life). Republican. Avocations: golf, travel, baseball. Office: Baxter Biosci 1700 Rancho Conejo Thousand Oaks CA 91320 Office Phone: 805-480-2925. Business E-Mail: timothy_bustillos@baxter.com.

BUSTIN, GEORGE LEO, lawyer; b. Perth Amboy, NJ, Feb. 10, 1948; s. George and Agnes W. (Bulvanoski) B.; m. Halina Orestovna Kaniuka, July 9, 1979; children: Michael G., Alexander G. AB summa cum laude, Princeton U., 1970; JD magna cum laude, Harvard U., 1973. Bar: N.Y. 1973, U.S. Dist. Ct. (so. dist.), U.S. Ct. Appeals ((2nd cir.), 1974. Assoc. Cleary, Gottlieb, Steen & Hamilton, NYC, 1973-81, ptnr., 1982-84, Brussels, 1984—90, 1992—2007, sr. counsel NYC, 2007—. Vis. prof. Princeton U., NJ, 1991, mem. adv. com. program law and pub. affairs, 2007—, sr. lectr. law and pub. affairs program, 2007—; dir. Sabre Found. (Europe) S.p.r.l.; chair Princeton Alumni Schs. Com., Belgium, 1998—2007; faculty assoc. Woodrow Wilson Sch. Pub., Internat. Affairs Princeton U., Princeton, NJ, 2007—. Author: Business Transactions with the USSR, 1975, International Business Transactions, 1980, International Financial Law Review, 1990, Insights, 1990. Recipient Spencer Reynolds award, Princeton U. Alumni Coun., 2005. Mem. ABA (vice chair European law com. 2003-06, co-chair fall meeting of sect. internat. law and practice 2003, sr. adviser 2006, Spl. Achievement award 2004), Cercle Gaulois Artistique et Litteraire, Harvard Law Sch. Assn. (sec. Brussels 1989-92), NY State Bar Assn. (chair Brussels chpt. internat. divsn. 1996-2007), Assn. Bar City NY (chair coms. on rels. with European bars 2001-04), Ordre Francais du barreau de Bruxelles (mem. commn. internat. rels. 2003-07), Brussels Sports Assn. (bd. dirs. 1996-98). Home: 310 Pennington-Titusville Rd Pennington NJ 08534 Office: 1 Liberty Plz #4300 New York NY 10006 Office Phone: 212-225-2070. Business E-Mail: gbustin@cgsh.com.

BUSTREO, FLAVIA, epidemiologist; b. Padua, Italy, Aug. 17, 1961; d. Lino and Maria Bustreo. Grad. in Communicable Disease Epidemiology, London Sch. of Hygiene and Tropical Medicine, 1994; grad., CUAMM Coll., Padova, Italy, 1993; postgrad. in sports medicine & rehab., U. Padova, Italy, 1990, grad. in Medicine and Surgery with honors, 1987. Clinician Italian Assn. of Physicians, 1987. Clinician in internal medicine Inst. Gris, Treviso, Italy, 1990—91; sports medicine and rehab. physician Ctr. di Medicina Dello Sport, Venice, Italy, 1990—93; clinician rschr. Regional U. Ctr. of Sports Medicine, Padova, Italy, 1990—93; med. officer in the integrated program on communicable diseases WHO, Copenhagen, 1994—95, med. officer in the global tb program Geneva, 1995—97, med. officer in child health Khartoum, Sudan, 1997—99; sr. pub. health specialist World Bank Hdqs., Washington, 1999—; dep. dir. Child Survival Partnership, NYC, 2004—. Presenter in field. Contbr. articles to profl. jours. Sec. of Venice sect. Interat. Physicians forPrevention of Nuc. War, Venice, 1990—2005; vol. Italian NGOs, Padova, 1992—93, Rijeka, Croatia, 1991—93; mem. of del. to Iraq to assess the situation of children in the country after the war and the sanctions Internat. Physicians for the Prevention of Nuc. War, Italy, 1992. Recipient Bank award for Capacity Bldg. for Sr. WHO and World Bank Staff, World Bank, 2000, Bank award for Senegal Cmty. Nutrition Project, 2002, Bank award for Preparation of the Healthy Start in Life Conf., 2002; scholar 3 Yr. Scholarship For Postgrad. Med. Studies, Italian Ministry of Universities and Sci. Rsch., 1988-1990. Avocation: languages.

BUSUTTIL, STEVEN JAMES, surgeon; s. John and Dolores Busuttil; m. Carmelina Grimaldi, June 16, 1990. BSEE, SUNY, Stony Brook, NY, 1983, MD, 1988. Diplomate in gen. surgery Am. Bd. Med. Surgery, 1996, in vascular surgery Am. Bd. Med. Surgery, 1997. Rschr. U. Md., Balt., 2003—06, vascular surgeon, 2003—; chief sect. vascular surgery VAMC, Balt., 2006—. Vol. pilot Angle Flights, Balt., 2006. Mem.: AAS, Flying Physicians Assn., SVS. Avocation: flying. Home: 1604 Gupowder Ridge Rd Joppa MD 21085 Office: University of Maryland 22 South Greene St Baltimore MD 21201 Home Phone: 410-679-1170; Office Phone: 410-328-3319. Office Fax: 410-328-0717; Home Fax: 410-679-3448. Personal E-mail: sbusuttil@comcast.net. Business E-Mail: sbusuttil@smail.umaryland.edu.

BUSWELL, ARTHUR WILCOX, physician, surgeon; b. Oklahoma City, Jan. 6, 1926; s. Albert Currier and Enid May (Scott) Buswell; m. Loleta JoAnn Sherrill, June 11, 1950; children: Arthur Lee, Robert Joseph, Barbara JoAnn, Brian A., Gayla, Richard; m. Jane Marie Fuksa, Mar. 1, 1969. BS in Medicine, U. Okla., 1950, MD, 1952; AA in Med. Svcs., U.S. Army, 1963, student, 1963, Army Command and Gen. Staff Coll., 1966; postgrad., U. So. Calif., 1969. Intern Fitzsimons Army Hosp., Aurora, Colo., 1952—53; surg. resident Wesley Hosp., Oklahoma City, 1954—55; practice medicine and surgery Hennessey, Okla., 1955—63; dep. surgeon Ft. Wainwright and Yukon Command, 1963—65; chief staff Kingfisher Cmty. Hosp., 1956—57; supt. health Kingfisher County, 1960—61; chief profl. svcs. Bassett Army Hosp., 1963—65; div. surgeon 1st Armored Div., Ft. Hood, Tex., 1965—67; 1st Inf. Div. Vietnam, 1967—68; med. project officer U.S. Army Combat Devels. Command Experimentation Command, Ft. Ord, Calif., 1968—72; also chief human factors div. and chief experimentation div. of experimentation command; chief profl. svcs. Reynolds Army Hosp., Ft. Sill, Okla., 1972—73; comdr. med. dept. activities Ft. Stewart, Ga., 1973—77; chief profl. svcs. Kenner Army Hosp., Ft. Lee, Va., 1977—78; comdr. med. dept. activities Alaska, 1979—83. Adj. asst. prof. med. scis. Baylor U., 1973—. Mem. Kingfisher Meml. Libr. Bd.; pres. Ft. Stewart Sch. Bd., 1977; bd. dirs. Ft. Stewart Fed. Credit Union, 1977, Chisholm Trail Mus., 1986—, Friends of Librs. in Okla., 1987—; pres. Friends of Libr. for Kingfisher County, 1984—88. With AUS, 1944—46, 1st lt. US Army, 1952—54, maj. to col. US Army, 1961—83. Decorated Legion of Merit with 2 oak leaf clusters, Soldier's medal, Bronze Star for Valor with oak leaf cluster, Meritorious Service medal, Air medal with 3 oak leaf clusters, Army Commendation medal, Gallantry cross with palm, Honor medal 1st class (both Vietnam); named Citizen of Yr., Kingfisher C. of C., 1988; named to Kingfisher H.S. Hall of Fame, 1987. Fellow: Royal Soc. Health; mem.: AMA, Garfield-Kingfisher County Med. Soc., Assn. Mil. Surgeons U.S., Army Aviation Med. Assn., Aerospace Med. Assn., Okla. State Med. Assn. Home: PO Box 703 Kingfisher OK 73750-0703

BUTCHART, MARK STEVEN, diplomat; b. Honolulu, Mar. 20, 1961; s. Edwward Winslow and Margot Gisela Butchart; m. Jenny Paige Potter, Jan. 13, 1989. Grad. h.s., Decatur, Ga. Info. mgmt. specialist US Consulate, Guangzhou, China, 1995—97; info. programs officer US Embassy, Mbabane, Swaziland, 1997—98, info. systems officer Tel Aviv, 1998—2001; info. mgmt. officer US Consulate, Lagos, Nigeria, 2001—03; systems mgr. US Dept. State, Washington, 2003—05, info. mgmt. officer, 2005—. Divsn. chief US Dept. State, 2005—06. Sgt USAF, 1981—86. Recipient Superior Honor award, US Dept. State, 2006. Mem.: Mensa (life). Independent. Avocations: motocycles, astronomy, performing music, carpentry, scuba. Office: United States Department of State 2201 C St NW Washington DC 20520 Home Phone: 410-286-3523; Office Phone: 202-647-5046.

BUTCHER, BOBBY GENE, retired military officer; b. Mineral Wells, W.Va., Apr. 30, 1936; s. John Franklin and Anna Pearl (Hersman) B.; m. Patricia Maureen O'Keefe, Dec. 15, 1961 (dec. Dec. 1996); 1 child, Lisa Lee Butcher Clardy. BS, W.Va. U., 1958; grad., USN Flight Sch., 1960;

postgrad., USMC Amphibious Warfare Sch., 1966-67, USMC Command and Staff Coll., 1973-74. Commd. 2d lt. USMC, 1959, advanced through grades to maj. gen., 1989; officer in charge USMC Officer Selection Office, Phila., 1971-73; ops. officer Marine Attack Tng. Squadron 102, Yuma, Ariz., 1974, exec. officer, 1974-76, comdg. officer, 1976-77; ops. officer Marine Corps Air Sta., Yuma, 1977-79; ops. plans officer 3d Marine Div., Camp Courtney, Okinawa, 1979-80; comdg. officer Marine Aviation Weapons and Tactics Squadron One, Yuma, 1980-82; participant Dept. State Sr. Seminar, Arlington, Va., 1982-83; asst. chief staff, plans and policy, comdr. Naval Striking and Support Forces, So. Europe, Naples, Italy, 1983-86; asst. wing comdr. 3d Marine Aircraft Wing, El Toro, Calif., 1986-87; comdg. gen. 6th Marine Expeditionary Brigade, Camp Lejeune, NC, 1987-89; dir. ops. U.S. Pacific Command, Honolulu, 1989-91; comdg. gen. Landing Force Command, Coronado, Calif., 1991-92. Cons. in field. Decorated Def. D.S.M., D.S.M., Def. Superior Svc. medal, Legion of Merit, DFC, Bronze Star with combat V, Air medals (15); recipient various other unit and personal medals and ribbons. Mem. Mil. Officers Assn. Am. (pres. Region of Calif. Coun.), Flying Leatherneck Hist. Found. (chmn. bd. dirs.), USS Midway Mus. (bd. dirs.), Early and Pioneer Naval Aviators' Assn. (bd. govs.), Golden Eagles, Marine Corps Aviation Assn. (bd. dirs.) Republican. Methodist. Home: 110 Carob Way Coronado CA 92118-2433 E-mail: thunderbgb@san.rr.com.

BUTCHER, EDWARD BERNIE, state senator; b. Lewistown, Mont., July 20, 1943; m. Pamela Butcher; children: Trevis, Ross, Becky. BA, Ea. Mont. State, 1965; MA, U. Mont., 1967; postgrad., U. Colo., 1967, N.D. State U., 1969. Asst. prof. Valley City State U., 1968-71; owner Rolling Hills Ranch, 1972—; lectr. Am. studies U. Great Falls, 1974-79; nat. sales dir. Evans Bio Corp, 1987-88; sr. regional mgr. Attco Assocs., 1988—; Rep. senator dist. 47 Mont. State Senate, 2000—05; Mont. State Ho. of Reps, 2005—. Mem. exec. com. Gov.'s Agr. Adv. Bd., 1980-84; chair Montanans for Term Limits, 1992; chmn. House Agriculture com., 2005-. Mem. Mont. Bd. Crime Control, 1976-80; chair Fergus County Review Commn., 1994-96. Lutheran. Office: PO Box 89 800 Butcher Rd Winifred MT 59489

BUTCHER, FRED R., biochemistry professor, academic administrator; b. Rochester, Pa., Aug. 11, 1943; s. Goble S. and Monnie (Gibson) B.; children: Allen Ray, Amy Jo. BS, Ohio State U., 1965, PhD, 1969. Postdoctoral fellow U. Wis., Madison, 1969-71; asst. prof. Brown U., Providence, 1971-76, assoc. prof., 1976-78; prof. W.Va. U., Morgantown, 1978—, chmn. dept. biochemistry, 1981-84, assoc. dean Sch. Medicine, 1984-89, dir. MBR Cancer Ctr., 1989-2000, sr. assoc. v.p., 1993—; exec. dir. Blanchette Rockefeller Neuroscis. Inst., Morgantown, 1998—2000. Home: Rt 1 Box 325 Bruceton Mills WV 26525 Office Phone: 304-293-1536. Business E-Mail: fbutcher@hsc.wvu.edu.

BUTCHER, JACK ROBERT (JACK RISIN), manufacturing executive, film producer, actor, artist; b. Akron, Ohio, Dec. 10, 1941; s. William Hobart and Marguerite Bell (Dalton) Butcher; m. Gloria Jean Hartman, June 1, 1963 (dec. July 1995); children: Jack R. II, William H.(dec.) , Charlotte Jean; m. Marilyn E. LoMedico, Oct. 2, 2005. BA in Math., Jacksonville U., 1964; cert. in mgmt. consulting, Akron U., 1979; cert. in paralegal, CCT Inst., 1990; cert. in radio broadcasting, Chaffey Coll., 1994. Pres. Portableacher Corp., Hesperia, Calif., 1977—; v.p. Nice Day Products, Hesperia, 1980—85; pres. Mark Profl. Mgmt. and Design Co., Hesperia, 1983—, Nice Day Products, Hesperia, 1985—; owner Movie Funding Without Risk Co., 1996—; pres. Vallivue Prodns., Phelan, Calif., 2000—; co-owner Rizinn Consolidated Holdings Corp., 2001—. Co-owner JB Scale Co., Hesperia, 1991—. Actor, voice-overs and commls.: Film Industry Workshop Sch. Acting, 1995—99; author: (poems) Something Good, 1978, Forever My Valentine, 1996. Mem.: SAG, Internat. Platform Assn. (bd. govs. 1996—, Silver Bowl award 1995), Royal Order of Jesters, Shriners, Masons. Achievements include patents in field. Avocations: hunting, travel, designing, acting, commercial voice-overs. Home and Office: 1817-11 Beacon Hill Cir Cuyahoga Falls OH 44221 Personal E-mail: jrbutcher5@yahoo.com.

BUTCHER, KAREN A., lawyer; b. Dec. 30, 1966; BS, U. Va, 1988; JD, U. Va. Sch. Law, 1993. Bar: Va. 1993, D.C. 1994. Ptnr. Morgan, Lewis & Bockius LLP, Washington, asst. leader intellectual property trademark/copyright practice group. Mem.: Internat. Trademark Assn.-Info. Resources Com. Office: Morgan Lewis & Bockius 1111 Pennsylvania Ave NW Washington DC 20004 Office Phone: 202-739-5526. Office Fax: 202-739-3001. Business E-Mail: kbutcher@morganlewis.com.

BUTCHER, LARRY L., neuroscientist, educator; b. Richmond, Ind., Feb. 21, 1940; s. Frederick L. Butcher and Ellen E. Jennings; m. Nancy J. Woolf, Dec. 24, 1983; children: Lawson, Ashley. BA, U. Mich., 1962, MS, 1964, PhD, 1967; postgrad., U. Goteborg, Sweden, 1967—69. Prof. UCLA, 1969—, dir., gerontology minor program, 1997—. Cons. Pilgrim Sch., LA, 2000—. Contbr. scientific papers to profl. jours. Mem.: Sigma Xi. Office: UCLA 405 Hilgard Ave Los Angeles CA 90095-1563 Business E-Mail: butcher@psych.ucla.edu.

BUTCHER, RUSSELL DEVEREUX, writer, photographer; b. Bryn Mawr, Pa., Feb. 8, 1938; s. Devereux and Mary Frances (Taft) B.; m. Pamela Richards, Apr. 12, 1967 (div. 1993); children: Pamela Marie (dec.), Neill Devereux, Wendy Nan; m. Karen T. Black, Nov. 29, 1997. BA, U. Colo., 1960; postgrad., U. Mich., 1960-61. Rsch. editor Sierra Club, San Francisco, 1961-65; editl. writer N.Y. Times, 1963-79; publicity writer Save-the-Redwoods League, San Francisco, 1963-65; conservation specialist Nat. Audubon Soc., NYC, 1965-66; chief pub. rels. and publs. Mus. of N.Mex., Santa Fe, 1967-69; freelance writer, photographer, author, 1969-80. Conservation zoning cons. Town of Mount Desert, Maine, 1978-79, S.W. and Calif. rep. Nat. Parks and Conservation Assn., 1980-90, Pacific S.W. regional dir., 1990-93. Author: Maine Paradise, 1973, New Mexico: Gift of the Earth, 1975, The Desert, 1976, Field Guide to Acadia National Park, Maine, 1977, rev. edit., 2005, Exploring Our National Parks and Monuments, 9th edit., 1995, Exploring Our National Historic Parks and Sites, 1997, America's National Wildlife Refuges: A Complete Guide, 2003; author, compiler: Guide to National Parks (8 regional guides), 1999; mem. editl. bd. Audubon mag., 1965-1966; manuscript editor KC Publs., 1985-88; contbr. articles to profl. jours. Mem. Ariz. Strip Dist. adv. coun. U.S. Bur. Land Mgmt., 1983—90; bd. dirs. Friends Saguaro Nat. Park, 1997—2002, Rincon Inst., 2002—05. Nat. Parks and Conservation Assn. fellow, 1993-99. Mem. Save-the-Redwoods League (life), Nat. Parks and Conservation Assn., Maine Audubon Soc. (pres. Down East chpt. 1978-80, trustee 1979-80), Friends of Lake Dist. Eng. (life), Sierra Club (life). Episcopalian (Vestryman 1978-81). Address: 5948 N Misty Ridge Dr Tucson AZ 85718-3438

BUTCHKO, HARRIETT HAYS, physician; b. Athens, Ga., Mar. 31, 1950; d. William Jackson and Carolyn Ross Hays; m. Gregory Michael Butchko, July 8, 1972; children: Karin Hayston, Jeffrey Maston. Student, Canal Zone Coll., Balboa, 1968—69; BS, U. Ga., 1972; MD, Northwestern U., 1982. Diplomate Nat. Bd. Med. Examiners, 1984. Intern, resident Northwestern U., 1982—85; assoc. dir. clin. rsch. G.D. Searle & Co., Skokie, Ill., 1985—86, The NutraSweet Co., Skokie, 1986—91, dir. clin. rsch. and regulatory affairs Deerfield, Ill., 1991—97, v.p. med. and sci. affairs and chief med. officer Chgo., 2000—03; sr. dir. global regulatory coordination Monsanto Co., Skokie, 1997—2000; prin. scientist Exponent, Inc., Wood Dale, Ill., 2003—06; prin., owner Hayston Consulting LLC, Lake Forest, Ill., 2006—. Editor: (book) The Clinical Evaluation of a Food Additive: Assessment of Aspartame; contbr. chapters to books, articles to profl. jours. Fellow: Am. Coll. Nutrition; mem.: AMA, Am. Soc. Nutrition Scis., Am. Soc. Clin. Nutrition, Am. Acad. Neurology (assoc.), Internat. Soc. Regulatory Toxicology and Pharmacology, N.Am. Assn. for Study of Obesity, Phi Beta Kappa. Republican. Avocations: creating stained glass windows, collecting American brilliant cut glass, collecting antiques. Office Phone: 847-420-0388. Personal E-mail: hbutchko@comcast.net. E-mail: hbutchko@exponent.com.

BUTEL, JANET SUSAN, virologist, department chairman, research scientist; b. Overbrook, Kans., May 24, 1941; d. Floyd Charles and Berniece (Humbert) B.; m. David Yates Graham, Mar. 31, 1967; children: Susan Kathleen, David Peter. BS summa cum laude, Kans. State U., 1963; PhD with honors, Baylor U., 1966. Postdoctoral fellow Baylor Coll. Medicine, Houston, 1966—68, asst. prof., 1968—72, assoc. prof., 1972—76, prof., 1976—95, Joseph L. Melnick prof. virology, 1986—, head divsn. molecular virology, 1989—2000, disting. svc. prof., 1995—, chmn. dept. molecular virology and microbiol., 2000—, leader molecular carcinogenesis prog. Dan L. Duncan Cancer Ctr., dir. Ctr. AIDS Rsch. Mem. study sect. NIH, Bethesda, Md., 1980—84; mem. bd. sci. counselors Nat. Cancer Inst., Bethesda, 1980—84; mem. coun. Nat. Inst. Arthritis and Infectious Diseases, 1994—98; mem. external adv. coun. Am. Cancer Soc., 1998—2001. Contbg. editor: Lange Med. Microbiol., 1987—; contbr. sci. articles to profl. jours. Grad. fellow NSF, 1963-66; rsch. grantee NIH, 1973—; recipient Women in Cancer Rsch.-Charlotte Friend Meml. Lectureship, Am. Assn. Cancer Rsch., 2007. Mem. AAAS, Am. Assn. Cancer Rsch., Am. Soc. Cell Biology, Am. Soc. Microbiol. (divsn. chair 1990-91, group IV rep. 1993-95), Am. Soc. Virology, Internat. Assn. Breast Cancer Rsch. (bd. govs. Lakewood, Colo. 1987-91), Sigma Xi. Achievements include contributing fundamental research to the biology of tumor viruses and their cancer-causing mechanisms. Office: Baylor Coll Medicine One Baylor Plz Houston TX 77030 Office Phone: 713-798-4443. Office Fax: 713-798-5019. E-mail: jbutel@bcm.tmc.edu.*

BUTENHOFF, SUSAN GRACE, public relations executive; b. NYC, Jan. 13, 1960; BA in Internat. Rels. with hons., Sussex U., 1982; MPhil, Wolfson Coll. Cambridge U., 1985. Account exec. Ellen Farmer Prodns., 1984-85, Ketchum Pub. Rels., NYC, 1988-90, v.p., account supr., 1990-91; prin., CEO Access Pub. Rels., San Francisco, 1991—, pres., CEO. Mem. Pub. Rels. Soc. Am. Office: Access Comm 101 Howard St Fl 2D San Francisco CA 94105-1629

BUTENIS, PATRICIA A., ambassador; b. NJ; BA in Anthropology, U. Pa.; MA in Internat. Rels., Columbia U. Vice consul US Dept. State, Karachi, 1980—82, vice consul and polit. officer San Salvador, El Salvador, 1982—85, desk officer, 1988—90, consul New Delhi, 1985—88, consul, chief Am. citizen svcs. Bogotá, Colombia, 1990—93, consul gen., 2001—04, field liaison Visa Office, 1994—97, consul gen. Warsaw, 1998—2001, dep. chief of mission Islamabad, Pakistan, 2004—06, US amb. to Bangladesh Dhaka, 2006—07.

BUTENKO, SERGIY, engineering educator; b. Yevpatoria, Crimea, Ukraine, June 19, 1977; s. Ivan and Natalia Butenko; m. Joanna Trussin, Jan. 21, 2001; children: Ekaterina, Tatiana. MS in Math., Kyiv Taras Shevchenko U., Ukraine, 1999; PhD in Indsl. and Sys. Engring., U. Fla., Gainesville, 2003. Grad. asst. U. Fla., 1999—2003; asst. prof. indsl. and sys. engring. Tex. A&M U., College Station, 2003—. Editor: (book) Economics, Management and Optimization in Sports, 2004; contbr. articles to profl. jours. Recipient Favorite Prof. of Yr. award, Tex. A&M U., 2005—06; grantee Rsch. grant, NSF, 2006—, Civilian Rsch & Devel. Found., 2006—. Office: Texas A&M Univ 236E Zachry Engring Ctr College Station TX 77843-3131

BUTER, IRWIN, lawyer; Ptnr. Buter, Buzzard & Dunaetz, LLP, LA. Lectr. LA County Family Law Symposium, 1979—93, Calif. Continuing Edn. of Bar, 1980—95. Mem.: LA County Bar Assn. (chmn. family law sect. 1986—87, mem. exec. com. family law sect. 1977—91). Office: Buter Buzzard & Dunaetz LLP Ste 820 11611 San Vicente Blvd Los Angeles CA 90049 Office Phone: 310-820-6700. Office Fax: 310-207-4612. E-mail: buter@bbdflaw.com.*

BUTERA, ANN MICHELE, consulting company executive; b. Bayside, NY, Apr. 27, 1958; d. Gaetano Thomas and Josephine (Inserro) B. BA, L.I. U., 1979; MBA, Adelphi U., 1982. Dept. mgr. Abraham & Straus Stores, Huntington, NY, 1978-80; mgmt. cons. Chase Manhattan Bank N.A., Lake Success, NY, 1980-83, Nat. Bankcard Corp., Melville, NY, 1983-84; pres. Whole Person Project, Inc., Elmont, NY, 1984—. Adv. bd. mem. LI Devel. Corp.; bd. dirs. Nassau County coun. Girl Scouts U.S., 1985—95. Recipient Bus. Achievement award Women on the Job, 1990. Mem. ASTD, Fin. Women Internat., L.I. Networking Entrepreneurs (pres. 1984-91), Inst. Internal Auditors, Assn. Govt. Auditors, L.I. Ctr. for Bus. and Profl. Women, World Futurists Soc. Republican. Roman Catholic. Avocations: tennis, dance, gardening. Home and Office: Whole Person Project Inc 82 Cerenzia Blvd Elmont NY 11003-3631 Home Phone: 516-354-7089; Office Phone: 516-354-3551. E-mail: annbutera@cs.com.

BUTH, CHRISTIAN, physicist, researcher; b. Monchengladbach, Germany, Feb. 15, 1975; arrived in US, 2006; s. Rainer Hermann and Ursula Amanda Buth. Diploma in physics, Ruprecht-Karls U., Heidelberg, Germany, 2002; grad. studies, Max Planck Inst, Dresden, Germany, 2002—05, Rsch. assoc. Max Planck Inst., 2005—06, Argonne Nat. Lab., Ill., 2006—. Fellow, Alexander von Humboldt Found., Bonn, Germany, 2006—. Mem.: Am. Chem. Soc., Am. Phys. Soc. Avocations: reading, jogging, horseback riding, computer games. Office: Argonne Nat Lab 9700 S Cass Ave Argonne IL 60439

BUTHMAN, MARK A., health products executive; m. Tammy Buthman; 3 children. Fin. assoc. in corp. acctg. and procedures and controls Kimberly-Clark Corp., Neenah, Wis., 1982, cost analyst Memphis, 1983, project analyst to sr. strategic analyst, dir. corp. strategic analysis Neenah, Wis., 1984—95, v.p. strategic planning and analysis Dallas, 1997—2002, v.p. fin. Irving, Tex., 2002—03, sr. v.p. fin., CFO Tex., 2003—. Office: Kimberly Clark Corp PO Box 619100 Dallas TX 75261-9100 Office Phone: 972-281-1200.*

BUTHOD, CRAIG, library director; Rsch. asst. Tulsa City/County Libr. Sys., Okla., 1972—79, head bus. and tech. dept., 1979—85, chief ctrl. libr., 1985; dep. city libr. Seattle Pub. Libr., 1992—96, acting dir., CEO, 1996—98; dir. Louisville Free Pub. Libr., 1998—. Bd. mem. Ams. for Libr. Coun. Office: Louisville Free Pub Libr 301 York St Louisville KY 40203 Office Phone: 502-574-1611.

BUTHOD, MARY CLARE, school administrator; b. Tulsa, Aug. 20, 1945; d. Arthur Paul and Mary Rudelle (Dougherty) B. MA in Teaching, Tulsa U., 1969; M Christian Spirituality, Creighton U., 1981. Joined Order of St. Benedict. Asst. tchr. HeadStart, Tulsa, 1966; tchr. Madalene Parish Sch., Tulsa, 1968-69, Monte Cassino Pvt. Sch., Tulsa, 1969-79; prin. Monte Cassino Elem. Sch., Tulsa, 1979-86; dir. Monte Cassino Sch., Tulsa, 1986—. Mem. convent coun. Benedictine Sisters, Tulsa, 1975-88, dir. formation programs, 1983—; examiner Okla. Quality Found., 2004. Active State Congl. Edn. Com., Tulsa, 1989-90; co-chair for edn. and human devel. Tulsa Coalition Against Illegal Use of Drugs, 1990-91; adv. com. Okla. State Schs. Attuned, 2002—, Tulsa Pub. Sch. Quality Bd., 2005-06; adv. bd. Ret. Sr. Vol. Program, 2004— Recognized for Excellence in Edn. U.S. Dept. Edn., 1993-94. Mem. Tulsa Reading Coun. (sec. 1975-77), Nat. Cath. Edn. Assn., Delta Kappa Gamma. Home: 2200 S Lewis Tulsa OK 74114-3117 Office: Monte Cassino Sch 2206 S Lewis Ave Tulsa OK 74114-3109 Home Phone: 918-746-4212; Office Phone: 918-746-4112. Business E-Mail: smc@montecassino.org.

BUTKA, PAUL C., retail executive; Sr. v.p. corp. systems, chief info. officer TJX Cos., Inc., Framingham, Mass., exec. v.p., chief info. officer. Mem. Northborough-Southborough Regional Sch. Dist. Com. Recipient Humanitarian of Yr. award, St. Coletta & Cardinal Cushing Schs. Mass., Inc., 2006. Office: TJX Cos Inc 770 Cochituate Rd Framingham MA 01701 Office Phone: 508-390-1000. Office Fax: 508-390-2091. E-mail: paul_butka@tjx.com.*

BUTKI, BRIAN DAVID, psychologist, educator; b. Dearborn, Mich., May 18, 1970; s. Alice Mary Gibson and Julius Jerome Butki; m. Erin Rae Chandler, Aug. 9, 1997; children: Camden Grace children: Alisha Rae. BS, U. Wyo., Laramie, 1988—92, MSEd, 1992—93; PhD, U. N.C., Greensboro, 1994—98. Asst. prof. So. Ill. U., Edwardsville, 1998—2003; therapeutic recreation dir. Youth Focus, Inc., Greensboro, NC, 1998—99; dir. youth sport camps, asst. prof. Colo. State U., Ft. Collins, 2004—. Owner and dir. P.E.A.K. Performance Cons., Ft. Collins, 1998—. Tng. dir. Spl. Olympics of Ill., Highland, 1999—; dir. Metro East Humane Soc., Edwardsville, Ill., 2000—. Recipient Greensboro Grad. Award, State of N.C., 1994—98. Mem.: ASPCA, Am. Alliance of Health, Phys. Edn., Recreation, and Dance, Soc. of Behavioral Medicine, Assn. for the Advancement of Applied Sport Psychology, Phi Beta Kappa. Avocations: bicycling, travel, music, reading, hiking.

BUTKIEWICZ, JAMES LEON, economics professor, researcher, consultant; b. Kingston, Pa., Sept. 8, 1949; s. Joseph Leon and Anne (Lawlor) B.; m. Mary Ellen Fischer, Aug. 14, 1971; children: Erica, Lauren. BA, Wilkes Coll., 1971; PhD, U. Va., 1977. Asst. prof. econs. U. Del., Newark, 1976-82, assoc. prof., 1982-94, prof. econs., 1994—, assoc. dean Coll. Bus. and Econs., 1984-88, 91-96, chmn. dept. econs., 1996—2001; dir. grad. studies U. Del., Dept. Econ., 2003—04. Asst. prof. U. Va., Charlottesville, 1975; econ. cons., Newark, 1978—; guest lectr. Am. Coll, Bryn Mawr, Pa., 1985-89; cons. Office Tech. Assessment, Washington, 1988-89; vis. prof. U. Lyon, France, 2001; commentator weekly radio program, 1980-82; econ. analyst local TV and radio stas., 1979—. Editor: Keynes Economic Legacy, 1986; acting editor Ea. Econ. Jour., 2004-05, mem. editl. bd., 2001—; contbr. articles to profl. jours. Mem. Cecil County (Md.) Comprehensive Planning Com., 1988-90; mem. Del. Ins. Commr.'s Task Force of the Future of Del. Agts. and Agys., 1991-92, Cecil County Econ. Devel. Com., Bus. Retention and Fin. SubCom., chair 2000-05. Recipient 1st place for teaching Joint Coun. on Econ. Edn., 1988; Rsch grant U. Del., 1989, Del. Dept. Devel. grant, 1988 Mem. Am. Econ. Assn., Econ. History Assn., So. Econ. Assn., Phi Kappa Phi (pres. U. Del. chpt. 1986-91). Republican. Roman Catholic. Avocations: skiing, basketball. Office: U Del Dept Econs Newark DE 19716 Office Phone: 302-831-1891. Business E-Mail: butkiewj@lerner.udel.edu.

BUTKIN, ROBERT A., former state treasurer, law educator; m. Nina Butkin; children: Olivia, Julia, Claire. BA in History magna cum laude, Yale Coll., Conn., 1975; JD, U. Pa. Law Sch., 1978. Assoc. atty. Hogan and Hartson, Washington; asst. atty. gen. State of Okla., 1987—93, treas. Oklahoma City, 1995—2006; dean, prof. law Univ. Tulsa Coll. Law, 2005—. Vis. fellow Univ. Philippines Law Ctr., Quezon City. Bd. dir. Jasmine Moran Children's Mus., Okla. Acad., Leadership Okla.; trustee Congregation B'nai Emunah Endowment; mem. Jewish Found. Okla. City, 1993—94, Duncan C. of C. Henry Luce Scholar, 1978. Mem.: Nat. Assn. State Treasureres (former chair, banking, collateral & cast mgmt. com), So. State Treasurers Assn. (former pres.), Okla. Independent Petroleum Assn., Okla. Sch. Sci. & Math. Found. (trustee). Office: Univ Tulsa Coll Law 3120 E 4th Pl Tulsa OK 74104 Office Phone: 91863. Office Fax: 918-631-3126.*

BUTLER, (JAMES) CARON, professional basketball player; b. Racine, Wis., Mar. 13, 1980; s. Mattie Paden; m. Andrea Pink; children: Mia Caron, Camary, Caron Jr. Student in Comm., U. Conn., 2000—02. Forward Miami Heat, 2002—04, LA Lakers, 2004—05, Washington Wizards, 2005—. Spl. dep. Phila. Sheriff's Dept., 2006. Named one of Top Good Guys in Sports, Sporting News, 2006; named to New Eng. Sports Hall of Fame, 2003, All-Rookie 1st Team, NBA, 2003, Ea. Conf. All-Star Team, 2007. Mailing: Washington Wizards Verizon Ctr 601 F St NW Washington DC 20004*

BUTLER, CHARLES RANDOLPH, JR., federal judge; b. NYC, Mar. 28, 1940; BA, Washington and Lee U., 1962; LLB, U. Ala., 1966. Assoc. Hamilton Butler Riddick and LaTour, Mobile, Ala., 1966-69; asst. pub. defender Mobile County, 1969-70, dist. atty., 1971-75; ptnr. Butler and Sullivan, Mobile, 1975-84, Hamilton Butler Riddick Tarlton and Sullivan P.C., Mobile, 1984-88; dist. judge US Dist. Ct. (so. dist.) Ala., Mobile, 1988-94, 2003—, chief dist. judge, 1994—2003, sr. dist. judge, 2005—. Adj. prof. criminal justice program U. So. Ala., 1972-76; mem. jud. coun. 11th cir., 1994-2003, jud. conf. com. on criminal law, 1993-99, jud. conf. com., 1999-2002; past liaison mem. to long-range planning com. of the AO; past mem. program and adminstrn. subcom., planning for the future and automation subcom., probaton and pretrial umbrella group; mem. exec. com. Jud. Conf. of U.S., 1999-2002. Lst lt. USAR, 1962-64. Recipient Jud. award of merit Ala. State Bar, 2003; named One of Outstanding Young Men of Am., Mobile County Jaycees, 1971. Office: US Dist Ct 113 Saint Joseph St Mobile AL 36602-3683

BUTLER, DAPHNE, lawyer; b. Washington, Oct. 18, 1965; BA in Econs. with honors, Yale U., 1987, JD, 1991. Bar: Conn. 1991, NY 1992, DC 1993., Calif. 1996. Assco. Arnold & Porter, Wash., 1991—95, Morrison & Foerster, San Francisco, 1996—2002; sr. atty. Qwest Comm. Internat. Inc., Denver. Address: Qwest Comm Internat Inc 1801 California St 10th Fl Denver CO 80202 Office Phone: 303-992-1400. Office Fax: 303-992-1742.

BUTLER, DAVID, lawyer; b. St. Paul, June 11, 1930; s. Francis David and Alida (Bigelow) B.; m. Diana Dodge Duffy, Aug. 29, 1952 (div. 1957); children: Anne, Lawrence David; m. Barbara Williams Clark, July 12, 1958; children: Molly Elizabeth, Peter, Katherine BA, Princeton U., 1952; LLB, Harvard U., 1957. Bar. Colo. 1958, U.S. Dist. Ct. Colo. 1958. Assoc. Holland & Hart, Denver, 1957-63, ptnr., 1963-95, chmn. mgmt. com., 1990-95; of counsel, 1996—. Gen. counsel 1st Interstate Bank Denver, 1984-86; bd. dirs. UMB Bank Colo., Denver. Mem. bd. editors Harvard Law Rev., 1955-57. Chmn. lawyers adv. com. United Way, Denver, 1989—94; trustee Graland Country Day Sch., Denver, 1971—79, Legal Aid Found., Colo., 1991—97, chmn., 1993—97, Colo. Planning Group for Legal Svcs. to the Poor, 1995—2002; bd. dirs. Met. Denver Legal Aid Soc., 1971—74; trustee Colo. Lawyers Trust Account Found., 2000—05, pres., 2005; chmn. Colo. Access to Justice Commn., 2003—04, sec., 2005—; bd. dirs. Colo. Ctr. Law and Policy. 1st lt. US Army, 1952—54. Mem. ABA, Colo. Bar Assn. (chmn. tax sect. 1970, Jacob V. Schaetzel pro bono award 2002), Denver Bar Assn. Office: Holland & Hart 555 17th St Ste 2900 Denver CO 80202-3979

BUTLER, DAVID J., newspaper editor; b. Taylorville, Ill., June 19, 1950; s. Donald and Jeanie B.; m. Kathryn Lee, Nov. 2, 1991. BS in Journalism and Photography, Southern Ill. U., 1972. Metro editor, reporter The Southern Illinoisan, Carbondale, Ill., 1972-78; asst. city editor The Sun-Sentinel, Fort Lauderdale, Fla., 1978; mng. editor The Messenger-Inquirer, Owensboro, Ky., 1978-81, Jacksonville (Fla.) Jour., 1981-83; asst. mng. editor Rocky Mountain News, Denver, 1983-88; editor New Haven

Register, New Haven, 1988-96, LA Daily News, 1997—2005; and v.p. LA Newspaper Group; editor, pub. Detroit News, 2005—. Office: Detroit News 615 W Lafayette Blvd Detroit MI 48226 Office Phone: 313-222-2247.

BUTLER, DAVID T., III, communications systems company executive; Grad., Villanova U., Pa. Various fin. positions Loral Corp.; contr. Fairchild Systems Lockheed Martin; dir. planning and strategic devel. L-3 Comm. Holdings, Inc., v.p. mergers, acquisitions and corp. strategy, 2000, sr. v.p. bus. ops. Office: L-3 Comm Holdings Inc 600 Third Ave New York NY 10016 Office Phone: 212-697-1111. Office Fax: 212-805-5477.*

BUTLER, DEBRA YVONNE, special education educator, small business owner; b. Mobile, Ala., June 25, 1961; d. Percy and Lucille Tensley Butler; children: Jerrod Ferrilando Lindsey, Jerrico Dewon Lindsey. AA, S.D-.Bishop State C.C., Mobile, Ala., 1989; BA, Mobile Coll., 1991; MEd, Ala. State U., Montgomery, 1997. Cert. Class A MA Special Edn. (047) grades p-12 Ala., 1977. Mental health technologist Albert P. Brewer Devel. Ctr., Mobile, 1980—84; med. sec. supr. Franklin Meml. Primary Health Ctr., Mobile/Prichard, 1984—88; news reporter intern Wala Action News-10, Mobile, 1988—90; news reporter/pub. affairs dir. WQLS Radio 101.3, Dothan, Ala., 1991—92; news reporter WDHN-TV-18, Dothan, 1991—93; alternative sch. tchr. Dothan City Sch., Ala., 1991—96; spl. educator Vivian B Adams Sch., Ozark, Ala., 1994—95; spl. educator/soccer coach Mobile County Sch., 1996—2000; spl. educator Columbus Edn. Orgn., Maui, Hawaii, 2000—04, Hawaii Dept. Edn., Wai'Anae, 2004—, Nanakuli High and Intermediate Sch. Music entrepreneur Raw Talent Dx, Bklyn., 2004—; exec. protection specialist Maui Arts And Cultural Ctr., Kahului, Hawaii, 2000—04; talk show host Akaku - Maui Cmty. Tv Inc., Kahului, Hawaii, 2000—04; motivational spkr. Les Brown Inc., Potomac, Md., 1998—2003. Prodr.: (photography) Infinite Illusions (Internat. Libr. of Photography award, 2003), Visions Of The Soul; dir.: (video) Young People Our Hope Is In You (Black History award, 2000); contbr. articles pub. to profl. jour. Pres. READ(Reading Educates All Diversity) Found. INC., Honolulu, 2000; acting v.p. Oprah 'S Book Club, Maui, Hawaii, 2004; del. Ala. Edn. Assn., Mobile, Ala., 1996—2000; boxing coach Ewa Beach Boxing Club; ea. star Order Of Ea. Star, Prichard/Dothan, Ala., 1977; bd. mem. Epileptic Found. Of Maui, Maui, Hawaii, 2000. Recipient Everyday Heroes Award, Pukalani Cmty. - Maui, Hi., 2003, Excellence In Services To Hawaii's Children With Disabilities, Columbus Edn. Orgn., 2000—04, Kingdom Of Hawaii Sovereign Nation Of God, King Akahi Nui And Cabinet, 2003—05, Wall Of Tolerance, Rosa Parks, 2000—02, Championship Award For Excellence In News Reporting, FAA, 1991; scholar Tchr. Edn., Dewitt Wallace - Reader's Digest Ctr., 1993—95, Ala. Assn. Of Women's Club, Inc. And Youth Affiliates, 1995—96. Mem.: Hawaii Assn. Of Sch. Psychology (assoc.), Nat. Assn. Of Sch. Psychology (assoc.), NEA (life; edn. policy and profl. practice commn. 1998—2003). Achievements include patents for Hair And Scalp Conditioner; invention of Breast Protection Shells For Female Boxers. Avocations: yoga, boxing, Tae Kwon Do, singing, dance. Home Phone: 808-685-1290; Office Phone: 808-685-3461. Office Fax: 808-697-7017; Home Fax: 808-685-1290. Business E-Mail: debrabutler1@aim.com.

BUTLER, DENISE ELIZABETH, primary school educator; b. Everett, Wash., July 12, 1957; d. Donald Frances Somes and Wilma Jean Collazo; m. Douglas Eugene Butler, Sept. 8, 1978; children: Brent Michael, Brianne Meredith. BEd, Western Wash. U., Bellingham, 1980; MEd, Antioch U., Seattle, 2002. Kindergarten tchr. Everett Sch. Dist. 2, 1st grade tchr. Mem. site coun. Cedar Wood Elem. Sch., Bothell, Wash., math. tchr. leader. Leader Boy Scouts Am., Mukilteo, 1989—92, Girl Scouts Am., Mukilteo, Wash., 1992—2004, mem. pub. rels. com.; chmn. assemblies, programs PTA, Bothell; summer counselor Camp Silverton, Monte Cristo, Wash.; sec. Cedar Wood Elem. Sch. PTA, Bothell; Sunday sch. tchr., mem. bell choir Ctrl. Luth. Ch., Everett. Recipient Golden Acorn award, PTA, Bothell, Outstanding Girl Scout Leader award, Girl Scouts Am.; grantee, Everett Found., 2000, 2002. Mem.: Delta Kappa Gamma (pres. Alpha Phi chpt. 1992—94, 2004—06, v.p., sec., programs chmn., state convention hostess). Democrat. Avocations: travel, reading, boating, fishing, baking.

BUTLER, DONALD PHILIP, electrical engineer, educator; s. Clifton Aubrey and Helen Eunice (Roy) B.; m. Zeynep Celik, Aug. 23, 1986; children: Melissa, Susan. BA in Sci., U. Toronto, 1980; MS, U. Rochester, 1981, PhD, 1986. Fellow U. Rochester, N.Y., 1980-83, rsch. asst. N.Y., 1983-85, rsch. assoc. N.Y., 1985-86; asst. prof. elec. engring. So. Meth. U., Dallas, 1987-93, assoc. prof., 1993—. Contbr. articles to Applied Physics Letters, Jour. Applied Physics, others. Mem. IEEE (sec.-treas. Dallas chpt. electron device soc. 1984—), Am. Phys. Soc. Achievements include investigation of nonequilibrium properties of superconductors, observing dynamic intermediate state, transient magnetic superheating and phase-slip, microbridge mixers, uncooled infrared detectors; patents.

BUTLER, DONNA MARCIA, retired mathematics educator; d. Donald Marshall and Delores Gladine Butler. BS in Math., So. Ill. U., Edwardsville, 1974. Cert. tchr. Ill. Math. tchr. Cahokia Sch. Dist., Ill., 1974—2007; ret., 2007. Trustee Cahokia Pub. Libr. Dist., 1996—2005. Mem.: Math. Assn. Am. Lutheran. Avocations: genealogy, crafts. Personal E-mail: butler.zon@gmail.com.

BUTLER, DOUGLAS JOHN, physician; b. Greensboro, NC, Nov. 23, 1954; s. John C. and Jeannette Douglas. BA magna cum laude, Miami Univ., 1975; MD, Ohio State, 1978. Diplomate Am. Bd. Family Practice. Family medicine resident Moses Cone Hosp., Greensboro, 1978-81; attending physician, pvt. practice Ashe Meml. Hosp., Jefferson, NC, 1981-93, chief staff, 1982—83; emergency dept. physician Lake Norman Reg. Medical Ctr., Mooresville, NC, 1993; emergency dept. medical dir. Alexander Cmty. Hosp., Taylorsville, NC, 1993-2000, chief staff, 1999; locum tenens physician Indian Health Svc., 2000—; attending physician Old Fort Med. Clinic/McDowell Hosp., Marion, NC, 2001—02. Author: Ashe County Discovering the Lost Province, 1993, A Walk Atop America-50 State Summits and a Dream to Reach Them All, 2007; contbr. articles to profl. jours. Chmn. Ashe County EMS Coun., Jefferson, 1986—91. Mem.: Am. Heart Assn. (pres. Ashe County chpt. 1986—91), Jefferson Rotary. Avocations: photography, mountain climbing, travel.

BUTLER, FREDERICK GEORGE, retired drug company executive; b. Greenwich, Conn., Mar. 25, 1919; s. Harold Nassau and Rosa (Rhinhart) Butler; m. Sarah Lou Allred Butler, Sept. 23, 1945 (dec.); children: Pamela Sue, Frederick Houston(dec.). AB, Middlebury Coll., Vt., 1941; MBA, Columbia U., 1947. CPA, N.Y. With Price Waterhouse & Co., 1941—42, 1947—49, McKesson & Robbins, Inc., NYC, 1949—63, asst. comptr., 1952—61, comptr., 1961—63; contr. Bristol-Myers Co., NYC, 1963—66, v.p., contr., 1966—69, v.p. ops., 1970—76; ret., 1976. Pioneered development of bar code (compatible universal product code and nat. drug code) for supermarket automated checkout scanning and inventory control. Village mayor, Briarcliff Manor, N.Y., 1969-71. Served to comdr. USNR, 1942-46, 51-52. Mem. Fin. Execs. Inst., Pres.'s Club, Hillsdale (Mich.) Coll., Chi Psi. Methodist. Home: 6825 Davis Blvd Apt 252 Naples FL 34104-5325 Personal E-mail: fbutler@swfla.rr.com.

BUTLER, GARY C., computer company executive; BS, Ga. Tech. Univ., 1968; MBA, Univ. Ga., 1970. With Automatic Data Processing, Inc., Roseland, NJ, 1975—, corp. v.p., 1983—89, group pres. dealer svc., 1989—95, group pres. employer svc., 1995—98, bd. dir., 1995—, pres., COO, 1998—2006, pres., CEO, 2006—. Bd. dir. CIT Group Inc., Liberty Mutual Ins. Office: Automatic Data Processing Inc 1 ADP Blvd Roseland NJ 07068-1728*

BUTLER, GAYLE, editor-in-chief; m. Scott Butler; children: Sarah, Ellen. BA, Univ. Richmond. With Potomac Elec. Power Co.; joined Meredith Corp., 1983, assoc. editor, Better Homes & Gardens Mag. to sr.home editor, Better Homes & Gardens Books, various positions Spl. Interest Pubs., editl. dir., Spl. Interest Pubs., 2004—06, editor-in-chief, Better Homes & Gardens Mag., 2006—. Bd. dir. Des Moines Libr. Found. Recipient Disting. Svc. award, Univ. Richmond Alumni Assn., 2005. Mem.: Phi Beta Kappa. Office: Better Homes & Gardens Meredith Corp 1716 Locust St Des Moines IA 50309 Office Phone: 515-284-3000.*

BUTLER, GEEZER (TERENCE MICHAEL JOSEPH BUTLER), musician; b. Birmingham, England, July 17, 1949; m. Gloria Butler. Co-founder, bassist Black Sabbath, 1969—84, 1987—94, 1997—; founder Geezer Butler Band, 1984—87, G/Z/R, 1995—. Musician: (albums) Plastic Planet, 1995, Black Science, 1997, Ohmwork, 2005; musician: (with Black Sabbath) Black Sabbath, 1970, Paranoid, 1970, Master of Reality, 1971, Volume 4, 1972, Sabbath Bloody Sabbath, 1973, Sabotage, 1975, We Sold Our Soul for Rock & Roll, 1975, Technical Ecstasy, 1976, Never Say Die!, 1978, Heaven & Hell, 1980, Mob Rules, 1981, Live Evil, 1982, Born Again, 1983, Dehumanizer, 1992, Cross Purposes, 1994, The Sabbath Stones, 1996, Reunion, 1998, Past Lives, 2002; musician: (with Ozzy Osbourne) Just Say Ozzy, 1990, Ozzmosis, 1995. Named to Rock and Roll Hall of Fame, 2006. Office: Sanctuary Records Group Ltd Sanctuary House 45-53 Sinclair Rd London W14 0NS England E-mail: gzrmusic@gmail.com.

BUTLER, GLORIA SINGLETON, state legislator; children: Felicia, Leslie. AS in Bus. Adminstrn., Perimeter Coll. Fiscal acctg. asst. Health Scis. Ctr., Emory U., Atlanta; mem. Ga. State Senate, Atlanta, 1999—, sec. pub. safety com., mem. edn., retirement and transp. coms. Leg. asst. to U.S. Congresswoman Cynthia McKinney, Washington, 1992; mem. USIA Speaker program, South Africa, Zimbabwe, Swaziland, 1994; asst. to dir. AmeriCorps Team for Nat. Svc., 1996 Olympics and paralympics; dir. operation Big Vote, Coalition for Black Voter participation, 4th Congrl. Dist., DeKalb County, 1996; pub. rels. dir. Martin Luther King Jr. March com., 1997; mem. exec. staff, staff of intergovtl. rels. Office DeKalb County Sheriff. Mem. NOW, NAACP (exec. bd. DeKalb County chpt.), Nat. Coun. Negro Women, DeKalb Women's Polit. Caucus, Nat. Women's Polit. Caucus. Democrat. Office: Ste 420D State Capitol Atlanta GA 30334-9003

BUTLER, GREGORY B., lawyer, utilities executive; b. Cazenovia, NY; m. Nancy Butler; children: Liza, Sarah. BA in Hist., SUNY, Stony Brook, 1980; JD, Union U., 1988. Bar: NY, US Ct. Appeals (9th cir.). Assoc. counsel NY State Assembly, 1988—90; sr. atty. adv. legal policy US Dept. Justice, 1990—92; sr. counsel Niagara Mohawk Power Corp., 1992—95; v.p. fed. affairs New Eng. Elec. Sys., 1995—96, v.p. govtl. affairs, 1997—2001; v.p., gen. counsel, sec. N.E. Utilities, Hartford, Conn., 2001—03, sr. v.p., gen. counsel, 2003—. Bd. adv. Govt. Law Ctr. Albany Law Sch.; bd. parole State of Conn., 1998—2004. Bd. dirs. N.E. Utilities Found., New Eng. Legal Found., 2004—. Mem.: Energy Bar Assn. Office: Northeast Utilities PO Box 270 Hartford CT 06141-0270 Office Phone: 860-665-5000. Office Fax: 860-665-5400. E-mail: butlegb@nu.com.*

BUTLER, JACK FAIRCHILD, electric power industry executive; b. El Centro, Calif., July 18, 1933; s. Jack Orval and Dorothy (Marsh) B.; m. Colette Alice Guerard, Sept. 6, 1959; children— Alice, Jack, Michael, Patricia. Student, San Jose State Coll., 1951-54; BS, U. Calif., Berkeley, 1959, MS, 1960, PhD, 1962. Research staff mem. Mass. Inst. Tech., Lincoln Lab., Lexington, Mass., 1962-68; staff scientist Gen. Dynamics Corp., Pomona, Calif., 1968-71; sr. staff mem. Arthur D. Little, Inc., Cambridge, Mass., 1971-74; co-founder, co-owner, dir., pres. Laser Analytics, Inc., Lexington, 1974-81; founder, owner, dir., pres. Butler Research and Engring., Inc., 1981-85; co-founder, co-owner, dir., pres. San Diego Semicondrs., Inc., 1985-91, Aurora Techs. Corp., 1991-95; co-founder, co-owner, pres. Digirad (formerly Aurora Techs. Corp.), 1995-98; ret., 1998. Contbr. articles to sci. jours. Served with USMC, 1954-57. Mem. IEEE (life), AAAS, Am. Inst. Physics (life), Gen. Soc. Mayflower Descs. (life).

BUTLER, JAMES NEWTON, retired chemist, educator; b. Cleve., Mar. 27, 1934; s. Clyde Henry and Margaret (Manor) B.; m. Nancy Elizabeth Close, Aug. 31, 1957 (div.); 1 son, Christopher J.; m. Rosamond Hatch Bee, Dec. 10, 1966; stepchildren: Alden G. Bee, Kenneth M. Bee. BS, Rensselaer Poly. Inst., 1955; PhD, Harvard U., 1959. Staff scientist NACA Lewis Lab., Cleve., summers 1952-57, MIT Lincoln Lab., summer 1958; instr. U. B.C., Vancouver, 1959-61, asst. prof., 1961-63; sr. scientist Tyco Labs., Inc., Waltham, Mass., 1963-66, dept. head, 1966-71; from lectr. to prof. emeritus Harvard U., Cambridge, Mass., 1970—2000, prof. emeritus, 2000—; cons. Tyco Labs., Inc., Waltham, Mass., 1962-63, 71-73. Mem. steering com. co-author report Petroleum in the Marine Environment, Nat. Acad. Scis.— NRC, 1973-75, 80-82; mem. tech. panel, report drafting com. Com. on Environ. Decision-Making, 1975-77; chmn. com. on effectiveness of oil spill dispersants, NRC, 1985-89; cons. EPA, 1978— , NOAA, 1981—. Author: Ionic Equilibrium, 1964, rev. edit., 1998, Solubility and pH Calculations, 1964, The Calculus of Chemistry, 1965, Problems for Introductory University Chemistry, 1967, Pelagic Tar from Bermuda and the Sargasso Sea, 1973, Carbon Dioxide Equilibria and Their Applications, 1982, 2d edit., 1991, Studies of Sargassum and the Sargassum Community, 1983, Using Oil Spill Dispersants on the Sea, 1989, The Exxon Valdez Oil Spill: Fate and Effects in Alaskan Waters, 1995; contbr. articles to profl. jours. Trustee Bermuda Biol. Sta., 1972-97, v.p., 1985-86, 89-93, pres., 1986-89, life trustee, 1997—. NSF Faculty Sci. fellow, 1977; Alumni scholar Relsselaer Poly. Inst., 1955, NSF fellow, GE fellow Harvard U., 1955-59. Mem. Am. Chem. Soc., AAAS, Am. Soc. Limnology and Oceanography, Internat. Soc. Electrochemistry, Electrochem. Soc. N.Y. (chmn. Boston sect.), Gordon Research Conf. on Electrochemistry (chmn.), Assn. Harvard Chemists (pres.), Sigma Xi, Phi Lambda Upsilon. Personal E-mail: jim-butler@att.net, butler@seas.harvard.edu.

BUTLER, JANET C., shop owner; b. Wilmington, Del., Dec. 20, 1935; d. Harold J. and Helen Stiwalt Butler; m. Peter J. Cooke, Sept. 15, 1974. Student, U. Del., Newark, 1973—74. Clk. Atlas Powder Co., Wilmington, 1953—56; flying squad Saks Fifth Ave., NYC, 1956—57; office asst. Conn. Gen. Life Ins. Co, Wilmington, 1957—81; owner Butler and Cooke Antiques, Odessa, Del., 1983—. Trustee Corbit Calloway Meml. Libr., Odessa, 1985—2007; commr. Odessa Hist. Commn., 1995—2005, Odessa Planning Commn., 2002—05. Mem.: Del. Doll and Toy Collectors Club (assoc.; sec. 2000—07). Avocations: collecting dolls, antiques and others, restoring pre-revolutionary house. Office: Butler and Cooke Antiques PO Box 58 Odessa DE 19730 Home Phone: 302-378-7033; Office Phone: 302-378-7022. Business E-Mail: butlercooke@delaware.net.

BUTLER, JOHN D., multi-industry company executive; BS in Econs., Mich. State U., East Lansing, MS in Labor and Indsl. Rels.; cert. in Advanced Pers. and Labor, Cornell U., Ithaca, NY; grad. Advanced Gen. Mgmt. Program, Harvard U. Cert. Textron Six Sigma Green Belt 2006. Positions in mfg. ops., labor rels., employee benefits and human resource mgmt. GM, 1969—97, v.p. pers. Internat. Ops. Zurich, Switzerland; exec. v.p. adminstrn., chief human resources officer Textron, Inc., Providence, 1997—. Mem. supervisory bd. Adam Opel A.G.; dir. Human Resources Policy Assn. Fellow: Nat. Acad. Human Resources (trustee). Office: Textron Inc 40 Westminster St Providence RI 02903-2596*

BUTLER, JOHN EDWARD, lawyer; b. Teaneck N.J., Dec. 8, 1946; s. John Edward and Alice Mary (Knorr) B.;children: Jennifer, Kathryn, John Michael; m. Elizabeth M. Fair, Mar. 12, 1994. Home: 120 E Washington St Ste 825 Syracuse NY 13202-4014

BUTLER, JOHN MUSGRAVE, financial consultant; b. Bklyn., Dec. 6, 1928; s. John Joseph and Sabina Catherine (Musgrave) Butler; m. Ann Elizabeth Kelly, July 9, 1955; children: Maureen, John, Ellen, Suzanne. BA cum laude, St. John's U., 1950; MBA, NYU, 1951. CPA N.Y., Ill. Sr. acct. Lybrand, Ross Bros. & Montgomery (CPAs), NYC, 1953-59; sr. auditor ITT Corp., NYC, 1959-62; asst. to contr. Dictaphone Corp., Bridgeport, Conn., 1962-63, contr. Bridgeport, Rye, NY, 1964—68; v.p. acctg. Chgo. & North Western Ry. Co., 1968-69, v.p. fin. and acctg., 1969-72, Chgo. and North Western Transp. Co., 1972-79, sr. v.p. fin. and acctg., 1979-89, dir., 1976-89, trustee, 1978-82, acting sr. v.p. fin. and acctg., 1994; sr. v.p. fin. and acctg., dir. CNW Corp., 1985-89; cons. in fin. and acctg. for bus., 1989—2005; instr. fin. DePaul U., Chgo., 1989—2001. Dir. Cath. Med. Mission Bd., NYC, 1998—2000. With USCGR, 1951—53. Roman Catholic.

BUTLER, J(OHN) S(COTT), economist, educator; b. Waco, Tex., Mar. 28, 1950; s. Roy Francis and Barbara Goehring (Scott) B. BA, Rice U., 1973; MA, Cornell U., 1980, PhD, 1982. Teaching asst. U. Houston, 1975-76; teaching asst., fellow Cornell U., Ithaca, N.Y., 1976-79, prof. policy analysis and mgmt., 1999-2003; rsch. assoc. Mathematica Policy Rsch., Princeton, N.J., 1979-82, rsch. economist, 1982; asst. prof. econs. Vanderbilt U., Nashville, 1986-88, assoc. prof. econ., 1988-96, prof. econs., 1996-99; prof. Cornell U., 1999-2003, U. Ky., 2003—; industry economist Commodity Futures Trading Commn., 1991. Contbr. articles to profl. jours.; Grantee Inst. for Research Poverty, 1983, 85, Dept Health and Human Services, 1983, Inst. Research Poverty, 1986-87, soc. sec. adminstr., 1988-91. Mem. Am. Econ. Assn., Econometric Soc., Am. Statis. Assn. Office Phone: 859-257-1432.

BUTLER, JOHN WILLIAM, JR., lawyer; b. Detroit, Feb. 18, 1956; s. John William Sr. and Lucille Elmira (Miller) B. AB magna cum laude, Princeton U., 1977; JD, U. Mich., 1980. Bar: Mich. 1980, US Dist. Ct. (ea. and we. dists. Mich.) 1981, US Ct. Appeals (6th cir.), Ill. 1992. Assoc. Honigman, Miller, Schwartz & Cohn, Detroit, 1980-81; ptnr. Butzel Keidan, Simon, Myers & Graham, Detroit, 1981-90; ptnr., co-leader corp. restructuring Skadden, Arps, Slate, Meagher & Flom, LLP, Chgo., 1990—. Chmn. bd. govs. Comml. Fin. Assn. Edn. Found.; co-chmn. INSOL 2005 World Congress; dir. Am. Bd. Certification, 1993—2003; group of Thirty-Six INSOL Internat., 1995—; chmn. Am. Bd. Certification, 1997. Contbr. chapters to books. Bd. govs. Hugh O'Brian Youth Leadership, 1998—; mem. exec. adv. coun. Children Affected by AIDS, 2003—; co-chair Renaissance American/BeardGroup Corp. Reorganizations Conf., 1999—, Healthcare Transactions Conf., 2000—. Named leader in the corp. restructuring and insolvency field, Chamber's Global, Chambers USA; named one of Top Dozen Restructuring Lawyers in Am., Turnarounds & Workouts, Top Ten Worldwide Restructuring Lawyers, Global Counsel, 2002, "Dealmakers of Yr.", The Am. Lawyer, 2004; named to Client Svc. All Star Team, BTI Consulting Group, 2004; recipient Chmn.'s award, Turnaround Mgmt. Assn., 2001. Fellow Am. Coll. Bankruptcy, 1997, Internat. Solvency Inst., 2002; mem. ABA, Am. Bankruptcy Inst.(dir. 1992-98), Comml. Law League Am., Fed. Bar Assn., Mich. Bar Assn., Oakland County Bar Assn., Detroit Bar Assn., Turnaround Mgmt. Assn. (dir. 1991-99 & 2001-, chmn. 1996-97, chmn. award 2001, chmn. anniversary convs., 10th (1998) and 15th (2003)); assoc. gen. counsel, Comml. Fin. Assn., 1998-2002. Republican. Presbyterian. Avocation: officiate HS and Coll. football teams. Office: Skadden Arps Slate Meagher & Flom 333 W Wacker Dr Chicago IL 60606 Office Phone: 312-407-0730. Office Fax: 312-407-8501. E-mail: jbutler@skadden.com.*

BUTLER, JON TERRY, computer engineering educator, researcher; b. Balt., Dec. 26, 1943; s. Herbert Harriss and Vera Esse (Buck) B.; m. Susan Beth Wood, Feb. 24, 1968 (div. Aug. 1996); 1 child, Anne Elizabeth; m. Fujiko Sakaguchi, Jan. 31, 1998. BEE, Rensselaer Poly. Inst., 1966, M in Engring., 1967; PhD, Ohio State U., 1973. Registered profl. engr., Ohio. NRC postdoctoral assoc. Air Force Avionics Lab., Wright-Patterson AFB, Ohio, 1973-74; sr. postdoctoral assoc. Naval Postgrad. Sch., Wright-Patterson AFB, Ohio, 1980-81; assoc. prof. Northwestern U., Evanston, Ill., 1974-87; prof. Naval Postgrad. Sch., Monterey, Calif., 1987—, Navalex Chair prof., 1985-87. Editor: Multi-Valued Logic in VLSI, 1991; contbr. articles to profl. jours. Capt. USAF, 1967—70. Recipient Faculty Performance award Naval Postgrad. Sch., 1990-93. Fellow IEEE; mem. IEEE Computer Soc. (chmn. multiple-valued logic com. 1980-81, Disting. vis. 1982-86, press editor 1986-90, editor-in-chief Computer mag. 1991-92, editor-in-chief Computer Soc. Press 1993-97, chmn. Computer Soc. fellows evaluation com. 1999, chmn. Computer Soc. transactions ops. com. 1998-99, chmn. Computer Soc. Press ops. com. 2000—, Meritorious Svc. award 1988, 92, TAB Pioneer award 1989, cert. appreciation 1982, 89, 91, 95, 96, 99, 2000, Disting. Svc. award 1995, Third Centennial medal 2000, bd. govs. 1991-97). Presbyterian. Office: Naval Postgrad Sch Dept Elec Computer Engring Code EC-BU Monterey CA 93943-5121 E-mail: Jon_Butler2@redshift.com.

BUTLER, JONATHAN PUTNAM, architect; b. Portchester, NY, June 6, 1940; s. Jonathan Fairchild and Mary Elizabeth (Putnam) Butler; m. Deborah Day Rogers, Mar. 18, 1967; children: Jonathan Rogers, Pauline Washburn, Benjamin Putnam, Cynthia Day. BA, Princeton U., 1962, MFA, 1965; MArch, Columbia U., 1966. Designer, programmer, planner Skidmore, Owings & Merrill, Architects, NYC, 1968—71; ptnr. Rogers, Butler, Burgun & Shahine, NYC, 1971—79; pres. Butler, Rogers & Baskett, NYC, 1979—2003; pvt. practice Jonathan P. Butler AIA LLC, Niantic, Conn., 2003—. Bd. dirs. Woodlawn Cemetary, Bronx, N.Y. Mem AIA, Nat. Coun. Archl. Registration Bds. (cert.), Union Club. Home: 14 West Ln Niantic CT 06357-3716 Office: Jonathan P Butler AIA LLC 14 West Ln Niantic CT 06357 Office Phone: 860-739-9180. Business E-Mail: jonb@butlerarch.com.

BUTLER, KERRY, actress; Actor: (Broadway plays) Les Miserables, 1987—2003, Blood Brothers, 1993—95, Beauty and the Beast, 1994—95, Hairspray, 2002—03, Little Shop of Horrors, 2003— (nominated best actress Outer Critics Cir.), Xanadu, 2007, (regional stage shows) Prodigal, Le Passe Muraille, Bat Boy The Musical, The "I" Word, The Folsom Head, Bright Lights, Big City, Oklahoma, The Man in the White Suit, 2005, The Opposite of Sex, 2006, The Miracle Brothers. Office: Abrams Artists Agy 26th Fl 275 Seventh Ave New York NY 10001 Office Phone: 646-486-4600. Office Fax: 646-486-0100.*

BUTLER, KEVIN M., electronics executive; B in Psychology, U. Notre Dame, 1977, M in Psychology, 1979. Various pos., including prodn. supr., plant pers. mgr., sr. adminstr. classified employee compensation, mgr. exec. compensation GM Chevrolet Motor Divsn., 1976—89; dir. human resources GM Hydramatic divsn., Ypsilanti, Mich., 1989—91; dir. GM Health Care Plans, 1991—95; gen. dir. GM Health Care initiative staff, 1995—97; gen. dir. human resources Delphi Corp., Troy, Mich., 1997—2000, v.p. human resource mgmt., 2000—, mem. strategy bd., exec. champion pers. team. Exec. com. Midwest Bus. Group on Health. Adv. bd.

Ind. U., Kokomo, Xavier U. Health Adminstrn.; bd. dirs. Am. Soc. Employers. Office: World Hdqrs Delphi Corp 5725 Delphi Dr Troy MI 48098-2815 Office Phone: 248-813-2000. Office Fax: 248-813-2670.

BUTLER, LESLIE ANN, artist, writer, editor; b. Salem, Oreg., Nov. 19, 1945; d. Marlow Dole and Lala Ann (Erlandson) Butler. Student, Lewis and Clark Coll., 1963-64; BS, U. Oreg., 1969; postgrad., Portland State U., 1972-73, Lewis and Clark Coll., 1991. Creative trainee Ketchum Advt., San Francisco, 1970-71; asst. advt. dir. Mktg. Systems, Inc., Portland, Oreg., 1971-74; prodn. mgr., art dir., copywriter Finzer-Smith, Portland, 1974-76; copywriter Gerber Advt., Portland, 1976-78; freelance copywriter Portland, 1983-84, 83-85; copywriter McCann-Erickson, Portland, 1980-81; copy chief Brookstone Co., Peterborough, NH, 1981-83; creative dir. Whitman Advt., Portland, 1984-87; prin. L.A. Advt., 1987—; portrait artist. Author: The Dream Road and Other Tales From Hidden Hills, 1997; editor (arts and antiques): Living mag.; designer of fence featured in Better Homes & Gardens, 2000; one-woman shows include Ocean Lodge, Cannon Beach Oreg., 2004, Fifth Ave. Stes., Porland, 2004, Lawrence Gallery, Portland, 2004, City Hall, 2005, Fifth Avenue Suites, 2006, exhibitions include Sikta Art Invitational, Portland, 2003, 2004, Rhodes Stingfellow Gallery, Cannon Beach, Oreg., 2004—06, Brodrick Gallery, Portland, 2004, Goitlieb Gallery, Portland, Oreg., 2005—, Associated Arts Regional Juried Fine Arts Show, Ocean Shores, Wash., 2005, Coos Art Mus., Richland, Wash., 2005, Oregon Art Beat, 2006, exhibitions include many others, exhibited in group shows at Grants Pass Mus. Art, 2006, Represented in permanent collections George and Barbara Bush, Houston, Rue McClanahan, Bevelry Hills, Michael Jackson, Hollywood, Gary Maffei and Marc Linter, Portland. Spokeswoman Nat. Alopecia Areata Found., San Rafeal, Calif., 2004; Co-founder, v.p., newsletter editor Animal Rescue and Care Fund, 1972—81; mem. Friends of the Performing Arts Ctr., Portland Art Mus., Oreg. Humane Soc.; pres. OMSI; bd. dirs. Portland Opera Assn., 2000—02, Oreg. Humane Soc., 2002—. Recipient Internat. Film and TV Festival N.Y. Finalist award, 1985, 86, 87, 88, Internat. Radio Festival of N.Y. award, 1984, 85, 88, Hollywood Radio and TV Soc. Internat. Broadcasting award, 1981, TV Comml. Festival Silver Telly award, 1985, TV Comml. Festival Bronze Telly, 1986, AVC Silver Cindy, 1986, Los Angeles Advt. Women LULU, 1986, 87, 88, 89 Ad Week What's New Portfolio, 1986, N.W. Addy award Seattle Advt. Fedn., 1984, Best in the West award, 1985, Portland Advt. Fedn. Rosey Finalist award, 1986, Nat. winner Silver Microphone award, 1987, 88, 89. Mem.: Portland Art Mus., Portland Inst, Contemporary Art, Nat. Oil and Acrylic Painters Soc., People for Ethical Treatment of Animals. E-mail: labartist@aol.com.

BUTLER, LOUIS BENNETT, JR., state supreme court justice, lawyer; b. Chgo., Feb. 15, 1952; s. Louis Bennett and Gwendolyn (Prescott) B.; m. Irene Marianne Hecht, Aug. 30, 1981; children: Jessica Marianne, Erika Nicole. BA, Lawrence U., 1973; JD, U. Wis., Madison, 1977. Bar: Ill. 1978, Wis. 1979, U.S. Dist. Ct. (no. dist.) Ill. 1978, U.S. Dist. Ct. (ea. dist.) Wis. 1979, U.S. Ct. Appeals (7th cir.) 1979, U.S. Supreme Ct. 1983. Teaching asst. legal writing U. Wis. Law Sch., Madison, 1974-76; patient rights adv. Bur. Mental Health, Madison, 1976; hearing examiner, 1976-77; legal intern Prisoner's Legal Assistance, Chgo., 1977-78; atty. Independence Bank, Chgo., 1978-79, appellate atty. Office State Pub. Defender, Milw., 1979-92, judge, Milw. Mcpl. Ct., 1992-2002, Milw. Cty. Circuit Ct., 2002-04; justice, Wis. Supreme Ct., 2004-; Active South Shore Community Orgn., Chgo., 1978; pres. adv. bd. Adaptive Behavior Ctr., Chgo. Reed Mental Health Ctr., 1978; mem. faculty Nat. Jud. Coll., Reno, Nev., 2001-04; adj. prof. Marquette U., 1991-92; bd. dirs. criminal law sect. State Bar Wis., individual rights and responsibilities sect. Mem. Wis. Bar Assn., Ill. State Bar Assn., Wis. Black Lawyer's Assn. (treas. 1984-85, bd. dirs. 1984—, pres. 1985-86), NAACP. Democrat. Roman Catholic. Office: Wisc Supreme Ct PO Box 1688 Madison WI 53701-1688 Home Phone: 414-963-9649; Office Phone: 608-266-1884. Business E-Mail: louis.butler@wiscourts.gov.*

BUTLER, MANLEY CALDWELL, retired lawyer; b. Roanoke, Va., June 2, 1925; s. W.W.S. Butler Jr.; m. June Nolde, June 26, 1950; children: Manley, Henry, James, Marshall. AB, U. Richmond, 1948; JD, U. Va., 1950; LLD (hon.), Washington & Lee U., 1978. Bar: Va. 1950. Mem. Va. Ho. Dels., 1962-72, minority leader; mem. 92d-97th Congresses from 6th Va. dist., Judiciary Com., Com. on Govt. Ops., Woods, Rogers & Hazlegrove, P.L.C., 1983—99; ret., 1999. Mem. Nat. Bankruptcy Rev. Commn., 1995-97. Fellow Am. Bar Found., Am. Coll. Bankruptcy, Va. Law Found.; mem. ABA, Va. Bar Assn., Va. State Bar Assn., Roanoke Bar Assn., Am. Bankruptcy Inst., Raven Soc., Order of Coif, Phi Beta Kappa, Tau Kappa Alpha, Omicron Delta Kappa, Pi Delta Epsilon, Phi Gamma Delta. Episcopalian. Home: 200 Glebe Blvd Unit 1024 Daleville VA 24083 Personal E-mail: nuniepapa@gleberes.net.

BUTLER, MARGARET KAMPSCHAEFER, retired computer scientist; b. Evansville, Ind., Mar. 7, 1924; d. Otto Louis and Lou Etta (Rehsteiner) Kampschaefer; m. James W. Butler, Sept. 30, 1951; 1 child, Jay. AB, Ind. U., 1944; postgrad., U.S. Dept. Agr. Grad. Sch., 1945, U. Chgo., 1949, U. Minn., 1950. Statistician U.S. Bur. Labor Statistics, Washington, 1945-46, U.S. Air Forces in Europe, Erlangen and Wiesbaden, Germany, 1946-48, U.S. Bur. Labor Statistics, St. Paul, 1949-51; mathematician Argonne (Ill.) Nat. Lab., 1948-49, 51-80, sr. computer scientist, 1980-92; dir. Argonne Code Ctr. and Nat. Energy Software Ctr. Dept. Energy Computer Program Exch., 1960-91; spl. term appointee Argonne Nat. Lab., 1993—2006. Cons. AMF Corp., 1956—57, OECD, 1964, Poole Bros., 1967. Author: Careers for Women in Nuclear Science and Technology, 1992; editor Computer Physics Communications, 1969-80; contbr. (chpt.) The Application of Digital Computers to Problems in Reactor Physics, 1968, Advances in Nuclear Sci. and Technology, 1976; contbr. articles to profl. jours. Treas. Timberlake Civic Assn., 1958; rep. mem. nomination com. Hinsdale Caucus, Ill., 1961-62; coord. 6th dist. ERA, 1973-80; elected del. Rep. Nat. Conv., 1980; bd. mgr. DuPage dist. YWCA Met. Chgo., 1987-90; computer and info. sys. adv. bd. Coll. DuPage, 1987-95; industry adv. bd. computer sci. dept. Bradley U., 1988-91; vice chair Ill. Women's Polit. Caucus, 1987-90; chair voters svc. LWV, Burr-Ridge-Willowbrook, 1991-93; vol. Morton Arboretum, 1996-2005, Friends of Indian Prairie Pub. Libr., 2000-02, LaGrange Park Friends Libr., 2002—; bd. dirs. Plymouth Place Residents Coun., 2003-05, recording sec., 2006—; treas. Plymouth Landing Gift Shoppe, 2004—, spl. fin. and program coms., 2005-06. Recipient cert. of leadership Met. YWCA, Chgo., 1985, Merit award Chgo. Assn. Technol. Socs., 1988; named to Fed. 100, 1991; named Outstanding Woman Leader of DuPage County Sci., Tech. and Health Care, 1992. Fellow Am. Nuclear Soc. (mem. publs. com. 1965-71, bd. dirs. 1976-79, exec. com. 1977-78, chmn. bylaws and rules com., 1979-82, profl. women in ANS com. 1991-93, reviewer for publs., spl. award math. and computer divsn. 1992); mem. Assn. Computing Machinery (exec. com., sec. Chgo. chpt. 1963-65, publs. chmn. nat. conf. 1968, reviewer for publs.), Assn. Women in Sci. (pres. Chgo. area chpt. 1982, nat. exec. bd. 1985-87), Nat. Computer Conf. (chmn. Pioneer Day com. 1985, tech. program chmn. 1987). Independent. Home: 107 Brewster Lane La Grange Park IL 60526-6003 *My goal is the removal of barriers restricting individuals from achieving their full potential and the furtherance of individual rights.*

BUTLER, MARIE GLADYS, nursing educator; b. Chester, Pa., June 12, 1951; d. Joseph Francis and Juanita Marie (Spear) B. Diploma, LPN, James Martin, 1983; AGS, C.C. of Phila., 1989; BSN, Thomas Jefferson U., 1991. LPN Care Pavillon of Walnut Park, Phila., 1983-84, Supior Care, Phila., 1984-85, Norrell, Jenkintown, Pa., 1986-87, Health Force, Jenkintown, 1987-91, Proto Call, Phila., 1990-91; staff nurse VA Med. Ctr., Phila., 1991-93; case mgr. Nursing Unlimited Homecare, 1993; RN staff nurse Brinton Manor Subacute Rehab., 1993-95, Nurse Power, 1993-97, Maxim Healthcare, 1995—; home care RN Absolute Nursing Care, Landsdown, Pa., 1995—96; PRN pool Taylor Hosp. Transitial Care Unit, 1995-96; RN Camp Sunshine, Thorton, Pa., 1995, 98; clin. nursing instr. James Martin Sch. of Practical Nursing, Phila., 1996; unit mgr. St. Ignatius Nursing Home, Phila., 1996-97; RN, unit mgr. CarePavilion, Phila., 1997; case mgr. Aspen Home Health Care, Phila., 1997—98; tele. svc. rep. TV Guide, Radnor, Pa., 1998—2001; CNA instr. Am. Trade Bus. Sch., Phila., 1999—2000; RN Ctrl. Health Svcs., Media, Pa., 2001—02, Pulmonary Care Inc., Havertown, Pa., 2002—03; instr. Harrison Career Inst., Phila., 2003—. Regional coord. Student Nurses Assn. Pa., Harrisburg, 1990-91; co-chair mentoring com. C.C. Phila. Alumni Assn., 1992; mem. mentor and shadowing program Thomas Jefferson U., Phila., 1992; RN Camp Sunshine, 1995. Mem. Ladies Aux. of VFW, Phi Theta Kappa (C.C. of Phila. chpt.), Sigma Theta Tau (membership com. Delta Rho chpt. 1992, 94, v.p. 1993-95, del. biannual conv. 1993, chmn. membership com. 1995—). Roman Catholic. Avocations: gardening, sewing, crocheting, walking, travel. Home: 5522 N Mascher St Philadelphia PA 19120-2918 Office: Harrison Career Inst 1619 Walnut St Philadelphia PA 19103 Home Phone: 267-243-5079; Office Phone: 215-640-0177 ext. 117. E-mail: prendienurse@netscape.net.

BUTLER, MARY K., prosecutor; b. 1956; AB, Vassar Coll.; JD, U. Wis. Bar: Fla. 1981. Atty. Hopkins and Sutter, Chgo.; asst. U.S. atty. (so. dist.) Fla. US Dept. Justice, Miami, 1987—99, chief corruption sect., 1997—98, atty. pub. integrity sect. Washington, 1999—. Spkr. in field. Office: US Dept Justice 950 Pennsylvania Ave NW Washington DC 20530

BUTLER, MERLIN GENE, physician, medical geneticist, educator; b. Atkinson, Nebr., Aug. 2, 1952; s. Garold Melvin and Berdena June (Sandall) B.; m. Ranae Ilene Kisker, Oct. 2, 1976; children: Michelle Ranae, Brian Gene. BA with very high distinction, Chadron State Coll., 1974, BS with very high distinction, 1975; MD, U. Nebr., Omaha, 1978; MS, U. Nebr., Lincoln, 1980; PhD, Ind. U., Indpls., 1984. Supervising physician Med. Info. Svcs., Omaha, 1978-80; rsch. assoc. dept. biology U. Notre Dame, South Bend, Ind., 1983-84; med. dir. North Ctrl. Ind. Regional Genetics Ctr., South Bend, 1983-84; dir. cytogenetics Meml. Hosp., South Bend, 1983-84; NIH postdoctoral fellow dept. med. genetics Sch. Medicine Ind. U., Indpls., 1980-83, adj. asst. prof. dept. med. genetics Sch. Medicine, 1984; asst. prof. dept. pediatrics Sch. Medicine Vanderbilt U., Nashville, 1984-90, dir. regional genetics program Sch. Medicine, 1984-98, dir. Cytogenetics Lab. dept. pediatrics Sch. Medicine, 1989-98, assoc. prof. dept. pediatrics, 1990-98, assoc. prof. dept. pathology, 1991-98, investigator John F. Kennedy Ctr. Rsch. on Edn. and Human Devel., Peabody Coll., 1987-98; assoc. dir. Inst. Behavior and Genetics; assoc. prof. dept. orthopedics Vanderbilt U., 1994-98. Adj. assoc. prof. dept. pediatrics Meharry Med. Coll., Nashville, 1988-98; genetics cons. Baptist Hosp., Nashville, 1985-98, Westside Hosp., Nashville, 1985-98, Nashville Gen. Hosp., 1985-98, chief, section of Med. Genetics and Molecular Medicine, Children's Mercy Hosp., Kansas City, Mo., 1998—, William R. Brown prof., chmn., 1998—, prof. dept. pediats., U. Mo.-Kansas City Sch. Medicine; mem. epidemiology genetic diseases subcom. Ind. State Bd. Health, 1983-84; faculty interviewer Vanderbilt U., 1987; peer reviewer Am. Jour. Human Genetics, Am. Jour. Med. Genetics, Clin. Genetics, Am. Jour. Diseases of Children, Dysmorphology and Clin. Genetics, Am. Jour. Mental Retardation, Jour. Pediatrics, So. Med. Jour., Human Mutations, Cancer Genetics and Cytogenetics, Pediatrics, Genomics, Prader-Willi Perspectives; mem. ad-hoc grant review com. NIH, 1990—, craniofacial assessment team Vanderbilt U., 1992-98; lectr., presenter in field. Author: Fragile X Syndrome: A Major Cause of X-Linked Mental Retardation, 1988, 1989; author: (with others) Genetics for the Medically Oriented, 1983, Novak's Textbook of Gynecology, 11th edit., 1988, Birth Defects Encyclopedia, 1990, Prader-Willi Syndrome and Other Chromosome 15q Deletion Disorders, 1992, Human Genetics: New Perspectives, 1994, 1992 International Fragile X Conference Proceedings, 1992, Prader-Willi and Angelman Syndromes Examples of Genetic Imprinting in Man, 1994, Prader-Willi Syndrome: A Guide for Parents and Physicians, 1995, Prader-Willi Syndrome: Clinical and Genetic Findings, 2000' editor: Genetics of Developmental Disabilities, 2005, Management of Prader-Willi Syndrome, 2005, Guide to America's Top Physicians, 2005; mem. editl. bd. Prader-Willi Perspectives, 1992—; contbr. numerous articles to profl. jours. including Nature and New England Jour. Medicine. Grant reviewer March of Dimes Birth Defects Found., 1985—. Recipient Disting. Svc. award Chadron State Coll., 1986, Teaching award Osler Inst., 1989; grantee Univ. Rsch. Coun., 1985, 92-93, Tenn. Dept. Mental Health and Mental Retardation, 1986-91, Clin. Nutrition Rsch. Unit, 1986-88, Joseph P. Kennedy, Jr. Found., 1988, Clin. Rsch. Ctr. Meharry Med. Coll., 1989-98, Dept. Pathology, 1992-93, Orthopedic Rsch. Edn. Found., 1993-95, NIH, 1995—; Cancer Rsch. grantee Ind. U. Med. Ctr., 1980, Biomed. Rsch. Support grantee, 1985, 88, 89—, Clin. Rsch. grantee March of Dimes Birth Defects Found., 1987, 88, 90-92, Lyle V. Andrews Meml. scholar, 1974. Fellow Am. Coll. Med. Genetics (founder, diplomate, lab. practice subcom. 1993); mem. AMA (Physician Recognition award 1984, 87, 00), AAAS, Am. Bd. Med. Genetics (cert. clin. genetics and clin. cytogenetics), Am. Genetics Assn., Am. Soc. Human Genetics (cytogenetics resource com. 1992-97), Am. Fedn. Clin. Rsch., Coll. Am. Pathologists (cytogenetics resource com. 1992-97, molecular pathology resource com. 1993-97), So. Med. Assn., Davidson County Pediatric Soc., Metro. Med. Soc., Prader-Willi Syndrome Assn. (med. rsch. task force 1985—, diagnostic task force 1991—, sci. adv. bd. 1991—, chair 2000—), N.Y. Acad. Scis., Sigma Xi, Phi Chi. Avocations: gardening, camping, fishing, collecting sports memorabilia. Home: 6410 Hillside St Shawnee KS 66218-9070 Office: Children's Mercy Hosp 2401 Gillham Rd Kansas City MO 64108-4698 E-mail: mgbutler@cmh.edu.

BUTLER, MICHAEL FRANCIS, lawyer; b. Pitts., Aug. 17, 1935; s. Frank J. and Mary M. (Montgomery) B. BA magna cum laude, Harvard U., 1957; LLB, Yale U., 1960. Bar: Pa., D.C. Mem. Kirkpatrick & Lockhart, Pitts., 1960-69; asst. gen. counsel for domestic and internat. bus., then dep. gen. counsel U.S. Dept. Commerce, Washington, 1969-73; v.p., gen. counsel Overseas Pvt. Investment Corp., Washington, 1973-75; gen. counsel Fed. Energy Adminstrn., Washington, 1975-77; ptnr. Andrews & Kurth, Washington, 1977-92. Bd. dirs., chmn. audit com. Three Rivers Bancorp, Inc., Three Rivers Bank & Trust Co.; mem. adv. com. Fagan & Co.; mem. panel of arbitrators Dispute Settlement Ctr., Internat. Energy Agy., Paris; past mem. or chmn. U.S. dels. to OECD coms., Berne Union, Adminstrv. Conf. of U.S. Contbr. articles to profl. publs. Past vice chmn. class spl. gifts com. Harvard Coll. and Yale Law Sch.; past bd. dirs., sec. Three Rivers Arts Festival, Pitts.; past bd. dirs. Bryce Harlow Found. Fellow Am. Bar Found. (life); mem. ABA (past chmn. com. on fgn. investment in U.S. internat. law sect.), Am. Arbitration Assn. (mem. comml. panel of arbitrators), Pa. Bar Assn., D.C. Bar Assn., Allegheny County Bar Assn., Am. Law Inst., Am. Judicature Soc., Am. Soc. Internat. Law, Internat. Bar Assn., Washington Fgn. Law Soc., Inter-Am. Bar Assn., Harvard Club West Pa. (past. sec.), Harvard Club of D.C. (past bd. dirs.), Met. Club, Rolling Rock Club (Ligonier, Pa.), Harvard-Yale-Princeton Club (Pitts.). Republican. Presbyterian. Home and Office: 2214 Massachusetts Ave NW Washington DC 20008-2812

BUTLER, ORTON CARMICHAEL, retired climatologist, educator; b. Millersburg, Ohio, June 9, 1923; s. Maxon Henry Butler and Atossa Ruth Carmichael; m. Betty Ellen Johnson, Sept. 15, 1951; children: Marilyn Jean, Kathryn Ellen. BA, Oberlin Coll., 1948; MA, Clark U., 1951; PhD, Ohio State U., 1969. Rsch. analyst, China specialist U.S. Army Engr. Strategic Intelligence, Washington, 1951-60; prof. Memphis State U. (now U. Memphis), 1960-81; prof. emeritus U. Memphis, 1981. Author: (book) An Introductory Soils Laboratory Handbook, 1979, other publs. Cpl. U.S. Army, 1942-46, PTO. Mem. Masons. Republican. United Ch. of Christ. Avocations: tree farming, gardening, golf.

BUTLER, PETER E., plastic surgeon; s. Norman P. and Ursula J. Butler; m. Annabel M Heseltine, July 25, 1963. MB, BAO, BCh, Royal Coll. Surgeons, Dublin, Ireland, 1987. Demonstrator in anatomy Royal Coll. Surgeons Ireland, Dublin, 1988—89; rsch. fellow Mass. Gen. Hosp. and Harvard Med. Sch., Boston, 1993—95; sr. registrar in plastic and reconstructive surgery London Regional Tng. Scheme, 1996—99; hon. sr. lectr. Royal Free and U. Coll. Med. Sch., London, 1999—; cons. plastic surgeon Royal Free Hosp., London, 1999—; cons. in plastic surgery Mass. Gen. Hosp., Boston, 2001—. Contbr. articles to profl. jours. Recipient Rsch. prize, European Congress of Surgery, 1993, Joseph E. Murray award, New Eng. Soc. Plastic and Reconstructive Surgeons, 1994, Rsch. award co-investigator, Northeastern Soc. Plastic and Reconstructive Surgeons, 1994; grantee, Am. Assn. Aesthetic Plastic Surgeons, 1995, Am. Assn. Hand Surgery, 1995. Fellow: Royal Coll. Surgeons, Ireland, Royal Coll. Surgeons, Eng. (Plastic Surgery, priming grant 2002); mem.: Plastic Surgery Rsch. Coun. (Peter J. Gingrass co-investigator 1997, 2000, basic sci. award 2000). Conservative. Office: Royal Free Hosp Pond St London NW3 2QG England Office Phone: 011 44 7797 767 595.

BUTLER, REX LAMONT, lawyer; b. New Brunswick, NJ, Mar. 24, 1951; s. Ekker and Beatrice (Curry) B.; m. Stephanie Butler; children: Nijel Jaibrun, Vikteria Lamontra, Octavia Reneè Lamontra, Synclaire Lamontra. AA with honors, Fla. Jr. Coll., 1975; BA, U. North Fla., 1977; JD, Howard U., 1983. Bar: Alaska 1983, U.S. Dist. Ct. Alaska 1983, U.S. Ct. Appeals (9th cir.) 1984, U.S. Ct. Appeals (D.C. cir.) 1984, U.S. Supreme Ct. 1996. Assoc. M. Ashley Dickerson, Inc., Anchorage, 1983-84; profl. legis. asst. State of Alaska, Juneau, 1984, asst. atty. gen. Anchorage, 1984-85; pvt. practice Anchorage, 1985—; owner Rex Attys. Video, Inc. (RAV, Inc.), 2000. Adj. prof. law Anchorage C.C., 1985, U. Alaska, Anchorage, 1990—; mem. State Ct. Criminal Pattern Jury Instructions Com., 1997; chmn. lawyer rep. com. Alaska 9th Cir. Judicial Conf., 1997-98; law analyst for the news. Pres. Alaska Black Caucus, Anchorage, 1986, bd. dirs., 1987-88; gen. counsel NAACP, Anchorage, 1985-87, life mem., v.p. Anchorange branch, 2002-04; commr. Anchorage Telephone Utility, 1985-87; trustee Anchorage Sr. Ctr., Inc., 1985-87, Shiloh Missionary Bapt. Ch., Anchorage, 1985-87; bd. dirs. Ctr. Drug Problems, Anchorage, 1985-86, Alaska Civil Liberties Union, 1987-88; active fin. com. Dem. Cen. Com. Alaska; founder Rights Advocacy Project, Inc. (RAP, Inc.), 2004. With USN, 1969-73. Named one of Outstanding Young Men Am., 1984; recipient Cert. Appreciation, African Relief Campaign, 1985. Mem. ABA, Nat. Bar Assn., Nat. Assn. Criminal Defense Lawyers, Alaska Bar Assn., Assn. Trial Lawyers Am., Anchorage Bar Assn., Alaska Trial Lawyers Assn., Lions Internat., Omega Psi Phi (dist. counselor 1995-96, 98-2002). Democrat. Home: PO Box 200025 Anchorage AK 99520-0025 Office: 745 W 4th Ave Ste 300 Anchorage AK 99501-2157 Office Phone: 907-272-1497. Fax: 907-276-3306. Business E-Mail: rexattys@alaska.net.

BUTLER, ROBERT LEONARD, retired sales executive; b. West Warwick, RI, Aug. 8, 1931; s. Leonard Thomas and Henrietta Marie (Theroux) B.; m. Rosemarie Ann D'Ambra, Nov. 5, 1955; children: Robert Arthur, David Paul. MS in Fin. Svcs., Am. Coll., 1982, MS in Mgmt., 1985. ChFC, CLU. With sales and dept. mgmt. Sears Roebuck & Co., Worcester, Mass., 1956-67; dir. investment, prodn., sales State Mut. Am., Worcester, 1976-86; asst. sec. SMA Life Assurance Co., Worcester, 1974-86; v.p. SMA Equities Inc., Worcester, 1976-86; sr. v.p. sales Phoenix Equity Planning Corp., Hartford, Conn., 1986-92. Spkr., workshop leader conf. Life Office Mgmt. Assn. Contbr. articles to ins. mags. Mem. Am. Soc. Life Underwriters, Am. Abritration Assn. (comml. arbitrator 1993), Internat. Assn. Fin. Planners, Ins. Affiliated Broker-Dealer Forum (chmn. 1978-81), Nat. Assn. Securities Dealers (mem. dist. bus. com., mem. ins. affiliated broker/dealer com. 1991-92), Limra Fin. Products and Svcs., KC. Roman Catholic. Avocations: golf, jogging, swimming, photography, sports cars.

BUTLER, ROBERT OLEN, writer, educator; b. Granite City, Ill., Jan. 20, 1945; s. Robert Olen Sr. and Lucille Frances (Hall) B.; m. Carol Supplee, Aug. 10, 1968 (div. Jan. 1972); m. Marylin Geller, July 1, 1972 (div. July 1987); 1 child, Joshua Robert; m. Maureen Donlan, July 21, 1987 (div. Mar. 1995); m. Elizabeth Dewberry, Apr. 23, 1995. BS summa cum laude in Oral Interpretation, Northwestern U., 1967; MA in Playwriting, U. Iowa, 1969; postgrad., New Sch. Social Rsch., 1979-81; LHD, McNeese State U., 1994. Editor-in-chief Energy User News, NYC, 1975-85; assoc. prof. fiction writing McNeese State U., Lake Charles, La., 1985—93, prof., 1993—2001; Francis Epps prof. Fla. State U., 2001—. Summer faculty Iowa Summer Writing Festival U. Iowa, Port Townsend (Wash.) Writers Conf., New Orleans Writers' Conf., Southampton Writers' Conf., Long Island U., N.Y., Hofstra U. Summer Writing Conf., Hempstead, N.Y., others, 1988—. Author: The Alleys of Eden, 1981 (also wrote screenplay 1991-92), Sun Dogs, 1982, Countrymen of Bones, 1983, Fragments, 1984, On Distant Ground, 1985, Wabash, 1987, The Deuce, 1989, (short story collection) A Good Scent from a Strange Mountain, 1992 (Pulitzer Prize for fiction 1993, Richard and Hinda Rosenthal Found. award Am. Acad. Arts & Letters 1993, nominee PEN/Faulkner award 1993, Notable Book 1993 Notable Books Coun. Am. Libr. Assn.), They Whisper, 1994, Tabloid Dreams, 1996, The Deep Green Sea, 1998, Mr. Spaceman, 2000, Silver Rose Anthology: Award-Winning Short Stories, 2001, 2002, Fair Warning, 2002, From Where You Dream: The Process of Writing Fiction, 2005; author numerous short stories; works translated to 12 langs.; contbr. articles, book reviews to jours., newspapers, screenplays. Sgt. U.S. Army, 1969-72, Vietnam. Recipient Emily Clark Balch award best work fiction, 1990 Va. Quar. Rev., 1991, TuDo Chinh Kien award outstanding contbns. Am. culture by Vietnam vet. Vietnam Vets. Am., 1987, Medal of Merit, Lotos Club, 1996; grantee NEA, 1994; fellow John Simon Guggenheim Found., 1993. Mem. PEN, WGAWest. Office: English Dept Fla State U 411 Williams Bldg Tallahassee FL 32306-1580 E-mail: rbutler@english.fsu.edu.

BUTLER, ROBERT THOMAS, retired advertising executive; b. Westmont, NJ, Feb. 22, 1925; s. John T. and Kathryn M. (Donehower) B.; m. Eleanore MacIndoe, May 4, 1950; children— R. Mark, Kathryn J., Elizabeth Anne. BS, Temple U., Phila., 1951. Market research mgr. James Lees Carpet Co., 1951-53; v.p. N.W. Ayer, Phila., 1953-74; pres. Gray & Rogers, Phila., 1975-90. Served with USCG, 1943-46. Mem.: St. David's (Pa.) Golf, Merion Cricket (Haverford, Pa.). Republican. Episcopalian.

BUTLER, SAMUEL COLES, lawyer; b. Logansport, Ind., Mar. 10, 1930; s. Melvin Linwood and Jane Lavina (Flynn) B.; m. Sally Eugenia Thackston, June 28, 1952; children: Samuel Coles, Leigh F., Elizabeth J. AB magna cum laude, Harvard U., 1951, LLB magna cum laude, 1954. Bar: D.C. 1954, Ind. 1954, N.Y. 1957. Law clk. to Justice Minton U.S. Supreme Ct., 1954; assoc. Cravath, Swaine & Moore LLP, NYC, 1956—60, ptnr., 1961—2003, spl. counsel, 2004—. Trustee Vassar Coll., 1969-77, NY Pub. Libr., 1979—, chmn. bd., 1999—2004; trustee Am. Mus. Natural History, 1989-93, The September 11 Fund, 2001-04; chmn. Harvard Coll. Fund, 1977-85; bd. overseers Harvard U., 1982-88, pres. bd., 1986-88; bd. dirs. Culver Ednl. Found., 1981-2001, v.p. bd. 1985-2001. With U.S. Army, 1954-56. Mem. Coun. Fgn. Rels. Home: 1220 Park Ave New York NY 10128-1733 Office: Cravath Swaine & Moore LLP 825 8th Ave New York NY 10019-7475

BUTLER, SUSAN LOWELL, educational association executive, writer; b. Bklyn., Feb. 10, 1944; d. John William and Catherine (Mauro) Yost; m. Horace Hamilton Lowell (div. 1982); m. James Thomas Butler, Feb. 12,

1983; stepchildren: James, Kevin, Michael. BA, Lycoming Coll., 1965; postgrad., U. Pa., 1965-67. Tchr. English and Journalism Bristol Twp. Schs., Levittown, Pa., 1967-70; field rep. Nat. Edn. Assn., Washington, 1970-74, dir. comm., 1974-80, dir. western states region Austin (Tex.) and Denver, 1980-84; acct. supr. Dale Chrisman & Assocs., Austin, 1984-86; pvt. cons. Austin, 1986-88; exec. v.p. Women in Comm., Inc., Washington, 1988-91; nat. exec. dir. Nat. Women's Hall of Fame, Seneca Falls, NY, 1991-96; dir. Coalition For America's Children, Washington, 1996—97; managing partner Butler Pub. Affairs, 1998—; sr. dir. pub. edn. Nat. Mental Assn., 2000—; v.p. comms. and public affairs The Hospices of Nat. Capital Region, Fairfax, Va., 2000—. Mem. bd. The Media Inst., Washington, 1989-91, mem. family lodge steering com. NIG, 2000—. Author: National Education Association: A Special Mission, 1987, Handbook of Association Communications, 1987, Pressing Onward: The Women's Historical Biography of the National Education Association, 1996. V.p. pub. affairs Mental Health Assn. of Tex., Austin, 1987-88; bd. dirs. Nat. Women's Hall of Fame, Ovarian Cancer Nat. Alliance, 1997—; co-chair Ovarian Cancer Coalition Greater Washington, 1997—; dirs. consumer liaison group Nat. Cancer Inst. Dirs. Consumer Liaison Group, 1997—; adv. bd. Nat. Archives History Project, 1995-96; active Alexandria (Va.) Commn. for Women, 1996—, 250th Anniversary Commn., 1997—; bd. dirs. co-founder, v.p. Ovarian Cancer Nat. Alliance, 1997—. Mem. Am. Soc. Assn. Execs., Pub. Rels. Soc. Am. (accredited), Women in Comm. Inc. Episcopalian. Avocations: skiing, photography. Home and Office: Butler Pub Affairs 406 Skyhill Rd Alexandria VA 22314-4920

BUTLER, TERENCE MICHAEL JOSEPH See BUTLER, GEEZER

BUTLER, THOMAS WILLIAM, retired health and social services administrator; b. Aiken, SC, Aug. 29, 1933; s. Eddie and Lillie Mae B.; BA, Adelphi U., 1958; MS in Social Work, Columbia U., 1964; MPA, NYU, 1970; children: Kathi Susan, Thomas William, Michael David. Case supr. Nassau County (NY) Dept. Social Svcs., 1959-67; exec. asst. Joint Legis. Com. on Problems of Public Health Svcs., Medicare, Medicaid and Compulsory Health Ins., N.Y. State, 1967-69; dir. cmty. affairs NYC Health and Hosps. Corp., 1969-72; with div. alcohol, drug abuse and mental health Public Health Service, Dept. Health and Human Svc., NYC, 1972-95, regional cons. for mental health, 1972-79, regional supr. substance abuse and mental health, 1979-81, co-acting dir. Region II, NYC, 1981, chief health services, 1981-85, chief primary care health services, 1985-86, chief planning, evaluation and data mgmt. services, 1986-95, acting dir. grants mgmt., 1987-88, dep. dir., Divsn. of Health Svcs. Delivery, 1992-95, ret., 1995; guest lectr. NYU, 1977, Grad. Sch. Mgmt. and Urban Professions, New Sch. for Social Rsch., 1977-95. Mem. alumni bd. Columbia U., 1964-67, 76-78, 81-84, Columbia U. Sch. of Social Work rep. Alumni Fedn., 1975-78; bd. dirs. NCCJ, NYC, 1978-80, 80-. Served with U.S. Army, 1954-56; ETO. Recipient Internat. Service award Salvation Army, 1978; univ. athletic scholar, 1952-54, 56-58, univ. acad. scholar, 1952-54. Mem. NASW, VFW, U. Alumni, Adelphi Alumni, Acad. Cert. Social Workers, Am. Legion., Vets. Fgn. Wars. Author: Community Organization: A Case Study, 1970; contbr. articles to profl. jours.; inventor in field. Home and Office: 14 N Ferndale Pl Montauk NY 11954 also: 52 Udal Dr Great Neck NY 11020-1530

BUTLER, VINCENT PAUL, JR., internist, educator; b. Jersey City, Feb. 16, 1929; s. Vincent Paul and Ruth Eilene (Lynch) B. AB, St. Peter's Coll., 1949; MD, Columbia U., 1954. Intern Presbyn. Hosp., NYC, 1954-55, resident, 1955-56, 58-59, asst. physician, 1963-68, asst. attending physician, 1968-71, asso. attending physician, 1971-74, attending physician, 1974—2004; trainee clin. immunology U. Rochester Med. Center, 1959-61; research fellow immunochemistry dept. microbiology Columbia U., 1961-63, asst. prof. medicine, 1963-70, assoc. prof., 1970-74, prof., 1974-98, prof. emeritus, 1999—, spl. lectr., 1999—. Asst. vis. physician 1st med. div. Bellevue Hosp., N.Y.C., 1963-68, Harlem Hosp., N.Y.C., 1968-88; mem. VA Merit Rev. Bd. in Immunology, 1974-77, chmn., 1976-77; mem. immunol. sci. study sect. NIH, 1979-83, chmn., 1980-83 Rsch. com. Arthritis Found., 1986-91, chmn., 1989-91; bd. trustees St. Peter's Prep. Sch., Jersey City, 1985-93, chmn., 1991-93. Lt. M.C. USN, 1956-58. Helen Hay Whitney Found. fellow, 1960-63; Arthritis Found. investigator, 1963-68; Josiah Macy, Jr. Found. scholar dept. zoology Univ. Coll., London, 1979-80; recipient Rsch. Career Devel. award NIH, 1968-73; Joseph Mather Smith prize Columbia U. Coll. Physicians and Surgeons, 1973; Irma T. Hirschl Charitable Trust Career Scientist, 1973-78 Fellow AAAS; mem. Assn. Am. Physicians, Am. Soc. Clin. Investigation, Am. Assn. Immunologists, Am. Soc. Pharmacology and Exptl. Therapeutics, Am. Heart Assn., N.Y. Heart Assn., Am. Fedn. Med. Research, Harvey Soc. Roman Catholic. Home: 66 Tulip St Summit NJ 07901 Office: 630 W 168th St New York NY 10032-3702 Office Phone: 212-305-4059. Business E-Mail: vpb2@columbia.edu.

BUTLER, WILLIAM BLAINE, dean, dental educator; b. Huntingdon, Tenn., Apr. 8, 1947; s. Hugh L. and Virgie L. (Parker) B. Student, U. Pitts., 1965-66; BS, Tenn. State U., Nashville, 1969; DDS, Meharry Med. Coll., 1973; MS, U. Mich., 1977. Diplomate Am. Bd. Prosthodontics, Tenn. Bd. Prosthodontics. Asst. prof. U. Mich. Sch. Dentistry, Ann Arbor, 1978—79; instr. Meharry Med. Coll. Sch. Dentistry, Nashville, 1973-74, asst. prof., 1979—84, asst. prof., chmn. dept. prosthodontics, 1984-86, assoc. prof. to prof., chmn. dept. prosthodontics, 1986—99, prof., assoc. dean academic affairs, 1999—2000, prof., dean, 2000—; pvt. practice prosthodontics Butler Dental Clinic, Nashville, 1981—. MARC faculty fellow Nat. Inst. Gen. Med. Sciences, 1974—77. Contbr. articles to profl. jours. Co-chmn. bldg. task force Met. Interdenominational Ch., Nashville, 1986-87, mem. eccles. coun., 1986-90; charter mem. 18th Ave Cmty. Ctr., Nashville, 1991. Fellow: Am. Coll. Prosthodontists, mem: ADA, Nat. Dental Assn., Am. Acad. Fixed Prosthodontics, Mich. Prosthodontic Soc., Capital City Dental Soc. (pres. 1993-95), Francis B. Vedder Soc. Crown and Bridge Prosthodontics, Omicron Kappa Upsilon (past pres.), Alpha Phi Alpha. Avocations: birding, including wildlife habitat for birds, photography, fishing, landscape gardening. Office: Meharry Med Coll Sch Dentistry Office of Dean 1005 Dr DB Todd Jr Blvd Nashville TN 37208-3599 Office Phone: 615-327-6207. Office Fax: 615-327-6213. Business E-Mail: wbutler@mmc.edu.

BUTLER, WILLIAM ELLIOTT, lawyer, educator; b. Mpls., Oct. 20, 1939; s. William Elliott and Maxine Swan (Elmberg) Butler; m. Darlene Mae Johnson, Sept. 2, 1961 (dec. Nov. 23, 1989); children: William III, Bradley; m. Maryann Elizabeth Gashi, Dec. 6, 1991. AA, Hibbing Jr. Coll., 1959; BA, Am. Univ., Washington, 1961; MA, Johns Hopkins U., 1963; JD, Harvard U., 1966; PhD, Johns Hopkins U., 1970; LLD, London U., 1979; LLM, Russian Acad. Scis., 1997. Bar: DC 1967, U.S. Supreme Ct. 1970, Uzbekistan 1996, Russia 1997. Rsch. asst. Johns Hopkins U., Washington, 1966-68; rsch. assoc. Harvard Law Sch., Cambridge, Mass., 1968-70; reader in comparative law U. London, 1970-76, prof. comparative law, 1976—2005, prof. emeritus, 2005—; ptnr. White & Case, London, 1994-96; resident ptnr. PricewaterhouseCoopers CIS Law Firm, Moscow, 1997—2001; sr. ptnr. Phoenix Law Assocs. CIS, Moscow, 2002—; John Edward Fowler disting. prof. law Pa. State U. Dickinson Sch. Law, Carlisle, 2005—. Of counsel Cole, Corelte & Abrutyn, 1989—92, Clifford Chance, 1992—94; dir. Vinogradoff Inst. Pa. State Dickinson; dean, M. M. Speranskii prof. internat. and comparative law Moscow Sch. Social and Econ. Scis., 1995—2004; prof., chair civil law Moscow State Legal Acad., 2002; vis. prof. Washington and Lee U. Law Sch., 2005; professorial rsch. assoc. Sch. Oriental and African Studies U. London, 2006—; sr. mem. commn. room St. Anthony's Coll., Oxford Univ., 2004—. Author: Russian Law, 2d edit., 2003, Civil Code of Russian Federation, 2003, Russian Company and Commercial Legislation, 2003, Russian Foreign Relations and Investment Law, 2006, Civil Code of Uzbekistan, 2007, others; editor: Bookplate Internat., 1994—, Russian Law, 2004—, Jour. Comparative Law, 2006—, Eastern European Yearbook International and Comparative Law, 2006—; contbr. articles to profl. jours. Trustee Hakluyt Soc., 2004—. Recipient G. I. Tunkin medal, Russian Assn. Internat. Law, 2003, Ivan Fedorov medal, Russian Assn. Bibliophiles, 2004; Rsch. fellow, Leverhulme Trust, London, 1991, FSA. Mem.: Internat. Acad. Comparative Law, Russian Acad. Legal Scis., Nat. Acad. Scis. Ukraine (academician 1992—), Russian Acad. Natural Sci. (academician 1992—), Internat. Fedn. Ex-Libris Socs. (exec. sec. 1986—). Avocations: book collecting, bookplate collecting. Home: 155 Mount Rock Rd Newville PA 17241 Office: Pa State Univ Dickinson Sch Law 150 S College St Carlisle PA 17013 Office Phone: 717-240-5227. Business E-Mail: web15@psu.edu. E-mail: webakademik@aol.com.

BUTLER, WILLIAM JOSEPH, lawyer, educator; b. Brighton, Mass., Mar. 22, 1924; s. Patrick Lawrence and Delia (Conley) B.; m. Jane Hays, Dec. 22, 1945; children: Arthur Hays, Patricia. Student, Harvard U., 1946, NYU, 1949; DHL (hon.), U. Cin., 1988; LLD (hon.), Washington Jefferson Coll., 2007. Bar: N.Y. 1950. Assoc. Hays, St. John, Abramson & Schulman, NYC, 1949-53; ptnr. Butler, Jablow & Geller, NYC, 1953—. A founder Arthur Garfield Hays Civil Liberties program NYU Sch. Law, 1958; spl. counsel in landmark case on school prayer tried in Supreme Ct. ACLU, Washington, 1962; lectr. Practicing Law Inst., 1966; sec., dir., gen. counsel Walco Nat. Corp., FAO Schwartz, NYC, 1961—85; internat. legal observer to South African Elections, 1994; mem. faculty Salzburg Seminar, Austria, 1989, UN Devel. Program, Poland, 1992, Woodrow Wilson Sch. of Pub. and Internat. Affairs, Princeton U., 2000—01; spl. regional adv. for N.Am. on human rights UN High Commr. Mary Robinson, 1998. Author: Human Rights and the Legal System in Iran, 1976, The Decline of Democracy in the Phillipines, 1977, Human Rights in United States and United Kingdom Foreign Policy, Guatemala, a New Beginning, 1987, Palau; A Challenge to the Rule of Law in Micronesia, 1988, The New South Africa - The Dawn of Democracy, 1994; contbr. papers to U. Cin. Law Libr., articles to profl. jours. Mem. commn. urban affairs Am. Jewish Congress, 1965-70; dir. emeritus N.Y. Civil Liberties Union, Internat. League for Human Rights; exec. com. League to Abolish Capital Punishment; standing com. human rights World Peace Through Law Ctr., Geneva; chmn. adv. com. Morgan Inst. Human Rights, U. Cin. Sch. Law; internat. legal observer Internat. Human Rights Orgn., Internat. Criminal Tribunal for Former Yugoslavia in the Hague, The Netherlands, 1996—, others; faculty Salzburg (Austria) Seminar, 1989; UN Devel. Prog. to Poland, 1992. With U.S. Merchant Marine Svc., 1942—45. Recipient Spl. Citation for contbn. to cause of religious freedom, 1962, William J. Butler Human Rights medal, Urban Morgan Inst. Human Rights, U. Cin., 1999—, Florinda Lasker Civil Liberties award, 2004, Gold medal, Ministry Fgn. Affairs, Slovak Republic, 2006. Mem. Internat. Commn. Jurists (Geneva) (chmn. exec. com. 1975-90, pres., dir. Am. Assn., UN rep.), Coun. on Fgn. Rels., ABA, Assn. Bar City N.Y. (bd. dirs. Ctr. Internat. Policy, chmn. com. internat. human rights), Inter-Am. Assn. Democracy and Freedom, Internat. Law Assn. (Am. br.), Am. Soc. Internat. Law, Harvard Club (N.Y.C.), U. Club Dublin.

BUTLER, WILLIAM THOMAS, academic administrator, physician, educator; b. Boston, Aug. 10, 1932; s. Albert Quigg and Elizabeth West (Viskniskki) B.; m. Marilou Beutel, Apr. 26, 1957; children: Marilyn West, Thomas Charles, Robin Eileen; m. Carol Ann Pike, Nov. 23, 1977. AB, Oberlin Coll., 1954; MD, Western Res. U., 1958; grad. program for health systems mgmt., Harvard U., 1974, A.M.P., 1979. Intern and asst. resident in internal medicine Mass. Gen. Hosp., Boston, 1958—61, clin. fellow in medicine, 1960—61, resident in internal medicine, 1964—65; rsch. fellow in bacteriology and immunology Harvard Med. Sch., 1960—61; clin. assoc. Lab. Clin. Investigations, Nat. Inst. Allergy and Infectious Diseases, NIH, Bethesda, Md., 1961—62, chief clin. assoc., 1962—63, clin. investigator, 1963—64, acting head clin. immunology sect., 1965—66; asst. prof. Baylor Coll. Medicine, Houston, 1966—68, assoc. prof., 1968—71, prof. microbiology and immunology, prof. internal medicine, 1971—2001, assoc. dean, 1973—74, dean admissions, 1974—77, acting exec. v.p., 1976—77, exec. v.p., dean, 1977—79, pres., 1979—96, chancellor, 1996—2004, chancellor emeritus, 2004—, prof. immunology, 2001—. Mem. spl. med. adv. group VA, 1981-91, chmn., 1984-91; bd. dirs. Lyondell Chem. Co., chmn. bd., 1997—; mem. Am. Quality and Productivity Ctr., 1991-2004, chmn. S.W. CEO Coun., 1997-98, mem., 1994—2004. Mem. forward planning com. Tex. Med. Ctr., 1981-96; bd. dirs. South Main Ctr. Assn., exec. com., 1980-94, chmn., 1989-91, coun. advisors, 1994—2004; past assoc. chmn. key group United Way Campaign, Flagship Divsn., group chmn., 1990; mem. Houston Econ. Summit Host Com., 1990; bd. dirs. Blvd. Oaks Civic Assn., 1982-85, Sci. Engring. Fair of Houston, 1985—, United Way Tex. Gulf Coast, trustee, 1993-99, exec. com. 1998-99; nat. bd. dirs. Points of Light Found., 1995-2004; mem. coordinating bd. Tex. Coll. and Univ. System, Health Professions Edn. Adv. Com., 1984-95, chmn., 1988-95, rsch. adv. com., 1987-90; mem. The Houston Forum, 1981—, bd. govs., 1983-92, 1996-2004; mem. Tex. Sesquicentennial Celebration Com., 1984-86; mem. bd. edn. blue ribbon com. Houston Ind. Sch. Dist., 1986; adv. bd. Covenant House Tex., 1987-90; HISD City-Wide Com., 1987; vice-chmn. health svcs., 1990 U.S. Savs. Bond Program. Mem. AMA, Am. Assn. Immunologists, Am. Soc. Clin. Investigation, N.Y. Acad. Scis., Infectious Diseases Soc. Am., Inst. Medicine, Nat. Acad. Scis. (membership com. 1992-96, sect. 12 1992—, vice chmn., 1992-94, chmn. 1994-96, com. on prevention and control of sexually transmitted diseases 1995-96, chmn. 1995-96), Assn. Acad. Health Ctrs., Assn. Am. Med. Colls. (chmn. coun. deans 1987-89, adminstrv. bd. 1983-90, exec. coun. 1984-92, mgmt. edn. programs planning com. 1986-96, chmn.-elect 1989-90, chmn. 1990-91, project 3000x2000 implementation com. chmn. 1991-2002, nominating com. chmn. 1982), Harris County Med. Soc., Houston Acad. Medicine, Tex. Med. Assn. (adv. coun. med. edn.), Houston C. of C. (bd. dirs. 1981-82, 83-89), Greater Houston Partnership, Inc. (bd. dirs. 1989, 92-99, co-chair healthcare task force 1994-97, bus. issues adv. com. 1994-99, govtl. rels. adv. com. 1995-97), Houston Mus. Nat. Sci. (ex officio 1989-94), River Oaks Country Club, Doctors' Club (bd. govs. 1980-84, pres. 1982), Harvard Bus. Sch. of Houston Club, Sigma Xi, Alpha Omega Alpha. Methodist. Achievements include research in numerous publs. on infectious disease and immunology. Office: Baylor Coll Medicine 1 Baylor Plz Ste 177A Houston TX 77030-3498*

BUTLER-PURRY, KAREN L., electrical engineer, educator; BS in Elec. Engring. (summa cum laude), Southern U., Baton Rouge, La., 1985; MS, U. Tex., Austin, 1987; PhD in Elec. Engring., Howard U., 1994. Registered profl. engr., La., Tex., Miss. Joined as vis. asst. prof. Tex. A&M Univ., 1994, assoc. prof., elec. engring. College Station, Tex., asst. dean grad. studies, Dwight Look Coll. Engring., asst. dir., Power System Automation Lab. Spkr. in field; dir., Coll. Engring. Undergraduate Rsch. program Tex. A&M Univ., initiated the engring. grad. invitational. Contbr. articles in profl. jours. Recipient Faculty Career award, NSF, 1995, Young Investigator award, Office of Naval Rsch., 1999, 2005 AAAS Mentor award, 2006; secured grants from the US Dept. Homeland Security, Sloan Found. and NSF. Mem.: Soc. Women Engineers (faculty advisor, Tex. A&M Univ. chpt.), Nat. Soc. Black Engineers (faculty advisor, Tex. A&M Univ. chpt.), La. Engring. Soc., Am. Soc. for Engring. Edn., IEEE, Power Engring. Soc. Office: Elec and Computer Engring Dept Tex A&M Univ 3128 TAMUS Office #216G ZEC 216G Zachry Engineering Ctr College Station TX 77843-3128 Office Phone: 979-847-9048. Office Fax: 979-845-6259. Business E-Mail: klbutler@ee.tamu.edu.

BUTNEV, VIKTOR YURIEVICH, research scientist; MD, N.I.Pirogov Moscow State Med. Sch., 1975—81; PhD, Inst. for Exptl. Endocrinology and Hormone Chemistry, 1981—86. Therapeutist State Exam. Bd. of N.I.Pirogov Moscow State Med. Sch., 1981. Jr. rsch. scientist Inst. for Exptl. Endocrinology and Hormone Chemistry, Moscow, 1981—88, sr. rsch. scientist, 1988—94; postdoctoral fellow dept. biol. scis. Wichita State U., Kans., 1994—98; protein hormone biochemist Nat. Hormone and Pituitary Program, Rsch. and Edn. Inst., Harbor-UCLA Med. Ctr., Torrance, Calif., 1998—99; postdoctoral fellow dept. physiology and biophysics U Iowa, Iowa City, 1999—2002; scientist Genzyme Glycobiology Rsch. Inst., Oklahoma City, 2002—. NIH grantee, 1999—2002. Mem.: AAAS, Soc. for Study of Reprodn., Endocrine Soc. Achievements include discovery, isolation, and characterization of glycosylated prolactin and its carbohydrate moiety. Office: Genzyme Glycobiology Rsch Inst 800 Research Pkwy Ste 200 Oklahoma City OK 73104 Personal E-mail: butnev@aol.com. Business E-Mail: viktor.butnev@genzyme.com.

BUTORAC, FRANK GEORGE, librarian, educator; b. Crosby, Minn., Feb. 12, 1927; s. Frank and Mary (Paun) B.; m. Mary Regis McGowan Ratigan, Apr. 8, 1972; stepchildren: Helen Elizabeth, Nicholas. AB, U. Mich., 1950, AM, 1956, AMLS, 1958; postgrad., Cornell Law Sch., 1950-51, Harvard U., 1953; postgrad. in philosophy, U. Notre Dame, 1959, 60-62; postgrad. in theology, Holy Cross Coll., 1962-66; postgrad., Cath. U., 1963, Georgetown U., 1965, NYU, 1968-70, 79-81, Cambridge U., 1975, postgrad., 2005, Oxford U., 1989, postgrad., 1995, postgrad., 2003, Trinity Coll., Dublin, 1990, Russian State U. Humanities, Moscow, 2006, Free U. Berlin, 2007. With exec. tng. program U.S. Rubber, Mishawaka, Ind., 1952-53; tchr. 6th grade Jefferson Sch., Wayne, Mich., 1953-54; tchr. social studies Slauson Jr. H.S., Ann Arbor, Mich., 1954-55; supervising tchr. social studies Lincoln Consol. H.S., Ea. Mich. U., Ypsilanti, 1955-57; circulation libr., engring. libr. U. Mich., Ann Arbor, 1958-59; joined Congregation of Holy Cross, 1959; postulant U. Notre Dame, 1959; seminarian and temporary profession, 1959-66; novice Sacred Heart Novitiate, Jordan, Minn., 1959-60; registrar Mercer C.C., Trenton, NJ, 1966-68, asst. dir. cmty. and ext. svcs., 1968-70, dir. evening and ext. ops., 1970-71, dir. spl. programs, 1971-74, dir. libr. svcs., 1974-84, chmn. libr. tech. program, 1974-84, dir. libr. devel., 1984-87, libr., 1987—. Cons. libr. edn., libr. mgmt. Pres. U. Mich. Clubs Coun. 2d Dist., 1991-93; chmn. U. Mich. Newman Ctr. Fund Drive, 1958; professed Secular Franciscan Order Monastery of St. Clare, Bordentown, NJ, 1984, professed Fraternities St. Domino, Villa of Our Lady Retreat Ho., Pa., 2007. Bd. dirs. U. Mich. Alumni Assn., 1995-98; chmn. Anna B. Stokes Found., Trenton, 1972; dean's adv. com. Cornell Law Sch., 1972-73; mem. N.J. State Adv. Com. on Aging, 1971; mem. Mich. State Ctrl. Com. Young Democrats, 1949-50. Served with USN, 1944-47. Recipient Tall Cedars of Lebanon award for Cmty. Svc., Trenton, 1974. Mem. ALA, N.J. Libr. Assn. (exec. bd. 1977-78), Purnell Sch. Parents Assn., Cornell Law Assn., Bennington Coll. Parents Assn., Pine Manor Coll. Parents Assn., U. Mich. Ctrl. N.J. (pres. 1987-91), Mensa, English Speaking Union, Nassau Club (Princeton, N.J.), Princeton Club (N.Y.C.), Trenton Lions Club (pres. 1972), Trenton Torch Club (pres. 1972), Cornell Club Ctrl. N.J. (pres. 1977-78), Marines' Meml. Club (San Francisco), Cath. Alumni Club Trenton (pres. 1968), Theta Delta Chi, Phi Delta Phi, Phi Delta Kappa, Kappa Delta Pi, Alpha Phi Omega. Republican. Roman Catholic. Home: 6 Mercer St Princeton NJ 08540-6808 Office: 1200 Old Trenton Rd Princeton Junction NJ 08550-3407 Office Phone: 609-586-4800. Personal E-mail: butoracf@yahoo.com.

BUTT, CHARLES CLARENCE, food service executive; b. Houston, 1938; BS in Econs., U. Pa., 1959; grad. advanced mgmt. program, Harvard U. Pres. H.E.B. Grocery Co., San Antonio, 1971-84; chmn., CEO H.E. Butt Grocery Co., San Antonio, 1984—. Dir. Tex. Commerce Bancshares, 1974—89. Mem. bd. overseers The Wharton Sch.; mem. bd. dirs. of the assocs, Harvard Bus. Sch.; chmn. adv. coun. U. Tex. Marine Sci. Inst., 1976-86; chmn. M.D. Anderson Cancer Hosp. ann. campaign, 1981; mem. coord. bd. Tex. Coll. and Univ. Sys., 1978-83, chmn. faculty salaries com.; mem. Harvard Bus. Sch.'s Bd. Dirs. of Assocs. Recipient Conservation award Winedale Hist. Ctr., U. Tex., Amanda Cartwright Taylor award San Antonio Conservation Soc., Mr. South Tex. award Washington's Birthday Celebration Assn., 1996; named one of Forbes' Richest Americans, 2006. Mem.: San Antonio German Club, Order of the Alamo, NY Yacht Club, Nantucket Yacht Club, Corpus Christi Yacht Club, Argyle Club. Avocations: sailing, historical preservation, photography. Office: H E Butt Grocery Co 646 S Main Ave San Antonio TX 78204-1210*

BUTT, P. LAWRENCE, lawyer; b. Indpls., 1941; BBA, U. Cinn., 1964; JD, Ind. U., 1968. Bar: 1968. With Marsh Supermarkets, Inc., Indpls., 1977—, v.p., counsel, sec., 1992—97, sr. v.p., counsel, sec., 1997—. Bd. dirs. Marsh Supermarkets, Inc. Office: Marsh Supermarkets Inc 9800 Crosspoint Blvd Indianapolis IN 46256-3350 Office Phone: 317-594-2100. Office Fax: 317-594-2704.

BUTTACY, ANTHONY, social studies educator; b. Islip, NY, Apr. 24, 1981; s. Laurence and Stephanie Buttacy; m. Donna Buttacy. BA in History and Social Sci., Evangel U., Springfield, Mo, 2003; M in Internat. Affairs, Mo. State U., Springfield. Substitute tchr. Patchogue (N.Y.)-Medford Schs., 2003—04; social studies tchr. Leonard E. Burket Christian Sch., Center Moriches, NY, 2004—05; gen. adminstr. outdoor adventures and games ctr. Mo. State U., Springfield, 2005—07; instr. Evangel U., Springfield, 2005—07; prof. Ozark Tech. Coll., 2007. Curriculum writer Leonard E. Burket Christian Sch., Center Moriches, 2004—05, gen. orgn. advisor, 2004—05. Exec. staff: discovery ranger coord. N.Y. Dist. Royal Rangers, 2005; dep. tng. coord. L.I. Sect. Royal Rangers, NY, 2004—05, color guard coord. NY, 2003—05; discovery ranger group comdr. Royal Rangers, Shirley, NY, 2003—05; ch. orch. Cen. Assembly of God, Springfield, 1999; ch. worship team Shirley Assembly of God, 2003—05; youth leader Shirley Assembly of God/The Way, 2003—05; internat. del. coord. Royal Rangers Internat., 2006—; vol. tutor NY, 2004—05. Recipient grad. asst. scholarship, Mo. State U., 2005—. Mem.: Pi Gamma Mu. Avocations: outdoors, reading, music. Office: Evangel Univ 1111 N Glenstone Springfield MO 65803 Home Phone: 417-894-8319; Office Phone: 417-865-2815. Personal E-mail: anthony_buttacy@yahoo.com.

BUTTARO, LUCIA, language educator, consultant; b. Bklyn., May 21, 1963; d. Giuseppe Buttaro and Maria Christina Vuotto-Buttaro. BS Inst. de Enseranza Superior Daguerre, Buenos Aires, 1986; MS in edn., Fordham U., NYC, 1996, PhD, 1999. Instr. English High Lyceum of English Culture, Buenos Aires, 1982—85, Cambridge Inst., Buenos Aires, Aeon Eng. Conversation Sch., Toyahoshi, Japan, 1990—91, Alpha English Sch., Toyahoshi, Japan, 1991—92; GED lectr. Spanish Bronx Coll. CUNY, 1992—98; adj. prof. Baruch Coll. CUNY, 1995—; literacy cons. NYC Dept. of Edn., Bklyn., 2001—; asst. prof. Fordham U., NYC, 1999—, Kingsborough Coll. CUNY, Bklyn., 1999—2004, Adelphi U., 2004—. Del. Acad. Scholars Program, Shanghai, 2002—03; ESL med. instr. Action for Russian Immigrants, Bklyn., 1994—; mem. writing across the curriculum com. CUNY; mem. com. on admissions Kingsborough Coll. CUNY, mem. academic standing com. Contbr. articles to profl. jours., presentations to profl. conferences, 2000. Recipient PSC CUNY Rsch award program, 2002—03; grantee Fulbright Tchr. and Adminstr. Exch. Program, 2002—03. Mem.: ENLACE (bd. dir. 1999—), Phi Delta Kappa. Democrat. Roman Catholic. Avocations: travel, photography. Home: 1395 E Second St Brooklyn NY 11230 Personal E-mail: drbuttaro@aol.com.

BUTTE, AMY S., brokerage house executive; b. Jan. 8, 1968; BA in Polit. Sci. and Psychology, Yale U.; MBA, Harvard U. Various positions Anderson Consulting, Merrin Fin., Bridge Trading Co., Inc., Merrill Lynch; sr. mng. dir. Bear Stearns, 1999—2002; CFO, chief strategist fin. svcs.

divsn. Credit Suisse First Boston, 2002—03; exec. v.p. NY Stock Exch. Inc., NYC, 2004—06, CFO, 2004—06; CFO, global ops. Man Financial, Inc., Chgo., 2006—. Co-chair corp. adv. bd. NYC Ballet; participant World Econ. Forum's Young Global Leader Program. Mem.: Nat. Orgn. Investment Professionals, NY Women's Found., New York Women's Found. Office: Man Financial Inc 717 5th Ave New York NY 10022*

BUTTENWIESER, LAWRENCE BENJAMIN, lawyer; b. NYC, Jan. 11, 1932; s. Benjamin Joseph and Helen (Lehman) Buttenwieser; m. Ann Harriet Lubin, July 13, 1956; children: William Lawrence, Carol Helen Sharp, Jill Ann Schloss, Peter Lubin. BA, U. Chgo., 1951, MA, 1955; JD, Yale U., 1956; DHL (hon.), Yeshiva U., 1974. Bar: N.Y. 1956. Assoc. Rosenman & Colin, NYC, 1956-66, ptnr., 1966—2002; of counsel Katten Muchin Rosenman LLP, NYC, 2002—. Past pres., past trustee Associated YM-YWHAs Greater N.Y.; past v.p., past dir. Citizens Housing and Planning Coun. N.Y.; past treas., dir. City Ctr. Music and Drama, Inc.; past dir. Coun. Social Work Edn.; past trustee Dalton Sch.; past hon. chmn. bd. dirs., trustee, past pres. Fedn. Jewish Philanthropies N.Y.; past chmn. bd. trustees Montefiore Med. Ctr.; past gen. campaign chmn. United Neighborhood Houses N.Y.; past trustee N.Y. Acad. Sci. UJA/Fed. Joint Campaign; past chmn., trustee Citizens Budget Commn.; dir. Playwrights Horizons Inc.; past chmn., past trustee Am. Jewish World Svc.; trustee U. Chgo. Mem.: Assn. Bar City of N.Y. Office: Katten Muchin Rosenman Fl 21 575 Madison Ave Fl 21 New York NY 10022-2585 Office Phone: 212-940-8560. E-mail: lawrence.buttenwieser@kattenlaw.com.

BUTTER, KAREN ANN, school librarian; b. Terre Haute, Ind., Feb. 11, 1948; d. George Nicholis and Florence Butter. AB, U. Calif., Berkeley, 1970; MLS, Emporia State U., Kans., 1972. Head pub. svcs. Eccles Libr., U. Utah, Salt Lake City, 1974—83, project mgr. integrated academic info. sys., 1983—85; dep. dir. Welch Med. Libr., Johns Hopkins U., Balt., 1986—92, U. Calif., San Francisco, 1992—2000, univ. libr. & asst. vice-chancellor, 2000—. Mem. site team Mid. States Assn. Colls. & Schs., 1990—2007; adv. bd. San Jose State Libr. Sch., Calif. Contbr. chapter to book, articles to profl. jours. Bd. pres. Libr. Bd., Alameda, Calif., 2001—07; pres., bd. position LWV, Alameda, Calif., 1996—98. Mem.: Assn. Academic Health Sci. Librs. (com. chair 2002—07), Med. Libr. Assn. (sect. coun. vice-chair, com. chair 1989—92, Thomson Sci. & Frank Bradway Rogers award 2007). Independent. Home: 1027 Foster St Alameda CA 94502 Office: Univ Calif 530 Parnassus Ave San Francisco CA 94143-0840

BUTTERBRODT, JOHN ERVIN, real estate company officer; b. Beaver Dam, Wis., Feb. 14, 1929; s. Ervin E. and Josephine M. (O'Mare) B.; m. June Rose Bohalter, Sept. 27, 1952; children— Claire, Daniel, Larry. U. Agriculture short course, 1946-47. Cert. tchr. real estate, rental weatherization inspector, real estate appraiser, sr. profl. appraiser; internat. cert. farm appraiser; cert. gen., lic. appraiser, Wis. Vice-pres. Pure Milk Assn., 1967-69; pres. Asso. Milk Producers, Inc. Chgo., 1969-75, State Brand Creameries, Madison, Wis., 1970—, Wis. Real Estate Co., Wis. Real Estate of Burnett Inc., 1978—, Sunset Hills Golf & Supper Club Inc., 1979—; chmn. bd. Realty World-Wis. Real Estate, Inc., 1985—; treas. Real Estate Cons., 1983—. Dir. Town Mut. Ins. Co., Central Milk Sales, Central Milk Producers Coop. Pres. Sch. Bd., 1968; bd. dirs. Nat. Milk Producers Fedn., Central Am. Coop. Fedn., World Dairy Expo. Recipient Am. Farmer degree Future Farmers of Am., 1949, hon. degree, 1973; Outstanding Wis. Farmer award, 1965; Outstanding Wis. 4-H Alumni award, 1973; named Realtor of Yr., 1979 Mem.: United Dairy Industry Assn. Republican. Office: 1708 N Spring St Beaver Dam WI 53916-1106 Office Phone: 920-887-1733. Business E-Mail: johnb@wisreal.com.

BUTTERFIELD, ALEXANDER PORTER, air transportation executive, former federal official; b. Pensacola, Fla., Apr. 6, 1926; s. Horace Bushnell and Susan A. (Alexander) B.; m. Charlotte Mary Maguire, Sept. 9, 1949 (div. Jan. 1985); children: Leslie Carter (dec.), Alexander Porter Jr., Susan Carter Holcomb, Elisabeth Gordon Buchholz. BS, U. Md., 1956; MS, George Washington U., 1967; MA, U. Calif., 2005; PhD (hon.), Embry-Riddle U., 1973. Commd. 2d lt. USAF, 1949, advanced through grades to col., 1966, pilot, fighter-gunnery instr., parachutist, weapons officer, mem. Skyblazers (U.S. jet aerobatic team Europe), 1949-53; aide to comdr. 4th Allied Tactical Air Force (NATO), 1954-55; ops. officer interceptor squadron, 1955-56; asst. prof. USAF Acad., 1957-59; sr. aide to comdr.-in-chief U.S. Pacific Air Forces, 1959-62; comdr. fighter squadron Okinawa, 1962-63; comdr. tactical reconnaissance task forces S.E. Asia, 1963-64; tactical air warfare policy planner USAF hdqrs., 1964-65; mil. asst. to spl. asst. sec. def., 1965-66; student Nat. War Coll., 1966-67; sr. U.S. mil. rep. and comdr. in chief Pacific rep. Australia, 1967-69; retired, 1969; dep. asst. Pres. Richard M. Nixon, 1969-73; sec. to Cabinet, 1969-73; adminstr. FAA, 1973-75; lectr. Ethics in Govt. Am. Program Bur., 1975-76; exec. v.p., COO Internat. Air Svc. Co. Ltd., 1977—79; pres., COO Calif. Life Corp., 1979—80. Chmn. GMA Corp., Global Network Inc., 1981—82; chmn., CEO Armistead & Alexander, Inc., 1983—94. Contbr. articles to profl. jours. and nat. mags.; mem. editl. bd. LA County Mus. Natural History mag. Terra, 1983-86. Presidentially apptd. mem. Nat. Armed Forces Mus. adv. bd. Smithsonian Instn., 1970—76; mem. mil.-sci. expdn. to South Pole, 1968; leader of US govt. and industry del. to Moscow for ministerial leval talks on tech. and trade, 1973; key witness select com.'s hearings on Watergate US Senate, 1973; key witness during deliberations of impeachment of Pres. Richard Nixon US Ho. of Reps. Jud. Com., 1974; chmn. Chancellor's Assocs. U. Calif., San Diego, 2005—06; bd. dirs. Internat. Flight Safety Found., 1976—81, LA County Mus. Natural History, 1981—85. Decorated Legion of Merit, DFC, Air medal with 3 bronze oak leaf clusters, Bronze Star. Mem.: SAG, Air Force Assn., Tailhook Assn., Coun. for Excellence in Govt., Am. Film Inst., Thunderbird Alumni Assn., Bel-Air Country Club (L.A.), Univ. Club (San Diego). Home: 5340 Toscana Way # 416 San Diego CA 92122

BUTTERFIELD, ANDREA CHRISTINE, elementary school educator; b. Phila., Nov. 17, 1953; Student study abroad program, U. Md., Munich, Germany, 1973; BA in Childhood Edn., U. Fla., 1975; MEd in Reading Edn., Arcadia U., Glenside, Pa., 1977; postgrad. reading supr. cert. program, Millersville U., 1985; DEd in Adult Edn., Pa. State U., 1995. Cert. supervisory I supr. reading, instrnl. II reading specialist-elem., prin. K-12, supt's. letter. Reading specialist Lauderdale Lakes Middle Sch., Fla., 1977-78; coord., oper. individual title I Roman Cath. HS for Boys Sch. Dist. Phila., 1978-85; supr. reading specialist interns and grad. instr., clin. practicum reading clinic Millersville U., Pa., 1985-86; reading specialist Ebenezer Elem. Sch. and Cedar Crest Mid. Sch., Cornwall-Lebanon Sch. Dist., Lebanon, Pa., 1985—98; K-12 lang. arts supr., dir. ESL, fed. program coord. Dover Area Sch. Dist., 1998—. Adj. instr. Camden County Coll., NJ, 1980; cons. to ednl. orgns., 1994—; part-time faculty ednl. psychology Pa. State U., Harrisburg, 1995—; speaker in field. Reviewer: book The Reading Teacher. Planning commr., bd. officer Derry Township, Hershey, Pa., 1992—, design rev. bd. mem., 1994—. Recipient Rsch. award, Phi Delta Kappa. Mem. ASCD, Pa. ASCD (pres. so. region, chmn. so. region profl. devel. com.), Internat. Reading Assn. Avocation: travel. Home: 440 Leearden Rd Hershey PA 17033-2140 Office: Dover Area Sch Dist 2 School Ln Adminstrn Bldg Dover PA 17315 Personal E-mail: acbutterfield@yahoo.com.

BUTTERFIELD, BRUCE SCOTT, executive, editor, author, educator, consultant; m. Karin; children: Elizabeth, Timothy BA cum laude, Amherst Coll.; MAT, Harvard U.; MBA, U. Conn.; advanced cert. in journalism and creative fiction, Newspaper Inst. Am. Mng. editor, adminstr. Golden Press/Western Pub. Co., NYC, 1972-77; v.p., pub. Scholastic Inc., NYC, 1978-83; pres. Longman-Addison Wesley Pub. Group/Pearson PLC, 1984—93, Prentice Hall Regents/Simon & Schuster/Viacom Inc., 1993—97; CEO, pres. VirtualEd, Inc., 2002—06, Wittfield Group LLC, 2006—; pres. Scotlyn Group LLC, 2007—; exec. v.p. The Guardian Group LLC, 2007—, also bd. dirs. Bd. dirs. Endowment for Bibl. Rsch. Author: Fantasy and the Free School Thought: E.B. White and His Literature for Children; Our Real Work Can't Be Drudgery; editor: ABC's Wide World of Sports, Buccaneers, Book of the Mysterious, Chroma-Schema, Calculator Games, Children's Bible Stories, Oh Heavenly Dog, The Watcher in the Woods Named Most Valuable Semi-Pro Pitcher, Bergen Highlanders, All New Eng. Baseball Pitcher, All Am. Baseball Pitcher, named to U. Conn. Bus. Sch. Hall of Fame; recipient Wall St. Jour. Achievement award; Nat. Fedn. Music award; J.F. Kennedy Brotherhood Essay award; Gardener Fletcher fellow; St. Clair Meml. fellow; Amherst Coll. fellow. Mem. Beta Gamma Sigma, Phi Delta Kappa, Phi Delta Sigma.

BUTTERFIELD, DEBORAH KAY, sculptor; b. San Diego, May 7, 1949; m. John Buck; 2 children. BA, U. Calif., Davis, 1971, MFA, 1973; DFA (hon.), Mont. State U., 1998, Rocky Mountain Coll., Billings, Mont., 1997, Whitman Coll., Walla Walla, Wash., 2004. Asst. prof. sculpture U. Wis., Madison, 1975-76, Mont. State U., Bozeman, 1979-81, adj. prof., 1981-84. One-man shows include Lowe Mus. Art U. Miami, Coral Gables, Fla., 1992, San Diego Mus. Art, 1996, Yellowstone Art Mus., Billings, Mont., 2003-04, The Contemporary Mus. Art, Honolulu, 2004, Appleton Mus. Art, Ocala, Fla., 2004, U. Art Mus., U. La., Lafayette, 2005, Neuberger Art Mus., Purchase N.Y., 2005, Norton Mus. Art, West Palm Beach, Fla., 2005; exhibited in groups shows U. Mus. Berkeley, Calif., 1974, Whitney Mus. Am. Art, N.Y., 1979, Albright-Knox Gallery, Buffalo, 1979, Israel Mus., Jerusalem, 1980, Arco Ctr. Visual Art, 1981, Walker Art Ctr., Mpls., 1982, Dallas Mus. Fine Arts, 1982, Oakland, 1983, Chgo., 1985, Contemporary Art Ctr., Honolulu, 1986, Whitney Mus., 1988, Contemporary Art Mus., Honolulu, 1993, Seattle Mus. Art, 1994, The White House, Washington, Yale U., New Haven, 1997; represented in permanent collections Whitney Mus. Am. Art, N.Y., San Francisco Mus. Contemporary Art, Israel Mus., Jerusalem, Walker Art Ctr., Mpls., Met. Mus. Art, N.Y., Hirshhorn Mus., Washington, Seattle Art Mus., UCLA Sculpture Garden, L.A. Mus. Contemporary Art; commd. Copley Square, Boston, Portland (Oreg.) Airport, Denver Art Mus., Kansas City (Mo.) Zoo, White House, Washington, 2000, Monte Carlo, Monaco, 2000, Smithsonian Instn., Washington, San Francisco Internat. Airport. Nat. Endowment Arts grantee, 1977, 80, Guggenheim grantee, 1980; Commission Portland Internat. Airport.

BUTTERFIELD, GEORGE KENNETH, JR., congressman, former state supreme court justice; b. Wilson, NC, Apr. 27, 1947; s. G. K. and Addie (Davis) Butterfield; children: Valeisha Monique, Jenetta Lenai. BS in Polit. Sci. and Sociology, NC Ctrl. U., 1971; JD, NC Ctrl. U. Sch. Law, 1974. Bar: NC 1975. Sr. ptnr. Butterfield, Fitch & Wynn, 1974—88; judge NC Resident Superior Ct. Dist. 7B, 1989—2001; justice NC Supreme Ct., 2001—02; judge NC Spl. Superior Ct., 2002—04; mem. US Congress from 1st NC dist., 2004—, mem. armed svcs. com., mem. agr. com. Pers. specialist US Army, 1968—70. Named one of Most Influential Black Americans, Ebony mag., 2006; recipient Lawyer of Yr. award, NC Assn. Black Lawyers. Mem.: NC Bar Assn. (v.p. 2003—). Democrat. Baptist. Office: US House Reps 413 Cannon House Office Bldg Washington DC 20515-3301 Office Phone: 202-225-3101. Office Fax: 202-225-3354.*

BUTTERFIELD, STEPHEN ALAN, education educator; b. Middlebury, Vt., Sept. 10, 1948; s. Stewart Ellsworth and Mary Elizabeth (Coursey) B.; m. Jeanne Allison Zong, June 20, 1970; children: Sarah, Jason, Scott. BS, Springfield Coll., Mass., 1971; MEd, Keene State Coll., 1980; PhD, Ohio State U., 1984. Tchr. 4th grade Whitingham Sch., Jacksonville, Vt., 1971-72; prin., tchr. Halifax Sch., West Halifax, Vt., 1972-73; tchr. phys. edn. Austine Sch. for the Deaf, Brattleboro, Vt., 1973-81; prof. edn. and spl. edn. U. Maine, Orono, 1984—. Project dir. Nat. Youth Sports Program, state coord.; chmn., mem. Maine Task Force on Adapted Phys. Edn. Editor Maine Jour. Health, Phys. Edn., Recreation and Dance, 1988-96; contbr. articles to profl. jours. Bd. dirs. Bangor YMCA, Maine, 1990-92; mem. Gov.'s Coun. Phys. Fitness and Sports, 1996-98, 2000—; nat. stds. com. Adapted Phys. Edn., 2000-02. Recipient Meritorious award for Exceptional Project Performance, Nat. Youth Sports Program; state, fedn. found. grantee. Fellow: Am. Alliance Health and Phys. Edn., Recreation and Dance Rsch. Consortium; mem.: AAHPERD (ea. dist. merit award for phys. edn. 1989), Am. Coll. Sports Medicine, Nat. Consortium Phys. Edn. Recreation Individuals with Disabilities (editor The Advocate 1994—96, bd. dirs. 1997—99), Phys. Edn., Maine Assn. Health, Phys. Edn., Recreation and Dance (pres. 1986—87, Honor award for disting. leadership 1989). Republican. Avocation: military history. Home: 277 14th St Bangor ME 04401-4454 Office: U Maine 5740 Lengyel Hall College Ave Orono ME 04469-5740 Home Phone: 207-945-3684; Office Phone: 207-581-2469. Business E-Mail: steve.butterfield@umit.maine.edu.

BUTTERFIELD, STEWART, Internet company executive; m. Caterina Fake. BA with honors, U. Victoria; MPhil, Cambridge U. Dir. Communicate.com; co-founder, CEO Ludicorp, Vancouver, 2002—05; co-founder Flickr.com, 2004; dir. product mgmt. Yahoo!, San Francisco, 2005—. Cons. Telus, CBC, The Economist; founder 5K competition. Speaker in field. Co-recipient with Caterina Fake, Webby Breakout of Yr. award, 2005; named one of 100 Most Influential People, Time mag., 2006, 50 Who Matter Now, CNNMoney.com Bus. 2.0, 2006. Mem.: Internat. Acad. Digital Arts & Scis. Office: Yahoo 701 First Ave Sunnyvale CA 94089 E-mail: stewart@ludicorp.com.*

BUTTERLY, KATHY, sculptor; b. Amityville, NY, 1963; BFA, Moore Coll. Art, Phila., 1986; MFA, U. Calif., Davis, 1990. Exhibited in group shows at Fourth Concorso Nazionale della Ceramica d'Arte: Savona-Fortezza Primiar, Savona, Italy, 1990, Contemporary Ceramics, Bennington Coll. Gallery, Vt., 1992, Talentborse Handwerk, Munich, 1994, Forms and Transformations of Clay, Queens Borough Pub. Libr. Gallery, Jamaica, NY, 1997, Byron Cohen Gallery Contemporary Art, Kans. City, Mo., 2000, 2002, 15th Anniversary Exhbn., Franklin Parrasch Gallery, NYC, 2001, Kanazawa World Craft Forum, Japan, 2003, Very Familiar: Celebrating 50 Yrs. of Collecting Decorative Arts, Carnegie Mus. Art, 2003, Couples, Ctr. Maine Contemporary Art, Rockport, 2004, Carnegie Internat., Carnegie Mus. Art, Pitts., 2004—05, one-woman shows include Moore Coll. Art, Phila., 1992, Clay Studio, 1993, Franklin Parrasch Gallery, NYC, 1994, 1995, 1996, 1997, 1998, 1999, Bernard Toale Gallery, Boston, 2000, Tibor de Nagy Gallery, NYC, 2002, 2004, Shoshana Wayne Gallery, Santa Monica, Calif., 2003. Recipient Anonymous Was a Woman Grant award, 2002; grantee Evelyn Shapiro Found. grant, 1993, Empire State Crafts Alliance grant, 1995, NY Found. for the Arts grant, 1999. Mailing: c/o Tibor de Nagy Gallery 724 Fifth Ave New York NY 10019

BUTTERS, JOHN PATRICK, travel company executive, educator; b. Janesville, Wis., Jan. 11, 1933; s. John William and Mary Helen (Tracey) B.; m. Collette Helen Jung, Apr. 20, 1963; children: Blair John, Laura Lisbeth. BA, U. Wis., 1955. cert. travel counselor. Traffic supr., field training Pan Am. Airways, Chgo., 1958-64; ops. mgr. incentives Lerios/E.F. MacDonald, San Francisco, 1964-67; retail agy. mgr. Bungey Travel, Palo Alto, Calif., 1967-68; dist. sales mgr. Lissonne Lindeman, San Francisco, 1968-71; group travel mgr., Wis. div. Am. Automobile Assn., Madison, 1971-75; owner, v.p., sec. Travel/ease Inc., Madison, 1975-88; owner, pres. Travel Learn, Ltd., Madison, 1981-90; sr. curriculum specialist Inst. Cert. Travel Agts., Wellesley, Mass., 1989-93; free lance tour coord., tour escort Gretchen Petersen Tours, Inc., Madison, Wis., 1993-2000, Van Galder Tour and Travel, Janesville, Wis., 1996—. Cons. Madison Area Tech. Coll., 1982-88, Rockford (Ill.) Bus. Coll., 1988-90; treas. Capital Area Travel Soc., Madison, 1973-77. Editor: Travel Industry Mktg., 1990, Travel Industry Bus. Mgmt., 1992, U.S.A.-Can., 1992, Pacific Rim, 1993, Latin Am., 1994; contbr. articles to profl. jours. Program chmn. The Travel Club, Madison, 1973-77; bd. trustees St. Andrew's Soc., Madison, 1976-88 (treas. 1975-79); chmn. mus. svc. coun. Rock County Hist. Soc., Janesville, Wis., 1985-89; trustee Schumacher Farm Conservancy, Waunakee, Wis., 1984—. Mem. Inst. Cert. Travel Agts. (life), U. Wis. Alumni, Madison Club. Avocations: travel, reading, genealogy, history, geography. Home: 1328 Oakland Ave Janesville WI 53545-4243 Office: Van Galder Tour and Travel 20 S Main St Janesville WI 53545-3959 E-mail: jbutters@merr.com.

BUTTERS, RONALD RICHARD, language educator; b. Cedar Rapids, Iowa, Feb. 12, 1940; s. Richard Orton and Dorothy Mae B.; children: Rebecca, Catherine, Rachel. BA, U. Iowa, 1962, PhD, 1967. Asst. prof. English Duke U., Durham, N.C., 1967-74, assoc. prof. English, 1974-90, prof. English, 1990—, prof. anthropology, 2000—. Editor Am. Speech Jour. Am. Dialect Soc., 1981-95; vis. scholar Ctr. Applied Linguistics, Washington, 1988-89; mem. editl. adv. bd. New Oxford American Dictionary. Author: The Death of Black English, 1989; co-author: Displacing Hompohobia, 1989 (CEW best spl. issue award 1989); chief editor Am. Dialect Soc. publs., 1996—. Recipient Rsch. grant NEH, 1973-74. Mem. Am. Dialect Soc. (v.p. 1997-99, pres. 2000-02), Internat. Assn. Forensic Linguists, Linguistic Soc. Am., Southeastern Conf. Linguistics (pres. 1983), Law and Soc. Assn., Dictionary Soc. N.Am. Office: Duke Univ PO Box 90015 Durham NC 27708-0015 Home: 1000 Lamond Ave Durham NC 27701-2021 Home Phone: 919-423-8866; Office Phone: 919-684-2741. Personal E-mail: ronbutters@aol.com.

BUTTERWORTH, PAUL, information technology executive; BS in Info., Computer Sci., MS in Info., Computer Sci., Univ. Calif., Davis. Chief architect, dir. product engring Ingres Corp.; co-founder, chief architect, sr. v.p., engring, customer svc. Forte Software; co-founder AmberPoint Inc., Oakland, Calif., 2001—. Named one of Top 25 Chief Tech. Officers, InfoWorld mag., 2007; recipient Disting. Alumnus award, Univ. Calif. Davis, 2005. Office: AmberPoint Inc 155 Grand Ave Ste 404 Oakland CA 94612 Office Phone: 510-663-6300.

BUTTERWORTH, S. KENDALL, lawyer; d. Charles Kenneth and Sue (Anderson) Butterworth. BA with honors, U. Va., 1991; JD cum laude, U. Ga., 1994. Bar: Ga. 1994, U.S. Dist. Ct. (no. dist.) Ga. 1994, U.S. Ct. Appeals (11th cir.) 1994. Assoc. Kilpatrick Stockton LLP, Atlanta, 1994—97; atty. Bellsouth Telecomm., 1997—98, Bellsouth Cellular Corp., 1999—2000; litigation coun. Bellsouth Corp., 2001; sr. litigation coun. AT&T Southeast (formerly Bellsouth Corp.), 2007—07, chief litigation coun., 2007—. Mem. adv. bd. Atlanta Legal Aid Soc., 2002—, chief litigation counsel; spl. asst. to chair Supreme Ct. Commn. on Indigent Def., Atlanta, 2001—04. Named Up and Comer Under 40, Atlanta Bus. Chronicle, 2004—05, Ga. Rising Star, Atlanta mag., 2005. Mem.: Ga. State Bar (mem. bd. govs. 1999—, pres. Young Lawyers divsn. Atlanta chpt. 2000—01), ABA (mem. Ho. of Dels., Chgo. 2000—04, mem. jury commn. 2004—05, named Star of the Quarter 1999, 2004, 2005), Atlanta Bar Assn. Avocations: running, travel, music. Office: AT&T South 1155 Peachtree St Ste 1700 Atlanta GA 30309 Office Phone: 404-249-3388. Office Fax: 404-249-5664. Business E-Mail: kendall.butterworth@bellsouth.com.

BUTTERY, CHRISTOPHER MALCOLM GEDDA, medical educator; b. Harrogate, England, July 1, 1930; s. James Thomas Buttery and Katerina Gedda; m. Elizabeth R. McGowan; children: Alexander Kevin, Nigel Christopher, Gail Leslie Grandela. B Medicine B Surgery, U. London, 1954; MPH, Johns Hopkins U., Balt., 1968. Diplomate Am. Bd. Preventive Medicine, 1971. Dir. pub. health City of Portsmouth, Va., 1968—75, City of Corpus Christi, Tex., 1980—86, City of Richmond, Va., 1991—95; assoc. prof. Ea. Va. Med. Sch., Norfolk, 1975—80; commr. health State of Va., Richmond, 1986—91; clin. prof. pub. health Va. Commonwealth U., Richmond, 1990—. Cons. Office Surgeon Gen., US Army, Washington, 1974—90. Fellow: Am. Coll. Preventive Medicine (bd. dirs. 1984—86); mem.: Am. Assn. Pub. Health Physicians. Home: 8606 Woodshill Ct Richmond VA 23235-4162 Office: Va Commonwealth U 1000 East Clay St PO Box 980212 Richmond VA 23298 Office Phone: 804-828-9785. Business E-Mail: cbuttery@vcu.edu.

BUTTIGIEG, JOSEPH J., bank executive; BBA, U. Notre Dame; JD, Mich. State U. Coll. Law. Various to sr. v.p. Manufacturer's Bank, Detroit, 1972-89, exec. v.p., 1989-91; exec. v.p. global corp. banking Comerica, Inc., Detroit, 1995-99, vice-chmn. bus. bank, 1999—. Office: Comerica Inc Comerica Twr/500 Woodward A Detroit MI 48226

BUTTLAR, RUDOLPH OTTO, retired college dean; b. Chgo., Dec. 31, 1934; s. Otto Robert and Lucille Ann (Blasnig) B.; m. Lois Jacqueline Mercier, June 5, 1955; children— Michael Robert, Andrew Scott, John David. BS in Chemistry, Wheaton Coll., Ill., 1956; PhD in Inorganic Chemistry, Ind. U., 1962. Mem. faculty Kent (Ohio) State U., 1962-96, asso. prof. chemistry, 1971-96; dean Kent (Ohio) State U. (Coll. Arts and Scis.), 1975-96. Adminstrv. cons., 1996—. Mem. Am. Chem. Soc., Am. Sci. Affiliation. Baptist. Home: 5936 Horning Rd Kent OH 44240-4140 E-mail: rbuttlar@neo.rr.com.

BUTTNER, JEAN BERNHARD, diversified financial services company executive; b. New Rochelle, NY, Nov. 3, 1934; d. Arnold and Janet (Kinghorn) Bernhard; m. Edgar Buttner, Sept. 13, 1958 (div.); 3 children. BA, Vassar Coll., 1957; cert. bus. adminstrn., Harvard-Radcliffe program, 1958; Montessori diploma, Coll. Notre Dame, Belmont, Calif., 1967; D Bus. Adminstrn. (hon.), U. Bridgeport, 1994. Past v.p. Buttner Cos., Oakland, Calif.; chmn., pres., CEO Value Line Inc. (subs. Arnold Bernhard & Co., Inc.), NYC, 1985; chmn., pres. Vanderbilt Advt., Inc., 1988—, Arnold Bernhard & Co., Inc., NYC, 1988—, Compupower, 1988—, Value Line Securities, Inc., 1988—, Value Line Pub., Inc., 1990, Value Line Distbn. Ctr., Inc., 1999—. Chmn., pres. Value Line Mut. Funds. Editor-in-chief Value Line Investment Survey. Past trustee Skidmore Coll.; past pres. Piedmont Sch. Bd.; past dir. Berkeley Montessori Sch.; past mem. NYC Partnership, Com. of 200; past adv. coun. Stanford Bus. Sch.; past mem. Presdl. Roundtable; past vis. com. for bd. overseers Harvard Bus. Sch.; past bd. dirs. Harvard Bus. Sch. Club Greater NY; past west coast admissions rep. Vassar Coll.; past trustee Radcliffe Coll., Williams Coll., Emma Willard Sch., Coll. Prep. Sch. Com. for Econ. Devel.; trustee Choate Rosemary Hall. Named one of NY's 75 Most Influential Women in Business, Crain's, 1996, One of NY's 100 Most Influential Women in Business, Crain's, 1999; recipient Alumni Achievement award, Harvard U. Grad. Sch. Bus. Adminstrn., 1995, Alumnae award Choate Rosemary Hall, Wallingford, Conn., 1995, Emma Lazarus award Associated Builders and Owners of NY, Inc., 1996; Life Achievement award Emma Willard Sch., 1998. Republican. Congregationalist. Avocations: reading, swimming, bicycling, tennis, skiing. Office: Value Line Inc 220 E 42nd St Fl 6 New York NY 10017-5891 E-mail: jbb@valueline.com.

BUTTON, RENA PRITSKER, public relations executive; b. Providence, Feb. 15, 1925; d. Isadore and Esther (Kay) Pritsker; m. Daniel E. Button, Aug. 16, 1969; children by previous marriage: Joshua, Bruce, David Posner. Student, Pembroke Coll., 1942—45; BS, Simmons Coll., 1948; postgrad., Union U., 1968—69. Spl. asst. to U.S. Rep., 1967-69; spl. projects coord. United Jewish Appeal, 1971-74; exec. dir. Nat. Coun. Jewish Women, Inc., NYC, 1974-76; pres. Button Assos., NYC, 1976—; exec. v.p. Catalyst, NYC, 1980-82; pres. Button & Button, Albany, NY, 1982—. Adv. coun. N.Y. State Senate Minority, 1980—; exec. dir. N.Y.

State Coun. on Alcoholism and Other Drug Addictions, 1990-93; pres., founder Two Together, A Pilot Reading Program for Young People, 1997-2003. Co-producer, moderator: (TV) Speak For Yourself, 1963-66. Chair pub. affairs com. Marymount Manhattan Coll.; past bd. dirs. Albany YWCA, Albany Coun. Chs. Devel. Corp., World Affairs Coun., Planned Parenthood Assn. Albany; trustee Jerusalem Women's Seminar, Citizens for Family Planning, N.Y. Com. Integrated Housing, Hist. Albany Found. Ctr. for Counseling, Town of Bethlehem Pub. Libr., 1999; pres. Sr. Svc. Ctr. Albany Area, Two Together, 1997; bd. dirs. Com. Modern Cts.; exec. dir. N.Y. Head Injury Assn., 1993-96; candidate N.Y. State Assembly 102d Dist., 1996; trustee Albany Symphony Orch., 2002—. Mem. Siasconset Casino Club, Univ. Club. Clubs: Siasconset Casino (Siasconset, Mass.), Univ. (Albany). Home and Office: 16 Spruce Ct Delmar NY 12054-2614 Personal E-mail: rbutton99@verizon.net.

BUTTREY, DONALD WAYNE, lawyer; b. Terre Haute, Ind., Feb. 6, 1935; s. William Edgar and Nellie (Vaughn) B.; children: Greg, Alan, Jason; m. Karen Lake, Mar. 23, 1985. BS, Ind. State U., 1956; JD, Ind. U., 1961. Bar: Ind. 1961, U.S. Dist. Ct. 1961, U.S. Ct. Appeals (7th cir.) 1972, U.S. Tax Ct. 1972, U.S. Supreme Ct. 1972. Law clk. to chief judge Steckler, US Dist. Ct. So. Dist. Ind., 1961-63; mem. McHale, Cook & Welch, P.C., Indpls., 1963—, pres., 1986-93, chmn., 1993—2001; of counsel Wooden & McLaughlin, LLP, 2001—. Chmn. Ctrl. Region IRS-Bar Liaison Com., 1984; jud. nominating com. Marion County Mcpl. Ct., 1993-96; mem. Estate Planning Coun. Indpls., 1990—. Note editor Ind. Law Jour., 1960-61. Trustee Ind. State U., 1992-2000, v.p. bd., 1997-2000; bd. dirs. Ind. State U. Found., 1991—. With AUS, 1956-58, Korea. Fellow Am. Coll. Tax Counsel, Am. Bar Found., Ind. State Bar Found., Indpls. Bar Found. (pres. 1993-96, Buchanan award 1999); mem. ABA (taxation, real property, probate and trust sect., liaison IRS-Bar Liaison com., taxation sect. 1995-96), Ind. State Bar Assn. (bd. govs. 1994-96, taxation, real property, probate and trust sect., chmn. taxation sect. 1982-83), Indpls. Bar Assn. (pres. 1990, mem. probate, taxation sects.), Highland Golf and Country Club, Columbia Club, Univ. Club (bd. dirs. 1997-2000). Presbyterian. Home Phone: 317-846-9290; Office Phone: 317-639-6151 ext. 309. Business E-Mail: dbuttrey@woodmaclaw.com.

BUTTRICK, HAROLD, architect; b. Bryn Mawr, Pa., Jan. 2, 1931; s. Charles Edgar and Constance (La Boiteaux) B.; m. Ann Octavia White, Sept. 3, 1955; children: John Ward, Jerome Chanler, Mary Constance, Sarah Elizabeth, Catherine. Student, The Sorbonne, Paris, 1950-51; AB, Harvard U., 1953, MArch, 1959. Cert. NCRB. With Harold Buttrick & Assocs., NYC, 1963-75; prin. Smotrich Platt & Buttrick, NYC, 1975-76, Buttrick White & Burtis, NYC, 1976-97, Murphy Burnham & Buttrick, NYC, 1998—. Prin archtl. works include Corpus Christi Monastery, Nairobi, Kenya, 1967, Green Vale Sch., Iselin Ctr., Glen Head, N.Y., 1971, Trans World Airlines 747 Hangar, John F. Kennedy Airport, 1971, Carter Giraffe House, Bronx Zoo, 1981, 42 Tower Records Stores, 1982-94, St. Thomas Choir Sch., N.Y.C., 1987, Central Park projects, Loeb Boathouse, 1986, Ballplayers Refreshment Stand, 1990, restoration of the Pulitzer Fountain and Grand Army Plz., 1990, The Charles A. Dana Discovery Ctr., 1993, Performance Stage, Bushnell Park, Hartford, Conn., 1995, Battery Park City Authority Offices, 1996, Trinity Mid. Sch., NYC, 1998, St. Bartholomew's Ch., Master Plan, NYC, 2004. Bd. dirs. N.Y. Soc. Libr., 1989-93. Recipient Preservation League of N.Y. State awards, 1990-91, 96, City Club of N.Y. Bard awards Loeb Boathouse, 1986, St. Thomas Choir Sch., 1990, Ballplayers Refreshment Stand, 1992, St. Patrick's Cathedral Master Plan, 2006. Fellow AIA (Brick in Architecture award 1991, 95), NY State Assn. Archs.; mem. Century Assn., New Yorkers for Parks. Office: Murphy Burnham & Buttrick 48 W 37th St New York NY 10018 Office Phone: 212-768-7676.

BUTTS, HERBERT CLELL, retired dentist, educator; b. Dover, Tenn., Aug. 24, 1924; s. Sidney Lewis and Georgia (Sawyer) B.; m. Quay Coker; children: Marla Lyce, April Chyrese, Dawn Denise, Sidney Coker. Student, U. Tenn. Jr. Coll., 1942-43, Memphis State U., 1946-47; DDS, U. Tenn., 1950; MS, U. Iowa, 1966. Pvt. practice dentistry, Memphis, 1950-58; mem. faculty Coll. Dentistry, U. Tenn., Memphis, part-time 1950-58, 58-60, assoc. dean acad. affairs, 1978-81, spl. advisor to dean, 1986-2000; ret., 2000; fgn. svc. officer, dental edn. advisor State Dept. Fgn. Aid program, San Salvador, El Salvador, 1960-64; assoc. prof. St. Louis U. Sch. Dentistry, 1966-67; prof., chmn. dept. operative dentistry Coll. Dental Medicine, Med. U. S.C., Charleston, 1967-70, asst. dean for admissions and student affairs, 1970, 72-74, acting dean, 1971; editor-in-chief ADA, Chgo., 1974-77; dean Sch. Dental Medicine So. Ill. U., Alton, 1981-86. Editor U. Tenn. Coll. Dentistry Bull., 1990-2000. With USNR, 1943-46. Recipient Outstanding Alumnus award U. Tenn. Coll. Dentistry, 1975. Mem. ADA, Tenn. Dental Assn. (fellowship award 1993), Memphis Dental Soc., Am. Coll. Dentists (pres. Tenn. sect. 1994, sec.-treas. Tenn. sect. 1995-98), Internat. Coll. Dentists, Am. Assn. Dental Schs., Ala. Dental Assn. (hon.), Am. Assn. Women Dentists (hon.), Omicron Kappa Upsilon. Home: 1360 Peabody Ave Memphis TN 38104-3636

BUTTS, HUGH FLORENZ, physician, psychiatrist, psychoanalyst; b. NYC, Dec. 2, 1926; s. Lucius Cornelius and Edith Eliza Butts; m. June Dobbs, June 9, 1953 (div. Dec. 1971); children: Lucia Irene, Florence, Eric Hugh; m. Clementine Riggsbee, Dec. 11, 1971; children: Sydney Clementine, Samantha Florenz, Heather Marguerita. BS, CCNY, 1949; MD, Meharry Med. Coll., Nashville, 1953. Diplomate Am. Bd. Psychiatry and Neurology. Intern Morrisania Hosp., 1956; resident Bronx VA Hosp., 1958; psychiatry instr. Columbia U., NYC, 1962-65, assoc. prof. psychiatry, 1965-67, asst. clin. prof. psychiatry, 1967-74; mem. faculty Columbia Psychoanalytic Clinic, NYC, 1962-87, supervising and tng. analyst, 1968-87; lectr. Columbia Coll., NYC, 1969-71; instr. Seek program CCNY, NYC, 1972-74. Prof. psychiatry Albert Einstein Coll. Medicine, Bronx, 1974-81; cons. Altanta U. Sch. Social Work, 1970-74; vis. prof. psychiatry Meharry Med. Coll., Nashville, 1980-82; dir. Bronx Psychiat. Ctr., 1974-79; 1st dept. commr. N.Y. State Office Mental Health, Albany, N.Y., 1975-76; chmn. adv. bd. The Med. Herald, 1991-02; presenter and lectr. in field; honoree, guest spkr. Vassar Coll. Program on African Studies, 2007. Pres., founder Clementine Pub. Co., 1989, Lit. Mind Assocs., 1989; author: The Blackness of Darkness, 1994; co-author: The Psychology of Black Language, 1973, 2d edit/, 1993; editor: Racism and Post Traumatic Stress Disorder, 2006; contbr. more than 300 articles to profl. jours. With USAAF, 1944-45. Recipient Spl. Merit award Assn. for Psychoanalytic Medicine, 1967, Nat. Med. Assn. award, 2005, Annual Dr. Eugene F. Williams Sr. Scholar of Distinction award Nat. Med. Assn., 2006; Travel fellow Ford Found., 1972. Fellow: NY Acad. Scis., Am. Psychiat. Assn. (Disting. Life fellow 2003); mem.: Am. Psychoanalytic Assn. Achievements include completed the NYC marathon in 1991, 94 and 95. Avocations: gardening, fishing, antiques, violin, writing. Office: 350 Central Park W New York NY 10025-6547 Office Phone: 212-864-6191. Personal E-mail: h7buttsmd@aol.com.

BUTTS, WILLIAM LESTER, entomologist, researcher; b. Reynoldsburg, Ohio, Dec. 7, 1931; s. Edward Donald and Mamie Olive (Minor) Butts; m. Barbara Baily; children: Nicholas Edward, Susan Lee, Thomas William. BS, Wilmington Coll., 1953; MS, Ohio State U., 1954, PhD, 1964. Assoc. prof. Purdue U., Lafayette, Ind., 1957—66; prof. SUNY, Oneonta, NY, 1967—95, prof. emeritus, 1995—. Field rschr. SUNY Oneonta Biol. Field Station, Cooperstown, NY, 1968—. Author: Scientific Guide to Post Control Operations, 1962. Mem.: Union of Concerned Scientists, Am. Mosquito Control Assn., Sigma Xi. Avocations: hunting, birdwatching. Office: Oneonta Biol Field Sta 5838 State Hwy 80 Cooperstown NY 13326

BUTTZ, CHARLES WILLIAM, outdoor advertising executive; b. Aberdeen, SD, Aug. 8, 1932; s. Ward Leland and Mary Baker (Eddy) B.; m. Teresa Margarita Castro, July 28, 1956; children: Jean, Teresa, Charles, William, James. BCE, Rensselaer Polytech Inst., 1956; MBA, U. Conn., 1974. Chief engr. Kuala Lumpur Transp. Study, Malaysia, 1963—64; project mgr. Tippetts Abbett McCarthy Stratton Engrs., NYC, 1956—65; mgmt. cons. Booz, Allen and Hamilton, NYC, 1965—67; dir. Knight, Gladieux and Smith Cons., NYC, 1967—74; group mgr. Boeing Computer Svcs. Cons., NYC, 1974—76; v.p. Middlesex Rsch. Ctr., Washington, 1976—77; pres. Ea. Shelter-All Inc., Mountainhome, Pa., 1977—, N.J. Shelter-All Inc., Columbia, 1980—, Regional Shelter-All Inc., Buck Hill Falls, Pa., 1985—. Instr. mktg. U. Conn., Stamford, 1975-76. Pres. St. Paul's Housing Corp., Norwalk, Conn., 1974-77; com. mem. Alfred Dater Coun. Boy Scouts Am., Stamford, 1970-77; v.p., camp chmn. Darien (Conn.) United Way, 1974; v.p., sec. Darien Young Mens Christian Assn., 1974-77; dir. United Way Monroe County, Tannersville, Pa., 1984-97. Maj. USAR, 1956-70. Scholar, Wall St. Jour., 1974. Mem. ASCE, Pa. Soc., Inst. Transp. Engrs., Am. Legion, Army and Navy Club. Episcopalian. Home: Cottage 266 Buck Hill Falls PA 18323 Office: Ea Shelter-All Inc PO Box 152 Mountainhome PA 18342

BUTZ, EARL LAUER, former secretary of agriculture, consultant; b. Albion, Ind., July 3, 1909; s. Herman L. and Ada (Lauer) B.; m. Mary Emma Powell, Dec. 22, 1937 (dec.); children: William, Thomas. BSA, Purdue U., 1932, PhD, 1937, LLD, 1973; DAgr, Tri-State Coll., 1976, Western Ill. U., 1976. Asst. prof. agrl. econs. Purdue U., Lafayette, Ind., 1937-42, assoc. prof., 1942-46, prof., head dept., 1946-54; asst. sec. USDA, Washington, 1954-57; dean agr. Purdue U., Lafayette, Ind., 1957-67, dean continuing edn., v.p. Rsch. Found., 1967-71; sec. USDA, Washington, 1971-76; pub. lectr., bus. cons. Lafayette, 1977—. Author: Production Credit System for Farmers, 1944; contbr. articles to profl. jours. Mem. several nat. coms. on agrl. policy; active in polit. campaigns. Ky. col.; named Sagamore of the Wabash, Gov. of Ind., 1958, 75, Admiral of Nebr., Gov. of Nebr., 1976. Mem. Am. Agrl. Econ. Assn. (v.p., sec. 1952-54), Alpha Gamma Rho (nat. pres. 1948-50, Hall of Fame 1981). Republican. E-mail: ebutz@purdue.edu.

BUTZ, GENEVA MAE, pastor; b. Emmaus, Pa., May 11, 1944; d. Edwin F. and Arlene E. (Engler) B. BA, Hood Coll., 1966; MRE, Union Theol. Sem., 1968; D Divinity (hon.), Ursinus Coll., 1994. Ordained clergywoman United Ch. of Christ, 1972. Dir. Christian edn. United Ch. of Christ, Palos Verdes, Calif., 1968-72; mng. editor Youth mag., United Ch. Bd. for Homeland Ministries, Phila., 1972-75; affiliate rep. Ecumenical Community of Taizé, France, New Zealand, Australia, Indonesia, India and others, 1975-77; parish worker Temple Presbyn. Ch., Phila., 1978-83; pastor Old First Reformed Ch., United Ch. Christ, Phila., 1984—2003; assoc. conf. minister Pa. SE Conf. United Ch. Christ, 2003—. Bd. dirs. Met. Christian Coun. of Phila., 1985-96, 98—; chair Ch. and Ministry Com., Phila. Assn. United Ch. Christ, 1983-86; cons. Auburn Theol. Sem., N.Y., 1988-89; coord. 5-Day urban seminar for incoming students Lancaster Theol. Sem., 1986-93, The Small Ch. and Cultural Change, Bangor Theol. Sem., 1988; mem. adv. com. on evangelism and membership growth priority United Ch. Christ, 1989=90; team chair Toward the 21st Century, A Church-wide Planning Process for the United Ch. Christ, 1990-93; spkr. Faith Journey, consultation XVI in Parish Ministry for United Ch. Christ Clergy, Orlando, Fla., 1991; guest preacher Nat. Cathedral, Washington, 1993; commencement spkr. Lancaster Theol. Sem., 1996; sabbatical visitor to ch. in Indonesia through Common Global Mission Bd. (Disciples of Christ/United Ch. Christ), 2001. Author: Color Me Well, 1986, Christmas Comes Alive, 1988, Christmas in All Seasons, 1995; contbr. Women Pray, Karen Roller, Ed, 1986. Bd. dirs. Bethesda Project, Inc., Phila., 1986-98, Phila. Religious Leadership Devel. Fund, 1988-98, Maternity Care Coalition, Phila., 1999—; del. Gen. Synod-United Ch. Christ, Cleve., Ft. Worth, Providence, Kansas City, 1987-89, 99-2001; ecumenical del. Gen. Assembly Presbyn. Ch. (USA), 1989; adv. bd. Seamen's Ch. Inst., Phila., 1992-2003; trustee Lancaster Theol. Sem., 1992—; 2d v.p. Met. Christian Coun. Phila., 1998—. Named One of 85 People to Watch, Phila. Mag., 1985, One of 7 Clergy Leading U.S. Constl. Bicentennial Parade, 1987, Valiant Woman of Yr., Ch. Women United, 1991; recipient Human Rels. award, NCCJ, Phila., 1985; fellow Merrill fellow, Harvard Div. Sch., 1993. Mem. Nat. Orgn. of Women, Ch. Women United of Greater Phila., Old Phila. Clergy, Assn. United Arts and Religion, Phila. Assn. (ministrial standing). Democrat. Office: Pa SE Conf United Ch of Christ 505 S 2d St Collegeville PA 19426 E-mail: gbutz@psec.org. *Being religious is so simple that as adults we find it hard to achieve. Children do it easily. We need to work with children so we don't destroy their natural religious inclination. The future of the faith lies in our ability to evoke the innate religious sensitivity in all people.*

BUTZ, JAMI LIPAN, psychiatric pharmacy specialist; d. James Harris and Tamara Gene Lipan; m. Steven Wayne Butz, Mar. 20, 1999. BS, U. Md., Catonsville, 1997; PharmD, U. Md., Balt., 2001. Cert. Geriatric Pharmacist Commn. for Cert. in Geriatric Pharmacy, 2004, Bd. Cert. Psychiatric Pharmacist Bd. Pharm. Specialties, 2005. Psychiat. pharmacy resident U. Md., Balt., 2001—02; cons. pharmacist NeighborCare, Annapolis Junction, Md., 2002—04; clin. psychiat. pharmacy specialist Sinai Hosp. Balt., 2004—. Clin. asst. prof. U. Md., Balt., 2005—; mem. ABC News Pharmacy Consensus Panel, 2005—. Reviewer Jour. Clinical Psychiatry, 2005—06. Participant Avon Breast Cancer 3-day Walks, Balt., 2001—02. Mem.: Am. Soc. Cons. Pharmacists, Am. Coll. Clin. Pharmacy, Am. Soc. Health-Sys. Pharmacists, Coll. Psychiat. and Neurologic Pharmacists. Avocations: reading, dance, travel.

BUTZ, NORBERT LEO, actor; b. St. Louis, Jan. 30, 1967; m. Sydney Butz; children: Clara Virginia, Maggie Lou. BFA, Webster U.; MFA, Ala. Shakespeare Theatre. Actor: (Broadway plays) Rent, 1996; (Broadway plays, nat. tour) Cabaret (Helen Hayes award, outstanding actor in a musical); (Broadway plays) Thou Shalt Not, 2001, Wicked, 2003, Dirty Rotten Scoundrels, 2005 (Tony award, best performance by a leading actor in a musical, 2005, Drama League award, disting. performance, 2005, Outer Critics Circle award, outstanding actor in a musical, 2005, Drama Desk award, oustanding actor in a musical, 2005); (plays, off-broadway) Buicks, The Last Five Years, 2002 (Drama League award, outstanding actor in a musical); (plays) Juno and the Paycock, Saved; (films) Went to Coney Island on a Mission from God.Be Back by Five, 1998, (voice) Looking for an Echo, 2000, Noon Blue Apples, 2002, West of Here, 2002.

BUTZ, STEFAN PETER, science association director; b. Haan, Germany, July 1, 1968; m. Katrin Petzoldt, Dec. 6, 1997; children: Jil Caroline, John Peter Maximilian. MBA, U. Bayreuth, Germany, 1994. Mgr. strategy competency accenture, Munich, 1997—2000; dir. corp. devel. TUV Sued AG, Munich, 2000—02; CEO, pres. TUV Am., Danvers, Mass., 2002—. Mem. Atlantik Bruecke e.v., Berlin. Home: 2 Avery St #27D Boston MA 02111 Office: TUV America Inc 5 Cherry Hill Dr Danvers MA 01923 Home Phone: 978-869-4816; Office Phone: 978-739-7000. Business E-Mail: sbutz@tuvam.com.

BUX, WILLIAM JOHN, lawyer; b. Wadsworth, Ohio, Nov. 10, 1946; s. William J. and Helen M. (Sybelnik) B.; m. Linda Alice Zenar, Feb. 13, 1971. BSME, Ohio State U., 1969, MS, 1970; JD cum laude, So. Meth. U., 1977. Bar: Tex. 1977, U.S. Dist. Ct. (so. dist.) Tex. 1978, U.S. Ct. Appeals (5th cir.) 1978, U.S. Dist. Ct. (no. dist.) Tex. 1980, U.S. Dist. Ct. (ea. and we. dists.) Tex. 1981, U.S. Ct. Appeals (11th cir.) 1981, U.S. Supreme Ct. 1982; cert. Labor & Employment Law Tex. Bd. Legal Specialization. Assoc. Vinson & Elkins, Houston, 1977-85; ptnr. Hughes & Luce, Dallas, 1985-93; shareholder Locke Purnell Rain Harrell, Dallas, 1994-97; ptnr. Liddell, Sapp, Zivley, Hill & La Boon, Houston, 1997-98, Locke, Liddell & Sapp, Houston, 1999—. Author: Developing and Enforcing Drug and Alcohol Abuse Work Rules: A Primer for Texas Employers, 1984. Sec. So. Meth. U. Law Sch. Alumni Council, Dallas, 1986-88. Capt. USAF, 1971-74. Mem. ABA, Tex. Bar Assn. (chmn. labor and employment law sect. 1992-93), Houston Bar Assn., Dallas Bar Assn., 5th Cir. Bar Assn. (named a Tex. Super Lawyer 2003-07, named one of Best Lawyers Am. 2006-07), Order of the Coif. Republican. Roman Catholic. Home: 2511 Westgate St Houston TX 77019-6609 Office: Locke Liddell & Sapp 600 Travis St 3400 JP Morgan Chase Twr Houston TX 77002-3095 Office Phone: 713-226-1275.

BUXBAUM, RICHARD M., lawyer, educator; b. 1930; AB, Cornell U., 1950, LLB, 1952; LLM, U. Calif., Berkeley, 1953; D (hon.), U. Osnabrück, 1992, Eötvös Lorand U., Budapest, Hungary, 1993, U. Cologne, 2006. Bar: Calif. 1953, NY 1953. Pvt. practice, Rochester, NY, 1957—61; prof. U. Calif., Berkeley, 1961—, dean internat. and area studies, 1993-99. Hon. prof. U. Peking, 1998. Editor-in-chief Am. Jour. Comparative Law, 1987-2004. Property commn. mem. Found. for Responsibility, Remembrance, and the Future, Germany, 2001—06. Recipient Humboldt prize, 1991, German Order of Merit, 1992, Officier Arts et Lettres, France, 1997, Order of Rio Branco, Brazil, 1998. Mem. AAAS, Am. Law Inst., Internat. Acad. Comparative Law, German Soc. Comparative Law (corr.), Coun. on Fgn. Rels. Office: U Calif Sch Law 888 Simon Hall Berkeley CA 94720-0001 Office Phone: 510-642-1771. Business E-Mail: bux@berkeley.edu.

BUXBAUM, ROBERT C(OURTNEY), internist; b. Milw., Dec. 16, 1930; s. Edwin C. and Lillian (Tousman) B.; m. Ann S. Shocket, Dec. 26, 1955; children: Laura, Carl, Paula, Margaret. AB, Harvard U., 1952; MD, U. Pa., 1956. Diplomate Am. Bd. Internal Medicine, Am. Bd. Hospice and Palliative Medicine. Intern Henry Ford Hosp., Detroit, 1956-57; officer USPHS, San Carlos Apache Res., Ariz., 1957-59; resident, rsch. fellow U. Wis. Hosp., Madison, 1959-63; from rsch. assoc. to instr. Harvard Med. Sch., Boston, 1963-69, asst. prof. medicine, 1969—2004, clin. assoc. prof. medicine, 2004—. Internist Harvard Cmty. Health Plan (now Harvard Vanguard Med. Assocs.), Boston, 1969—; cons. health policy; founding mem. Mass. Compassionate Care Coalition, 1999—, v.p., 2000, 2003, pres., 2003—. Author: Sports for Life, 1979; contbr. articles to profl. jours. Chmn. Gov.'s Com. on Fitness, Mass., 1975—80. Fellow ACP. Mem. Am. Acad. Hospice and Palliative Medicine. Avocations: playing oboe, swimming, skiing. Office: Harvard Vanguard Med Assocs Faulkner Hosp 1153 Centre St 6th Fl Boston MA 02130 Office Phone: 617-838-5437. Business E-Mail: robert_buxbaum@hms.harvard.edu.

BUXTON, DOUGLAS FRANCISCO, ophthalmologist, educator; b. NYC, Nov. 5, 1952; s. Jorge Norman and Amalia (Gonzalez) B. BA, Yale U., 1975; postgrad., Columbia U., 1977; MD, Cornell U., 1982. Diplomate Am. Bd. Ophthalmology, Nat. Bd. Med. Examiners; diplomate in cataract/implant surgery, penetrating keratoplasty, and laser in situ keratomileusis Am. Bd. Eye Surgery. Intern St. Vincent's Hosp. and Med. Ctr., NYC, 1982—83; resident N.Y. Eye and Ear Infirmary, NYC, 1983—86, fellow in cornea and external disease, 1986—88, attending surgeon, 1986—; asst. attending surgeon dept. ophthalmology Manhattan Eye, Ear and Throat Hosp., NYC, 1988—; clin. assoc. prof. ophthalmology N.Y. Med. Coll., 1991—. Contbr. articles to profl. jours. Fellow Am. Acad. Ophthalmology; mem. Am. Coll. Eye Surgeons, Am. Soc. Cataract and Refractive Surgeons, Castroviejo Cornea Soc., N.Y. Intra-Ocular Lens Implant Soc., Pan Am. Assn. Ophthalmology, N.Y. Keratorefractive Soc. Office: NY Eye and Ear Infirmary 310 E 14th St Ste 403 New York NY 10003-4201 Office Phone: 212-979-4410. Fax: 212-353-5772. Business E-Mail: dbuxton@nyee.edu.

BUXTON, MARGARET ROSE, human resources specialist, director; m. Bobby Lee Buxton, Feb. 23, 1980; children: Johnathan Martin, Justin Marcellous. BS, Hampton U., Va., 1972, EdM, 1987; EdD, George Wash. U., Washington, 1998. Tchr. Va. Beach Pub. Sch., Va., 1982—89, asst. prin., 1989—90, human resource specialist, 1990—2003; human resources dir. Portsmouth Pub. Sch., 2003—. Cons. JONJUS Diversity Consultants, Portsmouth, Va., 2000—. Chair Dept. of Behavioral Health Svcs., 1997—. Recipient President's award, PTA, 1995, Human Rights award, Human Rights Commn., 1999, 2001. Mem.: ASCD, Links, Inc., Jack and Jill of Am., Inc. (v.p. and sec. 1994—98, cert. of Appreciation 1998). Roman Catholic. Achievements include research in diversity for educators. Avocations: reading, youth mentor, jogging, travel. Home: 308 Dinwiddie St Portsmouth VA 23704 Office: Portsmouth Pub Sch PO Box 998 Portsmouth VA 23704 Home Phone: 757-397-0517. E-mail: margaret.buxton@pps.k12.va.us.

BUXTON, WILLIAM GLENTON, neurologist, director; b. Amory, Miss., Oct. 1971; s. George and Marion Buxton; m. Verna Buxton, Apr. 1998; 3 children. BS in Biochemistry, UCLA, 1989—93, MD, 1993—97. Cert. neurology with subspecialty in clinical neurophys. Am. Bd. Psychiatry & Neurology, 2003. Intern UCLA Med. Ctr., 1997—98, resident, 1998—2001; asst. prof. dept. neurology UCLA, Santa Monica, 2002—06, med. dir. neurodiagnostic lab., Santa Monica Med. Ctr., 2005—. Stewardship chair 1st United Meth. Ch., Santa Monica, 2005. Fellow, UCLA and Cedars-Sinai Med. Ctrs., 2001—02. Mem.: Rotary (dir. 2007—). Meth. Office: UCLA Santa Monica Neurological Assocs 1245 16th St Ste 309 Santa Monica CA 90404 Home Phone: 310-395-3862; Office Phone: 310-319-5098. Business E-Mail: wbuxton@ucla.edu.

BUYER, STEVEN EARLE, congressman, lawyer; b. Rensselaer, Ind., Nov. 26, 1958; m. Joni Geyer; children: Colleen, Ryan. BS in Bus. Adminstrn., The Citadel, 1980; JD, Valparaiso U., 1984. Officer Med. Svc. Corps U.S. Army, 1980, spl. asst. to U.S. Atty. Va., 1984-87; dep. atty. gen. Ind., 1987-88; atty., 1988—92; legal counsel 22nd Theater Army, Saudi Arabia, 1990-91; legal advisor U.S Armed Forces/Western Enemy Prisoner of War Camps/War Crimes Interrogations, Saudi Arabia, 1991; mem. U.S. Congress from 4th Ind. Dist., 1993—. Mem. com. on energy & commerce, U.S. Ho. of Reps.; mem. health, Energy and Air quality, environment & hazardous materials subcoms.; mem. com. on vet.'s affairs, chmn. subcom. oversights & investigations. Natl. Gaurd and Reserve Components Caucus Decorated Bronze Star. Republican. Office: US Ho Reps 2230 Rayburn Ho Office Bldg Washington DC 20515-1405*

BUYSE, MARYLOU, pediatrician, geneticist, medical administrator; b. NYC, June 27, 1946; d. George J. and Barbara M. (Sauer) B.; m. Carl N. Edwards, Jan. 22, 1982. AB, Hunter Coll., 1966; MD, Med. Coll. Pa., 1970; MS in Prev. Health and Med. Adminstrn., U. Wis., Madison, 1993. Diplomate Am. Bd. Med. Genetics. Intern U. Mich., 1970-71; resident in pediatrics L.A. County-U. So. Calif. Med. Ctr., 1971-73, fellow, 1973-75, U. So. Calif. Sch. Medicine, 1975-84, asst. prof. pediatrics, 1973—75, 2004—, Tufts U., 1976-84; coord. Myelodysplasia Clinic Tufts-New Eng. Med. Ctr., Boston, 1976-79; dir. Cystic Fibrosis Clinic, staff pediatrician Ctr. for Genetic Counseling and Birth Defects Evaluation, 1975-82; med. dir. Ctr. for Birth Defects Info. Service, 1978-82, dir. center, 1982-94; pres. Medx Ltd., 1985-94, Ctr. for Birth Defects Info. Scis., Inc., 1985-94; dir. clin. genetics Children's Hosp., Boston, 1985-86; mem. med. adv. bd. Mass. Cystic Fibrosis Found., 1977-79; med. dir. Fernald State Sch., 1988—94; assoc. med. dir. MassPRO, 1993-95; mem. Mass. Bd. Registration in Medicine, 1994-95; assoc. med. dir. Care Advantage Health Sys., Inc., med. dir., 1996-97, United Health Care of New England, 1997-98, consulting physician advisor, 1998-99, v.p. health affairs, 1999-2001; pres., CEO Mass. Assn. Health Plans, 2001—. Cons. in field. Assoc. editor Birth Defects Compendium, 2d edit., 1979; assoc. editor Syndrome Identification

Jour., 1977-82, editor, 1982; editor Jour. Clin. Dysmortpholgoy, 1982-86, Dysmorphology and Clinical Genetics, 1986-94; editor-in-chief Birth Defects Encyclopedia, 1990. Chair RI Folic Acid Coun., RI March of Dimes, 1999-2001; dir. Mass. Health Consortium, 2001-, Martin's Pt. Healtch Care, 2006-; pres. Mass. Health Coun., 2007—; chair Jane Doe Inc., Gala, 2007. Recipient Physicians Recognition award AMA, 1975, Alumni Achievement award Med. Coll. Pa., 1987; named to Alumni Hall of Fame, Hunter Coll., 1998. Fellow: Mass. Med. Soc. (asst. sec.-treas. 1991—94, trustee 1991—2000, sec.-treas. 1994—96, v.p. 1996—97, pres.-elect 1997—98, pres. 1998—99), Am. Acad. Pediat.; mem.: AAAS, Mass. Health Coun. (v.p. 2005—, pres. 2007—), Teratology Soc., Am. Coll. Physicians Execs., Soc. Craniofacial Genetics (pres. 1986), Am. Med. Writers Assn., Am. Soc. Human Genetics, Am. Mgmt. Assn., Am. Med. Women's Assn. (pres. Mass. br. 39 1986—91), Charles River Dist. Med. Soc. (pres. 1993—95), Alpha Omega Alpha. Office: Ctr Birth Defects Info Svcs Inc Box 1776 Dover MA 02030

BUYSSE, PAUL HENRI MARIA, manufacturing executive; b. Mar. 17, 1945; s. Eugene and Germain (Van Hecke) Buysse; children: Frank, Pia, Ann, Sophie, Thomas. Various mktg. and sales positions Ford Motor Co., 1966; dep. mng. dir. British Leyland Credit N.V., 1976; gen. mgr. car sales and mktg. British Leyland Belgium N.V., 1976; exec. dir. Tenneco Belgium, 1980; mng. dir. J.I. Case Benelux, 1980; gen. mgr. Europe North J.I. Case, Internat. Harvester and Poclain, 1984; group mng. dir. Hansen Transmissions Internat., 1988; group chief exec. BTR Automotive and Engrng. Group, 1989, BTR Engrng. and Dunlop Overseas, 1991; exec. dir. BTR plc, London, 1992; CEO Vickers plc, London, 1998; chmn. Bakaert, 2000. Group chief exec. BTR Industries Ltd., 1989, regional chief exec., 1994—98; dir. BTR Internat. Ltd., 1991; CEO Vickers plc, 1998—2000; chmn. Bekaert N.V., 2000, Videohouse, Prince Philippe Found., Coll. Censors Nat. Bank of Belgium, Internat. C. of C. Belgium, Ceasar Real Estate Fund, Family Bus. Network Belgium; bd. dirs. Fortis Bank Zone North-Ctr., Flemish Employers Assn.; mem. exec. com. Fedn. Belgian Industry; hon. consul-gen. Great Britain, Northern Ireland; mem. advisory bd. Transparency Internat.; mem. Belgian Coun. Insead, Fontainebleau, France; mem. Assn. for Continuity Fortis Bank, mem. merchant and private banking adv. bd. Mem. advisory bd. King Baudouim Found. Inc., USA; mem. internat. bd. overseers Sabanci U., Istanbul. Named a Knight, Order of Leopold, Belgium, 1988, Cmdr., 2001, Cmdr. of the Brit. Empire, 1997, Baron, King Albert II of Belgium, 1998, Hon. Citizen of New Orleans, Jianghia City, 2001; named an Officer in the Order of Orange-Nassau, The Netherlands, 1994, Hon. Dean of Labour, Belgium, 1994, Officer in the French Nat. Order of Merit, 1996; recipient Shanghai Magndia Gold award, 2003. Mem.: Royal Automobile Club Belgium (bd. dirs.). Home: Sparrendreef 104 8300 Knokke Belgium Office: Bekaert N V Diamant Bldg A Reyerslaan 80 1030 Brussels Belgium Office Phone: 32 2 706 84 54. E-mail: paul.buysse@bekaert.com.

BUZACOTT, JOHN ALAN, engineering educator; b. Sydney, N.S.W., Australia, May 21, 1937; emigrated to Can., 1967; s. Alan Ernest and Jean Elizabeth (Bingle) B.; m. Ursula Schulmerich, Sept. 7, 1963; children: Alan J., Kimberly A. BSc, U. Sydney, 1957, BE, 1959; MSc, U. Birmingham, Eng., 1962, PhD, 1967; Dr. honoris causa (hon.), Tech. U. Eindhoven, 2001. Engr. Associated Elec. Industries, Rugby, England, 1959-61; ops. research systems officer A.E.I. Hotpoint Ltd., London, 1963-64; asst. prof. U. Toronto, 1967-71, assoc. prof., 1971-77, prof., 1977-83, U. Waterloo, Ont., Canada, 1984-91, York U., North York, 1991—2002, prof. emeritus, 2002—. Author: Scale in Production Systems, 1982, Stochastic Models of Manufacturing Systems, 1993; corr. editor: Canadian Jour. Info. Processing and Ops. Research, 1974-78. Mem. Can. Operational Rsch. Soc. (pres. 1983-84), Inst. for Ops. Rsch. and Mgmt. Sci., Prodn. and Ops. Mgmt. Soc. (pres. 1999). Office: York U Schulich Sch Bus North York ON Canada M3J 1P3 Home: 203-955 Milwood Rd Toronto ON Canada M4G 4E3 Business E-Mail: jbuzacot@schulich.yorku.ca.

BUZAK, EDWARD JOSEPH, lawyer; b. Jersey City, Apr. 20, 1948; s. Edward and Nellie (Scalone) B.; m. Gail Marie Capizzi, July 24, 1971; children: Craig E., Lindsay T. BA, Union Coll., 1970; JD, Georgetown U., 1973. Bar: N.J. 1973, D.C. 1974. Assoc. Villoresi & Flanagan, Boonton, N.J., 1973-75; ptnr. Villoresi & Buzak, Boonton, 1976-82; pvt. practice, Montville, N.J., 1983—. Trustee Housing Partnership of Morris County, Morristown, NJ, 1992—. Contbr. articles to profl. jours. Chmn. affordable housing com., asst. counsel N.J. State League of Municipalities, Trenton, N.J., 1986-; asst. counsel N.J. Planning Ofcls., 1998-2000, 04—. Mem. Assn. Environ. Authorities (chmn. legis. com. 1986-2000), N.J. Inst. Local Govt. Attys.(pres. 2003-04), N.J. Bar Assn. (chmn. local gov. com. 1985-87). Roman Catholic. Avocations: running, skiing, music, reading. Office: 150 River Rd Ste N4 Montville NJ 07045-8920 Office Phone: 973-335-0600. Business E-Mail: ejblaw@njaccess.com.

BUZARD, A. VINCENT, lawyer; b. Sullivan, Ind., June 7, 1942; BA, Wabash Coll., 1964; JD cum laude, Univ. Mich., 1967. Corp. counsel, Rochester, NY, 1971—73; founder A.Vincent Buzard Law Firm (merged with Harris Beach & Wilcox), 1980—97; ptnr. Harris Beach & Wilcox, Rochester, 1997—. Mem. Spl. Commn. on Future of NY State Courts, 2006. Recipient Adolph J. Rodenbeck award, 1995. Mem.: ABA (ho. dels. 1993, 2004—), NY State Trial Lawyers Assn., Assn. of Trial Lawyers of Am., Monroe County Bar Assn. (pres. 1993—94), NY State Bar Assn. (v.p. 1997—2001, pres.-elect 2004, mem., Ho. of Del., pres. 2005), NY State Head Injury Assn. (bd. dir., sec. 1984—88, pres. 1990—92). Office: Harris Beach LLP 99 Garnsey Rd Pittsford NY 14534 Office Phone: 585-419-8605. Office Fax: 585-232-4400. Business E-Mail: vbuzard@harrisbeach.com.*

BUZARD, DAVID ANDREW, lawyer; b. Evanston, Ill., Dec. 8, 1961; s. Clifford Howard and Mary Louise (Dole) B.; children: Clémentine, Victor. Student, Carleton Coll., 1980-82; BA in Linguistics, Northwestern U., 1984; JD, Tulane U., 1990. Bar: Ill. 1991, Va. 1997, U.S. Ct. Mil. Appeals 1991, U.S. Ct. Appeals (4th cir.) 1991, U.S. Dist. Ct. (ea. dist.) Va. 1997, U.S. Dist. Ct. (no. dist.) Ill. 1998, U.S. Supreme Ct. 1998; cert. qualified guardian ad litem for incapacitated adults, Va. Supreme Ct. Law clk. U.S. Atty.'s Office, New Orleans, 1988-90; judge advocate U.S. Navy, 1990-97; assoc. Glasser & Glasser, PLC, Norfolk, Va., 1997-98, Bennett & Zydron, P.C., Virginia Beach, Va., 1998—. Adj. asst. prof. Old Dominion U., 2002; lectr. law and ethics U.S. Joint Forces Staff Coll., 2002-03; counsel Alliance Française Chapitre de Grasse, Norfolk, Va., 1996—; judge Jessup Internat. Law Moot Ct. Competition, 1998. Contbr. articles to profl. jours. Lt. USN, 1990-97; lt. comdr. USNR, 1998—. Nat. Merit scholar. Mem. ATLA (fed. tort liability and mil advocacy sect., nursing homes litigation group), Va. State Bar (bd. govs. mil. law sect.), Virginia Beach Bar Assn., Va. Trial Lawyers Assn. (del. 2003-), Norfolk and Portsmouth Bar Assn. (founder, chair mil. law and lawyers com. 1997-2002, Walter E. Hoffman award 2001), Judge Advocates Assn., DAV, Naval Res. Assn., Pan European Orgn. Personal Injury Lawyers, Mil. Officers Assn. Am. Avocations: civic activities, travel. Office: Bennett & Zydron PC 120 S Lynnhaven Rd Virginia Beach VA 23452 E-mail: dbuzard@bandzlaw.com.

BUZARD, JAMES ALBERT, healthcare management consultant; b. Warren, Ohio, Nov. 2, 1927; s. Milton Vogan and Mary Cora (Matthews) B.; m. Caroline L. Jansen, July 28, 1951; children: Catherine A. Sazdanoff, James M. BS, Kent State U., Ohio, 1949; MA, U. Buffalo, 1951, PhD, 1954. Rsch. biochemist, then dir. R & D Norwich (N.Y.) Pharmacal Co., 1954—68; dir. devel., then exec. v.p. G.D. Searle & Co., Skokie, Ill., 1968—79, also bd. dirs.; exec. v.p. Merrell Internat./Richardson Merrell Inc., Wilton, Conn., 1979—81, Merrell Dow Pharm., Inc., Cin., 1981—89; v.p. corp. affairs, mergers & acquisitions Marion Merrell Dow Inc., 1989-90; ret., 1990; mgmt.-health care cons., 1990—. Bd. dirs. Meridian Diagnostics Inc., Cin.; chmn. emeritus Biostart, Cin., Ohio. Contbr. 40 articles to profl. jours. With USNR, 1945-46, 51-55. Named Ohio Entrepreneur Yr., 1998. Republican. Roman Catholic. Avocations: woodworking, golf, gardening, painting.

BUZARD, KURT ANDRE, ophthalmologist; b. Lakewood, Colo., Apr. 9, 1953; s. Donald Keith and Sonja Marie (Vik) B. BA in Math. and Physics, Northwestern U., 1975; MA in Applied Physics, Stanford, U., 1976; MD, Northwestern U., 1980. Diplomate Am. Bd. Ophthalmology, Nat. Bd. Med. Examiners. Intern medicine L.A. County-U. So. Calif. Med. Ctr., 1980-81; resident Jules Stein Eye Inst. UCLA, 1982-85; fellow cornea/refractive surgery Richard C. Troutman, MD, 1985-86; ophthalmologist, corneal specialist Las Vegas, Nev., 1986—. Staff physician Rancho Los Amigos Hosp., 1981-82; clin. asst. prof. div. ophthalmology dept. surgery U. Nev. Sch. Medicine, 1988—; clin. asst. prof. dept. ophthalmol. medicine Tulane U. Med. Ctr., New Orleans, 1991; med. dir. S.W. Eye Procurement Ctr., Las Vegas, 1989—; affiliate Humana Hosp.-Sunrise, 1989—, Las Vegas Surg. Ctr., 1989—, Las Vegas Surg. Ctr., Med. Ctr. So. Nev., 1989—; assoc. staff Valley Hosp., Las Vegas, 1986—; mem. med. adv. bd. Donor Orgn. Referral Svc.; internat. hon. advisor Tung Wah Ea. Hosp., Hong Kong, 1999-2003. Author: (with Richard Troutman) Corneal Astigmatism: Etiology, Prevention and Management, 1992, (with Miles Friedlander and Jean Luc Febbraro) The Blue Line Incision and Refractive Phacoemulsification, 2000; mem. editorial bd. Refractive and Corneal Surgery, 1992—; contbr. articles to profl. jours. Mem. Las Vegas C. of C., 1989. Recipient Rsch. award Jules Stein Inst., L.A., 1985. Fellow Am. Acad. Ophthalmology (Honor award 1999), Am. Coll. Surgeons; mem. Am. Soc. Cataract and Refractive Surgery, AMA, Assn. for Rsch. in Vision and Ophthalmology, Castroviejo Soc., Colombian Soc. Ophthalmology (corr.), Eye Bank Assn. of Am.-Paton Soc., Internat. Soc. for Eye Rsch., Internat. Soc. Refractive Keratoplasty (long-range planning com., alternative rep. to Am. Acad. Ophthalmology, bd. dirs. 1992-94), Pan Am. Assn. Ophthalmology, Pan Am. Implant Assn., Phi Eta Sigma, Phi Beta Kappa. Avocations: computers, photography. Office: 7135 W Sahara Ave Las Vegas NV 89117-2828

BUZBEE, RICHARD EDGAR, retired newspaper editor; b. Fordyce, Ark., Aug. 16, 1931; s. Edgar Andrew and Helen Koester (Darling) B.; m. Marie Palmer, Apr. 16, 1955; children: Robert Edgar, William Bruce, James Palmer, John Richard. B.J., BA, U. Mo., 1954. Mgmt. intern Harris Newspaper Group, Chanute (Kans.) Tribune, Burlington (Iowa) Hawk-Eye, also Olathe (Kans.) News, 1957-63; editor, pub. Olathe News, 1963-79, Hutchinson (Kans.) News, 1979-93; ret. Hutchinson Pub. Co., 1993. Hon. chmn. bd. dirs. Hutchinson Pub. Co., 1993—; ptnr. Radine Enterprises, Olathe. Trustee William Allen White Found.; pres. Olathe C. of C., 1969, Olathe United Way, 1968, Johnson County chpt. ARC, 1978-79; chmn. Johnson County Scholarship Found., 1968; mem. Olathe Public Bldg. Commn. 1, 1964-65, 2, 1978-79; co-chmn. Olathe Home-for-Christmas from Vietnam Project, 1969-72; mem. bd. Hutchinson Public Library, 1980-87, chmn., 1982-83; bd. dirs. Hutchinson Symphony Assn., 1980-88, pres. 1987. Served to lt. (j.g.) USNR, 1954-57. Mem. Greater Hutchinson C. of C. (chmn. 1988), Rotary (bd. dirs. 1981-83), Phi Beta Kappa. Clubs: Rotary. (dir. 1981-83). Republican. Methodist. Home: 4 Crescent Blvd Hutchinson KS 67502-5541 Personal E-mail: dick@buzbee.net.

BUZZARD, JAMES A., paper, packaging and chemical company executive; BS in Pulp and Paper Tech., N.C. State U.; MBA in Fin., U. Pa. Joined WestVaco, 1978, purchasing mgr., Kraft Divsn., 1982—84, adminstrv. mgr., Container Divsn., 1984—86, area sales mgr., container plant Eaton, Ohio, 1986—88, corp. mktg. mgr., 1988—90, mgr., mktg. svcs., 1990—91, mgr., bus. planning, analysis, Envelope Divsn., 1991—92, mgr., Envelope Divsn., corp. v.p., 1992—94, interim mktg., sales mgr., Fine Papers Divsn., 1994—95, sales, mktg. mgr., 1995—98, asst. divsn. mgr., Fine Papers Divsn., 1998—99, sr. v.p., 1999—2000, mgr., Fine Papers Divsn., 1999—2000; exec. v.p. Westvaco Corp., 2000—02, MeadWestvaco Corp., Stamford, Conn., 2002—03, pres., 2003—. Mem.: Web Offset Assn. (mem. supplier adv. bd.). Office: MeadWestvaco 100 High Ridge Park Stamford CT 06905*

BUZZARD, STEVEN RAY, lawyer; b. Centralia, Wash., May 22, 1946; s. Richard James and Phylis Margaret (Bevington) B.; m. Joan Elizabeth Merrow, Nov. 11, 1967; children: Elizabeth Jane, Richard Wolcott, James Merrow. BA, Cen. Wash. State Coll., 1972; postgrad., U. Wash., 1973; JD, U. Puget Sound, 1975. Bar: Wash. 1975, U.S. Dist. Ct. (we. dist.) Wash. 1976, U.S. Supreme Ct. 1979, U.S. Tax Ct. 1983. Assoc. Shires, Kruse, Wallace, Roper & Kamps, Port Orchard, Wash., 1975-77; ptnr. Buzzard & O'Connell, Centralia, 1978-80, Buzzard & Tripp, Centralia, 1980-94, Buzzard & Assoc., Centralia, 1994—. City atty. Mossyrock, Wash., 1979-94, Vader, Wash., 1989-96, Bucoda, Wash., 1989-99; judge Centralia, 1980-84, Winlock, Wash., 1983—; sec. Consol. Enterprizes Inc., Centralia, 1986-88; judge Chehalis (Wash.) Mcpl. Ct., 1998—, Winlock Mcpl. Ct., 1983—, Napavine Mcpl. Ct., 2001—, Vader Mcpl. Ct., 2001—; past pres. Reliable Enterprises, Inc.; bd. dirs. Lewis County Dispute Resolution Ctr. Chmn. bd. dir. Lewis County Cmty. Svcs., Chehalis, Wash., 1981-84; bd. dir. Lewis County United Way, 1993-95; adv. bd. Centralia Sch. Dist., 1995—; founding mem., trustee, treas. Dollars for Scholars, Scholarship Found., 1997-2002; dir. Lewis County Dispute Resolution Ctr., 2006; adv. com. bd. dir. Lewis County Vets., VFW, 2006. Mem. ABA (rural judges com. 1986), Wash. State Bar Assn. (ct. rules com. 1992-, jud. selection com.), Lewis County Bar Assn. (past pres.), Assn. Trial Lawyers Am., Wash. State Trial Lawyers Assn., Wash. State Govt. Lawyers Bar Assn. (former trustee), Wash. State Dist. and Mcpl. Ct. Judges Assn. (dist. and mcpl. rural judges com.), Wash. Bd. Jud. Adminstrn. (best practices com. 2001—, ct. improvement com., 2001-), Dist. and Mcpl. Judges Assn. (dist. and mcpl. rural judges com., ct. improvement com., long range planning com.), Kiwanis (pres.-elect 1991, pres. 1992-93, Disting. Past Pres. award 1994), Elks (trustee Centralia 1981—). Avocations: running, boating, hiking, biking, fishing. Office: Buzzard & Assoc 314 Harrison Ave Centralia WA 98531-1326 Office Phone: 360-736-1108. Fax: (360) 330-2078.

BUZZELLI, CHARLOTTE GRACE, special education educator; b. Mar. 21, 1947; d. Edmund Albert and Sarah Agnes (Russo) Buzzelli. BS, U. Akron, Ohio, 1969, MS in Edn., 1976. Tchr. St. Anthony Sch., Akron, 1969-76; program coord., tchr. Akron Montessori Sch. Continuing Edn. Program, Eastwood Ctr., Akron, 1976-77; dir. edn. Fallsview Psychiat. Hosp., Ohio Dept. Mental Health, Cuyahoga Falls, 1977-92, developer job tng. partnership grant program and spl. needs handicapped grant program, 1992-97; tng. coord. N.E. regional & program educator children svcs. Ohio Dept. Mental Health State Operated Svcs., 1992—97. Spl. edn. svcs. developer and educator cmty svcs. divsn. North Coast Behavioral Health-care Sys., Ohio Dept. Mental Health, 1997-2002; tchr. adult basic lit. edn. program Akron City Sch. Dist., 1992—; developer Akron City Schs. Project Rise Homeless Youth Family Learning Literacy Program, 2001—; cons. in field; pioneered first spl. edn. program in Ohio for adult state psychiat. hosp.; developed 1st cmty.-based adult basic edn. program in state instn. in Ohio; program cons. state operated svcs. State of Ohio; participant U. Hawaii Study Tours Rsch. Projects, Internat. Edn. and East Asia Pi Lambda Theta Orient Study Tour, Manoa campus, 1990, spl. edn. rsch. U. Akron, 1976. Developer literacy evaluation program Project Rise Homeless Youth, Akron, 2000—; supr. Ctr. for Literacy, U. Akron Students Svs. Learners Program, Homeless Shelters Akron Pub. Schs. programs; supr. dept. ctr. lit. U. Akron; mem. gospel meets Symphony chorus Akron Symphony Orch. Gospel Choir, 1996—; mem. choir Diocese of Cleve., St. John's Cathedral, Mass of Jubilee Gospel Choir, 1998, 2000. Named Ohio Tchr. of Yr., 1979; recipient A Key award, U. Akron, Urban Light award for outstanding svc., 2001, Cmty. Svc. Achievement award, Italian Am. Soc., Cmty. Collaboration award, Summit County Housing Network, 2003, 2004. Mem. CEC (coun. pres.), ASCD, Assn. Children with Learning Disabilities, Internat. Reading Assn., U. Akron Alumni Assn. (Disting. Edn. award 2004), Univ. Club, Akron Women's City Club, Coll. Club of Akron, Pi Lambda Theta (pres.), Phi Delta Kappa, Delta Kappa Gamma, Gamma Beta (pres.), Kappa Kappa Iota. Avocations: pet therapy to children and adults with disabilities, reading, travel, writing, singing. Home: 662 Dayton St Akron OH 44310-2301 Office: Adult Basic Literacy Edn Profl Devel Acad 785 Carnegie Ave Akron OH 44314

BUZZENDORE, ROBERT L., lawyer; b. Columbia, Pa., Sept. 22, 1964; BA, Widener U., Chester, Pa., 1986; JD, Am. U., Washington, 1989. Bar: Pa. Supreme Ct. 1989, US Dist. Ct., Pa. (mid. dist.) 1991, US Ct. Appeals (fed. cir.) 1994. Atty. Robinson & Geraldo, Harrisburg, Pa., 1990—96, Hoffmeyer & Semmelman, LLP, York, Pa., 1996—. Mem., trustee Susquehanna Fire & Rescue Co, Columbia, Pa., 1980—; com. mem., former vice chair Columbia Borough Rep. Com., 1999—2005; councilman Columbia Borough Coun., 1998—2001, coun., 2004—, v.p., 2000—01, 2004—05, pres., 2006—; mem. St. James Luth. Ch., Columbia, 1979—, councilman, 1991—94, sec., 2000—06; bd. mem. Columbia K-9 Campaign, 1999—2007, York County Housing Coun., 2003—05. Recipient Adm. Herbert F. Leary award, Widener U., 1986. Conservative. Lutheran. Home: 1053 Central Ave Columbia PA 17512 Office: Hoffmeyer & Semmelman LLP 30 North George St York PA 17401 Home Phone: 717-684-9636; Office Phone: 717-846-8846. Business E-Mail: rbuzzendore@hoffsemm.com.

BUZZI, RUTH, comedienne; b. Westerly, RI, July 24, 1936; d. Angelo Peter and Rena Pauline (Macchi) B.; m. Kent Perkins, Dec. 10, 1979. Grad., Pasadena Playhouse Coll. of Theatre Arts, 1957. Appeared on Broadway in Sweet Charity; appeared in off-Broadway theater prodns. including Misguided Tour, A Man's a Man; network TV appearances include Garry Moore Show, Rowan and Martin's Laugh-In, Dean Martin Roasts, Trapper John, M.D., Medical Center, Alice, The Entertainers, Carol Burnett and Friends, Flip, Donnie and Marie, The Dean Martin Comedy Hour, Tony Orlando and Dawn, Day of Our Lives, Passions, 2003, The Jamii Foxx Show, Diagnosis Murder, The Muppet Show, Sesame Street, That Girl, The Monkees, Saved By the Bell, Love Boat, The Munsters Today, Masquerade, Adam 12, Major Dad, Here's Lucy, Come On Over; films include Freaky Friday, 1972, Skatetown, U.S.A., 1977, The Apple Dumpling Gang Rides Again, 1979, The Villain, 1979, The North Avenue Irregulars, 1979, Surf II, 1984, Bad Guys, 1986, Dixie Lanes, 1988, Diggin Up Business, 1990, Fallen Angels, 2007; TV movies In Name Only, 1969; featured commedienne in 19 mus. revues; filmed numerous TV and radio commls.; recorded hundreds of voice overs for cartoon series including Linus the Lionhearted, Pound Puppies and Berenstein Bears; club acts at MGM Grand Hotel and Sahara Hotel, Las Vegas. Recipient Golden Globe award, Image award NAACP, Northwoods U. Disting. Woman award; named to R.I. Hall of Fame; inducted into Broadcasting Hall of Fame; nominee 5 Emmy awards. Mem. DAR (hon.).

BYARS, MERLENE HUTTO, accountant, artist, writer; b. West Columbia, SC, Nov. 8, 1931; d. Gideon Thomas and Nettie (Fail) Hutto; m. Alvin Willard Byars, June 10, 1950 (dec.); children: Alvin Gregg, Robin Mark, Jay C., Blaine Derrick; m. Fred W. Klutzow, Dec. 10, 1999. Student, Palmer Coll., Midlands Tech., U. S.C., 1988—; diploma in Journalism, Internat. Corr. Sch., 1995, Longridge Writers Group, 1995. Acct. State of SC, 1964-93; ret., 1993; pres. Merlene Hutto Byars Enterprises, Cayce, 1993—. Designer Collegiate Licensing Co., US Trademark, 1989—; mem. Thinktank for Ret. Employees, U. SC Edn. Found., 1998—2003. Pub. Lintheads, 1986, Olympia-Pacific: The Way It was 1895-1970, 1981, Did Jesus Drive a Pickup Truck, 1993, Fate, Faith and Fortitude, 2003, Our British Heritage, 3 vols., 2006, The Plantation Era in South Carolina; pub., produr. (play) Lintheads and Hard Times, 1986; creator quilt which hung in SC State Capital for bicentennial celebration, 1988; designer Saxe Gotha Twp. Flag, 1993; author: The State of South Carolina Scrap Book, Orangeburg District, 1990, A Scrap Book of SC, Dutch Fork, Saxe Gotha, Lexington County, 1994, The Plantation Era of SC, 1996, Colonization , Plantations and More in South Carolina, 2004, A History of St. Luke's Lutheran Church within the Olympia-Pacific Community Columbia, South Carolina, 2004, Our British Heritage, 3 vols., 2007; exhibited art at Oxford (Eng.) U., 1997, Internat. Congress on Arts and Comm., 1997, Sonesta Hotel, New Orleans, 1998—; exhibited art and book From My Scrap Book of the State of SC; Xlibris publ. new book, 2003, Fate, Faith and Fortitude, Life of F.W. Klutzow, MD., Four Seasons, The Ritz, 1999—; exhibited genealogy and art work St. John's Coll., Cambridge U., 2001. Life mem. Women's Missionary Soc., United Luth. Ch., 1954—; mem. edn. found. U. SC, 1969-93; treas. Airport HS Booster Club, 1969-76; sec. Saxe Gotha Hist. Soc., Lexington County, 1994-96; mem. USC Edn. Found., Think-Tank for 2001 fundraising campaign/ret. faculty and staff, 1998-2001; rep. Cayce Hist. Com. at Am. Biographical Inst./Internat. Biographical Ctr. Congress, New Orleans, 1998. Recipient numerous awards for quilting SC State Fair, 1976—, Cert. for rose rsch. test panel Jackson and Perkins, 1982, Foremost Women in Comm. award, 1969-70, Cayce Amb. award, City of Cayce, 1994. Fellow Internat. Biog. Assn. (dep. dir. gen. 1999—), U.S.C. Caroliniana Soc., U. S.C. Thomas Cooper Libr. Soc.; mem. Cayce Mus. History (contbr. books, award for contribution 1987), SC State Mus., Town and Country Assn., Kiwanis Internat. Found. (disting. internat. sec. 2004-05, disting. Kiwinian 2005-06), Kiwanis Club Cayce-West Columbia. Avocations: history, genealogy, reading, sewing, travel. Home: PO Box 3387 West Columbia SC 29171-3387 Personal E-mail: needle1@msn.com.

BYARS, SAMUEL D., lawyer; b. La Feria, Tex., Aug. 18, 1954; BA with highest honors, U. Tex., 1975; JD, Harvard U., 1978. Bar: Tex. 1978. Briefing atty. Tex. Supreme Ct., 1978-79; mem. Strasburger & Price, L.L.P., Austin, Tex.; atty. Armbrust & Brown, LLP, Austin, Tex. Recipient Best Lawyers in Am., Tex. Super Lawyer, Tex. Monthly mag., Best Lawyers in Real Estate, Corp. Counsel mag. Mem. ABA, Tex. Bar Found., Coll. State Bar Tex., Travis County Bar Assn., Phi Beta Kappa. Office: Armbrust & Brown LLP 100 Congress Ave Ste 1300 Austin TX 78701 Office Phone: 512-435-2303. Office Fax: 512-435-2360. Business E-Mail: sbyars@abaustin.com.

BYARS, WALTER RYLAND, JR., lawyer; b. Birmingham, Ala., Oct. 5, 1928; s. Walter Ryland and Essie (Hopper) B.; m. Mildred Lucile Rhodes, Dec. 22, 1950; children: Debra Leigh Byars Patterson, Walter Ryland III, Rebecca Lynn Byars Pradat, John Baxter. BS, U. Ala., 1948, LLB, 1952, JD, 1969. Bar: Ala. 1952, U.S. Ct. Appeals (5th and 11th cirs.), U.S. Dist. Ct. (no., mid. and so. dists.) Ala., U.S. Supreme Ct. Pvt. practice, Troy, Ala., 1953-57; atty. legal dept. So. Bell. Tel. & Tel. Co., Atlanta, 1957-59, gen. atty. Birmingham, 1959-68; ptnr. Steiner, Crum & Baker, 1968—; city atty. Montgomery, Ala., 2002—; ptnr. Steiner, Crum & Byars, PC, Montgomery, 2003—. Bd. editors Ala. Law Rev., 1951-52. Lt. (j.g.) USNR, 1952-53. Fellow Am. Bar Found., Ala. Bar Found., Internat. Soc. Barristers (gov. 1977-83, sec.-treas. 1979-80, 2d v.p. 1980-81, 1st v.p. 1981-82, pres. 1982-83), Am. Coll. Trial Lawyers; mem. ABA (Young Lawyers past mem. exec. council, com. chmn.), Ala. Bar Assn. (pres.-elect 1983-84, pres. 1984-85, past pres. Young Lawyers, past sect. chmn., past com. chmn.), Pike County Bar Assn. (past pres.), Birmingham Bar Assn. (past com. chmn.), Montgomery County Bar Assn. (past com. chmn., bd. dirs. 1976-79, v.p. 1978, pres. 1979), Ala. Law Inst. (coun.), Montgomery Area Com. of 100, Masons, Sigma Chi, Phi Alpha Delta. Methodist. Home:

1744 Fairforest Dr Montgomery AL 36106-2602 Office: Regions Bank Bldg PO Box 668 Montgomery AL 36101-0668 Office Phone: 334-832-8800. Business E-Mail: wbyars@steinercrum.com.

BYATT, NANCY, psychiatrist; b. Sheffield, England, Feb. 25, 1976; d. Peter and Miranda Helen Black; m. Stephen James Byatt, June 16, 2001. BA with hons., Lehigh U., 1998; MBA, N.Y. Inst. Tech., 2003; DO, N.Y. Coll. Osteo. Medicine, 2003. Lic. physician Mass. Med. Bd., 2005. Resident psychiatrist U. Mass. Meml. Med. Ctr., Worcester, Mass., 2003—. Team capt. walk Nat. Alliance for the Mentally Ill, Woburn, Mass., 2004—05; mem. human rights com. Cmty. Health Link, Worcester, 2005—06. Recipient Stanley Scholar Award, L.I. (N.Y.) Jewish Hosp., 2002, Excellence in Behavioral Medicine award, N.Y. Coll. Osteo. Medicine, 2003, Team Capt. award, Nat. Alliance Mentally Ill, 2005, Emergency Psychiat. award, janssen Am. Assn., 2006; scholar, Lehigh U., 1998; Howard Hughes scholar, 1996. Mem.: Mass. Med. Soc., Am. Soc. Psychopharmacology, Am. Assn. Emergency Psychiat., Mass. Psychiat. Soc., Am. Psychiat. Assn. (mem. consultation-liaison emergency mental health interest group 2005—06, mem. pub. sector interest group 2005—06), Phi Eta Sigma. Democrat. Avocations: hiking, backpacking, skiing, tennis, mountain biking. Office: UMass Memorial Medical Center 361 Plantation St Worcester MA 01605 Home Phone: 617-875-9870; Office Phone: 508-856-8952.

BYBEE, JAY SCOTT, federal judge, former federal agency administrator; b. Oakland, Calif., Oct. 27, 1953; s. Rowan Scott and Joan (Hickman) B.; m. Dianna Jean Greer, Feb. 15, 1986; children: Scott, David, Alyssa, Ryan. BA, Brigham Young U., 1977, JD, 1980. Bar: DC 1981, US Ct. Appeals (4th cir.) 1983, US Supreme Ct. 1985, US Ct. Appeals (5th cir.) 1986, US Ct. Appeals (2d, 9th, 10th and DC cirs.) 1987. Law clk. to Hon. Donald Russell US Ct. Appeals (4th cir.), 1980-81; assoc. Sidley & Austin, Washington, 1981-84; atty., Office of Legal Policy US Dept. Justice, Washington, 1984—86, atty. civil divsn., 1986—89; assoc. counsel to Pres. The White House, Washington, 1989-91; prof. law La. State U., Baton Rouge, 1991-98, U. Nev., Las Vegas, 1999—2001; asst. atty. gen. Office Legal Counsel US Dept. Justice, Washington, 2001—02; judge US Ct. Appeals (9th cir.), San Francisco, 2003—. Contbr. articles to profl. jours. Missionary Mormon Ch., Santiago, Chile, 1973-75. Edwin S. Hinckley scholar, Brigham Young U., 1976-77. Mem. Phi Kappa Phi. Avocations: piano, all sports, reading. Office: US Ct Appeals Lloyd B George US Courthouse Ste 3099 333 Las Vegas Blvd Las Vegas NV 89101*

BYBEE, RODGER WAYNE, science administrator; b. San Francisco, Feb. 21, 1942; s. Wayne and Mary Genevieve (Mungon) B.; m. Patricia Ann Brovsky, May 28, 1966. BA, Colo. State Coll., 1966; MA, U. No. Colo., 1969; PhD, NYU, 1975. Tchr. sci. Greeley (Colo.) Pub. Schs., 1965-66; instr. sci. U. No. Colo., Greeley, 1966-70; teaching fellow NYU, NYC, 1970-72; instr. edn. Carleton Coll., Northfield, Minn., 1972-75, asst. prof., 1975-81, assoc. prof., chmn. dept., 1981-85; assoc. dir. Biol. Scis. Curriculum Study, Colorado Springs, 1986-95, acting dir., 1992-93; exec. dir. Ctr. Sci., Math. and Engring. Edn. NRC, Washington, 1995-99; exec. dir. BSCS, Colorado Springs, Colo., 1999—. Mem. adv. bd. for sci. assessment Nat. Assessment Ednl. Progress, Princeton, N.J., 1987-89, 92-93, 95-96; mem. adv. bd. Social Sci. Edn. Consortium, Boulder, Colo., 1987-90; chairperson working group on curriculum NRC project on Nat. Sci. Ednl. Stds., 1993-95; chmn. Sci. Framework 2006, Orgn. Econ. Coop. and Devel., Paris, France. Author: numerous books; contbr. numerous articles to profl. jours. NSF grantee, 1986—. Fellow AAAS (mem.-at-large 1987-90, chair sect. Q 1993-94, coun. del.), Nat. Assn. Rsch. Sci. Teaching (rsch. coord. 1986-89). Home: PO Box 563 Frisco CO 80443-0563 Office: BSCS 5415 Mark Dabling Blvd Colorado Springs CO 80918-3842 E-mail: rbybee@bscs.org.

BYBEL, MICHAEL JOHN, medical researcher; m. Celeste Pauline Vislusky, June 14, 1980; children: Charleen Julianna, Jeremy Michael. BS, Albright Coll., Reading, Pa, 1978. Supr. sterile filling and packaging Sanofi Pasteur, Swiftwater, Pa., 1987—89, tissue culture specialist, quality control serology, 1989—93, sr. rsch. asst., rsch. serology, 1993—95, mgr., rsch. clin. serology, 1995—99, rsch. scientist, clin. serology, 1999—2002, mgr., rsch. scientist, global clin. immunology, 2002—. Home: 600 E White Bear Dr Summit Hill PA 18250 Office: Sanofi Pasteur Inc 1 Discovery Dr Swiftwater PA 18370 Home Phone: 570-645-3536; Office Phone: 570-839-5015. Business E-Mail: mike.bybel@sanofipasteur.com.

BYCZYNSKI, EDWARD FRANK, lawyer, corporate financial executive; b. Chgo., Mar. 17, 1946; s. Edward James and Ann (Ruskey) B.; children: Stefan, Suzanne. BA, U. Wis., 1968; JD, U. Ill., 1972; Cert. de Droit, U. Caen, France, 1971. Bar: Ill. 1972, U.S.Dist. Ct. (no. dist.) Ill. 1972, U.S. Supreme Ct. 1976. Title officer Chgo. Title Inst. Co., 1972-73; ptnr. Haley, Pirok, Byczynski, Chgo., 1973-76; pres. Alderstreet Investments, Portland, Oreg., 1976-82, Nat. Tenant Network, Portland, 1981—. Asst. regional counsel SBA, Chgo., 1973-76; pres. Bay Venture Corp., Portland, 1984—. Contbr. articles to profl. jours. Mem. ABA, Ill. Bar Assn. Independent. Home: PO Box 2377 Lake Oswego OR 97035-0614 Office: 525 1st St Ste 105 Lake Oswego OR 97034-3100 Business E-Mail: efb@ntnonline.com.

BYE, KERMIT EDWARD, federal judge, lawyer; b. Hatton, ND, Jan. 13, 1937; s. Kermit Berthrand and Margaret B. (Brekke) Bye; m. Carol Beth Soliah, Aug. 23, 1958; children: Laura Lee, William Edward, Bethany Ann. BS, U. N.D., 1959, JD, 1962. Bar: ND 1962, US Dist. Ct. ND 1962, US Ct. Appeals (8th cir.) 1969, US Supreme Ct. 1974, Minn. 1981. Dep. securities commr. State of ND, 1962—64, spl. asst. atty. gen., 1964—66; asst. U.S. atty. US Atty.'s Office, Dist. ND, 1966—68; ptnr. Vogel Brantner Kelly Knutson Weir & Bye, Fargo, ND, 1968—2000; judge US Ct. Appeals (8th cir.), Fargo, 2000—. Mem. adv. com. appellate rules U.S. Jud. Conf., 2005—. Mem. editl. bd.: N.D. Law Rev., 1961—62. Chmn. Red River Human Svcs. Found., 1980—83; S.E. Mental Health and Retardation Ctr., Inc. Fellow: Am. Bar Found.; mem.: ABA (state del. 1986—95, bd. govs. 1999—2001, state del. 2002—), Minn. Bar Assn., Cass County Bar Assn., N.D. State Bar Assn. (pres. 1983—84). Lutheran. Office: 655 1st Ave N Ste 330 Fargo ND 58102 Business E-Mail: zhanna@ce8.uscourts.gov.*

BYE, RAYMOND ERWIN, JR., academic administrator; b. Mobile, Ala., Feb. 22, 1944; s. Raymond Erwin and Frances (Bain) Bye; m. Katherine Jackson, Dec. 28, 1971; children: Philip Jackson, Eleanor Ashley. BA, Rhodes Coll., Memphis, 1966; MA, Kent State U., 1968, PhD, 1974. Resident dir., 1966-68; area residence dir. Kent (Ohio) State U., 1968-69, asst. to pres., 1969-71, asst. to vice pres. student affairs, 1971-72; asst. to dir., deputy head, head congl. affairs NSF, Washington, 1973-83, dir. office of legis. and pub. affairs, 1983-94; assoc. v.p. rsch. Fla. State U., Tallahassee, 1994-98, v.p. rsch., 1999—2003, dir. fed. rels., 2004—. Adv. bd. Knight Found., 2002—; bd. dirs. Tallahassee Chamber, 1995—2005, Econ. Devel. Commn., 1995—98, TMH Hosp., 1998—2001; Oak Ridge Assn. Univs., 2001—03, Coun. Gov. Affairs, pres., 1998—2000, Fla. State U. Rsch. Found., 1998—2003; bd. dirs. Nat. Assn. State Univ. Land Grant Colls., 1999—2000, chair coun. govt. affairs, 1999—2001; bd. govs. Oak Ridge Nat. Lab., 2000—03. Recipient Disting. Svc. award, NSF, 1989, Pres. Meritorious Exec. award, 1991. Mem.: AAAS, Acad. Mgmt., So. Polit. Sci. Assn., Fla. Econ. Club (bd. dirs. 2002—). Office: Fla State U Westcott Bldg Tallahassee FL 32306-1330 Office Phone: 850-645-1410. Business E-Mail: rbye@mailer.fsu.edu.

BYEFF, PETER DAVID, hematologist, oncologist; b. Nov. 27, 1948; s. Herbert Isaac and Ruth Helen (Wolfe) B.; m. Gail Schneider, Apr. 2, 1982. BA, U. Pa., 1970; MD, Johns Hopkins U., 1974. Diplomate Am. Bd. Internal Medicine (subcert. in med. oncology and hematology), Nat. Bd. Med. Examiners. Intern Georgetown U. Hosp., Washington, 1974-75, resident in internal medicine, 1975-77; vis. fellow in hematology and oncology Columbia-Presbyn. Med. Ctr., NYC, 1977-81, Damon Runyon-Walter Winchell oncology fellow, 1977-81. Instr. Coll. Physicians and Surgeons, Columbia U., N.Y.C.; assoc. prof., attending physician U. Conn.; attending physician Bradley Meml. Hosp., Southington, Conn., New Britain (Conn.) Gen. Hosp., med. dir. George Bray Cancer Ctr.; sr. investigator Gynecologic Oncology Group; prin. investigator Eastern Cooperative Oncology Group, Nat. Surg. Bowel and Breast project. Office: Bradley Med Bldg 55 Meriden Ave Ste 1-a Southington CT 06489-3237 also: 40 Hart St New Britain CT 06052-1743 Office Phone: 860-621-9316.

BYER, DIANA, performing company executive; b. Trenton, NJ, Aug. 31, 1946; d. Fred and Norma (Handis) B. Student, Juilliard Sch., 1964—66. Soloist Manhattan Festival Ballet, NYC, 1972, Les Grands Ballet Canadiens, Montreal, Can., 1975; dir. Ballet Sch. of N.Y., NYC, 1978—, N.Y. Theatre Ballet, 1978—. Dir., founder Project LIFT scholarship program for children living N.Y.C. homeless shelters, 1989—. Helen Weiselberg scholar, Nat. Arts Club, 1988, 1990, 1993. Achievements include being subject of Lincoln Ctr. presentation Dreams on a Shoestring, 1992. Office: NY Theatre Ballet 30 E 31st St New York NY 10016-6825 Office Phone: 212-679-0401. Business E-Mail: dianabyer@nytb.org.

BYER, RENEE C., photographer; m. Paul Kitagaki. BS, Bradley U., Peoria, Ill. Staff photographer Peoria (Ill.) Jour. Star, Hartford (Conn.) Courant, Syracuse (NY) Newspapers, Oregonian, Statesman Jour., Salem, Oreg., Seattle Post-Intelligencer, 1999—2003; staff photographer & photo editor Sacramento (Calif.) Bee, 2003—. Mem. faculty Mountain Workshop for Photojournalism, Madison, Ky., 2006. Recipient Harry Chapin Media award, 2005, 1st place, Best of Photojournalism competition, Nat. Press Photographers Assn., 2005, President's award, McClatchy Co., 2005, Picture Story award, San Francisco Bay Are Press Photographers Assn., Sigma Delta Chi award, Soc. Profl. Journalists, 2006, Pulitzer Prize for Feature Photography, 2007. Mem.: Women in Photojournalism (nat. co-chair 1994—98). Office: Sacramento Bee PO Box 15779 Sacramento CA 95816 E-mail: rbyen@sacbee.com.*

BYER, THEODORE SCOTT, accountant; b. Trenton, NJ, Oct. 2, 1957; s. Fred and Norma (Handis) B.; m. Marcy Pam Steier, Aug. 8, 1981; children: Sarah, Tara, Hallie. BA, Muhlenberg Coll., 1979; MBA, Rider Coll., 1986. CPA, CFP. Auditor State of N.J., Trenton, 1979-80; staff acct. Louis H. Linowitz and Co., Trenton, 1980-82; supr. Amper, Politzner & Mattia, Flemington, NJ, 1982-88; tax mgr. Price Waterhouse, NYC, 1988-90; sr. mgr. Salomon & Co., P.C., NYC, 1990-94; ptnr. Mintz, Rosenfeld & Co., Fairfield, NJ, 1994—2006, J.H. Cohn LLP, 2006—. Co-author: Taxation of Foreign Nationals in the United States, 1990; editor: Selecting and Installing Medical Practice Computer Software, 1996. Fellow N.J. State Soc. CPAs (co-founder Hunterdon-Warren chpt.); mem. AICPA, N.Y. State Soc. CPAs. Avocations: avid reader, music, computers. Home: 87 Cedar Ln Berkeley Heights NJ 07922-2400 Office: JH Cohn LLP 4 Becker Farm Rd Roseland NJ 07068 Office Phone: 973-228-3500. Business E-Mail: tbyer@jhcohn.com.

BYERLEIN, ANNE P., human resources specialist, food products executive; Various positions PepsiCo.; v.p. corp. human resources, 1988—96; v.p. human resources Yum Brands, Inc. (formerly Tricon Global Restaurants), Louisville, 1997—2002; chief people officer KFC, 2000—02, Yum Brands, Inc., Louisville, 2002—. Past pres. Leadership Palm Beach County. Office: Yum Brands Inc 1441 Gardiner Ln Louisville KY 40213 Office Phone: 502-874-8300. Office Fax: 502-874-8790.

BYERLY, RADFORD, JR., science administrator; b. Houston, May 22, 1936; s. Radford and Garvis N. (Cook) B.; m. Kathryn Jester, May 13, 1960 (div. 1980), children: Laura, Hamilton, Charles; m. Carol Ann Ries, Apr. 10, 1987. BA, Williams Coll., 1958, MA, 1960; PhD, Rice U., 1967. Sr. engr. No. Rsch. & Engring. Co., Cambridge, Mass., 1961-63; postdoctoral fellow U. Colo., Boulder, 1967-69, dir. Ctr. for Space and Geoscis. Policy, 1987-91, vis. scholar Ctr. for Sci. and Tech. Policy Rsch., 2001—; physicist, mgr. Nat. Bur. Standards, Washington, 1969-75; mem. profl. staff com. on sci. and tech. U.S. Ho. of Reps., Washington, 1975-87, chief of staff, com. on sci. and tech., 1991-93; v.p. pub.policy U. Corp. for Atmosphere Rsch., Boulder, 1993-94; dir. Roberts Inst., Boulder, 1993-94. Space sta. adv. com. NASA, 1988-91, space sci. adv. com., 1987-91, 93-98; adv. com. on space launch industry OTA, 1993-95; bd. assessment NIST NAS, 1993-2000, NAS com. on Dept. Energy peer rev. 1997-98, com. environ. R&D, 2000-01, com. on staged respository strategies, 2001-03; space studies bd. NAS, 2001-06, efficiency com. EPA rsch., 2007; hon. lectr. Mid-Am. State Univs. Assn., 1988-89; trustee Rainbow Ranch Land Trust, SD, 2000-06. Editor Space Policy Reconsidered, 1989, Space Policy Alternatives, 1991, Prediction: Science, Decision Making, and the Future of Nature, 2000; contbr. articles to profl. jours. NSF fellow, 1965—67. Fellow AAAS (com. on sci. engring. and pub. policy 1998—); mem. AIAA (chmn. civil space subcom. 1988-89), Assn. Univs. Rsch. in Astronomy (bd. dirs. 1998—2004, pers. policy com. 2002-2004), Am. Phys. Soc., Phi Beta Kappa, Sigma Xi (pres. U. Colo. chpt. 1995-97). Avocations: skiing, hiking, gardening. Home: 1811 Columbine Ave Boulder CO 80302 Personal E-mail: hrbyerly@comcast.net.

BYERLY, STEVEN LEE, educational consultant; s. Jerry Sterling Byerly and Betty Jean Basile; m. Dora Jean Chriss, June 14, 1968; children: David, John. BA, Azusa Pacific Coll., Calif., 1970; MA, Calif. State U., San Bernardino, 1986; PhD, U. Calif.-Riverside, 1995. Asst. prin. Hesperia H.S., Calif., 1991—95; prin. Marysville H.S., Kans., 1995—97, Pierce H.S., Arbuckle, Calif., 1997—2000, San Jacinto H.S., San Jacinto, Calif., 2000—01; dir. curriculum and instrn. Sutter Union H.S. Dist., Sutter, Calif., 2001—. Adj. instr. Azusa Pacific U., 1990—91; columnist Marysville Advocate, 1995—97. Author: Poestricks, 1989, Linking Classroom Instruction to the Real World, The Kappan, 2001; contbr. columns in newspapers, articles to mags. Mem. CIF Realignment Com. of No. Calif., 1999; pres. Sacramento Valley League of No. Calif., 1998—2000; chair Sch. Bond Com., Hesperia, 1990, Affirmative Action Planning Com., Hesperia, 1993. Named History Tchr. of the Yr., DAR, 1991. Mem.: Am. Ednl. Rsch. Assn. Avocations: theater, quarter horses, model trains. Office Phone: 530-822-5161 ext. 234. Business E-Mail: sbyerly@suttenhigh.k12.ca.us.

BYERRUM, RICHARD UGLOW, college dean; b. Aurora, Ill., Sept. 22, 1920; s. Earl Edward and Florence (Uglow) B.; m. Claire Somers, Apr. 3, 1945; children: Elizabeth, Mary, Carey. AB, Wabash Coll., 1942, D.Sc. (hon.), 1967; PhD, U. Ill., 1947. Teaching asst. U. Ill., 1942-44; research asso. U.S. Chem. Corps, toxicity dept. U. Chgo., 1944-47; faculty Mich. State U., East Lansing, 1947—, prof. biochemistry, 1957-91, prof. emeritus, 1991—; acting dir. Mich. State U. (Inst. Biology and Medicine), 1961-62; dean Mich. State U. (Coll. Natural Sci.), 1962-86. Author: (with others) Experimental Biochemistry, 1956; Editorial bd.: (with others) Phytochemistry, 1961-81; Contbr. (with others) numerous articles to profl. jours. Mem. Project Hope, 1961—; Trustee Mich. Health Council, 1961—, pres., 1966. Travel grantee Internat. Congress Biochemistry, Vienna, 1958; Travel grantee Internat. Congress Biochemistry, Montreal, 1959 Mem. Am. Chem. Soc. (lectr. vis. scientist program, awards com., visitor for com. profl. tng.), N. Central Assn. Colls. and Secondary Schs., A.A.A.S., Am. Soc. Plant Physiologists (trustee, exec. com.), Am. Soc. Biol. Chemists, Soc. Exptl. Biology and Medicine, Mich. Acad. Arts, Sci. and Letters, Phi Beta Kappa (pres. local chpt. 1962), Sigma Xi (awards com., Jr. Research award Mich. State U. chpt. 1958), Phi Kappa Phi (pres. 1968-69), Phi Lambda Upsilon, Alpha Chi Sigma, Beta Theta Pi. Achievements include patent in cancer tumor inhibiting material. Home: 2407 Sapphire Ln East Lansing MI 48823-7264

BYERS, CHRISTOPHER GORDON, veterinarian; b. Dover, NH, May 12, 1977; s. William Gordon and Pamela Ann Byers. BS, Colo. State U., Fort Collins, 1999; DVM, Cornell U., Ithaca, NY, 2003. Vet. tech., asst. office mgr. Broadview Animal Hosp., Rochester, NH, 1991—2002; intern LI Vet. Specialists, Plainview, NY, 2003—04; resident VCA Vet. Referral Assocs., Gaithersburg, Md., 2004—. Med. supr. VCA Vet. Referral Assocs., 2004—. Author: (textbook) Handbook of Veterinary Emergency Protocols; contbr. articles to profl. jours.; actor: (vet players theatre group) Many Musicals And Plays; singer: (a capella music group) Ultrasound A capella group. Recipient Aux. to the AVMA prize, Cornell U., 2003, award Excellence Emergency/Critical Care Medicine, 2003. Mem.: AVMA (assoc.), Critical Care Soc. (assoc.), Vet. Emergency & Critical Care Soc. (assoc.). Conservative. Greek Orthodox. Avocations: swimming, travel, golf, hiking. Office: VCA Veterinary Referral Associates 15021 Dufief Mill Rd Gaithersburg MD 20878 Office Phone: 301-340-3224. Office Fax: 301-738-8845. E-mail: christopher.byers@vcamail.com.

BYERS, GEORGE WILLIAM, retired entomology educator; b. Washington, May 16, 1923; s. George and Helen (Kessler) B.; m. Martha Esther Sparks, Feb. 25, 1945 (div. 1953); children: George William, Carolyn Sylvia; m. Gloria B. Wong, Dec. 16, 1955; children: Bruce Alan, Brian William, Douglas Eric. BS, Purdue U., 1947; MS, U. Mich., 1948, PhD, 1952. Asst. prof. dept. entomology U. Kans., Lawrence, 1956-60, curator Snow Entomol. Mus., 1956-83, dir., sr. curator, 1983-88, assoc. prof., 1960-65, prof. entomology, 1965-88, prof. dept. systematics and ecology, 1969-88, chmn. dept. entomology, 1969-72, 84-87, ret., 1988. Vis. prof. Mountain Lake Biol. Sta. U. Va., alt. summers, 1961-92, U. Minn. biol. sta., 1970. Author: several book chpts.; contbr. articles to profl. jours. With U.S. Army, 1942-46, 53-56, WWII and Korea; lt. col. M.S.C., USAR, ret. Rackham fellow U. Mich., 1952-53; NSF grantee, 1958-87, 97-99. Mem. Entomol. Soc. Am. (editl. bd. Annals 1967-72, chmn. 1971-72), Entomol. Soc. Can., Ctrl. States Entomol. Soc. (pres. 1958-59), Entomol. Soc. Washington, Soc. Systematic Biology (editor Syst. Zool. jour. 1963-66), Phi Beta Kappa, Phi Kappa Phi, Sigma Xi. Avocations: invertebrate paleontology, photography, ornithology. Home: 909 Holiday Dr Lawrence KS 66049-3006 Office: U Kans Entomology Divsn Natural History Mus Lawrence KS 66049-2811 Office Phone: 785-864-4538. Business E-Mail: ksem@ku.edu.

BYERS, KEITH THOMAS, librarian; b. Laurel, Miss., Nov. 13, 1952; s. Theodore Kenneth and Alma Gladys B. ABA, Orangeburg-Calhoun Tech. Coll., 1973; BS in Mech. Engring., S.C. State U., Orangeburg, 1980, MEd in Maths., 1988; M in Libr. and Info. Scis., U. S.C., 1999; MDiv in Ministry, Erskine Theol. Seminary, 1997. Cert. librarian S.C. Libr. Bd. Security guard Pinkerton's Inc., Orangeburg, 1973-80; devel. mech. engr. Bell Telephone Labs., Norcross, Ga., 1980-84; libr. asst. Erskine Coll. and Sem., Due West, SC, 1997, Luth. Theol. So. Sem., Columbia, SC, 1998-99; libr. intern S.C. State U., Orangeburg, 1999; reference dept. Orangeburg Co. Pub. Libr., 2000—. Contbr. articles to Christian Observer; inventor test probe, hand tool. Mem.: ALA, S.E. Libr. Assn., Travelers Protective Assn., S.C. Libr. Assn., Am. Theol. Libr. Assn., Am. Forestry Assn. (life), Clowns of Am. (life), Alpha Kappa Mu. Presbyterian. Avocations: electronics, fishing, gardening, mechanics, woodworking. Home: 1635 Central St Orangeburg SC 29115-3321

BYERS, STEVEN N., anthropologist, educator, computer professional; b. S.Gate, Calif., Sept. 2, 1950; s. Leonard L. and Catherine A. Byers; m. Sue Ellen Carey, Dec. 29, 1976; 1 child, Jacob M. BA in Anthropology, Colo. State U., Ft. Collins, 1970—72, MA in Anthropology, 1972—75; PhD in Anthropology, U. N.Mex, Albuquerque, 1983—92. Instr. U. So. Co., Pueblo, 1975—77; social rschr. various orgns., Colo., 1977—81; computer programmer/analyst Bernalillo County Data Processing, Albuquerque, 1981—84, US Govt., Albuquerque, 1984—96; adj. faculty U. New Mex., Albuquerque, 1992—2000; rsch. assoc. Mus. Natural Sci., La. State U., Baton Rouge, 1996—97; computer programmer Santa Fe CC, 1997—2005; adj. faculty U. New Mex.-Valencia, Los Lunas, 2001—. Author: (textbooks) Introduction to Forensic Anthropology: A Textbook, 2002, 2nd edit., 2005, (lab manual) Forensic Anthropology Laboratory Manual, 2005; contbr. articles to profl. jours. Equipment Support for Huerfano County Multi-Purpose Sr. Citizens Ctr. grant, Title V of Older Am. Act of 1965, 1978, Displace Homemakers Needs Assessment grant, Colo. State Bd. Cmty. Coll. & Occupl. Edn., 1978, Cmty. Food & Nutrition Program grant, Cmty. Svcs. Adminstrn., 1979. Mem.: Paleopathology Assn. (annotated bibliography contbr. 2006—), Am. Acad. Forensic Scis., Am. Assn. Phys. Anthropology, Sigma Xi. Achievements include bioarchaeological study of the skeletal remains of 400+ individuals from prehistoric Louisiana; research in reconstruction of the skull and body of Gigantopithecus blacki, used to create a full-sized model for the San Diego Museum of Man; displaced homemakers in Colorado in 1979; Pueblo's poor in 1979. Avocations: travel, woodworking, exercise. Home: 1521 Sunset Gardens SW Albuquerque NM 87105 Office Phone: 505-925-8600. Personal E-mail: stevebyers2000@yahoo.com.

BYERS, WALTER, athletic association executive; b. Kansas City, Mo., Mar. 13, 1922; s. Ward and Lucille (Hebard) B.; children: Ward, Ellen, Frederick. Student, Rice U., 1939-40, U. Iowa, 1940-43. News reporter United Press Assn. (later U.P.I.), St. Louis, 1944, U.P.I., Madison, Wis., 1945, sports editor Chgo., 1945, asst. sports editor NYC, 1946-47; also fgn. sports editor; dir. Big Ten Conf. Service Bur., Chgo., 1947-51; exec. asst. NCAA, Chgo., 1947-51, exec. dir., 1951-52, Kansas City, Mo., 1952-73, Shawnee Mission, Kans., 1973-87, exec. dir. emeritus, 1988-90. Pres. Byers Seven Cross Ranch, Inc., Emmett, Kans., 1974—, Ironwood Seven Cross Ranch, Inc., Hatfield, Mo., 1992-2002, Volland, Kans., 2002-06, Byers Land and Cattle Co., Emmett, 1996—; mgr. Byers Ranches, Limited Liability Co., Emmett, 1997-. With M.C. AUS, 1944. Home and Office: 25707 Aiken Switch Rd Emmett KS 66422 Office Phone: 785-535-4044.

BYERS, WILLIAM D., engineering executive; BS in Chem. Engring., Oreg. State U., 1973; MBA, U. Oreg., 1981. Registered profl. engr., Oreg., 1982, Am. Acad. Environmental Engrs., 1982. Mem. staff CH2M Hill, 1981—94, v.p., 1994—, dir. tech. devel., 1994—. Mem.: AIChE (pres. 2004). Office: vp Technol Devel 2300 NW Walnut Blvd Corvallis OR 97330 Office Phone: 541-768-3510. Business E-Mail: bill.byers@ch2m.com.

BYERS-PEVITTS, BEVERLEY, college administrator, educator; b. Ohio County, Ky., Aug. 15, 1939; d. Stanley Beveridge and Vera Elizabeth (Amos) Byers; m. Robert Richard Pevitts, June 12, 1966; 1 child, Robert Stanley. BA, Ky. Wesleyan Coll., 1961; MA, So. Ill. U., 1967, PhD, 1980. Dir. theatre and faculty Dept. English, Speech, Drama Young Harris (Ga.) Coll., 1966-69; dir. theatre and asst. prof. speech and theatre arts Western Carolina U., Cullowhee, NC, 1969-71; coord. supplementary progr., asst. prof. Eng. and drama Pfeiffer Coll., Misenheimer, NC, 1972-74; dir. and prof. speech and theatre Ky. Wesleyan U., Owensboro, 1974-86; chair theatre arts U. Nev., Las Vegas, 1986-89, prof. and dir. grad. studies in theatre arts, 1986-90; dean coll. of humanities and fine arts, prof. U. No. Iowa, Cedar Falls, 1990-95; v.p. acad. affairs Tex. Woman's U., Denton, 1995—2001; pres. Park U., Parkville, Mo., 2001—. Lectr. in field; conductor workshops in field. Editor: Theatre Topics, 1990-93; contbr.

articles to profl. jours.; author: (plays) Reflections in a Window, 1982, rev., 1983, Beauty and the Beast, 1982, Time and the Rock, 1981, Family Haven, 1979, Take Courage, Stand Beside Us, 1977, A Strange and Beautiful Light, 1976-77; co-author: Epilogue to Glory, 1966. Bd. dirs. Waterloo/Cedar Falls Symphony Orch., 1990-94, Iowa Citizens for the Arts, 1991-94; coord. spl. drama programs WeCan, Inc., Las Vegas, 1986; tchr. Elderhostel Program; program coord. NOW. NEH Seminar grantee U. Wis.-Milw., 1983, NYU, 1977; recipient Outstanding Alumni award Ky. Wesleyan Coll., 1983; named Disting. Woman Am. Theatre Assn., 1977; grantee Ford Found., Exxon Corp.; elected to Nat. Theatre Conf., 1992—. Mem. Assn. for Theatre in Higher Edn. (founding pres. 1986-87, bd. govs. 1986-89), Assn. for Communication Adminstrn. (exec. com. 1988-91), Univ. and Coll. Theatre Assn. of Am. Theatre Assn. (pres. 1985-86), League Profl. Theatre Women N.Y., Internat. Coun. of Fine Arts Deans, Coun. of Colls. of Arts and Scis., Order of Oak and Ivy, Alpha Psi Omega. Avocations: gourmet cooking, travel, collecting antiques. Office: Park Univ 8700 NW River Park Dr Kansas City MO 64152 E-mail: president@mail.park.edu.

BYFIELD, BERT A., conservative humanitarian novelist; b. Lansing, Mich., Mar. 9, 1943; s. Virgil Albert and Frances Mary Pitts; m. Theresa Anne Baldassare, Dec. 2, 1972 (div. Dec. 1996); children: Cyndee, Maria, Catherine, Charity; m. Barbara Lloyd Scott, May 16, 1998. Author Caravela Books, Henrietta, NY, 1995—. Author: Rage of the Bear, 1995, Scream of the Eagle, 1999, Last Stand at Perekop, 2001, Father Gregory, 2003, Koba, 2003. Organizer Computer People for Peace, 1968-70. With USN, 1960-64. Russian Orthodox. Avocations: computer programming, computer games. Office: Caravela Books 134 Goodburlet Rd Henrietta NY 14467-9503 E-mail: bbyfieldww@caravelabooks.com.

BYLER, ANTHONY J., lawyer; b. Goshen, Ind., Oct. 12, 1968; BA, Ind. U., 1991; JD, Temple U., 1995. Bar: Pa. 1995, NJ 1995. With Van Syoc Law Offices, Cherry Hill, NJ, 1995—97; assoc. atty. Cohen, Seglias, Pallas & Greenhall, PC, Phila., 1997—2000; now ptnr. Shah & Byler, LLP, Phila. Mem.: Mech. Contrators Assn., Am. Soc. Highway Engrs., Contractors Assn. of Ea. Pa., Nat. Assn. of Demolition Contractors, NJ Bar Assn., Phila. Bar Assn. Office: Shah & Byler, LLP 510 Walnut St, 9th Fl Philadelphia PA 19106 Office Phone: 212-238-1045. E-mail: tbyler@shahbyler.com.

BYLINSKY, GENE MICHAEL, magazine editor; b. Belgrade, Yugoslavia, Dec. 30, 1930; s. Michael Ivan and Dora (Shadan) B.; m. Gwen Gallegos, Aug. 14, 1955; children: Tanya, Gregory. BA in Journalism, La. State U., 1955. Staff reporter Wall St. Jour., Dallas, 1957-59, San Francisco, 1959-61, NYC, 1961; sci. writer Nat. Observer, Washington, 1961-62, Newhouse Newspapers, Washington, 1962-66; bd. editors Fortune Mag., NYC, 1966—2001, contbg. writer, 2002—. Author: The Innovation Millionaires, 1976, Mood Control, 1978, Life in Darwin's Universe, 1981, Silicon Valley, High Tech Window on the Future, 1985. Served with AUS, 1956. Recipient 21st Ann. Albert Lasker Med. Journalism award, 1970, Deadline award Sigma Delta Chi, 1970, 72, 79, spl. commendation AMA, 1967, 68, 72, Journalism award, 1974, Claude Bernard Sci. Journalism award Nat. Soc. Med. Rsch., 1973, 74, James T. Grady award for interpreting chemistry to pub. Am. Chem. Soc., 1976, Am. Space Writers Assn. award, 1976-79, Bus. Journalism award U. Mo.-Columbia, 1984, Journalism award Am. Assn. Engring. Socs./Engring. Found., 1995, hon. mention award, 1970, 71, hon. mention award AAAS-Westinghouse Corp., 1975, 76, 77, hon. mention award Overseas Press Club, 1988. Mem. Nat. Assn. Sci. Writers, N.Y. Acad. Scis. Mem. Russian Orthodox Ch. Office: Fortune Magazine Time and Life Bldg Rockefeller Plz New York NY 10020-2002

BYMEL, SUZAN YVETTE, talent manager, film producer; b. Chgo. d. Howard Behr and Jacqueline Shirley (Richards) B. Student, U. Ill., Chgo. Exec. asst. Kenny Rogers Prodns., 1981; prodn. exec. Pinehurst Prodns., 1982; music mgmt. assoc. Frontline Mgmt., 1983; pres. Suzan Bymel & Assocs., 1985-94; oper. ptnr. Bymel/O'Neill Mgmt., 1995—, Meg Ryan Prodns. (a.k.a. Fandango Films), 1988-93, Bymel/O'Neill Mgmt., 1995-98; operating ptnr. Talent Entertainment Group, Beverly Hills, Calif., 1998—; founding ptnr. Management 360. Freelance screenwriter, actress. Mem. Hollywood Woman's Polit. Com., L.A. Office: Talent Entertainment 9111 Wilshire Blvd Beverly Hills CA 90210 Fax: 310-205-5385. E-mail: sbymel@mmbon.com.

BYNAGLE, HANS EDWARD, library director, philosophy educator; b. Ruurlo, The Netherlands, Feb. 24, 1946; came to U.S., 1956; s. Cornelius Adrian and Maria (Kalfsbeek) B.; m. Janet Mae Monsma, June 27, 1969; children: Maria Elizabeth, Derek Johannes. BA, Calvin Coll., 1968; PhD, Columbia U., 1973; MLS, Kent State U., 1976. Asst. prof. philosophy Union Coll., Schenectady, N.Y., 1972-73, Coll. Wooster, Ohio, 1974-75; dir. learning resources Friends U., Wichita, Kans., 1976-82; dir. library Eckerd Coll., St. Petersburg, Fla., 1982-83; dir. library, prof. Whitworth Coll./U., Spokane, Wash., 1983—. Author: Philosophy: A Guide to the Reference Literature, 1986, 3d edit., 2006; mem. editl. bd. Christian Scholar's Rev., 1992—; numerous rev. to profl. jours. Named one of Outstanding Young Men of Am., 1982. Mem. ALA, Assn. Coll. and Rsch. Librs. (chmn. Kans. chpt. 1980-81). Presbyterian. Avocation: music. Home: 1122 W Bellwood Dr Spokane WA 99218-2907 E-mail: hbynagle@whitworth.edu.

BYNES, AMANDA, actress; b. Thousand Oaks, Calif., Apr. 3, 1986; d. Rick and Lynn Bynes. Designer Dear clothing line, 2007—. Actor: (films) Big Fat Liar, 2002, What a Girl Wants, 2003, Lovewrecked, 2005, (voice) Robots, 2005, She's the Man, 2006, Hairspray, 2007; (TV series) All That, 1996—2000 (nominee Cable Ace award, 1997), The Amanda Show, 1999—2002, (voice) Rugrats, 2002—04, What I Like About You, 2002—06, (voice): (videos) Charlotte's Web 2: Wilbur's Great Adventure, 2003; appeared as herself/guest panelist (TV series) Figure It Out, 1997—2000. Recipient Favorite TV Actress, Kid's Choice Awards, 2001, 2002, 2003, Favorite Movie Actress, 2003. Achievements include discovered at age 10 at a kid's comedy showcase at the Laugh Factory, LA and signed immediately by Nickelodeon for TV series All That.*

BYNES, FRANK HOWARD, JR., physician; b. Savannah, Ga., Dec. 3, 1950; s. Frank Howard and Frenchye (Mason) B.; m. Janice Ratta, July 24, 1987; children: Patricia, Frenchye. BS, Savannah State Coll., 1972; MD, Meharry Med. Coll. Resident gen. surgery Staten Island (N.Y.) Hosp., 1978-82; resident internal medicine N.Y. infirmary Beekam Downtown Hosp., NYC, 1983-86; dir. medicine USAF Sheppard Regional Hosp., Sheppard AFB, Tex., 1986-87; pvt. practice internal medicine NYC, 1987-90; attending physician Bronx (N.Y.) Lebanon Hosp., 1990-93; pvt. practice internal medicine Savannah, Ga., 1994—. Maj. USAF, 1986-87. Mem. AMA, AAAS, ACP, N.Y. Acad. Scis., Assn. Mil. Surgeons of U.S., Alpha Phi Alpha. Home Phone: 912-354-5767; Office Phone: 912-354-0899.

BYNOE, PETER CHARLES BERNARD, real estate developer, lawyer; b. Boston, Mar. 20, 1951; s. Victor Cameron Sr. and Ethel May (Stewart) B.; m. Linda Jean Walker, Nov. 20, 1987. BA, Harvard U., 1972, JD, MBA, Harvard U., 1976. Bar: Ill. 1982; cert. real estate broker, Ill. Exec. v.p. James H. Lowry & Assocs., Chgo., 1977-82; chmn., chief exec. officer Telemat Ltd., Chgo., 1982—; exec. dir. Ill. Sports Facilities Authority, Chgo., 1988-92; mng. gen. ptnr. Denver Nuggets, 1989-92; ptnr., Land Use & Devel., Project Finance practices DLA Piper US LLP, Chgo., 1995—. Bd. dirs. Uniroyal Tech. Corp., Jacor Comms., Ind., Blue Chip Broadcasting. Chmn. Chgo. Landmarks Commn., 1985-87; vice chmn., chmn. exec. com. Goodman Theater; dir. Chgo. Econ. Club, 1993-2000, Ill. Sports Facilities Authority, 1993-2005; trustee Rush-Presbyn. St. Luke's Med. Ctr.; bd. overseers Harvard U., 1993-2002; mem. Chgo. Art Inst.; dir. The CORE Ctr. Named one of Am.'s Top Black Lawyers, Black Enterprise mag., 2003; named to Diversity 2005 Most Influential List, Fortune Mag., 2005. Mem.: Lawyers Club of Chgo., Chgo. Planning and Devel. Commn. (chmn. 1997—2004), Chgo. Coun. Foreign Relations (dir. 1995—2000), Econ. Club (dir. 1993—2000), East Bank Club. Democrat. Achievements include being the first African American owner of a National Basketball Association team. Avocations: squash, tennis, racquetball, skiing, travel, golf. Office: DLA Piper US LLP Suite 1900 203 N La Salle St Chicago IL 60601-1293 Office Phone: 312-368-4090. Office Fax: 312-630-7333. E-mail: peter.bynoe@dlapiper.com.

BYNUM, CAROLINE WALKER, history professor, writer; b. Atlanta, 1941; BA, U. Mich., 1962; PhD, Harvard U., 1969; LHD (hon.), U. Pa., 2007. Prof. Harvard U., 1969—76, U. Wash., 1976—88; faculty mem. Columbia U., NYC, 1988—2003, Morris A. and Alma Schapiro chair in history, 1990—98, dean Sch. Gen. Studies, assoc. v.p. undergrad. edn., 1993—94, univ. prof., 1999—2003; prof. European Medieval history Inst. Advanced Study, Princeton, NJ, 2003—. Author: Gender and religion: On the complexity of symbols, 1986, Holy Feast and Holy Fast: The Religious Significance of Food to Medieval Women, 1987 (Gov.'s Award, State Wash., Philip Schaff prize, Am. Soc. of Church History), Fragmentation and Redemption: Essays on Gender and the Human Body in Medieval Religion, 1990 (Trilling Prize, Award for Excellence in Study Religion, Am. Acad. Religion), Resurrection of the Body in Western Christianity, 200-1336, 1995 (Ralph Waldo Emerson Prize, Phi Beta Kappa, Jacques Barzun Prize, Am. Philos. Soc.), Metamorphosis and Identity, 2001, Wonderful Blood: Theology and Practice in Late Medieval Northern Germany and Beyond, 2006; co-author: Last Things: Death and the Apocalypse in the Middle Ages, 1999; contbr. articles to profl. jours. Recipient Centennial Medal, Harvard Grad. Soc., 2001, Disting. Career Award, Am. Soc. of Church History, 2005; MacArthur Fellow, 1986—93, Jefferson Lectr., 1999. Fellow: Am. Philos. Soc., Medieval Acad. Am. (pres. 1997—98); mem.: Am. Acad. Arts. Scis., Am. Hist. Assn. (pres. 1996). Office: Inst Advanced Study Sch Hist Studies Einstein Dr Princeton NJ 08540 Office Fax: 609-734-8199, 609-951-4435. E-mail: cwbynum@ias.edu.*

BYNUM, GRETCHEN LUEPKE, geologist; b. Nov. 10, 1943; d. Gordon Maas and Janice (Campbell) Luepke; m. Robert Flournoy Bynum, Oct. 2, 1999. Student, U. Colo., 1962; BS cum laude, U. Ariz., Tucson, 1965, MS, 1967. Registered geologist, Oreg. Geol. field asst. U.S. Geol. Survey, Flagstaff, Ariz., 1964, geologist Pacific br. marine geology Menlo Park, Calif., 1967—99, emeritus geologist br. coastal and marine geology, 1999—. Project coord. Hist. Marine Geology Program US Geol. Survey; mem. US Congress Office Tech. Assessment Workshop Mining and Processing Placers of EEZ, 1986; contr. on placer deposits Circum Pacific Map Project on Offshore Mineral Deposits US Geol. Survey, 1996—99. Editor: Stability of Heavy Minerals in Sediments, Economic Analysis of Heavy Minerals in Sediments, book rev. Earth Scis. History, 1989—2002; contbr. articles on heavy-mineral analysis to publs. including, Circum Pacific Map Project on offshore mineral deposits, chapters to books. Fellow: Geol. Soc. Am. (Interdisciplinary Perspectives on the Hist. Earth Scis., Penrose Conf. 1994, Cordilleran sect. com. on geology and pub. policy 1998—2002, nominating com. History of Geology Divsn. 2000—02, com. chair 2002); mem.: Internat. Marine Minerals Soc. (charter), Internat. Assn. Sedimentologists, History of the Earth Scis. Soc., Bay Area Mineralogists (chmn. 1979—80), Peninsula Geol. Soc., Ariz. Geol. Soc., Soc. Econ. Paleontologists and Mineralogists (chmn. com. librs. in developing countries 1988—91, mem. web com. 2007—), Am. Geophys. Union, Geospeakers Toastmasters Club (charter, Competent Toastmaster 1995, Advanced Toastmaster-Bronze Level 2001, Silver Level 2006), Tau Beta Sigma, Sigma Xi. Office: 345 Middlefield Rd Menlo Park CA 94025-3561 Personal E-mail: gluepke@aol.com.

BYNUM, TERRELL WARD, humanities educator, consultant; s. Terrell Waltham and Elizabeth Bynum; m. Aline W. Bynum, June 22, 1965; children: Timothy H., Andrew J. BS in Chemistry with honors and distinction, U. Del., Newark, 1963, BA in Philosophy with honors and distinction, 1963; MA in Philosophy, Princeton U., NJ, 1966; MPhil, CUNY, NYC, 1986, PhD in Philosophy, 1986. Asst. prof. philosophy Am. U., Washington, 1967—68, SUNY, Albany, NY, 1968—74, Ramapo Coll., Mah Wah, NJ, 1974—75, Dutchess Coll. of SUNY, Poughkeepsie, NY, 1975—78, assoc. prof. philosophy, 1978—87, So. Conn. State U., New Haven, 1987—89, prof. philosophy, 1989—. Exec. dir. Am. Assn. of Philosophy Tchrs., 1978—82, pres., 1984—86; dir. rsch. ctr. on computing & soc. So. Conn. State U., New Haven, 1987—; organizer and co-director Nat. Conf. on Computing and Values, New Haven, 1988—92; chair, com. on profl. ethics Assn. for Computing Machinery, NYC, 1993—96; chair com. on philosophy and computing Am. Philos. Assn., Newark, 1994—97; organizer internat. confs. on computer ethics. Translator (biographer and editor): Gottlob Frege, Conceptual Notation and Related Articles (Oxford U. Press Classic, 2002); co-editor (and author): Computer Ethics and Profl. Responsibility; co-editor: (with James H. Moor) Cyberphilosophy: The Intersection of Philosophy and Computing, The Digital Phoenix: How Computers Are Changing Philosophy; founder and editor-in-chief Metaphilosophy, 1968—94, host and assoc. prodr. What Is Computer Ethics?; contbr. articles to profl. jours. Fellow, Woodrow Wilson Found., 1963-1965, Danforth Found., 1963-1967, Andrew Mellon Found., 1982-1983; grantee Computer Ethics Rsch., NSF, 1989, 1991, 1992, 1993; Fulbright Fellow in Eng., US Govt., 1963-1964, Dartmouth Coll. Humanities Rsch. Fellowship, 1998. Mem.: Internat. Soc. for Ethics and Info. Tech., Internat. Assn. for Computing and Philosophy (bd. mem. 2001), Assn. for Computing Machinery, Am. Philos. Assn., Computer Profls. Social Responsibility (life). Achievements include development of computer ethics as a field of scholarly research and teaching. Avocations: travel, bird watching, walking, poetry writing, science reading. Office: So Conn State U 501 Crescent St New Haven CT 06515 Home Phone: 203-387-9389; Office Phone: 203-392-6790. Business E-mail: bynumt2@southernct.edu.

BYOWITZ, MICHAEL H., lawyer; b. Bklyn., Apr. 14, 1952; s. Ira and Shirley (Wexler) B.; m. Ruth Holzer, Aug. 8, 1976; children: Alice, David, Suzanne. AB, Columbia Coll., 1973; JD, NYU, 1976. Bar: DC 1976, US Supreme Ct. 1981, NY 1983, US Ct. Appeals (2d cir.) 1984, US Ct. Appeals (4th cir.) 1981, US Ct. Appeals (DC cir.) 1977, US Dist. Ct. DC 1977, US Dist. Ct. (ea. and so. dists.) NY 1984, US Dist. Ct. (ea. dist.) Va. 1981. Assoc. Arnold & Porter, Washington, 1976-78; trial atty., sr. trial atty. antitrust div. U.S. Dept. Justice, Washington, 1979-83; spl. asst. U.S. Atty. U.S. Dist. Ct. (ea. dist.) Va., Alexandria, 1981; with Wachtell, Lipton, Rosen & Katz, NYC, 1983—, ptnr., 1984—. Bd. dirs. Connaught Tower Corp., NYC., 1989-99, pres., 1997-99; pres., bd. dirs. Chesterfield Coop. Corp., Washington, 1979-83. Contbr. chpts. to books, articles to profl. jours. Mem.: ABA (past chair internat. law sect., del., House of Del.), Assn. Bar City of NY (chair, coun. on internat. affairs, past chair, antitrust and trade regulation com.), Order of the Coif. Office: Wachtell Lipton Rosen Katz 51 W 52nd St Fl 27 New York NY 10019-6150 Office Phone: 212-403-1268. Office Fax: 212-403-2268. Business E-mail: mhbyowitz@wlrk.com.

BYRD, ANDREW WAYNE, investment company executive; b. Nashville, Apr. 16, 1954; s. Benjamin F. and Allison (Caldwell) B.; m. Marianne Menefee; children: Marianne, Valere, Andrew Jr. BA, Vanderbilt U., 1976, JD, 1979; LLM, Georgetown U., 1981. Bar: Tenn., 1979, U.S. Dist. Ct. (mid. dist.) Tenn. 1979, U.S. Supreme Ct. 2001. Atty. Stokes & Bartholomew, Nashville, 1981-84; exec. v.p. Gen. Cap Am. Inc., 1987-94, Gen. Capital Corp., Nashville, 1984-89, pres., 1989-94, Andrew W. Byrd & Co., LLC, 1994—. Chmn., bd. dirs. Multi-Link, Inc., Lexington, Ky., Albertville (Ala.) Quality Foods, Inc., Precision Boilers, Inc., Morristown, Tenn., So. Quality Meats, Inc., Pontotoc, Miss., Indco, Inc., Louisville, Superior Highwall Miners, Inc., Beckley, W.Va. Mem. Leadership Nashville, 1984-85; deacon 1st Presbyn. Ch., 1982-92, elder, 2005—; bd. dirs. Tenn. divsn. Am. Cancer Soc., 1982-88, 92-97, Cheekwood, 1987-93; bd. dirs. Boy Scouts of Am., Mid. Tenn. Coun., 1995—, v.p. manpower, 2002-04, treas., 2005-06, v.p. fin., 2007—; bd. dirs. Exch. Club Charities, 2003-06, v.p. fin. 2007—; bd. dirs. Vanderbilt Children's Hosp., 1987-93, chmn., 1991-93; bd. dirs. Vanderbilt Cancer Ctr., 2007—. Recipient Silver Beaver award, Boy Scouts Am., 2006, Celtic Cross award, First Presbyn. Ch., 2007. Mem. ABA, Tenn. Bar Assn., Nashville Bar Assn., Nashville Area C. of C. (bd. dirs. 2003-), Exch. Club (pres. 1993-94). Democrat. Avocations: tennis, gardening, travel. Home: 4419 Harding Pl Nashville TN 37205-4530 Office: Andrew W Byrd & Co LLC 201 4th Ave N Ste 1250 Nashville TN 37219-2092 Office Phone: 615-256-8061.

BYRD, BETTY RANTZE, writer; b. Oklahoma City, July 8, 1949; d. Rolande Brown and Mary Louise Haner; m. Bill Byrd, Sept. 16, 1995; 1 child from previous marriage, Elizabeth Chase Rantze. Student, Ariz. State U., Tempe, Ohio State U., Columbus; BA in Creative Writing and French, U. Ariz, Tucson, 1974; legal asst. cert., Capital U. Law Sch., Columbus, 1975. Editor The Spectator Newspapers, Columbus, 1974—75; mng. editor Ohio State U. Dental Newsletter, 1974—75; paralegal, pub. defender Lewisburg, Pa., 1976—77. Author: Trinity's Daughter, 2002; actor: appeared in numerous commls., films, and TV, 1978—93. Vol. Salvation Army, Meals-on-Wheels, San Diego, Spl. Olympics, San Diego, San Diego Family Recovery Ctr. Recipient Best Fiction Writer's Guild award, Santa Barbara Writer's Conf., 2004. Mem.: AFTRA, SAG, Nat. Charity League, Rancho Lit. Soc. Avocations: photography, golf, travel, walking, scrapbooks. Home and Office: PO Box 2593 Rancho Santa Fe CA 92067 E-mail: bettybyrd@sbcglobal.net.

BYRD, CHRISTINE WATERMAN SWENT, lawyer; b. Oakland, Calif., Apr. 11, 1951; d. Langan Waterman and Eleanor (Herz) Swent; m. Gary Lee Byrd, June 20, 1981; children: Amy, George. BA, Stanford U., 1972; JD, U. Va., 1975. Bar: Calif. 1976, U.S. Dist. Ct. (ctrl., so. no., ea. dists.) Calif., U.S. Ct. Appeals (9th cir.) Law clk. to Hon. William P. Gray U.S. Dist. Ct., LA, 1975—76; assoc. Jones, Day, Reavis & Pogue, LA, 1976—82, ptnr., 1987—96; asst. U.S. atty. criminal divsn. U.S. Atty.'s Office, Ctrl. Dist. Calif., LA, 1982—87; ptnr. Irell & Manella, LA, 1996—. Mem. Calif. Law Revision Commn., 1992-97. Author: The Future of the U.S. Multinational Corporation, 1975; contbr. articles to profl. jours. Fellow: Coll. Comml. Arbitrators, Am. Coll. Trial Lawyers; mem.: ABA (vice chmn. ADR Advocacy in Litig. 2003—05), Assn. Bus. Trial Lawyers (bd. govs. 1996—99), 9th Jud. Cir. Hist. Soc. (pres. 1997—2002, bd. dirs. 1986—), Century City Bar Assn. (bd. govs. 2001—05), Stanford Profl. Women L.A. County, Am. Arbitration Assn. (large and complex case panel 1992—, nat. energy panel 1998—, class action panel 2004—, bd. dirs. 1999—), Women Lawyers Assn. L.A. County, L.A. County Bar Assn., Calif. State Bar (com. fed. cts. 1985—88), Stanford U. Alumni Assn. Republican. Office: Irell & Manella LLP 1800 Ave Of Stars Ste 900 Los Angeles CA 90067-4276 Office Phone: 310-277-1010. Business E-Mail: cbyrd@irell.com.

BYRD, DEBRA ANN, actor, theater producer, performing company executive; b. NYC, Oct. 26, 1965; d. Carlos Raymond Machicote and Marie Glenn; m. Nathan Robert Byrd, June 6, 1987 (div.); children: Martha Nicole Glenn, Joshua Alexander Glenn. BFA, Marymount Manhattan Coll., 2001. Cert. accounting clk., NY Bilingual Inst., NYC, 1986; arts leadership Tchr.'s Coll., Columbia U., 2004, prodr. Comml. Theatre Inst., 2007. Customer svc. rep. Banker's Trust Corp., NYC, 1986—87; sr. svc. rep. Barclay's Bank Of NY, NYC, 1987—89; sec. Phillips, Capiello, et al Esqs., NYC, 1989—90, Barish & O'Brien, CPAs, NYC, 1990—91; founder & chief exec. Take Wing And Soar Productions, Inc., NYC, 1991—; asst. to the prodr. Nat. Black Theatre, Inc., NYC, 2002—; assoc. prodr. 6-10 Productions, LLC, Kansas City, Mo., 2002—. Asst. to prodr. Am. Showcase Theatre, Bklyn., 1993—94; producing cons. Shining Star Productions, NYC, 1995—98; prodn. stage mgr. Nat. Black Touring Circuit, NYC, 2003. Actor: (theater) The Domestic, Brown Women Who Fly, Nzinga's Children, Love's Labor's Lost, For Colored Girls Who Have Considered Suicide, Antigone, Trifles, A Midsummer Night's Dream, Nobody Loves A Black Little Girl, The Importance Of Being Earnest, Aunt Vanya, Freedom Train, Say Yes To Jesus, Sweet Daddy & Amazing Grace, Looking For Love In Darkness, Once On This Island, The Bad Seed, You Shouldn't Have Told, (independant film) Da Projects; prodr.: (theater) Richard III, The Other Woman, The Women of Shakespeare, Coriolanus: The African Warrior, The TWAS Classical Lab Reading Series, The Darker Face of the Earth; prodr.: Medea; prodr.: Hamlet; prodr.'s asst. (theater) A Secret Lies Inside My Sister's Womb; make-up designer: (theater) The Making Of A Perfect Mate; prodr.: Serenade: The Music and Words of Oscar Brown Jr.; editor: (the griffin year book 2001) Journey To Success; author: (research publication) JURIES: An MMC Actor Prepares (Marymount Manhattan Honors Colloquium award, 2001). Festival devel. dir. Harlem Health Festival, Inc., NYC, 2002. Recipient Black Family Theatre award, In-A-Woman Productions, Inc., 1996, Women Of Excellence award, N.Y.C. Dist. Leader Hon. Theresa Freeman, 1997, Gold medal For Academic Excellence in Acting, Marymount Manhattan Coll., 2001, MMC Gold Cross award, 2001, Dorothy L. Stickney Theatre award, Zonta Womens Club of N.Y., 2001, Women's Forum Ednl. award, Women's Forum Inc., 2001, NY State Proclamation, NY State Senator David A. Paterson, 2003, Josephine Abady award, League Profl. Theatre Women, 2006; Madeline Burns scholarship, Marymount Manhattan Coll., 1999, William T. Morris Found. scholarship, 2000, Mary Colquhoun Acting scholarship, Joseph Papp Pub. Theatre Shakespeare Lab, 2001, Arts Mgmt. Tng. scholarship, Arts Leadership Inst., 2004, Nancy Quinn Fund grant, Alliance of Resident Theatres N.Y., 2004—05. Mem.: Theatre Comm. Group, Harlem Arts Alliance, Alliance Of Resident Theatres NY, Arts & Bus. Coun., AUDELCO, Theatre Devel. Fund, N.Y. Coalition of Profl. Women in Arts & Media, League Profl. Theatre Women (life), Actor's Equity Assn. (life), Omicron Delta Kappa (life), Am. Scholars Nat. Honor Soc. (life). Presbyterian. Avocation: arts and culture researcher, dramaturgy. Office: PO Box 5524 Manhattan Sta New York NY 10027 Office Phone: 212-696-6575. Business E-Mail: dabyrd@takewingandsoar.org.

BYRD, EVA WILSON, communications executive; Dir. media Bates Health World, New York, NY, 1994—, v.p., dir. media. Office: Girgenti Hughes Butler & McDowell Fl 8 100 Ave of the Americas New York NY 10013-1687

BYRD, GARY ELLIS, lawyer; b. Dothan, Ala., Mar. 8, 1957; m. Emily Marie Reid; children: Elizabeth, Virginia and Victoria (twins). BS in Pre-Law and Am. History summa cum laude, Troy State U., 1979; JD, U. Ala., 1982. Bar: Ga. (no. and middle dists.) 1983, U.S. Dist. Ct. (no. and so. dists), Ga., U.S. Ct. Appeals. Pntr. Bishoff & Byrd, Talbotton, Ga., 1982-86; assoc. Bunn & Kirby, Hamilton, Ga., 1993—, 1993-96; ptnr. Bunn & Byrd, Hamilton, Ga., 1996—2000; city atty. Woodland, Ga., 1986—, Geneva, Ga., 1988—, Shiloh, Ga., 1994—; ptnr. Bunn, Byrd, Newsom & Hix, 2001—, city atty. Junction City, Ga., 2002; pvt. practice, 2003—. Chmn. bd. dirs. Talbot County Law Libr., Talbotton, 1992-2004, 2001-2002; bd. dirs. Harris County Law Libr., Hamilton, 1998-2004. Contbr. numerous articles to newspapers and profl. jours., chpt. to book;

author City of Woodland city code, 1986, City of Geneva charter, 2000, City of Shiloh charter, 2001. Bd. dirs. Chattahoochie-Flint RESA, Americus, Ga., 1986-87, Pine Mountain Regional Arts Coun., Manchester, Ga., 1986-88; pres., chmn. exec. com. Talbot County 2000 Group, Talbotton, 1987-88; coach debate team dept. social studies Manchester (Ga.) H.S., 1982; chmn. appropriations com. Harris County YMCA, Hamilton, 1994-2000, 2002-03, bd. dirs. 1994-2000, 2002-03; mem. budget com. City of Talbotton, 1989-92, councilman, 1985-92, mem. policy adv. com., 1986-92, vol. fireman, 1982-93; ct. apptd. adminstr. City of Geneva, Ga., 1992; mem. adv. com. Am. Security Coun., Washington, 1976-82; dir. Harris County Indigent Def. Program, 1999-2004. Recipient Outstanding Svc. award Talbot County Jaycees, 1983, Mem. Ga. Bar Assn., Ga. Mcpl. Assn. (atty.'s sect.), Talbot County C. of C. (chmn. membership com. 1992-93, bd. dirs. 1993), Harris County C. of C. (bd. dirs. 2000-02), Troy State U. Alumni Assn. (membership com. East Ala./West Ctrl. Ga. chpt. 1993-99, Rotary (chmn. internat. svc. com. 2002-04), Phi Kappa Phi, Phi Alpha Theta (State Hist. Rsch. award 1979). Author, City of Geneva, GA Charter, 2000; Author, City of Shiloh, GA Charter, 2001. Avocations: model trains, stock car racing. Home: PO Box 119 Hamilton GA 31811-0119 Office: 103 N College St PO Box 489 Hamilton GA 31811-0489 Office Phone: 706-628-5511. E-mail: byrdgary@msn.com.

BYRD, HARRY FLOOD, JR., publishing executive, retired senator; b. Winchester, Va., Dec. 20, 1914; s. Harry Flood and Anne Douglas (Beverley) B.; m. Gretchen B. Thomson, Aug. 9, 1941 (dec. Oct. 1989); children: Harry, Thomas Thomson, Beverley. Student, Va. Mil. Inst., 1931—33, U. Va., 1933—35, LLD, LHD, U. Va., D (hon.) in Internat. Svc. Editor Winchester Evening Star, 1935—81; pub. Harrisonburg (Va.) Daily News-Record, 1937—2000; pres., dir. Rockingham Pub. Co., 1946—; dir. AP, 1950-66; v.p., mem. exec. com., mem. Va. Senate, 1947-65; mem. U.S. Senate from Va., 1965-83, chmn. subcom. on taxation. Author Va. automatic tax reduction law. Mem. Va. Dem. Ctrl. Com., 1940-66. Served to lt. comdr. USNR, 1942-46. Recipient Honor medal Freedoms Found.; named to Va. Comm. Hall of Fame. Mem. VFW, Va. Press Assn. (Man of Yr.), Am. Legion, Masons (33d degree, insp. gen. hon.), Rotarian Club, National Press Club, Army-Navy Club. Office: Rockingham Pub Co Inc 2 N Kent St Winchester VA 22601-5038 Office Phone: 540-662-7745.

BYRD, HENRY STEPHENSON (STEVE), plastic surgeon, educator; BA with honors, North Tex. State U., 1968; MD with honors, U. Tex., Galveston, 1972. Diplomate Am. Bd. Surgery, 1978, Am. Bd. Plastic Surgery, 1980, lic. Tex., Utah. Surg. intern U. Tex. Southwestern Med. Ctr., Dallas, 1972—73, resident plastic surgery, 1977—79, prof., vice chair plastic surgery, 1979—2000; resident gen. surgery U. Utah Med. Ctr., Salt Lake City, 1973—77; chief pediat. plastic surgery sect. Children's Med. Ctr., Dallas, 1979—. Sec.-treas., bd. mem. Selected Readings in Plastic Surgery, 1980—; treas. Rhinoplasty Soc.; chmn. Bd. Pediat. Surg. Alliance; bd. mem. Health Tex. Provider Network; sec. Preferred Surg. Specialist Tex.; attending staff Parkland Meml. Hosp., Dallas, U. Med. Ctr., Dallas; dir. plastic surgery svc., mem. cleft lip-craniofacial team Children's Med. Ctr., Dallas; chief plastic and reconstructive surgery svc. Baylor U. Med. Ctr., Dallas, 1996—2002, dir. Dallas Day Surgery, 1992—. Fellow: ACS; mem.: Plastic Surgery Ednl. Found. (bd. mem. 1993—, chmn. in-svc. exam com. 1989—91, mem. long range planning task force 1991, mem. mktg. com. 1991, bd. dirs. 1996—98, mem. select com. on forward planning 1996—), Dallas County Med. Soc., Dallas Soc. Plastic Surgeons (sec.-treas.), Tex. Soc. Plastic Surgeons, Tex. Med. Assn., Am. Cleft Palate Assn., Am. Soc. for Aesthetic Plastic Surgery (mem. edn. commn.), Am. Assn. Plastic Surgeons, Am. Soc. Plastic and Reconstructive Surgeons (mem. sci. program com. 1991, James Barrett Brown award 1984), Alpha Omega Alpha, Blue Key Honor Soc. Office: Dallas Plastic Surgery Inst 411 N Washington Ave Ste 6000 LB 13 Dallas TX 75246 Office Phone: 214-821-9662. Office Fax: 214-828-2609. Business E-Mail: info@drstevebyrd.com.

BYRD, ISAAC BURLIN, retired biologist; b. Canoe, Ala., Mar. 14, 1925; s. Isaac Britt and Mary Adline B.; m. Marjorie Fé Elmore, Sept. 24, 1949; children— Cathy Ann, Teresa Carol, Gary Curtis. BS, Auburn U., 1948, MS, 1950. Chief fisheries sect. Ala. Dept. Conservation, 1951-65; fed. aid coordinator fisheries research and devel. Bur. Comml. Fisheries, Dept. Interior, 1965-70; chief div. state-fed. relationships, fisheries research, devel. and mgmt. Nat. Marine Fisheries Service, St. Petersburg, Fla., 1970-85, asst. regional dir. S.E. Region, 1985-91, ret., 1991. Adminstr. Internat. Fisheries Agreement (for U.S. shrimp fishermen to fish Brazilian coastal waters), 1975-76; mem. adv. com. to organize 1st fishery mgmt. councils and to develop initial fed. policies under Fisheries Conservation and Mgmt. Act 1976 (for marine fisheries in fisheries conservation zone of U.S.); chmn. Gulf of Mexico State/Fed. Fisheries Mgmt. Bd., 1985-86, 88-89; chmn. South Atlantic State/Fed. Fisheries Mgmt. Bd., 1990-91 Contbg. author: McCanes Standard Fishing Ency., Internat. Angling Guide, 1965; contbr. articles to sci. jours. Served with USAAF, 1943-46. Recipient Gov. Ala. award outstanding tech. accomplishments conservation, 1964 Fellow Am. Inst. Fishery Research Biologists; mem. Am. Fisheries Soc. (pres. So. div. 1958, pres. 1965-66, asso. editor trans. 1955-58), World Mariculture Soc. (dir. 1972-73), Internat. Assn. Fish and Wildlife Agys., Gulf and Caribbean Fisheries Inst., Inland Comml. Fisheries Assn., Phi Kappa Phi, Omicron Delta Kappa, Gamma Sigma Delta, Alpha Zeta, Alpha Gamma Rho. Methodist. Achievements include initiating the 1st fisheries mgmt. and fisheries research program in state for Ala. Dept. Conservation. Home: 11105 7th St E Treasure Island Saint Petersburg FL 33706

BYRD, JAMES EVERETT, lawyer; b. Cin., Aug. 1, 1958; BS, U. Dayton, Ohio, 1980, JD cum laude, 1984. Law clk. U.S. Dist Ct. (so. dist.), Ohio, 1983; assoc. Smith & Schnacke, Dayton, 1984-89; v.p., gen. counsel Internat. Cargo Svcs., Virginia Beach, Va., 1989-91; assoc. Beale, Balfour et al., Richmond, Va., 1991-92; corp. counsel Huffy Corp., Dayton, 1992-94; ind. corp. legal cons., 1994-95; sr. dir., assoc. gen. counsel Lexis Nexis divsn. Reed Elsevier, Inc., Dayton, 1995—. Pres. Condominium Owners Assn., Dayton, 1995-99. Mem. ABA, Ohio Bar Assn., Va. Bar Assn. Office: Lexis Nexis 9443 Springboro Pike Miamisburg OH 45342-4425 E-mail: james.e.byrd@lexisnexis.com.

BYRD, JANICE ADELE, elementary school educator; d. James Earl and Deborah Ann Montgomery; m. Jeremy Byrd; children: Shelby, Riley. BA, MA, No. Ariz. U., Flagstaff, 1999. Cert. educator Ariz., 1998. Tchr. Tuscon Unified Sch. Dist., 1998—. Recipient Exemplary Tchr. award, Rodel, 2006. Office Phone: 232-7261.

BYRD, JOAN EDA, retired librarian; b. May 12, 1942; BFA, Howard U., 1965; MLS, Cath. U. Am., 1976; MA, New Sch. for Social Rsch. Reference libr. Bklyn. Pub. Libr., 1985—87, sr. libr., 1987—89; sr. film libr. N.Y. Pub. Libr., NYC, 1989—93, supervising libr., 1993—2004; ret.

BYRD, JOYCE MARIE, dentist; b. Florence, Miss., Oct. 18, 1955; d. Thomas Allen and Kathleen M. Byrd; m. David Howard Warnock, June 20, 1981 (div. Jan. 1, 2000). BS, Eckerd Coll., St. Petersburg, Fla., 1982; DDS, U. Tenn., Memphis, 1988. Lic. dentist Fla. Clk. Pulpit Pub., Jackson, Miss., 1970—73; sec. State of Miss., Jackson, 1974—78; pvt. practice Dunnellon, 1989—2000, Flowood, Miss., 2000—. Dentist St. Augustine Presbytery and Jamaica Ecumenical Mission, Kingston, Jamaica, 1994—; owner JMB Valplast Dental Lab., Florence, 2005—. Elder Dunnellon Presbyn. Ch., 1999; pres. acad. scholarship Dunnellon H.S., 1996; vol. Hist. Soc. Dunnellon, 1994—99. Mem.: ADA, Miss. Dental Assn., Am. Assn. Women Dentists (pres. U. Tenn. Dental Sch. 1986—87), Kiwanis Club of Dunnellon (coord. com. young children minority one - children's health fair 1995—97, bd. dirs. 1992—2000, Hixon award 1997, Prestigious Past Pres. award 1996). Avocations: piano, gardening. Office: 128 Riverview Dr Flowood MS 39232 Office Phone: 601-664-9981.

BYRD, KATHRYN SUSAN, psychologist, educator; d. George Washington Byrd and Josie Beth Mayes. BA, Centenary Coll., Shreveport, La., 1974; MS, Northwestern State U., Natchitoches, La., 1977; PhD, U. Tex. Richardson, 1995. Cert. mediator Tex., 2004. Coord. of academic advising, communication arts & tech. divsn. Eastfield Coll., Mesquite, Tex., 2001—, adj. faculty, 2001—. Acad. adv. Eastfield Coll., Mesquite, Tex., 1999—; apptd. to district-wide ednl. improvement coun. Garland Ind. Sch. Dist., 2004—05. Mem. of class of 2002, Eastfield Coll. rep. Leadership Garland, Mesquite, Tex., 2002. Mem.: APA, Romance Writers Am., Bluebonnet Bebes Doll Collectors Club. Republican. Southern Baptist. Office: Eastfield College 3737 Motley Dr Mesquite TX 75150 Office Phone: 972-860-7671. Business E-Mail: ksb4323@dcccd.edu.

BYRD, LARRY DONALD, behavioral pharmacologist; b. Salisbury, NC, July 14, 1936; s. Donald Thomas and Mildred (Gardner) B.; m. Corrinne Williams, Dec. 23, 1961; children: Kay, Lynn, Renee, Andrew. AB, E. Carolina U., Greenville, NC, 1962; MA, E. Carolina U., 1964; PhD, U. N.C., 1968; postgrad., Harvard U., 1967-70. Faculty E. Carolina U., 1962-64; tchg. and rsch. asst. exptl. psychology U. N.C., Chapel Hill, 1964-67; rsch. fellow pharmacology, instr. psychobiology Harvard Med. Sch., 1967-70; assoc. scientist Lab. Psychobiology New Eng. Reg. Primate Rsch. Ctr., 1969-74; psychobiologist, chmn. divsn. primate behavior Yerkes Primate Rsch. Ctr., Emory U., Atlanta, 1974-79, assoc. rsch. prof., chmn. divsn. primate behavior, 1979-80, lectr. dept. psychology, 1974-81, assoc. rsch. prof., chief divsn. behavioral biology, 1980-82, prof., chief divsn. behavioral biology, 1982-97, prof. dept. pharmacology, 1995-97; prof. emeritus, 1998. Adj. prof. dept. psychology Emory U., 1981-97; cons. Dept. Pharmacological and Physiol. Scis. U. Chgo., 1973, MIT Press, Cambridge, 1975, Nat. Ctr. for Toxicological Rsch. FDA, Jefferson, Ark., 1976-77, S.W. Found. for Rsch. and Edn., San Antonio, 1977, Naval Aerospace Med. Rsch. Lab. U.S. Naval Air Sta., Pensacola, Fla., 1977, G.D. Searle and Co., Skokie, Ill., 1986, Battelle Meml. Inst., Columbus, Ohio, 1989-94; mem. spl. rev. com. Contract Rev. Unit Nat. Inst. on Drug Abuse, Lexington, Ky., 1979-81, mem. spl. rev. com. biomed. rsch. rev. com., 1981-82, spl. rev. cons. clin., behavioral and psychosocial rsch. rev. com., 1981-82, mem., 1982-85, chmn., 1984-85, others; spl. rev. cons. dept. medicine and surgery VA, Washington, 1983, NSF, Washington, 1984, div. of rsch. resources NIH, Washington, 1983, mem. spl. study sect. div. rsch. grants, 1984, panel mem. Workshop on Implemenation of Pub. Health Svc. Policy on Humane Care and Use of Lab. Animals, 1989, others; panel mem. USPHS Animal Welfare Forum Alcohol, Drug Abuse and Mental Health Adminstrn., 1985; active numerous other career related orgns. Editorial bd. Jour. Exptl. Analysis of Behavior, 1969-79, 87-91; assoc. editor Jour. Exptl. Analysis of Behavior, 1970-76; cons. editor Am. Jour. Primatology, 1980-83; editor Psychopharmacology Newsletter, 1976-82; editorial advisor Jour. Pharmacology and Exptl. Therapeutics, Jour. Exptl. Analysis of Behavior, others; contbr. numerous articles to profl. jours. Mem. sci. adv. com. Nat. Families in Action, 1991—95. Recipient Outstanding Alumnus award, E. Carolina U., 1977, Disting. Alumnus award, U. N.C., 1987. Fellow AAAS, Am. Psychol. Assn. (exec. com. psychopharmacology divsn. 1976-95, neurobehavioral toxicity test standards com. 1980-97, coord. Young Psychopharmacologist award 1985-95, bd. sci. affairs com. on animals in rsch. and ethics 1990-93); mem. Assn. for Assessment and Accreditation Lab. Animal Care (trustee 1990-98, exec. com. 1991-98, sec. 1993, vice chmn. 1994-96, chmn. 1996-98), Am. Soc. Pharmacology and Exptl. Therapeutics, Nat. Families in Action (sci. adv. com. 1991-95), Am. Soc. Primatologist, Behavioral Pharmacology Soc. (pres. 1984-86), Soc. Exptl. Analysis of Behavior (v.p. 1975-76, bd. dirs. 1970-78), European Behavioral Pharmacology Soc., Southeastern Pharmacology Soc., Am Pub. Health Assn., Behavioral Toxicology Soc., Southeastern Assn. for Behavior Analysis, Internat. Study Group Investigating Drugs as Reinforcers, Emory Neurosci. Group, Phi Sigma Pi. Home: 2730 Camp Branch Rd Buford GA 30519-4455 Business E-Mail: lbyrd@emory.edu.

BYRD, LLOYD GARLAND, retired civil engineer; b. Atlanta, May 6, 1923; s. Lloyd Porter and Gladys Ardee (Daniell) B.; m. Jeanne Mae Parkhurst, Jan. 23, 1943; children: Gary Daniell, Donna Jeanne, Jeffrey Alan, Julie Anne. BCE, Ohio State U., 1950. Staff engr. Ohio Dept. Hwys., Columbus, 1949-52; maintenence engr. Ohio Turnpike Commn., Berea, 1952-60; assoc. editor Pub. Works Publs., Ridgewood, NJ, 1960-63; ptnr. Byrd, Tallamy, MacDonald & Lewis, Falls Church, Va., 1963-72; sr. v.p., mgr. Byrd, Tallamy, MacDonald & Lewis div. Wilbur Smith & Assocs., Falls Church, 1972-84; interim dir. Strategic Hwy. Rsch. Program, Washington, 1984-86; pvt. practice Washington, 1986-99; ret. Chmn. group 3 coun. Transp. Rsch. Bd., Washington, 1972-76, chmn. overview com.; ex-officio governing bd. NRC, Washington, 1989-95; mem. bd. cons. Eno Found., Westport, Conn., 1986-89; mem. report rev. com. NRC, 1997—. Co-author: Street and Highway Maintenance Manual: American Public Works Association, 1985; assoc. editor: Handbook of Highway Engrng., 1975; chmn. pub. affairs coun. Am. Assn. Engrng. Socs., 1992. Chmn. Fairfax County Human Rights Commn., Va., 1978-79; pres. Fairfax County C. of C., 1975-76; bd. dirs. Hospice of Carolina Foothills, Inc., 2002-07. Recipient Disting. Alumnus award Ohio State U. Coll. Engrng., 1978, Roy W. Crum award Transp. Rsch. Bd., Washington, 1986, P.D. McLean Meml. award Road Gang, Washington, 1989, Disting. Lectr. award, 1998, Transp. Rsch Bd. Fellow ASCE (pres. nat. capital sect. Washington 1976-77, nat. bd. dirs. N.Y.C. 1979-82, Wilbur S. Smith award 1985, Francis C. Turner Lecture award 1995); mem. NAE, Am. Pub. Works Assn., Univ. Club (Washington), Tryon (N.C.) Country Club, Rotary Club. Congregationalist. Avocations: golf, bridge. Personal E-mail: lgbyrd@alltel.net.

BYRD, MARC ROBERT, floral designer; b. Flint, Mich., May 14, 1954; s. Robert Lee and Cynthia Ann (Poland) B.; m. Bonnie Jill Berlin, Nov. 25, 1975 (div. June 1977). Student, Ea. Mich. U., 1972-75; grad., Am. Floral Sch., Chgo., 1978; BS, U. Redlands, 2002, MA in Mgmt., 2004. Gen. mgr., dir. floral shops; designer Olive Tree Florist, Palm Desert, Calif., 1978-79, Kayo's Flower Fashions, Palm Springs, 1979-80; owner, designer Village Florist, Inc., Palm Springs, 1980-85; pres. Mon Ami Florist, Inc., Beverly Hills, 1986-87; gen. mgr. Silverio's, Santa Monica, 1987; gen. mgr., hotel florist, creative dir. Four Seasons Hotel, Beverly Hills, 1988-90; pres. Marc Fredericks, Inc., Beverly Hills, 1990-97; event florist Marc Byrd of Floral Works, LA, 1997—2002, Marc Byrd Eventful Flower Design, 2002—. Author: Celebrity Flowers, 1989. Del., Dem. County Conv., 1972, Dem. County Conv., 1972, Dem. State Conv., 1972, Dem. Nat. Conv., 1972. Mem. Soc. Am. Florists, So. Calif. Floral Assn., Desert Mus., Robinson's Gardens, U. Redlands Alumni Assn. (bd. dirs.), Whitehead Leadership Soc. (bd. dirs.) Democrat. Episcopalian. Avocations: skiing, tennis, community service. Office Fax: 323-962-9275. Personal E-mail: marcbyrd@earthlink.net.

BYRD, MILTON BRUCE, academic administrator; b. Boston, Jan. 29, 1922; s. Max Joseph and Rebecca (Malkiel) B.; m. Susanne J. Schwerin, Aug. 30, 1953; children: Deborah, Leslie, David. AB cum laude, Boston U., 1948, MA, 1949; PhD, U. Wis., 1953; postgrad. (fellow), U. Mich., 1961-62. Teaching asst. English U. Wis., 1949-53; instr., asst. prof. English Ind. U., 1953-58; asst. prof., assoc. prof. humanities So. Ill. U., 1958-62, head div. humanities, 1958-60, supr. acad. advisement, 1959-60, asso. dean, 1960- 62; v.p. acad. affairs No. Mich. U., 1962-66; pres. Chgo. State U., 1966-74; provost Fla. Internat. U., 1974-78; pres. Adams State Coll., Alamosa, Colo., 1978—80; v.p. corp. devel. Frontier Cos., Anchorage, 1981-85; pres. Charter Coll., 1985—2005, pres. emeritus, 2005—. Bd. dirs Chgo. Council for Urban Edn., Union for Experimenting Colls. and Univs., Am. Assn. State Colls. and Univs., Resource Devel. Council Alaska, Alaska Commn. Econ. Edn.; v.p. Common Sense for Alaska, Inc.; former pres. Alaska Support Industry Alliance; pres. Alaska World Affairs Coun. Author: (with Arnold L. Goldsmith) Publication Guide for Literary and Linguistic Scholars, 1958; contbr. to profl. jours. Vice chmn. Alaska Commn. on Postsecondary Edn. With USAAF, 1943—46. Mem. MLA, Nat. Council Tchrs. English, Coll. English Assn., Am. Studies Assn., AAUP, Fla. Assn. Univ. Adminstrs. (former pres.), Rocky Mountain Athletic Conf. (former pres.), Assn. for Higher Edn., Pub. Relations Soc. Am., NEA, Alaska Press Club, Mich. Edn. Assn., Phi Beta Kappa, Phi Delta Kappa. Clubs: Rotary. Office: # 120 2221 E Northern Lights Blvd Anchorage AK 99508-4143

BYRD, ROBERT CARLYLE, senator; b. North Wilkesboro, NC, Nov. 20, 1917; s. Cornelius Sale and Ada (Kirby) B.; m. Erma Ora James (dec. March 25, 2006), May 29, 1937; children: Mona Carole (Mrs. Mohammad Fatemi), Marjorie Ellen (Mrs. John Moore). Student, Beckley Coll., Concord Coll., Morris Harvey Coll., 1950-51, Marshall U., 1951-52, BA in Polit. Sci., 1994; JD cum laude, Am. U., 1963. Mem. W.Va. Ho. of Reps., 1947-50, W.Va. Senate, 1951-52, US Congress from 6th W.Va. dist., 1953—59; US Senator from W.Va., 1959—; majority leader, 1977-80, 87-88; minority leader, 1981-86; pres. pro tempore, 2007—. Mem. appropriations com., armed svcs. com., rules and adminstrn. com., budget com., senate Dem. steering and coord. com. Author: The Senate, 1789-1989, 4 vols., 1989-94, The Senate of the Roman Republic: Addresses on the History of Roman Constitutionalism, 1995, Losing America: Confronting a Reckless and Arrogant Presidency, 2004, Robert C. Byrd: Child of the Appalachian Coalfields, 2005; contbr. articles to profl. jours. Recipient Disting. Svc award Radio and TV News Dirs. Assn. 1986, Montgomery award, Nat. Guard Bur. 2000, Robert J. Collier award Nat. Aeronautic Assn., 2001, Nat. Leadership award Civil War Preservation Trust, 2002, Edmund S. Muskie Disting. Public Svc. award Ctr. Nat. Policy, 2003, Freedom from Fear medal Franklin and Eleanor Roosevelt Inst., 2003, Theodore Roosevelt-Woodrow Wilson award civil svc. Am. Historial Assn., 2004, Wellstone award United Steelworkers Am., 2004; named Most Influential Mem. U.S. Senate, U.S. News and World Report Poll, 1979, Legislator of Yr. Nat. Coal Assn., 1986, West Virginian of the 20th Century, 2001, West Virginian of Twentieth Century, W. Va. House Delegates, 2001. Mem. Country Music Assn. (hon.) Lodges: Masons (33 degree). Democrat. Baptist. Achievements include holding the record for the longest period of service as a US Senator in 2006. Office: US Senate 311 Hart Senate Ofc Bldg Washington DC 20510-0001 also: District Office 300 Virginia St Ste 2630 Charleston WV 25301 Office Phone: 202-224-3954. Office Fax: 202-228-0002, 304-342-5855, 304-343-7144.*

BYRD, STEPHEN C., utilities executive; BBA in Fin., Coll. William and Mary, Williamsburg, Va.; LLD/MBA, U. Va., Charlottesville. Exec. dir. global energy and utilities group Morgan Stanley; sr. v.p. fin., bus. devel., strategy and M&A PSEG Svcs. Corp., 2007—. Mem.: NY State Bar Assn. Office: PSEG Svcs Corp PO Box 570 Newark NJ 07101 Office Phone: 973-430-7000.*

BYRD, STEPHEN FRED, human resource consultant; b. Charleston, SC, June 12, 1928; s. Paul Fred and Dorothy B.; m. Margaret A. McAulay, Apr. 15, 1955; children: Owen, Susan Student, CCNY, 1945—48; LLB, N.Y. Law Sch., 1951. Bar: N.Y. 1951. Corp. indsl. rels. rep. Pan Am. Airways, 1957—62, Sinclair Oil Corp., 1962—64; v.p. employee rels. indsl. chems. divsn. Allied Chem. Corp., 1964—68; v.p. indsl. rels. and pers. Internat. Nickel Co., Ltd., 1968—72; sr. v.p. human resources Schering-Plough Corp., Madison, NJ, 1973—88; cons. Right Assocs., Parsippany, NJ, 1988—90. Author: Front Line Supervisors Labor Relations Handbook, 1962, Management Strategy in Collective Bargaining, 1964 Bd. dirs. United Fund Morris County, N.J., Big Bros. Morris County, Morristown YMCA, 1962-63; chmn. Madison coun. Boy Scouts Am., 1975-76; trustee Drew U., Madison, 1976-80. With AUS, 1952-53, Korea Mem. Indsl. Rels. Rsch. Assn., N.Y. Law Sch. Alumni Assn Home and Office: 23 Academy Rd Madison NJ 07940-2001 Home Phone: 973-377-9174; Office Phone: 973-822-0507. E-mail: stevebyrd@att.net.

BYRD, WYATT, microbiologist, researcher; b. Panama City, Fla., June 23, 1958; s. Elizabeth and Isaac Byrd; m. Dagmar Beinenz, Sept. 18, 1962; children: Lewis, Fiona. PhD, U. of Ga., 1985—91. Rsch. assoc. Miami U., Oxford, Ohio, 1993—97; rsch. asst. Walter Reed Army Inst. Rsch., Silver Spring, Md., 1998—2004. Mem.: Am. Soc. for Microbiology (assoc.). Office: 18929 Fountain Hills Dr Germantown MD 20874 Office Phone: 301-515-0253. Personal E-mail: dagmarbyrd@comcast.net.

BYRNE, GABRIEL, actor; b. Dublin, May 12, 1950; m. Ellen Barkin, 1988 (div. 1993); children: Jack, Romy. Actor: (Broadway) A Moon for the Misbegotten, (Theatre World award), 2000, A Touch of the Poet, 2005 (Outer Critics' Cir. award, outstanding actor in a play, 2006); (films) On a Paving Stone Mounted, 1978, The Outsider, 1979, Excalibur, 1981, The Keep, 1983, Hannah K., 1983, Defence of the Realm, 1985, Gothic, 1985, Lionheart, 1987, Hello, Again, 1987, Siesta, 1987, Julia and Julia, 1988, A Soldier's Tale, 1988, The Courier, 1988, Miller's Crossing, 1990, Shipwrecked, 1991, Dark Obsession, 1991, Cool World, 1992, Point of No Return, 1993, A Dangerous Woman, 1993, A Simple Twist of Fate, 1994, Trial by Jury, 1994, Little Women, 1994, The Usual Suspects, 1995, Frankie Starlight, 1995, Past into Present, 1996, Mad Dog Time, 1996, Dr. Hagard's Disease, 1996, Somebody is Waiting, 1996, The End of Violence, 1997, Smillas Sense of Snow, 1997, The Man in the Iron Mask, 1998, Polish Wedding, 1998, Enemy of the State, 1998, This Is the Sean, 1998, Quest for Camelot (voice), 1998, The Brylcreem Boys, 1998, Stigmata, 1999, End of Days, 1999, Madigan Men, 2000, Ghost Ship, 2002, Shade, 2003, Vanity Fair, 2004, P.S., 2004, El Puente de San Luis Ray, 2004, Assault on Precinct 13, 2005, Wah-Wah, 2006; (TV movies) Wagner, 1983, Reflections, 1983, Mussolini: The Untold Story, 1985, Christopher Columbus, 1985, Buffalo Girls, 1995, (TV series) The Riordan's, Bracken; actor, co-exec. prodr. Spider, 2002; actor, assoc. prodr.: (films) Into the West, 1993; co-exec. prodr.: (films) In the Name of the Father, 1993; actor, exec. prodr. Last of the High Kings, 1996, Smilla's Sense of Snow, 1997, Weapons of Mass Destruction, 1996, Toby's Story, 1998, Polish Wedding, 1998, This is the Sea, 1998, The Man in the Iron Mask, 1998, (voice) Quest for Camelot, 1998, An Ideal Husband, 1999; dir. End of Violence, 1996, The Lark in the Clear Air, 1996; actor, writer Draiocht, 1996; narrator Irish Cinema: Ourselves Alone?, 1997; author: (book) Pictures in My Head, 2001. Office: United Talent Agy 9560 Wilshire Blvd Ste 500 Beverly Hills CA 90212

BYRNE, GEORGE MELVIN, physician; b. Aug. 1, 1933; s. Carlton and Esther (Smith) B.; m. Joan Stecher, July 14, 1956; children: Kathryne, Michael, David; m. Margaret C. Smith, Dec. 18, 1982; m. Barbara Barrett, May 19, 2001. BA, Occidental Coll., 1958; MD, U. So. Calif., 1962. Intern Huntington Meml. Hosp., Pasadena, Calif., 1962-63, resident, 1963-64; family practice So. Calif. Permanente Med. Group, 1964-81; physician-in-charge Pasadena Med. Office, 1966-81; asst. dir. family practice residency Kaiser Found. Hosp., LA, 1971-73; clin. instr. emergency medicine Sch. Medicine U. So. Calif., 1973-80; v.p. East Ridge Co., 1983-84, sec., 1984; dir. Alan Johnson Porsche Audi, Inc., 1974-82, sec., 1974-77, v.p., 1978-82. Mem. commn. disability LA Episc. Bishop, 2007. Bd. dirs. Kaiser-Permanente Mgmt. Assn., 1976-77; mem. regional mgmt. com. So. Calif. Lung Assn., 1976-77; mem. pres.'s cir. Occidental Coll., L.A. Drs. Symphony Orch., 1975-80; mem. profl. sect. Am. Diabetes Assn; apptd. Disabilities Commn. Episcopal Bishop LA, 2007. Fellow Am. Acad. Family Physicians (charter); mem. AMA, Calif. Med. Assn., L.A. County Med. Assn., Calif. Acad. Family Physicians, Internat. Horn Soc., Quarter

Century Wireless Assn., Am. Radio Relay League (Pub. Svc. award), Sierra (life), So. Calif. Dx Club. Home: 528 Meadowview Dr La Canada Flintridge CA 91011-2816 Personal E-mail: GMByrne@aol.com.

BYRNE, GERARD ANTHONY (GERRY), publishing executive, consultant; b. NYC, Apr. 27, 1944; s. Thomas Edward and Eileen (Reilly) B.; m. Elizabeth Julia Daly, Dec. 6, 1969; children: Megan, Gavin. BA in Econs., Fordham U., 1966. Advt. sales rep. NY Daily News, NYC, 1969-73, Advt. Age, NYC, 1973-77, internat. sales dir., 1977-80, ea. sales mgr., 1980-82; pub., v.p. Electronic Media, NYC, 1982-84; v.p./pub. Crain's N.Y. Bus., NYC, 1984-87; v.p., dir. corp. comm. Crain Comm., NYC, 1987-88; sr. v.p. corp. planning and internat. devel. Act III Pub., NYC, 1988-89; pub. Variety, NYC, 1990-92, v.p., dir. pub. ops., 1993-95; group v.p., pub. Daily Variety and Weekly Variety, NYC, 1996—2000; v.p., group pub. Variety, Inc., NYC, 1997—2000; pres., CEO Stagebill Media, 2000—02; CEO Gerry Byrne Media Ptnrs. LLC, 2002—. Sr. advisor Parade Mag.; chmn. exec. bd. Wash. Life Mag. Founder, chmn. The Quill Book Awards; bd. dirs. Am. Mus. Moving Image, The Intrepid Mus. Found., The Westhampton Beach Performing Arts Ctr., Am. Friend of the Nat. Film and TV Sch., London, Fisher House Found., Vets. Advantage, Reisenbach Found., NYC Police Mus., Armory Found., Creative Coalition; chmn. Quills Literacy Found. Capt. USMC, 1966-69, Vietnam. Recipient combat action ribbon, Navy achievement medal, Show East Salah Hassanein Humanitarian award, 1996. Mem. Internat. Radio and TV Soc., NY Athletic Club, VFW, Friendly Sons of St. Patrick. Roman Catholic. Avocations: fishing, tennis, photography, skiing, golf. Home: 6 Peter Cooper Rd New York NY 10010-6701 Home Phone: 212-533-9252; Office Phone: 212-450-7063. E-mail: gerrybyrnemp@aol.com.

BYRNE, GRANVILLE BLAND, III, lawyer; b. San Antonio, Jan. 26, 1952; s. Granville Bland and Mary (Dowling) B.; divorced; children: Peyton Smith, Fulton Buckner; m. Monique Renée Wise, 1999; 1 child, Monique Renée-Christienne. AB, U. N.C., Chapel Hill, 1974; JD, Harvard U., 1978. Bar: Ga. 1978, U.S. Dist. Ct. (no. dist.) Ga. 1978, U.S. Ct. Appeals (5th cir.) 1978, U.S. Ct. Appeals (11th cir.) 1981. Assoc. Swift, Currie, McGhee & Hiers, Atlanta, 1978-84, ptnr., 1984-94; prin. Byrne, Eldridge, Moore & Davis, P.C., Atlanta, 1994—99, Byrne, Moore & Davis, PC, Atlanta, 1999—2002, Byrne & Davis, PC, Atlanta, 2003, Byrne, Davis & Hicks, PC, Atlanta, 2003—. Bd. dirs. Cagle's, Inc. Elder, mem. session 1st Presbyn. Ch. Atlanta, 1993-96, 99-2002. Mem. ABA, Ga. Bar Assn., Atlanta Bar Assn. Democrat. Presbyterian. Home: 3555 Castlegate Dr NW Atlanta GA 30327-2601 Office: Byrne Davis & Hicks PC 3340 Peachtree Rd NE Atlanta GA 30326-1000 Home Phone: 404-262-7626; Office Phone: 404-266-7260. Personal E-mail: gbb3@bellsouth.net.

BYRNE, JAMES FREDERICK, banker; b. Fairmont, NC, July 30, 1931; m. Daphne Martin, July 22, 1955; children: Paula Jean, Daphne Ann, Laura. BS, Wake Forest U., 1953; MBA, U. NC, 1959. Ptnr. Byrne-Floyd Realty, Fairmont, NC, 1961-80; v.p., city exec. So. Nat. Bank, Fairmont, 1963-69, mgr. master charge Lumberton, NC, 1969-71, v.p., dir. mktg., 1971-77, sr. v.p., dir. customer services, 1977-83, exec. v.p., 1983, exec. v.p., dir. retail banking, 1985-89, sr. exec. v.p., chief adminstrv. officer, 1989-94. Mem. endowment bd. Pembroke State U., NC, 1985—87, chmn. libr. bd., NC, 1995—96. Pres. Am. Lung Assn. NC, Wilmington, 1971, Raleigh, 1972, NC rep. dir., NY, 1977-89, nat. v.p., 1989; pres. Robeson County Cmty. Found., 2005-06, 06-07. Recipient Vol. of Yr. award, Am. Lung Assn. of N.C., 1972—90, Nat. Humanitarian award, 1993. Mem. Bank Mktg. Assn., NC Bankers Assn., Shrine Club (pres. 1996-97), Rotary (pres. 1968), Masons. Home: 905 Dogwood Dr Fairmont NC 28340-2115

BYRNE, JOHN EDWARD (JEB BYRNE), retired federal official; b. NYC, Jan. 15, 1925; s. Harry Theodore and Mary Elizabeth (Whelen) B.; m. Beverly Ann McKinley, Mar. 31, 1951; children— Peter J., David F., John P., Michael T. BA, Marquette U., 1949; MA, George Washington U., 1973, PhD, 1987. News service corr. UPI, Milw., 1949-50, Albany, N.Y., 1951, Portland, Maine, 1951-56, Augusta, Maine, 1956-58; gov.'s press sec., state promotion ofcl. State of Maine, Augusta, 1959-60; exec. GSA, Washington, 1961-80; dir. fed. register Nat. Archives and Records Adminstrn., Washington, 1980-88. Fulbright scholar Alexander Turnbull Libr., Wellington, New Zealand, 1989. Served to 2d lt. USAAF, 1943-45 Roman Catholic. Home: 2104 Marthas Rd Alexandria VA 22307-1823

BYRNE, JOHN MICHAEL, energy and environmental educator; b. Chgo., Nov. 2, 1949; s. Michael Thomas and Mabel Victoria (Cranford) B.; m. Elizabeth Maria Garey, Aug. 9, 1975; children: Brian, Tara. BA in Econs., U. Del., 1971, MA, 1973, PhD in Urban Affairs and Pub. Policy, 1980. Asst. prof. Coll. Urban Affairs and Pub. Policy, U. Del., Newark, 1982-86, assoc. prof., 1986-92, prof., 1992—2004, dist. prof. of public policy, 2004—, dir. Energy Policy Rsch. Group, 1981-84, dir. Ctr. for Energy and Environ. Policy, 1984—, chair Urban Affairs and Pub. Policy grad. program, 1992-96. Apptd. environ. policy advisor Korea Nat. Assembly, 1998—; co-exec. dir. Joint Inst. for a Sustainable Energy and Environ. Future, 1999—; rsch. chair Internat. Solar Cities Initiative, 2004—. Co-editor: Energy and Cities, 1985, The Politics of Energy R&D, 1988, Energy and Environment: The Policy Challenge, 1992, Governing the Atom: The Politics of Risk, 1996, Environmental Justice, 2002, Transforming Power, 2006, Bull. Sci., Tech., and Soc., 2003—; co-author: Energy Revolution, 2004, Water Conservation-Oriented Rates, 2005. Bd. dirs. Urban Environ. Ctr., Environ. Market Solutions, Inc., Internat. Solar Cities Initiative. Grantee ESMAP/World Bank, 1990-91, U.S. Dept. Energy/Nat. Renewable Energy Lab., 1991-2001, UNIDEL Found., 1992, U.S. EPA, 1994, 97-2001, 05—, Asia Found., 1995, Inst. Internat. Edn., 1996-97, W. Alton Jones Found., 1997-2002, U.S. Dept. Energy, 2006—, U.S. NSF, 2006—, Blue Moon Fund, 2003—, Beyond Petroleum Found., 2004—; recipient Fulbright Sr. Lectr./Rschr. award, 1995. Mem.: Internat. Assn. Sci., Tech. and Soc. (pres.-elect). Avocations: music, woodworking, hiking. Office: U Del Ctr Energy & Environ Policy Newark DE 19716-7381 Office Phone: 302-831-8405.

BYRNE, JOHN VINCENT, educational consultant; b. Hempstead, NY, May 9, 1928; s. Frank E. and Kathleen (Barry) B.; m. Shirley O'Connor, Nov. 26, 1954; children: Donna, Lisa, Karen, Steven. AB, Hamilton Coll., 1951, JD (hon.), 1994; MA, Columbia U., 1953; PhD, U. So. Calif., 1957. Research geologist Humble Oil & Refinery Co., Houston, 1957-60; assoc. prof. Oreg. State U., Corvallis, 1960-66, prof. oceanography, 1966—, chmn. dept., 1968-72, dean Sch. Oceanography, 1972-76, acting dean research, 1976-77, dean research, 1977-80, v.p. for research and grad. studies, 1980-81, pres., 1984-95; adminstr. NOAA, Washington, 1981-84; U.S. commr. Internat. Whaling Commn., 1982—85; pres. Oreg. State U., 1984-95; higher edn. cons. Corvallis, 1996—. Program dir. oceanography NSF, 1966-67; exec. dir. Kellogg Commn. on Future of State and Land Grant Univs., 1996-2000; dir. Harbor Br. Ocean Inst., Oregon Coast Aquarium. Recipient Carter teaching award Oreg. State U., 1964. Fellow AAAS, Geol. Soc. Am.; mem. Geol. Soc. Am., Am. Geophys. Union, Sigma Xi, Chi Psi. Home: 3190 NW Deer Run St Corvallis OR 97330-3107 Office: Autzen House 811 SW Jefferson Ave Corvallis OR 97333-4506 Office Phone: 541-737-3542. Business E-Mail: john.byrne@oregonstate.edu.

BYRNE, LAURA G., music educator, theater educator, vocal coach; d. Edward and Gloria E. Gallagher; m. Barry E. Byrne; 1 child, Phineas Thomas. MusB, Shenandoah Conservatory Music, Winchester, Va., 1980—84. Cert. tchr. Mass., 2002. Chorus and drama tchr. Nantucket Pub. Schs., Mass., 2001—03; music and theater tchr. Nantucket Sch. Music, 2002—. Dir., children's theater dir. Theater Workshop Nantucket, 2001—. Musician: (exhibition) Jazz Ensemble; actor: (performance) I do, I do; dir.: (performances) I Hate Hamlet, Don't Count Your Chickens Until They Cry Wolf; dir., choreographer (performances) Oliver!, Really Rosie. Com. leader Island to Island, Nantucket, 2001—01; performer Nantucket Arts Coun., 2005—06; bd. mem. Jr. Miss, Nantucket, 2000—02; v.p. Theatre Workshop Nantucket, 1999—2003. Mem.: Nat. Assn. Tchrs. Singing (assoc.). Avocations: writing, cooking, yoga. Office: Nantucket Sch Music 31 Centre St Nantucket MA 02554 Home Phone: 508-228-3468. Home Fax: 508-325-7845. Personal E-mail: lauragbyrne@comcast.net. Business E-Mail: kim@comcast.net.

BYRNE, MICHAEL JOSEPH, manufacturing executive; b. Apr. 3, 1928; s. Michael Joseph and Edith (Lueken) Byrne; m. Eileen Kelly, June 27, 1953; children: Michael Joseph, Nancy, James, Thomas, Patrick, Terrence. BSC in mktg., Loyola U., Chgo., 1952. Sales engr. Emery Industries, Inc., Cin., 1952—59; with Pennsalt Chem. Corp., Phila., 1959—60; pres. Oakton Cleaners, Inc., Skokie, Ill., 1960—70, Datatax Inc., Skokie, Ill., 1970—74, Midwest Synthetic Lubrication Products, 1978—, Pure Water Sys., 1984—, Superior Tax Svc., 1984—. With US Army, 1946—48. Mem.: Am. Inst. Mgmt., Toastmasters Internat., VFW, Alpha Kappa Psi. Home: PO Box 916 Prospect Heights IL 60070-0916 Personal E-mail: mypaintlid@comcast.net.

BYRNE, NOEL THOMAS, sociologist, educator; b. San Francisco, May 11, 1943; s. Joseph Joshua and Naomi Pearl (Denison) B.; m. Dale W. Elrod, Aug. 6, 1989. BA in Sociology, Sonoma State Coll., 1971; MA in Sociology, Rutgers U., 1975, PhD in Sociology, 1987. Instr. sociology Douglass Coll., Rutgers U., New Brunswick, NJ, 1974-76, Hartnell Coll., Salinas, Calif., 1977-78; from lectr. to assoc. prof. dept. mgmt. Sonoma State U., Rohnert Park, Calif., 1978-94, chmn. dept. of mgmt., 1990-91, from. assoc. prof. to prof. sociology dept., 1994—, chmn. dept. sociology, 1997—2002; cons. prof. Emile Durkheim Inst. for Advanced Study, Grand Cayman, B.W.I., 1990-93. Chair of faculty Sonoma State U., 2002—03, chair acad. senate, 2002—03. Contbr. articles and revs. to profl. lit. Recipient Dell Pub. award Rutgers U. Grad. Sociology Program, 1976, Louis Bevier fellow, 1977-78. Mem. AAAS, Am. Sociol. Assn., Pacific Sociol. Assn., N.Y. Acad. Sci., Soc. for Study Symbolic Interaction (rev. editor Jour. 1980-83), Soc. for Study Social Problems, Commonwealth Club. Democrat. Home: 4773 Ross Rd Sebastopol CA 95472-2114 Office: Sonoma State U Dept Sociology Rohnert Park CA 94928 Home Phone: 707-829-8641; Office Phone: 707-664-2517. Business E-Mail: noel.byrne@sonoma.edu.

BYRNE, PATRICK J., information technology executive; BS, U. Calif., Berkeley; MS in Elec. Engring., Stanford U., 1988. V.p. product Generation Unit, Electronic Products and Solutions Group Agilent Technologies, Inc., Santa Clara, Calif., v.p., gen. mgr. Wireless Bus. Unit, 2001—05, sr. v.p., pres. Electronic Measurements Group, 2005—07; pres., CEO Intermec, Inc., West Everett, Wash., 2007—. Bd. dirs. Intermec, Inc., 2007—. Bd. mem. Samuel Ginn Coll. Engring., Auburn U. Office: Intermec Inc 6001 36th Ave Everett WA 98203-1264

BYRNE, RHONDA, television producer; b. Melbourne, Australia; Sr. prodr. Nine Network, Australia; co. prin. Prime Time Productions, Australia, 1994—. Prodr.: (TV films) The Secret; author, 2004; guest appearences on Larry King Live, The Ellen DeGeneres Show, Oprah. Named one of The World's Most Influential People, TIME mag., 2007. Office: Prime Time Productions PO Box 578010 Chicago IL 60657*

BYRNE, ROBERT WILLIAM, lawyer; b. Frankfurt, Germany, Dec. 12, 1958; s. Robert Patrick and Anne Lise (Brondelsbo) B. BA, Rutgers U., 1981; JD, Seton Hall U., 1984; LLM, Golden Gate U., 2002. Bar: N.J. 1984, U.S. Dist. Ct. N.J. 1984, D.C. 1986, U.S. Ct. Appeals (3d cir.) 1987, U.S. Ct. Appeals (D.C. and fed. cirs.) 1988, (11th cir.), 1993, U.S. Dist. Ct. D.C. 1989, U.S. Supreme Ct. 1989, N.Y. 1991, U.S. Dist. Ct. (so. and ea. dists.) N.Y. 1991, Fla. 1992, U.S. Dist. Ct. (no. and mid. dists.) Fla. 1992, Calif. 2001., U.S. Dist. Ct. (no. dist.) Calif. 2001, U.S. Ct. Appeals (9th cir.) 2001. Law clk. to Judge Sylvan G. Rothenberg, Superior Ct. Passaic County N.J., 1984-85; asst. prosecutor Bergen County, N.J., 1985-88; assoc. Harwood Lloyd, Hackensack, NJ, 1988-90, Mudge Rose Guthrie Alexander & Ferdon, NYC, 1990-91; sr. assoc. O'Connor, Reddy & Jensen, NYC, 1991-92; pvt. practice Panama City, Fla., 1992-94; v.p., gen. counsel Bay Bank & Trust Co., Panama City, Fla., 1994-2000; dep. atty. gen. Calif. Dept. Justice, San Francisco, 2002—. Contbr. Seton Hall Legis Jour., 1983-84. Mem. Phi Alpha Delta, Pi Sigma Alpha. Democrat. Lutheran. Home: 267 Roosevelt Way San Francisco CA 94114-1431 Office: 455 Golden Gate Ave Ste 11000 San Francisco CA 94102-7004 E-mail: robert.byrne@doj.ca.gov.

BYRNE, SHAUN PATRICK, lawyer; b. Atlantic City, Aug. 22, 1963; s. Warren Patrick and Donna Mae (Curlott) B. Student, Nat. Acad. Paralegals, Egg Harbor, NJ, 1991; AS, Cumberland County Coll., Vineland, NJ, 1994; BA in Criminal Justice, Stockton State Coll., Pomona, NJ, 1995; grad., Widener U. Sch. Law, 2000. Bar: (NJ, Pa.) 2000; ordained min. Universal Life Ch. Police officer Atlantic City Police Dept., 1984-85; with trade union, 1986-91; sr. detective Jamesway Corp., Secaucus, NJ, 1991-95; law clk. Atlantic County Pub. Def. Office, 1999-2000; assoc. Long & Assocs. LLC, Northfield, NJ. Security advisor P.S.I., Inc.; paralegal, 1991-92; mediation counselor Criminal Justice Inst., 1995-2000; deputy gen. dir. Internat. Biog. Ctr., 1999; mediator US Post Office, 1998-2000; assoc. in worker's compensation Long & Assocs., Northfield, NJ. Martial arts trainer/demonstrator Fighting Dragons Dojo, Atlantic City, 1980-97; high sch. presentations on violence/drugs, Vineland, 1995; Oceanville vol. firefighter, 2003—; firefighter Atlantic County Fire Tng. Ctr.; vol. Habitat for Humanity. Named Outstanding Person 20th Century Internat. Biog. Ctr., 1997; Am. Biog. Inst. fellow, 1998. Republican. Roman Catholic. Avocations: martial arts, kick boxing, scuba diving, weight training. Home: PO Box 1081 Absecon NJ 08201-5081 Office Phone: 609-745-8585. Personal E-mail: p8s2i2@earthlink.net.

BYRNE, THOMAS J., lawyer; b. Rochester, NY, June 17, 1944; m. Brenda C. Byrne, June 4, 1994; children: Thomas, David, Heather, Alexandra. AB, U. Rochester, 1967; JD, U. Denver, 1976. Bar: Colo. 1977, Calif. 1977, U.S. Ct. Appeals (10th cir.) 1977, U.S. Dist. Ct. Colo. 1977, U.S. Dist. Ct. (so. dist.) Tex. 1990, N.Y. 1990, U.S. Ct. Appeals (3d cir.) 1992, U.S. Dist. Ct. (ea. dist.) Pa. 1992, U.S. Dist. Ct. (ea. dist.) Va. 1992, U.S. Ct. Appeals (4th cir.) 1993, U.S. Dist. Ct. (no. dist.) Ill. 1993, U.S. Dist. Ct. Ariz. 1993, U.S. Dist. Ct. Utah 1996, U.S. Dist. Ct. (so. dist.) N.Y. 1997, U.S. Dist. Ct. Idaho 2003, U.S. Dist. Ct. Mont. 1999. Law clk. Dist. Ct. Colo., Denver, 1976-77; assoc. Ullstrom Law Offices, Denver, 1978-83; ptnr., Denver mgr. Conklin & Adler, Ltd., Denver and Chgo., 1983-86; mng. ptnr. Byrne, Kiely & White LLP, Denver, 1986—. Mem. fin. com. Citizens for Romer, Denver, 1990—. Capt. USAF, 1967-73. Mem. ABA (tort and ins. practice sect., vice chair aviation and space law com., litigation sect., forum on air and space law), Internat. Bar Assn., Colo. Bar Assn., Denver Bar Assn., State Bar Calif., N.Y. State Bar Assn., Def. Rsch. Inst., Colo. Def. Lawyers Assn., Nat. Bus. Aircraft Assn., Lawyer-Pilot Bar Assn., Aviation Ins. Assn., Nat. Air Transportation Assn., Flight Safety Found. Avocations: flying, travel, sports. Office: Byrne Kiely & White LLP 1120 Lincoln St Ste 1300 Denver CO 80203-2140 Office Phone: 303-861-5511.

BYRNE, WILLIAM ANDREW, historian, educator; b. Valparaiso, Fla., Jan. 19, 1944; s. William Andrew Byrne and Ramonde Ruckel Williams; m. Ute Johanna Byrne, Nov. 27, 1964; children: Drew, Sean. BA, Fla. State U., 1968, MA, 1971, PhD, 1979. Adj. asst. prof. Okaloosa Walton C.C., Niceville, Fla., 1982—85; adj. assoc. prof. U. West Fla., 1986—94; assoc. prof. Norfolk State U., 1994—2000, prof. and chair, 2000—03, asst. dean Sch. Liberal Arts, 2003—. Budget com. Norfolk State U., 1998—, black hist. month com., 2000—, coun. tchr. edn., 2000—, assessment adv. com., 2004—, coun. asst. deans, 2005. Contbr. articles to jours. Mem. Chrysler Mus., 1995, Va. Symphony, 1995, Norfolk Bot. Garden, 1995; bd. trustees Martin Luther King Jr. Living Hist. & Pub. Policy Ctr., Richmond, Va. Served with US Army, 1962—65, Germany. Mem.: Ga. Hist. Soc., So. Hist. Assn., Org. Am. Historians, Phi Kappa Phi, Phi Alpha Theta. Democrat. Avocation: golf. Home: 1209 Willow Creek Ct Chesapeake VA 23321 Office: Norfolk State U 700 Park Ave Norfolk VA 23504 Office Phone: 757-823-2082. Business E-Mail: wabyrne@nsu.edu.

BYRNE-DEMPSEY, CECELIA (CECELIA DEMPSEY), journalist; b. LA, Aug. 7, 1925; d. John Joseph and Margaret Agnes (Frakell) B.; m. John Dempsey, Mar. 25, 1951 (dec. June 1981); children: Margaret, Elizabeth, John, Cecelia, Cathrine, Patricia, Bridget, Charles, Mary Teresa. Student, Immaculate Heart Coll., 1944; BA in Psychology, Calif. State U., Northridge, 1975, BA in Journalism, 1978, MA in Mass Comm., 1992. Staff Lockheed Aircraft Corp., Burbank, Calif., 1943—, Office Naval Rsch., San Francisco, 1947—; with Sisters of Mercy, Burlingame, Calif., 1945—, Sisters of Presentation, San Francisco, 1949—; mem. staff Calif. State U., 1976—. Rschr., journalism historian early Am. newspapers, 1978—. Author: The Meaning Index: A Model for Early American Newspaper Indexing: a research guide, 1992. Mentor 4-H Club; past mem. Urban Corp., L.A Mem. Mensa, Kappa Gamma Delta. Republican. Jewish. Avocations: poetry, gardening, philosophical meditation.

BYRNES, BRUCE L., consumer products company executive; b. Columbus, Ohio, Mar. 29, 1948; BA in Philosophy of Religion, Princeton U., 1970. Brand asst. Procter & Gamble Co., Cin., 1970—71, sales trainee, 1971—72, asst. brand mgr., 1972—74, brand mgr., 1974—78, assoc. advt. mgr. paper products divsn., 1978—82, advt. mgr. coffee divsn., 1982—84, advt. mgr. packaged soap and detergent divsn., 1984—86, mgr. packaged soap and detergent divsn., 1986—87, v.p. packaged soap and detergent divsn., 1987—90, v.p. No. Europe, 1990—91, pres., paper and beverage products, Procter & Gamble Europe, group v.p., 1991—95, pres., paper products-U.S., Procter & Gamble N.Am., group v.p., 1995—96, pres., health care products-U.S., Procter & Gamble N.Am., group v.p., 1996—97, pres., health care products-N.Am., Procter & Gamble N.Am., group v.p., 1997—99, pres., global health care and corp. new ventures, 1999—2000, pres., global beauty care and global health care, 2000—02, vice chmn. & pres. global beauty, global feminine and global health care, 2002—04, vice chmn. household products, 2002—, vice chmn. baby care, family care and pet health & nutrition businesses, 2006—07, vice chmn. glob. brand bldg., 2007—. Bd. dir. Cin. Bell Inc., 2003—. Mem. steering coun. Success by 6, 2002—; bd. trustee Cin. Art Mus., 1996—; maj. firms chair 1999 Fine Arts Fund Campaign, 1998—99. Office: Procter & Gamble Co 1 Procter & Gamble Plz Cincinnati OH 45202*

BYRNES, CHRISTOPHER IAN, engineering educator; b. NYC, June 28, 1949; s. Richard Francis and Jeanne (Orchard) Byrnes; children: Kathleen, Alison, Christopher; m. Gwendolyn Renee Byrnes, Feb. 14, 2005. BS in math., Manhattan Coll., 1971; MS in math., U. Mass., 1973, PhD in math., 1975; D of Tech. (hon.), Royal Inst. Tech., Stockholm, 1998. Registered profl. engr., Mo. Instr. U. Utah, Salt Lake City, 1975-78; asst. prof. Harvard U., Cambridge, Mass., 1978-81, assoc. prof., 1981-85; rsch. prof. Ariz. State U., Tempe, 1985-89; prof. Washington U., St. Louis, 1989—, Edward H. and Florence G. Skinner prof., 1998—, chmn. dept. systems sci. and math., 1989—91, dean Sch. Engring. and Applied Sci., 1991—2006. Adj. prof. Royal Inst. Tech., Stockholm, 1985—90; cons. Sci. Sys., Inc., Cambridge, 1980—84, Sys. Engring., Inc., Greenbelt, Md., 1986; sci. advisor Sherwood Davis & Geck, 1996—98, Cernium Inc., 2002—, Midwest Bank Ctr., 2002—07; mem. NRC; bd. dirs., chmn. nominating and governance com. Belden Inc., 1995—2006; chmn. bd. dir. Ctr. Emerging Techs., 1993—2003, chmn. emeritus; pres., bd. dir. WUTA, Inc., 1991—2004; mem. bus. bd. adv. Newberry Group Inc., 2002—. Editor: (book series) Progress in Systems Control, 1988, Foundations of Systems and Control, 1998—2001; Nonlinear Synthesis, 1991, 13 other books; contbr. numerous articles to profl. jours., book revs. Recipient Best Paper award, IFAC, 1993. Fellow: IEEE (Geroge Axelby award 1991, 2003), Acad. Sci. St. Louis, Japan Soc. for Promotion Sci.; mem.: AIAA, AAAS, Regional Chamber for Growth Assn. (vice chmn. tech., chmn. Tech. Gateway Alliance 2000—03), Royal Swedish Acad. Engring. Sci. (fgn.), Am. Math. Soc., Soc. Indsl. Applied Math. (program com. 1986—89, Reid prize 2005), Tau Beta Pi, Sigma Xi. Avocations: cooking, fishing, travel. Office: Washington U Dept Elec and Sys Engring 1 Brookings Dr Saint Louis MO 63130-4899 Office Phone: 314-935-6067. Business E-Mail: chrisbyrnes@wustl.edu.

BYRNES, HOPE HUSKA, singer, volunteer; b. NYC, Sept. 17, 1939; d. Charles John and Irma Kapalla Huska; m. Paul Joseph Byrnes, July 20, 1968; children: Paul, Jr., Kate, Sean. BA in Polit. Sci., Stetson U., DeLand, Fla., 1961. Legis. asst. U.S. Ho. of Reps., Washington, 1961—64, press asst., 1964—65; asst. supt. U.S. Senate Radio and TV Gallery, Washington, 1965—68; adminstrv. asst. Am. Bankers Assn., Washington, 1968—70. Singer: Ritz Carlton Fine Arts Tea, 2007. Pres. Sarasota Opera Guild, Fla., 1990—92, Asolo Theatre Guild, Sarasota, Fla., 1992—94, Sarasota Sister Cities Assn., Fla., 1994—2001, Fla. West Coast Children's Chorus, 2003—; bd. mem. Jazz Club Sarasota, 2004—07; arts coun. cultural exec. com. rep. Broadcasters Club, 2005—; charter mem. Bus. Women's Network, Madrid, 1986—88. Recipient Mayor's award for Outstanding Cmty. Svc., Outstanding Achievement award, Fla. Sister Cities Assn., Martha Washington medal for disting. cmty. svc., Fla. Sons Am. Revolution, 2006. Mem.: All-Fla. News Media Exec. Roundtable, U.N. Assn., Sarasota County Openly Plans for Excellence, Am. Legion Aux. (Post 30). Achievements include chair, City of Sarasota 100th Anniversary Opening Dinner and founder, Asolo Theatre Guild Guilder Award for local HS that has done most to promote new and innovative theater; performer Sarasota Sr. Theater. Avocations: singing, volunteer work. Personal E-mail: 2byrnes@verizon.net.

BYRNES, JAMES BERNARD, museum director, consultant; b. NYC, Feb. 19, 1917; s. Patrick J.A. and Janet E. (Geiger) B.; m. Barbara A. Cecil, June 10, 1946; 1 son, Ronald L. Student, N.A.D., 1936-38, Am. Artist Sch., 1938-40, Art Students League, 1940-42, U. Perugia, Italy, 1951, Inst. Meschini, Rome, 1952. Art tchr. mus. activity program NYC Bd. Edn., 1936-40; indsl. designer Michael Saphier Assos., NYC, 1940-42; audio visual specialist USNR, 1944—45; with LA County Mus., 1946-47, assoc. curator modern contemporary art, 1947-48, curator, asst. to dir., 1948-53; dir. Colorado Springs Fine Arts Center, 1954-55; from assoc. dir. to dir. NC Mus. Art, 1956-60; dir. New Orleans Mus. Art, 1961-71, dir. emeritus, 1989—; dir. Newport Harbor Art Mus., Newport Beach, Calif., 1972-75. Vis. lectr. U. Fla., 1961, Newcomb Coll., Tulane U., 1963; art cons. Author: Masterpieces of Art, W.R. Valentiner Memorial, 1959, Tobacco and Smoking in Art, 1960, Fetes de la Palette, 1963, Edgar Degas, His Family and Friends in New Orleans, 1965, Odyssey of an Art Collector, 1966, Art of Ancient and Modern Latin America, 1968, The Artist as Collector of Primitive Art, 1975, also numerous mus. catalogs. Decorated knight Order Leopold II (Belgium); recipient Isaac Delgado Meml. award, New Orleans Mus. of Art, 1998. Mem. Am. Soc. Interior Design (hon. life), Am. Soc. Appraisers (sr.), Retired Appraisers Assn. Am. Office: James B Byrnes and Assocs 7820 Mulholland Dr Los Angeles CA 90046-1223

BYRNES, WILLIAM JOSEPH, lawyer; b. Bklyn., Apr. 11, 1940; s. William James and Margaret Mary (English) B.; m. Catherine Belle Rollings, Aug. 15, 1970 (dec. 2002); children: Jennifer, Suzanne; m. Mary Pat Collins, Feb. 17, 2007. BS, Fordham U., 1961; JD, Yale U., 1964. Bar: NY 1965, DC 1970, Va. 1992. Atty. AEC, Washington, 1964-68; internat. mgr. Comm. Satellite Corp., Washington, 1968-70; ptnr. Haley, Bader & Potts, Arlington, Va., 1970-95; of counsel Irwin Campbell & Tannenwald, Washington, 1995-96; pvt. practice, McLean, Va., 1997—; v.p. Shared Spectrum Co. Author: Telecom. Regulation: Something Old and Something New in the Comm. Act: A Legis. History of the Major Amendments, 1934-1996, 1999; co-author: The Common Carrier Provisions--A Product of Evolutionary Devel. in A Legis. History of the Comm. Act, 1989, Decency Redux: The Curious History of the New FCC Broadcast Indecency Policy, 1989, A New Telecom. Paradigm, 1993; actor: various local theater companies. Candidate Fairfax County Bd. Suprs., 1995; v.p., bd. dirs. McLean Citizens Assn., past pres. Recipient cert. U.S. AEC, 1967. Mem. Fed. Comm. Bar Assn., Va. State Bar, DC Bar Assn. Avocations: acting, videography. Office: 7921 Old Falls Rd Mc Lean VA 22102-2414

BYROM, FLETCHER LAUMAN, chemical manufacturing company executive; b. Cleve., July 13, 1918; s. Fletcher L. and Elizabeth (Collins) B.; m. Marie L. McIntyre, Feb. 17, 1945; children: Fletcher Lauman, Carol A. Byrom Conrad, Susan J. Byrom-Thomas. BS in Metallurgy, Pa. State U., 1940; graduate Advanced Mgmt. Program, Harvard U., Cambridge, Mass., 1952. Sales engr. Am. Steel & Wire Co., Cleve., 1940-42; procurement and adminstrv. coord. Naval Ordnance Lab., also Bur. Ordnance and Research Planning Bd., Navy Dept., 1942-47; from asst. to gen. mgr. Tar Products divsn. Koppers Co., Inc., Pitts., 1947-82, pres., 1960—70, chmn., 1970—82; mgr. Micasu Tungsten LLC, 2000—. Mem. Pitts. br. Fed. Res. Bd. Cleve., 1962-68, chmn., 1966-68, N.Y. Stock Exch., 1980-86; mem. bd. govs. Com. Devel. Am. Capital, 1989-2004; bd. dirs. Purecycle Corp., 1988-2004, pres., bd. dirs. Micasu Corp. Bd. dirs. Allegheny Conf. on Cmty. Devel., v.p., 1970-83; chmn. Hershey Med. Ctr. Subcom., 1970-73; chmn. Pres.'s Export Coun., 1974-79, Pub. Edn. Fund, 1980-85; chmn. bd. trustees Presbyn.-Univ. Hosp., 1972-83, internat. 1975-80, Kiskiminetas Springs Sch., 1971-82; trustee Carnegie Mellon U., 1975-81, Allegheny Coll., 1969-79, Pa. State U., 1970-73; former trustee, Inst. Advanced Study, Inst. for Future Mem., Hudson Inst., Keystone Ctr.; trustee Conf. Bd., 1962-82, lifetime chancellor, 1968—; mem. pres.'s circle NAS, chmn., 1999-2000; trustee Com. for Econ. Devel., chmn. bd. dirs., 1978-84, lifetime trustee. Recipient Disting. Civilian Service award U.S. Navy Dept., Disting. Alumnus Pa. State U., David Ford McFarland award Pa. State U., 1979, Alumni Achievement award Harvard U. Bus. Sch., 1981, William Metcalf award West Pa. Engring. Soc., 1985; Woodrow Wilson Edn. Found. vis. fellow, Pa. State U. fellow. Mem. Pa. State U. Alumni Assn. (pres. 1965-66), Coun. Retired CEO's, Duquesne Club Pitts., Phi Kappa Psi. Presbyterian. Home and Office: 305 Village Heights Dr Apt 328 State College PA 16801 Home Phone: 814-278-1200. Personal E-mail: fmicasu@aol.com.

BYRON, BEVERLY BUTCHER, retired congresswoman; b. Balt., July 27, 1932; d. Harry C. and Ruth Butcher; m. Goodloe E. Byron, 1952 (dec.); children: Goodloe E. Jr., Barton Kimball, Mary McComas; m. B. Kirk Walsh, 1986. Student, Hood Coll., 1962-64. Mem. 96th-102nd Congresses from 6th Md. dist., 1979-93; Presdl. appt. to base closing and realignment commn., 1993. Bd. dirs. McDonnell Douglas, Constellation Energy Group, Blue Cross/Blue Shield, UNC Corp., Farm and Mech. Nat. Bank, LMI, Def. Adv. Commn. on Women in the Mil.; exec. panel Chief of Naval Ops.; adv. bd. NASA, A.F. Meml. Found. State treas. Md. Young Dems., 1962, 65; bd. assocs. Hood Coll.; bd. visitors USAF Acad., 1980-87; trustee Mt. St. Mary's Coll.; bd. dirs. Frederick County chpt. ARC; sec. Frederick Heart Assn., 1974-79; mem. Frederick Phys. Fitness Commn.; chmn. Md. Phys. Fitness Commn., 1979-89; mem. Frederick County Landmarks Found.; bd. dirs. Am. Hiking Soc.; bd. dirs. Adventure Sports Inst., 1992—; bd. advisors Internat. Studies Frostburg State U., 1990—, Am. Volkssport Assn., 1991—; mem. bd. vis. U.S. Naval Acad., 1995—, chair, 1997-2002; chair TedCo. Recipient Pres.'s medal John Hopkins U. Democrat. Episcopalian. Home: 306 Grove Blvd Frederick MD 21701-4813 Office Phone: 202-333-4455.

BYRON, ERIC HOWARD, sculptor, museum researcher and administrator; b. NYC, Jan. 14, 1948; s. Melville and Ruth (Levine) Byron. BA, Beloit Coll., Wis., 1970; postgrad., Hunter Coll., NYC, 1972-75, YIVO Inst./Columbia U., 1972-76; MA, Goddard Coll., Plainfield, Vt., 1979; postgrad, NYU, 1985. Founder, dir. The Synagogue Rescue Project, Inc., NYC, 1974-85; mus. technician South St. Seaport Mus., NYC, 1992-93, Statue of Liberty Nat. Monument/Ellis Island Immigration Mus, NYC, 1993—. Lectr. sr. citizensNY Tech. Inst., 1982; coord. oral history project Brookdale Ctr. on Aging, Hunter Coll., 1982, discography project Ellis Island Mus. Immigration, 1997—. Exhibited in group shows at Ward-Nasse Gallery, 1975-76, Detail, NYC, 1989, Nathaniel's Music Box, NYC, 1989, Civilization, 1989, Am. Craftsman, 1989-90, Dinosaur Hill, NYC, 1990, Mus. Am. Folk Art, NYC, 1990, Mark Milliken Gallery, NYC, 1990, Faith Nightengale Gallery, San Diego, 1991-92, Whitney Mus., NYC, 1992; sculpture, performer Washington Sq. Pk., 1989-2001; featured on PBS Channel 13 City Arts, 1998, also on Nat. Pub. Radio, 1999; contbr. articles to profl. jours. Fellow Brookdale Ctr. on Aging, NYC, 1985; recipient archeology award Profl. Archeologists NYC, 1997. Mem.: League for Yiddish, Nat. Steroscopic Assn., Nat. Trust Historic Preservation. Home: 411 E 10th St Apt 15F New York NY 10009-4212 Office: Statue of Liberty Nat Mus Liberty Island New York NY 10004-1467 Office Phone: 212-363-3206 153. Business E-Mail: ericbyron@earthlink.net.

BYRON, WILLIAM JAMES, minister, retired academic administrator, finance educator; b. Pitts., May 25, 1927; s. Harold J. and Mary I. (Langton) B. AB in Philosophy, St. Louis U., 1955, Ph.L., 1956, MA in Econs, 1959; S.T.B., Woodstock Coll., 1960, S.T.L., 1962; PhD in Econs, U. Md., 1969; cert., Harvard U. Inst. Ednl. Mgmt., 1974. Joined S.J., 1950, ordained priest Roman Cath. Ch., 1961. Tchr. math. Scranton (Pa.) Prep. Sch., 1956-58; manpower rsch. fellow Dept. Labor, 1965-66; asst. prof. econs. Loyola Coll., Balt., 1967-69; assoc. prof. social ethics, rector Woodstock Coll., Woodstock Jesuit Community, 1967-73; dean Coll. Arts and Scis. Loyola U., New Orleans, 1973-75; pres. U. Scranton, 1975-82, Cath. U. Am., Washington, 1982-92; rsch. assoc. Georgetown U., 1992-93, Disting. prof. mgmt. Sch. of Bus. Washington, 1993—2000; rsch. prof. Sellinger Sch. Bus., Loyola Coll. in Md. Author: Toward Stewardship: An Interim Ethic of Poverty, Pollution and Power, 1975, Quadrangle Considerations, 1989, Take Your Diploma and Run, 1992, Finding Work Without Losing Heart, 1995, The 365 Days of Christmas, 1996, Answers from Within, 1998, Jesuit Saturdays, 2000; editor: Causes of World Hunger, 1982; contbr. numerous articles to profl. jurs. Bd. dirs. Fed. City Coun., Joint Commn. on Accreditation Healthcare Orgns., U. San Francisco, Loyola Coll. in Md., Balt. With U.S. Army, 1945-56. Mem. Am. Econs. Assn., Am. Soc. Christian Ethics, Assn. Cath. Colls. and Univs., Phi Beta Kappa, Alpha Sigma Nu Mailing: 4603 Millbrook Rd Baltimore MD 21212 Office Phone: 410-617-2121. Business E-Mail: wbyron@loyola.edu.

BYSIEWICZ, SUSAN, state official; b. New Haven, Sept. 29, 1961; m. David Donaldson; 3 children. BA magna cum laude, Yale Coll., 1983; JD, Duke U., 1986. Corp. atty. White & Case, NYC, 1986-88, Robinson & Cole, Hartford, Conn., 1988-92; with law dept. Aetna Life and Casualty, 1992-94; mem. Conn. State Ho. Reps. from 100th dist., 1993—99, chair govt. adminstrn. and elections com., 1995—99; sec. state State of Conn., 1999—. Author: Ella: A Biography of Governor Ella T. Grasso, 1984. Conn. Bar Assn., NY Bar Assn. Democrat. Address: Rm 104 State Capitol Hartford CT 06106 Office Phone: 860-509-6200. Office Fax: 916-653-4620. E-mail: susan.bysiewicz@po.state.ct.us.*

BYSTRYN, JEAN-CLAUDE, dermatologist, educator; b. Paris, May 8, 1938; arrived in U.S., 1949, naturalized, 1958; s. Iser and Sara Bystryn; m. Marcia Hammill, May 14, 1972; children: Anne, Alexander. BS, U. Chgo., 1958; MD, NYU, 1962. Diplomate Am. Bd. Dermatology, Am. Bd. Immunodermatopathology. Intern Montefiore Hosp., NYC, 1962-63, resident in medicine, 1963-64; resident in dermatology NYU Sch. Medicine, NYC, 1966-69, USPHS postgrad. tng. fellow in immunology, 1968-72, asst. prof. clin. dermatology, 1971—72, assoc. prof., 1976-84, prof., 1984—. Asst. dispensary physician Albany Med. Coll., 1964—66; asst. attending physician Univ. Hosp., NYC, 1969—; asst. vis. dermatologist Bellevue Hosp. Ctr., NYC, 1969—; dir. melanoma program NYU Kaplan Cancer Ctr., NYC; dir. Immunofluorescence Lab. NYU Med. Sch., NYC. Contbr. articles to profl. jours. Mem. adv. bd. Skin Cancer Found., Vitiligo Found., Nat. Alepecia Areata Found., Am. Skin Assn., Nat. Pemphigus Found. Lt. comdr. USPHS, 1964—66. Recipient Irma T. Hirschl Rsch. Career award, AOA; Ford Found. fellow, 1954—58, NIH grantee, 1970—. Mem.: N.Y. Dermatol. Soc. (dir.), Soc. Investigative Dermatology, Am. Assn. Cancer Rsch., Am. Assn. Immunologists, Am. Acad. Dermatology, Am. Dermatology Assn. Office: NYU Med Ctr U Hosp 530 1st Ave New York NY 10016-6402 Office Phone: 212-889-3846. E-mail: bystryn@nyu.edu.

BYTAUTAS, LAIMUTIS, chemist, educator; b. Kretinga, Lithuania, May 22, 1965; arrived in U.S., 1991; s. Vytautas Bytautas and Aldona Vasiliauskaite; m. Egle Adiklyte Bytautiene, Aug. 18, 1989; 1 child, Dominykas Vasaris. MS in Physics, Vilnius U., Lithuania, 1990; PhD in Phys. Chemistry, Vanderbilt U., 1996. Rsch. assoc. Inst. Theoretical Physics and Astronomy, Vilnius, 1990—91; postdoctoral rsch. assoc. Tex. A&M U., Galveston, 1996—99, Iowa State U., Ames, 1999—2003, asst. scientist, 2003—. Author: (novel) Theoretical Method Correlation Energy Etrapolation by Intrinsic Scaling for ab imitio computation of molecular energies, 2004; referee: jours. in field; contbr. articles to profl. jours. Mem.: Am. Chem. Soc. Avocations: basketball, soccer, travel. Office: Iowa State Univ Ames Lab USDOE Wilhelm Hall 307 Ames IA 50011 Office Phone: 515-294-9927. Business E-Mail: bytautas@scl.ameslab.gov.

BYTHER-SMITH, IDA W., social services administrator; d. Leroy and Josephine Wilson; children: James, Melissa, Lavinia, Branden Shirelle. BA in Edn., Gov. State U., Chgo., 1988. Renal technologist Renal Care Group, Chgo., 1984—2001; group counselor Alliance for Cmty. Empowerment, Chgo., 2002—05; founder, CEO Jo-Ray House, Inc., Chgo., 2003—. AIDS counselor Chgo. Women's AIDS Project, 2001—05. Co-author: A Woman's Story: Overcoming the Shame of HIV, 2002. Chair membership com. Planning Coun. for Mayor Chgo. Recipient Dr. Sherry E. Luck award, Alliance for Cmty. Empowerment, 2002, Gigi Nicks award, Let's Talk, Let's Test, 2004, Long Term Survivor award, Educate Adv. Support Empower Orgn., 2004. Office: Jo-Ray HOuse Inc 23 W 115th St Chicago IL 60628

BYTWERK, RANDALL LEE, communication educator; b. Grand Rapids, Mich., Apr. 13, 1950; s. Robert L. and Ruth E. Bytwerk; m. Sharon L. Van Haitsma, May 27, 1978; 1 child, David Paul. BA, Calvin Coll., 1971; MA, Northwestern U., 1973, PhD, 1975. Prof. Southern Ill. Univ., Carbondale, Ill., 1975-85, Calvin Coll., Grand Rapids, 1985—. Author: Julius Streicher, 2001 (Golden Anniversary award Speech Comm. Assn., 1984), Bending Spines, 2004; contbr. articles to profl. jours. Office: Calvin Coll 1810 East Beltline SE Grand Rapids MI 49546-5952 Home: 3530 Reeds Hill Ct SE Grand Rapids MI 49546 Home Phone: 616-974-0505; Office Phone: 616-526-6286. E-mail: bytw@calvin.edu.

BYUN, MICHAEL, plastic surgeon; b. Tokyo, May 2, 1965; s. Justine and Terresa Byun; 1 child, Hannah. BS cum laude, U. Calif., Irvine, 1988; MD with highest honors, Northwestern U., 1992. Cert. Am. Bd. Plastic Surgery, 2002. Clin. instr. Northwestern U., Chgo., 1997—98, chief resident, 1997—98; staff plastic surgeon 900 N Mich. Surgery Ctr., Chgo., 1998—2002; attending plastic surgeon Swedish Covenant Hosp., Chgo., 1998—, Rush Presbyterian Hosp., Chgo., 1999—; dir. Chgo. Cosmetic Surgery, Chgo. & Northbrook, 1998—; assoc. plastic surgeon Lutheran Gen. Hosp., Park Ridge, Ill., 1998—2002, dir. pediatric plastic surgery, 2002—. Instr. Northwestern Univ. Med. Sch., 1997—98; chief plastic surgery resident Northwestern Univ. Med. Sch., Shriner's Sock Children's Hosp., Chgo., 1997; asst. prof. plastic surgery Rush Med. Sch., 2000—02. Author: Consumer Plastic Surgery, 2003; contbr. articles to profl. jours. Attending plastic surgeon charitable orgn., Chgo., 2001. Recipient Young Scientist award, Iksong Found., 1988, award, Mayor of Chgo., 2001. Mem.: AMA, Korean Am. Physician Assn., Am. Soc. Plastic Surgeons, Chgo. Med. Soc. Avocations: skiing, golf. Office: Northbrook Office 1775 Walters Ste 100 Northbrook IL 60062

BYUN, SUNG HUN, research scientist; b. Pusan, Republic of Korea, Mar. 20, 1962; s. Haksoo Byun and Youngsook Woo, Oak-ja Um (Stepmother). BS, Korea Aviation U., 1985; MS, Korea Advanced Inst. of Sci. and Tech., 1987; PhD, U. of Tex., 1998. Rsch. staff Jet Propulsion Lab., Pasadena, Calif., 1999—. Recipient Spot award, Jet Propulsion Lab., 2004, Tech. award, NASA, 2004, Board Space Act award, 2006. Mem.: Inst. of Nav., Tau Beta Pi Engring. Honor Soc. Achievements include research in Developed satellite precise orbit determination method using Global Positioning System in a kinematic mode. Avocations: sailing, skiing. Home: 105 South El Molino Ave Pasadena CA 91101 Office: Jet Propulsion Lab 4800 Oak Grove Dr Pasadena CA 91109-8099 Home Phone: 626-584-7004; Office Phone: 818-393-5452. Office Fax: 818-393-5452. Personal E-mail: byun@caltech.edu. E-mail: sung.h.byun@jpl.nasa.gov.

BYUN, YOUNGJOO, research scientist; BS in Pharmacy, Seoul Nat. U., Republic of Korea, 1994, MS in Medicinal Chemistry, 1996; PhD, Ohio State U., Columbus, 2006. Rsch. scientist AmorePacific Corp., Seoul, 1996—2001. Fellow, Proctor & Gamble, 2004—05, Presdl. fellow, Ohio State U., 2006. Mem.: Am. Chem. Soc., Phi Kappa Phi. Achievements include patents for design and discovery of COX-2 selective inhibitors; discovery and development of boron delivery agents for boron neutron capture therapy.

BYWATER, DUNCAN, biologist, educator; PhD, U. Nebr., Lincoln, 1998. Asst. prof. Brigham Young U., Provo, Utah, 2003—. Mentor Mem. LDS Ch., Woodland Hills, Utah, 2003—06. Democrat. Office: Brigham Young University 775 WIDB Provo UT 84602-5253 Office Phone: 801-422-3132.

BYYNY, RICHARD LEE, former academic administrator, physician, educator; b. South Gate, Calif., Jan. 6, 1939; s. Oswald and Essa Burnetta (McGinnis) B.; m. Jo Ellen Garverick, Aug. 25, 1962; children: Kristen, Jan, Richard. BA in History, U. So. Calif., 1960, MD, 1964. Intern and resident in internal medicine Columbia Presbyn. Med. Ctr., NYC, 1964-66, chief resident, 1968-69; fellow in endocrinology Vanderbilt U., Nashville, 1969-71; asst. prof. medicine U. Chgo., 1971-74, head div. internal medicine, 1972-77, assoc. prof., 1975-77; prof. internal medicine U. Colo., Denver, 1977—, head divsn. internal medicine, 1977-94, vice-chmn. dept. medicine Health Scis. Ctr., 1977-85, exec. vice chancellor, 1994-95, v.p. acad. affairs, 1995-97, chancellor Boulder, 1997—2005; exec. dir. Ctr. for Health Policy U. Colo. Hosp., 2005—06. Med. dir. ambulatory care, 1990-92; mem. Coun. on Econ. Devel., Boulder, Colo., bd. dirs. Rocky Mtn. region Inst. Internal Edn., 2004—. Author: A Clinical Guide in the Care of Older Women, 1990, 2d edit., 1995; contbr. articles to profl. jours., chapters to books. Pres. Ill. Council Continuing Med. Edn., Ill., 1976-77; bd. dirs. Denver affiliate Am. Heart Assn., 1987-98 (pres. 1994-95), Boulder Com. Hosp., 1997-2007, Bank of Boulder, Boulder Econ. Coun., arm of Boulder C. of C., US Coun. on Competitiveness Big 12 Conf. Capt. USAF, 1966-68. Recipient Merck award U. So. Calif., 1964; Am. Coun. Edn. fellow, 1992-93. Fellow ACP; mem. AAAS, Soc. for Gen. Internal Medicine (pres. 1979-80), Am. Soc. Hypertension, Western Soc. Clin. Investigation, Endocrine Soc., Am. Fedn. for Clin. Rsch., Am. Coun. Edn. (commn. leadership instl. effectiveness), Boulder Country Club, Alpha Omega Alpha (bd. dirs. 1996—). Avocations: tennis, skiing, running, surfing, sailing. Home: 2900 Park Lake Dr Boulder CO 80301-5139 Office: 4200 E 9th Ave Box C299 Denver CO 80262 Home Phone: 303-665-3854. Business E-Mail: richard.byyny@uchsc.edu.

BZOCH, KENNETH RUDOLPH, speech and language educator, department chairman; b. Chgo., Nov. 6, 1927; s. Rudolph and Mildred (Novotny) B.; m. Lorrayne M. Cali, Oct. 29, 1950; children: Kathleen Marie, Kevin Jude. BA, DePaul U., Chgo., 1951; MA, Northwestern U., 1952, PhD, 1956. Cert. clin. competence-speech pathology, CCC-audiology; lic. speech pathologist, Fla. Asst. prof. Loyola U., Chgo., 1953—57, Northwestern U., Chgo., 1957—59; assoc. prof. U. Fla., Gainesville, 1960—64, prof., chair, 1964—96, prof. emeritus. Program dir. Communicative Disorders and Craniofacial Ctr., Shands Hosp., U. Fla.; researcher in field. Author: Communicative Disorders Related to Cleft Lip and Palate, 5th edit., 2004, Receptive-Expressive Language Test: A Method of Assessing Language Skills in Infancy, 3d edit., 2004, How Babies Learn To Talk: A Book for New Parents and Grandparents, 2004. Cpl. USMC, 1946-47. Fellow Am. Cleft Palate Assn. (past pres.), Fla. Cleft Palate Assn. (hon., past pres.), Fla. Speech Lang. and Hearing Assn. (hon., past pres.). Home and Office: 640 NW 57th St Gainesville FL 32607-6103 Home Phone: 352-331-7171; Office Phone: 352-331-7171. Personal E-mail: bzoch@aol.com.

BZYMEK, ZBIGNIEW MARIAN, engineering educator; b. Warsaw, Aug. 5, 1935; came to U.S., 1981; s. Stefan and Stefania (Turek) Bzymek; m. Danuta Jaworska, Oct. 22, 1966; children: Malgorzata, Dorota, Zbigniew Wojciech. MS in Engring., Politechnika Warszawska, Warsaw, 1959, PhD in Engring. Sci., 1967; MS in Engring., U. Mich., 1961. Asst. Politechnika Warszawska, 1961, sr. asst., 1961-67, adj., 1967-73, docent, 1973-81; assoc. prof., dir. CAD & CAM, Expert Sys. Lab. U. Conn., Storrs, 1981—. Cons. Head Mgmt. Ctr. for Hwy. Data Processing, 1978-81; designer bridge sect. Transproject, Warsaw, 1961-63. Author: (Hungarian and Polish) Application of Computers in Structural Analysis, 1966, others; translator (from Russian): Structural Analysis by Means of Digital Computers, 1970; sect. editor (monthly) Drogownictwo, 1977-81; head editor Rsch. Reports on Automatization of Structural Design, 1974-81; contbr. numerous articles to profl. jours. Recipient 1st Prize for Design Competition Soc. of Transp. Engrs., 1974, Hon. mention, 1974. Mem. ASME (2nd Nat. Design award), Internat. Orgn. for Sci. and Tech. (chmn. CAD/CAM com. 1987-92), N.Y. Acad. Scis., Assn. for Computers Machinery (spl. interest group graphics 1982), Polish Acad. of Sci. (mem. civil engring. com., computer graphics pioneer, award 1976), Soc. of Bldg. Engrs. (Stefan Bryla award 1977). Achievements include research in computer graphics, structural analysis, bridge and machine design and theory of engineering design and problem solving; introduced multithickness and multicolor computer graphics representation in structural analysis systems; introduced principles of miniaturization, nanotechnology and biotechnology in problem solving in engineering. Avocations: tennis, skiing, sailing, coin collecting/numismatics. Home: 260 Codfish Falls Rd Storrs Mansfield CT 06268-1407 Office: U Conn U-3139 ME 191 Auditorium Rd Storrs Mansfield CT 06269-9012 Office Phone: 860-486-2275. Business E-Mail: bzymek@uconnvm.uconn.edu.

CABALQUINTO, LUIS CARRAZCAL, freelance writer; b. Magarao, Camarines Sur, Philippines, Jan. 31, 1935; came to U.S., 1968; s. Geminiano and Irene (Carrazcal) C. BA in Journalism, U. Philippines, 1967; postgrad., Cornell U., 1968—71, NYU, 1982—84. Editor Office Philippine Pres., Manila, 1960—66; editor, instr. U. Phillipines, Los Baños, 1966—75; customer svc. rep. Pfizer Inc., NYC, 1980—90; pvt. practice NYC, 1990—. Author: The Dog-eater and Other Poems, 1989, The Ibalon Collection, 1991, Dreamwanderer, 1992, Bridgeable Shores, 2001, Moon Over Magarao, New and Selected Poems, 2003, Mannahatta Mahal, 2007. Recipient Dylan Thomas Poetry award New Sch. Social Rsch., 1979, Poetry prize Acad. Am. Poets, 1985, fiction prize Philippine Graphic Mag., 1992; fellow N.Y. Found. Arts, 1989. Mem. Poetry Soc. Am., Poets Writers, Am. PEN, Acad. Am. Poets. Avocations: sports, movies, photography, travel, horticulture. Home: 1 Stuyvesant Oval MF New York NY 10009-2101 Office: PO Box 618 P Stuyvesant Sta New York NY 10009-0618 Office Phone: 212-254-4514. Personal E-mail: DonLuisC@aol.com.

CABANA, ROBERT D., aerospace transportation executive, astronaut; b. Mpls., Jan. 23, 1949; m. Nancy Joan Shimer; children: Jeffrey, Christopher, Sarah. BS in Math., U.S. Naval Acad., 1971; grad., Naval Flight Officer Tng., Pensacola, Fla., 1972, U.S. Naval Test Pilot Sch., 1981. Commd. ensign USMC, advanced through grades to col., ret., 2000; bombardier/navigator Marine Air Wings, Cherry Point, NC and Iwakuni, Japan; naval aviator 2d Marine Aircraft Wing, Cherry Point; project mgr., X-29 advanced then. demonstrator project officer, test pilot Naval Air Test Ctr., Patuxent River, Md.; asst. ops. officer Marine Aircraft Group Twelve, Iwakuni, Japan; flight software coord Astronaut Office Space Shuttle, NASA, 1985—86, dep. chief aircraft ops. Johnson Space Ctr. Houston, 1986—89, lead astronaut Shuttle Avionics Integration Lab., spacecraft communicator, chief astronaut appearances, chief Astronaut Office, dep. dir. flight crew ops., mgr. internat. ops. Internat. Space Sta. Program, dir. Human Space Flight Programs, Russia, 2001—02, dir. Flight Crew Ops. Directorate, 2002—04, dep. dir., Johnson Space Ctr. Houston, 2004—. NASA lead rep. Russian Aviation and Spacy Agy. Decorated DFC, Def. Superior Svc. medal, Def. Meritorious Svc. medal, Meritorious Svc. medal; recipient award, DAR, 1976, De La Vaulx medal, Fedn. Aeronautique Internat., 1994, Nat. Intelligence Medal of Achievement. Mem.: Assn. Space Explorers, Soc. Exptl. Test Pilots (assoc.). Achievements include four space flights; logged over 1,010 hours in space; pilot on STS-41 Discovery (Oct. 6-10, 1990), STS-53 Disco (Dec. 2-9, 1992); mission comdr. STS-65 Columbia (July 8-23, 1994) and STS-88 Endeavour (Dec. 4-15, 1998). Avocations: jogging, softball, sailing, woodworking, bicycling. Office: Astronaut Office/CB NASA Johnson Space Ctr Houston TX 77058

CABANISS, JOHN TRIGG, lawyer; b. Houston, June 5, 1941; s. Weldon Burke Cabaniss and Eleanor Russell Flowers; m. Betty Sherleen Johnson, Sept. 25, 1964; children: Katherine Ann, Elizabeth Lynn. BA in Bus. Adminstrn., Rice U., Houston, 1963; JD, U. Tex., Austin, 1966. From assoc. to sr. ptnr. Andrews Kurth, LLP, Houston, 1966—. Avocations: travel, hunting, fishing. Home: 5769 Indial Cir Houston TX 77057 Office: Andrews Kurth LLP 600 Travis St Ste 4200 Houston TX 77002

CABCABIN, DIANA M., elementary school educator, consultant; b. Bethesda, Md. d. Faustino Colandog and Conchita Macapanas Cabcabin. BA in Geography, U. Calif., Berkeley, 1985; M in Internat. Adminstrn., Sch. Internat. Tng., Brattleburg, Vt., 1992. ESI tchr. YMCA, Taipei, Taiwan, 1985—86, Internat. Lang. Inst., Washington, 1987—88, Lado Inst., Washington, 1990—93; internat. coop. asst. US Agy. Internat. Devel., Washington, 1989—95; child protection specialist UN Chidlren's Fund,

Tashkent, Uzbekistan, 2000—01; substitute tchr. Oakland Unifed Sch. Dist., Calif., 2001—, ESL tchr., 2002—07, tchr., 2001—. Trainer, facilitator, character edn. Living Values, San Francisco, 2004—; facilitator, organizer devel. Orgnl. Devel. Network, Washington, 1987—2000; bd. mem. Women's Action Orgn., Washington, 1990—93. Editor: (newsletter) Women's Actin Orgn. Newsletter, 1990—93, DC Coalition Against Domestic Violence, 1991. Vol. Americorp Promise Project, San Francisco, 1998—99, Berkeley, 1998—99; bd. mem. UN Assn., Berkeley, 2002—04, Assn. Women Devel., Washington, 1992—94. Mem.: Am. Fedn. Tchrs. Oakland, Oakland Edn. Assn., Coalition Against Trafficking in Women. Avocations; meditation, writing, hiking, languages.

CABELA, RICHARD N., retail executive; b. Nebr. m. Mary A. Cabela; 9 children. Student, Regis Coll., 1956—58. Founder Cabela's Inc., 1961, chmn., dir., 1965—. Exec. com. Direct Marketing Ednl. Found. Regent Regis Univ., 1994—, bd. trustees. Recipient Small Businessman of the Yr. award, 1970, Nebr. Hall of Fame award, 1994, Alumni Achievement award, Regis Univ., 2003. Roman Catholic. Office: Cabela's One Cabela Dr Sidney NE 69160 Office Phone: 308-254-5505. Office Fax: 308-254-4800.

CABEZAS, HERIBERTO, chemical engineer, researcher; b. La Esperanza, Las Villas, Cuba; arrived in U.S., 1967, naturalized, 1974; s. Heriberto and Ana Rosa C.; m. Isaura Vazquez. BSChemE magna cum laude, NJ Inst. Tech., Newark, 1980; MSChemE, U. Fla., 1981, PhD in Chem. Engring., 1985. Asst. prof. chem. engring. U. Ariz., 1985-93; leader simulation and design team, sustainable tech. divsn. EPA Nat. Risk Mgmt. Rsch. Lab., Cin., 1994-2000; chief sustainable environ. br. sustainable tech, div. EPA Nat. Risk Mmgt. Rsch. Lab., Cin., 2000—. Cons. Nat. Inst. Stds. and Tech., Gaithersburg, Md., 1986-93, rschr. biotech. divsn., 1993-94; adj. prof. dept. civil and environ. engring. U Cinn., 2007-. Contbr. numerous articles to profl. jours., chapters to books. Chair environ. divsn. Am. Inst. Chem. Engrs., 1996; external adv. bd. Inst. Environ. Sci. and Policy U. Ill., Chgo., 2003—. With USN, 1971—75. Recipient Disting. Alumni Achievement award, NJ Inst. Tech. Alumni Assn. Mem. AIChE, AAAS, Tau Beta Pi, Omega Chi Epsilon. Roman Catholic. Achievements include development of Paris II solvent design software, waste reduction WAR algorithm for chemical process design, sustainable systems theory. Office: US EPA 26 W Martin Luther King Dr Cincinnati OH 45268-0001 Business E-Mail: cabezas.heriberto@epa.gov.

CABIALLAVETTA, MATHIS, insurance company executive; Joined Union Bank of Switzerland, 1971—, CEO; vice chmn. Marsh & McLennan Companies, NYC, 1999—; chmn. MMC Internat., 1999—. Bd. dirs. Philip Morris Cos., 2002—, Altria Group, Inc., HBM BioVentures AG, Swiss Am. Chamber of Commerce. Office: Marsh & McLennan Co Inc 1166 Ave of the Americas New York NY 10036-2774*

CABLE, CHARLES ALLEN, mathematician; b. Akeley, Pa., Jan. 15, 1932; s. Elton Thomas and Margaret (Fox) C.; m. Mabel Elizabeth Yeck, Dec. 19, 1955; children: Christopher A., Carolyn E. BS, Edinboro State Coll., 1954; M.Ed., U. N.C., 1959; PhD in Math., Pa. State U., 1969. Instr. math. Interlaken High Sch., NY, 1954-55, Tidioute High Sch., Pa., 1957-58; asst. prof. math Juniata Coll., Huntingdon, Pa., 1959-67; assoc. prof. dept. math. Allegheny Coll., Meadville, Pa., 1969-75, prof. dept. math., 1975-96, chmn. dept., 1970-90. Editorial reviewer: Math. Mag., 1975-80; assoc. editor: Focus, 1981-85. Served with AUS, 1955-57. Gen. Elec. fellow, 1958; NSF fellow, 1959, 61, 68, 73; NDEA fellow, 1969 Mem. Am. Math. Soc., Math. Assn. Am. (chmn. Allegheny Mountain chpt. 1973-75, bd. govs. 1981-84, mem. newsletter editorial com. 1981-85, com. on student chpts. 1987-93, publs. com. 1983-86), AAUP. Republican. Presbyterian.

CABLE, JOHN FRANKLIN, lawyer; b. Hannibal, Mo., Dec. 22, 1941; s. John William and Dorothy (Stanley) C.; m. Leslie Gibbs, Apr. 5, 1965; children: Coventry, Tory, John. AB, Stanford U., 1964; LLB, Harvard U., 1967. Bar: Oreg. 1967. Assoc. Miller, Nash, Wiener, Hager & Carlsen, Portland, Oreg., 1967-73, ptnr., 1973—2007; mng. dir. Obsidian Fin. Group, Portland, 2007—. Office: Obsidian Fin Group 10260 SW Greenburg Rd Ste 1150 Portland OR 97223 Business E-Mail: fcable@obsidianfinance.com.

CABOT, HUGH, III, painter, sculptor; b. Boston, Mar. 22, 1930; s. Hugh and Louise (Melanson) C.; m. Olivia P. Taylor, Sept. 8, 1967. Student, Boston Mus., 1948, Ashmolean Mus., Oxford, England, 1960, Coll. Ams., Mexico City, 1956, San Carlos Acad. Portrait, landscape painter. Author (illustrator): Korea I (Globe); one-man shows include U.S. Navy Hist. and Records Dept., U.S. Navy Art Gallery, The Pentagon, Nat. War Mus., Washington, La Muse de la Marine, Paris, exhibited in group shows at Tex. Tri-State, 1969, Represented in permanent collections Starmont Vail Med. Ctr., Topeka, Kans., Tucson Med. Ctr., Harwood Found., Taos, N.Mex., Washburn U., Topeka, U. Ariz., Tucson, Chandler Ctr. Arts, Ariz., Booth Western Mus. Art, Cartersville, Ga.; Ofcl. artist for Korean War. With USN, Korean War. Named Artist of Yr., Scottsdale, Ariz., 1978, 30th ann. Mem. Salmagundi Club (NYC). Office Phone: 520-398-2721.

CABOT, LEWIS PICKERING, manufacturing company executive, art consultant; b. Sept. 6, 1937; s. John Moors and Elizabeth (Lewis) C.; m. Judith Ogden, July 1, 1960 (div. 1974); children: Elizabeth Lewis, Edward Ogden, Timothy Pickering; m. Susan Knight, July 15, 1978; children: James Eliot, Alexander Lee. AB, Harvard U., 1961, MBA, 1964. Trainee F.S. Moseley & Co., Boston, 1961-62; analyst John P. Chase, Inc., Boston, 1964-68; prin. Gardner & Preston Moss, Boston, 1968-73; chmn., pres. Artcounsel, Inc., Portland, Maine, 1973—; chmn., CEO Southworth Internat. Group, Inc., Portland, Maine, 1977—; pres. ZY-AX Realty, Portland, Maine, 1977—. Chmn. Shellback Corp., 1984-93; pres., chmn. Maine Art Leasing, 1988—; bd. dirs. Material Handling Roundtable; trustee NE Pooled Common Fund, Princeton, N.J., 1972-94. Trustee, pres. Soc. Arts and Crafts, Boston, 1962-66; trustee Phila. Maritime Mus., 1963-68, Mus. Fine Arts, Boston, 1966-90, Mus. Am. Folk Art, N.Y.C., 1973-77, Maine Coll. Art, 1982-91, Portland (Maine) Mus. Art, 1994—, Storm King Art Ctr., Mountainville, N.Y., 1961-72, Maine Maritime Mus., 1997—. Mem. vis. com. Harvard U. Art Mus., Cambridge, Mass., 1982-88; bd. dirs. Maine State Music Theater, 1996-2001. Mem. Met. Club (Washington), Somerset Club (Boston), N.Y. Yacht Club (N.Y.C.). Office: Southworth Internat Group 11 Gray Rd Falmouth ME 04105-2027 Office Phone: 207-878-0700 4204. Business E-Mail: lcabot@southworthproducts.com.

CABOT, LOUIS WELLINGTON, foundation trustee; b. Boston, Aug. 3, 1921; s. Thomas Dudley and Virginia (Wellington) C.; m. Mabel Hobart Brandon, 1997. AB, Harvard U., 1943, MBA, 1948; LLD (hon.), Norwich U., 1961. With Cabot Corp., 1948-96, pres., 1960-69, chmn. bd., 1969-86; chmn. Brookings Instn., Washington, 1986-92, hon. trustee; chmn. Cabot Wellington, LLC; trustee Cabot Family Trust, VWC Found. Bd. dirs. Owens-Corning Fiberglas Corp., 1961-91, Wang Labs Inc., 1982-91, New Eng. Tel. & Tel., 1965-82, R.R. Donnelley & Sons Co., 1965-91; bd. dirs. Fed. Res. Bank Boston, 1970-78, chmn., 1975-78; U.S. rep. 15th Plenary Session UN Econ. Commn. for Europe, 1960; mem. bus. ethics adv. coun. Dept. Commerce, 1961-63; dir., New Eng. chmn. Nat. Alliance Businessmen, 1970-72, Boston chmn., 1968-69; chmn. Sloan Commn. on Govt. and Higher Edn., 1977-80; mem. Pres.'s Blue Ribbon Commn. on Def. Mgmt., 1985-86; mem. Def. Sec.'s Commn. on Base Realignment and Closure, 1988; dir. Nat. Coun. for U.S.-China Trade, 1978-82. Mem. bd. overseers Harvard U., 1970-76; chmn. Harvard Coll. Fund Coun., 1963-65; pres. Beverly (Mass.) Hosp., 1958-61; chmn. Com. Corp. Support Pvt. Univs., 1977-83; trustee Norwich U., 1952-77, Mus. of Sci., Boston; corp. mem. MIT; trustee Woods Hole Oceanographic Inst., Northeastern U Conservation Internat. & Island Inst. Fellow: Am. Acad. Arts and Scis. (v.p.); mem.: NAS (pres. cir., co-chmn. 1992—95), Coun. Fgn. Rels., NY Yacht Club, Met. Club, Comml. Club (Boston) (pres. 1970—72), Somerset Club, Harvard Club, Sigma Xi, Phi Beta Kappa. Office: Cabot-Wellington LLC 70 Federal St Boston MA 02110-1906 Home Phone: 617-491-3618; Office Phone: 617-451-1744.

CABRAL, ANNA ESCOBEDO, federal official; m. Victor Cabral; children: Raquel, Viana, Catalina, Victor Christopher. BA, UCLA, 1987; MPA, Harvard U., 1990; JD, George Mason U. Exec. staff dir. US Rep. Task Force on Hispanic Affairs, Washington, 1991—99; dep. staff dir. US Senate Com. on Judiciary, Washington, 1993—99; pres., CEO Hispanic Assn. on Corp. Responsibility, Washington, 1999—2003; US treas. US Dept. Treasury, Washington, 2004—. Dir. Smithsonian Ctr. for Latin Initiatives Smithsonian Inst., 2003—; gov., bd. mem. Am. Red Cross. Office: US Dept Treasury 1500 Pennsylvania Ave NW Rm 2134 Washington DC 20220 Office Fax: 202-622-6464.*

CABRAL, GLORIA MARIA, food service executive, educator; d. Arlindo Fernandes Dias Jr. and Gloria Margarita (Socarras) Dias; m. John Andrew Cabral Sr., May 17, 1980; children: John Andrew Jr., Michael Anthony. B in Baking and Pastry Arts, Johnson & Wales U., Providence, 2002; student, World Pastry Forum, Las Vegas, 2003, student, 2004, World Pastry Forum, Phoenix, 2005, student, 2006, Mold Making with Michael Joy, Chgo., 2004; MEd, Cambridge Coll., Mass., 2004; student, Am. Culinary Fedn. Regional Conf., Toronto, Can., 2006, Am. Culinary Fedn. Nat. Conf., Phila., 2006. Baker Wilhelmina's Catering, Little Compton, RI, 1999; pastry cook Le Meridien Hotel, Boston, 2000—02; chef caterer and owner Sinfully Delicious Catering, Westport, Mass., 2001—; pastry chef Catering Collaborative, Providence, 2002—03; prodn. chef supr. Marjorie Poore Prodns., San Francisco, 2001—. Lab asst. and adj. tchr. Bristol C.C., Fall River, Mass., 2002—03, chef instr. baking and pastry arts, 2003—06, asst. prof. baking and pastry arts, 2006—. Roman Catholic. Home: 139 Briggs Westport MA 02790 Office: Bristol CC 777 Elsbree St Fall River MA 02720 Office Phone: 508-678-2811 2940. Office Fax: 508-730-3290. Business E-Mail: gcabral@bristol.mass.edu.

CABRANES, JOSÉ ALBERTO, judge; b. Mayagüez, PR, Dec. 22, 1940; s. Manuel and Carmen López Cabranes; m. Kate Stith, Sept. 15, 1984; children: Alejo, Benjamin José;children from previous marriage: Jennifer Ann, Amy Alexandra. AB, Columbia U., 1961; JD, Yale U., 1965; MLitt in Internat. Law, Cambridge U., Eng., 1967; LLD (hon.), Colgate U., 1988, other univs. Bar: NY 1968, DC 1975, US Dist. Ct. Conn. 1976. Assoc. Casey, Lane & Mittendorf, NYC, 1967—71; assoc. prof. law sch. Rutgers U., Newark, 1971—73; spl. counsel to gov. P.R., head Office Commonwealth P.R., Washington, 1973—75; gen. counsel Yale U., New Haven, 1975—79; judge US Dist. Ct. Conn., New Haven, 1979—94, chief judge, 1992—94; judge US Ct. Appeals (2nd cir.), 1994—. Mem. Pres.'s Commn. White House Fellowships, 1993—96, Pres.'s Commn. Mental Health, 1977—78; US del. Conf. Security and Coop. in Europe, Belgrade, 1977—78; founding mem. P.R. Legal Def. and Edn. Fund, 1972, chmn. bd., 1977—80; cons. to sec. Dept. State, 1978; mem. Fed. Cts. Study Com., 1988—90; instr. history P.R. Colegio San Ignacio de Loyola, Rio Piedras, PR, 1962; supr. in internat. law Queens' Coll., Cambridge U., 1966—67. Author: Citizenship and the American Empire, 1979; co-author (with Kate Stith): Fear of Judging: Sentencing Guidelines in the Federal Courts, 1998 (Cert. of Merit, ABA); author: articles on law and internat. affairs. Trustee Yale U., 1987—99, Yale-New Haven Hosp., 1978—80, 1984—87, Colgate U., 1981—90, Century Found., NYC, 1983—2000, Columbia U., 2000—, Fed. Jud. Ctr., 1986—90; mem. Coun. on Fgn. Rels.; bd. dirs. Aspira of NY, chmn., 1971—73; bd. dirs. James Madison Meml. Fellowship Found., 1995—2003. Recipient Life Achievement award, Nat. P.R. Coalition, 1987, John Jay award, Columbia Coll., 1991, Life Achievement award student divsn., Nat. Hispanic Bar Assn., 1991, Learned Hand medal for excellence in fed. jurisprudence, Fed. Bar Coun., 2000; Kellett rsch. fellow, Columbia Coll. at Cambridge U., 1965—67. Fellow: ABA Found., Mex.-Am. Lawyers Assn. (Spl. Recognition award 1994); mem.: Nat. Hispanic Bar Assn., Am. Law Inst., Conn. Bar Assn. (Naruk Jud. award 1993). Roman Catholic. Office: US Ct of Appeals US Courthouse 141 Church St New Haven CT 06510-2030*

CABRASER, ELIZABETH JOAN, lawyer; b. Oakland, Calif., June 23, 1952; AB, U. Calif., Berkeley, 1975; JD, U. Calif., 1978. Bar: Calif. 1978, U.S. Dist. Ct. (no., ea., cen. and so. dists.) Calif. 1979, U.S. Ct. Appeals (2d, 3rd, 5th, 6th, 9th, 10th, and 11th cirs.) 1979, U.S. Tax Ct. 1979, U.S. Dist. Ct. Hawaii 1986, U.S. Dist. Ct. Ariz. 1990, U.S. Supreme Ct. 1996. Ptnr. Lieff, Cabraser, Heimann & Bernstein LLP, San Francisco, 1978—. Contbr., editor California Causes of Action, 1998, Moore's Federal Practice, 1999, editor-in-chief California Class Actions Practice and Procedures, 2003; contbr. articles to law jours. Named one of The 100 Most Influential Lawyers, Nat. Law Jour., 1997, 2000, The Top 50 Women Lawyers, 1998, The 100 Most Influential Lawyers, 2006, The 50 Most Influential Women Lawyers in Am., 2007, The Top Ten Lawyers in Bay Area, San Francisco Chronicle, 2003; recipient Presdl. Award of Merit, Consumer Attys. Calif., 1998, Matthew O. Tobriner Public Service Award, Legal Aid Soc., 2000, Disting. Jurisprudence Award, Anti-Defamation League, 2002, U. Calif., Berkeley Sch. Law Citation Award, 2003. Mem. ABA (tort and ins. practice sect., sect. litig. com. on class action and derivative skills, chair subcom. on mass torts), ATLA, Coun. Am. Law Inst., Calif. Constn. Rev. Commn., Nat. Ctr. for State Cts. (mass tort conf. planning com.), Women Trial Lawyer Caucus, Consumer Attys. Calif., Calif. Women Lawyers, Assn. Bus. Trial Lawyers, Nat. Assn. Securities and Comml. Attys., Bay Area Lawyers for Individual Freedom, Bar Assn. San Francisco (v.p. securities litig., bd. dirs.). Office: Lieff Cabraser Heimann & Bernstein LLP Embarcadero Ctr W 30th Fl 275 Battery St San Francisco CA 94111-3305 E-mail: ecabraser@lchb.com.*

CABRERA, ANGEL LEOPOLDO, professional golfer; b. Córdoba, Argentina, Sept. 12, 1969; m. Sylvia Cabrera, 1989; children: Federico, Angel. Profl. golfer, 1989—; mem. European Tour, 1996—; spl. temp. mem. PGA TOUR, 2001, 2006, mem., 2007—. Mem. Argentine team Alfred Dunhill Cup, 1997, 98, 2000, WGC World Cup, 1998—2006; mem. Internat. team Presidents Cup, 2005. Achievements include winning the 2007 US Open Championship on the PGA TOUR; winner, Paraguay Open, 1995, Colombia Open, 1995, Volvo Masters of Latin America, 1996, Torneo de Maestros Telefonica, 1999, 2001, Open de Argentina, 2001, Benson and Hedges International, 2002; winner, Argentine Open, 2002, Argentine PGA (tied), 2002, Abierto del sur de Argentina, 2004, BMW Championship, 2005, 18th Torneo de Maestros Copa Personal, 2005, Abierto Visa del Centro, 2005, 06, Abierto de Norte, 2005. Office: Av Colón 4276 Local 3 X5003DEN Córdoba Argentina Office Phone: 54 351 484 4721. E-mail: info@angelcabrera.com.*

CABRERA, MIGUEL (JOSE MIGUEL CABRERA), professional baseball player; b. Maracay, Venezuela, Apr. 18, 1983; m. Rosangel Cabrera; 1 child, Rosangel. Player Fla. Marlins, 2003—. Named to Nat. League All-Star Team, Maj. League Baseball, 2004—; recipient Silver Slugger award, 2005—06. Office: Fla Marlins Pro Player Stadium 2267 Dan Marino Blvd Miami Gardens FL 33056-2600*

CABRERA, ORLANDO J., federal agency administrator; m. Betty Cabrera; children: Orly, Stefan. BA, U. Mich., 1984; JD, U. Wis., 1989. Ptnr. Holland & Knight, LLP; citizen rep. Fla. Housing Bd. Dirs., 2000—01, vice chmn. to chmn., 2001—03; exec. dir. Fla. Housing Fin. Corp., 2003—05; asst. sec. pub. and Indian housing US Dept. Housing & Urban Devel., Washington, 2005—. Bd. dirs. Nat. Coun. State Housing Agencies; mem. advisory bd. North Fla. Fannie Mae Partnership; chmn. cmty. devel. and housing com., Miami, 2001. Office: US Dept Housing & Urban Devel 451 7th St SW Washington DC 20410

CABRERA-OTERO, SYLVIA, physician; b. San Juan, Jan. 15, 1945; d. Benigno Cabrera and Ana Otero; m. Antonio Nieves-Negron, Feb. 20, 1965; 1 child, Sylvianne. BS, U. PR, 1967, postgrad. in geriatrics, 1987-88, MPH, 1996; MD, U. Valencia, 1974. Diplomate Am. Bd. Sexology, 1995. Family medicine CDT Minillas, Bayamón, PR, 1978—2006, prin., owner, 1978—2006; staff San Pablo Hosp., Bayamón, 1985—2006; sex educator, therapist PR Coll. Physicians, 1987—2006. Sec. Found. Coll. Physicians, 2004—06; Sen. Pub. Health Coll. Physicians; pres. disciplines of pub. health Coll. of Physicians, 2006—. Fellow Am. Acad. Family Practice (past pres. PR chpt., postgrad. in fundamentals of mgmt.), Internat. Physicians; mem. AMA, Am. Acad. Sex Edn. (counselor and sex therapist), PR Med. Assn., World Assn. Sexology, Med. Found. P.R. Coll. Physicians (sec. 2004-06, pres. pub. health sect. 2006—), Bayamon P.R. Coll. Physicians (sec. 2006—). Avocations: writing, brewing, crocheting, guitar, teaching. Office: Z22 Ave Laurel Urb Lomas Verdes Bayamon PR 00956-3244 Office Phone: 787-798-5175.

CABROL, NATHALIE AGNES, research scientist; b. Bagneux, France, Aug. 30, 1963; d. Jean Cabrol and Michele Marcelle Quatre-Sols; m. Edmond Antoine Grin, Apr. 15, 2000. Masters in Planetary Sciences, U. Paris-Sorbonne and Obs. of Paris-Meudon, France, 1986, PhD in Planetary Sciences, 1991; Cert. on the list Maitre de Conferences in geology, Paris, France, 1995. Fellow NASA Ames Rsch. Ctr., Space Sci. Divsn., Moffett Field, Calif., 1996—98; prin. investigator SETI Inst., NASA Ames Rsch. Ctr., Space Sci. Divsn., Moffett Field, Calif., 1998—. Spkr. in field. Contbr. chapters to books, articles to profl. jours. Recipient Silver Medal for Rsch. Work, Obs. of Triel (France), 1992, Bronze Medal for Edn. and Pub. Outreach, Ecole des Mines de Douai (France), 1996, Silver Medal, Societe d'Encouragement au Progres, 1997, Gold medal Internat. Water and Sci. award, Unesco, European Parliament, 2000, Medal for Edn. and Pub. Outreach, City of Triel, France, 2000, ASIP, 2004, Women of Discovery: Air and Space Award, World Wings Quest, 2005; grantee Mars Exploration Rover Mission Participating Scientist, NASA, 2002—, NASA Ames Rsch. Ctr., 2002—03, NASA Astrobiology Inst., 2003—, NASA Astrobiology Sci. and Tech. for Exploring Planets, 2003—; Carey Fellow, Wings World Quest, 2005. Achievements include research in exploring the highest lakes on Earth as analogs to ancient Martian lakes in order to understand their potential for life inception and survival and study the limits of life on Earth; the Gusev crater as a landing site for the Mars Exploration Mission; first to free dive (without oxygen tanks) in high-altitude lakes (5, 916 m or 18, 500 ft) to study human physiological response and adaptation to high altitude; develop science exploration strategies for automated robotic vehicles (rovers) to search for habitable environments and life on Mars; being a member of the Mars Exploration Rover Science Team. Avocations: Climbing, hiking, diving, scientific high altitude mountaineering and free diving (without oxygen tanks), music, painting, visiting art galleries and mus. Office: SETI Inst 515 N Whisman Rd Mountain View CA 94043 also: NASA Ames Rsch Ctr Space Sci Divsn MS 245 3 Moffett Field CA 94035 Home Phone: 650-967-6981. Office Fax: 650-604-6779; Home Fax: 650-967-6981. Business E-Mail: ncabrol@mail.arc.nasa.gov.

CACACE, MICHAEL JOSEPH, lawyer; b. Apr. 20, 1952; s. Jerry F. and Margaret F. (Pesditsch) Cacace; m. Maureen R. Brown, May 24, 1975; children: Joseph M., Christine M. BA, Fordham U., 1974; JD, N.Y. Law Sch., 1978. Bar: Conn. 1978, N.Y. 1979, U.S. Dist. Ct. Conn. 1979, U.S. Ct. Appeals (2d cir.) 1981, U.S. Dist. Ct. (so. dist.) N.Y. 1982. Atty. Saxe, Bacon & Bolan, NYC, 1978—79, Abate, Fox & Farrell, Stamford, Conn., 1979—82; pvt. practice law Stamford, Conn., 1982—87; ptnr. D'Andrea & Cacace, Stamford, Conn., 1988—94, Cacace Tusch & Santagata, Stamford, Conn., 1994—. Co-chmn. 13th Charter Revision Com., Stamford, 1982—83; bd. dirs. The Vol. Ctr., Stamford, 1980—86, pres., 1984—86; v.p. Gateway Cmtys., Inc., Stamford, 1981—89; bd. dirs. Stamford Commn. on Aging, 1975—80, chmn., 1978—80; bd. dirs. Vis. Nurses Assn., Stamford, 1982—87, Shippan Point Assn., Stamford, 1980—83, Stamford Ctr. for the Arts, 1986—, v.p., 1989—2000, pres., 2000—; bd. dirs. Stamford Sr. Svcs., 1998—2004; exec. bd. Yankee coun. Boy Scouts Am., 2000—; bd. dirs. Italian Ctr. Stamford, 1989—, pres., 2005—07. Named one of Best Lawyers in Am.; recipient Cmty. Leader of Yr. award, The Stamford Adv., 1986, Good Scout award, Conn. Yankee coun. Boy Scouts Am., 2001, Dr. Max Reich award, N.Y. Law Sch., Humanitarian award, Southwestern Conn. Assn. Life Underwriters, 1987—88, Lawyers Co-op Book award, Lawyers Co-op Book Co., 1977, Thomas F. Richardson Pres.'s award, United Way Stamford, 1995, Citizen of Yr. award, The Fred Robbins Post #142 Jewish Vets. of U.S., 1995. Mem.: ATLA, Conn. Trial Lawyers Assn., N.Y. Bar Assn., Conn. Bar Assn. (chair planning and zoning sect. 1994—97), Stamford/Darien Bar Assn. (mem. exec. com. 1980—92, treas. 1986—87, sec. 1987—88, 2d v.p. 1988—89, 1st v.p. 1989—90, pres. 1990—91), Urban Inst., Am. Planning Assn. (Conn. chpt.), State St. Debating Soc., Stamford C. of C. (bd. dirs. 1999—2004), Landmark Club (bd. govs. 1995—2001), Roasters Club (Stamford). Democrat. Roman Catholic. Home: 316 Scofieldtown Rd Stamford CT 06903-4012 Office: Cacace Tusch Santagata 777 Summer St Ste 201 Stamford CT 06901-1022 Office Phone: 203-327-2000.

CACCAMISE, GENEVRA LOUISE BALL (MRS. ALFRED E. CACCAMISE), retired librarian; b. July 22, 1934; d. Herbert Oscar and Genevra (Green) Ball; m. Alfred E. Caccamise, July 7, 1974. BA, Stetson U., DeLand, Fla., 1956; MLS, Syracuse U., NY, 1967. Tchr. grammar sch., Sanford, Fla., 1956-57; tchr. elem. sch. Longwood, Fla., 1957-58; tchr., libr. Enterprise Sch., Fla., 1958—63; libr. media specialist Boston Ave. Sch., DeLand, Fla., 1963-83; head media specialist Blue Lake Sch., DeLand, 1983-87, ret., 1987. Author: Volusia County manual Instructing the Library Assistant, 1965, Echoes of Yesterday: A History of the DeLand Area Public Library, 1912-1995, 1995, A Quest for Beauty: A History of the Garden Club of DeLand, Florida, 1927-97, 1997, Index to Reflections: West Volusia County, 100 Years of Progress, 2002, (compilation) The Minutes and Memorials of the Old Settlers of DeLand, Fla., 1882-1926, 2003. Charter mem. West Volusia Meml. Hosp. Aux., DeLand, 1962—81; leader Girl Scouts USA, 1955—56; area dir. Fla. Edn. Assn., Volusia County, 1963—65; bd. dirs. Alhambra Villas Home Owners Assn., 1972—75; trustee DeLand Pub. Libr., 1977—86, sec., 1978—80, v.p., 1980—82, pres., 1982—84; v.p. Friends of DeLand Pub. Libr., 1987—88, 1998—2005, bd. dirs., 1987—, pres., 1989—90, 1995—97, 2006—, newsletter editor, 1992—95, 1999—2005; charter mem. Guild of the DeLand Mus. Art, 1988—, v.p., 1990, pres., 1991—92, co-rec. sec., 1997—98, rec. sec., 2005—, mus. bd. dirs., 1991—95; co-orgn. chmn. Friends of DeLand Mus. Art, 1993. Recipient Woman's Club Lit. award for contbns. to arts in West Volusia County, 1995. Mem.: DAR (asst. chief page Continental Congress, Washington 1962—65, chpt. registrar 1969—80, Excellence in Cmty. Svc. award 1995), AAUW (rec. sec. 1961—65, 2d v.p. chpt. 1965—67, rec. sec. 1978—80, pres. 1980—82, parliamentarian 1982—84), Volusia County Ret. Educators Assn. (pres. Unit II 1988—90, scholarship chmn. 1992—95, corr. sec. 2003—), Volusia County Assn. Media in Edn. (treas. 1977), Fla. Libr. Assn., Assn. Childhood Edn. (corr. sec. 1963—65, 1st v.p. 1965—66), Roots and Brs. Geneal. Soc. of West Volusia County (corr. sec. 2006—), Nat. League Am. Pen Women (corr. sec. 1996—98, pres. 1998—2000, corr. sec. 2000—04), Magna Carta Dames, Stetson U. Alumni Assn. (class chmn. for ann. fund dr. 1968), Soc. Mayflower Descendants (lt. gov. Francis Cook Colony

1988—90), Pilgrim John Howland Soc., Colonial Dames XVII Century, Nat. Soc. New Eng. Women (v.p. Daytona Beach Colony 1990—91), Nat. Soc. US Daus. of 1812 (rec. sec. Peacock chpt. 1989—90), Fla. Hist. Soc., West Volusia Hist. Soc. (libr. 1993—, sec. 1996, v.p. 2000—02, pres. 2002—03, bd. dirs., Vol. of Yr. 1999, Historian of Yr. 2002), Morning Glory Garden Cir., Hibiscus Garden Cir. (treas. 1988—89, v.p. 1990—93, 1996—97, pres. 1997—99, treas. 2001—03), DeLand Garden Club (corr. sec. 1993—95, editor newsletter 1993—95, v.p. 1997—99), Bus. and Profl. Women's Club (corr. sec. DeLand 1968—71, 2d v.p. 1969—70), Delta Kappa Gamma (pres. Beta Psi chpt. 1982—84). Address: PO Box 241 Deland FL 32721-0241

CACCIATORE, JOANNE, social worker; b. NYC, Nov. 16, 1965; d. John Louis and Josephine Cacciatore; children: Arman John Sadeghi, Cameron Michael, Stevie Jo, Joshua Cheyne, Cheyenne (Deceased). BS, Ariz. State U., Phoenix, 2001, MSW, 2004; PhD, U. Nebr., Lincoln, 2006. CEO MISS Found., Phoenix, 1996—; faculty Ariz. State U., 2005—. Dir. Elisabeth Kubler-Ross Found., Scottsdale, Ariz., 2004—. Author: (book) Dear Cheyenne, (manual/book) The Power of Compassion: A New Attitude in Healthcare; editor: (publication for agency) MISSing Angels; contbr. film by japanese public television, chapters to books. Vol. MISS Found., Glendale, 1996—2005; mem. Ariz. Domestic Violence Fatality Rev. Com., Phoenix, 2002—03; mem., past chair Ariz. Dept. Health Services, 1999—2006; founding mem. Elisabeth Kubler Ross Found., Scottsdale, Ariz., 2004—06, Internat. Stillbirth Alliance, Chgo., 2002—05; dir. Elisabeth Kubler Ross Found., 2004—; founder The Kindness Project, Peoria, 1997—2006. Recipient Laurel award, St. Luke's Charitable Health Trust, hon. Kachina award, 2007; fellow, Assn. Death Edn. and Counseling; grantee, St. Luke's Charitable Health Trust; scholar, Ariz. State U., 2001, 2003, 2004. Mem.: Compassionate Friends, Unexplained Infant Death Adv. Coun., Internat. Stillbirth Alliance (assoc.), Psi Chi, Golden Key Internat. Honor Soc. (hon.). Libertarian. Achievements include first to successfully lobby the Arizona legislature to pass the first MISSing Angels Bill in the United States, later successsfully spearheaded the same bill's passage in 16 other states since; successfully lobbied the federal government for first-time funding on stillbirth and maternal health through the National Institutes of Health; successfully lobbied the Arizona legislature in the creation of the Unexpected Infant Death Advisory Council, a formal, multidisciplinary team charged with research and education of infant deaths; successfully lobbied the Az legislature to pass SB1003, a one-time tax exemption for families after an infant's death to help offset funeral and birth costs; successfully rallied a team to lobby the Congress to sign National Children's Memorial Day Act. Avocations: reading, hiking, surfing, rock climbing. Home: 3642 W Magellan Anthem AZ 85086 Office: Arizona State University/MISS Foundation CHS/Dept of SW 4701 W Thunderbird Glendale AZ 85306 Home Phone: 623-979-1000; Office Phone: 602-543-6659. Home Fax: 623-979-1001. Personal E-mail: joanne727@cox.net. E-mail: joanne.cacciatore@asu.edu.

CACCIATORE, RONALD KEITH, lawyer; b. Donaldsville, Ga., Feb. 5, 1937; s. Angelo D. and Myrtice E. (Williams) C.; children: Rhonda, Donna, Rex. Student, Spring Hill Coll., 1955-56; BA, U. Fla., 1960; JD, 1963. Bar: Fla. 1963, U.S. Supreme Ct. 1969. Asst. state atty. 13th Jud. Cir., 1963-65; pvt. practice Tampa, Fla., 1967. Lectr. criminal law; mem. 13th Jud. Cir. Jud. Nominating Commn., 1976-80, chmn., 1980; mem. Fed. Judiciary Adv. Commn. Fla., 1987—. Trustee Hillsborough C.C., 1979-83, chmn., 1982-83. Recipient Jack Edmund Civility and Excellence in Practice Criminal Law award. Fellow Am. Coll. Trial Lawyers; mem. Hillsborough County Bar Assn. (pres. 1975-76, chmn. trial lawyers sect. 1983-85, Herbert G. Goldburg Meml. award 1991), Fla. Bar Assn. (chmn. criminal law sect. 1977-78), Fla. Coun. Bar Pres.'s (chmn. 1979-80), Fed. Bar Assn. (pres. Tampa Bay chpt. 1985-86, fed. jud. nominationcom. Fla. 1999—, George C. Carr Meml. award Tampa Bay chpt. 1996), Master of the Bar, White-Ferguson Inn, Herbert G. Goldburg Criminal Law Am. Inn of Ct. (pres. 2000—), Am. Inns of Ct., Palma Ceia Golf and Country Club, University Club.

CACCIATORE, S. SAMMY, lawyer; b. Tampa, Fla., Aug. 2, 1942; s. Sam and Margarita C.; m. Carolyn Michels, Aug. 10, 1963; children: Elaine Michel, Sammy Michel. BA, JD, Stetson U., DeLand, Fla., 1966. Bar: Fla. 1966, U.S. Ct. Appeals (5th cir.) 1967, U.S. Supreme Ct. 1971, U.S. Ct. Appeals (11th cir.) 1981, U.S. Dist. Ct. (mid. dist. 1966) Fla. Asst. public defender 9th jud. cir. State of Fla., Fla., 1966; assoc. firm Orlando, Fla., 1966-67; pvt. practice Melbourne, Fla., 1967—; ptnr. Nance, Cacciatore, Hamilton, Barger, Nance & Cacciotore, Melbourne, Fla., 1970—. Mem. 5th Dist. Appellate Nomination Commn., 1979-83; mem. Fla. Med. Malpractice Adv. Com., 1982; mem. jud. nominating commn. Fla. Supreme Ct. 1986-90, mem. Supreme Ct. Jury Instrn. Com., 2001—; bd. overseers Stetson U. Coll. Law, 1995-, chairperson, 2006-; trustee Stetson U., 2000—; lectr. in field. Contbr. articles to profl. jour., chpt. to books. Trustee A. Max Brewer Meml. Law Libr., Brevard County, Fla., 1972-76, chmn., 1972-75. Mem. ABA, Am. Assn. for Justice (formerly ATLA), Am. Law Inst., Internat. Acad. Trial Lawyers, Am. Bd. Profl. Liability Lawyers, Am. Bd. Trial Advocates, Nat. Bd. Trial Advocacy, Fla. Justice Assn. (formerly Acad. Fla. Trial Lawyers; bd. dir. 1970—, pres. 1984-85, Pres.'s award 1983), Fla. Bar (bd. govs. 1994-99, exec. com. 1995-99, vice chmn. advt. task force 1995-97, budget com. 1994-97, chmn. 1996, mem. exec. com. trial lawyer sect. 1975, chmn. constl. revision com. 1997—, mem. legis. com. 1995-99, chmn. 1998-99, mem. jury instrn. com. Fla. Supreme Ct., 2001—), So. Trial Lawyers Assn., Stetson Lawyers Assn. (1st v.p. 1992-93, pres.-elect 1994-95, pres. 1995-96), Brevard County Bar Assn. (bd. dir., Pres.'s award 1975, Lifetime Achievement award for professionalism), Vassar Carlton Inn of Ct. (emeritus), Eau Gallie Yacht Club (gov., vice commodore 1981-82, commodore 1983-84). Democrat. Roman Catholic. Avocations: fishing, boating, travel. Office: 525 N Harbor City Blvd Melbourne FL 32935-6837 Home Phone: 321-773-1711; Office Phone: 321-777-7777. Business E-Mail: sammy@nancelaw.com. *The law is a living, growing institution of our lives. Lawyers need to remember this and nurture its development as one would a child. It should grow straight and strong for the benefit of the people.*

CÁCERES, FRANKLIN THOMAS, retired writer; b. NYC, July 8, 1946; s. Frank Caceres and Louise Caamano; m. Magali Zayas; children: Anthony Caceres, German Gomez, Zaira Gomez. BBA, Manhattan Coll., 1969; MA, U. South Fla., 1998; PhD, Clayton Coll. Natural Health. Regional credit mgr. Carrier Air Conditioners, Inc., Clearwater, Fla., 1988—94; asst. acad. dean Hillsborough C.C., Mac Dill AFB, Fla., 1994—96; mgmt. sys. analyst Hillsborough County Bd. Commrs., Tampa, Fla., 1996—2005; ret., 2005. Cons. Hispanic Bus. Initiative Fund, Tampa, 1996—. Author: (novels) Because They Were, 2002, Chronic Nights, 2003, By Reason of Privilege, 2005, Bye the Book, 2006; contbr. articles to profl. jours. and newsletters. Mem. So. Poverty Law Ctr., Montgomery, 2000—, Hillsborough Alliance for Citizens with Disabilities, Tampa, 1996—, Nat. Coun. La Raza, Washington, 2000—. With US Army, 1969—71. Mem.: Fla. Writers Assn., Paralyzed Vets. Am., Mystery Writers Am., League United Latin Am. Citizens, Tampa Writers' Alliance, Nat. Multiple Sclerosis Soc., Phi Kappa Phi. Roman Catholic. Avocation: woodworking. Personal E-mail: caceresf@novel-guy.com.

CACIOPPO, JOHN TERRANCE, psychologist, educator, researcher; b. Marshall, Tex., June 12, 1951; s. Cyrus Joseph and Mary Katherine (Kazimour) Cacioppo; m. Barbara Lee Andersen, May 17, 1981 (div. 1998); children: Christina Elizabeth, Anthony Cyrus; m. Wendi L. Gardner, Sept. 8, 2001. BS in Econs., U. Mo., Columbia, 1973; MA in Psychology, Ohio State U., 1975, PhD in Psychology, 1977. Asst. prof. psychology U. Notre Dame, Ind., 1977-79, U. Iowa, Iowa City, 1979-81, assoc. prof., 1981-85, prof. psychology, 1985-89, Ohio State U., 1989-98, Univ. chaired prof. psychology, 1998-99; Tiffany-Margaret Blake disting. svc. prof. U. Chgo., 1999—. Vis. faculty Yale U., 1986, U. Hawaii, 1990, U. Chgo., 1998—99; tng. grant dir. NIMH Social Psychology, 1993—98; co-dir. Inst. for Mind and Biology, 1999—2004, dir. social psychology program, 1999—2005; dir. Ctr. Cognitive and Social Neurosci. U. Chgo., 2004—. Editor: Psychophysiology, 1994—97; contbr. articles to profl. jours. Active John D. and Catherine T. MacArthur Found. Network on Mid-Body Integrations, 1995-98; bd. dirs. Ohio State U. Rsch. Found., 1993-98 Recipient Early Career Contbn. award Psychophysiology, 1981, Troland Rsch. award NAS, 1989, Disting. Sci. Contbr. Psychophysiol., Soc. Psychophysiol. Rsch., 2000; NSF grantee, 1979—, Campbell award Soc. Personality and Social Psychology, 2000. Fellow: APA (past pres. 2 divsns., Disting. Sci. Contbn. award 2002), Acad. Behavioral Medicine Rsch., Am. Psychol. Soc. (keynote spkr. ann. meeting 2002, bd. dirs. 2002—); mem.: AAAS, Assn. for Psychol. Sci. (pres.-elect), Am. Acad. Arts and Scis., Soc. Exptl. Psychologists, Soc. Exptl. Social Psychology, Soc. Personality and Social Psychology (pres. 1995), Soc. Psychophysiol. Rsch. (bd. dirs. 1985—88, officer 1991—94, pres. 1992—93, bd. dirs. 1998—2000), Sigma Xi (nat. lectr. 1996—98). Office Phone: 773-702-1962.

CADDELL, FOSTER, artist; b. Aug. 2, 1921; s. Foster and Clara (Bamford) C.; m. June A. Kaufmann, Apr. 10, 1943 (dec. Feb. 1989); m. Gail L. Marchant, Feb. 14, 1993. Student, R.I. Sch. Design, Providence, 1940—43; pvt. study with, Peter Helck, Robert Brackman, Guy Wiggins. Artist Providence Lithograph Co., R.I., 1939-52; freelance illustrator, 1951—85; owner, instr. Foster Caddell's Art Sch., Voluntown, Conn., 1958—. One-man shows Providence Art Club, 1948, 63, South County (R.I.) Art Assn., 1967, Slater Mus., Norwich Acad., 1976, Heritage Plantations of Sandwich, 1985; group shows include Springfield Mus. Fine Arts, 1962-77, Am. Watercolor Soc., 1973, NAD, 1973, Am. Artists Profl. League (awards 1953, 71, 72, 89, 90, 91), Acad. Artists Am. (awards 1968, 73, 75), Slater Mus., Norwich Acad., 1975-80, Providence Art Club (award 1978, 79, 92), Nat. Arts Club, 1978, Internat. Soc. Artists (award 1978), Soc. des Pastellists de France, 1987, The Monmouth (N.J.) Mus., 1994, Brown U. Libr., Providence, 1995, Pastel Soc. No. Fla. (award 1996), Pastel Soc. Am. (elected Hall of Fame 1998, award 2005, 06), Beijing Acad. Fine Arts, 1997, others; specialist in portraiture, 1965—; author: Keys to Successful Landscape Painting, 1976, Keys to Successful Color, 1979, Keys to Painting Better Portraits, 1982, Oil Painting Techniques, 1983, Landscape Painting Techniques, 1984, Foster Caddell's Keys to Successful Landscape Painting, 1993, Pastel Interpretations, 1993, The Art of Pastel Portraiture, 1996, Best Pastels II, 1998, Best of Sketching and Drawing, 1998, Pastel Jour. 2000, Pastel Artists Internat. 2001, My Friends, Todays Great Masters, 2007; work on display at pastelsocietyofamerica-.org, artshow.com, Conn. Soc. Portrait Artists, ctpastelsociety.com; artist ofcl. portraits of father and son, U.S. Sen. Thomas J. Dodd, 1965, and U.S. Sen. Christopher J. Dodd, 2004; contbr. articles to profl. publs Served as artist USAAC, WWII. Recipient award, Norwich Acad., 1947, Ogunquit Art Ctr., 1949, Conservative Painters R.I., 1962, Salmagundi Club, 1973, 1980, No. Fla. Pastel Soc., 1996, Award of Excellence, Mystic Seaport Maritime Gallery, 1996, Best of Show award, Mystic Art Assn., 1997, award, Conn. Pastel Soc., 1990—94, 1998, 1999, Honor award, 2001, 2002, 2003, 2004, 2005, 2006. Mem. Oil Painters of Am., Washington Soc. of Portrait Artists (award 1998), Lyme Art Assn., Providence Art Club, Am. Artists Profl. League, Acad. Artists Am., Am. Soc. Portrait Artists, Salmagundi Club, Pastel Soc. Am. (award 1990, 91, 92, 93, 94, 98, 99, 2005), Internat. Soc. of Portrait Artists (award 2004), Conn. Soc. Portrait Artists (Best of Show 2003, Lifetime Achievement award 2005), New Eng. Plein Air Painters. Address: 47 Pendleton Hill Rd Voluntown CT 06384-1920 Home Phone: 860-376-9583; Office Phone: 860-376-9583. Personal E-mail: fcaddell@sbcglobal.net.

CADDELL, LYNN M., waste management executive; B in Hist., Jacksonville U., Fla.; M in Systems Engring., U. Ariz., Tucson; grad. Exec. Edn. Program, Harvard U. Engr. IBM, Inc.; engring. mgmt. positions Motorola, Inc.; dir. systems devel. Am. West Airlines; v.p. systems devel. Yellow Techs., Inc., Overland Park, Kans., pres., 1999—2004; sr. v.p., chief info. officer Waste Mgmt., Inc., Houston, 2004—. Named one of 25 Women Who Mean Bus., Kansas City Bus. Jour., 2003. Office: Waste Mgmt Inc 1001 Fannin Ste 4000 Houston TX 77002 Office Phone: 713-512-6200.*

CADDICK, SARAH J., medical association administrator, biomedical researcher; b. Wales, 1968; BSc, U. Portsmouth, UK, 1990; PhD in Neuroscience, U. Southampton, UK, 1993. Rsch. assoc. Duke U. Med. Ctr., 1993—97, Med. Coll. Va., 1997—98; dir. award programs Damon Runyon-Walter Winchell Found. Cancer Rsch. Fund, 1998—2000; dir. med. & sci. programs Steve & Michele Kirsch Found., 2000—03; exec. dir. Wadsworth Found., 2003; exec. v.p., chief sci. officer Faster Cures/Ctr. for Accelerating Med. Solutions, Milken Inst., Washington, 2003—05; exec. dir. Columbia U. Ctr. Neuroscience Initiatives, 2005—. Named one of 40 Under 40, Crain's NY Bus., 2007; fellow Am. Epilepsy Soc./Milken Found., 1996. Office: Hammer Health Sci Ctr Rm 2-205 701 W 168th St New York NY 10032 Office Phone: 212-342-1858. E-mail: sjc@columbia.edu.*

CADDY, MICHAEL DOUGLAS, lawyer; b. Long Beach, Calif., Mar. 23, 1938; s. Frank Edward and Tabitha (Miles) C. BS in Fgn. Svc., Georgetown U., 1960; JD, NYU, 1966. Bar: DC 1970, Tex. 1979. Practiced in, Washington and, Tex.; exec. dir. com. on pub. affairs McGraw-Edison Co., NYC, 1960-61; asst. to lt. gov. State of N.Y., 1962-65; asst. to exec. v.p. NAM, NYC, 1966-67; Washington liaison Gen. Foods Corp., 1968-70; assoc. Gall, Lane, Powell & Kilcullen, 1970-74; legis. counsel Nat. Assn. Realtors, Washington, 1975-76; atty. Office Tex. Sec. of State, Austin, 1980-81. Author: The Hundred Million Dollar Payoff, 1974, How They Rig Our Elections, 1975, Understanding Insurance, 1984, Legislative Trends in Insurance Regulation, 1985, Exploring America's Future, 1987. Mem. Rep. County Com., N.Y.C., 1965-66; nat. dir. Young Ams. for Freedom, 1960-62. Scholar Intercollegiate Studies Inst., 1957-59. Mem.: FBA, ACLU, ABA, ATLA, Nat. Lesbian and Gay Law Assn., Nat. Trust Hist. Preservation, People for Am. Way, Supreme Ct. Hist. Soc., Nat. Coun. Crime and Delinquency, Internat. Platform Assn., Am. Acad. Polit. and Social Sci., Am. Econ. Assn., Assn. Former Intelligence Officers, Am. Judicature Soc., Stonewall Lawyers Assn. Houston, Houston Bar Assn., Tikkun Cmty. Office: 7941 Katy Fwy Ste 296 Houston TX 77024-1924 E-mail: douglascaddy@justice.com.

CADE, GREGORY BRIAN, federal agency administrator, fireman; b. 1950; A.A. in Fire Sci., Prince George's Cmty. Coll., Maryland, 1979; BS in Fire Adminstrn., U. Md., 1994; M in Pub. Safety Leadership, Old Dominion U. Vol. firefighter Prince George's County, Md., firefighter Md., 1971—92, bur. chief Md., bur. chief fire suppression; fire chief City of Hampton, Md., 1992—98; fire chief/emergency mgmt. coord. City of Va. Beach, 1998—2007; adminstr. US Fire Adminstrn., US Dept. Homeland Security, Emmitsburg, Md., 2007—. Office: US Fire Adminstrn 16825 South Seton Ave Emmitsburg MD 21727 Office Phone: 301-447-1000. Office Fax: 301-447-1346.*

CADE, WALTER, III, artist, actor, musician, vocalist; b. NYC; s. Walter Cade and Helen (Henderson) Brehon. Student, Arts Students League, Inst. Modern Art. Appeared in (plays) Amen Corner, Hatful of Rain, Jim Pavone & the Buzz Bomb, Mary Mary, Don't Bother I Can't Cope, Harlequinade, The Story of Ulysses, Mateus, Which Way America, Poetry Now Subway Cinema, (films) Cotton Comes to Harlem, Education of Sonny Carson, Claudine, Now, Angel Heart, The Wiz, FX, (T.V.) Joe Franklin Show, Positively Black, Soul, Sammy Davis Telethon, June Rolands, Musical Chairs, Big Blue Marble; one man shows include: Ocean County Coll., 1977, Jackson State U., 1980, Phoenix Gallery, Atlanta, 1982, Olin Mus. Art, Bates Coll., Maine, 1993, U.S. Nat. Tennis Ctr., Arthur Ashe Stadium, U.S. Open, NY, 1997, 98, 99, Sande Webster Gallery, Pa., 2000, others; 2-man shows include: Lewiston-Auburn Coll., Maine, 1993, others; 3 man shows include: Suffolk CC, 1987; group shows include Whitney Mus., 1971, Corcoran Gallery, 1972, Black Expo, NYC, 1973, Miss. Mus. Fine Art, 1991, Roanoke (Va.) Mus. Fine Art, 1982, Tampa Mus., 1982, Hunter Mus. Art, 1983, Tucson Mus. Art, 1983, New Eng. Fine Arts Inst., Maine, 1993, Lewiston-Auburn Coll., 1994; represented in permanent collections Fine Arts Mus. South, Bruce Mus., Virginia Beach Art Mus., Rockefeller Found., Peter A. Juley and son Collection, Smithsonian Inst. Nat. Mus. Am. Art, others. Recipient Best in show award Las Olas Art Festival, 1980, Arts Festival Atlanta, 1981, Bruce Mus., 1983-84, 94, 1st prize Fine Arts Mus. South, 1982, others. Mem. SAG, Artists Equity. Home: 17203 119th Ave Jamaica NY 11434-2261 Office Phone: 718-527-5634. E-mail: zenbopwe@msn.com.

CADENA, FREDERICO EDUARDO, finance company executive; b. Mexico City; s. Frederico Marquez Cadena and Francis Carol Samame; m. Elizabeth Ann Kopplin, Dec. 14, 2002; 1 child, Samuel Joseph. BA in Econs., Rochville U., 2003; postgrad. in Fin., Heriot Watt U., Edinburgh, Scotland, 2004—. Registered rep. Series 7 Nat. Assn. of Securities Dealers, 2002, securities prin. Series 24 Nat. Assn. of Securities Dealers, 2004, options prin. Series 4 Nat. Assn. of Securities Dealers, 2004. Ops. mgr. Global Rsch. and Recovery, El Paso, Tex., 1997—99; svc. mgr. Excell Agt. Svcs., Las Cruces, N.Mex., 1999—2001; sales mgr. Providian Fin., El Paso, Tex., 2001—02; investment rep. Edward Jones Investments, El Paso, Tex., 2002—04; v.p. risk and margin OptionsXpress, El Paso, Tex., 2004—. Chmn. El Paso County Parks Bd., El Paso, Tex., 1998—98; v.p. Associacion de Lidres Mexicanos-Americanos, El Paso, Tex., 1999—99; dir. of club devel. Tex. Young Rep. Fedn., 1998—99; exec. dir. El Paso County Rep. Party, Tex., 1996—98; vestry mem. All Saints Episcopal Ch., El Paso, Tex., 2002—04. Recipient Vol. of the Yr. award, Rep. Party of Tex., 1998. Mem.: Profl. Risk Mgr.'s Internat. Assn., Global Assn. of Risk Profls. R-Consevative. Episcopalian. Avocations: investing/trading, cooking, fitness, wine tasting, travel. Office: OptionsXpress 4725 Ripley St El Paso TX 79922 Home Phone: 915-204-0999; Office Phone: 312-267-6482. Personal E-mail: fred@fredcadena.com. Business E-Mail: fcadena@optionsxpress.com.

CADENHEAD, ALFRED PAUL, lawyer; b. LaGrange, Ga., Oct. 14, 1926; s. Roy E. and Omie (Bishop) C.; m. Sara Davenport, Oct. 14, 1945; children: Steven Paul, David James. Jr. coll. certificate, W. Ga. Coll., 1944; LLB, Emory U., 1949. Bar: Ga. 1949. Sr. counsel, ptnr. Hurt, Richardson, Garner, Todd & Cadenhead, Atlanta; with Hurt, Richardson, 1977-92; of counsel Fellows La Briola, Atlanta, 1993—. Pres. Atlanta Legal Aid Soc., 1958. Pres. Met. Atlanta Mental Health Assn., 1964-65, Ga. Assn. Mental Health, 1968; past trustee Queens Coll., Charlotte, NC; lifetime trustee West Ga. Found. Served with paratroops US Army, 1944-46. Recipient West Ga. Coll. Disting. Svc. award, 1993, Emory U. Law Sch. Disting. Alumnus award, 1996, Ben F. Johnson Pub. Svc. award Ga. State U., 1999, Founders award State U. West Ga., 2001. Fellow Am. Bar Found., Am. Acad. Matrimonial Lawyers, Am. Coll. Trial Lawyers, Internat Soc. Barristers; mem. State Bar Ga. (past bd. govs.), Atlanta Bar Assn. (pres. 1970-71, Charles E. Watkins award for disting. and sustained svc. 1992, Leadership award 2000, Professionalism award, 2004), Atlanta Estate Planning Coun. (pres. 1976). Presbyterian. Home: 6305 Riverside Dr NW Atlanta GA 30328-3646 Office: South Tower Peachtre Ctr Ste 2300 225 Peachtree St NE Atlanta GA 30303-1731 Business E-Mail: acadenhead@fjl-law.com.

CADES, STEWART RUSSELL, lawyer, communications executive; b. Phila., Jan. 16, 1942; s. Ralph E. and Lillian G. (Mann) C. BS in Econs., U. Pa., 1964, LLB, 1967; MEd, Temple U., 1971. Bar: Pa. 1971. Sole practice, Phila. and Bala-Cynwyd, Pa., 1971—; chmn. bd. Porcupine Communications Co., Phila., 1971—. Pres. Nairn U.S. Holdings divsn. Stewart Nairn Group P.L.C., 1980-86; bd. dirs. Cloche Assocs., Inc., Andrews & Leith, Ltd., ACM Worldwide, Ltd.; mng. dir. Overseas Strategic Consulting, 1992—; chmn. bd. dirs. Towne Met., Inc., 1985-92, also pres. Election judge Montgomery County, Pa., 1975—77; ct. vol. probation dept. Ct. Common Pleas Phila. County, 1972—74; vice-chmn. Montgomery County Planning Commn., 1980—95; bd. dirs. Southeastern Pa. Transit Authority, 1991—97, trustee, 1991—97, pension com., 1991—97, chmn. real estate com., 1991—97; mem. adv. bd. City of Phila. Airport, 1994—, mem. exec. com., 2000—01; bd. dirs. Friends of Phila. Mus. Art, 1985—91, vice chmn., 1987—89; bd. dirs. Juvenile Law Ctr., 1983—98, pres., 1986—90; bd. dirs. SEPTA Transit Mus.; assocs. adv. bd. Phila. Mus. Art, 2001—, co-chair assoc. adv. bd., 2004—06, trustee, 2004—06, Pa. Acad. Fine Arts, 1992—2002; bd. dirs. Found. Arch., 1999—2002, Conservation Ctr. Art and Hist. Artifacts, 2000—; sec., sch. chmn. alumni undergrad admissions U. Pa., 1978—2001, alumni pres. Class of '64, 1975—90; v.p. Fabric Workshop and Mus., 1992—. Mem.: ABA, Montgomery County Bar Assn., Phila. Bar Assn. (ct. house and detention facilities com. 1983—86), Pa. Bar Assn., Phila. Club, Print Club (bd. govs. 1978—98, hon. bd. 1999—2004).

CADIEUX, CHESTER, retail executive; b. Tulsa, 1932; m. Debbie Cadieux; 6 children; 1 child, Chester III. BBA, U. Okla., 1954. Salesman Maneke-Kinzie Printing Co., Tulsa, Okla., 1954—58; co-founder (with Burt B. Holmes) QuikTrip, Tulsa, Okla., 1958, CEO. Bd. trustees U. Tulsa; pres. Nat. Assn. Convenience Stores; mem. bd. C. of C., Tulsa; chmn. Tulsa Area United Way, River Parks Authority; mem. bd. Nat. Benevolent Assn., Tulsa Cmty Found., Okla. Bus. and En. Coalition, Trust for Public Lands. Named Ernst and Young Southwest Retail-Wholesale Entrepreneur of Yr.; named to Okla. Commerce and Industry Hall of Fame. Avocations: reading, running. Office: QuikTrip Corp 4705 S 129th East Ave Tulsa OK 74134*

CADIEUX, ROGER JOSEPH, geriatrics services professional; b. Bay Shore, NY, Feb. 7, 1945; m. Kathryn Cadieux; children: Kevin, Kristin, Brooke, Michael. BS, Northwestern State U., 1973; MD, La. State U., 1977. Cert. geriatric psychiatrist, RN anesthetist. Intern, then resident in psychiatry Coll. Medicine Pa. State U., Hershey, 1977-81, psychogeriatric fellow, instr. Coll. Medicine Milton S. Hershey Med. ctr., 1980-81, asst. prof. dept. psychiatry, 1981-93, assoc. prof. psychiatry, 1993-99; clin. prof. psychiatry, 1999—; dir. geriatric assessment program Pa. State U. Coll. Medicine, 1992-98; psychiat. cons. Jewish Home of Harrisburg, 1985—, Homeland Ctr. of Harrisburg, 1993—; program dir. Pa. Dept. Aging, 1986—, physician cons., 1987—; pres. Commonwealth Affiliates, P.C., 1992—. Contbr. articles to profl. jours. Fellow Am. Bd. Psychiatry and Neurology (disting., diplomate); mem. Am. Psychiat. Assn., Am. Geriatric Soc., Am. Assn. for Geriatric Psychiatry, Acad. Sleep Disorders Medicine, Alpha Omega Alpha. Office: 2215 Forest Hills Dr Ste38 Harrisburg PA 17112-1099 Home Phone: 717-566-0333; Office Phone: 717-540-5353. Personal E-mail: rjcpsy@aol.com.

CADIEUX, RONALD CLAUDE, mathematics educator; b. Schenectady, NY, June 4, 1959; s. John Claude Cadieux and Wanda Jean Olszewski; m. Dorothy M. Hoffman, June 29, 1996. BS, SUNY, Plattsburgh, 1981; math. cert., SUNY, Albany, 1984, MA, 1986; coaching cert., Fulton-Montgomery CC, Johnstown, NY, 1987. Cert. nursery-12th grade math., social studies and developmental reading NY. Mid. sch. tchr. St. Joseph's Sch., Rensselaer, NY, 1981—82, St. Adalbert's Sch., Schenectady, 1982—83; HS tchr. Schenectady City Schs., 1984—, co-curriculum chmn., 1997—99. Adj.

faculty mem. Hudson Valley CC, Troy, NY, 1998—2000; tchr. leader People to People, 1995—. Ward capt. Schenectady Dem. Party, 2002—04. Named Tchr. of Yr. (5 times), Schenectady HS; recipient Golden Apple Outstanding Achievement award, Schenectady City Sch. Dist.; scholar, Radio Shack/Tandy. Mem.: Assn. Math. Tchrs. NY State, Nat. Coun. Tchrs. Math., Schenectady Fedn. Tchrs. (v.p. 1997—99), Pi Delta Kappa. Roman Catholic. Avocations: travel, camping, theater and performing arts. Office: Schenectady HS 1445 The Plaza Schenectady NY 12308

CADMAN, EDWIN CLARENCE, health facility administrator, retired educator; b. Bandon, Oreg., May 14, 1945; s. Edwin Herbert Cadman and Gloria (Ranellie) Wilson; children: Tim, Kevin, Brian. AB, Stanford U., 1967; MD, U. Oreg., 1971. Intern in internal medicine Stanford U. Hosp., Calif., 1971-74; fellow in oncology Yale U., New Haven, 1974-76, asst. prof. medicine, 1976-79, assoc. prof. medicine, 1979-83, prof., chmn. medicine, 1987-94, prof., 1994—99; prof. medicine, dir. Cancer Rsch. Inst. U. Calif., San Francisco, 1983-87, vice chmn. dept. medicine, 1985-87; chief of staff, sr. v.p. med. affairs Yale New Haven Hosp., 1994—99; dean, prof. John A. Burns Sch. of Med. Univ. of Hawaii, 1999—2005. Prof. Am. Cancer Soc., 1985-87. Contbr. over 300 articles to profl. jours. Basketball coach Novato (Calif.) Park and Recreation, 1985. Capt. USNG, 1972-78. Recipient Gold Headed Cane award U. Oreg. Med. Sch., 1971. Fellow AAAS, ACP; mem. AFCR (pres. 1984-86), ASCI, AAP, ASCO/AACR, AOA. Avocations: running, fishing, reading. Office: John A Burns Sch Med 1960 E West Rd Honolulu HI 96822 Office Phone: 808-692-0891. Business E-Mail: cadman@hawaii.edu.

CADMAN, WILSON KENNEDY, retired utilities executive; b. Wichita, Kans., Sept. 7, 1927; s. Wilson K. and Ethel Louise (Wheeler) C.; m. Mary Roslyn Rowley, Nov. 22, 1950; children: Elizabeth Louise, Cadman Haywood, Robert Wilson. AB, Wichita State U., 1951, postgrad., 1953, Okla. State U., 1965. With Kans. Gas & Electric Co., Wichita, 1951-92, mgr. Wichita divsn., 1967-70, v.p., 1970-79, pres., 1979-92, chief exec. officer, 1981-92, also chmn. bd. dirs.; ret., 1992. Sr. advisor Barr Devlin & Assocs. Investment Bankers, NYC; bd. dirs. Bank IV of Wichita, El Paso Electric Co., Tex., Columbia Energy Group, Herndon, Va., Clark/Bardes Inc., Dallas, Broadbande2e.com, Newport Beach, Calif., Ponca Products Mfg., Wichita, Kans. Bd. govs. Wichita State U. Endowment Assn.; bd. dirs. Wichita State U. Athletic Scholarship Orgn.; mem. Gov.'s Task Force on High Tech. Devel., Mayor's Econ. Adv. Council, Kans. Water Resources Council. Served with USN, 1945-46. Mem. Edison Electric Inst., Wichita Area Devel. (exec. com.), Wichita State U. Endowment Assn., Wichita Club, Wichita Country Club, Univ. Club, Crestview Country Club, Kiwanis, Phi Lambda Psi. Home and Office: The Cloisters 8905 E Douglas Wichita KS 67207

CADY, BLAKE, surgical oncologist; b. Washington, Dec. 27, 1930; s. John Parmalee and Elizabeth (Blake) C.; children: Brian, Suzanne, Pamela. AB, Amherst Coll., 1953; MD, Cornell U., 1957. Diplomate Am. Bd. Surgery; lic. physician, Mass., NY, RI. Intern Tufts Surg. Svc. Boston City Hosp., 1957-58, resident Tufts Surg. Svc., 1958-59, resident Harvard Surg. Svc., 1961-65; USPHS clinic cancer trainee Meml. Hosp. for Cancer and Allied Diseases, NYC, 1965-67; fellow in surgery Cornell U. Med. Coll., 1965-67; fellow Sloan-Kettering Inst., 1965-67; staff surgeon Lahey Med. Clinic, Burlington, Mass., 1967-81; mem. surg. staff New Eng. Deaconess Hosp., Boston, 1967-97; chief surg. oncology New Eng. Deaconess, Boston, 1982-97; prof. surgery Brown U. Med. Sch., Providence, 1997—. Surg. liaison Dana Farber Cancer Ctr., Boston, 1982—; cons. surgery Uganda Cancer Inst., Kampala, Uganda, East Africa, 1971; assoc. clin. prof. surgery Harvard Med. Sch., 1975-82, assoc. prof., 1982-91, prof. 1991-97, emeritus prof., 1997—; dir. Breast Health Ctr., Women and Infants Hosp., Providence, 1997-2003; interum dir. Comprehensive Breast Ctr., RI Hosp., 2003-. Editor emeritus: Surgical Oncology Clinic of North America; mem. editl. bd. several jours.; contbr. over 300 articles to profl. jours. Bd. dirs. Mass. div. Am. Cancer Soc., 1974, pres., 1991-93, nat. bd. dirs., 1993-99, chmn. tobacco policy com., 1991-93; chmn. bd. dirs. Tobacco Control Resource Ctr., 1994—, Planned Parenthood League Mass., 1984-85; chmn. Mass. Coalition for Healthy Future, 1991-93, Tobacco Control Oversight Coun. Mass.; pres. James Ewing Found., 1988. Lt. M.C., USN, 1959-61. Recipient Lemuel Shattuck medal Mass. Pub. Health Assn., 1983, 96; ann. nat. divsn. award Mass. divsn. Am. Cancer Soc., 1984, Disting. Svc. award, 2000. Mem. AMA, ACS (Mass. chpt., spl. rep. to regional cancer control com. subcom., regional cancer control com.), Am. Surg. Assn., Soc. Surg. Oncology (program chmn. nat. meetings 1980, 81, chmn. rsch. com. 1980-82, sec. 1984-86, v.p. 1986-87, pres.-elect 1987-88, pres. 1988, chmn. exec. com. 1989-90), Soc. Head and Neck Surgeons (program com. 1980, Hayes Martin lectr. 1998), Am. Assn. Endocrine Surgeons (v.p. 1982, local arrangements chmn. 1988, exec. coun. 1986-90, sec.-treas. 1991-94, pres. 1998), New Eng. Cancer Soc. (treas. 1976-83, sec. 1983-87, pres. 1991), New Eng. Surg. Soc. (recorder 1989, pres. 1995-96), Soc. for Surgery Alimentary Tract, Boston Surg. Soc. (pres. 1993), Halstead Soc. Avocations: sailing, travel. Home: 24 Walnut Pl Brookline MA 02445-6710 Office: Univ Surg Assocs APC-438 593 Eddy St Providence RI 02903 Office Phone: 401-444-6158. Business E-Mail: bcady@usasurg.org.

CADY, DONA M., humanities educator; b. Merced, Calif., Dec. 4, 1955; d. Donald Forrest and Mac Millheim; m. Edward J. Cady; children: Edward A., Elizabeth, Alexandra. BA, U. Pacific, Stockton, Calif., 1978; MA, U. Notre Dame, Ind., 1979; Diploma European Archeology, Oxford U., England, 1980. Prof. Middlesex CC, Bedford, Mass., 1981—. Achievements include development of COD Winner. Office: Middlesex CC Springs Rd Bedford MA 01730 Home Phone: 978-664-4428; Office Phone: 781-280-3721. Business E-Mail: cadyd@middlesex.mass.edu.

CADY, DUANE MAYNARD, surgeon; b. Endicott, NY, 1934; m. Joyce Cady; 5 children. BS in Chem., Atlantic Union Coll., Mass.; MD, Loma Linda U., 1959. Diplomate Am. Bd. Surgery. Intern SUNY-Syracuse Med. Ctr., 1959-60, resident in surgery, 1960-64, clin. assoc. prof. surgery; pvt. practice NYC. Apptd. chair N.Y. State Medicaid Managed Care Adv. Coun.; mem. N.Y. State Pub. Health Couns. Task Force on Pain Mgmt.; mem. med. staff pres., chair dept. surgery, bd. trustees St. Joseph's Hosp., Syracuse. Captain & army surgeon Medical Corps US Army. Fellow Am. Coll. Surgeons; mem. AMA (coun. med. svc., bd. trustees, chair bd. trustees 2005-, pres. AMA Found., 2004-), Med. Soc. of the State of NY (past pres. & chmn.), Am. Soc. Gen. Surgeons. Mailing: PO Box 137 La Fayette NY 13084

CADY, ELWYN LOOMIS, JR., medicolegal consultant; b. Ames, Iowa, Feb. 21, 1926; s. Elwyn Loomis Sr. and Annabel (Lacey) C.; m. Jane Carolyn Elliott, Jan. 27, 1964 (dec. Dec. 1989); children: James Anson, Kathryn Anne; stepchildren: Martin Norman Jensen III, Paul Elliott Jensen. JD, Tulane U., 1951; BS in Medicine, U. Mo., 1955. Bar: Mo. 1951, U.S. Supreme Ct. 1965. Sci. comml. tchr., athletic dir. and coach Vermillion (Kans.) Rural H.S., 1948-49; pvt. practice Kansas City, St. Louis, Independence, Mo., 1951—; dir. law-medicine program U. Kansas City, 1951-56; asst. dir. Law-Sci. Inst. U. Tex., Austin, 1956-57, sec. Law-Sci. Acad. Am., 1956-57; of counsel Koenig & Dietz, St. Louis, 1959-74; gen. counsel Elliott Oil, Inc., Independence, 1966—2004, Overland Park Dry Cleaners, Inc. Mem. com. on mgmt. Ea. Jackson County Planned Parenthood Clinics, Independence, 1970-75. Author: (book) Law and Contemporary Nursing, 1961, 1st rev. edit., 1963; author: (with others) Immediate Care of the Acutely Ill and Injured, 1974, Cardiac Arrest and Resuscitation, 1958, 4th rev. edit., 1974, West's Federal Practice Manual, 1960, rev. 2d edit., 1989, Gradwohl's Legal Medicine, 1954; book reviewer sci. books and films. Legal Counsel Friends of the Truman Campus, U. Mo.-Kansas City, Independence, 1987-97, Cmty. Assn. for the Arts, Independence, 1991—; charter mem. Friends of Nat. Frontier Trails Ctr., Independence, 1990—, Independence Hist. Trails City Com., 1991—. With U.S. Army, 1944-45, ETO. Fellow Harry S. Truman Libr. Inst. for Nat. and Internat. Affairs (hon.), Am. Acad. Forensic Sci. (ret.); mem. AAAS (life), Nat. Geog. Soc. (life), Am. Legion (past comdr., judge adv., chaplain, chmn. state blood donor program, chmn. dist. oratorical contest), Mo. Writers' Guild (past pres., historian), Soc. Mayflower Descs. (gov. Heart of Am. colony), Phi Alpha Delta (life), Phi Beta Pi, Tau Kappa Epsilon. Home and Office: 1919 Drumm Ave Independence MO 64055-1836 Office Phone: 816-252-2219.

CADY, MARK S., state supreme court justice; b. Rapid City, SD, July 12, 1953; married; 2 children. Undergrad. degree, Drake U., JD, 1978. Law clk. 2d Jud. Dist. Ct., 1978-79; asst. Webster County atty.; with law firm Ft. Dodge; dist. assoc. judge, 1983—86; dist. ct. judge, 1986—94; judge Iowa Ct. Appeals, 1994—98, chief judge, 1997—98; justice Iowa Supreme Ct., 1998—. Author: (book) Curbing Litigation Abuse and Misuse: A Judicial Response. Chmn. Supreme Ct. Task Force on Ct.'s and Cmty.'s Response to Domestic Abuse. Mem.: Webster County Bar Assn., Iowa State Bar Assn. Office: Iowa Supreme Ct 1111 E Ct Ave Des Moines IA 50319 E-mail: MarkS.Cady@jb.state.ia.us.*

CADY, SHERRY L., astrobiologist, educator; BA (with highest honors) in Geology, U. Calif. Berkeley, 1987, PhD in Geology, 1994. Office mgr., bus. products and supplies co., San Francisco, 1981—87; grad. student, dept. geology U. Calif. Berkeley, 1987—94; rsch. assoc., geomicrobiology NRC, NASA Ames Rsch. Ctr., Calif., 1994—96; prin. investigator, rsch. scientist SETI Inst., Menlo Park, Calif., 1996—98; asst. prof., dept. geology Portland State U., Oreg., 1998—2002, assoc. prof., dept. geology Oreg., 2002—. Mem. biosciences steering group NSF. Contbr. chapters to books, scientific papers, articles to profl. jours.; editor-in-chief Astrobiology, 2001—, mem. editl. bd. Geobiology. Mem.: Geological Soc. Am. (co-founder, vice chair geobiology and geomicrobiology divsn.), Environmental Biogeochemistry (mem. internat. com. 1999). Achievements include working on various projects connected to the search for life on Mars and the investigation of how microorganisms leave their biosignatures in extreme environments. Office: Dept Geology Portland State U PO Box 751 Portland OR 97207-0751 Address: Portland State U Dept Geology Rm 17 Cramer Hall 1721 SW Broadway Portland OR 97201 Office Phone: 503-725-3377. Office Fax: 503-725-3025. Business E-Mail: CadyS@pdx.edu.

CAETANO, RAUL, psychiatrist, educator; b. São Paulo, Brazil, May 5, 1945; came to U.S., 1978; s. Silvestre Vieira and Vera Vieira (Barbosa) C.; m. Patrice Vaeth, Sept. 30, 1995; children: Izabel, Lauren, Helena. MD, U. Rio de Janeiro, 1969, diploma in Psychiatry, 1971; MPH, U. Calif., Berkeley, 1979, PhD, 1983. Psychiatrist Pinel Hosp., Rio de Janeiro, 1969-73; asst. prof. State U., Rio de Janeiro, 1969-73; rsch. psychiatrist Inst. Psychiatry U. London, 1973-76; asst. prof. Inst. Psychiatry, Rio de Janeiro, 1976-78; vis. scholar Alcohol Rsch. Group, Berkeley, 1978-83, assoc. scientist to sr. scientist, 1983-94, dir., 1992—. Adj. prof. Sch. Pub. Health, U. Calif., Berkeley, 1991-98; assoc. dir. Calif. Pacific Med. Ctr. Rsch. Inst., San Francisco, 1992-93; prof., regional dean Sch. Pub. Health, U. Tex., 1998—, prof., dean Sch. Allied Health Scis., U. Tex. Southwestern Med. Ctr., 2006—. Contbr. articles to profl. jours. WHO fellow, 1973-76; rsch. grantee Nat. Inst. Alcohol Abuse and Alcoholism, 1985—. Mem. APHA, Am. Coll. Epidemiology, Rsch. Soc. Alcoholism. Roman Catholic. Office: V8112 5323 Harry Hines Blvd Dallas TX 75390-9128 Office Phone: 214-648-1080. Business E-Mail: raul.caetano@utsouthwestern.edu.

CAFARO, DEBRA A., real estate company executive; b. Dec. 15, 1957; m. Terrence Livingston; 2 children. BA in Govt., U. Notre Dame, 1979; JD, U. Chgo., 1982. Bar: Ill., Pa. Founding mem. Barack Ferrazzano Kirschbaum Perlman & Nagelberg LLP, Chgo., 1986—97; pres., dir. Ambassador Apartments, Inc., 1997—98; pres., CEO Ventas, Inc., Louisville, 1999—, chmn. bd., 2003—. Adj. prof. law Northwestern U. Law Sch., 1988—92; bd. dirs. Weyerhaeuser Co., 2007—. Named one of 50 Women to Watch, The Wall St. Jour., 2004. Mem.: Nat. Assn. of Corp. Dirs., Nat. Assn. of Real Estate Investment Trusts (bd. dirs.). Office: Ventas Inc Ste 300 10350 Ormsby Park Pl Louisville KY 40223*

CAFFARELLI, LUIS ANGEL, mathematician, educator; b. Buenos Aires, Dec. 8, 1948; came to U.S., 1973; s. Luis and Hilda Delia (Cespi) C.; m. Irene Andrea Martinez-Gamba; children: Alejandro, Nicolas, Mauro. MS, Univ. Buenos Aires, 1969, PhD, 1972; D (hon.), Ecole Normal Superieur, Paris, Univ. Autonoma de Madrid, Univ. del la Plata, Argentina. Postdoctoral asst., asst. prof. U. Buenos Aires, 1972-73; asst. prof. to prof. math. Univ. Minn., 1973-83; prof. math. Univ. Chgo., 1983-86, Courant Inst., NYU, 1980—82, 1994—97, Inst. for Advanced Study, Princeton, NJ, 1986—96, Univ. Tex., Austin, 1997—. Hon. prof. math. Univ. de Buenos Aires, Univ. de Mar del Plata. Contbr. articles to profl. jours. Recipient Stampacchia prize Scuola Normale de Pisa, 1983, Bocher prize Am. Math. Soc., 1984, Pius XI medal, 1988, Premio Konex, 2003, Rolf Schock prize, Royal Swedish Acad. Sciences, 2005; Guggenheim grantee. Mem. NAS, AAAS, Pontifical Acad. Sci., Am. Math. Soc., Accademia dei XL, Academia Argentina de Ciencias. Office: U Tex Dept Math 1 Univ Sta C1200 Austin TX 78712 Office Phone: 512-471-3160. Office Fax: 512-471-9038. Business E-Mail: caffarel@math.utexas.edu.

CAFFEE, LORREN DALE, lawyer; b. Decatur, Ind., Oct. 22, 1947; s. Howard Dale and Maxine Faye (Smith) C.; m. Mary Katherine Hostetler, May 25, 1968 (div. Apr. 1982); children: Liesl Katherine, Evan Dale, Colin Dale (dec.); m. Mary Jannice Dyer, June 14, 1986. BA, Bluffton Coll., Ohio, 1969; JD, Georgetown U., Washington, DC, 1972. Bar: Ind. 1972, US VI 1994, US Dist. Ct. (no. dist.) Ind. 1974. Pvt. practice, Decatur, 1972-73, 74-76; assoc. DeVoss & DeVoss Law Offices, Decatur, 1973-74; judge Adams County Ct., Decatur, 1976-84, Adams Superior Ct., Decatur, 1985-90, Adams Cir. Ct., Decatur, 1991-99; assoc. A.J. Weiss & Assoc. Law Office, 1999—2002; of counsel Law Offices of Norman P. Jones, St. Thomas, VI, 2003—04, Smock & Moorehead, 2004—05, Watts, Benham & Sprehn, St. Thomas, 2005—. Mem. county ct. com. Ind. Jud. Ctr., 1978-88, chmn., 1983-86; mem. juvenile benchbook com. Jud. Conf. of Ind., 1991-99, bd. dirs., 1995-99. Bd. dirs. Ind. Right to Life, 1974-76; mem. constn. and by-laws com. Ind. Young Reps. Fedn., 1974, of counsel, 1975-76; chmn. Adams County Young Reps., 1973-76. Mem. Ind. State Bar Assn., Adams County Bar Assn. (pres. 1975-76), Ind. Judges' Assn., Am. Judges Assn., Nat. Coun. Juvenile and Family Ct. Judges, Federalist Soc. Lutheran. Avocations: jazz music, aviation, sports cars, art, reading. Home: PO Box 11479 St Thomas VI 00801-4479 Office: Watts Benham & Sprehn PO Box 11720 St Thomas VI 00801-4720 Home Phone: 340-774-0315; Office Phone: 340-777-5737. Personal E-mail: caffeelaw@hotmail.com.

CAFFERTY, JACK, news anchor; Began career, Reno, 1960; news anchor WHO-TV, Des Moines; anchor, Strictly Business syndicated bus. program, 1977—89; originator Live at Five WNBC-TV, NYC; co-anchor Fox News at 7 WNYW, NYC; co-anchor WB11 News at Ten, NYC, 1992—98; anchor WPIX-TV Channel 11 News at 10, NYC; anchor, Before Hours CNN, NYC, co-host, American Morning, anchor, In the Money. Host Jack Cafferty's Newsline New York. Recipient numerous awards including Emmy award, Edward R. Murrow award.

CAFFERTY, PASTORA SAN JUAN, education educator; b. Cienfuegos, Las Villas, Cuba, July 29, 1940; arrived in US, 1947; d. Jose Antonio and Hortensia (Horruitiner) San Juan; m. Michael Cafferty, Apr. 13, 1971 (dec. 1973); m. Henry P. Russe, Aug. 18, 1988 (dec. 1991). BA, St. Bernard Coll., 1967; MA, George Washington U., 1969, PhD, 1971; DHC, Columbia Coll., 1987. Instr. George Washington U., Washington, 1967-69; asst. to sec. U.S. Dept. Transp., Washington, 1969-70, U.S. HUD, Washington, 1970-71; asst. prof. U. Chgo., 1971-76, assoc. prof., 1976-83, prof., 1983—2005, prof. emeritas, 2005—. Bd. dirs. Waste Mgmt. Inc., Houston, Harris Fin. Corp., Chgo., Integrys, Chgo. Author: The Politics of Language: The Dilemma of Bilingual Education for Puerto Ricans, 1981, Backs Against The Wall, 1983, The Dilemma of American Immigration, 1983, Hispanics in the U.S.A., 1985, 2d edit., 1992, Hispanics: An Agenda for 21st Century, 1999, 2d edit., 2002. Bd. dirs. Lyric Opera Assn., Chgo., 1990—, Rush Univ. Med. Ctr., 1993— White House fellow U.S. Govt., 1969-70. Mem. Chgo. Yacht Club. Democrat. Roman Catholic. Office: U Chgo 969 E 60th St Chicago IL 60637-2677 Office Phone: 773-702-8959. Business E-Mail: p-cafferty@uchicago.edu.

CAFFEY, HORACE ROUSE, academic administrator, agricultural company executive; b. Grenada, Miss., Mar. 24, 1929; s. C. Horace and Anna Belle (James) C.; m. Lois (Granger) Stevens, Mar. 13, 1999; children: Brenda, Jerry, Belle, Rex. BS, Miss. State U., 1951, MS, 1955; PhD, La State U., 1959. Agronomist in charge rice project Miss. Agrl. Exptl. Sta., Stoneville, 1958—62; supt. La. State U. Rice Sta., La. Agrl. Exptl. Sta., Crowley, 1962—70; assoc. dir., prof. La. State U., La. Agrl. Exptl. Sta., Baton Rouge, 1970—79; vice-chancellor adminstrn. La. State U. Agrl. Ctr., 1979—80, vice-chancellor internat. programs, 1980—81, chancellor, 1984—97, interim chancellor, 2007—; chancellor La. State U., Alexandria, 1981—84; pres., CEO Caffey Internat. Inc., 1997—; interim v.p. acad. affairs La. Coll., 2005. Internat. rice cons. AID, World Bank, other orgns., 1965—; mem. pub. health study team Nat. Acad. Sci., Washington, 1973-74; mem. adv. bd. Bd. Regents Masters Plan Higher Edn., Baton Rouge, 1977; Nat. co-chair joint coun. for Food and Agr., 1989-94, Internat. Sci. and Edn. Coun., 1986-90; chmn. Nat. Assn. State Univs. and Land Grant Colls. divsn. Agr. Budget Com., 1989; spring semester interim v.p. acad. affairs La. Coll., Pineville, 2005. Contbr. articles to profl. jours., chapters to books. Pres. Internat. Rice Festival, Crowley, 1968; bd. dirs. Boy Scouts U.S.A., United Way, others. Served to 1st lt. 82nd airborne US Army, 1951—54. Recipient Internat. award of Merit Gamma Sigma Delta, 1970, 81; honoree Internat. Rice Festival, 1974; named Man of Yr. Crowley C. of C., 1969-70, Progressive Farmer Man of Yr. in Svc. to La. Agr., 1986, Outstanding Alumnus Coll. Agr. of La. State U., 1992, Alumnus of Yr., La. State U., 1993, Outstanding Alumnus of Yr., Coll. Agr., Miss. State U., 1993. Mem. Sigma Xi, Gamma Sigma Delta, Phi Delta Kappa, Omicron Delta Kappa, Phi Delta Phi, Phi Zeta. Lodges: Masons; Rotary. Democrat. Baptist. Home: 10471 Barry Dr Baton Rouge LA 70809-3265 Office: Chancellor Emeritus La State U 4560 Essen Ln Baton Rouge LA 70809-3424 Office Phone: 225-763-3997. Personal E-mail: hrcaffey@aol.com.

CAFFREY, PATRICIA, diversified financial services company executive; With JP Morgan Chase & Co., NYC, 1993—, mng. dir. global syndicated fin. group, mng. dir. restructuring group, regional mgr. Chase Bus. Credit, 2006—. Office: JP Morgan Chase & Co 270 Park Ave New York NY 10017 Office Phone: 212-270-6000. Office Fax: 212-270-1648.

CAFRITZ, PEGGY COOPER, communications executive; b. Mobile, Ala., Apr. 7, 1947; d. Algernon Johnson and G. Catherine (Mouton) C.; married; 2 children. BA in Polit. Sci., George Washington U., 1968, JD, 1971. Bar: DC 1972. Founder Workshops for Careers in Arts, Washington, 1968; developer, chmn. bd. Duke Ellington Sch. Arts., Washington, 1968-84; dir. Arrowstreet, Architects and Planners Inc., Cambridge, Mass., 1972-74, Washington, 1972-74; spl. asst. to pres. Post-Newsweek Stas. Inc., Washington, 1974-77; programming exec., producer documentary films Sta. WTOP-TV, Washington, 1974-77; pres. DC Bd. Edn., Washington, 2000—. Cultural arts critic (PBS TV show) Around Town, 1986—. Mem. exec. com. D.C. Commn. Arts and Humanities, 1970-75, chmn., 1979-87, chmn. emeritus, 1987—; trustee Am. Film Inst., 1972-74, Pratt Inst., 1991; bd. govs. Corcoran Gallery Art, Washington, 1972-74; exec. dir. gt. issure program D.C. Bicentennial Commn., 1974; bd. dirs. Washington Performing Arts Soc., 1983—, Kennedy Ctr. Performing Arts, 1986—, Women's Project, 1987—, Nat. Guild Community Schs. of Arts, 1976-80, Pennsylvania Ave. Devel. Corp., Washington, 1979-87, Atlanta U., 1983-86, Washington, Am. Place Theater, N.Y.C.; co-chmn. Mayor's Blue Ribbon Task Force on Cultural and Econ. Devel., 1987-88; mem. exec. bd. Nat. Assembly State Arts Agys., 1979-86, planning com., 1986-87; mem. conv. staff Dem. Nat. Com., 1972, 76; mem. steering com. Carter-Mondale, Washington, 1976; mem. nat. panel Arts, Edn. and Ams., 1975-79; mem. internat. com. UNICEF, 1976-79; chair Smithsonian Cultural Edn. Com., 1989—; co-chair Smithsonian Cultural Equity Com., 1988—; mem. adv. bd. W.E.B. DuBois Inst., Harvard U., 1992-; mem. African-Am. Instnl. study adv. com. Smithsonian Instn., 1990— pres., D.C. St. Bd. of Education, 2001-. Fellow Woodrow Wilson Internat. Ctr. for Scholars, 1971; recipient John D. Rockefeller III award, 1972, George F. Peabody award U. Ga., 1976, Emmy award, 1977, 27th Ann. Broadcast Media award, 1977, Zeta Phi Beta award for outstanding contbn. in the arts, 1974, N.Y. Black Film Festival award, 1976, Women's Achievement award Pub. TV, 1984, Brava award for Outstanding Contbn. to Arts in Washington, 1988, Mayor's Art award for excellence in svc. to arts, 1991, 20th Malcolm X DayAnniversary award Arts Advocacy, 1991, Ann. Cultural Alliance award, 1992; named Washingtonian of Yr. Washingtonian mag., 1972, Woman of Yr. Mademoiselle mag., 1973, and numerous other awards. Mem.: DC Bar Assn., ABA. Home and Office: 3030 Chain Bridge Rd NW Washington DC 20016-3410 Office: DC Board of Ed 825 North Capitol St NE Nineth Floor Washington DC 20002 E-mail: peggy.cafritz@k12.dc.us. *Growing up black in the fully segregated city of Mobile, Alabama, instilled in me a youthful passion "to become the wind and not the blown." This passion, from which flows the energy that drives me to achieve has never abated; it has broadened: I do hope that I have done and will continue to do much to help others so that they too can become the wind.*

CAGE, JACK HAYS, executive search consultant; b. San Francisco, Mar. 15, 1953; s. James Gilliam and Audrey (Shade) C.; m. Laura E. Larson; children: Catherine, Anna. BS, U.S. Mil. Acad., 1975; MA, Columbia U., 1981, PhD, 1982. Commd. 2d lt. U.S. Army, 1975, advanced through grades to Col., 1995, ret., 1997; mng. dir. Sullivan & Co., NYC, 1997-99; ptnr. Heidrick & Struggles, NYC, 1999—2001, co-head global ins. tech. practice; sr. client ptnr. Global Tech. Markets Practice. Ptnr. Fin. Svcs. Info. Tech., NYC, 1997—; sr. client ptnr. Korn/Ferry Internat., 2001-06; pres. Cage Talent, NYC, 2007-; CIO, chief tech. officer Ins. Tech. Practice. Recipient Bronze Star U.S. Army, 3 Legion of Merit awards U.S. Army, Combat INfantryman's Badge, U.S. Army. Mem. Assn. Exec. Search Cons., Union League Club. Avocations: personal investment, information systems, travel, charity work. Office Phone: 646-284-7284. E-mail: jack@jackcage.com.

CAGE, NICOLAS (NICOLAS COPPOLA), actor; b. Long Beach, Calif., Jan. 7, 1964; s. August Coppola and Joy Vogelsang; m. Patricia Arquette, Apr. 8, 1995 (div. May 18, 2001); m. Lisa Marie Presley, Aug. 10, 2002 (div. May 16, 2004); m. Alice Kim, July 30, 2004; 1 child, Kal-el Coppola; 1 child, Weston. Grad., UCLA; DFA (hon.), Calif. State Fullerton, 2001. Actor: (feature films) Fast Times At Ridgemont High, 1982, Valley Girl, 1983, Rumble Fish, 1983, Racing with the Moon, 1984, Birdy, 1984, The Boy in Blue, 1986, The Cotton Club, 1984, Peggy Sue Got

Married, 1986, Raising Arizona, 1986, Moonstruck, 1988, Vampire's Kiss, 1989, Never on a Tuesday, 1989, Tempo di Uccidere, 1989, Fire Birds, 1990, Wild at Heart, 1990, Zandalee, 1991, Honeymoon in Vegas, 1992, Time to Kill, 1992, Amos & Andrew, 1993, Red Rock West, 1993, Deadfall, 1993, Guarding Tess, 1994, It Could Happen to You, 1994, Trapped in Paradise, 1994, Kiss of Death, 1995, Leaving Las Vegas, 1995 (Best Actor award L.A. Film Critics 1995, Best Actor award N.Y. Film Critics 1995, Golden Globe award for best actor 1996, Acad. award for best actor 1996), The Rock, 1996, The Funeral, 1996, Con Air, 1997, Face Off, 1997, Welcome to Hollywood, 1998, Snake Eyes, 1998, City of Angels, 1998, 8MM, 1999, Bringing Out the Dead, 1999, Gone in 60 Seconds, 2000, Family Man, 2000, Captain Corelli's Mandolin, 2001, Windtalkers, 2002, Adaptation, 2002, Matchstick Men, 2003, National Treasure, 2004, The Weather Man, 2005, (voice) The Ant Bully, 2006, World Trade Center, 2006, Ghost Rider, 2007, Grindhouse, 2007; actor, prodr.: (films) Sonny (also dir.), 2002, Lord of War, 2005, The Wicker Man, 2006, Next, 2007; prodr.: (films) Shadow of the Vampire, 2000, The Life of David Gale, 2003. Office: Saturn Films 9000 W Sunset Blvd Ste 911 West Hollywood CA 90069-5809 also: Creative Artists Agy 9830 Wilshire Blvd Beverly Hills CA 90212-1804*

CAGEAO, CAROLYNN FINNEN, language educator; b. Bronx, NY, Sept. 12, 1960; d. James J. and F. Joan Finnen; m. Kevin T. Cageao; 1 child, Allison M. Quirk. MS, Iona Coll., New Rochelle, NY, 1987. Tchr. Spanish Clarkstown Sr. HS South and North, New City and West Nyack, NY, 1982—83, Pascack Valley HS, Hillsdale, NJ, 1983—. Named Tchr. of Yr., Pascack Valley HS, 1990; recipient Gov.'s Tchr. Recognition, State of NJ, 1990. Mem.: Am. Coun. Tchg. Fgn. Langs. Home: 18 Mohawk Ln Pomona NY 10970 Office: Pascack Valley HS 200 Piermont Ave Hillsdale NJ 07642

CAGGIANO, JOSEPH, advertising executive; b. NYC, Oct. 22, 1925; s. Daniel Joseph and Lucia (Gaudiosi) C.; m. Catherine Marie Gilmore, Aug. 28, 1948; children— Cathleen, Mary Yvonne. BBA, Pace Coll., 1953. Chief accountant Criterion Advt. Co., NYC, 1947-57; treas. Emerson Foote, Inc., NYC, 1957-67; became sr. v.p. Bozell & Jacobs, Inc. (now Bozell, Jacobs, Kenyon & Eckhardt Inc.), NYC, 1967, exec. v.p. finance and adminstrn. Omaha, 1971-91, vice chmn. bd., chief financial officer, 1991-97; vice chmn. bd. dirs. emeritus Bozell, Jacobs, Kenyon & Eckhart Inc., 1991—, ret., 1998. Bd. dirs. St. Mary's Coll., Omaha Zool. Soc. Served with USNR, 1943-46, ETO, PTO. Mem. N.Y. Credit and Financial Mgmt. Assn., Omaha Zool. Soc. (dir.) Home: 9731 Fieldcrest Dr Omaha NE 68114-4932 *Luck in business is best defined as preparation meeting opportunity while always keeping a positive attitude. Dedication and fairness to a cause is mandatory. There are few short cuts to success in business or meaningful relationships with family and friends; and still fewer gray areas. It would have been impossible to achieve any degree of success without the help and understanding of my wife and family.*

CAGINALP, AYDIN S., lawyer; b. Ankara, Turkey, Aug. 2, 1950; AB, Ind. U., 1972; JD, Tulane U., 1974; LLM in Taxation, NYU, 1975. Bar: N.Y. 1976, U.S. Dist. Ct. (so. and ea. dists.) N.Y. 1976, U.S. Tax Ct. 1976. Ptnr. Alston & Bird LLP, NYC. Bd. editors Tulane U. Law Rev., 1973-74. Address: Alston & Bird LLP 90 Park Ave New York NY 10016-1387 Office Phone: 212-210-9414. Office Fax: 212-210-9444. Business E-Mail: acaginalp@alston.com.

CAGINALP, GUNDUZ, mathematician, educator, researcher; b. Ankara, Turkey, July 20, 1952; arrived in U.S., 1959; s. Nejat Tahsin and Munire Feyma (Deniz) C; m. Eva Keller, Aug. 14, 1992; children: Carey Allen, Reginald Jarrett, Ryan Lee. AB cum laude with distinction in all subjects, Cornell U., 1973, MA, 1976, PhD, 1978. Postdoctoral fellow Cornell U., Ithaca, NY, 1978; rsch. assoc. Rockefeller U., NYC, 1978-80; Zeev Nehari rsch. asst. prof. Carnegie-Mellon U., Pitts., 1980-83, vis. asst. prof., 1983-84; asst. prof. math. U. Pitts., Pitts., 1984-85, assoc. prof., 1985-90, prof., 1990—, group leader applied math., 1988-90. Mem. bd. advisers Internat. Found. for Rsch. in Exptl. Econ., 2002-. Editor Jour. Psychology and Fin. Markets, 2000-02, Jour. Behavioral Fin., 2003-04; mem. editl. bd. Applied Math. Fin., Internat. Jour. Computation and Math., Selcuk Jour. Applied Math.; contbr. articles to profl. jours. and papers in field. Fellow, Cornell U., 1973; grantee, NSF, 1980—2000; scholar, Fred Maytag Family Found., 2001. Mem. Am. Math. Soc., Am. Phys. Soc., Soc. for Indsl. and Applied Math., Econ. Sci. Assn., Phi Beta Kappa. achievements include proof of theorems on existence and properties of surface free energy; studied connections between statis. mechanics and quantum field theory; developed phase field methods for studying free boundary problems; rsch. on applying renormalization group methods to differential equations; analyzed experimental econ. using differential equations and time series; established that price patterns in finan. markets have predictive value. Office: U Pitts Dept Math Pittsburgh PA 15260 E-mail: caginalp@pitt.edu.

CAGLE, CASEY, lieutenant governor; b. Hall County, Ga., Jan. 12, 1966; m. Nita Cagle; children: Jared, Grant, Carter. Attended, Gainesvill Coll., Ga. Southern U. Senator Ga. State Senate, 1994—2006; pres. Casey Cagle Properties; lt. gov. State of Ga., 2007—. Mem. higher edn. com., appropriations com., corrections, correctional instns. and property com., sec. sci. and tech. industry com., chmn. senate rep. caucus Ga. State Senate. Ga. rep. environment com. Nat. Conf. State Legislatures. Republican. Office: Lieutenant Governor 240 State Capitol Atlanta GA 30334 Office Phone: 404-656-5030. Office Fax: 404-656-6739.*

CAGLE, MELINDA REEVES, editor; d. Harry Tillman Reeves and Lillie Mae Dunn; m. Carrol Dean Cagle, June 2, 1968; children: Jeffrey, Thomas, Andrew, David, Sarah, Caroline, Anne, John. Student, Tex. Tech. U., 1967—68; BFA, U. Houston, 1975; postgrad., No. Ill. U., 1976—77. Mem. history coun. Bapt. Gen. Conv. Tex., Dallas, 2003—05. Editor: (history jour.) The Herald, 2003—. Historian, ch. coun. First Bapt. Ch., Woodlands, Tex., 1998—. Mem.: Jr. League Houston, Inc. (chmn. The Goldfarb Project 1988—90), Montgomery County Geneal. and Hist. Soc. (bd. dirs. 2000—, Vol. of Yr. 2003, Hall of Fame 2006). Avocations: piano, painting, genealogy, writing. Home: 18 W Shaker Ct The Woodlands TX 77380

CAGLE, ROGER E., physician; b. Jan. 2, 1953; BS in Zoology, Ark. State U., Jonesboro, 1974; MD, U. Ark., Little Rock, 1978. Cert. Am. Bd. Family Medicine. Ptnr. Paragould Doctor's Clinic, Ark., 1981—2000, physician, 1981—2000; owner CR Doc PLLC, Paragould, Ark., 2003—06.

CAGLE, WILLIAM REA, retired librarian; b. Hollywood, Calif., Nov. 15, 1933; s. Howard Clinton and Eunice (Colcord Althouse) C.; m. Terry Lucinda Conrad, Jan. 17, 1975; children by previous marriage: Michael Stewart, Chantal Gabrielle, Mark Christopher, Monique Antoinette. AB in English, UCLA, 1956, MLS, 1962; postgrad., Oxford U., 1959—60. Asst. to libr. Henry E. Huntington Libr. and Art Gallery, San Marino, Calif., 1960—62; libr. for English Ind. U., Bloomington, 1962—67, asst. Lilly libr., 1967—75, acting Lilly libr., 1975—77, Lilly libr., 1977—97; ret., 1997. Dir.'s acad. adv. com. Harry Ransom Humanities Rsch. Ctr. U. Tex.; mem. adv. bd. U. S.C. Ctr. for Lit. Biography; adv. bd. Maine Women Writers Collection U. New Eng. Author: A Matter of Taste, 1990, revised and enlarged, 1999, Two Hundred and Fifty Years of the British Novel: 1740-1989, 1990, American Books on Food and Drink, 1998, 150 Years of the American Short Story, 1998, Lit Check: The Center for Literary Biography Online Checklist, University of South Carolina, www.cla.sc.edu/engl/litcheck.html; contbr. to Printing and the Mind of Man, 1967; editor Ind. U. Bookman, 1966-89; mem. adv. bd. Dictionary Lit. Biography. Cambridge edit. Joseph Conrad, Bibliography of United States Literature, Chadwyck-Healey American Poetry Full-Text Database; mem. editl. bd. Pitts. Series in Bibliography; contbr. articles to profl. jours. Trustee Carver Meml. Libr., Searsport, Maine, Camden Pub. Libr.; mem. collection adv. bd. Kinsey Inst. Sex, Gender and Reprodn. With US Army, 1956—59. Mem.: Assn. Internat. de Bibliophilie, Benjamin Franklin Guild (bd. govs.), Baxter Soc., Lincoln Soc., Caxton Club (Chgo.), Grolier Club (N.Y.C.), Century Club. Home: 65 Blvd Malesherbes 75008 Paris France Personal E-mail: cagletlc@yahoo.com.

CAGLE, YVONNE DARLENE, astronaut; b. West Point, NY, Apr. 24, 1959; BA in Biochemistry, San Francisco State U., 1981; PhD in Medicine, U. Wash., 1985. Cert. ACLS instr.; flight surgeon. Intern Highland Gen. Hosp., Oakland, Calif., 1985; resident in family practice Ghent FP Ea. Va. Med. Sch., 1992; dep. project mgr. Kelsey-Seybold Clinics NASA-JSC Occupl. Health Clinic, 1994—96; tech. astronaut office ops. planning br. NASA Johnson Space Ctr., 1996—. Clin. asst. prof. U. Tex., Galveston; cons. in field. Active Boys and Girls Club Am.; vol. family practice clinical faculty U. Calif., Davis; active Third Bapt. Ch. With USAF. Named one of Outstanding Young Women of Am.; recipient Disting. Scientist award, Nat. Tech. Assn., Commendation award, Marin County Bd. Supr., Novato Sch. Bd. Mem.: Aerospace Med. Assn., Am. Acad. Family Physicians. Avocations: jigsaw puzzles, juggling, skating, hiking, music. Office: NASA Johnson Space Ctr Mailcode JA Houston TX 77058

CAGLEY, SUSAN A., history professor; b. New Castle, Ind., July 21, 1962; d. D. Michael and R. Dorothy Cagley. BS in Music Edn., Bob Jones U., Greenville, SC, 1984; MA in History, U. Ctrl. Ark., Conway, 1993. Music tchr. Heritage Christian Sch., Canton, Ohio, 1984—86; social studies tchr. Ark. Bapt. HS, Little Rock, 1987—2000; assoc. prof. Bapt. Bible Coll., Clarks Summit, Pa., 2000—. Pianist Parker Hill Cmty. Ch., Clarks Summit; harpist Serenity, Clarks Summit, 2001—; pianist Interludes, Scranton, Pa., 2001—; tutor Masonic Learning Ctr. Children, Scranton, 2006—. Mem.: Nat. Coun. Social Studies, Christian Educators Assn. Internat. (assoc.). Avocations: needlework, reading, music, walking. Office: Baptist Bible Coll 538 Venard Rd Clarks Summit PA 18411

CAGLIUSO, NICHOLAS VINCENT, SR., public health service officer; b. 1974; BS cum laude, John Jay Coll., NYC; MPH, NY Med. Coll., Valhalla, NY; PhD candidate, Milano New Sch. Mgmt. & Urban Policy, NYC. EMT, Bklyn., 1992; rsch. asst. to med. dir. Fire Dept. NY, 1997—2001; with Port Authority NY/NJ, 2001—05, emergency pregaredness analyst, Office of Emergency Mgmt., mgr. exec. policy & analysis, Aviation Dir.'s Office; coord. emergency preparedness NY-Presbyn. Healthcare Sys. Mem. editl. bd. Jour. Homeland Security & Emergency Mgmt.; adj. asst. prof. MPA in Emergency & Disaster Mgmt. Program, Met. Coll. NY. Contbr. chapters to books, articles. Named one of 40 Under 40, Crain's NY Bus., 2007. Mem.: Am. Coll. Healthcare Execs. Office: NY-Presbyn Healthcare System 525 E 68th St New York NY 10021 Office Phone: 212-746-4036.*

CAGNEY, LAWRENCE K., lawyer; b. Feb. 2, 1957; AB, Fordham U., 1978; JD, Gerogetown U., 1981. Bar: NY 1982. Asst. counsel Warner Lambert, 1985—86; assoc. Milbank, Tweed, Hadley & McCloy, 1981—84, Debevoise & Plimpton LLP, NYC, 1986—90, ptnr., 1990—, chair Exec. Compensation and Employee Benefits Practice Groups. Mem.: ABA, Assn. Bar of City NY. Office: Debevoise & Plimpton LLP 919 Third Ave New York NY 10022 Office Phone: 212-909-6909. Office Fax: 212-909-6836. E-mail: lkcagney@debevoise.com.

CAGNEY, WILLIAM ROBERT, psychologist; b. Pitts., Oct. 7, 1937; s. Edward Patrick and Pearl Barbara (Sebastian) C.; m. Vivian Antoinette Tartaglia, June 26, 1965; children: Lori Anne, Julie Alissa, Melissa Beth. BS, Duquesne U., 1960, MA, 1965, PhD, 1968. Lic. psychologist, Pa.; cert. Nat. Register Health Svcs.; cert. profl. qualification in psychology Assn. State and Provincial Psychology Bds.; diplomate in clin. hypnotherapy NBCCH, Nat. Bd. cert. clin. Hypnotherapists. Psychology intern, staff psychologist Dixmont State Hosp., Glenfield, Pa., 1962-68; staff psychologist South Hills Child Guidance Ctr., Pitts., 1968-69; asst. dir., psychol. svcs. Woodville State Hosp., Carnegie, Pa., 1968-70; chief psychologist Counseling Ctr. of South Hills, Pitts., 1970-72; clin. dir. Chartiers MH/MR Ctr., Bridgeville, Pa., 1972-79; pvt. practice Pitts., 1971—. Cons. Outreach South, Mt. Lebanon, Pa., 1976-2004, South Hills Interfaith Ministries, Bethel Park, Pa., 1969-2003, Crisis Addiction Recovery Edn., Inc., Washington, Pa., 1984-88, YMCA South Hills, Pitts., 1977-78; field supr. dept. psychology U. Pitts., 1970-73, W.Va. U., Morgantown, 1973-78; resident psychologist Sta. KDKA-TV Pitts. Today, 1978-79; presenter seminars and workshops to profl. and cmty. groups, 1972—. Cons. Twp. Upper St. Clair Adminstrn., Police, Schs., Family Resource Program, Upper St. Clair, Pa., 1986-89. Fellow Pa. Psychol. Assn.; mem. APA, Greater Pitts. Psychol. Assn., Am. Group Therapy Assn. Avocations: exercise, art, music. Office: 1725 Washington Rd Ste 509 Pittsburgh PA 15241-1207 Home Phone: 412-833-6645; Office Phone: 412-833-9250. Business E-Mail: cagsfive@aol.com.

CAGUIAT, CARLOS JOSE, health facility administrator, priest; b. NYC, Jan. 23, 1937; s. Carlos C. and Carmen C.; m. Julianna Skomsky, Aug. 29, 1958; children: Stephen D., Jonathan J., Sarah E. Caguiat Borthwick. BA, CCNY, 1958; MDiv, Gen. Theol. Sem., 1965; MPA, NYU, 1976. Ordained priest Episcopal Ch., 1965. Curate St. Christopher Chapel, NYC, 1965—68; vicar St. Christopher's Chapel, NYC, 1968—71; exec. dir. project for human comm. Episcopal Diocese of N.Y., NYC, 1971-73; project mgr. ambulatory care/cmty. rels. N.Y.C. Health and Hosps. Corp., 1973-76, regional coord. for adminstrn./ops., 1975-76; assoc. dir. adminstrn./ops. Morrisania Neighborhood Family Care Ctr., Bronx, NY, 1976-78, adminstr., 1978-81; adminstrv. dir. Clin. Ctr., Mich. State U., East Lansing, 1981-90; regional v.p. St. Francis Acad., Lake Placid, NY, 1990—2002, strategic planning and ventures v.p. Saranac Lake, NY, 1999—2002. Chair decentralized unit of several parishes, N.Y.C.; mem. Diocese of N.Y. Pension Bd., Ecumenical Commn., Budget Com., 1967-81; vice chair North Country Behavioral Health Devel. Corp., 1997-98, chair, 1999-2002. Chair Two Bridges Settlement Housing Corp.; bd. dirs. Settlement Housing Fund., 1969-73; pres. Mid-Mich. South Health Sys. Agy., 1985-88; bd. trustees Adirondack Med. Ctr., 2004—. Infantry and Intelligence Officer, U.S. Army, St. Francis Acad., 2002— Fellow Am. Coll. Health Care Execs., Lake Placid Rotary (bd. dirs., v.p., 2002, pres. 2003-04, sec. 2004—), Lakeside House (bd. dirs. 2003—) Home: 20 Oakwood Rd Saranac Lake NY 12983 Home Phone: 518-891-5810. Business E-Mail: carlosc@capital.net.

CAHILL, CATHERINE FRANCES, environmental scientist, educator; b. Woodland, Calif., July 30, 1968; d. Thomas Andrew and Virginia Arnoldy Cahill. BS in Applied Physics, U. Calif., 1990; MS in Atmospheric Scis., U. Wash., 1994; PhD in Atmospheric Scis., U. Nev., 1996. Fulbright fellow Univ. Coll. Galway, Ireland, 1996—97; vis. asst. rsch. prof. Desert Rsch. Inst., Reno, 1997—98; prof. U. Alaska, Fairbanks, 1998—. Program chair for atmospheric sci. program U. Alaska Fairbanks, Alaska, 2000—01. Contbr. articles pub. to profl. jour. Mem. U.S. China Polar Sci. Panel. Fellow Fulbright Fellowship, Coun. for the Internat. Exch. of Students, 1996-1997. Mem.: Am. Assn. Aerosol Rsch., Am. Geophys. Union, Am. Chem. Soc. (chair alaska sect. 2000—01), Sigma Pi Sigma, Sigma Xi. Democrat-Npl. Achievements include research in long-range transport of aerosols to the Arctic. Avocations: travel, reading. Office: Univ Alaska Fairbanks 900 Yukon Dr Rm 182 Fairbanks AK 99775 Home Phone: 907-488-5512; Office Phone: 907-474-6905. Office Fax: 907-474-5640. Business E-Mail: ffcfc@uaf.edu.

CAHILL, CHARLES L., retired academic administrator, chemistry professor; b. El Reno, Okla., Feb. 23, 1933; m. Dorotha Ann Cleek, Feb. 14, 1954; children: Steven Charles, Terri Ann, Susan Beth. AB in Chemistry, Okla. Bapt. U., 1955; MS in Biochemistry, U. Okla., 1957, PhD in Biochemistry, 1961. Rsch. asst., biochemist Vets. Hosp., Sch. Medicine, U. Okla., Oklahoma City, 1955-57; NIH predoctoral fellow Sch. Medicine, U. Okla., Oklahoma City, 1957-60; clin. chemist med. arts labs. Oklahoma City U., 1960-61, asst. prof. chemistry, 1961-63, asst. prof., chmn. dept., 1963-67, assoc. prof., chmn. dept., assoc. dean Coll. Arts and Sci., 1967-69, prof. chemistry, assoc. dean, dir. rsch., 1970-71; vice chancellor for acad. affairs U. N.C., Wilmington, 1971—92, provost, vice chancellor acad. affairs, 1992-2000, prof. emeritus, 2000—; ret. Mem. Rotary. Avocations: bass fishing, hunting, golf.

CAHILL, GEORGE FRANCIS, JR., physician, educator; b. NYC, July 7, 1927; s. George Francis and Eva Marion (Wagner) C.; m. Sarah Townsend duPont, Dec. 20, 1949; children: Colleen Cahill Remley, Peter duPont, George Francis III, Sarah Rhett Cahill Zuckerman, Eva Wagner Cahill Georgaklis, Elizabeth Anglin Cahill Tiedemann. BS, Yale, 1949; MD, Columbia U., 1953; MA, Harvard U., 1966. Intern Peter Bent Brigham Hosp., Boston, 1953-54, resident, 1954-55, 57-58; rsch. fellow biol. chemistry Harvard U. Med. Sch., 1955-57; assoc. in medicine Peter Bent Brigham Hosp., 1962-65; practice medicine specializing in metabolism Boston, 1965-78; sr. physician Peter Bent Brigham Hosp., 1983—94; prof. medicine Harvard U., 1970-90, prof. emeritus, 1990—; prof. biol. scis. Darmouth Coll., Hanover, NH, 1990—97. Prin. cons. endocrinology, metabolism VA, 1972-75; investigator Howard Hughes Med. Inst., 1962-68, dir. rsch., 1978-85, v.p. sci. edn. and devel., 1985-89, sr. scientist, 1989-90, cons., 1991-1994; mem. rsch. tng. coms. NIH. Contbr. articles to profl. jours. Chmn. bd. dir. Greenwall Found., 1992-96; v.p. trustees Hotchkiss Sch., 1992-97; overseer Dartmouth Med. Sch. and the Everett C. Koop Inst., 1990-95. With USNR, 1945-47. Recipient Banting medal U.S., 1971, Banting medal Eng., 1974, J.P. Hoet award Belgium, 1973, Gairdner Internat. award Can., 1979. Fellow AAAS, Am. Acad. Arts and Scis.; mem. Am. Diabetes Assn. (pres. 1975, Lilly award 1965), Endocrine Soc. (Oppenheimer award 1963), Nat. Commn. on Diabetes, Am. Soc. Clin. Investigation, Assn. Am. Physicians, Am. Clin. Climatol. Assn., Am. Physiol. Soc. Home: PO Box 367 Stoddard NH 03464 E-mail: gcahill1@cheshire.net.

CAHILL, HARRY AMORY, diplomat, educator; b. NYC, Jan. 10, 1930; s. Harry Amory and Elaine Olga (Loumena) C.; m. Angelica Margarita Ravazzoli, Dec. 12, 1956; children— Alan, Daniel, Sylvia, Irene, Madeleine, Steven BA, Manhattan Coll., NYC, 1951; postgrad., Johns Hopkins U., 1964-65; MS, George Washington U., Washington, 1972. Sales exec. Johns Manville Corp., NY, 1954-56; fgn. service officer U.S. Dept. of State, Washington, 1956-59, Oslo, 1959-61, Warsaw, 1961-64, Belgrade, Yugoslavia, 1965-68, Montevideo, Uruguay, 1968-71, Lagos, Nigeria, 1975-78, Colombo, Sri Lanka, 1979-81; dir. comml. service U.S. Dept. Commerce, 1982-83; U.S. consul gen. Dept. of State, Bombay, 1983-87; U.S. Mission to UN, dep. U.S. rep. UN Econ. and Social Coun., NYC, 1987-89; pres. Amory Assoc., Inc., McLean, Va., 1990—, World of Film Found., NYC. Prof. Pepperdine U., 1992—, Georgetown U., 1995; cons. U.S. Dept. State, 1991—, U.S. Dept. Def., 1999—. Author: The China Trade and U.S. Tariffs, 1973. Pres. Hinduja Found., NYC, 1993—2002. Woodrow Wilson Nat. Fellowship found. fellow, 1990-93. Mem. Am. Fgn. Svc. Assn. Roman Catholic. Avocation: photography. Office: 1240 Daleview Dr Mc Lean VA 22102-1539

CAHILL, JOHN DONALD, emergency medicine physician, educator; b. NYC, May 17, 1967; s. John Donald and Elizabeth Anne Cahill; m. Rachel Whelan Kelly; 1 child, John. BA, Cath. U. Am., DC, 1985—89; MD, Mt. Sinai Sch. Medicine, NYC, 1996. Diplomate Am. Bd. Emergency Medicine, 2001. Attending physician RI Hosp., Providence, 2000—03, St. Luke's Roosevelt Hosp. Ctr., NYC, 2003—; exec. dir. Ctr. Global Collaboration & Health Initiatives, NYC, 2006—. Vis. lectr. Royal Coll. Surgeons, Dublin, 2000—; asst. prof. Brown U., Providence, 2000—, Columbia U., NYC, 2003—; cons. Glaxo Smith Kline, Phila., 2001. Author: (textbook) Handbook of Bioterrorism & Disaster Medicine. Med. advisor Global Pediatric Alliance, Calif., 2003—. Fellow: Royal Soc. Tropical Medicine & Hygiene, Am. Coll. Chest Physicians. Office: St Luke's Roosevelt Hosp Ctr 425 W 59th St Ste 8A New York NY 10019 Home Phone: 646-785-6441. Office Fax: 212-492-5505; Home Fax: 212-492-5505.

CAHILL, KIMBERLY M., lawyer; d. Florence Schoenherr-Warnez. BA, U. Mich., 1982, JD, 1985. Ptnr. Schoenherr Cahill and Warnez; pres. Schoenherr Developments Inc. Named Alexander Macomb Citizen of Yr., 1998. Mem.: Women Lawyers Assn. Mich. (pres. Macomb region 1989, pres. 1996), Macomb County Bar Found. (past pres.), Macomb County Bar Assn. (pres. 2001—02), Mich. State Bar Found. (bd. dirs.), State Bar Mich. (pres. 2006—07, chair Access to Justice campaign com.). Office: Schoenherr & Cahill PC 24735 Van Dyke Ave Center Line MI 48015 Office Phone: 586-757-0733. Office Fax: 586-757-2968.

CAHILL, LAWRENCE R., lawyer; b. Syracuse, NY, Apr. 17, 1947; BA, U. Rochester, 1969; JD, U. Chgo., 1972. Bar: Ill. 1973, Mass. 1977. Comml. real estate develop., Chgo.; atty. Goodwin, Procter & Hoar, Boston; ptnr., real estate group Goodwin Procter LLP, Boston, mem. diversity com.; chair, hiring ptnr. legal hiring com. Address: Goodwin Proctor LLP Exchange Pl 53 State St Boston MA 02109-2803 Office Phone: 617-570-1411. Office Fax: 617-523-1231. Business E-Mail: lcahill@goodwinprocter.com.

CAHILL, RICHARD FREDERICK, lawyer; b. Columbus, Nebr., June 18, 1953; s. Donald Francis and Hazel Fredeline (Garbers) C.; m. Helen Marie Girard, Dec. 4, 1982; children: Jacqueline Michelle, Catherine Elizabeth, Marc Alexander. Student, Worcester Coll., Oxford, 1973; BA with highest honors, UCLA, 1975; JD, U. Notre Dame, 1978. Bar: Calif. 1978, U.S. Dist. Ct. (ea. dist.) Calif. 1978, U.S. Dist. Ct. (cen. dist.) Calif. 1983, U.S. Dist. Ct. (so. dist.) Calif. 1992, U.S. Dist. Ct. (no. dist.) Calif. 2002, U.S. Ct. Appeals (9th cir.) 1992. Dep. dist. atty. Tulare County Dist. Atty., Visalia, Calif., 1978-81; staff atty. Supreme Ct. of Nev., Carson City, 1981-83; assoc. Acret & Perochet, Brentwood, Calif., 1983-84, Thelen, Marrin, Johnson & Bridges, LA, 1984-89; ptnr. Hammond Zuetel & Cahill, Pasadena, Calif., 1989-98, Pivo, Halbreich, Cahill & Yim, Irvine, Calif., 1999—2002; mng. sr. counsel Tenet Health Sys., Santa Ana, Calif., 2002—06; asst. v.p. The Doctors Co., Napa, Calif., 2007—. Mem. Pasadena Bar Assn., Los Angeles County Bar Assn., Assn. So. Calif. Defense Counsel, Notre Dame Legal Aid and Defender Assn. (assoc. dir.), Am. Health Lawyers Assn., Phi Beta Kappa, Phi Alpha Delta (charter, v.p. 1977-78), Pi Gamma Mu, Phi Alpha Theta (charter pres. 1973-74), Phi Eta Sigma, Sigma Chi. Republican. Roman Catholic. Avocation: tennis. Home: 201 Windwood Ln Sierra Madre CA 91024-2677 Office: The Doctors Co Law Dept 185 Greenwood Rd Napa CA 94558 Home Phone: 636-355-2721; Office Phone: 707-226-0360. Business E-Mail: ndlawyer78@aol.com.

CAHILL, THOMAS ANDREW, physicist, researcher; b. Paterson, NJ, Mar. 4, 1937; s. Thomas Vincent and Margery (Groesbeck) C.; m. Virginia Ann Arnoldy, June 26, 1965; children: Catherine Frances, Thomas Michael. BA, Holy Cross Coll., Worcester, Mass., 1959; PhD in Physics; NDEA fellow, UCLA, 1965. Asst. prof. in residence UCLA, 1965-66; NATO fellow, rsch. physicist Centre d'Etudes Nucleaires de Saclay, France, 1966-67; prof. physics U. Calif., Davis, 1967-94; acting dir. Crocker Nuc. Lab., 1972, dir., 1980—89. Dir. Inst. Ecology, 1972-75; cons.

NRC of Can., Louvre Mus. UN Global Atmospheric Watch, 1990—; mem. Internat. Com. on PIXE and Its Application, Calif. Atty. Gen., Nat. Audubon Soc., Mono Lake Com. Author: (with J. McCray) Electronic Circuit Analysis for Scientists, 1973; editor Internat. Jour. Pixe, 1989—; contbr. articles to profl. jours. on physics, applied physics, hist. analyses and air pollution. Prin. investigator IMPROVE Nat. Air Pollution Network., 1987-97; co-dir. Crocker Hist. and Archeol. Projects; head U. Calif. Delta Group, Davis, 1997-. OAS fellow, 1968, Japanese Nat. Rsch. fellow, Kyoto, 1992. Mem. Am. Phys. Soc., Air Pollution Control Assn., Am. Assn. Aerosol Rsch., Sigma Xi Democrat. Roman Catholic. Home: 1813 Amador Ave Davis CA 95616-3104 Office: U Calif Dept Physics One Shields Ave Davis CA 95616 Office Phone: 530-752-4674. Business E-Mail: tacahill@ucdavis.edu.

CAHILL, TIMOTHY P., state official; b. Norwood, Mass., Dec. 1, 1958; m. Tina Cahill; 4 children. BA, Boston Univ., 1981. Author; small bus. owner; treas. Norfolk County, 1997—2003; state treas., receiver gen. State of Mass., 2002—. City coun. Quincy City Coun., 1987—2003. Bd. overseers YMCA Greater Boston. Grantee Eisenhower Fellowship, 2007. Democrat. Cath. Office: State Treas State House Rm 227 Boston MA 02133 Office Phone: 617-367-6900.*

CAHIR, JOHN JOSEPH, meteorologist, educator, educational administrator; b. Scituate, Mass., Oct. 8, 1933; s. Jeremiah Francis and Mary Eleanor (Duggan) C.; m. Mary Anne Louise Schrott, Dec. 1, 1962; children: Ellen, William, Kathryn, Barton. BS in Meteorology, Pa. State U., 1961, PhD, 1971. Meteorologist trainee, meteorologist U.S. Weather Bur., 1956-64; from instr. to assoc. prof. meteorology Pa. State U., University Park, 1965—79, prof., 1980—2002, prof. emeritus, 2002—; assoc. dean Coll. Earth and Mineral Scis., Pa. State U., University Park, 1980-93; vice provost, dean for undergrad. edn. Pa. State U., University Park, 1993—2002. G.J. Haltiner rsch. chair in meteorology US Naval Postgrad. Sch., Monterey, Calif., 1983-84; vis. prof. St. Augustine's Coll., Va. State Coll.; cons. in field; mem. Commn. Atmospheric Scis., World Meteorol. Orgn. (UN), 1986-97, alt. prin. U.S. del. to 9th session, Sofia, Bulgaria, 1986, del. to 10th session, Offenbach, Fed. Republic Germany, 1990, 11th session, Geneva, 1994; com. on info. sys. for ports and harbors Marine Bd., NRC, 1985; Earth Sci. Adv. com. U. Space Rsch. Assn., 1987-93, convenor, 1992-93; olicy adv. com. Coop. Program for Meteorol. Edn. and Tng., U. Corp. Atmospheric Rsch., 1988-92, chair, 1996-99, adv. panel, 1996-00, vis. scientist, 2003—; instnl. mem. The Coll. Bd., 1993-02; planning com. Boro State Coll., 2003-07, chair, 20006-07. Co-author: Principles of Climatology, 1969, The Atmosphere, 1975, 78 81; editor: Monthly Weather Rev., 1977-80; contbr. articles to profl. jours. Bd. dirs. Pa. Coll. Tech., Williamsport, 1994—, Standards for Success, Washington, 2001-02. Served with USN, 1958-60. Recipient McKay Donkin award Pa. State U., 2003; Nat. Ctr. Atmospheric Rsch. fellow 1974. Fellow Am. Meteorol. Soc. (chmn. com. on weather forecasting and analysis 1979-80, seal of approval for TV weathercasting, nat. councillor 1986-89, chmn. com. on undergrad. awards 1986, nominating com. 1990-91, chmn. 1991, investment com. 1997—, chair 1999—); mem. Royal Meteorol. Soc., Am. Geophys. Union, Nat. Weather Assn. (pres. 1981-82, Svc. award 1979), Am. Assn. Univs. (task force on Undergrad. Edn. 1999-02). Office: 617 Walker Bldg University Park PA 16802-1505 Business E-Mail: jjc2@psu.edu.

CAHN, JAMES, lawyer, educator; b. Cleve., Apr. 16, 1946; s. Sherman D. and Barbara Cahn; m. Jean A. Johnson, May 20, 1978; children: Rachel, Lucy. BA, U. Pa., 1968; JD, Ohio State U., 1973; 7th Degree Black Belt, Oriental Martial Arts Coll., 2003. Bar: Ohio 1973. Assoc. Calfee, Halter & Griswold, Cleve., 1973-75; pvt. practice Cleve., 1975-77; ptnr. Hermann, Cahn & Schneider, Cleve., 1977—. Instr., Master Oriental Martial Arts Coll., Cleve. and Columbus, Ohio, 1975—; legal ounsel U.S. Taekwondo Union, Colorado Springs, Colo., 1977-81, 85-86; lectr. Ohio Jud. Coll., others. Founding mem. Ctr. for Principled Family Advocacy, pres., 2002. Named Ohio Superlawyer; named one of Best Lawyers in Am., 1992—. Fellow Am. Acad. Matrimonial Lawyers (pres. Ohio chpt. 1997-98, mem. arbitration com., bd. govs.); mem. ABA, Ohio State Bar Assn., Cuyahoga County Bar Assn. (chair family law sect. 1990-91), Cleve. Bar Assn. (family law sect.), US Taekwondo Aliance (officer), Beechmont Country Club. Office: Hermann Cahn & Schneider 1301 E 9th St Ste 500 Cleveland OH 44114-1876 Office Phone: 216-781-5515.

CAHN, JEFFREY BARTON, lawyer; b. NYC, Jan. 1, 1943; s. Harold Leon and Vivian (Loewy) C.; m. Miriam Epstein, Jan. 22, 1965; children: Lauren Samantha, Vanessa Shari. BA, Ind. U., 1964; JD, Rutgers U., 1967. Bar: N.J. 1967, U.S. Dist. Ct. N.J. 1967, U.S. Ct. Appeals (3d cir.) 1971, U.S. Supreme Ct. 1971, U.S. Tax Ct. 1973, U.S. Ct. Appeals (D.C. cir.), 1979, N.Y. 1980, U.S. Ct. Appeals (9th cir.) 1981, U.S. Claims Ct. 1981, U.S. Dist. Ct. (so. dist.) N.Y. 1992, U.S. Dist. Ct. (ea. dist.) N.Y. 1994, U.S. Ct. Appeals (2nd cir.) 1998. Law clk. to sr. presiding judge Appellate Div. N.J. Superior Ct., Trenton, NJ, 1967-68; assoc. Schapira, Steiner & Walder, Newark, 1968-72; ptnr. Sills, Cummis, Radin, Tischman, Epstein & Gross, Newark, 1972—. Author: (with others) New Jersey Transaction Guide, Vol. 12, 1993, The Use of Another's Trademark: A Review of the Law in The United States, Canada, and Western Europe, 1997; co-author, editor: Trademark Law Basics Coursebook, 2001; rsch. editor: Rutgers Law Rev., 1966-67; prin. editor Trademark Administration, 3d edit., 2006; contbr. articles to profl. jours. Mem. ATLA, ABA, N.J. State Bar Assn., Essex County Bar Assn., Internat. Trademark Assn. (projects editl. bd. 2001-, publs. bd. 2006), N.Y. State Bar Assn. (sect. intellectual property, chair copyright law com.), Am. Intellectual Property Law Assn., N.J. Intellectual Property Law Assn., Phi Delta Phi (Outstanding Grad. 1967). Jewish. Home: 72 Winged Foot Dr Livingston NJ 07039-8229 Office: Sills Cummis Epstein & Gross Legal Ctr 1 Riverfront Plz Fl 13 Newark NJ 07102-5401 Home Phone: 973-994-3055; Office Phone: 973-643-5858. Business E-Mail: jcahn@sillscummis.com.

CAHN, JOHN WERNER, metallurgist, educator; b. Germany, Jan. 9, 1928; arrived in U.S., 1939, naturalized, 1945; s. Felix H. and Lucie (Schwarz) C.; m. Anne Hessing, Aug. 20, 1950; children: Martin Charles, Andrew, Lorie Selma. BS, U. Mich., 1949; PhD, U. Calif., Berkeley, 1953; DSc (hon.), Northwestern U., 1990, U. d'Evry, France, 1996. Instr. U. Chgo., 1952-54; with rsch. lab. GE, 1954-64; prof. metallurgy MIT, 1964-78; ctr. scientist Nat. Inst. Stds. and Tech. (formerly Nat. Bur. Stds.), 1978—84, sr. fellow, 1984—2006, emeritus, 2006. Vis. prof. Isreli Inst. Tech., Haifa, 1971—72, 1980; cons. in field, 1986—; chmn. Gordon Conf. Phys. Metallurgy, 1964; affil. prof. physics and astronomy U. Wash., Seattle, 1984—; rsch. fellow Japan Soc. Promotion of Sci., 1981—82. Research and articles on surfaces and interfaces, thermodynamics, phase changes, quasicrystals. Recipient Dickson prize, Carnegie Mellon U., 1981, Gold medal, U.S. Dept. Commerce, 1982, Von Hippel award, Materials Rsch. Soc., 1985, Stratton award, Nat. Bur. Stds., 1986, Michelson-Morley prize, Case Western Res. U., 1991, William Hume-Rothery award, Minerals, Metals and Materials Soc., 1993, Harvey prize, Israel Inst. Tech., 1995, Nat. Medal of Sci., 1998, Bakhuis-Roozeboom medal, Netherlands Acad. Sci., 1999, Heyn medal, German Materials Soc., 2001, Bower award in Sci., Franklin Inst., 2002; fellow Guggenheim Found., 1960. Fellow: Am. Soc. Metals Internat. (Saveur award 1989), Am. Inst. Metallurg. Engrs., Am. Acad. Arts and Scis.; mem.: Japan Inst. Metals (gold medal 1994), Am. Ceramics Soc. (hon.), Indian Materials Rsch. Soc. (hon.), French Soc. for Metals and Materials (hon. medal 2005), NAE, NAS. Office: Univ Wash Dept Physics and Astronomy Seattle WA 98195-1580

CAHN, RICHARD CALEB, lawyer; b. Bklyn., June 11, 1932; s. Irving and Pearl (Abel) Cahn; m. Vivian Isabel Meksin, Dec. 24, 1961; children: Michael, Lisa, Daniel, Sara. AB, Dartmouth Coll., Hanover, NH, 1953; LLB, Yale U., New Haven, Conn., 1956, U. London, 1959. Bar: N.Y. 1956, Fla. 1966, U.S. Supreme Ct. 1960. Student asst. US Atty. So. Dist. NY, NYC, 1955; atty. US Dept. Justice, Washington, 1956—57; ptnr. Cahn & Cahn, LLP, Melville, NY, 1957—65; prin. asst. dist. atty. Suffolk County, NY, 1965—66; dep. atty. Town of Huntington, NY, 1966—68; spl. counsel Towns of Islip, Brookhaven, Babylon, Southampton, NY, 1967—68, 2005—, Amityville Sch. Dist., 1978—79, Village of North Hills, 1978—79, Huntington, NY, 1981—92, Towns East Hampton and Southampton, NY, 1997—, Merrick Pub. Libr., Smithtown, NY, 2005, Village of Sag Harbor, 2005; counsel Brentwood Sch. Dist., 1977—82, 1986—90, Syosset Sch. Dist., 2005—06. Adj. prof. Touro Coll., 1987—90, 1993—; hearing officer NY State Edn. Dept., Nassau and Suffolk Counties, 1971—77; spl. dist. atty. Suffolk County, 1972; participant World Peace Through Law Conf., 1967, Malpractice Mediation Panel, 2d dept., 1974—84, Gov.'s Jud. Nominating Com. 2d edpt., 1975—81; screening com. bankruptcy judges US Dist. Ct. (ea. dist.) N.Y., 1976—81; screening com. US Magistrate Judges, 1977—81, 2003—; regional counsel SUNY, Stony Brook, 1972—90; editl. bd. Yale Law Jour., 1954. Contbr. articles to profl. jours. Del. Moscow Conf. on Law and Jurisprudence, 1990; trustee Adelphi U., 1977—; bd. dirs. Stony Brook Found., 1974—86, Ea. Dist. Civil Litigation Fund, 1982—86. Fellow, Soc. Values in Higher Edn., 1984—96. Mem.: ABA, Fed. Bar Coun. (v.p. 1982—84, trustee 1984—89), Am. Judicature Soc., Fed. Bar Assn., Suffolk County Bar Assn. (pres. 1981—82), N.Y. Bar Assn. (ho. of dels. 1981—83, chmn. condemnation, zoning and property use com. 1989—90). Office: 445 Broadhollow Rd Ste 332 Melville NY 11747 Office Phone: 631-752-1600. Personal E-mail: rccahn@gmail.com. Business E-Mail: rcahn@cahnlaw.com.

CAHN, STEVEN MARK, philosopher, educator; b. Springfield, Mass., Aug. 6, 1942; s. Judah and Evelyn (Baum) C.; m. Marilyn (Ross), May 4, 1974. AB, Columbia U., 1963, PhD, 1966. Vis. instr. Dartmouth Coll., 1966; vis. prof. U. Rochester, NY, 1967; asst. prof. philosophy Vassar Coll., Poughkeepsie, NY, 1966-68, NYU, NYC, 1968-71, assoc. prof., 1971-73, dir. grad. studies, 1972, dir. under grad. studies, 1971-73; prof., chmn. dept. philosophy U. Vt., Burlington, Vt., 1973-80, adj. prof. philosophy, 1980-83; dean grad. studies, prof. philosophy Grad. Sch. and Univ. Ctr., CUNY, 1983—, provost, v.p. for acad. affairs, 1984-92, acting pres., 1991; program officer Exxon Edn. Found., NYC, 1978-79; assoc. dir. Rockefeller Found., NYC, 1979-81, acting dir. humanities, 1981-82; dir. div. gen. programs NEH, Washington, 1982-83. Pres. John Dewey Found., 1983—; cons., panelist NEH, 1975—82. Author: Fate, Logic, and Time, 1967, 3d edit., 2004, A New Introduction to Philosophy, 1971, 3rd edit., 2004, The Eclipse of Excellence: A Critique of American Higher Education, 1973, Education and the Democratic Ideal, 1979, Saints and Scamps: Ethics in Academia, 1986, rev. edit., 1994, Philosophical Explorations: Freedom, God and Goodness, 1989, Puzzles & Perplexities: Collected Essays, 2002, 2d edit., 2007, God, Reason, and Religion, 2005; editor (with Frank A. Tillman): Philosophy of Art and Aesthetics: From Plato to Wittgenstein, 1969; editor: The Philosophical Foundations of Education, 1970, Philosophy of Religion, 1970, Classics of Western Philosophy, 1977, 7th edit., 2006, New Studies in the Philosophy of John Dewey, 1977, Scholars Who Teach: The Art of College Teaching, 1978;: 2d edit., 2004;; editor: (with David Shatz) Contemporary Philosophy of Religion, 1982; editor: (with Patricia Kitcher and George Sher) Reason at Work: Introductory Readings in Philosophy, 1984, 3d edit., 1995; editor: Morality, Responsibility and the University: Studies in Academic Ethics, 1990, Affirmative Action and the University: A Philosophical Inquiry, 1993; editor: (with Joram G. Haber) Twentieth Century Ethical Theory, 1995; editor: The Affirmative Action Debate, 1995, 2d edit., 2002, Classic and Contemporary Readings in the Philosophy of Education, 1997, Classics of Modern Political Theory: Machiavelli to Mill, 1997; editor: (with Peter Markie) Ethics: History, Theory, and Contemporary Issues, 1998, 3d edit., 2005; editor: Classics of Political and Moral Philosophy, 2002; editor: (with David Shatz) Questions About God, 2002; editor: (with Tziporah Kasachkoff) Morality and Public Policy, 2003; editor: (with Maureen Eckert and Robert Buckley) Knowledge and Reality, 2003; editor: Philosophy for the 21st Century: A Comprehensive Reader, 2003, Ten Essential Texts in the Philosophy of Religion: Classics and Contemporary Issues, 2004, Political Philosophy: The Essential Texts, 2004, Exploring Philosophy: An Introductory Anthology, 2d edit., 2005, Seven Masterpieces of Philosophy, 2007; editor: (with Christine Vitrano) Happiness: Classic and Contemporary Readings in Philosophy, 2007; editor: (with Maureen Eckert) Philosophical Horizons: Introductory Readings, 2005; gen. editor: Issues in Acad. Ethics, 1994—, Critical Essays on the Classics, 1997—, Blackwell Philosophy Guides, 2001—, Blackwell Readings in Philosophy, 2001—. Chmn. standing com. on tchg. philosophy Am. Philos. Assn., 1985-90, del. Am. Coun. Learned Socs., 1998-2002. Home: 100 W 57th St New York NY 10019-3302 Office: CUNY Grad Sch U Ctr 365 5th Ave New York NY 10016-4334 Business E-Mail: scahn@gc.cuny.edu.

CAHOON, RICHARD STUART, biotechnologist, educator; b. Salt Lake City, Apr. 28, 1954; s. Reynolds Fehring and Margaret (Mothersill) C.; m. J'Nelle Hathaway, June 28, 1980; children: Lauren E., Lindsey M. BA, U. Utah, 1976, BS cum laude, 1977; MS, Mont. State U., 1983; PhD in Natural Resource Policy, Cornell U. R&D tech. Pax Co. (Cenex), Salt Lake City, 1974-78; rsch. tech. II Biology dept. U. Utah, Salt Lake City, 1978-80; rsch. specialist U.S. Geol. Survey, Salt Lake City, 1980-81; rsch. assoc. Inst. for Bioprocess Analysis Mont. State U., Bozeman, 1981-83; pres. Assoc. Biotechs., Inc., Salt Lake City, 1983-85; sales/process engr. Monroe Food Process Machinery, Inc., Salt Lake City, 1985-87; dir. bus. devel. CCE, Inc., Bozeman, 1987-88; tech. transfer dir. The R&D Inst., Bozeman, 1989—90; asst. dir. industrial rels. NSF Nat. Engring. Rsch. Ctr.; asst. dir. tech. mktg. Cornell Rsch. Found., 1990, v.p., 1993—2003, sr. v.p., interim dir., 2003—; assoc. dir. patents and tech. mktg. Cornell U., 1992—; acting exec. dir. Cornell Ctr. for Tech., Enterprise, and Commercialization, 2004—06. Program devel. Inst. for Bioprocess Analysis, 1988—; asst. dir. tech. mktg. Cornell U., 1990, assoc. dir. office of patents & tech. mktg., 1993; assoc. dir. indsl. rels. Nat. Engring. Rsch. Ctr. Mont. State U., 1989-90; v.p. Cornell Rsch. Found., 1993. Author (strategic plan) Tech./Transfer Devel., 1989, IPA , 1989; patentee in field. Vol. tchr. Montessori Sch., Bozeman, 1988—, Granite Sch. Dist., Salt Lake City, 1980-81; vol. therapist Children's Ctr. United Way, Salt Lake City, 1978-80; coord. Neighborhood Tree Planning Porject, Salt Lake City, 1978-81. Rsch. Commendation award U.S. Geol Survey, Salt Lake City, 1981; Rsch. fellow Chevron, Inc., Bozeman, 1981-83, Rsch. Creativity grantee, Mont. State U., Bozeman, 1982. Mem. Pi Kappa Alpha. Avocations: natural sciences, skiing, camping, celtic history, history of technology. Office: Cornell Ctr for Tech, Enterprise, and Commercialization 20 Thornwood Dr # 105 Ithaca NY 14850-1265 Office Phone: 607-257-1081. Office Fax: 607-257-1015. E-mail: rsc5@cornell.edu.*

CAHOUET, ANN P., lawyer; b. Annapolis, Md., Sept. 7, 1957; BA in comparative lit., Scripps Coll., 1980; JD, U. Pitts., 1991. Bar: Pa. 1991. Positions in book pub. and advt.; joined Reed Smith LLP, Pitts., 1991, named dir. pro bono and cmty. svc., 1996, now dir. cmty. support. Mentor Career Literacy for African Am. Youth program, Duquesne U. Recipient Children's Voice Award, Allegheny County Ct. Apptd. Spl. Advocates, 2002, Caritas Award for Pub. Svc., Cath. Charities of Pitts., 2003. Mem.: Allegheny County Bar Assn. (mem. adoption com.), Pa. Bar Assn., ABA. Office: Reed Smith LLP 435 Sixth Ave Pittsburgh PA 15219 Office Phone: 412-288-4198. Office Fax: 412-288-3063. Business E-Mail: acahouet@reedsmith.com.

CAI, GANGSHU, finance educator; b. ZhangZhou, FuJian, China, Feb. 23, 1973; s. GenChi Cai and ShuiYing Xu; m. Yu Cheng. BS in Physics, Peking U., Beijing, 1996, MS in Econs. and Applied Stats., 1999; PhD in Ops. Rsch. and Computer Sci., NC State U., Raleigh, 2005. Rsch. intern IBM, Hawthorne, NY, 2004; asst. prof. Coll. Bus. Adminstrn., Tex. A&M Internat. U., Laredo, 2005—. Contbr. research papers in e-commerce, auction theory, supply chain and operations management. Fellow, Peking U., 1997—98; scholar, Am. Assn. Artificial Intelligence, 2004, 2002, NC State U., 2000—05. Mem.: Am. Assn. Artificial Intelligence, Inst. Ops. Rsch. and Mgmt., Omega Rho. Achievements include patents pending for proxy algorithm for combinatorial auctions. Office: Tex A&M Internat U 5201 Univ Blvd Laredo TX 78041

CAI, MEI, materials engineer, researcher; b. Beijing; m. Jie Du; children: Allen Jerry Du, Jason Henry Du. PhD, Wayne State U., Detroit, 1999. Product engr. Engring. Design Inst., Beijing, 1988—91; staff rsch. engr. dept. R&D Gen. Motors, Warren, Mich., 1995—. Contbr. articles to profl. jours. Mem.: Detroit Chinese Engring. Assn., Electrochem. Soc., Materials Rsch. Soc. Achievements include over 20 patents in novel materials and processing. Office: Gen Motors Rsch & Devel 30500 Mound Rd Warren MI 48090-9055 Office Phone: 586-596-4392. Office Fax: 586-986-1910. Business E-Mail: mei.cai@gm.com.

CAI, MING ZHI, chemist, researcher, film producer; b. Changsha, China, Feb. 22, 1935; arrived in U.S., 1986; d. Xian Cai and Xian Jiao Du; m. Jing Yi Jin, Apr. 18, 1958; children: Ge Jin, Jun Jin. BS with hons. in Chemistry, Wu Han U., 1957. Tchr. polymer sci. U. Sci. and Tech. China, 1958—73; tchr. Raman spectroscopy Ctr. Instrumental Analysis Tsing Hua U., 1973—86; rschr. surface enhanced Raman spectroscopy UCLA, 1991—93. Rschr. Micro-Raman spectroscopy Sch. Chemistry Ga. Inst. Tech., Atlanta, 1986—89; rschr. Ultra Violet resonance Raman spectroscopy dept. chemistry Pitts. U., 1989—90. Prodr.: (video series for TV stas.) Local Conditions and Customs of America, 1998—; (films, TV stas.) The Stories of Chinese Americans, 2001—; (documentaries) Teacher of Ballet, 2003, Gymnastic Coaches, 2003, Mongolia Doctor in LA, 2003, World Basketball Invitational Tournament for Chinese, 2003, Joys of Spring, 2004, Paradise on the Sea, 2004, The Coast Cities of Mexico, 2004, I Love You China, 2004, Kentucky Derby, 2004, Magical Photographer, 2004, At Xmas Eve, 2004, Antique Cars, 2004, The Tournament of Roses Parade, 2005, Celebrate Lunar New Year, 2005, One Hundred Years of Las Vegas, 2005, Entrepreneur, 2006, Chinese Folk Dance, 2006, National Date Festival, 2006, Air Show, 2006, Hundred Years City - Whittier, 2006, Walk to L.A., 2006, Mission San Juan Capistrano, 2006; prodr.: (documentaries) Three Brothers Raise Cows, 2006, Dr. Phillips, 2006, Fifteen Years Birthday, 2006, Air Show, 2006, Crossing Guard, 2006, Painting the Town, 2006, Artist Dennis, 2006; prodr.: (documentaries) Richard's Philatelic Center, 2007, sci. and edn. films, —. Mem.: Internat. Artist Photographer Soc., Assn. Rsch. Vision and Opthalmology, Microbeam Analysis Soc., Internat. Soc. Eye Rsch., Sci. and Tech. Soc. China, Instrumental Measurement Soc. China, Chem. Soc. China, Nat. Mus. Women in Arts. Avocations: painting, photo design, film editing, travel, organic agriculture. Personal E-mail: mingzhicai@yahoo.com.

CAI, MINGSHUI, education educator; b. Shishi City, China, July 14, 1944; m. Jianrong Zhang, Aug. 15, 1944; 1 child, Shuofeng. PhD, Ohio State U., Columbus, 1992. Recipient Va. Hamilton Essay award, Kent State U., 1993, Rsch. award, U. No. Iowa, Coll. Edn., 2001, Charles B. Mendehall Meml. award, Ohio State U., 1992. Mem.: Internat. Reading Assn., Nat. Conf. Rsch. Lang. and Literacy, Nat. Coun. Tchrs. English. Home: 3821 South Lawn Rd Cedar Falls IA 50613 Office: College Rd Cedar Falls IA 50614 Home Phone: 319-277-7382; Office Phone: 319-273-5872.

CAI, TAO, biomedical researcher; arrived in U.S., 1994; m. Ping Yu; children: Wendy, Angelina. MD, Jiangxi Med. Coll., Jinjiang, China, 1981; PhD, Ctrl. South U., Changsha, China, 1990. Assoc. prof. Xiangya Hosp., Ctrl. South U., Changsha, 1993—95; assoc. prof., assoc. dir. Nat. Key Lab. Med. Genetics, Changsha, 1994—96; vis. scientist Georgetown U., Washington, 1995—98; rsch. fellow NIH, Bethesda, Md., 1998—2001, staff scientist, 2001—. Recipient Hunan Med. Sci. Progress award, 1993, 1999, 2000. Achievements include research in human 7p duplication sydrome mapped on chromosome 7p21.2; discovery of SCA1 gene mutation causes SCA diesease in Chinese patients; research in PJA1, encoding a RING-H2 finger ubiquitin ligase, is a novel human X chromosome gene abundantly expressed in brain; insulinoma-associated protein IA-2 (a vesicle transmembrane protein) affects neurosecretion in Caenorhabditis elegans; discovery of kynurenine aminotransferase III is a novel member of the KAT family. Office: NIH 30 Convent Dr Bethesda MD 20892 Office Phone: 301-402-5320. Business E-Mail: tcai@mail.nih.gov.

CAI, XINJIANG, cardiologist, researcher; b. Xinhua, Hunan, China, Feb. 6, 1975; s. Yiping Cai and Lan Ouyang; m. Yanhong Zhang, Aug. 10, 1999. MD, Hunan Med. U. (formerly Yale-China Med. Coll.), 1996; MSc Cardiology, Capital U. Med. Scis., Beijing, 1999; PhD, U. Calgary, Can., 2004. Med. intern Hunan Med. U. Yale-China Hosp., Changsha, 1995—96; cardiology fellow Capital U. Med. Scis., Beijing, 1997—99; rsch. assoc. depts. cell biology & cardiology Duke U. Med. Ctr., Durham, NC, 2004—. Contbr. articles to profl. jours. Scholarship for investigating potassium-dependent sodium-calcium exchangers, Alta. Heritage Found. for Med. Rsch., 2001—04, Postdoctoral Fellowship, Howard Hughes Med. Inst., 2004—05. Mem.: Joint Steering Com. Pub. Policy (Travel award 2007), Can. Soc. Biochemistry, Molecular and Cellular Biology (assoc.), Am. Soc. Cell Biology (assoc.), Am. Soc. Biochemistry and Molecular Biology (assoc.), Biophys. Soc. (assoc. Travel award 2003), Sigma Xi. Office: Duke University Medical Center Carl 447 Dumc 3187 Durham NC 27710 Home Phone: 919-383-5721. Office Fax: 919-684-6870. Business E-Mail: xinjiang.cai@duke.edu.

CAI, ZHIJUN, mechanical engineer; s. Guohua Cai and Yudi Qiu; m. Lin Lin; 1 child, Felicia. PhD, La. State U., Baton Rouge, 2005. Rsch. asst. Mech. Engring., Baton Rouge, 2001—05; rsch. fellow Sys. Lab., Iowa City, 2005—. Recipient First prize of YuCai, Shanghai JiaoTong U., 1997. Mem.: IEEE. Home Phone: 319-353-4871.

CAIAZZO, NICHOLAS R., lawyer; b. Bklyn., Jan. 28, 1963; BA, NYU, 1985; JD, St. John's U., 1988. Bar: NY 1988, NJ 1988. Ptnr. Wilson, Elser, Moskowitz, Edelman & Dicker LLP, NYC. Mem.: ABA, Def. Rsch. Inst., NY State Trial Lawyers Assn., NY State Bar Assn. Office: Wilson Elser Moskowitz Edelman & Dicker LLP 23rd Fl 150 E 42nd St New York NY 10017-5639 Office Phone: 212-490-3000 ext. 2121. Office Fax: 212-490-3038. Business E-Mail: caiazzon@wemed.com.

CAICEDO, PATRICIA, singer, musicologist, physician; b. Ibagué, Colombia, Feb. 19, 1969; d. Jorge Caicedo and Patricia Serrano de Caicedo; m. Paxton Helms, Feb. 16, 2001 (div. Sept. 0, 2005). MD, Colombian Sch. Medicine, 1992; MM in Musicology, U. Complutense de Madrid, 2006. Physician Ligue Against Epilespy, Ibagué, Colombia, 1992—93, Clinica Tolima, Ibagué, Colombia, 1994—96; dean students affairs U. El Bosque, Bogotá, 1996—98, tchr. epistemology and history sci., 1996—98; pres. Mundo Arts, Inc., Washington, 2001—. Founder Assn. for Promotion of Ibero Am. Muic and Arts, Barcelona, 2003—; founder and artistic dir. Barcelona Festival Song, 2005—; lectr. in field. Author: (book) The Latin American Art Song: A Critical Anthology and Interpretative Guide for Singers, 2006; singer: (CD) La Felicidad, 1998, Lied: Art Songs of Latin America Vol. 1, 2001, To My Native City, 2005; singer, author, dir.: DVD

Live Concert: The Doors of the Morning, 2004, The Art Song in Argentina and Colombia, 2005, The Brazilian Art Song, 2006, singer numerous performances for voice and piano, voice and guitar, voice and orch. Recipient First prize, Nat. Competition of Bambuco, 1993, SONY Music Competition, 1998, Colono de Oro Music Competition, 2003. Mem.: Assn. Promotion Ibero Am. Music and Arts (pres. 2003), Latin Am. Art Song Alliance (assoc.; bd. dirs. 2001—07). Personal E-mail: patricia.caicedo@gmail.com.

CAI-LEE, WENDY, entrepreneur; b. Shanghai, 1974; arrived in US, 1985; BA with honors, Rutgers U., 1996. Mktg. exec. Chase, Citibank, 1996—99; founder & CEO Hagglers.com, NYC, 1999—2002; dir. Chinese Svcs. Group Deloitte & Touche USA, LLP, NYC. Active in China Com. US Coun. Internat. Bus. Active in Cammy Lee Leukemia Found.; co-founder Leo Club of Chinatown, NYC. Named one of 20 Under 30, Working Women, 2000, 40 Under 40, Crain's NY Bus., 2007. Mem.: Asian Women in Bus. (bd. dirs., chmn. Corp. Leadership com., Entrepreneurial Achievement award 2000). Office: Deloitte & Touche 2 World Financial Ctr 225 Liberty St New York NY 10281-1414 Office Phone: 212-436-6773. Office Fax: 212-436-5000. E-mail: wcai@deloitte.com.*

CAIN, ALBERT CLIFFORD, psychologist, educator; b. Chgo., July 19, 1933; s. Edward Arthur and Fae Anita (Shafton) C.; m. Barbara Strean, Nov. 15, 1959; children: Steven, Kenneth. BA, U. Mich., 1954, PhD, 1962. From asst. prof. to assoc. prof. dept. psychology and psychiatry U. Mich., Ann Arbor, Mich., 1962-69, prof. dept. psychology, 1969—, chmn. dept. psychology, 1981-91; chief psychologist Child Psychiat. Hosp., Ann Arbor, Mich., 1964-69. Mem. rev. com. Ctr. Studies of Suicide Prevention NIMH, 1969—72; dir. U. Mich. Child Bereavement Project. Editor: Survivors of Suicide, 1972; contbr. articles to profl. jour. Recipient Young Contributor award Am. Assn. Suicidology, 1973. Fellow APA, Am. Orthopsychiatric Assn. (bd. dir. 1978-81, editor jour. 1983-88); mem. Phi Beta Kappa. Home: 1927 Hampton Ct Ann Arbor MI 48103-4521 Office: U Mich Dept Psychology 2251 East Hall 525 E University Ave Ann Arbor MI 48109-1109

CAIN, BURTON EDWARD, retired chemistry professor; b. Batavia, NY, Sept. 11, 1942; s. Burton Leo and Bettie S. (Williams) C. BA, SUNY, Binghamton, 1964; PhD, Syracuse U., NYC, 1971. Biochemist Onondaga County Pub. Health Labs., Syracuse, 1971-72, O'Brien & Gere Cons. Engrs., Inc., Syracuse, 1972-74; asst. prof. chemistry Nat. Tech. Inst. Deaf, Rochester, NY, 1974-80, assoc. prof. dept. chemistry, 1980—84, prof., 1984—2005; asst. chemistry dept. head Rochester Inst. Tech., 1981—87, 1988—2003, assoc. chemistry dept. head, 2003—05; prof. emeritus, 2005—; ret., 2005. Reader Advanced Placement chemistry exams. Ednl. Testing Svc., June 1987, 88, 89, 90, 91, 92. Author: The Basics of Technical Communicating, 1988; contbr. articles to profl. jours. Reviewer grant proposals coll. sci. instrument program NSF, 1987, instrumentation and lab. improvement program NSF, 1992; election insp. Monroe County, NY, 2005—. Recipient Eisenhart Outstanding Tchr. award, 1980. Mem. AAAS, NSTA, Am. Chem. Soc., Nat. Assn. Deaf, Conf. Am. Instrs. for Deaf, Registry of Interpreters for Deaf, Sigma Xi, Phi Lambda Upsilon, Gamma Epsilon Tau (Tchr. of Yr. award 1983). Home: 200 East Ave Apt 1105 Rochester NY 14604-2633 Business E-Mail: becsch@rit.edu.

CAIN, COLEEN W., writer, educator; b. Birmingham, Iowa, Sept. 2, 1916; d. Marida Irwin Cain and Effie Levina Walters; m. James Cazort McClurkin, Feb. 5, 1937 (dec. Jan. 1938); m. James Robert Cazort, Dec. 24, 1942 (div. Oct. 1970); 1 child, Sidney Cain; m. Eugene Everett Bauer, Nov. 3, 1974 (div. Feb. 1983). BA in Journalism, U. Ark., Fayetteville, 1938. Cert. real estate agt. Ark., 1946, Wash., 1963. Tech. writer Manpower, Inc., Huntsville, Ala., 1966—69; editor, arts reviews Huntsville Times, 1969—70; fgn. news corr. Beijing PRC Jour. Am., Bellevue, Wash., 1980—83; instr. Beijing Fgn. Langs. Inst., 1981—83; lectr. Continuing Edn. Bellevue & South Seattle C.C., 1983—88; pres., owner Cain-Lockhart Press, Issaquah, Wash., 1985; instr. Issaquah Cmty. Ctr., 1996, North Bellevue Cmty. Sr. Ctr., 1997—2006. Spkr. in field. Author: Beth Bauer's Enjoy China More, 1985, 2d printing, 1986, 115 Jet Stories for Your Briefcase, 2001, 2d printing, 2003, Wild Blue, 1st of WWII Series, 2002, 2d edit., 2005, Glory After the War, 2d of WWII Series, 2005, The Fourth Pillar, 2007. Singer Seattle Symphony Chorale, New Orleans Opera Soc., Cascadian Chorale, Huntsville Cmty. Chorus; mem. 41st dist. Democrats, Bellevue, 1972; alt. del. King County Democrats, Seattle, 1992; election judge Westlake Precinct, Issaquah, 1991—98; sec. Christian Writers Assn., Bellevue, Wash., 1986—88; mezzo soloist (35 yrs.), choirs (65 yrs.). Recipient cert. of excellence, City of Bellevue Parks and Cmty. Svcs. Dept., 2001. Mem.: Pacific Northwest Writers Assn. (critique editor 1995—99, 3rd place nonfiction award 1976). Democrat. Presbyterian. Avocation: music. Home: 19510 S E 51st St Issaquah WA 98027-9327 Personal E-mail: cwcain@peoplepc.com.

CAIN, DAVID H., lawyer, former state legislator; b. Pampa, Tex., Nov. 13, 1947; s. Don and Betty Anne C.; m. Sally Anne Haenelt; children: David, Jennifer. BA in History, McMurry Coll., 1970; JD, U. Tex., 1973. Bar: Tex. 1973. Assoc. Crowder & Mattox, Dallas, 1973-78; ptnr. Bennett & Cain, Dallas, 1979-82; pvt. practice Dallas, 1982-86; assoc. Burleson, Pate, and Gibson, Dallas, 1986—; mem. Tex. Ho. of Reps., Austin, 1977-95, chmn. transp. com., 1983-95; mem. Tex. Senate, Austin, 1995—2002, vice chmn. econ. devel. com., 1997-99, chmn. Senate subcom. on infrastructure, 1999, vice chmn. spl. com. on electric utility restructuring, 1999. Chair Tex. Sunset Adv. Commn., 1991-93, transp. com. So. Legis. Conf., 1991-93. Founder Clean Dallas East; mem. Parents as First Tchrs. Recipient Friend of Bus. award Tex. C. of C., 1993; named Outstanding Young Man of Am. by Jaycees, 1978, 81, Legis. Crime Fighter of Yr. by Greater Dallas Crime Commn., 1993, One of Ten Best Legislators by Tex. Monthly Mag., 1993. Mem. State Bar of Tex., Dallas Bar Assn., East Dallas Bar Assn., Nat. Conf. State Legislatures, Greater Dallas C. of C. Democrat. Methodist. Avocations: running, travel. Office: Burleson, Pate & Gibson 2414 N Akard Suite 700 Dallas TX 75201

CAIN, DAVID LEE, retired corporate executive; b. Morgantown, W.Va., Oct. 14, 1941; s. David Melvin and Dorothy Eleanor (Burchinal) C.; children: Diana Jo, Michael Allen, Mark Aaron. BSME, W.Va. U., 1965. Adminstrn. mgr. Value Engring. Co., Alexandria, Va., 1968-72; gen. mgr. Walker Iron Works, Woodbridge, Va., 1972-75; owner, mgr. Dyna Products, Richmond, Va., 1975-78; adminstrn. mgr. VSE Corp., Alexandria, 1978-83; sr. v.p. The Orkand Corp., Falls Church, Va., 1983—2004; v.p. Harris Corp., Falls Ch., Va., 2004—05; ret., 2005. Vol. youth progs., various orgns., 1965—; head coach freshman wrestling team, W.Va., U., Morgantown, 1965, asst. coach varsity wrestling team, 1965; judge various pageants in Va., N.C., S.C., Md., Del., Pa., 1984—; mem. Rep. Nat. Com., 1990—. Capt. U.S. Army, 1965-68. Recipient scholarship W.Va. U., 1961-64, Disting. Student grant, ROTC, 1963-64, Disting. Mil. Grad., 1964-65. Mem. Nat. Contracts Mgmt. Assn. Methodist. Avocations: gardening, sports, collections. Personal E-mail: caindavid@aol.com.

CAIN, DOUGLAS MYLCHREEST, lawyer; b. Chgo., Sept. 8, 1938; s. Douglas M. Jr. and Louise C. (Coleman) C.; m. Constance Alexis Adams Moffit, Apr. 18, 1970; children: Victoria Elizabeth Moffit, Alexandra Catherine Moffit. AB, Harvard U., 1960; JD with distinction, U. Mich., 1966; LL.M., N.Y. U., 1970. Bar: Colo. 1966, U.S. Ct. Appeals (10th cir.) 1972, U.S. Supreme Ct. 1972. Assoc. Sherman & Howard, L.L.C., Denver, 1966-72, ptnr., 1972-93; equity mem., 1993—; chmn. policy council Sherman & Howard, Denver, 1984-87; adj. prof. law U. Denver, 1972-78. Mem. Rocky Mountain Estate Planning Council, pres., 1976-77 Assoc. editor: Mich. Law Rev, 1964-66; contbr. articles to profl. jours. Bd. dirs. Craig Hosp. Found., 1980-86, v.p., 1984-85, pres., 1986-87, 88-89; bd. dirs. Colo. Jud. Inst., 1990-96, chmn., 1992-93; bd. dirs. Colo. chpt. Am. Diabetes Assn., 1993, Breathe Better Found., 1993—, Colo. Coun. Econ. Edn., 1996-98, Fortune Found., 1998—; mem. Estate Planning Seminar Group. With USN, 1960—63. Fellow Am. Coll. Tax Coun., Am. Coll. Trust and Estate Counsel; mem. ABA, Colo. Bar Assn. (gov. 1980-82), Greater Denver Tax Coun. Assn. (v.p. 1987, pres. 1988), Assn. Harvard Alumni (regional dir. 1978-81), Rocky Mountain Harvard Club (pres. 1977-78, 92-93), Denver Country Club, Mile High Club, Rotary. Home: 1960 Hudson St Denver CO 80220-1459 Office: Sherman & Howard LLC 633 17th St Ste 3000 Denver CO 80202-3665 Home Phone: 303-322-8161; Office Phone: 303-299-8122. Business E-Mail: dcain@sah.com.

CAIN, GEORGE HARVEY, lawyer, association administrator; b. Washington, Aug. 3, 1920; s. J. Harvey and Madeleine (McGettigan) C.; m. Patricia J. Campbell, Apr. 23, 1946 (div.); children: George Harvey, James C., John P., Paul J.; m. Constance S. Collins, Aug. 10, 1985 BS, Georgetown U., 1942; JD, Harvard U., 1948. Bar: N.Y. 1949, Ohio 1972, Conn. 1977, U.S. Supreme Ct. 1995. Practiced law, NY, 1949-71, 73-76; pvt. practice Ohio, 1972-73; sec., gen. counsel Nat. Carloading Corp., 1949-54; mem. firm Spence & Hotchkiss, 1954-55; gen. atty., asst. sec. Cerro Corp., 1955-68, sec., gen. atty., 1968-72; v.p., gen. counsel Pickands Mather Co., Cleve., 1971-73; v.p., sec., gen. counsel Flintkote Co., White Plains, NY, 1973-76, Stamford, Conn., 1976-80; spl. counsel Day, Berry & Howard, Hartford and Stamford, Conn., 1980-82, ptnr. Stamford, 1983-90, of counsel, 1991—. Sec. Cerro Sales Corp., 1955-71; bd. dirs., sec. Leadership Housing Sys., Inc., 1970-71; bd. dirs., gen. counsel Atlantic Cement Co., Inc., 1962-71; bd. dirs. Hajoca Corp., 1975-79, Polymer Bldg. Sys., Inc.; adj. prof. U. Bridgeport Law Sch., 1983-86. Author: Turning Points: New Paths and Second Careers for Lawyers, 1994, Law Firm Partnership: Its Rights and Responsibilities, 1995, 2nd edit., 1999, Law Partnership Revisited, 2002. Served to 1st lt. USAAF, 1942-46; to capt. USAF, 1951-52. Fellow Am. Bar Found.; mem. ABA (chair sr. lawyers divsn. 2002—), N.Y. State Bar Assn., N.Y.C. Bar Assn., Ohio Bar Assn., Conn. Bar Assn., Am. Law Inst., Am. Soc. Corp. Secs., Georgetown U. Alumni Assn. (mem. Alumni senate), Harvard Club N.Y., Dutch Treat Club. Office: Day Berry & Howard City Place I Hartford CT 06103-3499 Office Phone: 860-676-8535.

CAIN, JAMES NELSON, arts school and concert administrator; b. Arcadia, Ohio, Jan. 6, 1930; s. Alfred Ray and Gladys Eliza (Cruikshank) C.; m. Marthellen Jones, June 12, 1950; children— Nelson, Jennifer, Richard, Elizabeth. AB, Ohio State U., Columbus, 1955. Dir. Prestige Concerts, Inc., Columbus, 1948-62; exec. dir. Music Assos. Aspen, Inc., Colo., 1962-68; from asst. mgr. to mgr. St. Louis Symphony Orch., 1968-80; v.p. St. Louis Conservatory and Schs. Arts, 1980-94. Home: 2 Nantucket Ln Saint Louis MO 63132-4111 Personal E-mail: JNCain@prodigy.com.

CAIN, JAMES P., ambassador, lawyer; BA cum laude, Wake Forest U., JD cum laude, 1984. Bar: NC 1984. Atty., co-founder Kilpatrick Stockton, LLP, Raleigh, NC, 1985—2000, ptnr., 2002—05; pres., COO Carolina Hurricanes NHL/Gale Force Holdings, 2000—02; U.S. amb. to Denmark US Dept. State, Copenhagen, 2005—. NC vice chair Bush-Cheney campaign, 2004; mem. Rep. Nat. Com. Office: 5280 Copehagen Pl Washington DC 20521

CAIN, JUDITH SHARP, mathematics professor, consultant; d. Sturdy O. and Erna E. Sharp; children: Jason Charles, Crystal Heather, Jeffrey Ronald. MEd, U. La., Lafayette, 1989. Cert. tchr. 1-8, secondary math., mid. sch. math. La., tchr. leader La., 2007, supr. of instrn. La., adminstr. La., early adolescence tchr. math Mid. Sch. Nat. Bd. Profl. Tchg. Stds., 2005, cert. supr. of student tchrs. Estimator Sellers, Dubroc & Assoc., Inc., Civil Engrs., Lafayette, La., 1972—81; tchr. mid. sch. math. Lafayette Parish Sch. Bd., Cathedral Carmel Sch., 1986—99; lead tchr., mid. sch. math. Lafayette Parish Sch. Bd., 1999—, presenter workshops and inservices, 1997—. Math. workshop cons./tchr. trainer various sch. districts, La., 1999—; mem. com. grade level expectations and textbook adoption, intern rev. LEAP range finding, iLEAP rev. com., LAA2 com., LEAP item rev. com. La. Dept. Edn., 2003—; adj. instr. South La. CC, 1999—2004, U. La., Lafayette, 2004—06; applicant mentor Nat. Bd. Cert., 2006—. Author: An Evaluation of the Connected Math. Project. Active St. Anne's Cath. Ch., Youngsville, La. Named Outstanding Tchr., Diocese of Lafayette, 1993—94, Tchr. of Yr., Lafayette Parish, 2000. Mem.: NEA, ASCD, Nat. Coun. Suprs. Math., La. Tchrs. Math., Nat. Coun. Tchrs. Math. Office: Lafayette Parish Sch Bd PO Drawer 2158 Lafayette LA 70502 Office Phone: 337-501-7452. Personal E-mail: cain.judy@gmail.com.

CAIN, LAWRENCE EDWARD, small business owner, language educator, researcher; b. Sept. 28, 1941; BA, Mich. State U., East Lansing, 1965. Tchr. English, Detroit, 1965—68; process server, investigator ABC Legal Process Svc., San Francisco, 1978—82; onwer, operator Lawrence E. Cain Process Svc., San Francisco, 1982—89. Mem.: Mensa (life). Home: 606 S Williams St Apt 815 Royal Oak MI 48067-2649

CAIN, RUSSELL M., psychiatrist, educator, administrator; b. Pitts., Aug. 31, 1940; s. Ralph H. and Lillian (Noon) C.; m. Nancy Napier, Oct. 23, 1965; 1 child, Christine Elizabeth. BS, Ohio State U., 1962; postgrad., Coll. de France, Paris, 1962-63, Inst. de Neurophysiologie Gen.; MD, Ohio State U., 1967. Diplomate Am. Bd. Psychiatry and Neurology. Intern U. Wis., Madison, 1967-68, resident in psychiatry, 1968-71, fellow in family therapy, 1970—71; with U. Rochester, NY, 1973—2004, prof. emeritus NY, 2004. Lt. comdr. M.C., USNR, 1971-73. Recipient Recognition award Commn. on Accreditation Rehab. Facilities; gen. Univ. scholar in medicine Ohio State U., 1963-67; NIMH fellow in psychiatry, 1968-71, Falk fellow 1969-70. Fellow Am. Psychiat. Assn. (disting. life fellow); mem. Rochester Acad. Medicine, Med. Soc.of Monroe County, Genesee Valley Psychiat. Assn. (pres. 1995-97), U.S. Naval Inst., Genesee Conservation League, Marines Meml. Assn., U. Wis. Alumna Assn., The Oxford Alumni Assn. Avocations: sailing, photography, music, reading, travel. Office Phone: 585-461-3243. Personal E-mail: rmcain@frontiernet.net.

CAIN, THOMAS ROBERT, interventional radiologist; b. Sullivan, Mo., Sept. 4, 1951; s. Noble William and Evelyn (Scott) C.; m. Emily Hamlin, Mar. 7, 1984; children: Geoffrey, Amy, Natalie. BA, U. Calif., Berkeley, 1973; MPH, UCLA, 1974; MD, U. So. Calif., 1978. Diplomate in radiology and in cardiovasc. and interventional radiology Am. Bd. Radiology. Intern Cedars-Sinai Med. Ctr., LA, 1978-79; resident UCLA Med. Ctr., LA, 1980-83, Northridge Hosp. Med. Ctr., 1983-85; ptnr., mem. staff Western Roentgenologic Assocs., Northridge, Calif., 1985-94; dir. nonvascular interventional rdiology sect. Christ Hosp. and Med. Ctr., Oak Lawn, Ill., 1987—2003; ptnr. Oak Lawn Radiologists, S.C., 1994—2003; fellow Am. Coll. Nuclear Medicine, 2000—. Asst. prof. U. So. Calif.; dir. Advanced Med. Imaging Svcs., 1987-88, Panorama Cmty. Hosp., 1989-92, Northridge Diagnostic Ctr., 1992-94, Pacifica Hosp. of the Valley, Sun Valley, Calif., 1991-94; com. mem. Christ Hosp. Med. Ctr. Fellow Am. Coll. Nuc. Medicine; mem. AMA, Radiol. Soc. N.Am., Soc. Cardiovasc. and Interventional Radiology, Salerni Collegium, Chgo. Med. Soc. Office: Provena Mercy Med Ctr 1325 N Highland Ave Aurora IL 60506 Office Phone: 630-801-2692. E-mail: trcainmd@yahoo.com.

CAIN, TIM J., lawyer; b. Angola, Ind., July 12, 1958; s. Nancy J. (Nichols) C.; m. Debra J. VanWagner, Feb. 28, 1976; children: Christine M., Stephanie L., Katherine S., Jennifer A. BA in Polit. Sci. with honors, Ind. U., 1980; JD, Valparaiso U., 1984; MBA, Ind. Wesleyan U., 1991; LLM in Internat. Bus. and Trade with honors, John Marshall Law Sch., 2001. Bar: Ind. 1984, U.S. Dist. Ct. (no. and so. dists.) Ind. 1984, U.S. Supreme Ct., 2002. Assoc. Hartz & Eberhard, LaGrange, Ind., 1984-85; pub. defender LaGrange Cir. Ct., 1985-86; sr. assoc. Eberhard & Assocs., LaGrange, 1985-86; chief dep. to Pros. Atty.'s Office, LaGrange, 1986-87; ptnr. Eberhard & Cain, LaGrange, 1986-89; pvt. practice LaGrange, 1989-95; pros. atty. La Grange (Ind.) County, 1991—2002; ptnr. Williams and Cain, Ft. Wayne, Ind., 2002—. Asst. atty. La Grange County, La Grange; atty. Town of Shipshewana, Ind., 1984-93. Coach Orland (Ind.) Little League, 1977-79, Prairie Hts. Baseball, LaGrange, 1986-90; pres. Prairie Hts. H.S. Dollars for Scholars, LaGrange, 1989; active LaGrange County Coun. on Aging, 1989-91, Prairie Hts. At-Risk Students Com., 1989—, LaGrange County 4-H Fair Assn., 1993-97. Mem.Ind. Bar Assn., LaGrange County Bar Assn. (sec.-treas. 1986-87, v.p. 1987-89, pres. 1990-93). Clubs: Exchange (pres. 1988-89). Republican. Home: 360 S 900 E Lagrange IN 46761-9529 Office: PO Box 895 Angola IN 46703 Office Phone: 260-668-6251. Business E-Mail: tim@williams-cain.com.

CAIN, VERNON, retired diversified financial services company executive; b. Bisbee, Ariz., Jan. 5, 1947; BS, No. Ariz. U., 1969; MBA with honors, Roosevelt U., 1984. Pres. U.S. holdings Dawson Holdings PLC, Oregon, Ill., 1985-96, CEO, mng. dir. info. svcs. group, 1996-2000. Mem. Am. Libr. Assn. Home: 4505 W Sunset Dunes Pl Tucson AZ 85743-8345 Office Phone: 520-743-4696. Personal E-mail: verncain@aol.com, vwjec@msn.com.

CAIN, WILLIAM HOWARD, secondary school educator; b. Terre Haute, Ind., Sept. 19, 1949; s. Rush M. and Mary Margaret (Shepard) C. BS, Ind. State U., Terre Haute, 1971, MS, 1976. Choral tchr. Attica Sch. System, Ind., 1971-73, Schulte Sch., Terre Haute, 1973-75; ch. organist Centenary United Meth. Ch., Terre Haute, 1974—, pvt. tchr. piano, 1977—. Organist winter and spring commencements ISU, 1999—. Mem. Am. Guild Organists (dean 1974-84), Music Tchrs. Nat. Assn. Avocations: songwriting, walking, exercise, fossil collecting. E-mail: indycain553@ma.rr.com.

CAIN, WILLIAM STANLEY, experimental psychologist, educator, researcher; b. NYC, Sept. 7, 1941; s. William Henry and June Rose (Stanley) Cain; m. Claire Murphy, Oct. 30, 1993; children: Justin, Alison stepchildren: Michael, Jennifer, Courtney. BS, Fordham U., 1963; MSc, Brown U., 1966, PhD, 1968. From asst. fellow to fellow John B. Pierce Lab., New Haven, 1967—94; from instr. to assoc. prof. dept. epidemiology, pub. health, and psychology Yale U., New Haven, 1967—84, prof., 1984—94; prof. otolaryngology U. Calif., San Diego, 1994—. Mem. sensory disorders study sect. NIH, Bethesda, Md., 1991—95; mem. sci. adv. bd. Ctr. Indoor Air Rsch., Linthicum, Md., 1991—99. Mem. editl. bd. Chem. Senses, 1985—94, mem. editl. adv. bd. Indoor Air, 1990—2000, 2005—, Physiology and Behavior, 1995—96; editor: 5 books, 1971—; contbr. articles to profl. jours. Recipient Jacob Javits/Claude Pepper award, NIH, 1984, Sense of Smell Rsch. award, Fragrance Rsch. Fund, 1986. Fellow: ASHRAE (Crosby Field award 1984), APA, Acad. Indoor Air Rsch.; mem.: N.Y. Acad. Scis. (pres. 1986), Assn. Chemoreception Scis. (exec. chmn. 1983—84, Max Mozell award 2006). Home: 4459 Nabal Dr La Mesa CA 91941-7168 Office: U Calif Dept Surgery 9500 Gilman Dr Rm Mc957 La Jolla CA 92093-0957 Office Phone: 858-622-5831. Business E-Mail: wcain@ucsd.edu.

CAINE, ARNOLD, pharmaceutical executive; b. Phila., Oct. 24, 1954; s. Allen and Miriam Caine; m. Diana Karlin, June 16, 1991; children: Rachel Lauren, Marlee Elizabeth. BS in Pharmacy, Phila. Coll. Pharmacy and Sci., 1977. Registered Bd. Pharmacy Del., 1978, lic. real estate realtor Del., 2006. Global supply chain mgr. AstraZeneca Pharm., Alderley Edge, Cheshire, England, 1997—99, v.p. US bus. svc. Wilmington, Del., 1999—. Treas. TMA Del., Wilmington, 2001—06; sec., bd. advisors Pub. Allies Del., Wilmington, Del., 2002—07; bd. dirs. New Castle County Econ. Devel. Coun., Wilmington, 2003—07, Del. Ctr. Contemporary Arts, Wilmington, 2004—07. Mem.: New Castle County C. of C. (bd. dirs.), Mensa, Nat. Assn. Watch and Clock Collectors.

CAINE, FRANKLYN A., aerospace transportation executive; b. Plainfield, NJ, Mar. 1950; B in Chem. Engring., Princeton U., 1971; MBA in fin., internat. bus., U. Chicago, 1976. Mgmt. RCA Corp., Penn Central Corp., Exxon Corp.; sr. v.p. controller, dir. corp. devel. United Techs. Corp., Hartford, Conn.; exec. v.p., CFO Wang Global, 1994-99; sr. v.p., CFO Raytheon Co., Lexington, Mass., 1999—2002; dir. Phase Forward. Office: Phase Forward 880 Winter St Waltham MA 02451

CAINE, MICHAEL, actor; b. London, Mar. 14, 1933; s. Maurice and Ellen Frances Marie Micklewhite; m. Patricia Haines, 1954; children: Dominique, Natasha; m. Shakira Baksh, 1973. Asst. stage mgr. Westminster Repertory, Horsham, Sussex, England, 1953; actor Lowestoft Repertory, 1953-55, Theatre Workshop, London, 1955. Actor: What's It All About?: An Autobiography, 1993, (numerous TV appearances):, 1957—63,: (plays) Next Time I'll Sing for You, 1963; (films) A Hill in Korea, 1956, How to Murder a Rich Uncle, 1958, Zulu, 1964, The Ipcress File, 1965, Alfie, The Wrong Box, Gambit, 1966, Hurry Sundown, 1967, Woman Times Seven, 1967, Deadfall, 1967, The Magus, 1968, Battle of Britain, 1968, Play Dirty, 1968, The Italian Job, 1969, Too Late the Hero, 1970, The Last Valley, 1971, Get Carter, 1971, Zee & Co., 1972, Kidnapped, 1972, Pulp, 1972, Sleuth, 1973, The Black Windmill, 1974, Marseilles Contract, 1974, The Wilby Conspiracy, 1974, Peeper, 1975, The Romantic Englishwoman, 1975, The Man Who Would Be King, 1975, Harry and Walter Go to New York, 1975, The Eagle Has Landed, 1976, A Bridge Too Far, 1976, Silver Bears, 1976, The Swarm, 1977, California Suite, 1978, Beyond the Poseidon Adventure, 1979, Dressed to Kill, 1980, The Island, 1980, The Hand, 1981, Victory, 1981, Deathtrap, 1982, Educating Rita, 1983, Beyond the Limit, 1983, The Jigsaw Man, 1984, The Holcroft Covenant, 1984, Blame It On Rio, 1984, The Whistle Blower, 1985, Hannah and Her Sisters, 1986 (Acad. award for best supporting actor, 1987), Water, Sweet Liberty, 1986, Mona Lisa, 1986, Half Moon Street, 1986, Jaws The Revenge, Surrender, 1987, Without a Clue, 1988, Dirty Rotten Scoundrels, 1988, Shock to the System, 1989, Bullseye!, 1990, Jekyll and Hyde, 1990, Mr. Destiny, 1990, Noises Off, 1991, The Muppets Christmas Carol, 1992, On Deadly Ground, 1994, Bullet to Beijing, 1995, Blood and Wine, 1996, Curtain Call, 1997, Blue Ice, 1993, Little Voice, 1998 (Golden Globe), Debtors, 1999, Cider House Rules, 1999 (Acad. award for best supporting actor), Quills, 1999, Shiner, 2000, Get Carter, 2000, Miss Congeniality, 2000, Last Orders, 2001, Quicksand, 2001, The Quiet American, 2002 (Acad. award nomination, 2002), Austin Powers 3, 2002, The Actor, 2003, Secondhand Lions, 2003, The Statement, 2003, Around the Bend, 2004, The Weatherman, 2005, Batman Begins, 2005, Bewitched, 2005, Children of Men, 2006, Flawless; actor, exec. prodr.: (films) The Fourth Protocol, 1987; actor: (TV miniseries) Jack the Ripper, 1988, World War II: When Lions Roared, 1994 (Emmy nominee for Lead Actor in a Miniseries, 1994). Named Companion of Order of the Brit. Empire, 1992, Sir Michael Caine, 2000, Knight, Queen of Eng., 2000. Office: care Pam PR Inc 4401 Wilshire Blvd Los Angeles CA 90010-3728 also: Chelsea Harbour London England Business E-Mail: jerrypam1@aol.com.

CAINE, PAUL JASON, publishing executive; b. NYC, Apr. 21, 1964; s. Donald Ray and Pearl Jane (Silberstein) C. BA, Ind. U., 1986. Asst. media planner J. Walter Thompson Co., NYC, 1986, media planner, 1987—89; assoc. pub., Teen People Time Warner Inc., NYC, 1997—2001, assoc. pub., advt. sales, People mag., 2001—02, pub., Teen People, 2002—03, pub., Entertainment Weekly, 2003—, pub., People mag., 2004—05, People group pub., 2005—. Chmn. com. Union Bd. Concert. Named to Advertising Hall of Achievement, 2004. Mem. Tau Kappa Epsilon (pres. alumni chpt.). Avocation: piano. Office: Entertainment Weekly 1675 Broadway New York NY 10019*

CAINE, RAYMOND WILLIAM, JR., retired public relations executive; b. Fall River, Mass., June 30, 1932; s. Raymond W. and Emma (Gardella) C.; m. Sharon G. Henry, Nov. 10, 1956; children: Karen, Kimberly, Patrick, Peter. BS, Providence Coll., 1956. Sr. v.p. advt., pub. relations Creamer, Dickson, Basford, NYC and Providence, 1966-74; v.p. pub. rels. Blue Cross (Blue Shield), Providence, 1974-80; v.p. corp. communications Textron, Inc., Providence, 1980-94; ret. Contbr. articles to profl. jours. Bd. dirs. R.I. Commodores, 1987—, Newport Preservation Soc., Newport Hist. Soc.; trustee The Miriam Hosp. Recipient Bell Ringer award Publicity Club Boston, 1971, 72. Mem. Pub. Rels. Soc. Am. (bd. dir. 1971-73), Newport Reading Rm. Avocations: golf, home remodeling.

CAINE, STEPHEN HOWARD, data processing executive; b. Washington, Feb. 11, 1941; s. Walter E. and Jeanette (Wenborne) C. Student, Calif. Inst. Tech., 1958-62. Sr. programmer Calif. Inst. Tech., Pasadena, 1962-65, mgr. sys. programming, 1965-69, mgr. programming, 1969-70; pres. Caine, Farber & Gordon, Inc., Pasadena, 1970—; gen. mgr. Gatekeeper Systems, Pasadena, 1995—. Lectr. applied sci. Calif. Inst. Tech., Pasadena, 1965-71, vis. assoc. elec. engring., 1976, vis. assoc. computer sci., 1976-84; dir. San Gabriel Valley Learning Ctrs., 1992-95. Mem. AAAS, IEEE, Nat. Assn. Corrosion Engrs., Am. Ordnance Assn., Assn. Computing Machinery, Pasadena Tournament of Roses Assn. (vice-chmn. com. 1996-2000, chmn. com. 2000-07, bd. dirs. 2004-07, hon. dir. 2007—), Athanaeum Club (Pasadena), Houston Club. Home: 77 Patrician Way Pasadena CA 91105-1039

CAINE, VIRGINIA A., city health department administrator; BS, Gustavus Adolphus Coll., Minn., 1973; MD, N.Y. Upstate Med. Ctr., Syracuse. Resident U. Cin.; resident, infectious diseases U. Wash., Seattle; assoc. prof., medicine Ind. U. Sch. Medicine; dir. Marion Co. Health Dept., Indpls., 1993—. Mem., com. credentialing for pub. health workforce CDC, mem., bioterrorism and emergency preparedness com. Co-dir. Indpls. Campaign for Healthy Babies Initiative; bd. mem. Damien AIDS Ctr.; bd. mem., substance abuse Fairbanks Hosp.; bd. mem. Ind. AIDS Fund, Indpls. Alliance for Health Promotion, Ind. State Women's Health Com.; mem. Cmty. Drug Summit, Mayor's Commn. on Family Violence, City of Indpls. Mayor's Emergency Preparedness Task Force; mem. adv. bd. Women's Fund of Ctrl. Ind. Named one of Influential Women in Indpls., Indpls. Bus. Jour., The Ind. Lawyer; recipient Superstar award, Ind. AIDServe, 1998, Outstanding Svc. award, Indpls. Bus. Jour. Mem.: Ind. Pub. Health Assn., Nat. Med. Assn. (chair, infectious diseases, co-chair, AIDS sect., Internist of Yr. 1999), Nat. Assn. of County and City Health Officials, Am. Pub. Health Assn. (pres. 2004—, New Leadership award). Office: Marion Co Health Dept 3838 N Rural St Indianapolis IN 46205-2930

CAIRNS, DIANE PATRICIA, motion picture executive; b. Fairbanks, Alaska, Mar. 2, 1957; d. Dion Melvin and Marsha Lala (Andrews) C. BBA, U. So. Calif., 1980, MFA, 2003. Literary agt. Sy Fischer Agy., LA, 1980-85; sr. v.p. Internat. Creative Mgmt., LA, 1985-96; sr. v.p. prodn. Universal Pictures, LA, 1996-97, Cairns Co., LA, 2004—. Mem. NOW, Acad. Motion Picture Arts and Scis., Women's Action Coun., Amnesty Internat., L.A. County Mus. of Art Home and Office: 8231 Tuscany Ave Playa Del Rey CA 90293-7825

CAIRNS, ELTON JAMES, chemical engineering professor; s. James Edward and Claire Angele (Larzelere) C.; m. Miriam Esther Citron, Dec. 26, 1974; 1 dau., Valerie Helen; stepchildren: Benjamin David, Joshua Aaron. BS in Chemistry, Mich. Tech. U., Houghton, 1955, BSChemE, 1955; PhD in Chem. Engring., U. Calif., Berkeley, 1959. Phys. chemist GE Rsch. Lab., Schenectady, NY, 1959-66; group leader, then sect. head chem. engring. divsn. Argonne (Ill.) Nat. Lab., 1966-73; asst. head electrochemistry dept. GM Rsch. Labs., 1973-78; assoc. lab. dir., dir. energy and environment divsn. Lawrence Berkeley (Calif.) Nat. Lab., 1978-96, head Energy Conversion and Storage Program, 1982—98, head Berkeley Electrochemical Rsch. Coun., 1982—, C.D. Hollowell meml. lectr., 1996; prof. chem. engring. U. Calif., 1978—. Cons. in field; mem. numerous govt. panels. Author: (with H.A. Liebhafsky) Fuel Cells and Fuel Batteries, 1968; mem. editl. bd. Advances in Electrochemistry and Electrochem. Engring., 1974—, Internat. Jour. Electrochemical Sci., 2006-; divsn. editor Jour. Electrochem. Soc., 1968-91; regional editor Electrochimica Acta, 1984-99, editor, 2000-04; contbr. articles to profl. jours. Recipient IR-100 award, 1968, Centennial medal Case Western Res. U., 1980, R & D 100 award, 1992, Melvin Calvin medal of distinction Mich. Technol. U., 1998; named Croft lectr. U. Mo., 1979, McCabe lectr. U. NC, 1993; grantee DuPont Co., 1956; Dow Chem. Co. fellow, univ. fellow, NSF fellow, Std. Oil Co. Calif. grantee, U. Calif., Berkeley. Fellow Am. Insts. Chemists, Electrochem. Soc. (chmn. phys. electrochem. divsn. 1981-84, v.p. 1986-89, pres. 1989-90, Francis Mills Turner award 1963); mem. AIChE (chmn. energy conversion com. 1970-94), AAAS, Am. Chem. Soc., Internat. Soc. Electrochemistry (hon.; chmn. electrochem. energy conversion divsn. 1977-85, U.S. nat. sec. 1983-89, v.p. 1984-88, pres. 1999-2000), Intersoc. Energy Conversion Engring. Conf. (steering com. 1970-2003, gen. chmn. 1976, 90, 97, program chmn. 1983, co-chair internat. meeting on lithium batteries 2002), Sigma Xi (pres. Berkeley chpt. 2002-03). Achievements include patents in field. Home: 239 Langlie Ct Walnut Creek CA 94598-3615 Office: Lawrence Berkeley Nat Lab MS 70RO108B 1 Cyclotron Rd Berkeley CA 94720-0001 Office Phone: 510-486-5028. Personal E-mail: ejcairns@cal.berkeley.edu. Business E-Mail: ejcairns@lbl.gov, cairns@cchem.berkeley.edu.

CAIRNS, JAMES DONALD, lawyer; b. Chelsea, Mass., Aug. 7, 1931; s. Stewart Scott and Kathleen (Hand) C.; m. Alice Crout Cairns, June 18, 1988; children from previous marriage: Douglas S., Timothy H., Pamela S., Heather M. AB, Harvard U., 1952; JD, Ohio State U., 1958. Bar: Fla. 1974, Ohio 1958, US Dist. Ct. (no. dist.) Ohio 1975, US Tax Ct. 1963, Supreme Ct., 2000. Ptnr. Squire, Sanders & Dempsey, Cleve., 1958-95, Spieth, Bell, McCurdy & Newell, Cleve., 1995—. Served to lt. (j.g.) USNR, 1952-55. Mem. ABA, Am. Coll. Trust and Estate Counsel, Fla. Bar Assn., Ohio State Bar Assn., Bar Assn. Greater Cleve., Union Club, Edgewater Yacht Club, Shoreby Club. Democrat. Episcopalian. Office: Spieth Bell McCurdy Newell 2000 Huntington Bldg 925 Euclid Ave Cleveland OH 44115-1408 Home Phone: 216-451-6488; Office Phone: 216-696-4700. Personal E-mail: dcairns@att.net. Business E-Mail: dcairns@spiethbell.com.

CAIRNS, JAMES ROBERT, mechanical engineering educator; b. Indpls., Feb. 4, 1930; s. John Joseph and Agatha Bertha (Krebs) C.; m. Catherine I. DiCicco, Feb. 6, 1954; children: James Robert, Steven J., Michael P., Daniel F., Timothy E., Robert B. BS in Mech. Engring, U. Detroit, 1954; MS in Engring, U. Mich., 1959, PhD, 1963. Registered profl. engr., Mich. cert. energy mgr. Instr. U. Detroit, 1954-57, U. Mich., Ann Arbor, 1957-63, asst. prof. Dearborn, 1963-65, asso. prof., 1965-68, prof. mech. engring., 1968—, chmn. engring. div., 1964-73, acting dean, 1973-75, dean, 1975-81. Cons. and expert witness in product liability litigation. Contbr. articles to profl. jours. Ford Faculty fellow, 1960-63 Mem. ASME, ASHRAE, Assn. Energy Engrs., Am. Soc. Engring. Edn., Common Cause, Tau Beta Pi, Pi Tau Sigma. Roman Catholic. Home: 836 Dover Dr Dearborn Heights MI 48127-4144 Office: 4901 Evergreen Rd Dearborn MI 48128-2406 Personal E-mail: bobcairns@comcast.net. Business E-Mail: bcairns@umich.edu.

CAJORI, CHARLES FLORIAN, artist, educator; b. Palo Alto, Calif., Mar. 9, 1921; s. Florian Anton and Marion (Haines) C.; m. Barbara Grossman, June 23, 1967; children: Marion, Nicole. Student, Colo. Coll., 1939—40, Cleve. Art Sch., 1940—42, Columbia U., 1946—48, Skowhegan Sch., 1947, student, 1948. Instr. Notre Dame of Md., Balt., 1950-56, Cooper Union, NYC, 1956-59, 60-65; vis. artist U. Calif., Berkeley, 1959; instr. N.Y. Studio Sch., NYC, 1964—69, 1985—; prof. Queens Coll., NYC, 1965-86; instr. Yale U., Hew Haven, 1989. Co-founder Tanager Gallery, NYC, 1952, NY Studio Sch., NYC, 1964; one-man shows include Howard Wise Gallery, NYC, 1963, Bennington (Vt.) Coll., 1969, Landmark Gallery, NYC, 1974, 81, Ingber Gallery Ltd., NYC, 1976, Am. U., Washington, 1977, 88, Gross McCleaf Gallery, Phila., 1983, 85, N.Y. Studio Sch., NYC, 1988, Cen. Conn. State U., New Britain, Conn., 1992, Dartmouth Coll., NH, 1996, NY Studio Sch., 2000, Paessagio Gallery, West Hartford, Conn., 2002, Wright State U., Daytona, Ohio, 2004, Lohin Geduld Gallery, NYC, 2004, David Findlay Jr. Gallery, NYC, 2005, 07; exhibited in group shows including Chgo. Art Inst., 1964, Whitney Mus., NYC, 1965, Loeb Ctr., NYU, NYC, 1970, Artists Choice, 1977, Wadsworth Atheneum, Hartford, Conn., 1983, Bruce Mus., Greenwich, Conn., 1989, New Britain Mus., 1990, Nat. Acad., NYC, 2003-04, Inst. Arts and Letters, 2001, Frye Mus., 2002; represented in permanent collections including Am. U., Washington, Del. Art Ctr., Wilmington, Met. Mus. Art, NYC, Mitchner Collection, Austin, Tex., NYU, NYC, U. N.Mex., Albuquerque, Walker Art Ctr., Mpls., Whitney Mus., Geigy Chem. Corp. Ardsley, NY, Snite Mus., U. Notre Dame, Ind., Honolulu Art Acad., Hirshhorn Mus., Washington, Met. Mus. Art, NYC, Ark. Art Ctr., Little Rock, Denver Art Mus., Cin. Art Mus., Modern Museet, Stockholm. Served with USAAF, 1942-46. Recipient Distinction in Arts award Yale U., 1959, purchase awards Longview Found., 1962, purchase awards Ford Found., 1963, purchase awards Childe-Hassam, 1975, 76, 80, 2006, painting award Inst. Arts and Letters, N.Y.C., 1970, Louis Comfort Tiffany award, 1979, Altman Figure prize Nat. Acad., 1983, 87, 94, 2000, Purchase award Inst. Arts and Letters, 2006; Guggenheim fellow, 2001; Fulbright grantee, 1952-53, Nat. Endowment Arts grantee, 1981. Mem. NAD, Coll. Art Assn. Home: 2338 Litchfield Rd Watertown CT 06795-1005 Office: NY Studio Sch 8 W 8th St New York NY 10011-9002

CAKIR, HASAN, research analyst; b. Bursa, Turkey, Jan. 30, 1977; s. Ahmet and Berra Cakir. BS, Gazi U., Ankara, Turkey, 1998; MS, Ind. U., Bloomington, 2001, PhD, 2006. Tech. support Ind. U., Bloomington, 2002—04, rsch. analyst, 2004—.

CAKNIPE, CHRISTOPHER HOWARD, environmental health specialist; b. Alexandria, Va., Dec. 12, 1970; s. John William Caknipe and Kay Lightner Doreen; m. Amber Willis Caknipe, Feb. 7, 2005. B in Chemistry, U. of South Fla., Tampa, 2002, Grad. Cert. in Hydrogeology, 2004. Registered environ. profl. Nat. Registry Environ. Profls. Substitute chemistry tchr. Polk County Schs., Fla., 1999—2000; molecular biologist U. of South Fla., Tampa, 2000—01, tchr.'s asst., 2002—04; hydrologic technician U.S. Geologic Survey, Tampa, 2003—04; geochemist U.S. Labs., Ft. Myers, Fla., 2004—05; environ. health specialist Va. Dept. of Health, Boydton, 2005—. Recipient Eager Beaver award, U.S. Geologic Survey, 2004. Mem.: Mensa (life), Phi Theta Kappa. Libertarian. Achievements include research in Using Hydrogen and Oxegyn isotopes to discern baseflow and storm flow from total flow in low gradient streams. Avocations: hunting, basketball, collecting horror movies. Home: 1125 Barnes Rd Chase City VA 23924 Home Phone: 434-372-3895; Office Phone: 434-738-6815. Personal E-mail: ccaknipe@yahoo.com. Business E-Mail: christopher.caknipe@vdh.virginia.gov.

CALABRESE, CHARLES, radio station official; b. Steubenville, Ohio, June 3, 1951; s. A. Felix and Ann Frances (Golec) C. BA in Drama and English, Coll. of Steubenville, 1973. Tchr. lang. arts Steubenville City Schs., 1973; news dir. Sta. WEIR, Weirton, W.Va., 1974-76; tchr. religion Cath. Cen. High Sch., Steubenville, 1977; news dir., performing arts critic Sta. WSTV and WRKY, Steubenville, 1977—96. Lector Blessed Sacrament Ch., Wintersville, Ohio, 1965—, mem. liturgy com., cantor, 1979—; actor, dir., v.p. Brooke County (W.Va.) Arts Coun., 1974—, bd. dirs., 1980—; lectr. various civic orgns., Steubenville, 1977—. Avocations: theater, leathercraft, music, art, panelology. Office: 3375 County Rd 36 Bloomingdale OH 43912-7903

CALABRESE, JOSEPH A., lawyer; b. Paterson, NJ, 1956; BA summa cum laude, Boston Coll., 1978; JD cum laude, Cornell U., 1981. Bar: Calif. 1981, US Dist. Ct. (Central Dist. Calif) 1981. Chair, entertainment and media practice group O'Melveny and Myers LLP, LA, mng. ptnr., office head (Century City office). Spkr. in the field. Staff mem. Cornell Internat. Law Jour., 1979—80, articles editor, 1980—81. Dir. Educate the Children Found., Constitutional Rights Found. Mem.: Independent Film and Television Alliance (arbitrator), Century City Bar Assn., ABA (task force on alternative dispute resolution in entertainment industry). Office: O'Melveny & Myers LLP 1999 Avenue of the Stars 7th Fl Los Angeles CA 90067-6035 Office Phone: 310-246-6743. Office Fax: 310-246-6779. Business E-Mail: jcalabrese@omm.com.

CALABRESE, JOSEPH D., psychologist, educator; s. Joseph and Ann Calabrese; m. Tracey Calabrese. MusB, DePaul U., 1989; MA in Anthropology, U. Ill., 1993; PhD in Psychology, U. Chgo., IL, 2006. Rsch. assoc.dept psychiatry U. Chgo., 1999—2000, Bernice Neugarten lectr. com. on human devel., 2002—03; lectr. anthropology U. Ill., Chgo., 1996—97; clin. fellow Harvard Med. Sch., Cambridge Hosp., Mass., 2006—07; rsch. fellow dept. social medicine Harvard Med. Sch., 2007—. Contbr. articles various profl. jours., chapters to books. Recipient Bernice Neugarten prize on human devel., U. Chgo., 2003, Hayek Fund for Scholars award, Inst. for Humane Studies, 2003; Grad. fellowship, U. Chgo., 1994 through 1999, Human Rights Program fellowship, 2002, Coolidge Scholar fellowship, Assn. for Religion and the Intellectual Life, Columbia U., 2003. Mem.: APA, Am. Anthrop. Assn., Soc. Psychotherapy Rsch., Soc. Med. Anthropology, Soc. Psychol. Anthropology. Achievements include research in ritual healing and socialization in the Native American Church completed within the Navajo Nation; severe mental illness, including participant observation of a mutual help organization by and for persons with mental illness. Avocations: baroque, renaissance lute. Office: Cambridge Hosp Harvard Med Sch Behavioral Med 1493 Cambridge St Cambridge MA 02139 Personal E-mail: jdcalabr@uchicago.edu.

CALABRESE, KIRK ROBERT, medical transcriptionist; b. Geneva, NY, Nov. 3, 1964; s. Ralph Robert and Shirley Ann Calabrese; m. Candace Jean Bayliss, June 20, 1992; children: James Liliestedt, Julie Liliestedt. BA, U. Buffalo, NY, 1989; AA, Finger Lakes C.C., Canandaigua, NY, 1996; MA, Empire State Coll., Saratoga Springs, NY, 1999. Cert. Comptia, 2004; med. transcriptionist Calif., 2006. Med. transcriptionist Finger Lakes Health, Geneva, NY, 1996—2005, Execuscribe, Rochester, NY, 2005—06, Acuis, Santa Clara, Calif., 2006—. Composer: (songs) Black Dreams, 2000; contbr. articles to profl. jours. Vol. Finger Lakes Vis. Nurse Svc., Geneva, NY, 1992—2006. Recipient The Morton Orlov Edn. award, Finger Lakes Health, 2001. Mem.: AMA, Am. Assn. Med. Transcriptionists. Democrat. Methodist. Achievements include design of computer programs. Avocation: skiing. Home Phone: 315-781-5189. Personal E-mail: kirk_c_99@yahoo.com.

CALABRESE, MICHAEL RAPHAEL, manufacturing executive, lawyer, consultant; b. Atlantic City, May 28, 1956; s. Angelo William and Sally (Snyder) C.; m. Kitty R. Calabrese. BS in Fgn. Svc., Georgetown U., 1978; JD, U. Va., 1982. Law clk. to cir. judge U.S. Ct. Appeals (4th cir.), Washington, 1982—83; assoc. Mudge, Rose et al, Washington, 1983—84, Finley, Kumble et al, Washington, 1984—86, Morgan, Lewis & Bockius, Washington, 1986—92; ptnr. McKenna & Cuneo, Washington, 1992—95; asst. gen. counsel Lockheed Martin Corp., Bethesda, Md., 1995—99; ptnr. Coudert Bros., Washington, 1999—2003; cons. investment banking, corp. and internat., 2004—06; sr. v.p. Cajun Industries, LLC, 2006—. Mem.: Columbia Country Club, Univ. Club, Army and Navy Club, Phi Beta Kappa. Republican. Home: 17907 E Augusta Dr Baton Rouge LA 70810 Personal E-mail: calabresem@bellsouth.net.

CALABRESE, ROSALIE SUE, management consultant, writer; b. NYC, Feb. 17, 1938; d. Julius and Florence (Tuck) Hochman; m. Anthony J. Calabrese, June 15, 1960 (div.); 1 child, Christopher. BA in Journalism, CCNY, 1959. Asst. news editor Electronic News, NYC, 1960; asst. to publicist Abner Klipstein, NYC, 1963; asst. to producer Leonard Field, NYC, 1964; mgr. Am. Composers Alliance, NYC, 1969-85, exec. dir., gen. mgr., 1985-94; dir. Rosalie Calabrese Mgmt., NYC, 1983—. Music advisor Phyllis Rose Dance Co., NYC, 1987—, also bd. dirs.; sec. bd. dirs. Am. Composers Orch., NYC, 1987-93; pres., bd. dirs. 1st Ave. Ensemble, 1993—, Golden Fleece Ltd., 1994—, sec. 1996-; bd. dirs. Friends Am. Composers, treas., 1991-94; adv. bd. Downtown Music Prodns., 1991-2007, bd. dirs., 2007—; adv. bd. Joan Miller's Dance Players, NYC, 1991-94, Copland House, 1996-97; mem. editl. adv. bd. New Music Connoisseur Mag., 2002-05; mem. music com., Estate Project for Artists with AIDS, 2001-03. Author, lyricist: (musicals) A Hell of An Angel, Simone, Not in Earnest, Murdering Macbeth, Pop Life, Does Anyone Here Speak Arabic?, Friends and Relations, Double-Play, C-R; assoc. prodr., treas. box office: (play) Courtyard, 1959, The Mime and Me; co-prodr.: various plays at White Lake (N.Y.) Playhouse, also packaged tours for Prodn. Assocs.; dir. The Bagel Baker's Daughter, 1999, night club acts for Florence Hayle; contbr. short stories and poetry to lit., nat. mags. and anthologies. Mem.: Poetry Soc. Am., Poets and Writers, Broadcast Music Inc., Dramatists Guild. Office: Rosalie Calabrese Mgmt PO Box 20580 New York NY 10025-1521

CALABRESI, GUIDO, federal judge, educator; b. Milan, Oct. 18, 1932; s. Massimo and Bianca Maria (Finzi Contini) C.; m. Anne Gordon Audubon Tyler, May 20, 1961; children: Bianca Finzi Contini, Anne Gordon Audubon, Massimo Franklin Tyler BS in Analytical Econs., Yale U., 1953, LLB, 1958, MA (hon.), 1962; BA in Politics, Philosophy and Econs., Oxford U., 1955, MA in Politics, Philosophy and Econs., 1959; LLD (hon.), Notre Dame U., 1979, Villanova U., 1984, U. Toronto, 1985, Boston Coll., 1986, Cath. U. Am., 1986, U. Chgo., 1988, Conn. Coll., 1988, Chgo.-Kent-I.T.T., 1989, William Mitchell Coll. Law, 1992, Princeton U., 1992, Detroit Mercy Sch. Law, 1994, Seton Hall U., 1995, Albertus Magnus Coll., 1995, Lewis and Clark Coll., 1996, St. John's U., 1997, Pace U., 1998, Iona Coll., 1998, Roger Williams U., 1999, Hofstra U., 1999, N.Y. Law Sch., 1999, Skidmore Coll., 2000, Colby Coll., 2001, U. San Diego, 2001; Dott. Ius SD (hon.), U. Turin, Italy, 1982; JD (hon.), U. Pavia, Italy, 1987, U. Stockholm, 1993; PhD (hon.), U. Haifa, Israel, 1988; DPhil, U. Tel Aviv, 1998; LHD (hon.), U. New Haven, 1989, Williams Coll., 1991, Quinnipiac Coll., 1993; DSc in Politics (hon.), U. Padua, Italy, 1990; Dott. Jur. (hon.), U. Bologna, Italy, 1991, U. Milan, 1998. Bar: Conn. 1958. Asst. instr. dept. econs. Yale U., New Haven, 1955-56; law clk. to Hon. Hugo Black U.S. Supreme Ct., Washington, 1958-59; asst. prof. Yale U. Law Sch., 1959-61, assoc. prof., 1961-62, prof., 1962-70, John Thomas Smith prof. law, 1970-78, Sterling prof. law, 1978-95; prof. emeritus, lectr. Yale U., 1995—; dean Yale U. Law Sch., 1985-94, Sterling prof. law emeritus, lectr. New Haven, 1995—; judge US Ct. Appeals 2d cir., New Haven, 1994—. Fellow Timothy Dwight Coll., 1960—; vis. prof. Harvard U. Law Sch., 1969-70, Japan Am. Studies Seminar, Kyoto-Doshisha Univs., summer 1972, European U. Inst., Florence, Italy, 1979; Arthur L. Goodhart prof. legal sci. Cambridge U., also fellow St. John's Coll., 1980-81. Author: The Costs of Accidents: A Legal and Economic Analysis, 1970; (with P. Bobbitt) Tragic Choices, 1978; A Common Law for the Age of Statutes, 1983 (ABA citation of merit, Order of Coif Triennial Book award); Ideals, Beliefs, Attitudes and the Law: Private Law Perspectives on a Public Law Problem (Silver Gavel award ABA), 1985; contbr. articles to profl. jours. Hon. trustee Hopkins Grammar Sch., pres. 1976-80; trustee St. Thomas More Chapel, Yale U.; vice-chmn. bd. trustees Carolyn Found., Minn. Rhodes scholar, 1953; named one of Ten Outstanding Young Men Am., U.S. Jaycees, 1962; recipient Laetare Medal, U. Notre Dame, 1985, Marshall-Wythe medal Coll. William and Mary, 1985, award for outstanding rsch. in law and govt. Fellows of Am. Bar Found., 1998, Thomas Jefferson medal in law Jefferson Found./U. Va. Law Sch., 2000. Fellow Am. Acad. Arts & Scis., Associazione Italiana di Diritto Comparato, Brit. Acad. (corr.), Royal Swedish Acad. Scis. (fgn.), Nat. Acad. dei Lincei (fgn.), Acad. delle Sci. di Torino (fgn.); mem. Conn. Bar Assn., Assn. Am. Law Schs. (exec. com. 1986-89), Am. Philos. Soc. Home: 639 Amity Rd Woodbridge CT 06525-1206 Office: US Ct Appeals 2d Cir 157 Church St New Haven CT 06510-2100*

CALABRESI, STEVEN G., law educator; BA cum laude, Yale U., 1980, JD, 1983. Law clk. to Hon. Ralph K. Winter US Ct. Appeals (2nd cir.), New Haven, 1983—84; to Hon. Robert H. Bork US Ct. Appeals, DC cir., 1984—85; spl. asst. to atty. gen. US Dept. Justice, 1985—87; spl. asst. to asst. to Pres. for Domestic Affairs The White House, 1987; law clk. to Hon. Antonin Scalia US Supreme Ct., 1987—88; rsch. assoc. Am. Enterprise Inst. for Pub. Policy Rsch., 1988—90; speechwriter to Vice President Dan Quayle The White House, 1990; asst. prof. law Northwestern U. Sch. Law, Chgo., 1990—93, assoc. prof., 1993—96, prof., 1996—, George C. Dix prof. constitutional law, 1998—2001, 2004—. Co-founder, nat. co-chmn. The Federalist Soc. for Law and Pub. Policy Studies, 1982—2005. Contbr. articles to profl. jours. Office: Northwestern U Sch Law 357 E Chicago Ave Chicago IL 60611 Office Phone: 312-503-7012. E-mail: s-calabresi@law.northwestern.edu.

CALABRO, ALFRED A., lawyer; b. Hartford, Conn., Sept. 25, 1925; s. Antonio Joseph Calabro and Concettina Failia; m. Katherine Anne Larkin, July 14, 1980. A, LA City Coll.; JD, Southwestern U., LA. Atty, Calabro, Calabro & Calabro, Glendale, Calif. Office: Calabro Law Offices 124 S Isabel St Ste 200 Glendale CA 91205 Office Phone: 818-240-4812, 818-240-9137. Business E-Mail: calabrolaw@aol.com.

CALACANIS, JASON MCCABE, internet entrepreneur, blogger; b. Bklyn., Nov. 28, 1970; Attended, Fordham U. Founder, owner Rising Tide Solutions; co-founder, CEO Weblogs, Inc. (purchased by America On Line in 2005, but still maintains site); website gen. mgr. Netscape.com, 2005—06; entrepreneur-in-action Sequoia Capital, 2006—; founder, CEO Mahalo.com search engine, 2007—. Prodr., editor, CEO (publication) Silicon Alley Reporter (renamed Venture Reporter in 2001, eventually sold to another publishing comp.), 1996; prodr.: (publication) Digital Coast Reporter; cons., featured in The Center of the World, blogger (website) calacanis.com. Named one of Top 25 Web Celebs, Forbes mag., 2007. Address: 2200 Colorado Ave Ste 729 Santa Monica CA 90404 Office: Mahalo Inc 902 Colorado Ave Santa Monica CA 90401 Office Phone: 310-828-8284. Office Fax: 310-456-4900.*

CALAMAR, GLORIA, artist; b. NYC, Sept. 7, 1921; d. Louis B. and Dina (Cotter) Calamar; m. R.L. Redgate, Aug. 22, 1950 (div. 1972); children: Chris James, Steven Clay, Michael Cotter. Cert., Otis Art Inst., LA, 1943; student, Art Students League, NYC, 1944-45; BA in Art History, State Univ. Coll. N.Y. at New Paltz, 1970. Instr. art history and painting Orange County (N.Y.) Community Coll., 1964-69; instr. art history Mt. St. Mary Coll., Newburgh, NY, 1968-69; instr. painting Santa Barbara City Coll., 1975-80. Judge Hallmark Art Contest, N.Y., 1968; lectr. Woodstock (N.Y.) Sch. Art, 1994; color slide lectr. throughout world. Artist in water color, oil, pen and ink, 1946—; one woman shows include Georgetown U., 1974, Portland (Oreg.) C.C., 1973, Willamette U., 1972, U. Oreg., 1971-72, U. Calif. at Berkeley, 1969, Santa Barbara (Calif.) Mus. Art, 1950, Musèe d'Art Moderne de la Ville de Paris, 1967, Galèrie de la Madeleine, Brussels, Belgium, 1964, Landau Gallery, Beverly Hills, Calif., 1953, Parnassus Sq., Woodstock, N.Y., 1978, Ibiza, Balearic Islands, Spain, 1978, Santorini, Greece, 1980, Beaux Arts Ctr., Tunis, Tunisia, 1981, Alkamal Gallery, Jerusalem, Israel, 1981, Jaisalmer, India, 1984, Women's Cmty. Bldg., Santa Barbara, 1986, Jewish Cmty. Ctr., San Francisco, 1986; group shows include Delgado Mus., New Orleans, 1950, San Francisco Art Assn., 1953, L.A. County Mus. Art, 1954, Bertrand Russell Centenary Invitational, London, 1972-73, Woodstock Art Assn., 1978, Faulkner Gallery Santa Barbara, 1992, 93; curated Santa Barbara Visual Artists League Exhbn., 1993, 94; book, video Tar Pits Park Landmark Proposal, Portola Sycamore Tree Landmark Proposal, Carpinteria Airport Landmark Proposal, Juarez-Hosmer Adobe Landmark Proposal, Leaping Greyhound Bridge Landmark Proposal, Los Clavelitos Landmark Proposal, Los Cruces Adobe Landmark Proposal, De la Cuesta Adobe Landmark Proposal; painted the facade of Wells Cathedral, 1999-00; producer video TV program; author: Traveling Artist, 1995; prodr. TV video series Traveling Artist; contbr. articles to publs; prodr. (video) The Traveling Artist, 1996—. Curator Visual Artists League Exhbn., Santa Barbara, 1992, 93, 94, 95; mem. Santa Barbara County Hist. Landmark Adv. Commn. Nat. Endowment for Arts grantee, 1980-81; recipient Calif. Gov.'s Historic Preservation award Santa Barbara County Hist. Landmark Adv. Commn., 1999. Mem. Woodstock (N.Y.) Art Assn. (life), Alumni Assn. Otis Art Inst. (L.A.), Art Students League N.Y. (life), Santa Barbara Visual Artists League. *Many people have told me that I am a strong painter and add in the same breath— like a man. Others have asked me which comes first— my work or my children. I wonder how many male artists have been evaluated or interrogated in the same way. To the former I say thank you for the evaluation of strength but to be a woman artist does not preclude this ingredient. To the latter (I say) one interest supports the other and each is given priority at different times. Much in the same way that food and drink are necessary to the whole person and each is given priority at different times.*

CALAMARI, JOSEPH AUGUST, legal educator; b. NYC, Feb. 20, 1919; s. August Alexander and Margaret Elizabeth (Casella) C.; m. Marie Jean Sileo, June 30, 1951; children: Betty Jo, Ann-Marie, Maryellen, James. BA, Fordham U., 1939, LLB, 1942; M.Law, NYU, 1949. Bar: NY 1942, US Dist. Ct. (so. dist.) NY 1946, (ea. dist.) NY 1947, US Ct. Apls. (2d cir.) 1947, Va. 1952, US Supreme Ct. 1951, US Ct. Mil. Apls. 1951. Assoc. counsel Alexander Ash & Schwartz, NYC, 1946-50; post judge adv. Post Headquarters, Ft. Myer, Va., 1950-52; dep. gen. counsel/gen. counsel Mil. Sealift Command Atlantic, Bklyn., 1952-73; prof. law St. John's U. Sch. Law, Jamaica, NY, 1973—; hearing officer US EEO, Washington, 1979—. Contbr. articles to profl. jours. Mem. Western Property Owners of Garden City, NY, 1956—; sponsor Nat. Republican. Congl. Com., 1984; mem. Republican Nat. Com., 1983. Served to col., USAR, 1972-77. Decorated Bronze Star, Army Commendation medal. Mem. Fed. Bar Assn., ABA, Martime Law Assn. US, Bar Assn. Nassau County (arbitrator), Res. Officers Assn., Am. Judicature Soc., Garden City Country Club, Mast Hope Lodge. Roman Catholic. Home: 14 Glen Rd Garden City NY 11530-1012 Office Phone: 718-990-6009.

CALAMARO, RAYMOND STUART, lawyer; b. Cairo, May 28, 1944; came to U.S., 1947, naturalized, 1960; s. Albert and Charlotte (Golub) C.; m. Jaana Pirinen; 1 child, Alexander M. AB, Cornell U., 1966; JD, NYU, 1969. Bar: N.Y. State 1970, U.S. Supreme Ct. 1975, D.C. 1976. Legis. dir. Sen.Gaylord Nelson, Washington, 1973-75; exec. dir. Com. for Pub. Justice, NYC, 1975-76; adj. faculty New Sch. Social Rsch., NYC, 1976; staff profl. Carter/Mondale Transition Team, Washington, 1976-77; dep. asst. atty. gen. Office Legis. Affairs, Dept. Justice, Washington, 1977-79; pvt. practice Washington and Brussels, 1979-95; team leader Clinton-Gore Transition Team, 1992-93; ptnr. Hogan & Hartson, Washington, 1995—. U.S. vice-chmn. U.S.-Korea Com. on Bus. Coop., 1997-99. Recipient Royal Order of Polar Star King Carl XVI Gustav, Sweden, 1989. Mem. Met. Club (Washington), St. Albans Tennis Club (Washington). Home: 5073 Lowell St NW Washington DC 20016-2616 Office: Hogan & Hartson 555 13th St NW Ste 800W Washington DC 20004-1109 also: rue de l'Industrie 26 1040 Brussels Belgium E-mail: RSCalamaro@HHLaw.com.

CALAME, BYRON EDWARD, journalist; b. Appleton City, Mo., Apr. 14, 1939; s. Harry Franklin and Gladys Verl (Neal) C.; m. Kathryn Lee Boehm, June 9, 1962; children: Christine Lee, Jonathan David. BJ, U. Mo., 1961; MA in Polit. Sci, U. Md., 1966. Staff reporter Wall St. Jour., NY, LA, and Washington, DC, 1965-74, bur. chief Pitts., 1974—78, LA, 1978—85, asst. mng. editor, West Coast coverage, 1985-87, sr. editor NYC, 1987-92, dep. mng. editor, 1992—2004; ret., 2004; public editor NY Times, NYC, 2005—07. Thomas Jefferson disting. vis. lectr. U. Mo., Columbia, 1997. Participant (TV series) Genesis, A Living Conversation. Served to lt. USN, 1961—65. Recipient Faculty-Alumni award U. Mo., Columbia, 1996, nat. fraternity's Oxford Cup award for Disting. Svc. and Accomplishments in Chosen Field, Beta Theta Pi, 2004, Elliot V. Bell award, NY Fin. Writers Assn., 2005, Gerold Loeb Lifetime Achievement award, UCLA Anderson Sch. Mgmt., 2005, Bart Richards award for Media Criticism, Pa. State U. Coll. Comm., 2006. Mem. Am. Soc. Newspaper Editors, Soc. Am. Bus. Editors and Writers (bd. govs., Disting. Achievement award 2002); pres. Soc. Am. Bus. Editors and Writers, 2000-01. Personal E-mail: barney@calames.net.

CALAME, KATHRYN LEE, microbiologist, educator; b. Leavenworth, Kans., Apr. 23, 1940; d. Jay O. and Marjorie B.; m. Byron Edward Calame, June 9, 1962; children: Christine Lee, Jonathan David. BS, U. Mo., 1962; MS, George Washington U., Washington, DC, 1965, PhD, 1975. Asst. prof. biol. chemisty UCLA, 1980-85, assoc. prof., 1985-88, prof., 1988; prof. microbiology Coll. Physicians and Surgeons Columbia U., NYC, 1988—. Mem. sci. rev. bd. Howard Hughes Med. Inst., 2002—. Exec. editor: Nucleic Acids Rsch., 1992-98; mem. bd. rev. editors: Sci. Mag., 1988-2000; assoc. editor Jour. Clin. Investigation; contbr. articles to profl. jours. Trustee Leukemia Soc. Am., NYC, 1992—2001, chair grant rev. com., 1992-96; mem. bd. sci. counselors Nat. Inst. Child Health and Devel., 1999—2004. Recipient Stohlman award Leukemia Soc. Am., 1989, Faculty Alumni award U. Mo., Columbia, 1996; disting. lecture in basic sci., Columbia Physicians and Surgeons, 1998. Fellow: AAAS, Am. Acad. Arts and Sci.; mem.: Am. Assn. Biochemistry and Molecular Biology (chair pub. com. 1992—93). Democrat. Avocations: cooking, gardening, reading, antiques. Office: Columbia U Dept Microbiology 701 W 168th St New York NY 10032-2704 Business E-Mail: klc1@columbia.edu.

CALAMOS, JOHN PETER, SR., brokerage house executive; b. Aug. 28, 1940; s. Peter and Mary (Kyriakopoulos) Calamos; m. Jackie Calamos, Aug. 15, 1962; children: John Peter Jr. and Laura Lynn. BS in Econs., Ill. Inst. Tech., 1963, MBA in Fin., 1965. Registered rep. DuPont Walston Co., Chgo., 1971-74, Loeb Rhoades Co., Chgo., 1974, Bache & Co., Chgo., 1974-75, Hornblower-Weeks Co., Chgo., 1975-76; sr. v.p. Woodlard & Co., Chgo., 1976-77; pres., mng. dir. Calamos Asset Mgmt., Inc., Oak Brook, Ill., 1977—, CEO. Pres. Calamos Convertible Income Fund, Oak Brook, 1985—. Author: Investing in a Convertible Securities: A Guide to Their Risks and Rewards, 1988; contbr. articles to profl. jours. Served as maj. USAF, 1965-70, Vietnam. Named one of 400 Richest Am., Forbes mag., 2006. Mem. Internat. Assn. Fin. Planners, Chgo. Assn. Commerce and Industry, Assn. Investment Mgmt. Sales Execs., Inst. Investment Mgmt. Cons., Investment Mgmt. Cons. Assn. Clubs: Sky Haven (Aurora, Ill.) (pres.). Avocations: airplanes, tennis. Office: Calamos Asset Mgmt Inc 1111 E Warrenville Rd Naperville IL 60563-1405

CALARCO, VINCENT ANTHONY, specialty chemicals company executive; b. NYC, May 29, 1942; s. George Michael and Madeline J. Calarco; m. Linda Joyce Maniscalco, Apr. 10, 1971; children: David V., Christopher G. BS, Polytech. U. N.Y., 1963; MBA, Harvard U., 1970. With Crompton & Knowles Corp., NYC, pres., CEO, 1985—2004, chmn. bd., 1986—. Bd. dirs. Newmont Mining, Con Edison, The Hosp. of St. Raphael. Trustee Poly. U. With US Army, 1966—68. Mem.: Chem. Heritage Found. (chmn., exec. com., trustee), Am. Chemistry Coun. (chmn. bd. 1995—96), Am. Soc. Chem. Industry (chmn. Am. sect. 1998—99, pres. 1998—2000), Am. Chem. Soc., Harvard Bus. Sch. Club.

CALATRAVA, SANTIAGO, architect, structural engineer, artist; b. Valencia, Spain, July 28, 1951; Degree, Inst. Architecture, Valencia, 1974, Fed. Inst. Tech., Zürich, 1979; D of Tech. Sci., Fed. Inst. Tech., 1981; D (hon.), Poly U., Valencia, 1993, U. Seville, Spain, 1994; LittD in Environ. Studies (hon.), Heriot-Watt U., Edinburgh, Scotland, 1994; DSc (hon.), U. Coll. Salford, Eng., 1995, U. Strathclyde, Glasgow, Scotland, 1995—97, U. Tech., Delft, The Netherlands, 1995; D (hon.), Milw. Sch. Engring., Wis., 1995—97; D of Civil Engring. (hon.), U. degli Stugi di Cassino, Italy, 1999; D of Tech. (hon.), Lund U., Sweden, 1999; D (hon.), Technion, Israel, 2004. Lic. structural engr., Ill., profl. engr., Calif. Pvt. practice, Zurich, 1981—, Paris, 1989—, Valencia, Spain, 1991—. Prin. works include Stadelhofen Rlwy. Sta., Zürich, Switzerland, 1983—84 (City of Zürich award, 1991, Brunel award, 1992), Alamillo Bridge and La Cartuja Viaduct, Seville, Spain, 1987—92, Campo Volantin Footbridge, Bilbao, Spain, 1990—98, Sondica Airport, Bilbao, 1990—99, Alameda Bridge and Underground Sta., Valencia, 1991—95, Palace of the Arts, Valencia, Spain, 2001, City of Arts and Sci. Valencia, Valencia, Oriente Sta., Lisbon, Portugal, 1993—98, Lyon Airport Sta., Lyon, Turning Torso Tower, Malmö, World Trade Ctr. Transp. Hub, NYC, Milw. Art Mus. expansion, Milw., 2001, Tenerife Auditorium, Canary Islands, The Chicago Spire, 2007, exhibitions include Jamileh Weber Gallery, Zürich, 1985, Mus. of Architecture, Basel, Switzerland, 1985, traveling exhbn., NY, St. Louis, Chgo., LA, Toronto, Montreal, 1985, Suomen Rakennustaiteen Mus., Helsinki, Finland, 1991, Mus. of Design, Zürich, Switzerland, 1991, Dutch Inst. Architecture, Rotterdam, Holland, 1992, Royal Inst. Brit. Architects, London, Eng., 1992, ArkitekturMuseet, Stockholm, Sweden, 1992, Deutsches Mus., Munich, Germany, 1993, Mus. Modern Art, NYC, NY, 1993, La Lonja Mus., Valencia, Italy, 1993, Pavilion Overbeck Soc., Lübeck, Germany, 1993, Architecture Ctr., Gammel Dok, Copenhagen, Sweden, 1993, Bruton St. Gallery, London, Eng., 1994, Mus. Applied and Folk Art, Moscow, Russia, 1994, Ma Gallery, Tokyo, Japan, 1994, Arqueria de los Nuevos Ministerios, Madrid, Spain, 1994, Sala de Arte La Recova, Santa Cruz de Tenerife, 1994, Mus. of Design, Zürich, Switzerland, 1995, Ctr. Cultural de Belem, Lisbon, Portugal, 1995, Navarra Mus. Pamplona, 1995, Archivo Floral, Bilbao, 1995, Palazzo della Raggione, Padova, Italy, 1995, Dept. of Bldg., Basel, Switzerland, 1995, Milw. Art Mus., 1995, Britannic Tower, London, 1995, Israel Nat. Mus. of Sci., Haifa, 1995, Palazzo Strozzi, Florence, 2000—01, Met. Mus. Art, N.Y.C., 2005. Named Global Leader for Tomorrow, World Econ. Forum, Davos, Switzerland, 1993, Gold Master of the High Direction Forum, Madrid, 1995; named one of Time Mag. 100 Most Influential People, 2005; recipient Auguste Perret prize, Internat. Union Architects, 1979, Art prize, City of Barcelona, 1985, Press Assn. award, Valencia, 1985, prize, Internat. Assn. Bridge and Structural Engring., 1985, Fomento de las Artes y del Diseño, Spain, 1985, Fritz Schumacher prize for urbanism, architecture and engring., Hamburg, Germany, 1985, Silver medal for rsch. and technique, Found. Acad. Architecture, Paris, 1990, European Glulam award, Munich, 1991, Gold medal, Inst. Structural Engrs., London, 1992, II Honor prize, City of Pedreguer, 1993, Urban Design award, City of Toronto, 1993, medal of honor, Fundación Garcia Cabrerizo, Madrid, 1993, award for good bldg., Canton of Lucerne, Switzerland, 1995, Gold medal, Ministry of Culture, Granada, Spain, 1995, European award for steel structures, Berlin, 1995, art prize, Louis Vuitton-Moet Hennessy, Paris, 1995, Principe de ASTURIAS award for the arts, 1999, Gold medal, AIA, 2005, Eugene McDermott award in the arts, MIT, 2005, Gold Medal, Am. Inst. Architects, 2005, Golden Plate award, Acad. Achievement, 2004; fellow Fazlur Rahman Khan Internat. for architecture and engring., 1985. Fellow: Royal Incorporation of Architects (Scotland) (hon.); mem.: Royal Swedish Acad. Engring. Scis., Order of Arts and Letters (Paris), European Acad. (Cologne, Germany), Real Acad. Bellas Artes de San Carlos, Internat. Acad. Architecture, Union of Swiss Architects, Real Acad. Bellas Artes de San Fernando (hon.), Coll. Architects Mexico City (hon.), Royal Inst. Brit. Architects (hon.), Union of German Architects (hon.). Office: Santiago Calatrava SA Parkring 11 8002 Zurich Switzerland*

CALCANIS, JASON MCCABE, Internet company executive; b. Bklyn. BS in Psychology, Fordham Univ., NYC. Founder, CEO Rising Tide Studios; co-founder, creator Weblogs, Inc. (sold to AOL), 2004—05; sr. v.p. AOL, 2005—07, gen. mgr., Netscape, 2006—07; CEO Mahalo search engine, 2007—. Script cons., actor (films) Center of the World. Bd. dir. Bay Ridge Prep. Sch. Named one of 50 Who Matter Now, Business 2.0, 2007. Avocations: Tae Kwon Do, running marathons. Office: Mahalo Ste 729 2200 Colorado Ave Santa Monica CA 90404 Office Phone: 310-828-8284.*

CALCAVECCHIA, MARK, professional golfer; b. Laurel, Nebr., June 12, 1960; Student, U. Fla. Profl. golfer, 1981—. Mem. US team Ryder Cup, 1987, 89, 91, 2002, Dunhill Cup, 1989, 90, Presidents Cup, 1998. Named to Phoenix Open Hall of Fame, 2002. Achievements include winning the S.W. Classic, 1986, Honda Classic, 1987, 98, Bank of Boston Classic, 1988, Australian Open, 1988, LA Open, 1989, Phoenix Open, 1989, 92, 2001, British Open, 1989, Argentine Open, 1993, 95, BellSouth Classic, 1995; winner, Greater Vancouver Open, 1997, Subaru Sarazen World Open, 1997, Maekyung Open, 2004, Bell Can. Open, 2005, PODS Championship, 2007. Mailing: c/o PGA Tour 112 PGA Tour Blvd Ponte Vedra Beach FL 32082*

CALDEIRA, CHARLENE A., lawyer; b. New Bedford, Mass., Jan. 31, 1971; BA in Psychology, cum laude, Bridgewater State U., 1994; JD cum laude, Suffolk U., 1998. Bar: Mass. 1998, US Dist. Ct. (Dist. Mass.) 2000, US Ct. Appeals (1st Cir.) 2000. Law clk. to Assoc. Justice Neil L. Lynch Supreme Judicial Ct., 1998, rsch. asst. to Assoc. Justice Joseph R. Nolan; assoc. Family and Probate Law Group Todd & Weld, LLP; assoc. Family and Probate Law, Criminal Law and Appellate Law Group Casner & Edwards LLP, Boston. Adj. prof. family law New England Sch. Law. Mem.: ABA, Mass. Bar Assn., Boston Bar Assn. Office: Casner & Edwards LLP 303 Congress St Boston MA 02210 Office Phone: 617-426-5900. Office Fax: 617-426-8810. E-mail: caldeira@casneredwards.com.

CALDER, IAIN WILSON, publishing executive; b. Scotland, Feb. 27, 1939; arrived in U.S., 1967, naturalized; s. William and Charlotte G. (West) C.; m. Jane Brownlea Bell, Apr. 17, 1965; children: Douglas William, Glen Robert Bell. Student pub. schs., Falkirk, Scotland. Reporter Falkirk Sentinel, 1955-56, Stirling Jour., 1956, Falkirk Mail, 1956-60, Glasgow Daily Record, 1960-64; London bur. chief Nat. Enquirer, 1964-67, articles editor, 1967-73, exec. editor, 1973-75, editor, 1975-91, pres. Lantana, Fla., 1976-95, editor-in-chief, 1991-95, editor emeritus, 1995-97; exec. v.p. pub. Am. Media Inc., 1994-97. Dir. Am. Media, Inc./Nat. Enquirer; Disting. lectr Fla. Atlantic U. Bd. dirs. Bethesda Hosp. Found., 1997—.

CALDER, JAMES J., lawyer; b. NYC, Apr. 5, 1954; BA, U. Va., 1974, JD, 1977. Bar: NY 1978, US Ct. Appeals, 2nd and 3rd Cir., US Dist. Ct., Ea. and So. Dists. NY, US Supreme Ct. Ptnr. Katten Muchin Rosenman LLP, NYC. Mem.: ABA, Assn. Bar of City NY, Phi Beta Kappa. Office: Katten Muchin Rosenman LLP 575 Madison Ave New York NY 10022 Office Phone: 212-940-6460. Office Fax: 212-940-3817. Business E-Mail: james.calder@kattenlaw.com.

CALDER, KENT EYRING, political science professor, federal agency administrator; b. Salt Lake City, Apr. 18, 1948; s. Grant H. and Rose (Eyring) C.; m. Toshiko Matsuura; children: Mari, Ryan. BA with honors, U. Utah, 1970; AM, Harvard U., 1972, PhD, 1979. Staff mem. U.S. Ho. of Reps., Washington, 1968-69; tchg. fellow Harvard U. Dept. of Govt., Cambridge, Mass., 1972-74; rsch. economist U.S. Fed. Trade Commn., Washington, 1974-78; vis. fellow U. Tokyo, 1977—78; exec. dir. U.S.-Japan Program Harvard U., Cambridge, 1979-80, lectr., 1979-83; asst. prof. Woodrow Wilson Sch., Princeton (N.J.) U., 1983—89, tenured faculty, 1989—2003, dir. U.S.-Japan program, 1990—2003; Edwin O. Reischauer prof. East Asian Studies Johns Hopkins U., Washington, 2003—, dir. Reischauer Ctr. East Asian Studies Washington, D.C., 2003—. Internat. adv. bd. Japanese Ministry of Fin., Inst. of Fiscal and Monetary Policy, Tokyo, 1987-96; Japan chair Ctr. for Strategic and Internat. Studies, Washington, 1989-91, 96; spl. advisor to U.S. Amb. to Japan, 1996-2001; mem. Bretton Woods Com., 2001—; mem. nat. U.S. adv. bd. Japan Found., 2003—; vis. prof. Seoul (Rep. Korea) Nat. U., 2005—; adv. bd. Korea Econ. Inst., 2005—. Author: Crisis and Compensation, 1988 (Ohira and Arisawa Meml. prizes 1990), Japan's Changing Role in Asia, 1992, Strategic Capitalism, 1993, Pacific Defense, 1996 (Mainichi Asia-Pacific Grand prize 1997), Embattled Garrisons, 2007; co-author: The Eastasia Edge, 1982; mem. editl. bd. Asian Security, 2005—. Instr. Japan Soc. U.S.-Japan Leadership Program, N.Y.C., 1988-91, U. Pa. Wharton Sch. Internat. Forum, 1990—; trustee Princeton in Asia, 1987-95; mem. Coun. on Fgn. Rels., 1990—, internat. adv. bd. Waseda U. Sch. Asia-Pacific Studies, 1998—, World Econ. Forum East Asia Summits, 1998—, Bretton Woods Com., 2001—. 1st lt. U.S. Army, 1975-76. Graduate Prize fellow Harvard U., 1970-74, Faculty Rsch. fellow Japan Found., 1984, Fulbright Faculty fellow and Doctoral fellow, 1985-86, 75-76, Abe fellow US-Japan Ctr. for Global Partnership, 2005-07. Mem. Am. Polit. Sci. Assn., Assn. for Asian Studies, Phi Beta Kappa, Phi Kappa Phi (Sparks Fellow 1970-71, Gibbs Fellow 1970), OECD Tide 2000 Club. Avocations: stamp collecting/philately, collecting African musical instruments, tennis. Home: 197 Shadybrook Ln Princeton NJ 08540-4135 Office: Sch Adv Internat Studies 1619 Mass Ave NW Washington DC 20036-1984 Office Phone: 202-663-5812. Business E-Mail: kcalder@jhu.edu.

CALDER, ROBERT AUSTIN, preventive medicine physician, administrator; b. Beloit, Wis., May 21, 1954; s. John T. and Rosemary A. (Austin) Calder; m. Daphne R. Calder, Aug. 17, 1979 (div. June 2007); children: Heather, Joseph. BS, U. Wis., 1979; MD, Med. Coll. Wis., 1982; MS, U. Wis., Milw., 1984. Diplomate Am. Bd. Preventive Medicine. Chief, preventive medicine U.S. Army, Ft. Sill, Okla., 1985-87; epidemiologist Fla. Dept. Health, Tallahassee, 1987-90; assoc. dir. Merck & Co., Inc., West Point, Pa., 1990-91, dir., 1992-93, sr. dir., 1993-98, exec. dir., 1999—. Capt., U.S. Army, 1985-87. Eagle Scout, 1970. Fellow Am. Coll. Preventive Medicine. Roman Catholic. Avocations: sailing, bicycling. Home and Office: 137 E Wilson St Unit 512 Madison WI 53703 Office: Merck & Co Inc UG3AB-10 351 N Sumneytown Pk North Wales PA 19454

CALDERA, LOUIS EDWARD, former academic administrator, former federal official; b. El Paso, Tex., Apr. 1, 1956; s. Benjamin Luis Caldera and Soledad (Siqueiros); m. Eva Orlebeke Caldera; children: Allegra, Sophia, Camille. BS, U.S. Mil. Acad., 1978; JD, MBA, Harvard U., 1987. Bar: Calif. 1987. Commd. 2nd lt. US Army, 1978, advanced through ranks to capt., 1982, resigned commn., 1983, sec., 1998—2001; assoc. O'Melveny & Myers, LA, 1987-89, Buchalter, Nemer, Fields & Younger, LA, 1990-91; dep. county counsel County of LA, 1991-92; mem. Calif. State Assembly, 46th Dist., LA, 1992-97, chmn. banking and fin. com.; mng. dir., COO Corp. for Nat. Svc., Washington, 1997-98; vice chancellor, univ. advancement Calif. State U., 2001—03; pres. U. N.Mex, Albuquerque, 2003—06, prof. law, 2006—. Democrat. Roman Catholic.

CALDERBANK, ROBERT, engineering educator, researcher; m. Ingrid Daubechies. BS, Warwick U., 1975; MSc, Oxford U., 1976; PhD, Calif. Inst. Tech. Mem. tech. staff Bell Telephone Labs., 1980; v.p. info. scis. rsch. AT&T Labs, 1997—2002, v.p. rsch. and Internet and network sys., 2002—03; prof. elec. engring and math. Princeton U., NJ, 2003—. Fellow: IEEE (Info. Theory Prize Paper Award 1995, 1999, Millennium Medal 2000); mem.: NAE. Office: Princeton U Enging Quadrangle Olden St Princeton NJ 08544 Office Phone: 609-258-3500. Office Fax: 609-258-3745. E-mail: calderbk@princeton.edu.

CALDERON, RONALD, state official; b. Montebello, Calif., Aug. 12, 1957; m. Ana Calderon; children: Jessica, Zachary. Student, Western State U. Law; BA, UCLA, 1980. Owner fin. svcs. sales and mktg. firm; mgr. mfg. industry; mortgage banker; real estate agt.; chief of staff Assemblyman Ed Chavez; state assembly mem. Dist. 58 Calif. State Assembly, 2002—. Mem. appropriations com.; mem. banking and fin. com.; mem. govtl. orgn. com.; mem. ins. com.; mem. utilities and commerce com. Mem. La Merced Elem. Sch. PTA, 1998—; bd. dirs. L.A. Econ. Devel. Corp., 1998—, N.E. Cmty. Clinic, 1999—; mem. Gangs Out of Downey, 2001—. Democrat. Mailing: Rm 2179 PO Box 942849 Sacramento CA 94249 Office: Ste 100 400 N Montebello Blvd Montebello CA 90640

CALDERÓN, SILA MARIA, former governor; b. San Juan, Sept. 23, 1942; 3 children. B in Polit. Sci. with honors, Manhattanville Coll., degree (hon.); MPA, U. P.R.; degree (hon.), Boston U., New School U., Hunter Coll., Rutgers U., Manhattanville, Calif. Worked for Sec. of Labor; spl. asst. econ. devel. and labor for Gov. Hernández Colón, 1974; chief of staff Gov. Hernández Colón, 1985, sec. state, 1988; mayor City of San Juan, 1996—2000; gov. PR, San Juan, 2001—05. Bd. dirs. Banco Popular P.R., P.R. Pub. Broadcasting Corp., Pueblo Supermarkets. Named Outstanding Woman of Yr., PR C. of C., 1975, 1985, 1987, Puerto Rican Products Assn., 1986, PR chpt. Am. Assn. Pub. Works, 1988; recipient Harvard Found. award, Golden Plate award, Acad. Achievement, 2004. Mem.: Sister Isolina Ferré Found. Popular Democratic. Achievements include becoming first woman elected to office of governor of Puerto Rico; spearheaded the Special Communities Project for disadvantaged residents of Puerto Rico. Office Phone: 787-753-8310.*

CALDERONI, ROBERT M., software company executive; BS in Acctg. and Fin., Fordham U. CPA, Calif. Various fin. mgmt. positions IBM, Apple Computers, 1996-97; sr. v.p. fin., CFO Avery Dennison, Pasadena, Calif., 1997—2001; CFO Ariba, Inc., Sunnyvale, Calif., 2000—01, exec. v.p., CFO, 2001, pres., 2001—04, CEO, 2001—, chmn., 2003—. Bd. dirs. Ariba, Inc.; bd. dir. Juniper Networks, Inc. Office: Ariba Inc 807 11th Ave Sunnyvale CA 94089 Office Phone: 650-390-1000.

CALDICOTT, CATHERINE V., medical educator, researcher; AB, Princeton U., NJ, 1978; cert., U. Pa., Phila., 1987; MD, Dartmouth Med. Sch., Hanover, NH, 1991. Cert. Am. Bd. Internal Medicine, 1996. Intern Yale-New Haven Hosp., Conn., 1991—92; resident U. Mich. Hosps., Ann Arbor, 1992—94, clin. asst. prof., 1994—95; Robert Wood Johnson clin. scholar U. Mich., Ann Arbor, 1995—97; asst. prof. dept. medicine SUNY Upstate Med. U., Syracuse, NY, 1997—, asst. prof. bioethics and humanities, 2001—. Singer: opera, solo recitals, liturgical music, chamber music; author: published poetry (Dearing Writing award, 2006). Mem. Princeton Class of '78 Found., 1999—2007, sec., 2003—06. Recipient Mannix award for Excellence in Med. Edn., Med. Soc. NY, 2003—05. Fellow: ACP; mem.: Soc. Gen. Internal Medicine (co-chair qualitative rsch. abstract selection com. 2005), Am. Soc. Bioethics and Humanities (chair residency edn. interest group 1996—98). Office: SUNY Upstate Med Univ/CBH 725 Irving Ave Ste 406 Syracuse NY 13210 Business E-Mail: caldicoc@upstate.edu.

CALDWELL, ANN WICKINS, academic administrator; b. Rochester, NY, Dec. 3, 1943; d. Ralph Everett and Constance Ann (McCoy) Wickins; m. Herbert Cline Caldwell, Sept. 17, 1966; children: Constance Haley Blacklow, Robert James. BA in English Lit., U. Mich., 1965. Reporter Democrat & Chronicle, Rochester, 1961-64; asst. to dean Harvard Grad. Sch. of Edn., Cambridge, Mass., 1965-70, editor alumni quarterly, 1968-71; freelance editor, writer Harvard U. and Radcliffe, Cambridge, 1971-73; assoc. sec. Philips Acad., Andover, Mass., 1973—80; v.p. for planning and resources Wheaton Coll., Norton, Mass., 1980-90; assoc. dir. Mus. Fine Arts, Boston, 1990—91; v.p. for devel. Brown U., Providence, 1991—97; pres. MGH Inst. Health Professions, Boston, 1997—2007, pres. emerita, 2007—. Chair bicentennial com. Newburyport, Mass., 1974—76; citizens adv. com. Pub. Sch., Newburyport, 1979—80; bd. dirs. Am. Laryngological Voice Rsch. & Edn. Found., 1999—2005; trustee Women's Edn. and Indsl. Union, Boston, 1988—91, John Hope Settlement Ho., Providence, 1997—2007, Jr. Achievement of Ea. Mass., 2004—05, Am. Coll. of Greece, 2007—. Mem.: Am. Coun. Edn. (comm. status women in higher edn. 2005—, chair 2006—07), Women in Devel. Boston (pres. 1984—86, founder), Coun. for Advancement and Support of Edn. (trustee, sec. dist. 1 1985—87, trustee, sec. nat. 1987—89), Boston Club, Chilton Club, Phi Delta Kappa. Avocations: sailing, skiing, travel, reading. E-mail: acaldwell@mghihp.edu.

CALDWELL, BARRY H., waste management executive; Atty. Kutak Rock & Campbell, Washington, Cole Corette & Abrutyn, Washington; counsel to chief of staff US Senator Arlen Specter; v.p. fed. affairs Pharm. Rsch. and Mfrs. of Am.; v.p. govt. rels. CIGNA Corp., 2000—02; sr. v.p. govt. affairs and corp. comm. Waste Mgmt., Inc., 2002—. Bd. dirs. Keep Am. Beautiful, 2005. Office: Waste Mgmt Inc 1001 Fannin Ste 4000 Houston TX 77002 Office Phone: 713-512-6200.*

CALDWELL, BENJAMIN DALE, corporate financial executive, consultant; b. Columbus, Ohio, June 21, 1958; s. Roger Dale Caldwell and Kay June (Fulcomer) Shaw, John Shaw (Stepfather). Cert. in Internat. Rels., U. Rochester, NY, 1980, BA, 1980; diploma in Internat. Banking and Fin., City London U., 1981; MS in Pub. and Internat. Affairs, U. Pitts., Pa., 1982. Cert. lay spkr. United Meth. Ch., 1993; economic devel. fin. profl. Nat. Devel. Coun., 1991. Devel. rep. Pa. Dept. Commerce, Harrisburg, Pa., 1984—86, regional rep. Phila., 1987—88, regional mgr., 1989—95; prin., owner Caldwell Enterprises, Wayne, Pa., 1996—; dir. bus. devel. Somerset Industries, Inc., Spring House, Pa., 1998—2001, gen. mgr., 2002—. Mem. adminstrv. coun. Wayne United Meth. Ch., Pa., 1991—2007, chmn. adminstrv. coun., 1995—97; bd. dirs. Philabundance, Phila., 2006—07. Recipient Student Life award, U. Rochester, 1980; fellow, U. Pitts., 1981; scholar, U. Rochester, 1976—80, U. Pitts., 1982. Mem.: Am. Correctional Assn., North Am. Acad. Ecumenists. United Methodist Church. Achievements include established prison industry plant/program in Lovelock, Nevada. Avocations: golf, travel, singing, trombone. Home Phone: 610-989-0743. Personal E-mail: bdcald@comcast.net.

CALDWELL, BILLY RAY, geologist; b. Newellton, La., Apr. 20, 1932; s. Leslie Richardson and Helen Merle (Clark) C.; m. Carolyn Marie Heath; children: Caryn, Jeana, Craig. BA, Tex. Christian U., 1954, MA, 1970; PhD, Cambridge Grad. Sch., 2004. Cert. petroleum geologist, profl. geologist; lic. geoscientist, Tex. Geologist Geol. Engring. Svc. Co., Ft. Worth, Tex., 1954-60; sci. tchr. Ft. Worth and Lake Worth Sch. Dists., 1960-63; mgr. Outdoor Living, 1963-71; instr. geology Tarrant County Coll., Ft. Worth, 1971—. Petroleum and environ. geologist cons., Ft. Worth, 1971—. Bd. dirs. Ft. Worth and Tarrant County Homebuilders Assn., 1973; past mem. Ft. Worth Environ. Coun. Named Dir. of Yr. Ft. Worth Jaycees, 1966-67. Mem. Am. Inst. Profl. Geologists, Am. Assn. Petroleum Geologists, Geol. Soc. Am., Ft. Worth Geol. Soc. Republican. Baptist. Avocations: travel, church work, enrichment lecturing on cruise ships. Home: 305 Bodart Ln Fort Worth TX 76108-3804 Office: PO Box 150989 Fort Worth TX 76108-0989 Office Phone: 817-246-5477. Personal E-mail: bcgeology@sbcglobal.net.

CALDWELL, BRADLEY W., lawyer; b. Tyler, Tex., Sept. 28, 1978; BSEE, Tex. A&M U., 2000; JD with honors, U. Tex., Austin, 2003. Bar: Tex. 2003, US Dist. Ct. (no. and ea. dists. Tex.). Elec. engr. CIA, Langley, Va.; assoc. McKool Smith, P.C., Dallas. Named a Rising Star, Tex. Super Lawyers mag., 2006; named one of Best Lawyers Under 40, D Mag., 2006. Mem.: Dallas Assn. Young Lawyers, ABA, IEEE. Office: McKool Smith PC 300 Crescent Ct Ste 1500 Dallas TX 75201 Office Phone: 214-978-4201. E-mail: bcaldwell@mckoolsmith.com.*

CALDWELL, COURTNEY LYNN, lawyer, real estate consultant; b. Washington, Mar. 5, 1948; d. Joseph Morton and Moselle (Smith) Caldwell. Attended, Duke Univ., 1966-68, U. Calif., Berkeley, 1967, 1968-69; BA, U. Calif., Santa Barbara, 1970, MA, 1975; JD (hon.), George Washington Univ., 1982. Bar: DC, Wash. 1986, Calif. 1989. Jud. clk. U.S. Ct. Appeals for 9th Cir., Seattle, 1982-83; assoc. Arnold and Porter, Washington, 1983-85, Perkins Coie, Seattle, 1985-88; dir. western ops. Edn. Real Estate Svc., Inc., Irvine, Calif., 1988-91, sr. v.p., 1991-98; ind. cons., Orange County, Calif., 1998—. Bd. dir. Univ. Town Ctr. Assn., 1994; bd. dir. Habitat for Humanity, Orange County, 1993-94, chair legal com., 1994. Named Nat. Law Ctr. Law Rev. scholar, 1981—82. Mem.: Calif. Bar Assn. Avocation: fgn. languages. Home and Office: 140 Cabrillo St 15 Costa Mesa CA 92627 Office Phone: 949-650-8170. Personal E-mail: clcaldwell@earthlink.net.

CALDWELL, DALE GILBERT, management consultant; b. Boston, July 6, 1960; s. Gilbert Haven and Grace Estelle (Dungee) C.; m. Sharon Marie Richards, Aug. 16, 2003; 1 child, Ashley Marie. BA in Econs., Princeton U., 1982; MBA in Fin., U. Pa., 1988. Cert. fin. planner; cert. mgmt. cons.; cert. tennis tchg. profl. Sr. mgr., mgmt. cons. divsn. Deloitte & Touche, Parsippany, NJ, 1988—99; exec. dir. Newark Alliance, 1999—2002; dep. commr. N.J. Dept. Cmty. Affairs, Trenton, 2002—05; exec. dir. strategic partnerships Scholastic Inc., NYC, 2005—06; pres., CEO Tempus Mgmt. Consulting LLC, 2006—, Residential After Sch. Program, Inc. Author of hymns. Pres., bd. dirs. Middlesex County Ednl. Svcs. Commn., 1999—; v.p., bd. dirs. New Brunswick Bd. Edn., 1998—; pres. Ea. sect. USTA, 2004—; bd. commrs. Asbury Park Housing Authority, 2003—. Avocations: Hymn writing, coin collecting/numismatics, nationally ranked tennis player, nationally ranked triathelete, nationally ranked duathelete. Office: PO Box 793 New Brunswick NJ 08903 Home Phone: 732-249-4544. Personal E-mail: dalegcaldwell@aol.com. Business E-Mail: dcaldwell@tempusmc.com.

CALDWELL, DAVID ORVILLE, physics professor; b. LA, Jan. 5, 1925; s. Orville Robert and Audrey Norton (Anderson) C.; m. Miriam Ann Planck, Nov. 4, 1950 (div. Apr. 1978); children: Bruce David, Diana Miriam; m. Edith Helen Anderson, Dec. 29, 1984. BS in Physics, Calif. Inst. Tech., 1947; postgrad., Stanford U., 1947-48; MA in Physics, UCLA, 1949, PhD in Physics, 1953. From instr. to assoc. prof. physics MIT, Cambridge, 1954-63; vis. assoc. prof. physics Princeton U., NJ, 1963-64; lectr. physics dept. U. Calif., Berkeley, 1964-65, prof. physics Santa Barbara, 1965—94, prof. emeritus and rsch. prof., 1995—. Cons. U. Calif. Radiation Lab., Berkeley, 1957-58, 64-67, Am. Sci. and Engring., Boston, 1959-60, Inst. Def. Analyses, Washington, 1960-67; exec. dir. U. Calif. Intercampus Inst. for Rsch. at Particle Accelerators, 1984-95, dir. U. Calif. Inst. for Nuc. and Particle Astrophysics and Cosmology, 1995-2000. Contbr. numerous articles to profl. jours. Served to 2d lt. USAAF, 1943-46. Recipient von Humboldt Sr. Disting. Sci. award, 1987; rsch. grantee Dept. Energy, 1966-2002; Ford Found. fellow, 1961-62, NSF fellow 1953-54, 1960-61, Guggenheim fellow, 1971-72. Fellow Am. Phys. Soc.; mem. Phys. Soc. (exec. com. 1976-78). Democrat. Avocations: tennis, skiing. Office: U Calif Physics Dept Santa Barbara CA 93106 also: Stanford U Varian Physics Bldg Stanford CA 94305-4060 Business E-Mail: caldwell@slac.stanford.edu.

CALDWELL, ELWOOD FLEMING, food scientist, educator; b. Gladstone, Man., Can., Apr. 3, 1923; s. Charles Fleming and Frances Marion (Ridd) C.; m. Irene Margaret Sebille, June 13, 1949; children: John Fleming, Keith Allan; m. Florence Annette Zar, June 23, 1979. BS, U. Man., 1943; MA in Food Chemistry, U. Toronto, 1949, PhD in Nutrition, 1953; MBA, U. Chgo., 1956. Chemist Lake of the Woods Milling Co., Canada, 1943-47; research chemist Can. Breweries Ltd., Toronto, Ont., 1948-49; chief chemist Christie, Brown & Co. div. Nabisco, Toronto, 1949-51; research assoc. in nutrition U. Toronto, 1951-53; with Quaker Oats Co., Barrington, Ill., 1953-72, dir. research and devel., 1969-72; prof., head dept. food sci. and nutrition U. Minn., St. Paul, 1972-86, exec. assoc. to dean Coll. Agr., 1986-88; dir. sci. svcs. Am. Assn. Cereal Chemists, 1988-94, analysis svcs. coord., 1994-98; exec. editor Cereal Foods World, 1986-91; chmn. bd. Dairy Quality Control Inst., Inc., St. Paul, 1972-88, R. & D. Assocs. for Mil. Food & Packaging, Inc., San Antonio, 1970-71; chmn. evening program in food sci. Ill. Inst. Tech., Chgo., 1965-69. Contbr. articles to sci. jours. Chmn. North Barrington (Ill.) Bd. Appeals, 1966-69, mayor, 1969-72; vice-chmn. Barrington Area Council Govts., 1972; bd. dirs. Family Guidance Barrington, 1971-72. Recipient cert. of appreciation for civilian service U.S. Army Materiel Command, 1970. Fellow Am. Assn. Cereal Chemists (Geddes Meml. award 1996), Inst. Food Technologists (Chmn.'s Svc. award Chgo. sect. 1975, Chmn.'s award Minn. sect. 1977, Calvert L. Willey Disting. Svc. award 1991); mem. Kiwanis, Phi Tau Sigma (nat. pres. 1980-81), Gamma Sigma Delta (award of merit 1988), Phi Upsilon Omicron. Republican. Lutheran.

CALDWELL, GARNETT ERNEST, lawyer; b. Houston, July 2, 1934; s. William Ernest and Ethel Leona (Jones) C. BA, U. Houston, 1957, JD, 1959. Bar: Tex. 1958. Pvt. practice law, Houston, 1959-64; ptnr. Ginther, Erwin, Dillard & Caldwell, Houston, 1964-65, Prappas, Caldwell & Moncure, Houston, 1965-77, Caldwell & Baggott, Houston, 1977-82, Caldwell, Wallis, Pruitt & Baggott, Houston, 1982; pvt. practice Houston, 1982-85, 87-90, Houston and Galveston, 1990—; ptnr. Caldwell & Lareau, 1985-87. Lectr. govt. U. Houston, 1961—62. 2d lt. U.S. Army, 1957, lt. col. Res., 1977—. Decorated knight and knight comdr. Royal Yugoslavian Order St. John of Jerusalem. Mem. Galveston County Bar Assn. (dir. 2006-07), Houston Bar Assn., Houston Sr. Lawyers Forum, Houston Bankruptcy Conf., Res. Officers Assn., Houston Early Music Soc., K.C., Delta Theta Phi. Roman Catholic. Home and Office: 1619 Post Office St Galveston TX 77550-4813 Office Phone: 409-762-3500.

CALDWELL, IAN, writer; b. Washington, 1976; BA in History, Princeton U., 1998. Co-author: (novels) (with Dustin Thomason) The Rule of Four, 2004 (Publishers Weekly bestseller list, 2004, NY Times bestseller list, 2004, San Francisco Chronicle bestseller list, 2004, Boston Globe bestseller list, 2004, New York Post bestseller list, 2004). Mem.: Phi Beta Kappa. Office: c/o Dial Books 375 Hudson St New York NY 10014

CALDWELL, JOHN THOMAS, JR., communications executive; b. Sewickley, Pa., July 30, 1932; s. John Thomas and Helen Olive (Sheats) C.; m. Margery Eleanor Hill, Dec. 31, 1971. AB, U. Pitts., 1955; postgrad., Mich. State U., East Lansing, U. Mich., Ann Arbor, Harvard U. Sch. Bus., Cambridge, Mass. Mem. prodn. staff Sta. WKAR-TV, East Lansing, Mich., 1955-56, dir., 1957, prodr., 1958, prodn. mgr., 1959-62; distbn. mgr. Nat. Ednl. TV, Inc., Ann Arbor, Mich., 1962-64; v.p. distbn. and ops., 1964-66; ops. mgr. Sta. WGBH, Boston, 1966-70; gen. mgr. Sta. WGBY-TV, Springfield, Mass., 1971-79; pres., gen. mgr. Sta. WTVS-TV, Detroit, 1979-83; dir. electronic communication, corp. pub. affairs Ford Motor Co., Dearborn, Mich., 1983-86, dir. internal comm., pub. affairs, 1986-94; v.p. bus. comm. planning Convergent Media Systems, 1995-98; pres. The Caldwell Co., Grosse Pointe, Mich., 1998—. Bd. dirs. Public Broadcasting Service, 1977-81, Sta. WTVS-TV, 1979-92. Bd. dirs. Detroit Symphony Orch., 1979—87, Mich. Cancer Found., 1980—96, Boys and Girls Clubs Mich., 1981—84, Springfield Symphony Orch., Mass., 1975—79; mem. U. Mich. Cmty. Adv. Bd., 1979—88, Mich. State Film, TV and Rec. Arts Adv. Coun., 1984—86; bd. dirs. Karmanos Cancer Inst., 1986—2007, Mich. Info. Tech. Network, 1995—2001, Karmanos Cancer Found., 2002—07. Woodrow Wilson fellow, 1981 Mem. Nat. Acad. TV Arts and Sci., Mich. Corp. Public Broadcasting (dir. 1979-83), Internat. TV Assn., Economic (Detroit) Club, Grosse Pointe Yacht Club, Skyline Club, Marina Club at Jonathan's Landing, Jupiter, Fla. Home: 29 Windemere Grosse Pointe MI 48236-3078 Office Phone: 313-886-1800. Business E-Mail: jack@caldwellco.com.

CALDWELL, L. SCOTT, actress; b. Chgo., Apr. 17, 1944; Mem. Milw. Repertory Theatre, 1981-82. Mem. Negro Ensemble Co. Appeared in The Daughters of the Mock, 1978, A Season to Unravel, 1979, Old Phantoms, 1979, Plays from Africa, 1979, Home, 1979, 80, Boesman and Lena, 1981, Colored People's Time, 1982, About Heaven and Earth, 1983; other theater appearances include A Raisin in the Sun, Buffalo, 1982, A Play of Giants, 1984, Come and Gone, New Haven, 1985, Boston, 1986, N.Y.C., 1988 (Antoinette Perry award for best featured actress in a play, 1988), Proposals, A Month of Sundays, N.Y.C., 1987, Going to St. Ives, 2005 (Obie award, Village Voice, 2005); appeared in films Without a Trace, 1983, Exterminator 2, 1984, Up Against the Wall, 1991, Dutch, 1991, The Fugitive, 1993, The Switch, 1993, Soweto Green, 1995, The Net, 1995, Devil in a Blue Dress, 1995, Graham's Diner, 1999, Mystery , Alaska, 1999, Dragonfly, 2002, Gridiron Gang, 2006; TV films: God Bless the Child, 1988, Dangerous Passion, 1990, Love, Lies and Murder, 1991, Baby of the Bride, 1991, Extreme Justice, 1993, Darkness Before Dawn, 1993, For the Love of My Child: The Anissa Ayala Story, 1993, Down Came a Blackbird, 1995. Twilight Man, 1996, Dying to Be Perfect: The Ellen Hart Pena Story, 1996, Weapons of Mass Distraction, 1997, Intimate Betrayal, 1999, The Last Man On Planet Earth, 1999; TV series The Outsiders, 1990, Queens Supreme, 2003, recurring role in Judging Amy. Mailing: c/o Primary Stages 59 East 59th St New York NY 10022

CALDWELL, LESLIE RAGON, lawyer, former prosecutor; b. Pitts., Aug. 30, 1957; BA in economics summa cum laude, Pa. State U., 1979; JD with honors, George Washington U., 1982. Bar: NY 1983. Assoc. Cadwalader, Wickersham & Taft LLP, NYC, 1984—87; asst. US atty. US Atty.'s Office Ea. Dist. NY, Brooklyn, 1987—98, dep. chief Narcotics Sect., dep. chief General Crimes Sect., chief Violent Criminal Enterprises Sect., 1994—97, sr. trial counsel, 1997—98; asst. US atty. US Atty.'s Office No. Dist. Calif., San Francisco, 1998—2002, dep. chief Criminal Divsn., chief Econ. Crimes Unit, chief Securities & Fraud Sect., chief Criminal Divsn., 2001—02; ptnr. Morgan Lewis & Bockius LLP, NYC, 2004—. Dir. Enron Task Force, US Dept. Justice, 2002—04; adj. faculty NY Law Sch. Named one of The 50 Most Influential Women Lawyers in Am., Nat. Law Jour., 2007; recipient Henry L. Stimson Medal, Assn. Bar City NY, 1994, John Marshall Award for Trial of Litig., Atty. Gen., Award for Fraud Prevention, Spl. Achievement Award, US Dept. Justice. Office: Morgan Lewis & Bockius LLP 101 Park Ave New York NY 10178-0060*

CALDWELL, LINDA E., critical care nurse; b. Spencer, Iowa, June 23, 1954; d. George W. and Elaine Wava (Parks) D.; m. Bill Caldwell, June 25, 1988. ADN, Cumberland County Coll., 1984; EMT, Cumberland Adult Edn., 1986. RN; cert. EMT. Staff nurse Newcomb Med. Ctr., Vineland, NJ; head nurse Leesburg State Prison, Delmont, NJ; charge nurse, ICU South Jersey Hosp. Divsn., Millville, NJ, 1991—; co-owner P.S. & L. Emergency med. tech. Bridgeton Ambulance Svc. Mem. EOF (past pres.), AACN. Home: PO Box 976 Millville NJ 08332-0976 Office Phone: 877-724-6478. Personal E-mail: linda4847@aol.com. Business E-Mail: psl@painspray.com.

CALDWELL, LOUISE PHINNEY, historical researcher, community volunteer; b. Dallas, Sept. 19, 1938; d. Carl Lawrence and Louise (Snow) Phinney; m. Josef Caldwell, Sept. 8, 1962; children: Mattie Caldwell Roberts, Jane Barron Caldwell Jackson, Josef Caldwell Jr., Charles Phinney Caldwell. Grad., The Hockaday Sch., 1956; student, Sweet Briar Coll., 1956—57. Owner retail bus., Dallas, 1965-75; project chmn. Mus. of Dallas History, 1985—95; interim dir. Dallas Hist. Soc., 1990, chmn., 1991-93, pres., 1987-91, life trustee, 1991—, exec. com., 2005—; bd. Friends of the Dallas Publ. Libr., 2003—10. Membership chair trustee com. Tex. Assn. Mus., Austin, 1986-88; mem.-at-large Women's Coun. Dallas County, 1991—; adv. 36th Inf. Divsn. Mus. Com., Camp Mabry, Austin, Tex.; v.p., treas. Hist. Inquiry, Inc., 1992—. Author rsch. project 150 Years of Lone Star Cuisine, 1986. Mem. Dallas County Hist. Commn., 1989-90; chmn. Awards for Excellence in Cmty. Svc., Dallas, 1983-89; founding co-chmn. Jubilee Dallas! Celebrating 150 Years, 1990-91; mem. charter bd. dir. Friends of Fair Park, Dallas, 1985-91; mem. Crystal Charity Ball Com.; chmn. Festival Shakespeare, 1994. Recipient Heritage award Dallas County Heritage Soc., 1982. Fellow Dallas Hist. Soc. (chmn. Fellows 1982-84), Mayflower Soc., Nat. Soc. of Colonial Dames (chmn. Dallas town com.), Daus. of Republic of Tex. (chpt. v.p. 1991-92), Dallas Woman's Club, Dallas Garden club, Charter 100 Club, Belterling Found. Episcopalian. Avocations: collects & catalogues, antique glass trade beads, folk art of Hispanic southwest, history of early Texas families.

CALDWELL, NAOMI RACHEL, library and information scientist, educator, writer; b. Providence, Mar. 31, 1958; d. Atwood Alexander II and Juanita (Johnson) Caldwell; 1 child, William Earl Wood. BS, Clarion State Coll., 1980; MSLS, Clarion U. Pa., 1982; postgrad., Tex. A&M U., 1986—87, Providence Coll., 1990—92; PhD in Libr. and Info. Studies, U. Pitts., 2002. Cert. tchg. libr.; cert. libr. media specialist. Asst. dir., adult svcs. libr. Oil City Pub. Libr., 1984—85; microtext reference libr. Sterling C. Evans Libr., Tex. A&M U., College Station, 1985—87; libr. media specialist Nathan Bishop Mid. Sch., Providence, 1987—92; sch. library media specialist Feinstein High Sch. for Pub. Svc., Providence, 1994—99; asst. prof. U. R.I. Grad. Sch. Libr. Info. Studies, 2002—07, assoc. prof., 2007—. Mem. discovery award com. US Bd. on Books for Young People, 1994; mem. com. RI Children's Book award, 1990—92, RI Read-Aloud, 1990—92; participant Native Am. and Alaskan Native Pre-Conf. to White House Conf. on Librs. and Info. Scis., Washington, 1991, George Washington U. Nat. Indian Policy Ctr. Forum on Native Am. Librs. and Info. Svcs., Washington, 1991; participant, del., spkr. Internat. Indigenous Librs. Forum, Auckland, New Zealand, 1999, Santa Fe, 2003; hon. del. White House Conf. on Libr. and Info. Svcs., Washington, 1991; bd. dirs. Ocean State Freenet; mem. exec. bd. R.I. Ednl. Media Assn., 1996—97; mem. exec. bd. Native Am. child literacy program If I Can Read, I Can Do Anything, 2001—; mem. exec. bd. OYATE, 2001—05, mem. adv. bd., 1992—, Native Ams. Info. Dir., 1992, Gale Ency. Multicultural Am., Native N.Am. Reference Libr.; cons. Am. Coll. Testing, 1995—; mem. Coalition Libr. Advocates, 2002—; del., spkr. Internat. Indigenous Libr. Forum, Santa Fe, 2003; presenter in field. Mem. editl. adv. bd., reviewer: Multicultural Rev., 1991—; reviewer Clarion Books, Greenwood Press, Random House, Harcourt Brace Trade Divsn., Browndeer Press, Oryx Press; contbr. articles to profl. jours. Mem. State of RI Libr. Bd., 1996-97, Spl. Presdl. Adv. Com. on Libr. of Congress, 1996-97; mem. nominating com. R.I. chpt. Girl Scouts of Am., 1998-99; enrolled mem. Ramapough Lenape Tribe; bd. dirs. Tomaquaq Indian Mus., 2005—; mem. planning com. Joint Conf. Librarians of Color, 2006. Recipient scholarship, Joint Conf. Librs. of Color, 2006, Am. Libr. Assn. Advocacy award, 2006; libr. sci. doctoral fellow, dept. libr. sci. Sch. Libr. and Info. Sci., U. Pitts., 1992—94. Mem.: ALA (councilor-at-large 1992—96, chmn. com. on status of women in librarianship 1995—97, nominating com. 1996—97, legis. assembly 1996—98, councilor-at-large 1996—2000, assembly on planning and budget 1998—99, presdl. task force spectrum program, com. on coms. 1999—2000, spectrum jury com. 2001—02, com. on diversity 2001—04, pres.'s adv. com. 2003—04), R.I. Coalition of Libr. Advs. (sec. 2003), Native Am. N.E. Librs., Worcraft Cir. Native Writers and Storytellers, Windwalker Coalition, Libr. Adminstrn. Mgmt. Assn., Spl. Librs. Assn., Am. Assn. Sch. Librs., Am. Indian Libr. Assn. (new mems. round table publicity com. 1986, new mems. round table minority recruitment com. 1986—88, OLOS libr. svcs. for Am. Indian people subcom. 1986—88, ALCTS micropub. com. 1988—90, OLOS libr. svcs. for Am. Indian people subcom. 1990—91, pres. 1990—94, mem. coun. com. on minority concerns 1991—92, chmn. 1992—94, sec. 1994—96, mem. coun. com. on minority concerns 1994—96, chair book award task force 2004, chair youth book award com. 2005—), Alpha Kappa Alpha Inc. Home: 475 Sowams Rd Barrington RI 02806-2745 Office: U RI Grad Sch Libr and Info Studies 11 Rodman Hall Kingston RI 02881 Office Phone: 401-874-2278. Personal E-mail: inpeacencw@aol.com.

CALDWELL, PHILIP, retired automobile manufacturing and finance company executive; b. Bourneville, Ohio, Jan. 27, 1920; s. Robert Clyde and Wilhelmina (Hemphill) C.; m. Betsey Chinn Clark, Oct. 27, 1945; children: Lawrence Clark, Lucy Hemphill Caldwell-Stair (Mrs. Thomas O. Stair), Désirée Caldwell Armitage (Mrs. William F. Armitage, Jr.). BA in Econs., Muskingum Coll., 1940, HHD (hon.), 1974; MBA, Harvard U., 1942; DBA (hon.), Upper Iowa U., 1978; LLD (hon.), Boston U., 1979, Ea. Mich. U., 1979, Miami U., 1980, Davidson Coll., 1982, Ohio U., 1984, U. Mich., 1984, Lawrence Inst. Tech., 1984. Served to lt. USNR, 1942-46; civilian Navy Dept., 1946-53, dep. dir. procurement policy div., 1948-53; with Ford Motor Co., 1953-90, v.p., gen. mgr. truck ops., 1968-70; pres., dir. Philco-Ford Corp. subs., 1970-71, v.p. mfg. group N.Am. automotive ops., 1971-72; chmn., CEO Ford of Europe, Inc., 1972-73, exec. v.p. internat. automotive ops., 1973-77; dir. Ford of Europe Inc., Ford Latin Am., Ford Mideast and Africa, Ford Asia Pacific, 1973-85; vice chmn. bd. Ford Motor Co., 1977-79, dep. CEO, 1978-79, pres., 1978-80, CEO, 1979-85, chmn. bd. dirs., 1980-85, dir., 1973-90, Ford Motor Credit Co., Ford of Can., 1977-85; mem. Ford European Adv. Coun., 1976-88, chmn., 1987-88; sr. mng. dir. Lehman Bros. Inc., NYC, 1985-98. Bd. dirs. Castech Aluminum Group, Inc., 1994-96, Chase Manhattan Corp., Chase Manhattan Bank NA, 1982-85; Digital Equipment Corp., 1980-95, Federated Dept. Stores Inc., 1984-88, Russell Reynolds Assocs., Inc., 1984-05, The Kellogg Company, 1985-92, Shearson Lehman Bros. Holdings, 1985-93, Specialty Coatings Grp. Inc., 1991-93, The Mex. Fund, 1991-06, Zurich Am. Ins. Group, 1987-99, Zurich Reinsurance Ctr. Holdings, 1993-97, Waters Corp., 1994-05, Mettler-Toledo, Inc. 1998-05, chmn., 1996-98; Russel Reynolds Assocs., Inc., 1984-05, Waters Corp., 1994-05; mem. policy com. The Bus. Roundtable, 1980-85, Bus. Coun., 1980-01, Com. for Econ. Devel., 1979—, Conf. Bd., 1979—, Trilateral Commn., 1979-86; mem. U.S. Trade Rep. Adv. Com. for Trade Negotiations, 1983-85; mem. Pres.'s Export Coun., 1985-89; mem. Mex.-U.S. Bus. Com., 1985—; mem. adv. bd. Russell Reynolds Assocs, Inc., 2005—; adv. coun. Japan-U.S. Econ. Rels., 1981-85; dir. Japan Soc., 1983-89, vice chmn., chmn. exec. com. 1987-89; mem. motor truck com. Automobile Mfg. Assn., 1964-70; mem. transp. com. U.S. C. of C., 1968-77; mem. U.S. coun. Internat. C. of C., 1973-77, U.S. Coun. for Internat. Bus., 1977-85; mem. internat. adv. com. Chase

Manhattan Bank, 1979-85; mem. Coun. Fgn. Rels., 1985—; mem. Zurich Fin. Svcs. Group U.S. Adv. Bd., 1999-01. Trustee Muskingum Coll., 1967—, Winterthur Mus. and Gardens, 1986-2000; dir. Harvard Bus. Sch. Assocs., 1977-93; dir. Inst. Europeen de Adminstrn. des Affaires (INSEAD), 1978-81, chmn. U.S. adv. bd., 1979-84, mem. internat. coun., 1983-2002; bd. advisors The Jerome Levy Econs. Inst., 1988-2001; bus. adv. coun. Kent State U., 1968-70; mem. Merrill-Palmer Inst., 1971-81, New Detroit, Inc., vice-chair, 1977-85, Detroit Renaissance, 1979-85, dir. Detroit Symphony Orch., 1974-85; charter mem. Bus. Higher Edn. Forum, 1979-84; dir. Citizens Rsch. Coun. of Mich., 1980-85; hon. bd. mem. Plan Internat. USA, 1989—; dir. Econ. Club of Detroit, 1977-86. Recipient 1st William A. Jump Meml. award, 1950, Meritorious Civilian Svc. awardUS Navy Dept., 1953, Disting. Svc. Alumni award Muskingum Coll., 1978, Internat.Exec. of Yr. award Sch. Mgmt. Brigham Young U., 1983, Bus. Statesman of Yr. award Harvard Bus. Sch. Club Greater N.Y., 1984, Businessman of Yr. award Harvard Bus. Sch. Club Columbus, Ohio, 1984, Alumni Achievement award Harvard Bus. Sch.,1985; named Automotive Industry Leader of Yr. Automotive Hall of Fame, 1984; Harvard Bus. Sch. Philip Caldwell Professorship of Bus. Adminstrn. named in his honor, 1990; named Statesman of Yr. Harvard Bus. Sch. Club Detroit, 1991; elected laureate Nat. Bus. Hall of Fame, 1995. Mem. The Links, River Club (N.Y.C.). Office: Ford Motor Co W Bldg 225 High Ridge Rd Stamford CT 06905-3000 Fax: 203-357-8241.

CALDWELL, RICHARD H., lawyer; b. Pine Bluff, Ark., 1939; BS cum laude, U. Houston, 1960; LLB, Harvard Law Sch., 1963. Bar: Tex. 1963, US Ct. Appeals (5th Cir.), US Ct. Appeals (11th Cir.), US Dist. Ct. (No. Dist.) Tex., US Dist. Ct. (So. Dist.) Tex., US Dist. Ct. (Ea. Dist.) Tex., US Dist. Ct. (We. Dist.) Tex., US Supreme Ct. Ptnr., co-chmn. Litig. Sect. Andrews Kurth LLP, Houston, mem. mgmt. com. Named one of Best Lawyers in Am. Fellow: Internat. Acad. Trial Lawyers, Houston Bar Found., Tex. Bar Found.; mem.: State Bar Tex., ABA, Phi Kappa Phi, Omicron Delta Kappa. Office: Andrews Kurth LLP Ste 4200 600 Travis St Houston TX 77002-3090 Office Phone: 713-220-4712. Office Fax: 713-238-7361. Business E-Mail: rcaldwell@andrewskurth.com.

CALDWELL, TRACY ELLEN, surface chemist, researcher; b. Arcadia, Calif., Aug. 14, 1969; d. James and Mary Ellen C. BS in Chemistry, Calif. State U., Fullerton, 1993; PhD in Phys. Chemistry, U. Calif., Davis, 1997. Journeyman electrician J.C. Electric Co., Cherry Valley, Calif., 1987-92; environ. lab. asst. Rsch. and Instrnl. Safety Office Calif. State U., Fullerton, 1990-93, rsch. asst. chemistry, 1991-93; tchg. asst. chemistry U. Calif., Davis, 1993-94, rsch. asst. chemistry, 1994-96, rsch. asst. physics, 1996-97, Camille and Henry Dreyfus postdoctoral fellow in Environ. Sci. Irvine, 1997; astronaut, 1998—. Private pilot and conversational in Am. Sign Language (ASL) and Russian; Russian crusader Astronaut Office ISS Ops. Branch, 1999; prime crew support astronaut 5th Internat. Space Station (ISS) Expedition Crew; ISS spacecraft communicator (CAPCOM) inside mission control; with Astronaut Shuttle Ops. Branch assigned to flight software verification in the Shuttle Avionics Integration Lab, 2003; mission specialist STS-118 Mission (Endeavour) to Internat. Space Station. Contbr. articles to profl. jours. including Polyhedron, Jour. Am. Chem. Soc., Surface Sci., and Jour. Phys. Chemistry. Recipient U. Calif., Davis Graduate Rsch. award, 1996, U. Calif., Davis Grad. Student award for Scientific Travel, 1996, Pro Femina Rsch. Consortium Grad. Rsch. award, 1996, Pro Femina Rsch. Consortium Grad. award for Scientific Travel, 1996, Nellie Yeoh Whetten award, Am. Vacuum Soc., 1996, Grad. Rsch. award, 1996, NASA Superior Accomplishment Award, 2000, NASA Performance Award, 2001, 2002, NASA Group Achievement award-Russian Crusader Team, 2000, NASA Go the Extra Mile award, 2001; Patricia Roberts Harris Grad. Fellowship in Chemistry, 1993—97. Mem. Am. Chem. Soc., Am. Vacuum Soc. (Nellie Yeoh Whelton award 1996, Grad. Rsch. award 1996), Sigma Xi. Presbyterian. Achievements include mem. Russian Crusader Team, Office ISS Operations Branch, 1999; Crew Support Astronaut, 5th ISS Expedition crew, 2000. Avocations: running, weightlifting, hiking, softball, auto repair/maintenance. Office: NASA Johnson Space Ctr Astronaut Office Houston TX 77058*

CALDWELL, WESLEY STUART, III, lawyer, lobbyist; b. Teaneck, NJ, June 3, 1946; s. Wesley S. Jr. and Helen Skrek C.; m. Theresa Hale, Apr. 20, 1970 (div. Jan. 1988); children: Ashley Hale, Ferris Elena; m. J.R. Dillenback, May 27, 1988. BA in Liberal Arts, Fairleigh Dickinson U., 1968; JD, Rutgers U., 1975. Bar: N.J. 1975, U.S. Dist. Ct. N.J. 1975, U.S. Supreme Ct. 1992. Dep. atty. gen. N.J. Atty. Gen.'s Office, Trenton, 1975-78; assoc. gen. counsel Prudential Reins. Co., Newark, 1978-79; v.p. Am. Ins. Assn., NYC, 1979-86; ptnr. LeBoeuf, Lamb, Greene & MacRae, Newark, 1986-95, Caldwell Megna & Brewster, Trenton, 1995-97, Caldwell Megna, Trenton, 1997—2001; ins. regulatory atty. Wesley S. Caldwell III Law Offices, Trenton, 2002—06. With U.S. Army, 1969-72. Mem. N.J. Bar Assn. (past chmn. ins. law sect.). Avocations: golf, pocket billiards. Home: 180 Aqueduct Rd Washington Crossing PA 18977 Office: 224 W State St Trenton NJ 08608-1002 Office Phone: 609-396-2000.

CALDWELL, WILLIAM MACKAY, IV, cloning and stem cell research company executive; b. Boston, July 23, 1947; s. William Mackay, III and Mary Louise (Edwards) C.; m. Kathleen Fogwell, Mar. 19, 1977; children— William Mackay V, Blake Harrison, Tyler Robert BA, U. So. Calif., 1969; postgrad., Christ Coll., Cambridge, Eng., 1970; MBA, U. Pa., 1973. Mktg. adminstr. Sepulveda Properties/Standard Oil, Los Angeles, 1970-71; sr. assoc. Booz, Allen & Hamilton, Washington, 1973-75; v.p. mktg. Flying Tiger Line, Inc., Los Angeles, 1975-80; sr. v.p. fin. and mktg. Van Vorst Industries, Pasadena, Calif., 1981-83, pres., 1983-86; pres., chief exec. officer, chmn. Union Jack Group, Inc., 1986—93; v.p., corp. fin. Kidder, Peabody, 1986—93; pres. Digital Satellite Broadcasting Corp., 1993—97; vice-chmn. CAIS, Inc., 1997—99, Cleartel Comm., Inc., 1997—99; v.p. CAIS Internet, 1998—99; pres. CAIS Internet and CAIS Inc., 1999, CEO, 2000—01, Advanced Cell Technology, Inc., Alameda, Calif., 2005—, also bd. dir., 2005—. Dir. Cleartel Comm., 1995, CAIS, Inc., 1996, CAIS Internet, 1998, So. Cross Industries, Atlanta, Kyco, Inc., Pasadena, Englander Co., Inc., N.Y.C., U.S. Bedding, St. Paul, R.G.L. Trading Co., Los Angeles, Hoffman Travel Service, Inc., Beverly Hills, Alan Weston Communications, Inc., Burbank. Lee Pharm. and King Koil Franchising Corp. Vice pres., bd. dirs. Frat. of Friends Music Ctr., Los Angeles, 1981 Multi Nat. Enterprise fellow Wharton Sch., U. Pa., 1972 Mem. Newcomen Soc., World Trade Assn. Clubs: Calif., Jonathan (LA); Bel Air Bay (Pacific Palisades, Calif.). Episcopalian. Office: Advanced Cell Technology Inc 1201 Harbor Bay Pkwy Ste 120 Alameda CA 94502

CALDWELL, ZOE, actress, film director; b. Hawthorn, Victoria, Australia, Sept. 14, 1933; m. Robert Whitehead, 1968; 2 sons: Sam, Charlie. Attended, Meth. Ladies Coll., Melbourne, Australia. Dorothy F. Schmidt Vis. Eminent Scholar in Theatre, Fla. Atlantic U., 1989-93. Theater debut as mem. of Union Theatre Repertory Co., Melbourne, 1953; other appearances in The Madwoman of Chaillot, Goodman Theatre, Chgo., 1964, The Way of the World, The Caucasian Chalk Circle, Mpls., Slapstick Tragedy, N.Y.C., 1966 (Best Supporting Actress Tony award 1966), Antony and Cleopatra, Richard III, The Merry Wives of Windsor, Stratford, Ont., Can., Shakespeare Festival, 1967, The Prime of Miss Jean Brodie, 1967 (Best Actress Tony award 1968), Colette, N.Y.C., 1970, A Bequest to the Nation, London, 1970, The Creation of the World and Other Business, N.Y.C., 1972, Love and Master Will, Washington, 1973, The Dance of Death, N.Y.C., 1974, Long Day's Journey Into Night, N.Y.C., Washington, 1976, Medea, N.Y.C., 1982 (Best Actress Tony award), Lillian, 1986, Come A-Waltzing With Me, A Perfect Ganesh, 1993, Master Class, 1995 (Best Actress Tony award 1996), A Little Night Music, 2004, A Spanish Play, 2007; dir. (plays): An Almost Perfect Person, N.Y.C., 1977, Richard II, Stratford, Ont., 1979, These Men, off-Broadway, 1980, The Taming of the Shrew, Hamlet, Am. Shakespeare Theatre, 1985, Vita and Virginia, N.Y.C., 1995, Limonade Tours les Jours, Bay St. Theatre, Sag Harbor, N.Y., 2004, voice: Lilo & Stitch!, 2002, Stitch! The Movie, 2003. Decorated Order Brit. Empire; recipient Theatre World award, 1966, John Gielgud award Shakespeare Guild/Folger Shakespeare Libr., 1998, Linda Wilson Lifetime Achievement award for Excellence in the Theatre U. Fla., 1998, Bernard B. Jacobs Excellence in the Theatre award/U.J.A. Fedn. N.Y., 1999, medal of distinction Barnard Coll., 1999. Address: Whitehead Stevens 1501 BroadwaySte 1614 New York NY 10036*

CALE, CHARLES GRIFFIN, lawyer, real estate and corporate financial company executive; b. St. Louis, Aug. 19, 1940; s. Julian Dutro and Judith Hadley (Griffin) C.; m. Jessie Leete Rawn, Dec. 30, 1978; children: Whitney Rawn, Walter Griffin, Elizabeth Judith. BA, Principia Coll., Elsah, Ill., 1961; LLB, Stanford U., 1964; LLM, U. So. Calif., 1966. Bar: Calif. 1965. Pvt. practice, LA, 1965—81, 1985—90; ptnr. Adams, Duque & Hazeltine, LA, 1970—81, Morgan, Lewis & Bockius, LA, 1985—90. Bd. dirs., co-chmn., CEO World Cup USA 1994, Inc., L.A., 1991. Group v.p. sports L.A. Olympic Organizing Com., 1982-84; assoc. counselor U.S. Olympic Com., 1985, spl. asst. to pres., 1985-89, asst. to pres, dir. olympic del., 1989-92; bd. dirs. Century 21 Real Estate-Can. Ltd., 1995-97, Rapattoni Corp., 2001—, Foresters Equity Svcs. Corp., 2001—. Trustee St. John's Hosp. and Med. Ctr., Santa Monica, Marymount H.S., 1996-2004; asst. chief de mission U.S. Olympic Team, 1988; bd. dirs. Hallum Prevention of Child Abuse Fund, 1976-96. Recipient Gold medal of Youth and Sports, France, 1984. Mem.: State Bar Calif., Ind. Order Foresters (bd. dirs. 1993—2001), The Beach Club, L.A. Country Club, Calif. Club. Office: PO Box 688 Pacific Palisades CA 90272-0688

CALEGARI, MARIA, ballerina; b. NYC, Mar. 30, 1957; d. Richard A. and Marion (Gentile) C. Student, DuPons Dance Studio, Queens, 1960-66, Ballet Acad., 1966-71, Sch. Am. Ballet, 1971-74. Mem. corps de ballet N.Y.C. Ballet, 1974-81, soloist, 1981-83, prin., 1983-94; guest artist Richmond Ballet, 1996—; artistic dir. dance Conn. Conservatory of the Performing Arts, New Milford, 2002—; artistic dir. The Maria Calegari Schl of Ballet, New Milford, Conn., 2003—. Artist-in-residence Richmond Ballet, Richmond Ctr. for Dance, State Ballet of Va., 1997—98, Conn. Cons. of Performing Arts, New Milford, 1999—. Dancer in N.Y.C. Ballet's Balanchine Celebration, 1993, Celebrating Balanchine, Kennedy Ctr., 1995. Repétiteur George Balanchine Trust, Robbins Rights Trust. Recipient Alumni award, Profl. Children's Sch., 1986. E-mail: mcale50064@aol.com.

CALELLO, PAUL, diversified financial services company executive; b. NYC, Feb. 14, 1961; BA, Villanova U., Pa., 1983; MBA, Columbia U., 1987. With global mktgs. divsn. Bankers Trust Co., NYC, 1986, 87; v.p., sr. risk mgr. equity derivatives products (Asia) Derivative Products of Asia/Bankers Trust Internat., Tokyo, 1987-90; dir./mng. dir., head derivatives products trading Asia Credit Suisse First Boston (Japan) Ltd./Credit Suisse Fin., Tokyo, 1990-92; mng. dir., head N.Am. fixed income, global equities trading Credit Suisse Fin. Products, London, 1992-94; mng. dir., mem. global equity operating com. CS First Boston, NYC, 1994-95; pres. CSFP Capital Inc., NYC, 1994-99; mng. dir., mem. exec. bd., mgmt. co., co-head trading Credit Suisse Fin. Products, NYC, 1994-99, head mktg. for the Ams., 1994-99; mem. fixed income and equity mgmt. com. Credit Suisse First Boston, NYC, 1997, mng. dir., global head equity derivatives/convertibles, 1997—2002, mem. global oper. com. and firms exec. bd., 2000—02; chmn., CEO investment banking divsn. Credit Suisse Asia Pacific, 2002—06, chmn., CEO, 2006—; CEO investment banking Credit Suisse Group, NYC, 2007—, mem. exec. bd., 2007—. Bd. dirs. CSFB Long Term Capital Ptnrs., N.Y.C., 1998—. Trustee charitable contbns. Credit Suisse First Boston Found., N.Y.C., 1999—. Office: Credit Suisse First Boston 11 Madison Ave Fl 3D New York NY 10010-3629*

CALENDAR, RICHARD LANE, biochemistry educator; b. Hackensack, NJ, Aug. 2, 1940; s. Howard L. and Jean (Wappler) C.; m. Gunilla Viola Jansen, Jan. 6, 1969 (div. Sept. 1983); children: Hugo Raphael, Johanna Magdalena. BS in Chemistry, Duke U., 1962; PhD in Biochemistry, Stanford U., 1967. Helen Hay Whitney fellow Karolinska Inst., Stockholm, 1966-68; mem. faculty dept. cell and molecular biology U. Calif., Berkeley, 1968—, asst. prof. to prof., 1968—76. Alexander von Humboldt fellow, Munich, 1973, Guggenheim fellow, Stockholm, 1979-80. Home: 940 Euclid Ave Berkeley CA 94708-1436 Office: U Calif 401 Barker Hall Berkeley CA 94720-3208

CALFANO, BRIAN ROBERT, education educator; b. Marlton, NJ, Jan. 14, 1977; s. Albert Joseph and Cynthia Ann Calfano. BA, Rider U., Lawrenceville, NJ, 2000; PhD, U. N. Tex., Denton, 2007. Asst. pre-law advisor U. N. Tex., Denton, 2004—06; lectr. Tex. A&M U., College Station, Tex., 2006—07; asst. prof. Chatham Coll., Pitts., 2007—. Contbr. articles to profl. jours. Mem.: World Affairs Coun. Dallas/Ft. Worth, Southwestern Assn. Pre-Law Advisors, Western Assn. Pre-Law Advisors, Soc. Sci. Study Religion (Jack Shand Rsch. grantee 2005), Religious Rsch. Assn. (Constant H. Jacquet Rsch. grantee 2005), Am. Polit. Sci. Assn., Pi Sigma Alpha (Grad. Student Mentor award 2006). Office Phone: 979-845-0385. Business E-Mail: briacal@polisci.tamu.edu, bcalfano@chatham.edu.

CALFEE, ROBERT CHILTON, psychologist, educator; b. Lexington, Ky., Jan. 26, 1933; s. Robert Klair and Nancy Bernice (Stipp) C. BA, UCLA, 1959, MA, 1960, PhD, 1963. Asst. prof. psychology U. Wis., 1964-66, assoc. prof., 1966-69; assoc. prof. edn. Stanford U., 1969-71, prof., 1971-98, prof. emeritus, 1998—; assoc. dean research and devel., dir. Ctr. for Ednl. Rsch., 1976-80; with Sch. Edn. U. Calif., Riverside, 1998—2005. Cons. and speaker in field; vice-chmn. State of Calif. Commn. for Establishment of Acad. Content and Performance Stds., 1996-2002; mem. com. on equivalancy and linkage of ednl. tests NRC/NAS, 1998-2000, Energy and Edn. Task Force, 2005-; mem. ednl. adv. bd., Leapfrog Edn., 1997-. Author: Human Experimental Psychology, 1975, Cognitive Psychology and Educational Practice, 1982, Experimental Methods in Psychology, 1985, Handbook of Educational Psychology, Teach Our Children Well, 1995, (with Marilyn J. Chambliss) Textbooks for Learning, 1999; editor: Jour. Ednl. Psychology, 1984-90, Ednl. Assessment, 1992-2002. Trustee Palo Alto (Calif.) Sch. Dist., 1984-88; vice chair Calif. Commn. for Ednl. Stds.; chair ednl. adv. bd. Leapfrog Enterprises. Served with USAF, 1953—57. Guggenheim Meml. fellow, 1972; fellow Center for Advanced Study in Behavioral Scis., 1981-82 Fellow AAAS, APA; mem. Am. Ednl. Rsch. Assn., Internat. Reading Assn. (named to Hall of Fame), Nat. Conf. Rsch. in English, Psychonomic Soc., Nat. Coun. Tchrs. English, Nat. Soc. Study of Edn. (bd. trustees), Sigma Xi. Office: U Calif Sch Edn 1207 Sproul Hall Riverside CA 92521-0001 Home: 995 Wing Pl Stanford CA 94305 Office Phone: 951-533-0034. Business E-Mail: robert.calfee@ucr.edu.

CALHOUN, CRAIG JACKSON, social scientist, educator; b. Watseka, Ill., June 16, 1952; s. Jay Robert and Audrey Thelma (Jackson) C.; m. Pamela Frances DeLargy, Aug. 2, 1980. BA, U. So. Calif., 1972; MA, Columbia U., 1974, U. Manchester, Eng., 1975; D Phil, Oxford U., Eng., 1980. Rsch. assoc. Columbia U., NYC, 1972-74; instr. U. N.C., Chapel Hill, 1977-80, asst. prof. sociology, 1980-85, assoc. prof., 1985-89, prof. sociology and history, 1989-96; prof. NYU, 1996—, chair dept. sociology, 1996-99; pres. Social Sci. Rsch. Coun., NYC, 1999—. Tech. advisor U.S. AID, Govt. of Sudan, 1984-86; dir. program in social theory and cross-cultural studies U. N.C., 1989-95, office of internat. programs 1990-93, chmn. curriculum in internat. studies, 1990-93, dir. Univ. Ctr. for Internat. Studies, 1993-96; vis. prof. dept. sociology, U. Oslo, 1991-97; vis. fellow Swedish Collegium for Advanced Study in Social Scis., 1994; rsch. fellow Ctr. for Transcultural Studies-Ctr. for Psychosocial Studies, Chgo., 1983; Irene Flecknoe Ross lectr., UCLA, 1994-5; Harry Bridges lectr. U. Wash., 1995, Howard W. Beers lectr. U. Ky., 1997, Benjamin J. Meaker Disting. vis. prof. U. Bristol, 2000. Author: The Question of Class Struggle, 1982; co-author: Sociology, 1988, Neither Gods Nor Emperors: Students and the Struggle for Democracy in China, 1995, Critical Social Theory: Culture, History, and the Challenge of Difference, 1995, Nationalism, 1997; editor: The Anthropological Study of Education, 1976: Habermas and the Public Sphere, 1992, Sociological Theory, 1994-99, Hannah Arendt and the Meaning of Politics, 1997, Dictionary of the Social Science, 2002, Understanding September 11, 2002; contbr. numerous articles to profl. jours. Recipient Kellogg Found. fellow, 1982-85; R.J. Reynolds Fund award U. N.C. 1985, Disting. Contrbn. to Scholarship award Am. Sociol. Assn. Fellow Royal Anthrop. Inst.; mem. Am. Sociol. Assn. (chair sect. comparative hist. sociology 1984-85, chair com. on internat. sociology 1988-92, chair sect. on theoretics of sociology, 1991-92; coun. mem. 2000—), Sociol. Rsch. Assn., Soc. for Comparative Rsch. Address: SSRC 810 7th Ave New York NY 10019-5818 Office: NYU Dept Sociology 269 Mercer St New York NY 10003-6633 E-mail: craig.calhoun@nyu.edu.

CALHOUN, DAVID L., information and media company executive; Degree in Acctg., Va. Poly. Inst., 1979; completed the GE Fin. Mgmt. program. Joined the GE corp. audit staff Gen. Electric Co., 1981, mgr. of programs and planning GE Corp. audit staff, 1986, apptd. staff exec. at the GE Corp. Exec. office, 1989; mgr. of mktg. for the Americas GE Plastics, 1989; v.p. of audit staff Gen. Electric Corp.; pres. of the Pacific region GE Plastics, 1994—95; pres.,CEO GE Trans. Sys., 1995—97; pres., CEO GE Lighting, 1997—99; named pres., CEO GE Employers Reinsurance Co., 1999—2000; pres., CEO GE Aircraft Engines, 2000—03, GE Transp., 2003—05; vice chmn. GE Infrastructure, 2005—06; chmn. exec. bd., CEO VNU Group B.V., Haarlem, Netherlands, 2006—. Office: VNU Inc 770 Broadway New York NY 10003-9595

CALHOUN, JIM, men's college basketball coach; m. Patricia McDevitt; children: James, Jeffrey. BA in Sociology, Am. Internat. Coll., 1968. Asst. basketball coach Am. Internat. Coll., 1966-68; head coach basketball Old Lyme H.S., Conn., 1969, Westport (Mass.) H.S., 1970, Dedham H.S., Mass., 1971-72; head coach Northeastern U., U. Conn., 1986—. Author: (novels) Dare to Dream: Connecticut Basketball's Remarkable March to the National Championship, 1999. Past chair Ronald McDonald Houses, We. New England; hon. chmn. Conn. chpt. Am. Cancer Soc.; hon. chmn. New Haven Pub. Edn. Fund; mem. adv. staff we. region Big. Bros./Big Sisters; mem. nat. adv. bd. Ctr. for the Study of Sports in Soc.; hon. chmn. Conn. Sports Mus. and Hall of Fame, greater Hartford chpt. Juvenile Diabetes Found. Named Coach of the Yr.,1990, Big East Coach of the Yr., 1990, 1994, 1996, 1998; winner NCAA Big East Title, 1999; NCAA Divsn. I champs 1999, 2004; NIT Champions, 1988. Mem. Nat. Assn. Basketball Coaches (mem. nom. com. Hall of Fame), Big East Conf. Coaches Assn. (pres.). Office: Univ of Connecticut 2095 Hillside Rd Storrs Mansfield CT 06269-9017

CALHOUN, JOHN ALFRED, social services administrator; b. Phila., Dec. 1, 1939; s. John Alfred and Helen Fordham (Webster) C.; m. Ottilia Klenota, May 29, 1971; children: Byron, Hollis. BA, Brown U., 1962; M in Div., Episcopal Div. Sch., Cambridge, Mass., 1965; MPA, Harvard U., 1986; DHL (hon.), Heidelberg Coll., 2001. Tchr. Phila. pub. schs., 1965-66; program adminstr. Action for Boston Community Devel., 1966-70; v.p. Tech. Devel. Corp., Boston, 1970-73; exec. dir., founder Justice Resource Inst., Boston, 1973-76; commr. Mass. Dept. of Youth Svcs., Boston, 1976-79, U.S. Adminstrn. for Children, Youth and Families, Washington, 1979-81; v.p., dir. Ctr. for Govtl. Affairs Child Welfare League, Washington, 1981-83; pres., CEO Nat. Crime Prevention Coun., Washington, 1984—2004. Pres. Internat. Ctr. for the Prevention of Crime; bd. dirs. Ctr. for Internat. Leadership, D.C., OK Kids, Reclaiming Youth Internat.; assoc. in edn. Harvard U., 1978; moderator Aspen Inst., 1980—; founder Pre-trial Diversion Programs, Mass., Urban Ct. Mediation Cmty. Sentencing, Mass., Cmty. Responses to Drug Abuse, 10 Sites Across the U.S., 13 Calif. City Gang Prevention Network; mem. U.S. Atty. Gen.'s Coordinating Coun. on Juvenile Justice; founder Youth as Resources., Ctr. for Faith and Svc., Teens, Crime and the Cmty., Faith and Svcs. Tech. Edn. Network; mem. adv. bd. Nat. Coun. Chs. in Christ. Author: What, Me Evaluate?, 1986, Hope Matters: The World Story of How Faith Works in America, 2007; editor: Crime in Urban Communities, 1986, Making a Difference, 1985, Reaching Out: School-based Community Service Programs, Teen Crime and the Community, National Service and Public Safety: Partnerships for Safer Communities, Taking the Offensive: How Seven Cities Did It, Changing Communities Through Faith in Action:Crime Prevenation in the New Millenium, Philantrophy and Faith, Hope Matters: The Untold Story of How Faith Works in America; contbr. articles to profl. jours. Coach McLean (Va.) Youth; tchr. confirmation class Louisville Presbyn. Ch., McLean; state chmn. Mass. Adolescent Task Force, 1978; chmn. Mass. State of the Family Task Force, 1979; pres. Franklin Flaschner Found., 1978; treas. Met. Beaverbrook Area Mental Health Bd.; bd. advisors U. Mass. Coll. Cmty. Pub. Svc., 1979; bd. dirs. Edna Stein Acad., Boston, Pekinese Island Sch., Woods Hole, Mass.; mem. adv. bd. Va. Dept. for Children, 1990-94; mem. policy adv. com. Advt. Coun. Inc. Littauer fellow Harvard U. Kennedy Sch. of Govt., 1986; recipient award of Recognition Am. Arbitration Assn., 1978, award of Recognition, U.S. Office Juvenile Justice and Delinquency Prevention, 1998, Spirit of Crazy Horse award Reclaiming Youth Internat., 2002. Democrat. Presbyterian. Avocations: photography, tennis, gardening, skiing, writing poetry. Home: 921 Mackall Ave Mc Lean VA 22101-1617 Office Phone: 703-785-2312. Personal E-mail: hopematters@cox.net.

CALHOUN, JOHN C., JR., academic administrator; b. Betula, Pa., Mar. 21, 1917; s. John C. and Martha (Rowe) C.; m. Ruth Elizabeth Huston, June 10, 1941; children: John, Emily, Mary Beth, Ruth Ellen. BS in Petroleum and Natural Gas Engring., Pa. State U., 1937, MS, 1941, PhD, 1946; DSc (hon.), Ripon Coll., 1975. Research asst., instr. petroleum and natural gas engring. Pa. State U., 1937-46, prof., head dept. petroleum and natural gas engring., 1950-55; assoc. prof., then prof. Sch. Petroleum Engring., U. Okla., 1946-50, chmn., 1948-50; dean Sch. Engring. Tex. Agrl. and Mech. Coll., College Station, 1955-57; dir. Engring. Expt. Sta., Engring. Ext. Service Tex. Agrl. and Mech. U., College Station, 1955-57, v.p. engring., 1957-59, vice chancellor for engring., 1959-60, vice chancellor for devel., 1960-63, v.p. programs, 1965-71, Disting. prof. petroleum engring., 1965-83, dir. Office Sea Grant Programs, 1968-72, dean geoscis., 1969-71, v.p. acad. affairs, 1971-77, exec. vice chancellor for programs Tex. A&M U. System, 1977-80, dep. chancellor for engring., 1980-83; dir. Crisman Inst. Petroleum Reservoir Mgmt., 1984-87; dep. chancellor for engring. emeritus Tex. A&M U. Sys., College Station, 1983—; asst., sci. advisor to sec. Dept. Interior, Washington, 1963-65. Vice chmn. Engring. Coll. Rsch. Coun., 1959-62; mem. Fed. Coun. for Sci. and Tech., 1963-65, Presdl. Task Force on Oceanography, 1969, Nat. Adv. Coun. on Oceans and Atmosphere, 1971-72, Tex. Coastal and Marine Coun., 1972-83; acting dir. Office Water Resources Rsch., 1964; mem. environ. pollution panel Pres.'s Sci. Adv. Com., 1964-66; chmn. com. on oceanography NAS, 1967-70, chmn. ocean sci. affairs bd., 1970-72; chmn. Pres.'s Santa Barbara Oil Spill Panel and Panel on Union Oil Lease, 1969; mem. adv. panel Internat. Decade Ocean Exploration, NSF, 1970-72; mem. nat. adv. coun. on minorities in engring. Nat. Acad. Engring., 1973-74; mem. naval studies bd. Nat. Acad. Scis., 1974-79; bd. dirs. Inst. Nautical Archeology, 1976-86; dir. Tex. Petroleum Rsch. Com., 1978-82; cons. So. Regional Edn. Bd., 1953-54, Pa. Dept. Forests & Waters, 1955, World Bank, 1978-85, Coun. Internat. Edn. Exch., 1988-92; mem. rsch. coordination panel Gas Rsch.

Inst., 1977-82; mem. adv. com. on mining and mineral resources rsch. Dept. Interior, 1987-94. Author: Fundamentals of Reservoir Engineering, 1953; contbr. articles to profl. jours. Chmn. Coll. Sta. United Fund, 1961; trustee U. Corp. for Atmospheric Rsch., 1969-71, chmn. bd., 1968-71; trustee Tex. Agrl. and Mech. Rsch. Found., 1961-82, Tex. Inst. for Rehab. and Rsch., 1981-82; bd. dirs. EDUCOM, 1966-69, Houston Area Rsch. Ctr., 1982-83; exec. dir., pres. Gulf Univs. Rsch. Corp., 1966-69. Recipient 15th Sea Grant award Sea Grant Assn., 1984, Lifetime Achievement award Dwight Look Coll. Engring., Tex. A&M U., 2001; alumni fellow Pa. State U., 1976. Fellow AAAS, Marine Tech. Soc. (pres. 1975-76), Am. Soc. Engring. Edn. (v.p., dir. 1968-72, pres. 1974, Centennial medallion 1993, Collins award 1996); mem. Nat. Acad. Engring., Engrs. Coun. Profl. Devel. (bd. dirs. 1964-67), Engrs. Joint Coun. (bd. dirs. 1972-77), AIME (hon.), Soc. Petroleum Engrs. (pres. 1964, DeGolyer medal 1982, Anthony F. Lucas Gold medal 1997), Am. Assn. Engring. Socs. (mem. exec. com. internat. affairs coun. 1980-81), Tex. Acad. Medicine, Engring. and Sci., Sigma Xi, Tau Beta Pi, Sigma Gamma Epsilon, Phi Kappa Phi, Tau Kappa Epsilon. Presbyterian. Home: 2901 Shilling Rd Texarkana TX 75503

CALHOUN, JOHN JOSEPH (JACK), retail executive; b. Lafayette, Ind., May 27, 1964; s. Robert James and Elizabeth (Callaghan) C. BS, Purdue U., West Lafayette, Ind., 1987; MBA, Harvard U., 1992. Asst. brand mgr. Procter & Gamble, Cin., 1987-90, Hunt Valley, Md., 1992-93; cons. Corp. Decision, Boston, 1991; mktg. mgr. Levi Strauss & Co., San Francisco, 1993-94; account supr. Foote, Cone & Belding, San Francisco, 1994-95; v.p. dir. account mgmt. Citron Haligman Bedecarre, San Francisco, 1995-98; sr. v.p. group dir. Young & Rubicam, San Francisco, 1998, gen. mgr. San Francisco office; exec. v.p. brand mgmt. and advt. Charles Schwab & Co.; exec. v.p. merchandising and mktg. Banana Republic Gap, Inc., San Francisco, 2003, interim pres. Banana Republic. Office: Banana Republic Gap Inc 2 Folsom St San Francisco CA 94105 Office Phone: 650-952-4400.*

CALHOUN, JOHN R., lawyer; m. Elizabeth Calhoun; four children. BA in Polit. Sci., U. Iowa, 1956, JD, 1958. Bar: Iowa, 1958, Calif. 1960, U.S. Ct. Appeals (9th cir.) 1987, U.S. Ct. Appeals (fed. cir.) 1997, U.S. Dist. Ct. (cen. dist.) Calif. 1960, U.S. Supreme Ct. 1963, U.S. Ct. Mil. Appeals 1963. Commd. 2d lt. U.S. Army Res., 1958, advanced through grades to col., JAG Corp., ret., 1988; atty. U.S. Securities and Exch. Commn., 1960, Automobile Club of So. Calif., 1960-61; dep. dist. atty. L.A. Dist. Atty.'s Office, 1961-62; dep. city prosecutor Long Beach (Calif.) City Prosecutor's Office, 1962-67; dep. city atty. Long Beach City Atty.'s Office, 1967-78, asst. city atty., 1978-85, elected city atty., 1985—98; commr., pres. Long Beach Harbor Commn., 1999—2005. Decorated Legion of Merit, Meritorious Svc. medal. Mem. Calif. Bar Assn., Long Beach Bar Assn. (bd. govs. 1974-75, 87-88), Res. Officers Assn., Long Beach Area C. of C., Phi Delta Phi, Phi Delta Theta. Home: 4011 Chestnut Ave Long Beach CA 90807-3207

CALHOUN, JOHN VINCENT, research scientist; b. Columbus, Ohio, Apr. 8, 1961; s. John Michael and Sharon L. (Hahn) Calhoun; m. Laurel Anne Currie, June 27, 1998; 1 stepchild, Nicholas Breton 1 child, Jennifer Lynn; m. Julia Cornett, Nov. 5, 1985 (div. Sept. 1994). Student, Ohio State U., 1980—85. Quality control coord. Johnson & Johnson, 1990—92, product mgr., 1996—2000; product mgr., regulatory mgr. Sempermed USA Inc., Clearwater, Fla., 2000—. Rsch. assoc. Fla. State Collection Arthropods. Author: (book) Butterflies and Skippers of Ohio, 1992, Butterflies Through Binoculars: Florida, 2001; contbr. articles to profl. jours. Mem.: So. Lepidopterists' Soc. (chmn. 1992—93, 1996—98, John Abbot award 2002), Ohio Lepidopterists' Soc. (pres. 1988), Lepidopterists' Soc. (exec. coun. 1993—94, 2006—08). Achievements include research in Entomological artwork of John Abbot (1751-ca.1840), multiple papers. Avocations: hiking, natural history illustration, antiquarian books. Home: 977 Wicks Dr Palm Harbor FL 34684 Home Phone: 727-785-0715. Personal E-mail: bretcal1@verizon.net.

CALHOUN, JOSEPH PATRICK, economics professor, researcher; b. Elgin, Ill., Oct. 30, 1967; s. William Patrick Calhoun and Violet Lucille Mihevc; m. Kimberly Rose Rasmussen, Apr. 27, 1996; children: Tayla Rose, Savannah May, Kendra Miriam Joy. BS, Ill. State U., 1990; MBA, DePaul U., 1997; PhD, U. Ga., 2003. Underwriter The Travelers Ins. Co., Naperville, Ill., 1990—93; cons. Deloitte & Touche, San Francisco, 1993—94; sr. underwriter BlueCross BlueShield Ill., Chgo., 1994—97, United HealthCare, Schaumburg, Ill., 1997—99; grad. student instr. U. Ga., Dept. Econ., Athens, Ga., 1999—2005; lectr., asst. dir. Stavros Ctr. for Econ. Edn., Fla. State U., Tallahassee, 2005—. Asst. dir. Stavros Ctr. for Econ. Edn., Tallahassee, 2004. Recipient Grad. Tchg. award, U. Ga., 2003. Mem.: Nat. Assn. Econ. Educators (assoc.), Nat. Coun. Econ. Edn. (assoc.), Assn. for Instl. Rsch. (assoc.), Assn. for Study of Higher Edn. (assoc.), Am. Econ. Assn. (assoc.). Conservative. Methodist. Avocations: landscaping, construction, bicycling. Home: 2804 Shamrock St N Tallahassee FL 32309 Office: Fla State U 250 S Woodward Ave Tallahassee FL 32306 Home Phone: 850-893-9866; Office Phone: 850-644-7723. Home Fax: 850-644-7795. E-mail: jcalhoun@fsu.edu.

CALHOUN, NOAH ROBERT, oral maxillofacial surgeon, educator; b. Clarendon, Ark., Mar. 23, 1921; s. Noah and Della (Sherman) Calhoun; m. Cecelia Christopher, Oct. 19, 1950; children: Stephen Marc, Cecelia Noel. DDS, Dental Sch., Howard U., 1948; M.Dental Sci., Tufts Med. and Dental Sch., 1955. Oral surgeon VA Hosp., Tuskegee, Ala., 1950—52, Kessler AFB, Biloxi, Miss., 1952—53; chief dental service VA Hosp., Tuskegee, Ala., 1955—57, oral surgeon, asst. chief dental surgeon Washington, 1964—74; chief dental service, oral surgeon VA Med. Center, Washington, 1974—; prof. oral surgery Dental Sch., Howard U., Washington, 1966—92, Georgetown U., Washington, 1975—93; prof. emeritus Dental Coll. Howard U., 1992—. Dir. Tuskegee Red Cross, Ala., 1962—64; chmn. Nat. Concerned VA Dentists, 1975, Inst. Medicine-NAS, 1975. Sect. editor Current Lit. in Internat. Oral/Maxillofacial Surgery, 1986, mem. editl. bd. Jour. Oral and Maxillo-facial Surveys, 1993; contbr. articles to profl. jours. Mem. fin. com. St. Michael Ch., Silver Spring, Md. Mem.: NAACP (trustee D.C. chpt.), ADA, Inst. Medicine of NAS, Am. Coll. Dentistry, Internat. Coll. Dentistry, Am. Soc. Oral and Maxillofacial Surgeons (Audio Visual award 1978), Bridge Masters Washington (pres.), Omicron Kappa Upsilon. Roman Catholic. Office: Dental Coll Howard U Washington DC 20001 Office Phone: 202-882-1846. Personal E-mail: ncalh@aol.com.

CALHOUN, SCOTT DOUGLAS, lawyer; b. Aurora, Ill., May 1, 1959; s. Ellsworth L. Calhoun and Mary Louise (Mummert) Wire; m. Gloria Jean Fulvi, Aug. 1, 1987; 1 child, John Daniel. BA cum laude, Knox Coll., 1981; JD, Coll. of William and Mary, 1984. Bar: Ga. 1984, U.S. Dist. Ct. (no. dist.) Ga. 1984, U.S. Ct. Appeals (11th cir.) 1984. Assoc. Swift, Currie, McGhee & Hiers, Atlanta, 1984-90, ptnr., 1990-92; pvt. practice Atlanta, 1992-94; prin. Byrne, Eldridge, Moore & Davis, PC, Atlanta, 1994-95; ptnr. Mozley, Finlayson & Loggins, Atlanta, 1996—2006; of counsel Hendrick, Phillips, Salzman & Flatt, Atlanta, 2006—. Spkr. in field. Bd. dirs. Atlanta Symphony Assocs., 1991-97, Wildwood Civic Assn., Atlanta, 1991-98; elder Trinity Presbyn. Ch., Atlanta, 1994-97, 2001-04. Mem. Mortar Bd. Avocations: golf, music. Office: Hendrick Phillips Salzman Flatt 230 Peachtree St NW Ste 2500 Atlanta GA 30303 Home Phone: 404-355-1568; Office Phone: 404-522-1410. Business E-Mail: sdc@hpsf-law.com.

CALHOUN-BATES, CAROLYN E., social services administrator; b. Selma, Ala. d. Joe L. Calhoun and Catherin Calhoun Ellis; m. Harry Bates; children: Keyshe C. Ellis, Harry Joenathan Bates, Joe Calton Bates. Student, Selma U., 1977—79, Ala. U., Tuscaloosa, 2001, Auburn U., 2002—03. Founder, adv., vol. Selma Disabilities Adv. Program, Ala., 1999—. Co-founder Bates Rental Units, Selma, 1989—; educator State of Ala. Dept, Edn., Selma, 1989—2002; social security rep. SDAP-PAIRS Legal Svc. Coun., Selma, 1999—; ombudsman, cons., facilitator SDAP-BATES Alt. Ombudsman, Selma, 1999—; rehab. svc. agy. provider Dallas County Dept. Edn., Selma, 2004—; cmty. ctr. dir. U.S. Dept Edn., Office Spl. Edn., Selma, 2004—; jud. adminstrv. officer State of Ala. Unified Jud. Sys., Selma, 2005—; juvenile ct. monitor Dallas County Dist. Ct., Selma, 2005—. Nominee Woman of Yr., Selma-Dallas County C. of C., 2005, WAKA Television Giving Your Best award, 2006; named to Wall of Tolerance. Mem.: NAACP (ptnr. 2004—, Extraordinary Commitment award 2004), Dallas County Children's Policy Coun. (chairwomen 2004—), So. Poverty Law Ctr. (leadership coun. 2004—, Morris Dees and Rosa Parks Honors 2004). Baptist. Achievements include development of special education awareness; Selma's first disabilities multi needs center; policy for Alabama legislative; multi needs and alternative programs; youth disabilities and at risk programs; First Special Needs Day in the US. Avocation: reading. Office: Selma Disabilities Adv Program 701 Lauderdale St PO Box 268 Selma AL 36702 Office Phone: 334-875-6001. Business E-Mail: selmadisability@cs.com.

CALHOUN-SENGHOR, KEITH, lawyer; b. Richmond, Va., June 14, 1955; s. Clarence Calhoun Jr. and Senegal Senghor; m. Sharon White. AB with honors, Stanford U., 1977; JD, Harvard U., 1981. Bar: D.C. 1981, U.S. Ct. Appeals (4th cir.) 1982. Law clk. to judge U.S. Ct. Appeals for 4th Cir., Richmond, 1981-82; assoc. Gibson, Dunn & Crutcher, L.A. and Washington, 1983-85; fgn. legal fellow Kreuz, Niebler & Mittl, Munich, 1986; v.p., gen. counsel Tech. Applications, Inc., Alexandria, Va., 1986-90; pres. Noma Internat. Enterprises, Inc., Washington, 1990-93; of counsel Wood, Williams, Rafalsky & Harris, Washington, 1991-93; dir. Office of Space Commercialization U.S. Dept. Commerce, Washington, 1993-99; v.p. internat. and legal affairs, gen. counsel Edenspace Systems Corp., Reston, Va., 1999—2000; legal and fin. cons., 2000—. Fulbright scholar U. Bonn., 1977-78; German Acad. Exch. Svc. Fgn. fellow, 1985-86. Mem.: ABA, Md. State Bar Assn., DC Bar Assn. Office Phone: 202-425-4968.

CALIFANO, JOSEPH ANTHONY, JR., lawyer, former secretary of health education and welfare; b. Bklyn., May 15, 1931; s. Joseph Anthony and Katherine (Gill) C.; m. Hilary Paley Byers, 1983; children by previous marriage: Mark Gerard, Joseph Anthony III, Claudia Frances; stepchildren: Brooke A. Byers, John Fredric Byers IV. BA, Holy Cross Coll., 1952; LLB, Harvard U., 1955. Bar: N.Y. 1955, U.S. Supreme Ct. 1966, D.C. 1969. Atty. Dewey Ballantine LLP, NYC, 1958-61; spl. asst. to gen. counsel US Dept. Def., 1961-62, spl. asst. to sec. & dep. sec., 1964-65; spl. asst. to sec. US Dept. Army, 1962-63, gen. counsel, 1963-64; spl. asst. to Pres. The White House, 1965-69; ptnr. Arnold & Porter, Washington, 1969-71, Williams, Connolly & Califano, Washington, 1971-77; sec. US Dept. HEW, Washington, 1977-79; ptnr. Califano, Ross & Heineman, Washington, 1980-82; sr. ptnr. Dewey Ballantine LLP, Washington, 1983-92; prof. pub. health policy Columbia U. Schs. Medicine and Pub. Health, NYC, 1992—; chmn., pres. Nat. Ctr. on Addiction & Substance Abuse, Columbia U., NYC, 1992—. Bd. dirs. Viacom Inc., Willis Group Holdings, Ltd.; gen. counsel Dem. Nat. Com., 1971—72. Author: The Student Revolution: A Global Confrontation, 1969, A Presidential Nation, 1975, Governing America: An Insiders Report from the White House and the Cabinet, 1981, The 1982 Report on Drug Abuse and Alcoholism, America's Health Care Revolution, 1986, The Triumph and Tragedy of Lyndon Johnson, 1991, Radical Surgery: What's Next for America's Health Care, 1995, (memoir) Inside: A Public and Private Life, 2004, (with Howard Simons) The Media and the Law, 1976, The Media and Business, 1978. Trustee Urban Inst., Am. Ditchley Found., Century Fund, LBJ Found., Nat. Health Mus.; bd. govs. N.Y. and Presbyn. Hosp. Inc.; chmn. Inst. Social and Econ. Policy in Mid. East, Harvard U., 1983-98. Recipient Disting. Civilian Svc. award Dept. Army, 1964; Man of Yr. award Justinian Soc. Lawyers, 1966; Disting. Pub. Svc. medal Dept. Def., 1965; named One of Ten Outstanding Young Men of Am., 1966. Mem. N.Y. State Bar Assn., D.C. Bar Assn., Met. Club (Washington), Century Assn., Univ. Club. Office: Nat Ctr Addiction Substance Abuse Columbia U 633 3rd Ave 19th Fl New York NY 10017-6706 Office Phone: 212-841-5210. Business E-Mail: jcalifan@casacolumbia.org.

CALIGIURI, JOSEPH FRANK, retired engineering executive; b. Columbus, Ohio, Feb. 13, 1928; s. Frank and Angeline Josephine (Gentile) C.; m. Barbara Jane Delaney, June 15, 1948 (dec. 1996); children: Mark, Timothy, Jeffrey, Anderw; m. Tanya Alberta Condon, June 24, 1998. BSEE, Ohio State U., 1949, MSEE, 1951. Chief engr. Sperry Gyroscope Co., Great Neck, NY, 1966-69; v.p. engring. Guidance and Control Sys. divsn. Litton Industries, Inc., Woodland Hills, Calif., 1969-71, pres., 1971-77, v.p. parent co., 1974-77, sr. v.p., group head Beverly Hills, Calif., 1977-81, exec. v.p., head advanced electronics group, 1981-93; ret., 1993. Bd. dirs. Phillip Mark Cos. Home: 1353 Oak Grove Pl Westlake Village CA 91362-4248

CALIGUR, MATTHEW W., lawyer; BA, U. North Tex., 1989, MS, 1991; JD summa cum laude, South Tex. Coll. Law, 2001. Bar: Tex. 2001, US Dist. Ct. (no., ea. and so. dists. Tex.) 2002, US Dist. Ct. (we. dist. Tex.) 2003, US Ct. Appeals Fifth Cir. 2004, US Supreme Ct. 2004. Intern Staff of Ewing Werlein, Jr., US Dist. Ct., So. Dist. Tex.; assoc. litig. Baker Hostetler, Houston, 2003—. Past. mem. editl. bd.: The Houston Lawyer mag. Mem. Greater Houston Partnership. Named a Rising Star, Tex. Super Lawyers mag., 2005, 2006, 2007. Mem.: Fed. Bar Assn., Bar Assn. of Fed. Fifth Cir., Houston Bar Assn., Def. Rsch. Inst. Office: Baker Hostetler 1000 Louisiana Ste 2000 Houston TX 77002-5009 Office Phone: 713-646-1355. Office Fax: 713-751-1717. E-mail: mcaligur@bakerlaw.com.

CALINESCU, ADRIANA GABRIELA, curator, art historian; b. Bucharest, Romania, Dec. 30, 1941; came to U.S., 1973; d. Nicolae and Tamara Gane; m. Matei Alexe Calinescu, Apr. 29, 1963; children: Irena, Matthew. BA, Cen. Lyceé, Bucharest, 1959; MA in English, U. Bucharest, 1964; MLS, Ind. U., 1976, MA in Art History, 1983. Asst. prof. Inst. Theater and Cinema, Bucharest, 1967-73; rsch. assoc. Ind. U. Art Mus., Bloomington, 1979-83, Thomas T. Solley curator ancient art, assoc. scholar, 1992—. Vis. assoc. mem. Am. Sch. Classical Studies, Athens, Greece, 1984. Author: The Art of Ancient Jewelry, 1994, Egypt After Alexander, 2005; author, co-editor: Ancient Art from the V. G. Simkhovitch Collection, 1988; editor: Ancient Jewelry and Archaeology, 1996. NEA fellow, 1984; grantee Salzburg Seminar, 1970, NEA, 1987, 93, Kress Found., 1991, Internat. Rsch. and Exchanges Bd., 1991. Mem. Am. Inst. Archaeology, Classical Art Soc., Beta Phi Mu. Office: Ind U Art Mus E 7th St Bloomington IN 47405 Office Phone: 812-855-1033.

CALINGAERT, MICHAEL, non-profit organization executive; b. Detroit, Sept. 17, 1933; s. George and Dorothy C.; m. Efrem Funghi, June 20, 1962; children: Alexander, Daniel, Nicholas. BA, Swarthmore Coll., 1955; postgrad., U. Cologne, Fed. Republic Germany, 1955-56, U. Calif., Berkeley, 1963-64. Commd. fgn. svc. officer Dept. State, 1956, intelligence rsch. specialist Washington, 1957-58; vice consul Am. consulate gen. Mogadiscio, Somalia, 1959—61; econ. officer Am. consulate gen. Bremen, Germany, 1961-63; econ. officer Am. Embassy, Colombo, Sri Lanka, 1964-68; chief food policy div. Dept. State, Washington, 1968-72; econ. counselor Am. Embassy, Tokyo, 1972-75, econ./comml. min. Rome, 1975-79; dep. asst. sec. for internat. resources and food policy Dept. State, 1979-83; econ. min. Am. Embassy, London, 1983-87; vis. sr. fellow Nat. Planning Assn., Washington, 1987-89, sr. fellow, 1993-97; non-resident sr. fellow Atlantic Coun. U.S., 1989; dir. of European ops. Pharm. Mfrs. Assn. (U.S.), Belgium, 1989-93; dir. The Monnet-Madison Inst., Brussels, 1994-97; exec. dir. Coun. for U.S. and Italy, 1997—2003, exec. v.p., 2003—. Rsch. fellow Inst. for European Studies, Free U. Brussels, 1994-98, mem. polit. sect., 1998—2002; guest scholar The Brookings Inst., 1996-2004, vis. scholar Ctr. for the U.S. and Europe, 2004—. Author: The 1992 Challenge from Europe: Development of the European Community's Internal Market, 1988, European Integration Revisited: Progress, Prospects, and U.S. Interests, 1996; contbr. numerous articles to profl. jours. Recipient Meritorious Honor award Dept. State, 1971, Superior Honor award, 1981 Mem. Am. Fgn. Svc. Assn., Royal Inst. Internat. Affairs, Inst. Affari Internat. Office: The Brookings Inst 1775 Massachusetts Ave NW Washington DC 20036-2103 Office Phone: 202-797-6135. Business E-Mail: mcalingaert@brookings.edu.

CALINGER, RONALD STEVE, historian; b. Aliquippa, Pa., Apr. 6, 1942; s. Thomas H. and Mary (Blicha) Calinger; m. Betty Jeanne Mikulecky, Dec. 21, 1974; children: John Michael, Anne Sun Nyeo. AB summa cum laude, Ohio U., Athens, 1963; MA, U. Pitts., 1964; PhD, U. Chgo., 1971. Assoc. editor scis. A.N. Marquis Publ. Co., Chgo., 1966-68; mem. faculty Rensselaer Poly. Inst., Troy, NY, 1969-85, assoc. prof. history, 1975-85, chmn. dept. history and polit. sci., 1977-82, dean Undergrad. Coll., 1982-85; dean sch. arts scis. Cath. U. Am., Washington, 1985-87, assoc. to ordinary prof. history, 1987—. Author: Gottfried Wilhelm Leibniz, 1976, A Contextual History of Mathematics: Up to Euler, 1999; co-author: Dictionary of Twentieth Century World Politics, 1993; editor: Classics of Mathematics, 1982, rev. edit., 1995, Vita Mathematica, 1996, The Johns Hopkins University Press History of Mathematics Series, 2004—, Humanization of Social Life, vol. II, 2004, The John Zeender Festschrift, 2007; sect. editor: newsletter History and Pedagogy of Math., 1989—98; contbr. articles to profl. jours., chapters to books. Named Dibner Residential fellow, Smithsonian Inst., 2007; recipient Henry Schuman Prize, 1968, Austrian Cross Scis. & Arts 1st Class, 1996, Foley Outstanding Educator of the Yr. award, Nat. Bd. Dir. Aplha Delta Gamma, 2001, Dornan Meml. Tchr. of Yr. award, Cath. U., 2005; grantee German Marshall Fund, 1987, 1989, NSF, 1995, 1996, 1998, Hitachi, Internat. Virtual Inst. Hist. Studies Math., 1998—2001. Mem.: Math. Assn. Am. (hist. maths. com.), Atlantic Coun. (acad. assoc., mem. selection com. Mellon disseration grants, CLIR), History Sci. Soc. (Washington rep. 1991—2001), Euler Soc. (chancellor 2004—), Phi Beta Kappa. Roman Catholic. Achievements include research in the history of mathematics; biographies of Leonhard Euler and Gottfried Leibniz; development of Newtonian science and competing Leibnizian and Wolffian thought in 18th century Brandenburg-Prussia and Russia. Home: 12806 Lacy Dr Silver Spring MD 20904-2916 Office Phone: 202-319-5484. Business E-Mail: calinger@cua.edu.

CALIO, ANTHONY JOHN, research scientist, operations specialist; b. Phila., Oct. 27, 1929; s. Antonio and Mary Emma (Cappuccio) C.; m. Jenanne L. Murphy. BA, postgrad., U. Pa., 1953, Carnegie Inst. Tech., 1959; ScD (hon.), Washington U., St. Louis, 1974; postgrad. (Sloan fellow), Stanford U., 1974-75. With Westinghouse Electric Corp., Pitts., 1956-59; chief nuclear physics sect. Am. Machine & Foundry Co., Alexandria, Va., 1959-61; v.p. Mt. Vernon Rsch. Co., 1961-63; electronic rsch. task group NASA Hdqrs., Washington, 1963-64; chief rsch. engring. NASA (Electronics Rsch. Ctr.), Boston, 1964-65; chief instrumentation and systems integration br. NASA Hdqrs., Washington, 1965-67, asst. dir. planetary exploration, 1967-68; dir. sci. and applications NASA Johnson Space Ctr., Houston, 1969-75; dep. assoc. adminstr. office space scis. NASA Hdqrs., Washington, 1975-77, assoc. adminstr. Office of Space and Terrestrial Applications, 1977-81; dep. adminstrn. NOAA Dept. Commerce, 1981-84, under sec. for oceans and atmosphere, 1984-87; sr. v.p. Planning Rsch. Corp., McLean, Va., 1987-90; from exec. v.p. to sr. v.p. Hughes Info. Tech. Corp., Reston, Va., 1991-97; sr. v.p. Hughes Info. Tech. Sys., 1996-97; pres. Space Sys., 1996-97, Hughes Info. Tech. Sys., 1997-99; ret., 1999. With U.S. Army, 1954-56. Recipient Group Achievement award (2) NASA, 1969, Exceptional Service medal, 1969, Apollo Achievement award, 1970, Exceptional Sci. Achievement medal, 1971, Lunar Sci. Team award, 1973, Disting. Service medal, 1973, 81, presdl. rank of Disting. Exec., 1980 Fellow AIAA, Am. Astron. Soc.; mem. Am. Geophys. Union. Home: 4920 Scurlock Rd Freeland WA 98249-9632

CALIO, NICHOLAS E., diversified financial services company executive; b. Jan. 10, 1953; m. Lydia Keller; 3 children. BA, Ohio Wesleyan U., 1975; JD, Case Western U., 1978. Assoc. Santarelli & Gimer, 1978—81; of counsel Santarelli & Bond, 1981—84; litig. counsel Washington Legal Found., 1981—84; sr. v.p. govt. rels., exec. dir. wholesaler-distbr. polit. action com. Nat. Assn. Wholesaler-Distbrs., 1984—89; v.p. Duberstein Group, Inc., Washington, 1991—92; asst. to pres. for legis. affairs Pres. George H.W. Bush, 1992—93; ptnr. O'Brien & Calio, 1993—2001; asst. to pres. for legis. affairs Pres. George W. Bush, Washington, 2001—03; sr. v.p. global govt. affairs Citigroup, NYC, 2003—. Bd. trustee Ohio Wesleyan Univ., Georgetown Visitation Preparatory Sch. Office: Citigroup Inc 399 Park Ave New York NY 10043

CALIP, ROGER, writer, educator; b. Manila, Sept. 19, 1941; came to U.S. 1968; s. Generoso and Paula (Echalar) C. LittB in Journalism, U. Santo Tomas, Manila, 1961; cert. with hons. in Spoken French and French Lang., Alliance Française, Paris, 1964; cert. in Tchg. French, Inst. Overseas French Profs., Sorbonne, 1965; Lic. Ès Lettres, U. Paris, 1968; MA in Sociology, U. Conn., 1972, MA in French, 1977. Various positions in ins. cos., Greater Hartford Area, Conn., 1977—86; proofreader Robinson & Cole, Hartford, Conn., 1986-90; contbg. editor The Business Times, East Hartford, Conn., 1986-88; contbg. writer The Hartford News, Hartford, 1988-90; writing tchr. Manchester C.C., Conn., 1988—98, West Hartford Continuing Edn., 1999—, Windsor Continuing Edn., 2007—; freelance bus. writer Hartford Courant, Conn., 2001—03. Adj. instr. sociology and demography We. New Eng. Coll., Springfield, Mass., 1972-75, sociology Tunxis C.C., Farmington, Conn., 1992-94; adj. instr. French Mitchell Coll., New London, Conn., 1998-99. Editor Philippine Trade and Travel Guide, Orient Tours Mag., Manila, 1961-63; contbr. articles and essays to mags. and newspapers. Recipient Rank 14 Top 100 Articles Writer's Digest, 1980, 2d Pl. short story Hartford Advocate, 1996; scholar Alliance Française de Paris, 1963-64; fellow U. Conn., 1975-77. Mem.: Assn. Writers and Writing Programs. Roman Catholic. Avocation: reading. Home and Office: 19 Fennbrook Rd West Hartford CT 06119-2205

CALIPARI, JOHN V., men's college basketball coach; b. Feb. 10, 1959; m. Ellen Calipari; children: Erin Sue, Megan Rae, Bradley Vincent. Student, U. NC, Wilmington, Clarion State U., Pa., 1982. Asst. coach U. Kans., 1982-85; recruiting coord. U. Vt., 1983; asst. coach U. Pitts., 1985-88; head coach U. Mass., Amherst, 1988-96; head coach, exec. v.p. basketball ops. NJ Nets, East Rutherford, 1996—99; asst. coach Phila. 76ers, 1999; head coach U. Memphis, 2000—. Asst. Buckler Challenge All-Star Team, 1993, head coach, 1994; coach East squad US Olympic Festival, Denver. Vol. Camp Good Days and Spl. Times; chmn. Children's Miracle Network Telethon, Springfield. Named US Basketball Writers Assn. Dist. I Coach of Yr., 1993, Naismith Nat. Coach of Yr., 1996, The Sporting News Nat. Coach of Yr., 1996, Atlantic 10 Coach of Yr., 1996, Basketball Times East Region Coach of Yr., 1996, Conf. USA Coach of Yr., 2006; recipient Lombardi award UNICO Nat., 2003; named to Nat. Italian Am. Sports Hall of Fame, 2004, U. Mass. Athletic Hall of Fame, 2004. Office: U Memphis 230 Athletic Office Bldg Memphis TN 38152-3730 Office Phone: 901-678-2346. Office Fax: 901-678-5333. E-mail: jcalipar@memphis.edu.*

CALISE, NICHOLAS JAMES, lawyer; b. NYC, Sept. 15, 1941; s. William J. and Adeline (Rota) C.; m. Mary G. Flannery, Nov. 10, 1965; children: James R., Lori K. AB, Middlebury Coll., 1962; MBA, JD, Columbia U., 1965. Bar: N.Y. 1965, Conn., 1974, Ohio, 1986, Colo. 2000. Assoc., ptnr. Olvany, Eisner & Donnelly, NYC, 1969-76; corp. staff atty. Richardson-Vicks Inc., Wilton, Conn., 1976-82, div. counsel, dir. planning and bus. devel. home care products div. Memphis, 1982-84; staff v.p., sec., asst. gen. counsel The B.F. Goodrich Co., Akron, Ohio, 1984-89, v.p., sec., assoc. gen. counsel, 1989-99. Mem. Flood and Erosion Control Bd., Darien, Conn., 1976, Rep. Town Meeting, Darien, 1977-78; chmn. Zoning Bd. Appeals, Darien, 1978-82; Justice of the Peace, Darien, 1982; bd. dirs. Condillera Property Owners Assn., 2002-05, pres. 2005-06; bd. dirs. Mirabel Cmty. Assn., 2006-, pres., 2007-. Served to lt. USN, 1965—68, capt. JAGC USNR, 1984—96, ret. USNR, 1996. Mem.: ABA, Ohio Bar Assn., Colo. Bar Assn., N.Y. State Bar Assn., Am. Corp. Counsel Assn., Am. Soc. Corp. Secs. (bd. dirs. 1990—93, pres. Ohio chpt. 1991—92, chmn. nat. conf. com. 1997, mem. various coms.), U.S. Naval Inst., Naval Res. Assn. (life), Navy League (life), Res. Officers' Assn. (life), Judge Advs. Assn. (life), Mirabel Golf Club, Club Cordillera (bd. dirs. 2003—06, pres. 2003—05), Country Club of Hudson (bd. trustees 1996—99, sec. 1997—99, Bracebridge H. Young Disting. Svc. award 2001), Am. Legion. Roman Catholic. Home: 37184 N 102d St Scottsdale AZ 85262 Home Phone: 480-659-0724; Office Phone: 480-659-0725. Personal E-mail: caliselaw@yahoo.com.

CALISE, WILLIAM JOSEPH, JR., lawyer; b. NYC, May 22, 1938; s. William Joseph and Adeline (Rota) C.; m. Kathryn A. Verner; children: Kimberly Elizabeth, Andrea Elizabeth. BA, Bucknell U., 1960; MBA, JD, Columbia U., 1963. Bar: N.Y. 1963, D.C. 1981. Assoc., then ptnr. Chadbourne & Parke, NYC, 1967—94; sr. v.p., gen. counsel, sec. Rockwell Automation, Inc. (formerly Rockwell Internat.), Milw., 1994—2004. Bd. dirs. Henry St. Settlement, N.Y.C., 1977-94, Jr. Achievement Inc., 1999-2004; mem. Allendale (N.J.) Sch. Bd., 1977-80. Capt. U.S. Army, 1964-66. Mem. Assn. Bar N.Y.C., Assn. Gen. Counsel. Roman Catholic. Office Phone: 805-564-1888. Personal E-mail: casacalise@cox.net.

CALISSI, JEFFREY LUKE, music educator; b. Ramsey, NJ, July 1, 1976; s. Guy William and Judith Margaret Calissi. B of Music Edn., Radford U., 1999; MusM, U. NC, Greensboro, 2001, DMA, 2004. Lic. tchr., collegiate profl. tchr. Asst. prof. music Ea. Conn. State U., 2006. Percussionist. Composer: (mus. compositions) C. Alan Publs. Recipient tuition waivers and scholarships, U. N.C., 1999—2004. Mem.: Percussive Arts Soc., Coll. Music Soc. Office Phone: 860-465-5504. Business E-Mail: calissi@easternct.edu.

CALK, STEPHEN HAMILTON, environmentalist; b. Augusta, Ga., May 7, 1952; s. William Calk and Mary Margret Hamilton; m. Martha Lynn DeBerry, June 23, 1979; 1 child, William Robert. Environmentalist I SC Dept. Health Environ. Ctr., Charleston, SC, 1979—85, environmentalist III, 1985—90, environ. quality mgr., 1990—2004, regional compliance officer, 2004—. Contbr. articles to profl. jours. Advisor Children's Ministries, 1981—88. Mem.: SC Pub. Health Assn. (bd. dirs. 1980—83), Nat. Environ. Health Assn. (bd. dirs. 1983), SC Environ. Health Assn. (pres. 1983). Avocations: gold mining, woodworking. Office: SC Dept Health and Environ Control 2600 Bull St Columbia SC 29201

CALKINS, BENJAMIN, lawyer; b. Boston, Jan. 20, 1956; s. Evan and Virginia (Brady) C.; m. Lindsay Noble, July 4, 1981; children: Sarah Noble, Bradley Phillips, Patricia Noble, Haley McCormick. AB, Harvard U., 1978; JD, U. Mich., 1981. Bar: D.C. 1982, U.S. Dist. Ct. (ea. dist.) Mich. 1982, Ohio 1983, U.S. Dist. Ct. (no. dist.) Ohio 1983, U.S. Ct. Appeals (6th cir.) 1986, N.Y. 1990. Law clk. to presiding justice U.S. Dist. Ct. (ea. dist.) Mich., Detroit, 1981-83; assoc. Squire, Sanders & Dempsey, Cleve., 1983-89; ptnr. Benesch, Friedlander, Coplan & Aronoff, Cleve., 1989—96, Spieth, Bell, McCurdy & Newell Co., L.P.A., Cleve., 1996—2006; prin. Kahn Kleinman LPA, Cleve., 2006—. Assoc. editor U. Mich. Law Rev., 1979-80, sr. editor, 1980-81; contbr. articles to profl. jours. Sustaining mem. Rep. Nat. Com., Washington, 1985—; ballot issues com. Citizens League Greater Cleve., 1989-93, task force on edn. governance, 1991-92; fin. com. Ga. County Rep. Cen. and Exec. Coms., 1990—96; strategic planning com. West Geauga Sch. Dist., 1990-91; founder Newbury Ednl. Found.; treas. Friends of Newbury Schs., 1993-2006; grad. Leadership Geauga, 2002; chair mktg. com., livestock sales com. Geauga County Jr. Fair, 2000—; trustee Geauga County Far Bur., 2003—, chair policy devel. com., 2004—, treas., 2005—. Mem. ABA (corp., banking and bus. law sect.), Ohio Bar Assn. (mem. corp. law com.), Cleve. Bar Assn. (securities law sect., corp. banking and bus. law sect.), D.C. Bar Assn., Greater Cleve. Internat. Lawyers Group (sec. 1991-92, v.p. 1992—2006, membership chmn. 1992-2000), Assn. for Corp. Growth, Ohio Venture Assn. (v.p. 1996—, chmn. programs 2001-04, pres. 2004—), Union Club, Harvard Club (trustee 1985-88, 94—96, v.p. 1988-90, pres. 1990-94). Presbyterian. Avocations: sports, animal husbandry. Home: 11510 Music St Newbury OH 44065-9565 Office: Kahn Kleinman LPA 1301 E 9th St Ste 2600 Cleveland OH 44114 Office Phone: 216-736-3350, 440-564-7658. Business E-Mail: bcalkins@kahnkleinman.com.

CALKINS, EVAN, physician, educator; b. Newton, Mass., July 15, 1920; s. Grosvenor and Patty (Phillips) C.; m. Virginia McC. Brady, Sept. 9, 1946; children: Sarah Calkins Oxnard, Stephen, Lucy McCormick, Joan, Benjamin, Hugh, Ellen Rountree, Geoffrey, Timothy. Grad., Milton Acad., 1939; AB, Harvard U., 1942, MD, 1945. Intern, asst. resident medicine Johns Hopkins, 1946-47, 48-50; chief resident physician Mass. Gen. Hosp., 1951-52, mem. arthritis unit, 1952-61; NRC fellow med. scis. Harvard, 1950-51, instr., asst. prof. medicine, 1952-61; practice medicine, specializing in rheumatology Boston, 1951-61, Buffalo, 1961—; prof. medicine SUNY, Buffalo, 1961—90, prof. emeritus, 1990—, chmn. dept. medicine, 1965-77; head dept. medicine Buffalo Gen. Hosp., 1961-68; dir. medicine E.J. Meyer Meml. Hosp., 1968-78; head gerontology sect. Buffalo VA Med. Ctr., 1978-90; head div. geriatrics/gerontology SUNY-Buffalo, 1978-90. Founder, pres. Network in Aging of Western NY, Inc., 1980-83; cons. Nat. Inst. Arthritis and Metabolic Diseases Tng. Grants Com., 1958-62, Program Project Com., 1964-68, Nat. Instn. Spl. Study Sect. for Health Manpower, 1969-77, for Behavioral Medicine, 1978-79; acad. awards com. Nat. Inst. on Aging, 1979-80, nat. adv. coun., 1985-88; dir. Western NY Geriat. Edn. Ctr., 1983-88, co-dir., 1988-90; dir. Multidisciplinary Ctr. on Aging SUNY, Buffalo, 1989-90, prof. family medicine, 1987-94; sr. physician and coord. geriat. programs Health Care Plan, 1990-97; ptnr. Promedicus Health Group, 1998-2001; co-dir. WNY/Rochester Osteoporosis Ednl. Resource Ctr., 1999; pvt. practice rheumatology and geriatrics, 2001—. Editor: Yesterdays: Memoir from Six Generations of an American Family, 2006; editor: Handbook of Medical Emergencies, 1945, Geriatric Medicine, 1983, Practice of Geriatrics, 1986, 2d edit., 1991, New Ways to Care for Older People: Building Systems Based on Evidence, 1998, contbr. articles to profl. jours. Pres. Nat. Assn. Geriatric Edn. Ctrs., 1992-93. Capt. M.C. AUS, 1943-45, 46-48. Recipient Presdl. citation for Community Service, 1983 Fellow ACP (master 1989, Laureate award N.Y. Upstate chpt. 1998), Am. Coll. Rheumatology (founder, pres. 1967-68, master 1986), Gerontol. Soc. Am. (chair clin. med. sect. 1989, Freeman award 1991), Am. Geriatrics Soc. (Milo D. Leavitt award 1986); mem. Am. Clin. and Climatological Assn. (v.p. 1987), Am. Soc. Clin. Investigation, Assn. Am. Physicians, Soc. Medicine Argentina (hon.), Argentine Soc. Gerontology and Geriatrics (hon.), Soc. Fellows John Hopkins U., Alpha Omega Alpha. Home: 3799 Windover Dr Hamburg NY 14075-6338 Office: Village Rheumatology 17 Long Ave Ste 110 Hamburg NY 14075-6388 Office Phone: 716-646-5188.

CALKINS, HUGH, foundation executive; b. Newton, Mass., Feb. 20, 1924; s. Grosvenor and Patty (Phillips) C.; m. Ann Clark, June 14, 1955; children: Peter, Andrew, Margaret, Elizabeth. AB, LLB, Harvard U., 1949, D (hon.) in Law, 1985. Bar: Ohio 1950. Law clk. to presiding judge U.S. Ct. Appeals (2d cir.), NYC, 1949-50; law clk. to justice Felix Frankfurter U.S. Supreme Ct., Washington, 1950-51; from assoc. to ptnr. Jones, Day, Reavis & Pogue, Cleve., 1951-90; tchr. elem. schs. Cleve. City Sch. Dist., 1991-94. Contbr. articles on fed. income tax to profl. jours. Mem. Cleve. Bd. Edn., 1965-69; assoc. dir. Pres.'s Commn. on Nat. Goals, Washington, 1960; mem., pres., fellow Harvard U., 1968-85; mem. task forces Cleve. Summit on Edn., 1990-94; chair, treas., trustee Initiatives in Urban Edn., 1991—. Capt. USAF, 1943-46. Mem. ABA (chmn. tax sect. 1985-86), Am. Law Inst. (coun.), City Club, Cleve. Skating Club, Rowfant Club, Phi Beta Kappa. Democrat. Unitarian Universalist. Home and Office: 3345 N Park Blvd Cleveland OH 44118 Home Phone: 216-321-9338; Office Phone: 216-397-9749. Personal E-mail: calk2@adelphia.net.

CALKINS, RALPH NELSON, retired economics professor; b. Albuquerque, Apr. 28, 1926; s. Fred Myron and Luella (McDonald) C.; m. Ruth J. (Thatcher) Calkins, Jan. 8, 1949; children: Alison, Paul, Patricia. BBA, U. N.Mex., 1947, MA, 1949; PhD, Columbia U., 1963. Instr. econs. Bloomfield (N.J.) Coll., 1949-53, dean, 1953-67; assoc. prof. U. Alaska, Fairbanks, 1967-68; prof. dept. econs. and bus. adminstrn. Hanover (Ind.) Coll., 1968-91, prof. emeritus, 1991. Author: The Gradual Encroachment-Capitalism As We Know It, 2003. With USN, 1944—46. Mem. AAAS, Am. Econ. Assn., Am. Solar Energy Soc., Union of Concerned Scientists (sponsor), Ind. Acad. Social Scis. (bd. dirs. 1985-88). Democrat. Home: 7424 Edith Blvd NE Albuquerque NM 87113-1202 Personal E-mail: ralphnruth@aol.com.

CALKINS, STEPHEN, lawyer, educator; b. Balt., Mar. 20, 1950; s. Evan and Virginia (Brady) C.; m. Joan Wadsworth, Oct. 18, 1981; children: Timothy, Geoffrey, Virginia. BA, Yale U., 1972; JD, Harvard U., 1975. Bar: N.Y. 1976, D.C. 1977, U.S. Dist. Ct. D.C. 1979. Law clk. to FTC commr. S. Nye, Washington, 1975-76; assoc. Covington & Burling, Washington, 1976-83; assoc. law prof. Wayne State U., Detroit, 1983-88, prof., 1988—, dir. grad. studies, 2004—; gen. counsel FTC, Washington, 1995-97; of counsel Covington & Burling, Washington, 1997—, program dir. conf. bd. antitrust conf., 2001—. Vis. assoc. prof. law U. Mich., Ann Arbor, 1985, U. Pa., Phila., 1987; vis. prof. law U. Utrecht, Netherlands, 1989; chair career devel. Wayne State U., 1990-91. Author: (with Gellhorn and Kovacic) Antitrust Law and Economics in a Nutshell, 5th edit., 2004; editor: Antitrust Law Developments, 1984, 86, 88; editor legal book revs. The Antitrust Bull., 1986—; articles editor Antitrust, 1991-95. Co-chair Class of 1972 Yale Alumni Fund, 2004-07, chair 2007-; counsel Ind. Commn. on Admissions Practices in Cranbrook Sch., Detroit, 1984-85; mem. Northville Zoning Bd. Appeals, 1987-95; rep.-at-large Assn. Yale Alumni Assembly, 1989-92; bd. dirs. Yale Alumni Assn. of Mich., 2002-; elder First Presbyn. Ch. Northville, 1989-92. Rsch. fellow Wayne State U., 1984; USAID grantee, 1999-2004; recipient FTC award disting. svc., 1997, Donald H. Gordon Tchg. award, 2006. Fellow: Am. Bar Found., Am. Antitrust Inst. (sr.); mem.: ABA (counsel to com. on FTC 1988—89, coun. antitrust sect. 1988—91, 1997—2000, coun. adminstrv. law sect. 1999—2002, coun. antitrust sect. 2006—, Antitrust sect. 50th anniversary pub. award 2002), Am. Assn. Law Schs. (sec. antitrust sect. 1987—91, chair-elect 1991—93, chair 1993—95), Am. Law Inst., Anthony Wayne Soc., Northville Swim Club, Detroit Yale Club, Detroit Harvard Club. Presbyterian. Avocations: reading, skiing, rollerblading. Home: 317 W Dunlap St Northville MI 48167-1404 Office: Wayne State U Law Sch 471 W Palmer Detroit MI 48202 Office Phone: 313-577-3945. Business E-Mail: calkins@wayne.edu.

CALKINS, SUSAN W., state supreme court justice; Grad., U. Colo.; JD, U. Maine; M, U. Va. Sch. of Law. Staff atty., exec. dir. Pine Tree Legal Assistance; judge Maine Dist. Ct., 1980-90, chief judge, 1990—94; judge Maine Superior Ct., 1995—98; justice Maine Supreme Ct., 1998—. Ct. liaison Bd. of Bar Examiners, Jud. Ethics Com., Advisory Com. on Rules of Evidence. Fellow: Maine Bar Foundation; mem.: ABA (mem. Judges' Advisory Com. on Ethics & Professional Responsibility). Office: Maine Supreme Ct 142 Federal St PO Box 368 Portland ME 04112-0368*

CALKINS, SUSANNAH EBY, retired economist; b. Bucyrus, Ohio, Jan. 16, 1924; d. Samuel L. and Mae (McClure) Eby; m. G. Nathan Calkins, Nov. 19, 1949 (dec.); children: Helen E. (dec.), Margaret S. Van Auken, Sarah A. (dec.), Abigail Calkins Aguirre. AB, Goucher Coll., 1945; MS in Econs. (Univ. scholar 1946-47), U. Wis., 1947. Fiscal analyst U.S. Bur. Budget, 1945-50; economist U.S. Council Econ. Advisors, 1950-51, U.S. Office Price Stabilization, 1951-53, U.S. Bur. Budget, 1953-55; cons. U.S. Adv. Commn. on Intergovtl. Rels., Washington, 1972-73, 74-75, cons. on counter-cyclical aid programs, 1977-78, sr. analyst, 1979-87, exec. asst. to dir., 1987-89. Cons. revenue sharing Brookings Instn., Washington, 1973—74. Author (with R. Nathan and A. Manvel): Monitoring Revenue Sharing, 1975. Sponsor S.S. Goucher Victory, Balt., 1945; bd. dirs. Bread for the City, 1994—2002. Mem.: Am. Econs. Assn., George Towne Club (Washington), Cosmos Club (assoc.), Phi Beta Kappa. Presbyterian. Home: 6504 Dearborn Dr Falls Church VA 22044-1115

CALKINS, TIM, marketing professor; b. Buffalo, July 27, 1965; s. Evan Calkins and Virginia Brady; m. Carol Saltoun; children: Claire, Charles, Anna. BA, Yale U., New Haven, Conn., 1987; MBA, Harvard U., Cambridge, Mass., 1991. Rsch. assoc. Booz Allen and Hamilton, NYC, 1987—89; mktg. exec. Kraft Foods, Glenview, Ill., 1991—2002; prof. mktg. Kellogg Sch. Mgmt., Evanston, Ill., 1998—. Editor: (book) Kellogg on Branding. Office: Kellogg Sch Mgmt 2001 Sheridan Rd Evanston IL 60208 Office Phone: 847-467-3209. Business E-Mail: t-calkins@kellogg.northwestern.edu.

CALL, BRIDGET KAY, literature and language educator; B in Secondary Edn., Alderson Broaddus Coll., Philippi, W.Va.; MA, Marshall Univ., Huntington, W.Va. Tchr., 1975—; English, theater, writing tchr. Matewan (W.Va.) H.S. Named W.Va. Tchr. of Yr., 2006; recipient Arch Coal Tchr. Achievement award, 2001. Office: Matewan High Sch 100 Tiger Ln Matewan WV 25678 Business E-Mail: bkcall@access.k12.wv.us.*

CALL, CHARLES H., JR., civil engineer; s. C. Harvey and Jane M. Call; m. Robin Call, June 8, 1970; children: Kim, Kenyra, Kenton, Kaleb. BS, Brigham Young U., Provo, Utah, 1973, MS, 1974. Lic. profl. engr. Hydrologist and water rights engr. Woodward-Clyde Cons., Denver, 1974—76; engr. RBBG Engring, Provo, Utah, 1976—79; pres. Call Cons., Salt Lake City, 1979—81; engring. adminstr. Salt Lake Pub. Utilities, 1981—. Mem.: ASCE (pres. Utah sect. 1983—84), Am. Public Works Assn., Am. Water Works Assn. (life). Avocations: basketball, painting, photography, volunteering. Office: Salt Lake Pub Utilities 1530 S West Temple Salt Lake City UT 84115

CALL, DAVID ANDREW, meteorologist, educator; b. York, Pa., Mar. 3, 1977; s. Thomas F. and Verna L. Call; BS, Pa. State U., University Park, 1998; MA, Syracuse U., NY, 2004, PhD, 2007. Meteorologist WJET-TV, Erie, Pa., 1998—2002, WSTM-TV, Syracuse, 2002—07; lectr. meteorology Pa. State U., Erie, 2000—02; grad. asst. Syracuse U., 2002—07; asst. prof. Ball State U., Muncie, Ind., 2007—. Contbr. articles to profl. jours. Chmn. worship com. Pk. Ctrl. Presbyn. Ch., Syracuse, 2004—07. Fellow, Syracuse U., 2004—07; Roscoe Martin Dissertation Rsch. grantee, Maxwell Sch., Syracuse U., 2005. Mem.: Nat. Weather Assn. (Seal of Approval for TV 2002), Assn. Am. Geographers (Gilbert White award for Outstanding Thesis or Dissertation, Hazards Specialty Group 2005), Am. Meteorol. Soc. (Seal of Approval for TV 2000), Sigma Xi (Grad. Rsch. award Syracuse chpt. 2004). Avocations: restoring antique traffic signals, cello, trombone, piano. Office: Ball State U Dept Geography Muncie IN 47306 Office Phone: 765-285-1768.

CALL, GREGORY S., academic administrator, mathematics professor; AB in Math. summa cum laude, Dartmouth Coll.; MA, PhD, Harvard Univ. Prof. math. Amherst (Mass.) Coll., 1988—, dean new students, 2003—05, interim dean faculty, 2003—05, dean faculty, 2005—. Office: Dean of the Faculty Amherst Coll PO Box 5000 Amherst MA 01002-5000 Office Phone: 413-542-2334. Office Fax: 413-542-2621.

CALL, MERLIN WENDELL, lawyer; b. Long Beach, Calif., Nov. 25, 1931; s. True and Bernice (Johnson) C.; m. Kathryn J. Gage, Dec. 22, 1956 (div.); children: Christopher, Lori. AB, Stanford U., 1951, JD, 1953. Bar: Calif. 1953. Assoc. Tuttle & Taylor, LA, 1955-60, ptnr., 1960-2000; sr. counsel Shapiro, Borenstein & Dupont, Santa Monica, Calif., 2000—02. Bd. visitors Stanford Sch. Law, 1987-90. Chmn. bd. trustees Westmont Coll., Santa Barbara, Calif., 1988—94, The Fuller Found., Pasadena, Calif., 1987—94, Mission Aviation Fellowship, Redlands, Calif., 1974—78, Gospel Broadcasting Assn., 1967—78, De Pree Leadership Ctr., 2001—; mem. Town Hall Calif., LA, 1958—; trustee Fuller Theol. Sem., Pasadena, 1963—78, 1983—, chmn., 2001—06; trustee China Connection, 2001—, Westmont Coll., Santa Barbara, Calif., 1984—, The Fuller Found., 1987—, Mission Aviation Fellowship, Redlands, Calif., 1963—78. Mem. Phi Beta Kappa, Order of Coif. Home: 1660 La Loma Rd Pasadena CA 91105-2158 Office: 225 S Lake Ave Ste 300 Pasadena CA 91101- E-mail: mwcall@earthlink.net, mwcalllaw@polarisnet.net.

CALL, NEIL JUDSON, manufacturing executive; b. Detroit, June 15, 1933; s. Judson Francis and Glennys Jean (Amluxen) C.; m. Jane E. Rathslag, Feb. 4, 1956; children: Laura, Keith; m. Eleanor Ann King, Nov. 23, 1978. BBA, U. Mich., 1955, MBA, 1956. C.P.A., Mich. With Hogan Juengel & Harding, CPAs, Detroit, 1956-61, Ford Motor Co., Dearborn, Mich., 1961-65; with Ford Motor Credit Co., Dearborn, 1965-67, Gulf & Western Industries Inc., NYC, 1968-86, v.p., 1970-79, sr. v.p., 1979-83, exec. v.p., 1983-84, D.F. King & Co., Inc., NYC, 1986-89, Dewe Rogerson Inc., NYC, 1990-92, Mackenzie Ptnrs., Inc., NYC, 1992—. Bd. dirs. Sona Bank. Bd. dirs. Lower Fla. Keys Hosp. Dist., 2000—, Performing Arts Ctr. of Key West, 2005—. Served with U.S. Army, 1956-58. Home: 1500 Atlantic Blvd Apt 307 Key West FL 33040-5071 Office: Mackenzie Ptnrs Inc 105 Madison Ave New York NY 10016-7002 Personal E-mail: nandecall@aol.com.

CALLAGY, JOHN M., lawyer; b. NYC, 1944; AB, Georgetown U., 1966; JD, NYU, 1969. Bar: N.Y. 1969, Conn. 1977. Ptnr. Kelley, Drye & Warren LLP, NYC, chmn., 1993—. Office: Kelley Drye & Warren LLP 101 Park Ave Fl 30 New York NY 10178-0062 E-mail: jcallagy@kelleydrye.com.

CALLAHAN, BILL, college football coach; b. Chgo., July 31, 1956; m. Valerie Callahan; 4 children. Offensive line coach Northern Arizona U., 1987—88; offensive coord. So. Ill. Univ., 1989; offensive line coach Univ. Wis., 1990—94, Phila. Eagles, 1995—97, Oakland Raiders, 1997—2000, tight ends coach, 1998, offensive coordinator, 1998—2002, head coach, 2002—03, Univ. Neb., Lincoln, 2004—. Office: Univ Neb 103 S Stadium Lincoln NE 68588*

CALLAHAN, CONSUELO MARIA, federal judge; b. Palo Alto, Calif., June 9, 1950; married; 2 children. BA, Leland Stanford Jr. Univ., 1972; JD, McGeorge Sch. Law, Univ. Pacific, 1975; LLM, Univ. Va., 2004—. Bar: Calif. 1975. Dep. city atty. City of Stockton, Stockton, Calif., 1975—76; dep. dist. atty. Dist. Atty. Office, San Joaquin County, Calif., 1976—82, sup. dist. atty., 1982—86; ct. comm. Mcpl. Ct. of Stockton, Stockton, Calif., 1986—92; judge San Joaquin County Superior Ct., San Joaquin, Calif., 1992—96; assoc. judge Ct. Appeal , State of Calif., Calif., 1996—2003; judge US Ct. Appeals (9th cir.), 2003—. Recipient Award for Criminal Justice Programs, Gov., Susan B. Anthony Award for Women of Achievement, Stockton Peacemaker of the Yr., 1997, Mexican-Am. Hall of Fame, San Joaquin County, 1999. Achievements include first hispanic, first woman named to San Joaquin Co. Superior Ct. Office: US Ct Appeals 501 I St Sacramento CA 95814 Office Phone: 916-930-4160.*

CALLAHAN, DANIEL J., lawyer; b. Chgo., Sept. 13, 1949; children: Caitlin, Michael. BA magna cum laude, Western Ill. U., 1976; JD with honors, U. Calif., Davis, 1979. Bar: Calif. 1980, Hawaii 1980, US Tax Ct. 1981, US Ct. Appeals (9th cir.) 1981, US Dist. Ct. (dist. Hawaii) 1981, US Dist. Ct. (all dist. Calif.) 1983, US Supreme Ct. 1997. Editor U. Calif. at Davis Law Rev., 1978; founder, mng. ptnr. Callahan & Blaine, Santa Ana, Calif., 1984—. Sponsor Elizabeth Glaser Pediatric Aids Found., YMCA, Orange County, Braille Inst., CHOC found. Children & Good Sheppard Luth. Charities. Named Trial Lawyer of Yr., OCTLA, 2000, Orange County, 2004, Calif. Bus. Litig. Trial Lawyer of Yr., Calif. Lawyer Mag., 2003; named one of Hot 25, OC Metro Mag., 2000, Top 10 Trial Lawyers in Am., Nat. Law Jour., 2004; recipient Pres. Pro Bono award, Calif. State Bar, 1994. Mem.: Pi Sigma Alpha, Am. Inns of Ct., Assn. Bus. Trial Lawyers, Assn. Trial Lawyers of Am., Consumer Attys. Calif., Orange County Trial Lawyers Assn., ABA, Fed. Bar Assn., Hawaii State Bar Assn., LA County Bar Assn., Orange County Bar Assn. (chair Law Practice Mgmt. Sect. 1993—95, chair Bus. Litig. Sect. 1996, voted Top Gun 2000, 2004), Phi Kappa Phi. Office: Callahan & Blaine Ste 900 3 Hutton Centre Dr Santa Ana CA 92707 Office Phone: 714-241-4444.*

CALLAHAN, DANIEL JOHN, biomedical researcher; b. Washington, July 19, 1930; s. Vincent Francis and Anita (Hawkins) Callahan; m. Sidney Cornelia de Shazo, June 5, 1954; children: Mark Sidney, Stephen Daniel, John Vincent, Peter Thorn, Sarah Elisabeth, David Lee. BA, Yale U., 1952; MA, Georgetown U., 1957; PhD, Harvard U., 1965; DSc (hon.), U. Medicine and Dentistry of N.J., 1981; DHL (hon.), U. Colo., 1990, Williams Coll., 1992, Oreg. State U., 1997, SUNY, 2006. Exec. editor The Commonweal, NYC, 1961—68; staff assoc. Population Council, 1969—70; co-founder, pres. The Hastings Ctr., 1969—96, dir. internat. programs, 1997—; resident scholar Aspen Inst. Humanistic Studies, 1975. Vis. asst. prof. religion Temple U., 1964; vis. asst. prof. religious studies Brown U., 1965; vis. prof. theology Marymount Coll., 1966; vis. prof. U. Pa., 1970; sr. fellow Harvard Ctr. for Population and Devel. Studies, 1996; cons. med. ethics, jud. coun. AMA, 1972—82, ACP, 1979—86; spl. cons. Commn. on Population Growth and Am. Future, 1970—71, NEH, 1979; hon. prof. Charles U. Med. Sch., Prague, 1997—; sr. lectr. Harvard Med. Sch., 1998—; sr. rsch. scholar Yale U., 2004—. Author: The Mind of the Catholic Layman, 1963, Honesty in the Church, 1965, The New Church, 1966, Abortion: Law, Choice and Morality, 1970, Ethics and Population Limitation, 1971, The Tyranny of Survival, 1973, The Teaching of Ethics in the Military, 1982, Setting Limits: Medical Goals in an Aging Society, 1987, What Kind of Life: The Limits of Medical Progress, 1990, The Troubled Dream of Life: Living with Morality, 1993, False Hopes: Why America's Quest for Perfect Health is a Recipe for Failure, 1998, What Price Better Health: Hazards of the Research Imperative, 2003, Medicine and the Market Equity v. Choice, 2006; also essays, articles:; co-editor: Christianity Divided: Protestant and Roman Catholic Theological Issues, 1961, Ethical Issues in Human Genetics, 1973; editor: Federal Aid and Catholic Schools, 1964, Secular City Debate, 1966, The Catholic Case for Contraception, 1969, The American Population Debate, 1971, Science, Ethics and Medicine, 1976, Knowledge, Value and Belief, 1977, Morals,

Science and Sociality, 1978, Knowing and Valuing, 1979, Ethics Teaching in Higher Education, 1980, Ethical Issues in Population Aid, 1980, The Roots of Ethics, 1981, Ethics in Hard Times, 1981, Ethics, the Social Sciences and Policy Analysis, 1983, Abortion: Understanding Differences, 1984, Applying the Humanities, 1985, Representation and Responsibility, 1985, A World Growing Old, 1995, What Price Mental Health?, 1995, Promoting Healthy Behavior, 2000, The Role of Complementary and Alternative Medicine, 2002, Medicine and the Market, 2006; mem. editl. adv. bd.: Tech. in Soc., 1981—, mem. adv. bd.: Ency. of Life Scis., 1982, Sci., Tech. and Human Values, 1979—, Bus. and Profl. Ethics, 1981, Criminal Justice Ethics, 1982, Environ. Ethics, 1982, Jour. Bioethics, 1985—96. Mem. nat. adv. bd. Health Promotion Program, Henry J. Kaiser Family Found., 1987—91, N.Y. Panel and HIV Screening, 1987; adv. com. to dir. Ctr. for Disease Control, DHHS; mem. N.Y. Coun. for Humanities, 1975—79, Nat. Book Award Com., 1975, N.Y. State Health Adv. Coun., 1975—76; selection com. Ford-Rockefeller Program in Population Policy, 1975—78, Rockefeller Found. Program in Humanities, 1980; elector Nat. Medal for Lit., 1979—83; pub. mem. Am. Bd. Med. Specialties, 1982—87, N.Y. Sci. Policy Assn., 1985—91; mem. N.Y. Task Force on Life and Law, 1985—87; trustee U. Pa. Med. Ctr., 1987—91; mem. adv. com. on sci. integrity HHS, 1991—93. Named one of 200 Outstanding Young Men Leaders, Time mag., 1974; recipient Thomas More medal, 1970, Daryl J. Mase Disting. Leadership award, 1987, Book of Yr. award, Am. Jour. Nursing, 1987, Henry Knowles Beecher award, The Hastings Ctr., 1989, James H. Hamilton Book award, Am. Coll. Health Care Execs., 1990, Pres. Cabinet award, U. Tex., 1995, Scientific Freedom and Responsibility award, AAAS, 1995, Joseph Leiter award, Nat. Libr. of Medicine, 1999, ARCHON award, Sigma Theta Tau Internat. Honor Soc. of Nursing, 1999, Washington Irving Book award for Fals Hopes, 1999, Career Achievement award, Soc. Bioethics and Med. Humanities, 2001, Morrison prize, MIT, 2002, Centennial medal, Harvard Grad. Sch. Arts and Scis., 2006, Bioethics Leadership award, Johns Hopkins U., 2006; Tekolste scholar, Ind. Hosp. Assn., 1986, Bus. Enterprise Trust fellow, 1989—95. Fellow: AAAS (Sci. Freedom and Responsibility award 1996); mem.: Soc. for Study Social Biology (bd. dirs. 1987—95), Inst. Medicine of NAS, Am. Assn. for Advancement Humanities, Harvard Grad. Sch. Arts and Scis. (Centennial medal 2006), Harvard Grad. Soc. (coun. 1989—92, Sr. scholar 1994—). Home: PO Box 260 Ardsley On Hudson NY 10503-0260 Office: The Hastings Ctr 21 Malcolm Gordon Rd Garrison NY 10524-5555 Business E-Mail: callahan@thehastingscenter.org.

CALLAHAN, DEBRA JEAN, political organization worker; b. Burbank, Calif., June 4, 1958; d. Robert Bascom and Betty Jean Callahan; m. Kenneth A. Cook. Student, Calif. State Poly. U., San Luis Obispo, 1976-79; BA magna cum laude, U. Calif., Santa Barbara, 1981. Legal asst. Loo, Merideth & McMillan, LA, 1982-83; field staff Mondale for Pres., Washington, 1984; dep. state campaign mgr. Mondale-Ferraro Com., Kansas City, Mo., 1984; regional polit. dir. League of Conservation Voters, Portsmouth, NH, 1985-86; dep. campaign mgr. Kent Conrad for U.S. Senate, Bismarck, ND, 1986; exec. asst. to Senator Kent Conrad, Washington, 1986-87; dep. nat. polit. dir. Gore for Pres., Washington, 1987-88; exec. dir. Ams. for the Environment, Washington, 1988-90; campaign mgr. Re-election Rep. Howard Wolpe (D-Md.), 1990; policy cons. Nat. Toxics Campaign, 1991—; program dir. W. Alton Jones Found., 1992-95; exec. dir. Brainerd Found., Seattle, 1995-96; pres. League of Conservation Voters, Washington, 1996—2006. Polit. cons. League of Conservation Voters, 1988. Field dir. Hands Across Am., St. Louis, 1986; bd. dir. World Resources Inst., 1998—, Earth Day Network, 1999-2003. U. Calif. Dept. Environ. Studies scholar, Santa Barbara, 1981, Alumni award, 1998. Avocations: travel, reading, scuba diving, bicycling, music. Office: League of Conservation Voters 1920 L St NW Ste 800 Washington DC 20036-5045

CALLAHAN, DENNIS S., insurance company executive; BA in Math., NYU. V.p. global ops. and tech. Goldman, Sachs & Co., NYC, 1971—91; chief info. officer Wellington Mgmt. Co., Boston, 1991—95; sr. v.p. Fidelity's Asset Svcs. Group, Boston, 1995—97; chief info. officer Am. Internat. Group, NYC, 1997—2000; sr. v.p., chief info. officer Guardian Life Ins. Co. Am., NYC, 2000—03, exec. v.p., chief info. officer, 2003- -. Named one of Premier 100 IT Executives, Computerworld mag., 2003. Office: Guardian Life Ins Co 7 Hanover Sq New York NY 10004-2616

CALLAHAN, EDWARD WILLIAM, chemical engineer, retired manufacturing executive; b. NYC, July 17, 1930; s. William Patrick and Clara (Schultz) C.; m. Barbara Jane Willmarth, Nov. 23, 1985; children: Susan Lynne, Kevin Foster. B.Ch.E., Cornell U., 1953. Engr. Solvay div. Allied Chem. Corp., Syracuse, NY, 1953-65, dir. comml. devel., 1965-66; asst. to pres. Allied Signal Corp., NYC, 1966-70, gen. mgr. environ. services Morristown, NJ, 1970-78, v.p. health, safety and environ. scis., 1978-95; ret. Bd. dirs. Am. Cancer Soc., Morristown, 1982-84; trustee Ind. Coll. Fund. of N.J., 1988-94. Mem.: Chem. Mfrs. Assn. (chmn. environ. mgmt. com. 1978—82), Am. Indsl. Health Coun. (dir. 1978—91), Chem. Industry Inst. Toxicology (dir. 1974—91, Conf. Bd. environ. com. chmn. 1994—95), World Environ. Ctr. (bd. dirs. 1992—98), Internat. Environ. Forum (chmn. 1986—94), Quantuck Beach Club, Quogue Field Club, Shinnecock Yacht Club, Union Club, F & AM (Holland Lodge No. 8). Home: 389 S Lake Dr Apt 4C Palm Beach FL 33480

CALLAHAN, JACK F., JR., food products executive; With McKinsey & Co., GE; v.p. strategy and planning Frito Lay North Am. PepsiCo Inc., CFO Frito Lay Internat., sr. v.p. investor relations; exec. v.p., CFO Dean Foods, 2006—. Office: Dean Foods 2515 McKinney Ave Ste 1200 Dallas TX 75201-1945*

CALLAHAN, JAMES MICHAEL, physician, educator; b. Ilion, NY, July 24, 1959; s. Joseph R. and Eileen R. Callahan; m. Irene G. Gazetos, June 26, 1982; children: Peter J., Katherine E., Christine S. BS, St. Lawrence U., Canton, NY, 1977—81; MD, SUNY Upstate Med. U., Syracuse, 1981—85. Diplomate Am. Bd. Pediat., 1989, in Pediat. Emergency Medicine Am. Bd. Pediat., 1994. Clin. asst. prof., pediat. U. Pa. Sch. Medicine, Phila., 1995—96; asst. prof., pediat. Ohio State U. Coll. Medicine, Columbus, 1996—97; asst. prof., emergency medicine and pediat. SUNY Upstate Med. U., Syracuse, 1997—2002, assoc. prof., emergency medicine and pediat., 2002—06, dir. pediatric emergency medicine fellowship program, 2004—06; assoc. prof. clin. pediat. Sch. Medicine, U. Pa., 2006—; dir. med. edn. divsn. emergency medicine Children's Hosp. Phila., 2006—. Office: Children's Hosp Philadelphia Divsn Emergency Medicine 34th St and Civic Ctr Blvd Philadelphia PA 19104 Home: 2220 Walnut St Apt 924 Philadelphia PA 19103 Office Phone: 215-590-1944. Office Fax: 215-590-4454. Business E-Mail: callahanj@email.chop.edu.

CALLAHAN, J(OHN) WILLIAM (BILL CALLAHAN), judge; b. Rockville Centre, NY, Feb. 8, 1947; s. Peter Felix and Catherine L. C. BA, Mich. State U., 1971, JD cum laude, 1974. Atty. Bank of Commonwealth, Detroit, 1974-76; assoc. Hopps & Hudson, P.C., Detroit, 1976-79, Tyler & Canham, P.C., Detroit, 1979-80, Stark & Reagan, P.C., Troy, Mich., 1980-81; pvt. practice Farmington Hills, Mich., 1981-86; mem. Plunkett & Cooney, P.C., Detroit, 1986-96; judge Wayne County Cir. Ct., Detroit, 1996—. Bd. dirs. Vietnam Vets. Am. Chpt. 9, Detroit, 1981-85. With USMC, 1967-69, Vietnam. Mem. Detroit Bar Assn. Office: 1813 City-County Bldg Detroit MI 48226

CALLAHAN, KIM VERSPRILLE, special education educator; b. Tallahassee, Fla., June 30, 1959; d. Patrick John and Mary Fay Versprille; m. Patrick Murray Callahan, Nov. 24, 1988; children: Patrick Versprille, Veronica Murray, Caroline Rose. BA, Old Dominion U., Norfolk, Va., 1985; MA in Edn., Regent U., Virginia Beach, Va., 1999; EdS, Regent U., Virginia Beach Va., 2007. Cert. Instl. tech. Old Dominion U., 2001; trainer content enhancement organizer U. Kans., 2005, trainer Wilson Reading Sys., 2007. Spl. educator Norfolk Pub. Sch., Va., 1998—2007; coord. mid. coll. Norfolk Pub. Sch., Tidewater C.C., Va., 2004—06. Adj. prof. Regent U., Virginia Beach, Va., 2002—07. Mem. Alhambra, Norfolk, 2001—07. Mem.: Cir. of Friends (assoc.). D-Conservative. Roman Catholic. Avocations: swimming, cooking. Home: 1356 Kilmer Ct Norfolk VA 23502 Office: Norfolk Pub Sch Granby High 7101 Granby St Norfolk VA 23505 Home Phone: 757-853-1824; Office Phone: 757-451-4113. Personal E-mail: kcallahan@regent.edu. Business E-Mail: kvcallah@nps.k12.va.us.

CALLAHAN, LEEANN LUCILLE, psychologist; b. San Diego, Calif., Dec. 7, 1950; d. Charlie A. Olsen and Dolores A. (Libke) Turner; m. Chuck Callahan, Oct. 31, 1970; children: Clint, Devin, Chet. BS/MS in Psychology, San Diego State U., 1983; PhD in Psychology, USIU, San Diego, 1990. Lic. clin. psychologist. Clin. dir. Sharp Cabrillo Hosp., San Diego, 1989-91, Charter Hosp., San Diego, 1991-93; psychologist San Diego, 1989—. Preferred provider Charter Hosp., San Diego, 1990—, speakers bur., 1990—; staff psychologist Sharp Cabrillo Hosp., San Diego, 1989-92. Editor Parentteen Mag.; contbr. articles to profl. jours. Pres. PTA, San Diego, 1985; citizen adv./city coun. City of San Diego, 1987; vol. Poway Unified Sch. Dist., San Diego, 1975—; speaker Rotary, San Diego, 1994. Recipient Citizen of Yr. award, Sigma Chi, 1997. Mem. APA, Calif. State Psychol. Assn. Office: 9320 Carmel Mountain Rd Ste D San Diego CA 92129-2159

CALLAHAN, LEIGH FLEMING, medical educator, researcher; b. Rutherfordton, NC, Feb. 24, 1957; d. George Arthur and Ruth Fleming Callahan; m. John Buckner Winfield. BS, U. N.C., Chapel Hill, 1979; PhD, Vanderbilt U., Nashville, 1992. Rsch. asst. Wistar Inst., Phila., 1979—81; rsch. assoc. Vanderbilt U., Nashville, 1981—93; epidemiologist Ctrs. Disease Control and Prevention, Atlanta, 1993—95; asst. prof. U. N.C., Chapel Hill, 1995—99, assoc. prof., 1999—. Assoc. dir. Thurston Arthritis Rsch. Ctr., Chapel Hill, 1995—2000; rsch. fellow Cecil B. Sheps Ctr., Chapel Hill, NC, 1996—. Editor: Arthritis Care and Rsch.; contbr. articles to profl. jours. Trustee Arthritis Found., Atlanta, 1989—2006, sr. vice chair, 1999—2000, treas., 1997—98, vice chair, 1995—96, chair Tenn. chpt. Nashville, 1994, chair Carolinas chpt. Charlotte, NC, 2004—06. Recipient Disting. Scholar award, Assn. Rheumatology Health Profls., 1995, Harding award, Arthritis Found., 2006, Addie Thomas Svc. award, Assn. Rheumatology Health Profls. Mem.: APHA, Assn. Health Svcs. Rsch., Soc. Epidemiologic Rsch., Am. Coll. Rheumatology. Avocations: scuba diving, reading, travel, bicycling, music. Home: 102 Greenwood Ln Chapel Hill NC 27514 Office: U NC 3300 Thurston Bldg CB 7280 Chapel Hill NC 27599 Home Phone: 919-968-7230; Office Phone: 919-966-0564. Office Fax: 919-966-1739. Business E-Mail: leigh_callahan@med.unc.edu.

CALLAHAN, MICHAEL J., lawyer, retail executive; b. 1963; BA, Rutgers U.; JD, U. Va. Bar: NJ 1988. With Real Estate Dept. Bed Bath & Beyond, Union, NJ, v.p., corp. counsel. Office: Bed Bath & Beyond 650 Liberty Ave Union NJ 07083

CALLAHAN, MICHAEL JOHN, lawyer; m. Dana Weintraub; 2 children. BS in Internat. Affairs and Arab Studies, Georgetown U., 1990; JD with honors, U. Conn., 1995. Bar: Calif. Atty. Skadden, Arps, Slate, Meagher & Flom, LLP, 1995—99; mgr. bus. devel., corp. counsel electronics Electronics for Imaging Inc., 1999; corp. counsel Yahoo!, Inc., Sunnyvale, Calif., 1999—2000, sr. corp. counsel, 2000, assoc. gen. counsel, 2000—01, dep. gen. counsel, asst. sec., 2001—03, gen. counsel, sec., 2003—, also sr. v.p., 2003—. Office: Yahoo Inc 701 First Ave Sunnyvale CA 94089 Office Phone: 408-349-3300. Office Fax: 408-349-3301.*

CALLAHAN, MICHAEL R., lawyer; b. NYC, Apr. 11, 1953; BA, No. Ill. U.; JD, DePaul U., 1979. Bar: Ill. 1979. Law clerk to Justice Daniel P. Ward Ill. Supreme Ct., 1979—81; ptnr. head Health Care Practice group Katten Muchin Zavis Rosenman, Chgo. Adj. prof. DePaul Coll., Masters in Health Law Prog. Mem.: ABA, Am. Health Lawyers Assn., Ill. Assn. of Hosp. Attys., Chgo. Bar Assn. Office: Katten Muchin Zavis Rosenman 525 W Monroe St Chicago IL 60661 Office Phone: 312-902-5634. Office Fax: 312-577-8945. Business E-Mail: michael.callahan@kattenlaw.com.

CALLAHAN, MICHAEL THOMAS, arbitrator, consultant, construction executive, writer; b. Kansas City, Mo., Oct. 7, 1948; s. Harry Leslie and Venita June (Yohn) Callahan; m. Stella Sue Paffenbach, Mar. 21, 1970; children: Molly Leigh, Michael Kroh. BA, U. Kans., 1970; JD, U. Mo., 1973, LLM, 1979; postgrad., Temple U., 1976-77. Bar: Kans. 1973, N.J. 1975, Mo. 1977. V.p. T.J. Constrn., Inc., Lenexa, Kans., 1973-74; sr. cons. Wagner-Hohns-Inglis, Inc., Mt. Holly, NJ, 1974-77, v.p. Kansas City, Mo., 1977-86; exec. v.p. CCL Constrn. Cons., Overland Park, Kans., 1986-88, pres., 1988—. Adj. prof. U. Kans., Iowa State U.; arbitrator; lectr. in field; chmn. CCL Pacific Corp.; pres. Handcrafted Wines Kans., Inc. Home: 9011 Delmar St Shawnee Mission KS 66207-2343 Office: CCL Constrn Cons 4600 College Blvd Ste 104 Overland Park KS 66211-1606 Office Phone: 913-491-8626. Business E-Mail: cclcon@ix.netcom.com.

CALLAHAN, PATRICIA R., bank executive; BSME, MIT, M in Mgmt. and Fin. Various mgmt. positions Crocker Nat. Bank, 1977—84, sr. v.p., mgr. corp. svcs., 1984—93; dir. human resources Wells Fargo & Co., 1993—97, exec. v.p. wholesale banking sys. fin. and ops., 1997—98, exec. v.p., dir. human resources, 1998—2005, exec. v.p. compliance & risk mgmt., 2005—. Bd. dirs. United Way Bay Area; bd. trustees Dominican U. Calif. Office: Wells Fargo & Co 420 Montgomery St San Francisco CA 94163*

CALLAHAN, ROBERT F., JR., media company executive, former broadcast executive; m. Janice Callahan; children: Elizabeth, Claire, Helen. BS in Journalism, Univ. of Kansas. Media planner Young & Rubicam advt., from 1976; then positions in acct. mgmt. with McCann-Erickson and Wells, Rich, Greene, Inc.; Eastern Sales Mgr. Fairchild Pubs., from 1981, various sales and pub. positions; then sr. v.p., group pub. Fairchild Pubs. Capital Cities/ABC Pub., sr. v.p. diversified pub. group, 1990; pres. ABC Radio Divsn., NYC, 1990-99; pres. broadcasting ABC Inc., NYC, 1999-2000; pres. ABC Broadcast Group, NYC, 2000—01; chmn., CEO Ziff Davis Media, NYC, 2001—. Mem.: Am. Bus. Media, Mag. Pubs. Assn., Mus. Broadcasting, Internat. Radio and TV Soc., Radio Network Assn., Nat. Assn. Broadcasters, Edn. Corp. Am. Office: Ziff Davis Media Inc 28 E 28th St New York NY 10016 Office Phone: 212-503-3500.*

CALLAHAN, SONNY (H.L. CALLAHAN), former congressman; b. Mobile, Ala., Sept. 11, 1932; m. Karen Reed; children: Scott, Patrick, Shawn Cushing, Chris, Cameron (dec.), Kelly Thomas. Grad., McGill Inst. Pres., chmn. bd., chief exec. officer Finch Cos., Mobile and Montgomery, Ala., 1964-84; mem. Ala. Ho. of Reps., 1970-78, chmn. Mobile County delegation; mem. Ala. Senate, 1978-82, U.S. Congress from 1st Ala. dist., 1985—2002; mem. appropriations com.; chmn. subcom. on energy and water devel.; pres. Sonny Callahan and Assoc. Served with USN, 1952-54 Mem. Mobile Area C. of C., Ala. Movers Assn., Ala. Trucking Assn., Kiwanis, Optimists, Ala. Port Authority Bd. Republican.

CALLAHAN, THOMAS JAMES, lawyer; b. Cleve., Jan. 21, 1957; s. Thomas Joseph and Lucille Dorothy (DeVries) Callahan; m. Laura Jean Schwartz, Oct. 13, 1979; children: Thomas, Michael. BS in Acctg. cum laude, Duke U., 1979; JD cum laude, Case Western Reserve U., 1985. CPA Ohio, 1981; bar: Ohio 1985, US Ct. Appeals (6th cir.) 1987, US Tax Ct. 1987, US Dist. Ct. (no. dist.) Ohio 1987, US Ct. Fed. Claims 1987, US Ct. Appeals (fed. cir.) 2000, US Supreme Ct. 2000. Staff sr. acct. Price Waterhouse, Cleve., 1979-82, mgr., 1985-86; assoc. Thompson Hine LLP, Cleve., 1986-96, ptnr., 1997—, leader tax practice. Mem. adv. bd.: Jour. Tax Practice Procedure. Vice chair allocations com. United Way Svcs., Cleve., 1992—96; mem. arbitration com. Cuyahoga Ct. Common Pleas, Cleve., 1989—. Mem.: AICPA, ABA (tax sect., chair adminstrv. practice com.), Am. Coll. Tax Counsel (regent), Cleve. Tax Inst. (exec. com. 1999—2005, chair 2001, 2004), Cleve. Bar Assn. (spkr. 1994—, chmn. gen. tax com. 1999), Tax Club Cleve. (bd. dir. 2000, treas. 2001, v.p. 2002—03, pres. 2004, mem. advisory bd. Jour. Tax Practice and Procedure). Office: Thompson Hine LLP 3900 Key Ctr 127 Pub Sq Cleveland OH 44114-1216 Office Phone: 216-566-5612. E-mail: tom.callahan@thompsonhine.com.

CALLAHAN, TIMOTHY T., real estate company executive; BA, Notre Dame U., Ind.; student in Bus. Adminstrn., NYU. Sr. v.p. Chem. Realty Corp., 1974—88; from dir. devel to v.p. fin. Edward J. DeBartolo Corp., Youngstown, Ohio, 1988—92; sr. v.p. EGI, 1992—95; pres., CEO Equity Office Properties Trust, 1996—2002; pres. Trizec Properties, Inc., Chgo., 2002—, CEO, 2002—, bd. dir. Office: Trizec 10 S Riverside Plz Ste 1100 Chicago IL 60606-3708

CALLAHAN, VINCENT FRANCIS, JR., state legislator, publishing executive; b. Washington, Oct. 30, 1931; s. Vincent Francis and Anita (Hawkins) C.; children from previous marriage: Vincent Francis III, Elizabeth Lauren, Anita Marie, Cynthia Helen, Robert Bruce; m. Yvonne Weight, Feb. 15, 2006. BS in Fgn. Svc., Georgetown U., 1957; LHD (hon.), No. Va. C.C., 1997. Pres. Callahan Publs., 1957-2000; mem. Va. Hos. of Dels., 1968—, minority leader, 1982-85, chmn. appropriations com. Author eight books including: Missle Contracts Guide, 1958, Space Guide, 1959, Underwater Defense Handbook, 1963, Military Research Handbook, 1963. Candidate for lt. gov. Va., 1965; state fin. chmn. Rep. Party of Va., 1966-68; candidate for U.S. Congress, 1976; chmn. No. Va. Cmty. Found.; chmn. Jamestown-Yorktown Found. With USMC, 1950-53; as lt. USCGR, 1959-63. Mem. U.S. Naval Inst., Nat. Press Club, Kiwanis (past pres. McLean, Va.). Republican. Roman Catholic. Office: PO Box 1173 Mc Lean VA 22101-1173 Office Phone: 703-356-1925. Personal E-mail: dcalla5475@aol.com.

CALLAHAN, VIVIAN, broadcast executive; d. Albert Lewis and Gloria Elaine (Gentry) Snyder; m. Gregory James Callahan, June 1, 1996. Grad. H.S., Redondo Beach, Calif. Singer New Christy Minstrels, LA, 1973, USO, LA, 1973—74; writer/prodr. Ken Belsky Prodns., Studio City, Calif., 1981—82, CBS TV Network, LA, 1983—88, assoc. dir., 1988—92; dir. Fox Broadcasting Co., LA, 1992—96, exec. dir., 1996—. Mem., gold ribbon judge, presenter/spkr. PROMAX, Internat., LA, 1993—97; mem. Mayor Riordan's Arts Adv. Com., LA, 1996—97; pres., founding mem. Fox Talkz (Toastmasters), Century City, Calif., 1997—2000. Prodr., writer: 16-episode TV series Join The Group, TV spl. The Best Moments of 90210, The Rock and Roll Skating Special; prodr.: (TV spl.) Love Thy Neighbor: The Baddest and Best of Melrose Place. Founding mem. The Story Project, Culver City, Calif., 1996—2000; mem./mentor L.A. Maritime Inst., San Pedro, Calif., 2002—05; founding mem. Soc. Women Adventurers, 2005. Recipient Cert. of Merit, Internat. Film and TV Festival of N.Y., 1990, Hollywood Radio and TV Soc., 1990, award, Columbus Internat. Film and TV Festival, 1991, Mobius Advt. Com., 1991. Mem.: Acad. TV Arts and Scis., Soc. Women Adventurers (founding mem.), Del Rey Yacht Club. Avocations: sailing (transoceanic), travel, reading, creative writing, skiing. Home Phone: 310-540-1148; Office Phone: 310-369-4976. Business E-Mail: vivian.callahan@fox.com.

CALLAHAN KERN, GENE MARIE C., soprano, music educator; b. Glens Falls, NY, June 2, 1950; d. Eugene Leonard Callahan and Loise Edna Ellithorpe; m. Mike Kern, Apr. 28, 1948. MusB, Hope Coll., Holland, Mich., 1973; postgrad., Lyric Opera Ctr. for Am. Artists, Chgo., 1980—83, Am. Inst. Musical Studies, Graz, Austria, 1983, Goethe Inst., Chgo., 1985—87. Pvt. voice and piano instr., Rensselaer, NY, 1973—; music tchr. Luth. Parochial Sch., Jersey City, 1976—77; dir. fine arts The Bergen Sch., Jersey City, 1978—80; tchr. Sawyer Secretarial Sch., Chgo., 1983—84; substitute music tchr. Ft. Plain Ctrl. Sch. Dist., NY, 1993—94; tchr. Fulton-Montgomery C.C. Coll.; Enrichment Experience, Johnstown, NY, 1994; adj. prof. voice and music Castleton State Coll., Vt., 2003—04; adj. prof. music and voice Mass. Coll. Liberal Arts, North Adams, 2004—05; vocal instr. Emma Willard Sch., Troy, NY, 2005—. Singer: (Operas) La Forza del Destino and Don Giovanni, Verdi Requiem, The Tales of Hoffmann, I Pagliacci, (oratorio) Midland Music Soc., NW Ind. Symphony, Fox River Valley Symphony, Lake Forest Symphony, Bklyn. Contemporary Chorus, Friends of Music, Battenkill Chorale, The Univ.-Cmty. Chorale SUNY, (oratorio/recital) Trinity on Wall Street Recital Series, Glens Falls Symphony, Capitol Hill Choral Soc., Burnt Hills Oratorio Soc.; condr.: Handel's Messiah, musical dir.: Colonial Little Theater, Johnstown, NY; singer: (CD recording) A Tribute to James Levine by the Chicago Symphony; Verdi's Macbeth, 1981. Leader, program chair Girl Scouts, Jersey City, 1975—78; active Planned Parenthood, Jersey City, 1974—76; organist, choir dir. Wicker Park Luth. Ch., Chgo., First Reformed Ch., Canajoharie, NY, North Main St. United Meth. Ch., Gloversville, NY; choir dir. Ninth St. Christian Reformed. Finalist, OperaAmerica, 1982, Met. Opera, 1983; named one of, Outstanding Young Women Am., 1979; recipient Prix d'Honneur, Nat. Assn. French Tchrs., 1967, Svc. award, Second Ref. Ch., Zeeland, Mich., 1974; grantee Study in Austria (AIMS), Austrian Consulate Gen., 1983, Sullivan Found., 1985; scholar Carol Fox Meml. scholar, Chgo. Lyric Opera, 1981; Grace Marguerite Browning Voice scholar, Hope Coll., 1972—73. Mem.: Am. Guild Musical Artists, Coll. Music Soc. (program com. mem. Ea. regional conf. 2004—05), Music Tchrs. Nat. Assn., Nat. Assn. Tchrs. Singing (Ea. NY chpt. mem. art song festival com. 2005). Achievements include development of low budget fine arts program for The Bergen School, Jersey City, NJ. Avocations: knitting, reading, travel. Home Phone: 518-449-1659. Personal E-mail: gmckern@nycap.rr.com.

CALLAN, JOSI IRENE, museum director; b. Yorkshire, Eng., Jan. 30, 1946; came to U.S., 1953; d. Roger Bradshaw and Irene (Newbury) Winstanley; children: James, Heather, Brett Jack; m. Patrick Marc Callan, June 26, 1984. BA in Art History summa cum laude, Calif. State U., Domingues Hills, 1978, MA in Behavioral Scis., 1981. Dir. community rels./alumni affairs Calif. State U., Dominguez Hills, adminstrv. fellow office chancellor Long Beach, assoc. dir. univ. svcs. office chancellor, 1979-85; dir. capital campaign, assoc. dir. devel. Sta. KVIE-TV, Sacramento, 1985-86; dir. project devel. Pacific Mountain Network, Denver, 1986-87; dir. mktg. and devel. Denver Symphony Orch., 1988-89; assoc. dir. San Jose (Calif.) Mus. Art, 1989-91, dir., 1991-99, Mus. of Glass, Tacoma, Wash., 1999—. Asst. prof. sch. social and behavioral scis. Calif. State U., Dominguez Hills, 1981—; mem. adv. com. Issues Facing Mus. in 1990s JKF U., 1990-91. Mem. com. arts policy Santa Clara Arts Coun., 1990-92; chair San Jose Arts Roundtable, 1992-93; active ArtTable, 1992—, Community Leadership San Jose, 1992-93, Am. Leadership Forum, 1994, bd. dirs., 2000—; mem. adv. bd. Bay Area Rsch. Project, 1992—; mem. Calif. Arts Coun., Visual Arts Panel, 1993-95, Santa Clara Arts Coun. Visual Arts Panel, 1993; bd. dirs. YWCA, 1993—. Recipient Leadership award Knight Found., 1995; Women of Vision honoree Career Action Ctr., 1998; fellow Calif. State U., 1982-83. Mem. AAUW, Am. Assn. Mus., Nat. Soc. Fund Raising Execs. (bd. dirs. 1991), Colo. Assn.

Fund Raisers, Art Mus. Devel. Assn., Assn. Art Mus. Dirs., We. Mus. Assn., Calif. State U. Alumni Coun. (pres. 1981-83), Rotary Internat. Office: Museum of Glass 1801 E Dock St Tacoma WA 98402-3217

CALLAND, ALBERT M., III, information technology executive, former federal official, retired military officer; b. 1952; Grad, US Naval Acad., 1974; MS, Indsl. Coll. of Armed Forces, 1996. Advanced through ranks to vice admiral USN, assoc. dir. ctrl. intelligence for military support, 1987—92, comdr. SEAL Team One, 1992—95, comdr. Naval Spl. Warfare Devel. Group, 1997—99; comdr. Spl. Ops. Command US Ctrl. Command, 2000; joint forces spl. ops. component command Operation Enduring Freedom USN, 2001, comdr. naval spl. warfare command, 2002—04; assoc. dir. ctrl. intelligence for military support CIA, 2004—05, acting dep. dir., 2005, dep. dir., 2005—06; dep. dir. for strategic operational planning, Nat. Counterterrorism Ctr. Office Nat. Intelligence, Washington, 2006—07; exec. v.p. security & intelligence integration CACI Internat. Inc., Arlington, Va., 2007—. Decorated Disting Svc. Medal, Superior Svc. Medal (two awards), Legion of Merit, Bronze Star Medal, Def. Meritorious Svc. Medal (two awards), Meritorious Svc. Medal (five awards), Navy Comendation Medal, others. Office: CACI Internat Inc Three Ballston Plz 1100 N Glebe Rd Arlington VA 22201*

CALLANDER, BRUCE DOUGLAS, journalist, freelance writer; b. Malone, NY, Dec. 23, 1923; s. Douglas Newton and Blanche Keller (Redfield) C.; m. Imogene A. O'Malley, Nov. 23, 1979; children by previous marriage— Richard Scott, John Byron AB with cert. in Journalism, U. Mich., Ann Arbor, 1948. Indsl. editor Kaiser Frazer Co., Willow Run, Mich., 1948-50; pub. relations officer U.S. Air Force, Ohio, Md., 1951-52; assoc. editor Air Force Times, Washington, 1952-67, mng. editor, 1967-72, editor Springfield, Va., 1972-85; freelance writer, mil. historian Mullett Lake, Mich., 1986—. Served to capt. USAF, 1942-45, 51-52; Italy. Recipient Hopwood awards U. Mich., 1945, 48; Freedom Found. award, 1982. Mem.: St. Andrews Soc. (Washington). Avocations: painting, sculpting, woodworking, flute. Personal E-mail: brucal@hmo.net.

CALLANDER, KAY EILEEN PAISLEY, business owner, retired education educator, writer; b. Coshocton, Ohio, Oct. 15, 1938; d. Dalton Olas and Dorothy Pauline (Davis) Paisley; m. Don Larry Callander, Nov. 18, 1977. BSE, Muskingum Coll., New Concord, Ohio, 1960; MA in Speech Edn., Ohio State U., Columbus, 1964, postgrad., 1964-84. Cert. elem., gifted, drama, theater tchr., Ohio. Tchr. Columbus Pub. Schs., Ohio, 1960-70, 80-88, drama specialist Ohio, 1970-80, classroom, gifted/talented tchr. Ohio, 1986-90, ret. Ohio, 1990; sole prop. The Ali Group, Kay Kards, 1992—. Coord. Artists-in-the Schs., 1977-88; ednl. cons. Innovation Alliance Youth Adv. Coun., 1992—; cons., presenter in field. Producer-dir., Shady Lane Music Festival, 1980-88; dir. tchr. (nat. distbr. video) The Trial of Gold E. Locks, 1983-84; rep., media pub. relations liason Sch. News., 1983-88; author, creator Trivia Game About Black Americans; presenter for workshop by Human Svc. Group and Creative Edn. Coop., Columbus, Ohio, 1989. Benefactor, Columbus Jazz Arts Group; v.p., bd. dirs. Neoteric Dance and Theater Co., Columbus, 1985-87; tchr., participant Future Stars sculpture exhibit, Ft. Hayes Ctr., Columbus Pub. Schs., 1988; tchr. advisor Columbus Coun. PTAs, 1983-86, co-chmn. reflections com., 1984-87; mem. Columbus Mus. Art, Citizens for Humane Action, Inc.; upt.'s adv. coun. Columbus Pub. Schs., 1967-68; presenter Young Author Seminar, Ohio Dept. Edn., 1988, Illustrating Methods for Young Authors' Books, 1986-87; cons. and workshop leader seminar/workshop Tchg. About the Constitution in Elem. Schs., Franklin County Ednl. Coun., 1988; sponsor Minority Youth Recognition Awards, 1994. Named Educator of Yr., Shady Lane PTA, 1982, Columbus Coun. PTAs, 1989, winner Colour Columbus Landscape Design Competition, 1990; Sch. Excellence grantee Columbus Pub. Schs.; Commendation Columbus Bd. Edn. and Ohio Ho. of Reps. for Child Assault Prevention project, 1986-87; first place winner statewide photo contest Ohio Vet. Assn., 1991; recipient Muskingum Coll. Alumni Disting. Svc. award, 1995. Mem. ASCD, AAUW, Assn. for Childhood Edn. Internat., Ohio Coun. for Social Studies, Franklin County Ret. Tchrs. Assn., Nat. Mus. Women in the Arts, Ohio State U. Alumni Assn., US Army Officers Club, Navy League, Liturgical Art Guild Ohio, Columbus Jazz Arts Group, Columbus Mus. Art, Nat. Coun. for Social Studies, Columbus Art League, Columbus Maennerchor (Damen sect.). Republican. Avocations: painting, photography, swimming, golf, playing piano and organ. Home: 9131 Indian Mound Rd Pickerington OH 43147 Personal E-mail: paiscallander@embarqmail.com.

CALLARD, DAVID JACOBUS, investment company executive; b. Boston, July 14, 1938; s. Henry Hadden and Clarissa Cooley (Jacobus) C.; m. Deborah Winston, 1960 (div. 1982); children: Owen Winston, Francis Jacobus, Anne Lloyd, Elizabeth Hadden, Samuel Porter; m. Mary R. Morgan, July 14, 1990. AB, Princeton U., 1959; postgrad., Union Theol. Sem., 1964—65; JD, NYU, 1969. With Morgan Guaranty Trust Co., NYC, 1959-61, asst. v.p., 1965-69, v.p., 1970-72; gen. ptnr. Alex Brown & Sons, Balt., 1972-84; mng. dir., 1984-89; bd. dirs. Alex Brown Inc., Balt., 1984-89; pres. Wand Ptnrs. Inc., NYC, 1990—; chmn. Pelican Investment Mgmt., Inc., Boston, 2002—. Bd. dirs. Fulcrum Analytics, Inc., Seedworks, Inc., Jacent Tech. Inc., eLaw Forum, Inc. Chmn. bd. dirs. Union Theol. Sem., NYC; dep. exec. dir. Pres.'s Commn. on All Vol. Armed Forces, 1969-70. Lt. USMC, 1961-64. Boothe Ferris fellow, 1964-65 Mem. Union Club, Knickerbocker Club, Elkridge (Balt.). Democrat. Episcopalian. Office Phone: 212-949-1936.

CALLAWAY, BEN ANDERSON, journalist; b. Oakland, Calif., Mar. 16, 1927; s. Owen M. and Aulis (Anderson) C.; m. Patricia Hurd, Apr. 7, 1951; children: Randall Owen, Karen Callaway Franks. Student, Stanford, 1946-47; BA, Denison U., 1950. Sports writer, wildlife editor Denver Post, 1950-57; with Phila. Daily News, 1957-80, sports editor, 1961-70, outdoor columnist, 1961-80; outdoor editor Phila. Inquirer, 1980-91, editor fishing reports, 1992—2000; outdoor columnist Courier-Post, 1992—2001. Exec. editor Metro East Outdoor News, 1973-77; co-editor Penn-Jersey Outdoor Sportsman, 1976-77; free-lance mag. writer-photographer; commentator Sta. KYW, 1972-95. Sports chmn. Phila. United Fund, 1966-70; active local Boy Scouts Am., Eagle, 1942. Served with USNR, 1945-46. Recipient Henshall award Am. Fishing Tackle Mfrs. Assn., 1964, Old Salt award N.J. Resort Assn., 1967, Johnson Deep Woods award, 1977; gold medal Pa. Fish and Game Protective Assn., 1978; McCulloch Outdoor Writing award, 1978 Mem. Phila. Sports Writers Assn. (pres. 1968-70), Denver Sports Writers and Broadcasters Assn. (pres. 1957), Outdoor Writers Am. (dir. 1976-79, 89—92, Pa. Outdoor Writers, Boating Writers Internat. (dir. 1976-85), Met. N.Y. Rod and Gun Editors, N.J. Outdoor Writers Assn. (v.p. 1982-86, pres. 1988-91), Blue Key, Beta Theta Pi, Pi Delta Epsilon, Omicron Delta Kappa. Presbyn. (elder) and Meth. Address: 146 Buckingham Dr Southampton NJ 08088 E-mail: callaben@comcast.net.

CALLAWAY, CLIFFORD WAYNE, physician; b. Easton, Md., May 28, 1941; s. Charles Herschel and Anna Agnes (Stradley) C.; 1 child, David Wayne; m. Jackie Chalkley. BA, U. Del., Newark, 1963; MD, Northwestern U., Evanston, Ill., 1967. Diplomate Am. Bd. Internal Medicine, Am. Bd. Endocrinology, Diabetes and Metabolism, Am. Bd. Nutrition. Resident in internal medicine Northwestern U. Med. Ctr., Chgo., 1967—69, Mayo Grad. Sch. Medicine, Rochester, Minn., 1971—73, advanced clin. resident in endocrinology, 1973—75; assoc. cons. Mayo Clinic, 1975—78, cons. endocrinology, 1978—85, dir. nutrition and lipid clinics, 1980—85; rsch. assoc. Harvard Med. Sch., Boston, 1976—78; dir. ctr. clin. nutrition George Washington U., Washington, 1986—88; sr. sci. cons. Food & Nutrition Bd., NRC/NAS, Washington, 1987—88; pvt. practice Washington, 1988—. Contbr. articles to profl. jours.; co-author (with Catherine Whitney): The Callaway Diet: Successful Permanent Weight Control for Starvers, Stuffers, and Skippers, 1990, Surviving with AIDS: A Comprehensive Program of Nutritional Co-Therapy, 1991; co-author: (with Michael B. Alleert) Clinical Nutrition for the House Officer, 1992; co-author: (with Melanie Barnard, Brooke Dojny and Mindy Herman) Am. Med. Assn. Family Cookbook Good Food That's Good for You, 1997; co-author: (with Melanie Barnard and Brooke Dojny) Family Healthy Cookbook Good Food that's Good for You, 1997. Acting exec. sec. nutrition coordinating office HHS, Washington, 1980. Mayo Found. scholar, 1976-78. Mem. Am. Soc. Clin. Nutrition (treas. 1988), Am. Bd. Nutrition (bd. dirs. 1983-89, 95-98, sec.-treas. 1984-86, v.p. 1986-88), Am. Inst. Nutrition (chair and various coms.), Am. Dietetics Assn. (hon.), Am. Osler Soc. (bd. dirs.), Am. Assn. Clin. Endocrinologists (bd. dirs. 1992-95), Ctrl. European Ctr. for Health and Environment (bd. dirs.), Wash. Acad. Medicine. Achievements include development and writing of dietary guidelines for Americans (USDA/DHHS). Office: 2311 M St NW Ste 301 Washington DC 20037-1468 Office Phone: 202-331-3330. Personal E-mail: cwcallaway@aol.com. Business E-Mail: cwcallaway@doctorcallaway.com.

CALLAWAY, HOWARD HOLLIS, resort executive; b. La Grange, Ga., Apr. 2, 1927; s. Cason Jewell and Virginia (Hand) C.; m. Elizabeth Walton, June 11, 1949; children: Elizabeth Callaway Considine, Howard Hollis Jr., Edward Cason, Virginia Callaway Martin, Ralph Walton. Student, Ga. Inst. Tech., 1944-45; BS, U.S. Mil. Acad., 1949. Commd. 2d lt. AUS, 1949, advanced through grades to 1st. lt., 1952; resigned, 1952; mem. 89th Congress from 3d Ga. dist.; U.S. Sec. Army Washington, 1973-75; campaign mgr. Pres. Ford Com., 1975-76; dir. Crested Butte (Colo.) Mountain Resort, 1975—94. Pres. Nat. 4-H, svc. com.; former chmn. bd. trustees Ida Cason Callaway Found., Pine Mountain, Ga., Freedoms Found. at Valley Forge; former bd. regents U. Sys. Ga.; Rep. candidate for Gov. of Ga., 1966; candidate Rep. primary for U.S. Senate from Colo., 1980; chmn. Colo. Rep. Com., 1981-87, chmn. GOPAC, 1987-93; mem. Def. Base Realignment and Closure Commn., 1992; active com. Ga. Dept. Econ. Devel., 2001. 1st lt. inf. U.S. Army, 1949-52. Mem. World Pres.' Orgn. (past pres.), Young Pres.' Orgn. (past pres.), Chief Execs. Orgn., Capital City Club (Atlanta), Piedmont Driving Club (Atlanta), Bohemian Club (San Francisco), Phi Delta Theta, Phi Kappa Phi. Republican. Episcopalian. Home: PO Box 1326 Pine Mountain GA 31822 Office Phone: 706-663-5075. Business E-Mail: bocallaway@callawaygardens.com.

CALLAWAY, JAMES W. (JIM), telecommunications industry executive; BBA, Ark. State U., 1968. Various mgmt. positions Southwestern Bell Tel., 1968—96, pres. Kans. divsn., v.p. mktg. St. Louis, v.p., gen. mgr. so. Tex.; pres., CEO Southwestern Bell Telecom.; pres., COO Southwestern Bell Mobile Systems; sr. v.p. strategic planning SBC Comm., 1996—97, pres. Calif., 1997, grp. pres. SBC svcs., grp. pres. internat. ops., directory ops., sterling commerce, 2000—05; grp. pres. SBC-AT&T merger integration planning and transition AT&T, Inc. (merger of SBC Comm. & AT&T Corp.), San Antonio, 2005; sr. exec. v.p. bus. devel. AT&T, Inc., 2006—07, sr. exec. v.p., exec. ops., 2007—. Chmn. Free Trade Alliance San Antonio; bd. mem. St. Mary's U., Ark. State U. Found., Cancer Therapy Rsch. Ctr., San Antonio Bowl Assn.; chmn. bd. Golf San Antonio. Office: AT&T Inc 175 E Houston St PO Box 2933 San Antonio TX 78299-2933*

CALLAWAY, MARK CLAYTON, investment company executive; b. Dayton, Ohio, June 16, 1956; s. Fuller Earle Callaway 3d and Wanda (Vogt) Warren; m. Debra Cerniglia, Jan. 16, 1982; children: Fuller Earle IV, Mary Hollis, Joseph Hayes. BA, La Grange Coll., 1981; postgrad., NYU, 1982—82. Adminstrv. asst. Hills & Dales, La Grange, Ga., 1982; investment broker Johnson, Lane, Space, Smith & Co., 1983; v.p. Lamon-Callaway, Inc., Atlanta, 1983—89; pres. Lamon-Callaway Fin. Svcs., Inc., 1984—89; ptnr. Lamon-Callaway Group., 1984—89, mng. dir., 1985—89; dir., chmn. investment and fin. com. Bank of Troup County, La Grange, Ga., 1984—90. Trustee Callaway Found., Inc., 1981—, Fuller E. Callaway Found, Inc., 1982—; bd. dirs. Alliance Theatre Co., Atlanta, 1983—86, Ga. Bot. Gardens, Athens, 1980—87; mem. exec. com. fin. com. Ga. Pub. End. Found., 1986; bd. dirs. Ga. Trust for Historic Preservation, 1985, La Grange United Way, Ga., 1984—86, chmn., 1986—87. Named One of the Outstanding Young Men of Am., 1986, Mem.: La Grange C. of C. (dir. 1984—), Planning Am. Assn. Individual Investors, Internat. Ass. Fin. Planners, La Grange Rotary Club, Highland Country Club, Piedmont Driving Club. Republican. Roman Catholic. Office: Robinson-Humphrey Shearson Lehman Hutton PO Box 1007 Lagrange GA 30241-0018 Home: 902 Lenox Hill Ct NE Atlanta GA 30324-2957

CALLÉ, CRAIG R.L., finance company executive; b. Greenwich, Conn., Dec. 17, 1959; s. Hans Martin Erich and Mary Ann (Sadtler) C.; m. Catherine Maechling, June 18, 1993. BA, BS in Econ., U. Pa., 1981; MBA, Harvard U., 1985. Fin. analyst Salomon Bros. Inc., NYC, 1981-83, assoc., 1985-88, v.p., 1988-91; treas. Crown Cork & Seal Co., Inc., 1991, v.p. & treas., 1991-95, sr. v.p. fin., treas., 1995—2004; exec. v.p., CFO IPWireless, Inc.; founder, CEO common.net, 2001—06; v.p., treas., v.p. fin. prof. and direct segments Gateway, Inc., Irvine, Calif., 2006—. Mem. Harvard Club NYC, Phila. Cricket Club. Republican. Office: Gateway Inc 7565 Irvine Center Dr Irvine CA 92618 Business E-Mail: craig.calle@gteway.com.

CALLEN, JAMES DONALD, plasma physicist, nuclear engineer; b. Wichita, Kans., Jan. 31, 1941; s. Donald Dewitt and Bonnie Jean (Walton) C.; m. Judith Carolyn Chinn, Aug. 26, 1961; children: Jeffrey Scott, Sandra Jean. BS in Nuclear Engring., Kans. State U., 1962, MS in Nuclear Engring., 1964; PhD in Nuclear Engring., MIT, 1968. Postdoctoral fellow Inst. for Advanced Study, Princeton, NJ, 1968-69; asst. prof. aeros. and astronautics MIT, Cambridge, 1969-72; mem. rsch. staff fusion energy divsn. Oak Ridge (Tenn.) Nat. Lab., 1972-74, group leader, 1974-75, head plasma theory sect., 1975-79; prof. nuc. engring. and physics U. Wis., Madison, 1979-86, D.W. Kerst prof. engring. physics and physics, 1986—. Mem. editor. bd. Nuc. Fusion Jour., 1978-97; assoc. editor divsn. plasma physics Phys. Rev. Letters Jour., 1980-85; contbr. over 165 articles to profl. jours. Recipient Dept. of Energy Disting. Assoc. award, 1988, Disting. Career award Fusion Power Assocs., 2002; named to Coll. Engring. Hall of Fame, Kans. State U., 1991; Fulbright fellow Tech. Hogesch., Eindhoven, Netherlands, 1962-63; Guggenheim fellow, 1986. Fellow Am. Phys. Soc. (chmn. divsn. plasma physics 1986), Am. Nuc. Soc.; mem. NAE, AAAS. Office: U Wis 1500 Engineering Dr Madison WI 53706-1609 Business E-Mail: callen@engr.wisc.edu.

CALLEN, JEFFREY PHILLIP, dermatologist, educator; b. May 30, 1947; s. Irwin R. and Rose P. (Cohen) C.; m. Susan B. Manis, Dec. 21, 1968; children: Amy, David. BS, U. Wis., 1969; MD, U. Mich., 1972. Diplomate Am. Bd. Internal Medicine, Am. Bd. Dermatology. Intern, resident in internal medicine U. Mich., Ann Arbor, 1972-75, resident in dermatology, 1975-77; from asst. clin. prof. to dir. residency tng. program U. Louisville Sch. Medicine, 1977-84, dir. residency tng. program, 1984-88; chief dermatology svc. Louisville VA Hosp., 1984-93, prof., chief dermatology divsn., 1988—. Author: Manual of Dermatology, 1980, Cutaneous Aspects of Internal Disease, 1981, Neurology Clinics North America, 1987, Dermatologic Signs of Systemic Disease, 1988, 3d edit., 2003, Color Atlas of Dermatology, 1993, 2d edit., 2000, Current Practice of Dermatology, 1995; editor: Clinics in Rheumatic Disease, 1982, Dermatologic Clinics, 1985, 89, 2002, Medical Clinics of North America, 1982, 84, 86, 89, Dermatologic Therapy, 2007; editor-in-chief Dermavision video program; mem. editl. bd. Internat. Jour. Dermatology, 1990-95; asst. editor Internat. Jour. Dermatology, 1993-95, Jour. Am. Acad. Dermatology, 1995-2003; assoc. editor Archives Dermatology, 2003— Bd. dirs. Actor's Theater of Louisville, 1982-98, 2000—, sec., 1986-87, Ky. Arts and Crafts Found., 1991-97; bd. govs. JB Speed Art Mus., 1995-2003 Fellow ACP, Am. Acad. Dermatology (chmn. audio/visual edn. com., task force therapeutic agts., internal med. symposium 1978-83, chmn. sci. and tech. exhibits 1986-89, dir. various symposiums, mem. coun. sci. assembly 1993-98, chair 1997-98, chair com. to evaluate ann. meeting, 1999-2003, vice chair coun. on edn. 2002-2003, chair coun. on edn. 2003-07, v.p. elect 2003-04, v.p. 2004-05, bd. dirs. 1995-99, mem. exec. com. 1997-99, 2003-05, co-chair program for 21st century 1999-2000, chair psoriasis edn. conf. 2002, chair unity summit, chair task force on psoriasis edn. 2005, com. on maintenance cert. 2006—), Am. Coll. Rheumatology (founder, chair skin disease study group 1996-98, 2000-02); mem. AMA, Am. Fedn. Clin. Rsch., Am. Dermatol. Assn., Dermatology Found. (trustee 1984-90), Louisville Theatrical Assn. (bd. dirs. 1999-2002). Achievements include research on condition in which systemic disease has cutaneous manifestations, lupus erythematosus, psoriasis, dermatomyositis. Office: U Louisville Dept Dermatology 310 E Broadway Ste 200 Louisville KY 40202-1745 Office Phone: 502-583-1749. Personal E-mail: jefca@aol.com.

CALLENBACH, ERNEST, writer, editor; b. Williamsport, Pa., Apr. 3, 1929; m. Christine Leefeldt, May 19, 1978; children: Joanna, Hans. Ph.B., U. Chgo., 1949, MA, 1953. Editor Film Quar., U. Calif. Press, Berkeley, 1958-91, editor books, 1958-91. Author: Living Poor With Style, 1971, rev. as Living Cheaply With Style, 2000, Ecotopia, 1975, Ecotopian Ency. for the Eighties, 1981, Ecotopia Emerging, 1981, Publisher's Lunch, 1989, Earth's Ten Commandments, 1990, Bring Back the Buffalo!, 1995, Ecology: A Pocket Guide, 1998; co-author: The Art of Friendship, 1979, Citizen Legislature, 1985, Humphrey the Wayward Whale, 1986, EcoManagement, 1993. Mem. Nat. Writers Union. Address: care Banyan Tree Books 1963 El Dorado Ave Berkeley CA 94707-2441

CALLENDER, CLIVE ORVILLE, surgeon; b. NYC, Nov. 16, 1936; s. Joseph and Ida (Burke) C.; m. Fern Irene Marshall, May 25, 1968; children: Joseph, Ealena, Arianne. AB, Hunter Coll., 1959, DSc (hon.), 1998; MD, Meharry Med. Coll., 1963. Diplomate Am. Bd. Surgery, 1970. Intern U. Cin., 1963-64; asst. resident Harlem Hosp., NYC, 1964-65, Howard U. and Freedmans Hosp., Washington, 1965-66, 67-68, chief resident, 1968-69, instr. dept. surgery, 1969-71; asst. resident Meml. Hosp. for Cancer and Allied Diseases, NYC, 1966-67; cons. surgery Port Harcourt Gen. Hosp., Nigeria, 1970, 71; med. officer D.C. Gen. Hosp., 1970-71; NIH postdoctoral rsch. and clin. transplant fellow U. Minn., 1971-73; asst. prof. surgery Howard U. Med. Coll., Washington, 1973-76, assoc. prof., 1976-81, prof. surgery, 1981—, vice-chmn. dept. surgery, 1980-95, chmn. dept. surgery, 1996—, LaSalle D. Leffall, Jr. prof. surgery, 1996—, dir. transplant ctr., 1973—. Transplantation cons., Bermuda, 1977, V.I., 1978, 82-86; cons. Ethiopian Surg., Amenity Med. Sch., 1984; G.P.A. Ford Meml. lectr., 1978; mem. task force on organ procurement and transplantation HEW, 1984; testifier com. on labor and human resources U.S. Senate, 1983; mem. end stage renal disease study com. Inst. of Medicine, 1989-90, mem. com. on xenograft transplantation: ethical issues and pub. policy, 1995-96, com. on non-heart-beating organ transplantation II, 1999, mem. com. to increase rates of organ donation, 2005-06; fellowship in liver transplantation Pitts. U., 1986-87; founder, prin. investigator Nat. Minority Organ and Tissue Transplant Edn. Program, 1991—; mem., increasing organ donation com. Inst. Medicine, 2005-06. Mem. editl. adv. bd. New Directions, 1974-91, Contemporary Dialysis and Nephrology Jour., 1993-95, Clin. Transplant Proceedings, 1998—, Am. Jour. Kidney Disease, 2001—); contbr. articles to med. jours. Testified for Ho. of Reps. Com. on Appropriation, U.S. Congress, 1992, others; councillor Soc. Organ Sharing, 1993, sec., 1995; chmn. tissue com. D.C. chpt. ARC, 1993-95; trustee Hunter Coll. Found., 2000. Recipient Hoffman LaRoche award, 1961, Charles Nelson Gold medal, 1963, Hudson Meadows award, 1963, Charles R. Drew Rsch. award, 1969, Daniel Hale Williams award, 1969, William Alonzo Warfield award, 1977, Howard U. Faculty Outstanding Unit award, 1982, 1st Humanitarian award Cmty. of Caring Ctr., 1990, Disting. Svc. award Surg. Sect. Nat. Med. Assn., 1990, Howard U. Health Affairs Disting. Svc. award, 1984, Outstanding Svc. award Dialysis and Transplant Support, Inc., 1993, Howard U. Legacy of Leadership in Health award, 1995, 11th ann. Minds in Motion award Sci. Skills Ctr., 1993, Edler Garnet Hawkins Humanitarian award Bronx Urban League, 1993; appreciation plaque for 1st renal transplant in V.I., Gov. St. Thomas, 1983, plaque for outstanding contbns. V.I. Legislature, 1984; named to Hunter Coll. Hall of Fame, 1989, Practitioner of Yr., Nat. Med. Assn., 1989, Scroll of Merit, Nat. Med. Assn., 1998, 1 of 10 Outstanding African Am. Male, WHMM-TV, Washington, 1994, 1 of 133 Gifts to the World Alumni Achievers, CUNY, 1995, Pearl Watson Meml. award for excellence in health care delivery Caribbean Am. Intercultural Orgn., Inc., 1995, Pioneer in Edn. award Inst. for Ind. Edn., 1995, Kidney Patients medal of Excellence 2nd Am. Assn., 1997, Leadership Edn. award Shiloh Bapt. Ch., 2002, Prof. Achievement award Hunter Coll. Hall Fame, 2002, Masons Pub. Svc. award, 2003, Humanitarian Svc. award Julia West Hamilton League, 2005, others. Fellow ACS (bd. govs. 1994-2000, LaSalle D. Leffall, Jr. award 1998, Mary McLeod Bethune Legacy award 2000); mem. D.C. Med. Soc. (past vice chmn., chmn. surg. sect. 1994—, trustee 1995), Internat. Soc. Organ Sharing (sec. 1993—), Transplantation Soc., Am. Soc. Transplantation Surgeons (chmn. membership com. 1986, organ placement com. 1991, mem. ethics com. 1995-97), N.Y. Acad. Medicine, Am. Assn. Kidney Patients (bd. dirs. 1998), Nat. Assn. Former Foster Care Children Am. (bd. dirs. 1998-99), Nat. Kidney Found. (nat. bd. dirs. 1991-94, nat. capital area 1977-90), Am. Surg. Assn., Am. Coun. on Transplantation (bd. dirs.), Nat. Med. Assn., Soc. Surg. Assn., Inst. Cellular Therapeutics (adv. bd.), United Network of Organ Sharing (vice-chair 1996-98, chair 1998-00), Soc. Black Acad. Surgeons (pres. 2001—), Alpha Omega Alpha, Alpha Phi Omega, Alpha Phi Alpha. Office: 2041 Georgia Ave NW Washington DC 20060-0001 Office Phone: 202-865-1441. E-mail: ccallender@howard.edu.

CALLENDER, JOHN FRANCIS, lawyer; b. Jacksonville, Fla., May 3, 1944; s. Francis Louis and Ethel (McLean) C.; children: John Francis Jr., Susanna McLean. AB cum laude, Davidson Coll., 1966; MA, U. N.C., 1969; JD with distinction, Duke U., 1976. Bar: Fla. 1976, U.S. Supreme Ct. 1982, bd. cert. civil trial lawyer: Fla. Bar. Asst. states atty. State of Fla., Jacksonville, 1980-81; ptnr. Turner, Ford & Callender, P.A., Jacksonville, 1981-84; pvt. practice Jacksonville, 1984—. Pres. Mental Health Clinic Jacksonville, Inc., 1985; bd. dirs. Vol. Jacksonville, Inc., 1981-84, AANR Edn. Found., Inc., 2003—, FANR, 2004-2007. Served with U.S. Army, 1970-73. Fellow Am. Soc. Papyrologists, 1969. Mem.: ABA, Jacksonville Bar Assn., Fla. Bar, Fla. Justice Assn., Am. Assn. Justice, Phi Beta Kappa Alumni Assn. N.E. Fla. (treas. 1996—99, pres. 1999—2000), Am. Mensa Ltd., Fla. Yacht Club, Rotary Club (pres. 1997, asst. dist. gov. 1999—2002, dist. sec. 2002—03). Democrat. Episcopalian. Avocations: sailing, windsurfing, fishing, tennis, swimming. Office: 1301 Riverplace Blvd Ste 2105 Jacksonville FL 32207-9027 Office Phone: 904-398-8833. Business E-Mail: jcallend@fdn.com.

CALLENDER, NORMA ANNE, counselor, public relations executive; b. Huntsville, Tex., May 10, 1933; d. C.W. Carswell and Nell Ruth (Collard) Hughes Bost; m. B.G. Callender, 1951 (div. 1964); remarried 1967 (div. 1973); children: Teresa Elizabeth, Leslie Gemey, Shannah Hughes, Kelly Mari; m. E Purfurst, June 1965 (div. Aug. 1965). BS, U. Houston, Clear Lake, 1969, MA, 1977; postgrad., Tex. So. U., Houston, 1971, Lamar U., Beaumont, Tex., 1972-73, U. Houston-Clear Lake, 1979, 87, 89-93, postgrad., 1998, St. Thomas U., 1985-86, Aerospace Inst., NASA, Johnson Space Ctr., 1986, San Jacinto Coll., Houston, 1988—99, postgrad., 2001—03; PhD, Cornerstone U., 1998. Cert. profl. reading specialist, Tex.; lic. profl. counselor; approved supr. lic. profl. interns. Tchr. Houston Ind. Schs., 1969-70; co-counselor, instr. Ellington AFB, Houston, 1971; tchr.

Clear Creek Schs., League City, Tex., 1970-86; owner, dir. Bay Area Tutoring and Reading Clinic, Clear Lake City, Tex., 1970—, Bay Area Tng. Assocs., 1982-98, Bay Area Family Counseling, 1995—, Bay Area Speech and Lang., 2003—; cons., LPC intern Guidance Ctr., Pasadena Ind. Sch. Dist., Tex., 1993-95; prin., dir. pub. rels. Gateway Supplies, Inc., 2005—. Instr. San Jacinto Coll., Pasadena, 1980-81, 91-93; adj. instr. U. Houston, Clear Lake, 1986-91; founder, editor BATA Books Pub., 1997—. Author: numerous poems. State advisor U.S. Congl. Adv. Bd., 1985-87; vol., bd. dirs. Family Outreach Ctr., 1989-92; vol. Bay Area Coun. on Drugs and Alcohol, Nassau Bay, Tex., 1993-94; bd. dirs. Ballet San Jacinto, 1985-87; adv. bd. Cmty. Ednl. TV, 1990-92; charter mem. Nat. Women's History Mus., Washington, 2005. Recipient Franklin award U. Houston, 1965-67; Delta Kappa Gamma/Beta Omicron scholar, 1967-68, PTA scholar, 1973, Berwin scholar, 1976, Mary Gibbs Jones scholar, 1976-77, Found. Econ. Edn. scholar, 1976, Insts. Achievement Human Potential scholar, Phila., 1987. Mem.: ACA, The NET: Bay Area Mental Health Providers Network, Clear Creek Educators Assn. (past, honorarium 1976, 1977, 1985), Sam Houston Chpt., Daughters of Am. Revolution, Houston Symphony League, Bay Area, Houston Symphony League of Bay Area, Leadership Clear Lake Alumni Assn. (charter, program and projects com. mem. 1986—87, edn. com. 1985), U. Houston Alumni Assn. (life), Phi Theta Kappa, Phi Delta Kappa, Kappa Delta Pi, Psi Chi (life), Phi Kappa Phi (life). Mem. Life Tabernacle Ch. Office: 16815 Royal Crest Ste 110 Houston TX 77058-2538

CALLEO, DAVID PATRICK, history professor, political scientist; b. Binghamton, NY, July 19, 1934; s. Patrick and Gertrude (Crowe) C.; m. Avis Thayer Bohlen. BA, Yale U., 1955, MA, 1957, PhD, 1959. Instr. polit. sci. Brown U., Providence, 1959-60; from instr. to asst. prof. polit. sci. Yale U., New Haven, 1961-67; rsch. fellow Nuffield Coll., Oxford U., 1966—67; cons. to undersec. for polit. affairs U.S. Dept. of State, Washington, 1967-68; prof., dir. European studies Nitze Sch. Advanced Internat. Studies Johns Hopkins U., Washington, 1968—, Dean Acheson chair Nitze Sch. Advanced Internat. Studies, 1988—, Univ. prof., 2001—; sr. Fulbright lectr. Fed. Republic Germany, 1975; assoc. fellow Jonathan Edwards Coll, Yale U., New Haven, 1972—; v.p. Lehrman Inst., NYC, 1972-87; project dir. The Twentieth Century Fund, NYC, 1981-85. Project dir. The 20th Century Fund, N.Y.C., 1993-99; assoc. Centre d'Etudes et de Rsch. Internat., 1993-94; enseignant invité Inst. d'études politiques de Paris, 1993-94; invited prof. Inst. U. de hautes études Internat., Geneva, 1999, adv. prof. East China Normal U., Shanghai, 2004—. Author: Europe's Future, 1965, Coleridge & The Idea of the Modern State, 1966, Britain's Future, 1968, The American Political System, 1968, The Atlantic Fantasy, 1970, America and the World Political Economy, 1973 (Gladys M. Kammerer award Best Book Analyzing Am. Nat. Policy, Am. Polit. Sci. Assn. 1973), The German Problem Reconsidered, 1978, The Imperious Economy, 1982, Beyond American Hegemony, 1987, The Bankrupting of America, 1992, Rethinking Europe's Future, 2001. Trustee, Jonathan Edwards Trust, 1972—. Guggenheim fellow, 1966-67, George Herbert Walker Bush fellow Am. Acad., Berlin, 2005. Mem. Am. Polit. Sci. Assn., Coun. on Fgn. Rels., Brooks' (London), Met. Club Washington, Century Assn. (NYC), Internat. Inst. Strategic Studies, Literary Soc. (Washington). Avocations: gardening, squash, opera. Office Phone: 202-663-5796. Business E-Mail: dcalleo@jhu.edu.

CALLERY, GRANT, financial industry regulatory authority general cousel; Grad., Marietta Coll.; JD, Georgetown Law Sch. Staff mem. Gen. Counsel's Office (OGC), Nat. Assn. of Securities Dealers , Inc. (NASD), 1979—90, dep. gen. counsel, 1990—93, gen. counsel, 1993—2007; exec. v.p., gen. counsel Fin. Industry Regulatory Authority (FINRA), 2007—. Author: (legal publications) Children of War, Problems of Amerasian Children in Vietnam, 1973, Participation Coverage & Vesting Under the Pension Reform Act, 1975; co-editor: Mortgages & Trust Deeds, 1980; author: NASD Disciplinary Proceedings - Recent Developments, 1993. Mem.: Bus. and Securities Law Committees, ABA. Office: Fin Industry Regulatory Authority Inc 1735 K St NW Washington DC 20006-1516 Office Phone: 202-728-8000.*

CALLERY, T. GRANT, lawyer; b. White Plains, NY, Oct. 12, 1946; s. Thomas Ricker and Jean Grant Callery; m. Jacqueline Ann Machan, May 11, 1949; children: Megan Elizabeth-Callery Peluso, Brian Matthew. BS, Marietta Coll., 1968; JD, Georgetown U., 1973. Bar: DC 1973, U.S. Supreme Ct., U.S. Ct. Appeals (D.C. cir.), U.S. Tax Ct., U.S. Dist. Ct. D.C. Atty. US CSC, Washington, 1973—74; assoc. Winkelman & Delaney, 1974—79; various NASD, 1979—93, exec. v.p., gen. counsel, 1993—. Trustee Marietta Coll., Ohio, 2003—, vice chmn. bd. trustees, 2006—. Contbr. articles to profl. jours., chapters to books. With US Army, 1969—71, Vietnam. Decorated Bronze Star medal US Army, Good Conduct medal. Mem.: ABA, Fed. Bar Assn. (chair young lawyers divsn. 1977—78). Avocations: boating, photography. Office: NASD Inc 1735 K St NW Washington DC 20006 Home Phone: 301-652-5974; Office Phone: 202-728-8285.

CALLESEN-GYORGAK, JAN ELAINE, special education educator; b. Manistee, Mich., Sept. 21, 1959; d. Carl Wayne and Patsy Arlene (Haglund) Callesen; m. Gregg Gyorgak, Oct. 27, 1990; children: Danielle Marie, Nathaniel Charles, Kristen Lynn, Wayne Anthony, Raymond Jacob. BS in Edn., Bowling Green State U., 1981; M in Curriculum and Instrn., Cleve. State U., 1988. Lic. elem. edn., spl. edn., libr. and media scis. Montessori tchr. Children's Home of Parma, Ohio, 1981-82; kindergarten tchr., coord. Murton's Child Devel. Ctr., Fairview Park, Ohio, 1983-85; spl. edn. tchr.-learning disabilities Cleve. Pub. Schs., 1985—. Advisor Safety Patrol, Cleve., 1986-99. Mem. Cleve. Tchrs. Union, Coun. for Exceptional Children (divsn. learning disabilities). Avocations: needlepoint, embroidery, collecting precious moments figurines, scrapbooks. Home: 6283 Surrey Dr North Olmsted OH 44070-4813 Office: Walton Elem Sch 3409 Walton Ave Cleveland OH 44113-4942

CALLETON, THEODORE EDWARD, lawyer, educator; b. Newark, Dec. 13, 1934; s. Edward James and Dorothy (Dewey) C.; m. Elizabeth Bennett Brown, Feb. 4, 1961; children: Susan Bennett, Pamela Barritt, Christopher Dewey.; m. Kathy E'Beth Conkle, Feb. 22, 1983; 1 child, James Frederick. BA, Yale U., 1956; LLB, Columbia U., 1962. Bar: Calif. 1963, U.S. Dist. Ct. (so. dist.) Calif. 1963, U.S. Tax Ct. 1977. Assoc. O'Melveny & Myers, LA, 1962-69, Agnew, Miller & Carlson, LA, 1969, ptnr., 1970-79; pvt. practice LA, 1979-83; ptnr. Kindel & Anderson, LA, 1983-92, Calleton & Merritt, Pasadena, Calif., 1992-99, Calleton & Trytten, Pasadena, 1999—2002; pvt. practice Pasadena, 2002—06; ptnr. Calleton, Merritt, DeFrancisco & Real-Salas, Pasadena, 2006—. Academician Internat. Acad. Estate and Trust Law, 1974—; lectr. Calif. Continuing Edn. Bar, 1970—96, U. So. Calif. Tax Inst., 1972, 76, 91, Calif. State U., LA, 1974—93, Practicing Law Inst., 1976—86, Am. Law Inst., 1985; bd. dirs. UCLA/Continuing Edn. of Bar Estate Planning Inst., 1979—; adj. prof. Golden Gate U. Law Sch., 1997—2000, Loyola U. Sch. Law, 2002—. Author: The Short Term Trust, 1977, A Life Insurance Primer, 1978, Calleton's Wills and Trusts, 1992—2003; co-author: California Will Drafting Practice, 1982, Tax Planning for Professionals, 1985, California Estate Planning, 2002, California Revocable Trusts, 2003; contbr. articles to profl. jours. Chmn. Arroyo Seco Master Planning Comm., Pasadena, Calif., 1970-71; bd. dirs. Montessori Sch., Inc., 1964-68, chmn., 1966-68, Am. Montessori Soc., N.Y.C., 1967-72, chmn., 1969-72; trustee Walden Sch. of Calif., 1970-86, 90-94, chmn., 1980-86; trustee Episc. Children's Home of L.A., 1971-75; bd. dirs. L.A. Master Chorale Assn., 1989-94, San Gabriel Valley Coun., Boy Scouts of Am., 2002-05. Lt. USMC, 1956-59. Fellow Am. Coll. Trust and Estate Counsel; mem. L.A. County Bar Assn. (chmn. taxation sect. 1980-81, chmn. probate and trust law sect. 1981-82, Dana Latham Meml. award 1996), Aurelian Honor Soc., Elihu, Beta Theta Pi, Phi Delta Phi. Home: 301 Churchill Rd Sierra Madre CA 91024-1354 Office: 131 N El Molino Ave Ste 300 Pasadena CA 91101 Office Phone: 626-395-0860. Business E-Mail: ted@cmdrlaw.com.

CALLEY, JOHN, former motion picture company executive, film producer; b. NJ, 1930; m. Olinka Schoberova, 1972 (div.); m. Meg Tilly, 1995 (div.); 1 child, Sabrina; stepchildren: Emily, David, Will. Dir. nighttime programming, dir. programming sales NBC, 1951-57; prodn. exec. and TV producer Henry Jaffe Enterprises, 1957; v.p. radio and TV Ted Bates Advt. Agy., 1958; exec. v.p., film producer Filmways, Inc., 1960-69; with Warner Bros., Inc., Burbank, Calif., 1969-87, exec. v.p. world-wide prodn., 1969-75, pres., 1975-80, vice chmn. bd., 1977-80, cons., 1980-87; independent film prodr., 1987—93; pres., COO, United Artists Pictures, 1993-96; pres., CEO, Sony Pictures Entertainment, Inc., Culver City, Calif., 1996—98, chmn., CEO, 1998—2003. Prodr. (films): Face in the Rain, 1963, The Loved One, 1965, Eye of the Devil, 1967, Don't Make Waves, 1967, Ice Station Zebra, 1968, Castle Keep, 1969, Catch-22, 1970, Fat Man and Little Boy, 1989, Postcards from the Edge, 1990, The Remains of the Day, 1993, Closer, 2004, The Da Vinci Code, 2006, The Jane Austen Book Club, 2007.

CALLEY, TRANQUIL HUDSON, retired travel consultant, educator; b. New Amsterdam, Guyana, Nov. 27, 1937; arrived in US, 1938; d. Adrian Wilfred Maurice Hudson and Nancy Hilda Turner; m. John Edward Calley, Sept. 17, 1971; stepchildren: John James, Griffyd Adams; m. Loren Rue Smith, June 17, 1957 (div. June 1970); children: Loren Adrian Smith, Kalyn David Smith-Tranquil'son(dec.). AA in Liberal Studies, West Valley CC, Campbell, Calif., 1970; BA in English, Calif. State U., Fresno, 1976; MA in English Lit., U. Calif., Riverside, 1989. Tchg. credential Calif., cert. c.c. tchr. State of Calif., travel agt. Inst. of Cert. Travel Agts., destination specialist (Europe and Latin America) Inst. of Cert. Travel Agts. Fit travel cons. Travel Planners, San Jose, Calif., 1969—70; travel cons. Bashford Travel, Fresno, Calif., 1974—77; mgr. Giselle Travel, Fresno, Calif., 1977—78, Travel Network, Hemet, Calif., 1978—82; travel cons. Travel by George, Riverside, 1982—90; instr. Mt. San Jacinto Coll., Calif., 1989—92; travel agent outside sales Unique Vacations, Riverside, 1990—92; advisor, counselor dept. liberal studies U. Redlands, 1999—2002, ret., 2002. ESL instr. Mt. San Jacinto CC, Hemet, 1989—92; trainer sexual harassment in the workplace Riverside County Office Edn., Calif., 1996—99; adv. counselor U. Redland, 1999—2002; adj. prof. U. Redlands, 2002—06. Editor: (books of poetry) Whispers in the Gale: An AIDS Journal; dramatist: (dramatic poetry performance piece) Whispers in the Gale: Living and Dying with AIDS, 2004. Vol. for AIDS awareness; rep. to Sacramento Riverside Alumni Advocacy Com., Riverside, 2000—05; mem. local spiritual assembly Baha'i Faith, Fresno, 1975—78, sec., 1975—78; dir. Advocates Sch. for Underperforming Students, Grand Terrace, Calif., 1997—2000; mem. scholarship com. U. Calif.-Riverside Alumni Assn., Riverside, 2004—05. Recipient Supporting U. Calif.-Riverside Lesbian Gay Bisexual Transgender students award, Chancellor's Adv. Com. Status of Lesbians, Gays, Bisexuals, Transgenders, June 3 2004. Mem.: U. Calif. Alumni Assn. (bd. dirs. 2005). Home: 23715 Coldwater Ct Moreno Valley CA 92557-2864 Home Phone: 951-247-4940. Personal E-mail: tcalley747@aol.com.

CALLIES, DAVID LEE, lawyer, educator; b. Chgo., Apr. 21, 1943; s. Gustav E. and Ann D. Callies; m. Laurie Breeden, Dec. 28, 1996; 1 child, Sarah Wayne Callies. AB, DePauw U., 1965; JD, U. Mich., 1968; LLM, U. Nottingham, England, 1969. Bar: Ill. 1969, Hawaii 1978, U.S. Supreme Ct. 1974. Spl. asst. states atty., McHenry County, Ill., 1969; assoc. firm Ross, Hardies, O'Keefe, Babcock & Parsons, Chgo., 1969-75, ptnr., 1975-78; prof. law Richardson Sch. Law, U. Hawaii, Honolulu, 1978—; Benjamin A. Kudo prof. law U. Hawaii, Honolulu, 1995—. Mem. adv. com. on planning and growth mgmt. City and County of Honolulu Coun., 1978-88, mem. citizens adv. com. on State Functional Plan for Conservation Lands, 1979-93. Author: (with Fred P. Bosselman) the Quiet Revolution in Land Use Control, 1971 (with Fred P. Bosselman and John S. Banta) The Taking Issue, 1973, Regulating Paradise: Land Use Controls in Hawaii, 1984, (with Robert Freilich and Tom Roberts) Cases and Materials on Land Use, 1986, 4th edit., 2004, Preserving Paradise: Why Regulation Won't Work, 1994 (in Japanese 1994, in Chinese 1999), Land Use Law in the United States, 1994; editor: After Lucas: Land Use Regulation and the Taking of Property Without Compensation, 1993, Takings: Land Development Conditions and Regulatory Takings After Dolan and Lucas, 1995, (with Hylton, Mandelker and Franzese) Property Law and the Public Interest, 1998, 2nd edit., 2003, 3rd edit., 2004, (with Kotaka) Taking Land, 2002, (with Curtin and Tappendorf) Bargaining For Development: A Handbook, 2003, (with Bosselman, et al) Customary Law & Sustainable Development, 2005; co-editor Environ. and Land Use Law Rev., 2000—. Named Best Prof., U. Hawaii Law Sch., 1990-91, 91-92; Mich. Ford Found. fellow U. Nottingham (Eng.), 1969, life mem. Clare Hall, Cambridge U., 1999. Fellow: Am. Coll. Real Estate Lawyers, Am. Inst. Cert. Planners; mem.: ABA (chmn. com. on land use, planning and zoning 1980—82, coun. sect. on state and local govt. 1981—85, sec. 1986—87, exec. com. 1986—90, chmn. 1989—90, coun. sect. on state and local govt. 1995—, Lifetime Achievement award 2006), Internat. Bar Assn. (coun. Asia Pacific Forum 1993—96, co-chair Acads. Forum 1994—96, chair 1996—98), Ill. Bar Assn., Am. Bar Found., Am. Assn. Law Schs. (chair, state & local gov. sect. 2004), Hawaii State Bar Assn. (chair, real property and fin. svc. sect. 1997), Am. Planning Assn., Am. Law Inst., Lambda Alpha Internat. (pres. Aloha chpt. 1989—90, internat. v.p. Asia-Pacific region 2001—, Internat. Mem. of Yr. 1994). Home: 4620 Sierra Dr Honolulu HI 96816 Office: U Hawaii Richardson Sch Law 2515 Dole St Honolulu HI 96822-2328 Office Phone: 808-956-6550. Business E-Mail: dcallies@hawaii.edu.

CALLIGAN, WILLIAM DENNIS, retired life insurance company executive; b. Hibbing, Minn., Mar. 21, 1925; s. Raymond George and Ann Matilda (Olson) C.; m. Aletha E. Cornelius, Dec. 21, 1949; children— Ann M., Timothy M. BA, Yankton Coll., SD, 1949. With NY Life Ins. Co., 1953—, dir. mass market products, 1963-77, v.p. pensions, 1977-87; ret., 1987. Mem. Internat. Found. Employee Benefit Plans, Inc. Served with USMC, World War II. Home: 3535 7th Ave E Hibbing MN 55746 Personal E-mail: calligan@mchsi.com.

CALLINAN, TOM, editor-in-chief; b. 1948; m. Maureen Callinan; 3 children. Corr. St. Cloud (Minn.) Daily Times, 1975; various positions Little Falls (Minn.) Daily Transcript, 1977—83; from asst. city editor to mng. editor Argus Leader, Sioux Falls, Minn., 1983—86; editor Lansing (Mich.) State Jour., 1986—91; exec. editor Fort Myers News-Press, 1991—94; editor Dem. and Chronicle and Times-Union, Rochester, NY, 1994—2000, v.p. news, 1994—2000; editor The Ariz. Republic, Phoenix, 2000—02; editor & v.p. Cin. (Ohio) Enquirer, 2002—. Named Gannett's Editor of Yr., 1997; recipient six Gannett Pres.'s Rings in News. Office: Cincinnati Enquirer 312 Elm St Fl 18 Cincinnati OH 45202-2724 Office Phone: 513-768-8551. E-mail: tcallinan@enquirer.com.*

CALLISON, JAMES W., retired lawyer, air transportation executive; b. Jamestown, NY, Sept. 8, 1928; s. J. Waldo and Gladys A. C.; m. Gladys I. Robinson, Oct. 3, 1959; children: Sharon Elizabeth, Maria Judith, Christopher James. AB with honors, U. Mich., 1950, JD with honors (Overbeck award 1952, Jerome S. Freud Meml. award 1953), 1953. Bar: D.C. 1954, Ga. 1960, U.S. Supreme Ct., 1961. Atty. Pogue & Neal, Washington, 1953-57; with Delta Air Lines, Inc., Atlanta, 1957-93, v.p. law and regulatory affairs, 1974-78, sr. v.p., gen. counsel, 1978-81, sr. v.p., gen. counsel, corp. sec., 1981-88; sr. v.p. legal and corp. affairs, sec. Delta Air Lines Inc., 1988-90; sr. v.p. corp. and external affairs Delta Air Lines, Inc., 1990-91, sr. v.p. corp. affairs, 1991-93; ret., 1993. Contbr. articles to legal jours.; asst. editor: Mich. Law Rev, 1952-53. Recipient Papal Pro Ecclesia Et Pontifice award, 1966. Mem. State Bar Ga. (chmn. corp. counsel sect. 1989-90, mem. emeritus), Atlanta Bar Assn. (life), Atlanta Athletic Club, Order of Coif. Home: 2034 Dunwoody Club Way Dunwoody GA 30338-3024

CALLISON, RUSSELL JAMES, lawyer; b. Redding, Calif., Sept. 4, 1954; s. Walter M. and Norma A. (Bruce) C. BA in Polit. Sci., U. of Pacific, 1977, JD cum laude, 1980. Bar: Calif. 1980, U.S. Dist. Ct. (ea. dist.) Calif. 1981, U.S. Dist. Ct. (no. dist.) Calif. 1986, U.S. Ct. Appeals (9th cir.) 1989. Assoc. Memering & DeMers, Sacramento, 1980-85; pres. DeMers, Callison & Donovan, P.C., Sacramento, 1985-95; ptnr. Lewis Brisbois Bisgaard & Smith, San Francisco, 1995—. Spl. master Calif. State Bar, 1991—; arbitrator, judge pro tem Calif. Superior Cts., 1986—. Co-author: Premises Liability in California, 1996. Mem. ABA (litig. sect.), SAR (chpt. pres. 1992-93), Am. Arbitration Assn. (panel of arbitrators), Assn. Def. Counsel No. Calif., Commonwealth Club, Natomas Racquet Club, Order of Coif, Phi Alpha Delta. Republican. Episcopalian. Avocations: golf, hunting, fishing, antique restoration. Home: 3889 20th St San Francisco CA 94114-3018 Office: Lewis Brisbois Bisgaard & Smith LLP One Sansome St Ste 1400 San Francisco CA 94104-4431 Home Phone: 415-509-9980; Office Phone: 415-362-2580. Business E-Mail: callison@lbbslaw.com.

CALLISTER, LOUIS HENRY, JR., lawyer; b. Aug. 11, 1935; s. Louis Henry and Isabel (Barton) C.; m. Ellen Gunnell, Nov. 27, 1957; children: Mark, Isabel, Jane, Edward, David, John Andrew, Ann. BS, U. Utah, 1958, JD, 1961, LLD (hon.), 2002. Bar: Utah 1961. Asst. atty. gen., Utah, 1961; sr. ptnr. Callister Nebeker & McCullough, Salt Lake City, 1961—2002, of counsel, 2002—. Bd. dirs. Goldman Sachs Bank USA, 2004-; vice-chmn. Salt Lake City Zoning Bd. Adjustment, 1979-84; bd. govs. Salt Lake Valley Hosps., 1983-91; treas. exec. com. Utah Rep. Com., 1965-69; chmn. Utah chpt. Rockefeller for Pres. Com., 1964-68; sec., trustee Salt Lake Police/Sheriff Hon. Cols., 1982-97; trustee, mem. exec. com. Utah Econ. Devel. Corp., 1992—, chmn., 1998-00; trustee U. Utah, 1987-99, vice-chmn., 1989-99, bd. dirs. U. Utah Hosp., 1993-99; trustee Grand Canyon Trust, 2001—, chmn. bd., 2006—; mem. nat. adv. coun. U. Utah, 2004—. Recipient Recognition award, U. Utah, 1999, Cicero award, Utah Atty Gen., 2005. Mem. Lds Ch. Home: 3860 Highland Ct Bountiful UT 84010-3365 Office Phone: 801-530-7322. Business E-Mail: Lhcallister@cnmlaw.com.

CALLO, JOSEPH FRANCIS, writer; b. NYC, Dec. 16, 1929; s. Joseph Francis and Mary Ellen (Brennan) C. (Mary Walsh C. stepmother); m. Susan Catherine Jones, June 10, 1952 (div. Nov. 1978); children: Joseph Francis III, James D., Mary Ellen, Kathleen E., Patricia A.; m. Sally Chin McElwreath, Mar. 17, 1979; 1 stepson, Robert Joseph McElwreath. BA, Yale U., 1952. Account exec. firm Joseph F. Callo Inc., NYC, 1952-58; v.p. Potts-Woodbury Inc., NYC, 1958-60, also dir., 1958-60; pres. Callo & Carroll Inc., NYC, 1960-74; chmn. bd. dirs., creative dir. Callo Berger Albanese Inc., NYC, 1974-75; TV prodr. NBC-TV, also PBS, 1976-78; exec. v.p. Albert Frank/FCB, Inc., NYC, 1978-81; sr. v.p. Grey Advt., 1981-83, Muir Cornelius Moore, Inc., 1983-84. Ptnr. Leeward Islands Yacht Charters, 1980-83; adj. assoc. prof. comm. arts St. John's U., N.Y.C., 1965-78; mem. mktg. rev. group USN, 1973-74. Author: Legacy of Leadership: Lessons from Admiral Lord Nelson, 1999, Nelson Speaks, 2001, Nelson in the Caribbean, 2002, John Paul Jones: America's First Sea Warrior, 2006 (Samuel Eliot Morison award). Bd. advisors Nat. Maritime Hist. Soc. Rear adm USN, 1952—54. Mem.: Soc. Nautical Rsch. (Gt. Britain), Surface Navy Assn. (founding pres. greater NY chpt.), The Naval Club (London), Yale Club of N.Y. Home: 330 E 38th St Apt 25A New York NY 10016-2727 Office Phone: 212-972-8651. Personal E-mail: jfc1952@aol.com.

CALLOW, ALLAN DANA, surgeon; b. W. Somerville, Mass., Apr. 9, 1916; s. Edward Rol and Carrie (Fowles) C.; M. Eleanor Magee (dec. 1986); children: Beverly Ann Callow Nelson, Susan Diane Callow Moseley, Allan Dana Jr.; m. Una Scully Ryan, May 26, 1989; stepchildren: Tamsin Smith, Amy Ryan. BS, Tufts U., 1938, MS, 1948, PhD in Physiology, 1952; MD, Harvard, 1942, DSc (hon.), 1987. Intern Boston City Hosp., 1942-43; rsch. fellow, resident in gen. and vascular surgery Tufts New Eng. Med. Ctr., Boston, 1947-51, vice chmn. dept. surgery, 1966-82; cons. vascular surgery, dir. Vascular Surgery Rsch. Group, TNEMC, 1982-90; prof. surgery vascular div. Washington Univ Sch Medicine, St. Louis, 1990-94; rsch. prof. medicine, surgery Boston U. Med. Ctr., 1995—. Mem. Whitaker Inst. Advanced Cardiovascular Rsch.; spl. fellow vascular diseases Mayo Clinic, Rochester, Minn., 1948-49; instr. to prof. surgery Tufts U. Sch. Medicine, Boston, 1948-64; cons. to surgeon gen. Med. Corps, U.S. Navy, also civilian community hosps.; mem. study com. div. med. scis. NRC, 1969-72 Author: Carotid Surgery, 1996; editor: Vascular Surgery, 1995; assoc. editor Jour. Vasc. Surgery, 1969—; contbr. articles on vascular surgery, gen. surgery, med. edn. to profl. jours. Trustee Tufts U., 1971— , chmn. bd., 1977-87; trustee Civic Edn. Found., Lincoln Filene Center; chmn. bd. deacons Wellesley Congl. Ch., 1962-66. With M.C. USNR, 1943-46, PTO; rear adm. Res. (ret.). Decorated Legion of Merit; recipient award Hellenic Internat. Red Cross, Predl. medal Tufts U. Mem. Internat. Cardiovascular Soc. (sec.-gen. 1967-77, pres. 1977-79, pres. N.Am. chpt. 1974-75), A.C.S. (gov. 1974— , pres. Mass. chpt. 1973), New Eng. Surg. Soc., AMA (ho. dels. 1966-70), New Eng. Soc. Vascular Surgery (pres. 1977-78), Soc. Vascular Surgery (pres. 1986), Soc. Biomaterials (Clemson award 1988), Boston Surg. Soc. (pres. 1978), Mass. Med. Soc., Mass. Soc. Med. Rsch. (pres. 1988—), Am. Surg. Assn., European Soc. Vascular Surgery, So. Vascular Assn., Assn. Med. Consultants to Armed Forces, Navy Inst., Navy League, Navy Res. Officers Assn., Phi Beta Kappa, Sigma Xi, Delta Upsilon, Alpha Omega Alpha; hon. mem. Hellenic, Mexican, Argentine socs. angiology, Italian, Belgian surg. socs., European Soc. Cardiovascular Surgery. Clubs: Union (Boston), Wardroom (Boston). Office: Boston U Med Ctr 80 E Concord St Boston MA 02118-2307 Office Phone: 617-638-5692. Personal E-mail: allancallow@peoplepc.com.

CALLOW, WILLIAM GRANT, retired judge; b. Waukesha, Wis., Apr. 9, 1921; s. Curtis Grant and Mildred G. C.; m. Jean A. Zilavy, Apr. 15, 1950; children: William G., Christine S., Katherine H. PhB in Econs, U. Wis., 1943, JD, 1948. Bar: Wis.; cert. for Fla. mediation. Asst. city atty. City of Waukesha, 1948—52, city atty., 1952—60; county judge Waukesha, 1961—77; justice Supreme Ct. Wis., Madison, 1978—82; ret., 1992. Asst. prof. U. Minn., 1951-52; mem. faculty Wis. Jud. Coll., 1968-75; Wis. commr. Nat. Conf. Commrs. on Uniform State Laws, 1967—; arbitrator Wis. Employment Rel. Commn.; arbitrator-mediator bus. disputes; arbitration and mediation nat. and internat. res. judge, 1992—. With USMC, 1943-45; with USAF, 1951-52, Korea. Recipient Outstanding Alumnus award U. Wis., 1973 Fellow Am. Bar Found.; mem. ABA, Dane County Bar Assn., Waukesha County Bar Assn. Episcopalian. Personal E-mail: justicehi@aol.com.

CALLOWAY, GARY R., choral director, music director; b. Oak Ridge, Tenn., Oct. 24, 1950; s. Velma Davis; m. Mary Ann Hughes, June 1, 1972; children: Joshua, Rachel. MS in Music Edn., U. Tenn., 1979. Cert. tchg. S.C. Choral dir. Lexington HS, SC, 1991—; music dir. Lexington Presbyn. Ch., 2003—. Pres. S.C. Music Educators Assn. Choral Divsn., SC, 2002—04. Mem.: MENC. Home: 406 Wise Ferry Rd Lexington SC 29072 Office: Lexington HS 2463 Augusta Hwy Lexington SC 29072 Home Phone: 803-957-0831; Office Phone: 803-358-1868. Personal E-mail: grcall@earthlink.net. Business E-Mail: gcalloway@lexington1.net.

CALLOWAY, STEPHANIE MICHELLE, secondary school educator; m. Brian S. Calloway; 1 child, Cammi E. BS, MEd, U. SC, Converse, 2006. Cert. tchr. SC Dept. Edn., 2006. Tchr. James F. Byrnes H.S., Duncan, SC, 2000—06. Home: 8 Lantern Ln Greer SC 29651 Office: 150 E Main St Duncan SC Home Phone: 864-350-4048; Office Phone: 864-949-2355. Personal E-mail: calloway96@charter.net.

CALLSEN, CHRISTIAN EDWARD, health products executive; b. 1938; married. AB, Miami U., 1959; MBA, Harvard U., 1966. With Cole Nat. Corp., Cleve., 1966-87, various mgmt. and v.p. positions, 1966-87, exec. v.p., 1983-87; pres. Hyatt Legal Svcs., Cleve., 1987-90, Profl. Vet. Hosps., Detroit, 1991, Profl. Med. Mgmt., Cleve., 1992—2000, Applied Med. Tech., Cleve., 1993-96; chmn., CEO Allen Med. Sys., Cleve., 1995-99; pres. Polymer Concepts, Inc., 1999; chmn. TAGA Med. Techs., Inc., 2000—05. Lt. USN, 1959-64. Office: 7561 Tyler Blvd Ste 8 Mentor OH 44060-4867 Home: 21 Clinton St Hudson OH 44236 Office Phone: 440-953-9605. Personal E-mail: cec235@aol.com.

CALLUM, MYLES, magazine editor, writer; b. Lynn, Mass., Apr. 4, 1934; s. Abraham Edward and Ann Edith (Caswell) C.; m. Suzanne Connellis, Apr. 22, 1967 (div. 1974); children— Deborah, Jennifer. Student, U. Conn., 1951-53, N.Y. U., 1958-61. Pvt. investigator, Stamford, Conn., 1958-59; assoc. editor Leisure mag., NYC, 1959-60; asst. editor Good Housekeeping mag., NYC, 1961-63, assoc. editor, 1963-69, dir. spl. publs. divsn., 1969-70; mng. editor Better Homes and Gardens, Des Moines, 1971-75; assoc. editor TV Guide, Radnor, Pa., 1977-86, sr. editor., 1986-91, sr. writer NYC, 1991-96, contbg. editor, 1996-97. White Ho. cons., writer Fed. health programs, 1968; constructor crossword puzzles, 1998—. Author: Body-Building and Self-Defense, 1961, Body Talk, 1972, also articles. Served with CIC AUS, 1955-57. Home: 2367 Julio Ln Santa Rosa CA 95401-5725

CALMAN, CRAIG DAVID, actor, writer; b. Riverside, Calif., June 11, 1953; Student, Pacific U., Forest Grove, Oreg., 1971-72, U. de Querétaro, Mex., 1972-73; BA in Motion Picture/TV, UCLA, 1975. Sr. admitting worker UCLA Med. Ctr., 1974-76; actor/playwright Old Globe Theatre, San Diego, 1977-78, Off Broadway and regional, NYC and East Coast, 1979-86; exec. asst. various film/TV studios and law firms, LA, 1986-89, Orion Pictures Corp., LA, 1989-90; dir. staged readings LA, 1991—, The Transcription Co., 1998—. Actor with starring roles (TV and film) ADP Industrial, Teamwork, Macbeth, Flesteron in Amazonia, co-starring roles in Commercial Break, Sullivan's Travels; actor with co-starring/lead roles (theatre) in Book of the Dead, Dark Lady of the Sonnets, Hamlet, Rosencrantz and Guildenstern are Dead, Much Ado About Nothing, Too True to be Good, Henry V, Richard III, The Rivals, Merchant of Venice, A Day for Surprises, The Tavern, The Earrings of Madame De., The Firebugs, Christophe: For the Love of Freedom Part III, and others; columnist FilmZone, 1995-97. Author play/screenplays: The Turn of the Century, Strangled Nocturne, Skidoo Ruins, Life Without Father, Patterns Woven In A Park; author: The Turn of the Century; author one-act plays, screenplays, full-length plays, poetry; writer asst. Hal Roach, Bel Air, Calif., 1987-88; writer, dir., prodr. The Calista Zipper Story, 2007. Vol. book reader Recording for the Blind, L.A., 1991—. Recipient Old Globe Theatre Atlas award for best actor in a comedy role for Too True to be Good, 1977-78; Helene Wurlitzer Found. of N.Mex. Writers Residency grantee, 1988; finalist Walt Disney fellowship program, 1992, Chesterfield Film Writers Project, 1997. Mem. SAG, Actors Equity Assn., Actors Studio West (playwright/dir. unit 2000-2005, Mark Rydell's Director's Unit, 2003-04). Office Phone: 323-906-8886. Personal E-mail: craigcalman@earthlink.net.

CALMAN, ROBERT FREDERICK, mining executive; b. Mineola, NY, May 14, 1932; s. William Arthur and Ida (Albersworth) C.; m. Susan Jean Raphael, June 20, 1959 (div. 1978); children: Andrew Frederick, Camille, Matthew Alexander; m. Doris Sumerson, June 9, 1979. BA, Yale U., 1954; MS, MIT, 1967. With Chase Manhattan Bank, NYC, 1954-61, asst. treas., 1961; with Mobil Oil Corp., NYC, 1961-70, treas. N.Am. div., 1964-68, treas. Internat. div., 1968-69; v.p. finance, treas. IU Internat. Corp., Phila., 1970-72, group v.p. devel., 1972-74, exec. v.p., 1974-78, vice chmn., 1978-85, chmn. fin. com., dir., 1986-88; chmn., dir. Echo Bay Mines Ltd., Edmonton, Alta., Canada, 1981-96. Bd. dirs. Corp. Cons. Group, Ltd., Bank of N.Y. Trust Co. of Fla., The Gold Inst., Am. Mining Congress; lectr. NYU, 1968-69. Author: Linear Programming and Cash Management/Cash Alpha, 1968. Pres., Phila. chpt. Nat. Found. for Ileitis and Colitis, Inc., 1974-75; pres., mem. bd. govs. Soc. Alfred P. Sloan Fellows; dir. alumni fund, mem. corp. devel. com. Mass. Inst. Tech. Served to 1st lt., arty. AUS, 1955-57. Recipient E.P. Brooks prize Mass. Inst. Tech., 1967. Mem. Phi Beta Kappa, Phi Gamma Delta. Republican. Christian Scientist. Office: 241 S 6th St Apt 2302 Philadelphia PA 19106-3736 E-mail: bobcalman@cs.com.

CALMAN, SANDRA GOGINS, physician, researcher; b. Salt Lake City, May 18, 1961; d. Laird Barnett and Dorene Coral (Taylor) Gogins. BS with honors, U. Utah, Salt Lake City, 1984, MD with honors, 1988. Dir. clinical rsch. Premier Eye Care, San Francisco, 1998—2004, Dow Pharm., Petaluma, Calif., 2004—05; dir. clinical rsch., acting chief med. officer Johnson & Johnson, Fremont, Calif., 2005—06; chief med. officer Dey, LP, Napa, Calif., 2006—07; chief med. officer, v.p. clinical devel. Isolagen, Inc., Exton, Pa., 2007—. Mailing: PO Box 371527 Montara CA 94037-1527

CALOGERO, PASCAL FRANK, JR., state supreme court justice; b. New Orleans, Nov. 9, 1931; s. Pascal Frank and Louise (Moore) C.; children— Deborah Ann Calogero Applebaum, David, Pascal III, Elizabeth, Thomas, Michael, Stephen, Gerald, Katie, Chrissy. Student, Loyola U., New Orleans, 1949-51, JD, 1954; LLM in Jud. Process, U. Va., 1992; LLD (hon.), Loyola U., New Orleans, 1991. Bar: La. Law clerk Civil Dist. Ct.; ptnr. Landrieu, Calogero & Kronlage, 1958-69, Calogero & Kronlage, 1969-73; gen. counsel La. Stadium and Expn. Dist., 1970-73; assoc. justice Supreme Ct. La., New Orleans, 1973-90, chief justice, 1990—. Mem. La. Democratic State Central Com., 1963-71; mem. subcom. on del. selection La. Dem. Party, 1971; del. Dem. Nat. Conv., 1968; bd. directors Conference Chief Justices, 1997-; lecturer U. New Orleans, Harvard Law Sch., Loyola Sch. of Law. Served to capt. US Army, 1954—57. Recipient Disting. Jurist award La. Bar Founds., 1991; Judge Bob Jones Meml. award, Am. Judges Assn., 1995, Justice Albert Tate, Jr. award La. Assn. Criminal Defense Lawyers, 1997, Outstanding Jud. award Victims & Citizens Against Crime, Inc., 1999. Mem. ABA, La. Bar Assn., New Orleans Bar Assn., Greater New Orleans Trial Lawyers Assn. (v.p. 1967-69), Order of the Coif. Office: Supreme Ct La 400 Royal St New Orleans LA 70130 Business E-Mail: icaloger@lasc.org.

CALORE, PAUL, writer, retired government agency administrator; b. Providence, Apr. 5, 1938; s. Enrico and Ida Calore; m. Cecilia Ferreira, Apr. 18, 1964; children: Vickie Noel, Stephen, Cheryl Calore-Abatacola. BA magna cum laude, Johnston & Wales U., 1976. Ops. br. chief Def. Logistics Agy., Needham, Mass., 1981—93. Author: Land Campaigns of the Civil War, 2000, Naval Campaigns of the Civil War, 2002. Mem.: Civil War Ctr., Civil War Preservation Trust. Avocations: collecting Civil War memorabilia, travel. Personal E-mail: paulcalore@comcast.net.

CALVA, ROBERT BARAQUIEL, music educator; b. Witchita, Sept. 15, 1959; s. Erma Mae and Robert Calva. Cert. Musicians Inst., Hollywood, 1992, Svc. Calif., 2002. Music instr. Delian Music, Culver City, Calif.; git instr. Musicians Inst., Hollywood, Calif.; instr. music So. Calif. Conservatory of Music, West Hills, Calif. Musician Lincoln St., LA. Author: (book) Texas Blues Guitar, Blues - Rock Soloing for Guitar. Conservative. Avocations: reading, exercise, natural healing, history, movies. Home: 12300 Sherman Way # 164 North Hollywood CA 91605 Personal E-mail: rbcalva@aol.com. E-mail: robertc@mi.edu.

CALVANI, TERRY, lawyer; b. Carlsbad, N.Mex., Jan. 29, 1947; s. Torello Howard and Mary Virginia (Hawkins) C.; m. Mary Virginia Anderson, May 3, 1969; m. Judith Thompson, Aug. 28, 1980; children: Dominic Mario, Torello Howard; m. Sarah Holter Hill, June 19, 2003. BA, U. N.Mex., 1969; JD with distinction, Cornell U., 1972. Bar: N.Mex. 1972, Calif. 1972, Tenn. 1978, D.C. 1992, U.S. Dist. Ct. N.Mex. 1972, U.S. Dist. Ct. (no. dist.) Calif. 1972, U.S. Dist. Ct. (mid. dist.) Tenn. 1978, U.S. Dist. Ct. D.C. 1994, U.S. Ct. Appeals (9th cir.) 1972, U.S. Ct. Appeals (6th cir.) 1977, U.S. Ct. Appeals (5th cir.) 1981, U.S. Ct. Appeals (11th cir.) 1981, U.S. Ct. Appeals (D.C. cir.) 1994, U.S. Supreme Ct. 1985. Tchg. fellow Stanford U. Law Sch., 1972-73; asst. prof. law Vanderbilt U. Sch. Law, Nashville, 1974—77, assoc. prof., 1977—80, prof., 1980—83; assoc. Pillsbury, Madison & Sutro (now Pillsbury Winthrop LLP), San Francisco, 1973-74, ptnr., 1990—2002; mem. The Competition Authority Republic of Ireland, 2002—05, 2005; of counsel Freshfields Bruckhaus Deringer, Washington, 2005—. Vis. prof. law U. Va., Charlottesville, 1981—82; of counsel Haksell Slaughter & Young, Birmingham, 1980—83; commr. U.S. F.T.C., 1983—90, acting chmn., 1985—86; lectr. Harvard U. Sch. Law, 1998—2002, Trinity Coll., Dublin, 2004—05; sr. lecturing fellow Duke U. Sch. Law, 2000; adj. prof. law Cornell Law Sch., 2006. Author: (with John Siegfried) Economic Analysis and Antitrust Law, 1979, 2d edit., 1988; mem. editl. bd. Antitrust Bull., 1982—, Bur. Nat. Affairs RICO Report, 1986-96. Mem.: ABA (chmn. spl. com. to study antitrust penalties and damages antitrust sec 1979—82, chmn. Robinson-Patman com. antitrust sect. 1981—83, coun. mem. 1985—86), 6th Jud. Conf. (life), Am. Law Inst. (life), Lagunitas Country Club (Ross), Olympic Club (San Francisco), Colonnade Club (Charlottesville), G.C. Club Tenn. (Nashville), The Club (Birmingham), Pacific Union Club (San Francisco), Richland Country Club (Nashville), Stephen's Green Club (Dublin), Order of the Coif. Roman Catholic. Office: Freshfields Bruckhaus Deringer Ste 600 701 Pennsylvania Ave Washington DC 20004 Office Phone: 202-777-4505. Office Fax: 202-777-4555. Business E-Mail: terry.calvani@freshfields.com.

CALVER, RICHARD ALLEN, retired dean; b. Chillicothe, Ohio, Feb. 16, 1939; s. Robert K. Calver and Catherine Mae (Roush) Bryan; m. Susan Jane Yost, Oct. 9, 1988; children: Mark R. Fortney, Sherry Sue Skinner, Alan D. Fortney. Student, U. Hawaii, 1959-61; BSBA, W.Va. U., 1963; MS in Bus., Va. Commonwealth U., 1970; C.A.G.S.E., Va. Tech. U., 1983, EdD in C.C. Edn., 1984. Mgmt. trainee Sears Roebuck & Co., 1963, Reuben H. Donnelley Corp., 1963-64, state publs. and customer rels. mgr., 1964-68; state job analyst Va. Divsn. pers., Richmond, 1968-70; dean adminstrv. svcs. S.W. Va. C.C., Richlands, 1970-88, Thomas Nelson C.C., Hampton, Va., 1988—2002, interim pres., 1994-95, ret., 2002, spl. asst. to pres., 2002—05. Accreditation team So. Assn. Colls. and Schs., 1976-95, Mid. States Assn., 1983-94. Active. Lebanon (Va.) Town Coun., 1978-82; spl. edn. adv. com. Russell County Sch. Bd., 1984-88, Va. Peninsula Inst. Leadership Inst. Program, 1989; planning com. Greater Williamsburg Area Crossroads, 1999-2005; bd. mem. Thomas Nelson C.C., 2005-07. With USAF, 1957-61. Mem. Nat. Coun. C.C. Bus. Officers (Regional Outstanding Bus. officer 1990, nat. bd. dirs. 1985-94), So. Assn. Coll. and Univ. Bus. officers, Ea. Assn. Coll. and U. Bus. Officers, Coll. and Univ. Pers. Assn., Lions (pres. Lebanon club 1976-77), Shriners (pres. club 1974-75), Scottish Rite (32d degree), Masons, Delta Tau Delta, Phi Kappa Phi, Phi Theta Kappa (hon.). Methodist. Home: 5509 N Mallard Run Williamsburg VA 23188-9415

CALVERT, C. EMMETT, former state agency administrator; b. Lexington, Ky., Feb. 24, 1937; s. Emmett I. and Minnie (Hall) C.; m. Violet Stafford, Sept. 22, 1962; children: Emmett Bradford, Eric Brandon. BS in Commerce and Acctg., U. Ky., 1959. Rsch. asst. U. Ky., Lexington, 1959; from auditor to audit mgr. Ky. Revenue Cabinet, Lexington, 1959-87, sec. Frankfort, 1987-91. Bd. dirs. Ky. Housing Corp., Frankfort, Ky. Workers Compensation Funding Commn., Frankfort, State Property and Bldg. Commn., Frankfort, Commonwealth Venture Fund, Ky. Employees Deferred Compensation System, Frankfort, 1991-94. Mem. tax com. Ky. Farm Bur., Louisville, 1991; vol. non-profit schs., Lexington; coach, league ofcl. various sport orgns., Lexington, 1975-86. Recipient Cert. of merit, Office Vocat. Rehab., 1990. Mem. Southeastern Assn. Tax Adminstrs., Fedn. Tax Adminstrs., Lexington Yacht Club. Democrat. Presbyterian. Avocations: boating, woodworking, brick laying. Home: 3536 Castlegate Wynd Lexington KY 40502-7701 E-mail: emmettcalvert@insightbb.com.

CALVERT, DAVID VICTOR, soil science educator; b. Chaplin, Ky., Feb. 26, 1934; s. Stanford Byron and Willia Neal Calvert; m. Joyce Faye LeMay, July 27, 1957; children: Victor Neal Calvert, Yvonne Carole Calvert. BS, U. Ky., 1956, MS, 1958; PhD, Iowa State U., 1962. Cert. profl. soil scientist, Am. Registry of Cert Profls. in Agronomy, Crops and Soils, Ltd. Grad. rsch. asst. U. Ky., Lexington, 1956-58, Iowa State U., Ames, 1958-62; asst. prof. soil and water sci. U. Fla., Ft. Pierce, 1962-68, assoc. prof., 1968-76, prof., 1976—2003, prof. emeritus, 2003—, dir. Indian River Rsch. & Edn. Ctr., 1979-94. Ofcl. collaborator S.E. region USDA, Athens, Ga., 1965-79; cons. World Bank, Jamaican Sch. Agr., Kingston, 1970-71; cons. soil sci. Coun. for Agrl. Sci. and Tech., St. Louis. Contbr. over 175 articles to profl. jours. including Soil Sci. Soc. Am. Proceedings, Jour. Agrl., Food Chem., Jour. Environ. Quality, Soil Sci., Proceedings Internat. Soc. Citriculture. Recipient Soil-Water-Air-Plant grant USDA Agrl. Rsch. Svc., Fla., 1968-80; grantee EPA, 1970-73, Water Quality Rsch. City of Okeechobee, Fla., 1990-93, St. Johns and South Fla. Water Mgmt. Dists., Palatka and West Palm Beach, 1993-96; award Fla. Dept. Agr. and Consumer Svcs., Tallahassee, 1996—; recipient Rsch. Achievement award Fla. Fruit and Vegetable Assn., 1979, Agrl. Hall of Fame award Saint Lucie County Farm Bur., 1997; U. Ky. fellow; named Outstanding Conservationist of Yr., Soil Conservation Svc. USDA, Fla., 1983, Disting. Out-of-State Alumnus for the U. Kys. Coll. of Agrl., 1997. Fellow Am. Soc. Agronomy; mem. Soil Sci. Soc Am., Internat. Soc. Soil Sci., Am. Soc. Hort. Sci., Coun. of Agrl. Sci. and Tech., Soil and Crop Sci. Soc. Fla. (pres. 2000, hon. membership award, 2006), Fla. State Hort. Soc. (hon. membership award 1997), Internat. Soc. Citriculture, Rsch. Ctr. Adminstrs. Soc., Am. Soc. Agronomy, Farmhouse Fraternity, Scovell Soc. U. Ky. (charter mem.), Sigma Xi, Gamma Sigma Delta, Alpha Zeta. Achievements include contbns. to development and deployment of working water quality standards to guide growers using low-volume sprinkler and micro irrigation systems; development of a soil and water management strategy for control of nitrates and phosphates leaching from citrus groves into surface water and ground water. Home: 1007 Grandview Blvd Fort Pierce FL 34982-4323 Office Phone: 772-468-3922. Personal E-mail: cgator1@bellsouth.net.

CALVERT, DELBERT WILLIAM, retired energy executive; b. Bosworth, Mo., Jan. 29, 1927; s. William McKinley and Ruby Leona (Berrier) Calvert; m. Mary Lee Brown, Feb. 10, 1947 (div. Mar. 1971); children: Gary D., Danial L.; m. Melva Allen Hurst, Sept. 4, 1971; stepchildren: Holly Hurst, Allen Hurst. BSCE, U. Mo., 1952. Asst. mgr. supply and transp. divsn. Phillips Petroleum Co., Bartlesville, Okla., 1952-63; asst. to v.p. Tex. Ea. Transmission Corp., Houston, 1963-65; mgr. diversification dept. No. Natural Gas Co., Omaha, 1965-68; pres. Williams Bros. Pipe Line Co., Tulsa, 1968-71; exec. v.p. The Williams Cos., Tulsa, 1971-85, also bd. dirs.; chmn. bd. Williams Energy Co., 1975-79, also bd. dirs.; chmn., CEO, Agrico Chem. Co., Tulsa, 1977-85, also bd. dirs.; ret. Pres. Wiliams Techs., Inc., 1992—97; chmn. bd. dirs. Black Mesa Pipeline Co., 1996—97, adv. dir., 1997—98. Apptd. to gov.'s agroindustry policy commn., 1987—; mem. exec. bd. Indian Nations coun. Boy Scouts Am., 1969—, pres., 1974—76; mem. U. Mo. Devel. Fund, 1969—, chmn., 1972—73; bd. dirs. Goodwill Industries Tulsa. With AUS, 1945—47. Mem.: Potash and Phosphate Inst. (dir. 1982—85), Fertilizer Industry Assn. (chmn. bd.), Am. Petroleum Inst. (gen. com. div. transp. 1971), Okla. Petroleum Coun. (dir. 1968—, pres. 1977—78), Mo. U. Civil Engring. Acad. Disting. Alumni (Pipe Liner of Yr. 1998), Garden of Gods Club (Colorado Springs, Colo.), Univ. Club (Columbia, Mo.), Waikoloa (Hawaii) Village Golf Club, Pi Mu Epsilon, Chi Epsilon, Tau Beta Pi. Home: PO Box 384690 Waikoloa HI 96738 E-mail: tinkanbill@aol.com.

CALVERT, GORDON LEE, retired legal association executive; b. Wardensville, W.Va., Sept. 2, 1921; s. Aaron Lee and Ada (Brill) C.; m. Margaret James, June 9, 1945; children— Gordon R., Roger L., Walter R. BA with distinction, George Washington U., 1943, JD with distinction, 1945. Bar: D.C. 1946. Assoc. firm Covington & Burling, Washington, 1944-46; with Investment Bankers Assn. Am., Washington, 1946-71, exec. dir., gen. counsel, 1966-71; exec. v.p., gen. counsel Securities Industry Assn., 1972; v.p., gen. counsel N.Y. Stock Exchange, Washington, 1973-76; exec. dir. comml. collection agy. sect. Comml. Law League Am., Washington, 1976-92. Author: Fundamentals of Municipal Bonds, 1959, Digest of Investments of State Pension Funds, 1960, Digest of State Laws Regulating Debt Collection Agencies, 1977, 81. Mem. ABA, Order of Coif, Pi Kappa Alpha, Phi Delta Phi, Omicron Delta Kappa, Met. Club (Washington), Columbia Country Club (Chevy Chase, Md.). Presbyterian. Home: 3100 N Leisure World Blvd Apt 526 Silver Spring MD 20906

CALVERT, JACK GEORGE, atmospheric chemist, educator; b. Inglewood, Calif., May 9, 1923; s. John George and Emma (Eschstruth) C.; m. Doris Arlene Breimon, Nov. 8, 1946; children: Richard John, Mark Steven. BS in Chemistry, UCLA, 1944, PhD, 1949. Mem. faculty Ohio State U., 1950-81, prof. chemistry, 1960-81, Kimberly prof. chemistry, 1974-81, prof. emeritus, 1981—, chmn. dept., 1964-68; sr. scientist Nat. Ctr. Atmospheric Rsch., Boulder, Colo., 1982-94, sr. rsch. assoc., 1994—2002, sr. scientist emeritus, 2002—. Vis. scientist Oak Ridge (Tenn.) Nat. Lab., Environ. Scis. Divsn., 2002—; cons. air pollution tng. com. USPHS, 1964-66; cons. World Innovation Found., 2001—; mem. Nat. Air Pollution Control Manpower Devel. Com., 1966-69, chmn., 1968-69; bd. dirs. Gordon Rsch. Confs., 1969-71; mem. air pollution control rsch. grants com. EPA, 1970-72, chmn., 1971-72, mem. chemistry and physics adv. com., 1973-75; chmn. air pollution com. Conservation Found., 1968-70; mem. air conservation commn. Am. Lung Assn., 1973-75; chmn. EPA environ. chemistry/physics grants rev. panel, 1979-83; mem. State of Colo. Air Quality Control Commn., 1987-90, Disting. Acad. Adv. Group of Auto/Oil Air Quality Improvement Rsch. Program, 1989-96; mem. panel on atmospheric effects of aviation NRC/NAS, 1995-98, mem. com. on ozone potential of reformulated gasoline, 1997-99; atmospheric chemistry tech. implementation panel Am. Chem. Coun., 1998-2004. Author: (with J. N. Pitts, Jr.) Photochemistry, 1966, Graduate School in the Sciences, 1972; also articles. Ensign USNR, 1944-46. Named Honor Prof. of Year Coll. Arts and Scis., Ohio State U., 1957; recipient Alumni award for disting. tchg., 1961, Disting. Rsch. award, 1981; fellow NRC Can., 1949; Guggenheim fellow, 1977-78 Fellow Ohio Acad. Sci., Am. Inst. Chemists, Am. Geophys. Union; mem. AAUP, Am. Chem. Soc. (award for creative rsch. in environ. sci. and tech. 1981, Columbus sect. award 1981), Air Pollution Control Assn. (Chambers award 1986), Phi Beta Kappa, Sigma Xi, Pi Mu Epsilon, Phi Lambda Upsilon, Alpha Chi Sigma. Achievements include research on photochemistry, reaction kinetics, atmospheric chemistry, mechanisms free radical reactions.

CALVERT, JAY H., JR., lawyer; b. Charleston, SC, Mar. 19, 1945; m. Ann E., June 14, 1969; children: Amanda, Emily, Sarah. BA, Amherst Coll., Mass., 1967; JD, U. Va., 1970. Bar: Pa. 1970, U.S. Dist. Ct. (ea. dist.) Pa. 1970, U.S. Ct. Appeals (3d cir.) 1971, U.S. Dist. Ct. (mid. dist.) Pa. 1973, U.S. Ct. Appeals (2d cir.) 1980, U.S. Ct. Appeals (8th cir.) 1987, U.S. Supreme Ct. 1989, U.S. Dist. Ct. Ariz. 1994, U.S. Dist. Ct. (we. dist.) Pa. 2000. Assoc. Morgan, Lewis & Bockius LLP, Phila., 1970—78, ptnr., 1978—, exec. ptnr., 1987—90; mem. firm governing bd. Morgan Lewis & Bockius LLP, Phila., 1989—94; mng. ptnr. Morgan, Lewis & Bockius LLP, Phila., 1990—94, mem. exec. com., 1997—98, sr. ptnr. litigation sect., 1990—, mgr. litigation sect., 1996—99. Trustee Agnes Irwin Sch., Rosemont, Pa., 1988-94; mem. bd. dirs. St. David's Nursery Sch., Wayne, Pa., 1980-94; mem. ann. fund campaign com. Inglis House, 1998-04; chmn. devel. com. Phila. Zoo, 1993-96, chmn. facilities, exhibits and safety com., 1997-2001, bd. dirs., 1992—, vice-chmn. bd. dirs., 1994-96, 2004—. 2nd lt. USAR, 1970—72, 1st lt. USAR, 1972—76, capt. USAR, 1976—78. Mem. ABA, Pa. Bar Assn., Phila. Bar Assn., Lawyers Club Phila., Leukemia and Lymphoma Soc. Am. (trustee Phila. chpt. 1982—, pres. bd. dirs. 2005—), Pyramid Club (mem. bd. govs. 2004—) Avocations: bicycling, gardening, hiking, horseback riding, animal husbandry. Office: Morgan Lewis & Bockius LLP 1701 Market St Philadelphia PA 19103-2903 Home Phone: 610-687-0245; Office Phone: 215-963-5462. Business E-Mail: jcalvert@morganlewis.com.

CALVERT, KEN, congressman; b. Corona, Calif., June 8, 1953; AA, Chaffey Coll., 1973; BA Econs., San Diego State U., 1975. Corona/ Norco youth chmn. for Nixon, 1968, 82; county youth chmn. rep. Vesey's Dist., 1970, 43d dist., 1972; congl. aide to Rep. Vesey, Calif., 1975-79; gen. mgr. Jolly Fox Restaurant, Corona, Calif., 1975-79, Marcus W. Meairs Co., Corona, Calif., 1979-81; pres., gen. mgr. Ken Calvert Real Properties, Corona, Calif., 1981—; Reagan-Bush campaign worker, 1980; co chmn. Wilson for Senate Campaign, 1982, George Deukmejian election, 1978, 82, 86, George Bush election, 1988, Pete Wilson senate elections, 1982, 88, Pete Wilson for Gov. election, 1990; mem. U.S. Congress from 43rd Calif. dist., 1993—2003, U.S. Congress from 44th dist., 2003—; mem. armed svcs., resources, sci. com. Former v.p. Corona/ Norco Rep. Assembly; chmn. Riverside Rep. Party, 1984-88, County Riverside Asset Leasing; bd. realtors Corono/ Norco Exec. bd. Corona Community Hosp. Corp. 200 Club; mem. Corona Airport adv. commn.; adv. com. Temescal/ El Cerrito Community Plan. Mem. Riverside County Rep. Winners Circle (charter), Lincoln Club (co-chmn., charter, 1986-90), Corona Rotary Club (pres. 1991), Elks, Navy League Corona Norco, Corona C. of C. (pres. 1990), Noroco C. of C., Monday Morning Group, Corona Group (past chmn.), Econ. Devel. Ptnrship., Silver Eagles (March AFB support group, charter). Republican. Office: US Ho Reps 2201 Rayburn Ho Office Bldg Washington DC 20515-0544 also: Office of Ken Calvert Ste 200 3400 Central Avenue Riverside CA 92506*

CALVERT, WALTER RANDOLPH, lawyer; b. Takoma Park, Md., Jan. 7, 1958; s. Gordon Lee and Margaret (James) C.; m. Cynthia Thomas, Apr. 22, 1989. BS in Commerce, U. Va., 1980; JD, Coll. William & Mary, 1983. Bar: Md. 1983, DC 1989, admitted to practice: US Dist. Ct. (Dist. Md.) 1984, US Ct. Fed. Claims 1993, US Ct. Appeals (Fed. Cir.) 1994, US Tax Ct. 1994. From assoc. to sr. assoc. Semmes, Bowen & Semmes, Balt., 1983—; ptnr., Taxation Dept. Venable LLP, Balt. Lectr. in field. Contbr. articles to mags. Eagle scout Boy Scouts Am., 1976. Recipient Mero Award, Md. State Bar Assn. (Taxation Sect.). Mem. ABA (Taxation Sect., State & Local Govt. Law Sect., Bus. Law Sect.), Md. State Bar Assn. (chmn. taxation sect. publs. and state legis. coms. 1984-90), Nat. Assn. Bond Lawyers. Office: Venable LLP 1800 Mercantile Bank & Trust Bldg 2 Hopkins Plz Baltimore MD 21201 Office Phone: 410-244-7726. Office Fax: 410-244-7742. Business E-Mail: wrcalvert@venable.com.

CALVERT, WILLIAM PRESTON, radiologist; b. Warrensburg, Mo., July 2, 1934; s. William Geery and Elizabeth (Spaulding) C.; m. Mary Kay Kersh, Apr. 4, 1976. BS, MIT, 1956; MD, U. Pa., 1960. Diplomate Am. Bd. Nuclear Medicine, Am. Bd. Radiology. Intern Pa. Hosp., Phila., 1960-61, resident in medicine, 1961-62, 64-66, chief med. resident, chief resident physician, 1965-66; resident in gastroenterology U. Miami, 1966-67, NIH fellow in gastroenterology, 1967-68, resident in radiology, 1968-71; radiologist Meml. Hosp., Hollywood, Fla., 1971-72; chief dept. radiology Larkin Gen. Hosp., South Miami, Fla., 1972-80, radiologist, 1980-89, Jackson Meml. Hosp., U. Miami, 1989-93, Univ. Hosp., Tammarac, Fla., 1993-95; part-time radiologist Northern Navajo Med. Ctr., Shiprock, N.Mex., 1995-2000; ret., 2000. Clin. instr. radiology U. Miami Sch. Medicine, 1971-76, clin. asst. prof. radiology, 1984-88, clin. assoc. prof. radiology, 1988-94. Bd. dirs. Wediko Farms Children's Svcs., Carbondale, Ill. Served with M.C., USAF, 1962-64. Mem. AMA, Fla. Med. Assn., Fla., Greater Miami radiol. socs., Soc. Nuclear Medicine, Radiol. Soc. N.Am., Explorers Club. Personal E-mail: calvertb12@aol.com.

CALVIN, CHARLES D., lawyer; b. Evanston, Ill., Apr. 9, 1948; BA cum laude, Pomona Coll., 1969; JD, Yale U., 1972. Bar: Colo. 1972, Utah 1989. Mem. Davis, Graham & Stubbs, Denver; ptnr. Faegre & Benson LLP, Denver. Contbr. articles to profl. jours. Named Am's. Leading Bus. Lawyers, by Chambers USA, 2005, 2006, Super Lawyers, 2006, Best Lawyers Am., 2006, 2007. Mem.: Colo. Bar Assn. (real estate coun., law office tech. com. mem.). Office: Faegre & Benson LLP 3200 Wells Fargo Ctr 1700 Lincoln St Denver CO 80203-4532 Office Phone: 303-607-3677. Office Fax: 303-607-3600. Business E-Mail: ccalvin@faegre.com.

CALVIN, DONALD LEE, stock exchange official; b. Mount Olive, Ill., Nov. 10, 1931; m. Louise Elinor Peterson, Mar. 28, 1952; children: Jane Calvin Palasek, Sally Anne Calvin Salvaterra. Student, Ea. Ill. U., 1950-54, LLD, 1990; LLB, U. Ill., 1956. Bar: Ill. 1956. Atty. Office Sec. of State of Ill., Springfield, 1957-58, securities commr., 1959-62; syndicate mgr. A.C. Allyn & Co., Chgo., 1962-63; atty. F.I. DuPont & Co., Chgo., 1963-64; exec. asst. civic and govt. affairs NY Stock Exch., NYC, 1964-65, v.p., 1966-77, sr. v.p., 1977—86, exec. v.p., 1986—87; chmn. Internat. Bus. Enterprises, Inc., NYC, 1987—. Advisor to chmn. Chgo. Bd. Options Exch., Geneva Stock Exch., 1987—96; advisor to pres. Fedn. Internat. des Bourses de Valeurs, Paris, 1989—98, Kuala Lampur Stock Exch., 1991—2000, São Paulo (Brazil) Stock Exch., 1993—98, Stock Exch. of Hong Kong, 1995—98, Cairo and Alexandria, Egypt Stock Exchs., 1997—; bd. dirs. Internat. Fin. Ctr. and Exch. of Curacao, bd. dirs. SEC Hist. Soc.; bd. dirs. Nat. Coun. on Econ. Edn.; chmn. Nat. Stock Exch., Chgo., 2002—. With USMCR, 1951-56. Mem. ABA, Internat. Bar Assn., Ill. State Bar Assn., Chgo. Bar Assn., Am. Law Inst., Met. Club NYC, India House Club, Manhasset Bay Yacht Club (Port Washington, NY). Home: 4 Knolls Ln Manhasset NY 11030-1630 Personal E-mail: calvindonaldl@aol.com.

CALVIN, JAMES WILLARD, thoracic and vascular surgeon; b. Oakland, Calif., Dec. 7, 1929; s. George Fairchild and Mary Norris Calvin; m. Claudine Deprez (div. 1971); m. Carrie Carman, 1973; children: Carolyne, Frances, Sophie. BA, Stanford U., 1951; MD, MChir, McGill U., 1955. Diplomate Nat. Bd. Med. Examiners, Am. Bd. Surgery, Am. Bd. Thoracic Surgery, spl. qualifications gen. vascular surgery. Lectr. in astronomy Menlo Coll., Menlo Park, Calif., 1951; intern Stanford (Calif.) U., 1955-56, resident dept. surgery, 1959-63, chief resident dept. surgery, 1963-64; group practice Sansum Med. Clinic, Santa Barbara, Calif., 1964-66; pvt. practice Thoracic and Cardiovascular Med. Group, Inc., Ventura, Calif., 1966—95. Bd. dirs. Rehab. Inst. Santa Barbara, bd. trustees; scientific adv. coun. Ramus Med. Techns., Carpinteria, Calif., 1996-01; hosp. staff Cmty. Meml. Hosp., Ventura; chief staff Cmty. Meml. Hosp., Ventura, 1994; hosp. staff County Med. Ctr., Ventara Hosp., 1959-95. Contbr. articles to profl. jours. Quality of care reviewer Medicare, 1985—95; bd. dirs. Friends of the Libr., La Quinta, Calif., 1999—. With USAF, 1956—58. NIH rsch. fellow, 1960-61. Fellow ACS (rep. hosps. of Ventura County 1980-87), Am. Coll. of Chest Physicians; mem. AAAS, AMA, Am. Cancer Soc. (Ventura county chpt., bd. dirs. 1969-72), Am. Heart Assn. (coun. on cardiovascular diseases), Am. Lung Assn., Am. Thoracic Soc., Calif. Med. Assn., Internat. Cardiovascular Soc. (N.Am. chpt.), N.Am. Soc. for Pacing and Electrophysiology, Samson Thoracic Surg., Soc. for Clin. Vascular Surgery, Soc. for Thoracic Surgeons, Soc. Vascular Surgeons, So. Calif. Vascular Surg. Soc., Ventura County Heart Assn. (pres. 1965), Ventura County Med. Soc. (pres. 1979, bd. govs. 1975-81). Home: 47-515 Via Florence La Quinta CA 92253 Personal E-mail: jcalvin@dc.rr.com.

CALVO, ROQUE JOHN, professional society administrator; b. Allentown, Pa., Sept. 26, 1958; s. Rocco John and Ruth Hattie (Zimpfer) C.; m. Marianne Willever, Feb. 27, 1982; children: Amy Elizabeth, Roque John. BS, Lebanon Valley Coll., 1980; MBA, Rider U., 1986. Acctg. supv. Electrochem. Soc., Inc., Pennington, NJ, 1980-82, asst. exec. dir., 1982-91, exec. dir., 1991—. Adv. bd. Fedn. Materials Socs., Washington, 1991—; meeting adv. bd. Starwood Hotels and Resorts Worldwide. Mem. Am. Soc. Assn. Execs., Coun. Engring. and Sci. Society Execs. (bd. dirs. 1995-2002, pres. 2000-01), N.J. Soc. Assn. Execs. Avocations: golf, basketball, reading. Office: Electrochemical Soc Inc 65 S Main St Pennington NJ 08534-2827 Office Phone: 609-737-1902. E-mail: rcalvo12@aol.com, roque.calvo@electrochem.org.

CAMACCI, MICHAEL A., real estate broker and developer, consultant; b. Youngstown, Ohio, Feb. 6, 1951; s. Martin B. and Viola F. (Conti) Camacci; m. Susan Hawkins, Oct. 18, 1985; 1 child, Michael Philip. BBA, Youngstown Coll., 1974. Cert. bus. analyst. Acct. U.S. Steel Corp., Youngstown, 1969-80; mgr. sales Soc. Realty, Boardman, Ohio, 1980-81; dir. sales Pop-ins Maid Services, Columbiana, Ohio, 1981-82; bus. broker Eranco Assocs., Girard, Ohio, 1982-86; pres. JMC Realty, Inc., Youngstown, 1986-99; pres., broker Camacci Real Estate, 1986—; pres. Hillview Nursing Home, 1988-99, Valley View Nursing Home, 1990-99, Pyramid Printing, Inc., 1991-99; dir. Crestview Nursing & Rehab. Facility, 1999—2002; CEO Van Fossan & Assoc., 2000—. Pres. CRE Holding Corp., 1996, Wedgewood Property Mgmt., Inc., 4682 North, LLC, 55 West, LLC, 1997—2002, 19th Hole Investments, 1997—2002, Goldco Internat., 1997—, 20 West, LLC, 1998—2007, Downtown Partners, 1998—2005, Landmark Real Estate Svcs., Inc., 1998—, CPR, LLC, 2003—; mgr. 48 North, LLC, 1408 South, LLC, 2005—; broker, mgr. LandQuest Comml. Real Estate ILC; mgr. JLB Gunn LLC; broker/pres. Level 3 Real Estate, LLC, 2007—. Mem. Youngstown-Warren Regional Growth Alliance; v.p. Austintown Growth Found., 1994—96. With US Army, 1971—77. Mem.: BBB, Downtown Ptnrs., Mahoning County Home Builders Assn., Internat. Coun. Shopping Ctrs., Nat. Assn. Printers and Lithographers, Ohio Health Care Assn., Fla. Gulf Coast Area Realtors, Am. Health Care Assn., Westshore Alliance, Columbiana Area C. of C., Youngstown-Warren Area C. of C. Democrat. Roman Catholic. Office: Camacci Real Estate Inc 5533 Mahoning Ave Youngstown OH 44515-2316 E-mail: broker8400@landmarkohio.com, mikec@levebre.com.

CAMACHO, CHARLOTTE DLG, principal, elementary school educator; m. Mike Camacho; 3 children. BA in Early Childhood Edn., San Diego State Univ. Kindergarten, first grade tchr., Saipan, No. Marianas; prin. Gregorio T. Camacho Elem. Sch., Saipan, No. Marianas. Named No. Marianas Islands Tchr. of Yr., 2006. Office: Gregorio T Camacho Elem Sch PO Box 501370 Saipan MP 96950*

CAMACHO, FELIX PEREZ, governor; b. Camp Zama, Japan, Oct. 30, 1957; s. Carlos G. and Lourdes Perez Camacho; m. Joann Gumataotao Garcia Camacho; children: Jessica Lourdes, Felix James, Maria Amparo. BBA in Fin., Marquette U., 1980. Ins. mgr. property casualty divsn. Pacific Fin. Corp.; account adminstr. IBM; dep. dir. Pub. Utility Agy., Guam, 1988—92; senator Commonwealth of Guam, 1992—2002, majority whip, chmn. com. on tourism, 2000—02, gov., 2002—. Mem.: Nat. Coun. State Legislators, Asian Pacific Parliamentarian Union, Knights of Columbus. Republican. Roman Catholic. Office: Office of the Governor PO Box 2950 Hagatna GU 96932*

CAMACHO, GEORGE, internist; b. Savannah, Ga., Nov. 20, 1952; s. D. F. and Carmen Camacho; m. Dolores Knight, Dec. 27, 1974; children: Christopher George, Heather Ashley. BS, U. Houston, 1977; MD, Tex. Tech. Health Scis. Ctr., 1980. Cert. Am. Bd. Internal Medicine. Internal medicine intern Shands Hosp., Jacksonville, Fla., 1984-85, resident, 1985-87. Mem. internal medicine adv. bd. Specialty Hosp., Jacksonville, Fla., 1994—, mem. hosp. bd., 1997-98, ethics com., 1994-97; pharmacy and therapeutics Meml. Hosp., Jacksonville, 1994-96. Fellow ACP; mem. AMA (Physicians Recognition award 1998, 99, 2002, 03), Fla. Med. Soc. Republican. Roman Catholic. Avocations: baseball, basketball, water sports, kids. Office: Internal Medicine Assocs 3627 University Blvd S Ste 415 Jacksonville FL 32216-4299 Office Phone: 904-398-5123. E-mail: gcamach@bellsouth.net.

CAMACHO, PHILIP BRUCE, insurance company executive; CPA. Acct. Pricewaterhouse Coopers LLP; mgmt. positions from v.p. info. systems to exec. v.p. investor rels. Am. Bankers, 1990—99; exec. v.p. sales & mktg. Assurant Group, 1999—2000; pres. Assurant Solutions, 2000—03, pres., CEO, 2003—05; exec. v.p., CFO Assurant Inc., NYC, 2005—07, on adminstrv. leave, 2007—. Office: Assurant Inc 1 Chase Manhattan Plz New York NY 10005*

CAMARA, DAVID JOHN, school librarian; b. Lakewood, NJ, June 3, 1963; s. Michael Armando and Juanita Camara; m. Junko Marlene Kihara, May 2, 1999. BA, Rowan U., Glassboro, NJ, 1986; MA, U. Ga., Athens, 1992; MS, Pratt Inst., Bklyn., 2003. Sr. libr. Bklyn. Pub. Libr., 2003—. Recipient Acad. Achievement award, Pratt Inst. Mem.: Phi Alpha Theta. Avocations: reading, book collecting, travel.

CAMARA, VINCENT ANTONIN REGINALD, statistician, educator, researcher; arrived in U.S., 1992; s. Athanase and Lucie Camara; m. Gislhaine Claire P. Soivilus. BSc Math., U. Dakar, 1984, MS Pure Math., 1986; MS Applied Math., U. North Fla., 1994; PhD Math. and Option Statis., U. South Fla., 1997. Educator stats. U. NC, Charlotte, 1997—98; educator math. and stats. U. South Fla., Tampa, 1998—2001, St. Leo U., Largo, Fla., 2001—. Assoc. dir., rschr. Rsch. Ctr. for Boyesian Applications, Inc., 2003—; presenter in field. Contbr. articles to profl. jours.; mem. editl. bd.: Jour. Modern Applied Statis. Methods. Mem.: The Risk Analysis Soc., The Bayesian Statis. Soc., Am. Statis. Assn., Phi Kappa Phi, Pi Mu Epsilon. Personal E-mail: gvcamara@ij.net. Business E-Mail: vincent.camara@saintleo.edu.

CAMARDA, CHARLES J., astronaut; b. Queens, NY, May 8, 1952; s. Jack and Ray Camarda; m. Melinda Miller; 4 children. BS in Aerospace Engring., Poly. Inst. Bklyn., 1974; MS in Engring. Sci., George Washington U., 1980; PhD in Aerospace Engring., Va. Poly. Inst. and State U., 1990. Rsch. scientist thermal structures br., divsn. structures and materials Langley Rsch. Ctr., NASA, Hampton, Va., 1974—89, head structures and materials tech. maturation team, Nat. Aero-Space Plan program, 1989—94, head thermal structures br., 1994—96; astronaut, mission specialist NASA, Johnson Space Ctr., Houston, 1996—. Assigned tech. duties in the Astronaut Office Spacecraft Systems/Ops. Br.; served on Expedition-8 back-up crew; mission specialist 5 (MS-5), STS-114 (Discovery) Return to Flight mission NASA, 2005. Recipient NASA Cert. Recognition (12), Sustained Superior Performance awards (2), Spl. Achievement awards (2), Technology Commercialization awards(2), Space Station Program Team Excellence award, NASA Group Achievement award, NASA Superior Accomplishment award, NASA Honor award, Rsch. and Devel. 100 award for one of the top Tech. Innovations, Indsl. Rsch. Mag., 1983. Fellow: AIAA (assoc.). Achievements include Holds 7 Patents; development of heat-pipe-cooled sandwich panel. Avocations: racquetball, running, weightlifting, boxing. Office: Astronaut Office/CB NASA Johnson Space Ctr Houston TX 77058

CAMARDO, MICHAEL F., retired aerospace transportation executive; b. Jan. 17, 1942; BS in Econ., Villanova U. With RCA Service Company (merged w/ GE), 1964—90; pres. GE Government Svc. (merged w/ Martin Marietta), 1990—93, Martin Marietta Services Group (merged w/ Lockheed Martin), 1993—95, Lockheed Martin Services Group (now Technology Services Group), 1995—99; exec. v.p., info., tech. svcs. Lockheed Martin Corp, 1999—2006. Bd. of dir. exec. advisory council, Rutgers Univ.; class B dir. Fed. Res. Bank Phila., 2007—. Bd. of dir. American Red Cross. Office: Federal Reserve Bank of Philadelphia 10 Independence Mall Philadelphia PA 19106-1574*

CAMARGO, ANTHONY, jewelry designer; Co-owner, designer (with Nak Armstrong) Anthony Nak, 1998—. Work featured in Vogue, Harper's Bazaar, Town and Country, WWD, Glamour, InStyle, Elle, W, Marie Claire, People, Nat. Jeweler, Basel Mag., and Jewelry Connoisseur. Recipient Fashion Group Internat. Rising Star award, 2003, Town & Country Editors Choice award, 2004, Swarovski Perry Ellis award for accessory design, Council of Fashion Designers of Am., 2005, Couture Internat. Jeweler Retail Design award, Nat. Jeweler and Couture Internat. Jeweler mag., 2005.

CAMAROTTO, DAVID EARLE, lawyer; BA, St. John's U., 1997; JD, William Mitchell Coll. Law, 2000. Bar: Minn. 2001, US Dist. Ct. (dist. Minn.). Jud. law clk. to Hon. John J. Sommerville Hennepin County, Minn.; atty. Johnson & Lindberg, Mpls., Bassford Remele, P.A., Mpls. Named a Rising Star, Minn. Super Lawyers mag., 2006. Mem.: Minn. Def. Lawyers Assn., Hennepin County Bar Assn., Minn. State Bar Assn. Office: Bassford Remele PA 33 S 6th St Ste 3800 Minneapolis MN 55402-3707 Office Phone: 612-376-1618. E-mail: davidc@bassford.com.*

CAMBEIRO, ARTHUR MICHAEL, plastic surgeon; b. Las Vegas, Nev., Aug. 5, 1972; BS in Psychobiology, U. So. Calif., Los Angeles, 1994; MD, U. Colo. Sch. Medicine, Denver, 1998. Cert. Am. Bd. Plastic Surgery, Am. Bd. Surgery. Chief surgery resident, gen. surgery & vascular trauma surgery Phoenix Integrated Surgical Residency Program, 1998—2003; fellow, cosmetic, plastic and reconstructive surgery Mayo Clinic, Rochester, Minn., 2003—05; staff mem., plastic reconstructive surgery St. Rose Hosp., Henderson, Nev., 2005—; private practice SurgiSpa, Henderson, Nev., 2005—. Med. physician treating local population, La Ceiba, Honduras, 1998; plastic surgeon treating children with facial deformities Global Health Outreach, Hanoi, Vietnam, 2005; bd. dir. St. Rose Hosp., Las Vegas, Nev., 2005—. Featured in Profl. Outlook 2006, Luxury Las Vegas, WomensCare. US intern Nev. Senator Harry Reid, Washington, 1990; guest lectr. Bishop Gorman HS, Las Vegas, 1997, Arturo Cambeiro Elementary Sch., Las Vegas, 1997—. Named Best in Beauty, Las Vegas Life, 2005; named one of 210 Top Doctor, 2006, Doctors (Med. Guide), 2006, Top Doc, 2006, 2007, Las Vegas' Top Docs, Beauty, Health, Fitness Mag., 2005—06, Top 40 Under 40, In Business Las Vegas, America's Top Plastic Surgeon 2006-The Guide to America's Top Plastic Surgeons; recipient Excellence in Rsch. award-Outstanding Promise in Surgery, 1998, Owens-Swan award-Outstanding Promise in Surgery, 1998. Mem.: Minn. Med. Assn., Zumbro Valley Med. Soc., Mayo Clinic Fellows' Assn., AMA, Nev. State Med. Assn., Clark County Med. Soc., Am. Soc. Plastic Surgeons, Alpha Epsilon Delta, Psi Beta, Phi Sigma. Office: 2821 W Horizon Ridge Pkwy Ste 100 Henderson NV 89052 Office Phone: 702-566-8300.*

CAMBER, DIANE WOOLFE, museum director; b. Miami Beach, Fla. m. Isaac Camber. BA in Art History, Barnard Coll.; postgrad., Columbia U., Mass. Coll. Art; MEd in Arts Edn., Boston State Coll. Mus. lectr., pub. rels. specialist Albright-Knox Art Gallery, Buffalo, 1962—64; mus. educator De Cordova and Dana Mus., Lincoln, Mass., 1967—68; mus. lectr. Mus. Fine Arts, Boston, 1968—69; art specialist L.A. Pub. Schs., 1970—77; instr. Ft. Lauderdale (Fla.) Art Inst., 1978—79; assoc. dir. Miami (Fla.) Design Preservation League, 1978—80; acting dir. Bass Mus. Art, Miami, 1980—82, exec. dir., chief curator, 1982—2007, dir. emeritus, 2007—. Co-author: Frank Lloyd Wright: Decorative Objects, Prints, Drawings, Florida Projects, 1984. Campaigned to place Miami's Art Deco Dist. on the Nat. Register of Historica Places; bd. dirs. Chaim Gross Found., NY. Recipient Chevalier des Arts et Lettres, French Govt., 1989. Mem.: Fla. Art Mus. Dirs. Assn. (v.p. 1984—86, pres. 1986—), Mus. Trustees Assn. (mem. adv. coun. dirs.), Am. Assn. Art Mus. Dirs. Office: Bass Mus Art 4474 Sheridan Ave Miami Beach FL 33140

CAMBONE, STEPHEN ANTHONY, former federal agency administrator; b. Bronx, NY, 1952; m. Margaret T. Cambone. BA in Polit. Sci., Cath. U., 1973; MA in Polit. Sci., Claremont U., 1977, PhD in Polit. Sci., 1982. Staff mem. Office of Dir. Los Alamos Nat. Lab., 1982—86; dep. dir. strategic analysis SRS Techs. (Washington ops.), 1986—90; dir. for strategic def. policy US Dept. Def., 1990—93; sr. fellow in polit.-mil. studies Ctr. for Strategic and Internat. Studies, 1993—98; staff dir. Commn. to Assess the Ballistic Missile Threat to U.S., 1998; dir. rsch. Inst. for Nat. Strategic Studies, Nat. Def. U., 1998—2000; staff dir. Commn. to Assess U.S. Nat. Security Space Mgmt. and Orgn., 2000—01; spl. asst. to sec. & dep. sec. US Dept. Def., Washington, 2001, prin. dep. under sec. for policy, 2001—02, dir program analysis & evaluation, 2002—03, under sec. for intelligence, 2003—06. Author: NATO's Role in European Stability, Center for Strategic and International Studies, 1995, A New Structure for National Security Policy Planning. Center for Strategic and International Studies, 1998. Recipient Employe of the Yr. award, SRS Technologies (Washington ops.), 1988, Sec. Def. award for Outstanding Svc., US Dept. Def., 1993, Disting. Public Svc. medal, Dept. the Navy, 2003, Disting. Svc. medal, Dept. Def., 2006, Nat. Intelligence. Disting. Svc. medal, 2006.

CAMBOU, BERTRAND, information technology executive; Engring. Degree, Supelec, Paris; D in Elec. Engring., Paris XI U. With Motorola, 1984—99; COO, co-pres., bd. dirs. Gemplus; mng. dir., bd. dirs. Ingenico, 1999—2002; sr. v.p. memory group Advanced Micro Devices, Sunnyvale, Calif., 2002—03, exec. v.p., & pres., CEO Spansion, 2003—05; pres., CEO Spansion Inc., Sunnyvale, Calif., 2005—. Achievements include patents in field. Office: Spansion Inc PO Box 3453 915 Deguigne Dr Sunnyvale CA 94088-3453*

CAMBRIA, CHRISTOPHER C., lawyer, communications systems company executive; b. July 1958; CPA. Assoc. Cravath, Swaine & Moore, 1986—93, Fried, Frank, Harris, Shriver & Jacobson, 1993—97; sr. v.p., sec., gen. counsel L-3 Comm. Holdings, Inc., 1997, sr. v.p., spl. counsel mergers and acquisitions. Office: L-3 Comm Holdings Inc 600 Third Ave New York NY 10016 Office Phone: 212-697-1111. Office Fax: 212-805-5477.*

CAMBRICE, ROBERT LOUIS, lawyer; b. Nov. 23, 1947; s. Eugene and Edna Bertha (Jackson) Cambrice; m. Christine Jackson, Jan. 7, 1972; children: Bryan, Graham. BA cum laude, Tex. So. U., 1969; JD, U. Tex., 1972. Bar: Tex. 1973, U.S. Dist. Ct. (so. dist.) Tex. 1975, U.S. Ct. Appeals (5th cir.) 1975, U.S. Ct. Appeals (11th cir.) 1981, U.S. Supreme Ct. 1981. Asst. atty. City of Houston, 1974-76, 1986—, sr. trial atty. legal dept., 1990-92, chief def. litigation dept., 1992—; pvt. practice Houston, 1976-81; asst. atty. Harris County, Tex., 1981-85; asst. atty. Legal Dept. City Houston, 2005—. Earl Warren fellow, 1969—72. Mem.: NAACP, ABA, Nat. Bar Assn., Alpha Kappa Mu. Roman Catholic. Business E-Mail: Robert.Cambrice@cityofhouston.net.

CAMBY, MARCUS D., professional basketball player; b. Hartford, Conn., Mar. 22, 1974; EdB, U. Mass., 1996. Forward Toronto Raptors, 1996—98, NY Knicks, 1998—2002, Denver Nuggets, 2002—. Tutor math. and English to pub. sch. students. Founder Cambyland Found. Recipient John R. Wooden award, 1996, Naismith award, 1996; named to NBA All-Rookie First Team, 1997, NBA All-Defensive First Team, 2007; named Athlete of Yr. NY mag., 1999, NBA Defensive Player of Yr., 2007. Office: Denver Nuggets 1000 Chopper Cir Denver CO 80204*

CAMDEN, CARL T., human resources company executive; BA in Psychology/Speech, Southwest Baptist Coll., 1975; MA in Clin. Psychology/Speech Comm., Central Mo. State U., 1977; DCom., Ohio State U., 1980. Assoc. prof. comms. Cleve. State U.; co-founder, co-owner North Coast Behavioral Rsch. Group; co-pres. Wyse Advt.; sr. v.p., dir. corp. mktg. KeyCorp.; sr. v.p. corp. mktg. Kelly Svcs. Inc., Troy, Mich., 1995—97, exec. v.p. mktg. & strategy, 1997—98, exec. v.p., field ops. sales & mktg., 1998—2001, exec. v.p., COO, 2001, COO, 2001—06, pres., 2001—, CEO, 2006—. Mem. labor adv. bd. Fed. Reserve Bank Chgo.; mem. ERISA adv. council, 2000—02. Mem. bd. vis. Fuqua Sch. Bus., Duke Univ., Sch. Nursing, Oakland Univ. Recipient William J. Heartwell award, NASWA, 2004. Office: Kelly Svcs Inc 999 W Big Beaver Rd Troy MI 48084-4782*

CAMERA, NICHOLAS J., lawyer; b. NYC, Jan. 12, 1947; s. Anthony Joseph and Cecile Elizabeth (Merritt) C.; m. Barbara Danko, July 10, 1971 (div. 1986); children: David Merritt, Lauren Anne; m. Susan Salorio, June 30, 2001. BS in Econs., Wagner Coll., Staten Island, NY, 1969; JD, Bklyn. Law Sch., 1972; MBA, Fordham U., 1980; MA in Am. Studies, Columbia U., 1997. Bar: NY 1973, US Dist. Ct. (so. and ea. dists. NY) 1973, US Ct. Appeals (2nd cir.) 1973. Assoc. Bigham, Englar, Jones & Houston, NYC, 1972-78; gen. atty. Phelps Dodge Industries, Inc., NYC, 1978-82; asst. gen. counsel Congoleum Corp., Kearney, NJ, 1982, Avon Products, Inc., NYC, 1982-91; positions up to sr. v.p., gen. counsel, sec. Interpublic Group of Cos., NYC, 1993—. Mem. ABA, Assn. of Bar of City of NY, Am. Soc. Corp. Secs. Office: Interpublic Group of Cos 1114 Avenue Of The Americas Fl 19 New York NY 10036 Office Phone: 212-704-1343. Office Fax: 212-704-2236. E-mail: ncamera@interpublic.com.*

CAMERIUS, JAMES WALTER, marketing educator, corporate researcher; b. Chgo., June 14, 1939; s. Wilbert Albert and Violet Elna (Johnson) C. BS, No. Mich. U., 1961; MS, U. N.D., 1963; postgrad., U. Okla., 1974-77. From instr. to assoc. prof. No. Mich. U., Marquette, 1963-90, prof. mktg., 1990—. Lectr. in field; adv. bd. S.E. Advanced Tech. Edn. Consortium. Mem. editl. bd. Bus. Case Jour., Jour. SMET Edn. Cir. lay rep. Luth. Ch.-Mo. Synod, 1987-89; pres. Redeemer Luth. Ch., Marquette, 1989-90, sec. to ch. coun., 1990-92, bd. elders, 1993-98, v.p., 2000-2001, pres. 2001-02; mktg. track chair N.Am. Case Rsch. and Mktg. Assn., 1997-2003. Recipient MAGB Disting. Prof. award, 1995; Rsch. grantee Direct Selling Edn. Found., 1987-2002, Walker L. Cisler Sch. No. Mich. U., 1990, Filene Rsch. Inst., 1994; named Outstanding Case Reviewer, Case Rsch. Jour., 1998. Fellow: Acad. Mktg.; mem.: World Assn. Case Method Rsch. and Application (case colloquium dir. 1997—, adv. bd., global case amb. 2006), N.Am. Case Rsch. Assn. (bd. dirs. 2003—, newsletter editor), Soc. Case Rsch. (v.p. 1990—91, case workshop dir. 1999, pres.-elect 2000, pres. 2001—02, archivist, Phil Fisher Svc.

award 2006, Disting. Svc. award 2007), Am. Mktg. Assn., Econ. Club, Alpha Kappa Psi (Alumni award). Democrat. Home: 171 Lakewood Ln Marquette MI 49855-9543 Office: No Mich U Mktg Dept Marquette MI 49855 Office Phone: 906-227-1245. Business E-Mail: jcameriu@nmu.edu.

CAMERON, ALEX BRIAN, accountant, educator; b. Fresno, Calif., Nov. 20, 1943; s. Alexander Archer and Francette (Maize) C.; m. Judy Lea Helphrey, June 7, 1969; children: Michelle, Michael. BA, Eastern Wash. U., 1969, MBA, 1970; PhD, U. Utah, 1982. Cert. in mgmt. acctg. Mgr. prodn. planning Bunker Hill Mining Co., Kellog, Idaho, 1970-77; asst. prof. Wash. State U., Pullman, 1978-79; assoc. prof. Eastern Wash. U., Cheney, 1981-87, prof., 1987—, chmn. dept. acctg., 1988-89, assoc. dean, 1990-97, interimm v.p. bus. and fin., 1998-99, interim dean Coll. Bus. and Pub. Adminstrn., 1999-2001. Contbr. articles to profl. jours. Avocations: sailing, golf, volleyball. Home: 15212 Pinnacle Ln Veradale WA 99037-9163 Office: 668 N Riverpoint Blvd Spokane WA 99202-1677 Home Phone: 509-921-5815. Personal E-mail: jcameron55@comcast.net. Business E-Mail: acameron@ewu.edu.

CAMERON, CAM (MALCOLM CAMERON), professional football coach; b. Chapel Hill, NC, Feb. 6, 1961; m. Missy Cameron; children: Tommy, Daniel, Christopher, Elizabeth BS in bus. mgmt., Ind. U., 1983. Grad. asst. football coach U. Mich., 1984-85, wide receivers coach, 1986—89, quarterbacks & receivers coach, 1990—93; quarterbacks coach Wash. Redskins, 1994-96; head football coach Ind. U., 1997—2001; offensive coord. San Diego Chargers, 2002—06; head coach Miami Dolphins, 2007—. Recipient Trester award for mental attitude, 1979; named Vigo County's Athlete of Yr., 1978-79, Nat. Athlete of Yr., Fellowship Christian Athletes, 1979 Office: c/o Miami Dolphins 7500 SW 30th St Fort Lauderdale FL 33314*

CAMERON, CARL (KARL LAMBERG-KARLOVSKY), political correspondent; b. New Haven, Sept. 22, 1961; s. C.C. and Martha Lamberg-Karlovsky; children: Kyle, Ryan. With Sta. WFEA, Manchester, NH, 1985, Sta. WZID, Manchester, NH, 1985; polit. dir. Sta. WMUR-TV, Manchester, NH; chief congl., polit. corr. FOX News Channel, Washington, 1996—2005, chief White House corr., 2005—. Recipient numerous AP awards, 1987-95, Assn. of Broadcasters awards, 1987-99. Office: FOX News Channel 400 N Capitol St NW Ste 550 Washington DC 20001 E-mail: cameron@foxnews.com.

CAMERON, DAVID RONALD, entrepreneur, historian, researcher; b. Jamaica, NY, June 21, 1941; s. David Campbell and Geraldine Norene Cameron; m. Ellie Kantartzis, Jan. 26, 1969; children: Nicole Elizabeth Cameron Mikolak, James David. Clk. Triple S. Stamp Redemption, South Glens Falls, NY, 1963—64; shipping clk. Shell Oil Co., Cleve., 1964—68; asst. traffic mgr. Krogers, Solon, Ohio, 1968—71; transp. mgr. Glidden-Durkee, Cleve., 1972—76; procurement analyst Ford Motor Co., Brookpark, Ohio, 1977—2001; prin., owner Dave's Record Den, Strongsville, Ohio, 1985—. Airmen 1st class USAF, 1959—63. Mem.: Clan Cameron Ohio, Strongsville Soc. Model RR Engrs. (founder, pres. 1980). Avocations: record collecting, WWII naval history, writing. Office: Daves Record Den PO Box 360948 Strongsville OH 44136-1020

CAMERON, DONALD B., JR., lawyer; BA, Kenyon Coll., 1971; JD, Vanderbilt U., 1974; LLM, Vrije Universiteit Brussels, 1975. Bar: DC 1979, US Ct. Internat. Trade, Ct. Appeals, Fed. Cir. Ptnr. litig., co-chair Internat. Trade Group Kaye Scholer LLP, Washington, DC. Mem.: ABA. Office: Kaye Scholer LLP McPherson Bldg 901 Fifteenth Street, NW, Ste 1100 Washington DC 20005 Office Phone: 202-682-3630. E-mail: dcameron@kayescholer.com.

CAMERON, DONALD JOHN, retired commodities trader; b. St. Louis, Aug. 17, 1928; s. James and Florence Frances Cameron; m. Beverly Frances Rapp, Dec. 27, 1952; children: John Braden, Paul James. BS in Bus. Adminstrn., Washington U., St. Louis, 1952. Grain buyer Ralston Purina Co., St. Louis, 1954—56, Charlotte, NC, 1956—61; owner and founder Cameron Brokerage Co., Charlotte, 1965—99; ret. Arbitrator arbitration appeals com. Nat. Grain and Feed Assn., Washington, 1988—98. Chmn. blood program com. Red Cross, Charlotte, 1958—60; chmn. Catawba Valley Scottish Soc., Huntersville, NC, 1992—96; chieftan Clan Cameron N.Am., 1987—2005; comdr. Knights Templar, NC, 1999—2007. 2nd lt. US Army, 1952—53, ETO. Mem.: Sr. Forum (assoc.). Conservative. Roman Catholic. Avocations: golf, bridge, travel. Home: 5413 Stallworth Dr Charlotte NC 28226 Home Phone: 704-540-0164. Personal E-mail: doncameron@bellsouth.net.

CAMERON, DORT, electronics executive; b. 1945; m. Elizabeth Cameron. Grad., Middlebury Coll. With Drexel Burnham Comml. Paper, Inc., Dallas, 1966—84, pres.; with Investment Ltd. Partnership, Greenwich, Conn., 1984—99, mng. gen. ptnr.; chmn. Entex Info. Svcs., Rye Brook, NY, 1993—99; trustee emeritus Middlebury Coll. Bd. mem. Rippowan Cisqua Sch. Westchester Land Trust; dir. First Marblehead Corp. Office: Airlie Group 115 E Putnam Ave Greenwich CT 06830-5643

CAMERON, DOUGLAS E., lawyer; b. Wheeling, W.Va., Feb. 19, 1959; BA in economics/acctg. summa cum laude, Bethany Coll., W.Va., 1981; JD magna cum laude, U. Pitts., 1984. Bar: Pa. 1984, US Ct. Appeals 2nd Cir., US Ct. Appeals 3rd Cir., US Ct. Appeals 7th Cir., US Ct. Appeals Fed. Cir., US Dist. Ct. We. Dist. Pa., US Dist. Ct. Mid. Dist. Pa., US Dist. Ct. Ea. Dist. Pa., Supreme Ct. Pa., Supreme Ct. Appeals W.Va., US Supreme Ct. Assoc. Reed Smith LLP, Pitts., 1984—93, ptnr., 1993—; practice group leader ins. coverage group, 2003—. Office: Reed Smith LLP 435 Sixth Ave Pittsburgh PA 15219 Office Phone: 412-288-4104. Office Fax: 412-288-3063. Business E-Mail: dcameron@reedsmith.com.

CAMERON, DUKE EDWARD, cardiac surgeon, educator; b. Miami, Fla., Mar. 9, 1952; s. Edward John and Joanne (Abbott) C.; m. Claudia Oppenheim; children: Danielle, Nicole. AB, Harvard Coll., 1974; MD, Yale U., 1978. Resident gen. surgery Yale-New Haven Hosp., 1978-84, resident cardiothoracic surgery, 1984-87; prof. surgery, dir. pediatric cardiac surgery Johns Hopkins Hosp., Balt. Fellow ACS; mem. Soc. Thoracic Surgeons, So. Thoracic Surg. Assn., Am. Assn. Thorac Surg. Home: 2209 South Rd Baltimore MD 21209-4437 Office: Johns Hopkins Hosp Blalock 618 600 N Wolfe St Baltimore MD 21287 Home Phone: 410-542-9047; Office Phone: 410-955-2698. Business E-Mail: dcameron@jhmi.edu.

CAMERON, FRANCES MARILYN, elementary school educator; b. Denison, Tex., July 19, 1936; d. Cornelius McLeod and Duressie Amelia Andersno; m. Leo Samuel Cameron, Apr. 6, 1963 (dec. Feb. 8, 1973); children: Reginald Eugene, Derrick Leon. BS, Prairie View A&M U., Tex., 1954—58, MEd, 1959—63. Cert. tchr., elem. & secondary edn. Tex. Dept Edn. 4th grade tchr. Floydada Pub. Schs., Tex., 1958—59; 3rd grade tchr. Denison Ind. Sch. Dist., 1959—62; tchr., 8th grade & typing Bonham Ind. Sch. Dist., 1962—64; 3rd grade tchr. Denison Ind. Sch. Dist., 1965—94; reading Edison-Sherman, Sherman, 1995—2000; remedial reading tchr. Sherman Ind. Sch. Dist., 2000—. Mem., rep. Texoma Coun. of GDU, Sherman, 1992—2002; sec., mem. Denison Ind. Sch. Dist. Bd., 1997—, Texoma Edn. Fed. Credit U., Sherman, 1997—. Mem. N. Town Shalom Corp., Denison, 1992, NAACP, Sherman & Dennison, 1999. Recipient State Retiree of Yr. award, Tex. Classroom Tchr. Assn., Austin, 1995, Dream Maker award, Tex. House of Rep., Denison, 1999, Edn. award, NAACP, Sherman, 1999. Mem.: Delta Kappa Gamma. Avocations: travel, working with youth, reading, stage plays. Home: 800 W Elm St Denison TX 75020

CAMERON, HEATHER ANNE, publishing executive; b. Montreal, Quebec, Can., Mar. 12, 1951; came to U.S., 1981; d. Douglas George and Jeanne Sutherland (Thompson) C.; m. Ward Eric Shaw, Dec. 20, 1980; 1 child, Geoffrey Cameron. BA, Queen's U., Kingston, Ont., Can., 1973; MLS, McGill U., Montreal, 1977. Head reference and bibliography sect. Nat. Libr. Can., Ottawa, 1977-80; head editl. dept. Librs. Unltd., Inc., Denver, 1981-86; v.p. acquisitions and editl. devel. ABC-CLIO, Inc., Santa Barbara, Calif., 1986-92, pres., pub. Santa Barbara, Denver and, Eng., 1992-97; v.p., gen. mgr. Westgroup, San Francisco, 1997—. Bd. dirs. Friends of Librs. U.S.A., v.p., 1996, pres., 1997—. Mem. ALA (com. chair 1993—), Friends of Librs., USA (dir. 1994—, pres. 1997-2000), Amnesty Internat., Phi Beta Mu. Office: Thomson-West 425 Market St San Francisco CA 94105 Office Phone: 415-344-5010. Business E-Mail: heather.cameron@thomson.com.

CAMERON, JAMES, film director, screenwriter, producer; b. Kapuskasing, Ont., Can., Aug. 16, 1954; s. Philip and Shirley Cameron; m. Sharon Williams, 1974 (div. 1985); m. Gale Ann Hurd, 1985 (div. 1989); m. Katheryn Bigelow, 1989 (div. 1991); m. Linda Hamilton, 1997 (div. 1999), 1 child, Josephine Archer Cameron; m. Suzy Amis, 2000; children, Clair and Elizabeth Rose. Grad. in Physics, Calif. State U., Fullerton. Head Lightstorm Entertainment, Burbank, Calif., 1992—; CEO Digital Domain, 1993—. Art dir. Battle Beyond the Stars, 1980, prodn. designer Galaxy of Terror, 1981, creator spl. effects Escape from New York, 1981; dir.: (films) Piranha II: The Spawning, 1981, Terminator 2 3-D, 1996; (TV films) Earthship, 2001; screenwriter Rambo: First Blood Part II, 1985, Strange Days, 1995, exec. prodr. Point Break, 1991, dir., screenwriter Xenogenesis, 1978, The Terminator, 1984, Aliens, 1986, The Abyss, 1989, dir., prodr., editor (films) Titanic, 1997 (Academy award for Best Picture and Best Dir., 9 others, 1997), dir., prodr. Ghosts of the Abyss, 2002, (TV) Expedition Bismarck, 2002, dir., prodr., screenwriter Terminator II: Judgement Day, 1991 (6 Academy award nominations, Ray Bradbury award for dramatic screenwriting, 5 Saturn awards Acad. Sci. Fiction, 5 MTV Movie awards, People's Choice award), True Lies, 1994, writer, exec. prodr. (TV series) Dark Angel, 2000—; author: (films) Terminator 3: Rise of the Machines, 2003; prodr.: (films) Volcanos of the Deep Sea, 2003, Aliens of the Deep, 2005; (TV films) Titanic Adventure, 2005, Last Mysteries of the Titanic, 2005; (documentaries) The Lost Tomb of Jesus, 2007. Mem. adv. bd. Science Fiction Mus. and Hall of Fame. Mem.: Am. Cinema Editors. Office: Lightstorm Entertainment 919 Santa Monica Blvd Santa Monica CA 90401-2704*

CAMERON, JEFFREY M., lawyer; b. June 1970; Assoc. Vinson & Elkins LLP, 1996—2004; v.p., legal counsel, sec. Group 1 Automotive, 2004—06. Office Phone: 713-647-5700. Office Fax: 713-647-5800. Business E-Mail: jcameron@group1auto.com.*

CAMERON, JOHN CLIFFORD, lawyer, health science association administrator; b. Phila., Sept. 17, 1946; m. Eileen Duffy, July 12, 1975; children: Christopher, Meghan. BA, U. Pitts., 1969; MBA, Temple U., 1972; JD, Widener U., 1976; LLM, NYU, 1980. Bar: Pa. 1977, N.J. 1977, Md. 1995. Asst. adminstr. Phila. Psychiatric Ctr., 1972-76; jud. clk. to presiding justice N.J. Superior Ct., Newark, 1976-77; asst. adminstr. St. Elizabeth Hosp., Elizabeth, NJ, 1977; v.p. corp. legal affairs Methodist Hosp., Phila., 1978-94; legal cons. North Penn Hosp, Lansdale, Pa., 1994-95; counsel, legal adminstr. Hodes, Ulman, Pessin & Katz, P.A., Towson, Md., 1995-96; asst. to pres. Temple U. Health Sys., Phila., 1996—; asst. sec. Neumann Med. Ctr., Phila., 1997—2002, Jeanes Hosp., Phila., 1997—, Northwood Nursing Home, Phila., 1997—2002, Temple Physicians, Inc., Phila., 1997—, Temple Univ. Hosp., Phila., 1997—, Lower Bucks Hosp., Bristol, Pa., 1997—2002, Episcopal Hosp., Phila., 1997—, Temple U. Children's Med. Ctr., Phila., 1997, Northeastern Hosp., Phila., 1997—, Temple Continuing Care Ctr., Phila., 1997—2002. Sec. Suthbrelt Properties, Ltd., Phila., 1981-94, Asbury Corp., Wilmington, Del., 1982-94, Healthmark, Inc., Moorestown, N.J., 1982-94, Meth. Hosp. Nursing Ctr., Phila., 1983-94; asst. sec. various hosps. and nursing homes, 1997—, instr. Grad. Sch. Mgmt., Pa. State U., 1991—; instr. mgmt. dept. Neumann Coll., 1991-96; instr. bus. divsn. Rosemont Coll., 1995-96. Contbr. articles to profl. jours. Mem. campaign United Way, Phila., 1979-94; mem. health and welfare com. United Meth. Eastern Pa. Conf., 1978-94; advisor Explorer Post, Boy Scouts Am., 1988-94; mem. steering com. Golden Cross, Phila., 1984-94; sec. Tredyffrin Twp. Park and Recreation Bd., 1987-95; alumni rep. Widener U.; mem. environ. adv. com. and open space task force Tredyffrin Twp., 1991-95. Fellow Am. Coll. Healthcare Execs. (chmn. bylaws com. 1995-96); mem. ABA, N.J. Bar Assn., Pa. Bar Assn., Phila. Bar Assn., Am. Hosp. Assn., Hosp. Assn. Pa., Swedish Colonial Soc. (bd dirs. 1992—, gov. 1993-95), Sons of Union Vets. of Civil War, SAR. Avocations: swimming, music. Home: 1410 Church Rd Malvern PA 19355-9714

CAMERON, JOHN M., nuclear scientist, educator, administator; b. Aug. 9, 1940; BSc, Queens U., Ireland, 1962; MSc, UCLA, 1965, PhD, 1967. Tech. asst. U.K. Atomic Energy Authority, Eng., 1962-63; asst. prof. UCLA, 1967-68; rsch. assoc. U. Wash., Seattle, 1968-70; asst. prof. to prof. U. Alta., 1970-87; dir. Cyclotron Facility, prof. dept. physics Ind. U., Bloomington, 1987—. Asst. dir. initial ops. TRIUMF, Vancouver, 1973-74; vis scientist U. Paris, SIN Switzerland, 1977-78; staff scientist Nat. Saturne Lab., France, 1981-82; dir. Nuclear Rsch. Ctr., U. Alta., 1985-87. Fellow Am. Phys. Soc. Office: IN Univ Bloomington Cyclotron Facility 2401 Milo Sampson Ln Bloomington IN 47408-1368 Office Phone: 812-855-3316.

CAMERON, JOSEPH ALFRED, III, pharmacist; b. Kans. City, Mar. 31, 1974; s. Roger Williams and Lauren Sue (Bennett) C.; m. Diana Frances Cline, May 22, 1999; children: Christopher Joseph, Catherine Frances. BS in Biology, Lincoln U., Jefferson City, 1995—98; PharmD, U. Mo., Kans. City, 1999—2004. Cert. pharmacotherapy specialist Bd. Pharm. Specialits, DC, 2006. Pharmacy practice resident U. Mo. Health Care, Columbia, 2004—05, ICU critical care pharmacist, 2005—. Contbr. articles to profl. jours. Recipient Patient Care award for recognition of outstanding performance during pharmacy rotations, GlaxoSmithKline, 2003—04. Mem.: Mid-Mo. Soc. Health Sys. Pharmacy (pres. 2007), Mo. Soc. Health Sys. Pharmacy, Am. Coll. Clin. Pharmacy, Am. Soc. Health Sys. Pharmacy. Meth. Avocations: reading, swimming, movies, volleyball, hiking. Home Phone: 573-445-7747. Business E-Mail: cameronj@health.missouri.edu.

CAMERON, KAY, conductor, composer; b. Robbins, NC; d. Joe and Gladys Cameron. MusB, U. N.C., 1972, MusM, 1973. Music dir. Kennedy Ctr. For the Performing Arts, Washington, 1994—; condr. Words and Music, Musicals in Concert; music supr. Sondheim Celebration. Tchr. Richmond Pub. Schs., Va., 1973-77; music dir., condr. broadway and nat. tours, N.Y., 1978-1996; arranger, orchestrator musicals and TV, 1979-1996; vis. lectr. U. N.C., Wilmington, 1997-98; condr. concert featuring Cy Coleman, Kennedy Ctr. Opera House Orch. Music dir., condr. State Fair, The Will Rogers Follies, Phantom, The King and I, On The 20th Century, Sugar Babies, Showboat, The Sound of Music, Salute To The Broadway Composer, The Sound Of Rodgers And Hammerstein, New Moon, La Cage Aux Folles (opera) Amelia Goes To The Ball, Candide, Die Fledermaus, Hansel and Gretel, The Medium, Madama Butterfly, The Telephone, others; arranger, orchestrator Show Boat on PBS, United Nations 40th Anniversary, Herman & Soundheim Together, (compositions) A Christmas Carol, Heroes, others. Mem. Am. Fedn. Musicians. Home: 121 Loder Ave Wilmington NC 28409 E-mail: kcameron@kennedy-center.org.

CAMERON, KENZIE ALYNN, medical researcher, educator; BS in Speech, Northwestern U., Evanston, Ill., 1988—92; MA, Mich. State U., E. Lansing, 1994—96, PhD, 1996. Asst. prof., dept. speech comm. U. Ga., Athens, 1998—2003; asst. prof., rsch., Ctr. Comm. and Medicine/Gen. Internal Medicine Northwestern U. Feinberg Sch. Medicine, Chgo., 2003—. Participant summer Inst. on Randomized Controlled Trials Involving Behavioral Interventions NIH, 2005. Contbr. articles to profl. jours. Recipient Excellence in Tchg. citation, Mich. State U., 1998, Outstanding Faculty Academic Advisor award, U. Ga., 2002, J. Hatten Howard III Tchg. award, 2003; grantee Faculty Mentoring Fellowship, Inst. Behavioral Rsch., U. Ga., 1999—2000; Lilly Tchg. Fellowship, U. Ga., 2000—02, grant, Ctr. Disease Control & Prevention, Northwestern U., 2004—07. Mem.: APHA, European Assn. Comm. Healthcare, Nat. Comm. Assn. (student rep. 1996—97, Disting. Article award, Applied Comm. Divsn. 1996), Phi Beta Delta, Phi Kappa Phi Honor Soc. (life). Office: Northwestern Univ 676 N St Clair St Ste 200 Chicago IL 60611 Home Phone: 773-276-7198.

CAMERON, KIRK MACGREGOR DRUMMOND, statistician; b. Glendale, Calif., Oct. 27, 1962; s. Paul Drummond and Virginia May (Rusthoi) C.; m. Kelly Mitchell, May 21, 1994; chilre: Kaitlyn Gray, Kit MacGregor, Kyle Henry, Kristyn Virginia, Kieran Timothy. BS Math., U. Nebr., 1984; MS Statis., Stanford U., 1989, PhD Statis., 1990. Statis. cons. Family Rsch. Inst., Colorado Springs, Colo., 1983—; sr. statis. Sci. Applications Internat. Corp., McLean, Va., 1990—95; pres., statis. cons. Macstat Cons., Colorado Springs, 1995—. Bd. dirs. Family Rsch. Inst., editor, 1995—; cons. and nat expert on groundwater monitoring optimization to USAF, EPA, and Dept. Energy; tech. peer reviewer to USEPA; expert legal witness regarding stats. of groundwater monitoring; reviewer jours. in field; expert witness in field. Contbr. articles to profl. jours.; contbr. scientific papers. Youth counselor McLean Bible Ch., 1991-94; Sunday sch. leader Village Seven Presbyn., Colorado Springs, 1995—2002, 2005-07; county del. El Paso County Rep. Conv., Colorado Springs, 1998; judge sci. fair Classical Acad., Colorado Springs, 2005, 07. Fellow NSF, 1984, Pew Found., 1990; grantee Dept. Def. Environ. Security Tech. Cert. Program, 2006. Mem. ASCE (task com. on long term groundwater monitoring design, 2001), Am. Statis. Assn., Inst. Math. Stats., Rand Alumni Assn., Phi Beta Kappa. Achievements include development of groundwater monitoring optimization software. Avocations: rock collecting, guitar, hiking, camping, tennis. Office Phone: 719-532-0453. Personal E-mail: kcmacstat@qwest.net.

CAMERON, LUCILLE WILSON, retired dean; b. Nashua, NH, Dec. 21, 1932; d. Hugh Alexander and Louise Perham (Baldwin) C.; m. James Robert Doris, Aug. 19, 1976; children: Glenn A. Browning, Gail W. Browning, Valerie B. Cruickshank. BA, U. R.I., 1964, MLS, 1972. Social case worker R.I. Dept. Pub. Assistance, Providence, 1964-70; asst. circulation libr. U. R.I. Libr., Kingston, 1970-72, reserve libr., 1972-73, reference/bibliographer, 1973-88, head reference unit, 1983-86, chair pub. svcs., 1988-89, interim dean, 1989-90, dean, 1990—, dean emerita. Bd. trustees North Scituate (R.I.) Pub. Libr., 1995, pres., 1996. Co-author: Labor and Industrial Relations Journals and Serials, 1989; contbr. articles to profl. jours. Bd. trustees North Scituate (R.I.) Pub. Libr., 1995—, pres., 1996—. Recipient Computerized Intergrated Libr. System award Champlin Founds., Providence, 1989, 90, 91, Coll. Tech. Libr. Program award U.S. Dept. Edn., Washington, 1990, Disting. Alumna award Grad. Sch. Libr. and Info. Studies, U. R.I., Kingston, 1991. Mem. ALA, Assn. Coll. and Rsch. Librs., Consortium R.I. Acad. and Rsch. Librs., Higher Edn. Libr. Info. Network (chair), Univ. Press New England (gov.), North Scituate (R.I.) Pub. Libr. Assn. (bd. trustees 1995—, pres. 1996—), Alpha Kappa Delta.

CAMERON, NICHOLAS ALLEN, manufacturing executive; b. Phila., Jan. 6, 1939; s. Nicholas Guyot and Katherine (Rogers) C.; m. Leslie Wood, Dec. 14, 1974; children: Christopher Wilson, Pamela Wilson. BS, Yale U., 1960. Treas. Allied Corp., Morristown, NJ, 1979-81, v.p. and treas., 1981-82, v.p. fin., 1982-83, v.p. planning and devel., 1983-85; sr. v.p. planning, devel. and adminstrn. Allied-Signal Inc., Morristown, NJ, 1985-86; sr. v.p. tech. and bus. devel. Bendix Aerospace-Allied-Signal, Inc., Arlington, Va., 1986-87; group pres. Allied-Signal Aerospace, 1988; sr. v.p. ops. svcs. Allied-Signal, Inc., Morristown, NJ, 1988-90, sr. v.p., gen. mgr. chem. intermediates, 1990-95. Bd. dirs. Morristown Meml. Health Found., 1996—2001, United Way of Morris County, Morristown, 1980-86, 90-98, campaign chmn., 1991, chief vol. officer, 1993-95, bd. chmn., 1996-98; bd. dirs. Morris 2000, 1990-97, 99-2003, chmn., 1993-96; adv. bd. Morristown Hosp., 1998—; mem. Morris County Park Commn., 1999—, pres., 2005-07. Mem. Morris County C. of C. (bd. dirs. 1975-86, 1990-98), Tau Beta Pi. Clubs: St. Elmo Soc. (New Haven); Morris County Golf. Republican. Episcopalian. Home and Office: 20 Pippins Way Morristown NJ 07960 Office Phone: 973-683-0344. Personal E-mail: ncame1639@aol.com.

CAMERON, PAUL DRUMMOND, health facility administrator; b. Pitts., Nov. 9, 1939; s. Nelson Drummond and Veronica (Witco) C.; m. Virginia May Rusthoi; 3 children. BA, L.A. Pacific Coll., 1961; MA, Calif. State U., LA, 1962; PhD, U. Colo., 1966. Asst. prof. psychology Stout State U., Menomonie, Wis., 1966-67, Wayne State U., Detroit, 1967-69; assoc. prof. psychology U. Louisville, 1970-73, Fuller Grad. Sch. Psychology, Pasadena, Calif., 1976-79; assoc. prof. marriage and family U. Nebr., Lincoln, 1979-80; pvt. practice psychologist Lincoln, 1980-83; chmn. Family Rsch. Inst., Washington, 1982-95, Colo. Springs, 1995—. Reviewer Am. Psychologist, Jour. Gerontology, Psychol. Reports, Brit. Med. Jour., Can. Med. Assn. Jour.; presenter, expert witness, cons. in field. Author: Exposing the AIDS Scandal, 1988, The Gay 90's, 1993; contbr. articles to profl. jours. Mem. Ea. Psychol. Assn. Republican. Lutheran. Achievements include pioneer investigation of health effects of second-hand tobacco smoke; investigator of first comprehensive national random sample of sexuality. Office: Family Rsch Inst PO Box 62640 Colorado Springs CO 80962-2640 Home Phone: 303-681-3124; Office Phone: 303-681-3113. E-mail: pdcameron@juno.com.

CAMERON, RITA GIOVANNETTI, writer, publishing executive; b. Washington; d. Joseph Angelo and Adeline Katherine (Fochett) C. BS with honors, U. Md., 1957; MEd, Am. U., Washington, 1962; DEd, Nova U., 1978. Tchr. D.C. pub. schs., Washington, 1959-64; prin. Prince George's County (Md.) Pub. Schs., 1964-73, 76-84; supr. instrn. K-12 Prince George's County pub. schs., 1973-76; free-lance writer ednl. materials Media, Materials Inc., Balt., 1965-75, Learning Well, Balt., 1995, World Class Learning Materials, Inc., Balt., 2000—; free-lance writer travel articles AAA, Washington, 1978-83; owner, pub. Sch. House Global Enterprises, Fort Washington, Md., 1980—. Presenter, cons. to sch. systems and ednl. orgns., 1985—. Author: Let's Learn About Maryland and Prince George's County, 1970, Let's Learn About Maryland, 1972, 95, Super Sub! Or How to Substitute Teach in Elementary School, 1974, AAA Travel articles and Traffic Safety Teacher Guide Grades 4-6, 1982, 83; author, pub.: The Master Teacher's Plan and Record Book, 1985, The School House Encyclopedia of Educational Programs and Activities, 1991; author, publisher and nat. marketer of 89 social studies and sci. ednl. materials for students grades 4-10; developer/owner School House Global Enterprises Pub. Co. Food preparer So Others Might Eat, Washington, 1985—, food preparer for Missions of Charity Home for AIDS Victims, Washington, 1992—, sponsor Christian Found. for Children and Aging, 1998—. Recipient Outstanding Citizenship award DAR, 1954, Nat. Tchr. award Expedition Nat. Tchr. Awards Program, 1960-61, Outstanding Tchr. Sci. award D.C. Coun. Engring. and Archtl. Soc. and Washington Acad. Scis., 1964, Outstanding Educator of Yr. award Prince George's County Bd. Edn., 1982-83, Am. Hist. award DAR, 1987, Outstanding Contbn. to Bicentennial Leadership Project award Couns. for Advancement of Citizenship, 1989. Mem.: Mt. Vernon Assn., Kennedy Ctr. Stars, Ford Theater, Smithsonian Assocs. (contbg. mem. Smithsonian), Phi Kappa Phi. Roman

Catholic. Avocations: art, music, theater, antiques, travel. Office: Sch House Global Enterprises PO Box 441028 Fort Washington MD 20749-1028 Office Phone: 301-292-8877. Office Fax: 301-292-9744. Business E-Mail: dawn@schoolhouseglobalenterprises.com. *In one form or another, I have been a teacher all my life. It's been an enormous responsibility, matched only by enormous satisfaction. The knowledge, skills, love for learning, and feelings of self-worth given to students are among the finest gifts they will ever receive.*

CAMERON, THOMAS WILLIAM LANE, investment company executive; b. Newton, Mass., Feb. 19, 1927; s. Percy G. and Mary W.D. (Mitchell) C.; m. Carol Louise Soliday, June 17, 1950; children: Helen Delone, Thomas Mitchell (dec.). AB cum laude, Harvard, 1948, MBA, 1951. With sales dept. Procter & Gamble, Boston, 1951-53; with Hopper, Soliday, & Co., Inc., Phila., 1953-66, ptnr., 1961—, pres., 1966-72, chmn., 1972-83; dir. Hopper, Soliday & Co., Inc., 1983-86; sr. v.p. Interstate/Johnson Lane, Johns Island, SC, 1986—99; chmn. Sovereign Investors Inc., 1979-91; vice chmn. John Hancock Sovereign Investors, 1991-96; chmn. Cameron & Assocs., Inc., 1999—, Rising Dividend Growth Fund, 2004—. Chmn. Phila.-Balt.-Washington Stock Exch., 1970-74, bd. govs., 1963-75; chmn. Dividend Growth Advisers, 2004—. Bd. mgrs. Franklin Inst., 1970-90, chmn., 1978-81; bd. dirs. Holling Cancer Ctr., Med. U. S.C., 1992—2002. Served with USNR, 1944-46. Mem.: Waynesborough Country (Paoli, Pa.) (pres. 1965-67); Harvard (Phila.) (pres. 1965-66), Harvard Bus. Sch. (Phila.) (pres. 1962-64). Office: Cameron & Assocs Inc 1894 Andell Bluff Blvd Johns Island SC 29455-8222

CAMERON, TIMOTHY G., lawyer; b. Auckland, New Zealand, May 6, 1971; B.Com., LLB, Univ. Auckland, 1994, M.ComLaw, 1997; LLM, Univ. Chgo., 1998. Bar: New Zealand 1994, NY 1999, lic.: US Tax Ct. 2003. Assoc. Russell McVeagh McKenzie Bartleet & Co., Auckland, New Zealand, 1994—97, Cravath, Swaine & Moore LLP, NYC, 1998—2005, ptnr., litig., 2005—. Mem.: ABA, NY State Bar Assn., Auckland and New Zealand Dist. Law Societies. Office: Cravath Swaine & Moore LLP Worldwide Plz 825 Eighth Ave New York NY 10019-7475 Office Phone: 212-474-1120. Office Fax: 212-474-3700. Business E-Mail: tcameron@cravath.com.

CAMERON-MICKENS, VERTRELLE DIANE, singer, conductor, voice educator; b. Florence, SC, May 15, 1956; d. Rudolph Norman and Mary Elizabeth Cameron; m. Hayward Ivan Mickens, Oct. 6, 1984; children: Regina Allyson Mickens, Regina Allyson Mickens. B of Music Performance, Fisk U., Nashville, 1978; M of Music in Vocal Performance, Johnson Hopkins U., Balt., 1983; D of Musical Arts, U. Ky., Lexington, 2005. Dir. music, condr. Second Presbyn. Ch., Lexington, Ky., 1996—; voice faculty Ea. Ky. U., Richmond, 1999—. Artistic dir. Repertory Theatre Co. of the VI, St. Thomas, VI, 1989—93. Singer (soprano soloist): Akron Symphony, Lexington Philharmonic, Altenburg Festival Symphony; singer: Jubilee Singers, 1974—78, (Broadway plays) Porgy and Bess. Lymon T. Johnson Rsch. Assoc. fellow, U. Ky., 1996—2000. Fellow: IBM Watson Found. (life); mem.: Nat. Assn. Tchrs. Singing (cert.). Avocations: travel, swimming. Home: 916 Woodglen Ct Lexington KY 40515 Home Phone: 859-420-6560; Office Phone: 859-254-7768. Office Fax: 859-252-3857; Home Fax: 859-252-3057. Personal E-mail: vertrelle.mickens@eku.edu. Business E-Mail: vertrelle@2preslex.org.

CAMERY, JOHN WILLIAM, computer engineer; b. Cin., Feb. 5, 1951; s. Donald Otis and Mary Lynne (Edgington) C. *In July, 1997, using his frequent flyer miles, he organized the family vacation. His parents, well known in amateur radio and Army MARS, his Aunt Emily Leslie, his sisters, Amy Sue and Marianne, their husbands, Moussa Abdallah and John Meyer, and their children, Kristen, Matthew, John and Mary Elizabeth flew to Hawaii, staying at Puamana, Maui and the Imperial. They traversed the islands, up Haleakela and Diamond Head and even underseas courtesy of his friend Maily Schara at Atlantis Submarines. Kristen and Matthew snorkeled at Hanauma Bay and learned to train dolphins at Sea Life Park. Matthew learned to surf.* BA, U. Cin., 1972; MS, Carnegie-Mellon U., 1974. Mathematician US Army Material Sys. Analysis Agy., Aberdeen Proving Grounds, Md., 1973, US Army Comms. Electronics-Engring. Agy., Washington, 1975-83, Def. Comms. Agy., Washington, 1983-86; student asst. engring. spectrum analysis task force Fed. Comms. Commn., Park Ridge, Ill., 1974; computer specialist US Army Mgmt. Sys. Analysis Agy., Washington, 1983; programmer, analyst Gen. Scis. Corp., Laurel, Md., 1986-87; software engr. Sygnetron Protection Systems, Timonium, Md., 1987-88, Automation Cons., Inc., Balt., 1988-89, RDA Logicon, Leavenworth, Kans., 1989-2001; lead application sys. analyst Battle Commd. Tng. Ctr. Gen. Dynamics Info. Tech., Schofield Barracks, Hawaii, 2001—07; ind. distbr. Herbalife, Mililani, Hawaii, 2007—. Cons. Martin Marietta Ocean Systems Ops., Glen Burnie, Md., 1988-89. *He was instrumental in designing the system to consolidate the "genser" message traffic centers for the Pentagon. During the pre-INF Treaty period, he supported the software maintenance effort on the Theater Mission Planning System and Mission Data Preparation System for TLAM-N and GLCM. He has collected data for the FCC to evaluate their Automated Frequency Assignment Model, enhanced the Data Systems Dynamic Simulator for NASA at Goddard Space Flight Center, developed the communication software for the Global Telemetered Seismograph Network and provided technical support for the "Corps Battle Simulation" warfighter exercises world-wide for the Battle Command Training Program, participated in Keris Strike 2004-06.* Carnegie-Mellon U. fellow, 1972—73. Mem. IEEE, Am. Math. Soc., Societe Mathematique de France, IEEE Computer Soc., IEEE Comm. Soc., European Math. Soc., Belgian Math. Soc., Nat. Defense Indsl. Assn., Imperial Hawaii Vacation Club, Greater Cin. Amateur Radio Club. Republican. Mem. Christian Ch. Avocations: music, dance, swimming, electronics, travel. Home: 94-647 Kauakapuu Loop Mililani HI 96789-1832 Office Phone: 513-322-5150. Personal E-mail: john.camery@gmail.com.

CAMI, RUSSELL, lawyer; b. Bronx, NY, Apr. 26, 1967; BA cum laude, Harvard U., 1989; JD, Rutgers U., Newark, 1993. Bar: NY 1994. Law clk., Hon. Kevin Thomas Duffy US Dist. Ct., So. Dist. NY; assoc. Cravath, Swaine & Moore LLP, NYC & London, 1994—2001, ptnr., corp. NYC, 2001—. Sr. articles editor Rutgers Law Rev. Mem.: Order of Coif. Achievements include sr. articles editor, Law Rev., Rutgers U. Office: Cravath Swaine & Moore LLP Worldwide Plz 825 Eighth Ave New York NY 10019-7475 Office Phone: 212-474-1048. Office Fax: 212-474-3700. Business E-Mail: rcami@cravath.com.*

CAMIC, DAVID EDWARD, lawyer; b. Indpls., June 11, 1954; s. Edward Franklin Camic and Carolyn (Hooker) Camic-Longland. BA, Aurora U., 1982; postgrad., DePaul U., 1982-83; JD cum laude, John Marshall Law Sch., 1987. Bar: Ill. 1987, U.S. Dist. Ct. (no. dist.) Ill. 1990, N.Y. 1996. Ptnr. Camic, Johnson, Wilson & McCulloch P.C., Aurora, Ill., 1987—, managing ptnr., 1990—. Mem. faculty, lectr. Aurora U., 1993-98; lectr. in criminal law Regional Police Tng., Aurora, 1987-95. Contbr. articles to profl. jours. Chmn. Rape Def. Seminar, Aurora, 1986. Named Man of Yr. Todays Orgn. Youth, 1987. Mem. ABA, Ill. Bar Assn. (past-chair criminal justice sect.), Kane County Bar Assn. (past chair criminal law com., bd. dirs. 2000-01, sec./treas. 2005, 2d v.p. 2006), Nat. Assn. Criminal Lawyers, Phi Delta Phi. Office: Camic Johnson Wilson & McCulloch PC 546 W Galena Blvd Aurora IL 60506-3855 Home Phone: 630-670-0640; Office Phone: 630-859-0135.

CAMILLERI, LOUIS C., consumer goods company executive; b. Alexandria, Egypt, 1957; m. Marjolyn Camilleri. Grad. econ. and bus. adminstrn., Lausanne University, 1976. Bus. analyst W.R. Grace and Co., Laussane, Switzerland; bus. develop. analyst Philip Morris Europe, 1978—82; dir. bus. develop. & planning Philip Morris Internat., 1982—86, v.p. Ea. Europe, Middle East & Africa, 1986—90, v.p. Central & Ea. Europe region, 1990—93, sr. v.p. European Union region, 1993—95; sr. v.p. corp. planning Philip Morris, 1995, pres., CEO Kraft Foods Internat., 1995—96; chmn., Kraft Foods Philip Morris (now Altria Goup), 2002—; sr. v.p., CFO Altria Group, 1996—2002, chmn., CEO, 2002—. Bd. dir. SABMiller plc; mem. bd. exec. NYSE; trustee U.S. Council for Internat. Bus. Office: Altria Group 120 Park Ave New York NY 10017-5592*

CAMILLERI, MICHAEL, lawyer, educator; b. NYC, July 16, 1953; s. Joseph and Lena (Calatozzo) C.; m. Debralyn Fisher, Aug. 5, 1989; children: Bryan, Brandon, Brooke. BA, L.I. U., 1974; JD, Fordham U., 1977. Bar: N.Y. 1978. Sr. v.p., gen. counsel Nat. Coun. Compensation Ins., NYC, 1978-91; ptnr. Adorno & Zeder, Miami, Fla., 1991-99; pres. AmTrust Ins. Group, Boca Raton, Fla.; prin. Preferred Ins. Capital Cons., Boca Raton, 2001—; pres. Newport Star Reins. Co., Columbia, SC, 2003—; CEO USA Title Co., 2006—. Pres. Ins. Data Resources, 1997-2000; cons. Family Counseling Ctr., Bklyn., 1980-85; adj. prof. law Coll. Ins., NYC, 1981-91; arbitrator civil ct., NYC, 1983-91; bd. dirs., gen. counsel First Comml. Co., 2001—. Author: Matthew Bender's Accident and Health Law, 1989; editor: Werbel's N.Y. Worker's Compensation Law, 1986-94. Mem. ABA, N.Y. State Bar Assn., D.C. Bar Assn., Profl. Bowlers Assn. Home Phone: 561-703-0457; Office Phone: 561-241-9974.

CAMINITI, DONALD ANGELO, lawyer; m. Holly Caminiti; children: David, Christian, Matthew, Courtney. BA magna cum laude, Rutgers U., 1973, JD, 1976. Bar: NJ 1976, DC 1977, NY 1980; cert. civil trial atty. NJ Supreme Ct., cert. trial lawyer Nat. Bd. Trial Advocacy, Am. Bd. Trial Advocates. Ptnr. Breslin & Breslin, P.A., Hackensack, N.J., 1977—; counsel Housing Authority of Bergen County, 1977—; asst. counsel Twp. of River Vale, 1977-80; counsel Housing Devel. Corp. Bergen County, 1978—, North Bergen Rent Leveling Bd., 1980—, North Bergen Housing Authority, 1980-84, Passaic Housing Authority, 1990—, Paramus Affordable Housing Corp., 2006—; spl. counsel Dept. Housing and Urban Devel., NJ, 1990—96. Master Morris Pashman Inns Ct., 1998—; speaker in field. Co-author: (with others) Recreation and Sports Equipment Products Liability Practice Guide, 1988. Exec. bd. mem. Tomorrow's Children's Fund. With USAF, 1966-70. Mem.: ATLA (parliamentarian 1984—85, seminar com. chmn. 1984—87, chmn. edn. com. 1990—91, v.p. 1990—91, 2d v.p. 1991—92, 1st v.p. 1992—93, pres.-elect 1993—94, pres. 1994—95, bd. govs. NJ chpt. 2001—), ABA, Italian Am. Bar Assn., Am. Assn. Justice (bd. gov. 2001—, mem. Million Dollar Advocay forum), Bergen County Bar Assn., NY Bar Assn., DC Bar Assn., NJ Bar Assn., Phi Beta Kappa. Office: Breslin and Breslin PA 41 Main St Hackensack NJ 07601-7087 Home: 7 Parkwood Ln Mendham NJ 07945-2201 Office Phone: 201-342-4014. Business E-Mail: dcaminiti@breslinandbreslin.com.

CAMINKER, EVAN H., dean, law educator; BA summa cum laude, UCLA; JD, Yale Law Sch. Faculty mem. UCLA, 1991—99; prof. U. Mich. Sch. Law, Ann Arbor, 1999—, assoc. dean, 2001—03, dean, 2003—. Clerk for Justice William J. Brennan U.S. Supreme Court; for Judge William A. Norris Ninth Cir. Ct. of Appeals; atty. Ctr. for Law in Pub. Interest, Los Angeles, Wilmer, Cutler & Pickering, Washington, DC; dep. asst. atty. gen. Office of Legal Coun., U.S. Dept. Justice, 2000—01. Sr. editor Yale Law Jour.; contbr. articles to law jours. Recipient Benjamin Scharps Prize, Disting. Profs. Award for Civil Liberties Edn., ACLU; Coker Fellow. Office: U Mich Law Sch 324 Hutchins Hall 625 S State St Ann Arbor MI 48109-1215 Office Phone: 734-764-0514. Office Fax: 734-763-1055. Business E-Mail: caminker@umich.edu.*

CAMMAKER, SHELDON IRA, lawyer; b. NYC, Apr. 26, 1939; s. Jack Robert and Anne (Benjamin) C.; children: Joshua, Meredith. BA magna cum laude, Brandeis U., Waltham, Mass., 1961; JD cum laude, Harvard U., 1964. Bar: N.Y. 1965, U.S. Dist. Ct. (so. dist.) N.Y. 1961. Assoc. Botein Hays & Sklar, NYC, 1964—70, ptnr., 1971—87; exec. v.p., gen. counsel Emcor Group, Inc., Norwalk, Conn., 1987—. Office: Emcor Group Inc 301 Merritt Seven Norwalk CT 06851-6214 Office Phone: 203-849-7831. Business E-Mail: scammaker@emcorgroup.com.

CAMMARATA, ANGELO, surgical oncologist; b. Italy, 1936; s. Giuseppe and Giuseppina (Ruggiero) C.; m. Diane M. Donner, Apr. 25, 1965; children: Joseph, Marisa, Michael, Christina. BA, Upsala Coll., 1958; MD, N.Y. Med. Coll., 1962. Diplomate Am. Bd. Surgery. Intern N.Y. Polyclin. Hosp., NYC, 1962; resident, chief resident Met. Hosp. N.Y.C., 1963-67, asst. surgeon, 1968—; resident in surgery Meml. Hosp. Cancer and Allied Diseases, NYC, 1967-68; assoc. surgeon, attending surgeon, chief breast surgery Cabrini Med. Ctr., NYC; attending surgeon Beth Israel North Hosp., NYC; instr. surgery N.Y. Med. Coll., NYC, 1968-74, clin. asst. prof. surgery, 1974—. Vis. attending surgeon Met. Hosp. Ctr., N.Y.C. Contbr. articles to profl. jours. Fellow ACS, Internat. Coll. Surgeons; mem. AMA, N.Y. Cancer Soc., N.Y. Met. Breast Cancer Group, N.Y. Acad. Scis., Meml. Alumni Soc., Alpha Club. Office: 55 E 87th St New York NY 10128-1043 Office Phone: 212-427-2131.

CAMMARATA, BERNARD, retail executive; b. 1940; Mdse. mgr. J. W. Mays, NYC, 1962-67, Wilmington Dry Goods, Del., 1967-70; v.p., gen. mdse. mgr. Marshalls Dept. Store, Woburn, Mass., 1976; founder TJ Maxx, 1976; pres., CEO TJX Oper. Cos., 1976-89, TJX Cos., Inc., Framingham, Mass., 1989—2000, acting CEO, 2005—07, chmn., 1999—. Dir. Heritage Property Investment Trust Inc. With US Army, 1959—62. Office: TJX Cos Inc 770 Cochituate Rd Framingham MA 01701 Office Phone: 508-390-1000.*

CAMMARATA, RICHARD JOHN, financial advisor; b. Boston, June 29, 1950; s. Dominic Joseph and Anna Mary (Masone) C. BA, Stonehill Coll., 1972. Mgr. Ace Fence Co., South Boston, 1972-83; fin. advisor, investor self-employed Randolph, Mass., 1983—. Mem. Am. Security Coun., Nat. Adv. Bd., Boston, Va., 1988—. Mem. Rep. Presdl. Task Force, Washington, 1987—, Rep. Nat. Com., Washington, 1984—, GOPAC, Washington, 1984—. Mem. N.Y. Acad. Scis., AAAS. Republican. Roman Catholic. Home and Office: 47 Eugenia St Randolph MA 02368-1950

CAMMISA, FRANK P., JR., surgeon, educator; b. Waterbury, Conn., Jan. 18, 1956; m. Gail Ann McGovern, Sept. 28, 1991; children: Anne Katherine, Frank P. III, John Patrick. BS summa cum laude, Tufts U., 1978; MD, Columbia U. Coll. Physicians and Surgeons, 1982. Diplomate Nat. Bd. Med. Examiners, Am. Bd. Orthop. Surgery. Resident, gen. surgery The Presbyn. Hosp., Columbia-Presbyn. Med. Ctr., NYC, 1982-83; fellow, spinal surgery U. Miami-Jackson Meml. Med. Ctr., Fla., 1987-88; resident, orthop. surgery The Hosp. for Spl. Surgery, NYC, 1983-87, asst. scientist rsch. divsn., 1988-99, assoc. scientist rsch. divsn., 2000—, asst. attending orthop. surgeon, 1988-99, assoc. attending orthop. surgeon, 2000—, chief spine svc., 1995—, dir., Spine Care Inst., 1999—. Vis. clin. fellow surgery Coll. of Physicians and Surgeons, Columbia U., N.Y.C., 1982-83; clin. assoc. surgery Cornell U. Med. Coll., N.Y.C., 1983-87, instr. orthopaedic surgery, 1988-89, asst. prof. orthopaedic surgery, 1990-99, assoc. prof. clin. orthopaedic surgery, 2000—; attending surgeon VA Hosp., Miami, 1987-88; asst. attending surgeon The N.Y. Hosp., N.Y.C., 1988-99; attending surgeon spinal cord injury svc. Burke Rehab. Ctr., White Plains, N.Y., 1988—; attending surgeon VA Hosp., Bronx, N.Y., 1988—; assoc. attending surgeon N.Y. Presbyn. Hosp., 2000—; presenter in field; cons. Meml. Sloan Kettering Cancer Ctr., N.Y.C., 1988—; spinal cons. St. John's U. Athletic Teams, 1988—, N.Y. Knights World League of Am. Football, 1991-92, Phoenix Alliance, 1993, N.Y. Racing Assn., 1993; cons. Spinal Cord Injury Unit. Editorial bd.: Orthopaedic Product News, 1990-91; contbr. chpts. to books and articles to profl. jours. Grantee The Hosp. for Spl. Surgery, 1986, Acromed Corp., 1988, Orthop. Rsch. and Edn. Found., 1991-92; recipient Harvard Book prize Harvard Club So. Conn., 1974, Tufts Psychology Soc. Rsch. award Tufts U., 1978, Resident award N.Y. Acad. Medicine, Sect. Orthop. Surgery, 1986, 87, Lewis Clark Wagner award Hosp. for Spl. Surgery, N.Y.C., 1986; N.Am. Traveling fellowship Am. Orthop. Assn., 1989; Ofcl. citation Gen. Assembly State of Conn., 1992; named one of Best Doctors, NY Mag., 2004. Fellow ACS; mem. ACP, Am. Acad. Orthop. Surgeons, Internat. Coll. Surgeons, Am. Coll. Spine Surgery; mem. AMA, N.Am. Spine Soc., Am. Spine Soc., Am. Spinal Injury Assn., Internat. Soc. for Study of Lumbar Spine, Cervical Spine Rsch. Soc., Scoliosis Rsch. Soc., Med. Soc. State N.Y., N.Y. State Soc. Orthop. Surgeons, N.Y. County Med. Soc., Alumni Assn. The Hosp. for Spl. Surgery, Assn. of the Alumni, Coll. Physicians and Surgeons, Columbia U., The Irish-Am. Orthop. Soc., Ea. Orthop. Assn. (Fellow scholar award 1988, Spinal Rsch. award 1989), Groupe Internat. Cotrel-Dubousset, N.Y. Athletic Club, Winged Foot Golf Club, Phi Beta Kappa, Psi Chi, Alpha Omega Alpha, Delta Tau Delta. Office: East River Professional Bldg 523 E 72nd St New York NY 10021 also: 143 Sound Beach Ave Old Greenwich CT 06870 Address: Hosp for Special Surgery 535 E 70th St New York NY 10021 Office Phone: 212-606-1946. Office Fax: 212-472-1486.*

CAMNER, HOWARD, writing educator, writer, poet; b. Miami, Fla., Jan. 14, 1957; s. Edward I. and Ida (Puldy) C.; m. Susan Clara Camner, July 29, 2000; 2 children. BA in English, Fla. Internat. U., 1982; LittD (hon.), London Sch. Applied Rsch., 1995. Cert. English tchr., Fla. Editor Southwind Mag., Miami, Fla., 1976-78; performance poet Writers' Exch., NYC, 1979-81; freelance writer various publications, Miami, 1982-84; screenwriter Harris Prodns., LA, 1985-89; TV prodr., host Century Cable, LA, 1986-88; writing instr. Dade County Schs., Miami, 1990—. Author: (poems) Notes from the Eye of a Hurricane, 1979, Transitions, 1980, Scattered Shadows, 1980, Road Note Elegy, 1980, A Work in Progress, 1981, Poetry from Hell to Breakfast, 1981, Midnight at the Laundromat, 1983, Hard Times on Easy Street, 1987, Madman in the Alley, 1989, Stray Dog Wail, 1991, Banned in Babylon, 1993, Jammed Zipper, 1994, Bed of Nails, 1995, Brutal Delicacies, 1996, Hiss, 2000, Cheating the Sphinx, 2005; co-author: Southern Gothic, Taj Mahal Review: Florida in Poetry, 1995, also over 100 lit. collections. Named Best Poet in Miami, New Times Newspaper, 2007; recipient Literary award, MiPo, 2004. Mem. Nat. Writers Assn., Acad. of Am. Poets, Poets and Writers, Inc., Poetry Soc. of Am., So. Fla. Poetry Inst., Authors Guild. Home: 14910 SW 127th Ct Miami FL 33186 Personal E-mail: hcamner@aol.com.

CAMOUGIS, GEORGE, health, safety and environmental consultant; b. Concord, Mass., May 10, 1930; s. Charles George and Angeliki (Georgekopoulou) C.; m. Irene Andreson, Nov. 18, 1961; children: Caroline A., Elizabeth M., Sarah A. BS magna cum laude, Tufts U., 1952; MA, Harvard U., 1957, PhD, 1958. Asst. prof. physiology Clark U., 1958—62, assoc. prof., 1962—64, affiliate prof., 1964—79; sr. neurophysiologist Astra Pharm. Products, Inc., Worcester, Mass., 1964—66, head sect. neuropharmacology, 1966—68; pres., rsch. dir., dir. New Eng. Rsch., Inc., Worcester, 1968—88; sr. cons. New Eng. Indsl. Waste, Inc., 1988—89; 19v.p., compliance officer Am. Reclamation Corp., 1989—96. Cons. Bd. Radioactive Wast Mgmt. NAS, 1987-92, numerous state and fed. agys. including Army C.E., Fed. Hwy. Adminstrn., U.S. Dept. Interior, EPA; cons. Mass. Dept. Mental Health, 1997—; affiliate prof. Worcester Poly. Inst., 1970-82; adj. prof. toxicology Tufts U. Sch. Vet. Medicine, 1981-84; panelist NSF; mem. corp. Bermuda Biol. Sta. for Rsch., 1968-85; lectr. in field, U.S., Can.; mem. Worcester Sci. Ctr. Planning Com., 1963. Author: Nerves, Muscles and Electricity, 1970, Environmental Biology for Engineers, 1981; contbr. numerous articles to profl. jours., 1959—; patentee drug; cons. editor Acad. Press, Inc., 1978; mem. editl. adv. bd. Hazardous Waste Mgmt., 1983-90. Bd. dirs. Worcester Children's Friend Soc., 1968-92, v.p. 1978-84, pres. 1984-87. With USNR, 1952-54, Korea. Virginia B. Gibbs scholar, 1954-55; E.L. Mark fellow, 1956, USPHS fellow, 1957-58; NIH grantee, 1962-64, Office Naval Rsch. grantee, 1963-64; recipient Sci. Achievement award Worcester Engring. Soc., 1985. Mem. AAAS, Biophys. Soc., Am. Physiol. Soc., N.Y. Acad. Scis., ASTM, Soc. Environ. Toxicology and Chemistry, Harvard Club (Boston), Phi Beta Kappa, Sigma Xi. Republican. Greek Orthodox. Home and Office: 7 Wheeler Ave Worcester MA 01609-1707 Office Phone: 508-798-0047.

CAMP, ALICE ANN, medical transcriptionist; b. Fremont, Ohio, Apr. 19, 1957; d. Donald Paul and Mary Catherine Camp. Cert., Davis Coll. Bus., Toledo, 1984; at, Lourdes Coll., Sylvania, Ohio, 1998—. Cert. med. transcriptionist Ohio, 1994. Lab. sec. Meml. Hosp., Fremont, Ohio, 1975—79, sec., med. transcriptionist, 1979—89, med. transcriptionist, 1991—2000, Humana Hosp., Aurora, Colo., 1989—91, Toledo Hosp., 2000—02, Arrowhead Plastic Surgeons, Maumee, 2002—. Naturalist vol. Toledo Metro Parks, 2002—; participant holiday outreach project Lourdes Coll., 2004, 2005, greenhouse vol., 2005. Grantee, Lourdes Coll., 1999. Mem.: Am. Assn. Med. Transcriptionists. Roman Catholic. Avocations: rollerblading, hiking, travel. Home: 3942 Sylvanwood Dr Sylvania OH 43560-3928

CAMP, DAVID LEE, congressman, lawyer; b. Midland, Mich., July 9, 1953; m. Nancy Keil, Sept. 10, 1994; children: Andrew, David, Lauren. BA magna cum laude, Albion Coll., Mich., 1975; JD, U. San Diego, 1978. Bar: Mich., Calif., DC, admitted to practice: US Supreme Ct., US Dist. Ct. (Ea. Dist.) Mich., US Dist. Ct. (So. Dist.) Calif. With Riecker, Van Dam, Looby & Barker, 1978-90; spl. asst. atty. gen. Mich., 1980-84; adminstrv. asst. to Congressman Bill Schuette, 1985-87; state rep. 102nd Dist. Mich., 1989-91; mem. U.S. Congress from 10th (now 4th) Mich. dist., 1991—, mem. ways and means com., asst. minority whip, mem. select com. on homeland security. Chmn. Spkrs. Correction Day Com. Mem.: Midland County Bar Assn., ABA. Republican. Office: US Congress 137 Cannon Bldg Washington DC 20515-2204 also: District Office 135 Ashman Dr Midland MI 48640 Office Phone: 202-225-3561, 989-631-2552. Office Fax: 202-225-9679, 989-631-6271.*

CAMP, DELPHA JEANNE, counselor; b. Yakima, Wash., Apr. 20, 1937; d. George Emerson and Emilie Loraine (Rivard) Stevens; m. George Ernest Mills, Aug. 13, 1960 (dec. 1975); children: Adriene Phillips, Stacey Harcus, Ryan, Tiffany Morrison; m. James Clell Camp, June 24, 1978 (dec. 2004); children: Catherine Thompson (dec.), Wayne (dec.), Darla Coolman, John, Janna Barnes. BEd, Gonzaga Univ., 1959; MS, Univ. Oreg., 1977. Lic. profl. counselor; cert. in death, dying and bereavement. Tchr. Riverside Sch. Dist., Milan, Wash., 1959-61, Cheney (Wash.) Sch. Dist., 1968-70; asst. prof. Univ. Oreg., Eugene, 1979-92; pvt. practice Eugene, 1992—. Mem. faculty Marylhurst (Oreg.) U., 1992—2002. Mem. Assn. for Death Edn. and Counseling (bd. dirs. 1990-93, co-chair conf. 1994, 2002, 1st v.p. 1998-99, pres. 1999-00, Svc. award 1990), Am. Mental Health Counselors Assn., Oreg. Mental Health Counselors Assn. Avocations: reading, classical music. Home: 440 E 39th Ave Eugene OR 97405-4722 Office: 541 Willamette St Ste 102 Eugene OR 97401 Office Phone: 541-341-3477. Personal E-mail: deljcamp@aol.com.

CAMP, DONALD EUGENE, experimental photographer, educator; b. Meadville, Pa., July 28, 1940; s. Ira Guy and Martha Gladys (Irving) C.; m. Marie Josephé Dumont, Nov. 26, 1966; children: Stephanie Martha Helené, Dorothea Rae. BFA, Tyler Sch. Art, Phila., 1987; MFA, Tyler Sch. Art, 1989. Staff photographer Phila. Bulletin, 1972-81; asst. prof. Tyler Sch. of

Art, Phila., 1989-91, Slippery Rock (Pa.) U., 1992—. Dir. Future Faculty Fellowship program Temple U., Phila., 1990—91; vis. asst. prof. Ursinus Coll., Collegeville, Pa., 2000—, artist in-residence, vis. asst. prof. art, 2002—06; mem. bd. overseers Inst. Contemporary Art, U. Pa., 2002—. One person exhbns. include Nat. Mus. The Gambia, 2000, Smithsonian, 2000, Anacostia Mus. and Ctr. for African Am. History and Culture, 2000, Reflections In Black. 1840-Present, 2000, The Chemistry of Color, Sorgenti Collection Pa. Acad. Fine Art, 2005; photographs have appeared in many popular magazines including Ebony, News Week, People; represented in numerous pub. collections including ARCO collection, Phila. Mus. Art, and Schaumberg Ctr. for Black Culture, N.Y.C., Pa. Conv. Ctr., U. Mich. Mus. of Art; appeared in Face to Face Exhbn. Nat, Jewish Am. Mus. in Phila., U. Mich. Mus. Art, 1998, Inst. Contemporary Art, U. Pa., 1999. Mem. Spiritual Assembly of Bahais of Phila., 2003—, Interfaith Support Group, Phila., 1989-92. Recipient Future Faculty fellowship Temple U., Phila., 1988, Eugene Feldman award The Print Club, 1983; named Pa. Visual Artist fellow, 1990, Smithsonian Am. Artist Oral History, 1991, PEW Charitable Trust resident artist to the Am. Acad. in Rome, 1994; John Simon Guggenheim Found. fellow, 1995-96, fellow NEA, Pew Charitable Trust fellow, Pa. Coun. for the Arts fellow. Mem. Soc. Photographic Educators (bd. dirs. 1990-94, chmn., founder multicultural caucus, 1990-93), Recherche. Avocations: baha'i promotion, magic. Home: 4511 Spruce St Philadelphia PA 19139-4526 Business E-Mail: doncamp@cartel.net.

CAMP, JOHN BLISS, journalist, television producer; b. Nashville, Nov. 2, 1935; s. William Eledge and Lena Marie Camp; m. Cecile Annette Giles, Dec. 13, 1986. Student, Columbia Coll., LA, 1960. Dir. investigative reporting Sta. WCKT-TV, Boston, 1976—82; investigative prodr., reporter Sta. WBRZ-TV, Baton Rouge, 1982—89; sr. investigative corr. Cable News Network (CNN), Atlanta, 1989—2000; ind. reporter, prodr. Atlanta, 2000—. Freelance reporter, prodr., Baton Rouge. Prodr., reporter (TV documentary) Give Me That Big Time Religion, 1983 (George Foster Peabody award Columbia Dupont, 1984), (investigative documentary) The Best Insurance Commissioner Money Can Buy, 1988 (George Foster Peabody award Columbia Dupont, 1988), Mafia Influence on South Florida (George Foster Peabody award, 1976). Founder O'Brien Ho., Baton Rouge, 1971—2004. With USAF, 1957. Recipient Nat. Headliners award, 1983, 1985, 1990, SDX Excellence in Journalism award, Soc. Profl. Journalists, 1984, 1988. Mem.: Investigative Reporters and Editors, Inc., Baton Rouge Press Club (pres. 1972—73). Democrat. Avocation: golf. Home: 32 Beechgrove Ln The Bluffs LA 70748 Office: John Camp Prodns 643 St Charles St Baton Rouge LA 70802 Home Phone: 225-634-9948; Office Phone: 225-343-4974. Office Fax: 225-343-5136; Home Fax: 225-634-9948. Personal E-mail: jblisscamp@aol.com.

CAMP, JOHN ROSWELL See SANDFORD, JOHN

CAMP, JOSEPH SHELTON, JR., film producer, director, writer; b. St. Louis, Apr. 20, 1939; s. Joseph Shelton and Ruth Wilhelmena (McLaulin) C.; m. Andrea Carolyn Hopkins, Aug. 7, 1960; children: Joseph Shelton III, Brandon Andrew. BBA, U. Miss., 1961. Jr. account exec. McCann-Erickson Advt., Houston, 1961-62; owner Joe Camp Real Estate, Houston, 1962-64; account exec. Norsworthy-Mercer, Dallas, 1964-69; dir. TV commls. Jamieson Film Co., Dallas, 1969-71; founder, pres., writer, producer, dir. feature films Mulberry Square Prodns., Inc., Dallas, 1971-90, Gulfport, Miss., 1991-94, Chapel Hill, N.C., 1994—. Producer, dir., writer films including Benji, 1974, Hawmps, 1976, For the Love of Benji, 1977, The Double McGuffin, 1979, Oh Heavenly Dog, 1980, Benji The Hunted, 1987; TV spls. The Phenomenon of Benji, 1978, Benji's Very Own Christmas Story, 1978, Benji at Work, 1980, Benji (Takes a Dive) at Marineland, 1981; TV series Benji, Zax and the Alien Prince, 1983; author: Underdog, 1993. Bd. trustees Piney Woods Country Life Sch., Warren Wilson Coll.; adv. bd. N.C. Sch. of Arts, Sch. of Film Making. Mem. Dir.'s Guild Am., Writer's Guild Am. Office: 29067 Aerie Rd Valley Center CA 92082-5728 *I hope that I have been able to help people in a troubled time to lose themselves for a moment in a piece of entertainment and, when it's over, to feel better for having done so, to have a new respect for persistence in achieving objectives and a new feeling of hope and happiness in their lives. I hope to inspire others to follow their dreams with passion and persistence, to reach further than they might have otherwise.*

CAMP, KIMBERLY N., museum administrator, artist; b. Camden, NJ, Sept. 11, 1956; d. Hubert E. and Marie (Dimery) C.; m. Seydou Coulibaly, Apr. 1997 (div. June 2006). BA, U. Pitts., 1978; MS, Drexel U., 1986. Dir. artistic design project City Camden, 1984-86; program dir. Pa. Coun. on Arts, Harrisburg, 1986-89; dir. exptl. gallery Smithsonian Instn., Washington, 1989-94; pres. Charles H. Wright Mus. African Am. History, Detroit, 1994-98; pres., CEO Barnes Found., Merion, Pa., 1998—2005. Evaluator Am. Assn. Mus., Washington, 1994—; panel chair Nat. Endowment for Arts, Washington, 1991-92; vice chair, bd. dirs. Assn. Am. Cultures, Washington, 1987-89. One-woman shows include Clifton Art Ctr., N.J., Glouchester County Coll., Deptford Township, N.J., Passaic Count C.C., Paterson, N.J., Diggs Gallery, Winston-Salem, N.C., Galerie Francois, Washington, Banneker Douglass Mus., Annapolis, Md., 3d Bienniel Nat. Black Arts Festival, Atlanta, Manchester Craftsmen's Guilde, Pitts., Caribbean Cultural Ctr., N.Y.C., Jr. Black Acad. Arts and Letters, Dallas, Walt Whitman Ctr. Arts and Humanities, Camden, Longwood Gardens, Kennett Square, Pa., Art Mus. Western Va., Raonoke, Harrison Mus. African Am. Culture, Roanoke, 1994; represented in permanent collections J.B Speed Art Mus., Manchester Craftsmen's Guild, Reader's Digest, Camden Hist. Soc.; mng. editor Nat. Conf. Artists Phila. Chpt. newsletter, 1980-84. Bd. dirs. Bus. Vols. for Arts, 1994-97. Recipient Nat. Svc. award Nat. Conf. Artists, 1984, Arts Achievement award City of Camden, 1984, Cmty. Svc. award Assn/ Negro Bus. and Profl. Women, 1985, Builders of Cmty. award Camden County Cultural and Heritage Commn., 1986, Purchase award J.B. Speed Art Mus., 1988, Spirit of Detroit award Detroit City Coun., 1994; Arts Internat. grantee Ctr. Internat. Exch. Scholars, 1994, Roger L. Stevens Nat. Arts award Carnegie Mellon U. H. John Heinz Sch. Mgmt., 1999; fellow Kellogg Nat. Leadership Program, 1997-2000. Mem. Assn. Am. Cultures (bd. dirs. 1989—91), Am. Assn. Museums (bd. dirs. 1995-97), Links, Inc., N.J. Coun. on Arts. Address: 1202 Yarmouth Rd Wynnewood PA 19096 Office Phone: 610-658-0944. Business E-Mail: kcamp911@msn.com.

CAMP, SHARON L., reproductive health organization administrator; B. with honors, Pomona Coll.; MA, PhD, Johns Hopkins U. Sr. v.p. Population Action Internat., 1975—93; coord. Internat. Consortium for Emergency Contraception, 1993—98; pres., CEO Women's Capital Corp., 1998—2003, Guttmacher Inst., NYC, 2003—. Sr. lectr. Columbia U. Mailman Sch. Pub. Health; former chair Family Health Internat., Nat. Coun. Internat. Health, Internat. Ctr. Rsch. on Women; founding chair Reproductive Health Technologiess Project; former dir. Nat. Family Planning & Reproductive Health Assn., AVSC Internat. (name changed to EngenderHealth, 2001), Mgmt. Sciences for Health, Population Action Internat. Office: Guttmacher Inst 21st Fl 120 Wall St New York NY 10005 Office Phone: 800-355-0244.

CAMP, WILLIAM H., agricultural products executive; BS in Bus. Adminstrn., U. Ill., 1977. V.p. Archer Daniels Midland Co., Decatur, Ill., 1993—99, group v.p. and pres. S.Am. oilseed processing divsn., 1999—2000, group v.p. and pres. N.Am. oilseed processing divsn., 2000—01, sr. v.p. oilseeds processing and cocoa, 2001—05, exec. v.p. global processing, 2005—. Office: Archer Daniels Midland Co 4666 Faries Pkwy Decatur IL 62526*

CAMPAGNOLO, MARY FRANCES, physician; b. Teaneck, NJ, 1956; MD, George Washington U., 1982. Diplomate with qualification in geriat. Am. Bd. Family Medicine. Intern Overlook Hosp., Summit, NJ, 1982—83, resident in family practice, 1983—85; staff physician Virtua-Meml. Hosp. of Burlington County, Mt. Holly, NJ, 1987—; chief dept. family practice Virtua-Meml. Hosp. Burlington County, 1993—. Named an Outstanding Woman of Burlington County, 2006; named one of Top Drs. 2003, N.J. Monthly Mag., Del. Valley Consumer, Top Drs. for Women, N.J. Living, Top Drs., Phila. Mag., 2004, South Jersey Mag., 2005, Top Doctors, 2006; recipient Virtua Health Star award, 2006. Mem.: N.J. Acad. Family Physicians (Lifetime Achievement Chair award 2005). Office: Lumberton Family Physicians LLC Independence Plaza 1561 Rte 38 Ste 6 Lumberton NJ 08048 Office Phone: 609-267-2100. Business E-Mail: mcampagnolo@lumbertonfp.com.

CAMPANELLI, JOSEPH P., bank executive; b. 1956; m. Carolyn Campanelli; 3 children. BSBA, Babson Coll., 1979. Mgmt. positions Hartford Nat. Bank, Shawmut Bank, Fleet Bank, 1979—97; joined Sovereign Bancorp Inc., Boston, 1997, vice-chmn., 2002—06, pres., CEO, 2006—; pres., COO New England divsn., Sovereign Bancorp Inc., Boston, 1999—2005, pres., CEO, 2005—06. Mem. bd. overseers Babson Coll., Boston Mus. Sci.; chmn. bd. trustees Floating Hosp., Boston; dir. Mass. Bus. Develop. Corp.; chmn., trustee Tufts-New England Med. Ctr. Office: Sovereign Bancorp Inc 75 State St Boston MA 02109 E-mail: jcampane@sovereignbank.com.

CAMPANELLI, RICHARD M., federal agency administrator; m. Shannon Campanelli; 3 children. BS in Economics, U. Va., JD. Trial atty. spl. litig. sect. of civil right divsn. US Dept. Justice, 1983—86; mem. S. Africa Working Group US Dept. State, 1986—87, sr. spl. asst. to atty. gen., 1987—89; atty. Gammon & Grange, PC, McLean, Va., 1989—2002; dir. Office for Civil Rights US Dept. Health and Human Services, 2002—. Past adj. prof. George Mason U. Office: Office for Civil Rights US Dept Health and Human Svcs 200 Independence Ave SW Rm 509F HHH Bldg Washington DC 20201

CAMPANO, RUWANTHI, surgeon; b. Colombo, Sri Lanka, Oct. 17, 1969; d. T. Nandasiri and Silverine D. Samaranayake; m. Angelo Felice Campano, Sept. 4, 1999. BA, Franklin & Marshall Coll.; MS, MD, U. Md., Balt. Dept. head & neck surgery Kaiser Permanente, San Francisco, 2002—03; otolarynogology Drummond Med. Group, Ridgecrest, Calif., 2003—05; pvt. practice Golden State Otolaryngoloty Med. Corp., Lancaster, Calif., 2005—. Mem.: Am. Acad. Facial Plastic Reconsturctive Surgery, Am. Acad. Otolaryngology & Head & Neck Surgery. Office: 44105 15th W. Ste 202 Lancaster CA 93534

CAMPANY, KAY HUDKINS, biology educator, assistant principal; d. Roger Jay Hudkins and Edna Church Elrod; m. Donald Campany; children: Courtney Eugene, Stacy Nicole. BS in Biology, Piedmont Coll., Demorest, Ga., 1974; MA in Edn. and Biology, Western Carolina U., Cullowhee, NC, 1979; postgrad., Appalachian State U., Boone, NC, 2004—06. Nat. bd. cert. tchr. sci., adolescent - young adult Nat. Bd. for Profl. Tchg. Stds., 2003. Resident social worker therapist Youth Help Inc., Wilmington, NC, 1975—76; sci. tchr. Savannah H.S., Ga., 1979—80; environ. educator Oatland Island Edn. Ctr., Savannah, 1980; biology tchr. Fairmount H.S., Ga., 1981—83, Glynn Acad. H.S., Brunswick, Ga., 1983—86, Shelby H.S., NC, 1986—88, Avery County H.S., Newland, NC, 1990—, asst. prin. for curriculum, 2006—. Leader Girl Scouts Am., Boone, NC, 1991—2004. Named Grad. Rsch. award, Appalachian State U., 1990, Girl Scout Leader of Yr., Watauga Girl Scout Svc. Unit, 2000; Intel's Teach for Tomorrow grantee, Intel, 2003—06. Mem.: Nat. Assn. for Profl. Devel. Schs., NC Sci. Tchrs. Assn., NC Assn. for Rsch. in Edn., Appalachian State U. Pub. Sch. Partnership Coordinating Coun. (corr.), Sigma Xi, Phi Kappa Phi. Democrat. Baptist. Achievements include research in habitat preservation for an endangered plant, fringed gentian, in North Carolina. Home: 255 Northridge Dr Boone NC 28607 Office: Avery County High School 401 High School Rd Newland NC 28657 Home Phone: 828-264-4048; Office Phone: 828-733-0151. Business E-Mail: kaycampany@avery.k12.nc.us.

CAMPASINO, ELLEN MARIE, elementary school educator; b. Titusville, Pa., Aug. 30, 1950; d. Frank and Helen (Lowicki) Campasino. BS in Elem. and Early Childhood Edn., Edinboro U., 1972, cert. in elem. and early childhood edn., 1978. 1st grade tchr. St. Titus Sch., Titusville, 1975-76, 4th grade tchr., 1976-77, 3rd grade tchr., 1977—. Coaching tchr. St. Titus Tchr. Induction Program, Titusville, 1989—90, asst. to prin., 1993—. Mem. ministry tng. program Diocese of Erie; min. hospitality St. Walburga Parish, Roman Cath. Ch., Titusville. Recipient Svc. award, Diocese of Erie, 1988, 1990, 1996, 25 Yrs. of Svc. award, 2000—01, 30 Yrs. of Svc. award, St. Titus Sch., 2006. Avocations: reading, doll collecting, embroidery. Office: St Titus Sch 528 W Main St Titusville PA 16354-1598

CAMPBELL, ALAN, actor; b. Homestead, Fla., Apr. 22, 1957; s. Edward John and Audrey Carolyn (Griner) C. BBA, U. of Miami. Performer Urban Arts Corps, New York, NY, 1982; founding member H.O.L.A. (Heart of Los Angeles) Youth Theater, Los Angeles, CA. Stage appearances include: I Love My Wife (Coconut Grove Theatre, FL), Boogie-Woogie Rumble of Dream Deferred (Urban Arts Corp), On Shiloh Hill (Ford Theatre, Wash. DC) The Nerd (Birmingham Theatre, Detroit, MI), Sunset Boulevard (L.A. and Broadway - Tony nomination, Lead Actor in a Musical, 1995), Contact, 2000, Beauty and the Beast, 2005, Adrift in Macao, 2007; TV appearances include: (series) The Facts of Life, Throb, B.J. and the Bear, Counterattack: Crime in America, 1982, Three's a Crowd, 1984-85, Jake and the Fatman, 1987-92, Matlock, Another World, (movie) Red Flag: The Ultimate Game, 1981; film appearances include: Smokey and the Bandit II, 1980, The Final Terror, 1983, Weekend Warriors, 1986, Hollywood Air Force Base.*

CAMPBELL, ALEX, mobile marketing executive; b. 1976; BS in Econs., U. Pa. Wharton Sch. Co-head paging co., Chgo., 1998; co-founder, CEO Vibes Media, Chgo., 1998—. Named one of Top 40 Under 40, Crain's Chgo. Bus., 2006. Mem.: Mobile Mktg. Assn. (mem. mobile strategies and best practices com.). Office: Vibes Media 205 W Wacker Dr 23rd Fl Chicago IL 60606*

CAMPBELL, ALLAN MCCULLOCH, bacteriology educator; b. Berkeley, Calif., Apr. 27, 1929; s. Lindsay and Virginia Margaret (Henning) C.; m. Alice Del Campillo, Sept. 5, 1958; children— Wendy, Joseph. BS in Chemistry, U. Calif., Berkeley, 1950; MS in Bacteriology, U. Ill., 1951; PhD, 1953; PhD (hon.), U. Chgo., 1978, U. Rochester, 1981. Instr. bacteriology U. Mich., 1953-57; research asso. Carnegie Inst., Cold Spring Harbor, NY, 1957-58; asst. prof. biology U. Rochester, NY, 1958-61, assoc. prof. NY, 1961-63, prof. NY, 1963-68; prof. biol. sci. Stanford U., Calif., 1968—, Barbara Kimball Browning prof. humanities and sciences Calif., 1992—. Author: Episomes, 1969; co-author: General Virology, 1978; editor Gene, 1980-90, mem. editl. bd., 1990—; assoc. editor Virology, 1963-69; assoc. editor Ann. Rev. Genetics, 1969-84, editor, 1984—; spl. editor Evolution, 1985-88; editl. bd. Jour. Bacteriology, 1966-72, Jour. Virology, 1967-75, New Biologist, 1989-92. Served with AUS, 1953-55. Recipient Research Career award USPHS, 1962-68 Mem. NAS, Am. Soc. Microbiology (Abbott-ASM Lifetime Achievement award 2004), Soc. Am. Naturalists, Genetics Soc. Am.; fellow AAAS, Am. Acad. Microbiology, Am. Acad. Arts and Scis. Democrat. Home: 947 Mears Ct Stanford CA 94305-1041 Office: Stanford U Herrin Labs RM 339A Mail Code 5020 Dept Biol Scis Stanford CA 94305-5020 Home Phone: 650-493-6153. Business E-Mail: AMC@stanford.edu. *I've always thought that each individual has some contribution to human knowledge that he is uniquely suited to make. So I try to be organized and to avoid doing things that I expect will get done, anyway, by others. And, of course, everything worthwhile requires hard work.*

CAMPBELL, ALMA JACQUELINE PORTER, elementary school educator; b. Savannah, Ga., Jan. 5, 1948; d. William W. and Gladys B. Porter. BS in Elem. Edn., Savannah State Coll., 1969; MEd, SUNY, Brockport, 1971, cert. advanced study in adminstrn. magna cum laude, 1988. Cert. permanent elem. tchr., N.Y. Elem. tchr., Savannah, 1969-70, 71-74; tchr. intern project unique Rochester (N.Y.) City Sch. Dist., 1970-71, tchr., 1974-88, adminstrv. intern chpt. 1 office, 1988; mem. student progress task force, 1994; mem. coun. elem. leadership, mem. instrnl. com.; basic skills cadre Francis Parker Sch., Rochester, 1988—, lead tchr. mentor, 1991—; lead tchr., mentor tchr., basic skills cadre John Walton Spencer Elem. Sch. No. 16, 1992—; vice prin. Theodore Roosevelt Sch. # 43, 1993—94, prin., 1994—2003; dir. Newburn Fellowship Learning Ctr. Pre-Schoolers, 2006. Demonstration tchr., 1987-88; active Effective Parenting Info. and Children program, 1987-89; active coop. tchr. program Nazareth Coll. and Rochester City Sch. Dist., 1987; mem. policy bd. Rochester Tchr. Ctr., 1994, adminstrv. rep. to policy bd., 1995-97; adv. com. N.Y. State Systemic Iniative, 1994, sch. quality reviewer; coord., presenter ednl. workshops; apptd. mem. Student Progress Task Force, 1995; asst. WXXI Broadcasting Partnership and Sch. Number 43; coord. Sch. Quality Rev. Initiative, 1996-97; establisher partnership with Urban Schs. Inst. in conjunction with U. Rochester, 1996-97; mem. Supt. Janey's Profl. Devel. Focus Group, 1997; apptd. Profl. Devel. Acad. Adv. Bd., 1999, vis. practitioner Prin.'s Ctr. Harvard U., 2000; mem. Oxford Round Table, St. Anthony's Coll.; advisor F.C.D. Hall of Fame, Inc., Rochester; dir. New Burn Child Care Ctr., Rochester. Author: (with McGriff) Quick Reference Manual for Teachers, 1989-90; co-author: A Quick Reference Manual for Teachers and Absolutely Jam-Packed With Super Teaching Tips, 1991-92. Mem. Martin Luther King Commn. on Edn., Rochester, 1988-89, Francis Parker Sch. PTA, 1988—; mental health asst. Curriculum Task Force, Rochester City Sch. Dist., 1991, coop. learning tchr., trainer, 1990, 91-92; asst. dir. Meml. A.M.E. Zion Ch., 1979-82, dir. summer camp, 1982-85, asst. sec. bd. Christian edn., 1987-89; bd. dirs. Hamm House, Jefferson Area Child Devel. Ctr., 1990-91, Save Our Sisters; bd. trustees Dr. William J. Knox, 2005—; active United Way; mem steering com. African Am. Devel. Program; exec. bd., Dem. Women's Leadership Coun Mem. ASCD (assoc.), NAFE (sub-adv. com. Strong Mus. sch. programs), Am. Assn. Sch. Adminstrs., Internat. Reading Assn., Rochester Coun. Elem. Leadership, Rochester Early Childhood Assn., Children's Inst. Rochester, Kiwanis Internat., Phi Delta Kappa (treas. 1996-97), Alpha Kappa Alpha (chair nominating com. 1988-89, Ivy Leaf reporter 1992—, Cert. of Achievement 1988). Democrat. Avocations: reading, travel, collecting mugs, visiting amusement parks. also: Meml AME Zion Ch Clarissa St Rochester NY 14604 also: Harvard U 536 Leverett House Mail Ctr 28 De Wolfe St Cambridge MA 02138 Home: 268 Applewood Dr Rochester NY 14626 Office Phone: 585-342-5020, 585-342-7270. Personal E-mail: ACampbel43@frontiernet.net.

CAMPBELL, ANDREW WILLIAM, immunotoxicology physician; b. Beirut, Apr. 3, 1948; s. William Alexander and Gisela (Landes) C.; children: Denia Giselle, Michelle Elise, Colin Alexander, Ian William. BA in Pre-med., Psychology, Franklin Piere Coll., Rindge, NH, 1970; MD, U. Autonoma de Guadalajara, Mex., 1974. Diplomate Am. Bd. Family Practice, Am. Bd. Forensic Examiners, Am. Bd. Forensic Medicine. Intern Pediat. Hosp. Infantil, Ob-gyn., Clin. Santa Monica, Guadalajara, Mex., 1974-75, Pub. Health Dept., Guadalajara, Mex., 1975-76; resident gen. surgery Orlando (Fla.) Regional Med. Ctr., 1977-78; resident family practice Med. Coll. Ga., Augusta, 1978-81; pvt. practice family physician Two Physician Practice, Sarasota, Fla., 1981, with former chief surgeon Eisenhower Med. Ctr., Augusta, Ga.; pvt. practice Augusta, Wrens and Louisvlle, Ga., 1983-84, Houston, 1985—; med. dir. Med. Ctr. for Immune and Toxic Disorders, Houston, 1993—. Staff mem. Meml. City Med. Ctr., Spring Branch Med. Ctr.; chmn. dept. family practice Sam Houston Meml. Hosp., Houston, 1987, chmn. credentials com., 88, exec. com., 1987—89; lectr. and spkr. at Artificial Implants and Toxic Exposure Symposia; faculty U. Tex. Sch. Medicine, 1993—98; cons., presenter in field. Author (with others): Health Effects of Toxic Chemicals, 1994, Textbook of Nephrology (2 vols.), 1995; co-editor: Internat. Jour. Occupl. Medicine and Toxicology, 1992—95; mem. editl. bd.: Toxicology and Indsl. Health, 1994—96; contbr. articles to profl. jours., chapters to books. Founder Clinic for the Indigent, St. John Vianney Ch., Houston, 1987; bd. trustees Sam Houston Meml. Hosp., 1987-93. Recipient Consumer's Choice award Am. Nurses in Bus. Assn., Houston, 1994. Fellow: Am. Acad. Family Physicians; mem.: AMA, AAAS, Am. Assn. Immunologists, Indoor Air Quality Assn. of Tex., Tex. Med. Assn., Am. Bd. Forensic Examiners, Harris County Med. Soc., Soc. Mucosal Immunology, Internat. Soc. Neuroimmunology, Am. Acad. Clin. Toxicology, Am. Coll. Occupl. and Environ. Medicine, Tex. Acad. Family Physicians. Republican. Avocations: golf, collecting pipes, collecting pens. Office Phone: 281-681-8989. Business E-Mail: md@immunotoxicology.com.

CAMPBELL, ARTHUR ANDREWS, retired federal agency administrator; b. Bklyn., Feb. 8, 1924; s. Arthur Monroe and Jo Ethel (Andrews) C.; m. Nancy Elizabeth Pyle, Jan. 28, 1961; children— Julia, Tay. AB, Antioch Coll., 1948; postgrad., Columbia U., 1947-50. Editorial clk. Met. Life Ins. Co., NYC, 1950-52; statistician U.S. Bur. of Census, Washington, 1952-56; asso. research prof. Scripps Found. for Research in Population Problems, Miami U., Oxford, Ohio, 1956-64; chief natality stats. br. Nat. Center for Health Stats., Washington, 1964-68; dep. dir. Center for Population Research, NIH, Bethesda, Md., 1968-94; ret., 1994. Co-author: Family Planning, Sterility, and Population Growth, 1959, Fertility and Family Planning in the U.S, 1966, Trends and Variations in Fertility in the U.S, 1968, Manual of Fertility Analysis, 1983. Served with USN, 1943-46. Recipient Meritorious Service award U.S. Dept. Commerce, 1957; Dir.'s award NIH, 1976 Fellow Am. Statis. Assn.; mem. Population Assn. Am. (pres. 1973-74), Internat. Union for Sci. Study Population.

CAMPBELL, BEN NIGHTHORSE, former senator; b. Auburn, Calif., Apr. 13, 1933; s. Albert and Mary Vierra Campbell; m. Linda Aline Price, 1966; children: Colin Lee, Shanan Lee. BA, Calif. U., San Jose, 1957; spl. rsch. student, Meiji U., Tokyo, 1960—64. Educator Sacramento Law Enforcement Agy.; mem. Colo. Gen. Assembly, 1983-86, U.S. Ho. Reps., 1987-93; US senator from Colo., 1993—2005. Chair, Com. on Indian Affairs, 2001; rancher, jewelry designer, Ignacio, Colo. Chief No. Cheyenne Tribe. Served in USAF, 1951—54. Named Outstanding Legislator Colo. Bankers Assn., 1984, Man of Yr. LaPlata Farm Bur., Durango, Colo., 1984; named one of Ten Best Legislators Denver Post/Channel 4, 1986. Mem. Am. Quarter Horse Assn., Am. Brangus Assn., Am. Indian Edn. Assn. Republican. Avocation: silversmithing, jewelry-making.

CAMPBELL, BENTON J., federal agency administrator; BA, Yale U.; JD, U. Chgo. Law Sch. Litig. assoc. Kirkland & Ellis LLP; asst. US atty. ea. dist. NY US Dept. Justice, Bklyn., 1994—, dep. chief violent enterprises sect., chief violent enterprises sect., dep. chief criminal divsn., acting counselor to asst. atty gen. criminal divsn., 2005—06, dep. asst. atty. gen. criminal divsn., 2006, acting chief of staff, prin. dep. asst. atty. gen. criminal divsn., 2006—. Ex-officio commr. US Sentencing Commn. Office: Dept Justice Criminal Divsn 950 Pennsylvania Ave Washington DC 20530 Office Phone: 202-514-9351. E-mail: criminal.division@usdoj.gov.

CAMPBELL, BOBBY JACK, academic administrator; b. Ft. Worth, Oct. 12, 1929; s. Jack Bryan and Ruby Opal (Lamberth) C.; m. Frances Carol Alexander, Aug. 24, 1957; children: Carol Stuart Davis, John William Campbell. BA, Tex. Christian U., 1951, MA, 1953; PhD, U. N.C., 1960. Asst. dir. U. N.C. Inst. of Govt., Chapel Hill, 1957-59; chief accident rsch. br. Cornell U. Aero. Lab., Buffalo, 1959-66; dir. U. N.C. Hwy. Safety Rsch. Ctr., Chapel Hill, 1966-91, sr. investigator, dir. emeritus, 1992—. Chmn. com. accident stats. Nat. Safety Coun., 1964-68; chmn. nat. motor vehicle safety adv. coun. U.S. Dept. Transp., 1975-76, mem., 1987-89, chmn. nat. driver register adv. com., 1983-86; chmn. panel on automotive assessment into 21st century U.S. Congress Office Tech. Assessment, 1976-77; chmn. com. to study CB radios on buses NRC, 1983-84, mem. com. to identify measures to improve safety of sch. bus transp., 1987-88; chmn. Global Traffic Safety Trust, Melbourne, Australia, 1988-92; lectr. or cons. in Australia, Azerbaijan, Brazil, Can., China, Denmark, Dominica, France, India, Hong Kong, Japan, Republic of Korea, Malawi, Malaysia, New Zealand, Russia, Saudi Arabia, Spain, Switzerland, Uruguay. Author: Driver Improvement: The Point System, 1958, Reducing Traffic Injury: A Global Challenge, 1988; (with others) Reflections on the Transfer of Highway Safety to Developing Nations, 1998, Collier's Encyclopedia, 1962, Human Factors in Technology, 1963, Trauma and the Automobile, 1966, Traffic Safety: A National Problem, 1967, Key Issues in Highway Loss Reducation, 1970, Restraint Technologies: Rear Seat Occupant Protection, 1987; contbr. numerous articles to profl. jours. SFC US Army, 1948—49. Recipient Leadership award Nat. Gov. Safety Rep. Orgn., 1997, Gerin Medal for Rsch. Internat. Assn. for Accident and Traffic Medicine, 1992, Gustafson Leadership award Hwy. Users Fedn., 1989, Volvo Internat. Traffic Safety prize, 1988, Volvo Pub. Safety award 1984, Disting. Svc. award Am. Assn. for Automotive Medicine, 1978, N.C. Pub. Health Assn., 1972, Alvah Lauer award Human Factors Soc., 1976, Met. Rsch. prize, 1960, Commendation Nat. Safety Coun., 1971, 60. Avocations: astronomy, classical music, opera, sports, history. Home: 502 Belmont St Chapel Hill NC 27517-3000

CAMPBELL, BRADFORD P., government agency administrator; BA, Harvard U.; JD, Georgetown U. Law Ctr. Legis. dir. Ernest Fletcher; sr. legis. asst. SEC Chmn. Christopher Cox; sr. legis. officer Dept. of Labor, Office of Congl. and Intergovernmental Affairs, 2001—04; dep. asst. sec. for policy Employee Benefits Security Adminstrn., 2004—06, acting asst. sec., 2006—07, asst. sec., 2007—. Office: Employee Benefits Security Adminstrn 200 Constitution Ave NW Ste S-252 Washington DC 20210 Office Phone: 202-693-8300. Office Fax: 202-219-5526.*

CAMPBELL, BRUCE ALAN, corporate coach; b. Washington, Jan. 19, 1944; s. Albert Angus and Jean Lorraine (Winter) C.; m. Jennifer Lee Drew, May 3, 1968 (div. Dec. 1986); children: Kirsten, Robert; m. Lorna Marion Wise Ekholm, Aug. 21, 1993. BA, Oberlin Coll., 1966; MA, U. Mich., 1968, PhD, 1971. Asst. prof. to assoc. prof. U. Ga., Athens, 1971-83, dir. survey rsch. ctr., 1981-83; v.p. Marktrend Mkt. Rsch., Vancouver, B.C., Canada, 1983-84; pres., CEO Campbell Goodell Traynor Consul, Vancouver, B.C., Canada, 1984—2000; sr. cons. CGT Rsch. Internat. (formerly named Campbell Goodell Traynor Consul), Vancouver, B.C., Canada, 2000—02; v.p. Corp. Insights, Inc., Vancouver, 1992-96; pres. Argus Strategies, Ltd., Vancouver, B.C., 1988—. Dir. Downtown Vancouver Assn., 1989-96, pres., 1994-96, mem. adv. bd., 1996—; dir. Parking Corp. of Vancouver, 1992-2000, v.p., 1994-96, chmn. bd., 1996-98; bd. dir s. Downtown Vancouver Bus. Improvement Assn., 1994-96; mem. Vancouver Econ. Devel. Commn., 1996. Author: The American Electorate, 1979, profl. jours. Avocations: musical theatre, minor hockey officiating. Office: Argus Strategies Ltd 2224 W 15th Ave Vancouver BC Canada V6K 2Y7 Office Phone: 604-732-8865.

CAMPBELL, BRUCE CRICHTON, hospital administrator; b. Balt., July 21, 1947; s. James Allen and Elda Shaffer (Crichton) C.; m. Linda Page Cottrell, June 28, 1969; children: Molly Shaffer, Andrew Crichton. BA, Lake Forest Coll., 1969; M.H.A., Washington U., St. Louis, 1973; DPH, U. Ill., 1979. Adminstrv. asst. Passavant Meml. Hosp., Chgo., 1970-71; adminstrv. resident Albany (N.Y.) Med. Center Hosp., 1972-73; adminstrv. asst. Rush-Presbyn.-St. Luke's Med. Center, Chgo., 1973-75, asst. adminstr., 1975-77, asst. v.p., 1977-79, v.p. adminstrv. affairs, 1979-83; chmn. dept. health systems mgmt. Rush U., Chgo., 1977-81, dean Coll. Health Scis., 1981-83; exec. dir. U. Chgo. Hosps. and Clinics, 1983-85; lectr. Grad. Sch. Bus., U. Chgo., 1983-85; pres. Campbell Assocs., Chgo., 1985-92; exec. v.p. Ill. Masonic Med. Ctr., Chgo., 1993, pres., 1993-2000, Advocate Luth. Gen. Hosp., Park Ridge, Ill., 2000—. W.K. Kellogg Found. fellow, 1977; Leadership Greater Chgo. fellow, 1984-85 Fellow Am. Coll. Healthcare Execs.; mem. Young Adminstrs. Chgo. (pres. 1977), Assn. Univ. Programs in Health Adminstrn., Am. Hosp. Assn., Ill. Hosp. Assn., Chgo. Hosp. Council. Office: Advocate Luth Gen Hosp 1775 Dempster St Park Ridge IL 60668

CAMPBELL, BYRON CHESSER, newspaper publishing executive; b. Evanston, Ill., Feb. 6, 1934; s. Chesser Milburn and Hallie (Calhoun) C.; m. Barbara Mace, Aug. 16, 1958 (div. Apr. 1982); children: Evan Chesser, Aimee Campbell Wood; m. Meta Pierce, Aug. 13, 1983; stepchildren: Marc Wise, Meier Wise, Matthew Wise, Miles Wise. BA, Yale U., 1955; MBA, Harvard U., 1959. Various positions Burlington (Vt.) Free Press, 1959-61; prodn. engr., asst. labor rels. mgr. Chicago Tribune, 1961-68, prodn. mgr., 1970-73; bus. mgr. Chicago Today, 1968-70; asst. to pres. Tribune Co., 1973-75; pres., gen. mgr. Area Publs. Corp., Merrill Printing Co., Chgo., 1975-77; pres., chief exec. officer News and Sun-Sentinel Co., Ft. Lauderdale, Fla., 1977-83; pres., pub. L.A. Daily News; pres., chief exec. officer Tribune Newspapers West, Inc., LA, 1983-87; pres., pub. The Record, Hackensack, NJ; v.p. Macromedia Inc., Hackensack, 1988-91. Bd. dirs. Home News Pub. Co., New Brunswick, N.J., Newspapers of New Eng., Concord, N.H., George W. Prescott Pub. Co., Quincy, Mass., Journal-Star Printing Co., Lincoln, Nebr., Freedom Comm., Inc., Irvine, Calif. Bd. dirs. Lyric Opera Chgo., Newberry Libr. Chgo., Sta. WPBT, Miami, Fla., Rush-Presbyn.-St. Luke's Med. Ctr., Chgo.; bd. dirs., campaign chmn. United Way of Bergen County, 1989-91; adv. bd. Bergen 2000; bd. dirs., pres., campaign chmn. United Way of Broward County, Fla.; bd. dirs., chmn. San Fernando Valley Cultural Found., L.A.; bd. dirs., pres. Chgo. Youth Ctrs., Broward Community Blood Ctr.; bd. dirs., exec. com. Broward Workshop; bd. dirs. United Way, L.A., campaign chmn. San Fernando Valley; bd. dirs., 1st v.p. Ft. Lauderdale Symphony. Lt. USNR, 1955—57. Mem. AP (nominating com.), Am. Newspaper Pubs. Assn. (govt. affairs com., newsprint com. 1989-92), Am. Press Inst. (bd. dirs. 1984-93), Inland Press Assn. (pres., bd. dirs.), Greater L.A. C. of C. (bd. dirs.), Econ. Club (Chgo.), Yale Club (Chgo., bd. dirs., pres.), Lotos Club (N.Y.C.), Univ. Club (Chgo., bd. dirs., admissions com.), Saddle and Cycle Club (Chgo., bd. dirs., admissions com.), Lauderdale Yacht Club (Ft. Lauderdale, Fla.), Ristigouche Salmon Club (Matapedia, Que.). Congregationalist. Avocations: tennis, wine, fly fishing, travel, golf.

CAMPBELL, CASEY JOSEPH, chaplain; b. Ardmore, Okla., May 27, 1972; s. Timothy Joe and Sherry Kay Campbell; m. Kimberly Christine Hanover, Sept. 4, 1993; children: Kitana Janae children: Gracie Danae, Christine Elizabeth, Derek Wayne, Carson Alexander, Kathryn Victoria, Stormy Leigh. BA, Southeastern Okla. State U., Durant, 1993; MDiv, Southwestern Bapt. Theol. Sem., Ft. Worth, 1997. Pastor First Bapt. Ch., Thackerville, Okla., 1994—97, Southside Bapt. Ch., Gainesville, Tex., 1997—2004; br. chaplain US Army, Fort Sill, 2004—07; chaplain Fed. Bur. Prisons, USP Hazelton, Bruceton Mills, W.Va., 2006—; br. chaplain Army Reserve, Charleston, 2007—. Capt. US Army, 2004—. Decorated Global War on Terrorism Svc. medal US Army, Nat. Def. Svc. medal, Army Achievement, Commendation medal. Mem.: The Order St. Barbara, Am. Mensa. Republican. Baptist. Home: 312 Williams Ave Kingwood WV 26537 Home Phone: 304-329-0867. Personal E-mail: uspchaplain@verizon.net.

CAMPBELL, CATHERINE LYNN, elementary school educator; b. Lynchburg, Va., Mar. 16, 1961; d. Tomie Eawell Campbell and Barbara (Arthur) McCraw. BA, Sweet Briar Coll., Va., 1983; MEd in Admnistrv. and Supervision, U. Va., Charlottesville, 2003. Cert. elem. tchr., NK-8 tchr. VA. Tchr. Amherst County Pub. Schs., Va., 1984—. Mem. Va. Real Estate Bd. Common Interest Properties. Mem.: NEA, ASCD, Nat. Coun. Tchrs. English, Internat. Reading Assn., Va. Edn. Assn., Nat. Honor Soc. Avocations: horseback riding, raising quarter horses. Home: 139 Cedar Crest Dr Ste 107 Madison Heights VA 24572-2366 Office: Amherst County Pub Schs Amherst VA 24521 Office Phone: 434-946-0691. Business E-Mail: ccampbell@amherst.k12.va.us.

CAMPBELL, CHAD, professional golfer; b. Andrews, Tex., May 31, 1974; Degree, UNLV, 1996. Winner The Tour Championship, 2003, Bay Hill Invitational, 2004, Bob Hope Chrysler Classic, 2006. Mem. US Team Ryder Cup, 2004, 06. Named Rookie of Yr. (Hooters Tour), 1997, First Team Jr. Coll. All-Am. Achievements include three time Hooters Tour Player of Yr. Avocation: hunting. Office: c/o PGA Tour 112 PGA Tour Blvd Ponte Vedra Beach FL 32082*

CAMPBELL, CHARLES ALTON, transportation executive; b. Brunswick, Ga., Mar. 10, 1944; s. Rayford Monroe and Cecelia Elizabeth (Camilla) C.; m. Mary Alla Traber, Aug. 15, 1970; children: Christine Beensen, Elizabeth Traber, Charles Traber. B Indsl. Engring., Ga. Inst. Tech., 1966; MBA, Harvard U., 1973. Mgr. ops. projects Camak Lumber Ops., ITT Rayonier, Thomson, Ga., 1974-75, mgr. ops. projects Wood Products Group NYC, 1975-77, dir. chems. devel. parent co., 1977-79, dir. operational planning and control Seattle, 1979-80; pres. Fox Mfg. Co., Rome, Ga., 1980-81, Camtec, Inc., Rome, 1981-88; chmn. bd. Universal Ceramics, nc., Adairsville, Ga., 1984-87; exec. v.p. Saunders, Inc., Birmingham, Ala., 1987-88, pres. CEO, 1988-90; pres. N.Am. Tech. Corp., Birmingham, 1990—. Lt. CE, USNR, 1967-69. Mem. Downtown Rotary (Birmingham, Ala.) Plantation Club at Reynolds Plantation, The Club. Episcopalian. Office: NAm Tech Corp PO Box 43462 Birmingham AL 35243-0462 Home: 1060 Early Pl Greensboro GA 30642

CAMPBELL, CHARLES TAYLOR, chemistry educator; b. Beaumont, Tex., Apr. 30, 1953; married; 1 child. BS, U. Tex., Austin, 1975, PhD, 1979. Summer grad. student Sandia Nat. Labs, N.Mex., 1977; postdoctoral rsch. assoc. U. Munich, 1979-81; staff mem. Los Alamos Nat. Lab., N.Mex., 1981-86; assoc. prof. Ind. U., Bloomington, 1986-89, U. Wash., Seattle, 1989-92, prof. chemistry, 1992—, adj. prof. physics, 1994—, co-dir., Ctr. for Nanotechnology, 1997—2003, dir., Ctr. for Nanotechnology, 2003—04, Lloyd E. and Florence M. West Endowed Professorship in Chemistry, 2004—; co-dir. Pacific Northwest Nat. Lab., 2001—, U. Wash. Joint Inst. for Nanoscience, 2001—. Mem. Dept. Energy Labs Tech. Rsch. Program Review, Catalysis/Chem. Conversion, 1996, Dept. Energy/Oak Ridge Nat. Lab Chem. Sciences Program Review, 1997, Lawrence Berkeley Nat. Lab, Materials Sci. Review, 1998; mem. scientific adv. com., Pacific Northwest Nat. Labs EMSL, 2003-; mem. internat. scientific adv. bd., Fritz Haber Inst., Max Planck Soc., Berlin, Germany, 2005-; scientific adv. bd. Prolinx, Inc., Bothell, Wash., 2001-2003, Lumera, Inc., Bothell, Wash., 2004-, Asemblon, Inc., Seattle, Wash., 2005-; bd. dir., Wash. Tech. Ctr., 1997-2000, Internat. Workshop on Oxide Surfaces, 2006-; presenter in field. Mem. editl. bd. Jour. of Catalysis, 1991-93, Jour. Chem. Physics, 2002-2004, Current Topics in Catalysts, 2004-; chief editor Surface Sci., 2002-; patentee in field; contbr. articles to profl. jours. Recipient DuPont Young Faculty award, 1988-89, Camille and Henry Dreyfus Found. Tchr./Scholar award, 1988-92, John Yarwood Meml. award Brit. Vacuum Coun., 1989, Alexander von Humboldt Rsch. award, 2001; NSF NATO postdoctoral fellow U. Munich, 1979-80, Alexander von Humboldt fellow U. Munich, 1980-81, Alfred P. Sloan rsch. fellow, 1986-88; Lubrizol Found. scholar U. Tex., 1973-74, Alcoa and Dean's Office scholar U. Tex., 1974-75. Mem. Am. Chem. Soc. (treas. colloid & surface divsn. 1984-89, vice-chmn. 1991, chmn.-elect 1992, chmn. 1993, co-chmn. continuing symposium on surface and colloid chemistry of advanced materials 1988-91, Am. Chem. Soc. Colloid and Surface Chemistry award, 2001, Arthur W. Adamson award for Disting. Svc. in the Advancement of Surface Chemistry, 2007), N.Am. Catalysis Soc. (Pacific Coast Catalysis Soc. Repr., 2006-), Am. Vacuum Soc. (exec. com. N.Mex. chpt. 1983-84), Phi Eta Sigma (pres. Lamar U. chpt. 1971), Phi Lambda Upsilon (nat. v.p., 1999-2002, nat pres., 2002-2005). Office: Dept Chemistry U Wash Bagley 36 Box 351700 Seattle WA 98195-1700 Office Phone: 206-616-6085, 206-616-4270, 206-616-2969, 206-616-2967. Office Fax: 206-616-6250. Business E-Mail: campbell@chem.washington.edu.*

CAMPBELL, CHRISTIAN BETHUNE, actor; b. Toronto, Ontario, Canada, May 12, 1972; s. Gerry Campbell and Marnie Neve; m. Erin Matthews, May 12, 2001 (div. 2003). Cofounder Blue Sphere Alliance, LA; ptnr. Rebellion Productions LLC. Actor: (films) Next Time, 1998, Hairshirt, 1998, Cold Hearts, 1999, Trick, 1999, Angels!, 2000, Thank You, Good Night, 2001, Who is A.B.?, 2001, The Good Things, 2001, Plead, 2001, Red Faction II, 2002, Chaos Legion, 2003, Max Steel: Endangered Species, 2004, Pretty Dead Girl, 2004, Max Steel: Forces of Nature, 2005, Reefer Madness: The Movie Musical, 2005; (TV films) School's Out, 1991, City Boy, 1992, Born to Run, 1993, Seduced by Madness: The Diane Borchardt Story, 1996, I've Been Waiting for You, 1998, Cruel Justice, 1999, The Piano Man's Daughter, 2003, Banshee, 2006; (TV series) Degrassi High, 1990, Tek War, 1996, Malibu Shores, 1996, Seventh Heaven, 1996, The Street, 2000, Max Steel, 2001, Jeremiah, 2002, Blue Murder, 2003, All My Children, 2004—05, The Book of Daniel, 2006; (plays) Reefer Madness, 1999 (LA Drama Critics Cir. award best lead performance, 1999), Nagasaki Dust, Tick, Tick.BOOM!, Great Expectations, 2006. Mailing: c/o Forster Entertainment 12533 Woodgreen St Los Angeles CA 90066

CAMPBELL, CHRISTIAN LARSEN, lawyer; b. Chgo., Nov. 21, 1950; s. William Joseph and Marie Agnes (Cloherty) C.; m. Heather Gilchrist, Mar. 7, 1987; children: Christian Jr., Brent, Amelia. BA, MA in Econ., Northwestern U., 1972; JD, Harvard U., 1975. Bar: Ill. 1975, U.S. Dist. Ct. (no. dist.) Ill. 1975, U.S. Ct. Appeals (7th cir.) 1975, U.S. Ct. Appeals (5th cir.) 1980, U.S. Supreme Ct. 1980. Assoc. Sidley & Austin, Chgo., 1975-83, ptnr., 1983—90; v.p., gen. counsel, sec. Nalco Chem. Co., Naperville, Ill., 1990—94; sr. v.p., gen. counsel, sec. Owens Corning, 1995—97, Yum! Brands, Louisville, 1997—, chief franchise officer, 2003—. Mem. ABA, Ill. State Bar Assn., Ky. Bar Assn., Chgo. Bar Assn., Louisville Bar Assn., Am. Mgmt. Assn. (lectr.1976—). Clubs: Barclay (Chgo.). Avocations: tennis, jogging. Office: Yum! Brands 1441 Gardiner Ln Louisville KY 40213-1914 Office Phone: 502-874-2467.*

CAMPBELL, COLIN GOETZE, foundation president; b. NYC, Nov. 3, 1935; s. Joseph and Marjorie (Goetze) C.; m. Nancy Nash, June 20, 1959; children: Elizabeth, Jennifer, Colin, Blair. AB, Cornell U., 1957; JD, Columbia U., 1960; LLD (hon.), Amherst Coll., 1972, Williams Coll., 1973, Dickinson Coll., 1982, U. Hartford, 1983, Wesleyan U., 1989, Conn. Coll., 1990, Fairfield U., 1999; DHL (hon.), Trinity Coll., 1981, Georgetown U., 1984; PhD in Pub. Sci. (hon.), Cedar Crest Coll., 1997. Bar: Conn. 1961. Atty. Cummings & Lockwood, Stamford, Conn., 1960-62; asst. to pres. Am. Stock Exch., NYC, 1962-63, sec., 1963-64, v.p., 1964-67; adminstrv. v.p. Wesleyan U., Middletown, Conn., 1967-69, exec. v.p., 1969-70, pres., 1970-88, pres. emeritus, 1988—; pres. Rockefeller Bros. Fund, 1988-2000; chmn., pres. Colonial Williamsburg (Va.) Found., 2000—. Bd. dirs. Pitney Bowes, Sysco Corp. Bd. dirs. Rockefeller Fin. Svcs. Mem. Am. Acad. Arts and Scis., Coun. on Fgn. Rels., Century Assn., Knickerbocker Club, Psi Upsilon, Phi Delta Phi. Episcopalian. Home: Coke-Garrett House 465 E Nicholson St Williamsburg VA 23185 Office: Colonial Williamsburg Found PO Box 1776 Williamsburg VA 23187-1776 Office Phone: 757-220-7200. E-mail: ccampbell@cwf.org.

CAMPBELL, COLIN HERALD, former mayor; b. Winnipeg, Man., Can., Jan. 18, 1911; s. Colin Charles and Aimee Florence (Herald) C.; m. Virginia Paris, July 20, 1935; children: Susanna Herald, Corinna Buford, Virginia Wallace. BA, Reed Coll., 1933. Exec. sec. City Club of Portland, 1934-39; alumni sec., dir. endowment adminstrn. Reed Coll., 1939-42; exec. sec. NW Inst. Internat. Rels., 1940-42; supr. contract, engr. Kaiser Co., Inc., 1942-45; asst. pers. dir. Portland Gas & Coke Co., 1945-48; dir. indsl. rels. Pacific Power & Light Co., Portland, 1948-76. Mem. Oreg. Adv. Com. on Fair Employment Practices Act, 1949-55; trustee, chmn., pres. Portland Symphonic Choir, 1950-54; trustee Portland Civic Theater, 1941-54; bd. dirs. Portland Symphony Soc., 1957-60, Cmty. Child Guidance Clinic, 1966-68; active United Way, 1945-75; bd. dirs. Contemporary Crafts Assn., 1972-76, treas., 1975-76; bd. dirs. Lake Oswego Corp., 1961-65, 71-73, 74-76, corp. sec., 1964, pres., 1973-74, treas., 1975-76; mem. Com. on Citizen Involvement, City of Lake Oswego, 1975-77; chmn. Bicentennial Com., Lake Oswego, 1975-76; sec.-treas. Met. Area Comms. Commn., 1980-85; treas. Clackamas County Cmty. Action Agy., 1980-82, chmn., 1982-85; fin. adv. com. West Clackamas County LWV, 1974-76, 78-80; councilman City of Lake Oswego, 1977-78, mayor, 1979-85, chmn. libr. growth task force, 1987-89, chmn. hist. rev. bd., 1990-92; chmn. energy adv. com. League Oreg. Cities, 1982-84; adv. bd., chmn. fin. com. Lake Oswego Adult Cmty. Ctr., 1985-88; pres. Oswego Heritage coun., 1992-95, sec., 1995-96, treas., 1997-99, dir., 2000, dir. emeritus, 2001—; mem. County Blue Ribbon Com. on Law Enforcement, 1987-89; fee arbitration panel Oreg. State Bar Assn., 1995-2000; mem. resident coun. Mary's Woods at Marylhurst, 2001—06. Mem. Lake Oswego C. of C. (v.p. 1986-87, chmn. land use com. 1990-91), Nat. Trust for Hist. Preservation, Hist. Preservation League Oreg., Oreg. Hist. Soc., McLoughlin Meml. Assn., Oswego Heritage Coun. (pres. 1992-94, 95-96, treas. 1997-99, editor 1992-2003), Clackamas County Hist. Assn., Rotary (treas. Lake Oswego chpt. 1990-93). Republican. Presbyterian. Home: Apt 306 17440 Holy Names Dr Lake Oswego OR 97034-5143 Personal E-mail: colinhc@comcast.net.

CAMPBELL, COLIN KYDD, electrical and computer engineering educator, researcher; b. St. Andrews, Fife, Scotland, May 3, 1927; s. David Walker and Jean (Hutchison) C.; m. Vivian Gwyn Norval, Apr. 17, 1954; children— Barry, Gwyn, Ian BSc in Engring. with honors, St. Andrews U., 1952, PhD, 1960; MS, MIT, 1953; DSc, U. Dundee, 1984. Registered profl. engr., Ont. Comm. engr. Fgn. Office and Diplomatic Wireless Svc., London, 1946—47, Brit. Embassy, Washington, 1947—48; electronics engr. Atomic Instrument Co., Cambridge, Mass., 1954—57; asst. prof. elec. and computer engring. McMaster U., Hamilton, Ont., Canada, 1960—63, assoc. prof. elec. and computer engring., 1963—67, prof. elec. engring., 1967—89, prof. elec. and computer engring., 1989—2005, prof. emeritus, 2005. Vis. scholar Ctr. for Power Electronic Sys., Va. Poly. Inst. and State U., Blacksburg, 2000, 02. Author: Surface Acoustic Wave Devices and Their Signal Processing Applications, 1989, Surface Acoustic Wave Devices for Mobile and Wireless Communication, 1998; contbr. numerous articles to profl. jours. Served with Brit. Army, 1944-46 Recipient The Inventor insignia Can. Patents and Devel. Ltd., 1973, invitation fellow Japan Soc. for Promotion of Sci., 1995, rsch. fellow Rand Afrikaans U., South Africa, 1995. Fellow Royal Soc. Can. (Thomas Eadie medal 1983), Engring. Inst. Can., Royal Soc. Arts London, IEEE (life); mem. Sigma Xi, Royal Can. Mil. Inst. Club Toronto Avocation: fishing. Home: 160 Parkview Dr Ancaster ON Canada L9G 1Z5 Office: McMaster U Elec Computer Engring 1280 Main St W Hamilton ON Canada L8S 4K1 Business E-Mail: colin.kydd.campbell@sympatico.ca.

CAMPBELL, CYNTHIA, consumer products company executive; Grad., U. Kans. Various positions up to v.p., gen. mgr. GTE Info. Svcs., 1976—95; regional v.p. Bus. Svcs. Group SE Region Office Depot, Inc., Delray Beach, Fla., 1995—2000, sr. v.p. sales Fla. and Ga., 2000, sr. v.p. sales Bus. Svcs. Group East Region, exec. v.p. Delivery Sales N.Am., 2003, exec. v.p. bus. solutions divsn. Office: Office Depot Inc 2200 Old Germantown Rd Delray Beach FL 33445*

CAMPBELL, DAVID, lawyer, utilities executive; BA, Yale Univ.; JD, Harvard Univ.; M, Oxford Univ. Prin. McKinsey & Co., Dallas; exec. v.p. corp. planning & strategy TXU Corp., Dallas, 2004—06, exec. v.p., CFO, chief risk officer, 2006—. Trustee Dallas Theater Ctr.; past. mem. Rhodes Scholarship selection com. Rhodes Scholar. Mem.: Council on Fgn. Rels., Dallas Assembly. Office: TXU Corp Energy Plz 1601 Bryan St Dallas TX 75201*

CAMPBELL, DAVID D., consumer products company executive; BS, McMaster U., Hamilton, Ont.; M in Bus., York U., Toronto, Ont. Various mktg. and mgmt. positions Molson Industries, Canada; pres. Constrn. Products bus. Ill. Tool Works, Canada, 1983; pres. ACCO Can. ACCO World, 1989, sr. v.p. ACCO USA, 1992, pres., CEO, 2000—05; head Hardware Group Fortune Brands, 1995; chmn., CEO ACCO Brands Corp., 2005—. Office: ACCO Brands Corp 300 Tower Pky Lincolnshire IL 60069 Office Phone: 800-222-6462.*

CAMPBELL, DAVID GWYNNE, petroleum executive, geologist; b. May 2, 1930; s. Lois Raymond Henager and La Vada (Ray) Henager Campbell; m. Janet Gay Newland, March 1, 1958; 1 child, Carl David. BS, Tulsa U., 1953; MS, U. Okla., Norman, 1957. Geologist Lone Star Producing Co., Oklahoma City, 1957-65; dist. geologist, geol. cons. Tenneco Oil Co., Oklahoma City, 1965-77; exploration mgr. Leede Exploration, Oklahoma City, 1977-80; pres. Earth Hawk Exploration, Inc., Oklahoma City, 1980—. Divsn. exploration mgr. PetroCorp., Inc., Oklahoma City, 1983-92, divsn. gen. mgr. 1992-96; cons. Jr. Achievement, Oklahoma City, 1996-2005; active U. Okla. Sch. Geology and Geophysics Alumni 1985—, bd. dirs. adv. coun. 1988-90, sec. 1990-91, vice chmn., 1991-92, chmn., 1992-93, life mem., 1994, centennial com., 2000-01, U. Okla. Trailblazer award com., 2003—. Contbr. articles to Jour. Cherokee Studies. Active Last Frontier Coun. Boy Scouts Am., 1960-73, edn. chmn. Eagle Dist. 1963-67; gubernatorial appointee Native Am. Cultural and Edn. Authority, 2002—; Okla. Cultural Coalition Gala com., 1999. Recipient cert. of appreciation, Nat. Exch. Club, Oklahoma City, 1999, Okla. Gov.'s Arts award for cmty. svc., 2003. Mem. AAAS, Internat. Assn. Energy Economists, Soc. Ind. Profl. Earth Scientists (pres. Okla. chpt. 1988, chmn. 1989, 91), Soc. Profl. Well Log Analysts, Am. Assn. Petroleum Geologists (hon. mem. 1995, chmn. house of dels. 1981-82, ho. of dels. 1982—, exec. com. 1981-82, 90-91, found. trustee assoc. 1983—, corp. mem. Am. Assn. Petroleum Geologists Found. 1996—, mem. adv. coun. 1984-87, councillor mid-continent sect. 1984-87, nominating com. 1984-85, 86-87, astrogeology com. 1984-2004, honors and awards com. 1984-85, 85-86, adv. bd. Treatise of Petroleum Geology 1986-91, nat. membership adv. coun. 1987-90, membership com. chmn. mid-continent sect. 1987-90, Disting. Svc. award 1989, nat. v.p. 1990-91, mid-continent councillor energy minerals divsn. 1992-94, chmn. com. of coms. 1992-98, charter mem. divsn. Environ. Geoscis. 1992, candidate for nat. pres. 2001), Oklahoma City Geol. Soc. (hon. life mem. 1992, pub. rels. chmn. Spkrs. Bur. 1963-64, chmn. stratigraphic code com. 1967-68, presdl. appointee 1969-70, advt. mgr. Shale Shaker 1969-71, bylaws and incorp. rev. com. 1986), Oklahoma City Geol. Found. (founding pres. 1993-98, bd. dirs. 1993-2001), Ind.

Petroleum Assn. Am. (Okla. chpt. regulatory affairs com. 1991-93), Houston Geol. Soc., Tulsa Geol. Soc., Petroleum Exploration Soc. Great Britain, Oklahoma City Petroleum Club (bd. dirs. 1987-90, 1995-98, sec. 1989, 2d v.p. 1990, chmn. membership com. 1988-90), Geol. Soc. Moscow, NY Acad. Scis., Oklahoma City C. of C., Okla. Hist. Soc., Cherokee Nat. Hist. Soc. (devel. com. 1987-95, trustee nat. soc. 1983-96), Ctr. Am. Indian (bd. dir. 1988-92), Red Earth Indian Ctr. (bd. dirs. 1992—, co-founder Red Earth Amb. of Yr. award, v.p. 1994-97, pres. 1997-98, Spirit award, 1999), Nat. Mus. Am. Indian, Am. Indian Cultural Soc., Houston Mus. Fine Arts, Okla. Pilots Assn., Exptl. Aircraft Assn., Aircraft Owners and Pilots Assn., First Families of Twin Ters., Clan Campbell N.Am., Sigma Xi, Pi Kappa Alpha. Home: 6109 Woodbridge Rd Oklahoma City OK 73162-3220 Office: Earth Hawk Exploration Inc PO Box 2396 Oklahoma City OK 73101-2396 Office Phone: 405-236-3030.

CAMPBELL, DAVID KELLY, theoretical physicist, engineering educator; b. Long Beach, Calif., July 23, 1944; s. S. Kelly and Elizabeth (Platt) C.; children from previous marriage: Jean-Pierre N., Michael C.; m. Claude Hobson, May 25, 2002; stepchildren: Alex, Jeremy, Nicola, Oliver, Gabriel, Sophie and Theodora Hobson. BA in chemistry and physics, Harvard U., 1966; PhD in theoretical physics and applied math., Cambridge U., Eng., 1970. Instr. and rsch. assoc. U. Ill., Urbana, 1970-72; mem. Inst. for Advanced Study Princeton U., 1972-74; J.R. Oppenheimer Fellow Los Alamos Nat. Lab., 1974—77, staff mem., 1977—92, dir. Ctr. for Nonlinear Studies, 1987—92; prof., head. dept. physics U. Ill., 1992—2000; dean Coll. Engrng. Boston U., 2000—05, provost ad interim, 2004—. Editor: Order in Chaos, 1981, Interactive Electrons in Reduced Dimensions, 1989, Chaos/XAOC: Soviet-American Perspectives in Nonlinear Science, 1990—. Named Disting Lectr. Assn. Western U., Dept. Energy, 1989-90, Dept. Edn., Peoples Republic China, 1986; Eminent scholar State of N.Mex., 1989. Fellow AAAS, Am. Phys. Soc. Office: Boston U Office of the Provost One Sherborn St 8th Fl Boston MA 02215 E-mail: dkcampe@bu.edu.

CAMPBELL, DEMAREST LINDSAY, artist, writer, interior designer; d. Peter Stephen III and Mary Elizabeth (Edwards) C.; m. Dale Gordon Haugo, 1978. BFA in Art History, MFA in Asian Art History, MFA in Theatre Design. Designer interiors, historic renovation, mural art Demarest Campbell Art and Interiors, San Francisco, 1975—; chargeman scenic artist Am. Conservatory Theatre, 1976—. Designed, painted and sculpted over 300 prodns. for Broadway, internat. opera, motion pictures. Mem. NOW, Asian Art Mus. Soc., San Francisco. Mem. Internat. Alliance of Theatrical Stage Employees, Art Dirs. Guild and Scenic, Title and Graphic Artists (Local 800), Sherlock Holmes Soc. London, Amnesty Internat., Nat. Trust for Hist. Preservation (Gt. Britian and U.S.A. chpt.), Shavian Malthus Soc. (charter Gt. Britian chpt.), Humane Soc. of U.S. (millennium mem.), The Drones Club. Avocations: medical history, pre-twentieth century military history.

CAMPBELL, DENNIS MARION, academic administrator, educator, theologian; b. Dalhart, Tex., Aug. 23, 1945; s. Francis Marion and Margaret (Osterberg) C.; m. Leesa Heydenreich, June 13, 1970; children: Margaret Heyden, Robert Trevor. AB, Duke U., 1967, PhD, 1973; BD, Yale U., 1970; DD (hon.), Fla. So. U., 1986. Ordained to ministry United Meth. Ch., 1974. Min. Trinity United Meth. Ch., Durham, NC, 1973-74; chmn. dept. religion Converse Coll., Spartanburg, SC, 1974-79; dir. continuing edn. Div. Sch. Duke U., Durham, 1979-82, prof. theology, 1982—, dean. Div. Sch., 1982-97; headmaster Woodberry Forest (Va.) Sch., 1997—. Mem. Oxford (Eng.) Inst. Theol. Studies, 1982, 87, 92, Denver, 1996; gen. conf. United Meth. Ch., Balt., 1984, St. Louis, 1988, Louisville, 1992; del. World Meth. Coun., Nairobi, Kenya, 1987, World Coun. Chs. 7th Assembly, Canberra, Australia, 1991. Author: Authority and the Renewal of American Theology, 1976, Doctors, Lawyers, Ministers: Christian Ethics in Professional Practice, 1982, The Yoke of Obedience: The Meaning of Ordination in Methodism, 1988, Who Will Go For Us?, 1994. Chmn. Protection of Human Subjects Com.; bd. dirs. Family Health Internat., Research Triangle Park, 1986—, Internat. Coalition Boys Schs; bd. visitors Perkins Sch. Theology So. Meth. U., Dallas, 1987—; overseers com. Harvard U., 1992—; trustee Duke Endowment, 2004-. Mem. Am. Theol. Soc., Am. Acad. Religion, Soc. Christian Ethics, Assn. Theol. Schs. (accrediting com. 1986—), Phi Beta Kappa, Omicron Delta Kappa. Methodist. Home: PO Box 48 Woodberry Forest VA 22989-0048 Office: The Residence Woodberry Forest VA 22989-0048

CAMPBELL, DONALD G., retail executive; b. 1951; With TJX Cos., Inc., 1973—85, v.p., corp. contr. Framingham, Mass., 1985—87, sr. fin. exec., 1988—89, CFO, 1989—2004, sr. v.p., fin., 1989—96, exec. v.p. fin., 1996—2004, sr. exec. v.p., chief adminstrv. bus. devel. officer, 2004—07, vice chmn., 2007—; sr. v.p. fin. & adminstrn. Sayres Stores divsn., 1987—88. Office: The TJX Cos Inc 770 Cochituate Rd Framingham MA 01701-4672*

CAMPBELL, EDWARD ADOLPH, judge, electrical engineer; b. Boonville, Ind., Jan. 16, 1936; s. Revis Allen and Sarah Gertrude C.; m. Nancy Colleen Keys, July 26, 1957; children: Susan Elizabeth Campbell Frisse, Stephen Edward, Sara Lynne Campbell Dillman. BEE, U. Evansville, 1959; JD, Ind. U., 1965; grad. Nat. Coll. Dist. Attys., U. Houston, 1972; grad. Nat. Jud. Coll., U. Nev., 1978; grad. Am. Acad. Jud. Edn., U. Va., 1979; grad., Ind. Jud. Coll., 1981; grad. Ind. Grad. Program for Judges, Ind. Jud. Ctr., 1999. Bar: Ind. 1965, U.S. Dist. Ct. (so. dist.) Ind. 1965, U.S. Ct. of Customs and Patent Appeals 1967, U.S. Supreme Ct. 1973, U.S. Ct. Appeals (fed. cir.) 1982. Patent examiner U.S. Patent Office Digital Computer Divsn., Washington, 1959-60; patent adv. U.S. Naval Avionics, Indpls., 1960-65; patent atty. Gen. Elec. Co., Ft. Wayne, Ind., 1965-66; ptnr. Weyerbacher & Campbell, attys., Boonville, Ind., 1966-71; pros. atty. 2nd Jud. Cir., Warrick County, Ind., 1971-77; judge Warrick Superior Ct. No. 1, 1977-2001; sr. judge Ind. State Trial Cts., 2001—. Fellow, Ind. Bar Found.; mem. IEEE, Ind.State Bar Assn., Evansville Bar Assn., Warrick County Bar Assn., Ind. Judges Assn., Warrick County C. of C. (bd. dirs. 1978-84, 97-04), Lions Club, Sigma Pi Sigma, Phi Delta Phi. Democrat. Methodist. Home: 911 Julian Dr Boonville IN 47601-9556

CAMPBELL, EDWARD JOSEPH, retired machinery company executive; b. Boston, Feb. 21, 1928; s. Edward and Mary (Doherty) C.; divorced; children: Gary, Kevin, Diane. BSME, Northwestern U., 1952, MBA, 1959. With Am. Brakeshoe Co., 1952-58, Whirlpool Corp., 1958-65; gen. mgr. Joy Mfg. Co., 1965-67; exec. v.p. J.I. Case Co. subs. Tenneco, Inc., 1968-78; pres., chief exec. officer Newport News Shipbuilding & Dry Dock Co. subs. Tenneco, Inc., Va., 1979-91; pres. J.I. Case Co. subs. Tenneco Inc., Racine, Wis., 1992-94. Bd. dir. Global Marine, Zurn Industries, Titan Internat., ABS Group; chmn. Campbell Enterprises. Mem. bd. and adv. coun. Webb Inst., Northwestern U., William & Mary Coll., U. Wis. Vet. Medicine Sch., Hampden & Sydney Coll.; chmn. Navy League US Found., elected ato NAE 1986 (Nat. Acad. of Engrng., With USNR, 1946-48. Home: 1 Deepwood Dr Unit A1 Racine WI 53402-2868 Office: PO Box 8 Racine WI 53401-0008

CAMPBELL, EDWARD WALLACE, nutritionist; b. Elizabeth, NJ, June 29, 1939; s. Edward Wallace Sr. and Dorothy Mae (Fairchild) C.; m. Phyllis A. Vecere, Sept. 27, 1959 (div. 1985); children: Diane Theresa, Christina Marie. PhD, Am. Coll., 1988; DLitt, Wellington U., 1990; MD, Open Internat. U., 1991, DSc, 1992; diploma, Lyons Med. Lab. Sch. Diplomate Internat. Coll. Acupuncture, Am. Coll. Manipulation and Nutrition, Inst. for Human Biomechanics, Am. Bd. Nutrition and Clin. Nutrition; cert. wellness counselor; Australian postgrad. cert. in acupuncture. Pvt. practice, 1974-94; dean of students Nat. Nutrition Inst., Oak Park, Ill., 1988-92; exec. dir. Am. Bd. Nutritional and Naturopathic Cert., Toms River, NJ, 1989-92; dir. R & D Vitagenics Rsch., Brick, NJ, 1990-95; dir. rsch. World AIDS Rsch. Inc., 1995—2006; CEO www.Nutriprotocols.com, 2006—. Spkr. Nat. Health Fedn., 1987-93; prof. Open Internat. U. Author: Orthomolecular Protocol for Morbid Obesity with Adjunctive Congestive Heart Failure, 1987, Orthomolecular Protocols for the Physician, 1988, The Etiology of Hyperlipoproteinemia, 1990, Nutritional Management of Peripheral Vascular Diseases, 1991; contbg. editor: Am. Nutrition Cons. Assn. Jour., 1988-93. Assoc. mem. Am. Mus. Nat. History; mem. Nat. Arbor Day Found., Rep. Nat. Com., Washington, 1980—; del. Rep. Party Platform Planning Com., Washington 1991-92, Presdl. Trust, Washington, 1992; campaign trustee Rep. Presdl. Task Force, Washington, 1987, 93. Fellow Found. Complementary Medicine, Commonwealth (U.K.) Inst. Natural Medicine, Medicina Alternativa Sci. Soc., The Homeopathic Found.; mem. Internat. Assn. Holistic Health and Medicine, Am. Nutrition Cons. Assn., Nat. Health Fedn., Am. Assn. of Nutritional Cons., Wilson Ctr. Assocs., Homeopathy and Homotoxicology Symposium, Va. Sheriffs Inst., Law Enforcement Alliance Am., Am. Legion, Senators Club, Clan Campbell Soc. Methodist. Avocations: hunting, fishing, chess, numismatism. Personal E-mail: dr@nutriprotocols.com. *One's achievements are of no importance when accomplished without regard for morality and ethics.*

CAMPBELL, EDWIN DENTON, educational association administrator, consultant, accountant; b. Boston, June 25, 1927; s. William Edwin and Mildred (Altmiller) C.; m. Crystal Cousins, 1973; children: Geraldine, Linda, David, Sean, Jennifer. Grad., Bentley Coll., Boston, 1948; CAS, Harvard U., Cambridge, Mass., 1971; EdD, 1975. CPA, Mass. Mgr. Arthur Andersen & Co. CPAs, Boston, 1948-53; v.p. Lab. for Electronics, Inc., Boston, 1953-62, also dir.; exec. v.p. Itek Corp., Lexington, Mass., 1962-70, dir., 1962-83; pres. Edn. Devel. Ctr., Newton, Mass., 1971-76, trustee, 1971—2004; pres. Gulf Mgmt. Inst. div. Gulf Oil Corp., Boston, 1976-83; on loan as exec. v.p. Nat. Alliance of Bus., Washington, 1983-86; dean sch. bus. Adelphi U., Garden City, NY, 1986-87; trustee Edn. Testing Svc., Princeton, NJ, 1983-87, v.p., 1987-89; exec. dir. Coalition of Essential Schs., Annenberg Inst. for Sch. Reform, Brown U., Providence, 1990-96; prin. Padanaram Assocs., Inc., 1996—2001. Interim exec. dir. Plimoth Plantation, 1997; bd. dirs. Artworks!, 1993-2003; mem. faculty Bentley Coll., Boston, 1956-58. Cons. editor: Change, 1980-98. Trustee Bentley Coll., 1963—, New Bedford Whaling Mus., 1996—2003, Friends Acad., 1996—2002, Ptnrs. in Edn., Inc., 1997-99; v.p. Mass. Assn. Mental Health, 1965-68, bd. dirs., 1962-73; mem. Mass Commn. Vocat. Rehab., 1966-68, Coll. Bd. Commn. on Pre-coll. Counseling, 1984-86; mem. vis. com. Harvard Sch. Edn., 1977-83; mem. fin. com. Town of Carlisle, Mass., 1965-68; trustee Boston Urban Found., 1969-75, Mass. Taxpayers Found., 1962-68, Fenn Sch., 1970-75, OSTI, Inc., 1971-76, Lesley Coll., 1972-76, Mass. Advocacy Ctr., 1975-76. Served with USMC, 1943-45, PTO. Mem. Assn. Industries Mass. (pres. 1967-69, now dir.), Harvard Club Boston, Cosmos Club Washington (D.C.), New Bedford Yacht Club.

CAMPBELL, EILEEN M., oil industry executive; married; 2 children. Bachelor's, U. Md. Lobbyist Gov. NJ; with Nat. Assn. Mfrs.; lobbyist United Gas Pipe Line Co.; mgr. govt. affairs Marathon Oil Corp., Houston, 1991—98, v.p. human resources, 2000—; dir. state govt. affairs USX, 1998—2000. Office: Marathon Oil Corp Corp Hdqrs 5555 San Felipe Rd Houston TX 77056-2723

CAMPBELL, ELLEN FEYK, elementary school educator; b. Glen Cove, NY, Oct. 17, 1955; d. Richard Peter and Joan Marian Feyk; m. Declan Francis Miney (dec. 1994); children: Ryan Feyk-Miney, Kyle Feyk-Miney, Jillian Feyk-Miney; m. Peter Eugene Campbell, June 21, 1997. BSN cum laude, Adelphi U., 1977; MA in Edn. with honors, U. LaVerne, 2004. Noon-duty aide, tchrs. aide Claremont (Calif.) Unified Sch. Dist., 1996, substitute tchr., 1996—97; music tchr. grades K-6 Condit Elem. Sch., Claremont, 1997—98; music tchr. grades 7-8 St. Merks Sch., Upland, Calif., 1997—98, 4th grade tchr., 1998—99, Carnelian Elem., Alta Loma, Calif., 1999—, grade level leader 4th grad., 2000—05, gifted and talented edn. coord., 2004—. Childbirth educator Richmond Childbirth Educators Assn., 1973—92; dir., owner Positive Expectations Childbirth Classes, 1992—96; music tchr. traditional piano Claremont Cmty. Sch. Music, Calif., 1996—; presenter in field. Mem., coord. Claremont Presbyn. Ch., 1996—, family led ch. svc., 2001—05; soloist Claremont Presbyn. Choir. Regents scholar, N.Y., 1972. Mem.: Claremont H.S. Band Boosters, Claremont PTA, Alta Loma PTA, Music Tchrs. Calif., Calif. Tchrs. Am. Avocations: singing, swimming, diving, piano, flute. Home: 1963 Rosemount Ave Claremont CA 91711 Office: Carnelian Elem Sch 7105 Carnelian St Alta Loma CA 91701

CAMPBELL, F(ENTON) GREGORY, academic administrator, historian; b. Columbia, Tenn., Dec. 16, 1939; s. Fenton G. and Ruth (Hayes) C.; m. Barbara D. Kuhn, Aug. 29, 1970; children: Fenton H., Matthew W., Charles H. AB, Baylor U., 1960; postgrad., Philipps U., Marburg/Lahn, Germany, 1960-61; MA, Emory U., 1962; postgrad., Charles U., Prague, Czechoslovakia, 1965-66; PhD, Yale U., 1967; postgrad., Harvard U., 1981. Rsch. staff historian Yale U., New Haven, 1966-68, spl. asst. to acting pres., 1977-78; asst. prof. history U. Wis., Milw., 1968-69; asst. prof. European history U. Chgo., 1969-76, spl. asst. to pres., 1978-87, sec. bd. trustees, 1979-87, sr. lectr., 1985-87; pres., prof. history Carthage Coll., Kenosha, Wis., 1987—. Fellow Woodrow Wilson Internat. Ctr. Scholars, Smithsonian Instn., Washington, 1976-77; participant Japan Study Program for Internat. Execs., 1987; bd. dir. Thrivent Mut. Funds, Johnson Family Mut. Funds., Prairie Sch., United Health Systems, Wis. Author: Confrontation in Central Europe, 1975; joint editor Akten zur deutschen auswartigen Politik, 1918-1945, 1966-96; contbr. articles and revs. to profl. jours. Fulbright grantee, 1960-61, 73-74; Woodrow Wilson fellow, 1961-62; U.S.A.-Czechoslovakia Exch. fellow, 1965-66, 73-74, 85. Mem. Mid-Day Club (Chgo.), Coun. on Fgn. Rels. (NYC), Phi Beta Kappa, Omicron Delta Kappa. Office: Carthage Coll Kenosha WI 53140-1360 Home Phone: 262-551-8087; Office Phone: 262-551-5858. Business E-Mail: poc@carthage.edu.

CAMPBELL, FINLEY ALEXANDER, geologist, consultant; b. Kenora, Ont., Can., Jan. 5, 1927; s. Finley McLeod and Vivian (Delve) C.; m. Barbara Elizabeth Cromarty, Oct. 17, 1953; children— Robert Finley, Glen David, Cheryl Ann. B.Sc., Brandon Coll., U. Man., Can., 1950; MA, Queen's U., Kingston, Ont., 1956; PhD, Princeton U., 1958. Exploration and mining geologist Prospectors Airways, Toronto, 1950-58; asst. and asso. prof. geology U. Alta., Can., Edmonton, 1958-65; prof., head dept. geology U. Calgary, Alta., 1965-69, v.p. capital resources, 1969-71, v.p. acad., 1971-76, prof. geology, 1976-84, v.p. priorities and planning, 1984-88, prof. emeritus, 1988—; geol. cons., 1988—. Bd. dirs., vice chmn. Can Energy Research Inst. Contbr. articles on geol. topics to profl. jours. Bd. dirs. Calgary Olympic Devel. Assn.; mem. minister's adv. bd. Tyrrell Mus. Palaeontology. Decorated Queen's Jubilee medal Can.; recipient Commemorative medal for 125th Anniversary of Can., Geology medal Brandon U. Honor Soc.; Sir James Dunne fellow, 1955-56; Princeton Alumni fellow, 1957-58. Fellow Royal Soc. Can.; mem. Assn. The Univ. of Calgary (pres. emeritus), Geol. Assn. Can., Mineral Assn. Can., Soc. Econ. Geologists, Assn. Profl. Geologists Alta., Am. Mineral Soc. Royal Soc. Can., Can. Inst. Mining and Metallurgy, Brandon Univ. Alumni Assn. (reg. dir., Disting. Svc. award Hockey Hall of Fame 1994), Glenmore Yacht Club, Silver Springs Golf and Country Club, Clearwater Bay Yacht Club. Home: 3408 Benton Dr NW Calgary AB Canada T2L 1W8 Office: U Calgary Dept Geology and Geophysics Calgary AB Canada T2N 1N4 Business E-Mail: campbelf@ucalgary.ca.

CAMPBELL, FRANCES ALEXANDER, psychologist; b. Greensboro, NC, Feb. 3, 1933; d. Norman and Nancy Miriam (Spoon) Alexander; m. Bobby Jack Campbell, Aug. 24, 1957; children: Carol Stuart, John William BA, U. N.C., Womans Coll., 1955; MA, U. N.C., 1958, PhD, 1963. Lic. psychologist, N.C. Asst. prof. Rosary Hill Coll., Williamsville, NY, 1964—65; asst. prof., rsch. assoc. U. N.C. Sch. Medicine, Chapel Hill, 1968—71; rsch. assoc. Child Devel. Inst. U. N.C., Chapel Hill, 1972—78, investigator, 1975—80, coord. psychol. assessment, 1980—90, sr. investigator, 1990—93, fellow, 1994—99, sr. scientist, 2000—. Chmn. Acad. Affairs Internal Rev. Bd. on Human Subjects U. N.C., 1993—97. Keynote spkr. Spearman Conf., Sydney, 2001; contbr. articles to profl. jours. Recipient Disting. Svc. award, U. NC, 2007. Fellow Am. Orthopsychiat. Assn.; mem. APA, Soc. Rsch. Child Devel., Soc. Rsch. Adolescence Office: U NC Child Devel Ctr Cb # 8180 Chapel Hill NC 27599-0001

CAMPBELL, FRANCIS JAMES, retired chemist; b. Toledo, July 29, 1924; s. Herbert J. and Florence E. C.; m. Elizabeth P. Savage, Aug. 21, 1948; children: Nancy, MaryLou, Joan, Kathryn, Janice, James, Daniel. BSChemE, U. Toledo, Ohio, 1948. Cert. profl. chemist. Chemist Dow Chem. Co., Midland, Mich., 1948-53; chemist Dow Corning Corp., Midland, 1953-58, Naval Rsch. Lab., Washington, 1958-93; retired, 1993. Chmn. radiation effects on elec. insulation com. Internat. Electrotech. Commn., Geneva, 1974-85 House com. mem. Ind. Living for Handicapped, Inc., Washington, 1983-92; No. Va. chmn. Joint Bd. on Sci. and Engrng. Edn., Washington, 1965-92. With U.S. Army, 1943-45. Recipient Research Publs. award Naval Research Lab., 1982, USN Meritorious Civilian Svc. award, 1997; decorated D.F.C., Air medal with 2 oak leaf clusters, Asiatic-Pacific Theater ribbon, WWII victory medal; inducted into Edward Drummond Libbey High Sch. Hall of Fame, Toledo, 1996; inducted as hon. fellow Washington Acad. Scis., 1999. Fellow IEEE (life); mem. IEEE Dielectrics and Elec. Insulation Soc. (Eric O. Forster award for Disting. Svc. 1992), Am. Chem. Soc., Am. Legion, Sigma Xi. Achievements include patents on thermal control coatings and battery packaging to prolong satellite life; research in thermal aging and multi-factor effects on reliability of electrical insulation of wire and cable, radiation curing of polymer matrix composites and adhesives, and in radiation damage in organic materials; in identifing the failure mechanisms in Kapton insulated wires that were responsible for a high number of electrical fires in Naval aircraft. Home: 7406 Spring Village Dr Apt 113 Springfield VA 22150 Personal E-mail: franklib@verizon.net.

CAMPBELL, FREDERICK HOLLISTER, retired lawyer, historian, retired military officer; b. Somerville, Mass., June 14, 1923; s. George Murray and Irene Ivers (Smith) C.; m. Amy Holding Strohm, Apr. 14, 1951; 1 child, Susan Hollister. AB, Dartmouth Coll., 1944; JD, Northwestern U., 1949; postgrad., Indsl. Coll. Armed Forces, 1961-62; MA in History, U. Colo., 1984, PhD in History, 1993. Bar: Ill. 1950, U.S. Supreme Ct. 1967, Colo. 1968. Joined USMCR, 1942, USMC, 1953, advanced through grades to lt. col., 1962; asst. editor Callaghan and Co., Chgo., 1949-50; pvt. practice Colorado Springs, Colo., 1968-88; ptnr. Gibson, Gerdes and Campbell, 1969-79; pvt. practice, 1980-88; gen. counsel 1st Fin. Mortgaage Corp., 1988-96; vice-chmn., corp. sec. 1st Fin. Mortgage Corp., 1993-96, ret., 1996; hon. instr. history U. Colo., Colorado Springs, 1986—99. Judge adv. USMC, Camp Lejeune, N.C., Korea, Parris Island, S.C., 1950-67, El Toro, Calif., Vietnam, Washington, 1950-67; vis. instr. Colo. Coll., 1993-95, asst. prof., 1996-97. Author: John's American Notary and Commissioner of Deeds Manual, 1950; contbr. articles to profl. jours. Mem. Estate Planning Coun., Colorado Springs, 1971—81, v.p., 1977—78; trustee Frontier Village Found., 1971—77; precinct committeeman Rep. Party, 1971—86; del. Colo. State Conv., 1972, 1974, 1976, 1980; bd. dirs. Rocky Mountain Nature Assn., 1975—2001, pres., 1979—92; bd. dirs. Rocky Mountain Nat. Park Assocs., 1986—2001, v.p., 1986—92, sec., 1992—95; bd. dirs. Colorado Springs Symphony Assn., 2002—03. Officer USMC. Mem. Colo. Bar Assn., El Paso County Bar Assn. Am. Arbitration Assn., Marines Meml. Club, Phi Alpha Theta. Congregationalist.

CAMPBELL, GAVIN ELLIOTT, real estate investor and developer; m. Diana McClain, May 31, 1997; 2 children. BA in Polit. Philosophy magna cum laude, Yale U., 1982; MBA in Fin., U. Chgo., 1989. Analyst internat. trade Ill. Dept. Agr., Springfield, 1982—83; asst. to gov. State of Ill., Springfield, 1983—85; dep. dir. Civic Com., Chgo., 1985—90; assoc. acquisitions LaSalle Investment Mgmt., Inc., Chgo., 1990—92; v.p. acquisitions LaSalle Investment Mgmt., Chgo., 1992—93, exec. v.p. acquisitions, 1994—95, prin., acquisitions, 1996—98, mng. dir., acquisitions, 1999—2002; pres. Fla. Office Property Co., 1998—. Mng. prin. Steelbridge Capital, 2003-. Pres. Latino Chgo. Theater Co., Chgo., 1990-96, Leadership Fellows Assn., Chgo., 1996-98; dir. Yale Coll. Alumni Schs. Com., Chgo., 1991-95; com. rep. A.N. Pritzker Local Sch. Coun., 1993-98; co-founder, mem. exec. com. Young Leader's Fund, 1994-96; bd. dirs., chmn. Landmarks Preservation Coun. Ill., 2004—; fellow Nat. Tropical Bot. Garden; founder Yankeedoodle.org. Gov.'s fellow, Springfield, 1982, fellow Leadership Greater Chgo., 1987. Mem.: Economic Club Chgo. Avocation: historic building restoration. Office: Steelbridge Capital 4064 N Lincoln Ave Ste 178 Chicago IL 60618 E-mail: gcampbell@steelbridgecapital.com.

CAMPBELL, GEORGE, JR., physicist, university administrator; s. George Washington and Lillian (Britt) C.; m. Mary Schmidt Campbell, Aug. 24, 1968; children: Garikai, Sekou, Britt. BS in Physics, Drexel U., 1968; PhD in Theoretical Physics, Syracuse U., 1977; postgrad., Yale U., 1988; D (hon.), Drexel U., 2000, Coe Coll., 2002, Syracuse U., 2003. Sr. faculty Nkumbi Internat. Coll., Kabwe, Zambia, 1969-71; staff scientist AT&T Bell Labs., Holmdel, NJ, 1977-83, third level mgr., 1983-89; pres., CEO Nat. Action Coun. for Minorities in Engrng., Inc., NYC, 1989-2000; Porth disting. lectr. U. Mo.-Rolla, 1993, 99; pres. Cooper Union for the Advancement of Sci. and Art, NYC, 2000—. Mem. adv. bd. NRC Com. on Women in Sci. and Engring., 1991-95, Sta. WGBH-TV Discovering Women series, 1993-94, Merck Inst. Sci. Edn., 1993-99, US Sec. Energy, 1990-93; nat. commn. Ill. Inst. Tech., 1994; pres. Coalition for Equity and Access to Sci., Tech., Engrng. and Math., 1996-97; regular guest commentator, PBS-TV Nightly Bus. Report; Morella Commn., US Congress, 1999-2000. Co-editor: Access Denied: Race, Ethnicity and the Scientific Enterprise, 2000, contbr. chpts. to books, articles to profl. jours. including Phys. Rev. D, Jour. Math. Physics, Issues in Sci. and Tech., Procs. IEEE Globecom, Black Issues in Higher Edn., Black Collegian, Chronicle of Higher Edn., NACME Rsch. Letter, AAAS Sci. and Tech. Policy Yearbook, 1995; commentator Nightly Bus. Report, 1993-2000. Bd. dirs. NY Hall of Sci., 1994—, Oak Ridge Assoc. Univs., 1993-99, Crossroads Theater Co., 1990-95, Consolidated Edison, Inc., 2000—, Montefiore Med. Ctr., 2001-; NSF adv. bd. Comprehensive Regional Ctr. for Minorities, NY chmn., 1990-93; trustee, exec. com. Rensselaer Poly. Inst., Troy, NY, 1991—, Woodrow Wilson Nat. Fellowship Found., 2004—, Regional Plan Assn., 2006—; chmn. NYC Chancellor's Task Force on Sci. Edn., 1992-93; task force on minorities in sci. Nat. Inst. Environ. Health Scis., 1994; bd. govts. All Nations Alliance for Minority Participation in Sci. and Engring., 1995-2000; trustee Poly. U., Bklyn., 1997-2000, Consolidated Edison, Inc., NY, Commission on Independent Colleges and Universities, 2004-, Regional Plan Assn., Inc., 2006-; mem. Pres.' Info. Tech. Adv. Com. Socio-Econ. and Workforce Panel, 1998—. Recipient George Arents Pioneer medal in physics Syracuse U., 1993, Drexel U. Centennial medal, 1992, US Presdl. award for excellence in math., sci. and engring. mentoring, 1996, EPIC award US Dept. Labor, 1998, Disting. Svc. award for sci. and tech. Poly. U., 1999, Leon J. Obermeyer award City Phila. Bd. Edn.; named Black Achiever in Industry, YMCA, NYC, 1987; Simon Guggenheim scholar Guggenheim Found., Phila., 1963-67. Fellow AAAS (com. on sci., engrng. and pub. policy 1990-96), NY Acad. Scis. (pres.

coun. 1991-2003); mem. Am. Phys. Soc. (pres. cir. 1997-2002), Nat. Acad. Scis., Nat. Acad. Engring. and Inst. Medicine, Nat. Acad. Engring. (steering com. on engr. of 2020), Sigma Pi Sigma. Achievements include extending bootstrap model to SU(4)-symmetric strong interaction physics; responsible for third generation satellite 3 power system development. Office: The Cooper Union for Advancement of Sci & Art 30 Cooper Sq New York NY 10003-7120 Home Phone: 212-254-7474; Office Phone: 212-353-4240. E-mail: campbell@cooper.edu.

CAMPBELL, GEORGE EMERSON, lawyer; b. Piggott, Ark., Sept. 23, 1932; s. Sid and Mae (Harris) C.; m. Anna Claire Janes, June 22, 1960 (dec. Mar. 1971); children: Dianne, Carole; m. Joan Stafford Rule, Apr. 7, 1973. JD, U. Ark., Fayetteville, 1955. Bar: Ark. 1955, U.S. Supreme Ct. 1971. Law clk. to judge Ark. Supreme Ct., 1959-60; mem. Rose Law Firm, P.A., Little Rock, 1960—; Del. 7th Ark. Constl. Conv., 1969-70; regional v.p. Nat. Mcpl. League, 1974-86. Mem. Ark. Ednl. TV Commn., 1976-92, chmn., 1980-82, 88-91. Chmn. bd. Pulaski County Law Libr., 1980—; bd. dirs. Ark. Arts Ctr., 1991-95, sec. 1992-93), Ark. Symphony Orch. Soc., 1982-87, Ark. Capital Corp., pres. 2001-03, chmn. 2003-05; bd. dirs. Ark. Cert. Devel. Corp., Downtown Partnership, 1978-2002, Youth Home Inc., 1986-92, pres., 1991-92; bd. dirs. Ark. Ednl. TV Found., 1984-92, chmn., 1988-91. With USNR, 1955-77, comdr. ret. Fellow Am. Bar Found.; mem. ABA, Ark. Bar Assn., Pulaski County Bar Assn., Am. Law Inst. (life mem.), Nat. Assn. Bond Lawyers Office Fax: 501-375-1309. E-mail: gcampbell@roselawfirm.com.

CAMPBELL, GILBERT SADLER, surgeon, educator; b. Toronto, Ont., Can., Jan. 4, 1924; s. Gilbert S. and Ellen (Thorson) Campbell; m. Dorothy Jean Nugent, Sept. 18, 1947 (div. 1960); children: Kathryn Elln, Rebecca Sadler, Thomas Kim, William Riley; m. Joan Louise Hancock, Sept. 28, 1961; children: Susan Muffin, John Gilbert. Student, Hampden-Sydney Coll., Va., 1939-40; BA, U. Va., Charlottesville, 1943, MD, 1946; MS, U. Minn., Mpls., 1949, PhD, 1954. Intern U. Minn. Hosps., Mpls., 1946-47, tchg. asst., 1947-49, researcher Am. Cancer Soc., 1951-53, sr. surgery resident, 1953-54; instr. physiology U. Minn., Mpls., 1948-49, instr. surgery, 1954-55, asst. prof., 1955-58; prof. surgery U. Okla., Oklahoma City, 1958-65; prof. surgery and thoracic surgery U. Okla. Med. Ctr., Oklahoma City, 1958-65; prof. surgery, chief thoracic surgery U. Ark. for Med. Scis., Little Rock, 1965-90; cons. surgery Little Rock VA Hosp, 1965-90, Ark. Children's Hosp., Little Rock, 1973-90; mem. courtesy staff Ark. Bapt. Med. Ctr., Little Rock, 1972-90; prof. emeritus, 1990—. Contbr. articles in field to med. jours. Served to capt. US Army, 1949-51. Decorated Purple Heart, Bronze Star with oak leaf cluster, Silver Star with oak leaf cluster US Army; Mary R. Markle scholar, 1954-59; recipient Horsley prize U. Va., 1954; named Surgery Alumnus of Yr. U. Minn., 1983; named to U. Ark. Medicine Hall of Fame. Mem. Am. Assn. Thoracic Surgery, AMA (ho. of dels. 1976-82), Am. Physiol. Soc., Am. Surg. Assn., Halsted Soc. (pres. 1978), Internat. Cardiovascular Soc. (v.p. N. Am. Chpt. 1973), Societe Internationale de Chirurgie, Soc. Thoracic Surgeons, Soc. Univ. Surgeons, Soc. Vascular Surgery, So. Surg. Assn. (1st v.p. 1981), Western Surg. Assn., S.W. Surg. Congress (pres. 1980), Raven Soc., Alpha Omega Alpha Home: 66 River Ridge Rd Little Rock AR 72227-1526

CAMPBELL, HENRY CUMMINGS, librarian; b. Vancouver, BC, Can., Apr. 22, 1919; s. Henry and Margaret (Cummings) C.; m. Sylvia Woodsworth, Sept. 13, 1943; children— Shiela (Mrs. David Macrae), Bonnie, Robin. BA, U. B.C., 1940; BLS, U. Toronto, 1941; MA, Columbia U., 1949. Librarian, film producer Nat. Film Bd., Canada, Ottawa, 1941-46; with Secretariat UN, NY, 1946-48, UNESCO, Paris, 1949-56; chief librarian Toronto (Can.) Pub. Library, 1956-78; gen. mgr. Cinfolink Svcs., Toronto, 1994—. Lectr. U. Toronto Sch. Libr. Sci., 1970-71; cons. on info. systems and libr. svcs. Canadian Govt. Social Sci. Rsch. Coun. Can., UNESCO; active State Sci. and Tech. Commn., Beijing, China, 1991—, China Internet Info. Svcs., 1997—. Author: How To Find Out About Canada, 1967, Canadian Libraries, 1972, rev. edit., Early Days on the Great Lakes, 1971, The Public Library in the Urban Metropolitan Setting, 1973, Development of Public Library Systems and Services, 1982, Computer Information Systems in the People's Republic of China, Cinfolink Directory of Information Services in China and Hong Kong, 1993-94, 1993, Cinfolink Annual Review of Information Services in China, 1995-96, 1996, Looking for Harrison, 1993, Cinfolink China Internet Directory, 2002, (with Joachim Wieder) IFLA: A History 1927-2002, 2002. Recipient Prof. Kawla award for Library and Info. Sci., 1984 Fellow IFLA (hon.); mem. Internat. Assn. Met. City Librs. (pres. 1971-74), Canadian Libr. Assn. (pres. 1973-74), Ont. Continuing Edn. Assn. (pres. 1966), Fedn. Can.-China Friendship Socs. (pres. 1985-88), Ex Libris Assn. (pres. 2002—).

CAMPBELL, HUGH BROWN, JR., judge; b. Charlotte, NC, Feb. 19, 1937; s. Hugh Brown and Thelma Louise (Welles) C.; m. Mary Irving Carlyle, Nov. 3, 1962; children: Hugh B. III, Irving Carlyle, Thomas Lenoir. AB, Davidson Coll., NC, 1959; JD, Harvard U., Cambridge, Mass., 1962. Atty. Craighill, Rendleman, Charlotte, 1964-77, Weinstein & Sturges, Charlotte, 1977-94, Cansler Lockhart Charlotte, 1994—2000; judge NC Ct. Appeals, Raleigh, 2000—02, 26th Jud. Dist. Ct., Charlotte, 2003—. Chmn. Jury Commn., Mecklenburg County, NC, 1985-97; exec. com. County Bar Assn., Mecklenburg County, 1989-92, civil cts. com. chair, 1990-92. Rep. NC House Reps., Raleigh, 1969-71; legis. liaison Charlotte/Mecklenburg County, Raleigh, 1971-72; state chmn. NC Zoo Bond Campaign, 1972; chmn. Carolinas Med. Ctr. Bond Campaign, 1976. Col. JAG US Army, 1962-64, Res., 1964-92. Decorated Legion of Merit, Meritorious Svc. medal (2); Honored Order of Hornet, Mecklenburg County, 1976. Mem. NC Bar Coun. (exec. com., chair ethics 1981-90), Planned Parenthood Charlotte (bd. dirs., chmn. 1980-81), YMCA Charlotte (adv. bd. 1992—), Rotary Club East Charlotte (pres. 1976-77). Democrat. Episcopalian. Avocations: tennis, swimming, hiking, reading, politics. Home: 1428 Scotland Ave Charlotte NC 28207-2561 Office: 26th Jud Dist 832 E 4th St Ste 9600 Charlotte NC 28202 Office Phone: 704-686-0101. Office Fax: 704-686-0339. Business E-Mail: hugh.b.campbell@nccourts.org.

CAMPBELL, IAN DAVID, opera company director; b. Brisbane, Australia, Dec. 21, 1945; came to U.S., 1982; m. Ann Spira; children: Benjamin, David. BA, U. Sydney, Australia, 1967. Prin. tenor singer The Australian Opera, Sydney, 1967-74; sr. music officer The Australia Council, Sydney, 1974-76; gen. mgr., stage dir. The State Opera of South Australia, Adelaide, 1976-82; asst. artistic adminstr. Met. Opera, NYC, 1982-83; gen. dir., artistic dir. San Diego Opera, 1983—. Guest lectr. U. Adelaide, 1978; guest prof. San Diego State U., 1986—; cons. Lyric Opera Queensland, Australia, 1980-81; bd. dirs. Opera Am., Washington, 1986-95, 1997-01, chmn., 2001-04; chmn. judges Met. Opera Auditions, Sydney, 1989, Masterclasses, Music Acad. of the West, 1993-96. Prodr., host San Diego Opera Radio Program, 1984-01, At the Opera with Ian Campbell, 2001-05; stage director La Bohème, 1981, 05 (San Diego opera), The Tales of Hoffmann, 1982 (both in South Australia), Falstaff (San Diego opera), 1999, Cavalleria Rusticana/Pagliacci (Santa Barbara Grand opera), 1999, Il Trovatore (San Diego opera), 2000, Tosca (San Diego opera), 2002, Katya Kabanova and La Traviata (San Diego opera), 2004, La Bohème (San Diego opera), 2005. Mem., bd. dirs. San Diego Conv. and Visitors Bur., 1997-2002. Recipient Peri award Opera Guild So. Calif., 1984; named Headliner of Yr., San Diego Press Club, 1991, Father of Yr., San Diego, 1997. Fellow: Australian Inst. Mgmt.; mem.: Rotary, San Diego Press Club. Avocation: golf. Office: San Diego Opera 1200 3rd Ave Fl 18 San Diego CA 92101-4112 Office Phone: 619-232-7636. Business E-Mail: ian.campbell@sdopera.com.*

CAMPBELL, JACQUELYN C., community health nurse; b. Camden, NJ, Aug. 2, 1946; d. Joseph and Dorothy (Cutler) Bowman; 1 child, Christina, Bradley. BSN, Duke U., 1968; MSN, Wright State U., 1980; PhD in Nursing, U. Rochester, 1986. RN, Mich. Instr. Sinclair Community Coll., Dayton, Ohio, 1976-79, Wayne State U. Coll. Nursing, Detroit, 1980-82, mem. faculty, 1984—, assoc. prof., 1988—; teaching asst. U. Rochester (N.Y.) Sch. Nursing, 1982-84; Anna D. Wolf Endowed Prof., Sch. Nursing Johns Hopkins U., associate dean for the Ph.D. program and res., Sch. Nursing. Bd. dirs. Family Violence Prevention Fund, House of Ruth; mem. violence rev. panel NIMH, Washington. Co-author: Nursing Care of Victims of Family Violence, 1984 (AJN Book of Yr.); author: To Have & To Fit, Cultural Perspectives on Wife Beating, 2d edit., 1999, Assessing Dangerousness: Violence by Sexual Offenders, Batterers and Child Abusers, 1994, Ending Domestic Violence: Changing Public Perceptions/Halting the Epidemic, 1997, Empowering Survivors of Abuse: Health Care for Battered Women and their Children, 1998, Family Violence and Nursing Practice, 2003, Nursing Care Survivors of Family Violence 2d edit., 1993; mem. editorial bd. to sci. jours.; contbr. articles to profl. jours. V.p., bd. dirs. Women's Justice Ctr., Ann Arbor, Mich., 1987—; pres. Coun. on the Status of Women, Detroit, 1988-92; support group facilitator My Sister's Place, Detroit, 1989-92; mem. adv. bd. Wayne County Adv. Bd. Interpersonal Violence, Detroit, 1991-92, adv. panel Robert Wood Johnson Found., Princeton, N.J., 1990-92; prin. investigator NIH, NCNR, 1990—; mem. Dept. Defense Task Force on Domestic Violence. Recipient First ward NIH, 1987-92; W.K. Kellogg Found., 1990-93. Mem. ANA (chair task force on violence 1991-92), APHA, Am. acad. Nursing, a.A.N. award 1988), Inst. Medicine, Midwest Nursing Rsch. Soc. (Helen Werley new investigator 1992), Nursing Rsch. Consortium on Violence and Abuse, Nursing Network on Violence Against Women. Democrat. Avocation: tennis. Office: Johns Hopkins Univ Sch Nursing 525 N Wolfe St Baltimore MD 21205-2110

CAMPBELL, JAMES, philosopher, educator; b. Phila., Mar. 1, 1948; s. Francis Patrick and Marie (Reinhardt) Campbell; m. Linda Marie Frank, Dec. 23, 1972; children: Annamarie, Julie Elizabeth. BA, Temple U., Phila., 1973; MA in Philosophy, SUNY, Stony Brook, 1978, PhD in Philosophy, 1979. Asst. prof. philosophy U. Maine, Orono, 1980—81, U. Ky., Lexington, 1981—82, U. Toledo, 1982—87, assoc. prof. philosophy, 1987—93, prof. philosophy, 1993—2001, Disting. Prof. philosophy, 2001—. Fulbright Exch. prof. U. Innsbruck, 1990—91, U. Munich, 2003—04; Mellon rsch. fellow, 1995—96. Author: (book) The Community Reconstructs: The Meaning of Pragmatic Social Thought, 1992, Understanding John Dewey: Nature and Intelligence, 1995, Recovering Benjamin Franklin: An Exploration of a Life of Science and Service, 1999, A Thoughtful Profession: The Early Years of the American Philosophical Association, 2006; editor: Selected Writings of James Hayden Tufts, 1992; editor: (with R.E. Hart) Experience as Philosophy: On the Work of John J. McDermott, 2006. Pres. Am. Assn. Philosophy Tchrs., 1996—98. Mem.: Am. Philos. Assn. Office: University of Toledo 2801 W Bancroft St Toledo OH 43606 Office Fax: 419-530-6189. Business E-Mail: james.campbell@utoledo.edu.

CAMPBELL, JAMES P., manufacturing executive; b. New York, NY, Sept. 14, 1957; BS in Mktg., St. John's U.; MBA, Hofstra U. Sales/mktg. rep. GE Appliances, 1981, mgr. microwave cooking products Louisville, 1992—99; v.p. sales/mktg. GE, 1999—2001; pres., CEO GE Appliances, 2001—02; CEO GE Consumer Products, 2002—04; pres., CEO GE Consumer & Indsl. Americas, 2004—05, GE Consumer & Indsl., 2005—. Bd. mem. NAM. Bd. mem. Frazier Internat. Hist. Mus.*

CAMPBELL, JAMES ROBERT, retired bank executive; b. Rochester, Minn., May 24, 1942; s. Donald William and Alice Marie (Gray) Campbell; m. Carmen Dawn Starkson, July 11, 1964; children: Peter Ian, Kathryn Ann. BS in Bus, U. Minn., 1964. Comml. banking officer Norwest Nat. Bank Mpls., 1964-67, asst. v.p., 1967-71, sr. v.p. nat. dept., 1976-79, pres., COO, 1984-86; pres., dir. Lease N.W., Inc., Mpls., 1971-75, Norwest Bank Omaha N.A., 1979-82; regional pres. Norwest Corp.-Norwest Banks, 1982-84; pres., CEO Wells Fargo Bank, Mpls., 1986-95, chmn. bd. dirs., 1995—2002; chmn. bd. Norwest Bank Minn. N.A., Mpls., 1995-98; ret., 2002; interim dean Carlson Sch. Mgmt. U. Minn., 2005—06. Group exec. v.p. Wells Fargo & Co., 1998—2002; exec. v.p. Norwest Corp.; bd. dirs. Marvin Lumber & Cedar Co., Lifetouch, Inc., Forsythe Appraisals, Inc., Ryan Companies. Chmn. The Itasca Project; bd. dirs. U. Minn. Found. Mem.: World Pres. Orgn., Minn. Exec. Orgn., Royal Poinciana Golf Club, Bay Colony Golf Club, Spring Hill Golf Club, Mpls. Club, Minikahda Club. Presbyterian. Home: 5521 Woodcrest Dr Edina MN 55424-1651 Office Phone: 612-667-9141. Business E-Mail: James.r.campbell@wellsFargo.com.

CAMPBELL, JAMES T., history professor; BA in Hsitory, Yale U., New Haven, Conn., 1980; MA in History, Stanford U., 1983, PhD in History, 1989. Jr. lectr. in History U. Witwatersrand, South Africa, 1986—87; instr. History Stanford U., 1988—89; asst. prof., dept. History Northwestern U., Chgo., 1989—96; sr. rsch. officer Inst. Advanced Social Rsch., U. Witwatersrand, South Africa; assoc. prof., Am. Civilization, Africana Studies, History Brown U., Providence, 1999—. Historical cons. This Far by Faith: African American Spiritual Journeys Film Series. Author: Songs of Zion: The African Methodist Episcopal Church in the United States and South Africa, 1995 (Organization of American Historians' Frederick Jackson Turner Prize, 1996, Carl Sandburg Literary Award for Non-Fiction, 1996), Middle Passages: African American Journeys to Africa, 1787-2005, 2006 (Mark Lynton History Prize, 2007); author articles in profl. jours., anthologies, incl. Dissent, Wash. Post, LA Times. Grantee Stanford U. Grad. Fell., 1981—85, Rotary Found. Grad. Travel Fell., 1985—86, NEH Summer Stipend, 1992, Fullbright African Rsch. Fell., 1992—93, Charles Warren Ctr. Am. History, Harvard, 2000—01, Ctr. Comparative Study Race and Ethnicity, 2003—04. Office: Brown U History Dept PO Box 1892 82 Waterman St Providence RI 02912 Office Phone: 401-863-2896.*

CAMPBELL, JANE LOUISE, former mayor; b. May 19, 1953; d. Paul and Joan (Brown) C.; m. Hunter Morrison, Dec. 8, 1984; children: Jessica Elizabeth, Catherine Joanna. BA in History, U. Mich., 1974; MS in Urban Studies, Cleve. State U., 1980. Mem. State of Ohio Ho. of Reps. 11th dist., Columbus, 1984—92, majority whip, 1992—2000; mayor City of Cleve., 2001—05. Apptd. mem. Nat. Com. on Welfare Reform; mem. Cuyahoga County Plan Commn., Fin. and Appropriations Com., Ways and Means Com., Aging and Housing Com.; active Nat. Coun. State Legislators, vice-chair Human Svcs. Com., Children, Families and Youth Com., past pres. Women's Network, mem. Federal Budget and Taxation Com.; chair Abused, Neglected Children Oversight Com.; vice-chair Select Com. on Child Abuse and Juvenile Justice, 1989; mem. gov. task force on Adolescent Sexuality and Pregnanacy, 1986, com. to Study Ohio's Sch. Found. Program Distribution of State Funds to Sch. Dists., 1991; exec. dir. Friends of Shaker Square, 1982-84; nat. field dir. ERAmerica, 1979-82; founding dir. Womenspace, 1975-79. Elder Heights Christian Ch. Recipient Legislative Leadership award Ohio Psychological Assn., 1986, Legislative award Ohio Hunger Task Force, 1987, Recognition award Ohio Primary Care Assn., 1987, Dean's Disting. Alumni award Cleve. State Univ., 1987, Hall of Fame award Nat. Senior Citizens, 1988, State Public Official of the Year award Ohio Chpt. Nat. Assn. of Social Workers, 1988, Found. award Ohio Chpt. ACLU, 1988, Legislative award Ohio Assn. of Counseling and Devel., 1989, Ohio Assn. of County Bds. of Mental Retardation/Developmental Disabilities award, 1989, Cancer Fighter award Ireland Cancer Ctr., 1990, Legislative award Ohio Human Svcs. Dirs. Assn., 1990, Hosephine Irwin award Womenspace, 1991, Spcl. Recognition award Providence House, 1991, Citizen award Ohio Assn. for the Edn. of Young Children, 1991, Legislator of the Year award Greater Cleve. Nurses Assn., 1991, Legislative award Nat. Assn. of Sch. Psychologists, 1992, Outstanding Svc. award Public Children's Svcs. Assn., 1992., numerous others. Democrat. Office: Cleveland City Hall 601 Lakeside Ave Rm 202 Cleveland OH 44114 Office Phone: 216-664-3990. Business E-Mail: mayorcampbell@city.cleveland.oh.us.

CAMPBELL, JANET CORAL, architect; b. Albuquerque, Nov. 24, 1953; d. Ovid Sylvester Campbell II and Evelyn Grace (Kistler) Campbell London; m. Rodney Lee Pope, June 12, 1977 (div. 1991). BS, Ga. Inst. Tech., Atlanta, 1975, MArch, 1977; MS in Real Estate, Ga. State U., Atlanta, 1989. Registered architect, Ga. Assoc. planner Metro Atlanta Rapid Transp. Authority, 1977-78; project designer Toombs, Amisano & Wells, Atlanta, 1978-80; project arch., designer Thompson, Ventulett & Steinback, Atlanta, 1980-84; project arch. Dimery, Corbet & West, Atlanta, 1984; arch., renderer Dan Harmon & Assocs., Atlanta, 1984-85; pres. Chantilly Properties, Inc., Atlanta, 1985-91; prin. Campbell Pope & Assocs., Atlanta, 1985-91; arch. J.D. & Assocs., Burlingame, Calif., 1991; sr. arch. U. Calif., San Francisco, 1991—99; prin. Campbell and Assoc., San Francisco, 1992—; arch. Skidmore, Owings & Merrill, 2002, Soga and Assoc., 2003—05. Exhibitions include High Mus., Atlanta, 1982. Elected mem. 12th dist. Rep. Party Ctrl. Com., San Francisco, 2005—06, 2007—; vice chair spl. events San Francisco Rep. Party, 2007—. Recipient Nat. Inst. for Arch. Edn. award, 1975. Mem. AIA (bd. dirs. Ga. chpt. 1989-91, Excellence of Studies award 1977). Mem. Plymouth Brethren Ch. Avocations: painting, reading. Office Phone: 415-261-2613.

CAMPBELL, JEFFREY C., health products executive; b. July 16, 1960; m. Susan Campbell; children: Grace, Eric, Patrick. BA in Econs., Stanford U., 1985; MBA, Harvard U., 1990. CPA Deloitte, Haskins & Sells, 1986—88; sr. analyst fin. Am. Airlines, 1990—92, mgr. fin. planning, 1992—93, mng. dir. internat. planning, 1993—95, mng. dir. corp. fin. and banking, 1995—98, v.p. corp. devel., treas., 1998—2000, v.p. Europe, 2000—02, sr. v.p. fin., CFO, 2002—03; sr. v.p., CFO McKesson Corp., San Francisco, 2003, exec. v.p., CFO, 2004—. Office: McKesson Corp One Post St San Francisco CA 94104*

CAMPBELL, JOAN VIRGINIA LOWEKE, secondary school and language educator; b. Detroit, Nov. 8, 1942; d. George Paul and Lolamae (Weians) L.; m. James Bachelder Campbell, July 26, 1975; 1 child, James Bachelder Loweke. BA in German, French, Hope Coll., 1965; student, Cologne U., Germany, 1964, Salzburg U., Austria, 1968, Stuttgart U., Germany, 1970-71, Sampere Inst., Madrid, 1982, Millersville U., Pa., 1983, 84, 90, Va. Poly. Inst. and State U., 1976-77, 80-84, U. Va., 1996-97, 98-99. Cert. secondary tchr., Mich., Kans., Va. Tchr. French and German I, II Grand Haven (Mich.) Jr. H.S., 1965-69; asst. instr. elementary and intermediate German U. Kans., Lawrence, 1969-70, 71-72; tchr. German I, II Ctrl. Jr. H.S., Lawrence, Kans., 1972-74; tchr. French I, II, sr. English Oskaloosa (Kans.) H.S., 1974-75; tchr. German I-IV Highland Park H.S., Topeka, 1975-76; tchr. French I-V, Spanish I and II Blacksburg (Va.) H.S., 1977—. Tchr. French, Spanish YMCS, YMCA evening courses, Blacksburg, Va., 1976-80; mem. audio visual com. Montgomery County Fgn. Lang. Collaborative Group, Blacksburg, 1984-87; chaperone Am. Inst. Fgn. Study, Germany, France, Spain, 1968-82, area adminstr. summer and winter programs abroad, Western Mich., 1968-69; chaperone Ednl. Adventures, Quebec City, Montreal, 1984, 90-91, 93-94, 98, Montgomery County Schs.; presenter in field. Author: The Gothic Cathedral, 1995. Mem. Internat. Host Family Orgn. Va. Poly. Inst. and State U., Blacksburg, 1977— Fulbright exch. fellow U. Kans., 1970-71, Fulbright fellow Goethe Insts., 1976, Rockefeller fellow Rockefeller Assn. and Nat. Endowment Humanities, 1986, NDEA fellow, 1966; recognized as Va. Gov.'s Sch. Outstanding Educator, 1990. Mem. Am. Assn. Tchrs. French (state and region IV U.S. Recognition effort, dedication and high scores on nat. French exams, 1988, 96, 97, founder La Soc. Hon. de Français for Outstanding Students in French Blacksburg chpt. 1977, state com., dist. adminstr. Le Grand Concours-Nat. French Exams 1980—), Am. Assn. Tchrs. Spanish and Portuguese, Am. Assn. Tchrs. German (life, Va. exec. com. sec. 1977-83, co-chmn. nat. German exams Va. chpt. 1984-87, state nominating com. 1984-87, chmn. 1984-85, life), Nat. Assn. Edn. (Blacksburg H.S. rep. 1980-82), Va. Assn. Edn., Montgomery County Assn. Edn., Fgn. Lang. Assn. Va. (life). Republican. Presbyterian. Avocations: gardening, hiking, travel, classical music, art history. Home: 3003 Mclean Ct Blacksburg VA 24060-8110 Office: Blacksburg HS 520 Patrick Henry Dr Blacksburg VA 24060-3106 Personal E-mail: jayhawk@vt.edu.

CAMPBELL, JOHN, former ambassador; b. Washington, 1944; BA, MA, U. Va.; PhD, U. Wis., 1970. Prof. British and French Hist. Mary Baldwin Coll., Staunton, Va., 1970—75; fgn. svc. officer US Dept. State, 1975—, polit. counselor Lagos, Nigeria, 1988—90, polit. counselor Pretoria/Cape Town, South Africa, 1993—96, dep. asst. sec., Bur. Human Resources, US amb. to Nigeria, 2004—07. State Dept. sr. fellow Princeton U. Woodrow Wilson Sch., 1990—91.

CAMPBELL, JOHN, philosopher, educator; b. Glasgow, Scotland, Nov. 2, 1956; s. Roderick and Catriona Campbell. BA, Stirling U., Scotland, 1978; MA, Calgary U., Can., 1979; BPhil, Oxford U., Eng., 1981, DPhil, 1986. Rsch. lectr. Christ Church Coll., Oxford, 1983—86; fellow and tutor in philosophy New Coll., Oxford, 1986—2001; Wilde prof. mental philosophy Oxford U., 2001—04; Willis S. and Marion Slusser prof. philosophy U. Calif., Berkeley. Author: (academic monograph) Past, Space and Self, Reference and Consciousness. Named Reader in Philosophy, U. Oxford, 1997—2001; fellow, Ctr. for Advanced Study in the Behavioral Scis., Stanford, 2003—04; Rsch. Readership, Brit. Acad., 1995—97. Mem.: European Soc. for Philosophy and Psychology (pres. 2003—06). Office: UC Berkeley Dept Philosophy 314 Moses Hall Berkeley CA 94720-2390 Office Fax: 510-642-4164. Business E-Mail: jjcampbell@berkeley.edu.

CAMPBELL, JOHN B. T., III, congressman, former state senator; b. LA, July 19, 1955; m. Catherine Campbell; children: Taylor, Logan. BA, UCLA, 1976; MS, U. So. Calif., 1977. Tax acct. Ernst & Young; pres., CEO Campbell Automotive Group, 1985—95, Saturn of Orange County, 1990—99; chair, CEO Saab of Orange County, 1999—; mem. Dist. 70 Calif. State Assembly, Sacramento, 2000—04; mem. Calif. State Senate, Sacramento, 2004—05, US Congress from 48th Calif. dist., 2005—. Chair Orange County Overall Econ. Devel. Program Com.; mem. Calif. Rep. State Cen. Com.; vice-chair budget com. Mem. Turtlerock Sch. Site Coun.; pres. Young Pres. Orgn. Mem.: Nat. Automobile Dealers Assn., Calif. Soc. CPAs. Republican. Presbyterian. Mailing: US Ho Reps 1728 Longworth House Office Bldg Washington DC 20515-0548

CAMPBELL, JOHN MORGAN, retired chemical engineer; b. Virden, Ill., Mar. 24, 1922; S. John M. and Ione Marie (Whittler) C.; m. Gwendolyn Thompson, Aug. 27, 1945; children: John Morgan, Robert, Charles. BS in Chem. Engring, Iowa State U., 1943; MS, U. Okla., 1948, PhD, 1951. Devel. engr. and supr. E.I. duPont de Nemours & Co., Inc., 1943-46; spl. instr. chem. engring. U. Okla., 1946-50; tech. adviser to v.p. Black Sivalls and Bryson, Oklahoma City, 1951-54; mem. faculty U. Okla. Sch. Petroleum Engring., 1954-69, chmn. dept., 1956-63, Erle P. Halliburton prof., 1963-69, dir., 1969, Petroleum Research Center, 1964-69. Pres. John M. Campbell & Co. (engring. counselors, mgmt. consultants), 1968-82; chmn. bd. Petrotech Ltd., Petroleum Learning Programs Ltd. Author: Oil Property Evaluation, 1959, Effective Technical Communications, 1969, Decision Methods For Petroleum Investments, 1969, Gas Conditioning and Processing, 2 vols., 1970, 6th edit., 2000, The Professional - From Puberty to Senility, 1970, Effective Communication for the Technical Man, 1972,

Petroleum Reservoir Property Evaluation, 1973, Mineral Property Economics (3 vols.), 1978, Petroleum Evaluation for Financial Disclosures, 1983, Analysis and Management of Petroleum Investments, 1987, Successful Communication Strategies and Practices, 2000, Analysis and Management of Risky Investments, 2001; also numerous articles, chpts. in books. Recipient Hanlon award Gas Processors Assn., 1987, Disting. Achievement award Iowa State U., 1988, Disting. Grad. award Okla. U. Mem. NAE, AIME (hon. mem. 1994, exec. com. coun. edn., mineral industries econs. award 1989), Soc. Petroleum Engrs. (hon. mem. 1994, J.F. Caril award 1978, Arps award 1989), Am. Arbitration Assn. (arbitration panel), Internat. Petroleum Inst. (pres. 1968-82), Sigma Alpha Epsilon, Phi Lambda Upsilon, Pi Epsilon Tau. Clubs: Lion. Home: 6 Rustic Hills St Norman OK 73072-7411

CAMPBELL, JOHN RICHARD, pediatric surgeon; b. Pratt, Kans., Jan. 16, 1932; s. John Ross and Laura (Harkrader) C.; m. Susan Charlotte Baker, June 9, 1962; children: Kathryn, John Richard, George Ridgway. BA, U. Kans., 1954, MD, 1958. Diplomate Am. Bd. Surgery with cert. of spl. qualifications in pediatric surgery. Rotating intern Hosp. U. Pa., 1958-59; resident in gen. surgery U. Kans. Hosp., 1959-63; resident in pediatric surgery Children's Hosp. of Phila., 1965-67; asst. instr. U. Pa. Med. Sch., 1965-67; mem. faculty U. Oreg. Health Scis. Ctr., Portland, 1967—, prof. surgery emeritus, 2000, prof. surgery and pediatrics emeritus, 2000—, chief pediatric surgery, prof. emeritus surgery and pediats., 2000—; surgeon-in-chief Doernbecher Children's Hosp., Portland, 1967-99. Cons. VA, Shriners Crippled Children's hosps., Alaska Native Med. Ctr., Anchorage. Served to lt. comdr. M.C. USNR, 1963-65. Mem. A.C.S., Soc. Acad. Surgeons, Am. Acad. Pediatrics, Am. Pediatric Surg. Assn., Pacific Assn. Pediatric Surgeons, North Pacific Pediatric Soc., North Pacific Surg. Assn., Pacific Coast Surg. Assn., Portland Acad. Pediatrics, Portland Surg. Soc. Presbyterian. Office: Oreg Health Scis Univ 745 SW Gaines St # Cdw7 Portland OR 97239-2901 Office Phone: 503-494-7764. Business E-Mail: campbell@ohsu.edu.

CAMPBELL, JOSEPH JOHN, technology and financial company executive; b. Harrisburg, Pa., May 24, 1947; s. John Patrick and May (Murray) C.; m. Susan Jane Ott, Jan. 28, 1966; children: John William, Allison Susan. BA in Econs., Allentown Coll. of St. Francis de Sales (now DeSales U.), 1970; Advanced Mgmt. Cert., U. Pitts., 1980. Computer and systems profl. Gen. Acceptance Corp., Allentown, Pa., 1968-70; v.p. sys. planning and devel. Fin.Am. Corp. (Bank Am. Corp.), 1970-83; v.p. sys. devel. and strategic planning Chrysler First, 1983-87; sr. v.p., chief info. officer Dollar Dry Dock Bank, NYC, 1987-90; sr. v.p., retail bank opers. and tech. Citicorp/Citibank, NYC, 1990-91, sr. v.p. mortgage opers. and tech. St. Louis, 1991-93; exec. v.p. Home Ins. Co., NYC, 1993-95; exec. v.p., chief info. officer Zurich Risk Mgmt. Svcs./Zurich Fin. Group, NYC, 1995—2004; ret., 2004; CEO, pres. Clear Data Strategies, Inc., Danbury, Conn., 2006—. Mem. Pres.'s Coun. Allentown Coll. of St. Francis de Sales, 1988—; owner Breakthrough Fitness Ctrs., Hilton Head Island and Bluffton, S.C., Pilates of Hilton Head. Inventor computer system in fin. field. Mem. investment com. DeSales U., 2006—. Mem. Allentown Coll. of St. Francis de Sales Alumni Assn. (pres. 1981-85, Alumnus of Yr. award 1986). Avocations: golf, tennis, raquetball.

CAMPBELL, JOYCE S., language educator, department chairman; BA in French Edn., Mich. State U., Lansing, 1976; MA in Curriculum Devel., U. Mich., Ann Arbor, 1982. French tchr. Mercy HS, Farmington Hills, Mich., 1976—, chmn. lang. dept., 1989—. Named Tchr. of Yr., Mich. Fgn. Lang. Assn., 1995. Mem.: Mich. World Lang. Assn., Am. Assn. Tchrs. French. Business E-Mail: jacampbell@mhsmi.org.

CAMPBELL, JUDITH E., retired insurance company executive; BA, Chestnut Hill Coll., 1969. With Chem. Bank, N.Y., sr. v.p. consumer sales and svc. delivery N.Y., head ops. and adminstrn. consumer banking NY, sr. v.p., 1991—92; with Consumer Banking, 1992—97; sr. v.p., chief info. officer, bd. dirs. N.Y. Life Ins. Co., NYC, 1997—2007; ret. Bd. trustees Drew U. Office: NY Life Ins Co 51 Madison Ave New York NY 10010-1603

CAMPBELL, KEVIN P., oil industry executive; B in Computer Sci., Tex. A&M U. With Atlantic Richfield Co.; dir. info. sys. Tex. Industries, Inc.; v.p., CIO Hunt Oil, Dallas, 2002—. Mem.: Am. Heart Assn. (nat. info. tech. expert panel), Dallas/Ft. Worth Soc. Info. Mgmt. (chmn. exec. bd.), Nat. Eagle Scout Assn. (life). Office: Hunt Oil 1445 Ross at Field Fountain Place 1 Dallas TX 75202

CAMPBELL, KEVIN PETER, physiology and biophysics educator; b. Bklyn., Jan. 19, 1952; s. Miller Jerome and Anna L. (Telesco) C.; m. Anna A. Derragon, Jan. 5, 1974; children: Colleen, Kerry, David. BS in Physics, Manhattan Coll., 1973; MS, U. Rochester, 1976, PhD, 1979. Grad. fellow U. Rochester, NY, 1973-77, teaching asst. NY, 1976-78; Elon Huntington Hooker fellow dept. radiation biology and biophysics, U. Rochester (N.Y.), 1977-78; Med. Rsch. Coun. postdoctoral fellow U. Toronto, Ont., Canada, 1978-81; asst. prof. dept. physiology and biophysics U. Iowa, Iowa City, 1981-85, assoc. prof., 1985-88, prof., 1988—, Found. Disting. prof., 1989—, Howard Hughes Med. Inst. investigator, 1989—. Mem. editorial bd. Jour. Biol. Chemistry, Circulation Rsch., Cell Calcium; reviewer for Nature, Jour. Clin. Investigation, Jour. Cell Biology, Proc. NAS, Archives Biochem. and Biophysics, Molecular Pharmacology, Biophys. Jour.; contbr. numerous articles and abstracts to profl. jours. Patentee immunogen conjugates and use; co-patentee in field. Grantee NIH, NSF, NATO, Muscular Dystrophy Assn., 1981—; recipient Amgen award Am. Society Biochemistry and Molecular Biology, 1994, Internat. Albert Fleckenstein award, G. Conte prize, Elsevier Sci. award. Mem. AAAS, Biophys. Soc. (officer 1988—), N.Y. Acad. Scis., Soc. Gen. Physiologists, Am. Physiology Soc., Am. Soc. Cell Biology, Am. Soc. Biochem. Chemists, Am. Heart Assn. (established investigator, coun. high blood pressure rsch., cell transport and metabolism rsch. study com. 1989—), Inst. Medicine, NAS, Sigma Xi (Bendix award), Phi Beta Kappa; fellow Am. Acad. Arts and Sciences Roman Catholic. Office: U Iowa HHMI 400 Eckstein Med Rsch Ctr Iowa City IA 52242

CAMPBELL, KRISTIN A., lawyer, retail executive; JD, Cornell U. Sch. Law, Ithaca, NY. Atty. Goodwin Proctor LLP, Boston; real estate counsel Staples, Inc., 1993, head internat. legal matters Europe, Asia and S.Am., sr. v.p., dep. gen. counsel, 2005—07, sr. v.p., gen. counsel, sec., 2007—. Office: Staples Inc 500 Staples Dr Framingham MA 01702 Office Phone: 508-253-5000.

CAMPBELL, LAURA ELIZABETH, library administrator; BA, Pa. State U., 1973; MA in mgmt., U. Maine, 1979; MS in Accounting, Georgetown U., 1983. Staff cons., mgr., prin. Arthur Young & Co. (now Ernst and Young), 1984—89; project mgr. strategic planning review Libr. of Congress, Washington, 1988—89, dir. libr. distribution svcs., 1992, dir. Am. Memory Program, 1993, co-chair Digital Futures Group, 1998, dir. Nat. Digital Libr. (NDL) Program, assoc. libr. strategic initiatives, 2000—. Pvt. cons., v.p. QueTel Corp, 1989—92. Office: Libr of Congress 101 Independence Ave, SE Washington DC 20540 Office Phone: 202-707-3300. E-mail: lcam@loc.gov.*

CAMPBELL, LEONARD M., lawyer; b. Denver, Apr. 12, 1918; s. Bernard Francis and May (Moran) C.; m. Dot J. Baker, Sept. 23, 1944; children: Brian T., Teri Pat, Thomas P. AB, U. Colo., 1941, LLB, 1943. Bar: Colo. 1943. With Gorsuch, Kirgis, 1948-88, sr. ptnr., 1951-88; city atty. Denver, 1951-53; of counsel Gorsuch, Kirgis LLC, 1989—2004. Cons. pub. utility matters Colo. Mcpl. League. Mem. Denver Charter Com., 1947; mgr. Safety and Excise for Denver, 1947-48; chmn. Denver Com. Human Relations, 1954; mem. Denver Planning Bd., 1950-51; mem. Bd. Water Commrs., Denver, 1965-70, pres., 1968-69; mem. Gov.'s Com. on Jud. Compensation, 1972; chmn. U. Colo. Law Alumni Devel. Fund, 1962. Served with USAAF, 1943-46. Mem. ABA, Colo. Bar Assn. (pres. 1978-79, Award of Merit 1967), Denver Bar Assn. (pres. 1969), Am. Coll. Trial Lawyers, Cath. Lawyers Guild Denver (pres. 1962, St. Thomas More award 1978), Nat. Inst. Mcpl. Law Officers (v.p. 1952), Colo. Judicial Inst. (Chancellor Chester Alter award 1987), Denver Athletic Club (sec. 1960-61, pres. 1962). Democrat. Roman Catholic. Home and Office: 3447 S Birch St Denver CO 80222-7212

CAMPBELL, LESLIE CAINE (CAINE CAMPBELL), writer, historian; b. New Orleans, June 5, 1932; s. George Alexander and Nell Ruble C.; m. Bettye Bryan, June 10, 1961; children: Cathryn Campbell Jordan, Roxane Campbell Rose. BS in Bus., Miss. State U., 1954; MA in History, U. Miss., 1964, PhD in History, 1967. Chmn. div. humanities Ark. Coll., Batesville, 1967-68; assoc. dean Sch. Arts and Scis. Auburn (Ala.) U., 1968-86, dean Coll. Liberal Arts, 1986-88, prof. history and journalism, 1988-92. Hartman lectr. U. Miss., 1983. Author: Two Hundred Years of Pharmacy, 1976 (Am. Inst. History of Pharmacy award 1977), A Reminder of Stones, 2001, Mickey, Do You Hear Them Singing?, 2004; contbg. author: Research Institutions and Learned Societies, 1982, Foundations, 1984; contbg. editor Nat. Forum, 1987-92; newsman NBC News-TV and Radio, 1962-66. With USN, 1955—58. NSF fellow, 1966; Challenge grantee NEH, 1980. Mem. Am. Assn. Univ. Adminstrs. (bd. dirs. 1987-90), Assn. Ala. Coll. Adminstrs. (pres. 1988). Office: 126 Summerhill Hoschton GA 30548 Home Phone: 706-654-9066.

CAMPBELL, LEVIN HICKS, federal judge; b. Summit, NJ, Jan. 2, 1927; s. Worthington and Louise (Hooper) Campbell; m. Eleanor Saltonstall Lewis, June 1, 1957; children: Eleanor S., Levin H., Sarah H. AB cum laude, Harvard U., 1948, LLB, 1951; postgrad., Nat. Coll. State Judiciary, 1970; LLD (hon.), Suffolk U., 1975; LLD (hon.), Colby Coll., 1982. Bar: D.C. 1951, Mass. 1954. Assoc. firm Ropes & Gray, Boston, 1954—64; mem. Mass. Ho. of Reps., 1963—64; asst. atty. gen. State of Mass., 1965—66, spl. asst. atty. gen., 1966—67, 1st asst. atty. gen., 1967—68; assoc. justice Superior Ct. of Mass., 1969—72; judge US Dist. Ct. Mass., Boston, 1972, US Ct. Appeals (1st cir.), Boston, 1972—, chief judge, 1983—90, sr. judge, 1992—. Fellow Inst. of Politics J.F. Kennedy Sch. Govt. Harvard U., 1968—69, study group leader, 1980; faculty chmn. law sessions Salzburg Seminar in Am. Studies, 1981. Pres. Cambridge 9 Neighborhood Assn., 1960—62; treas. Cambridge Ctr. for Adult Edn., 1961—64; campaign chmn. Cambridge United Fund, 1965; mem. bd. overseers Boston Symphony Orch., 1969—75, 1977—80; pres. bd. overseers Shady Hill Sch., 1969—70; mem. vis. com. Harvard U. Press, 1958—64; v.p. Cambridge Cmty. Svcs.; corp. mem. SEA Endl. Assn., 1982—; trustee Colby Coll., Waterville, Maine, 1981—90, 1991—99, Asheville (N.C.) Sch., 1987—98; overseer U.S. Constn. Mus. 1st lt. (j.g.) US Army, 1951—54, Korea. Mem.: ABA, Mass. Hist. Soc. (coun. 1993—96, v.p. 1996—99, pres. 2000—02, coun. 2003—), U.S. Jud. Conf. (ct. adminstrn. com. 1975—83, chmn. subcom. on supporting pers. 1980—83, exec. com. 1985—90, ad hoc com. study jud. conf. 1987, fed. ct. study com. 1988—90, chmn. com. to rev. cir. coun. conduct and disability orders 1989—94, nat. commn. on jud. discipline and removal 1991—93), Boston Bar Assn., Mass. Bar Found. (long range planning com. 1999—2000), Am. Bar Found., Am. Law Inst. Office: US Ct of Appeals US Courthouse 1 Courthouse Way Ste 6720 Boston MA 02210-3008*

CAMPBELL, LEWIS B., multi-industry company executive; b. Winchester, Va., May 18, 1946; m. Mary Campbell; 3 children. BS in Mech. Engring., Duke U., 1968. Various mgmt. positions Gen. Motors, 1968-88, v.p., gen. mgr. Flint automotive divsn. Buick-Oldsmobile-Cadillac group, 1988-91, v.p., gen. mgr. GMC truck divsn., 1991-92; exec. v.p. Textron Inc., 1992-94, COO, 1992—98, pres., 1994-98, 2001—, CEO, 1998—, chmn., 1999—. Bd. dirs. Bristol-Myers Squibb, Dow Jones & Co. Office: Textron Inc 40 Westminster St Providence RI 02903*

CAMPBELL, LINZY LEON, molecular biology researcher, educator; b. Panhandle, Tex., Feb. 10, 1927; s. Linzy Leon and Eula Irene (McSpadden) C.; m. Alice P. Dauksa, Feb. 7, 1953. BA in Bacteriology and Chemistry, U. Tex., 1949, MA, 1950, PhD, 1952. Rsch. scientist U. Tex., 1947—51; predoctoral rsch. fellow NIH, 1951—52; postdoctoral rsch. fellow Nat. Microbiol. Inst., U. Calif. Berkeley, 1952—54; asst. prof., then assoc. prof. Wash. State U., 1954—59; assoc. prof. We. Res. U. Sch. Medicine, 1959—62; sr. rsch. fellow USPHS, 1959—62; prof. microbiology U. Ill. Urbana, 1962—72, head dept., 1963—71, dir. Sch. Life Scis., 1971—72; prof. microbiology, provost and v.p. acad. affairs U. Del., Newark, 1972—88, rsch. prof. molecular bioscis., 1988—89, Hugh M. Morris rsch. prof. molecular bioscis., 1989—. Editorial bd.: Jour. Bacteriology, 1961-65; editor, 1964-65, editor-in-chief, 1965-77; Contbr. articles to profl. jours. Served with USNR, 1944-46. Fellow AAAS; mem. Am. Soc. Microbiology (chmn. publ. bd. 1965-80, councilor at large 1962-64, v.p. 1972-73, pres. 1973-74), Am. Soc. Biochemistry and Molecular Biology. Office: U Delaware Dept Biology 400 Morris Library Newark DE 19717 Office Phone: 302-831-6767. Business E-Mail: campbell@udel.edu.

CAMPBELL, MAGDA, retired child psychiatrist, researcher, educator; b. Subotica, Yugoslavia, Jan. 22, 1928; arrived in U.S., 1957; d. Bela and Marija (Lipoženčic) Pijuković; m. Francis P. Campbell, July 2, 1961; children: Maria D., John F. MD, U. Belgrade, Yugoslavia, 1953. Diplomate in psychiatry and child psychiatry Am. Bd. Psychiatry and Neurology. From tchg. asst. to prof. psychiatry NYU, NYC, 1963-95, prof. emeritus, 1995—; dir. divsn. child adolescent psychiatry, 1987-91; dir. tng. edn., 1990—91; ret., 1995. Co-author: Child and Adolescent Psychopharmacology, 1985, Clinical Evaluation of Psychotropic Drugs for Psychiatric Disorders, 1993; contbr. over 225 articles to profl. jours., chpts. to books. Grantee NIMH, 1973-95. Fellow: Am. Coll. Neuropsychopharmacology (life; emeritus), Am. Acad. Child Adolescent Psychiatry (life), Am. Psychiatric Assn. (life). Office: NYU Med Ctr Dept Psychiatry 550 1st Ave New York NY 10016

CAMPBELL, MARIA BOUCHELLE, lawyer, consultant; b. Mullins, SC, Jan. 23, 1944; d. Colin Reid and Margaret Minor (Perry) C. Student, Agnes Scott Coll., 1961-63; AB, U. Ga., 1965, JD, 1967. Bar: Ga. 1967, Fla. 1968, Ala. 1969. Pvt. practice law, Birmingham, Ala., 1968-94; law clk. U.S. Cir. Ct. Appeals, Miami, Fla., 1967-68; assoc. Cabaniss, Johnston and Gardner, 1968-73; sec., counsel Ala. Bancorp., Birmingham, 1973-79; sr. v.p., sec., gen. counsel AmSouth Bancorp., 1979-84, exec. v.p., gen. counsel, 1984-94, AmSouth Bank, 1984-94; exec. asst. to rector Parish of Trinity Ch., NYC, 1994-99; lawyer, mediator Sirote & Permutt, 1999-2001; cabinet ofcl., supt. of banks State of Ala., Montgomery, 2001—03; chmn. fin. svcs. SC& B Strategic Solutions, Montgomery, 2003—; of counsel Steiner Crum & Byars, Montgomery, 2003—. Bd. trustees Ptnrship for Women's Health Columbia U., 1996-2000; bd. dirs. Leake and Watts Childrens Svcs., Inc., 1997-99; lectr. continuing legal edn. programs; cons. to charitable orgns. Exec. editor Ga. Law Rev, 1966-67. Bd. dirs. St. Anne's Home, Birmingham, 1969-74, chancellor, 1969-74; bd. dirs. Children's Aid Soc., Birmingham, 1970-94, 1st v.p., 1988-90, pres., 1990-92; trustee Canterbury Cathedral Trust in Am., 1992—, Discovery 2000 Children's Mus., 1991-94, Soc. for Propagation of Christian Knowledge, 1991-93; bd. dirs. NCCJ, 1985-94, 99-2002, state chair, 1990-93; bd. dirs. Positive Maturity, 1976-78, Mental Health Assn., 1978-81, YWCA, 1979-80, Op. New Birmingham, 1985-87, pers. com., 1987-90, v.p., 1990-94; bd. dirs. Soc. for the Fine Arts U. Ala., 1986-89, Baptist Hospital Found. of Birmingham Inc., 1994-95, Alliance for Downtown N.Y., 1995-99; chair affordable housing initiative region 2020, 2000-01, Habitat for Humanity of Birmingham, 2000-02; commr. Housing Authority, Birmingham Dist., 1980-85, Birmingham Partnership, 1985-86, Leadership Birmingham, 1986—, program com., 1989-90, co-chair program com., 1990-91, mem.'s coun., 1999-2002; mem. pres. adv. coun. Birmingham So. Coll, 1988-92, chair bd. overseers Masters Program, 1990-94; mem. pres.'s cabinet U. Ala., 1990-95; trustee Ala. Diocese Episcopal Ch., 1971-72, 74-75, mem. canonical revision com., 1973-75, 89-91, liturg. commn., 1976-78, treas., chmn. dept. fin., 1979-83, 2000-03; mem. coun., 1983-87, chancellor, 1987-91, cons. on stewardship edn., 1981-94, dep. to gen. conv., 1985, 88, 91; mem. Standing Commn. on Constn. and Canons, 1988-94, mem. investment com., 2000—, vice chmn., 2003—; vestryman St. Luke's Episcopal Ch., 1991-94; bd. advisors So. region of Am. Soc. Corp. Secs., pres., 1992-94; cmty. advisor Jr. League Birmingham, 1992-93; mem. adv. bd. Cahaba River Soc., 1991-94; trustee St. Andrew's Sewanee Sch., 1998—; commr. Ala. Securities Commn., 2001-03; bd. dirs. Ala. Agrl. Commn., 2001-03; bd. dirs. Ala. Housing Fin. Authority, 2001-03; bd. regents Univ. of the South, 2002—; bd. dirs. Housing Enterprise Ctrl. Ala., 2003—, Fin. Investors of South, 2003—04, Associated Long Term Care Ins. Co., 2004—. Named One of Top 10 Women in Birmingham, 1989, One of Top 5 Women in Bus., 1993. Mem. ABA, State Bar Ga., Fla. Bar, Ala. Bar Assn., Birmingham Bar Assn., Am. Corp. Counsel Assn. (bd. dirs. Ala. 1984-89), Assn. Bank Holding Cos. (chmn. lawyers com. 1986-87), Greater Birmingham C. of C. (bd. dirs. 1988-94, exec. com. 1992-94, vice chmn., gen. counsel 1993-94), Kiwanis, The Church Club N.Y., Order of St. John of Jerusalem, Summit Club. Office: PO Box 668 Montgomery AL 36101 Home Phone: 205-714-7766; Office Phone: 334-956-6800. Personal E-mail: mcampbell@scbstrategic.com.

CAMPBELL, MARY ELIZABETH, retired primary school educator; b. Mt. Pleasant, Pa., Oct. 12, 1952; d. John Jacob and Hazel Marie Luckey; m. Alexander Murray Jr. Campbell, Dec. 28, 1984; 1 stepchild, Whitney Alexander. BS in Elem. Edn., Calif. U., Pa., 1974, BA in Philosophy, 1976, MEd, 1978. Kindergarten tchr. Northcumberland Co. Pub. Schs., Heathville, Va., 1974—84; organist St. John's Episcopal Ch., Warsaw, Va., 1974—75, Fairfield's Bapt. Ch., Burgess, Va., 1976—78, St. Stephen's Episcopal Ch., Heathsville, 1978—83; kindergarten tchr. Chesterfield Co. Pub. Schs., Va., 1984—2005; ret., 2005. Sec. Enterprise Sale & Design, Richmond, 2005—. Composer: (songs) Little Tiny Baby, 2006. Mem.: Am. Guild Organists (Richmond chpt.), Delta Kappa Gamma Soc. for Women Educators (Alpha Alpha chpt.). Avocations: pipe organ, reading, boating, RVing. Home: 918 Westham Pkwy Richmond VA 23229

CAMPBELL, MARY SCHMIDT, dean; b. Phila., Oct. 21, 1947; d. Harvey Nathaniel and Elaine Juanita (Harris) S.; m. George Campbell, Jr., Aug. 24, 1968; children: Garikai, Sekou, Britt Jackson. BA in English Lit., Swarthmore Coll., 1969; MA in Art Hist., Syracuse U., 1973, PhD in Humanities, 1982; ArtsD (hon.), Pace U., 1991; DFA (hon.), CCNY, 1992; PhD (hon.), Colgate U., 1994, Coll. New Rochelle, 2001. Art editor Syracuse New Times, NY, 1973—77; guest curator, curator Everson mus., Syracuse, 1974—76; exec. dir. Studio Mus. Harlem, NYC, 1977—87; commr. cultural affairs City of NY, 1987—91; dean Tisch Sch. Arts NYU, NYC, 1991—. Bd. mgrs. Swarthmore Coll., Pa., 1987-99; mem. fine arts vis. com. bd. overseers, Harvard Coll., Harvard U., Cambridge, Mass., 1991-95; mem. Tony nominating com., 1996-98, 2000-02. Co-author: Harlem Renaissance: Art of Black America, 1987, Memory & Metaphor, 1991; prodr. (film) Sembene: A Biography, 1994. Mem. NYC Mayor's Adv. Commn. on Culture, 1991-94; co-chmn. subcommittee on culture Dem. Nat. Conf., NYC, 1992; bd. dirs. NY Shakespeare Festival, 1993—, Harlem Sch. Arts, 1997-2001; bd. trustees Am. Acad. Rome, 1999—, Bklyn. Mus. Art, 1999-2002, mem. bd. trustees, UN Internat. Sch., 2001-. Recipient George Arents award Syracuse U., 1993, Project of Yr. award NY Coun. Humanities; Tisch Sch. fellow Am. Acad. Arts & Scis.; named to The Ebony Power 150, Ebony mag., 2007. Democrat. Baptist. Avocations: jogging, writing. Office: Tisch Sch of the Arts NYU 721 Broadway 12th Fl New York NY 10003-6862 Office Phone: 212-998-1801. Office Fax: 212-995-4064. E-mail: Mary.Campbell@nyu.edu.*

CAMPBELL, MARY STINECIPHER, retired chemist; b. Chattanooga, Feb. 26, 1940; d. Jesse Franklin and Florence Gladys (Marshall) S.; m. John David Fowler Jr. (div. Mar. 1979); children: John Christopher, Jesse David; m. Billy M. Campbell (dec. 2006), Jan. 1995. BA, Earlham Coll., 1962; PhD, U. N.C., 1967. Cert. organic fruit grower. Postdoctoral researcher Research Triangle Inst., Research Triangle Park, NC, 1966-68, 74-76; staff Los Alamos (N.Mex.) Nat. Lab., 1976—2004; ret., 2004. Adj. prof. organic, inorganic and phys. chemistry U. N.Mex. Grad. Ctr., Los Alamos, 1989—, instr. chemistry lab., 1989; vis. scientist AFOSR (AFATL), Eglin AFB, Fla., 1980-81. Contbr. articles to profl. jours.; inventor ammonium nitrate explosive systems and other explosive salts. Commr. Acequia Sancochada Cmty. ditch; mem. Habitat for Humanity. Mem. Am. Chem. Soc., N.Mex. Network Women in Sci. and Engring. (v.p. 1985-86, pres. 1986-87, No. chpt. pres. 1999), Bio-Integral Rsch. Ctr., N.Mex. Apple Coun. Democrat. Unitarian Universalist. Avocations: skiing, dog training, hiking, singing, gardening. Personal E-mail: bmcampbell@newmexico.com.

CAMPBELL, MELISSA LYNNSIMMONS, music educator; d. Ralph Thorton and Barbara Fay Simmons; m. Donald James Dwight Campbell, Jan. 1, 1998. MusB in Edn., Susquehanna U., Selingsgrove, Pa., 1978; MEd, Cambridge Coll., Mass., 1990. Substitute tchr. Ctrl. Berkshire Regional Sch. Dist., Dalton, Mass., 1978—79, tchr. elem. gen. and instrumental music, dir. band, 1979—80, tchr. instrumental music, gifted and talented class Dalton Jr. H.S., 1980—81, tchr. music, dir. chorus, concert and marching band, drill and flag team, all classroom music classes Wahconah Regional H.S., 1981—84, tchr. all dist. elem. instrumental music, dir. band, 1984—. With cleaning and maintenance crew Camp Danbee, Peru, Mass., 1975—92, instr. horseback riding r., 1989—92. Designed and compiled (method book for each band instrument:) My Flute's Band-Aid, My Clarinet's Band-Aid, My Saxophone's Band-Aid, My Trumpet's Band-Aid, My Trombone's Band-Aid, My Drum's Band-Aid. Mem. United Meth. Ch. of Lenox, Mass., 2003; sustaining mem. Doris Day Animal League, Washington, 1998; sustaining mem./adopted animal guardian Farm Sanctuary, Watkins Glen, NY, 2000; sustaining mem. Physicians Com. For Responsible Medicine, Washington, 2000; percussionist Eagles Band, Pittsfield, Mass., 1978—83. Recipient William Manning award, Marion Manning, 1974; Orff Music Workshop grant, Berkshire Taconic Found., 2004. Mem.: Mass. Tchrs.' Assn., Music Educators Nat. Conf. Achievements include development of Horseback riding program at Camp Danbee; First full high school marching Color Guard and Drill Team in Berkshire County; Co-founded a music collaborative for professional development of area music and arts teachers. Avocation: veganism. Personal E-mail: gmpsbell@msn.com.

CAMPBELL, MICHAEL H., air transportation executive; Grad., U. Richmond, 1971; law degree, U. Va., 1974. Ptnr. Ford & Harrison LLP, Atlanta, 1978—96; of counsel Ford & Harrison, 2005—06; sr. v.p. human resources and labor rels. Continental Airlines, Inc., 1997—2004; exec. v.p. human resources and labor rels. Delta Air Lines, Inc., Atlanta, 2006—. Mem.: Phi Beta Kappa. Office: Delta Air Lines Inc PO Box 20706 Atlanta GA 30320-6001 Office Phone: 404-715-2600.*

CAMPBELL, MICHAEL L., recreational facility executive; Co-founder Premiere Cinemas Corp., 1982—89; founder, CEO Regal Cinemas, 1989—; co-chmn., co-CEO Regal Entertainment Group, Knoxville, Tenn., 2002—05, chmn., CEO, 2005—. Bd. dir., mem. exec. com. Nat. Assn.

Theatre Owners; bd. dir. Fandango, Inc., NCM Inc., Nat. CineMedia. Mem.: Nat. Assn. Theatre Owners (exec. com., bd. dir.). Office: Regal Entertainment Group 7132 Regal Ln Knoxville TN 37918*

CAMPBELL, MILDRED CORUM, business owner, nurse; b. Warfield, Va., Feb. 24, 1934; d. Oliver Lee and Hazel King (Young) Corum; m. Hugh Stuart Campbell, Dec. 2, 1972. BSN, U. Va., Charlottesville, 1956. Head nurse plastic surgery U. Va. Med. Ctr., Charlottesville, 1956-58, head nurse cardio-surg., 1958-61; staff nurse oper. rm. NIH Heart Inst., Bethesda, Md., 1961-62; supr. oper. and recovery rms. Med. Univ. of S.C., Charleston, 1962-64; head nurse cardio operating rms. Meth. Hosp., Tex. Med. Ctr., Houston, 1964-67; supr. oper. and recovery rms. Cedars of Lebanon Med. Ctr., LA, 1967-68; product-nurse cons. Ethicon, Inc., Somerville, N.J., 1968-69; nurse cons. Johnson & Johnson, New Brunswick, N.J., 1969-70; gen. mgr. Ariz. Heart Inst., Phoenix, 1970-72; owner, pres., bd. dirs. Highland Packaging Labs., Inc., Somerville, 1983—2002; ret., 2002. Mem., moderator Nat. Ass. Operating Rm. Nurses, Denver, 1963-76; pres. Aux. Orgn., Muhlenberg Hosp., Plainfield, N.J., 1979-80; chmn. Assn. for Retarded Citizens Fund Raising Ball, Somerset County, N.J., 1982. Mem.: Inst. Packaging Profls. Home: 29 Lambert Dr Princeton NJ 08540-2304 Personal E-mail: hs.cam@verizon.net.

CAMPBELL, NANCY DUFF, lawyer; b. 1943; BA, Barnard Coll., 1965; JD, NYU, 1968. Bar: DC 1975, N.Y. 1968. Atty. Ctr. Social Welfare Policy and Law; prof. Cath. U. Sch. Law, Georgetown U. Law Ctr.; founder, co.-pres. Nat. Women's Law Ctr. Mem. US Commn. on Child and Family Welfare. Author: jour. articles on women's legal issues. Bd. adv. Princeton U. Ctr. for Rsch. on Child Wellbeing, Cmty. Tax Law Report, Alliance Nat. Def., Inst. Women's Policy Rsch.; mem. Nat. Conf. State Legis. Child Care Adv. Com., Campaign Family Leave Income Adv. Com.; bd. dirs. Low Income Investment Fund. Named Woman of Genius, Trinity Coll.; named one of 25 Heroines, Working Woman mag.; recipient Lifetime Achievement award, US Dept. Health and Human Svcs., William J. Brennan award, DC Bar. Fellow: ABA. Office: National Women's Law Ctr 11 DuPont Cir NW Ste 800 Washington DC 20036 Office Phone: 202-588-5180. Business E-Mail: campbell@nwlc.org.

CAMPBELL, NAOMI, model; b. London, May 22, 1970; d. Valerie Campbell. Attended, London Acad. Performing Arts. With Elite Model Mgmt., NYC, 1987-93, Elite Premier, London, Ford Models, Inc., Paris, 1991, NYC, 1993, Women Model Mgmt., NYC, IMG Models, NYC, 2007. Owner NC.Connect co., 2002—; organizer Fashion for Relief, 2005; amb. Rio de Janeiro, 2007—; with Dalai Lama Found., UNESCO. Appearances include (TV series) The Fresh Prince of Bel Air, The Cosby Show, (videos) George Michael's Freedom, Michael Jackson's In the Closet, (book) Madonna's Sex, 1992, (films) Cool As Ice, 1991, The Night We Never Met, 1993, Ready to Wear, 1994, Miami Rhapsody, 1995, Unzipped, 1995, To Wong Foo, Thanks for Everything, Julie Newmar, 1995, Catwalk, 1995, Absolutely Fabulous: Jealous, 1995, Girl 6, 1996, Invasion of Privacy, 1996, An Alan Smithee Film: Burn Hollywood Burn, 1997, Beautopia, 1998, Trippin, 1999, Prisoner of Love, 1999, Destinazione Verna, 2000, Intimate Portrait, Naomi Campbell, 2001, (TV film) Naomi Conquers Africa, 1998; author: Swan, 1997, Naomi; album: Love and Tears, 1994, Babywoman, 1995. Recipient Outstanding Contbn. award, Glamour Women of Yr. awards, 2007. Achievements include first black model to appear on the cover of French and Brit. Vogue and Time Mag. Office: IMG Models NY 304 Park Ave South 12Fl New York NY 10010*

CAMPBELL, NAOMI, artist; Student, Art Students League NY, Nat. Acad. Design, Sch. Visual Arts, U. Guelph, Can. Adj. Salmagundi Ctr. Am. Art, NYC, Lehman Coll., NYC, Maimonides Hosp., NYC. Represented in permanent collections Art Students League NYC, City of NY Arts for Transit, NY Pub. Libr., Trenton City Mus., NJ, Am. Soc. Prevention of Cruelty to Animals, NYC, Soc. Worldwide Interbank Fin. Telecom., exhibited in group shows at Exhbn. Butler Mus. Am. Art., 2001, Tokyo Met. Mus. Art, 2003, Heidi Cho Gallery, 2003, Paine Webber UBS Gallery, NYC, 2005, Lehman Coll. Gallery, 2006—, Susan K. Black Fedn., Tex., 2007—, Trenton City Mus., 2007—. Recipient, Am. Soc. Portrait Artists, 2002, NYC Merit award, 3 Gold Medals of Honor for Pastels, nat. juried exhbn., 2003—04. Mem.: Allied Artists Am., Audubon Artists Am., Transparent Watercolor Soc. Am., Nat. Watercolor Soc., Pastel Soc. Am. (signature, Pastel Jour. award 2006), Catherine Lorillard Wolfe Art Club. Home: 177 7th Ave #3L Brooklyn NY 11215

CAMPBELL, NEAL FRANKLIN, music educator; b. Pittsboro, NC, Jan. 27, 1953; s. Owen Riley and Aline Grey (Mangum) C.; m. Gwynn McLaurine Callis, May 13, 1996. MusB, Manhattan Sch. Music, 1983, MusM, 1985, D of Mus. Arts, 1996. Asst. organist All Saints' Ch., Chevy Chase, Md., 1973-76; organist, choirmaster St. Peter's Ch., Phila., 1976-77, St. George's By the River, Rumson, NJ, 1977-80, Christ Ch., Bloomfield, NJ, 1980-85, St. Stephen's Ch., Richmond, Va., 1985—2006; adj. asst. prof. music U. Richmond, 1997—2006; dir. music, organist St. Luke's Ch., Darien, Conn., 2006—. Author: Music and Life of Harold Friedell, 1996; performer recordings, radio and TV. Recipient Bronson Ragan award Manhattan Sch. Music, 1983. Mem. Am. Guild Organists (dean 1989-90, chair recital com. 1995-96, nat. coun. 2000-2006), Assn. Anglican Musicians, Organ Hist. Soc., Royal Coll. Organists (London), Ch. Club N.Y. Episcopalian. Office Phone: 203-655-1456. Business E-Mail: neal.campbell@saintlukesdarien.org.

CAMPBELL, NEVE, actress; b. Guelph, Ont., Can., Oct. 3, 1973; m. Jeffrey Colt, Apr. 3, 1995 (div. May 8, 1998); m. John Light, May 5, 2007 Student, Nat. Ballet Sch. Can. Actress: (films) Paint Cans, 1994, The Passion of John Ruskin, 1994, The Dark, 1994, Love Child, 1995, Scream, 1996 (Saturn award for Best Actress, MTV Movie award nomination, MTV Movie award for Best Female Performance), The Craft, 1996, Scream 2, 1997 (Blockbuster Entertainment award for Favorite Actress-Horror, MTV Movie award for Best Female Performance), 54, 1998, Wild Things, 1998, (voice only) Lion King II: Simba's Pride, 1998, Three to Tango, 1999, Scream 3, 2000, Drowning Mona, 2000, Panic, 2000, Investingating Sex, 2001, Lost Junction, 2003, Blind Horizon, 2004, When Will I Be Loved, 2004, Churchill The Hollywood Years, 2004, Reefer Madness: The Movie Musical, 2005, Relative Strangers, 2006, Partition, 2007; (TV movies) I Know My Son Is Alive, 1994, The Forget-Me-Not Murders, 1994, The Canterille Ghost, 1996, Last Call, 2002; (TV series) Catwalk, 1992-93, Part of Five, 1994-2000; (TV appearances) My Secret Identity, 1991, The Kids in the Hall, 1992, Are You Afraid of the Dark?, 1994, Kung Fu: THe Legend Continues, 1994, Adventures dans le Grand Nord, 1994, Mad TV, 1995 actor, prodr. (films) Hairshirt, 1998, The Company, 2003; actor (theatre) Resurrection Blues, 2006, Love Song, 2006 Named one of 50 Most Beautiful People, People mag., 1998. Office: Creative Artists Agy 9830 Wilshire Blvd Beverly Hills CA 90212-1825*

CAMPBELL, PATRICK D., manufacturing executive; b. Douglas, Mich., July 15, 1952; BS in Mgmt., Walsh Coll., 1975; MS in Mgmt., Saginaw Valley State Coll., 1980. Trainee Gen. Motors, Saginaw, Mich., 1976—82, various fin. positions, 1982—86, dir., capital and program analysis Zurich, Switzerland, 1986—87, comptroller, Adam Opel AG Tech. Devel. Ctr. Rüsselsheim, Germany, 1987—89, with Cadillac Motor Divsn., GM Elec. Vehicles, 1989—94, CFO, internat. opers., 1994—99, v.p., fin., GM Europe, 1994—95, exec. dir., investor relations and worldwide benchmarking analysis, 2000—01, v.p., fin., 2001—02; sr. v.p., CFO 3M Co., St. Paul, 2002—. Office: 3M Co 3M Ctr Saint Paul MN 55144 Office Phone: 651-736-0042. Office Fax: 651-733-9973.*

CAMPBELL, PAUL, III, lawyer; b. Chattanooga, Feb. 1, 1946; children: Paul IV, Kolter M. BA, Vanderbilt U., 1968; MA, Middlebury Coll., 1972; postgrad., So. Meth. U., 1971-72, Emory U., 1972-73; JD, U. Tenn., 1975. Bar: Tenn. 1976, Ga. 1977. Tchr. English St. Mark's Sch., Dallas, 1968-72; ptnr. Campbell & Campbell, Chattanooga, 1976-98; mem. Witt, Gaither & Whitaker, Chattanooga, 1998—2002, Shumacker Witt Gaither & Whitaker, Chattanooga, 2002—. Adj. prof. English, U. Tenn., Chattanooga, 1976, adj. prof. law, 1979-81, adj. prof. pre-trial litigation, Knoxville, 1996, adj. prof. pol. sci., 2002-; mem. Tenn. Ct. of Judiciary, 1995-2003; mem. Tenn. Jud. Evaluation Guidelines Commn., 1994-95. Author: Tennessee Admissibility of Evidence in Civil Cases, 1987; co-author: Tennessee Automobile Liability Insurance, 1986, 95, 96, 99, 2002; editor-in-chief Tenn. Law Rev., 1975; contbr. articles to profl. jours. Bd. mgrs. YMCA Youth Residential Ctr., 1977-80; mem. McCallie Sch. Alumni Coun., 1987-93, U. Tenn. Dean's Alumni adv. coun. law coll., 1979—; trustee, Harbison Found., 1994-96; bd. Cmty. Found. Greater Chattanooga, 2002-. Recipient Am. Jurisprudence award U. Tenn., 1974, U. Ten. Coll. Law Pub. Svc. award, 1995; Alumni Achievement award McCallie Sch., 1994. Mem. ABA (ho. del. 2002—), Am. Bar Found., Tenn. Bar Assn. (bd. govs. 1985-94, pres. 1992-93), Tenn. Bar Found., Chattanooga Bar Found., Chattanooga Bar Assn. (bd. govs. 1983-85), State Bar Ga., Fed. Bar Assn. (dir. chpt. 1983-88), Fed. Defense and Corp. Counsel, Def. Rsch. Inst., Internat. Assn. Def. Counsel, Order of Coif, Phi Kappa Phi. Office: Shumacker Witt Gaither & Whitaker 736 Market St Ste 1100 Chattanooga TN 37402-4856

CAMPBELL, RAYMOND, III, publication director; b. Dallas, June 4, 1948; s. Raymond Jr. and Ruth F. (Carroll) C.; m. Sarah Elizabeth Cooper; children: Dana, Raymond IV, William Thomas, Benjamin. BA in Comm., Dallas Bapt. U., 1970. Rep. polit. pub. rels. VanCronkhite & Maloy Pub. Rels., Dallas, 1971-72; promoter, film prodr. Praxcine Film Prodn., Dallas, 1972-74; account exec. Wieting-Fitzgerald Advt., Dallas, 1974-75; dir. pub. info. Eastfield Coll., Mesquite, Tex., 1975-81; dir. pub. rels. Sta. KERA-FM, Dallas, 1981-82; gen. mgr. Sta. K18AL-TV, Tex., 1983; publs. dir. Dallas County C.C., 1984—. Cons. Magic, Dallas, 1987-88, Texasuccess Co., 1988—; mem. adv. com. DCC-PAC, 1990—. Editor Coll. mag., 1986, Bus. and Profl. Inst., 1987, CC mag., 1989-95, Change, Power Moves Mag., 1996—; exec. editor Chancellor's Report, 2007. Vice-chmn. Am. Heart Assn., Mesquite, Tex. 1976-79; chmn. publicity com. Bedford Hist. Found., 1999-2000; chmn. County Fair at The Old Bedford Sch., 2000; mem. Selective Svc. Bd., 2003—. With Tex. N.G., 1971-77 Mem. Nat. Guard Assn. Tex. (life), Coun. For Advancement and Support of Edn., Nat. Coun. Mktg. and Pub. Rels., Dallas Bapt. U. Alumni Assn. (pres. 1974), Univ. and Coll. Designers Assn., Tex. Longhorn Breeders Assn. Democrat. Baptist. Office: Dallas County CC 701 Elm St Ste 500 Dallas TX 75202-3200 Office Phone: 214-860-2135.

CAMPBELL, RICHARD BRUCE, lawyer; b. Phila., Jan. 5, 1947; s. George B. and Edith (Neithammer) C.; m. Patricia Ann James, Mar. 7, 1981; children: Ron Martin, Rebecca Joi. BA, U. S.C., 1968, JD, 1974. Bar: U.S. Dist. Ct. S.C. 1975, U.S. Ct. Appeals (4th cir.) 1976, U.S. Ct. Appeals (5th cir.) 1983, Colo. 1985, U.S. Dist. Ct. Colo. 1986, U.S. Ct. Appeals (fed. cir.) 1989, Fla. 1989, U.S. Dist. Ct. (mid. dist.) Fla., U.S. Ct. Appeals (11th cir.) 1992. Law clk. to presiding justice U.S. Dist. Ct., Columbia, SC, 1975; ptnr. Henderson & Salley, Aiken, SC, 1975—80; atty. TVA, Knoxville, 1980—85; ptnr. Wells, Love & Scoby, Boulder, Colo., 1986—89; shareholder Carlton Fields PA, Tampa, Fla., 1989—2005, Carey, O'Malley, Whitaker and Manson PA, Tampa, 2005—. Lectr. in field. Contbr. articles to profl. jours. Served to capt. USAF, 1968—72. Mem. ABA, Am. Arbitration Assn. (panelist), Fla. Bar Assn., Colo. Bar Assn., Hillsborough County Bar Assn. Avocations: travel, skiing, photography. Office: Carey O'Malley Whitaker and Manson PA 712 S Oregon Ave Tampa FL 33606 Office Phone: 813-250-0577. Business E-Mail: rcampbell@cowmpa.com.

CAMPBELL, RICHARD LYNN, research engineer; b. Jackson, Mich., Mar. 30, 1952; s. Paul Burton and Lucile Irene Campbell; m. Sara Emma Rankinen, Aug. 4, 1990; children: Lena Johanna Mower, Ana Sara Rugani, Richard L. Campbell, Jr. BS in Physics, Seattle Pacific U., 1973—75; MSEE, PhD, U. Wash., Seattle. 2d class radioman USN, Phila., 1971—73; sr. tech. assoc. Bell Labs., Murray Hill, NJ, 1975—79; assoc. prof. Mich. Technol. U., Houghton, 1983—96; prin. engr. TriQuint Semiconductor, Hillsboro, Oreg., 1996—2003, Cascade Microtech, Inc., Beaverton, Oreg., 2003—. Chmn. microwave theory & techniques soc. com. 17 Inst. Elec. & Electronic Engrs., NYC, 2007—. Author: (technical book) Experimental Methods in RF Design; contbr. articles to profl. jours. Recipient Tech. Excellence award, 1989, Tech. Excellence Award, 1993, Prof. of Yr. award, HKN Student Br., 1991, 1996, DeMaw Tech. Excellence award, 1999. Mem.: Inst. Elec. & Electronic Engrs. United Meth. Achievements include patents for in microwave technology; design of Gallium Arsenide radio frequency integrated circuits widely used in cell phones; research in microwave signal propagation in random environments. Avocations: amateur radio, sailing. Office: Cascade Microtech Inc 2430 NW 206th Ave Beaverton OR 97006 Home Phone: 503-617-0558. Business E-Mail: kk7b@ieee.org.

CAMPBELL, ROBERT, architect, writer; b. Buffalo, Mar. 31, 1937; s. R. Douglas and Amy (Armitage) C.; m. Janice Jaye Gold, Feb. 2, 1969 (div. 1990); 1 child, Nicholas. AB magna cum laude with highest honors, Harvard U., 1958, MArch, 1967; MS in Journalism, Columbia U., 1960. Registered architect, Mass. Writer, editor Parade mag., 1960-63; designer Benjamin Thompson Assocs., 1968-69; assoc. Sert Jackson & Assocs., 1967-75; architecture critic Boston Globe, 1973—; pvt. practice architecture Cambridge, Mass., 1975—. Cons. Am. Acad. Arts and Scis., Whitehead Inst., Boston Symphony Orch., Isabella Stewart Gardner Mus., Mayors Inst. for City Design, City of San Francisco; lectr. in field; mem. vis. faculty U. N.C. Sch. Architecture, Charlotte, 1979-94; Sam Gibbons Eminent scholar U. South Fla., 1993-2002; vis. scholar MIT, 1991-94; Max Fisher vis. prof. U. Mich., 2002; artist-in-residence Am. Acad. Rome, 1997. Author: Cityscapes of Boston: An American City Through Time; contbg. editor Architectural Record mag.; contbr. articles to profl. jours.; published poet, photographer. Mem. Mid-Cambridge Neighborhood Assn.; propr. Boston Athenaeum. Recipient Francis Kelley prize, 1967, Pulitzer Prize for Criticism, 1996; named Julia Amory Appleton traveling fellow, 1967, Nat. Endowment for Arts design fellow, 1975; Nat. Arts Journalism Program sr. fellow Columbia U., 2003; grantee Graham Found., 1991, 2003. Fellow AIA (nat. design com., medal for criticism 1980), Am. Acad. Arts and Scis.; mem. Boston Archtl. Ctr. (hon. life), Boston Soc. Architects (award of honor 2004), Cambridge Club, Tavern Club, Examiner Club, Century Assn. (N.Y.C.), Saturday Club, Phi Beta Kappa. Democrat. Address: 54 Antrim St Cambridge MA 02139-1102 Fax: 617-576-4784. E-mail: Robert@RCampbell.net.

CAMPBELL, ROBERT CHARLES, minister, theology studies educator; b. Chandler, Ariz., Mar. 9, 1924; s. Alexander Joshua and Florence (Betzner) C.; m. Lotus Idamae Graham, July 12, 1945; children: Robin Carl, Cherry Colleen. AB, Westmont Coll., 1944; BD, Eastern Baptist Theol. Sem., 1947, ThM, 1949, ThD, 1951, DD (hon.), 1974; MA, U. So. Calif., 1959; postgrad., Dropsie U., 1949-51, U. Pa., 1951-52, NYU, 1960-62, U. Cambridge, Eng., 1969; DLitt (hon.), Am. Bapt. Sem. of West, 1972; HHD (hon.), Alderson-Broaddus Coll., 1979; LHD (hon.), Linfield Coll., 1982; LLD (hon.), Franklin Coll., 1986. Ordained to ministry Am. Bapt. Ch., 1947; pastor 34th St. Bapt. Ch., Phila., 1945-49; instr. Eastern Bapt. Theol. Sem., Phila., 1949-51; asst. prof. Eastern Coll., St. Davids, Pa., 1951-53; assoc. prof. N.T. Am. Bapt. Sem. of West, Covina, Calif., 1953-54, dean, prof., 1954-72; gen. sec. Am. Bapt. Chs. in U.S.A., Valley Forge, Pa., 1972-87; pres. Eastern Bapt. Theol. Sem., Phila., 1987-89, ret. Vis. lectr. Sch. Theology at Claremont, Calif., 1961-63, U. Redlands, Calif., 1959-60, 66-67, Fuller Theology Seminary, Calif., 1992-97; Bd. mgrs. Am. Bapt. Bd. of Edn. and Publ., 1956-59, 65-69; v.p. So. Calif. Bapt. Conv., 1967-68; pres. Am. Bapt. Chs. of Pacific S.W., 1970-71; Pres. N.Am. Bapt. Fellowship, 1974-76; mem. exec. com. Bapt. World Alliance, 1972-90, v.p., 1975-80; mem. exec. com., gov. bd. Nat. Council Chs. of Christ in U.S.A., 1972-87; del. to World Council of Chs., 1975, 83, mem. central com., 1975-90. Author: Great Words of the Faith, 1965, The Gospel of Paul, 1973, Evangelistic Emphases in Ephesians, Jesus Still Has Something To Say, 1987. Baptist. Home: 1763 Royal Oaks Dr No Apt D20 Bradbury CA 91010

CAMPBELL, ROBERT DAVID, manufacturing and metal products executive; b. Teaneck, NJ, May 5, 1947; s. Robert Wesley and Phyllis May Julich; m. Elizabeth I. Young, June 15, 1978; 1 child, Ariel. BS, Syracuse U., 1969. Trader C. Tennant Sons & Co., NYC, 1969—73, Cargill, NYC, 1974—75; mng. dir. Amalgamated Metal Corp., Zug, Switzerland, 1975—80; pres. Amalgamet Inc., NYC, 1978—80; v.p. Samincorp Inc., NYC, 1980—84; pres. RST Resources, Inc., NYC, 1984—93; pres., CEO Global Minerals & Metals Corp., NYC, 1993—. Mem.: Cannon Point South (bd. dirs. 1983—95), Metropolitan Club, NY Copper Club. Avocations: tennis, scuba, sailing, skiing. Home: 45 Sutton Pl S New York NY 10022-2444 Personal E-mail: gmmcllc@aol.com.

CAMPBELL, ROBERT EMMETT, retired health products executive; b. Passaic, NJ, Oct. 24, 1933; Grad., Fordham U., 1955, Rutgers U., 1962; PhD (hon.), Fordham U., U. Medicine & Dentistry of NJ. Joined Johnson & Johnson, New Brunswick, NJ, 1955, corp. gen. controller & assist. treasurer, 1971—75, v.p. finance, 1975—76, bd. mem., treasurer, 1976—80, v.p. finance, 1980—83; vice chmn. exec. com. IMPATH, 1985—; vice chmn., dir. Johnson & Johnson, New Brunswick, NJ, 1989—95, ret., 1995. Mem. advisory council U. Notre Dame Coll. Sci.; bd. mem. Parker Memorial Home; mem. bd. of overseers Robert Wood Johnson Med. Sch.; bd. chmn. New Brunswick Affiliated Hospitals. Chmn. bd. trustees Fordham U., 1992-98, bd. dir. Robert Wood Johnson Found., 1994- (chmn. 1999—2005); chmn. bd. dirs. Cancer Inst. N.J., 1995—. Served USAF. Address: Robert Wood Johnson Found Rte 1 & College Rd E PO Box 2316 Princeton NJ 08543-2316

CAMPBELL, ROBERT HEDGCOCK, investment banker, lawyer; b. Ann Arbor, Mich., Jan. 16, 1948; s. Robert Miller and Ruth Adele (Hedgcock) C.; m. Katherine Kettering, June 17, 1972; children: Mollie DuPlan, Katherine Elizabeth, Anne Kettering. BA, U. Wash., 1970, JD, 1973. Bar. Wash. 1973, Wash. State Supreme Ct. 1973, Fed. 1973, U.S. Dist. Ct. (we. dist.) Wash. 1973, Ct. Appeals (9th cir.) 1981. Assoc. Roberts & Shefelman, Seattle, 1973-78, ptnr., 1978-85; sr. v.p. Lehman Bros., Inc., Seattle, 1985-87, mng. dir., 1987—. Bd. dirs. Pogo Producing Co., 1999—; dir., treas. Nat. Assn. Bd. Lawyers, Hinsdale, Ill., 1982-85; pres., trustee Wash. State Soc. Hosp. Attys., Seattle, 1982-85; mem. econs. dept. vis. com. U. Wash., 1995-97; mem. Law Sch. dean's adv. bd. U. Wash., 1999—. Contbr. articles to profl. jours. Trustee Bellevue (Wash.) Schs. Found., 1988-91, pres., 1989-90; nation chief Bellevue Eastside YMCA Indian Princess Program, 1983-88; trustee Wash. Phikeia Found., 1983-91, Sandy Hook Yacht Club Estates, Inc., 1993-98; mem. Wash. Gov.'s Food Processing Coun., 1990-91. Mem. U. Wash. Varsity Swimming Alumni Bd. Republican. Avocations: skiing, wind surfing, bike riding, physical fitness, golf. Home: 8604 NE 10th St Medina WA 98039-3915 Office: Lehman Bros Bank of America Tower 701 5th Ave Ste 7101 Seattle WA 98104-7016 Home Phone: 425-454-0228; Office Phone: 206-344-5888. Personal E-mail: ibe2ski@msn.com. Business E-Mail: rhcampbe@lehman.com.

CAMPBELL, ROBERT MURRAY, JR., surgeon, researcher; b. Nashville, May 7, 1951; s. Robert Murray and Betty Ann (Kennedy) Campbell; m. Corey Le Campbell, Mar. 31, 2001; children: Abigail Le, Noah Robert. Studied, Vanderbilt U., Nashville, 1969—71; BA, Johns Hopkins U., Balt., 1973; MD, Georgetown U., 1977. Diplomate Nat. Bd. Med. Examiners, 1978, cert. in Orthopedics Am. Bd. Orthopedic Surgery, 1982. Resident in orthop. surgery Fitzsimmons Army Med. Ctr., Denver, 1978—81; orthopedist U.S. Army, Fort Meade, Md., 1981—85; fellow in pediatric orthops. A.I. Dupont Inst., Wilmington, Del., 1985—86; pvt. practice in pediatric orthops. San Antonio, 1986—92; from asst. prof. to assoc. prof. orthops. U. Tex. Health Sci. Ctr., San Antonio, 1992—2002, prof., 2003—. Cons. U.S. Consumer Product and Safety Commn., 2000; mem., med. adv. com. Nat. Orgn. of Rare Disorders, 2000—; dir. Thoracic Inst., Christus Santa Rosa Children's Hosp., San Antonio, 2001—. Cons., reviewer Jour. of Bone and Joint Surgery, 1987—, Jour. Pediat. Orthop., —; contbr. articles to profl. jours. Participant Orthop. Edn. in Third World Countries, 1999—. Maj. US Army, 1983—85. Named to San Antonio (Tex.) Sci. and Tech. Hall Fame, 2005; recipient Imagineer Award, Mind Sci. Found. of San Antonio, 1993, Miracle Maker Award, A.H. Robins/Wyeth Pediat., 1994, Therapeutic Achievement award, Nat. Org. Rare Diseases, 2005, Endowed Chair in Pediat. Orthopedics, Dielmann Pres. Coun., 2005; grantee, Nat. Orgn. Rare Disorders, 1992—93, FDA Office Orphan Products Devel., 1994—2000. Fellow: Scoliosis Rsch. Soc. (chmn., growing spine com. 2002); mem.: Am. Acad. Pediat. (mem. task force pediatric device devel.), Pediatric Orthop. Soc. of N.Am. (edowed chair, pres. coun. 2004, Arthur H. Huene Excellence and Promise award 2006), Clin. Orthop. Soc. (pres. 2005). Achievements include invention of verticle expandable prosthetic titanium rib and the FDA approval of this device as a humanitarium use device; apparatus and method for effecting surgical incision through use of a fluid jet; co-invention of bioabsorbable intramedullary rod implant system. Avocations: white-water rafting, bicycling, running. Office: U Tex Health Sci Ctr Dept Orthops Mailcode 7774 7703 Floyd Cir San Antonio TX 78229 Office Phone: 210-567-5125. Business E-Mail: campbellr@uthscsa.edu, rcampbell.thoracic.institute@christushealth.org.

CAMPBELL, RONALD NEIL, retired graphics designer; b. Morristown, NJ, Mar. 7, 1926; s. Carroll Francis and Emily Ruth (Peters) C.; m. Jule Gallina, Sept. 22, 1956; 1 son, Bruce G. BFA, R.I. Sch. Design, 1951. With Fortune mag., NYC, 1952—82, dir. art, 1974—82; ret., 1982. Freelance writer Sports Illustrated, CASE Currents, Graphis mag.; freelance graphic designer, lectr., 1951—; mem. adv. bd. Internat. Editorial Design Forum; designer Merrill Lynch, 1970-72, Time Inc., 1984; designer, art dir. Inside Time Inc., 1984-86; design cons. Harvard Mag., 1985-95, Harvard Bus. Rev., 1987-90. Served with USNR, 1944-46. Recipient merit awards Art Dirs. Club NY, merit awards Comm. Arts Mag., merit awards Art Direction Mag., Page One award Am. Newspaper Guild, 2 Silver awards Editl. Design Forum, NJ State Disting. Svc. medal, 2003. Mem. Soc. Illustrators (Gold and Silver medals), Am. Inst. Graphic Arts (merit awards), Soc. Publ. Designers (hon. bd. dirs., merit awards), Univ. and Coll. Designers Assn., USS Bon Homme Richard Assn. Home: 37 Barton Hollow Rd Flemington NJ 08822-5929 Office: 136 Waverly Pl Apt 8A New York NY 10014-6822 Office Phone: 212-924-1953.

CAMPBELL, SCOTT ROBERT, lawyer, former food products executive; b. Burbank, Calif., June 7, 1946; s. Robert Clyde and Jenevieve Anne (Olsen) C.; Patricia Marie Bovan, Dec 30, 2003; 1 son, Donald Steven. BA, Claremont Men's Coll., 1970; JD, Cornell U., 1973. Bar: Ohio 1973, U.S. Dist. Ct. (so. dist.) Ohio 1974, Minn. 1976, Calif. 1989, U.S. Dist. Ct. (no. dist.) Calif. 1989, U.S. Ct. Appeals (9th cir.) 1989, U.S. Dist. Ct. (cen. and so. dists.) Calif. 1990, U.S. Ct. Appeals (5th cir.) 1991, U.S. Tax Ct. 1991, U.S. Ct. Appeals (fed. cir.) 2001, U.S. Ct. Appeals (11th cir.) 2004, U.S. Dist. Ct. (ea. dist.) Calif. 2005. Assoc. Taft, Stettinius & Hollister, Cin., 1973—76; atty. Mpls. Star & Tribune, 1976—77; sr. v.p., gen. counsel, sec. Kellogg Co., Battle Creek, Mich., 1977—89; ptnr. Furth Fahrner Mason, San Francisco, 1988—2000, Zelle, Hofmann, Voelbel, Mason & Gette,

LLP, San Francisco, 2000—. U.S. del. ILO Food and Beverage Conf., Geneva, 1984; participant, presenter first U.S.-USSR Legal Seminar, Moscow, 1988; speaker other legal seminars. Mem. ABA, Ohio Bar Assn., Minn. Bar Assn., Calif. Bar. Assn. Office: Zelle Hofmann Voelbel Mason & Gette LLP 44 Montgomery St Ste 3400 San Francisco CA 94104 Office Phone: 415-633-1903. Personal E-mail: srclaw@ix.netcom.com. Business E-Mail: scampbell@zelle.com.

CAMPBELL, SELAURA JOY, lawyer; b. Oklahoma City, Mar. 25, 1944; d. John Moore III and Gyda (Hallum) C. AA, Stephens Coll., 1963; BA, U. Okla., 1965; MEd, Chapel Hill U., 1974; JD, N.C. Cen. U., 1978; postgrad. atty. mediation courses, South Tex. Sch. of Law, Houston, 1991, Atty. Mediators Inst./Dallas, Dallas, 1992. Bar: Ariz 1983; lic. real estate broker, N.C.; cert. tchr. N.C. With flight svc. dept. Pan Am. World Airways, NYC, 1966-91; lawyer Am. Women's Legal Clinic, Phoenix, 1987. Charter mem. Sony Corp. Indsl. Mgmt. Seminar, 1981; guest del. Rep. Nat. Conv., Houston, 1992; judge all-law sch. mediation competition for Tex., South Tex. Sch. Law, Houston, 1994. Mem. N.C. Cen. U. Law Rev., 1977-78. People-to-People del. People's Republic of China, 1987; guest del. Rep. Nat. Conv., Houston, 1992. Mem. Ariz. Bar Assn., Humane Soc. U.S., Nat. Wildlife Fedn., People for the Ethical Treatment of Animals, Amnesty Internat., Phi Alpha Delta. Republican. Episcopalian. Avocations: mountain climbing, horseback riding, photography. Home: 206 Taft Ave Cleveland TX 77327-4539

CAMPBELL, STEWART FRED, foundation administrator, consultant; b. St. Louis, June 29, 1931; s. Archibald Stewart and Charlotte (Ehrmann) C.; m. Ann Abbey Hudson, Dec. 18, 1954; children: Karen Ann, Deborah Ann. BS, Lehigh U., Bethlehem, Pa., 1954; MBA, NYU, 1961. With Mfrs. Hanover Trust Co., NYC, 1958-64, asst. sec., 1962-64; with Duke Endowment, NYC, 1964-79, asst. treas., 1967-73, treas., 1973-79; sec.-treas. Alfred P. Sloan Found., NYC, 1979-86, fin. v.p., sec., 1986—2004. Treas. Doris Duke Trust, 1973-79, Angler B. Duke Meml., Inc., 1973-79, Nanaline H. Duke Fund, 1973-79; asst. treas. Duke Power Co., 1968-75; bd. dirs. Skytop Lodge, Inc., 1992—, v.p., 1993-95, chmn. bd., 1995-2000. Treas. Essex unit N.J. Assn. Retarded Children, 1967-72, trustee, 1966-74; trustee Meml. Home of Upper Montclair, 1987-96, pres., 1990-95; trustee COPE Ctr., Inc., 2004—, treas., 2005—. Mem. Delta Phi. Clubs: Montclair Golf, Skytop (Pa.). Home: 3 Wendover Rd Montclair NJ 07042-3031 E-mail: campbell@sloan.org.

CAMPBELL, THOMAS DOUGLAS, business executive; b. NYC, Jan. 5, 1951; s. Edward Thomas and Dorothy Alice (Moore) C.; m. Mary Anne Makin, Dec. 22, 1978; 1 child, Kristen Anne. BA, U. Del., 1972; JD, U. Pa., 1976. Bar: Del. 1977. Law clk. Law Offices Bayard Brill & Handleman, Wilmington, Del., 1974-77; govt. affairs rep. Northeastern U.S. Standard Oil Co. Ind., 1977-78; Washington rep. Std. Oil Co., Ind., 1978-85; pres. Thomas D. Campbell and Assocs., Inc., Alexandria, Va., 1985—; chmn. bd. dirs. Compressus, Inc., 2001—. With U.S. Army, 1968-69, Del. Air N.G., 1969-77. Elected to Wall of Fame, U. Del., 2000; recipient US Congress Congl. Leadership award, 2003, Presdl. Call to Svc. award, 2004. Mem. ABA, Congl. Awards Found. (chmn. bd. dirs. 1995-03), Duke of Edinburgh's Internat. Award Assn. (internat. trustee 2001-03), Phi Beta Kappa, Phi Kappa Phi, Omicron Delta Epsilon, Omicron Delta Kappa. Republican. Episcopalian. Home: PO Box 37 Cruz Bay St John VI 00831

CAMPBELL, TIMOTHY R., insurance company executive; b. Sparta, Ill. s. Floyd and Dorothy Campbell; m. Sara Campbell; children: Timothy Scott, Catherine Elizabeth. AB, MacMurray Coll., Jacksonville, Ill., 1968; postgrad., U. Ill., Urbana, 1968-69, U. Hartford, West Hartford, Conn., 1972; MA in Adminstrn., U. Ill., Springfield, 1975; grad., Pub. Affairs Inst., Tucson, 1995. V.p. govt. affairs Travelers Ins. Cos., Hartford; v.p. govt. rels. Travelers Group, NYC, v.p. state govt. rels.; sr. v.p., dir. state govt. rels. divsn. Citigroup, 1998-2000, sr. v.p. state govt. rels. divsn., 2000—02; sr. v.p. govt. rels. Travelers Property Casualty Corp., Hartford, Conn., 2002—04, The Travelers Companies, Inc., Hartford, 2004—. Mem. exec. com. Nat. Conf. State Legislatures, Denver, 1976-78; chair governing bd. Manifesto Ins. Group, Tallahassee, Fla., 1992-98. Trustee MacMurray Coll., Jacksonville, Ill., 1976-83, 94-99; dir. Sci. Mus. Conn., West Hartford, 1994, 97-2000; apptd. by gov. to Conn. Adv.Commn. on Intergovtl. Rels., 1996-2004. Inducted into Samuel K. Gove Ill. Legis. Internship Hall of Fame, 1995. Mem. Am. Soc. Pub. Adminstrn., Ins. Fedn. Pa. (bd. dirs. 1988-2003), Ins. Assn. Conn. (bd. dirs.), Am. Ins. Assn. (govt. affairs com.). Avocations: reading, travel. Office: The Travelers Companies Inc 1 Tower Sq Hartford CT 06183-0001 Office Phone: 860-954-3716.

CAMPBELL, TOM, state agency administrator, dean, former congressman; b. Chgo., Aug. 14, 1952; s. William J. and Marie Campbell; m. Susanne (Martin) Campbell. BA, MA in Econs. with highest honors, U. Chgo., 1973, PhD in Econs. with highest dept. fellowship, 1980; JD magna cum laude, Harvard U., 1976. Law clk. to Judge George E. MacKinnon U.S. Ct. Appeals (D.C. cir.), 1976-77; law clk. to Justice Byron R. White U.S. Supreme Ct., Washington, 1977-78; assoc. Winston & Strawn, Chgo., 1978-80; White Ho. fellow Office Chief of Staff, Washington, 1980-81; exec. asst. to dep. atty. gen. Dept. Justice, Washington, 1981; dir. Bur. Competition FTC, Washington, 1981-83; mem. 101st, 102nd, 104th, 105th, 106th Congresses from Calif. 12th Dist., 1989—93; mem. com. on sci., space and tech., com. on judiciary, banking, fin. and urban affairs; mem. Calif. State Senate, 1993-95, 104th-106th Congresses from Calif. 15th Dist., 1995-2001; mem. com. internat. rels., com. on banking, joint econ. com.; dean Haas Sch. Bus. U. Calif., Berkeley, 2002—; dir. dept. fin. State of Calif., 2004—. Prof. Stanford Law Sch., 1983-2002; bd. dirs., DEMOS. Referee Jour. Polit. Economy, Internat. Rev. Law and Econs. Nat. adv. bd. Haas Ctr. Pub. Svc., Stanford U. Mem. ABA (antitrust sect., coun. 1985-88, program chmn. 1983-84), Coun. on Fgn. Rels., World Affairs Coun. No. Calif. (chair 2003-). Republican. Office: State of Calif Dept Fin 915 L St Sacramento CA 95814 Office Phone: 914-445-4141.*

CAMPBELL, VINCENT BERNARD, judge, lawyer; b. Rochester, NY, Nov. 1, 1943; s. Paul and Lucy C.; m. Geraldine Miceli, July 4, 1970; children: Dina, Tracy. BS, Syracuse U., 1965, LLD, 1968. Bar: N.Y. 1969. Lawyer Goldman and Shinder, Rochester, NY, 1970—74, Vincent B. Campbell Law Firm, Rochester, 1974—; businessman Flower City Builders Supply Corp., Rochester, 1974—; real estate developer V.R.J.D. Devel. Inc., 40 West Ave. Properties, Rochester, 1970—; judge Town of Greece, NY, 1994—. V.p. Monroe County Legislature, Rochester, 1976-88; N.Y. state committeeman Rep. Party, Rochester, 1988-93; town councilman Town of Greece, 1990-94; bd. trustees N.Y. Chiropractic Coll., Seneca Falls, N.Y., 1992; econ. devel. com. Nazareth Coll., Rochester, 1991-93. Recipient Robert Roantree award Syracuse Credit Mfrs. Assn., 1965, Am. Jurisprudence award Lawyers Coop., 1969; named Legislator of the Yr., Monroe County Conservative Party, 1983-84. Mem. ABA, N.Y. State Bar Assn., N.Y. State Magistrate's Assn., Rochester Yacht Club. Avocations: sailing, golf, hunting, winemaking. Office Phone: 716-621-1820.

CAMPBELL, WALTER EVERETT, adult education educator; b. Brockton, Mass., Mar. 28, 1930; s. Walter and Vera Campbell; m. Phoebe Ann Campbell, Aug. 30, 1954; children: Eric, Brian, Robin, Scott, Laurie. B, Bridgewater State Coll., Mass., 1952; M, U. So. Calif., LA, 1968; D, George Washington U., 1975. Commd. 2d lt. USAF, 1952, advanced through grades to maj., 1971, ret., 1990. Cons. in field. Dist. commr. Boy Scouts Am., Germany, 1970—72; vol. Meals on Wheels, Severna Park, Md., 1990—2005. Mem.: Mil. Officers Assn. (life). Independent. Unitarian. Avocations: bicycling, hiking, antiques, classical music. Home: 1201 Severnview Dr Crownsville MD 21032

CAMPBELL, WILLIAM BERNARD, cardiologist; b. Nov. 18, 1946; MD, U. Wis. Med. Sch., Madison. Cert. Am. Bd. Internal Medicine, Am. Bd. Internal Medicine, subspecialty Cardiovascular Disease. Resident, internal medicine Akron Gen. Med. Ctr., Ohio; fellow, cardiology Cleve. Clinic, Ohio; cardiologist Borgess Cardiology Group, Kalamazoo. Pres. Heart Ctr. for Excellence. Achievements include specializing in angioplasty and pioneered the use of peripheral and coronary stents in Kalamazoo. Office: Borgess Cardiology Group 1717 Shaffer St Ste 232 Kalamazoo MI 49048 Office Phone: 269-226-5050.*

CAMPBELL, WILLIAM EDWARD, mental hospital administrator; b. Kansas City, Kans., June 30, 1927; s. William Warren and Mary (Bickerman) C.; m. Joan Josselyn Larimer, July 26, 1952; children: William Gregory, Stephen James, Douglas Edward. Student, U. Nebr., 1944-45, MS, 1975; student, U. Mich., 1945, Drake U., 1948; BA, U. Iowa, 1949, MA, 1950; PhD in Psychology, U. Nebr., Lincoln, 1980. Psychologist Dept. Pub. Instrn., State of Iowa, 1951-52; hosp. adminstr. Mental Health Inst., Cherokee, Iowa, 1952-68; dir. planning and rsch. Dept. Social Svcs., State of Iowa, 1968-69; supt. Glenwood Rescource Ctr. (formerly Glenwood State Hosp. Sch.), Iowa, 1969—, Clarinda Mental Health Inst., Iowa, 1979—; assoc. prof. mental health adminstrn. Northwestern U., Chgo., 1982—; pres. River Bluffs Cmty. Mental Health Ctr., 1971—, also bd. dirs. Dir. Shared Mental Health Svcs., Clarinda/Glenwood; founder, chmn. Regional Drug Abuse Adv. Coun.; adj. prof. Sch. Pub. Health U. Minn., also preceptor grad. students in mental health adminstrn.; vis. faculty Avepane U., Caracas, Venezuela; adj. prof. Coll. Medicine and Health Adminstrn. Tulane U.; mem. vis. staff dept. psychiatry U. Nebr. Med. Ctr.-Creighton U. St. Joseph Med. Ctr.; apptd. State of Iowa Dept. Human Svcs. Exec. Mgmt. Team, 1997; doctoral advisor U. Neb., 2000—. Author works in field. UN spl. cons. to Venzuela for UNESCO; bd. dir. Polk County Mental Health; v.p., bd. dir. Mercy Hosp., Coun. Bluffs, Iowa; state pres. United Cerebral Palsy; charter mem., bd. dir. Pub. Broadcasting Sta. KIWR, Council Bluffs, Iowa, Glenwood-Mills County Econ. Devel. Found., Inc., 1985—; charter mem., bd. dir. Mills County Econ. Devel., 1987, Glenwood Resource Ctr., 1993—; bd. dir. On-With-Life, adminstr., 2005-; bd. dir., mem. human rels. and fin. coms. On-With-Life Found., bd. dir. Glenwood C. of C.; charter mem., organizer Loess Hills Alliance, 1998—, mem. land protection, econ. devel. and long range planning coms., 1999—; mem. Glenwood City Tree Bd.;vol. at hosps., also in mental health and substance abuse, and long term care orgns. Served with AUS, 1944-46; col. Res. Decorated Army Commendation medal; recipient Meritorious Service medal U.S. Army, 1982. Fellow Assn. Mental Health Adminstrs. (nat. com. chmn. 1970); mem. Assn. Med. Adminstrs., Am. Hosp. Assn. (nat. governing bd. psychiat. services sect., charter panelist nat. adv. panel on mental health services, mem. governing body psychiat. services sect.), Iowa Hosp. Assn., Health Planning Council of Midlands, Assn. Univ. Programs in Health Adminstrn. (mem. nat. task force on edn. of mental health adminstrs. 1969—), Am. Assn. on Mental Deficiency (chmn. adminstrn. sect. Region 8), Nat. Rehab. Assn., Assn. Retarded Children, Mental Health Assn., Phi Beta Kappa. Home: 307 Louise Ave Glenwood IA 51534

CAMPBELL, WILLIAM HENRY, JR., rail transportation executive, former federal agency administrator; b. Quincy, Mass., Mar. 12, 1947; s. William Henry and Alice Elizabeth (Cleary) C.; m. Pamela Jeanne Beall, Mar. 29, 1974; children: Jennifer Anne, John Matthew. BS in Engring., Mass. Maritime Acad., 1967; Dipl. Mgmt., Indsl. Coll. Armed Forces, Washington, 1984; MS in Tech. Mgmt., Johns Hopkins U., Balt., 1987. Chief engr. U.S. Merchant Marine, 1967-73; chief main propulsion br. George G. Sharp, Inc., Hyattsville, Md., 1973-75; sr. mech. engr. USCG, Washington, 1975-77, chief sys. tech. div., 1980-85; investigator-in-chg. Nat. Transp. Safety Bd., Washington, 1977-80; dep. comdr. engring. quality Naval Supply Sys. Command, Washington, 1985-91; chief procurement mgmt. and sr. competition advocate USCG, 1991—2000; dep. asst. sec. for finance, dep. CFO US Dept. Veterans Affairs, Washington, 2000—02, asst. sec. mgmt., CFO, 2002—05, acting asst. sec for human resources & adminstr., 2003—05; v.p. Aon Consulting, Chgo., 2005; dir. Fed. CFO Advisory Services practice KPMG LLP, Washington; CFO Amtrak, Washington, 2007—. Contbr. articles to profl. jours. Recipient Engring. award Brotherhood of Marine Officers, 1967, Disting. Svc. award Nat. Transp. Safety Bd., 1980, Equal Opportunity award U.S. DOT, 1983, Superior Civilian Svc. medal USN, 1991. Mem. Mass. Maritime Acad. Alumni Assn., Indsl. Coll. Armed Forces Alumni Assn., Johns Hopkins U. Alumni Assn. Democrat. Avocations: history, philosophy, economics. Office: Nat Railroad Passenger Corp 60 Massachusetts Ave NE Washington DC 20002*

CAMPBELL, WILLIAM J., JR., lawyer; b. Nov. 5, 1948; BA, U. Chgo., 1970; JD, U. Mich., 1973. Bar: Ill. 1973, U.S. Dist. Ct. (no. dist.) Ill. 1973, U.S. Ct. Appeals (7th cir.) Calif. 1974, U.S. Dist. Ct. (ctrl. dist.) Calif. 1974, U.S. Ct. Mil. Appeals 1976, U.S. Supreme Ct. 1978, U.S. Dist. Ct. (ctrl. dist.) Ill. 1979, U.S. Ct. Appeals (2nd, 5th and 9th cirs.) 1980, U.S. Dist. Ct. (no. dist.) Calif. 1983. Ptnr. Rudnick & Wolfe, Chgo.; ptnr., comml. litig. DLA Piper Rudnick Gray Cary, Chgo. Lt. USN, 1973-76; JAGC, USNR, 1970-82. Office: DLA Piper Rudnick Gray Cary 203 N La Salle St Ste 1900 Chicago IL 60601-1210 Office Phone: 312-368-7050. Office Fax: 312-236-7516. Business E-Mail: william.campbell@piperrudnick.com.

CAMPBELL, WILLIAM O'NEAL, retired physician; b. McCaysville, Ga., May 22, 1928; s. Martin Hoyt Campbell and Pauline Kimsey; m. Reba Kathern Hughes, June 14, 1961; 1 child, Martin Lee. AA, Tenn. Wesylan Coll., 1948; MD, U. Tenn. Memphis, 1962. Diplomate Am. Acad. Family Physicians. Resident Carraway Meth. Hosp., Birmingham, Ala., 1965; family physician Copperhill, Tenn., 1965—77; staff physician Tenn. Valley Authority, Chattanooga, 1977—94; ret., 1994. Cons. U. So. Ala. Med. Mus., Mobile, Med. Mus., Foley, Ala. Mem.: AMA, Med. Collectors Assn., Chattanooga and Hamilton County Med. Soc., Alpha Omega Alpha, Alpha Epsilon Delta. Home: 4900 Bal Harbor Dr Chattanooga TN 37416

CAMPBELL, WILLIAM V., computer company executive; b. Pitts. married; 1 son. BS in Econs., MS in Econs., Columbia U. V.p. J. Walter Thompson, NYC; dir. mktg. film divsn. Eastman Kodak Co.; v.p. mktg. Apple Computer Inc., 1983, v.p. sales, 1984, v.p. distgn. svc. and support, exec. v.p., 1984, group exec. of U.S.; founder, pres., CEO Claris Corp. (purchased by Apple Computer), 1990; pres., CEO GO Corp., 1990-94, Intuit, 1994-98, 1999—2000, chmn. bd., 1998—. Bd. dirs. Great Plains Software, SanDisk, Apple Computer Inc. Dir. Nat. Football Found. and Hall of Fame. Named to InfoWorld's Top 25 CTOs, 2004. Office: Intuit Inc 2535 Garcia Ave Mountain View CA 94043-1111

CAMPBELL-ALSTON, DEIRDRE ADINA, anatomist, physiologist, researcher; b. Queens, NY, Apr. 10, 1976; d. Kenneth Campbell and Susan Dorothy Smith-Sligh; m. Kinard Ivron Alston, Oct. 8, 2002. BS in Biology, Salisbury U., Md., 1998; MS magna cum laude in Natural Health, Clayton Coll. Natural Health, Birmingham, Ala., 2003. Cert. EMT Md., 1999. Intern Environ. Careers Orgn., Washington, 2001; tchr. sci. Gwynn Pk. Mid. Sch., Brandywine, Md., 2001—03; prof. anatomy and physiology Sanford Brown Inst., Landover, Md., 2003—04, Howard CC, Columbia, Md., 2004—06; donor coord. Transplant Resource Ctr. Md., Balt., 2004—05; clin. rschr. Pharm. Product Devel., Columbia, Md., 2005—. Vol. Food & Friends, Washington, 2001—02, Stop the Silence, Washington, 2005—07; christian missionary Campus Crusade for Christ, Takoradi, Ghana, 1998, Accra, 1999; spkr. at missions conf. New Birth Ministries, Atlanta, 1999; leader bible study Impact, Salisbury, Md., 1997—98; tchr. vacation bible sch. Union Bethel African Meth. Epsicopal Ch., Brandywine, Md., 1998—98, tchr. sunday sch., 1998—99. Mem.: Aplastic Anemia and Myelodysplastic Syndromes Found. (life). Independent. Christian. Avocation: travel. Office: Pharmaceutical Product Development 9881 Broken Land Parkway Columbia MD 21046 Office Fax: 919-654-9800.

CAMPBELL-SMITH, PATRICIA, federal official; Grad. in Elec. Engring. with honors, Duke U., 1987; grad. with honors, Tulane Law Sch., 1992. Bar: La., Md. Extern to Judge John Minor Wisdom 5th Cir. Ct. Appeals, 1991; clk. to Judge Martin L.C. Feldman US Dist. Ct. (ea. dist. La.), 1992—93, clk. to Judge Sarah S. Vance, 1996—97; atty. Liskow & Lewis, New Orleans, 1993—96, 1997—98; clk. to Judge Emily C. Hewitt US Ct. Fed. Claims, 1998—2005, spl. master Washington, 2005—. Office: Office of Spl Masters US Ct Fed Claims 717 Madison Pl NW Washington DC 20005*

CAMPER, JOHN JACOB, writer, academic administrator; b. Toledo, Sept. 8, 1943; m. Cleraine Uguccioni, Mar. 27, 1971 (div. May 1981); 1 child, Sarah; m. Mary C. Galligan, Jan. 9, 1988; 1 child, Joseph. BA, Kenyon Coll., 1964. Reporter Detroit News, 1965-68; reporter, critic Chgo. Daily News, 1968-78; editorial writer Chgo. Sun-Times, 1979-84; dept. head external relations Regional Transp. Authority, Chgo., 1984-85; media coord. Chgo. World's Fair Authority, 1985; reporter Chgo. Tribune, 1985-90; assoc. chancellor for pub. affairs U. Ill., Chgo., 1990-97; dep. press sec., speech writer Mayor of Chgo., 1997—; v.p. Chgo. Pub. Rels. Forum, 1995-97, pres., 1997-98. Bd. dirs. Family Svc. Mental Health Ctr. of Oak Park and River Forest, 1990-97. Recipient Peter Lisagor award Chgo. Headline Club, 1983, UPI award, Chgo., 1983, Stick-O-Type, Chgo. Newspaper Guild, 1983, Nat. Assn. Black Journalists award, 1987. Home: 1846 W Newport Ave Chicago IL 60657-1024 Office: 550 City Hall 121 N Lasalle St Chicago IL 60602-1202 E-mail: jcamper@cityofchicago.org.

CAMPION, EDMUND JOSEPH, composer, educator; b. Dallas, Tex., July 9, 1957; s. James Timothy Campion and Mary Louise Kucera; m. Danielle De Gruttola. BA, U. Tex., 1984; MA, Columbia U., 1987, DMA, 1993. Prof. music U. Calif., Berkeley, 1996—, Jerry and Evelyn Hemmings Chambers Chair Music, 2005—. Co-dir. Ctr. New Music and Audio Technologies, Berkeley, 1996—; interviewee Computer Music Jour., 2004. Composer: Losing Touch, 1994, Domus Aurea, 2000, L'Autre (The Other), 2000. Recipient Lili Boulonger Composition award, U. Mass., 1993, Rome prize, Am. Acad. in Rome, 1995, Hinrichsen award, Am. Acad. of Arts and Letters, 1999, Commande d'Etat, French Min. Culture, 2005. Achievements include works published by Billaudot Editions and Henry Lemoine, Paris, Peters Editions, N.Y. Avocations: computers, music. Office: U Calif Dept Music #1200 104 Morrison Hall Berkeley CA 94720-1200 Fax: 510-642-7918. E-mail: campion@cnmat.berkeley.edu.

CAMPION, JANE, film director, screenwriter; b. Wellington, New Zealand; d. Richard and Edith Campion. BA in Anthropology, Victoria U., Wellington, 1975; Diploma of Fine Arts, Chelsea Sch. Arts, London, 1979; degree, Sydney Coll. Arts, 1979; Diploma in Direction, Australian Film and T.V. Sch., Sydney, 1984; DLitt (hon.), Victoria U., 1999. Adj. prof. Sydney Coll. Arts, 2000. Dir., screenwriter Peel: An Exercise in Discipline, 1982 (also editor, Palme d'Or short film category Cannes Internat. Film Festival 1986, Diploma of Merit Melbourne Film Festival, 1983, finalist Greater Union awards, Australian Film Inst. awards 1983-84), A Girl's Own Story, 1983 (with Gerard Lee, Rouben Mamoulian award 1984, Best overall short film Sydney Film Festival 1984, Unique Artist Merit Melbourne Film Festival 1984, Best Direction, Best Screenplay, Best Cinematography Australian Film Inst. 1984, First Prize Cinestud Amsterdam Film Festival, 1985, Best Film Cinestud 1985, First Prize Festival and Press prize), writer/dir. Mishaps of Seduction and Conquest, 1984-85, Passionless Moments (also prodr., dir., writer, with Gerard Lee and dir. photography, Unique Artist Merit Melbourne Film Festival 1984, Best Exptl. Film Australian Film Inst. 1984, Most Popular Short Film Sydney Film Festival 1985), screened at Cannes Un Certain Regard, 1986, After Hours, 1984 (XL Elders award Best Short Fiction, Best Short Fiction Melbourne Internat. Film Festival 1985), Dancing Daze (TV series), Two Friends (TV movie), 1986 (Golden Plaque TV category Chgo. Internat. Film Festival 1987, Best Dir., Best Telemovie, Best Screenplay Australian Film Inst. awards 1987, screened at Cannes in Un Certain Regard, 1986, Edinburgh Film Festival, Sydney and Melbourne Film Festival, 1986), Sweetie, co-writer, dir. 1988, (Georges Sadoul prize Best Fgn. Film, Best Dir., Best Actress, Best Film Australian Critics awards 1990, New Generation award L.A. Film Critics, 1990, Best Fgn. Film Spirit of Independence awards 1990), An Angel at my Table, 1990 (Byron Kennedy award Australian Cinema 1990, Spl. Jury prize, Elvira Notari award Best Woman Dir., Agia Scuola Italian Min. Culture, Best Film Si presci award Panel Internat. Critics, Best Film O.C.I.C. award Christian journalists, Best Film for Young Audiences Cinema e Ragazzi Italian film critics prize, Critics award Toronto Film Festival, Most popular film in the Forum, Otto Debelius prize Berlin Film Festival, Best Fgn. Film, Spirit of Independence Awards, Venice Film Festival, World Premiere, 1990); writer, dir. The Piano, 1993 (Palme d'Or Cannes Internat. Film Festival 1993, Academy Award Best Original Screenplay 1994, Best Picture, Best Dir., Best Cinematography nominations, Acad. Awards, Australian Film Inst. awards, Australia Film Critics, Southeastern Film Critics Assn., others, Best Fgn. Film Chgo. Film Critics, Caesar awards (2000 WIN award, Wimfemme Film Festival Women's Image Network); composer: Feel the Cold, 1983, (play) The Portrait of A Lady, 1996; co-writer, dir.: Holy Smoke, 1998-99 (Best Film Francesco Pasinetti award, pres. Internat. jury Mostra Internat. Art Cinematogrophy Festival Venice Film Festival, 1997, Nat. Union Film Journalists, nominated Best Costume Acad. awards 1997, nominated Best Supporting Actress Acad. awards 1997); dir. In the Cut, 2002-03, 8-The Water Diary, 2005. Office: HLA Mgmt Pty Ltd 87 Pitt St Redfern NSW 2016 Australia also: PO Box 1536 Strawberry Hills NSW 2012 Australia Office Phone: 612 9310 4948. E-mail: hla@hlamgt.com.au.

CAMPION, KATHLEEN FRANCIS, lawyer, gifted and talented educator; b. Middletown, NY, Dec. 13, 1952; d. William Aloysius Campion and Margaret Johanna Roll; m. Conard Morris Smith, Dec. 28, 1988; 1 child, Anthony Daniel Campion-Smith. JD, U. N.Mex, Albuquerque, 1991, MA, 2005. Bar: N.Mex 1991. Pvt. practice atty., Corrales, N.Mex., 1991—; tchr. Albuquerque Pub. Schs. Advanced placement coord. Eisenhower Sch., Albuquerque, 2003—, instrnl. com. Leader Boy Scouts, Corrales, N.Mex., 2001; com. mem. sr. affairs Village of Corrales. Mem.: N.Mex State Bar (mem. com. delivery legal svc. to mentally ill 1994—97), Golden Key. Democrat. Avocations: reading, debate, travel, gardening, travel. Home: PO Box 957 Corrales NM 87048 Home Phone: 505-897-1476.

CAMPION, ROBERT THOMAS, manufacturing executive; b. Mpls., June 23, 1921; s. Leo P. and Naomi (Revord) C.; m. Wilhelmina Knapp, June 8, 1946; 1 son, Michael. Student, Loyola U., Chgo., 1939-41, 46-48. C.P.A., Ill. With Alexander Grant & Co., Chgo., 1946-57, ptnr., 1954-57; with Lear Siegler, Inc., Santa Monica, Calif., 1957—, pres., 1971-85, chief exec. officer, dir., 1971-86, chmn., 1974-86; pvt. investor, 1987—. Served with AUS, 1942-46. Mem. AICPA, Ill. Soc. CPAs, Bel Air Country Club, Jonathan Club, La Quinta Country Club. Republican. Office: Blair House # 406 10490 Wilshire Blvd Los Angeles CA 90024-4646

CAMPION, THOMAS FRANCIS, lawyer; b. Bklyn., Aug. 15, 1935; s. Thomas Francis and Genevieve Agnes (Schantz) C.; m. Virginia Grosscup, Aug. 21, 1965; children: Caroline, Michael. AB, Fordham U., 1957; LLB, Cornell U., 1961. Bar: N.J. 1961, U.S. Supreme Ct. 1966, N.Y. 1988. Law clk. to judge Appellate Div.-Superior Ct. N.J., 1961-62; assoc. Shanley & Fisher, Newark and Morristown, NJ, 1962-67, ptnr. Morristown, 1968-99, Drinker, Biddle & Shanley, LLP, Florham Park, NJ, 1999—2002; ptnr., litig. Drinker, Biddle & Reath, LLP, Florham Park, NJ, 2003—. Bd. on trial atty. cert. N.J. Supreme Ct., 1982—89, chmn., 1987—89, chmn. disciplinary oversight com., 1994—2001, vice chmn. commn. on rules of profl. conduct, 2001—03. Contbr. articles to profl. jours. Mem. N.J. Gov.'s Mgmt. Commn., 1970. 1st lt. USAR, 1957-61. Fellow Am. Bar Found., Am. Coll. Trial Lawyers; mem. ABA, N.J. Bar Assn. (past chmn. jud. and county prosecutor appointments com., civil cts. task force), Essex County Bar Assn., Morris County Bar Assn., Assn. Fed. Bar N.J. (pres. 1980-82), Univ. Club (N.Y.C.). Home Phone: 973-377-9513; Office Phone: 973-549-7300. Business E-Mail: thomas.campion@dbr.com.

CAMPISE, JAMES F., lawyer; s. James Vincent and Anna Campise; m. Annie Ling; children: Michael, Thomas, Jasmine. BS, Bklyn. Poly., 1967; JD, NY Law Sch., NYC, 1974. Bar: NY 1975, NJ 1978, Fla. 2003. Data mgr. ITT Avionics, Nutley, NJ, 1968—71; ptnr. Weiss & Campise, NYC, NJ, 1976—86, Mandel Weiss Campise, NYC, NJ, 1986—88, Marcieliano & Campise, NYC, NJ, 1988—2000, Nicoletti, Hornig, Campise & Sweeney, NYC, 2000—07, Cozen O'Connor, NYC, 2007—. Lectr. Recovery Forum, NYC, 2003, Marine Claims Mgrs. Group, NYC, 2004, London Shipping Centre, 2005. Contbr. articles to profl. jours. Named Super Lawyer, NY Times, 2006—07; recipient Property Law award, Am. Jurisprudence, 1972. Mem.: ABA. Office: Cozen O'Connor 45 Broadway New York NY 10006

CAMPO, DAVE, professional football coach; b. July 18, 1947; m. Kay Campo; 6 children. Student, Ctrl. Conn. State. Football coach various Colls., 1971-89; asst. coach to head coach Dallas Cowboys, 1989—2002; defensive coord. Cleve. Browns, 2003—04; asst. head coach/secondary coach Jacksonville Jaguars, 2005—. Office: Jacksonville Jaguars 1 Alltel Stadium Pl Jacksonville FL 32202

CAMPO, DAVID WAYNE, conductor, educator, composer; b. Baton Rouge, Oct. 3, 1957; s. Bernard Luke and Eva Mae Campo; m. Donna Lynn Landry; children: Brandon Joseph Barrilleaux, McKenzie Eve. MusB, La. State U., 1985, MusM in Composition, 1995; MusD, U. Okla., Norman, 2003, MA, 2007. Assoc. dir. bands U. La., Lafayette, 1998—2000, Stephen F. Austin State U., Nacogdoches, Tex., 2003—. Cons., Tex., 2003—06. Composer: (music) Westport Overture. Mem.: Phi Kappa Phi, Tau Beta Sigma, Kappa Kappa Psi, Phi Beta Mu, Phi Mu Alpha (former province gov.). Home: 110 Lakeview Ln Nacogdoches TX 75965 Office: Stephen F Austin State U PO Box 13043 SFA Station Nacogdoches TX 75965 Home Phone: 936-468-1046. Office Fax: 936-462-1744.

CAMPOFRANCO, SALVATORE, real estate company executive; married; 2 children. BS in Acctg., St. John's U., NYC, 1980. CPA N.Y. Mgr. Kenneth Leventhal Real Estate Group, NY; sr. v.p. fin. and ops. Towermarc Corp.; sr. v.p., mng. dir. Westchester and Conn. divsn. Reckson Assocs. Realty Corp., 1996—2003, exec. v.p., COO Melville, NY, 2003—. Trustee St. Luke's Sch., New Canaan, Conn. Recipient Westchester County Bus. Leader of Yr. award, 2000. Mem.: Westchester County Assn. (trustee, mem. exec. com.). Office: Reckson Assocs Realty Corp 225 Broadhollow Rd Melville NY 11747-4833

CAMPOLETTANO, THOMAS ALFRED, international contract manager; b. Long Island City, NY, Feb. 13, 1946; s. Barney and Mary (Felner) C.; m. Kathy Lee Clemons, Mar. 19, 1989; 1 stepchild, Christopher; children by previous marriage: Lisa, Jennifer, Tricia. AAS, Nassau Coll., 1971; BA, U. South Fla., 1977; postgrad., Am. Grad. U., 1980-85, Touro Coll., 1980-85; internat. contracting cert., George Washington U., 1998. Cert. profl. contract mgr. Cost/price analyst Grumman Aero. Corp., Bethpage, N.Y., 1963-70; sr. cost/price analyst Potter Instrument Co., Plainview, N.Y., 1970-73; prin. fin. analyst, govt. liaison Space Systems div. Honeywell, Inc., Clearwater, Fla., 1973—2007, sr. contracts mgr. Honeywell Aerospace and Electronics, 2002—. Prof. Honeywell Fed. Contracting Tng. program Author: Profit Proposal Initiatives, 1990; co-author: Weighted Guidelines Profit, 1984. With USN, 1963-66, Vietnam, 7th Fleet Flag Commendation, Combat Air Ops., 1965. Recipient Apollo Space Program commendation, NASA, 1969, Honeywell Fin. Achievement award, 1992 Mem. Nat. Contract Mgmt. Assn., Fin. Exec. Inst. (mem. com. on govt. bus. 1985), Def. Industry Offset Assn. Republican. Roman Catholic. Avocation: golf. Office: Honeywell Inc 13350 Us Highway 19 N Clearwater FL 33764-7290 Personal E-mail: bulltmp@aol.com. Business E-Mail: tom.a.campolettano@honeywell.com.

CAMPOS, FERNANDO, editor-in-chief; b. Santiago, Dominican Republic, May 30, 1934; came to U.S., 1949; s. Manuel DeJesus and Luz (Navarro) C. Grad. high sch., Commerce, NY. Trademark and patent clk. Haseltine & Lake, NYC, 1953-55; gen. clk. Everywoman's Mag., NYC, 1955-56, Rexall, LA, 1956-57; legal rsch. libr. U.S. Army, Ft. Dix, N.J., 1957-59; legal clk. Lucke & Lucke, NYC, 1959-62; mgr. list dept. St. John Assocs., NYC, 1962-68; feature writer Temas Mag., NYC, 1968-77; editor-in-chief Canales Mag., NYC, 1977—2000; entertainment editor La Voz Hispana, 2000—. Fgn. corres. Cinema Mag., Havana, Cuba, 1956-57, El Redondel, Mexico City, 1985-87. Translator: 1001 Ideas of Interior Decoration, 1969; illustrator several pubs. Recipient Hispanic Columnist of Yr. award, Record World Mag., 1977, Press award, Inst. Puerto Rico, 1978, Media award Latin Exch., 1979, Silver medal Arts-Scis.-Lettres, Paris, 1979, Outstanding Dominican award, 2003. Mem. Assn. Hispanic Critics (founder 1967, pres. 1976-78, 81-83, hon. pres. 1983—). Avocation: travel. Home and Office: Canales Mag Apt 8E 215 W 92nd St New York NY 10025-7444 E-mail: acc215@hotmail.com.

CAMPOS, LUIS, puzzle writer; arrived in U.S., 1948; s. Manuel de Jesus Campos and Luz Navarro; 1 child, Larry. Grad., Benjamin Franklin H.S., NYC, 1952. Mem. adv. and inventory staff House of Fabrics, Inc., Sherman Oaks, Calif., 1963—82; puzzle creator United Feature Syndicate, NYC, 1984—. Editor: (magazine) VOL.NO. Poetry Mag., 1983. With US Army, 1952—54. Roman Catholic. Achievements include patents in field; has published over 11,000 puzzles. Avocations: poetry, drawing. Mailing: PO Box 15866 North Hollywood CA 91615-5866 Office Phone: 818-768-5053. E-mail: poempoema@aol.com.

CAMPOS, LUÍS MANUEL BRAGA DA COSTA, mathematics, physics, acoustics and aeronautics educator; b. Lisbon, Portugal, Mar. 28, 1950; s. Elmano Neves and Francelina (dos Reis Braga) da Costa Campos; m. Maria Isabel Carreira de Vila-Santa, Aug. 8, 1978; children: Nuno Luis, Ana Isabel. Diploma Mech. Engring., Inst. Superior Tecnico, Lisbon Tech. U., 1972, ScD, 1982; PhD, Cambridge U., 1977. Lectr. applied mechanics and math. Inst. Superior Tecnico, Lisbon Tech. U., 1972-78, aux. prof., 1978-80, assoc. prof., 1980-85, prof., 1985—, coord. aerospace engring., 1992—. Counsellor Nat. Inst. Sci. Rsch., 1985—; sr. Rouse Ball scholar Trinity Coll., Cambridge U., 1979; Alexander von Humboldt scholar Max-Planck Inst. for Aeronomie, 1992. Author: Funcoes Complexas e Campos Potenciais, Forms of Existence, Aircraft Design Integration and Affordability, Mecanica Aplicada; contbr. articles to profl. jours. and aerospace sects. of Encyclopedia Verbo. Recipient Von Karman medal, Rsch. and Tech. Orgn., 2002. Fellow AIAA (assoc.), Cambridge Philos. Soc.; mem. ASME, Am. Math. Soc., Am. Astron. Soc., European Astron. Soc. (founding mem.), European Math. Soc., London Math. Soc., Soc. Indsl. and Applied Math., Internat. Astron. Union, Adv. Group for Aerospace Rsch. and Devel. (chmn. Flight mechanics panel), Rsch. and Tech. Orgn. (vice chmn. sys. concepts and integration panel), Acoustic Soc. Am., European Sci. Found. (mem. space sci. com.), NSF (liaison mem. space sci. bd.), Societe Francaise d'Acoustique, Internat. Coun. for Aero. Scis., Aero. Rsch. and Tech. (v.p., mgmt. com. European Community Aero. program), Portuguese Acad. Engring. (bd. dirs.). Avocations: classical music, plastic arts, photography, swimming. Office: Inst Superior Tech Av Rovisco Pais 1049 001 Lisbon Portugal Business E-Mail: aero@popsrv.ist.utl.pt.

CAMPOS, ROEL C., lawyer, former commissioner; b. Harlingen, Tex., 1949; m. Mini Villarreal; children: David, Daniel. BS, USAF Acad., 1971; MBA, UCLA, 1972; JD, Harvard Law Sch., 1979. Asst. US atty. (So dist.) Calif. US Dept. Justice, Los Angeles, 1985—89; atty. pvt. practice, 1990—95; pres., gen. counsel El Dorado Comm. Inc., Houston, 1995—2002; commr. SEC, Washington, 2002—07; ptnr. Cooley Godward Kronish LLP, Washington, 2007—. Officer USAF. Office: Cooley Godward Kronish LLP 1200 19th St NW 5th Fl Washington DC 20036*

CAMPOS-ORREGO, NORA PATRICIA, lawyer, consultant; b. Lima, Peru, Sept. 3, 1959; d. Victor M. Campos and Ofelia A. Orrego. BA, Cath. U. Peru, 1979, LLB, 1983, Lawyer, 1984; JD magna cum laude, InterAm. U. P.R., San Juan, 1989. Bar: PR 1989, Peru 1984, U.S. Supreme Ct. 2003. Legal asst. women's affairs commn. PR Gov.'s Office, San Juan, 1988-89, lawyer women's affairs commn., 1989-93, PR Gov.'s Office/Immigration Law Practice, Miami, Fla., 1993-94; women's discrimination cons. San Juan, 1994-95; pvt. practice specializing in immigration law Miami, 1996—. Editor: Law Sch. Mag., 1988—89. All Am. scholar U. PR, 1988-89. Mem. ABA, FBA, Am. Immigration Lawyers Assn., PR Bar Assn., Peru Bar Assn. Roman Catholic. Avocations: sightseeing, reading, dance, walking.

CANADA, GEOFFREY, social welfare administrator, writer; b. Harlem, NY, Jan. 13, 1952; BA, Bowdoin Coll.; MA, degree, Harvard U., Williams Coll. Founder Chang Moo Kwan Martial Arts Sch., 1983; supr. Camp Freedom, Center Ossipe, NH; dir. Robert White Sch., Boston; head children's program Rheedlen Ctrs. for Children and Families, NYC, 1983; pres., CEO Harlem Children's Zone, Inc. (formerly Rheedlen Ctrs. for Children and Families), NYC, 1990—. Author: Fist Stick Knife Gun: A Personal History of Violence in America, 1995, Reaching Up For Manhood: Transforming the Lives of Boys in America, 1998, two video essays. Bd. trustees the City Project, Geel Inc., The NY Black Child Devel. Inst., The Door, The Neighborhood Family Svcs. Coalition, Harlem Children's Zone Sch. Named one of NY Influentials, NY Mag., 2006; recipient Heinz award, 1994, Hero of the Yr. award, Robin Hood Found., Spirit of the City award, Cathedral of St. John Divine, Common Good award, Bowdoin Coll., Brennan Legacy award, NYU. Office: Harlem Childrens Zone 35 E 125th St New York NY 10035*

CANADA, MARY WHITFIELD, retired librarian; b. Richmond, Va., June 13, 1919; d. Waverly Thomas and Ruth Bradshaw (Smith) C. BA magna cum laude, Emory and Henry Coll., 1940; MA in English, Duke U., 1942; BS in LS, U. NC, 1956. Asst. circulation dept. Duke U. Libr., 1942-45, undergrad. libr., 1945-55, reference libr., 1956-65, asst. head reference dept., 1967-79, head dept., 1979-85, ret., 1985. Contbr. articles to profl. jours. Duke U. grantee Can., 1979, 81. Mem. ALA (life; initiated performance evaluation discussion group), Southeastern Libr. Assn. (sec. coll. and univ. sect., chmn. nominating com. reference svcs. divsn., also chmn. divsn.), NC Libr. Assn. (chmn. nominating com., chmn. newspaper com., chmn. coll. and univ. sect.), Alumni Assn. Sch. Libr. Sci. U. NC (pres.), Va. Hist. Soc. (life), Va. Geneal. Soc., DAR (chpt. regent), Friends of Va. State Archives, Campus Club (Duke U.), Va. Mus. Fine Arts, Duke U. Hosp. Aux., Beta Phi Mu. Methodist. Home: 1312 Lancaster St Durham NC 27701-1132

CANADA, W. RALPH, JR., lawyer; b. Dallas, July 16, 1955; BA with highest honors, U. Tex., 1976; JD cum laude, Harvard U., 1979. Bar: Tex. 1979, US Dist. Ct., (no., ea., we. & so. dists.) Tex., US Dist. Ct. (no. dist.) Ill., US Ct. of Appeals, (2nd, 5th, & 9th cirs.). Ptnr. Hopkins & Sutter, Dallas, Deary Montgomery DeFeo & Canada LLP, Dallas. Mem. ABA, State Bar Tex., Dallas Assn. Young Lawyers, Dallas Bar Assn., Phi Beta Kappa, Dallas & Am. Bar Assns. Office: Deary Montgomery DeFeo & Canada LLP 2515 McKinney Ste 1565 Dallas TX 75201 Office Phone: 214-292-2600. Business E-Mail: rcanada@dmdclegal.com.

CANADAY, DORIS CHARLENE, retired traffic representative; b. Island Branch, W.Va., Aug. 4, 1932; d. Doy A. and Virgie (Haynes) Nichols; m. Frederick M. Canaday, Mar. 27, 1958 (div. 1963); 1 child, Tammy J. Canaday-Slike. Grad. high sch., Charleston, W.Va. With selecting dept. Owens-Illinois, Inc., Charleston, 1950-56, packer selecting dept./clk. typist various adminstrv. depts., 1956-58, steno clk. adminstrv. svc., 1958-62, clk. typist corrugated dept. Forest Products div., 1962, steno clk. svc. dept. Clarion, Pa., 1963-74; traffic mgr. Owens-Brockway GC, a Unit of Owens Illinois, Clarion, 1974-93; ret., 1993. Former mem. supervisory com. OnIzed Fed. Credit Union, Clarion, 1976. Mem. DAR, North-Cen. Pa. Traffic Club (bd. dirs. 1989-92), OnIzed Club, Clarion OnIzed Quarter Century Club, Gold Emblem Club. Republican. Presbyterian. Avocations: international travel, network marketing. Home: 32 Woodlawn Ave Clarion PA 16214-1250

CANADY, ALEXA IRENE, pediatric neurosurgeon, educator; b. Lansing, Mich., Nov. 7, 1950; d. Clinton Jr. and Hortense (Golden) C.; m. George Davis, June 18, 1988. BS, U. Mich., 1971, MD cum laude, 1975; DHL (hon.), Marygrove Coll., 1994, U. Detroit, 1997; DSc (hon.), Ctrl. Mich. U., 1999, U. So. Conn., 1999, U. W. Fla., 2006. Diplomate Am. Bd. Neurol. Surgery. Intern in surgery Yale U., New Haven, 1975-76; resident in neurosurgery U. Minn., Mpls., 1976-81; fellow in pediatric neurosurgery Children's Hosp. Pa., Phila., 1981-82; instr. neurosurgery U. Pa., Phila., 1981-82; staff neurosurgeon, instr. neurosurgery Henry Ford Hosp., Detroit, 1982-83; asst. dir. neurosurgery Children's Hosp. Mich., Detroit, 1986-87, chief of neurosurgery, 1987-97; assoc. prof. neurosurgery Wayne State U., Detroit, 1988-91, vice chmn. neurosurgery, 1991—2001; prof. neurosurgery Sacred Heart Hosp., Pensacola, Fla., 1997—2001; prof. pediat. in neurosurgery Fla. State U., 2006—. Clin. instr. neurosurgery Wayne State U. Sch. Medicine, 1985, mem. internal rev. com. dept. anatomy, 1988, chmn. search com. dept. neurosurgery, 1989, internal rev. com. dept. neurology, 1991-92, 125th anniversary celebration com., 1992, internal rev. com. dept. pediat., 1993, chmn. search com. dept. ophthalmology, 1992-93, internal rev. com. dept. neurosurgery, 1994; chmn. neurobiol. devices panel, FDA, cons. neurol. devices panel Med. Devices Adv. Com., 1994—, chmn., 1998-2000, co-chair ctr. devices and regulatory health enhanced sci. rev., 2001; vis. prof. Med. Coll. S.C., 1990; clin. prof. dept. clin. scis., pediatric neurosurgery Fla. State Coll. Medicine, 2007-; mem. surg. com. Children's Hosp. Mich., chmn. operating room subcom. surg. com., intensive care unit com., med. record com., med. exec. com.; mem. med. staff Children's Hosp. Mich., William Beaumont Hosp, Royal Oak and Troy, Mich., Harper-Grace Hosps., Detroit, Hutzel Hosp., Detroit, Sinai Hosp., Detroit, Huron Valley Hosp., Milford, Mich., Crittenton Hosp., Rochester Hills, Mich., St. John Hosp. and Med. Ctr., Detroit; presenter various profl confs. in U.S. and internat. Contbr. chpts. to books. Mem. Mich. Head Injury Alliance, Mich. Myelodysplasia Assn.; bd. dirs. Inst. Am. Bus., 1986-88. Recipient citation Women's Med. Assn., 1975, Candace award Nat. Coalition 100 Black Women, N.Y., 1986, Golden Heritage award, 1989, Leonard F. Sain Esteemed Alumni award U. Mich., 1990, Disting. Alumni award Everett H.S., Pres.'s award Am. Med. Women's Assn., 1993, Variety Heart award for Med., Sci. and Tech. Variety Club, 1994, Shining Star award Colgate-Palmolive Co./Starlight Found., 1994, Golden Apple award Roeper Sch., 1995, Athena award Alumni Assn. U. Mich., 1995, Golden Apple Faculty Tchg. award U. Fla. Pediat. Residents, 2004, Chmn. Recognition award Fla. Bd. Medicine, 2005; named Outstanding Young Woman in Am., 1977, Top 100 Bus. & Profl. Women of Am., 1985, Woman of Yr. Detroit Club Nat. Assn. Negro Bus. & Profl. Women's Club, Inc., 1986; named to Mich. Woman's Hall of Fame, 1989; grantee Am. Cancer Soc., 1979, Minn. Med. Found., 1979, Am. Cancer Soc., 1981-82, Widman Found. Early Intervention Treatment and Follow-Up of Infants with Post-hemorrhagic Hydrocephalus, 1984-85, Neuropsychol. Recovery and Family Adaptation to CHI Children's Hosp. Mich., 1987-88, Hydrocephalus Induced Endocrinopathies: Morphologic Correlates Children's Hosp. Mich., 1989, 91; finalist Inst. Medicine African Am. Portrait Gallery, 2006; poster placed in Nat. Acad. Medicine Gallery African Am. Physicians, 2006. Mem. AMA, ACS, Am. Assn. Neurol. Surgeons, Congress Neurol. Surgeons, Am. Soc. Pediatric Neurosurgery, Nat. Med. Assn. Detroit Med. Soc., Mich. Assn. Neurol. Surgeons (sec. 1992-93, v.p. 1994-95, pres. 1995-96), Transplantation Soc. Mich. (adv. bd. 1993-94), Mich. State Med. Soc. (child abuse and neglect divsn. 1986), Southeastern Mich. Surg. Soc. (sec. 1986-87), Soc. Crit. Care Medicine, Wayne County Med. Soc. (ethics com., pub. affairs com., law com.), U. Mich. Med. Ctr. Alumni Soc., Delta Sigma Theta. Office: 6064 Forest Green Rd Pensacola FL 32505 Office Phone: 850-416-7101. Personal E-mail: alexacanady@aol.com.

CANADY, RICHARD WARREN, lawyer; b. Boone, Iowa, Dec. 7, 1934; s. Cecil M. and Myra N. (Shurtz) Canady; m. Carol Jean Canady, Feb. 1, 1960; children: Michael Warren, Kelly Lynn. BS, Iowa U., 1956, JD with distinction, 1959; LLM, Georgetown U., 1962. Bar: Iowa 1959, Calif. 1962. With Navy JAG, 1960—62; law clk. to judge US Ct. Appeals 9th Cir., 1962—63; assoc. White, Froelich & Peterson, San Diego, 1963—64; ptnr. Howard, Rice, Nemerovski, Canady, Falk & Babkin, San Francisco, 1968—, mng. ptnr., 1968—74, 1986—90. Trustee, pres. Iowa Law Sch. Found., 1991—2001. Named a No. Calif. Super Lawyer, 2005, 2007; named one of Best Lawyers in Am., 2007, Top 10 Mergers and Acquisitions Lawyers, US Lawyer Rankings, 2006, 2007; recipient No. Calif. Super Lawyer, 2006. Mem.: ABA, San Francisco Bar Assn., Iowa Bar Assn., State Bar Calif., Mission Hills Country Club, Olympic Club, San Francisco Golf Club, Pacific Union Club, Order of Coif. Presbyterian. Office: Howard Rice Nemerovski Canady Falk & Rabkin 3 Embarcadero Ctr Fl 7 San Francisco CA 94111-4024 E-mail: rcanady@howardrice.com.

CANALES, DENISE NILES, software company executive; b. San Antonio, Jan. 31, 1968; d. Dennis Wesley Niles and Sylvia Amend Batha; m. Roberto R. Canales Jr., Aug. 21, 1993; 1 child, Olivia Elise. Student, Tex. Luth. U., 1986—87; BA, U. Tex., 1992; MA, Trinity U., San Antonio, 1994. Sr. rsch. intern Psychol. Corp., San Antonio, 1993—94; sr. rsch. asst. U. Tex. Med. Sch., Houston, 1994—97; dir. compliance Baylor Coll. Medicine, Houston, 1997—2000, dir. rsch. informatics, 2000—02; dir. rsch. and ops. API, Lexington, Ky., 2002—04, pres., CEO, 2004—. Spkr. in field. Contbr. chpt. to book. Mem.: Applied Rsch. Ethics Nat. Assn. (regional rep. coun. 1998—2003). Republican. Baptist. Avocations: painting, gardening, golf, reading, writing. Office: API Inc 167 W Main St Ste 210 Lexington KY 40507 Office Phone: 859-233-2006.

CANALES, HERBERT GLENN, library director; b. Corpus Christi, Tex., June 19, 1954; s. Humberto G. and Irene (Reyna) C. BA, U. Tex., 1976; MS with honors, Columbia U., 1979. Libr. Corpus Christi Pub. Librs., 1980—85, dir. librs., 1985—. Mem. ALA, Tex. Libr. Assn. Roman Catholic. Office: Corpus Christi Pub Librs 805 Comanche St Corpus Christi TX 78401-2715 Office Phone: 361-826-7070. Office Fax: 361-826-7046.

CANALES, JAMES EARL, JR., foundation president; b. San Francisco, Nov. 6, 1966; s. James Earl Canales Sr. and Maritsa M. (Solorzano) Espinoza. BA, Stanford U., 1988, MA, 1989. English tchr., class dean San Francisco Univ. H.S., 1989-91, dir. admissions, 1991-93; program assoc. The James Irvine Found., San Francisco, 1993-95, program officer, spl. asst. to pres., 1995-97, chief adminstrv. officer, corp. sec., 1997-99, v.p., corp. sec., 1999—2003, pres. and CEO, 2003—. Bd. dirs. Nat. Ctr. Nonprofit Bds., Washington, 1996—2003, Stanford U., Calif., 2006—, Coll. Access Found. Calif. Chair bd. dir. Larkin St. Youth Ctr., San Francisco, 1992—99; bd. dirs. Nat. Assn. Cmty. Leadership, Indpls., 1994—97, KQED, Inc., San Francisco, 1999—2005, Monterey Bay Aquarium, San Francisco; trustee San Francisco Day Sch., 1996—99; bd. regents St. Ignatius Coll. Preparatory, 2001—03. Andrew W. Mellon Edn. Found. fellow, 1988-89. Mem. Stanford Alumni Assn. (bd. dir. 1997-05, vice chmn. 2001-03, chmn. 2003-05). Democrat. Roman Catholic. Home: 21 Carmel St San Francisco CA 94117-4332 Office: 575 Market St Ste 3400 San Francisco CA 94105 E-mail: jcanales@irvine.org.

CANARY, LEURA GARRETT, prosecutor; m. William J. Canary; children: William James, Margaret Garrett. Grad., Huntington Coll.; JD, U. Ala. Asst. atty. gen State of Ala., 1981—90; trial atty. civil divsn. US Dept. ustice, 1990—94; asst. US atty. (mid. dist.) Ala. US Dept. Justice, 1994—2001, US atty. (mid. dist.) Ala., 2001—. Office: US Attys Office One Ct Sq Ste 201 Montgomery AL 36104*

CANARY, NANCY HALLIDAY, lawyer; b. Cleve., Apr. 21, 1941; d. Robert Fraser and Nanna (Hall) Halliday; m. Sumner Canary, Dec. 1975 (dec. Jan. 1979). BA, Case Western Res. U., 1963; JD, Cleve. State U., 1968. Bar: Ohio 1968, Fla. 1972, US Dist. Ct. (no. dist.) Ohio 1975, US Supreme Ct. 1974, US Dist. Ct. (so. dist.) Fla. 1994. Law clk. to presiding judge Ohio Ct. Appeals, Cleve., 1968—69; ptnr. McDonald, Hopkins & Hardy, Cleve., 1969—83; ptnr. managing Palm Beach office Thompson, Hine, LLP, Cleve., 1984—2002; sole practitioner Palm Beach, Fla., 2003—. Trustee Beck Ctr. for Cultural Arts, Lakewood, Ohio, 1980—90, Ohio Motorists Assn., 1989—95, Ohio Chamber Orch.; trustee, mem. devel. adv. com. Fairview Gen. Hosp., Cleve., 1980—96; chairperson Sumner Canary Lectureship com. Case Western Res. U. Law Sch.; sec. bd. govs. Churchill Ctr., Washington, 2000—02; bd. dirs. Comerica Bank & Trust Co., F.S.B., 1993—2000. Mem. Ohio State Bar Assn., Cleve. Bar Assn., Palm Beach County Bar Assn., Estate Planning Coun. Cleve., Estate Planning Coun. Palm Beach County, Gulf Stream (Fla.) Golf Club, Westwood Country Club (Cleve.). Republican. Avocations: music, horseback riding, collecting Churchill books. Home: Unit 1806 12500 Edgewater Dr Cleveland OH 44107-1677 also: 200 N Ocean Blvd Delray Beach FL 33483-7126 Office: 125 Worth Ave # 117 Palm Beach FL 33480 Office Phone: 216-226-7466.

CANATSEY, KEN, nurse; b. Kansas City, Mo., Oct. 26, 1943; s. Kary and Lillian Canatsey; m. Susan Montas, June 13, 1954; 1 child, Brian. BA, U. Calif., Santa Barbara, 1966; A, Southwestern Coll., Calif., 1989. English tchr., Katmander, Nepal, Italy, 1969; ESL tchr. Sch. of English, Athens, Greece, 1969—70; park ranger Calif. State Pks. Sys., Anza-Borrego Desert, 1971—73; salesman Heritage Fan Co., Pacific Beach, Calif., 1975—81, Camarillo State Hosp., Calif., 1987—89; RN VA Med. Ctr., LA, 1989—. Author poetry. Mem.: Am. Fedn. Govt. Employees (v.p. local 3943 1996—99). Democrat. Roman Catholic. Avocations: reading, writing, swimming, hiking. Home: 6278 Pisces St Agoura Hills CA 91301

CANAVAN, CHRISTINE ESTELLE, state legislator; b. Dorchester, Mass., Jan. 25, 1950; m. Paul Canavan; 2 children. Grad., Massasoit C.C., 1983; BS summa cum laude, U. Mass., 1988. RN. Mem. Mass. Ho. of Reps., Boston, 1993—, chair second fl. divsn., spl. legis. com. on foster care. Mem. Brockton (Mass.) Sch. Com., 1990-94, vice chmn., 1992-2000, Brockton (Mass.) Libr. Found. Mem. Polish White Eagles, Brockton (Mass.) Hist. Soc. Democrat. Roman Catholic. Home: 29 Mystic St

Brockton MA 02302-2825 Office: Mass Ho of Reps Mass State House Rm 122 Boston MA 02133 Office Phone: 617-722-2006. Business E-Mail: rep.christinecanavan@hou.state.ma.us.

CANBY, WILLIAM CAMERON, JR., federal judge; b. St. Paul, May 22, 1931; s. William Cameron and Margaret Leah (Lewis) Canby; m. Jane Adams, June 18, 1954; children: William Nathan, John Adams, Margaret Lewis. AB, Yale U., 1953; LLB, U. Minn., 1956. Bar: Minn. 1956, Ariz. 1972. Law clk. US Supreme Ct. Justice Charles E. Whittaker, 1958—59; assoc. firm Oppenheimer, Hodgson, Brown, Baer & Wolff, St. Paul, 1959—62; assoc., then dep. dir. Peace Corps, Ethiopia, 1962—64, dir. Uganda, 1964—66; asst. to US Senator Walter Mondale, 1966; asst. to pres. SUNY, 1967; prof. law Ariz. State U., 1967—80; judge US Ct. Appeals (9th cir.), Phoenix, 1980—96, sr. judge, 1996—; chief justice High Ct. of the Trust Ter. of the Pacific Islands, 1993—94. Bd. dirs. Ariz. Ctr. Law in Pub. Interest, 1974—80, Maricopa County Legal Aid Soc., 1972—78, D.N.A.-People's Legal Svcs., 1978—80; Fulbright prof. Makerere U. Faculty Law, Kampala, Uganda, 1970—71. Author: American Indian Law, 2004; note editor: Minn. Law Rev., 1955—56; contbr. articles to profl. jours. Precinct and state committeeman Dem. Party Ariz., 1972—80; bd. dirs. Ctrl. Ariz. Coalition for Right to Choose, 1976—80. 1st lt. USAF, 1956—58. Mem.: Maricopa County Bar Assn., State Bar Ariz., Order of Coif, Phi Beta Kappa. Office: Sandra Day O'Connor US Courthouse 401 W Washington St SPC 55 Phoenix AZ 85003-2156 Office Phone: 602-322-7300.*

CANCRO, ROBERT, psychiatrist, educator; b. NYC, Feb. 23, 1932; s. Joseph and Marie E. (Cicchetti) C.; m. Gloria Costanzo, Dec. 8, 1956; children: Robert, Carol. Student, Fordham U., 1948-51; MD, SUNY, 1955. Intern Kings County Hosp., Bklyn., 1955-56, resident in psychiatry, 1956-59; attending staff Gracie Sq. Hosp., NYC, 1959-66; clin. instr. SUNY Downstate Med. Ctr., Bklyn., 1959-66; staff psychiatrist Menninger Found., Topeka, 1966-69; cons. Topeka State and VA Hosps., 1967-69; prof. dept. psychiatry U. Conn. Health Ctr., Farmington, 1970-76; prof., chmn. dept. psychiatry NYU Med. Ctr., 1976—2005; dir. N.S. Kline Inst. Psychiat. Rsch., 1982—2005. Cons. psychiat. edn. br. NIMH; biol. scis. sect. NIMH. Editor 10 books.; Contbr. articles on schizophrenia to profl. jours. Recipient Freida Fromm-Reichmann award, 1975, Strecker award, 1978, Dean award, 1981, Lehmann award, 1992. Fellow A.C.P., Am. Coll. Psychiatrists, Am. Psychiat. Assn.; mem. Am. Psychol. Assn., Assn. Am. Med. Colls., Am. Assn. Social Psychiatry (pres. 1984-86), N.Y. Acad. Scis., AAAS, AMA. Home: 118 Mclain Rd Mount Kisco NY 10549-4932 Office: NYU Med Ctr 550 1st Ave MHL-HN416 New York NY 10016-6402 Home Phone: 914-241-1131; Office Phone: 212-263-5744. Business E-Mail: robert.cancro@med.nyu.edu.

CANDELORA, DEBORAH MICHAEL, engineer, sculptor; b. Flint, Mich., Mar. 10, 1955; d. Sidney R. and Helen S. Michael; m. Raymond Michael Candelora, Aug. 26, 1978; children: Rachel, Danielle. BSEE, U. Wis., Madison, 1976; MS in Engring., U. Mich., Ann Arbor, 1977; AA in Fine Arts, Brookdale CC, Lincroft, NJ, 2007. Mem. tech. staff AT&T Bell Labs., Lincroft, 1976—84, engr. supr., 1984—92; engring. cons., 1992—96; founder, chief arch. R2D2 Enterprises, LLC, 2000—; artist-in-residence Continuity Sculpture, Colts Neck, 2006—. Author: Learning Center Activities - Science; designer (software program) EasyOrg Website Management Software. Curriculum devel. Colts Neck Sch. Dist., 1993—99; coach, program dir. Colts Neck Sports Found., 1991—2003, bd. mem., 2000—03. Recipient Excellence Edn. award, Colts Neck Sch. Dist., 1995, K12 Curriculum Eisenhower Nat. Clearning House award, K-12 Hands-On Sci. Program, 1998. Mem.: Monmouth County Arts Coun., Tau Beta Pi, Eta Kappa Nu. Avocations: horseback riding, martial arts, flute, travel. Home and Office: 36 Mulberry Ln Colts Neck NJ 07722 Office Phone: 732-598-4972. Personal E-mail: info@ContinuitySculpture.com.

CANDES, EMMANUEL JEAN, mathematics professor; b. Paris, Apr. 27, 1970; s. Paul Etienne Candes, Sylvie Christiane Reboul; m. Chiara Sabatti; children: David children: Gabrielle. Earned degrees from, Ecole Polytechnique, Univ. Paris IV, Univ. Paris IX; PhD in Math. and Computer Sci., Stanford U., 1998. Asst. prof. Stanford U., 1998—2000; asst. prof., applied and computational math. Calif. Inst. Tech., Pasadena, 2000—05, prof., applied and computational math., 2005—, Ronald and Maxine Linde prof., 2006—. Recipient Vasil Popov prize in approximation theory, Dept. Energy Young Investor award, James H. Wilkinson prize in numerical analysis and scientific computing, Best Paper award, European Assn. for Signal, Speech and Image Processing, Alan T. Waterman award, NSF, 2006; Alfred P. Sloan Rsch. Fellow, 2001. Office: Calif Inst Tech Applied & Computational Math MC 217-50 1200 E California Blvd 300 Firestone Pasadena CA 91125 Office Phone: 626-395-4560, 626-395-2291. Office Fax: 626-578-0124. Business E-Mail: emmanuel@acm.caltech.edu, ecandes@acm.caltech.edu.

CANDIB, MURRAY A., retail executive, consultant; b. Chelsea, Mass., Sept. 16, 1915; s. Jacob and Fannie (Einbinder) C.; m. Claudette Aggie, Oct. 8, 1972 (dec. Dec. 1991); children: Nancy, Rachel, David, Caroline; m. Maureen Davis, July 30, 1995. BA, Boston U., 1950. Founder King's Dept. Store Inc., 1949; pres. Canco Enterprises, Worcester, Mass. Founder, life trustee, soc. mem. Mt. Sinai Hosp., Miami Beach, Fla.; benefactor Miami Heart Inst.; charter mem. Rep. Presdl. Task Force, 1981-, U.S. Senatorial Club, 1981-, Nat. Rep. Senatorial Com.; mem. Fla. Victory Com. Brandeis U. fellow, 1966; recipient Human Relations award Am. Jewish Com., Nat. Community Service award Jewish Theol. Sem. of Am., 1965, Man of Yr. award Mental Health Clinic, Mt. Sinai Hosp., N.Y.C., Man of Yr. award Boys Wear Industry of N.Y., Hall of Fame award U. Mass. Mem. Am. Heart Assn., Shriners, Masons, Westview Country Club Miami. Jewish. Founded the first self-service department stores and pioneered the industry; subject of articles in Fortune Mag., Harvard Bus. Rev. and other professional journals. Office: 306 Main St Worcester MA 01608-1550 Personal E-mail: maggsmom@aol.com.

CANDIDO, ARTHUR ALDO, publishing and distribution company executive; b. Corona, Queens, N.Y., June 6, 1960; BA, CUNY, 1982. Ordained to permanent diaconate Diocese Rockville Centre, NY, 2007. Ops. mgr. Scholium Internat. Inc., Port Washington, NY, 1982-91, pres., 1991—. Mem. Spl. Librs. Assn., Am. Booksellers Assn. Office: Scholium Internat Inc PO Box 1519 Port Washington NY 11050-7519

CANDLAND, D. STUART, lawyer; b. Madison, Wis., Sept. 6, 1942; s. Don Charles and Dorothy Jane (Nelson) C.; m. Evelyn McComber, Dec. 3, 1982; children: Ashley, Tara Lynn, Brett. BA with honors, Brigham Young U., 1967; JD, U. Calif., Berkeley, 1970. Bar: Calif. 1971, U.S. Dist. Ct. (no. dist.) Calif. 1971, U.S. Ct. Appeals (9th cir.) 1971. Dep. atty. gen. State of Calif., San Francisco, 1970-73; dep. dist. atty. Solano County Dist. Atty.'s Office, Fairfield, Calif., 1973-75; assoc. Law Offices of M. Craddick, Walnut Creek, Calif., 1976-78; ptnr. Craddick, Candland & Conti, Danville, Calif., 1979—. Asst. prof. law Armstrong Sch. Law, Berkeley, 1971-77. Mem. ABA, Assn. Def. Counsel, Contra Costa County Bar Assn. (Calif. med-legal com.). Office: Craddick Candland & Conti Ste 260 915 San Ramon Valley Blvd Danville CA 94526-4021 Business E-Mail: scandland@ccclawfirm.com.

CANDLAND, DOUGLAS KEITH, psychology professor; b. Long Beach, Calif., July 9, 1934; s. Horace George and Erma Louise (Downing) C.; m. Mary Homrighausen, June 18, 1959; children: Kevin, Christopher, Ian. AB, Pomona Coll., 1956; PhD, Princeton U., 1959. Postdoctoral rsch. fellow U. Va., 1959-60, Delta Primate Ctr., 1967-68, Pa. State U., 1968—70; vis. prof. U. Stirling, Scotland, 1972-73, Cambridge U., England, 1978—79; Fulbright fellow U. Mysore, India, 1983; asst. prof. psychology Bucknell U., 1960-64, assoc. prof., 1964-67, prof., 1967—85, prof. animal behavior, 1985—2002, Presdl. prof., 1973-80, head program in animal behavior, 1968—2002, pres. div. teaching of psychology, 1976-77, head dept. psychology, 1970-75, Class of 1956 lectr., 1971, Homer P. Rainey prof. emeritus psychology and animal behavior, 2004—. Vis. scholar U. Calif., Berkeley, 1996-97. Author: Exploring Behavior, 1961, Psychology: The Experimental Approach, 1968, 2d edit., 1978, Emotion, Bodily Change, 1961, Emotion, 1979, Feral Children and Clever Animals, Reflections on Human Nature, 1993, Handbook of Comparative Psychology, 1998, Archeopsychology of the Modern Mind, 2007; editor: Rev. Gen. Psychology, 2002—; contbr. chpts. to profl. books; editor The Primates, 1968-78, Animal Behaviour, 1979-89; assoc. editor Animal Learning and Behavior, 1976-84, Teaching of Psychology, 1976-84, Am. Jour. Primatology, 1980-84; cons. editor Jour. Comparative Psychology, 1988-94; documentary film featured scientist: The Boy Who Was Raised With Monkeys, 1999, The Rise of Animal Rights, 2001, Le Compagnie Taxi Brousse, Artes, French TV, 2005, Sci. and Insight, Russian State TV, 2005, Feral Children, Nat. Geographic TV, 2007. Chmn. conservation Wildlife Preservation Trust Internat., 1989—94, bd. dirs. Recipient award Lindback Found., 1971, Harriman award Bucknell U., 1979. Fellow Am. Psychol. Assn. (Disting. Contbn. to Edn. award 1978), Am. Psychol. Soc.; mem. Brit. Psychol. Assn., Psychonomic Soc., Internat. Soc. Primatologists, Animal Behavior Soc. (chmn. policy and planning, Disting. Contbn. to Edn. award 1999), Phi Beta Kappa. Home: 125 Stein Ln Lewisburg PA 17837-1742 Office: Bucknell U Lewisburg PA 17837 Office Phone: 570-577-1200. Business E-Mail: dcandlan@bucknell.edu.

CANDLER, FAXON DAVID, small business owner; b. Reidsville, NC, Oct. 13, 1934; s. Faxon Douglas Candler and Inez Levenior Echols. Student, Presbyn. Jr. Coll., Maxton, NC, 1953, Guilford Coll., 1961. Draftsman, machinist Newman Machine Co., Greensboro, 1961; owner Candler Instruments, Greensboro, NC, 1962; with ECT, Salisbury, NC, 1963—94; owner Lab Links Engring. Lab, Salisbury, 1994—. Composer: Fantasy Impromptu, 1953. Vol. VA Med. Ctr., Salisbury, 1995—; mem. Rep. Nat. Com., Washington, 1976—78. With Signal Corp US Army, 1954—57. Independent. Baptist. Achievements include patents pending in field. Avocation: piano. Home and Office: 517 N Cedar St Salisbury NC 28144

CANDLER, JAMES NALL, JR., lawyer; b. Detroit, Jan. 25, 1943; s. James Nall and Lorna Augusta (Blood) C.; m. Jean Ward McKinnon, Mar. 8, 1974; children: Christine, Elizabeth, Anne. AB, Princeton U., 1965; JD, U. Mich., 1970. Bar: Mich. 1970. Assoc. Dickinson Wright PLLC, Detroit, 1970-77, ptnr., 1977—. Adj. prof. real estate planning U. Detroit Sch. of Law, 1975-80. Bd. dirs. Detroit Inst. Ophthalmology, 1983—, chmn., 1994—. Lt. USNR, 1965-67. Mem. Internat. Assn. Attys. and Execs. in Corp. Real Estate, State Bar Mich. (chmn. real property law sect. 1998-99), Am. Coll. of Real Estate Lawyers, Grosse Pointe Club (chmn. 1987-89), Country Club of Detroit. Republican. Avocations: sailing, golf, platform tennis. Home: 211 Country Club Dr Grosse Pointe Farms MI 48236-2901 Office: 500 Woodward Ave Ste 4000 Detroit MI 48226-3425 Office Phone: 313-223-3513. E-mail: jcandler@dickinson-wright.com.

CANDLISH, MALCOLM, manufacturing executive; b. Liverpool, Eng., Aug. 23, 1935; came to U.S., 1963; s. Norman Dennis and Jane Jefferson (Grieves) C.; m. Jasmine Rosemary Cresswell, Apr. 15, 1963; children: Fiona, Vanessa, Sarah, John. BSc, London Sch. Econs., 1956. Mgr. mktg., asst. mgr. prodn. Beecham Products, Brazil, England, 1958-63; product mgr. Colgate Palmolive, NYC, 1963-65; prin. McKinsey and Co., NYC, Cleve., Toronto, Melbourne and Sydney, Australia, 1965-77; pres., sr. v.p. mktg. Wilson Sporting Goods, Chgo., 1977-83; pres. Samsonite Corp., Denver, 1983-89; chmn., CEO Sealy, Inc. (formerly Ohio Mattress Co.), Cleve., 1989-92, First Alert, Inc., Aurora, Ill., 1992-98. Bd. dirs. Mile High United Way, Denver, 1985-89. Lt. British Army, 1956-58. Mem. Luggage and Leather Goods Mfrs. Am. (bd. dirs. 1984-89), Econ. Club (founding mem.). Avocations: literature, philosophy, sports. Personal E-mail: candlish@aol.com.

CANDOTTI, FABIO, pediatrician; MD summa cum laude, U. Brescia, Italy, 1987. Diplomate in pediats. and pediat. allergy and immunology; lic. physician, Italy. Med. staff fellow dept. pediatrics U. Brescia, Italy, 1988-89; enlisted Italian Army Sch. of Medicine, Florence, 1989; resident in pediatrics U. Brescia, 1989-92, staff mem. Bone Marrow Transplantation Unit Italy, 1990-91, postdoctoral fellow Lab. of Biotechnology, 1991-92; postdoctoral fellow Metabolism Br. NCI, NIH, Bethesda, Md., 1992-94; postdoctoral fellow Clin. Gene Therapy Br. NHGRI/NIH, Bethesda, 1994-96. Lectr. Italian Nat. Health Svc. Nursing Sch., Brescia, 1991-92; asst. prof. dept. pediatrics U. Brescia, 1996-97; tenure-track investigator NHGRI/NIH, Bethesda, 1998-2004, sr. investigator, 2004-; mem. animal care and use com. NHGRI, 1998-2002, vice chair animal care and use com., 2003-06 , head NIH gene therapy interest group, 1998—, NHGRI liaison to NIH Office of Biotech. Activities, 1999—; mem. instnl. rev. bd. NHGRI, 2005-06, chmn. instnl. rev. bd., 2006—; attending physician dept. pediatrics Brescia City Hosp., Italy, 1996-97, Clin. Ctr., NIH, Bethesda, 1998—; investigator in field. Co-author: (book) The Child: Health and Disease, 1993; mem. editl. bd. Exptl. Hematology, 2003-05; contbr. articles to profl. jours., books, and publs. Physician, lt. Italian Army, 1988—. Recipient fellowship Italian Nat. Health Svc., 1988, Assn. for Child with Cancer, Brescia, 1990-91, Fondazione Golgi, Brescia, 1992-94; recipient awards nat. Ctr. for Human Genome Rsch. Scientific Retreat, Airlie, Va., 1995, 96, NIH Merit award, 1999, 05, others; grantee in field. Mem. Italian Soc. Pediatrics, Working Group on Human Genetics, Italian Soc. Pediatric Immunology and Allergy, Am. Soc. Gene Therapy (hematopoietic cell gene therapy com. 2004—07, gene therapy of genetic diseases com. 2007—), European Soc. Immunodeficiencies, Pan Am. Group for Immunodeficiency, Clin. Immunology Soc. (membership com. 2004-06, chmn. membership com. 2006—), Am. Soc. Clin. Investigation, Am. Soc. Hematology, Am. Soc. Hematology. Office: 49 Convent Dr 49/3A04 Bethesda MD 20892 Business E-Mail: fabio@nhgri.nih.gov.

CANDRIS, LAURA A., lawyer; d. Charles M. and Dorothy (King) Sutton; m. Aris S. Candris, Dec. 22, 1974. AB with honors and distinction in polit. sci., Transylvania Coll., 1975; postgrad., U. Pitts., 1975-77, JD, 1978; postgrad., U. Fla., 1977-78; grad. in mediation, Harvard Law Sch. Program on Negotiation, 2006; grad. in conflict resolution and mediation, Pitts. Mediation Ctr., 2006. Bar: Fla. 1978, US Dist. Ct. (mid. dist.) Fla. 1978, US Ct. Appeals (4th cir.) 1980, Pa. 1981, US Dist. Ct. (we. dist.) Pa. 1982, US Ct. Appeals (3d cir.) 1983. Assoc. Coffman, Coleman, Andrews & Grogan, Jacksonville, Fla., 1978-80, Manion, Alder & Cohen, Pitts., 1981-85, Eckert, Seamans, Cherin & Mellott, Pitts., 1985-86, ptnr., 1987-96, vice chmn. labor and employment law dept, mem. practice mgmt. com., mem. strategic planning com.; ptnr. Meyer Unkovic & Scott, LLP, Pitts., 1996—, chair labor, employment law and employee benefits sect., mem. dispute resolution group. Apptd. mediator, early neutral evaluator US Dist. Ct. (we. dist.) Pa. Contbr. over 30 articles to profl. jours. including Compensation and Benefits Rev., Forum Reporter, Employment Law Inst. manuals, Ref. Manual for the 34th Ann. Mid-West Labor Law Conf. Dynamic Bus. Bd. dirs. Tri State Employers Assn, 1991—93; elected mem. O'Hara Twp. Coun., 1986—90; mem. O'Hara Twp. Planning Commn., 1990; bd. dirs. Parent and Child Guidance Ctr., 1991—2001, v.p., 1998—99, mem. exec. com., 1998—2001, pres., 1999—2000, sec., 2000—01; treas., mem. exec. com. SMC Bus. Couns., 1993—94, bd. dirs., 1993—96, Big Bros. and Big Sisters Greater Pitts., 1998—, v.p. planning, 2001—02, mem. exec. com., 2001—05, v.p. adminstrn., 2003—04, pres., 2004, 2005; bd. dirs. The Whale's Tale, 2000—01, Mediation Coun. Western Pa., 2006—; bd. dirs., mem. exec. com. FamilyLinks, 2000—01. Nat. Merit Found. scholar 1972-75; named Ky. Col., 1974. Fellow: Allegheny County Bar Found.; mem.: ABA (dispute resolution sect., employment law sect.), Meditation Coun. W. Pa., Pa. Coun. Mediators, Allegheny County Bar Assn. (coun. on professionalism 1990—2000, newsletter editor, fed. ct. sect. 2003—07, mem. counsel fed. cts. sect. 2003—, vice chair 2004—05, chair-elect 2005—06, nominating com. 2006, mem. coun. employment sect. 2006—, chair fed. ct. sect. coun. 2006—07, nominating com. 2007, women in the law divsn., alternate dispute resolution com., hqrs. com. and pers. subcom.), Pa. Bar Assn. (employment sect., coun. women in profession com., alternative dispute resolution com.), Fla. Bar. Republican. Avocations: skiing, travel, bicycling, reading. Office: Meyer Unkovic & Scott LLP 1300 Oliver Bldg 535 Smithfield St Pittsburgh PA 15222 Office Phone: 412-456-2891. Business E-Mail: lac@muslaw.com.

CANE, JEFFREY, editor; Assignment editor, markets editor bus. day sect. New York Times. Office: New York Times 229 W 43d St New York NY 10036 Office Phone: 212-556-1474. Office Fax: 212-556-1448. Business E-Mail: cane@nytimes.com.

CANE, MARILYN BLUMBERG, law educator; b. Rockville Center, NY, Feb. 26, 1949; d. Howard Godfrey and Lilly Ruth (Goldberg); m. Edward M. Cane, Dec. 24, 1970 (div.); children: Daniel Eric, Jonathan Marc Howard; life ptnr. Karen E. Michaels, June 18, 2001. BA magna cum laude, Cornell U., 1971; JD cum laude, Boston Coll., 1974. Bar: N.Y. 1975, U.S. Dist. Ct. (so. dist.) N.Y. 1975, U.S. Ct. Appeals (2d cir.) 1976, Conn. 1977, Fla. 1981. With Reavis & McGrath, NYC, 1974-76, Badger, Fisher & Assocs., Greenwich, Conn., 1977-80; counsel Corp Components divsn. GE, Fairfield, Conn., 1980-81; with Gunster, Yoakley & Assocs., Palm Beach, Fla., 1981-83; asst. prof. law Nova Southeastern U., Fort Lauderdale, Fla., 1983-85, assoc. prof. law, 1985-88, prof. law, 1988—. Author: Securities Arbitration: Law and Procedure, 1991; contbr. articles to profl. jours. Dir. Jewish Cmty. Day Sch. Palm Beach County, West Palm Beach, Fla., 1983-88; mem. adv. com. Conn. Banking Commn., Hartford, 1979-81; trustee Temple Beth Torah, Wellington, Fla., 1985-87, 92-98, Sta. WXEL, 1992—. Fellow Am. Bar Found.; mem. ABA (bus. law sect., bank holding cos. subcom.), Fla. Bar Assn., (advisor exec. coun. bus. law sect. 1988—, chair corp./securities com. bus. law sect. 1992-93, vice chair 1999-2000), Am. Law Inst., Order of Coif, Human Rights Campaign. Home: 1580 NW 100th Terr Plantation FL 33322 Office: Nova Southeastern U Law Ctr 3305 College Ave Fort Lauderdale FL 33314-7721 Home Phone: 954-533-2865; Office Phone: 954-262-6153. Personal E-mail: marilyncane@yahoo.com.

CANEDY, DANA, editor; BA, Univ. Ky., 1960. Reporter Palm Beach Post; reporter & editor Cleveland Plain Dealer, 1988—96; reporter, Miami bureau chief New York Times, 1996—2003, day editor, nat. desk, 2003—. Recipient Pulitzer prize, 2000. Office: New York Times 229 W 43d St New York NY 10036 Office Phone: 212-556-7356. Office Fax: 212-556-7614.

CANELAS, DALE BRUNELLE, retired library director; b. Chgo., Jan. 13, 1938; d. Ralph Everley and Margaret Barbara (Clark) Brunelle; m. L. Marcelo Canelas, June 17, 1961; 1 child, Cathryn Margaret. BS in Humanities, Loyola U., Chgo., 1960; MLS, Rosary Coll., 1966; cert. in mgmt., U. Md., 1971. Asst. dir. Palatine Pub. Libr., Ill., 1966-68; asst. dir. adminstrv. svcs. Northwestern U. Libr., Evanston, Ill., 1969-75; assoc. dir. Stanford U. Libr., 1975-84; dir., univ. libr. U. Fla. Librs., Gainesville, 1985—2007. Vice pres. Freedom to Read Found., Chgo., 1977-78. Mem. ALA (various coms. and offices), Libr. Adminstrn. and Mgmt. Assn. (pres. 1978-80), Assn. Rsch. Librs. (bd. dirs. 1992—, various coms. 1985—). Office Phone: 904-392-0342. E-mail: dcanelas@ufl.edu.

CANELLI, JEANNE, early childhood educator; b. Framingham, Mass., June 9, 1948; d. Francis J. and Jeanne T. (Landry) Keefe; m. Gerard P. Canelli, Aug. 5, 1972; children: Gerry Jr., Jill, Jennifer. BS in Elem. Edn., Framingham State Coll., 1970; MS, Wheelock Coll., 1987; PhD, Lesley Coll., 1999. Cert. tchr. in elem. edn., moderate spl. needs, young children with spl. needs, Mass. Tchr. Holliston Pub. Schs., 1970—73, Bellingham Pub. Schs., Mass., 1980—81; dir., head tchr. ECDC Sherborn Pre sch., Mass., 1981—87; assoc. prof. dept. edn., dir. child devel. lab. Framingham State Coll., 1987—, chmn. Dept. Edn., 2005—. Validator Nat. Acad. Early Childhood Programs, 1993—; tchg. fellow Lesley Coll. Grantee Mass. Dept. Edn. Mem. Nat. Assn. Edn. Young Children (founder, pres. Framingham chpt.), Mass. Assn. Early Childhood Educators Office Phone: 508-626-4761. Personal E-mail: jccdl@comcast.net. Business E-Mail: jcanell@frc.mass.edu.

CANELLOS, GEORGE PETER, hematologist, oncologist, educator; b. Boston, Nov. 1, 1934; s. Peter and Pota C. (Coronios) C.; m. Jean H. Speare, July 27, 1958; children: Peter, George, Andrew Phillip. AB, Harvard U., 1956; MD, Columbia U., 1960; Doctor Honoris Causa, Nat. and Kapodestrian U. Athens, Greece, 1997. Diplomate Am. Bd. Internal Medicine, 1967, Am. Bd Internal Medicine, Hematology, 1972, Am. Bd. Internal Medicine, Medical Oncology, 1973; lic. Mass., 1962. Intern surgery Mass. Gen. Hosp., 1961—62, asst. resident medicine, 1962—63, sr. resident medicine, 1965—66, clin. rsch. fellow medicine, 1962, physician in medicine, 1966—, attending physician, hematology-oncology svc., 1997—; rsch. fellow Royal Postgraduate Med. Sch., London, 1966—67; active staff Children's Hosp. Med. Ctr., Boston, 1978—96, attending physician, 1977—78; clin assoc., medicine branch Nat. Cancer Inst., Bethesda, Md., 1963—65, sr. investigator, 1967-74, attending physician, medicine branch, 1967—75, clin. dir. Bethesda, Md., 1974-75; chief divsn. med. oncology Sidney Farber Cancer Inst./Dana-Farber Cancer Inst., Boston, 1975—95; med. dir. for network devel. Dana-Farber/Partners CancerCare, 1995—2004; attending physician Dana-Faber Cancer Inst., 1975—; cons. physician medicine Georgetown U. Hosp., Wash., 1971—75; sr. assoc. medicine Peter Bent Brigham Hosp., Boston, 1975—82; rsch. fellow medicine Harvard Med. Sch., 1962—63, assoc. prof. medicine Boston, 1975-83, prof., 1983-88, William Rosenberg prof. medicine, 1988—; physician Beth Israel Hosp., Boston, 1988—; attending physician, medical svc. Brigham and Women's Hosp., Boston, 1976—78, sr. physician, 1983—, physician, 1982—83, attending physician, hematology-oncology svc., 1997—. Asst. clin prof. med. Georgetown U. Sch. Medicine, Wash., 1971—74, assoc. clin. prof. medicine, 1974—75; assoc. prof. medicine Harvard Med. Sch., 1975—83, prof. medicine, 1983—88; sr. investigator and attending physician, medicine branch Nat. Cancer Inst., Bethesda, Md., 1967—73, head sect. on hematology investigations and asst. chief medicine branch, 1973—74, acting clin. dir., acting assoc. dir. for med. oncology, divsn. cancer treatment, 1974—75; oncologic drugs adv. com. Food and Drug Adminstrn., Wash., DC, 1984—88; vis. prof. U. Colo., 1976, Mayo Clinic, 1977, UCLA, 1978, Wadsworth VA Ctr., 1978, U. Fla., 1979, St. Bartholomew's Hosp., London, 1980, U. Rochester, 1981; McIlrath vis. prof. Sydney U., Australia, 1989; Ruitingavan Swieten Found. prof. Amsterdam Med. Ctr., 1989; Semler vis. prof. Boston U. Med. Ctr., 1992; Shenson vis, prof. Stanford U., 1992; vis. prof. McGill U., 1994; several other vis. prof. positions; prin. investigator Dana-Farber Cancer Inst., 1982—, mem. lymphoma com., 1982—, chair, lymphoma com., 1998—2003. Editor: Neoplastic Diseases of the Blood, 1985, 2d edit., 1991; editor in chief Jour. Clin. Oncology, 1988-2001, Oncology Up-to-Date, 2000-, The Lymphomas, 1998, 2nd edit., 2006, Lymphoma, the Oncologist, 2005-; editl. bd. European jour. of Cancer and Clin. Oncology, 1983-, Jour. Internal Medicine, 1989-, Current Opinion in Oncology, 1989-, Hematology/Oncology Clinics N.Am., 2004-. Am. Cancer Soc. Trust, Inc., 1986—; external review com. Wash. U. Cancer Ctr., St.

Louis, 1996—; Med. Oncology Fellowship Selection Dana-Farber Cancer Inst./Dana-Farber Ptnrs. CancerCare, 1975—; Internat. Adv. Com. Specialty Care Exec. Com. Partners HealthCare Sys., 1997—; Clin. Rsch. Coordinating Com. Dana-Farber/Ptnrs. Cancer Care, 2001—. Recipient Achievement award, Nat. Conf. of Christians and Jews, 1984, Hippocratic award, AHEPA, 1985, Disting. Physician award, Hellenic Med. Soc. NY, 1988, Leonideion award, Pan-Laconian Fedn. US and Can., 1993, Disting. Svc. award for Sci. Achievement, Am. Soc. Clin. Oncology, 1996, Disting. Sci. award, HSCO, 1996, Lifetime Achievement award, Alpha Omega Coun., 1999, Key to the Cure award, Cure for Lymphoma Found., 1999, George Papanicolaou award, New England Hellenic Med. and Dental Soc., 2000, Perez-Santiago award lecture, Puerto Rican Soc. Hematology, 2003, Ellis Island Medal of Honor, NECO, 2004, San Salvatore award, Internat. Lymphoma Conf., 2005, Frank Moran award, U. Mich., 2006, Fishcher lecture, Yale, 2006. Fellow ACP, Royal Coll. Physicians London and Scotland; mem. Am. Soc. for Clin. Investigation, Assn. Am. Physicians, Am. Soc. Clin. Oncology (pres. 1993-94), Am. Assn. Cancer Rsch., Am. Fedn. for Clin. Rsch., Am. Soc. Hematology, Mass. Soc. Clin. Oncology. Office: Dana-Farber Cancer Inst 44 Binney St Boston MA 02115-6084 Home Phone: 781-237-1835; Office Phone: 617-632-3470.*

CANELLOS, PETER C., lawyer; b. NYC, Mar. 24, 1944; s. Constantine and Helen (Demetracopoulos) C.; m. Connie Salaoutis, Dec. 28, 1969; children: Sophia, Eleni. BA summa cum laude, Columbia U., 1964, LLB magna cum laude, 1967. Bar: N.Y., 1967. Law clk. Judge Charles D. Breitel, N.Y.S. Ct. Appeals; assoc. Cravath, Swaine & Moore, NYC, 1969-77; of counsel Wachtell, Lipton, Rosen & Katz, NYC, 1977—2006, chmn. tax dept. Editor (in chief): Columbia Law Rev.; contbr. articles to profl. jours. Fulbright scholar Univ. Amsterdam, The Netherlands, 1968-69. Mem. Am. Law Inst., N.Y. State Bar Assn. (chair tax sect.), Assn. of Bar of City of N.Y, Phi Beta Kappa. Office: Wachtell Lipton Rosen & Katz 51 W 52nd St Fl 29 New York NY 10019-6150 Office Phone: 212-403-1241. Office Fax: 212-403-2241. Business E-Mail: pcanellos@wlrk.com.

CANES-WRONE, BRANDICE, political scientist, educator; b. Washington, Jan. 25, 1971; d. Michael and Mary Pat Canes; m. David A. Wrone. PhD, Stanford U., 1998; AB, Princeton Univ., 1993. Asst. prof. of polit. sci. MIT, Cambridge, Mass., 1998—2002; vis. asst. prof. of polit. sci. Calif. Inst. of Tech., Calif., 2001—02; assoc. prof. of polit. sci. Northwestern U., Ill., 2002—. Editl. bd. mem. Presdl. Studies Quar. Author: (scholarly articles) American Political Science Review, American Journal of Political Science, Journal of Politics, among other journals (Patrick J. Fett Award, 1997). Fellow EPA Sci. to Achieve Results Fellowship, EPA, 1997—98. Mem.: Midwest Polit. Sci. Assn., Am. Polit. Sci. Assn.

CANFIELD, ANDREW TROTTER, lawyer, writer; b. NYC, Apr. 30, 1953; s. Edward Francis and Janet Powell (Trotter) C.; m. Marguerite Southworth Dove, May 30, 1987; children: Augusta Phillips, Lilian Sinclair. BA in History, U. Va., 1976; JD, Am. U., 1991. Bar: Pa. 1991, D.C. 1993. Rsch. assoc. Planning Rsch. Corp., McLean, Va., 1977-79; legal asst. Casey, Scott and Canfield P.C., Washington, 1979-88, law clk., 1988-91, assoc., 1991-93, Canfield and Smith, Washington, 1993-94, of counsel, 1994—. Technical and legal writer on solar energy, environ. law, manufactured housing, computer products liability and govt. timber contracts, 1976—. Republican. Episcopalian. Avocations: history, audio, photography, poetry, skiing. Home: PO Box 819 1117 Webster Rd Shelburne VT 05482 E-mail: andrewtcanfield@mac.com.

CANFIELD, JACK, writer, speaker, trainer; b. Ft. Worth, Aug. 19, 1944; s. Elmer Elwyn and Ellen Waterhouse (Taylor) C.; m. Judy Ohlbaum, 1971 (div. Nov. 1976); children: Oran, Kyle; m. Georgia Lee Noble, Sept. 9, 1978 (div. dec. 1999); 1 child, Christopher. BA, Harvard U., 1966; MEd, U. Mass., 1973; PhD, U. Santa Monica, 1981. Educator Clinton (Iowa) Job Corps Ctr., 1968-69; dir. edn. W.C. Stone Found., Chgo., 1969-70; co-dir. New Eng. Ctr., Leverett, Mass., 1971-77; instr. U. Mass., Amherst, 1978-80; dir. ednl. svcs. Insight of Tng. Seminars, Santa Monica, Calif., 1981-83; pres. Self-Esteem Seminars, Culver City, Calif., 1983—, Santa Barbara, Calif., 1983—; CEO Chicken Soup for the Soul Ent., Santa Barbara, 1998—. Pres. Inst. Holistic Edn., Amherst, 1975-81; mem. adv. bd. The Wyland Found., Laguna, Calif., 1997—. Author: Personalized Learning: Confluent Processes in the Classroom, 1976, Self-Esteem and Peak Performance: A Transcript, 1991, Los Angeles Dodgers Team Esteem Program: A Self-Esteem Curriculum Guide, 1992; co-author: (with H.C. Wells) About Me: A Curriculum for a Developing Self, 1971, Japanese edit., 1977, 100 Ways to Enhance Self-Concept in the Classroom: A Handbook for Teachers and Parents, 1976, rev. edit., 1993, (with others) Self-Esteem in the Classroom: A Curriculum Guide, 1986, (with A. Mecca, et al) Toward A State of Esteem: The Final Report of the California Task Force to Promote Self-Esteem and Personal and Social Responsibility, 1990, (with. F. Siccone) 101 Ways to Develop Student Self-Esteem and Responsibility in the Classroom, Vol. II: The Power to Succeed in School and Beyond, 1992, vol. I, 1994, (with M.V. Hansen) Chicken Soup for the Soul: 101 Stories to Open the Heart and Rekindle the Spirit, 1993, large print edit., 1996, various translations (Abby award Am. Booksellers Assn. 1995, other awards, #1 N.Y. Times Best Seller List over 2 years, #1 Pubs. Weekly Best Seller List over 2 years, others), Dare to Win, 1994, various translations, 1996—, (with K. Goldberg) Follow Your Dreams: A Goals Setting Workbook, 1994, (with M.V. Hansen) A 2nd Helping of Chicken Soup for the Soul: 101 More Stories to Open the Heart and Rekindle the Spirit, 1995, large print edit., 1996, various translations (various awards), The Aladdin Factor: How to Ask for and Get Everything You Want in Life, 1995, various translations, (with M.V. Hansen and D. Von Welanetz Wentworth) Chicken Soup for the Soul Cookbook: Stories and Recipes from the Heart, 1995, (with M.V. Hansen) A 3rd Serving of Chicken Soup for the Soul: 101 More Stories to Open the Heart and Rekindle the Spirit, 1996, (with J. Miller) Heart at Work: Stories and Strategies for Building Self-Esteem and Reawakening the Soul at Work, 1996, various translations, (with M.V. Hansen) The Chicken Soup for the Soul Journal, 1996, (with M.V. Hansen, P. Aubery, and N. Mitchell) Chicken Soup for the Surviving Soul: 101 Stories of Courage and Inspiration from Those Who Have Survived Cancer, 1996, various translations, (with M.V. Hansen and B. Spilchuk) A Cup of Chicken Soup for the Soul, 1996, (with M.V. Hansen and P. Hansen) Condensed Chicken Soup for the Soul, 1996, Chicken Soup for the Kid's Soul, 1998, (with M.V. Hansen, M. Shimoff, and J. Hawthorne) Chicken Soup for the Woman's Soul: 101 Stories to Open the Heart and Rekindle the Spirits of Women, 1996, various translations, Chicken Soup for the Mother's Soul: 101 Stories to Open the Hearts and Rekindle the Spirits of Women, 1997, (with M.V. Hansen, M. Rutte, M. Rogerson, and T. Clauss) Chicken Soup for the Soul at Work: 101 Stories of Courage Compassion and Creativity in the Workplace, 1996, (with M.V. Hansen, H. McCarty, and M. McCarty) A Fourth Course of Chicken Soup for the Soul: 101 Stories to Open the Heart and Rekindle the Spirit, 1997, (with M.V. Hansen and K. Kirberger) Chicken Soup for the Teenage Soul: 101 Stories About Life, Love and Learning, 1997, (with M.V. Hansen and P. Aubery) Chicken Soup for the Christian Soul: 101 Stories to Open the Hearts and Rekindle the Spirits of Christians, 1997, (with M.V. Hansen) A Little Sip of Chicken Soup for the Soul: Inspiring Stories of Self-Affirmation, 1997, Another Sip of Chicken Soup for the Soul: Heartwarming Stories of the Love Between Parents and Children, 1997, A Fifth Portion of Chicken Soup for the Soul: 101 Stories to Open the Heart and Rekindle the Spirit, 1998, (with M.V. Hansen, M. Becker, DVM, and C. Kline) Chicken Soup for the Pet Lover's Soul: 101 Stories to Open the Hearts and Rekindle the Spirits of Pet Lovers, 1998, (with M.V. Hansen and R. Camacho) Chicken Soup for the Country Soul: 101 Stories Served up Country Style and Straight from the Heart, 1998, (with M.V. Hansen, P. Hansen and I. Dunlap) Chicken Soup for the Kid's Soul, 1998, (with M.V. Hansen, M. Shimoffand J. Hawthorne) A 2nd Chicken Soup for the Woman's Soul, 1998, (with M.V. Hansen and K. Kirberger) Chicken Soup for the Teenage Soul II, 1998, Chicken Soup for the Teenage Soul Journal, 1998, (with M.V. Hansen, M.& C. Donnelly and B. DeAngelis) Chicken Soup for the Couple's Soul, 1999 (with M.V. Hansen, J. Aubery and M.& C. Donnelly) Chicken Soup for the Golfer's Soul, 1999, (with M.V. Hansen, Ki. Kirberger and D. Clark) Chicken Soup for the College Soul, 1999 (with M.V. Hansen and H. McNamara) Chicken Soup for the Unskinkable Soul, 1999, (with M.V. Hansen, M. Shimoff and J. Hawthorne) Chicken Soup for the Single Soul, 1999, (with M.V. Hansen, M. Becker and Carol Kline) Chicken Soup for the Cat and Dog Lover's Soul, 1999 (with M.V. Hansen and Don Dible) Chicken Soup for the Dental Soul, 1999, (with P. Meyer, B. Chesser, M.V. Hansen and A. Seeger) Chicken Soup for the Golden Soul, 2000, (with Janet Switzer) The Success Principles: How to Get From Where You Are to Where You Want to Be, 2005, (with M.V. Hansen, P. Aubery and N. Autio) Chicken Soup for the Christian Family Soul, 2000. Named Outstanding Young Man of Am., US Jaycees, 1978; recipient So. Calif. Book Publicist of the Yr. award, L.A., 1995, Body Mind Spirit Book award Body Mind Spirit Mag., 1996, Chancellor's Medal, U. Mass., 1998, Promise to the Earth award Nat. Arbor Day Found., 1998, Oprah's Angel Network award, 1999, Golden Plate award, Acad. Achievement, 2004. Mem. Nat. Coun. for Self-Esteem (founder, bd. dirs. 1986-98, adv. bd. 1986—, Nat. Leadership award 1993), Nat. Spkrs. Assn. (Cert. Speaking Profl. award 1989). Democrat. Avocations: tennis, travel, guitar. Office: The Jack Canfield Cos PO Box 30880 Santa Barbara CA 93130 Office Phone: 805-563-2935. Office Fax: 805-563-2945.*

CANGANELLI, VINCENT GUGLIELMO, retired psychiatrist; b. Indpls., Sept. 3, 1927; s. Benedetto Antonio and Mary Ethel Canganelli; m. Beverly Janice Neal (div.); children: Michael Antonio, Patrick William, Theresa Ann, Joanne Leah, Janice Maria, Mark Angelo, Monica Louise. MD, Ind. U., Indpls., 1952. Lic. psychiatrist Ind. Intern St. Vincent's Hosp., Indpls., 1953; psychiatrist pvt. practice, Ind., 1952—69, NY, 1969—77, Iowa, 1977—83, Nebr., 1983—89, Ky., 1989—93, Ky., 1996—97, Va., 1994—95, Wyo., 1995—96; ret., 1997. Cons. in field. With USN, 1946. Mem.: Am. Psychiat. Assn. (life). Roman Catholic. Avocation: writing. Home: 1151 Park Ave Apt 1016 Valparaiso IN 46385

CANGEMI, JOSEPH PETER, psychologist, consultant, educator; b. Syracuse, NY, June 26, 1936; m. Amelia Elena Santaló, Oct. 6, 1962; children: Michelle, Lisa Ann. BS, SUNY, Oswego, 1959; MS, Syracuse U., 1964; EdD, Ind. U., 1974; LittD (hon.), William Woods U., 1996; DHC (hon.), Moscow State U., 2001. Diplomate Am. Bd. Forensic Examiners, Am. Coll. Counselors, in profl. counseling Internat. Acad. Behavioral Medicine, Counseling and Psychology, cert. sch. psychologist, counselor NY; diplomate Am. Bd. Vocat. Experts. Instr. Syracuse Pub. Schs., 1959-60, vocat. rehab. coord., rsch. assoc., 1961-65; instr., asst. dir. Carol Morgan Sch., Santo Domingo, Dominican Republic, 1960-61; asst. head basketball coach SUNY C.C., Syracuse, 1962-63, lectr., chmn. dept. psychology evening-extension divsn., 1962-65, vis. lectr., 1966; supr. edn. Orinoco Mining divsn. U.S. Steel Corp., Ciudad Piar, Venezuela, 1965-66, supr. tng. and devel. Puerto Ordaz and Ciudad Piar, Venezuela, 1966-68; asst. prof. psychology Western Ky. U., Bowling Green, 1968-75, assoc. prof., 1975-79, prof., 1979—2005, prof. emeritus, 2006—; dir. Inst. Leadership, Inc., Inst. for Creative Leadership Strategies, Inc., 1970—. Project dir. U. Los Andes, Merida, Venezuela, Inter-Am. Devel. Bank, Washington, Western Ky. U., 1975—77; cons. R. R. Donnelley & Sons, Coca Cola, Gould Corp., Eaton Corp., Firestone Tire and Rubber Co., Uniroyal/Goodrich Tire and Rubber Co., Gen. Tire and Rubber Co., Jefferson Smurfit, Std. Products, Tyson Foods, others. Host conversation program Wester Ky. U. divsn. Radio, TV Film, 1968—71; author: Higher Education and the Development of Self-Actualizing Personalities, 1977, La Administracion Participative, 1983, Higherd Education in the United States and Latin America, 1983; author: (with Casimir Kowalski) Perspectives in Higher Education, 1983, Andersonville Prison, Lessons in Organizational Failure, 1993; author: (with George Guttschalk) Effective Management, 1980; author: (with Casimir Kowalski and Jeffrey Claypool) Participative Management: Employee Management Cooperation, 1985, Chinese edit., 1990; author: (with Mario Noronha) Marketing Y Venda, Portuguese edit., 1992; author: (with Carl Kreisler) Raymond C. Gibson-Distinguished Kentuckian, Renowned Educator and Statesman: An Anthology, 1996; author: (with Mario Noronha, Casimir Kowalski, George Guttschalk) Falhas Organizaciones, Protuguese edit., 1996; author: (with Tatyana Ushakova and Casimir Kowalski) Leadership for the 21st Century, Russian edit., Russian Academy of Sciences; author: (with Casimir Kowalski and Habib Khan) Leadership Behavior, 1998; author: (with R. Miller, C. Kowalski, T. Hollopeter) Developing Trust in Organizations, 2005; editor: Educator's Svc. Bull., 1971—72; editor, exec. editor: Psychology and Edn.: An Interdisciplinary Jour., 1977—, Jour. Human Behavior and Learning, 1983—90, Orgn. Devel. Jour., 1983—89; mem. editl. bd. Archivos Panamenos de Psicologia, 1968—88, Coll. Student Jour., 1973—2004, Edn., 1976—, Faculty Rsch. Bull. Western Ky. U., 1977—78, Jour. Instrnl. Psychology, 1977—90, Counseling and Values, 1979—84, Technol. Horizons Edn. Jour., 1979—92, Jour. Fgn. Psychology, Russia, 1996—2003, Forensic Examiner, 1998—2004; contbr. articles to profl. jours., chapters to books. Past mem. House of Goa, Lisbon, 1996—97; trustee William Woods U., 1988—; past bd. dirs. Cooperative de Ensino Superior de Technicas Avancadas de Gestao e Informatica Technol. U., Lisbon, Portugal. Recipient certs. and awards, US Army Armor Sch., 1974, Eaton Corp., 1974, 1976, Nat. Autonomous U. Nicaragua, 1976, ICETEX, Colombia, 1977, Colobian Nat. Assn. Indsl. Engrs., 1977, Decreto City of Bucaramanga, Colombia, 1976, 1977, Quality Control Assn., 1979, Decreto award, State of Santander, Colombia, 1977, Excellence in Productive Tchg. award, Western Ky. U. Coll. Edn., 1979, 1991, 1999, Fireston Tire and Rubber Co. award, 1978, 1981, 1991, Profl.-Tech. Socs. award, 1983, Coll. Student Jour. and Models of Excellence award, 1983, Disting. Pub. Svc. award, Western Ky. U., 1983, Excellence in Pub. Svc. award, Coll. Edn., 1983, Disting. Alumnus award, SUNY, Oswego, 1983, award, Uniroyal-Goodrich Tire and Rubber Co., 1986, Excellence in Rsch. and Creativity award, Coll. Edn., Wester Ky. U., 1987, United Rubber Workers/Internat. Brotherhood Elec. Workers award, 1991, Jour. Edn. award, Project Innovation, 1992, Bridgestone-Firestone award, Valencia, Venezuela, 1994, Outstanding Contbn. award, Southeastern divsn. Redman Industries, 1996. Mem.: RODP, ACA (life; regional chmn. com. internat. edn. 1976), Soc. Psychology Mgmt., Acad. Mgmt., InterAm. Soc. Psychology, Intenrat. Registry Ogn. Devel. Profls., Nat. Assn. Gifted (bd. dirs. 1973), Internat. Assn. Edn. and Vocat. Guidance, Assn. Specialists Group Work (charter), Internat. Coun. Psychologists (past area chmn. Ky.), Nat. Vocat. Guidance Assn. Profl., Colombian Nat. Soc. Indsl. Engrs. (hon.), Panamanian Psychol. Assn. (hon.), Ky. Acad. Arts and Scis. (life), Alumni Assn. SUNY, Oswego, Capitol Arts Assn., Ind. U. Alumni Assn. (life), Olde Stone Country Club, Gold Key, Phi Delta Kappa, Sigma Tau Delta, Sigma Delta Psi, Psi Chi, Pi Kappa Delta. Home: 1409 Mt Ayr Cir Bowling Green KY 42103-4708 Office: Western Ky U Dept Psychology Bowling Green KY 42101 Home Phone: 270-842-3436; Office Phone: 270-842-3436. Fax: 270-842-0432. Personal E-mail: jpcnbg@aol.com. Business E-Mail: joseph.cangemi@wku.edu, joseph.cangem@insight.bb.

CANGEMI, LISA LYNNE, art director, graphics designer; b. Bklyn., May 20, 1963; d. Robert A. and Elizabeth J. (Kopter) C. BFA in Graphic Design with honors, Sch. Visual Arts, NYC, 1985. Owner C&C Graphic Design, 1985—; art direction accounts for Amerchol, Associated Bus. Pub., AT&T Corp., Briarcliffe Coll., Cablevision, Cahners Pub., CMP Media, Condé Nast, CTB Pub., Deloitte, Touche & Tomatsu, Dover Pub., Earnshaw Pub., Famous Brands, Gattefossé, Grey Advt., Miller Freeman, Nassimi Corp., New Phase Tech., NJ Savvy, Patchogue Theatre, PCI Animal Health, Petrolite Corp., TalkAIDS, United-Guardian, Verizon Wireless, VNU Pub., Walker and Co. Prof. Graphic Design Briarcliffe Coll., NY, 2002—. One-woman shows include painting exhbns. NY galleries and librs., 1993—2006 (GD USA, Folio, Creativity, and Davey awards, over 3 dozen graphic design awards). Recipient Lifetime award for excellent in field of graphic design, Alpha Beta Kappa, 2007. Avocations: photography, painting, travel. Office: PO Box 782 Lynbrook NY 11563-0782 Office Phone: 516-295-0936. Personal E-mail: CCGraphics85@aol.com.

CANGEMI, MICHAEL PAUL, accountant, author, consultant; b. Bklyn., May 5, 1948; s. Ignatius and Mary (Chimento) C.; m. Maria D. Ruscitti, Nov. 23, 1974; children: Michael Jason, Marc Ignatius. BBA, Pace U., 1970. CPA, NY; cert. info. sys. auditor. Asst. to v.p. ops. Blair & Co., NYC, 1966—70; prin. Arthur Young & Co., NYC, 1970—80; v.p. Phelps Dodge Corp., NYC, 1980—88; ptnr., nat. dir. EDP auditing BDO Seidman, 1988—92; sr. v.p., CFO, CEO Etienne Aigner Inc., Edison, NJ, 1992—2000; pres., CEO, bd. dirs. Etienne Aigner Group, Edison, 2000—04; founder, pres. MC Comm., 2004, Cangemi Co. LLC, 2005—; pres., CEO Fin. Executives Internat., Florham Park, NJ, 2007—. Lectr. field. Author: Managing the Audit Function-A Corporate Audit Department Procedures Guide, 1993, 3d edit., 2003, Managing the Audit Function Chinese lang. edit., 2005; contbg. author: The Handbook for EDP Auditing, 1986; co-author: Auditing in an EDP Environment; contbr. articles to profl. jours. Trustee, vice chmn. bd., chair governance and audit com. NJ Reads, Inc.; mem. adv. bd. Rutgers U. Continuous Auditing Rsch. Lab.; chmn. The Edison Project, 2006—. Recipient Alumni Achievement award, Pace U. Lubin Sch. Bus., 2003. Mem. AICPA, NY State Soc. CPA (data processing com. 1979-80, computer usage and data processing com. 1980-82), EDP Auditors Assn. (internat. bd. dirs. 1982-89, trustee 1982-89, v.p. edn. 1982-84, exec. v.p. 1984-85, assn. found. pres. 1985-86, pres. NY chpt. bd. dirs. 1978-86, 2d v.p., 1979-80, 1st v.p. 1983, nominating com. 1982-86, conf. site selection com. 1981-82, editor Info. Sys. Control Jour., 1987—, editor-in-chief, 1992-94, assoc. editor EDPACS newsletter, The EDP Audit, Control and Security, 1988-94, J.J. Wasserman award 1987, Eugene M. Frank award 1989, Michael P. Cangemi best article-best book award, 1996), Pace U. (Lubin Alumni Achievement award, 2003), Inst. Internal Auditors (Thomas Johnson Lifetime Achievement award, 2006, Lubin Sch. Legacy award, 2006, Fin. Execs. Internat. (mem. intervention com. on fin. and tech. 2006-), Inst. Internal Auditors (program devel. com. for 1986 conf. 1984-86, bd. govs. NY chpt. 1986-92, bd. rsch. advisors 1987-93, pres. NY chpt. 1989-90, trustee rsch. found. 1994-2000), Soc. Info. Sys. Quality (bd. dirs. 1987-88), Arthur Young Businessmen's Assn. (bd. dirs. 1982-89, v.p. 1985-89), Info. Systems Audit & Control Assn. (dir., internat. pres.), Metuchen (NJ) Golf Country Club. Roman Catholic. Office: Financial Executives International 200 Campus Dr Florham Park NJ 07932-0674 E-mail: mpcangemi@canco.us.

CANHAM, PRUELLA CROMARTIE NIVER, music educator; b. Statesboro, Ga., Dec. 4, 1924; d. Esten Graham and Mary Lee (Jones) Cromartie; m. Robert G. Niver June 4, 1946 (div. 1965) m. David L. Canham July 26, 1985; 1 child, Peddy Niver Hayhurst Moran. BS in Bus. and Music, Ga. So. U., 1944; postgrad., various univs. tchr. voice, piano, chorus and bus. career maths. North Ft. Myers H.S., Fla.; former sec. Statesboro Air Base, Ga., Warner Robbins Air Base, Macon, Ga.; former tchr. Westside Sch., Bulloch County, Ga., Southside Sch., Opelika, Ala. Mem. Singers Club of L.I.; guest spkr., panelist various cultural orgns. in Fla. and so. states; soloist various chs. and schs.; music cons. local theater groups; mem. Fla. State Secondary Music Instructional Materials Coun. Nominee Gannett Found. Heart of Gold Humanatarian award, 1981; named Vocal Solo. Lit. Music Specialist State of Florida, Lee County Florida Tchr. of the Year, 1987, nominee Nat. Tchr. Hall of Fame, 1998; recipient Nat. Libr. Poet's Editor's Choice award, 1994; cert. Appreciation Nat. Park Trust, 1995, Lee County Sch. Dist. Fla., 1991, numerous awards in 2002, including: ABI Hall of Fame, Poet of Year, Internat. Poet Merit and Honored Mem., Living Legions, Worlds Lifetime Achievement award, Companion of Honor, Internat. Peace Prize, Am. Medal of Honor; Nobel Prize for Oustanding Achievement and Contbr. to Humanity, 2002; recipient Congl. Medal of Excellence, 2004. Mem. AAAS, Am. Ch. Dirs. Assn., Fla. Music Educator Assns., Music Educators Nat. Conf., Lee County Alliance of the Arts (charter), Fla. Vocal Assn. (past coord., state bd.), Nat. Assn. of Tchrs. of Singing in Am. and Cand., So. Fla. Symphony and Chorus Assn., Am. Guild of Organists, Fla. League of the Arts (past pres. and bd. dirs., hon. life, 1998—), Lee County Ret. Tchrs. Assn., Fla. Vocal Assn., Am. Choral Assn., Internat. Soc. Poets (disting. mem. 1994, merit award, 1995), Profl. Women's Adv. Bd., others. Home: 1271 Burtwood Dr Fort Myers FL 33901-8711

CANIANO, DONNA ANNE, surgeon, educator; b. Albany, NY, July 21, 1950; d. Mary Lombard and James Joseph Caniano; m. Richard A. Flores, July 28, 2004; children: Christopher Flores, Matthew Flores. BA, Vassar Coll., Poughkeepsie, NY, 1972; MD, Albany Med. Coll., 1976. Diplomate Am. Bd. Surgery, 1984. Asst. prof. surgery U. Md., Baltimore, Md., 1983—85, Johns Hopkins U., Balt., 1983—85, Ohio State U., Columbus, 1985—90, assoc. prof. of surgery, 1991—98, prof. surgery, 1999—. Dir. residency in pediatric surgery Columbus Children's Hosp., Ohio, 1999—, surgeon-in-chief, 1999—. Mem. Recreation Unlimited, Columbus, Ohio, 2006—07. Recipient Woman of Achievement award, YWCA, Columbus, 2006. Fellow: ACS; mem.: Am. Acad. Pediat. (chiarperson 2005), Am. Surg. Assn., Am. Pediat. Surg. Assn. Avocations: gardening, reading, piano, opera. Office: Children's Hosp Dept Surgery ED 379 700 Children's Dr Columbus OH 43205 Home Phone: 614-463-1675.

CANIPAROLI, VAL WILLIAM, choreographer, dancer; b. Renton, Wash., Sept. 12, 1951; s. Francisco and Leonora (Marconi) C. Student, Wash. State U., Pullman, 1969—71, San Francisco Ballet Sch., 1971—72. Dancer San Francisco Opera, 1973, San Francisco Ballet, 1973—; co-dir. OMO, San Francisco, 1985; resident choreographer San Francisco Ballet, 1983—, Ballet West, 1993—97, Tulsa Ballet, 2001—. Choreographer (ballets) Street Song, 1980, Pacific Northwest Ballet, Seattle, 1980, 91, The Bridge, 1998, Love-lies-Bleeding, 1982, Aria, 1998, Slow, 1998, Ciao Marcello, 1997, Hamlet and Ophelia, 1985, In Perpetuum, 1990, Aubade, 1985 (Isadora Duncan award 1986), Narcisse, 1987, Ririe Woodbury Dance Co., 1988, Ritual, 1990, A Door is Ajar, 1990, Jacob's Pillow Dance festival, 1990, Pulcinella, 1991, Concerto Grosso, 1992, Seeing Stars, 1993, Lady of the Camellias, 1993, Ballet West, 1994, Lambarena, 1995, Capriccio, Chgo. Lyric Opera, 1994, Bow Out, 1995, San Francisco Symphony Pops, 1995-96, Prawn Watching, 1996, Djangology, 1997, Open Veins, 1998, Book of Alleged Dances, 1998, Going for Baroque, 1999, Attention Please, 1999, The Nutcracker, 2001, Torque, 2001, Jaybird Lounge, 2001, Death of a Moth, 2001, Unspoken, 2002, No Other, 2002, boink!, 2002, Gustave's Rooster, 2003, Vivace, 2003, Sonata for Two Pianos and Percussion, Boston Ballet, 2004, A Doll's House, San Francisco, 2004, A Christmas Carol, ACT, 2005, Songs, 2005, Violin, 2006, Richmond Ballet Suite, 2007, others. Recipient Isadora Duncan award, 1987, 97, 2001, Choo-San Goh and H. Robert Magee Found. award for choreography, 1994, 97; Nat. Endowment Arts fellow, 1981-88. Fellow Calif. Arts Coun. Choreographers. Avocations: music, theater, dance. Office: San Francisco Ballet 455 Franklin St San Francisco CA 94102-4471

CANIZARES, CLAUDE ROGER, astrophysicist, educator; BA, Harvard U., 1967, MA, 1968, PhD, 1972. Postdoctoral fellow MIT, 1971—74, prof., 1974—84, Bruno Rossi prof. exptl. physics, 1984—, dir. Ctr. for Space Rsch., 1990—2001, assoc. provost, 2001—06, v.p. rsch., 2006—. Assoc. dir. NASA-Chandra X-ray Obs. Ctr.; chair NRC Space Studies Bd.,

1994-00; chair space sci. adv. com. NASA, 1993-94, mem. Space Earth Sci. Adv. Com., Washington, 1986-88; mem. adv. coun. NASA, 1992-00; mem. astron. and astrophysics survey com. NRC, Washington, 1989-91; trustee Assoc. Univs., Inc., 1997-05; mem. Air Force Sci. Adv. Bd., 1999-2003; mem. bd. on physics and astronomy NRC, 2001-03. Contbr. over 210 articles to profl. jours. Royal Soc. vis. fellow, Cambridge, Eng., 1981-82, Alfred P. Sloan Found. fellow, 1980-84; NASA grantee, 1975—; recepient NASA public svc. medal, 2000, Goddard medal, Am. Astronautical Soc., 1997. Fellow Am. Phys. Soc., Am. Acad. Arts & Sci. 2004; mem. NAS (mem. governing coun. 2005-), AAAS, Am. Astron. Soc., Internat. Astron. Union, Internat. Acad. Astronautics, Phi Beta Kappa, Sigma Xi. Achievements include first implementation of studies in x-ray spectroscopy and plasma diagnostics of supernova remnants, clusters of galaxies. Office: MIT 77 Massachusetts Ave 3-234 Cambridge MA 02139-4309 Office Phone: 617-253-3206.

CANMANN, MICHAEL, investment banker; b. 1967; Degree in Eng. and Hist., Amherst, 1989. Fin. analyst Prudential Bache Securities, NYC; v.p. Salomon, Smith, Barney Investment Banking, Chgo.; mng. dir. Citigroup Global Markets Inc., Chgo. Mem. Lincoln Park Zoo, Art Inst., Mus. Contemporary Art. Mem.: Old Masters Soc. Office: Citigroup Global Markets Inc 1448 N Lake Shore Dr Chicago IL 60610*

CANN, SHARON LEE, retired health science librarian; b. Ft. Riley, Kans., Aug. 14, 1935; d. Roman S. and Cora Elon (George) Foote; m. Donald Clair Cann, May 16, 1964. Student, Sophia U., Tokyo, 1955-57; BA, Calif. State U., Sacramento, 1959; MSLS, Atlanta U., 1977; EdD, U. Ga., 1995. Cert. health scis. libr. Recreation worker ARC, Korea, Morocco, France, 1960-64; shelflister Libr. Congress, Washington, 1967-69; tchr. Lang Ctr., Taipei, Taiwan, 1971-73; libr. tech. asst. Emory U., Atlanta, 1974-76; health sci. libr. Northside Hosp., Atlanta, 1977-85, libr. cons., 1985-86; libr. area health edn. ctr., learning resource ctr. Morehouse Sch. Medicine, 1985-86; edn. libr. Ga. State U., 1986-93; dir. libr. svcs. Ga. Bapt. Coll. Nursing, 1993-99, ret., 1999. Author: Life in a Fishbowl: A Call To serve, 2003; editor Update, publ. Ga. Health Scis. Libr. Assn., 1981; contbr. articles to profl. jours. Chmn. Calif. Christian Youth in Govt. Seminar, 1958. Named Miss Far East Air Force, 1956, Alumni Top Twenty, Calif. State U., Sacramento, 1959; recipient Miss Meiji Bowl Tokyo, 1956. Mem. ALA, Med. Libr. Assn. (hon. life; bookkeeper So. chpt. 1996-98, credentialing com. 1996-2000, 05, nursing and allied health sect. continuing edn. chair 1998-2000), Spl. Libr. Assn. (dir. South Atlantic chpt. 1985-87), Ga. Libr. Assn. (spl. libr. divsn. chmn. 1983-85), Ga. Health Scis. Libr. Assn. (hon. life, chmn. 1981-82), Atlanta Health Sci. Libr. (chmn. 1979, 95), Am. Numis. Assn., ARC Overseas Assn., Audubon Soc., Women in Mil. Svc. for Am., Suncity Hilton Head Computer Club (v.p. 2003). Home: 69 Plymouth Ln Bluffton SC 29909-5062 E-mail: sharoncann@aol.com.

CANNADAY, BILLY K., JR., school system administrator; B in Health and Physical Edn., Va. Tech U., 1972, EdD in Ednl. Adminstrn., 1990; M in Ednl. Adminstrn., Hampton U., 1980. Prin. Huntington Middle Sch., Newport News, Va.; dir. secondary edn., asst. supt. instruction Hampton Pub. Schs., 1986—94, supt., 1994—2000, Chesterfield County Pub. Schs., 2000—06; supt. pub. instruction Va. Dept. Edn., Richmond, 2006—. Mem. State Standard Setting Adv. Com., Va. Standards of Learning, 1999—2000; disting. leader in residence Jepson Sch. Leadership, U. Richmond, 2004—05. Mem. Coll. William & Mary Gifted Adv. Bd., U. Va. Tchr. Edn. Adv. Com.; bd. dirs. Greater Richmond Cmty. Found. Named William & Mary Profl. Educator of Yr., 2000, Va. Supt. of Yr., 2005. Office: Va Dept Edn PO Box 2120 Richmond VA 23218 Office Phone: 804-225-2023.*

CANNAVALE, BOBBY (ROBERTO CANNAVALE), actor; b. Union City, NJ, May 3, 1971; m. Jenny Lumet, 1994 (div. 2003); 1 child, Jacob. Mem. Circle Repertory Theatre, Lab Theatre Co. Actor: (films) I'm Not Rappaport, 1996, Night Falls on Manhattan, 1997, Gloria, 1999, The Bone Collector, 1999, The Devil and Daniel Webster, 2001, 3 A.M., 2001, Washington Heights, 2002, The Guru, 2002, The Station Agent, 2003, Fresh Cut Grass, 2004, Haven, 2004, Shall We Dance, 2004, The Breakup Artist, 2004, Happy Endings, 2005, Romance & Cigarettes, 2005, The Night Listener, 2006, Fast Food Nation, 2006, Snakes on a Plane, 2006, The Ten, 2007; (TV films) When Trumpets Fade, 1998, The Exonerated, 2005, Recipe for a Perfect Christmas, 2005; (TV series) Third Watch, 1999—2001, 100 Centre Street, 2001, (TV mini series) Kingpin, 2003; guest appearances include Trinity, 1998—99, Sex and the City, 2000, Law & Order: Special Victims Unit, 2002, Ally McBeal, 2002, Law & Order, 2002, Oz, 2003, Law & Order: Criminal Intent, 2003, Will & Grace (several episodes), 2004—05 (Creative Arts Primetime Emmy award for guest actor in a comedy series, 2005), Six Feet Under, 2004.*

CANNELL, JOHN REDFERNE, lawyer; b. Cambridge, Mass., Apr. 3, 1937; s. John and Thyra (Larson) C.; m. Elizabeth Ann May, May 28, 1960; children: John R. Jr. (dec.), James C., William H. AB, Princeton U., 1958; LLB, Columbia U., 1961. Bar: NY 1961. Assoc. Simpson Thacher & Bartlett, NYC, 1961-70, ptnr., 1970-95, ret., 1996—. Gov. Am. Bus. Coun., Singapore, 1982-85, vice chmn., 1984-85; dir. Mattapoisett Casino, 2002-04. Trustee Kessler Inst. for Rehab., West Orange, NJ, 1986-97, vice chmn., 1989-92, chmn., 1992-95; trustee Henry H. Kessler Found., 1992—, chmn., 1996-99; trustee Marcus Ward Home, Maplewood, NJ, 1996-2006; dir. Kessler Rehab. Corp., 1992-2003, Kessler Med. Rehab. Rsch. and Edn. Corp., 1997-2006; bd. dir. New Alternatives for Children, Inc., 1996—. Mem. Montclair Golf Club (trustee 2001-07), Univ. Club, Bay Club (Mattapoisett). Episcopalian. Avocations: squash, golf. Office: Simpson Thacher & Bartlett 425 Lexington Ave Fl 17 New York NY 10017-3903

CANNING, DAVID, economist; b. Strabane, Ireland, Mar. 16, 1958; s. James and Ann Canning; m. Hyesun Canning, Apr. 15, 1993; children: Sacha, Sophia. BA, Queen's U., Belfast, 1979; MA, Harvard U., 2003; PhD, Cambridge U., 1983. Lectr. London Sch. Econ., 1988—89, Cambridge U., 1989—92; assoc. prof. Columbia U., NYC, 1992—93; prof. Queen's U., Belfast, 1993—2002; prof. econ. and internat. health Harvard U., Boston, 2002—. Co-author: The Demographic Dividend: A New Perspective on the Economic Consequences of Population Change, 2003. Office: Harvard Univ 665 Huntington Ave Boston MA 02459 Business E-Mail: dcanning@hsph.harvard.edu.

CANNIZZARO, LINDA ANN, geneticist, researcher; b. S.I., NY, Aug. 4, 1953; BS, St. Peter's Coll., 1975; MS, Fordham U., 1977, PhD, 1981. Postdoctoral fellow Dartmouth U. Med. Sch., Hanover, N.H., 1981-83; fellow in human genetics Children's Hosp. Phila., 1983-84; co-dir. cytogenetics Milton S. Hershey (Pa.) Med. Ctr., 1984-86; dir. gene mapping S.W. Biomed. Rsch. Inst., Scottsdale, Ariz., 1986-89; asst. prof. Fels Inst. Temple U. Med. Sch., Phila., 1989-91; asst. prof. Jefferson Cancer Inst., Phila., 1991-93; assoc. prof. Albert Einstein Coll. Medicine, Bronx, NY, 1993—2001; dir. cancer and molecular cytogenetics Albert Einstein Coll. Medicine and Montefiore Hosp., Bronx, N.Y., 1993—; prof. pathology Albert Einstein Coll. Medicine, 2001—; prof. Montefiore Med. Ctr. and Albert Einstein Coll. Medicine, 2006—. Co-editor-in-chief Cytogenetics and Genome Rsch., 1995—; contbr. articles to profl. jours. Grantee Am. Cancer Soc., 1989-90, 94-97; Kriser awardee in Lung Cancer Rsch., 1999-2001. Mem. AAAS, AAUW, Am. Soc. Human Genetics. Avocations: painting, hiking, reading, writing. Office Phone: 718-405-8103. Personal E-mail: cannizza@earthlink.net. Business E-Mail: cannizza@aecom.yu.edu.

CANNON, BEVERLY J., deaf education educator, interpreter; d. Robert Hamilton Cannon and Dorothea Alta Collins. PhD, UCLA, 1990. Lectr. in German Gallaudet U., Washington, 1976; asst. prof. lang. arts Ohlone Coll., Fremont, Calif., 1977—85; asst. prof. deaf studies Calif. State U., Northridge, 1990—99; assoc. prof. deaf edn. Western Oreg. U., Monmouth, 1999—, coord. tchr. preparation deaf edn. program, 2001—. Lectr. in interpreting U. Iceland, Rekjavik, 1996—97. Author: (novels) The Connecticut River has Flooded the Fields. Bd. deaf ministry Diocese of Oreg., Portland, 2000. Pers. Preparation grantee, Office Spl. Edn. Programs, 1999—2002, 2004—. Mem.: Accosiation Coll. Educators of the Deaf and Hard of Hearing. Office: Western Oregon University 345 N Monmouth Ave Monmouth OR 97361 Home Phone: 503-838-8077; Office Phone: 503-838-8077. Office Fax: 503-838-8228. Business E-Mail: cannonb@wou.edu.

CANNON, CARL M., reporter; b. San Francisco; s. Lou Cannon; m. Sharon Cannon; 3 children. B. in journalism, U. Colo. Reporter, Washington bur. Knight-Ridder Newspapers, Washington, 1982—93; White House corr. Baltimore Sun, 1993—98, Nat. Jour., Washington, 1998—. Reporter San Jose (Calif.) Mercury News, 1989. Co-author: Boy Genius: Karl Rove, the Brains Behind the Remarkable Political Triumph of George W. Bush, 2003; author: The Pursuit of Happiness in Times of War, 2003. Recipient Gerald R. Ford journalism prize, 1999, Aldo Beckman award, White House Corrs. Assn., 2006. Office: National Journal 600 New Hampshire Ave NW Washington DC 20037 Office Phone: 202-739-8400. Office Fax: 202-833-8069. E-mail: ccannon@nationaljournal.com.

CANNON, CARL N., publishing executive; b. Ga. Grad., U. Ga., 1965. Advt. mgr. Morris Comm., Augusta, Ga., advt. dir. Lubbock, Tex., gen. mgr. Amarillo, Tex., mgr. corp. group Augusta, publ. Jacksonville, Fla., 1990—; v.p. Morris Comm., Fla. Group, Augusta, Ga., 1990—; pub. The Fla. Times-Union, Jacksonville, Fla., 1995—. Avocations: golf, fishing, pro sports. Office: Fla Times-Union PO Box 1949 Jacksonville FL 32231-0053 Office Phone: 904-359-4151.

CANNON, CHRISTOPHER BLACK, congressman, lawyer; b. Salt Lake City, Oct. 20, 1950; m. Claudia Fox, 1978; 8 children. BS, Brigham Young U., 1974; attended, Harvard Bus. Sch., 1975—76; JD, Brigham Young U., 1980. Bar: Utah 1980. Atty., Provo; asst. assoc. solicitor Dept. Interior, 1983—84, assoc. solicitor, 1984—86; cons. to asst. sec. productivity, tech. and innovation Dept. Commerce, 1986—87; co-owner Geneva Steel, Orem, Utah, 1987—90; owner Cannon Industries, Inc., 1990—95; fin. chmn. Utah Rep. Party, 1991—92; Utah fin. chmn., 1992; mem. nat. fin. com. Lamar Alexander for Pres., 1995—96; mem. US Congress from 3rd Utah dist., 1997—, mem. judiciary com., chmn. comml. and adminstrv. law subcommittee, mem. govt. reform com., mem. resources com., chmn. Western Caucus, 2003—. Del. Rep. Nat. Conv., 1992, 1996. Republican. Office: US Ho Reps 2436 Rayburn Ho Office Bldg Washington DC 20515-4403 Office Phone: 202-225-7751.*

CANNON, DAVID JOSEPH, lawyer; b. Milw., Aug. 6, 1933; s. George W. and Florence (Dean) c.; m. Carol Nevins, Mar. 10, 1962; children: Charles, Courtney. BS, Marquette U., 1955, JD, 1960. Bar; Wis. 1960, U.S. Dist. Ct. (ea. dist.) Wis. 1960, U.S. Ct. Appeals (7th cir.) 1969, U.S. Ct. Appeals (8th cir.) 1976, U.S. Dist. Ct. (we. dist.) Wis. 1976, U.S. Ct. Appeals (5th cir.) 1978, U.S. Ct. Appeals (4th cir.) 1997. Atty. Cannon & Cannon, Milw., 1960-66; asst. dist. atty. Milw. County Dist. Atty., 1966-68, dist. atty., 1968; U.S. atty. Dept. Justice Ea. Dist. Wis., Milw., 1969-73; ptnr. Michael, Best & Friedrich, Milw., 1973—. Office: Michael Best & Friedrich 100 E Wisconsin Ave Ste 3300 Milwaukee WI 53202-4108 Home: 13600 Park Cir N Elm Grove WI 53122-2557 Home Phone: 262-786-4565; Office Phone: 414-225-4978.

CANNON, FRANK See MAYHAR, ARDATH

CANNON, GARLAND, linguist, educator; b. Fort Worth, Dec. 5, 1924; m. Patricia Richardson, 1947; children— Margaret, Elizabeth, Jennifer. BA in English, U. Tex., 1947, PhD in English Linguistics, 1954; MA in English, Stanford U., 1952. Instr. U. Hawaii, Honolulu, 1949-52; instr. U. Tex., Austin, 1952-54, U. Mich., Ann Arbor, 1954-55; asst. prof. speech U. Calif.-Berkeley, 1955-56; acad. dir. Am. U. Lang. Ctr., Bangkok, 1956-57; asst. prof. English U. Fla., Gainesville, 1957-58; vis. prof. linguistics U. P.R., 1958-59; asst. prof. linguistics Columbia U., NYC, 1959-62; dir. English lang. program for Afghanistan, Kabul, 1960—62; assoc. prof. Northeastern Ill. U., Chgo., 1962-63, Queens Coll., CUNY, 1963-66; assoc. prof. English Tex. A&M U., College Station, 1966-68, prof. English, 1968—; vis. prof. humanities U. Mich., 1970-71; vis. prof. linguistics Kuwait U., 1979-81. Vis. prof. linguistics Inst. Teknologi Mara, Kuala Lumpur, 1987; vis. summer prof. Cambridge U., 1980, Oxford U., 1974, MIT, 1969, U. Wash., 1967; lectr. throughout world Author: Sir William Jones, Orientalist: A Bibliography, 1952, Biography, 1964, A History of the English Language, 1972, An Integrated Transformational Grammar of the English Language, 1978, Sir William Jones: A Bibliography of Primary and Secondary Sources, 1979, Historical Change and English Word-Formation, 1987, Oriental Jones: The Life and Mind of Sir William Jones, 1990, Arabic Loanwords in English, 1994, 2d edit. e-publ., 2007, (with A. Pfeffer) German Loanwords in English, 1994, Japanese Loanwords in English, 1996, (with A. Kaye) Persian Loanwords in English, 2001; editor: The Letters of Sir William Jones, 1970 (Book of Yr. Sunday London Telegraph 1970); editor: The Collected Works of Sir William Jones, 1993, Objects of Enquiry: The Life and Influences of Sir William Jones, 1995; contbr. numerous articles to profl. jours. Recipient Disting. Achievement award Tex. A&M U., 1972; Indian Govt. grantee, 1984; Linguistic Soc. Am./Am. Council Learned Socs. grantee, 1984; Am. Philos. Soc. grantee, Eng., 1964, 66, 74 Mem. MLA (exec. com. gen. linguistics discussion group 1982-85, chmn. 1984, 85, exec. com. present-day-English 1986-89, 94-97, exec. com. lexicography 1986-89, chmn. 1989, rep. to del. assembly 1985-88), Am. Dialect Soc. (exec. coun. 1989-93), Dictionary Soc. N.Am., South Asian Lit. Assn. (pres. 1979-85). Office: Tex A&M U Dept English College Station TX 77843-0001

CANNON, GEORGE W., JR., judge; Atty. priv. practice, St. Croix; magistrate judge V.I. Dist. Ct., St. Croix Div., 2004—. Office: VI Dist Ct St Croix Div Almeric L Chritian Fed Bldg 3013 Estate Golden Rock St Croix VI 00820 also: PO BOX 1548 Frederiksted VI 00841-1548 Office Phone: 340-773-1601, 340-773-2743.

CANNON, GRACE BERT, retired immunologist; b. Chambersburg, Pa., Jan. 29, 1937; d. Charles Wesley and Gladys (Raff) Bert; m. W. Dilworth Cannon, June 3, 1961 (div. 1972); children: Michael Quayle Cannon, Susan Radcliffe Cannon Antolin, Peter Bert Cannon. AB, Goucher Coll., Towson, Md., 1958; PhD, Washington U., St. Louis, 1962. Fellow Columbia U., NYC, 1962—64, Columbia U. Coll. Physicians and Surgeons, NYC, 1964—65; staff fellow Nat. Cancer Inst. NIH, Bethesda, Md., 1966—67; cell biologist Litton Bionetics, Inc., Kensington, Md., 1972—80, head immunology sect., 1980—85; dir. sci. ImmuQuest Labs., Inc., Rockville, Md., 1985—88; pres. Biomed. Analytics, Inc., Rockville, 1988—2001; mgr. ATLIS Fed. Svcs., Inc., Rockville, 1991—95, dir. Silver Spring, Md., 1995—97; sr. assoc. United Info. Sys., Inc., Bethesda, 1998—2000; ret., 2000. Mem. contract rev. coms. Nat. Cancer Inst., 1983-87 Contbr. articles to profl. jours Mem. Pub. Health Svcs. Club, Bethesda, 1984-2006, sec., 1990-2000. Grantee USPHS, 1959-65, NSF, 1959 Mem. AAAS, Am. Assn. Cancer Rsch., N.Y. Acad. Sci., Sigma Xi Home and Office: 1908 Nero Ct Walnut Creek CA 94598 Personal E-mail: gracecannon@astound.net.

CANNON, JOE LOUIS, retired orthodontist; b. Jan. 27, 1929; MS, DDS, U. Tenn., 1957. Pvt. practice orthodontist, Memphis, 1957—98; ret., 1998. Col. USAF, 1949—53, Korea. Decorated Purple Heart, Legion of Merit, DFC, Air Medal with three oak leaves. Home: 4834 Fleetview Ave Memphis TN 38117-3225

CANNON, JOHN, III, lawyer, insurance company executive; b. Phila., Mar. 19, 1954; s. John and Edythe (Grebe) Cannon. BA, Denison U., Granville, Ohio, 1976; JD, Dickinson Sch. Law, 1983. Bar: Pa. 1983, Hawaii 1986, US Dist. Ct. (ea. dist. Pa.) 1983, US Ct. Appeals (3rd cir.) 1985. Account exec. PRO Svcs., Inc., Flourtown, Pa., 1976-79, br. officer mgr. Pitts., 1979-80; law clk. Montgomery County Ct. Common Pleas, Norristown, Pa., 1983-84; assoc. Rawle & Henderson, Phila., 1984-88; comml. litig. counsel CIGNA Corp., Phila., 1988-90, sr. v.p. pub. affairs, assoc. gen. counsel, 2003—06, sr. v.p., dep. gen. counsel, 2006—; counsel fin. svcs. divsn. CIGNA Internat., Phila., 1990-93, sr. counsel, 1993-95, v.p., sr. counsel, 1995-97, sr. v.p., chief counsel, 1997-2000, CIGNA Healthcare, Bloomfield, Conn., 1999—2003, Conn. Gen. Life Ins. Co., Bloomfield, Conn., 1999—2003. Trustee US-China Legal Coop. Fund, Washington, 1998—. Comments editor Dickinson Internat. Law Ann., 1983. Pres. CIGNA Found., Phila., 2003—06. Mem. ABA, Pa. Bar Assn., Hawaii State Bar Assn., Greater Phila. C. of C. (bd. dirs. 2003), Kappa Sigma (pres. 1975-76), Gamma Xi (v.p., trustee 1982-86). Republican. Episcopalian. Office: CIGNA Corp Two Liberty Pl 1601 Chestnut St Philadelphia PA 19192-1550 Office Phone: 215-761-1000.

CANNON, KIM DECKER, lawyer; b. Salt Lake City, Oct. 15, 1948; s. Morris Nibley Cannon and Bette Jeanne (Decker) Sage; m. Jane B. Howard, June 10, 1972 (div. Sept. 1985); children: Sage, Meredith; m. Susan Margaret Clinch, Sept. 6, 1986; 1 child, Grace. AB, Dartmouth Coll., 1970; JD, U. Colo., 1974. Bar: Wyo. 1974, U.S. Dist. Ct. Wyo. 1974, U.S. Ct. Appeals (10th cir.) 1974. Ptnr. Burgess & Davis, Sheridan, Wyo., 1974-90, Burgess, Davis, Carmichael & Cannon, Sheridan and Cheyenne, Wyo., 1990-94, Davis & Cannon, Sheridan and Cheyenne, 1994—. Pres. Sheridan County Fulmer Pub. Librs., 1980-85, Wyo. Theater, Inc., Sheridan, 1986-91, Wyo. Outdoor Coun., Lander, 1987-91; chmn. Wyo. Environ. Quality Coun., 1992-96; mem.Commn. on Jud. Conduct and Ethics, 1997-2001, chair, 2001-03; chmn. Rhodes Scholarship Selection Com., Wyo., 1998-2005. Mem. Sheridan Bar Assn. (pres. 1982), Dartmouth Lawyers Assn. (v.p. 1998), Wyo. Trial Lawyers Assn. (bd. dirs.), Internat. Acad. Trial Lawyers. Avocations: polo, training horses, fly fishing, skiing. Home: PO Box 401 Big Horn WY 82833-0401 Office: Davis & Cannon 40 S Main St Sheridan WY 82801-4222 Home Phone: 307-672-8388; Office Phone: 307-672-7491. Business E-Mail: cannon@davisandcannon.com.

CANNON, L. KINDER, III, lawyer; b. Tallahassee, Oct. 19, 1942; BA, Duke U., 1964; JD, U. Fla., 1966. Bar: Fla. 1967. Gen. counsel Holland & Knight, Jacksonville, Fla. Exec. editor U. Fla. Law Review, 1966. Mem. ABA, Fla. Bar, Fla. Bar, Jacksonville Bar Assn., Fla. Bar Examiners (mem. 1990-95, chmn. 1995), Fla. Bar Grievance Com.; Fellow Am. Bar Found. Office: Holland & Knight LLP 50 N Laura St Ste 3900 Jacksonville FL 32202-3622 Office Phone: 904-798-5477. Business E-Mail: kinder.cannon@hklaw.com.

CANNON, LOUIS SIMEON, journalist, writer; b. NYC, June 3, 1933; s. Jack and Irene (Kohn) C.; m. Virginia Oprian, Feb. 2, 1953 (div. 1983); children: Carl, David, Judy, Jack; m. Mary L. Shinkwin, Sept. 7, 1985. Student, U. Nev., 1950-51, San Francisco State U., 1951-52. Reporter Lafayette Sun, Calif., 1957; editor Newark (Calif.) Sun, 1957-58, Merced Sun Star, Calif., 1958-60, Contra Costa Times, Calif., 1960-61, San Jose (Calif.) Mercury News, Calif., 1961-69; Sacramento corr. San Jose Mercury News, Calif., 1965-69; Washington corr. Ridder Pubs., Washington, 1969-72; reporter The Washington Post, 1972-96, spl. corr., 1997-99. Author: Ronnie and Jesse, 1969, The McCloskey Challenge, 1972, Reporting: An Inside View, 1977, Reagan, 1982, President Reagan: The Role of a Lifetime, 1991, rev. and updated 2000, Official Negligence: How Rodney King and the Riots Changed Los Angeles and the LAPD, 1998, The Presidential Portfolio: Ronald Reagan, 2001, Governor Reagan: His Rise to Power, 2003. Recipient Gerald R. Ford prize Gerald Ford Libr., 1988, Merriman Smith award White House Corrs. Assn., 1986, Aldo Beckman award, 1984, Washington Journalism Rev. award, 1985, Disting. Reporting of Pub. Affairs award Am. Polit. Sci. Assn., 1968, Lifetime Achievement award Ctr. for Calif. Studies at Calif. State U., Sacramento, 2001. Mem. Soc. of Profl. Journalists, Authors Guild. Home: PO Box 436 Summerland CA 93067-0436 Personal E-mail: cannonlou@hotmail.com.

CANNON, MARK WILCOX, retired government official; b. Salt Lake City, Aug. 29, 1928; s. Joseph Jenne and Ramona (Wilcox) C.; m. Ruth Marian Dixon, Dec. 28, 1956 (div. Jun. 1992); children: Lucile Cannon Critchley, Mark, Kristen Cannon Brown. m. Betty Ann Schomann, June 25, 1993. Student, Deep Springs Coll., 1944-46; BA, U. Utah, 1949; MA, Harvard U., 1954, MPA, 1955, PhD, 1961. Missionary Ch. Jesus Christ of Latter-Day Saints, Argentina, 1949-52; rsch. analyst Utah Found., 1953; sec. Utah Sch. Merit Study Com., 1954; instr. Brigham Young U., 1955, chmn. dept. polit. sci., 1961-64; mem. staff U.S. Senator W.F. Bennett, 1961, 62-63; adminstrv. asst. to U.S. congressman Henry A. Dixon, 1956-61; mem. staff Inst. Pub. Adminstrn., NYC, 1964-72, dir. urban devel. program Venezuela, 1964-65, dir. internat. programs NYC, 1965-68, dir., 1968-72; adminstrv. asst. to chief justice of U.S., 1972-85; staff dir. Commn. on Bicentennial of U.S. Constn., 1985-88; vice chmn., bd. dirs. Geneva Steel; exec. v.p. Geneva Devel., 1988-89; vice chair Cannon Industries, 1989-96. Venture capitalist, 1989—; guest scholar Woodrow Wilson Internat. Ctr. for Scholars, 1989. Author: (with R. Joseph Monsen) The Makers of Public Policy: American Power Groups and Their Ideologies, 1965; (with others) Partnership for Progress: Atlanta-Fulton County Consolidation, 1969, Urban Government for Valencia, 1973, Views From The Bench: The Judiciary and Constitutional Politics, 1985; contbg. author: Development Administration in Latin America, 1973; contbr. articles to profl. jour.; mem. editorial bd. Judicature, 1975-76. Trustee Inst. Pub. Adminstrn. Recipient ann. award Western Polit. Sci. Assn., 1963 Mem. Nat. Acad. Pub. Adminstrn., Internat. Studies Assn. (sec. 1962-63). Home: 8360 Greensboro Dr Apt 917 Mc Lean VA 22102-3543 E-mail: mwcannon@verizon.net. *Much of my motivation, orientation, and values stem from a conviction of the masterful leadership of a perfect personal God who is exemplary in His knowledge and utilization of eternal laws to promote the eternal progress and happiness of each human being, partially by providing a complicated earthly learning environment and by permitting people to deal freely with individual and social problems, thereby providing laboratory opportunities for the flourishing of character, knowledge, and wisdom.*

CANNON, MICHAEL R., computer company executive, former electronics executive; b. 1953; BA in Mech. Engring., Mich. State U.; attended, Harvard Bus. Sch. Various positions in engring. & mgmt. Boeing Co.; v.p. S.E. Asia ops. Imprimis Tech.; sr. v.p. Syquest Tech. Inc.; various positions including v.p. mobile & desktop bus. unit IBM, v.p. product design, v.p. worldwide ops.; pres., CEO Maxtor, 1996—2003, Solectron Corp., Milpitas, Calif., 2003—07; pres. global ops. Dell, Inc., Round Rock, Tex., 2007—. Bd. dirs. Maxtor Corp., 1996—2006, Adobe Systems, 2003—, Silicon Valley Mfg. Group. Office: Dell Inc 1 Dell Way Round Rock TX 78682-2222*

CANNON, PATRICK FRANCIS, public relations executive; b. Braddock, Pa., Mar. 2, 1938; s. Peter J. and Kathleen (Donnelly) C.; children by previous marriage: Patrick F. Jr., Elizabeth Kathleen; m. Jeanette Krema, Nov. 22, 1986. BA, Northwestern U., 1969. Ops. mgr. Compact Industries,

Albert Lea, Minn., 1968-72; pub. info. dir. Dept. Pub. Works, Chgo., 1970-72; acct. exec. Humes & Assocs., Chgo., 1972-77; freelance journalist, cons. Oak Park, Ill., 1977-79; mgr. pub. rels. and prodn. Lions Clubs Internat., Oak Brook, Ill., 1979-2001; pvt. comms. cons., writer, 2001—. Author: Hometown Architect--The Complete Buildings of Frank Lloyd Wright in Oak Park and River Forest, Illinois, 2006; editor: Water in Rural America, 1973, Wastewater in Rural America, 1974, We Serve: A History of the Lions Clubs, 1991; exec. prodr., writer (pub. TV documentaries) With Very Little.Blindness Prevention in Developing Countries, 1991, The Search for Light, 1993, A Dangerous Time for Kids, 1997; contbr. articles to profl. jours. and mags. Exec. dir. Civic Arts Coun. Oak Park, 1977-79; vol. svc. com. Frank Lloyd Wright Preservation Trust, 1988-94, pub. programs com., 1995-96, chmn. Wright Plus Housewalk, 1996, tour com., 2004—; bd. adv. U.S. Internat. Film and Video Festival; internat. bd. adv. World Media Festival. Named PR All Star 1996, Inside PR Mag.; recipient awards Publicity Club of Chgo., PRSA, Internat. Assn. of Bus. Comms., U.S. Film and Video Festival, others. Mem. Lions (pres. 1983-84). Roman Catholic. Avocations: history, horse racing. Home and Office: 243 Iowa St Oak Park IL 60302-2347 Office Phone: 708-383-0579. E-mail: patnette@comcast.net.

CANNON, ROBERT EUGENE, library director; b. Dec. 20, 1945; s. Wendell Eugene and Louise Marie (Bredehoeft) C.; m. Miriam Ruth Hillson, May 25, 1974; 1 child, Alexander. BA in Music, Calif. State U., LA, 1967; postgraduate student, Ariz. State U., 1967-68; MS in Libr. Sci., U. So. Calif., 1970; MPA, San Diego State U., 1978. Adult svcs. libr. Tucson Pub. Libr., 1969-70, Altadena Libr. Dist., 1970-71; head tech. processing, regional coord. San Diego County Libr., 1971-76; asst. dir. Tulare County Libr., Visalia, Calif., 1976-78; dir. Kern County Libr., Bakersfield, Calif., 1978-86; exec. dir. Pub. Libr. of Charlotte and Mecklenburg County, 1986—2003; dir. Broward County Libr., Ft. Lauderdale, Fla., 2003—; exec. bd. Southeast Libr. Info. Network, 2003—; bd. dirs. Broward County Libr. Found., 2003—. Bd. dirs. Mecklenburg County Law and Govt. Libr., Inc., 1992-2003; sec., treas. Pub. Libr. Charlotte and Mecklenburg County, 1986-2003; sec. Mus. New South, 1991-93, bd. dirs., 1991-97, pres.'s coun. Fla. Atlantic U., 2003—. Former mem. Leadership Charlotte; founder Novello Festival of Reading, 1991—2003, ProSearch Info. Svc., 1991—96, Internat. Bus. Libr., 1994—2003, Virtual Libr., 1995—2000, Virtual Village Comm. Ctr., 2000—03, BizLink, 1998—2003, Readers Club website, 1999—2003, StoryPlace, 2000—03, Brarydog.net, 1999—2003, BookHive, 1999—2003; co-founder Charlotte's Web, 1995—2000; bd. visitors Sch. Info. and Libr. Sci. U. NC, Chapel Hill; bd. visitors Johnson C. Smith U., 2002—03; mem. steering com. Charlotte Alliance Info. Referral Svcs., 1995—97; mem. Internat. Network Pub. Librs. Bertelsman Found., Germany, 1996—2003; mem. leadership group Charlotte Reads, 2001—03; mem. steering com. Leave a Legacy, 1998—2003; mem. Leadership Cir. United Way Ctrl. Carolinas, 1997—2003; co-founder Novello Festival Press, 2000—03, ImaginOn: The Joe and Joan Martin Ctr., 2003; founder ImginOn.org, 2003; bd. dirs. Smart Start of Charlotte Mecklenburg, 2000—03. Named NC Libr. Dir. of Yr., NC Pub. Libr. Dirs. Assn., 1995, Local Hero, Creative Loafing newspaper; recipient Pegasus award, Pub. Rels. Soc. Am., 1998, Bridge Builders award, Partnerships for Livable Cmtys., 2003. Mem. ALA, Fla. Libr. Assn., Charlotte/Mecklenburg Coalition for Literacy, 1988-89, Kern County Hist. Records Commn. (vice chmn. 1978-86), Southeastern Libr. Assn. (treas., chmn. conf. com. 1993-95), Mecklenburg Hist. Assn., Cultural Edn. Collaboration (bd. dirs. 1998-2000), Broward County Libr. Found. (exec. bd.), S.E. Libr. Info. Network (pres.). Office: Broward County Libr 100 S Andrews Ave Fort Lauderdale FL 33301-1830 Office Phone: 954-357-7377.*

CANNON, ROBERT HAMILTON, JR., aerospace engineering educator; b. Cleve., Oct. 6, 1923; s. Robert Hamilton and Catharine (Putnam) C.; m. Dorothea Alta Collins, Jan. 4, 1945 (dec. Apr. 1988); children: Philip Gregory, Douglas Charles, Beverly Jo, Frederick Scott. David John, Joseph Collins, James Robert; m. Vera Berlin Crie, May 27, 1989. BS, U. Rochester, 1944; Sc.D. (du Pont fellow), MIT, 1950. Rsch. engr. Baker Mfg. Co., Evansville, Wis., 1946-50; instr. MIT, 1949-50; research engr. Bendix Aviation Research Labs., Detroit, 1950-51; with Autonetics div. N.Am. Aviation Inc., Downey, Calif., 1951-57, supr. automatic flight control systems, 1951-54, systems engr. inertial nav. instruments and systems, 1954-57; assoc. prof. mech. engring. MIT, 1957-59; mem. faculty Stanford U., 1959-74, prof. aeros. and astronautics, 1962-74, founder Guidance and Control Lab., 1960—69; chief scientist USAF, 1966-68; asst. sec. U.S. Dept. Transp. Washington, 1970-74; chmn. div. engring. and applied sci. Calif. Inst. Tech., Pasadena, 1974-79; Charles Lee Powell prof. aeronautics and astronautics Stanford U., 1979—, chmn. dept., 1979-90, founder aerospace robotics lab., 1980—97, dir. emeritus, 1997—; chmn. sci. adv. com. to CEO GM, 1979-84. Mem. Draper Corp., 1975—; vice chmn. sci. adv. bd. USAF, 1968-70; chmn. assembly engring. NRC, 1974-75, chmn. energy engring. bd., 1975-81, mem. com. on nuc. and alt. energy sources, 1975-78, aeros. and space engring. bd., 1975-79, 1985-92, governing bd., 1976-78, commn. underwater vehicles, ocean studies bd., 1991-94; chmn. Gen. Electric Space Sta. Adv. Bd., 1985-87; chmn. Pres.'s Com. on Nat. Medal of Sci., 1984-88; chmn. NASA Flight Telerobotic Servicer Commn., 1987-91; tech. adv. coun. Boeing Corp., 1984-94, R.R. Donnelley, 1984-89, Comsat, 1985-87, United Techs. Corp., 1989-92. Author: Dynamics of Physical Systems, 1967; also articles. Served to lt. (j.g.) USNR, 1944-46. Fellow AIAA (dir. 1968-70), Am. Acad. Arts and Scis., Internat. Acad. Astronautics; mem. Nat. Acad. Engring. (councillor 1975-81), Sigma Xi, Theta Chi (chpt. pres. 1943-44), Tau Beta Pi. Achievements include development of hydrofoil boats, automatic flight control, inertial guidance instruments and systems, space vehicle control, drag-free satellite; co-founder of Einstein experiment gravity probe b gyro test of gen. relativity in orbiting satellite; technical assessment of climatic impact of stratospheric flight; research in wave-actuated upwelling pump, flexible-robot and space-robot control systems, autonomous underwater robots and automonous task-commanded helicopters. Office: Stanford U Dept Aeronautics & Astronautics Durand Bldg Rm 356 Stanford CA 94305-8468

CANO, MARGARITA, artist, consultant, retired librarian; b. Havana, Cuba, Feb. 27, 1932; arrived in US, 1962; d. Rafael Fernandez Ruenes and Margarita Villaurrutia Suarez; m. Pablo Cano, Oct. 6, 1952; children: Isabel, Pablo. D in Physics and Chemistry, U. Havana, Cuba, 1956, MLS, 1961. Libr. Miami Dad Pub. Libr., Fla., dir. cmty. rels.; ret., 1999. Bd. dirs. Friends of Libr., Miami, Cintas Found., NYC. Democrat. Roman Catholic. Home: 501 SW 24th Ave Miami FL 33135-2933

CANO, MARIO STEPHEN, lawyer; b. Miami, Fla., Sept. 2, 1953; s. Mario Arturo Cano and Irene H. Moreno; m. Johanna Marie Van Rossum, Oct. 13, 1979. AA, Miami Dade Jr. Coll., 1973; BA, Fla. Internat. U., 1975; JD, U. Santa Clara, 1978. Bar: Fla. 1979, US Dist. Ct. (so. dist.) Fla. 1979, US Ct. Claims 1979, US Tax Ct. 1979, US Ct. Mil. Appeals 1979, US Ct. Appeals (9th cir.) 1979, US Dist. Ct. (no. and mid. dists.) Fla. 1980, US Dist. Ct. (no. dist.) Calif. 1980, US Ct. Appeals (3d cir.) 1980, US Ct. Internat. Trade 1981, US Ct. Appeals (11th cir.) 1981, US Ct. Appeals (6th and 10th cirs.) 1983, US Supreme Ct. 1983, Nebr. 1984, US Dist. Ct. Nebr. 1984, US Dist. Ct. (no. dist.) Okla. 1984, US Dist. Ct. Hawaii 1984, US Ct. Appeals (2d, 4th, 5th, 7th 8th and DC cirs.) 1984, NY 1985, US Dist. Ct. (no., we., ea. and so. dists.) NY 1985, US Ct. Appeals (1st cir.) 1987, US Dist. Ct. (no. and so. dist.) Tex. 1988, US Dist. Ct. (ea. dist.) Wis. 1988, US Dist. Ct. (we. dist.) Pa. 1988, US Dist. Ct. (no. dist.) Ill. 1991, Mass., 1998, US Dist. Ct. Mass. 1999. Assoc. Orta and Assocs., Miami, 1979-80, Law Office of J. Ramirez, Coral Gables, Fla., 1980, Law Office of I.G. Lichter, Miami, 1980-82, Gelb & Spatz, Miami, 1982; pvt. practice Coral Gables, 1982—. Mem.: Am. Immigration Lawyers Assn., Cuban Am. Bar Assn. Democrat. Office: 2121 Ponce De Leon Blvd Ste 950 Coral Gables FL 33134-5217 Office Phone: 305-442-2121. Office Fax: 305-567-0423. Business E-Mail: mcano@canolawmiami.com.

CANO, ROBINSON JOSE, professional baseball player; b. San Pedro de Macoris, Dominican Republic, Oct. 22, 1982; s. Jose Cano and Claribel Mercedes. Second baseman NY Yankees, 2005—. Named to Am. League All-Star Team, 2006; recipient Silver Slugger award, 2006. Achievements include having a 13 game hitting streak in 2005, the longest hitting streak by an American League rookie that season; concluding the 2006 season with a 13 game hitting streak, the longest hitting streak to conclude a season by a Yankee since Reggie Jackson in 1980. Mailing: Yankee Stadium 161st St and River Ave Bronx NY 10451 Office Phone: 718-293-4300.*

CANONERO, MILENA, costume designer; b. Turin, Italy; m. Marshall Bell. Costume designer: (films) A Clockwork Orange, 1971, (with Ulla-Britt Soderlund) Barry Lyndon, 1975 (Academy award best costume design 1975), Midnight Express, 1978, The Shining, 1980, Chariots of Fire, 1981 (Academy award best costume design 1981, British Academy award best costume design 1982), The Hunger, 1983, The Cotton Club, 1984, Give My Regards to Broad Street, 1984, Out of Africa, 1985 (Academy award nomination best costume design 1985, British Academy award nomination best costume design 1986), Haunted Summer, 1988, Tucker: The Man and His Dream, 1988 (Academy award nomination best costume design 1988), Dick Tracy, 1990 (Academy award nomination best costume design 1990), The Godfather, Part III, 1990, Damage, 1992, (with Elisabetta Beraldo) Camilla, 1993, The Love Affair, 1994, Death and the Maiden, 1994, Bullworth, 1998, Titus, 1999, The Affair of the Necklace, 2001, Solaris, 2002, The Life Aquatic, 2004, Oceans Twelve, 2004, Marie Antoinette, 2006 (Academy award, Best Costume Design, 2007), (TV series) Miami Vice, 1986-89; costume designer, visual cons.: (films) Barfly, 1987; assoc. prodr.: (films) Good Morning Babylon, 1987, Mamba, 1988; costume design cons.: (films) Lost Angels, 1989, Reversal of Fortune, 1990. Recipient Coty Am. Fashion Critics' award 1984, Career Achievement award in Film from Costume Designers Guild, 2001. Office: care Marc H Glick Glick and Weintraub 1501 Broadway New York NY 10036-5601*

CANONI, JOHN DAVID, lawyer; b. Newton, Mass., May 11, 1939; s. John Joseph and Olga Elizabeth (Mangini) C.; m. Katherine Ariadna Bryant, Aug. 18, 1962; children: Lisa Ann, Peter Christopher, John Charles, Scott Francis. BA cum laude, Amherst Coll., 1960; LLB, Yale U., 1963. Bar: NY 1964, U.S. Ct. Appeals (2d cir.) 1966, US Ct. Appeals (3d cir.) 1967, US Ct. Appeals (4th cir.) 1968, US Ct. Appeals (1st cir.) 1969, US Supreme Ct. 1971, US Ct. Appeals (7th cir.) 1972. Assoc. Townley & Updike, NYC, 1963-71, ptnr., 1971-95, Nixon Peabody LLP, NYC, 1995—. Mem. Lt. Gov.'s Task Force on Plant Closings, NY, 1984-85. Mem. ABA, NY State Bar Assn. (chmn. labor & employment law sect. 1983-84), CPR Inst. Dispute Resolution, Yale Club. Republican. Roman Catholic. Home: 20 High Meadows Mount Kisco NY 10549-3847 Office: Nixon Peabody LLP 437 Madison Ave New York NY 10022-7001 Home Phone: 914-666-4177; Office Phone: 212-940-3169. Office Fax: 866-947-2320. Personal E-mail: jcanoni@aol.com.

CANSECO, JOSE, retired professional baseball player; b. Havana, Cuba, July 2, 1964; m. Esther Haddad (div. 1991); m. Jessica Sekely (div. 1999). With Oakland (Calif.) Athletics, 1982—92, 1997, Tex. Rangers, 1992-94, Boston Red Sox, 1994-96, Toronto Bluejays, 1998, Tampa Bay Devil Rays, 1999—2000, NY Yankees, 2000, Chgo. White Sox, 2001, San Diego Surf Dogs Amateur Baseball Team. Appeared in instructional video, Jose Canseco's Baseball Camp, 1989; author: Juiced: Wild Times, Rampant 'Roids, Smash Hits and How Baseball Got Big, 2005. Named Am. League Rookie of the Yr., 1986, Am. League Most Valuable Player, 1988; named to Am. League All-Star team, 1986, 1988—90, 1999; recipient Am. League Silver Slugger Award, 1988, 1990—91, 1998. Mem. Am. League All-Star Team, 1986, 88, 89, 90, 92. Achievements include being first player to have 40 home runs and 40 stolen bases in same season, 1988; member of World Series Champion, Oakland Athletics, 1989, New York Yankees, 2000; led American League in Home Runs (42), 1988, (44), 1991, RBI's (124), 1988. Office: Regan Books HarperCollins 10 E 53rd St New York NY 10022

CANSEV, MEHMET, physician, researcher; b. Denizli, Turkey, Nov. 19, 1975; s. Suleyman and Saide Cansev; m. Asuman Uslu, Oct. 4, 2003; 1 child, Zeynep. MD, Uludag U., Bursa, Turkey, 1999, PhD, 2003. Postdoctoral fellow MIT, Cambridge, 2004—. Achievements include research in finding treatments that help prevent neurodegenerative diseases. Office: MIT 43 Vassar St 46-5027 Cambridge MA 02139 Office Phone: 617-253-8371. Business E-Mail: mcansev@mit.edu.

CANSLER, LESLIE ERVIN, retired newspaper editor; b. Hickory, NC, Sept. 16, 1920; s. Leslie Ervin and Mabel Pearl (Braswell) C.; m. Marie Muriel Olwell, Aug. 19, 1944 (dec.); children: David, Robert, James.; m. Elizabeth Marie Walters (dec.); 1 child, Leslie Anne. BA, Wake Forest U., 1941. News editor Daily Advance, Elizabeth City, N.C., 1941; reporter Raleigh (N.C.) Times, 1941-42, 46, city editor, 1946-47; with News-Jour. Co., Wilmington, Del., 1947-88, day mng. editor, 1966-68, mng. editor, 1968-76, assoc. Sunday editor, 1976-79, Sunday editor, 1979-80, assoc. editor, 1980-89. Served with USNR, 1942-45. Mem. Sigma Phi Epsilon. Republican. Episcopalian. Home: 11 Bristol Way New Castle DE 19720-3906

CANTARELLA, PAOLO, former automotive executive; b. Vercelli, Italy, 1944; Grad., Turin Polytechnic. With Fiat S.p.A, Turin, Italy, 1977—2002, asst. to the CEO, 1980—83; mng. dir., Comau, 1983; dir., supply & distribution Fiat Auto, 1989—90, gen. mgr., 1990, CEO, 1990—96; pres., CEO Fiat S.p.A., Turin, Italy, 1996—2002. Pres. European Automobile Mfrs. Assn., 2000; bd. dirs. Polaroid Group, 2003—. Office: Polaroid Corp Corp Hdqts 1265 Main St Bldg W3 Waltham MA 02451

CANTELON, PHILIP LOUIS, historian; b. Ft. Wayne, Ind., Nov. 7, 1940; s. Philip Eccles and Marie (Gehrke) C.; m. Eileen S. McGuckian, Feb. 14, 1989. AB, Dartmouth Coll., 1962; MA, U. Mich., 1963; PhD, Ind. U., 1971. Asst. prof. Williams Coll., Williamstown, Mass., 1968-77; Fulbright prof. Kyushu Nat. U./Seinan Gakuin U., Fukuoka, Japan, 1978-79; pres., CEO, History Assocs. Inc., Rockville, Md., 1980—. Adj. prof. Cath. U., 2002; exec. sec. Nat. Coun. Pub. History, Washington, 1979-81; sec.-treas. Soc. History in Fed. Govt., Washington, 1979-80, pres., 1995-96; chmn. Montgomery County Hist. Preservation Commn., 1985-91; pres. Montgomery County Hist. Soc., Rockville, 1991-95, Peerless Rockville Historic Preservation, Ltd., 1996-2002. Author: Crisis Contained, 1980, The History of MCI, 1993, The Roadway Story, 1996, Never Stand Still: The History of Consolidated Freightways and CNF Transportation Inc., 1999, The History of Mere Point: 1878-2003, 2003; editor: The American Atom, 1989, Corporate Archives and History, 1993. Trustee Am. U. of Rome, 2005—. Recipient Franklin D. Roosevelt award, Soc. for History of Fed. Govt., 2004. Mem.: Oral History Assn., Orgn Am. Historians (chmn. com. on rsch. and access to his. documentations 1999), Cosmos Club (admissions com. 1993—94, chair, bd. mgmt. 1995—99, v.p. 1999—2000, pres. 2000—01, bd. mgmt. 2001—02, awards com. chair 2005—). Home: 11807 Dinwiddie Dr Rockville MD 20852-4459 Office: History Assocs Inc 300 N Stonestreet Ave Rockville MD 20850 E-mail: pcantelon@historyassociates.com.

CANTER, CHARLES W. (NICK), retail executive; With Lowe's Cos., Inc., 1974—, regional v.p., store ops., 1993—98, v.p., merchandising-millwork, 1998, sr. v.p. and gen. mdse. mgr., bldg. materials, 1998—99, sr. v.p., store ops.-no. divsn., 1999—2005, exec. v.p. store ops., 2005—06, exec. v.p. merchandising, 2006—. Office: Lowes Cos Inc 1605 Curtis Bridge Rd Wilkesboro NC 28697*

CANTERBURY-COUNTS, W. DOUGLAS, psychologist; b. Lancaster, Pa. s. William L. Jr. and Marion E. (Winters) Counts; m. Belinda Jaya Canterbury, Mar. 12, 1977; 1 child, William Andrew Hanuman. BA, So. Calif. Coll., 1979; MDiv, Ea. Bapt. Theol. Sem., 1983; PhD, Temple U., 1989. Pvt. practice roofing contractor, Calif. & Pa., 1976-88; counselor Pathways Counseling Svc., Swarthmore, Pa., 1985-86; psychotherapist, clin. coord. dept. medicine Temple U., Phila., 1985-88; pvt. practice clin. psychologist Lake Worth and Sebastian, Fla., 1989—. Lectr. Temple U., Coll. Edn., Phila., 1983-86; adj. prof. Fla. Atlantic U., Boca Raton, 1990—; cons. Goodwill Industries, Inc., West Palm Beach, Fla., 1995—, River Sch., Sebastian, 1995—; founder, dir. Ctr. for Sacred Psychology, 1992. Contbr. articles to profl. jours. County del. Delaware County Crisis Intervention and Suicide Prevention, Media, Pa., 1981-83; chairperson bereavement com. Fla. chpt. NAMES Project AIDS Meml. Quilt, Sebastian, 1997—; bd. dirs. River Fund, Sebastian, 1997—; mem. Coun. Interfaith Call, World Tibet Day Found. Sgt. USMC, 1969-75. Mem. APA, Nat. Acad. Neuropsychology, Fla. Psychol. Assn., Ctr. for Jungian Studies SE Fla, Inc. (v.p. 1990-96). Democrat. Avocations: t'ai chi ch'uan, advocacy, camping, white water rafting. Office Phone: 772-569-2239. E-mail: sacredpsyc@aol.com.

CANTERO, RAOUL G., III, state supreme court justice; b. Madrid, Aug. 1, 1960; m. Ana Maria Cantero; 3 children. BA in English and Bus., Fla. State U.; JD cum laude, Harvard U. Bd. cert. in appellate practice:. Law clk. to Hon. Edward B. Davis U.S. Dist. Ct. (so. dist.) Fla.; shareholder, head appellate divsn. Adorno & Yoss, Miami; justice Fla. Supreme Ct., Tallahassee, 2002—. Lectr. in field. Contbr. articles to legal jours., short stories to anthologies; author: Non-Final Review of Insurance Coverage Issues: Wading through the Quagmire, 1995, Changes to the Florida Rules of Appellate Procedure, 1997, Discovery from Medical Experts: How Much is Too Much?, 1997, Certifying Questions to the Florida Supreme Court: What's So Important?, 2002. Mem. planning and zoning bd. City of Coral Gables, 1993—2001; mem. pastoral coun. St. Augustine Ch., 1990—97, chmn., 1997—2001, head Men's Retreat Ministry, 1994—2000; bd. dirs. Legal Svcs. of Greater Miami, Inc., 1991—95. Mem.: Dade County Bar Assn. (mem. appellate ct. com. 1998—99), Fla. Bar Assn. (mem. appellate rules com. 1993, sec. 1997—99, treas. appellate practice sect. 1999—2000, vice-chair 2001—02, sec. appellate practice sect. 2000—01, mem. 11th jud. cir. jud. nominating commn. 2001—02). Office: Fla Supreme Ct 500 S Duval St Tallahassee FL 32399*

CANTIE, JOSEPH S., automotive executive; BS in Bus. Adminstrn. and Acctg., SUNY, Buffalo, 1985. CPA. Acct. KPMG Peat Marwick, 1985—95; mgr. fin. and bus. analysis Lucas Varity (U.K.), 1995, v.p., corp. contr., 1998—99; v.p. investor rels. TRW, Inc., 1999—2001, v.p. fin., 2001—02; v.p., CFO TRW Automotive, Livonia, Mich., 2002—04, exec. v.p., CFO, 2004—. Adj. prof. acctg. SUNY, Buffalo, 1993—95. Mem.: AICPA. Office: TRW Automotive 12025 Tech Center Dr Livonia MI 48150*

CANTILLI, EDMUND JOSEPH, safety engineer, educator, translator, writer, consultant; b. Yonkers, NY, Feb. 12, 1927; s. Ettore and Maria (deRubeis) C.; m. Nella Franco, May 15, 1948; children: Robert, John, Teresa. AB, Columbia U., 1954, BS, 1955; cert., Yale Bur. Hwy. Traffic, 1957; PhD in Transp. Planning and Engring., Poly. Inst. Bklyn., 1972; postgrad. in urban planning and pub. safety, NYU, 1968-71. Registered profl. engr., N.Y., N.J., Calif.; profl. planner, N.J.; bd. cert. safe ty profl. (BCSP); bd. cert. planner (AICP); bd. cert. forensic engr. (BCFE). Supervising engr. safety rsch. and studies Port Authority of N.Y. & N.J., 1955-69; prof. transp. and safety engring. Poly. U., NYC, 1969-90, prof. emeritus, 1990—; pres. Urbitran Assocs., 1973-81; exec. dir., chmn. bd. Internat. Inst. for Safety Trans., Inc., 1977—; pres. EJC Safety Assocs., Inc., 1989—95. Tchr. Italian, algebra, traffic engring., urban planning, transp. planning, urban and transp. geography, land use planning, aesthetics, environment, indsl., traffic and transp. safety engring., human factors engring., ethics for engrs.; cons. transp. and traffic safety engring., community planning, traffic engring., transp. planning, accident reconstrn., environ. impacts, 1969—; vis. prof. transp. safety engring. Inst. Superior Técnico, Lisbon, 1987-97; advisor to doctorate students Poly. U., CUNY, 1969-94, Politecnico di Milano, U. Trieste, Italy, 1980-98; consulting forensic engr., accident reconstructionist, expert witness transp. accident litigation including hwy. traffic, railroad, rail rapid transit, pedestrian accidents, 1969—. Translator (Italian-English autobiog. Joseph Tusiani): The Difficult Word; The New Word; The Ancient Word, 1988; author: Programming Environmental Improvements in Public Transportation, 1974, Transportation and the Disadvantaged, 1974, Transportation System Safety, 1979; editor: Transportation and Aging, 1971, Pedestrian Planning and Design, 1971; editor, contbr.: Traffic Engineering Theory and Control, 1973; editor and calligrapher There Is No Death That Is Not Ennobled by So Great A Cause, 1976; contbr. over 200 articles to profl. jours. and trade jours.; developer daylight running lights, methods of severity evaluation of accidents, identification, priority-setting and treatment of roadside hazards, transp. system safety methodology; expert systems for improving traffic safety; introduced diagrammatic traffic signs, collision energy-absorption devices. With U.S. Army, 1945-49, 50-51. Fellow ASCE, Inst. Transp. Engrs., Nat. Acad. Forensic Engrs.; mem. NSPE, Am. Planning Assn. (charter), Am. Inst. Cert. Planners (cert.), Am. Soc. Safety Engrs., N.Y. Acad. Scis., Nat. Assn. Profl. Accident Reconstrn. Specialists, Internat. Assn. for Accidents and Traffic Medicine, Human Factors Soc., N.Y. Acad. Scis., System Safety Soc., Sigma Xi. Home: 134 Euston Rd West Hempstead NY 11552-1024 Office: PO Box 63 Franklin Square NY 11010-0063 E-mail: ejcsafety@aol.com, insafetran@aol.com, cantoxxv@aol.com.

CANTLIFFE, DANIEL JAMES, horticulture educator; b. NYC, Oct. 31, 1943; s. Sarah Lucretia Keesler C.; m. Elizabeth F. Lapetina, June 5, 1965; children: Christine, Deanna, Danielle, Cheri. BS, Delaware Valley Coll., Doylestown Pa., 1965; MS, Purdue U., West Lafayette, 1967, PhD, 1971. Asst. prof. horticulture U. Fla., Gainesville, 1974-76, assoc. prof., 1976-81, prof., 1981—2007, asst. chair dept., 1983-84, acting chair dept., 1984-85, chmn. dept., 1985-92, acting chair dept. fruit crops, 1991-92, chair dept. hort. scis., 1992—, prof. rsch. found., 2005, disting. prof., 2007—. Vis. prof. U. Hawaii, Honolulu, 1979-80; sci. cons. Sun Seeds Genetics, Hollister, Calif., 1987, Pillsbury Co., 1987—, Teltech Inc., Bloomington, Minn., 1988—, DNAP, Monsanto, Seed Dynamics, Ball Seed Co., Sybron Chem., Dow Agro Scis. Contbr. articles to profl. jours. and conf. procs., chpts. to books. Recipient rsch. award Fla. Fruit and Vegetable Assn., Orlando, 1986, Alumni Achievement award Delaware Valley Coll., Doylestown, 1990, Distinguished Agrl. Alumni award Purdue Univ., 1999, Group Hon. award USDA, 1997; fellow U. Fla., 2005, named Disting. Internat. Educator, 2005. Fellow: Crop Sci. Soc. Am. (pres. 1991—92, Seed Sci. award 1997), Am. Soc. Hort. Sci. (v.p. hort. sci. 1991—92, pres.-elect 1993—94, pres. 1994—95, chmn. 1995—96, mem. outstanding rsch. award selection com. 2003—06, chair outstanding rsch. award selection com. 2006, task force on the future hort. sci. 2004—, Outstanding Grad. Educator award 1991, Best Paper Vegetable Sect. 1992, Membership Recruitment award 1996, Outstanding Rsch. award 1997, vegetable publ. award 1997, So. Region Leadership and Adminstrn. award 2000); mem.: Inst. Food and Agrl. Scis., Plasticulture Soc. Am., N. Am. Strawberry

Growers Assn., Bot. Soc. Am., Internat. Soc. Tropical Horticulture, Fla. State Hort. Soc. (hon.; v.p. vegetable sect. 1984—85, pres. 1991—92, chmn. exec. com. 1992—93, best paper vegetable sect. 1991, 1993, profl. execellence program award 1996, best paper vegetable sect. 1999, 2001, 2002, 2004, best paper garden and landscape sect. 2005, Profl. Excellence Program award 1996), Am. Soc. Agronomy, Am. Soc. Plant Physiologists, Internat. Soc. Horticulture, Fla. Seed Assn., Crop Sci. Soc. Am., Internat. Soc. Hort. Sci. (chair sect. of vegetables 1998—, veg sect. chair 2002—06, coun. rep., nominations and award com. 2003—), Phi Beta Delta, Gamma Sigma Delta (Disting. Leadership award 2003, Dist. Svc. Agr. award 2005), Phi Kappa Phi, Delta Tau Alpha, Sigma Xi. Office: U of Fla Hort Scis Dept PO Box 110690 1251 Fifield Hall Gainesville FL 32611-0690 Office Phone: 352-392-1928 x203. Business E-Mail: djcant@ufl.edu.

CANTOR, ALAN BRUCE, management consultant, application developer; b. Mt. Vernon, NY, Apr. 30, 1948; s. Howard and Muriel Anita C.; 1 child, Alec Brandon. BS in Social Scis., Cornell U., 1970; MBA, U. Pa., 1973. Mgmt. cons. M & M Risks Mgmt. Svcs., NYC, 1974-78; nat. svcs. officer spl. projects divsn. Marsh & McLennan Risk Mgmt. Svcs., LA, 1980-81; sr. v.p. sr. cons. prin. Warren, Mc Veigh & Griffin, Inc., 1981-82; founder, pres. Cantor & Co., 1982—; ptnr. BDE Entertainment, 2006—; ptnr., prodr. DeBrino/Cantor Entertainment, 2007—. Co-mgr. Air Travel Rsch. Group, NYC, 1977-79; instr. risk mgmt. program Am. Mgmt. Assn.,; lectr. Risk and Inst. Mgmt. Soc. Conf., 1975-87, Med. Edn. Spkrs. Bur. So. Calif., 1990—; seminars How to Use Spreadsheets in Risk Mgmt., 1986-89, How to Use Computers in Risk Mgmt., 1989-93. Contbr. articles to profl. jours. Cons., vol. Urban Cons. Group, N.Y.C.; elder Beverly Hills Presbyn. Ch., 1991—; co-project dir. East European Orphans Toy Ministry, 1999—2000. Mem. Cornell Alumni Assn. N.Y.C. (bd. govs., program chmn.), Cornell Alumni Assn. So. Calif., Wharton Bus. Sch. Club (N.Y.C., chmn., mem. adv. com. L.A.), L.A. Athletic. Achievements include design of airline industry model; development of Riskmap risk mgmt. software products; Riskmap Windows version, Exposure Base Mgmt. Sys., patient care monitoring sys., Med. Quality Mgmt. Sys. Plus, Med. Quality Mgmt. Sys. Plus Windows version, MQMS Plus; Qualworx; patents for risk financing simulation model. Office: Cantor & Co 9100 Wilshire Blvd Beverly Hills CA 90212-3415 Office Phone: 310-859-7277. Business E-Mail: acantor@cantorandco.com.

CANTOR, BERNARD JACK, lawyer; b. NYC, Aug. 18, 1927; s. Alexander J. and Tillie (Henzeloff) Cantor; m. Judith L. Levin, Mar. 25, 1951; children: Glenn H., Cliff A., James E., Ellen B., Mark E. BME, Cornell U., 1949; JD, George Washington U., 1952. Bar: DC 1952, U.S. Patent Office 1952, Mich. 1952, registered: U.S. (patent atty.), Can. Examiner U.S. Patent Office, Washington, 1949-52; pvt. practice Detroit, 1952-88; ptnr. firm Harness, Dickey & Pierce, Troy, Mich., 1988—. Lectr. in field. Contbr. articles to profl. jours. Mem. nat. bd. govs. Am. Jewish Com.; mem. exec. coun. Detroit area Boy Scouts Am., 1972—. With US Army, 1944—46. Recipient Ellsworth award patent law, George Washington U., 1952, Shofar award, Boy Scouts Am., 1975, Silver Beaver award, 1975, Disting. Eagle award, 1985. Fellow: Mich. State Bar Found.; mem.: ABA, Am. Technion Soc. (nat. bd. regents), Cornell Engring. Soc., Am. Arbitration Assn. (arbitrator), Am. Intellectual Property Law Assn., Mich. Patent Law Assn., Oakland Bar Assn., Detroit Bar Assn., Mich. Bar Assn. (dir. econs. sect., arbitrator State of Mich. grievance com.), Beta Sigma Rho, Phi Delta Phi, Pi Tau Sigma. Home: 5685 Forman Dr Bloomfield Hills MI 48301-1154 Office: Harness Dickey & Pierce 5445 Corporate Dr Troy MI 48098-2683 Home Phone: 248-626-5259; Office Phone: 248-641-1600. Personal E-mail: bjcantor@aol.com. Business E-Mail: cantor@hdp.com.

CANTOR, CHARLES ROBERT, biochemistry professor; b. Bklyn., Aug. 26, 1942; s. Louis and Ida Dianne (Banks) C. AB summa cum laude, Columbia U., 1963; PhD, U. Calif., Berkeley, 1966. Asst. prof. chemistry Columbia U., NYC, 1966-69, assoc. prof. chemistry and biol. scis., 1969-72, prof., 1972-81, prof., chmn. genetics and devel., dep. dir. Comprehensive Cancer Ctr. Coll. Physicians and Surgeons, 1981-89; dir. Human Genome Ctr. Lawrence Berkeley Lab. 1988-90; prof. molecular biology U. Calif., Berkeley, 1989-92; prof. biomed. engring. Boston U., 1992—, chmn., 1994-98, dir. Ctr. for Advanced Biotech., 1992—, prof. pharmacology, 1995—; prin. scientist human genome project Dept. Energy, 1990-92; chief sci. officer Sequenom, Inc., 1998—; also bd. dirs., 2000—. Sherman Fairchild vis. scholar Calif. Inst. Tech., 1975-76; mem. biophysics and biophys. chemistry study sect. NIH, 1971-75; mem. cell and molecular basis of disease rev. com. Nat. Inst. Gen. Med. Scis., 1977-81, coun. mem., 1986-89; mem. ozone update com. NRC, 1983, mem. rsch. opportunities in biology com., 1985-89, com. on the human genome, 1986-89, com. on bits of power, 1995-96; trustee Cold Spring Harbor Lab., 1977-83; mem. proposal rev. panel Stanford Sychrotron Radiation Lab., 1976-88; mem. U.S. Nat. Commn., Internat. Union Pure & Applied Biophysics, 1986-94, vice chmn., 1988-91, chmn., 1991-94; sci. adv. bd. Hereditary Disease Found., 1987-89; mem. coun. Human Genome Orgn., 1989-92, v.p. 1990-92, pres. America's, 1991-98; chmn. Department of Energy Human Genome Coordinating com., 1989-92; adv. com. Searle Scholars program, 1987-93, chair, 1993-94, mem. adv. com. program in parasite biology MacArthur Found., 1990-93; mem. sci. adv. coun. Roswell Park Cancer Inst. 1992-98; sci. adv. com. European Molecular Biology Lab., 1989-94; bd. sci. counselors Nat. Ctr. for Biotechnology Info., Nat. Libr. Medicine, 1990-95; cons. Incyte Pharm. Inc., 1992-98, Genelabs, Inc., 1988-, Samsung Advanced Inst. Tech., 2000-; mem. coun. Internat. Union Pure and Applied Biophysics, 1993-99; vis. com. biology Brookhaven Nat. Lab., 1986-89; bd. dirs. and chair sci. adv. com. Avitech Diagnostics, Inc. (formerly ATGC Inc.), 1992-1997; mem. nomenclature com. IUBMB, 1989-; chair adv. com. European Bioinformatics Inst., 1993-94; mem. USDA Genome Adv. Com., 1992-98; co-chair biotech. adv. coun. Fisher Sci., 1994—; mem. biology adv. com. Lawrence Livermore Nat. Lab., 1995-, chair 2000-04; chair sci. adv. com. Sequenom, Inc., Sequenom Instruments GmbH, 1995-, mem. sci. adv. com., Aclara, Inc., 1996-2003, Caliper, Inc., 1996-; bd. dirs. ExSar, Inc. (formerly Carta, Inc., formerly Thermaphore, Inc.), 1999-2004, SIGA Inc. (formerly Plexus Inc.), The Molecular Scis. Inst., Selectxpharmaceuticals, 2003-2004(chair sci adv. bd., 2003-); mem. sci. adv. com., Odyssey Inc., 2002-; pres. Biochemist, Inc., 2001-2002; mem. FASEB consensus conf. on fed. funding, 1995-2000; quest scholar Quest Diagnostics, Inc., 1997-99; mem. biotech. coun. Dept. of Energy, 1996-99; mem. unconventional pathogen countermeasures adv. com. DARPA (Def. Advanced Projects Rsch. Agy., 1996-2000; mem. adv. com. Uppsala Bio-X, 2004-06; adj. prof. biomed. engring., U. Calif., San Diego, 2002—. Author: (with Paul R. Schimmel) Biophysical Chemistry, I, II, III, (with Cassandra L. Smith) Genomics; assoc. editor Ann. Rev. Biophysics, 1983-93. Trustee Assoc. Univs. Inc., 1999-2000; bd. dirs. Keystone Confs., 1999-2006. Recipient Fresenius award Phi Lambda Upsilon, 1972; Eli Lilly award in biol. chemistry Am. Chem. Soc., 1978; Alfred P. Sloan fellow, 1969-71; Guggenheim fellow, 1973-74; Nat. Cancer Inst. outstanding investigator grantee, 1985, Analytica prize, 1988; ISCO prize, 1989, Sober prize ASBMB, 1990. Fellow AAAS, Biophys. Soc. (mem. coun. 1977-81, Emily Gray prize 2000, fellow 2000); mem. Am. Acad. Arts and Scis., NAS, Am. Soc. Biol. Chemists, Am. Chem. Soc., Soc. Analytical Cytology, Harvey Soc., Am. Soc. Human Genetics, Biomed. Engring. Soc., Japanese Biochem. Soc. (hon.). Home: 526 Stratford Ct Apt E Del Mar CA 92014-2767 Office: Sequenom Inc 3595 John Hopkins Ct San Diego CA 92121 Office Phone: 858-202-9012. E-mail: ccantor@sequenom.com.

CANTOR, ERIC I., congressman, lawyer; b. Richmond, Va., June 6, 1963; m. Diana Marcy Fine; children: Evan, Jenna, Michael. BA, George Washington U., 1985; JD, Coll. William & Mary, Williamsburg, Va., 1988; MS, Columbia U., NYC, 1989. Mem. Va. State Ho. Dels., 1992-2001, co-chair claims com., 1992-2001, mem. cts. of justice, 1992-2001, mem. gen. laws com., 1992-2001, mem. corp. ins. & banking com., 1992-2001, mem. sci. & tech. com., 2000-2001; mem. US Congress from 7th Va. dist., 2001—, chief dep. majority whip, 2002—, mem. ways and means com., chmn. Congl. Task Force on Terrorism and Unconventional Warfare, 2001—. Republican. Jewish. Office: US Ho Reps 329 Cannon Ho Office Bldg Washington DC 20515-4607 Office Phone: 202-225-2815.*

CANTOR, HERBERT I., lawyer; b. NYC, Dec. 10, 1935; s. David and Ethel C.; m. Lynn Hardie, July 8, 1972; children: David, Susan. BA in Chemistry, NYU, 1965; JD, Cath. U. Am., 1970. Bar: Md. 1970, U.S. Dist. Ct. Md. 1970, D.C. 1971, U.S. Dist. Ct. D.C. 1971, U.S. Ct. Appeals (5th, D.C. and fed. cirs.) 1971, U.S. Supreme Ct. 1974, U.S. Ct. Appeals (4th cir.) 1981, U.S. Ct. Claims 1987. Patent examiner U.S. Patent Office, Washington, 1965-67; agt. Jacobi, Davidson & Jacobi, Washington, 1967-68; pvt. practice Washington, 1968-70; with Kraft, Cantor & Singer, Cantor & Lessler, Washington, 1971-85; ptnr. Cantor & Lessler, Washington, 1982-85, Wegner, Cantor, Mueller & Player, Washington, 1985-94; Evenson, McKeown, Edwards & Lenahan, Washington, 1994-2001; Crowell & Moring, 2001—. Adj. prof. Law Ctr. Georgetown Univ., Washington, 1988-89. Assoc. editor Cath. U. Law Rev., 1969-70. Mem. Am. Chem. Soc., Fedn. Internat. des Conseils Propriete Industrielle, Am. Intellectual Property Assn. Office: Crowell & Moring 1001 Pennsylvania Ave NW Washington DC 20004 Office Phone: 202-624-2500. E-mail: hcantor@crowell.com.

CANTOR, JAMES ELLIOT, lawyer; b. Detroit, Mar. 14, 1958; s. Bernard J. and Judith (Levin) C.; m. Susan Elaine Finger, Dec. 26, 1983; children: Tilly Samantha, Brian Alexander. BS in Natural Resources, U. Mich., 1980; JD, Cornell U., 1986. Bar: Alaska 1986. Assoc. Perkins Coie, Anchorage, 1986-91; asst. atty. gen. environ. sect. Alaska, Atty. Gen.'s Office, Anchorage, 1991-98, supervising atty. transp. sect., 1998—, chief asst. atty. gen., 2003—. Mem. Eagle River (Alaska) Pk. and Recreation Bd. of Suprs., 1989-95, chmn., 1991-92; dir. Anchorage (Alaska) Trails and Greenways Coalition, 1994-97; commr. Municipality of Anchorage, The Municipality of Anchorage Heritage Land Bank Adv. Commn., 1999—2005, chmn., 2002-03; trustee Congregation Beth Sholom, 2004—. Avocation: dog sled racing. Office: Atty Gen Office 1031 W 4th Ave Ste 200 Anchorage AK 99501-5903

CANTOR, JEROME OWEN, surgical pathologist, educator, researcher; b. NYC, Nov. 14, 1949; s. Morris and Helen C.; m. Bronislava Shteyngart, April 3, 2003. BA, Columbia U., 1971; MD, U. Pa., 1975. Diplomate Am. Bd. Pathology, Nat. Bd. Med. Examiners. Fellow Roche Inst. Molecular Biology, Nutley, N.J., 1975; intern Presbyn. Hosp., NYC, 1975-76, resident, 1976-80; asst. prof. Coll. Physicians and Surgeons Columbia U., NYC, 1980-95; rsch. assoc. St. Luke's/Roosevelt Inst. for Health Scis., NYC, 1987—; attending pathologist Arden Hill Hosp., Goshen, N.Y., 1990-95, Horton Meml. Hosp., Middletown, N.Y., 1990-95, St. Joseph's Med. Ctr., Paterson, N.J., 1992-95, The Bklyn. Hosp. Ctr., 1995—99, Maimonides Med. Ctr., 1999—2002, St. John's U., 2002—; co-founder Cotherix Biopharm. Co., 1999—. Cons. dept. pediatrics U. Medicine and Dentistry of N.J., Newark, 1987-91. Editor: Handbook of Animal Models of Pulmonary Diseases, 1989; contbr. numerous articles to profl. jours.; patentee in field. Grantee Measey Found., 1973, NIH, 1976-78, 80-86, 90-93, 2001-2003, Alpha-One Found., 2004-2006, Am. Lung Assn., 1978-80, 87-90, Stony Wold-Herbert Fund, 1982-84; recipient Bausch and Lomb Sci. award, 1967; fellow Armed Forces Inst. Pathology, Washington, 1980. Fellow Coll. Am. Pathologists. Avocation: golf. Office: St Johns U SAH 128 8000 Utopia Pky Jamaica NY 11439 Office Phone: 718-990-7495. Personal E-mail: jocantor@pol.net.

CANTOR, MELVYN LEON, retired lawyer; b. Boston, Aug. 13, 1942; s. Manuel and Adeline (Raffel) C.; m. Susan Gershen, June 7, 1964 (div. Jan. 1981); children: Matthew, Douglas; m. Kathryn Gabler, Jan. 3, 1982; 1 child, Joanna. BA, U. Vt., 1964; LLB magna cum laude, U. Pa., 1967. Bar: N.Y. 1969, U.S. Dist. Ct. (so. and ea. dists.) N.Y. 1971, U.S. Ct. Appeals (2nd cir.) 1971, U.S. Ct. Appeals (3d cir.) 1974, U.S. Ct. Appeals (5th cir.) 1986, U.S. Supreme Ct. 1987. Law clk. to Hon. Stanley A. Weigel U.S. Dist. Ct., San Francisco, 1967-68; assoc. Simpson, Thacher & Bartlett, NYC, 1968-74, ptnr., 1974-97; of counsel, 1998—. Adj. prof. Yeshiva U. Benjamin Cardozo Sch. Law, N.Y.C., 1977-81, lectr. in law, Columbia U. Contbr. numerous articles to profl. jours. Fellow Am. Coll. Trial Lawyers; mem. Bar Assn. of City of NY Office: Simpson Thacher & Bartlett 425 Lexington Ave Fl 14 New York NY 10017-3903 Home Phone: 203-869-1167; Office Phone: 212-455-3070. Business E-Mail: mcantor@stblaw.com.

CANTOR, NANCY, academic administrator; b. NYC; m. Steven Brechin; children: Maddy, Archie. AB, Sarah Lawrence Coll., 1974; PhD in Psychology, Stanford U., 1978. Faculty, chair dept. psychology Princeton (NJ) U., 1991—96; dean Horace H. Rackham Sch. Grad. Studies, vice provost for acad. affairs U. Mich., Ann Arbor, 1996—97, provost, exec. v.p. acad. affairs, 1997—2001; chancellor U. Ill.-Urbana-Champaign, 2001—04; chancellor, pres. Syracuse U., NY, 2004—, disting. prof. psychology and women's studies. Mem. adv. bd. NSF; mem. com. on nat. needs in biomed. and behavioral sci. rsch. NRC, mem. com. on women in sci. and engring. Co-author (or co-editor): 3 books; contbr. 50 articles to profl. jours., chpts. to books. Recipient Woman of Achievement award, Anti Defamation League. Fellow: Soc. for Personality and Social Psychology, APA (Disting. Sci. award for early career contbn. in psychology), Am. Psychol. Soc.; mem.: Am. Assn. for Higher Edn. (vice chair bd. dirs.), Am. Acad. Arts and Sci., Inst. of Medicine of NAS. Office: Syracuse U 300 Tolley Adminstrm Bldg Syracuse NY 13244-1100 E-mail: cancellor@syr.edu.*

CANTOR, RICHARD IRA, physician, corporate health executive; b. NYC, Jan. 25, 1944; s. Jacob Alvin and Sarah Cantor; m. Patricia Ann Honeycutt, June 7, 1970. AB, NYU, 1965; MD, Med. Coll. Va., 1970; postgrad., Bellevue Hosp. Ctr., NYC, 1970-73. Diplomate Am. Bd. Internal Medicine. Intern Bellevue Hosp. Ctr., NYC, 1970-71, resident, 1971-73; internist N.Y. Med. Group, NYC, 1973-76; asst. med. dir. substance abuse programs Bellevue Hosp., 1973-76, med. dir. substance abuse programs, 1976-79; med. dir. Med Plan, NYC, 1979-84; employee health unit Equitable Life Assurance Soc. U.S., NYC, 1984-87; v.p., dir. health and med. svcs. Citibank, NYC, 1988-89, v.p., dir. health, med. and staff svcs., 1989-91, v.p., corp. med. dir., 1991-98, Citigroup, NYC, 1998—. Teaching asst. in medicine NYU Med. Ctr., NYC, 1970-73, asst. prof. clin. medicine, 1983—; attending physician Cabrini Med. Ctr., NYC, 1973-76, Bellevue Hosp. Ctr., 1973—; chmn. policy adv. bd. NYC Methadone Maintenance Treatment Programs, 1976-77; med. cons. Am. Fedn. State, County, and Mcpl. Employees, NYC, 1979-84. Columnist Ask Your Med Plan Doctor, Pub. Employee Press, 1980-84. NIH trainee in endocrinology Med. Coll. Va., 1968. Mem. ACP, AMA, Am. Coll. Occupl. and Environ. Medicine, Royal Soc. Medicine (London), Am. Coll. Physician Execs., NY Occupl. Med. Assn. (exec. com. 1997), Med. Execs., Med. Soc. County NY, Med. Soc. State NY, Nat. Corp. Med. Assocs., Internat. Soc. Travel Medicine, Med. Dirs. Forum, Phi Beta Kappa, Alpha Omega Alpha, Sigma Zeta. Office: Citibank 399 Park Ave New York NY 10022-4699 Office Phone: 212-559-0032.

CANTRELL, DUANE L., retail executive; Degree in Econs., Kans. State U., 1978; postgrad., U. Va. From merchandiser to exec. v.p. ops., sr. v.p. retail ops., sr. v.p. merchandise distbn. and planning Payless ShoeSource, Inc., Topeka, 1978—99; exec. v.p. retail ops. Payless ShoeSource, 1999—2002, pres., dir., 2002—. Trustee Kansas State U. Found.; chmn. adv. bd. Coll. Bus. Adminstrn. Kans. State U., mem. Mike Ahearn adv. bd. Office: Payless ShoeSource Inc 3231 SE 6th Ave Topeka KS 66607-2207

CANTRELL, GEORGIA ANN, realtor; b. Hall , Ky., May 26, 1950; d. Melvin Johnson and Liza Ann (Collins) Johnson; children: David Cantrell, Jr., Mary Elizabeth Cantrell Riley. Grad. h.s., Fedcreek, Ky. Cert. realtor Ky. Owner Cantrell Supply, Winchester, Ky., 1979—2000; realtor Coldwell Banker Mc Mahan, Winchester, Ky., 1995—2005; co-owner Ensor/Cantrell Real Estate LLC, Winchester, 2005—. Recipient Leadership award, Winchester-Clark Co. C. of C., 1996. Mem.: Boonesboro Lions Club, Million Dollar Club (life). Baptist. Avocations: travel, reading, walking. Home: 330 Runnymeade Dr Winchester KY 40391 Office: 3503 Lexington Rd Winchester KY 40391 Personal E-mail: georgia@georgiacantrell.com.

CANTRELL, JOSEPH SIRES, chemistry professor; b. Parker, Kans., July 31, 1932; s. Joseph Sires and Alta Fern (Collins) C.; m. Margaret Joyce Herr, Aug. 17, 1958; children: Mark Alan, Kenneth Aaron, Keith Floyd. AB, Emporia U., Kans., 1954; MS, Kans. State U., 1958, PhD, 1961. Scientist, chemist Procter and Gamble Co., Cin., 1961—65; asst. prof. chemistry Miami U., Oxford, Ohio, 1965—68, assoc. prof., 1968—80, prof., 1980—2002, emeritus prof., 2002—. Cons. Mound Lab. EG and G, Miamisburg, Ohio, 1982—, Lawrence Livermore (Calif.) Nat. Lab., 1984—; cons. space shuttle program NASA, New Orleans, 1954—. Co-author: (book) Antarctica - The Land of Ice, 2001; contbr. articles to profl. jours. Cubmaster pack 937, Boy Scouts Am., Hamilton, Ohio, 1978-80, com. chmn. troop 956, 1980-86, scoutmaster troop 930, Oxford, 1986-89, chart orgn. rep.troop 930, 2000-, dist. commr. Dan Beard coun., 1970—, dist. chmn. Sgt. U.S. Army, 1954-56. Fellow Ohio Acad. Sci., 1981, Inst. Environ. Sci., 1988. Mem. AAAS, Am. Chem. Soc. (chmn. Cin. sect. 1983-84), Electrochem. Soc. (Masons (master Oxford 1969, 76), Sigma Xi (pres. Miami U. chpt. 1980-81). Methodist. Achievements include a scientific expedition to Antarctica to sample water from lake Hoar along the Trans-Antarctic mountains for the National Science Foundation. Avocations: camping, hiking, stamp collecting/philately, painting, amateur radio. Home and Office: 206 Pearl River Trace Pearl River LA 70452 Personal E-mail: joecantrell@bellsouth.net.

CANTRELL, LANA, actress, lawyer, singer; b. Sydney, Aug. 7, 1943; d. Hubert Clarence and Dorothy Jean (Thistlethwaite) C. JD, Fordham Law Sch., 1993. Bar: N.Y. 1994. Former of counsel Ballon Stoll Bader & Adler, NYC; assoc. Sendroff & Assocs. PC, NYC, 1996—. Singer supper clubs, TV programs, Australia, 1958-62; U.S. debut: TV show The Tonight Show, NBC, 1962; rec. artist RCA and Polydor Records, 1967— (Grammy award as Most Promising New Female Artist, Nat. Assn. Rec. Arts and Scis. 1967); recs. include Lana!, Act III, And Then There Was Lana, The Now of Then! Pres. Thrush, Inc.; U.S. rep. Internat. Song Festival, Poland, 1966, UN Internat. Women's Year Concert, Paris, France, 1975. Decorated Order of Australia, 2003; recipient 1st prize Internat. Song Festival Poland, 1966; 1st Internat. Woman of Yr. award Feminist Party, 1973 Office: 300 E 71st St New York NY 10021-5234

CANTRELL, LUTHER E., JR., lawyer; b. Nashville, Aug. 6, 1933; s. Luther E. and Hattie Mai (Cassetty) C.; m. Barbara Ann Richardson, Oct. 4, 1960; children: Luther III, Timothy Richard, Christopher Thomas. BS in fin. and econs., U. Tenn., 1960; LLD, Nashville Sch. Law, 1965. Bar: Tenn., U.S. Dist. Ct. (mid. dist.) Tenn., U.S. Ct. Appeals (6th cir.), U.S. Supreme Ct. Assoc. Smith, Ortale & Smith, Nashville, 1965-70, Taylor, Schlater & Smith, Nashville, 1970-72; ptnr. Smith, Smith & Cantrell, Nashville, 1972-73, Smith, Davies, Smith & Cantrell, Nashville, 1973-84, Davies, Cantrell, Humphreys & McCoy, Nashville, 1984-96; pvt. practice Nashville, 1997—. Mem. staff Nashville Sch. of Law, 1966—. Cpl. U.S. Army, 1954-55. Named Disting. Alumni Nashville Sch. Law, 1996. Mem. Tenn. Def. Lawyers Assn., Def. Rsch. Inst., Atlanta Claims Assn., Nashville Bar Assn., Tenn. Bar Assn., U.S. Supreme Ct Historical Soc., U. Tenn. Alumni Assn., Nashville Sch. Law Alumni Assn. (pres. 1971), Shriners, Am. Legion, Masons, Scottish Rite Masons, Optimist Club (pres. 1969, lt. gov. 1970-71, Honor Club 1969), Crime Stoppers Inc. (bd. dirs.), Royal Order Jesters (order of Quetzalcoatl). Avocations: music, photography, bowling, reading. Home: 2813 Glenoaks Dr Nashville TN 37214-1605 Office: Law Offices Luther E Cantrell Jr 3d Fl Court Square Bldg 300 James Robertson Pkwy Nashville TN 37201-1107

CANTRELL, ROBERT WENDELL, otolaryngologist, head and neck surgeon, educator; b. Neosho, Mo., Apr. 25, 1933; s. Lloyd L. and Ruby R. (Moffett) Cantrell; m. Young Hi Lee, Feb. 6, 1964; children: Mark L., Elizabeth L., Victoria L., Robert Wendell, Jr. Student, US Naval Acad., 1952—55; AB, George Wash. U., Washington, DC, 1956, MD, 1960. Diplomate Am. Bd. Otolaryngology 1969. Intern N.Y. Hosp-Cornell U., 1960—61; resident in otolaryngology Nat. Naval Med. Center, Bethesda, Md., 1965—69; chmn. dept. otolaryngology Naval Regional Med. Center, San Diego, 1969—76; chair dept. otolaryngology-head and neck surgery U. Va., Charlottesville, 1976—96; acting v.p., provost U. Va. Health Scis. Ctr., 1995—96, v.p., provost, 1996—2001; dir. Va. Health Policy Ctr., Charlottesville, 2001—04. Bd. dirs. Am. Bd. Otolaryngology, 1980—98, exec. v.p., 1990—98. Mem. editl. bd. Laryngoscope, 1976—88, Annals of Otology, Rhinology and Laryngology, 1977—88, Am. Jour. of Otolaryngology, 1978—82, Archives of Otolaryngology, 1979—88. Mayor City of Oakmont, Md., 1968—69. Capt. USN, 1961—76, capt. USNR, 1976—91. Recipient Huron W. Lawson prize, 1960; fellow, Am. Heart Assn., 1959. Mem.: Am. Otol. Soc., Am. Laryngol. Assn. (coun. 1988—90, treas. 1990—95, pres.-elect 1995, pres. 1996—97), Am. Broncho-Esophagological Assn. (pres. 1988—89), Soc. Univ. Otolaryngologists (pres. 1982), Am. Soc. Head and Neck Surgery (pres. 1985—86), Triological Soc. (v.p. So. sect. 1989—90, Mosher award 1974), Am. Acad. Facial Plastic and Reconstructive Surgery (v.p. So. sect. 1980—83), Am. Acad. Otolaryngology-Head and Neck Surgery (pres. 1987), AMA, Alpha Omega Alpha. Home: 1925 Owensville Rd Charlottesville VA 22901-8824

CANTRELL, SCOTT, newspaper music critic; b. Ft. Smith, Ark., Nov. 14, 1949; s. Bert Thomas and Elizabeth Winstel (Scott) C. BFA, So. Meth. U., 1971; MS, Rensselaer Poly. Inst., 1974. Prodr., announcer Sta. WMHT, Schenectady, N.Y., 1973-86; music critic Times Union, Albany, N.Y., 1981-87, Rochester, N.Y., 1987-90; classical music editor Kansas City (Mo.) Star, 1990-99; music critic Dallas Morning News, 1999—. Freelance contbr. N.Y. Times, High Fidelity, Musical Am., Ovation, Classical and various other publs., 1973—; organist, choirmaster various chs., Albany, 1971-87. Recipient Deems Taylor award ASCAP, 1987, 89. Mem. Am. Guild of Organists, Music Critics Assn. N.Am. (exec. bd. 1989-2001, pres. 1993-97). Episcopalian. Avocations: travel, art, architecture, reading, cuisines. Office: The Dallas Morning News PO Box 655237 Dallas TX 75265-5237 E-mail: scantrell@dallasnews.com.

CANTRELL, SHARRON CAULK, principal; b. Columbia, Tenn., Oct. 2, 1947; d. Tom English and Beulah (Goodin) Caulk; m. William Terry Cantrell, Mar. 18, 1989; 1 child, Jordan; children from previous marriage: Christopher, George English, Steffenee Copley. BA, George Peabody Coll. Tchrs., 1970; MS, Vanderbilt U., 1980; EdS, Mid. Tenn. State U., 1986. Tchr. Ft. Campbell Jr. High Sch., Columbia, Tenn., 1970-71, Whitthorne Jr. High Sch., Columbia, Tenn., 1977-86, Spring Hill (Tenn.) High Sch., 1986—. Mem. NEA, AAUW (pres. Tenn. divsn. 1983-85), Maury County Edn. Assn. (pres. 1983-84), Tenn. Edn. Assn., Assn. Preservation Tenn.

Antiquities, Maury Alliance, Friends of Children's Hosp., Rotary (bd. dirs.), Phi Delta Kappa. Mem. Ch. of Christ. Home: 5299 Main St Spring Hill TN 37174-2495 Office: Spring Hill High Sch 1 Raider Ln Columbia TN 38401-7346

CANTRILL, THOMAS H., lawyer; b. Springfield, Mo., Apr. 5, 1948; BBA with honors, So. Meth. U., 1970; JD with honors, U. Tex., 1973. Bar: Tex. 1973. Shareholder Jenkens & Gilchrist, P.C., Dallas, firm leader estate planning practice group, firm pres. & chmn., 2004—. Fellow Tex. Bar Found.; mem. ABA, Am. Coll. Trusts and Estate Counsel, Tex. State Bar Assn., Dallas Bar Assn., Internat. Acad. Estate and Trust Law, Order Coif, Beta Alpha Psi, Beta Gamma Sigma. Office: Jenkens & Gilchrist PC 1445 Ross Ave Ste 3200 Dallas TX 75202-2799 Office Phone: 214-855-4324. Office Fax: 214-855-4300. Business E-Mail: tcantrill@jenkens.com.

CANTU, IMELDA M., theater educator; b. Falfurrias, Tex., July 4, 1956; d. Joe C. and Olinda Perez Salas; m. Omar Cantu, June 17, 1978; children: Omarr Idden, Ivah Marie, Osman Alvarr. BS, Tex. A & I U., Kingsville, 1977, MA, 1982. Tchr. reading/English Falfurrias Jr. Sch., Tex., 1977—83; tchr. speech/theater Falfurrias H.S., 1983—. Theatre dir. Falfurrias H.S., 1983—, fine arts dept. chair, 2000—, coord., 2002—; prose and poetry state judge U. Interscholastic League, 2002—07. Dir.: numerous theatrical performances. Spl. activity dir. Boys & Girls Club, Falfurrias, 2003—05, Teen Awareness, Falfurrias, 2004—05; youth choir dir. Sacred Heart Ch., Falfurrias, 1995—2006. Named Tchr. of Yr., Wal-Mart, 2000; named one of Outstanding Young Women of Am., 1983; recipient Sponsor award, U. Interscholastic League, 1999—2000, U. Interscholastic League Sponsor Excellence award, Southwestern Bell, 2000—01, Tchr. of Yr., Walmart & Sam's Club, 2007. Mem.: Ednl. Theatre Assn., Nat. Forensics Assn., Assn. of Tex. Profl. Educators, Tex. Ednl. Theatre Assn., Alpha Chi, Alpha Lambda Delta (pres. & sr. advisor), Sigma Delta Pi. Democrat. Roman Catholic. Avocations: swimming, travel, crafts. Home: 901 S Center Falfurrias TX 78355 Office: Falfurrias HS 100 Jersey Dr Falfurrias TX 78355 Office Phone: 361-325-5681. Office Fax: 361-325-9284. Personal E-mail: imcantu@hotmail.com. Business E-Mail: imcantu@bcisd.esc2.net.

CANTU, JENNIFER ST. JOHN, gifted and talented educator; b. Washington, June 21, 1969; d. James E. and Carolin M. G. St. John; m. Christopher G. Cantu, May 27, 2006. BA, U. Va., 1992, M in Tchg., 1992. Lic. tchr. Va. Classroom tchr. Fairfax County Pub. Schs., Centreville, Va., 1992—96, gifted and talented specialist Fairfax Station, Va., 1996—2006, web curator, 2004—06. Mem.: NEA, ASCD, Fairfax Edn. Assn., Va. Edn. Assn., Nat. Assn. for Gifted Children, U. Va. Alumni Assn. (life), Kappa Delta Pi, Alpha Delta Pi (life; guard 1988—89). Roman Catholic. Home: 6832 Austin Harbor Loop Sherwood AR 72120 Personal E-mail: jkstjohn@prodigy.net.

CANTÚ, NORMA V., law educator, former federal official; b. Brownsville, Tex., Nov. 2, 1954; BS summa cum laude, Pan Am. U., 1973; JD, Harvard U., 1977. Bar: Tex. 1978, U.S. Dist. Ct. (so. dist.) Tex. 1979, U.S. Dist. Ct. (we. dist.) Tex. 1981, U.S. Ct. Appeals (5th and 11th cirs.) 1982, Calif. 1985, U.S. Ct. Appeals (10th cir.) 1986, U.S. Dist. Ct. (no. dist.) Tex. 1992. Tchr. English, Brownsville, 1974, San Antonio, 1979; intern Office of Atty. Gen. Tex., 1977-78; atty. Mex. Am. Legal Def. and Ednl. Fund, 1979—93, regional counsel, 1985-93; asst. sec. for civil rights Office for Civil Rights U.S. Dept. of Edn., Washington, 1993—2001; prof. law and edn. U. Tex., Austin, Tex., 2001—. U.S. rep. OAS Commn. on Children, 1999—2001. Officer Avance Parent Child Tng. Program, 1990; bd. dirs. Hispanic Health Policy Devel. Program, 1992, Leadership San Antonio, 1992—93, MALDEF, 2001—02, Mex. Am. Leadership Coun., 2002—. Named to San Antonio Women Hall of Fame, Women in Sports Edn. Hall of Fame. Office: U Tex at Austin Sch Law Townes Hall Rm 3118M 727 E Dean Keeton St Austin TX 78705 Home: 140 Twinleaf Ln San Antonio TX 78213 Office Phone: 512-232-7111. Business E-Mail: ncantu@law.utexas.edu.

CANTWELL, BRIAN, aeronautical engineer, educator; BA, U. Notre Dame, 1967, BS, 1968; diploma, Von Karman Inst. for Fluid Dynamics; MS, Calif. Inst. Tech., 1971, PhD, 1976. Faculty mem. Stanford U., 1978—, chair Aeronautics and Astronautics Dept., 2001—, Edward C. Wells prof. Sch. Engring. Fellow: AIAA, Royal Aeronautical Soc., Am. Physical Soc.; mem.: NAE, Sigma Xi. Office: Dept of Aeronautics and Astronautics Stanford U 379 Durand Bldg, 496 Lomita Mall Stanford CA 94305-4035 Office Phone: 650-723-4825. Office Fax: 650-723-3018. E-mail: cantwell@stanford.edu.

CANTWELL, CHRISTOPHER WILLIAM, artist; b. Atwater, Calif., Dec. 24, 1960; s. Donald Byron and Ann Louise Cantwell; m. Susan Rebecca Moore, Sept. 19, 1982 (div. 1997); children: Claire Elyse Moore, Katie Lynn Moore. Owner, artist Christopher W. Cantwell Woodworks, Modesto, Calif., 1979-82, Oakhurst, Calif., 1982—. Cons. Internat. Union for conservation of Natural Resources, Cambridge, Eng., 1991—. Contbr. art book Jewelry Boxes, 1996; one-man shows include Houston Ctr. for Contemporary Craft, 2004; exhibited at Del Mano Gallery, 1990, 98, 99, Furniture Soc. Conf., San Francisco, 1998, Del Mano, 1999, Laguna Art Mus., 1999, Orange County Mus. Art, 2000, OXO Tower, London, England, 2001, Collins Gallery, Glasgow, Scotland, 2002, Jeffrey Weiss Gallery, 2003, L.I. Beach Mus. Art, 2003; represented in permanent collections Irving Lipton Collection, Robert Bohlen Collection, White House Ornament Collection. Youth advisor Oakhurst Luth, Ch., 1992-96. Mem. Am. Craft Coun., World Wildlife Fund, Program for Belize, Good Wood Alliance (CITES Liaison 1994—), Box Art Soc. (pres. 1999—). Democrat. Avocations: rock climbing, skiing, surfing. Home and Office: PO Box 1736 Oakhurst CA 93644-1736 Personal E-mail: cwcw@sti.net.

CANTWELL, DON, artistic director; b. Charleston, SC, July 10, 1935; s. James Richard Jr. and Helen (Thompson) C.; m. Patricia Downs; children: Kimberly S., Dewey S. Jr., Joshua Paul. Grad. high sch., Charleston. Dir. Charleston Ballet Sch., 1969—; artistic dir. Charleston Ballet Theatre, 1969—. Mem. Southeastern Ballet Assn. (v.p. 1981-82, 85-86, pres. 1983-84, 86-87, chmn. bd. 1984-85, 87-88). Office: Charleston Ballet Theatre 477 King St Charleston SC 29403-6231 Home Phone: 843-849-7814; Office Phone: 843-723-7334.

CANTWELL, JOHN WALSH, advertising executive; b. Fall River, Mass., July 16, 1922; s. William J. and Esther (Walsh) C.; m. Evelyna Dyson; children from previous marriage: Sharon, Peter, Paul. BS in Econs., Holy Cross Coll., 1944; MA, Georgetown U., 1945; postgrad., Columbia U., 1949-50. Asst. sales mgr. Internat. Milling Co., 1947-48; v.p. mgmt. supr. Compton Advt., NYC, 1948-60; sr. v.p. mgmt. supr. Sullivan, Stauffer Colwell & Bayles, NYC, 1960-65; pres., CEO Pritchard, Wood (advt.), NYC, 1965-68, Parkson Advt. Agy., Inc., 1968-69; sr. v.p. J.B. Williams Co., Inc., 1968-69; pres. Jack Cantwell, Inc., 1970—; chmn., CEO Dolphin Med. Acoustics, Ltd., 1997-99; CEO Byrd Walsh Internat. LLP, 2004—. Office: Essex Towers 340 Sunset Dr Ste 1405 Fort Lauderdale FL 33301-2653

CANTWELL, MARIA E., senator; b. Indpls., Oct. 13, 1958; d. Rose and Paul Cantwell. BA in Public Adminstrn., Miami U., Ohio, 1981. Public relations cons. Cantwell and Associates, 1981—87; state repr. Dist. 44 Wash., 1987—92; mem. 103rd Congress from 1st Wash. dist., Washington, 1993—95; v.p. mktg. Progressive Networks, Seattle, 1995—97; sr. v.p. consumer and e-commerce Real Networks (formerly Progressive Networks), Seattle, 1997—2000; US Senator from Wash., 2001—. Mem. com. commerce, sci. and transp. US Senate, com. energy and natural resources, com. Indian affairs, com. small bus. and entrepreneurship. Bd. dirs. Wash. Econ. Develop. Fin. Authority. Named Woman of Yr., KING-TV Evening Mag., 2001; recipient Cyber Champion award, Bus. Software Alliance, 2003, Friend of Blues, Experience Music Project-Vulcan, Inc., 2003. Democrat. Roman Catholic. Office: US Senate 717 Hart Senate Bldg Washington DC 20510 also: District Office Ste 3206 915 Second Ave Seattle WA 98174-1011 Office Phone: 202-224-3441, 206-220-6400. Office Fax: 202-228-0514, 206-220-6404.*

CANTY, DAWN M., lawyer; b. Chgo., June 21, 1964; AB, U. Chgo., 1986; JD, U. Mich., 1989. Bar: Ill. 1989. Ptnr. Katten Muchin Zavis Rosenman, Chgo. Mem.: ABA, Am. Bar Assn., Trial Bar of No. Dist. of Ill. Office: Katten Muchin Zavis Rosenman 525 W Monroe St Chicago IL 60661 Office Phone: 312-902-5253. Office Fax: 312-577-8607. E-mail: dawn.canty@kmzr.com.

CANU, WILLIAM HENRY, psychology professor; s. Pierre H. and Victoria K. Canu; m. Rebekah Canu; 1 child, Owen. PhD in clin. Psychology, U. Tex., Austin, 2004. Asst. prof. U. Mo., Rolla, 2004—07, Appalachian State U., Boone, 2007—. Contbr. articles to profl. jours. Recipient Janet T. Spence Tchg. award, U. Tex., Austin, 2003, Outstanding Tchg. award, U. Mo., 2005. Mem.: APA, Sigma Xi, Assn. Behavioral and Cognitive Therapies, Internat. Soc. Rsch. Child and Adolescent Psychopathology, Assn. Psychol. Sci., Omicron Delta Kappa, Psi Chi. Business E-Mail: canuwh@appstate.edu.

CANUP, ROBIN M., astrophysicist, science administrator; BS magna cum laude in Physics, Duke U., NC; MS in Astrophysy., Planetary and Atmospheric Scis., PhD in Astrophysy., Planetary and Atmospheric Scis., U. Colo., Boulder. Rsch. assoc. lab. atmospheric and space physics U. Colo., 1995—98; sr. rsch. scientist S.W. Rsch. Inst. Dept. Space Studies, 1998—99, asst. dir., 1999—2005, dir., 2005—07, exec. dir., 2007—. Vis. prof. divsn. geol. and planetary scis. Calif. Inst. Tech., 2005; mem. planetary sci. subcommittee NASA Adv. Coun., 2006—. Contbr. articles to sci. jours.; mem. editl. bd.: Icarus, 2003—06. Named an Brilliant 10, Popular Sci. mag., 2004; recipient Harold C. Urey prize, Am. Astron. Soc. (Divsn. Planetary Scis.). Fellow: Am. Geophys. Union (Macelwane medal 2004); mem.: Phi Beta Kappa. Avocation: ballet. Office: Dept Space Studies SW Rsch Inst 1050 Walnut St Ste 300 Boulder CO 80302 E-mail: robin@boulder.swri.edu.

CANZANO, DANIEL A., information technology executive; b. Rochester, NY; m. Kathy Canzano; 4 children. BS in Econ., History, Univ. Dayton, MA; MBA. Mkting dept. NCR, Dayton, Ohio, computer sys. sales Phila.; sales to dir. to gen. mgr., mfg. sys. divsn. Martin Marietta, NJ; zone sales mgr. Paychex Inc., Cherry Hill, NJ, 1989—92, info. tech. dept. head Rochester, NY, 1992—93, v.p. info. tech., 1993—. Named one of Top 25 Chief Tech. Officers, InfoWorld mag., 2006. Office: Paychex Inc 911 Panorama Trail S Rochester NY 14625-0397 Office Phone: 716-385-6666.*

CANZONERI, LOIS H., retired church musician; b. Detroit, May 3, 1931; d. Charles Bronson Seymour and Mary Ruth Coon; m. Robert Dominic Canzoneri, July 8, 1951; 1 child, Ruth Jane. BA, San Diego State U., 1953; M of Holistic Healing, The Tree Of Light Inst., Utah, 1993. Cert. svc. playing Am. Guild Organists, 1963. Organist/choir dir. St. Dunstan's Episcopal Ch., San Diego, 1951—76; elem. sch. tchr. La Mesa-Spring Valley Sch. Dist., La Mesa, Calif., 1953—55, Gospel Of Life Christian Sch., 1962—63; ind. distbr. Nature's Sunshine Products, 1980—. Pvt. tchr. piano, La Mesa, Calif., 1965—80; subdean and dean San Diego chpt. Am. Guild Organists, 1973—75; adjudicator Lawrence Waddy scholarship, San Diego, 1983—95. Judge Exch. Club Talent Awards, La Mesa, 2000—03; mem. and contbr. Young America's Found., Herndon, Va., 2000—07. Named Weight loss leaderw, Prism Christian Weight Loss Program, 1998—2003. Mem.: Spreckels Organ Soc., Delta Zeta (officer 1949—53). Episcopalian. Avocations: exercise, travel, square dancing, round dancing, music. Home: 8019 Shadow Hill Dr La Mesa CA 91941 Personal E-mail: blcanzoneri@sbcglobal.net.

CANZONIER, WALTER JUDE, shellfish aquaculturist; b. New Brunswick, NJ, Feb. 6, 1936; s. Joseph V. and Mary M. (Patterson) C. BS, St. Peter's Coll., Jersey City, 1957; postgrad., Rutgers U., 1957-64. Teaching asst. dept. zoology Rutgers U., New Brunswick, NJ, 1958-59, rsch. asst. dept. oyster culture, 1960-67, rsch. assoc., 1968-71, 81-87; rsch. fellow Inst. Marine Biology, CNR, Venice, Italy, 1971-77; dir. Coastal Resources Applied Rsch. Lab., Venice, 1977-80; dir. R & D, Aquarius Assocs., Port Noris, NJ, 1987—. Mem. tech. coms. Italian Ministry Sanità and Ministry Merchant Marine, 1974-80, Interstate Shellfish Sanitation Conf., 1980—; cons. on marine sci. UNESCO, France, 1978—. Contbr. articles to profl. jours. Organizer, treas. Point Pleasant Beach Taxpayers Assn., NJ, 1963-70; bd. dirs. N.E. Regional Aquaculture Ctr., 1992-2005, mem. exec. com., 1993-96, 2001-05; mem. NJ Taskforce for Revitalization of Shellfish Industry, 1997, NJ Aquaculture Adv. Coun., 2000-04. Recipient numerous grants from pub. agys. in N.Am. and Europe, 1971—. Mem. Nat. Shellfisheries Assn., Soc. Invertebrate Pathology, World Aquaculture Soc. N.J. Aquaculture Assn. (trustee 1989—, pres. 1991-2006). Achievements include development of shellfish sanitation guidelines and regulations for state and national health agencies in North America and Europe; design of marine research and aquaculture facilities in Asia, Europe and North America; advocacy for legis. to promote comml. aquaculture devel. Home: 44 Cowart Ave Manasquan NJ 08736-3102 Office: Aquarius Assocs PO Box 662 Port Norris NJ 08349-0662 Home Phone: 732-223-5229; Office Phone: 856-785-0402. Personal E-mail: garugala@att.net.

CAO, DENGFENG, pathologist; arrived in U.S., 1996; s. Hongling Cao and Yunying Guo; m. Zhikai Zhu, Feb. 18, 2004. MD, Peking Union Med. Coll., Beijing, China, 1996; PhD, U. Pitts., 2001. Diplomate Am. Bd. Pathology. Pathology resident Johns Hopkins Hosp., Balt., 2001—05, sr. clin. fellow, 2005—. Recipient Joseph Eggleston award for Excellence in Surg. Pathology, Johns Hopkins Hosp., 2004, Sixth Pathology Young Investigator award, 2004; Grad. Student scholar, U. Pitts., 1996—2001. Mem.: Internat. Assn. Chinese Pathologists (Best Abstract award 2004), U.S. and Can. Acad. Pathology, Coll. Am. Pathologists. Office: Johns Hopkins Hosp Weinberg 2242 401 North Broadway Street Baltimore MD 21231 Home Phone: 410-585-1232; Office Phone: 410-955-3580. Office Fax: 410-614-7726. Business E-Mail: dcao1@jhmi.edu.

CAO, GUOPING, research scientist; arrived in US, 2001; BS, Ctrl. South U., Hunan, China, 1993; MS, Inst. Chem. Metallurgy, Chinese Acad. Sci., Beijing, 1996; PhD, U. Wis., Madison, 2006. Rsch. asst. U. Wis., 2001—06, rsch. assoc., 2006—. Recipient Warren F. Savage Meml. award, Am. Welding Soc., 2006, William Spraragen Meml. award, 2007. Achievements include patents for arc-enhanced friction stir welding; research in advanced materials processing and welding. Office: U Wis Madison 1500 Engineering Dr Madison WI 53706 Office Phone: 608-262-3490. Business E-Mail: gcao@wisc.edu.

CAO, HANQIANG, science educator, researcher; b. Wuhan, Hubei, China, Nov. 7, 1953; s. Biwu Cao and Shiyun Feng; m. Jianmin Zhang; 1 child, Chao. BS, Wuhan U., 1978. Cert. tchr. Rschr., educator Huazhong U Sci. and Tech., Wuhan. Contbr. articles to profl. jours. Office: Huazhong U Sci and Tech Luoyu Rd Wuhan Hubei 430074 China Fax: 86-27-87547655. E-mail: itd@mail.hust.edu.cn.

CAO, HUI, physics and astronomy professor; BS, Peking U., 1990; MA in Mech. and Aerospace Engring., Princeton U., 1992; PhD in Applied Physics, Stanford U., 1997. Asst. prof., physics and astronomy Northwestern U., 1997—2002, assoc. prof., physics and astronomy, 2002—. Contbr. articles to profl. publs., chapters to books; reviewer Nature, Science, Physical Review/Physical Review Letters, Applied Physics Letters, Journal of Optical Society of America, Optical Express, Optics Communications, Applied Optics, Photonics Technology Letters, IEEE, Journal of Selected Topics in Quantum Electronics, NSF, Am. Chem. Soc. Petroleum Rsch. Fund, US Civilian R&D Found., Rsch. Corp., Australian Rsch. Coun., and Sci. Found. Ireland. Recipient NSF Career award, 2001, Outstanding Young Researcher award, Overseas Chinese Physics Assn., 2004, Friedrich Bessel Rsch. award, Alexander von Humboldt Found., 2004; Guang-Hua Fellowship, 1989, Zonta Internat. Found. Amelia Earhart Fellowship, 1992, Karel Urbanek Grad. Fellowship, 1997, David and Lucille Packard Fellow, 1999, Alfred P. Sloan Fellow, 2000. Mem.: IEEE, Optical Soc. Am. (mem. Max Born prize com. 2005, vice-chair, technical group on waves in random and periodic media 2004—06), Am. Phys. Soc. (Maria Goeppert-Mayer award 2006). Office: Dept Physics and Astronomy Northwestern U 2145 Sheridan Rd Evanston IL 60208-3112 Office Phone: 847-467-5452. Office Fax: 847-491-9982. Business E-Mail: h-cao@northwestern.edu.

CAO, NANNAN, research scientist; BS, U. Sci. and Tech. China, Hefei, Anhui; PhD, Wash. U., St. Louis. Rsch. asst. U. Ill., Chgo., 2003—05, Wash. U., St. Louis, 2006—. Mem.: IEEE, Women in Optics, Women in Engring., Internat. Soc. Optical Engring. Office: Washington Univ Campus Box 1127 One Brookings Dr Saint Louis MO 63130 Home Phone: 312-399-7838; Office Phone: 314-935-9350. Office Fax: 314-935-4146. Business E-Mail: ncao4@ese.wustl.edu.

CAO, SHOUSONG, medical researcher, educator; b. Longhai, Hunan, China, Dec. 20, 1957; s. Guanwen Cao and Baiyu Xiao; m. Joann Juan Liu, Sept. 27, 1987; children: Felicia, Joshua. MS, Peking Union Med. U., Beijing, 1987; MD, Xiangya Med. Coll., Changsha, China, 1983. Diplomate Shousong Cao Med. Diplomate Com., China, 1983. Vis. rsch. prof. Peking Union Med. U., Beijing, 2000—; vis. prof., Ctrl. South U., Changsha, Hunan, China, 2006—; sr. scientist Roswell Pk. Cancer Inst., Buffalo, 2003—. Bd. dir. PrimaNova BioSci., Inc, Medford, NY, 2006—; evaluator Current Drugs Ltd., London. Reviewer Jour. Gastroenterology; contbr. numerous articles to profl. jours. Recipient Advanced and Technol. award, Chinese Academy Med. Scis., 1991, First prize, Ministry Public Health, 1995. Achievements include research in new anticancer drug discovery and development. Made major contribution to 5-fluorouracil/leucovorin and 5-fluorouracil/Irinotecan combinations, Xeloda, and selenium development; three US patents for method of reducing toxicity of anticancer agents and for method of augmenting the antitumor activity of anticancer agents; two US patents pending. Home: 8771 Millcreek Dr East Amherst NY NY 14 Office: Roswell Park Cancer Inst Elm & Carlton Sts Buffalo NY NY 14 Home Phone: 716-741-0242; Office Phone: 716-845-1638. Office Fax: 716-846-8221. Personal E-mail: shousongc@yahoo.com. Business E-Mail: shousong.cao@roswellpark.org.

CAO, XINHUA, medical researcher; b. Suzhou, Anhui Province, China, Sept. 30, 1957; arrived in U.S., 1998; s. Xianzhi Cao and Wenshu Zhang; m. Wei Xiong; 1 child, Yifan. BSEE, Xi'an Jiaotong U., China, 1982, MSEE, 1989, PhD, 1996. Assoc. prof. Xi'an (China) Jiaotong U., Shaanxi Province, 1989—98; rsch. fellow, vis. scholar U. Calif. San Francisco, 1998—2003; rsch. scientist Harvard Med. Sch., Boston, 2003—. Recipient Silver Medal, Beijing Internat. Invention Exhbn. Fair, 1996, First-grade Award of Sci. & Tech. Progress, Nat. Edn. Com. of China, 1991. Mem.: IEEE. Achievements include patents for a digital x-ray radiography imaging device with a scanning table; a stereo display and stereo observation device for medical imaging. Office: Harvard Medical School 220 Longwood Avenue Boston MA 02115

CAOUETTE, DAVID PAUL, public relations executive; b. Sanford, Maine, Aug. 6, 1960; s. Paul Henry and Barbara (Stackpole) C. BA with distinction, U. Maine, Orono, 1983. Editor employee communications Union Mutual Life Ins. Co., Portland, Maine, 1981-84, pub. rels. acct. exec., 1984-85; mgr. employee communications UNUM Life Ins. Co., Portland, 1985-87; v.p., mgr. communications Integrated Resources, Inc., NYC, 1987-89; asst. dir. corp. communications Fin. Guaranty Ins. Co., NYC, 1989—; a.v.p. corp. comms. GE Capital/FGIC, NYC, 1989-94; corp. comms. dir. AT&T Capital, Morristown, N.J., 1994-98; fin. comm. dir. AT&T Corp., Basking Ridge, NJ, 1998—2001; v.p. corp. media rels. and fin. comms. AT&T Wireless Svcs. Corp., Redmond, Wash., 2001—05; v.p. corp. commn. The Walt Disney Co., Burbank, Calif., 2005—. Ptnr., co-founder Interactive Communications, Inc., Merrick, N.Y., 1989—. Recipient Grand award ARC awards, 2002, Best of Show NIRI, Seattle, 2002, 2003, Nicholson Annual Report award, 2004 Mem. Internat. Assn. Bus. Communicators, Pub. Rels. Soc. Am., Nat. Investor Rels. Inst. Democrat. Roman Catholic. Office: The Walt Disney Co 500 S Buena Vista St Burbank CA 91521 Home: 1450 N Genesee Ave Los Angeles CA 90046-3930 E-mail: david.caouette@disney.com.

CAPALBO, CARMEN, theater director, producer; b. Harrisburg, Pa., Nov. 1, 1925; s. Joseph and Concetta (Riggio) C.; m. Patricia McBride, July 9, 1950 (div. June 1961); children: Carla, Marco. Student, Yale Sch. Drama. Prodns. include: dir., co-prodr. (plays) Juno and the Paycock, Shadow and Substance, Dear Brutus, Awake and Sing!, The Threepenny Opera, The Potting Shed, A Moon for the Misbegotten, The Cave Dwellers, The Rise and Fall of the City of Mahagonny; dir. (opera) The Good Soldier Schweik, (plays) A Connecticut Yankee, Seidman and Son, The Strangers, Enter Solly Gold, Slowly, By Thy Hand Unfurled; original dir.: The Sign in Sidney Brustein's Window, The Chosen; also TV prodn. The Power and the Glory; story cons.: Studio One, 1951-52; cons. The Bronx: After the Fires, Conversation with Eddie, 1983; prodn. mgr. Emlyn Williams as Charles Dickens, 1952-53, Jean-Louis Barrault-Madeleine Renaud Co., 1952; dir., prodr., writer 200 radio plays. With US Army, 1944—45. Decorated Bronze Star, Purple Heart; recipient spl. Tony award 1956, Obie award 1956. Mem. League N.Y. Theatres, Dirs. Guild Am., Soc. Stage Dirs. and Choreographers, Dramatists Guild, League OffBroadway Theatres (co-founder 1958, exec. bd. 1958-60). Address: 500 2nd Ave New York NY 10016-8606

CAPALDI, ELIZABETH ANN DEUTSCH, psychological sciences professor; b. NYC, May 13, 1945; d. Frederick and Nettie (Tarasuck) Deutsch; m. Egidio J. Capaldi, Jan. 20, 1968 (div. May 1985) AB, U. Rochester, 1965; PhD, U. Tex., 1969. Asst. prof. dept. psychol. scis. Purdue U., West Lafayette, Ind., 1969-74, assoc. prof., 1974-78, prof., 1979-86, asst. dean Grad. Sch., 1982-86, head dept. psychol. scis., 1983-88, sec.-treas. council of grad. dept. psychology, 1986-88; prof. U. Fla., Gainesville, 1988-2000, provost, v.p. acad. affairs, 1996-99; provost SUNY, Buffalo, 2000—04; vice chancellor SUNY Albany, 2004—; chief of staff SUNY, 2004—. Spl. asst. to pres., U. Fla., 1991-96. Author: Psychology, 1989, 4th edit., 1996; cons. editor Jour. Exptl. Psychology, 1991-96; assoc. editor Psychonomic Bull. Rev., 1993-98; contbr. articles to profl. jours. NIMH grantee, 1984-94, NSF grantee, 1995-98. Fellow AAAS, APA, Am. Psychol. Soc. (mem. governing bd. 1991-96, pres. 1999); mem. Psychonomic Soc. (mem. governing bd. 1992-97), Midwestern Psychol. Assn. (sec.-treas. 1988-90, pres. 1991), Sigma Xi. Office: SUNY State University Plz T-12 Albany NY 12246 Office Phone: 518-443-5538. Business E-Mail: betty.capaldi@suny.edu.

CAPALDINI, LISA CLAIRE, physician, educator; b. Bluefield, W.Va., Dec. 19, 1955; MD, U. Calif. San Francisco, 1982; M in Pub. Health, U.

Calif. Berkeley, 1983. Intern San Francisco Gen. Hosp. U. Calif., 1983—84, resident, 1983—86; assoc. clin. prof. medicine U. Calif. San Francisco, course dir. nursing sch., 1998—; pvt. practice internal medicine, 1998—. Contbr. articles to profl. jours. Office: 45 Castro St Ste 227 San Francisco CA 94114-1033 Office Phone: 415-861-3366.

CAPALDO, GUY, obstetrician, gynecologist; b. Bisaccia, Italy, Jan. 1, 1950; came to U.S., 1958; s. Arturo Nunziante and Maria Carmela (Ciani) C.; m. Kathy Nicita, Apr. 20, 1985. BSEE magna cum laude, U. Dayton, 1972; MS, Ohio State U., Columbus, 1973; MD, Med. Coll. Ohio, 1978. Diplomate Am. Bd. Ob-Gyn; cert. clin. densitometrist Internat. Soc. Clin. Densitometry. Research asst. Ohio State U., 1973-75; resident in ob-gyn Med. Coll. Ohio, Toledo, 1978-82; practice medicine specializing in ob-gyn Mansfield, Ohio, 1982—. Chief ob-gyn. dept. Mansfield Gen. Hosp., 1985—; lab. dir. Mansfield (Ohio) Ob-Gyn Assocs. Contbr. articles to profl. jours. Clinic physician Plan Parenthood, Mansfield, 1982—. Pres. scholar U. Dayton, 1968-72, Univ. fellow Ohio State U., 1972-75. Fellow Am. Coll. Ob-Gyn; mem. AMA, Ohio State Med. Assn., Richland County Med. Soc. Avocations: reading, fishing, travel, golf. Office: Mansfield Ob-Gyn Assocs 500 S Trimble Rd Mansfield OH 44906-3483 Office Phone: 419-756-6000.

CAPARRO, JAMES, entertainment industry executive; b. Bklyn., Dec. 26, 1951; s. Vincent and Clara (Curran) C.; m. Mary Judith Senna; children: Daniel, James Michael, Kristin. BA, William Paterson Coll., 1973; postgrad., Golden State U., 1974—76, New Sch. for Social Rsch., 1978—80. Several sales and mktg. positions Epic Records; with Sony Music, 1973, CBS Records, NYC, 1973-79, sales rep., 1979-80, sales mgr., 1980-83, Mid Atlantic, 1983-87, v.p. sales NYC, 1987-88; with PolyGram Group Distbn., NYC, 1988—98, exec. v.p., 1990-92, pres., CEO, 1992—98; chmn., CEO Island Def Jam Music Group (divsn. of Universal Music Group), 1998—2001; CEO WEA Corp., 2002—03; pres., interim CEO Atari Inc., 2004—05; founder, pres., CEO Entertainment Distbn. Corp. (divsn. of Glenayre Techs. Inc.), 2005—. Bd. dirs. Glenayre Techs., Atari Inc., 2002—, Prana Found., T.J. Martell Found. Originator, exec. in charge prodn. (TV spl.) Michael Jackson-The Magic Returns, 1987. Active PTA , Rockville, Md., 1983-86. Recipient Masterworks Branch of Yr. award CBS Records, N.Y., 1984, Columbia Branch of Yr. CBS Records, N.Y., 1985; named CEO of Yr., S.I.N. Mag., 2001. Mem. Country Music Assn., Nat. Assn. Rec. Merchandisers (bd. dir., recipient Distributor of Yr., 1993-97). Republican. Roman Catholic. Avocations: golf, reading, music, jogging. Office Phone: 212-333-8545. Business E-Mail: jim.caparro@edcllc.com.

CAPASSO, FEDERICO, physicist; b. Rome, June 24, 1949; came to U.S., 1976; D in Physics summa cum laude, U. Rome, 1973; D in Electronic Engring. (hon.), U. Bologna, Italy, 2003. Rschr. Fondazione Bordoni, Rome, 1974-76; vis. scientist Bell Labs., Holmdel, NJ, 1976-77, mem. tech. staff, Lucent Techs. (formerly AT&T), Murray Hill, NJ, 1978-87, head quantum phenomena and device rsch. dept., 1987-97, head semiconductor physics rsch. dept., 1997-2000, v.p. phys. rsch., 2000—02; Robert L. Wallace prof. applied physics, Vinton Hayes sr. rsch. fellow elec. engring. Harvard U., 2003—. Co-chmn. Internat. Semiconductor Device Rsch. Symposium, Charlottesville, Va., 1995; chmn. Internat. Conf. on Advances in Semiconductors and Superconductors, Newport Beach, 1988, 90; program co-chmn. Picosecond Electronics and Optoelectronics Conf., Lake Tahoe, 1987; program com., mem. of 20 internat. confs.; invited lectr. at over 160 internat. confs. Editor 4 books; mem. editl. bd. Il Nuovo Cimento, Applied Physics Letters, Semiconductor Sci. and Tech.; holder 46 U.S. patents, more than 54 fgn. patents; contbr. over 300 articles to profl. jours. Recipient award N.Y. Acad. Scis., 1993, Gold medal Heinrich Welker Meml., 1994, Vinci Excellence award LMVH, 1995, medal Materials Rsch. Soc., 1995, Electronics Letters Premium award Inst. of Elec. Engrs. (London), 1995, Bell Labs. fellow award, 1997, John Price Wetherill medal Franklin Inst., 1997, Rank prize, 1998, Capitolium prize, 1998, Alessandro Volta Meml. medal, 1999, Willis Lamb medal in laser physics, 2000, Goff Smith Prize, U. of Mich., 2003, Tommassoni Internat. prize U. Roma, 2004, Pres. Italy gold medal for culture, arts and sci., 2005; co-recipient King Faisal Internat. prize (Sci.), King Faisal Found., 2005; named hon. mem. Franklin Inst., 1997, Meritourious Achievement in Culture, Arts, and Sci. Gold medal, Pres. Italy, 2005. Fellow AAAS (Newcomb Cleveland prize 1995), Am. Acad. Arts and Scis., IEEE (David Sarnoff award 1991, W. Streifer Sci. Achievement award 1998, Edison Medal 2004), Am. Phys. Soc. (Arthur Schawlow prize in laser sci. 2004), Optical Soc. Am. (Robert Wood prize 2001), Internat. Soc. for Optical Engring., Inst. of Physics (Duddell medal 2001); mem. NAE, NAS, European Acad. Sci. Business E-Mail: capasso@deas.harvard.edu.

CAPDEVILA, JORGE H., medical educator, biochemistry educator; b. Santiago, Chile, Oct. 6, 1940; arrived in US, 1971; s. Jorge Capdevila and Carmen Honorato; m. Antonieta M. Maturana, June 26, 1971; children: Christian, Andres. B, U. Chile, Santiago, 1959, MS, 1965; PhD, U. Ga., Athens, 1974. Postdoctoral fellow Karolinska Inst., Stockholm, 1974—75; assoc. prof. Vanderbilt U. Med. Sch., Nashville, 1986—90, prof., 1991—. Fellow: Am. Heart Assn. (Novartis award for hypertension rsch. 2004). Roman Catholic. Achievements include patents for Cyp2c and Hypertension. Office: Vanderbilt University Medical School 1161 21st Ave South Nashville TN 37232 Home Phone: 615-322-4968; Office Phone: 615-322-4968.

CAPDEVILLE, ALEX, academic administrator; b. Opheim, Mont. A, B, M, Mont. State U. - Northern; PhD, Colo. State U. CEO Helena Coll. Tech., 1978—2000; chancellor Mont. State Univ. Northern, Havre, 2000—. Mem.: Northwest Assn. Schools and Colleges. Mailing: Montana State Univ Northern PO Box 7751 Havre MT 59501*

CAPE, JAMES ODIES E., fashion designer; b. Detroit, Nov. 18, 1947; s. Odies E. and Juanita K. (Brandon) C. Student, Henry Ford C.C., 1973-75, Am. Acad. Dramatic Arts, NYC, 1975-76, Pace U., 1977-78. Trapeze artist Mills Bros. Circus, 1962; skater Ice Capades, 1971-72; creator, dir., instr. skating program City of Southfield, Mich., 1972, 73; haute couture designer James E. Cape & Assocs., Dearborn, Mich., 1986—. Mem. Marji Kunz scholarship award com. Wayne State U., Detroit. Film reviewer Times-Herald Newspapers, 1989-90; clothing designs pub. in various mags. and newspapers; creations for TV and stage including the Emmys, The Am. Music Awards, Dick Clark-ABC Prodns., Showtime Spl. Aretha, Trump Castle, Atlantic City, The Chgo. Theater, Kennedy Ctr., Washington, Radio City Music Hall; co-prodr. Eartha Kitt, A Night in Paris; spl. commd. designs various celebrities; spl. publicity creations for Detroit Inst. Arts, Am. Lung Assn.; producer, host TV show "Town Talk." Recipient Pre-silver, bronze medals U.S. Figure Skating Assn., 1969, Citation award City of Dearborn, 1994, Wayne County (Mich.) Resolution award, 1993, Spl. Tribute award State of Mich. Ho. of Reps., 1994, Page award Herald Newspapers, 1999-2000. Mem. AFTRA, Actors Equity, Soc. for Cinephiles. Home: James E Cape & Assocs 500 N Rosevere Dearborn MI 48128 Office Phone: 313-561-4575. E-mail: JamesECape@aol.com.

CAPECCHI, MARIO RENATO, genetics educator; b. Verona, Italy, Oct. 6, 1937; BS, Antioch Coll., 1961; PhD in Biophysics, Harvard U., 1967. Soc. fellows, jr. fellow biophysics Harvard U., 1966-69, from asst. prof. to assoc. prof. biochemistry med. sch., 1969-73; prof. Biology U. Utah, 1973-88; prof. human genetics U. Utah Sch. Medicine, Salt Lake City, 1989—; investigator Howard Hughes Inst./U. Utah, Salt Lake City, 1988—; disting. prof. human genetics Howard Hughes Inst./U.Utah, 1993—. Mem. bd. sci. counselors Nat. Cancer Inst. Recipient Biochemistry award, Am. Chem. Soc., 1969, Intrnat award, Gairdner Found., Can., 1990, Alfred P. Sloan Jr. prize, Gen. Motors Corp., 1994, Molecular Bioanalytics prize, 1996, Kyoto Prize in Basic Schs., 1996, Franklin medal, Franklin Inst., 1997, Baxter award, AAMC, 1988, Horace Mann Disting. Alumni award, Antioch Coll., 2000, Premio Phoenix-Anni Verdi award, Associazione Anni Verdi, 2000, 33d Jimenez-Diaz prize, Fundacion Concita Rabago de Jiminez-Diaz, 2001, Albert Lasker award Basic Med. Rsch., 2001, Laureate of the Nat. Medal of Sci. award, 2001, Utah Gov.'s Medal of Sci. and Tech. award, 2002, Wolf prize in Medicine, 2002—03, Pezcollar Found. Internat. Cancer Rsch. award, Am. Assn. Cancer Rsch., 2003, March of Dimes prize in devel. biology, 2005. Mem. NAS, Am. Biochem. Soc., Am. Soc. Biol. Chemistry, Am. Soc. Microbiology, Molecular Med. Soc., N.Y. Acad. Sci., Soc. Devel. Biology, Internat. Genome Soc., Genetics Soc. Am., Am. Acad. Microbiology, European Acd. Scis. Achievements include research in gaining an understanding of how the information encoded in the gene is translated by the cell, elucidating the mechanism of genetic recombination in mouse embryo-derived stem (ES) cells, developing gene targeting in the mouse, gaining an understanding of embryonic and neuronal mammalian development through the use of gene targeting. Office: Howard Hughes Med Inst Univ Utah 15 N 2030 E Rm 5100 Salt Lake City UT 84112-5331 Office Phone: 801-581-7096. Business E-Mail: mario.capecchi@genetics.utah.edu.

CAPECE, MICHELLE RENÉ, elementary school educator; b. Augsburg, Germany, Oct. 25, 1965; arrived in U.S., 1967; d. Jonathan Bennett and Judy Gibson Capece. BS in Edn., Ga. So. U., Statesboro, 1993. Tchr. pre-K, Jenkins County Primary, Millen, Ga., 1994—96, Sikes Schs., Snellville, Ga., 1996—97, Rainbow Express, Dublin, Ga., 1998—2000; tchr. lang. arts Dry Branch Elem., Ga., 2000—01; tchr. pre-K, Danville Elem. Sch., Ga., 2001—02, Jeffersonville Elem. Sch., Ga., 2002—03, tchr. K-6th sci., 2003—. Aftersch. tchr. Jeffersonville Elem. Sch., 2002—. Team capt. Relay for Life, Twiggs County, 2002—; football coach Twiggs Recreation Dept., Twiggs County, 2005, soccer coach, 2006. Recipient Apple award, Jenkins County Primary Sch., 1996. Home: 409 Irish Lake Rd Dublin GA 31027 Office: Twiggs County Bd Edn 952 Main St Jeffersonville GA 31044 Personal E-mail: michellecapece@yahoo.com.

CAPEHART, BARNEY LEE, industrial and systems engineer, educator; b. Galena, Kans., Aug. 20, 1940; s. Samuel Alfred and Mary Jane (Bliss) Capehart; m. Lynne Carol Fowler, Sept. 2, 1961; children: Thomas David, Jeffrey Donald, Cynthia Diane. BSEE, U. Okla., 1961, MEE, 1962, PhD, 1967. Instr. elec. engring. U. Okla., Norman, 1965—67; mem. tech. staff Aerospace Corp., San Bernardino, Calif., 1967—68; asst. prof. indsl. and sys. engring. U. Fla., Gainesville, 1968—72; assoc. prof. indsl. engring. U. Tenn., 1972—73; assoc. prof. indsl. and sys. engring. U. Fla., Gainesville, 1973—79, prof., 1979—, asst. chmn., 1987—88. Cons. Martin Marietta Corp., U.S. Naval Tng. Device Ctr., State of Fla., Hicks and Assocs., Casazza, Schultz & Assocs., U.S. Dept. Energy, Dep. Ass. Sec. Bldg. Techs., Washington, 1989—90; nat. lectr. Assn. Energy Engrs.; expert witness in energy and safety cases; chmn. Regional Energy Action Com., 1977—79; mem. Region IV adv. group appropriate tech. Dept. Energy, 1978—80; mem. Local Energy Action Program, 1980—81. Author: books in field; editor: Internat. Jour. Energy Sys., 1985—88; contbr. articles to profl. jours. Pres. Fla. League Conservation Voters, 1984—86; dir. Energy Analysis and Diagnostic Center U. Fla., Fla., dir. Indsl. Assessment Ctr., 1995—99; grad. leadership Gainesville, 1984. Decorated USAF Commendation medal; named May 26, 1987, Barney Capehart Day in his honor, Alachua County, Fla.; named to Assn. Energy Engrs. Hall of Fame; recipient Palladium medal, Am. Assn. Engring. Socs., 1988. Fellow: IEEE (mem. energy com. 1988—90), AAAS, Inst. Indsl. Engrs. (dir. energy mgmt. divsn. 1986—87); mem.: Assn. Energy Engrs., Fla. Conservation Found., Audubon Soc. (Fla. chpt. Conservationist of the Yr. 1987), Sigma Xi, Fla. Blue Key, Eta Kappa Nu, Tau Beta Pi, Alpha Pi Mu, Sigma Tau. Home: 1601 NW 35th Way Gainesville FL 32605-4846 Office: U Fla Dept Indsl & Systems Engring 303 Weil Hall Gainesville FL 32611-2083 Office Phone: 352-392-1464 ext. 2008. Business E-Mail: capehart@ise.ufl.edu.

CAPEHART, BONNIE, language educator; d. Kenneth James and Marion June Hawkins; m. Donn Robert Holmer (div.); 1 child, Robert James Holmer; m. David Harold Capehart, Aug. 22, 1992. BA in Applied Arts and Scis. Art, San Diego State U., 1987; M in Tchg., Nat. U., San Diego, 2005. Cert. tchr. Calif. Avid coord. S.W. Mid. Sch., San Diego, 1999—2006, English tchr., 1999—2006; tchr. Bonita Vista Mid. Sch., Chula Vista, Calif., 2006—. Mem.: NEA, Calif. Tchrs. Assn., Nat. Coun. Tchrs. English. Avocations: genealogy, reading. Office: Bonita Vista Mid Sch Sweetwater Union HS Dist 650 Otay Lakes Rd Chula Vista CA 91910 Office Phone: 619-397-2200.

CAPELLAS, MICHAEL D., telecommunications industry executive; b. Aug. 19, 1954; m. Marie Capellas; 2 children. BBA Kent St. U., 1976. With Republic Steel Corp., 1976—81; corp. dir. for info. systems, contr. and treas. of Asia Pacific ops. Schlumberger Ltd., 1981—96; founder, mng. ptnr. Benchmarking Partners, Cambridge, Mass., 1996; dir. supply chain mgmt. SAP Am., 1996—97; sr. v.p., gen. mgr. for global energy bus. Oracle Corp., 1997—98; chief info. officer Compaq Computer Corp., Houston, 1998-99, acting COO, 1999, pres., CEO, 1999—2000, chmn., CEO, 2000—02; pres. Hewlett-Packard Co., 2002; chmn., CEO WorldCom Inc. (now MCI), 2002—04; pres., CEO MCI, Inc., Ashburn, Va., 2004—06; acting pres & CEO Serena Software, Inc., 2006—07; sr. adv. Silver Lake Partners, 2007—. Bd. dirs. Cisco Systems, 2006—. Bd. govs. Boys & Girls Clubs Am.; bd. trustees Am. U., Washington. Recipient Hope Technology Award, ctr. for Missing and Exploited Children. Mem.: bd. of Trustees of American University in Wash. DC. Avocations: travel, golf, running, music. Mailing: Cisco Systems Bd Directors 170 W Tasman Dr San Jose CA 95134-1706 Office Phone: 703-886-5600. Office Fax: 212-885-0570.*

CAPELLE-FRANK, JACQUELINE AIMEE, writer; b. Fond du Lac, Wis., Dec. 23, 1935; d. Ira Richard and Aimee Cecilia (Dignin) Capelle; divorced; children: P. Malachi, Tamara, Daria Frank-Weber. AA, Edison C.C., Naples, Fla., 1986; cert., U. Cambridge, Eng., 1991, U. Oxford, 1992, Paris Am. Acad., 1992; BA, Fla. Internat. U., 1994. Part-time instr. Internat. Coll., 1999. Author: (children's book) What's a Library, 1974, (anthologies) Poetic Voices of America, 1996, 97. Mem. adv. bd. Greater Naples Leadership, Inc., 1999-2000. Mem. AAUW, DAR, Soc. Mayflower Descendants, Nat. Mus. Women, Collier County Hist. Soc. (bd. dirs. 1994-2002, pres. 1997-2001), Nat. Trust for Hist. Preservation, Mus. Trustee Assn., Antiques Automobile Club Am. Republican. Presbyterian. Avocations: reading, travel, country walks, gardening, swimming. Home: 143 4th Ave N Naples FL 34102-8421

CAPELLI, JOHN PLACIDO, nephrologist, educator; b. Hammonton, NJ, May 23, 1936; s. John L. and Marie C.; m. Patricia Ann Verna, Nov. 4, 1961; children: John L., Elizabeth Ann, David S. BS in Biology, Villanova U., 1958; MD, Jefferson Med. Coll., 1962. Diplomate: Am. Bd. Internal Medicine (Nephrology). Intern Michael Reese Hosp., Chgo., 1962-63; resident Thomas Jefferson U. Hosp., 1963-65, NIH fellow in nephrology, 1965-67, Martin E. Rehfuss chief resident internal medicine, 1967-68; practice medicine specializing in nephrology Haddonfield, NJ, 1968—; clin. prof. medicine U. Medicine and Dentistry N.J., 1995—; pres. Lourdes Med. Assn., P.A. and Health Mgmt. Svcs. Orgn., Inc., 1995—, Nephrology Network for N.J., P.C., 1995—. Dir. div. clin. pharmacology Jefferson Med. Coll., Phila., 1968-69; dir. hemodialysis unit Our Lady of Lourdes Med. Ctr., Camden, N.J., 1969— , dir. div. nephrology and transplantation, 1974— , chief of staff, 1980-86, v.p. med. affairs, 1987-2001, sr. v.p. med. affairs, 2002—; clin. prof. medicine Thomas Jefferson U., Phila., 1974—; mem. chronic renal disease adv. com. N.J. Dept. Health, 1969-79, chmn., 1971-73, 74-75; pres. Health Mgmt. Svcs. Orgns., Inc., 1995—, N.J. Renal Mgmt., 1996—. Discovered extra-renal source of renin in uterus, 1968; contbr. articles to med. jours. Named to Order of Knights St. Gregory, 1995. Mem. Am. Soc. Nephrology, Internat. Soc. Nephrology, Renal Physicians Assn. (pres. 1977-79), AMA, Med. Soc. N.J., Am. Soc. Artificial Internal Organs, Southeastern Organ Procurement Found., Nat. Kidney Found. Home: Office: Haddon Renal Med Specialists 35 Kings Hwy E Haddonfield NJ 08033-2009 Office Phone: 856-757-3903. Personal E-mail: jpcapelli@aol.com.

CAPELLO, WILLIAM NALDO, surgeon; b. Tarentum, Pa., Feb. 22, 1942; s. Americus and Neila Capello; children: Gregory, Susan Sockel. BA, Rutgers State U., New Brunswick, NJ, 1964; MD, U. Pitts., 1968. Cert. orthop. surgeon Am. Bd. Orthop. Surgeons, 1974. Orthop. surgery residency U. Iowa, 1970—73; asst. prof. orthop. Ind. U. Sch. Medicine, Indpls., 1975—80, assoc. prof. orthop., 1980—87, prof., 1987—. Contbr. articles to profl. and med. jours. Orthop. surgeon US Army, 1973—75, Indpls. Mem.: AMA (assoc.), Soc. Arthritic Joint Surgery, Am. Assn. Hip and Knee Surgeons, Am. Acad. Orthop. Surgeons, Orthop. Rsch. Soc. (shands cir. mem. 2000—), Am. Orthop. Assn. (assoc.), Internat. Hip Soc. (assoc.), Hip Soc. (assoc.; pres. 1992—93). Achievements include patents for acetabular shell with supplemental support and method. Office: Ind U Sch Medicine 541 Clinical Dr Room 600 Indianapolis IN 46202 Office Phone: 317-274-8617. Office Fax: 317-274-3702.

CAPELLOS, CHRIS SPIRIDON, chemist; b. Athens, Greece, Oct. 22, 1934; came to US, 1966, naturalized, 1976; s. Spiridon Em. and Melpo Christou (Christidou) C.; m. Helen Nicholaou Sakkoulas, Dec. 3, 1959; children: Melina, Maria. BS in Chemistry, Athens, 1959; DIC in Nuc. Tech., Imperial Coll., London U., 1962; PhD, London U., 1965. Rsch. assoc. Brookhaven Nat. Lab., NY, 1966-68, assoc. chemist NY, 1968, vis. assoc. chemist NY, 1968-72; sr. rsch. chemist energetic materials divsn. Armament R&D Command, Dover, NJ, 1968—, sr. scientist, 1972—. Vis. scientist Davy Faraday Lab., Royal Inst., 1970-71; NRC rsch. advisor; bd. dirs. NATO Advanced Study Inst., 1980, 85; tech. adv. panel to Army Rsch. Office for Univ. Rsch. Initiative, 1987—; vice-chmn. Gordon Rsch. Conf. on Energetic Materials for 1990, chmn., 1992. Author: Kinetic Systems, 1972, Japanese transl., 1978; editor NATO Conf. Procs., 1980, 86; contbr. writings to sci. jours.; contbr. numerous sci. papers to nat. and internat. meetings. Served with Greek Army, 1965-66. Recipient NATO award, 1979-80, 86, R&D awards for tech. excellence Sec. US Army, 2004, 05; USAF Office Sci. Rsch. fellow, 1962-65. Mem. Am. Chem. Soc., Radiation Rsch., NY Acad. Scis., Sigma Xi (pres. Picatinny chpt.). Home: 11 Cambridge Rd Morris Plains NJ 07950-1529 Office Phone: 973-724-3550. Personal E-mail: cristeleni@aol.com.

CAPEN, CHARLES CHABERT, veterinary pathology educator; b. Tacoma, Sept. 3, 1936; s. Charles (Kenneth) and Ruth (Chabert) C.; m. Sharron Lee Martin, June 27, 1968. DVM, Wash. State U., Pullman, 1960; MS, Ohio State U., Columbus, 1961, PhD, 1965. Diplomate Am. Coll. Veterinary Pathologists. Instr. dept. vet. pathology Ohio State U., Columbus, 1962—65, asst. prof. dept. vet. pathology, 1965—67, assoc. prof., 1967—70, prof., 1970—, prof. endocrinology Coll. Medicine, 1972—, chmn. dept. vet. pathobiology, 1981—94, chmn., 1982—94, interim chmn. dept. bioscis., 1994—97, chmn., 1997—2002, disting. univ. prof., 2001—. Israel Doniach Meml. lectr. Brit. Endocrine Soc. meeting, Manchester, 1989; plenary lectr. Italian Soc. Endocrinology Congress, Pisa, 1995. Editor: (series) Animal Models of Human Disease, 1979—96; mem. editl. bd.: Lab. Investigation, 1988—2006; Vet. Pathology, 1986—87; Am. Jour. Pathology, 1984—88; Exptl. and Toxicologic Pathology, 1990—2005; Food and Chem. Toxicology, 1993—2000; Drug and Chem. Toxicology, 1994—97; Toxicology and Ecotoxicology News, 1993—2006; Handbook on Rat Tumor Pathology WHO/IARC, 1991—96. Mem. Opera Columbus, 1982—, Columbus Symphony Assn., 1972—. Named Disting. U. Prof., Ohio State U., 2001; recipient Disting. scholar award, 1993, Dean's Tchg. Excellence award for grad. edn., Coll. Vet. Medicine, 1993, Disting. Vet. Alumnus award, Wash. State U., 1997, Career Achievement award in canine rsch., Am. Vet. Med. Found., 1997. Fellow: Am. Assn. Advancement of Sci.; mem.: AVMA (Nat. Borden rsch. award 1975, small animal rsch. award 1984, Gaines rsch. award 1987, excellence in canine rsch. award 1995, George Scott Meml. award of Toxicology Forum 1997), Am. Assn. Clin. Chemistry (Outstanding Contbns. Animal Clin. Chemistry award 2004), Soc. Toxicol. Pathologists (pres. 1997—98, Career Achievement award 2006, 2006), U.S. Can. Acad. Pathology (coun. 1989—92), Inst. Medicine/NAS, Am. Coll. Vet. Pathologists (coun. 1975—81, pres. 1978—79, diplomate, disting. mem.). Avocations: travel, wildlife and nature photography. Office: The Ohio State U Dept Vet Bioscis 1925 Coffey Rd Columbus OH 43210-1005 Office Phone: 614-247-6206. Business E-Mail: capen.2@osu.edu.

CAPENER, REGNER ALVIN, minister, electronics engineer, writer; b. Astoria, Oreg., Apr. 18, 1942; s. Alvin Earnest and Lillian Lorraine (Lehtosaari) C.; divorced; children: Deborah, Christian, Melodie, Ariella; m. Della Denise Melson, May 17, 1983; children: Shelley, Danielle, Rebekah, Joshua. Student, U. Nebr., 1957-58, 59-60, Southwestern Coll., Waxahachie, Tex., 1958-59, Bethany Bible Coll., 1963-64; BA Sales and Mktg., Gen. Motors Inst., 1968; student Greek and Hebrew studies, Fuller Theol. Sem., 1974—75; EE diploma, Panasonic's Elec. Engring. Inst., 1983. Ordained minister Full Gospel Assembly Ch., 1971. Rsch. engr. Lockheed Missiles & Space Corp., Palo Alto, Calif., 1962-64; engr., talk show host Sta. KHOF-FM, Glendale, Calif., 1966-67; youth min. Bethel Union Ch., Duarte, Calif., 1966-67; pres. Intermountain Electronics, Salt Lake City, 1967-72, Christian Broadcasting Network-Alaska, Inc., Fairbanks, 1977-83, R & DC Engring., Anchorage, 1991—, R & DC Ministries, 2005—, Capener Ministries, 2006—; assoc. pastor Full Gospel Assembly, Salt Lake City, 1968-72, Long Beach Christian Ctr., 1972-76; v.p. Refuge Ministries, Inc., Long Beach, 1972-76; gen. mgr. Action Sch. Broadcasting, Anchorage, 1983-85; pres., pastor House of Praise, Anchorage, 1984-93; chief engr. KTBY-TV, Inc., Anchorage, 1988-93, KTLM-TV, McAllen, Tex., 1999—2003; sr. pastor House of Praise and Worship, 2005—06, River Worship Ctr., 2006—; pres. Capener Ministries, 2006—. Area dir. Christian Broadcasting Network, Virginia Beach, 1977-83; cons., dir. Union Bond and Trust Co., Anchorage, 1985-86; author, editor univ. courses, 1984-85; dep. gov. Am. Biog. Inst. Rsch. Assn., 1990—. Author: Spiritual Maturity, 1975, Spiritual Warfare, 1976, The Doctrine of Submission, 1988, A Vision for Praise, 1988, Ekklesia, 1993, For the Marriage of the Lamb Has Come, 1996, Open Letters to the Ekklesia, 1997, Another Coffee Break, 2005; author, composer numerous gospel songs. Sec., Christian Businessmen's Com., Salt Lake City, 1968-72; area advisor Women's Aglow Internat., Fairbanks, 1981-83; local co-chmn. campaign Boucher for Gov. Com., Fairbanks, 1982; campaigner for Boucher, Anchorage, 1984, Clark Gruening for Senate Com., Barrow, Alaska, 1980; TV producer Stevens for U.S. Senate, Barrow, 1978; fundraiser City of Refuge, Mex., 1973-75; statewide rep. Sudden Infant Death Syndrome, Barrow, 1978-82; founder Operation Blessing/Alaska, 1981; mem. resch. bd. advisors Am. Biog. Inst., 1990—; advisor Anchorage chpt. Women's Aglow Internat., 1990-91, bd. dirs., v.p., 2001-04, Hidalgo County Children's Adv. Ctr.; candidate for U.S. Ho. of Reps., 2003-04; mem. Coun. Nat. Policy, 2004—. Mem. IEEE, Soc. Broadcast Engrs. (sec. Rio Grande Valley chpt. 2001-05, Anchorage chpt. 1989, 90, CBNT cert.), Internat. Soc. Classical Guitarists (sec. 1967-69), Nat. Assn. Broadcasters, Tex. Assn. Broadcasters, McAllen C. of C. Republican. Achievements include invention of broadcasting and electronic instruments. Avocations: music, languages, history. Office: River Worship Ctr 700 S 6th St Sunnyside WA 98944-2113 Home Phone: 509-837-2887; Office Phone: 509-837-4657. Business E-Mail: capenerministries@embarqmail.com. *The word "impos-*

sible" need never be a part of the vocabulary of one whose life is intertwined with the Lord Jesus Christ. I have learned that there are no problems in life which do not have clear and definitive solutions when approached from the standpoint of a personal relationship with Jesus Christ.

CAPERS, DOM (DOMINIC CAPERS), professional football coach; b. Cambridge, Ohio, Aug. 5, 1950; BS in Psychology and Phys. Edn., Mount Union Coll.; MA in Adminstrn., Kent State U. Grad. asst. Kent State U., 1972-74, U. Wash.; defensive backs coach U. Hawaii, 1975, defensive coach, 1976; defensive asst. coach San Jose State, 1977, U. Calif., 1978-79; defensive backs coach U. Tenn., 1980-81, Ohio State, 1982-83, Phila. Stars (USFL), 1984, Balt. Stars (USFL), 1985, New Orleans Saints, 1986-91; defensive coord. Pitts. Steelers, 1992-94; head coach Carolina Panthers, 1995-98; defensive coord. Jacksonville Jaguars, 1999-2001; head coach Houston Texans, 2001—05; spl. asst. to head coach Miami Dolphins, 2006—07, def. coord., 2007—. Named NFC Coach of the Yr., 1996. Office: Miami Dolphins 7500 SW 30th St Davie FL 33314*

CAPERS, GREGG, secondary school educator, musician; b. Bronx, NY, Jan. 21, 1961; s. Joe Simon and Evelyn Delores Capers; m. Alberta Amber Lloyd, Jan. 21, 1966; children: George Steven Bush, Christina Lillian Bush, Anthony Tony Burno. MusB, Bowie State U., 1983; Assoc. Degree, Comml. Programming Unlimited, NYC, 1985; cert., Trident Tech. Coll., Charleston, SC, 1988. Min. praise and worship God's Positive Minds, Phila., 1998—2003; tchr. Del. Valley Charter H.S., Phila., 1999—. Musical and choir dir. Inspirational Words for Life, Phila., 1999—. Min. music Ministers of Praise, Phila. Recipient John Phillip Sousa Award For Music Excellence, USMC, 1980. Democrat. Home: 6740 Old York Rd Philadelphia PA 19126 Office: Inspirational Words Of Life 6740 Old York Rd Philadelphia PA 19126 Office Phone: 215-424-7003. Personal E-mail: greg.alberta@verizon.net.

CAPERTON, (WILLIAM) GASTON, (III), educational association administrator, former governor; b. W.Va., Feb. 21, 1940; m. Rachael Worby; children: Gat, John. BA, U. NC, 1963. Ins. agent, Charleston, W.Va.; pres. McDonough Caperton Ins. Group, 1976; gov. State of W.Va., Charleston, 1989—97; dir. Inst. Edn. & Govt. Columbia U., NYC, 1997—99; pres. Coll. Bd., 1999—. Tchg. fellow John F. Kennedy Inst. Politics Harvard U., 1997; founder, mgr. tchr. Inst. Edn. and Govt. Columbia U. Mem. Intergovernmental Policy Adv. Com. on US Trade; founder, past pres. W.Va. Edn. Fund.; chmn. Appalachian Regional Commn., So. Regional Edn. Bd., So. Growth Policy Bd. Mem.: Nat. Governors Assn. Exec. Com., Dem. Governors' Assn. Office: The Coll Bd 45 Columbus Ave New York NY 10023*

CAPICE, PHILIP CHARLES, retired broadcast executive; b. Bernardsville, NJ, June 24, 1931; s. Philip Joseph and Angelina Mary (Togno) C. BA, Dickinson Coll., 1952; M.F.A., Columbia U., 1954. Production supr., assoc. program dir. Benton & Bowles Inc., NYC, 1954-64, Vice pres. in charge program devel., 1965-69; dir. spl. programs CBS-TV Network, NYC, 1969-74; sr. v.p. creative affairs Lorimar Prodns., Burbank, Calif., 1974-78; pres. Lorimar TV, Burbank, Calif., 1978-79; ind. producer Lorimar Productions, Culver City, Calif., from 1979; pres., chief exec. officer Raven's Claw Productions, Los Angeles, Calif. Since 1974, exec. producer Dallas, Eight Is Enough, The Blue Knight, Two Marriages, Helter Skelter, Sybil (Emmy Award, 1977, Peabody Award, 1977), Green Eyes (Peabody Award, 1978, Humanitas Prize, 1978), Eric, Widow, Studs Lonigan, A Man Called Intrepid, The Runaways, The Prince of Central Park, A Question of Guilt, Some Kind of Miracle (Christopher Award, 1978), Returning Home, Conspiracy of Terror, Hunter, Married: The First Year, The Rivermen, Mary and Joseph: A Love Story, The Stranger Within, A Matter of Life and Death, Bunco, Some People Like Us, Private Sessions, others. Trustee Dickinson Coll. Recipient Emmy award, 1977, Peabody award, 1977, 78, Disting. Alumni awrd for profl. achievements Dickinson Coll., 2003. Mem. Acad. TV Arts and Scis., The Caucus for Producers, Writers and Dirs, Producers-Writers Guild.

CAPITAN, WILLIAM HARRY, university president emeritus; b. Owosso, Mich., Feb. 7, 1933; s. Harry and Anthe (Sarris) C.; m. Dolores Marie Randolph, Sept. 19, 1959; children: Rita, Edwin. BA, U. Mich., 1954; postgrad., Queens U.; postgrad. (Ulster Am. fellow), 1954-55; MA, U. Minn., 1958, PhD, 1960. Registered mediator 2001, lic. Capt. USCG, auxiliary USCG, 2001, comdr. flotilla, 2005. Instr. philosophy U. Minn., 1959-60, U. Md., 1960-62; asst. prof., assoc. prof., chmn. dept. Oberlin (Ohio) Coll., 1962-70; dean fine arts, v.p. acad. affairs, acting pres. Saginaw Valley State U., U. Ctr., Mich., 1970-74; v.p. acad. affairs, dean faculty, acting pres. W.Va. Wesleyan Coll., Buckhannon, 1974-79; pres. Ga. Southwestern State U/, Americus, 1979-95; pres. emeritus Ga. Southwestern Coll., Americus, 1996—. Adj. prof. U. Ga., 1996. Author: Introduction to the Philosophy of Religion, 1972, Speak For Yourself, 1987; editor: (with D.D. Merrill) Metaphysics and Explanation, Art, Religion, and Mind, 1967, The Ethical Navigator, 2000. Trustee Charles L. Mix Meml. Fund, Inc., 1979—96; pres. Americus Sumter County C. of C., 1985; v.p. Hellenic-Am. C. of C., Atlanta; lay reader Episcopal Ch., Americus, Ga.; bd. dir. Saginaw Symphony Orch., 1970—74; Project Save; Buckhannon C. of C.; Sumter County United Way. Vice capt. USCG Aux., comdr. USCG Aux., 2004—06. Am. Council Lerned Socs. fellow Paris, 1967-68 Mem. Am. Soc. Aesthetics, Am. Philos. Assn., Rotary (pres. 1990-91), Beta Theta Phi, Omicron Delta Kappa, Phi Kappa Phi, Phi Delta Kappa. Episcopalian. Office: GA Southwestern State U Americus GA 31709 *Clarity of objectives, persistence, and Christian respect for persons have guided me in whatever of value I have accomplished. My failures came when I wasn't very clear about what I was doing. America rewards, supports, and buoys up those with initiative. This is why my parents were able to go from "rags to riches" and I from illiterate to lettered. We Americans help one another, and we shape our institutions to help, too. May we ever remain so.*

CAPITO, SHELLEY MOORE, congresswoman; b. Glen Dale, W.Va., Nov. 26, 1953; m. Charles L. Capito, Jr.; children: Charles, Moore, Shelley. BS in Zoology, Duke U., 1975; MEd, U. Va., 1976. Career counselor W.Va. State Coll.; dir. Edn1. Info. Ctr. W.Va. Bd. Regents; mem. W.Va. State Ho. Dels. from 30th Dist., 1996—2000, US Congress from 2nd W.Va. dist., 2001—, mem. rules com. Mem. YWCA (past pres.), Cmty. coun., Kanawha Valley, West Va. Interagency Coun. Early Intervention. Republican. Presbyterian. Office: US Ho Reps 1431 Longworth Ho Office Bldg Washington DC 20515-4802 Office Phone: 202-225-2711.*

CAPIZZI, MICHAEL ROBERT, lawyer, former prosecutor; b. Detroit, Oct. 19, 1939; s. I.A. and Adelaide E. (Jennelle) C.; m. Sandra Jo Jones, June 22, 1963; children: Cori Anne, Pamela Jo. BSBA, Ea. Mich. U., 1961; JD, U. Mich., 1964. Bar: Calif. 1965, U.S. Dist. Ct. (so. dist., cent. dist.) Calif. 1965, U.S. Ct. Appeals (9th cir.) 1970, U.S. Supreme Ct. 1971, U.S. Ct. Fed. Claims 2001, U.S. Dist. Ct. (east. dist.) Calif. 2004. Dep. dist. atty., Orange County, Calif., 1965-68; head writs, appeals and spl. assignments sect., 1968-71; asst. dist. atty., dir. spl. ops., 1971-86; legal counsel, mem. exec. bd. Interstate Organized Crime Index, 1971-79, Law Enforcement Intelligence Unit, 1971-95, chief asst. dist. atty., 1986-90, dist. atty., 1990-99; pvt. practice, 1999—. Instr. criminal justice Santa Ana Coll., 1967-76, Calif. State U., 1976-87. Commr. City Planning Commn., Fountain Valley, Calif., 1971-80, vice chmn. 1972-73, chmn. 1973-75, 79-80; candidate for Rep. nomination Calif. Atty. Gen., 1998. Fellow Am. Coll. Trial Lawyers; mem. Nat. Dist. Attys. Assn. (bd. dirs. 1995-96, v.p. 1996-99), Calif. Dist. Attys. Assn. (outstanding prosecutor award 1980, v.p. 1995, pres. 1996), Calif. Bar Assn., Orange County Bar Assn. (chmn. cts. com. 1977, chmn. coll. of trial advocacy com. 1978-81, bd. dirs. 1977-81, sec.-treas. 1982, pres. 1984). Republican. Office: PO Box 1938 Santa Ana CA 92702-1938 Office Phone: 714-283-1878. Business E-Mail: mrclaw@socal.rr.com.

CAPKA, J. RICHARD (JOSEPH RICHARD CAPKA), federal agency administrator, retired military officer; m. Susan Capka; children: David, Richard. BS, U.S. Mil. Acad., 1967; MS in Engring., U. Calif. Berkeley; MBA, Chaminade U.; Grad., Nat. War Coll., 1991. Commd. 2d lt. U.S. Army, 1967, advanced through grades to brig. gen., various assignments with Army Corps Engrs. including comdr., dist. engr., Balt. Engring. Dist., spl. asst. to Chief of Engineers for Internat. Activities, capt., then maj. Pacific Ocean Divsn., 1980-84; comdr., divsn. engr. South Pacific Divsn. U.S. Army CE, Hawaii, comdr., divsn. engr. South Atlantic Divsn.; CEO, exec. dir. Mass. Turnpike Authority, 2001—02; dep. adminstr. Fed. Highway Adminstrn., US Dept. Transp., Washington, 2002—06, acting adminstr., 2005—06, adminstr., 2006—. Decorated DSM, Def. Superior Svc. medal, Army Commendation medal, Legion of Merit. Office: US Dept Transp Fed Highway Adminstrn 400 Seventh St SW Rm 4218 Washington DC 20590 E-mail: capka@fhwa.dot.com.

CAPLAN, ALLAN HART, lawyer; BA, U. Manitoba, 1966; JD, William Mitchell Coll. Law, 1974. Bar: Minn. 1974, Wis. 1988, Fed. Ct. Former asst. atty., Hennepin County; former pub. defender; ptnr. Caplan Law Firm P.A., Minn., 1983—. Spkr. in field. Named Minn. Super Lawyer Criminal Def., Mpls.-St. Paul Mag., Minn. Law and Politics. Mem.: NACDL (life), Minn. State Bar Assn., Hennepin County Bar Assn. Office: Caplan Law Firm PA 525 Lumber Exchange Bldg 10 S 5th St Minneapolis MN 55402 Office Phone: 612-341-4570. Office Fax: 612-341-0507. E-mail: acaplan@caplanlaw.com.*

CAPLAN, ARTHUR LEONARD, university program director, educator; b. Boston, Mar. 21, 1950; s. Sidney and Natalie (Fluke) C.; m. Margaret Brennan; 1 child, Zachary. BA in Philosophy, Brandeis U., 1971; MA in Philosophy, Columbia U., 1973, MPhil, 1975, PhD in History and Philosophy of Sci., 1979; seven degrees (hon.), colls. and med. schs. Tchr. U. Pitts., Columbia U.; staff assoc. in ethical issues in sci. and medicine The Hastings Ctr., 1975-76, assoc. for humanities, 1977-84, assoc. dir., 1984—87; instr. Sch. Pub. Health, Columbia U., NYC, 1977-78, assoc. for social medicine, 1978-81; prof. philosophy, surgery, dir. Ctr. for Biomedical Ethics U. Minn., Mpls., 1987-94; Emmanuel and Robert Hart prof. bioethics, chair dept. med. ethics, dir. Ctr. Bioethics U. Pa., Phila., 1994—. Vis. prof. U. Pitts., 1986: adv. bd. Poynter Inst., Nat. Marrow Donor Program, ARC; chair adv. com. UN on Human Cloning, Dept. Health and Human Svcs. on Blood Safety and Availability; mem. Presdnl. Adv. Com. on Gulf War Illnesses; mem. spl. adv. com. Internat. Olympic Com. on Genetics and Gene Therapy; mem. ethics com. Am. Soc. Gene Therapy; spl. adv. panel NIMH on Human Experimentation on Vulnerable Subjects; columnist MSNBC.com; frequent guest and commentator Nat. Pub. Radio, CNN, MSNBC, NY Times, Washington Post, Phila. Inquirer, and others; cons. in field many corps., non-profit orgns. and consumer orgns.; mem. nat. and internat. coms.; chair Nat. Cancer Inst. Biobanking Ethics Working Group; mem. bd. dirs. The Keystone Ctr., Tengion, The Nat. Ctr. Policy Rsch. on Women and Families, Octagon, Iron Disorders Found. and the Nat. Disease Rsch. Interchange. Author: Moral Matters, 1995, Prescribing Our Future: Ethical Challenges in Genetic Counseling, 1993, If I Were a Rich Man Could I Buy a Pancreas and Other Essays on Medical Ethics, 1992, When Medicine Went Mad: Bioethics and the Holocaust, 1992, Everyday Ethics: Resolving Dilemmas in Nursing Home Life, 1990, Beyond Baby M, 1990, Smart Mice, Not So Smart People, 2006; editor (with J. McCartney and D. Sisti) The Case of Terri Schiavo: Ethics at the End of Life, 2006; contbr. over 500 papers to profl. jours.; contbr. over 500 papers in refereed jours. medicine, sci., philosophy, bioethics and health policy; columnist bioethics MSNBC.com.; frequent guest, commentator Nat. Pub. Radio, CNN, MSNBC, The NY Times, Washington Post, Phila. Inquirer and many other media outlets. Mem. Clin. Health Care Task Force, Wash. (vice chmn. ethics working group 1993-94); cons. Office of Tech. Assessment U.S. Congress, Minn. Dept. Health, Am. Found. for AIDS Rsch., NIH, Dept. Health and Human Svcs., Nat. Marrow Donor Program, Lifesource-Organ Procurement Org., Nat. Acad. Scis.-Inst. Medicine, state legis. Pa., Minn., NY, NJ Recipient Commr.'s award Dept. Health and Human Svcs., 1993, McGovern medal Am. Med. Writers Assn.; named Person of Yr. USA Today, 2001; named One of the Fifty Most Influential People in Am. Health Care Modern Health Care mag., One of the Ten Most Influential People in Am. in Biotech. Nat. Jour., One of the Ten Most Influential People in Ethics of Biotech. Nature Biotech. Jour. Fellow: AAAS, Coll. Physicians Phila., NY Acad. Medicine, The Hastings Ctr.; mem.: Am. Assn. Bioethics (pres. 1993—95), Aspen Inst. (Mellon fellow), Am. Philos. Assn. (Centennial Prize), Ctrl. Soc. Clin. Rsch. Avocation: tennis. Office: U Pa 3401 Market St Philadelphia PA 19104-3318 E-mail: caplan@mail.med.upenn.edu.

CAPLAN, EDWIN HARVEY, retired dean, finance educator; b. Boston, Aug. 24, 1926; s. Henry and Dorothy (Nathanson) C.; m. Ramona Hootner, June 20, 1948; children— Gary, Dennis, Jeffrey, Nancy BBA, U. Mich., 1950, MBA, 1952; PhD, U. Calif., 1965. CPA, Calif., Mich. Ptnr. J.J. Gotlieb & Co., CPAs, Detroit, 1953-56; prof. acctg. Humboldt State U., 1956-61, U. Oreg., 1964-67; prof. U. N.Mex., Albuquerque, 1967-91, assoc. dean Sch. Mgmt., 1982-83, dean Sch. Mgmt., 1989-90; ret., 1991. Cons. in field. Contbr. articles to profl. jours. 1st lt. U.S. Army, 1944-46. Mem. AICPA, Am. Acctg. Assn., Inst. Mgmt. Accts. Home: 8201 Harwood Ave NE Albuquerque NM 87110-1517

CAPLAN, GERALYN MARIE, biology professor; b. Chicago, May 8, 1961; d. Frank and Loretta Mostaccio; m. Larry Caplan, Mar. 30, 1985; children: Joshua Alan, Jessica Marie. BS, No. Ill. U., 1982; MS, U. of Ill., 1984; BS, U. of So. Ind., 1999. Cert. tchr. Ind., Ky. Sci. and art history tchr. Union County H.S., Ky., 1999—2000; asst. prof. of biology Owensboro Cmty. and Tech. Coll., Ky., 2001—. Vol. Wesselman Woods Nature Preserve, Evansville, Ind., 1986—2006, Vanderburgh County Humane Soc., Evansville, Ind., 2002—05; mem. 2+2 Ednl. Sci. Com., Frankfurt, Ky., 2006; bd. chair New Beginnings Rape Crisis Ctr., Owensboro, Ky., 2003—. Recipient Bd. Mem. of The Yr., New Beginnings, 2004. Mem.: NSTA, Am. Assn. of Women in Cmty. Colls. (assoc.), Nat. Biology Tchr.'s Assn. (assoc.), Human Anatomy and Physiology Soc. (assoc.). Office: Owensboro Cmty and Tech Coll 4800 New Hartford Rd Owensboro KY 42303-1899 Home Phone: 812-867-1459; Office Phone: 270-686-4636. Business E-Mail: geralyn.caplan@kctcs.edu.

CAPLAN, LOUIS ROBERT, neurologist, educator; b. Balt., Dec. 31, 1936; s. Carl Clarence and Bess Pauline (Cohen) C.; m. F. Brenda Fields, Nov. 28, 1963; children: Laura, Daniel, Jonathan, David, Jeremy, Benjamin. BA cum laude, Williams Coll., 1958; MD summa cum laude, U. Md., 1962. Diplomate Am. Bd. Internal Medicine, Am. Bd. Psychiatry and Neurology. Intern to jr. asst. resident Boston City Hosp., 1962-64; resident Harvard Neurol. Unit, Boston, 1966-69; cerebrovascular fellow Mass. Gen. Hosp., Boston, 1969-70; neurologist Beth Israel Hosp., Boston, 1970-78; asst. prof. Harvard Med. Sch., Boston, 1970-78, prof. neurology, 1999; chief neurologist Michael Reese Hosp., Chgo., 1978-84; prof. neurology U. Chgo., 1980-84; chief neurologist New England Med. Ctr., Boston, 1984-97; prof., chmn. dept. neurology Tufts U., Boston, 1984-97, prof. medicine, 1989-97; neurologist Beth Israel Deaconess Med. Ctr., Boston, 1998—; prof. neurology Harvard Med. Sch., 1999—. Author: stroke: A Clinical Approach, 1986, 3rd edit., 2000, Consultations in Neurology, 1987, The Effective Clinical Neurologist, 2nd edit., 2001, Vertebrobasilar Arterial Disease, 1993; author: (with others) Cerebral Small Artery Disease, 1993; author: Management of Persons with Stroke, 1993, Brainstem Localization and Function, 1993, Intercerebral Hemmorhage, 1994, Family Guide to Stroke, 1994, Brain Ischemia-Basic Concepts and Clinical Relevance, 1995, Stroke Syndromes, 2nd edit., 2001, Posterior Circulation Disease, 1996, Neurologic Disorders: Course and Treatment, 1996, 2d edit., 2003, Primer on Cerebrovascular Diseases, 1997; author: (with others) Clinical Neurocardiology, 1999; author: Uncommon Causes of Stroke, 2001, Striking Back at Stroke--A Doctor-Patient Journal, 2003, Stroke, 2005, Brain Embolism, 2006; contbr. more than 500 articles to profl. jours. Bd. dirs. Solomon Schecter Day Sch., Boston, 1977-78, Chgo., 1983-85. Capt. U.S. Army, 1962-64. Recipient House Officer Tchg. prize Michael Reese Hosp., 1980. Fellow Am. Acad. Neurology, Am. Neurol. Assn., Stroke Coun. Am. Heart Assn. (chmn. 1987-89, sci. adv. com. 1990—), Royal Soc. of Medicine; mem. Coun. Med. Specialties Socs. (rep. 1982-90), Chgo. Neurol. Soc. (chmn. 1984-85), Boston Soc. Neurology and Psychiatry (pres. 1988-89), Chgo. Heart Assn. (chmn. stroke com. 1979-84), Australian Neurol. Soc. (hon.), German Neurol. Assn. (hon.), Phi Beta Kappa, Alpha Omega Alpha. Democrat. Jewish. Office: Beth Israel Deaconess MC Dept Neurology 330 Brookline Ave Palmer 127 Boston MA 02215-5400 Office Phone: 617-632-8911. Business E-Mail: lcaplan@bidmc.harvard.edu.

CAPLAN, MITCHELL H., diversified financial services company executive; b. Va; AB, Brandeis U., 1979; MBA, JD, Emory U. Assoc. Shearman & Sterling, 1985—90; with Strategic Devel. Dept. Telebanc Fin. Corp., 1990—2000; from chief fin. products officer, mng. dir. to CEO E*Trade Fin. Corp., Menlo Pk., Calif., 2000—03, CEO, 2003—. Bd. dirs. Juvenile Diabetes Found. Capitol Charter, The Am. Com. Weizmann Inst. Sci. Office: ETRADE Financial Corp 671 Glebe Road N 11th Fl Arlington VA 22203*

CAPLAN, RONALD MERVYN, obstetrician, gynecologist; b. Montreal, Dec. 12, 1937; came to U.S., 1971; s. Philip and Betty (Gamer) C.; m. Marilyn Gail Amdur, Dec. 23, 1962; children: Randy Sue, Gordon. BSc, McGill U., Montreal, 1958, MD CM, 1962. Resident Royal Victorial Hosp., Montreal, 1963-67; instr. ob-gyn McGill U., 1968-71; practice medicine specializing in ob-gyn Montreal, 1968-71, NYC, 1971—; mem. attending staff Royal Victoria Hosp., Montreal, 1968-71; asst. attending physician in ob-gyn N.Y. Hosp., NYC, 1971, now assoc. attending physician. Clin. assoc. prof. ob-gyn NY Weill Cornell Med. Coll. Editor: (with William J. Sweeney, III) Advances in Obstetrics and Gynecology (Williams, Wilkins), 1978, Principles of Obstetrics, 1982. Fellow ACS, Am. Coll. Obstetricians and Gynecologists, Royal Coll. Surgeons (Can.); mem. AMA, N.Y. Med. Soc., Soc. Reproductive Surgeons, Griffis Faculty Club of Cornell U. Office: 955 Old Quaker Hill Rd Pawling NY 12564 Personal E-mail: rcaplanmd@gmail.com.

CAPLAN, SHARON M., real estate company executive; b. Beloit, Wis., Apr. 18, 1943; m. Irvin N. Caplan; 3 children. BS, U. Wis., 1964; MS, Johns Hopkins U., Balt., 1975. Lic. real estate broker Md. Econ. asst. Balt. County Econ. Devel. Commn., 1979—83; positions up to sr. v.p. Manekin, L.L.C., Balt., 1983—. Vol. tutor Md. Dyslexic Soc.; bd. mem. Levindale Hebrew Geriatric Ctr. and Hosp. Named Broker of Yr., Greater Balt. Bd. Realtors, 1997; named one of Md.'s Top 100 Women, Daily Record, 1996, 1998, Top 3 Real Estate Brokers, Balt. Bus. Jour., Top 50 Women in Bus., Balt. Mag.; recipient Sustained Achievement award, Daily Record. Mem.: Soc. Indsl. and Office Realtors (office mem., nat. tenant rep. instr.), Comml. Real Estate Women (past nat. bd. mem.), Network 2000, Women's Giving Cir. Office: Manekin LLC 120 E Baltimore St Ste 2200 Baltimore MD 21202 Office Phone: 410-385-5771. E-mail: scaplan@manekin.com.*

CAPLES, LINDA GRIFFIN, retired secondary school educator; d. Melvin Mack and Inez (Watkins) Griffin; m. Thomas Ray Caples, Apr. 7, 1962; children: Thomas David, Gina Lynn Stegenga BA, U. Ala., 1962, MA, 1965; MS, So. Ill. U., 1975. Tchr. math. Tuscaloosa City Schs., 1962—64, Anniston City Schs., Ala., 1965—66, Demopolis City Schs., Ala., 1966—67, St. Charles Sch. Dist., Mo., 1969—70, 1974—97; ret., 1997. Spkr. profl. orgns Contbr. Active Calvary Evang. Free Ch.; tchr. vol. Child Evangelism Fellowship of Greater St. Louis. Mem. NEA, Nat. Coun. Tchrs. Math., Mo. Coun. Tchrs. Math., Mo. Edn. Assn., Math. Educators Greater St. Louis Avocations: travel, camping, bicycling. Home: 14 Wendy Ln Saint Peters MO 63376-2135 Personal E-mail: lcaples@charter.net.

CAPLES, RICHARD JAMES, performing company executive, lawyer; b. Balt., June 7, 1949; s. Delphin Delmas and Louise Skinner (Leigh) C. BA, Yale U., 1971; MA, Johns Hopkins U., 1974; JD, Cornell U., 1977. Bar: N.Y. 1978, U.S. Dist. Ct. (so. and ea. dists.) N.Y. 1978. Assoc. Donovan Leisure Newton & Irvine, NYC, 1977-81, Shearman & Sterling, NYC, 1981-83; exec. dir. Santa Fe Festival Theater, 1983-84, Lar Lubovitch Dance Co., NYC, 1984—; dir. Doug Varone and Dancers, NYC, 1995—, Dance/USA, Washington, 1995—2002, also sec. bd., 1998-2000, treas., 2000—02, dir., 2004—, vice chmn., 2004—; sec.-treas. Project Ballet Theater, 2000—. With Park 58 Corp., N.Y.C., 1989-2006, pres., 1994-2004; bd. dir. Artists Cmty. Fed. Credit Union, 2003-06, sec., 2004, asst. treas., 2005-06; mentor Pentacle Help Desk Program, 2000—06. Mem. Am. Soc. Internat. Law, N.Y. State Bar Assn., Assn. Bar City of N.Y. (com. on copyright 2002-03, com. on art law 2003-06, com. on entertainment law 2006—), Am. Coun. on Germany, Johns Hopkins Alumni Assn. (bd. dir. N.Y.C. chpt. 1988-92), Univ. Club, Yale Club, Johns Hopkins Club (Balt.). Episcopalian. Home: 470 Park Ave New York NY 10022-1903 Office: Lar Lubovitch Dance Co 229 W 42d St 8th Fl New York NY 10036-7299 Office Phone: 212-221-7909. Personal E-mail: DickCaples@aol.com. Business E-Mail: Lubovitch@aol.com.

CAPLICE, CHRISTOPHER, engineering educator; BS in Civil Engring., Va. Military Inst.; MS in Civil Engring., U. Tex.; PhD, MIT, 1996. V.p. product mgmt. and profl. svcs. Logistics.com, Burlington, Mass.; v.p. transp. planning Chainalytics; prin. rsch. assoc. ctr. transp. and logistics MIT, exec. dir. master engring. in logistics program. Contbr. articles to profl. jours. including Jour. Bus. Logistics, Internat. Jour. Logistics Mgmt., Transportation Rsch. Capt. Army Corps Engrs. Office: MIT Bldg E40-363 77 Massachusetts Ave Cambridge MA 02139-4307 Office Phone: 617-258-7975. Business E-Mail: caplice@mit.edu.

CAPLIN, JERROLD LEON, health physicist; b. Phila., Jan. 25, 1930; s. Samuel Harry and Katherine (Socloff) C.; children: Sally C. Daniels, Patricia Graham Reed. AB, Temple U., 1951, postgrad., 1952—53. Supervisory health physicist U.S. Army C.E., Ft. Belvoir, Va., 1959—61; health physicist radiation protection stds. AEC, U.S. Nuc. Regulatory Commn., Washington, 1961—81, project mgr. respirator R&D, nuc. reactor environ. assessments, 1961—81; ret., 1981; cons., 1981—. Guest lectr. radiation sci. Georgetown U. Grad. Sch., 1987-97; sr. scientist Advanced Sys. Tech., Inc., 1993-97; photographer, newspaper editor, sci. writer, 1983—; sr. tech. editor Advanced Technologies and Labs. Internat., Inc., 2000-03. Co-author, editor Manual Respiratory Protection Against Airborne Radioactive Materials, 1976. Active Nat. Mus. of Women in Arts, Friends of the Nat. Zoo, Friends of the Kennedy Ctr. Lt. USNR, 1953-58. AEC Radiol. Physics fellow, Vanderbilt U., Oak Ridge Nat. Lab., 1951—52. Mem. AAAS, ASTM, Am. Nat. Stds. Inst., Am. Conf. Gov. Indsl. Hygienists (chmn. com. 1977-83), Am. Assn. Physics Tchrs., Am. Film Inst., Nat. Ctr. Sci. Edn. (assoc.), Internat. Radiation Protection Assn., U.S. Naval Inst., Nat. Wildlife Fedn., Nat. Geog. Soc., Nat. Trust for Hist. Preservation, Health Physics Soc., Smithsonian Instn. (resident assoc. 1970—), Wilderness Soc., Libr. Congress Assocs., Com. Sci. Investigation of Claims of the Paranormal Assoc. Home and Office: 9 Goodport Ln Gaithersburg MD 20878-1001 Personal E-mail: jcaplin001@aol.com.

CAPLIN, MORTIMER MAXWELL, lawyer, educator; b. NYC, July 11, 1916; s. Daniel and Lillian (Epstein) C.; m. Ruth Sacks, Oct. 18, 1942; children: Lee Evan, Michael Andrew, Jeremy Owen, Catherine Jean. BS, U. Va., 1937, LLB, 1940; JSD, NYU, 1953; LLD (hon.), St. Michael's Coll., 1964. Bar: Va. 1941, N.Y. 1942, D.C. 1964. Law clk. to Hon. Armistead M. Dobie U.S. Ct. Appeals (4th cir.), Richmond, 1940-41; assoc. Paul, Weiss, Rifkind, Wharton & Garrison, NYC, 1941-42, 45-50; prof. law U. Va., Charlottesville, 1950-61, vis. prof. law, 1965-87, prof. emeritus, 1988—; ptnr. Perkins, Battle & Minor, Charlottesville, 1952-61; U.S. commr. IRS, Washington, 1961-64; founding mem., sr. ptnr. Caplin & Drysdale, Washington, 1964—. Mem. Pres.'s Task Force on Taxation, 1960; bd. dirs. Danaher Corp., Washington, Fairchild Corp., McLean, Va., Presdl. Realty Corp., White Plains, N.Y., Environ. and Energy Study Inst.; mem. pub. rev. bd. Arthur Andersen & Co., Chgo., 1980-88; reorgn. trustee Webb & Knapp, Inc., 1965-72. Author: Proxies, Annual Meetings and Corporate Democracy, 1953, Doing Business in Other States, 1959; editor-in-chief Va. Law Rev., 1939-40; contbr. numerous articles on tax and corp. matters to profl. jours. Past chmn. bd. dirs. Nat. Civic Svc. League, Am. Coun. on Internat. Sports; past chmn. nat citizens adv. com. Assn. Am. Med. Colls.; trustee Arena Stage, U. Va. Law Sch. Found., Wolf Trap Found. Performing Arts, Shakespeare Theatre, Washington, Arena Stage, Washington, Peace Through Law Found., Washington; bd. overseers U. V.I.; chmn. adv. bd. Hospitality and Info. Svc., Washington; hon. chmn. Coun. for Arts, U. Va.; past pres. Atlantic Coast Conf.; emeritus trustee George Washington U.; mem. bd. visitors U. Va., 1992-97; pres., bd. dirs. Indigent Civil Litigation Fund; mem. governing coun. U. Va. Miller Ctr. Pub. Affairs. Decorated mem. initial landing force Normandy Invasion USN; recipient, Va. State Bar and Va. Soc. CPAs award, 1960, Achievement award, Tax Soc. of NYU, 1962, Judge Learned Hand Human Rels. award, Am. Jewish Com., 1963, Pub. Svc. award, VFW, 1963, Judge Learned Hand Human Rels. award, Am. Jewish Com., 1993, Alexander Hamilton award, U.S. Treasury Dept., 1964, Disting. Svc. award, Tax Execs. Inst., 1964, medal in law, U. Va. Thomas Jefferson Found., 2001. Fellow Am. Bar Found. (bd. dirs. 2003—), Am. Tax Policy Inst., Am. Coll. Tax Counsel; mem. ABA (ho. of dels. 1980-92, mem. fed. jud. com. 1993-96, ALI-ABA com. continuing profl. edn. 1997-2000, chair DC Fellows), Nat. Conf. of Lawyers and CPAs, Am. Law Inst. (life), N.Y. State Bar Assn., Va. Bar Assn., D.C. Bar Assn., Am. Bar Fedn. (bd. dirs. 2003-), D.C. Bar Found. (adv. com.), Univ. Club (Washington), Fed. City Club (bd. govs.), Colonnade Club (Charlottesville), Order of Coif, Phi Beta Kappa, Phi Beta Kappa Assocs., Omicron Delta Kappa. Democrat. Jewish. Avocations: swimming, tennis, hiking. Home: 5610 Wisconsin Ave Apt 18E Chevy Chase MD 20815-4415 Office: One Thomas Circle NW Washington DC 20005-5802 Office Phone: 202-862-5050. E-mail: mmc@capdale.com.

CAPLIN, OLGA YERYOMINA, psychiatrist; b. Kamensk-Uralsky, Russia, July 6, 1967; d. Stanislav Alexandrovich Yeryomin and Ludmila Pavlovna Yeryomina; m. Herbert M Caplia, Feb. 24, 1996. MD, Blagoveschensk State Med. Inst., 1984—90. Psychiatry resident Acad. Physicians, 1992—94, fellow, 1994—95; psychiatry resident So. Ill. U. Psychiatry Dept., 2000—04. Mem.: Am. Psychiat. Soc. Avocations: painting, skiing, kayaking. Personal E-mail: caplin6@hotmail.com.

CAPLOE, ROBERTA, magazine editor; b. Framingham, Mass., Mar. 24, 1962; d. Robert Coleman and Jeanne Adele (Goldburg) Caploe. BA, Barnard Coll., 1984. Sr. prodr. Phone Programs Inc., NYC, 1985—88; exec. editor Soap Opera Digest Presents, NYC, 1988—89; West Coast editor Soap Opera Digest, LA, 1989—95; exec. editor Seventeen mag., NYC, 1997—2000; editor-in-chief Youth Entertainment Group, Primedia, 2000—03; exec. editor Ladies Home Jour., NYC, 2003—. Co-author (with Jamie Caploe): Melrose Confidential. Assoc. mem. Acad. TV Arts and Scis. Avocation: tennis. Office: Ladies Home Jour 20th Fl 125 Park Ave New York NY 10017

CAPLOW, TED, environmental engineer; b. NYC, Dec. 14, 1969; s. Theodore Caplow and Christine Allen, Margaret Pettit Caplow (Stepmother); m. Pascale van Kipnis, Aug. 4, 1996. BA, Harvard U., Cambridge, Mass., 1992; MPhil, PhD, Columbia U., NYC, 2004; MS in Engring., Princeton U., NJ, 1998. Mng. dir. Soma Soup LLC, NYC, 1999—2001; exec. dir. NY Sun Works, NYC, 2004—. Cons. Capital-E, LLC, Washington, 2002—04. Contbr. articles to profl. jours. Grantee grad. fellow, Link Found., 1997—98; Guggenheim fellow, Princeton U., 1996—98, grad. fellow, NSF, 1999—2003, U. Presdl. fellow, Columbia U., 2001—04. Office: New York Sun Works 1841 Broadway Ste 200 New York NY 10023 Office Phone: 212-757-7560. Business E-Mail: info@nysunworks.org.

CAPLOW, THEODORE, sociologist; b. NYC, May 1, 1920; s. Samuel Nathaniel and Florence (Israel) C.; m. Margaret Mary Pettit, 1981. AB, U. Chgo., 1939; PhD, U. Minn., 1946; LLD, Ball State U., 2003. Mem. faculty U. Minn., 1945—60; prof. sociology Columbia U., 1961—70; Commonwealth prof. U. Va., Charlottesville, 1973—2005, chmn. dept. sociology, 1970—78, 1984—86, prof. emeritus, 2005—. Vis. prof. U. Bordeaux, France, 1950, U. Aix-Marseille, France, 1951, U. Utrecht, Netherlands, 1954-55, Stanford, 1957, P.R., 1959, U. Bogota, Colombia, 1962, Sorbonne, Paris, France, 1968-69, Institut d'Etudes Politiques, Paris, 1983, U. Rome, 1984, U. Oslo, 1986; pres. Mendota Research Group Inc., 1957-65 Author: Sociology of Work, 1954, Principles of Organization, 1964, Two Against One, 1968, L'Enquête Sociologique, 1970, Toward Social Hope, 1975, Peace Games, 1989, American Social Trends, 1991, Perverse Incentives, 1994; sr. author: The Academic Marketplace, 1957, The Urban Ambience, 1964, Middletown Families, 1982, All Faithful People, 1983, Recent Social Trends in the United States, 1960-90, 1991, Systems of War and Peace, 1995, Sociologie Militaire, 2000, The First Measured Century, 2001, Leviathen Transformed, 2002, Forbidden Wars, 2007. With AUS, 1943-45, PTO. Decorated Purple Heart. Mem. Tocqueville Soc. (pres. 1979-83), Am. Sociol. Assn. (sec. 1983-86), Farmington Hunt Club, Albemarle Yacht Club,(Charlottesville), Century (N.Y.C.), Tarratine Club (Dark Harbor, Maine). E-mail: tc@virginia.edu.

CAPODILUPO, ELIZABETH JEANNE HATTON, public relations executive; b. McRae, Ga., May 3, 1940; d. Lewis Irby and Essee Elizabeth (Parker) Hatton; m. Raphael S. Capodilupo, Jan. 21, 1967. Grad., Dale Carnegie Inst., 1976. Sec. A.R. Clark Acct., Fernandina Beach, Fla., 1958-59; receptionist, girl Friday Sta. WNDT-TV, NYC, 1960-62, Coy Hunt and Co., NYC, 1962-69; clk. Woodlawn Cemetery, Bronx, N.Y., 1969-71, historian, cmty. affairs coord., 1971-84, editor newsletter, 1979—, asst. to pres., 1984-99, dir. pub. rels., 1984; grad. asst. Dale Carnegie Inst., 1977-78. Rschr. Woodlawn Cemetery's Hall of Fame; contbr. articles to Collier Encyclopedia, 1985; contbr. articles to profl. jours. Chmn. ann. Adm. Farragut Honor Ceremony, Bronx, 1976—; founder, chmn. Toys for Needy Children, 1983-97; bd. dirs. Bronx Mus. Arts, v.p., 1983-84; pres. Bronx Coun. Arts, 1987-90, Network Orgn. Bronx Women, 1997-98; adv. bd. Salvation Army, 1985, Bronx Arts Ensemble, 1985; bd. mgrs. Bronx YMCA, 1985, vice-chmn., 1989—; bd. dirs. Bronx Urban League, 1985, Bronx Coun. on Arts, 1985, pres. 1987-90; active Bronx Landmarks Task Force, 1994—. Recipient award citation VFW, 1976, Voice of Democracy Program judge's citation, 1980, Disting. Community Svc. award N.Y.C. Council, Il Leone di Sanmarco award Italian Heritage & Culture Com. Bronx, 1989, Lifetime Achievement Humanitarian award Bronx Coun. on Arts, 1999-2000; named Woman of Yr., YMCA, Bronx, 1986, Network Orgn. Bronx Women, 1986, Jeanne and Ray Capodilupo named as Mr. & Mrs. Bronx 1989-90 proclaimed by Borough Pres., named Pioneer of the Bronx, 1992, Citizen of Yr. Bronx Club, 1995; recipient cert. appreciation Dale Carnegie Inst., 1977, Outstanding Citizenship award Bronx N.E. Kiwanis Club, 1981, Service to Youth award YMCA of Bronx, 1983; recipient proclamation City Council of N.Y., Italian Heritage and Culture Com. of the Bronx, 1989; Outstanding Cemeterian award Am. Cemetery Assn., 1987-88; Citation of Merit Bronx Borough Pres.'s Office, 1988; Spl. Hons. for Outstanding Vol. Work Ladies Aux. Our Lady of Mercy Med. Ctr.; named Hon. Grand Marshall Bronx Columbus Day Parade, 1987-89, Bronx Meml. Day Parade, 1989; apptd. to commn. celebrating 350 yrs. of the Bronx by Borough Pres., recipient Pioneer award for Women's History Month for Outstanding Humanitarian Svcs., 1991, Lifetime Achievement award Bronx YMCA, 1999-2000, Role Model award Columbus Alliance, 2000; Jeanne Hatton Capodilupo Day proclaimed by Bronx Borough Presdl. Proclamation, 1999. Mem. Bronx County Hist. Soc., Network Orgn. Bronx Women (pres. 1997-99), Women in Communication, Bronx C. of C. (sec. 1988), YMCA (life mem.), N.Y. Press Club, Italian Big Sisters Club, Women's City Club, Order Eastern Star. Methodist. Office: 371 Scosdale Rd Yonkers NY 10707 Personal E-mail: smilerjean@aol.com.

CAPOLARELLO, JOE R., photojournalist; b. Bklyn., Sept. 6, 1961; s. Carmelo and Grace (Auditore) Capolarello. Cert. in news prodn. and tech., Inst. New Cinema Artists, NYC, 1981; cert. in TV news video workshop, U. Okla., Norman, 1986; cert. in TV news feature workshop, Internat. Film & TV Workshops, Rockport, Maine, 1987; cert. in leadership in broadcast photojournalism, Poynter Inst. Media Studies, St. Petersburg, Fla., 1992. Photojournalist, videotape editor, field producer W.Va. Jour. Sta. WSWP-TV, Beckley, W.Va., 1982-83; photojournalist Eyewitness News Sta. WABC-TV, NYC, 1983; photojournalist Bus. Times, ESPN, NYC, 1984, Broadcast News Svc., NYC, 1984, Cable News Network, Inc., NYC, 1984—, Entertainment Tonight, Paramount Pictures Corp., NYC, 1988-91, Fox News at Seven, Ten O'Clock News, Sta. WNYW-TV, NYC, 1988-91, USA Today: The Television Show, Grant Tinker/Gannett East Prodns. Inc., NYC, 1988-89, Preview: the best of the new, TV Program Enterprises, NYC, 1990; photojournalist Personalities Twentieth Century Fox Film Corp., NYC, 1991. Mem.: Nat. Press Photographers Assn., TV and Radio Working Press Assn., Nat. Hon. Broadcasting Soc., Acad. TV Arts and Scis. Democrat. Avocation: travel. Home: 1 Liberty St Little Ferry NJ 07643-2303 Office: Cable News Network 1 Time Warner Ctr New York NY 10019-8012 Office Phone: 212-275-7835. Personal E-mail: JoeCapolarello@hotmail.com.

CAPON, EDWIN GOULD, retired religious organization administrator, minister; b. Boston, Apr. 1, 1924; s. Gould and Helen (Wood) C.; m. Norma Jean Wilcoxson (div. Jan. 1971); children: Peter Lawrence, Jonathan Edwin; m. Esther Constance Nicastro, Sept. 5, 1975. AB, Harvard U., 1947; STM, Andover-Newton Theol. Sem., 1949. Ordained to ministry Swedenborgian Ch., 1949. Min. Bridgewater (Mass.) New Ch., 1948-51, Elmwood (Mass.) New Ch., 1949-55, Detroit New Ch., Royal Oak, Mich., 1977-79; v.p. Swedenborg Sch. Religion, Cambridge, Mass., 1953-55, pres. Cambridge and Newton, Mass., 1955-77; pastor San Francisco Swedenborgian Ch., 1979-90; interim min. St. Paul Swedenborgian Ch., 1991-92, min., 1992-94; pres. The Swedenborgian Ch., Newton, 1992-98, chmn. coun. mins., 1956-67. Trustee Urbana (Ohio) U., 1966-80, 92-99; v.p. Mass. Coun. Chs. Mem. Swedenborgian Ch. Avocations: hiking, mountain climbing in new england.

CAPONIGRO, JEFFREY RALPH, public relations counselor; b. Kankakee, Ill., Aug. 13, 1957; s. Ralph A. and Barbara Jean (Paul) C.; m. Ellen Colleen Kennedy, Oct. 15, 1982; children: Nicholas J., Michael J. BA, Ctrl. Mich. U., 1979. Sports reporter Observer and Eccentric newspaper, Rochester, Mich., 1974-75, Mt. Pleasant (Mich.) Times, 1975-77, Midland (Mich.) Daily News, 1977-79; acct. exec. Desmond & Assocs., Oak Park, Mich., 1979-80; v.p. Anthony M. Franco, Inc., Detroit, 1980-84; chmn., pres., CEO Shandwick USA (formerly Casey Comm. Mgmt., Inc.), Southfield, 1984—95; founder & CEO Caponigro Public Relations Inc., Detroit, 1995—. Contbr. author: Best Sports Stories, 1978. Mem. Pub. Rels. Soc. Am. (accredited, Detroit chpt., nat. accrediation bd.). Home: 5790 Springbrook Dr Troy MI 48098-5352 Office: #1750 4000 Town Ctr Southfield MI 48075-1411

CAPONNETTO, MARIANNE, information technology executive; b. NYC, June 29, 1951; married; 2 children. BA in English Lit., Romance Lang., U. Calif. Berkeley, 1972; student, NYU. Media rsch. asst. McCann-Erickson Worldwide; sr. v.p., dir. media svcs. Lord Einstein O'Neill & Ptnrs., 1975-89; dir. strategic mktg. then dir. corp. mktg. Dow Jones & Co., 1989—94; v.p., worldwide media and digital media IBM Corp., 1994, v.p., publishing, global media & entertainment; chief sales and mktg. officer DoubleClick, Inc., 2006—. Bd. dir. Audit Bur. Circulations (ABC), 1995—2001, chair, bd. dirs.; bd. dir. Ad Club NY, Bus. Publs. Assn., Assn. Nat. Advertisers CASIE Com.; mem. steering com. Fast Forward; spkr. in field. Bd. dir. Family Friendly Forum; mem. YWCA Acad. Women Achievers. Office: DoubleClick Inc 111 Eighth Ave 10th Fl New York NY 10011

CAPORALE, D. NICK, lawyer; b. Omaha, Sept. 13, 1928; s. Michele and Lucia Caporale; m. Margaret Nilson; children: Laura Diane Stevenson, Leland Alan. BA, U. Nebr.-Omaha, 1949, MSc, 1954; JD with distinction, U. Nebr.-Lincoln, 1957. Bar: Nebr. 1957, U.S. Dist. Ct. Nebr. 1957, U.S. Ct. Appeals 8th cir. 1958, U.S. Supreme Ct. 1970. Judge Nebr. Dist. Ct., Omaha, 1979—82, Nebr. Supreme Ct., Lincoln, 1982—98; of counsel Baird Holm LLP, 1998—. Lectr. U. Nebr., Lincoln, 1982—84, 2000—03. Pres. Omaha Community Playhouse, 1976. Served to 1st lt. US Army, 1952—54, Korea. Decorated Bronze Star; recipient Alumni Achievement U. Nebr.-Omaha, 1978; Disting. Alumni Award, U. Nebr. Coll. Law, 2004. Fellow Am. Coll. Trial Lawyers, Internat. Soc. Barristers; mem. Order of Coif. Office: Baird Holm LLP 1500 Woodmen Tower Omaha NE 68102 Office Phone: 402-344-0500. Business E-Mail: dncaporale@bairdholm.com.

CAPORIZZO, A. WILLIAM, lawyer; b. 1960; BS magna cum laude, Univ. Pa., 1982; JD magna cum laude, Boston Univ., 1985. CPA; bar: Mass. 1985, Conn. 1992. Ptnr., co-chmn. Tax dept., mem. Joint Venture & Fund Formation group Wilmer Cutler Pickering Hale & Dorr, Boston. Mem.: ABA, Mass. Bar Assn., Boston Bar Assn. Office: Wilmer Cutler Pickering Hale & Dorr 60 State St Boston MA 02109 Office Phone: 617-526-6411. Office Fax: 617-526-5000. Business E-Mail: william.caporizzo@wilmerhale.com.

CAPOZZI, LOU, public relations executive; Formerly with Hill & Knowlton, 1968; pres., CEO Manning, Selvage & Lee (subs. Publicis Groupe), NYC, 1995—2005; exec. chair Publicis PR and Corp. Comm. Group, NYC, 2005—. Chmn. Coun. PR Firms. Office: Publicis Group PR & Corp Comm 1675 Broadway New York NY 10019

CAPP, DAVID A., prosecutor; Criminal divsn. chief US Atty.'s Office, Dyer, 1988-91; 1st asst. atty. US Dept. Justice, Dyer, US atty. (no. dist.) Ind., 1999—2001, acting US atty (no. dist.) Ind., 2007—. Office: US Attys Office 5400 Federal Plz #1500 Hammond IN 46320-1843*

CAPP, MICHAEL PAUL, pediatrician, educator; b. Yonkers, NY, July 1, 1930; s. Michael and Mary (Bybel) Capp; m. Constance Whitehead, Jan. 4, 1989; children: Marianne, Michael, Steven, John. BS, Roanoke Coll., Salem, Va., 1952; MD, U. N.C., 1958. Diplomate Am. Bd. Radiology. Lab. instr. physics Roanoke Coll., 1952; tchg. asst. Grad. Sch. Physics, Duke U., 1952—54; intern in pediat. Duke U. Med. Ctr., 1958—59, resident in radiology, 1959—62, assoc. in radiology, 1962, asst. prof., 1963—66, assoc. prof., 1966—70, dir. diagnostic divsn., dept. radiology, 1967—70, asst. prof. pediat., 1968—70, radiologist in charge pediatric cardiology, 1962—70; dir. Duke U. Med. Ctr. (Pediatric Radiology Program), 1965—70, Duke Med. Center (Med. Students Teaching Program Diagnostic Radiology), 1965-66; prof., chmn. dept. radiology U. Ariz. Coll. Medicine, Tucson, 1970—93, prof. emeritus, 1993—; chief of staff Ariz. Med. Ctr., Univ. Hosp., 1971—73; exec. dir. Am. Bd. of Radiology, Tucson, 1993—2001. Mem. NRC com. on Radiology James Picker Found., 1972. Contbr. articles to profl. jours. Mem.: NAS, AMA, Inst. Medicine, Soc. for Chmn. Acad. Radiology Depts. (pres. 1977), Soc. for Pediatric Radiology, Eastern Radiol. Soc. (sci. program chmn. 1967, v.p. 1973—), Pima County Med. Soc., N.Y. Acad. Scis., N.Am. Soc. Cardiac Radiologists (pres. 1975), Radiol. Soc. N.Am. (chmn. sci. exhibits com. 1976—79), Am. Bd. Radiology (treas. 1982—85, v.p. 1985, pres. 1987—89, exec. dir. 1993—), Am. Heart Assn. (pres. coun. on cardiovasc. radiology 1976—78), Am. Assn. Univ. Radiologists (exec. com. 1970, Gold medal 1988), Am. Roentgen Ray Soc. (pres. 1990), Am. Coll. Radiology, Sigma Pi Sigma. Office: U Arizona Coll Med 1501 N Campbell Ave PO Box 245017 Tucson AZ 85724

CAPPEL, CONSTANCE, editor, writer; b. Dayton, Ohio, June 22, 1936; d. Adam Denison and Mary Louise (Henry) C.; m. R.A. Montgomery Jr., June 16, 1962 (div. Apr. 1980); children: Raymond A. Montgomery III, Anson Cappel Montgomery. Grad., The Masters Sch., Dobbs Ferry, NY, 1955; BA, Sarah Lawrence Coll., 1959; MA, Columbia U., NYC, 1961; PhD, Union Inst. & Univ., Cin., 1991. Editor Newsweek, NYC, 1961—63, Vogue, NYC, 1964—66; mem. faculty Pine Manor Coll., Chestnut Hill, Mass., 1968—72, prof.; grad. prof. Goddard Coll., Plainfield, Vt., 1975—80; founder, CEO, pub. Vt. Crossroad Press, Waitsfield, 1972—82; comml. realtor Investmark, Dayton, 1983—85; prin., founder, CEO Cappel Cons., San Francisco, 1986—94; bus. advisor U.S. Peace Corps, Lodz, Poland, 1994—96; mgr. Price Waterhouse Real Estate, Warsaw, 1996—97; dir. devel. Conflict Resolution Catalysts, Montpelier, Vt., 1997; tchr. trainer U.S. Peace Corps., Kazakhstan, 1998; pres. Newport (N.H.) Earth Inst., 1999; faculty Norman Rockwell Mus., 2000—02. Adj. faculty PhD program Union Inst. and U., 2002—05. Author: Hemingway in Michigan, 1966, paperback 1977, 99, Vermont School Bus Ride, 1977, Utopian Colleges, 1999, Sweetgrass and Smoke, 2002, A Stairwell in Lodz, 2004, A Union of Voices: Accounts of the Union Institute & University, 2004; editor: Odawa Language and Legends: Andrew S. Blackbird and Raymond Kiogima, 2006, Deva Poetry, 2007. Founder Women's Rights Project/ACLU, Vt., 1973-74; grad. alumni/ae bd. The Union Inst. and Univ., 1992-94, 1999-2006, sec., 1993, pres., 2004-06; bd. dirs. Chief Andrew Blackbird Mus., 2002-05; trustee Harbor Springs Hist. Soc., 2002-05 McDowell Colony fellow, Peterborough, N.H., 1972, 1974. Mem.: Petoskey Audabon Soc., New Eng. Antiquities Rsch. Assn., Soc. Strang Studies (treas. 2005—06), Archaeol. Conservancy, Audubon Soc., Mich. Hemingway Soc., Ernest Hemingway Soc., Great Lakes Lighthouse Keepers Assn., PEN Am. Ctr. Democrat. Office: 524 Pine St Harbor Springs MI 49740

CAPPEL, HARRY W., lawyer; b. Salem, Oreg., May 25, 1970; BA in Polit. Sci., U. Cin., 1993; JD, U. Cin. Coll. Law, 1996. Bar: Ohio 1996, Ky. 2002, Ind. 2003. Ptnr. Graydon Head & Ritchey LLP, Cin. Vol. St. Lawrence Sch.; mentor U. Cin.; vol. coach Dearborn County YMCA. Named one of Ohio's Rising Stars, Super Lawyers, 2005, 2006. Mem.: Elder Bus. Professionals Assn., Ind. State Bar Assn., Ky. Bar Assn., Ohio State Bar Assn., Cin. Bar Assn. Office: Graydon Head & Ritchey LLP 1900 Fifth Third Ctr Cincinnati OH 45202 Office Phone: 513-629-2709. Office Fax: 513-651-3836.

CAPPELLANO, ROSEMARIE ZACCONE, small business owner; b. Council Bluffs, Iowa, Apr. 1, 1952; d. Carl Paul and Marianna (Urbano) Zaccone; m. Al Cappellano, June 23, 1940; children: Marco, Mario. Degree in bus., U. Nebr., 1978. Owner Al's Angels and Gifts, Omaha, 1996—. Spkr. in field; exhibitor An Event With Angels. Named Columbus Day Queen, Sons of Italy, 1976. Mem.: Cath. Daus. Democrat. Roman Catholic. Avocations: travel, gourmet cooking, music, movies. Office: Al's Angels and Gifts 12105 W Center Rd # 132 Omaha NE 68144 Home Phone: 402-493-4832; Office Phone: 402-330-1333. Office Fax: 402-333-4325. E-mail: alsangels291@aol.com.

CAPPELLAZZO, AMY, art appraiser, writer; BA in Fine Arts, NYU; MA in Urban Design and City Planning, Pratt Inst., NYC. Dir. Rubell Family Collection & Found.; Miami; internat. co-head, post-war and contemporary art dept. Christie's, NYC. Bd. dir. LA Contemporary Exhbns.; lectr. in field. Co-editor In Company: The Collaborations of Robert Creeley, 1999. Bd. dir. Miami Light Project. Named one of 40 Under 40, Crain's New York Bus. Journal, 2006. Office: Christie's/NY 20 Rockefeller Plz New York NY 10020 Office Phone: 212-636-4932. Office Fax: 212-636-4932. Business E-Mail: acappellazzo@christies.com.*

CAPPELLO, A. BARRY, lawyer; b. Bklyn., Feb. 21, 1942; s. Gus and Ann (Klukoff) C.; children: Eric Rheinschild, Blythe, Brent, Dominic, Vincent. AB, UCLA, 1962, JD, 1965. Bar: Calif. 1966, U.S. Dist. Ct. (cen. dist.) Calif. 1966, U.S. Ct. Appeals (9th cir.) 1974, U.S. Dist. Ct. (no. dist.) Calif. 1981, U.S. Ct. Appeals (7th cir.) 1983, U.S. Supreme Ct. 1983, U.S. Dist. Ct. (ea. dist.) Calif. 1986, U.S. Ct. Appeals (10th cir.) 1986, U.S. Dist. Ct. (so. dist.) Calif. 1988. Dep. atty. gen. State of Calif., LA, 1965—68; chief trial dep., asst. dist. atty. Santa Barbara County, 1968—70, city atty., 1971—77; mng. ptnr. Cappello & Noel, Santa Barbara, 1977—. Lectr. complex bus. litigation, lender liability, adv. trial techniques. Author: Lender Liability, 3d edit., 2004, Lender Liability: A Practical Guide, 1987, AmJur Model Trials and Proofs of Facts; contbr. more than 200 articles to profl. legal and bus. jours. Named Best Lawyer in Am. Woodard/White, Inc., 1992-, One of Am.'s Best Lawyers Forbes Radio, 2005. Mem. ABA, ATLA, Consumer Attys. Calif. Avocation: triathalons. Office: Cappello & Noël 831 State St Santa Barbara CA 93101-3227 Office Phone: 805-564-2444. Business E-Mail: abc@cappellonoel.com.

CAPPIELLO, FRANK ANTHONY, JR., investment advisor; b. Trenton, NJ, Jan. 5, 1926; s. Frank A. and Rose Marie (Clapis) C.; m. Marie Therese Rhodes, June, 1954; children: Frank Rhodes, Annmarie, Elaine. AB, U. Notre Dame, 1949; postgrad., Cornell U. Law Sch., 1949-50; MBA, Harvard U., 1954. Supr. rate research Va. Electric and Power Co., Richmond, 1954-61; mgr. research dept. Alexander Brown & Sons, 1961-67; v.p. Securities Monumental Life Ins. Co., 1968-74; fin. v.p. Monumental Corp., 1970-80; pres. Monumental Capital Mgmt., Inc., Balt., 1974-80, Dowbeaters, Inc., Summit, N.J. and Balt., 1981-83, McCullough, Andrews and Cappiello, Inc., Balt. and San Francisco, 1983—2003; founder, dir. Bank of Md., 1985-90; chmn. Cappiello-Rushmore Mutual Funds, Bethesda, Md., 1993—2000; chmn., mng. dir. Montgomery Bros., Cappiello, LLC, 2003—. TV panelist Wall St. Week, 1970—2002; disting. visiting prof. fin. Loyola Coll., Balt., 1986—; mem. adv. investment com. Md. State Retirement Systems. Author: Finding the Next Super Stock, 1982, From Main Street to Wall Street, 1988. Trustee Balt. City Pension System; mem., commr. Md. State Econ. and Community Devel. Commn., 1977-80. Served with U.S. Marine Corps, 1950-52. Mem. Fin. Analysts Fedn. (chmn., dir.), Balt. Security Analysts Soc. Clubs: Univ., Harvard (N.Y.C.); Hamilton Street (Balt.). Roman Catholic. Home: 19 Buchanan Rd Baltimore MD 21212-1013 Office: 10751 Falls Rd Ste 250 Lutherville Timonium MD 21093-4552 Office Phone: 410-337-2255. E-mail: cappiello@aol.com.*

CAPPO, JOSEPH C., journalist, writer; b. Chgo., Feb. 24, 1936; s. Joseph V. and Frances (Maggio) Cacioppo; m. Mary Anne Cappo, May 7, 1967; children: Elizabeth, John. BA, DePaul U., 1957. Reporter Hollister Publs.,

Wilmette, Ill., 1961-62, Chgo. Daily News, 1962-68, bus. columnist, 1968-78; columnist Crain's Chgo. Bus., 1978—, pub., 1979-89, editor at large, 2003—; v.p. Crain Comm., Inc., 1981-89, sr. v.p. group pub., 1989-95, sr. v.p. internat., 1996—2003; pres. Crain Comms. of Mex., 2001—02. Pub. Advt. Age, 1989—92, publishing dir., 1992—99; dir. Assn. Area Bus. Publs., 1982—88, pres., 1985—86. Author: Future Scope: Success Strategies for the 1990's and Beyond, 1990, The Future of Advertising: New Clients, New Media, New Consumers in the Post Television Age, 2003. Bd. dirs. Off the Street Club, Chgo., 1981—, Chgo. Advt. Fedn., 1987-93, Mus. Broadcast Comm., 1984-90, Ill. Coun. on Econ. Edn., 1990-95. With U.S. Army, 1959-61. Recipient award Ill. Press Assn., 1962, (with other Daily News staffers) Nat. Headliner award, 1966, Disting. Alumni award DePaul U., 1975, Page One award Chgo. Newspaper Guild, 1978, Peter Lisagor award Sigma Delta Chi, 1978, Outstanding Achievement award in comm., Justinian Soc. Lawyers, 1979, Champion award YWCA of Met. Chgo., 1984, Media Svc. award Chgo. Lung Assn., 1990, Dante award Joint Civic Com. Italian-Ams., 2003. Mem.: Bus. and Econ. Writers (bd. govs. 1984—89), Econ. Club (Chgo.), Internat. Advt. Assn. (world bd. 1994—, sr. v.p. 1996—98, world pres. 1998—2000), Delta Mu Delta (hon.). Roman Catholic. Office: Crain Communications Inc 360 N Michigan Ave Chicago IL 60601-3806

CAPPS, JAMES LEIGH, II, lawyer, military officer; b. Brunswick, Ga., 1956; s. Thomas Edwin Sr. and Betty Marie C.; m. Nancy Ann Fisher, 1978; children: Bonnie Lynn, James Leigh III. AA, Seminole C.C., Sanford, Fla., 1976; BA in History, U. Cen. Fla., 1981; JD, U. Fla., 1987. Bar: Fla. 1987, U.S. Ct. Mil. Appeals 1988, Colo. 1990, U.S. Ct. Appeals (4th cir.) 1997. Enlisted USAF, 1976, advanced through grades to maj., 1995, med. svc. specialist MacDill AFB, Fla., 1977-79, air weapons dir. Germany, 1982-84, claims officer Homestead AFB, Fla., 1987-88, area def. counsel, 1988-90, dep. staff judge adv. Onizuka AFB, Calif., 1990-93; ret. USAFR, 2005; atty. office of state atty. 18th Jud. Ct., Sanford, Fla., 1994; assoc. Dominick Salfi Law Offices, Maitland, Fla., 1993-94, of counsel, 1994—98; res. judge adv. Moody AFB, Ga., 1993-99; pvt. practice, 1996—; res. judge adv. Patrick AFB, Fla., 2000—05; civilian contract specialist for Naval Air Warfare Ctr. USN, Orlando, Fla., 1999—; contract specialist Flight Sch. XXI Simulation Svcs. Assigned to 16th Air Force Hdqs., Aviano AFB, Italy, Operation Joint Endeavor, 1996; implementation force Dayton Peace Accords UN. Atty. Vietnam Vets. Ctrl. Fla., 1998—99. Maj. USAFR. Recipient McCarthy award for legal svc. Air Combat Command, 1995. Mem.: VFW, DAV (JAG Chpt. 30 2006—), Nat. Order Tranchrats (life), Moose (lodge 1851), Am. Legion. Democrat. Office: Law Office of James Capps PO Box 2551 Sanford FL 32773 Office Phone: 407-380-4174. Personal E-mail: cappslegal@aol.com.

CAPPS, JOHN EDWARD, lawyer, consumer products company executive; BA, Vanderbilt U., 1986, MBA in Fin., 1989, JD, 1994. Bar: NY 1995, Wash. 1996. Assoc. Cravath, Swaine & Moore, 1994—97, Sullivan & Cromwell, 1998—2003; joined Jarden Corp. (formerly Am. Household, Inc.), Rye, NY, 2003, sr. v.p., gen. counsel, sec., 2007—. Office: Jarden Corp Ste B302 555 Theodore Fremd Ave Rye NY 10580 Office Phone: 914-967-9400.*

CAPPS, LOIS RAGNHILD GRIMSRUD, congresswoman, former school nurse; b. Ladysmith, Wis., Jan. 10, 1938; d. Jurgen Milton and Solveig Magdalene (Gullixson) Grimsrud; m. Walter Holden Capps, Aug. 21, 1960 (dec.); children: Lisa Margaret, Todd Holden, Laura Karolina. BSN with honors, Pacific Luth. U., 1959; MA in Religion, Yale U., 1964; MA in Edn., U. Calif., Santa Barbara, 1990. RN, Calif.; cert. sch. nurse, Calif.; jr. coll. instr., Calif. Asst. instr. Emanuel Hosp. Sch. Nursing, Portland, Oreg., 1959-60; surgery flr. nurse Yale/New Haven Hosp., 1960-62, head nurse, out patient, 1962-63; staff nurse Vis. Nurse Assn., Hamden, Ct., 1963-64; sch. nurse Santa Barbara Sch. Dists., Calif., 1968-70, 77-98; dir. teenage pregnancy and parenting project Santa Barbara, 1985-86; mem. U.S. Congress from 23rd Calif. dist., Washington, 1998—; mem. Budget com. and Energy and Commerce com. Mem. commerce com., former mem. sci. com., internat. rels. com; mem U.S. Congress, campaign finance reform task force, budget task force, Calif. ISTEA task force, congrl. caucus women's issues, congrl. task force tobacco and health, diabetes caucus, congrl. caucus on the arts, House com. on the budget; instr. Santa Barbara City Coll., 1990—. Bd. dirs. Am. Heart Assn., Santa Barbara, 1989—, The Adoption Ctr., Santa Barbara, 1986-90, Family Svc. Agy., Santa Barbara, 1994—, Stop AIDS Now, Santa Barbara, 1994—, Santa Barbara Women's Polit. Com., 1991—; instr. CPR, first aid, ARC, Santa Barbara, 1985—; bd. dirs. Pacific Luth. Theol. Sem. Democrat. Lutheran. Office: US House of Reps 1707 Longworth Ho Office Bldg Washington DC 20515-0523 Home: 1216 State Street Suite 403 Santa Barbara CA 93101 Fax: 202-225-5632. E-mail: lois.capps@mail.house.gov.*

CAPPS, RICHARD HENRY, retired minister; b. Columbia, SC, June 22, 1944; s. Henry Eddie and Maude Cecile (Simpson) Crapps; m. Joyce Dianne Wood, Aug. 2, 1968; children: Richard Henry (Hank) Jr., Elizabeth Cecille. AA, North Greenville Coll., 1965; BA, Furman U., 1967; ThM with honors, New Orleans Bapt. Theol. Sem., 1970, DMin, 1978. Ordained min. So. Bapt. Ch., 1965. Pastor Fairfield Bapt. Ch., Winnsboro, SC, 1964-68, Soc. Hill Bapt. Ch., Oakvale, Miss., 1969-71, First Bapt. Ch., Gaston, SC, 1971-79, interim pastor Cheraw, SC, 1968; sr. pastor Laurel Bapt. Ch., Greenville, SC, 1979-82; dir. missions South Roanoke Bapt. Assn., Greenville, 1982-93, Liberty Bapt. Assn., Thomasville, NC, 1993-98; area dir. Piedmont/Western NC Prison Fellowship, Winston-Salem, 1999; min. missions and outreach Forsyth Park Bapt. Ch., Winston-Salem, 2000, sr. pastor, 2000—03; sr. pastor, missions min. Marketplace Ministries Fellowship, SBC, Winston-Salem, 2003—; agy. monitor Second Harvest Food Bank N.W. NC, Winston-Salem, 2004—. S.S. enlargement campaign cons. SC Bapt. State Conv., 1981-82; PACT cons. N.Am. Mission Bd., Atlanta, 1988-95; state disaster relief coord. NC Bapt. Min., Cary, 1989-93; ch. growth cons. Bapt. State Conv. of NC, Cary, 1996-98. Contbr. articles to profl. publs. Bd. dirs. Greenville Boys Choir, 1986-90, Transplant Recipient Suport Sys., Pitt County Meml. Hosp., Greenville, 1991-93; mem. Greenville Choral Soc., 1990-93; mem. religion in schs. task force Pitt County Schs., Greenville, 1993; vice chmn. chaplains bd. Davidson Correction Ctr., Lexington, NC, 1996-98; vol. greeter ARC, 2000—; bd. dirs., chmn. program com., mem. exec. com. Smart Start of Davidson County, 2004—; bd. dirs. Svcs. for Deaf and Hard of Hearing, Davidson County, Lexington, 2005. Recipient Am. Legion award, 1965; named Vol. of Yr., Davidson Correctional Ctr., 1997, Northwestern NC chpt. ARC, 2000. Mem. Dir. of Missions Conf. (pres. 1986-87, treas. 1987-98), Thomasville C. of C., Lexington Ministerial Assn., Gaston Ruritan Club (chaplain 1973-77), Am. Numis. Assn., Nat. Probation and Parole Assn., Sierra Club. Democrat. Avocations: antiques, walking, stamp collecting/philately, gardening, coin collecting/numismatics. Home: 198 Creekside Dr High Point NC 27265-9209 Office: PO Box 5808 Winston Salem NC 27113-5808 Office Phone: 336-749-1221.

CAPPS, THOMAS EDWARD, utilities company executive, lawyer; b. Wilmington, NC, Oct. 31, 1935; s. Edward S. Jr. and Agnes (Rhodes) C.; m. Jane Paden, Sept. 13, 1963; children: Ashley R., Leigh C. AB, U. N.C., 1958, JD, 1965. Bar: Fla. 1975, N.C. 1966. Sr. counsel Carolina Power & Light Co., Raleigh, N.C., 1970-74; v.p., gen. counsel Boston Edison Co., 1974-75; sr. ptnr. Steel Hector & Davis, Miami, Fla., 1975-84; exec. v.p. Va. Power, Richmond, 1984-86; pres. Dominion Resources, Inc., Richmond, 1986—2003, chief exec. officer, 1990—, chmn. bd. dirs., 2001—. Bd. dirs. Amerigroup Corp., Assoc. Elec. & Gas Ins. Svc. Bd. dirs. Va. Blood Svcs., 1986. Lt. USCG, 1959-62. Mem. ABA, Bd. of Bar Overseers, N.C. Bar Assn., Fla. Bar Assn., Mass. Bar Assn. Episcopalian. Office: Dominion Resources Inc PO Box 26532 Richmond VA 23261-6532

CAPPUCCIO, PAUL T., lawyer, communications executive; b. West Peabody, Mass., June 5, 1961; AB, Georgetown U., 1983; JD, Harvard U. Sch. Law, 1986. Bar: Ohio 1989, DC 1990. Law clk. to Hon. Alex Kozinski US Ct. Appeals (9th cir.), Pasadena, Calif., 1986—87; law clk. to Hon. Antonin Scalia US Supreme Ct., 1987—88, law clk. to Hon. Anthony M. Kennedy, 1988—89; assoc. Jones, Day, Reavis & Pogue, 1989—91; assoc. dep. atty. gen. US Dept. Justice, 1991—93; ptnr. Kirkland & Ellis, 1993—99; sr. v.p., gen. counsel Am. Online, Inc., 1999—2001; exec. v.p., gen. counsel Time Warner Inc., NYC, 2001—. Adj. prof. U. Calif., Berkeley, 1990, 91, Georgetown U. Law Ctr., Washington, 1991, 93, Columbia U. Sch. Law, NYC, 1996, 97. Bd. dir. Inst. Jud. Adminstrn., NYU Sch. Law. Office: Time Warner Inc Law Dept One Time Warner Ctr New York NY 10019 Office Phone: 212-484-8000.

CAPPY, RALPH JOSEPH, state supreme court chief justice; b. Pitts., Aug. 25, 1943; s. Joseph R. and Catherine (Miljus) C.; m. Janet Fry, Apr. 19, 1985; 1 child, Erik. BS in Psychology, U. Pitts., 1965, JD, 1968. Bar: Pa. 1968, U.S. Dist. Ct. (we. dist.) Pa. 1968, U.S. Supreme Ct. 1975. Law clerk to president judge Ct. of Common Pleas of Allegheny County, 1968—70; atty. civil and family court litigation priv. practice, 1968—78; trial defender, first asst. homicide atty., dep. dir. Office of Public Defender of Allegheny County, 1970—75; public defender Allegheny County, 1975—78; judge Family and Juvenile Ct. Ct. of Common Pleas, Allegheny County, 1978—89, judge criminal div., 1979—85, judge civil div., 1985—86, presiding admin. judge civil div., 1986—90; justice Pa. Supreme Ct., 1989—, chief justice, 2003—. Lectr. constl. law U. Pitts., 1970-72; instr. criminal law and trial tactics City of Pitts. Police Acad., Allegheny County Police Acad., 1970-74; liaison justice to Supreme Ct. Appellate Procedural Rules Com., 1990-94, Minor Judiciary of Pa., 1990-94, Pa. Bd. of Law Examiners, 1990-94, First Jud. Dist., 1990-94, Supreme Ct. Civil, Domestic Relations & Orphans' Ct. Procedural Rules Com., 1994-96, Pa. Bd. of Law Examiners, 1994-96, Civil Procedural Rules Com., Pa. Bd. of Law Examiners, Pa. Continuing Legal Education Bd., 1996-. Mem. Pitts. Health and Welfare Planning Agy., 1984—; mem. jud. ethics com. Pa. Law Jour., 1980-82; trustee U. Pitts., 1992—, bd. visitors, 1992—. Named Man of Yr., Sons of Italy; recipient Acad. of Trial Lawyers award, Citation of Merit, Mothers Against Drunk Driving, Man of Yr., Italian Am. Heritage Found., Pa. State Police, Pa. Fraternal Order of Police. Fellow Am. Bar Found.; mem. ABA, Pa. Bar Assn. (Jud. award 1997), Allegheny Bar Assn., Pa. Conf. State Trial Judges (legis. and planning com. 1978-83, legis. com., zone rep. 1984—, chmn. edn. com. 1985-88), Pa. Coll. Judiciary (lectr. 1983—, treas. 1987—, sec. 1988—), NACCP (life), Pitts. Athletic Assn. Office: Pa Supreme Ct 1 Oxford Ct Ste 3130 Pittsburgh PA 15219-1407*

CAPRARO, FRANZ, accountant; b. Uder-Eichsfeld, Thuringia, Germany, Nov. 19, 1941; came to U.S., 1959; s. Ernst Capraro and Lia (Loeschmann) Baeuscher; m. Daniela DiPauli, Dec. 26, 1964; 1 child, Monica L. BBA cum laude, U. Miami, 1964. CPA Fla. Ptnr. Deloitte Haskins & Sells (name now Deloitte & Touche), Miami, 1966-84; exec. v.p. The Wolfson Initiative Corp., Miami, 1984-95; v.p. The Novecento Corp., Miami, 1984-95, Washington Storage Co., Miami, 1984-95, The Foundlings, Inc., Miami Beach, 1984-95, The Hampton Roads, Inc., Miami Beach, 1984-95; pvt. practice acctg. Davie, Fla., 1995-96; ptnr. Grau & Co., P.A., Miami, 1996—. Treas. The Jour. of Decorative and Propaganda Arts, Miami, 1986-98; attended Nat. Security Forum, U.S. Air War Coll., Montgomery, Ala., 1993. Mem. exec. com. U. Miami Citizens Bd., Coral Gables, 1987—; treas. Mitchell Wolfson Family Found., Miami, 1985—; bd. dirs. Louis Wolfson II Media History Ctr., Miami, 1987-95; trustee Greater Miami Opera Fin. Com., 1991-96. 1st lt. U.S. Army Fin. Corps, France, 1965-66. Recipient Certificate of Appreciation City of Miami Beach, 1987; named Honorary Conch City of Key West, 1987. Mem. AICPA, Fla. Inst. CPAs, Schlaraffia Costa Aurea (treas. 1986-87), U.S. Air War Coll. Alumni Assn. (life). Roman Catholic. Avocations: reading, travel. Home: 2821 SW 116th Ave Fort Lauderdale FL 33330-1418 Office: Grau & Company PA PH 2 1110 Brickell Ave Miami FL 33131

CAPREZ, JUDITH V., social worker, director; b. Oil City, Pa., Jan. 7, 1940; m. Lionel Preston Caprez, Dec. 31, 1967; children: Cassandra Caprez Davis, Adam Preston. MSW, Ohio State U., Columbus, 1963. LSCSW Kans., 1975; cert. mediator Kans., 2001. Dir. social work High Plains Mental Health Ctr., Hays, Kans., 1970—75; dir. staff devel. Hadley Regional Med. Ctr., 1981—92; dir. baccalaureate social work Ft. Hays State U., 1992—. Adminstrn. dir. nursing Hadley Regional Med. Ctr., Hays, 1975—81. Contbr. articles to profl. jours. Screening com. Big Bro./Big Sisters, Hays; diplomate Am. Coll. Forensic Examiners Inst., Inc., Springfield, Mo., 1999—; v.p. bd. First Call Help, 2003—; bd. mem. Kans. Legal Svcs., 2005—. Recipient Social Worker Yr., Kans. Nat. Assn. Social Work, 2001. Mem.: ACSW (assoc.), NASW (assoc.), Kans. Coun. Social Work Edn. (assoc.), Baccalaureate Program Directors (assoc.), Coun. Social Work Edn. (assoc.). Office: Fort Hays State University 600 Park Hays KS 67601 Office Phone: 785-628-4469. Office Fax: 785-628-4426. Personal E-mail: jcaprez@fhsu.edu.

CAPRIATI, JENNIFER MARIA, professional tennis player; b. NYC, Mar. 29, 1976; d. Stefano and Denise (Deamicis) Capriati. Profl. tennis player, 1990—. Mem. U.S. Wightman Cup Team, 1989, U.S. Fed Cup Team, 1990—91, 1996, 2000. Winner: (jr. singles) French Open, 1989, U.S. Open, 1989, (jr. doubles, with McGrath) Italian Open, 1989, Wimbledon, 1989, Championships: Roland Garros, 2001, Australian Open, 2001, 02, Gold medal, U.S. Women's Singles, Barcelona Olympic Games, 1992, Espy award as Comback Athlete of Yr., 2002; named Comback Player of Yr., WTA, 1996, Female Athlete of Yr., AP, 2001, Singles Champion of Yr., Internat. Tennis Fedn., 2001, Sportswoman of the Year by US Olympic Comm., 2001. Avocations: dance, swimming, reading, music, golf. Address: Ste 1500 One Progress Plaza Saint Petersburg FL 33701 Office: International Management Group 420 W 45th St New York NY 10036-3503*

CAPRIO, ANTHONY S., academic administrator; b. Providence, Apr. 12, 1945; s. Salvatore and Esther (Iafrati) C. BA, Wesleyan U., 1967; MA, Columbia U., 1969, PhD, 1973; BA (hon.), Western New Eng. Coll., 2000. Asst. prof. langs. and fgn. studies Lehman Coll., CUNY, Bronx, 1971-76; assoc. prof. Cedar Crest Coll., Allentown, Pa., 1976-80; prof., adminstr. Am. U., Washington, 1980-89; provost Oglethorpe U., Atlanta, 1989-96; pres. Western New Eng. Coll., Springfield, Mass., 1996—. Corporator Hampden Bank, 2004—; mem. Nat. Humanities Faculty, 1977—. Author: Reflets de la femme, 1973, En Français, 1976, 3d edit., 1985; contbr. over 100 articles to profl. jours., chpts. to books. Trustee Willie Ross Sch. for the Deaf, 1999—, Springfield Symphony Orch., 1998-2004; bd. dirs. Springfield Adult Edn. Coun., 1999-2002, Greater Springfield Convention and Visitors Bur., 1999—, Pioneer Valley Econ. Devel. Coun., 2000—, Springfield Sch. Vols., 2000—, Tuition Exch. Inc., 1994—, Mass. Mentoring Partnership, 2001—; exec. com. Assn. Ind. Colls. and Univs. in Mass., 1999-2002; mem. cabinet Cmty. United Way of Pioneer Valley, 1998—; co-chair Leadership Coun. of Springfield Mentoring Partnership, 1998—2004; corporator Springfield Libr. and Mus. Assn., 1998—; task force on workforce devel. Pioneer Valley Planning Commn., 1998—2003; pres. Cooperating Colls. of Greater Springfield, 2000—; accreditation com. ABA, 2002—. Recipient Adminstr.-Faculty award Am. U., 1984, Disting. Adminstr. and Educator award Greater Washington Assn. Fgn. Lang. Educators, 1986. Mem. Am. Translators Assn., Am. Assn. Higher Edn., Am. Assn. Univ. Adminstrs., Soc. Coll. and Univ. Planning, Phi Beta Kappa, Omicron Delta Kappa, Phi Beta Delta, Phi Beta Kappa (fellow), others. Office: Western New Eng Coll Office of President 1215 Wilbraham Rd Springfield MA 01119-2612 Office Phone: 413-782-1243. Business E-Mail: acaprio@wnec.edu.

CAPRIO, FRANK THOMAS, state official, lawyer; b. Providence, May 10, 1966; s. Frank and Joyce Elaine (Tibaldi) C.; 1 child, Ashley Nicole. BA, Harvard U., 1988; JD, Suffolk U., 1991. Ptnr. Caprio and Caprio, Providence, 1991—; RI State Rep., Dist. 14 RI Ho. of Reps., Providence, 1991—94; RI State Sen, Dist 8 RI Senate, Providence, 1995—2002, RI State Sen., Dist 5, 2003—06; Gen. Treas. State of RI, Providence, 2007—. Bd. dir. Chase Wiggin Develop. Del. Dem. Nat. Convention, Atlanta, 1988. Mem. RI Bar Assn., Mass Bar Assn., Aurora Civic Assn.(bd. dir. & pres.), Harvard Club of Boston & RI, Harvard Varsity Club, KC, Italo-Am Club RI, Am. Corp. Counsel Assn., Justinian Law Soc. Democrat. Roman Catholic. Office: Caprio and Caprio One Center Pl Providence RI 02903-1614 also: State House Rm 102 Providence RI 02903*

CAPRON, ALEXANDER MORGAN, lawyer, educator, bioethicist; b. Hartford, Conn., Aug. 16, 1944; s. Willaim Mosher and Margaret (Morgan) Capron; m. Barbara A. Brown, Nov. 9, 1969 (div. Dec. 1985); 1 child, Jared Capron-Brown; m. Kathleen West, Mar. 4, 1989; children: Charles Spencer West Capron, Christopher Gordon West Capron, Andrew Morgan West Capron. BA, Swarthmore Coll., 1966; LLB, Yale U., 1969; MA (hon.), U. Pa., 1975. Bar: D.C. 1970, Pa. 1978. Law clk. to presiding judge U.S. Ct. Appeals, Washington, 1969—70; lectr., rsch. assoc. Yale U., 1970—72; asst. prof. law U. Pa., 1972—75, assoc. prof., 1975—78, vice dean, 1976, prof. law and human genetics, 1978—82; exec. dir. Pres.'s Commn. for Study of Ethical Problems in Med. and Biomedical and Behavioral Rsch., Washington, 1980—83; prof. law, ethics and pub. policy Law Ctr. Georgetown U., Washington, 1983—84, inst. fellow Kennedy Inst. Ethics, 1983—84; Topping prof. law, medicine and pub. policy U. So. Calif., LA, 1985—89, prof., 1989—, prof. medicine and law, 1991—, Henry W. Bruce prof. equity, 1991—2006, Scott H. Bice chair in healthcare policy, ethics and law, 2006—; co-dir. Pacific Ctr. for Health Policy and Ethics, LA, 1990—; dir. ethics and health WHO, 2002—03, dir. ethics, trade, human rights and health law, 2003—06. Mem. bd. advisors Am. Bd. Internal Medicine, 1985—95, chmn., 1991—95; cons. NIH, mem. subcom. on human gene therapy, 1984—92, mem. recombinant DNA adv. com., 1990—95; chmn. Congrl. Biomedical Ethics Adv. Commn., 1987—91; mem. Joint Commn. on Accreditation of Healthcare Orgns., 1994—, mem. ethics adv. com., 1984—85; mem. Nat. Bioethics Adv. Commn., 1996—2001. Author (with Katz): Catastrophic Diseases: Who Decides What?, 1976; author: (with others) Genetic Counseling: Facts, Values and Norms, 1979, Law, Science and Medicine, 1984, supplements, 1987, 1989, 2d edit., Treatise on Health Care Law, 1991; contbr. articles to profl. jours. Bd. mgrs. Swarthmore Coll., 1982—85; bd. trustees The Century Found. Fellow: AAAS, Hastings Ctr. (bd. dirs. 1975—98, Inst. Soc., Ethics and Life Scis.), Am. Coll. Legal Medicine (hon.); mem.: AAUP (exec. com. Pa. chpt.), Internat. Assn. Bioethics (mem. bd. 1992—96, 2001—, v.p. 2003—05, pres. 2005—), Am. Soc. Law, Medicine and Ethics (pres. 1988—89), Inst. Medicine of NAS (bd. dirs. 1985—90), Swarthmore Coll. Alumni Soc. (v.p. 1974—77). Office: U So Calif Gould Sch Law Los Angeles CA 90089-0071 Home Phone: 310-450-1815; Office Phone: 213-740-2557. Business E-Mail: acapron@law.usc.edu.

CAPRONI, VALERIE E., lawyer, federal agency administrator; BA in Psychology magna cum laude, Tulane U., New Orleans, 1976; JD summa cum laude, U. Ga., 1979. Clk. Hon. Phyllis Kravitch, U.S. Ct. Appeals, 11th cir., 1979—80; assoc. litigation dept. Cravath, Swaine & Moore, NYC, 1980—85; asst. U.S. atty. Criminal divsn. U.S. Atty.'s Office, Ea. Dist. N.Y., 1985—89; gen. counsel N.Y. State Urban Devel. Corp., 1989—92; chief of spl. prosecutions, chief organized crime and racketeering sect. U.S. Atty.'s Office, 1992—94, chief criminal divsn., 1994—98; regional dir. Pacific Regional office SEC, L.A. and San Francisco, 1998—2001; counsel Simpson Thacher & Bartlett, NYC, 2001—03; gen. counsel Office of Gen. Counsel, FBI, Washington, 2003—. Office: FBI J Edgar Hoover Bldg 935 Pennsylvania Ave NW Washington DC 20535-0001

CAPSHAW, KATE (KATHY SUE NAIL), actress; b. Ft. Worth, Nov. 3, 1953; m. John Capshaw (div.); 1 child: Jessica; m. Steven Spielberg, Oct. 12, 1991; children: Theo, Sasha, Sawyer, Mikaela, Destry. MA in Learning Disabilities, U. Mo. Actress: (feature films) A Little Sex, 1982, Indiana Jones and the Temple of Doom, 1984, Best Defense, 1984, Dreamscape, 1984, Windy City, 1984, Power, 1986, Spacecamp, 1986, Ti Presento un'Amica, 1988, Black Rain, 1989, Love at Large, 1990, My Heroes Have Always Been Cowboys, 1991, Love Affair, 1994, Just Cause, 1995, How to Make an American Quilt, 1995, Duke of Groove, 1995, The Locusts, 1997, Life During Wartime, 1997, No Dogs Allowed, 1996; (TV series) The Edge of Night, Black Tie Affair, 1993, (TV movies) Missing Children: A Mother's Story, 1982, The Quick and the Dead, 1987, Her Secret Life, 1987, Internal Affairs, 1988, Next Door, 1994, Due East, 2002; (TV miniseries) A Girl Thing, 2001; actress, prodr.: The Love Letter, 1999. Mem. Screen Actors Guild, AFTRA. Office: Creative Artists Agy care Kevin Huvane 9830 Wilshire Blvd Beverly Hills CA 90212-1804

CAPSHAW, TOMMIE DEAN, judge; b. Oklahoma City, Sept. 20, 1936; m. Dian Shipp; 1 child, Charles W. BS in Bus., Oklahoma City U., 1958; postrad., U. Ark., 1958-59; JD, U. Okla., 1961. Bar: Okla. 1961-2000, Wyo. 1971, Ind. 1975. Assoc. Looney, Watts, Looney, Nichols and Johnson, Oklahoma City, 1961-63, Pierce, Duncan, Couch and Hendrickson, Oklahoma City, 1963-70; trial atty., v.p. Capshaw Well Service Co., Liberty Pipe and Supply Co., Casper, Wyo.; adminstrv. law judge Evansville, Ind., 1973-75, 96-99; hearing office chief adminstrv. law judge, 1975—96; acting regional chief adminstrv. law judge Chgo., 1977—78; sr. adminstrv. law judge, 1999—. Acting appeals coun. mem., Arlington, Va., 1980, acting chief adminstrv. law judge, 1984; mem. faculty U. Evansville, 1977, So. Ill. U. Sch. Law, 1988—, So. Ind. U., 1990; lectr. in field. Author: A Manual for Continuing Judicial Education, 1981, Practical Aspects of Handling Social Security Disability Claims, 1982, Judicial Practice Handbook, 1990, A Quest for Quality, Speedy Justice, 1991; contbr. numerous articles to profl. jours., chpt. to textbook. Adv. coun. Boy Scouts Am., scoutmaster, den leader, 1969—2003, Nat. Jud. Coll. U. Nev.; bd. dirs. Casper Symphony, 1972-73, Casper United Fund, 1972-73, Midget Football Assn., Casper, 1972-73, German Twp. Water Dist., 1984-85; pres. Evansville Unitarian Universalist Ch., 1984-86; performer Evansville Philharm. Orch., 1986-98; bd. dirs. German Twp. Vol. Fire Dept., 1998-2003, vol. Hospice, 2000—. Recipient Kappa Alpha Order Ct. of Honor award, 1962, Silver Beaver award Boy Scouts Am., 1980, presentation for vol. svc. contbg. betterment of cmty. Office Hearings and Appeals, 1992, presentation outstanding jud. mentor tng. Supreme Ct. Iowa, 1992, presentation disting. mentor tng. Fla. Jud. Coll., 1992, Robert V. Pagant award Nat. Jud. Coll., 2002. Mem. Okla. Bar Assn., Okla. County Bar Assn. (v.p. 1967), Wyo. Bar Assn., Evansville Bar Assn. (jud. rep. 1986-87, James Bethel Gresham Freedom award 1988), Young Lawyers Assn., Assn. Adminstrv. Law Judges HHS (bd. dirs. 1979-82, Tic Vickery award 1998), Oklahoma City U. Alumni Assn. (bd. dirs. 1965). Home: 6105 School Rd # 6 Evansville IN 47720

CAPUANO, MICHAEL EVERETT, congressman, lawyer; b. Somerville, Mass., Jan. 9, 1952; s. Andrew and Rita (Garvey) C.; m. Barbara Teebagy, 1974; children: Michael, Joseph. BA in Psychology, Dartmouth Coll., 1973; JD, Boston Coll., 1977; postgrad., Boston U. Bar: Mass. 1977. Former atty. Mass. Legislative Aide; Alderman Ward 5 Somerville,

1977-79; alderman-at-large, 1985-89; mayor, 1990-99; mem. US Congress 8th Mass. dist., 1999—. Mem. Ho. Dem. Leadership team (regional whip), com. fin. svcs., subcoms. on Captial Mkts., Securities and Govt. Sponsored Enterprises, banking subcom. housing and cmty. mem. Ho. Dem. steering and policy com., com. transp. and infrastructure, subcom. allocation, hwys. and transit and aviation. Democrat. Office: US Ho Reps 1530 Longworth Ho Office Bldg Washington DC 20515-2108 also: Dist Office 110 First St Cambridge MA 02141*

CAPUS, STEVE, broadcast executive; b. Pa., 1963; m. Sophia Faskianos; 2 children; 1 child from previous marriage. BA in Journalism, Temple Univ., Phila., 1986. With WCAU-TV, Phila., 1986; writer, prodr. KYW-TV, Phila., 1987—90, exec. prodr., 1990—92; sr. prodr., Nightside NBC News, Charlotte, NC, 1993—94, broadcast prodr., NBC News Sunrise NYC, 1994, supervising prodr., Today, 1995; sr. broadcast prodr., daytime news coverage MSNBC, NYC, 1996—97, exec. prodr., The News with Brian Williams, 1997—2001; exec. prodr., Nightly News NBC News, NYC, 2001—05, sr. v.p., 2005, pres., 2005—. Recipient DuPont Columbia award, 3 Emmys, 6 Edward R. Murrow awards, 6 Nat. Headliner awards. Office: NBC News 30 Rockefeller Plz New York NY 10112

CAPUTE, COURTNEY G., lawyer; b. Granville, Ohio, Sept. 20, 1954; BA, Ohio Wesleyan U., 1977; JD, U. Md., 1986. Bar: Md. 1987. Ptnr., Real Estate Dept, Comm. Dept. Venable LLP, Balt., compensation com., assoc. evaluation com., chiar, partnership selection com. Notes & comments editor Md. Law Rev., 1985—86. Pres. Turnaround Inc., Balt., 2002—06; pro bono counsel Manna House, Balt. Mem.: ABA, Md. State Bar Assn., Bar Assn. Balt. City. Office: Venable LLP 1800 Mercantile Bank & Trust Bldg 2 Hopkins Plz Baltimore MD 21201 Office Phone: 410-244-7531. Office Fax: 410-244-7742. Business E-Mail: cgcapute@venable.com.

CAPUTO, DAVID ARMAND, academic administrator, political scientist, educator; b. Brownsville, Pa., Aug. 30, 1943; s. Armand and Marie E. (Smalstig) C.; m. Alice M. Glotfelty, June 27, 1964; children— Christopher, Elizabeth, Jeffrey. BA, Miami U., Oxford, Ohio, 1965; MA, Yale U., 1967, MPhil, 1968, PhD, 1970. Mem. faculty Purdue U., 1969—, prof. polit. sci., 1977—, head dept., 1978-87, dean Sch. Liberal Arts, 1987-95; pres. Hunter Coll., CUNY, NYC, 1995-2000, Pace U., NYC, 2000—. Author: Urban America: The Policy Alternatives, 1976; co-author: Urban Politics and Decentralization, 1974; editor: Politics of Policy-Making in America, 1977. Trustee Madison Ave. Presbyn. Ch., NYC, 2000—03; ruling elder Ctrl. Presbyn. Ch., Lafayette, Ind., 1981—87. Woodrow Wilson nat. fellow, 1965-66; NSF faculty fellow, 1977; Fulbright fellow, Italy, 1985; Lilly fellow, 1985; Bologna chair Fulbright sr. fellow, Italy, 1993. Mem. Am. Polit. Sci. Assn., Am. Soc. Public Adminstrn., Midwest Polit. Sci. Assn., So. Polit. Sci. Assn., Phi Beta Kappa, Omicron Delta Kappa. Office: Pace Univ One Pace Plz New York NY 10038 Home Phone: 212-541-5551; Office Phone: 212-346-1097. Business E-Mail: president@pace.edu.

CAPUTO, GREGORY MICHAEL, internist, educator; b. May 18, 1954; s. Joseph Vincent and Mary (Pisapia) C.; m. Leesa, June 10, 1978; children: Jennifer, Michael. BA in Biol. Sci., U. Del., Newark, 1976; MD, U. Md., 1980. Diplomate Am. Bd. Internal Medicine, Am. Bd. Infectious Disease. Intern Thomas Jefferson U. Hosp., Phila., 1980-81, clin. asst. prof. dept. medicine, 1987—90; from asst. prof. to prof. medicine Pa. State U., Hershey, 1990—98, prof., 1998—; resident Milton S. Hershey Med. Ctr., Pa. State U. Coll. Medicine, 1981—83, fellow divsn. infectious diseases, 1983—84; chief divsn. gen. internal medicine Milton S. Hershey Med. Ctr., 1996—2004, vice-chair dept. medicine, 2002—04, interim chair dept. emergency medicine, 2004—06, chief quality officer, 2006—, Robert Dye endowed prof. medicine, 2006—. Mem. staff Med. Ctr. Del., Wilmington, 1990—95, Alfred I. duPont Med. Ctr., 1990—, med. dir. diabetes amputation prevention program, 1993—99; dir. Cecil County Lyme Disease Clinic, Elkton, 1988—90; cons. Assn. Acad. Health Ctrs., Am. Lyme Disease Found., 1992—; vis. scholar Johns Hopkins Ctr. Preventive Cardiology, 2001—02; lectr. in field. Author: (chpt.) Comprehensive Textbook of Pulmonary Medicine, 1991, The Foot in Diabetes, 2d edit., 1994; co-author: (chpt.) Comprehensive Textbook Pulmonary Medicine Update, 1995, (computer program) The Prevention Guides for Clinicians and Patients, 1996; co-editor: Medical Consultation, 1997; reviewer New Eng. Jour. Medicine, Internal Medicine Jour., Clin. Infectious Diseases, Diabetes Care; contbr. articles to profl. jours. Recipient Fletcher Brown award, 1975, Disting. Physician award, Pa. State U. Coll. Medicine, 1995, Disting. Educator award, 2006; fellow, Harvard Med. Sch., 1984—85, C. Everett Koop Inst. Dartmouth Coll., 1996; vis. scholar, Johns Hopkins Med. Instns., 2001—02. Fellow ACP; mem. Am. Soc. Microbiology, Soc. Gen. Internal Medicine, Am. Diabetes Assn., Phi Beta Kappa, Phi Kappa Phi, Beta Beta Beta, Alpha Omega Alpha. Avocations: music, tennis, hiking. Office: Milton S Hershey MC Divsn Gen Int Med MC HU15 500 University Dr Hershey PA 17033

CAPUTO, KATHRYN MARY, paralegal; b. Bklyn., June 29, 1948; d. Fortunato and Agnes (Iovino) Villacci; m. Joseph John Caputo, Apr. 4, 1976. AS in Bus. Adminstrn., Nassau C.C., Garden City, NY, 1989. Legal asst. Jacob Jacobson, Oceanside, NY, 1973—77; legal asst., office mgr. Joseph Kaldor, P.C., Franklin Square, 1978—82, William H. George, Valley Stream, 1983—89; exec. legal asst., office adminstr. Katz & Bernstein, Westbury, 1990—93; sr. paralegal and office adminstr. Blaustein & Weinick, Garden City, NY, 1993—2004, Mark R. Blaustein, P.C., 2004—. Instr. adult continuing edn. legal sec. procedures Lawrence (N.Y.) H.S., 1992—. Spl. events coord. Bklyn.-Queens Marriage Encounter, 1981, 82, 83, 85, 86; mem. Lynbrook Civic Assn., St. Raymond's R.C. Ch. Pastoral Coun., 1999-2002, sec. 2000-02, Renew 2000, mem. rev. bd.; mem. St. Vincent DePaul Soc., sec., 2001—. Mem. L.I. Paralegal Assn. Avocations: travel, reading, theater, gardening. Office: Mark R Blaustein PC 1325 Franklin Ave Garden City NY 11530-1629 Business E-Mail: kcaputo@mrbpclaw.com.

CAPUTO, LISA M., finance company executive; b. Wilkes-Barre, Pa. d. A. Richard and Rosemary (Shea) C. BA in French and Polit. Sci. magna cum laude, Brown U., 1986; MS in Journalism with highest honors, Northwestern U., 1987. Press sec., fed. grants coord. U.S. Rep. Bob Traxler, Washington, 1987-89; press sec. nat. issues Dukakis-Bentsen Campaign, Boston, 1988; press sec. U.S. Senator Tim Wirth, Washington, 1989-92; dir. vice presdl. media ops. Dem. Nat. Conv., NYC, 1992; press sec. to Hillary Rodham Clinton Clinton-Gore Campaign and Presdl. Transition, Little Rock, 1992; dep. asst. to Pres., press sec. to First Lady The White House, Washington, 1993-96; v.p. corporate comm. CBS, 1996—98; v.p., global comm. and synergy Disney Pub. Worldwide, 1998—99; pres., CEO, Women and Co. Citigroup Inc., 2000—, mng. dir., bus. ops. and planning, global consumer div., 2003—05; sr. mng. dir. bus. ops. and planning Globe Consumer Group, 2005, chief mktg., advt. and cmty. rels. officer, 2005—. Contbg. editor George Mag., 1997—2000; co-host, Crossfire CNN; co-host, Equal Time CNBC, MSNBC; mem. Coun. Foreign Relations, Fin. Women's Assn. Office: Citigroup Inc 399 Park Ave New York NY 10022

CAPUTO, LUCIO, trade company executive; b. Monreale, Italy, May 22, 1935; arrived in U.S., 1967; s. Giuseppe and Gioacchina C.; m. Maria Luisa Mayr, Oct. 5, 1967; 1 child, Giorgio. Law degree, Palermo U., 1957, journalism degree, 1958, degree in polit. sci., 1960, postgrad. in econs., 1961. Bar: Italy, 1961. Journalist, Italy, 1950—65; assoc. Studio Legale Caputo-Orlando, Palermo, Italy, 1960—62; ofcl. Italian Fgn. Trade Inst., 1962—82; market rschr. Libya, Cyprus, 1963; dep. trade commr. London, 1964—67; dir. study mission S.E. Asia, 1967; Italian trade commr. Phila., 1967—71, NYC, 1972—82; founder Italian Wine Promotion Ctr., NYC, 1975—, Italian Tile Ctr., NYC, 1979—, Italian Fashion Ctr., NYC, 1980—, Italian Shoe Ctr., NYC, 1981—, ITAL Trade Ctr., NYC, 1981—. Pres. Ital Trade USA Corp., 1982-86, Italian Wine and Food Inst., 1984—; organizer ann. Italian Week on 5th Ave., NYC; pres., bd. dirs. Gruppo Esponenti Italiani, 1974—. Signer agreement between Italy and People's Republic of China, 1967; editor trade mags.: Italy Presents, Quality (English, French, Spanish, German), 1962-64; contbr. articles to popular mags. and newspapers. Adv. bd. mem. Italy-Am. C. of C., 1972-82; U.S. rep. Verona Fair Orgn., 1980—; chmn. Internat. Trade Ctr., Inc., 1987—; exec. dir. Gruppo Ristoratori Italiani, 1988-90; vice-chmn., bd. dirs. Nat. Wine Coalition, 1990-95, NIAF, 2005; chmn. bd. dirs. European Wine Coun., 1993—, chmn. bus. adv. coun. for gov., 1996—; adv. coun. Princeton U.; Lt. Italian Air Force, 1959-61 Named Cavaliere Ufficiale nell'Ordine al Merito della Republica Italiana, 1972, Commendatore, 1981, Grande Ufficiale, 1996, Cavaliere di Gran Croce, 2003. Mem. Sommelier Soc. Am., Italian Sommelier Soc., Italian Bar Assn., Italian Journalist Assn., Fgn. Consular Assn. Phila., Soc. Fgn. Consuls NY, Am. Soc. Italian Legions of Merit (chmn. bd. dirs.), Assn. Pres. of Maj. Italian-Am. Orgns. (sec., bd. dirs.), Confedn. Imprenditori Italiani Nel Mondo (v.p. N. Am.) Office: Lincoln Bldg 60 E 42d St Ste 1341 New York NY 10165 Mailing: PO Box 789 New York NY 10150 Office Phone: 212-867-4111. Office Fax: 212-867-4114. Business E-Mail: iwfi@aol.com.

CAPUTO, PHILIP JOSEPH, writer, journalist; b. Chgo., June 10, 1941; s. Joseph and Marie Ylonda (Napolitan) C.; m. Jill Esther Ongemach, June 21, 1969 (div. 1982); children: Geoffrey Jacob, Marc Antony.; m. Marcelle Lynn Besse, Oct. 30, 1982 (div. 1985); m. Leslie Blanchard Ware, June 4, 1988. BA in English, Loyola U., Chgo., 1964. Mem. staff Chgo. Tribune, 1968-72; fgn. corr. Europe, Middle East, USSR, 1972-77; freelance writer, 1977—. Author: A Rumor of War, 1977, Horn of Africa, 1980, Del Corso's Gallery, 1983, Indian Country, 1987, Means of Escape, 1991, Equation for Evil, 1996, Exiles, 1997, The Voyage, 1999, Ghosts of Tsavo, 2002, Acts of Faith, 2005, 13 Seconds: A Look Back at the Kent State Shootings, 2005, 10,000 Days of Thunder, 2005; contbr. to NY Times, LA Times, Boston Globe, Nat. Geog. Adventure, others. Served with USMCR, 1964-67, Vietnam. Recipient award Ill. AP, Ill. United Press award, Green Gavel award ABA, Overseas Press Club award, Pulitzer prize, Sidney Hillman award, others. Mem. Authors Guild. Democrat. Roman Catholic. Address: care Aaron Priest Lit Agy 708 3rd Ave New York NY 10017-4201

CARABIAS LILLO, JULIA, government official; b. Mexico City, 1954; BA, MA, Nat. Autonomous, 1981. Sec. Environ., Natural Resources & Fisheries, Mexico, 1998—2000. Prof. sci. Nat. Autonomous U., 1981, U. Coun. UNAM, 1989-93, 2000—; pres. Nat. Ecol. Inst.; mem. Coun. Nat. Solidarity Program; mem. adv. coun. Nat. Conservation Fund. Recipient 23rd Annual J. Paul Getty Wildlife Conservation prize, WWF, 2001, Internat. Cosmos prize, 2004. Office: Nat Autonomous U Mexico Av Universidad 3000 Circuito Escolar Ciu 04510 Mexico

CARABIN, DANA A., lawyer; JD. Gen. counsel, sec. Quanta Services, Inc., 2001—05, EGL Inc., Houston, 2005—, chief compliance officer, 2006—. Office: EGL, Inc 15350 Vickery Dr Houston TX 77032 Office Phone: 281-618-3100.*

CARACCIOLO, JOSEPH M., film producer; Exec. prodr., prodr: (films) A Chorus Line, 1985, Brighton Beach Memoirs, 1986, The Glass Menagerie, 1987, The Secret of My Success, 1987, Biloxi Blues, 1988, The Dream Team, 1989, Parenthood, 1989, Second Sight, 1989, My Blue Heaven, 1990, Tune in Tomorrow, 1990, True Colors, 1991, My Girl, 1991, Hero, 1992, Lost in Yonkers, 1993, My Girl 2, 1994, To Die For, 1994, The Sun Chaser, 1995, Courage Under Fire, 1996, 8MM, 1999, Big Daddy, 1999, Charlie's Angels, 2000, Mr. Deeds, 2002, Spider-Man 2, 2004, Guess Who, 2005, Spider-Man 3, 2007. Office: PO Box 690-178 Orlando FL 32869-0178*

CARADONNA, STEPHANIE ANN, dermatologist; d. Richard and Laura Caradonna; m. James T. Cannon, June 24, 2000; 1 child, Gabrielle. BS in Neurosci. and Psychology, U. South Fla., Gainesville, 1995, MD, 1999; postgrad., Fla. State U., Tallahassee, 1995—96. Intern U. South Fla. Coll. Medicine, Gainesville, 1999—2000; resident in dermatology U. NC, Chapel Hill, 2000—03; pres., owner Sarasota Skin and Cancer Ctr., Osprey, Fla., 2003—. Author: Treatment for Scleoompxederia, 2000. Office: Sarasota Skin and Cancer Ctr 2179 S Tamiami Tr Osprey FL 34229

CARAGINE, LOUIS PHILIP, JR., neurosurgeon; married; 3 children. BS in Biology, Georgetown U., Washington, DC, 1987, MS in Physiology and Biophysics, 1989, MD with honors, 1992; PhD in Physiology, Wayne State U., Detroit, 1998. Diplomate Am. Bd. Neurol. Surgery. Gen. surg. intern Detroit Med. Ctr., 1992—93; resident dept. neurol. surgery Sch. Medicine Wayne State U., Detroit, 2000; fellow U. Calif., San Francisco, 2000—02; assoc. Geisinger Med. Ctr., 2002—05, dir. Endovascular Neurosurg. Ste., 2002—05, dir. Vascular and Endovascular Neurosurgery and Interventional Neuroradiology, 2002—05; assoc. prof. Med. Ctr. The Ohio State U., 2005—, dir. Endovascular Neurosurgery, 2005—, dir. Neurol. Surgery Intensive Care Unit, 2006. Head by-laws com. cerebrovascular section Congress of Neurol. Surgery, 2007; primary investigator Wingspan HDE Stent Sys. for Intracranial Atherosclerotic Disease, 2007; sec. Ohio State Neurosurg. Soc.; presenter in field; lectr. in field. Reviewer: profl. jours.; contbr. articles to profl. jours. Recipient The Galbraith award, Cong. Neurol. Surgeons, 1998, Scholarly Activities Excellence award, Wayne State U. Sch. Medicine, 1998; fellow, NIH, 1989, Target, 2000—02; scholar, The Rhone-Poulenc Rorer Cong. Neurol. Surgeons, 1999. Mem.: AMA, Am. Surg. Assn., Am. Coll. Radiology, Neurocritical Care Soc., Am. Heart Assn. (stroke coun. 2003—05), Am. Assn. Neurol. Surgeons (mem. young neurosurgeons com. 1999—, liaison 2005—, mem. coun. state neurosurgical socs. 2005—), Am. Soc. Interventional Neuroradiology (sr.). Office: Dept Neurol Surgery The Ohio State Univ Med Ctr N 1011 Doan Hall 410 West Ave Columbus OH 43210 Office Phone: 614-293-7190. Business E-Mail: Louis.Caragine@osu.mc.edu.

CARALEY, DEMETRIOS JAMES, political science professor, writer, editor; b. NYC, June 22, 1932; s. Christopher and Stella (Psaras) Caraley; m. Vilma Mairo Bornemann; 1 child, Lisa Anne;children from previous marriage: James Christopher(dec.) , David Andrew. BA summa cum laude, Columbia U., 1954, MPhil, PhD, 1962. Mem. faculty Barnard Coll. and Columbia U., NYC, 1959—, prof. polit. sci., 1968—, Janet H. Robb prof. social scis., 1980—; editor Polit. Sci. Quar., 1973—; dir. Grad. Program in Pub. Policy and Adminstrn. Columbia U., 1978-85, chmn. Barnard dept. polit. sci., 1965-95; pres. Acad. Polit. Sci., 1992—. Vis. scholar Russell Sage Found., 1995—96. Author: Politics of Military Unification, 1966, New York City's Deputy Mayor & City Adminstrator, 1966, Party Politics and National Elections, 1966; author: (with R. H. Connery) Governing the City, 1969, National Security and Nuclear Strategy, 1983; author: City Governments and Urban Problems, 1977, American Political Institutions in the 1970's, 1976; author: (with M. A. Epstein) The Making of American Foreign and Domestic Policy, 1978; author: Doing More with Less, 1982, The President's War Powers, 1984, Volatilities in the New World Politics, 1993, Critical Issues for Clinton's Domestic Agenda, 1994; author: (with B. B. Hartman) American Leadership, Ethnic Conflict, and the New World Politics, 1997; author: The New American Interventionism, 1999, September 11, Terrorist Attacks and U.S. Foreign Policy, 2002, American Hegemony: Preventive War, Iraq, and Imposing Democracy, 2004; co-author: American Politics and Public Policy, 1978, Urban Policymaking, 1979. Mem. North Tarrytown Zoning Bd. Appeals, 1970—71, North Tarrytown Bd. Trustees, 1971—73; chmn. North Tarrytown Planning Bd., 1977—79; dep. mayor and acting mayor City of North Tarrytown, 1972—73. With USNR, 1954—56. Mem.: Acad. Polit. Sci. (bd. dirs., pres. 1992—), Am. Polit. Sci. Assn., Univ. Club (N.Y.C.), Phi Beta Kappa. Democrat. also: Acad Polit Sci/Polit Sci Quar 475 Riverside Dr Ste 1274 New York NY 10115-1299 Office Phone: 212-870-2504. Business E-Mail: jc1@psgonline.org, dc121@columbia.edu.

CARAM, DOROTHY FARRINGTON, educational consultant; b. McAllen, Tex., Jan. 14, 1933; d. Curtis Leon and Elena (Santander) Farrington; m. Pedro C. Caram, June 7, 1958 (dec. Aug. 2000); children: Pedro M., Juan D., Hector L., Jose M. BA, Rice U., 1955, MA, 1974; EdD, U. Houston, 1982; postgrad., U. Madrid, 1957. Tchr. Houston Ind. Sch. Dist., 1955-56, 56-60, St. Mark's Episcopal Ch., Houston, 1964-65; substitute tchr. St. Vincent De Paul Cath. Sch., Houston, 1965-68; mgr. med. office Houston, 1983; dir. Fed. Home Loan Bank, Little Rock, 1976-82; pres. Inst. Hispanic Culture, Houston, 1983, 93, chmn. bd. and pres., 1984; with Houston Ednl. Excellence Program, 1980. Mem. task force Tex. Edn. Agy., 1981-83; adv. coun. Nat. Inst. Neurol. and Communicative Disorders and Stroke, 1972-76; pres. IDM Satellite Comm. of Tex. Divsn., Inc., 1990, chmn. bd., 1998—99 asst. to pres. U. Houston, 1991-94, ret., 1994. Mem. coun. Miller Theater, Houston, 1976—, adv. bd. emeritus, 2000-; bd. dir. Houston Pops, 1983-87, United Way Tex., 1991-94; mem. task force Quality Integrated Edn., Houston, 1972; bd. dirs. United Way Tex., Gulf Coast, 1989-95, exec. bd., sec.; mem. Civil Svc. Commn. Houston, 1983-85; bd. mgrs. Harris County Hosp. Dist., 1988-90; founder, mem. Houston Hispanic Forum, bd. dirs., 1985, 2006—, pres., 1989-90; chmn. bd. Teatro Bilingue de Houston, 1989-90; pres. Mexican Cultural Inst. Houston, Inc., 1997; bd. dirs. Southmain Ctr. Assn., 1998-2005, Harris County Hosp. Dist. Found., 1997-2005, emeritus mem., 2005—; bd. dirs. Houston Ind. Sch. Dist. Found., 1996-2002, chmn. peer com. magnet and vanguard schs., 1996-2002; adv. bd. Theater Under Stars, Career and Recovery, Jobs for Progress of Tex. Gulf Coast, Inc., AAMA; bd. dirs. Majestic Seas Aquarium, 1998-99, U. St. Thomas, 2004—; bd. dir., treas. Colonial Homes Found. for Youth, 1999; mem. Mil. and Hospitler Order of St. Lazarus of Jerusalem, 1982-; pres. Braes Rep. Women, 2002-03, precinct judge, 1998-2006; v.p. edn. bd. Houston Grand Opera, 2001-05; commr. Tex. Commn. on Arts, 2004—; Rice alumni 50th graduation com., 2001-05, alumni coun. U. Houston, 2003; appointments chmn. Tex. Fedn. Rep. Women, 2003-05; advisor Amb. Internat. Ballet Folklorico, 2003—; trustee U. St. Thomas, Houston, 2005—; bd. dirs. Houston C.C. Found., 2004-06. Recipient Willie Velasquez Outstanding Hispanic Citizenship award, 1994, Dorothy F. Caram Leadership award Blueprint-United Way Tex. Gulf Coast, 2000-, Woman of Vision award Delta Gamma Found., 2003; named Vol. of Yr., United Way Tex. Gulf Coast, 1992, Outstanding Alumnus, Coll. Edn. U. Houston, 2000, Rice U., 2005, Extraordinary Eucharistic Min., St. Vincent de Paul Cath. Ch., 2003—; decorated Lady in Court of Isabel La Catolica by King Carlos (Spain), 1984; Oustanding Sr. fellow Am. Leadership Forum, 2004. Mem. Cedars Club (pres. 1978), Tex. Commn. Arts (commr. 2005—). Roman Catholic. Home: 2603 Glen Haven Blvd Houston TX 77025-2132 Personal E-mail: dcaram@worldnet.att.net.

CARAM, EVE LA SALLE, language educator, writer; b. Hot Springs, Ark., May 11, 1934; d. Raymond Briggs and Lois Elizabeth (Merritt) La Salle; m. Richard George Caram, Apr. 19, 1965 (div. Apr. 1978); 1 child, Bethel Eve. BA, Bard Coll., 1956; MA, U. Mo., 1977. English instr. Stephens Coll., Columbia, Mo., 1974,79-82; fiction writing grad. instr. Sch. Profl. Writing U. So. Calif., LA, 1982-87; English lit. and writing instr. Calif. State U., Northridge, 1983—; sr. fiction writing instr. The Writers' Program UCLA, 1983—. Fiction contest judge Calif. State U., Long Beach, 1992, 94, writer's conf. spkr., 1985-87, 94; spkr., mem. panel Tex. Am. Studies Assn., Wichita Falls, 1998. Author: Dear Corpus Christi, 1991, 2d edit., 2001, Wintershine, 1994, Rena, A Late Journey, 2000, The Blue Geography, 2005; editor: Palm Readings, Stories from Southern California, 1998; fiction editor West/Word, 1991. Recipient Outstanding Instr. in Creative Writing award, UCLA Ext. Writers' Program, 2006. Mem.: AAUP, Assn. Calif. State Profs., Nat. Assn. Tchrs. English, Poets and Writers, PEN Ctr. U.S.A. West, Inst. Noetic Scis., Greenpeace. Democrat. Avocations: swimming, beach walks, outdoors. Home: 3400 Ben Lomond Pl Apt 121 Los Angeles CA 90027-2952 Office: UCLA Ext The Writers' Program 10995 Le Conte Ave Los Angeles CA 90095-3001 also: Calif State U English Dept 1811 Nordoff Northridge CA 91330-0001 E-mail: ecaram1@earthlink.net.

CARAPEZZI, WILLIAM R., JR., telecommunications industry executive, lawyer; BA in Acctg., Fairfield U., 1979; JD, Western New Eng. Sch. Law; LLM in Taxation, NYU. Conn. pub. acct. Tax mgr. Arthur Andersen & Co., Hartford, Conn., 1983—89; treas. AT&T, sr. tax atty., 1989—98; v.p., Global Tax & Trade Lucent Technologies Inc., sr. v.p., gen. counsel, corp. sec., 1998—. Spkr. in field. Conn. Bar Assn., ABA, Conn. Society CPA's. Office: Lucent Technologies Inc 600 Mountain Ave New Providence NJ 07974-0636

CARASSO, ALFRED SAM, mathematician; b. Alexandria, Egypt, Apr. 9, 1939; arrived in US, 1962; s. Samuel and Renee (Ades) Carasso; m. Beatrice Kozak, June 12, 1964; children: Adam Leonard, Rachel Lisa. BSc in Physics, U. Adelaide, Australia, 1960; PhD in Math., U. Wis., 1968. Meteorologist Bur. Meteorology, Adelaide, 1960-62; rsch. asst. grad. sch. U. Wis., Madison, 1962-68; asst. prof. math. Mich. State U., East Lansing, 1968-69, U. N.Mex., Albuquerque, 1969-72, assoc. prof., 1972-76, prof., 1976-81; mathematician Nat. Inst. Standards and Tech., Gaithersburg, Md., 1982—. Vis staff mem Los Alamos Nat Lab, N.Mex., 1972—81; cons. Inst Def Analyses's Ctr Computing Scis, 1996—2003. Contbr. articles to profl jours. Mem.: Soc Indust and Applied Math, Am Math Soc, Cosmos Club. Jewish. Achievements include significant contributions to the deconvolution problem; and to such related areas of mathematical analysis as ill-posed continuation, time-reversed parabolic equations, holomorphic semigroup theory, and first kind integral equations; invention of slowly divergent schemes and backward beam formalism for solving inverse diffusion equations; invention of APEX and BEAK methods in blind image deconvolution; development of slow evolution constraint for extensive class of ill-posed PDE problems; creation of singular integral method in Lipschitz space characterization of non smooth imagery; applications in system identification, nondestructive evaluation, inverse heat transfer, image reconstruction; discovery of useful property of heavy-tailed Lévy stable laws in blind deconvolution of wide classes of images, incuding Hubble space telescope, Landsat, and electron microscope imagery, MRI and PET brain scans; patented image reconstruction procedures. Office: Nat Inst Stds and Tech Math & Computational Scis Gaithersburg MD 20899-0001 E-mail: alfred.carasso@nist.gov.

CARAVAN, RONALD L., music educator, composer; b. Pottsville, Pa., Nov. 20, 1946; s. Vincent R. and Isabelle Slater Caravan; m. Nancy Carol Nelsen, June 28, 1989; children: Michelle, Adrienne, Lisa. BS in music edn., State U. of NY, 1968; MA in music theory, Eastman Sch. of Music, 1973, MusD in music edn., 1974. Cert. in clarinet performance 1974. Music prof. State U. NY, Potsdam, NY, 1975—76, Oswego, NY, 1977—78, Fredonia, NY, 1978—79, Syracuse U., Syracuse, NY, 1980—; writer, editor The Valley News, Fulton, NY, 1974—. Pres. No. Am. Saxophone Alliance, 1986—88, jour. editor, 1978—84; woodwind review editor NY State Sch. Music Assn., 1986—. Contbr. articles various prof. jour.; composer mus. compositions, pedagogic collections, and music arrangements. With US Army, 1968—70. Recipient Amy Writing award, The Amy Found., 2000, 2001. Mem.: NY Press Assn. Home: PO Box 376 Phoenix NY 13135 Office: Syracuse U Setnor Sch of Music Syracuse NY 13244 Office Phone: 315-598-6397. Business E-Mail: rlcarava@syr.edu. E-mail: rcaravan@twcny-rr.com.

CARAVATT, PAUL JOSEPH, JR., communications executive; b. New Britain, Conn., Dec. 13, 1922; s. Paul Joseph and Bessie (Avery) C.; m. B. Laura Bennett, June 22, 1946; children— Cynthia Diane, Suzanne Laura. AB, Dartmouth, 1945, MBA, 1947. With Nat. Dairy Assn., 1947-49, Young & Rubicam, 1949-50; advt. mgr. Hunting and Fishing mag., 1950-52, Biow Co., 1952-56; v.p. Ogilvy, Benson & Mather, 1956-59; sr. v.p. Foote, Cone & Belding, 1960-64, LaRoche, McCaffrey & McCall (advt. agy.), NYC, 1964-66; pres. Carl Ally, Ind. (advt. agy.), NYC, 1966-67; chmn. bd., chief exec. officer Marschalk Co., Inc. (mem. Interpublic Group of Cos.), NYC, 1967-69; sr. v.p., dir. Interpub. Group Cos., NYC, 1970-72; pres., chief exec. officer, dir. Caravatt Communications, 1971-86, Newtel World Communications, NYC, 1971-86; pres., chief exec. officer Caravatt Mktg., Wilton, Conn., 1986—; pres. Caravatt Mktg. Group, 1998—. Exec. dir. Vision Fund, The Lighthouse, 1994—97. Mem. SAR, Spl. Interest Video Assn. (pres., exec. dir. 1988-97), Newcomen Soc., Univ. Club (N.Y.C.), Ednl. Found. of Spl. Interest Marketers and Prodrs. (pres. 1997—), Zeta Psi. Congregationalist. Home: 512 Burr Rd Southbury CT 06488 Office Phone: 203-264-7680. Personal E-mail: caravattmkg@yahoo.com.

CARAWAY, STEPHANIE SCHANKERMAN, prosecutor; b. Indpls., Oct. 17, 1969; d. Abraham Clifford and Dolores Levy Schankerman; 1 child, Avraham Hart Forrest. BA, Ind. U., Bloomington, 1991, JD, 1994. Bar: Ind. 1994. Dep. pros. atty. Marion County Prosecutor's Office, Indpls., 1995—99; assoc. Lewis & Kappes, P.C., Indpls., 1999—2000; dep. pros. atty. Marion County Prosecutor's Office, 2000—01, Johnson County Prosecutor's Office, Franklin, Ind., 2001—04, Marion County Prosecutor's Office, 2005—. Mem. faculty Nat. Advocacy Ctr., Columbia, SC, 2003—. Editor: Ind. Jour. Global Legal Studies. Vol. Humane Soc. Indpls., 1995—2002; mem. Congregation Beth-El Zedeck, 1969—2006. Fellow, Ind. U. Sch. Law, 1991—94. Mem.: Dist. Attys. Assn., Am. Mensa. Jewish. Avocations: skiing, reading. Office Phone: 317-327-5336. Personal E-mail: stephanie.caraway@yahoo.com.

CARBALLO, BERNARD A., computer company executive; Exec. v.p. Seagate Tech. Inc., Oklahoma City, Okla., 1997—. Office: Seagate Tech Inc 10321 W Reno Ave Oklahoma City OK 73127-7140

CARBALLO, JUAN-ANTONIO, research scientist; b. Madrid, Nov. 29, 1970; s. Juan-Antonio Carballo-Gallego and Maria-Cruz Herrero. BS, MS in Telecomms. Engring., Poly. U. Madrid, 1994; MBA, Coll. des Ingenieurs, Paris, 1995; PhD, U. Mich., 2000. Info. sys. cons. Andersen Cons., Madrid, 1992—93; bus. cons. Electricite de France, Paris, 1994—95; staff mem. rsch. divsn. IBM Corp., Austin, Tex., 2000—. Mem. voting com. Virtual Socket Interface Alliance, Los Gatos, 2001; mem. Design Automation Tech. Com., Poughkeepsie, NY, 2001—; mem. program com. Electronic Design Processes Workshop, Monterey, 2001—. Contbr. paper to conf. proceedings. Fellow, Coll. des Ingenieurs, 1994—95. Mem.: IEEE. Home Phone: 5123883746; Office Phone: 512-838-8914. Office Fax: 603-754-5754; Home Fax: 6037545754. Business E-Mail: jantonio@us.ibm.com.

CARBINE, JAMES EDMOND, lawyer; b. Scotts Bluff, Nebr., June 3, 1945; s. Edmond Horace Carbine and Mabel (Porterfield) Hukle; m. Marianne Lemly, Aug. 5, 1972; 1 child, Matthew. BA, Mich. State U., 1967; JD, U. Md., 1972. Bar: Md. 1972. Assoc. Weinberg and Green, Balt., 1972-79, ptnr., 1980-96, chmn. litigation dept., 1985-95; pvt. practice Balt., 1996—. Panel mem. Nat. Press Club Symposium, 1974. Reporter Govs. Landlord Tenant Commn., Md., 1973-76; mem. Mayor's Bus. Roundtable, Balt., 1983-85; bd. dirs. Greater Homewood Community Corp., Balt., 1980-82; trustee Roland Park Found., 1986-87; bd. dirs. Md. Vol. Lawyers Svc., 1991-2002. With U.S. Army, 1968-70. Named one of Outstanding Young Men Am., Jaycees, 1977. Mem. ABA (computer litigation com., corp. coun. com., co-chair trial practice com. 1994-97), Md. Bar Assn., Balt. City Bar Assn., Nat. Press Club (panelist 1974). Avocation: outdoor sports. Office: 111 S Calvert St Ste 2700 Baltimore MD 21202-6143 Home Phone: 410-235-2531; Office Phone: 410-385-5300. Business E-Mail: jcarbine@trialaw.com.

CARBO, TAMMERA MELISSA, counselor, counseling administrator; b. Waco, Oct. 6, 1959; d. Levy and Norma Yon; m. Bernardo Carbo; children: Bernardo Christopher, Shianne Sommer, Tyler Christopher, Skilar Carmen. MA in Clin. Psychology, Wheaton Coll., Ill., 1989. Lic. Mental Health Counselor Fla., 1990, Profl. Counselor Ala., 1998. Profl. counselor Diamond Club Ministry, Mobile, 1994—; sch. counselor Adams Mid. Sch., Saraland, Ala., 2001—. Counseling Lighthouse Bapt. Ch., Theodore, Ala., 2006—. Named Employee Yr., Circles Care Inc., 1994. Mem.: AACA (licentiate). Independent Baptist. Home: 6352 Woodside Dr S Theodore AL 36582 Office: Adams Mid Sch 401 Baldwin St Theodore AL 36582 Home Phone: 251-653-5621; Office Phone: 251-221-2000. Personal E-mail: bcarbo75@aol.com. Business E-Mail: tmcarbo@mcpss.com.

CARBO, TONI (TONI CARBO BEARMAN), information scientist, educator; b. Middletown, Conn., Nov. 14, 1942; d. Anthony Joseph and Theresa (Bauer) Carbo; m. David A. Bearman, Nov. 14, 1970 (div. Nov. 1995); 1 child, Amanda Carole Bearman Rochon; m. Clark Coolidge, July 7, 1962 (div. Oct. 1966). AB, Brown U., 1969; MS, Drexel U., 1973, PhD, 1977. Bibliog. asst. Am. Math. Soc., Math. Revs., 1962-63; supr. Brown U. Phys. Scis. Library, Providence, 1963-66, 67-71; subject specialist U. Wash. Engring. Library, Seattle, 1966-67; teaching and research asst. Drexel U., Phila., 1971-74; exec. dir. Nat. Fedn. Abstracting and Info. Svcs., Phila., 1974-79; cons. for strategic planning and new product devel. Instn. Elec. Engrs., London, 1979-80; exec. dir. U.S. Nat. Commn. on Libraries and Info. Sci., Washington, 1980-86; prof. U. Pitts. Sch. Info. Sci., 1986—, dean, 1986—2002. Adv. com. U.S. Dept. Commerce, Patent and Trademark Office, 1987—90; Lazerow lectr. U. Ind., 1984, U. Toronto, 1999; Schwing lectr. La. State U., 1988; Cunningham lectr. Vanderbilt U., 2002; Sigma chpt. lectr. Drexel U., Phila.; numerous other lectureships; bd. dirs. Pa. Info. Hwy. Consortium; chair jury Senator John Heinz Award for Technology, the Economy and Employment, 2001. Co-editor: Internat. Info. and Libr. Rev., 1989—92; editor, 1993—; mem. editl. bds. profl. jours.; contbr. articles to profl. jours. Mem. presdl. adv. com. Carnegie Libr. Pitts.; mem. adv. coun. Women and Girls Found. Western Pa., 2004—; chair Bd. Policy Archive, 2004—; bd. dirs. Greater Pitts. Literacy Coun.; mem. libr. adv. coun. Brown U., 2006—. Named Disting. Dau. Pa., Gov. Penn. Edward Rendell, 2004; recipient Disting. Alumni award, Drexel U. Coll. Info. Studies, 1984, 100 Most Disting. Alumni award, 1992, 100th Anniversary medal, Drexel U., 1992, Silver Anniversary award, U.S. Nat. Commn. Librs. & Info. Sci., 1996, Leadership award in Sci. and Tech., YWCA Greater Pitts., 2000, Innovation in Sci. award, Women and Girls Found. Western Pa., 2005; fellow Madison Coun., Libr. Congress, 2002—03. Fellow: AAAS (chmn. sect. T 1992—93, coun. 1997—99), Spl. Librs. Assn. (rsch. com. 1987—92, internat. rels. com. 1991), Inst. Info. Scientists, Nat. Fedn. Abstracting and Info. Svcs. (hon.); mem.: ALA (coun. 1988—92, 50th Anniversary Honor Roll 1996), Internat. Women's Forum Western Pa., Assn. Libr. and Info. Sci. Edn. (bd. dirs. 1996—2000, pres. 1997—98, chair conf. planning com. 1997—98, 1999—2000, governance com. 2005, Profl. Contbn. to Libr. and Info. Sci. Edn. award 2002, 2005), Internat. Fedn. Info. and Documentation (co-chair U.S. nat. com. 1990—2000, chair global info. infrastructure and superhighways taskforce 1993—96, mem. coun., chair info. structures and policies com. 1997—2000), Nat. Info. Stds. Orgns. (bd. dirs. 1987—90), Pa. Libr. Assn. (Disting. Svc. award 1996), Am. Soc. Info. Sci. and Tech. (chmn. networking com., chmn. 50th ann. conf., pres. 1989—90, chmn. planning and nominations com. 1990—91, Watson Davis award 1983), 3 Rivers Connect (bd. dirs., exec. com. 1998—2004, vice chair 1999—2004, SIG III cabinet rep. 2005—, mem. internat. rels. com. 2007—), Ctr. Democracy and Tech. (bd. dirs. 1996—2007, chair 1999—2002, chmn. audit com. 2006—07, mem. of pres. libr. adv. coun. 2006—), Laurel Initiative (bd. dirs. 1990—93). Home: 263 Maple Ave Pittsburgh PA 15218-1523 Office: 135 N Bellefield Ave Pittsburgh PA 15213-2609 Office Phone: 412-624-9310. Business E-Mail: tcarbo@mail.sis.pitt.edu.

CARBONARI, BRUCE A., consumer products company executive; b. 1955; BS, Boston Coll., 1977, MA; MS, Rensselaer Poly. Inst., 1984. With Price Waterhouse & Co., NYC, 1977-81; various managerial positions Moen, Inc., North Olmsted, Ohio, 1981-84, asst. contr., 1984-85, corp. contr., CFO, 1985-90, pres., COO, 1990; pres., CEO home and hardware divsn. Fortune Brands, Inc., Deerfield, Ill., 2001—05, chmn., CEO home and hardware divsn., 2005—07, pres., COO, 2007—. Office: Fortune Brands Inc 520 Lake Cook Rd Ste 400 Deerfield IL 60015-5633*

CARBONE, ANTHONY J., chemicals executive; m. Patricia; children: Christopher, Carolyn. BS in Mech. Engring., Yale U.; MBA, Ctrl. Mich. U. Various tech. svc. and devel. positions Dow Chem. Co., Midland, Mich., 1962-67, sect. head, 1967-69, group mgr. TS&D, 1969-70, product sales mgr. laminated and coated products, 1970-72, mktg. mgr. laminated and coated products, 1972-74, group v.p. Dow Plastics, Chems., Plastic bus. group, 1993-95; also bd. dirs., mem. exec. com.; mktg. dir. Dow Lat. Am., Coral Gables, Fla., 1974-76; bus. mgr. STYROFOAM brand functional products adn sys. dept. Dow U.S.A., Midland, 1976-80, dir. mktg. functional products and sys., 1980-83, gen. mgr. coatings and resins dept., 1983-87, gen. mgr. separation sys. dept., 1983-86, v.p. Dow Plastics, 1987-91; group v.p. Dow Plastics Dow N.Am., 1991-93; exec. v.p. Dow Chem. Co., Midland, 1996—2000, vice chmn., 2000—. Bd. dir. Rockwell Collins. Mem. adv. coun. Heritage Found. Mem. Am. Plastics Coun.(mem. bd., exec. com.), Am. Chem. Soc., Soc. Plastic Industries. Office: The Dow Chem Co 2030 Dow Ctr Midland MI 48674

CARBONE, RICHARD J., insurance company executive; b. 1948; Mng. dir., chief adminstrv. officer Pvt. Client Group Bankers Trust Co., 1993—95, mng. dir., controller, 1988—93; controller Bankers Trust NY Corp.; global controller, mng. dir. Salomon, Inc., 1995—97; sr. v.p., CFO Prudential Ins., Newark, 1997—; CFO Prudential Fin., Newark, 2000—, sr. v.p., 2001—. Office: Prudential 751 Broad St Newark NJ 07102-3714*

CARBONE, TRACY, pediatrician, educator; b. Jersey City, Nj, Aug. 7, 1956; d. Joseph and Marie Carbone; m. Kimon Violain; children: Joseph, Alexa. BS, Georgetown U., Washington, DC, 1978; MD, U. Padua, Italy, 1984. Bd. cert. pediat., bd. cert. neonatal perinatal medicine. Asst. prof. pediat. Robert Wood Johnson Med. Sch., New Brunswick, NJ, 1990—97; dir. Ctr. for Pediat. Sleep Disorders The Valley Hosp., Ridgewood, NJ, 1998—; asst. prof. pediat. Columbia U., NYC, 2000—. Assoc. prof., pediat. Columbia U., New York, NY. Fellow: Am. Acad. Pediat.; mem.: Am. Assn. SIDS Prevention Physicians (pres.-elect), Am. Assn. Sleep Medicine. Office: The Valley Hosp 505 Goffle Rd Ridgewood NJ 07450-4120

CARBONELL, JOAQUIN R., III, telecommunications industry executive, lawyer; b. Camaguey, Cuba, 1952; arrived in US, 1961; BA summa cum laude, Boston Coll.; JD, Duke U.; MS in Mgmt., Stanford U., 1989. Bar: Fla. 1978. Joined BellSouth Enterprises Inc., 1980; gen. atty. BellSouth, Fla., 1986—90, named gen. atty. DC office, 1990; v.p. Latin Am. BellSouth Internat., pres. Latin Am.; pres. BellSouth Europe; v.p., group counsel wireless svcs. BellSouth Enterprises, Inc.; exec. v.p., gen. counsel of regulatory and legal Cingular Wireless, 2001—04; exec. v.p., gen. counsel Cingular Wireless (after merger with AT&T Wireless), 2004—. Alfred P. Sloan Fellow, 1989. Mem.: Phi Beta Kappa. Office: Cingular Wireless Glenridge Highlands Two 5565 Glenridge Connector Atlanta GA 30342*

CARBONELL, JOSEFINA G., federal agency administrator; b. Cuba; 1 child, Alfredo. Grad., Fla. Internat. U. With Little Havana Activities and Nutrition Centers, Dade County, Fla., 1972—2001, pres., CEO, 1982—2001; asst. sec. for aging HHS, Washington, 2001—. Named one of the Most Influential Hispanic Women, Hispanic Bus., 2003; recipient Citizen of Yr. award, Miami, 1992, Charles Whited Spirit of Excellence award, Miami Herald, 1993, Cmty. Svc. award, Nat. Alliance for Hispanic Health, 1995, Monsignor Bryan Walsh Outstanding Human Svc. award, United Way, 1997, Commrs. Team award, Social Security Adminstrn., 1997, Claude Pepper Cmty. Svc. award, 2001; Kellogg Fellowship in Health Mgmt., John F. Kennedy Sch. Govt., Harvard U. Office: HHS Adminstrn Aging 1 Massachusetts Ave NW Washington DC 20201

CARBONNEAU, GUY, professional hockey coach, former professional hockey player; b. Sept-Iles, Que., Can., Mar. 18, 1960; Center Montreal Canadiens, 1979—94, St. Louis Blues, 1994—95, Dallas Stars, 1995—2000, asst. gen. mgr., 2002—06; supr. prospect devel. Montreal Canadiens, 2000, asst. coach, 2000—02, assoc. coach, 2006, head coach, 2006—. Recipient Frank J. Selke Trophy, 1988, 1989, 1992. Achievements include being a member of Stanley Cup Champion, Montreal Canadiens, 1986, 1993, Dallas Stars, 1999. Office: c/o Montreal Canadiens 1275 St Antoine St W Montreal PQ Canada H3C 5L2

CARBULLIDO, F. PHILIP, judge; b. Tamuning, Guam, Feb. 5, 1953; s. Francisco Chaco and Maria Salas (Castro) Carbullido; m. Fay Diana Lizama Garrido; children: Brandon Philip, Kristina Joy, Adam Philip, Steven Philip. BS in Polit. Sci., U. Oreg., 1975; JD, U. Calif., Davis, 1978. Intern to asst. atty. gen. Office Atty. Gen.; assoc. Arriola and Lamorena, Arriola & Cowan, ptnr., Carbullido & Pipes, P.C., 1983—97, Carbullido Bordallo & Brooks, LLP, 1997, Carbullido & Brooks LLP; justice Guam Supreme Ct., Hagåtña, 2000—, chief justice, 2003—. Recipient award of Merit, Pacific Jaycees, 1983; Profl. Tech. scholar, Govt. of Guam. Office: Supreme Ct Guam Jud Ctr Ste 300 120 W O'Brien Dr Hagatna GU 96910 Business E-Mail: justice@guamsupremecourt.com.*

CARCIERI, DONALD L., governor; b. East Greenwich, RI, Dec. 16, 1942; s. Nicola and Marguerite Carcieri; m. Suzanne Owren; children: Matthew, Alison, Jill, Sarah. BA in Internat. Rels., Brown U., 1965. Tchr.; various positions including exec. v.p. Old Stone Bank; head West Indies ops. Cath. Relief Svcs., Kingston, Jamaica, 1981—83; various positions including CEO Cookson Am., RI, 1983, joint mng. dir. Cookson Group Worldwide RI; gov. State of RI, 2002—. Mem. Cath. Relief Svcs. Leadership Coun.; former chair R.I. Math./Sci. Edn. Coalition; co-founder Acad. Children's Sci. Ctr., East Greenwich; dir. Providence Ctr., RI. Republican. Roman Catholic. Office: Office of the Gov State House Rm 115 Providence RI 02903*

CARD, ANDY (ANDREW HILL CARD JR.), former White House Chief of Staff; b. Brockton, Mass., May 10, 1947; s. Andrew Hill and Joyce (Whitaker) C.; m. Kathleene Marie Bryan, 1968; children: Tabetha, Rachel, Drew. BS in Engring., U. S. C., 1971; MA, LLD (hon.), Mount Ida Coll. and Assumption Coll.; MA, DPA (hon.), Curry Coll.; postgrad., Mass. Maritime Acad. Structural design engr. Maurice Reidy Engrs., Inc., 1971-72, David M. Berg, Inc., 1972-75; mem. Mass. Ho. Reps., 1975—83; v.p. CMIS Corp., Vienna, Va., 1983; N.H. campaign mgr. for George Bush, 1987-88; spl. asst. to for inter-govtl. affairs The White House, 1983-87, dep. asst. to Pres., dir. Office of Intergovernmental Affairs Washington, 1988, asst. to Pres. & dep. chief of staff, 1989-92; sec. US Dept. Transp., Washington, 1992—93; pres., CEO Am. Automobile Mfrs. Assn., Washington, 1992—98; v.p. govt. relations GM, 1999—2000; chief of staff to Pres. The White House, Washington, 2000—06. Mem. adv. commn. on intergovtl. relations, 1988; head of task force Federal relief effort Hurricane Andrew So. Fla., 1992; bd. dirs. Union Pacific Corp. 2006-. Candidate for gov., Mass., 1983. Served in USN, 1965—67. Named one of Nation's Outstanding Legislators, Nat. Rep. Legislators' Assn., 1982.

CARD, DEBORAH R., orchestra administrator; b. Pottstown, Pa., Sept. 30, 1956; d. Marshall Anthony and Winifred (Hitz) R. BA, Stanford U., 1978; MBA, U. So. Calif., 1985. Orch. mgr. LA Philharm., 1978-86; exec. dir. LA Chamber Orch., 1986-92, Seattle Symphony Orch., 1992—2003; pres. Chgo. Symphony Orch. Bd. dirs. AIDS project LA, 1985-92; active Jr. League LA, 1982-92. Mem. Am. Symphony Orch. League, Assn. Calif. Symphony Orchs. (pres. 1988-91), Assn. N.W. Symphony Orchs. (bd. dirs. 1993—), Chamber Music Soc. LA (bd. dirs. 1987-92), Ojai Festival (pres.'s coun.). Democrat. Episcopalian. Avocations: skiing, tennis, gardening, reading. Home: 1536 W Nelson St Chicago IL 60657-3104 Office: Chgo Symphony Orch Assn 220 S Michigan Ave Chicago IL 60604 Office Phone: 213-294-3205.*

CARD, ORSON SCOTT (BYRON WALLEY), writer; b. Richland, Wash., Aug. 24, 1951; s. Willard Richards and Peggy Jane (Park) C.; m. Kristine Allen, May 17, 1977; children: Geoffrey, Emily, Charles, Zina, Erin. BA in Theater, Brigham Young U., 1975; MA in English, U. Utah, 1981. Editor Brigham Young U. Press, Provo, Utah, 1974-76; assoc. editor Ensign mag., Salt Lake City, 1976-78; sr. editor Compute! Publs., Greensboro, NC, 1983; game design cons. Lucasfilm Games, 1989-92. Instr. Brigham Young U., U. Utah, U. Notre Dame, Appalachian State U., Clarion West Writer's Workshop, Cape Code Writers Conf., Antioch Writers Workshop; columnist "You Got No Friends In This World", Science Fiction Review, 1979-86, "Book to Look For", Fantasy and Science Fiction, 1987—, "Gameplay", Compute!, 1988—. Author: (fiction) Capitol, 1978, Hot Sleep, 1978, A Planet Called Treason, 1979, Songmaster, 1980 (Hamilton/Brackett award 1981), Unaccompanied Sonata and Other Stories, 1980, Hart's Hope, 1982, The Worthing Chronicle, 1983, A Woman of Destiny, 1983, Ender's Game, 1985 (Nebula award 1985, Hugo award 1986, Hamilton/Brackett award 1986), Speaker For The Dead, 1986 (Nebula award 1986, Hugo award 1987, Locus award 1987), Hatrack River, 1986 (Hugo award nomination 1986, World Fantasy award 1987), Wyrms, 1987, Seventh Son, 1987 (Locus award best fantasy 1988, Hugo award nomination 1988, World Fantasy award nomination 1988), Cardography, 1987, Eye for Eye, 1987 (Hugo award 1988, Locus award nomination 1988), Treason, 1988, Red Prophet, 1988 (Locus award 1989), Prentice Alvin, 1989, Folk of the Fringe, 1989, The Abyss, 1989, Maps in a Mirror, 1990, The Worthing Saga, 1990, Xenocide, 1991, The Memory of Earth, 1992, Lost Boys, 1992, The Call of Earth, 1992, The Changed Man, 1992, Flux, 1992, Cruel Miracles, 1992, Monkey Sonatas, 1993, The Ships of Earth, 1993, A Storyteller in Zion, 1993, Earthfall, 1994, (with David Dollahite) Turning Hearts, 1994, (with Kathryn H. Kidd) Lovelock, 1994, Earthborn, 1995, Alvin Journeyman, 1995 (Locus award 1996), Pastwatch: The Redemption of Christopher Columbus, 1996, Children of the Mind, 1996, Treasure Box, 1996, Stone Tables, 1997, Homebody, 1998, Heartfire, 1998, Enchantment, 1999, Ender's Shadow, 1999, Magic Mirror, 1999, Sarah, 2000, Shadow of the Hegeman, 2001, Rebekah, 2001, Shadow Puppets, 2002, The Crystal City, 2003, First Meetings: in the Enderverse, 2003, Shadow of the Giant, 2005 (Publishers Weekly Bestseller list), Magic Street, 2005; (nonfiction) Listen, Mom and Dad, 1978, Saintspeak, 1981, Ainge, 1982, Characters and Viewpoint, 1988, How to Write Science Fiction and Fantasy, 1990 (Hugo award for non-fiction 1991); (plays) The Apostate, 1970, In Flight, 1970, Across Five Summers, 1971, Of Gideon, 1971, Stone Tables, 1973, A Christmas Carol, 1974, Father, Mother, Mother, and Mom, 1974, Liberty Jail, 1975, Rag Mission, 1977, Fresh Courage Take, 1978, Elders and Sisters, 1979, Wings, 1982; editor: Dragons of Darkness, 1981, Dragons of Light, 1983; author numerous audio and videoplays; contbr. short stories and essays to Fantasy & Sci. Fiction, Windows Sources and other mags. Recipient John W. Campbell award World Sci. Fiction Conv., 1978, Hugo award nominations World Sci. Fiction Conv., 1978, 79, 80, Nebula award nominations Sci. Fiction Writers of America, 1979, 80, Utah State Inst. of Fine Arts prize, 1980. Mem. Sci. Fiction Writers Am., Authors Guild. Democrat. Mem. Lds Ch. Address: c/o Tor Books 175 5th Ave Fl 14 New York NY 10010-7703 also: Barbara Bova Lit Agy PO Box 770365 Naples FL 34107

CARD, STUART KENT, psychologist, researcher; b. Detroit, Dec. 21, 1943; s. Stuart Llewellyn and Kathleen Marie (Wolfe) C.; m. Josefina Bulatao Jayme, Jan. 26, 1972; children: Gwyneth Megan, Tiffany Heather. AB in Physics, Oberlin Coll., Ohio, 1966; MS, Carnegie Mellon U., 1970, PhD in Psych., 1978. Acting dir. Oberlin Coll. Computer Ctr., 1967; mem. rsch. staff Xerox Palo Alto Rsch. Ctr., Calif., 1974-86, prin. scientist, 1986-90, mgr. user interface rsch., 1988—2007, rsch. fellow, 1990, sr. rsch. fellow. Cons. Psychol. Svc. Pitts., 1968-73; adh. assoc. prof. dept. psych. Stanford U., 1983; chmn. human factors summer study on automation in combat aircraft for the 1990s Air Force/NRC, Woods Hole, Mass., 1980; charter mem. Bd. on Army Sci. and Tech., NRC, Washington, 1982-85; group leader NATO Advanced Workshop on Man-Machine Sys., Loughborough, Eng., 1983; blue ribbon com. on Army aviation aircrew integration NASA/Army, Moffitt Field, Calif., 1983. Editl. bd. Behavioral and Info. Tech., London, 1984, Human-Computer Interaction, 1984, ACM Transactions on Office Info. Sys., 1988-90, Cambridge U. Press, 1991; assoc. editor ACM Transactions on Human-Computer Interaction, 1992; co-author: The Psych. of Human-Computer Interaction, 1983; co-editor: Human Performance Models for Computer-Aided Engring., 1990; co-designer computer sys.: Rooms, 1986, Info. Visualizer, 1991; author: Readings in Information Visualization, 1999. Troop leader Girl Scouts US, Palo Alto, Calif., 1985-86; coach Odyssey of the Mind, Palo Alto, 1993-94; chair cognition models NAS Panel on Pilot Performance Models for Computer-Aided Engring., Washington, 1987-89. Recipient Bower award and prize for Achievement in Sci., Franklin Inst., 2007. Fellow Assn. Computing Machinery (prog. chair conf. on human factors in software 1991, program com., 1983-94, faculty doctoral consortium 1985, 88, Computer-Human Interaction Lifetime Achievement award, 2000), World Tech. Network; mem. IEEE, Cognitive Sci. Soc., Human Factors Soc., Computer-Human Interaction Acad., Sigma Xi, NAE. Achievements include patents in field. Office: Xerox Palo Alto Rsch Ctr 3333 Coyote Hill Rd Palo Alto CA 94304-1314 Office Phone: 650-812-4362. E-mail: stuart.card@parc.com.

CARD, WESLEY ROY, apparel and footwear company executive; b. East Hartford, Conn., Dec. 29, 1947; s. Harriet (Curtis) C.; m. Dianne Kenny; children: W. Scott, Geoffrey W., Stephen A. BS in Acctg., U. R.I., 1970. CPA, Mass., Conn. Sr. acct. Price Waterhouse & Co., Boston, 1970-75, audit mgr. Syracuse, N.Y., 1975-77; asst. contr. Bank of Boston, 1977-79; v.p. fin. Hathaway div. Warnaco Inc., Waterville, Maine, 1979-84; exec. v.p. fin. & adminstrn., CFO Warnaco Knitwear div. Warnaco, Inc., Altoona, Pa., 1984-86; v.p., corp. contr., asst. sec. Warnaco, Inc., Bridgeport, Conn., 1986-88; exec. v.p., CFO Carolyne Roehm, Inc., NYC, 1988-90; CFO Jones Apparel Group, Inc., Bristol, Pa., 1990—2007, COO, 2002—07, pres., CEO, 2007—. Bd. dir. Am. Apparel & Footware Assn., chmn., 2005—07. Served to staff sgt. USAR, 1965-72. Mem. AICPA, N.J. Soc. CPAs. Baptist. Avocations: golf, skiing, running. Office: Jones Apparel Group Inc 250 Rittenhouse Cir Bristol PA 19007-1616*

CARDAMONE, RICHARD J., federal judge; b. Utica, NY, Oct. 10, 1925; s. Joseph J. and Josephine (Scala) Cardamone; m. Catherine Baker Clarke, Aug. 28, 1946. BA, Harvard U., 1948; LLB, Syracuse U., 1952. Bar: NY 1952. Pvt. practice, Utica, 1952—62; judge NY State Supreme Ct., 1963—71, judge appelate divsn. 4th dept., 1971—81; judge US Ct. Appeals (2nd cir.), Utica, 1981—93, sr. judge, 1993—. Pres. NY State

Assn. Supreme Ct. Justices, 1977—78. Lt. (j.g.) USNR, 1943—46. Mem.: Oneida County Bar Assn., NY State Bar Assn., Am. Law Inst. Roman Catholic. Office: US Ct Appeals 10 Broad St Utica NY 13501-1233*

CARDEN, ALAN L., hospital chaplain; b. Prattville, Ala., Dec. 21, 1953; s. Ocie Omer and Eloise Sanford Carden, Barbara Carden (Stepmother); m. Janice Virden Carden, Sept. 23, 2000; children: Matthew Marshall, Casey Elizabeth, Lauren Bethany Frazier, Annie Jean Frazier. MusB, Miss. Coll., Clinton, 1976; M of Ch. Music, New Orleans Bapt. Theol. Sem., 1979, MRE, 1988; D of Ministry, Columbia Theol. Sem., Atlanta, 2000. Bd. cert. chaplain Assn. Profl. Chaplains, 1993. Min. music Shiloh Bapt. Ch., Saraland, Ala., 1980—85, First Bapt. Ch., Theodore, Ala., 1987—88; staff chaplain Bapt. Regional Med. Ctr., Corbin, Ky., 1991—92, Bapt. Health Sys., Jackson, Miss., 1992—98, clin. ministries mgr., 1998—2003, hosp. chaplain dir., 2003—. Vol. Habitat for Humanity, Jackson, 1992—, bd. mem., 1995—. Fellow: Am. Assn. Pastoral Counselors. Republican. Baptist. Avocations: bicycling, travel, photography. Office: Baptist Health Sys 1225 N State St Jackson MS 39202 Home Phone: 601-672-0775; Office Phone: 601-968-1000.

CARDENAS, DIANA DELIA, academic administrator, retired physician, educator; b. San Antonio, Apr. 10, 1947; d. Ralph Roman and Rosa (Garza) C.; m. Thomas McKenzie Hooton, Aug. 20, 1971; children: Angela, Jessica. BA with highest honors, U. Tex., 1969; MD, U. Tex., Dallas, 1973; MS, U. Wash., 1976, MHA, 2001. Diplomate Nat. Bd. Med. Examiners, Am. Bd. Phys. Medicine & Rehab., Am. Bd. Electrodiagnostic Medicine. Asst. prof. dept. rehab. medicine Emory U., Atlanta, 1976-81; instr. dept. rehab. medicine U. Wash., Seattle, 1981-82, asst. prof. dept. rehab. medicine, 1982-86, assoc. prof. dept. rehab. medicine, 1986-92, prof. rehab. medicine, 1992; chair Dept. Rehab. Medicine U. Miami, Fla., 2006—. Med. dir. rehab. medicine clinic U. Wash. Med. Ctr., Seattle, 1982—99; project dir. N.W. Regional Spinal Cord Injury Sys., Seattle, 1990—; mem. Accreditation Coun. for Grad. Med. Edn. Residency Rev. Com., 1995—96; chief of svc. rehab medicine U. Wash. Med. Ctr., 2002—. Editor: Rehabilitation & The Chronic Renal Disease Patient, 1985, Maximizing Rehabilitation in Chronic Renal Disease, 1989; acad. editor Archives of Phys. Medicine and Rehab., 1997-99; contbr. articles to profl. jours. Co-chairperson Lakeside Sch. Auction Student Vols., Seattle, 1991; bd. dirs. CONSEJO Counseling & Referral Svc; elected to Inst. Medicine of Nat. Acad., 2004. Mem.: Inst. of Medicine Nat. Acad. Sci. (com. on assessing rehab. sci. and engring. 1996—97, com. on injury prevention and control 1997—99), Nat. Inst. Child Health and Human Devel. (rsch. subcom. 1996—99), Am. Assn. Electrodiagnostic Medicine, Am. Congress of Rehab. Medicine (chairperson rehab. practice com. 1981—83, bd. govs. 2003, Ann. Essay Contest winner 1976), Am. Acad. Phys. Medicine and Rehab. (chairperson rsch. adv. and advocacy com. 1997—99), Am. Spinal Injury Assn. (chairperson rsch. com. 1990—94, bd. dirs. 1994—2000, co-chair internat. rels. com. 1995—98, chair internat. rels. com. 1999—, chair mktg. com. 2000—03), Assn. Acad. Physiatrists (chair awards com. 1993—99). Avocations: art collecting, sewing, painting. Office: U Miami Dept Rehab Medicine PO Box 016960 (D461) Miami FL 33101

CARDENAS, RAUL RODOLFO, JR., engineering executive, educator, consultant; b. Galveston, Tex., Feb. 5, 1929; s. Raul Rodolfo and Clementina (Munoz) C.; m. Mary R. Gaglio, Nov. 23, 1961; children: Dianne, Randolph, Patricia. BA, U. Tex.-Austin, 1951, postgrad., 1955-57; MS in Environ. Health Sci., NYU, 1963, PhD, 1970. Asst. rsch. scientist NYU, NYC, 1961-63, asst. prof., 1966-72; rsch. assoc. Manhattan Coll., 1963-66; prof. dept. civil engring. Poly. Inst. N.Y., Bklyn., 1972-87; pres. Internat. Technol., Inc., Northvale, N.J., 1997—, also bd. dirs. Northvale, N.J., Tel Aviv, Israel. Bd. dirs. Advanced Compost Technol (ACT), v.p., tech. dir.; lab. dir. sewage dist. Rockland County; adj. prof. Hunter Coll., Polytech U., Cooper Union Coll., CCNY; lectr., cons. in field. Contbr. articles to profl. jours. and books. First chmn. elect PCB Settlement Com., N.Y. State, 1974-76; chmn. bd. dirs., pres. Carpenter Environ. Assoc., Inc., 1980-91; gov.'s tech. adv. bd. State of N.J., 1985; mem. pres. adv coun. Dominican Coll. 1st lt. U.S. Army, 1952-54. Fellow Scientists Inst. for Pub. Info.; mem. Water Environ. Assn. (Outstanding Analyst Achievement award 1996), Am. Soc. Microbiology, AAAS, Interam. Assn. San. Engrs., N.Y. Explorers Club, Sigma Xi. Home and Office: 66 Pine Tree Ln Tappan NY 10983-2112 Home Phone: 845-359-1184; Office Phone: 845-359-1184. Personal E-mail: enviroraul@yahoo.com.

CARDENAS-VALENCIA, ANDRES MANUEL, chemical engineer, researcher; b. Morelia, Michoacan, Mex., Jan. 27, 1974; s. Luis Felipe Cardenas-Padilla and Luz Maria Valencia-Gonzalez; m. Michelle Lynn Janowiak, July 17, 2004. BChemE, Universidad de Guadalajara, Guadalajara, Mex., 1996; M in Engring., U. S. Fla., 1998, PhD, 2001. Intern Polyurethanos del Occidente de Mex., POM. S.A., Guadalajara, Jalisco, Mexico, 1994—96; salesman Fabricas de Francia, Guadalajara, Jalisco, Mexico, 1994—95; rsch. and grad. asst. chem. engring. dept. U. S. Fla., Tampa, 1997—2001, mems sr. devel. engr. Ctr. Ocean Tech. St. Petersburg, 2002—. Postdoctoral fellow Ctr. Ocean Tech. U. S. Fla., St. Petersburg, 2001—02. Contbr. articles to profl. jours. Scholar, Consejo Nacional de Ciencia y Tecnologia, 1997-2001; Rsch. scholar, Universidad de Guadalajara, 1994—96. Mem.: ACS, Omega Chi Epsilon (sec., pres. 1998—2000), Phi Kappa Phi. Roman Catholic. Achievements include patents for spectrophotometric system and method for the identification and characterization of a particle in a bodily fluid; patents pending for method and Apparatus for Continuous Measurement of the Refractive Index of a Fluid; aluminum galvanic cell; actuated electrochemical power source; micro-aluminum galvanic cells and method for constructing the same. Avocations: travel, exercise, collecting Star-wwrs action figures. Office: U S Fla COT 140 Seventh Ave S Saint Petersburg FL 33701 Home Phone: 813-854-1653; Office Phone: 727-553-1198.

CARDENES, ANDRES JORGE, musician, educator; b. Havana, Cuba, May 2, 1957; came to U.S., 1958; s. Andres Manuel and Arlene (Cuevas) C. Student, Ind. U., 1975-80; diploma, Meisterkurse Zurich, Switzerland, 1977. Asst. prof. music Ind. U., Bloomington, 1980-82; prof. music Espoo Festival, Helsinki, Finland, 1982; prof. U. Utah, Salt Lake City, 1982-85; prof. music U. Mich., 1987-89; concertmaster Utah Symphony, 1982—85, San Diego Symphony, 1985—86, Pitts. Symphony, 1989—. Mem. artistic com. Utah Symphony, Salt Lake City, 1983-85; cons. in field; bd. dirs. Intermountain-West Music Festival, Salt Lake City, 1984-88; artistic dir. Strings in the Mountains Chamber Music Festival, Steamboat Springs, Colo.; founder & music dir. Culver City Chamber Orch.; Dorothy & Richard Starling & Alexander C. Speyer prof. music Carnegie Mellon U., 1989—. Concert violin soloist, 1981—; 1985-86; editor: Concerto by Ramiro Cortes, 1983; performer worldwide Nuclear Arms Freeze, 1980; recordings: Arensky & Tchaikovsky Piano Trios (with Jeffrey Solow & Mona Golabek) (Grammy nomination 1991); Saint-Saëns' Sonatas for Violin & Piano (with Doris Stevenson); It's Peaceful Here (with Luz Manriquez); Made in the USA, 1997; A Cuban Blues Man, 2004. Cultural amb. UNICEF, 1980—; chmn., co-founder Underprivileged Arts Student San Diego Soc.; cultural chmn. Make-a-Wish Found. of Pitts. Recipient Bronze medal Queen Elizabeth Internat. Violin Competition, Brussels, 1980, Bronze medal Sibelius Internat. Violin Competition, Helsinki, 1980, Bronze medal Tchaikovsky Internat. Violin Competition, Moscow, 1982, Bronze medal Internat. Violin Competition, Indpls., 1986, Pitts. Classical Artist of Yr., 1998, Starling Found. endowed chair Carnegie-Mellon U., 1998, Shalom awrd Kollell Found. Mem. Young San Diegans Soc. (bd. dirs.). Clubs: Machista (Bloomington) (pres. 1978—). Roman Catholic. Office: Pittsburgh Symphony Orch Heinz Hall 600 Penn Ave Ste 1 Pittsburgh PA 15222-3259

CARDER, PAUL CHARLES, retired advertising executive; b. Oak Park, Ill., Jan. 27, 1941; arrived in Can., 1967; s. Lawrence E. and Irene (Zahler) C.; m. Jacqueline MacNeil, 2005; children from previous marriages: Greg Lawrence, Tracy Allison, Leigh Rebecca Kamping-Carder, Amanda Rachel Kamping-Carder. BA, U. Mich., 1962; MBA, Harvard U., 1964. Account exec. Ogilvy & Mather, NYC, 1964-65; v.p. Ogilvy & Mather Can., Ltd., Toronto, Ont., Canada, 1966-73; v.p., dir. client svcs. Doyle Dane Bernbach, Toronto, 1974-77; sr. v.p., mng. dir. Vicker & Benson, Ltd., Toronto, 1978-83; pres., CEO Carder Gray Advt., Inc., Toronto, 1983-90, DDB Needham Worldwide, Toronto, 1990-94; ret., 1994; dean, faculty Bus. and Creative Arts George Brown Coll., Toronto, 1999—2002. Adj. prof. Queen's U. Sch. Bus., 1995—96; prin. Paladin Co.; dir. mktg. and bus. devel. Davies, Ward, Phillips & Vineberg, 2003—. Bd. dirs. Nat. Ballet Can., Toronto, 1984-90, Thousand Islands Playhouse, 1995—2004, Heart and Stroke Found. of Ont., 1997—2005, Toronto Cmty. Found., 2000—2006, Soulpepper Theatre Co., 2003—, Young Centre for the Performing Arts, 2005—, Ballet Jorgen Can., 2003—. Mem. Inst. Can. Advt. (dir., treas. 1988-90), Harvard Bus. Sch. Club of Toronto (dir.). Liberal party of Ontario. Avocations: tennis, skiing. Personal E-mail: paul@paulandjacqueline.com.

CARDIFF, ROBERT DARRELL, pathology educator; b. San Francisco, Dec. 5, 1935; s. George Darrell and Helen (Kohfield) C.; m. Sally Joan Bounds, June 23, 1962; children: Darrell, Todd, Shelley. BS, U. Calif., Berkeley, 1958, PhD, 1968; MD, U. Calif., San Francisco, 1962. Intern King's County Hosp., Bklyn., 1962-63; resident in pathology U. Oreg., Portland, 1963-66; NIH fellow U. Calif., Berkeley, 1966-68, mem. faculty med. sch. Davis, 1971—, prof. pathology Med. Sch., 1977—2005, disting. prof., 2005—, chair dept. pathology, 1990-96; dir. Ctr. for Med. Informatics U. Calif. Davis Healthcare Sys., 1996-98, faculty Ctr. for Comparative Medicine; chair Med. Informatics Grad. Group, 2002—04; dir. Ctr. Genomic Pathology, 2007—. Mem. sci. adv. bd. Contra Costa Cancer Fund, Walnut Creek, Calif., 1985-99; mem. Univ.-Wide AIDS Task Force, Berkeley, 1984-87; vis. prof. Sun-Yat Sen U. Med. Sci., Peoples Republic of China, 1985, 93, Harvard Med. Sch., 1990, U. Calif. San Diego, 1998-99. Mem. editl. bd. Human Pathology, 1992-2004, Tumor Markers, 1992—, Internat. Jour. Oncology, 1992—, Jour. Mamgland Biol. and Neoplasia, 1998—; contbr. articles to profl. jours Lt. col. US Army, 1968—71. Recipient Triton Rsch. award, Triton Bioscis., Inc., 1985, Sadusk award, Peralta Cancer Inst., 1986, Dist. Prof. award, 2005. Master: AAUP (exec. com. 1983—85); fellow: AAAS; mem.: No. Calif. Pathology Soc. (pres. 1990—96), Sacramento Pathology Soc. (bd. dirs. 1985—96), Internat. Assn. Breast Cancer Rsch. (bd. dirs. 1984—96, pres. 2003—06, chair 2006—, chair, bd. govs. 2006—), Internat. Acad. Pathology, Pluto Soc., Sigma Xi. Avocations: basketball, skiing, jogging. Office: U Calif-Davis Ctr for Comparative Medicine 98 County Rd & Hutchison Dr Davis CA 95616 Office Phone: 530-752-2726. Business E-Mail: rdcardiff@ucdavis.edu.

CARDILE, PAUL JULIUS, fine arts dealer; b. NYC, July 30, 1948; s. Julius Joseph and Mary Lola (Contrucci) C. BA, Queens Coll., NYC, 1969, MA, 1971; MPhil, Yale U., 1974, PhD, 1976. Asst. prof. SUNY, Albany, 1975-76, Newcomb Coll., New Orleans, 1976-77, Cleve. State U., 1977-78; asst. prof., mus. dir. Denison U., Granville, Ohio, 1978-84; owner Cardile Galleries, NYC, 1984—. Appraiser Assn. of Am., N.Y.C., 1985—, bd. dirs., 1995—. Author: Paintings in Churches and Sacred Places in Cortona, 1982; contbr. articles to profl. jours. Historian Orthodox Knights Hospitaller of St. John of Jerusalem. Humanities fellow NEH, 1982-83. Mem. Portuguese Heritage Found. (adv. coun. 1991—). Republican. Roman Catholic. Home: 880 5th Ave # 6H New York NY 10021-4951 Office: RF Stuart 444 Park Ave S New York NY 10016

CARDILLO, JAMES G., automotive executive; Grad. in Bus. Adminstrn., Cleve. State U. Mgmt. positions Rockwell Corp.; with Peterbilt Motors Co., 1990—99, sr. exec.; chmn., pres. DAF Trucks N.V. PACCAR, England, 1999—2004, sr. v.p. Bellevue, Wash., 2004—06, exec. v.p. Office: PACCAR PO Box 1518 Bellevue WA 98009 Office Phone: 425-468-7400. Office Fax: 425-468-8216.*

CARDIMONA, KIMBERLY MARIE, language educator; b. Wilkes-Barre, Pa., Aug. 15, 1961; d. Andrew Joseph and Marlene Kratz; m. Jeffrey Nicholas Cardimona, Nov. 6, 2002; children: Tia Marie Hartenfels, Tara Kimberly Hartenfels, Jeffrey Nicholas. AA in Edn., Luzerne County CC, Nanticoke, Pa., 1981—81; BS in Edn., Clarion U., Pa., 1983; MS in Edn., Wilkes U., Pa., 2002—03, MS in Instrnl. Tech., 2004; PhD in Curriculum and Instrn., Pa. State U., University Park, 2004. Cert. German Pa., 2002, ESL Pa., 2002. Propr. It's A Small World Internat. Kindergarten, Dusseldorf, Germany, 1993—2001; ESL tchr., German instr. Tamaqua Area Sch. Dist., Pa., 2002—; adj. faculty Coll. Misericordia, Dallas, Pa., 2003—; half time faculty Bloomsburg U., Pa., 2005—. Mem.: TESOL, Assn. Instl. Rsch. (assoc.). Home: 555 Pond Hill Mountain Rd Wapwallopen PA 18660 Office: Tamaqua Area Sch Dist Broad St Wapwallopen PA 18660 Home Phone: 570-379-1263. Personal E-mail: kmc342@psu.edu, kcardimona@tamaqua.k12.pa.us.

CARDIN, BENJAMIN LOUIS, senator, former congressman; b. Balt., Oct. 5, 1943; s. Meyer M. and Dora (Green) C.; m. Myrna Edelman, Nov. 24, 1964; children: Michael, Deborah. BA cum laude, U. Pitts., 1964; JD, U. Md., 1967; LLD (hon.), U. Balt., 1990, U. Md., 1993, Balt. Hebrew U., 1994, Goucher Coll., 1996. Bar: Md. 1967. Pvt. practice law, Balt., 1967-87; mem. Md. Ho. of Del., 1967-86, chmn. ways and means com., 1974-79, spkr. of house, 1979-86; mem. US Congress from 3d Md. Dist., Washington, 1987—2007, standards. and ofcl. conduct com., 1991-97, ways and means com., 1999—2005, human resources and social security subcoms., 1991—2007, steering com. Dem. caucus, 1991—2007, chair orgn., study and review com. of Dem. caucus, 1997—2007, mem. homeland security com.; US Senator from Md., 2007—. Chmn. MD Legal Svc. Corp., 1988-95; commr. Commn. on Security and Cooperation in Europe, 1993—. Contbr. Bd. visitors U. Md. Sch. Law, 1993—; trustee St. Mary's Coll., 1988-99, Goucher Coll., 1999—. Recipient Small Bus. Coun. of Am. Congrl. award, 1993, 99, Jacob K. Javits award Am Psychiat. Assn., 1999, Md. Psychiatric Soc. Friend of Psychiatry Award, 1988; Common Cause of Md. Ann Hogan Meml. Award, 1087; Rep. of Yr. award Nat. Assn. Police Orgn., 1998, Md. Bar Found. Vernon Eney award, 1996, Md. Save Our Streams' Living Stream award, 1996, Digestive Disease Nat. Coalition Publ. Policy Leadership award, 1996, The Coalition for a Lead Safe Environment, Alliance to End Childhood Lead Poisoning: the H. John Heinz III Nat. Leadership Award, 1994; ABA Pro Bono Publico Award, 1989; Hunting S. Williams award, 1995, H. John Heinz III Nat. Leadership award, 1994, Nat. Multiple Sclerosis Soc. Rep. of the Yr. award, 1993, Israel Freedom award, 1992, U. Md. Law Sch. Alumni Assn. Cardin Pro Bono award, 1990, Congl. Advocate of Yr. award Child Welfare League of Am., 2000; named to Concord Coalition's Deficit Hawk Honor Roll, 1998, 99, The Am. Med. Assoc. Dr. Nathan Davis Award for Publ. Svc., 1999; Congressional Advocate of the Yr. Award, Child Welfare League of Am, 2000; Nat. Leadership Award for Svc. to Children and Families, Casey Family Svc., 2000; Congressional Leadership Award, the Am. Coll. of Emerg. Physicians, 2001; Congressional Champion Award, The Nat. coalition for Cancer Rsch., 2002; Legislator of the Yr., Am. Assoc. of Health Plans, 2003. Mem.: Md. Bar Assn., ABA (Pro Bono Pub. award 1989), Balt. City Bar Assn. Democrat. Jewish. Office: US Senate 2207 Rayburn House Office Bldg Washington DC 20515*

CARDIN, PIERRE, fashion designer; b. San Biagio di Callalta, Italy, July 2, 1922; Student, St. Etienne, France. Tailor Manby, Vichy, France, 1939-40; adminstr. with French Red Cross, Paris, 1940-45; designer Paquin, Paris, 1946—47, Elsa Schiaparelli, Paris, 1946—47, House of Dior, Paris, 1947—50; founder, designer Pierre Cardin, Paris, 1950—. Mem. Chambre Syndicale de la Haute Couture et du Prêt-à-Porter, 1953—93, Maison du Haute Couture, 1953—93; founder, dir. Theatres des Ambassadeurs-Cardin (now Espace Cardin), Paris, 1970—; owner, chmn. Maxim's Restaurant, Paris, 1981—; goodwill ambassador UNESCO, 1991—. Designer costumes for films including La Belle et la bête, 1946, A New Kind of Love, 1963, The V.I.P.s, 1963, Eva, 1964, The Yellow Rolls Royce, 1965, Mata Hari, Agent H-21, 1967, A Dandy in Aspic, 1968, The Immortal Story, 1969, You Only Love Once, 1969, Little Fauss and Big Halsy, 1970 Decorated Officier Legion d' Honneur, France, 1983, les insignes de Comdr. de l'Ordre du Mérite de la République Italienne, 1976; recipient Basilica Palladiana prize, 1973, le prix de l'EUR (Italian theatre Oscar), 1974, Gold Thimble awards for most creative high fashion collections, 1977, 79, 82, Career Achievement award, Cutty Sark Men's Fashion Awards, 1984, Prize of Found. for Garment & Apparel Advancement, Tokyo, 1988, Internat. award, Coun. Fashion Designers Am., 2007 Office: 59 rue du Faugourg-St Honoré 75008 Paris France also: 27 Ave Marigny 75008 Paris France*

CARDINALE, GERALD P., retail executive; With Rite Aid Corp., 1970—, v.p. merchandising, v.p. info. systems devel., 1996—98, sr. v.p. category mgmt., 1998—. Mem. adv. bd. Nat. Assn. Chain Drug Stores. Recipient Pres. award, Rite Aid Corp., 2000. Office: Rite Aid Corp 30 Hunter Lane Camp Hill PA 17011 Office Phone: 717-761-2633. E-mail: jcardinale@riteaid.com.*

CARDINALE, KATHLEEN CARMEL, retired health facility administrator; b. Donegal, Ireland, July 13, 1933; came to U.S., 1958, naturalized, 1966; d. Denis and May (Cannon) O'Boyle; m. Anthony Cardinale, Aug. 28, 1965. BA, Jersey City State Coll., 1971, MA, 1973. RN, N.Y., U.K.; cert. nursing adminstr. advanced; nat. managed care cert., 1996. Nurse Walton Hosp., Liverpool, Eng., 1955; staff nurse, acting-in-charge Manhattan Gen. Hosp., NYC, 1958-59; charge nurse, acting-in-charge Met. Hosp., NYC, 1959-60; charge nurse, relief supr. Manhattan Gen. Hosp., NYC, 1960-64, asst. dir. nursing, 1964-68, staffing coord., 1968-70; acting assoc. dir. nursing Bernstein Inst., NYC, 1970; clin. supr., clin. specialist Beth Israel Med. Ctr., NYC, 1971-73; asst. dir. nursing Cabrini Med. Ctr., NYC, 1974-77, assoc. DON, 1977-78, v.p. nursing svcs., 1978-94, sr. v.p. nursing svcs., 1994-2000; ret., 2000. Mem. ANA, Greater N.Y. Hosp. Assn. (mental hygiene com.), Am. Hosp. Assn., Am. Orgn. Nurse Execs., Dean and Dirs., N.Y.C. Inc. (sec. 1993-94), Am. Coll. Health Care Execs. (assoc.). Home: 545 E 14th St New York NY 10009-3020 Personal E-mail: nungie0713@yahoo.com.

CARDMAN, LAWRENCE SANTO, physics professor, researcher; b. Mt. Vernon, NY, Oct. 7, 1944; s. Michael L. and Alice (Willis) C.; m. Helen-Andrea Fox; children: Andrew Lawrence, Michael Allan, Zena Maria. BA, Yale U., 1966, PhD in Physics, 1972. Instr. physics Yale U., New Haven, 1971—72, rsch. assoc., 1972; NAS/NRC postdoctoral fellow Nat. Bur. Stds., 1972—73; asst. prof. U. Ill., Urbana, 1973—78, assoc. prof., 1978—82, prof., 1982—95, adj. prof., 1995—, co-prin. investigator nuc. physics lab. Champaign, 1982—89, 1992; dep. assoc. dir. physics Continuous Electron Beam Accelerator Facility, Newport News, Va., 1993—96; assoc. dir. for physics Thomas Jefferson Nat. Accelerator Facility, Newport News, Va., 1996—; prof. U. Va., Charlottesville, 2002—. Vis. scientist Centre D'Etudes Nucleaire Saclay, France, 1980-81, Continuous Electron Beam Accelerator Facility, Newport News, Va., 1989-90; adj. prof. Coll. William and Mary, Williamsburg, Va., 1995—. Contbr. over 90 articles to profl. jours. Nat. Acad. Scis.-NRC Postdoctoral Rsch. fellow, 1972-73. Fellow Am. Phys. Soc.; mem. Sigma Xi. Avocations: woodworking, electronics, computers, cooking. Office: Jefferson Lab 12000 Jefferson Ave Newport News VA 23606 Office Phone: 757-269-7032. Business E-Mail: cardman@jlab.org.

CARDONA, JULIO JOSE, student affairs director, educational researcher; b. Martinez, Calif., Mar. 24, 1980; s. Ramon Cardona and Lucia Raya. AS, Johnson and Wales U., Providence, 2000; BA, Calif. State U., Seaside, 2003; MA, Stanford U., Calif., 2004. Sr. acad. tutor Johnson and Wales U., Providence, 1998—2000; rsch. assoc. Calif. State U., Monterey Bay, Seaside, 2001—03; rsch. asst. Stanford U., Stanford, Calif., 2003—04, sch. programs coord., 2004—05; asst. dean U. Calif., Santa Cruz, 2005—; lectr. Calif. State U., Monterey Bay, 2006—. Co-founder and vice-chair L.E. Raya Scholarship Edn. Found., Marina, Calif., 2001—; guest lectr. Stanford U., 2004—, Calif. State U., Monterey Bay, 2003—; steering com. mem. Citizen Schools at MIT, Redwood City, Calif., 2004—; peer reviewer Am. Ednl. Rsch. Assn., Washington, 2005—, Assn. for the Study of Higher Edn., Mich. Contbr. book, articles to profl. jours. Vol. ARC, Washington, 1994; mem. Pacifica Found., Berkeley, Calif., 2005, Downtown Planning Com., Marina, Calif., 2001—04; vol. mem. Cmty. Events Com., Marina, 2000—02; mem. League of United Latin Am. Citizens, Monterey, Calif., 1998—2004. Recipient Achievement award in edn., Bank of Am., 1998, Vigil Honor Membership, Order of the Arrow, Boy Scouts of Am., 1998; grantee Ft. Ord Alumni Assn. E.O.C., Calif. State U., Monterey Bay, 2002; scholar Nat. scholar, League of United Latin Am. Citizens, 1998. Mem.: Nat. Latino Ednl. Assn., Assn. for the Study of Higher Edn., Am. Ednl. Rsch. Assn., Boy Scouts of Am. (Eagle Scout 1996), Nat. Eagle Scout Assn. (life), Alpha Gamma Sigma. Achievements include research in The usage of multicultural education theories in the college classroom; first to The impact of federal TRIO programs in California State Universities. Avocations: travel, camping, cooking. Personal E-mail: jcardona@stanfordalumni.org.

CARDONA, MANUEL, physics professor; b. Barcelona, Catalonia, Spain, July 9, 1934; s. Juan and Angela (Castro) C.; m. Inge Hecht; children: Michael, Angela, Steven. Licenciado en Ciencias, U. Barcelona, 1955; DSc, U. Madrid, 1958; MSc, Harvard U., 1958, PhD, 1959; degree (hon.), Brown U.; Dr. (hon.), U. Autónoma de Madrid, 1985, U. Autónom de Barcelona, 1985, U. Regensburg, Germany, 1994, Sherbrooke U., Can., 1994, U. La Sapienza, Roma, 1995, U. Toulouse, 1998, U. Thessaloniki, 2001, Masaryk U., Brno, 2002, Valencia U., 2004, U. La Laguna, 2006. Mem. tech. staff RCA Labs, Zurich, Switzerland, 1959-61, Princeton, NJ, 1961-64; assoc. prof. physics Brown U., Providence, 1964-66, prof. physics, 1966-71; dir. Max Planck Inst. for Solid State Rsch., Stuttgart, Germany, 1971-2000, emeritus, 2000—. Adj. prof. U. Stuttgart, 1973—, U. Konstanz, 1990—; lectr. Air New Zealand, 2001; mem. French Nat. Com. for Evaluation Sci. Rsch., 1999—2001. Editor-in-chief Solid State Comm., Oxford, Eng., 1992-2004; mem. bd. editors Physica Status Solidi, Berlin, 1971—; assoc. editor Phys. Rev. Letters, Upton, N.Y., 1989-92; editor Solid State Sci. Series Springer, 1975—; author: Modulation Spectroscopy, 1969, Fundamentals of Semiconductors, 1995, 3d edit., 2001; others; contbr. numerous articles to profl. jours. Recipient N. Monturiol medal, Govt. of Catalonia, 1984, Great Cross of Order of Alfonso X el Sabio, Spain, 1987, Principe de Asturias Found. award, 1988, J.M. Marci von Kronland medal, Czechoslovak Spectroscopic Soc., Prague, 1989, Sci. prize, Catalonian Sci. Found., 1990, Medaglia Tenesiana, U. Pavia, Italy, 1992, Italgas prize, 1993, Max Planck Rsch. prize, 1994, Ernst Mach medal, Czech Phys. Soc., 1999, Sir Nevill Mott medal and prize, Inst. Physics, London, 2001, Medaglia Matteucci, Italian Acad. Scis., 2004, Blaise Pascal medal in Physics, European Acad. Scis., 2004; fellow, World Innovation Found., 2001. Fellow: Inst. of Physics (London), Am. Phys. Soc. (Frank Isakson prize 1984, John Wheatley award 1997); mem.: NAS of U.S. (ordinary mem.), Internat. Union Pure and Applied Physics (chmn. semiconds. commn. 1996—2002), Royal Acad. Scis. of Spain (corr. mem.), Academia Europaea, Mex. Acad. Scis. (corr.), German Phys. Soc.,

European Phys. Soc., Acad. Scis. of Barcelona (corr. mem.), A.F. Ioffe Inst. (hon.). Lutheran. Office: Max Planck Inst Solid State Rsch Heisenbergstr 1 D-70569 Stuttgart Germany Business E-Mail: m.cardona@fkf.mpg.de.

CARDONA, RODOLFO, Spanish language and literature educator; b. San Jose, Costa Rica, Jan. 17, 1924; came to U.S., 1943, naturalized, 1950; s. Jose Ismael and Julia (Cooper) C.; m. Electra Ducas, Aug. 1, 1954; children: Eleni Maria, Alexander Xavier, Michael Anthony, Christopher Pericles. BA, La. State U., 1946; PhD, U. Wash., 1953. Consul of Costa Rica, San Diego, 1943-44; asst. instr. fine arts and Spanish La. State U., 1946-47; asst. prof. Am. Inst. Fgn. Trade, Phoenix, 1947-48; instr. U. Wash., 1948-53; hon. consul Costa Rica, Seattle, 1948-53, asst. prof. Western Res. U., also hon. consul Cleve., 1953-56; asst. prof., then assoc. prof. Chatham Coll., Pitts., 1956-60; prof., then chmn. dept. Hispanic langs. U. Pitts., 1961-69; hon. consul Costa Rica, Pitts., 1956-69; prof. Spanish, chmn. dept. Spanish and Portuguese U. Tex., Austin, 1969-78; Univ. prof., dir. Univ. Profs. Program Boston U., 1978-88, prof. emeritus, 1991—. Resident dir. Internat. Inst., Madrid, 2000—02; acad. coord. Residencia de Estudiantos, Madrid, 2002-05. Author: Ramón: A Study of Gómez de la Serna and His Works, 1957, Galdos ante la literature y la historia, 1998, Del Heroismo a la Caquexia: Los Episodios Nacionales de Galdos, 2005; co-author: Visión del esperpento; editor: Novelistas españoles de hoy, 1959, La sombra de Benito Pérez Galdós, 1964, Doña Perfecta, 9th edit., 1984, Greguerias, 9th edit., 1997, La viuda blanca y negra by R. Gomez de la Serna, 1988; Novelistas españoles de postguerra, 1977; co-editor: Teatro selecto de Galdós, 1973; founder, editor: Anales galdosianos; contbr. articles to profl. jours. Andrew Mellon postdoctoral fellow, 1960-61; grantee Am. Council Learned Socs., 1967-68; grantee Univ. Rsch. Inst., 1973-74; fellow Nat. Endowment Humanities, 1973-74. Mem. Assn. Theatre Dirs. (hon.), Phi Beta Kappa, Phi Kappa Phi, Pi Mu Epsilon, Phi Sigma Iota. Mem. Easthern Orthodox Ch. Home: 56 Bay State Rd Boston MA 02215-3108 Home Phone: 617-522-2662; Office Phone: 617-522-2662. Personal E-mail: rcardona56@comcast.net.

CARDONE, BONNIE JEAN, freelance/self-employed photojournalist; b. Chgo., Feb. 21, 1942; d. Frederick Paul and Beverly Jean Rittschof; m. David Frederick Cardone, June 9, 1963 (div. 1978); children: Pamela Susan, Michael David. BA, Mich. State U., 1963. Editorial asst. Mich. State Dental Assn. Jour., Lansing, 1963-64; asst. editor Nursing Home Adminstr. mag., Chgo., 1964-65, Skin Diver Mag., LA, 1976-77, sr. editor, 1977-81, photographer, 1981—, exec. editor, 1981-97, editor, 1997-99; mystery novelist, 1999—. Author: Fireside Diver, 1993; co-author: Shipwrecks of Southern California, 1989. Named Woman Diver of Yr. Women's Scuba Assn., 1999; recipient Calif. Scuba Svc. award St. Brendan Corp., 1999; named to Women Diver's Hall of Fame, 2000, Women's Scuba Assn. Mem. Calif. Wreck Divers Club (Wreck Divers Hall of Fame, 2003), Hist. Diving Soc. (bd. dirs. 1997-2001). E-mail: bjcardone@hotmail.com.

CARDOSO, ANTHONY ANTONIO, artist, educator; b. Tampa, Fla., Sept. 13, 1930; s. Frank T. and Nancy (Mesina) C.; m. Martha Rodriguez, 1954; children: Michele Denise, Toni Lynn. BS in Art Edn., U. Tampa, 1954; BFA, Minn. Art Inst., 1965; MA, U. South Fla., Tampa, 1975; PhD in Art, Elysion Coll., Calif., 1981. Art instr., head fine arts dept. Jefferson H.S., Tampa, 1952-67, Leto H.S., Tampa, 1967—; supr. art and humanities Hillsborough County Sch., Tampa, 1985—91. Bd. dirs., supr. art Hillsboro County Schs.; rep. Tampa Art Coun.; artist, 1952-87. One-man shows include Warren's Gallery, Tampa, 1974, 75, 76, Tampa Realist Gallery, Tampa, 1975, Kotler Gallery 2005; group shows include Rotunda Gallery, London, End., 1973, Raymon Duncan Galleries, Paris, France, 1973, Brussells Internat., 1973; represented in permanent collections Minn. Mus., St. Paul, Tampa Sports Authority Art Collection, Tampa Arts' Coun.; executed murals Tampa Sports Authority Stadium, 1972, Suncoast Credit Union Bldg., Tampa, 1975, Kotler Gallery Exhibit, Tampa, 2004, Centro Asturiano Ball Room Gallery, 2004. Recipient Prix de Paris Art award Raymon Duncan Galleries, 1970, Salon of 50 States award Ligoa Duncan Gallery, NYC, 1970, Latham Found. Internat. Art award, 1964, XXII Bienniel Traveling award Smithsonian Instn., 1968-69, Purchaase award Minn. Mus., 1971, 1st award Fla. State Fair, 1967, Gold medal Accademia Italia, 1981-82, Medallion Merit, Internat. Parliament, Italy, 1984, Statue of Vittoria award for centro studi and richerche, Italy, 1988, Accademia D'Europa, Premio Palma D'Oro D' Europa, Italy, 1989—, El Prado Gallery, 1990—, Merit award Festival Arts Hillsborough County Tampa, 1994-2002, El Prado Gallery, Tampa, 1999-2004, Koetler Gallery Tampa, 2005, Internat. Photographers award, 2007. Democrat. Roman Catholic. Home Phone: 813-876-3629; Office Phone: 813-876-3629. Personal E-mail: cardoso@verizon.net.

CARDOSO, CARLOS M., metal products executive; 2 children. BS, Fairfield U., Conn.; MS, Hartford Grad. Ctr., Conn. Various engring., mfg., mgmt. positions Internat. Nickel Corp., Caval Tool & Machine Co.; v.p. mfg. ops. Colt Mfg. Co., Hartford, Conn.; with Allied Signal (became Honeywell); pres., pump divsn. Flowserve Corp.; v.p., pres. metalworking solutions & services group Kennametal Inc., Latrobe, Pa., 2003—05, v.p., COO, 2005, pres., CEO, 2005—. Office: Kennametal Inc 1600 Technology Way Latrobe PA 15650 Office Phone: 724-539-5000.*

CARDOZA, DENNIS, congressman; b. Atwater, Calif., Mar. 31, 1959; m. Kathleen McLoughlin; children: Joey, Brittany, Elaina. BA, U. Md., 1983. Intern Rep. Martin Frost, Washington; mem. Calif. Assembly, 1996—2002, US Congress from 18th Calif. dist., 2003—, mem. agr. com., mem. com. on resources, mem. com. on sci. Mem. Atwater City Coun., 1984, Merced City Coun., 1994. Named Legis. of Yr., Calif. Sheriff's Assn., 2001, Calif. Sherrif's Assn., 2002, U. Calif., 2001, Small Bus. Roundtable, 2001, Small Bus. Assn., 2001. Democrat. Office: US Ho Reps 435 Cannon Ho Office Bldg Washington DC 20515-0518*

CARDOZO, ARLENE ROSSEN, writer; b. Mpls., Jan. 12, 1938; d. Ralph and Beatrice (Cohen) Rossen; m. Richard Nunez Cardozo, June 29, 1959; children: Miriam, Rachel (dec.), Rebecca. B.A., U. Minn., 1958, M.A., 1982, PhD, 1990. Founder, dir. Writers Unlimited, Mpls., 1972-76, Woman at Home Workshops, Mpls., 1976-81; lectr. U. Minn. Summer Arts Study Ctr., 1981-85; artist-in-residence Split Rock Arts Ctr., Duluth, Minn., 1984-85, Dept. Mass Communications U. Minn., 1990-97, Augsburg Coll., 1994-96, St. Cloud State U., 1994, U. Miami, 1998-2000; cons. Sequencing Mothers, 1986—, manuscript and pub. industry. Author: The Liberated Cookbook, 1972, Woman at Home, 1976, Jewish Family Celebrations, 1982, Sequencing, 1986, 89, 96; editor, pub. The Read-Aloud Rev.; contbr. essays, articles, reviews to Chgo. Sun Times, Mpls. Star/Tribune, Cleve. Plain Dealer, Newsday; L.I. Journalism Quar.; prodr., narrator (radio) Once Upon a Time; guest lectr. Harvard-Radcliffe U., 1982; others; guest appearances Today Show, Phil Donahue Show, Dr. Ruth Show, CBS News Nightwatch, Attitudes, radio and TV, U.S. and Can.; featured in NY Times, Washington Post, Mpls. Star Tribune, Redbook Mag. Founder, Harvard Neighbors, Cambridge, 1963-64; vol. Mpls. pub. schs., 1972-82; pres. Rachel Liba Cardozo Children's Found., 1992-; dir. Brownstone Distbg., 1991-. Mem. Authors Guild, Authors League Am., Nat. Press Club, Nat. Book Critics Circle (charter), Hadassah (life). Jewish. Home: 202A Sunrise Dr Key Biscayne FL 33149 also: 1007 Pine Tree Trl Stillwater MN 55082 E-mail: arcardozo@worldnet.att.net.

CARDOZO, BENJAMIN MORDECAI, lawyer; b. NYC, May 15, 1915; s. Sidney Benjamin and Eva Cecile (Mordecai) C.; m. Barbara Ruth Schaffer, Sept. 21, 1941; children: Enid Cardozo Lamcn, Ellen Cardozo Sonsino. BA, Dartmouth Coll., 1937; postgrad., Columbia U., 1938; JD, NYU, 1941. Bar: N.Y. State bar 1942, U.S. Supreme Ct. bar 1947, Conn. bar 1954. Mem. staff Moreland Commn. Workmen's Compensation Investigation, NY, 1941, Office Alien Property, U.S. Dept. Justice, Washington, 1946-49; assoc. Cardozo & Nathan, NYC, 1949-51, Cardozo & Cardozo, P.C., NYC, 1952—; pvt. practice, NYC. Mem. ABA, New York County Lawyers Assn., Assn. Bar City N.Y., Yale Club, Met. Club. Home: 325 E 79th St New York NY 10021-0954 Office: 488 Madison Ave Rm 1100 New York NY 10022-5702 Office Phone: 212-838-6120.

CARDOZO, MICHAEL A., lawyer; b. NYC, June 28, 1941; s. Harmon and Lucile Cardozo; children: Hedy, Sheryl. AB, Brown U., 1963; JD, Columbia U., 1966. Bar: N.Y. 1966, U.S. Dist. Ct. (so. dist.) N.Y. 1967, U.S. Ct. Appeals (1st cir., 2d cir., 7th cit., 9th cir. and 3d cir.), U.S. Supreme Ct. Law clk. to Hon. Edward C. McClean US Dist. Ct. (so. dist.) NY, NYC, 1966—67; assoc. Proskauer Rose LLP, NYC, 1967—74, ptnr., 1974—2001; corp. counsel NYC Law Dept., NYC, 2002—. Chair Columbia U. Law Sch. Bd. Visitors, 1999. Fellow: Am. Coll. Trial Lawyers; mem.: Fund for Modern Courts (chair 1999—2000), Assn. Bar City N.Y. (pres. 1996—98). Democrat. Jewish. Office: Office of Corporation Counsel 100 Church St New York NY 10007-2601 Office Phone: 212-788-0800. Business E-Mail: mcardozo@law.nyc.gov.*

CARDOZO, RICHARD NUNEZ, marketing professional, educator, entrepreneur; b. Mpls., Feb. 13, 1936; s. William Nunez and Miriam (Honig) C.; m. Arlene Rossen, June 29, 1959; children: Miriam, Rachel (dec.), Rebecca. AB, Carleton Coll., 1956; MBA, Harvard U., 1959; PhD, U. Minn., 1964. Asst. prof. bus. adminstrn. Harvard U., 1964-67; assoc. prof. mktg. U. Minn., 1967-71, prof., 1971—2000, Curtis L. Carlson chair in entrepreneurial studies, 1987-2000, prof. entrepreneurial studies, strategic mgmt., 2000—02, prof. emeritus, 2002—; dir. Ctr. for Exptl. Studies in Bus., 1969-73, chmn. dept. mktg., 1975-78; dir. Case Devel. Ctr., 1980-2000, Entrepreneurial Studies Ctr., 1987-2000. Dir. Nat. Presto Industries, Brownstone Distbg., Valspar Corp., 1976-96, Best Buy Co., 1985-92; Fulbright lectr. Hebrew U., Jerusalem, 1980; vis. prof. bus. adminstrn. Harvard U., Grad. Sch. Bus., 1982-83; adj. prof. U. Miami, 2003—; cons. in field; mem. editl. bd. Jour. Mktg., 1976-93, Jour. Mktg. Rsch., 1976-82, Jour. Bus. Venturing, 1987-2002. Author: Product Policy: Cases and Concepts, 1979; co-author: (with others) Problems in Marketing, 4th edit, 1968, New Product Forecasting, 1981, Business Financing, 1999; contbr. articles to profl. jours. Dir. Kids, Inc., 1971—76. Fellow, Ford Found., Kaiser, 1961—63; Fulbright fellow, London Sch. Econ., 1956—57. Mem. Am. Mktg. Assn. (entrepreneurship rsch. award 2006), AAAS, Product Devel. and Mgmt. Assn., Acad. Mgmt. Home: 202A Sunrise Dr Key Biscayne FL 33149 Personal E-mail: dickcardozo@aol.com.

CARDUCCI, DONALD JOSEPH, music educator; b. Syracuse, NY, Mar. 2, 1955; s. Alfred and Elda Carducci. MusB in Edn., SUNY, 1977; MusM in Edn., Ithaca Coll., NY, 1990. Tchr. band Liverpool (N.Y.) Ctrl. Schs., 1977—81, West Genesee Ctrl. Schs., Camillus, NY, 1982—88, Oswego (N.Y.) City Schs., 1989—90, Dryden (N.Y.) Ctrl. Schs., 1990, Orchard Pk. (N.Y.) Ctrl. Schs., Orchard Pk., 1991—. Bd. dirs. Orchard Pk. (N.Y.) Coun. Arts, 1991—, Orchard Pk. (N.Y.) Symphony Orch., 1999—. Recipient Excellence award, Buffalo (N.Y.) Philharmonic, 2003. Mem.: N.Y. State Band Dirs. Assn. (bd. dirs. 1985—95, 2005—). Home: 85 Ashwood Ln Orchard Park NY 14127 Office: Orchard Park Ctrl Schs 4040 Baker Rd Orchard Park NY 14127 Office Phone: 716-209-6321. Business E-Mail: dcarducci@opschools.org.

CARDUCCI, JUDITH WEEKS BARKER, artist, retired social worker; b. Norwood, Mass., Feb. 25, 1935; d. Harold O. and Catherine E. (Stone) Barker; m. Dewey J. Carducci, June 22, 1961; 1 child, David E.B. BA, U. Maine, Orono, 1956; MS, Columbia U., NYC, 1958. Coor. psychiatry and social work programs Cleve. VA Med. Ctr., Brecksville, Ohio, 1964-94; now artist, 1994—. Instr. art workshops, Cuyahoga Valley Art Ctr., Cuyahoga Falls, Ohio, Orange Art Ctr., Pepper Pike, Ohio, France, Italy, Andreeva Portrait Acad., Santa Fe, Charleston Art Club, NC; mem. faculty Portrait Soc. Am. One-woman shows include Gallery 732, Akron Women's City Club, 1997, Hudson (Ohio) Galleries, 1997, Akron Jewish Cmty. Ctr., 1997, Moos Gallery, Western Res. Acad., Ohio, mag., Am. Artists Mag., 1997, 2001, Artist's Mag., 1998, 2000, book, The Best of Portrait Painting, 1998, Internat. Artist, 1999, 2000, Pastel Artist Internat., 1999, 2001, mag., 2003, Pastel Jour., 2003, 1999, book, Beautiful Things, 2000, Paint! Figure & Portrait, 2000, Exhibited in group shows at Churski Gallery, Bath, Ohio, 1996—, State Tchrs. Retirement Sys., 1997—98 (Purchase award, 1997), Pastel Soc. Am., Nat. Arts Club, Am. Artists Profl. League, Salmagundi Club, Hilton Head Art League, Grand Exhbn., Akron, Portrait Soc. Am., Reston, Va., Degas Pastel Soc., New Orleans, Pastel Soc. of the West Coast, Calif., Butler Inst. Am. Art, Youngstown, Ohio, KLH Fine Art Competition, Bennington (Vt.) Ctr. Fine Art, Cahoon Mus. Am. Art, Mass., Lexington (Ky.) Art League (Best of Show), Cin. Art Club (3d prize, 2003), Veerhoff Gallery, Georgetown, Va., Cin. Art Club Nat. Show, 2003, exhibitions include Butler Inst. Am. Art, Youngstown, Ohio, Spaces Gallery, Cleve., Summit Art Space, Akron, Ohio, Represented in permanent collections Ohio Edn. Assn., State Tchrs. Retirement Sys., Rep. Sav. Bank, Hudson Libr. and Hist. Soc., Cuyahoga Valley Youth Ballet, Hudson C. of C., City of Hudson, Case-Barlow Hist. Farm, Cleve. State U., Hosp. for Spl. Surgery., NYC, U. Maine Mus. Art, represented in book, How Did You Paint That--100 Ways to Paint People, 2004 (Internat. Artist award), The Best of Pastel, 2006; co-author: The Caring Classroom-A Guide for Teachers Troubled by the Difficult Student & Classroom Description, 1984. Recipient Best of Show nat. pastel competition LaFond Galleries, Portrait Soc. Am. Internat. Competition, Best of Show, 2005; named Artist of Yr., Akron Life & Leisure Mag., 2007. Mem.: Hudson Soc. Artists (pres. 1996—97), Am. Artists Profl. League, Portrait Soc. Am. (charter, bd., faculty), Akron Soc. Artists (Best of Show award), Degas Pastel Soc. (award of Excellence 1998, Patrons Purchase award 2001, Daler-Rowney award 2001, Award of Merit 2002), Pastel Soc. Am. (Art Times award, David B. Korostoff Purchase award, Silberman Purchase award 2005), Cin. Art Club, Salmagundi Club, Phi Kappa Phi, Phi Beta Kappa. Home: 197 Sunset Dr Hudson OH 44236-3347 Office Phone: 330-650-4069. E-mail: djcarducci@aol.com.

CARDWELL, DIANE, journalist; Reporter The New York Times. Author: (articles) Tactics By Police Mute The Protesters and Their Messages, 2004, Mayor Vows a Bigger Role in Rebuilding at Ground Zero, 2005. Office: The New York Times 229 W 43rd St New York NY 10036 Office Fax: 212-556-3690.

CARDWELL, HAROLD DOUGLAS, SR., retired rehabilitation services professional; b. Varnell, Ga., July 17, 1926; s. Arlie Amber and Hettie Ellen (Eledge) C.; m. Priscilla Dean Rumley, July 3, 1954; children: Harold Douglas, Jr., Ruth Ellen Cardwell-Lindau. AA, Daytona Beach C.C., 1972; student, U. Fla., 1970; BA, Fla. Tech. U., 1974; postgrad., Clemson U., 1975. Registered landscape architect Fla. Chem. operator Fercleve Chem. Corp., Oak Ridge, Tenn., 1945-46; draftsman C.M. Price Constrn. Co., Daytona Beach, Fla., 1947-48; bookkeeper, expediter W.A. Cardwell Constrn. Co., Gatlinburg, Tenn., 1948-49; office mgr., sales rep. J.H. Gordon Lumber Co., St. Augustine, Fla., 1949-51; asst. mgr. King Bros. Lumber Co., St. Augustine, 1951-56; pvt. practice landscape architect Port Orange, Fla., 1956-67; sr. rehab. specialist State of Fla. Divsn. of Blind Svcs., Daytona Beach, 1967-99, ret., 1999. Vice chmn. Daytona Beach Preservation Bd., 1987-98; adv. task force Daytona Beach City Govt., 1987; vice chmn. Volusia County Hist. Commn., Deland, Fla., 1989-92; mem. adv. bd. Volusia County Hist. Preservation Bd., Deland, 1992-94; adv. mem. Flagler Centennial Com., Tallahassee, Fla., 1986; pres. Fla. Anthropol. Soc., Gainesville, 1988-89; chmn. Daytona Beach Preservation Bd., 1998-2006. Recipient Historian of Yr. award Volusia County Hist. Commn., 1988, Lazarus award for Preservation, Fla. Anthropol. Soc., 1988. Mem. Am. Hort. Therapy Assn. (registered hort. therapist, nat. treas. 1978-80), Fla. Nurserymen and Growers Assn. (bd. dirs. 1963-64, 68-69), Halifax Hist. Soc. (bd. dirs. 1974—), Fla. Hist. Soc. (bd. mem., 2000—), Lions (Pres.' award in leadership Port Orange/South Halifax club 1988). Democrat. Methodist. Avocations: history, anthropology, historical tools, pre-historic tools, writing, research. Home: 1343 Woodbine St Daytona Beach FL 32114-5740

CARDWELL, JAMES A., SR., service company executive; Founder Petro Stopping Ctrs., El Paso, Tex., 1975, chmn., CEO. Trustee Archstone Smith Trust, 1980—, bd. dirs., mem. audit com., Colo.; bd. dirs. El Paso Electric Co., 1990—2004, State Nat. Bank, 1999, mem. audit and compensation coms. Office: Petro Stopping Ctrs 6080 Surety Dr El Paso TX 79905 Office Phone: 915-779-4711.*

CARDWELL, KENNETH HARVEY, architect, educator; b. LA, Feb. 15, 1920; s. Stephen William and Beatrice Viola (Duperrault) C.; m. Mary Elinor Sullivan, Dec. 30, 1946; children: Kenneth William, Mary Elizabeth, Ann Margaret, Catherine Buckley, Robert Stephen. AA, Occidental Coll.; AB, U. Calif.-Berkeley; postgrad., Stanford U. Lic. architect, Calif. Draftsman Thompsen & Wilson Architects, San Francisco, 1946-48, Michael Goodman, Architect, Berkeley, Calif., 1949; architect W.S. Wellington, Architect, Berkeley, 1950-59; prin. Kolbeck, Cardwell, Christopherson, Berkeley, 1960-66; prof. dept. arch. U. Calif.-Berkeley, 1950-82; prin. Kenneth H. Cardwell Architect, Berkeley, 1982—. Author: Bernard Maybeck, 1977. Pres. Civic Art Commn., Berkeley, 1963-65; mem. Bd. Adjustments, 1967-69, Alameda County Art Commn., 1969-72. Served to 1st lt. USAAF, 1941-45. Decorated D.F.C.; decorated Air medal with 3 oak leaf clusters; Rehman fellow, 1957; Graham fellow, 1961; recipient Berkeley citation U. Calif., 1982. Fellow: AIA; mem.: Berkeley Hist. Soc. (pres. 1997—2000), Alpha Rho Chi. Home and Office: 1210 Shattuck Ave Berkeley CA 94709-1413 E-mail: cardwell@berkeley.edu.

CARDWELL, NANCY LEE, editor, writer; b. Norfolk, Va., Apr. 2, 1947; d. Joseph Thomas Cardwell and Martha (Bailey) Underwood BA in Econs., Duke U., 1969; MS in Journalism, Columbia U., 1971. Copy editor Wall Street Jour., NYC, 1971-73, reporter, 1973-76, editor fgn. dept. and Washington bur., 1977-80, night news editor, 1981-83, nat. news editor, 1983-87, asst. mng. editor, 1987-89; sr. editor Bus. Week mag., NYC, 1989-91; editor Habitat World, Habitat for Humanity Internat., Americus, Ga., 1991-94; freelance editor/writer, 1994—. Episcopalian.

CARDWELL, SUE WEBB, psychology professor; d. Frank Elbert Webb and Susie Josephine Rankin Webb; m. Walter Douglas Cardwell, May 15, 1938; children: Walter Jr., Janet Sue, Mary-Ann, David Webb, Elbert Hugh. MS, Butler U., 1962, EdS, 1965; STM with spl. distinction, Christian Theol. Sem., Indpls., 1970; Phd, Ind. U., 1978. Cert. psychology pvt. practice Ind. State Bd. Psychology, lic. psychologist Ind., health svc. provider in psychology Ind. State Psychology Bd.; ordained missionary United Christian Missionary Soc. Missionary, Indpls. and the Congo, 1945—57; psychometrist, adminstrv. asst. Christian Theol. Sem., Indpls., 1962—76, psychologist, rsch. assoc., 1976—79, assoc. then dir. I Pastoral Counseling Svc., 1981—88, asst. prof. psychology and counseling, 1979—84, assoc. prof. psychology and counseling, 1984—88, prof. psychology and counseling emerita, 1988—. Mem. theol. sch. inventory com. Ministry Inventories, Dallas, 1971—98; mem. adv. coun. Buchanan Counseling Ctr., Indpls., 1981—2001, interim dir., 2000—01; mem. editl. com. Jour. Pastoral Care, 1990—; cons., mem. Commn. on Ministry, Christian Ch., Indpls., 1967—80; mem. planning com. Ann. Conf. on Ministry with Aging, Zionsville, Ind., 1996—2005. Author: (manual) Guide to Interpreting the TSI, 1991; contbr. articles to profl. jours. Fellow: Am. Assn. Pastoral Counselors (diplomate, v.p., pres. 1984—88); mem.: APA (life), Ind. Psychol. Assn., Commn. on Ministry, Christian Ch., Ind. Depressive and Manic-Depression Assn. (bd. dirs. 1999—2001), Theta Phi. Disciples Of Christ. Home: Apt 265 5354 W 62d St Indianapolis IN 46268

CAREK, DONALD J(OHN), child psychiatry educator; b. Sheboygan, Wis., Aug. 10, 1931; s. Peter and Rose (Gergisch) C.; m. Frances M. Schaefer, Jan. 28, 1956; children: Carla, Thomas, Therese, Peter, Mary Beth, Christopher MD, Marquette U., 1956. Diplomate Am. Bd. Psychiatry and Neurology (examiner in child psychiatry, psychiatry). Intern Walter Reed Army Hosp., 1956-57; resident U. Mich. Hosps., 1959-63; pediatrician Fort Meyer Dispensary, Arlington, Va., 1958-59; instr. psychiatry U. Mich., Ann Arbor, 1962-65, asst. prof., 1965-66; dir. day care Children's Psychiat. Hosp., Ann Arbor, 1965-66; assoc. prof. psychiatry and pediatrics Med. Coll. Wis., Milw., 1966-74, acting chmn. div. human behavior, 1970-73, prof. psychiatry, 1974-76; pres. med. staff Milw. Psychiat. Hosp., 1971-73; prof. psychiatry and pediatrics, chief youth divsn. Med. U. S.C., Charleston, 1976-96, emeritus prof. psychiatry, 1996—; staff psychiatrist Vols. in Medicine, Hilton Head, SC, 2004—. Co-author: Guide to Psychotherapy, 1966; author: Principles of Child Psychotherapy, 1972; mem. editorial bd. Am. Jour. Child & Adolscent Psychiatry, 1988-93; contbr. articles to profl. jours. Bd. dirs. Cedarcrest Girls Residential Treatment Ctr., 1969-71. Capt. USAR, 1956-59. Named Best Doctors in America Southeast Region, 1995. Fellow Am. Acad. Child Psychiatry (life, com. on adolscent psychiatry 1979-85, com. on psychotherapy 1986-90), Am. Psychiat. Assn., Am. Coll. Psychiatrists (membership com. 1991-98); mem. AMA, AAAS, Am. Orthopsychiatry Assn., Am. Psychosomatic Soc., Soc. Profs. Child Psychiatry, S.C. Med. Assn. (mental health com. 1992-93), S.C. Dist. Cr. Am. Psychiat. Assn., Charleston County Med. Soc., S.C. State Bd. Med. Examiners (med. disciplinary commn. 1992-95), Alpha Omega Alpha, Alpha Sigma Nu. Roman Catholic. Home: 97 Nightingale Ln Bluffton SC 29909 Office: Med Univ SC 171 Ashley Ave Charleston SC 29425-0001 Home Phone: 843-705-7343; Office Phone: 843-792-2436. Personal E-mail: djfmcarek@davtv.com.

CARELL, STEVE, comedian, actor; b. Acton, Mass., Aug. 16, 1963; m. Nancy Walls, 1995; children: Elizabeth Anne, John. Grad., Denison U. Performed with theater groups including Second City, Chgo., The Goodman, Wisdom Bridge. Actor: (films) Curley Sue, 1991, Over the Top, 1997, Tomorrow Night, 1998, Suits, 1999, Street of Pain, 2002, Bruce Almighty, 2003, Sleepover, 2004, Anchorman, 2004, Melinda and Melinda, 2004, Bewitched, 2005, Little Miss Sunshine, 2006 (Outstanding Performance by a Cast in a Motion Picture, SAG, 2007), Evan Almighty, 2007, (voice) Over the Hedge, 2006,: (TV films) Life As We Know It!, 1991, H.U.D., 2000; (TV series) Saturday Night Live, 1996—2002, (and writer) The Dana Carvey Show, 1996, Over the Top, 1997, The Daily Show with Jon Stewart, 1999—2004, Watching Ellie, 2002—03, Come to Papa, 2004, The Office, 2005— (Best Performance by an Actor in TV Series-Musical or Comedy, Hollywood Fgn. Press Assn. (Golden Globe award), 2006, SAG award outstanding performance by an ensemble in a comedy series, 2007, Episodic Comedy (Casino Night), Writers Guild Am., 2007, Choice TV Actor: Comedy, Teen Choice Awards, 2007); actor, writer, prodr.: (films) The 40-Year-Old Virgin, 2005 (Best Comedic Performance, MTV Movie awards, 2006). Named one of 50 Most Powerful People in Hollywood, Premiere mag., 2006.*

CARELLI, MARIO DOMENICO, nuclear engineer; b. Taggia, Italy, Feb. 6, 1942; came to U.S. 1969; s. Giuseppe and Rosita (Cichero) C.; m. Maria Sabina Viti, Mar. 29, 1969; children: Eric Viti, Eliana Jennifer. BS, U. Florence, Italy, 1962; PhD in Nuclear Engring. summa cum laude, U. Pisa, Italy, 1966. Researcher U. Pisa, 1966-67; engr. Atomic Energy Authority, Bologna, Italy, 1967-69; engr., sr. engr. to prin. engr. Westinghouse Adv. Reactors, Madison, Pa., 1969-77; fellow engr. Westinghouse Adv. Energy Systems, Madison, Pa., 1977-84, div. patent chmn., 1984-88, mgr. ALMR engring., 1988-89, mgr. thermofluids systems and safety, 1989—. Adj. assoc. prof. U. Pitts., 1978—. Contbr. over 80 articles to profl. jours. U. Pisa fellow, 1966. Mem. Am. Nuclear Soc. (mem. power div. exec. com. 1987-90, 91—, publs. steering com. 1991—, thermal hydraulic div. exec. com. 1984-87, Outstanding Session Organizer 1990), Internat. Assn. Hydraulic Rsch. (sect. chmn. 1990—). Achievements include patents on advanced nuclear reactors core design; international authority on fast reactors core design and liquid metals thermalhydraulics. Office: Westinghouse Sci and Tech Ctr 1310 Beulah Rd Pittsburgh PA 15235-5098

CAREN, ROBERT POSTON, aerospace scientist; b. Columbus, Ohio, Dec. 25, 1932; s. Robert James and Charlene (Poston) C.; m. Linda Ann Davis, Mar. 27, 1963; children: Christopher Davis, Michael Poston. BS, Ohio State U., 1953, MS, 1954, PhD, 1961. Sr. physicist N.Am. Aviation, Columbus, 1959-60; assoc. research scientist research and devel. div. Lockheed Missiles and Space Co., Inc., Palo Alto, Calif., 1962-63, research scientist, 1963-66, sr. mem. research lab., 1966-69, mgr. def. systems space systems div., 1969-70, mgr. infared tech. R & D div., 1970-71, research dir., 1972-76, chief engr., 1976-86, v.p. gen. mgr. R & D div., 1986—, corp. v.p. sci. and engring., 1987-98; chmn. LITEX Inc., 1998—2000. Bd. dirs. LITEX Corp.; mem. U.S./Israel Sci. and Tech. Commn., 1997—. Contbr. articles to profl. jours.; patentee in field. Fellow AIAA, AAAS, AAS, Soc. Automotive Engrs.; mem. NAE, IEEE (sr.), Am. Def. Preparedness Assn. (past chmn. rsch. divsn.), Am. Phys. Soc., Aerospace Industries Assn. (past chmn. tech. and ops. coun.), Calif. Coun. on Sci. and Tech., Sigma Pi Sigma, Pi Mu Epsilon. Home: 6039 Gleneagles Cir San Jose CA 95138-2372 Office: 1220 Ventura Blvd Ste 2250 Sherman Oaks CA 91403-5338 Personal E-mail: rcaren@comcast.net.

CARET, ROBERT LAURENT, academic administrator; b. Biddeford, Maine, Oct. 7, 1947; s. Laurent J. and Anne (Santorsola) C.; m. Elizabeth Zoltan; children: Colin Caret, Katherine Caret, Katalyn Ford, Kellen Ford. BA in Chemistry & Math., Suffolk U., Boston, 1969, DSc (hon.), 1996; PhD in Organic Chemistry, U. NH, Durham, 1974; DHL (hon.), Nat. Hispanic U., San Jose, Calif., 1997, San Jose U., 2004. Dean Coll. Natural and Math. Scis. Towson State U., 1981-87, prof. chemistry, 1994—, assoc. v.p., 1985-86, exec. asst. to pres., 1986-87, provost, exec. v.p., 1987-95, pres., 2003—, San Jose State U., Calif., 1995—2003. Bd. dirs. Coll. Bound Found., Md. Bus. Coun. Author: (with A.S. Wingrove) Quimca Organica, 1984, Organic Chemistry, 1981, (with P. Plante) Myths and Realities in Higher Education Administration, 1990, (with K. Denniston and J.J. Topping) Principles and Applications of Organic and Biological Chemistry, 1995, 2d edit., 1997, Principles and Applications of Inorganic, Organic and Biological Chemistry, 1992, 4th edit. (General, Organic and Biochemistry), 2004, Foundations of Inorganic, Organic and Biological Chemistry, 1995; contrb. chpts. to monographs and articles to profl. jours. Chmn. Baltimore County Higher Edn. Adv. Bd., Towson, 1989-1994; co-chmn. Balt. Sci. Fair/Kiwanis, Towson, 1983-88; bd. dirs. San Jose Repertory Theater, 1995-2001, San Jose Opera, Calif. State U. Inst., 1995-2003, Franklin Square Hosp., 2005—; apptd. Md. Gov.'s Workforce Investment Bd. Named one of Silicon Valley's 100 Power Brokers, San Jose Mag., 2003; named to Chamber Bus. Hall Fame, Balt. County, 2006; recipient Employee Incentive award, State of Md., 1987, Outstanding Chemistry Tchr. award, Md. Inst. Chemists, 1971, Award for Excellence, Suffolk U. Gen. Alumni Assn., 1986, Tomas Rivera Leadership award, Nat. Hispanic U., 1999, Univ. Partnership award, 2002, Outstanding Pres. award, All Am. Football League, 2001, Achievement award, Italian-Am. Heritage Found., 2001; Albert W. Diniak fellow, U. N.H., 1972, Lester A. Pratt fellow, 1972. Mem. AAUP (chpt. exec. com. 1978-81, v.p. 1975-80, divsn. and dept. rep. 1975-80), NCAA (presdl. adv. com. 2004—, coun. pres. 2004—), Am. Assn. Higher Edn., Am. Assn. Univ. Adminstrs. (Md. membership rep. 1986-1989), EDUCOM (instl. rep. 1986-87), Am. Chem. Soc. (Chesapeake sect. alt. counselor 1979-87, exec. com. 1978-87, com. mem. 1978-87, George L. Braude award 2005), Am. Coun. Edn. (Leadership Commn. 2000, Internat. Commn. 1997), Am. Assn. State Colls. and Univs. (adv. bd. 1986—, Kellogg Leadership bd., state rep. 1989-1989, joint venture Silicon Valley bd. dirs. 1997-2003, co-chair econ. devel. team 1996-98, co-chair econ. prosperity coun. 1998-2000, bd. dirs. 2004—, rep. to ACE bd. dirs. 2005—, chair nominating com. 2006-07), Coalition Met. Univs. (v.p. bd. dirs. 2004—, program and pub. policy com. 2005—, chair nominating com. 2006-07), Silicon Valley Mfg. Group (bd. dirs. 1988-2003), San Jose C. of C. (bd. dirs. 1995-2001, Leadership in Excellence award 1999), 1st Mariner Bank (bd. dirs. 2006-), Center Club Balt. (bd. govs., mem. Md. Gov.'s Workforce investment bd.), Balt. Area Convention and Visitor's Assn., Sigma Xi (chpt. pres. 1975-76), Sigma Zeta, Phi Beta Chi, Omicron Delta Kappa. Avocations: jogging, tae kwan do, cross country skiing, golf. Office: Towson Univ 8000 York Rd Towson MD 21252-0001 Office Phone: 410-704-2356.

CARETTI, ANN M., school system administrator; d. Anthony S. Caretti and L. Caretti Cristina. BA, U. RI, 1976; MEd, RI Coll., 1981; PhD, Capella U., 2005. Cert. spl. edn. adminstr. Mass., dir. spl. edn. RI. Spl. edn. resource tchr. Pawtucket (RI) Sch. Dept., 1986—96, asst. dir. spl. edn., 1994—95; dir. spl. edn. East Providence (RI) Sch. Dept., 1997—2000; dir. spl. svcs. Beacon Edn. Mgmt., Westboro, Mass., 2000—01; dir. student svcs. Nauset Pub. Schs., Orleans, Mass., 2001—. Adj. instr. Providence Coll., 1991—. Mem. Lower Cape Coalition, Eastham, Mass., 2001—02; bd.dirs. Conservation Commn., Bristol, RI, 1994—97, Nat. Alliance for Mentally Ill Cape Cod, Hyannis, Mass., 2002—05. Mem.: ASCD, Coun. Exceptional Children, Assn. Spl. Edn. Dirs. Mass. Avocations: photography, tennis, gardening. Home: 3 Glenwood Dr Harwich MA 02645 Home Phone: 508-430-0940. Personal E-mail: acaretti@earthlink.net.

CAREY, ARTHUR BERNARD, JR., editor, columnist; b. Phila., May 16, 1950; s. Arthur Bernard and Mary Louise (Lynch) C.; m. Katherine Ann White, Apr. 14, 1973 (div. Feb. 1980); m. Tanya Marie Walters, July 17, 1982; 1 child, Edward Lynch AB, Princeton U, 1972; MS, Columbia U., 1975. Editor Fedn. Telephone Workers of Pa., Phila., 1972-74; reporter Bucks County Courier Times, Levittown, Pa., 1975-77, Phila. Inquirer, 1977—. Author: In Defense of Marriage, 1984, The United States of Incompetence, 1991; editor: That's Livin', 1984 Term trustee The Episcopal Acad., Merion, Pa., 1982-88, alumni trustee, 1990-93; mem. com. to nominate alumni trustees Princeton U., 1989-92. Recipient Edward J. Meeman Conservation award Scripps-Howard Found., 1977, Best Story of the Yr. award Nat. Conf. Sunday Mags., 1983, George Washington Honor medal Freedoms Found., 1984, Disting. Journalism award Epilepsy Found. Am., 1997, Robert Joplin Sci. Writers award Am. Orthopedic Foot and Ankle Soc., 1998; Robert E. Sherwood Traveling fellow Columbia U., 1975; best feature story Pa. Soc. Newspaper Editors, 1986, 91. Mem. Soc. Profl. Journalists (best newsfeature N.J. chpt. 1979) Democrat. Episcopalian. Avocations: running, weightlifting, carpentry. Home: 928 Clover Hill Rd Wynnewood PA 19096-1631 Office: Phila Inquirer 400 N Broad St Philadelphia PA 19130-4099 Office Phone: 610-701-7623. Business E-Mail: acarey@phillynews.com.

CAREY, CHARLES P., mercantile exchange executive; b. Chgo., 1954; MBA, We. Ill. U. Mem. MidAmerica Commodity Exchange, 1976—78, Chgo. Bd. Trade, 1978—2007, exch. dir., 1990—96, full-mem. dir. exch., 1996, first vice chmn., 1999—2001, chmn., 2003—07; vice chmn. CME Group Inc., 2007—. Served on numerous exec. and spl. fin. committees. Office: CME Group Inc 20 S Wacker Dr Chicago IL 60606*

CAREY, CHASE (CHARLES G.), broadcast executive; BA, Colgate U., Hamilton, NY, 1976; MBA, Harvard U., 1981. Sr. v.p. Columbia Pictures, 1981—88; exec. v.p., CFO Fox Inc., 1988—92, COO, 1992—94; chmn., CEO Fox TV Group, 1994—2000; co-COO News Corp., 1997—2002; dir., pres., CEO Sky Global Networks, Inc., 2001—02; pres., CEO DIRECTV Group, El Segundo, Calif., 2003—, bd. dirs., 2005—. Bd. dirs. Fox Entertainment Group, Inc., 1992—2002, News Corp., 1996—, NDS Group, Inc., 1996—2002, News Am. Inc., 1998—2002, Gemstar-TV Guide Internat., Inc., 2000—02, Brit. Sky Broadcasting plc, 2003—, Gateway, Inc., Yell Fin. B.V. Bd. trustees Colgate U. Office: DIRECTV Group 2230 E Imperial Hwy El Segundo CA 90245 Office Phone: 310-964-5000.*

CAREY, DAVID, publishing executive; BA, UCLA. Founding pub. Smart Money Mag.; pub. House & Garden Conde Nast Pubs., NYC, 1996—98, pub. The New Yorker, 1998—2001; CEO bus. info. group Gruner & Jahr Pub., NYC, 2001; v.p. & pub. The New Yorker Conde Nast Pubs., NYC, 1998—2005, pres. Bus. Group, pub. dir., 2005—. Office: Conde Nast Pubs 4 Times Sq New York NY 10036*

CAREY, DAVID P., judge, career military officer; married; 1 child. Grad., Tulane U., Ohio No. U. Law Sch., Army Command Gen. Staff Coll., Army War Coll. Entered active duty U.S. Army, 1977, advanced through ranks to brigadier gen., legal assistance officer, chief mil. justice Fort Devons, Mass., def. counsel Republic of Korea, internat. law specialist we. command Fort Shafter, Hawaii, officer-in-charge br. VII Corps office staff judge advocate Ludwigsburg, Germany, 1985—88, with litigation divsn. Pentagon, exec. officer for judge advocate Europe, 1992—94, staff judge advocate 101st Airborne Divsn. (air assault) and Ft. Campbell, 1994—97, chief litigation divsn., 1997—2000, judge advocate Europe and Seventh Army Heidelberg, Germany, 2000, asst. JAG civil law and litigation Arlington, Va., comdr., chief judge legal svcs. agency. Decorated Legion of Merit with two oak leaf clusters, Meritorious Svc. Medal with three oak leaf clusters, Army Commendation Medal with oak leaf cluster, Army Achievement Medal.

CAREY, DREW, actor; b. Cleve., May 23, 1958; Attended, Kent State U.; PhD (hon.), Cleve. State U., 2000. Acting debut on The Tonight Show, 1991; actor: (films) Coneheads, 1993; prodr.: The Big Tease, 1999; actor(voice): Robots, 2005,: (TV films) Freaky Friday, 1995, Sex, Drugs and Freedom of Choice, 1998; (TV series) The Drew Carey Show, 1995—2004; exec. prodr.: Drew Carey's Green Screen Show, 2004—; host, prodr. (TV series) Whose Line Is It Anyway?, 1998—2005, exec. prodr. (TV movie) Geppetto, 2000, TV guest appearances include The Torkelsons, 1991, Late Night with Rita Sever, 1998, Star Search, 1988, George Carlin Show, 1995, Lois & Clark: The New Adventures of Superman, 1993, Home Improvement, 1991, Ellen, 1994, Sabrina, the Teenage Witch, 1996, Weird Al Show, 1997, Dharma & Greg, 1997, Larry Sanders Show, 1992, star comedy spls. for Showtime: Full Frontal Comedy, Drew Carey, Human Cartoon; author: Dirty Jokes and Beer, 1997; host 25th Ann. Am. Music Awards, 1999, (game show) The Power of 10, 2007—, The Price of Right, 2007—. Formerly with USMC. Recipient Editor's Choice award, TV Guide, 1999, People's Choice award for best actor in a new series, CableACE award. Mem.: Delta Tau Delta.

CAREY, EDWARD JOHN, utilities executive; b. NYC, Jan. 16, 1944; s. Edward John and Mary Elizabeth (Hopkins) C.; m. Maureen A. McCullough, June 4, 1977; children: Christine, Caroline. BA, Fordham U., 1971. With N.Y. Central R.R., 1962-68; with Consol. Edison Co., NYC, 1968-99; ret., 1999. Past bd. dirs. Salvation Army, Greater N.Y. Adv. Bd. Home: 17 Richmond Hills Irvington NY 10533-2301

CAREY, EDWARD JOHN, insurance company executive; b. Kansas City, Aug. 12, 1947; s. Joseph George and Nelda (Roy) C.; m. Dana Marie LeMay, Mar. 30, 1985; children: Bridget C., Edward J. Jr., William T. BS in Polit. Sci., Rockhurst Coll., 1973. Multi line claims adjuster Safeco Ins. Co., Kansas City, 1973-79; risk mgr. Dolphin Titan Internat., Houston, 1980-85, Pennzoil Co., Houston, 1985-89; ins. broker Arthur J. Gallagher Co., Houston, 1989-99; mng. dir. John L. Wortham & Son LP, Houston, 1999—. Instr., assoc. risk mgmt. designation Risk and Ins. Mgmt. Soc., Houston, 1985-95. Charter mem., bd. dirs. Offshore Energy Ctr. Soc., Galveston, Tex., 1996, Tex. Ind. Oil Prodrs. and Royalty Owners Assn.; scout leader Boy Scouts Am., Houston, 1999; com. Houston Livestock Show and Rodeo, 1990, founder's coun. mem. James ick Found. for Performing Arts, Internat. Fest. Inst. at Round Top, 2005; founder, pres. Sis. Angela Mary Carey Found., San Paulo, Brazil. With USMC, 1966-70. Mem. Houston City Club, Univ. Club, Lakeside Country Club. Roman Catholic. Avocations: golf, private pilot, collecting books on albrecht durer.

CAREY, FRANCIS JAMES, investment banker; b. Balt., Mar. 24, 1926; s. Francis James and Marjorie (Armstrong) C.; m. Mary Crozer Page, 1947 (dec.); children: Francis James III, Elizabeth Page; m. Emily Norris Large, June 8, 1956 (dec. Apr. 1997); children: Henry Augustus, Emily Norris, Frances Carey MacMaster. Student, Princeton, 1944; AB, U. Pa., 1945, JD, 1949. Bar: Pa. 1950. Law sec. to justice Supreme Ct. Pa., 1950-51; with firm Reed Smith Shaw & McClay, Phila., 1951-87, ptnr., 1956—87, counsel, 1987-92; pres. bd. dir. W.P. Carey & Co., Inc., 1987—98, 2000—; chmn., CEO, bd. dir. Carey Diversified LLC, NYC, 1998—2000; vice chmn., chmn. exec. com., bd. dir. W.P. Carey & Co. LLC, 2000—, chmn. exec. com., bd. dir., 2006—. Mem. faculty U. Pa., 1946-47; bd. mgrs., mem. exec. com. Western Savs. Bank, 1970-82; mem. bus. adv. com. Bus. Coun. for UN, 1994—2002; trustee Investment Program Assn., 1990-2000, chmn., 1998-2000; mem. Senatorial Trust, 1992—. Mem. Com. of Seventy, Phila., 1957-58; mem. Lower Gwynedd Twp. (Pa.) Planning Commn., 1962-75, sec., 1962-65; trustee Germantown Acad., Fort Washington, Pa., 1961—, pres., 1966-72; overseer Sch. Arts and Scis., U. Pa., 1983-90; mgr. Law Alumni Soc., U. Pa., 1962-66; jr. warden St. Martin's in the Field, Biddeford Pool, Maine, 2003-04, chmn., sr. warden, 2004—; trustee Md. Hist. Soc., 2002—, v.p., 2007—. Served to lt. USNR, 1943-45, PTO. Mem. ABA, Pa. Bar Assn. (chmn. real property, probate and trust law sect. 1966-67, chmn. conf. group to cooperate with Pa. Land Title Assn. 1970-77), Phila. Bar Assn. (chmn. com. on civil legis. 1962), Soc. Mayflower Descs. in State of N.Y., Fourth Street Club, St. Anthony Club (Phila.), Sunnybrook Golf Club (Plymouth Meeting, Pa.), The Brook Club, St. Anthony Club (N.Y.), Abenakee Club (Biddeford Pool, Maine), Biddeford Pool Yacht Club, Md. Club (Balt.). Republican. Episcopalian. Home: 485 Lewis Ave Ambler PA 19002 Business E-Mail: fcarey@wpcarey.com.

CAREY, JAMES HENRY, banker; b. Elizabeth, NJ, May 22, 1932; s. Charles C. and Adelyne (Bilyeu) C.; m. Nancy Mershon Ferrenz, Aug. 14, 1954; children: Jane Meredith, Christopher James, George Mershon, David James. BA cum laude, Brown U., Providence, RI, 1953; postgrad. Sch. Bus. Adminstrn., NYU, 1956-59. With Chase Manhattan Bank, NYC, 1955-86, asst. v.p., 1961-63, v.p., 1963-68, exec. v.p., 1976-86, Hambro Am. Bank & Trust Co., NYC, 1968-69, pres., 1969-72, also bd. dirs.; pres., chmn. bd. First Empire Bank NY (formerly Hambro Am. Bank & Trust Co.), NYC, 1972-75; exec. v.p. Chase Manhattan Corp., NYC, 1976-86; pres., CEO The Berkshire Bank NY, NYC, 1989-92; mng. dir. Briarcliff Fin. Assocs., NYC, 1992—2002; chmn., dir. ABX Air, Inc., Wilmington, Ohio, 2002—. Bd. dirs. Midland Co. Bd. dirs. The Rayburn Found., Am. Mus. Flyfishing. Lt. (j.g.) USNR, 1953-55. Mem. The Dorset Field Club (Vt.), Mid Ocean Club (Bermuda), Phi Beta Kappa, Delta Tau Delta. Episcopalian. Office: PO Box 859 Manchester VT 05254-0859 Personal E-mail: jhcarey@verizon.net.

CAREY, JANA HOWARD, lawyer; b. Huntsville, Ala., Apr. 20, 1945; d. Ernest Randall and Mary Regna (Baites) Howard; m. James Johnston Hale Carey, Jan. 15, 1983. BS in Home Econs., Auburn U., 1967; MS in Audiovisual Communications, Towson State U., 1973; JD, U. Balt., 1976. Bar: (U.S. Ct. Appeals (4th cir.)) 1977, (U.S. Dist. Ct. (Md. dist.)) 1978, (U.S. Ct. Appeals (3d cir.)) 1994, (U.S. Supreme Ct.) 1995, (U.S. Ct. Appeals (Md. cir.)) 1996. Tchr. Hampton High Sch., Melbourne, Australia, 1967; home economist U. Ga., Athens, 1967-70, devel. specialist state youth program, 1970-72, U. Md., College Park, 1972-73; clk. appellate div. Pub. Defender's Office, Balt., 1974; assoc. Venable, Baetjer & Howard, Balt., 1975, 76-84, ptnr., 1994—2003, past chair labor and employment group, 1995-97. Spkr in field. Co-author: (book) Legal Aspects of the Employment Relationship: An Introduction for the General Practitioner, 1978; mem ed bd: Employment Testing Law and Policy Reporter, Nat Employment Law Inst Adv Bd, Am Employment Law Coun Adv Bd; contbr. articles to profl jours. Chair dean's adv coun U. Balt. Law Sch.; pres. U. Balt. Edn. Found., U. Balt. Bd. Visitors; past mem pres adv coun St Mary's Col, Pension Oversight Comn Anne Arundel County. Named Top 100 Women for Outstanding Achievement, Daily Record, 1997, 2000, 2002; recipient Circle of Excellence, 2002, Univ. Baltimore Alumnae of Yr., 1999, Distinguished Alumnae Award, 2004. Mem.: ABA (past chair sect. coun. labor and employment law sect., past mgt. co-chair insts. and meetings com., EEOC liaison com. sects. com. equal employment opportunity law, mem. standing com. CLE, dep. chair labor & employment law com. sect. pub utility, comm, transp, health law forum, commn. on women in the profession), Univ. Baltimore Women's Bar Assn., Nat Asn Women Lawyers (past mem. gender bias com.), Am Col Labor and Employment Lawyers, Nat Labor Lawyers Adv Comt CUE. Home Phone: 410-349-3949. Personal E-mail: janahowardcarey@comcast.net.

CAREY, JOHN, judge; b. Phila., June 11, 1924; s. Henry Reginald and Margaret Howell (Bacon) Carey; m. Patricia F. Frank, Feb. 24, 1951; children: Henry Frank, John, Douglas, Jennifer Patricia. Grad., Milton Acad., 1942; BA, Yale U., 1947; LLB, Harvard U., 1949; LLM in Internat. Law, N.Y.U., 1965; LLD, U. W.I., 1985. Bar: Pa. 1950, N.Y. 1957. Practiced in, Phila., 1949-55; asst. dist. atty., 1952-54; cons. spl. com. fed. loyalty-security program Assn. Bar City N.Y., 1955-56; ptnr. Coudert Bros., 1961-87; justice N.Y. Supreme Ct., 1987; judge Westchester County Ct., White Plains, N.Y., 1988-94; mem. faculty NYU Law Sch., 1966-73; jud. hearing officer N.Y. State, 1995—. Author: UN Protection of Civil and Political Rights, 1970; editor: United Nations Law and Reports, 1966—. Alt. mem. subcommn. promotion and protection human rights UN, 1966—91, alt. rep. human rights commn., 1968; mem. Rye (N.Y.) City Coun., 1964—68, 1972—74, mayor, 1974—82; trustee Little Harbor Chapel, Portsmouth, NH. Mem.: ABA, Coun. Fgn. Rels., Am. Soc. Internat. Law (v.p. 1987—88), Assn. Bar City of N.Y., N.Y. State Bar Assn., Phi Beta Kappa. Home and Office: 860 Forest Ave Rye NY 10580-3145 Office: County Ct House White Plains NY 10601 Office Phone: 914-967-1290. Personal E-mail: jncarey@westnet.com.

CAREY, JOHN, language educator, critic; b. London, Apr. 5, 1934; s. Charles William and Winifred Ethel (Cook) C.; m. Gillian Mary Booth, Aug. 13, 1960; children: Leo, Thomas. BA, St. John's Coll., Oxford, Eng., 1957; PhD, Oxford U., 1960. Lectr. Christ Church Coll., Oxford, 1958-59; rsch. fellow Balliol Coll., Oxford, 1959-60; tutorial fellow Keble Coll., Oxford, 1960-64, St. John's Coll., 1964-75; Merton prof. English lit. Oxford U., 1976-2001. Prin. book reviewer Sunday Times, London, 1977—; hon. fellow St. John's Coll., Balliol Coll., Oxford, fellow British Acad., 1996. Author: Milton, 1969, The Violent Effigy, 1973, Thackeray: Prodigal Genius, 1977, John Donne: Life, Mind and Art, 1981, Original Copy: Selected Reviews and Journalism, 1987, The Faber Book of Reportage, 1987, The Intellectuals and the Masses, 1992, The Faber Book of Science, 1995, The Faber Book of Utopias, 1999, Pure Pleasure, 2000, What Good Are the Arts?, 2005. Served to lt. Brit. Army, 1953-54. Fellow Royal Soc. Lit. Avocations: bee-keeping, gardening, swimming. Home: 57 Stapleton Rd Headington Oxford England Office: Merton Coll Oxford England Personal E-mail: john.carey53@ntlworld.com.

CAREY, JOHN ANDREW, investment company executive; b. Glendale, Calif., May 27, 1949; s. John Nelson and Dorothea Ruth (Bordwell) C.; m. Harriet Ruth Stolmeier, June 19, 1982; children: Julia Scott, Elizabeth Bordwell. BA, Columbia U., 1971; AM, Harvard U., 1972, PhD, 1979. Chartered fin. analyst. Teaching fellow Harvard U., Cambridge, Mass., 1973-78; sr. council rep. Yankelovich, Skelly & White, Stamford, Conn., 1977-79; analyst Pioneer Investment Mgmt., Inc., Boston, 1979-81, sr. analyst, 1981-83, v.p., 1983-98, sr. v.p., 1998—2002, exec. v.p., 2002—. V.p. Pioneer Scout, Inc., Boston, 1984-89, v.p. Pioneer Fund, 1987—, Pioneer Equity-Income Fund, 1992—, Pioneer Income Fund, 1994-96, Pioneer Variable Contract Trust, 1995—; mem. bd. visitors New Eng. Conservatory of Music. Author: Judicial Reform in France before the Revolution of 1789, 1981. Treas. Newton Hist. Soc., Mass., 1983—87, Musicians of the Old Post Rd, 1998—; trustee Longy Sch. Music, 2001—. Mem.: Cambridge Soc. for Early Music (bd. dirs.), CFA Inst., Boston Security Analysts Soc., Boston Athenaeum, Harvard Club of Boston. Republican. Episcopalian. Home: 14 Yarmouth Rd Wellesley Hills MA 02481-1249 Office: Pioneer Investment Mgmt Inc 60 State St Fl 18 Boston MA 02109-1800 Office Phone: 617-742-7825.

CAREY, JOHN CLAYTON, pediatrician, educator, medical geneticist; b. Balt., 1946; MD, Georgetown U., 1972; MPH, U. Calif., Berkeley, 1976. Diplomate Am. Bd. Med. Genetics, Am. Bd. Pediatrics. Prof. pediat. U. Utah Med. Ctr., Salt Lake City, vice chmn. Dept. Pediat. Co-author: Medical Genetics, 3d edit., 2003, Care of the Child with Trisomy 18/13, 1996, rev. edit. 2000. Softly Written, Softly Spoken, 2002; editor-in-chief Am. Jour. Med. Genetics; contbr. over 200 articles to profl. jours. Med. advisor Support Orgn. Trisomy 18, 13 and Related Disorders, Utah Birth Defects Network, Pregnancy Risk Line. Office: U Utah Med Ctr Pediatrics 2C412 SOM 50 N Medical Dr Salt Lake City UT 84132-0001 Office Phone: 801-581-8943.

CAREY, JOHN EDWARD, communications executive; b. Albany, NY, Sept. 21, 1949; s. John Edward and Lillian Rose (Murdock) C.; m. Nicolette Anne Yianilos, Oct. 26, 1974; children: Theodore, Anna. BA, Tulane U., 1971. Pres. FOI Svcs., Inc., Rockville, Md., 1976-95, Gaithersburg, Md., 1995—. Office: FOI Svcs Inc 704 Quince Orchard Rd Ste 275 Gaithersburg MD 20878-1770 Office Phone: 301-975-9400. E-mail: jcarey@foiservices.com.

CAREY, JOHN LEO, lawyer; b. Morris, Ill., Oct. 1, 1920; s. John Leo and Loretta (Conley) C.; m. Rhea M. White, July 15, 1950; children: John Leo III, Daniel Hobart, Deborah M. BS, St. Ambrose Coll., Davenport, Ia., 1941; JD, Georgetown U., 1947, LLM, 1949. Bar: Ind. 1954, DC 1947, Ill. 1947. Legis. asst. Senator Scott W. Lucas, 1945-47; spl. atty. IRS, Washington, 1947-54; since practiced in South Bend; ptnr. Barnes & Thornburg, 1954—, now of counsel; law prof. taxation Notre Dame Law Sch., 1968-90. Trustee LaLumire Prep. Sch., Laporte, Ind. Served with USAAF, WW II; to lt. col. USAF, Korean War. Decorated D.F.C., Air medal. Mem. ABA (bd. govs. 1986-89, treas. 1990-93), Ind. Bar Assn. (pres. 1976-77), St. Joseph County Bar Assn., Signal Point Country Club, Quail Valley City Club. Office: 600 1st Source Bank Ctr 100 N Michigan St South Bend IN 46601-1630 Home: 940 St Annes Ln Vero Beach FL 32967

CAREY, KATHRYN ANN, retired foundation administrator, editor, consultant; b. LA, Oct. 18, 1949; d. Frank Randall and Evelyn Mae (Walmsley) Carey; m. Richard Kenneth Sundt, Dec. 28, 1980. BA in Am. Studies with honors, Calif. State U., LA, 1971; postgrad., Georgetown U., DC, Boston Coll. Cert. comml. pilot instrument rated, advanced cert. corp. cmty. rels. Tutor Calif. Dept. Vocat. Rehab., LA, 1970; tchg. asst. U. So.

Calif., LA, 1974-75, UCLA, 1974-75; claims adjuster Auto Club So. Calif., San Gabriel, 1971-73; corp. pub. rels. cons. Carnation Co., LA, 1973-78; cons., adminstr. Carnation Cmty. Svc. Award Program, 1973-78; pub. rels. cons. Vivitar Corp., 1978; sr. advt. asst. Am. Honda Motor Co., Torrance, Calif., 1978-84; exec. dir. Am. Honda Found., 1984—2006, Honda Philanthropy, Office of the Ams., 1996—2006. Adminstr. Honda Involvement Program; mgr. Honda Dealer Advt. Assns., 1978—84; cons. in field. Asst. editor: Friskies Rsch. Digest, 1973—78; editor: Vivitar Voice, 1978, Honda Views, 1978—84, Found. Focus, 1984—, Instrument Pilots' Survival Manual (Rod Machado), 1991; contbg. editor: Newsbriefs and Momentum, 1978—. Dir. devel. The Spencer Theater, 2006—; mem. Lincoln County Sheriff's Posse. Recipient Silver award, Wilmer Shields Rich award, Coun. Founds. Excellence in Comm., 1995, 2003, Gold award, 1997, 2001, Bronze award, 2005, award of Excellence, Soc. Tech. Comm., 1995, Merit award, 1996, 1997, 1999, 2001, Apex award, Excellence in Comm., 1997—2001, 2003, Bronze award, 2004; scholar, Calif. Life Scholarship Found., 1967. Mem.: Affinity Group on Japanese Philanthropy (pres.), Coun. on Founds., So. Calif. Assn. Philanthropy, Pub. Rels. Soc. Am., Advt. Club LA, Elsa Wild Animal Appeal, Humane Soc. US, Am. Humane Assn., Ocicats Internat., Greenpeace, LA Soc. Prevention of Cruelty to Animals, Aircraft Owners and Pilots Assn., Am. Quarter Horse Assn., Ninety-Nines. Office Phone: 505-336-0015. Personal E-mail: kcarey@spencertheater.com.

CAREY, LEVENIA MARIE, counselor; d. Easy Mae Evans; m. Robert William Carey, June 15, 1991; children: Danielle LaTrice, Shontrice Nicole, Robert William Carey, II. EdM, East Ctrl. U., Ada, Okla., 1998. Lic. profl. counselor Okla. State Dept. Mental Health, 2001. Pvt. lic. profl. counselor, McAlester, 2001—; project dir. campus violence prevention project Ea. Okla. State Coll., Wilburton, 2005—. Cons., trainer, educator Dept. Def., McAlester, 2001—. Bd. mem. Pittsburg County Child Abuse Response Effort, McAlester, 2005. Recipient Okla. Collegiate State Champion Informative Speaking award, East Ctrl. U., 1996, Outstanding Pub. Spkr. award, 1995, 1996. Mem.: ACA (assoc.). Republican. Mem. Church Of Christ. Avocations: church youth activities, mentoring, travel. Office: Eastern Oklahoma State College 1301 West Main Wilburton OK 74578 Home Phone: 918-429-8184; Office Phone: 918-465-1757. Office Fax: 918-465-4436. Business E-Mail: lcarey@eosc.edu.

CAREY, LISA ANNE, oncologist, educator; b. Red Bank, NJ, June 21, 1962; m. Matthew Glaize Ewend, 1990. BA in Biology & Art History, Wellesley Coll., 1984; MS in Physiology, U. Ky., 1986; MD, John Hopkins U., 1990; ScM in Clinical Investigation, John Hopkins Sch. Pub. Health, 1994—98. Cert. Internal Medicine and Med. Oncology. Intern, internal medicine John Hopkins U., Balt., 1991, resident, oncology, 1990—93, fellow, med. oncology, 1993—98; attending physician U. NC, Chapel Hill, 1998, asst. prof., 1998—2005, assoc. prof., dept. medicine, divsn. hematology-oncology, 2005—; med. dir. U. NC Breast Ctr., Chapel Hill, 2003—; protocol office exec. com. breast disease group leader, protocol review com. breast cancer chair U. NC Lineberger Cancer Ctr. Researcher in clinical/translational rsch. in breast cancer; named to Cancer & Leukemia Group B (CALGB) Breast Core Com., 2003; prin. investigator of several clinical trials, including a multicenter inter-SPORE (Specialized Prog. of Rsch. Excellence), Nat. Cancer Inst Phase II study of targeted theraphy in metastatic basal-like breast cancer; spkr. in field. Contbr. articles to profl. jours. Recipient Doris Duke Clinician Scientist award, 1999, Career Develop. award, Nat. Cancer Inst., 2000. Mem.: Am. Soc. Clinical Oncology (mem. scientific prog. com., faculty for the annual mtg.). Office: U NC Sch Medicine Divsn Hematology/Oncology Dept Medicine 3009 Old Clinic Bldg Cb-7305 Chapel Hill NC 27599*

CAREY, MARTIN CONRAD, gastroenterologist, molecular biophysicist, educator, medical geneticist; b. Clonmel, Ireland, June 18, 1939; came to U.S., 1967; s. John Joseph and Alice (Broderick) C.; m. Antonieta Fernandez, July 1, 1972 (div. 1987); children: Julian Albert, Dermot Martin. MB, BCh BAO with 1st class honors, Nat. U. Ireland, 1962, MD, 1981, DSc, 1984, LLD (hon.), 1992; AM (hon.), Harvard U., 1989. Intern St. Vincent's Hosp., Dublin, 1962-63, resident, 1965-67, Nat. Maternity Hosp., Dublin, 1963, St. Luke's Hosp., Dublin, 1964, Queen Charlotte's Hosp., London, 1964; asst. prof. medicine Boston U. Sch. Medicine, 1973-75, Harvard U. Med. Sch., Boston, 1975-79, assoc. prof., 1979-88, Lawrence J. Henderson assoc. prof. health sci. & tech., 1979-88, 88-91, faculty mem. Grad. Sch. Arts & Scis., 1983—, assoc. mem. dept. cellular & molecular physiology, 1983—, prof. medicine, 1988—, prof. health sci. & tech., 1991—. Mem. staff Brigham and Women's Hosp., Boston, 1975—; McIlrath guest prof. Royal Prince Alfres Hosp., U. Sydney, 1987; cons. Gipharmex S.A., Milan, 1984—87, Dow Chem. Co., Midland, Mich., 1984—87, Merix, Inc., Needham, 1986—96, Oculon, Cambridge, 1987—95, Ciba-Gigey, Summit, NJ, 1988—93, Labs. Fournier, Dijon-Diax, 1992—93, Aventis, Frankfurt, 1993—2002, Genzyme, 1993—2002, Merck & Co., 2001—03, Dublin Molecular Medicine Centre, 2001—, Mpex Biosci., Inc., San Diego, 2002—03, Chrysalis Biotech., Inc., Galveston, Tex., 2003—04, Peptimmune, Inc., Cambridge, Mass., 2006—, Daiichi-Sankyo Inc., Parsippany, NJ, 2007—. Author: Bile Salts and Gallstones, 1974, Hepatic Excretory Function, 1975; assoc. editor Jour. Lipid Rsch., 1978-81; mem. editl. bd. Am. Jour. Physiology, 1976-81, Gastroenterology, 1983-88, Hepatology, 1981-84; contbr. articles to profl. jours Recipient Acad. Career Devel. award NIH, 1976, MERIT award, 1986, 2004, Adolf Windaus prize Falk Found., 1984, Huddinge Sikhuis medal Karolinska Inst., Stockholm, 1992, Fitzgerald medal U. Coll., 1993, Ismar Boas medal German Soc. for Digestive and Metabolic Diseases, 2002; hon. fellow med. faculty Nat. U. Ireland, Dublin, 2003; postdoctoral fellow Boston U. Sch. Medicine, 1968-73, Guggenheim Found. fellow, 1974, Fogarty Internat. fellow NIH, 1968, Fulbright fellow, 1967-68. Fellow AAAS, Royal Coll. Physicians Ireland; mem. Gastroenterology Rsch. Group (vice-chmn., steering com.), Am. Soc. Clin. Investigation, Am. Gastroent. Assn. (Disting. Achievement award 1990, William Beaumont prize 2000), Am. Oil Chemists Soc., Biophys. Soc., Interurban Clin. Club, Am. Assn. Physicians, Royal Irish Acad. (hon.), St. Botolph Club, The Club of Odd Volumes, Harvard Musical Assn. Roman Catholic. Achievements include patents in field. Office: Brigham and Womens Hosp Div Gastroenterology 75 Francis St Boston MA 02115-6106 Home Phone: 781-237-8581; Office Phone: 617-732-5822. Business E-Mail: mccarey@rics.bwh.harvard.edu.

CAREY, PAUL RICHARD, biophysicist; b. Dartford, Kent, Eng., June 17, 1945; arrived in Can., 1969; s. Charles Richard and Winifred Margaret (Knight) C.; m. Julia Smith, Sept. 4, 1966 (div. May 1991); children: Emma, Sarah, Matthew; m. Marianne Pusztai, Mar. 7, 1992. BS in Chemistry with honors, U. Sussex, Eng., 1966, PhD, 1969. Postdoctoral fellow Nat. Rsch. Coun., Ottawa, Ont., Canada, 1969-71, rsch. officer, 1971-94; mgr. Ctr. for Protein Structure Design, head protein lab. Inst. for Bio. Scis., Ottawa, Ont., Canada, 1987-93; prof. dept. biochemistry Case Western Res. U., 1995—, dir. Cleve. Ctr. Structural Biology, 2000—. Adj. prof. Dept. Biochemistry, U. Ottawa, 1987-94, prof., 1994; prof. dept. biochemistry Case Western Reserve U. Author: Biochemical Applications of Raman and Resonance Raman Spectroscopies, 1982; contbr. over 220 articles to profl. jours.; patentee in field. Fellow Chem. Inst. Can.; mem. Am. Chem. Soc., Can. Protein Engring. Network (Adminstrv. body 1990-93), Internat. Network Protein Engring. Ctrs. Achievements include first demonstration of resonance Raman spectroscopy providing vibrational spectrum of a substrate or drug in active site of an enzyme; generation of first quantitative relationship between active site bond lengths and reactivity by combining resonance Raman spectroscopy, enzyme kinetics and x-ray crystallography; using a Raman micoscope to follow chemical reactions in protein and RNA crystals; elucidation of mechanism of sunlight degradation of biological insecticide from B. thuringiensis; research on use of lasers in fingerprint detection. Office: Case Western Res U Dept Biochemistry Cleveland OH 44106-4935 Business E-Mail: paul.carey@case.edu.

CAREY, PETER KEVIN, reporter; b. San Francisco, Apr. 2, 1940; s. Paul Twohig and Stanleigh M. (White) C.; m. Joanne Dayl Barker, Jan. 7, 1978; children: Brendan Patrick, Nadia Marguerite. BS in Econs., U. Calif., Berkeley, 1964. Reporter San Francisco Examiner, 1964, Livermore (Calif.) Ind., 1965-67, editor, 1967; aerospace writer, spl. projects and investigative reporter San Jose (Calif.) Mercury, 1967—. Pulizer prize juror, 2002—03. Recipient Pulitzer prize for internat. reporting Columbia U., 1986, George Polk award L.I. U., 1986, Investigative Reporters and Editors award, 1986, staff Pulitzer prize for gen. reporting, Columbia U., 1990, Thomas L. Stokes award Washington Journalism Ctr., 1991, Malcolm Forbes award Overseas Press Club of Am., 1993, Gerald Loeb award UCLA Grad. Sch. Mgmt., 1993; NEH profl. journalism fellow, Stanford U., 1983-84. Mem. Internat. Consortium of Investigative Journalists, Soc. Profl. Journalists, Investigative Reporters and Editors. Avocation: piano. Office: San Jose Mercury-News 750 Ridder Park Dr San Jose CA 95190 Business E-Mail: pcarey@mercurynews.com.

CAREY, PETER PHILIP, writer; b. Bacchus Marsh, Victoria, Australia, May 7, 1943; 2 children. LittD, U. Queensland, Australia, 1989; LHD, The New Sch., 1998; DHC, Monash U., Australia, 2000. Dir. creative writing program Hunter coll. CUNY, 2007—. Tchr. creative writing NYU, Princeton (NJ) U., Columbia U., NYC; dir. creative writing program Hunter Coll., NYC. Author: The Fat Man in History, 1974, War Crimes, 1979 (Miles Franklin award 1979, New South Wales Premier's Lit. award 1980), Bliss, 1981 (Miles Franklin award 1981, Nat. Book Coun. award 1982, New South Wales Premier's Lit. award, 1982, Australian Film Inst. best adapted screenplay, best film 1985), Illywhacker, 1985 (Book Coun. award, 1985, shortlist Booker prize for fiction 1985, The Age Book of Yr. award 1985, Ditmar award Best Australian Science Fiction Novel 1986, Vance Palmer prize for fiction 1986, Victorian Premier's Lit. award 1986) Oscar and Lucinda, 1988 (Booker prize 1988, Book Coun. award 1988, Miles Franklin Award 1989), (with Wim Wenders) Until the End of the World, 1990, The Tax Inspector, 1991, The Unusual Life of Tristan Smith, 1994 (The Age Book of Yr. award, 1994), The Big Bazoohley, 1995, Jack Maggs, 1997 (The Age Book of Yr. award 1997, Commonwealth prize best book 1998), True History of the Kelly Gang, 2000 (Commonwealth prize 2001, Booker prize 2001, Vance Palmer prize for fiction, 2001), My Life as a Fake, 2003, Wrong About Japan, 2005, Theft - A Love Story, 2006. Recipient NSW Premier's Lit.award, Miles Franklin award (3), Nat. Book Coun. award (2), Age Book of Yr. award (3), Victorian Premier's Literary award, 1986. Fellow Royal Soc. Lit. Office: c/o Binky Urban ICM 40 W 57th St New York NY 10019-4001

CAREY, ROBERT MUNSON, physician, educator; b. Lexington, Ky., Aug. 13, 1940; s. Henry Ames and Eleanor Day (Munson) C.; m. Theodora Vann Hereford, Aug. 24, 1963; children: Adonice Ames, Alicia Vann, Robert Josiah Hereford. BS, U. Ky., 1962; MD, Vanderbilt U., 1965; Doctor Honoris Causa, Fed. U. Ceara, Brazil, 1998. Diplomate Am. Bd. Internal Medicine, Am. Bd. Endocrinology and Metabolism, Nat. Bd. Med. Examiners. Intern in medicine U. Va. Hosp., Charlottesville, 1966; jr. asst. resident in medicine N.Y. Hosp.-Cornell Med. Ctr., NYC, 1968-69, sr. asst. resident, 1969-70; instr. endocrinology, dept. medicine Vanderbilt U. Sch. Medicine, Nashville, 1970-72; postdoctoral fellow in medicine St. Mary's Hosp. Med. Sch., London, 1972-73; asst. prof. internal medicine, endocrinology and metabolism U. Va. Sch. Medicine, Charlottesville, 1973-76, assoc. prof., 1976-80, prof., 1980—, James Carroll Flippin prof. medical sci. and dean, 1986—2002, prof. u., 2002—, David A. Harrison III disting. prof. medicine, 2002—, assoc. dir. Clin. Rsch. Ctr., 1975-86, prof., dean emeritus, 2002—, head. div. endocrinology and metabolism, dept. internal medicine, 1978-86, chmn. gen. faculty, chmn. med. adv. com., chmn. exec. com., 1986—. Attending staff U. Va. Hosp., Charlottesville, 1973—, pres. clin. staff, 1977-79, vice chmn. med. policy com., 1986—, adv. bd. 1986—; mem. study sect. on exptl. cardiovascular scis. NIH, 1982-85; mem. cardiovascular and renal adv. com. USDA, 1988—; vis. prof. div. nephrology, U. Miami Med. Sch., Fla., 1979, 83, 84, Hosp. das Clinicas da Univ., Fed. do Ceara, Forteleza, Brazil, 1981, hypertension div. Mt. Sinai Sch. Medicine, N.Y.C., 1981, div. pediatric endocrinology N.Y. Hosp.-Cornell Med. Ctr., 1981, dept. endocrinology St. Vincent's Hosp., Univ. Coll., Dublin, Ireland, 1982, depts. physiology and endocrinology Mayo Grad. Sch. Medicine, Rochester, Minn., 1984, div. rsch. Cleve. Clinic Found., 1984, Genentech, Inc., San Francisco, 1984, divs. endocrinology and metabolism U. Mass., U. Pa. Sch. Medicine, Boston U. Med. Sch., 1984, U. N.C. Sch. Medicine, 1985, Harvard Med. Sch., Boston, 1987, Jefferson Med. Coll., 1988; Bley Stein vis. prof. endocrinology U. So. Calif., 1987; Pfizer vis. prof. in pharmacology U. Chgo., 1988; coorganizer 3d Internat. Meeting on Peripheral Actions of Dopamine, Charlottesville, 1989; v.p. Va. Ambulatory Surgery, Inc., 1986—; speaker, presenter numerous nat. and internat. profl. meetings and congresses. Author: (with E.D. Vaughn) Adrenal Disorders, 1988; co-editor: Hypertension: An Endocrine Disease, 1985; mem. editorial bd. Jour. Clin. Endocronlogy and Metabolism, 1981-84, Hypertension jour., 1983-84, Am. Jour. Physiology: Heart and Circulatory Physiology, 1987-89, Am. Jour. Hypertension, 1987—; author over 150 articles, revs., papers for profl. jours., contbr. 19 chpts. to books. Mem. exec. com. and fin. com. U. Va. Health Services Found., 1986—; bd. dirs. Va. Kidney Stone Found., Inc., 1986—, The Harrison Found., Inc. U. Va., 1986—, Dyslexia Ctr., Charlottesville, 1986—. Surgeon (lt. comdr.) USPHS, 1966-68, res., 1968—. Recipient Attending Physician of Yr. awrd dept. internal medicine U. Va. Med. Ctr., 1983-84, Disting. Alumnus award and Founder's medal Vanderbilt U.; USPHS fellow Vanderbilt U., 1970-72; recipient numerous NIH grants as co-prin. and prin. investigator, 1972—; named to Hall Disting. Alumni, U. Ky., 2000. Master ACP (program com. regional meeting 1987); fellow Coun. for High Blood Pressure Rsch. AHA (program com. 1984-86, exec. and long rang planning coms. 1992—; chair-elect 2002-); mem. Inst. Medicine of NAS, Am. Heart Assn. (established investigator 1975-80), Va. affiliate Am. Heart Assn. (bd. dirs. 1977-83, pres. 1979-80, Disting. Service award), The Endocrine Soc. (fin. com. 1988—, chair devel. com. 1991-92), Am. Fedn. Clin. Rsch. (so. sect. councilor 1978-81, nominating com. 1982), So. Soc. Clin. Investigation (nominating com. 1982, sec.-treas. 1985-86), Inter-Am. Soc. for Hypertension, Am. Soc. Clin. Investigation, Am. Clin. and Climatol. Assn., Am. Soc. Hypertension (intersocietal affairs com. 1986—), Internat. Soc. Hypertension, Assn. Am. Physicians, AMA, Albemarle County Med. Soc., Med. Soc. Va., Assn. Am. Med. Coll.s Coun. of Deans, Inst. of Medicine, Nat. Acad. of Scis., The Raven Soc., Alpha Omega Alpha (Disting. Med. Alumnus award Vanderbilt U. 1994). Home: Pavilion Vi East Lawn Charlottesville VA 22903 Office: U Va Sch Medicine PO Box 801414 Charlottesville VA 22908-1414

CAREY, SARAH COLLINS, lawyer; b. NYC, Aug. 12, 1938; d. Jerome Joseph and Susan (Atlee) Collins; m. James J. Carey, Aug. 28, 1962 (div. 1977); 1 child, Sasha; m. John D. Reilly, Jan. 27, 1979; children: Sarah Reilly, Katherine Reilly. BA, Radcliffe Coll., 1960; LLB, Georgetown U., 1965. Bar: D.C. 1966, U.S. Supreme Ct. 1977. Soviet specialist USIA/U.S. Dept. State, 1961-65; assoc. Arnold & Porter, Washington, 1965-68; asst. dir. Lawyers Com. for Civil Rights, Washington, 1968-73; ptnr. Heron, Burchette, Ruckert & Rothwell/predecessor firms, Washington, 1973-90; chair CIS Practice Steptoe and Johnson, Washington, 1990-99; chair CIS Practice, sr. ptnr. internat. Squire, Sanders & Dempsey, Washington, 1999—. Cons. Ford Found., 1975—83; bd. dirs. Yukos Oil Co., 2001—05, Akbars Bank, 2006—. Bd. dirs. Acad. for Ednl. Devel., 2004—; chair bd. dirs. Eurasia Found., 1994—; bd. dirs. Russia-Am. Enterprise Fund, 1993—95, Def. Enterprise Fund, 1994—2001, Georgetown U. Sch. Law Inst. Pub. Representation, 1971—85, Am. Arbitration Assn., 1975—82. Mem.: Internat. Women's Forum, Atlantic Coun., Coun. Fgn. Rels. Democrat. Office: 1201 Pennsylvania Ave NW Washington DC 20004-2401 Business E-Mail: scarey@ssd.com.

CAREY, STEPHANIE L., systems engineer, educator; b. Miami, Fla., July 31, 1973; d. Stephen C. and Joan D. Lutton; m. Craig E. Carey, Oct. 7, 2000; 1 child, Jack Donald. B, U. Fla., 1996; M, U. Miami, 2000; PhD in Biomedical Engring., U. South Fla., 2003—. Rsch. assoc. U. Miami, Fla., 1996—2000; sys. engr. Peak Performance, Denver, 2001—03; instr. U. South Fla., 2003—, tech. support Motion Analysis Lab., 2005—. Adj. instr. Front Range C.C., Boulder, Colo., 2002—03. Vol. Denver Children's Hosp., 2002—03. Mem.: IEEE. Business E-Mail: scarey3@eng.usf.edu.

CAREY, STEVENS ANTHONY, lawyer; b. Santa Monica, Calif., Mar. 30, 1951; s. Edward Macdonald and Elizabeth Crosby (Heckscher) Carey; m. Indy Shriner, Mar. 20, 1987; children: Lauren, Meagan. BA, U. Calif. Berkeley, 1973, MA, 1975, JD, 1978. Bar: Calif. 1978, NY 1988. Assoc. Lawler, Felix & Hall, LA, 1977, 1978—83; rsch. asst. Appellate Conf. IRS, San Francisco, 1977—78; ptnr. Pircher, Nichols & Meeks (formerly Lawler, Felix & Hall), LA, 1983—. Contbr. articles to profl. jours. Bd. mem. Calif. Trust Pub. Schs. Mem.: ABA, LA County Bar Assn. (real estate sect.), Calif. State Bar Assn. Avocations: swimming, music. Home: 1110 Benedict Canyon Dr Beverly Hills CA 90210 Office: Pircher Nichols Meeks 1925 Century Park E #1700 Los Angeles CA 90067 Business E-Mail: scarey@pircher.com.

CAREY, SUSAN R., lawyer; b. 1977; BA, Okla. State U., Stillwater, 2000; JD, U. Okla., Norman, 2003. Bar: Okla. 2003. Assoc. DeBee Gilchrist, Oklahoma City, 2003—. Mem.: ABA, Okla. Bar Assn. Home: 3229 NW 68th St Oklahoma City OK 73116 Office: DeBee Gilchrist 100 N Broadway Ste 1500 Oklahoma City OK 73102 Office Phone: 405-232-7777.

CAREY, WILLIAM BACON, pediatrician, educator; b. Phila., Dec. 6, 1926; s. Henry Reginald and Margaret (Bacon) Carey; m. Ann Lord McDougal, July 21, 1956; children: Katharine Blayney, Laura Bacon, Elizabeth McDougal. BA, Yale U., New Haven, Conn., 1950; MD, Harvard U., Boston, 1954. Diplomate Am. Bd. Pediatrics. Intern Phila. Gen. Hosp., 1954-55; resident in pediatrics Children's Hosp. of Phila., 1955-57, 59-60; dir. sect. on behavioral pediatrics Children's Hosp. Phila., 1989—; practice medicine specializing in pediatrics Media, Pa., 1960-89. Instr. pediat. U. Pa. Sch. Medicine, Children's Hosp. Phila., 1961—73, assoc. in pediat., 1973—79, clin. asst. prof., 1979—82, clin. assoc. prof., 1982—90, clin. prof., 1990—. Co-editor: (book) Developmental-Behavioral Pediatrics, 1983, 1992, 1999, Clinical and Educational Applications of Temperament Research, 1989, Prevention and Early Intervention: Individual Differences as Risk Factors for the Mental Health of Children, 1994; author (with S. C. McDevitt): Coping with Children's Temperament: A Guide for Professionals, 1995; author: (with M. Jablow) Understanding Your Child's Temperament, 1997, revised edit., 2005; contbr. articles to profl. jours.; developer Infant Temperament Questionnaire, 1970, co-developer Toddler Temperament Scale, 1978, Behavioral Style Questionnaire, 1976, Middle Childhood Temperament Questionnaire, 1980, Early Infancy Temperament Questionnaire, 1990, BASICS Behavioral Adjustment Scale, 2002. Pres. Friends of Wyck (House), Germantown, Phila., 1980—; bd. dirs. Benchmark Sch., Media, Pa., 1989—. Capt. M.C. US Army, 1957—59. Recipient Wistar-Haines award, 2001. Fellow: Am. Acad. Pediat. (Rsch. grantee 1975, 1980, 1985, Aldrich award 1991, Practitioner Rsch. award 1992); mem.: Coll. Physicians Phila., Phila. Pediatric Soc. (bd. dirs. 1969—71), Soc. Devel. and Behavioral Pediat. (exec. coun. 1983—85, pres-elect 1989—90, pres. 1990—91), Ambulatory Pediatric Assn., Soc. Rsch. Child Devel., Am. Pediat. Soc., Inst. Medicine NAS, Penn Club, Franklin Inn Club, Phi Beta Kappa. Home: 511 Walnut Ln Swarthmore PA 19081-1140 Office Phone: 215-590-1467. Personal E-mail: wbcarey@att.net. Business E-Mail: carey@email.chop.edu.

CAREY, WILLIAM POLK, investment banker; b. Balt., May 11, 1930; s. Francis J. and Marjorie A. (Armstrong) C. Grad., Pomfret Sch., 1948; student, Princeton, 1948—50; BS in Econs., Wharton Sch., U. Pa., 1953; ScD (hon.), Ariz. State U., 1998; DCS (hon.), CUNY, 2003; DCL (hon.), U. of the South, Sewanee, Tenn., 2006. V.p., gen. mgr. A. J. Orbach Co., Plainfield, NJ, 1955—58; prin. W.P. Carey & Co., Bloomfield, NJ, 1958—63; pres., dir. W.P. Carey & Co. and affiliates, NYC, 1973—83, chmn., 1983—; pres., dir. Internat. Leasing Corp., NYC, 1959—89; chmn. exec. com., dir. Hubbard, Westervelt & Mottelay, Inc. (now Merrill Lynch), NYC, 1964—67; dept. head Loeb, Rhoades & Co. (now Lehman Bros.), NYC, 1967—71; vice chmn. investment banking bd., dir. corp. fin. duPont Glore Forgan, 1971—73; gen. ptnr. Corp. Property Assocs., NYC, 1978—97, chmn. CPA series of pub. ltd. partnerships and real estate investment trusts, 1979—. Chmn. Carey Instnl. Properties, NYC, 1991-2004, W.P. Carey & Co. LLC, W.P. Carey Internat. LLC, 2000—; chmn. exec. com. Carey Diversified LLC, 1997-2000; adv. com. US Treasury Dept., 1986-92; exec. in residence Harvard Bus. Sch., 1999; advisor W.P. Carey Sch. Bus., Ariz. State U. Trustee Johns Hopkins U., Newcomen Soc.; adv. bd. Johns Hopkins Sch. Advanced Internat. Studies, Carey Bus. Sch.; life trustee Gilman Sch. Balt., Pomfret Sch., Conn.; trustee, exec. com. Rensselaerville Inst., NY, 1979—; chmn. bd. trustees Oxford Mgmt. Ctr. Assocs. Coun., 1984-94, hon. trustee 1994—; coun. mgmt. Templeton Coll., Oxford U., 1970-95; chm. St. Elmo Found., W.P. Carey Found., Pa. Inst. for Econ. Rsch., 2001—; hon. dir. Edmund Niles Huyck Preserve; leadership com. James A. Baker III Inst. for Pub. Policy Rice U., coun. on fgn. rels.; gov. Nat. Assn. Real Estate Investment Trusts, 1993-97; chmn. bd. overseers Rensselaerville Inst. Conf. Ctr., 2000—; 1st lt. USAF, 1953-55. Estab. W.P. Carey program in entrepreneurship and mgmt. Johns Hopkins U., William Polk Carey prize in econs., Carey term chairs in econs. and fin. U. Pa., Carey chair in math. Pomfret Sch., Carey prize in math. Calif. Inst. Tech., Armstrong law prize Ariz. State U. Mem. Soc. Mayflower Descs. (gov. emeritus), White's (London), The Pilgrims, The Brook, Newcomen Soc., Racquet and Tennis Club, Univ. Club, Penn Club (NY), St. Elmo Club (Phila. and NYC), Maryland Club (Balt.), Harvard Faculty Club (Cambridge), NE Harbor Fleet (NE Harbor, Maine), Johns Hopkins Club, Delta Phi. Episcopalian. Home: 525 Park Ave New York NY 10065 also: Fullerlea Rensselaerville NY 12147 Office: 50 Rockefeller Plz New York NY 10020-1605

CARFAGNA, PETER A., lawyer; b. Cleve., Feb. 15, 1953; AB summa cum laude, Harvard U., 1975; MA with honors, Oxford U., 1977; JD magna cum laude, Harvard U., 1979. Bar: Ohio 1979. Mem. Jones, Day, Reavis & Pogue, Cleve., 1979—94; gen. counsel IMG, 1994—2005; counsels Calfee, Halter & Griswold LLP, Cleve., 2005—. Adj. prof. Western Reserve U. Sch. Law's; disting. vis. Harvard Law Sch. Covington & Burling. Past bd. chair St. Ignatius High Sch.; bds. govs. Club Key Ctr. and Ave Maria Sch. Law; mem. Cleveland Museum Art's Corp. Coun. Rhodes scholar. Mem. Phi Beta Kappa, Harvard Alumni Assn., Nat. Bd. Assn. Am. Rhodes Scholars, Ohio Rhodes Scholarship Selection Com. Office: Calfee Halter & Griswold LLP 800 Superior Ave 1400 McDonald Investment Ctr Cleveland OH 44114 Office Phone: 216-622-8868. Office Fax: 216-241-0816. Business E-Mail: pcarfagna@calfee.com.

CARFINE, KENNETH E., government agency administrator; m. Deborah Carfine; 2 children. BS Acctg., U. of Baltimore. Banking, cash mgmt., payments, check claims, govt.-wide acctg. positions Dept. of the Treasury,

1973—2003, dep. asst. sec. for Fiscal Ops. and Policy, 2003—07, fiscal asst. sec., 2007—. Office: Dept of the Treasury 1500 Penn Ave NW Washington DC 20220 Office Phone: 202-622-2000.*

CARFORA, JOHN MICHAEL, economics professor, academic administrator; b. New Haven, July 24, 1950; s. John Michael and Rose Mary (Mitro) C.; m. Linda Louise Palmer, July 22, 1972; 1 child, Rachel Ellen. BS, U. New Haven, Conn., 1973, MPA, 1975; MS in Econs. and Polit. Sci., London Sch. Econs., 1978; AM, Dartmouth Coll., Hanover, NH, 1985; EdM, Harvard U., Cambridge, Mass., 1993; EdD, Columbia U., 2007. Rsch. asst. London Sch. Econs. and Polit. Sci., 1980-81; lectr. polit. sci. Albertus Magnus Coll., New Haven, 1982-83; lectr. econs. and quantitative analysis U. New Haven, 1982-83; program cons. Dartmouth Coll., 1984-85, assoc. prof. internat. econ. Sch. Internat. Tng., 1985-90; v.p. rsch. and acad. affairs, dir. Soviet-Am. projects Global-Genesis, Internat. Cons., 1989-91, dir. east and west projects, 1992-94; asst. dean for rsch. and sponsored programs Ind. State U., Terre Haute, 1994-95; dir. grants and sponsored programs Simmons Coll., Boston, 1995-97; assoc. dir. grants and contracts Dartmouth Coll., Hanover, NH, 1997—2002; dir. office rsch. & sponsored programs Boston Coll., 2002—07; dir. office sponsored rsch. Amherst Coll., Amherst, 2007—. Ednl. cons. USSR Acad. Mgmt., Moscow, 1991-92; vis. asst. prof. U.S. Dept. Def., Europe, 1979-80; vis. sr. lectr. Poly. of Ctrl. London, 1980; vis. asst. prof. internat. rels. So. Conn. State U., New Haven, 1982; cons. Commonwealth Acad. Mgmt., Moscow, 1992-94. Mem. editl. bd. Rsch. Mgmt. Rev.; contbr. articles to profl. jours. With USAR, 1970-76. Recipient Roy E. Jenkins award, 1972; fellow Radio Free Europe-Radio Liberty, 1979, Internat. Rsch. and Exchs. Bd., 1981-84. Mem. ASTD, AAUP, Am. Assn. Advancement Slavic Studies, Assn. Jesuit Colls. and Univs. (chmn. conf. on rsch. and sponsored programs 2005-07), Nat. Assn. Fgn. Student Advisors (internat. educators), Am. Acad. Polit. Sci., Am. Econ. Assn., Am. Polit. Sci. Assn., Am. Assn. for Higher Edn., Am. Assn. for Adult and Continuing Edn., Nat. Coun. Univ. Rsch. Adminstrs. (bd. dirs., chmn. internat. commn. on rsch. adminstrn. 2004—), Acad. Polit. Sci., N.E. Slavic Assn., Soc. Rsch. Adminstrs., Royal Acad. Pub. Adminstrn. (Eng.), Atlantic Econ. Soc., Am. Friends of the London Sch. Econs. (Conn. program chmn. 1981-85, N.H.-Vt. program chmn. 1985-87, alumni bd. dirs. 1983-92). Personal E-mail: johncarfora@yahoo.com. Business E-Mail: jcarfora@amherst.edu.

CARGILL, JENNIFER S., library director, dean, educator; MLS, La. State U. Dean librs., prof. libr. and info. scis. La. State U. Coun. mem. Online Computer Libr. Ctr.; chair mems. coun. del. Southeastern Libr. Network. Contbr. articles to profl. jours. Mem.: ALA (adv. com. Am. Librs. online 2006—, mem. com. on accreditation), Assn. Southeastern Rsch. Librs. (bd. dirs.). Office: La State U Librs Baton Rouge LA 70803 Office Phone: 225-578-2217. E-mail: cargill@lsu.edu.*

CARGILLE, CHARLES M., internist, educator; s. Ralph Phillips Cargille and Esther Anna Malmsten; m. Frances C. Johnson, June 11, 1961; children: James Royal, Christopher Allan, Jonathan Morell, David Lee, Robin Thomas. Grad., Bucknell U., 1954, U. Aberdeen, Scotland, 1955; BA, Bucknell U., 1956, U. Djakarta, Indonesia, 1960; MD, John Hopkins U. Sch. Med., 1961; MS, Am. U., DC, 1973, MA, 1976. Lic. Md., 1961, NJ, 1965, ND, 1975, Minn., 1978, La., 1980, registered DEA. Intern Barnes Hosp., St. Louis, 1961—62; resident in internal medicine Mountainside Hosp., Montclair, NJ, 1962—63, NJ Coll. Medicine, Jersey City, 1963—64, Mountainside Hosp., Montclair, NJ, 1964—65; fellow in rsch., endocrine div. NJ Coll. Medicine, Jersey City, 1965—66; sr. investigator, attending physician Nat. Cancer Inst., Bethesda, Md., 1966—70; guest worker Nat. Inst. Child Health and Human Devel., 1971, Interagency Com. Population Rsch., 1971; acting dep. dir. FDA, 1972; med. officer US Civil Svc., 1969—74; sr. investigator, attending physician Nat. Inst. Child Health and Human Devel., Bethesda, Md., 1970—74; asst. dean Area Health Edn. Ctr., dir. U. ND Sch. Medicine, Minot, 1974—76, asst. prof. medicine, 1974—80, dir. div. population studies, 1976—78; staff physician VA Hosp., Fargo, 1978—79; pvt. practice La., 1980—90; physician, house officer I LSU Med. Ctr., Shreveport, La., 1990—92; physician New Gen. Hosp., La. State Penitentiary, Angola, La., 1992—93; physician, health care authority Winn Parish Correctional Ctr., Winnfield, La., 1993; pvt. practice Riverland Hosp., Ferriday, La., 1994; staff physician Metropolitan Devel. Ctr., Belle Chasse, La., 1995—2003; pvt. practice Gretna and Hammond, La., 2003—04, Harvey and Mandeville, La., 2004—06, Mandeville, La., 2005—07. Cons. in field; spkr. in field; bd. dirs. Cargille Sci., Inc., 1965, R.P. Cargille Labs., Inc., 1965; mem. radioimmunoassay task force Nat. Pituitary Agy., Balt., 1967—69; mem. radiation com. NIH, 1967—69; lectr. Am. U., Washington, 1973—74; mem. advisory bd. Cath. U. Am., 1974—75; sec., bd govs. Family Practice Residency Program, Minot, 1975; mem. Scholastic Standards Com., U. ND Sch. Medicine, 1976—79; physician Monroe Mental Health Ctr., La., 1989, Shreveport Mental Health Ctr., La., 1992, Rapides Hosp. Outpatient Clinic Convenient Care Ctr., Alexandria, La., 1994. Contbr. articles to profl. jours., chapters to books; author: Global Dialogue of the Disciplines on Population, 1974, Key Issues in Population Policy:, 1976. Founder, pres. The World Population Soc., Washington, 1972—76; chmn. ad hoc com. on population US Nat. Com. for UNESCO, 1973—74; founder, pres. Population Food Fund, 1976—80; bd. dirs. Ctr. Econ. and Social Justice, Washington, 2003—. Sr. surgeon US Pub. Health Svc., 1966—69, surgeon US Pub. Health Svc. Res., 1969—, lt. col. US Nat. Guard, 1982—86, La., lt. col. USAR, 1984—87. Grantee Josiah Macy Jr. Found. scholarship, Johns Hopkins Med. Ctr., 1957—58, Rsch. fellow, NIH, 1965—66, Sunnen Found., 1975, Claudia Gips Found., 1974, Scherring Corp., 1974, Del Mar Found., 1975; Elected fellow, Am. Acad. Reproductive Medicine, 1971. Mem.: So. Pain Soc., Am. Chronic Pain Assn., Am. Pain Found., Am. Pain Soc., Am. Acad. Pain Medicine. Roman Catholic. Achievements include research in med. field. Home: 1222 Springwater Dr Mandeville LA 70471 Personal E-mail: charles.cargille@gmail.com.

CARGO, DAVID FRANCIS, lawyer, former governor; b. Dowagiac, Mich., Jan. 13, 1929; s. Francis Clair and Mary E. (Harton) C.; children: Veronica Ann, David Joseph, Patrick Michael, Maria Elena Christina, Eamon Francis. AB, U. Mich., 1951, M of Pub. Adminstrn., 1953, JD, 1957. Bar: Mich. 1957, N.Mex. 1957, Oreg. 1974. Pvt. practice, Albuquerque, 1957; asst. dist. atty., 1958-59; mem. N.Mex. Ho. of Reps., 1962; gov. N.Mex., 1967-71; practice law Santa Fe, 1970-73, Portland, Oreg., 1973-83. Bd. dirs. N.Mex. State Lottery Authority; mem. Interstate Compact; bd. mem. Fort Stanton Found. Chmn. Four Corners Regional Commn., 1967-71, Oil and Gas Conservation Commn., N.Mex. Lottery Authority, Cumbres & Toltec RR Commn.; chmn. N.Mex. Young Reps., 1959-61, Clackamas County Rep. Ctrl. Com.; mem. Israel Bond Com.; former mem. bd. govs. St. John Coll.; bd. dirs. Albuquerque Tech. Vocat. Sch.; chmn. governing bd. Albuquerque Tv.I. C.C.; mem. Albuquerque City Pers. Bd., N.Mex. State Lottery Authority; adv. bd. mem. N.Mex. State Fair; exec. bd. Found. for Open Govt.; bd. dirs. N.Mex. State Libr. Found.; elected state chair libr. bond chmn., 2002; bd. dirs. N.Mex. State Lottery, Cumbres and Toltec R.R.; chmn. bd. commrs. Cumbres and Toltec Scenic Rlwy.; founder David F. Cargo Cmty. Libr., Mora, N.Mex.; mem. Albuerque City Labor Bd. With U.S. Army, 1953-55. Named Man of Yr. Albuquerque Jr. C. of C., 1964, Congregation Albert Brotherhood Man of Yr., 2001, 2002; recipient Outstanding Conservationist award N.Mex. Wildlife Assn., 1969, 70; David F. Cargo Libr., Mora, N.Mex., named in his honor. Mem. NAACP (life), KC, Mich. Bar Assn., Oreg. Bar Assn., N.Mex. Bar Assn., Albuquerque Bar Assn., Isaac Walton League (past v.p. N.Mex.), World Affairs Coun. Oreg. (pres.), Interstate Oil and Gas Compact, Isaak Walton League Oreg., Hispano C. of C., Am. Leadership Conf. (bd. dirs.), Nat. Fedn. Blind, Oreg. State Film Commn. Home: 6422 Concordia Rd NE Albuquerque NM 87111-1228

CARHART, HOMER WALTER, retired research scientist; b. Orange, Calif., May 21, 1914; s. Walter D. and Ethel (Shepherd) C.; m. Julia M. Holzapfel, June 15, 1940; children: Martha Jean, David Henry. BS, Dakota Wesleyan U., 1934; MA, U. S.D., 1935; PhD in Organic Chemistry, U. Md., 1939; LD (hon.), Hood Coll., Frederick, Md., 2007. Asst. prof. Gallaudet Coll., Washington, 1939-42; rsch. chemist Naval Rsch. Lab., Washington, 1942-52, head fuels br., 1952-70, head chem. dynamics br., 1970-86, dir. Navy Tech. Ctr. for Safety and Survivability, 1986-94, sr. scientist emeritus, 1994—. Mem. sec. of treas. Blue Ribbon Com. on Tanker Hazards, 1962-63; USN mem., del. Am., Brit., Can., and Australian Quadripartite Coms. on Fuels, 1964-94; mem. USN Working Group in Submarine Atmosphere Control, 1966-71; mem. Nat. Acad. Scis./NRC Com. on Hazardous Materials, 1966-75, chmn. Elec. Hazards Panel, 1966-75, chmn. Electrostatics Panel, 1969-75, chmn. indsl. hazards com., 1982-89; fire panel mem., spl. cons. NASA Apollo 204 (Fatal) Fire Rev. Bd., 1967; mem. exec. group, dir. Navy Labs. Planning Panel for Enhanced Aircraft Carrier Survivability, 1967-68; chmn. USN Panel on Hydrogen as a Potential Fuel, 1973, USN Inter-Labs. Com. on Pers. Adminstrn., 1973-75; chmn. dir. Navy Labs. Advanced Tech. Objectives Working Group for Fire Rsch., 1973-76; mem. Coordinating Rsch. Coun. Diesel Com., 1950-66; chmn. Ignition Quality Investigation Group, 1956-66, Compression Ignition Adv. Group, 1960-65; chmn. Aviation Fuel Safety Task Force (Adv. to FAA), 1974-76; chmn. NAS/NRC Com. on Indsl. Hazards, 1982-89; mem. Dept. of Labor Joint Soviet/Am. Task Force on Safety in the Chem. Industry, 1991. Contbr. articles to profl. publs.; patentee in field. Recipient USN Meritorious Civilian Svc. award, 1945, Dept. of Navy Recognition of Achievement award, 1975, USN Superior Civilian Svc. award, 1965, USN Disting. Civilian Svc. award, 1979, Winning Team, Federally Employed Women, Inc. award, 1989, Robert Dexter Conrad award for outstanding achievemnet in naval sci. and engring., 1991, Naval Rsch. Lab. Lifetime Achievement award, 1994, Harry C. Bigglestone award for excellence in written comm. of fire protection concepts, 1990, Jack Bono Engring. Comms. award, 1995, Ann. Homer W. Carhart award for excellence in damage control/fire protection established by Chief of Naval Ops; elevated to rank of Meritorious Sr. Exec. by Pres. Bush, 1989, Naval Rsch. Lab. Award for Innovation, 1998. Mem. Am. Chem. Soc. (alt. councilor 1954-56), Chem. Soc. Washington (mgr. 1953, mem. com. on rels. and status com. 1954, chmn. budget com. 1957, chmn. edn. com. 1965-66, chmn. long range planning com. 1967-70), Combustion Inst. (charter), U.S. Naval Inst., Naval Submarine League, Surface Navy Assn., Navy League U.S., Phi Kappa Phi, Sigma Xi. Avocations: musical composition, plant hybridization, photography. Office: Naval Rsch Lab Code 6108 Washington DC 20375-0001

CARHART, MARK MONROE, investment company executive; b. Landstuhl, Germany, Feb. 14, 1966; arrived in U.S., 1968; s. Isaac Whitfield and Mary Shigley Carhart; m. Sabrina Michelle Coons, Feb. 7, 1998; 1 child, Adrienne. BA in Econs., Tale, 1988; PhD in Bus. Fin., U. Chgo., 1995. CFA. Analyst Clifford Mgmt., NYC, 1988—91; lectr. Grad. Sch. Bus., U. Chgo., 1991—95; asst. prof. Marshall Sch. Bus., U. So. Calif., LA, 1995—97; v.p. Goldman Sachs Asset Mgmt., NYC, 1997, mng. dir., 1999—, co-head quantitative strategies, 1998—. Sr. fellow Wharton Fin. Instns. Ctr., Phila., 1996—97; mem. inv. com. Mercer Global Advisors, Santa Barbara, Calif., 1996—97; cons. Dimensional Fund Advisors, Santa Monica, Calif., 1994—97. Contbr. articles to profl. jours. Mem.: Western Fin. Assn., Chgo. Quantitative Alliance, Q-Group. Avocations: bicycling, skiing, eating. Office: Goldman Sachs Asset Mgmt 17th Fllor 85 Broad St New York NY 10004 E-mail: mark.carhart@gs.com.

CARIDES, GEORGE WARREN, health economic statistics director; s. Peter and Constance Carides; m. Alexandra Doina Carides, Aug. 18, 1993; 1 child, Aliona Maria. BS in Econs., Coll. NJ, Ewing, 1983; AM in Econs., U. Chgo., 1985; PhD in Stats., Temple U., Phila., 1998. Cons. Merck & Co., Blue Bell, Pa., 1994—98, health econ. stats. North Wales, Pa., 1998—. Mem.: Am. Statis. Assn. (assoc. Student Paper award 1997). Achievements include research in estimation of mean treatment cost in the presence of right-censoring. Office Phone: 267-305-7946.

CARINO, AURORA LAO, psychiatrist, health facility administrator; b. Angeles, Philippines, Jan. 11, 1940; arrived in U.S., 1967; d. Pedro Samson and Hilaria Sanchez (Paras) Lao; m. Rosalito Aldecoa Carino, Dec. 2, 1967; children: Robert, Edwin, Antoinette. AA, U. of the East, Manila, 1961; degree in Medicine, U. of the East, Quezon City, Philippines, 1966. Lic. psychiatrist NY, Va., Conn., Fla.; cert. Am. Bd. Psychiatry and Neurology. Resident in pediat. U. of the East-R.M. Meml. Hosp., Quezon City, 1966-67; rotating intern Stamford Hosp., Conn., 1967-68; resident in psychiatry Norwich Hosp., Conn., 1968-71, staff psychiatrist, 1971-75; staff psychiatrist, unit chief, acting clin. dir. Harlem Valley Psychiat. Ctr., Wingdale, NY, 1975-80; svc. chief Fla. State Hosp., Chattahoochee, 1982-83; unit chief Hudson River Psychiat. Ctr., Poughkeepsie, NY, 1983-89, dep. med. dir., acting clin. dir., 1989-90, asst. to clin. dir., 1990-93, dep. med. dir.-admissions, 1993-97. Cons. Dept. Mental Hygiene, Dutchess County, Poughkeepsie, 1976—. Mem.: Am. Psychiat. Assn. Republican. Roman Catholic. Avocations: gardening, country music, recording/listening to spiritual enhancement. Home: 10 Millbank Rd Poughkeepsie NY 12603-5112 Office Phone: 845-486-3700.

CARIO, JEFFREY PETER, lawyer; b. Patchogue, NY, Sept. 17, 1962; s. Peter and Linda (DeMarsico) C.; m. Lisa Marie Hilbish, June 12, 1988; children: Jeffrey Robert, Alexandra Elizabeth. BS, U. Fla., 1984; JD, Nova U., 1987. Bar: Fla. 1987, Ga. 2006, US Dist. Ct. (mid. dist.) Fla. 1988, US Ct. Appeals (11th cir.) 1991, US Supreme Ct. 1992; family law mediator; bd. cert. family law specialist. Asst. state atty. State Atty.'s Office 5th Jud. Cir., Brooksville, Fla., 1987-89; ptnr. Hogan & Cario, Brooksville, Fla., 1989-90, Hogan, Levine, Unice & Cario, Brooksville/Clearwater, Fla., 1990-92; sole practice Spring Hill, Fla., 1992-95; ptnr. Tew, Zinober, Barnes, Zimmet & Unice, Spring Hill/Clearwater, Fla., 1995-2000; pvt. practice Spring Hill, 2000—. Chmn. Hernando County Rep. Exec. Com., 1990-91; v.p. Hernando County chpt. Am. Heart Assn., 1997—, pres. Hernando/Pasco County divsn., 1999—; dir. Hernando County chpt. St. Jude's Children's Rsch. Hosp., Spring Hill, 1996—, Hernando County Rape Crisis/Spouse Abuse Shelter, Brooksville, 1997—; bd. dir. Hernando County C. of C., BLighthouse for the Blind. Mem. Fla. Bar Assn. (family law divsn.), Hernando County Bar Assn., Inns of Ct., Sons of Italy, Kiwanis. Republican. Roman Catholic. Office: Jeffrey P Cario PA Ste 201 12435 Cortez Blvd Brooksville FL 34613 Business E-Mail: icario1@tampabay.rr.com.

CARIOLA, ROBERT JOSEPH, artist; b. Bklyn., Mar. 24, 1927; Grad., Pratt Inst. Art Sch., 1954; student, Pratt Graphic Ctr., 1958-59. Instr. art La Salle Acad., Oakdale, NY, 1963-65. Instr. creative painting workshop Nat. Art League, Douglaston, Queens, N.Y.; condr. art workshops in mixed media painting Bd. Continuing Edn. One-man shows include Long Beach Mus., NY, 1985, East Meadow Libr. Gallery, 1990, Merrick Symphony Performance Lobby of Hall, 1990, Vatican Pavilion-NY World's Fair, 1964; exhibited in group shows at Boston Mus., 1962, Corcoran Gallery Art, Washington, 1963, Pa. Acad. Fine Arts, Phila., 1963, Nat. Acad. Design, NYC, 1970, Signature Gallery, Va., 1986, Cath. Mus. Arts and Antiquities, Olympic Towers, NYC, 1995-96; represented in permanent collections Landing Gallery, Woodbury, Soundview Gallery, Pt. Jefferson, NY; contbr.: Illustrator Writer's Ann., 1958, Sign Mag., 1971, others; executed murals in Sr. Citizen Ctr., Wantagh, NY, 1989, cmty. Rm. St. Johns Luth. Ch., Merrick, NY, 1992, others; created, installed 4-sided Indian Monument dedicated to Meroke Tribe Indians-1643, Merrick, NY, 1993; painted murals and mosaics in 4 chapels; created metal, wood, and concrete sculptures, faceted stained glass windows St. Johns Cemetery Mausoleum, Queens, NY created 3 large bronze and brass wall sculptures, 2 mosaics and 3 large etched glass windows and doors at St. Raymonds Cemetery Mausoleum, Bronx NY, painted life sized horse casting for Nassau County's Horses of a Different Color fund raising project, installed at Wheatley Plaza in Greenvale, LI, NY 2003, created 4 foot bronze statue of Mother Theresa holding a baby, donated to Our Lady of Lourdes Ch., Massapequa, NY, dedicated June 2004. Recipient Ann. Painting prize Hofstra, 1957, Purchase award Hofstra, 1957, Operation Democracy prize Locust Valley, N.Y., 1958, 1st prize for painting John Kennedy Cultural Ctr. Bankers Trust, 1971, Grumbacher Cash award Silvermine Artists Guild, New Canaan, Conn., 1976, Best in Show award Bayshore C. of C. Art Festival, 1979, 1st prize Long Beach (N.Y.) Mus., 1984; grnatee Tiffany Grants, 1965, 66, N.Y. State Creative Arts Program, 1988, Nassau County, 1989, Wantagh Creative Arts Program, 1992; subject of feature article in Equine Images, fall, 1991. Address: 1844 Gormley Ave Merrick NY 11566-3009 Home Phone: 516-541-4080; Office Phone: 516-378-5379. E-mail: artist@robertcariola.com.

CARIUS, MICHAEL LEE, emergency medicine physician; b. Peoria, Ill., July 5, 1947; s. Marvin W. and Geraldine E. (Rapp) C.; m. Maura Ann Dugan (div. Apr. 1990); m. Kathleen Patricia Cilimberg, Feb. 24, 1996; children: Lauren, Jennifer, Brandon. BS in Biology, Trinity Coll., 1969; MD, U. Colo., 1973. Diplomate Am. Bd. Emergency Medicine, recert., Am. Bd. Family Practice, recert., Nat. Bd. Med. Examiners; lic. physician, Conn.; cert. ACLS instr. and provider, ATLS provider, APLS provider and instr. Rotating intern Naval Regional Med. Ctr., San Diego, 1973-74; resident in emergency medicine dept. emergency medicine U. So. Calif.-L.A. County Med. Ctr., 1981-83; staff emergency physician Middlesex (Conn.) Meml. Hosp., 1983-87, assoc. emergency dept. dir., 1985-87; chmn. dept. emergency medicine St. Vincent's Med. Ctr., Bridgeport, Conn., 1988-94; staff emergency physician Hosp. of St. Raphael, New Haven, Conn., 1994-95; chmn. dept. emergency medicine Norwalk (Conn.) Hosp., 1995—. Assoc. clin. prof. dept. traumatology and emergency medicine U. Conn. Sch. Medicine, Farmington, 1994—. With USN, 1974-77, with USAF, 1977-81. Fellow Am. Coll. Emergency Physicians (bd. dirs. 1996-2004); mem. AMA, Conn. State Med. Soc., Conn. Coll. Emergency Physicians (sec., treas., pres.-elect, pres., bd. dirs. 1984—), Fairfield County Med. Assn. Office: Norwalk Hosp 34 Maple St Norwalk CT 06850 Address: American College of Emergency Physicians 1125 Executive Cir Irving TX 75038-2522

CARIUS, ROBERT WILHELM, mathematics professor, retired military officer; b. Peoria, Ill., Jan. 4, 1929; s. Henry Clarence and Mary Magdalen (Wilhelm) C.; m. Geraldine Mary Sullivan, Mar. 16, 1957; children: Patricia, Mary, Linda, Robert, Daniel, Sara. BS in Naval Sci, U.S. Naval Acad., 1951; BS in Aero. Engring, U.S. Naval Postgrad. Sch., 1958; MS in Nuclear Engring, Iowa State Coll., 1959. Commd. ensign USN, 1951, advanced through grades to rear adm., 1977, served with Fighter Squadron 74, 1953-56, served with U.S.S. Bennington, 1959-61, project mgr. U.S. AEC, 1964-65, served with Air Anti-Submarine Squadron 33, 1962-63, command officer Air Anti-Submarine Squardon 29, 1966-68, exec. officer U.S.S. Princeton, 1968-70, R & D br. head Dept. Navy, 1970-71, command officer U.S.S. New Orleans San Diego, 1971-73, mem. staff Anti-Submarine Wing Pacific, 1973-77, comdr. Anti-Submarine Wings Atlantic, Naval Air Sta. Jacksonville, Fla., 1977-79, with aviation programs Dept. Navy, from 1979; instr. physics Ark. Coll., Batesville, 1983-85, asst. prof. physics, 1986—. Bd. govs. USO, Jacksonville. Mem. exec. bd. United Way of Jacksonville, N.E. Fla. coun. Boy Scouts Am.; pres. Independence County United Way. Decorated Legion of Merit, Air medal, Meritorious Service medal; recipient Spl. award United Way of Jacksonville, 1979 Mem. U.S. Naval Acad. Alumni Assn., Assn. Naval Aviation, Ret. Officers Assn., Ark. Hist. Soc., Batesville Symphony Assn., Naval Helicopter Assn., U.S. Naval Inst., Jacksonville C. of C. (gov.) Clubs: Rotary. Roman Catholic. Home: 2630 Antioch Rd Cave City AR 72521-9249 Office: Lyon Coll Batesville AR 72501 *Personal integrity and honesty to oneself have been key elements in my life's philosophy. Attempting to understand the people you work with and treating them as you prefer to be treated were other essential principles. Lastly, always do your very best in all endeavors, and you never have to look over your shoulder with regret.*

CARL, ALLEN LAURENCE, surgery educator; b. Queens, NY, Apr. 14, 1953; s. O. Edward and Muriel (Lerner) C.; m. Susan A. Ross, Dec. 26, 1981; children: Alissa, Andrew, Scott, Danielle. BA with honors, SUNY, Binghamton, 1975; MD, SUNY, Buffalo, 1979. Diplomate Nat. Bd. Med. Examiners, Am. Bd. Orthopaedic Surgery; lic. surgeon, N.Y. Intern in gen. surgery Albert Einstein Hosp., Bronx, N.Y., 1979-80; resident in orthop. surgery, clin. instr. SUNY, Stony Brook, 1980-81; resident in orthop. surgery Bellevue Hosp., NYC, 1981-85; fellow in spinal surgery Toronto (Ont., Can.) Gen. Hosp., 1985-86; asst. prof. orthop. surgery Albany Med. Coll., 1986-91, assoc. prof. orthop. surgery, 1991-97, prof. orthopedic surgery, 1997—, vice chmn. orthop. surgery, 1993—, assoc. prof. pediat., 1994—. Cons. and presenter in field; mem. N.Y. State Spinal Cord Injury Rev. Bd. Contbr. articles to Head and Neck Surgery, Contemporary Orthops., Foot and Ankle, Spine, Jour. of Bone Joint Surgery Am., Jour. Trauma, Med. Outlook for Orthop. Surgeons, Jour. Orthop. Trauma, Current Opinions in Orthops., Jour. Orthop. Techniques. Fellow ACS, Am. Acad. Orthop. Surgeons, Acad. Pain Mgmt., The Spine Jour., Am. Orthop. Assn.; mem. Am. Spine Injury Assn., Am. Spinal Injury Soc., N.Am. Spine Soc. (mem. prof. and tech. liaison com., mem. subcom. materials and devices), New Eng. Spine Study Group, Ea. Orthop. Assn., Internat. Soc. Minimal Intervention in Spinal Surgery, Scoliosis Rsch. Soc. (mem. instrumentation com., internat. traveling fellow), Acad. Orthop. Soc., Group Internat. Cotrel-Dubousset, Cervical Spine Rsch. Soc Achievements include patents for Dynamized Anterior Vertebral Body Fixation Device (concept and structure), Shape Memory Scoliosis and Limb Implant; patents pending for virtual reality 3-D spinal imaging and implant placement. Office: Albany Med Coll Divsn Orthopaedic Surgery A 61 OR Albany NY 12208 Office Phone: 518-489-2644. Personal E-mail: alcsar@nycop.rr.com.

CARL, ROBERT E., retired marketing company executive; b. Sept. 1, 1927; s. Elmer T. Carl and Marion R. (Pack) C.; m. Linda Arlene Sutton, Aug. 30, 1967; children: Melanie Ruth, Robert Brady, Camber Carlene. BS, U. Kans., 1950; grad. in real estate, So. Meth. U., 1965; cert. in investment analysis, NY Inst. Fin., 1967. V.p. sales promotion Wm. S. Henson, Inc., Dallas, 1951—54; pres., COO Jones-Carl, Inc., Dallas, 1954-62; v.p. mktg. comms. Modern Am. Corp., Dallas, 1962-70; v.p. sales Dunn Properties of Tex., Inc., Dallas, 1970-71; sr. v.p. mktg. svcs. Vantage Cos., Dallas, 1971-84; pres. Mktg. Mgmt. Sys., Dallas, 1984-90; v.p. The Premium Group, Inc., 1990-92; mem. Dallas Cable TV Bd., 1981-83; v.p. mktg. Availent Mortgage Co., 2000—02. Co-founder Liberty Christian HS, Dallas, 1995; co-founder, exec. dir. Prestin Ctr. Assn. Contbr. articles to profl. jours. Dir. comms. Rep. Party Dallas County; precinct chmn. Dallas County Grand Jury, election judge. Recipient Chevalier and Legion of Honor Degrees Internat. Supreme Coun. of Order of De Molay, 1957, Silver Anvil award Pub. Rels. Soc. Am., 1958, Eagle Scout with four palm awards. Mem. Sales and Mktg. Execs. Dallas (pres. 1976-77, Disting. Salesman's award 1954), SW Found. Free Enterprise (pres. 1975-76), Tex. Indsl. Devel. Coun., Nat. Assn. Corp. Real Estate Execs., Sales and Mktg. Execs. Internat. (sr. v.p.), Tex. Econ. Coun., Nat. Assn. Indsl. and Office Parks, Internat. Platform Assn., Dallas Advt. League, U. Kans. Alumni Assn. (life), Big D Toastmasters Club (pres. 1966), Press Club Dallas, Greater Dallas Pachyderm Club (chmn.), Park City Club (bd. govs. 1989-92), Masons (32d degree), Shriners, Dervish Club, Dallas Jr. C. of C. (bd. dir.). Home: 6337B Diamondhead Cir Dallas TX 75225

CARLE, MATT, professional hockey player; b. Anchorage, Sept. 25, 1984; Defenseman U. Denver Pioneers, 2003—06, San Jose Sharks, 2006—. Named NCAA Defenseman of Yr., Inside College Hockey.com; recipient Hobey Baker Meml. Award, 2006. Achievements include being a member of NCAA National Championship Team, U. Denver, 2004, 2005. Avocations: hiking, fishing. Office: San Jose Sharks 525 W Santa Clara St San Jose CA 95113

CARLESIMO, P.J. (PETER J. CARLESIMO), professional basketball coach; b. Scranton, Pa., May 30, 1949; m. Carolyn Carlesimo; children: Kyle, Casey. Grad., Fordham U., 1971. Asst. basketball coach Fordham U., Bronx, N.Y., N.H. Coll., Manchester; mem. staff Wagner Coll., Staten Island, N.Y.; head coach Seton Hall U., South Orange, N.J., 1982-94, Portland Trailblazers, 1994-97, Golden State Warriors, Oakland, Calif., 1997-99; asst. coach San Antonio Spurs, 2002—07; head coach Seattle SuperSonics, 2007—. Head coach USA Basketball Olympic Trials, 1988, World Championships, 1990, Goodwill Games, 1990, World University Games, 1991, Olympic Games, 1992. Office: Seattle SuperSonics Ke-yArena 305 Harrison St Seattle WA 98109*

CARLESON, LENNART A.E. (LENNART AXEL EDVARD CARLESON), mathematics professor; b. Stockholm, Mar. 18, 1928; BSc, MSc, Uppsala U., 1949, PhD, 1950; post-graduate studies, Harvard U., 1950—51; PhD (hon.), U. Helsinki, 1982, U. Paris, 1988, Royal Inst. Tech., Stockholm, 1989. Lectr. Uppsala U., 1950, 1951—54, prof., 1955—93, U. Stockholm, 1954—55; prof., dept. math. UCLA, 1991—, now prof. emeritus, dept. math. Vis. rsch. scientist MIT, 1957, guest prof., 1974—76, Stanford U., 1965—66; mem. Inst. for Advanced Studies, Princeton, NJ, 1961—62; dir. Mittag-Leffler Inst., Stockholm, 1968—84; mem. Salem prize com., 1971—; mem. scientific com. Institut des Hautes Etudes Scientifiques, Paris, 1983—; invited spkr. Internat. Congress Math., 1962, 90, keynote spkr., 66. Editor: Acta Mathmatica, 1956—79. Recipient Leroy Steel prize, Am. Mathematical Soc., 1984, Wolf prize in math., Wolf Found., Israel, 1992. Mem.: Hungarian Acad. Sciences, Finnish Acad. Sciences and Letters, Royal Norwegian Soc. Sciences and Letters, Norwegian Acad. Sciences and Letters (Abel prize 2006), Royal Danish Acad. Sciences and Letters, French Acad. Sciences, Royal Soc., London (Sylvester medal 2003), Russian Acad. Sciences (Lomonosov Gold medal 2002), Am. Acad. Arts & Sciences, Royal Acad. Sciences, Internat. Math. Union (pres. 1978—82), NAS (assoc.). Office: UCLA Math Dept Office MS 6363 Box 951555 Los Angeles CA 90095-1555 Office Phone: 310-825-4701. Business E-Mail: carleson@math.ucla.edu.

CARLETON, DON EDWARD, academic administrator, writer; b. Dallas, Jan. 22, 1947; s. Edward Preston and Wilma Jo (Smith) C.; m. Suzanne Marie Young, Jan. 2, 1974; children: Ian Alexander, Aunna Fleur. BS, U. Houston, 1969, MA, 1974, PhD, 1978. Tchr. Friendswood Ind. Sch. Dist., Tex., 1969-71; teaching fellow U. Houston, 1971-75; research asst. Southwest Ctr. for Urban Research, Houston, 1974-75; dir. Houston Met. Research Ctr., 1975-79, Barker History Ctr., Austin, 1979-91, Ctr. for am. History, U. Tex., Austin, 1991—. Urban adv. editor Handbook of Tex., Austin, 1983—95; sr. lectr. dept. history U. Tex., Austin, 1985—, dept. journalism, 1997—; J.R. Parten chair in Archives Am. History, 1989—; cons. Amon Carter Mus., Ft. Worth, 1983, Birmingham (Ala.) Pub. Libr., 1978, Nat. Archives Romania, 1998, 99, Brooklands New Media, Ltd., England, 2005—06. Editorial bd. Southwestern Hist. Quar., 1980-90; author: Who Shot the Bear?, 1984, Red Scare!, 1985, (Coral Tullis best book award Tex. Hist. Assn. 1986), A Breed So Rare: The Life of J.R. Parten, Liberal Texas Oilman, 1896-1992, 1998 (Tex. Inst. Letters Book award 1998), Being Rapoport: Capitalist With a Conscience, 2002; editor: Focus on America Series, 1999-; oral hist., mem. bd. advs. Pioneers of Television Project, Acad. Television Arts and Scis., L.A., 1998-; contbr. articles to profl. jours. Recipient Presdl. Excellence award, U. Tex., Austin, 1982; grantee, Parten Found., 1982, O'Connor Found., 1982. Fellow: Tex. Inst. Letters, Tex. State Hist. Assn. (grantee 1983); mem.: Philos. Soc. Tex., Headliners Club Austin. Democrat. Avocations: reading, travel. Office: U Tex Ctr Am History ANB Austin TX 78713-7330 Office Phone: 512-495-4684. Business E-Mail: d.carleton@mail.utexas.edu.

CARLETON, JOSEPH GEORGE, JR., lawyer, state legislator; b. Bklyn., July 21, 1945; s. Joseph G. and Ellen (Gabriel) C. AB, Dartmouth Coll., 1969; JD, Boston U., 1972. Atty. Calderwood & Ouellette, Dover, NH, 1972-79; pvt. practice Wells, Maine, 1979-83, 88—; atty., ptnr. Patterson Carleton & Mongue, Wells, 1983-88; mem. Maine Ho. of Reps., Augusta, 1990-98, asst. Rep. leader, 1994-96; commr. Gov.'s Blue Ribbon Commn. on Health, 2000, Maine Health Performance Coun., 2001—02. Chmn. Wells Site Rev. Bd., 1985-86; town meeting moderator Town of Wells, 1983—; mem. adv. bd. York County Tech. Coll., 1996-2003. Sgt. N.H. Air N.G., 1966-74. Mem. Wells C. of C. (pres. 1984), Elks, Masons. Republican. Avocations: golf, history, politics. Home and Office: PO Box 369 Wells ME 04090-0369 E-mail: atty@maine.rr.com.

CARLETON, WILLARD TRACY, retired finance educator; b. Boston, May 3, 1934; s. Frank Nagle and Margaret Lally (Parker) C.; married; children: James, Sarah, Leslie, Julia. AB, Dartmouth Coll., 1956, MBA, 1957, MA (hon.), 1971; MA in Econs., U. Wis., 1961, PhD in Econs., 1962. Assoc. C.F. Rittenhouse & Co., Boston, 1956; mem. labs. staff Bell Telephone Labs., Inc., NYC, 1957-58; teaching asst. econs. dept. U. Wis., 1958-59, research asst., 1959-61; economist Fed. Res. Bank St. Louis, 1961-63; asst. prof. fin. Grad. Sch. Bus. Adminstrn., NYU, 1963-65, assoc. prof., 1965-66; assoc. prof. quantitative methods and managerial econs. Sch. Bus., Northwestern U., 1966-67; assoc. prof. fin. and econs. Amos Tuck Sch. Bus. Adminstrn., Dartmouth Coll., 1967-70, prof. fin. and econs., 1970-73, Leon E. Williams prof. banking and fin., 1973-74; William R. Kenan Jr. prof. bus. adminstrn. U. N.C., Chapel Hill, 1974-84; Karl Eller prof. fin. U. Ariz., Tucson, 1984—99, Donald R. Diamond prof. fin., 1999—2001, prof. fin emeritus, 2001. Author: A Theory of Financial Analysis, 1966, Corporate Finance, 1985; contbr. articles to profl. jours. Trustee Coll. Retirement Equities Fund, NYC, 1980—84, Tchrs. Ins. and Annuity Assn., NYC, 1984—2003, Coll. Retirement Equities Fund, 2003—06. Mem. Fin. Mgmt. Assn. (pres. 1977-78), Western. Fin. Assn. (bd. dir. 1986-89), Am. Fin. Assn. (bd. dir. 1973-75), Am. Econ. Assn., Fin. Economist Roundtable. Episcopalian. Avocations: fishing, reading, music. Home: 4911 E Parade Ground Loop Tucson AZ 85712

CARLEY, GEORGE H., state supreme court justice; b. Jackson, Miss., Sept. 24, 1938; s. George L. Jr. and Dorothy (Holmes) C.; m. Sandra M. Lineberger, 1960; 1 child, George H. Jr. AB, U. Ga., 1960, LLB, 1962. Bar: Ga. 1961. Pvt. practice, Atlanta and Decatur, Ga., 1961-71; ptnr. McCurdy & Candler, Decatur, Ga., 1971-79; also spl. asst. atty. gen. Office. Atty. Gen.; judge Ct. Appeals Ga., 1979-89, chief judge, 1989-91, presiding judge, 1991-93; justice Ga. Supreme Ct., Atlanta, 1993—. Chmn. bd. visitors U. Ga. Law Sch., 1995-96. Past pres. U. Ga. Law Sch. Assn. Coun., 1989-90, active, 1986-91; trustee Ga. Legal History Found., Inc.; active Holy Trinity Episc. Ch., Decatur. Mem. ABA, State Bar Ga., Ga. Bar Found., Lawyers Club Atlanta, Old Warhorse Lawyers Club (pres. 1997-98), Joseph Henry Lumpkin Am. Inn of Ct. (pres. 1994-95), Pythagoras Lodge, Scottish Rite. Office: Ga Supreme Court State Office Annex Bldg 244 Washington St Atlanta GA 30334-9007*

CARLEY, KATHLEEN M., computer scientist, educator; d. Wilber Wray and Birdie Lou Parker; m. Larry Rick Carley, June 30, 1978; children: Cassandra Mariette, Arianna Nichole. PhD, Harvard U., Boston, 1984. Dir. Casos Ctr. Carnegie Mellon U., Pitts., 1998—, prof., 2002—. Panel mem. Nat. Rsch. Coun., Washington, 2005—06. Author: (monograph) Defense Modeling, Simulation, and Analysis: Meeting the Challenge. Grantee IGERT in CASOS, NSF, 1999—2007. Mem.: Am. Sociol. Assn. (pres. sociology sect. 1999—2000, Lifetime Achievement award sociology and computers sect. 2001). Office: Carnegie Mellon Univ 5000 Forbes Ave Wean 1323 Pittsburgh PA 15213 Business E-Mail: kathleen.carley@cs.cmu.edu.

CARLEY, KURT, actor; b. Greenville, Pa., Sept. 26, 1962; s. William Frederick and Eleanor Odessa (Scott) C. BFA in Theater cum laude, Point Park Coll., 1986. Actor Pitts. Playhouse Profl. Co., 1985-86, Portable Theater Co., Pitts., 1986; actor off-Broadway Little Shop of Horrors, NYC, 1986-87; film actor Dominick & Eugene, Monkey Shines, Pitts., 1987. Creature movement specialist (films) Godzilla, 1997, motion capture performer Dungeons & Dragons, Meggiddo-Omega Code II, Underworld, 2003, recurring co-star (TV series) Special Unit 2, motion capture performer Starship Troopers, 1999—2000; actor: (films) Batman: Dead End, 2003, Underworld, 2003, Star Trek: New Voyages, 2004, Skinned Deep, 2004, World's Finest, 2004, Underworld: Evolution, 2006, Lady in the Water, 2006. Mem. Actors Equity Assn., Screen Actors Guild. Clubs: Drama (Pitts.). Personal E-mail: kurtcarley@gmail.com.

CARLILE, JANET LOUISE, artist, educator; b. Denver, Apr. 28, 1942; d. Jessie Crawford and Alice Essie (Williams) Carlile. BFA, Cooper Union, 1966; MFA, Pratt Inst., 1971. Prof. Bklyn. Coll., CUNY, 1971—; prin., owner, dir. Red Mountain Gallery, Ouray, Colo., 2001—. Founder Incline Village (Nev.) Fine Arts Ctr., 1966—68; instr. Sch. Visual Arts, NYC, 1968—70, Printmaking Workshop, NYC, 1971, Scarsdale (N.Y.) Studio Workshop, 1971—73, SUNY-Stony Brook, LI, 1976, Bard Winter Coll., Rhinebeck, NY, 1980; head printmaking, asst. dir. Bklyn. Mus. Art Sch., 1971—77; dir. Bklyn. Coll. Press, 1977—2003; cons. Woodstock (N.Y.) Sch. Art, 1980—84; judge Alpine Artists Show, Ouray, Colo., 1989; judge Landscape Painting Show Woodstock Art Assn., 1995; owner, dir. virtual gallery www.artinouray.com, 2003—. One-woman shows include Blue Mountain Gallery, N.Y.C., 1980, Stetson U., Deland, Fla., 1995, Fairleigh Dickinson Coll., Teaneck, N.J., 1995, exhibited in group shows at Associated Am. Artists Gallery, N.Y., 1971—81, Bklyn. Mus., 1976, Ulster County Artists Show, N.Y. State Coun. Show, 1984, Alpine Artists Show Ouray County, 1987, IRT Bklyn. Mus. Sta., work appears in, Libr. of Congress Collection, Washington. Sec. San Juan Vista Landowners Assn., Ridgway, Colo., 1980—86. Recipient Hirshorn Purchase prize, Soc. Am. Graphic Artists, 1969, Best of Show award, Alpine Artists Show Ouray County, 1987, Creative Incentive award, Rsch. Found., CUNY, 1992—2004, Pollack/Krasner Found. award, 2002—03; fellow, Pratt Inst., Bklyn., 1971; grantee NEA workshop, Colo. Coun. Arts; full scholarship, Cooper Union, N.Y.C., 1962—66. Mem.: Ouray County Arts Assn. (pres. 1991—93). Avocation: Avocations: hiking, backpacking, skiing, yoga, rock climbing.

CARLIN, CLAIR MYRON, lawyer; b. Sharon, Pa., Apr. 20, 1947; s. Charles William and Carolyn L. (Vukasich) C.; children: Eric Richard, Elizabeth Marie, Alexander Myron. BS in Econs., Ohio State U., 1969, JD, 1972. Bar: Ohio 1973, Pa. 1973, U.S. Dist. Ct. (so. dist.) Ohio 1973, U.S. Dist. Ct. (no. dist.) Ohio 1975, U.S. Supreme Ct. 1976, U.S. Ct. Claims, 1983, U.S. Tax Ct. 1985. Staff atty. Ohio Dept. Taxation, Columbus, 1972-73; asst. atty. City of Warren, Ohio, 1973-75; assoc. McLaughlin, DiBlasio & Harshman, Youngstown, Ohio, 1975-80; ptnr. McLaughlin, McNally & Carlin, Youngstown, 1980-98, Carlin & Vasvari, LLC, Poland, Ohio, 1998-2000, Clair M. Carlin, LLC, 2000—. Mem. editl. bd. Ohio Trial mag. Mem. Trumbull County Bicentennial Commn., Ohio, 1976; v.p. Svcs. for the Aging, Trumbull County, 1976-77; mem. Pres.' Club Ohio State U., Polit. Action Com. Maj. Ohio NG, 1972-82. Fellow Ohio State Bar Found.; mem. ATLA (bd. govs. 1996-2002, trustee PAC 1996-98), ABA, Ohio State Bar Assn. (negligence law com. 1991—), Ohio State Bar Coll., Mahoning County Bar Assn. (chmn. legal edn. com. 1985-86, counsel 1986-87, trustee 2000—, pres.-elect 2003-04, pres. 2004—), Ohio Acad. Trial Lawyers (trustee 1988-92, polit. action com. chmn. 1991, exec. com. 1991-97, treas. 1992-93, sec. 1993-94, pres.-elect 1994-95, pres. 1995-96), Mahoning-Trumbull Acad. Trial Lawyers (pres. 1991), Ohio State U. Alumni Assn. (pres. Trumbull County chpt. 1985—), Cath. War Vets. (Ohio state commdr., Vet. of Yr. 1988), Rotary, Million Dollar Advocate Forum. Democrat. Roman Catholic. Home: 8100 Via Billagio Poland OH 44514-5303 Office: Clair M Carlin LLC PO Box 5369 Youngstown OH 44514-0369 Office Phone: 330-707-0377. Business E-Mail: cmc@carlin-law.com.

CARLIN, DAVID H., lawyer; b. NYC, Mar. 18, 1943; AB, Columbia U., 1964; JD, NYU, 1967. Bar: N.Y. 1967. With Hall, Dickler, Lawler, Kent & Friedman, NYC; joined Loeb and Loeb, NYC, 1985, mng. ptnr., NY office, 1992—96, mng. ptnr. LA, 1996—98, co-chmn. NYC, 1998—2002, ptnr., Reed Smith LLP, NYC, 2005—. Frequent lecturer on advertising issues; adjunct prof., grad. program in direct mktg. Mercy Coll. Mem.: Am. Advertising Federation (legal affairs com.). Office: Reed Smith LLP 599 Lexington Ave 29th Fl New York NY 10022 Office Phone: 212-549-0400. Office Fax: 212-521-5450. Business E-Mail: dcarlin@reedsmith.com.

CARLIN, DENNIS J., lawyer; b. Chgo., Aug. 23, 1941; s. Herbert E. and Lillian (Schneider) C.; children: Gregory A., H. David, Stuart B. BBA, U. Wis., 1963; JD, DePaul U., 1967; LLM in Taxation, Georgetown U., 1971. Bar: Ill. 1967; CPA. Auditor Checkers, Simon & Rosner, Chgo., 1963-67; assoc. tax ct. litigation divsn. IRS, Washington, 1967-71; ptnr. Frankel, McKay, Orlikoff, Denten & Kostner, Chgo., 1971-77, Horwood & Carlin, Chgo., 1977-82, Biddle Drinker Gardner Carton (formerly Gardner, Carton & Douglas), Chgo., 1982—; vice-chmn. Gardner, Carton & Douglas, Chgo., 1998—2003. Contbr. articles to profl. jours. Mem. atty. divsn. Jewish United Fund; bd. dirs., exec. com., chmn. Coun. Jewish Elderly. Mem. ABA, Am. Coll. Tax Counsel, Chgo. Bar Assn. (former chmn. fed. tax com.), Nat. Strategy Forum, NYU Inst. Fed. Taxation, DePaul U. Alumni Coun., Am. Israeli C. of C., Twin Orchard Country Club. Avocations: golf, skiing, reading, music, theater. Office: Biddle Drinker Gardner Carton 191 N Wacker Dr Ste 3400 Chicago IL 60606-1698 Office Phone: 312-569-1245. Business E-Mail: dennis.carlin@dbr.com.

CARLIN, DONALD WALTER, retired food products executive, consultant; b. Gary, Ind., Aug. 27, 1934; s. Walter Joseph and Mabel (Ebert) C.; m. Kathleen Susan McCone, Jan. 21, 1961; children: Michael Scott, Karen Mary, Mark Steven. BS in Engring, U. Notre Dame, 1956; LLB, U. Mich., 1959; grad., Advanced Mgmt. Program, Harvard U., 1978. Bar: Ind. 1959, Ill. 1960. Assoc. to ptnr. Soans, Anderson Luedeka & Fitch, Chgo., 1960-72; sr. atty. Kraft Inc., Glenview, Ill., 1972-73, v.p., asst. gen. counsel, 1974-79, sr. v.p., gen. counsel, 1979-81, sr. v.p., gen. counsel, sec., 1981-86, v.p., assoc. gen. counsel, 1986-89; v.p., dep. gen. counsel Kraft Gen. Foods, Northfield, Ill., 1989-92. Bd. visitors Sch. Medicine, U. Calif., Davis, 1990—; bd. dirs. Monterra Homeowners Assn., v.p. bd. dirs. 2004, pres. 2005-07. Mem. ABA (hon.; com. corp. law depts. sect. bus. law), Assn. Gen. Counsel (emeritus), Westmoreland Country Club (bd. dirs. 1989-94, pres. 1993-94), Notre Dame Club (Chgo.), Ironwood Country Club (pres. 2000-03, bd. dirs. 2000-03). Home and Office: 333 Regentwood Rd Northfield IL 60093-2762 also: 73-930 Carriage Tr Palm Desert CA 92260

CARLIN, GEORGE DENIS, comedian, actor; b. NYC, May 12, 1937; m. Brenda Hosbrook, 1961 (dec. May 11, 1997); 1 child, Kelly Radio announcer Sta. KJOE, Shreveport, La., Sta. WEZE, Boston, Sta. KXOL, Ft. Worth, Sta. KDAY, LA. Numerous TV appearances on Merv Griffin Show, Mike Douglas Show, Tonight Show (over 130), numerous other TV variety shows; regular on TV programs, Away We Go, 1967, John Davidson Show, 1966, Shining Time Station, 1992, The George Carlin Show, sitcom on Fox TV, 1994-95; syndicated TV spl. The Real George Carlin, 1973; miniseries Streets of Laredo, 1995; Actor (films) With Six You Get Eggroll, 1968, Car Wash, 1976, Americathon, 1979, Outrageous Fortune, 1987, Justin Case, 1988, Bill & Ted's Excellent Adventure, 1989, Working Trash, 1990, Bill and Ted's Bogus Journey, 1990, Prince of Tides, 1991, Dogma, 1999, Jay and Silent Bob Strike Back, 2001, Scary Movie 3, Happily N'Ever After, 2003, Jersey Girl, 2004, (voice only) Cars, 2006, Happily N'Ever After, 2007; TV specials include Drawing on My Mind, 1985, George Carlin: Playin' with Your Head, 1986, The Envelope, 1986, What Am I Doing In New Jersey?, 1988, Doin' It Again, 1990, Jammin' In New York, 1992, Back In Town, 1996, George's Best Stuff, 1996, George Carlin: 40 Years of Comedy, 1997, You Are All Diseased, 1999, Personal Favorites, 2001, Complaints and Grievances, 2001, Life Is Worth Losing, 2006; albums include Burns & Carlin at the Playboy Club Tonight, 1960, Take-Offs and Put-Ons, 1967, FM & AM, 1972 (Grammy for best comedy recording), Occupation: Foole, 1973, Class Clown, Toledo Window Box, An Evening with Wally Londo Featuring Bill Slaszo, 1975, Indecent Exposure, On the Road, 1977, A Place for My Stuff, 1982, The Carlin Collection, Carlin on Campus, Playin' With Your Head, What Am I Doin' in New Jersey?, Parental Advisory: Explicit Lyrics, Jammin' in New York, 1993 (Grammy for spoken comedy album), The Little David Years: 1971-1977, 2000, Brain Dropping, 2000, (Grammy for spoken comedy album), Napalm & Sillyputty, 2001, (Grammy for spoken comedy album); author Sometimes A Little Brain Damage Can Help, 1983, Brain Droppings, 1997, Napalm and Silly Putty, 2001, When Will Jesus Bring the Pork Chops?, 2004.*

CARLIN, HERBERT J., electrical engineering educator, researcher; b. NYC, May 1, 1917; s. Louis Aaron and Shirley (Salzman) C.; children: Seth Andrew, Elliot Michael; m. Mariann J. Hartmann, June 29, 1975 B.E.E., Columbia Coll., 1938, M.E.E., 1950; PhD in Elec. Engring., Poly. Inst. N.Y., 1947. Engr. Westinghouse Corp., Newark, 1940-45; from asst. to assoc. prof. Poly. Inst. Bklyn., 1945-60, prof., head electrophysics, 1960-66; J. Preston Levis prof. engring. Cornell U., Ithaca, NY, 1966—, dir. elec. engring., 1966-75. Mem. adv. panel Nat. Bur. Standards, Boulder, Colo., 1967-70; mem. rev. com. Lehigh U., Bethlehem, Pa., 1966-74, U. Pa., Phila., 1979-82; vis. prof. Ecole Normale Superieure, Paris, 1964-67, MIT, Boston, 1973-74; vis. scientist Nat. Ctr. for Telecommunications, Issy Les Moulineaux, France, 1979-80; vis. lectr. U. Genoa, Italy, summer 1973, U. London, Dec. 1979, The Technion, Haifa, Israel, Mar. 1980, Tianjin U., China, summer 1982, Univ. Coll., Dublin, Ireland, summer 1983, Polytech. of Turin, Italy, summer 1985, 91, Fed. Polytech., Lausanne, Switzerland, summer 1992. Co-author: Wideband Circuit Design, 1997. Fellow NSF, 1964; recipient Outstanding Achievement award U.S. Air Force, 1965 Fellow IEEE (chmn. profl. group on circuit theory 1955-56, Centennial medal 1985) Home: 3274 Ptarmigan Dr Apt 1B Walnut Creek CA 94595 Business E-Mail: hjc2@cornell.edu.

CARLIN, JOHN WILLIAM, educator, retired governor; b. Salina, Kans., Aug. 3, 1940; s. Jack W. and Hazel L. (Johnson) C.; m. Ramona Hawkinson, 1962 (div. 1980); children: John David, Lisa Marie; m. Lynn Lady, 1997. BS in Agr., Kans. State U., 1962, PhD (hon.), 1987. Farmer, dairyman, Smolan, Kans., 1962-79; mem. Kans. Ho. of Reps., 1971-79, speaker of ho., 1977-79; gov. State of Kans., Topeka, 1979-87; pres. Econ. Devel. Assocs., Inc., 1987-92; partner Carlin & Associates, Topeka, 1989-95; vice-chmn. Midwest Superconductivity, Inc., Lawrence, Kans., 1990-94; partner Clark Publishing, Inc., Topeka, 1991-95; archivist of the U.S. Nat. Archives & Records Admin., Washington, 1995—2005; vis. prof., exec. in residence Kans State U., 2005—. Vis. prof. pub. adminstrn. and internat. trade Wichita State U., 1987-88, Kans. U., 2005—, exec. residence dept. polit. sci., 2005—; chmn. Nat. Govs. Assn., 1984-85, Midwestern Govs. Conf., 1982-83; mem. Biosci. Authority, 2006—; chair Nat. Commn. Industrialized Farm Animal Prodn., 2006—. Democrat. Lutheran.

CARLIN, MARIAN P., secondary school educator; b. NYC, July 7, 1949; d. Gerard Richard and Wanda Priscilla (Duglin) Preville; m. Howard Sandy Carlin, Aug. 9, 1969; children: Jonathan, Jason, Jennifer, Jillian. BS History, Mercy Coll., 1985; MSED, LI U., 1993. Profl. diploma ednl. adminstrn. Long Island U., 2000. Tchr. Lakeland High Sch., Shrub Oak, NY, 1991—2001, CW Stanford Mid. Sch., Hillsborough, NC, 2002—. Tutor Lakeland Sch. Dist., Scrub Oak, 1991—99, pvt. practice, Mohegan Lake, 1991—97. Editor: Substitute Teacher's Handbook, 1997. Mem.: NCMSA, NCAE, NSTA, ASCD. Avocations: mentoring, travel, reading, music, exercise.

CARLIN, PAUL VICTOR, legal association executive; b. McKeesport, Pa., Nov. 11, 1945; BA, Grove City Coll., 1967; JD, Dickinson Law Sch., 1970. Bar: Pa. 1971, D.C. 1978, U.S. Dist. Ct. (we. dist.) Pa. 1971, U.S. Dist. Ct. D.C. 1978, U.S. Supreme Ct. 1979. Asst. atty. gen. Pa. Atty. Gen.'s Office, 1971; exec. dir. Balt. City Bar Assn., 1981—84, Conn. Bar Assn., Rocky Hill, 1984—85, Md. State Bar Assn., Balt., 1985—. Exec. v.p. Pro Bono Resource Ctr., 1990—; asst. sec. treas. Md. Bar Found.; founder Sr. Law Ctr., Phila., 1978, 59th St. Legal Clinic, Phila., 1977. Editor: CCH Government Contracts Reporter, 1972. Named to Hall of Fame, McKeesport, 2005; recipient Legal Excellence award for Advancement of Profl. Competence, Md. Bar Found., 2005. Mem. Am. Soc. Assn. Execs. (devel. com. 1995-97, legal sect. coun. 1997—), Legal Mut. Liability Soc. Md. (charter, bd. dirs.), Phila. Bar Assn. (dir. legal svcs. 1975-77), ABA (standing com. lawyer referral 1977-80, standing com. delivery of legal svcs. com. 1987-89, standing com. assn. com. 1992-96, standing com. on legal assts. 1996-99), D.C. Bar (dir. pub. svc. activities 1977-81), Nat. Assn. Bar Execs. (state del. 1987-89, treas. 1989-91, v.p. 1991, pres. elect 1992, pres. 1993, Bolton award for profl. excellence), Internat. Inst. Law Assn. Chief Execs., Mid.-Atlantic Bar Conf., So. Conf. Bar Pres.'s Office: Md State Bar Assn Inc 520 W Fayette St Baltimore MD 21201-1781 Office Phone: 410-685-7878. Business E-Mail: pcarlin@msba.org.

CARLIN, SYDNEY, state representative; b. Wichita, Kans., Nov. 20, 1944; m. John Carlin; 4 children. BS in Social Sci. City commr. City of Manhattan, Kans., 1993—96, mayor, 1996—97; state rep. Dist. 66, Kans., 2003—. Democrat. Roman Catholic. Office: 521-S State Capitol 300 SW 10th Ave Topeka KS 66612 Office Phone: 785-296-7651. Business E-Mail: carlin@house.state.ks.us.

CARLINER, DAVID, lawyer; b. Washington, Aug. 13, 1918; s. Louis and Cassie (Brooks) C.; m. Miriam Kalter, Jan. 24, 1944 (dec. Aug. 9, 1994); children: Geoffrey Owen, Deborah Joan (Mrs. Robert Remes). Student, Am. U., 1935-36, U. Va., 1936-38, student in law, 1938-40; LLB, Nat. U., 1941. Bar: Va. 1940, D.C. 1946. Atty. JAG Office Army Dept., Washington, 1946; Washington rep. New Coun. Am. Bus., Washington, 1946-48; pvt. practice, 1948-50; ptnr. Wasserman and Carliner, 1950-67; of counsel Chapman Duff and Lenzini, 1968-74; ptnr. Carliner and Gordon, 1974-84, Carliner and Remes, Washington, 1984—. Vis. lectr. Fgn. Svc. Inst., Dept. State, USIA, Harvard U., 1985. Author: Rights of Aliens, 1977; co-author The Rights of Aliens and Refugees, 1990. Nat. bd. dirs. ACLU, 1965-83, gen. counsel, 1976-79; chmn. Internat. Human Rights Law Group, 1978-86, Washington Home Rule Com., 1966-70; co-chmn. D.C. Com. for Re-Orgn. Plan, 1967-68; chmn. Washington chpt., mem. nat. exec. coun. Am. Jewish Com., 1969-71; mem. nat. adv. coun. Amnesty Internat., 1969—; Bd. dirs. Am. Coun. for Nationalities Svcs., 1977-89, Internat. League for Human Rights; trustee Washington Inst. Values in Pub. Policy, 1984-88. With AUS, 1941-45. Recipient Oliver Wendell Holmes award, 1966, Human Rights award Ctr. for Human Rights and Constl. Law, 1994, Isaiah award Am. Jewish Com., 1998. Mem. ABA (chmn. immigration and nationality com. adminstrv. law sect. 1979-83, mem. coun. administrv. law sect. 1983-87, Brookings Instn. coun., Washington 1995—), Fed. Bar Assn. (chmn. com. immigration and naturalization 1961-62), D.C. Bar (vice chmn. opinions com. ethics 1974-76, bd. dir. 1980-83), Va. State Bar, Am. Law Inst., Am. Immigration and Nationalization Lawyers Assn. (Jack Wasserman Meml. award 1994), Cosmos Club (Washington). Office: 1150 Connecticut Ave NW Ste 610 Washington DC 20036-3817 E-mail: dcarliner@remes.com.

CARLINER, GEOFFREY OWEN, economist, director; b. Washington, Sept. 21, 1944; s. David and Miriam (Kalter) C.; m. Astrid Synnove Skrikerud, July 31, 1971; children: Anders Benjamin, Hannah Emily Brooke. AB cum laude, Harvard U., 1966; MA, U. Calif., Berkeley, 1968, PhD, 1972. Rsch. assoc. U. Wis., Madison, 1971-73; asst. prof. U. Western Ont., London, Ont., Canada, 1974-80; sr. staff economist Coun. of Econ. Advisors, Washington, 1980-83, staff dir., 1983-84; exec. dir. Nat. Bur. of Econ. Rsch., Cambridge, Mass., 1984-95; dep. dir. Inst. for Internat. Econs., Washington, 1995-97; prin. Charles River Assocs., Boston, 1997—2001. Vis. asst. prof. U. Calif., Berkeley, 1976-77, vis. prof. Babson Coll., Wellesley, 2001-06, Boston U., 2004-2005, Fletcher Sch., Tufts U., Medford, Mass., 2007—. Co-editor: Politics and Economics in the Eighties, 1991; contbr. articles to profl. jours. Recipient Joint Coun. of Econ. Edn. award, 1976. Mem. Am. Econ. Assn., Boston Com. Fgn. Rels. (exec. dir. 2001—), Boston Econ. Club (exec. com.), Conf. for Rsch. on Income and Wealth (exec. com. 1985-95), Internat. Seminar on Internat. Trade (steering com. 1988-95). Personal E-mail: gcarliner@gmail.com.

CARLINI, JAMES, management consultant; b. Berwyn, Ill., Aug. 27, 1954; s. Harvey Reno and Helen Dorothy (Stan) C.; m. Holly R. Haupin, Sept. 29, 1979. MusB, Roosevelt U., 1976, BS in Computer Sci., 1978; MBA in Mgmt. Info. Systems and Mktg., DePaul U., 1982. Info. systems designer Western Electric div. Bell Labs., Naperville, Ill., 1977-79; software engr. Motorola, Schaumburg, Ill., 1979-81; mgr. Ill. Bell, Chgo., 1981-83; dir. telecommunications and computer hardware cons. Arthur Young & Co., Chgo., 1983-86; pres. Carlini & Assocs., Inc., Hinsdale, Ill., 1986—. Adj. prof. Technol. Inst. Sch. Speech Northwestern U., Evanston, Ill., 1986—, grad. sch. bus. DePaul U., Chgo., 1986-89; dir. Teledata Hong Kong; mem. adv. bd. COMDEX. Editorial adv. bd. mem. Cabling Bus. Mag.; editl. columnist MidwestBusiness.com; contbr. articles to profl. jours. Pres. Mental Health Bd., Berwyn, 1983; village trustee East Dundee, Ill., 2005—; apptd. mem. Fox Valley Cable Commn., East Dundee Liquor Commn., 2007- Recipient Northwestern U. Alumni Prof.'s award, 1995, Disting. Tchg. award Northwestern U., 1996. Mem. Assn. Cabling Profls. (dir. End User Coun., infrastructure cons., cabling facilities integrator, network cabling and applications integrator), Internat. Trade Assn., Data Processing Mgmt. Assn. (bd. dirs. 1988-96, Chgo. chpt. pres. 1994-96, Spkrs. award, Outstand Instrs. award 1993), Intelligent Bldg. Inst. (chmn. definitions com.), DAV (citation 1979), East Dundee Econ. Devel. Commn., Federal Comms. Bar Assn. Roman Catholic. Avocations: yachting, golf. Office: Carlini & Assocs Inc 445 Greenwood Ave Dundee IL 60118-1011 Office Phone: 773-370-1888. Personal E-mail: carlini@carlinij.com.

CARLINO, PETER M., gaming company executive; b. Phila., Pa. m. Marshia Carlino; 4 children. BA, Pa. State Univ., 1969. Positions through pres. Penn Title Ins. Co., 1969—72; pres. Mountainview Thoroughbred Racing Assn., 1972—76, Carlino Fin. Corp., 1976—83; founder, head Carlino Develop. Group, 1983—; chmn., CEO Penn Nat. Gaming Inc., Wyomissing, Pa., 1994—. Bd. dir. Mooring Fin. Corp., Am. Gaming Assn. Bd. dir. Milton S. Hershey Med. Ctr. Named Best Performing CEO, Casino Journal, 2004; recipient Disting. Alumni award, Pa. State Univ., 2003. Office: Penn Nat Gaming Inc Ste 200 825 Berkshire Blvd Reading PA 19610*

CARLISLE, DALE L., lawyer; b. Walla Walla, Wash., Apr. 24, 1935; BA, U. Idaho, 1957; JD, George Washington U. School of Law, 1960. Judge advocate USAF, 1960—63; asst. U.S. atty. Wash. State (western dist.), 1964—66; with Gordon, Thomas, Honeywell, Malanca, Peterson & Daheim PLLC, Tacoma, 1966—; gen. counsel Levitt West, Inc., 1970—73; mng. ptnr. Gordon, Thomas, Honeywell, Malanca, Peterson & Daheim PLLC, Tacoma, 1990—2000, of counsel. Mem.: Wash. State Bar Assn. (pres.-elect 2000—01, pres. 2001—02, bd. govs. 1999—2002). Address: 1201 Pacific Ave Ste 2200 Tacoma WA 98402-4314 Mailing: PO Box 1157 Tacoma WA 98402 Office Phone: 253-620-6401. E-mail: dcarlisle@gth-law.com.

CARLISLE, DOUGLAS R., health facility administrator; Former mgr. fin. Vt. Am. Corp.; former COO Belknap Hardward, Louisville; contr. health care divsn. Humana, Inc., 1986—91, v.p. Fla. region, 1991—97, regional v.p., 1997—99, sr. v.p. market ops., 1999—2002, sr. v.p. Sr. Products, 2002—. Office: Humana Inc 500 W Main St Louisville KY 40202

CARLISLE, ERVIN FREDERICK, university provost, educator; b. Delaware, Ohio, Mar. 20, 1935; s. Ervin Frederick C. and Winnifred (Lucas) Pope; children: Lindy, Rebecca, Ginna, Jana; m. Barbara, Sept. 28, 1973. BA, Ohio Wesleyan U., 1956; MA, Ohio State U., 1957; PhD, Ind. U., 1963. Mem. faculty Ohio U., Athens, 1962-63, DePauw U., Greencastle, Ind., 1963-66; asst. prof. dept. English Mich. State U., East Lansing, 1966-68, assoc. prof., assoc. chmn. dept. English, 1968-72, prof., 1972-79, chmn. dept. English, 1979-81, asst. to pres., 1981-85; provost, exec. v.p. for acad. affairs Miami U., Oxford, Ohio, 1985-89; sr. v.p., provost Va. Poly. Inst. and State U., Blacksburg, 1989-94, William E. Lavery prof., 1995-2000, William E. Lavery prof., sr. v.p. and provost emeritus, 2000—; spl. advisor to minister of higher edn. and the v.p, Zayed U., United Arab Emirates, 2001—. Author: The Uncertain Self, 1973, Loren Eiseley, 1983, Searching for Ervin, 2006; editor: American Poetry and Prose, 1970. Served to 1st lt. USAF, 1957-60. NEH fellow, 1972-73; NEH grantee, 1978, 80 Home: 1227 N Lakeside Dr Lake Worth FL 33460 E-mail: efredcarlisle@bellsouth.net.

CARLISLE, JAMES PATTON, entrepreneur; b. Miami Beach, Fla., May 7, 1946; s. William Olin and Evelyn Obie (Ogden) C.; m. Kirstina Laima Launags; children: Alexandra Ji-Anne, Erika Li, Wendy Laubach, Scott Reidenbach. BA, Auburn U., 1969; MDiv, Emory U., 1976. Ordained to ministry Meth. Ch., 1975. Adminstrv. asst. Radney for Lt. Gov. Ala. campaign, 1969-70; asst. adminstr. Lee County Head Start, Auburn, Ala., 1970-72; assoc. pastor 10th St United Meth. Ch., Atlanta, 1974-76; dir. continuing edn. No. Ga. Ann. Conf. United Meth. Ch., Atlanta, 1975-78; program dir. Ctr. Profl. Devel. in Ministry, Lancaster, Pa., 1978-80; pres. Carlisle Leadership Group, 1989-99, The de Bono Group, 2000—; program master trainer Edward de Bono Thinking Methods, 2000—; pres. The Edward de Bono Grad. Inst., 2007—. Dir. Ctr. for Profl. Devel. in Ministry, Lancaster Theol. Sem., 1980—90; exec. dir. Ctr. for Creative Ch. Leadership, 1990—2004; cons. on devel. of distributorships and trainers in S.Am. to deBono Thinking Sys. global distbr. for Edward de Bono Thinking Methods; distbr. Edward de Bono Thinking Methods, Mex., Argentina, Brazil, Colombia; dir. programs and continuing edn. events; pres. Edward deBono Grad. Inst., 2004—. Contbr. articles to profl. jours. Leader career planning events for clergy Uniting Ch. of Australia, Australia and N.Z.; elder N.Y. Ann. Conf. United Meth. Ch.; bd. dirs. Phila. Human Resources Planning Group; clergy mem. N.Y. Ann. Conf. of United Meth. Ch. Mem. OD Network,Soc. Advancement Continuing Edn. for Ministry, Omicron Delta Kappa. Achievements include first to introduce debono methods to corporations in China. Home and Office: 1722 Niblick Ave Lancaster PA 17602-4826 Office Phone: 717-299-5811. Business E-Mail: jpc@debonogroup.com.

CARLISLE, JAY CHARLES, II, lawyer, educator; b. Washington, Apr. 8, 1942; s. Jay C. and Opal Fiske C.; m. Frances Bell, Nov. 22, 1970 (div.); 1 child, Marie Bell; m. Janessa C. Nisley, June 22, 1984. AB, UCLA, 1965; JD, U. Calif., Davis, 1969; postgrad., Columbia U., 1969-70. Bar: N.Y. 1970, N.Mex. 1972, U.S. Dist. Ct. (so., ea. and we. dists.) N.Y. 1971, U.S. Ct. Appeals (2d cir.) 1975, U.S. Supreme Ct. 1975. Asst. trial counsel ITT, Hartford, 1970-71; assoc. Bigbee, Bryd, Carpenter & Crout, Santa Fe, 1971-73; pvt. practice law, 1973-75; asst. dean faculty of law SUNY, 1975-78; from asst. prof. to prof. of law Pace Univ., White Plains, N.Y., 1978—. Spl. master N.Y. Supreme Ct., 1980—; commr. N.Y. Task Force on Women and Cts., 1984-86; adj. prof. Fordham U., 1987-88, 90-91, N.Y. Law Sch., 1993-2002, Quinnipiac U. Law Sch., 2001-07; referee N.Y. State Commn. on Jud. Conduct, 1999—; bd. editors Weinstein, Korn & Miller, NY Civil Practice, 2004—; pres. Bklyn. chpt. N.Y. Civil Liberties Union, 1987-1988. Contbr. articles to profl. jours. Apptd. chair pub. adv. coun. NY Temp. Commn. on Local Govt. Ethics, 1992-94; mem. Yonkers Police Profl. Stds. Rev. Bd., 1993-95; commr. NY Task Force on Cameras In the Cts., 1996-97; dir. Spl. Needs, Inc., 2002-07; mem. vestryman Christ Episcopal Ch., Hudson, NY, 2004-07. Recipient Harrison Tweed award ABA/Am. Law Inst., Disting. Svc. award Pace Law Alumni, 2007. Fellow: NY Bar Found., Am. Bar Found. (life); mem.: Assn. Bar City N.Y., N.Y. State Bar Assn., Rotary (v.p., pres.-elect, pres., dir. Hudson Chpt., Paul Harris fellow). Republican. Episcopalian. Office: Pace U Sch Law 78 N Broadway White Plains NY 10603-3796 Office Phone: 914-422-4234. Business E-Mail: jcarlisle@law.pace.edu.

CARLISLE, LINDA ELIZABETH, lawyer; b. San Antonio, Dec. 17, 1948; d. Charles and Elizabeth (Chalkley) Herrera; m. Charles Larry Carlisle, Aug. 22, 1969; 1 child, Zachary Charles. BA in Biology, U. Tex., 1970; JD, Cath. U., 1980; MLT, Georgetown U., 1984. Bar: D.C. 1980, U.S. Ct. Appeals (D.C. cir.) 1980, U.S. Tax Ct. 1981, N.Y. 1990. Assoc. Cadwalader, Wickersham & Taft, Washington, 1980-84, ptnr., 1987-91; atty., adv. office tax legislation Dept. Treas., Washington, 1984-85, spl. asst. to asst. sec. tax policy, 1985-87; shareholder McClure, Trotter & Mentz, Washington, 1991-95; ptnr. White & Case, Washington, 1995—. Mem. bd. contbrs. Jour. of Taxation of Investment. Mem. ABA (sect. taxation, fin. transactions com.), Fed. Bar Assn., Am. Law Inst., Bar Assn. Dist. Columbia (tax sect., chair fin. products com.), N.Y. State Bar Assn. (sec. taxation and fin. instruments com.), Internat. Fiscal Assn. Republican. Home: 3215 Newark St NW Washington DC 20008-3346 Office: White & Case LLP 701 13th St NW Washington DC 20005 Office Phone: 202-626-3666.

CARLISLE, RICK (RICHARD PRESTON CARLISLE), former professional basketball coach, retired professional basketball player; b. Ogdensburg, NY, Oct. 27, 1959; m. Donna Carlisle; 1 child, Abigail Claire. Student, U. Maine; BA in Psych., U. Va., 1984. Profl. basketball player Boston Celtics, 1984—87, NY Knicks, 1987—88, NJ Nets, 1989, asst. coach, 1989—94, Portland Trail Blazers, 1994—97, Ind. Pacers, 1997—2000; head coach Detroit Pistons, 2001—03, Ind. Pacers, 2003—07, exec. v.p. basketball ops., 2006—07. Named Coach of Yr., NBA, 2002. Achievements include teams that have ranked no lower than 16th in the league in scoring and have ranked in the top-10 during four of those seasons; won NBA Championship as a member of the Boston Celtics, 1986. Avocations: golf, piano.*

CARLISLE, SHEILA A., judge; b. Michigan City, Ind., Jan. 16, 1963; d. Andrew Thomas Gembala and Beverly Kay Gregory; m. William A. Rogers, Mar. 26, 2004; children: Alexander, Kelsey. BS in Criminal Justice, Ind. U., Bloomington, 1985, JD, 1987. Intern Marion County Prosecutor, Indpls., 1987—88, dep. prosecutor, 1988—90; chief dep. prosecutor Johnson County Prosecutor, Franklin, 1991—95; felony chief prosecutor Marion County Prosecutor, 1996—97, chief trial dep., 1997—2000; judge domestic violence divsn. Marion Superior Ct., 2001—03, judge criminal divsn., 2004—. Bd. trustees Ind. Criminal Justice Inst., Indpls., 2005—06; mem. jury com. Supreme Ct. Adminstrn., 2001—. Mem. adv. bd. Protective Order Project, 2002—; mem. bd. Christian edn. St. Johns United Ch. Christ, Indpls., 2005—06. Recipient Trial Process award, Lawyers Coop. Pub. Co., Bloomington, 1987, Lugar Excellence in Pub. Svc. Series Grad., 2006. Fellow: Ind. Bar Found.; mem.: Indpls. Bar Assn., Nat. Assn. Women Judges. Republican. Office: Marion Superior Ct Criminal Rm #3 W242 City County Bldg Indianapolis IN 46204

CARLOCK, JOHN BRUCE, JR., language educator; b. Pitts., Sept. 21, 1925; s. John Bruce and Sydney Jane (Whiteside) C.; m. Ruth Olive McCardle, Oct. 19, 1948; children: Elizabeth Kehl, Rebecca Riley, John Bruce III, David Matthew (dec.). BA, Wesleyan U., 1951; PhD, U. S.C., 1973. Prof. English, Erskine Coll., Due West, SC, 1973—, chmn. dept. English. Dir. theatre studies Erskine Coll., Due West, 1973-91. Editor: (jour.) Voice of Sanity, 1988—. Bd. dirs. Upstate S.C. chpt. ACLU, Abbeville (S.C.) Opera House, pres., 1995-96. Served USAF, 1943—46, Maj. USAF, 1951—69, Vietnam. Decorated Bronze Star USAF, Air Force Commendation medal. Mem. MLA, Beta Theta Pi. Democrat. Avocations: reading, writing, speaking, orcharding. Home: Burning Tree Farm 247 Arborville Rd Donalds SC 29638 Office: Erskine Coll PO Box 458 Due West SC 29639

CARLOCK, SANDRA LYNN, musician, educator; b. Oklahoma City, Nov. 5, 1944; d. Kenneth Lynn Carlock and Edith Ruth Lavers. MusB, Oberlin Coll. Conservatory, Ohio, 1965; MusM, SUNY, Stony Brook, 1971; postgrad. study, Juilliard Sch. Music, 1965—66. Arthur Judson Disting. Faculty Chair in piano, tchr. by spl. arrangement Settlement Music Sch., Phila., 1970—. Internat. concert pianist, 1989—; lectr., recitalist specializing in piano music of Clara Schumann and Edward MacDowell. Musician: (recs.) Sandra Carlock in Recital, 1999, Piano Music by Edward MacDowell, 2005 (Classical CD of the Week Pick, London Evening Std., 2005, Pianist Recommended Stamp of Approval, Pianist Mag., 2005). Recipient prize, 1st Internat. Emma Feldman Meml. Competition, Phila., 1967, exclusive concert mgmt., Nat. Music League, NYC, 1967. Mem.: Music Tchrs. Nat. Assn., Pi Kappa Lambda. Avocations: reading, photography, travel. Personal E-mail: carlock@voicenet.com.

CARLOTTI, RONALD JOHN, food scientist; b. Martins Ferry, Ohio, Sept. 20, 1942; s. John Peter and Mary Rose (Pilla) C.; m. Eileen Theresa Dorsey, May 17, 1969; children: Lori Ann, Christina Maria, Jennifer Ann, Theresa Maria. Student, Wheeling Jesuit U., W.Va., 1960—63; BS, Ohio State U., 1964; MS, W.Va. U., 1966, PhD, 1970; MM, Aquinas Coll., 1996. Postdoctoral fellow dept. biochemistry U. Iowa, Iowa City, 1971—72, asst. rsch. scientist dept. pediats., 1973—74; corp. nutritionist Kellogg Co., Battle Creek, Mich., 1974—77; mgr. nutrition/basic rsch. Frito Lay divsn. Pepsico, Dallas, 1977—82, prin. scientist new products Frito Lay divsn., 1982—85; sr. rsch. scientist Amway Corp., Ada, Mich., 1985—89; dir. food sci. and tech. Country Home Bakers, Grand Rapids, Mich., 1990—93; pres. Carlotti and Assocs., Grand Rapids, 1994; pres., CEO Natura Inc., Lansing, Mich., 1995—2001; regulatory affairs and devel. specialist Ranir Corp., Grand Rapids, 2002—05. Tech. rep. Snack Food Assn., Crystal City, Va., 1978-82, Grocery Mfrs. Am., Washington, 1975-77; nutritionist Am. Frozen Food Assn., Washington, 1990-93; vis. asst. prof. chemistry Grand Valley State U., Allendale, Mich., 2002; adj. faculty Davenport U., 2004—, Baker Coll., Muskegon, Mich, 2005—, Allen Pk., Mich., 2006—. Contbr. articles to profl. jours. Pres. Mary Immaculate Sch. Bd., Dallas, 1981-83. Recipient Lovable Spud award, Nat. Potato Promotion Bd., Denver, 1981. Mem. Am. Chem. Soc., Am. Assn. Cereal Chemists, Inst. Food Tech. Roman Catholic. Achievements include start-up of new biotechnology-based food and chemical ingredients company, development of patented taste-appealing shelf-stable blend of fruit juice and milk, development of patented antioxidant system protecting food, pharmaceuticals and plastics against air and/or photo-oxidation, development of nutritionally improved (low fat/low calorie) prototype of Tostitos Baked tortilla chips, of high potency dry dog food, of nutritionally improved fruit pies for diabetics, of specially formulated pumpkin pie which will not allow for the growth of pathogenic bacteria innoculated after baking in testing required to verify that the product can be stored at ambient temperature for up to five days; initiation of tech. and regulatory functions for corporate products. Home: 6921 Maplecrest Dr SE Grand Rapids MI 49546-9208

CARLOTTI, STEPHEN JON, lawyer; b. Providence, Apr. 28, 1942; s. Albert Edward and Rose C.; m. Nancy Ann Arnold, Sept. 16, 1961; children: Stephen J., Cristina C. AB, Dartmouth Coll., 1963; LLB, Yale U., 1966. Bar: R.I. 1966, U.S. Ct. Mil. Appeals 1967, U.S. Ct. Appeals (9th cir.) 1969, U.S. Dist. Ct. R.I. 1970, U.S. Supreme Ct. 1972. Assoc. Hinckley, Allen, Salisbury & Parsons, Providence, 1966, 70-72; ptnr. Hinckley, Allen, & Snyder, Providence, 1972-89, 91, mng. ptnr., 1986-89, 92-96; with The Mut. Benefit Life Ins. Co., Newark, 1989-91. Chmn. Town Com., 1975-76; trustee Roger Williams U., 1978-93; chmn. Healthcare Provider Svcs.; dir. R.I. Pub. Expenditures Coun. Capt. JAGC, U.S. Army, 1967-70. Mem. ABA, R.I. Bar Assn., R.I. Country Club (pres.), Univ. Club Republican. Roman Catholic. Avocations: golf, sailing. Office: Hinckley Allen & Snyder 50 Kennedy Plz Ste 1500 Providence RI 02903 Office Phone: 401-274-2000. Business E-Mail: scarlotti@haslaw.com.

CARLOW, KATHLEEN M., lawyer; b. Denver, Aug. 18, 1968; JD, U. Iowa, Iowa City, 1997. Cert.: JAMS, The Resolution Experts (advanced mediation) 2002. ESL instr. Japanese Ministry of Edn., Kuwana, Mie-Ken, Japan, 1990—92; atty. Constantine & Assocs., P.C., Albuquerque, 1998—2000, 2005—; mgr. JAMS, The Resolution Experts, Irvine, Calif., 2001—05. Office: Constantine & Assocs PC 7850 Jefferson NE Ste 140 Albuquerque NM 87109 Office Phone: 505-244-0011. Office Fax: 505-244-0020. Business E-Mail: kcarlow@rt66.com.

CARLOZZI, CATHERINE L., corporate communications consultant, writer; b. Berea, Ohio, July 25, 1953; d. Charles Henry and Carol Louise (Jones) Bader; m. Nicholas Carlozzi, Jan. 4, 1975. BA in English summa cum laude, Denison U., 1975; MA in English with distinction, U. Wis., 1976. Tchg. asst. U. Wis., Madison, 1976-77; editor Visual Edn. Cons., Madison, 1977-78; copywriter advt. Walnut Equipment Leasing, Ardmore, Pa., 1978-79; assoc. nat. dir. publs. Laventhol & Horwath, Phila., 1979-84; sr. assoc., mgr. spl. projects, v.p. Brown Boxenbaum, NYC, 1984-91; prin. Carlozzi Comm. Cons., Cedar Grove, NJ, 1991—. Trustee Montclair, N.J. Art Mus., 1993-2004. Recipient Dir.'s award Montclair Art Mus., 1994, 2000. Mem. N.Y. Women in Comm. (v.p. membership 1999-2002, co-v.p. programs 2002-05, Liz Hoover award 1999), N.Y. Women in Comm. Found. Bd., Phi Beta Kappa. Avocation: sailing. Home and Office: 334 Crestmont Rd Cedar Grove NJ 07009-1908

CARLS, ALICE CATHERINE, history professor; b. Mulhouse, France, June 14, 1950; came to U.S., 1977; d. Victor Adrien Clement and Lise Simone (Ebersolt) Maire; m. Stephen Douglas, June 25, 1977; children: Philip, Elizabeth, Paul. BA, Sorbonne U., Paris, 1970, MA, 1972, PhD, 1976. Asst. prof., polit. sci. Lambuth Coll., Jackson, 1985-88, asst. prof., history, polit. sci., 1988-92; asst. prof. history U. Tenn., Martin, 1992-96, chmn. dept. history, 1997-2000, assoc. prof. history, 1996-2001, prof. history, 2001—05, Tom Elam Disting. prof. history, 2005—, chmn. civil rights conf., 2001—07. Ea. European corr. Ctr. Pub. Justice, Washington, 1981—97, mem. editl. bd., 1998—, World History Connected, 2005—, Poésie Première, 2005—. Author: La Ville Libre de Dantzig en crise ouverte, 1938-1939, 1982; translator (Wladyslaw Grzedzielski): Le Cavalier Polonais, 1991; translator: (Jan Kochanowski) La Vie qu'il faut choisir, 1992; translator: (Jozef Wittlin) La saga du patient fantassin, 2000; translator: (Stephen D. Carls) Louis Loucheur, ingénieur, homme d'Etat, modernisateur de la France 1872-1931, 2003; translator: (Anna Frajlich) Le Vent, à nouveau me cherche, 2003; contbr. articles to profl. jours. Mem. Bicentennial Com., Ad-hoc Bicentennial Com., Jackson, 1987; alt. dir. Ad-hoc Com. Memories Life Bemis Jackson, 1991-92; dir. Ad-hoc Com. Polish Week, Sterling, Kans., 1982. Grantee Herbert Hoover Instn. for War, Revolution and Peace, 1984, Herbert Hoover Pub. Libr. 1979, Deutscher Akademischer Austausch Dienst 1975, French Ministry Fgn. Affairs 1973-75; recipient Internat. Scholar award U. Tenn., Martin, 1999. Cunningham award U. Tenn., Martin, 2002; featured scholar U. Tenn., Martin, 1999, Legacy award U. Tenn., 2004. Mem.: Am. Hist. Assn., Ctr. for Pub. Justice, So. Hist. Assn. (Simpson and Smith awards com. of the European history sect. 2001—, sec.-treas. European history sect. 2002—), Polish Inst. Arts and Sci., Am. Assn. for Advancement of Slavic Studies, Polish-Am. Hist. Assn. (exec. com. 1989—91, mem. editl. bd. 1991—93), UN Assn.-USA, Am. Hist. Assn., Phi Alpha Theta, Pi Delta Phi, Phi Kappa Phi. Presbyterian. E-mail: accarls@utm.edu.

CARLSEN, JAMES CALDWELL, retired musicologist; b. Pasco, Wash., Feb. 11, 1927; s. Theodore N. and Eunice (Caldwell) C.; m. Mary Louisa Baird, May 1, 1949; children: Philip C., Douglas A., Susan A., Kristine L. BA, Whitworth Coll., 1950; MA, U. Wash., 1958; PhD, Northwestern U., 1962. Pub. sch. tchr., Almira, Wash., 1950-53; pub. sch. tchr. Portland, Oreg., 1953-54; mem. faculty Whitworth Coll., 1954-63, U. Conn., 1963-67; prof. music U. Wash., Seattle, 1967-92, head div. systematic musicology, 1968-92, ret., 1992, emeritus prof. music, 1992—. Rsch. assoc. Stäatliches Institut für Musikforschung, West Berlin, Germany, 1973-74; adj. prof. psychology U. Wash., 1979-92; vis. lectr. Instituto Investigaciones Educativas, Buenos Aires, 1981, Ind. U., 1985, Centro de Investigacion en Educacion Musical del Collegium Musicum, Buenos Aires, 1994; vis. scholar U. Bergen, Norway, 1986; disting. vis. prof. music Aichi U. Edn., Japan, 1992; Housewright eminent scholar chair in music Fla. State U., 1998. Author: Melodic Perception, 1965; editor Jour. Research in Music Edn, 1978-81; assoc. editor Psychomusicology, 1980-01; cons. editor Jour. Music Perception and Cognition, Japan, 1998—. Condr. Spokane Symphonic Band, Wash., 1957-60; music dir. Walla Walla Choral Soc., 1997. Served with AUS, 1945-47. Danforth Tchr. Study grantee, 1960-61; grad. fellow Presbyn. Ch., 1961-62; Fulbright-Hays grantee, 1973-74; recipient Soc. Rsch. in Music Edn. Sr. Researcher award, 1994. Mem. AAUP, Music Educators Nat. Conf., Music Edn. rsch. Coun. (past chmn.), Coll. Music Soc., Soc. for Music Perception and Cognition, Internat. Soc. Music Edn. (chmn. rsch. commn. 1976-80), Internat. Soc. Music Edn. Rsch. Commn. Seminars (hon. life), Internat. Soc. Music Edn. (hon. life), Walla Walla Symphony Soc. (bd. dirs. 1997-2003). Home: 845 Fern Ct Walla Walla WA 99362-8857

CARLSEN, MARY BAIRD, clinical psychologist; b. Salt Lake City, Utah, Aug. 31, 1928; d. Jesse Hays and Susannah Amanda (Bragstad) Baird; m. James C. Carlsen, May 1, 1949; children: Philip, Douglas, Susan, Kristine. Student, St. Olaf Coll., 1946-47; BA, Whitworth Coll., 1950; MA, U. Conn., 1967; PhD, U. Wash., 1973. Profl. organist, piano tchr., Wash., Oreg., Ill., Conn., 1949-68; staff counselor Presbyn. Counseling Svc., Seattle, 1976-79; pvt. practice clin. psychologist, marriage therapist, cognitive, devel. psychology, career devel. Seattle, 1978-95; cons. creative aging Walla Walla, 1996—. Chmn. sr. adult adv. coun. Seattle Parks Dept., 1975-76; adv. bd. Northwest Ctr. for Creative Aging, 1995-98; mem. steering com. Quest Learning Inst., Walla Walla, Wash., 1997-2001, mem.

faculty, 1997—; mem. nat. adv. bd. Ctr. for Creative Retirement, Asheville, N.C., 1998-2001. Author: Meaning-Making: Therapeutic Processes in Adult Development, 1988, Creative Aging: A Meaning-Making Perspective, 1991, 2d edit., 1996, Transformational Meaning-Making and the Practices of Career Counseling, 1991; contbr. chpts. to books and articles to profl. jours. Grantee PEO Rsch., 1972, U. Wash. Women's Guidance Ctr., 1972. Mem. AAUW, APA, Am. Soc. Aging, Nat. Coun. on Aging.

CARLSMITH, CHRISTOPHER, history professor; s. J. Merrill and Lyn K. Carlsmith. AB, Stanford U., 1986; MA, U. Va., 1995, PhD, 1999. History dept. chair, head residence The Am. Sch. Switzerland (TASIS), Lugano, 1989—92; instr. U. Va., Charlottesville, 1995—97; history faculty Noble & Greenough Sch., Dedham, Mass., 1999—2000; asst. prof. history dept. U. Mass., Lowell, 2001—06, assoc. prof., 2006—. Contbr. articles to profl. jours., chpts. to books. Steering com. Cmty. Teamwork, Inc., Lowell, 2004—. Recipient History Dept. Tchg. award, U. Mass. Lowell, 2002—03, Exceeding Expectations Faculty award, U. Mass. Lowell Student Govt. Assn., 2003—04; I-HUM Program fellow, Stanford U., 2000—01, Delmos Found. rsch. grantee, 2006. Mem.: Renaisssance Soc. Am., Am. Hist. Assoc., Stanford Club New Eng. (bd. dirs. 2001—05). Office: U Mass History Dept 850 Broadway St Lowell MA 01854-3099 Office Phone: 978-934-4277. Office Fax: 978-934-3023.

CARLSMITH, ROGER SNEDDEN, chemistry and energy conservation researcher; b. NYC, Oct. 2, 1925; s. Leonard Eldon and Hope (Snedden) C.; m. Thelma Kathleen Sutton, July 31, 1954; children: David, Nancy Lynn. AB in Chemistry cum laude, Harvard, 1948; MSCE, MIT, 1960. Rsch. engr. Oak Ridge Nat. Lab., Oak Ridge, Tenn., 1950—62, group leader, 1962—70, sect. mgr., 1970—78, prog. dir. conservation and renewable energy, 1978—94; ret., 1994. Mem. Gov.'s Energy Task Force, Tenn., 1972-74, adv. com. Fed. Power Commn., Washington, 1973; bd. dirs. Am. Coun. Energy Efficient Economy., Washington, Tenn. Citizens Wilderness Planning. Author: (book with others) World Energy Conference Survey of Energy Resourses, 1974. Sgt. USAF, 1943-46. Recipient Sadi Carnot medal for achievements in energy conservation rsch. Dept. Energy, 1996. Mem. AAAS, Sierra Club, The Wilderness Soc. Achievements include research and development of advanced technology for improved energy efficiency, alternative energy sources, environmental impacts of energy, energy and the economy. Home: 1052 W Outer Dr Oak Ridge TN 37830-8641

CARLSON, ARNE HELGE, former governor; b. NYC, Sept. 24, 1934; s. Helge William and Kerstin (Magnusson) C.; children by previous marriage: Arne H. Jr., Anne Davis; m. Susan Shepard, July 12, 1985; 1 child, Jessica Shepard. BA, Williams Coll., 1957; postgrad., U. Minn., 1957-58. Mem. advt. staff Control Data, Bloomington, Minn., 1962-64; councilman Mpls. City Council, 1965-67; ind. businessman Mpls., 1968-69; legislator Minn. Ho. Reps., St. Paul, 1970-78; state auditor State of Minn., St. Paul, 1978-90, gov., 1991-99; chmn. bd. RiverSource Funds, Mpls., 1999—2006, bd. mem., 2006—. Bd. dirs. Minn. Land Exch. Bd., St. Paul, FloMet LLC, Rideau Recog Solutions; trustee Minn. State Bd. Investment, St. Paul, 1979-99. Bd. dirs. Exec. Coun., St. Paul, KidsFirst Scholarship Fund Minn., 1999-2002, Fairview Lakes Regional Health Care, 2002-04; sec. Minn. Housing Fin. Agy., St. Paul, 1979-91; past pres. Pub. Employees Retirement Assn., St. Paul, 1985-88; adv. bd. mem. Nat. Heritage Acad., 2001—; mem. Nat. Gov.'s Assn., Midwest Gov.'s Assn., Great Lakes Govs.; mem. Nat. Ednl. Goals Panel of Nat. Gov.'s Assn. Bush Found. Leadership fellow, 1971; recipient Children's Champion award Minn. Children's Def. Fund, Nat. Audubon Soc. award, Small Bus. Guardian award Nat. Fedn. Ind. Businesses, 1994, Great Blue Heron award N.Am. Waterfront Mgmt. Plan/U.S. Fish & Wildlife Svc., 1995; named Rep. of Yr. Nat. Ripon Soc., 1993; finalist Outstanding Mutual Fund Trustee of Yr., 2004, 06. Republican. Avocations: reading, squash, sports. Office: RiverSource Funds 901 Marquette Ave Ste 2810 Minneapolis MN 55402-3268 Home: 145 Holly Ln N Minneapolis MN 55447 Home Phone: 763-249-0310; Office Phone: 612-330-9284.

CARLSON, BRUCE MARTIN, anatomist; b. Gary, Ind., July 11, 1938; s. Martin E. and Esther (Granquist) C.; m. Jean Ann Hyslop, Aug. 18, 1968; children: Martin, James. BA, Gustavus Adolphus Coll., 1959; MS, Cornell U., 1961; MD, PhD, U. Minn., 1986. Exchange scientist Inst. of Devel. Biology, Moscow, 1965-66; Fulbright fellow Hubrecht (Netherlands) Inst., 1973-74; Joshiah Macy scholar U. Helsinki, Finland, 1981-82; exchange scientist Inst. of Physiology, Prague, Czechoslovakia, 1971; asst. prof. of anatomy to prof. U. Mich., Ann Arbor, 1966—2006, prof. biology, 1979—2006, prof. emeritus, 2006—, chmn. dept. anatomy and cell biology, 1988-2000, rsch. scientist Inst. Gerontology, 1989—2006, dir. Inst. Gerontology, 2000—04. Fellow Fetzer Inst., Kalamazoo, Mich., 1990-96, trustee, 1998—; mem. study sects. NIH, 1986-90, Nat. Bd. Med. Examiners, 1994-96; NIH Fogerty fellow, U. Otago, Dunedin, New Zealand, 1999-00. Author: The Regeneration of Minced Muscles, 1972, Patten's Foundations of Embryology, 1974, 4th edit., 1981, 5th edit., 1988, 6th edit., 1996, Regeneration (in Russian), 1986, Human Embryology and Developmental Biology, 1994, 3d edit., 2004, Principles of Regenerative Biology, 2007, Beneath the Surface, 2007; editor: From Message to Mind, 1988, Regeneration and Transplantation, 1990, others. Recipient Disting. Alumni award Gustavus Adolphus Coll., 1979, Newcomb-Cleveland prize AAAS, 1972, 650th Anniversary medal, Charles U., Prague, silver medal Russian Acad. Nat. Scis., 2004, Henry Gray award Am. Assn. Anatomists, 2004. Fellow: AAAS, Russian Acad. Natural Scis.; mem.: Gerontol. Soc. Am., Internat. Soc. Devel. Biology, Soc. Devel. Biologists, Assn. of Anatomy, Cell Biology and Neurobiology Chairpersons (pres. 1995), Am. Soc. Ichthyologists and Herpetologists, Am. Soc. Zoologists (divsn. chmn. 1987—89), Am. Assn. Clin. Anatomists, Am. Assn. Anatomists (nominating com. 1991, exec. com. 1994, pres. 1997—99). Lutheran. Achievements include invention of techniques of free muscle transplantation. Home: 3838 Curlew Ln Ann Arbor MI 48103-9404 Office: U Mich Inst of Gerontology Ann Arbor MI 48109

CARLSON, BRUCE WILLIAM, diversified holding company executive; BS in Acctg., U. Buffalo, 1969. CPA, N.Y. Mgr. Arthur Andersen & Co., Rochester, N.Y., 1969-77; v.p. fin. Andco Inc., Buffalo, 1977-86; v.p., corp. contr. Delaware North Cos., Inc., Buffalo, 1986—. Mem. AICPA, Beta Gamma Sigma. Office: Delaware North Cos Inc 40 Fountain Plz Buffalo NY 14202 Business E-Mail: bcarlson@dncinc.com.

CARLSON, BURFORD ARLEN, retired military officer, pilot; b. Jamestown, NY, Nov. 27, 1929; s. Stanley Carlson and Violet Imogene Carlson-Hehan; m. Joan Elizabeth Townend, Feb. 25, 1972; children: Brent A., Kristen D., Drew C. Student in Engring. Physics, Cornell U., Ithaca, NY, 1949; MS in Metorology, Naval Postgrad. Sch., Monterey, Calif., 1960. Enlisted USN, 1947, flight tng. Pensacola, Fla., 1949, midshipman, 1950, commd., 1961, advanced through grades to capt., 1971, with naval air transport command Moffat Field, Calif., 1951—53, flight instr. NAAS Whiting Field, 1953—55, mem. airborne early warning squadron NAS Barber's Point, Hawaii, 1955—58, with fleet weather facility NAS Alameda, Calif., 1960—63, meteorologist CVA-43 Coral Sea, 1962—64, commanding officer Fleet Weather Faculty Yokosuka, Jamaica, 1962—67, meteorologist staff operation, 1969—72, commanding officer fleet weather facility Quinsey Point, RI, 1972—74, officer-in-charge naval weather svc. enrivon. detachment, 1974—75; owner, aircraft broker Piper, Beechcraft Aircraft Dealership, Salinas, Calif., 1975—78; bd. mem. Carmel Valley Chapel Thrift Shop, Calif., 1985—. Cmmdg. officer Fleet Weather Facility, Yokosuka, Japan, 1967—69, Quonsey Port, RI, 1972—74; officer in charge Naval Weather Svc. Environ. Detachment, Bensacola, 1975. Bd. mem. Carmel Valley Vintage Airport Com., Calif., 1995—2004; pres., bd. mem. Impact, Pacific Grove, Calif., 1997—. Mem.: Montery County Airport Land Use Commn., Monterey County Elections (inspector 1995—), Carmel Valley Cmty. Youth Ctr. (bd. mem. 1999—). Independent. Unitarian. Avocations: tennis, travel, flying, juggling.

CARLSON, CATHERINE KOSSAN, secondary school educator; b. Freeport, Pa., Oct. 26, 1933; d. Joseph Bill Kossan and Edith Thelma (Robinson) Hill; m. Leonard Merton Carlson, July 2, 1955; children: Sue Ann Carlson Fucilla, Richard Eugene, Laura Jean Carlson Bieritz. BS in Biology, Chemistry, English, Marion Coll., Ind., 1956. Cert. tchr. Ind., Mich., Tex., Conn. Tchr. Roseburg Elem. Sch., Ind., 1957—60, Litchfield Cmty. HS, Mich., 1962—63, Hillsdale Jr. HS, Mich., 1964—67, Bethel Mid. Sch., Conn., 1967—70, Naperville Ctrl. HS, Ill., 1972—79, Richardson Jr. HS, Tex., 1979—82, Parkhill Jr. HS, Dallas, 1982—2005; tchr., secondary sci. specialist Richardson Ind. Sch. Dist., Tex., 2005—07. Presenter in field. Co-author: Holt Science Plus Blue Version, 1987. Leader Girl Scouts U.S.; life mem. PTA; mem. ch. coun., sec. Luth. Ch. Sci. Curriculum fellow, ASCD, 1992—95. Mem.: NEA, Tex. Assn. Biology Tchrs., Richardson Edn. Assn., Sci. Tchrs. Assn. Tex. (pres.), Nat. Sci. Tchrs. Assn. Republican. Avocation: travel. Home: 192 Belmont Ln Van Alstyne TX 75495 Office: Richardson Ind Sch Dist Richardson TX 75080 Personal E-mail: lmckcarl@earthlink.net.

CARLSON, CURTIS EUGENE, orthodontist, periodontist; b. Mar. 30, 1942; m. Dona M. Seely; children: Jennifer Ann, Gina Christine, Erik Alan. BA in Divisional Scis., Augustana Coll., 1965; BDS, DDS, U. Ill., 1969; cert. in periodontics, U. Wash., 1974, cert. in orthodontics, 1976. Dental intern Oak Knoll Navy Hosp., Oakland, Calif., 1969-70; dental officer USN, 1970-72; part-time dentist VA Hosp., Seattle, 1972-73; part-time periodontist Group Health Dental Coop., Seattle, 1973-76, part-time orthodontist, 1976-78; clin. instr. U. Wash., 1976; prin. Bellevue (Wash.) Orthodontic and Periodontic Clinic, 1976—; clin. instr., trainer Luxar Laser Corp., Bothell, Wash., 1992—. Presenter in field. Master of ceremonies Auctioneer Friendship Fair, Augustana Coll., 1965, orientation group leader, 1965, mem. field svcs. com. for high sch.recruitment, 1965; orthodontic advisor Seattle Study Clubs, 2001-. Fellow Am. Coll. Dentists; mem. ADA, Am. Acad. Periodontology, Am. Assn. Orthodontics, Western Soc. Periodontology (bd. dirs. 1984-85, 86, program chmn. 1986, v.p. 1988, pres. elect 1989, pres. 1990), Seattle King County Dental Soc. (grievance, ethics and pub. info. coms.), Wash. State Dental Assn., Wash. State Soc. Periodontists (program chmn., pres. elect 1987, pres. 1988, 89), Wash. Assn. Dental Specialists (com. rep. 1987, 88, 89), Wash. State Orthodontic Soc., Wash. State Soc. Periodontists, Pacific Coast Soc. Orthodontics, Omicron Kappa Upsilon (dental hon. fraternity), Pi Upsilon Gamma (social chmn. 1964, pres. 1965). Home: 16730 Shore Dr NW Seattle WA 98155-5634 Office: Bellevue Orthodontic/ Periodontic Clinic 1248 112th Ave NE Bellevue WA 98004-3712 Home Phone: 206-364-7923; Office Phone: 425-453-1202. E-mail: orthoperio@aol.com.

CARLSON, CURTIS R., electronics research industry executive; b. 1945; BS in Physics, Worcester Polytechnic Inst., 1967; MS, Rutgers U., PhD, 1973; DSc (hon.), Worcester Polytechnic Inst., 2006. Mem. tech. staff RCA Lab. (became Sarnoff Corp. and part of SRI, 1987), Princeton, NJ, 1973-1981; founder, leader high definition TV program Sarnoff Corp. subs. SRI Internat., Princton, NJ, 1981-84; dir. Info. Systems Lab, 1984-90; vp, info. systems Sarnoff Corp., 1990-95; exec. v.p. Sarnoff Corp. subs. SRI Internat., Princton, NJ, 1995-98, head ventures and licensing; pres., CEO SRI Internat., Menlo Park, Calif., 1998—. Co-founder, exec. dir. Nat. Info. Display Lab., 1990; past mem. adv. bd. USAF; past mem. rsch. lab. tech. assessment bd. U.S. Army; active Joint. Civilian Ops. Conf., 1996; vis. disting. scientist, U. Wash., 1998; served on several govt. task forces; cons. and presenter in field. Author 15 U.S. patents in the fields of image quality, image coding and computer vision; co-author (with William Wilmot) Innovation: The Five Disciplines for Creating What Customers Want, 2006 Co-recipient Otto Schade prize for display performance and image quality, Soc. for Info. Display, 2006; recipient Dr. Robert H. Goddard award for profl. achievements, Worcester Polytechnic Inst., 2002. Mem. IEEE, Soc. Motion Picture and TV Engrs., Highlands Group (charter mem.), Sigma Xi, Tau Beta Pi. Avocation: violin. Address: SRI Internat 333 Ravenswood Ave Menlo Park CA 94025 E-mail: inquiry.line@sri.com.

CARLSON, CYNTHIA JOANNE, artist, educator; b. Chgo. d. Ivan Morris and Ruth (Holmes) Carlson. BFA, Sch. Art Inst., Chgo., 1965; MFA, Pratt Inst., Bklyn., 1967. Instr. Phila. Coll. Art., 1967-72, U. Colo., Boulder, 1972-73; asst. prof. painting Phila. Coll. Art., 1973; assoc. prof. Phila Coll. Art., 1979-82; prof. Phila. Coll. Art., 1982-87, Queens Coll., CUNY, 1987—. One-woman shows include Allen Meml. Art Mus., Oberlin, Ohio, 1980, Milw. Art Mus., 1982, Pam Adler Gallery, NYC, 1983, Albright-Knox Art Gallery, Buffalo, 1985, Queens Mus., Flushing, NY, 1990, Charles More Gallery, Phila., 1990—96, AIR Gallery, NYC, 1992, Neuberger Mus., Purchase, NY, 1999, exhibited in group shows at Contemporary Art Ctr., Cin., 1980, Whitney Mus. Art, NYC, 1980, Hayden Art Gallery, MIT, Cambridge, 1981, Jacksonville Art Mus., Fla., 1982, Represented in permanent collections Guggenheim Mus., NYC, Bklyn. Mus. Art, Phila. Mus. Art, Richmond Mus. Fine Arts, Denver Art Mus., Allen Meml. Art Mus., commn., LA Metro Rail Sys., 1992—93, Criminal Justice Ctr., Phila., Dept. Arts and Culture, 1995. Grantee, NEA, 1975, 1978, 1981, 1987, Creative Artists Pub. Svc., 1978. Home: 139 W 19th St New York NY 10011-4105 Office: CUNY Queens Coll Art Dept Klapper # 172 Flushing NY 11367-0904 Personal E-mail: ccarlson607@yahoo.com. Business E-Mail: ccyncyn@earthlink.net.

CARLSON, DALE ARVID, retired dean; b. Aberdeen, Wash., Jan. 10, 1925; s. Edwin C.G. and Anna A. (Anderson) C.; m. Jean M. Stanton, Nov. 11, 1948; children: Dale Ronald, Gail L. Carlson Manahan, Joan M. Carlson Lee, Gwen D. Carlson Lundgren. AA, Grays Harbor Coll., 1947; BSCE, U. Wash., 1950, MSCE, 1951; PhD, U. Wis., 1960. Registered profl. engr., Wash., 1955. Water engr. City of Aberdeen, 1951-55; asst. prof., assoc. prof., prof., chmn. dept. civil engring. U. Wash., Seattle, 1955-76, dean Coll Engring., 1976-80, dean emeritus, 1980—, dir. Valle Scandinavian Exch., 1980—2002; chmn. dept. civil engring. Seattle U., 1983-88, acting dean sci. and engring., 1990, dean sci. and engring., 1990-92. Vis. prof. Tech. U. Denmark, Copenhagen, 1970, Royal Coll. Agr., Uppsala, Sweden, 1976, Uppsala, 78; adv. com., dept. Scandinavian studies U. Wash., 2003—, adv. com. dept. civil and environ. engring., 2006—, adv. com. Valle Scandinavian exch. program, 2006—. Contbr. articles to profl. jours. Exec. bd. Pacific N.W. Synod Luth. Ch. in Am., chmn. fin. com., 1980-84, treas., 1986-87, bd. edn., fin. com. Evang. Luth. Ch. in Am., 1987-91; v.p. Nat. Luth. Campus Ministry, 1988-91; treas. N.W. Washington synod Evang. Luth. Ch. in Am., 1996-2000, mem. synod candidacy com., 2001—; exec. bd. Nordic Heritage Mus., 1981-86; bd. dirs. Hearthstone Retirement Ctrs., 1984-93, Evergreen Safety Coun., 1980-86. With AUS, 1943-45. Named Outstanding Grad. Weatherwax H.S., Aberdeen, 1972, Outstanding Grad. Grays Harbor Coll., 1947; guest of honor Soppeldagene, Trondheim, 1978. Mem. ASCE, Internat. Water Acad., Am. Soc. Engring. Educators, Am. Acad. Environ. Engring., Am. Water Works Assn., Am. Scandinavian Found., Swedish Am. C. of C. (bd. dirs. 1994-99), Norwegian Am. C. of C., Rainier Club, Rotary, Phi Beta Kappa, Sigma Xi, Chi Epsilon. Home: 9235 41st Ave NE Seattle WA 98115-3801 Business E-Mail: dcarlson@engr.washington.edu.

CARLSON, DALE BICK, writer; b. NYC, May 24, 1935; d. Edgar M. and Estelle (Cohen) Bick; children: Daniel, Hannah. BA, Wellesley Coll., 1957. Lic. wildlife rehabilitator. Founder, pres. Bick Pub. House, 1993—. Author young adult books, adult books, Perkins the Brain, 1964, The House of Perkins, 1965, Miss Maloo, 1966, The Brainstormers, 1966, Dracula, 1967, Frankenstein, 1968, The Electronic Teabowl, 1969, Warlord of the Genji, 1970, The Beggar King of China, 1971, The Mountain of Truth, 1972 (Spring Festival Honor book, named Am. Libr. Assn. Notable Book), Good Morning Danny, 1972, Hannah, 1972, The Human Apes, 1973 (named ALA Notable Book), Girls Are Equal Too, 1973;: 2d edit., 2000 (named ALA Notable Book), Baby Needs Shoes, 1974, Triple Boy, 1976, Where's Your Head?, 1971 (Christopher award), The Plant People, 1977, The Wild Heart, 1977, The Shinning Pool, 1979, Lovingsex for Both Sexes, 1979, Boys Have Feelings Too, 1980, Call Me Amanda, 1981, Manners That Matter, 1982, The Frog People, 1982, Charlie the Hero, 1983—85, The Jenny Dean Science Fiction Mysteries, The Mystery of the Shining Children, The Mystery of the Hidden Trap, The Secret of the Third Eye, The James Budd Mysteries, The Mystery of Galaxy Games, The Mystery of Operation Brain, 1985, Miss Mary's Husbands, 1988, Wildlife Care for Birds & Mammals, 1997, Living With Disabilities, 1997, Stop the Pain: Mediations for Teenagers, 1998 (N.Y. Pub. Libr. Best Books, 2000), Confessions of a Brain-Impaired Writer: A Memoir, 1998; Stop the Pain: Adult Meditations, 2000; editor: What Are You Doing With Your Life, 2001, In and Out of Your Mind: Teen Science, Human Bites, 2002 (named Best Book, N.Y. Pub. Libr., 2003), Who Said What? Philosophy Quotes for Teens, 2003 (Voya Honor award, 2003), The Teen Brain Book, 2004 (Book of Yr. Bronze award Foreword Mag., 2004), Talk, Teen Art of Communication, 2006 (Book of Yr. award ForeWord Mag.6, 2007). Mem. Authors League Am., Authors Guild. Address: 307 Neck Rd Madison CT 06443-2755 Office: Agent Hagenbach-Bender 20 Gutenbergstrasse Bern Switzerland Office Phone: 203-245-0073. Business E-Mail: bickpubhse@aol.com.

CARLSON, DAVID BRET, retired lawyer; b. Jamestown, NY, Aug. 16, 1918; s. David Albert and Gertrude (Johnson) C.; m. Jane Tapley, Apr. 12, 1947; children: Christopher Tapley, David Kurt, Nancy Berners-Lee. AB, Brown U., 1940; LL.B., Harvard U., 1947. Bar: N.Y. 1947, U.S. Supreme Ct. 1972. Assoc. Debevoise & Plimpton, NYC, 1947-53, ptnr., 1953-87. Contbr. articles to profl. publs. Mem. ABA, N.Y. State Bar Assn., Bar Assn. City of N.Y. Home: PO Box 32 275 W Falmouth Hwy West Falmouth MA 02574

CARLSON, DAVID EDWARD, journalism educator, journalist, consultant; b. Duluth, Minn., June 25, 1951; s. Carl Alfred Carlson and Frances Rita Gueroult; m. C. Jeanne Reynolds, May 27, 1984; children: Christopher Troy Reynolds, Laura Catherine Reynolds, Kelly Anne Reynolds. BJ, Drake U., 1973. Regional editor Chronicle-Tribune, Marion, Ind., 1973—81; editor The Kingman Daily Miner, Kingman, Ariz., 1984—87, The Albuquerque Tribune, 1987—93, dining critic, 1989—93, The Gainesville Sun, Gainesville, Fla., 1999—; new media columnist Am. Journalism Rev., College Park, Md., 1999—2000; dir., interactive media lab, Coll. Journalism and Comm. U. Fla., Gainesville, 1993—, prof. new media journalism, 2002—. Pres. The Albuquerque (N. Mex.) Press Club, 1991—92; lectr. in field. Contbr. columns to magazines, columns in newspapers. Scoutmaster Boy Scouts of Am., Thoreau, N.Mex., 1983—85; mem. Kirkwood Environ. Improvement Assn., Gainesville, Fla., 1996—98. Recipient Dozens of journalism awards, 1993-present; fellow, The Poynter Inst., 1994, 2004, Am. Press Inst., 1995, 1996; grantee, Russian Ctr. for Cyberjournalism, 1994, 1995, 1996, 1997, The NY Times Co., 1995, 1996, 1997, US Dept. State, 1998, 2003, 2006. Mem.: Am. Soc. Newspaper Editors, Online News Assn., Investigative Reporters and Editors, Soc. Profl. Journalists (mem. exec. com. 1997—, nat. sec.-treas. 2003—04, nat. pres. elect 2004—05, pres. 2005—06), The Albuquerque Press Club. Achievements include development of first journalism-related site on the World Wide Web; first interactive newspaper based on a personal computer. Avocations: cooking, piloting small aircraft, computing, woodworking, sports car racing. Office: U Fla 3219 Weimer Hall Gainesville FL 32611 Home Phone: 352-846-0171; Office Phone: 352-846-0171.

CARLSON, DAVID EMIL, physicist, researcher; b. Weymouth, Mass., Mar. 5, 1942; s. Emil Algot and Anne Alice (Salomaa) C.; m. Mary Ann Lewinski, June, 1966; children: Eric, Darcey. BS in Physics, Rensselaer Poly. Inst., 1963; PhD in Physics, Rutgers U., 1968. Research scientist U.S. Army Nuclear Effects Lab., Edgewood Arsenal, Md., 1968-69; head photovoltaic device research RCA Labs., Princeton, NJ, 1970-83; dep. gen. mgr., dir. research Solarex Thin Film Div., Newtown, Pa., 1983-86, gen. mgr., 1986-88, v.p., 1988-98; chief scientist BP Solar, 1999—. Contbr. articles to profl. jours.; patentee in field. Served to capt. Signal Corps U.S. Army, 1968-70, Vietnam. Decorated Bronze Star medal; recipient Ross Coffin Purdy award Am. Ceramic Soc., 1976, Outstanding Achievement award RCA Labs., 1973, 76, Walton Clark medal Franklin Inst., 1986, Karl W. Boer Solar Energy medal of merit U. Del. and Internat. Solar Energy Soc., 1995. Fellow IEEE (co-recipient Morris N. Liebmann award 1984, William R. Cherry award 1988); mem. Am. Phys. Soc., Am. Vacuum Soc., Sigma Xi. Achievements include inventor amorphous silicon solar cell, 1974. Home: 217 Yorkshire Dr Williamsburg VA 23185-3912 Office: BP Solar 630 Solarex Ct Frederick MD 21703 Office Phone: 301-698-4256. Business E-Mail: dave.carlson@bp.com. *My career in science has resulted from a curiosity about the workings of nature and a desire to use the phenomena and materials of nature to benefit society.*

CARLSON, DAVID HAROLD, library director, dean; b. New Haven, May 27, 1954; s. Harold E. and Marion R. (Bennett) C.; m. Sherry A. Murray, June 5, 1976; children: Karen A., Alison M. BA, U. Conn., 1977; MLS, U. Mich., 1979; MS, U. Evansville, 1983. Bibl. instrn. libr. U. Evansville, Ind., 1979-84; systems analyst libr. U. RI, Kingston, 1984-87; dir. libr. systems U. Louisville, 1987-91; exec. dir. Triangle Rsch. Librs. Network, Chapel Hill, NC, 1991—94; dir. librs. Bridgewater State Coll., Mass., 1994—2001, acting asst. v.p. acad. info. resources Mass., 1995—97; dean libr. affairs So. Ill. U., Carbondale, 2001—. Presenter in field. Contbr. articles to profl. jours. Mem. ALA (Assn. Coll. and Rsch. Librs. 1981—, Libr. and Info. Tech. Assn. 1983—), Electronic Frontier Found. Office: So Ill U Morris Libr 605 Agriculture Dr, Mailcode 6632 Carbondale IL 62901 Office Phone: 618-453-2522. E-mail: dcarlson@lib.siu.edu.*

CARLSON, DESIREE ANICE, pathologist; b. Clinton, Iowa, June 10, 1950; d. Donald Richard and Bernice Elfriede (Jacobs) C. MD, Duke U., 1975. Diplomate in anat. and clin. pathology, blood banking and cytopathology Am. Bd. Pathology. Resident in pathology U. Wash., Seattle, 1975-76, N.E. Deaconess Hosp., Boston, 1976-77, Peter Bent Brigham Hosp., Boston, 1977-79; pathologist W. Roxbury VA Med. Ctr., Boston, 1979-82; med. dir. blood bank Univ. Hosp., Boston, 1982-90; assoc. chief pathology N.E. Meml. Hosp., Stoneham, Mass., 1990-93; chief pathology Brockton (Mass.) Hosp., 1993—, sec., treas. med. staff, 2001—02, v.p. med. staff, 2003—04, pres. med. staff, 2005—07. Asst. prof. pathology Boston U. Sch. Med., 1983—; cons. pathology Brigham and Women's Hosp., Boston, 1984-95; mem. adv. bd. ARC, Dedham, 1982-96. Contbr. chapters to books, articles to profl. jours. Recipient Outstanding Contbd. Article award Med. Lab. Observer, 1988. Mem. Coll. Am. Pathologists (N.E. regional commr. 1991—), Am. Med. Women's Assn., Am. Assn. Blood Banks, Mass. Med. Soc. (coms.), Mass. Pathology Soc., N.E. Pathology Soc. (sec. 1996-98, treas. 1998-2000, pres.-elect 2000-01, pres. 2001-02, joint sponsored activities coord. 2002-04). Republican. Presbyterian. Avocations: dance, aerobics. Office: Brockton Hosp 680 Centre St Brockton MA 02302-3395 Home Phone: 508-785-9082; Office Phone: 508-941-7321. Business E-Mail: dcarlson@brocktonhospital.org.

CARLSON, DEVON MCELVIN, architect, educator; b. Topeka, Dec. 1, 1917; s. Gustave Elvin and Gertrude M. (Swanson) C.; m. Mary E. Ackley, June 14, 1949; children: Mitchell Lans, Martha Sue, Judith Ann, Peter DeVon. BS in Architecture, U. Kans., 1941; BS in Archtl. Engring. with honors, U. Colo., 1947; MS in Architecture, Columbia U., 1949. Mem. faculty U. Colo., 1943-81, prof., chmn. dept. architecture and archtl. engring., 1959-62, dean Sch. Architecture, 1962-70, dean Coll. Environ. Design, 1970-71, dean emeritus, 1981—, mem. steering com. Creative Arts Program, 1959-80. Lectr. civic and profl. groups; past mem. Colo. Bd. Examiners Architects, pres., 1964-65. Co-author: An Approach to Architectural Design, 1950, Architecture/Colorado, 1966; contbr. articles to profl. jours. Past mem. Boulder Landmarks Bd.; advisor emeritus Nat. Trust for Hist. Preservation; mem. Colo. Hist. Preservation Rev. Bd., 1980-84, 85-93. Recipient Stearns award 1972, Disting. Alumnus award U. Kans., 1984; Columbia U. scholar, 1948. Fellow AIA (bd. dirs. Colo. chpt. 1966-67, pres. 1969, nat. scholarship com. chmn. 1977-78, mem. nat. com. on hist. resources 1978—, Silver medal Western Mountain region 1980, Carlson Lecture series established in his honor 1981); mem. Nat. Coun. Archtl. Registration Bds. (exam-devel. com. 1962-76, 87-93, chmn. 1975, editor Handbook 1976), Colo. Soc. Architects (pres. 1980), Assn. Coll. Schs. Architecture, Am. Soc. Engring. Edn. (past chmn. Colo. chpt.), Boulder C. of C., Rocky Mountain Liturg Art Assn., Hist. Boulder, Hist. Denver, Soc. Archtl. Historians, Scarab Club, Triangle Club, Rotary (bd. dirs.), Tau Beta Pi, Delta Phi Delta, Chi Epsilon.

CARLSON, DONALD OTTO, magazine publisher, editor; b. Gary, Ind., Oct. 4, 1926; BA in Journalism, History, English, Ind. U., 1949. Spot news reporter Walla Walla (Wash.) Union Bulletin; mem. staff Inside Mich., Vance Pub. Corp., Chgo.; editor various, Chgo. and NYC; prin., owner CMN Assocs., Inc., Calif., 1964—. Editor (pub.): Automated Builder, 1974—; observed: Automated Builder mags. 40th Anniversary with edit. no. 392, Feb. 2004, —; author: Dictionary/Ency. of Industrialized Housing, 1995—, How to Start an Inner City Housing Plant, 1999—, Shelter All Victims of Emergencies and Disasters, 2000—, How and Why to Buy a Factory Built Home, 2001—. Founder Automated Builders Consortium, 1993, ABC Saved shelter, 1999. Recipient five nat. journalism awards; named Factory-Built Housing's Man of the 20th Century, Allen Newsletter, Indpls., 2000; charter mem. Hall of Fame, Modular Bldg. Inst., 2001. Mem. Soc. Profl. Journalists, Wood Truss Council Am. (hall of fame 1988), Wood Found. Inst. (co-founder 1980). Office Phone: 805-642-9735.

CARLSON, DONNA, art association administrator, director; b. Grand Junction, Colo., Jan. 16, 1936; d. Vincent Grasso and Evalyn Eileen Holley; m. Leslie M. Carlson (div.). BA, U. Denver, 1956; MFA, U. S.D., 1957. Founder theater Thresholds, NYC, 1962—69; dir. adminstrn. Art Dealers Assn. Am., NYC. Mem.: Phi Beta Kappa. Office: Art Dealers Association America 575 Madison Ave New York NY 10022 Office Phone: 212-940-8590. Business E-Mail: adaa@artdealers.org.

CARLSON, EDWARD C., anatomy educator, cell biologist, department chairman; b. Iron Mountain, Mich., Feb. 22, 1942; s. Clarence H. and Rachel O. (Olsen) C.; m. Pam R. Carlson, 1995; children: Scott Edward, Susan Rebecca. BA, Bethel Coll., 1964; PhD, U. N.D., 1970. Spl. instr. dept. biology Bethel Coll., St. Paul, 1964-66; instr. anatomy U. Ariz., Tucson, 1970-72, asst. prof., 1972-77; assoc. prof. human anatomy U. Calif., Davis, 1977-81, prof., 1981—; chmn. dept. anatomy and cell biology U. N.D., Grand Forks, 1981—. Rsch. anatomist Calif. Primate Rsch. Ctr., Davis, 1982-85; co-dir. N.D. Diabetes Ocular Rsch. Ctr., Grand Forks, 1988—. Contbr. articles to profl. jours. Rsch. grantee Juvenile Diabetes Found., Am. Heart Assn., NIH, EPSCOR, NSF. Mem. Am. Assn. Anatomists, Am. Soc. for Investigative Pathology, Am. Soc. Cell Biology, Microcirculatory Soc. Avocations: running, fishing. Office: U ND Dept Anatomy & Cell Biol Grand Forks ND 58202 Home Phone: 701-272-8360; Office Phone: 701-777-2101. Business E-Mail: ecarlson@medicine.nodak.edu.

CARLSON, ERIK B., lawyer; b. 1947; BA, Dartmouth College; JD, George Washington U. Law Sch. Sr. atty. Western Crude Oil Inc.; asst. gen. counsel Davis Oil Co.; sr. v.p., gen. counsel, sec. Duke Energy Field Svcs. (formerly Associated Natural Gas Corp.), 1983—98, TransMontaigne Inc., Denver, 1998—. Office: TransMontaigne Inc 370 17th St Ste 2750 PO Box 5660 Denver CO 80217 Office Phone: 303-626-8265. Office Fax: 303-626-8228. Business E-Mail: ecarlson@transmontaigne.com.*

CARLSON, GEORGE ARTHUR, artist; b. Elmhurst, Ill., July 3, 1940; s. William Emanuel and Mathilda Katherine (Jorgensen) C.; m. Pamela Gustavson Hatzenbiler, May 9, 1981; children: Solon Emil, Andra Sean, Erin Hatzenbiler Vaughan, Eric Hatzenbiler. Student, Am. Acad. Art, Chgo., Art Inst. Chgo., U. Ariz.; DFA (hon.), U. Idaho. Lectr. 1st U.S./Soviet Art Summit, Tretyakov Mus., Moscow, 1989. One man exhbns. include Indpls. Mus. Art, 1979, 85, Smithsonian Inst., Washington, 1982, Southwest Mus., L.A., 1988, Autry Western Heritage Mus., 1993, Gilcrease Mus., Tulsa, 1994, Ft. Worth Zoo Art Gallery, 1995-96, Denver Art Mus., 2007; one man shows include Saks Gallery, Colorado Springs, Colo., 1972, Kennedy Galleries, N.Y.C., 1976, Bishop Galleries, Scottsdale, Ariz., 1977, Stremmel Galleries, Reno, 1978, 81, Grand Cen. Galleries, N.Y.C., 1980, O'Grady Galleries, Chgo., 1977, 83, Gerald Peters Gallery, Santa Fe, N.Mex., 1977, 85, 88, 92, Gerald Peters Gallery, Dallas, 1987, Farber Gallery Fine Arts, Indpls., 1989, Kneeland Gallery, Sun Valley, Idaho, 1990, 93, 94, Fenn Galleries, 1993, The Art Spirit Gallery, 2001, Nicholas Gallery, Billings, Mont., 2002, Matthew -Chase Gallery, Santa Fe, 2002; featured in group exhbns. including Phoenix Art Mus., Denver Art Mus., Denver Natural History Mus., Penrose Library at U. Denver, Gillette Pub. Libr., Wyo., Nat. Acad. We. Art, Oklahoma City, 1973-90, The Peking Exhibit, Beijing, China, 1981, Artists of Am. Show, Denver, 1981-2000, Nat. Sculpture Soc., N.Y.C., 1982-83, 86, 90, Mus. Western Art, Denver, 1985, Gilcrease Mus., Tulsa, 1985, Ft. Smith (Okla.) Art Ctr., 1986, Kyoto (Japan) World Expn. Hist. Cities, 1987, Sonoma County Mus., Santa Rosa, Calif., 1987, We. & Wildlife Mus., Jackson Hole, Wyo., 1988, Amerika Haus, Berlin, 1990, Nat. Acad. Design, N.Y.C., 1990, Hubbard Mus., Riudoso, N.Mex., 1990, Hakone Open-Air Mus.,Tokyo, 1991, Denver 7 Show Nat. Cowboy Hall of Fame, 1992, 93, others; represented in pub. and corp. collections including Indpls. Mus., Genesee Mus., Rochester, N.Y., Denver Pub. Libr., Denver Natural History Mus., L.A. Athletic Club, Cherokee Nat. Hist. Soc., Chakota, Okla., Corning (N.Y.) Mus., Anshutz Collection, Denver, Autry Nat. Mus., L.A., Outdoor Mus. Art, Denver, Rockwell Mus., Pitts., Bank of Am., Las Vegas, Boatmans Bankshare, Inc., St. Louis, Brownsville (Tex.) Nat. Bank, Mountain States Bank, Denver, Rocky Mountain Bank, Denver, Nev. Mus. Art, Reno, Nat. Cowboy and We. Heritage Mus., Oklahoma City, Mobile Oil Corp.; represented in various pvt. corp. and mus. collections, including U.S. Embassy, Copenhagen, Tucson Mus. Art, Manville Corp., Denver, L.A. Athletic Club, Rockwell Internat., others; sculptures include Bill Cosby, 1979, Bill Harrah, 1981, Early Day Miner, Washington Park, Denver, 1980, Of One Heart, Genesee Country Mus., 1982, Of One Heart, Mus. of Outdoor Arts, Englewood, Colo., 1985, I'm the Drum, Bank Am., Las Vegas, 1987, The Greeting, Genesee Mus., 1988, Eiteljorg Mus., 1989, Paul Robeson Cen. State U., Wilberforce, Ohio, 1990, Phylicia Rashad, 1991, I'm the Drum, Colo. Springs Fine Arts Ctr., 1994, Old Blue, Amon Carter Mus., Ft. Worth, 1995, Ennis Cosby, 1997, Mane of Wind-Neck of Thunder, Kirkland, Wash., 1999, Conqueror, Leanin' Tree Mus., Boulder, Colo., 2005, Autry Mus. We. Heritage, 2005, Denver Art Mus., 2007, Colo. Sch. Mines, Golden, 2007; featured in various bibliographies and films. Served with USAR, 1963-69. Recipient gold medal Nat. Acad. Western Art, 1974, 78, 80, 85, 89, Prix de West, 1975, Silver medal, 1976, 81, 88, Robert Lougheed award, 1989, Gold medal, 1989; Merit award We. Rendezvous Show, 1983, Kenneth T. and Eileen Morris Found. award Sculpture, Autry Nat. Mus., 2003, Masters of Am. West award, 2005, John J. Geraghty award, 2005, Gold medal Sculpture, Calif. Art Club, 2003, Mary Bell Grant award, Coors Invitational, 2003 Mem. Nat. Sculpture Soc., Nat. Acad. Western Art (Gold medal 1974, 78, 80, 85, (2) 1989, Best of Show 1975, Silver medal 1976, 81, 88). Address: PO Box 28 Harrison ID 83833-0028

CARLSON, GEORGE CLARENCE, JR., state supreme court justice; b. Greenwood, Miss., May 23, 1946; s. George Clarence and Gusta Christine (Wooley) C.; m. Jane Ivy Russel, July 25, 1970; children George Russel, Meredith Christine. BS in History, Miss. State U., 1969; JD, U. Miss., 1972; grad., Nat. Jud. Coll. U. Nev., Reno, 1982. Bar: Miss. 1972, U.S. Dist. Ct. (no. dist.) Miss. 1972. Practiced law, Panola County, Miss., 1972—82; cir. ct. judge 17th Jud. Dist. Miss., Batesville, 1982—2001; justice Miss. Supreme Ct., 2001—. Sch. bd. atty. S. Panola Sch. Dist., 1972-82; state chmn. Miss. Sch. Bds. Assn. Coun. of Sch. Bd. Attys., 1980-81; mcpl. judge pro tem City of Batesville, 1979-82; atty. 2d ct. dist. Indsl. Devel. Authority, Panola County, 1980-82; mem. Govs'. Criminal Justice Task Force, 1991, Commn. on the Cts. in the 21st Century, 1992-93; vice-chair Miss. Circuit Judges Conference, 1998-99, chair 1999-2000. Elected del. precinct, county, congl. dist. caucuses and to state Dem. conv., 1976. Named Boss of Yr. Panola County Legal Secs. Assn., 1981; elected King Batesville Jr. Aux. Charity Ball, 1985. Fellow Miss. Bar Found.; mem. ABA, Miss. Bar Assn. (bd. dirs. young lawyers divsn. 1975-78), Panola County Bar Assn. (pres. 1975-76), Am. Judges Assn., William C. Keady Am. Inns of Ct. (past pres.). Presbyterian. Avocations: golf, skiing. Office: Miss Supreme Ct PO Box 779 Batesville MS 38606-0779 Home Phone: 662-563-2511. Business E-Mail: jcarlson@mssc.state.ms.us.

CARLSON, GRETCHEN, news correspondent; b. Anoka, Minn. married; 2 children. Grad., Stanford U., 1990; attended, Oxford U. Anchor, polit. reporter WRIC-TV, Richmond, Va., 1990—92; anchor, reporter WCPO-TV, Cinn., 1992—94, WUAB-TV, Cleve., 1995—96, WOIO-TV, Cleve., 1996—98; weekend anchor, reporter KXAS-TV, Dallas, 1998—2000; CBS Newspath correspondent CBS TV, 2000—02, co-anchor Saturday Early Show, 2002—05; anchor Fox News Channel, 2005—, co-host Fox & Friends, 2006—. Nat. celebrity spokesperson March of Dimes. Named Miss Minnesota, 1989, Miss America, 1990; recipient 3 Am. Women in Radio and TV Nat. awards, two Ohio Press Club awards, award for Best Newscast in Ohio, Emmy award, 1994, 1996, First Place citation for pub. svc. reporting, 1997. Office: Fox News Channel 1211 Avenue of the Americas New York NY 10036*

CARLSON, JAMES G., healthcare services executive; Grad., Rider Univ. Mgmt. positions through pres. we. group ops. Prudential Ins. Co.; CEO Workscape Inc.; exec. v.p., pres. United Healthcare UnitedHealth Group Inc.; pres., COO AMERIGROUP Corp., Va. Beach, Va., 2003—07, pres., CEO, 2007—. Bd. dir. Nat. Kidney Found.; bd. mem. Va. Aquarium & Marine Sci. Ctr., Va. Beach Neptune Festival; mem. health sector adv. bd. Fuqua Sch. Bus. Duke Univ. Office: Amerigroup Corp 4425 Corp Ln Virginia Beach VA 23462*

CARLSON, JANET FRANCES, psychologist, educator; b. Newport, RI, Oct. 3, 1957; d. Robert Carl and Alice Marion (Orina) Carlson; m. Kurt Francis Geisinger, Sept. 22, 1984. BS summa cum laude, Union Coll., Schenectady, 1979; MA in Clin. Psychology, Fordham U., 1982, PhD in Clin. Psychology, 1987. Lic. psychologist NY and Tex., cert. sch. psychologist NY. Clin. psychology intern Conn. Valley Hosp., Middletown, Conn., 1983-84; rsch. fellow Schering-Plough Found., Bronx, NY, 1984-85; psychologist I Creedmoor Psychiat. Ctr., Queens Village, NY, 1985-86; psychologist Hallen Sch., Mamaroneck, NY, 1986-88; asst. prof. psychology Fordham U., Bronx, NY, 1988-89; asst. prof. sch. and applied psychology Fairfield (Conn.) U., 1989-93, dir. sch. and applied psychology programs, 1989-90; from asst. prof. counseling and psychol. svcs. to prof. SUNY, Oswego, 1993—2002, assoc. dean Sch. Edn., 1998-2001; prof. psychology, head dept. gen. academics Tex. A&M U., Galveston, 2002—06. Cons. N.Y.C. Bd. Edn. Office Rsch., Evaluation and Assessment, 1988—92; vis. asst. prof. psychol. LeMoyne Coll., Syracuse, NY, 1992—93; dir. Office Tchg. Resources in Psychol., 2001—; vis. prof. ednl. psychology and psychology U. Nebr., Lincoln, 2006—. Recipient Sugarfree scholarship, 1984—85; grantee Sigma Xi, 1984—85. Fellow: APA; mem.: NASP, NY Assn. Sch. Psychologists, Northeastern Ednl. Rsch. Assn. (ed newsletter 1988—91, bd dirs. 1990—93, pres. 1995—96), Am. Ednl. Rsch. Assn., Sigma Xi, Psi Chi, Phi Kappa Phi (pres. 1995—96). Avocations: wildlife preservation, conservation issues.

CARLSON, JEANNIE ANN, writer; b. Bklyn., Jan. 13, 1955; d. Lloyd Arthur and Ruth Frances (Riley) C.; m. Kenneth D. Williams, May 15, 1976 (div. 1981); 1 child, Carl Philip; m. H. Daniel Hopkins, Dec. 16, 1987 (div. 1994); m. Timothy R. Burns, Mar. 21, 1998. BA, Randolph-Macon Woman's Coll., 1977. Mktg./editing rep. Harris Pub., White Plains, NY, 1982; adminstrv. asst. Ray Fried Assocs., Inc., Eastchester, NY, 1980—84; proofreader Nat. Pennysaver, Elmsford, NY, 1983—84; chief writer Profl. Resume and Writing Svc., St. Petersburg, Fla., 1984—87; exec. writer, pres. Viking Comm., Inc., 1987—98; v.p. comm. Technifax Svcs. Inc., St. Petersburg, 1998—2001, exec. v.p., 2001—04; dir. comm. Nat. Risk Svcs. Inc., St. Petersburg, 2004—07. Staff corr. Tampa Bay Newspapers Inc., Largo, 1998—; feature writer Asbury News, Crestwood, NY, 1983-84; editl. asst. Children's Rights Am., Largo, 1984; pub. rels. coord. The Renaissance Cultural Ctr., Clearwater, Fla., 1985; com. mem. work area on commn. Pasadena Cmty. Ch., St. Petersburg, 1986-88, 2000—, Christian edn. bd. Our Savior Luth. Ch., St. Petersburg, 1991-93; editl. advisor Grief Recovery Ctrs., Fla., 1992; columnist Believer's Bay Online mag., St. Petersburg, 2000-02 Recipient Golden Poet award World of Poetry, 1985, 88, 89, 91, 92, Silver Poet award, 1986, 90, Merit award, 1983 (2), 85, 87, 88 (2). 91, 92, Recognition award Nat. Soc. Poets, 1979, poetry awards Internat. Publs., 1976-77, Editor's Choice award Nat. Libr. Poetry, 1994, Woman of Yr. award ABI, 1995, 96, 97 Mem. Nat. League Am. Pen Women, Profl. Assn. Resume Writers, Phi Beta Gamma Methodist. Avocations: theater, culinary arts, music. Office: Nat Risk Svcs Inc 6170 Central Ave Ste 100 Saint Petersburg FL 33707

CARLSON, JENNIE PEASLACK, bank executive; b. Ft. Thomas, Ky., June 11, 1960; d. Roland A. and Shirley (Willen) Peaslack; m. Charles I. Michaels, Aug. 13, 1983 (div. May 1989); m. Richard A. Carlson, May 2, 1992. BA in English, Centre Coll., 1982; JD, Vanderbilt U., 1985. Bar: Ohio 1985, Minn. 2002. Atty. Taft, Stettinius & Hollister, Cin., 1985-91; sr. v.p., dep. gen. counsel Star Banc Corp., Cin., 1991—95; gen. counsel Star Bank Corp., Firstar Corp, 1995—2001; dep. gen. counsel U.S. Bancorp, 2001, exec. v.p., human resources Mpls., 2002—. Office: US Bancorp US Bancorp Ctr 800 Nicollet Mall Minneapolis MN 55402 Office Phone: 612-303-7699. E-mail: jennie.carlson@usbank.com.

CARLSON, JON GORDON, lawyer; b. Wakefield, Mich., June 25, 1943; s. John Edwin and Irene Anne (Erickson) C.; m. Jane McCann, June 17, 1965; children: Christine, Eric, Susan. BA, U. Ill., 1965, JD, 1967. Bar: Ill. 1967, Mo. 1990. Assoc. Edward F. O'Malley, East St. Louis, Ill., 1967-68, Kassly, Weihl & Bone, Belleville, Ill., 1968-70; ptnr. Kassly, Weihl, Bone, Becker & Carlson, Belleville, 1970-78, Chapman & Carlson, Ill., 1978-84, Talbert, Carlson & Mallon, Ill., 1985-86, Carlson & Alfeld, Edwardsville, Ill., 1986-87; prin. Jon G. Carlson & Assocs., P.C., Edwardsville, Ill., 1987-94, Carlson, Wendler & Assocs., P.C., Edwardsville, Ill., 1994-99, St. Louis, 1996-99, Carlson & Carlson, P.C., 1999—. Finalist Trial Lawyer of the Yr., Trial Lawyers for Pub. Justice, 1998. Fellow Am. Bar Found.; mem. ATLA, Ill. Trial Lawyers Assn. (pres. 1987-88, Leonard Ring Lifetime Achievement award 2004), Mo. Trial Lawyers Assn. Ill. Bar Assn., Mo. Bar Assn. Democrat. Avocations: flying, walking, hiking. Office: 90 Edwardsville Profl Park PO Box 527 Edwardsville IL 62025-0527 Home Phone: 618-659-2389; Office Phone: 618-656-0066. E-mail: jcarl568@yahoo.com.

CARLSON, KATHLEEN BUSSART, law librarian; b. Charlotte, NC, June 25, 1956; d. Dean Allyn and Joan (Parlette) Bussart; m. Gerald Mark Carlson, Aug. 15, 1987. BA in Polit. Sci., Ohio State U., 1977; JD, Capital U., 1980; MA in Libr. and Info. Sci., U. Iowa, 1986. Bar: Ohio (inactive) 1980. Editor Lawyers Coop. Pub. Co., Rochester, NY, 1980-83; asst. state law libr. State of Wyo., Cheyenne, 1987-88, state law libr., 1988—. 2d v.p., bd. dirs. Wyo. coun. Girl Scouts US, Casper, 1990—92, 1st v.p., bd. dirs., 1993—96; bd. adjustment City of Cheyenne, 2001—07, chair, 2006—07. Mem.: Bibliog. Ctr. Rsch. (trustee 1991—95), Wyo. Libr. Assn. (sec. acad. and spl. librs. sect. 1990—92, pres. 1994—95), Western Pacific Assn. Law Librs. (pres. 1996—97, 2003—04), Am. Assn. Law Librs. (mem. edn. com. state and county librs. sect. 1991—92, sec.-treas. 1992—95, mem. indexing legal periodical lit. adv. com. 1993—96, chair 1994—96, mem. scholarship com. 1996—98, chair grants com. 1997—98, mem. nominating com. 1998—99, mem. citatition format com. 1998—2000, co-chair membership com., chair edn. com. 2000—01, mem. fair bus. practices com. 2000—04, mem. citatition format com. 2007—, exec. bd. 2003—06), Zonta (pres. local club 2002—03), Beta Phi Mu, Kappa Delta. Avocations: arts and crafts, baking, travel. Home: 911 E 18th St Cheyenne WY 82001-4722 Office: State Law Libr 2301 Capitol Ave Cheyenne WY 82002-0001 Home Phone: 307-635-5324; Office Phone: 307-777-7509. Business E-Mail: kcarlson@courts.state.wy.us.

CARLSON, LAWRENCE ARVID, retired English language educator, real estate agent; b. San Diego, Dec. 29, 1935; s. Arvid Fritiof and Ruth Mathilda (Hedman) C.; m. Patricia Catherine Barlow, Sept. 8, 1963; children: Lawrence Stephen, Janine Catherine. BA in History, Roanoke Coll., 1957; MS in Edn., S.D. State U., 1962; MA in English, Calif. State U., Fullerton, 1966; grad., Realtor Inst., 2002. Cert. e-PRO Internet Profl. Tchr. Edison Jr. H.S., LA, 1962—63, Anaheim H.S., Calif., 1963—66; prof. English Orange Coast Coll., Costa Mesa, Calif., 1966—2001; ret., 2001; instr. karate Orange Coast Coll., Costa Mesa, 1984—95. Sales assoc. Real Estate Offices, San Juan Capistrano, Calif., 1994—. Host, writer (ednl. TV show) Creative Writers Viewpoint, 1975. Horseback riding tour leader Rock Creek Pack Sta., Bishop, Calif., 1990-95; leader 4-H, Orange County, Calif., 1983-93; vol. Liberty Walk, Dana Point, Calif., 1997. Maj. USMCR, 1957-67. Recipient Excellence award Nat. Inst. Staff Orgnl. Devel., 1993, President's Club award, Re/Max of Calif. and Hawaii, 2003, 05. Mem. Nat. Assn. Realtors, Calif. Assn. Realtors, Orange County Assn. Realtors, Faculty Assn. Calif. C.C.'s, San Juan Capistrano C. of C. Democrat. Lutheran. Avocations: horseback riding, Karate, surfing. Office: Ste A-102 32241 Camino Capistrano San Juan Capistrano CA 92675 Mailing: PO Box 1266 San Juan Capistrano CA 92693 Office Phone: 949-487-6567. Personal E-mail: ranchcarlson@earthlink.net. Business E-Mail: carlsons@larandpat.com.

CARLSON, LEROY THEODORE, JR., telecommunications industry executive; b. 1946; AB, Harvard U., 1968, MBA, 1971. Fin. analyst, mgr. fin. analysis and planning, mgr. acctg. Singer Corp., 1971-74; v.p. Telephone and Data Systems, Inc., 1974-78, exec. v.p., 1978-81, pres., 1981-86, pres., CEO, 1981—; chmn. bd. Am. Paging Sys., Inc., 1998. Chmn. bd. Am. Paging, Inc., TDS Telecomm., U.S. Cellular Corp., Am. Portable Telecom. Mem. U.S. Telephone Assn. (bd. dirs.), Nat. Rural Telecom. Assn. (bd. dirs.). Office: Telephone & Data Sys Inc 30 N La Salle St Ste 4000 Chicago IL 60602-2587*

CARLSON, MARVIN ALBERT, theater educator; b. Wichita, Kans., Sept. 15, 1935; s. Roy Edward and Gladys (Nelson) C.; m. Patricia Alene McElroy, Aug. 20, 1960; children— Geoffrey, Richard. BS, U. Kans., 1957, MA, 1959; PhD, Cornell U., 1961; Doctorate (hon.), U. Athens, 2005. Instr. speech and drama Cornell U., Ithaca, NY, 1961-62, asst. prof., 1962-66, assoc. prof. theatre arts, 1966-73, prof., 1973-79, chmn. dept., 1966-68, 73-78; dir. Cornell U. (Univ. Theatre), 1963-64, 65-66; prof. theatre and drama Ind. U., Bloomington, 1979-86, prof. comparative lit., 1984-86, disting. prof., 1986—; exec. officer PhD program in theatre Grad. Ctr. CUNY, 1986-95; Sidney E. Cohn chair in theatre CUNY, 1988—. Walker-Ames lectr. U. Wash., 1994. Author: Andre Antoine's Memories of the Theatre-Libre, 1964, The Theatre of the French Revolution, 1966, The French Stage in the Nineteenth Century, 1972, The German Stage in the Nineteenth Century, 1972, Goethe and the Weimar Theatre, 1978, The Italian Stage from Goldoni to D'Annunzio, 1981, Theories of the Theatre, 1984, The Italian Shakespearians, 1985, Places of Performance, 1989, Theatre Semiotics, 1990, Deathtraps, 1993, Performance, 1996, Voltaire and the Theatre of the Eighteenth Century, 1998, The Haunted Stage, 2001, The Arab Oedipus, 2005, Speaking n Tongues, 2006. Recipient George Jean Nathan award, 1994, ATHE Career Achievement award, 1995, Calloway prize, 2001; Guggenheim fellow, 1968, Ind. U. Soc. for Humanities fellow, 1993. Mem. Am. Soc. Theatre Rsch. (Outstanding Achievement award 2000), Internat. Assn. Theatre Critics, Am. Theatre in Higher Edn., Internat. Fedn. Theatre Rsch., Nat. Theatre Conf. Home: 20 E 35th St New York NY 10016 Office: CUNY Grad Grad Ctr Program in Theatre 365 Fifth Ave New York NY 10016-4334 Office Phone: 212-817-8877. Business E-Mail: mcarlson@gc.cuny.edu.

CARLSON, NATALIE TRAYLOR, publisher; b. St. Paul, Feb. 15, 1938; d. Howard Ripley and Maxine Smith; m. James S. Carlson, Oct. 6, 1990; children: Drew Michael, Dacia Lyn, Dana Ann. BA with honors, Jacksonville State U., Ala., 1975. Dir. Madison County Assn. of Mental Health, Huntsville, Ala., 1966-67; campaign mgr. U.S. Senatorial Race, No. Ala., 1968; pub. rels. Ingraham Acad., 1970-76; journalist The Anniston Star, 1970-74, The Birmingham News, 1972-76; dir. Ala. affiliate, Am. Heart Assn., Birmingham, 1976-77; mgr. San Vincent New Home div., San Diego County Estates Realty, 1978-79; dir. sales Blake Pub. Co., San Diego, 1980-86; CEO, owner Century Publ., San Diego, 1986—. Alternate del. at large Rep. Nat. Conv., San Francisco, 1964; fin. chmn. Madison County Rep. Exec. Com., Huntsville, Ala., 1966-69; pres. Madison County Rep. Women, Huntsville, 1967, 68; Diocesan Conv. del. Grace Anglican Ch., Ala., 1975; active Nat. Rep. Party, 1962—; mem. St. James Anglican Ch., Newport Beach, 1990—, mem. scholarship com., mem. welcomer's com.; mem. Nat. Rep. Pres.'s Club, 1996-97, 2000, 2001, 04. Recipient 1st Pl. AP Newswriting award, 1971, 72, 73, 1st place So. Heart Assn. Profl. Staff award for profl. paper Am. Heart Assn., 1977; nominee Outstanding Woman of Yr., Huntsville Area Jaycees, 1967. Mem. Am. C. of C. (56 Award for Comm. Excellence, 2000-07), Palm Springs C. of C. (Spl. Svc. plaque), Glendale C. of C., Huntington Beach C. of C. (Nat. Athena award 2004), Redding C. of C., Santa Clarita Valley C. of C., Santa Rosa C. of C., Walnut Creek C. of C., Newport Beach C. of C., Yuma County C. of C., Greater Redding C. of C., Visalia C. of C., Ariz, Soroptimist Internat. (rec. sec. Huntington Beach 2001, co-chair charity holiday gala, 1998), Kappa Kappa Gamma. Avocations: reading, travel. Office Phone: 858-486-7700.

CARLSON, NORMAN A., retired federal agency administrator; b. Sioux City, Iowa, Aug. 10, 1933; s. Albert N. and Esther (Hollander) C.; m. Patricia Helen Musser, Sept. 8, 1956 (dec. Feb. 1994); children: Lucinda M., Gary N.; m. Phyllis J. Rohan, May 23, 1997. BA, Gustavus Adolphus Coll., 1955; MA, State U. Iowa, 1957, Princeton U., 1966. Parole officer Dept. Justice, U.S. Penitentiary, Leavenworth, Kans., 1957-58; casework supr. Fed. Correctional Inst., Ashland, Ky., 1958-60; asst. supr. instl. programs Fed. Bur. Prisons, Dept. Justice, Washington, 1960-62, project officer, 1962-65, exec. asst. to dir., 1966-70; dir. Fed. Bur. Prisons, 1970-87; sr. fellow Hubert Humphrey Inst. Pub. Affairs, U. Minn., Mpls., 1987-88; prof. dept. sociology U. Minn., Mpls., 1988-98. Nat. Inst. Pub.

Affairs fellow Princeton U., 1965-66; recipient Arthur S. Flemming award, 1972, Roger W. Jones award for exec. leadership, 1978, Atty. Gen.'s award for exceptional service, 1981 Mem. Am. Correctional Assn. (past pres., mem. exec. com., E.R. Cass award 1981) Home: 15745 W Vale Dr Goodyear AZ 85338-8757 E-mail: ncarl123@aol.com.

CARLSON, P(ATRICIA) M(CELROY), writer; b. Guatemala City, Guatemala, Feb. 3, 1940; (parents Am. citizens); d. James Benjamin and Alene (Jones) McElroy; m. M.A. Carlson, Aug. 20, 1960; children: Geoffrey, Richard. BA, Cornell U., 1961; MA, Cornell, 1966, PhD, 1974. Instr., lectr. psychology and human development Cornell U., Ithaca, NY, 1973-78. Mem. bd. dirs. Bloomington Restorations, Inc., 1982-84. Author: (with M. Potts, R. Cocking and C. Copple), Structure and Development in Child Language, 1979, Audition for Murder, 1985, Murder is Academic, 1985, Murder is Pathological, 1986; (with Richard Darlington) Behavioral Statistics, 1987, Murder Unrenovated, 1988, Rehearsal for Murder, 1988, Murder in the Dog Days, 1991, Murder Misread, 1991, Bad Blood, 1991, Gravestone, 1993, Bloodstream, 1995, Renowned Be Thy Grave, 1998, Deathwind, 2004, Crossfire, 2006; contbr. chpts. to books, short stories. Chair Ithaca Environ. Commn., 1975-78; bd. dirs. Historic Ithaca, 1976-77. Mem. Mystery Writers Am. (bd. dirs. 1990-92, editor Mystery Writers Ann. 1993-96, 98-2000), Sisters in Crime (internat. sec. 1990-91, v.p. 1991-92, pres. 1992-93). Address: Vicky Bijur Literary Agy 333 W End Ave New York NY 10023-8128 E-mail: readermail@pmcarlson.net.

CARLSON, RICHARD A., interior designer; m. Helen Carlson (dec.). BA, Pratt Inst.; postgrad., Oxford U., Eng. Joined Swanke, Hayden, Connell Archs., NYC, 1968, prin., 1979, prin.-in-charge interior design, 1979—, mem. exec. com. Bd. mem. Creative Ctr. for Women with Cancer Chips Soup Kitchen. Named to, Interior Design Mag. Hall of Fame; recipient Nat. Hist. Preservation award, 1992, Gold medal award, Nat. Arts Club, 2001. Fellow: Inst. Bus. Designers (pres. N.Y.C. chpt.), Internat. Interior Design Assn. (Ron Wallin Disting. Merit award). Roman Catholic. Office: SHCA 295 Lafayette St New York NY 10012

CARLSON, RICHARD WARNER, journalist, broadcast executive, federal agency administrator, diplomat; b. Boston, Feb. 10, 1941; adopted s. W.E. and Ruth Miriam (Rafuse) C.; m. Patricia Caroline Swanson; children: Tucker McNear, Buckley Peck. Student, U. Miss., 1961-62; LLD (hon.), Calif. Western U., 1988. Editl. asst. L.A. Times, 1962-63; writer, columnist UPI, San Francisco, Sacramento, 1963-66; investigative reporter, anchorman ABC-TV, San Francisco, 1966-71, anchorman, polit. editor LA, 1971-75; anchorman Sta. KFMB-TV (CBS), San Diego, 1975-77; prodr., writer, dir. documentary films NBC-TV, Burbank, Calif., 1974; anchorman, host Carlson & Co., CBS-TV, San Diego, 1975-76; sr. v.p. Gt. Am. First Bank, San Diego, 1977-84; dir. USIA/Voice of Am., Washington, 1985-91; U.S. amb. to Republic Seychelles, 1991-92; pres., CEO Corp. for Pub. Broadcasting, 1992-97; CEO Kingworld Pub. TV, Washington, 1997-99; vice chmn. Found. for the Def. of Democracies, Washington, 2003—; columnist The Hill Newspaper, Washington, 2003—. Vice chmn. Found. for the Def. of Democracies; bd. dirs. Exec. Info. Svc., Radio Voyager, Inc.; pres. Gately-Carlson Cons.; lectr., cons. in field. Chmn. San Diego Coalition, 1980-81; gov. Scripps Meml. Hosps., La Jolla, 1981-90, Banff (Can.) TV Festival, 1996—, Am. Ctr. Children's TV, 1996—; mem. Calif. State Rep. Ctrl. Com., 1982-85; appointed Pres.'s Coun. Peace Corps, 1982-84; mem. La Jolla Planned Dist. Bd., 1982-84; bd. dirs. Sharp Hosp. Found., 1983—, Scripps Inst. Medicine and Sci., 1995—; mem. La Jolla Town Coun., 1983-85; mem. San Diego Crime Commn., 1984-85; trustee Fund for Am. Studies, 1988-91; mem. Rosalind Russell Arthritis Found., 1985-91; dir. Georgetown Club, 1995—. Recipient investigative reporting awards AP, 1968, 76, 77, awards news analysis, 1968, 69, 75, Nat. Headliners award, 1968, Emmy award best investigative reporting, 1977, Golden Mike award best documentary, 1972, investigative reporting, 1975, best commentary, 1975, George Foster Peabody award, 1976, L.A. Press Club Grand award, 1976, San Diego Press Club award, 1976, 77, 79, Friend of Lithuania award Knights of Lithuania, 1988, Jose Marti award Cuban Am. Polit. Soc., Miami, Fla., 1988, Broadcast Pioneer award, 1997. Mem. Nat. Press Club, Thunderbird Country Club (Rancho Mirage, Calif.), Mid-Ocean Club (Tuckerstown, Bermuda), Georgetown Club, Met. Club, Diplomatic and Consular Officers Retired, The Pilgrims (N.Y.C.), Am. Ambs. Episcopalian. Office Phone: 202-207-0185. Business E-Mail: rwc@defenddemocracy.org.

CARLSON, ROBERT CHARLES, financial planner, writer; BS in Fin. Mgmt. with high honor, Clemson U., 1979; MS in Acctg., U. Va., 1982, JD, 1982. CPA Md.; bar: DC 1982. Law clk. US Dept. Justice, Washington, 1982, US Dept. Edn., Washington, 1982-83; editor Tax Savs. Report, Balt., 1983-85, Fin. Independence, Balt., 1983-85, Tax Wise Money (formerly Tax Avoidance Digest), Balt., 1985—97, Bob Carlson's Retirement Watch, 1991—; prin. R.C. Carlson Adv., Fairfax, Va., 1988-94; pres. Ctr. for Retirement Security, Inc., Fairfax, 1992—; mng. mem. Carlson Wealth Advisors, LLC. Mem. Va. Fiscal Alternative Commn., Richmond, 1989-91; trustee, vice chmn. Fairfax County, Va. Employees' Retirement System, 1992—, chmn. 1995—; trustee Va. Retirement Sys., 2000-05 Author: Tax Savings Through Short-Term Trusts, 1985, 199 Loopholes That Survived Tax Reform, 1987, How to Handle and Win a Federal Tax Appeal, 1988, Retirement Tax Guide, 1989, rev. 4th edit. 1994, How to Slash Your Mutual Fund Taxes, 1990, 2d rev. edit. 1991, Tax Wise Money Strategies, 1995, Estate Planning Strategies, 2d edit., 1998, New Rules of Estate Planning, 2003, New Rules of Retirement, 2005, Invest Like a Fox.Not Like a Hedgehog, 2007. Treas. 10th Dist. Rep. Com., Fairfax, 1988-92; treas. No. Va. Rep. Bus. Forum, Alexandria, 1990—, Atoka Country Supper Com., Springfield, Va., 1989-92; chmn. Fairfax Area Young Reps., Annandale, Va., 1989-91; treas. Wahlquist for Senate, 1988-94, Butler for Congress, 1992-94; chmn. Sully Dist. Rep. Com., Fairfax County, Va., 2004—. Named one of Outstanding Young Men of Am., U.S. Jaycees, 1983. Mem. DC Bar Assn., Conservative Club, Sully Dist. Rep. Com. (chmn., 2004-), Phi Kappa Phi, Phi Gamma Sigma. Home: PO Box 222070 Chantilly VA 20153-2070 Personal E-mail: bcarlson@retirementwatch.com.

CARLSON, ROBERT CODNER, industrial engineering educator; b. Granite Falls, Minn., Jan. 17, 1939; s. Robert Ledin and Ada Louise (Codner) C.; children: Brian William, Andrew Robert, Christina Louise. BSME, Cornell U., 1962; MS, Johns Hopkins U., 1963, PhD, 1976. Mem. tech. staff Bell Tel. Labs., Holmdel, NJ, 1962-70; asst. prof. Stanford (Calif.) U., Stanford, 1970-77, assoc. prof., 1977-82, prof. indsl. engring., 1982-2000, prof. mgmt. sci. & engring., 2000—. Program dir., lectr., cons. various spl. programs U.S., Japan, France, 1971—; cons. Japan Mgmt. Assn., Tokyo, 1990—, Boeing, L.A., 1998—, GKN Automotive, London, 1989—, Rockwell Internat., L.A., 1988—; vis. prof. U. Calif., Berkeley, 1987-88, Dartmouth Coll., Hanover, N.J., 1978-79; vis. faculty Internat. Mgmt. Inst., Geneva, 1984, 88. Contbr. articles to profl. jours. Recipient Maxwell Upson award in Mech. Engring. Cornell U., 1962; Bell Labs. Systems Engring. fellow, 1962-63, Bell Labs. Doctoral Support fellow, 1966-67. Mem. INFORMS (chmn. membership com. 1981-83), Inst. Indsl. Engrs., Am. Soc. Engring. Edn., Am. Prodn. and Inventory Control Soc. (bd. dirs. 1975-81), Confrerie des Chevaliers du Tastevin, Tau Beta Pi, Phi Kappa Phi, Pi Tau Sigma. Avocations: wine tasting, travel. Home Phone: 650-327-9179; Office Phone: 650-723-9110. Business E-Mail: r.c.carlson@stanford.edu.

CARLSON, ROBERT EDWIN, lawyer; b. Bklyn., Oct. 11, 1930; s. Harry Victor and Lenore Marie (Hanrahan) C.; m. Maureen Eleanor Donnelly, Aug. 24, 1963; children: John T., Katherine L., Elizabeth A., Robert E. Jr. BS, U. Oreg., 1953; JD, U. Calif., San Francisco, 1958; LLM, Harvard U., 1963. Bar: Calif. 1959, U.S. Dist. Ct. (ctrl. dist.) Calif. 1959, U.S. Ct. Appeals (9th cir.) 1959. Assoc. Kindel & Anderson, LA, 1958-63, ptnr., 1963-67, Agnew, Miller & Carlson, LA, 1967-80, Hufstedler, Miller, Carlson & Beardsley, LA, 1980-88, Paul, Hastings, Janofsky & Walker LLP, LA, 1988—, chmn. corp. practice group investment mgmt., 1988—2001. Pres. Constl. Rights Found., LA, 1978-80, LA County Bar Found., 1988-89; exec. com. bus. sect. LA Bar Assn., 1982-89; bd. dirs. Legal Aid Found., LA. Bd. dirs. Westridge Sch. for Girls, Pasadena, Calif., 1985-91, Trust for Pub. Land, San Francisco, 1987—; chair bd. Skid Row Housing Trust, LA, 1989-2000; mem. Pasadena Cmty. Found., 2001—; bd. visitors Santa Clara Law Sch., 1986-92. With U.S. Army, 1953-55. Recipient Griffin Bell award Dispute Resolution Svcs., Inc., 1992, Katherine Krause award Inner City Law Ctr., 1996. Mem. ABA (securities com., co-chair com. devel. investment svcs., task force to prepare guidebook for dirs. mut. funds 1995, chair youth edn. for citizenship, Chgo. 1982-85), Calif. State Bar (corp. com. 1990-94), Valley Hunt Club, Chancery Club, Calif. Club. Democrat. Avocations: hiking, tennis, reading, skiing. Office: Paul Hastings Janofsky & Walker LLP 515 S Flower St Fl 23 Los Angeles CA 90071-2300 Office Phone: 213-683-6299. Office Fax: 213-627-0705. Business E-Mail: robertcarlson@paulhastings.com.

CARLSON, ROBERT JAMES, bishop; b. Mpls., June 30, 1944; s. Robert James and Jeanne Catherine (Dorgan) C. BA, St. Paul Sem., 1964, MDiv, 1976; JCL, Catholic U. Am., 1979. Ordained priest Roman Catholic Ch., 1970. Asst. St. Raphael Ch., Crystal, 1970—72; assoc. St. Margaret Mary Ch., Golden Valley, 1972—73, adminstr., 1973—76; vice chancellor Vocation Office, 1976—79, dir., 1977; chancellor Archdiocese, 1979—84; pastor St. Leonard of Port Maurice, Mpls., 1982—84; aux. bishop St. Paul and Mpls., Mpls., 1983—94, Archdiocese of St. Paul and Mpls., Mpls., 1984—94; apptd. coadjutor Bishop of Sioux Falls, SD, 1994—95, Sioux Falls, SD, 1995—; bishop of Sioux Falls, 1995—2005; bishop of Saginaw Mich., 2005—. Author: Going All Out: An Invitation to Belong, 1985. Pres. Nat. Found. Cath. Youth Ministry, Washington, 1989—97; bd. govs. N.Am. Coll. Rome, 1997—2001; active Sioux Falls Humane Soc., 2003—05; Episcopal moderator Nat. Cath. Com. on Scouting, 1993—97, USA/Can. Coun. Serra Internat., 1996—2001; bd. dirs. St. Paul Sem., 1984—2000; bd. trustees Sacred Heart Sem., Detroit, 2005—; bd. dirs. Mt. Angel Sem., Portland, Oreg., 1995—2001, St. John V. Coll. Sem., U. St. Thomas, St. Paul, 1997—2001, Hennich-Glennon Sem., St. Louis, 1998—2001. Decorated Papal Knight, Knight Comdr. with star Holy Sepulchre of Jerusalem; recipient Friendship award, Knights and Ladies of St. Peter Claver, 1990, St. De LaSalle Meml. award, Cretin H.S. Alumni Assn., 1990, Humanitarian of Yr. award, SD Right to Life, 1998, Dist. Svc. award, Serra Internat., 2002, Cosmopolitan Club Sioux Falls, 2002, Our Lady of Guadalupe medal, Inst. for Priestly Formation, 2003, Hon. Canon, Ch. of Holy Sepulchre, Jerusalem, 2003, Pat Mackan award, Network Inclusive Cath. Educators, 2006. Mem.: US Conf. Cath. Bishops (chair ad hoc com. cath. charismatic renewal 2005—, chair life and ministry com. 2006—), Canon Law Soc. Am. Roman Catholic. Avocation: hunting. Office: The Chancery 5800 Weiss St Saginaw MI 48603 Office Phone: 989-797-6615. Business E-Mail: rcarlson@dioceseofsaginaw.org.

CARLSON, ROBERT MARSHALL, health facility administrator; b. Jamestown, NY, Oct. 6, 1950; s. Marshall Lawrence and Alice (Christine) C.; m. Robin Shankey, May 29, 1987; children: Todd Marshall, Scott Thomas. BS, Bowling Green State U., Ohio, 1972; postgrad. in pub. health, U. Utah, 1972; ME in Health Edn., U. Toledo, 1977. Planning analyst, then found. dir. Riverside Hosp., Toledo, 1975-78; hosp. planning coord. Med. Coll. Ohio, Toledo, 1978-80, asst. hosp. dir. for ambulatory programs, 1980-81; cons. P.M.S. (Planning & Mgmt. Services) Inc., Bloomington, Minn., 1981-82; dir. health tech. mktg., sr. cons. Ellerbe Cons. Group, Bloomington, 1983-85; mktg. dir. Ellerbe Assocs. Inc., Mpls., 1986; v.p. Ellerbe Assocs., 1987-89, Export USA Publs., Mpls., 1989-91; dir. physician svcs. HealthEast, St. Paul, 1991-95; exec. adminstr. OSF Med. Group, OSF Healthcare Systems, Peoria, Ill., 1995-99; dir. clin. svcs. Phycor, Inc., Nashville, 1999-2000; sr. assoc. Progressive Healthcare, Inc., Nashville, 2000—02; adminstr. Medicine Patient Care Ctrs., Vanderbilt U. Med. Ctr., Nashville, 2003—06; v.p., exec. dir. ambulatory clinics Tulane U. Hosp. and Clinic, New Orleans, 2007—. Served to commdr., Med. Svc. Corps., USNR, 1972-98. Mem. Med. Group Mgmt. Assn., Am. Coll. Med. Practice Execs., Assn. Mil. Surgeons of U.S., Profl. Ski Instrs. Am., Res. Officers Assn., Phi Kappa Phi, Kappa Sigma. Lutheran. Office: Tulane U Hosp and Clinic 1415 Tulane Ave Ste 6122 New Orleans LA 70112

CARLSON, ROBERT MICHAEL, artist; b. Bklyn., Nov. 19, 1952; s. Sidney Carlson and Vickey (Mihaloff) Woodward; m. Linda Schneider; m. Mary Elizabeth Fontaine, Feb. 24, 1984; 1 child, Nora. Student, CCNY, 1970-73; studied with Flora Mace and Joey Kirkpatrick, Pilchuck Glass Sch., 1981, studied with Dan Dailey, 1982. Teaching asst. Pilchuck Sch., Stanwood, Wash., 1986, 88, mem. faculty, 1989-90, 92, 95, Pratt Fine Arts Ctr., Seattle, 1988-90, Penland (N.C.) Sch. Crafts, 1994, Bild-Werk Sch., Germany, 1996-2000. Mem. artists adv. com. Pilchuck Sch., 1989, 90; vis. artist Calif. Coll. Arts and Crafts, Oakland, 1989, Calif. State U., Fullerton, 1991, blossom summer program Kent State U., Ohio, 1991, U. Ill., Urbana-Champaign, 1993, Toledo Mus. of Art Sch., 1994; visual-artist-in-residence Centrum Found., Port Townsend, Wash., 1992; prof. artist-in-residence Pilchuck Sch., Wash.; faculty The Glass Furnace, Riva, Turkey, 2005 One-man shows include Foster White Gallery, Seattle, 1987, 90, 92, The Glass Gallery, Bethesda, Md., 1988, Heller Gallery, N.Y.C., 1989, 95, Betsy Rosenfield Gallery, Chgo., 1991, 92, MIA Gallery, Seattle, 1994, Habitat Gallery, Florida, 1998, 2001, 06, William Traver Gallery, Seattle, 2000, 04, others; exhibited in group shows at Traver Gallery, Seattle, 1984, 89, Mindscape Gallery, Evanston, Ill., 1984, 86, Tucson Mus. Art., 1984 (Purchase award), 86 (Award of Merit), Hand and Spirit Gallery, Scottsdale, Ariz., 1985, 86, Craftsman Gallery, Scarsdale, N.Y., 1985, Robert Kidd Gallery, Birmingham, Mich., 1985, 88, Gazebo Gallery, Gatlinburg, Tenn., 1985, The Glass Gallery, Bethesda, Md., 1986 (Jurors award), 91, 92, 94, Artists Soc. Internat., San Francisco, 1987 (Critics Choice award), William Traver Gallery, Seattle, 1987, 90, 91, 92, Japan Glass Artcrafts Assn., Tokyo, 1987, Heller Gallery, 1988, 89, 90, 91, 93, 94, 95, 96, 97, Washington Sq. Ptnrs., 1988, Foster White Gallery, 1988, 90, Bellvue Art Mus., Wash., 1988, 91, 94, Am. Arts and Crafts Inc., San Francisco, 1989, Mus. Craft and Folk Art, San Francisco, 1989, Great Am. Gallery, Atlanta, 1989, Dorothy Weiss Gallery, San Francisco, 1989, Habitat Gallery, Farmington Hills, Mich., 1990, 93, Philabaum Gallery, Tucson, 1990, Greg Kucera Gallery, Seattle, 1990, Connell Gallery, Atlanta, 1990, Net Contents Gallery, Bainbridge Island, Wash., 1991, Seattle Tacoma Internat. Airport Installation, 1991, 95, Pratt Fine Arts Ctr., Seattle, 1991, Crystalex, Novy Bor, Czechoslovakia, 1991, Whatcom County Mus., Bellingham, Wash., 1992, Art Gallery West Australia, 1992, 1004 Gallery, Port Townsend, 1992, Bainbridge Island Arts Coun., 1992, MIA Gallery, 1993, Betsy Rosenfield Gallery, Chgo., 1993, Blue Spiral Gallery, Asheville, N.C., 1995, Huntington Mus., 1996, Salem Art Assn., 1996, Judy Yovens Gallery, Houston, 1997, Internat. Glass Art Exchange, Tucson, 1997, Habitat Gallery, Boca Raton, Fla., 1998, 2000, 06, Habitat Gallery, Farmington Hills, Mich., 1998, Tampa (Fla.) Mus. Art, 1998, 2005, Traver Gallery, 2001, Glass Gallery, 2001, Glasmus., 2000, Kentucky Art & Luak Gall., 2000, Fine Arts Mus. San Francisco, 2004, Soc. Arts and Crafts, Boston, 2005, Chantagua Ctr. Visual Arts, N.Y., 2005, L.A. County Mus. Art, 2006, Soc. Contemporary Craft, Pitts., 2007; represented in permanent collections Corning (N.Y.) Mus. Glass, Tucson Mus. Art, Toledo Mus. Art, Mus. Glass, Tacoma, Wash., Tampa Mus. Art, Glasmuseum Frauenau, Germany, Glasmuseum Ebeltoft, Denmark, Valley Nat. Bank, Phoenix, Fountain Assocs., Portland, Oreg., Iceland Air Co., Reykjavik, Iceland, Crocker Banks, L.A., Davis Wright Tremain, Seattle, Meiwa Trading Co., Tokyo, Safeco Ins. Corp., Seattle, Crystalex Corp., L.A. County Mus. Art, Indpls. Mus. Art. Bd. dirs. Am. Craft Coun., 1997-99. Fellow Tucson Pima Arts Coun., 1987, NEA, 1990; John Hauberg fellow, 2000. Mem. Glass Art Soc. (conf. lectr. 1991, bd. dirs. 1992-97, v.p. 1994-95, pres. 1995-97, Lifetime Mem. award 2004). Office: PO Box 11590 Bainbridge Island WA 98110 Home Phone: 206-892-3206; Office Phone: 206-842-3206. E-mail: bobway@robertcarlson.net.

CARLSON, RONALD LEE, law educator; b. Davenport, Iowa, Dec. 10, 1934; s. Arthur A. and Louise (Sehmann) C.; m. Mary Murphy, Apr. 10, 1965; children: Michael, Andrew. BA, Augustana Coll., 1956; JD (Clarion DeWitt Hardy law scholar), Northwestern U., 1959; LL.M. (E. Barrett Prettyman law scholar), Georgetown U., 1961. Bar: Ill. 1959, Iowa 1959, D.C. 1960, U.S. Supreme Ct. 1966. Mem. firm Betty, Neuman, McMahon, Hellstrom & Bittner, Davenport, Iowa, 1961-65; U.S. commr. So. Dist. Iowa, 1964—65; prof. law U. Iowa, Iowa City, 1965-73, Washington U., St. Louis, 1973-84; John Byrd Martin prof. law U. Ga., 1984-95, Fuller E. Callaway prof. law, 1995—. Vis. prof. Wayne State U., Detroit, 1974, Detroit, 1976—77, Detroit, 1979, U. Tex., 1978, St. Louis U., 1982—86, 1988, U. Iowa, 1986—87, 1996, Ohio State U., 2003, U. Tenn., Knoxville, 2006; cons. Legis. Com. Criminal Code Revision Iowa, 1969—73; moderator Robert Vance Forum on The Bill of Rights, 1990—96, 2002—03; Founder's Day lectr. U. Ga., 2005. Author: Criminal Law Advocacy, 1982, Successful Techniques for Civil Trials, 1983, rev. edit., 1992, Pocket Proof of Facts, 1993, Trial Handbook for Georgia Lawyers, 2003, Student's Guide to Elements of Proof, 2004, Criminal Justice Procedure, 2005; author: (with D. Brown and S. Crump) Adjudication of Criminal Justice, 2007; author: (with M. Ladd) Cases on Evidence, 1972; author: (with J. Yeager) Criminal Law and Procedure, 1979; author: (with M. Bright) Maine Objections at Trial, 1991, New Hampshire Objections at Trial, 1992, Oregon Objections at Trial, 1992; author: (with A. Montgomery and M. Bright) Minnesota Objections at Trial, 1992; author: (with R. Aronson and M. Bright) Washington Objections at Trial, 1992; author: (with J. Young, K. Curtis, and M. Bright) Virginia Objections at Trial, 1998; author: (with M. Bright and E. Imwinkelried) Objections at Trial: A Concise Guide, 2002; author: (with E. Imwinkelried) Dynamics of Trial Practice: Problems and Materials, 2002; author: (with E. Imwinkelried, E. Kionka and K. Strachan) Evidence Teaching Materials for an Age of Science and Statutes, 2007. V.p. alumni bd. Augustana Coll., Rock Island, Ill., 1968; com. mem. Found. of Freedom Comm'n. Recipient Roscoe Pound Found. Jacobson award, ATLA, 1987. Mem.: ABA (Harrison Tweed award 2000), Ga. State Bar Assn. (founds. freedom com. 2005—06), Ga. Trial Lawyers Assn. (Lifetime Achievement award 2005), Am. Inns. of Ct., Fed. Practice Inst. (dir. 1980—83, dean 1985—89), Iowa Bar Assn., Fed. Bar Assn. (chmn. law sch. divsn. 1978—79, nat. coun. 1994—95, Earl W. Kintner award 1992), Am. Assn. Law Schs. Republican. Office: U Ga School of Law Sch of Law Athens GA 30602 Office Phone: 706-542-5186. Business E-Mail: mlfield@uga.edu. *Proper application of law provides the key to resolution of disputes: local, national, and international. As a teacher of law to judges, lawyers and students, it is my goal to educate in a manner which contributes to this needed resolution of conflict in a positive way.*

CARLSON, SHAWN ERIC, physicist, educator; b. San Francisco, Mar. 11, 1960; s. Devere Milfred Carlson Jr. and Beverly Ann Bennett; m. Michelle Lynn Tetreault, 1994; children: Katherine Joanne, Erik Philip, Jennifer Elizabeth. BS in Physics, Applied Math., U. Calif., Berkeley, 1981; MS in Physics, UCLA, 1983, PhD in Physics, 1989. V.p. R & D Flowgram Software Assocs., San Francisco, 1989-91; rsch. physicist, astrophysicist Lawrence Berkeley Labs., 1982-94; founder, exec. dir. Soc. Amateur Scientists, 1994—; co-founder Tinkers Guild Pubs., 1999; chief tech. officer Personal Genetics, 2000—01; founder, CEO Bright Sci., LLC, 2003—; creator labrats.org, 2005, scifair.org, 2005; ind. cons. sci. and tech., 1995—. Adj. prof. physics, San Diego State U., 1995—; sci. and tech. cons. CSICOP 1985—; vis. scholar Brown U., 2002--; speaker in field. Author: Satanism in America, 1989, Core Concepts in Physics, 1997, The Amateur Scientist-The Complete 20th Century Collection (CD-Rom), 2000, The Amateur Astronomer, 2000, The Amateur Biologist, 2001; columnist Sci. Am. Mag., 1995-2001; Humanist Mag., Buffalo, 1991-93, MAKE Mag., 2005—; numerous radio and TV appearances. Investigator faith-healers, Satanism, religious miracles, astrology for Com. Scientific Examination of Religion, Buffalo, 1987, 89. Fellow MacArthur Found., 1999; named Headliner of Yr., San Diego Press Club, 2000; recipient San Diego State U. Svc. award, 2000. Mem. AAAS, Am. Astron. Soc., Nat. Assn. Sci. Writers, Sigma Xi, Labrats Sci. Club. Office: Soc Amateur Scientists 5600 Post Rd Ste 114-341 East Greenwich RI 02818 Office Phone: 401-398-7001. Business E-Mail: scarlson@sas.org.

CARLSON, SUZANNE OLIVE, architect; b. Worcester, Mass., Aug. 20, 1939; d. Sigfrid and Helga (Larson) C. BS, RI Sch. Design, 1963. Jr. ptnr. Dingnam-Fauteux & Ptnrs., Worcester, 1969-70; ptnr. Richard Lamoureux Assoc., Worcester, 1970-75, Herron & Carlson (AIA), Worcester, 1975-96; arch. Edgecomb, Maine, 1997—. Guest lectr. Holy Cross Coll., 1969-70. Chmn. Worcester Hist. Commn., 1976-88; trustee Worcester Heritage Soc., 1982-88, Park Spirit of Worcester Inc., 1987—, Friends of Ft. Edgecomb, 2005-; v.p. Lincoln County Hist. Assn., 2001—; trustee Worcester Girls Inc. of Worcester, pres. 1989-92, 95-2002, sec. 1994-95; trustee Performing Arts Sch. Worcester, 1977-86, v.p. 1980-85; trustee Cultural Assembly Greater Worcester, 1981-86, v.p., 1982-83; pres. Edgecomb Hist. Soc., 1997—. Recipient European Honors Program grant Rome, Italy, 1961-62; recipient AIA School medal for excellence, 1963. Mem. AIA (exec. bd. Ctrl. Mass. chpt. 1969-71, sec.-treas. 1970-71, v.p. 1971-72, pres. 1972-73), Mass. Soc. Archs. (exec. bd. 1972-74, v.p. 1975, pres. 1976), New Eng. Regional Coun. Archs. (pres. 1977), New Eng. Antiquities Rsch. Assn. (membership chair 1982-84, 90-94, resource devel. chair 1994—, graphics dir. jours. 1982—, publs. chair 1995—, trustee 1990—). Home and Office: Suzanne O Carlson Architect 94 Cross Point Rd Edgecomb ME 04556-3208 Office Phone: 207-882-8155. E-mail: krosspt@lincoln.midcoast.com.

CARLSON, TERRANCE L., lawyer, aerospace transportation executive; b. Superior, Wis., Jan. 21, 1953; s. Einar August and Carol (McAuley) C.; m. Jeanette Michele Leehr, Mar. 13, 1987; children: Aurora Brita Leehr, Henry Einar, Stephen Michael. BS in Bus. with high distinction, U. Minn., 1975; JD cum laude, U. Mich., 1978. Bar: Calif. 1978, U.S. Dist. Ct. (cen. dist.) Calif. 1978. With Gibson, Dunn & Crutcher, 1978-94, London, 1981-87, ptnr.-in-charge Hong Kong, 1987-89; v.p., gen counsel Allied Signal Aerospace, Torrance, CA, 1994; dep. gen. counsel AlliedSignal (now Honeywell Internat.); sr. v.p. bus. devel., gen. counsel, sec. PerkinElmer Inc., 1999—2001; sr. v.p., gen. counsel, corp. sec. Medtronic Inc., Mpls., 2001—. Adj. prof. London Law Ctr. U. Notre Dame, 1983-87, Pepperdine U., London, 1984; exec. dir. Annual Multi-Species Invitational (Since 1973). Contbr. articles to legal publs. Mem. Soc. English and Am. Lawyers (com. 1985-87), Royal Auto. Club, Am. Club. Avocations: fishing, guitar. Office: Allied Signal Aerospace 2525 W 190th St Torrance CA 90504-6002 also: Medtronic Inc 710 Medtronic Pky NE Minneapolis MN 55432-5604*

CARLSON, THOMAS JOSEPH, real estate developer, lawyer; b. St. Paul, Jan. 12, 1953; s. Delbert George and Shirley Lorraine (Willardson) C.; m. Chandler Elizabeth Campbell, July 15, 1973; 1 child, Thomas Chandler. BA, George Washington U., 1975; JD, U. Mo., Kansas City, 1979. Reporter Springfield (Mo.) News-Leader, 1975-76; editor Buffalo (Mo.) Reflex, 1976-77; assoc. Woolsey Fisher, Springfield, 1980-83; pvt. practice law Springfield, 1983-86; ptnr. Carlson & Clark, 1986-93, Carmichael, Carlson, Gardner & Clark, Springfield, 1993-94; mayor City of Springfield, 1987-93, 2001—; U.S. Bankruptcy trustee Springfield, 1982-98; pvt. practice, 1994-98. CEO, Resorts Mgmt., Inc., 1995—; bd. dirs.

ITEC Attractions, Inc., Great So. Bancorp; lectr. in field. Contbr. articles to profl. jours. Mem. Ozark Trail coun. Boy Scouts Am.; mem. Springfield City Coun., Mo., 1983—87, 1997—2001, Airport Bd. Springfield, 1994—97; chmn. Springfield-Branson Leadership Com., Springfield, 1993—; bd. dir. Mo. Cmty. Devel. Corp. Iniative, Mo. Commn. on Intergovtl. Cooperation; mem. bd. govs. Mo. State U., 2003—05; adv. coun. Fannie Mae Southwestern Regional Housing and Cmty. Devel.; Bd. mem. Mo. Health and Ednl. Facilities Authority, 2005—. Mem.: Mo. Mcpl. League (bd. mem. 2003—), Nat. League of Cities (bd. mem. 2005—), Mo. Bar Assn. (Disting. Young Lawyer award 1989). Presbyterian. Office: 205 W Walnut Ste 200 Springfield MO 65806-2115

CARLSON, TUCKER, political analyst, writer, television host; b. San Francisco, May 16, 1969; s. Richard and Patricia Buckley (Stepmother); m. Susie Andrews, 1991; children: Lillie, Buckley, Hopie. Attended, Trinity Coll., Conn. Writer Policy Review, Wash., DC; staff writer Arkansas Democrat-Gazette, Little Rock; co-host Spin Room CNN, 2000—01, co-host Crossfire, 2001—05, political analyst Wash. bureau; host & mng. editor Tucker Carlson: Unfiltered PBS, 2004—05; anchor MSNBC, 2005—, host The Situation With Tucker Carlson, 2005—. Regular contributor to The Weekly Standard & Esquire; articles in NY Times, NY Mag., Reader's Digest, Wall Street Journal, Forbes, GQ. Author: Politician, Partisans and Parasites: My Adventures in Cable News, 2003. Office: One MSNBC Plaza Secaucus NJ 07094

CARLSON, WALTER CARL, lawyer; b. Chgo., Sept. 14, 1953; s. LeRoy T. and Margaret (Deffenbaugh) C.; m. Debora M. DeHoyos, June 20, 1981; children: Amanda, Greta, Linnea. BA magna cum laude, Yale U., 1975; JD magna cum laude, Harvard U., 1978. Bar: Ill. 1978, US Dist. Ct. (no. dist.) Ill. 1980, (ea. dist.) Wis. 1992, US Supreme Ct. 1991. Law clk. to presiding justice U.S. Dist. Ct. No. Dist., Chgo., 1978-80; ptnr. securities litig. Sidley Austin LLP, Chgo., 1986—, mem. exec. com., 2002—. Bd. dirs. Telephone and Data Sys., Inc., Chgo. (non-exec. chmn.), mem. and former chmn. audit com. 1989-2001, chmn., 2002-; bd. dirs. U.S. Cellular Corp., 1989—, chmn. audit com. 1989-2001; bd. dirs. Aerial Comm., Inc., 1996-2000. Mem. Dist. 65 Sch. Bd., Evanston, Ill., 1993-2001, pres., 1997-2001. Mem. ABA, US Supreme Ct. Hist. Soc., Am. Judicature Soc., Seventh Cir. Bar Assn., Chgo. Hist. Soc., Chgo. United. Office: Sidley Austin LLP One South Dearborn Chicago IL 60603 Home Phone: 847-864-6869; Office Phone: 312-853-7734. Business E-Mail: wcarlson@sidley.com.

CARLSON, WILLIAM CLIFFORD, retired defense industry executive, military officer; b. Detroit, Feb. 7, 1937; s. William and Marion Lucille Carlson; m. Jane Elder, Jan. 28, 1960 (div. Jne 1987); children: David, Scott, Jennifer Carlson-Burns; m. Linda Darlene Reid, June 6, 1991. BS in Edn., U. N.Mex., Albuquerque, 1959; MS in Physics, U.S. Naval Postgrad. Sch., Monterey, Calif., 1965; MS equivalent, U.S. Naval War Coll., Newport, RI, 1975. Commd. U.S. Navy, 1959, advanced through ranks to rear admiral, officer, 1959-92, mgr. ASW combat sys. Naval Sea Sys. Command Washington, 1982-88, asst. dep. cmdr. Naval Sea Sys. Command, 1988-91, cmdr. Naval Undersea Warfare Ctr., 1991-92, ret., 1992; dir. advanced programs Scientific Atlanta Instrumentation Group, 1993-94; v.p. mktg. & sales Scientific Atlanta SPS Group, 1994-95; dir. surface ship ASW combat system programs Lockheed Martin, Syracuse, NY, 1995—2002. Mem. Acoustical Soc. Am., U.S. Naval Inst., U.S. Navy League, Surface Warfare Assn. Avocations: trout fishing, fly tying, skiing. Home: 3996 Pompey Hollow Rd Cazenovia NY 13035-9523 E-mail: wcarlso1@twcny.rr.com.

CARLSON ARONSON, MARILYN A., language educator; b. Gothenburg, Nebr., July 24, 1938; d. Harold N. and Verma Elnora (Granlund) C.; m. Paul E. Carlson, July 31, 1959 (dec. Sept. 1988); 1 child, Andrea Joy; m. David L. Aronson, July 8, 1995. BS in Edn., English and Psychology, Sioux Falls Coll., 1960; MA in History, U. SD, Vermillion, 1973, MA in English, 1992, EdD in Ednl. Adminstrn., 1997. Tchr. English and social scis. curriculum coord. Beresford Pub. Sch., SD, 1960-78; tchr. English and social scis. Sioux Empire Coll., Hawarden, Iowa, 1979-85; instr. English and ESL, Midwest Inst. for Internat. Studies, Sioux Falls, S.D., 1985-89; asst. prof. English Augustana Coll., Sioux Falls, 1989-97, asst. prof. English and edn., 1997-2000; acad. affairs coord. acad. evaluation U. SD, Vermillion, 2000—02; assoc. acad. dean Nat. Am. U., Sioux Falls, 2002—03, acad. dean, 2003—. Part time instr. psychology Northwestern Coll., 1985; part time instr. English and lit. Nat. Coll., 1985-88; part time instr. English and history Augustana Coll., 1986-89; mem. exec. com. SD Humanities Coun., 2007-. presenter in field. Author: Visions of Light: Flannery O'Connor's Themes and Narrative Method, 1992, A Higher Education Perspective: Themes and Narrative Methods of Flannery O'Connor and Eudora Welty, 1997; Plains Goddesses: Heroines in Willa Cather's Prairie Novels, 1995; contbr. articles and revs. to profl. publs. including The Social Sci. Jour., others. Humanities Scholar evaluator Rainbow Project and Increasing Cultural Understanding Seminar, 2000; evaluator Profl. Devel. Conf. Native Am. Curriculum, Rapid City, SD, 2001; mem. SD Humanities Coun., 2003—, sec. exec. bd., 2007—. Recipient Internat. Prof.'s Exch. award Sor Trondelag Coll., Trondheim, Norway, Jan. 1999; named Tchr. of Yr. Beresford Pub. Schs., 1976; SD Humanities scholar, 1993—; Bush mini-grantee, 1993, Internat. Studies grantee, 1994, 98, 99, SD Humanities Spkr.'s Bur. grantee, 1996—,. Mem.: Delta Kappa Gamma. Home: 29615 469th Ave Beresford SD 57004-6457 Office: Nat Am U 2801 S Kiwanis Ave Sioux Falls SD 57105

CARLSON-RUKAVINA, PATRICIA ANN, small business owner; b. St. Paul, Minn., Oct. 9, 1945; d. Frank Ludomil and Bertha Mahala (Patterson) Loss; m. Thomas Arnold Carlson (div.); children: Christina Marie Carlson Shadwick, Erick Michael Carlson; m. Carl Robert Rukavina, Sept. 6, 1980. BA, Sch. of Associated Arts, 1978. Lic. cosmetology Oliver Thein Beauty Sch., 1970, diploma Mind Control Inst. Inc., 1972, cert. honorary Rufus Hays cert. Acad. of Hairdressing, 1970, lic. life insur. Minn. State Bd. Insurance agent Western Fraternal Life Assoc., Cedar Rapid, Iowa, 1984—87; sales assoc. Host Internat., Mpls./St Paul, Minn., 1987—88; owner 1st Impressions Photography, St. Paul, 1989—91; sales Avon, 1987—91, Herbalife Internat., Los Angeles, Calif., 2001—03; sales assoc. Silver Gallery, Colo., 1980—2004; owner, artist Lone Bird Studio, St. Paul, 1991—. Asst. dir. Minn. State Fine Arts Bd., St. Paul, 1979; art tchr. Guadalupe Primary Sch., Puerto Vallarta, Mexico, 1978. Exhibitions include visual arts Just for the Season Gallery, 2004—05, Represented in permanent collections Minn. Mus. Art. Disaster response team Am. Red Cross, St. Paul, 1998; fund raiser Naomi House Woman's Shelter, St. Paul, 1991; fund raiser, trade ambassador Minn. World Trade Ctr., St. Paul, 1996; fundraiser, participant Minn. Leukemia Soc. Marathon, 1996; deaconess Park Baptist Ch., St. Paul, 1980. Mem.: Mpls. Inst. Art, Minn. Inst. Art, Sokol Minn. (delegate 1995—), ZCBJ Lodge #69 Orel-Western Fraternal Life (treas. 1994—). Baptist. Avocations: reading, gardening, travel, sports, religion.

CARLSSON, BO AXEL VILHELM, economics professor; b. Ulricehamn, Sweden, July 22, 1942; arrived in U.S., 1984; s. Carl Axel Valentin and Dagmar Elisabet (Karlsson) C.; m. Glenda Joyce Bishop, Dec. 28, 1965; children: Eric, Mark, Amy. BA, Harvard U., 1968; MA, Stanford U., 1970, PhD, 1972; Docent, Uppsala U., Sweden, 1980. Sr. rsch. assoc. Indsl. Inst. Econ. and Social Rsch., Stockholm, 1972-84, dep. dir., 1977-81; Umstattd prof. indsl. econs. Case Western Res. U., Cleve., 1984-2000, de Windt prof. indsl. econs., 2000—, chmn. dept. econs., 1984-87, assoc. dean rsch. and grad. programs Weatherhead Sch. Mgmt., 1996—2001, dir. PhD programs and rsch., 2001—05, faculty dir., exec. doctor mgmt. program, 2005—. Vis. scholar MIT, 1982; cons. World Bank, Washington, 1983-87, Swedish Fedn. Industries, Stockholm, 1984-89; min. of fin. Stockholm, 1993-94, Econ. Commn. for L.Am., 1996; project dir. Sweden's Tech. Sys., Stockholm, 1987—; mem. Indsl. and Sci. Coun., Nat. Bd. Tech. Devel., 1987-98; chair sci. adv. bd. Danish Rsch. Unit for Indsl. Dynamics, 1996—; mem. internat. evaluation panel Acad. of Finland, 2004. Author: Technology and Industrial Structure, 1979, Industrial Subsidies, 1980, Swedish Industry Facing the 80s, 1981; editor: Industrial Dynamics, 1989, Technological Systems and Economic Performance, 1995, Technological Systems and Industrial Dynamics, 1997, Technological Systems in the Bio Industries: An International Study, 2002. Mem. Swedish cultural orgns. Mem. Europe Assn. Rsch. Indsl. Econs. (pres. 1983-85, exec. com.), Am. Econ. Assn., Ea. Econ. Assn. (bd. dirs. 1989-92), Internat. J.A. Schumpeter Soc. (prize selection com. 1988-90, 94-96, 2002-04), Assn. Christian Economists. Methodist. Home: 2708 Rochester Rd Cleveland OH 44122-2167 Office: Case Western Res Univ Weatherhead Sch Mgmt Dept Econs Cleveland OH 44106-7235 Home Phone: 216-464-1774; Office Phone: 216-368-4112. Business E-Mail: Bo.Carlsson@case.edu.

CARLSTON, JOHN A., allergist; b. NYC, Nov. 9, 1932; s. Ramon R. and Genevieve P. (Poss) C.; m. Jean L. Lawson, June 21, 1958; children: Ann, Kimberly, Susan. BS in Biology and Philosophy, Coll. of Holy Cross, 1954; MD, Yale U., 1958. Diplomate Am. Bd. Allergy and Immunology. Intern Akron (Ohio) Gen. Hosp., 1958-59, resident in internal medicine, 1959-61; fellow in allergy U. Pitts., 1961-62; instr. medicine in allergy U. Ill., Chgo., 1962-64; assoc. in medicine Northwestern U., Chgo., 1964-69; active staff in medicine Virginia Beach (Va.) Gen. Hosp., 1969—; assoc. prof. in medicine Eastern Va. Med. Sch., Norfolk, Va., 1974—. Bd. cert. Allergy, 1974, 77, 80, 83, 87, 93. Contbr. articles to profl. jours. Lt. col. U.S. Army Med. Corps, 1967-69. Fellow Am. Coll. Allergy and Immunology, Am. Acad. Allergy and Immunology; mem. Va. Allergy Assn., S.E. Allergy Assn., Va. Beach Med. Soc. (pres. 1976), Allergy Rehab. Found. (cons.). Republican. Episcopal. Avocations: Go, travel, skiing, golf, tennis. Office: Asthma and Allergy Specialists Ltd 1704 Sir William Osler Dr Virginia Beach VA 23454-3003

CARLTON, ALFRED PERSHING, JR., lawyer; b. Raleigh, NC, Aug. 27, 1947; s. Alfred P. and Katherine (Singleton) C.; m. Blair Creech Carlton, Apr. 21, 2001; children: Mary Elizabeth, Troy Eugene. BSBA, U. N.C., 1969, JD, 1975; MPA, U. Dayton, 1973; LLD, Stetson U., 2002, U. Denver, 2003. Bar: N.C. 1975, U.S. Dist. Ct. (ea. dist.) N.C. 1975, U.S. Ct. Appeals (4th cir.) 1976, U.S. Supreme Ct. 1993. Pvt. practice, Raleigh, 1975-77; counsel N.C. Bankers Assn., Raleigh, 1977-79; sec., gen. counsel Bancshares N.C., Inc., Raleigh, 1979-82; adj. prof. law Campbell U., Buies Creek, NC, 1979-82; ptnr. Sanford, Adams, McCullough & Beard, Raleigh, 1983-89; shareholder McNair & Sanford, Raleigh, 1990-95; ptnr. The Sanford Holshouser Law Firm, Raleigh, 1995—2001, Kilpatrick Stockton LLP, 2002—. Active City of Raleigh Hist. Properties and Hist. Dists. Commn., 1978-82; exec. bd. Occoneechee coun. Boy Scouts Am., 1983-94; trustee U. N.C. at Wilmington, 1997-2005, chmn. 2004-05; bd. advisors Elon U. Law Sch., 2004—; mem. Chief Justice's Commn. on Professionalism, 1998-2001. 1st lt. Med. Svc. Corps, USAF, 1970-73 Fellow Am. Bar Found.; mem. ABA (ho. of dels. 1982-84, 1987—, chmn. of the house 1996-98, bd. govs. 1996-98, chmn. standing com. on jud. independence 1998-2001, pres.-elect 2001-02, pres. 2002-2003), N.C. Bar Assn. (bd. govs. 1981-82, 92-95), Am. Law Inst., N.C. Legis. Rsch. Commn. (study com. on pub. financing 1985-88). Democrat. Episcopalian. Avocations: tennis, gardening. Office: Kilpatrick Stockton LLP 3737 Glenwood Ave Ste 400 Raleigh NC 27612 Home Phone: 919-755-6915; Office Phone: 919-420-1831. E-mail: apcarlton@kilpatrickstockton.com.

CARLTON, BUZZ (CLYDE GORDON CARLTON JR.), singer, songwriter, entertainer, recording artist; b. Richmond, Va., Aug. 8, 1962; Student, Fork Union Mil. Acad., 1978—80, Coastal Carolina U., Conway, SC, 1997, Va. Commonwealth U., Richmond, 1999. Owner Millhouse Records. Instr. music United Meth. Ch., Richmond, 1998—99. Performances include Nat. Anthem, Richmond Braves Baseball Game, 1989, 90, also TV, radio, and concerts; singer Freedom of Speech, 2001; albums include: Blame It On the Blues, 2004, Just This Side of the Blues, 2006, Somebody Get Me My Guitar, 2007; author (song) What a Lie. Vol. Salvation Army, Richmond, 1996—99. Mem.: Recording Acad., ASCAP. Democrat. Avocations: nature, psychology, philosophy. Office: Buzz Carlton LLC PO Box 8382 Richmond VA 23226-0382 Office Phone: 804-840-6640. Business E-Mail: buzz@buzzcarlton.com.

CARLTON, DONALD MORRILL, retired research, development and engineering executive; b. Houston, July 20, 1937; s. Spencer William and Ruth (Morrill) C.; m. Elaine Yvonne Smith, Jan. 28, 1961; children: Donna Kay, Spencer Frank, Monica Elaine. BA, U. St. Thomas, Houston, 1958; PhD, U. Tex., Austin, 1962. Mem. staff, then group leader Sandia Corp., Albuquerque, 1962-65; with Tracor, Inc., Austin, 1965-69, asst. dir. research, 1968-69; pres., chmn. bd. Radian Corp., Austin, 1969-95; pres., CEO Radian Internat., LLC, Austin, 1996-98, ret., 1998. Bd. dir. Am. Elec. Power Co., Smith Barney Investment Series Trust, Nat. Instruments Corp., Temple-Inland, Crystatech Corp.; mem. mgmt. com. Signature Sci.; past chmn. natural sci. adv. coun. U. Tex., Austin; mem. Engring. Found. adv. coun.; former mem. adv. coun.; past chmn. Electric Power Rsch. Inst.; mem. Inst. Nuc. Power Ops., 1984-2004, chmn., 1998-2004. Mem. Am. Chem. Soc., Tex. Taxpayers and Rsch. Assn. (past chmn.), Austin C. of C. (past dir.), Tex. C. of C. (past chmn.). Home: 403 N Weston Ln Austin TX 78733 Office: URS/RADIAN PO Box 201088 Austin TX 78720-1088

CARLTON, JANE M.R., geneticist; b. Edinburgh, Jan. 7, 1967; came to US, 1997; d. Hugh Ian and Judith (Gaynor) C. BS in Genetics, U. Edinburgh, Scotland, 1990, PhD, 1995. Postdoct. assoc. U. Edinburgh, Scotland, 1995-97, U. Fla., Gainesville, 1997-99, asst. scientist, 1999—2000; vis. scientist Nat. Ctr. for Biotechnology Info., NIH, Bethesda, Md., 2000—01; assoc. investigator, Parasite Genomics Group The Inst. for Genomic Rsch., Rockville, Md., 2001—; assoc., dept. molecular microbiology and immunology John Hopkins Sch. Pub. Health, Balt., 2004—. Contbr. articles to profl. jours. Recipient SUMP Jr. Investigator award, Kindrogan, Scotland, 1993; Med. Rsch. Coun. Post Grad. Fellowship, 1990, NIH Postdoctoral Fellowship, 1997. Mem. Am. Soc. Tropical Medicine and Hygiene. Office: The Inst for Genomic Rsch 9712 Medical Center Dr Rockville MD 20850 Office Phone: 301-795-7000. Office Fax: 301-838-0208. Business E-Mail: carlton@tigr.org.*

CARLTON, JOHN L., lawyer; AB summa cum laude, UCLA, 1973, JD, 1979. Bar: Calif. 1979, US Dist. Ct. (ctrl. dist. Calif.) 1980, US Ct. Appeals (9th cir.) 1981, US Ct. Appeals (5th cir.) 2006. Atty. Kadison, Pfaelzer, Woodard, Quinn & Rossi, LA; asst. US atty. Ctrl. Dist. Calif., LA, 1987—98; ptnr. Arnold & Porter LLP, LA. Named a So. Calif. Super Lawyer, Law & Politics and LA Mag., 2005, 2006. Office: Arnold & Porter LLP 44th Fl 777 S Figueroa St Los Angeles CA 90017-5844 Office Phone: 213-243-4101. Office Fax: 213-243-4199. E-mail: John.Carlton@aporter.com.

CARLTON, PAUL KENDALL, JR., physician; b. Roswell, N.Mex., May 13, 1947; s. Paul Kendall and Helen C. (Sweat) C.; m. Dorothea Janice Prichard, July 5, 1969; children: Paul Kendall III, Christianne Joy, Stephanie Jill, Luke Jeffrey. BS, USAF Acad., 1969; MD, U. Colo., 1973, DSc (hon.), 2003. Diplomate Am. Bd. Surgery, 1980, 1990, 2000. Commd. 2d lt. USAF, 1969, advanced through grades to lt. gen., 1999; resident in surgery Wilford Hall Med. Ctr., San Antonio, 1973-78; comdr. USAF Hosp. Torrejon, Madrid, 1985-88, Scott Med. Ctr., Scott AFB, Ill., 1988-91; command surgeon Air Edn. and Tng. Command, San Antonio, 1991-94; comdr. Wilford Hall Med. Ctr., San Antonio, 1994-99, surgeon gen., 1999—2002; prof., dir. Homeland Security Health Sci. Ctr. Tex. A&M, 2002—. Decorated Air medal, Legion of Merit (2), Def. Disting. Svc. medal, Airman's medal; recipient Hoekton Silver award AMA, 1978, Nathan Davis award, AMA, 2001. Fellow ACS (gov. 1992-96). Avocations: hunting, flying. Office: Tex A&M U Health Sci Ctr Homeland Security Dir College Station TX 77845 also: 7th Fl 301 Tarrow St College Station TX 77840-7896

CARLTON, ROBBIN BRILEY, elementary school educator; b. South Boston, Va., Jan. 22, 1973; d. David Clifton and Gwen Godwin Briley; m. Daniel Ray Carlton, June 26, 1999; children: Dillon Ray, Madison Lynn. BS in Elem. Edn., E.Carolina U., Greenville, NC, 1997, MEd in Instrnl. Tech., 2004. Tchr. 6th grade lang. arts & math / 7th grade sci. S.W. Snowden Elem. Sch., Beaufort County Schs., Aurora, NC, 1997—99; tchr. 5th grade North Rowan Elem. Sch., Rowan-Salisbury Schs., Spencer, NC, 1999—2002; tchr. 7th / 8th grade math and sci. Extended Day Sch., Davidson County Schs., Lexington, NC, 2002—. Named North Rowan Elem. Tchr. of Yr., Rowan-Salsibury Sch. Sys., 2001—02, Extended Day Sch. Tchr. of Yr., Davidson County Schs., 2004—05; Mini-Grant Winner Ecosystems in Our Own Backyard, Title VI, 2001—02, Project Based Learning Grant Team, Davidson County Schs. / Buck Inst., 2002—03. Mem.: NSTA (assoc.), Nat. Coun. Tchrs. Math. (assoc.), N.C. Assn. Educators (assoc.). Methodist. Achievements include Middle School Conference Committee Member - Current; Chair, Project Wild 1998-1999; Assistant Coach, Girls Volleyball Team 1997-1999; Yearbook Committee 1998-1999; Mentor / Lead Mentor - Extended Day School - Current; Technology Leadership Team - Extended Day School - Current; NCETC Technology Showcase Presenter - 2000-2001, Representing Rowan-Salsibury Schools; Grade Level Chairperson 2000-2002; Point of Contact for the National Science Education Standards K-5 1999-2002; Science Fair Committee 1997-2002; Chair, School Climate Committee (SACS) 1998-1999; Chair, Science Olympiad 1997-1999. Avocations: arts & crafts, photography, web page design, reading, cooking. Home: 163 O'Farrell Street Winston Salem NC 27107 Office: Extended Day School 2065 E Holly Grove Road Lexington NC 27292 Home Phone: 336-769-0398; Office Phone: 336-242-1459. Office Fax: 336-242-1456. E-mail: rcarlton@davidson.k12.nc.us.

CARLTON, TERRY SCOTT, retired chemist, educator; b. Peoria, Ill., Jan. 29, 1939; s. Daniel Cushman and Mabel (Smith) C.; m. Claudine Fields, 1960; children: Brian, David. BS, Duke U., 1960; PhD (NSF grad. fellow 1960-63), U. Calif., Berkeley, 1963. Mem. faculty Oberlin (Ohio) Coll., 1963—, prof. chemistry, 1976-2001, prof. emeritus, 2001—, chmn. dept., 1980-83. Vis. prof. chemistry U. N.C., Chapel Hill, 1976. Co-author: Composition, Reaction and Equilibrium, 1970. Home: 143 Kendal Dr Oberlin OH 44074-1906 Office: Oberlin Coll Dept Chemistry and Biochemistry Oberlin OH 44074-1097 E-mail: terry.carlton@oberlin.edu.

CARLUCCI, DAVID R., information technology executive; BA in Polit. Sci., Univ. Rochester. With IBM, 1976—2002; v.p. mktg., channel mgmt IBM Personal Computer Co. NA, 1990—92; v.p. sys., industries, svcs. IBM Asia Pacific, 1993—95; gen. mgr. IBM Printing Sys. Co., 1995—97; chief info. officer IBM, 1997—98, gen. mgr., S/390 divsn., 1998—2000; gen. mgr. IBM Americas, 2000—02; COO IMS Health, Norwalk, Conn., 2002—04, pres., 2002—, CEO, 2004—, chmn., 2006—. Office: IMS Health Ste 612 901 Main Ave Norwalk CT 06851 Office Phone: 203-319-4700.*

CARLUCCI, FRANK CHARLES, III, former secretary of defense; b. Scranton, Pa., Oct. 18, 1930; s. Frank Charles, Jr. and Roxanne (Bacon) C.; m. Marcia Myers, Apr. 15, 1976; children: Karen, Frank, Kristin. AB, Princeton U., 1952; postgrad., Sch. Bus. Adminstrn., Harvard U., 1956; postgrad. hon. dr. degree, Wilkes Coll., Kings Coll., 1973; LLD (hon.), U. Scranton, 1989. With Jantzen Co., Portland, Oreg., 1955-56; fgn. svc. officer US Dept. State, 1956—69, vice consul, econ. officer Johannesburg, 1957-59, second sec., polit. officer Kinshasa, Democratic Republic of Congo, 1960-62, officer in charge Congolese polit. affairs, 1962-64, consul gen. Zanzibar, 1964-65, counselor for polit. affairs Rio de Janeiro, 1965-69; asst. dir. Office Econ. Opportunity, Washington, 1969, dir., 1971; assoc. dir. Office Mgmt. & Budget, Exec. Office of the Pres., Washington, 1971—72, dep. dir., 1971—72; undersec. US Dept. Health, Edn. & Welfare, Washington, 1972-74, 1977—78; US amb. to Portugal US Dept. State, Lisbon, 1974—77; dep. dir. CIA, Washington, 1978-81; dep. sec. US Dept. Def., Washington, 1981—83, sec., 1987-89; asst. to the Pres. for national security affairs NSC, Washington, 1986-87; pres. Sears World Trade, Inc., Washington, 1983-84, chmn., CEO, 1984-86; vice chmn. Carlyle Group, Washington, 1989-93, chmn., 1993—2003, chmn. emeritus, 2003—05. Mem. Coun. on Fgn. Rels.; trustee RAND Corp.; co-chair RAND Ctr. for Middle East Pub. Policy; chmn. emeritus Acad. Diplomacy; bd. dir. Quaker Oats Co., SunResorts, Ltd., N.V., Encysive Pharms. Served as lt. (j.g.) USNR, 1952-54. Recipient Superior Honor award, 1969, Superior Svc. award Dept. State, 1971, HEW Disting. Civilian Svc. award, 1975, Def. Dept. Disting. Civilian award, 1977, Disting. Intelligence medal, 1981, Nat. Intelligence Disting. Svc. medal, 1981, Presdl. Citizens award, 1983, Woodrow Wilson award, 1988, James Forrestal Meml. award, 1988, Herbert Roback Meml. award, 1989, George C. Marshall award, 1989.*

CARLUCCI, JOSEPH P., lawyer; b. Port Chester, NY, Aug. 21, 1942; m. Elizabeth Smith; children: Susan Elizabeth, Kathleen Ann BS Econs., Georgetown U., 1964; JD, Fordham U., 1967. Bar: NY 1969. Ptnr. Pierro & Carlucci, Port Chester, NY, 1969—76; pvt. practice Rye, NY, 1977—78; mng. ptnr. Cuddy & Feder LLP, White Plains, NY, 1979—99. Chief legis. counsel to NY senator from Westchester County, 1971-73; chief counsel NY State Select Com. on State's Economy, 1973-74 Co-founder, v.p. Rye Town-Port Chester Rep. Club, 1972; trustee Village of Port Chester, 1974-77; chmn. Port Chester Indsl. Devel. Agy., 1974-76; mem. Westchester County Econ. Devel. Coun., 1976-80, Narcotics Guidance Coun. Port Chester, 1970-74; chmn. Met. NY YMCA Key Leaders Conf., 1984; active Parent's Coun., Wheaton Coll., 1986-87; bd. dirs. Port Chester YMCA, 1970-79, sec., 1972-77, v.p., 1978; mem. Port Chester Govt. Study Commn., 1971-73; commr. appraisal White Plains and Greenburgh Urban Renewal; counsel to South Shore Hotline, 1973-74; mem. Port Chester Pub. Employees Rels. Bd., 1973-77; adv. bd. bd. dirs. Salvation Army, 1973-77; adv. bd. Security Title and Guaranty Co., 1986-90; bd. dirs. Rye YMCA, 1979-87, pres., 1982-85, trustee, 1989—; trustee Rye Hist. Soc., 1979-83, 90-96, sec., 1980-81, v.p., 1982-83, 92-94, pres., 1994-96; interviewer alumni admissions program Georgetown U., 1988-96; bd. visitors Pace U. Sch. Law, 1990—; bd. dirs. Vol. Ctr. United Way Westchester County, 1991-97; mem. Westchester divsn. Cardinal's Com. for Laity, 1991-2001, vice chmn., 1992, chmn., 1993-95; paralegal curriculum adv. com. SUNY-Westchester CC, 1994; bd. dirs. March of Dimes Birth Defects Found., 1994-96, Westchester Bus. Partnership, 1995-98, Westchester Partnership for Econ. Devel., 1996-97, Jacob Burns Film Ctr., Inc.; bd. dirs. Mercy Coll., vice-chmn., 2006—; trustee Westchester Arts Coun., 2000-04. Capt. MPC, US Army, 1967-69 Recipient Golden R award Renaissance Project, Inc., Gold Man award YMCA, 1985, Cmty. Svc. award Rotary Internat. Club, 1995, Corp. Leadership award Andrus Children's Ctr., 2006. Mem. ABA (vice-chmn. econs. law practice com. on lawyering skills 1984-85), N.Y. State Bar Assn., Westchester County Bar Assn. (real property com. 1978-82), Port Chester-Rye Bar Assn. (sec. 1970-75, pres. 1976-77, bd. dirs. student assistance svcs. alcohol and drug abuse prevention program 1989-95, adv. bd. 1995—), Westchester C.C. Found. (bd. dirs.), Real Estate Fin. Assn. (bd. dirs. 2000-03), Coveleigh Club (bd. govs. 1978-86, sec. 1979, v.p. 1980, pres. 1981-84), Georgetown U. Met. Club (bd. dirs. 1980-82), Hundred Club Westchester (bd. dirs.) Office: Cuddy & Feder LLP 445 Hamilton Ave 14th Fl White Plains NY 10601 Office Phone: 914-761-1300. Business E-Mail: jcarlucci@cuddyfeder.com.

CARLUCCI, PAUL V., publishing executive; b. 1947; Various sales positions NY Daily News, mgr. account sales Retail City; advt. mgr. N.Y. divsn. R.H. Macy, Inc., 1979-80, councilor, 1979-80, adminstr., advt. dir., 1981-83, sr. v.p. sales promotion Midwest divsn. Kansas City, Mo., 1983-85; sr. v.p. sales promotion Macy's NJ, 1985-89; sr. v.p., dir. mktg. Caldor, Inc., Norwalk, Conn., 1989—91; exec. v.p. News Am. FSI, Inc., subs. News Corp. Ltd., NYC, 1991—92; pres. News Am. FSI, Inc. subs. News Corp. Ltd., NYC, 1993-95; CEO, News Am. Pub., Inc., NYC, 1995-97; chmn., CEO News Am. Mktg., NYC, 1997—, and pub., NY Post, 2005—. Office: News Am Mktg NY Post 1211 Ave of America New York NY 10036*

CARLUCCI, WILLIAM PHILIP, lawyer; b. Scranton, Pa., Sept. 26, 1955; m. Christine Vanderlin; 3 children. AB, Lycoming Coll., 1976; JD, Temple U., 1979. Bar: Pa. 1979, Lycoming County 1979, U.S. Dist. Ct. Md. 1980, U.S. Dist. Ct. Pa. 1980, U.S. Supreme Ct. 1988. Ptnr. Elion, Wayne, Grieco, Carlucci, Shipman & Irwin, Williamsport, Pa. Mem.: Lycoming Law Assn. (treas. 1986—87, mem. exec. com. 1988—90, v.p., pres.-elect 1991, pres. 1992), Pa. Bar Assn. (v.p. 2003—04, pres.-elect 2004—, mem. bd. govs. 1993—96). Office: Elion Wayne Grieco Carlucci Shipman & Irwin 125 E Third St Williamsport PA 17701 Office Phone: 570-326-2443. Office Fax: 570-326-1585. E-mail: elionwayne@suscom.net, ewcarlucci@suscom.net.*

CARLUZZO, LEWIS R., federal judge; b. NJ, 1949; Diploma, Villanova U., 1971, JD, 1974. Bar: NJ 1974. Law clk. NJ Superior Ct. Judge; assoc., city prosecutor Bridgeton, NJ, 1975; atty., office of chief counsel, dist. counsel's office IRS, Washington, 1977—83, spl. trial atty. litig., 1983—92, spl. trial atty. large case, 1992—94; spl. trial judge US Tax Ct., 1994—. Office: US Tax Ct 400 Second St NW Washington DC 20217*

CARLYLE, BOBBIE KRISTINE, sculptor; b. Idaho, 1948; d. Howard and Ethel Seelos Carlyle; children: K. Justin Lawyer, Jennifer Crosby, Jared Lawyer, Jessika Tora, Joshua Lawyer, Jacob Lawyer, Jonas Lawyer. BFA, Brigham Young U., Provo, Utah, 1989. Sculptor Bobbie Carlyle Sculpture Studios, Loveland, Colo., 1967—. Sculptor (bronze sculpture) Diadems, Buffalo Soldier, Day's Catch, Chief's Daughter, For Love of the Game, Endeavor, Yield Curve, Balance and Harmony, Espirit de Corps, The Fabric of Her Soul, Stretch the Limits, Descent Into Night, Hard to Leave, Hunter, In Progress, Jennifer, Lorelei, Moses, Mounting Relief, On the Brink of Tomorrow, One Point Landing, Pace the Wind, Phoenix Rising, Priority Mail, Puppy Dog Tales, Reeds, Self Made Woman, Storyteller, Sunriser, Self Made Man, Upper Limits, La Vendemia, Aviator, Puppy Dog Tales, #1 Handicap, A State of Grace, Ariel, At The Well. Recipient Ettel Grant award, Allied Artists of Am., 1990. Mem.: Nat. Sculpture Soc. Home Phone: 970-622-0213; Office Phone: 970-622-0213. Personal E-mail: bobbiecarlyle@att.net.

CARLYLE, RANDY, professional hockey coach, retired professional hockey player; b. Sudbury, Ont., Can., Apr. 19, 1956; m. Corey Carlyle; children: Craig, Derek, Alexis. Defenseman Toronto Maple Leafs, 1976—78, Pitts. Penguins, 1978—84, Winnipeg Jets, 1984—93, asst. coach, 1995—96, Manitoba Moose, 1996—97, head coach, 1997—2001, 2004—05; asst. coach Washington Capitals, 2002—04; head coach Anaheim Ducks (formerly Mighty Ducks of Anaheim), 2005—. Achievements include being the head coach of Stanley Cup Champion, Anaheim Ducks, 2007. Office: Anaheim Ducks 2695 E Katella Ave Anaheim CA 92806*

CARLYON, DAVID JAMES, writer, theater director; b. Lincoln, Nebr., July 24, 1949; s. Donald and Betty Carlyon; m. Barbara Whitman, Oct. 19, 1986; children: Daniel, Will. BA, U. Mich., 1971; JD, U. Calif., Berkeley, 1976; PhD, Northwestern U., Evanston, Ill., 1993. Circus clown Ringling Bros. and Barnum & Bailey Circus, National Tours, DC, 1976—79; actor NYC, 1980—89; asst. prof. theater U. Mich., Flint, 1993—96; writer Larchmont, NY, 1996—. Author: Dan Rice: The Most Famous Man You've Never Heard Of, 2001 (Wash. Irving Book Award, 2001). Vol. schs., Mamaroneck, NY, 1996—2006; baseball coach Little League / Babe Ruth, Mamaroneck, NY, 1997—2005. With US Army, 1971—73. Mem.: Am. Hist. Assn., Calif. Bar Assn., Orgn. Am. Historians, Assn. Theatre in Higher Edn., Am. Soc. for Theatre Rsch., SAG, AFTRA, Dramatists Guild, Actors Equity Assn., Circus Hist. Soc. Personal E-mail: carlyon@aol.com.

CARMACK, CATHERINE ELISE, archives administrator; b. Nashville, Sept. 13, 1956; d. John Douglas and Mildred Harrell Carmack. BA in History, U. Tenn., Knoxville, 1983; BS in Comm., Mid. Tenn. State U., Murfreesboro, 1986, MA in History, 1995. Archival asst. Tenn. State Libr. and Archives, Nashville, 1986—95, archivist, 1995—2006, dir. Archival Tech. Svcs., 2006—. Active MoveOn.org, 2003—, Nashville Symphony Chorus, 1989—; vol. Nashville Humane Assn., 2005—. Mem.: Soc. Am. Archivists, Soc. Tenn. Archivists (webmaster 1995—), Delta Gamma (life). Liberal. Avocations: music, working with animals, jewelry-making. Office: Tennessee State Library and Archives 403 Seventh Ave North Nashville TN 37243-0312 Home Phone: 615-833-4410; Office Phone: 615-253-3468. Office Fax: 615-532-5315. Business E-Mail: cathi.carmack@state.tn.us.

CARMACK, MILDRED JEAN, retired lawyer; b. Folsom, Calif., Sept. 3, 1938; d. Kermit Leroy Brown and Elsie Imogene (Johnston) Walker; m. Allan W. Carmack, 1957 (div. 1979); 1 child, Kerry Jean Carmack Garrett. Student, Linfield Coll., 1955-58; BA, U. Oreg., 1967, JD, 1969. Bar: Oreg. 1969, U.S. Dist. Ct. Oreg. 1980, U.S. Ct. Appeals (9th and fed. cirs.) 1980, U. S. Claims Ct. 1987. Law clk. to Hon. William McAllister Oreg. Supreme Ct., Salem, 1969-73, asst. to ct., 1976-80; asst. prof. U. Oreg. Law Sch., Eugene, 1973-76; assoc. Schwabe, Williamson & Wyatt, Portland, Oreg., 1980-83, ptnr., 1984-96, ret., 1996. Writer, lectr., legal educator, Oreg., 1969—; mem. exec. bd. Appellate sect. Oreg. State Bar, 1993-95. Contbr. articles to Oreg. Law Rev., 1967-70. Mem. citizen adv. com. State Coastal Planning Commn., Oreg., 1974-76, State Senate Judiciary Com., Oreg., 1984; mem. bd. visitors Law Sch. U. Oreg., 1992-95; mem. Oreg. Law Commn. Working Group on Conflict of Laws, 2000. Mem. Oreg. State Bar Assn., Order of Coif.

CARMAN, CAROL A., psychologist, educator; d. Nora and Martin Carman. BS Psychology, Tex. A&M U., 1999, MS Ednl. Psychology, specializing in Creativity and Giftedness, 2000; PhD Ednl. Psychology specializing in Stats. and Measurement, U. Kans., 2005. Grad. tchg. asst. U. Kans., Lawrence, 2001—05; asst. prof. U. Houston - Clear Lake, 2005—. Mem.: APA, Am. Ednl. Rsch. Assn., Nat. Assn. for Gifted Children (life). Avocations: reading, computers, gaming, cooking, travel. Office: Univ Houston - Clear Lake 2700 Bay Area Blvd Houston TX 77058 Home Phone: 281-990-9950.

CARMAN, GARY OLEN, child welfare consultant; b. Binghamton, NY, Oct. 27, 1935; s. George Earl and Ann (Bell) C.; m. Judith Florence Haight, Mar. 22, 1963; children: Virginia Eve, Monica Lou. BS, SUNY, Buffalo, 1962, MS, 1965; cert. in advanced study, Syracuse U., 1968, PhD, 1972; MSW, Fordham U., 2002. Tchr. Lakeshore Sch. Dist., Eden, NY, 1962-64, Gateway Treatment Ctr., Williamsville, NY, 1964-66; dir. Edn. Gateway Pub. Sch., Williamsville, NY, 1967-70; supr. Spl. Edn. North Syracuse (N.Y.) Pub. Schs., 1971-72; dir. spl. svcs. Yonkers (N.Y.) Pub. Schs., 1972-75; CEO Julia Dyckman Andrus Meml., Yonkers, 1975—2003. Mem. Coun. on Accreditation, Tex. Edn. Dept., Austin, 1971-72, N.Y. State Edn. Dept., 1973-74, Bd. Coop. Ednl. Svcs., North Westchester, Putnam, Yorktown Heights, N.Y., 1992. Author: Permanence & Family Support, 1988, Evaluation Criteria for Special Education in Residential Schools, 1991, Quality Indicators in Residential Treatment, 1994; contbr. articles to profl. jours. Chmn. bd. dirs. Salvation Army-Citadel Corp., Yonkers, 1977-88; mem. Mayor of Yonkers Blue Ribbon Task Force for selection of Bd. Edn., 1988-90; mem. Yonkers 2000 com., 1989-91; bd. dirs. YMCA, Yonkers, 1987-89, Nat. Commn. on Accreditation for Spl. Edn. Svcs., 1991—; bd. dirs. Alliance for Children and Families, 1997-2000; chair Westchester Behavioral Healthcare Network, 1996-98; governing bd. Internat. Coun. Exceptional Children, 1980-83. Recipient Nordlinger Child Welfare Leadership award, 1999; U.S. Office of Edn. fellow, 1966-67, 70-72, Paul Harris fellow Rotary Internat., 1988. Mem. Nat. Assn. Homes and Svcs. for Children (bd. dirs. 1984-87, pres. 1997), Child Welfare League of Am.), Internat. Inst. Edn. Spl. (bd. dirs. 1990—, chmn. internat. congress, chmn. Am. del. to internat. congress in Vienna 1992-96), Phi Kappa Phi. Avocations: golf, birdwatching, travel. Office: Carman Consulting 11 Timber Trail South Windsor CT 06074 Office Phone: 860-432-7737, 860-916-9785. Personal E-mail: Goc63@aol.com.

CARMAN, GREGORY WRIGHT, federal judge; b. Farmingdale, NY, Jan. 31, 1937; s. Willis B. and Marjorie (Sosa) C. Exch. student, U. Paris, 1956-57; BA, St. Lawrence U., 1958; JD, St. John's U., 1961; Judge Adv. Gen. honors grad., U. Va. Law Sch., 1962. Bar: N.Y. 1961. Atty. Carman, Callahan & Sabino, Farmingdale, N.Y., 1964-83; councilman Town of Oyster Bay, N.Y., 1972-81; mem. 97th Congress from 3d Dist. N.Y., 1981-82; U.S. Congl. del. I.M.F. Cong., 1982; judge U.S. Ct. Internat. Trade, NYC, 1983—96, 2003—, acting chief judge, 1991, chief judge, 1996—2003. Statutory mem. Jud. Conf. U.S., 1991. Capt. AUS, 1962-64. Fellow Am. Bar Found.; mem. ABA, N.Y. State Bar Assn. (cts. and cmty. com.), Nassau County Bar Assn., Nassau Lawyers Assn., St. John's Law Rev. Republican. Episcopalian. Office: US Ct Internat Trade 1 Federal Plz New York NY 10278-0001*

CARMAN, JUDITH ELAINE, music educator, writer; b. Mayfield, Ky., Dec. 4, 1940; d. Roscoe Vernon Carman and Mary Jewell Caldwell. MusB, George Peabody Coll., Nashville, 1963, MusM, 1965; DMA, U. of Iowa, 1973. Instr. in music and voice Shenandoah Conservatory of Music, Winchester, Va., 1966—69; grad. asst. in voice U. of Iowa Sch. of Music, Iowa City, 1970—73; asst. prof. music Cen. Mich. U., Mt. Pleasant, 1973—74; pvt. voice tchr. Houston, 1979—2007. Adj. instr. in music Houston Bapt. U., 1978—79; vis. prof. of voice Tex. So. U., Houston, 2005—06; yoga tchr. pvt. classes, Houston, 1999—. Editor: (annotated bibliography) Art Song in the United States: An Annotated Bibliography, 1976, Art Song in the United States, 1759-1999: An Annotated Bibliography, 2001; author: Art Song in the United States, 1987, (column) Music Review in Journal of Singing, 1997—. Mem.: Nat. Assn. of Tchrs. of Singing (pres. Greater Houston chpt. 1990—92), Calif. Yoga Tchrs. Assn. (corr.). Liberal. Episcopalian. Avocations: bicycling, reading, writing, cooking, hiking and camping. Home Phone: 713-789-7606. Personal E-mail: jecarman@earthlink.net.

CARMANY, GEORGE WALTER, III, finance company executive, consultant; b. NYC, Mar. 21, 1940; s. George Walter Carmany, Jr. and Merle (Harrold) Carmany; m. Judith Jermain Lawrence, Apr. 27, 1968; children: George W. W., Elizabeth C. Perreten. BA, Amherst Coll., 1962. V.p. Bankers Trust Co., NYC, 1966—71; sr. v.p. Am. Express Co., NYC, 1975—81; sr. exec. v.p. Am. Express Bank, Ltd., NYC, 1981—90, The Boston Co., 1990—93; pres. G.W. Carmany & Co., Inc., Boston, 1994—. Vice chmn. Computerized Med. Systems, St. Louis, 2001—; sr. advisor EnGeneIC Pty. Ltd., Sydney, 2003—; dir. SunLife Fin., Inc., Toronto, Ontario, Canada, 2004—, Macquarie Infrastructure Co., NYC, 2004—; chmn. Helicon Therapeutics, Farmingdale, NY, 1999—2005. Mem. pres.'s cir. The Nat. Acads., Wash., 2002—; chmn. The New Eng. Med. Ctr. Hosps, Boston, 1996—97; vice chmn. Lifespan, Inc., Providence, 1997—2002; chmn. bd. assocs. The Whitehead Inst., Cambridge, Mass., 2001—03; mem. exec. com. alumni coun. Amherst Coll., 2007—, mem. exec. com coun., 2007—; trustee Bentley Coll., Waltham, Mass., 1990—. Lt. USNR, 1962—66. Recipient Disting. Svc. award, Amherst Coll., 2001. Mem.: Racquet and Tennis Club, Ft. Worth Boat Club, Shinnecock Yacht Club (commodore 1983—87), Royal Sydney Yacht Squadron, Somerset Club, N.Y. Yacht Club (trustee 1996—). Avocations: ocean racing, game fishing, hunting. Home: 4 Lime St Boston MA 02108 Office: GW Carmany and Co Inc 1 Liberty Sq Ste 1200 Boston MA 02109 Home Phone: 617-720-2824; Office Phone: 617-542-5918.

CARMELI, MOSHE, theoretical physicist; b. Baghdad, Iraq, June 15, 1933; arrived in Israel, 1951; naturalized US citizen, 1973; s. Eliaho and Neomi Carmeli-Chitayat; m. Elisheva Cohen, Aug. 17, 1961; children: Eli, Dorith, Yair. MSc, Hebrew U., Jerusalem, 1960; DSc, Technion-Israel Inst. Tech., Haifa, 1964. Rsch. assoc. Lehigh U., Bethlehem, Pa., 1964-65, Temple U., Phila., 1964-65, U. Md., Coll. Pk., Md., 1965-67, asst. prof., 1967-68; rsch. physicist USAF Lab., Dayton, Ohio, 1967-72; assoc. prof. Ben Gurion U., Beer Sheva, 1972-74, head physics dept., 1973-77, prof. physics, 1974—, Albert Einstein prof. physics, 1979—2004, emeritus prof. theoretical physics, 2004—, head Theoretical Physics Ctr., 1980-89. Vis. prof. Inst. for Theoretical Physics, SUNY, Stony Brook, 1977-78, 81, U. Md., Coll. Pk., 1985-86, Inst. Henri Poincaré, Paris, 1975, Internat. Ctr. for Theoretical Physics, Trieste, 1977, 78, 79, 80, 81, 82, 85, 87, 88, Max-Planck Inst., Munich, 1980, U. Mass., Amherst, 1985, Colgate U., Hamilton, NY, 1987, Queen Mary Coll., U. London, 1988, State U. Campinas, São Paulo, Brazil, 1998, Churchill Coll. U Cambridge, 2000, Inst. of Astrophysics U. Cambridge, 2000. Author: Group Theory and General Relativity, 1977, Classical Fields: General Relativity and Gauge Theory, 1982, Statistical Theory and Random Matrices, 1983, Cosmological Special Relativity: The Large-Scale Structure of Space, Time and Velocity, 1997, 2d edit., 2002, Cosmological RElativity: The Special and General Theories for the Structure of the Universe, 2006; co-author: Representations of the Rotation and Lorentz Groups, 1976, Gauge Fields: Classification and Equations of Motion, 1989, Gravitation: SL (2,C) Gauge Theory and Conservation Laws, 1990, Theory of Spinors, 2000; co-editor: Relativity, 1970; mem. editl. bd. Weizmann Sci. Press, 1978-80; referee Phys. Rev., Phys. Rev. Latt., Found. Phys., Gen. Relativity Gravitation, Jour. Math. Phys., Internat. Jour. Theoretical Physics, Nuovo Cimanto, Classical Quantatum Gravity, NSF, NRC, US-Israel Binat. Sci. Found. Rev.; reviewer Math. Reviews; contbr. more than 100 articles to profl. jours. Fellow AAAS, Am. Phys. Soc. (jour. referee); mem. Israel Phys. Soc. (pres. 1982-85), Internat. Soc. for Gen. Relativity and Gravitation, NY Acad. Sci., Sigma Xi. Home: 19 Erez St Omer Israel Office: Ben Gurion U Dept Physics Be'er Sheva 84105 Israel Office Phone: 972-8-6461647. Business E-Mail: carmelim@bgu.ac.il.

CARMELLINI, ANDREW, chef; Student, Culinary Inst. Am., 1991. Commis position San Domenico, Imola, Italy, chef tournant NYC; chef de partie with Gray Kunz Lespinasse, 1993—96; sous chef Le Cirque 2000; exec. chef Cafe Boulud, NYC, 1998—. Named Best New Chef, Food and Wine Mag., 2000; recipient Best Chef: NYC, The James Beard Found., 2005. Office: Cafe Boulud 20 East 76th St New York NY 10021-2688*

CARMEN, IRA HARRIS, political scientist, educator; b. Boston, Dec. 3, 1934; s. Jacob and Lida (Rosenman) Carmen; m. Sandra Vineberg, Sept. 6, 1958 (div. June 1999); children: Gail Deborah, Amy Rebecca; m. Lawrence Lowell Putnam, Mar. 16, 2000. BA, U. N.H., 1957; MA, U. Mich., 1959, PhD, 1964. Asst. prof. Ball State U., 1963-66; assoc. prof. Coe Coll., 1966-68; prof. polit. sci. U. Ill., 1968—. Mem. Inst. Genomic Biology U. Ill., 2004—; mem. recombinant DNA adv. com. NIH, 1990—94; vis. lectr. Tamkang U., Taiwan, 1991; participant numerous internat. meetings. Author: Movies, Censorship, and the Law, 1966, Power and Balance, 1978, Cloning and the Constitution, 1986, Politics in the Laboratory: The Constitution of Human Genomics, 2004; contbr. articles to profl. jours. Sr. advisor Bush-Quayle Nat. Jewish Campaign Com., 1988; mem. Pres. George Bush's Inaugural Educators Adv. Com., 1989; guest del. Rep. Nat. Conv., 1992; mem. Rep. Nat. Com., Rep. Jewish Coalition, Straight Talk Am. Grantee, NSF; vis. scholar, Yale Law Sch., 1981. Mem.: AAAS, Assn. Politics and Life Scis. (chmn. coun. 2000—03), Am. Soc. Gene Therapy, Human Genome Orgn., Phi Beta Kappa. Office: U Ill Dept Polit Sci Urbana IL 61801 Home Phone: 217-373-5814; Office Phone: 217-333-3880. Business E-Mail: icarmen@uiuc.edu.

CARMICHAEL, DAN R., insurance company executive; Chmn., pres., CEO Anthem Casualty Ins. Group; CEO Shelby Ins.; pres., CEO IVANS, Inc., 1994—2000; pres., CEO, dir. Ohio Casualty Corp., Fairfield, Ohio, 2000—07; exec. cons. Liberty Mutual Agency Markets, 2007. Bd. dir. Alleghany Corp., Platinum Underwriters Holdings Ltd. Mem.: Griffith Found. for Ins. Edn. (trustee), Ins. Inst. Am. (trustee), Am. Inst. Chartered Property Casualty Underwriters (trustee). Office: Ohio Casualty Corp 9450 Seward Rd Fairfield OH 45014 Office Phone: 513-603-2400. Office Fax: 513-603-7900.*

CARMICHAEL, DAVID BURTON, physician; b. Santa Ana, Calif., Sept. 12, 1923; s. David Burton and Phyllis (Adams) Carmichael; m. Ava Louise Smith, Dec. 26, 1944; children: Catherine Ann, Heather Sue, Linda L., Ava L. Student, Graceland U., 1940-42; BA, MD, U. Iowa, 1946; postgrad., Harvard U., 1949-50; LL.D. (hon.), Graceland U., Iowa, 1985. Diplomate Am. Bd. Internal Medicine. Clin. and research fellow medicine Mass. Gen. Hosp., Boston, 1949-50; cons. cardiovascular diseases U.S. Naval Hosp., San Diego, Camp Pendleton, 1956-86, U.S. VA, 1960-82; chief dept. medicine Scripps Meml. Hosp., La Jolla, Calif., 1961-63, 65-67, chief staff, 1970-71. Clin. prof. medicine U. Calif. at San Diego, 1968—; pres. De Anza Lab. Corp., 1962-72, Carmichael-Carson Med.-Clin. Lab. Corp., 1962-75; sr. ptnr. Med. Clinic; founding med. dir. Cardiovascular Inst. Scripps Meml. Hosps., 1985-96; pres. Orange County Pioneer Coun., 1993-94; trustee GDE Systems, Inc., 1992-94. Contbr. articles to profl. jours. Trustee Millicent Rogers Mus., Taos, N.Mex., 1986—90, Graceland U., Iowa, 1987—, Rancho de las Golondrinas Mus., Santa Fe, 1989—. Rear adm. med. insp. gen. USNR. Decorated Legion of Merit; recipient Alumni Disting. Service award Graceland U., 1967. Master ACP (gov. So. Calif. region III 1972-76, Laureate award 1991); fellow Am. Coll. Cardiology (dir., sec. 1975, trustee 1979-85, Disting. Fellow award 1994, Mastership 2001), Am. Coll. Chest Physicians, Am. Heart Assn., Am. Heart Assn. (fellow); mem. AMA (chmn. specialty soc. and service delegation 1985-87, 93-96, mem. grad. med. edn. adv. com. 1983—89, chmn., 1985-87, chmn. sect. council on clin. cardiology, Disting. Svc. award 1997), San Diego County Heart Assn. (pres. 1959-60), San Diego Biomed. Rsch. Inst. (pres. 1958-59, 62-63, vice chmn. residency rev. com. internal medicine 1971-78), Soc. Med. Cons. to the Armed Forces, San Diego Soc. Internal Medicine (pres. 1959-61). Republican. Mem. Community Ch. of Christ. Home: 8333 Calle Del Cielo La Jolla CA 92037-3033 Personal E-mail: ascdbc@aol.com. *This country, with its Christian heritage, gives to the vast majority the opportunity to serve and often, the chance to excel. The guidance of parents and instructors should never be forgotten, nor should the sacrifices of those who have allowed us to preserve our freedom.*

CARMICHAEL, DAVID RICHARD, lawyer, insurance company executive; b. Sept. 4, 1942; BS, UCLA, 1964, JD, 1967. Bar: Calif. 1968. Assoc. Adams, Duque & Hazeltine, LA, 1967-72; gen. counsel The Housing Group, Irvine, Calif., 1972-77; assoc. counsel Pacific Mut. Life Ins. Co., 1977-81, v.p., assoc. gen. counsel, 1981-89, corp. sec., 1981—83, 2nd v.p., assoc. gen. counsel, 1983—92, v.p., investment counsel, 1989-92, sr. v.p., gen. counsel, 1992—. Dir. & chmn. Ca. Life & Health Ins. Guarantee Assn.; dir. Assn. Ca. Life Ins. Companies, Assn. Life Ins. Counsel. Office: Pacific Life Ins Co 700 Newport Center Dr Newport Beach CA 92660-6307

CARMICHAEL, DONALD SCOTT, retired lawyer, corporate financial executive; b. Toledo, Feb. 19, 1912; s. Grey Thornton and Edna Earle (Jaite) C.; m. Mary Glenn Dickinson, May 28, 1940; children: Mary Brooke McMurray, Pamela Hastings Keenan. AB, Harvard U., 1935, student Sch. Law, 1935-37; LLB, U. Mich., 1942. Bar: Ohio 1942. Staff dept. law City of Cleve., 1938-40; chief renegotiation br. Cleve. Ordnance Dist., War Dept., 1942-46; practiced in Cleve., 1946; asst. sec. Diamond Alkali Co., 1946-48, sec., 1948-57, gen. counsel, 1957-58; v.p.-gen. counsel Stouffer Corp., 1959-60, exec. v.p., 1960-64; practiced in Cleve., 1964-71; pres. Schrafft's divsn. Pet, Inc., NYC, 1971-75, Sportsvc. Corp., Buffalo, 1975-80, Del. North Cos., Inc., Buffalo, 1980-89, vice chmn., 1989; officer, dir. various corps.; dir., cons. Editor: F.D.R; Columnist, 1947; Contbr. to law revs. Mem. Cuyahoga County Charter Commn., 1959; chmn.; mem. Cleve. Met. Services Commn., 1957-59, President's Task Force on War Against Poverty, 1964; Del. Democratic Nat. Conv., 1960, 64; mem. Cuyahoga County Dem. Exec. Com.; Chmn. bd. trustees Cuyahoga County Hosps., 1958-64, Urban League, Karamu House. Mem. ABA, Ohio Bar Assn., Cleve. Bar Assn., Union Club Cleve., Chagrin Valley Hunt Club, Harvard Club N.Y.C., River Club N.Y.C., Buffalo Club, Phi Gamma Delta. Home: 21 Hardscrabble Ln Lyme NH 03768

CARMICHAEL, GARY ALAN ALAN, social studies educator; b. Missoula, Mont., May 7, 1964; s. Glen Alan Carmichael and Jerri Ruth (Haines) Maclay. BA, U. Mont., 1989. Cert. tchr., Mont. Telecommunication specialist, social studies chmn., libr. media specialist Saco Pub. Schs., 1990-93; libr. media specialist Great Falls Pub. Schs., 1993—97; now social studies tchr. White Fish (Mont.) H.S., 1997—. Mem. adv. com. No. Mont. Curriculum Consortium, 1990-93; coach speech, debate, drama team, Saco, 1990-93; trainer, online resource, Discovery Channel Sch. Pres. Circle K Internat., U. Mont., 1986, gov. Mont. dist., 1984. Named Mont. Tchr. of Yr., 2007. Mem. Mont. Libr. Assn., Mont. Coun. for Social Studies, Theta Chi (pres.), U. Mont. Alumni Assn.; Whitefish Edn. Assn. (past v.p.). Office: Whitefish HS 600 East 2nd St Whitefish MT 59937*

CARMICHAEL, GREG D., bank executive; BS, Univ. Dayton; MS, Ctrl. Mich. Univ. Mgmt. positions GE; v.p., CIO Emerson Elec. Co.; exec. v.p. info. tech. & ops., CIO Fifth Third Bancorp, Cin., 2004—06, exec. v.p., COO, 2006—. Office: Fifth Third Bancorp Fifth Third Ctr 38 Fountain Sq Plz Cincinnati OH 45263*

CARMICHAEL, JESSE ROYAL, musician; b. Boulder, Colo., Apr. 2, 1979; Band mem. Kara's Flowers (name changed to Maroon 5, 2001), LA, 1994—; signed to Reprise Records, 1997—99, Octone Records, 2001—. Musician (as Kara's Flowers): (albums) Fourth World, 1997; musician: (as Maroon 5) Songs About Jane, 2002, 1.22.03.Acoustic, 2004, Live Friday the 13th, 2005, It Won't Be Soon Before Long, 2007, (songs) Harder to Breathe, 2003, This Love, 2004 (MTV Video Music award for Best New Artist, 2004, Grammy award for Best Group Pop Performance, 2006), She Will Be Loved, 2004, Shiver, 2005, contbr. to Spider-Man 2 soundtrack, 2004. Recipient World Music award for Best New Group, 2004, MTV Europe award for Best New Act, 2004, Grammy award for Best New Artist (with Maroon 5), 2005. Address: Maroon 5 PO Box 884564 San Francisco CA 94188 Office: Octone Records Rm 500 560 Broadway New York NY 10012 Office Phone: 646-613-0200. E-mail: maroon5@maroon5.com.

CARMICHAEL, JUDY LEA, record industry executive, concert jazz pianist; b. Lynwood, Calif., Nov. 27, 1952; d. John Alvin and Jeanne Pauline (Boock) Hohenstein. Student, Calif. State U., Long Beach, 1970-73, Calif. State U., Fullerton. Owner C&D Prodns., NYC, 1989—. Chmn. jazz fellowships com. NEA, Washington, 1990-91; featured on Nat. Pub. Radio, Marian McPartland's Piano Jazz, 1990, Morning Edition Nat. Pub. Radio, also TV programs Entertainment Tonight, CBS, Sunday Morning with Charles Kuralt, 1993; host, prodr. Pet Syle Radio with Judy Carmichael, 2007. Performed as pianist at Breda Jazz Festival, The Netherlands, 1986, Carnegie Hall, N.Y.C., 1988, 89, Rio de Janeiro, 1989, Peggy Guggenheim Mus., Venice, Italy, 1990, Am. Acad., Rome, 1990, 91, USIA Tour, Portugal, 1991, Spain, 1991, India, 1988, China, 1992, Singapore, 1994, S. Am., 1996, major U.S. tours 1993-95, also L.A., Zurich, Switzerland, Paris, Cannes, France; performer Stanford Symphony Pops with Skitch Henderson, 1997; author (music) Judy Carmichael's Complete Book of Stride Piano, 1987, You Can Play Stride Piano, 1996; prodr., artist (LP's) Jazz Piano, 1983, Two Handed Stride, 1980, (CD's) Trio, 1989, Old Friends, 1991, Pearls, 1985, ...And Basie Called Her Stride, 1993, Judy, 1994, Chops, 1995, PianoDisc, 1995, QRS piano rolls, 1996, (CD and player piano formats) High on Fats and Other Stuff, 1997; featured on CBS Sunday Morning with Charles Osgood, Entertainment Tonight, Prairie Home Companion, Nat. Pub. Radio's Morning Edit.; jazz editor Sheet Music mag., 1989-90; host, creator, prodr. Judy Carmichael's Jazz Inspired, Nat. Pub. Radio, 2000—, Pub. Radio Internat. on Sirius Satellite Network; stage show with Steve Ross 2000-2003 aboard QEII and throughout Europe and U.S., and QEII, Canary Islands, Lisbon, Atlantic crossing; tour of Australia and New Zealand, 2004; performer Robert Redford's Sundance Cantata, 2004, Sundance Film Festival, 2005, QMII concerts, 2005; co-host, prodr. (radio show) Dog Talk, 2005-06, prodr., host Pet Style Radio with Judy Carmichael, PetStyle.com and Sirius Satellite Radio, 2007—; contbr. numerous articles to profl. jours. NEA fellow, grantee; Grammy award nominee, 1980; chosen to be Steinway artist, 1986; nominated for Mac award Manhattan Assn. Cabarets and Clubs for Stage Show with Steve Ross, 1996. Avocations: golf, softball, tennis, skiing. Office Phone: 631-725-3603. Personal E-mail: judy@judycarmichael.com.

CARMICHAEL, ROBERTA KAY, writer; b. Daytona Beach, Fla., Dec. 11, 1956; d. James Lawton and Barbara Kent Coward; m. Del Carmichael, July 5, 1974; 1 child, Joseph. Grad. H.S., Crescent City, Fla.; Breaking into Print Diploma, Long Ridge Writers Group, West Redding, Conn., 2000. Tchr. Kiddie Korner Nursery Sch., Crescent City, 1972—77; freelance writer Homosassa, Fla., 2000—. Contbr. articles to publs. Phys. therapy vol. Citrus Meml. Hosp., Inverness, Fla., 1992—93. Mem.: Pisgah Camping Club. Avocations: writing, reading, woodcarving, hiking, dulcimer. Home: 3610 S Springbreeze Way Homosassa FL 34448

CARMICHAEL, SALLY W., volunteer; b. Jackson, Ms., Jan. 14, 1925; d. Benton McMillin and Adele Rhodes Wakefield; m. Charles Ellis Carmichael; children: Chris, Charles E. Jr. Student, Hollins U., Roanoke, Va., 1942—44; BA in Sociology, U. Ga., Athens, 1946. With Ms. Sch. Supply Co.; radio commentator. Advisor Miss. Childrens Mus., 2004—06; pres. Miss. Symphony Found., 1986, sec., 1990—2005; bd. govs. Miss. Symphony Orch., 1974—83, 1985—2001, sec., 1976, search com., 2000; pres. Jackson Symphony League, 1974, bd. dirs., 1974—2005; exec. v.p. Miss. Assn. Symphony Orchs., 1979—83; pres. nat. vol. coun. Am. Symphony Orch. League, 1982—83, mem. exec. com., 1982—83, nat. coun. panelist, 1979—86, 1990, vol. cons., 1986—91, chair S.Ea. regional conf. Jackson, 1981, newsheet editor nat. vol. coun., 1976—80; sec. of bd. Arts Alliance, 1987—88, mem. exec. com., 1988—91; pres. Gallery Guild Miss. Mus. Art, 1982, mem. aux. bd., 1989—97; mem. exec. com. Miss. Friends of the Arts, 1980—86; mem. adv. coun. Jackson Pub. Sch. Dist. Acad. and Peforming Arts Complex, 1991—2000; commr. Miss. Arts Ctr./Planetarium, 1983—91; docent Govs. Mansion, 1989—; panelist S.Ea. Mus. Conf., 1991; bd. dirs. Miss. Meth. Rehab. Ctr., 1990—2006; pres. and bd. advisor So. Christian Svcs. for Children and Youth, 1990—2006; sec., bd. dirs., advisor Jr. League Jackson, 1956—66; active Wilson Found. Bd., 2000—06; past pres. Jackson chpt. Goodwill Industries Vol. Svcs., v.p. nat. chpt. Named Vol. of Yr., Goodwill Industries, 1993, Ms. Mus. Art, 1993; recipient Nat. Cmty. Arts award for first concert at a rehab. hosp., 1979, Miss. Govs. award for the arts, 2002. Mem.: Nat. Mus. Women in Arts (Miss. State Com.). Home: 4730 Old Canton Rd Jackson MS 39211 Personal E-mail: ccarmic525@aol.com.

CARMICHAEL, WILLIAM DANIEL, management consultant, educator; b. Denver, Sept. 5, 1929; s. Fitzhugh Lee and Anna Devona (Sullivan) C.; m. Faith Young, June 21, 1958; children: Amy, Philip Fitzhugh, Daniel Owen. AB, Yale, 1950; MA, MPA, Princeton, 1952, PhD, 1959; BLitt (Rhodes scholar), U. Oxford, Eng., 1955; LLD (hon.), U. W.I., 1989. Legislative analyst U.S. Bur. Budget, 1955-56, budget analyst, 1956-57; lectr. econs. and pub. affairs Princeton, 1957-60, asst. prof., 1960-62; dir. undergrad. program Woodrow Wilson Sch. Pub. and Internat. Affairs, 1958-62; prof. econ. policy, dean Grad. Sch. Bus. and Pub. Adminstrn., Cornell U., 1962-68; rep. Ford Found., Brazil, 1968-71, head Latin Am. and Caribbean, 1971-77, Middle East and Africa, 1977-81, v.p. for developing country programs, 1981-89; exec. dir. Ea. European programs Inst. Internat. Edn., NYC, 1989-93. Cons. on edn. and econ. devel., 1993—. Bd. dirs. emeritus Human Rights Watch; bd. dirs. So. African Legal Svcs.; chmn. Future Generations. Mem. Coun. on Fgn. Rels., Assn. Am. Rhodes Scholars, Phi Beta Kappa. Home and Office: 603 W Lyon Farm Dr Greenwich CT 06831-4363 Home Phone: 203-532-1461; Office Phone: 203-532-1461. Personal E-mail: wdcarm@optonline.net.

CARMODY, ARTHUR RODERICK, JR., lawyer, director; b. Shreveport, La., Feb. 19, 1928; s. Arthur R. and Caroline (Gaughan) C.; m. Renee Aubry, Jan. 26, 1952 (div. 1980); children: Helen Bragg, Renee, Arthur Roderick, Patrick, Timothy, Mary, Virginia, Joseph; m. Mary Wells, Sept. 1, 1990. Grad. with honors, N.Mex. Mil. Inst.; BS, Fordham U., 1949; LLB, La. State U., 1952. Bar: La. 1952, U.S. Supreme Ct. 1971. Mem. firm Wilkinson, Carmody & Gilliam and its predecessors, Shreveport, 1952—. Bd. dirs. Kansas City So. Transport Co., Kansas City, Shreveport and Gulf Terminal Co., Shreveport Braves Baseball Club (Tex. League), Sta. KDAQ-FM Pub. Radio, pres., 1991, chmn., 1992, RED River Pub. Radio Network; mem. Shreveport Steamer (World Football League) Partnership; pres. Touchdown Club of Shreveport, 1960; pres. Loyola Coll. Prep., 1982-1986. Author: Legal Problems in the Development and Mining of Lignite, 1976; legal history columnist Shreveport Bar Review, 1995—; La. adv. editor The Insurance Bar, 1961—. Chmn. Met. Shreveport Zoning Bd. Appeals, 1959—72; mem. gov.'s ad hoc com. for preparation rules and regulations for mining and reclamation of lignite in State of La., Dept. Conservation, 1978—79; mem. select com. for rev. stds. juc. conduct Supreme Ct. La., 1994—; pres. bd. trustees Jesuit H.S., 1976—82; chmn. bd. govs. Loyola Found., Shreveport, 1991—94; trustee Schumpert Med. Ctr., 1965—85; adv. bd. La. State U., Shreveport, 1982—86, La. State U. Found., Baton Rouge, Agnew Day Sch., Shreveport, 1970—82; bd. dirs. Ridgewood Montessori Sch., Christus Schumpert Health Sys. Found.; bd. trustees La. State Paul M. Hebert Law Ctr. 1st lt. USAR, 1948—50. Recipient Alumni Achievement award Fordham U., 1995; named Hon. Alumnus, elected to Hall of Honor Loyola Coll. Prep., 1993; named to N.Mex. Mil. Inst. Hall of Fame, 1994. Master: Am. Inns of Ct.; fellow: La. Bar Assn. (mem. com. on lawyer and judicial conduct 1996—), Am. Coll. Trial Lawyers, La. Bar Found. (life); mem.: ABA, Mil. Order Stars and Bars, Crossed Saber Soc., Soc. for Civil War History, Soc. for Mil. History, U.S. Horse Cavalry Assn., North La. Civil War Round Table, Res. Officers Assn., La. Civil Svc. League, Soc. Hosp. Counsel, Rlwy. and Locomotive Hist. Soc., Kansas City So. Hist. Soc., Shreveport C. of C. (dir. 1968—70), Pub. Affairs Rsch. Coun., Nat. Legal Ctr. for the Pub. Interest, La. Assn. Bus. and Industry, Tarshar Soc., La. R.R. Assn. (exec. com. 1992—), Mid-Continent Oil and Gas Assn. (exec. com. 1984—), Am. Arbitration Assn. (panel arbitrators), Nat. Acad. Law and Medicine, La. Assn. Def. Counsel, Internat. Assn. Def. Counsel, Nat. Assn. R.R. Trial Counsel, Trial Attys. Am., Coll. Master Advocates and Barristers, La. Law Inst., Am. Judicature Soc., Assocs. of La. State U., Supreme Ct. of La. Hist. Soc., Scribes Soc., Nat. Soc. SAR (pres. Galvez chpt. 1997), Confederate Meml. Lit. Soc., La. Hist. Assn., North La. Hist. Soc., Federalist Soc., Fifth Fed. Cir. Bar Assn., U.S. Supreme Ct. Hist. Soc., Shreveport Bar Assn. (pres. 2003), Fed. Bar Assn., Kappa Alpha Order, Sovereign Mil. Order of Malta, Phi Delta Phi. Home: 255 Forest Ave Shreveport LA 71104-4506 Office: Wilkinson Carmody & Gilliam 1700 Beck Bldg 400 Travis St Shreveport LA 71101-3108 Office Phone: 318-221-4196. Personal E-mail: artcarmody@aol.com. Business E-Mail: Acarmody@wcglawfirm.com.

CARMODY, CAROL JONES, transportation executive, former federal agency administrator; BA, U. Okla.; M in Pub. Adminstrn., Am. U. Aviation staff member Senate Commerce Comm., 1988—94; U.S. rep. to the Council Internat. Civil Aviation Org., Montreal, 1994—99; mem. Nat. Transportation Safety Bd. (NTSB), Washington, DC, 2000—05, vice chmn., 2001—02; dir. transp. initiatives Nat. Acad. Pub. Adminstrn., 2005—. Office: Nat Acad Pub Adminstrn Ste 1090 E 1100 New York Ave, NW Washington DC 20005-3934 Office Phone: 202-204-3666. E-mail: ccarmody@napwash.org.

CARMODY, MARGARET JEAN, retired social worker; b. Wauwatosa, Wis., Aug. 5, 1924; d. Peter and Gertrude Francelia (Brown) Galijas; m. James Matthew Carmody, Apr. 3, 1971 (dec. May 2005). BA, Marquette U., 1945; MA, U. Chgo., 1949. Social worker Denver Gen. Hosp., 1950-51; Fulbright fellow France, 1951-52; med. social work cons. U. Ill., Chgo., 1954-60; health scientist, adminstr. USPHS, Washington, 1960-96; ret., 1996. Mem. Acad. Cert. Social Workers. Democrat. Roman Catholic. Home: 40 Riverside Ave Apt 11 I Red Bank NJ 07701 Personal E-mail: gertrude8@verizon.net.

CARMODY, RICHARD PATRICK, lawyer; b. Chgo., June 2, 1942; s. Thomas Francis and Margaret (Tully) C.; m. Alison Pierce Cutter, Dec. 27, 1968; children: Elizabeth Carmody Gonzalez, Emily Pierce Carmody. BA, U. Ill., 1964; JD, Vanderbilt U., 1975. Bar: Ala. 1975, U.S. Dist. Ct. (no., mid. and so. dists.) Ala. 1975, U.S. Ct. Appeals (11th cir.) 1985, U.S. Supreme Ct. 1988. Assoc. Lange, Simpson, Robinson & Somerville, Birmingham, Ala., 1975-81, ptnr., 1981—2002; chmn. exec. com. Lange, Simpson Robinson & Somerville, Birmingham, Ala., 1987-93; ptnr. Adams and Reese/Lange Simpson LLP, Birmingham, 2003—. Mem. Am. Bankruptcy Inst., Washington, 1985—, co-chair ethics com. 1999-2005; bd. dirs. Am. Bd. Cert., 2000-05, mem. exec. com., 2001-03, mem. faculty com., 2004-05. Bd. dirs. Birmingham Coun. Campfire Boys and Girls Inc., 1978-90, pres., 1983-85, mem. standing com. 2006-; bd. dirs. Ala. region NCCJ, 1995—, state chair, 2000-02; bd. dirs. St. Vincent's Hosp. Foudn., 2002—; active Leadership Birmingham, 1998—. Fellow Am. Coll. Bankruptcy, 1999—. Mem. Ala. Bar Assn. (chmn. bankruptcy and comml. law sect. 1985, exec. com. 1986-93), Greystone Golf & Country Club, Kiwanis. Roman Catholic. Avocations: golf, sports, travel. Office: Adams & Reese LLP 2100 3d Ave N Ste 1100 Birmingham AL 35203 Office Phone: 205-250-5033. Business E-Mail: richard.carmody@arlaw.com.

CARMONA, RICHARD HENRY, former Surgeon General of the United States; b. NYC, Nov. 22, 1949; m. Diana Sanchez; 4 children. AA, Bronx Cmty. Coll., CUNY; BS in biology and chemistry, U. Calif., San Francisco, 1977, MD, 1979; MPH, U. Ariz., 1998. Surgical resident U. Calif., San Francisco; prof. surgery, pub. health and family and cmty. medicine U. Ariz., 1985—2002; dir., trauma services Tucson Med. Ctr., 1985—93; surgeon, dep. sheriff Pima County Sheriff's Dept., 1986—2002; CEO Kino County Cmty. Hosp., 1995—96, Pima Health Care System, 1997—99; chmn. State of Ariz. So. Regional Emergency Med. Sys., 1990—2002; surgeon gen. US Dept. Health & Human Services, Washington, 2002—06; vice chmn. Canyon Ranch, Tucson, 2006—, CEO health divsn., 2006—; pres. Canyon Ranch Inst., Tucson, 2006—; prof. pub. health, Mel & Enid Zuckerman Coll. Pub. Health U. Ariz., Tucson, 2006—. With US Army, 1967—70. Named one of Top 10 Latinos in Healthcare, LatinoLeaders mag., 2004. Fellow: Am. Coll. Surgeons.*

CARMONA, WAYNE, television producer; 4 children. BFA, Art Ctr. Coll. Design. Art. dir. Doyle Dane Bernbach, NYC. Prodr.: (TV series) Grosse Point, Leap of Faith, Karen Sisco, Entourage, 2004— (Producers Guild award, 2006), (comml.) over 5,000 commercials, (2d unit): (films) Con Air. Mailing: Home Box Office Entourage 1100 Ave of the Americas New York NY 10036

CARNABUCI, FRANK J., III, headmaster; b. Nov. 23, 1951; BA, Drew U., 1973; MA in Edn., Columbia U., Harvard U. Asst. headmaster Dalton Sch., NYC; headmaster Birch Wathen Lenox Sch., 1992—. Contbr. (book) The Dalton School, 1992, Founding Mothers and Others, 2002. Office: Birch Wathen Lenox Sch 210 E 77th St New York NY 10021 Office Phone: 212-861-0404. Office Fax: 212-879-5309.

CARNAHAN, BRICE, chemical engineer, educator; b. New Philadelphia, Ohio, Oct. 13, 1933; s. Paul Tracy and Amelia Christina (Gray) C. BS, Case Western Res. U., 1955, MS, 1957; PhD, U. Mich., 1965. Lectr. in engring. biostats. U. Mich., Ann Arbor, 1959-64, asst. prof. chem. engring. and biostatics, 1965-68, assoc. prof., 1968-70, prof. chem. engring., 1970—. Vis. lect. Imperial Coll., London, England, 1971-72; vis. prof. U. Pa., 1970, U. Calif.-San Diego, 1986-87; mem., chmn. Curriculum Aids for Chem. Engring. Edn. com. Nat. Acad. Engring., 1974-75 Author: (with H.A. Luther and J.O. Wilkes) Applied Numerical Methods, 1969, (with J.O. Wilkes) Digital Computing and Numerical Methods, 1973; Editorial bd.: Jour. Computers and Fluids, 1971—, Computers and Chemical Engineering, 1974—. Mem. communications com. Mich. Council for Arts, 1977—. Recipient Chem. Engr. of Yr. award Detroit Engring. Soc., 1987, 3M award Am. Soc. for Engring. Edn., 1990. Fellow AIChE (Computers in Chem. Engring. award 1981, chmn. CAST div. 1981); mem. AAAS, Assn. for Computing Machinery, Soc. for Computer Simulation, Sigma Xi, Sigma Nu. Office Phone: 734-764-3366. Business E-Mail: carnahan@umich.edu.

CARNAHAN, GEORGE RICHARD, retired finance educator; b. Zanesville, Ohio, May 20, 1935; s. George Edwin and Anna Eloise (Beymer) Carnahan; m. Mary Linn Burbage, June 14, 1958; children: Elizabeth, George, Glenn, John. BS, Juniata Coll., 1957; MBA, Miami U., Oxford, Ohio, 1962; PhD, Ohio State U., 1967. Prof. mgmt. No. Mich. U., Marquette, 1964-2001, prof. mgmt. emeritus, 2003—, dept. head, 1985-93. Bd. dirs. Bay Mills CC, Brimley, Mich., 1985—. Co-author: T.I.M.E. to Improve Management Effectiveness, 1986; contbr. articles to profl. jours. Ruling elder 1st Presbyn. Ch., Marquette; sec. bd. dirs. Med. Care Access Coalition. Mem.: Alpha Kappa Psi (v.p. 1983—87, pres. 1987—89). Democrat. Home: 1530 W Ridge St Apt 22 Marquette MI 49855-5703 Personal E-mail: gcarnahan@tourvilles.com.

CARNAHAN, JOHN ANDERSON, retired lawyer; b. Cleve., May 8, 1930; s. Samuel Edwin and Penelope (Moulton) C.; m. Katherine A. Halter, June 14, 1958; children: Peter M., Allison E., Kristin A. BA, Duke U., 1953, JD, 1955. Bar: Ohio 1955. Pvt. practice, Columbus, Ohio, 1955-78; ptnr. Arter & Hadden, Columbus, 1978-99; in-house counsel The XLO Group, Cleve., 2000—04; ret. Lectr. Ohio Legal Ctr. Inst., 1969, 73-74. Editor Duke Law Jour., 1954-55; chmn. bd. editors Ohio Lawyer, 1986-91; contbr. articles to profl. jours. Chmn. UN Day, Columbus, 1960; pres. Capital City Young Republican Club, 1960; bd. dirs. Columbus Cancer Clinic, pres., 1978-81; bd. dirs. Columbus chpt. ARC, 1979-87; mem. governing bd. Hannah Neil Mission, Inc., 1974-78; chmn. Duke Alumni Admissions Adv. Com., 1965-79. Named one of Outstanding Young Men of Columbus, 1965. Fellow Am. Bar Found. (life, chmn. Ohio fellows 1988-95), Columbus Bar Found. (life); mem ABA (ho. of dels. 1984-95), Ohio State Bar Found. (trustee 1986-90), Nat. Conf. Bar Pres., Ohio State Bar Assn. (coun. of dels. 1965-67, exec. com. 1977-81, 82-85, pres.-elect 1982-83, pres. 1983-84, Ritter award for outstanding contbns. adminstrn. justice 1987), Columbus Bar Assn. (bd. govs. 1970-72, sec.-treas. 1974-75, pres. 1976-77, Professionalism award 1996), Kit Kat Club (past pres.), Crichton Club. Presbyterian. Home and Office: 767 S 5th St Columbus OH 43206-2145 Office Phone: 614-648-9442. Personal E-mail: jac5830@aol.com.

CARNAHAN, ORVILLE DARRELL, retired state legislator, academic administrator; b. Elba, Idaho, Dec. 25, 1929; s. Marion Carlos and Leola Pearl (Putnam) C.; m. Colleen Arrott, Dec. 14, 1951; children: Karen, Jeanie, Orville Darrell, Carla. BS, Utah State U., 1958; MEd, U. Idaho, 1962, EdD, 1964. Vocat. dir., v.p. Yakima (Wash.) Valley Coll., 1964; chancellor Eastern Iowa C.C. Dist., Davenport, 1969—71; pres. Highline Coll., Midway, Wash., 1971—76; assoc. Utah Commn. for Higher Edn., Salt Lake City, 1976—78; pres. So. Utah U., Cedar City, 1978—81, Salt Lake C.C., Salt Lake City, 1981—90, pres. emeritus, 1990—; mem. Utah Ho. of Reps., 1993—99; ret., 1999. Cons. in field. Active Boy Scouts Am. Served with U.S. Army, 1952-54, Korea. Mem. Am. Vocat. Assn., NEA, Idaho Hist. Soc., Utah Hist. Soc., Alpha Tau Alpha, Phi Delta Kappa, Rotary Internat. Mem. LDS Ch. Home: 1653 Cornerstone Dr South Jordan UT 84095-5501 Office: Salt Lake CC 4600 S Redwood Rd Salt Lake City UT 84123-3197 Personal E-mail: odcarn@comcast.net.

CARNAHAN, ROBERT PAUL, civil engineer, educator, researcher, consultant; b. Bradenton, Fla., July 22, 1936; s. Robert Dewey and Marion (Wilbur) C.; m. Geraldine Schott, July 30, 1938; children: Robert P. Jr., Christopher T., Sean P. BCE, U. Fla., 1959; MS in Sanitary Engring., U. N.C., 1964; PhD, Clemson U., 1973. Registered profl. engr., Fla., Va., Md. Commd. 2d lt. US Army, 1959, advanced through grades to lt. col., 1975; co. comdr. 92d Engring. Battalion, Ft. Bragg, NC, 1960-61; project officer US Environ. Hygiene Agy., Edgewood Arsenal, Md., 1961—63; instr. Med. Field Svc. Sch., San Antonio, 1966—68; sr. environ. engr. 20th Pvt. Med. Unit, Vietnam, 1968-69; project officer US Army Med. R&D Command, Washington, 1973—75; project devel. officer US Army Material Devel. and Rsch. Ctr., Ft. Belvoir, Va., 1975—79; divsn. chief EPA br. US Army Med. Bioengring. R&D Lab., Frederick, Md., 1979—80; asst. prof. dept. civil engring. and mechs. U. South Fla., Tampa, 1980—84, assoc. prof. dept. civil engring. and mechs., 1984—89, prof. dept. civil engring. and mechs., 1989—93, assoc. dean rsch., 1993—2007, prof. emeritus, 2007; prin. Enviroprogress, Inc., 2007—. Adj. rsch. prof. dept. chemistry Am. U., 1976-77; adj. prof. dept. civil, mech. and environ. engring. George Washington U., 1979-80. Contbr. numerous articles to profl. jours. Decorated Legion of Merit, Bronze Star with oak leaf cluster, Meritorious Service Medal with oak leaf cluster, Army Commendation medal with oak leaf cluster; recipient Silver medal for research and devel. Am. Def. Preparedness Assn., Rsch. award U.S. Dept. of Army Rsch., Comdr.'s award for tech. Meradcom. Mem. ASCE, Nat. Soc. Profl. Engrs., Am. Inst. Chem. Engrs., Am. Chem. Soc., Water Pollution Control Fedn., Am. Water Works Assn., N.A. Membrane Soc., Internat. Desalination Assn., Am. Desalting Assn. (Hall of Fame 1998), Fla. Engring. Soc., Internat. Assn. Water Pollution Research, Am. Acad. Environ. Engrs. (cert.), Sigma Xi, Chi Epsilon, Tau Beta Pi. Democrat. Roman Catholic. Home: 506 Terrace Hill Dr Tampa FL 33617-3850 Office: 5470 E Busch Blvd 431 Tampa FL 33617 Office Phone: 813-988-6257. Personal E-mail: gcarnahan@msn.com. Business E-Mail: robert.carnahan@enviroprocess.com.

CARNAHAN, ROBIN, state official; b. Mo., Aug. 4, 1961; d. Mel and Jean Carnahan. BA in Economics with honors, William Jewell Coll., Liberty, Mo., 1983; JD, U. Va. Sch. Law, 1986. Atty., corp. & bus. law Thompson & Mitchell, St. Louis; spl. asst. to chmn. Export-Import Bank of US; sec. state State of Mo., Jefferson City, 2004—. Mem. Nat. Dem. Inst. Democrat. Baptist. Office: Office Sec State 600 W Main PO Box 1767 Jefferson City MO 65101 Office Phone: 573-751-4936. Fax: 573-751-2490. Business E-Mail: sosmain@sos.mo.gov.*

CARNAHAN, RUSS (JOHN RUSSELL CARNAHAN), congressman, lawyer; b. Rolla, Mo., July 10, 1958; m. Debra Carnahan; children: Austin, Andrew. Student, U. Mo., Rolla, 1976—77, Richmond Coll., London, 1978; BS in Pub. Adminstrn., U. Mo., Columbia, 1979; JD, U. Mo. Sch. Law, Columbia, 1983. Atty. BJC Healthcare, 1995—; mem. Mo. State Ho. Reps., 2000—04, US Congress from 3rd Mo. dist., 2005—. Mem. transp. & infrastructure com., fgn. affairs com. and sci. & tech. com. US Congress, vice chmn. subcommittee on internat. orgns., human rights and oversight, sr. majority whip. Mem. Compton Heights Neighborhood Assn., Landmarks Assn. St. Louis, State Hist. Soc. Mo., St. Louis Regional Commerce and Growth Assn., Pub. Policy Com.; mem. Friends Tower Grove Pk. Mo. Bot. Gardens and DeMenil Mansion; mem. govt. rels. com. United Way Greater St. Louis; chmn. Miss. River Pky. Commn. Recipient Lewis & Clark Statesman award, St. Louis Regional C. of C., 2002, Legis. award, St. Louis Bus. Jour., 2002. Mem.: Bar Assn. Mo. (Legis. award 2002), Bar Assn. Met. St. Louis. Democrat. Office: US House Reps 1710 Longworth House Office Bldg Washington DC 20515 Office Phone: 202-225-2671, 202-225-7452.*

CARNALL, GEORGE HURSEY, II, lawyer; b. Ft. Smith, Ark., Feb. 19, 1947; s. George and Kathleen (Browne) C.; m. Janet Spaulding, Aug. 28, 1971; children: Clayton Wilson, Abigail Browne, Kevin Joseph. BS in Econs. and Bus. Adminstrn., Millikin U., Decatur, Ill., 1969; JD, Vanderbilt U., 1974. Bar: Tenn. 1974, U.S. Dist. Ct. (we. dist.) Tenn. 1974. Assoc. Arnoult & May, Memphis, 1974-76, Watson Cox & Arnoult, Memphis, 1976-79; gen. counsel S.M.R. Enterprises, Memphis, 1980-82, pres., 1982-87; pres. internat. divsn. Fantastic Sam's Internat., Inc., Memphis, 1987-91; pres. LP Svcs., Inc., Memphis, 1992-97, Mid South FS, Inc., Olive Branch, Miss., 1997—, Carnall Franchise Group, Memphis, 1991—. Sec. Lil Pals Pet Photography, Inc., 2005—; dir. devel. SBEC Sch., 2002—. Contbr. articles to legal jours., mags., newspapers. Bd. dirs. Teen Challenge, Memphis, 1982-87. Served with U.S. Army, 1969-71. Mem. Cornerstone Assembly of God Ch. Office: Carnall Franchise Group 6375 Nellwood Olive Branch MS 38654 Home Phone: 662-895-7325; Office Phone: 662-349-5003. Personal E-mail: gandj@midsouth.rr.com.

CARNALL, TIMOTHY W., music educator; b. Ft. Wayne, Ind., Mar. 12, 1967; s. Jerry Wayne and Donna Rae (Bercot) Carnall; m. Sandra Elizabeth Carnall, July 19, 1997; 1 child, Samuel William Wayne. BS in Music Edn., Ball State U., 1990. Tchr., band dir. N. Decatur Jr./Sr. H.S., Greensburg, Ind., 1990—91, Ft. Wayne, Ind., Elkhart (Ind.) Ctrl. H.S. Pvt. music tchr., 1990—; judge ISSMA, Ind., 1995—. Mem.: Ind. Music Educators, Ind. Band Masters. Home: 1302 Briarwood Dr Elkhart IN 46514 Office: Elkhart Ctrl High Sch 1 Blazer Blvd Elkhart IN 46516

CARNASE, THOMAS PAUL, graphics designer, consultant; b. Bronx, NY, Sept. 15, 1939; BFA, NYC CC, 1959. Assoc. designer Sudler & Hennessey, Inc., NYC, 1959-64; pres., designer Bonder & Carnase Studio, Inc., NYC, 1964-68; v.p., ptnr. Lubalin, Smith, Carnase, Inc., NYC, 1969-79; pres. Carnase, Inc., NYC, 1979—, Carnase Computer Typography, NYC, 1979—, World Typeface Ctr., Inc., NYC, 1981—. Adv. com. NYC CC, 1977—; guest lectr., juror in field. Exhibited in group show Whitney Mus. Am. Art, NYC; editor Ligature jour., 1981—; designer numerous typefaces; represented in permanent collection at Cooper Hewitt Nat. Design Mus. Recipient award of Excellence, Communication Arts mag.; cert. of Distinction Creativity mag.; archived drawings and records gifted to The Cary Graphic Arts Collection at Rochester Inst. Tech., 2004. Mem. NY Art Dirs. Club, NY Type Dirs. Club, Soc. Publ. Designers, Am. Inst. Graphic Arts Office: Carnase Inc 1577 Bay Rd Miami Beach FL 33139

CARNEAL, GEORGE UPSHUR, lawyer; b. NYC, May 31, 1935; AB, Princeton U., 1957; LLB, U. Va., 1961. Bar: Va. 1961, D.C. 1962. Law clk. to judge U.S. Ct. Appeals, D.C. Circuit, 1961-62; assoc. Hogan & Hartson, Washington, 1962-68, ptnr., 1973—, dir. aviation practice group. Spl. asst. to sec. Dept. Transp., Washington, 1969-70; gen. counsel FAA, Washington, 1970-73; lectr. Georgetown U. Law Ctr., 1965-68; chmn. bd. trustees D.C. Bar Clients Security Trust Fund, 1973-78; gen. counsel Nat. Aeronautic Assn., 1984—. Decisions editor: Va. Law Rev, 1960-61; contbr. articles to legal jours. Bd. govs. Flight Safety Found., 1982-95; mem. exec. com. Princeton U. Alumni Coun., 1984-87; bd. dirs. Nat. Aviation Rsch. Inst., 2001-03. Mem. ABA, Fed. Bar Assn., Raven Soc., Order of Coif. Clubs: Princeton (pres. 1984-86), Aero (pres. 1982) (Washington), Metropolitan, Chevy Chase. Office: Hogan & Hartson 555 13th St NW Washington DC 20004-1161 Home Phone: 703-893-9158; Office Phone: 202-637-6546. Office Fax: 202-637-5910. Business E-Mail: gucarneal@hhlaw.com.

CARNEIRO, ROBERT LEONARD, curator, anthropologist; b. NYC, June 4, 1927; s. Anthony Mario and Serafina (Garrigo) Carneiro; m. Barbara Ora Bode, Aug. 7, 1980; 1 child, Brett Rodrigo. BA, U. Mich., 1949, MA, 1952, PhD, 1957. Instr. anthropology U. Wis., Madison, 1956-57; asst. curator anthropology Am. Mus. Natural History, NYC, 1957-63, assoc. curator anthropology, 1963-69, curator anthropology, 1969—. Ethnographic field work Kuikuru Indians, Brazil, 1953—54, Brazil, 1975, Amahuaca Indians, Peru, 1960—61, Yanomamo Indians, Venezuela, 1975; vis. prof. UCLA, 1968, Pa. State U., University Park, 1973, U. Victoria, BC, Canada, 1977; adj. prof. anthropology Columbia U., 1992—. Co-editor: Essays in the Science Culture, 1960, Leslie A. White: Ethnological Essays, 1987; editor: Herbert Spencer: The Evolution of Society, 1967; author: The Chiefdom: Precursor of the State, 1981, The Muse of History and the Science of Culture, 2000, Evolutionism in Cultural Anthropology: A Critical History, 2003. Recipient Monks Meml. prize, Inst. Humane Studies, 1973;, Robert L. Carneiro Disting. Univ. professorship in anthropology established in his name U. Mich., 2005. Fellow: AAAS (chmn. nominating com. sect. H 1982—83), Am. Anthrop. Assn., N.Y. Acad. Scis. (vice chmn., chmn. anthropology sect. 1981—83, 1983—85), Linnean Soc. London; mem.: Nat. Acad. Scis. Achievements include proposal of one of the leading theories of the origin of the state. Office: Am Mus Natural History Central Pk W At 79th St W New York NY 10024 Office Phone: 212-769-5897. Business E-Mail: carneiro@amnh.org.

CARNELL, KENT I., lawyer; b. Phila., Dec. 10, 1945; m. Barbara J. McFarland, June 1, 1996; children: Sarah Dailey, Amy Williams, Mara Chambers, Kevin. BS, U. Wis., Madison, 1967, JD, 1970. Bar: Wis. 1970, Fed. Dist. Ct. (ea. dist. Wis.) 1970, Fed. Dist. Ct. (we. dist. Wis.) 1970, 7th Cir. Ct. Appeals 1977, cert.: Nat. Bd. Trial Advocacy (in civil trial advocacy) 2001. Atty. Lawton & Cates, Madison, Wis., 1970—, pres., 2004—. Chmn. bd. dirs. Salvation Army, 2001—03, bd. dirs., 1979—, Second Harvest Foodbank, 1986—99, founder, 1986. Mem.: Dane County Bar Assn. (Pro Bono Publico Disting. Svc. award 2005), Wis. Acad. Trial Lawyers, Am. Inns Ct., Am. Assn. Justice, State Bar Wis (chmn. bd. 2005—06, bd. govs. 2001—06, Pres.'s award 2005). Avocations: golf, travel. Office: Lawton & Cates SC 10 E Doty St Madison WI 53703 Office Phone: 608-282-6200. Office Fax: 698-282-6252.

CARNELL, TERESA BURT, lawyer; b. Phila., Sept. 15, 1964; BA cum laude, U. Del., 1986; JD, U. Md., 1992. CPA; bar: Md. 1992, US Ct. Appeals (4th cir.), US Dist. Ct. (dist. Md.). Legis. counsel Md. Gen. Assembly's Dept. Legis. Svcs.; assoc. Ballard, Spahr, Andrews & Ingersoll, LLP; of counsel Venable, LLP, Baltimore, 2004—. Mem. Econ. Matters Com.; lectr. in field. Contbr. articles to profl. jours. Named one of Balt.'s Top Lawyers: The Next Generation, Balt. Mag., 2003; recipient Cunningham award. Mem.: ABA, Md. State Bar Assn. (co-chair Com. Corp. Laws, formerly, Bus. Law Sect.), Omicron Delta Kappa, Pi Sigma Alpha. Office: Venable LLP 1800 Merc Bank & Trust Bldg 2 Hopkins Plz Ste 1800 Baltimore MD 21201 Office Phone: 410-244-7526. Office Fax: 410-244-7742. E-mail: tcarnell@venable.com.*

CARNER, DOROTHY ANN, financial advisor; b. Spokane, Wash., Mar. 23, 1937; d. Theodore Baza LaRue and Florence Irene (Jaeger) Innes; m. Peter L. Sbarbaro Sr., May 16, 1959 (div. 1973); children: Peter L. Jr., David A., John E.; m. Robert Carner, Jan. 9, 2007. AS in Acctg., Napa Valley Coll., 1974; BS, Calif. State U., Sacramento, 1977. Cert. fin. planner. Acctg. asst. Napa (Calif.) County Counsel for Econ. Opportunity, 1972-73; owner, cons. Dash Enterprises, American Canyon, Calif., 1973-78; owner, bookkeeper Reliable Meats, American Canyon, 1973-74; fin. planner IDS Fin. Svcs., Napa, 1983-94, Am. Express Fin. Advisors, Napa, 1995—2005, Ameriprise Fin., Napa, 2005—. Vol. Boy Scouts Am., Am. Canyon PTA, Little League, Pop Warner Football; sponsor T-ball and Babe Ruth Bambino and Babe Ruth League Teams; tax preparer Vita, Napa, 1973-74. Mem. Order Ea. Star, Women of Moose. Office Phone: 707-257-3980.

CARNER, GEORGE, foreign service executive, economic strategist; b. NYC, Sept. 2, 1945; s. Joseph Carner Ribalta and Esther Cadefau; m. Michele Colette Delamotte, Apr. 20, 1968; children: Shawn L., Deric A. BA in Internat. Affairs, U. N.C., 1965; postgrad., Inst. Polit. Sci. La Sorbonne, Paris, 1966; MA in Internat. Affairs, George Washington U., 1971; student, Fgn. Svc. Inst., 1975. Internat. trade specialist U.S. Dept. Commerce, Washington, 1967-71; asst. program officer Agy. for Internat. Devel., Rabat, Morocco, 1971-75, dep. program officer Kabul, Afghanistan, 1976-79, program planning officer Manila, 1979-82, officer-in-charge India Washington, 1982-84, chief policy plan/eval. DP/AFR, 1984-86, dep. mission dir. Dakar, Senegal, 1986-88, mission dir. Tunis, Tunisia, 1988-91, Antan, Madagascar, 1991-94, Managua, Nicaragua, 1994-98, Guatemala City, Guatemala, 1998—2002; U.S. rep to OECD/DAC Paris, 2003—. Speaker, panelist Nat. Assn. of Schs. Pub. Affairs and Adminstrn., Honolulu and N.Y.C., 1981, 83, Harvard U., Boston, 1984. Contbr. articles to profl. jours. and procs. Recipient Superior Honor award Agency for Internat. Devel., Washington, 1978, Presdl. Meritorious Svc. awards The White House, 1987, 2000. Mem. Am. Fgn. Svcs. Assn. Avocations: listening to jazz, art, scuba diving, nature walks. Address: USOECD PSC116 OECD/AID APO 09777 United States

CARNES, EDWARD E., federal judge; b. Albertville, Ala., June 3, 1950; BS, U. Ala., Tuscaloosa, 1972; JD cum laude, Harvard U., 1975. Asst. Ala. atty. gen. Office Atty. Gen., 1975—92; cir. judge US Ct. Appeals (11th cir.), Montgomery, Ala., 1992—. Mem.: Jud. Conference Adv. Com on Criminal Rules, 1997- (chmn, 2001-), Fed. Judges Assn. Office: 500-D Federal Courthouse Annex 1 Church St Montgomery AL 36104-4096 also: Elbert P Tuttle US Ct Appeals Bldg 56 Forsyth St NW Atlanta GA 30303*

CARNES, JAMES DONALD, real estate manager; b. Marietta, Ga., Nov. 25, 1933; s. James Davis and Melba Holland Carnes. BA, Ga. State U., 1964; MA, Fla. State U., 1965, PhD, 1976. Contracts adminstr. Lockheed Ga., Marietta, 1951—72; inst. hist. U. Md., Nurnberg, 1976—81; real estate devel. mgmt. Marietta, Ga., 1982—. Cpl. US Army, 1954—56, Germany. NDEA fellowship, Tulane U., 1964. Mem.: Kennesaw Mt. Hist. Assn. Republican. Bapt. Avocations: travel, photography, genealogy, history. Home and Office: 1670 Burnt Hickory Rd Marietta GA 30064 Office Phone: 770-428-0701.

CARNES, JAMES EDWARD, retired electronics executive; b. Cumberland, Md., Sept. 27, 1939; s. Roy Clifton and Alta (Wigfield) C.; m. Nancy Louise Zolto, Nov. 27, 1977; 1 child, Gillian. BS in Engring. Sci., Pa. State U., 1961; MA in Elec. Engring., Princeton U., 1967, PhD in Elec. Engring., 1970; PhD (hon.), Thomas Edison State Coll., 1994, Kean U., 1998. Mem. tech. staff RCA Labs., Princeton, NJ, 1969-77; mgr. tech. application RCA Consumer Electronics, Indpls., 1977-80, dir. new products lab, 1980-82, div. v.p. engring., 1982-87; v.p. consumer electronics and info. scis. David Sarnoff Rsch. Ctr. (subs. SRI Internat.), Princeton, NJ, 1987-90, pres., COO, 1990-93, pres., CEO, 1993—2002, sr. advisor, 2002—03; sr. v.p. SRI Internat., 1990-95; chmn. bd. Sensar, Inc., Princeton, NJ, 1992-2000, Orchid Biocomputer Inc., 1995-97, Sarnoff Digital Comm., Inc., 1996-97. Dir. Sarnoff Real Time Inc., Sarif, Inc., Delsys Pharm. Corp., Orchid Biocomputer, Inc., Sarnoff Digital Comms., Nova Corp., SRI Internat., C-Cor Inc., 2002—; Village at Pa. State, 2004—; short course lectr. UCLA, 1978-81, Am. U. Washington, 1976, Ctrl. Poly. Inst., London, 1974. Contbr. articles to profl. jours. Campaign chmn. Princeton Area United Way, 1992, bd. dirs., 1992-94, 1st v.p., 1993-94; chmn. bd. trustees United Way Greater Mercer County, 1994-96; chmn. sci. adv. bd. Rider Coll., 1990-92; trustee Rider U., 1993-2002, Ind. Coll. Fund. N.J., 1990-96, Thomas Edison State Coll. Found., 1992—, Am. Boychoir Sch., 1995-2002, Regional Planning Partnership, 1997-2002; mem. bd. overseers N.J. Inst. Tech., 1993-98; co-chair Prosperity N.J., 2000-02; bd. mem. Village at Penn State, 2004—. Lt. USN, 1961-65. Recipient David Sarnoff Outstanding Achievement award RCA, 1981, Engr. of Yr. award Ctrl. N.J. Engring. Coun., 1991, Humanitarian award NCCJ, 1994, Citizen of Yr. award Mercer County C. of C., 1996, N.J. Tech. Coun. High Tech. Hero award, 1999, N.J. Network Chmn.'s award, 2000; named to Jr. Achievement Bus. Hall of Fame, 1998, Am. Electronics Assn. N.J. High Tech Hall of Fame, 1999, Acad. Digital TV Pioneers, 2002. Fellow IEEE (Centennial medal 1984, Region 1 award 1993); mem. Am. Electronics Assn., Nat. Acad. Engring. (com. on mem., 2004—), Pa. State U. Alumni Assn. (coun., exec. com., Outanding Engr. Alumnus award 1992, Pres. and Exec. dir. award 1995, Disting. Alumnus award 1996, v.p. 1997-99, pres. 1999-2001, alumni fellow 2003). Achievements include inventor in field. Avocations: flying, golf. Home: 7038 Kingsmill Ct Bradenton FL 34202 Home Phone: 941-907-1597. Personal E-mail: jim.carnes@psualum.com.

CARNES, JOSEPH SYDNEY, clergyman; b. Memphis, Dec. 2, 1929; s. Samuel Leslye and Marion Rachel (Weaver) C.; m. Annie Frank Rutledge, June 22, 1952; children: Jane Ann, Joseph Sydney Jr., James Rutledge, John David. BS, Memphis State U., 1956; MDiv, Tex. Christian U., 1962, D Ministry, 1979. Ordained to ministry Christian Ch. (Disciples of Christ), 1949; cert. pastoral counselor Parkland Hosp., Dallas. Min. of membership 1st Christian Ch, Eugene, Oreg., 1962-65, sr. min. Nampa, Idaho, 1965-72, Lakeview Christian Ch., Dallas, 1972-81, Oak Cliff Christian Ch., Dallas, 1981—. Pres. Christian Chs. in Idaho, Boise, 1971. Co-author: Communion Meditations, 1966. Founding dir. Nampa Christian Housing, 1967; bd. dirs. Mercy Hosp., Nampa, 1968-72, Idaho Mental Health Dept., 1969-72. Col. Tex. State Guard, chief chaplains, 1972-94. Recipient Disting. Min. of Yr. award, Tex. Christian U., 2003. Mem. Mil. Chaplains Assn. U.S.A. (local pres. 1972—), Masons (33d degree, chaplain 1988-95), Lions (local pres. 1981-82), Order Ea. Star. Republican. Avocations: fishing, hunting, world travel. Home: Wedgewood Twr Apt 615 2511 Wedglea Dr Dallas TX 75211-2041 Office: 1222 W Kiest Blvd Dallas TX 75224-3233 E-mail: jsydney1@aol.com.

CARNES, JULIE ELIZABETH, judge; m. Stephen S. Cowen. AB summa cum laude, U. Ga., 1972, JD magna cum laude, 1975. Bar: Ga. 1975. Law clk. to Hon. Lewis R. Morgan U.S. Ct. Appeals (5th cir.), 1975-77; spl. counsel U.S. Sentencing Commn., 1989, commr., appellate chief, 1990-96; asst. U.S. Atty. U.S. Dist. Ct. (no. dist.) Ga., Atlanta, 1978-90, judge, 1992—. Office: US Courthouse 75 Spring St SW Ste 2167 Atlanta GA 30303-3309

CARNES, TARA LEA BARKER, music educator; d. Blaine Byers and Arlene Quesillon Barker; m. Thomas Paul Carnes, May 23, 1987 (div. Sept. 15, 1995); 1 child, Emma Louise. Student, Bartlesville Wesleyan U., Okla., 1981—82; MusB, U. S.D., Vermillion, 1982—85; MA in Musicology, U. N.Tex., Denton, 1986—91. Cert. tchr. Tex. Dept. Edn. Pianist, choir dir., organist Krum UMC, Tex., 1987—88; organist St. Paul UMC, Hurst, Tex., 1988—89; music tchr. Holy Family Sch., Ft. Worth, 1988—89; music tchr., band dir. Fonville Mid. Sch., Houston, 1989—92; music tchr. Holy Spirit Episcopal Sch., Houston, 1992—94, Duchesne Acad. of the Sacred Heart, Houston, 1994—, chair, fine arts dept. Pvt. music instr., Pierre, SD, 1985; presenter in field. Organist, choir dir. Bethel Ch., Houston, 1989—, chair, choir robe come., 1995, mem., pastoral search com., 2000, chair, hymnal com., 2004. Mem.: Chorusters Guild, Am. Guild Organists, Tex. Choral Dir.'s Assn. Roman Catholic. Avocations: piano, reading, gardening, composing. Office: Duchesne Acad of the Sacred Heart 10202 Memorial Dr Houston TX 77024 Business E-Mail: tara.carnes@duchesne.org.

CARNESALE, ALBERT, engineering educator, former academic administrator; b. Bronx, NY, July 2, 1936; m. Robin Gerber, Apr. 6, 2002; children: Keith, Kimberly. BME, Cooper Union, 1957; MS, Drexel U., 1961, LLD (hon.), 1993; PhD, NC State U., 1966, LLD (hon.), 1997; AM (hon.), Harvard U., 1979; ScD (hon.), NJ Inst. Tech., 1984. Prof. NC State U., Raleigh, 1962—69, 1972—74, John F. Kennedy Sch. Govt., Harvard U., Cambridge, Mass., 1974—97, acad. dean, 1981—91, dean, 1991—95; provost, Lucius N. Littauer prof. pub. policy and adminstrn. Harvard U., 1994—97; chief def. weapons sys. US Arms Control and Disarmament Agy., Washington, 1969—72; chancellor UCLA, 1997—2006, prof. pub. policy, mechanical and aerospace engring., 2006—. Author: Nuclear Power Issues and Choices: Report of the Nuclear Energy Policy Study Group, 1977, Living with Nuclear Weapons, 1983, Hawks, Doves and Owls: An Agenda for Avoiding Nuclear War, 1985, Superpower Arms Control: Setting the Record Straight, 1987, Fateful Visions: Avoiding Nuclear Catastrophe, 1988; co-author: New Nuclear Nations: Consequences for US Policy, 1993. Recipient Gano Dunn award Outstanding Profl. Achievement, Cooper Union, NYC. Fellow: Am. Acad. Arts and Scis.; mem.: LA World Affairs Coun., Internat. Inst. for Strategic Studies, Coun. on Fgn. Rels. Business E-Mail: acarnesale@ucla.edu.

CARNEY, BRADFORD GEORGE YOST, lawyer, educator; b. Oct. 25, 1950; s. Blanchard Donald and Anne Carolyn (Yost) C.; m. Gail Elaine Hasson, Jan. 6, 1973; children: Jason Bradford, Brandon Burroughs. BA, Washington Coll., 1972; JD, U. Balt., 1976. Bar: Md. 1977, U.S. Dist. Ct. Md. 1978, U.S. Supreme Ct. 1982. Ptnr. Callahan, Calwell, Laudeman, Balt., 1982—87, Weinberg and Green, Balt., 1987—96; of counsel Royston, Mueller, McLean & Reid LLP, Towson, Md., 1996—. Asst. prof. law Villa Julie Coll., Stevenson, Md., 1983-97, assoc. prof., 1997-2000, adj. prof. law, 2000-06. Bd. trustees Boys' Latin Sch., Md., 1988-93. Mem. ABA, Nat. Assn. Criminal Def. Lawyers, Md. State Bar Assn., Md. Criminal Def. Attys. Assn., Balt. County Bar Assn., Balt. City Bar Assn., U. Balt. Alumni Assn. (bd. govs. 1984-87), Boys' Latin Sch. Alumni Assn. (bd. dirs. 1983-, pres. 1986-88). Home: 474 Five Farms Ln Lutherville Timonium MD 21093-2954 Office: Royston Mueller McLean & Reid LLP 102 W Pennsylvania Ave Towson MD 21204-4526 Office Phone: 410-823-1800. Personal E-mail: bcarney@rmmr.com.

CARNEY, CHRISTOPHER PAUL, congressman, political science educator; b. Cedar Rapids, Iowa, Mar. 2, 1959; s. Paul A. and Jane (Greiner) C.; m. Jennifer Lynn Graves, June 27, 1987; children: Ryne, Sean, Seth, Keeley, Brett B in Spl. Studies, Cornell Coll., 1981; MA, U. Wyo, 1983; PhD, U. Nebr., 1993. Teaching asst. dept. polit. sci. U. Wyo., Laramie, 1981-83, 85-86, U. Nebr., 1986-89; instr. dept. social sci. Laramie County C.C., Cheyenne, 1983-85, Houston C.C. System, summer 1988; instr. dept. polit. sci. Creighton U., Omaha, 1989-90; asst. prof. Kearney (Nebr.) State Coll., 1990-91; rsch. assoc., vis. instr. Ctr. Internat. Programs U. Wyo., 1991-92; assoc. prof. polit. sci. Pa. State U., Dunmore, 1992—2007; mem. US Congress from 10th Pa. dist., 2007—, mem. homeland security com., transp. & infrastructure com. Presenter numerous confs. in field; participant NATO Study Tour, Belgium, The Netherlands, Federal Republic Germany, German Democratic Republic, 1989. Contbr. articles to profl. publs. Lt. comdr. USNR, 1995—. Decorated: Def. Meritorious Svc. medal, Joint Svc. Achievement medals (3), USN & Marine Corps Achivement medal, Outstanding Volunteer Svc. medal; Named Outstanding Young Man Am., U.S. Jaycees, 1984; Regents fellow U. Nebr., 1989. Mem. Internat. Studies Assn. (sec./treas. comparative interdisciplinary studies sect. 1991-94), Assn. Third World Studies, Am. Polit. Sci. Assn., Atlantic Coun. Democrat. Roman Catholic. Office: US House Reps 416 Cannon House Office Bldg Washington DC 20515 also: 233 Northern Blvd Ste 4 Clarks Summit PA 18411 Office Phone: 570-585-9988. Office Fax: 570-585-9977.*

CARNEY, DAVID JOHN, computer scientist, music theorist; b. Bklyn., Aug. 22, 1942; s. Francis John and Edith (Murphy) C. MusB, Cath. U. of Am., 1963; MusM, U. So. Calif., 1966; D of Musical Arts, Boston U., 1981, MS, 1985. Instr. Oberlin Conservatory, Ohio, 1967-69; asst. prof. Boston U., 1972-79; software engr. Intermetrics, Inc., Cambridge, Mass., 1984-87; mem. rsch. staff Inst. for Def. Analysis, Alexandria, Va., 1987-92; sr. mem. tech. staff Software Engring. Inst., Pitts., 1992—. Dir. enterprise mgmt. divsn. US Air Force, 2006—. Author: Principles of CASE Tool Integration, 1994, Quotations from Chairman David, 1998, The Adventures of Ricky & Stick, 2006; contbr. articles to profl. jours.; composer choral and orchestral compositions, 1970-77; staff organist King's Chapel, Boston, 1969-74; asst. condr. Handel & Haydn Soc., Boston, 1973-76. Dir. Omnibus Concerts, Boston, 1974-77; premiered significant vocal works Kings Chapel, Boston, 1998, 99, vocal and instrumental works, Boston, Lexington, Omsk, Russia, 2000 London, 2003; chmn. Eugene Green Meml. Found., 1994—; keynote addresses Internat. Cons., U.S., Europe, 2001, 02, 04. Mem. Phi Beta Kappa. Office: Engring Dept Hanscom Afb MA 01731 Home Phone: 617-482-0450; Office Phone: 781-377-4226. Personal E-mail: dockjr@hotmail.com.

CARNEY, DEBORAH LEAH TURNER, lawyer; b. Great Bend, Kans., Aug. 19, 1952; d. Harold Lee and Elizabeth Lura Turner; m. Thomas JT. Carney, Mar. 20, 1976; children: Amber Blythe, Sonia Briana, Ross Dillon. BA in Human Biology, Stanford U., 1974; JD, U. Denver, 1976. Bar: Kans. 1977, U.S. Dist. Ct. Kans. 1977, U.S. Ct. Appeals (10th cir.) 1982, Colo. 1984, U.S. Dist. Ct. Colo. 1984, U.S. Supreme Ct. 1989, U.S. Claims Ct. 1990. With Turner & Boisseau, Great Bend, 1976-84, of counsel, 1984-93; assoc. Lutz & Oliver, Arvada, Colo., 1984-85; prin. Deborah Turner Carney, P.C., Golden and Lakewood, Colo., 1985-92; shareholder Carney Law Office, Golden, Colo., 1992-95, owner, 1995—. Author (newsletter) Profl. Solutions, 1984, (chpt.) Courtroom Handbook, 1998; editor Apple Law newsletter, 1984-86; contbr. articles to profl. jours. Pres. Canyon Area Residents for the Environment (C.A.R.E.), 1998. Mem. Genesee Daytime Bookclub (co-chair 1997-98), Kiwanis (bd. dirs. Denver club 1988-90, trustee 1990-92, sec. 1992-93). Republican. Avocations: horses, dance, computers. Office: 21789 Cabrini Blvd Golden CO 80401-9488 Home Phone: 303-526-0214; Office Phone: 303-526-9666. Business E-Mail: deb@carneylaw.net.

CARNEY, J. W., JR., lawyer; b. New Bedford, Mass., Apr. 28, 1952; s. James William and Lucille (Parent) C.; m. Joy B. Rosen; children: Julia, Nathaniel. BA, Holy Cross Coll., 1975; JD, Boston Coll., 1978. Bar: Mass. 1978, U.S. Dist. Ct. Mass. 1979, U. S. Ct. Appeals (1st cir.) 1982, U.S. Supreme Ct. 1991. Trial lawyer Mass. Pub. Defenders Com., Boston, 1978-83; asst. dist. atty. Middlesex Count Dist. Atty's. Office, Cambridge, Mass., 1983-88; ptnr. Carney & Bassil, Boston, 1989—. Chmn. adv. bd. Nat. Mock Trial Competition, Boston, 1987—. Contrbg. author: Massachusetts Courtroom Evidence, 1988, Massachusetts Criminal Defense, 1990. Fellow Am. Coll. Trial Lawyers; mem. Nat. Assn. Trial Lawyers, Mass. Assn. Criminal Defense Lawyers, Mass. Bar Assn., Boston Bar Assn., Boston Coll. Law Sch. Alumni Assn. (sec. 1987-89, treas. 1989—), Lawyers Assistance Strike Force (co-chmn. 1992-), Fed. Ct. Criminal Justice Act Bd (2001-), Mass. Judicial Nominating Com. (2002-, vice chmn. 2002-2003), Women's Lunch Place (Homeless Shelter) (bd. dirs. 1996-). Avocations: music, basketball. Office: Carney And Bassil 20 Park Plz Ste 1405 Boston MA 02116-4311 Office Fax: 617-338-5587. Business E-Mail: jcarney@CarneyBassil.com.

CARNEY, JOHN C., JR., lieutenant governor; b. Claymont, Del. m. Tracey Quillen; children: Sam, James. BA in English, Dartmouth Coll., 1978; MPA, U. Del. Assoc. dir. Cath. Youth Orgn., Wilmington; staff asst. U.S. Senator Joseph R. Biden, 1986-89; dep. chief adminstrv. officer New Castle County, 1989-94, acting dir. pub. works; dep. chief of staff to Gov. State of Del., 1994-97, sec. fin. Dover, 1997-2000, lt. gov., 2000—. Bd. dirs. Cath. Youth Orgn. Democrat. Office: Office Lt Governor Third Floor Tatnall Bldg Dover DE 19901 also: Office Lt Governor Carvel State Office Bldg 820 North French St Wilmington DE 19801 Office Phone: 302-744-4333, 302-577-8787. Office Fax: 302-739-6965. E-mail: ltgov@state.de.us.

CARNEY, JOHN F., III, academic administrator; m. Patricia Carney; children: Anna, Catherine. BA in Civil Engring., Merrimack Coll., 1963; MA, Northwestern U., 1963, PhD, 1966. Rsch. scientist Northwestern U., 1966; asst. prof. U. Conn., 1966—69, assoc. prof., 1969—74, prof., 1974—81; prof., head Auburn U., 1981—83; prof. civil engring. Vanderbilt U., 1983—96, assoc. dean for grad. affairs, 1993—96, assoc. dean for rsch. and grad. affairs, 1993—96; provost, v.p. for acad. affairs Worcester Poly. Inst., Mass., 1996—2005; chancellor U. Mo., Rolla, 2005—. Editor: Effectiveness of Highway Safety Improvements, 1986; contbr. articles to profl. jours. Fellow: Am. Soc. of Civil Engrs.; mem.: ASCE, Soc. Automotive Engrs. Office: U Mo 206 Parker Hall 1870 Miner Circle Rolla MO 65409-0910 Office Phone: 573-341-4416. E-mail: jfc3@umr.edu.*

CARNEY, JOSEPH BUCKINGHAM, lawyer; b. Greensburg, Ind., July 8, 1928; s. Edward O. and Grace Rebecca (Buckingham) C.; m. Constance J. Caylor, July 8, 1950; children: Elizabeth, Joseph Buckingham Jr., Julia, Sarah. AB, DePauw U., 1950; LLB, Harvard U., 1953. Bar: D.C. 1953, Ind. 1953, U.S. Dist. Ct. (so. dist.) Ind. 1953, U.S. Supreme Ct. 1957, U.S. Ct. Appeals (7th cir.) 1961; ind. cert. mediator. Assoc. Hogg, Peters & Leonard, Ft. Wayne, Ind., 1953-54, Baker & Daniels, Indpls., 1957-62, ptnr., 1962—95, mem. mgmt. com., 1993-94, sec., 1994, of counsel, 1996—. Mem. lawyers com. Nat. Ctr. State Cts., Williamsburg, Va., 1985—; assoc. Environ. Law Inst., Washington. Co-chmn. bd. dirs. Parkinson Awareness Assn. Ctrl. Ind., Inc.; past pres. Interfaith Homes, Inc., Indpls.; past chmn., elder Northwood Christian Ch., Indpls. 1st lt. U.S. Army, 1954-57. Recipient Disting. Alumni award DePauw U., 1984. Mem. ABA, Ind. Bar Assn., Indpls. Bar Assn., Am. Judicature Soc., 7th Cir. Bar Assn. (pres. 1983-84), Univ. Club, Columbia Club, Contemporary, Lawyers Club Indpls. (past pres.), Phi Eta Sigma, Phi Gamma Delta (bd. dirs.

1974-78, sec. 1976-78, pres. 1980-82), Phi Gamma Delta Ednl. Found. (bd. dirs. 1994-2005, pres. 1996-98). Avocations: scuba diving, travel, photography. Office: Baker & Daniels 300 N Meridian St Ste 2700 Indianapolis IN 46204-1782 Home Phone: 317-848-5199; Office Phone: 317-237-0300.

CARNEY, KAREN ROSE, music educator, pianist; b. Canton, Ohio, Dec. 9, 1940; d. Alex and Ruby (Berky) Winkelman; 1 child, Miles. BMus, Baldwin-Wallace Coll., 1961; postgrad., Case Western Res. U., 1961; MA in Music Edn., Ohio State U., 1980, PhD in Music Edn., 1983. Cert. music tchr., N.C., Ohio. Accompanist, staff musician dance dept. Ohio State U., Columbus, 1983-85; asst. prof. N.C. Wesleyan Coll., Rocky Mount, 1985-87, U. S.D., Vermillion, 1987-88; pianist, spl. events Ohio State U., Columbus, 1988-90; lectr., choir accompanist Fayetteville (N.C.) State U., 1990-91; instr. performing arts Meth. Coll., Fayetteville, NC, 1990-91; asst. prof. Lincoln U., Pa., 1991-93; assoc. prof. Paine Coll., Augusta, Ga., 1993-95, Winston-Salem (N.C.) State U., 1995-99; elem. music tchr. New Hanover County Schs., Wilmington, NC, 1999-2000; lectr. U. Ctrl. Ark., Conway, 2000-01; music tchr. K-8 Franklin Local Schs., Duncan Falls, Ohio, 2001—04; asst. prof. Fayetteville State U., 2004—. PRAXIS item writer Ednl. Testing Svc., Princeton, N.J., 1997; com. music edn. UNC/NCCC Articulation Agreement, Chapel Hill, N.C., 1997; clinician Nat. Group Piano Symposium, U. Okla., Norman, 1985; judge music contests, Ohio, N.C., S.D. Vol. tchr., performer Winston-Salem/Forsyth County Pub. Schs., 1997-99; vol. pianist Baltic (Ohio) Country Manor, 1992-2000, nursing and retirement homes, Winston-Salem, 1995-98; guest organist, pianist various chs., N.C. and Ohio. Rsch. grantee Lilly-Lincoln U., 1992; recipient Cert. of Recognition Winston-Salem State U. Friends of O'Kelly Libr., 1997. Mem.: Music Tchrs. Nat. Assn. (profl. cert. in piano), Nat. Assn. Music Edn., Coll. Music Soc., Am. Fedn. Musicians, Am. Mensa, Pi Kappa Lambda, Mu Phi Epsilon. Home: 320 Fairwood Ct Fayetteville NC 28305-4904 Home Phone: 910-480-0656; Office Phone: 910-672-1571. E-mail: kcarney@uncfsu.edu.

CARNEY, KEVIN, principal; b. 1969; Prin. Desert Sky Middle Sch., Vail Sch. Dist., Tucson. Mem. Boy Scouts and Girl Scouts of Am., sch. partnerships with Rita Ranch, YMCA and Southwest Youth Sports, Citizen Sch. Prog., Oasis Ch. Named one of 40 Under 40, Tucson Bus. Edge, 2006. Mem.: Homeowners Assn. Office: Desert Sky Middle School 9850 E Rankin Loop Tucson AZ 85747 Office Phone: 520-762-2704.

CARNEY, MICHELLE CATHERINE, assistant principal; b. Atlantic City, Feb. 22, 1971; d. James Arthur and Jacqueline Elenor Carney. BA, The Coll. of William and Mary, Williamsburg, Va., 1989—93; MS in Edn., Old Dominion U., Norfolk, Va., 1994—96; MEd, Widener U., Chester, Pa., 2004—05. Tchr. of Handicapped Va. Dept. Edn., 1996, N.J. Dept. Edn., 1997, Learning Disability Tchr./Cons. N.J. Dept. Edn., 2001, cert. Prin. N.J. Dept. Edn., 2005. Tchr. of the handicapped SECEP, Norfolk, Va., 1995—97; tchr. of handicapped Brigantine Pub. Schools, NJ, 1997—2002; learning disability tchr./cons. Galloway Twp. Pub. Schools, 2002—05; asst. prin. Egg Harbor Twp. Mid. Sch., 2005—; asst. coach-varsity Holy Spirit HS, Absecon, 2001—04; asst. coach-varsity The Richard Stockton Coll. of NJ., Pomona, 2004—05. Recipient Golden Key Nat. Honor Soc., Old Dominion U., 1996. Mem.: Nat. Assn. Secondary Sch. Principals, ASCD, Phi Delta Kappa. Democrat. Roman Catholic. Avocations: singing, music, travel, basketball/crew/working out, dance. Office: Egg Harbor Twp Mid Sch 4034 Fernwood Ave Egg Harbor Township NJ 08234 Home Phone: 609-926-0650; Office Phone: 609-383-3355 1503. Business E-Mail: carneym@eht.k12.nj.us.

CARNEY, ROBERT ARTHUR, restaurant executive; b. Haddonfield, NJ, Aug. 20, 1937; s. George Albert and Margeret (Hollworth) C.; m. Janellen Sockol, may 31, 1996; 1 child, Lynn Ann. BA, Ursinus Coll., 1963. Procurement agt. Campbell Soup Co., Paris, Tex., 1963-69, mgr. procurement Salisbury, Md., 1969-72, dir. procurement Camden, NJ, 1972-78; v.p. procurement Burger King Corp., Miami, 1978-82; v.p. purchasing Pizza Hut, Inc., Wichita, 1982-95; sr. v.p. procurement & distbn. Long John Silver's, Inc., Lexington, Ky., 1995-99; ret., 1999. Mem. editl. adv. bd. Supplier Selection and Mgmt. Report. Mem. dean's adv. bd. Ala. State U. Capt. U.S. Army, 1958-60. Mem.: Nat. Restaurant Assn. Roman Catholic. Home: 4384 Laurel Park Hwy Hendersonville NC 28739

CARNEY, ROBERT THOMAS, lawyer; b. Youngstown, Ohio, Mar. 28, 1947; s. Thomas P. and Mildred B. (Keeling) C.; m. Victoria L. Schrecengost, May 21, 1977; children: Brian, Michael. BS in Physics, Northwestern U., 1969; JD, Georgetown U., 1972. Bar: Ohio 1972, D.C. 1974, U.S. Ct. Appeals (fed. cir.), U.S. Ct. Fed. Claims, U.S. Tax Court, U.S. Patent and Trademark Office, U.S. Supreme Ct. Law clk. U.S. Dist. Ct., Cleve., 1972-73; trial atty. tax divsn U.S. Dept. Justice, Washington, 1973-79; ptnr. tax atty. Lee, Toomey & Kent, Washington, 1979-88, Dow, Lohnes & Albertson, Washington, 1988-90, Rogers & Wells, Washington, 1990-96; ptnr. Fulbright & Jaworski, Washington, 1996-98, Ernst & Young, Washington, 1998—2005, O'Melveny & Myers LLP, Washington, 2005—. Adj. prof. Georgetown U. Law Sch., Washington, 1987—. Mem. Murdoch Inn of Ct. (master, sec.-treas.). Office: O'Melveny & Myers LLP 1625 I St NW Washington DC 20006 Home Phone: 703-883-8922; Office Phone: 202-383-5317. Business E-Mail: rcarney@omm.com.

CARNEY, ROGER FRANCIS XAVIER, retired military officer; b. Bklyn., Oct. 20, 1933; s. Frank Clement and Clara Helen (Muller) Carney; m. Linda Ann Bowlus, Aug. 11, 1963 (div. Mar. 1993); children: Kevin James, Stephen Jason, Brian Andrew. BS, Purdue U., 1960, MS in Indsl. Adminstrn., 1963; grad., U.S. Army Command and Gen. Staff Coll., 1975, U.S. Army War Coll., 1979; MA, U. Conn., 1992. Commd. 2d lt. U.S. Army, 1960, advanced through grades to lt. col., 1976; comdr. 583d Ordnance Co., Muenster, Germany, 1969-72; R&D coord. Army Material Comman Field Office, Kirtland AFB, N.Mex., 1972-74; logistic staff officer CENTAG Signal Support GP (NATO), Seckenheim, Germany, 1975-78; chief nuc. weapons logistic element G4 CENTAG (NATO), Seckenheim, 1978; comdr. 15th Ordnance Bn., Darmstadt, West Germany, 1978-80; prof. mil. sci. head dept. Worcester (Mass.) Poly. Inst., 1980-84; prof. mil. sci., head dept. Fitchburg (Mass.) State Coll., 1980-84, Nichols Coll., Dudley, Mass., 1982-84, dean student affairs, 1985-98, dir. Robert C. Fischer Inst., 1998—2004; ret., 2004. Mem. Worcester Com. Fgn. Rels. Decorated Legion of Merit, Bronze Star. Mem.: DAV, Purdue Alumni Assn., Mil. Officers Assn. Am., U. Conn. Alumni Assn., Assn. Former Intelligence Officers, Assn. U.S. Army, Am. Legion, Pi Lambda Theta, Alpha Sigma Pi (pres. Purdue U. chpt. 1959—60). Democrat. Home: 7 Thayer Pond Dr Apt 11 North Oxford MA 01537-1134 Personal E-mail: rcarney3093@charter.net.

CARNEY, SHANNON MAUREEN, small business owner, educator; b. Lansdale, Pa., Oct. 29, 1975; d. James Patrick and Patricia Dorothy (Somers) Gillespie; m. Kevin Patrick Carney, July 27. BA, DeSales U., Allentown, Pa., 1998. Dance instr. Buckingham Dance, Pa., 1998—2001, Conservatory of Music and Dance, Harleysville, Pa., 1998—2006, asst. choreographer, 1998—2006; owner, instr. Shannon Carney Dance Acad., Silverdale, Pa., 2005—. Office: Shannon Carney Dance Academy PO Box 370 Silverdale PA 18962 Office Phone: 215-257-2292.

CARNEY, STEPHEN PATRICK, lawyer, retired insurance company executive; b. Morristown, NJ, Aug. 14, 1950; s. Stephen M. and June K. Carney; m. Patricia Ann Davis, Oct. 29, 1989. BS, Coll. William & Mary, 1972, JD, 1980. Bar: Md. 1981. Law clk. to Hon. J. Calvitt Clarke, Jr. U.S. Dist. Ct. (ea. dist.) Va., Norfolk, 1980-81; labor assoc. Venable, Baetjer & Howard, Balt., 1981-84, assoc. real estate, 1984-88; gen. counsel, sec. Med. Mut. Liability Ins. Soc. Md., Hunt Valley, 1988-89, v.p., gen. counsel, sec., 1989-99, sr. v.p., gen. counsel, sec., 1999—2005; of counsel Funk & Bolton, 2005—. Bd. dirs. Mid-Atlantic Med. Ins. Co., Health Liability Alliance; mem. Gov.'s Adv. Com. on Practice Parameters, Balt., 1993-2001; adj.prof. law Coll. William and Mary, 2006-. Bd. dirs. Md. chpt. March of Dimes, Balt., 1990—, mem. exec. com., chair pub. affairs com., 1993—2003, chair bd. dirs., 2003—06. Recipient Alumni Svc. award Coll. William & Mary, 1998; named Pub. Affairs Com. Mem. of Yr. March of Dimes, White Plains, N.Y., 1998. Mem. ABA, Am. Corp. Counsel Assn., Physician Insurers Assn. Am. (legal sect.), Md. State Bar Assn., William and Mary Law Sch. Found. (bd. dirs., pres. 2003-05). Avocations: sailing, golf, travel, classic cars. Office: Funk & Bolton 36 S Charles St 12th Fl Baltimore MD 21201-3111 Office Phone: 410-659-7700. Business E-Mail: scarney@fblaw.com.

CARNEY, THOMAS DALY, lawyer; b. Detroit, Mar. 28, 1947; s. William C. and Mary L. (Daly) C.; m. Anne C. Filson; children: Thomas, David, Kristen. BA, U. Mich., 1969, JD, 1972. Bar: Mich. 1972. Assoc., Cross, Wrock, Miller & Vieson, Detroit, 1973-77, mem. firm, 1977-79; corp. counsel Hoover Universal, Inc., Ann Arbor, Mich., 1979-81, sec., gen. counsel, 1981-83, v.p., sec., gen. counsel, 1983-86; counsel Dickinson, Wright, Moon, Van Dusen & Freeman, Detroit, 1986-87, ptnr., 1988—94; named v.p., gen. counsel, sec. Borders Group Inc., Ann Arbor, Mich., 1994, now sr. v.p. gen. counsel, sec. Mem. ABA, Mich. Bar Assn., Am. Soc. Corp. Secretaries, Assn. Corp. Counsel. Club: Barton Hills Country (Ann Arbor). Office: Borders Group Inc 100 Phoenix Dr Ann Arbor MI 48108*

CARNEY, TIMOTHY ALAN, lawyer; b. Indpls., June 19, 1960; s. Chauncey F. and Mavis E. Carney; m. Cathy Denise Griggs, Aug. 10, 1985; children: Matthew A., Stephen M., Michelle E. BS in Fin., Mo. State U., Springfield, 1983; JD, U. Tulsa, Okla., 1986. Bar: Okla. 1986, US Ct. Appeals (10th cir.) 1986, US Supreme Ct. 1989. Atty. GableGotwals, Tulsa, 1986—. Adminstrv. coun. Asbury United Meth. Ch., Tulsa, 2004—07; bd. dirs. Tulsa Boys Home, Sand Springs, Okla., 1993—2007. Named one of Best Lawyers in Am., Woodward/White, Inc., 2006. Avocations: running, golf. Office: GableGotwals 1100 Oneok Plz 100 W Fifth St Tulsa OK 74103 Office Phone: 918-595-4800. Office Fax: 918-595-4990. Business E-Mail: tcarney@gablelaw.com.

CARNEY, TIMOTHY MICHAEL, ambassador; b. St. Joseph, Mo., July 12, 1944; s. Clement Egan Carney and Jane (Byrne) Booth; m. Tep Demaz Baker, 1973 (div. 1983); 1 child, Anne; m. Victoria Anne Butler, May 28, 1983. BS, MIT, 1966; postgrad., Cornell U., 1975-76. Joined Fgn. Svc., 1966; 3d sec., vice consul Am. Embassy, Saigon, Maseru, Phnom Penh, 1967-75, first sec. Bangkok, 1980-83, counsellor of embassy for polit. affairs Pretoria, South Africa, 1983-86, counsellor of embassy in polit. affairs Jakarta, Indonesia, 1987-90; prin. officer, consul U.S. Consulate, Udorn, Thailand, 1978-80; dir. Asian affairs NSC, Washington, 1991-92; dir. info./edn. divsn. UN Transitional Authority for Cambodia, Phnom Penh, Cambodia, 1992-93; cons. to UN UNOSOM, Somalia, 1993-94, UNOMSA, South Africa, 1993-94; dep. asst. sec. for South Asian affairs US Dept. State, Washington, 1994-95, US amb. to Sudan Khartoum, 1995-97, US amb. to Haiti Port-au-Prince, Haiti, 1998—99; sr. authority Ministry Industry & Metals Coalition Provisional Authority, Baghdad, 2003—04; chmn. Haiti Democracy Project, 2005; charge d'affaires Am. Embassy, Port-au-Prince, 2005—06; coord. for econ. transition in Iraq US Dept. State, Baghdad, 2007—. Author: Kampuchea: Balance of Survival, 1981; and monograph; contbr. articles to profl. jours. Mem. ethnozoology working group of species survival commn. Internat. Union for Conservation of Nature, Switzerland, 1987-90; life mem. Mzuri Wildlife Found., Zambia, Zimbabwe E. and South Africa Wildlife Socs. Mem. Siam Soc. (life). Avocations: photography, hunting.

CARNEY NELSON, ELLEN B., elementary school educator; b. Soda Springs, Idaho, June 11, 1936; d. Clarence Lyle and Benda Gladys (Petersen) Burton; m. Earl J. Carney Jr., Mar. 17, 1954 (div. 1981); children: Dennis (dec.), Phyllis, Maureen, Wade, Gary; m. Lewis G. Nelson, June 7, 1996. Student, U. Alaska, 1965; BA in Edn., U. Ariz., 1972; postgrad., Brigham Young U., 1975; MEd, U. Utah, 1976; postgrad., Idaho State U., 1990. Cert. elem. tchr., Ariz., Idaho, Utah. Tchr. Kiddie Club Kindergarten, Ft. Walton Beach, Fla., 1967; substitute tchr. Tucson (Ariz.) Dist. Schs., 1971-72; tchr. Jordan Sch. Dist., Sandy, Utah, 1973-79, Promised Horizons Pvt. Sch., Sandy, 1981; owner, operator Smart Start Preschool, Draper, Utah, 1978-81; tchr. Soda Springs Sch. Dist., 1981-90; grad. asst. Idaho State U., Pocatello, 1990-91; substitute tchr. Tooele Sch. Dist., 1991-95; tchr. Tooele Jr. H.S., 1996-2000, Grantsville Mdid. Sch., 2000-01. Sch. bicentennial chmn. South Jordan (Utah) Elem. Sch., 1976; mem. GEMS program devel. team Jordan Sch. Dist., 1976-79; owner Wayan (Idaho) Cash Store, 1985-90. Author: Dr. Ellis Kackley-Best Damn Doctor in the West, 1989, Flora Whittemore, 1990, The Mountain: Carriboo and Other Gold Camps in Idaho, 1990, Way Out in Grays Lake, 1992, The Oregon Trail: Ruts, Rogues and Reminiscences, 1993, River of Beaver, Stream of Gold, 1994, Historic Soda Springs: Oasis on the Oregon Trail, 1998, Mavericks in Calico, Vol. 1, They Rewrote Women's Role, 2003, Mavericks in Calico, Vol. 2, Powerful Mormon Women, 2003, Edie, 2006, (plays) 200 Years Too Late, 1976; corr.: Soda Springs Sun, Idaho State Jour., 1983—. Den mother, cub scout leader, fin. coun. Boy and Girl Scouts Am., Anchorage, 1965-66, Ft. Walton Beach, 1967-68, Sandy, 1973-75; neighborhood chmn. ARC, Sandy, 1979-80, hosp. vol., Tucson, 1970; bd. dirs. Caribou County Hist. Preservation Commn., Soda Springs, 1988-94, chmn., 2004—06; v.p. Caribou Hist. Soc., 2001-05. Named Bicentennial Contest Winner, Utah Edn. Assn., 1976. Mem. Lds Ch. Avocations: reading, writing, fishing, handicrafts, quilting. Home: 23 Grays Lake Rd Wayan ID 83285

CARNICERO, JORGE EMILIO, aeronautical engineer, transportation executive; b. Buenos Aires, July 17, 1921; arrived in US, 1942, naturalized, 1950; s. Alberto and Ana (Sulimeau) C.; m. Jacqueline Joanne Damman, Feb. 22, 1946; children— Jacqueline Denise, Jorge Jay. Student, U. LaPlata, Argentina, 1939—41, Rensselaer Poly. Inst., 1945. Chief engr. Dodero Airlines, Argentina, 1945, Flota Aerea Mercante, Argentina, 1945-46; v.p. Air Carrier Svc. Corp., Washington, 1946, exec. v.p., 1947-55, chmn. bd. dirs., dir., 1955-88; ret., 1988. Past chmn., bd. Dyncorp (formerly Calif. Ea. Aviation, then Dynalectron Corp.); pres., bd. dirs. Blue Cove, Inc., N.Y., Inter-Properties, Inc., Del., Trans-Am. Aero. Corp., Del., Round Hill Devel. Ltd., Jamaica. Bd. visitors Sch. Fgn. Service, Georgetown U., Washington; mem. council Rensselaer Poly. Inst., Troy, N.Y., mem. adv. bd. mech., aero. and mechanics dept. Fellow Royal Aero. Soc.; mem. Argentine-Am. C. of C. (bd. dirs.), Univ. Club, Met. Club, Congl. Country Club, Georgetown Club. Home: 3949 52d St NW Washington DC 20016-1925 Office: 1313 Dolley Madison Blvd Mc Lean VA 22101-3926 Home Phone: 202-966-8139. Personal E-mail: jccarjc@aol.com.

CARNIE, KAY C., artist, educator; b. NYC, June 8, 1942; d. James Ogden and Allegra MacCulloch Combes; m. Donald Ross Carnie, June 6, 1964; children: David, Michael. BA, Fla. So. Coll., 1964; MA, San Jose State U., 1988, MFA, 1993. Profl. artist, Cupertino, Calif., 1993—; instr. Palo Alto Art Ctr., Calif., 1996—99, San Mateo Cmty. Edn., Calif., 1999; tchr. Coll. of San Mateo, 2000—. Juror fine arts Santa Clara County Fair, San Jose, 1991, 97. Splash 4, 1996, Painting Great Pictures from Photographs, 1999, Capturing Texture, 2002, Splash 8, 2004. Mem. Nat. Watercolor Soc. (signature), Midwest Watercolor Soc. (signature), Calif. Watercolor Assn. (signature), Watercolor West (juried mem.). Avocations: piano, photography, travel. Home and Office: 10439 Heney Creek Pl Cupertino CA 95014 Personal E-mail: kccarnie@aol.com.

CARNIOL, PAUL J., plastic and reconstructive surgeon, otolaryngologist; b. NYC, Sept. 26, 1951; s. David A. and Diane (Hadler) C.; m. Renie Rich, Jan. 3, 1976; children: Michael P., Alan R., Eric T. BA, NYU, 1972; MD, U. Pa. Sch. Medicine, 1976. Diplomate Am. Bd. Otolaryngology, Am Bd. Facial Plastic and Reconstructive Surgery, Am. Bd. Cosmetic Surgery, Am. Bd. Med. Examiners. Resident, surgery U. Pa., Phila., 1976-77, resident, plastic and reconstructive surgery, 1981-83; resident, surgery North Shore U. Hosp., Manhasset, NY, 1977-78; resident, surgery and otolaryngology, clin. tchg. fellow Mass. Eye and Ear Infirmary, Harvard Med. Sch., Boston, 1978-81; attending plastic surgery, head and neck surgery Overlook Hosp., Summit, NJ, 1983—; instr. with U. Medicine and Dentistry of NJ, Newark, 1994—, clin. assoc. prof., surgery, 2000—. Instr. courses on lasers in plastic surgery, facial rejuvenation; chief sect. otolaryngology Overlook Hosp., 1992-97; courtesy staff, St. Barnabus Hosp., 1996-; mem. Univ. Hosp. staff 1998-; police surgeon, Summit, NJ, 1997-, New Providence, NJ, 1997-; mem. bd. health New Providence, 2002-, emergency response team, 2003-; mem. Union County emergency response team, 2004; vis. prof. dept. otolaryngology U. Pa. Sch. Medicine, 2006; cons., lectr., presenter in field. Editor: Laser Skin Rejuvenation, 1998, Facial Rejuvenation, 2001; spl. editor: Am. Jour. Cosmetic Surgery, mem. editl. bd.: Jour. Cosmetic and Laser Therapy, Facial Plastic Surgery Times, Plastic Surgery Products, 1999, Jour. Aesthetic Dermatology and Cosmetic Dermatologic Surgery, 1992—94, Jour. Cutaneous Laser Surgery, 2000; contbr. articles to profl. jours., chapters to books. Interviewer for admissions com. U. Pa., Phila., 1987—. Named Top Cosmetic Surgeons, NJ Savvy Mag., 2006, 2007, Top Plastic Surgeons, Consumer's Rsch. Coun., 2006, Top Physician in NY Met. Area, Castle Connolly Ltd., 2006; named one of Top Cosmetic Surgeons in NJ, NJ Life Magazine and Castle Connelly Med., Ltd., 2004; recipient Cmty. Svc. award, Ciba-Geigy, Summit, 1978, Found. award, NYU, 1972, Alumni Gold Medal award, 1972, Silver Shield, PBA 55, 2003. Fellow: ACS (coun. mem. NJ chpt. 2004—), Am. Acad. Cosmetic Surgery (chmn. edn. com. 1995—97), Am. Acad. Facial Plastic and Reconstructive Surgery (dir. courses lasers, facial plastic surgery and cosmetic surgery 1996—98, care com., chmn. new tech. and surg. devices com. 1997—2000, v.p. R & D 2001—03, pres. 2002—), Am. Acad. Otolaryngology, Nead and Neck Surgery (bd. dir. 1991—); mem.: AMA, Am. Rhinologic Soc., NJ Acad. Facial Plastic Surgery (pres. 2003—), Med. Soc. N.J. (trustee 2005—, bd. dirs.), Union County Med. Soc. (planning com. 1986—89, exec. com. 1995—97, chmn. program com. 1995—, exec. bd. 1997—, treas. 1999—2000, v.p. 2000—02, pres.-elect 2002—03, pres. 2003—04), NJ Acad. Otolaryngology (pres. 1993—96, 1997—), NJ Med. Soc. (mem. coun. comm. 1996—2002, coun. on med. svcs. 2002—, mem. coun. legislation 2004—, mem. bd. trustees), Internat. Soc. Cosmetic Laser Surgery (bd. dir. 1998—2001, v.p. 2001—03, trustee 2005—), Phi Beta Kappa. Avocations: golf, fishing, bicycling, Karate. Office: 33 Overlook Rd Ste 202 Summit NJ 07901 Address: 8 Mountain Blvd Warren NJ 07059 Office Phone: 908-598-1400.

CARNOCHAN, WALTER BLISS, retired humanities educator; b. NYC, Dec. 20, 1930; s. Gouverneur Morris and Sibyll Baldwin (Bliss) C.; m. Nancy Powers Carter, June 25, 1955 (div. 1978); children— Lisa Powers, Sarah Bliss, Gouverneur Morris, Sibyll Carter; m. Brigitte Hoy Fields, Sept. 16, 1979. AB, Harvard, 1953, A.M., 1957, PhD, 1960. Asst. dean freshmen Harvard U., 1954-56; successively instr., asst. prof., assoc. prof., prof. English, Stanford (Calif.) U., 1960-94, prof. emeritus, 1994—, chmn. dept. English, 1971-73, dean grad. studies, 1975-80, vice provost, 1976-80, dir. Stanford Humanities Ctr., 1985-91, Anthony P. Meier Family prof. humanities, 1988-91, Richard W. Lyman prof. humanities, 1993-94, Richard W. Lyman prof. emeritus, 1994—, acting dir. Stanford Humanities Ctr., 1999. Mem. overseers com. to visit Harvard Coll, 1979-85, mem. bd. advisors Ehrenpreis Ctr. for Swift Studies, 1984—. Author: Lemuel Gulliver's Mirror for Man, 1968, Confinement and Flight: An Essay on English Literature of the 18th Century, 1977, Gibbon's Solitude: The Inward World of the Historian, 1987, The Battleground of the Curriculum: Liberal Education and American Experience, 1993, Momentary Bliss: An American Memoir, 1999, The Sad Story of Burton, Speke and the Nile; or was John Hanning Speke a Cad: Looking at the Evidence, 2006, Golden Legends: Images of Abyssinia, Samual Johnson to Bob Marley, 2007. Trustee Mills Coll., 1978-85, Athenian Sch., 1975-88, Berkeley (Calif.) Art Mus., 1983-96, 98-2001. Home: 138 Cervantes Rd Portola Valley CA 94028-7725 Business E-Mail: carnoch@stanford.edu.

CARNWATH, SQUEAK, artist, educator; b. Abington, Pa., May 24, 1947; d. Samuel Carnwath and Shirley Howlan Carnwath; m. Gary Knecht. MFA, Calif. Coll. Arts & Crafts, Oakland, 1977. Artist Carnwath Studio, Oakland, 1971—; prof. in residence, dept. art practice U. Calif., Berkeley, 1998—. Pres. Artists' Legacy Found., Oakland, 2000—07. Recipient Visual Artists award, Flintridge Found., 2002; fellow, Guggenheim Found., 1994; grantee Individual Artist fellowship, Nat. Endowment Arts, 1985;, 1980. Personal E-mail: info@squeakcarnwath.com.

CARO, IVOR, dermatologist; b. Johannesburg, June 2, 1946; came to U.S., 1975; s. Herbert and Rachel (Eisenstein) C.; m. Sheryl Helaine Marsden, Dec. 14, 1969; children: Howard Seth, Glen. MB, BCh, U. Witwatersrand, 1969. Diplomate, Am. Bd. Dermatology. Resident U. Witwatersrand, Johannesburg, 1971—74; fellow St. John's Hosp., London, 1974—76; asst. prof. U. N.C., Chapel Hill, 1975—78; pvt. practice Seattle, 1978—99; dir. internat. program dermatology Harvard Med. Sch., Boston, 1999—2003; dir. dermatol. clin. investigation unit Mass. Gen. Hosp./ Harvard Med. Sch., 2000—03; med. dir. dermatology Genentech, South San Francisco, 2003—. Clin. prof. U. Wash., Seattle, 1978-99; chief of dermatology, attending dermatologist Va. Mason Med. Ctr., Seattle, 1978-99. Contbr. to profl. publs. and textbooks. Fellow: Am. Acad. Dermatology; mem.: Pacific Dermatol. Soc., New Eng. Dermatol. Soc., Noah Worcester Dermatol. Soc. (sec., treas. 2000—04, pres. 2004—05), Seattle Dermatol. Soc. (pres. 1987—88). Office: Genentech 1 DNA Way MS 84 South San Francisco CA 94080 Office Phone: 650-225-6370. E-mail: icaro@gene.com.

CARO, ROBERT ALLAN, historian, writer; b. NYC; s. Benjamin and Cele (Mendelow) C.; m. Ina Joan Sloshberg, June 9, 1957; 1 child, Chase Arthur. AB cum laude, Princeton U., 1957; DLitt (hon.), Merrimack Coll., 1983, L.I. U., 2003, New Sch. for Social Rsch., 1997. Reporter New Brunswick Home News, NJ, 1957-59, Newsday, Garden City, NY, 1960-66; Nieman fellow Harvard U., Cambridge, Mass., 1965-66. Historian, biographer, 1967—. Author: The Power Broker: Robert Moses and the Fall of New York, 1974 (Pulitzer prize for biography 1975, Francis Parkman prize Soc. Am. Historians 1975, Selected by Modern Libr. as 1 of 100 Best Nonfiction Books Written in English during the 20th Century), The Years of Lyndon Johnson: The Path to Power, 1982 (Nat. Book Critics award for biography 1983, Tex. Inst. Arts and Letters award for non-fiction 1983), The Years of Lyndon Johnson: Means of Ascent, 1990 (Nat. Book Critics Cir. award for biography 1991), The Years of Lyndon Johnson: Master of the Senate, 2002 (Nat. Book award for non-fiction 2002, Pulitzer prize for biography 2003, L.A. Times Book prize for biography 2003, Carl Sandburg award in Lit. 2004, award Chgo. Pub. Libr. Found. 2003). Bd. dir. Fund for City NY, NY Soc. Libr., Theatre for New Audience, John Simon Guggenheim Meml. Found. Recipient Soc. of Silurians award, 1964, Deadline Club, 1964, 65, spl. citation NY chpt. AIA, 1975, Pulitzer Prize for biography, 1975, 2003, Nat. Book Critics Cir. award Biography, 1983, 91, H.L. Mencken prize Free Press Assn., 1983, award in lit. Am. Acad. and Inst. Arts and Letters, 1986, Lifetime Achievement in Arts award Guild Hall Acad. Arts, 1992, John Steinback award Southampton Coll., 2004, Disting. Achievement award English-Speaking Union, 2004, Gold medal in biography Am. Acad. and Inst. Arts and Letters, 2006; co-recipient ann. polit. book award Washington Monthly, 1975, 83, 91. Fellow Soc. Am.

Historians (Francis Parkman prize); mem. Authors Guild Am. (bd. dir. 1976—, pres. 1980-82), PEN Am. Ctr. (mem. exec. bd. 1986-88, v.p. 1989-92), Century Club. Office: Robert A Caro Inc 250 W 57th St Ste 2215 New York NY 10107-2209 Office Phone: 212-582-4845. E-mail: Randeltracy@aol.com.

CARO, WILLIAM ALLAN, physician, educator; b. Chgo., Aug. 16, 1934; s. Marcus Rayner and Adeline Beatrice (Cohen) Caro; m. Ruth Fruchtlander, June 15, 1959 (dec.); children: Mark Stephen, David Edward; m. Joan Peters, Oct. 18, 1997. Student, U. Mich., 1952-55; BS in Medicine, U. Ill., 1957, MD, 1959. Intern Cook County Hosp., Chgo., 1959-60; resident in internal medicine U. Ill. Rsch. and Ednl. Hosps., 1960-61; resident in dermatology Hosp. U. Pa., 1961-62, 64-66; Earl D. Osborne fellow dermal pathology Armed Forces Inst. Pathology, Washington, 1966-67; asst. in medicine U. Ill. Coll. Medicine, 1960-61; asst. instr. U. Pa. Med. Sch., 1961-62, 64-66; from asst. prof. to assoc. prof. dermatology Northwestern U. Med. Sch., 1967—81, prof., 1981—; pvt. practice specializing in dermatology Chgo., 1967—. Chief dermatology sect. MacDonald Army Hosp., Ft. Eustis, Va., 1962—64; attending physician Chgo. Wesley Meml. Hosp., 1969—72, Northwestern Meml. Hosp., 1972—, mem. med. exec. com., 1977—79; cons. Rehab. Inst. Chgo., Mcpl. Tb Sanitarium Chgo., 1968—74. Mem. editl. bd. Cutis, 1975—; assoc. editor: Year Book Pathology and Clin. Pathology, 1977—80. Mem. medicine adv. bd. U. Ill. Coll. Medicine, 1988—; trustee Northwestern Meml. Hosp. Chgo., 1986—87, bd. dirs., 1988—91, Northwestern Meml. Corp., 1987—2000, mem. exec. com., 1988—91. Served as capt. M.C. USAR, 1962—64. Mem.: AMA, Am. Bd. Dermatology (diplomate 1966, bd. dirs. 1981—91, v.p. 1989—90, pres. 1990—91), Dermatology Found. (Clark W. Finnerud award 2002), Pacific Dermatol. Assn., Internat. Soc. Dermatology, Am. Soc. Dermatopathology (pres.-elect 1995—96, bd. dirs. 1995—2000, pres. 1996—97), Am. Dermatol. Assn. (bd. dirs. 1993—98, v.p. 2004—05), Chgo. Dermatol. Soc. (editor trans. 1971—73, pres. 1983—84, Founders award 1992), Am. Acad. Dermatology (Gold award sci. exhibit 1970), U. Ill. Med. Alumni Assn. (exec. bd. 1977—80), Phi Kappa Phi, Alpha Omega Alpha. Office: 676 N Saint Clair St Ste 1840 Chicago IL 60611-2927

CAROLAND, WILLIAM BOURNE, structural engineer; b. Clarksville, Tenn., July 9, 1929; s. Enoch Arden and Jennie Wimberly (Bourne) C.; m. Eloise Joyce Crickard, June 3, 1957; children: Richard Bradley, Jennifer Dorothy. Student, U. Tenn., 1947-52. Registered surveyor, Ky., 1967-2000; profl. engr., Ky., 1967-, Tenn., 1972-2004, Fla., 1972-2001, W.Va., 1972-2004, Mich., 1972-2004, Ind., 1974-2004. Survey party chief King & Clark Engrs., Clarksville, 1955-56, Michael Baker Jr., Inc., Jackson, Miss., 1956-57, asst. designer Charleston, W.Va., 1957-62, project supr. Louisville, 1962-63, designer Charleston, 1963-64; bridge designer Vogt, Ivers & Assocs., Cin., 1964-65; sr. structural engr. Brighton Engring., Frankfort, Ky., 1965-73; chief bridge engr. Beam, Longest & Neff, Indpls., 1973-79; with Am. Cons. Engrs., Lexington, Ky., 1979—2001, chief bridge engr., 1988—2001; ret., 2001; cons. Am. Cons. Engrs., 2001—03. Cons. in field; mem. Am. Cons. Engrs. Coun. Contbr. papers to profl. publs. With U.S. Army, 1952-55. Recipient Welded Steel Design award Lincoln Arc Welding Found., 1974, Welded Steel Design hon. mention, 1975, silver award 1999; Bridge Design award Prestressed Concrete Inst., 1977, 92, Grand Conceptor award Am. Consulting Engrs. Coun., 2001. Avocations: woodworking, photography. Home: 114 Christal Dr Georgetown KY 40324 *When I was growing up my father always told me there is no such word as can't. Over the years I have come to agree with this. If we believe and work hard it can be done.*

CAROLEO, LINN E., mathematician, writer; b. Oslo, Dec. 6, 1968; d. Lawrence S. Damon and Barbra M. Enger; m. Wayne A. Caroleo, May 5, 2001. BA, U. Calif., San Diego, 1997; MS, Calif. State U., San Marcos, 1999; EdD, U. West Fla., Pensacola, 2005. Master Farrier Am. Horseshoeing Assn., 1988. Math. prof. Calif. State U., San Marcos, 1997—2001; adj. prof. Northeastern U., Boston, 2001—02; math. prof. Emmanuel Coll., Boston, 2001—02; adj. math. prof. U. West Fla., Pensacola, 2002—04; grad. and tchg. asst. Office of Juvenile Studies, Pensacola, 2003—04; spl. projects reporter The Sun, Yuma, Ariz., 2004—05; regulatory scientist Gowan Co., Yuma, Ariz., 2005—06. Dir. edn. Cocopah Indian Tribe, Somerton, Ariz., 2006—07. Author (reporter): (newspaper articles) Blue Heaven (Second Pl., Ariz. Newspaper Assn., 2005). Aviation structural mechanic egress sys. petty officer USN, 1989—93. Office Phone: 928-225-9498. E-mail: linn@aikorn.com.

CAROLINA, MONTEIRO, ecologist; b. Sao Paulo, Brazil, Dec. 4, 1978; d. Carlos and Marilena Monteiro; m. Nicholas Haertle, July 3, 2006. BS in Biology, U. Mogi Cruzes, San Pablo, 2001; M in Biology, U. Ark., Fayetteville, 2006. Rsch. asst. U. Ark., Fayetteville, Ark., 2002—06; ecol. technician, CEET U. La., Lafayette, 2007—. Tchg. asst. U. Ark., 2004—06. Achievements include research in rattlesnake. Office: CEET Ctr Ecology Univ La 703 Thoroughbred Dr Lafayette LA 70507 Personal E-mail: karol_monteiro@yahoo.com. Business E-Mail: ceet@louisiana.edu.

CARON, JACQUES, professional hockey coach; b. Noranda, Que., Can., Apr. 21, 1940; m. Marjorie Caron. Goalie LA Kings, St. Louis Blues, 1971—73; mem. coaching staff Hartford Whalers, 1980—92; goalie coach NJ Devils, 1996—. Office: NJ Devils 33 Fl 744 Broad St Newark NJ 07102*

CARON, WILFRED RENE, retired lawyer; b. NYC, July 23, 1931; s. Joseph Wilfred and Eva Caron; m. Anne Theresa Flanagan, AUg. 2, 1958. JD, St. John's U., 1956. Bar: N.Y. 1956, D.C. 1977, U.S. Dist. Ct. D.C. 1977, U.S. Dist. Ct. (no. dist.) N.Y. 1957, U.S. Dist. Ct. (so. and ea. dists.) N.Y. 1961, U.S. Ct. Appeals (2d cir.) 1965, U.S. Ct. Appeals (3d cir.) 1973, U.S. Ct. Appeals (5th cir.) 1977, U.S. Ct. Appeals (6th cir.) 1973, U.S. Ct. Appeals (8th cir.) 1975, U.S. Ct. Appeals (9th cir.) 1976, U.S. Ct. Appeals (D.C. cir.) 1975, U.S. Supreme Ct. 1961. Law clk. to chief judge N.Y. State Ct. Appeals, 1956-59; spl. asst. atty. gen. N.Y., 1959-60; assoc. Goldman & Drazen, 1960-64, Corner, Finn, Cuomo & Charles, NYC, 1964-69; asst. gen. counsel Ronson Corp., Woodbridge, N.J., 1969-71; assoc. gen. counsel Securities Investor Protection Corp., Washington, 1972-80; gen. counsel U.S. Cath. Conf., Inc., Washington, 1980-87, Nat. Conf. Cath. Bishops, 1980-87, Cath. Telecom. Network Am., Inc., NYC, 1981-88; ptnr. O'Connor & Hannan, Washington, 1987-88; sr. advisor Office of Policy Devel., U.S. Dept. of Justice, Washington, 1988-90; appellate counsel Travelers Ins. Co., 1990-92; ret., 1992. Contbr. articles to profl. jours. Adv. bd. St. Thomas More Inst. Legal Rsch., St. John's U. Sch. Law, N.Y.C., 1981-92; exec. bd. Ctr. for Ch.-State Studies, DePaul U. Law Coll., Chgo., 1982-2003. Served to 1st lt. U.S. Army, 1952-54, Korea. Mem.: ABA, D.C. Bar Assn., Am. Legion, VFW. Roman Catholic. Home: 44 Old Main Rd Little Compton RI 02837-1321

CARONE, NICOLAS, artist; b. NYC, June 4, 1917; Student, Nat. Acad. of Design, Art Students League, Hans Hoffman Sch. Fine Arts, 1931—41. Founding mem. New York Studio School, Stable Gallery; tchr., painting Yale U., Columbia U., Brandeis U., Cornell U., Cooper Union, Sch. Visual Arts, Skowhegan Sch. Solo exhibitions, Lohin Geduld Gallery, Frumkin Gallery, Stable Gallery, Staempfli Gallery, group exhibitions, Mus. Modern Art, Rome, Brussel's World Fair, The Venice Biennale, The Tate Gallery, Guggenheim Mus., Mus. Modern Art, Nat. Acad. Design, Hunter Coll. Gallery, Baruch Coll. Gallery, Sewell Art Gallery Rice U., Rose Art Mus., Brandeis U., Ninth St. Show, Geitain Group, Japan, Represented in permanent collections, Whitney Mus., Mus. Am. Art, Hirschhorn Mus., Minn. Mus. Am. Art, Norton Mus. Art, Balt. Mus. Art. Named National Academician, 2001; recipient The Rome Prize, Andrew Carnegie prize, Nat. Acad. Mus.; fellow Fullbright Fellowship; grantee William Copely Grant, Childe Hassam Grant, NY State Coun. on Arts, Longview Found. Office Phone: 212-675-2656. Personal E-mail: info@lohingeduld.com.

CARONIS, GEORGE JOHN, insurance executive; b. Columbus, Ohio, Dec. 8, 1933; s. John George and Effie (Zarafonetis) C.; m. Shirley Ann Milburn, June 7, 1958; 1 child, Kevin M. BA, Ohio State U., 1955, MA, 1960. CLU; ChFC; chartered property and casualty underwriter; CFP. Asst. dean of men Ohio State U., Columbus, 1957-60; assoc. gen. agt. Tice Ins. Co., Columbus, 1960-74; v.p. pensions and estate planning Midland Mut. Life Ins. Co., Columbus, 1974-77; v.p. bus. devel. Bank One Trust Co., Columbus, 1977-79; v.p. fin. svcs. Kientz and Co., Columbus, 1979-82; dir. mktg. Nationwide Ins. Cos., Columbus, 1982-87; mktg. mgr. Aetna Life and Casualty Co., Columbus, 1987-89; v.p. advanced underwriting Western Res. Life Assurance Co., Clearwater, Fla., 1989-91, v.p. mktg., 1991—2001; sr. v.p. Asset Accumulation Group, Aegon U.S.A., 1994-98; exec. v.p. Aegon Equity Group, 1998—2001; registered prin. ProVise Mgmt. Group, LLC, 2002—. Bd. dirs. Mass. Fidelity Trust Co. 1st lt. U.S. Army, 1955-57. Recipient Thomas Arkle Clark award Alpha Tau Omega, 1955, Alumni Centennial award Ohio State U., 1970, Ralph D. Mershon award Ohio State U., 1990. Fellow Life Mgmt. Inst.; mem. Ohio State Alumni Assn. (nat. pres. 1983-85), Ohio State U. Found. (nominating com.), Nat. Assn. Life Underwriters, Am. Soc. CLUs and ChFCs. Home: 1371 River Oaks Ct Oldsmar FL 34677-4829 Office: Western Res Life Assurance 1371 River Oaks Ct Oldsmar FL 34677-4829

CAROOMPAS, CAROLE JEAN, artist, educator; b. Oregon City, Nov. 14, 1946; d. John Thomas and Dorothy Lietta (Dirks) Caroompas. BA, Calif. State U., Fullerton, 1968; MFA in Painting, U. So. Calif., 1971. Instr. El Camino Coll., Torrance, Calif., 1971—72; vis. artist Calif. State U., Northridge, 1972—75; instr. Immaculate Heart Coll., LA, 1973—76; vis. artist Calif. State U., Fullerton, 1976—78; instr. U. Calif., Irvine, 1976—80, Claremont Grad. Sch., Calif., 1976—79, Art Ctr. Coll. Design, Pasadena, Calif., 1978—86, UCLA Ext., 1984—93; prof. fine arts Otis Coll. Art and Design, LA, 1981—. Vis. artist Anderson Ranch Art Ctr., Aspen, Colo., 1996, Aspen, 98, Aspen, 2005. One-woman shows include Jan Baum Art Gallery, LA, 1978—82, Karl Bornstein Gallery, 1985, LA Contemporary Exhbns., 1989, U. Calif., Irvine, 1990, Sue Spaid Fine Art, LA, 1992, 1994, P.P.O.W., NYC, 1994, Otis Coll. Art and Design Art Gallery, 1997—98, Mark Moore Gallery, Santa Monica, 1997, 1999, 2000, Western Project, Culver City, Calif., 2004, 2007, exhibited in group shows at Pasadena Mus. Art, 1972, Whitney Mus. Art, 1978, Mus. Modern Art1976, NYC, LA County Mus., 1982, Corcoran Gallery Art, Washington, 1993, Under Constrn. Armory Ctr. Arts, Pasadena, 1995, UCLA Hammer Mus. Art, 1996, 2000, LA County Mus. Art, 1996, Beaver Coll., 1996, LA Mcpl. Art Gallery, 1997, Calif. State U., Fullerton, 2001, San Jose Mus., 2002, Rosamund Felson Gallery, Santa Monica, 2003, Lewis and Clark Coll., Portland, Oreg., 2003, San Luis Obispo Art Ctr., 2003, Western Project, Culver City, 2006, 2006, The Lab., San Francisco, 2006, LA Mcpl. Art Gallery, 2007, Riverside Mus., Calif., 2007, Track 16, Santa Monica, 2007; singer: 2 individual albums, (albums) The Record: 13 Vocal Artists; contbr. articles to profl. jours. Grantee, NEA, 1987, 1993, Visual Arts Funding Initiative, Calif. Cmty. Found., 2005, Peter S. Reed Found., 2006; Faculty Devel. grantee, New Sch. Social Rsch., 1989, Support grantee, Esther and Adolph Gottlieb Found., 1993, Guggenheim Meml. fellow, 1995, Individual Artist's fellow, City of L.A. Cultural Affairs Dept., 2000, Peter S. Reed Found. grantee, 2006. Office: Otis Coll Art and Design 9045 Lincoln Blvd Los Angeles CA 90045-3505 Office Phone: 310-838-0609.

CAROTHERS, DOUGLAS EDWARD, special education educator; b. Akron, Ohio, Oct. 10, 1959; s. Loris Carothers. EdD, Fla. Atlantic U., Boca Raton, 2002. Asst. prof. Radford U., Va., 2002—03, Fla. Gulf Coast U., Fort Myers, 2003—. Mem.: Coun. Exceptional Children. Achievements include research in asperger syndrome and assessment. Home: 7155 Pine Manor Dr Lake Worth FL 33467 Office: Florida Gulf Coast Univ 10501 FGCU Blvd S Fort Myers FL 33965 Home Phone: 561-602-9592; Office Phone: 239-590-7787. Office Fax: 239-590-7801; Home Fax: 239-590-7801. Business E-Mail: dcarothe@fgcu.edu.

CAROTHERS, ROBERT LEE, academic administrator; b. Sewickley, Pa., Sept. 3, 1942; s. Robert Fleming and Mary (Skinner) C.; children: Robert Kennedy, Shelley Rye, Matthew K. BA in English, Edinboro U., 1965; MA, Kent State U., 1966, PhD, 1969; JD, U. Akron, 1980. Bar: Pa. 1981. Prof. English, dean, v.p. Edinboro U., 1968-83; pres. S.W. State U., Marshall, Minn., 1983-86; chancellor Minn. State U. Sys., St. Paul, 1986-91; pres. U. R.I., Kingston, 1991—. Author: Freedom and Other Times, 1972; John Calvin's Favorite Son, 1980. Served with AUS, 1960-68. Recipient Humanitarian award, Urban League RI, 2000, Jean Hicks award, RI Nat. Conf. for Cmty. and Justice, 2000, History Makers Salute, RI Historical Soc., 2001, Silver Anniversary Honor Roll award, Am. Cancer Soc., Coun. Fellows Mentor award, Am. Coun. Edn., 2005. Mem.: Nat. Inst. Alcohol Abuse and Alcoholism (com. campus drinking 1999—2002). Avocation: fishing. Home: 56 Upper College Rd Kingston RI 02881-2022 Office: URI Office of the Pres Green Hall 35 Campus Ave Kingston RI 02881-1303 Office Phone: 401-874-2444. Office Fax: 401-874-7149. E-mail: muskrat@uri.edu.

CAROVANO, JOHN MARTIN, not-for-profit developer; b. Tacoma, May 9, 1935; s. John and Elda C. (Martin) C.; m. Barbara Bevins, June 14, 1958; children: Kristen, Kathryn. BA, Pomona Coll., 1957, LL.D., 1979; MA, U. Calif., Berkeley, 1961, PhD, 1965; LL.D., Hamilton Coll., 1974. Research asst., teaching fellow U. Calif. at Berkeley, 1959-63; instr. econs. Hamilton Coll., Clinton, NY, 1963-65, asst. prof., 1965-68, asso. prof., 1969-74, acting provost, 1971-72, provost, 1972-74, pres. coll., 1974-88; dir. N.Y. office The Nature Conservancy, 1988-94, planned giving officer, 1994—. Financial economist Office Tax Analysis, U.S. Dept. Treasury, Washington, 1968-69; chmn. N.Y. Com. of Selection, Rhodes Scholarship Trust, 1978-82; trustee Commn. on Ind. Colls. and Univs. N.Y., 1980-83 Mem. Democratic Com., Clinton, 1970-74. Served with AUS, 1957-58. Home: 87 Railroad Pl # 407 Saratoga Springs NY 12866 Office: Nature Conservancy 112 Spring St Ste 105 Saratoga Springs NY 12866 E-mail: carovano@nycap.rr.com.

CARP, DANIEL A., former consumer products company executive; b. Wytheville, Va., May 4, 1948; BBA in Quantitative Methods, Ohio U., 1970; MBA, Rochester Inst. Tech., 1973; MS in Mgmt., MIT, 1988. Stats. analyst Eastman Kodak Co., Rochester, NY, various positions in market rsch. and mgmt., gen. mgr. sales Kodak Can., gen. mgr. consumer electronics divsn., asst. gen. mgr. Latin Am. region, 1986-88, v.p., gen. mgr., 1988-90, gen. mgr. European Mktg. Cos., 1990—95, exec. v.p., asst. COO, 1995-97, pres., COO, 1997-2000, pres., CEO, 2000, chmn., pres., CEO, 2000—01, chmn., CEO, 2001—05, chmn., 2005. Bd. dirs. Eastman Kodak Co., 1997—2005, Tex. Instruments Inc.; mem. Bus. Council; mem. bd. trustees George Eastman House; mem. adv. coun. MIT Sloan; mem. Alumni Hall of Distinction, N.Y. State Commn. on Ind. Colls. & Univs. Sloan fellow Sloan Sch. of Mgmt., MIT; recipient Leadership award, 2001, Person of the Yr. award, 2004, PhotoImaging Manufacturers & Distributors Assn., Corning award for Excellence, 2005, Diversity Best Practices CEO award, 2005.

CARP, JEFFREY N., lawyer, investment company executive; BS in Math. and Econs. magna cum laude, Tufts U.; JD with honors, George Washington U. Atty. Hale & Dorr, LLP, 1982—2004, sr. ptnr., 1989—2004; exec. v.p., gen. counsel Mass. Fin. Svcs., 2004—05; exec. v.p., chief legal officer, sec., mem. oper. grp. State St. Corp., Boston, 2006—. Dir. ICI Mut. Ins. Co. Bd. dirs. Project Bread - The Walk for Hunger. Mem.: DC Bar Assn., Mass. Bar Assn., ABA. Office: State St Corp 1 Lincoln St Boston MA 02111*

CARP, LARRY, lawyer; b. St. Louis, Jan. 26, 1926; s. Avery and Ruth C. Student, U. Mo., Columbia, 1944; cert., Sorbonne U., Paris, 1946; BA, Washington U., St. Louis, 1947; postgrad., Grad. Inst. Internat. Studies, Geneva, 1949; JD, Washington U., St. Louis, 1951. Bar: Mo. 1951, U.S. Dist. Ct. (ea. dist.) Mo. 1951. Mem. U.S. Dept. of State, Washington, 1951-53; mem. staff Senator Paul H. Douglas (Dem. Ill.), Washington, 1953-54; assoc. Fordyce, Mayne, Hartman, Renard, and Stribling, St. Louis, 1954-63; sole practice St. Louis, 1963-68; ptnr. Carp & Morris, St. Louis, 1968-90, Carp, Sexauer and Carr, St. Louis, 1990-94, Carp and Sexauer, St. Louis, 1994—. Assoc. counsel, acting chief counsel U.S. Senate Subcom. on Constitutional Rights, Washington, 1956; life mem. bd. trustees Acad. Sci., St. Louis, 1984—; mem. St. Louis Regional U.S. Export Expansion Coun., 1964-74; mem. Mo. Commn. on Human Rights, 1966-78, vice chmn., 1977-78; vice chmn., bd. dirs. Pastoral Counselling Inst. for Greater St. Louis, 1964-91; mem. adv. bd. George Engelmann Math. and Science Inst., 1992-96; bd. dirs. St. Louis Ctr. for Internat. Rels., 1998-2006; legal advisor Image, Inc., St. Louis, 1998-2003. Co-author: (musicals) Pocahontas, The Pied Piper, Androcles; author: (musicals) For the Love of Adam, The Red Ribbon, Famous Last Words, GOD KNOWS!; contbr. articles on immigration law to newspapers and profl. jours. Mem. Common Cause, 1966-78, chmn. Mo. chpt., 1973-75; bd. dirs. Internat. Inst. of Metro St. Louis, 1980-86, English Speaking Union, St. Louis, 1985—, Mo. Prison Arts Program, 1999-2003; U.S. presdl. appointee as sr. adviser and U.S. pub. del. to UN 55th Gen. Assembly, 2000-2001; bd. trustee Acad. of Sci., St. Louis. With U.S. Army, 1944-46, ETO. Decorated (2) Battle Stars; Rotary Internat. fellow Grad. Inst. Internat. Studies, Geneva, 1948-49; award Outstanding Svc. Recognition of Spl. Needs Hispanic Community IMAGE, St. Louis, 1984; named to Best Lawyers in Am., 1994—. Fellow Am. Acad. Matrimonial Lawyers; mem. ABA (immigration law coord. com., 1989, chmn. immigration law com. gen. practice sect. 1981-86), Mo. Bar Assn., Bar Assn. Met. St. Louis (chmn. internat. law and trade com. 1973-79, chmn. immigration law com. 1989-92), Am. Immigration Lawyers Assn., UNA-USA Assn. (bd. dirs. St. Louis chpt. 1999-2003), Phi Delta Phi. Office: Carp and Sexauer 225 S Meramec Ave Ste 325 Saint Louis MO 63105-3511 Home Phone: 314-991-7727; Office Phone: 314-863-4300. Office Fax: 314-727-0308. E-mail: carpandsexauer@msn.com.

CARPAN, ANN CAROLYN, school librarian, educator; b. Halifax, Can., Apr. 19, 1971; arrived in U.S., 2000, naturalized, 2005; d. William Edward Carpan and Ann Eileen O'Connell. BA, Dalhousie U., 1994; MA, Meml. U. Newfoundland, 1996; MA in Libr. and Info. Studies, Dalhousie U., 1998. Libr. Can. Broadcasting Corp., Halifax, N.S., Canada, 1998—99; reference libr. Rollins Coll., Winter Park, Fla., 2000—, asst. prof., 2000—06, assoc. prof., 2006—. Author: Rocked by Romance: A Guide to Teen Romance Fiction, Jane Yolen. Mem.: ALA, Ctrl. Fla. Libr. Coop. (bd. dirs. 2005—), Assn. Coll. and Rsch. Librs., Beta Phi Mu (life). Office: Olin Library Rollins College 1000 Holt Avenue Box 2744 Winter Park FL 32789-4499 Home Phone: 407-894-5483; Office Phone: 407-646-2683. Office Fax: 407-646-1515. Business E-Mail: acarpan@rollins.edu.

CARPENETI, WALTER L., state supreme court justice; b. San Francisco, Dec. 01; m. Anne Dose, 1969; children: Christian, Marianna, Lia, Bianca. AB in History with distinction, Stanford U., 1967; JD, U. Calif., Berkeley, 1970. Law clk. Justice John H. Dimond Alaska Supreme Ct., 1970-71; partner Carpeneti & Carpeneti, San Francisco, 1972-74; supervisor Alaska Public Defender Agency, Juneau, Alaska, 1974-78; partner Carpeneti & Council, Juneau, 1978-81; judge Alaska Superior Ct., Juneau, 1981-98; justice Alaska State Supreme Ct., Juneau, 1998—. Mem. Alaska Judicial Council, 1980—81, Alaska Commn. on Judicial Conduct, 1992—95. Office: Alaska Supreme Ct PO Box 114100 Juneau AK 99811-4100 Office Phone: 907-463-4771.

CARPENITO, FRANK ANTHONY, principal, educator; b. Bklyn, June 24, 1945; s. Frank Gerard and Carmela Julia Carpenito; children: Danielle Antonia Carpenito-Caccese, Frank Richard, Christopher Michael. B in History, Fordham Coll., Bronx, NY, 1967; MS, CUNY, NYC, 1969, M in Ednl. Adminstrn., 1974. Elem. sch. prin. NYC Bd. Edn., SI, 1990—2003; ret. Mem.: Ret. Suprs. Assn (sec. 2006—). Democrat. Roman Catholic. Avocations: travel, jogging. Home: 72 Savo Ln Staten Island NY 10305 Home Phone: 718-816-0661.

CARPENTER, ANGIE M., former small business owner, editor, county legislator; b. Bay Shore, NY, Sept. 30, 1943; d. Joseph and Ida (Gullo) Linarello; m. Joe David Carpenter, Apr. 13, 1964; children: Richard, Robert. AAS in Bus. & Mktg., Suffolk County C.C. Office mgr., graphic designer, typographer Merrick (N.Y.) Typographers and Maverick Pubs., 1966-76; founder, v.p. AC Typesetters and Printing, Inc., West Islip, NY, 1976-93; dep. presiding officer Suffolk County Legislature. Editor, pub., co-founder West Islip Record, 1986-91; columnist The Graphic, The Beacon, 1985-87. Chmn. publicity com., trustee Babylon/West Islip Windmill Com., Inc., Babylon, NY, 1986—, ASK US, 1987-98; trustee West Islip After-Sch.-Care program, 1987-97, Our Lady of Consolation Geriatric Care Ctr.; chmn. West Islip Youth Enrichment Svcs., 1986-87; mem. govt. action coun. LI Assn., 1987; mem. recycling panel Town of Islip, 1987; chairperson TOI Blue Ribbon Com. on Recycling, 1987-88; trustee Suffolk County Vanderbilt Mus., 1990-93; vice chair Salvation Army adv. bd., Suffolk County, mem. legis., 1993-05, dep. presiding officer, chmn. pub. safety com., vice chmn. budget and fin., county treas., 2005—; elected treas. Suffolk County, 2006—. Mem. West Islip C. of C. (v.p., mchts. dir. 1982-84, pres. 1985, 86, 87, 88), Govt. Fin. Officer's Assn. Republican. Roman Catholic. Office: 330 Center Dr Riverhead NY 11901-3311 Office Phone: 631-852-1500. Personal E-mail: angiecarp930@aol.com. Business E-Mail: angie.carpenter@co.suffolk.ny.us.

CARPENTER, BRUCE WILLIAM, information technology manager, director; s. William Hoxie and Bertha Billings Carpenter; m. Carol Marie Nasiatka, Aug. 10, 1968; children: Jennifer Marie, Stephen Patrick. BA, Quinnipiac U., 1969; MS, U. Bridgeport, 1972. Coord. audiovisual services Quinnipiac U., Hamden, Conn., 1969—86, dir. media services, 1986—95, dir. instrnl. tech. svcs., 1995—99; dir. tech. support Conn. Coll., New London, Conn., 1999—. Mem., del. to New Zealand and Australia for visual and instrnl. edn. People to People Citizen's Amb. Program. Chmn. Mystic Mid. Sch. Bldg. Com., Stonington, Conn., 1998—2001; pres. Mystic Lion's Club, Mystic, Conn., 1998—99; trustee DNA EpiCenter, New London, Conn., 2003—06; bd. sec. DNA EpiCEnter, New London, Conn., 2004—07. Mem.: Conn. Higher Edn. Tech. Assn. (pres. 1995—97, 1989—93), New Eng. Dirs. Adminstrv. Computing, Am. Coll. and U. Telecom. Assn. Avocations: antiques, genealogy, local history, gourmet cooking. Home: 108 Cove Rd Stonington CT 06378 Office: Conn Coll 270 Mohegan Ave New London CT 06320 Home Phone: 860-536-7770; Office Phone: 860-439-5242. Business E-Mail: bwcar@conncoll.edu.

CARPENTER, CAROLYN, elementary school educator; b. Passaic, NJ, Apr. 24, 1948; d. Roman and Mary Petrisin; m. John Burnett Carpenter, Jr.; 1 child, Sarah Mary. BA, Paterson State U., 1970. Tchr. Netcong (N.J.) Elem. Sch., 1970—. Title I coord. Netcong Elem. Sch., affirmative action officer, 1979, 2004—05. Leader, vol. Girl Scouts of Am., Netcong, 1973, 1991—93; vol. Booster Club Bangor (Pa.) H.S., 1996—98, mem. Band

Parents, 1996—98. Named Tchr. of Yr., Netcong Elem. Faculty, 1991. Mem.: N.J. Edn. Assn., Netcong Tchr.'s Assn. (pres. 1973—74). Democrat. Lutheran. Avocations: cooking, crocheting, travel. Home: 208 Frutchey Ct Mount Bethel PA 18343

CARPENTER, CHARLES COLCOCK JONES, internist, educator; b. Savannah, Ga., Jan. 5, 1931; s. Charles Colcock Jones and Alexandra (Morrison) C.; m. Sally R. Fisher, Nov. 29, 1958; children— Charles Morrison, Murray Douglas, Andrew Fisher. AB, Princeton, 1952; MD, Johns Hopkins, 1956. Diplomate: Am. Bd. Internal Medicine (mem. bd. 1976— , exec. com. 1980— , chmn. 1983-84). Intern Johns Hopkins Hosp., Balt., 1956-57, resident, 1957—59, 1961—62, practice medicine, specializing in infectious disease, 1962-73; asst. prof. medicine Johns Hopkins, 1962-67, assoc. prof., 1967-69, prof., 1969-73; physician-in-chief Balt. City Hosps., 1969-73; prof., chmn. dept. medicine Case Western Res. Sch. Medicine, 1973-86; physician-in-chief Case Western Res. Univ. Hosp., 1973-85; prof. medicine Brown U., 1986—, dir. Internat. Health Inst., 1993—98, dir. AIDS Ctr., 2006—. Dir. Cholera Research Program, Johns Hopkins Center Med. Research and Tng., Calcutta, India, 1962-64; chmn. cholera panel U.S.-Japan Coop. Med. Sci. Program, 1965-72; mem. U.S.-Japan Coop. Med. Sci. Program (U.S. del.), 1973—2000, chmn., 1990-2000; mem. adv. bd. Sch. Medicine Johns Hopkins U., 1982-97; mem. Nat. Adv. Coun. Allergy and Infectious Diseases, 1985-89; chmn. extramural cons. AIDS exec. com. NIH, 1986-87, nat. adv. com. for AIDS, NIH, 1992-93; chmn. adv. coun. AIDS Rsch., NIH, 1995-2000; dir. Lifespan/Tufts/Brown Ctr. for AIDS Rsch., 1998-. Trustee Internat. Ctr. for Infectious Disease Rsch., Bangladesh, 1979-83, Internat. Child Health Found., 1985-96, Miriam Hosp., 1992-97. Sr. asst. surgeon USPHS, 1959-61. Recipient John E. Fogarty Internat. Health Recognition Award, NIH, 2003, John H. Chafee Award for Leadership in Healthcare, Am. Heart Assn., 2004, Disting. Chair Medicine award, Assn. Profs. Medicine, 2007. Fellow ACP (master 1992, Disting. Physician award, 2003), AAAS (chmn. med. scis. sect. 1994-96); mem. Inst. Medicine NAS, Am. Soc. Clin. Investigation, Assn. Am. Physicians (sec. 1975-81, councillor 1981-86, v.p. 1986-87, pres. 1987-88), Infectious Diseases Soc. Am. (Smadel medal 1991), Johns Hopkins Soc. Scholars, Johns Hopkins Med. and Surg. Assn. (pres. 1995-97), Order of the Sacred Treasure (Japan). Home: 12 Half Mile Rd Barrington RI 02806-4104 Office Phone: 401-793-4025.

CARPENTER, CHARLES ELFORD, JR., lawyer; b. Greenville, SC, Nov. 3, 1944; s. Charles Elford and Mary Charlotte (Campbell) C.; m. Nancy Townsend, June 8, 1968; children: Charlotte Elizabeth, John Morrison. BA, Furman U., Greenville, SC, 1966; JD, U. Va., Charlottesville, 1969; MPA, U. SC, 1976. Bar: Va. 1969, SC 1972, US Dist. Ct. SC 1974, US Ct. Appeals (4th cir.) 1978, US Supreme Ct. 1983, US Ct. Appeals (11th cir.) 1984. Assoc. Leatherwood, Walker, Todd & Mann, Greenville, 1969, Richardson, Plowden, Grier & Howser, Columbia, SC, 1974-78; ptnr. Richardson, Plowden, Carpenter & Robinson, P.A., Columbia, 1978—. Mem. com. on grievances and discipline SC Supreme Ct., 1986-89, 1996; spkr. Law Seminars, Inc., Columbia, 1987, Outline for Post-Trial Practice, 1988, 89, 90; mem. SC Supreme Ct. Bd. Law Examiners, 1995-2001; spkr. in field. Editor Appeal and Error, SC Jurisprudence; contbr. articles to legal jours. Mem. bd. visitors Presbyn. Coll., Clinton, SC, 1983-87; trustee James H. Hammond Sch., Columbia, 1986-89, Trinity Presbytery; founding mem. bd. trustees St. John's Prepatory Sch., 2007; elder Eastminster Presbyn. Ch. Capt. US Army, 1969-72. Fellow Am. Acad. Appellate Lawyers (bd. dirs., pres. 2006-07); mem. ABA (spkr. appellate process program 1990, editor Appellate Practice Jour. 1989-2000, co-chair oral argument subcom. litig. sect., mem. task force on unreported opinions 1996—), SC Bar Assn. (mem. Richland County fee dispute com. 1984-88, spkr. 1987, appellate practice, panel mem. proposed rules of appellate practicefor SC Bar ann. meeting 1989, mem. practice and procedure com., health and hosp. law subcom., appellate rules subcom., chmn. merit selection of judges subcom., alternative dispute resolution com. 1993—), Richland County Bar Assn., SC Def. Trial Attys. (chmn. amicus curiae com. 1981-85), Forest Lake Club, St. Andrews Soc., Tarantella Club, Columbia Ball Club, Torch Club (pres. 2000-01). Avocations: reading, hunting, hiking. Office: Richardson Plowden Carpenter & Robinson PA PO Box 7788 1900 Barnwell St Columbia SC 29201 Office Phone: 803-576-3707. Personal E-mail: charlie.ccclaw@gmail.com. Business E-Mail: ccarpenter@rpcrlaw.com.

CARPENTER, CHARLES FRANCIS, lawyer; b. Raleigh, NC, Apr. 3, 1957; s. William Lester and Mattie Frances (Wallace) C.; m. Heidi Ann Athanas, June 14, 1980 BA honors, U. N.C., 1979, JD, 1982. Bar: N.C. 1982, U.S. Dist. Ct. (mid. dist.) N.C. 1982, U.S. Dist. Ct. (ea. dist.) N.C. 1986, U.S. Ct. Appeals (4th cir.) 1986, U.S. Dist. Ct. (we. dist.) N.C. 1988; cert. superior ct. mediator. Assoc. Newsom, Graham, Hedrick, Murray, Bryson & Kennon, Durham, NC, 1982—87; ptnr. Newsom, Graham, Hedrick, Bryson & Kennon, Durham, 1988—93; pvt. practice Charles F. Carpenter, P.A., Durham, 1993—98; ptnr. Pulley, Watson, King & Lischer, PA, Durham, 1998—. Trustee N.C. Conf. United Meth. Ch., 1993-2002; mem. exec. bd. Occoneechee Coun. Boy Scouts Am., 1988-2000, mem. adv. bd., 2001— Mem. ABA, N.C. State Bar, N.C. Bar Assn., Durham County Bar Assn. (medico-legal com. 1994-2002, bd. dirs. 1998-2003), Order of Old Well, Hon. Order Ky. Cols., Phi Beta Kappa Democrat. Avocations: Karate (black belt), golf, jogging, skiing. Home: 1100 W Forest Hills Bvd Durham NC 27707-1601 Office: 905 W Main St Ste 21 F Durham NC 27701-2076 Home Phone: 919-489-3868; Office Phone: 919-682-9691. Business E-Mail: cfc@pwkl.com.

CARPENTER, CHRIS, professional baseball player; b. Exeter, NH, Apr. 27, 1975; m. Alyson Carpenter; 1 child, Sam. Pitcher Toronto Blue Jays, 1997—2002, St. Louis Cardinals, 2002—. Named Nat. League All-Star Starting Pitcher, 2005, NL Pitcher Yr., Players Choice awards, 2006; recipient NL Cy Young award, MLB, 2005. Office: St Louis Cardinals 250 Stadium Plz Saint Louis MO 63102-1722 Home: Bedford NH*

CARPENTER, DAVID ALLAN, lawyer; b. Cambridge, Mass., May 16, 1951; s. David Lawrence and Jane (Boucher) C.; m. Nancy Joan Surdyka, Apr. 29, 1973. BS in Bus. Adminstrn., Bucknell U., Lewisburg, Pa., 1972; MBA in Fin., Temple U., Phila., 1975; JD, Rutgers U., 1981. Banking officer Girard Bank, Phila., 1972-77, mng. ptnr., 1983-85, mng. ptnr. Mid Atlantic region, 1985-89, mng. ptnr. Atlantic region, 1989-92; nat. dir. litigation and claims svcs. Coopers & Lybrand, Phila., 1987-92, nat. dir. fin. adv. svcs. Boston, 1992-94; founding ptnr. Ptnrs. for Mkt. Leadership, Inc., Atlanta, 1995—. Co-editor: Proving and Pricing Construction Claims, 1990, Environmental Dispute Handbook, 1991; contbr. articles to profl. jours., chpts. to books. Mem. Inst. Mgmt. Consultants, Turnaround Mgmt. Assn., Beta Gamma Sigma. Office: Ptnrs for Mkt Leadership Inc 400 Galleria Pkwy SE Ste 1500 Atlanta GA 30339-3122 Office Phone: 800-984-1110.

CARPENTER, DAVID ERWIN, retired county official, land use planner; b. Appleton, Wis., Oct. 20, 1939; s. Erwin Carl and Othilia Mary (Killian) Carpenter; m. Linda Louise Simkins, June 22, 1961 (div. Apr. 15, 1983); children: Bradley John, Robert Anthony, Paige Elizabeth; m. Mary Starr Griffin, May 18, 1991 (div. Feb. 22, 2006). BS, U. Wis., 1962, MS, 1979. Planner Wis. Dept. Devel., Madison, 1963-66, Fond du Lac County, Wis., 1966-68; supr. county planning Wis. Dept. Devel., Madison, 1968-69; assoc. dir. Southeastern Wis. Health Systems Agy., Milw., 1969-77; dir. planning St. Mary's Hosp. Med. Ctr., Madison, 1977-84; dir. mktg. St. Mary's Svcs., Madison, 1984-86; pres. David Carpenter Assocs., Madison, 1986-89; dir. planning Dodge County Planning and Devel., Juneau, Wis., 1989-95, exec. dir., 1995—2006; ret., 2006. Author: Solid Waste Recycling Plan, 1991, Outdoor Recreation Plan, 1995. Sec.-treas. Ice Age Pk. and Trail Found., Madison, 1990; mgr. Dodge County Heritage Preservation, Beaver Dam, 1991—97; vol. Columbus Main St. Program, 1992—95; mem. exec. com. Flyway Area Labor-Mgmt. Coun., Horicon, 1993—98; mem. Columbus Ad Hoc Econ. Devel. Com., 1994, Skilaufers, Inc., 2001—, Seth Peterson Cottage Conservancy, Inc., 2002—. Friends of Cherokee Marsh, 2006, Northside Planning Coun., 2007—; bd. dirs. Skilaufers, Inc., 2002—, pres., 2003—05, Rock River Coalition, Watertown, 1995—97, chmn. comm. com., 1997—98; docent Monona Terr. Cmty. and Conv. Ctr., Madison, 1999—; active City of Columbus Planning Commn., 2000—05; bd. dirs. Columbus Area Aquatic Ctr., 2000—03; vol. Wis. Pub. TV, 2002—; trustee Columbus United Meth. Ch., 1992—2003, pres., 1998—2003. Recipient Foward Wis. award, 1994, Elmer Kohlbeck Friend of Tourism award, 1994, 2006, Svc. award, Rock River Coalition, 1998. Mem.: Western Pa. Conservancy, Wis. Hist. Soc., League Am. Bicyclists, Olbrich Bot. Soc., Charles E. Brown Archeol. Soc. (pres. 1992—95), Wis. Archeol. Soc. (Eileen Swiggum award for Contbn. 2001), Am. Planning Assn., Phi Sigma Kappa. Avocations: archaeology, art, history, gardening, bicycling. Personal E-mail: dcarpenter3@charter.net.

CARPENTER, DAVID WILLIAM, lawyer; b. Chgo., Aug. 26, 1950; s. William Warren and Dorothy Susan (Jacobs) C.; m. Jane Ellen French, Aug. 18, 1973 (div. Jan. 2001); children: Johanna Lindsay, Julie Rachel; m. Orit Karni, Mar. 26, 2004. BA cum laude, Yale U., 1972; JD magna cum laude, Boston U., 1975. Bar: Mass. 1975, Ill. 1979, DC 1980, US Ct. Appeals (1st cir.) 1977, US Dist. Ct. (no. dist.) Ill. 1979, DC 1995, US Ct. Appeals 3rd. cir. 1981, DC cir. 1982, 7th cir. 1982, 10th cir. 1985, 8th cir. 1986, 9th cir. and 11th ciruits 1987, 2nd, 5th and 6th circuits, 1990, 4th cir. 2000, US Supreme Ct. 1981. Law clk. to presiding justice US Ct. Appeals (1st cir.), Portland, Maine, 1975-77; US Supreme Ct., Washington, 1977-78; assoc. Sidley & Austin (now Sidley Austin LLP), Chgo., 1978-82; ptnr. Sidley Austin LLP, Chgo., 1982—, and mem. exec. com., 1994—. Lectr. Ill. Inst. Tech., Chgo., 1980—82. Bd. dirs., sec. Chgo. Coun. for Young Profls., 1985-90; bd. dirs., exec. com. Brennan Ctr. for Justice, NYC, 1995-2004; bd. dirs. Lyric Opera Chgo., 1999—. Democrat. Mem. United Ch. Christ. Office: Sidley Austin LLP One S Dearborn St Chicago IL 60603 Office Phone: 312-853-7237. Business E-Mail: dcarpenter@sidley.com.

CARPENTER, DELBERT STANLEY, educational administration educator; b. Wichita Falls, Tex., May 18, 1950; s. Delbert Stanley Sr. and Nancy (Williams) S.; m. Noralyn Gray, July 13, 1973 (div. Mar. 1986); m. Janet Ann Stewart, July 15, 1989 (div. June 1993); m. Linda Jan Meerdink Evans, June 25, 1994; 1 child, Susanne Gray Carpenter; stepchildren: Robert Scott Evans, Peter Clark Evans. BS, Tarleton State U., 1972; MS, East Tex. State U., 1975; PhD, U. Ga., 1979. Actuarial technician A.S. Hansen, Inc., Dallas, 1972-74; grad. asst. ctrl. housing office East Tex. State U., Commerce, 1974-75; men's resident dir. Oglethorpe U., Atlanta, 1975-77; grad. asst. rsch., tchg., counseling and human devel. dept. U. Ga., Athens, 1977-79; dean students U. Ark., Monticello, 1979-81; asst. dir. devel. Tex. A&M U., College Station, 1982-84, from asst. prof. ednl. adminstrn. to assoc. prof., 1985-95, prof., 1995—2003; prof., chair ednl. adminstrn. and psychol. svcs. dept. Tex. State U., San Marcos, 2003—. Mem. editl. bds. various profl. jours.; contbr. articles to profl. jours. Named Outstanding Doctoral Alumnus, Students Affairs Adminstrn. U. Ga., 1995, Disting. Tchg. award Assn. Former Students Coll. of Edn., 1996. Mem. Assn. for the Study Higher Edn. (exec. dir. 1987-98, Disting. Svc. award 1996), Am. Coll. Pers. Assocs. (Annuit Coeptis award 1995, Sr. Scholar 2000, chair 2001-04, Esther Lloyd-Jones Profl. Svc. award 2004), Nat. Assn. Student Pers. Adminstrn. (mem.-at-large nat. bd. 2001-03), South Assn. for Coll. Student Affairs (Melvene Hardee award 1997), Alpha Phi Omega (pres., bd. dirs. 1986-90, Nat. Disting. Svc. award 1990, trustee endowment fund 1996—, chair 1997—2005), Alpha Chi. Avocations: golf, reading, travel. Home: 10909 Olympia Fields Loop Austin TX 78747 Office Phone: 512-245-8851. Business E-Mail: stanc@txstate.edu.

CARPENTER, DERR ALVIN, retired landscape architect; b. Sunbury, Pa., Jan. 18, 1931; s. Alvin Witmer and Katharine C. (Rockefeller) Carpenter; m. Helen Longden Hedge, Apr. 10, 1954; children: Mary Katharine Carpenter Denault, Melissa Sue Carpenter Sclumbata. BS, Pa. State U., 1953. Registered landscape arch. Chief landscape architect La. State Parks, Baton Rouge, 1955-58; asst. dir. City Parish Planning Com., Baton Rouge, 1958-62; chief planning and engring. Pa. State Parks, Harrisburg, 1962-67; pres. Derr A. Carpenter & Assocs., Camp Hill, Pa., 1967-73; v.p. Smith, Miller & Assocs. Inc., Camp Hill and Kingston, Pa., 1973-86, Rettew Assocs. Inc., Mechanicsburg and Lancaster, Pa., 1987-90; self employed landscape architect Mechanicsburg, 1990—2003. Lectr. Pa. State U., Harrisburg Area CC, 1973—2003, Susquehanna U. Mem. legis com. Pa. Recreation and Pk. Soc., University Park, 1982—90; mem. Camp Hill Shade Tree Commn., 1968—87; bd. dirs. Pk. Adv. Bd., Cumberland County, Pa., 1978—84, YMCA, Harrisburg, 1974—80, Capital Region Econ. Devel. Corp., 1988—93; chair Zoning Commn., 1989, Dauphin County Open Space Commn., 1989—92; councilman Tree of Life Luth. Ch., Linglestown, 1994—98, mem. bldg. com., mem. fellowship com., mem. social ministry com.; bd. dirs. Pa. State Arts and Architecture Alumni Bd., University Park, 1985—95. With US Army, 1953—55. Pa. State U. Alumni fellow, 1984. Fellow: Am. Soc. Landscape Archs. (dir. legis. 1968—90, pres. chpt. 1973—77, trustee 1977—80, 1983, nat. ethics com. chmn. 1984—87, Disting. Svc. award 1981, cert. appreciation 1984); mem.: Pa. Nursery Mktg. Adv. Coun. (chmn. 1976—77, bd. dirs., Outstanding Achievement award 1972), Susquehanna River Tri-State Assn. (pres. 1980—82, bd. dirs., Leadership award 1982), Pa. State Alumni Assn. Harrisburg (pres. 1983—85, bd. dirs., Leadership award 1985), Masons, Rotary (bd. dirs. 1968—82), Torch (bd. dirs. 1976—81). Republican. Lutheran. Avocations: gardening, hiking, reading, printing, massage. Personal E-mail: laguy3@juno.com.

CARPENTER, EDMUND NELSON, II, retired lawyer; b. Phila., Jan. 27, 1921; s. Walter S. and Mary (Wootten) C.; m. Carroll Morgan, July 18, 1970; children: Mary W., Edmund Nelson III, Katherine R.R., Elizabeth Lea; stepchildren: John D. Gates, Ashley du Pont Gates. AB, Princeton U., 1943; LLB, Harvard U., 1948; LLD (hon.), Widener U., 1985, U. Del., 1999. Bar: Del. 1949, U.S. Supreme Ct. 1957. Assoc. Richards, Layton & Finger, Wilmington, Del., 1949-53, ptnr., 1953-78, dir., 1978-91, pres., 1982-85; ret., 1991. Dep. atty. gen. State of Del., 1953-54, spl. dep. atty., 1960-62; chmn. Del. Superior Ct. Jury Study Com., 1963-66, Del. Supreme Ct. Cts. Consol. Com., 1985-87; mem. Del. Gov.'s Commn. Law Enforcement and Adminstrn. Justice, 1969; chmn. Del. Supreme Ct. Adv. Com. on Profl. Fin. Accountability, 1974-75, Del. Jud. Nominating Commn., 1977-83, Del. Superior Ct. Study Com., 1991-92; mem. Long Range Cts. Planning Com., 1976-89, Del. Ct. Common Pleas Study Com., 1992, Del. Supreme Ct. Com. on Judicial Code of Conduct, 1991-93; co-chmn. Del. Justice Ctr. Com., 1994-97; mem. lawyers adv. com. U.S. Ct. Appeals (3d cir.) 1975-80, chmn., 1975-77; chmn. local rules com. U.S. Dist. Ct. Del., 1978-83, Del. Ct. on the Judiciary Rules Com., 1996-98; bd. dirs. Bank of Del., Barclay's Bank. Trustee Wilmington Med. Ctr., 1965—, U. Del., 1971-77, Princeton U., 1974-85, 86-91, Winterthur Mus., 1991-99, World Affairs Coun. Wilmington, 1968-80, Woodrow Wilson Found., 1985—, Lawrenceville Sch., 1953-74, trustee emeritus, 1974—; trustee Nat. Humanities Ctr., 1995-98, U.S. Supreme Ct. Hist. Soc., 2004—, U. Del. Libr. Assocs., 2006—; bd. dirs. Good Samaritan Inc., 1973—, pres., 1998—; mem. Del. Health Care Injury Ins. Study Commn., 1976-80. With U.S. Army, 1942-46, 50-52 Decorated Bronze Star, Soldier's medal, Chinese Order of the Flying Cloud with four battle stars; recipient 1st State Disting. Svc. award, Del. State Bar Assn., 1984, Josiah Marvel Cup award Del. State C. of C., 1990, Benjamin Franklin Disting. Pub. Svc. award Am. Philos. Soc., 1996, Am. Inns of Ct. Professionalism award U.S. Ct. Appeals, 3d cir., 2003, Sister Eva Fink award Ministry of Caring, 2003, Ellis Island medal of honor Nat. Ethnic Coalition Orgns., 2006. Fellow Am. Coll. Trial Lawyers, Am. Bar Found.; mem. ABA (ho. of dels. 1979-86), Del. State Bar Assn. (pres. 1971-72, Presdl. citation 1987), ATLA, Am. Judicature Soc. (bd. dirs. 1974-83, exec. com. 1978-80, v.p. 1980-81, pres. 1981-83, Justice award 1991). Home and Office: 600 Center Mill Rd Wilmington DE 19807-1502

CARPENTER, GENE BLAKELY, crystallography and chemistry educator; b. Evansville, Ind., Dec. 15, 1922; s. Leland A. and Juanita (Blakely) C.; m. Elizabeth E. Corkum, Apr. 15, 1949; children: Jonathan R., Anne E. BA, U. Louisville, 1944; MA, Harvard U., 1945, PhD, 1947. NRC fellow Calif. Inst. Tech., 1947-48, research fellow, 1948-49; instr. Brown U., 1949-52, asst. prof., 1952-56, asso. prof., 1956-63, prof., 1963-88, prof. emeritus, 1988—. Guggenheim fellow U. Leeds, Eng., 1956-57; vis. prof. U. Groningen, The Netherlands, 1963-64; Fulbright-Hayes lectr. U. Zagreb, Yugoslavia, 1971-72; vis. scientist Oak Ridge Nat. Lab., 1980, U. Göttingen, Fed. Republic of Germany, 1987, U. Canterbury, Christchurch, New Zealand, 1989. Author: Principles of Crystal Structure Determination, 1969; Contbr. articles to sci. jours. Mem. Am. Crystallographic Assn., Am. Chem. Soc. Home: 229 Medway St Apt 309 Providence RI 02906-5300 Office: Brown U Dept Chemistry Providence RI 02912-0001 E-mail: gene_carpenter@brown.edu.

CARPENTER, JAKE BURTON See BURTON, JAKE

CARPENTER, JAMES, glass innovator; BFA in Sculpture, RI Sch. of Design, 1972. Cons. Corning Glass Works, Corning, NY, 1972—82; pres. James Carpenter Design Assoc., Inc., NYC, 1978—. Named a MacArthur Fellow, 2004; recipient Inst. Honor, Am. Inst. of Arch., 1991, DuPont Benedictus award (hon. mention), 2003. Office: James Carpenter Design Assoc 4th Fl 145 Hudson St New York NY 10013 Office Phone: 212-431-4318. Office Fax: 212-431-4425.

CARPENTER, JOANN DEAKIN, history professor; b. Bangor, Maine, Aug. 9, 1955; d. Donald Frederick and Sylvia Hanson Deakin; m. Bruce Michael Carpenter, June 15, 1984; 1 child, Michael Hanson. BA, Wofford Coll., 1977; MA, PhD, Emory U., 1987. Prof. history Fla. C.C., Jacksonville, Fla., 1988—. Author supplements Prentice-Hall, Upper Saddle, NJ, 1999—; faculty dir. NEH-Faces of America Fla. C.C., Jacksonville, 2001—02. Cons. Boys and Girls Club, Jacksonville, 2003—. Mem.: Orgn. American History, So. Hist. Assn. (recruiting officer 1988—), Am. Hist. Assn. Democrat. Luth. Avocations: reading, needlecrafts, cooking. Office: Florida Community Coll Jacksonville 11901 Beach Blvd Jacksonville FL 32246 Office Phone: 904-646-2415. Office Fax: 904-646-2315. Business E-Mail: jcarpent@fccj.edu.

CARPENTER, JOHN HOWARD, director, screenwriter; b. Carthage, NY, Jan. 16, 1948; s. Howard Ralph and Milton Jean (Carter) C; m. Adrienne Barbeau, Jan. 1, 1979 (div. 1984); m. Sandra Ann King, Dec. 1, 1990; 1 child, John Cody. Student, U. So. Calif., 1972. Co-writer, editor, composer: (short film) The Resurrection of Bronco Billy, 1970 (Academy award best live action short subject 1970); writer, prodr., dir., composer: (films) Dark Star, 1974; writer, dir., composer: (films) Assault on Precinct 13, 1976, Halloween, 1978, The Fog, 1980, Escape from New York, 1981, Prince of Darkness, 1987, They Live, 1988, Escape from L.A., 1996, Ghosts of Mars, 2001; writer, prodr., composer: (films) Halloween II, 1981; prodr., composer: (films) Halloween III: Season of the Witch, 1982; writer, prodr.: (films) The Fog, 2005; dir.: (films) The Thing, 1982, Starman, 1984, Memoirs of an Invisible Man, 1992, In the Mouth of Madness, 1994, Escape from L.A., 1996, Vampires, 1998, Halloween H2O, 1998; (TV movies) Elvis, 1979; dir., composer: (films) Christine, 1983, Big Trouble in Little China, 1986; exec. prodr.: (films) The Philadelphia Experiment, 1984, (TV movies) John Carpenter Presents Body Bags, 1993; writer: (films) The Eyes of Laura Mars, 1978, Black Moon Rising, 1986, (TV movies) Zuma Beach, 1978, Better Late Than Never, 1979, El Diablo, 1990, Blood River, 1991; writer, dir.: (TV movies) Someone's Watching Me!, 1978; composer: (films) Halloween V: The Revenge of Michael Myers, 1989. Mem. ASCAP, Dirs. Guild Am. West, Writers Guild Am. West. Avocations: music, helicopter piloting. Office: ICM 8942 Wilshire Blvd Beverly Hills CA 90211-1934

CARPENTER, MARGARET S. (MOLLY CARPENTER), artist; b. Wilmington, Del., Jan. 21, 1960; d. Richard Paulett and Margaret Marvel Sanger; m. Samuel Preston Carpenter, Oct. 4, 1981; children: Benjamin Sanger, Margaret Paulett. Student, Pa. Acad. Fine Arts, Phila., 1978—79, Frudakis Acad. Fine Arts, 1978—81. Apprentice Charles Cropper Parks , Wilmington, 1977-80; sculptor, Salem, 1981—. One-woman shows include Gallery 50, Bridgeton, N.J., 1983, 86, 92, Gloucester C.C., 1988, Vineland Pub. Libr., 1988; exhibited in group shows, including Wilmington Christmas Shop Artists' Gallery, 1981-2000, Glassboro State Coll., 1989, Longwood Gardens, Kennett Square, Pa., 1993, Rockfeller Ctr., 1996, Independence Seaport Mus., Phila., 1996, The Coliseum, N.Y.C., 1996, Ronald McDonald House, 1996-98, 2003, Nat. Sculpture Soc., 1997, Catherine Lorillard Wolfe Art Club, Nat. Arts Club, N.Y.C , 1999, Del. Art Mus., 1999, Olympic Regional Devel. Assn., Mus., 2000, Goodwill Games Mus., 2000; represented in permanent collections Independence Seaport Mus., Du Pont Children's Hosp., Wilmington, 1989; commns. include Constl. Compass Rose, Del. Heritage Commn. for U.S. Constn. Bicentennial, Legis. Hall, Dover, 1987, bas relief sculpture to honor Judge Samuel Desimone, Bar Assns. Cumberland, Salem and Gloucester Counties, N.J., 2000; portrait sculptures include Vince Gioaya, Robert Kasey, Dr. Martin Luther King Jr.; designer rooms class Phila. Flower Show, 1990-2001. Bd. dirs. Salem County Arts Alliance, 1997—, v.p., 2000—; mem. arts com. Salem County Cultural and Heritage Commn., 1998—; bd. dirs. Salem County Cultural and Heritage, 1998—. Recipient numerous best of show awards, award sculpture AIDS Del., 1998; creator of Achievement Award in Sculpture, Creative Grandparenting Del., 2000. Mem. Nat. Sculpture Soc. Home: 465 Kings Hwy Salem NJ 08079 E-mail: sculptor@mollycarpenter.com.

CARPENTER, MARK WARREN, social sciences educator; b. Long Beach, Calif., Nov. 11, 1949; s. Philip Benham and Nancy Anne C. BA in Comm., Calif. State U., Fullerton, 1974, MPA, 1977; MA in Behavioral Sci., Calif. State U., Dominguez Hills, 1982; MA in Edn., U. Calif., Riverside, 1994. Life cert. tchr. cmty. coll. sociology; life cert. FCC. Editor, rsch. analyst, project coord. Govt. Edn. Ctr., LA, 1975—76; rsch. fellow Calif. State U., Dominguez Hills, 1980-81, mem. staff registrar's office Fullerton, 1984-87; tchg. asst. U. Calif., Riverside, 1987-88; lectr., mem. faculty dept. sociology Riverside C.C., 1989—. Founder, World Citizens Institute, 1986. Author/compiler: (ednl. directory) After Work in Los Angeles, 1976; author, editor: (gen. plan element) Torrance Energy Awareness Monograph, 1978. Sgt. U.S. Army, 1969-71, Vietnam. Mem. Am. Ednl. Rsch. Assn., Am. Soc. Pub. Adminstrn. (mem. higher edn. and govt. rels. com.), Sociology of Edn. Assn., Assn. Environ. Profls., Calif. Coop. Edn. Assn., Internat. Assn. Cognitive Edn., Internat. Platform Assn., Com. for Expanded Ednl. Opportunity, So. Calif. Assn. Govts., Mensa. Avocations: surfing, writing. Home: PO Box 8116 Moreno Valley CA 92552-8116 Office: Riverside C C 4800 Magnolia Ave Riverside CA 92506-1242 Business E-Mail: mark.carpenter@rcc.edu.

CARPENTER, MICHAEL A., diversified financial services company executive; b. London, Mar. 24, 1947; came to U.S., 1971; s. Walter and Kathleen Mary C.; m. Mary Aughton, Mar. 1, 1975; children: Nicholas James, Abigail Lee. BSc with joint honors, U. Nottingham, Eng., 1968; LLD (hon.), U. Nottingham; MBA, Harvard U., 1973. Bus. analyst Mond div. Imperial Chem. Industries, Runcorn, England, 1968-71; cons., mgr. Boston Cons. Group, 1973-78, v.p., 1978-83; v.p. bus. devel. and planning GE Corp., Fairfield, Conn., 1983-86, exec. v.p. Stamford, Conn., 1986—89, GE Financial Services Inc., 1986—89; chmn., pres., CEO Kidder Peabody & Co. Inc., 1989—94; exec. v.p. Travelers Group, Hartford, 1994—98, chmn., CEO, pres. life and annuity, 1995—98, vice chmn., 1998; chmn., CEO Salomon Smith Barney, NYC, 1998—2002; chmn., CEO, Global Corp. and Investment Bank Citigroup, NYC, 1998—2002; chmn., CEO Citigroup Alternative Investments, NYC, 2002—06; prin., owner Southgate Holdings, LLC, NYC, 2006—. Bd. dirs. NYC Investment Fund, Mikronite Techs., Inc. Baker scholar Harvard Bus. Sch., 1973 Office Phone: 212-223-4623. Business E-Mail: carpenterm@southgatealternativeinvestments.com.

CARPENTER, MICHAEL H., lawyer; b. Huntington, W.Va., Mar. 3, 1953; BA, Ohio State U., 1974, JD, 1977. Bar: Ohio 1977. Former ptnr. Jones, Day, Reavis & Pogue, Columbus, Ohio; ptnr. Carpenter & Lipps LLP, Columbus, 1994—. Mem. Order of Coif, Phi Beta Kappa. Office: Carpenter & Lipps LLP 280 Plaza Ste 1300 280 N High St Columbus OH 43215 Office Phone: 614-365-4100. Business E-Mail: carpenter@carpenterlipps.com.

CARPENTER, NANCY E., mathematics professor; m. John W. Carpenter, June 6, 1985; 1 child, Erin A. MA in Math. Edn., U. Mo., Kansas City, 1986. Prof. math. Johnson County C.C., Overland Park, Kans., 1988—. Recipient Disting. Svc. award, Johnson County C.C., 2005-2006. Mem.: NEA. Office: Johnson County CC 12345 College Blvd Overland Park KS 66210 Home Phone: 913-441-8510; Office Phone: 9134698500 3500. E-mail: nancyc@jccc.edu.

CARPENTER, NANCY J., health science association administrator; Assoc. dir. H.A. Chapman Inst. Med. Genetics, Tulsa, Okla.; pres. Am. Bd. Med. Genetics, 2001—. Adj. prof. biochemistry Okla. State U. Office: H A Chapman Inst Med Genetics 4502 E 41st St Tulsa OK 74135-2553 Business E-Mail: ncarpenter@hillcrest.com.

CARPENTER, PAUL LYNN, cardiologist; b. Fairmont, Minn., Jan. 14, 1946; s. Orlo Earnest and Mae Elizabeth (Poulson) C.; m. Rhoda Ann Jordeth, Mar. 15, 1969; children: Amy Elizabeth, Emily Anne, Abigail Lynn. BSChE, U. Minn., 1968, MD, 1974. Diplomate Am. Bd. Internal Medicine. Chem. engr. 3M Co., St. Paul, 1968-69, USPHS, Cin., 1970-71; extern So. Bapt. Hosp., Ailoun, Jordan, 1975; resident in internal medicine Northwestern Hosp. U. Minn., Mpls., 1975-78, fellow in cardiology, 1978-80; invasive cardiologist Ctrl. Plains Clinic, Sioux Falls, SD, 1980-81, North Ctrl. Heart, Ltd., Sioux Falls, 1981—; asst. clin. prof. dept. medicine U. S.D. Sch. Medicine, Sioux Falls, 1982-90, assoc. clin. prof. dept. medicine, 1990-98, clin. prof. medicine, 1998—; dir. cardiovascular tng. Avera Heart Hosp., Sioux Falls, 2006—. Chmn. cardiac care com. Mckennan Hosp., Sioux Falls, 1984-98, co-dir. cardiac catheterization lab., 1988—, dir. cardiac rehab., 1990—, dir. cardiology, 2003-; pres. North Ctrl. Heart, Ltd., 1984-85; dir. cardiovasc. tng. Avera Heart Hosp., 2006—. Girls basketball coach YMCA, Sioux Falls, 1987-96; girls coach Sioux Falls Soccer Assn., 1991-94; Sunday sch. tchr. Ctrl. Bapt. Ch., Sioux Falls, 1987-94. Fellow Am. Coll. Cardiology (gov. S.D. 1987-90), Am. Coll. Chest Physicians; mem. ACP, AMA, S.D. State Med. Assn., Christian Med. Soc. (life), Alpha Omega Alpha, Tau Beta Pi. Avocations: civil war and native american history, travel, sports, fishing. Office: No Ctrl Heart Ltd 4520 W 69th St Sioux Falls SD 57108 Home Phone: 605-339-3924; Office Phone: 605-977-5000. Business E-Mail: pcarpenter@ncheart.com.

CARPENTER, RANDLE BURT, lawyer; b. Raleigh, NC, Oct. 19, 1939; s. Randle Burt and Adonis (Watson) C.; m. Suzanne Gronemeyer, Aug. 21, 1965; children: Randle III, Christine. BA in Internat. Rels., Duke U., 1962, LLB, 1965; LLM in Fgn. Law, NYU, 1969. Bar: N.Y. 1967, N.C. 1965, U.S. Supreme Ct., U.S. Ct. Appeals (2d cir.), U.S. Dist. Ct., U.S. Ct. Internat. Trade. Official asst. First Nat. City Bank, NYC, 1965-67; with Exxon Internat. Inc., NYC, 1967-68; gen. counsel Occidental Crude Sales Inc., NYC, 1968-75; v.p. law Wesco Internat. Inc., NYC, 1975-76; gen. counsel A. Johnson & Co., Inc., NYC, 1976-81; ptnr. Davidson Dawson & Clark, NYC, 1981-84, Schoeman, Marsh & Updike, NYC, 1984-97, Jackson & Nash, NYC, 1997—. Adj. prof. law Pace U., White Plains, N.Y., 1984—. Contbr. articles to profl. jours. Angier B. Duke scholar Duke U., 1958. Mem. Am. Arbitration Assn., Assn. of Bar of City of N.Y. (inter-Am. affairs com.), Maritime Law Assn., Church Club N.Y., Colonial Order of the Acorn (companion). Home: 29 Hazel Ln Larchmont NY 10538-4007 Office: Jackson & Nash 330 Madison Ave Rm 1800 New York NY 10017-5001

CARPENTER, RAY WARREN, engineering educator, materials engineer; b. Berkeley, Calif., 1934; s. Fritz Josh and Ethel Thordis (Davisson) C.; m. Ann Louise Leavitt, July 10, 1955; children: Shannon R., Sheila A., Matthew L. BS in Engring., U. Calif., Berkeley, 1958, MS in Metallurgy, 1959, PhD in Metallurgy, 1966. Registered profl. engr., Calif. Sr. engr. Aerojet-Gen. Nucleonics, San Ramon, Calif., 1959-64; sr. metallurgist Stanford Rsch Inst., Menlo Park, Calif., 1966-67; mem. sr. rsch. staff Oak Ridge (Tenn.) Nat. Lab., 1967-80; prof. Solid State Sci. & Engring. Ariz. State U., Tempe, 1980—, prof. chem. and materials engring., 2003—, dir. Facility for High Resolution Electron Microscopy, 1980-83, dir. Ctr. for Solid State Sci., 1985-91, also bd. dirs. Ctr. for Solid State Sci. Chmn. doctoral program on sci. and engring. of materials, 1987-90, 94-98; vis. prof. U. Tenn., 1976-78; adj. prof. Vanderbilt U., Nashville, 1979-81. Contbg. author books; contbr. articles to profl. rsch. jour. and symposia; editor Phys. and Material Scis., Jour. of the Microscopy Soc. of Am., 1994-97; editor Microscopy and Microanalysis, 1995-2000; dep. editor Acta Materialia, 2001-2006. Recipient awards, Internat. Metallographic Soc. and Am. Soc. for Metals competition, 1976, 77, 79; Faculty Disting. Achievement award Ariz. State U. Alumni Assn., 1990. Mem. ASM Internat. (chpt. officer, vice chair 2005-06), Electron Microscopy Soc. Am. (pres. 1989, dir. phys. sci. 1980-83), Metall. Soc. of AIME, Materials Rsch. Soc., Am. Phys. Soc., Am. Ceramic Soc., Sigma Xi. Office: Ariz State U Ctr Solid State Sci Tempe AZ 85287-1704 Home Phone: 480-354-5299; Office Phone: 480-965-4549. Business E-Mail: carpenter@asu.edu.

CARPENTER, RICHARD NORRIS, retired lawyer, energy consultant; b. Cortland, NY, Feb. 14, 1937; s. Robert P. and Sylvia (Norris) C.; m. Elizabeth Bigbee, Aug. 1961 (div. June 1975); 1 child, Andrew Norris; m. Leslie Nordby, July, 1991. BA magna cum laude, Syracuse U., NY, 1958; LLB, Yale U., New Haven, 1962. Bar: NY 1962, N.Mex. 1963, US Dist. Ct. (no. dist.) NY, US Dist. Ct. N.Mex., US Ct. Appeals (DC and 10th cirs.), US Supreme Ct. Assoc. Breed, Abbott & Morgan, NYC, 1962, Bigbee & Byrd, 1963—67; ptnr. Bigbee Law Firm et al., 1967—78, Carpenter et al. Law Firm, 1978—97; ptnr., co-owner Carpenter & Nixon, 1997—2000; owner Carpenter Law Firm, 2000—02; ret., 2002. Spl. asst. atty. gen., State of N.Mex., 1963-74, 90-96; sec. Bokum Corp., Miami, Fla., 1969-70; bd. dirs. Bigbee Cattle Co., 1978-86, Sandia TV Corp., 1975. Adv. bd. Interstate Mining Compact, N.Mex., 1981-88; elder 1st Presbyn. Ch., Santa Fe, 1978-80, 86-89, bd. trustees, 1975-77, pres., 1977; bd. dirs. Santa Fe Cmty. Coun., 1965-67, v.p., 66-67; bd. dirs. Santa Fe Prep. Sch., 1981-84, pres., 1982-84; bd. dirs. St. Vincent Hosp. Found., Santa Fe, 1980-82, v.p. 1980-82; bd. trustees St. Vincent Hosp., 1980-86, 1987-2001, chmn. 1985-86, 90-93, 1998-2000; bd. dirs. Santa Fe YMCA, 1964-69, pres., 1969; trustee Santa Fe Prep. Permanent Endowment Fund., 1987-90; bd. trustees, treas. Con Alma Health Found., 2002-07; bd. regents N.Mex. Inst. Mining and Tech, 2003—, sec., treas., 2004-06, pres., 2006—; bd. dirs. N.Mex. Edn. Assistance Found., 2003—, vice-chmn., 2005—; bd. trustees Archdiocese of Santa Fe Cath. Found., 2003—; mem. jt. city-county Santa Fe Energy Task Force, 2004-05; mem. governing bd. adv. com. N.Mex. Higher Edn. Dept., 2006—. Rotary Found. fellow, Panjab U., Pakistan, 1959-60; named to Best Lawyers of Am. natural resources, pub. utility, 1989-2002. Mem. Phi Beta Kappa, Pi Sigma Alpha, Phi Kappa Phi. Home and Office: 1048 Bishops Lodge Rd Santa Fe NM 87501-1009 Personal E-mail: rncarpenter@aol.com.

CARPENTER, ROBERT C., state legislator, retired banker; b. Franklin, NC, June 18, 1924; m. Helen Carpenter. Student, Ind. U., Kokomo, 1947, Purdue U., 1950, U. Va., 1964, Western Carolina U. V.p. bank, 32 yrs.; ret.; mem. N.C. Senate, Raleigh, 1988—. Ranking minority mem. appropriations com. on Dept. Transp., judiciary I com., mem. appropriations/base budget com., commerce com., pensions and retirement and aging com., vice chmn. transp. com. Mem. Am. Legis. Exch. Coun.; commr. Macon County, N.C., 1978-82. Pilot USN, 1943-45. Mem. Am. Legion, KC, Rotary. Republican. Roman Catholic.

CARPENTER, RUSSELL H., JR., lawyer; b. Providence, May 17, 1941; AB, Princeton U., 1963; BPhil in Politics, Oxford U., Eng., 1965; LLB, Yale U., 1968. Bar: D.C. 1968. Law clk. to Hon. David Bazelon U.S. Ct. Appeals (D.C. cir.), 1968-69; mem. Covington & Burling, Washington. Contbr. articles to profl. jours. Rhodes scholar. Mem. Order Coif. Office: Covington & Burling PO Box 7566 1201 Pennsylvania Ave NW Washington DC 20004-2401 Office Phone: 202-662-5172. Business E-Mail: rcarpenter@cov.com.

CARPENTER, SHEILA JANE, lawyer; b. Kyoto, Oct. 16, 1950; d. Chester Elwin and Betty (Boulger) C.; m. William Joseph McCarthy, May 26, 1973; 1 child, Diana Elizabeth. BA, Purdue U., 1972; JD, Yale U., 1975. Bar: Md. 1975, U.S. Dist. Ct. Md. 1976, D.C. 1977, U.S. Dist. Ct. D.C. 1978, U.S. Supreme Ct. 1980, U.S. Dist. Ct. (no. dist.) Ohio 1980, U.S. Claims Ct. 1982, U.S. Ct. Appeals (D.C. cir.) 1983, U.S. Ct. Appeals (4th and Fed. cirs.) 1984, U.S. Ct. Appeals (8th cir.) 2000, U.S. Ct. Appeals (5th cir.) 2004. Assoc. Weinberg & Green, Balt., 1975-77, Sutherland, Asbill & Brennan, Washington, 1977-82, ptnr., 1982-96, Jorden Burt LLP, Washington, 1996—. Pub. svc. com. Sutherland, Asbill & Brennan, 1990-94, chair, 1990-92, chair litig. group Washington office, 1991-93; web chair steering com. 2000-, life, health and disability com. Def. Rsch. Inst. Contbr. articles to profl. jours. Fellow Am. Bar Found.; mem. ABA (mem. excess surplus lines and reins. com. TIPS sect., vice chmn. 1992-94, chair 1995-96, vice chair pub. regulation ins. commn. TIPS sect. 1995-00, mem. life ins. com. TIPS sect., vice chair 2004-), Am. Arbitration Assn. (arbitrator large complex case panel), Md. Bar Assn., Phi Beta Kappa. Office: Jorden Burt LLP Ste 400E 1025 Thomas Jefferson St NW Washington DC 20007-5208 Office Phone: 202-965-8165. E-mail: sjc@jordenusa.com.

CARPENTER, STANLEY DEAN MACDONALD, military officer, educator; b. Raleigh, NC, Aug. 28, 1953; s. William Lester and Mattie Frances (Wallace) Carpenter; m. Linda Ann Lannie, July 15, 2005; children: Christopher Kenneth Wells Carpenter, William Gerald Wells Carpenter, Samantha Theresa Wells Carpenter. BA, U. NC, 1975; MLitt, U. St. Andrews, Scotland, 1978; PhD, Fla. State U., 1998; Diploma in Strategic Studies, US Naval War Coll., 2000. Real Estate Broker's Lic. NC State, 1987. Advanced through grades to capt. USN, 1979—; task leader Booz Allen & Hamilton, Inc., Arlington, Va., 1984—87; dep. program mgr. LSA, Inc., Arlington, 1988—90; grad. student/instr. Fla. State U., 1991—98; prof. of strategy/policy US Naval War Coll., 1998—, command historian, strategy/policy divsn. head, Coll. of Distance Edn. Adj. prof. of history Am. Mil. U., Manassas Pk., Va., 1996—, Salve Regina U., Newport, RI, 1999—. Author: (book) Mil. Leadership in the Br. Civil Wars: "The Genius of this Age", 2005; contbr. numerous articles in ency., conf. papers, and book reviews. Vol. Boy Scouts of Am., 1961, Portsmouth Cmty. Theater, RI, USS NC Hist. Detachment, Wilmington, NC, 1998—. Recipient Phi Alpha Theta, FSU Delta Chpt., 1992; grantee Clan Donald Ednl. and Charitable Trust scholarship, 1975—77, Richard C. Maguire scholarship, Rock Island Arsenal Hist. Soc., 1992—95, Henry J. Reilly Mem. Grad. scholarship, Res. Officers Assn. of the US, 1992—94. Fellow: Res. Officers Assn.; mem.: Navy League of the US, RI Employer Support to the Guard and Res., Naval Res. Assn., Royal United Services Inst., US Naval Inst., Triangle Inst. for Security Studies, Fla. Conf. of Historians, Armed Forces Comm. and Electronics Assn., Hist. Soc., Am. Hist. Assn. Avocations: cmty. theater, reenacting, scouts. Office: US Naval War Coll 686 Cushing Rd Newport RI 02841

CARPENTER, STEPHEN HAYES, JR., lawyer; BA, U. Va., 1990; JD, U. Oreg., Eugene, 1995. Bar: Oreg. Supreme Ct. 1995, Wash. State Supreme Ct. 1996, U.S. Ct. Appeals Armed Forces 2003, U.S. Dist. Ct. Oreg. 1996, cert.: U.S. Dept. Justice (criminal trial advocacy) 2003. City atty. City Wheeler, Oreg., 1997—99; pvt. practice Rockaway Beach, Oreg., 1995—99; asst. U.S. Army Judge Adv. Corps, Friedberg, Hessen, Germany, 1999—2004; asst. atty. gen. Atty. Gen.'s Office, Olympia, Wash., 2005—. Adj. lectr. trial advocacy U. Washington Law Sch., 2006—. Contbr. articles to profl. jours. City counselor, Manzanita, Oreg., 1998—99; del. overseas bar Oreg. State Bar, 2001—02. Capt. judge adv. gen.'s corps US Army, 1999—2004, Germany and Kosovo. Office: 1201 Third Ave 28th Fl Seattle WA 98101 Home Phone: 206-326-0803. Business E-Mail: scarpenter@blankenshiplawfirm.com.

CARPENTER, SUSAN KAREN, defender; b. New Orleans, May 6, 1951; d. Donald Jack and Elise Ann (Diehl) C. BA magna cum laude with honors in English, Smith Coll., 1973; JD, Ind. U., 1976. Bar: Ind. 1976. Dep. pub. defender of Ind. State of Ind., Indpls., 1976-81, pub. defender of Ind., 1981—; chief pub. defender Wayne County, Richmond, Ind., 1981. Bd. dirs. Ind. Pub. Defender Coun., Indpls., 1981—; Ind. Lawyers Comm., Indpls., 1984-89; trustee Ind. Criminal Justice Inst., Indpls., 1983—. Mem. Criminal Code Study Commn., Indpls., 1981—, Supreme Ct. Records Mgmt. Com., Indpls., 1983—, Ind. Pub. Defender Commn., 1989—, Ind. Supreme Ct. Commn. on Race and Gender Fairness, 2000—. Mem. Ind. State Bar Assn. (criminal justice sect.), Nat. Legal Aid and Defender Assn., Nat. Assn. Defense Lawyers, Phi Beta Kappa. Office Phone: 317-232-2475. Business E-Mail: scarpenter@iquest.net.

CARPENTER, TED GALEN, political scientist; b. Ladysmith, Wis., Oct. 1, 1947; s. Jay Dee and Magdalene (Stuner) C.; m. Barbara Lynette Bethke, May 11, 1968; children: Lara, Amber, Brian. BA, U. Wis., Milw., 1970, MA in History, 1971; PhD in History, U. Tex., 1980. Rsch. assoc. ideas and action project U. Tex., Austin, 1980-83; fgn. policy analyst Cato Inst., Washington, 1985-87, dir. foreign policy studies, 1987-95, v.p. def. and fgn. policy studies, 1996—. Cons. Profl. Mgmt. Resources, Austin, Tex., 1983-84. Author: A Search for Enemies: America's Alliances After the Cold War, 1992, Beyond NATO: Staying Out of Europe's Wars, 1994, The Captive Press: Foreign Policy Crises and the First Amendment, 1995, Peace & Freedom: Foreign Policy for a Constitutional Republic, 2002, Bad Neighbor Policy: Washington's Futile War on Drugs in Latin America, 2003, America's Coming War With China: A Collision Course Over Taiwan, 2006; co-author: The Korean Conundrum: America's Troubled Relations with North and South Korea, 2004; editor: Collective Defense or Strategic Independence: Alternative Strategies for the Future, 1989, NATO at 40: Confronting a Changing World, 1990, America Entangled: The Persian Gulf Crisis and Its Consequences, 1991, The Future of NATO, 1995, Delusions of Grandeur: The United Nations and Global Intervention, 1997, NATO's Empty Victory: A Postmortem on the Balkan War, 2000, NATO Enters the 21s Century, 2001; co-editor: The U.S.-South Korean Alliance; Time for a Change, 1992, NATO Enlargement: Illusions and Reality, 1998, China's Future: Constructive Partner or Emerging Threat?, 2000; contbg. editor National Interest, 2005—; meml. editl. bd.: Jour. Strategic Studies, meml. editl. adv. bd.: Mediterranean Quar.; contbr. articles to profl. jours. Mem.: Coun. on Fgn. Rels., Acad. Polit. Sci. Mem. Unitarian Ch. Office: Cato Institute 1000 Massachusetts Ave NW Washington DC 20001-5400 Business E-Mail: tcarpenter@cato.org.

CARPENTER, WILL DOCKERY, chemicals executive; b. Moorhead, Miss., July 13, 1930; s. Horace Aubrey and Celeste (Brian) C.; m. Hellen E. Dodd, Mar. 26, 1960; children: Celeste, Bill. BS in Agronomy, Miss. State U., 1952; MS in Plant Physiology, Purdue U., 1956, PhD in Plant Physiology, 1958, DSc (hon.), 1999; grad. exec. program in bus. adminstrn., Columbia U., 1980; DSc (hon.), Miss. State U., 2005. Research biochemist Monsanto Co., St. Louis, 1958-60, agrl. research chemist, 1960-61, staff agrl. devel., 1961-65; mgr. market devel. Monsanto Agrl. Div., St. Louis, 1965-71; dir. product devel. Monsanto Agrl. Products Co., St. Louis, 1971-77, dir. environ. ops., 1977-80, dir. environ. mgmt./environ. policy staff, 1980-84, gen. mgr. tech., 1984-86; v.p. technology Monsanto Agrl. Co., St. Louis, 1986-90, v.p., gen. mgr. new products, 1990-92; chmn., bd. dirs. Agridyne Techs. Inc. Served to capt. U.S. Army, 1952-54, Korea. Fellow Weed Sci. Soc. Am. (treas. 1975, pres. 1980); mem. Indsl. Biotech. Assn. (bd. dirs. 1986—), Chem. Mfrs. Assn. (chmn. environ. mgmt. com. 1982-84, chmn. chem. warfare disarmament com. Washington 1985—), North Cen. Weed Control Conf. (pres. 1977, hon. mem. 1982). Office: 456 Conway Meadows Dr Chesterfield MO 63017-9625 E-mail: wdchdc@aol.com.

CARPENTER, WILLIAM F., III, hospital management company executive, lawyer; BA, JD, Vanderbilt Univ. Ptnr. Waller Lansden Dortch & Davis, Nashville, 1983—98; gen. counsel Am. group HCA, 1998—99; sr. v.p. to exec. v.p., gen. counsel, corp. sec. LifePoint Hospitals Inc., Brentwood, Tenn., 1999—2006, pres., CEO, 2006—. Bd. dir. Psychiatric Solutions Inc., 2004—, Fedn. Am. Hospitals. Office: Lifepoint Hospitals Inc Ste 200 103 Powell Ct Brentwood TN 37027*

CARPENTER, WILLIAM MORTON, language educator, writer; b. Cambridge, Mass., Oct. 31, 1940; s. James M. and Dorothy N. (Sauer) C.; m. Joanne Laventis, 1962 (div. 1987); 1 child, Matthew; m. Donna Gold; 1 child, Daniel. BA, Dartmouth Coll., 1962; PhD, U. Minn., 1967. Instr. U. Minn., Mpls., 1963-67; asst. prof. U. Chgo., 1967-72; mem. faculty dept. lit. Coll. of Atlantic, Bar Harbor, Maine, 1972—, faculty dean, 1983-89. Bd. dirs. Maine Acad. Coalition, Augusta. Author: The Hours of Morning, 1981, Rain, 1986, Speaking Fire at Stones, 1992, A Keeper of Sheep, 1994, Wooden Nickel, 2002. Recipient Neruda prize U. Okla., 1979, Contemporary Poetry award Assoc. Writing Program, 1981, Black Warrior Rev. prize U. Ala., 1984, Morse prize Northeastern U., 1985; NEA fellow, Venice, Italy, 1985, Inst. for Human Ecology fellow 1989—, Yaddo Ctr., fellow 1984, MacDowell Colony fellow, 1985. Office: Coll of Atlantic 105 Eden St Bar Harbor ME 04609-1105 Home Phone: 207-567-4172; Office Phone: 207-288-5015. E-mail: carpentr@coa.edu.

CARPENTER, WOODROW WILSON, manufacturing executive, ceramics engineer; b. Snyder, Ill., Sept. 11, 1915; s. Marion Ernest and Margaretta (Fawver) Carpenter; m. Fay D. Turner, Nov. 24, 1939 (div. 1959); 1 child, Gay M. Caldwell; m. Irmgard K. Toberg, Sept. 3, 1960. BS in Ceramic Engring., U. Ill., 1939. Rsch. engr. Ingram Richardson Mfg. Co., Frankfort, Ind., 1939-54; dir. rsch. Barrows Porcelain Enamel Co., Cin., 1954-58; chmn. bd. Ceramic Coating Co., Newport, Ky., 1958-97, Thompson Enamel, inc., Bellevue, Ky., 1997—. Founder mag. Glass On Metal, 1982, W.W. Carpenter Enamel Found., 2003. Lt. col. AUS, 1941-46, PTO Mem. Enamelist Soc. (founder). Avocations: magic, puzzles, golf. Home: PO Box 7 Cold Spring KY 41076 Office: 650 Colfax Ave Bellevue KY 41073-1621 Office Phone: 859-291-3800.

CARPENTER III, HARRY EVERETT, social sciences educator, history professor; b. Cherry Point Marine Base, NC, Aug. 25, 1952; s. Harry Everett Carpenter Jr. and Adele Kaleel Carpenter; children: Harry Everett Carpenter IV, Meredith LeighAnn Eller. B in Ceraminc Engring., Ga. Inst. Tech., Atlanta, 1974; MA in History, U. NC, Charlotte, 1993. Engr., foreman Acme Brick Co., Tulsa, 1974—76; engr. Hyalyn Ltd., Hickory, NC, 1976—80; self-employed acct., fin. planner Hickory, 1980—90; adj. instr., history Catawba Valley CC, Hickory, 1998—2002; instr., history, social scis. Western Piedmont CC, Morganton, NC, 2002—. Youth coord. Reagan-Bush NC Campaign, 1980; 10th congl. dist. chmn. NC Young Reps., Conover, 1978—80, chmn., 1980—81; mem. bd. dirs. Catawba County Sheltered Workshop, Conover, 1984—87; parent rep. NC Coun. Hearing Impaired, Raleigh, NC, 1985—87. Recipient Outstanding Young Rep., Catawba County Rep. Party, 1978. Mem.: Toastmasters Internat. (divsn. dir. 1985—87, Toastmaster Yr. 1986—87, 1987—88), Econ. and Bus. Hist. Soc., Soc. Automotive Historians, Inc. Independent. Orthodox Church Of America. Home: Coll 114 B Rhyne St Morganton NC 28655 Office: Western Piedmont Cmty Coll 1001 Burkemont Ave Morganton NC 28655 Home Phone: 828-413-9640; Office Phone: 828-430-7284. Business E-Mail: hcarpenter@wpcc.edu.

CARPENTER-MASON, BEVERLY NADINE, quality assurance professional, medical/surgical nurse, pediatric nurse practitioner, consultant, writer; d. Frank Carpenter and Thelma Deresa (Williams) Carpenter Smith; m. Sherman Robert Robinson Jr., Dec. 26, 1953 (div. Jan. 1959); 1 child, Keith Michael Robinson; m. David Solomon Mason Jr., Sept. 10, 1960; 1 child, Tamara Nadina Mason. Grad., Shadyside Hosp. Sch. Nursing, Pitts.; BS, St. Joseph Coll., North Windham, ME, 1979; MS, So. Ill. U., 1981; PhD, Columbia Pacific U., 1995. RN Pa., DC, Fla., cert. PNP; state ombusman long term care North Pinellas Pasco County Long Term Care Ombudsman Coun., parish nurse 2004, lay spkr. 1999, lay del. Fla. Conf. United Meth. Ch., 1998. Staff nurse med. surgery, ob-gyn neonatology and pediat. Pa., NY, Wyo., Colo. and Washington, 1954—68; mgr. clinician dermatol. svcs. Malcolm Grow Med. Ctr., Camp Spring, Md., 1968—71; PNP Dept. Human Resources, Washington, 1971—73; asst. DON Glenn Dale Hosp., Md., 1973—81; nursing coord. medicaid divsn. Forest Haven Ctr., Laurel, Md., 1981—83, spl. asst. to supr. for med. svcs., 1983—84; spl. asst. to supt. for quality assurance Bur. Habilitation Svcs., Laurel, 1984—89; exec. asst. quality assurance coord. Mental Retardation Devel. Disabilities Adminstrn., Washington, 1989—91, also bd. dirs.; owner, prin. BCM Assocs., 1992—; coord. quality assurance health svcs. divsn. UPARC, Clearwater, Fla., 1993—94. Mem. exec. com. Am. Found. Edn. Healthcare Quality, 1995—97; bd. dirs. Dist. V, Fla. Dept. HHS, 1997—2002; cons., lectr. in field. Author: Quality Assurance: Toward a Paradigm of Universality, 1995; mem. editl. bd., case study editor: Am. Jour. Quality Assurance, 1985—2005; contbr. articles to profl. jours. Mem., star donor ARC Blood Dr., Washington, 1975—91; mem. health and human svcs. bd. Fla. Dept. Children and Families, 1997—2000, cons. Dist. XI, 1998; bd. dirs. Pinellas County (Fla.) Coun., Pinellas County WAGES Coalition, 1999; mem. Parish Nurse Assn., 2004—; vol. chief cons. Am. Bd. Med. Quality 2005 Cert. Examination Devel., 2005—; vol. curriculum specialist cons. Accreditation Coun. for Edn. and Tng., 2001—; lay del. United Meth. Ch. Fla. Conf., 1998—; bd. ordained ministry apptd. by the bishop of United Meth. Ch., 2004—; bd. dirs. North Pinellas divsn. Am. Cancer Soc., 2002—04; bd. trustees, dir. Upper Pinellas Assn. Retarded Citizens Bd./Found., 2002—; chair nominations com. Prince Georges Nat. Coun. Negro Women, Md., 1984—85; exec. sec. Pipers Meadow Home Owners Assn., 1993—2001; mem. Long Term Care Fla. State Ombudsman Coun., 2000—05. Named Woman of the Yr., 1990—96; recipient awards, Dept. Air Force and DC Govt., 1966—92, Della Robbia Gold medallion, Am. Acad. Pediat., 1972, John P. Lamb Jr. Meml. Lectureship award, E. Tenn. State U., 1988, Outstanding Svc. award, U.S. Congress Adv. Bd. Svc., 1991. Fellow: Am. Coll. Med. Quality (mem. jour. editl. bd.

1985—2004, chmn. publs. com. 1987—2003, asst. treas. 1988—93, Disting., case study editor, Svc. award 1999); mem.: NAFE, Internat. Platform Assn., Healthcare Quality Inst., Assn. Retarded Citizens, Am. Bd. Quality Assurance and Utilization Rev. Physicians (asst. treas. 1988—94, chair exam. com. 1990—93, chief proctor exam. com. 1995—97, Chmn. of the Yr. award 1992, presdl. citation, Calvin R. Openshaw Svc. award 1993), Am. Assn. Mental Retardation (conf. lectr. 1988), Top Ladies Distinction (1st v.p. 1986—91), World Cir. Lang. Club (1st v.p. 2003—05, corr. sec. 2005—), Soroptimists Internat. (sec. Pinellas chpt. 1999, Achievement in Healthcare award 1997), Order Ea. Star (Achievement award Deborah chpt. 1991). Democrat. Avocations: studying languages, travel, reading, writing, collecting antiques. Personal E-mail: drbevearpmason@aol.com.

CARPENTIERI, CAROL ELLEN, artist, educator; b. Bklyn., Nov. 3, 1941; d. Nicholas Francis and Marie Ann Mecchella; m. Frank Dominick Carpentieri, Oct. 20, 1962; children: Diane P. Michaeli, Frank N., Marc J. AB, Westchester Bus. Sch., 1960; student, Fashion Inst. Tech., 1986. Tchr. art West Patent Elem. Sch., Bedford Hills, NY, 1972—82. Author: A November Walk, 2004, Winter in South Salem, 2005; exhibitions include West Side Art Coalition, 2004, Katonah Mus., 2005, Cork Gallery, Avery Fisher Hall, Licnoln Ctr. Plaza, 2005, Licht Blick Studios Gallery, 2005, Armonk United Meth. Ch., 2005, 96th St. Gallery, 2005. Vol. kitchen help God's Love We Deliver, NYC, 1993—99. Recipient Tri State Art Competition award, Katonah Art Mus., 2005, Hon. Mention award, Westchester Land Trust, 2006. Mem.: Katonah Mus. Artist Assn., West Side Arts Coalition, Nat. Mus. Women in Arts, Lewisboro Garden Club. Democrat. Avocations: horseback riding, kayaking, gardening, yoga, knitting. Home: 29 Hoyt St South Salem NY 10590

CARPENTIERI, SARAH C., neuropsychologist, researcher, clinical psychologist; m. James F. Asbury; 2 children. BBA/BA, U. Notre Dame, 1989; MS, U. Memphis, 1991, PhD, 1994; postgrad., Northeastern U., Boston, 1999—2001, U. Houston, 2001—02. Lic. psychologist, neuropsychologist, healthcare provider Mass., 1997, Tex., 2003. Rschr. St. Jude Children's Hosp., Memphis, 1990—94; psychology intern Harvard Med. Sch. /Children's Hosp., Boston, 1994—95; neuropsychology post-doctoral fellow Harvard Med. Sch., 1995—97, instr., asst. psychology and neuropsychologist, 1997—2003; assoc. rsch. and neuropsychologist Children's Hosp., Boston, 1997—2003; asst. prof. Baylor Coll. Medicine, Houston, 2003—; pediat. neuropsychologist Tex. Children's Hosp., Houston, 2003—. Lead investigator pediatric brain tumor rsch. program Children's Hosp., Boston, 1998—; reviewer various med. jours., 1998—; cons. Dana Farber Cancer Inst., Boston, 2001—04; prin. investigator Pediat. Oncology Rsch. Studies, 2003—; neuropsychology and psychology cons., 2003—. Contbr. articles to profl. jours., chapters to books. Fellow VanVleet, U. Memphis, 1993—94; grantee Rsch., Pitino Found., 1999—2000, Murphy Child's Trust, 1999—2000, S&S Found., 1997—2003. Mem.: APA, Tex. Psychol. Assn., Mass. Psychol. Assn., Nat. Acad. Neuropsychology, Internat. Neuropsychology Soc. Achievements include research in area of neurocognitive functioning and polymorphisms. Business E-Mail: sarah.carpentieri@carpenburymed.com.

CARPER, FERN GAYLE, small business owner, writer; b. Pitts., Jan. 28, 1934; d. Phillip Jack and Jean Edith (Epstein) Whitman; m. Robert S. Carper, Aug. 3, 1958; children: Pamela Hope, Bruce Alan. Diploma, Taylor Alderdice H.S., 1952. Exe. sec. J.J. Gumberg & Co., Pitts., 1952—58; author, owner Pete The Toad Enterprises, Potomac, Md., 2000—. Author: Pete The Toad and Friends, 2002. Democrat. Achievements include development of line of Pete The Toad stuffed animals and tee shirts. Avocations: oil and acrylic art, still life painting, singing. Home: 18003 Mateny Rd Germantown MD 20874

CARPER, GERTRUDE ESTHER, small business owner, real estate developer; b. Jamestown, NY, Apr. 13, 1921; d. Zenas Mills and Virgie (Lytton) Hanks; m. J. Dennis Carper, Apr. 5, 1942; children: David Hanks, John Michael Dennis, Michelle Kristen. Student violinist, Nat. Acad. Mus., 1931-41; diploma fine arts, Md. Inst. of Art, 1950; voice student, Frazier Gange, Peabody Inst. Music, 1952-55. Interior decorator O'Neill's (Importers), Balt., 1942-44; auditor Citizens Nat. Bank, Covington, Va., 1945-46; owner, developer Essex Yacht Harbour Marina, Balt., 1955—, owner, developer St. Michael's Sanctuary wildlife preserve, 1965—. Jewelry designer, 1987—; portrait artist, 1947—; exhibited one-woman shows Ferdinand Roten Gallery, Balt., 1963, Highfield Salon, Balt., 1967, Le Salon des Nations a Paris, 1985, Ducks and Geese of North Am., 1986, Series of Lighthouses, 1991; exhibited group shows Md. Inst. Alumni Show, 1964, Essex Libr., 1981, Hist. Preservation of Am., Hall of Fame, 1989, others; works included in collections including Prestige de la Peinture d'Aujourd'hos dans le Monde, 1990, Artists and Masters of the Twentieth Century, 1991; author: Expressions for Children, 1985, Fidere, 1993, Mentation, 1993; contbr. articles and poetry to ch. publs. and newspapers. Vol. tchr. of retarded persons, 1942—; leader Women's Circle at local Presbyn. chs., 1952-87, mem. 40 yrs. of choir svc. Mem. Md. Inst. Art Alumni Assn. (life), Grand Coun. World Parliament of Chivalry (Nobless of Humanity citation), Nat. Mus. Women in the Arts (charter, Washington). Avocations: raising orchids, reading, writing essays and poetry. Office: Essex Yacht Harbour Marina 500 Sandalwood Rd Baltimore MD 21221-5830

CARPER, THOMAS RICHARD, senator, former governor; b. Beckley, W.Va., Jan. 23, 1947; s. Wallace Richard and Mary Jean (Patton) C.; m. Martha Ann Stacy, Jan. 1, 1986; children: Christopher Thomas, Benjamin Michael. BA in Economics, Ohio State U., 1968; MBA, U. Del., 1975. Indsl. devel. specialist Del. Divsn. Econ. Devel., Dover, 1975-76; state treas. State of Del., Dover, 1977—83; mem. 98th-102nd Congresses from Del., Washington, 1983-93; governor of Del., 1993-2001; US Senator from Del., 2001—. Vice chmn. Democratic Leadership Coun.; mem. com. banking, housing, and urban affairs US Senate, com. environment and public works, com. homeland security and govtl. affairs, spl. com. aging. Fundraising chmn. Big Bros.-Big Sisters of Del., 1985, 93; hon. chair Del. Spl. Olympics, 1987—; adv. bd. Delmarva Coun., Boy Scouts of Am.; bd. dirs. Am. Legacy Found., Amtrak, vice chair Jobs for America's Grads, 1996-. Lt. USN, 1968—73, comdr. Res. USN, 1973—91. Decorated Achievement award, Vietnam Campaign Ribbon, Air medal, Commendation medal; recipient Am. Fin. Leadership award, Fin. Services Roundtable, 2002, Magnificent Mentor award, Del. Mentoring Coun., 2002, Rook of Yr., Rehoboth Beach-Dewey Beach, Del. C. of C., 2002, Early Stage East Founders' award, 2003, George Falcon Golden Spike award, Nat. Assn. Railroad Passengers, 2004. Mem. Nat. Govs. Assn. (vice chmn. 1997-98, chmn. 1998-99), Nat. Governors Assn. (chmn. 1998). Democrat. Presbyterian. Office: US Senate 513 Hart Senate Office Bldg Washington DC 20510 also: One Christina Ctr Ste 102 L-1 301 North Walnut St Wilmington DE 19801-3974 Office Phone: 202-224-2441, 302-573-6291. Office Fax: 202-228-2190.*

CARR, ARTHUR CHARLES, psychologist, educator; b. Buffalo, Nov. 27, 1918; s. John E. and Katherine (Haas) C. BS, Buffalo State Tchrs. Coll., 1941; MA, Tchrs. Coll. Columbia U., 1946; PhD, U. Chgo., 1952; postgrad., William Alanson White Inst., 1953-54, Inst. Group Therapy, 1957-58, N.Y. Soc. Clin. Psychologists, 1954-60. Diplomate: Am. Bd. Examiners in Profl. Psychology, N.Y. State Edn. Dept. Trainee clin. psychology VA, 1947-52; sr. clin. psychologist Creedmoor State Hosp., Queens Village, N.Y., 1952-56; prin. clin. psychologist N.Y. State Psychiat. Inst., NYC, 1956—; ret.; asst. prof. psychology Adelphi Coll., Garden City, N.Y., 1952-56; asso. prof. med. psychology, dept. psychiatry Coll. Physicians and Surgeons, Columbia U., 1956-71, prof., 1971-78, prof. emeritus, 1978—; prof. psychology in psychiatry Cornell U. Med. Coll., 1978-89. Author: (with Shervert Frazier) Introduction to Psychopathology, 1964, (with Herbert Hendin, William Gaylin) Psychoanalysis and Social Research, 1965; author, editor: (with others) Loss and Grief, 1970, Psychosocial Aspects of Terminal Care, 1972, The Terminal Patient, 1973, Anticipatory Grief, 1974, Bereavement: Its Psychosocial Aspects, 1975, Grief, Selected Readings, 1975, The Mouth in Critical and Terminal Illness, 1980, Education of the Medical Student in Thanatology, 1981, Adolescent Marijuana Abusers and their Families, 1981, Bernard Schoenberg: Contributions to Psychiatry, Education of the Health Professional, Thanatology and Ethical Values, 1984, Principles of Thanatology, 1987, Psychodynamic Psychotherapy of Borderline Patients, 1989; editor-in-chief: Man and Medicine, 75-80; cons. editor, 1980—; editorial bd., cons. editor: Jour. Projective Techniques, 1967-73; asso. editor: Jour. Abnormal Psychology, 1966 70, Jour. Thanatology, 1971—; contbr. articles to profl. jours. Served to maj. AUS, 1941-46. Fellow Am. Psychol. Assn., Soc. Projective Techniques (dir. 1961-64, pres. 1971-72); mem. Eastern, N.Y. State psychol. assns., N.Y. Soc. Clin. Psychologists. Home: 560 Riverside Dr New York NY 10027-3202

CARR, BERNARD FRANCIS, hospital administrator; b. Wilkes-Barre, Pa., July 13, 1919; s. John Daniel and Marjorie Veronica (Gallagher) C.; m. Mary Ann Reiss, Dec. 30, 1945; children: Bernard, Cathy, Irene, Patricia, Mary Ann. Grad., Rockland State Hosp. Sch. Nursing, 1942; BS, NYU, 1949; MBA in Hosp. Adminstrn., U. Chgo., 1951; student, We. State U. Coll. Law, 1981—81. R.N., Calif., Pa., Va.; lic. nursing home adminstr., Va.; lic. real estate agt., Calif.; lic. comml. aviator. Commd. USMCR, 1945; adminstrv. resident Ind. U. Med. Ctr., Indpls., 1950—51, adminstrv. asst., 1951—52, asst. adminstr., 1952—53; supt. Altoona Hosp., Pa., 1953—72; adminstr. South Coast Cmty. Hosp., South Laguna, Calif., 1972—78, Bedford County Meml. Hosp., Va., 1978—79; exec. dir. South Coast Cmty. Hosp. Found., South Laguna, 1976—77; dir., sec.-treas. Bedford Meml. Hosp. Found., 1978—79; regional mgr. Calif., Charter Med. Corp., Macon, Ga., 1978—81, divsn. mgr., 1981—84; adminstr., CEO Kellogg Psychiat. Charter Hosp., Corona, Calif., 1981—82; pres., CEO New Riyadh Internat. Airport Hosp., Saudi Arabia, 1980—81; assoc. dir. corp. quality assurance, dir. physician rels. Charter Med. Corp., 1981—84. Committeman Hosp. Coun. So. Calif., 1981; coord. home nursing svc. Kimberly Quality Svc., Costa Mesa, Calif., 1992-96. Mem. Altoona Redevel. Authority, 1964-70, vice chmn., 1966-70; exec. com. Coordinating Coun. on Continuing Edn. in Health Care Sys., Pa. State U., 1971-73; mem. Blair County Child Welfare, Blair County Soc. for Crippled Children adv. bds., 1965-72; Blair County Human Devel. Task Force; mem. tech. adv. com. Altoona Cmty. Renewal Program, 1971-73; fund raising chmn. Bedford area Piedmont divsn. Am. Heart Assn., 1978, White House Coun. on Aged. Served at naval aviation cadet, 1943-45; cadet regimental comdr. Rensselaer Polytech. Inst., Chapel Hill, Glenview NAS, Pensacola, Fla. and Corpus Christi, Tex. 1st lt. USMCR, 1945-52. Fellow Am. Coll. Nursing Home Adminstrs., Am. Coll. Health Care Execs. (life); mem. APHA, Am. Hosp. Assn. (life, del. 1970—, regional adv. bd., coun. hosp. schs. nursing 1968-72), Calif. Hosp. Assn., Va. Hosp. Assn. (coms.), Hosp. Assn. Pa. (v.p. 1969-70, pres.-elect 1970-71, pres. 1971-72), Nat. League for Nursing (agy. rep. 1959—), Am. Health Care Assn., Va. Health Care Assn., Assn. Mental Health Adminstrs., Hosp. Fin. Mgmt. Assn., Nat. Coun. Cmty. Hosps., Roanoke Area Hosp. Coun., Laguna Beach C. of C. (dir.), VFW (Saddleback Valley, El Toro chpt., life, quartermaster 2000—, post comdr. 2001-02), USMC 1st Divsn. Assn., Marine Corps League (life), Order of Cootie (life), Rotary (pres. elect Bedford 1979-80, pres. South-Laguna-Niguel 1976-77), First Marine Divsn. Assn Home: 31291 E 9th Dr Laguna Niguel CA 92677-2907 Personal E-mail: boxiemary1@cox.net. *Throughout my career I've made it clear to my subordinates that I would never stand in the way of their career opportunities, even if I were hard pressed to replace them. Over the years this attitude became a trademark for me and has resulted in an eager supply of key associates. Each has learned a basic philosophy: "What you do is a reflection on you; what your adversaries do is a reflection on them".*

CARR, BOB, congressman, lawyer; b. Janesville, Wis., Mar. 27, 1943; s. Milton Raymond and Edna (Blood) C.; m. Kathleen Smith; 1 child, Alexandra Anne; stepchildren: Jennifer McCloskey, Christopher McCloskey. BS, U. Wis., 1965, JD, 1968; postgrad., Mich. State U., 1968—69. Bar: Wis. 1968, Mich. 1969, U.S. Supreme Ct. 1973. Mem. staff of minority leader Mich. State Senate, 1968-69; adminstrv. asst. to atty. gen. State of Mich., Lansing, 1969-70, asst. atty. gen., 1970-72; counsel to spl. joint com. on legal edn. Mich. Legislature, Lansing, 1972; mem. 94th-96th, 98th-103rd Congresses from 6th (now 8th) Mich. Dist., Washington, 1975-80, 83; appropriations com., 1983-95; chmn. transp. subcom. appropriations, 1993-95; sr. v.p. The Jefferson Group, Inc., 1996-98, Henry J. Kaufman & Assocs., Washington, 1997-99, Carr Sherman Minjack, Washington, 1999—2005; of counsel Dow Lohnes, PLLC, Washington, 2005—. Mgmt. cons., 1995-; sr. fellow UCLA Sch. Pub. Policy, 2000-01. Mem. U.S. Assn. Former Mems. Congress (bd. dirs. 2001—), Supporters Civil Soc. Russia (bd. dirs. 2003—) Democrat. Office: Dow Lohnes PLLC 1200 New Hampshire Ave NW Washington DC 20036-6802 Office Phone: 202-776-2065. Business E-Mail: bcarr@dowlohnes.com.

CARR, CAROLYN KINDER, art gallery director; b. Providence; BA in Art History, Smith Coll.; MA in Art History, Oberlin Coll.; PhD in Art History, Case Western Reserve U. Instr. art history Kent (Ohio) State Univ., 1963-65, 67-68; art critic Akron (Ohio) Beacon Jour., 1968-73; chief curator Akron Art Mus., 1978—83; asst. dir. for collections Nat. Portrait Gallery, Washington, 1984-90, dep. dir., chief curator, 1991—. Vis. lectr. Akron U., Spring 1975, '76; organizer numerous art exhbns. Akron Art Mus., 1978—83, Nat. Portrait Gallery, 1984—. Contbr. articles to art publs. including Nat. Portrait Gallery, The Dictionary of Art, Am. Art, The Am. Art Jour., Dialogue, Currier Gallery of Art Bull.; author: art catalogs for exhibitions at Akron Art Mus., Chrysler Mus. of Art, Nat. Portrait Gallery and Smithsonian Instn. Office: Nat Portrait Gallery 750 9th St NW Box 37012 Washington DC 20013-7012 Home Phone: 202-244-0492; Office Phone: 202-275-1867. Business E-Mail: carrc@si.edu.

CARR, CHARLES F., orthopedist; b. Coronado, Calif., May 17, 1957; s. Robert Turner Carr and Marjorie (Carr) Dillon; m. Carol Anne LaCasse, May 7, 1985; children: Matthew, Daniel, Christopher. BA, Dartmouth Coll., 1979; MD, Dartmouth Med. Sch., 1981. Diplomate Am. Bd. Orthop. Surgery. Assoc. prof. Orthop. Surgery Dartmouth Med. Sch., Hanover, NH, 1989—; dir., sports medicine Dartmouth-Hitchcock Med. Ctr., Lebanon, NH. Head team physician Dartmouth Coll., Hanover, 1990—; dir. residency Darthmouth Hitchcock Med Ctr, Lebanon, NH, 1997—. Contbr. articles to profl. jours. Office: Dept Orthopaedics Dartmouth-Hitchcock Med Ctr One Medical Ctr Dr Lebanon NH 03756*

CARR, CHARLES LOUIS, retired religious organization administrator; b. Rockport, Ind., Sept. 9, 1930; s. Louis E. and Loris B. (Lindsey) C.; m. Shirley R. Cron, Nov. 15, 1950; children: Kathleen Carr Wright, Charles Stephen, Jeffrey Louis, David Wayne. Student, Ind. State U., 1949-50, So. Bapt. Theol. Sem., 1965-67; BS, Oakland City U., 1978, DD, 1994. Ordained to ministry Gen. Assn. Gen. Bapts., 1957. Pastor East Oolitic Gen. Bapt. Ch., Bedford, Ind., 1959-63, Mt. Zion Gen. Bapt. Ch., Indpls., 1963-65, Hunsinger Lane Gen. Bapt. Ch., Louisville, 1965-67; missionary to Saipan Mariana Islands, 1967-73; exec. dir. Gen. Bapt. Fgn. Mission Soc., Poplar Bluff, Mo., 1973-96; ret., 1996; pastor Wyatt United Meth Ch., 1997—, Dogwood United Meth Ch., 1997—; ret., 2005. Author: Seed, Soil and Seasons, 1988; contbr. articles to various publs. Home: 706 S 9th St Poplar Bluff MO 63901-5639 Personal E-mail: carrsson@sbcglobal.net.

CARR, CYNTHIA, lawyer; b. San Antonio, Nov. 4, 1953; d. Robert Claude Carr and Alta Mae (Bletsch) Holmes; m. Marc Allan Wallman; children: Lydia Michael, Aidan Holmes BA, Austin Coll., 1975; JD, Harvard U., 1984; LLM, NYU, 1990. Bar: N.Y. 1985, Conn. 1988. Coord. Cambodian sect. Internat. Rescue Com., Bangkok, 1980—81; legal intern Mental Health Legal Advisers Com., Boston, 1982—83; assoc. White & Case, NYC, 1984—87; assoc. gen. counsel, exec. dir. planned giving Yale U., New Haven, 1988—2000; gen. counsel Save the Children, Westport, Conn., 2000—06, v.p., gen. counsel, 2006—. Vis. lectr. Yale U. Law Sch., New Haven, 1988-90 Vol. Peace Corps, West Africa, 1975-77, 79-80; bd. dirs. Yale Law Sch. Early Learning Ctr., 1990-95; trustee Yale U. Hong Kong Charitable Trust, 1997-2000, Oak Leaf Endowment Trust for Yale, 1997-2000 Mem. ABA (vice chair lifetime and charitable gift planning com. 2000—, probate and trust divsn. 2000-01), Conn. Bar Assn. (charitable giving exempt orgns. subcom.), Trusts and Estates Mag. (charitable giving mini bd. mem. 1996-99), Jewish Found. New Haven (tax and legal com. 1999—), Conn. Planned Giving Group (bd. dirs. 2000-01) Home: 30 Hawley Rd Hamden CT 06517-2128 Office: Save the Children 54 Wilton Rd Westport CT 06880-3131 Office Phone: 203-221-4035. Business E-Mail: ccarr@savechildren.org.

CARR, DANIEL BARRY, anesthesiologist, endocrinologist, researcher, pharmaceutical executive; b. NYC, Apr. 6, 1948; s. Andrew Joseph and Florence (Glassman) C.; m. Justine M. Meehan, Nov. 11, 1978; children: Nora, Rebecca, Andrew. BA, Columbia U., 1968, MA, 1970, MD, 1976. Diplomate Am. Bd. Internal Medicine (subsplty. bds. Endocrinology and Metabolism, Anesthesiology, Pain Mgmt.). Intern Columbia-Presbyn. Med. Ctr., NYC, 1976-78; resident med. svc. Mass. Gen. Hosp., Boston, 1978-79, endocrine fellow, 1979-82, staff physician endocrine unit, 1982-94, clin. assoc. physician, clin. rsch. ctr., 1982-84, fellow in anesthesiology, 1984-86, dir. analgesic peptide rsch. unit, 1986-94, staff physician anesthesia svc., co-dir. anesthesia pain unit, 1986-91, dir. divsn. pain mgmt., 1991-94; anesthetist, 1992-94; instr. medicine Harvard U. Med. Sch., 1982-84, asst.prof., 1984-88, assoc. prof., 1988-94; rsch. staff Shriners Burn Inst., Boston, 1986-94; Saltonstall prof. Pain Rsch. in anesthesia and medicine Tufts-New England Med. Ctr., 1994—; dir. pain mgmt. rsch. Caritas St. Elizabeth's Med. Ctr., 1998—; CEO, CMO Javelin Pharms., Cambridge, Mass. Co-chair acute and cancer pain mgmt. guideline panels Agy. for Health Care Policy and Rsch., U.S. Dept. HHS, 1990—94; vice chair rsch. dept. anesthesia New Eng. Med. Ctr., 1994—; pain rev. editor Cochrane collaboration rev. group Pain, Palliative and Supportive Care, 1998—; mem. Gov. Mass. Spl. Commn. Pain Mgmt., 1993—98; tech. expert Agy. Healthcare Rsch. and Quality, 1999—2002; chair pain outcomes expert com. JCAHO-AMA-NCQA, 2002—03. Editor-in-chief IASP Pain: Clinical Updates, 1993—; mem. editl. bd. Clin. Jour. Pain, 1988—, Jour. Clin. Anesthesia, 1995—, Anesthesia and Analgesia, 1996-99, Acute Pain, 1998—, Jour. Pain, 1999—, Pain Medicine, 1999—, Pain, 2001-; contbr. articles, rsch. reports, essays, revs. to profl. librs. Daland fellow Am. Philos. Soc., 1980-83. Mem. Am. Pain Soc. (bd. dirs. 1994-97), Am. Acad. Pain medicine (bd. dirs. 1995-98, sec. 2003-), France-Am. Pain Soc. (pres. 1996-98), Am. Soc. Anesthesiologists, Internat. Assn. for Study Pain (coun. 1996-99), Endocrine Soc., Soc. for Neurosci., Internat. Anesthesia Rsch. Soc., Assn. Univ. Anesthetists, Alpha Omega Alpha. Achievements include development of specialty pharmaceuticals and novel chemical entities for pain control; research on pain, analgesic peptides and stress responses; relationship between analgesia and clinical outcome; systematic reviews and guidelines for improved pain treatment in hospital, hospice and home care settings. Office: Javelin Pharmaceuticals 125 CambridgePark Dr Cambridge MA 02140 Office Phone: 617-349-4500. Business E-Mail: dcarr@javelinpharmaceuticals.com.

CARR, DAVID, professional football player; b. Bakersfield, Calif., July 21, 1979; s. Roger and Sherry Carr; m. Melody Tipton, Mar. 27, 1999; children: Austin, Tyler. Grad., Fresno State U. Quarterback Houston Texans, 2002—07, Carolina Panthers, 2007—. Named WAC (We. Athletic Conf.) Player of Yr., NCAA, 2001; recipient Johnny Unitas Golden Arm award, 2001, Sammy Baugh award, 2001. Achievements include being the first overall selection in 2002 NFL Draft. Office: Carolina Panthers 800 S Mint St Charlotte NC 28202*

CARR, DAVID TURNER, physician; b. Richmond, Va., Mar. 12, 1914; s. John Ernest and Mary Lela (King) Carr; m. Rosemary Rudow, June 18, 1948 (div. 1953); 1 child, Caroline Anne Carr Oderkirk; m. Christine Nadeau, Dec. 27, 1979. Student, U. Richmond, 1931-33; MD, Med. Coll. Va., 1937; MS in Medicine, Mayo Grad. Sch. Medicine, 1947. Intern, then asst. resident Grady Hosp., Atlanta, 1937-39; resident chest diseases Bellevue Hosp., NYC, 1940-41; fellow medicine Mayo Clinic, 1943-47, cons. medicine, 1947-79, chmn. dept. oncology, 1975; dir. Mayo Comprehensive Cancer Ctr., 1975; assoc. dir. Ctr. Cancer Control, 1976-79; prof. medicine Mayo Med. Sch., 1964-79, M.D. Anderson Hosp. and Tumor Inst., Tex. Med. Ctr., Houston, 1979-92; med.-legal cons., 1992—. Mem.-at-large bd. dirs. Am. Lung Assn., 1959—74, v.p., 1971—72; bd. dirs. Rochester Civic Theatre, 1951—70, pres., 1965—67; bd. dirs. at large Am. Cancer Soc., 1967—74, pres. Minn. divsn., 1974—75, mem. am. joint com. cancer, 1971—79, chmn. am. joint com. cancer, 1979—82. Fellow: AAAS, ACP; mem.: Am. Thoracic Soc. (v.p. 1963—64), Internat. Assn. Study Lung Cancer (v.p. 1974—76, pres. 1976, treas. 1976—82), Ctrl. Soc. Clin. Rsch., Peruvian Atni-Tb Assn. (hon.), Rochester C. of C. (pres. 1959—60). Achievements include research in pulmonary diseases. Home and Office: PO Box 9300 Rancho Santa Fe CA 92067 Office Phone: 858-759-1798.

CARR, DAVIS HADEN, lawyer; b. Richmond, Va., July 21, 1940; s. Frederick and Bernice (Haden) Carr; m. Judith A. Guerry, Aug. 1959 (div. Apr. 1979); children: Wendy, Julia Carr Stewart; m. Martha Cash, Feb. 12, 1983. BEE, U. Va., 1961; JD, Vanderbilt U., 1970. Bar: Tenn. 1970, Ky. 1989. Assoc. Boult, Cummings, Conners & Berry PLC, Nashville, 1970-74, ptnr., 1974—; mng. ptnr. Boult, Cummings, Conners & Berry, Nashville, 1984-94, chmn., 1995-99. Active Leadership Nashville, 1977-78, chmn. alumni assn., 1978-79, trustee, 1997—, fin. chair 2000-01; pres. Cumberland Museums, Nashville, 1978-80; bd. dirs. Greater Nashville Arts Found., 1991-97; bd. dirs. Jr. Achievement Mid. Tenn., 1991-99, chmn., 1995-97; trustee Vol. State Horsemen's Found., 1988-, Houghland Found., 1988—, The Bright Hour Trust, 2000—; trustee, exec. com. Fisk U., 1996-2004, vice-chmn., 2000-03; bd. dirs. Nashville Downtown Partnership, 1994-99, chmn., 1994-95, exec. com., 1997-99. Mem. ABA, Tenn. Bar Found., Tenn. Bar Assn., Nashville Bar Found., Nashville Bar Assn., Vanderbilt U. Law Alumni Assn. (bd. dirs.), Cumberland Club (pres. 1986-87), Belle Meade Country Club, Nashville Area C. of C. (gen. counsel, mem. exec. com. 1992-96, bd. govs.). Office: Boult Cummings Conners & Berry PO Box 340025 Nashville TN 37203 Home: 4401 Beacon Dr Nashville TN 37215 Office Phone: 615-252-2319. Business E-Mail: dcarr@bccb.com.

CARR, E. BARBARA, librarian; d. George Albert Jr. and Ella Mae (Carter) Buckner; m. Richard Lenard Carr, Feb. 12; children: Richard Lenard Jr., Eric Antonio, Lakelsha Reneé(dec.). BS in Food and Nutrition, Lincoln U., Jefferson City, Mo., 1966. Cert. libr. Mo., home economist Mo. Caseworker Mo. Divsn. Family Svc., St. Louis, 1966—73; tchr. St. Louis Pub. Schs., 1986—88, libr., 1988—. Sec. Sherman Cmty. Sch. Edn. Bd., St. Louis. Editor, designer: AKA Souvenir Fashionetta, 1993. Sec., v.p. St. Charles U. Extension, Mo., 1980—85; mem. St. Peters Betterment Coun., Mo., 1980—86, St. Peters Planning and Zoning Commn., 1980—85. Mem.: AAUW, One Hundred Black Women, Alpha Kappa Alpha. Episcopalian. Avocations: crafts, knitting, computer design, piano, sewing.

CARR, EDWARD A., lawyer; b. Borger, Tex., July 31, 1962; AB with honors and distinction, Stanford U., Calif., 1984; JD, UCLA, 1987. Bar: Tex. 1988, DC 1989, US Dist. Ct. (so. dist.) Tex. 1989, US Ct. Appeals (5th cir.) 1989, US Ct. Appeals (fed. cir.) 1989. Assoc. Vinson & Elkins, Houston, 1988—97, ptnr., 1997—. Lectr. in field; spkr. in field. Contbr. articles to profl. jours.; contbg. author Texas Legal Ethics in the American Legal Ethics Library, Cornell Law School, 1998, Business and Commercial Litigation in Federal Courts, 2005, mem. UCLA Law Rev., 1985—87, mem. editl. bd., 1986—87. Fellow Tex. Bar Found. (life), Coll. State Bar Tex.; mem. ABA (sects. antitrust law, litigation), Am. Judicature Soc. (life), D.C. Bar, Fed. Bar Assn., State Bar Tex. (chair dist. 4B grievance com. 2003-04), Houston Bar Assn. Address: Vinson & Elkins LLP First City Tower 1001 Fannin St Ste 2300 Houston TX 77002-6760

CARR, EDWARD ALBERT, JR., pharmacologist, educator, physician; b. Cranston, RI, Mar. 3, 1922; s. Edward Albert and Florence (Hodge) C.; m. Nancy Albosta, Dec. 27, 1952; children: Sharon L., Cynthia F. AB summa cum laude, Brown U., 1942; MD cum laude, Harvard U., 1945. Rsch. fellow, instr. pharmacology Harvard Med. Sch., 1948-51; exch. fellow St. Bartholomew's Hosp., London, 1952-53; mem. faculty U. Mich. Med. Sch., Ann Arbor, 1953-74, prof. pharmacology, 1962-74, prof. internal medicine, 1967-74, dir. program investigative clin. pharmacology, 1962-74; mem. sr. staff Univ. Hosp., 1957-74; dir. Upjohn Ctr. Clin. Pharmacology, 1966-74; prof. medicine, prof. and chmn. dept. pharmacology Med. Sch., U. Louisville, 1974-76; prof. medicine, pharmacology and therapeutics Med. and Dental Sch., SUNY, Buffalo, 1976-92, emeritus prof. medicine, pharmacology and therapeutics, 1992—, chmn. dept. pharmacology and therapeutics, 1976-88. Mem. sr. staff, chmn. therapeutics com. Louisville Gen. Hosp., 1974-76; lectr. U. Helsinki, 1972, Autonomous U. Barcelona, 1974, Japan Med. Assn., 1977, Swedish Acad. Pharm. Sci., Stockholm, 1977, Esteve Found. Symposium, Mallorca, 1988; cons. Ann Arbor VA Hosp., 1954-74, Louisville VA Hosp., 1974-76, Buffalo VA Hosp., 1976-2002, Erie County Med. Ctr., 1978-92; mem. pharmacology-toxicology program com. NIH, 1971-75; hon. vis. prof. Prince Henry and Prince of Wales Hosp., Sydney, Australia, 1973. Co-author: Radioisotopes in Biology and Medicine, 1964; also articles. Mem. Nat. Joint Commn. on Prescription Drug Use, 1976-80; mem. coop. studies evaluation com. US VA, 1980-83; chmn. pharmacology com. Am. Inst. Biol. Sci., Walter Reed Army Inst. Rsch., 1985-86; vol. Niagara Hospice, 1992-2002, bd. dir., 1992-95, 1996-2002. Fellow ACP (emeritus); mem. Am. Thyroid Assn. (emeritus), Am. Soc. Pharmacology and Exptl. Therapeutics (emeritus) (exec. com. clin. pharmacology div. 1984-86), Am. Soc. Clin. Pharmacology and Therapeutics (emeritus, pres., 1974-75, Henry W. Elliott award 1981), Soc. Nuclear Medicine (emeritus), Ctrl. Soc. Clin. Rsch. (emeritus), Endocrine Soc. (emeritus), Phi Beta Kappa, Sigma Xi, Alpha Omega Alpha. Home: 2 Gothic Ledge Lockport NY 14094-9702

CARR, EDWARD GARY, psychology professor; b. Toronto, Aug. 20, 1947; came to U.S., 1969; s. Saul Isaac and Anne (Goldsmith) C.; m. Ilene Wasserman, Aug. 2, 1987; 1 child, Aaron. BA, U. Toronto, 1969; PhD, U. Calif., San Diego, 1973. Lic. psychologist, N.Y. Asst. prof. psychology SUNY, Stony Brook, 1976—81, assoc. prof., 1981—85, prof., 1985—2000, leading prof., 2000—. Dir. rsch. and continuing edn. Devel. Disabilities Inst., Smithtown, N.Y., 1976—. Author: In Response to Aggression, 1981, How to Teach Sign Language, 1982, Communication-Based Intervention for Problem Behavior, 1994; author monograph. Recipient Disting. Rsch. award Assn. for Retarded Citizens, Cert. of Commendation, Autism Soc. Am.; Woodrow Wilson fellow. Fellow: APA (Applied Rsch. award in Behavior Analysis); mem.: Autism Soc. Am. (panel profl. advisors), Assn. for Positive Behavior Support (pres. 2003—06). Office: SUNY Dept Psychology Stony Brook NY 11794-2500 Home Phone: 631-751-6508; Office Phone: 631-632-7839. Business E-Mail: edward.carr@sunysb.edu.

CARR, FIRPO WYCOFF, bible scholar, educator, writer; b. LA, Sept. 17, 1954; s. Oscar James and Ophelia Priscilla Carr; m. Mary Bethe Richards, June 17, 1979 (div. Nov. 22, 1989); 1 child, Danielle Corrin. B Info. Sys. Mgmt., U. San Francisco, 1984—86; M in Mgmt., U. Redlands, 1986—88; PhD, Pacific Western U., 1988—90. Adj. prof. U. Phoenix, Los Angeles, Calif., 1994—, UCLA, 1994—; prof. Mt. St. Mary's Coll., Brentwood, Calif., 2002—03. Author: (book) Germany's Black Holocaust: 1890-1945 (Nat. Best Seller, 2004), The Divine Name Controversy (Vol. I), Wicked Words: Poisoned Minds (Nat. Best Seller), Search for the Sacred Name, A History of Jehovah's Witnesses (Nat. Best Seller), Jehovah's Witnesses: African American, Are Gays Really Gay?. Min. Christian Congregation, 1975—2004; bd. dirs. Cri-Help Drug Rehab., North Hollywood, Calif., 1994—2004. Achievements include first to photograph, in color, and digitize pages from the oldest most complete Hebrew Bible located at the time in the Soviet Union; research in biblical manuscripts, written in Hebrew and other ancient languages, known as the Dead Sea Scrolls; discovery of the obscured divine name of God using an advanced IBM computer. Office: Scholar Tech Institute of Research Inc 4067 Hardwick St #330 Lakewood CA 90712 Office Phone: 800-501-2713. Personal E-mail: firpocarr@aol.com.

CARR, GARY THOMAS, lawyer; b. El Reno, Okla., July 25, 1946; s. Thomas Clay and Bobbye Jean (Page) C.; m. Ann Elizabeth Smith, Jan. 5, 1985. AB, Washington U., St. Louis, 1968, BSCE, 1972, JD, 1975. Bar: Mo. 1975, U.S. Dist. Ct. (ea. and we. dists.) Mo. 1975, U.S. Ct. Appeals (8th cir.) 1977, U.S. Ct. Appeals (fed. cir.) 1980, U.S. Ct. Appeals (5th cir.) 1991, U.S. Ct. Fed. Claims, 2004. Jr. ptnr. Bryan, Cave, McPheeters & McRoberts, St. Louis, 1975-83, ptnr., 1984-99. Lectr. law Washington U., 1978-82, adj. prof., 1982-85; sec., dir. Bruton-Stroube Studios, Inc., 1978—. Trustee Parkview Subdiv. Assn., St. Louis, 1982-90, 2003—. 1st lt. U.S. Army, 1968-71, Vietnam. Mem. ABA, Mo. Bar Assn., St. Louis Bar Assn., Order of Coif. Avocations: woodworking, hunting, fishing, automobiles. Office: PO Box 300129 Saint Louis MO 63130-0430 Home Phone: 314-725-3726; Office Phone: 314-725-6464. E-mail: gtc10485@aol.com.

CARR, GERALD FRANCIS, language educator; b. Pitts., Dec. 29, 1930; s. James Patrick and Hannah (Sweeney) C.; m. Irmengard Rauch, June 12, 1965; children: Christopher, Gregory. EdB, Duquesne U., 1958; MA, U. Wis., 1960, PhD, 1968. Instr. in German Duquesne U., Pitts., 1960-62, asst. prof. German, 1964-68; tchg. asst. U. Wis., Madison, 1962-64; asst. prof. German Ea. Ill. U., Charleston, 1968-70, assoc. prof. German, 1970-75, prof. German, 1975-87, Calif. State U., Sacramento, 1987—. Co-editor: Linguistic Method: Essays in Honor of Herbert Penzl, 1979, The Signifying Animal: The Grammar of Language and Experience, 1980, Language Change, 1983, The Semiotic Bridge, 1989, On Germanic Linguistics, 1992, Insights in Germanic Linguistics I, 1995, Insights in Germanic Linguistics II, 1996, Semiotics Around the World, 1996, Essays for Irmengard Rauch, 1998, New Insights in Germanic Linguistics I, 1999, New Insights in Germanic Linguistics II, 2000, New Insights in Germanic Linguistics III, 2002; series editor: Studies in Old Germanic Languages and Literatures, assoc. editor: Interdisciplinary Jour. for Germanic Linguistics and Semiotic Analysis. Cpl. USMC, 1951—54. Dist. tchg. fellow, U. Wis., 1966. Mem. MLA, Internat. Assn. for Semiotic Studies (co-dir. 5th congress 1994), Am. Coun. Tchrs. Fgn. Lang., Semiotic Soc. Am., Am. Assn. Tchrs. of German, Soc. German Philology, Calif. Fgn. Lang. Tchr. Assn., Semiotic Circle Calif., Kappa Phi Kappa, Delta Phi Alpha. Avocations: books, antiques. Office: Calif State U 6000 J St Sacramento CA 95819-2605 Home Phone: 707-746-7480; Office Phone: 916-278-6379.

CARR, GERALD PAUL, retired astronaut, engineer, marketing professional, military officer; b. Denver, Aug. 22, 1932; s. Thomas Ernest and Freda (Wright) C.; divorced; children: Jennifer, Jamee, Jeffrey, John, Jessica, Joshua; m. Patricia Musick, Sept. 14, 1979 BS in Mech. Engring., U. So. Calif., 1954; BS in Aero. Engring., U.S. Naval Postgrad. Sch., 1961; MS in Aero. Engring., Princeton U., 1962; DSc (hon.), St. Louis U., 1976. Registered profl. engr., Tex. Commd. 2d lt. USMC, 1954, advanced through grades to col., 1974, ret., 1975; jet fighter pilot U.S., Mediterranean, Far East, 1956-65; astronaut NASA, Houston, 1966-77; comdr. 3d Skylab Manned Mission, 1973-74; sr. v.p. CAMUS, Inc., Manchester Center, Vt.; ret. Adv. bd. Nat. Space Soc., Space Dermatology Found. Bd. trustees U. of the Ozarks. Recipient Group Achievement award NASA, 1971, Distinguished Service medal, 1974; Gold medal City of Chgo., 1974; Gold medal City of N.Y., 1974; Alumni Merit award U. So. Calif., 1974; Distinguished Eagle Scout award Boy Scouts Am., 1974; Robert J. Collier Trophy, 1974; Robert H. Goddard Meml. trophy, 1975; FAI Gold Space medal; others; inductee Astronaut Hall of Fame, 1997. Fellow Am. Astronautical Soc. (Flight Achievement award 1975); mem. NSPE, Marine Corps Assn., Marine Corps Aviation Assn., Soc. Exptl. Test Pilots, U. So. Calif. Alumni Assn., Tau Kappa Epsilon. Presbyterian. Home and Office: 49 Maple St # 123 Manchester Center VT 05255 Business E-Mail: camusinc@verizon.net.

CARR, GILBERT RANDLE, retired railroad executive; b. Rockford, Ill., Jan. 4, 1928; s. Audra Clifford and Marjorie (Lantz) C.; m. Marion Minnie Heinemann, Mar. 28, 1953; children: John W., James M. BS in Accounting and Mgmt, U. Ill., 1950. With Arthur Andersen & Co., Chgo., 1950—57; with C.& N. W. Transp. Co., 1957-88, comptroller, 1967-79, v.p., comptroller, 1979-88; ret., 1988. Served with AUS, 1946-47. Lutheran. Home: 1425 Linden Ave Park Ridge IL 60068-5545

CARR, GLADYS JUSTIN, publishing executive, consultant, editor, writer; b. NYC; d. Jack and Mollie (Marmor) Carr. BA, MA, Smith Coll.; postgrad., Cornell U. Sr. editor Prentice-Hall, Inc., Englewood Cliffs, NJ, 1969; exec. editor Cowles Comm., Inc., NYC, 1969-71; editl. dir., editor-in-chief Am. Heritage Press, NYC, 1971-75; sr. editor McGraw-Hill, Inc., NYC, 1975-81, editor in chief, editorial dir., chmn. editorial bd., 1981-89, v.p., pub., 1988-89, HarperCollins Pubs., Inc., NYC, 1989-2000; mng. dir. GJ Carr Assocs., NYC, 2000—. Contbr. articles, fiction and poetry to literary and profl. jours. Marjorie Hope Nicholson trustee fellow, Smith Coll., Ford Found., Walter Francis Wilcox fellow, Cornell U. Mem. PEN Am. Ctr., Women's Media Group, Acad. Am. Poets, Poetry Soc. Am., Nat. Arts Club, Exec. and Chemists Club, Smith Coll. Club (N.Y.C.), Phi Beta Kappa. Home and Office: 920 Park Ave New York NY 10028-0208 also: 1 Boulder Ln East Hampton NY 11937-1047

CARR, HAROLD NOFLET, investment company executive; b. Kansas City, Kans., Mar. 14, 1921; s. Noflet B. and Mildred (Addison) C.; m. Mary Elizabeth Smith, Aug. 5, 1944; children: Steven Addison, Hal Douglas, James Taylor, Scott Noflet. BS, Tex. A&M U., 1943; postgrad., Am. U., 1944-46. Asst. dir. route devel. Trans World Airlines, Inc., 1943-47; exec. v.p. Wis. Central Airlines, Inc., 1947-52; mem. firm McKinsey & Co., 1952-54; pres. North Central Airlines, Inc., Mpls., 1954-69, chmn. bd., 1965-79; chmn. Republic Airlines, Inc., 1979-84, chmn. exec. com., 1984-86; chmn. Carr and Assocs., 1986—. Professorial lectr. mgmt. engring. Am. U., 1952-62; mem. bd. nominations Nat. Aviation Hall of Fame; mem. exec. adv. com. Minn. Aviation Hall of Fame. Trustee Tex. A&M Rsch. Found.; mem. pres.'s coun. of advisors Tex. A&M U. Mem. Nat. Aero. Assn., World Bus. Coun., Am. Mgmt. Assn., Nat. Trust Historic Preservation, Pine Beach Peninsula Assn., Am. Econ. Assn., Tex. A&M Former Students Assn., Nat. Aviation Club, Aero Club (Washington),Mpls. Club, Twelfth Man Found. (dir., Coll. Sta., Tex.), Tex. A&M Century Club, Gull Lake Yacht Club (Brainerd, Minn.), Wings Club (N.Y.C.), Stearman Alumnus (Wichita, Kans.), Briarcrest Country Club, Beta Gamma Sigma. Episcopalian. Office Phone: 979-846-1765.

CARR, JAMES GRAY, federal judge; b. Boston, Nov. 14, 1940; s. Edmund Albert and Anna Frances C.; m. Eileen Margaret Glynn, Dec. 17, 1966; children: Maureen M., Megan A., Darrah E., Caitlin E. AB, Kenyon Coll., 1962; LLB, Harvard U., 1966. Bar: Ill. 1966, Ohio 1972, US Dist. Ct. (no. dist.) Ill. 1966, US Dist. Ct. (no. dist.) Ohio 1970, US Supreme Ct. 1980. Assoc. Gardner & Carton, et al., Chgo., 1966-68; staff atty. Cook County Legal Asst. Found., Evanston, Ill., 1968-70; prof. U. Toledo Law Sch., 1970-79; magistrate judge US Dist. Ct. (no. dist.) Ohio, Toledo, 1979-94, judge, 1994—, chief judge, 2005—; judge Fgn. Intelligence Surveillance Ct., 2002—. Adj. prof. law Chgo. Kent Law Sch., 1969, Loyola U., Chgo., 1970; reporter, juvenile rules com. Ohio Supreme Ct., Columbus, 1971-72; reporter, mem. nat. wiretap com. US Congress, Washington, 1976-77. Contbr. articles to profl. law jours. Founder, bd. dirs. Child Abuse Ctr., Toledo, 1970-84; active Lucas County Mental Health Bd., Toledo, 1984-89, Lucas County Children Svcs. Bd., Toledo, 1989-94. Fulbright fellow, 1977-78. Mem. ABA (reporter, elec. survey stds. 1979-80, mem. task force on tech. and law enforcement 1995-99, mem. task force on jury initiatives 1995-98), Toledo Bar Assn. (bd. dirs.), Phi Beta Kappa. Roman Catholic. Office: US Dist Ct 203 US Courthouse 1716 Spielbusch Ave Toledo OH 43624-1363 Office Phone: 419-259-6420. E-mail: james_g_carr@ohnd.uscourts.gov.*

CARR, JAMES REVELL, writer, curator, retired museum director; b. Bryn Mawr, Pa., Aug. 11, 1939; s. Clinton DeWitt and Asta Marie (Knudsen) C.; m. Mary Elizabeth Bump, June 25, 1963 (div. Oct. 1986); children: James Revell III, George McKelvy; m. Barbara Palmer, Apr. 15, 1989. BA, Rutgers U., 1962; MA, U. Pa., 1969. Tchg. asst. U. Pa., Phila., 1968—69; archeologist N.J. State Mus., Trenton, 1968—69; rsch. assoc. Mystic Seaport Mus. Inc., Conn., 1969—70, chief curator, 1970—78, dir., 1978—2001, pres., 1988—2001, dir. emeritus, 2001—. Pres. Internat. Congress Maritime Mus., Liverpool, Eng., 1984-87, Coun. Am. Maritime Mus., 1981-84; trustee Nat. Trust for Historic Preservation, Washington, 1983-92; accreditation commr. Am. Assn. Mus., Washington, 1988-94; chmn. Nat. Maritime Heritage Task Force, Washington, 1981-84. Author: American Ship Portraits, 1976, Seventy Days, 13 Million Tons, 2500 Ships, 50,000 Lives, All Brave Sailors, 2004; contbr. chpts. to books, articles to profl. jours.; TV commentator Operation Sail, WBZ-TV, Boston, 1976, with Peter Jennings on ABC-TV, 1986, Columbus Celebration, Pub. Broadcast Sta., 1992. Corporator Lawrence and Meml. Hosp., New London, Conn., 1979-86; mem. vestry Calvary Ch., Stonington, Conn., 1978-81; mem., sec. Navy Adv. Com. Naval History. Lt. USNR, 1962-67. Mem. Am. Antiquarian Soc., Century Assn., Newcomen Soc. Avocations: running, skiing, sailing. Mailing: 75 Seawood Park Rd New Harbor ME 04554

CARR, JAMES RUSSELL, engineering educator; b. Fairfield, Calif., July 30, 1957; s. Russell Elwood and Elsie Estrid Carr; m. Janice Ivy Freeman, Sept. 4, 1987; children: Anna Elise, Russell James. BS, U. Nev., Reno, 1979; MS, U. Ariz., Tucson, 1981; PhD, U. Ariz., 1983. Cert. profl. engr., State Nev. Bd. Registered Profl. Engrs. and Land, 1987. Asst. prof. U. Mo., Rolla, 1983—86, U. Nev., Reno, 1986—89, assoc. prof., 1989—94, prof., 1994—. Author: (textbook) Numerical Analysis for the Geological Sciences, Data Visualization in the Geosciences. City supr. Washoe-Storey Conservation Dist., Reno, Nev., 2001—05. Recipient Disting. Tchr., U. of Nev., Reno, 1993, President's prize, Internat. Assn. for Math. Geology, 1987. Mem.: Am. Soc. for Photogrammetry and Remote Sensing, Internat. Assn. for Math. Geology. Democrat-Npl. Avocations: hiking, camping, collecting minerals and fossils. Office: Univ of Nevada Reno Mail Stop 172 Reno NV 89557-0138 Home Phone: 775-356-9303; Office Phone: 775-784-4244. Office Fax: 775-784-1833; Home Fax: 775-784-1833. Business E-Mail: carr@unr.edu.

CARR, JAMES T., publishing executive; Grad., U. Miami, Fla., 1985. Account exec. Country Am. mag. Meredith Corp., 1989—91, various positions including NY advt. mgr., 1991—94, advt. dir. Midwest Living, 1995—99, pub. Mature Outlook, 1999—2001, pub. Midwest Living, 2001—05, v.p., pub. Family Circle mag., 2005—. Office: Meredith Corp Family Circle Mag 375 Lexington Ave 9th Fl New York NY 10017-5514 Office Phone: 212-551-7110. Office Fax: 212-499-2000. E-mail: James.Carr@Meredith.com.*

CARR, JEFFREY W., lawyer, manufacturing executive; BA in Govt. and Fgn. Affairs, U. Va.; JD with honors, Georgetown U. Law Ctr. Founder, mgr. Internat. Adv. Svcs. Group, Ltd.; law clk. Judge Schwartz, U.S. Dist. Ct., Del.; atty., internat. trade Willkie Farr & Gallagher, Washington; atty. Wald Harkrader & Ross, Washington; internat. counsel FMC Technologies, Phila., 1993—97, assoc. gen. counsel, energy & airport sys. bus. groups, 1997—2001, v.p., gen. counsel Chgo., 2001—. Office: FMC Technologies 200 E Randolph Dr Chicago IL 60601 Office Phone: 312-861-6000.*

CARR, LARRY DEAN, not-for-profit executive; b. Mt. Vernon, Ill., Apr. 22, 1947; s. Jewell Dean and Mary Janet (Lawrence) C.; m. Kathleen; 1 child, Lisa Diane. BS in Fin., U. Ill., 1969. CPCU. Analyst Allstate Ins. Co., Northbrook, Ill., 1970-75, controller Svc. Rev. Arlington Heights, Ill., 1975-76, regional controller Rochester, NY and Murray Hiil, NJ, 1976-80, exec. info. dir. Northbrook, 1980-82, dir. mktg., 1982-83; v.p. Crum and Forster Personal Ins. Co./U.S. Fire Ins. Co., Basking Ridge, NJ, 1983-84, sr. v.p., 1984-85, exec. v.p., 1985-86, chmn. bd. dirs., pres., CEO, 1986-90, also bd. dirs.; CEO Viking Inc. Co., 1986-90, Nat. Gen. Ins.Co., 1986-91; exec. v.p. Motors Ins. Corp., 1991; pres., CEO Presbyn. Ch. Found., 1993-99; pres., founding dir., chmn. bd. dirs. New Covenant Trust Co., N.A., 1997-99; pres. case mgmt. divsn. Concentra Managed Care, Inc., Waltham, Mass., 2000—02; COO Greater Boston Aid to the Blind, Inc., 2002—03, Jewish Guild for the Blind, 2003—. Treas., bd. dirs. Somerset Hills YMCA, Basking Ridge, 1984-85; trustee Kent Place Sch., 1989-90; mem. adv. bd. Resource Ctr. for Women and Their Families, 1989-90; dir. Jarvie Commonweal Svc., 1994-99, Ky. Shakespeare Festival, 1997, Presbyn. Outlook Found., 2000-06; elder Madison Ave. Presbyn. Ch., 2005—. Served with USAR, 1969-74. Mem. Pres.' Assn., Am. Mgmt. Assn., Delta Sigma Pi. Republican. Presbyterian. Avocations: swimming, skiing. Home Phone: 631-269-2701; Office Phone: 212-712-9957. Business E-Mail: carrl@jgb.org.

CARR, LAWRENCE EDWARD, JR., lawyer; b. Colorado Springs, Colo., Aug. 10, 1923; s. Lawrence Edward and Lelah R. (Rubert) C.; m. Agnes Isabel Dyer, Dec. 26, 1946; children— Mary Lee, James Patrick, Lawrence Edward III, Eileen Louise, Thomas Vincent. BS, U. Notre Dame, 1948, LL.B., 1949; LL.M., George Washington U., 1954. Bar: Colo. 1949, D.C. 1952, Md. 1961. With Travelers Ins. Co., 1949-51; practiced in Washington, 1952—; sr. ptnr. Carr Goodson, PC, Washington, 1984—2001, Carr Maloney, PC, 2001—. Mem. adv. coun. U. Notre Dame Coll. Law, 1985—. With USMCR, 1943-46, 51-52; col. Res.; ret. Fellow Am. Bar Found.; mem. ABA (ho. of dels. 1973-75), Bar Assn. D.C. (dir. 1969-71, pres. 1974-75), D.C. Def. Lawyers Assn. (pres. 1978-79), Bar Assn. D.C. Rsch. Found. (pres. 1985-86). Office: Carr Maloney PC 1615 L St NW Ste 500 Washington DC 20036-5652 Home: 420 Oyster Cove Rd Grasonville MD 21638 Office Phone: 202-310-5501. Personal E-mail: leadcarr@aol.com. Business E-Mail: lec@carmaloney.com.

CARR, LEILA S., bank executive; b. 1961; 2 children. BA in Hist., U. Va., 1983. With First Union Nat. Bank; sr. v.p., dir., Sales, Mktg. and Product Devel. Synovus Fin. Corp., Columbus, Ga., 2000—04, sr. v.p., Retail Banking, 2004—05, exec. v.p., Retail Banking, 2005—. Bd. mem. St. Luke Early Learning Ctr., Girls, Inc., Columbus, Ga. Named one of 25 Women to Watch, US Banker, 2006. Office: Synovus Financial Corp PO Box 120 Columbus GA 31902 Office Phone: 706-649-5850.*

CARR, LES, psychologist, educator; b. Bklyn., Mar. 7, 1935; s. Sam and Sara (Berman) Carr; children: Lincoln Damian, Sharon Rose, Lewis Wade, Faith Theresa. BA, NYU, 1957; MA, New Sch. for Social Rsch., NYC, 1959; PhD, Vanderbilt U., 1963. Diplomate Am. Bd. Med. Psychotherapists (fellow), lic. psychologist Calif., cert. psychologist, R.I. Rsch. and clin. intern Rockland State Hosp., N.Y.C. Dept. Mental Hygiene, 1958-59; cons. clin. psychologist to sr. clin. psychologist Ctrl. State Hosp., Nashville, 1962-64; sr. coord. psychol. svcs. U. R.I., Providence, 1963-68; prof., chmn. psychology dept., dean Summer Sch., Salve Regina Coll., Newport, R.I., 1966-70, v.p. acad. affairs, 1969-71; project dir. Newport Hosp., 1967-71; pres. Lewis U., Lockport, Ill., 1971-76; dean of faculty Columbia Pacific U., San Rafael, Calif., 1977—2000; pres. Columbia Commonwealth U., 2000—. Staff psychologist San Quentin State Prison, 1989—2000, No. Calif. Women's Facility, 2000—03; former ednl. cons. to sultan and min. of edn., Oman. Past chmn. R.I. Gov.'s Task Force on Mental Health Rehab.; chmn. bd. dirs. Sr. U., Richmond, Can.; mem. nat. adv. coun. Profl. Children's Sch., N.Y.C.; past chmn. adv. bd. dirs. Comprehensive Mental Health Ctr., Newport; past bd. dirs. Regional Ballet Soc., Joliet, Ill., R.I. Rehab. Assn.; past chmn. bd. trustees St. Mary's Acad., Nauvoo, Ill.; past mem. exec. com. R.I. Gov.'s Commn. on Vocat. Rehab.; mem. Am. Endurance Ride Conf. With U.S. Army, 1958. Home: 7900 Shenandoah Ln Somerset CA 95684-9597 Office Phone: 530-620-1112. Office Fax: 530-620-6427. E-mail: Elder100@bigplanet.com.

CARR, LLOYD H., college football coach; m. Laurie McCartney; children: Melissa, Brett, Jason, Ryan, Emily, Jarrett. Student, Univ. Mo.; BS in Edn., No. Mich. Univ., 1968, MEd, 1970. Asst. coach Ea. Mich. Univ., 1976—77, Univ. Ill., 1978—79; defensive secondary coach Univ. Mich., 1980—87, defensive coord., 1987—94, also asst. coach, 1990—94, head football coach, 1995—. Mem. bd. NCAA Rules Com. Chmn. WJR/Special Olympics Golf Outing, Mich.; co-chmn. United Way Campaign, Washtenaw Co., 2002. Recipient Paul "Bear" Bryant award, Nat. Sportscasters & Sportswriters Assn., 1997. Mem.: Am. Football Coaches Assn. (mem. bd. trustees). Office: Univ Mich Athletics 1000 So State St Ann Arbor MI 48109-2201

CARR, MARCUS EUGENE, JR., internist; b. Greensboro, NC, Mar. 9, 1949; s. Marcus Eugene and Alsie May (Barham) C.; m. Sarah Martin, Oct. 17, 1975 (div. June 1992); children: Joseph, Jonathan, Ashley, Mary Katherine, Christian, Stephen; m. Sheryl L. Zekert, Nov. 1993. BS in Physics, Davidson Coll., 1971; PhD in Biomed. Engring., U. N.C., 1975, MD, 1979; postgrad, U.S. Army War Coll., 1999. Diplomate Am. Bd. Internal Medicine, Am. Bd. Hematology. Commd. 2nd lt. USAR, 1971, advanced through grades to capt., 1978; ret., 1979; intern N.C. Meml. Hosp., Chapel Hill, 1980-81, jr. resident internal medicine, 1981-82, sr. asst. resident in internal medicine, 1982-83, chief resident, 1983-84; asst. prof. medicine Med. Coll. Va., Richmond, 1985-91, asst. prof. pathology, 1988-91, assoc. prof. pathology, internal medicine, 1991—98; founder, pres. Hemodyne, Inc., Richmond, Va., 1993—; comdr. U.S. Army Hosp., 1995—97, 2000—02; prof. medicine pathology VCU Sch. Medicine, 1998—2005, clin. prof. medicine, 2005—; prof. biomed. engring. VCU Sch. Engring., 2005—; exec. dir. clin. rsch. hemostasis Novo Nordisk, Inc., Princeton, NJ, 2005, v.p. U.S. rsch., 2005—. Tissue and transfusion com., rsch. and devel. com., McGuire V.A. Med. Ctr., M-III med. curriculum com., admissions com. Sch. of Medicine, promotions com. dept. of pathology, Med. Coll. Va.; presenter in field. Contbr. articles to profl. jours. Mem. Richmond Blood Club, Bon Air Bapt. Ch., Richmond. Recommd. maj. M.C., USAR, 1987, advanced to col., 1999, served in Desert Storm, Operation Enduring Freedom, also in Kosovo. Recipient med. student rsch. fellowship, 1977; grantee: So. Med. Assn., 1983, Med. Coll. Va., 1985, A. D. Williams Faculty, 1985, VA Rsch. Adv. Group, 1985, '86. 88-91,

Massey Ctr. Instl. grant 1987-88, Burroughs-Wellcome , 1989, 90-91, 92—. Fellow Am. Heart Assn., Am. Coll. Physicians, Am. Coll. Angiology, Internat. Coll. Angiology, Internat. Coll. Hematology; mem. Am. Coll. Physicians, Am. Soc. Hematology, Am. Fedn. Clin. Rsch. (coun. on thrombosis), Am. Heart Assn., Internat. Soc. Thrombosis and Haemostasis, Internat. Soc. Exptl. Hematology, Nat. Haemophelia Found., N.Y. Acad. Scis., Assn. Military Surgeons of U.S., So. Soc. Clin. Investigation, Am. Soc. Clin. Pathologists, Internat. Fibrinogen Rsch. Soc., Sigma Xi. Achievements include patents in field of hematology. Home: 12 Appaloosa Trl Holland PA 18966-2593 Office: Novo Nordisk Inc 100 Coll Rd W Princeton NJ Personal E-mail: mecarrjr@msn.com. Business E-Mail: mcrr@novonordisk.com.

CARR, OSCAR CLARK, III, lawyer; b. Apr. 9, 1951; s. Oscar Clark Carr Jr. and Billie (Fisher) Carr Houghton; m. Mary Leatherman, Aug. 4, 1973; children: Camilla Fisher, Oscar Clark V. BA in English with distinction, U. Va., 1973; JD with distinction, Emory U., 1976. Bar: Tenn. 1976, U.S. Dist. Ct. (we. dist.) Tenn. 1977, (no. dist.) Miss. 1977, U.S. Ct. Appeals (6th cir.) 1985, (5th cir.) 1995, U.S. Dist. Ct. (so. dist.) Miss. 2000; cert. mediator Tenn. Assoc. Glankler Brown, PLLC (formerly Glankler, Brown, et al, Memphis, 1976-82, ptnr., 1982—, chief mgr., 1998-00. Mem. Emory Law Coun., 2004—. Treas., vestryman St. John's Episcopal Ch., Memphis, 1988—91, sr. warden, 1991; mem. Commn. on Ministry Diocese of West Tenn., 1987—90; King of Carnival Memphis, 1994; bd. dirs. West Tenn. chpt. Juvenile Diabetes Found., 1998—2004, dir., 1998—2002; bd. dirs. Memphis Ballet Soc., 1980, Memphis-Shelby County Unit Am. Cancer Soc., Memphis Oral Sch. Deaf, 1988—91, Carnival Memphis. Recipient Living and Giving award, West Tenn. chpt. Juvenile Diabetes Rsch. Found., 2002. Fellow Tenn. Bar Found., Litig. Counsel Am.; mem. ABA, Tenn. Bar Assn. (we. dist. coun. environ. law 1992-2000), Memphis-Shelby County Bar Assn. (bd. dirs. 1985-87), Memphis Country Club (atty. 2004-), Lawyers Jour. Club of Memphis. Office: Glankler Brown PLLC 1700 One Commerce Sq Memphis TN 38103 Office Phone: 901-525-1322. Business E-Mail: ocarr@glankler.com.

CARR, PATRICIA ANN, community health nurse; b. Teaneck, NJ, Dec. 6, 1949; d. John O. and Elizabeth (Nestor) Olsen. Diploma, Mt. Sinai Hosp. Sch. Nursing, NYC, 1970. RN, Ga., Fla.; AIDS cert. RN; cert. clin. rsch. coord. Asst. DON Taylor Meml. Hosp., Hawkinsville, Ga., 1979-81; staff nurse ICU Shands Teaching Hosp., Gainesville, Fla., 1981-82; staff nurse Venice Hosp., 1982-84; field nurse Fla. Home Health Svcs. Sarasota Inc., 1986-93; regulatory compliance coord. Fla. Home Health Svcs., Sarasota, 1993-96; program clin. coord. Cmty. AIDS Network, Inc., Sarasota, 1996-98; clin. studies coord. Infectious Diseases Assocs., Sarasota, 1998—. Contbr. articles to publs. Mem. APHA, Assn. Nurses in AIDS Care, Home Health Nurses Assn., Intravenous Nurses Soc., Assn. Practitioners in Infection Control, Assn. Clin. Rsch. Profls. Office: Infectious Diseases Assocs 1425 S Osprey Ave Ste 1 Sarasota FL 34239-2900 Office Phone: 941-366-0776. Personal E-mail: patcarr2@verizon.net.

CARR, PETER WILLIAM, chemistry professor; b. Bklyn., Aug. 16, 1944; s. Peter V. and Kathleen T. Carr; m. Leah Phillips, 1966; children: Sean, Erin, Kelly. BS in Chemistry, Polytech Inst. Bklyn., 1965; PhD in Analytical Chemistry, Pa. State U., 1969. Rsch. asst., assoc. Brookhaven Nat. Lab., 1965, 66; postdoctoral assoc. Stanford U. Med. Sch., 1968; faculty mem. U. Ga., 1969-77; prof. chemistry U. Minn., 1977—. Cons. Leeds and Northrup, Hewlett Packard, 3M Co., Cabot Inc.; pres. ZirChrom Separations, Inc., 1995-2002; pres. Symposium Analytical Chemistry in Environment, 1976. Mem. editl. adv. bd. Analytical Chemistry, Talanta, Jour. Chromatography, LC/GC, Chromatographia, Separation Sci. and Tech.; contbr. over 350 articles to profl. jours. Recipient L.S. Palmer award Minn. Chromatography Forum, 1984, Benedetti-Pichler award Am. Microchem. Soc., 1990, award in Fields Analytical Chemistry Ea. Analytical Symposium, 1993, S. Nogare award Del. Valley Chromatography Forum, 1996, award in chromatography ISCO, 1997, award in separation sci. Ea. Analytical Symposium, 2000, Pitts. Conference award in analytical chemistry, 2004. Mem. Am. Chem. Soc. (chmn. subdivsn. chromatography and separation sci. of Analytical Chemistry divsn. 1988-89, Chromatography award 1997), Minn. Chromatography Forum. Office: U Minn Dept Chemistry 207 Pleasant St SE Minneapolis MN 55455-0431 Office Phone: 612-624-0253. Business E-Mail: carr@chem.umn.edu.

CARR, RICHARD WILLIAM, federal program manager; b. Montgomery, Ala., Aug. 16, 1944; s. Walter Thomas Jr. and Maude Carr; m. Susan Lane Seckman, Sept. 30, 1967; 1 child, Richard II. AA in Computer Sci. and Elec. Engring., Miami-Dade Coll., 1972. Cert. Internet security specialist. Fed. computer/network sys. analyst Fed. Comms. Commn., Washington, 1972-79; fed. dir. info. tech. security Gen. Svcs. Adminstrn., Washington, 1979-85; fed. info. tech. project mgr. Dept. Justice, Washington, 1985-86; fed. info. tech. security program mgr. Dept. Energy, Germantown, Md., 1986-89, NASA, Washington, 1989—2003. Charter and founding mem. steering com. Forum of Incident Response and Security Teams, Washington, 1992-94; mem. Presdl. Com. on Nat. Security Telecomms. and Info. Sys. Security, Washington, 1986-94; mem. Presdl. Info. Infrastructure Task Force, Washington, 1993-96; mem. Nat. Security Policy Bd., Wash., 1993-96; mem. Sr. Fed. Adv. Coun. on Advanced Info. Tech. Security R&D Issues, Washington, 2000-03. Recipient Unsung Hero of Computer Security award Fed. Computer week, Congress, OMB (Office of Mgmt. and Budget Exec. Office of the Pres.), NIST (Nat. Inst. of Standards and Tech.), 1991. Mem. Ops. Security Profls. Soc. Achievements include founded first centralized IT security vulnerability and incident handling capability in the federal government; established and directed NASA's first IT security incident response center. Home: PO Box 472 Polk City FL 33868-0472 Personal E-mail: rcarr1@peoplepc.com.

CARR, RUTH MARGARET, plastic surgeon; b. Waco, Tex., July 2, 1951; MD, U. Okla., 1977. Intern U. Okla. Med. Sch., Oklahoma City, 1977-78; resident U. Okla. Health Sci. Ctr., Oklahoma City, 1978-81, UCLA, 1981-83; plastic surgeon St. John's Hosp., 1989—. Clin. asst. prof. UCLA, 1983—, U. So. Calif., 1984-. Mem.: Bay Surgical Soc. (pres. 2004), Calif. Soc. Plastic Surgeons (parliamentarian 2004—05), Am. Soc. Plastic Surgeons. Office: 1301 20th St Ste 470 Santa Monica CA 90404-2082 Home Phone: 310-284-8321; Office Phone: 310-315-0222. Business E-Mail: rcarr@ucla.edu.

CARR, SCOTT, technology educator; b. Doylestown, Pa., Feb. 16, 1969; s. Dale J. and Lillian M. (Knight) Carr; m. Nancy L. Caruso. BA in Psychology, Temple U., Phila., 1993. Counselor Voyage House, Phila., 1992—94; lab. coord. Nat. Disease Rsch. Interchange, Phila., 1995—99; instrnl. tech. specialist St. Joseph's U., Phila. Mem.: ICIA, Mensa. Avocations: astronomy, genealogy, stamp collecting/philately, cooking. Office: Tapehiss Recordings PO Box 525 Glenside PA 19038 Home Phone: 215-886-8306; Office Phone: 215-886-8306. Business E-Mail: scott@tapehissrecordings.com.

CARR, STEPHEN HOWARD, materials engineer, educator; b. Dayton, Ohio, Sept. 29, 1942; s. William Howard and Mary Elizabeth (Clement) C.; m. Virginia W. McMillan, June 24, 1967; children: Rosamond Elizabeth, Louisa Ruth. BS, U. Cin., 1965; MS, Case Western Res. U., 1967, PhD, 1970. Coop. engr. Inland divsn. GM, Dayton, 1960-65; asst. prof. materials sci. and engring. and chem. engring. Northwestern U., Evanston, Ill., 1970-73, assoc. prof., 1973-78, prof., 1978—, dir. Materials Rsch. Ctr., 1984-90, asst. dean engring., 1991-93, assoc. dean engring., 1993—. Cons. in field. Contbr. articles to profl. jours. Recipient Outstanding Alumni Achievement award U. Cin. Coll. Engring., 1993. Fellow Am. Soc. for Metals Internat., Am. Phys. Soc.; mem. AIChE, Soc. Automotive Engrs. (Ralph R. Teetor award 1980), Plastics Inst. Am. (Ednl. Svc. award 1975), Am. Chem. Soc., Soc. Plastics Engrs., Materials Rsch. Soc. Achievements include patents in plastics and textiles fields. Home: 2704 Harrison St Evanston IL 60201-1216 Office: Northwestern U 2145 Sheridan Rd Evanston IL 60208-0834 Business E-Mail: s-carr@northwestern.edu.

CARR, THOMAS A., lawyer; BA in Sociology, St. John's U., NY, 1979; JD with highest honors, NY Law Sch., 1984. Former asst. US atty., NY; former partner Barrett, Gilman & Ziker; city atty. Seattle, 2001—. Mem. King County Bd. Developmentally Disabled, Wash., 1995—97, Metro S.W. Sounding Bd., Wash., 1997—98, Elevated Transp. Co. Coun., Seattle, 1998—, chmn., 1998—2001; mem. King County Metro Transit Adv. Com., 1999—. Mem.: King County Bar Assn. Office: 600 4th Ave 4th Fl PO Box 94769 Seattle WA 98124-4769 E-mail: thomas.carr@seattle.gov.

CARR, TRACY A., musician, educator; d. Raymond H. and Naomi B. Carr. MusB, U. R.I., 1987; MusM, Miami U., Oxford, Ohio, 1990; D of Musical Arts, U. So. Calif., 1994. Assoc. prof. music Ea. N.Mex U., Portales, 1999—. Oboist Trio Encantada, Portales, N.Mex., 1999—, Eisenstadt Classical Music Festival Orch., 2007—. Musician: (solo, chamber, orchestral musician) various national and international performances. Mem.: Am. Musicological Soc., Coll. Music Soc., Internat. Double Reed Soc. Office: Music Ea NMex Univ Station 16 Portales NM 88130 Home Phone: 505-356-6539; Office Phone: 505-562-2681. Personal E-mail: tracy.carr@enmu.edu.

CARR, WALTER JAMES, JR., research physicist, consultant; b. Knob Noster, Mo., May 6, 1918; s. Walter James and Alice Frances (Koch) C.; m. Winifred Walker Schultz, Mar. 21, 1953; children: James Lawrence, Robert David. BSEE, U. Mo., Rolla, 1940; MEE, Stanford U., 1942; DSc in Physics, Carnegie-Mellon U., 1951. Engr. Westinghouse Electric R&D, Pitts., 1942-51, section mgr., 1951-57, adv. physicist, 1957-65, mgr. solid state theory, 1965-70, cons., 1970-85; ind. cons. Pitts., 1985—. Physicist Atomic Energy Establishment, Harwell, Eng., 1962. Author: AC Loss and Macroscopic Theory of Superconductors, 1983, 2d edit., 2001. Named to Acad. Elec. Engring., U. Mo., Rolla, 1981. Fellow: IEEE, Am. Phys. Soc.; mem.: Pitts. Athletic Assn. Avocation: tennis. Home: 1460 Jefferson Heights Rd Pittsburgh PA 15235-5220 Business E-Mail: wjamescarrjr@att.net.

CARR, WALTER STANLEY, lawyer; b. Chgo., May 5, 1945; s. Robert Adams and Margaret (Wiley) C.; m. Mary Baine, Sept. 20, 1969. BS, U. Pa., 1967; JD, U. Chgo., 1970. Bar: Ill. 1970. From assoc. to ptnr. McDermott, Will & Emery, Chgo., 1970-86; v.p. Miami Corp., Chgo., 1987—. Pres. Hull House Assn., Chgo., 1989; bd. dirs. Planned Parenthood Assn. Chgo. Area, 1980—. Mem. ABA, Ill. Bar Assn., Chgo. Bar Assn., Chgo. Estate Planning Council. Clubs: Univ. (Chgo.). Home: 507 W Briar Pl Chicago IL 60657-4633 Office: Miami Corp 410 N Michigan Ave Ste 590 Chicago IL 60611-4252

CARR, WILLARD ZELLER, JR., retired lawyer; b. Richmond, Ind., Dec. 18, 1927; s. Willard Zeller and Susan (Brownell) C.; m. Margaret Paterson, Feb. 15, 1952; child: Jeffrey Westcott. BS, Purdue U., 1948; JD, Ind. U., 1951. Bar: Calif. 1951, U.S. Supreme Ct. 1963. Ptnr. Gibson, Dunn & Crutcher, Los Angeles, 1952—. Mem. nat. panel arbitrators Am. Arbitration Assn.; former labor relations cons. State of Alaska; lectr. bd. visitors Southwestern U. Law Sch.; mem. adv. council Southwestern Legal Found., Internat. and Comparative Law Ctr. Trustee Calif. Adminstrv. Law Coll.; bd. dirs. Employers' Group, Calif. State Pks. Found., L.A. coun. Boy Scouts Am.; mem. Mayor's Econ. Devel. Policies Com.; past chmn. Pacific Legal Found.; past chmn. men's adv. com. Los Angeles County-U. So. Calif. Med. Ctr. Aux. for Recruitment, Edn. and Service; past chmn. bd. Wilshire Republican Club; past mem. Rep. State Ctrl. Com.; past mem. pres.'s coun. Calif. Mus. Sci. and Industry; mem. Nat. Def. Exec. Res., L.A. World Affairs Coun.; chmn. bd. councilors Andrus Sch. Gerontology, U. So. Calif.; bd. dirs., sec. L.A. Police Meml. Found.; past chmn. L.A. sect. United Way; mem. adv. com. Los Angeles County Human Rels. Commn., past commr., Calif. State World Trade Commn.; former chmn. L.A. chpt. ARC. Fellow Am. Bar Found.; mem. Internat. Bar. Assn. (past chmn. labor law com. of bus. law sect., past chmn. labor employment practice group), The Federalist Soc., Calif. Bar Assn., L.A. County Bar Assn., L.A. C. of C. (past chmn. 1980), Calif. C. of C. (past chmn., 1991) Office: Gibson Dunn & Crutcher 333 S Grand Ave 49th Fl Los Angeles CA 90071-3197 Office Phone: 213-229-7238. Business E-Mail: wcarr@gibsondunn.com.

CARR, WINIFRED WALKER, artist, historian; b. Shanghai, June 8, 1925; d. Lawrence Henry Schultz and Ann Winifred Walker; m. Walter James Carr, Mar. 21, 1953; children: James Lawrence, Robert David. BFA, Carnegie Mellon U., 1948. Lectr. AAUW, Pitts., 1960—. One-woman shows include (Alumna of Yr. award, 1992). Vol. schs., YWCA, galleries, mus., Pitts., 1953—2000; arranger polit. awareness programs AAUW, Pitts., 1994—2004. Mem.: AAUW (pres. 2004—06). Democrat. Unitarian. Home: 1460 Jefferson Heights Rd Pittsburgh PA 15235 Home Phone: 412-824-3456. E-mail: wjamescarrjr@att.net.

CARRABBA, CHRISTOPHER ENDER, singer; b. West Hartford, Conn., Apr. 10, 1975; Lead singer The Vacant Andies, Further Seems Forever, 1998—2001; founder & singer Dashboard Confessional, 1997—. Singer: (albums) (with Dashboard Confessional) The Swiss Army Romance, 2000, The Places You Have Come to Fear the Most, 2001, A Mark, a Mission, a Brand, a Scar, 2003, Dusk & Summer, 2006, (with Further Seems Forever) The Moon is Down, 2001. Office: c/o Vagrant Records Ste 361 2118 Wilshire Blvd Santa Monica CA 90403*

CARRABBA, JOSEPH A., mining executive; BS, Capital Univ.; MBA, Frostburg State Univ. Mgmt. positions Rio Tinto plc, 1983—2000; gen. mgr. bauxite ops. Comalco Aluminum (Rio Tinto plc), 2000—03; pres., COO Diavik Diamond Mines (Rio Tinto plc), 2003—05, Cleveland-Cliffs Inc., Cleve., 2005—06, pres., CEO, 2006—07, chmn., pres., CEO, 2007—. Bd. dir. Newmont Mining Co. Office: Cleveland-Cliffs Inc 1100 Superior Ave Cleveland OH 44114*

CARRADINE, DAVID, actor, director; b. Hollywood, Calif., Dec. 8, 1936; s. John Arthur Carradine; m. Donna Lee Becht, Dec. 1960 (div.); 1 child, Calista Miranda; m. Linda Gilbert Feb. 2, 1977 (div. 1983); 1 child, Kansas; m. Gail Jensen Dec. 4, 1988 (div. 1997); m. Coco d'Este Feb. 20, 1998 (div. Dec. 12, 2001); m. Annie Bierman Dec. 26, 2004. Attended, Oakland Jr. Coll., San Francisco State Coll. TV appearances in: series Shane, 1966, Kung Fu, 1972, Kung Fu, The Legend Continues, 1993-97; others; TV films include Maybe I'll Come Home in the Spring, 1971, Mr. Horn, 1978, Gaugin the Savage, 1980, High Noon, Part II: The Return of Will Kane, 1980, A Distant Scream, 1983, Jealousy, 1984, North and South, 1985, The Bad Seed, 1985, Oceans of Fire, 1986, North and South II, 1986, Kung Fu the Movie, 1986, Six Against the Rock, 1987, I Saw What You Did, 1987, The Cover Girl and the Cop, 1988, Deadly Surveillance, 1991, Luck of the Draw: The Gambler Returns, 1991, Brotherhood of the Gun, 1991, Last Stand at Saber River, 1997, Lost Treasure of Dos Santos, 1997, Martian Law, 1998, Nosferatu: The First Vampire, 1998, By Dawn's Early Light, 2000, Largo Winch: The Heir, 2001, Warden of Red Rock, 2001, The Defectors, 2001, Out of the Wilderness, 2001, The Outsider, 2002; Broadway plays The Deputy, 1963, The Royal Hunt of the Sun, 1965; motion pictures include Taggart, 1965, Bus Riley's Back In Town, 1965, Too Many Thieves, The Violent Ones, 1967, Heaven With A Gun, 1969, Young Billy Young, 1969, The Good Guys and the Bad Guys, 1969, The McMasters, 1970, Macho Callahan, 1970, Boxcar Bertha, 1972, Mean Streets, 1972, The Long Goodbye, 1973, Death Race 2000, 1975, Cannonball, 1976, Bound for Glory, 1976, Thunder and Lightning, 1977, The Serpent's Egg, 1977, Fast Charlie - The Moonbeam Rider, 1978, Gray Lady Down, 1978, Deathsport, 1978, The Silent Flute, 1978, Circle of Iron, 1979, Cloud Dancer, 1980, The Long Riders, 1980, Safari 3000, 1981, "Q", 1981, Trick or Treat, 1982, Lone Wolf McQuade, 1983; The Warrior and the Sorceress, 1984, Rio Abajo, 1984, POW: The Escape, 1986, Armed Response, 1986, Tropical Snow, 1986, The Misfit Brigade, 1986, Marathon, 1987, Project Eliminator, 1989, Crime Zone, 1989, Nowhere to Run, 1989, Night Children, 1989, Wizards of the Lost Kingdom II, 1989, Sundown, 1989, Sauf votre respect, 1989, Fatal Secret, 1990, Midnight Fear, 1990, Sonny Boy, 1990, Think Big, 1990, Bird on a Wire, 1990, Martial Law, 1990, Dune Warriors, 1991, Future Zone, 1991, Future Force, 1992, Evil Toons, 1992, Night Rhythms, 1992, Roadside Prophets, 1992, Double Trouble, 1992, Animal Instincts, 1992, Distant Justice, 1992, Field of Fire, 1992, Waxwork II: Lost in Time, 1992, Omega Cop II: The Challenge, 1993, Kill Zone, 1993, Dead Center, 1994, Macon County Jail, 1997, Full Blast, 1997, The New Swiss Family Robinson, 1998, The Effects of Magic, 1998, Sublet, 1998, Lovers and Liars, 1998, Light Speed, 1998, Knocking on Death's Door, 1999, Zoo, 1999, Shepherd, 1999, Dangerous Curves, 2000, Natural Selection, 2000, Down 'n Dirty, 2000, The Donor, 2000, G.O.D., 2001, Wheatfield with Crows, 2002, Bala perdida, 2002, Kill Bill: Vol. 1, 2003, American Reel, 2003, Kill Bill: Vol. 2, 2004, (voice) Hair High, 2004, Last Goodbye, 2004, Max Havoc: Curse of the Dragon, 2004, Brothers in Arms, 2005, Miracle at Sage Creek, 2005, Last Hour, 2006, The Last Sect, 2006, Final Move, 2006, Homo Erectus, 2007, Epic Movie, 2007; Off-Broadway The Transgressor Rides Again, 1969, The Ballad of Johnnny Pot, 1970; director You & Me, 1975, Americana, 1981; Author: Spirit of Shaolin, David Carradine's Tai Chi Workout, Endless Highway, 1995. Office: Encanta Entertainment care Camden Agy PO Box 1836 Studio City CA 91614-0836*

CARRADINE, KEITH IAN, actor, singer, composer; b. San Mateo, Calif., Aug. 8, 1949; s. John Richmond Reed and Sonia (Sorel) C.; m. Sandra Will, Feb. 6, 1982, 2 daughters: Martha Campbell Plimpton, Sorel; 1 son, Cade Richmond. Student in drama, Colo. State U., 1967. Appeared on Broadway in Hair, 1969-70, L.A. prodn., 1969, Foxfire, 1982-83 (Outer Critics Circle award 1983), L.A. prodn., 1985-86, The Will Rogers Follies, 1991-92 (Tony nomination best performance leading actor in a musical 1991), Dirty Rotten Scoundrels, 2006; N.Y. Shakespeare Festival prodn. Wake Up, It's Time to go to Bed, 1979; film appearances include: A Gunfight, 1970, McCabe and Mrs. Miller, 1970, Idaho Transfer, 1971, Grasslands, 1971, Emperor of the North, 1972, Antoine and Sebastian, 1973, Joe and Margherito, 1973, Thieves Like Us, 1973, Nashville, 1975 (Acad. and Golden Globe awards, Best Original Song for "I'm Easy" 1975), Lumiere, 1975, (also contbr. music) Welcome to L.A., 1976, Old Boyfriends, 1976, The Duellists, 1977, Pretty Baby, 1978, An Almost Perfect Affair, 1979, The Long Riders, 1980, Southern Comfort, 1981, Choose Me, 1983, Maria's Lovers, 1984 (lyricist Maria's Story), Trouble in Mind, 1986, The Inquiry, 1986, Backfire, 1986, The Moderns, 1987, Street of No Return, 1988, Cold Feet, 1988, The Bachelor, 1989, Daddy's Dyin, Who's Got the Will?, 1990, Criss Cross, 1991, The Ballad of the Sad Cafe, 1991, Andre, 1994, Wild Bill, 1994, The Tie That Binds, 1994, 2 Days in the Valley, 1995, A Thousand Acres, 1996, Standoff, 1998, The Hunter's Moon, 1999, Out of the Cold, 1999, The Hunters Moon, 1999, Cahoots, 2000, The Angel Doll, 2000, Wooly Boys, 2001, Mending Fences, 2002, Falcons, 2002; TV films include: Man on a String, 1972, The Godchild, 1974, Scorned and Swindled, 1984, Blackout, 1984, A Winner Never Quits, 1985, Half a Lifetime, 1985, Eye on the Sparrow, 1987, Stones for Ibarra, 1987, My Father, My Son, 1988, The Revenge of Al Capone, 1988, The Forgotten, 1989, Confessional, 1989, Judgment, 1990, Payoff, 1990, Is There Life Out There?, 1994, Journey to Mars, 1995, Trial by Fire, 1995, The Last Stand At Saber River, 1996, The Oath, 1996, Keeping The Promise, 1997, Hard Time: Hostage Hotel, 1999, Enslavement: The True Story of Fanny Kemble, 2000, Baby, 2000, The Diamond Jeru, 2001, The Outsider, 2002, Monte Walsh, 2003, Coyote Waits, 2003(TV series) Outreach, 1999, Metropolis, 2001, Deadwood, 2004, Complete Savages, 2004; (mini-series) A Rumour of War, 1980, Chiefs, 1983 (Emmy award nominee 1983), Murder Ordained, 1986, Confessional, 1989, In the Best of Families: Bitter Blood, 1994, Dead Man's Walk, 1995, (pilot movie) Last Chance, 1995; narrations include: Hot on the Trail: The Untold West, 1993, Baseball Documentary Series, 1994, The West Documentary Series, 1995, Sirens, 1999; (composer TV) Willa, 1979; (prodr.) The Forgotten, 1989; albums include: I'm Easy, 1976, Lost and Found, 1978. Presented a star on Hollywood Walk of Fame, 1993. Mem. Acad. Motion Picture Arts and Scis., Greenpeace Found., Cousteau Soc., Sierra Club. Democrat. Episcopalian.

CARRAHER, MARY LOU CARTER, art educator; b. Cin., Mar. 9, 1927; d. John Paul and Martha Leona (Williams) Carter; m. Emmett Carraher, Nov. 6, 1943 (div. July 1970); children: Candace Lou Holsenbeck-Smith, Michael Emmett (dec.), Cathleen C. Kruska. Student, U. Cin., 1946-48, Calif. State U., 1973-74. Lifetime credential in adult edn.: art, ceramics, crafts, Calif. Substitute tchr. Cobb County Schs., Smyrna, Ga., 1961-63; art tchr. pvt. lessons Canyon Country, Calif., 1968-72; adult edn. art tchr. Wm. S. Hart HS Dist., Santa Clarita, Calif., 1973-97; children's art and calligraphy cmty. svcs. Coll. of the Canyons, Santa Clarita, Calif., 1976-96. Fine arts coord. Santa Clarita Sr. Ctr., 1998—; founder, bd. dirs. Santa Clarita Art Guild, 1972-80; art dir. European tours Continental Club, Canyon Country, 1977-81; art tour guide, travel cons. Northridge Travel, Calif., 1981-91; vol. art tchr. stroke patients Henry Newhall Meml. Hosp., Valencia, Calif., 1993-96; craft tchr. for respite care program, Newhall, Calif., 1995-96, Respite Care Ctr., Santa Clarita Valley Sr. Ctr., 1995-96; Celebration of Life vol. Am. Cancer Soc., 2006—. Artist, author History of Moreland School District, San Jose, Calif., 1965; exhibitions include Art Walk, Arts Coun., 2002—, Represented in permanent collections Paintings for each season of Church Year, 1970's, Sr. Ctr. Watercolors Ctr. Scenes, Watercolors of Christmas Charity Home Tour, Henry Mayo Newhall Meml. Hosp., Christian Ch. and Sr. Ctr. Tchr., Santa Clarita United Meth. Ch., 1966-96; judge for art contests and exhibits, Santa Clarita, 1973-96; leader art tours to Spain, 1997, 99, 2002, Italy, 2001, Portugal, 2002, Australia, New Zealand and Fiji, 2003, Budapest, Hungary, 2007; designer certs. with scenes of Sr. Ctr., Cir. of Friends certs; leader art tour Rhine River Cruise, France, 2003-2004, Rhone River Tour, 2003-04, Budapest to Black Sea, 2007. Recipient Bravo award nomination for Outstanding Achievement in Art, 1995, Sr. of Yr. Santa Clarita Valley Sr. Ctr. and Svc. Newspaper "The Signal", 1995, Christian Svc. award Santa Clarita United Meth. Ch., 1988; invited by Citizen Amb. Program of People to People Internat. to join US del. to assess bus. and trade opportunities of the craft industry in China. Mem. Santa Clarita Valley Arts Coun., Hosp. Home Tour League, Nat. Women in the Arts (charter, Washington). Republican. Methodist. Avocations: travel, art, reading.

CARRAHER, SHAWN MICHAEL, investment company executive, management educator; b. Kansas City, Kans., Nov. 9, 1966; s. Charles E. and Loyalea Velda (Zimmerman) C.; m. Sarah Carlene Laine, July 6, 2001; children: Shawn Michael, Charles. BBA with honors, Fla. Atlantic U., 1987; MBA, U. Cin., 1988; PhD, U. Okla., 1992. Delivery specialist Dayton Daily News, Beavercreek, Ohio, 1980-85; pres., owner Carraher & Sons, Beavercreek, 1982-87; tchr. U. Kans., Lawrence, 1988; rschr. Fla. Atlantic U., Boca Raton, 1989-90, U. Okla., Norman, 1990-92; vis. asst. prof. U. Wis., Milw., 1992-94; assoc. prof. Calif. State U., Chico, 1994-95, Ind. State U., Terre Haute, 1995-98, Ind. U., Bloomington, 1998-2000; prof. mgmt. and global entrepreneurship Tex. A&M U., Commerce,

2000—04; Virginia Brewczynski Endowed chair entrepreneurial studies, dir. Ctr. Emerging Tech. and Entrepreneurial Studies, Cameron U.; prof. mgmt. and global entrepreneurship Cameron U., Lawton, Okla., 2004—. Pres. Carraher & Carraher Cons. Group, 1997—; cons. City of Norman, 1990-91, USAF, 1990-92, Pratt & Whitney, West Palm Beach, Fla., 1990; spkr. at more than 600 profl. presentations on goal-setting and mgmt. devel., including U. Okla., Norman, 1992; dir. Internat. Family Bus. Ctr., Tex. A&M U., 2002— Author: (12 video tapes) Industrial Psychology, 1992; contbr. 80 articles to profl. jours. Pres. Christians In Action, Beavercreek, 1984-85; treas. Campus Crusade for Christ, Norman, 1991-92 Shuman fellow U. Okla., 1991; recipient Outstanding Reviewer award for Careers Divsn. of the Acad. of Mgmt., SW Acad. Mgmt. Disting. Reviewer award, 1997, 2000, Midwest Acad. Mgmt. Disting. Reviewer award, 2000, Southern Mgmt. Assn. Outstanding Reviewer award, 2000, Outstanding Educator award internat. divsn. US Assn. Small Bus. and Entrepreneurship, 2004. Mem. Acad. Mgmt. (chair elect 2000-01), Am. Ednl. Rsch. Assn., Am. Psychol. Soc., So. Mgmt. Assn.(bd. dir. 2000-03, program chmn., 2002-03, chmn. mgmt. history and future trends track), S.W. Acad. Mgmt (rep at large 1998-2001, program chair elect, 2001-02, pres. 2004-05), U.S. Assn. Small Bus. and Entrepreneurship (program chair, chair elect, sec. 2000-01, program chair internat. divsn., 2001-02, pres. 2006—. Fulbright sr. specialist 2002, 2004, Outstanding Educator award), Acad. Internat. Bus., Internat. Small Bus. Inst. Assn. (pres.), Acad. Internat. Bus. (chmn. international mgmt. and bus. track, asst. v.p. program chair, divns. chmn., 2002-03, competitive papers chmn., 2003—) Avocations: research, speaking on goal-setting, martial arts, weight-lifting, cooking. Home: 5012 Malcolm Rd Lawton OK 73505 Office: Ctr Emerging Tech and Entrepreneurship Studies Sch Bus Cameron U 2800 W Gore Blvd Lawton OK 73505 Business E-Mail: scarraher@cameron.edu.

CARRANZA, JOVITA, federal agency administrator, retired delivery service executive; b. Chgo., June 29, 1949; m. Joel Roque; 1 child, Klaudene. Undergraduate, U. Miami, Calif. State U., LA; MBA for exec., U. Miami. Night-shift hub clerk UPS, LA, 1976; supr. UPS, Metro LA Hub Oper., 1976—79; human resources supr. UPS, Metro LA, 1979—85, workforce planning mgr., 1985—87, bus. mgr., 1987; dist. human resources mgr. UPS, Cent. Tex., 1987—90, UPS, Ill., 1990—91, divsn. mgr. hub, packer, and feeder opers. Ill., 1991—93, ctrl. Fla. dist. mgr., 1993—96, divsn. mgr. hub, packer, and feeder opers. Wis., 1996—99, mgr. Am. regions (including Mexico, PR, Dominican Rep., Virgin Islands), 1999—2000, region mgr. internat. opers. Miami, 2000—03, v.p. air ops. Louisville, 2003—06; dep. adminstr. SBA (Small Bus. Adminstrn.), Washington, 2006—. Vol. Habitat for Humanity; bd. mem. Libr. Found., Louisville. Named Woman Yr., Hispanic Bus. Mag., 2004; named one of 50 Most Important Hispanics in Tech. & Bus., Hispanic Engr. & Info. Tech. mag., 2005. Mem.: Nat. Coun. La Raza. Achievements include first female internat. region pres. in UPS history; highest ranking Hispanic female at UPS; expanded UPS in Latin Am. Office: SBA 409 3rd St SW Rm 7000 Washington DC 20416*

CARRASCO, JOSÉ ANÍBAL, recreational therapist; b. San Juan, Sept. 11, 1964; s. Aníbal Carrasco and Rosa Margarita Ayala; m. Nora Liz O'Neill, Oct. 27, 1990; children: Jonathan Andrés, Mario Alejandro. BA, U. PR, 1988; M in music therapy, Fla. State U., 1994. Rehab. therapist, music therapist Alzheimer's Unit 16, Fla. State Hosp., Chattahoochee, Fla., 1993—95; rehab. therapist, music therapist Ctrl. Forensic Unit, Fla. State Hosp., Chattahoochee, Fla., 1995—; vis. asst. prof. Coll. of Music, Fla. State U., Tallahassee, 2002—. Grad. asst., music dir. Salsa Fla. Caribbean Ensemble, Ctr. for Music of The Americas, Fla. State U. Coll. of Music, Tallahassee, 1988—91; latin music ensemble dir. Colonial H.S., Orlando, Fla., 1990—91; dir. Latin Jazz Band Latin Attitude, Tallahassee, 1993—. Musician (musical dir., co-producer): Feel The Rhythm; musician: Trompetas Con Trovadores by Elías Lopés & Co., Huellas by Tony Croatto, Tony Croatto. Student mem. Fla. State U. Equal Opportunity Com., Tallahassee, 1989—90. Recipient Dist. Performance as Dir. of Salsa Fla., Ctr. for Music of The Americas, Fla. State U. Sch. of Music, 1988-1990, Davis Productivity award, State of Fla., 1997, 5 Years Svc. award, Fla. Dept. of Children and Families, 1998. Avocations: music arranging, electronic music and keyboards, computers, outdoors cooking, classical music. Home: 2198 Foster Dr Tallahassee FL 32303 Office: Fla State Hospital Ctrl Forensic US Hwy 90 PO Box 1000 Chattahoochee FL 32324 Home Phone: 850-386-3701; Office Phone: 850-663-7632. Home Fax: 850-386-3701. Personal E-mail: papo@latinattitude.com.

CARRAU, RICARDO L., otolaryngologist, educator; b. Mayagüez, PR, Jan. 6, 1959; MD, U. PR Sch. Medicine, San Juan, 1981. Cert. Am. Bd. Otolaryngology, 1987. Resident internal medicine VA Hosp., San Juan, 1981—82; resident gen. surgery Univ. Hosp., San Juan, 1982—84, resident otolaryngical head & neck surgery, 1984—87; fellow head & neck surgery, oncology U. Pitts. Sch. Med., 1989—90, asst. prof. dept. otolaryngology, 1992, assoc. prof. dept. otolaryngology-head and neck surgery; dir., maxillofacial trauma svc. U. Pitts. Med. Ctr., dir., consult svc., dir., tracheotomy and swallowing care unit; with Keesler Air Force Med. Ctr., Ill., 1990—92. Guest lectr. in field. Contbr. articles to profl. jours., chapters to books; co-editor (with Thomas Murry): Comprehensive Management of Swallowing Disorders, 2006. Major in active reserve, med. corps USAFR, 1987—92. Recipient Best Physicians in Pitts. award, 1996. Mem.: ACS, Pa. Med. Soc., European Skull Base Soc., Am. Soc. Head and Neck Surgery, Am. Acad. Otolaryngology-Head and Neck Surgery, Am. Rhinologic Soc., North Am. Skull Base Soc. Office: Eye & Ear Inst 203 Lothrop St Ste 300 Pittsburgh PA 15213 Office Phone: 412-647-2100. Office Fax: 412-647-7964.*

CARREL, MARIANNE EILEEN, music educator; b. Greenville, Pa., Aug. 28, 1957; d. Francis Raymond Cremi, Betty Hutton Cremi; m. Marion Lee Carrel. Student, Clarion U. Pa., 1975—76; BS, Edinboro U., 1979, MEd, 1985. Cert. elem. tchr. Ohio. Substitute tchr. Greenville and Reynolds Sch. Dists., Greenville, Pa., 1979—80; tchr. music Webster County Schs., Cowen, W.Va., 1980—84; grad. asst. Edinboro U., Edinboro, Pa., 1984—85; tchr. music Madison Local Schs., Madison, Ohio, 1985—86; tchr. music Geneva Area City Schs., Geneva, Ohio, 1986—. Sec. All-Am. Judges Assn., Ohio, 1989—. Named Assoc. of Yr., Am. Bus. Women's Assn., 2000-2001. Mem.: NEA, Internat. Double Reed Soc., Music Educators Nat. Conf., Ohio Edn. Assn., Kappa Delta Pi, Sigma Alpha Iota (life). Home: 4850 Boughner Rd Rock Creek OH 44084 Office: Geneva Area Schs 839 Sherman St Geneva OH 44041 Office Phone: 440-466-4831 ext. 134. Personal E-mail: mandmcarrel@hughes.net.

CARRELL, DANIEL ALLAN, lawyer; b. Louisville, Jan. 2, 1941; s. Elmer N. and Mary F. (Pfingst) C.; m. Janis M. Wilhelm, July 3, 1976; children: Mary Monroe, Courtney Adele. AB, Davidson Coll., 1963; BA, Oxford U., 1965, MA, 1969; JD, Stanford U., 1968. Bar: Va. 1972, U.S. Dist. Ct. (ea. dist.) Va. 1972, U.S. Ct. Appeals (4th cir.) 1975, U.S. Dist. Ct. (we. dist.) Va. 1985. Asst. prof. U.S. Mil. Acad., West Point, N.Y., 1968-71; assoc. Hunton & Williams, Richmond, Va., 1971-79, ptnr., 1979-95; prin. Carrell, Rice & Rigsby, Richmond, Va., 1996—. Hearing officer Commonwealth of Va., 2000—. Active Richmond Rep. Com., 1974—; co-counsel Dalton for Gov. campaign, Richmond, 1977; counsel Obenshain for Senate campaign, Richmond, 1978; treas. Va. Victory '92; state fin. chmn., fin. com., state ctrl. com. and budget com. Rep. Party Va., 1993-96; bd. dirs. Southampton Citizens Assn., 1985-2001; pres. Davidson Coll. Alumni Assn., 1987-88; trustee Davidson Coll., 1987-88; bd. dirs. Needle's Eye Ministries, 1986-90, adv. bd., 1990-, bd. dirs. U-Turn, Inc., 2001-; elder, trustee Stony Point Reformed Presbyn. Ch., 1993—; moderator James River Presbytery Presbyn. Ch. Am., 1998, 2001, 06; chmn. com. constl. bus. Presbyn. Ch. Am., 2003-05. Rhodes scholar, 1962; recipient Merit award Sports Illustrated Mag., 1963. Mem. ABA (chmn. exemption and Noerr Doctrine com. 1986-87, antitrust sect.), Va. Bar Assn. (chmn. young lawyers joint law-related edn. com. 1978-79, young lawyers fellow award 1980), Va. State Bar (chmn. com. on legal edn. and admission to bar 1984-91, bd. govs. sect. edn. lawyers 1992-99. dist. com. discipline 2001-03), Richmond Bar Assn., Christian Legal Soc., Westwood Club. Presbyterian. Avocations: tennis, basketball, theater, concerts. Home: 3724 Custis Rd Richmond VA 23225-1102 Office: Carrell Rice & Rigsby 7275 Glen Forest Dr Ste 310 Richmond VA 23226-3772 Office Phone: 804-285-7900. Personal E-mail: lexrex3dac@aol.com.

CARRELL, JANEEN BROWN, retired psychologist; b. Elkton, Md., Oct. 3, 1940; d. Harry Todd and Janith George Brown; m. Donald Frederick Eipper, Apr. 21, 1962 (div. Oct. 28, 1968); m. William (Bill) Douglas Carrell, May 23, 1971; 1 child, Ashley Carrell Habsburg (dec.). PhD, Kent State U., 1971; MDiv, Ashland Sem., 1995. Pvt. practice Dr. Janeen Carrell-Brown and Assocs., Garrettsville, Ohio, 1980—96; psychologist, spiritual dir. Faith Formation Assocs., Sebring, Fla., 1997—2002, Hiram, Ohio, 2002—05, Pleasant Hill, Tenn., 2005—; psychol. assessor Bair Found., Ashtabula, Ohio, 2003—05. Vice-chair, commn. ministry Fla. United Ch. Christ, Orlando, 1997—2000. Actor: (cmty. presentations) Women of Merit; artist, photographer (exhibitions) Snow Season in Amish Country, My Signature, Made By Me. Vol. Avalon's Second Chance, Crossville, Tenn., 2006—07; labyrinth presenter Hiram Coll., Ohio, 2005. Mem.: Am. Assn. Sex Educators, Counselors, and Therapists (life), Amnesty Internat. Democrat. Congregationalist. Avocations: travel, photography, quilting, reading. Office: Bair Found 5021 State Rd Ashtabula OH 44004 also: The Bair Foundation PO Box 1415 Ashtabula OH 44005-1415

CARRELL, TERRY EUGENE, manufacturing executive; b. Monmouth, Ill., July 1, 1938; s. Roy Edwin and Caroline Hilma (Fillman) Carrell; m. Bonnie Lee Clements, July 11, 1964; children: Philip Edwin, Andrew David. AB, Monmouth Coll., 1961; MBA, Calif. State U., LA, 1967; D in Bus. Adminstrn., U. So. Calif., 1970; AAS, Ivy Tech. State Coll., 1991. Engr. Argonne Nat. Lab., 1957—59, Mass. Inst. of Tech. Rsch. and Engring., 1959—62; from sr. engr. to prin. engr. reconnaissance and comm. N.Am. Aviation, 1962-67; mgr. avionics analysis and techs. B-1 divsn. Rockwell Internat., 1967-73; dir. engring. Morse Controls divsn., 1973-74; gen. mgr. Morse Controls divsn. Incom Internat. Inc., 1974-78; pres. Morse Controls, 1978—82, Heim Bearings, 1982—85; gen. mgr. Stewart-Warner Corp., 1985-88; pres. Stewart Warner South Wind Corp., 1988-95, Stewart Warner Electronics Corp., 1991-95; pres., COO Nartron Corp., 1995-97; pres. Image Moulding and Frame, Inc., Image Arts, Inc., 1997-99, TECorp, Inc., 1997—, Best Weld, Inc., 1998—2007. Cons. in field; lectr. U. So. Calif., 1967—70. Contbr. articles to profl. jours. Nat. coun. Boy Scouts Am., 1980—85; active Hudson (Ohio) Econ. Devel. Com., 1979—82; mem. svc. rev. panel United Way Summit County, 1980; bd. dirs., coun. commr. Boy Scouts Am., 1980—85. NDEA fellow, 1961—63. Mem.: Boating Industry Assn. (chmn. steering task force 1974—85), Am. Boat and Yacht Coun. (dir. 1980—88), Hudson C. of C. (trustee 1976—78). Achievements include patents in field. Office: 1315 W 18th St Anderson IN 46016-3800 Personal E-mail: tcarrell@insightbb.com.

CARREN, JEFFREY P., lawyer; b. Chgo., Oct. 8, 1946; AB with high honors, U. Ill., 1968; JD, Northwestern U., 1972. Bar: Ill. 1973, U.S. Dist. Ct. (no. dist.) Ill. 1973, U.S. Ct. Appeals (7th cir.) 1976, U.S. Supreme Ct. 1980. Formerly ptnr. Winston & Strawn, Chgo.; ptnr. Laner, Muchin, Dombrow, Becker, Levin & Tominberg Ltd., Chgo., 1994—. Editor notes and comments Northwestern U. Law Rev., 1971-72/ Edmund James scholar. Mem. ABA (tax and bus. sects.), Ill. State Bar Assn. (employee benefits sect.), Chgo. Bar Assn. (employee benefits com), Am. Arbitration Assn. (panel arbitrators), Phi Eta Sigma. Office: Laner Muchin et al 515 N State St Chicago IL 60610-4324 Office Phone: 312-467-9800. E-mail: jcarren@lanermuchin.com.

CARRERA, JAGANATH, acupuncturist, yoga educator; b. Elizabeth, NJ, Jan. 23, 1950; s. Peter Daniel and Maria Felicita Carrera; m. Mary Ellen Janaki Schmidt, June 28, 1980. B in Religious Studies, SUNY, NYC, 1995; M in Acupuncture, Tri State Coll. Acupuncture, 1998. Diplomate Nat. Coun. for Cert. Acupuncture and Oriental Medicine, 1998, cert. acpuncturist N.J., Va., N.Y., 1998, Swedish Inst. of Massage and Allied Sci., 1978; Raja yoga instr. Integral Yoga Internat., 1987; instr. Integral Yoga Internat., 1975, tchr. trainer Integral Yoga Internat., 1980, registered tchr. Yoga Alliance, 2002. Exec. dir. Integral Yoga Inst., New Brunswick, NJ, 1975—87; vice pres., adminstr. Satchidananda Ashram-Yogaville, Buckingham, Va., 1987—94; dean studies Ea. Sch. Acupuncture and Traditional Medicine, Montclair, NJ, 1997—2002, v.p. Monclair, NJ, 2002—, clinic supr.; hatha yoga instr. Integral Yoga Internat., 1974—, raja yoga instr., 1975—, meditation instr., 1974—, yoga tchr. trainer, 1976—. Hatha yoga instr. Integral Yoga Ministry, 1974—, mediation instr., 1974—, raja yoga instr., 1975—, exec. dir., 1975—87, yoga tchr. trainer, 1976—, bd. mem., 1980—; adv. bd. New Sem., NYC, 1998—; spiritual advisor One Spirit Learning Alliance, NYC, 2000—; bd. govs. Ea. Sch. Acupuncture, Montclair, NJ. Contbr. articles to profl. jours. Recipient Guru Tattwa Ratnam award, Integral Yoga Internat., 1986. Achievements include originator and devloper of Integral Yoga Ministry; development of co-developer of Integral Yoga Raja Yoga and Integral Yoga meditation teacher trainings. Home Phone: 973-523-8206; Office Phone: 201-796-7585. Personal E-mail: revjaganath@yahoo.com. E-mail: iyiyoga@aol.com.

CARRERA, VICTOR MANUEL, lawyer; b. Rio Grande City, Tex., Nov. 20, 1954; s. Eladio and Ines Olivia (Guerra) C. BS, U. Tex., 1975, BA with honors, 1976, JD, 1979. Bar: Tex. 1979, U.S. Dist. Ct. (so. dist.) Tex. 1980, U.S. Dist. Ct. (we. dist.) Tex. 1996, U.S. Dist. Ct. (no. dist.) Tex. 2001, U.S. Ct. Appeals (5th cir.) 1986; cert. civil trial law, personal injury trial law, civil appellate law, Tex.; cert. mediator Inst. Conflict Mgmt. Assoc. Cardenas & Whitis, McAllen, Tex., 1979-80; briefing atty. U.S. Dist. Ct. (so. dist.) Tex., Brownsville, 1980-81; assoc. Keys, Russell & Seaman, Corpus Christi, Tex., 1981-84, Wood, Boykin, Wolter & Keys, Corpus Christi, 1984-86, ptnr., 1987-88; participating mem. Law Offices of Ramon Garcia, P.C., Edinburg, Tex., 1988-90; ptnr. Munoz, Hockema & Reed, McAllen, Tex., 1990-96, Reed & Carrera, Edinburg, Tex., 1997, Reed, Carrera & McLain, 1997—2004; pvt. practice, 2004—. Lectr. South Tex. Coll. Law, Houston, 1987, U. Houston, 1989-90, 96-99, State Bar Tex., 1992. Mng. editor: Tex. Internat. Law Jour., 1978—79. Recipient Outstanding Individual Contbn. Award Vol. Lawyers of Coastal Bend, 1985, Tex. Super Lawyer award Jour. Law and Politics and Tex. Monthly, 2003, 04, 06. Mem.: Hidalgo County Bar Assn. (lector 2000, 2002, 2003), Tex. Bar Assn. Democrat. Avocations: history, archaeology. Home: 5400 N 1st St Mcallen TX 78504-2211 Office: Law Office Victor M Carrera PC 1 Paseo Del Prado Ste 103-B Edinburg TX 78539 Office Phone: 956-661-8100. Business E-Mail: vmc@carreralaw.com.

CARRERAS, FRANCISCO JOSÉ, retired academic and foundation administrator; b. San Juan, May 13, 1932; s. Francisco and Antonia (Muriente) C.; m. Ana Elisa Carreras, Mar. 29, 1964; children: Inés María, María Soledad, Irene María, Marianne, Francisco José, María del Pilar. Student, Instituto Superior de Estudios Clásicos, Havana, Cuba, 1954-57; BA, Universidad Pontificia de Comillas, Santander, Spain, 1959; MA, Fordham U., Bronx, NY, 1960; PhD, Universidad Pontificia Gregoriana, Rome, 1966. Mem. faculty U. P.R., Rio Piedras Campus, 1962-69, acad. asst. to dir., 1967-69, dir. humanities dept., 1967-68; pres. Cath. U. P.R., Ponce, 1969-81; academician P.R. Acad. Arts and Scis., 1970; exec. dir. Angel Ramos Found., Inc., San Juan, 1984—; mem. P.R. State Commn. on Post-Secondary Edn., 1973. Dir. Banco Popular de P.R. Author: Filosofía de la Coordinación de José Vasconcelos, 1971, Incógnita y Revelación, 1981; also articles. Adv. Sociedad Puertorriqueña UNESCO, 1973; pres. P.R. Endowment for Humanities, 1977; bd. dirs. Angel Ramos Found., 1977; bd. dirs. Damas Hosp., 1978, P.R. Acad. Arts and Scis., 1980; adv. bd. dirs. Orgns. Universidades Católicas de América Latina, 1976. Recipient Pres.'s medal Ana G. Mendez Univ. Sys.-P.R., 2000; named Knight of St. Gregory the Great, 2007. Mem. Fundación Puertorriqueña Humanidades (pres. 1977), Ponce Sales and Mktg. Execs. Assn., Alpha Phi Omega, Phi Delta Kappa. Clubs: Rotary, Lions. Roman Catholic. Home: 1 St C-16 Villas Del Pilar San Juan PR 00926-5448 Office: Angel Ramos Found Inc PO Box 362408 San Juan PR 00936-2408 Business E-Mail: fcarreras@farpr.org.

CARRERE, CHARLES SCOTT, judge, educator; b. Dublin, Ga., Sept. 26, 1937; 1 son, Daniel Austin. BA, U. Ga., Athens, 1959; LLB, Stetson U., 1961. Bar: Ga. 1960, Fla. 1961. Law clk. US Dist. Judge, Orlando, Fla., 1962—63; asst. US Atty. Mid. Dist. Fla., 1963—66, 1968—69, chief trial atty., 1965—66, 1968—69; ptnr. Harrison, Greene, Mann, Rowe & Stanton, 1970—80; judge Pinellas County, Fla., 1980—96; vis. prof. law Stetson Coll. Law, 1997—98, Cumberland Law Sch., 1998—99. Recipient Jud. Appreciation award St. Petersburg Bar Assn., 1996, Alumnus of Yr. award Stetson Student Bar Assn., 1998. Mem. State Bar Ga., Fla. Bar, Phi Beta Kappa. Presbyterian. Address: PO Box 7177 Seminole FL 33775-7177

CARRETO-CHAVEZ, GERARDO, lawyer; s. Martha Chavez-Avina. JD with spl. honors (hon.), Universidad Iberoamericana, Mexico City, 2001; LLM, NYU, NYC, 2004. Lic.: Mex. (lawyer) 2001. Sr. assoc. Barrera, Siqueiros y Torres Landa, S.C., Mexico City, 1998—; fgn. assoc. intern Jenner & Block, LLP, Chgo., 2004—05; fgn. intern Miller Nash, LLP, Portland, Oreg., 2004; in-house counsel Global Crossing, Mexico City, 2001; summer legal intern Centro Mexicano De Derecho Ambiental (Cemda), Mexico City, 2000. Adj. law faculty. Universidad Iberoamericana - Sch. of Law, Mexico City, 2002—06. Translator (official translator for the english lang): (official translator and interpreter) Render official translations; contbr. articles to profl. jours. Free translator and advisor to co-citizens residing in Chgo. IND, Chicago, 2004—06. Fellow, "Teléfonos de México" (TELMEX), 1996—2001; scholar, Universidad Iberoamericana - Sch. of Law, 1996—2001. Mem.: Barra Mexicana-Colegio de Abogados, A. C. Avocations: swimming, music, computers. Office: Barrera Siqueiros Y Torres Landa Sc Montes Urales 470 1er Piso Col Lomas Mexico City 11000 Mexico Home Phone: (011) (52 55) 5540-8040; Office Phone: (011) (52 55) 5540-8040. Office Fax: (011) (52 55) 5520-5115. E-mail: gcc@bstl.com.mx.

CARREY, JIM, actor; b. Newmarket, Ont., Can., Jan. 17, 1962; s. Percy and Kathleen Carrey; m. Melissa Womer, Mar. 28, 1987 (div. Dec. 11, 1995); 1 child, Jane; m. Lauren Holly Sept. 23, 1996 (div. July 29, 1997). Actor: (films) Finders Keepers, 1984, Once Bitten, 1985, Peggy Sue Got Married, 1986, The Dead Pool, 1988, Earth Girls Are Easy, 1989, Pink Cadillac, 1989, High Strung, 1991, Ace Ventura: Pet Detective, 1993 (also screenwriter), The Mask, 1994, Dumb and Dumber, 1994, Batman Forever, 1995, Ace Ventura: When Nature Calls, 1995, The Mask's Revenge, 1996, Liar, Liar, 1996, The Cable Guy, 1996, The Truman Show, 1997 (Golden Globe award for best performance by an actor in a motion picture 2000), Simon Birch, 1998, Man on the Moon, 1999 (Golden Globe for best performance by an actor in a motion picture 2000), Me, Myself and Irene, 2000, How the Grinch Stole Christmas, 2000, The Majestic, 2001, Bruce Almighty, 2003, Eternal Sunshine of the Spotless Mind, 2004, Lemony Snicket's A Series of Unfortunate Events, 2004, The Number 23, 2007; actor, prodr. (films) Fun with Dick and Jane, 2005; actor (TV series) The Duck Factory, 1984, In Living Color, 1990-94; (TV movies) Mike Hammer: Murder Takes All, 1989, Doing Time on Maple Drive, 1992 Star on the Hollywood Walk of Fame, 2000, Muhammad Ali Celebrity Entertainer award, 2006; named one of 50 Most Powerful People in Hollywood, 2004-06. Office: Creative Artists Agy 9830 Wilshire Blvd Beverly Hills CA 90212*

CARREY, NEIL, lawyer, educator; b. Bronx, NY, Nov. 19, 1942; s. David L. and Betty (Kurtzburg) Carrey; m. Karen Krysher, Apr. 9, 1980; children: Jana, Christopher;children from previous marriage: Scott, Douglas, Dana. BS in Econs., U. Pa., 1964; JD, Stanford U., 1967. Bar: Calif. 1968. Mem. firm, v.p. corp. DeCastro, West, Chodorow, Inc., LA, 1967-97; of counsel Jenkens & Gilchrist, LA, 1998—2007, Baker & Hostetler LLP, LA, 2007—. Instr. program legal paraprofls. U. So. Calif., 1977—89, lectr. Dental Sch., 1987—; lectr. Employee Benefits Inst., Kansas City, Mo., 1996. Author: Nonqualified Deferred Compensation Plans-The Wave of the Future, 1985. Treas. Nat. Little League, Santa Monica, 1984—85, pres., 1985—86, coach, 1990—95; referee, coach Am. Soccer Youth Orgn., 1989—95; officer Vista Del Mar Child Care Ctr., LA, 1968—84; coach Bobby Sox Softball Team, Santa Monica, Calif., 1986—88, bd. dirs., 1988, umpire in chief, 1988; pres. Gail Dorin Music Found., 1994—; bd. dirs. Santa Monica Youth Athletic Found., 1995—2004, Santa Monica Police Activities League, 1995—, pres., 1999—2001; dir. Small Bus. Coun. Am., 1995—, Santa Monica HS Booster Club, 1995—97; v.p. Sneaker Sisters, 1996—2001; pres. Santa Monica Jr. Rowing, 1997—2002; legal cons. 33d Dist. Calif. PTA, 1997—99; sec. Santa Monica Leaders Club, 1999—2000; women's sports adv. bd. U. Pa., 1998—2003; pres. Chris Carrey Charitable Found., 2000—; v.p. bd. Ivan and Sam Found., 2002—05; active Cir. of Care Children's Hosp., 2003—; chair coms. Santa Monica-Malibu Sch. Dist., 1983—2004, prop 39 bond oversight com., 2007; recreation and parks commr. City of Santa Monica, 1999—; bd. dirs. Padres Contra el Cancer, 2001—03, v.p., 2002—03, pres., 2003—05, pres. emeritus, 2005—06. Mem.: LWV (dir. 1997—2003), Acad. Country Music, Country Music Assn., Children's Hosp. L.A. (adv. coun. 2001—, new hosp. com. 2007), U. Pa. Alumni Soc. (pres. 1971—79, dir. 1979—87), Mountaingate Tennis Club, Alpha Kappa Psi (life). Jewish. Home: 616 23d St Santa Monica CA 90402-3130 Office: 12100 Wilshire Blvd Fl 15 Los Angeles CA 90025-7120 Office Phone: 310-442-8835. Business E-Mail: ncarrey@bakerlaw.com.

CARRICK, RICHARD DAVID, composer, performing company executive, music educator; s. Richard John and Suzanne Carrick. BA, Columbia U., NYC, 1993; MA, U. Calif., San Diego, 1995, PhD, 2001. Dir. music tech., composition faculty Hoff Barthelson Music Sch., Scarsdale, NY, 2002—; artistic dir. Either/Or Music, NYC, 2003—. Composer: (multimedia concert performance) Cosmicomics, The Fall, (orchestra) Two Moments, (chamber music) L'idee sans l'ideal, FmlrSmblNcs, In Flow, Masculin Feminin, (chamber orchestra) The Veins of Marble (selection to ISCM World Music Days, Switzerland, 2004), (films) Solidarity (Mayor's award Heart of Gold Internat. Film Festival, Australia, 2006). Grantee Grane award, Eiler Found., 2002, Composer Assistance Program, Am. Music Ctr., 2004; Arthur Rose Tchg. fellow, Columbia U., 1993, Arthur Gleish Tchg. fellow, U. Calif., San Diego, 1993. Mem.: BMI. Office: Hoff Barthelson Music School 25 School Ln Scarsdale NY 10583 Office Phone: 914-723-1169. Business E-Mail: mail@richardcarrick.com.

CARRICO, HARRY LEE, retired judge; b. Washington, Sept. 4, 1916; s. William Temple and Nellie Nadalia (Willett) C.; m. Betty Lou Peck, May 18, 1940 (dec. 1987); 1 child, Lucretia Ann; m. Lynn Brackenridge, July 1, 1994. Jr. cert., George Washington U., 1938, JD, 1942; LLD (hon.), U. Richmond, 1973, George Washington U., 1987; LLD, Coll. William & Mary, 1993; LLD (hon.), Shenandoah U., 2004. Bar: Va. 1941. With Rust & Rust, Fairfax, Va., 1941-43; trial justice Fairfax, Va., 1943-51; pvt. practice, 1951-56; judge 16th Jud. Cir., Va., 1956-61; justice Va. Supreme Ct., Richmond, 1961-81, chief justice, 1981—2003, sr. justice, 2003—.

Chmn. bd dirs. Nat. Ctr. for State Cts., 1989-90; vis. prof. law and civic engagementU. Richmond, 2004-. With USNR, 1945—46. Recipient Alumni Profl. Achievement award George Washington U., 1981, Hill-Tucker Pub. Svc. award, 1999, Pub. Svc. award Va. Mil. Inst., 2003. Mem. McNeill Law Soc., Conf. Chief Justices (bd. dirs. 1985-91, 1st v.p. 1987, pres.-elect. 1988, pres. 1989-90, co-chmn. nat. jud. coun. 1991-97), Order of Coif, Phi Delta Phi, Omicron Delta Kappa. Episcopalian. Office: Supreme Court of Va 100 N 9th St 4th Fl Richmond VA 23219 Home Phone: 804-740-8693; Office Phone: 804-786-2023. Business E-Mail: hcarrico@courts.state.va.us.

CARRICO, STEPHEN J., construction company executive; b. 1954; Grad., Ctrl. Mich. U., 1977. CPA. With Straka, Jarackas & Co., Detroit, 1977-84; various positions Hensel Phelps Constrn. Co., Greeley, Colo., 1984—, now v.p. fin. Office: Hensel Phelps Construction 420 Sixth Ave Greeley CO 80632

CARRICO, VIRGIL NORMAN, physician; b. Cumberland, Md., Aug. 28, 1940; s. Virgil Norman and Lucille E. Carrico; m. Nina Lois Lemper, Aug. 17, 1963; children: Pamela Beth Carrico-Miller, Sandra Kelly (dec.). BA, Wabash Coll., 1962; MD, Ind. U., 1966. Diplomate Am. Bd. Family Practice. Intern Marion County Gen. Hosp., Indpls., 1966-67; resident in family practice Akron (Ohio) City Hosp., 1970-72, chief resident in family practice, 1972, assoc. dir. family practice residency, 1972; chief family practice Bryan Cmty. Hosp., chief of staff, 1977-78, preceptor Bryan Area Health Edn. Ctr.; past preceptor cmty. medicine Med. Coll. Ohio, Toledo, clin. asst. prof. family medicine, clin. prof. family medicine; past preceptor preventive medicine and family practice Ohio State U.; med. dir. Bryan Area Health Edn. Ctr. Past pres., bd. dirs. Bryan Med. Group, Inc. Contbr. articles to profl. jours. Trustee YWCA, Bryan, Ohio, v.p., 1990-92; bd. dirs. United Fund, pres., 1990-92; bd. dirs. Jr. Achievement, 1981-83, Bryan Area Found. Capt. USAF, 1967-70. Fellow Am. Acad. Family Physicians (bylaw coms. 1989, 90, 91, 92, nat. chmn. 1993, chmn. patient care svcs. commn. 1988-89, chmn. mem. svcs. commn. 1989-90); mem. Soc. Tchrs. Family Medicine, Ohio Acad. Family Medicine, Am. Acad. Family Medicine, Williams County Med. Soc. (rpes. 1976-79, sec.-treas., v.p. 1980-83), Ohio Acad. Family Physicians (del. to ho. of dels. 1972-85; pres. Fulton County chpt. 1973-85, chmn. resident affairs subcom., nominating com., student awards, fin. com., ref. com. of the ho. of dels.; treas. 1985-87, v.p. 1987-89, bd. dirs. 1983-92, pres.-elect 1990-91), Rotary Internat. Avocations: golf, travel, reading. Office: Bryan Med Group 442 W High St Bryan OH 43506-1681 Office Phone: 419-636-4517. Personal E-mail: bmg@bright.net.

CARRIER, CELINE A., psychologist; b. Plattsburgh, NY, Jan. 13, 1951; d. Paul J. and Doreen A. George; m. Paul A. Carrier, June 26, 1971; children: Jonathan P, Justin P. BA, Notre Dame Coll., 1972, MEd, 1995; degree, Fitchburg State Coll., Mass., 2003. Lic. sch. psychologist N.H., 2003, counselor N.H., 1995, cert. educator N.H., 1972. Educator secondary sch. City Manchester (N.H.) Sch. Dept., 1985—95, counselor, 1995—2003, sch. psychologist, 2003—. Dir. Sch. to Careers Partnership, Manchester, 1998—2000. Recipient Contbn. to Edn. award, Manchester Sch. Dept., 1997, Excellence in Edn. award, Manchester C. of C., 1998; grantee, Norwin S. and Elizabeth L. Bean Found., 1994. Mem.: NEA, Nat. Assn. Sch. Psychologists, Manchester Edn. Assn., N.H. Edn. Assn. Roman Catholic. Avocations: writing, travel, reading. Office: Manchester NH School District 186 Commercial Street Manchester NH 03101 Home Phone: 603-472-5550; Office Phone: 603-624-6300. Home Fax: 603-624-6361. Personal E-mail: ccarrier@mansd.org.

CARRIER, FRANCE, medical educator; b. Beauport, Que., June 9, 1961; d. Philippe Carrier and Therese Pare; m. Steven I. Hirschfeld; 1 child, Joshua Samuel. PhD, U. Montreal, 1988. Postdoctoral fellow Biotechnology Rsch. Inst., Montreal, Que., 1988—89; vis. assoc. NIH, Bethesda, Md., 1989—91; vis. scientist Nat. Cancer Inst. NIH, Bethesda, 1991—98; prof. medicine U. Md., Balt., 1998—. Mem. Greenebaum Cancer Ctr., Balt. Contbr. articles to profl. jours., chapters to books. Grantee Rsch. grantee, NIH, 2007—; Internat. fellow, Human Frontier Sci. Program Orgn., 1990, Rsch. grantee, NIH, 1999—2003, Am. Cancer Soc., 2000—02, 2004—07, A-T Children's Project, 2003—06. Mem.: Am. Assn. for Cancer Rsch. (sponsor, Brigid Leventhal award 2002), N.Y. Acad. Scis., Cosmos Club (Elected mem. 1999). Achievements include patents for methods for determining the presence of functional p53 in mammalian cells and for inhibitors of the S100-p53 protein-protein interaction and methods of inhibiting cancer employing the same; research in genotoxic stress-response, cancer progression, chromatin remodeling. Office: U Md 108 N Greene St Baltimore MD 21201-1503 Office Phone: 410-706-5105. Business E-Mail: fcarr001@umaryland.edu.

CARRIER, RONALD EDWIN, academic administrator, director; b. Bluff City, Tenn., Aug. 18, 1932; s. James Murphy and Melissa (Miller) C.; m. Edith Marie Johnson, Sept. 7, 1955; children: Michael Lavon, Linda Lois Carrier Frazee, Jennine Marie. BS, Ea. Tenn. State U., Johnson City, 1955; MS in Econs., U. Ill., Champagne-Urbana, 1957, PhD in Econs., 1960; Doctorate (hon.), William and Mary Coll., Williamsburg, Va., Bridgewater Coll., Va., Jacksonville State U., Ala., Francis Marion U., Florence, SC. Assoc. prof. econs. U. Miss., Oxford, 1960-63; dir., prof. Bur. Bus. and Econ. Rsch., Memphis U., 1963-66, provost, v.p. acad. affairs, 1966-71; pres., chancellor James Madison U., Harrisonburg, Va., 1971—2002, pres. emeritus, 2002—; pres. Ctr. Innovative Tech., Herndon, Va., 1986-87. Chancellor Romanian Am. U. Author: Plant Locations: A Theory and Explanations, 1968; contbr. articles to profl. jours. Mem. White House Conf. Balance Econ. Growth, Va. Indsl. Facilities Study Commn., 1972—75; chmn. Va. Land Use Adv. Com., 1974—77, Va. Gov.'s Electricity Costs Commn., 1975—; mem. Va. Gov.'s Energy Resource Adv. Commn., 1975—76, Gov.'s Regulatory Reform Adv. Bd., 1983, Joint Subcom. to Study Coal Slurry Pipeline Feasibility 2002., 1983; ethics com. Senate Va., 1999; mem. Va. Higher Edn. Steering Commn., 2002; mem. bd. visitors Va. State U., 2002—04. Earheart fellow, 1958-60; recipient Ben Franklin award Memphis Printing Industry, 1966, Faculty award East Tenn. State U., 1955, Disting. Svc. award Jr. C. of C., 1965; named Outstanding alumni award East Tenn. State U., 1975, Disting. Alumnus in Higher Edn., 1999, Virginian of Yr. award Va. Assn. Broadcasters, 1982, cultural laureate Va., Outstanding Virginian FFA, 1991. Mem.: Sigma Phi Epsilon, Omicron Delta Gamma, Omicron Delta Kappa. Methodist. Office: James Madison U MSC 5730 Harrisonburg VA 22807 Home: 209 Divot Dr Harrisonburg VA 22802 Office Phone: 540-568-8181. Business E-Mail: carriere@jmu.edu.

CARRIER, WARREN PENDLETON, retired university chancellor, writer; b. Cheviot, Ohio, July 3, 1918; s. Burly Warren and Prudence (Alfrey) C.; m. Marjorie Jane Regan, Apr. 3, 1947 (dec.); 1 child, Gregory Paul; m. Judy Lynn Hall, June 14, 1973; 1 son, Ethan Alfrey. Student, Wabash Coll., 1938-40; AB, Miami U., Oxford, Ohio, 1942; MA, Harvard U., 1948; PhD, Occidental Coll., 1962. Asst. prof. English U. Iowa, 1949-52; assoc. prof. Bard Coll., 1953-57; lit. faculty Bennington, 1955-58; vis. prof. Sweet Briar (Va.) Coll., 1958-60; prof. Deep Springs (Calif.) Coll., 1960-62, Portland (Oreg.) State U., 1962-64; prof., chmn. English dept. U. Mont., Missoula, 1964-68; assoc. dean. prof. English and comparative lit., chmn. comparative lit. Livingston Coll., Rutgers U., 1968-69; dean Coll. Arts and Letters, San Diego State U., 1969-72; v.p. acad. affairs U. Bridgeport, Conn., 1972-75; chancellor U. Wis., Platteville, 1975-82. Author: The Hunt, 1952, Bay of the Damned, 1957, Toward Montebello, 1966, Leave Your Sugar for the Cold Morning, 1977, The Diver, 1986, Death of a Chancellor, 1986, An Honorable Spy, 1992, Murder at the Strawberry Festival, 1993, An Ordinary Man, 1997, Death of a Poet, 1999, Justice at Christmas, 1999, Risking the Wind, 1999, Coming to Terms, 2004; founder Quar. Rev. of Lit.; editor: Guide to World Literature, 1980; co-editor: Reading Modern Poetry, 1955, 68, Literature from the World, 1981; assoc. editor: Western Rev., 1949-51; contbr. articles, poems, revs. to lit. mags. Mem. Jud. Commn. Wis. Vol., Am. Field Service attached to Brit. Army, India-Burma, 1944-45. Recipient award for poetry Nat. Endowment for Arts, 1972; Colladay prize for poetry, 1986 Mem. Nat. Coun. Tchrs. English, Royal Soc. Arts, Wis. Acad. Arts and Scis., Phi Beta Kappa. Home: 2201 L St NW # 7 Washington DC 20037-1413

CARRIERE, BROTHER WILLIAM JOSEPH, school system administrator; b. Detroit, Mar. 26, 1943; s. Leon Simon and Josephine Mary (Diguigno) C. BA, Loyola U., Chgo., 1970; MA, Seton Hall U., 1973; PhD, U. Ariz., 1982. Cert. tchr., sch. adminstr. Tchr. various Cath. schs., 1965-75, adminstr., 1975-80; prof. St. Mary's Coll., Moraga, Calif., 1983-86; assoc. supt. Diocese of Orange, Calif., 1986-90, supt. Calif., 1990—. Dir. tchr. edn. for Christian brs. St. Mary's Coll., Moraga, 1983-86, sch. adm. master's program dir. Cath. schs., 1983-86. Recipient Disting. Svc. to Cath. Edn., Today's Cath. Tchr. Mag., 1987. Mem. Nat. Cath. Ednl. Assn. (exec. com. 1989-93). Roman Catholic. Office: Dept Cath Schs PO Box 14195 Orange CA 92863-1595 Home: PO Box 429 Anaheim CA 92815-0429

CARRIERI, ARTHUR HELMUT, physicist, researcher; b. Phila., June 15, 1953; s. Philip and Margot Carrieri. AB, Temple U., 1976; MS, Pa. State U., 1978. Sr. rsch. physicist U.S. Army Rsch., Devel. and Engring. Command, Edgewood Chem. Biol. Ctr., Aberdeen Proving Ground, Md., 1983—. Contbr. articles to profl. jours. Recipient R&D Devel. Achievement awards, U.S. Army, 1994, 1999, 2001. Roman Catholic. Achievements include patents for neural network pattern recognition systems; infrared Mueller matrix detection and ranging system, thermal luminescence sensor, chemical imaging sensor and laser beacon, earth monitoring satellite system, others. Avocation: scuba diving. Home: 3105 K Cardinal Way Abingdon MD 21009 Office: US Army Edgewood Chem & Biol Ctr 5183 Blackhawk Rd Aberdeen Proving Ground MD 21010-5424 Office Phone: 410-436-5943. Personal E-mail: ahcarrie@verizon.net. Business E-Mail: arthur.carrieri@us.army.mil.

CARRIG, JOHN A., oil industry executive; b. 1952; BA, Rutgers U., 1976; JD, Temple U., 1977; LLM Tax Law, NYU Sch. Law, 1978. Tax atty. Phillips Petroleum Co., London, 1978—81, Bartlesville, Okla., 1981—93, finance mgr., 1993—95, treasurer, 1995, v.p., treasurer, 1996—2000, senior v.p., treasurer, 2000, senior v.p., CFO Houston, 2001—02; exec. v.p. fin., CFO ConocoPhillips, Houston, 2002—. Mem. fin. com. Am. Petroleum Inst. Mem. overseers council Jesse H. Jones Grad. Sch. of Mgmt., Rice U.; mem. fin. com. Awty Internat. Sch.; bd. dirs. Alley Theatre, Houston. Mem.: Phi Beta Kappa. Office: ConocoPhillips PO Box 2197 Houston TX 77252-2197*

CARRIG, KENNETH J., food products executive; m. Lisa Carrig; 3 children. BS in Labor Econs., Cornell U., 1981. With PepsiCo; head human resources Continental Airlines, 1995—97; global practice leader human capital practice Andersen Cons.; v.p., chief adminstrv. officer Sysco Corp., Houston, 1998—99, sr..v.p. adminstrn., 1998—2004, exec. v.p., chief adminstrv. officer, 2004—. Fellow: Nat. Acad. of Human Resources. Office: Sysco Corp 1390 Enclave Pky Houston TX 77077-2099

CARRIGAN, DAVID OWEN, history educator; b. New Glasgow, NS, Can., Nov. 30, 1933; s. Ronald and Marion Constance (Hoare) C.; m. Florence Catherine Nicholson, June 21, 1958; children: Nancy, Janet, David, Glen, Sharon, Douglas. BA, St. Francis Xavier U., 1954; MA, Boston U., 1955; PhD, U. Maine, 1966. Asst. prof. history St. Francis Xavier U., 1957-61, assoc. prof., 1961-67; assoc. prof. history Wilfred Laurier U., 1967-68; prin., dean arts Kings Coll., U. Western Ont., 1968-71; pres. St. Mary's U., Halifax, N.S., 1971-79, prof., 1979-99, prof. emeritus, 1999—. Author: Canadian Party Platforms, 1867-1968, 1968, Crime and Punishment in Canada: A History, 1991, Juvenile Delinquency in Canada a History, 1998; contbrs. articles to profl. jours. Former trustee Inst. Research on Public Policy; past mem. Can. Council; past bd. dirs. Can. Assn. for Treatment and Study of Families Mem.: Phi Kappa Phi.

CARRIGAN, JIM R., arbitrator, mediator, retired judge; b. Mobridge, SD, Aug. 24, 1929; s. Leo Michael and Mildred Ione (Jaycox) C.; m. Beverly Jean Halpin, June 2, 1956. PhB, JD, U. N.D., 1953; LLM in Taxation, NYU, 1956; LLD (hon.), U. Colo., 1989, Suffolk U., 1991, U. N.D., 1997. Bar: N.D. 1953, Colo. 1956. Asst. prof. law U. Denver, 1956—59; vis. assoc. prof. NYU Law Sch., 1958, U. Wash. Law Sch., 1959—60; Colo. jud. adminstr., 1960—61; prof. law U. Colo., 1961—67; ptnr. Carrigan & Bragg (and predecessors), 1967—76; bd. regents U. Colo., 1975—76; justice Colo. Supreme Ct., 1976—79; judge U.S. Dist. Ct. Colo., 1979—95. Mem. Colo. Bd. Bar Examiners, 1969-71; lectr. Nat. Coll. State Judiciary, 1964-77, 95; bd. dirs. Nat. Inst. Trial Advocacy, 1971-2006, chmn. bd. 1986-88, also mem. faculty, 1972—; adj. prof. law U. Colo, 1984, 1991—; bd. dirs. Denver Broncos Stadium Dist., 1996—; mem. steering com. new U. Colo. Law Bldg., 2005-. Editor-in-chief: N.D. Law Rev., 1952-53, Internat. Soc. Barristers Quar., 1972-79; editor: DICTA, 1957-59; contbr. articles to profl. jours. Bd. visitors U. N.D. Coll. Law, 1983-85. Recipient Disting. Svc. award Nat. Coll. State Judiciary, 1969, Outstanding Alumnus award U. N.D., 1973, Regent Emeritus award U. Colo., 1977, B'nai Brith Civil Rights award, 1986, Thomas More Outstanding Lawyer award Cath. Lawyers Guild, 1988, Oliphant Disting. Svc. award Nat. Inst. Trial Advocacy, 1993, Constl. Rights award Nat. Assn. Blacks in Criminal Justice (Colo. chpt.), 1992, Disting. Svc. award Colo. Bar Assn., 1994, Amicus Curiae award ATLA, 1994, Colo. Trial Lawyers Assn. Lifetime Achievement award, 2000. Fellow Colo. Bar Found., Boulder County Bar Found.; mem. ABA (action com. on tort system improvement 1985-87, TIPS sect. long range planning com., 1986-97; coun. 1987-91, task force on initiatives and referenda 1990-92, size of civil juries task force 1988-90, class actions task force 1995-97), Colo. Bar Assn., Boulder County Bar Assn., Denver Bar Assn., Cath. Lawyers Guild, Inns. of Ct., Internat. Soc. Barristers, Internat. Acad. Trial Lawyers (bd. dirs. 1995—), Fed. Judges Assn. (bd. dirs. 1985-89), Am. Judicature Soc. (bd. dirs. 1985-89), Tenth Circuit Dist. Judges Assn. (sec. 1991-92, v.p. 1992-93, pres. 1994-95), Order of Coif, Phi Beta Kappa. Roman Catholic. Office: Judicial Arbiter Group 1601 Blake St Ste 400 Denver CO 80202-1328 Office Phone: 303-572-1919, 303-494-1444. Personal E-mail: carrigan2350@earthlink.net. Business E-Mail: info@jaginc.com.

CARRIKER, ROBERT CHARLES, history professor; b. St. Louis, Aug. 18, 1940; s. Thomas B. and Vivian Ida (Spaunhorst) C.; m. Eleanor R. Gualdoni, Aug. 24, 1963; children: Thomas A., Robert M., Andrew J. BS, St. Louis U., 1962, AM, 1963; PhD, U. Okla., 1967. Asst. prof. Gonzaga U., Spokane, Wash., 1967-71, assoc. prof., 1972-76, prof. history, 1976—2002, disting. prof. Coll. Arts and Scis., 2003—. Author: Fort Supply, Indian Territory, 1970, 90, The Kalispel People, 1973, Father Peter De Smet, 1995, 1998, (with Harry Fritz) America Looks West, 2002, Ocian in View!, 2005; editor: (with Eleanor R. Carriker) Army Wife on the Frontier, 1975, (with William L. Lang) Great River of the West, 1999; book rev. editor Columbia mag., 1987—. Mem. Wash. Lewis and Clark Trail Com., 1978-99; commr. Wash. Maritime Bicentennial, Olympia, 1989-92; bd. dirs. Wash. Commn. for Humanities, Seattle, 1988-94. Burlington No. Found. scholar, 1985, 96; recipient Disting. Svc. award Lewis and Clark Trail Heritage Found., 1989. Mem. Wash. State Hist. Soc. (trustee 1981-90, v.p. 1993-2000), Western Hist. Assn., Phi Alpha Theta (councilor 1985-87). Roman Catholic. Avocations: travel, photography, cartography. Office: Gonzaga U 502 E Boone Ave Spokane WA 99258-0001 Business E-Mail: carriker@gonzaga.edu.

CARRILLO, ELPIDIA, actress; b. Michoacan, Mexico, 1963; Actor: (films) The Border, 1982, The Honorary Consul, 1983, Salvador, 1986, Predator, 1987, Cita con el Destino, 1988, The Assassin, 1989, Predator 2, 1990, City of the Blind, 1991, Daughter of the Puma, 1994, Casa del Abuelo, 1995, My Family, 1995, The Brave, 1997, Un Embrujo, 1998, They Come at Night, 1998, The Other Conquest, 1998, A Day Without a Mexican, 2004, Nine Lives, 2005 (ALMA award, Nat. Coun. La Raza, for outstanding supporting actress in a motion picture, 2006), Tortilla Heaven, 2006, (TV films) Lightning Field, 1991, (TV series) Christopher Columbus, 1985, La Otra, 2002, Kingpin, 2003, (TV appearances) To Have and To Hold, 1989, Miami Vice, 1989, Midnight Coller, 1990, 21 Jump Street, 1990, Reasonable Doubts, 1991, Charlie Grace, 1995, Lazarus Man, 1996, The Pretender, 1997, ER, 2000, Law & Order SVU, 2001-2002; Writer, dir., editor, actor: Killer Snake, 2004. Mailing: care Nat Coun La Raza Ste 840 523 W 6th St Los Angeles CA 90014

CARRINGER, ROBERT, language educator; b. Knoxville, Tenn., May 12, 1941; m. Sonia Raysor, Sept. 7, 1968. AB, U. Tenn., 1962; MA, Johns Hopkins, 1964; PhD, Ind. U., 1968. Asst. prof. English U. Ill., Urbana, 1970-76, assoc. prof. English, 1976-84, disting. prof., 1985, prof. English and film, 1985—2003, prof. emeritus. Vis. humanities scholar, U. Colo., 1981; assoc. Ctr. Advanced Study, 1983-1984. Mem. editl. bd.: Am. Studies, Quar. Rev. Film and Video, Cinema Jour.; co-author: Ernst Lubitsch, 1978 (Choice Outstanding Acad. Book award, 1979), The Making of Citizen Kane, 1985, rev. edit., 1996, Magnificent Andersons: A Reconstruction, 1996; editor: The Jazz Singer, 1979; contbr. articles to profl. jours.; prodr.: (laserdiscs). Recipient Instrnl. Tech. awards Amoco Corp., 1980, Apple Computer, 1988; Rsch. grantee NEH, 1986-87; fellow in cognitive psychology U. Ill., 1990-91; NEH Rev. Panels scholar, 1993, 96, Getty scholar Getty Rsch. Inst., 1996-97. Mem.: MLA (chmn. film divsn. exec. com. 1981), Phi Beta Kappa, Phi Kappa Phi. Home: 50 County Rd 1675N Seymour IL 61875 Business E-Mail: fergus@uiuc.edu.

CARRINGTON, BESSIE MEEK, librarian; b. Houston, Oct. 17, 1931; d. James H. and Bessie B. Meek; m. Paul D. Carrington, Aug. 2, 1952; children: Clark, Mary, William J., Emily. BA, U. Tex., 1956; MLS, U. Mich., 1972. Libr. HUD, NYC, 1972-73; reference libr. Detroit Pub. Libr., 1973-76; asst. br. libr. Ann Arbor (Mich.) Pub. Libr., 1976-78; reference libr. Duke U., Durham, N.C., 1979-94. Adj. prof. U. Mich., Ann Arbor, 1976, U. N.C., Chapel Hill, 1989, 91, 92. Contbr.: Guide to Reference Books, 11th edit., 1996; contbr. articles to profl. jours.; reviewer. Mem. ALA, Am. Econs. Assn., Am. Soc. for Info. Sci., N.C. Libr. Assn., Alpha Lambda Delta, Phi beta Kappa. Home: 1616 Pinecrest Rd Durham NC 27705-5832 E-mail: bessiec@mindspring.com.

CARRINGTON, MICHAEL DAVIS, criminal justice and security consultant; b. South Bend, Ind., Mar. 9, 1938; s. Herman Lakin and Margaret (Davis) C.; m. Lynn Ogden, Feb. 8, 1958; children: Michael O. (dec.), Jill A., Elizabeth A., Gretchen L. BA, Ind. U., 1970; MALS, Valparaiso U., 1971. Parole officer State of Ind., South Bend, 1970-71; chief probation officer St. Joseph County, South Bend, 1971-74; dir. pub. safety City of South Bend, 1974-76, mayor's asst., 1976-80; adj. assoc. prof., dir. safety, security, police Ind. U., South Bend, 1979-94; presdl. appointment as U.S. Marshal Northern Dist. of Ind., South Bend, Ind., 1994—2002; ret. U.S. Marshall's Svc., 2002—. Cons. in pvt. security Pan Am. Games, Indpls., 1987; cons. on Bur. Motor Vehicles security study Gov. of Ind., 2003-04; security advance agt. Olympic Torch Relay, Ind., 1984, Hands Across Am., Ind., 1986; mem. alcoholic beverage bd. St. Joseph County, South Bend, 2007—. Mem. Ind. Parole Bd., 2004—05. Named Ky. Col., 1984, Hon. Big Bro. of Yr., 1974; recipient Sagamore of the Wabash award, 1984, 2002, 2004, Disting. Alumnus award, Coll. Arts and Scis., Ind. U., South Bend, 2002. Mem.: Assn. of Threat Assessment Profls. Presbyterian. Avocations: travel, reading, walking, working. Office: Box 96 South Bend IN 46624 Home Phone: 574-272-5857; Office Phone: 574-210-8575. E-mail: carringtonconsulting@comcast.net.

CARRINGTON, PAUL DEWITT, lawyer, educator; b. Dallas, June 12, 1931; s. Paul and Frances Ellen (DeWitt) C.; m. Bessie Meek, Aug., 1952; children: Clark DeWitt, Mary Carrington Coults, William James, Emily Carrington. BA, U. Tex., 1952; LLB, Harvard U., 1955. Bar: Tex. 1955, Ohio 1962, Mich. 1967. Practice, Dallas, 1955; teaching fellow Harvard U., 1957-58; asst. prof. law U. Wyo., 1958-60, Ind. U., 1960-62; assoc. prof. Ohio State U., 1962-65; prof. U. Mich., 1965-78; dean Duke U. Sch. Law, Durham, NC, 1978-88, prof., 1978—. Reporter civil rules adv. com. Jud. Conf. of U.S., 1985-92. Author (with Meador and Rosenberg): Justice on Appeal, 1977, Appeals, 1994; author: (with Babcock) Civil Procedure, 1977, 3d edit., 1983; author: Stewards of Democracy, 1999, Spreading America's Word, 2005; author: (with Cramton) Reforming the Supreme Court, 2006; author: (with Jones) Law and Class in America, 2006. Trustee Ann Arbor (Mich.) Bd. Edn., 1970-73; pres. Pvt. Adjudication Ctr., Inc., 1988-94, chmn., 1995-2002. With US Army, 1955—57, with USAR, 1957—61. Guggenheim fellow, 1988-89. Fellow: Am. Acad. Appellate Lawyers, Am. Acad. Arts and Scis., Am. Bar Found.; mem.: ABA, Am. Law Inst. Office: Duke U Sch Law Durham NC 27708-0362 Home Phone: 919-489-8668; Office Phone: 919-613-7040. Business E-Mail: pdc@law.duke.edu.

CARRION, RICHARD L., bank executive; b. San Juan, P.R., 1952; BS, U. Penn.; MS in Mgmt. Info. Systems, MIT. Pres. Ban Ponce Corp.; chmn., CEO Banco Popular de P.R.; chmn., pres., CEO Popular Inc. Bd. dirs. Nynex Corp., 1995—97, Verizon Comm., 1997—, Wyeth, 1997—; mem. exec. bd. Internat. Olympic Com., 2004—. Office: Banco Popularde Puerto Rico 209 Munoz Rivera Avenue Hato Rey PR 00918*

CARRITHERS, JOSEPH EDWARD, English composition and literature educator; b. Red Bay, Ala., July 28, 1963; s. Edward Walden and Dessie Lee McClure. BA in Comm./Journalism, Miss. State U., Starkville, 1985, BA in English/History, 1987, MA in English, 1990, U. So. Calif., 1992, PhD in English, 2003. Reporter Comml. Dispatch, Columbus, Miss., 1985-88; mng. editor Starkville Daily News, 1988-90; asst. lectr. U. So. Calif., LA, 1990-94; ESL instr. Don Martin Coll., Monterey Park, Calif., 1991; part-time prof. Mt. San Antonio Coll., Walnut, Calif., 1991-94; lectr. Woodbury U., Burbank, Calif., 1993-94; prof. English Fullerton (Calif.) Coll., 1994—. Mem. faculty senate Fullerton Coll. 1996-2002, pres. 1998-2001, mem. Planning and Consultative Coun., Fullerton Coll., 1997-2005 Contbr. poetry to Forum; contbr. articles to Frontiers, Men's Fitness, Jour. Popular Film and TV Named Tchr. of Yr., Fullerton Coll., 2004. Mem. MLA, United Faculty, Nat. Coun. Tchrs. English, Am. Studies Assn., Gay and Lesbian Assn. Dist. Employees, Lambda Soc. (advisor). Office: Fullerton Coll 321 E Chapman Ave Fullerton CA 92832-2011

CARRO, ERIC F., neurosurgeon; b. San Juan, P.R., Dec. 1, 1949; BS, U. P.R., 1970, MD, 1974. Diplomate Am. Bd. Neurol. Surgery. Assoc. prof. U. P.R., San Juan, 1982—; pvt. practice neurosurgery, 1981—. Mem.: Caribbean Assn. Neurol. Surgeons, Am. Assn. Neurol. Surgeons. Office: 73 Santa Cruz St Office 207 Bayamon PR 00961 Office Phone: 787-740-2166.

CARROL, EDWARD NICHOLAS, psychologist; b. Newark, June 22, 1943; s. Wilfred and Ruth (Gluck) C.; m. Anne Marie McDonald, May 27, 1973 (div. May 1989); 1 child, Abbe Galen; m. Virginia Paisley Herbruck, Oct. 6, 1996. BA, Columbia U., 1965; MA, NYU, 1970, U. Del., 1975,

PhD, 1979. Diplomate Am. Acad. Pain Mgmt. Dir. Pain Clinic, VA Med. Ctr., Cleve., 1979—2003, dir. pain psychology Pain Mgmt. Ctr., 2003—. Mem. Internat. Assn. Study of Pain, Midwest Pain Soc. Republican. Jewish. Avocations: dogs, classical and country music. Home: 21490 Claythorne Rd Shaker Heights OH 44122-1964 Office: VA Med Ctr Pain Mgmt Ctr 10701 East Blvd Cleveland OH 44106-1702 Home Phone: 216-932-3460; Office Phone: 216-791-3800 x 4480.

CARROLL, ANDREW PATRICK KEATING, writer; b. Washington, Sept. 27, 1969; s. Thomas Edmund and Marea Grace Carroll. BA, Columbia U., 1992. Exec. dir., co-founder The Am. Poetry and Literacy Project, Washington, 1993—. Bd. dirs. Literacy Vols. of Am., Washington, 1994—. Author: Volunteer USA, 1991, Golden Opportunities: A Volunteer Guide for Americans over 50, 1994, War Letters: Extraordinary Correspondence from American Wars, 2001, Behind the Lines: Powerful and Revealing American and Foreign War Letters--and One Man's Search to Find Them, 2005. Named Tomorrow's Leaders Today, Pub. Allies, 1993, Person of the Week, ABC World News Tonight, 1994; recipient Pres. award IONA Sr. Svcs., 1994. Office: The Am Poetry & Lit Project PO Box 53445 Washington DC 20009-9445

CARROLL, BARRY JOSEPH, manufacturing and real estate executive; b. Highland Park, Ill., Jan. 22, 1944; s. Wallace Edward and Lelia (Holden) C.; m. Barbara Ann Pehrson, July 16, 1965; children: Megan, Sean, Deirdre, Colleen, Oona. Student, Boston Coll., 1961-63; AB, Shimer Coll., 1966; MBA, Harvard U., 1969. Lic. real estate broker, Ill. Account rep. Amerad Advt. Service, Chgo., summers 1966, 67; staff analyst Jamesbury Valve Co., Worcester, Mass., 1968; asst. to pres. Am. Gage & Machine Co., Elgin, Ill., 1969; pres. J.C. Deagan Co., Chgo., 1969-77; v.p. Internat. Metals & Machines, Des Plaines, 1977-92, bd. dir.; v.p. Katy Industries, Elgin, 1984-94, bd. dir.; pres. Katy Comm., Inc. (WIVS-AM, WXRD-FM, WAIT AM/FM), 1986-92, Sta. W45AJ-TV, Rockford, Ill., 1989-92. V.p., bd. dir. Pehrson-Long Assocs., Real Estate Mgmt., Am. Machine & Sci. Inc., CRL Inc., Carroll Internat. Corp. (chmn. 1992), GFS Holdings Co.; bd. dir. XPS Mktg. Inc. Author: (monograph) Talking with Business, 1986; author of appendix/editor: What I Do Best: The Biography of Wallace Edward Carroll, 1992; editor/author: Private Means/Public Ends, 1987; author: Lake Forest, A Very Special Place, 1996; producer, dir. indsl. films, including In There Punching, 1965, The Story of Mallet Instruments, 1975, Digging Lake County, 1999; dir./host (cable TV series) Area Arts, 2000—. Spl. asst. U.S. Sec. Edn., Washington, 1983-84; Presdl. Exch. exec., Washington, 1983-84; bd. govs. United Rep. Fund, Chgo., 1986-92; mem. Nat. Inst. Edn. Commn. Edn. and Tech., U.S. Dept. Edn., 1984-85; trustee Shimer Coll., 1970—, chmn. bd. trustees, 1975-78; trustee Barat Coll., Lake Forest, 1983—2001, life trustee, 1999—; trustee St. Xavier U., Chgo., 1988-94, Lake County Regional Sch. Bd., 1993—; trustee Am. Ireland Fund, 1982-2001, sec., 1991-99; bd. dirs. Lake Forest Symphony, 1970—, Pageant of Peace/Nat. Christmas Tree, 1987-2000, Lake Forest Symphony Sch. of Music. , 1991—, Roosevelt U., Chgo., 1996-2005, U. Ill. Eye Rsch. Inst., 1996—; bd. dirs. Chgo. Crime Commn., 1993—, treas., 1994-98; mem., chmn. Lake Forest Cultural Arts Commn., 1997—; chair adv. bd. Inst. Metro. Affairs Roosevelt U., 1998—; trustee Auditorium Theatre Roosevelt U., 2003—, chmn. fin. com., 2003—; mem. pres.'s coun. U. Ill., 1996—. Shimer fellow Shimer Coll., Mt. Carroll, Ill., 1972, Shimer Hero award Shimer Coll., Waukegan, Ill., 1980, Dr. Letters, 1995. Mem. Woods Hole Oceanographic Inst. Assn., Ill. Mfrs. Assn. (bd. dir. 1989-2005, treas. 1991-95), Am. Inst. Aeronautics and Astronautics, Assn. for Mfg. Tech. (bd. dir. chmn. pub. affairs com. 1988-93), Elawa Farm Commn.(dir.), Lake Forest, Lake Forest Onwentsia Club, Chgo. Club, Washington Met. Club , East Chop Beach Tennis and Yacht Clubs, Edgartown Yacht Club, West Palm Beach Bath and Tennis Club, Soc. Colonial Wars in the State of Ill. (treas. 1988-94, gov. 1998-2000), Nat. Soc. Colonial Wars (dep. gov. gen. 2002—05) Soc. Cin. Avocations: flying, sailing, scuba diving, photography. Office: Wildwood LLC 60 N Stonegate Lake Forest IL 60045 Business E-Mail: bcarroll@carrollintl.com.

CARROLL, BETTY JEAN, retired application developer; b. San Antonio, Dec. 5, 1930; d. Jesse Irvin Casbeer and Nelda Martha Blum; m. John D. Kissack, Oct. 5, 1957 (div. Oct. 0, 1963); m. Richard Andrew Carroll, Oct. 3, 1946 (div. Mar. 0, 1954); children: Peggy Jean Choka, Martha Ann Scott, Betty Jacquelyn, Richard Andrew, Michael Neil. AA, San Antonio Coll., Tex., 1956; BA in Liberal Arts, Wright State U., Dayton, Ohio, 1976. Office mgr. and acct. Civilian Bldg. and Supply, Ft. Wayne, Ind., 1963—66; staff acct. Rignanese, Shannon & Horn CPA, 1966—67; cost acct. Air Flow Heating and Air Conditioning, 1967—70; computer specialist/programmer Wright-Patterson AFB, Dayton, Ohio, 1970—95; office mgr. and acct. So. Ohio Growth Partnership, Portsmouth, 1995—98; computer programmer STAR Fin. Bank, Ft. Wayne, Ind., 2000—03. Author: The Foothill Spirits-Book One: Frontier Life & the Shawnees, 2001, rev., 2005, The Foothill Spirits-Book Two: Shawnees & Runaway Slaves, 2006, The Mystery of the Red-Brick House, 2002. Sec.-treas. Gingerbread Ho. Day Care, Fort Wayne, Ind., 1999—2003; mem. speaker's collective and women's ctr. task force Dayton Women's Liberation, Ohio, 1970—75; v.p. Women's Internat. League Peace and Freedom, 1974—75, Miami Valley Freedom of Choice, 1979—80; co-chair Women Racial & Econ. Equality, 1987—91; bd. mem. Midway Day Care Ctr., 1969—70; charter mem. Federally Employed Women, Fairborn, 1973; sec.-treas. AFGE Coun. 214, Dayton, 1980—82; charter mem. Coalition of Labor Union Women, Fairborn, 1985; pres. Am. Fedn. Govt. Employees AFL-CIO Local 1138, Dayton, 1991—95. Mem.: The Scribes. Unitarian-Universalist. Avocations: reading, book discussion groups, writer's group mentor, history, book collecting. Home: 7109 Lower Huntington Rd Fort Wayne IN 46809-9615

CARROLL, CHARLES A., manufacturing executive; Sales rep. Rubbermaid, 1971, pres., gen. mgr. housewares product divsn., 1990, pres., COO, 1993-99; pres., CEO Amana Appliances, 2000—04, Goodman Global Inc., Houston, 2004—. Office: Goodman Global Inc Ste 400 2550 North Loop West Houston TX 77092*

CARROLL, CHARLES MICHAEL, music educator; b. Otterbein, Ind., Mar. 5, 1921; s. James William and Catherine Doretta (Bohan) C.; m. Mary Lipford Rosenbush, Sept. 4, 1951; children: Charles Michael, Mary Catherine, Theresa Jane, William Rosenbush. BM, Ind. U., Bloomington, 1949; MM, Fla. State U., Tallahassee, 1951, PhD, 1960. Asst. coordinator music services Ind. U., 1949-50; instr. music Fla. State U., 1950-53; concert mgr. symphony orchs. Toledo, Washington, Savannah, Ga., 1953-58; prof. music Pensacola (Fla.) Jr. Coll., 1960-64; prof. St. Petersburg (Fla.) Jr. Coll., 1964-89, chmn. communications dept. Music critic Tallahassee Democrat, 1950-53, St. Petersburg Evening Independent, 1976-86. Author: The Great Chess Automaton, 1975; contbr. articles to profl. jours., and encyclopaedias. Served to capt., AUS, 1942-46, ETO. Mem. Am. Symphony Orch. League (v.p. 1955-56), Am. Musicol. Soc. (nat. council 1974-77, chmn. 1974-76), Am. Soc. Eighteenth-Century Studies (exec. bd. region 1974-82, regional pres. 1979-80), Coll. Music Soc. (editor 1979-83, nat. council 1978-81, chmn. chpt. 1979-80), Société d'Etudes Philidoriennes (conseiller bibliographique 1988—). Home: 1701 80th St N Saint Petersburg FL 33710-3703

CARROLL, CONSTANCE MARIE, pianist, music educator; b. Hartford, Conn., May 6, 1945; d. Joseph Deglan and Elizabeth Tracy Carroll; 1 child, Jackson William Blossom. MusB magna cum laude, U. Hartford, 1968; MusM, Manhattan Sch. Music, 1980; postgrad., Ind. U., 1981—84. Pvt. tchr. piano, Conn. and NY, 1965—. Organist, Union Congl. Ch., Torrington, Conn.; accompanist Lubeck Ballet and Musical Theatre, Germany, 1992—93, Luzern Ballet, Switzerland, 1993—94, Basel Ballet, Switzerland, 1994—96; pianist Imperial Sch. of Ballet, East Lyme, Conn., Hartford U. Sch. of Ballet. , NY State PTA scholar, 1983. Mem.: Am. Guild Organists, Music Tchrs. Nat. Assn., Conn. State Music Tchrs.' Assn. Home and Office: 41 Ridge Ct Oakville CT 06779 Office Phone: 860-274-4198.

CARROLL, CYNTHIA B., mining executive; b. Phila., Pa. married; 4 children. BS in Geology, Skidmore Coll., 1978; MS, U. Kansas, 1982; MBA, Harvard U., 1989. Geologist Amoco, 1982—87; bus. analyst, asst. to the pres. Alcan Inc., 1988, bus. analyst rolled products group, 1989—91, v.p., gen. mgr. US foil products, 1991—95, mng. dir. Aughinish Alumina subs. Ireland, 1996—98, pres. bauxite, Alcan's alumina and specialty chemicals group, 1998—2001, pres., CEO primary metal group, 2002—06; CEO Anglo American plc, 2007—. Bd. dirs. Sara Lee Corp., 2006—07, Anglo American plc, 2007—, BP plc, 2007—. Named one of 50 Women to Watch, Wall St. Jour., 2006. Mem.: Internat. Aluminum Inst. (bd. dirs.), Am. Aluminum Assn. (bd. dirs.). Office: Anglo American plc 20 Carlton House Terr London SW1Y 5AN England

CARROLL, DAVID, writer, illustrator; b. 1942; BFA, Tufts Univ., 1965. Lectr., cons. to conservation inst. New England Region. Exhibitions include Hunt Inst. Botanical Documentation, Dartmouth Coll. Mus. Galleries, Univ. Conn. Thomas J. Dodd Rsch. Ctr.; author: (science books) Trout Reflections, 1993, The Year of the Turtle, 1996, Swampwalker's Journal, 1999, Self-Portrait With Turtles, 2004. MacArthur Fell., John D. and Catherine T. MacArthur Found., 2006. Office: c/o John D and Catherine T MacArthur Found 140 S Dearborn St Chicago IL 60603-5285

CARROLL, DAVID PAUL, social welfare administrator; b. NYC, Nov. 22, 1935; s. Hugh Felix Carroll and Gertrude Jordan. BA in Physics, Cath. U. Am., Washington, 1958; M in Physics, Brown U., 1963; PhD in Sci. Edn., NYU, 1978. Data processing cons. Diocese Bklyn., 1965-68; founder, dir. Data Sys. Ctr. Archdiocese N.Y., NYC, 1968-79, asst. to chancellor, 1979-82; dir. rsch. Pope John Paul II Ctr., NYC, 1982-85; asst. to sec. gen. Cath. Near E. Welfare Assn., NYC, 1985—, under sec. gen. Cnewa, 2004—. Adj. asst. prof. St. John's U., Jamaica, N.Y., 1978-86; adj. prof. NYU, 1981-97; mid. east advisor Holy See Permanent Mission to UN, N.Y.C., 1985—. Co-author: The Ethics of Nuclear Deterrence, 1991; contbr. over 70 articles to profl. publs. Co-chair Muslim/Roman Cath. Dialogue, N.Y.C., 1985—; treas. Bros. of Christian Schs. Found., Oak Brook, Ill., 1987—; bd. dirs. Future Millenium Found., Arlington, Va., 1996—, St. Thomas Aquinas Coll., Sparkill, N.Y., 1998—, chmn. bd., 2006. Recipient Cross Pro Ecclescia Pro Pontifice Roman Cath. Pontiff, 1995. Mem. Cath. Acad. Scis. (founder, sec. 1987—, pres. elect, 2005), Equestrian Order Holy Sepulchre Jerusalem (knight comdr. with star 1987), Cath. Assn. Scientists & Engrs., Scholars Social Justice, Knight Grand Cross. Avocations: model railroading, canoeing, hiking, backpacking, classical music. Office: Cath Near E Welfare Assn 1011 1st Ave Ste 1552 New York NY 10022 Business E-Mail: b2d@cnewa.org.

CARROLL, DAVID WILLIAM, psychology professor; b. Floral Park, NY, July 28, 1950; s. Patrick Edwin and Mary Mammolite Carroll; m. Debora Panietz, July 8, 1973; children: Michael Adam(dec.) , Rachel Marie. BA, U. Calif., Davis, 1972; MA, Mich. State U., East Lansing, 1973; PhD, Mich. State U., 1976. Asst. prof. psychology U. Wis., 1976—82, assoc. prof. psychology, 1982—90, psychology prof., 1990—, chair, dept. of human behavior and diversity, 1995—2000, chair of faculty, 2004—06. Author: (textbook) Psychology of Language. Donor Duluth-Superior Cmty. Found., Minn., 2005—06. Recipient Faculty Scholarship award, U. of Wis.-Superior, 1987, Outstanding Student Orgn. Advisor, 2000, Tchg. Excellence award, 2005, Honors in Philosophy, U. of Calif. at Davis, 1972; NIMH Traineeship in Exptl. Psychology, Mich. State U., 1972—75. Mem.: APA, Soc. Gen. Psychology, Soc. for Tchg. of Psychology, Midwestern Psychol. Assn., Assn. for Psychol. Sci. Avocations: music, sports, gardening, cooking, history. Office: Univ Wis-Superior Psychology Program Belknap and Catlin Superior WI 54880-4500 Office Phone: 715-394-8323. Office Fax: 715-394-8493. Business E-Mail: dcarroll@uwsuper.edu.

CARROLL, DEIRDRE HOLDEN, psychiatric nurse practitioner, educator, medical researcher; b. Lake Forest, Ill., Jan. 1, 1973; d. Barry Joseph and Barbara Pehrson Carroll. BSN, Boston Coll., Chestnut Hill, Mass., 1995; MSN, Yale U., 2000; student, Boston Coll., 2003—. Cert. psychiatric-mental health clinical nurse specialist, Conn., adult nurse practitioner, Conn., lic. advanced practice RN, Conn., RN Conn., Ill. Staff nurse Lake Forest Hosp., 1996, Rush North Shore Med. Ctr., Skokie, Ill., 1996—98, Ariaù (Brazil) Jungle Towers, 1998; clin. faculty Yale U. Sch. of Nursing, New Haven, 2002—04, clin. preceptor. Co-investigator/clin. rsch., clin. faculty Yale U. Sch. Medicine, Child Study Ctr., New Haven, 2000—; psychiat. nurse practitioner Yale U. Sch. of Medicine, Child Study Ctr., New Haven, 2000—04; co-investigator Rsch. Units in Pediatric Psychopharmacology, New Haven, 2000—; presenter in field. Contbr. articles to profl. jours. Mem. Am. Ireland Fund. Mem.: DAR, Nat. League for Nurses, Am. Psychiatric Nurses Assn., Ea. Nursing Rsch. Soc., Coun. Fgn. Rels. Ill., Boston Coll. Nurses Assn., Ill. Nurses Assn., Conn. Nurses Assn., Am. Coll. of Nurse Practitioners, Internat. Soc. of Psychiatric-Mental Health Nurses, Irish-Georgian Soc., Yale Alumnae Assn., Landmarks Preservation Soc. Ill., Boston Coll. Alumni Assn., USTA, PA of Diving Instructors, Women's Athletic Club of Chgo., Yale Club of NYC, Boston Coll. Honor Soc., Sigma Theta Tau Internat. (named to Yale U. Honor Soc. 2001, named to Boston (Mass.) Coll. Honor Soc. 2004). Achievements include research in psychopharmacology and behavioral interventions for the treatment of children and adolecents with serious mental illness and developmental disorders. Avocations: international travel, classical piano, tennis/squash, photography, scuba diving. Home: 34 Chesterton Rd Wellesley Hills MA 02481 Home Fax: 781-489-5256. Personal E-mail: dcerulkar@yahoo.com.

CARROLL, DENNIS JEROME, aerospace transportation executive; b. Washington, Mo., Jan. 4, 1947; s. Kenneth Leroy and Nettie Lorainne Carroll; m. Barbara Louise Schild, Mar. 3, 1973; children: Matthew Griswald, Jeremy Walwyn, Barbara Renee Lilley. Assoc., Wentworth Mil. Acad., Lexington, Mo., 1966; BA, Drury Coll., Springfield, Mo., 1968; MS, Naval Post Grad. Sch., Monterey, Calif., 1975. Lic. aviator USN, 1969. Commd. ensign USN, 1968, advanced through grades to comdr., 1988, naval aviator Pensacola, Fla., 1968—88; tech. mgr. Gen. Dynamics, Ontario, Calif., 1988—93; dir. bus. devel. Hughes Aircraft, Tucson, 1993—97, dir. phalanx systems, 1997—2002; dep. guided projectiles products Raytheon Missile Systems, Tucson, 2002—04, v.p. bus. devel., 2004—. Cno strategic studies group V USN, Newport, RI, 1985—86. Decorated NCM USN, Air medal with Combat V. Achievements include 172 combat missions. Home: 6181 E Country Club Vista Dr Tucson AZ 85750-1986 Office: Raytheon Missile Systems Hermans Rd Tucson AZ 85734-1337 Home Phone: 520-299-4414; Office Phone: 520 794-3457. Business E-Mail: djcarroll@raytheon.com.

CARROLL, DONNA M., academic administrator; MA, U. Cin., 1977, PhD in Edn., 1981. Program dir. U. Cin.; dean of students Fairleigh Dickenson U., Madison, NJ, Mt. Vernon Coll., Washington, v.p. devel.; sec. Fordham U., 1991—94, exec. sec. Bd. Trustees, 1991—94; pres. Dominican U., River Forest, Ill., 1994—. Recipient Chief Exec. Leadership award, Coun. Advancement and Support of Edn., 2004. Office: Dominican U 7900 W Division River Forest IL 60305

CARROLL, EARL HAMBLIN, federal judge; b. Tucson, Mar. 26, 1925; s. John Vernon and Ruby (Wood) C.; m. Louise Rowlands, Nov. 1, 1952; children: Katherine Carroll Pearson, Margaret Anne BSBA, U. Ariz., 1948, LLB, 1951. Bar: Ariz., US Ct. Appeals (9th and 10th cirs.), US Ct. of Claims, US Supreme Ct. Law clk. Ariz. Supreme Ct., Phoenix, 1951-52; assoc. Evans, Kitchel & Jenckes, Phoenix, 1952-56, ptnr., 1956-80; judge US Dist. Ct. Ariz., Phoenix, 1980—, sr. judge, 1994—. Spl. counsel City of Tombstone, Ariz., 1962-65, Maricopa County, Phoenix, 1968-75, City of Tucson, 1974, City of Phoenix, 1979; designated mem. US Fgn. Intelligence Surveillance Court by Chief Justice US Supreme Ct., 1993-99; chief judge Alien Terrorist Removal Ct., 1996-01, 2001—06. Mem. City of Phoenix Bd. of Adjustment, 1955-58; trustee Phoenix Elem. Sch. Bd., 1961-72; mem. Gov.'s Council on Intergovtl. Relations, Phoenix, 1970-73; mem. Ariz. Bd. Regents, 1978-80. Served with USNR, 1943-46; PTO Recipient Nat. Service awards Campfire, 1973, 75, Alumni Service award U. Ariz., 1980, Disting. Citizen award No. Ariz. U., Flagstaff, 1983, Bicentenial award Georgetown U., 1988, Disting. Citizen award U. Ariz., 1990, Sidney S. Woods Alumni Svc. award, 2000, Disting. Alumnus award, 2007. Fellow Am. Coll. Trial Lawyers, Am. Bar Found.; mem. ABA, Ariz. Bar Assn., U. Ariz. Law Coll. Assn. (pres. 1975), Sigma Chi (Significant Sig award 1991, Hall of Fame award 2007), Phi Delta Phi. Democrat. Office: US Dist Ct US Courthouse Ste 521 401 W Washington SPC 48 Phoenix AZ 85003-2151 Home Phone: 602-258-2028; Office Phone: 602-322-7530.

CARROLL, FRANK EDWARD, JR., radiologist, researcher; b. Phila., Oct. 25, 1941; s. Frank Edward Sr. and Marie Elizabeth (Mullin) C.; m. Saramae Dorothy Dever, Sept. 4, 1965; children: Frank Leonard, Mark Edward. BS in Biology, St. Joseph's Coll., 1963; MD, Hahnemann Med. Coll., 1967. Diplomate Am. Bd. Radiology. Rsch. asst. Hahnemann Med. Coll. and Hosp., Phila., 1965-66; rotating intern U.S. Naval Regional Med. Ctr., Oakland, Calif., 1967-68; submarine med. officer U.S. Submarine Med. Sch., U.S. Naval Submarine Base, Gorton, Conn., 1968, SSBN 659 Will Rogers Polaris Nuclear Submarine, 1968-69; staff physician Armed Forces Staff Coll., Norfolk, Va., 1969-70; diagnostic radiology resident St. Mary's Hosp. and Med. Ctr., San Francisco, 1970-72; resident, fellow, rschr. U. Calif. San Francisco Sch. Medicine, 1972-73; asst. prof. diagnostic radiology Yale U. Sch. Medicine, New Haven, 1973-74; staff radiologist Broadway Hosp., Vallejo, Calif., 1974-75, Franklin (Pa.) Regional Med. Ctr., 1975-83; asst. prof. diagnostic radiology Vanderbilt U. Med. Ctr., Nashville, 1983-87, chief sect. pulmonary imaging, 1983—2000, assoc. dir. divsn. diagnostic radiology, 1984, dir. lab. radiologic rsch., 1984-85, assoc. prof. diagnostic radiology, 1987-94, dir. diagnostic radiology, 1985-89, assoc. prof. physics and astronomy, 1993-99, prof. diagnostic radiology, 1994—2004, emeritus prof. diagnostic radiology, 2004—, prof. physics and astronomy, 1999—; founder Mxisystems, Inc., Nashville. Adj. asst. prof. diagnostic radiology Duke U. Med. Ctr., Durham, N.C., 1981-83; cons. in field; referee jours. in field, including Investigative Radiology, Acad. Radiology, Radiology, Chest, Jour. Applied Physiology, Archives of Internal Medicine, Am. Jour. Neuroradiology, others; grant reviewer NIH, Washington. Contbr. articles to profl. jours., chpts. to books. Bd. dirs. Nashville Opera, 1988-94, Franklin Emergency Ambulance Svc., 1975-83, St. Patrick's Sch. Bd., 1975-83; asst. scoutmaster Boy Scouts Am., Franklin, 1975-83, physician and merit badge counselor, Nashville, 1983—; pres. Am. Cancer Soc., Franklin, 1975-83; design prodn. vol. Cheekwood Fine Arts Mus., Nashville, 1995—. Lt. comdr. USNR, 1963—73, submarine med. officer USNR, 1968—71, base physician Armed Forces Staff Coll., 1970—71. Fellow Am. Coll. Radiology, Am. Coll. Chest Physicians; mem. Am. Soc. Laser Medicine and Surgery, Soc. Photo-Optical Instrumentation Engrs., Soc. for Magnetic Resonance Imaging, Assn. Univ. Radiologists, Radiol. Soc. N.Am., Soc. thoracic Radiology, Tenn. Radiologic Soc., Mid. Tenn. Radiologic Soc. Achievements include production of pulsed, tunable, monochromatic X-rays by the free electron laser; designed and commissioned dedicated tabletop laser tunable, synchrotron source for monochromatic 3-D mammography without breast compression, k-edge imaging, auger cascade radiotherapy, phase contrast imaging, time-of flight imaging and protein crystallography; evaluation of lung water by magnetic resonance imaging. Home: 1216 Vintage Pl Nashville TN 37215-4707 Office: Vanderbilt U Med Ctr Emeritus Office 211 Oxford House Nashville TN 37232-4245 Business E-Mail: frank.carroll@vanderbilt.edu.

CARROLL, FRANK JAMES, lawyer, educator; b. Albuquerque, Feb. 10, 1947; s. Francis J. and Dorothy (Bloom) C.; m. Marilyn Blume, Aug. 9, 1969; children: Christine, Kathleen, Emily. BS in Acctg., St. Louis U., 1969; JD, U. Ill., 1973. Bar: Iowa 1973, U.S. Dist. Ct. Iowa, U.S. Tax Ct., U.S. Ct. Appeals (8th cir.); CPA, Mo., Iowa. Acct. Arthur Young & Co., St. Louis, 1969-70; shareholder Davis, Brown, Koehn, Shors & Roberts, P.C., Des Moines, 1973—. Lectr. law Drake U. Law Sch., Des Moines, 1976-86, lectr. Sch. Bus., 1988-92; bd. dirs. Iowa Agr. Devel. Authority, Iowa State Bar Assn.; adj. prof. Drake U. Law Sch., 2007—. Mem. commr.'s adv. group Internal Revenue Svc., Washington, 1989; mem. U. Mo. Kansas City Sch. Law, 1995. Mem. ABA, Iowa Bar Assn. (chmn. bus. law sect. 1995-98, chmn. corp. counsel sect. 2001-2003, bd. govs. 2003-07), Polk County Bar Assn. (bd. dirs. 2003-07), Des Moines C. of C., Wakonda Club, Des Moines Variety Club (bd. dirs. 1998), Beta Gamma Sigma. Home: 5725 Harwood Dr Des Moines IA 50312-1203 Office: Davis Brown Koehn Shors Roberts PC 666 Walnut St Ste 2500 Des Moines IA 50309-3904 Office Phone: 515-288-2500. Business E-Mail: frankcarroll@lawiowa.com.

CARROLL, GEORGE JOSEPH, pathologist, educator; b. Gardner, Mass., Oct. 14, 1917; s. George Joseph and Kathryn (O'Hearn) C. BA, Clark U., Worcester, Mass., 1939; MD, George Washington U., 1944. Diplomate Am. Bd. Pathology. Intern Worchester City Hosp., 1944-45; resident in medicine Doctors Hosp., Washington, 1945-46; resident in pathology Sibley Hosp., Washington, 1948-49, VA Hosp., Washington, 1949-50; asst. pathologist D.C. Gen. Hosp., 1950-51, assoc. pathologist, 1951-52; pathologist Louise Obici Meml. Hosp., Suffolk, Va., 1952—, sec. med. staff, 1956-59, chief of staff, 1959-60, 67-69; pathologist Chowan Hosp., Edenton, NC, 1952-71, Southampton Meml. Hosp., Franklin, Va., 1952—, Greensville Meml. Hosp., Emporia, Va., 1961—. Instr. pathology Georgetown U. Sch. Medicine, 1950-52; instr. bacteriology Am. U., Washington, 1950-51; assoc. clin. prof. pathology Med. Coll. Va., Richmond, 1968-70; clin. prof. pathology Va. Commonwealth U., 1970—; prof. dept. pathology Eastern Va. Med. Sch., Norfolk, 1974—; sec.-treas. Va. Bd. Medicine, 1967-86, treas., 1971-86. Contbr. articles to med. jours. Served with U.S. Army, 1946-48. Fellow ACP, Coll. Am. Pathologists, Am. Soc. Clin. Pathologists (bd. dirs. 1969—, pres. 1977—), Internat. Acad. Pathology; mem. AMA, So. Med. Assn. (Va. councilor 1965-70, pres. 1973-74), Med. Soc. Va., 4th dist. Med. Soc. (pres. 1968-70), Seaboard Med. Soc. (pres. 1957), George Washington Med. Soc., Tri-County Med. Soc. (pres. 1971-73), Am. Soc. Clin. Pharmacy Therapeutics, Va. Soc. Pathology (pres. 1973-74), Soc. Nuclear Medicine, Am. Assn. Blood Banks, Am. Cancer Soc. (bd. dirs. Va. div. 1955-62), Va. Med. Svc. Assn. (bd. dirs. 1960-71), Rotary. Home: 219 Northbrooke Ave Suffolk VA 23434-6647

CARROLL, HOWARD WILLIAM, state legislator; b. July 28, 1942; s. Barney M. and Lyla (Price) C.; m. Eda Stagman, Dec. 1, 1973; children: Jacqueline, Barbara. BBA, Roosevelt U., 1964; postgrad., Loyola U., 1964-65; JD, DePaul U., 1967. Bar: Ill. 1967. Staff atty. Chgo. Transit Authority, 1967-71; pvt. practice, 1971—; ptnr. Carroll & Sain, Chgo., 1974—; mem. Ill. Senate, Springfield, 1973-99, asst. minority leader, 1993-99, chmn. appropriations com., 1977-93. Mem. Legis. Info. System Commn., Ill. Comprehensive Health Ins. Bd.; vice chmn. State Employees Suggestion Award Bd.; mem. fed. budget and taxation com. State-Fed.

Assembly; mem. Assembly Com. on State's Legis. Fiscal Affairs and Oversight; prof. complemental faculty Rush U. Coll. Health Scis., Chgo.; lectr. in field. Mem. Ill. Ho. of Reps., 1971-72; chmn. fin. com. Chgo. and Cook County Dem. Crtl. Com., 1982-84, treas., 1984-2000; committeeman 50th Ward Dem. Orgn., 1980-2000; mem. platform com. Ill. Dem. Com., 1974—; former mem. youth adv. bd. Dem. Nat. Com.; del. nat. and Ill. Dem. convs.; v.p. Young Dem. Clubs Am., 1971-73, also former gen. counsel; mem. exec. bd. Atlantic Alliance Young Polit. Leaders, 1970-73; active numerous civic orgns.; mem. exec. com., vice chmn. Jewish United Fund, 1977—; vice chmn. bd. trustees Weiss Meml. Hosp. Found.; officer Jewish Cmty. Rels. Coun.; former chair govt. affairs Jewish Fedn. Met. Chgo., now vice chmn.; founder Howard W. Carroll Found.; vice chmn. Jewish Found. Met. Chgo., Jewish United Found, Northshore Ctr. Performing Arts Found. Recipient numerous awards, including cert. of appreciation Decalogue Soc. Lawyers, 1972, Hemophilia Found. Ill., 1988, City Colls. Chgo., 1992, Disting. Svc. award State of Israel Bonds, 1974, Self-Help Assn., 1986, citation for meritorious svc. DAV, 1986, Legislator of Yr. award Child Care Assn. Ill., 1988, Ill. Coun. on Long Term Care, 1988, Outstanding Legislator award Am. Acad. Ophthalmology, 1989, Legis. Advocacy award Ill. Coun. for Gifted, 1991, Founders medal Montay Coll., 1992, Peace Advocate award Ill. Coalition Against Domestic Violence, 1998, Spl. award Comprehensive Health Ins. Plan, Chgo., 1998, award Northshore Ctr. Performing Arts, 1999, Spl. Svc. award Anti Defamation League, 2001, Ytshak Rabin Visionary award State of Israel, 2003; named Ill. Health Care Outstanding Legislator of Yr., 1995. Mem. Chgo. Bar Assn. (Disting. Lawyer and Legislator award 1974), Zionist Orgn. Chgo., Masons (32d degree), B'nai B'rith (bd. dirs. West Rogers Park). Office: 7250 N Cicero Ave Lincolnwood IL 60712 Home: 31 Indian Hill Rd Winnetka IL 60093-3940 Office Phone: 847-568-7000. Business E-Mail: senhwc@carrollandsain.com.

CARROLL, JAMES EDWARD, lawyer; b. Milford, Mass., July 9, 1952; s. James William and Anna (Bertoni) Carroll; children: Jonathan Patrick, Benjamin James, Jeremy David. BS, Fairfield U., 1974; MA, U. R.I., 1977; JD cum laude, Suffolk U., 1983. Bar: Mass. 1983, N.Y. 1999, U.S. Dist. Ct. Mass. 1984, U.S. Ct. Appeals (1st cir.) 1984, U.S. Tax Ct. 1989, U.S. Supreme Ct. 1995, N.Y. (U.S. Dist. Ct.) 2002. Tchr. Prout Meml. High Sch., Wakefield, R.I., 1974-76, Walpole (Mass.) High Sch., 1976-83; assoc. Gaston Snow & Ely Bartlett, Boston, 1983-86; trial atty. U.S. Dept. Justice, Washington, 1986-88; assoc. Hale & Dorr, Boston, 1988; ptnr. Peabody & Arnold, Boston, 1988-95; founding ptnr. Cetrulo & Capone, LLP, Boston, 1995—. Mem. criminal justice panel, U.S. Dist. Ct. Mass., 1993—. Contbr. articles to law rev. Bd. dirs. Am. Cancer Soc. Mem.: ABA, Supreme Jud. Ct. Hist. Soc., Nat. Assn. Criminal Def. Attys., Assn. Bar City N.Y., N.Y. State Bar, Boston Bar Assn., Mass. Bar Assn. (spkr. 1991—92), Phi Delta Phi. Roman Catholic. Avocations: running, baseball, football, children's soccer. Home: 23 Forest Edge Rd Easton MA 02375 Office: 2 Seaport Ln Boston MA 02210-2001 Office Phone: 617-217-5500. Business E-Mail: jcarroll@cefcap.com.

CARROLL, JAMES EDWIN, child neurologist, researcher; b. Joplin, Mo., May 15, 1945; s. George Henry and Sarah Frances (Montee) C.; m. Shirley Ann Carol Rohlander, July 1, 1967; children: John, Peter, Ruth, Rebecca, Timothy, Matthew, Lydia, Elizabeth. BS, U. Louisville, 1966, MD, 1969. Diplomate Nat. Bd. Med. Examiners, Am. Bd. Pediat., Am. Bd. Psychiatry and Neurology. Resident in pediat. Louisville (Ky.) Children's Hosp., 1969-71; resident in child neurology U. Colo., Denver, 1973-76; fellowship, faculty Washington U., St. Louis, 1976-84; chief child neurology, prof. Med. Coll. Ga., Augusta, 1984-88; prof., dir. pediat. tng. program Kuwait U., 1988-90; prof., dir. child neurology, vice chmn. neurology Med. Coll. Ga., Augusta, 1990—. Co-dir. Jerry Lewis Neuromuscular Rsch. Ctr., Washington. U., 1982-84; dir. Muscular Dystrophy Clinic, Med. Coll. Ga., 1991—; mem. Ga. Myasthenia Gravis Med. Adv. Bd., 1985-88. Author book chpts.; contbr. over 60 articles to profl. jours. Mem. exec. bd. United Cerebral Palsy of Ctrl. Savannah River Area, Augusta, 1985-88. Served to lt. comdr. USN, 1971-73. Recipient Investigator award NIH, 1979-83, grant NIH, 1986-89, Meritorious Honor award for scv. in Embassy in Kuwait, U.S. Dept. State, 1990. Fellow Am. Acad. Pediat., Am. Acad. Neurology; mem. Soc. for Pediat. Rsch., Am. Neurol. Assn. Republican. Presbyterian. Achievements include characterization of biochemical findings in a number of neuromuscular diseases. Home: 2711 Hunters Xing Augusta GA 30907-4710 Office: Med Coll Ga Child Neurology CJ2103 Augusta GA 30912 Home Phone: 706-860-7426; Office Phone: 706-721-3371. E-mail: jcarroll@mail.mcg.edu.

CARROLL, JAMES P., lawyer; b. Washington, Aug. 22, 1952; BA with honors, Georgetown Univ., 1974; JD with honors, Catholic Univ., Washington, 1977. Bar: Md. 1977, D.C. 1978, US Dist. Ct. D.C. 1978, US Ct. Appeals D.C. cir. 1978, N.C. 1996. Ptnr. real estate dept., mng. ptnr. Charlotte office & mem. mgmt. com. Cadwalader Wickersham & Taft, Charlotte, NC. Adj. prof. George Washington Univ., 1985—96. Mem.: ABA (chmn., Real Property Probate & Trust Law sect. Securitization com. 2002—04). Office: Cadwalader Wickersham & Taft LLP 227 W Trade St Charlotte NC 28202 Office Phone: 704-348-5116. Office Fax: 704-348-5200. Business E-Mail: james.carroll@cwt.com.

CARROLL, JILL, freelance journalist; b. Ann Arbor, Mich., 1977; d. Jim and Mary Beth Carroll. BA in Journalism, Univ. Mass., Amherst, 1999. Reporter covering Wash., DC Wall Street Journal; network commentator MSNBC; freelance contbr. Boston Globe; journalist States News Svc., Christian Science Monitor. Released 82 days after being kidnapped by Iraqi Insurgency group, Brigades of Vengeance, 2006; US Marines arrested four Iraqi men for participating in the kidnapping in August, 2006. Feature for the 11 part series Hostage: The Jill Carroll Story, Christian Science Monitor, 2006; contbr. articles to numerous profl. jours. Office: The Christian Sci Monitor One Norway St Boston MA 02115 Office Phone: 617-450-2000.

CARROLL, JOHN DOUGLAS, mathematical and statistical psychologist, educator; b. Phila., Jan. 3, 1939; s. John Joseph and Nolie Fay (Godwin) C.; m. Sylvia Stevens Booma, Jan. 2, 1965; children: Gregory Alan, Steven Douglas BS honors, U. Fla., 1958; PhD, Princeton U., 1963. Rsch. asst. dept. psychology Yale U., 1961—63; math., statis. psychologist Bell Labs., Murray Hill, NJ, 1963—65, 1966—89; Bd. Govs., prof. mgmt. and psychology Rutgers Bus. Sch., Newark, 1990—. Asst. prof. indsl. engring. and ops. rsch. NYU, 1965-66, adj. assoc. prof. stats., 1968-70; acting prof. psychology U. Calif. San Diego, 1975-76; acting prof. social sci. U. Calif. Irvine, 1975-76, vis. rsch. prof. cognitive sci., 1993; adj. prof. stats. Baruch Coll., CUNY, 1971; adj. prof. mktg. U. Pa., 1978-79, Procter & Gamble adj. prof. mktg., 1987-89 Contbr. numerous articles and chpts. to profl. publs.; author computer programs for multidimensional analysis of behavioral sci. data; assoc. editor: Psychometrika, 1973—, Jour. Exptl. Psychology, 1978-88; mem. editl. bd. Jour. Classification, 1984—, Jour. Mktg. Rsch., 1994—; editor Methodika, 1987-93 Ednl. Testing Svc. psychometric fellow, 1958-61; NIMH fellow, 1959-61 Fellow AAAS, APA (active Divsn. 5, pres.-elect 1990-91, pres. 1991-92, Disting. Sci. Contbn. award 1989), Am. Psychol. Soc. (William James fellow 1989), Am. Statis. Assn. (program chair stats. in mktg. sect. 1992, chair stats. in mktg. sect. 1993-94, exec. com. 1991-95); mem. Psychometric Soc. (trustee 1971-77, 81-83, 84-87, 93-96, pres. 1975-76, editl. coun. 1975-81), Classification Soc. N.Am. (governing coun. 1974-77, pres. 1980-83, bd. dirs. 1984-96), Internat. Fedn. Classification Socs. (rep. to coun. 1984—, v.p./pres.-elect 1995, pres. 1996—), Soc. Multivariate Exptl. Psychology (editl. adv. bd. 1980-81, pres. 1982-83), Ea. Psychol. Assn., Psychonomic Soc., Soc. Math. Psychology, Am. Mktg. Assn., Assn. Consumer Rsch., Soc. Consumer Psychology, Inst. for Ops. Rsch. and Mgmt. Scis., Phi Beta Kappa, Sigma Xi, Beta Gamma Sigma Home: 14 Forest Dr Warren NJ 07059-5802 Office: Rutgers U Rutgers Bus Sch Mktg Dept 111 Washington St Newark NJ 07102-3027 Office Phone: 973-353-5814. Business E-Mail: dcarroll@rci.rutgers.edu.

CARROLL, JOHN MILLAR, computer science and psychology educator; b. Bethlehem, Pa., Oct. 10, 1950; s. John Millar and Jane (Morris) C.; m. Mary Beth Rosson, Feb. 12, 1983; 1 child, Erin Marissa. BA in Math. and Info. Sci., Lehigh U., 1972; MA in Psychology, Columbia U., 1974, PhD in Psychology, 1976. Scientist IBM Rsch., Yorktown Heights, N.Y., 1976-83, mgr., 1983-94; prof., dept. head Va. Poly. Inst. and State U., Blacksburg, 1994—2003, dir. Ctr. for Human-Computer Interaction, 1995—2003, Edward M. Frymoyer chair prof. info. scis. and tech., 2003—, dir. Ctr. for Human-Computer Interaction, 2003—. Author 12 books; mem. numerous editl. and adv. bds.; contbr. over 200 articles to profl. jours. Recipient Rigo award Assn. for Computing Machinery, 1994. Fellow: IEEE (Goldsmith award 2004), Assn. Computing Machinery (spl. interest group computer-hu7man interaction), Human Factors and Eroonomics Soc. (hon.); mem.: Assn. Computing Machinery, SIGCHI Rsch. Acad. (Lifetime Achievement award 2003).

CARROLL, JOHN SAWYER, educator, former newspaper editor; b. NYC, Jan. 23, 1942; s. John Wallace and Margaret (Sawyer) C.; m. Kathleen Kirk, May 1, 1971 (div. Sept. 1982) children: Kathleen Louise, Margaret Adriane; m. Lee Huston Powell, Nov. 1985. BA in English lit., Haverford Coll., 1963. Reporter Providence Jour.-Bull., 1963-64, Balt. Sun, 1966-72, fgn. corr. Vietnam, 1967-69, fgn. corr. Mid. East, 1969, reporter Washington, 1969-72; city editor, met. editor Phila. Inquirer, 1973-79; exec. v.p., editor Lexington Herald-Leader, Ky., 1979-91; editor, sr. v.p. Balt. Sun, 1991—2000; v.p. Times Mirror Co., 1998—2000; editor LA Times, 2000—05, exec. v.p., 2000—05; Knight Vis. Lectr., Shorenstein Ctr. on Press, Politics and Public Policy JFK Sch. Govt., Harvard Univ., 2006. Pulitzer Prize juror, 1987, 89, 94; mem. Pulitzer Prize Bd., 1994-2003, chmn., 2002. Served with U.S. Army, 1964-66 Recipient Leadership Award Am. Soc. Newspaper Editors, 2004, Burton Benjamin Meml. Award Com. to Protect Journalists, 2004; named Nat. Press Found. Editor of Yr., 1998; Nieman Fellow Harvard U., 1971-72; vis. journalist fellow Queen Elizbeth House, U. Oxford, 1988. Fellow: Am. Acad. Arts & Sciences.

CARROLL, JOSEPH J(OHN), lawyer; b. NYC, Sept. 18, 1936; s. James J. and M. Catherine (Molloy) C.; m. Barbara Ann Lediger, May 16, 1959; 1 child, Barbara Ann (dec.). BS, Manhattan Coll., 1958; LLB, St. John's U., 1963; LLM, NYU, 1968. Bar: NY 1964, US Supreme Ct. 1967. Ins. underwriter Atlantic Mut. Ins. Co., NYC, 1959-63; pub. adminstrn. intern N.Y. State Housing Fin. Agy., NYC, 1963-64, adminstrv. asst., 1964-67; assoc. Mudge, Rose, Guthrie, Alexander & Ferdon, NYC, 1967-77, ptnr., 1977-95; of counsel Sullivan Donovan & Gentile, P.C., NYC, 1995—2004, Centilman, Balin, Alder & Hyman LLB, 2004—. Mem. nat. coun. trustees Nat. Jewish Med. and Rsch. Ctr., Denver; trustee Manhattan Coll., NYC, Baldwin Pub. Libr. Mem.: Nat. Assn. Coll. and Univ. Attys., Am. Health Lawyers Assn., N.Y. State Bar Assn. (mcpl. health law sects.). Home Phone: 516-379-8448; Office Phone: 516-546-8233. Personal E-mail: jjbacarroll@juno.com.

CARROLL, JULIAN MORTON, lawyer, retired governor, state senator; b. Paducah, Ky., Apr. 16, 1931; s. Elvie B. and Eva (Heady) C.; m. Charlann Harting, July 22, 1951; children: Kenneth Morton, Iva Patrice, Bradley Harting, Ellyn Kriston. AA, Paducah Jr. Coll., 1952; AB, U. Ky., 1954, LLB, 1956. Bar: Ky. 1956. Ptnr. Emery & Carroll, Paducah, 1960—68; mem. Ky. Ho. of Reps., 1962-71, speaker, 1968-71; lt. gov. State of Ky., 1971-74, gov., 1974-79; of counsel Reed, Scent & Walton, Paducah, 1968-71; ptnr. Carroll & Assocs., Frankfort, Ky., 1980—; mem. Ky. State Senate, 2004—. Chmn. Nat. Conf. Lt. Govs., 1974, Nat. Govs. Assn., 1978-79. Trustee Paducah Jr. Coll., Regency U. Lt. USAF, 1956-59. Recipient Minerva award U. Louisville, 1977, Man of Yr. award Advt. Club Louisville, 1978. Mem. ABA, Ky. Bar Assn., Franklin County Bar Assn., Optimist Club, Phi Delta. Democrat. Avocation: golf. Office: Carroll & Assocs 413 Shelby St Frankfort KY 40601-1942 Home Phone: 502-695-4459; Office Phone: 502-223-8806. Personal E-mail: jmc75farm@aol.com, julian.carroll@lrc.ky.gov.

CARROLL, KAREN COLLEEN, pathologist, epidemiologist; b. Balt., Nov. 7, 1953; d. Charles Edward and Ida May (Simms) C.; m. Bruce Cameron Marshall, Feb. 13, 1982; children: Kevin Charles Marshall, Brian Thomas Marshall. BA, Coll. Notre Dame of Md., 1975; MD, U. Md., 1979. Diplomate Am. Bd. Internal Medicine, Am. Bd. Infectious Diseases, Am. Bd. Pathology. Intern U. Md., 1979-80, U. Rochester, AHP, 1980-82, chief med. resident in internal medicine, 1982-83; fellow infectious diseases U. Mass., 1984-86; fellow med. microbiology Health Scis. Ctr. U. Utah, 1989-90; asst. prof. pathology U. Utah Med. Ctr., Salt Lake City, 1990-97, adj. asst. prof. infectious diseases, 1990-97, assoc. prof. pathology, adj. assoc. prof. infectious disease, 1997—; dir. microbiology lab. Associated Regional and Univ. Pathologists, Inc., Salt Lake City, 1990—. Contbr. articles to profl. jours. Fellow Am. Acad. Microbiology, Coll. Am. Pathologists; mem. Am. Soc. for Microbiology, Infectious Diseases Soc. Am. Avocations: skiing, hiking, reading. E-mail: carrolkc@aruplab.com.

CARROLL, KENNETH G., lawyer; b. Winston-Salem, NC, Feb. 1, 1952; BA, Wake Forest Univ., NC, 1982, JD, 1985. Bar: NC 1985. Mem. mgmt. com. Womble Carlyle Sandridge & Rice, PLLC, mem. recruiting com., mem. professionalism com., mng. mem. Research Triangle, NC, chmn. assocs. com., chmn. salaried mem. com. Notes and comments editor Wake Forest Law Review, 1984—85. Mem. United Way-Triangle; Habitat for Humanity. Mem.: ABA, NC Bar Assn. (mem. curriculum com., bus. law sect.), Wake County Bar Assn. Mailing: Womble Carlyle Sandridge & Rice PLLC PO Box 13069 Research Triangle Park NC 27709 Office: Womble Carlyle Sandridge & Rice PLLC 2530 Meridian Pwky Ste 400 Durham NC 27713 Office Phone: 919-484-2318. Office Fax: 919-484-2368. Business E-Mail: kcarroll@wcsr.com.

CARROLL, KENT JEAN, retired naval officer; b. Newton, Iowa, Aug. 22, 1926; s. Lee A. and Mabel E. (McCormick) C.; m. Betty M. Harrington, Mar. 29, 1947; children: Craig, Debra Carroll Rollins, Lance S., Maureen Burt. BS in Naval Sci., U. Notre Dame, 1946; grad., U.S. Naval Postgrad. Sch., 1955, Naval War Coll., 1960, Army War Coll., 1965; BA in Internat. Affairs, George Washington U., 1965. Ensign USN, 1946, advanced through grades to vice adm., 1979; svc. in Korea and Vietnam; comdr. U.S.S. Sablefish, 1959-60, Submarine Divsn. 81, Divsn. 82, 1968-69, 69, U.S.S. Blue Ridge, 1970-72, Amphibious Squadron 10, 1972-73, Task Force 65, 1974-75, Naval Inshore Warfare Command, Atlantic Fleet, 1974-75, U.S. Naval Forces Marianas, 1975-77; dir. J-4 OJCS, Washington, 1977-81; comdr. Mil. Sealift Command, Washington, 1981-83. Decorated Navy D.S.M. with cluster, Def. D.S.M., Legion of Merit with 2 clusters; recipient John Paul Jones award Navy League, 1977; Presdl. citation for humanitarian svc., 1976, Rev. William Corby C.S.C. award U. Notre Dame, 1995. Mem. English Speaking Union. Home: Country Club NC 1600 Morganton Rd X 30 Pinehurst NC 28374-6862 E-mail: kcarroll@nc.rr.com.

CARROLL, LA SHUN LA RUE, dentist; b. NYC, Mar. 1, 1977; s. Marggio Carroll. BA in Philosophy and Natural Sci., magna cum laude, CUNY Bernard Baruch Coll., NYC, 2000; MS in Gen. Studies, Suffield Coll. and U., 2004; DDS cum laude, SUNY Buffalo Sch. Dental Medicine, 2005; JD, William Howard Taft Sch. Law, 2006—. Lic. info. sys. tech. h.s. level N.Y.C. Bd. of Edn.; BLS: CPR-AED for primary healthcare providers Am. Heart Assn., EMT-B Emergency Med. Svcs., N.J., cert. adv. cardiac life support healthcare Practitioners 2005, med. emergencies in dentistry Albert Einstein Coll. Medicine, 04. Retail salesperson Edison Bros., Inc., World Trade Ctr., 1994—95; med. libr. NYU Sch. of Medicine, 1994—95, info. sys. technologist, 1995—96; adminstr. Aux. of Tisch Hosp., NYU. Med. Ctr., 1996—97; staff rsch. pathology NYU Sch. of Medicine, 1997—2000; founder, exec. dir., CEO ELMA FAE Found., 2006—; assoc. prof. dept. biological sci. Northampton CC, Bethlehem, Pa., 2006. Student rschr. NYU Med. Ctr. Honors Program, NYC, 1993—95; adminstr. symposia on hydrocephalus and spina-bifida Aux. at Tisch Hosp., NYC, 1996—97; rschr. NASA Specialized Ctr. for Rsch. and Tng., Raleigh, NC, 1997; chemistry tchg. asst. for visually impaired students Bernard M. Baruch Coll., NYC, 1998—99; asst. instr. nat. jour. of chem. edn. conf. workshop Jour. of Chem. Edn., Sacred Heart U., Conn., 1999; vol. NYU Med. Ctr., NYC, 1996—97; vol. guest spkr. sr. oral health awareness at local nursing home U. at Buffalo Sch. of Dental Medicine, 2002, vol. guest spkr. local and inner-city pub. elem. schs. for ann. Children's Smile Day, 2002—; mem., vol. minority affairs com. U. Buffalo Sch. of Dental Medicine, Buffalo, 2003—; oral cancer screener SUNY Buffalo Sch. of Dental Medicine Oral Health Screening Program, 2003—; specialty endodontic residency program, NYC, 2005—. Author: When Death Becomes Us All, 2006, Corresponding with Christie, 2006, Different Slant: An Introspective Enquiry, 2006; contbr. articles and reports to profl. jours. Vol. student dr. oral cancer screening of physically and/or developmentally disabled Spl. Olympics, Buffalo, 2002; vol. EMT Emergency Med. Svcs., Monroe County, Pa., 2004—05; vol. comm. outreach program Buffalo Zoo, NY, 2004; organizer, presenter Healthcare Career Days Pocono Family YMCA. Recipient Spl. Recognition award for peer mediation, Murry Bergtraum H.S., NY, NY, 1993, Excellence Scholarship in Philosophy, CUNY, 2000, Arthur A. Schomburg fellowship, SUNY, Buffalo, 2001—05, Barrett scholarship, 2001—02, Class of 1964 scholarship for outstanding scholastic achievement, 2002, Tucker scholarship for top 25 students, SUNY Buffalo Sch. of Dental Medicine, 2002, SUNY, Buffalo, 2003, U. Buffalo Sch. of Dental Medicine Gen. scholarship, SUNY Buffalo Sch. of Dental Medicine, 2003, Outstanding Volunteerism award, Murry Bergtraum H.S., N.Y.C., 1994, Spl. Recognition award for peer mediation, 1995, CRC Press Chemistry Achievement award for outstanding scholastic achievement in chemistry, CRC Press, 1999, N.Y.C. Alliance for Minority Participation in Rsch. scholarship, NYC Alliance, CUNY, 1999; scholar Robert C. Weaver Incentive Scholarship, Bernard M. Baruch Coll. (CUNY), 1999. Mem.: Braille Sch./Blindness Related learning, Nat. Assn. Emergency Med. Techs., Nat. Registry Emergency Med. Techs., Am. Student Dental Assn., Acad. of Gen. Dentistry (assoc.), Internat. High IQ Soc. (life), Bernard M. Baruch Alumni Assn. (life), N.Y.C. Alliance for Minority Participation (scholarship 1999), Golden Key Nat. Hon. Soc. (life), Nat. Scholars Hon. Soc. (life), Student Hon. Soc. (life), Delta Epsilon Iota (life). Avocations: drawing, philosophy and logic, biblical hebrew and linguistics, science and medicine, writing. Office: Cmty Health Ctrs Rutland Region Dental Office 71 Grove St Rutland VT 05701

CARROLL, LINDA LOVELL, elementary school educator; d. Claude Jasper and Jessie Lula Couch Lovell; m. Edward H Carroll, July 18, 1969; 1 child, Laura Laine. BA, West Ga. Coll., Carrollton, 1970, MEd, 1974. Lic. Profl. Stds. Commn., 1970. Tchr. Carroll County Sch., Carrollton, Ga., 1970—. Mem.: CCAE. Avocations: exercise, reading. Home: 3346 NE Hickory Level Rd Temple GA 30179 Office: Villa Rica Elem Sch Peachtree St Villa Rica GA Home Phone: 770-214-2367; Office Phone: 770-459-5762. Home Fax: 770-214-8504.

CARROLL, LUCY ELLEN, theater director, educator; b. NYC, Oct. 11; d. Edward Joseph and Lucy Sophie (Czapszys) C. B in Music Edn., Temple U., Phila., 1968; MA, Trenton State Coll., NJ, 1973; D in Musical Arts, Combs Coll. Music, Phila., 1982. Cert. tchr. music, NJ, Pa., Nat. Cert., 1991. Tchr. music Log Coll. Jr. H.S., Pa., 1968-72, Ind. H.S., Pa., 1972-73, William Tennent H.S., Warminster, Pa., 1973-98, dir. mus. theater, 1973-98; choir dir. St. John Bosco Parish Choir, 1999—2001; organist, dir. Carmelite Monastery, Phila., 1996—. Music coord. Centennial Schs., 1991-98; founder, dir. Madrigal Singers, Warminster, Pa., 1971-98; choral dir. Cabrini Coll., Radnor, Pa., 1974-77, First Day Singers, Phila., 1979-83, Combs Coll. Music, Phila., 1981-84, 87-88; choral adjudicator various Music festivals, 1973-98; theatre dir., Villa Joseph Marie (Holland), 1998-99; del. Internat. Arts Conf., Cambridge, Eng., 1992; adj. assoc. prof. Westminster Choir Coll., Princeton, 2002—; lectr. in field. Singer (operas Ambler Festival): Street Scene, 1970, Death of Bishop of Brindisi (premiere) (Robin Hood Dell) La Boheme; dir. (jazz theater piece NYC): Murder of Agamemnon, 1980, (drama) Power of Love (1705), 1986, (outdoor music theater) Vorspiel (Pa. Historic Commn. 1989); editor: The Monastery Hymnal, 2002, Music of the Ephrata Cloister, 2003, Kelpius: Method of Prayer, 2007; columnist: Polyphony mag., Adoremus Bulletin, 2002—; creator: Churchmouse Squeaks cartoons, Monastery Mice cartoons; author: The Music of EPHRATA, 2003, The Bastet Worry-Stone and Other Tales, 2004, Monastery Mice: Life in the Loft, 2006, Monastery Mice: The Organist, 2006, Introduction to Music of the Wissahickon Glen, 2007; contbr. articles to profl. jours. and mags. Recipient awards Writers of Future, 1985, 87, Andrew Ferraro award Combs Coll. Music, 1989, plaque for svc. to music Bucks County Commr., 1991, Disting. Citizen medal Southampton Twp., 1994, Harmony award Country Gentlemen Nat. Soc. for Preservation and Encouragement Barbershop Quartet Singing in Am., 1994; Scholar-In-Residence, Pa. Hist. and Museum Commn.; named Humanities Spkr. for 2000, Pa. Humanities Coun. Mem. Am. Choral Dirs. Assn., Sci. Fiction Fantasy Writers of Am., Am. Musicol. Soc., Am. Guild Organists, Organ Hist. Soc., Latin Liturgy Assn., Del. Valley Composers (choral cons. 1988-90), Hist. Soc. Pa., Musical Fund Soc. of Phila., Soc. for Am. Music, Pa. Music Educators Assn. (adv. bd. 1986-87, contbg. writer Spotlight on Tchg. Chorus 2003), Nat. Assn. State Tchrs. of the Yr., Ephrata Cloister Assocs., Kelpius Soc. (editor newsletter 2004—, v.p., chair rsch. publs. 2005—), Sigma Alpha Iota. Republican. Roman Catholic. Avocation: travel. Home: 712 High Ave Hatboro PA 19040-2418 Personal E-mail: lucycarroll@att.net.

CARROLL, M(ARGARET) LIZBETH CARR, art educator, graphics designer, photographer; b. Washington, Feb. 9, 1936; d. J. Franklin and Dorothy Mae (Colborn) Carr; m. Eugene R. Carroll, Jr., June 2, 1979 (div. May 2000); children: Kyung Soo Kim, Whan Kim. BFA in Studio Art, U. DC, 1979; MFA in Visual Comm. & Photography, George Washington U., 1984; postgrad., Union Inst. and U., 2004—. Visual info. specialist US Fed. Govt., Washington, 1966—84; graphics designer Office of the Comptr. of the Currency, Dept. of the Treasury, Washington, 1984—94, sr. graphics designer, 1994—99; adj. prof. fine arts U. DC, Washington, 1989—; asst. prof. lectr. in art George Washington U., Washington, 2001—06. Adv. for Native Am. artists/pvt. cons. ArtDirections, Washington, 1994—. Author, photographer: Native Peoples Mag., 1995, Piecework Mag., 1998, Am. Rivers, Pres.'s Coun. Environ. Quality, US Congl. Record, Friends of the Earth, US Nat. Pk. Svc., Nat. Pks. Conservation Assn., Sierra Club, Wilderness Soc. in support of conservation and wilderness legis.; Represented in permanent collections US Dept. Interior, Grand Canyon Nat. Pk., exhibitions include Gallery 42, U. DC, 2003, exhibited in group shows at Martin Luther King, Jr. Libr., Washington, 2003, U. DC, 1976—79, Cath. U. Am., 1979, Dimock Gallery, Washington, DC, 1984. Home: 3313 Runnymede Pl NW Washington DC 20015-2415 Office: U DC Dept Mass Media Visual and Performing Arts 4200 Connecticut Ave NW Washington DC 20008

CARROLL, MARIE-JEAN GREVE, retired artist, educator; b. Paterson, NJ, Dec. 19, 1930; d. William John and Charlotte Marie (Kranich) McGill; m. Theodore R. Greve, 1950 (div. 1979, dec. 2005); 3 children; m. William P. Carroll, 1981 (dec. 2002). BA in Art Edn., William Paterson Coll., 1971, MA in Visual Art, 1976. Cert. art tchr., N.J. Tchr. art Ramapo HS, Franklin Lakes, NJ, 1986—2000; ret., 2000. Juried shows NW Bergen Art Ctr., 2005. Works exhibited at shows in Fla. galleries, 1983, Longboat Key Art Gallery, 1983-84, Manatee Art Gallery, 1984, Pike County Art Show, Milford, Pa., 1994-96, NJ Printmakers Coun., Sommerville, Paterson Pub. Libr., 1998, Mommouth County Mus., 2004, Bergen Sr. Art Exhibit, 2005. Recipient art awards. Mem. NEA, Bergen County Edn. Assn., NJ Edn. Assn., Nat. Art Edn. Assn., Watercolor Soc. NJ (assoc.), Chaucer Guild NJ Poetry Group. Avocations: poetry, swimming laps, golf.

CARROLL, MARK THOMAS, lawyer; b. Queens, NY, May 12, 1956; s. Bernard James and Thalia (Antypas) C.; m. Joanne Mary Grinnell, Aug. 4, 1979; children: Stephen, Thomas. BA, Columbia U., 1977; JD, Harvard U., 1980. Bar: Pa. 1980, U.S. Ct. Appeals (3d cir.) 1980, U.S. Dist. Ct. (ea. dist.) Pa. 1980. Assoc. Duane, Morris & Heckscher, Phila., 1980-82; asst. dir. ALI-ABA, Phila., 1982-85, dir. office of publs., 1985—. Bd. dirs. Bradford Glen Homeowners Assn., 1988-90; founding mem. Joseph's People Com. Mem. ABA, Assn. for Continuing Legal Edn. (pres. 2003-04). Republican. Roman Catholic. Home: 1402 Ashcom Dr Downingtown PA 19335-3566 Office: ALI-ABA 4025 Chestnut St Ste 500 Philadelphia PA 19104-3099 Office Phone: 215-243-1656. Business E-Mail: mcarroll@ali-aba.org.

CARROLL, MARY COLVERT, not-for-profit developer, consultant; b. Milw., June 5, 1940; d. Frederick Rolfing and Helen (McCall) Colvert; m. Andrew David Carroll; children: Sherri L. Oberg, Andrew David Carroll III. BA mgna cum laude, U. Miami, Fla., 1966. Bd. dirs. Aqua Am. Inc., Bryn Mawr, 1979—; chmn. bd. Friends Independence Nat. Hist. Park, Phila., 1978-81; bd. dirs. Urban Affairs Coalition, Phila., 1979-90, advisor, 1990—; pres., founder Friends Conversation Hall, Phila., 1982-83; bd. dirs. Internat. House, Phila., 1982—98; chmn., founder Nat. Parks Mid-Atlantic Council, Phila., 1982—2004; vice chmn. bd. Nat. Parks and Conservation Assn., Washington, 1982-88; bd. dirs. Phila. First Econ. Devel. Coalition, 1983-90; chmn., founder, bd. dirs. Phila. Hospitality, Inc., 1998—2000; bd. dirs. World Affairs Council, Phila., 1984-88; bd. trustees Bryn Mawr (Pa.) Presbyn. Ch., 1984-90; mem. bd. advisors Independence Hall Assn., Phila., 1984-86; vice chair Phila. Hist. Preservation Corp., 1986-93; vice chmn. bd. Fort Mifflin on Del., Inc., Phila., 1986—2001; trustee William Penn Found., Phila., 1987-93. Hon. trade rep. of Nepal, 2002—; cons. in field. Bd. dirs. Met. YMCA, Preservation Action, 1993-97, Friends of Patan Hosp., Kathmandu, 2005—; chair Nepal Found., 2003—. Recipient Civic Environ. award Found. for Architecture, 1983, Conservation Service award U.S. Dept. Interior, 1978, Friend of Nepal award Assn. Nepalis in the Americas, 2002, Woman of Distinction award Lake Forest Acad., 2005. Mem. Merion Cricket Club. Presbyterian.

CARROLL, MEGAN, lawyer, educator; b. Lake Forest, Ill., Sept. 7, 1967; d. Barry Joseph and Barbara (Pehrson) C.; m. Timothy J. Shea II. Student, Middlebury Coll., Paris, 1987-88; BA in Philosophy, French Lit., Boston Coll., 1989, JD, 1992. Bar: Mass., 1993, Ill. 1994, D.C. 1995. Law clk. Middlesex County Probate & Family Ct., Cambridge, Mass., 1990-91; assoc. Powers & Hall, Boston, 1991; asst. dist. atty. Norfolk County, Mass., 1992; prin., owner Carroll Assocs., Counsel for the Arts, Boston, 1994—. Bd. dirs. Carroll Internat. Corp., Des Plaines, Ill.; adj. prof. law New Eng. Sch. Law, 1998—; adj. prof. bus. law Wallace E. Carroll Sch. Bus., Boston Coll., 2001—. Arts review writer various publs. Mem. Am. Ireland Fund, Boston, Chgo., 1985—, Phillips Acad. Alumni Coun., Andover, Mass., 1991-95; trustee Regency Pk. Condominiums, Brookline, Mass., 1989-91; sec. Phillips Acad. Alumni Class of 1985, Andover, 1989-95; bd. overseers Boston Ballet, 2000—; mem. exec. com. capital campaign Boston Coll., 1998—;Bd. Overseers Mem. The Alliance Française Boston and Cambridge, MA; and The French Library and Cultural Center, Boston, MA (now merged); Boston Coll. Law Sch. Loan Forgiveness Development Bd.; Boston Coll. Museum of Art Council (Founder and Chairperson) and Boston Coll. Arts Council; Boston Dance Alliance; Boston Liturgical Dance Ensemble (Mem and Pro Bono Attorney); Cardinal Cushing School Development Board, Hanover, MA; Crescendo (Boston Symphony Orchestra Volunteers); Exe. Com. Boston Coll. President's Circle; Folk Arts Network of New England (FAN); Founding Board of Governors of the Boston Coll. Club; Greater Boston Chamber of Commerce (GBCC). Recipient Golden Key Nat. Honor Soc., Boston Coll., 1989, Order of the Cross and Crown, Scholar of the Coll., 1989; Daughters of the American Revolution; Wellesley Regent, Junior American Citizens State Chair, MA DAR State Outstanding Junior Member Award presented at Constitution Hall, Washington, D.C. 2003. Mem. ABA, Arts and Media Law Assn. Boston Coll. (pres., founder), Am., Mass., Ill., Dist. Columbia, and Boston Bar Assn., Social Register, Woman's Athletic Club Chgo., Order of Malta Aux. Boston, MA; DAR (vice regent Wellesley, Mass. 1999—), Jr. Internat. Club Lauterbach (Germany), East Chop Beach Club, East Chop Yacht Club, East Chop Tennis Club, Boston Coll. Club (bd. dirs. 1998—), Phi Delta Phi; Inst. Contemporary Art Coun., Boston, MA; Mass. Assn. Women Lawyers (MAWL); Mass. Media Alliance, Boston, MA; Mass. Orgn. Vying for the Industry of Entertainment (M.O.V.I.E.); Mass. Soc. Prevention of Cruelty to Children (MSPCC); Museum of Fine Arts Coun., Boston, MA; Nat. Soc. Fundraising Exec. (NSFRE); Small Bus. Assn. New England (SBANE); Vol. Lawyers for the Arts, Boston, MA; Wang Ctr. Mets., Boston, MA (Young at Arts prog.); Women's Bar Network (WBN). Republican. Roman Catholic. Avocations: ballet, scuba diving, diving, flying. Office: Carroll Assocs 396 Washington St Ste 322 Wellesley Hills MA 02481-6209 Office Fax: 617-542-7555. E-mail: mec@carrollassoc.com.

CARROLL, MICHAEL F., lawyer; b. Evergreen Park, Ill., July 31, 1963; s. Lucille M. Carroll; m. Jennifer L. Gobeille, Sept. 11, 1998; children: Kevin J., Daniel W. BA, No. Ill. U., DeKalb, 1985; JD, John Marshall Law Sch., Chgo., 1995. Bar: Ill. 1995. Atty. Law Office Michael F. Carroll, Orland Park, Ill., 1995—2005; ptnr. Carroll & Truesdale, P.C., Orland Park, 2005—. Mem. Orland Pk. Law Enforcement Orgn., 1999. Mem.: SW Bar Assn. (dir. 1998—), Will County Bar Assn. (mem. 2006), Frankfort Sportsmans Club (mem. 2006). Avocations: golf, music, skeet shooting. Office: Carroll & Truesdale PC 11516 W 183rd St Suite NE Orland Park IL 60467 Office Phone: 708-478-0200. E-mail: mfc@carrolltruesdale.com.

CARROLL, MILTON, oil industry executive; b. Houston, 1950; m. Cynthia Carroll; 3 children. BS in Indsl. Tech., Tex. So. Univ., 1973. Various positions Schlumberger Well Services; founder, chmn., CEO Instrument Products Inc., Houston, 1977—; bd. dir. CenterPoint Energy Inc., Houston, 1992—, chmn., 2002—. Commr. Port of Houston, 1987—93; former dir. Blue Cross and Blue Shield of Tex., 1994, Seagull Energy Corp., 1997, Texas Eastern Products Pipeline Co. (TEPPCO), 1997, Devon Energy Corp., 2003—05; bd. dirs. EGL Inc., 2003—, DCP Midstream Partners, 2005—. Dir. Houston Endowment Inc., Ocean Energy, Health Care Svcs. Corp. Mailing: CenterPoint Energy PO Box 1700 Houston TX 77251-1700*

CARROLL, PETE, college football coach; b. San Francisco, Sept. 15, 1951; m. Glena Carroll; children: Brennan, Nathan, Jaime. BS in Bus. Adminstrn., Univ. Pacific, 1973, MS in Physical Edn., 1976. Grad. asst., wide receivers coach Univ. Pacific Tigers, 1974—75, grad. asst., secondary coach, 1975—77; grad. asst., secondary Univ. Ark. Razorbacks, 1977—78; secondary coach Iowa St. Univ. Cyclones, 1978, Ohio St. Univ. Buckeyes, 1979; def. coord., secondary coach North Carolina St. Wolfpack, 1980—82; asst. head coach, offensive coord. Univ. Pacific Tigers, 1983; def. backs coach Buffalo Bills, 1984—85, Minn. Vikings, 1985—90; def. coord. N.Y. Jets, 1990—94, head coach, 1994; defensive coord. San Francisco 49ers, 1995—97; head coach New England Patriots, 1997-99; head coach, defensive coord. U. So. Calif. Trojans, LA, 2001—. Recipient Coach of Yr. award, Am. Football Coaches Assn., 2003. Achievements include coaching U. So. Calif. to the 2003-04 BCS Nat. Championship. Office: U So Calif 203 Heritage Hall Los Angeles CA 90089*

CARROLL, RAY DEAN, SR., retired veterinarian; b. Barry, Tex., Oct. 19, 1927; s. James William and Blanche Estelle (Jordan) C.; m. Lula Pearl Mayfield, June 6, 1957; children: James William, Ray Dean Jr. Assoc., Hillsboro Jr. Coll., 1948; BS in Animal Sci., Tex. A&M U., 1950, DVM, 1957. Vet. Carroll & Harpe Animal Hosp., Corsicana, Tex., 1957—2006; instr. Navarro Coll., Corsicana, 1970-95; ret., 2007. Author: Beef Cattle Science Handbook, vol. 16, 1979. Mem. found. bd. Navarro Coll., 1985—, vice-chmn., trustee, 1990. With USN, 1945-46, 51-52. Mem. AVMA, Tex. Polled Hereford Assn. (pres. 1992-96), Navarro County Ext. Beef Commn. (chmn. 1960—). Democrat. Methodist. Home: 2203 Highland Cir Corsicana TX 75110-1611

CARROLL, ROBERT LYNN, biology professor, paleontologist, curator, museum director; b. Kalamazoo , May 5, 1938; s. John Henry and Arvella Mae (Wickerham) Carroll; m. Helen Louise Swaim, June 22, 1961 (dec. Jan. 1972); 1 child, David Lynferd; m. Anna Di Turi, Sept. 26, 1987. BS, Mich. State U., 1959; MA, Harvard U., 1961, PhD, 1963. NRC postdoctoral fellow McGill U., Montreal, Que., Canada, 1962-63, asst. prof. zoology, 1964-69, assoc. prof. biology, 1969-74, prof. biology, 1974—, Strathcona prof. zoology, 1987—; curator vertebrate paleontology Redpath Mus., McGill U., 1965—, dir., 1985-90, 98-99, chmn. dept. biology, 1990-95. Vis prof biol Sir George Williams Univ, Montreal, 1965—66. Author: (book) Vertebrate Paleontology and Evolution, 1987, Patterns and Processes of Vertebrate Evolution, 1997; co-author: Paleontology - The History of Life, 1989; editor: Leposondyli, 1998; co-editor: Paleontology, The Evolutionary History of Amphibians, 2000; editor (assoc ed): Can Jour Earth Scis, 1984—93, Jour Vertebrate Paleontology, 1989—92; editor: (consulting ed) Trans Royal Soc Edinburgh: Earth Scis, 1993—; editor: (technical ed) Jour Paleontology, 2000—. Mem educ bd Linn Soc London, 1999—. Recipient Billings Medal for contbns to paleontology, Geological Asn Can; fellow NSF Postdoctoral, Brit Mus, London, 1963—64. Fellow: Paleontological Soc. (Schuchert award 1978), Linnean Soc., Royal Soc. Can. (Miller medal 2001); mem.: World Congress Herpetology (treas. 1989—94), Soc. Vertebrate Paleontology (hon.; pres. 1982—83, Romer-Simpson medal 2004), Am. Soc. Zoologists, Soc. Study Evolution. Avocations: hiking, singing. Office: Redpath Mus/McGill Univ 859 Sherbrooke St W Montreal PQ Canada H3A 2K6 Home Phone: 514-733-7939; Office Phone: 514-398-4086 ext. 4090. E-mail: robert.carroll@mcgill.ca.

CARROLL, ROBERT W., retired management consultant; b. Ossining, NY, May 29, 1923; s. John Francis and Catherine Veronica (Coyne) C.; m. Mary Bernardine Dugan, June 1, 1946; children: Kevin, Dennis, Terrence, Maura, Monica. Student, Sch. Commerce, NYU, 1952-56, Mgmt. Inst., 1957. With N.Y. Cen. R.R., 1942-68, asst. to sec., 1953-54, asst. sec., 1954-59, sec., 1959-68; sr. asst. sec. Penn Cen. Transp. Co., 1968-70, sec., 1971-76, also former v.p., sec., dir. several railroad, real estate, trucking and fin.-oriented subsidiaries, 1971-76; exec. dir. adminstrn. Law Offices La Brum and Doak, Phila., 1976-88; prin. Robert W. Carroll & Assoc., Mgmt. Cons., Radnor, Pa., 1989-93. Corp. sec. Pitts. and Lake Erie R.R. Co., 1959-79; v.p., sec., dir. Montour R.R. Co., Montour Land Co., Youngstown and So. Ry. Co., 1959-79; rep. Kissel Blake Orgn., Inc., 1983-89. Served with USCGR, 1942-46. Recipient Legion of Honor Chapel of the Four Chaplains, 1984. Mem. ABA (law office adminstrv. assoc. 1985-89), Internat. Assn. Legal Adminstrs. (bd. dirs. 1987-88, v.p. 1987—, pres.-elect Phila. chapter 1988), VFW, Soc. Friendly Sons St. Patrick, Pa. Soc. K.C. (4), World Affairs Coun. Phila., Am. Soc. of Corp. Secs., Inc., Overbrook Golf Club (Bryn Mawr, Pa.). Home: 9 Ridgewood Rd Wayne PA 19087-3713

CARROLL, ROBERT WAYNE, mathematics professor; b. Chgo., May 10, 1930; s. Walter Scott and Dorothy (Le Monnier) C.; m. Berenice Jacobs, Sept. 7, 1957 (div. June 1974); children: David Leon, Malcolm Scott; m. Alice von Neumann, Sept. 1974 (div. Mar. 1977); m. Joan Miller, Jan. 1979 (dec. Apr. 2001), m. Denise Bredt, May 2003. BS, U. Wis., 1952; PhD, U. Md., 1959. Aero. research scientist NASA, Cleve., 1952-54; NSF postdoctoral fellow, 1959-60; asst. prof. Rutgers U., 1960-63, assoc. prof., 1963-64; assoc. prof. math. U. Ill., Urbana, 1964-67, prof., 1967-97, prof. emeritus, 1997—. Author: Abstract Methods in Partial Differential Equations, 1969, Transmutation and Operator Differential Equations, 1979, Transmutation, Scattering Theory and Special Functions, 1982, Transmutation Theory and Applications, 1985, Mathematical Physics, 1988, Topics in Soliton Theory, 1991, Quantum Theory, Deformation and Integrability, 2000, Calculus Revisited, 2002, Fluctuations, Information, Gravity, and the Quantam Potential, 2006; co-author: Singular and Degenerate Cachy Problems, 1976; assoc. editor Jour. Applicable Analysis, 1970—; contbr. over 200 articles to profl. jours. Served with U.S. Army, 1954-57. Mem. Am. Math. Soc., Am. Phys. Soc. Avocations: foreign languages, cello. Home: 1314 Brighton Dr Urbana IL 61801-6417 Office: Univ Ill Math Dept Urbana IL 61801 Business E-Mail: rcarroll@math.uiuc.edu.

CARROLL, ROSEMARY FRANCES, historian, educator, lawyer; b. Providence, Oct. 15, 1935; d. Francis Edward and Katherine Loretta (Graham) C. AB, Brown U., Providence, 1957; MA, Wesleyan U., Middletown, Conn., 1962; PhD, Rutgers U., New Brunswick, NJ, 1968; JD, U. Iowa, Iowa City, 1983. Bar: Iowa 1983. Asst. prof. history Notre Dame Coll., NYC, 1968-70; vis. asst. prof. history Denison U., Granville, Ohio, 1970-71; asst. prof. history Coe Coll., Cedar Rapids, Iowa, 1971-75, assoc. prof. history, 1975-84, prof. history, 1984—2000, Henry and Margaret Haegg disting. prof. history, 2000—01, Henry and Margaret Haegg disting. prof. history emerita, 2001—, chair dept. history, 1988—2000, affirmative action officer, 1973-98, prelaw advisor, 1988-98, rep. Truman Found., 1988—98, faculty rep. Rhodes Scholarship Trust, 1993-98, faculty rep. Brit. Marshal Scholarship, 1996-98. Contbr. articles to profl. jours. Vol. lawyer Legal Svcs. Corp. Iowa, Cedar Rapids, 1984-2003, mem. adv. coun., 1985-2003. Olmsted fellow Hoover Presdl. Libr. Assn., 1987-92, Hoover grantee, 1992-94, NEH grantee, 1992-93. Mem. ABA, AAUP, AAUW (Stuart, Fla. br. pres. 2006—), Iowa Bar Assn. (legal heritage com. 1988—), Linn County Bar Assn. (continuing legal edn. com. 1990-2002), Linn County Women Atty. (treas. 1990-91), Orgn. Am. Historians (membership com. 1978), So. Hist. Assn. (membership com. 1986-87, 88-89, 96-98), So. Assn. Womens Historians (pres. 1975-76, membership com. 1987-88, 89-90, 96-98, Taylor Prize com. 2005), Am. Hist. Assn., Phi Kappa Phi. Roman Catholic. Avocations: bicycling, swimming. Home (Summer): 33 Nicholson Crescent Middletown RI 02842-5409 Home Phone: 401-846-3908. Personal E-mail: rfcarroll1@aol.com.

CARROLL, ROY, retired academic administrator; b. England, Ark., Dec. 8, 1929; m. Eleanor Kate Moorefield, 1953; children: Jane, Linda. BA cum laude, Ouachita Bapt. U., 1951; MA, Vanderbilt U., 1959, PhD, 1964. Math. tchr. Baker H.S., Columbus, Ga., 1955; asst. prof. history and polit. sci. Mercer U., Macon, Ga., 1959-65; prof. history, chmn. dept. history and polit. sci. Armstrong State Coll., Savannah, Ga., 1965-69; prof. history, chmn. dept. history Appalachian State U., Boone, NC, 1969-79; v.p. planning gen. adminstrn. U. NC Sys., 1979-90, 91-96, sr. v.p., v.p. acad. affairs, 1996-99, ret., 1999; interim chancellor U. NC, Asheville, 1990-91. Mem. NC Justice Edn. and Tng. Stds. Commn., 1979-90, chmn. planning com., 1981-88; mem. adv. bd. Inst. Transp. Rsch. and Edn., Rsch. Triangle Park, 1980—; bd. dirs. Western NC Devel. Assn., 1990-91, NC State Employees Credit Union, 1990-91, Rsch. Triangle Inst., 1996-2000; trustee Appalachian State U., 2000-05. Contbr. articles to profl. jours. Inf. officer U.S. Army, 1951-53, Japan, Korea. Fulbright scholar, Eng., 1958-59. Home: 6811 Huntingridge Rd Chapel Hill NC 27517-8673 Office: U NC Gen Adminstrn PO Box 2688 Chapel Hill NC 27515-2688 E-mail: rcl@ga.unc.edu.

CARROLL, SEAN B., geneticist, biologist, educator, researcher, writer; b. Sept. 17, 1960; m. Jamie Carroll; 2 children; 2 stepchildren. BA in Biology, Washington U., St. Louis; PhD in Immunology, Tufts U., 1983. Postdoctoral rschr. U. Colo., Boulder; faculty mem. to prof. molecular biology, genetics and med. genetics U. Wis., Madison, 1987—; investigator Howard Hughes Med. Inst., 1990—. Contbr. articles to sci. jours.; co-author: From DNA to Diversity: Molecular Genetics and the Evolution of Animal Design, 2004; author: Endless Forms Most Beautiful: The New Science of Evo Devo and the Making of the Animal Kingdom, 2005, The Making of the Fittest, 2006. Named one of 50 Future Leaders 40 and Under, Time mag., 1994; recipient Presdl. Young Investigator award, NSF, Shaw award, Milw. Found., Herbert W. Dickerman award, Wadsworth Ctr., NY State Dept. Health. Mem.: NAS, AAAS. Office: U Wis 201a RM Bock Labs 1525 Linden Dr Madison WI 53706 Office Phone: 608-262-7898. E-mail: sbcarrol@wisc.edu.*

CARROLL, WILLIAM, publishing company executive; Mgr., dir. Auto Book Press, Coda Publs.; dir., N.Mex. Books Coda Publs., Raton, N.Mex. Office: New Mex Books Coda Publs PO Box 71 Raton NM 87740-0071

CARROLL, WILLIAM J., municipal official; b. Aug. 24, 1944; BS in Acctg., Univ. Toledo, 1969; grad. Adv. Mgmt. Program, Harvard Bus. Sch., 1994. Gen. mgr., after market prodn. divsn. Hayes-Dana, 1987—89, v.p., after market prodn. divsn., 1989—93, pres., 1993—95, Dana Distribution Svc. Group, 1995—96, pres., diversified products and distribution, 1996—97, pres., automotive sys. group, 1997—2004, pres., COO, 2004; dir., econ., cmty. devel. City of Toledo, Ohio, 2004—. Office: City of Toledo Ste 1710 One Government Ctr Toledo OH 43604 Office Phone: 419-245-1286.

CARROLL, WILLIAM KENNETH, lawyer, educator, psychologist, theologian; b. Oak Park, Ill., May 8, 1927; s. Ralph Thomas and Edith (Fay) C.; m. Frances Louise Forgue; children: Michele, Brian. BS in Edn., Quincy Coll., Ill., 1950, BA in Philosophy, 1950; MA, Duquesne U., 1964; STL, Cath. U., 1965; PhD, U. Strasbourg, France, 1968; JD, Northwestern U., 1972. Bar: Ill. 1972, U.S. Dist. Ct. (no. dist.) Ill 1972, U.S. Ct. Appeals (7th cir.) 1973; lic. clin. psychologist, Ill. Asst. editor Franciscan Press, Chgo., 1955-60; asst. prof. psychology and religion Carlow Coll., Pitts., 1962-65, Loyola U., Chgo., 1968-70; staff atty. Fed. Defender Program, Chgo., 1972-75; prof. law John Marshall Law Sch., Chgo., 1975—. Bd. dirs. Am. Inst. Adlerian Studies; law reporter ABA Criminal Justice Mental Health Stds. Project, 1981-83; cons. legal issues Am. Psych. Assn.; standing com. on mental health law, Ill. Author: (with Kosnik et al.) Human Sexuality, 1977; Eyewitness Testimony, Strategies and Tactics, 1984, 2d edit., 2003; contbg. author: By Reason of Insanity, 1983, Law for Illinois Psychologists, 1985, Law and Mental Health Professionals, 2002. Bd. dirs. Chgo. Sch. Profl. Psychology, 1978-82; bd. adv. Ill. Sch. Profl. Psychology, 1985. Recipient Am. Juris award, 1970; U. Chgo. scholar, 1968-69. Fellow Inst. Social and Behavioral Pathology (chmn. 1987—); mem. ABA, AAUP, APA (Outstanding Contbn. to Psychology award 1998, com. on legal issues 1995—), Ill. Psychol. Assn., Cath. Theol. Soc. Am. Avocation: flying. Office: John Marshall Law Sch 315 S Plymouth Ct Chicago IL 60604-3968 Business E-Mail: 7carroll@jmls.edu.

CARROTHERS, CAROL ANN, special education services professional, educator; b. Seattle, Dec. 26, 1955; d. Murray Everett and Ann Cumming; m. David Wayne Carrothers, June 30, 1984; children: Erick David, Ryan David. BS in Spl. Edn., Ctrl. Wash. U., 1977; MS in Deaf Edn., We. Oreg. U., 1980. Tchr. spl. edn. Elm Lake Sch. Dist., Kirkland, Wash., 1978—79; tchr. deaf edn. North Thurston Sch. Dist., Olympia, Wash., 1980—82; asst. prof. Ctrl. Wash. U., Ellensburg, 1984—2000; state coord. deaf svc. Wash. Sensory Disabilities Svc., Ellensburg, 2000—. Deaf edn. specialist Ellensburg Sch. Dist., 1997—2000; bd. dirs. Coun. Am. Instrn. of Deaf, 2003—. Bd. dirs. Ellensburg Christian Sch., 1990—96; dir. family retreat Lazy F. Camp and Retreat, Ellensburg, 2001—; bd. dirs. Young Life, Ellensburg, 2003—. Mem.: Coun. Exceptional Childen, Nat. Registry Interpreters of Deaf, Nat. Assn. Deaf (cert. sign lang. interpreter). Avocations: knitting, horseback riding, fly fishing. Office: Wash Sensory Disabilities Svc/CWU 7409 400 E University Ave Ellensburg WA 98926

CARROTHERS, GERALD ARTHUR PATRICK, environmental and city planning educator; b. Saskatoon, Sask., Can., July 1, 1925; BArch, U. Man., Can., 1948, MArch, 1951; MCP, Harvard U., 1953; PhD, MIT, 1959. Lectr. architecture U. Man., Winnipeg, 1948-52; research asst. regional sci. Mass. Inst. Tech., Cambridge, 1953-56; asst. prof. town and regional planning U. Toronto, Ont., Can., 1956-60; assoc. prof. to prof. city planning U. Pa., Phila., 1960-67, chmn. dept. city planning, 1961-65; founding dir. Inst. Environ. Studies, 1965-67; prof. York U., Downsview, Ont., 1968—, founding dean faculty environ. studies, 1968-76. Chmn. U. Toronto-York U. Joint Program in Transp., 1971-78; adviser Central Mortgage and Housing Corp., Can., 1967-77; vis. prof. U. Nairobi, Kenya, 1978-80; mem. founding bd. dirs. Can. Urban Inst., 1988. Fellow World Acad. Art and Sci., Royal Archtl. Inst. Can., Can. Inst. Planners (founding editor Plan Can., 1959, councillor 1968-70); mem. Am. Inst. Cert. Planners (life), Am. Planning Assn. (charter), Regional Sci. Assn. (founding mem., founding editor Papers 1955, pres. 1970-71), Ont. Assn. Architects (life), Ont. Profl. Planners Inst. (founding registrar, founding bd. dirs. 1986). Home: 24 Bertmount Ave Toronto ON Canada M4M 2X9 Office: York U Fac Environ Studies 4700 Keele St Toronto ON Canada M3J 1P3

CARROW, JOHN C., computer company executive; b. Crystal City, Mo. BS, US Mil. Acad., 1966; MS in EE and Computer Sci., U. Ill., 1973. Commd. 2d lt. U.S. Army, advanced through grades, ret.; sys. engr., large scale info. sys. Gen. Electric; various sr. mgmt. positions GE Aerospace Info. Mgmt. Systems/Mgmt. Data Systems; chief info. officer, history City of Phila., 1993—96; chief info. officer Unisys Corp., 1996—, v.p., worldwide info. tech., 1996—. Chmn. bd. Red Cross (Southeastern Pa. Chpt.). Served to major US Army. Named Pub. Ofcl. of Yr., Governing mag., 1996. Office: Unisys Corp Unisys Way Blue Bell PA 19424

CARROW, MILTON MICHAEL, law educator; b. NYC, Sept. 13, 1912; s. Samuel and Ethel (Berlin) Carrow; m. Betsey Wood Hall, Nov. 2, 1940 (div. 1968); children: David M, Thomas E, Deborah, James H, Emily W; m. Eve Wagner Cooper, Feb. 28, 1969 (div. 1986); m. Barbara M Barski, Nov. 2, 1996. AB, Syracuse U., 1933, postgrad., 1933-34; JD, Harvard U., 1937. Bar: NY 1938. Assoc. Legal Aid Soc., Rochester, NY, 1937-38, Lincoln Epworth & Nathan Sweedler, 1938-42, Emil Schlesinger, 1946-48; pvt. practice, 1948-53; ptnr. Lavine & Carrow, NYC, 1953-59, Landis, Carrow, Benson & Tucker, NYC, 1959-70, Carrow, Bernson, Hoeniger, Freitag & Abbey, 1970-73; dir. Ctr. for Adminstrv. Justice, ABA, 1973-77, Nat. Center for Adminstrv. Justice, Consortium of Univs. of Washington Met. Area, 1977-79; pres. Nat. Center for Adminstrv. Justice, 1979-82. Adj. asst. prof. Law Sch. NYU, 1964—68; cons. Nat. Adv. Com. Civil Disorders, 1967; mem. faculty appellate judges seminar Inst. Jud. Adminstrn., 1969—70; vis. prof. Nat. Law Ctr. George Washington U., 1973—80; adj. prof. Georgetown U., 1980—81, rsch. prof. pub. policy, 1983—2005; vice chmn. Weston Charter Comm., Conn., 1965—66; counsel UN We Believe, 1962—72; vis. intervenor XVIII Internat. Congress Adminstrv. Scis., Madrid, 1980; US rep. to standing com. law and sci. pub. adminstrn. Internat. Inst. Adminstrv. Scis., 1982; cons. Block Island Charter Commn., 1988—89. Author: (book) Background of Administrative Law, 1948, The Licensing Power in New York City, 1968; author: (with J D Nyhart) Law and Science in Collaboration, 1983; editor (with Robert Paul Churchill and Joseph J Cordes): Democracy, Social Values and Public Policy, 1998; contbr. articles to profl jours; editor: Working Paper series, Grad Program in Pub Policy, 1985—. Dir. Washington Cir. George Washington U., 1988—94. With AUS, 1943—46. Mem.: ABA (chmn. sect. adminstrv. law 1971—72), Assn. Bar City NY (chmn. com. adminstrv. law 1964—67), Arts Club Washington (trustee, endowment com. 2001—04). Home: 224 Chandler St Milton DE 19968 Office Phone: 302-684-5746.

CARROZZA, VINCENT A., investment company executive; b. NYC, Jan. 15, 1972; s. Rocco Carrozza and Barbara DeLuca; m. Anne Reeves Carrozza, Jan. 10, 1954; children: Fay, Lynn, Robert. BA, Columbia U., NYC, 1949. Gen. mgr. Midnight Sun Broadcasting Co., Fairbanks, Alaska, 1954—56; dir. Alaska Statehood Campaign, Fairbanks, 1956; exec. v.p. Dallas Tex. Corp., 1958—69; real estate developer Ctr. City Inc., Dallas, 1969—90; chmn., CEO Carrozza Investments, Dallas, 1990—. Trustee Monyreit, NYC, 1986—90. Trustee, pres. Dallas Mus. Art, 1976—90; trustee, vice chmn. St. John's Coll., Santa Fe, 1984—89, Anapolis, Md., 1984—89; trustee Columbia U., NYC, 1990—93; trustee, exec. com. Am. Acad. Rome, NYC, 1984—90; trustee Italian Acad. Advanced Studies, NYC, 1992—95; world coun. mem. Internat. Ho., NYC; founding mem. Goals For Dallas; bd. dirs. Alzheimer's Disease and Related Disorders. Sgt. inf. US Army, 1942—45, Europe. Recipient Order Merit, Rep. Italy, 1987. Mem.: Century Assn., Idlewild. Avocation: tennis. Office: Carrozza Investments 2714 Routh St Dallas TX 75201

CARRUTH, HAYDEN, poet; b. Waterbury, Conn., Aug. 3, 1921; s. Gorton Veeder and Margery Tracy Barrow (Dibb) C.; m. Sara Anderson, Mar. 14, 1943; 1 child, Martha Hamilton; m. Eleanore Ray, Nov. 29, 1952; m. Rose Marie Dorn, Oct. 28, 1961; 1 child, David Barrow II; m. Joe-Anne McLaughlin, Dec. 29, 1989. AB, U. N.C., 1943; MA, U. Chgo., 1948; LLD, New Eng. Coll., 1987, Syracuse U., 1993. Editor-in-chief Poetry mag., 1949-50; assoc. editor U. Chgo. Press, 1950-51; project adminstr. Intercultural Publs. Inc., NYC, 1952-53; poetry editor Harper's mag., 1977—88. Poet-in-residence Johnson State Coll., 1972-74; adj. prof. U. Vt., 1975-78; prof. English Syracuse (N.Y.) U., 1979-91, prof. emeritus, 1991—. Author: The Crow and the Heart, 1959, Journey to a Known Place, 1961, Norfolk Poems, 1962, Appendix A, 1963, North Winter, 1964, Nothing for Tigers, 1965, Contra Mortem, 1967, After the Stranger, 1965, For You, 1970, The Clay Hill Anthology, 1970, The Voice That Is Great Within Us, 1970, The Bird-Poem Book, 1970, From Snow and Rock, from Chaos, 1973, Dark World, 1973, The Bloomingdale Papers, 1975, Loneliness, 1976, Aura, 1977, Brothers, I Loved You All, 1978, Almanach du Printemps Vivarois, 1979, Working Papers, 1982, The Mythology of Dark and Light, 1982, The Sleeping Beauty, 1982, If You Call This Cry a Song, 1983, Effluences from the Sacred Caves, 1983, Asphalt Georgics, 1985, Lighter than Air Craft, 1985, The Oldest Killed Lake in North America, 1985, The Selected Poetry of Hayden Carruth, 1986, Mother, 1986, Sitting In: Selected Writings on Jazz, Blues & Related Topics, 1986, Sonnets, 1989, Tell Me Again How the White Heron Rises and Flies Across the Nacreous River at Twilight Toward the Distant Island, 1989, Collected Shorter Poems, 1946-91, 92, Suicides and Jazzers, 1992, Collected Longer Poems, 1994, Selected Essays and Reviews, 1995, Scrambled Eggs and Whiskey, 1996, Reluctantly, 1998, Beside the Shadblow Tree, 1999, Faxes to William, 2000, Doctor Jazz, 2001, Letters To Jane, 2004, Toward the Distant Islands, 2006; mem. editl. bd. Hudson Rev., 1971—. Sr. fellow N.Y. Found. Arts, 1993. Recipient Vachel Lindsay prize, 1954, Bess Hokin prize, 1956, Levinson prize, 1958, Ann. Poetry award Brandeis U., 1959, Harriet Monroe Poetry prize U. Chgo., 1960, Helen Bullis prize U. Seattle, 1962, Carl Sandburg prize, 1963, Emily Clark Balch prize, 1964, Gov.'s medal State of Vt., 1974, Shelley award Poetry Soc. Am., 1978, Lenore Marshall prize, 1979, Morton Zabel prize, 1968, Whiting Writers award, 1986, Sarah Josepha Hale award, 1988, Ruth Lilly Poetry prize, 1990, Nat. Book Critics Circle award in poetry, 1993, Lannan award for poetry, 1995, Nat. Book award for Poetry, 1996; named Vt. poet laureate, 2002; fellow Bollingen Found., 1962, John Simon Meml. Guggenheim Found., 1965, 79, sr. fellow Nat. Endowment for Arts, 1988; grantee Nat. Found. on Arts and Humanities, 1967, 74. Home: 4788 Bear Path Rd Munnsville NY 13409 Personal E-mail: jomclaug@dreamscape.net.

CARRUTHERS, THOMAS NEELY, lawyer; b. Columbia, Tenn., Oct. 11, 1928; s. Thomas Neely and Ellen Douglas (Everett) Carruthers; m. Dale Gilder Jones, Feb. 7, 1959; children: Thomas Neely III, Virginia Carruthers Smith, Catherine Everett. AB, Princeton U., 1950; LLB, Yale U., 1955. Assoc. Bradley, Arant, Rose & White, Birmingham, Ala., 1955-63, ptnr., 1963—, chair exec. com. and mng. ptnr., 1990-95. Mem. editl. bd. Yale Law Jour., 1953—55. Trustee Ala. Shakespeare Festival, Leadership Ala., pres., 1995—96, chmn., 1996—97; trustee Birmingham Mus. Art, chmn., 1995—2002; bd. dirs. 2020 Birmingham Com., Ala. Dept. Archives and History; bd. advisors Cumberland Law Sch., chmn., 1993—95, Constl. Reform Task Force, 2005—; chmn. exec. com. Ala. Acad. Honor, 1999—; active Boy Scouts Am., Birmingham, exec. bd. Birmingham Coun.; chmn. fin. com. Lakeshore Found., 2005—; chancellor Episcopal Diocese Ala., 2003—06; trustee Children's Hosp., Ala., pres. Ala., 1996—97. Named Humanitarian of Yr., 1997; recipient Silver Beaver award, Boy Scouts Am., Thurmond Arnold Appellate Competition prize, Yale U., 1954, Birmingham-So. Coll. medal Honor, 1992, Pub. Svc. award, Birmingham Bar, 1996, Brotherhood and Sisterhood award, NCCJ, 2000, Justice Pub. Svc. award, Ala. Appleseed Ctr. Law, 2007, commendations, State Ala., Ala. Commn. Higher Edn., Jacksonville State U. Fellow: Am. Bar Found.; mem.: ABA, Birmingham Bar Assn. (Outstanding Lawyer of Yr. award 2001), Ala. Bar Assn., Am. Law Inst., Am. Tax Policy Inst. (past trustee), Am. Coll. Tax Counsel, So. Fed. Tax Inst. (pres. 1993—94, trustee, past chmn.), Internat. Bar Assn., Mountain Brook Club, Rotary (pres. 1992—93, Spain-Hickman award 2003). Episcopalian. Office: Bradley Arant Rose & White One Federal Pl 1819 5th Ave N Birmingham AL 35203 Home Phone: 205-879-0986; Office Phone: 205-521-8263. E-mail: tcarruthers@bradleyarant.com.

CARSBERG, SCOTT, chef; b. 1964; m. Jyun Joo Paek. Chef Le Pavillon, Wash., DC, Ritz-Carlton Buckhead, Atlanta; head chef Villa Mozart, Merano, Italy, Settebello, Seattle; owner, exec. chef Lampreia, Seattle. Named one of Rising Stars, Restaurant Hospitality Mag., 1994; recipient Best Chef: Northwest/Hawaii award, James Beard Found., 2006. Office: Lampreia Restaurant 2400 First Ave Seattle WA 98121 Office Phone: 206-443-3301.*

CARSON, ALICE HINES, secondary school educator; d. Melvin K. and Barbara F. Hines; m. Shawn Allen Carson, June 29, 1986; children: Allen Tyler, Lindsay Grey. AS, Mt. Olive Coll., NC, 1980; BS, E. Carolina U., Greenville, NC, 1982; MEd, U. SC, Columbia, 1990. Tchr. Plymouth HS, NC, 1982—84, Wellcome Mid. Sch., Greenville, 1984—85, McCants Mid. Sch., Anderson, SC, 1985—87, Pucolet Jr. HS, Sparntanburg, SC, 1987—91, S. Doyle HS, Knoxville, 1991—2001, Karns HS, Knoxville, 2001—. Leader Girls Scouts US, Knoxville, 2001—06; mem. leadership edn. com. Knoxville C. of C., 2000—01. Mem.: Nat. Coun. Tchrs. Math., Smoky Mountain Math. Assn. (pres. 2001—02).

CARSON, ANDREW DOYLE, applied psychologist; b. Dallas, Aug. 3, 1960; s. Doyle Irvin and Sarah Louise (Simmons) C.; m. Victoria Hutchinson McCain; children: Emily, Nathaniel. AB cum laude, Harvard U., 1982; MS in Human Devel., U. Tex. at Dallas, Richardson, 1986; PhD in Ednl. Psychology, U. Tex., Austin, 1990; cert. webmaster, Ill. Inst. Tech., 1999. Tchr. spl. edn. Highland Acad., Dallas, 1983-85; athletic dept. tutor U. Tex., Austin, 1985-88; cognitive rehab. therapist St. David's Hosp., Austin, 1988-89; psychol. intern Counseling Ctr., U. Md., College Park, 1989-90; asst. prof. counseling psychology Boston U., 1990-91, McGill U., Montreal, 1991-94; rsch. assoc. The Ball Found., Glen Ellyn, Ill., 1995-96, sr. rsch. assoc., 1996-97, dir. rsch., 1997-99; pres. Charter Sch. Assn., Wheaton, 1997; dir. Ball Labs., 1999; project coord. Britannica.com, 2000; prin. Andrew Carson Assoc., 2000—. Contbr. articles to profl. jours. and chpts. to books. Chmn. grants com. New 200 Found., Wheaton, Ill., 1997-98; pres. Charter Sch. Assn., Wheaton, 1997. FCAR Que. New Rschr. grantee, 1992, Strong Rsch. Adv. Bd. grantee, 1989, 94, 95. Mem. APA (divsns. 1, 10, 15, 17), Soc. for Vocat. Psychology, Nat. Career Devel. Assn., Am. Ednl. Rsch. Assn. (career devel. spl. interest group program chair 1995-98, pres. 1998—, chair multiple intelligences spl. interest group comm. 1999-2000). Presbyterian. Avocations: swimming, writing, drawing.

CARSON, BENJAMIN LEEDS, composer, educator; b. Raleigh, NC, Aug. 24, 1971; s. Robert James Carson and Mary Clare Hankel; m. Jennifer Jade Li, Aug. 13, 2005. BA, Willamette U., Oreg., 1993; MusM, U. Wash., Seattle, 1995; PhD, U. Calif., San Diego, 2001. Artist in residence Inst. Rsch. et Coord. d'Acoustique Musique, Paris, 1999; assoc. in composition U. Calif., San Diego, 1999; lectr. in writing Thurgood Marshall Coll., U. Calif., La Jolla, 2002; lectr. in music theory U. Calif., Riverside, Calif., 2002; asst. prof. U. Calif. Dept. Music, Santa Cruz, 2003—. Composer: Four Short Pieces for Orchestra, 2000, (chamber orch. ensemble) Detalér, 1999 (First prize. Brtish Internat. Bass Found., London, 2000). Inst. for Adv. Feminist Studies Internat. Socialist Orgn., 2004—; steering com. mem. UAW Acad. Union, San Diego, 1998—2001; organizer Internat. Socialist Orgn., Santa Cruz, 2003—. Grantee, Arts Rsch. Inst., U. Calif., 2005. Mem.: Am. Musicological Soc., Soc. Music Theory, Soc. for Music Perception and Cognition. Socialist. Avocation: languages. Office: U Calif Music Ctr Faculty Svcs 1156 Hight St Santa Cruz CA 95064

CARSON, BENJAMIN SOLOMON, neurosurgeon; b. Detroit, Sept. 18, 1951; s. Robert Solomon and Sonya (Copeland) C.; m. Lacena Rustin, July 6, 1975; children: Murray Nedlands, Benjamin Solomon Jr., Rhoeyce Harrington. BA, Yale U., 1973; MD, U. Mich., 1977; DSc (hon.), Gettysburg Coll., 1988, N.C. A&T, 1989, Andrews U., 1989, Sojourner-Douglas Coll., 1989, Shippenburg U., 1990, Jersey City State Coll., 1990, Southwestern Adventist Coll., 1992, U. Mass., Boston, 1992, Marygrove Coll., 1993, U. Detroit Mercy, 1994, Spalding U., 1994, Western Md. Coll., 1994, Morgan State U., 1994, Long Island U., 1994, N.C. State U., 1994, Tuskegee U., 1995, Yale U., 1996, Del. State U., 1996, Med. U. South Africa, Medunsa, 1997, GMI Engring. and Mgmt. Inst., 1997, U. Del., 1997, Coll. William and Mary, 1998. Diplomate Am. Bd. Neurol. Surgery. Surg. intern Johns Hopkins Hosp., Balt., 1977-78, neurosurg. resident, 1978-82, chief resident, 1982-83; sr. registrar Sir Charles Gairdner Hosp., Perth, W. Australia, 1983-84; dir. pediatric neurosurgery, prof. neurosurgery, plastic surgery, oncology & pediatrics Johns Hopkins Hosp., Balt., 1984—; co-dir. Johns Hopkins Craniofacial Ctr., Balt. Bd. dirs. Kellogg Co., Costco Wholesale Corp., Yale Corp.(emeritus fellow), Am. Promise; mem. President's Coun. on Bioethics, 2004; mem. governing body, Yale U.; invited spkr. in field. Author: Pediatric Neurooncology, 1987, Achondroplasia, 1988, Gifted Hands, 1989, Think Big, 1996, The Big Picture, 1999; contbr. jour. articles. Mem. med. adv. bd. Children's Cancer Found., Balt., 1987—; hon. med. chmn. Md. Red Cross, Balt., 1987—; co-founder, pres. Carson Scholars Fund, 1994, Benevolent Endowment Network (BEN) Fund. Recipient Am. Black Achievement award Ebony mag., Hollywood, Calif., 1988, Cum Laude award Am. Radiol. Soc., Chgo., 1982, Candle award Morehouse U., Atlanta, 1989; Paul Harris fellow Rotary Internat., 1988; Named one of Top 100 Black Physicians in Am. by Black Enterprise Mag., 2001, America's top 20 physicians and scientists, CNN and Time Mag., 2001; named one of 89 Living Legends, Libr. Congress. Mem. Am. Assn. Neurol. Surgeons, Congress Neurol. Surgeons, AAAS, Pediatric Oncology Group, Nat. Med. Assn., Am. Acad. Achievement, Horatio Alger Soc. of Distinguished Americans, Alpha Omega Alpha. Seventh Day Adventist. In 1987, gained world-wide recognition as the principal surgeon in the 22-hour separation of the Binder siamese twins from Germany. This was the first time occipital craniopagus twins had been separated with both surviving; in 1997, was the primary surgeon in the team of South African and Zambian surgeons that separated type-2 vertical craniopagus twins (joined at the top of the head) in a 28-hour operation. It represents the first time such complexly joined siamese twins have been separated with both remaining neurologically normal; participated in the noble, but unsuccessful, humanitarian effort to separate adult Iranian craniopagus twins in Singapore. Office: Johns Hopkins Hosp 600 N Wolfe St #811 Baltimore MD 21287-0005*

CARSON, BRAD ROGERS, former congressman; b. Winslow, AZ., Mar. 11, 1967; m. Julie. BA with honors, Baylor U., 1967; MA in politics, philospophy and econ., Oxford; JD, U. Okla. Coll. Law, 1994. Atty. pvt. practice, Crowe & Dunlevy, 1996; White House fellow, spl. asst. to Sec. Defense Spl. Projects, 1997-98; mem. US Ho. of Reps. (2nd dist.) Okla., 2001—05. Vice-chair Congl. Native Am. Caucus. Awarded Rhodes Scholarship. Mem. Phi Beta Kappa. Mem. Blue Dog Coalition, New Democrat Coalition; mem. First Baptist Ch. Claremore.*

CARSON, CHARLES MICHAEL, composer, musician; b. Fairfield, Calif., Nov. 24, 1959; s. Robert and Alene (Holleman) Carson; m. Olivia Sel Rush, May 19, 1984; children: Ciara, Mika, Jere. B Music Composition, U. So. Miss., Hattiesburg, 1983; M Music Composition, North Tex. State U., Denton, 1987; D Music Composition, U. North Tex., Denton, 1994. Dir. music Keystone Acad., Plano, Tex., 1992—93; min. music Bethany Bible Ch., Plano, 1993—95; resident composer 1st Bapt. Ch. Wylie, Tex., 1995—2000, 1st Bapt. Ch. Lavon, Tex., 2000—, assoc. pianist, 2002—, prin. organist, 2003—. Composer: (opera) Ryders to the Sea, 1994, (symphony) Adoration of the Christ, 2006, (CD) Psalms and Alleluias, 2002, Biblical Portraits and Musical Offerings, 2003, Miracles of Enchantment and Wonder, 2004, Transcendental Christmas Carols, 2005, Symphony No. 1 Adoration of the Christ, 2006. Founder Music for Missions, Lavon, 2002—; deacon 1st Bapt. Ch. Lavon, 2005—. Recipient Outstanding Performance of Yr. award, Sanden Internat. Am., 1979, Founders Day award, Sarden Internat. Japan, 2000, 2005. Mem.: Mensa, Phi Mu Epsilon, Phi Kappa Phi. Avocations: astronomy, chess. Home: 18280 FM 1778 Nevada TX 75173 Office: Sanden Internat Am 601 Sanden Blvd Wylie TX 75098

CARSON, CHRISTOPHER LEONARD, retired lawyer; b. Washington, Dec. 28, 1940; s. Leonard O. and Evelyn (Watters) C.; m. Cynthia Caffey, Dec. 27, 1963; 1 dau., Melissa Ann. AB, Duke U., 1962; JD, U. Mich., 1965. Bar: N.Y. 1965, Fla. 1968, Ga. 1970. Assoc. Olwine, Chase, O'Donnell & Weyher, NYC, 1965-66; ptnr. Hansell & Post, Atlanta, 1969-89, Jones Day, Atlanta, 1989—2006; ret., 2006. Contbg. author: Modern Real Estate Transactions; contbr. articles to legal publs. and mags. Bd. dirs., adv. coun. Atlanta Area Boy Scouts Am., 1974-80; bd. dirs. Young Life Urban Atlanta, 1983—87. Lt. sr. grade USNR, 1966-69. Fellow Am. Coll. Coml. Fin. Lawyers; mem. ABA (Uniform Comml. Code Com., Subcoms. on Secured Transactions and Letter of Credit 1982-95), Southeastern Bankruptcy Law Inst. (dir. 1973—, pres. 1980-81, chmn. 1981-82), Atlanta Bar Bankruptcy Sect. (chmn. 1981-82), Ga. Bar Uniform Code Com. (chmn. 1984-87), Cherokee Club. Republican. Baptist. Avocations: running, reading, travel. Home Phone: 904-373-0909.

CARSON, CULLEY CLYDE, III, urologist, educator; b. Westerly, RI, Feb. 25, 1945; s. Culley Clyde Jr. and Dorothy (Scarborough) C.; m. Mary Jo McDonald, Aug. 10, 1970; children: Culley Clyde IV, Hilary. BS, Trinity Coll., 1967; MD, George Washington U., 1971. Diplomate Am. Bd. Urology. Intern Dartmouth Med. Ctr., 1971-72, resident surgery, 1971-73; fellow urology Mayo Clinic, Rochester, Minn., 1975-78; instr. urology U. Minn. Mayo Med. Sch., Rochester, 1978; asst. prof. urology Duke U. Med. Ctr., Durham, NC, 1978-84, assoc. prof., 1984-88, prof., 1988-93, Rhodes Disting. chair, 1993—; prof., chmn. urology U. N.C., Chapel Hill, 1993—, Rhoads disting. prof., 2000—. Chief urology Durham VA Hosp.; mem. new drug panel U.S. FDA; mem. exec. com. U.S. Pharmacopea. Author: Endourology, 1985, Atlas of Urologic Endoscopy, 1986, Impotence, 1992, 98, Complications of Invasive Procedures, 1995, Textbook of Erectile Dysfunction, 1999; editor-in-chief Mediguide to Urology, 1994—, Contemporary Urology, 1997—; contbr. chpts. to urol. texts. Maj. M.C., USAF, 1973-75. Named Command Flight Surgeon of Yr., USAF, 1974, Healthcare Hero, Rsch. Triangle, 2007; recipient Calvin Klopp Rsch. award, 1971, Friedman rsch. prize, 1971, Cristol Mayo Alumni award, 1992, Jesse H. Neal award, 2001; rsch. fellow Am. Heart Assn., 1969, O'Dea travel fellow, 1978. Fellow ACS, Am. Surg. Assn.; mem. AMA, AAAS, Am. Assn. Genitourinary Surgeons, Am. Urol. Assn. (pres. Southeast sect. 2006), Sexual Medicine Soc. (pres. 2003), Internat. Soc. Urology, Am. Fertility Soc., Soc. Urol. Pros Surgery (pres. 2006), N.Y. Acad. Scis., Mayo Alumni Assn., Gov.'s Club, Carolina Club, Trinity Club (Hartford), Sigma Xi, Psi Chi, Alpha Omega Alpha. Home: 2719 Spencer St Durham NC 27705-5720 Office: UNC 2140 Bioinformatics Bldg Chapel Hill NC 27599-7235 Office Phone: 919-966-2574. Personal E-mail: culleyccarson3@hotmail.com. Business E-Mail: carson@med.unc.edu.

CARSON, DENISE WILKINSON, retired gifted and talented educator; b. Providence, Dec. 29, 1946; d. Thaddeus Archiebald and Helen Gautier Wilkinson; m. Keith Robert Carson, Sept. 9, 1967; children: Jeanne-Marie, Corwin Keith. BS in Math. and Govt., Fla. State U., Tallahassee, 1967—69; MAEd, Coll. William and Mary, Williamsburg, Va., 1988—89. Am. Montessori Soc. Montessori Tchr. Edn. Ctr., Mich., 1980, Gifted Cert. Shenandoah U., Va., 1998. Statistician Fla. Bd. Regents, Tallahassee, 1969—70; mathematician RCA, Alexandria, Va., 1971—72; budget officer Arlington Sch. Sys., Va., 1972—74; tchr. of students & tchrs. Troy Montessori/Montessori Tchr. Ed Ctr., Troy/West Bloomfield, Mich., 1978—83; tchr./adminstr. It's A Small World Sch., Tacoma, Wash., 1984—85; tchr. St. Patrick's Cath. Sch., Tacoma, 1985—87; elem. tchr. Armstrong Fundamental Sch., Hampton, Va., 1990—2001; tchr. gifted South Morrison Elem., Newport News, Va., 2001—06; ret., 2006. Chmn. Gifted Adv. Bd., Tacoma, 1985—86. Author (compiler): (student books used in school) Jamestown/Early American History, Government, Explorers & Simple Machines; co-author (academic units for gifted) Maps Skills; Ancient Greece & Ancient Rome. Grantee Va. Art grant, Va. Art Coun., 1992—93. Mem.: DAR (dist. press book chair), Newport News Ret. Tchrs. Assn. (fin. chmn. 2007—), Presch. Ptnrs. (mentor), Nat. Sci. Tchr. Assn., Va. State Reading Assn., Nat. Math. Tchr. Assn., Beta Sigma Phi (life; chpt. pres. 1999—2000, pres. peninsula coun. 2000—02, chpt. pres. 2006—07, Woman of Yr. 1991—92, 1994—95, 1999—2000, Peninsula Woman of Yr. 2001—02, Woman of Yr. 2006—07). Roman Catholic. Avocations: travel, reading, needlecrafts.

CARSON, HARRY, retired professional football player; b. So. Carolina, Nov. 26, 1953; Grad., So. Carolina St. Univ., 1975. Linebacker NY Giants, 1976—88. Named to NFL Pro Football Hall of Fame, 2006. Achievements include being named to Mid-East Athletic Conference (MEAC) first-team all-conference; two-time MEAC defensive player yr., 1974-1975; first team selection, All-American coll. team, 1975; 9 NFL Pro-Bowl appearances. Office: Pro Football Hall of Fame 2121 George Halas Dr NW Canton OH 44708 Office Phone: 330-456-8207.

CARSON, JAMES WOOD, psychologist; b. Greensboro, NC, Dec. 19, 1951; s. Nancy Wood and George Washington Mordecai (Stepfather); m. Kimberly Maynard Carson, May 16, 1998. PhD, U. NC, 2002. Lic. Psychologist NC, 2003. Postdoctoral fellow Duke U. Med. Ctr., 2002—05, asst. clin. prof., 2005—. Swami in Saraswati Order Gurudev Siddha Peeth, Ganeshpuri, Maharashtra, India, 1982—93. Pres. Heart of It Found., Durham, NC, 2005. Mem.: APA, Assn. for Behavioral and Cognitive Therapies, Soc. of Behavioral Medicine. Achievements include research in first study examining effect of mindfulness meditation on couples' relationships; first study examining effects of loving-kindness meditation. Avocation: Carolina basketball. Home Phone: 919-490-1605; Office Phone: 919-416-3407. Office Fax: 919-416-3458. Personal E-mail: jim@yogaatthethreshold.com. E-mail: jim.carson@duke.edu.

CARSON, JAY WILMER, pathologist, educator; b. Ki-Jang, Korea, Oct. 6, 1933; came to U.S., 1960; s. Han Kyu and Jin Chan (Son) Cha; m. Jennifer C. White, June 28, 1968 (dec. Aug. 1990); m. Teresa M. Alberda, July 14, 1995. MD, Seoul Nat. U., 1958. Diplomate Am. Bd. Pathology. Intern Bellevue Hosp. Ctr., NYC, 1961-62; resident in pathology Albert Einstein Coll. Medicine, NYC, 1963-66; fellow U. Montreal, Que., Canada, 1967-68; chief anatomic pathology VA Hosp., Martinez, Calif., 1969-91; dir. cytopathology VA Med. Ctr., San Francisco, 1992-96; assoc. clin. prof. U. Calif. Med. Sch., San Francisco, 1992—. Aviation med. examiner FAA, Oklahoma City, 1987-96; assoc. clin. prof. U. Calif., Davis, 1985—; hosp. comdr. 347th Gen. Hosp., Sunnyvale, Calif., 1992-1993, 6253d Army Hosp., Santa Rosa, Calif., 1994-96. Patentee needle aspiration device. Mem. chmn.'s adv. bd. Nat. Rep. Com., Washington, 1995-96. Col. USAR, 1971-96. Decorated Order of Military Med. Merit, Meritorious Svc. Medal with one oakleaf cluster, Sr. Flight Surgeon Badge. Fellow Coll. Am. Pathologists; mem. Internat. Acad. Pathology, Assn. Mil. Surgeons U.S. (life), Res. Officers Assn. (life), U.S. Army War Coll. Alumni Assn. (life), Soc. U.S. Army Flight Surgeons (life). Avocations: skiing, sailing, music. Home: 1550 Sorrel Ct Walnut Creek CA 94598-4800 Personal E-mail: jntcarson@astound.net.

CARSON, JEFFREY L., internist; b. Phila., Oct. 11, 1951; s. Albert Carson and Jackie Zeitz; m. Susan Carson, June 1977; children: Josh, Jennie, Rachael, Dylan. BA in Polit. Sci., U. R.I., 1973; MD, Hahnemann Med. Coll., 1977. Diplomate Am. Bd. Internal Medicine. Chief med. resident Hahnemann Med. Coll. and Hosp., Phila., 1979-80; Henry J. Kaiser fellow U. Pa./Hosp., Phila., 1981-82; asst. prof. medicine UMDNJ - Rutgers Med. Sch., Camden, NJ, 1982-87; assoc. prof. medicine UMDNJ - Robert Wood Johnson Med. Sch., New Brunswick, NJ, 1987-94, chief, Divsn. of GIM, 1987—, prof. of medicine, 1987—, Richard G. Reynolds chair, 1996—. Sr. internat. fellow U. Oxford, U.K., 1995-96; mem. epidemiology study sect. NIH, Bethesda, 1990-94, reviewers res., 1994-98; adhoc reviewer Agy. for Health Care Policy and Rsch., Bethesda, 1990—. Rsch. grantee Agy. for Health Care Policy and Rsch., 1993, NIH, 1990-95, Ortho-Biotech, Bridgewater, N.J., 1995. Fellow am. Coll. Physicians; mem. Soc. Gen. Internal Medicine (chair mid-atlantic sect. 1990-91, other offices)l. Avocations: sailing, coaching little league baseball. Office: UMDNJ-RWJ Med Sch 125 Paterson St New Brunswick NJ 08901-1962 Business E-Mail: carson@umdnj.edu.

CARSON, JOANNE, artist, educator; BA, U. Ill.; MFA, U. Chgo. Prof. & chairperson art dept. U. at Albany, SUNY. One-woman shows include, Bklyn. Mus., 2002, Plus Ultra Gallery, Bklyn., 2001, Sylvia Schmidt Gallery, New Orleans, 1994, Ruth Siegel Gallery, N.Y.C., 1990, Options,

Mus. Contemporary Art, Chgo., 1985, exhibited in group shows at Spring Exhibit, AAAL, 2002, New Works on Wood, Fleming Mus., Burlington Vt., 2001, Frederick Weisman Collection, New Orleans Mus., 1997, Whitney Biennial, Whitney Mus. Am. Art, N.Y.C., 1985. Recipient Purchase Prize Sculpture, AAAL, 2002; Rome Prize Fellowship Painting, Am. Acad. Rome, Artists Fellowship, Nat. Endowment Arts. Office: University at Albany, SUNY Art Dept 1400 Washington Ave FA 216 Albany NY 12222 Office Phone: 518-442-4020. Office Fax: 518-442-4807.

CARSON, JOHN ROBERT, lobbyist, secondary school educator; b. St. Joseph, Mo., Feb. 11, 1936; s. Robert Lee and Ellen Victoria Carson; m. Janet Carol Carson, Aug. 17, 1957; children: John William, Paul Frederick. BA, Midland Luth. Coll., Fremont, Nebr., 1958; MA, Drake U., Des Moines, 1963; LLD (hon.), Ohio Col. Pediat. Medicine, Cleve., 1984; DSc (hon.), Calf. Coll. Pediat. Medicine, San Francisco, 1994. High sch. tchr. Corwith Wesley Cmty. Schs., Corwith, Iowa, 1958—61, Earlham Cmty. Schs., Iowa, 1961—63; dir. Earlham Care Program Age, 1963—65; spl. asst. gov. State Nebr., Lincoln, Nebr., 1965—69; dir. govt. agy. Am. Podiatric Med. Assn., Washington, 1969—2001; ret. Recipient Disting. Svc. award., Am. Pediat. Med. Assn., 1968, Disting. Svc. award, 1993. Mem.: Am. League Lobbyists (life), Nat. Exchange Club (pres., nat. bd. mem. 1975—), Elks. Republican. Lutheran. Avocations: golf, travel, reading, Spanish.

CARSON, JOHNNIE, former ambassador, academic administrator; b. Chgo., Apr. 7, 1943; s. Dupree and Aretha (Rhodes) C.; m. Anne Diemer; Feb. 8, 1969; children: Elizabeth, Michael Dupree, Katherine Anne. BA, Drake U., 1965; MA in Internat. Rels., U. London, 1975. Tchr., vol. U.S. Peace Corps, Tanzania, 1965-68; fgn. svc. officer U.S. Dept. State, Washington, 1969—; polit. officer U.S. Embassy, Lagos, Nigeria, 1969-71; internat. rels. officer U.S. Dept. State, Washington, 1971-74; dep. chief of mission U.S. Embassy, Maputo, Mozambique, 1975-78; staff dir. fgn. affairs com. subcom. on Africa U.S. Ho. of Reps., Washington, 1979-82; dep. polit. counselor U.S. Embassy, Lisbon, Portugal, 1982-86, dep. chief of mission Gaborone, Botswana, 1986-90; Am. amb. Am. Embassy, Kampala, Uganda, 1991-94, Am. amb. to Zimbabwe Harare, 1995-97; prin. dep. asst. sec. for African Affairs Dept. of State, Washington, 1997-99, U.S. amb. to Kenya Nairobi, Kenya, 1999—2003; sr. v.p. Nat. Def. Univ., 2003—. Contbr. to numerous Congl. Studies on Africa, also to books; author articles on Africa and refugees. Mem. NAACP, African Studies Assn. Baptist. Avocations: tennis, reading, cross country skiing, hiking, fishing. Office: 257 2d Ave SW Fort Lesley J McNair Washington DC 20034-5123

CARSON, JULIA M., congresswoman; b. Louisville, July 8, 1938; 2 children. Student, Ind. U., 1960-62, St. Mary the Woods, 1976-78. Mem. Ind. Ho. of Reps., Indpls., 1972-76, Ind. Senate, 1976-90, U.S. Congress from 7th Ind. dist. (formerly 10th), 1997—. Mem. fin. svcs. com., 1997—, Vets. Affairs com., 1997—. V.p. Greater Indpls. Prog. Com.; nat. Dem. committeewoman; trustee YMCA; bd. didrs. Pub. Svc. Acad. Recipient Woman of Yr. Ind. award, 1974, Outstanding Leadership award AKA, Humanitarian award Christian Theol. Sem.; named one of Most Influential Black Americans, Ebony mag., 2006. Mem. NAACP, Urban League, Nat. Coun. Negro Women. Democrat. Baptist. Office: US Ho Reps 1535 Longworth Ho Office Bldg Washington DC 20515-1410 Office Phone: 202-225-4011. Office Fax: 202-225-5633.*

CARSON, LEONARD ALLEN, lawyer; b. Lorain, Ohio, Nov. 6, 1940; s. Frank and Josephine (Sulewski) Guzewicz. BS in Bus. Adminstrn., U. Fla., 1963, JD, 1966. Bar: Fla. 1967. Staff acct. Peat, Marwick, Mitchell & Co., NYC, 1963-64; mem. firm Kates and Ress, P.A., Miami, Fla., 1967-70; corp. counsel, asst. to exec. v.p. and treas. Cordis Corp., Miami, 1970-73; judge Indsl. Claims Ct., Ft. Lauderdale, Fla., 1973; mem. Fla. Indsl. Rels. Commn., Tallahassee, 1973-74, chmn., 1974-76, Fla. Pub. Employees Rels. Commn., Tallahassee, 1976-80; of counsel Seyfarth, Shaw, Fairweather & Geraldson, Tallahassee and Miami, 1980-83; pres. Carson & Adkins, Tallahassee, 1983—. Mem. Fla. Law Revision Coun., 1976-77, Internat. Assn. Indsl. Accident Bds. and Commns., 1974-76 Served with USMCR, 1960-66. Mem. ABA, Am. Arbitration Assn. (nat. panel 1968-73). Clubs: Governors, Capital Tiger Bay. Republican. Roman Catholic. Home: 233 Rose Hill Dr N Tallahassee FL 32312-9022 Office: Ste 200 2958 Wellington Cir N Tallahassee FL 32309-6888 Home Phone: 850-893-8906; Office Phone: 850-894-1009. E-mail: guzewicz@aol.com.

CARSON, LOFTUS C., II, law educator; b. 1946; BS, Cornell U., 1968; M of Pub. Affairs, Princeton U., 1970; JD, Harvard U., 1973; MBA, Pa. U., 1980. Bar: Pa. 1973. Assoc. Dechert, Price & Rhoads, Phila., 1973-75; atty., adviser SEC, D.C., 1975-76; counsel U.S. Senate, D.C., 1976-77; law clk. U.S. Ct. Appeals (3d cir.), Wilmington, Dela., 1977-78; counsel FTC, D.C., 1978-80; assoc. prof. U. Maine, 1980-86, prof. law, 1986-88; prof. law, Strasburger & Price centennial faculty U. Tex., Austin, 1988—, Ronald D. Krist prof. Contbr. Fellow U. Tex. Office: U Tex 727 E Dean Keeton St Austin TX 78705 Office Phone: 512-232-1355. Office Fax: 512-471-6988. Business E-Mail: lcarson@mail.law.utexas.edu.

CARSON, MARY KAY, writer; b. Everett, Wash., Nov. 18, 1964; d. George Arthur and Vicky Sue Carson, Mary Lou Carson (Stepmother); m. Thomas Mark Uhlman, Mar. 4, 2003. BS in Biology, U. Kans., Lawrence, 1987. Author: Wright Brothers for Kids, 2003, The Underground Railroad for Kids, 2005, Exploring the Solar System, 2006, Emi and the Rhino Scientist, 2007, Alexander Graham Bell: Giving Voice to the World, 2007, Weather Projects for Young Scientists, 2007. Mem.: Soc. Children's Book Writers and Illustrators, Nat. Assn. Sci. Writers. Avocations: outdoor pursuits, travel.

CARSON, RANDY W., manufacturing executive; BSEE, Valparaiso U., Ind. Various positions in sales, mktg. and distbn. Allen-Bradley, 1972—88, v.p. Intelligent Sensing bus., 1988, sr. v.p. Automation Group, exec. v.p. Reliance Elec. Group; exec. v.p. Rockwell Automation; corp. v.p. Growth Initiatives Eaton Corp., Cleve., 1999—2000, sr. v.p., pres. Elec. Group, 2000—. Vice chmn. Nat. Elec. Mfrs. Assn.; mem. adv. bd. Questra Corp. Office: Eaton Corp Eaton Ctr 1111 Superior Ave Cleveland OH 44114-2584 Office Phone: 216-523-5000.*

CARSON, REGINA E., healthcare administrator, pharmacist, educator, geriatric specialist; b. Washington; BS in Pharmacy, Howard U., Washington, DC; MBA in Mktg., Loyola Coll., Balt., 1987, MBA in Health Care Adminstrn., 1987. Asst. prof., asst. dir. pharmacy U. Md., Balt., 1986-88; asst. prof., coord. profl. practice Howard U., Washington, 1988-95; prin. Marrell Cons., Randallstown, Md., prin., mng. ptnr., 1993—; exec. dir. Sunrise Assisted Living, Fairfax, Va., 1997-99. Drug utilization rev. cons. Md. Pharmacy Assn., Balt., 1986—90; cons. pharmacist Balt. County Adv. Coun. Drug Abuse, Towson, Md., 1984—86; edn. cons. Assn. Black Women in Higher Edn., Accra, Ghana, 2000; program evaluator Train Pharm., U. Medicine and Pharmacy Cluj, Romania, 1999—2002; master gardener U. Md., College Park, 2001—. Bd. dirs. N.W. Hosp. Ctr. Aux., Randallstown, Joshua Johnson Coun., Balt. Mus. Art, Alzheimers Assn. Ctrl. Md.; trustee C.C. of Baltimore County, 1997—. Named Outstanding Alumni, Howard U. Coll. Pharmacy, 1992; recipient Grigore T. Popa medal, U. Medicine and Pharmacy, Iasi, Romania, 2000. Fellow: Am. Soc. Cons. Pharmacists; mem.: Nat. Assn. Retail Druggists (adv. com. , long-term care com.), Nat. Pharm. Assn. (life, Outstanding Women in Pharmacy 1984), Am. Assn. Colls. Pharmacy, Nat. Assn. Health Svc. Execs. Avocations: pharmacognosy, gardening, American art.

CARSON, RON, investment company executive; m. Jeanie Carson, 1986; 3 children. CFP, CFS, ChFC. Founder, pres. Carson Wealth Mgmt., Omaha, 1983—; founder PEAK Productions. Commentator CNBC Power Lunch, co-host Financial Focus radio prog. Named one of Top 250 Fin. Advisors, Worth Mag., 1996—2002, Top 100 Fin. Advisers, Barron's Mag., 2007. Office: Carson Wealth Mgmt 101 S 108th St Omaha NE 68154 Office Phone: 402-330-0808. Business E-Mail: rcarson@carsonwealth.com.*

CARSON, SAMUEL GOODMAN, retired bank executive; b. Glens Falls, NY, Oct. 6, 1913; s. Russell M.L. and Mary (Goodman) C.; m. Alice Williams, Oct. 14, 1939; children: Russell L., Frances Elizabeth (Mrs. Thomas E. Brady Jr.), Mary Goodman (Mrs. John A. Fedderke), Kathryn Williams (Mrs. Robert Richards), Samuel Goodman. BA magna cum laude, Dartmouth Coll., 1934. With Aetna Life Ins. Co., 1934-68; with Toledo Trust Co., 1967-84, exec. v.p., 1968, pres., 1969-84, chief exec. officer, 1970-84, chmn., 1976-84; chmn., dir. Toledo Trustcorp, Inc., 1976-84, ret., 1984. Dir. Kiemle-Hankins Co., Plastic Technologies, Inc., Carson Assocs., Inc. Mem. Ottawa Hills Bd. Edn., 1954-64; pres. United Appeal Greater Toledo Area, 1969, campaign chmn., 1964; Bd. dirs., trustee Toledo chpt. ARC, 1950— , chmn., 1959-61; trustee Toledo Hosp., 1960— , v.p., 1963-65, pres., 1966-69; bd. dirs. Community Chest Greater Toledo, 1962-65, pres., 1965; pres. Boys' Club Toledo, 1961-64, trustee, 1957—; trustee Toledo Mus. Art, 1967— , sec.-treas., 1969, v.p., 1973-78, pres., 1978-80. Recipient Service to Mankind award Sertoma Club Toledo, 1965, Man and Boy award Boys' Clubs Am., 1966, Pacemaker of Yr. award U. Toledo Coll. Bus. Adminstrn. Alumni Assn., 1969 Mem. Toledo Area C. of C. (trustee 1961-62, 73-76, pres. 1974-75), Phi Beta Kappa, Phi Gamma Delta. Clubs: Rotarian, Toledo Country, Toledo. Lodges: Rotary. Republican. Congregationalist. Office: 425 Madison Ave Toledo OH 43604-1229

CARSON, SCOTT E., aerospace transportation executive; b. Aug. 8, 1946; BBA, MBA, Wash. State U. Fin. analyst B-1 Bomber Avionics Program The Boeing Co., 1973, mgmt., 1976, exec. v.p. bus. resources Boeing Info., Space & Defense Sys., 1997, head Connexion by Boeing, 2000, mem. exec. coun., 2000—, sr. exec. Pacific N.W., exec. v.p., 2006—; v.p., CFO Boeing Comml. Airplanes, 1998, v.p. sales, 2004—06, pres., CEO, 2006—. Boeing exec. focal Wash. State U., chair nat. bd. advisors Coll. Bus. and Econs., advisory bd. Coll. Engrng. and Architecture; bd. govs. Wash. State U. Found. Recipient Bus. Leadership award, U. Wash. Exec. MBA Program, 2002. Fellow: Royal Aeronautical Soc. Office: Boeing Comml Airplanes PO Box 3707 Seattle WA 98124 Office Phone: 206-655-2121, 312-544-2000.*

CARSON, SOL KENT, artist, educator; b. Phila., June 7, 1917; s. Philip Pasach and Sarah Carson; m. Thelma Clearfield-Carson; 1 child, Kent Steven. MD, Zeckwer-Hahn Acad., Phila., 1937; BFA with honors, Temple U., Phila., 1944; BS in Edn. with honors, Temple U., 1945, MEd in Fine Arts with distinction, 1946, postgrad., 1957, NYU, 1958; PhD, U. Italy, 1960. Asst. Temple U., Phila., 1940—45, dir. dept. visual edn., 1944—47, dir. dept. art Eckels Coll., 1946—55, prof., 1946—55; cons. art Bristol Twp. Sch. Dist., Pa., 1956—66; prof. art dept. Wis. State U., Superior, 1965; assoc. prof. art dept. Millerville State U., Lancaster, Pa., 1966—79, assoc. prof. emeritus, 1979—. Mus. cons. U. Pa., 1945—46; art tchr. Phila. (Pa.) Bd. Edn., 1947—58; commn. Los Gatos (Calif.) Art Selection Panel. Represented in permanent collections Phila. Mus. Art Archives, Phila. Libr., Temple U., exhibitions include Mus. Modern Art, Acad. Fine Arts, Fed. Arts Galleries, Internat. League for Peace and Freedom, Tyler Galleries, Temple U., Millersville State Coll., Civic Ctr. Mus., Phila., Harrisburg State Bldg., Pa., Wis. State U., Superior. Fellow, Temple U.; scholar, Barnes Found. Mem.: NEA, AAUP, Pa. State Ednl. Assn., Artist Equity, Assn. Higher Edn., Phi Delta Kappa. Achievements include development of Visual Edn. and Printmaking depts. at Temple U; established and designed printmaking dept. at Millervile U., Pa. Avocations: music, poetry. Home: 447 Alberto Way C128 Los Gatos CA 95032

CARSON, STEVEN LEE, newspaper publisher; b. NYC, Mar. 23, 1943; s. Harold and Mathilde (Seidel) C.; m. Yvonne DeDrozizhki, Aug. 8, 1971 (dec. Feb. 1980). BA, NYU, 1964, MA, 1965. Archivist, conf. dir. Nat. Archives, Washington, 1967—73; chmn. White House Conf. Pres. & Children, Washington, 1974; conf. dir. The Manuscript Soc., 1974—80; editor, writer Manuscript Soc. News, Washington, 1987—2003, The Lincoln Forum Bull., 2004—. Dir. history pavilion Hall of Fame Great Am., NYC, 1964; editor US Pres. Commn. Civil Disorders, Washington, 1968; mem. (charter) Hildene Robert Todd Lincoln estate; TV commentator; spkr. in field. Author: Maximilien Robespierre, 1988; (plays) The Last Lincoln, Princess Alice; contbr. articles to profl. jours. Speechwriter The White House, US Congress, Md. Ho. Dels., 1974—; historian Rock Creek Cemetery, Washington, 1997—; timeline historian Woodrow Wilson House, Washington, DC, 2006-. Recipient NYU Heights Daily News Alumni award, 1964, medal, NY Civil War Roundtable, 1969, Archival medal, Republic of Korea, 1972, Internat. Psychohistory Assn. award, 1983, Lincoln Group of NY award, 1988, 1992, Man of the Month award, Washington Bus. Jour., 1989, Surratt Soc. award, 1993, award, Rowfant Club, 1996, Smithsonian lectr., 1999—; grantee, Md. Commn. Humanities, 1986, 1987, US Dept. Interior, 1985; Ford Found. fellow, 1964, Johns Hopkins U. Chas Carroll Fulton fellow, 1965. Fellow: The Manuscript Soc.; mem.: Washington Ind. Writers, Nat. Writers Union, Nat. Press Club (chmn. White Ho. panel 2006), Walt Whitman Leaves of Grass Sesquicentennial Comn., US Abraham Lincoln Bicentennial Com. (trustee 2003—), Abraham Lincoln Inst. (trustee 1997—), Lincoln Group D.C. (pres. 1985—88, Lincoln Recognition award 2003), Lincoln Forum (trustee 1997—), Lincoln Group III (trustee 1986—91), NYU Soc. of the Torch, NYU Perstare et Praestare, NYU Hon. Soc. Achievements include delivered official Lincoln Day Address, Ford's Theatre, Washington, 1996, 2005, National Defense University, 2006, Army-Navy Club, Washington, 2007; delivered Bicentennial Lincoln Address to University of Maryland Medical Center, 2007. Avocation: collecting historic manuscripts & letters. Office: 8811 Colesville Rd Ste 506 Silver Spring MD 20910-4332

CARSON, THOMAS BODE, bank executive, consultant; b. Washington, May 30, 1932; s. Thomas D. and Margaret (Bode) C.; m. Anne Conover; 1 child, Natalie Ambrose. BA, Princeton U., 1954; MA, Georgetown U., 1998. V.p. Chase Manhattan Bank, NYC, 1960-68; sr. ops. officer Inter-Am. Devel. Bank, Washington, 1969-89; cons. Washington, 1990—. Author: Beyond the American Dream: Work and Wealth in the 21st Century, 1998. 1st lt. U.S. Army, 1955-57. Fellow Woodrow Wilson Found., 1955. Mem. World Future Soc. (lectr.), Met. Club Washington, Chevy Chase Club, Knickerbocker Club, Phi Beta Kappa. Democrat. Episcopalian. Avocations: futurism, classical music. Home: 3323 Nebraska Ave NW Washington DC 20016

CARSON, VAN, lawyer; BA, Mt. Union Coll., 1963; LLB, Duke U., 1966. Bar: Ohio 1966, registered: Supreme Ct. Ohio 1966, US Ct. Appeals (6th cir.) 1976, US Supreme Ct. 1981, US Ct. Appeals (7th cir.) 1993, US Ct. Appeals (DC cir.) 1993, US Dist. Ct., DC 1996. Ptnr. Squire, Sanders & Dempsey LLP, Cleve., chmn., Environ., Health & Safety Practice Group. Exec. com. mem. & vice chmn. of bd. dir. Ohio C. of C. Mem.: Ohio State Bar Assn. (environ. law com.), Cleve. Bar Assn. (environ. law com.), ABA (Litig. Sect.), Order of Coif. Office: Squire Sanders & Dempsey LLP 4900 Key Tower 127 Public Sq Cleveland OH 44114-1304 Office Phone: 216-479-8559. Office Fax: 216-479-8780. Business E-Mail: vcarson@ssd.com.

CARSON, WALLACE PRESTON, JR., retired state supreme court justice; b. Salem, Oreg., June 10, 1934; s. Wallace Preston and Edith (Bragg) C.; m. Gloria Stolk, June 24, 1956; children: Scott, Carol, Steven (dec. 1981). BA in Politics, Stanford U., 1956; JD, Willamette U., 1962. Bar: Oreg. 1962, U.S. Dist. Ct. Oreg. 1963, U.S. Ct. Appeals (9th cir.) 1968, U.S. Supreme Ct. 1971, U.S. Ct. Mil. Appeals 1977; lic. comml. pilot FAA. Pvt. practice law, Salem, Oreg., 1962-77; mem. Oreg. House of Reps., 1967—71, majority leader, 1969—71; mem. Oreg. State Senate, 1971—77, minority floor leader, 1971—77; judge Marion County Cir. Ct., Salem, 1977-82; assoc. justice Oreg. Supreme Ct., Salem, 1982—2006, chief justice, 1992—2005. Dir. Salem Area Community Council, 1967-70, pres., 1969-70; mem. Salem Planning Commn., 1966-72, pres., 1970-71; co-chmn. Marion County Mental Health Planning Com., 1965-69; mem. Salem Community Goals Com., 1965; Republican precinct commiteeman, 1963-66; mem. Marion County Rep. Central Exec. Com., 1963-66; com. predinct edn. Oreg. Rep. Central Com., 1965; vestryman, acolyte, Sunday Sch. tchr., youth coach St. Paul's Episcopal Ch., 1935—; task force on cts. Oreg. Council Crime and Delinquency, 1968-69; trustee Willamette U., 1970—; adv. bd. Cath. Ctr. Community Services, 1976-77; mem. comprehensive planning com. Mid-Willamette Valley Council of Govts., 1970-71; adv. com. Oreg. Coll. Edn. Tchr. Edn., 1971-75; pres. Willamette regional Oreg. Lung Assn., 1974-75, state dir., exec. com., 1975-77; pub. relations com. Williamette council Campfire Girls, 1976-77; criminal justice adv. bd. Chemeketa Community Coll., 1977-79; mem. Oreg. Mental Health Com., 1979-80; mem. subcom. Gov's Task Force Mental Health, 1980; You and Govt. Adv. Com. Oreg. YMCA, 1981—. Served to col. USAFR, 1956—59. Recipient Salem Disting. Svc. award, 1968; recipient Good Fellow award Marion County Fire Svc., 1974, Minuteman award Oreg. N.G. Assn., 1980; fellow Eagleton Inst. Politics, Rutgers U., 1971 Mem. Marion County Bar Assn. (sec.-treas. 1965-67, dir. 1968-70), Oreg. Bar Assn., ABA, Willamette U. Coll. Law Alumni Assn. (v.p. 1968-70), Salem Art Assn., Oreg. Hist. Soc., Marion County Hist. Soc., Stanford U. Club (pres. Salem chpt. 1963-64), Delta Theta Phi.*

CARSON, WILLIAM CHARLES, sales and marketing executive; b. Palmyra, NJ, Nov. 9, 1924; s. William and Carrie (Forderer) C.; m. Jean Gingerich, Apr. 1, 1950; children: William Scott, Colleen Jean, Caroline Grace. BA, Gettysburg Coll., 1949. Sales rep. Nat. Sugar Refinery Co., Phila., 1949-60; account exec. Metal Edge Industries, Barrington, N.J., 1960-70, sales mgr., 1970-80; gen. mgr. Metal Edge div. Lydall, Inc., Hartford, Conn., 1980-83; mktg. and sales mgr. Mefco, North Wales, Pa., 1983-90; ret. Campaign chmn. United Way, Berkeley Heights, N.J., 1966, bd. dirs. Burlington County, N.J., 1985-2003, sec., bd. dirs. Moorestown, N.J., 1984—. Served to cpl. U.S. Army, 1943-45, ETO. Decorated Bronze Star with oak leaf cluster, Purple Heart, Combat Inf. badge. Mem. Am. Mgmt. Assn. (seminar chmn. 1972), Sales & Mktg. Execs. So. Jersey (v.p., bd. dirs. 1974-78), Am. Def. Preparedness Assn. (cons. 1984—, bd. dirs.), Def. Fire Protection Assn. (bd. advisors 1987—), Phi Kappa Psi (sec.). Republican. Avocation: golf. Home: 125 Somers Ct S Moorestown NJ 08057-3419

CARSON, WILLIAM MORRIS, manpower planning and development advisor; s. Edward Belmont and Frances Lucretia (Powell) C.; children: Lincoln Bruce Carson, Adrien Lee Allen, Anthony Lunt Carson, Karen Tracy Carson. BS, Columbia U., 1949; MA, Johns Hopkins U., 1951; postgrad., U. Chgo., 1955, London Sch. Econs., 1956; diploma in Arabic, Middle East Ctr. Arab Studies, 1969. Cairo corr. MBS, 1951-53; asst. prof. Mid. East Studies, SAIS, 1955-56; tng. officer U.S. AID, 1958-64; indsl. rels. staff analyst ARAMCO, Dhahran, Saudi Arabia, 1964-70; mgr. mgmt. deve. and tng. Saudi Arabian Airlines, Jeddah, 1970-72; chief tng. sect. UN Devel. Programme, NYC, 1973-75; mgr. mgmt. devel. and tng. Sulvania Tng. Ops., Waltham, Mass., 1975-76; dir. tng. Ingersoll-Rand Constrn. Svcs., Winston-Salem, N.C., 1977-79; sr. advisor manpower planning and devel. Internat. Human Resources Devel. Corp., Boston, 1979-83; gen. mgr. ITECO divsn. Saudi Tng. Svcs., Riyadh, Saudi Arabia, 1983-84; mng. dir. Arab Resources Devel. Corp., Mass., 1984-87; mgr. Turkish tech. projects GE Internat. Svc. Corp., 1987-92; prin. Carson & Assocs., Balt., 1992-96, Nat. Manpower Strategies, 1997—. Cons. UN; Middle East Inst. fellow; Ford Found. area fellow. Co-author: International Manpower Planning: The Developing World, 1982; also articles. Recipient Outstanding Performance award AID. Fellow Royal Anthrop. Inst. Gt. Britain and No. Ireland, Inst. Comml. Mgmt.; mem. Ineamus Meloria Honor Soc. Address: 1908 C St Forest Grove OR 97116-2308 E-mail: wlmcrsn@prodigy.net.

CARSTAIRS, SHARON, legislator; b. Halifax, NS, Can., Apr. 26, 1942; d. Vivian and Harold Connolly; m. John Esdale Carstairs, 1966; children: Catherine, Jennifer. BA in Polit. Sci. and History, Dalhousie U., 1962; MA in Tchg. of History, Smith Coll., 1963; postgrad., Georgetown U., 1964, U. Calgary, 1968; LLD (hon.), Brandon U., 2003. Tchr. Dana Hall Sch. for Girls, Wellesley, Mass., 1963-65, Calgary (Alta.) Separate Sch. Bd., 1965-71; chmn. bd. referees Unemployment Ins. Commn., 1973-77; tchr. St. John's Ravenscourt Sch., Winnipeg, Man., 1978-81, St. Norbert (Man.) Collegiate, 1982-84; elected leader Liberal Party in Man., 1984; elected mem. Man. Legis. Assembly, River Heights, 1986—; elected leader Ofcl. Opposition, 1988-90; apptd. to Senate, 1994—; apptd. dep. leader of the govt. in the Senate, 1997-99; leader of the govt. in the Senate, 2001—03; minister with spl. responsibility for palliative care, 2001—03. Scriptwriter, narrator Calgary and Region Ednl. TV, 1967-69. Brownie leader, Halifax and Winnipeg; mem. Parks and Recreation Bd., City of Calgary; fund-raiser Manitoba Heart Found.; canvasser Can. Cancer Soc., Alta., Man., Alta. Soc. for the Mentally Retarded; vol. Man. Mus. of Man and Nature; bd. mem. Women and the Arts, Nursing Coun. Man.; campaign worker provincial elections, Nova Scotia, 1948, 52, 56, 60; exec. positions Dalhousie U. Liberal Club, Nova Scotia, 1958-62; nat. exec. Univ. Liberals, Nova Scotia, 1960-62, others; poll capt. Fed. elections, Alta. 1965, 68, 72, 74; exec. Alta. Women's Liberal Assn., 1965-68; sec. Liberal Party, Alta., 1968-70, v.p., 1972-74, pres., 1975-77, nat. exec. 1975-77; Calgary Regional v.p., Liberal Party Alta., 1970-72; mem. Fed. Campaign com., Alta. 1972, 74, Man. 1983—; candidate Provincial Liberal, Alta. 1975; poll worker Ft. Rouge Provincial constituency, Man., 1977, Ft. Garry Fed. constituency, Man., 1979-80; office mgr. Tuxedo Provincial constituency, Man., 1981; exec., River Heights Provincial constituency, Man., 1983—; mem. Man. Legislative Assembly 1986—; elected leader Official Opposition, Man., 1988-90. Recipient Dalhousie U. Entrance scholarship, Dalhousie U. scholarship, Smith Coll. Grad. fellowship. Mem. Winnipeg C. of C. Liberal Party Can.

CARSTEN, JACK CRAIG, venture capitalist; b. Cin., Aug. 24, 1941; s. John A. and Edith L. C.; m. Mary Ellis Jones, June 22, 1963; children: Scott, Elizabeth, Amy. BS in Physics, Duke U., 1963. Mktg. mgr. Tex. Instruments, Dallas, Houston, 1965-71, integrated circuits gen. mgr. Houston, 1971-75; v.p. sales and mktg. Intel Corp., Santa Clara, Calif., 1975-79, v.p., microcomputer gen. mgr., 1979-82, sr. v.p., components gen. mgr., 1982-87; gen. ptnr. U.S. Venture Ptnrs., Menlo Park, Calif., 1988-90; venture capitalist Tech. Investments, Los Altos, Calif., 1990-99, Horizon Ventures LLC, Los Altos, 2000—. Bd. dirs. several privately held firms. Contbr. articles to profl.jours. Office: Horizon Ventures LLC 4 Main St Los Altos CA 94022-2998 E-mail: jack@carsten.com.

CARSTENS, DAVID HENRY, military officer; b. Fort Wayne, Ind., Sept. 29, 1966; s. Rose Mariam and Karl Heinz Carstens; m. Aida Gabriela Starcov, July 15, 2004. BA in Polit. Sci., Kent State U., 1988; MA in Strategic Studies, Naval War Coll., 2000. Collection platoon leader 106th M.I. Bn., Fort Richardson, Alaska, 1990—91; asst. intelligence officer 2d Brigade, 6th Inf. Divsn., Fort Richardson, 1991—92; intelligence officer 1-22 Inf. Bn., 1st Brigade, 10th Mountain Divsn., Fort Drum, NY, 1993—94, 1st Brigade Combat Team, 10th Mountain Divsn., Fort Drum, 1994—95; direct support co. comdr. A/110th M.I. Bn., 10th Mountain

Divsn., Fort Drum, 1995—96; observer, contr. Joint Readiness Tng. Ctr., Fort Polk, La., 1997—98; chief ops. g2 (intelligence) Eighth US Army G2, Yongsan, Republic of Korea, 2000—01; ops. officer Task Force 202, Kandahar, Afghanistan, 2001—02; fusion chief coalition forces land component command 513th M.I. Brigade, INSCOM, Baghdad, Iraq, 2003; chief-of-staff program mgmt. office Nat. Security Agy., Fort Meade, Md., 2003—05; comdr. 524th M.I. Bn., 501st M.I. Brigade, Yongsan, Republic of Korea, 2005—. Lt. col. US Army, 1988—2005, Korea. Decorated Bronze Star US Army; recipient DOD Defense Meritorious Service medal, Nat. Security Agency, Knowlton award, Military Intelligence Corps, 1995. Republican. Roman Catholic. Avocations: travel, running, skiing, piano, hiking. Home Phone: 410-571-9010. Office Fax: 010-9049-7665. Business E-Mail: david.carstens@us.army.mil.

CARSTENS, JANE ELLEN, retired library science educator; b. New Iberia, La., Apr. 19, 1922; d. Charles John and Marie Claudia (Blanchet) C. BA in Elem. Edn., U. Southwestern La., 1942; BS in LS, La. State U., 1945; MS in LS, Columbia U., 1955, DLS, 1975. Asst. libr. Hamilton Lab. sch. and instr. libr. sci. U. Southwestern La., Lafayette, 1942-54, asst. prof., 1954-65, assoc. prof., 1965-75; children's librarian/storyteller N.Y. Pub. Libr., NYC, 1947, 48-49; vis. lectr. U. Minn., Mpls., 1955-56, summer 59, La. State U., Baton Rouge, summer 1958, State Coll. Iowa, Cedar Falls, summer 1963; prof. libr. sci. U. Southwestern La., Lafayette, 1975-94. Vis. lectr. Syracuse U., summers 1962, 64, U. Tex., Austin, summers 1976-86, 89. Trustee Our Lady of Wisdom Cath. Ch., 1995-2007. Named Tchr. of Yr., Amoco, 1982, Outstanding Alumna, U. Southwestern La., 1986; recipient Essae Culver Disting. Svc. award La. Libr. Assn., 1987, Alumni Faculty Excellence award Blue Key, 1990, Faculty Advisor of Yr. award U. Southwestern La. Student Govt. Assn., 1992, Point of Excellence award Kappa Delta Pi, 1992, Outstanding Tchr. award USL Found., 1994; Blue Key Faculty/Student Staff Directory dedicated to her, 1994-95; Lifetime Achievement award, Coll. Edn.Chpt., ULL Alumni Assn., 2005. Mem. ALA, La. Libr. Assn. (pres. 1959-60), Phi Kappa Phi (pres. USL chpt. 1984-85), Delta Kappa Gamma (pres. Alpha chpt. 1988-90). Roman Catholic. Home: 214 Saint Joseph St Lafayette LA 70506-4535 also: ULL La Lafayette PO Box 40298 Lafayette LA 70504-0001

CARSTENSEN, EDWIN LORENZ, retired biomedical engineer, biophysicist; b. Oakdale, Nebr., Dec. 8, 1919; s. August Hans and Opal Lois (Norwood) C.; m. Pam McDonald, Aug. 1, 1947; children: Richard Lorenz, Allen Brent, Laura Lee, Loretta Dee, Christina Marie. BS, Nebr. State Tchrs. Coll., 1941; MS, Case Inst. Tech., 1947; PhD, U. Pa., 1955. Mem. sci. staff div. war rsch. Columbia U., 1942-45; head lab. sect. U.S. Navy Underwater Sound Reference Lab., Orlando, Fla., 1945-48; rsch. assoc. Moore Sch. Elec. Engring., U. Pa., 1948-55, asst. prof. elec. engring., 1955-56; prin. investigator U.S. Army Biol. Lab., Fort Detrick, Frederick, Md., 1956-61; assoc. prof. elec. engring. U. Rochester, 1961-73, prof., 1973-88, Arthur Gould Yates prof. engring., 1988-90, Arthur Gould Yates prof. engring. emeritus, 1990—, dir. biomed. engring., 1971-83, prof. biophysics, 1981-90, univ. mentor, 1982—, sr. scientist in elec. engring., 1990—. Dir. Rochester Ctr. for Biomed. Ultrasound, 1986-90. Author: Biological Effects of Transmission Line Fields, 1987; contbr. numerous articles to profl. publs. Fellow Acoustical Soc. Am., IEEE, Am. Inst. Ultrasound in Medicine; mem. Biophys. Soc., Biomed. Engring. Soc., Nat. Acad. Engring. Democrat. Home: 103 Eastland Ave Rochester NY 14618-1027 Office: U Rochester Dept Elec/Computer Engring Rochester NY 14627 Personal E-mail: ecarsten@rochester.rr.com.

CARSWELL, JANE TRIPLETT, retired family physician; b. Raeford, NC, Feb. 26, 1932; d. Arthur Dula and Madeline Mapp (Warburton) C. Student, Flora Macdonald Coll., 1950-52; AB in Chemistry, U. N.C., 1954; MD, Med. Coll. Va., 1958. Diplomate Am. Bd. Family Practice. Resident Med. Coll. Va., Richmond, 1958-61; practice medicine specializing in family medicine Harlan, Ky., 1961-62, Lenoir, NC, 1962—. Chmn. Lenoir Human Relations Com., N.C., 1962-64; vice-chmn. Caldwell County Council Status of Women, Lenoir, 1976-78 Mem. Caldwell County Med. Soc. (pres. 1965), N.C. Acad. Family Physicians (N.C. Family Physician of Yr. award 1983), N.C. Med. Soc., Am. Acad. Family Practice (Nat. Family Dr. of Yr. award 1984) Presbyterian. Avocations: hiking, backpacking, skiing, photography.

CARSWELL, LOIS MALAKOFF, botanical garden executive, consultant; b. NYC, Mar. 2, 1932; d. Arthur and Dora (Krechevsky) Malakoff; m. Donald Carswell, Oct. 12, 1957; children: Anne Carswell Tang, Alexander, Robert Ian. AB magna cum laude, Radcliffe Coll., 1953; cert. in bus. adminstrn., Harvard U. and Radcliffe Coll., 1954. Editor Dell Pub. Co., NYC, 1954-56; publicist Ruth E. Pepper Co., NYC, 1957-58; vol. Bklyn. Botanic Garden, 1964—, co-chmn. plant sales, 1967—, co-chmn. capital campaign, 1984-88, chmn. bd. dirs., 1989-98, chmn. emeritus, 1998—; Chmn. Coalition Living Mus. N.Y. State, N.Y.C., 1980—; cons. N.Y. State Natural Heritage Trust, 1982—. Office: Bklyn Botanic Garden 1000 Washington Ave Brooklyn NY 11225-1008 Home Phone: 718-789-9140; Office Phone: 718-623-7225. E-mail: loiscarswell@bbg.org.

CART, JON ROBERT, music educator, musician; MusB, DePauw U.; MusM, Ind. U.; D of Musical Arts, U. Md., 2001. Chair dept. music and theater arts Shippensburg (Pa.) U., 2000—. Tchg. artist apprentice Domingo-Cafritz young artist program Washington Nat. Opera, 2004—. Mem. SHAPE, Shippensburg, 2000—02. Mem.: Coll. Music Soc. Avocations: swimming, bicycling, hiking. Office: Shippensburg U 1871 Old Main Dr Shippensburg PA 17257 Home Phone: 717-532-3276; Office Phone: 717-477-1638.

CARTER, ANNETTE WHEELER, state legislator; b. May 24, 1941; divorced. Grad., Ala. State Coll. Mem. Conn. Ho. of Reps., Hartford, 1988—, mem. pub. safety, cmty. and exportation coms., vice chmn. appropriations com., asst. majority leader, mem. black caucus; assembly dist. 7 rep. Conn. House of Reps., Hartford; housing advisor Capitol Region Conf. Chs. Spkr. in field. Recipient Outstanding Accomplishments award Hope SDA Ch., 1990, Crispus A. Tucks award, 1991, Conn. State Black Dem. award, 1992. Mem. NAACP (award 1993), Greater Hartford Black Dem. Club. Democrat. Episcopalian. Home: 207 Branford St Hartford CT 06112-1406 Office: Conn Ho of Reps Legislative Office Bldg Hartford CT 06106

CARTER, ASHTON BALDWIN, former federal agency administrator; b. Phila., Sept. 24, 1954; s. William Stanley and Ann Baldwin C.; m. Ava Clayton Spencer, Aug. 6, 1983; children: William A., Ava Clayton. BA in Physics, Yale U., 1976, BA in Medieval History, 1976; PhD in Theoretical Physics, Oxford U., Eng., 1979. Analyst Office of Technology Assessment, Washington, 1980-81; rsch. analyst, Office of Sec. Def. US Dept. Def., Washington, 1981-82; rsch. fellow MIT, Cambridge, Mass., 1982-84; asst. prof. John F.Kennedy Sch. Govt., Harvard U., Cambridge, Mass., 1984-86, assoc. prof., 1986-88, Ford Found. prof. Sci. and Internat. Affairs, assoc. dir. Ctr. for Sci. and Internat. Affairs, 1988-90, dir. Ctr. for Sci. and Internat. Affairs, 1990-93, Ford Found. prof. sci. & internat. affairs, 1996—; asst. sec. for internat. security policy US Dept. Def., Washington, 1993-96. Mem. Def. Sci. Bd., Washington, 1990-93, 97—, Def. Polit. Bd., Washington, 1997—; advisor NAS, 1990—, AAAS, 1988—, White House Office of Sci. and Technology Policy, 1990-93, Joint Chiefs Staff; co-dir., Preventive Def. Project, JFK Sch. Govt.; trustee MITRE Corp. Author: Directed Energy Missile Defense in Space, 1984; co-author: Ballistic Missile Defense, 1984, Managing Nuclear Operations, 1987, Beyond Spinoff: Military and Commercial Technologies in a Changing World, 1991, Soviet Nuclear Fission: Control of the Nuclear Arsenal in a Disintegrating Soviet Union, 1991, A New Concept of Cooperative Security, 1992, Cooperative Denuclearization: From Pledges to Deeds, 1993, Global Engagement: Cooperation and Security in the 21st Century, 1994, Preventive Defense: A New Security Strategy for America, 1999; contbr. articles to profl. jours. Rhodes scholar, 1976; named Outstanding Young Man of Am., U.S. Jaycees, 1987; recipient, Disting. Svc. medal (2), US Dept. Def., Def. Intelligemce medal,Forun award, Am. Physical Soc. Mem. Am. Phys. Soc. (Forum award 1988), Coun. Fgn. Rels., Internat. Inst. Strategic Studies, Phi Beta Kappa. Office: Harvard U JFK Sch of Govt 79 JFK St Cambridge MA 02138-5801 E-mail: ashton_carter@harvard.edu.

CARTER, BARRY EDWARD, law educator; b. LA, Oct. 14, 1942; s. Byron Edward and Ethel Catherine (Turner) C.; m. Kathleen Anne Ambrose, May 17, 1987; children: Gregory Ambrose, Meghan Elisabeth. AB with great distinction, Stanford U., 1964; MPA, Princeton U., 1966; JD, Yale U., 1969. Bar: Calif. 1970, DC 1972. Program analyst Office of Sec. Def., Washington, 1969—70; mem. staff NSC, Washington, 1970—72; rsch. fellow Kennedy Sch., Harvard U., Cambridge, Mass., 1972; internat. affairs fellow Coun. on Fgn. Rels., 1972; assoc. Wilmer, Cutler & Pickering, Washington, 1973—75; sr. counsel Select Com. on Intelligence Activities, U.S. Senate, Washington, 1975; assoc. Morrison & Foerster, San Francisco, 1976—79; assoc. prof. law Georgetown U. Law Ctr., Washington, 1979—89, prof., 1989-93, 96—; dir. internat. and transnational programs Georgetown U. Law Ctr, Washington, 2005—; exec. dir. Am. Soc. Internat. Law, Washington, 1992—93; acting undersec. for export adminstrn. U.S. Dept. Commerce, Washington, 1993—94, dep. undersec., 1994—96. Mem. UN Assn. Soviet-Am. Parallel Studies Project, 1976—87; vis. prof. law Stanford U., 1990; chmn. adv. bd. Def. Budget Project, 1990—93; bd. dirs. Nukem, Inc., 1998—; adv. coun. Zurich Emerging Markets Solutions, 2001—; editl. advisor Kluwer Law Internat., 2007—, Aspen Pubs., 2007—. Author: International Economic Sanctions: Improving the Haphazard U.S. Legal Regime, 1988 (Am. Soc. Internat. Law Cert. of Merit, 1989); co-author: International Law, 5th edit., 2007; editor: International Law: Selected Documents, 2007—08; contbr. articles to profl. jours. With US Army, 1969—71. Mem.: ABA, Am. Soc. Internat. Law (hon. v.p. 1993—99, counselor 1999—2000), Coun. on Fgn. Rels., DC Bar Assn., Calif. Bar Assn., Am. Law Inst., Phi Beta Kappa. Democrat. Roman Catholic. Home: 2922 45th St NW Washington DC 20016-3559 Office: Georgetown U Law Ctr 600 New Jersey Ave NW Washington DC 20001-2075 Office Phone: 202-662-9322. Business E-Mail: carter@law.georgetown.edu.

CARTER, BETSY L., editor, writer; b. NYC, June 9, 1945; d. Rudy and Gerda Cohn; m. Gary Hoenig. BA, U. Mich., 1967. Editorial asst. McGraw Hill, 1967—68; editor co. mag. Am. Security and Trust Co., 1968—69; editorial asst. Atlantic Monthly, 1969—70; researcher Newsweek, NYC, 1971—73, asst. editor, 1973—75, assoc. editor, 1975—80; sr. editor Esquire Mag., NYC, 1980—81, exec. editor, 1981—82, sr. exec. editor, 1982—83, editorial dir., 1983—85; creator, editor-in-chief New York Woman, NYC, 1988; editor-in-chief New Woman mag., NYC, 1994—97; founding editor-in-chief AARP's My Generation, 1999—2003. Author: Nothing to Fall Back On, 2002, (novels) Orange Blossom Special, 2005, Swim to Me, 2007; contbr. articles to popular mags. including Atlantic, Washington Post, Glamour, Oprah, NY Mag. Mem.: Am. Soc. Mag. Editors (exec. com. 1988—91, v.p. 1997—). E-mail: bcarter@nyc.rr.com.

CARTER, C. MICHAEL, lawyer; b. Apr. 18, 1945; BS in Acctg., U. Calif., Berkeley, 1967; JD, George Washington U., 1973. Atty. Winthrop, Stimson, Putnam & Roberts; divsn. counsel Singer Co., 1981—83; sr. corp. counsel, asst. sec. R.J. Reynolds Inc., 1983—87; sr. v.p., opers., bd. mem. Concurrent Computer Corp., 1987—94; exec. v.p., gen. counsel, corp. sec. Pinkerton's, Inc., 1994—2000; sr. v.p., gen. counsel, corp. sec. Dole Food Co., Westlake Village, Calif., 2000—. Bd. dirs. Dole Food Co., Inc., Westlake Village, Calif. Bd. trustees George Washington U. Office: Dole Food Co One Dole Dr Westlake Village CA 91362 Office Phone: 818-879-6600, 818-879-6810. Office Fax: 818-874-4893. E-mail: michael_carter@na.dole.com.*

CARTER, CALVIN H., JR., materials engineer; married; 2 children. BS in Materials Engring., NC State U., 1977, MS in Materials Engring., 1980, PhD in Materials Engring., 1983. Co-founder Cree Inc. (formerly Cree Rsch. Inc.), Durham, NC, 1987—, exec. pres., dir., 1987—2000, dir. materials tech., 1987—. Recipient Nat. Medal of Tech. award, US Dept. Commerce, 2002. Office: Cree Inc 4600 Silicon Dr Durham NC 27703

CARTER, CHARLENE ANN, psychologist; b. Marshall, Mich., Apr. 7, 1941; d. Charles V. F. and Eva L. (Hesling) Hampton.; m. Ross E. Carter, Jan. 15, 1966; children: Laura, Paul. BA in Psychology and Sociology, Albion Coll., Mich., 1962; MA in Clin. Psychology, Mich. State U., East Lansing, 1964, PhD in Clin. Psychology, 1968. Lic. psychologist, Wis. Clin. intern VA Hosp., Battle Creek, Mich., 1963-65, Psychol. Clinic Mich. State U., East Lansing, 1965—66, Counseling Ctr. Mich. State U., 1966—68, asst. prof., 1968—69; pvt. practice Bangor, Maine, 1971, Media, Pa., 1974-75; assoc. clin.prof. dept. psychiatry Med. Coll. Wis., Milw., 1983—; pvt. practice, 1988—. Dir. clin. tng. Wis. Sch. for Girls, Oregon, Wis., 1969—70; staff psychologist The Counseling Ctr., Cmty. Mental Health Ctr., Bangor, Maine, 1971; mem. staff Aurora Psychiat. Hosp., 1992—, Rogers Hosp., 2001—; psychologist cons. Office of Hearing and Appeals, Social Security Adminstrn., Milw., 1986—91; lectr. in field. Contbr. articles to profl. jours. USPHS fellow, 1962, 65, 66. Mem. APA. Office: Maplewood Exec Ctr 250 N Sunnyslope Rd Ste 290 Brookfield WI 53005 Office Phone: 262-754-9460.

CARTER, CHARLES CONRAD, medical educator; b. Seattle, July 20, 1924; s. John Hempstead Carter and Thea Turner; m. Marylu Hopper, June 20, 1948; children: Charles Conrad Jr., Christopher Richard, John Hempstead II, Ronald Lynn. BA, Reed Coll., Portland, Oreg., 1946; MD, U. Oreg., Portland, 1948. Diplomate Am. Bd. Psychiatry and Neurology, 1957. Clin. instr. U. Oreg. Med. Sch., Portland, 1956—62, asst. prof. neurology, 1962—67, assoc. prof. neurology, 1967—70, prof. neurology, 1970—79; chief of neurology VA Hosp., Roseburg, Oreg., 1981—88; clin. prof. neurology Oreg. Health Scis. U., Portland, 1988—. Vis. assoc. prof. Washington U. Sch. Medicine, St. Louis, 1969—70. Bd. dirs. Western EEG Soc., 1972—79, Psychosurg. Bd., Salem, Oreg., 1973. Capt. med. corps USAF, 1951—53. Spl. NINDS fellow, NIH, 1969. Mem.: Am. Acad. Neurology, Alpha Omega Alpha. Home: 4884 NW Promenade Ter Unit 211 Portland OR 97229 Office: Oregon Health Scis U 3181 SW Sam Jackson Park Rd L226 Portland OR 97239 Home Phone: 503-629-9948; Office Phone: 503-494-8181. Office Fax: 503-494-7242. Business E-Mail: fehringe@ohsu.edu.

CARTER, CHRISTOPHER SCOTT, health facility administrator; b. Agana, Guam, Apr. 15, 1969; s. Ronald Thomas and Janice Joene Carter. BA, Lewis and Clark Coll., 1989; MD cum laude, Oreg. Health Scis. U., Portland, 1995. Resident internal medicine Mayo Clinic, Rochester, Minn., 1995—98; fellow pulmonary/critical care U. Minn., Mpls., 1998—2001, asst. prof., 2002—03, U. Miami, Fla., 2001—02; pvt. practice Pulmonary Physicians South Fla., Miami, 2003—05; dir. surg. ICU Malcom Randall VA Med. Ctr., Gainesville, Fla., 2005—, chief Surg. Inpatient Care, 2007—. Dir. Alpha-1 program U. Miami, 2002; chief surg. inpatient care sect. Malcolm Randall VA Med. Ctr.; asst. prof. surgery U. Fla., 2006—, asst. prof. anesthesia, 2007—. Contbr. chpts. to textbook. Fellow: Am. Coll. Chest Physicians; mem.: Fla. Med. Assn. (Fla. Disting. Physician 2007), Airline Owners and Pilots Assn., Alpha Omega Alpha. Avocation: flying. Office: Malcolm Randall VA Med Ctr 1601 SW Archer Rd Gainesville FL 32608 Home: 5818 NW 45th Dr Gainesville FL 32653

CARTER, CURTIS WILLIAM, communications executive; b. Cleve., Dec. 9, 1969; s. Vivian Marie Townsell; m. Janet Sue Schuesler, Oct. 14, 1999. BS in Bus. Mgmt., David N. Myers U., 1999. Pres. and owner Carter's Tax Svc., Bedford Heights, Ohio, 1993—97; prof. basketball player Can. Harlem Kings, Toronto, 1997—98; legal adminstr. Adv.'s Legal Ctr., Inc., Santa Ana, Calif., 1999—2002; profl. basketball player Sugar Land Sharks, Houston, 2002, KB Drita, Gjilan, Kosovo, 2003, Orange County Crush, Am. Basketball Assn., 2004—05; v.p. and bd. dirs. New Soul Records, Inc., Irvine, Calif., 2002—03; pres., CEO, chmn. of bd. Crossover Broadcast Network, Inc., Santa Ana, 2003—. Author: The Road to the NBA: The Other Side, vols. I and II, 2005. Mem. Nat. Ct. Apptd. Spl. Advocates. Mem.: Internat. Soc. Poets, Acad. Am. Poets, Ohioana Libr. Assn., Orange County Paralegal Assn., Songwriters Club of Am. (life). Avocations: writing, sports, travel, reading. Office: Crossover Broadcast Network Inc 2781 W MacArthur Blvd # B 608 Santa Ana CA 92704 Office Phone: 714-540-5028. Personal E-mail: ceocbn@aol.com. Business E-Mail: info@theroadtothenba.com.

CARTER, CYNTHIA (CINDY) LYNN, writer; m. Thomas Kenneth Carter, June 5, 1993. BA in Radio, TV & Film, U. Md., College Park, MD, 1989—93; MA in Film and Video, Am. U., Washington, DC, 1993—95. Film reviewer (as Cindy Rowse) Creative Screenwriting Mag., Los Angeles, Calif., 1995—2001, bd. script reviewers, 1998—2001; freelance writer Millsboro, Del., 2002—; screenplay writing cons. ScriptFix, Kensington, Md., 1999—2001. Author: (screenplays) Home (Hon. Mention Writer's Digest Writing Contest, 1995), The Willing Prey (aka The Cult) (Quarter Finalist Quantum Quest Screenplay Search, 1998, Semi-Finalist Lone Star Screenplay Competition, 1996, Quarter Finalist The Writer's Network Screenplay & Fiction Competition, 1997), The Actor (Quarter Finalist Lone Star Screenplay Competition, 1997, Semi-Finalist America's Best Screenplay Competition, 1997), (short stories) Lists, (short film) Three Days Later. Named a Semi-Finalist, Nat. Merit Scholars, 1978. Mem.: Golden Key Nat. Honor Soc. (life). Personal E-mail: cindylynncarter@aol.com.

CARTER, DAVID GEORGE, SR., academic administrator; b. Dayton, Ohio, Oct. 25, 1942; s. Richard Walter and Esther Mae (Dunn) C.; children: Ehrika Aileen, Jessica Faye, David George Jr. BS, Cen. State U., 1965; MEd, Miami U., 1968; PhD, Ohio State U., 1971. Cert. elem. tchr., Ohio. Prin. Dayton Pub. Schs., 1969-70, supr., 1970-71, unit facilitator, dist. supt., 1971-73; asst. and assoc. prof. Pa. State U., State College, 1972-77; assoc. dean and prof. edn. U. Conn., Storrs, 1977-82, assoc. v.p. acad. affairs, 1982-88; pres. East Conn. State U., Willimantic, 1988—2006; chancellor Conn. State U. Sys., Hartford, Conn., 2006—. Corporator Liberty Bank, 1999—, dir., 2000—; chair bd. visitors Marine Corps Univ., 2003-04. Contbr. articles to profl. jours. Bd. dirs. New England Regional Exch., Framingham, Mass., 1981-86, Haitian Health Found.; mem. Gov.'s Task Force on Jail and Prison Overcrowding. Named Young Man of Yr. Dayton C. of C., 1973, Disting. Alumnus Ctrl. State U., Wilberforce, Ohio, 1988, Man of Yr., African Am. Affairs Commn., 2000—; inducted into Donald K. Anthony Achievement Hall of Fame Ctrl. State U., 1993; recipient Roy Wilkins Civil Rights award NAACP, 1994; 39th Americanism award Conn. Am. Legion, 1994; recipient Greater Hartford NAACP award of honor, 2001, Good Citizen award, Conn. Grand Lodge Order Sons of Italy in Am., 2001, Educator of Yr. award Greater Hartford Assn. of Negro Bus. and Profl. Woman's Club, 2003, Whitney M. Young Jr. Svc. award Urban Scouting Com. Conn. Rivers Coun. Boy Scouts Am., 2003. Mem. Nat. Orgn. Legal Problems of Edn. (bd. dirs. 1980-83), NCAA (chair pres.' commn. divsn. III 1995-97, pres.'s commn. 1991-97), Am. Ednl. Rsch. Orgn., Am. Coun. on Edn. (bd. mem. 1999-2005, exec. com. 2001-03, chair fin. and audit com. 2002-05), Am. Assn. State Colls. and Univs. (dir. 2001—, chair bd. dirs. 2002-03, chair elect 2002, past chair 2004), Internat. Assn. U. Pres. (chair N.Am. council 2004-05), Phi Delta Kappa, Pi Lambda Theta, Phi Kappa Phi, Sigma Pi Phi. Home: 215 Stimson Rd New Haven CT 06511-1671 Office: Conn State Univ Sys 39 Woodland St Hartford CT 06105

CARTER, DENNIS LEE, marketing professional; b. Louisville, Oct. 23, 1951; s. Bernard Lee and Opal Delores (Jaggers) C.; m. Janice Lea Herbert, Dec. 31, 1976; children: Serra Kimberly, Scott Winston. BSEE, BS in Physics, Rose Hulman Inst., Terre Haute, Ind., 1973; MSEE, Purdue U., 1974, DSc (hon.), 1996; MBA, Harvard U., 1981. Instr. elec. engring. tech. Purdue U., West Lafayette, Ind., 1975; collateral engr. Rockwell-Collins, Cedar Rapids, Iowa, 1975-76, design engr., 1976-79; product mktg. engr. Intel Corp., Santa Clara, Calif., 1981-83, software products mktg. mgr., 1983-85, tech. asst. to pres., 1985-89, end-user mktg. mgr., 1989-90, gen. mgr. end-user components divsn., 1990-91, dir. corp. mktg., 1991-92, v.p., dir. corp. mktg., 1992-98, v.p., dir. strategic mktg., 1998—. Inventor radio reception path monitor for a diversity sys., 1985. Episcopalian. Avocation: baseball.

CARTER, DONALD PATTON, retired advertising executive; b. Richmond, Mo., July 30, 1927; s. R. D. and Lillian (Patton) Carter; m. Susan Virginia Wurst, Apr. 22, 1950 (dec. Apr. 1980); children: Jeffrey, Stephen, Carol; m. Carol Helen Holzrichter, Dec. 27, 1983. Student, U. Louisville, 1945-46; BS, U. Mo., 1948; MBA, U. Pa., 1950. With Continental Color Press, Inc., Kansas City, Mo., 1950-52; pres. Nasco, Inc., Kansas City, Kans., 1953-54; from v.p. to pres. Biddle Co., Bloomington, Ill., 1955-68; pres. Post Keyes Gardner Inc., Chgo., 1968-78, also bd. dirs.; chmn., pres. Cunningham & Walsh Inc., Chgo., 1978-83, exec. v.p. NY, 1978-83, also bd. dirs. NY; chmn. bd. dirs. Modu-line Industries, 1982-97; ret., 1997. Instr. econs., bus. adminstrn. Kansas City (Mo.) Jr. Coll., 1950—52; trustee Thomson-McKinnon Mut. Funds, 1983—96, PIMCO & ALLIANZ Multi-Mgr. Mut. Funds, 1996—2005. With USN, 1945—47. Named Young of the Yr., Jr. C. of C., 1961. Mem.: Bob O'Link Golf Club, Knollwood Country Club, Phi Kappa Psi. Home: 950 Gloucester Crossing Lake Forest IL 60045-4900

CARTER, DUDLEY ROCHELLE, lawyer; b. Franklinton, La., Sept. 10, 1950; s. James Cecil and Mildred Grace (Stennis) R. BA in Polit. Sci., La. State U., 1972; JD, Yale U., 1975. Bar: Ga. 1976, US Dist. Ct. (no. dist.) Ga. 1976, US Ct. Appeals (5th cir.) 1976, US Ct. Appeals (11th cir.) 1997. Vista atty. Atlanta Legal Aid Soc., 1975-76; law clk. to Hon. Joel J. Fryer Fulton County Superior Ct., Atlanta, 1976-77; trial atty. U.S. Dept. Labor, Atlanta, 1977-82; assoc. Hendrick Spanos & Phillips PC, Atlanta, 1982-88, shareholder (ptnr.), 1988-94, Spanos & Rochelle, P.C., Atlanta, 1994-97; shareholder Littler Mendelson, P.C., Atlanta, 1997—. Mem. adv. bd. Coverdell Leadership Inst., Atlanta, 1996—; mem. Ga. Commn. on Equal Opportunity; bd. dirs. Ga. Pub. Policy Found., 1996—. So. Inst. Bus. and Profl. Ethics, 2001—, Midtown Alliance, Atlanta, 1982—92. Mem. State Bar Ga. (mem. labor sect.), Atlanta Bar Assn. (mem. labor/employment sect., chairperson alt. dispute resolution com. 1986-92, mem. bench and bar com. 1986-87), Christian Legal Soc., Federalist Soc., Yale Club Ga. (bd. dirs. 1982-86), So. Inst. Bus. and Profl. Ethics (bd. dirs.). Republican. Avocations: outdoor activity, music. Home: 2769 Brook Grove Ln Atlanta GA 30339-5331 Office: Littler Mendelson PC 3348 Peachtree Rd NE Ste 1100 Atlanta GA 30326-1447 Office Phone: 404-233-0330. Business E-Mail: DRochelle@littler.com.

CARTER, E. KENNEDY, JR., bank executive; BBA, Campbell U., Buies Creek, NC. Various supervisory positions consumer fin. affiliate Chem. Bank; ops. mgr. Chem. Mortgage; sr. v.p. indirect home equity production Chase Manhattan Bank; with Nat. City Corp., Cleve., 1998—, exec. v.p. Nat. Home Equity. Office: Nat City Corp Nat City Ctr 1900 E Ninth St Cleveland OH 44114-3484 Office Phone: 216-222-2000.*

CARTER, EDYTHE L. (EDIE CARTER), mathematics educator; d. Fred H. and Shirley L. Cariker; m. S. Clay Carter; children: Elizabeth M., Coleman C. M, West Tex. A&M U., Canyon, Tex., 1988; BS, Tex. Tech U., Lubbock, 1979. Mid Management Certification State of Tex., 1988. Pub. sch. educator Amarillo Ind. Sch. Dist., 1979—88; pvt. math tutor Amarillo, Tex., 1989—2001; adj. faculty mem. Amarillo Coll., 1989—2000, instr. devel. math., 2000—05, asst. prof. devel. math., 2005—, coord. devel. math., 2002—. Com. Amarillo Ad Hoc Devel. Studies, Tex., 2002—; com. mem. Amarillo Coll. Assessment and Remediation, 2002—; com. Amarillo Coll. Instl. Rev., 2004—05; program chair Amarillo Coll. Commencement Com., 2002—03; spkr. in field. Vol. Jr. League, Amarillo, Tex., 1988; exec. sec., bd. mem. West Tex. A & M U., Canyon, Tex., 2001. Mem.: Women's Forum (assoc.; exec. bd. mem. 2006), Nat. Assn. Of Devel. Educators (assoc.), Tex. Cmty. Coll. Tchr. Assn. (assoc.). Home: 2601 Juniper Amarillo TX 79109 Office: Amarillo Coll Po Box 447 Amarillo TX 79178 Home Phone: 806-353-7783; Office Phone: 806-371-5335. Office Fax: 806-345-5571. Personal E-mail: elcarter@suddenlink.net. Business E-Mail: carter-el@actx.edu.

CARTER, ELLIOTT COOK, JR., composer; b. NYC, Dec. 11, 1908; s. Elliott Cook and Florence (Chambers) Carter; m. Helen Frost-Jones, July 6, 1939; 1 child, David. AB, Harvard U., 1930, AM, 1932, MusD (hon.), 1970, New Eng. Conservatory Music, 1961, Swarthmore Coll., 1956, Princeton U., 1967, Boston U., 1970, Yale U., 1970, Oberlin Coll., 1970, Cambridge U., Eng., 1983. Music dir. George Balanchine's Ballet Caravan, 1936—40; tchr. St. John's Coll., Annapolis, Md., 1940—42; cons. O.W.I., 1943—44; tchr. Greek and math.; tchr. music theory and composition Peabody Conservatory, Balt., 1946—48; dir., pres. Am. sect., Internat. Soc. Contemporary Music, 1946—52; assoc. prof. music Columbia U., NYC, 1948—50, Queen's Coll., NYC, 1955—56; tchr. Am. studies Salzburg (Austria) Seminars, 1958; lectr. music seminar Princeton (N.J.) U., 1959—60; prof. of composition Yale U., New Haven, 1960—62; Am. del. East-West Encounter, Tokyo, 1962; composer in residence Am. Acad. in Rome, 1963, 1967, Am. Sch., West Berlin, 1964; prof. of composition Julliard Sch. Music, NYC, 1967—84; Andrew D. White Prof.-at-Large Cornell U., Ithaca, NY, 1967—68. Composer: (symphonies/orchestral) Symphony, Suite from Pocahontas, 1939 (Juilliard pub. award, 1940), Symphony No. 1, 1942, Holiday Overture, 1944 (1st prize Ind. Music Publishers Contest, 1945), Suite, From the Minotaur, 1947, Elegy, 1952, Variations for Orchestra, 1954—55, Double Concerto (Sibelius medal, 1961, Critics' Cir. award, 1961), Piano Concerto, 1964—65, Concerto for Orchestra, 1968—69, A Symphony of Three Orchestras, 1976, Penthode, 1984—85, A Celebration of Some 100 x 150 Notes, 1986, Oboe Concerto, 1988, Remembrance, 1988, Anniversary, 1989, Violin Concerto, 1990 (Grammy award Best Contemporary Composition, 1994), Allegro Scorrevole, 1996 (Prince Rainier Found. Music award, 1998), Clarinet Concerto, 1997, (symphony) Sum fluxae pretium spei, 1996, Asko Concerto, 2000, Cello Concerto, 2000 (commissioned by the Chgo. Symphony Orch.), Boston Concerto, 2002 (commissioned by Boston Symphony), Dialogues, 2003, Reflexions, 2004, (chamber/instrumental) Canonic Suite, 1939 (BMI pub. prize, 1945), Pastoral, 1940, Elegy, 1941, Piano Sonata No. 1, 1945—46, Woodwind Quintet, 1948, Cello Sonata, 1948, Eight Études and a Fantasy, 1949—50, Eight Pieces for Four Timpani/Recitative and Improvisation, 1950—66, String Quartet No. 1, 1950—51 (1st prize Internat. Quartet Competition, Liège, Belgium, 1953), Sonata, 1952, String Quartet No. 2, 1959 (Pulitzer prize for music, 1960, Critics'Cir. award, UNESCO award, Naumburg award, 1956), String Quartet No. 3, 1971 (Pulitzer prize for music, 1973), Canon for Three: In Memoriam Igor Stravinsky, 1971, Duo, 1973—74, Brass Quintet, 1974, A Fantasy About Purcell's Fantasia Upon One Note, 1974, Birthday Fanfare for Sir William Glock's 70th, 1978, Night Fantasies, 1980, Triple Duo, 1982—83, Changes, 1983, Canon for Four: Homage to William, 1984, Esprit rude/Esprit doux, 1984, Riconoscenza per Goffredo Petrassi, 1984, String Quartet No. 4, 1986, Enchanted Preludes, 1988, 1994, Con Leggerezza Pensosa (Omaggio a Italo Calvino), 1990, Scrivo in Vento, 1991, Quintet for Piano and Winds, 1991, Trilogy for Harp and Oboe, 1992, Gra for clarinet alone, 1993, Figment for cello alone, 1994, Fragment for string quartet, 1994, esprit rude/esprit doux II, 1995, String Quartet No. 5, 1995, more than 90 for piano, A Six-Letter Letter (for Paul Sacher's 90th Birthday) for English Horn alone, 1996, Luimen, 1997, Quintet for Piano and String Quartet, 1997, Tempo e tempi, 1999, Mosaic, 2004, (vocal, choral) My Love is in a Light Attire, 1928, Tarantella, 1936, Harvest Home, To Music, Let's Be Gay, Heart Not So Heavy As Mine, Tell Me Where is Fancy Bred?, The Defense of Corinth, 1941, Three Poems of Robert Frost, 1943, The Difference, The Harmony of Morning, 1944, Musicians Wrestle Everywhere, 1945, Emblems, 1947, A Mirror on which to Dwell, 1975, Syringa, 1978, In Sleep, In Thunder, 1981, Of Challenge and Of Love, 1995, Two Diversions for piano, 1999, (statement) Remembering Aaron, for violin alone, 1999, (fantasy) Remembering Roger for violin alone, 1999, Rhapsodic Musings for violin alone, 2000, (ballet) Pocahontas, 1936, The Minotaur, 1947, (opera) What Next?, 1998, (incidental music) Philocetes, 1931, Mostellaria, 1936. Trustee Am. Acad. in Rome. Named Commandeur dans l'Ordre des Arts et des Lettres, France, 1987, Commendatore in the Order of Merit of the Republic of Italy, 1991; recipient Am. Composers' Alliance prize, 1943, Acad.-Inst. award in Music, Am. Acad. and Inst. of Arts and Letters, 1950, Guggenheim fellowships, 1945, 1950, Prix de Rome, 1953, Harvard Glee Club medal, 1967, Gold medal, Am. Acad. and Inst. of Arts and Letters, 1971, Handel medallion, 1978, Ernst von Siemens Musik-Preis, Munich, 1985, MacDowell medal, 1983, George Peabody medal, 1984, Nat. Medal of Arts, Nat. Endowment for the Arts, 1985. Mem.: Acad. Santa Cecilia (Rome), Acad. der Kunste (Berlin), Am. Composers Alliance (bd. dirs. 1939—52, treas. 1949—50), Am. Acad. Arts and Scis., Nat. Inst. Arts and Letters, Internat. Soc. Contemporary Music (bd. dirs. 1946—52, pres. U.S. sect. 1952), League Composers (bd. dirs. 1939—52). Address: Boosey & Hawkes Inc 35 E 21st St New York NY 10010-6212

CARTER, EMILY ANN, physical chemist, researcher, educator; b. Los Gatos, Calif., Nov. 28, 1960; d. David and Rebecca (Blumberg) C.; m. Bruce E. Koel, 1994; children; Adam, Brent (step), Jacqueline (step). BS in Chemistry, U. Calif., Berkeley, 1982; PhD in Chemistry, Calif. Inst. Tech., 1987. Postdoctoral rsch. assoc. U. Colo., Boulder, 1987—88; asst. prof., physical chemistry UCLA, 1988—92, assoc. prof., 1992—94, prof., 1994—2002, prof. chemistry and materials sci. and engring., 2002—04; prof. mech. engring. and applied math. Princeton U., NJ, 2004—06, Arthur W. Marks prof. mech. engring. and applied math., 2006—. Mem. Def. Sci. Study Group, 1996-97; cons. Inst. for Def. Analysis, 1998-, Los Alamos Nat. Lab., 2000-2005; mem. theoretical divsn. rev. com., 2000-05, DOE-BES coun. chem. sci., 2006-; vis. scholar in physics Harvard U., 1999; vis. scholar in aeronautics Calif. Inst. Tech., 2001; UCLA dir. modeling and simulation Calif. Nano Systems Inst., 2000-04; McDowell lectr. U. B.C., 2002, Merck-Frosst lectr., Concordia U., 2005. Mem. editl. bd. Jour. Phys. Chemistry, 1995-00, Surface Sci., 1994-99, Ency. Chem. Physics and Phys. Chemistry 1996-01, Chem. Phys. Letters, 1998-, Phys. Chem. Comm., 1998-2002, Chem. Phys. Chem., 2000-, Jour. Chem. Phys., 2000-02, Modeling and Simulation in Materials Sci. and Engring., 2001-, SIAM Multiscale Modeling and Simulation Jour., 2001-; guest editor Jour. Phys. Chem., 1999-2000. MPS theory steering com. NSF, 2004—05; chmn. Am. Conf. Theoretical Chemistry, 2005. Recipient New Faculty award Camille and Henry Dreyfus Found., 1988, NSF Presdl. Young Investigator award, 1988, Rsch. Innovation Recognition award Union Carbide Co., 1990-91, Dreyfus Tchr. Scholar award, 1992, Alfred P. Sloan fellow, 1993, Internat. Acad. of Quantum Molecular Sci. medal, 1993, Exxon faculty fellow, 1993, Glen T. Seaborg Rsch. award, 1993, Herbert Newby McCoy Rsch. award, 1993, Peter Mark Meml. award Am Vacuum Soc., 1995, Dr. Lee's vis. rsch. fellow Oxford U., 1996, UCLA Hanson-Dow award, 1998, UCLA Dean's Recognition award for rsch., 2002. Fellow AAAS, Am. Vacuum Soc., Am. Phys. Soc. (chmn. divsn. chem. phsyics 2004-05), Inst. Physics; mem. Am. Chem. Soc.(Award for Computers in Chemical and Pharma. Rsch. 2007), Sigma Xi, Phi Beta Kappa. Avocations: theater, films, cooking, reading, tennis. Office: Princeton U Dept MAE E Quad Rm D404A Princeton NJ 08544-5263 Office Phone: 609-258-5391. Business E-Mail: eac@princeton.edu.

CARTER, ETHEL ILENE, secondary school educator; b. Colorado Springs, Aug. 2, 1947; d. Delbert William and Vera Lauretta Lacy; m. James Dale Carter, Dec. 27, 1969 (div. Dec. 9, 1996); children: James Dale Jr., Heidi Jo. BS in Secondary Edn., Olivet Nazarene U., Ill., 1970; MA in Ednl. Theatre, NYU, 1999. Cert. Tchg. Type 09 Ill., 1970. Tchr. home econs. St. Anne Cmty. HS, Ill., 1970—73, Ill. Valley Ctrl. HS, Chillicothe, 1981—84; owner, mgr. Monical's Pizza, Canton, Ill., 1984—96; tchr. coop. vocat. edn., English, family and consumer sci. Canton HS, Ill., 1990—2000; tchr. theatre and family and consumer sci. Kaneland HS, Maple Park, Ill., 2000—. Dept. head home econs. St. Anne HS, Ill., 1970—73; judge-speech team Canton HS, Ill., 1991—97, tech prep-bus. ptnrs. in edn. com., 1991—2000, sponsor-nat. hon. soc., 1994—97, asst. coach-speech team, Maple Park, Ill., 1996—97, play dir., 1996—2000; play dir., thespian sponsor Kaneland HS, Maple Park, Ill., 2001—, speech team coach, 2004—, discipline com., 2004—, curriculum com., 2005—. Dir.: (over 35 sch. and cmty. plays, musicals, and children's theatre); co-dir.: (prodn. Creative Arts Team) Youth Theatre Co., 1998. Contemporary worship svc. com. First Christian Ch., Canton, Ill.; children's ch. dir., Snday sch. tchr., vacation bible sch. tchr., christian edn. com. Ch. of the Nazarene, Peoria, Ill.; bible sch. dir., play dir. Evang. Free Ch., Canton, Ill.; mem. Fulton County Playhouse, Canton, Ill., 1993—95; com. mem. Kaneland Found. Fine Arts Festival, Maple Park, Ill., 2004—06. Mem.: Ednl. Theatre Assn. Office: Kaneland Unit Sch Dist 47W326 Keslinger Rd Maple Park IL 60151 Home Phone: 630-845-4028; Office Phone: 630-365-5100 320. Business E-Mail: icarter@kaneland.org.

CARTER, EVELYN, retired elementary school educator; d. James Kyle and Mable Kuykendall; m. Willie James Carter (dec.). BS, Prairie View Coll., Tex., 1939, MEd, 1952. Tchr., Karnes City, Tex., 1939—41, Roosevelt HS, Luling, Tex., 1941—44, Newton, Tex., 1944—45, Jasper County, Tex., 1945—47, Camden, Tex., 1948—64, Nacogdoches, Tex., 1964—70; elem. tchr., 1970—76; ret., 1976. Lectr. various schs., Nacogdoches. Musician nursing homes in Nacogdoches; musician, vol. Bapt. Ch., Nacogdoches, Tex., 2006—. Named to Hall of Fame, Asberry HS, Yoakum, Tex., 1992; recipient Silver Fawn award, Boy Scouts Am., 1973. Mem.: AAUW (historian 2000—07), Nacogdoches Ret. Tchrs. Assn. (musician 2006—), Tex. Ret. Tchrs. Assn. (life). Baptist. Avocations: reading, piano, dance, singing. Home: 2533 Woden Rd Nacogdoches TX 75961

CARTER, FRANCES TUNNELL (FRAN), fraternal organization administrator; b. Springville, Miss. d. David Atmond and Mary Annie (McCutcheon) Tunnell; m. John T. Carter; children: Wayne, Nell Branum. BS, U. So. Miss., 1946; MS, U. Tenn., 1948; EdD, U. Ill., 1954. Tchr. elem. sch., Thaxton, Miss., 1942—43, Cumberland, Miss., 1943—44; tchr. h.s. home econs. Randolph, Miss., 1944—45, Maben, Miss., 1946—47; instr. Wood Coll., Mathiston, Miss., 1947—48, East Ctrl. Jr. Coll., Decatur, Miss., 1948—49; prof. home econs. Clarke Coll., Newton, Miss., 1950—56; prof. Samford U., Birmingham, Ala., 1956—84; editor, children and youth products and resources Woman's Missionary Union, Birmingham, 1983—85; pres. CarterCraft, Inc., Birmingham, 1983—89, Carter and Carter Consultants, 1987—2004; nat. exec. dir. Kappa Delta Epsilon, Birmingham, 1987—2003; founder, exec. dir. Am. Rosie the Rivater Assn. Vis. prof. Hong Kong Bapt. U., 1965-66, Anhui Normal U., People's Republic of China, 1987; medical/dental mission team mem. Honduras, Mex., 1983, 84, 89, 1994; tchr. workshops in China, 1988, 90, 92, 95, 97, 2000; tchr. workshops in Indonesia, 1993; lectr. in symposium at invitation of Russian Edn. Ministry, Moscow, 1994, U. Nanjing, People's Republic of China, 1997; curriculum writer Bapt. Brotherhood Commn., 1986-90; writer N.Am. Mission Bd., 1995-98. Author: Sammy in the Country, 1960, Tween-Age Ambassador, 1970, Ching Fu and Jim, 1978; co-author: Sharing Times Seven, 1977, also short stories, articles; feature writer: Crusader Mag., 1986-95, The Current, 1987-2003; editor 103 Rosie Stories, 2001. Tchr. Sunday sch. Bapt. Ch., Birmingham, 1980—; mem., lt. col. CAP, 1968—1996, bd. dirs. Aerospace Edn. Ala. Wing, 1991-94, dir. pub. affairs regional S.E., 1994-95; v.p. Women's Civic Club of Birmingham, 1997-98, 2002-03; placement officer ESL Sch., 1995-98, pres., 1982-83, Test of English as a Fgn. Lang. tchr., 1998-; Silver rep. Dist. 6 Ala. Nat. Silver Haired Congress, 1991-96, Ala. Silver Haired Legislator Dist. 55 Jefferson County, 1996—; alt. Dist. 6, Nat. Silver Haired Congress, 2000—. Recipient Career Achievement award Profl. Fraternity Assn., 1988, Outstanding Alumnae award Wood Coll., 1992, Outstanding award Kappa Delta Pi, 1992, Brewer award for Aerospace Edn. Southeast region CAP, 1994, Vol. of Yr. award Nat. Profl. Fraternity Assn., 1999, Lillian K. Keil award WWII Vets. Com., Washington, DC, 2004, cert. Rosie the Riveter reunion, Little White House, Warm Springs, Ga., 1997; named Birmingham's Woman of Yr., 1977, Birmingham's Vol. of Yr., 1980; named to Sr. Citizen Hall of Fame, 2002. Mem. AARP (local pres. 1988-89, asst. state dir. 1989-93, Nat. Cmty. award 1992), Birmingham's Women C. of C. (pres. 1975-76, 2003-04), Nat. League Am. Pen Women (3rd v.p. 1988-90, nat. pres. 1994-96), Ala. League Pen Women (pres. 1970-72), Birmingham League Am. Pen Women (pres. 1968-70, 76-78), Ala. Writers Conclave (pres. 1978-79), Ala. State Poetry Soc. (pres. 1979-82), Ala. Federated Women's Clubs (dist. dir. 1988-90, Outstanding Woman of Ala. Club award 1988), Freedoms Found. Valley Forge (pres. Birmingham area chpt. 1990-91), Nat. Fellowship Bapt. Educators (sec. 1987-93), Birmingham Bus. and Profl. Club (pres. 1986-87), Am. Rosie the Riveter Assn. Inc. (founder 1998, pres. 1998-2003, nat. exec. dir. 2003—), Kappa Delta Epsilon (nat. pres. 1980-85, exec. dir. 1987-2003, co-dir. ESL Sch. 1994-98), Alpha Delta Kappa, Delta Kappa Gamma, Phi Delta Kappa (Nat. Profl. Fraternity Assn. award 1999, cert. emeritus 2000), Birmingham Civic Club (pres. 1982-83, v.p. 2003-04, 06-07), Birmingham Women's C. of C. (pres. 2003-04), Samford U. Ret. Faculty Assn. (pres. 2004-06). Home and Office: 3470 Loch Ridge Dr Birmingham AL 35216 Office Phone: 205-822-4106. E-mail: fran.carter@juno.com.

CARTER, GENE, judge; b. Milbridge, Maine, Nov. 1, 1935; s. K.W. and S. Loreta (Beal) C.; m. Judith Ann Kittredge, June 24, 1961; children: Matthew G., Mark G. BA, U. Maine, 1958, LLD (hon.), 1985; LLB, NYU, 1961. Bar: Maine 1962. Ptnr. Rudman, Winchell, Carter & Buckley (and predecessors), Bangor, Maine, 1965-80; assoc. justice Maine Supreme Jud. Ct., 1980-83; from judge to sr. dist. judge U.S. Dist. Ct. Maine, 1983—2003, sr. dist. judge, 2003—. Chmn. adv. com. on rules of civil procedure Maine Supreme Jud. Ct., 1976-80. Chmn. Bangor Housing Authority, 1970-77. Mem. Am. Law Inst., Internat. Soc. Barristers, Am. Coll. Trial Lawyers. Office: US Dist Ct 156 Federal St Portland ME 04101-4152

CARTER, GENE RAYMOND, professional association executive; b. Staunton, Va. BA, Va. State U.; MA, Boston U.; EdD, Columbia U., 1973; LLD (hon.), Va. State U.; LittD, Old Dominion U. Tchr. & adminstr. Norfolk Pub. Schools, Va., 1962—92, supt. Va., 1983—92; exec. dir. Assn. for Supervision and Curriculum Develop., 1992—2000, CEO, 2000—. Dir. Norfolk Southern Corp., 1992—; edn. adv. com. Am.-Israel Friendship League; adv. commn. on pub. edn. ABA; active Nat. Commn. on Svc. Learning, Nat. Commn. on Asia in the Schools; adv. bd. Edn. Commn. of States; bd. dirs. Longview Found. Named Outstanding Sch. Supt. in Va., 1985, Nat. Supt. of Yr., An. Assn. Sch. Administrators, 1988; recipient Brotherhood Citation, Nat. Conf. of Christians and Jews, 1985, Presdl. Citation, Nat. Assn. Equal Opportunity in Higher Edn., 1985, Annual Leadership for Learning award, An. Assn. Sch. Administrators, 1990, Disting. Alumni award, Columbia U. Teacher's Coll., 1991. Office: ASCD 1703 N Beauregard St Alexandria VA 22311-1714 Home: 11516 Little Bay Harbor Way Spotsylvania VA 22553 E-mail: gcarter@ascd.org.

CARTER, GRAYDON (EDWARD GRAYDON CARTER), editor-in-chief; b. Canada, July 14, 1949; s. E.P. and Margaret Ellen Carter; 4 children; m. Anna Scott, May 21, 2005. Student, Carleton U., U. Ottawa. Editor The Can. Rev., 1973—77; writer Time, 1978—83, Life, NYC, 1983—86; founder, editor Spy, 1986—91; editor NY Observer, 1991—92; hon. editor Harvard Lampoon, 1989; editor in chief Vanity Fair, NYC, 1992—. Exec. prodr. (documentary) 9/11, CBS, 2002; prodr.: (documentary) The Kid Stays in the Picture, 2002; author: Vanity Fair's Hollywood, 2000, What We've Lost, 2004, Oscar Night: 75 Years of Hollywood Parties, 2004, Spy: The Funny Years, 2006. Named Editor of Yr., Advertising Age, 1996, Adweek mag., 1997, 2003; recipient Nat. Mag. award for Gen. Excellence for mags. with circulation over 1,000,000, 1997, 1999, Nat. Mag. award for Photography, 2000, 2002, 2000, Nat. Mag. award for Reviews and Criticism, 2003, Nat. Mag. award for Essays, 2005, 2 Nat. Mag. awards for Pub. Interest journalism & for Columns & Commentary, 2007. Mem.: Brook Club, Washington (Conn.) Club. Avocations: fly fishing, canoeing. Office: Conde Nast Media Group Vanity Fair Mag 4 Times Sq Fl 22 New York NY 10036-6522*

CARTER, HARRY ROBERT, fire protection consultant; b. Neptune, NJ, July 29, 1947; s. Harry Barringer and Stella (Napiorkowski) C.; m. Jacalyn Roberta Miller, Apr. 29, 1972; children: Ellen, Kathleen, Todd. AA, Brookdale Coll., 1971; BA, Thomas Edison State Coll., 1975; BS magna cum laude, Jersey City State Coll., 1976; MA, Rutgers U., 1979; PhD, Western States U., 1984, Capella U., 2005. Fire fighter Rahway (N.J.) Fire Dept., 1972-73, Newark (N.J.) Fire Dept., 1972-77, fire capt., 1977-90, battalion fire chief, 1990-97, dep. to divsn., 1997-99, ret., 1999. Assoc. prof., Mercer County Coll., West Windsor, N.J., 1999—; adj. prof. Ocean County Coll., Toms River, N.J., 1977-81; pres. Carter Fire Protection, Inc., Adelphia, N.J., 1980—; fire marshal N.J. Army Nat. Guard, 1981-91. Author: Management in the Fire Service, 1989, Managing Fire Service Finances, 1989, Understanding Fire Behavior, 1995, Strategic Planning and Fire Protection, 1996, Tactics in Fire Department Management, 1997, Firefighting Strategy and Tactics, 1998, Management in the Fire Service, 3d edit., 1998, It's All About Me, 2002, Living My Dream, 2006, Leadership: A View from the Trenches, 2006; contbr. articles to profl. jours. Vol. firefighter, officer Howell Twp. Fire Co. # 1, Adelphia, NJ, 1971—, tng. officer, 1978—91, fire chief, 1991; fire commr. fire dist. # 2 Howell Twp. Bd. Fire Commrs. Mem. ISFSI (bd. dirs. 1989-2001, pres. bd. dirs. 1999, chmn. bd. commrs.), N.J. Soc. Fire Instrs. (bd. dirs. 1978-80, pres. 1980-82), Nat. Fire Protection Assn. (adv. coun. 1975-90), Internat. Assn. Fire Chiefs (scholarship 1975-76), Internat. Assn. Fire Fighters, Masons (past master lodge), VFW, Am. Legion, Optimist Internat. Republican. Avocations: military music, playing the tuba, poetry, collecting military medals. Home: PO Box 100 Adelphia NJ 07710-0100

CARTER, HENRIETTA MCKEE, music educator, department chairman; d. Horace Adolphus and Thelma Henrietta McKee; m. William Grandvil Carter (dec. Dec. 1993); children: Darius Grandvil, Grandvil Elliott, Jonathan Grandvil. BS in Biology, Northeastern U., Boston, 1959; MM in Voice, New Eng. Conservatory, 1964; MS in Edn., Nat. U., LaJolla, Calif., 1988. Dir. music Walnut Hill Sch., Natick, Mass., 1964-68; instr. voice and music theory Inner City Inst., LA, 1972-74; instr. voice Univ. So. Calif. Preparatory Sch. of Arts, LA, 1970-74; rsch. fellow Univ. Ghana, Legon, Accra, Ghana, 1974-75; prof. voice, music Golden West Coll., Huntington Beach, Calif., 1976—, chair music and dance, 1993-98, chair performing arts, 1998—2006, chair visual and performing arts, 2006—. Pvt. voice studio, Huntington Beach, Calif., 1976—, Rossmoor, Calif., 1999—, voice cons., Southern Calif., 1976—, pvt. voice studio, Legon Accra, Ghana, 1974-75, voice cons., 1974-75; profl. soprano soloist and chorister for recitals, opera, media, choirs, 1957-86; study abroad instr., Florence, 2002. Bd. dirs. Scout Trail Homeowners Assn., 1992, Friends of Choral Music, 2007; mem. Friends of Pacific Theater, 2000-, Friends of LA Opera, 2000-, The Wagner Soc., 2005-. Recipient Woman of Yr. award Northeastern U., 1959; recipient numerous fellowships. Mem. Music Assn. Calif. C.C. (v.p. 1980-81), Music Tchr.'s Assn. Calif., Music Tchr.'s Nat. Assn., Nat. Assn. Tchrs. of Singing, Soc. for Ethnomusicology, Delta Sigma Theta. Democrat. Avocations: photography, theatre and concerts, reading, travel. Office: Golden West Coll 15744 Golden West St Huntington Beach CA 92647 Office Phone: 714-895-8753. Business E-Mail: hcarter@gwc.cccd.edu.

CARTER, HENRY MOORE, JR., retired foundation executive; b. Portsmouth, Va., Mar. 10, 1932; s. Henry and Debbie (McCoy) C.; m. Martha Rhea Greene, Aug. 21, 1954; 1 dau., Ann Clair. BA, Randolph-Macon Coll., 1953; MA, Vanderbilt U., 1954. Tchr. English, Norfolk County Public Schs., Portsmouth, 1954-59, head dept. English, 1957-59; headmaster Bollingbrook Sch., Petersburg, Va., 1959-66; dir. public relations Randolph-Macon Coll., Ashland, Va., 1966-68; dir. Randolph-Macon Fund, 1968-69, dir. devel., 1969-77; pres. Winston-Salem (N.C.) Found., 1977-97. Pastmem. adv. com. Kate B. Reynolds Trust for Poor and Needy; former chair bd. dirs. N.C. Ctr. for Nonprofits; former sec. Winston-Salem Campaign Coordinating Com. Past chmn., bd. dirs. coord. com. Winston-Salem Crime Stoppers; past chmn. Emergency Loan Fund, Southeastern Coun. Founds., N.C. Assn. Cmty. Founds., Forsyth Common Vision Coun., Old Salem Inc; past mem. adv. bd. Mary Baldwin Coll.; former sec.-treas. Twin City Devel. Corp; past bd. dirs. Crosby Scholars Cmty. Partnership, Hospice Found., Forsyth Tech. Coll. Found.; ret. pres. Waccamaw Cmty. Found. Carnegie fellow, 1953-54. Mem. Litchfield Country Club, Rotary. Republican. Methodist. Home Phone: 443-237-2674. Personal E-mail: grants1sc@verizon.net.

CARTER, HODDING, III, (WILLIAM), retired foundation executive, journalist, commentator, educator; b. New Orleans, Apr. 7, 1935; s. William Hodding and Betty Brunhilde (Werlein) C.; m. Margaret A. Wolfe, June 21, 1957 (div. 1978); children: Catherine Ainsworth, Elizebeth Fearn, William Hodding IV, Margaret Lorraine; m. Patricia M. Derian, 1978. BA, Princeton U., 1957; LLD (hon.), Stetson Coll., 1980, Kenyon Coll., 1984; LittD (hon.), Tusculum Coll., 1983; LLD (hon.), George Washington U., 1986, N.Y. Inst. Tech., 1987; LHD (hon.), U. Maine, 1985, U. San Diego, 1991, Millsaps Coll., 1998, U. SC, 2004. Reporter Delta Democrat-Times, Greenville, Miss., 1959-62, mng. editor, 1962-66, editor, pub., 1966-77; asst. sec. state for pub. affairs, dept. spokesman US Dept. State, Washington, 1977-80; vis. prof. Am. U., 1980; anchorman and chief corr. Inside Story, PBS, 1981-84; chief corr., exec. editor Capitol Jour., PBS, 1985-86; pres. MainStreet TV Prodn. Co., 1985-95; Knight chair in pub. affairs journalism U. Md., 1995-98; pres., CEO John S. and James L. Knight Found., Miami, 1998—2005; prof. leadership and pub. policy U. NC, Chapel Hill, 2006—. Vis. prof. Duke U., 1990; op. ed. columnist Wall St. Jour., 1980-91. Author: The South Strikes Back, 1959, The Reagan Years, 1988; contbr. to books, newspapers and mags.; commentator on TV and radio; columnist Newspaper Enterprise Assn., 1992-95. Co-chmn. Young Dem. Clubs Miss., 1965-68; founding mem. Loyal Dems. of Miss., 1968; mem. Charter Commn. Dem. Party, 1973-74; del. Dem. Conv., 1968, 72, 76, Dem. Mini Conv., Kansas City, Mo., 1974; mem. campaign staff Johnson for Pres., 1964, Carter for Pres., 1976; mem. exec. com. So. Regional Coun., 1969-75, Miss. Dem. Party, 1976-79; trustee Princeton U., 1983-98; dir. Dreyfus Corp. Funds; bd. dirs. Enterprise Corp. of the Delta, Ctr. Pub. Integrity, Americans for Campaign Reform; mem. Knight Found. Commn. on Intercollegiate Athletics; former chmn. Action Coun. for Peace in the Balkans, Am. Com. for US-Soviet Rels. Recipient Editl. award, Soc. Profl. Journalists, 1961, 4 Emmy awards for pub. affairs TV, 1984—85, Edward R. Murrow award for best fgn. documentary, 1984; Nieman fellow, Harvard U., 1965—66. Mem.: Pen/Am., Nat. Press Club, Coun. Fgn. Rels., Princeton Club NY, Tarratine Club. Episcopalian. Office Phone: 919-843-3236. Business E-Mail: hoddingcarter@umc.edu.

CARTER, JAINE M(ARIE), human resources specialist, director; b. Chgo., Oct. 29, 1946; m. James Carter, Apr. 8, 1970; children: Paul, Todd. BS, Northwestern U., 1968; PhD, Walden U., 1988. Mgmt. cons. to bus., 1969; chmn. bd. Pers. Devel., Inc., Palatine, Ill., 1969—; dir. women's divsn. Lake Forest Coll. Advanced Mgmt. Inst., Ill., 1970—. Writer, lectr., tchr., cons. mgmt. devel. programs; faculty AMA; speaker weekly cable TV series Life Skills; pres. bd. dirs. Family Renewal Inst., 1991—96. Author: How to Train for Supervisors, 1969, Career Planning Workshop for Women, 1975, Training Techniques That Bring About Positive Behavioral Change, 1976, Assertive Management Role Plays, 1976, Understanding the Female Employee, 1976, Rx for Women in Business, 1976, New Directions Needed in Management Training Programs, 1980, The Burnout of Retirement, 1983, Successfully Working with People, 1984, Assertiveness Training for Supervisors, 1985, Successfully Managing People, 1986, The New Success, 1986, Employee Assistance Program Handbook, 1988, Stay Out of Your Own Way-And Get the Job You Want, 1989, He Works/She Works-Successful Strategies for Working Couples, 1996; columnist: Scripps- Howard News Svc., Balancing Work and Family, 1996—2004; columnist Scripps-Howard News Svc. He Works/She Works, 1996—2004; moderator, content expert (TV spl.) Commitment to Quality, Nat. Tech. U., 1989; author: (TV series) Executive Communications, 1988 prodr.: (TV series) Relationships, 1992; creator, prodr., host (TV series) Choices, 1992, 1993, host (radio talk show), 1992—96, co-host Your Own Business!, 1993—97. Mem.: Pres.'s Forum (exec. dir. 1998—). *People can only be free when they are able to take personal responsibility for their actions, turn their back on the expectations of others, and confidently pursue their own unlimited realitites.*

CARTER, JAMES C., lawyer, apparel executive; b. Pendleton, Oreg., Aug. 7, 1948; m. Julie Carter; children: Emily, Tyler. AB in Econs., Stanford U., 1971; JD, U. Oreg., 1976. Bar: Oreg. 1976, US Fed. Ct. 1978. With Schulte, Anderson, Downes & Carter, Portland, Oreg.; gen. counsel US and Ams. Nike, Inc., Beaverton, Oreg., 1998—2003, v.p., gen. counsel, 2003—, chief legal officer, 2003—. Chair Classroom Law Project; mem. dean's adv. coun. U. Oreg. Law Sch. Mem.: Oreg. Assn. Def. Counsel. Avocations: travel, golf, running, bicycling. Office: Nike Inc 1 Bowerman Dr Beaverton OR 97005-6453*

CARTER, JAMES CLARENCE, pastor, educator; b. NYC, Aug. 1, 1927; s. James Clarence and Elizabeth (Dillon) C. BS in Physics, Spring Hill Coll., 1952; MS in Physics, Fordham U., 1953; STL in Theology, Woodstock Coll., 1959; PhD in Physics, Cath. U. Am., 1956. Ordained priest Roman Cath. Ch., 1958. Instr., asst. prof. Physics Loyola U., New Orleans, 1966-67, assoc. prof. of Physics, 1967—, v.p., 1970-74, pres., 1974-95, chancellor, 1995-2001; pastor Immaculate Conception Parish, New Orleans, 2001—04. Bd. dirs. Met. Area Com.; mem. higher edn. facilities com. State La., 1971-73, Am. Council's Commn. on Leadership in Higher Edn., 1975-78; bd. trustees Loyola U. Chgo., 1981-90; chmn. Mayor's Com. Ednl. Uses CATV, 1972. Contbr. articles to profl. jours. Mem. adv. com. New Orleans Pub. Library for the NEH Grant, 1975; bd. dirs. Greater New Orleans Area United Way, 1976-82, La. Ednl. TV Authority, 1977-83, 95-; bd. trustees Regis U., 1980-90, 94-98; lifetime trustee U. San Francisco, 1991-00, St. Joseph's U., 1993-04. Recipient Torch of Liberty award Anti-Defamation League of B'nai B'rith, 1983. Mem. Palmes Academiques, So. Assn. of Colls. and Schs. (exec. council of the commn. on colls.), Am. Phys. Soc., Am. Assn. Physics Tchrs., Assn. Jesuit Colls. and Univs. (chmn. acad. v.p. conf. 1971-74, chmn. 1991-94, exec. dir. 1996), Nat. Assn. Ind. Colls. and Univs. (bd. dirs. 1977-82), Am. Council Edn., Sigma Xi. Office: Loyola U New Orleans New Orleans LA 70118 Home Phone: 504-864-7415; Office Phone: 504-865-2168. E-mail: jcarter@loyno.edu.

CARTER, JAMES HAL, JR., lawyer; b. Ames, Iowa, Sept. 25, 1943; s. James H. Sr. and Louise (Benge) Carter; m. Theresa Carter; children: Janet, Faith, Katherine. BA, Yale U., 1965, LLB, 1969. Bar: NY 1971, US Ct. Appeals (2d cir.) 1971, US Dist. Ct. (so. dist.) NY 1972, US Dist. Ct. (ea. dist.) NY 1975, US Supreme Ct. 1976, US Ct. Internat. Trade 1980, US Dist. Ct. Conn. 1981, US Ct. Appeals (1st and 5th cirs.) 1984, US Ct. Appeals (fed. cir.) 1988, US Ct. Appeals (3d cir.) 1990, US Dist. Ct. (no. dist.) NY 1992, US Dist. Ct. (we. dist.) Mich. 1992. Law clk., Hon. Robert Anderson US Ct. Appeals (2d cir.), 1969-70; with Sullivan & Cromwell, LLP, NYC, 1970—77, ptnr., 1977—. Lectr. internat. comml. arbitration Practicing Law Inst. Corr. editor: Internat. Legal Materials; contbr. articles to profl. jours. Mem. adv. bd. Ctr. for Am. and Internat. Law; former mem., bd. dirs. Am. Bar Found. Fulbright scholar, Cambridge (Eng.) U., 1965—66. Mem.: ABA (past chair internat. law and practice sect., former co-chmn. internat. comml. arbitration com.), Am. Arbitration Assn. (chmn. bd. dirs. 2004—07), Coun. Fgn. Rels., Assn. Bar City of NY (former chmn. internat. affairs coun.), NY State Bar Assn. (former chmn. internat. dispute resolution com.), Am. Law Inst., Am. Soc. Internat. Law (pres. 2004—06), US Coun. Internat. Bus. (mem. com. arbitration). Office: Sullivan and Cromwell LLP 125 Broad St 32d Fl New York NY 10004-2498 Office Phone: 212-558-4000. Business E-Mail: carterj@sullcrom.com.

CARTER, JAMES HARVEY, retired state supreme court justice; b. Waverly, Iowa, Jan. 18, 1935; s. Harvey J. and Althea (Dominick) C.; m. Jeanne E. Carter, Aug. 1965; children: Carol, James. BA, U. Iowa, 1956, JD, 1960. Law clk. to judge U.S. Dist. Ct. 1960-62; assoc. Shuttleworth & Ingersoll, Cedar Rapids, Iowa, 1962-73; judge 6th Jud. Dist., 1973-76, Iowa Ct. Appeals, 1976-82; justice Iowa Supreme Ct., Des Moines, 1982—2006, sr. justice, 2006—. Office: Iowa Supreme Ct Judicial Branch Bldg 1111 E Ct Ave Des Moines IA 50319 Home Phone: 319-366-0027; Office Phone: 319-398-3920 500. Business E-Mail: james.carter@jb.state.ia.us.

CARTER, JAMES HARVEY, psychiatrist, educator; b. Maysville, NC, May 11, 1934; s. Thomas and Irene (Barber) C.; m. Jettie Lucille Strayhorn, Aug. 21, 1957 (dec. Sept. 1987); 1 child, James Harvey; m. Elsie Richardson, Aug. 26, 1988; 1 child, Saunia Carter-Wilson BS, N.C. Ctrl. U., Durham, 1956; MD, Howard U., 1966; MDiv, Shaw U., Raleigh, NC, 1999. Diplomate Am. Bd. Psychiatry and Neurology, Am. Bd. Forensic Examiners. Rotating intern Walter Reed Army Hosp., Washington, 1967; resident in gen. adult psychiatry Dorothea Dix/Duke Med. Ctr., Raleigh-Durham, NC, 1969-70; assoc. dept. psychiatry Duke U., Durham, 1971-74, asst. prof., 1974-78, assoc. prof., 1978-83, prof., 1983—; sr. psychiatrist Dept. Correction, Raleigh, 1974—. Lectr. N.C. Found. for Alcohol and Drug Studies, U. N.C., Wilmington, 1989-95. Editor Epikrisis. Bd. dirs. Gov.'s Inst. on Alcohol and Substance Abuse, 1992-94; co-founder Drug Action of Wake County, Raleigh. Served to Col. M.C., U.S. Army, 1958-94. Decorated Order of Mil. Merit; recipient Profl. Designation A, U.S. Army Surg. Gen., 1985, Order of the Oak Leaf Pine Gov.'s award, 1999, Salomon Carter Fuller award, Am. Psychiatric Assn., 2003; E.Y. Williams clin. scholar, 1994; Josiah Macy Faculty fellow, 1970-74; Falk fellow, 1971-72. Fellow Am. Psychiat. Assn. (life; disting.; Solomon Carter Fuller award 2003); vice chair com. on chronic mental illness), Orthopsychiat. Assn.; mem. AMA, N.C. Med. Soc. (life), Alpha Kappa Mu, Alpha Omega Alpha. Achievements include founding of various drug awareness programs. Office: Duke U Med Ctr PO Box 3106 Durham NC 27715-3106 Home Phone: 919-231-7350. Office Fax: 919-681-7504. Personal E-mail: jcarter511@bellsouth.net.com. Business E-Mail: carte049@mc.duke.edu.

CARTER, JAMES THOMAS, contractor, pilot; b. NYC, Dec. 27, 1952; s. Wendell Green and Carolyn Elizabeth (Smith) C.; m. Mary Jane Zellers, Oct. 8, 1985. Cert. airline transport pilot, flight instr., FAA, advanced open water diver, PADI. Charter pilot, flight instr. Pompano Air Ctr., Pompano Beach, Fla., 1976-78; profl. pilot Profl. Pilot Svcs., Ft. Lauderdale, Fla., 1978-79; aviation operative CIA, 1978-79; pres., pilot Carter Charter Co., Inc., Ft. Lauderdale, 1979-92; novelist Ft. Lauderdale, 1992-94; account exec. Power Line Components, Inc., Lighthouse Point, Fla., 1994-96; exec. dir. Advanced Tech., Inc., Ft. Lauderdale, 1996-99; v.p. Advanced Mgmt. Svcs. Inc., Ft. Lauderdale, 1999. Mem. missile program Lockheed Missile and Space, Huntsville, Ala., 1995-99, HRC program Smithsonian Astrophys. Obs., Cambridge, Mass., 1995-96, MIL-STAR program Electromagnetic Scis., Norcross, Ga., 1995-99, J-STARS program, 1996-99, Raytheon Missile Sys., Tucson, 1997-99, GEC Marconi, Norcross, Ga., 1997, airline capt. Profl. Air Charter, Ft. Lauderdale, Fla., 2000—. Author: Operation: Deepcover, 1994, A Twist of Fate, 1995, Stiletto, 1996, (poetry) Twilight, 1995, Christmas in the Snow, 1996. Recipient Editor's Choice award Nat. Libr. Poetry, 1996, 97. Mem. Aircraft Owners and Pilots Assn., Internat. Soc. Poets (disting.). Democrat. Presbyterian. Avocations: scuba diving, sailing, motorcycling, sea planes, skiing. Office: Profl Air Charter 1885 W Commercial Blvd Ste 120 Fort Lauderdale FL 33309-3066 E-mail: jtcatp@bellsouth.net.

CARTER, JANE FOSTER, agricultural industry executive; b. Stockton, Calif., Jan. 14, 1927; d. Chester William and Bertha Emily Foster; m. Robert Buffington Carter, Feb. 25, 1952 (dec. Dec. 1994); children: Ann Claire Carter Palmer, Benjamin Foster; m. Frank Anthony Bauman, Aug. 15, 1998 (div. Aug. 2003). BA, Stanford U., 1948; MS, NYU, 1949. Pres. Colusa (Calif.) Properties, Inc., 1953—; owner Carter Land and Livestock, Colusa, 1965—; pres. Sartain Mut. Water Co., Inc., 1992—2003, Carter Mut. Water Co. Inc., 2003—, J&B Rice Farms, Inc., Colusa, 1996—. Sec./treas. Carter Farms, Inc., Colusa, 1975—94, pres., 1994—2002; bd. dirs. Colusa Bean Growers, Inc., 1996—2002, sec., 1998—2002. Author: If the Walls Could Talk, Colusa's Architectural Heritage, 1988; author, editor: Colusa County Survey and Plan for the Arts, 1981—83, Implementing the Colusa County Arts Plan, 1984—86. Adv. mem. Calif. Gov.'s Commn. Agr., Sacramento, 1979—82; trustee Calif. Hist. Soc., 1979—89, regional v.p., 1984—89; mem. Calif. Reclamation Bd., 1982—96, sec., 1986—96; mem. Calif. Hist. Resources Commn., 1994—2001, vice chair, 1996—97, chair, 1997—99; mem. Colusa Heritage Preservation Com., 1976—2000, chmn., 1977—83, vice chmn., 1983—91, sec., 1997—2000; bd. dirs. Colusa Cmty. Theatre Found., 1980—99; trustee Calif. Preservation Found., 1989—95; del. Rep. Nat. Conv., Kans. City, Mo., 1976, Detroit, 1980, Dallas, 1984; mem. Calif. Rep. Ctrl. Com., 1976—94; bd. dirs. English-Spkg. Union U.S., NYC, 1995—2001, English-Spkg. Union, San Francisco, 1992—, pres., 1993—95, v.p., 1995—; bd. dirs. Leland Stanford Mansion Found., Sacramento, 1992—; bd. dirs. Colusa County br. Am. Cancer Soc., 1960—86, chmn., 1964—86; mem. exec. com. Sacramento River Water Contractors' Assn., 1974—2003, sec., 1992—2003. Recipient award of Merit for Hist. Preservation, Calif. Hist. Soc., 1989, Design award, Calif. Preservation Found., 1990, Pres.'s award, 2001, Citizens award, English-Speaking Union U.S., 2002, Congl. Order Merit, Nat. Rep. Congl. Com., 2003. Mem.: Francisca Club (San Francisco), Kappa Alpha Theta. Episcopalian. Avocations: travel, the arts, historic preservation. Home and Office: 4746 River Rd Colusa CA 95932-4200

CARTER, JEAN GORDON, lawyer; b. Fort Belvoir, Va., July 30, 1955; d. Thomas Laney and Cleone (Hunter) Gordon; m. Michael L. Carter, Sept. 17, 1977; children: Christina Jean, William Gordon. BS in Accountancy magna cum laude with honors, Wake Forest U., 1977; JD with high honors, Duke U., 1983. Bar: N.C. 1983; CPA; bd. cert. specialist in estates. Acct. Arthur Andersen & Co., Charlotte, NC, 1977-80; atty. Moore & Van Allen, Raleigh, NC, 1983-90; ptnr. Hunton & Williams, Raleigh, NC, 1990—. Mem. Am. Coll. Trusts and Estates Coun., N.C. Bar Assn., Wake County Estate Coun. (pres. 1991-92), Order of Coif, Phi Beta Kappa. Democrat. Presbyterian. Avocation: reading. Home: 3913 Stratford Ct Raleigh NC 27609-6351 Office: Hunton & Williams One Bank of America Plz Raleigh NC 27601-2947 Home Phone: 919-510-0112; Office Phone: 919-899-3088. Business E-Mail: jcarter@hunton.com.

CARTER, JEANIE, performing company executive; b. Decatur, Ill., May 16, 1950; children: James L. Cook, Abigail G. Cook, Sarah E. Mason;. B in music, Millikin U., 1972. Cons. Hewitt Assoc., Lincolnshire, Ill., 1989—2000; vocal instr. Willow Creek Arts Ctr., South Barrington, Ill., 2002—03; pres., artistic dir. Bel Canto Studios, Barrington, Ill., 2001—. Voice lessons Clare Kittner, Northbrook, Ill., 1972—85, Willow Creek Arts Ctr., South Barrington, 2002—03; mem. Willow Creek, McHenry County vocal team, 2005. Composer: Footprints, 2002. Soprano soloist 1st Presbyn. Ch., Libertyville, Ill., 1972—92; vocal ministry Willow Creek Cmty. Ch., South Barrington, 2002—03. Mem.: Nat. Assn. Tchr.'s Singing, Music Tchr.'s Nat. Assn. Office: 217 Park Ave Barrington IL 60010 Office Phone: 847-382-2560, 847-682-9601. Business E-Mail: jeaniecarter@belcantostudios.com.

CARTER, JEANNE WILMOT, lawyer, publishing executive; b. Iowa City, Iowa, Oct. 25, 1950; d. John Robert and Adelaide Wilmot (Briggs) Carter; m. Daniel Halpern, Dec. 31, 1982; 1 child, Lily Wilmot. BA cum laude, Barnard Coll., NYC, 1973; MFA, Columbia U., 1977; JD, Yeshiva U., NYC, 1982. Bar: N.Y. 1987. Assoc. Raoul Lionel Felder, P.C., NYC, 1986—; pres., co-owner, dir. Ecco Press, Hopewell, NJ, 1992—. Panelist trade secret law and alternate dispute resolution India project George Washington Law Sch., Mumbia, Bangalore and Goa, 2007. Author: Dirt Angel, 1997, Tales from the Rain Forest, 1997; editor: On Music, 1994; contbr. articles to profl. jours. and books including Reading the Fights, N.Am. Rev., O'Henry Prize Stories 1986, Antaeus, Antioch Rev., Arts and Entertainment Law Jour., Ont. Rev., Denver Quar., Jour. Blacks in Higher Edn., others. Bd. dirs. Nat. Poetry Series, 1981—, AIDS Helping Hand, N.Y.C., 1987-95, Planned Parenthood of Mercer County, 1998—; vol. litigator Womanspace, Princeton, N.J., 1994; mem. Jr. League of N.Y.C., 1980-91; chmn. Princeton Alcohol and Drug Alliance, 2000—; pres. bd. Corner House Found., 2004—. N.Y. Found. of the Arts fellow, 1989. Mem. ABA, N.Y. State Bar Assn.

CARTER, JEFFREY RICHARD, music educator; b. New Orleans, July 17, 1961; s. Vincent Richard Carter and F. Marie Blocher; 1 child, AJ. MA, U. Ctrl. Mo., Warrensburg, 1996; D in Musical Arts, U. Kans., Lawrence, 2000. Owner Carter Studios, Blue Springs, Mo., 1989—99; musical dir. The Jacomo Chorale, Blue Springs, Mo., 1990—99; asst. prof. music Ky. Wesleyan Coll., Owensboro, Ky., 1999—2000; assoc. prof. music performance; dir. u. singers Ball State U., Muncie, Ind., 2000—, coord. undergrad. programs in music, 2004—06, assoc. dir. Sch. Music, 2006—. Youth and student activities chmn. Am. Choral Dirs. Assn. (Nat.), Okla. City, 2005—. Composer: (choral composition) Phos Hilaron (Opus Award (Mo. Choral Dirs. Assn.), 1999), The Oxen; contbr. articles pub. to profl. jour. Choirmaster Grace Episcopal Ch., Muncie, Ind., 2002—05; dir. music First Presbyn. Ch., Lawrence, Kans., 1997—99. Named Student Orgn. Outstanding Leader, Ball State U., 2005; grantee Enriching the Four-Year Choral Experience, Lilly Found./Ball State U., 2003-2005. Mem.: Elgar Soc., Music Educators Nat. Conf., Am. Choral Dir. Assn. (divisional bd. mem. 2004—05, Nat. Student Chpt. of Yr. 2005), Herbert Howells Soc., Pi Kappa Lambda, Phi Mu Alpha Sinfonia (hon.). Episcopalian. Home Phone: 765-760-3812. E-mail: jrc@jeffreycarter.us.

CARTER, JEROME N., human resources specialist, paper company executive; With Union Camp Internat. Paper Co., Stamford, Conn., 1980—81, plant indsl. rels. mgr. to asst. divsn. mgr. indsl. and pub. rels., 1981—87, dir. indsl. rels., 1987—97, sr. v.p. human resources, 1999—. Spkr. in field. Office: Internat Paper Co 400 Atlantic St Stamford CT 06921 Office Phone: 203-541-8000.

CARTER, JIMMY (JAMES EARL CARTER JR.), 39th President of the United States; b. Plains, Ga., Oct. 1, 1924; s. James Earl and Lillian (Gordy) C.; m. Rosalynn Smith, July 7, 1946; children: John William, James Earl III, Donnel Jeffrey, Amy Lynn. Student, Ga. Southwestern Coll., 1941-42, Ga. Inst. Tech., 1942-43; BS, U.S. Naval Acad., 1946 (class of 1947); postgrad., Union Coll., 1952-53; LLD (hon.), Morris Brown Coll., 1972, Morehouse Coll., 1972, U. Notre Dame, 1977, Emory U., 1979, Kwansei Gakuin U., Japan, 1981, Ga. Southwestern Coll., 1981, N.Y. Law Sch., 1985, Bates Coll., 1985, Centre Coll., 1987, Creighton U., 1987; DEng (hon.), Ga. Inst. Tech., 1979; PhD (hon.), Weizmann Inst. Sci., 1980, Tel Aviv U., 1983, Haifa U., 1987; DHL (hon.), Cen. Conn. State U., 1985. Farmer, warehouseman, Plains, Ga., 1953-77; mem. Ga. Senate, 1963-67; gov. State of Ga., Atlanta, 1971-75; President of United States, 1977-81; disting. prof. Emory U., Atlanta, 1982—. Leader internat. observer teams Panama, 1989, Nicaragua, 1990, Dominican Republic, 1990, Haiti, 1990, Guyana, 1992, Venezuela, 1998, Nigeria, 1999, Indonesia and East Timor, 1999, Mexico, 2000, China, 2001, Jamaica, 2002, Guatemala, 2003; host peace negotiations Ethiopia, 1989; conflict mediator North Korea, Liberia, Haiti, Bosnia, Sudan, 1994, Sudan, Uganda, 1999, Venezuela, 2002-2003 Author: Why Not the Best?, 1975, A Government as Good as Its People, 1977, Keeping Faith/Memoirs of a President, 1982, Negotiation: The Alternative to Hostility, 1984, The Blood of Abraham, 1985, An Outdoor Journal, 1988, Turning Point: A Candidate, A State, and a Nation Come of Age, 1992, Talking Peace: A Vision for the Next Generation, 1993, Always a Reckoning, 1995, Living Faith, 1996, Sources of Strength: Meditations on Scripture for a Living Faith, 1997, The Virtues of Aging, 1998, An Hour Before Daylight: Memoirs of Rural Boyhood, 2001, Christmas in Plains: Memories, 2001, The Hornet's Nest: A Novel of the Revolutionary War, 2003, Sharing Good Times, 2004, Our Endangered Values: America's Moral Crisis, 2005 (No. 1 on Publishers Weekly hardcover bestseller list, Grammy award for Best Spoken Word Album, 2007), Palestine: Peace Not Apartheid, 2006; co-author: with Rosalynn Carter) Everything to Gain: Making the Most of the Rest of Your Life, 1987 Mem. Sumter County (Ga.) Sch. Bd., 1955-62, chmn., 1960-62; mem. Americus and Sumter County Hosp. Authority, 1956-70; mem. Sumter County (Ga.) Library Bd., 1961; chmn. congl. campaign com. Dem. Nat. Com., 1974; founder Carter Ctr. Emory U., 1982; bd. dirs. Habitat for Humanity, 1984-87; chmn. bd. trustees Carter Ctr., Inc., 1986—, Carter-Menil Human Rights Found., 1986—, Global 2000 Inc., 1986—; chmn. Coun. of Freely-Elected Heads of Govt., 1986—; chmn. Coun. Internat. Negotiation Network, 1991—. Served to lt. USN, 1946-53. Recipient Gold medal Internat. Inst. Human Rights, 1979, Internat. Mediation medal Am. Arbitration Assn., 1979, Martin Luther King Jr. Nonviolent Peace prize, 1979, Internat. Human Rights award Synagogue Coun. Am., 1979, Conservationist of Yr. award, 1979, Harry S. Truman Pub. Svc. award, 1981, Ansel Adams Conservation award Wilderness Soc., 1982, Disting. Svc. award So. Bapt. Conv., 1982, Human Rights award Internat. League for Human Rights, 1983, World Meth. Peace award, 1985, Albert Schweitzer prize for Humanitarianism, 1987, Edwin C. Whitehead award Nat. Ctr. for Health Edn., 1989, Jefferson award Am. Inst. Pub. Svc., 1990, Phila. Liberty medal, 1990, Spirit of Am. award Nat. Coun. for Social Studies, 1990, Physicians for Social Responsibility award, 1991, Aristotle prize Alexander S. Onassis Found., 1991, Félix Houphouet-Boigny Peace prize UNESCO, 1995, Nobel Peace prize, 2002. Democrat. Office: Carter Ctr 1 Copenhill 453 Freedom Pkwy NE Atlanta GA 30307-1406*

CARTER, JOHN CHARLTON See HESTON, CHARLTON

CARTER, JOHN D., recycling company executive; Ptnr. law firm, San Francisco; various sr. mgmt. positions including exec. v.p., dir. and pres. Bechtel Enterprises, Inc. Bechtel Group, Inc., 1982—2002; cons., 2002—05; pres., CEO Schnitzer Steel Industries, Inc., 2005—. Dir. NW Natural Gas Co., FLIR Systems, Inc.; chmn. bd. Kuni Automotive. Office: Schnitzer Steel Industries Inc PO Box 10047 Portland OR 97296-0047 Office Phone: 503-224-9900.*

CARTER, JOHN DALE, organizational development coordinator; b. Tuskegee, Ala., Apr. 9, 1944; s. Arthur L. and Ann (Bargyh) C.; m. Veronica Louise Helen Hopper, Oct. 12, 1986; children: Annelise Grace, Hopper Carter. AB, Ind. U., 1965, MS, 1967; PhD (NDEA fellow), Case Western Res. U., 1974. Dir. student affairs Dental Sch. Case Western Res. U., Cleve., 1974-75, asst. prof. applied behavioral sci., 1974-90, asst. dean orgn. devel. and student affairs, 1975-78; pres. John D. Carter and Assocs., Inc., Cleve., 1969—; former ptnr. Portsmouth Cons. Group, 1984. Chmn. bd. Gestalt Inst. Cleve., 1974-80, chmn. orgn. and systems devel. program, 1980—, program dir., fin. dir. 1981-86, dir. corp. svcs., 1989-95, dean of faculty, 1992-96; pres. Orgn. and Systems Devel. Ctr., 1996—; mem. exec. bd. Nat. Tng. Labs., 1975-78; faculty Am. U., 1980-90, 94-96; mem. Nat. Tng. Labs., 1976—; bd. dirs. Behavioral Sci. Found., Cleve., Orgn. Devel. Network, 1999—; exec. bd. Fielding Inst., 1987-89; preceptor Shri Ram Chandra Mission, Sahag Marg Meditation, 1993—; Gestalt Inst. Cleve., 1996—; bd. mem. ODN Orgn. Devel. Network, 1999—. Author: Counselling the Helping Relationship, 1975, Managing the Merger Integration Process, 1986, Institutionalizing Change, 1995. Hon. fellow Gestalt Inst. Cleve., 1999. Fellow Gestalt Inst. of Cleve. (hon.); mem. Internat. Assn. Applied Social Scientists (cert. cons. Internat.), Kappa Alpha Psi (pres. Alpha chpt. 1964-65), Alpha Phi Omega. Home and Office: 2232 Harcourt Dr Cleveland OH 44106-4622

CARTER, JOHN FRANCIS, II, lawyer; b. Washington, Dec. 21, 1939; s. John F. and Majorie (Thomas) C.; children: J. F. III, Marion; m. Catherine Dulany Turner, 2000. AB, Princeton U., 1963; JD, U. Tex., 1970. Bar: Tex. 1970, US Supreme Ct. 1977. Analyst Rotan Mosle, Houston, 1967-68; ptnr. Hutcheson & Grundy, Houston, 1970-90, mng. ptnr., 1990-94; sr. counsel Akin, Gump, Strauss, Hauer & Feld, Houston, 1996-98; atty. pvt. practice, Houston, 1998—. Mem. State Bar Grievance Commn., Houston, 1976-79; internat. sr. advisor to dep. sec. U.S. Dept. Energy, 1994-96. Co-author: Incorporation in Texas, 1980. Chmn. Tex. Arts Alliance, 1981-82, Mcpl. Art Commn., Houston, 1988-90; pres. Arts Coun., Houston, 1983-84; chmn., sec. Harris County Dem. Party, Tex., 1988-90; mem. host com. Econ. Summit, Houston, 1989-90; chair Planned Parenthood of Southeastern Va., 2005—; bd. dirs. Va. Coll. Bldg. Authority, 2005—; Capt. Spl. Forces, US Army, 1963-67, Panama, Vietnam. Named a Tex. Super Lawyer, 2003—05; named one of Best Lawyers in Am., 1996—; recipient Cert. Outstanding Svc. award, US Dept. State, 1996. Mem. ABA (com. chair 1987-94), Houston Club, Tejas Breakfast Club, Univ. Cottage Club, Princeton Club NY, Princeton Club Hampton Roads (pres.), Phi Delta Phi. Avocations: music, ballet, history. Office: The Carter Law Office 3417 Milam St Houston TX 77002-9531 Office Phone: 713-724-5440, 757-963-2195. Personal E-mail: jackcarter@aol.com.

CARTER, JOHN LOYD, lawyer; b. Clayton, N.Mex., Oct. 2, 1948; s. John Allen and Ruth (Laughlin) C.; m. Dorel Susan Payne, Sept. 20, 1975; children: Matthew, Caroline, Susan. BA, So. Meth. U., 1970, JD cum laude, 1973. Bar: Tex. 1973, U.S. Ct. Appeals (5th and 11th cirs.) 1975, U.S. Ct. Appeals (D.C. cir.) 2004, U.S. Supreme Ct. 1976, U.S. Dist. Ct. (so. dist.) Tex. 1974, U.S. Dist. Ct. (no. dist.) Tex. 1978, U.S. Dist. Ct. (ea. dist.) Tex. 1985, U.S. Dist. Ct. (we. dist.) Tex. 1999. Assoc. Vinson & Elkins, Houston, 1973-80, ptnr., 1980—. Editor-in-chief: Southwestern Law Jour., 1972—73. Fellow Am. Coll. Trial Lawyers, Am. Bar Found., Tex. Bar Found., Houston Bar Found., Order of the Coif, Barristers. Office: Vinson & Elkins 2500 First City Tower Houston TX 77002-6760 Home Phone: 713-627-1410; Office Phone: 713-758-2124. Business E-Mail: jcarter@velaw.com.

CARTER, JOHN RICE, congressman, lawyer; b. Houston, Nov. 6, 1941; s. John James and Elizabeth (Rice) Carter; m. Erika Theodora Van Bruegel, June 15, 1968; children: Gilianne, John, Theodore, Danielle. BA in Hist., Tex. Tech U., 1965; JD, U. Tex. Sch. of Law, 1969. Bar: Tex. 1969. Counsel Tex. Legis. Coun., Austin, 1969—72; lawyer pvt. practice, Round Rock, Tex., 1973—81; mcpl. judge Round Rock, Tex., 1978—80; judge Williamson County 277th Dist. Ct., Georgetown, 1981—82, dist. judge, 1982—2002; mem. US Congress from 31st Tex. dist., 2003—, mem. appropriations com. Chmn. planning com., Round Rock, Tex., 1975—78. Mem.: Williamson County Bar Assn. (pres. 1976), Round Rock Jaycees (pres. 1975, Jaycee of Yr. 1975). Republican. Office: US Ho Reps 408 Cannon Ho Office Bldg Washington DC 20515 Office Phone: 202-225-3864.*

CARTER, JOHN ROBERT, retired physician; b. Buffalo, Apr. 21, 1917; s. John Harvey and Gertrude Ann (Buckpitt) C.; m. Adelaide Briggs, May 8, 1943; children— Marilyn Anne, Jeanne Catherine. BS, Hamilton Coll., 1939; MD, U. Rochester, 1943. Diplomate: Nat. Bd. Med. Examiners. Intern State U. Iowa, 1943-44, resident, 1944-48, asst. dept. pathology, 1944, from instr. to asso. prof., 1944-55, prof., 1955-59; prof., chmn. dept. pathology and oncology U. Kans. Med. Center, 1960-66; prof. pathology dept. orthopedics Case Western Res. U., Cleve., 1981—2001, dir. Inst. Pathology, chmn. dept. pathology, 1966-81; prof. emeritus, 1987—; ret., 1995. Cons. VA Hosp., U.S. Army Hosp., U.S. Penitentiary, Watkins Meml. Hosp.; Past chmn. pathology study sect. NIH; mem. pathology tng. grant com. Nat. Inst. Gen. Med. Scis.; mem. pathology adv. council Central VA Office; mem. sci. adv. bd. Armed Forces Inst. Pathology.; Bd. dirs. Univs. Asso. Research and Edn. Pathology; past pres. Mem. editorial bd.: Am. Jour. Pathology. Served to lt. USNR, 1946-48. Mem. AMA, AAAS, Cleve. Acad. Medicine, Path. Soc. Gt. Britain and Ireland, Am. Assn. Pathologists and Bacteriologists (past pres.), Internat. Acad. Pathology, Am. Soc. Clin. Pathology, Am. Soc. Exptl. Pathology, Am. Soc. Investigative Pathology, Coll. Am. Pathologists, Soc. Exptl. Biology, AAUP, Central Soc. Clin. Research, Phi Beta Kappa, Sigma Xi, Alpha Omega Alpha. Home: 36570 Ridge Rd Willoughby OH 44094-4106 Personal E-mail: jrcarter51@hotmail.com.

CARTER, KAREN ZEPP, music educator, elementary school educator; b. Medford, Mass., Sept. 12, 1957; d. Ira Gilbert and Mary Dodd Zepp; 1 child, Rachael Elizabeth. MusB in Edn., Shenandoah Conservatory of Music, Winchester, Va., 1979; MusM, U. of Md., College Park, 1982. Tchg. Md. State Dept. Edn. Tchr.'s aide Montessori Sch., Westminster, Md., 1994—96; substitute tchr. Carroll County Pub. Schs., Wesminster, Md., 1996—98, tchr. instrumental music Westminster, Md., 1998—2003, Bryant Woods Elem. Sch., Columbia, Md., 2003—. Chairperson cultural arts com. LFES, Columbia, 2000—01; sch. rep. Howard County Parents for Sch. Music, Columbia, 2000—02; adjudicator Md. State Band, Balt., 2004—, Howard County Elem. Band, Columbia, 2004—, Balt. County Solo and Ensemble Festival, Balt., 2006—. Musician: Chamber Music on the Hill Concert Series, Carroll County Concert Band Sousa Series, McDaniel College Flute Choir. Recipient Homer Ulrich award, U. of Md., 1982, Music Educator of the Yr. nomination2006, Howard County Parents for Sch. Music, 2006, Outstanding Tchr. nomination, Carroll County Chamber of Commerce, 2003. Mem.: NEA, Music Educators Nat. Conf. Democrat. Methodist. Avocations: reading, performing, entertainment news. Office: Bryant Woods Elem Sch 5450 Blue Heron Ln Columbia MD 21044 Home: 5632 Vantage Point Rd Columbia MD 21044 Home Phone: 410-997-9544; Office Phone: 410-313-6859. Office Fax: 410-313-6864. Personal E-mail: k12rdygo@comcast.net. Business E-Mail: sean_martin@hcpss.org.

CARTER, KATHRYN GIBSON, education educator, consultant; b. Mullins, SC, Sept. 20, 1950; d. Mathew Brunson and Viola Faile Gibson; m. Harry Carlisle Carter, Apr. 4, 1982. Student, Winthrop U., 1968—70; BA, U. SC, 1972, MEd, 1976, MEd, 1978, EdD, 1995. Cert. tchr./prin. S.C., 1972. Tchr. Lexington Dist. Four, Swansea, SC, 1972—77; cmty. sch. dir. Florence (SC) Sch. Dist. One, 1977—78; coord. Richland Sch. Dist. One, Hopkins, 1978—92; cmty. edn. coord. SC. Dept. Edn., Columbia, 1992—98; exec. dir. S.C. Commn. Nat. & Cmty. Svc., Columbia, 1998—2005; CEO Carter's Leasing and Cons., LLC, Columbia, 2005—. Adj. faculty U. S.C., Columbia, 1999—2002. Editor: (spl. issue on svc. learning) Nat. Cmty. Edn. Jour.; author: (book) Hooking Out of School Youth Through Service Learning; co-author: Powerful Allies: Afterschool Programs, Service Learning and Community Education; dir.: (30 minute video for TV) Serving to Learn. Bd. mem. Nat. Cmty. Edn., Alexandria, Va., 1986—89, Family Shelter, Columbia, SC, 1992—96; mem. /bd. mem. Leadership Columbia Alumni Assn., 1989—2005; bd. mem. Capital Sr. Ctr., 2005—. Recipient Palmetto Pride award, Palmetto Project, 1995, Frank Manley Lectr., Nat. Cmty. Edn. Assn., 1997, Lamplighter award, Youth Svc. Charleston, 1997, Disting. Svc./Lifetime Membership award, S.C. Assn. Cmty. Edn., 1998, Disting. Alumni award, U. SC Coll. Edn., 2005;, Delta Kappa Gamma Internat. scholar, 1995, Paul Harris fellow, Rotary Internat., 1997, Internat. Cmty. Edn. Conf. Nairobi, Kenya scholarship, Pendell Pub. Co., 1987. Mem.: AAUW (bd. dirs. 2006), USC Alumni Soc. (bd. mem. 2006), Low County Women in Philanthropy, Delta Kappa Gamma (past pres. 1990—92, Alpha Delta chpt.), Phi Delta Kappa (past bd. mem. 1998—99). Baptist And Presbyterian. Achievements include development of. Avocations: reading, travel, golf, college football, politics. Office: Carters Leasing and Cons LLC 412 Vets Rd Ste K Columbia SC 29209 Office Phone: 803-776-7161. Personal E-mail: kathycarter@earthlink.net.

CARTER, KATHY DEONNE, language educator; d. Virginia Lee Tingley; m. Terry Grant Carter, Sept. 23, 1972; 1 child, Tilly Rae Gambill. BA, Howard Payne U., Brownwood, Tex., 1970—74; MEd, Henderson State U., Arkadelphia, Ark., 1992—94; MA in ESL, U. Ark., Little Rock, 1996—97. Cert. ESL tchr. Ark. Dept. Edn., 1998. Social worker Dept. Human Resources, Ft. Worth, 1974—80; ednl. cons. European Bapt. Conv., Wiesbaden, Hessen, Germany, 1984—91; instr. Ouachita Bapt. U., Arkadelphia, 1993—2003; ESL instr. Arkadelphia Pub. Schs., 1995—; instr. Yan Tai U., China, 2001—04. Vol., coord. Meals on Wheels; vol. ESL adults; vol. Human Soc.; mem. Vol. Coun. Arkadelphia, 2003—06. Mem.: TESOL (life; state office 2003—04), Delta Kappa Gamma (life; pres. local chpt. 2000—06, pres. 2003—06), Rotary Internat. (cmty. chair 2004—06). Home Phone: 870-246-3011.

CARTER, KENNETH CHARLES, geneticist; b. Flagstaff, Ariz., Nov. 28, 1959; s. James Frank and Norma (Barker) C. AA, AS, York Coll., 1980; BS in Biology, Abilene Christian U., 1983; PhD in Genetics, U. Tex. Med. Br., 1989. Grad. asst. U. Tex. Med. Br., Galveston, 1984-89; postdoctoral fellow U. Mass. Med. Sch., Worcester, 1989-93; scientist Human Genome Scis., Inc., Rockville, Md., 1993-98; pres. Internat. Genetics Assocs., Inc., Rockville, Md., 1998-99; CEO, pres. Avalon Pharms., Inc., Rockville, Md., 1999—. Contbr. articles to profl. jours. Recipient award for outstanding rsch. on aging Rose and Harry Walk Found., 1989, Muscular Dystrophy Assn., 1990, award for outstanding alumnus U. Tex. Med. Br., 1999; Kempner fellow J. B. Kempner Found., 1989, Human Genome fellow NIH, 1991. Mem. Am. Soc. for Cell Biology, AAAS, Microscopy Assn. Am., Thursday Group.

CARTER, LONNIE TYRONE, playwright, educator; b. Chgo., Oct. 25, 1942; s. Harold Walter and Evelyn Victoria Carter; children: Eve La Roche, Calpurnia Ann. BA, MA, Marquette, Milw.; MFA, Yale, New Haven, Conn., 1969. Tchr. NYU, NYC, 1979—. Author: (play) The Sovereign State of Boogedy Boogedy, The Romance of Magno Rubio (Obie award, 2003), Wheatley (Joseph Jefferson Nomination Best New Play, 2006). Bd. mem. Matha Boschen Fund Artists, Sharon, Conn.; bd. dirs. Falls Village Children's Theater, Conn. Grantee, Nat. Endowment Arts, 1975, 1985; John Simon Guggenheim Playwriting fellow, 1971. Mem.: Yale Club NYC (life). Democrat. Avocations: tennis, jazz enthusiast and collector, book collector. Office: NYU 721 Broadway New York NY 10003 Home Phone: 860-824-8011; Office Phone: 212-998-1940. Business E-Mail: lc25@nyu.edu.

CARTER, MAJORA J., urban planner; b. Bronx, NY, Oct. 27, 1966; BA, Wesleyan U., 1988; MFA, NYU, 1997. Project dir. The Point Cmty. Develop. Corp., 1997—98, assoc. dir. cmty. develop., 1998—2001; founder and exec. dir. Sustainable South Bronx (SSB), NY, 2001—. Open Soc. Inst. Cmty. Fellow, 2002, Drum Major Inst. Fellow, 2005, MacArthur Fellow, John D. and Catherine T. MacArthur Found., 2005. Office: Sustainable South Bronx 890 Garrison Ave 4th Floor Bronx NY 10474*

CARTER, MARGARET L., legislator; b. La., Dec. 29, 1935; d. Emma Carter; 9 children. BA, Portland State U., 1972; MEd, Oreg. State U., 1973; postgrad., Washington State U. Community organizer, asst. dir. Community Action Agy., Shreveport, La.; tchr. Albina Youth Opportunity Sch., Portland; counselor Portland Community Coll.; mem. Oreg. Ho. of Reps., Salem, 1984-98, Oreg. Senate from 22nd dist., Salem, 2001—. Mem. Joint Com. on Ways & Means, 2003, Spl. Senate Com. on Budget, 2003, Spl. Senate Com. on Oreg. Health Plan, 2003, Ways & Means Subcom. on Transp. & Econ. Devel., 2003; co-chair Human Resources com., 1985, vice chair, 87, Edn. com., 1985, 87, 89, Conf. com. on Dr. Martin Luther King State Holiday, co-chair, 1985, Joint Health Care com. 1986. Founder, mus. dir. Joyful Sound Singers Piedmont Ch. Christ; vol. counselor various juvenile detention ctrs. and women's prisons, voter registration drives in Portland's black neighborhoods, Project Pride; organizer Oreg. chpt. of Sickle Cell Anemia Found.; founder Oreg. Black Leadership Conf.; mem. Oreg. State Commn. on Post Secondary Edn. and the Oreg. Alliance for Black Sch. Educators, Spl. Commn. for the Parole Bd. on the Matrix System; mem. Gov.'s Task Force on Pregnancy and Substance Abuse, 1989—, Coun. on Alcohol and Drugs, 1989—, bd. dirs. ARC, Emanuel Med. Ctr. Found. Recipient Jeanette Rankin Award Oreg. Women's Polit. Caucus, 1985. Mem. Nat. Organ. Black Legis. Elected Women (v.p. 1985), Nat. Black Caucus (exec. com.), Blacks in Gov. (regional pres.), Alpha Kappa Alpha. Democrat. Home: 2948 NE 10th Ave Portland OR 97212-3240 Office: Oreg State Senate State Capitol S310 Salem OR 97301

CARTER, MARSHALL NICHOLS, stock exchange executive; b. Newport News, Va., Apr. 23, 1940; s. Marshall Sylvester and Préot (Nichols) C.; m. Mary Meehan, June 20, 1964; children: Christina Ann, Marshall William. BSCE, U.S. Mil. Acad., 1962; MS in Ops. Rsch., Systems Analysis, USN Postgrad. Sch., 1970; MA in Internat. Affairs, George Washington U., 1976. Commd. 2d lt. USMC, 1962, advanced through grades to maj., 1975; served in Vietnam, 1966-67, 70-71; ret., 1976; White House fellow US Dept. State, Washington, 1975-76; v.p. internat. dept. Chase Manhattan Bank, NYC, 1976-78; dir. budgeting Chase Manhattan Corp., NYC, 1978-81; product and prodn. risk mgmt. exec., div. exec. internat. trade procucts Chase Manhattan Bank, NYC, 1981-84, sr. v.p. global securities svcs., 1988-91; exec. v.p. banking, sales and svcs. Chase Lincoln First Bank, Rochester, NY, 1985-88; pres., COO State St. Bank & Trust Co., Boston, 1991, CEO, 1992—2000, chmn., 1993—2001; fellow, Ctr. for Pub. Leadership Harvard U., 2001—05; chmn. NY Stock Exch., NYC, 2005—06, NYSE Group, Inc., NYC, 2006—. Chmn. bd. trustees, Boston Med. Ctr.; bd. dirs. NY Stock Exch., 2003-06, Am. Bankers Assn., CEDEL, Euroclear & Nat. Securities Clearing Corp.; mem. exec. com. Livraison Valeurs Mobilieres, Luxembourg; co-chair, Working Group Group of Thirty, London, 1988-95; mem. Sinai peacekeeping surveillance del. Dept. State, 1975, mem. internat. relief efforts, Guatemala, Italy, Mali., 1975; chair, Mass. Gov.'s Spl. Advisory Task Force on Massport folowing the events of Sept. 11, 2001 Sr. coord. Tri-State United Way, N.Y.C., 1989. Col. USMCR, 1985. Decorated Navy Cross, Bronze Star, Purple Heart. Mem. Internat. Soc. Securities Adminstrs.; fellow Am. Acad. Arts and Sciences, 2006 Republican. Roman Catholic. Avocations: flying, tennis, skiing. Office: NYSE Group Inc c/o Corp Sec 11 Wall St New York NY 10005

CARTER, MARY ANDREWS, paralegal; b. Greenville, SC, Sept. 27, 1958; d. Harold M. Andrews and Mary Nancy Dollar; m. Donald P. Carter, Aug. 1, 1982 (div. Sept. 27, 1986); children: Christina Marie, Jason Paul. Diploma in paralegal, Greenville Tech., 1988. Paralegal Alan. O Campbell, P.E., Inc., Sullivan's Island, SC, 1995—99; pvt. practice, 1999—2001; paralegal Campbell, Schneider & Assocs., John's Island, SC, 2001—. Mem. adv. coun. Clark Acad., Charleston, 1998—2000; guardian ad litem State of S.C., Charleston, 1999—. Office: Campbell Schneider and Assocs 3690 Bohicket Rd Ste 1D Johns Island SC 29455

CARTER, MELVA JEAN, retired medical technician; b. Pitts., Aug. 24, 1942; d. William Skinner and Gladys Gaines; m. Samuel Edward Carter, June 15, 1965; 1 child, Daphne Denise. Bus. cert., Detroit Inst. Comms., 1962; AS, Wayne County C.C., 1979; postgrad., Wayne State U., 1982. Cert. med. lab. technician bd. eligible. Teletype oper. N.Y. Telephone Co., NYC, 1963—65; credit cons. Creditors Svc., Detroit, 1965—68; med. lab. technician Profl. Labs., Detroit, 1977—80; exec. office mgr. ARC, Detroit, 1969—77, med. lab. technician II, 1980—2004. Taught first aid various pub. schs.; pvt. tchr. music and voice. Observer search and rescue CAP-Aux. USAF, Selfridge AFB, Mich.; vol. neighborhood watch Mayor's Anti-Arson Com., Detroit, 2001—; neighborhood canvasser Dept. Elections, Detroit, citywide insp., 2006; manned several first aid stas.; poll challenger Mich. Dept. Elections, Detroit, 1983; dir. bibl. plays at various chs. Recipient Name placed on Wall of Tolerance, Montgomery, Ala., Spirit of Detroit award, City Coun. Detroit, 1989, Comty. Svc. cert., Mayor's Com., 2004, Cert. Recognition, House of Miracles, 2004. Mem.: So. Poverty Law Ctr., Murray Hill Block Club (block patrol 2000—). Democrat. Pentacostal. Avocations: bowling, drawing, music, reading, coin collecting/numismatics.

CARTER, MICHAEL ALLEN, nursing educator; b. Springfield, Mo., Feb. 13, 1947; s. William Franklin and Mary Alyne Kelly; m. Sarah Ann Jennings, July 4, 1969; 1 child, Elizabeth Ruth. BS in Nursing, U. Ark., 1969, MS in Nursing, 1973; D of Nursing Sci., Boston U., 1979. Cert. family nurse practitioner. Instr. U. Ark., Little Rock, 1972-73; nurse practitioner VA Hosp., Bedford, Mass., 1974-75; asst. prof. Boston U., 1975-76, U. Colo., Denver, 1976-79, assoc. prof., 1979-82; prof., coll. dean U. Tenn., Memphis, 1982-2000, univ. disting. prof., 2000—. 1st lt. Nurse Corps, U.S. Army, 1969-71. Named Vol. of Yr. Salvation Army, Denver, 1978; recipient Better Life award Tenn. Health Care Assn., 1988. Fellow Am. Acad. Nursing; mem. Nat. Acads. Practice (Disting. practitioner). Home: 369 Belmont Acres Cir Tumbling Shoals AR 72581 Office: U Tenn Coll Nursing 877 Madison Ave Memphis TN 38103-3408 Home Phone: 501-362-0763; Office Phone: 901-448-6128. Business E-Mail: mcarter@utmem.edu.

CARTER, MIKELE STANDER, lawyer; b. NYC, Aug. 31, 1933; d. Lionel and Lucy Dietz Stander; m. Adam Paul Carter, Nov. 9, 1969; children: Peter Christopher Aydelotte, Cindy Jo Collins. BA, Hunter Coll., NYC, 1960; JD, U. Miami, Coral Gables, Fla., 1973. Bar: Fla. 1973, Ga. 1983. Policewoman, sgt. police Miami Police Dept., 1961—83; asst. city atty. City Miami Law Dept., 1971—83; atty. civil svc. bd. City Hollywood, 1983—84; sole practitioner Blairsville, Ga., 1985—99; pro bono atty. Brevard County Legal Aid, Rockledge, Fla., 1999—. Docent Union County Hist. Soc., Blairsville, Ga., 1989—92; vol. Union County Animal Control, Blairsville, 2002—04. Named Outstanding Assistant City Atty. US, Nat. Inst. Mcpl. Law Officers, 1983; scholar, Law Enforcement Assistance Adminstrn., 1970—73. Mem.: Ga. Bar Assn. (assoc.), Fla. Bar Assn. (assoc. Pres.'s Pro Bono award 2000). Avocations: travel, bridge, reading, crossword puzzles. Home: 129 Treetop Dr Melbourne Beach FL 32951 Office Phone: 321-722-3875.

CARTER, NANETTE CAROLYN, artist; b. Columbus, Ohio, Jan. 30, 1954; d. Matthew Gameliel and Frances (Hill) C. BA, Oberlin Coll., 1976; MFA, Pratt Inst. of Art, 1978. Tchr. art Dwight Englewood Prep Sch., Englewood, NJ, 1978-87; profl. artist, 1987-92, CCNY, 1992-93; vis. lectr. Pratt Inst. of Art, Bklyn., 2001—. Artist-in-residence Triangle Workshop, Pine Plains, NYC, 1991. One-woman shows include Ericson Gallery, NYC, 1983, G.R. N'Namdi Gallery, Detroit, 1984, 86, 92-2002, Birmingham, Mich., 1989, 92, 96, 99, Chgo., 1999-2002, Cinque Gallery, NYC, 1985, Montclair (NJ) Art Mus., 1988, Jersey City (NJ) Mus., 1990, June Kelly Gallery, NYC, 1990, 94, 97, 2000, 04, Southampton (NY) Coll., 1991, Franklin Marshall Coll., Lancaster, Pa., 1992, Kebede Fine Arts, LA, 1992, Sande Webster Gallery, Phila., 1993, 95, 97, 99, 2001, 03, Alitash Kebete, LA, 1995, Hodges-Taylor Gallery, Charlotte, NC, 1997, Noel Gallery, Charlotte, N.C., 2004; exhibited in group shows at Bklyn. Mus., 1981, Newark Mus., 1985, Pa. Acad. Fine Arts, Phila., 1986, Clocktower Gallery, NYC, 1986, Associated Am. Artists Gallery, NYC, 1986, Wennigger Gallery Boston, 1987, Kenkelaba Gallery, NYC, 1987, Fashion Moda Gallery, Bronx, NY, 1988, Studio Mus. in Harlem, NY, 1988, Louisa McIntosh Gallery, Atlanta, 1990, Sande Webster Gallery, 1990, East Hampton Ctr. for Contemporary Art, NY, 1990, Space Gallery, Cleve., 1991, Mary Ryan Gallery, NYC, 1991, New Visions Gallery, Ithaca, NY, 1991, Bennington (Vt.) Coll., 1991, The Rifle Gallery, Columbus, Ohio, 1991, Bristol-Myers Squibb Co., Princeton, NJ, 1992, The Nat. Mus. of Woman in the Arts, Washington, 1992, The Paine Webber Art Gallery, NYC, 1993, Mus. Art, R.I. Sch. of Design, Providence, 1994, 98, Pratt's Inst.'s Manhattan Ctr., NYC, 1995, Skoto Gallery, NYC, 1995, Phila. Mus. Art, 1996, Wayne State U., Detroit, 1996, Pitts. Ctr. for Arts, 1996, W.Va. Wesleyan Coll., Buckhannon, 1996, Yale U. Art Gallery, New Haven, 1996, Spelman Coll. Mus. Fine Art, Atlanta, 1996, Rush Art, NYC, 1997, The Schomburg Ctr., NYC, 1998, Louis Ross Gallery, NYC, 1998, Nabisco, East Hanover, NJ, 1998, The Parish Art Mus., Southampton, NY, 1998, Elise Goodheart Gallery, Sea Harbor, NY, 1998, RI Sch. Design, Providence, 1998, Arlene Bujese Gallery, East Hampton, NY, 1999, Nat. Arts Club, NYC, 1999, Concordia Coll., Ann Arbor, Mich., 2000, Ark. Arts Ctr., Little Rock, 2000, Lambert Gallery, Atlanta, 2004, Rongio Gallery, Bklyn., 2004, and numerous others; represented in permanent collections Planned Parenthood, NYC, Jane Zimmerli Art Mus., Rutgers U., New Brunswick, NJ, Jersey City Mus., Libr. of Congress, Washington, ARCO, Phila., Reader's Digest, Pleasantville, NY, Schomburg Libr., NYC, Salomon Bros., NYC, Newark Mus., Herbert Johnson Mu., Art, Cornell U., Ithaca, NY, Studio Mus. Harlem, NY, MCI Telecomm., Chgo., Times Mirror, NYC, AT&T, NJ, IBM, Stamford, Conn., Lang Comm., Randolph, Vt., Merck Pharm. Co., Phila., Johnson & Johnson, Inc., New Brunswick, Pepsi-Cola, NYC, Motown Corp., L.P., LA, Am. Express, Mpls., Mus. Art RI Sch. Design, Providence, Yale Gallery of Art, New Haven, Conn., USA Assurance, San Antonio, Tex., Nextel Corp., LA, GE, Fairfield, Conn., Cochran Found., La Grange, Ga., Rutgers Grad. Sch. Mgmt., Newark, ARCO, Phila., Magic Johnson Enterprises, LA, Nissho Iwai Am. Corp., NYC, Pa. Acad. Fine Arts, Phila., Lucent Tech., Basking Ridge, NJ, Butler Inst. Am. Art, Youngstown, Ohio, Conkling Gallery, Minn. State Univ., Mankato, MN, 2002; Group shows: Jacktilton Gallery, NYC; Exhibit A Gallery, NYC; Pfizer Incorp., NYC, 2002; and numerous others. Grantee Nat. Endowment for Arts, 1981, The Jerome Found., 1981, NJ Coun. on Arts, 1985, NY Found. for Arts, 1990, The Pollock-Krasner Found., 1994, Wheeler Found., NYC, 1996, Fellowship, Lower East Side Printshop, NYC, 1997, Fellowship, Brandywine Workshop, Philadelphia, 1999

CARTER, NEVILLE LOUIS, geophysicist, educator; b. LA, Aug. 21, 1934; s. Herman Louis and Maribelle (Sheller) C.; m. Susan Ruth Orton, Aug. 1, 1987; children from previous marriage: James Neville, Lindsay Louis, Jenifer June. AB, Pomona Coll., 1956; MA, UCLA, 1958, PhD, 1963; postgrad. (Fulbright fellow), U. Oslo, Norway, 1958-59. Research assoc. Inst. Geophysics, UCLA, 1963; research geologist Shell Devel. Co., Houston, 1963-66; assoc. prof. geology and geophysics Yale U., New Haven, 1966-71; prof. geophysics SUNY-Stony Brook, 1971-78; prof., head dept. geophysics, faculty assoc. Ctr. for Tectonophysics, Tex. A&M U., College Station, 1978-83, dir., 1984-89; faculty assoc. Geodynamics Rsch. Inst., Tex. A&M U., 1984-96; prof. emeritus geology and geophysics Tex. A&M U., 1996—. Author, editor numerous publs. in field. Mem. Am. Geophys. Union (pres. tectonophysics sect. 1974-76), Sigma Xi. Home: PO Box 1442 Crescent City CA 95531-1442 Personal E-mail: nevillelcarter@aol.com.

CARTER, PEYTON FRANKLIN, III, accountant; b. NYC, Oct. 17, 1969; s. Peyton Franklin Carter, II and Elizabeth Ann Scott; m. Elizabeth Clayton Ketterson, Sept. 26, 1998; children: Parker Upshur, Peyton Franklin IV. BA in Polit. Sci., New Eng. Coll., 1994. Fund acct. State St. Bank & Trust, Boston, 1994—95, auditor, 1995—96, client svc. mgr., 1996—96, account mgr., 1997—99, corp. trainer, 1999—2001, acctg. officer, 2001—01; acctg. oversight mgr. Columbia Mgmt. Group - Fleet Bank, Boston, 2001—03; group mgr. Bisys Hedge Fund Svc., Boston, 2003—04; dir. fund acctg. Anchorage Capital Group, NYC, 2005—. Author: Who Was Richard Brayne?, 2002, Hitherto Above Reproach, 2003, The Bartons' Quest For Liberty, 2003, The Carters of Amelia County, Virginia, 2003. Trustee New Eng. Coll., 2005—; elected town meeting mem. Town Legislature, Brookline, Mass., 2000—02. Mem.: SAR, US Coast Guard Auxilliary, Soc. War of 1812, Union Club Boston, Soc. Colonial Wars, Mason. Unitarian Universalist. Avocations: tennis, travel, musical composition, baseball. Home (Winter): 9 Sentry Place SR Scarsdale NY 10583 Office: Anchorage Capital Group Llc 610 Broadway # 6 New York NY 10012-2601 Home (Summer): 39 Elm St Richfield Springs NY 13439

CARTER, REGINA, jazz violinist; b. Detroit, 1962; d. Grace Louise Carter. Violin performance student, New Eng. Conservatory Music; BA, Oakland U., Rochester, Mich., 1985. Musician: (albums) Regina Carter, 1995, Something for Grace, 1997, Rhythms of the Heart, 1998, Motor City Moments, 2000, Freefall, 2001, Paganini: After a Dream, 2003, I'll Be Seeing You: A Sentimental Journey, 2006, (with Straight Ahead) Look Straight Ahead, 1991, Body & Soul, 1993, (with String Trio of NY) Octagon, 1992, Blues.?, 1993, Live au Petit Faucheux, 1993, (with Mary J. Blige) My Life, 1994, (with Patti LaBelle) Flame, 1997, (with Cassandra Wilson) Traveling Miles, 1999, (with Danilo Perez) Motherland, 2000, (films) I Shot Andy Warhol, 1996, (documentaries) Jazz, 2001, (Operas) Wynton Marsalis' Blood on the Fields. MacArthur fellow, John D. & Catherine T. MacArthur Found., 2006. Office: c/o Michelle Taylor NIA Entertainment Ltd 90 Amsterdam Ave Teaneck NJ 07666 Office Phone: 201-837-0596. Office Fax: 201-837-0597.

CARTER, RICHARD DENNIS, lawyer, educator; b. Newburgh, NY, Feb. 17, 1949; s. Edward Francis and Catherine Florence (Harding) C. BA, Pace U., 1977; JD, George Washington U., 1980. Bar: DC 1980, Va. 1991, Md. 1991, U.S. Dist. Ct. DC 1981, U.S. Supreme Ct. 1987, U.S. Dist. Ct. Md. 1990, U.S. Ct. Appeals (4th cir.) 1991, U.S. Dist. Ct. (ea. dist.) Wis. 1994, U.S. Dist. Ct. Ariz. 1994. Supervising atty., adj. prof. law DC Law Students in Ct., Washington, 1980—90, dep. dir., 1981—85, exec. dir., 1985—90; adj. prof. trial advocacy Georgetown U., Washington, 1982—2000; ptnr. Cunningham and Hudgins, Alexandria, Va., 1990, Hudgins, Carter & Coleman, Alexandria, 1990—98, Carter & Coleman, Alexandria, 1998—. Contbr. articles to profl. jours. Mem. ABA, DC Bar Assn., Washington Bar Assn., Alexandria Bar Assn., Am. Inns of Ct. Episcopalian. Avocation: motor sports. Home: 1802 Jamieson Ave Alexandria VA 22314 Office: Carter Lay 803 Prince St Alexandria VA 22314 Home Phone: 703-299-0161; Office Phone: 703-549-0076. E-mail: rich@carterlay.com.

CARTER, RICHARD DUANE, management educator; s. Herbert Duane and Edith Irene (Richardson) Carter; m. Nancy Jean Cannell; 1 child, Erich Richardson. AB, Coll. William and Mary; MBA, Columbia U.; PhD, UCLA. Sr. advisor, dir. Taiwan Metal Industries Devel. Ctr. (under auspices of ILO), 1966-67; dir. UNDP, cons. svcs., Taiwan, 1966-67; chief exec. officer Human Resources Inst., Baton Rouge, 1968-70; liaison advisor Internat. Inst. Applied Systems Analysis, Vienna, 1975; U.S. rep., dir. indsl. mgmt. and cons. svcs. program UN Indsl. Devel. Orgn., Vienna, 1970-75; mem. East-West Trade and Mgmt. Commn., 1973-75; sr. advisor, dir. Korean Inst. Sci. and Tech. (under auspices of UN), Seoul, 1974-75; dean Sch. Bus. Quinnipiac Coll., Hamden, Conn., 1977-80; chmn. bd. TCG Industries, Inc., NYC, 1980—; prof. mgmt., program coord. Fairfield (Conn.) U., 1980-84; founder, mng. dir. Internat. Mgmt. Consortium, Vienna, Westport and Millerton, NY, 1975—; assoc. mem. Seminar on Orgn. and Mgmt. Columbia U., 1975-89, vice-chmn. Seminar on Orgn. and Mgmt., 1976-89, chmn. rsch. and publ. com. Seminar on Orgn. and Mgmt., 1983-89; mng. dir. Wainwright & Ramsey Securities, Inc., NYC, 1985—2005. Mem. editorial bd. Indian Adminstrv. and Mgmt. Rev., New Delhi, 1974-76; author: Management: In Perspective and Practice, 1970, The Future Challenges of Management Education, 1981; also numerous articles and revs. Trustee Dingletown Community Ch., Greenwich, Conn., 1978-87; mem. adv. coun. Calif. Coll. Tech., L.A., 1978—. Recipient Disting. Alumni medallion (Olde Guarde), Coll. William and Mary, 2001. Fellow Internat. Acad. Mgmt.; mem. Acad. Mgmt., Am. Mgmt. Assns. (pres.'s council, dir. 1976-77), N.Am. Soc. Corp. Planning, N.Am. Mgmt. Coun. (bd. dirs. 1983-87), Soc. Internat. Orgn. Devel., Mensa, Triple Nine Soc., Explorers Club, Sharon (Conn.) Country Club, Beta Gamma Sigma, Kappa Sigma, Rotary (chair, pres. internat. svcs. 2006-07). Office: Ste 250 Fish Rock The Sea Ranch CA 95497 Personal E-mail: carters@mcn.org. *Success depends upon the art of optimizing the skills of confrontation, compromise and cooperation.*

CARTER, ROBERT B., delivery service executive; b. Taiwan, 1959; B, U. Fla.; MBA, U. South Fla. V.p. info. and telecomm. FedEx Corp., 1993—98, chief tech. officer, 1998—2000, exec. v.p., chief info. officer Memphis, 2000—. Bd. dir. Saks Inc. Named Chief Tech. Officer of Yr., Infoworld, 2000, Chief of Yr., Information Week, 2005. Office: FedEx 942 S Shady Grove Rd Memphis TN 38120

CARTER, RONALD MARTIN, SR., pharmaceutical executive; b. Chgo., Nov. 18, 1925; s. Jack Edward and Anna (Press) C.; m. Joy Wolf, Nov. 14, 1946; children: Ronald M. Jr., Craig Alan. Student, U. Ill., 1942-43, 45-46. Sales mgr. Preston Labs., Inc., Chgo., 1948-52; v.p. Myers-Carter Labs., Inc., Phoenix, 1952-69, pres., 1969-75, Carter-Glogau Labs., Inc., Glendale, Ariz., 1975-86, Steris Labs., Inc., Phoenix, 1987—, The Pharmikon Co., 1987—. Cons. Internat. Exec. Service Corp., Stamford, Conn., 1985—. Served as cpl. U.S. Army, 1943-45. Mem. Drug, Chem. Allied Trades, Generic Pharm. Industry Assn., Nat. Assn. Pharm. Mfrs., Nat. Pharm. Alliance (pres. 1983-84). Clubs: Arizona, Plaza (Phoenix). Democrat. Jewish. Avocations: hunting, fishing. Home: 5707 N 40th St Phoenix AZ 85018-1108 Personal E-mail: roncar@cox.net.

CARTER, ROSALYNN SMITH (ELEANOR ROSALYNN CARTER), former First Lady of the United States; b. Plains, Ga., Aug. 18, 1927; d. Edgar and Allie (Murray) Smith; m. James Earl Carter, Jr., July 7, 1946; children: John William, James Earl III, Donnel Jeffrey, Amy Lynn. Attended, Ga. Southwestern Coll., 1944—46; DHL (hon.), Morehouse Coll., 1980; LLD (hon.), U. Notre Dame, 1987. First Lady of U.S., Washington, 1977—81; disting. centennial lectr. Agnes Scott Coll., Decatur, Ga., 1988—92; disting. fellow, Women's Studies Dept. Emory U., Atlanta, 1990—. Author: First Lady from Plains, 1984; co-author (with Jimmy Carter) Everything to Gain: Making the Most of the Rest of Your Life, 1987, (with Susan Golant) Helping Yourself Help Others: A Book for Caregivers, 1994, (with Susan Golant) Helping Someone With Mental Illness: A Compassionate Guide for Family, Friends and Caregivers, 1998. Co-founder Every Child by Two Campaign for Early Immunization; co-founder (with Jimmy Carter) The Carter Ctr., 1982, trustee, creator and chair Mental Health Task Force; ann. host Rosalynn Carter Symposium on Mental Health Policy; founder Rosalynn Carter Fellowships for Mental Health Journalism, 1996; chair Internat. Com. of Women Leaders for Mental Health; adv. bd. mem. Habitat for Humanity; mem. Ga. Gov.'s Commn. to Improve Svcs. for Mentally and Emotionally Handicapped, 1971; pres. bd. dir., Rosalynn Carter Inst. for Caregiving Ga. Southwestern State U.; hon. chair Pres.'s Commn. on Mental Health, 1977—78; deacon Maranatha Bapt. Ch., Plains, Ga., 2006—. Recipient Vol. of Decade award Nat. Mental Health Assn., 1980, Presdl. Citation APA, 1982, Nathan S. Kline medal of merit Internat. Com. Against Mental Illness, 1984, Disting. Alumnus award Am. Assn. State Colls. and Univs., 1987, Dorothea Dix award Mental Illness Found., 1988, Dean's award Columbia U. Coll. Physicians and Surgeons, 1991, Notre Dame award for internat. humanitarian svc., 1992, Eleanor Roosevelt Living World award Peace Links, 1992, Nat. Caring award The Caring Inst., 1995, Kiwanis World Svc. medal Kiwanis Internat. Found., 1995, Jefferson award Am. Inst. for Pub. Svc., 1996, Presdl. Medal of Freedom, 1999; named to Nat. Women's Hall of Fame, 2001. Fellow: Am. Psychiat. Assn. (hon.). Democrat. Avocations: fly fishing, birdwatching, swimming, bicycling. Office Phone: 404-331-3900.

CARTER, SCOTT, television producer; m. Bebe Carter; children: Calla, Cary. Writer (TV series) MTV's Mouth to Mouth, 1988, Night After Night with Allen Havey, 1989—92, SportsMonster, 1990—91, The Olympiacs, 1992, exec. prodr., writer Politically Incorrect, 1993—2000, Exhale with Candice Bergen, 2000—02, Earth to America, 2005, Real Time with Bill Maher, 2006—, co-exec. prodr. Ain't It Cool News, 2001, exec. prodr. The Conspiracy Zone, 2002, author & performer (one-man shows) Heavy Breathing, Suspension Bridge. Named one of 50 Creatives to Watch, Variety, 1997; recipient CableACE award for Talk Show Series for Politically Incorrect, 1995, 1996, Johnny Carson Prodr. of Yr. award for Real Time with Bill Maher, Prodrs. Guild Am., 2007.*

CARTER, SHAWN COREY See JAY-Z

CARTER, SHAWN DAVID, protective services official; b. Wilmington, Del., Dec. 12, 1968; s. Harry Charles Eastburne and Marilyn Elizabeth Foley, Paul Raymond Widmayer Jr. (Stepfather); m. Kathleen Jeanette Jones, June 9, 2001; children: Kristyn Leanne, Kevin Joseph. Student in Adminstrv. Justice, Del. County CC, Media, Pa., 2005; grad., US Army Tng. Sch., Ft. Jackson, SC, 1987, Signal and Comm. Sch., Ft. Gordon, Ga, 1987. Cert. police tng. Del. County CC, 2000, FBI evidence collection and handling Aberdeen Proving Grounds, Md., 2005, weapons intelligence tng. Aberdeen Proving Grounds, 2005, combat livesaving course cert. Aberdeen Proving Grounds, 2005. Fgn. weapons intelligence analyst 203rd Mil. Intelligence Bn., Aberdeen Proving Grounds, Md., 2000—; police officer Valley Twp. Police Dept., Coatesville, Pa., 2003—. Fire fighter Prospect Pk. Fire Co., 1994—96, Good Will Fire Co., West Chester, Pa., 1999—; asst. coach girls rugby Dowingtown HS, 1999—2002; asst. rugby coach East HS, 1999—2002; asst. treas. Prospect Pk. Fire Co., Pa., 1994—95. Staff sgt., weapons intelligence team leader US Army, 1987—, seved in Operation Desert Shield, Storm, Sword US Army, 1990—91, served in Operation Iraqi Freedom US Army, 2003, served in Operation Iraqi Freedom US Army, 2005—06, active USAR, 1987—. Decorated Bronze Star medal US Army, Purple Heart medal, Army Commendation medal, Army Achievement medal (9th award), Good Conduct medal, Combat Action Badge medal; recipient Fireman Rookie Yr., Prospect Pk. Fire Co., 1994, Samuel Sharp Ordnance medal, 2007. Mem.: VFW, West Chester U. Rugby Club, Am. Legion, Mil. Order Purple Heart. Avocations: rugby, running, baseball card collecting, mentoring kids. Home: 202 North Penn St West Chester PA 19380 Personal E-mail: shawn.carter1@us.army.mil.

CARTER, STEPHEN M., telecommunications manufacturing industry executive; b. London; m. Elizabeth Carter; 2 children. M, City Univ. Bus. Sch., London. Mng. dir. Gazelle Group plc, London; gen. mgr. consumer products div. Sony UK; mng. dir. SW Bell Telecom UK, 1987—90; pres. Freedom Phone SW Bell Telecom, 1990—93, pres., CEO, 1993—94; pres. strategic & spl. markets, pres. SBC Wireless SBC Corp., 1994—2000; pres., CEO Cingular Wireless, 2000—02; CEO Superior Essex Inc., Atlanta, 2003—, pres., CEO, 2004—04. Bd. dir. True Position Inc. Trustee Woodruff Arts Ctr.; bd. dir. Atlanta Spl. Olympics. Fellow: Chartered Inst. Mgmt. Accountants. Office: Superior Essex Inc 150 Interstate North Pkwy Atlanta GA 30339*

CARTER, STEVE, state attorney general; b. Lafayette, Ind., 1954; m. Marilyn Carter; 3 children. BA in Econs., Harvard U., 1976; JD, Ind. U., 1983, MBA. Chief city-county atty. Indpls.-Marion County; chief of staff Former Mayor Stephen Goldsmith Ind.; legis. counsel Ind. State Senate; chief of staff, agrl. asst. Ind. Lt. Gov. John Mutz; atty. gen. State of Ind., 2001—. Mem.: Nat. Assn. Attys. Gen. (pres., mem. Exec. Working Grp., Internal Rels. Com., Exec. Com., Fin. Com., bd. dirs., Mission Found. 2006—07). Republican. Office: Office Atty Gen Ind Govt Ctr S 5th Fl 402 W Washington St Indianapolis IN 46204

CARTER, SYLVIA, journalist; b. Keokuk, Iowa; d. Charles Sylvester and Frances Elizabeth (Smith) C. B of Journalism, U. Mo., 1968. Intern Quincy (Ill.) Herald-Whig, 1966, Detroit Free Press, 1967; reporter The N.Y. Daily News, 1968-70; successively gen. assignment reporter, edn. reporter, food writer, restaurant critic, food columnist Newsday, Melville, NY, 1970—; food writer, restaurant critic N.Y. Newsday, NYC, 1985-95; founder, editor Kidsday Newsday, Melville, columnist, 2005—. Author: Eats: The Best Little Restaurants in New York, 1988, Eats N.Y.C.: A Guide to the Best, Cheapest, Most Interesting Restaurants in Brooklyn, Queens and Manhattan, 1995; contbr. to Family Circle and other publs. Trustee Anne O'Hare McCormick Scholarship Fund, N.Y.C., 1988—; bd. dirs. Art Inst. N.Y., 2003-05. Recipient Feature Writing award U. Mo., 2000; nominee James Beard Journalism awards, 2001. Mem. Newswomen's Club N.Y. (pres. 1990-92, bd. dirs., Front Page award 1982). Democrat. Presbyterian. Avocations: reading, collectibles, hiking, music, cooking. Home: 46 Crescent Bow Ridge NY 11961-2915 Home Phone: 212-475-4821; Office Phone: 631-775-9534. Personal E-mail: sylviacarter@optonline.net.

CARTER, TERRY, retail executive; Grad., Univ. Okla., 1971. With QuikTrip Corp., Tulsa, Okla., 1980—, CFO, dir. Bd. chmn. Tulsa Area United Way. Office: Quick Trip PO Box 3475 Tulsa OK 74101-3475

CARTER, T(HOMAS) BARTON, law educator; b. Dallas, Aug. 6, 1949; s. Sydney Hobart and Josephine (Wren) C.; m. Eleonore Dorothy Alexander, June 3, 1978 (div. 1988); 1 child, Richard Alexander. BA in Psychology, Yale U., 1971; JD, U. Pa., 1974; MS in Mass Communication, Boston U., 1978. Bar: Mass. 1974, U.S. Dist. Ct. Mass. 1975, U.S. Ct. Appeals (1st cir.) 1975. Asst. prof. law Boston U., 1979-85, assoc. prof., 1985-96, prof., 1996—; pvt. practice Boston, 1974—. Pres. Tanist Broadcasting Corp., Boston, 1981—2001. Co-author: The First Amendment and the Fourth Estate, 1985, 9th edit., 2004, The First Amendment and the Fifth Estate, 1986, 6th edit., 2003, Mass Communications Law in a Nutshell, 1988, 6th edit., 2007. Mem. ABA, Assn. for Edn. in Journalism and Mass Comm. (clk. 1981-82, asst. head 1982-83, head 1983-84), Broadcast Edn. Assn. (chair law and policy divsn. 1989-90), Fed. Comm. Bar Assn., Univ. Club. Avocation: bridge. Home: 109 Commonwealth Ave Apt 6 Boston MA 02116-2345 Office: Boston U 640 Commonwealth Ave Boston MA 02215-2422 Office Phone: 617-353-3482. E-mail: comlaw@bu.edu.

CARTER, THOMAS SMITH, JR., retired rail transportation executive; b. Dallas, June 6, 1921; s. Thomas S. and Mattie (Dowell) C.; m. Janet R. Hostetter, July 3, 1946 (dec. 1981); children: Diane Carter Petersen, Charles T., Carol Carter Koehler. BSCE, So. Meth. U., 1944; MS in Engring. Mgmt., Kans. U., 1991. Registered profl. engr., Mo., Kans., Okla., Tex., La., Ark. With Mo. Kans. Tex. RR, 1946-54, chief engr., 1954-61, v.p. ops., 1961-66; v.p. Kansas City So. Rlwy. Co., La. and Ark. Rlwy. Co., 1966-74; pres. Kansas City So. Rlwy. Co., 1973-86, chmn. bd., 1981-91; pres. La. and Ark. Rlwy. Co., 1974-86, chmn. bd., 1981-91, CEO, 1981-91; ret., 1991. With U.S. Corps of Engrs., 1944-46. Fellow ASCE; mem. NSPE, Am. Rlwy. Engring. and Maintenance Assn. (life), Chi Epsilon, Hide-A-Way Lake Club. Home: 131 Clubview Dr Lindale TX 75771-5054

CARTER, TIMOTHY HOWARD, biochemist, educator; b. LA, Nov. 6, 1944; s. Everett and Cecile (Doudna) C.; m. Jocklyn Armstrong, Dec. 31, 1976; children: Benjamin, Jonathan. AB, Harvard U., 1966; PhD, Princeton U., 1972. Postdoctoral fellow U. Pa. Med. Sch., Phila., 1972-74, Columbia U. Coll. Physicians and Surgeons, NYC, 1974-75; asst. prof. Coll. Medicine Pa. State U., Hershey, 1975-78; asst. prof. St. John's U., Jamaica, N.Y., 1978-81, assoc. prof., 1981-92, prof. biochemistry, 1992—, chmn. dept. biol. scis., 1992—95. Investigator Feinstein Inst. Med. Rsch. North Shore-LI Jewish Health Sys., Manhasset, NY, 2000—. Contbr. articles, chpts. to sci. publs. Pa. Plan Scientist, U. Pa., 1973; Mattheson fellow Columbia U., 1974; grantee NIH, 1978-2007, NOAA, 1984-88, Am. Cancer Soc., 1991—. Mem. Am. Assn. Cancer Rsch., N.Y. Acad. Scis. (conf. com. 1991), Am. Soc. Microbiology, Am. Soc. Biochemistry and Molecular Biology, Am. Soc. Cell Biology, Sigma Xi. Avocations: performing chamber music, cello. Home: 71 Dover Pky Stewart Manor NY 11530-3805 Office: St Johns U Dept Biol Sci 8000 Utopia Pkwy Jamaica NY 11439-0001

CARTER, TONYA M., science educator; b. Cleveland, Miss., Dec. 21, 1969; d. Clarence and Earlene (Jackson) Davis, David Henry and Jacquelyn (Wallace) Carter (Stepmother), Ruthie Jean Carter. BS, Alcorn State U., Lorman, Miss., 1993; MS Natural Scis., Delta State U., Cleveland, 1996. Tchr., dept. head Greenville Pub. Schs., Miss., 1995—. Aux. dir. Greenville Weston Band, 2001—; sponsor Nat. Beta Club Greenville Weston H.S., 2002—, acad. tutor, 1999—; coord. Small Learning Cmty. Greenville Pub. Sch., 2001—05. Leader Youth Dept. Poplar Grove Ch., Shaw, Miss., 2002. Named, Who's Who Among H.S. Tchrs., 2003—04, 2005—06, Outstanding Sci. Tchr., Delta Sci. Tchrs., 1999—2000, Tchr. of Month-Aug., Greenville Weston H.S., 2005, Tchr. of Month-Dec., 2004, Tchr. of Month-Apr., 2003; recipient Biology Inst. award, Millsaps Coll., 1999. Mem.: Miss.Sci. Tchrs. Assn., Miss. Assn. Biology Educators, Order Ea. Stars, Alpha Kappa Alpha, Tau Beta Sigma (v.p. 1990—92, Outstanding Svc. award). Baptist. Avocations: travel, reading. Office Fax: 662-334-7081; Home Fax: 662-334-7091. E-mail: tmcarteraka@hotmail.com, tcarter@gville.112.ms.us.

CARTER, VINCE, professional basketball player; b. Jan. 26, 1977; BA in African Am. Studies, U. NC, 2001. Forward Toronto Raptors, 1998—2004, NJ Nets, 2004—. Pres. Visions in Flight Inc.; mem. Ea. Conf. All-Star Team, 2000, 01, 02, 03, 04, 05, 06, 07. Established Embassy of Hope Found. Named mem., 1995 USA Basketball Jr. Team, World Championships, Goodwill Amb., Big Bros./Big Sisters Am.; named to NCAA Tournament All-East Regional Team, 1997, 1998, Schick All-Rookie 1st Team; recipient Schick Rookie of Yr. award, 1998—99. Office: c/o NJ Nets 390 Murray Hill Parkway East Rutherford NJ 07073

CARTER, WILFRED WILSON, retired finance company executive, controller; b. Providence, Feb. 22, 1923; s. Leo and Florence (Wilson) C.; m. Elsa Aulisio, June 17, 1950; children— Linda J., Donald J., Paul J., Gregory J. AA, Roger Williams Coll., 1951; student, Bryant Coll., 1958-62. Sec., tax mgr. Nicholson File Co., East Providence, 1940-73; controller Columbia Chase Corp. (name changed to Chase Corp.), Braintree, Mass., 1973-84, v.p. fin., controller, 1984-88, CEO, pres., treas., CFO, 1988-91, chmn. bd. dirs., CEO, treas., 1991-93, chmn. bd. dirs., 1993-94; ret., 1994. Vestryman All Saints Meml. Ch., Providence, R.I., 1968-76, 94-2000, treas., 1968-76. With USAAF, 1942-46. Mem. Tax Exec. Inst. Episcopalian (vestryman 1968-76, 94-2000, treas. 1968-76). Home: 720 Putnam Pike Unit 607 Greenville RI 02828-1448

CARTER, WILLIAM G., lawyer; b. Oct. 1940; m. Barbara Carter; children: Elizabeth, Andrew. BS, U. Oreg., 1962, LLB, 1965. Bar: Oreg. 1965. Prosecutor Douglas County, Oreg.; gen. trial practice Medford, Oreg.; mcpl. judge; pro tem circuit judge Jackson County, Oreg.; prin. William G. Carter Mediation & Arbitration, Medford, Oreg. Mem. State Professional Responsibility Bd., 1993—95, chmn., 1995; mem. Minimum Continuing Legal Edn. Bd., 1995—97, chmn., 1997. Mem.: Jackson County Bar Assn. (pres.), Oreg. State Bar Assn. (mem. disciplinary bd. 1998—2000, regional chmn. disciplinary bd. 2000, bd. gov. 2001—04, pres. 2004). Office: William G Carter Arbitration and Mediation 10 Crater Lake Ave PO Box 70 Medford OR 97501 Office Phone: 541-773-8471. Office Fax: 541-245-6674. Business E-Mail: wilcar@aol.com.*

CARTER, WILLIAM GERALD, non-profit corporation executive; b. Bethany, Mo., Jan. 12, 1929; s. William Young and Leah Genevieve (Cover) C.; m. Geralyn Gail Finlay, July 22, 1951; children: Kathryn Carter Gee, Karen Carter Winn, William Ralph. BSc, U. Mo., Columbia, 1950. Assoc. editor Nat. Livestock Prodr., Chgo., 1950-51; comm. specialist Farmland Industries, Kansas City, Mo., 1953-54; advt. dir. MFA Oil Co., Columbia, Mo., 1954-58; ptnr. Neds & Wardlow Advt. Agy., Springfield, Mo., 1958-68; chmn., pres. Tri-State Pharm Co., Oklahoma City, 1968-81; real estate broker W.G. Carter Real Estate, Oklahoma City & Foster City, Calif., 1981-96; founder, chmn. Am. Acad. Vols. in Edn., Foster City, Calif., 1994-2000; advt. dir. The John Knox Village Voice, Lee's Summit, Mo., 2005—. Spl. agent intelligence U.S. Army, 1951-53. Named Young Man of Yr., C. of C., Springfield, 1964. Mem. Optimist Internat. (mem. various coms. 1981-89, v.p., bd. dirs. 1984, chair coms. 1985-87, v.p. Optimist Vols. for Youth, Inc. 1992-99). Republican. Methodist. Avocations: reading, writing. Home and Office: 1909 NW Quail Trl Lees Summit MO 64081-1614

CARTER, WILLIAM H., chemicals executive; Ptnr. Price Waterhouse LLP, 1975—95; exec. v.p., CFO Borden Chemical Inc., Columbus, Ohio, 1995—2005; interim pres., CEO BCP Mgmt. (sub. of Borden), 2000; exec. v.p., CFO Hexion Specialty Chemicals (merger of Borden & RRP LLC), Columbus, Ohio, 2005—. Office: Hexion Specialty Chemicals 180 E Broad StFl 30 Columbus OH 43215*

CARTER, WILLIAM HAROLD, SR., physicist, researcher, electrical engineer; b. Houston, Nov. 17, 1938; s. William Henry and Fannie Augusta (Simpson) Carter; children: William Harold Jr., Elizabeth Lee. BSEE, U. Tex., 1962, MSEE, 1963, PhD, 1966. Rsch. asst. U. Tex., Austin, 1962-66; program dir. Office of R&D, CIA, Washington, 1966—69; rsch. assoc. U. Rochester, NY, 1969-70; rsch. physicist Naval Rsch. Lab., Washington, 1971-93; prof. U. Nebr., Lincoln, 1981-82; instr. Johns Hopkin's U., Balt., 1989-93; program dir. NSF, Arlington, Va., 1993—95. Vis. rsch. fellow U. Reading, Eng., 1976-77; vis. scientist applied physics lab. Johns Hopkin's U., Columbia, Md., 1991-92. Contbr. articles to profl. jours. Cellist Alexandria (Va.) Symphony, 1979-88, Georgetown Symphony, 1981-2003. Capt. U.S. Army, 1967-69. Fellow Optical Soc. Am. (topical editor jour. 2000-03), Internat. Soc. for Optical Engring. (chmn. tech. coun. 1980-82, chmn. pub. com. 1981-83, chmn. fellows com. 1986); mem. IEEE (sr., conf. chmn. 1988), Am. Phys. Soc., Cosmos Club, Sigma Xi, Tau Beta Pi, Eta Kappa Nu. Achievements include co-discovery of the quasi-homogeneous source model; research in optical coherence, in applications of speckle phenomena, and in processing images and data from optical sensors. Home: 8301 Cherry Valley Ln Alexandria VA 22309-2117 E-mail: wcarter1@wwcom.net.

CARTER, WILLIAM JOSEPH, lawyer; b. Balt., Sept. 1, 1949; s. Henry Merle and Florence (Rogan) C.; m. Monica Anne Urlock, July 17, 1976. BS in Psychology, Va. Poly. Inst., 1971; JD, Coll. William and Mary, Williamsburg, Va., 1974. Bar: Va. 1974, Pa. 1974, Md. 1980, DC 1980, Colo. 2004, US Dist. Ct. DC 1981, US Dist. Ct. Md. 1983, US Dist. Ct. (ea. dist.) Va. 1985, US Ct. Claims 1977, US Tax Ct. 1977, US Ct. Mil. Appeals 1975, US Ct. Appeals (DC and 4th cirs.) 1979, US Ct. Appeals (fed. cir.) 1982, US Ct. Appeals (6th cir.) 1988, US Ct. Appeals (3d and 5th cirs.) 1992, US Ct. Appeals (11th cir.) 2002, US Supreme Ct. 1977, US Dist Ct. (we. dist.), Va., 2004. Commd. 2d lt. US Army, 1971, advanced through grades to capt., 1974, served with JAGC, 1971-79, resigned, 1979; assoc. Carr, Jordan, Coyne & Savits, Washington, 1979-84; shareholder Carr, Goodson & Lee, PC, 1984-95, Carr Goodson Lee & Warner Profl. Corp., Washington, 1996-98, Carr Goodson Warner Profl. Corp., Washington, 1999-2000, Carr Goodson, PC, Washington, 2000—01, Carr Maloney, PC, Washington, 2001—. Mem. Deans adv. roundtable Coll. Sci., Va. Poly. Inst. Author: Appellate Practice Handbook for Maryland, Virginia and District of Columbia, 1996; editor: Appellate Practice Manual for the District of Columbia Court of Appeals, 1992. Named Top Washington DC Lawyer, Ins. Coverage, Superlawyers website, 2007. Mem.: ABA, D.C. Bar Assn. (chair 1998—2001, cts. and adminstrn. of justice sect., ct. rules com.), Counsellors, Bar Assn. D.C., Rotary (pres. Olney, Md. chpt. 1999—2000, 2005—06). Episcopalian. Avocations: ice hockey, tennis, music, scuba diving, skiing. Office: Carr Maloney PC Ste 500 1615 L St NW Washington DC 20036 Home Phone: 301-774-5235; Office Phone: 202-310-5502. Business E-Mail: wjc@carrmaloney.com.

CARTER, WILLIAM WALTON, physicist, researcher; b. Pensacola, Fla., Nov. 7, 1921; s. Eugene Hudson and Nannie (Ledyard) C.; m. Elizabeth Jean Dedick, June 11, 1945; children— Carolyn A., Susan J., Judith J., Paul W. BS, Carnegie Inst. Tech., 1943; MS, Calif. Inst. Tech., 1948, PhD, 1949. Atomic and thermonuclear weapon R&D group leader weapons physics group, weapons div. Los Alamos Sci. Lab., 1949-59, mem. joint working com.; chief scientist Army Missile Command, Redstone Arsenal, 1959-67; asst. dir. nuclear programs, def. research and engring. Office Sec. Def., Washington, 1967-71; assoc. dir. Harry Diamond Labs. U.S. Army, 1971-74, tech. dir., 1975-84, also chmn. staff devel. council; sr. scientist Pacific-Sierra Rsch., Arlington, Va., 1984-94; scientific cons. nuclear treaty monitoring, 1994—. Designer, deployer instruments to verify nuclear treaties; chmn. steering com. Huntsville Rsch. Inst. Served to lt. USNR, 1944-46. Asso. fellow AIAA; mem. AAAS, Am. Phys. Soc., Am. Inst. Physics. Achievements include design of air samplers for worldwide network of sensors to monitor non-proliferation and nuclear test ban treaties; installation first unit in Turkmenistan; being project leader for first thermonuclear weapon to enter regular national stockpile. Home: 250 Pantops Mountain Rd Apt 5219 Charlottesville VA 22911 Office Phone: 434-972-2454, 434-972-2454. Personal E-mail: wwcarter@wcbr.us.

CARTER, YVONNE BREAUX, retired librarian; b. Crowley, La., Aug. 3, 1922; d. Valentin D. and Annie H. (Oertling) Breaux; m. Walter R. Carter, Apr. 23, 1943. BS in Edn. with high distinction, U. Southwestern La., 1943; BS in Libr. Sci., George Peabody Coll. Tchrs., 1950, MA, 1960, EdS, 1966. Cert. tchr. La., libr. La.. Tchr. Calcasieu Parish, Lake Charles, La., 1942—43; prin. Sardis H.S., Tenn., 1944—45; tchr. Gueydan H.S. Vermillion Parish Sch. Bd., Abbeville, La., 1945—63, 1964; libr. Vermillion Parish Sch. Bd., Abbeville, 1948—64, 1965—66, U.S. Office of Edn. Dallas Region, 1967—69; adminstrv. libr. U.S. Dept. of Edn., Washington, 1969—93; ret., 1993. Asst. prof. Northwestern State U., Natchitoches, La., 1963—64, Southwestern La. U., Lafayette, 1965—67. Mem. Lafayette Pub. Libr. Found. Bd. Kappa Kappa Iota scholar, Delta Kappa Gamma Epsilon scholar. Mem.: DAR (regent Galvez chpt. 1998, State of La. libr. 2003—, regent Galvez chpt. 2004), AAUW, ALA, La. Libr. Assn., Am. Assn. Sch. Librs., La. DAR (state libr. 2004—07), Women in Arts, Attakapas Hist. Assn., Women's Club Lafayette, Nat. Soc. Daus. War 1812 (state historian 2002—03, chpt. pres. 2004—), United Daus. Confederacy (chpt. pres. 2001—03), Beta Phi Mu, Delta Kappa Gamma, Kappa Delta Pi. E-mail: ycarter@bellsouth.net.

CARTER, ZACHARY W., lawyer; BA, Cornell U., 1972; JD, NYU, 1975. Bar: N.Y., U.S. Dist Ct. (ea. dist.) N.Y., U.S. Dist. Ct. (so. dist.) N.Y., U.S. Ct. Appeals (2d cir.), U.S. Supreme Ct. Asst. U.S. atty. U.S. Dist. Ct. (ea. dist.) N.Y., 1975-80; mem. Patterson, Belknap, Webb & Tyler, 1980-81; exec. asst. dist. atty. King County Dist. Atty's. Office, Bklyn., 1982-87; exec. asst. to dep. chief adminstrv. judge N.Y. City Cts., 1987; judge criminal ct. City of N.Y., 1987-91; U.S. magistrate judge E.D.N.Y., 1991-93; U.S. atty. ea. dist. N.Y. U.S. Dept. Justice, Bklyn., 1993-99; ptnr., trial, regulatory & tech. group Dorsey & Whitney, NYC, 1999—, and chair, white collar crime & civil fraud group. Bd. dirs. Marsh & McLennan Cos. Inc., 2004—, Cablevision Systems Corp., 2006—. Chmn., bd. dir. Hale House. Mem. N.Y. Bar Assn. (chmn. Mayor's adv. com. on jud. selection). Office: Dorsey & Whitney LLP 250 Park Ave New York NY 10177-1500 Office Phone: 212-415-9345. Office Fax: 212-953-7201. E-mail: carter.zachary@dorseylaw.com.*

CARTER-JOHNSON, JEAN EVELYN, management consultant; b. Front Royal, Va., Sept. 22, 1956; d. William Robert Carter and Hilda Mae Jett; m. Ronald Malcolm Johnson, Sept. 27, 1985; 1 child, Sherard Akeem Johnson. Dental Assistance Cert., Montgomery Jr. Coll., Takoma Park, Md., 1977, AA, 1978; BSBA, Southeastern U., Washington, 1990; MBA, U. Md., Coll. Pk., 2006. Licensing info. asst. Nuc. Regulatory Commn., Silver Spring, Md., 1982—86; freedom info. act/privacy act specialist U.S. Info. Agy., Washington, 1986—88; paralegal Fed. Trade Commn., Washington, 1988—2001; mgmt. analyst Dept. Commerce, Silver Spring, Md., 2001—. Freedom info. act/privacy act program mgr. Nat. Oceanic and Atmospheric Adminstrn., Silver Spring, Md., 2001—. Songwriter: CD America, 2005, In The Beginning, 2006. Mentor Young Adult Orgn., 2004. Fellow: Md. State Bd. Dental Examiners (lic. 1977). Avocations: reading, writing, cooking, piano, coin collecting/numismatics. Home: 7510 Somerset Terr Frederick MD 21702 Office: Dept Commerce 1315 Eastwest Hwy Silver Spring MD 20901 Personal E-mail: jeancj@adelphia.net.

CARTER-MILLER, JOCELYN, former retail executive; b. 1957; BSc in Acctg., U. Ill., Urbana-Champaign, 1979; MBA in Mktg. & Fin., U. Chgo., 1981. CPA. Various sr. level positions Mattel, Inc., 1984—91; corp. v.p., chief mktg. officer Motorola, Inc., 1992—2002; exec. v.p., chief mktg. officer Office Depot, Inc., 2002—04; pres. TechEdventures, Inc., 2005—. Bd. dirs. Prin. Fin. Group, Inc, 2001—, The Interpublic Group of Cos. Inc., 2007—. Author (with Melissa Giovagnoli): Networlding: Building Relationships and Opportunities for Success, 1998.*

CARTER PEREIRA, CLAUDINE RENEE, forensic specialist; d. Ronald Kallip and Joy Rita Carter; m. Rodrigo Miranda Batista Pereira, Oct. 12, 2002; 1 child, Arianna Lillie Pereira. BS, Loyola Coll., Balt., Md., 1995; MS, Va. Commonwealth U., Richmond, Va., 1997. Cert. latent print examiner Internat. Assn. Identification, 2000, tchr. Dance Educators Am., 2001. Technician crime lab. Balt. (Md.) City Police Dept., 1997—99; examiner latent prints Broward Sheriff's Office, Ft. Lauderdale, Fla., 1999—2000, sr. examiner latent prints, 2000—04, supr. latent prints, 2004—. Asst. dance instr. Lois Seiler Acad. Dance, Freeport, Bahamas, 1988—89; dance instr. Anna Appicella Sch. Dance, Balt., 1992—95; asst. artistic dir. Jubilee Dance Theatre, Inc, Ft. Lauderdale, 2003—. Dancer Don Quixote, 2000, 2003, The Nutcracker, 2000—02, Cinderella, 2001, Peter and the Wolf/Sleeping Beauty, 2004, MLK Gala Awards, 2004, dancer, asst. artistic dir. Out of The Box, 2003, dancer, artistic dir. NBC 6 South Fla. Today Show, 2004, dancer, asst. artistic dir. No Boundaries, 2004, asst. artistic dir. Pan African Bookfest, 2005, Arts Express, 2005, dancer, asst. artistic dir. Sounds of Freedom, 2006, Louder Than Words, 2006. Tchr. adult ballet classes African Am. Rsch. LIbr. and Cultural Ctr., Jubilee Dance Theatre, Inc., 2004—; ballet instr. Morton St. Dance Ctr., Balt., 1997—99, Regency Dance Acad., Richmond, Va., 1995—97, St. Frances HS, Balt., 1992—93. Mem.: Internat. Assn. Identification (assoc.), Alpha Phi Sigma. Avocation: dance. Office: Broward Sheriff's Office Crime Lab 201 SE 6th Street N Wing Rm 1799 Fort Lauderdale FL 33301 Home Phone: 954-977-9355; Office Phone: 954-831-3578. Business E-Mail: claudine_pereira@sheriff.org.

CARTIER, BRIAN EVANS, consumer products company executive; b. Providence, Apr. 12, 1950; s. Clarence Joseph and Mary Anna (Evans) C. BA, RI Coll., 1972; MEd, Springfield Coll., Mass., 1973. Exec. dir. Arthritis Found. Conn., Hartford, 1976-78, dep. exec. dir. N.Y. chpt. NYC, 1979; exec. dir. Found. for Chiropractic Edn. and Rsch., Arlington, Va., 1979-90, Nat. Ct. Reporters Assn., 1990-98; CEO Nat. Assn. Coll. Stores, Oberlin, Ohio, 1998—. Mem. Am. Mgmt. Assn. (cert. assn. exec.), Am. Soc. Assn. Execs., US C. of C. Republican. Roman Catholic. Office: NACS 500 E Lorain St Oberlin OH 44074-1238

CARTLEDGE, RAYMOND EUGENE, retired paper company executive; b. Pensacola, Fla., June 12, 1929; s. Raymond H. and Meddie (Brookins) C.; m. Gale Perry, June 30, 1962; children: John R., Perri Ann, Susan R. BS, U. Ala., 1952; postgrad., Harvard Bus. Sch., 1970. With Procter & Gamble Co., 1955-56, Union Camp Corp., Wayne, NJ, 1956-70, 80-94, pres., COO, 1983-86, chmn., pres., CEO, 1986-94; pres., CEO Clevepak Corp., White Plains, NY, 1971-79; chmn. Savannah Foods, 1996-97. Past chmn. Am. Paper Inst.; trustee Am. Enterprise Inst.; trustee, life councillor The Conf. Bd.; bd. dirs. Blount Internat., Graftec Internat.; past chmn. Inst. Paper Sci. and Tech. Served with U.S. Army Airborne Infantry, 1952-55. Office: 15 Lake St #235 Savannah GA 31411-2913 Office Phone: 912-598-3214. Personal E-mail: recart1929@aol.com.

CARTLIDGE, EDWARD SUTTERLEY, mechanical engineer; b. Trenton, NJ, Feb. 5, 1945; s. Leon James and Agnes Jean (Cinkay) C.; m. Marilyn Spinuzza, July 21, 1979. BS in Marine Engring., U.S. Mcht. Marine Acad., 1968; MSME, N.J. Inst. Tech., 1971; MBA, Temple U., 1982; MA, Biblical Theol. Sem., 2001. Registered profl. engr., Pa., Ill., Del., Md., N.J., Va., Wis., Calif., Fla. Marine engr. Seatrain Lines, 1968-69; performance engr. Foster Wheeler Corp., Livingston, N.J., 1969-71; cons. engr. Fluor, Sargent & Lundy, and Kuljian Corp., 1971-75; chief engr. Gimpel Corp., Langhorne, Pa., 1976-79; sr. R&D engr. Yarway Corp., Blue Bell, Pa., 1979-82; sr. project process engr. and power utilities supr. Merck & Co., Inc., West Point, Pa., 1982-91; sr. project mgr. Conmec, Inc., Bethlehem, Pa., 1992-93, Edward S. Cartlidge, PE and Assocs., Blue Bell, Pa., 1993—2000; mgr. facilities engring. Cardinal Health, Inc., Softgel Pharm. Mfg., St. Petersburg, Fla., 2000—04; mfr.'s rep. Tom Evans Environ. Water/Waste Water Products Inc., Lakeland, Fla., 2005; utilities mgr. All Star Svcs., FAA Tech. Ctr., Pomona, NJ, 2005—. Cons. Pharm., Facilities Mgmt., Utilities, Semiconductor, Steel Fab., Gideon; Christian fin. counselor, lectr., seminar leader. Bd. dirs. Grand Old Gospel Fellowship. Served to comdr. USNR, 1968-91. Mem. NSPE (chpt. pres.), ASME, ASHRAE, AWWA, Pa. Soc. Profl. Engrs. (Young Engr. of Yr. 1980), Nat. Fire Prevention Assn., Gideons Internat. (camp pres.). Home: 37 Able's Run Dr Absecon NJ 08201 Personal E-mail: edcartlidge@netzero.com.

CARTMELL, ELIZABETH BAYLEY (LIZA), hospitality and food services executive; b. Red Bank, NJ, Jan. 27, 1957; d. Peter and Constance (Wingerter) Cartmell; m. Paul Henry Zoubek, Aug. 15, 1981; children: Sarah, Brian. BA in Econs., Wellesley Coll., Mass., 1979; MBA in Fin., Columbia U., NYC, 1982. Analyst Citibank N.Am., NYC, 1979-80; banking officer to v.p. Mellon Bank, Phila., 1982-89; mgr. cash and banking ARAMARK, Phila., 1989; CFO to pres. stadiums and arenas to pres. sports and entertainment grp. ARAMARK Sports and Entertainment, Phila., 1994—2004, grp. pres., 2006—. Mem. Wellesley-in-Phila. (rec. sec. 1988-90). Office: ARAMARK 1101 Market St Philadelphia PA 19107-2934*

CARTMELL, NATHANIEL MADISON, III, lawyer; b. NYC, Oct. 22, 1951; s. Nathaniel Madison Jr. and Ruth Kincer (Davies) C.; m. Suzanne Cameron Pettus, Jan. 3, 1981; children: Nathaniel Madison IV, Edmund Winston, Samuel Chapman Davies. BA, Yale U., 1973; JD, Vanderbilt U., 1978. Bar: Calif. State 1983, D.C. 1980, Va. State 1978. Mem. faculty Williston Northampton Sch., Easthampton, Mass., 1973-75; assoc. Hunton & Williams, Richmond, Va., 1978-80, Washington, 1980-81; atty. U.S. Synthetic Fuels Corp., Washington, 1981; assoc. Pillsbury Madison & Sutro LLP, Washington, 1982-83, San Francisco, 1983-86; ptnr. Pillsbury Winthrop Shaw Pittman, LLP, San Francisco, 1987—, mgr. corp. and securities group, 1994-96, chmn. mergers and acquisitions specialty team, 1999—. Alumni bd. dirs. Vanderbilt Law Sch., 1998-2001; alumni coun. Phillips Acad., 1997-2000; bd. govs. Phelps Assn., 2004—; bd. dirs. YMCA, San Francisco, 2004—. Mem. ABA (mem. fed. regulation of securities com., bus. law sect. 1990—), Calif. State Bar (mem. corps. com., bus. law sect. 1989-91). Episcopalian. Office: Pillsbury Winthrop Shaw Pittman LLP 50 Fremont St San Francisco CA 94105 Home Phone: 510-848-2999; Office Phone: 415-983-1570. Office Fax: 415-983-1200. Business E-Mail: nathaniel.cartmell@pillsburylaw.com.

CARTON, LONNIE CAMING, educational psychologist; b. Balt. d. Daniel and Shirley (Cooper) Caming; m. Edwin B. Carton; children: Evan, Deborah, Paula. BS, Johns Hopkins U.; MS, U. Md.; PhD, Pa. State U. Tchr. Laurel (Md.) H.S.; instr. Pa. State U., State College, Temple U., Phila.; newspaper columnist Delaware County Times, Chester, Pa.; instr., then asst. prof. Tufts U., Medford, Mass., 1964—80; learning sys. cons. Tufts New Eng. Med. Ctr., Boston, 1968—73. Broadcast journalist CBS Radio, N.Y.C., 1974—; family support sys. cons. Boston Ptnrs. in Edn., 1985—; ind. cons., lectr., workshop leader in field; guest appearances of various radio and TV shows; family lit. cons. Mass. Dept. Edn., 2001—; v.p., dir. teen and family resources Warm 2 Kids, Inc., 2003—; adv. panel SeaWorld Entertainment. Author: Mommies, 1960, Daddies, 1963, Raise Your Kids Right, 1980, No is a Love Word, 1992, (cassette tapes) Parenting Preschoolers from the Park Bench, 1999; sr. editor Edn. Today, Boston, 1992-98; broadcast journalist Voice of Am., 1995-98; contbr. articles to profl. publs. Grantee Gannet Found., U.S. Dept. Edn., Mass. Dept. Edn., U.S. Dept. Hwy. Safety, Mass. Gov.'s Alliance Against Drugs; recipient Nat. Media award APA, 1978, 80, San Francisco State Broadcast Media award, 1983, Contbn. to Lives of Children award UNICEF, Margaret Sanger Soc. award Planned Parenthood, 1985, Don Bosco Friend of Youth award Salesian Soc., awards from Mass. Psychol. Assn., Nat. Commn. Against Drunk Driving, Gabriel Broadcaster's and Allied Communicators, Mass. Soc. Against Cruelty to Children, 1988; named to One Hundred Most Remarkable Women in Mass., Boston Woman's Mag., 1989, Freedoms Found., George Washington medal for pub. comms., 1998. Avocations: tennis, spectator football, reading. Personal E-mail: ebclcc@aol.com.

CARTWRIGHT, BRIAN GRANT, federal agency administrator, lawyer; b. Seattle, May 29, 1947; s. John Brydonne and Helen Ruth (Engman) C.; m. Jean Claudia Libby, Jan. 5, 1975; children: Grant, Eliot, Bryce. BS, Yale U., 1967; PhD, U. Chgo., 1971; JD, Harvard U., 1980. Bar: D.C. 1981, U.S. Dist. Ct. D.C. 1981, U.S. Ct. Appeals (D.C. cir.) 1981, Calif. 1984. Rsch. physicist U. Calif., Berkeley, 1973—77; law clk. U.S. Ct. Appeals (D.C. cir.), Washington, 1980-81, U.S. Supreme Ct., Washington, 1981-82; assoc. Latham & Watkins LLP, LA, 1982-88, ptnr., 1988—2005, mem. exec. com., 1994-98; lectr. U. Calif., Los Angeles, 1999—2005; gen. counsel SEC, Washington, 2006—. Mem. Los Angeles County Bar Assn. (mem. exec. com., bus. and corps. law sect. 1992-99), Inst. Corp. Counsel (bd. govs. 2004-2005). Office: SEC 100 F St NE Washington DC 20549

CARTWRIGHT, CAROL ANN, retired academic administrator; b. Sioux City, Iowa, June 19, 1941; d. Carl Anton and Kathryn Marie (Weishapple) Becker; m. G. Phillip Cartwright, June 11, 1966; children: Catherine E., Stephen R., Susan D. BS in Early Childhood Edn., U. Wis., Whitewater, 1962; MEd in Spl. Edn., U. Pitts., 1965, PhD in Spl. Edn., Ednl. Rsch., 1968. From instr. to assoc. prof. Coll. Edn. Pa. State U., University Park, 1968-72, from assoc. prof. to prof., 1972-79, dean acad. affairs, 1981-84, dean undergrad. program, vice provost, 1984-88; vice chancellor acad. affairs U. Calif., Davis, 1988-91, prof. human devel., 1988-91; pres. Kent State U., Ohio, 1991—2006. Bd. dirs. First Energy Corp. (formerly Ohio Edison), Akron, 1992—, KeyCorp., Cleve., PolyOne Corp., The Davey Tree Expert Co., Kent; exec. bd. Nat. Coun. for Accreditation Tchr. Edn., 2002—; chair NCAA Exec. Com.; mem. N.E. Ohio Coun. Higher Edn., Knight Commn. Intercollegiate Athletics, 2000. Editorial bd. Topics in Early Childhood Special Education, 1982-88, Exceptional Education Quarterly, 1982-88. Pres., bd. dirs. Child Devel. Coun. of Center County, Title XX Day Care Contractor, 1977-80; bd. dirs. Center County United Way, State College, Pa., 1984-88, Urban League of Greater Cleve., 1997—; bd. mem. Davis (Calif.) Art Ctr., 1988-91, Davis Sci. Ctr., 1989-91; bd. dirs. Ohio divsn. Am. Cancer Soc., 1993-2000, nat. bd. dirs., 1993—; mem. nat. bd. First Ladies Libr.; bd. trustees Woodrow Wilson Internat. Ctr. for Scholars, 1999—; bd. dirs. Ctr. for Rsch. Librs., 2002—. Named to Ohio Women's Hall of Fame; recipient Disting. Alumni award, U. Wis.-Whitewater, U. Pittsburgh Sch. Edn., Clairol Mentor award, Women of Achievement award, YWCA of Greater Cleve., Franklin Delano Roosevelt award for Excellence, March of Dimes. Mem. AAUW, Am. Coun. Edn. (Commn. on Women in Higher Edn., 2003-), Am. Ednl. Rsch. Assn., Am. Assn. for Higher Edn., Nat. Assn. State Univs. and Land-Grant Colls., Coun. for Exceptional Children, the Greater Akron Chamber, Cleve. Tomorrow. Roman Catholic. Avocations: walking, reading, travel. Home: 1703 Woodway Rd Kent OH 44240-5917 E-mail: carol.cartwright@kent.edu.

CARTWRIGHT, JAMES E., career military officer; b. Rockford, Ill., Sept. 22, 1949; Grad., U. Iowa, 1971, Naval Flight Sch., 1973; grad. with distinction, Air Command and Staff Coll., 1986; MA in Nat. Security and Strategic Study, Naval War Coll., 1991. Commd. 2d lt. USMC, 1971, advanced through grades to gen., 2004; line divsn. officer VMFA-333 USS NIMITZ, 1975—77; aircraft maintenance officer VMFA-235, 1979—82; adminstrn. officer, officer-in-charge deployed carrier ops. VMFAT-101, 1983—85; asst. program mgr. for engring. F/A 18 Naval Air Systems Command, 1986—89; comdr. Marine Aviation Logistics Squadron 12, Iwakuni, Japan, 1989-90, Marine Aircraft Group 24, Kanoehe Bay, Hawaii, 1991-92; dep. aviation plans, policy, and budgets Marine Hdqrs., Washington, 1992-94; fellow MIT, 1994; comdr. Marine Aircraft Group 31, 1994-96; assigned to Dir. Force Structure, Resources, and Assessment, The Joint Staff, Washington, 1996-97, dep. dir., 1997-98; dep. comdr. USMC Forces Atlantic, 1999—2000; commdg. gen. 1st Marine Aircraft Wing, 2000—02; dir., force structure, resources & assessment (J-8) The Joint Staff, The Pentagon, 2002—04; comdr. US Strategic Command, Offutt AFB, 2004—07; vice chmn. Joint Chiefs of Staff, US Dept. Def., Washington, 2007—. Office: US Dept Def 9999 JCS Pentagon Washington DC 20318*

CARTWRIGHT, KEROS, hydrogeologist, researcher; b. LA, July 25, 1934; s. Eugene Ewing and Charlotte Lucy (Searle) C.; m. Sharon Miller, July 5, 1955 (dec.); children: Sylvia, Jennifer; m. Jenifer Elizabeth Moberley, Mar. 9, 1962 (div. Sept. 1988); children: David, Bridget; m. Madalene Rose Tierney, Feb. 16, 1990. AB in Geology, U. Calif., Berkeley, 1959; MS in Geology, U. Nev., Reno, 1961; PhD in Geology, U. Ill., Urbana-Champaign, 1973. Cert. profl. geologist, profl. hydrologist. Hydrogeologist Humboldt River Rsch. Project, Winnemucca, Nev., 1959—61, Ill. State Geol. Survey, Champaign, 1961—2000, head hydrogeology and geophysics sect., 1975—84, prin. scientist and head gen. and environ. geology group, 1984—88, prin. rsch. scientist, 1988—99, chief scientist emeritus, 1999—; adj. prof. geology No. Ill. U., DeKalb, 1979—2004, U. Ill., Urbana, 1985—2004. Cons. pvt. practice in hydrogeology, N.Am. and Europe, 1968—, U.S. Environ. Protection Agy. Sci. Adv. Bd., Washington, 1983-2005, Savannah River Site Environ. Adv., Aiken, S.C., 1988-05. Mem. editl. bd. Elsevier Sci. Publ. Jour. of Hydrology, 1982-85; contbr. articles to profl. jours. Named Disting. Lectr. Assn. Groundwater-Water Scientists and Engrs., 1987; recipient Cert. Appreciation U.S. Environ. Protection Agy., 1988. Fellow: Geol. Soc. Am. (officer hydrogeology sect. 1975—78, chmn. 1978—79, Bull. 1981—83, mem. governing coun. 1993—97, chmn. publs. com., Birdsall disting. lectr. 1987—88, George B. Maxey Disting. Svc. award 1991), Explorers Club; mem.: ASTM (vice chmn. subcom. D-14 1984—88), Internat. Assn. Hydrogeologists (U.S. com. 1985—89), Am.Water Resources Assn., Am. Geophys. Union (assoc. editor 1975—81), Am. Inst. Hydrology (mem. editl. bd. Jour. Hydrol. Sci. and Tech. 1985—2005). Avocation: farming. Office: Ill Geol Survey 615 E Peabody Dr Champaign IL 61820-6918 Business E-Mail: redoaks@soltec.net.

CARTWRIGHT, NANCY, actress, television producer; b. Kettering, Ohio, Oct. 25, 1957; d. Frank and Miriam Cartwright; m. Warren Murphy, Dec. 24, 1988; children: Lucy Mae, Jackson. Student, Ohio U., 1976—77; BA in theatre, UCLA, 1981. Founder Cartwright Entertainment Inc. Author: (biography) My Life as a 10-Year-Old Boy, 2000; prodr.: (animated internet series) The Kellys, 2001—; actor(voice): (TV series) The Richie Rich/Scooby-Doo Hour, 1980, Richie Rich, 1981, Monchichis, 1983, Saturday Supercade, 1983, Alvin & the Chipmunks, 1983, The Shirt Tales, 1983—85, The Snorks, 1984, Galaxy High School, 1986, My Little Pony and Friends, 1986, Pound Puppies, 1986, Popeye and Son, 1987, (voice of Bart Simpson) The Tracy Ullman Show, 1987—89, (voice) Fantastic Max, 1988, (voice, Bart Simpson/Nelson/Todd Flanders/Ralph Wiggum/others) The Simpsons, 1989— (Emmy award outstanding voice-over performance, 1992), (voice) Dink, the Little Dinosaur, 1989, Goof Troop, 1992, Raw Toonage, 1992, Bonkers, 1993, Animaniacs, 1993 (Daytime Emmy awards honors for contbg., 1996), Problem Child, 1993, The Pink Panther, 1993, Aladdin, 1993, 2 Stupid Dogs, 1993, The Critic, 1994, Timon and Pumbaa, 1995, The Twisted Adventures of Felix the Cat, 1995, Toonsylvania, 1998, Pinky, Elmyra & the Brian, 1998 (Daytime Emmy awards honors for contbg., 1999), Mike, Lu & Og, 1999, Big Guy and Rusty the Boy Robot, 1999—, God, the Devil and Bob, 2000, (voice of Chuckie) Rugrats, 2001—04, (voice of Rufus) Kim Possible, 2002, (voice of Chuckie) All Grown Up, 2003, (voice): (videos) The Land Before Time VI: The Secret of Saurus Rock, 1998, Wakko's Wish, 1999, Timberwolf, 2002, Kim Possible: The Secret Files, 2003; (TV films) Kim Possible: A Stitch in Time, 2003; (films) The Chipmunk Adventure, 1987, The Little Mermaid, 1989, Petal to the Metal, 1992, Rugrats Go Wild!, 2003, The Simpsons Movie, 2007,: (TV films) Marian Rose White, 1982, The Rules of Marriage, 1982, Deadly Lessons, 1983, Not My Kid, 1985, Yellow Pages, 1988, On Hollywood Blvd., 1988, Precious Victims, 1993, Vows of Deception, 1996, Suddenly, 1996; (films) Twilight Zone: The Movie, 1983, Flesh & Blood, 1985, Godzilla, 1998; (plays) The Transgressor, 1980, Guys and Dolls, 1984, Coming Attractions, 1985, In Search of Fellini, 1995 (DramaLogue award best performance one-person show, 1996), Cat's Meow, 1998. Co-founder Neko Tech Learning Ctr., Ghana, W. Africa, 2000; mem., commr. Citizens Commn. on Human Rights, 1996—; active with Famous Fone Friends, The World Literacy Crusade, Make A Wish Foundation, The Way to Happiness Internat. Recipient Am. Libr. Assn. award, 1992, Elizabeth Andersch award, 1992, County of LA Pub. Libr. award, 1994, Annie award for outstanding individual achievement for voice acting field of animation, Internat. Animated Soc., 1995, PMA Star Power award, 2000. Mem.: Screen Actors Guild. Office: Cartwright Entertainment Inc 9420 Reseda Blvd #572 Northridge CA 91324*

CARTWRIGHT, TALULA ELIZABETH, leadership consultant, educator; b. Asheville, NC, Oct. 25, 1947; d. Ralph and Sarah Helen (Medford) C.; m. Edwin Byram Crabtree, May 23, 1976 (div. Sept. 1984); children: Charity, Baxter; m. Richard Thomas England, Apr. 27, 1986; 1 child, Isaac. BA, U. NC, Greensboro, 1971, MEd, 1974, EdD, 1988. Instr. McDowell Tech. Inst., Marion, NC, 1972-73, Guilford Tech. CC, Jamestown, NC, 1973-89, Guilford Coll., Greensboro, NC, 1982-87, U. NC-Greensboro, 1982-87; instr. leadership NC A&T State U., Greensboro, 1984-85. With Communication Assocs., Lenoir, Shelby, Asheboro, Greensboro, 1981—; dean continuing edn. Caldwell C.C., Lenoir, N.C., 1989-92; v.p. acad. programs Cleve. C.C., 1992-95; sr. faculty and program mgr. Ctr. for Creative Leadership, Greensboro, N.C., 1996—; chmn. bd. dirs. Cleve. Abuse Prevention Coun., 1993-95. Bd. dirs. Family Crisis Ctr., 2003—. Tchr. of Yr. award Guilford Tech. C.C. Edn. Assn., 1982, Edn. Honor Roll award 1989; winner Human Rights Writing Contest, 1988, 89. Mem. NCAE (pres. local unit 1988-89, chmn. higher edn. commn. 1989-90, 92-95), Am. Assn. Women in C.C., Women's Adminstrs. in N.C. (exec. bd. 1995). Office Phone: 336-286-4509.

CARTY, AMOS W., lawyer; b. V.I., 1966; m. Verna Carty. Chief legal counsel Legis., V.I.; counsel to Gov., V.I., 1997; COO Roy Lester Schneider Hosp. Mem.: V.I. Bar Assn. (ABA del. 2003, pres.-elect 2003—04, pres. 2004—05). Office: Roy Lester Schneider Hosp PO Box 307223 VDS Charlotte Amalie St Thomas VI 00802 Office Phone: 340-714-6331. Office Fax: 340-714-6316. E-mail: awcarty@rlhospital.org.*

CARTY, ARTHUR JOHN, science policy advisor, research administrator; b. Hookergate, County Durham, Eng., Sept. 12, 1940; arrived in Can., 1965; naturalized, 1969. George M. and Evelyn Carty; m. Helene Cloutier, Sept. 3, 1967; children: Richard, Stephane, Roxanne. BSc, U. Nottingham, Eng., 1962, PhD, 1965; DSc honoris causa, U. Rennes, France, 1986,

Carleton U., Ottawa, Can., 1997, U. Waterloo, Can., 1997; Prof. Honoris Causa, Nat. Chiao-Tung U., Taiwan, 1998; DSc honoris causa, Acadia U., NS, Can., 1999, McMaster U., Hamilton, Can., 2000, Queen's U., Kingston, Can., 2001, U. Ottawa, Can., 2002, St. John's Meml. U. Nfld., 2003, Okanagan U., 2004, U. Calgary, 2004, U. Nottingham, Eng., 2006. Asst. prof. chemistry Meml. U. Nfld., St. John's, Can., 1965-67, U. Waterloo, Ont., Canada, 1967-69, assoc. prof. chemistry Ont., 1969-75, prof. chemistry Ont., 1975-94, chmn. dept. chemistry Ont., 1983-89, dean rsch. Ont., 1989-94; pres. Nat. Rsch. Coun. Can., Ottawa, Ont., 1994—2004; mem. Sch. Grad. Studies and Rsch. U. Ottawa, 1995—; nat. sci. advisor to Govt. of Can., 2004—. Dir. Guelph-Waterloo Ctr. for Grad. Work in Chemistry, 1975—79; mem. internat. adv. bd. Asia Pacific Econ. Coop. Ctr. for Tech. Foresight, Thailand, 1998—, numerous others. Mem. Math. Info. Tech. and Complex Systems, 1999—, Can. Stroke Network, 2000-04, Genome Can., 2000-04, Communitech Assn. Inc., 2000-03; chmn. Can. Light Source Inc., 1999—; mem. Can. Space Agy. Adv. Coun., 2000-. Decorated officer Ordre Nat. du Mérite (France), officer Order of Can.; recipient Royal Soc. award Nuffield Found., 1974, Purvis award Soc. Chem. Industry, 1997, Queen Elizabeth II jubilee medal, 2002, Walter Hitschfeld award Can. Assn. Univ. Rsch. Adminstrs., 2006. Fellow Royal Soc. Can.; mem. Am. Chem. Soc., Can. Soc. for Chemistry (v.p. 1989-90, pres. 1990-91, Alcan award 1984, E.W.R. Steacie award 1995), Chem. Inst. Can. (Montreal medal 1996), Can. Inst. Chemistry (hon. fellow), Fields Inst. Rsch. in Math. Scis. (hon. fellow), Engring. Inst. Can. (hon.). Office: Nat Sci Adv to the Govt of Can Industry Canada 235 Queen St Ottawa ON K1A 0H5 Canada

CARTY, DONALD J., computer company and former air transportation executive; b. Toronto, July 23, 1946; m. Ana Carty; 3 children. Grad., Queen's U., Kingston, Ont., 1968, Harvard U., 1971. With Air Canada, 1971—73, Canadian Pacific Rwy.; gen. mgr. Montcel Distbrs. unit Celanese Can. Ltd., Montreal, 1973—78; sr. v.p. fin. Americana Hotels, 1978—79; v.p., ops. rsch. American Airlines, 1979—80, v.p. profit improvement, 1980—81, v.p., controller, 1981—83, sr. v.p., controller, 1983—85, sr. v.p. airline planning, 1987-89; pres., CEO CP Air, 1985—87; exec. v.p. fin. and planning AMR and Am. Airlines, DFW Airport, Tex., 1989-95; pres. AMR Airline Group and Am. Airlines, Inc., DFW Airport, Tex., 1995-98; chmn., pres., CEO AMR Corp., Ft. Worth, 1998—2002, chmn., CEO, 2002—03; chmn. Virgin Am., Inc., VAI Partners, LLC, San Francisco, 2006; vice chmn., CFO Dell Inc., 2007—. Bd. dirs. Dell computer Corp., 1992-, Sears, Roebuck & Co., 2001-05.; mem. Nat. Infrastructure Adv. Coun., Office of Sec., US Dept. Homeland Security. Bd. trustees Queen's U.; gov. Dallas Symphony Assn., Inc.; trustee So. Methodist U. Recipient The Order of Canada, 2003. Office: Dell Inc 1 Dell Way Round Rock TX 78682*

CARTY, MARY ELLEN, psychologist; b. NYC, Aug. 7, 1958; d. Walter Vincent and Sally Rita (Clarke) C. BA, Coll. of New Rochelle, 1980, MS, 1991; PsychD, Yeshiva U., 1997. Cert. sch. psychologist, N.Y.; lic. psychologist., N.Y. Grad. asst. Coll. of New Rochelle, NY, 1989-90, rsch. asst. NY, 1990-91; sch. psychologist intern Pawling (N.Y.) Ctrl. Sch. Dist., 1990-91; sch. psychologist Pawling Jr./Sr. H.S., 1991-93, Clarkstown H.S. South, West Nyack, NY, 1993-94; behavior specialist, psychologist Esperanza Ctr., NYC, 1993-96; clin. psychology intern, postdoctoral fellow Ctr. Preventive Psychiatry, 1996-98; program psychologist So. Westchester Bd. Coop. Ednl. Svcs., Harrison, 1998—2002; sch. psychologist Rye Neck Middle/H.S., Mamaroneck, NY, 2002—04, NYC Dept. Edn., 2004—. Acad. counselor Iona Coll., New Rochelle, N.Y., 1990-94, 96-97; adj. instr. psychology Coll. New Rochelle, 2004— Vol. English tchr. Immaculate Conception H.S., Jamaica, 1983—85, West Indies, 1983—85; mem. grad. sch. adv. bd. Coll. of New Rochelle, 1999—2000; co-pres. alumni assn. Ferkauf Grad. Sch. Psychology, Yeshiva U., 2000—03; dir. Alumni Assn. Coll. of New Rochelle, 2001—04; trustee, mem. ch. coun. St. Pius X Ch., Jamaica, 1983—85. Recipient Ursula Laurus citation, 2000; Empire Challenger fellow N.Y. State Edn. Dept., 1988-89. Mem.: APA, NY Assn. Sch. Psychologists (Ted Bernstein award 1996), Psi Chi. Democrat. Roman Catholic. Avocations: bicycling, meditation, travel. Home: 434 N High St Mount Vernon NY 10552-3103 Office Phone: 718-292-4742. Personal E-mail: carty434@earthlink.net.

CARTY, PAUL VERNON, lawyer; b. Uchitomari, Okinawa, Aug. 2, 1954; s. Leo Sylvester and Dolores Iola (Inniss) C.; m. Kimberly Ann Fickett, Jan. 23, 1982; children: Rachel Lee, Paul Jr., Trevor Dudley. BA, Wesleyan U., Middletown, Conn., 1977; JD, U. Conn., 1985. Bar: Conn. 1985, U.S. Dist. Ct. (Conn.) 1992, Mashantucket Pequot Tribal Ct. 1995. Claims adjustor Liberty Mut. Ins. Co., Bklyn., 1977-80; sr. claims rep. Cigna Corp., Farmington, Conn., 1980-85; assoc. Farren & King, New Haven, 1985-97; solo practitioner New Haven, 1997—. Chmn. West Haven (Conn.) Bd. Ethics, 1987-90; bd. dirs. Chem. Abuse Svcs. Agy., Inc., 1998—, West Haven Cmty. Ho., Inc., 2006—; bd. dirs. Tang Soo Do Mi Guk Kwan Assn., Inc., 2002—, chmn. 2004-06. Mem. ABA, Nat. Bar Assn., Conn. Bar Assn., Conn. Trial Lawyers Assn., Conn. Criminal Def. Lawyers Assn., New Haven County Bar Assn., West Haven Bar Assn., George Crawford Law Assn. Episcopalian. Avocations: Karate, photography. Home: 20 Swampscott St West Haven CT 06516-1424 Office: PO Box 3192 233 Orange St New Haven CT 06515-0292 Office Phone: 203-387-5400. E-mail: PVCartyEsq@aol.com.

CARUS, MILTON BLOUKE, children's periodicals publisher; b. Chgo., June 15, 1927; s. Edward H. and Dorothy (Blouke) C.; m. Marianne Sondermann, Mar. 3, 1951; children: Andre, Christine, Inga. BS in Elec. Engring, Calif. Inst. Tech., 1949; postgrad. in Chemistry, U. Freiburg, Germany, 1949-51; postgrad., Sorbonne U., Paris, 1951. Devel. engr. Carus Chem. Co., Inc., LaSalle, Ill., 1951—55, asst. gen. mgr., 1955—61, exec. v.p., 1961—64, chmn., CEO, 1964—90, Carus Corp., Peru, 1990—; editor Open Ct. Pub. Co., 1962—67, pub., pres., 1967—88, pub., 1988—89, sr. cons., 1989—; pub. Cricket mag., 1973—89; sr. cons. Cricket mag. group, 1989—2000, chmn., 2000—. Treas. Bookbird Internat. Bd. Books Young People, 1994-1996. Chmn. Ill. Valley Cmty. Coll. Com., 1965-67; pres. Internat. Baccalaureat N.Am. Inc., 1977, chmn., 1980-89; mem. IBO Coun., Geneva, 1977-94; co-trustee Hegeler Inst., 1968-89, chmn., 1989-; mem. employment and tng. com. U.S. Chamber, 1981-85; mem. Nat. Coun. on Ednl. Rsch. Nat. Inst. Edn., Dept. Edn., 1982-85, vice chmn., 1983-85; trustee Parliament of World's Religious, 1988—; mem. Ill. Gov.'s Task Force on Sch.-to-Work, 1994-96. Mem. Ill. Valley Indsl. Assn. (pres. 1970—), Chem. Mfrs. Assn. (dir. 1977-80), Ill. Mfrs. Assn. (dir. 1972-77, 1988-99, chmn. edn. com. 1988—), LaSalle County Hist. Soc. (dir. 1979-85), Phila Soc., Ill. State C. of C. (edn. com. 1973-75). Avocations: reading, travel, music, gardening, languages. Office: Carus Corp Hdqrs 315 5th St Peru IL 61354-2859 Office Phone: 815-224-6674. Business E-Mail: mbcarus@caruschem.com.

CARUSO, ADRIENNE IORIO, retired language educator; b. Saratoga Springs, NY, May 30, 1926; d. Andrew and Josephine Pompay Iorio; m. Carl Thomas Caruso, June 27, 1953 (dec. Feb. 2, 2001). BA, N.Y. State Coll. Tchrs., Albany, 1948, MA, 1951. Cert. tchr. N.Y. Dept. Edn. Tchr. English, French, art and libr. Oppenheim Ephratah Ctrl. Sch., NY, 1948—50; tchr. English Corinth H.S., 1951—52, Saratoga Springs Secondary Sch. Complex, 1952—82. Practice tchr. supr. Saratoga Springs City Sch. Dist.; faculty advisor Nat. Honor Soc.; faculty advisor yearbook, book club, others Saratoga Springs Secondary Complex. Permanent mem. Saratoga Performing Arts Ctr.; donor U. at Albany Found., NY; v.p. Saratoga Springs Ret. Tchrs. Assn., 1985—97; pres. Ladies Aux. BPOE Lodge 161, 1985—86; past bd. mem. and treas. LWV. Mem.: AAUW (life; pres. Saratoga Springs br. 1983—85, 1990—91), Catholic Daughters of Am., N.Y. State Retired Tchrs. Assn. (life; pres. Ea. zone 1995—98, honoree 1990), Hist. Soc. Saratoga Springs, Friends Saratoga Springs Pub. Libr., U. Albany Alumni Assn. (life; bd. dirs. 2000—). Republican. Roman Catholic. Avocations: art, dance, music, photography, travel. Home: 280 Lake Ave Saratoga Springs NY 12866-3735

CARUSO, DANIEL F., lawyer, judge, former state legislator; b. Greenwich, Conn., Dec. 12, 1957; s. Frederick A. Caruso and Ruth Collins. BA, U. Conn., 1980; JD, U. Vt., 1983. Bar: Conn. 1983, U.S. Dist. Ct. Conn. 1984. Atty. Paul M. Tymniak & Assocs., Fairfield, Conn., 1984-88; sole practice Fairfield, 1988-97; mem. Conn. Gen. Assembly, Hartford, 1989-94, asst. house minority leader, 1992-94, ranking mem. gen. law com., 1991; judge of probate Probate Dist. of Fairfield, 1995—; adminstrv. judge Probate Dist. of New Cannan, 2001, Probate Dist. of Greenwich, 2002, chmn. Conn. siting coun., 2006—; atty. Owen, Schine & Nicola, P.C., Fairfield, Conn., 1997—. Co-chmn. House Rep. Policy Group on Drug Control Strategy; mem. gen. law com. Conn. Gen. Assembly, 1991-94, mem. judiciary com., 1989-94, mem. regulation rev. com., 1989-94; 2d v.p. Conn. Probate Assembly, 2004—. Mem., advisor Nat. Heritage Trust Adv. Bd., 1990-91; treas. Town of Fairfield, 1993-95, mem. bd. fin., 1985-89; del. Rep. Nat. conv., Houston, 1992. Mem. Kiwanis, Eagle Scouts Am., Pi Sigma Alpha, Phi Alpha Theta, Alpha Phi Omega. Roman Catholic. Home: 160 Fairfield Woods Rd Apt 61 Fairfield CT 06825-3348 Office: 53 Sherman St Fairfield CT 06824-5821

CARUSO, DAVID, actor; b. Forest Hills, NY, Jan. 7, 1956; s. Charles and Joan C.; m. Cheri Maugans, Mar. 30, 1979, (div. Feb. 21, 1984); m. Rachel Ticotin, 1984 (div. 1987); m. Margaret Buckley, May 4, 1996 (div. Aug. 14, 2005); children: Greta, Marquez Anthony. Co-owner Steam home furnishings store, Miami. Appearances include (film) An Officer and a Gentleman, 1982, First Blood, 1982, Thief of Hearts, 1984, Blue City, 1986, China Girl, 1987, Twins, 1988, King of New York, 1990, Hudson Hawk, 1991, Mad Dog and Glory, 1993, Kiss of Death, 1994, Jade, 1995, The Split, 1997, Cold Around the Heart, 1997, The Split, 1998; (TV movies) Crazy Times, 1981, The First Olympics-Athens 1896, 1984, Into the Homeland, 1987, Rainbow Drive, 1990, Mission of the Shark, 1991, Judgement Day: The John List Story, 1993, Gold Coast, 1997; (TV series) N.Y.P.D. Blue, 1993-94 (Best Actor - Drama Golden Globe award 1994, Best Actor in Drama series Emmy award nominee 1994), Michael Hayes, 1997, CSI: Miami, 2002-; (TV miniseries) Baseball, 1994, Gold Coast, 1997. Office: William Morris Agy c/o Scott Lambert 151 S El Camino Dr Beverly Hills CA 90212-2775

CARUSO, MARK JOHN, lawyer; b. LA, Apr. 27, 1957; s. John Mondella and Joyce Dorothy C.; m. Judy F. Velarde, Aug. 15, 1987. BS cum laude, Pepperdine U., 1979, JD cum laude, 1982. Bar: Calif. 1982, N.Mex. 1987, U.S. Dist. Ct. (ctrl. dist.) Calif. 1982, U.S. Dist. Ct. N.Mex. 1987, U.S. Dist. Ct. (no. and so. dists.) Calif. 1995, U.S. Ct. Appeals (9th cir.) 1983, U.S. Ct. Appeals (10th cir.) 1987. Law clk. Fed. Trade Commn., LA, 1980—82; pvt. practice, Burbank, Calif., 1982—, Albuquerque, 1987—. Mem. N.Mex. Ho. of Reps., 1990-95, labor com., consumer and pub. affairs com., workers compensation oversight interim com., ct. correction and justice interim com., jud. com., labor com.; lobbyist Nat. Right to Work Com., 1984-86, Employee Rights Campaign Com., 1984-86; exec. dir. N.Mex. Citizens Right to Work, 1984-86, Okla. Freedom to Work Com., 1985-86; lectr. breast implant and diet drug litig.; expert witness drug litig. malpractice actions. Col., aide de camp to gov. State N. Mex., 1987; chmn. N. Mex. Mcpl. Boundary Commn., 1988—; del. Rep. Nat. Conv., 1988, 92; Sandoval county chmn. George Bush for Pres., 1988; campaign mgr. Boulter US Congress, Tex., 1975-82, Coll. Rep., 1975-82; staff mem. Ronald Reagan for Pres., 1979,80; mem. Young Am. for Freedom LA chpt., 1979-82. Recipient Am. Jurisprudence award, 1981, Platinum award, N.Mex. Free Enterprise Adv., 1986. Mem. ATLA, Breast Implant Litigation Group, Consumer Attys. Calif., Assn. Trial Lawyers Am., Albuquerque Hispano C. of C., Greater Albuquerque C. of C. Office: 4302 Carlisle Blvd NE Albuquerque NM 87107-4811 Office Phone: 505-883-5000. Office Fax: 505-883-5012.

CARUSO, NICK J., energy executive; BA in Acctg., La. State U. Various positions, including controller, gen. auditor to v.p. fin., CFO Shell Oil Co., Houston, 1969—2001; exec. v.p., CFO Dynegy, Inc., Houston, 2002—. Office: Dynegy Ste 5800 1000 Louisiana Houston TX 77002-5050 Office Phone: 713-507-6400.

CARUTHERS, LOYCE ELLENOR, education educator; d. Demancy and Ethel Lee Joiner; 1 child, Kenneth. B Elem. Edn. and History, U. Mo., Kansas City, 1972, MPA, 1974, Ednl. Specialist In Edn. Adminstrn., 1992, EdD, 2000. Cert. tchr. Mo. Staff devel. coord. Kansas City Mo. Sch. Dist., 1981—84, coord. spl. projects, 1984—87, asst. supt., 1996—98; project dir. Mid-Continent Regional Ednl. Equity Ctr., Aurora, Colo., 1987—93; sr. program assoc. Mid-Continent Regional Ednl. Lab., Aurora, 1993—96; assoc. prof. U. Mo., Kansas City, 2001—. Scorer sch. supt. assessment Ednl. Testing Svc. Contbr. articles to profl. jours. Con. Mo. 4H After Sch. Program, Kansas City, 1991—2002, mem. adv. bd., 1999—2002; mem. Coun. Black Edn., Urban League, Kansas City, 2006; bd. dirs. Niles Home for Children, Kansas City, 2004—06, KCMC Child Devel. Corp., Kansas City, 2004—05; mem. chancellor's bd. U. Mo., Kansas City, 1999—2003. Fellow, Am. Soc. Pub. Adminstrn., 1974; Chancellor Doctoral fellow, U. Mo., Kansas City, 1993. Mem.: ASCD, Nat. Staff Devel. Coun., Nat. Mid. Sch. Assn., Nat. Assn. Multicultural Edn., Nat. Alliance Black Sch. Educators, Am. Ednl. Studies Assn., Am. Edn. Rsch. Assn. (chmn. nomination com. 2004, mem. program com. 2003). Democrat. Achievements include research in First Things First implementation and early outcomes study; attendance, dropout prevention. Avocations: reading, walking, bargain shopping, collecting African art. Home: 2800 Parkwood Kansas City KS 66104

CARUTHERS, MARVIN HARRY, biochemistry educator; b. Des Moines, Feb. 11, 1940; s. Harry A. and Eva D. (Schultz) C.; m. Jennie Mary Smoly, Oct. 9, 1971; children: Jonathan, Andrew. BS in Chemistry, Iowa State U., 1962; PhD in Biochemistry, Northwestern U., 1968. Postdoctoral fellow U. Wis., Madison, 1968-70; sr. research scientist MIT, Cambridge, 1970-72; from asst. prof. to prof. biochemistry U. Colo., Boulder, 1973—, chmn. dept. chem. and biochem., 1992—95, disting. prof. biochemistry and bioorganic chemistry, 1999—; venture ptnr. Boulder Ventures, 1995—. Co-founder, former mem. sci. adv. bd., Amgen, Inc., scientific cons., Thousand Oaks, Calif. and Boulder, 1980-; co-founder Applied Biosystems, Inc. 1981; founding investor Genomica, Array BioPharma (bd. dir. 1998-, serves on compensation com.) and Dharmacon. Mem. editl. bd. Jour. Biotechnology, Jour. Molecular Recognition, Jour. Protein Engring; contbr. articles to profl. jours. Guggenheim fellow, 1981; recipient career devel. award USPHS, 1975-80, Nat. Biotechnology Ventures award, 1992, Elliott Cresson medal Franklin Inst., 1994, The Bonfils-Stanton Found. award in field of sci., 1994, Prelog medal, Zurich, Switzerland, 2004, Promega Biotechnology Research award, 2006; named 2006 Nat. Medal Sci. Laureate, NSF, 2007. Mem. AAAS, NAS (Award for Chemistry in Svc. to Soc., 2005), Am. Chem. Soc., Am. Soc. Biol. Chemists, Am. Acad. Arts and Scis. Achievements include invention and development of chemical reagents and methods currently used for the automated synthesis of DNA oligonucleotides; inventor of the gene machine; patents in field. Office: Dept Chemistry and Biochemistry Univ Colorado at Boulder Cristol Chemistry 355 Boulder CO 80309-0215 also: Boulder Ventures 1900 Ninth St Ste 200 Boulder CO 80302 Office Phone: 303-492-6095. Fax: 303-492-5894. E-mail: marvin.caruthers@colorado.edu.*

CARVALHO, JULIE ANN, psychologist; b. Washington, Apr. 11, 1940; d. Daniel Henry and Elizabeth Cecilia (Gardiner) Schmidt; children: Alan R., Dennis M., Melanie D., Celeste A., Joshua E. BA with high honors, U. Md., 1962, postgrad., 1962-63, 68-73, Va. Poly. Inst., 1979-88, Argosy U., 2003—04; MA, George Washington U., 1966. Social sci. rsch. analyst Mental Health Study Ctr., NIMH, Adelphi, Md., 1963-67; edn. and tng. analyst Computer Applications, Inc., Silver Spring, Md., 1967-68; edn. program specialist, program analyst Nat. Ctr. for Ednl. R&D, U.S. Office of Edn., Washington, 1969-73; equal opportunity specialist Office of Sec., HEW, Washington, 1973-77; legis. program, civil rights analyst Office for Civil Rights Dept. Health and Human Svcs., Washington, 1977-85; ind. cons. Adj. lectr. No. Va. C.C., George Mason U., Montgomery Coll., Strayer U., Park U., Shepherd Coll., Germanna Coll., U. Md. U. Coll., Va. Internat. U., Prince William Hosp., Fairfax County Pub. Schs., Fairfax County Dept. Social Svcs., all Washington area, 1986—; proposal evaluator HUD, HHS, 1989—; presenter in field. Contbr. articles to profl. jours. Bd. dirs. Child Care Ctrs., 1970—76, HEW Employees Assn., 1973—78; steering com. Alliance for Child Care, 1975—80. Mem.: ASPA (condr. panels 1975, 1991), APA (panel condr. 1969, 1975, editor Bull. of Peace Psychology 1991—97, divsn. 48), Unitarian Universalists for Social Justice (bd. dirs. Balt.-Washington region 2003—07), Federally Employed Women (nat. editor 1975—79), Psychologists Soc. Responsibility (cons., chair action com. on status of women), Capitol Area Social Psychologists Assn. (conf. chmn. 1985, 1993), Fairfax County Assn. for the Gifted (pres. 1980), Phi Alpha Theta, Psi Chi, Alpha Sigma Lambda (hon.). Home and Office: 4931 Americana Dr #203 Annandale VA 22003 Office Phone: 703-354-0838.

CARVEN, JOHN WINSLOW, priest; b. NYC, Jan. 20, 1932; s. Christopher Coleman and Mary Winslow Carven. BA, Mary Immaculate Seminary, 1956; MA, St. John's U., 1964; PhD, State U. of NY at Buffalo, 1972. Tchr. St. John's Preparatory Sch., Bklyn., 1960—64; assoc. prof. Niagara U., NY, 1964—76; assoc. dean St. John's U., Queens, NY, 1978—80; chaplain St. Joseph Provincial House, Emmitsburg, Md., 1985—95; annotation editor Vincentian Translation Project, Queens, 1980—; provincial archivist Ea. Province of the Congregation of the Mission, Phila., 1995—. Editor (annotation editor): St. Vincent de Paul, 1980—. Mem.: Del. Valley Archivists Group, Soc. Am. Archivists. Home and Office: St Vincents Seminary 500 E Chelten Ave Philadelphia PA 19144

CARVER, DAVID HAROLD, retired pediatrician; b. Boston, Apr. 18, 1930; s. Elias and Lottie (Jaffe) C.; m. Patricia Jo Nair, Aug. 2, 1963; children: Randolph Nair, Rebecca Lynn, Leslie Allison. AB magna cum laude, Harvard U., 1951; MD, Duke U., 1955. Intern Johns Hopkins Hosp., 1955-56; rsch. fellow pediatrics Cleve. Met. Hosp./Case We. Res. Med. Sch.), 1956-58; jr. asst. resident Children's Hosp. Med. Center, Boston, 1958-59, sr. asst. resident, 1959-60, chief resident, 1960-61, USPHS spl. rsch. fellow Harvard Med. Sch., 1961-63; asst. prof. pediatrics Albert Einstein Coll. Medicine, 1963-66; from assoc. prof. to prof. pediatrics Johns Hopkins U. Med. Sch., 1966-76; prof. pediatrics U. Toronto Med. Sch., 1976-88; physician-in-chief Hosp. Sick Children, Toronto, 1976-86; chmn. dept. pediatrics U. Toronto, 1976-86; prof. pediat. Robert Wood Johnson Med. Sch., New Brunswick, NJ, 1988—2005, chmn. dept. pediatrics, 1988—2000, assoc. dean faculty affairs, 2000—04, spl. advisor to the dean, 2004—05; chief pediats. Robert Wood Johnson U. Hosp., 1988—2000; ret., 2005. Mem. study sect. USPHS Ctr. Disease Control, 1971-73; mem. provincial research grants rev. com. Ont. Ministry Health, 1977-83, chmn., 1981-83 Assoc. editor: Textbook of Pediatrics, 14th edit, 1968, 15th edit., 1972, 16th edit., 1977; mem. editl. bd. Pediatrics, 1973-79. With USPHS, 1956-58. Recipient Schaffer award clin. teaching Johns Hopkins U. Med. Sch., 1973, Bain Clin. Tchg. award Hosp. Sick Children, 1978, Hon. award Robert Wood Johnson U. Hosp., 1997; Kennedy scholar, 1966-73 Mem. Am. Acad. Pediatrics (com. on infectious diseases 1973-79), Infectious Disease Soc. Am., Am. Soc. Virology, Internat. Soc. Interferon Research, Canadian Infectious Disease Soc., Am. Soc. Microbiology, Soc. Pediatric Research, Am. Pediatric Soc., Can. Pediatric Soc., Harvard Club Princeton. Home: 2416 Windrow Dr Princeton NJ 08540

CARVER, GEORGE ALLEN, JR., retired lawyer; b. Washington, Nov. 8, 1940; s. George Allen and Barbara Ellen (Bristol) C.; m. Joan Page, Dec. 13, 1964; children: George Allen III, Robert William. BS, U.S. Mil. Acad., 1964; JD, U. Va., 1972. Bar: Va. 1972, D.C. 1978, U.S. Ct. Appeals (D.C. cir.) 1979, U.S. Ct. Appeals (9th cir.) 1986, U.S. Ct. Appeals (4th cir.) 1988. Trial atty. gen. crimes sect. Criminal divsn. U.S. Dept. Justice, Washington, 1972-76, trial atty. pub. integrity sect., 1976-81, dir. conflicts of interest crimes br., pub. integrity sect., 1981-88, dep. chief fraud sect., 1988-92, prin. dep. chief fraud sect., 1992-95, sr. counsel to chief asset forfeiture/money laundering sect., 1995-96, dep. chief, sr. counsel to the chief, 1996-2000; ret., 2000. Capt. inf. U.S. Army, 1964-69. Decorated Silver Star, Bronze Star, Purple Heart, Vietnamese Gallentry Cross. Avocations: photography, fishing, boating, walking, reading. Home: 6049 Makely Dr Fairfax Station VA 22039-1324

CARVER, KENDALL LYNN, insurance company executive; b. Spencer, Iowa, Nov. 4, 1936; s. Marion and Letha G.; m. Carol Lee Spiers, July 1, 1961; children: Merrian, Kendra, Lee, Christine. BS, U. Iowa, 1958. Rep. field sales Washington Nat. Ins. Co., Evanston, Ill., 1958-73, regional dir., 1974-77, pres. NYC, 1977—, CEO, 1978-94; mng. dir. Kendall Carver and Assocs. LLC, 1996-98; chmn. fin. com. First Benefit Ins. Co. of Phoenix, 1996-98; also bd. dirs. First Benefit Inst. Co. of Phoenix, 1997; founder, pres., CEO Confirmation-Plus LLC, 1998—. Chmn. bd. dirs. Security Adminstrs. Inc., Binghamton, NY, 1999-2001; exec. com. Gt. Am. Life Ins. Co. NY, 1999-2001; founder, chmn. Exec. Men's Group, 2001-04; cons. in field. Founder, pres. Internat. Cruise Victims, 2006. Fellow Life Mgmt. Inst.; mem. Am. Coll. Life Underwriters. Republican.

CARVER, NORMAN FRANCIS, JR., architect, photographer; b. Jan. 27, 1928; m. Joan Willson, Aug. 15, 1953; children: Norman F. III, Cristina. Grad., Yale. Practice architecture, Kalamazoo; prof. advanced photography Kalamazoo Inst. Arts, 1971-86. Vis. lectr., critic Carnegie Inst. Tech., Mich. State U., Yale U., MIT, So. Ill. U.; guest lectr. King Faisal U., Saudi Arabia, 1981; co-owner The Carver Gallery, 2006. Exhibited photography U.S. and abroad; photographs published in Aperture, House Beautiful, Horizon, others; author: Form and Space of Japanese Architecture, 1955, 3d edit., 1993, Silent Cities of Mexico and the Maya, 1966, rev. edit., 1986, Italian Hilltowns, 1979, rev. edit., 1995, Iberian Villages - Spain and Portugal, 1981, Japanese Folkhouses, 1984, rev. edit., 2003, North African Villages, 1989, Greek Island Villages, 2001. Recipient Fulbright awards to Japan, 1953-54, 64, silver medal Archtl. League, 1962, award Archtl. Record, 1960, 61, 62, Robert Hastings award Mich. Soc. Architects, 1987. Home: 3201 Lorraine Ave Kalamazoo MI 49008-2003

CARVER, STEPHEN D., publishing executive, former broadcast executive; b. Oct. 5, 1954; m. Janice Carver; 2 children. BA in English Literature, Fairleigh Dickinson U. Asst. coord. sales dept. CBS TV Network, 1976-82; account exec. Sta. WCBS-FM, NYC, 1976-82, nat. sales mgr., 1982-83, retail sales mgr., 1983-85, gen. sales mgr., 1985-89; v.p., gen. mgr. Sta. WOGL-FM, Phila., 1989-90, Sta. WOGL-AM and Sta. WOGL-FM, Phila., 1990-93, Sta. WBBM, Chgo., 1993-98, Sta. WGN-AM, Chgo., 1998—2003, WATL-TV, Atlanta, 2003—06; v.p. radio Tribune Broadcasting, 1999—2001; regional v.p. Tribune TV, 2002—06; pres. Hartford (Conn.) Courant, 2006, pres., pub. & CEO, 2007—. Adv. bd. dirs.

LaSalle St. Coun.; mem. exec. com. Better Bus. Bur. Mem. Ill. Broadcasters Assn. (treas.), Chicagoland C. of C. (bd. dirs.). Office: Hartford Courant 285 Broad St Hartford CT 06115 Office Phone: 860-241-6200.*

CARVETTE, ANTHONY M., construction executive; V.p. fin., assoc. pub. N.Y. Mag.; contr. Harper's Mag.; acct. Peat Marwick & Mitchell; exec. v.p., COO Georgette Klinger; former COO Structure Tone Orgn., NYC, now pres. Mem. bd. trustees Alvin Ailey Am. Dance Found. Office: Structure Tone Orgn 770 Broadway 9th Fl New York NY 10003

CARVEY, DANA, actor, stand up comedian; b. Missoula, Mont., Apr. 2, 1955; m. Paula Zwaggerman. Student communication arts, San Francisco U. Appeared in TV films Alone at Last, 1980, Whacked Out, 1981, Hot Shots, 1986; TV series One of the Boys, 1982, Blue Thunder, 1984, Saturday Night Live, 1986— (Emmy award Outstanding Individual Performance in Variety or Musical Program 1989, 90, 91, 93); appeared in films including Halloween II, 1981, Racing with the Moon, 1984, This is Spinal Tap, 1984, Tough Guys, 1986, Moving, 1988, Opportunity Knocks, 1990, Wayne's World, 1992, Wayne's World II, 1993, Clean Slate, 1994, The Road to Wellville, 1994, Trapped in Paradise, 1994, The Shot, 1996, Little Nicky, 2000, The Master of Disguise, 2002; (TV series) The Dana Carvey Show, 1996; appeared on TV: Saturday Night Live, 25th Anniversary, 1999, Saturday Night Live: Best of Phil Hartman, 1998. Recipient Am. Comedy award, 1990.

CARVILLE, JAMES, JR., (CHESTER JAMES CARVILLE), political scientist, consultant; b. Fort Benning, Ga., Oct. 25, 1944; s. Lucille Carville; m. Mary Matalin, Nov. 25, 1993; 2 children. Grad., La. State Univ. Litigator, Baton Rouge, 1973—79; cons. Bob Casey's 1986 Penn. gubernatorial race, Sen. Harris Wofford's 1991 campaign; chief strategist, cons. Bill Clinton's 1992 presdl. campaign; cons. Gov. Jim Florio's 1993 re-election campaign, NJ, Ehud Barak's campaign for Prime Min. Israel, 1999. Co-host CNN's Crossfire; ptnr. Hawthorne Lane Restaurant, San Francisco; adj. prof. No. Va. CC, Alexandria, 2005—; spkr. in field. Author: We're Right, They're Wrong: A Handbook for Spirited Progressives, 1996, ...And the Horse He Rode in on: The People vs. Kenneth Starr, 1998, Stickin': The Case for Loyalty, 2000; co-author (with Mary Matalin): All's Fair: Love, War and Running for President, 1994; (with Paul Begala) Buck Up, Suck Up, and Come Back When You Foul Up, 2003, Take It Back: Our Country, Our Party, Our Future, 2006, (with Jeff Nussbaum) Had Enough?, 2003, (with Patricia C. McKissack) Lu and the Swamp Ghost, 2004; actor: (films) The People vs. Larry Flynt, 1996, Old School, 2003, Wedding Crashers, 2005, Man of the Year, 2006; (TV series) Boston Common, 1996, Arli$$, 1997, (voice only) King of the Hill, 1997, Mad About You, 1998, Spin City, 1999, (voice only) Family Guy, 2000; appearance (documentaries) The War Room, 1993, The Hunting of the President, 2004, (TV-polit. series) K Street. Named Campaign Mgr. of the Year, Am. Assn. of Political Consultants, 1993. Avocation: watching reruns of the andy griffith show. Office: Gaslight Inc 424 S Washington St Lower Level Alexandria VA 22314 Office Phone: 703-739-7777. Business E-Mail: james@carville.info.*

CARWELL, HATTIE VIRGINIA, health physicist; b. Bklyn., July 17, 1948; d. George and Fannie (Tunstall) Carwell. BS in Chemistry/Biology, Bennett Coll., Greensboro, NC, 1970; MS in Radiation Sci., Rutgers U., 1971; postgrad., U. Calif., Berkeley, 1973-75. Rsch. asst. Thomas Jefferson U. Hosp., Phila., 1970-72; health physicist AEC, Upton, NY, 1972-73, Energy Rsch. Adminstrn., Oakland, Calif., 1973-80; internat. nuclear safeguards insp. and group leader Internat. Atomic Energy Agy., Vienna, 1980-85; health physicist US Dept. Energy, Oakland, Calif., 1985-90, program mgr. for high energy and nuclear programs, 1990-91, program mgr. Berkeley, Calif., 1991-93, ops. team head, 1992—, ops. br. chief, 1993-94. Asst. environ. survey team leader Dept. Energy, Washington, 1987; lectr. U. Calif.-Berkeley, Stanford U., Cabrillo Coll., Can. Coll., Tougaloo Coll; dir. Mus. African Am. Tech. Sci. Village. Author: Blacks In Science: Astrophysicist to Zoologist, 1977, In Pursuit of Excellence: Dr. Warren Henry - World Class Scientist, 1998, Solar Cooker Design Training Guide, 1996, African American Achievements in Air and Space, 2003; contbr. sci. articles to profl. jours. Co-founder, chmn. Devel. Fund for Black Students in Sci. and Tech., Washington, 1983—; dir., co-founder Mus. African Am. Tech. Sci. Village, 2000—; bd. dirs. Nat. Inventors Hall of Fame Found., 2001—07; treas. Nat. Coun. Black Scientists and Engrs., 2001—07. Named inductee, Black Coll. Hall of Fame, 1991, included in exhibit, The African Am. Presence in Physics, 1999; named one of 101 Outstanding Women in the Cmty., Black Bus. Listing, 2006; recipient Fed. Cmty. Svc. award, 1977, Elijah McCoy award, 1989, vol. recognition, Dept. Energy, 1990, Disting. Alumni award, 1992, Image award, Bennett Coll., 1997, Outstanding Women in Sci. award, Nat. Tech. Assn., 1998, Inspiring Scientist award, Jr. Ctr of Art and Science of Oakland, 2002, Outstanding African Am. Women award, 2006. Fellow: African Sci. Inst.; mem.: NAACP (life), No. Calif. Coun. Black Profl. Engrs. (pres. 1986, 1987, sec. 1988, pres. 1994, 1995, sec. 1996—99, pres. 2000—05, mem. bd. 2006—07), Inst. Materials Mgmt. (treas. Vienna chpt. 1985), Nat. Health Physics Soc., Nat. Tech. Assn. (James C. Jones Humanitarian award 2000, Outstanding Woman Scientist Award 1998). Avocations: writing, travel. Home: 4622 Meldon Ave Oakland CA 94619-2646

CARY, GEORGE S., lawyer; b. San Francisco, Oct. 2, 1951; AB with honors in Econs., U. Calif., Santa Cruz, 1973; JD, U. Calif., Berkeley, 1976. Bar: Calif. 1976, DC 1979. Ptnr. Irell & Manella, LA; trial atty. FTC Bur. Competition, 1976—84, dep. dir., 1995—98; ptnr. Cleary, Gottlieb, Steen & Hamilton, LLP, Washington, 1998—. Mem.: ABA. Office: Cleary Gottlieb Steen & Hamilton LLP Ste 9000 2000 Pennsylvania Ave NW Washington DC 20006-1801 Office Phone: 202-974-1920. Office Fax: 202-974-1999. E-mail: gcary@cgsh.com.*

CARY, WILLIAM STERLING, retired church executive; b. Plainfield, NJ, Aug. 10, 1927; s. Andrew and Sadie C.; m. Marie B. Phillips; children: Yvonne, Denise, Sterling, Patricia. BA, Morehouse Coll., 1949, also D.D.; MDiv, Union Theol. Sem., 1952; LL.D., Bishop Coll.; D.D., Elmhurst Coll.; L.H.D., Allen U., Ill. Coll.; MDiv, Union Theol. Sem. Ordained to ministry Baptist Ch., 1948; pastor Butler Meml. Presbyn. Ch., Youngstown, Ohio, 1953-55, Interdenominational Ch. of Open Door, Bklyn., 1955-58, Grace Congl. Ch., NYC, 1958-68; area min. Met. and Suffolk assns. N.Y. Conf. United Ch. Christ, 1968-75; pres. Nat. Coun. Chs., NYC, 1972-75; conf. min. Ill. Conf. United Ch. Christ, 1974—94, conf. min. emeritus, 2001. Chmn. United Ch. Christ Council Conf. Execs., Council Religious Leaders Met. Chgo., 1986-92; mem. governing bd. Nat. Council Chs.; mem. rep. consultation on ch. union United Ch. of Christ; mem. exec. council United Ch. of Christ; mem. Council on Ecumenism, Ch. World Service, Pres.'s Adv. Com. Vietnam Refugees; lectr. in field. Named One of 100 Most Influential Blacks in Am. for 1974-75 Ebony mag. Home: 2344 Vardon Ln Flossmoor IL 60422-1363

CASAD, ROBERT CLAIR, legal educator; b. Council Grove, Kans., Dec. 8, 1929; s. Clair L. and Eula Imogene (Compton) C.; m. Sally Ann McKeighan, Aug. 20, 1955; children: Benjamin Nathan, Joseph Story, Robert Clair, Madeleine Imogene. AB, U. Kans., 1950, MA, 1952; JD with honors, U. Mich., 1957; S.JD, Harvard U., 1979. Bar: Kans. 1957, Minn. 1958, U.S. Dist. Ct. Kans. 1957; U.S. Ct. Appeals (10th cir.) 1985. Instr. law U. Mich., Ann Arbor, 1957-58; assoc. firm Streater & Murphy, Winona, Minn., 1958-59; asst. prof. law U. Kans., Lawrence, 1959-62, assoc. prof., 1962-64, prof., 1964-81, John H. and John M. Kane prof. law, 1981-97; John H. and John M. Kane prof. law emeritus, 1997. Vis. prof. UCLA, 1969—70, U. Ill., 1973—74, U. Calif., Hastings, 1979—80, U. Colo., 1982, U. Vienna, 1986, U. Mich., 1986, U. Valladolid, 1988, Chuo U., 1992, U. Salamanca, 1995, Emory U., 2001—02. Author: Jurisdiction and Forum Selection, 1988, 2nd edit., 1999, Jurisdiction in Civil Actions, 1983, 2d edit., 1991, (with Richman) 3d edit., 1998, Expropriation Procedures in Central America and Panama, 1975, (with others) Kansas Appellate Practice, 1978, Civil Judgment Recognition and the Integration of Multiple State Associations, 1982, Res Judicata in a Nutshell, 1976; (with Fink and Simon) Civil Procedure: Cases and Materials, 2d edit., 1989, (with Gard) Kansas Code of Civil Procedure Annotated, 4th edit., 2003, (with Clermont) Res Judicata: A Handbook on its Theory, Doctrine and Practice, 2001; contbr. numerous articles to legal jours. Mem. civil code adv. com. Kans. Jud. Coun. 1st lt. USAF, 1952-53. Recipient Coblentz prize Sch. Law, U. Mich., 1957, Rice prize U. Kans. Law Sch., 1976, 83, 84, 88, 89, medal Dana Fund for Internat. and Comparative Legal Studies, 1981, Balfour Jeffrey Rsch. prize U. Kans., 1984; Ford fellow, 1965-66, fellow in law Harvard U., 1965-66, OAS fellow, 1976, NEH fellow, summer 1978; grantee Dana Fund for Internat. and Comparative Legal Studies. Mem. Am. Law Inst., ABA, Kans. Bar Assn., Order of Coif. Democrat. Home: 1130 Emery Rd Lawrence KS 66044-2515 E-mail: casad@ku.edu, casad@sunflower.com.

CASADA, HILAREE A., lawyer; b. Nov. 29, 1971; BA cum laude in Broadcast Journalism, So. Meth. U., 1993; JD magna cum laude, So. Meth. U. Sch. Law, 2000. Bar: Tex., US Dist. Ct. (ea., no. and so. dists. Tex.), 5th, 9th and 11th Cir. Ct. Appeals, US Supreme Ct. Sr. assoc. Hermes, Sargent & Bates, L.L.P., Dallas. Named a Rising Star, Tex. Super Lawyers mag., 2006. Mem.: Dallas Bar Assn. (mem. appellate sect., mem. judiciary com.), State Bar Tex. (mem. appellate sect.), Dallas Assn. Young Lawyers (co-chair women in the law com., named a Rising Star 2004). Office: Hermes Sargent Bates LLP 901 Main St Ste 5200 Dallas TX 75202 Office Phone: 214-749-6512. E-mail: hilaree.casada@hsblaw.com.*

CASADESUS, PENELOPE ANN, advertising executive, film producer; b. Calcutta, India, Sept. 20, 1940; came to U.S., 1980; d. Francis John and Betty (Walker) Copeland; m. Jean-Claude Casadesus, Jan. 20, 1960; children: Caroline, Sebastian. Gen. Cert. of Edn., Godolphin Sch., Eng. Head of prodn. S.S.C.B. Lintas, Paris, 1975—78, Grey-France, Paris, 1978—80, Grey Worldwide, NYC, 1980, exec. producer Internat. Health and Beauty divsn., 1991—, sr. v.p., group prodr. Ind. film producer, 1984—. Author, producer (screenplays) Transvaal Episode, The Cuckoo.

CASALE, ALFRED STANLEY, thoracic and cardiovascular surgeon; b. Passaic, NJ, Nov. 28, 1955; s. Alfred Stanley and Regina Josephine (Cembor) C.; m. Mary Louise Cavell, Aug. 1, 1976; 1 child, Katherine. BA, Johns Hopkins U., 1976, MD, 1980. Diplomate Am. Bd. Surgery, Am. Bd. Thoracic Surgery; cert. Surg. Critical Care. Intern Johns Hopkins U., Balt., 1980-81, resident in surgery, 1981-85, resident in thoracic surgery, 1985-88, asst. prof., 1988-90; surgeon Mid Atlantic Surg. Assocs., Morristown, NJ, 1990-2000, ptnr., 1993—2000; chief cardiac surgery U. Hosp., UMD N.J., Newark, 2000—01; dir. cardiothoracic surgery Geisinger Wyoming Valley Med. Ctr., Wilkes-Barre, Pa., 2001—; surg. dir. Heart Inst., Geisinger Health Sys., Danville, PR, 2002—. Assoc. chief cardiac surgery Atlantic Health Sys., Florham Park, NJ; chief cardiac surgery Gen. Hosp. Ctr., Passaic, NJ, 2000; mem. cardiovasc. health adv. panel N.J. Dept. Health, Trenton; assoc. prof. N.J. Med. Sch., UMD N.J., 2000—01. Contbr. articles to profl. jours. Dir. Madison YMCA, N.J., 1990-96, Am. Heart Assn., Morristown, 1990-2001, Luzerne County, 2002—, Kirby Child Care Ctr., Madison, 1992-96. Fellow Am. Coll. Surgeons, Am. Coll. Cardiology, Am. Coll. Chest Physicians; mem. Assn. Acad. Surgery (Resident Rsch. award 1984), Internat. Soc. Heart Transplantation, Soc. Thoracic Surgery. Avocations: skiing, tennis, fishing, shooting. Office: Geisinger Wyo Valley Med Ctr 1000 E Mountain Blvd Wilkes Barre PA 18711 Office Phone: 570-820-6017. Business E-Mail: ascasale@geisinger.edu. E-mail: al@casale.org.

CASALE, THOMAS BRUCE, medical educator; b. Chgo., Apr. 21, 1951; m. Jean M. Casale; 1 son, Jeffrey G. BS cum laude, U. Ill., 1973; MD, Chgo. Med. Sch., 1977. Diplomate Am. Bd. Internal Medicine, Am. Bd. Allergy and Immunology. Resident in internal medicine Baylor Coll. Medicine, Houston, 1977-80; med. staff fellow lab. clin. investigation NIAID, NIH, Bethesda, Md., 1980-84; from asst. prof. to prof. internal medicine U. Iowa, Iowa City, 1984-94, prof. internal medicine, 1994-96; dir. Nebr. Med. Rsch. Inst., 1996-99; adj. prof. pediatrics Coll. Medicine U. Nebr., 1996—; clin. prof. medicine Creighton U., Omaha, 1997-99, prof., assoc. chair dept. medicine, dir. clin. rsch., 1999—, chief allergy/immunology, 2001—. Chief med. staff fellow lab. clin. investigation, NIAID, NIH, Bethesda, 1982-83; attending physician VA Med. Ctr., Iowa City, 1984-96, staff physician, 1986-96, clin. investigator, 1991-96; asst. dir. tchg. allergy/immunology divsn. dept. internal medicine U. Iowa, Iowa City, 1989-92, acting dir., 1992, dir., 1993-96, faculty inerdisciplinary immunology grad. degree program U. Iowa, 1993-96; bd. dirs. Am. Bd. Allergy and Immunology, Am. Acad. Allergy, Asthma and Immunology; reviewer over 15 profl. and sci. jours. Contbr. over 200 articles to profl. publs.; mem. editl. bd. Jour. Allergy Clin. Immunology, 1988-93, clin. asthma revs., 1996-99, Allergy & Clinical Immunology Internat., 1997-2002, Jour. World Allergy Org., 2003—; editor Respiratory Digest, 1999—, Ann. Allergy, Asthma & Immunology, 1999—. Mem. asthma technical adv. group Am. Lung Assn., 1989-96. Lt. commdr. USPHS, 1980-83, USPHS Res., 1983—. Recipient Dr. John J. Sheinin Rsch. award Chgo. Med. Sch., 1977, Clin. Investigator VA, 1991-96, Am. Soc. Clin. Investigation, 1992; grantee NIH, 1986-91, 87-90, 92-93, 93-94, VA Merit Rev., 1986-89, 89-92, 92-96, Environ. Health Sci. Core Ctr., 1990-96, Novartis Pharms., 1997—, Sepracor, Inc., 1997, Immune Tolerance Network, 2003—, others. Fellow ACP, Am. Acad. Allergy Immunology (cutaneous allergy com. 1985-90, postgrad. edn. com. 1988-91, chmn. 1989-90, program com. dermatologic diseases sect. 1988-93, sec. 1989-90, vice chmn. 1990-91, chmn. 1991-92, prof. edn. coun. 1998—, chair 1998—, sec. 1993-95, vice chair 1995—, chmn. bronchoalveolar lavage com. 1991-95, 98—, others), Am. Coll. Allergy Immunology (profl. allergy/immunology edn. com. 1989-94); mem. Am. Acad. Allergy Asthma Immunology (bd. dirs. 2001—, sec., treas. 2004—, pres.-elect 2006-07, pres. 2007-), Am. Fedn. Clin. Rsch., Am. Thoracic Soc. (sec. allergy immunology and inflammation scientific assembly 1990-91, chair-elect 1991-93, chair program com. 1992-93, chair 1993-95, long-range planning and policy com. sci. assembly on allergy immunology and inflammation 1991-96, sci. conf. com. 1991-93, bd. dirs. 1993-95, chair asthma adv. com. 1995-99), Am. Bd. Allergy and Immunology (bd. dirs. 1999—, co-chmn. 2003-04, chmn. 2005-), Iowa Soc. Allergy Immunology (pres. 1987-89), Am. Assn. Immunologists, Midwest Sect. Am. Fedn. Clin. Rsch., Ctrl. Soc. Clin. Rsch., Am. Soc. Clin. Invest., Am. Lung Assn. (mem. rsch. coordinating com. 1996-99), European Respiratory Soc. Office: Creighton U Dept Medicine 601 N 30th St Ste 5850 Omaha NE 68131-2137 Fax: 402-280-4115. Business E-Mail: tbcasale@creighton.edu.

CASAMASSIMA, CHRISTOPHER T., lawyer; b. LA, Oct. 5, 1975; m. Lindsay Dinn Casamassima, Aug. 31, 2003; children: Nathan Thomas, Spencer Dinn. BA, U. Pa., Phila., 1997; JD, U. Calif., LA Sch. Law, 2000. Bar: Calif. 2000, U.S. Ct. Appeals (9th cir.) 2000, U.S. Dist. Ct. 2001. Assoc. Kirkland & Ellis LLP, 2000—06, ptnr., 2006—. Mentor Everybody Wins, 2002—. Named Rising Star, So. Calif. Super Lawyers, 2004—07. Mem.: ABA (mem. criminal procedure com. antitrust sect. 2002—), LA County Bar Assn., Italian Am. Lawyers Assn. Home: 2294 Ronda Vista Dr Los Angeles CA 90027 Office: Kirkland & Ellis LLP 777 S Figueroa St #3700 Los Angeles CA 90017 Office Phone: 213-680-8353. Business E-Mail: ccasamassima@kirkland.com.

CASANOVA, ALDO JOHN, sculptor; b. San Francisco, Feb. 8, 1929; s. Felice and Teresa (Papini) C.; children: Aviva, Liana, Anabelle. BA, San Francisco State U., 1950, MA, 1951; PhD, Ohio State U., 1957. Asst. prof. art San Francisco State U., 1951-53; asst. prof. Antioch (Ohio) Coll., 1956-58; asst. prof. art Tyler Sch. Art, Temple U., Phila., 1961-64, Tyler Sch. Art, Temple U. (Italy campus), Rome, 1968-70; prof. art Scripps Coll., Claremont, Calif., 1966—, chmn. art dept., 1971-73; vis. prof. SUNY, 1981; faculty mem. Skowhegan Sch. Painting and Sculpture, Maine, summers 1973-74. One-man shows include Esther Robles Gallery, L.A., 1967, Santa Barbara (Calif.) Mus., 1967, Calif. Inst. Tech., 1972, Carl Schlosberg Fine Arts, L.A., 1977, SUNY, 1981, Casanova Retrospective Williamson Galleries, Claremont Colls., Calif. 2002; represented in permanent collections Whitney Mus., San Francisco Mus. Art, San Diego Mus. Sculpture Garden, Hirshhorn Collection, Cornell U., Columbus (Ohio) Mus., UCLA Sculpture Garden, Calif. Inst. Tech., Pasadena, Univ. Judaism, L.A., Air and Space Mus., Washington, Collection of Nat. Acad. of Design, N.Y.C., 1993, Robert Feldmuth Meml. Commn., W.M. Keck Sci. Ctr., Claremont, Calif., 1995, Orange County Mus., Calif., 1996, Rancho Santa Ana Botanic Gardens, Claremont, Calif., Palm Springs Mus., Calif., Brookgreen Gardens, Pawley's Island, SC. Recipient Prix-de-Rome Am. Acad. in Rome, 1958-61; Louis Comfort Tiffany award, 1970 Fellow: Am. Acad. in Rome; mem.: NAD, Nat. Sculpture Soc. Democrat. Roman Catholic.

CASARES, FEDERICO M., science educator; b. Buenos Aires, July 1, 1969; s. Carlos Alberto Casares and Raquel Nuria Valido y de Martí; m. Natalia Cecilia Re, Aug. 9, 2000; 1 child, Maximo Tomas. BS, SUNY, Old Westbury, 1996; MS in Marine Environ. Sci., SUNY, Stony Brook, 2000, PhD in Marine & Atmospheric Sci., 2005. Rsch. faculty SUNY, Old Westbury, 2005—; assoc. Marine Sci. Rsch. Ctr., Stony Brook U., 2006—. Sci. cons. LI Conservatory, Albertson, NY, 2003—. Recipient Cert. of Acad. Excellence in Rsch., SUNY, Old Westbury, 1996, Cert. of Acad. Achievement, award, Ednl. Opportunity Program, SUNY, 1996, Cert. of Acad. Achievement, Office of Spl. Programs, SUNY, 1996, W.B. Turner fellow, Stony Brook U., 2005; fellow Turner Postdoc Faculty Traineeship award, 2006—07; grantee, NIH and Nat. Inst. Drug Abuse, 1999—2003; Fogarty Internat. fellow, NIH, 1994, W.B. Turner fellow, Stony Brook U., 2003—05. Mem.: Alumni Assn. SUNY. Office: Neurosci Rsch Inst SUNY OW 231 Store Hill Rd Old Westbury NY 11568 Office Phone: 561-876-4883 ext. 2732. Office Fax: 516-876-2727. Business E-Mail: fcasares@sunynri.org.

CASAREZ, RUEBEN CHARLES, lawyer; b. El Paso, Tex., Sept. 26, 1953; s. Ramon and Irene (Lucero) C.; m. Nicole J. Bremner, Nov. 13, 1982. AB in Psychology, Stanford U., 1975; JD, U. Tex., 1979. Bar: Tex. 1979. Assoc. Butler & Binion, Houston, 1979-87, ptnr., 1988-95; sr. counsel Wells Fargo Bank, Houston, 1995—. Pres. Houston Housing Fin. Corp., 1992-94. Mem. Houston Housing Authority, 2006—. Mem. ABA, Hispanic Bar Assn. Houston (pres. 1991-92), Mexican Am. Bar Assn. Houston, Assn. for Advancement Mexican Ams. (gen. counsel 1992-98), Am. Law Inst. Democrat. Roman Catholic. Office: Wells Fargo Bank PO Box 3326 MAC T5008-022 Houston TX 77253-3326

CASAS, LAURIE ANN, plastic surgeon; b. May 26, 1956; married; 2 children. BS, BA, U. Ill., Champaign/Urbana, 1974—78; MD, Northwestern U. Med. Sch., Chgo., 1978—82. Diplomate Am. Bd. Plastic Surgery. Resident, gen. surgery Northwestern U. Med. Ctr., Chgo., 1982—85, resident, plastic surgery, 1985—88; microsurgery rsch. fellow So. Ill. U., Springfield, 1988; aesthetic plastic surgery fellow NYU, NYC, 1989; breast aesthetic and reconstruction fellow St. Joseph Hosp., Atlanta, 1989; clin. instr., surgery Northwestern U. Med. Sch., Chgo., 1987—88, asst. prof., surgery, 1990—2001, assoc. prof., surgery, 2001—; adj. staff, asst. attending in plastic/reconstructive surgery Evanston Northwestern Healthcare, Ill., 1990; assoc. attending in plastic/reconstructive surgery Evanston Hosp., Ill., 1992, attending in plastic/reconstructive surgery, 1996; co-dir., ctr. for plastic and aesthetic surgery Glenbrook Hosp., Glenview, Ill., 1990—95, adj. staff, asst. attending in plastic/reconstructive surgery, 1990, assoc. attending in plastic/reconstructive surgery, 1992, attending in plastic/reconstructive surgery, 1996; acting head, divsn. plastic surgery Evanston Hosp. Corp., Ill., 1993—96; head, divsn. plastic surgery Evanston Northwestern Healthcare, Glenbrook Hosp., Glenview, Ill., 1996—. Mem. editl. bd. Plastic Surgery Today, 2000, Guide to Aesthetic Plastic Surgery, 2000, Your Image, 2002—03, editor-in-chief Aesthetic Soc. News, 2000—; editor: Aesthetic Surgery Jour., 2005—. Bd. dirs. Plastic Surgery Edn. Found. Fellow: Am. Coll. Surgeons; mem.: AMA, Aesthetic Soc. Edn. Found. (bd. dirs. 2006—), Ill. Med. Soc., Plastic Surgery Rsch. Coun., Internat. Soc. Aesthetic Plastic Surgery, Midwestern Assn. Plastic Surgeons, The Rhinoplasty Soc., Chgo. Med. Soc., Chgo. Plastic Surgery Soc., Am. Soc. Plastic Surgery, Am. Soc. Aesthetic Plastic Surgery (bd. dirs. 2003—). Office: 2050 Pfingsten Ste 270 Glenview IL 60026 Office Phone: 847-657-6884. Business E-Mail: lcasas@casas.md.

CASAS, MARTHA, education educator; b. Huntington Pk, Calif. d. Roberto Rubio and Enriqueta Garcia Casas. BS in Edn., U. Tex., El Paso, 1978; MA in edn., U. Tex. at El Paslo, 1991; EdD, Harvard Grad Sch. of Edn., 1997. Elem. sch. tchr. El Paso Ind. Sch. Dist., 1978—91; doctoral student Harvard Grad. Sch. Edn., 1991—95; curriculum specialist El Paso Ind. Sch. Dist., 1993—99; asst. prof. in tchr. edn. U. Tex. at Permian Basin, Odessa, 1999—2001, U. Tex., El Paso, 2001—. Author: (book) Grolier's Encyclopedia Latina, 2003. Grant, Hervey Found., 2003, Univ. Tex. at El Paso, 2004. Mem.: Assn. Edn. Rsch. Assoc., Assoc. for Supervision of Curriculum Develop., Phi Delta Kappa Internat. Avocations: dance, gardening, swimming, travel. Home: 1213 Cambria Cove El Paso TX 79912 Office: Univ Tex at El Paso 500 W University El Paso TX 79968 Office Phone: 915-747-7616. Business E-Mail: mcasas@utep.edu.

CASASENT, DAVID PAUL, electrical engineer, educator, data processing executive; b. Washington, Dec. 8, 1942; s. Harold Kane and Delta (Fletchall) C.; m. Paula Timko; children: Candace, Erin, Maureen, Tod, Jon. BSEE, U. Ill., Urbana, 1964, MS, 1965, PhD, 1969. Prof. elec. engring. Carnegie Mellon U., Pitts., 1969—; pres. Unicorn Sys., Inc., Pitts., 1983—. Dir. Ctr. for Optical Data Processing, Pitts. Editor: Optical Data Processing, 1978; contbr. more than 700 articles to tech. jours. Recipient Thomas K. Benedict award AIAA, 1979; named George Westinghouse prof. Carnegie-Mellon U., 1980. Fellow IEEE (local pres. 1971-72, Barry Carlton award 1976), Optical Soc. Am. (local pres. 1975-77), Soc. Photo-Optical Instrumentation Engrs. (gov. 1982-85, 87-90, pres. 1993, exec. bd.), Internat. Neural Network Soc. (gov. 1992-95, 1998-00, pres. 1999). Republican. Roman Catholic. Avocations: travel, basketball, volleyball. Home: 133 Woodland Farms Rd Pittsburgh PA 15238-2021 Office: Carnegie Mellon U Dept Elec & Computer Engring Pittsburgh PA 15213-3890 Office Phone: 412-268-2464. E-mail: casasent@andrew-cmu.edu.

CASAS-MELLEY, ADELA TERESA, pediatrician, surgeon; b. Havana, Cuba, Jan. 2, 1963; arrived in US, 1964; d. Magdalena and Oscar Casas; m. Peter Clemens Melley, Nov. 10, 2000; children: Daniel Ryan Melley children: Peter Jonathan Melley, Matthew James Melley, Patrick Sean Melley. B in Chemistry and History, Emory U., 1985, M in Med. Sci., 1987; MD, Med. Coll. Ga., Augusta, 1991. Diplomate Am. Bd. Surgery. Internship Med. Coll. Ga., Augusta, residency; pediat. surgery fellowship St. Christopher Hosp. for Children, Phila.; clin. dir. divsn. solid organ transplant AI duPont Hosp. for Children, Wilmington, Del., 2000—06; assoc. prof. surgery Sanford Sch. Medicine, U. SD, 2006—. Fellow: ACS; mem.: Phila. Surg. Soc., Am. Pediat. Surgery Assn., Am. Soc. Transplantation, Am. Soc. Transplant Surgeons, Alpha Omega Alpha. Roman Catholic. Office: Sanford Children's Hosp 1305 W 18th St PO Box 5039 Sioux Falls SD 57117-5039 Office Phone: 605-333-7188. Business E-Mail: casasa@sanfordhealth.org.

CASATI, FABIO, engineer; b. Como, Italy, Jan. 28, 1971; s. Giulio Casati and Antonia Zocca; m. Lone Sorensen, Aug. 24, 1974. PhD, Politecnico di Milano, Milan, Italy, 1998. Engineer, Italy, 1996, cert. engr. With Hewlett-Packard, Palo Alto, Calif., 1998, sr. rsch. scientist, 1999—. Adj. prof. U. New South Wales, Australia; prof. U. Trento, Italy; mem. Orgn. Econ. Cooperation. Author: Web Services, 2003. Achievements include initiated research in bus. process intelligence and web services. Home: via Bonardi 1 22100 Como Italy Office Phone: +39 0461 882044.

CASATI, GIULIO, theoretical physics professor; b. Brenna, Italy, Dec. 9, 1942; m. Antonia, Sept. 1, 1968; children: Davide, Fabio. Laurea in Fisica, Milan U., Italy, 1968. Asst. prof. physics dept. Milan U., 1971-74, assoc. prof. physics dept., 1974-87, prof. physics dept., 1987—, dean sci. faculty, 1993—98; dep. rector U. Dell' Insubria, Como, 1999—2001; dir. Internat. Ctr. for Complex Sys., 2001—. Sci. sec. Centro di Cultura Scientifica A. Volta, Como, Italy, 1981—; mem. exec. coun. European Sci. Found., Strasbourg, France, 1987—. Editor several vols. on classical and quantum chaos. Recipient Italian prize for physics Francesco Somaini Found., 1991. Mem. Acad. Europaea, Internat. Union Pure and Applied Physics (internat. commn. C3), Italian Phys. Soc., European Phys. Soc., Am. Phys. Soc., Rotary. Office: Centro A Volta Villa Olmo 22100 Como Italy Business E-Mail: giulio.casati@uninsubria.it.

CASAZZA, JOHN ANDREW, electrical engineer, energy executive; b. Bklyn., Jan. 3, 1924; s. John Andrew and Jane (Granata) C.; m. Madeline Russo, Apr. 24, 1949; children: John Anthony, Joan Bernadette Casazza Fram. Student, Cooper Union, 1941-43; BEE, Cornell U., 1945. Registered profl. engr., N.J. Successively system planning and devel. engr., gen. mgr. planning and rsch., v.p. planning and rsch. Pub. Svc. Electric & Gas Co., Newark, 1946-77; v.p. Stone & Webster Mgmt. Cons., NYC, 1977-79; pres. Casazza, Schultz & Assocs., Inc., Arlington, Va., 1979-90; chmn. bd. CSA Energy Cons., 1991-97; pres. Am. Edn. Inst., 1994—. Mem. energy engrng. bd. NRC, 1988—94; mem. rsch. adv. com. Elec. Power Rsch. Inst., Palo Alto, Calif., 1976—77; mem. U.S. Energy Assn. World Energy Conf., 1983—92; bd. dirs. Ga. Sys. Ops. Co.; mem. Power Engineers Supporting Truth, 2003—. Contbr. numerous articles to profl. publs. Pub. trustee N.J. Marine Scis. Consortium, 1973-79; treas. N.J. Energy Rsch. Inst., 1977; mem. N.J. Gov.'s Panel on Solar Energy, 1975-77. Ensign USN, 1943-45. Fellow IEEE (life, chmn. energy policy com. 1981-82, chmn. environ. quality com. 1984-85, U.S. activities bd. citation of honor 1985, Herman Halperin award 1990, U.S. activities bd. dirs. VII profl. leadership award 1992); mem. Internat. Conf. on Large High Voltage Electric Sys. (Exec. com. U.S. nat. com. 1974-93, Atwood assoc. 1986—, spl. citation 1982, Philip Sporn award 1994), Springfield Golf and Country Club. Roman Catholic. Avocations: golf, writing. Office: Am Edn Inst 8208 Donset Dr Springfield VA 22152-1810 Office Phone: 703-569-3579. Personal E-mail: jackcasazza@aol.com.

CASAZZA, WILLIAM JAMES, insurance company executive, lawyer; b. Cambridge, Mass., 1955; BA, Tufts U., 1977; MBA, U. Notre Dame, 1979; JD, Cornell U., 1985. Bar: NY 1985, Conn. 1993; CPA, Pa. 2001. With Ernst & Whinney, CPA, 1979—83, Sullivan & Cromwell, 1985—92, Aetna Inc., Hartford, Conn., 1992—, v.p., dep. gen. counsel, 1997, corp. sec., 1999—, sr. v.p., 2004—05, sr. v.p., gen. counsel Hartford, 2005—. Mem. ABA Office: Aetna Inc 151 Farmington Ave Hartford CT 06156-0002 Office Phone: 860-273-1773. Business E-Mail: casazzawj@aetna.com.*

CASCARILLA, RICHARD A., lawyer; A in Bus., Lansing C.C., Mich., 1974; BS, Grand Valley State Coll., Allendale, Mich., 1976; JD, 1980. Gen. counsel Nev. Energy Co., Reno, 1990—98; atty. Murphy, Brenton & Spagnuolo P.C., East Lansing, Mich., 2002—. Mem.: Ingham County Bar Assn. Office: Murphy Brenton & Spagnuolo PC 4572 S Hagadorn Rd East Lansing MI 48823 Home Phone: 517-676-7081.

CASCIANO, DANIEL ANTHONY, biologist, educator; b. Buffalo, Mar. 1, 1941; s. Frederick James and Rose Ann C.; m. Gertrude Ann Tara, Aug. 22, 1964; children: Anne, Jonathan. BS, Canisius Coll., 1962; PhD in Cell Biology, Purdue U., 1971. Rsch. asst. Roswell Park Meml. Inst., Buffalo, 1963—64; rsch. asst. dept. biol. scis. Purdue U., West Lafayette, Ind., 1965—66, tchg. asst., 1969, rsch. trainee, 1966—71; trainee NIH, 1966—71; postdoctoral investigator U. Tenn., Oak Ridge Nat. Labs., 1971—73; assoc. prof. dept. biochemistry and molecular biology U. Ark. for Med. Scis., Little Rock, 1974—90, prof. dept. biochemistry and molecular biology, 1990—, prof. dept pharmacology and toxicology, 1990—; rsch. biologist Nat. Ctr. Toxicology Rsch., Jefferson, Ark., 1973, program dir. divsn. mutagenesis rsch., 1976—78, dir. divsn. genetic toxicology, 1979—97, dir. divsn. genetic and reproductive toxicology, 1997—99, dep. dir. for rsch., 1999—2000, acting dir., 1999—2000, dir., 2000—06; pres. Dan Casciano and Assocs., 2006—. Contbr. articles to profl. jours. Mem. Tissue Culture Assn., Environ. Mutagen Soc., AAAS, Beta Beta Beta. Home and Office: 47 Marcella Dr Margeux Pl Little Rock AR 72223-9172 Office Phone: 501-837-2401. Business E-Mail: dcasciano@sbcglobal.net.

CASCINO, ANTHONY ELMO, JR., lawyer, insurance company executive; b. South Bend, Ind., Aug. 21, 1948; s. Anthony E. and Lorayne (Allegretti) C.; m. Mary Anne Dory, July 28, 1973; children: Anthony Elmo III, Christine Anne, Caroline Stephanie BA, Loyola U., Chgo., 1970; JD, Ill. Inst. Tech., 1974; M Mgmt., Northwestern U., 1987. Bar: Ill. 1974, U.S. Dist. Ct. (no. dist.) Ill. 1974, U.S. Supreme Ct. 1996. Divsn. counsel CF Industries, Inc., Long Grove, Ill., 1974—79; sec., gen. counsel Energy Coop., Inc., Rosemont, Ill., 1979—83; v.p., gen. counsel GHR Energy Corp., Good Hope, La., 1983; dep. gen. counsel AM Internat., Inc., Chgo., 1983—86; v.p. bus. devel. Multigraphics divsn. AM Internat., Mt. Prospect, Ill., 1986—88; exec. v.p., sec., gen. counsel, bd. dirs. United Fin. Group Inc. Ill., Oak Brook, 1988—96; ptnr., exec. v.p. Tait Adv. Svcs., 1997—2000; v.p. Corp. Legal Warrior Ins. Group, 2000—02, Cascino & Assocs. PC, 2002—; sec., gen. counsel Echelon Property and Casualty Ins. Co., Chgo., 2004—. Bd. dirs. Oak Brook Property and Casualty Ins. Co., First Oak Brook Corp. Syndicate, United Comml. Affiliated, Inc., Combined Adjustment Co., Inc., Ctrl. State Ins. Co., Inc., Echelon Property and Casualty Ins. Co.; mem. inquiry bd. Atty. Registration and Disciplinary Commn., 1992-96; alt. trustee Ill. Ins. Exch., 1988-97; arbitrator Cook County Mandatory Arbitration Program, 1997—; lectr. Ill. Inst. Continuing Edn., 1986, Corp. Goverance Conf., 2004 Contbg. author: Commercial Damage, 1984; contbr. articles to profl. jours Bd. dirs. Chgo. Cmty. Loon Fund, 1999—; bd. advisors St. Joseph Sem. Coll., Archdiocese Chgo., 1999—; mem. adv. com. postgrad. programs Ill. Inst. Tech., 1987-88; hon. chmn. Tony C. and Carole Segal Patient Assistance Fund; mem. bd. adv. Cath. Charities Archdiocese Chgo., 2004 Mem. ABA, Fed. Energy Bar Assn., Ill. State Bar Assn., Chgo. Bar Assn. (vice chmn. ins. law com., 2004, chmn. ins. law com., 2004-2005), Dupage County Bar Assn., Art Inst. Chgo., Lyric Opera Chgo. (Glencoe chpt.), Bar and Gavel Soc., DuPage Club, Union League Club (Chgo.), Club Internat. (Chgo.), Bob O'Link Golf Club Democrat. Roman Catholic. Home: 385 Lincoln Ave Glencoe IL 60022-1521 Office: 875 N Michigan Ave Ste 1430 Chicago IL 60611 Office Phone: 312-654-6183. Business E-Mail: tcascino@eisgroup.net.

CASDEN, ANDREW MICHAEL, orthopedist; b. Bklyn., June 13, 1957; s. Daniel D. and Hannah L. (Bernstein) C.; m. Jeri Casden, Aug. 3, 1981; children: Jared, Ryan. BA, Cornell U., 1979; MD, Cornell U. Med. Coll., 1983. Bd. cert. Am. Bd. Orthop. Surgery; diplomate Nat. Bd. Med. Examiners; lic. NY. Intern gen. surgery The NY Hosp., Cornell Med. Ctr., NYC, 1983-84; Chgo. Spine Fellowship Rush Presbyn.-St. Luke's Med. Ctr., 1988—89; resident orthop. surgery Hosp. for Joint Diseases, Orthop. Inst., NYC, 1984-88; chief spine surgery., dept. orthop. Mount Sinai Med. Ctr., NYC, 1989—98; asst. prof. orthop. surgery Mount Sinai Sch. Medicine, NYC, 1989—98, asst. prof. neurosurgery, 1994—98; asst. prof. orthop. surgery Albert Einstein Coll. Medicine, Yeshiva Univ., NYC, 1999—; assoc. dir., spine surgery Spine Inst. NY, Beth Israel Med. Ctr., NYC, 1998—. Dir. (coarse) Pedicle Screw Fixation of the Thoracic Spine, 2002, 2003; presenter in field. Contbr. articles to profl. jours. Mem. Am. Acad. Orthop. Surgeons (com. on evaluations 1995), Am. Spinal Injury Assn., N.Am. Spine Soc., Scoliosis Rsch. Soc. Office: Mt Sinai Med Ctr 5 E 98th St New York NY 10029-6501 also: Beth Israel Med Ctr Spine Inst NY Phillips Ambulatory Care Ctr 10 Union Square E # 5P New York NY 10003 Office Phone: 212-844-8696, 212-844-8674, 914-934-0027. Business E-Mail: acasden@bethisraelny.org.*

CASE, CHARLES DIXON, lawyer; b. Manning, SC, Mar. 23, 1952; s. James E. and Jennie (Stout) C.; m. Margie Toy, Aug. 28, 1982; children: J. Everett II, Elliot T. BS in Physics, N.C. State U., 1973; JD, Harvard U., 1977. Bar: N.C. 1977, U.S. Dist. Ct. (ea., mid. and we. dists.) N.C., U.S. Supreme Ct. Environ. atty., ptnr. Moore & Van Allen, 1977-92; ptnr. Hunton & Williams, Raleigh, NC, 1992—. Adj. prof. law Campbell U., Buies Creek, N.C., 1981-84; hearing officer N.C. OSHA Safety and Health Rev. Bd., Raleigh, 1981-84; chmn. Wake County Bd. Adjustment, Raleigh, 1979-83; mem. N.C. Hazardous Waste Study Commn., 1982. Co-author: Toxic Tort and Hazardous Substance Litigation, 1995; contbr. articles to profl. jours. Pres. Coll. Phys. and Math. Scis. Found., N.C. State U. 1994-95, bd. dirs., 1991-98, 2000—; bd. dirs. Jr. Achievement Ea. N.C., 1994-98, Camp Kanata, 1997—; mem. bd. visitors N.C. State U., 1995—, chmn., 1999-2000. Home: 1540 Carr St Raleigh NC 27608-2302 Office: Hunton & Williams PO Box 109 Raleigh NC 27602-0109 Home Phone: 919-828-2199; Office Phone: 919-899-3045. E-mail: ccase@hunton.com.

CASE, DAVID BARTLETT, internist, educator; b. Plainfield, NJ, Mar. 17, 1942; s. George and Caroline (Bartlett) C.; m. Jean Brookhart, Aug. 2, 1969; children; Thayer Stimson, Nelson Chipman. AB, Princeton U., 1964; MD, Columbia U., 1968. Intern, then asst. resident Johns Hopkins Hosp., Balt., 1968-70; fellow Columbia Presbyn. Hosp., NYC, 1972-75; asst., then assoc. prof. Cornell U. Med. Coll., 1975-84, clin. assoc. prof., 1984—. Mem. Council on High Blood Pressure Research, 1979—; vis. lectr. Columbia U. Coll. of Physicians and Surgeons, 1997—. Contbr. chapters to books, articles to profl. jours. Recipient Andrew Mellon Tchr. Scientist award Cornell U., 1978. Master ACP (gov. downstate I); fellow Am. Coll. Clin. Pharmacology, Am. Heart Assn. Achievements include research in hypertension. Office: 635 Madison Ave New York NY 10022-1009 Office Phone: 212-857-4660. Personal E-mail: dbmdny@aol.com.

CASE, DAVID KNOWLTON, management consultant; b. Worcester, Mass., Mar. 26, 1938; s. Frederic Howard and Frances Mary (Knowlton) C.; m. Caroline Porter Richards, Feb. 2, 1974; children— Elizabeth, Sarah BA, Yale U., 1961; grad. mktg. mgmt. program, Harvard U., 1973. Pub. rels. rep. U.S. Steel Corp., Pitts., 1962-66; comms. dir. John Hancock Ins. Co., Boston, 1966-70; asst. v.p. Shawmut Bank, Boston, 1970-76; devel. dir. Boston Ctr. for the Arts, 1977; dir. Plimoth Plantation, Plymouth, Mass., 1977-90, pres., CEO, 1990-96; owner, CEO Case Consulting, Norwell, Mass., 1997—; ptnr. Case & Mann, Osterville, Mass., 2000—. Bd. assocs. ARTS/Boston, 1988—; pres. emeritus, hon. dir. English-Speaking Union, Boston; pres. emeritus, dir. Plymouth County Devel. Coun., 1988—; mem. adv. bd. S.E. Mass. Am. Automobile Assn., 1988—, Three Bays Preservation, Inc., Osterville; mem. external rels. com. Milton Acad. Recipient Golden Coin award Bank Mktg. Assn., 1973, Nat. award Bus. Com. Arts, N.Y., 1975, Leadership award Soc. Mayflower Descendants, 1994, Jackson Bowl award Milton Acad., 1995, Silver medal SAR, 1996, Lifetime Achievement award Mass. Office Travel and Tourism, 1997. Mem. Am. Assn. Mus., New Eng. Mus. Assn., Colonial Soc., Soc. Colonial Wars in Commonwealth of Mass., Yale Club (Boston and N.Y.), Harvard Club (Boston), The Beach Club (Centerville, Mass.). Republican. Episcopalian. Home and Office: 378 River St Norwell MA 02061-2205 also: PO Box 361 205 Seapuit Rd Osterville MA 02655-1819 Office Phone: 508-540-8169. Personal E-mail: dkcrcase@aol.com.

CASE, DAVID LEON, lawyer; b. Lansing, Mich., Sept. 22, 1948; s. Harlow Hoyt and Barbara Jean (Denman) C.; m. Cynthia Lou Rhinehart, Jan. 28, 1968; children: Beau, Ryan, Kimberly, Darren, Stephanie. BS with distinction, Ariz. State U., 1970, JD cum laude, 1973. Bar: Calif. 1973, US Dist. Ct. (cen. dist.) Calif. 1973, US Tax Ct. 1974, Ariz. 1976, US Supreme Ct. 1997. Assoc. Willis, Butler & Scheifly, LA, 1973—75; from assoc. to mem. Ryley, Carlock & Applewhite, Phoenix, 1975—. Mem. adv. bd. Ariz. Cmty. Found., 2006—. Fellow: Am. Coll. Trust and Estate Counsel, Ariz. Bar Found.; mem.: ABA (tax sect., corp. sect., probate and trust sect.), Ctrl. Ariz. Estate Planning Coun. (bd. dirs., pres. 1988—89), Calif. Bar Assn., Ariz. Bar Assn., Beta Gamma Sigma. Republican. Presbyterian. Avocations: guitar, sports. Office: Ryley Carlock & Applewhite PO Box 634 Phoenix AZ 85001-0634 Office Phone: 602-440-4808. Business E-Mail: dcase@rcalaw.com.

CASE, DONNI MARIE, investment company executive; b. Chgo., Feb. 20, 1948; d. Donald Milton and Felecia Virginia (Krantz) Schuette; m. Lawrence Lee Hewitt, Apr. 20, 1996. BA in Econs., U. Ill., 1970. Pres. FRB/Weber Shandwick, Chgo., 1972—. Bd. dirs. Inst. Bus. and Profl. Ethics Depaul U. Mem.: Chicago Network, TEC Internat. Home: 2417 N Geneva Ter Chicago IL 60614-5914

CASE, DOUGLAS MANNING, lawyer; b. Cleve., Jan. 3, 1947; s. Manning Eugene and Ernestine (Bryan) Case; m. Marilyn Cooper, Aug. 23, 1969. BA, U. Pa., 1969; JD, MBA, Columbia U., 1973. Bar: N.Y. 1974, N.J. 1975, Calif. 1980, Ohio 1991, Fla. 2000. Assoc. Brown & Wood, NYC, 1973-77; corp. counsel PepsiCo Inc., Purchase, NY, Irvine, Calif., 1977—83, Nabisco Brands Inc., NYC, East Hanover, N.J. and London, 1983-89; asst. gen. counsel Chiquita Brands Internat., Inc., Cin., 1989-92; pvt. practice Cin., Vero Beach, Fla., 1993—. Lectr. numerous seminars. Contbr. articles to profl. jours. Chmn. Olde Colonial Dist., 1986—88; active Morris-Sussex area coun. Boy Scouts Am., 1986—88; sec., trustee Marble Scholarship Com., NYC, 1983—88; trustee Cin. Opera Guild, 1994—99, pres., 1997—98, chmn., 1998—99, hon. trustee, 1999—; chmn. Indian River Dist. Boy Scouts Am., 2006—, active Gulfstream coun., 2006—; bd. dirs., mem. exec. com. Cin. Opera Assn., 1997—98. Mem.: ABA, Quality in Law (chmn. 1996—98), Cin. Bar Assn. (continuing legal edn. chair internat. law com. 1994—96, chair solo and small firm practitioners com. 1995—97, sec. 1996—97, vice chair 1997—98, chair 1998—2000), Fla. Bar Assn., Internat. Bar Assn., Munich Sister City Assn. Greater Cin. (chmn. econ. devel. com. 1995—96), Vero Beach Yacht Club (dir. 2006—), Bent Pine Golf Club, Kenwood Country Club, Columbia Bus. Sch. Club (N.Y.C.) (pres., bd. dirs. 1974—79), Morris County Golf Club, Met. Club (N.Y.C.), Lawyers Club Cin. (mem. exec. com. 1995—2000, treas. 1996, sec. 1997, 2d v.p. 1998, 1st v.p. 1999, pres. 2000). Avocation: golf. Office: 501 Bay Dr Vero Beach FL 32963-2163 Personal E-mail: dcaselaw@bellsouth.net.

CASE, EDWARD E., former congressman, lawyer; b. Hilo, Hawaii, Sept. 27, 1952; m. Audrey Case; children: David, Megan, James, David. BA, Williams Coll., 1975; JD, U. Calif., 1981. Aide to US Rep. Spark Matsunaga from Hawaii, Washington, 1975—78; clk. to Hon. William Richardson Hawaii Supreme Ct., 1981—82; clk. Hawaii State. Dept. Labor; from assoc. to mng. ptnr. Carlsmith Ball, Honolulu, 1983—; mem. Hawaii Ho. Reps., 1994—2002, majority leader, 1999—2000; mem. US Congress from 2nd Hawaii dist., Washington, 2002—06, mem. edn. and workforce com., agr. com., small bus. com. Mem. Manoa Neighborhood Bd., Honolulu, 1985—89. Named Legislator of Yr., Honolulu Weekly, 1995, Small Bus. Hawaii, 2000, New Economy Legislator of Yr., Hawaii Tech. and Trade Assn., 2000. Democrat. Office: 5104 Prince Kuhio Fed Bldg Honolulu HI 96850

CASE, ELDON DARREL, materials science educator; b. Logan, Kans., Aug. 23, 1949; s. Eldon George and Ila Marie (Lewis) C.; m. Linda Lee Lubken, Aug. 29, 1975 (div. Mar. 1993); 1 child, Carl Allen; m. Rebecca J. Ervin, 1996. BA in Physics and Math., U. Colo., 1971; MA in Physics, U. No. Colo., 1975; PhD in Materials Sci., Iowa State U., 1980. Rsch. asst. dept. materials sci. Iowa State U., Ames, 1976—80; NRC postdoctoral assoc. Nat. Bur. Stds., Gaithersburg, Md., 1980—82; rsch. engr. materials sci. and mining engrng. U. Calif., Berkeley, 1982—85; asst. prof. metallurgy, mechanics and materials sci. Mich. State U., East Lansing, 1985—89, assoc. prof., 1988—99, prof., 1999—. Cons. Indsl. Tech. Inst., Ann Arbor, Mich., 1990, Westinghouse, West Mifflin, Pa., 1991-92; judge Nat. Am. Indian Sci. and Engrng. Fair, 1993-2001; grand awards judge Internat. Sci. and Engrng. Fair, 2000; mem. internat. sci. com. ACUN-3 Advanced Composites, Sydney, Australia, 2000-01; mem. external adv. bd. Dept. Materials Sci. and Engrng. Iowa State U., 2004-; mem. editl. bd. Jour. Materials Engrng. and Performance, 2005- Assoc. editor Internat. Jour.of Applied Ceramics Tech., 2003—; contbr. more than 135 articles to profl. jours. and conf. proc. including Jour. Materials Sci., Materials Sci. Engrng., Applied Physics Letters. Spkr. sch. groups Okemos (Mich.) Pub. Schs., 1986-90; asst. with middle-sch. activities Episcopal Ch., East Lansing, 1988-92; judge Nat. Am. Indian Sci. and Engrng. Fair, 1993-2001. Recipient Tchr.-Scholar award Mich. State U., 1989, Withrow Excellence in Tchg. award Engrng. Coll. Mich. State U., 1993, 95, 98, 2006; Regents scholar U. Colo., 1967-71; grantee NASA, 1987, NSF, 1987-90, Mich. State U., 1989, AFOSR, 2001-04, Dept. Energy, 2004—, Office of Naval Rsch., 2005—, NSF, 2007—; Rsch. Instrumentation Program grantee Def. U., 2007—. Fellow ASM (chair advanced joining tech. com. 1999—2001, tech. programming bd. for joining critical tech. sector 1999-2004), Am. Ceramic Soc. (pres. Mich sect 1998-2004, chair organizing com. symposium); mem. AAUP, ASTM, Nat. Inst. Ceramic Engrs., The Metall. Soc. (sec. structural materials div. 1988-91, chair non-metall. com. 1988-91), Sigma Xi (chair organizing com. for bioceramics and biocomposites symposium Advanced Ceramics Conf. 2006—, mem. organizing com. thermoelectric materials symposia 2006—). Democrat. Achievements include first neutron scattering study from microcracks in a polycrystalline ceramic; statistical analysis of water drop impact damage cracks in infrared windows; microwave sintering and joining of ceramics and ceramic composites; adhesion studies of diamond thin-films on brittle substrates; thermal-shock and thermal fatigue studies on ceramics and ceramic composites, processing and mechanical property characterization of ceramids, bioceramics and thermoelectric materials. Home: 4469 Fairlane Dr Okemos MI 48864-2407 Office: Materials Sci and Mechanics Sci Dept East Lansing MI 48824 Office Phone: 517-353-6715. Business E-Mail: casee@egr.msu.edu.

CASE, ELIZABETH JOY, psychology and educational assessment director; b. Phila., Oct. 12, 1948; d. Edward N. and Helene (LeBlanc) C. BS in Edn./Spl. Edn., Ashland Coll., 1970; MA in Spl. Edn., Fairfield U., 1975; PhD, U. N.Mex., 1985. Cert. tchr. spl. edn. K-12, regular edn. K-12, adminstr. Tchr. second grade Mansfield (Ohio) Pub. Schs., 1969-70; supr., tchr. spl. edn. Greenwich (Conn.) Pub. Schs., 1970-78; cons. Nat. Learning Disabilties Assistance Project, Washington, 1976-78; instr. Fairfield (Conn.) U., 1975-79; grad. asst., fellow U. N.Mex., Albuquerque, 1978-81, instr., 1980-85; cons. IBM, White Plains and Arwork, N.Y., 1976-81; asst. prin. Albuquerque Pub. Schs., 1981-82, coord. spl. edn., 1989—93; with Minn. Dept. Edn., 1993—97; dir. rsch. Harcourt Assessment, Inc., 1997—. Cons. Office of Spl. Edn., U.S. Dept. Edn., Washington, 1980—; dir. regional large sch. testing programs, mid-continent Harcourt Edn. Measurement, 1999—, grants and devel. Minn. Dept. Children, Families, and Learning, Minn. Assessment Project, Rsch. on Spl. Populations Harcourt Assessment, Inc./The Psychol. Corp.; presenter in field. Contbr. articles to profl. jours./publs. Chmn. Gov.'s Com. on the Concerns of the Handicapped, Santa Fe, N.Mex., 1988-92; pres. Civitan/Sierra Vista, Albuquerque, 1989, Albuquerque Wheelchair Tennis Assn., 1985; pres., CEO World Inst. on Disabilities, 1997-98; adv. bd. Protection and Advocacy, Albuquerque, 1988-90; vice-chmn. N.Mex. Vols. for the Outdoors, Albuquerque, 1988-91; bd. dirs. Very Spl. Arts, 1984—. Easter Seal Fundraiser, 1976—, Spl. Olympics, 1986—. Named Vol. of the Yr., N.Mex. Vols. for the Outdoors, 1988, Nat. Woman's Single Champion/Nat. Wheelchair Tennis Assn., Irvine, Calif., 1985, Most Inspirational Tennis Player, 1985, Outstanding Leader in Elem. Edn., Ashland, Ohio, 1976, Conn. Outstanding Young Woman, Hartford, 1976. Mem. N.Mex. Coun. Exceptional Children (treas. 1990-92), Am. Ednl. Rsch. Assn., Phi Delta Kappa (pres. local chpt. 1990-91). Business E-Mail: betsy_case@harcourt.com.

CASE, GREGORY C., insurance company executive; BA summa cum laude, Kans. State Univ., 1985; MBA, Harvard Univ., 1989. With Fed. Reserve Bank Kansas City; investment banker Piper, Jaffray and Hopwood; ptnr., head fin. svc. & global ins. practices McKinsey & Co., 1988—2005; pres. & CEO Aon Corp., Chgo., 2005—. Bd. dir. Discover Fin. Services, 2007—. Mem.: Economic Club of Chgo., Fin. Services Roundtable, Internat. Ins. Society, Inc. Office: Aon Corporation 200 E Randolph St Chicago IL 60601*

CASE, JAMES HEBARD, lawyer; b. Lihue, Hawaii, Apr. 10, 1920; s. Adrial Hebard and Elizabeth (McConnell) C.; m. Suzanne Catherine Espenett, Sept. 18, 1948; children: Edward E., John H. (dec.), Suzanne D., Russell L., Elisabeth C. Marguleas, Bradford Case. AB, Williams Coll., 1941; JD, Harvard U., 1949. Bar: Hawaii 1949, U.S. Supreme Ct. 1985. Assoc. Pratt, Tavares & Cassidy, Honolulu, 1949-51, Carlsmith & Carlsmith, Hilo, Hawaii, 1951-59; ptnr. Carlsmith Ball, Honolulu, 1959—2002, of counsel, 2002—. Bd. dirs. ML Resources, Hilo, 1986-2006. Trustee Hanahauoli Sch., Honolulu, 1970-82, Ctrl. Union Ch., Honolulu, 1984-88, Arcadia Retirement Residence, Honolulu, 1985-91. Lt. comdr. USNR, 1943-46, PTO. Mem. ABA, Hawaii Bar Assn., Hawaii Yacht Racing Assn. (bd. dirs. 1994-2000), Pacific Club (bd. dirs. 1978-82), Kaneohe Yacht Club (Honolulu). Republican. Congregationalist. Avocations: sailing, tennis. Home: 3757 Round Top Dr Honolulu HI 96822-5043 Office: Carlsmith Ball PO Box 656 Honolulu HI 96809-0656 Home Phone: 808-949-8272; Office Phone: 808-523-2501. Business E-Mail: jcase@carlsmith.com.

CASE, JANICE CHANG, trust officer, property manager, naturopathic physician, psychologist, lawyer; b. Loma Linda, Calif., May 24, 1970; d. Belden Shiu-Wah and Sylvia (Tan) Chang; m. Steven Lewis Case, Sept. 12, 2004. BA, Calif. State U., San Bernardino, 1990, cert. paralegal studies, 1990, cert. creative writing, 1991; JD, LaSalle U., Phila., 1993; D in Naturopathy, Clayton Sch. Natural Healing, 1993; DFA in Creative Writing: Poetry, Am. Internat. U., 1999; MD in Alternative Medicines, Open Internat. U., 2001; D of Psychology, Calif. Coast U., 2002; LLM in Taxation, Wash. Sch. Law, 2006. Bd. cert. alternative med. practitioner, lic. naturopath DC; cert. loan signing agt., notary pub. Calif., lic. real estate salesperson Calif. Victim/witness contact clk.-paralegal Dist. Atty.'s Office

Victim/Witness Assistance Program, San Bernardino, Calif., 1990; gen. counsel JMC Enterprises, Inc., Riverside, Calif., 1993—2005; adj. law prof. LaSalle U., Mandeville, La., 1994-97; corp. counsel, CFO, JDS Assocs., Inc., Loma Linda, 1998-99, DJS, L.P., Loma Linda, 1998-99; trust officer/trust svcs. Southeastern Calif. Conf. Seventh-Day Adventists, Riverside, 1998—; CFO, gen. counsel Stanberden Properties, LLC, 2001—, SJD Enterprises, LLC, 2005—06. Contbr. poetry to anthologies, including Am. Poetry Anthology, 1987-90, The Pacific Rev., 1991, The Piquant, 1991, River of Dreams, 1994, Reflections of Light, 1994, Musings, 1994 (Honorable Mention award 1994), Treasured Poems of America, 1994, Windows of the Soul, 1995, Best Poems of 1995 (Celebrating Excellence award 1995, Inspirations award 1995), Am. Poetry Annual, 1996, 99, Best New Poems of 1996, Interludes, 1996, Meditations, 1996, Perspectives, 1996 (Honorable Mention award 1996), Keepsakes, 1997 (Honorable Mention award 1997), Best Poems of 1997, Poetic Voices of America, 1997, The Isle of View, 1997, The Other Side of Midnight, 1997, Treasures, 1998, Best Poems of 1998, Writingscapes: Insights & Approaches to Creative Writing, 1998, Mirrors, 1999 (Pres.'s Lit. Excellence award), Pieces of the Heart, 2000, The Silence Within, 2001, Nature's Echoes, 2001, The Best Poems and Poets of 2001, The Best Poems and Poets of 2002; contbr. to Internat. Libr. Photography: Tapestry of Dreams, 1999, Mystical Seasons, 1999, Candid Captures, 2001, The Mirror's Reflection, 2003. Vol. Health Fair Expo La Sierra U., 1988, 1989, Path of the Just Tree Project, 1998; vol. first aid, CPR, other classes ARC, 1994—; sponsor Student Employment Recognition Banquet La Sierra U., Riverside, Calif., 1999—2003. Recipient Poet of Merit award, Am. Poetry Assn., San Francisco, 1989, Golden Poet award, World of Poetry, Washington, 1989, Publisher's Choice award, Watermark Press, 1990, Pres.'s award for lit. excellence, Iliad Press, 1995—99. Fellow Am. Coll. Internat. Physicians; mem. ABA, Am. Coll. Legal Medicine, Am. Naturopathic Med. Assn., Nat. Notary Assn., Brit. Guild Drugless Practitioners (life). Republican. Seventh-Day Adventist. Avocations: poetry writing, photography, music, drama, literature, coin collecting/numismatics. Home: 1025 Crestbrook Dr Riverside CA 92506-5662 Office: Southeastern Calif Conf 7th-Day Adventists PO Box 8050 11330 Pierce St Riverside CA 92515-8050 Office Phone: 951-509-2229. Business E-Mail: casejm@secc-sda.org.

CASE, KAREN ANN, lawyer; b. Milw., Apr. 7, 1944; d. Alfred F. and Hilda M. (Tomich) Case. BS, Marquette U., 1963, JD, 1966; LLM, NYU, 1973. Bar: Wis. 1966, U.S. Ct. Claims 1973, U.S. Tax Ct. 1973. Ptnr. Meldman, Case & Weine, Milw., 1973-85, Meldman, Case & Weine divsn. Mulcahy & Wherry, S.C., 1985-87; Sec. of Revenue State of Wis., 1987-88; ptnr. Case & Drinka, S.C., Milw., 1989-91, Case, Drinka & Diel, S.C., Milw., 1991-97, CoVac, 1997—. Lectr. U. Wis., Milw., 1974-78; guest lectr. Marquette U. Law Sch., 1975-78; dir. WBBC, 1998—. Contbr. articles to legal jours. Mem. gov.'s Commn. on Taliesin, 1988, gov.'s Econ. Adv. Commn., 1989-91, pres.'s coun. Alverno Coll., 1988-94, nat. coun., 1998-2000; bd. dirs. WBCC, 1998—. Fellow Wis. Bar Found. (dir. 1977-90, treas. 1980-90); mem. ABA, Milw. Assn. Women Lawyers (founding mem., bd. dirs. 1975-78, 81-82), Milw. Bar Assn. (bd. dirs. 1985-87, law office mgmt. chair 1992-93), State Bar Wis. (bd. govs. 1981-85, 87-90, dir. taxation sect. 1981-87, vice chmn. 1986-87, 90-91, chmn. 1991-92), Am. Acad. Matrimonial Lawyers (bd. dirs. 1988-90), Nat. Assn. Women Lawyers (Wis. del. 1982-83), Milw. Rose Soc. (pres. 1981, dir. 1981-83), Friends of Boerner Bot. Gardens (founding mem., pres. 1984-90), Profl. Dimensions Club (dir. 1985-87), Tempo Club (sec. 1984-85). Office: CoVac 9803 W Meadow Park Dr Hales Corners WI 53130-2261 Home Phone: 941-387-4352; Office Phone: 414-425-5672. *Delegate tasks for responsibility and accountability. then spend the resulting freed time nourishing your soul. Resign yourself to the fact that the tasks will not be completed as you would have but they will be done, sometimes with more creativity. Give credit and praise always.*

CASE, KENNETH EUGENE, industrial engineering educator; b. Oak Ridge, Tenn., Aug. 12, 1944; s. Richard Thaddeus and Vera Lavone (Peyton) C.; m. Frances Lynn Curlee, Jan. 21, 1966; children: Kristin Lynn, David Rex. BSEE, Okla. State U., 1966, MS in Indsl. Engring., 1967, PhD in Indsl. Engring., 1969. Lic. profl. engr., cert. quality engr., Am. Soc. Quality, reliability engr., Am. Soc. Quality, quality auditor, Am. Soc. Quality, quality mgr., Am. Soc. Quality, prodn. and inventory mgmt., Am. Prodn. and Inventory Control Soc., 1990, six sigma black belt, Am. Soc. Quality. Asst. prof. indsl. engring. Va. Poly. Inst., Blacksburg, 1969-73, assoc. prof. indsl. engring., 1973-74; mgmt. scientist GTE Data Services, Tampa, Fla., 1974-75; assoc. prof. indsl. engring. Okla. State U., Stillwater, 1975-78, prof., head indsl. engring., 1980-82, prof. inden. engring., 1978-87, regents prof. inden. engring., 1987—, dir. MS in Engring. and Tech. Mgmt. Program, 1997—2002. Dir. MS in Engring. and Tech. Mgmt. Program Okla. State U., Stillwater, Okla., 1997—2002; sr. examiner Malcolm Baldridge Nat. Quality award Dept. of Commerce, 1988, 89, 90, panel of judges, 91, 92, 93. Co-author: Principles of Engineering Economic Analysis, 1977, 4th edit., 1998, Introduction to Industrial and Systems Engineering, 1977, 3d edit., 1993 (IIE Book of Yr. 1979), Profit Through Quality, 1978. Com. chmn. troop 828 Boy Scouts Am., Stillwater, 1985-88. Named Outstanding Engring. Prof. Okla. State U., 1983, Disting. Eagle Scout Boy Scouts Am., 1986; recipient L.E. Tinker award Boy Scouts Am., Albert Holzman Disting. Edn. award, 1991, Regents Disting. Teaching award Okla. State U., 1992, Silver Beaver award Boy Scouts Am., 1994. Fellow: Am. Soc. Quality (editl. bd. Jour. Quality Tech. 1979—97, editl. bd. Quality Mgmt. Jour. 1993—, nat. dir. 1999—2001, treas. 2001—02, pres.-elect 2002—03, pres. 2003—04, chmn. of bd. 2004—, past sect. chmn., Berg award 1978, Eugene L. Grant medal 2003), Inst. Indsl. Engrs. (internat. pres. 1986—87, Award of Excellence 1980, Disting. Svc. award 1984, Frank and Lillian Gilbreth Indsl. Engring. award 2002); mem.: NSPE, NAE (peer com. chair sect. 8, membership com., nominating com.), Am. Prodn. and Inventory Control Soc., Internat. Acad. Quality (academician 1990—, bd. dir., editor IAQ Contact), Am. Soc. Engring. Edn. (George Westinghouse award 1989), Okla. Soc. Profl. Engrs. (Okla. Outstanding Engr. 1987), Am. Radio Relay League (Conn. chpt.), Order of Arrow, Sigma Chi. Home: 2416 Tanglewood Cir Stillwater OK 74074-1717 Office: Okla State U Sch Indsl Engring and Mgmt Stillwater OK 74078-5018 Home Phone: 405-377-7586; Office Phone: 405-744-6952. E-mail: kcase@okstate.edu.

CASE, LARRY D., agricultural education specialist; b. Norborne, Mo., Aug. 8, 1943; s. Burr Jr. and Eva Marie (Harper); m. Joy Leona Vandivort, June 18, 1966; children: Jeffrey Dale, Rebecca Joy, Matthew Edward. BS in Agriculture, U. Mo., 1966, MEd, 1972, EdD, 1983; LHD (hon.), SUNY, Cobleskill, 1990. Life cert. agriculture tchr. Tchr. Northwestern High Sch., Mendon, Mo., 1966, Orrick (Mo.) Sch. Dist., 1966-69, Lexington (Mo.) R-V Sch. Dist., 1969-73, vocat. dir., 1973-74; dir. vocat. edn. Lexington La-Ray Area Vocat. Sch., 1974-77; supr. agrl. edn. Mo. Dept. Elem. & Sec. Edn., Jefferson City, 1977-78, state dir. agrl. edn., 1978-84; ednl. program specialist-agriculture U.S. Dept. Edn., Washington, 1984—. Chmn. bd. Future Farmers Am., Alexandria, 1984, Nat. Coun. for Vocat. Tech. Edn. in Agr., Alexandria, 1984-93, Nat. Postgrad. Agrl. Students Orgn., Alexandria, 1984; pres. Future Farmers Am. Found., Alexandria, 1984; adj. prof. Pa. State U., University Park. Contbr. articles on agrl. edn. and internat. travel related to agrl. edn. Active deacon Fredericksburg (Va.) Bapt. Ch., 1984—, Sunday sch. tchr., 1984—; pres. Motts Row Property Owners Assn., 1988-89. Recipient Hon. Am. Farmer degree Future Farmers Am., 1984, Citation of Merit, U. Mo. Coll. of Agr., 1990. Mem. Future Farmers Am. Alumni Assn. (life), Am. Vocat. Assn., Nat. Assn. State Suprs. Agrl. Edn. (sec. 1980-84), Nat. Vocat. Agr. Tchrs. Assn. (life), Nat. Planning Assn. (food and agr. com.), Phi Delta Kappa, Alpha Gamma Rho (nat. hon. mem.). Office: US Dept Edn OVAE 330 C St SW Washington DC 20202-0001

CASE, PAUL WATSON, JR., communications executive; b. Elmira, NY, Dec. 4, 1949; s. Paul Watson and Josephine Pharr (Pollock) C.; m. Laura Lee Sweet, Dec. 12, 1972; 1 child, Brian M. BA, U. Colo., 1971. Cert. in computer programming, cert. in data processing, Inst. Cert. Computer Profls. Programmer analyst Boulder Daily Camera, Colo., 1968—73; v.p. Mr. Steak Inc., Denver, 1973—83, United Cable TV Corp., Denver, 1983—88, United Artists Entertainment Corp., Denver, 1988—90; pres. Caspen, Inc., Larkspur, Colo., 1990; CEO Interactive TV Network Inc., Denver, 1991—97; founding prin. Spectralliance LLC, Denver, 1998—; mng. dir. Case Ventures, 2001—; pres. Kolani Distillers, 2002—. Mem. Colo. Open Systems Consortium (founder., chmn. 1992-95), Cable Data User Com. (chmn. 1986-88). Home: 6561 Pike Cir Larkspur CO 80118-9713 Office: Spectralliance LLC Ste 700 4600 S Ulster St Denver CO 80237 Office Phone: 303-681-3325. E-mail: pcase@spectralliance.com.

CASE, RICHARD W., sports association executive; m. Barbara Case; two children. Sec. gen. USA Baseball (formerly U.S. Baseball Fedn.), 1980—. Bd. dirs. U.S. Olympic Com.; cons., advisor and dir. in field; producer instrnl. videotapes, books and brochures with a concentration in the areas of player and coach tng., vol. enlistment, accident prevention, juv. delinquency, and youth tournament operation in all sports. Recipient USA Baseball Pres.'s award, Am. Baseball Coaches Assn. award of honor, Centenary medal Juan Antonio Samaranch, Internat. Olympic Com. Pres., others; inducted into Nat. Jr. Coll. Athletic Assn. Hall of Fame, Nat. Assn. Intercollegiate Athletics Hall of Fame, Nat. Police Assn. Hall of Honor; recipient numerous hon. citizenship and commendation awards. Mem. Internat. Baseball Assn. (sec. gen.). Office: Usa Baseball 403 Blackwell St Durham NC 27701-3972

CASE, ROBERT BROWN, physician; b. Columbus, Ohio, July 19, 1920; s. William Lyman and Margaret (Brown) C.; m. Nan Barkin, Nov. 9, 1973; 1 child, Lisa Case. BA, Ohio Wesleyan, 1943; BS, MIT, 1943; MD, Columbia U., 1948. Diplomate Am. Bd. Internal Medicine. Intern and resident St. Luke's Hosp., NYC, 1948-52, chief lab. of exptl. cardiology, 1956-95, sr. attending physician, 1971-95; rsch. fellow Harvard Sch. of Pub. Health, Boston, 1952-54; rsch. assoc. Nat. Heart Inst., Bethesda, Md., 1954-56; prof. emeritus medicine Columbia U., NYC, 1991—. Chief cardiac consultation clinic N.Y.C. Dept. Health, 1962-70; mem. cardiovascular study sect. Nat. Heart Inst., 1970-74. Mem. editl. bd. Circulation Rsch., 1977-85; contbr. articles to profl. jours. With USPHS, 1954-56. Rsch. Career devel. grant NIH, 1962-72. Felow Am. Physiol. Soc., N.Y. County Med. Assn., N.Y. State Med. Assn., Am. Heart Assn., Am. Fedn. for Clin. Rsch. Home and Office: 130 E 75th St New York NY 10021-3277 Home Phone: 212-249-5613; Office Phone: 212-249-5613. E-mail: rcasemd@nyc.rr.com.

CASE, STEVE (STEPHEN M.), healthcare investment company executive, former media and entertainment company executive; b. Honolulu, Aug. 21, 1958; m. Joanne Case (div.); 3 children; m. Jean Case. BA in Polit. Sci., Williams Coll., 1980. With mktg. dept. Procter & Gamble, 1980—82; mng. new pizza devel. Pizza Hut divsn. PepsiCo, 1982—83; with Control Video, 1983—85, Quantum Computer Svcs., 1985—92; co-founder, CEO America Online, 1992—2001, chmn., 1995—2001, AOL Time Warner, NYC, 2001—03, Exclusive Resorts LLC, Denver, 2004—; chmn., CEO Revolution Health Group, 2005—. Bd. dirs. America Online, 1992—2001, Time Warner Inc. (previously AOL Time Warner), 2001—05; launched Revolution Health.com, 2007—; investor RediClinic, 2006—. Named Named Entrepreneur of Yr., Inc. Mag., 1994. Avocation: reading political science and social history. Office: Exclusive Resorts LLC Ste 500 1530 16th St Denver CO 80202*

CASE, THOMAS LOUIS, lawyer; b. Dallas, June 14, 1947; s. Donald L. and Ellen (Hanson) C.; m. Bonnie Nally, July 8, 1972. BA, Vanderbilt U., 1969, JD, 1972; cert. civil trial law, Tex. Bd. Legal Specialization. Bar: Tex. 1972, U.S. Dist. Ct. (no. dist.) Tex. 1973, U.S. Dist. Ct. (we. and ea. dists.) Tex. 1978, U.S. Dist. Ct. (so. dist.) Tex. 1979, U.S. Dist. Ct. (ea. dist.) Ark. 1981, U.S. Ct. Appeals (5th cir.) 1977, U.S. Supreme Ct. 1978, U.S. Ct. Appeals (8th cir.) 1984, U.S. Ct. Appeals (11th cir.) 1981. Assoc. Johnson, Bromberg, Leeds & Riggs, Dallas, 1972-77; ptnr. Bickel & Case, Dallas, 1977-84, St. Claire & Case, Dallas, 1984-93, Thomas L. Case & Assocs., P.C., Dallas, 1993-2000; shareholder Case Carter Salyers & Henry, Dallas, 2000—01; ptnr. Bell, Nunnally & Martin, Dallas, 2002—. Mem. ABA, Tex. Bar Assn., Tex. Assn. Def. Coun., Dallas Assn. of Def. Counsel, Dallas Bar Assn. Office: Bell Nunnally & Martin 3232 McKinney Ave Ste 1400 Dallas TX 75204 Office Phone: 214-740-1422. Business E-Mail: tomc@bellnunnally.com.

CASEI, NEDDA, mezzo soprano; b. Balt. d. Howard Thomas and Lyda Marie (Graupman) Casey; m. John A. Wiles, Jr., 1971 (div. 1979); m. Samuel Strasbourger, 1983 (dec. 1987). Cert., Mozarteum, Salzburg, Austria, 1959; B in Performing Arts Adminstrn. magna cum laude, Fordham U., 1982; studied voice with, William P. Herman, NYC, Vittorio Piccinini, Milan, Italy, Loretta Corelli, NYC; also student piano, langs., modern dance, pilates, ballet. Tchr. master classes, lectr. univs. and festivals. Judge vocal competitions for Met. Opera, Fulbright Scholarship, Rosa Ponselle Internat. Competition, Savannah Festival, George London Found. Competition, First Internat. Vocal Competition, Baku, Azerbaijan, Nagakute Internat. Coval Competition, and others; vis. prof. Aichi Prefectural U. Fine Arts and Music, Nagoya, Japan, 1993-95, 2003—; guest prof. Flaine Festival/Paris Conservatory, Haut Savoie, France, Mannes Coll. Music, New Sch. Social Rsch., N.Y.C., Internat. Vocal Arts Inst., Tel Aviv; pvt. tchr. Operatic debut Theatre Royal de la Monnaie, Brussels, 1960, with La Scala, Milan, Met. Opera, N.Y.C., 1964; operatic performances at Met. Opera, 1964-86, Basel Stadttheater, Gran Liceo, Barcelona, Teatro Carlo Fenice, Genova, San Remo Festival, Trieste Opera, Opera du Rhin, Strasbourg, Salzburg Festspielhaus, Teatro San Carlo, Naples, Chgo. Lyric Opera, Bogota Opera, Caracas Opera, Pitts. Opera, Vancouver Opera, Cape Town Opera, Brno Opera, Bratislava Opera, Kosice Opera, Prague Opera, Miami Opera, Houston Opera, San Diego Opera, Hartford Opera, Phila. Opera, Toledo Opera, Dayton Opera, Memphis Opera, Mobile Opera, Los Angeles Opera, Boston Opera, N.J. Opera, Taipei Opera, Opera of Mexico City; performances in numerous mus. festivals, concerts, recitals and operatic guest appearances in Europe, South Africa, Cen. Am., S.Am., Can., U.S., Far East, Middle East and Australia, including Detroit Symphony, Cin. Orch., Toronto Symphony, Liepzig Gewandhaus Philharm., Phila. Orch., Brussels Philharm., NY Philharm.; performed on radio and TV in Holland, Belgium, Leipzig, Japan, U.S., German Dem. Republic, Fed. Republic of Germany, Hong Kong, Manila, Singapore; performed at White House, Washington; made various recs. Supraphon, Everest, Nonesuch, Concert Hall, Vanguard, CETRA, VAI, others; contbr. articles to profl. jours.; guest editor Opera Quar. Coord. mus. events and benefits for Internat. Ctr. for Disabled, Morningside Home, Aging in Am. Gerontol. Acad.; mem. adv. bd. Fordham U at Lincoln Ctr., 1984—; bd. dirs. Theatre for a New Audience, Am. Coun. for Arts, Nat. Cultural Alliance, Songs of Love; mem. Career Transition for Dancers Nat. Adv. Bd. Recipient Outstanding Young Singers award, 1959, Martha Baird Rockefeller Found. award, 1962, 1963, 1964, Woman of Achievement award, 1969, Cmty. Leaders and Noteworthy Americans, 1975—76, Outstanding Achievement award on behalf of Arts and Edn., Opera Music Theater Internat. and Children's Emergency Med. Fund, 2000, Outstanding Lifetime Achievement award, Licia Albanese/Puccini Found., 2001, Extraordinary Women award, 2000, honors at, 100 Year Verdi Celebration by Met. Opera, Mozart Celebration at Met Opera, 2006. Mem. AFTRA, Actors Equity, Am. Guild Mus. Artists (nat. pres. 1983-93. chmn. Emergency Relief Fund 1983-94), Nat. Assn. Tchrs. Singing (bd. govs.), N.Y. Singing Tchrs. Assn., The Players, James Beard Found. Personal E-mail: neddanewyork@nyc.rr.com. Business E-Mail: neddanagoya@guitar.ocn.ne.jp.

CASEIRAS, JO ANN STRIGA, artist, educator; b. Bklyn., Dec. 17, 1950; d. Michael Striga and Stella Mary Lango; m. Frank Caseiras, May 21, 1983; children: Michael Allen, Kevin Frank, Amanda Beth, Robert Anthony. BFA, St. John's U., Jamaica, NY, 1972; MFA, SUNY, New Paltz, 1975. Tchr. continuing edn. SUNY, New Paltz, 1974-75, prof. Buffalo, 1976-78; tchr. Marlboro (N.Y.) Elem. Continuing Edn., 1980-82; parent advocate Rondout Valley Ctrl. Sch. Dist., Accord, N.Y., 1992-97, tchr. program for the handicapped, 1999—. Exhibited in shows at Reavin Gallery, New Paltz, N.Y., 1976, Benjamin's Works of Art, Buffalo, 1977, Art Zone 208, New Paltz, 1979, Mamaroneck Artists Guild, White Plains, N.Y., 1979, Womanart Gallery, N.Y.C., Schenectady (N.Y.) Mus., 1980, New Rochelle (N.Y.) Art Assn., 1994, Heritage Art Gallery, Poughkeepsie, N.Y., 1995, St. John's U., Jamaica, N.Y., 1996, Heritage Gallery, Rhinebeck, N.Y., 1997, Highland (N.Y.) Cultural Art Ctr., 1996-98, Coffey Gallery, Kingston, N.Y., 1998, Woodstock (N.Y.) Art Assn., 1995—, First Union Bank, New Paltz, 2000, Marbletown Arts Assn., 2002, Marbletown Tricentennial Exhbn., 2003. Recipient Mortimer L. Medrich Meml. award, 1979. Mem.: Woodstock Art Assn., Art Soc. Kingston, Downs Syndrome Assn. Democrat. Roman Catholic. Avocations: sports, swimming, piano, photography. Personal E-mail: striga17@yahoo.com.

CASELE, HOLLY, obstetrician; b. Abington, Pa., Jan. 4, 1966; d. Joseph and Mary Elizabeth Casele; m. Robert Emmet Holden, Mar. 17, 1999; children: Nicholas Holden, Casey Holden, Aidan Holden. BA, Brown U., Providence, 1987; MD, Northwestern U., Chgo., 1991. Physician, asst. prof. Northwestern U. Med. Sch., Evanston, Ill., 1997—2006; physician maternal fetal medicine specialist San Diego Perinatal Ctr., 2006—. Contbr. articles to profl. jours. Grantee, Aventic Pharms., 1997—2006. Fellow: Am. Coll. Ob-gyn.; mem.: Internat. Soc. Thrombosis and Hemostasis (assoc.), Am. Inst. Ultrasound Medicine (assoc.), Soc. Maternal Fetal Medicine (assoc.; mem. pubs. com. 2004), Sigma Xi (life), Alpha Omega Alpha (life). Achievements include research in thromboembolic disease in pregnancy. Avocations: travel, skiing, running, golf. Office Phone: 858-939-6880.

CASELLA, ANTHONY JOHN, cardiologist; b. NYC, Mar. 8, 1945; s. Anthony Daniel and Benedetta Ann Casella; m. Kathleen Ann Barrs, Aug. 31, 1986; children: Daniel Edward, Eric Michael; 1 child from previous marriage, Joseph Anthony. BA, NYU, 1966; MD, N.Y. Med. Coll., 1970. Diplomate Am. Bd. Internal Medicine. Intern, resident N.Y. Hosp.-Meml. Hosp., 1970-73; fellow cardiology Columbia-Presbyn. Med. Ctr., NYC, 1975-77; cardiologist Diagnostic and Clin. Cardiology PA, West Orange, NJ, 1977—. Cardiologist St. Barnabas Med. Ctr., Livingston, NJ, 1977—, Clara Maass Med. Ctr., Belleville, NJ, 1977—; assoc. St. Michaels Med. Ctr., Newark, 1984—. Mem.: AMA, Essex County Med. Soc., Alpha Omega Alpha. Republican. Roman Catholic. Office: Diagnostic and Clin Cardiology PA 769 Northfield Ave West Orange NJ 07052-1198 Office Phone: 973-731-9442.

CASELLA, JIM, publishing executive; CEO Round1; 1st pres., CEO PennNet (now called PennEnergy); CEO Reed Bus. Info. U.S., 2002—05; vice chmn. Reed Bus. Info., 2005—. Sr. position pub. co. Harcourt; pres. ABC Mag.; COO IDG. Office: Reed Internat Bus US 18th Fl 360 Park Ave S New York NY 10010-1710 Business E-Mail: jcasella@reedbusiness.com.

CASELLA, PETER F(IORE), patent and licensing executive; b. June 5, 1922; s. Fiore Peter and Lucy (Grimaldi) C.; m. Marjorie Eloise Enos, March 9, 1946 (dec. Aug. 1989); children: William Peter, Susan Elaine, Richard Mark. BChE, Poly. U., Bklyn., 1943; student in chemistry, St. John's U., NYC, 1940. Registered to practice by the U.S. Patent and Trademark Office, Can. Patent and Trademark Offices. Head patent sect. Hooker Electrochem. Co., Niagara Falls, NY, 1943-54; mgr. patent dept. Occidental Chem. Corp. (formerly Hooker Chem. Corp.), Niagara Falls, NY, 1954-64, dir. patents and licensing, 1964-81, asst. sec., 1966-81, ret., 1981. Pres. TFA Products, Inc., Houston, Intra Gene Internat., Inc., Lewiston, N.Y., 1981-92; chmn. bd. In Vitro Internat., Inc., Linthicum, Md., 1983-86; cons. patents and licensing, Lewiston, N.Y., 1981—; Dept. Commerce del. on patents and licensing exchange, USSR, 1973, 90, Poland and German Dem. Rep., 1976. Editor: Drafting the Patent Application, 1957. Mem. Lewiston Bd. Edn., 1968-70. With AUS, 1944-46, Mediterranean Theater of Operation. Recipient Centennial citation Poly. U., Bklyn., 1955, Golden Jubilee Soc., 1993. Mem. ACS, AIChE, Assn. Corp. Patent Counsel (emeritus, exec. com. 1974-77, charter mem.), N.Y. Intellectual Property Law Assn. (Niagara Frontier chpt. pres. 1973-74, founder award 1974), Licensing Execs. Soc. (v.p. 1976-77, Trustees award 1977), Chartered Inst. Patent Agts. Gt. Britain (emeritus), Patent and Trademark Inst. Can., Internat. Patent and Trademark Assn. (emeritus), U.S. Trademark Assn., Nat. Assn. Mfrs. (patent com.), Mfg. Chemists Assn., Pacific Indsl. Property Assn., U.S. Patent Office Soc. (assoc.), U.S. Trademark Office Soc. (assoc.), Chemists Club (emeritus N.Y.C. chpt.), Niagara Club (Niagara Falls pres. 1973-74).

CASELLA, RUSSELL CARL, physicist; b. Framingham, Mass., Nov. 6, 1929; s. Rosario and Lena Casella; m. Marilyn Smith, Jan. 27, 1952; children: Sheryl M., Cynthia L. Conturie. BS in Physics, MIT, 1951, MS in Physics, 1953; PhD in Physics, U. Ill., 1956. Physicist Cambridge (Mass.) AF Rsch. Ctr., 1951-52; teaching and rsch. asst. physics dept. U. Ill., Urbana, 1953-55, rsch. fellow physics dept., 1955-56, rsch. assoc. physics dept., 1956-58; theoretical physicist IBM T.J. Watson Rsch. Ctr., Yorktown Heights, NY, 1958-65, Nat. Inst. Standards and Tech., Gaithersburg, Md., 1965-95. Contbr. articles to profl. jours. Recipient Silver medal U.S. Dept. Commerce, 1973. Mem. Am. Phys. Soc., Sigma Xi. Achievements include development of theory of condensed-matter and of elementary-particle physics; research in (broken) symmetries; neutron scattering; Bose condensation of excitons; tests of time reversal and CPT symmetries in Kaon physics; neutrino scattering; topology in neutron interferometry; high-temperature superconductivity; hydrogen in metals; quark-parton-sea content of the nucleon in deep-inelastic electroweak scattering.

CASELLAS, GILBERT F. F., lawyer; b. Tampa, Fla., Aug. 2, 1952; s. John G. and Yolanda (Panier) C.; m. Ada Garcia-Casellas, Aug. 1, 1981; 1 child, Marisa Astrid. BA, Yale U., 1974; JD, U. Pa., 1977. Bar: Pa. 1977, US Dist. Ct. (ea. dist.) Pa. 1979, US Ct. Appeals (3rd cir.) 1980, US Supreme Ct. 1988, US Dist. Ct. (mid. dist.) Pa. 1989. Assoc. Montgomery, McCracken, Walker & Rhoads, Phila., 1977-78, 80-85, ptnr., 1985-93; law clk. to Hon. Leon Higginbotham US Ct Appeals (3rd cir.), Phila., 1978-80; gen. counsel Dept. of Air Force, Washington, 1993-94; chmn. US EEOC, Washington, 1994-98; ptnr. McConnell Valdés LLP, Washington, 1998-99; pres., COO The Swarthmore Group, Inc., West Chester, Pa., 1999—; pres. Casellas & Associates, LLC; counsel Mintz Levin Cohn Ferris Glovsky and Popeo, Washington. Lectr. U. Pa. Law Sch., Phila., 1985-89, 92-93; spl. counsel Phila. Human Rels. Commn., Phila., 1990-91; judge pro tem Phila. Ct. Common Pleas, 1992; chmn. bd. overseers Sch. Social Work, U. Pa., 1996—; bd. dirs. Prudential Fin., Inc. Trustee U. Pa., 1996—; sec., trustee Free Libr. Phila., 1990-93; bd. dirs. P.R. Legal Def. and Edn. Fund, 1998—, Hispanic Fedn., 1999—, Nat. Constitution Ctr., 1999—; co-chair US Census Monitoring Bd., 1999—. Recipient Citation award City Phila., 1986, Clarence Farmer Svc. award Phila. Commn. on Human Rels., 1995; named one of Boardroom Elite, Hispanic Bus. Mag., 2007-. Mem. ABA (mem. ho. dels. 1986-91, Spirit of Excellence award 1999), Am. Law Inst., Am. Arbitration Assn. (bd. dirs. 1998—), Hispanic Nat. Bar Assn. (nat.

pres. 1984-85, Citation award 1985), Pa. Bar Assn. (mem. ho. dels. 1987-83), Phila. Bar Assn. (chmn. bd. govs. 1990), Phila. Bar Found. (trustee 1991). Office: Mintz Levin Cohn Ferris Glovsky and Popeo PC 701 Pennsylvania Ave NW Washington DC 20004 Office Phone: 202-434-7413.*

CASELLAS, JOACHIM, art gallery executive; b. Gerona, Spain, Aug. 1, 1927; came to U.S., 1954; s. Juan and Dolores Farres (Carrera) C.; m. Elizabeth Reed Brannon, Mar. 17, 1952 (dec. Dec. 1984); m. Janice Mary Bezverkov, May 29, 1990 (dec. Apr. 2002). BA, Gerona Coll., 1948; MA, Sacred Heart Coll., 1953. Curator Mus. Provincial, Gerona, Spain, 1952; art appraiser Feist Co., NYC, 1952-68, Mahan Co., New Orleans, 1968-72; pres. Casell Gallery, New Orleans, 1972—. One-man shows include Ft. Walton (Fla.) Beach Mus. Art, 1987. Mem. Ocean Springs Yacht Club. Republican. Episcopalian. Avocations: photography, gardening, travel, antiques, boating. Office: Casell Gallery 818 Royal St New Orleans LA 70116-3115 Home: 203 Lakeside Villa Diamondhead MS 39525 Office Phone: 504-524-0671. Personal E-mail: joaquin_cas@msn.com. Business E-Mail: casellartgallery@bellsouth.net.

CASELLAS, SALVADOR E., judge; b. 1935; BS in Fgn. Svc. cum laude, Georgetown U., 1957; LLB magna cum laude, U. P.R., 1960; LLM, Harvard U., 1961. Ptnr. Fiddler, Gonzalez & Rodriguez, 1962-72, 77-94; sr. judge U.S. Dist. Ct. P.R., San Juan, 1994—. Mem. P.R. Acad. Jurisprudence, P.R. Commn. on Bicentennial of U.S. Constn., 1987-89; aide to Sec. of U.S. Army, 1985-89, emeritus, 1990—. Dir. Alliance for Drug Free P.R., 1993-94. 1st lt. U.S. Army, 1961-62, Res., JAGC, 1963-67. Recipient Comdrs. medal Second U.S. Army, 1990, P.R. Nat. Guard medal, 1990. Mem. ABA, Am. Bar Found., P.R. Bar Assn., Caparra Country Club, Banker's Club. Office: US Courthouse Ste 342 Viejo San Juan PR 00901 Office Phone: 787-977-6060.

CASERTA, JENNIFER, communications executive; b. 1971; Mktg. positions Radio Advt. Bur., Westwood One, Oxygen Media, The Food Network; v.p., ad sales mktg. Court TV; sr. v.p. mktg. Ind. Film Channel, NYC, 2004—. Named one of 40 Executives Under 40, Multichannel News, 2006. Office: Independent Film Channel 323 6th Ave New York NY 10014

CASEY, BOB See CASEY, ROBERT JR.

CASEY, DANIEL ARTHUR, lawyer; b. Pitts., May 8, 1956; s. Robert Louis and Rosemary (Doran) C.; m. Maria Cristina Pena, Aug. 1, 1981; children: Patricia, Robert, Andrew. BS, Wheeling Coll., 1978; JD, Georgetown U., 1981. Bar: Fla. 1981, U.S. Dist. Ct. (so. dist.) Fla. 1986, U.S. Ct. Appeals (11th cir.) 1986, U.S. Dist. Ct. (mid. dist.) Fla. 1989. Asst. State Atty. Dade County State Atty., Miami, Fla., 1981-86; assoc. Kirkpatrick and Lockhart, Miami, 1986-89, ptnr., 1990—2004; adminstrv. ptnr. & mem. exec. com. Kirkpatrick & Lockhart Nicholson Graham LLP, Miami, 2005—. Adj. prof. law Nova U. Law Sch., 1989-96. Contbr. articles to profl. publs. Nat. bd. dir. YMCA of the USA; past pres. YMCA So. Broward County; mem. Ins. Info. Council; past pres. Greater Hollywood C. of C. Mem.: Dade County Bar Assn. (bd. dir.), Alpha Sigma Nu. Office: Kirkpatrick & Lockhart Nicholson Graham LLP Ste 2000 201 S Biscayne Blvd Miami FL 33131-2399 Office Phone: 305-539-3324. Office Fax: 305-358-7095. Business E-Mail: dcasey@klng.com.

CASEY, DANIEL E., psychiatrist, educator; b. West Springfield, Mass., Jan. 24, 1947; s. Arthur and Gloria Casey. BA in Psychology, U. Va., 1969, MD, 1972. Diplomate Am. Bd. Psychiatry and Neurology. Resident in psychiatry U. Oreg., Portland, 1973-74, Brown U., Providence, 1974-76; staff psychiatrist VA Med. Ctr., Portland, 1976—2003, chief psychiatry rsch., psychopharmacology, 1980—2003; affiliate sci. Oreg. Regional Primate Rsch. Ctr., Portland, 1980—; prof. psychiatry Oreg. Health and Sci. U., Portland, 1985—, prof. neurology, 1992—. Pres., bd. dirs. Danicas Found., Portland. Author books; Contbr. over 200 articles to profl. jours. Office: Oreg Health and Sci U GH249 Psychiatry Rsch 3181 SW Jackson Park Rd Portland OR 97239 Office Phone: 503-418-1291. E-mail: caseyd@ohsu.edu.

CASEY, DWANE L., former professional basketball coach; b. Morganfield, Ky., Apr. 17, 1957; m. Brenda Casey. BS in Bus. Admin., U. Ky., 1979. Grad. asst. U. Ky., 1979, asst. coach, 1985—90, U. Western Ky., 1980—85; head coach Japanese Nat. Team, 1990—94; assoc. head coach Seattle Supersonics, 2001—05, asst. coach, 1994—2005; head coach Minn. Timberwolves, 2005—07.

CASEY, EDWARD PAUL, manufacturing executive; b. Boston, Feb. 23, 1930; s. Edward J. and Virginia (Paul) C.; m. Patricia Pinkham, June 23, 1950 (dec. Nov. 1996); children: Patricia Estes Casey Shepherd, Tyler, Jennifer Paul, Sheila Pinkham Casey McManus, Virginia Louise Casey Pettengill; m. Mary Ann Patton, Mar. 28, 1998. AB, Yale U., 1952; MBA, Harvard Coll., 1955. With Davidson Rubber Co., Dover, NH, 1950-65; COO McCord Corp., Detroit, 1965-78, pres., 1965-78; COO Ex-Cell-O Corp., Troy, Mich., 1978-81, CEO, pres., 1981-86, chmn., 1983-86; vice chmn. Textron Inc., 1986-87; pres. E. Paul Casey Assocs., 1987-89; mng. gen. ptnr. Metapoint Ptnrs., Peabody, Mass., 1989-97, chmn., 1997—2004, chmn. emeritus, 2004—. Trustee Henry Ford Health Care Sys., Detroit; dir. Hobe Sound Cmty. Chest, Fla. Mem. Chief Execs. Orgn., Harvard Bus. Sch. Club So. Fla., N.Y. Yacht Club (N.Y.C.), Yondotega Club (Detroit), Ea. Yacht Club (Marblehead, Mass.), Yale Club (N.Y.C.), Jupiter Island Club, Hobe Sound Yacht Club (Jupiter Island, Fla.). Home: 330 S Beach Rd Hobe Sound FL 33455-2606

CASEY, GENEVIEVE M(ARY), librarian, educator; b. Mpls., July 13, 1916; d. Eugene James and Cecelia (Malerich) C. BS, Coll. St. Catherine, St. Paul, 1937; MA, U. Mich., 1956. Mem. staff Detroit Pub. Library, 1937-46, 48-61, chief extension dept., 1948-61; Mich. State librarian Lansing, 1961-67; prof. library scis. Wayne State U., 1967-83. Fulbright prof. U. Brasilia, 1979; librarian U.S. Army Librs., ETO, 1946-47; scholar in residence U. Mo. Sch. Libr. Informational Sci., 1985; bd. dirs., mem. curriculum com. Lay Theol. Acad., 2000—. Author: Library Service to the Aging, 1983, Father Clem Kern, Conscience of Detroit, 1989. Named Mich. Librarian of Yr. 1978. Mem. ALA (pres. Assn. Hosp. and Instn. Libraries 1961-62, pres. library edn. div. 1970-72), Pub. Library Assn. (pres. 1976-78), Mich. Library Assn., Am. Assn. Library Schs. (pres. 1979) Home and Office: 1121 Torrey Rd Grosse Pointe MI 48236-2358

CASEY, GEORGE WILLIAM, JR., career military officer; b. Sendai, Japan, July 22, 1948; s. George William Casey; m. Sheila Casey. BS in Internat. Rels., Georgetown U., 1970; MA in Internat. Rels., U. Denver. Commd. 2nd lt. US Army, 1970, advanced through grades to gen., 2003, various positions, 1970-82, exec. officer 1st Battalion, 10th Infantry, 4th Divsn. Ft. Carson, Colo., 1982-84, sec. gen. staff 4th Infantry Divsn., 1984-85; comdr. 1st Battalion, 10th Infantry, 4th Divsn. U.S. Army, Ft. Carson, Colo., 1985-87; congl. program coord. Office of the Chief of Legis. Liaison, Washington, 1988-89; spl. asst. to chief of staff US Army, Washington, 1989-91, chief of staff 1st Cavalry Divsn. Ft. Hood, Tex., 1991-93, comdr. 3rd Brigade, 1st Cavalry Divsn., 1993-95; asst. chief of staff G-3 (ops.), V Corps. US Army Europe, 1995; chief of staff V Corps. US Army Europe & Seventh Army, Germany, 1995-96, asst. divsn. comdr. 1st Armored Divsn., 1996-97; asst. dep. dir. politico-mil. affairs J-5 The Joint Staff, The Pentagon, Washington, 1997-99; comdg. gen. US Army Europe, 1st Armored Divsn., 1999—2001; dir. for strategic plans, policy The Joint Staff, The Pentagon, Washington, 2001—03, dir., 2003; vice chief of staff US Army, Washington, 2003—04, chief of staff, 2007—; comdr. Multi-Nat. Force-Iraq, Baghdad, 2004—07. Decorated Legion of Merit with 2 Oak Leaf Clusters, Def. Meritorious Svc. medal, Meritorious Svc. medal, Army Commendation medal with Oak Leaf Cluster, Army Achievement medal with Oak Leaf Cluster, Disting. Svc. medal with Oak Leaf Cluster, Def. Disting. Svc. medal (2). Office: US Army 200 Army Pentagon Rm 3E528 Washington DC 20310-0200*

CASEY, GERARD WILLIAM, retired food products executive, lawyer; b. NYC, Nov. 12, 1942; s. William Gerard and Bridget (Carmody) C.; m. Lani St. John; children: Jennifer, William, Thomas, Andrew, Patrick. BS in History, Fordham Coll., 1963; MA in History, NYU, 1966; JD, Fordham U., 1967. Bar: NY 1969. Criminal investigator U.S. Army, U.S., Korea, 1967-69; v.p., gen. counsel Pepsi Cola Co., PepsiCo, Inc., Puchase, NY, 1969—2001. Mem. Friendly Sons of St. Patrick, White Plains, 1987—; dir., chmn. bd. mgrs. Lincoln Hall Sch., Lincolndale, NY, 1988-91. Mem. ABA, NY State Bar Assn., Am. Corp. Counsel Assn., VFW. Roman Catholic. Home: 45 E 72nd St New York NY 10021

CASEY, H(ORACE) CRAIG, JR., electrical engineering educator; b. Houston, Dec. 4, 1934; s. H.C. and Mae (Walls) C.; m. Jean Anne Merritt, June 14, 1960 (div. 1983); children: Anne, Michael; m. Jacqueline Lucas, Jan. 22, 1983. BSEE, Okla. State U., 1957; MSEE, Stanford U., 1959, PhD, 1964. Devel. engr. Hewlett-Packard, Palo Alto, Calif., 1957-62; mem. tech. staff Bell Labs., Murray Hill, NJ, 1964-79; chmn. dept. elec. engring. Duke U., Durham, NC, 1979-94, prof. elec. engring., 1979—. Mem. Dept. of Def. Adv. Group Electron Devices, Washington, 1975-79; bd. dirs. Acme Elec., 1984-91. Author: Heterostructure Lasers, 1978, Devices for Integrated Circuits: Silicon and III-V Compounds, 1999. Fellow IEEE (pres. Electron Devices Soc. 1988-89, editor centennial issue Trans. on Electron Devices 1984); mem. Am. Phys. Soc. Office: Duke U Dept Elec Engring Durham NC 27706 Business E-Mail: hcc@ee.duke.edu.

CASEY, JAMES, engineering educator; b. Tipperary, Ireland, Sept. 15, 1949; s. William Casey and Winifred O'Dwyer; m. Irena Herszkowicz, 1984; children: David A., Eoghan, Daniel A.; m. Ita O'Connor, 1971 (div. 1980). B in Engring., Nat. U. Ireland, Dublin, 1971; PhD in Engring. Sci., U. Calif., Berkeley, 1980. Prof. U. Houston, 1980—90, U. Calif., Berkeley, 1990. Achievements include research in continuum mechanics. Office: U Calif 6125 Etcheverry Hall Berkeley CA 94720-1740

CASEY, JOHN ALEXANDER, lawyer; b. Wisconsin Rapids, Wis., Apr. 7, 1945; s. Samuel Alexander and Ardean A. AB, Stanford U., 1967; JD, U. Mich., 1970. Ptnr. Quarles & Brady, Milw., 1970—. Office: Quarles & Brady 411 E Wisconsin Ave Ste 2040 Milwaukee WI 53202-4497 Office Phone: 414-277-5383. Business E-Mail: jac@quarles.com.

CASEY, JOHN DUDLEY, writer, language educator; b. Worcester, Mass., Jan. 18, 1939; s. Joseph Edward and Constance (Dudley) C.; m. Jane Barnes, June 10, 1967 (div. 1980); children: Maud, Nell; m. Rosamond Pinchot Pittman, June 27, 1982; children: Clare, Julia. BA, Harvard U., 1962, LLB, 1965; MFA, U. Iowa, 1968. Prof. English U. Va., Charlottesville, 1972-92, U. Iowa, 1998, U. Va., 1999—. Lit. executor Estate of Breece D'J Pancake, 1979—; resident scholar Am. Acad. in Rome, 1990-91. Author: An American Romance, 1977 (runner up Ernest Hemingway award 1977), Testimony and Demeanor, 1979 (Friends Am. Lit. award 1980), Spartina, 1989 (Nat. Book award 1989), Supper at the Black Pearl, 1995, The Half-life of Happiness, 1998; co-translator: You're an Animal, Viskovitz (by A. Boffa), 2002, Enchantments (by L. Ferri), 2005; contbr. stories (O. Henry award 1989), essays maj. nat. mags. including New Yorker, Esquire. With USAR, 1959-60. Guggenheim fellow, 1979-80, Nat. Endowment for Arts fellow, 1983, resident Am. Acad. in Rome, 1990-91; grantee Strauss living AAAL, 1992-97. Mem. PEN. Avocation: rowing. Office: U Va Dept English Bryan Hall Charlottesville VA 22903-3289: Michael Carlisle Inkwell 521 5th Ave New York NY 10175

CASEY, KAREN ANNE, banker; b. Bklyn., Oct. 5, 1955; d. Stanley Joseph and Helen Katherine (Kosowski) Mozeleski; m. Dennis Joseph Casey, May 14, 1977; children: Christopher Sean, Erin Michelle. BBA, Baruch Coll., CUNY, 1977. CPA, NY, CFP. Jr. acct. Coopers & Lybrand, NYC, 1977-78, sr. acct., 1978-79, supr., 1979-81; asst. fin. contr. Gulf Internat. Bank, NYC, 1981-82, fin. contr., 1982; v.p., fin. contr. Allied Irish Banks plc, NYC, 1982-87, sr. v.p., fin. contr., 1988-89, sr. v.p. mgmt. support svcs., 1989-92, sr. v.p., CFO, 1992-94, sr. v.p., head pvt. fin. svcs., 1994-2001, sr. v.p., head retail and bus. banking, 2001—04; sr. v.p. Greater Cmty. Svcs. Inc., Little Falls, NJ, 2004; exec. v.p. Greater Cmty. Bank, Little Falls, 2005—. Mem. AICPA. Roman Catholic. Avocations: gardening, golf, tennis, reading. Office: Greater Cmty Bk 7 Ctr Ave Little Falls NJ 07424 Personal E-mail: kcasey55@aol.com.

CASEY, KATHLEEN L., commissioner; b. Tripoli, Libya; BA in Internat. Politics, Penn State U., 1988; JD, George Mason U., 1993. Bar: DC, Va. Staff dir. Subcom. on Fin. Institutions and Regulatory Relief U.S. Senate Banking Com. US Senate, 1994—96, legis. asst. to Senator Richard Shelby, 1993—94, legis. dir., chief of staff, 1996—2003, staff dir., counsel, Banking, Housing, and Urban Affairs Com., 2003—06; commr. SEC, 2006—. Mem.: Va State Bar Assn., DC Bar Assn. Office: SEC Hdqs 100 F St NE Washington DC 20549 Office Phone: 202-551-6551.

CASEY, KENNETH LYMAN, neurologist; b. Ogden, Utah, Apr. 16, 1935; s. Kenneth Lafayette and Lyzena (Payne) C.; m. Jean Louise Madsen, June 21, 1958; children— Tena Jeanette, Kenneth Lyman, Teresa Louise. BA, Whitman Coll., Walla Walla, Wash., 1957; MD with honors, U. Wash., Seattle, 1961. Diplomate Am. Bd. Neurology and Psychiatry. Intern in medicine Cornell U. Med. Center-N.Y. Hosp., 1961-62; USPHS officer lab. neurophysiology NIMH, 1962-64; fellow in psychology McGill U., Montreal, Que., Canada, 1964-66; mem. faculty U. Mich. Med. Sch., Ann Arbor, 1966—, prof. neurology and physiology, 1978—2005, prof. emeritus neurology, prof. emeritus molecular and integrative physiology, 2005—; resident in neurology U. Mich Hosp., 1971-74; chief neurology svc. VA Med. Center, Ann Arbor, 1979—2002, cons. in neurology, 2002—. Sci. adv. com. Santa Fe Neurol. Inst., 1984—. Assoc. editor Clin. Jour. Pain, 1984—, Pain, 1991—; editor-in-chief Am. Pain Soc. Jour. Pain Forum, 1991-99; contbr. articles to profl. jours., chpts. to books. Grantee, NIH, 1966—; Spl. fellow, 1964—66, Bristol-Myers rsch. grantee, 1988—93. Fellow: Am. Acad. Neurology; mem.: Internat. Assn. Study Pain (hon. life mem.), Wayne County Med. Soc. (Rhoades lectr. and medalist 2002), Am. Pain Soc. (pres. 1984—85, F.W.L. Kerr Basic Sci. Rsch. award and lecture 1998, named hon. life mem. 2005), Soc. Neurosci., Am. Neurol. Assn., Am. Acad. Neurology, Am. Physiol. Soc., Alpha Omega Alpha (J.J. Bonica disting. lectr. and award 1991), Sigma Xi, Phi Beta Kappa. Unitarian Universalist. Achievements include named lectureship established in his honor by Pfizer Co. in 2002. Home: 2775 Heatherway St Ann Arbor MI 48104-2852 Office: VA Med Ctr Neurology Svc 2215 Fuller Rd Ann Arbor MI 48105-2300 Business E-Mail: kencasey@umich.edu.

CASEY, MICHEAL WILLIAM, portfolio manager; b. Indpls., Oct. 4, 1955; s. Robert Ellsworth and Mildred Jane (Holland) C.; m. Christine McCarthy, Apr. 11, 1991 (div. Sept. 1997); children: Kathleen Maura, Thomas Robert, James Patrick. AB, Ind. U., 1978; MS, London Sch. Econs., 1985; PhD, New Sch. Social Rsch., 1996. Translator U. Graz, Austria, 1978-80; tchr. math. Peace Corps, Sierra Leone, 1981-83; economist McCarthy, Crisanti & Matthei, NYC, 1986—90; internat. economist Maria Ramierz, Inc., NYC, 1990—96; portfolio mgr. Federated Investors, NYC, 1996—2002; pres. Discretionary Global Mgmt., NYC, 2002—. Mem.: Am. Fin. Assn., Am. Econ. Assn., Downtown Economists Club, Forecasters Club. Office Phone: 646-775-4819. Personal E-mail: mcasey@discretionaryglobal.com.

CASEY, PAT, college baseball coach; b. McMinnville, Oreg., 1959; m. Susan Casey; children: Jonathan, Brett, Ellie, Joseph. Student, U. Portland, 1978—80; BA in Interdisciplinary Studies, George Fox Coll., 1990. Minor league baseball player San Diego Padres Orgn., 1980—86; head coach George Fox Coll., 1988—94, Oreg. State U., Corvallis, 1995—. Named Pac-10 Coach of Yr., 2005. Achievements include coaching team to school record in wins, 1997; coaching Nat. Champion NCAA Coll. World Series Winners, 2006, 07. Office: Oreg State U Athletics 646 Kerr Adminstrn Bldg Corvallis OR 97331-2106*

CASEY, PATRICK ANTHONY, lawyer; b. Apr. 20, 1944; s. Ivanhoe and Eutimia (Casados) C.; m. Gail Marie Johns, Aug. 1, 1970; children: Christopher Gaelen, Matthew Colin. BA, N.Mex. State U., 1970; JD, U. Ariz., Tucson, 1973. Bar: N.Mex. 1973, Ariz. 1973, US Dist. Ct. N.Mex. 1973, US Ct. Appeals (10th cir.) 1979, US Supreme Ct. 1980, US Dist. Ct. Ariz. 1999. Assoc. Bachicha & Casey, Santa Fe, 1973-76; Patrick A. Casey, P.A. Santa Fe, 1976—. Bd. dirs. Cath. Charities of Santa Fe, 1979-82, Old Santa Fe Assn., 1979-88, Santa Fe Fiesta Coun., 1982—, United Way 1986-89, N.Mex. State U. Found., 1985-93. With USN, 1961—67. Fellow: Am. Coll. Trial Lawyers; mem.: VFW, ABA, Am. Assn. Justice (formerly ATLA) (state del. 1988—89, bd. govs. 1990—91, 1993—95), Hispanic Bar Assn., Bar Assn. 1st Jud. Dist. (pres. 1980), N.Mex. Trial Lawyers Assn. (dir. 1977—79, treas. 1979—83, pres. 1983—84, dir. 1985—, treas. 2000—01), Western Trial Lawyers Assn. (gov. 1987—90, bd. dirs. 1988—91, officer 1990—95, pres. 1996—97, treas. 2000—04, pres. 2004—05), Vietnam Vets. Am., Am. Legion, Elks. Office: 1421 Luisa St Ste P Santa Fe NM 87505-4073 Office Phone: 505-982-3639. Personal E-mail: pacpalaw@msn.com.

CASEY, PAUL ARNOLD, writer, producer, photographer, composer, director; b. Inglewood, Calif., Dec. 10, 1934; s. Paul Franklyn and Orilee Corinne (Gray) C. AA, BA, UCLA. Pres., genetics cons. CSCA Internat., Sun Valley, Calif.; pres., tech. advisor Solenz Corp., Wilmington, Del. Dramaturg L.A. Playwrights Group, 1996; dir., CEO L.A. Playwrights Group. Author: Open the Coffin, 2005, (poetry) Songs of Youth, 1951; writer TV show Lassie, 1969; photographer wildlife: Girl Scouts Calendar, 1995; developer breed of cat: Calif. Spangled, 1971-86; inventor power lens, 1967; prodr. (theatrical) Original Sins; dir.: (film and theatrical prodn.) Smoke Screen; playwright: Anna & Ylenna; playwright Jewel Box Theatre Ctr. for Performing Arts, 1998-02. With USN, 1953-54. Recipient Nat. Humane Soc. award, 1965, Meritorious Achievement award Contbn. to Sci., 1998; scholar U.S. Govt. scholar, 1954. Mem. L.A. Playwrights Group (gen. sec. 1995-96, bd. dirs. 1998-2006). Achievements include invention of wind driven desalination and water purification plant. Avocations: wildlife photography, astronomy, archaeology, natural power systems technology. Office: CSCA International PO Box 368 Sun Valley CA 91353-0368 Home Phone: 818-768-9516. Personal E-mail: paulcasey8@yahoo.com. Business E-mail: casey.paul@sbcglobal.net.

CASEY, ROBERT PATRICK, JR., (BOB CASEY), senator; b. Scranton, Pa., Apr. 13, 1960; s. Robert Patrick and Ellen Theresa (Harding) Casey; m. Terese Foppiano, 1985; children: Elyse, Caroline, Julia, Marena. BA, Coll. Holy Cross, Springfield, Mass., 1982; JD, Catholic U., DC, 1998. Bar: Penn. 1991. Pvt. law practice, Scranton, Pa., 1991—96; auditor gen. State of Pa., Harrisburg, 1996—2005, state treas., 2005—06; US Senator from Pa., 2007—. Democrat. Office: US Senate B-40C Dirksen Senate Office Bldg Washington DC 20510*

CASEY, ROBERT REISCH, lawyer; b. New Orleans, May 19, 1946; s. Robert Taylor Casey and Merlyn Lucille (Reisch) Weilbaecher. BBA magna cum laude in Acctg., U. Notre Dame, 1968; JD, Tulane U., 1971; LLM in Taxation, NYU, 1973. Bar: La. 1971; cert. La. Bd. Legal Specialization (tax law). Ptnr. Jones, Walker, Waechter, Poitevent, Carrère & Denègre, LLP, Baton Rouge, 1971—. Mem. bd. editors Tulane Law Rev., 1970-71. Named one of Top 100 Attys., Worth mag., 2005—06, 2006—07. Mem. ABA (chmn. partnerships com. tax sect. 1982-84, mem. coun. 1985-88, sec. 1988-89, vice chmn. 1989-91), La. State Law Inst., Am. Coll. Tax Counsel, Order of Coif, Beta Gamma Sigma, Beta Alpha Psi, Phi Delta Phi. Avocations: golf, French horn. Office: Jones Walker Waechter Poitevent Carrere & Denegre LLP 4 United Plz 8555 United Plaza Blvd Ste 500 Baton Rouge LA 70809-7028 Office Phone: 225-248-2090. Office Fax: 225-248-3090. Business E-Mail: rcasey@joneswalker.com.

CASEY, SUE (SUZANNE MARGUERITE PHILIPS), actress, real estate broker; b. LA, Apr. 8, 1926; d. Burke Dewey and Mildred Louise (Hansen) Philips; children: Colleen O'Shaughnessy, John Joseph Durant III, Christopher Kent Durant, Diane M. Kelly; m. Jack Hoffmann (div.); stepchildren: Joy Hoffmann Molloy, Kristen Hoffmann Blutman. Student, UCLA Extension, 1972-75. Lic. real estate broker and saleswoman, Calif. With Coldwell Banker, Beverly Hills, Calif. Appeared in numerous movies, including swimming in 5 Esther Williams films, singing and dancing in over 20 films, Goldwyn Girl, 1945-47; Star Is Born, Surf Terror, 1965, Catalina Caper, 1967, Happy Ending, Secrets of Monte Carlo, The Family Jewels, Marriage Young Stockbroker, The Big Circus, The Errand Boy, Two Weeks in Another Town, Paint Your Wagon, Camelot, Evil Speak, 1981, Swamp Country, Ladies Man, Lucky Lady, Annie Get Your Gun, Show Boat, Carpetbaggers, Rear Window, Breakfast at Tiffany's, The Scarf, Main Event, Brady Bunch Sequel, 1996, American Beauty, 1999; appeared in TV shows, including Hunter, Hotel, Hart to Hart, White Shadow, Sunny Valley, Lucy, Gunsmoke, Arnie, Marcus Welby, Sky Terror, Dallas, Days of Our Lives, Unsolved Mysteries, Rosie O'Neill, Haggerty, Emergency, California Fever, I Love Lucy, Farmer's Daughter, Beverly Hillbillies, Delta House, Bodies of Evidence, The Faculty, Divorce Court, Colgate Comedy Shows, Carol Burnett Shows, Red Skelton Show, Roy Bolger Show, All Star Revues, Bob Hope Specials, Ann Southern Show, Family Medical Center, Red Shoe Diaries, What Love Sees, Boy Meets World, 1997, Diagnosis Murder, 1999; has appeared in over 200 TV commls.; stage appearances include Picnic, Goodnight Ladies. Ball chmn. The Footlighters, Inc., 1971-73, 93-94, press chmn., 1972-73, pres., 1982-83, 98-99, parliamentarian, 1983-94, 99-00,02-03, hospitality chmn., 1992-93. Named Ms. Sr. Am. of L.A., 1993. Mem. AFTRA, SAG, Actors Equity Assn. Office: Coldwell Banker 301 N Canon Dr Beverly Hills CA 90210-4722 Home Phone: 310-275-2685; Office Phone: 310-777-6344. E-mail: suecaseyla@yahoo.com.

CASEY, THOMAS CLARK, retired trust company executive, investment advisor; b. Akron, Ohio, Dec. 17, 1929; s. Thomas W. and Portia (Clark) C.; m. Tanya Seely, July 2, 1958 (dec.); children: Tate, Doug, John, Gary, Brad, Nina, Mimi, Tom W.; m. Suzanne Rhodes, Apr. 5, 1997. BA, Bowdoin Coll.; MBA, Stanford U.; CFSC, Northwestern U. Registered investment advisor, SEC, 1995. Sales rep. Acushnet Co., New Bedford, Mass., 1953-55, Reeves Rubber Co., San Clemente, Calif., 1957-59; gen. mgr. Polymer Corp., Santa Ana, Calif., 1959-61; from trust officer to pres. 1st Am. Trust Co., Santa Ana, 1965-95; registered investment advisor pvt. practice, 1995—. Bd. dir. First Am. Trust F.S.B., 1999—. Trustee Bowdoin Coll., 1989—2001; bd. dirs. Hoag Meml. Hosp., 1982—95; chmn. Orange County com. So. Calif. Bldg. Fund, 1986—94; co-chmn. capital expenditure rev. com. United Way, 1982—; chair bd. dirs. Hoag Hosp. Found., 1995—99; bd. dirs. Newport Ctr. Assn., 1976—2002, pres., 1979; trustee Newport-Mesa Unified Sch. Dist., 1969—77, pres., 1975—77; bd. dirs.

Orange County Bar Found., 1995—2001; bd. dirs., mem. exec. com. Alzheimers Assn. Orange County, 2000—06; bd. dirs. Adult Day Svcs., 2007—. Named Outstanding Vol. of Yr., Orange County, Calif., 2003. Mem.: Orange County Soc. Investment Mgrs., Calif. Bankers Assn., L.A. Soc. Fin. Analysts, Soc. Preservation New Eng. Antiquities. Avocations: golf, skiing, snorkeling, travel. Office: Ste 1100 620 Newport Ctr Dr Newport Beach CA 92660-8011

CASEY, THOMAS JEFFERSON, clean energy industry executive and entrepreneur, environmental activist; Student, U.S. Naval Acad., 1964; MBA, Harvard U., 1970; postgrad., U. London/Am. U., 1997. Pres., COO New Eng. Furniture Group, Boston, 1968—71; chmn., CEO Commonwealth Industries, Inc., NYC, 1971—75, Quantum Renewable Energy, NYC, 1991—; pres., gen. mgr. Damson Oil Corp. AMEX, NYC, Houston, 1975—80; founder, chmn., CEO Sovereign Group, Ltd., NYC, 1980—90. Guest lectr. Wharton Grad. Sch. Bus. Adminstrn.; former mem. faculty internat. mgmt. Northeastern U. Sch. Mgmt. and Adminstrn., Boston; sr. fin., investment advisor several Fortun 500 cos., sovereign fgn. govts. and internat. fin. instns. Environ. activist. Avocations: golf, tennis, sailing, skiing, flying. Office: Quantum Renewable Energy Inc 730 5th Ave Ste 900 New York NY 10019-4105

CASEY, TOM (THOMAS W. CASEY), bank executive; BS in Acctg., Kings Coll., Wilkes-Barre, Pa. Audit supr. Coopers & Lybrand, 1984—90; with Citicorp, 1990—92; from advisor/contr., to analyst GE Capital Corp., 1992—99, sr. v.p., CFO GE Fin., 1999—2002; exec. v.p., CFO Washington Mut., Inc., Seattle, 2002—. Mem. Pres.'s Coun. Washington Mut., Inc. Office: Washington Mut Inc 1201 Third Ave Seattle WA 98101 Office Phone: 206-461-2000. Office Fax: 206-554-2790.*

CASEY WALL, HOLLY, plastic surgeon; b. Denver, Nov. 28, 1968; m. Simeon Wall, Jr. BS in Nutrition, Brigham Young U., Provo, Utah; MD, U. Utah, Salt Lake City, 1996. Lic.: La.; cert. Am. Bd. Plastic Surgery, 2002, lic. Calif. Intern gen. surgery Stanford U., Calif., 1996—97, resident plastic surgery, 1997—99, resident, 1999—2001; assoc. active staff Christus Schumpert Hosp., Shreveport, La., 2001; asst. court staff Willis Knighton Hosp., Shreveport, 2001; assoc. staff mem. Dr.'s Hosp., Shreveport, 2001; plastic surgeon Wall Ctr. Plastic Surgery, Shreveport, 2001—. Vol. Interplast; bd. dir. Goodwill Industries Northwest La. Mem.: Am. Soc. Aesthetic Plastic Surgeons, La. Soc. Plastic Surgeons, La. State Med. Soc., Shreveport Med. Soc., Zedplast (Stanford U. Plastic Surgery Alumni Assn.). Office: Wall Ctr Plastic Surgery 1400 E Bert Kouns Ste 106 Shreveport LA 71105 Office Phone: 318-795-0801. Office Fax: 318-795-9492.

CASH, JAMES IRELAND, JR., retired business educator; b. 1948; s. Juanita Cash; m. Clemmie Cash; 2 children. BS in math., Tex. Christian U., 1969; MS in computer sci., Purdue U., PhD in mgmt. info. systems; LLD (hon.), Babson Coll., 2003. Mem. faculty Harvard Bus. Sch., 1976—2003, prof., 1985—2003, James E. Robison Prof. Bus. Adminstrn., chmn. MBA Program, 1992—95, sr. assoc. dean., chmn. HBS Pub., 1998—2003. Bd. dirs. Phase Forward Inc., Chubb Corp., 1996—, GE, 1997—, Sci.-Atlanta Inc., 2001—, Microsoft Corp., 2001—, Wal-Mart Stores Inc., 2006—; bd. advisors Egenera Inc.; dir. Cash Concours program The Concours Group; part-owner Boston Celtics, 2003—. Co-author: (books) Global Electronic Wholesale Banking, 1990, Corporate Information Systems Management: Issues Facing Senior Managers and Corporate Information Systems Management: Text and Cases, 1992, Building the Information-Age Organization: Structure, Control and Information Technology, 1994; author: Business Decision Making with Lotus 1-2-3, articles in acctg. and info. tech. journals; co-editor: The Information Systems Challenge: Survey Research Methods, 1991. Bd. trustees Harlem Children's Zone, Babson Coll., Mass. Gen. Hosp., Partners Healthcare, Newton-Wellesley Hosp.; overseer Boston Mus. Sci.; founding mem. coun. Nat. Mus. African Am. History and Culture, Smithsonian Instn., 2004—. Recipient Bert King Award for Svc. to the Cmty., Afro-Am. Student Union, Harvard Bus. Sch., 2002. Office: Harvard Bus Sch Soldiers Field Boston MA 02163

CASH, JEANIE MARITTA, educational association administrator; b. Nashville, Ark., Dec. 18, 1948; d. Roy M. and Doris M. Reed; m. Ronald David Cadh, Apr. 17, 1971; children: Brandon Reed, Kristofer Robert. BA, Whittier Coll., 1971; MA, U. La Verne, 1985. Cert. adminstr. Calif., 1985, nat. curriculum auditor Calif., 2000. Prin. Bellflower Unified Sch. Dist., Calif., 1985—99, Los Alamitos, Calif., 1995—99; assoc. supt. Chino Unified Sch. Dist., Calif., 1999—2005; asst. supt. Placentia-Yorba Linda Unified Sch. Dist., Calif., 2005—. Com. of practitioners State Dept. Edn., Sacramento. Contbr. articles to profl. jours. Curriculum writer Am. Bapt. Assn., Texarkana, Tex., 1980—2005. Mem.: State Dept of Edn., Assn. Calif. Sch. Adminstrs. (pres., curriculum coun. 2005), Delta Kappa Gamma, Phi Delta Kappa (assoc.). Republican. Baptist. Avocations: music, rollerblading, travel. Home: 9352 Julie Beth Cypress CA 90630 Office: Placentia-Yorba Linda Unified Sch Dist 1301 E Orangethorpe Placentia CA 92870 Home Phone: 714-821-4237; Office Phone: 714-985-8650. Office Fax: 714-577-8104. Business E-Mail: jcash@pylusd.org.

CASH, JOSEPH CARL, history educator, government educator; b. Aug. 26, 1982; Cert. tchr. Ga. Tchr. Am. history and govt. White County 9th Grade Acad., Cleve., Ga., 2004—07. Mem. Nat. Soccer Coaches Assn. Am., 2005—06. Named Tchr. of Yr., White County 9th Grade Acad. Bd. Edn., 2006. Mem.: Nat. Coun. Social Studies.

CASH, MARY FRANCES, minister, retired civilian military employee; d. Hugh Lester and Myrtle Victoria (Byrd) Flucas; m. William Hadley Cash, May 7, 1966; children: Aleta Grace Pearson, William Anthony, Antonio Hadley. Diploma, Atlantic Bus. Coll., 1961; Assoc. in Religious Edn., Washington Saturday Coll., 1996; Masters Degree in religious edn., Bethel Bible Coll./Seminary, 2003. Ordained elder African Meth. Episcopal Ch., 1999. Sec., stenographer Dept. Human Resources, Washington, 1964—77; adminstr. Flu-Bea Enterprises, Landover, Md., 1977—80; substitute tchr. Pineview Elem. Sch., Valdosta, Ga., 1980—81; sec. Moody AFB, Valdosta, 1981—82, Andrews AFB, Camp Spring, Md., 1982—92, Dept. Def., Va., 1992—94; pastor Cmty. African Meth. Episcopal Ch., Whitehall, Ark., 1998—. Dean bd. examiners East Northeast Ark. Conf., sec. annual conf., trustee ann. conf. Leader, trainer Girl Scout Coun. Am., Washington, 1971—79, Valdosta, Ga., 1980—82, Washington, 1982—96; mem. adv. bd. Duke Ellington Sch. Art, Washington, 1986; instr. Summer Tchg. Program for Children, Jonesboro, 1996—2000; dir. Saturday Sch. Brown Meml. African Meth. Episcopal Ch., Washington, 1990—96. Named Mother of the Yr., Brown Meml. African Meth. Episcopal Ch., 1988; recipient Spl. Svc. award, Girl Scout Coun. Nations Capitol, 1994, Superior award, Young and Adult Missionary Soc., 1996. Mem.: East No. Ark. Annual Conf. of the 12th Episcopal Dist. (Sec. 2002—).

CASH, ROSANNE, singer, songwriter; b. May 1955; d. John R. Cash and Vivian (Liberto) Distin; m. Rodnay J. Crowell, Apr. 7, 1979 (div. 1992); children: Caitlin Rivers, Chelsea Jane, Carrie Kathleen; m. John Leventhal, Apr. 30, 1995; 1 child: Jakob William. Student, Vol. State C.C., 1974, Vanderbilt U., 1976, Lee Strasberg Theatre Inst., 1977. Rec. artist Ariola Records, Europe, 1978-84, CBS Records, worldwide, 1979—95; chair Earth Comm. Office, 1989—91; rec. artist Capitol Records, 1995—. Songwriter Blue Moon with Heartache, 1979, Seven Year Ache, 1980 (Gold Record award Rec. Industry Assn. Am. 1981), I Don't Know Why You Don't Want Me, 1984, (Grammy award 1985), Hold On (Robert J. Burton award 1987), others; Albums: Right Or Wrong, 1979, Seven Year Ache, 1980, Somewhere in the Stars, 1982, Rhythm & Romance, 1985, King's Record Shop, 1987, Hits 1979-89, 1989, Interiors, 1990, The Wheel, 1993, 10 Song Demo, 1996, Retrospective, 1997, What Kinda Girl Live, 1999, Rules of Travel, 2003, Black Cadillac, 2006; composer (films) Mariners & Musicians, 2006. Bd. advisors Nashvillians for Nuclear Arms Freeze, 1987-90; mem. PAX, 2001-. Mem. AFTRA, Nat. Acad. Rec. Arts and Scis. (Grammy award 1985), Am. Fedn. Musicians, Screen Actors Guild, Broadcast Music, Inc. (Spl. Achievement awards), Nashville Songwriters Assn. Internat., Pen American Ctr. Democrat. Mailing: c/o Danny Kahn Cross Road Mgmt 45 West 11th St Ste 7B New York NY 10011

CASH, ROY DON, retired gas and petroleum company executive; b. Shamrock, Tex., June 27, 1942; s. Bill R. and Billie Mae (Lisle) C.; m. Sondra Kay Burleson, Feb. 20, 1966; 1 child, Clay Collin. BS in Indsl. Engring., Tex. Tech U., 1966. Former engr. Amoco Prodn. Co.; v.p. Mountain Fuel Supply, Salt Lake City, 1976-79; pres. Wexpro Co., Salt Lake City, 1979-80; pres., CEO Mountain Fuel Supply Co., Salt Lake City, 1980-84, Questar Corp., Salt Lake City, 1984-85, pres., chmn., CEO, 1985—2003, now bd. dirs. Bd. dirs. Zions Bancorp., Aegis Ins. Svcs., Inc., Nat. Fuel Gas, TODCO. Trustee Holy Cross Hosp., 1987-90, Salt Lake Organizing Com. of 2002 Olympic Winter Games, 1991—2002, So. Utah U., 1992-97; bd. dirs. Utah Symphony Orch., Salt Lake City, 1983-86, 93—2004, Gas Rsch. Inst., 1991-93, Lubbock Symphony Orch., 2003—, Tex. Tech Found., 2002—. Mem. Soc. Petroleum Engrs., Rocky Mountain Oil and Gas Assn. (bd. dirs., pres. 1982-84), Utah Mfrs. Assn. (bd. dirs. 1983-89, chmn. 1986), Pacific Coast Gas Assn. (bd. dirs. 1981-85, 87-97, chmn. 1993-94), Am. Gas Assn. (bd. dirs. 1989-95), Am. Petroleum Inst. (bd. dirs. 1986-91), Nat. Petroleum Coun., Ind. Petroleum Assn. of Am., Salt Lake Area C. of C. (bd. dirs. 1981-84, 89-92, chmn. 1991-92), Alta Club, Jeremy Ranch Golf and Country Club. Avocations: boating, skiing, tennis, fishing, hunting. Office: Questar Corp PO Box 45433 Salt Lake City UT 84145-0433

CASH, SWIN (SWINTAYLA MARIE CASH), professional basketball player; b. McKeesport, Pa., Sept. 22, 1979; d. Kevin Menifee (Stepfather) and Cynthia Cash. Grad., U. Conn., 2002. Basketball player McKeesport High Sch., McKeesport, Pa., U. Conn., 1998—2002; basketball player, forward Detroit Shock, WNBA, 2002—; founder Swin Cash LLC. Mem. USA Basketball Women's Senior Nat. Team, 2004. Named Parade Magazine, USA Today and Street & Smith All-Am. first team, 1998, Gatorade Pa. Player of the Yr., 1998, Kodak/WBCA All-District I, 2002, Final Four Most Outstanding Player, 2002; named to All-Big East third team, 2000, All-Big East second team, 2001, All-Big East first team, 2002, AP All-American second team, 2001, Kodak/WBCA & US Basketball Writers Assn. All-Am. first team, 2002, WNBA All-Star Team, 2003, all-WNBA second team, 2003. Achievements include mem. NCAA Divsn. 1 Nat. Championship Team, U. Conn., 2000, 2002; mem. WNBA Championship Team, Detroit Shock, 2003; mem. US Women's Basketball Team, Athens Olympic Games, 2004. Office: USA Basketball 5465 Mark Dabling Blvd Colorado Springs CO 80918-3842

CASH, W. LARRY, health products executive; CPA AICPA. With Humana Inc., 1973—96; v.p., group CFO Columbia/HCA, 1996—97; exec. v.p. Cmty. Health Sys., Brentwood, Tenn., 1997—, CFO, 1997—. Bd. dir. Cmty. Health Sys., Cross Country, Inc. Mem.: Healthcare Fin. Mgmt. Assn., Am. Assn. Health Plans, Tenn. Soc. CPAs.

CASHIN, RICHARD M., JR., diversified financial services company executive; AB in East Asian Studies, Harvard Coll.; MBA, Harvard U. Fellow Trinity Coll., Cambridge, England; mem. staff to pres. Citicorp Venture Capital, Ltd., 1980—2000; mng. ptnr. One Equity Ptnrs. LLC J.P. Morgan Chase & Co., 2001—. Dir. Quintiles Transnational Corpn.; bd. mem. Last Mile Connections, Inc., Remy Internat., Fairchild Semiconductor, Titan Internat., Inc., Telerate, Inc. Chmn. Nat. Rowing Found.; trustee Boys Club NY, American U., Cairo. Office: One Equity Ptnrs 320 Park Ave 18th Fl New York NY 10022

CASHMAN, BRIAN M., professional sports team executive; b. NY, July 3, 1967; s. John and Nancy Cashman; m. Mary Cashman, 1995; children: Grace, Teddy. BA, Catholic U., DC, 1989. With NY Yankees, 1989—93, asst. gen. mgr. baseball adminstrn., 1992—98, gen. mgr., 1998—, v.p., 2000—01, sr. v.p., 2001—. Achievements include administrating five world championship teams. Office: NY Yankees E 161st and River Ave Bronx NY 10452

CASHMAN, GIDEON, lawyer; b. NYC, Sept. 10, 1929; s. Abba Morris and Rachel (Cashman) Cashman; m. Kathryn Batchelder, 1985; children: Adam Parker, Lindsey Avril, Emily Parker Hyle. AB, NYU, 1951; JD, Columbia U., 1954. Bar: D.C. 1954, N.Y. 1954. Asst. counsel Waterfront Commn. N.Y., 1954-55; asst. U.S. atty. criminal divsn. So. Dist. Ct. N.Y., 1958-61, chief criminal apls., 1959-61; assoc. Christy Perkins & Christy, NYC, 1961-63; sr. ptnr. Pryor, Cashman, Sherman & Flynn LLP, NYC, 1963—. Lectr. trial tactics Practicing Law Inst.; bd. dirs. Irvington Inst. for Med. Rsch. Trustee Friars Found., Heart Rsch. Found., Eugene O'Neill Teatre Ctr. 1st lt. U.S. Army, judge advocate Gen.'s Corps, 1955-58. Mem. ABA, N.Y. State Bar Assn., Assn. Bar City N.Y., N.Y. County Lawyers Assn., Friars Club (N.Y.C.). Jewish. Home: 812 Park Ave New York NY 10021-2759 Office: 410 Park Ave New York NY 10022-4441 Office Phone: 212-326-0172.

CASHMAN, MICHAEL RICHARD, small business owner; b. Owatonna, Minn., Sept. 26, 1926; s. Michael Richard and Mary (Quinn) C.; m. Antje Katrin Paulus, Jan. 22, 1972 (div. 1983); children: Janice Katrin, Joshua Paulus, Nina Carolin. BS, U.S. Mcht. Marine Acad., 1947; BA, U. Minn., 1951; MBA, Harvard U., 1953. Regional mgr. Air Products & Chems., Inc., Allentown, Pa., 1959-64, then pres. so. div. Washington, 1964-68; mng. dir. Air Products & Chems., Inc. Europe, Brussels, 1968-72; internat. v.p. Airco Indsl. Gasses, Brussels, 1972-79; pres. Continental Elevator Co., Denver, 1979-81; assoc. Moore & Co., Denver, 1981-84; prin. Cashman & Co., Denver, 1984—. Committeeman Denver Rep. Com., 1986—, congl. candidate, 1988; chmn. "Two Forks or Dust" Ad Hoc Citizens Com. Lt. (j.g.) USN, 1953-55. Mem. Bldg. Owners and Mgrs. Assn., Colo. Harvard Bus. Sch. Club, Am. Rights Union, Royal Golf de Belgique, Belgian Shooting Club, Rotary, Soc. St. George, Phi Beta Kappa. Avocations: skiing, golf, sailing, guitar, opera. Home: 2512 S University Blvd Apt 802 Denver CO 80210-6152

CASHMAN, WAYNE, professional athletics coach; b. Kingston, Ont., Can. m. Lyn Cashmar; children: Scott, Becky. NHL vet. Bruins NHL, 18 seasons; scout to asst. coach N.Y. Rangers, 1986-92; assoc. coach Tampa Bay Lightning, 1995—. Mem. two Stanley Cup Championship teams/Bruins, Boston, 1970, 72, five Stanley Cup Finals appearances; currently ranks third on Bruins and 80th on the NHL all-time list in games played, with 1,027. Office: Philadelphia Flyers First Union Ctr 3601 S Broad St Ste 2 Philadelphia PA 19148-5297

CASIANO, KIMBERLY, publishing executive; b. NY; m. Juan Woodroffe; children: Natalia, Juan Antonio. BA in politics and Latin Am. studies, Princeton U.; MBA, Harvard. Founded Caribbean Mktg. Overseas Corp., 1981—88; v.p. Casiano Comm., 1988—94, pres., CEO, 1994—. Bd. mem. Ford Motor Co., 2003—, mem. fin. bd. com., mem. nom. com., mem. corp. governance com., mem. environ. and pub. policy com. Mem. Access Am. Com. US C. of C.; bd. trustees Hispanic Coll. Fund; mem. bd. dirs. Young Pres. Orgn. (YPO) PR chpt., Mutual of Am. Named one of Elite Women, Hispanic Bus. mag., 2004. Achievements include apptd. to US Savings Bond Nat. Com. by US Treas. Sec. Office: Casiano Comm 1700 Ave Fernandez Juncos San Juan PR 00909-2938 Office Phone: 787-728-3000. Office Fax: 787-268-1216.

CASIDA, JOHN EDWARD, toxicology and entomology professor; b. Phoenix, Dec. 22, 1929; s. Lester Earl and Ruth (Barnes) Casida; m. Katherine Faustine Monson, June 16, 1956; children: Mark Earl, Eric Gerhard. BS, U. Wis., 1951, MS, 1952, PhD, 1954; D (hon.), U. Buenos Aires, 1997. Research asst. U. Wis., 1951-53, mem. faculty, 1954-63, prof. toxicology & entomology, 1959-63, U. Calif.-Berkeley, 1964—; scholar-in-residence Bellagio Study and Conf. Center, Rockefeller Found., Lake Como, Italy, 1978. Messenger lectr. Cornell U., 1985; Sterling B. Hendricks lectr. USDA and Am. Chem. Soc., 1992; dir. Environ. Chemistry and Toxicology Lab., U. Calif., Berkeley, 1964—; William Muriece Hoskins chair in chem. and molecular entomology U. Calif., Berkeley, 1996—, faculty rsch. lectr., 1998; lectr. in sci. Third World Acad. Scis., Buenos Aires, 1997. Author: rsch. publs. With USAF, 1953. Named Jeffery lectr., U. New South Wales, Australia, 1983; recipient medal, 7th Internat. Congress Plant Protection, Paris, 1970, Disting. Svc. award, USDA, 1988, Wolf prize in agr., Wolf Found., Isreal, 1993, Koro-Sho prize, Pesticide Sci. Soc. Japan, 1995; fellow Haight traveling fellow, 1958—59, Guggenheim fellow, 1970—71. Fellow: Entomol. Soc. (Bussart Meml. award 1989); mem.: NAS, European Acad. Scis., Soc. Environ. Toxicology and Chemistry (Founder's award 1994), Pesticide Sci. Soc. Japan (hon.), Soc. Toxicology (hon.), Am. Chem. Soc. (Internat. award rsch. pesticide chemistry 1970, Spencer award in agrl. and food chemistry 1978), Royal Soc. UK (fgn.). Home: 1570 La Vereda Rd Berkeley CA 94708-2036

CASILLAS, MARK, lawyer; b. Santa Monica, Calif., July 8, 1953; s. Rudolph and Elvia C.; m. Natalia (Settembrini), June 2, 1984. BA in History, Loyola U., LA, 1976; JD, Harvard U., Cambridge, Mass., 1979. Bar: NY 1982, Calif. 1983. Clk. to chief judge US Ct. Appeals (10th cir.), Santa Fe, 1979—80; assoc. Breed, Abbott, and Morgan, NYC, 1980—82; counsel Bank of Am. Nat. Trust and Savings Assn., San Francisco, 1982—84; assoc. Lillick and Charles, San Francisco, 1984—87, ptnr., 1988—95, Russin and Vecchi, LLP, San Francisco, 1995—96; of counsel LeBoeuf, Lamb, Greene, and MacRae, LLP, San Francisco, 1997—2000, Wilson, Sonsini, Goodrich, and Rosati, Palo Alto, Calif., 2000—03; chmn. Casillas Law Group, San Francisco, 2003—, Belvedere Investment Group, Tiburon, Calif., 2003—. Counsel Internat. Bankers Assn. in LA, 1984-89, 94-97; bd. regents John F. Kennedy U., 2005—; bd. dirs. Innovative Bank. Co-author: California Limited Liability Company: Forms and Practice Manual, 1994; mng. editor Harvard Cvil Rights, Civil Liberties Law Rev., 1978-79. Bd. regents John F. Kennedy U., 2005—. Mem. ABA (apptd. mem. airfin. subcom. 1991—), NY Bar Assn., Calif. Bar Assn. (vice-chmn. fin. instn. com. 1987-88), Internat. Bar Assn., The Japan Soc., Bankers Club (bd. dir. 1996—, pres. 2003), Innovative Bank (bd. dirs. 2007-). Avocations: skiing, travel. Business E-Mail: mark@casillaslaw.com.

CASIMIRE-ETZIONI, ATHEMA LOUISE, veterinary pathologist; b. New Orleans, Nov. 4, 1976; d. Rodney Omar Gerard and Celestine Bernade Casimire; m. Baruch Nisan Etzioni, May 30, 2003; children: Akebalan Yao Etzioni, Nyela Aziza Etzioni. BS in Biology Pre-medicine, Chemistry, Xavier U. La., New Orleans, 1997; DVM, Tuskegee U., Ala., 2001; MS in Vet. Clin. Pathology, Purdue U., West Lafayette, Ind., 2005. Vet. clin. pathologist Tuskegee U., 2001—. Mem.: AAHA, AVMA, Am. Soc. Vet. Clin. Pathology, Omega Tau Sigma, Phi Zeta, Sigma Xi (life). Avocations: dance, Capoeira, needlecrafts, reading. Office: Tuskegee U Sch Vet Medicine Dept Pathobiology Tuskegee Institute AL 36088 Office Phone: 334-724-4104. Office Fax: 334-724-4110. Personal E-mail: acasimire@tuskegee.edu.

CASINI, JANE SLOAN, wholesale distribution executive; b. Richmond, Va., Sept. 22, 1947; d. James Turner and Jane Patrick (Coleman) Sloan; m. Mauro Casini (div.). Student, Villa Mercede, Florence, Italy. Owner, Richmond and Washington; retailer; leather salesman Florence. Bd. dirs. Va. Home for Boys, Richmond, 1991. Office: Jane Casini 5407 Lakeside Ave Richmond VA 23228

CASKEY, CAROLINE T., lab administrator; b. 1967; m. Sam Goodner. BA, Duke U.; MBA, Rice U., Houston, 1993. V.p. Laboratories for Genetic Svcs.; founder, pres., CEO Identigene Corp., Houston, 1993—. Bd. dir. Tex. Lyceum. TV appearances Dateline NBC, NBC Nightly News, Today Show. Mem.: Young Entrepreneur's Orgn. Office: Identigene Corp 5615 Kirby Ste 800 Houston TX 77005*

CASKEY, CHARLES THOMAS, biotechnology executive, biology and genetics educator; b. Lancaster, SC, Sept. 22, 1938; m. Peggy Ann Pearce, 1960; children: Clifton, Caroline. Student, U. S.C., 1956-58; MD, Duke U., 1963; DSc (hon.), U. S.C., 1993. Diplomate Am. Bd. Internal Medicine. Intern, resident dept. medicine Duke Med. Sch., 1963-65; rsch. assoc. Nat. Heart & Lung Inst., Bethesda, Md., 1965-67, head sect. med. genetics, 1970-71; sr. investigator Lab. Biomed. Genetics NIH, Bethesda, 1967-70; chief sect. med. genetics, prof. medicine, prof. biochemistry Baylor Coll. Medicine, Houston, 1971—, investigator Howard Hughes Med. Inst., 1976—, dir. Robert J. Kleberg, Jr. Ctr. for Human Genetics, 1980-94, dir. med. scientist tng. program, 1982-93, prof. cell biology, 1982-94, dir. and prof. molecular genetics Inst. Molecular Genetics, 1985-92, prof. molecular genetics Inst. Molecular Genetics, 1985-94, Henry and Emma Meyer chmn. molecular genetics, 1987-94, dir. Human Genome Ctr., 1991-94, chmn. dept. molecular and human genetics, 1994-95; sr. v.p. rsch. Merck Rsch. Labs., 1995-99; adj. prof. Baylor Coll. Medicine, Houston, 1995—; pres., CEO Cogene BioTech Ventures, Houston, 2000—; disting. prof., inst. molecular medicine U. Tex. Health Sciences Ctr., Houston. Josiah Macy, Jr. faculty scholar Med. Rsch. Coun. Cambridge (Eng.) U., 1979-80; dir. NATO ASI on Somatic Cell Genetics, 1980-81, NATO/EMBO/FEBS Spetsai European Molecular Biology Course, 1983, 87; Bernard Sachs lectr. Child Neurology Soc., 1993; Roy E. Moon disting. lectr. sci. Angelo State U., 1994; Samuel Rudin disting. vis. prof. Columbia U., N.Y.C., 1994; mem. biochem. test com. Nat. Bd. Med. Examiners, 1977-81, chmn. biochem. test com., 1981-84, mem. coord. com. for FLEX, 1984-86, mem.-at-large, 1984-88; chmn. sci. adv. bd. Xytronyx Inc., 1984-90; acad. assoc. Nichols Inst., 1987-92; liason mem. program adv. com. on human genome NIH, 1989-92; chair adv. panel forensic uses DNA tests U.S. Congress Office Tech. Assessment, 1989-90; mem. mapping the human genome adv. com. U.S. Dept. Energy, 1986-89; mem. adv. panel mapping the human genome U.S. Congress Office Tech. Assessment, 1987-88; mem. human genome coord. com. Dept. Energy, 1989-94, gov.'s bd. Texas Academy of Sci., Engring. and Medicine, 2004; trustee, pres. Merck Genome Rsch. Inst., Inc., 1996—; pres. Academy of Medicine, Engring. and Sci. of Texas; chmn. bd. Lexicon Genetics Inc., Odessey Thera Corp.; bd. dirs., Kodiak Technologies, EnVivo Pharmaceuticals, Athersys Corp. Author: Somatic Cell Genetics, 1982; author: (with others) Prebiotic and Biochemical Evolution, 1971, Frontiers of Biology: The Mechanism of Protein Synthesis and Its Regulation, 1972, The Enzymes, 1974, The Kidney in Systemic Disease, 1976, Protein Synthesis, 1976, Molecular Mechanisms of Protein Biosynthesis, 1977, Tay-Sachs Disease Screening and Prevention, 1977, Nonsense Mutations and tRNA Suppressors, 1979, Strauss and Welt Diseases of the Kidney, 3d edit., 1979, Gene Amplification, 1982, Internal Medicine, 1983, Advances in Gene Technology: Human Genetic Disorders, 1984, After Barney Clark: Reflections on the Utah Artificial Heart Program, 1984, Pediatric Neurology, 1986, Clinical Endocrinology, 1986, Gene Transfer, 1986, Molecular Biology of Homo Sapiens, 1986, Medical and Experimental Mammalian Genetics: A Perspective, 1987, Human Genetics, 1987, Molecular Neurobiology in Neurology and Psychiatry, 1987, Current Neurology, vol. 9, 1988, Textbook of Internal Medicine, 1988, Nucleic Acid Probes in Diagnosis of Human Genetic Diseases, 1988, Molecular Genetics of Brain, Nerve, and Muscle, 1989, Molecular Genetics of Diseases of Brain, Nerve, and Muscle, 1989, The Metabolic Basis of Inherited Disease, 6th edit., 1989, PCR Technology: Principles and Applications of DNA Amplification, 1989, The Polymerase Chain Reaction, 1989, PCR Protocols: A Guide to Methods and Applications, 1989, Genetic Engineering, Principles and Methods, vol. 11, 1989, The Science and Practice of Pediatric Cardiology, vol. 1, 1990, Ribosomes and Protein Synthesis: A Practical Approach, 1990, Etiology of Human Disease at the DNA Level, 1991, PCR: A Practical Approach, 1991, Neurodegenerative Disorders: Mechanisms and Prospects for Therapy, 1991, Reproductive Risks and Prenatal Diagnosis, 1991, Antisense RNA and DNA, 1991, Biomonitoring and Carcinogen Risk Assessment, 1991, Legal and Ethical Issues Raised by the Human Genome Project, 1991, Advances in Forensic Haemogenetics, 1992, Gene Mapping - Using Law and Ethics as Guides, 1992, The Code of Codes, 1992, Antisense Strategies, 1992, Molecular Basis of Neurology, 1993, Genetic Engineering, Principles and Methods, 1993, Genetics and Society, 1993, numerous other chpts. to books; mem. editorial bd. Archives Biochemistry and Biophysics, 1975-78, Jour. Biol. Chemistry, 1978-83, Annals Intenal Medicine, 1980-83, Molecular Biology and Medicine, 1982-90, Somatic Cell and Molecular Genetics, 1983-94, Trends in Genetics, 1985-90, Genomics, 1987-90, Molecular and Cell Biology, 1988-90, Human Gene Therapy, 1990—, Jour. AMA, 1991-94, Genetic Epidemiology, 1992-94, Human Mutation, 1992—, Circulation, 1993—; mem. bd. reviewing editors Sci., 1991—. Mem. Human Genome Orgn., 1988—, pres., 1993—; mem. task force on genetics Muscular Dystrophy Assn., 1989-94. With USPHS, 1965-67. Recipient Borden Rsch. award, Disting. Alumnus award Duke U. Med. Sch., 1991, Wadsworth award N.Y. State Dept. Health, 1992, Svc. Merchandise Leadership award Muscular Dystrophy Assn., 1992, Basic Biomed. Rsch. prize Giovanni Lorenzini Med. Found., 1993, Lucy Wortham James Basic Rsch. award Soc. Surg. Oncology, 1994, Norberto Montalbetti Milan award, 1994, The Coriell medal Coriell Inst., 1995, 5th Milano award in memory of Norberto Montalbetti, 1995. Fellow AMA (founding), AAAS (sci. innovation program com. 1991-93), Am. Coll. Physicians, Am. Acad. Microbiology, Royal Soc. Medicine Found.; mem. Nat. Acad. Scis., Am. Fedn. Clin. Rsch., Am. Soc. Biochemistry and Molecular Biology, Am. Soc. Clin. Investigation, Am. Soc. Human Genetics, Am. Soc. Cell Biology, Am. Coll. Med. Genetics, Assn. Am. Physicians, Fedn. Am. Socs. for Exptl. Biology, N.Y. Acad. Scis., So. Soc. Clin. Investigation, Soc. Inherited Metabolic Disorders, Inst. Medicine Nat. Acad. Scis., Royal Soc. Medicine, Baylor Med. Alumni Assn. (disting. faculty mem. 1993), Alpha Omega Alpha.

CASKIE, GRACE I. L., statistics professor; b. Pine Grove, Pa., Aug. 15, 1971; d. Glenn A. Lehman and Linda L. Miller; m. Stephen J. Caskie, Oct. 22, 1994; 1 child, Julianna L. BA, Millersville U., 1993; MA, U. NC, Chapel Hill, 1996, PhD, 1998. Rsch. assoc. Pa. State U., University Park, 1998—2004; asst. prof. Lehigh U., Bethlehem, 2004—. Cons. Pa. State U. Gerontology Ctr., State College, 2004—. Mem.: Ea. Psychol. Assn., Gerontol. Soc. Am., Am. Psychol. Assn. Office: Lehigh University 111 Research Drive Bethlehem PA 18015 Office Phone: 610-758-6094. E-mail: caskie@lehigh.edu.

CASNER, TRUMAN SNELL, lawyer; b. Balt., Oct. 9, 1933; s. A. James and Margaret (Snell) Casner; m. Elizabeth Lyons, June 12, 1954 (dec. Aug. 1997); children: Richard Dana, Elizabeth Anne, Abigail Lee; m. Cynthia Ferris Evans, May 29, 1999. BA cum laude, Princeton U., 1955; LLB cum laude, Harvard U., 1958. Bar: Mass. 1958. Law clk. to Chief Justice Raymond Wilkins, Mass. Supreme Judicial Ct., 1958-59; assoc. firm Ropes & Gray LLP, Boston, 1959-68, partner, 1969—, mng. ptnr., 1994-99. Bd. dirs. State St. Corp., State St. Bank and Trust Co. Active Belmont Town Meeting, 1971—95; trustee, exec. com. Belmont Hill Sch., 1966—94, pres., 1985—89, chmn., 1989—2001; sec., trustee, mem. exec. com. Pine Manor Coll., 1973—79; overseer, trustee Boston Mus. Sci., 1981—; trustee Old Dartmouth Hist. Soc. (New Bedford Whaling Mus.), 2000—; mem. corp. Woods Hole Oceanographic Inst. Fellow: Am. Bar Found.; mem.: Boston Bar Assn., ABA, Am. Law Inst., Tavern Club, Cruising Club of Am. (sec., mem. governing bd.), Kittansett Club (pres.), Comml. Club of Boston, New Bedford Yacht Club. Episcopalian. Home: 54 Fairgreen Pl Chestnut Hill MA 02467-2710 Office: Ropes & Gray LLC One International Pl Boston MA 02110-2624 Office Phone: 617-951-7382. Office Fax: 617-951-7050. E-mail: truman.casner@ropesgray.com.

CASNOCHA, BENEDICT T., entrepreneur; b. Mar. 1, 1988; Grad., Univ. HS, San Francisco, 2006. Founder & chmn. Comcate, Inc., San Francisco, 2000—. Former mem. adv. bd. BizWorld Found. Author: Ben Casnocha: The Blog, 2004— (named one of Top 25 Blogs in Silicon Valley, San Jose Bus. Jour., 2005), My Start-Up Life: What a (Very) Young CEO Learned on His Journey Through Silicon Valley. Named one of 25 Who are Changing the World of Internet & Politics, PoliticsOnline, 2003, Best Entrepreneurs Under 25, Bus. Week, 2006. Office: Comcate Inc Ste 4200 44 Montgomery St San Francisco CA 94104 Office Phone: 415-517-1547. Office Fax: 415-249-4901. E-mail: ben@comcate.com.

CASO, ANTHONY T., lawyer; b. 1955; BA in Polit. Sci., magna cum laude, La Verne Coll., 1976; MBA, Golden Gate U.; JD, U. Pacific, McGeorge Sch. Law. Bar: Calif. 1979. Joined Pacific Legal Found., Sacramento, sr. v.p. and gen. counsel. Adj. prof., McGeorge Sch. Law U. Pacific. Office: Pacific Legal Foundation 3900 Lennane Dr Sacramento CA 95834 Office Phone: 916-419-7111. Business E-Mail: atc@pacificlegal.org.

CASON, ALAN C., lawyer; b. Havre de Grace, Md., 1958; BS, U. Md., College Park, 1980; JD, U. Md., Balt., 1983. Bar: Md. 1984, DC 1985, US Dist. Ct. Dist. Md. Dep. county atty. Harford County, Md., 1988—90; assoc. Shapiro & Olander, 1990—93, McGuireWoods LLP, Balt., 1993—95, ptnr., 1995—, mng. ptnr. Balt. office, 2003—. Bd. mem. N.E. Md. Waste Disposal Authority, 1990—93. Adv. bd. U. Md. Cancer Ctr., 1996—2000. Named U. Md. Sch. Law Alumnus of Yr. Mem.: Monumental City Bar Assn., Balt. City Bar Assn. (chmn. minority clerkship program), Nat. Assn. Bond Lawyers, Nat. Bar Assn., Md. State Bar Assn. (mem. coun. bus. law sect.), U. Md. Alumni Assn. (mem. exec. com., fin. com.), Terrapin Club (bd. mem.), M Club. Office: McGuireWoods LLP Ste 1000 7 St Paul St Baltimore MD 21202-1671 Office Phone: 410-659-4433. Office Fax: 410-659-4481. Business E-Mail: acason@mcguirewoods.com.

CASON, JAMES CALDWELL, ambassador; s. Arthur and Marion C.; m. Carmen Aguiluz, Aug. 1972; children: James, William. BA in Internat. Rels., Dartmouth Coll., 1966; MA, Johns Hopkins U., 1968; grad. with distinction, Nat. War Coll., 1991. With US Fgn. Svc., numerous locations, Portugal, 1969—; trade promotion officer US Trade Ctr., Milan, 1979-81; polit. counselor US Embassy, Montevideo, Uruguay, 1981-82, polit. officer Panama City, Panama, 1982-83; desk officer Guatemala US Dept. State, Washington, 1983-87; polit. counselor US Embassy, La Paz, Bolivia, 1987-90, dep. chief of mission Tegucigalpa, Honduras, 1991-95; polit. advisor, comdr.-in-chief US Atlantic Command/Supreme Allied Comdr. Atlantic NATO, 1995-97; dep. chief of mission US Embassy, Kingston, Jamaica; dir. policy, planning & coord., Bur. We. Hemisphere Affairs US Dept. State, Washington, chief of mission, US Interests Section Havana, Cuba, 2002—05, US amb. to Paraguay Asuncion, 2005—. Fulbright scholar, 1968-70; Recipient Superior Honor award, US Dept. State, Dept. Disting. Honor award, Joint Chiefs of Staff Best Essay award, Def. Intelligence Agy. Writing award, Chmn. of the Joint Chiefs of Staff Joint Meritorious Svc. medal, Nat. Humint Intelligence award, 1991, Coast Guard's Disting. Pub. Svc. award, Presdl. Rank, award, 2006. Mailing: Am Embassy 3020 Asuncion Pl Washington DC 20521 Office: 1776 Mariscal Lopez Ave Asuncion Paraguay Office Phone: 213-715-9521. Business E-Mail: casonjc@state.gov. E-mail: jimccason@cs.com.

CASPER, CHARLES B., lawyer; b. Boise, Idaho, June 9, 1952; s. John Blaine and Joyce Lucile (Mercer) C.; m. Brenda Cheryl Bowers, Aug. 28, 1976; children: Timothy L., Jonathan B. BA, Yale U., 1974; JD, U. Va., 1977; MDiv, Princeton Theol. Sem., 1985. Bar: Utah 1977, U.S. Dist. Ct. Utah 1977, U.S. Ct. Appeals (10th cir.) 1978, U.S. Supreme Ct. 1982, Pa. 1985, U.S. Dist. Ct. (ea. dist.) Pa. 1989, U.S. Ct. Appeals (3d cir.) 1989, U.S. Dist. Ct. N.J. 1990, N.J. 1990. Assoc. Fabian & Clendenin, Salt Lake City, 1977-82, shareholder, 1982; assoc. pastor Arch St. United Meth. Ch., Phila., 1985-89; assoc. Montgomery, McCracken, Walker & Rhoads, LLP, Phila., 1989-92, ptnr., 1992—, vice chmn. litigation dept., 1996-98, 2002—04. Bd. dirs. Ptnrs. Sacred Places, 1999-2003, 06—, chmn., 2003-06, Evangelical Svcs. for the Aging Found., 1996-99, United Meth. Neighborhood Svcs., Phila., 1987-93, Parent-Infant Ctr., Phila., 1990-93; com. chair Utah Heritage Found., Salt Lake City, 1979-82; mem. local bd. Emergency Food and Shelter Program, 1988-98, chair, 1998—. Recipient Svc. award Utah Heritage Found., 1982, United Way Committed Cmty. Vol. award, Pa., 2005. Mem. ABA, Utah State Bar Assn., N.J. Bar Assn., Pa. Bar Assn., Phila. Bar Assn. Republican. Office: Montgomery McCracken Walker and Rhoads LLP 123 S Broad St Fl 24 Philadelphia PA 19109-1099 Office Phone: 215-772-1500.

CASPER, LEONARD RALPH, American literature educator; b. Fond du Lac, Wis., July 6, 1923; s. Louis and Caroline (Eder) C.; m. Linda Velasquez-Ty, June 2, 1956; children: Gretchen Gabrielle, Kristina Elise. BA, U. Wis., 1948, MA, 1949, PhD, 1953. Grad. asst. U. Wis., 1949-51; instr. Cornell U., 1952-53; asst. prof. U. Philippines, 1953-56, Fulbright lectr., 1962-63, summer 1973; mem. faculty Boston Coll., 1956—, prof. contemporary Am. lit., 1963-93, prof. emeritus, 1993—99; lectr. RSVP/SOAR, 2001—. Dir. creative writing U. RI, 1958; lectr. in field. Author: Robert Penn Warren: The Dark and Bloody Ground, 1960, The Wayward Horizon: Essays on Modern Philippine Literature, 1961, The Wounded Diamond: Studies in Modern Philippine Literature, 1964, New Writing from The Philippines: A Critique and Anthology, 1966, A Lion Unannounced: 12 Stories and a Fable, 1971, Firewalkers: Concelebrations 1964-1984, 1987, In Burning Ambush: Essays, 1985-90, 1991, The Opposing Thumb: Decoding Literature of the Marcos Regime, 1995, Sunsurfers Seen from Afar: Critical Essays, 1991-96, 1996, The Blood Marriage of Earth and Sky: The Later Novels of Robert Penn Warren, 1997, The Circular Firing Squad, 1999, Green Circuits of the Sun: Studies in Philippine and American Literature, 2002; editor: Six Filipino Poets, 1955, Modern Philippine Short Stories, 1962; co-editor (with T.A. Gullason): The World of Short Fiction: An International Collection, 1962; contbg. editor Panorama, Manila, 1955—61, Drama Critique, 1956—62, Solidarity, Manila, 1966—78, Literature East and West, 1969—81, Aquila, 1975—79, Pilipinas, 1987—2002. Served with F.A., AUS, 1943-46. Recipient Ford Found. Pub. award, Nat. Coun. on Arts award, 1970, Rockefeller Found. Residency award, Bellagio, Italy, 1994; Stanford Creative Writing fellow, 1951-52; Bread Loaf Creative Writing scholar, 1961; rsch. grantee Am. Coun. Learned Socs.-Social Sci. Rsch. Coun., 1965, Asia Soc., 1965; Creative Writing grant Boston Coll.; rsch. travel grantee Am. Philos. Soc., 1968-69. Home: 54 Simpson Dr Framingham MA 01701-4076

CASPER, RICHARD HENRY, lawyer; b. Chgo., Nov. 4, 1950; s. Edson Lee and Dorothy Ellen (Klemp) C.; m. Betty Gene Ward, Aug. 26, 1972; children: Terrance, Laura, Russell, Jeremy. AB, Bowdoin Coll., 1972; JD, Northwestern U., 1975. Bar: Wis. 1975, U.S. Dist. Ct. (ea. dist.) Wis. 1975. Assoc. Foley & Lardner LLP, Milw., 1975-82, ptnr., 1982—. Pres. Milw. Chamber Orchestra, 1988—90; bd. dirs. Florentine Opera Co., 1998—. James Bowdoin scholar Bowdoin Coll, 1972. Mem. Wis. Bar Assn., Milw. Bar Assn., Order of the Coif. Office: Foley & Lardner LLP Firstar 777 E Wisconsin Ave Milwaukee WI 53202-5367 Office Phone: 414-297-5612. Business E-Mail: rcasper@foley.com.

CASPERSEN, FINN MICHAEL WESTBY, diversified financial services company executive; b. NYC, Oct. 27, 1941; s. Olaus Westby and Freda Caspersen; m. Barbara Caspersen, June 17, 1967. BA in Econs. with honors, Brown U., 1963; LLB cum laude, Harvard U., 1966; DHL (hon.), Johns Hopkins U., 1999; various hon. degrees. Assoc. Dewey, Ballantine, Bushby, Palmer & Wood, NYC, 1969-72; chmn. bd., chief exec. officer, mem. exec. com. Beneficial Corp., Wilmington, Del., 1976-98; chmn. bd. dirs., CEO Knickerbocker LLC; chmn. Hodson Trust, 1976—. Past bd. dirs., mem. exec. com. Beneficial Nat. Bank; chmn. bd. dirs. Beneficial Bank, Plc; bd. advisors Inst. Law and Econs., U. Pa.; past chmn. Coalition for Better Transp.; past co-chair Prosperity NJ; commr., dir. Hosp. for Spl. Surgery. Emeritus trustee Brown U.; former chmn. Save Ellis Island; moderator, bd. dirs. Shelter Harbor Fire Dist., Jupiter Island; pres. O.W. Caspersen Found.; chmn. bd. trustees Peddie Sch., Hightstown, NJ; former chmn. bd. trust Gladstone Equestrian Assn. Inc.; past bd. dirs. Drumthwacket Found.; charter mem. Partnership for NJ, New Brunswick; mem. Martin County Econ Devel. Coun.; bd. dirs. Coalition of Svc. Industries, Inc., Washington, 1982-95, vice chair, 1995; chmn. World Pair Championship, 1993, chmn. Princeton World Cup Regatta, 2000, Westby Corp., The Hudson Trust; dir. chmn. emeritus Princeton Nat. Rowing Assn.; dir. Nat. Rowing Found.; mem. corp. Cardigan Mountain Sch.; mem. exec. com. Harvard Resources Com.; former trustee John Carter Libr.; chmn. dean's adv. bd. Harvard Law Sch., Harvard Law Sch. Campaign; past dir. Clay Math. Inst. Lt. USCG, 1966-69; commr. Jupiter Island. Recipient Pres.'s medal Johns Hopkins U., Ethics in Bus. award BBB, 1992, Gov.'s award Alexander Hamilton Econ. Devel., 1997, President's medal Brown U., 1997, Brightest Star award Boys and Girls Clubs Newark, Inc., 1997, Humanities Citizen of Yr. award NJ Coun. for Humanities, 1999; named Civic Leader of Yr., YMCA, 1982, Citizen of Yr., Morristown Meml. Hosp., 1993. Mem. Am. Fin. Svcs. Assn. (bd. dirs., chmn. govt. affairs com., chmn. membership com., adminstrn. com., past chmn.), Fla. Bar Assn., NY Bar Assn., Harvard Club, Knickerbocker Club, Univ. Club, Wilmington Club, Shelter Harbor Golf Club (founder, chmn.). Office: Knickerbocker LLC Hobe Sound Office Plz 11450 SE Dixie Hwy Hobe Sound FL 33455

CASPERSEN, SIDNEY J., state agency administrator; BS in Law Enforcement, Jacksonville State U., Jacksonville, Ala.; studied advanced criminal investigation, U. Ala.; studied undercover and pub. corruption in-svc. tng., FBI Acad., Quantico, Vir. Police officer, Anniston, Ala., 1969; sr. spl. agent Nat. Automobile Theft Bur., 1974—78; with FBI, NYC, spl. agt., organized crime unit Birmingham, Ala., program mgr., supervisory agt. NYC, supervisory spl. agt., violent fugitive task force and the pub. corruption unit, asst. chief, spl. ops.; supervisory spl. agt. Russian Counter-Intelligence; asst. dir. intelligence NY State Office Pub. Safety, 2002, dep. dir., 2002; dir. NJ Office Counter-Terrorism, Trenton, NJ, 2002—. Recipient Outstanding Contbn. to Law Enforcement award, Marine Corps Law Enforcement Found. Office: NJ Office Counter Terrorism 25 Market St PO Box 091 Trenton NJ 08625-0091 Office Phone: 609-341-3434. Office Fax: 609-341-2958.

CASPILLO, CAROL A., secondary school educator; b. Newark, Ohio, Dec. 12, 1945; d. Edmond L. and Hilda G. Bonham; m. Maurice F. Caspillo, June 18, 1972; children: Carrice N., Eric J. BS in Edn., Ohio State U., 1967; MA in Adminstrn. and Curriculum, Gonzaga, U., 1999. Cert. novice data modeling and SQL instr., Java instr. Oracle Internet Acad., Java Instructor Oracle Internet Acad., 2004, cert. internet and computing Certiport. Math. educator Lincoln Jr. HS, Newark, 1968—72, Kapa'a (Hawaii) HS, 1978—. Mem.: ASCD (assoc.), NEA (assoc.), Hawaii State Tchrs. Assn., Nat. Coun. Tchrs. Math. (assoc.), Phi Delta Kappa (assoc.). Avocations: exercise, reading. Home: PO Box 181 Kilauea HI 96754 Office: Kapa'a HS 4695 Mailihuna Rd Kapaa HI 96746 Office Phone: 808-821-4400. Home Fax: 808-826-6313. Business E-Mail: ccaspill@notes.k12.hi.us. E-mail: ccaspillo@hawaiiantel.net.

CASS, RONALD ANDREW, lawyer, former dean; b. Washington, Aug. 12, 1949; s. Millard and Ruth Claire (Marx); m. Susan Nezamian; children: Laura Rebecca, Alexander Stephan, Daniella Helena. BA with high distinction, U. Va., 1970; JD with honors, U. Chgo., 1973. Bar: Md. 1973, D.C. 1974, U.S. Dist. Ct. D.C. 1974, U.S. Ct. Appeals (D.C. cir.) 1974, U.S. Supreme Ct. 1977, Va. 1979. Law clk. to chief judge U.S. Ct. Appeals (3d cir.), Wilmington, Del., 1973-74; assoc. Arent, Fox, Kintner, Plotkin & Kahn, Washington, 1974-76; asst. prof. law U. Va. Sch. Law, Charlottesville, 1976-81; assoc. prof. law Boston U., 1981-83, prof., 1983-95, dean Law Sch., 1990—2004, dean emeritus, 2004—, Melville Madison Bigelow prof., 1995—2004; legal advisor Office Plans and Policy, FCC, Washington, 1987-88; mem. U.S. Internat. Trade Commn., Washington, 1988-90, vice chmn., 1989-90; pres. Cass & Assoc., PC, 2004—, chmn. ctr. rule law, 2005—. Cons. comm. program Aspen (Colo.) Inst., 1977-78, Adminstrv. Conf. U.S. Washington, 1980-87, Helsell, Fetterman, Martin, Todd & Hokanson, Seattle, 1984-85, Assn. Trial Lawyers Am., Phila., 1985-87, UN Conf. Trade and Devel., Geneva, 1991, U.S. Dept. Justice, 1998, Microsoft Corp., 1998-2004, TransKaryotic Therapies, 2004-05; spl. cons. Nat. Econ. Rsch. Assn., Cambridge, Mass., 1990-94; arbitrator Biogen v. Schering-Plough, 1999-2000, Telesisa Sistemas v. Lucent Tech., 2000-2002, UPS v. Canada, 2001-07; adj. scholar Am. Enterprise Inst., Washington, 1993-2005; sr. fellow Internat. Ctr. Econ. Rsch., Turin, 1996-97, 99-2002, 04—; sesquicentennial assoc. Ctr. Advanced Studies U. Va. Law Sch., 1980-81; mem. nat. adv. bd. Case Western Res. U. Sch. Law, 1996-97; disting. lectr. U. Francisco Marroquin, Guatemala City, 1996, IMADEC Internat. Bus. Sch., Vienna, 2000, U. Aix-Marseille, 2002, 06—, Boston U. London Program, 2002; vis. prof. U. Lyon, 2004-05. Author: Revolution in the Wasteland: Value and Diversity in Television, 1981, (with Colin S. Diver) Administrative Law: Cases and Materials, 1987, (with Colin S. Diver and Jack M. Beermann) Administrative Law: Cases and Materials, 2nd edit., 1994, 5th edit., 2006, (with John R. Haring) International Trade in Telecommunications, 1998, The Rule of Law in America, 2001, (with Michael Knoll) International Trade Law, 2003; contbr. articles and essays to profl. jours., also chpts. to books. Bd. dirs. Northwestern Va. Health Systems Agy., Culpeper, 1980; bd. govs. Sightsavers Internat., Washington, 1989-91; bd. dirs. Telecomm. Policy Rsch. Conf., Washington, 1989-91, sec.-treas. 1989-90, vice chmn., 1991-92; bd. dirs. New Eng. Legal Found., 1994-2002, New England Coun., 1995-2004, Ralph Papitto Sch. Law, Roger Williams U., 2005—, Mass. 9/11 Fund, 2002-05; bd. overseers Boston Bar Found., 1992-94, Supreme Jud. Ct. Hist. Soc., 1997-2000; sr. Europe Discussion Group, Ctr. for Strategic and Internat. Studies, 1989-96; bd. advisors George Mason U. Law Sch. Law & Econs. Ctr., 1996-99, Inst. Dem. Comm., Boston, 1991-92, Fundación de la Commn. Social, Madrid, 1995—, IMADEC Internat. Bus. Sch., Vienna, 1999-2001, Legal Issues in Econ. Integration, Amsterdam, 2000—, Competition Policy Internat., 2005—. Fellow Am. Bar Found.; mem. ABA (adminstrv. law and regulatory practice sect., coun. 1993-95, chair 1998-99, legal edn. and admission bar sect., review commn. 1994-95, ho. of dels. 2000-02), Am. Law Inst., Am. Law Deans Assn. (bd. dirs. 1995-2004, pres. 1995-97), Mont Pelerin Soc., Boston Bar Assn. (coun. 1992-95), Adminstrv. Conf. U.S. (pub. mem. 1990-95, govt. mem. 1988-90), Transatlantic Policy Network (U.S. Working Group), Order of Coif, Federalist Soc. (internat. law, exec. com. 2001—, chmn. 2004—), Phi Beta Kappa. Republican. Jewish. Home and Office: 10560 Fox Forest Dr Great Falls VA 22066 Business E-Mail: roncass@cassassociates.net.

CASSAR, JON FRANCIS, television director, film director; b. Malta, Apr. 27, 1958; arrived in Can., 1963; s. Frank and Elda (Segona) C.; m. Kristina Francis Kinderman; children: Alexis, Zak. Student, Algonquin Coll., Ottawa, Ont., Can., 1983. Instr. Algonquin Coll., 1984-87, Maine Internat. Film and TV Workshops, 1986, 87; pres. J.F.C. Steadicam Photography, Ottawa, Ont., 1986—; v.p. Gen. Assembly Prodns., Ottawa, 1986—. Cameraman: (TV series and spls.) Gemini Awards (Can. TV), Nations Business (CBC), New Years Eve Special (Can. Broadcasting Co.), Rights and Freedoms (Can Broadcasting Co.), The Elephant Show (CBC and TVO); (commls.) Bradson's Business Center, Budget Rent-A-Car, Canadian Heart Foundation, Delisle Automobiles, Demers Automobiles, Ramada Inn Hotel, Sleep Shop, Toy World, United Way; (music videos) 39 Steps, David Gibson, Downchild Blues Band, Eight Seconds, Kyana, Peter Stewart Band, Sherry Keen, Screaming Bamboo, The Republic, Zoo Train; (documentaries) Airport Security, Energy Management Comes Home, Export With Care, Four Equity, Street Kids, The Queen's Printer, Winterlude 1986; (short dramas) Goodbye Heart, Kids, Three Rogers; steadicam operator 1988 Winter Olympics for Can. TV and ABC-TV; director: (TV) CHiPs '99, 1998, 24 (Emmy award Outstanding Directing for a drama series, 2006 Outstanding Directorial Acheivement in Dramatic Series Night, Directors Guild Am., 2007). Recipient Excellence awards Avt. and Sales Assn. Ottawa, 1987. Mem. Can. Assn. Motion Pictures and Electronic Recording Artists, Can. Soc. Cinematographers. Avocations: cinema, reading, soccer, volleyball. Office: 24 TV Series 21050 Lassen St Chatsworth CA 91311 Address: care Jeffrey Benson Paradigm Talent & Lit Agy 360 N Crescent Dr Beverly Hills CA 90210*

CASSARA, FRANK, artist, educator, printmaker; b. Partinico, Italy, Mar. 13, 1913; came to U.S., 1913, naturalized, 1936; s. Gaspare and Rosalia (Savarino) C.; m. Gretchen Jean Grathwohl, Dec. 28, 1946; children: Christina, Francesca. Student, U. Iowa, summer 1956, Atelier 17, Paris, summer 1958; MS in Design, U. Mich., 1954. Supr. easel painting sect. WPA, 1937; instr. Detroit Sch. Art, 1935-36, Soc. Arts and Crafts, Detroit, 1946-47; prof. U. Mich., Ann Arbor, after 1947, prof. emeritus. Instr. Nat. Music Camp, Interlochen, Mich., summers 1948-49 Illustrated manuscript published in Artists Proof, A Collectors Edition, 1963; one-man shows include: U. Man., Can., Winnipeg, Flint (Mich.) Inst. Arts, Toledo Mus., 1983, Kalamazoo Art Ctr., U. Maine, Orono, U. Ill., Urbana, U. Oreg., Corvallis, U. Nebr., Lincoln; group shows include: 7th Internat. Prints, Chgo. Art Inst., Mus. Palace Legion of Honor, San Francisco, Gallerie Nees Morphes, Athens, Greece, Bklyn. Mus., Achenbach Found. Graphic Arts, San Francisco, Okla. Art Ctr., Oklahoma City, Internat. Conf. Hand Papermakers, Boston, 1980, Internat. Papermakers, Birmingham Art Assn., Ella Sharp Mus. and Slusser Gallery; represented in permanent collections at Bibliotecque Nationale, Paris, Stadelijk Mus., The Netherlands, Libr. of Congress, USIA Agy., Nat. Mus. Am. Art, Smithsonian Instn., Washington; mural executed East Detroit Post Office, 1939, Sandusky (Mich.) Post Office, 1941, Lansing (Mich.) Water Conditioning Plant, 1941, renovated, 1989, Palio, Ann Arbor, 1996. Served with U.S. Army, 1942-46. Decorated 2 Bronze Stars.; Grantee Rackham Research Found., U. Mich., 1957-61, 68; Recipient over 50 awards in National and regional exhibitions. Mem. Ann Arbor Art Assn. (past pres., dir. 1954-62), Nat. Acad. Design. Achievements include being the innovator of two white grounds for etching.

CASSAVETES, NICK, film director, actor; b. NYC, May 21, 1959; s. John Cassavetes and Gena Rowlands; m. Heather Wahlquist; children: Sasha, Virginia. Dir.: (films) She's So Lovely, 1997, John Q, 2002, The Notebook, 2004; exec. prodr. (TV movies) The Incredible Mrs. Ritchie, 2003; writer (films) Blow, 2001, Whatever We Do, 2003; dir., writer: (films) Unhook the Stars/Décroche les étoiles, 1996, Alpha Dog, 2006; actor: A Woman Under the Influence, 1974, Mask, 1985, The Wraith, 1986, Quiet Cool, 1986, Black Moon Rising, 1986, Under the Gun, 1988, Assault of the Killer Bimbos, 1998, Blind Fury, 1989, Desperation Rising, 1989, Object of Desire, 1990, Backstreet Dreams, 1990, Delta Force 3: The Killing Game, 1991, Sins of the Night, 1993, Sins of Desire, 1993, Body of Influence, 1993, Broken Trust, 1993, Mrs. Parker and the Vicious Circle, 1994, Twogether, 1994, Class of 1999 II: The Substitute, 1994, Black Rose of Harlem, 1996, Me and the Gods, 1997, Face/Off, 1997, Conversations in Limbo, 1998, Life, 1999, The Astronaut's Wife, 1999, (TV movies) Reunion, 1980, Shooter, 1988, Just Like Dad, 1995. Office: c/o DGA 7920 W Sunset Blvd Los Angeles CA 90046-3300*

CASSCELLS, SAMUEL WARD, III, federal agency administrator, cardiologist, educator; b. Wilmington, Del., Mar. 18, 1952; s. Samuel Ward and Oleda (Dyson) C.; m. Roxanne Bell, Feb. 10, 1990; children: Sam, Henry, Lillian. BS cum laude, Yale U., 1974; MD magna cum laude, Harvard U., 1979. Intern then resident Beth Israel Hosp., Boston, 1979-82; cardiology fellow Mass. Gen. Hosp., Boston, 1982-85; Kaiser fellow clin. epidemiology Brigham and Women's Hosp. and Harvard Sch. Pub. Health, 1984-85; rsch. fellow Nat. Heart, Lung, and Blood Inst., Bethesda, Md., 1985-91; vis. scientist Scripps Inst. Medicine and Sci., LaJolla, Calif., 1991-92; chief cardiology, T.R. and M. O'Driscoll Levy prof. medicine U. Tex. Med. Sch., Houston, 1994-2000; John E. Tyson Disting. prof. medicine and public health U. Tex. Health Scis. Ctr., Houston, 2000—07, v.p. biotech., 2000—02; asst. sec. for health affairs US Dept. Def., Washington, 2007—. Chief cardiology Hermann Hosp., Houston, 1994-2001; dir. clin. rsch. Tex. Heart Inst., 2004—; co-founder Prizm Pharms., La Jolla, 1992—, Selective Genetics, La Jolla, Volcano Found., Sacramento, Calif., LifeSentry Inc., Houston, Claritas Capital, Nashville; founder Pres. Bush Ctr. Cardiovasc. Health, Houston, Alliance for Nano Health; bd. dirs. Lifeline Systems; adv. bd. U. Houston Law Ctr. Health Law and Policy Inst., 1999-2001; adv. Bio Houston; adv. bd. GE, Spectrocell, Lifeline Sys. Mem. editl. bd. Circulation, 1992—, Am. Jour. Cardiology, 1992—, Tex. Heart Inst. Jour., 1992—, Vascular Medicine, 1995-2001, U.T. Lifetime Newsletter, 1996—, Jour. Royal Soc. Medicine 1999—, Heart Watch, 2001--; contbr. articles to profl. jours. Mem. Bush-Cheney HHS Transition Adv. Com., 2001—; pres. George W. Bush Healthcare Adv. Com., 2001—; mayor's adv. com. to Med. Strike Force, 2001--; task force on bioterrorism Ctr. for Strategic and Internat. Studies, 2001--; bd. dirs. CapCURE; prostate cancer adv. bd. M.D. Anderson Cancer Ctr.; founder Alliance for Nano Health, Houston, 2004. Decorated Meritorious Svc. medal U.S. Army, Joint Svc. Commendation medal; named Hero of the Flood, Meml. Hermann Healthcare Sys., Houston, 2002; recipient First Harvard/CIMIT award for med. innovation, 2001, Gen. Maxwell Thurman award, Am. Telemedicine Assn., 2004. Mem.: Am. Clin. and Climatological Assn., Assn. Profs. Cardiology (bd. dirs.), Assn. Univ. Cardiologists, Am. Coll. Cardiology, Houston Cardiology Soc. (pres. 1995—96), Soc. Vascular Biol. Medicine (bd. dirs. 1997—2000), Am. Heart Assn. (Houston bd. dirs. 1992—2001), Met. Club, Met. Club (Washington), Sankaty Head Golf Club, The Siasconset Casino Assn., The Dancers, Tejas Breakfast Club, Bidermann Golf Club, Coronado Club, Houston Country Club, City Tavern Club, Farmington Country Club, Vicmead Hunt Club, Union Boat Club, Chevy Chase Club. Office: US Dept Def 1200 Def Pentagon Rm 3E1082 Washington DC 20301

CASSEL, CHRISTINE KAREN, physician; b. Mpls., Sept. 14, 1945; d. Charles Moore and Virginia Julia (Anderson) Cassel. BA, U. Chgo., 1967; MD, U. Mass., 1979. Diplomate Am. Bd. Internal Medicine (chmn. 1998-99). Intern, resident in internal medicine Children's Hosp., San Francisco, 1976—78; fellow in bioethics Inst. Health Policy Studies, U. Calif., San Francisco, 1978—79; fellow geriatrics Portland (Oreg.) VA Hosp., 1979—81; asst. prof. medicine and public health U. Oreg. Health Scis. U., 1981—83; asst. prof. geriatrics and medicine Mt. Sinai Med. Ctr., NYC, 1983—84; prof. medicine, prof. pub. policy U. Chgo., 1989—95, chief gen. internal medicine, 1985—95; chmn. and prof. geriatrics and medicine Mt. Sinai, 1995—2002; dean sch. of medicine Oreg. Heatlh and Sci. U., 2002—03; pres., CEO Am. Bd. Internal Medicine and ABIM Found., 2003—. Adj. prof. medicine U. Pa., 2004—. Author: Ethical Dimensions in the Health Professions, 1981, 2nd edit., 1993, Geriatric Medicine: Principles and Practice, 1984, 4th edit., 2003, Nuclear Weapons and Nuclear War: A Sourcebook for Health Professionals, 1984, Geriatric Medicine, A Practical Guide to Aging, 1997, Medicine Matters: What Geriatric Medicine Can Teach American Health Care, 2005. Bd. dirs. Greenwall Found., 1999—2004, chmn., 1999—2004. Henry J. Kaiser Family Found. faculty scholar, 1982—85, Hastings Ctr. fellow. Master: ACP (regent 1989—98, pres. 1996—97); fellow: Am. Geriatrics Soc.; mem.: Am. Soc. Law and Medicine (bd. dirs. 1988—94), Soc. Health and Human Values (pres. 1986), Physicians for Social Responsibility (dir. 1983—86, pres. 1988—89), Inst. of Medicine (coun. 2002—). Office: Am Bd Internal Medicine Ste 1700 510 Walnut St Philadelphia PA 19106-3699 Business E-Mail: ccassel@abim.org.

CASSEL, MARC, chef; Degree, El Centro Coll., Dallas, 1991. Sous chef Baby Routh; opening chef Star Canyon; exec. sous chef Azalea, Atlanta; with Mansion on Turtle Creek, Dallas; exec. chef The Green Room, Dragonfly, Hotel ZaZa, Dallas, 2005—. Named one of Dallas' Rising Stars, StarChefs.com, 2007. Office: Dragonfly Hotel ZaZa 2332 Leonard St Dallas TX 75201*

CASSEL, ROBERT URIAH, chemist; b. Phila., Nov. 26, 1914; s. Christian Uriah and Laura Elsie Cassel; m. Carol Ann Stanton, Sept. 22, 2001; m. Eva Perian, Oct. 4, 1941 (dec. 1994); children: Judith Kathleen, Claire Lorraine. BS in Sci., Lebanon Valley Coll., Annville, Pa., 1936. Cert. substitute tchr. NJ, 1931. Electrician NY Shipyard, Camden, NJ, 1937; process operator Socony Vacuum Oil Co., Paulsboro, NJ, 1937—38, control lab. technician, 1938—41, refinery equipment chem. inspector, 1945—48, employee rels. journalist, 1948—65; chemist Mobil Oil Corp, Paulsboro, 1965—81; ret. Plant journalist Mobil Oil Co., Paulsboro, plant photographer, 1954—64. Editor: Hoodlum News (301st Infantry Assn.), 1981—; contbr. articles to profl. jours. Councilman Paulsboro Boro Coun., 1950—53; sch. bd. mem. Mantua Twp. Bd. Edn., NJ, 1953—56; chmn., deacon, elder Christ Presbyn. Ch., Gibbstown, NJ. With US Army, 1941—45, capt. USAR, 1946—57. Decorated Bronze Star with three oak leaf clusters US Army; recipient NJ. Svc. medal, 1999, Svc. medal, Gloucester County, 2001. Mem.: Gloucester County Nature Club (pres.), 94th Infantry Divsn. Assn. (pres. 1996—97), Gloucester County Nature Club (program chair). Avocations: gardening, birding.

CASSELL, ERIC JONATHAN, physician; b. NYC, Aug. 29, 1928; s. Hyman William and Anne (Lake) Goldstein; m. Joan M. Fishman, Oct. 17, 1957 (div. 1987); children: Justine, Stephen; m. Patricia M. Owens, May 26, 1990. BA, Queens Coll., 1950; MA, Columbia U., 1950; MD, NYU, 1954; DHL (hon.), Med. Coll. Pa., 1985. Intern 3d med. divsn. Bellevue Hosp., NYC, 1954—55, asst. resident 3d med. divsn., 1955—56, physician 3d, 4th med. divsn., 1965—66; USPHS trainee in infectious diseases Weill Med. Coll., Cornell U., NYC, 1959—61; clin. prof. pub. health Cornell U., NYC, 1971—; attending physician French Hosp., NYC, 1961—74; assoc. attending physician Mt. Sinai (N.Y.) Hosp., 1966—71; assoc. dir. ambulatory care Community Med., Mt. Sinai, 1966—68; attending physician N.Y. Presbyn. Hosp., 1984—; asst. resident 3d med. divsn. Bellevue Hosp., NYC, 1958—59. Clin. assoc. prof. medicine NYU, 1965—66, Mt. Sinai Hosp., 1966—71; bd. dirs. Hasting's Ctr., Garrison, NY, 1973—2006; commr. Nat. Bioethics Adv. Commn., 1997—2001; vis. investigator Meml. Sloan Kettering Cancer Ctr., 1999—; adj. prof. medicine McGill U., Montreal, Canada, 2005—. Author: Healer's Art, 1976, Place of Humanities in Medicine, 1984, Talking with Patients (2 vols.), 1985, The Nature of Suffering, 1991, 2d edit., 2004, Doctoring: The Nature of Primary Care Medicine, 1997; editor: Changing Values in Medicine, 1979. Capt. M.C. US Army, 1956—58. Master: ACP; fellow: N.Y. Acad. Medicine; mem.: Inst. of Medicine of NAS. Democrat. Jewish. Avocations: woodworking, metalworking. Personal E-mail: eric@ericcassell.com.

CASSELL, KAY ANN, librarian; b. Van Wert, Ohio, Sept. 24, 1941; d. Kenneth Miller and Pauline (Zimmerman) C. BA, Carnegie-Mellon U., 1963; MLS, Rutgers U., 1965; MA, Bklyn. Coll., 1969; PhD, Internat. U. Grad. Studies, 2005. Reference librarian Bklyn. Coll. Library, 1965-68; adult svcs. cons. NJ State Libr., Trenton, 1968-71; libr. cons.-vol. Peace Corps, Rabat, Morocco, 1971-73; adult svcs. cons. Westchester Libr. System, White Plains, NY, 1973-75; dir. Bethlehem Pub. Libr., Delmar, NY, 1975-81, Huntington (N.Y.) Pub. Libr., 1982-85; exec. dir. Coordinating Coun. Lit. Mags., NYC, 1985-87; univ. libr. New Sch. Social Rsch., 1987-88; assoc. dir. collections and svcs. br. librs. NY Pub. Libr., 1989—2006; asst. prof. Sch. Communication, Info., and Libr. Studies, Rutgers U., 2006—. Adj. faculty Grad. Sch. Libr. Sci., SUNY, Albany, 1976-78, Palmer Sch. Libr. and Info. Scis., LI U., 1986-90, Grad. Sch. Info. and Libr. Sci., Pratt Inst., 1994—2006; chmn. cmty. adv. com. Capital Dist. Humanities Program, Albany, 1980-81; bd. dirs. Literacy Vols. of Suffolk, Bellport, NY, 1981-85; chmn. NYC Sch. Libr. Sys. Coun., 1991-94; treas. Libr. Pub. Rels. Coun., 1993-98, pres., 1999-2000. Mem. ALA (pres. reference and adult svcs. divsn. 1983-84, chair membership com. 1991-95, coun. 1992—, chair pub. com. 1999-01, chair human resources com., 2003-04), Freedom to Read Found., NY Libr. Assn. (pres. reference and adult svcs. sect. 1975-76), Feminist Press (bd. dirs.), Beta Phi Mu.

CASSELL, SAMUEL JAMES, professional basketball player; b. Balt., Nov. 18, 1969; Grad., Dunbar H.S., Balt., San Jacinto Coll., 1993. Co-owner shoe store, Houston; basketball player Houston Rockets, 1994-96, Pheonix Suns, 1996, Dallas Mavericks, 1996-97, NJ Nets, East Rutherford, 1997-99, Milw. Bucks, 1998—2005, LA Clippers, 2005—. Mem. NBA championship team, 1994,95; won Fleer ShootAround during the 1996 All-Star Weekend, San Antonio, Tex; named NBA Player of Week from Apr. 6-12, 1998. Office: LA Clippers Staples Ctr 1111 S Figueroa Los Angeles CA 90015

CASSELL, WILLIAM COMYN, retired college president; b. Vallejo, Calif., Oct. 8, 1933; s. Comyn R. and Emily E. (Duckwith) C.; m. Jeanne Taylor, Dec. 27, 1955; children: Paul, Susan, David. BA, Pomona Coll., 1956; MA, Claremont Grad. Sch., 1969; LHD (hon.), Lakeland Coll., 1977; LLD, William Penn Coll.; D in Bus. Adminstn., Won Kwang U.; MBA, DLitt, Heidelberg Coll. Broker Hornblower and Weeks, Inc., Orange, Calif., 1958-64; asst. to treas. Claremont (Calif.) Coll., 1964-65; dir. income trusts and bequests Calif. Inst. Tech., Pasadena, 1965-69; dir. devel. and pub. relations Menninger Found., Topeka, 1969-70; dir. devel. U. Denver, 1970-74; pres. Coll. of Idaho, Caldwell, 1974-80, Heidelberg Coll., Tiffin, Ohio, 1980-96, pres. emeritus, 1996—. Cons. Ford Found., Phelps-Stokes Fund, Congress of No. Marianas Islands, others; hon. consul gen. Nepal; bd. dirs. Fifth-Third Bank No. Ohio. Author: The Case for Deferred Giving, 1966, Deferred Giving Programs: Administration and Promotion, 1972; editorial adv. bd.: Ednl. Record. Active Parks and Recreation Commn., Claremont, 1967-69, City Coun., Bow Mar, Colo., 1967-69; adv. bd. Salvation Army, Caldwell, Western Electric Fund; trustee Caldwell Meml. Hosp., chmn., 1976; mem. Idaho newspaper carrier scholarship selection com.; mem. Missions on Am. Mgmt. and Ednl. Techniques to Indonesia and Jamaica; mission leader Thailand on Edn. and Mgmt.; mem. White House Adv. Com. on Libr. and Tech., White House Conf.; active Ohio Higher Edn. Facilities Commn., Depository Libr. Commn. of U.S.; adv. com. chmn. bd. Western Ind. Coll. Funds; bd. dirs. Tiffin YMCA, Wood River Cmty. YMCA, 2005-; chair Ketchum/Sun Valley Transit Authority; jr. warden St. Thomas Episcopal Ch.; chair adv. bd. Minn. Pub. Radio of Wood River Valley, 2000—; sec., bd. dirs. Arts Found. for the Wood River Valley, Croj Canyon Ranch Found. Capt. USAR, 1957-58. Recipient Brakeley award for Outstanding Coll. Devel. Am. Alumni Coun., 1968, Nat. Fund Raising Coun. award, 1969; named Outstanding Young Man of Yr., Claremont, Calif., 1967, an Idaho Disting. Citizen, 1977, hon. VIP Sta. KIDO, Boise, Citizen of Yr. City of Tiffin, 1991. Mem. Coun. for Advancement of Support of Edn., Caldwell C. of C. (exec. bd. dir.), Tiffin C. of c. (bd. dirs., v.p.), Internat. Assn. Univ. Pres. (exec. com.), World Bus. Coun., North Cen. Accreditation Assn. (commr.), Am. Coun. on Edn. (commn. internat. edn.), Rotary (fellows selection com. dist., Citizen of Yr., Tiffin, Ohio 1991), Ketchum Sun Valley Rotary Club (mem. internat. projects com. Rotary dist.). Home: PO Box 1688 Sun Valley ID 83353-1688

CASSELL, WILLIAM WALTER, retired accounting operations consultant; b. Chgo., Apr. 10, 1917; s. Charles F. and E. Margaret (Jackson) C.; m. Rosamond Mary Fisher, May 13, 1944; children: Anne, Gerald, Douglas, Mary. Student, U. Wash., 1936-38, Syracuse U., 1943-44; grad., Am. Inst. Banking, 1957, Grad. Sch. Savs. Banking, 1965, Savs. Banks Mgmt. Devel. Program, U. Mass., 1970. Officer's asst. Syracuse (N.Y.) Savs. Bank, 1959-66, treas., 1966-71, v.p., 1971-75, sr. v.p., controller, 1975-77, exec. v.p., 1977-83, cons., 1983, also dir.; dir. State Bank of Chittenango, 1963—73, 1983—2005, Credit Bur. Syracuse, 1976-83, Consumer Credit Counseling Service, 1979-83. Chmn. bd. dirs. State Bank of Chittenango, 1993-2005, SBC Fin. Corp., 1993-2005 Bd. dirs. Syracuse Symphony Orch., 1979-81, Opera Theater of Syracuse, 1982-84; pres. Madison County Hist. Soc., 1982-84. Served with U.S. Army, 1941-45, ETO. Decorated Bronze Star Mem. Am. Inst. Banking, Fin. Execs. Inst. (pres. Syracuse chpt. 1971-72). Clubs: Men's Garden of Am, Monarch of Syracuse. Republican. Methodist. Home: 131 W Genesee St Chittenango NY 13037-1501 *To find happiness in little things each day; to be all I am capable of being, judged within the framework of my own real values and to make others glad I came this way— this is the measure of a life worthwhile: contentment, not complacency.*

CASSELLA, DENNIS GENE, retired county official; b. Pratt, Kans., Oct. 24, 1946; s. Barney Joseph and Norma Jeanne Cassella. AA, Sacramento C.C., 1970; BA in History/Polit. Sci., U. Calif., Davis, 1971; MPA, East Tex. State U., 1975. City pers. dir. City of Texarkana, Ark., 1971—75; dir. adminstrv. svcs. Ark. Dept. Local Svcs., Little Rock, 1975—76; dir. gen. svcs. County of Nevada, Calif., 1977—2002; ret., 2002. Dir. emergency svcs. County of Nevada, 1988-2003; sr. adj. prof. Golden Gate U., Sacramento, 1979-2000. Commr. Grass Valley Pers. Com., Calif., 2003—; mem. Nevada City Police Cmty. Rels. Commn., 1991—93, Nevada City Bicentennial of the Constn. Commn., Calif., 1986—; bd. mem. Nev. County Fire Safe Coun., 2006—. Mem. Nevada County Libr. Found. (pres. 1998-99), Gold Country Lions (pres. 1987, 2004), Hospice of the Foothills (bd. mem.). Home: 205 Cypress Hill Dr Grass Valley CA 95945 E-mail: henryv@nccn.net.

CASSELLA, WILLIAM NATHAN, JR., retired not-for-profit organization executive; b. Alton, Ill., July 14, 1920; s. William Nathan and Martha (Stanly) C.; m. Margaret Powers Crowley, June 22, 1946 (dec. Nov. 1987); children: John Woodson, Stephen Rowan, Mark Crowley, William Kent. AB, U. Ill., 1942; MS, Syracuse U., 1943; AM, Harvard U., 1951, PhD, 1953. Rsch. asst. Pub. Adminstrn. Clearing House, Washington, 1946; instr., then asst. prof. polit. sci. U. Mo., 1948—54; with Nat. Mcpl. League, 1953—90, exec. dir., 1969—85, project coord., 1985—90; sr. assoc. Inst. Pub. Adminstrn., 1988—2004. Rsch. assoc. Govt. Affairs Found., 1954-57; vis. assoc. prof. pub. adminstrn. Columbia, 1957; sr. rsch. assoc. Columbia (Met. Region Program), 1957-61; mem. adv. com. state and local govt. stats. Bur. Census, 1962-65, chmn., 1963-65; mem. area devel. adv. bd. Com. Econ. Devel., 1964-66; cons. Adv. Commn. Intergovtl. Rels., 1967-89. Author: Constitutional Aspects of Metropolitan Government, 1961, also articles; contbg. editor Nat. Civic Rev., 1954-85, chmn. editorial bd., 1969-85. Mem. Greenburgh (N.Y.) Bd. Edn., 1961-64; mem. Westchester County Planning Bd., 1962-97, vice chmn., 1967-72, chmn., 1973-97, Hudson River Valley Greenway Compact Commn., 1997—2005, Conservation Adv. Bd., Dobbs Ferry, N.Y., 1997—2005; bd. dirs. Westchester County Indsl. Devel. Agy., 1976-83; trustee Pub. Adminstrn. Service, 1969-76; governing bd. Governmental Affairs Inst., 1969-76. Served to lt. USNR, 1943-46. Mem. Am. Polit. Sci. Assn., Am. Soc. Pub. Adminstrn., Govtl. Rsch. Assn., Internat. City/County Mgmt. Assn., Nat. Acad. Pub. Adminstrn., Regional Plan Assn. N.Y., Phi Beta Kappa, Alpha Kappa Lambda, Delta Sigma Pi, Omicron Delta Kappa, Pi Alpha Alpha. Episcopalian. Home: 7 Ridgedell Ave Hastings On Hudson NY 10706 Personal E-mail: wncassella@aol.com.

CASSELLE, CORENE, pre-school educator; b. Chgo., Jan. 26, 1943; d. Lawrence Edward Walker and Dorothy Monterie Sims; children: Lawrence Walter Kwakou, Anika Fani Foreman, Omowale Khalfani, Adjovi Abeeku Austin. BS, No. Ill. U., 1964; MEd, U. Ill., Urbana-Champaign, 1970; EdD, U. Nev., Las Vegas, 1977. Cert. std. spl. tchr./reading Ill., gen. adminstrn./supervision Ill. Reading specialist, adminstr. Sch. Dist. #299, Chgo., 1992—. Curator BENIZRT, Justice, Ill., 1986—. Author: Country of the Black People, 1975. Achievements include invention of peppermill filler. Home: 8651 S 87th Ave Ste 201 Justice IL 60458-2020 Office Phone: 708-475-0200. Personal E-mail: ccasselle@yahoo.com.

CASSELLI, HENRY CALVIN, JR., artist, painter; b. New Orleans, Oct. 25, 1946; m. Donna Madden, June 5, 1971; 1 child, Dana Nicole. Student, John McCrady Sch. Fine and Applied Arts, 1967. Solo shows include Smithsonian Inst., Washington, 1968, 71, Lauren Roberts Mus., 1972, Far Gallery, N.Y.C., 1974-77, Hunter Mus., Tenn., 1981, Am. Watercolor Soc., 1971-86, Greenville (S.C.) Mus., 1980, others; permanent collections include New Orleans Mus., Albany Mus., Ga., The White House, Lauren Rogers Mus., Grover M. Herman Fine Arts Ctr, Libr. Congress, N.Y. Pub. Libr., Nat. Portrait Gallery, Washington. Served with USMC, 1967-70. Decorated Bronze Star medal with combat V.; named offical NASA artist for space shuttle. Mem. NAD, Am. Watercolor Soc. (v.p. 1979-80, nat. juror 1979, High Winds medal 1976, 77, 79, 88, Silver medal 1986, Gold medal 1987.) Office: 4015 N Labarre Rd Metairie LA 70002-1820

CASSELMAN, FREDERICK LEE, computer artist, printmaker; b. Columbus, Ohio, Jan. 5, 1940; s. Carroll Dean Casselman and Marjory Evelyn Howard; m. Carol Esther Puffer, Nov. 23, 1968; children: Amy, Aaron. BEE, Ohio State U., 1963, MSEE, 1965. Sr. engr. GTE Corp., Needham, Mass., 1966-94. Exhibited in one-man shows at Boston Cyberarts Festival, 1999, Chelsea (Mass.) Waterfront Gallery, 2000, Sonoma Mus. Visual Art, 2002, Ctrl. Wyo. Coll., 2002, Wayland Mass. Pub. Libr., 2003, Inst. Noltic Scis., Petaluma, Calif., 2005; author website The Earth Echo Galleries, 1996—; artist on-line-exhbn. Digital Americana, Orlando Mus. Art, 1998. Publicity dir. Framingham (Mass.) Cultural Coun., 1996-2001; vol. Mass. Correctional Instn., Framingham, 1999—; active Art and Sci. Collaborations, Inc. Home: 48 Florissant Ave Framingham MA 01701-4224 E-mail: fred@earthecho.com.

CASSELMAN, WILLIAM E., II, lawyer; b. Washington, Pa., July 8, 1941; s. William E. and Lucy B. Casselman; m. Mia Kang, June 15, 1993; children: Katharine Carr, Lee Wilson. BA, Claremont-McKenna Coll., 1963; postgrad., U. Madrid, 1963-64; JD, George Washington U., 1968. Bar: Va. 1968, DC 1972, US Supreme Ct. 1975. Legis. asst. to Robert McClory US Ho. of Reps., 1965-68; staff asst. Office of Pres., 1969, dep. spl. asst. to Pres., 1969-71, counsel to Pres., 1974-75; gen. counsel Gen. Svcs. Adminstrn., 1971-73; legal counsel to Vice Pres. U.S., 1973-74; ptnr. Ambrose & Casselman, P.C., 1975-79; pvt. practice Washington, 1979-82; ptnr. Dorsey & Whitney, 1982-84, Popham, Haik, Schnobrich & Kaufman, Ltd., Washington, 1985-93; of counsel Stairs Dillenbeck & Finley, NYC, 1993—; pvt. practice Washington, 1993—. Mem. adminstrv. conf. US, 1971-73; adv. mem. Nat. Conf. Commrs. on Uniform State Laws, 1975; mem. Gerald R. Ford Commemorative Com., 1977-82; bd. dirs. gen. counsel, mem. fin. com., fellow Georgetown U. Ctr. for Internat. Bus. and Trade (formerly Nat. Ctr. Export-Import Studies), 1983-93. Recipient Disting. Alumni Achievement award George Washington U., 1975. Mem. ABA, Fed. Bar Assn. (chmn. gen. counsels com. 1973-74, nat. coun. 1974-79, Disting. Svc. commendation 1974), George Washington Law Assn. (bd. dirs. 1976-81), Nat. Trust for Hist. Preservation (mem. com. on legal svcs. 1978-80), Delta Theta Phi, Theta Chi. Republican. E-mail: weclawfirm@aol.com.

CASSELS, MARTHA BEASLEY, realtor, investor; b. Greenwood, SC, Oct. 22, 1932; d. Hugh Alton and Ora Faith (Mitchell) Beasley; m. Marion Carlyle Crenshaw, Jr., June 25, 1953 (div. 1979); children: Marion Carlyle III, William Frank, Hugh Charles, Faith Byrd; m. Samuel Jones Cassels, III, Oct. 6, 1979 (div. 1999). BA, Converse Coll., 1953. Cert. residential specialist Realtors Nat. Mktg. Inst., 1979. Tchr. Carr Jr. H.S., Durham, N.C., 1953-55, 1st Congl. Pre Sch., Branford, Conn., 1964-66; dir. Barfield Kindergarten, Durham, 1966-68, Duke Meml. Pre Sch., Durham, 1968-74; sec. corp. Bob Gunter Realty, Inc., Durham, 1972-77; owner Crenshaw Co., Inc., Durham, 1977-79, Cassels Real Estate, Montgomery, Ala., 1980—. Pres. Hampton Killingsworth, Inc. 1990—, Montgomery Area Bd. Realtors, Ala. Bd. Realtors, 1979—, Nat. Bd. Realtors, Chgo., 1974—. Mem. County Bd. Edn., Durham, 1972—79; patron theatre dept. Ala. State U., Montgomery, 1994—; active Montgomery Zoo; bd. dirs. Scott and Zelda Fitzgerald Mus., Montgomery, 1986—, sponsor statewide lit. contest for high schs. and colls. Named Top Prodr., Montgomery Area Bd. Realtors, 1981; recipient 10 Consecutive Yrs. of Multi Millions award Montgomery Area Bd. Realtors, 1990, Top Residential award Montgomery Area Bd. Realtors, 1992. Mem.: YMCA, AAUW, Greater Montgomery Home Builder Assn., Prattville C. of C., Montgomery Area C. of C., C.E.O. Roundtable, Jr. Twentieth Century Club, Mobile Yacht Club. Methodist. Avocations: reading, swimming, sailing. Office: Cassels Real Estate 623 S Perry St Montgomery AL 36104-5890 Office Phone: 334-269-9400.

CASSENS WEISS, DEBRA SUE, professional association administrator, publishing executive; b. Chgo., Nov. 2, 1956; d. Kenneth Henry and Geraldine Cassens; m. Dean J. Moss, Aug. 9, 1981 (div. 1996); m. David Weiss, Aug. 23, 2003. BA in English, U. Ill., 1978; JD, DePaul U., 1983. Bar: Ill. Newscaster WMRO, WAUR Radio, Aurora, Ill., 1979-81; reporter, editor City News Bur., Chgo., 1984-85; consumer news rschr. WMAQ-TV News, Chgo., 1985-86; from reporter to asst. mng. editor ABA, Chgo., 1986—; mng. editor ABA Jour., Chgo. Office: ABA Jour 321 N Clark St Chicago IL 60610

CASSERLY, CHARLEY, former professional football team executive; b. River Edge, NJ, Feb. 27, 1949; m. Bev Casserly; 1 daughter, Shannon. BS in Edn., Springfield Coll., M. in Guidance, Ph.D in Humanics, 2005. Asst. coach Cathedral H.S., Springfield, Mass., 1969-72, athletic dir., 1974-75; asst. Springfield Coll., 1973-74; tchr., football coach Minnechaugh H.S., Mass., 1975-76; joined Washington Redskins, 1977, asst. gen. mgr., 1982—89, gen. mgr., 1989—2000; sr. v.p., gen. mgr. football ops. Houston Texans, 2000—06. Named to The Springfield Coll. Sports Hall of Fame.

CASSERLY, JAMES LUND, lawyer; b. Norfolk, Va., Dec. 26, 1951; s. James Robert and Patricia (Lund) C.; m. Kathleen Ann Flynn, Apr. 25, 1981; 1 child Laura Flynn. AB magna cum laude, Tufts Coll., 1973; JD, Columbia U., 1976. Bar: D.C. 1976, U.S. Dist. Ct. D.C. 1980, U.S. Ct. Appeals (D.C. cir.) 1981. Law clk. to trial judges U.S. Ct. Fed. Claims, Washington, 1976-77; law clk. to judge Marion Bennett U.S. Ct. Appeals Fed. Cir., Washington, 1977-78; assoc. Wilkinson, Cragun & Barker LLP,

Washington, 1978-82, Squire Sanders & Dempsey, Washington, 1982-85, ptnr., 1985-94; sr. legal advisor to Commr. Susan Ness FCC, Washington, 1994-99; ptnr. Mintz Levin Cohn Ferris Glovsky & Popeo PC, Washington, 1999—2002, Willkie Farr & Gallagher LLP, Washington, 2003—. Home: 2839 Allendale Pl NW Washington DC 20008 Office: Willkie Farr & Gallagher LLP 1875 K St NW Washington DC 20006-1238 Office Phone: 202-303-1119. Personal E-mail: jlcasserly@aol.com. Business E-Mail: jcasserly@willkie.com.

CASSERLY, MICHAEL DAVID, educational association administrator; b. Portland, Oreg., May 12, 1948; s. William Ryan and Shirley (Dean) C.; m. Mary Janet Stith, June 9, 1973; 1 child, Jeannette. BA, Villanova U., 1970; PhD, U. Md., 1982. Rsch. asst. Am. Insts. Rsch., Washington, 1973—76; rsch. assoc. RMC Rsch., Bethesda, Md., 1976; legis. and rsch. assoc. Coun. Gt. City Schs., Washington, 1977—91, exec. dir., 1992—. Served in US Army, 1970—73. Roman Catholic. Office: Coun Grt City Schs 1301 Pennsylvania Ave NW Ste 702 Washington DC 20004 Office Phone: 202-393-2427. Office Fax: 202-393-2400.*

CASSIDY, DAVID MICHAEL, lawyer; b. Amityville, NY, May 31, 1954; s. Paul Francis and Theresa Alice (Britts) C.; children: Daniel B., Caitlin E. BA, SUNY, Stony Brook, 1981; JD, St. John's U., Jamaica, NY, 1985. Bar: N.Y. 1986. Assoc. Rivkin Radler LLP, Uniondale, NY, 1985-92, ptnr., 1992—. Mem. Suffolk County Bar Assn., L.I. Assn. Office: Rivkin Radler LLP Eab Plz Uniondale NY 11556-0001

CASSIDY, DENIS ANDREW, artist, architect; b. Bklyn., Mar. 9, 1961; s. John Joseph Cassidy and Monica Mary Gallagher. BA, Cath. U., 1984; postgrad., Pratt Inst., 1987-88. Registered arch., NY. Student intern The White House, Washington, 1982-84; account exec. Telephone Mktg. Programs, NYC, 1985; illustrator Gen. Rsch., Teaneck, NJ, 1985-86; arch., planner Port Authority of N.Y. and N.J., NYC, 1986-94; arch., ptnr. Paul S. Marchese and Assocs., Greenwich, Conn., 1996—2001; prin. D.A. Cassidy Arch., LLC, Stamford, Conn., 2001—. Author: My Life as a Cartoon, 1996. Mem. Snug Harbor Cultural Ctr., Upper Catskill Cultural Coun., The Whitney Mus. of Am. Art. Recipient Exceptional Svc. medal Port Authority of N.Y. and N.J., 1993. Mem. Am. Inst. Archs., Schoharie Artists Coun. Office: 25 Bank St Stamford CT 06901 Home: 84 Southridge Dr Waterbury CT 06708-3328 Office Phone: 203-316-9332. E-mail: dac.architect@adelphia.net.

CASSIDY, EUGENE PATRICK, pathologist; b. NYC, July 21, 1940; s. Eugene Zachary and Anita Hilda (Corsi) C.; m. Hollis Elizabeth Ward, Sept. 25, 1965; 1 child, Meredith. BA, Williams Coll., 1962; MD, Yale U., 1966. Diplomate Am. Bd. Pathology. Intern Yale-New Haven Hosp., Conn., 1966-67; resident then fellow in pathology and lab. medicine Yale U. Med. Ctr., 1967-70; dir. pathology Appalachian Lab. for Occupational Respitory Disease, Morgantown, Wis., 1970-72; pathologist Clarkson Hosp., Omaha, 1972-78, Scripps Hosp., Encinitas, Calif., 1978-84; dir. pathology Marshalltown (Iowa) Med. and Surgical Ctr., 1984—. Asst. prof. W.Va. U. Sch. Medicine, Morgantown, 1970-72, U. Nebr. Sch. Medicine, Omaha, 1974-78. Contbr. articles to profl. jours. Served with USPHS, 1970-72. Fellow Internat. Acad. Pathology, Coll. Am. Pathologists, Am. Soc. Clin. Pathologists; mem. AMA, Am. Assn. Blood Banks. Republican. Avocations: music, architecture. Home: 505 Craig Cir Marshalltown IA 50158-6303 Office: Marshalltown Med & Surg Ctr 3 S Fouth Ave Marshalltown IA 50158-2924 Home Phone: 641-753-9192. Business E-Mail: ecassidy@marshmed.com.

CASSIDY, JACK, academic administrator, educator; b. Phila., Mar. 12, 1941; married; 2 children. BA in English, Gettysburg Coll., Phila., 1962; MEd in Secondary Edn., Temple U., Phila., 1965, PhD in Ednl. Psychology, 1975. Tchr. Hawaii Dept. Pub. Instrn., Island Kauai, Lihue, 1965-69; instr. Temple U., 1970-71; reading supr. Newark Sch. Dist., Del., 1972—78; prof. Millersville U., Pa., 1998; assoc. dean Coll. Edn. Tex. A&M U., Corpus Christi, 1998—. Spl. cons. Ednl. Testing Svc., 1977-93. Sr. author: Basic Life Skills, Macmillan Lit. Series, Read-Reason-Write, Scribner Reading Series; contbr. articles to profl. jours. Coach Cmty. Swim Teams, Kapaa, Hawaii, 1967-68. Mem. Internat. Reading Assn. (legis. com. 1975-76, dir. 1976-79, pres. 1982-83), Diamond State Reading Assn. (pres. 1974-75), Nat. Coun. Tchrs. English, Assn. for Supervision and Curriculum Devel., Nat. Coun. Accreditation Tchr. Edn. (exec. bd. 1986-88, chmn. 1988-89, 1997-2000), Coll. Reading Assn. (dir. 1994-97, pres. 1999-2000), Phi Delta Kappa. Home: 322 Santa Monica Pl Corpus Christi TX 78411-1612 Office: Early Childhood Devel Ctr Tex A&M Univ 6300 Ocean Dr Corpus Christi TX 78412-5503 Office Phone: 361-825-5611. Business E-Mail: jack.cassidy@tamucc.edu.

CASSIDY, JAMES MARK, construction company executive; b. Evanston, Ill., June 22, 1942; s. James Michael and Mary Ellen (Munroe) C.; m. Bonnie Marie Bercker, Aug. 1, 1964 (div. Dec. 1981); children: Micaela Marie, Elizabeth Ann, Daniel James; m. Patricia Margaret Mary Murphy, Sept. 15, 1984. BA, St. Mary's Coll., 1963. Estimator Cassidy Bros., Inc., Rosemont, Ill., 1963-65, project mgr., 1965-67, v.p., 1967-71, exec. v.p., 1971-77, pres., 1978—. Trustee Plasterer's Health & Welfare Trust, 1971-92; chmn. labor liaison com. Laborers Internat. Union N.Am. and Assn. Wall and Ceiling Industries, 1982-85, chmn. labor-mgmt. group, 1985-88; chmn. Chicagoland Assn. Wall and Ceiling Contractors' Carpenters Union Negotiating Team, 1983—; trustee, vice chmn. laborers dist. coun. Chgo. and Vicinity Laborers-Employers Cooperation and Edn. Trust Fund, 1999—. Area fund leader Constrn. Industry Salute to Boy Scouts Am., 1975; mem. president's coun. St. Mary's Coll. With U.S. Army, 1963-64, N.G., 1964-69. Mem. Chgo. Plastering Inst., Builder Uppers Club (pres. 1973-74), Chicagoland Assn. Wall and Ceiling Contractors (pres. 1976-79), Great Lakes Coun., Internat. Assn. Wall and Ceiling Contractors (chmn. 1977), Constrn. Employers Assn. Chgo. (bd. dirs. 1976—, pres.-elect 1989-90, pres. 1991-93, chmn. com. labor-mgmt. rels. 1983-93), Chicagoland Safety Coun. (bd. dirs. 1988-92), Joint Conf. Bd. Cook County (chmn. 1996-97, 98-99, 2003-04, 06—), Assn. Wall and Ceiling Industries Internat. (bd. dirs. 1978-81, 88-89, fin. v.p. 1990, 2d v.p. 1991, pres.-elect 1992, pres. 1993), Park Ridge County Club (Ill.) (bd. dirs. 1994-97), Eagle Creek Country Club (Naples, Fla.).

CASSIDY, JOHN HAROLD, lawyer; b. St. Louis, June 18, 1925; s. John Harold and Jennie (Phillips) C.; m. Marjorie Blair, Nov. 26, 1947; children: Patricia, John, Brian. AB, Washington U., 1949, JD, 1951. Bar: Mo. 1951, U.S. Dist. Ct. (ea. dist.) Mo. 1951, U.S. Ct. Appeals (8th crct.) 1951, U.S. Supreme Ct. 1955. Atty. U.S. Govt., St. Louis, 1951-56; pvt. practice St. Louis, 1956-59; atty. Crown Zellerbach Corp., San Francisco, 1959-61, Ralston Purina Co., St. Louis, 1961-89, v.p., 1975-85, v.p., sec., sr. counsel, 1985-89. Served with U.S. Mcht. Marine, 1943-45. Mem.: ABA, Am. Soc. Corp. Secs., St. Louis Bar Assn., Mo. Bar Assn. Republican.

CASSIDY, MIKE, online game company executive; Student in piano, Berkelee Coll. Music, Boston; BS in Aerospace Engring., MIT, 1985, MS in Aerospace Engring., 1986; MBA, Harvard Bus. Sch., 1991. Co-founder, CEO Stylus Innovation (acquired by Artisoft in 1996), Direct Hit (acquired by Ask Jeeves in 2000), Ultimate Arena (now Xfire, Inc). Spkr. in fields of tech. and online gaming. Office: Xfire Inc 200 Middlefield Rd Ste 102 Menlo Park CA 94025

CASSIDY, ROBERT CHARLES, JR., lawyer; b. Beaumont, Tex., May 16, 1946; s. Robert Charles and Peggy (Timken) C.; m. Leslie Fleming Iben, Sept. 2, 1949; children: Robert Charles III, Thomas Reinhard, Leslie Anne Vallandingham. BA, Johns Hopkins U., 1968; JD, U. Pa., 1973; LLM, Georgetown U., 1977. Bar: Pa. 1973, US Dist. Ct. DC 1975, US Ct. Appeals (DC cir.) 1975, US Ct. Internat. Trade 1982, US Ct. Appeals (fed. cir.) 1982. Asst. counsel Office of Legis. Counsel U.S. Senate, 1973-75, internat. trade counsel Com. on Fin., 1975-79; gen. counsel Office of U.S. Trade Rep., Exec. Office of Pres., Washington, 1979-81; ptnr. Kaye, Scholer, Fierman, Hays & Handler, Washington, 1982-83, Wilmer Cutler Pickering Hale and Dorr, Washington, 1983—, trade group leader, 1985—2001, internat. practice group leader, 1995—2000. With US Army, 1968—70. Mem.: ABA (chmn. internat. trade law com. 1986—89, mem., bd. govs. 2004—), Am. Soc. Internat. Law., D.C. Bar Assn. Office: Wilmer Cutler Pickering Hale and Dorr 1875 Pennsylvania Ave NW Washington DC 20006 Office Phone: 202-663-6740. Business E-Mail: Robert.Cassidy@wilmerhale.com.

CASSIDY, WILLIAM ARTHUR, geology and planetary science educator; b. NYC, Jan. 3, 1928; s. John and Nellie (Briel) C.; m. Beverly J. Griffith, Aug. 29, 1959; children: Shauna Lynne, Laura Dawn, Brian John. BS in Geology, U. N. Mex., 1952; PhD in Geochemistry, Pa. State U., 1961. Seismic computer Superior Oil Co. of Calif., Midland, Tex., 1952-53; research scientist Lamont Geol. Obs., Palisades, NY, 1961-67; assoc. prof. geology and planetary sci. U. Pitts., 1968-80, prof., 1981-98, prof. emeritus, 1998—. Trustee Univ. Space Research Assn., Columbia, Md., 1975-82, chmn., 1978-79; chmn. meteorite working group Lunar and Planetary Sci. Inst., Houston, 1977-83 Author: Meteorites, Ice and Antarctica, 2003; contbr. articles to profl. jours. Served with USNR, 1945-46. Recipient Antarctic Svc. medal NSF, 1978; Fulbright student, 1953-54; grantee NSF, NASA. Mem. Am. Geophys. Union, Meteoritical Soc. (Barringer award 1995), Antarctican Soc. (Washington). Office: U Pitts 200 Space Research Coordination Ctr Pittsburgh PA 15620-3332 Home Phone: 412-373-0457. Business E-Mail: ansmet@pitt.edu.

CASSILL, HERBERT CARROLL, artist; b. Percival, Iowa, Dec. 24, 1928; s. Howard Earl and Mary Elizabeth (Glosser) C.; m. Jean Kuniko Kubota, Aug. 23, 1951; children: Sarah Eden, J. Aaron. Student, Purdue U., 1944-45; B.F.A., State U. Iowa, 1948, M.F.A., 1950. Instr. printmaking State U. Iowa, Iowa City, 1953-57; prof., head dept. printmaking Cleve. Inst. Art, 1957-91, prof. emeritus, 1991—. One man shows include Oakland Art Mus., Calif., Ohio State U., Columbus, Cleve. Inst. Art, U. Wis., William Busta Gallery, 1990, 93, 96, 2001; group shows include Library of Congress, Washington, Bklyn. Art Mus., Bradford Internat. Invitational, 1984; represented in permanent collections, Mus. Modern Art, NYC, Cleve. Mus. Art, Oakland Art Mus., San Francisco Art Mus., and others. Tiffany fellow printmaking, 1953 Home: 3084 Coleridge Rd Cleveland OH 44118-3556 Office: 11141 East Blvd Cleveland OH 44106-1710 Personal E-mail: hcprint@hotmail.com.

CASSIMATIS, PETER JOHN, economics professor; b. Greece, Jan. 30, 1928; came to U.S., 1946, naturalized, 1946; s. John G. and Coula N. (Lourantos) C.; m. Margaret Ann Nell, Nov. 30, 1958; 1 son, Gregory. BCE, CUNY, 1953, MBA, 1961; PhD, New Sch. Social Research, 1967. Registered profl. engr., N.Y.; cert. cost analyst. Project mgr. several mgmt. and engring. cons. firms, 1953-64; prof. econs. and finance Fairleigh Dickinson U., Teaneck, NJ, 1964-99, emeritus prof. econs. and finance, 1999—. Vis. prof. Center for Planning and Econ. Research, Athens, Greece, 1972-73 Author: Economics of the Construction Industry, 1970, Construction and Economic Development, 1975, The Construciton Industry in Greece, 1976, Engineering Economics, 1988, Managerial Economics, 1996; contbr. articles to profl. jours. With US Army, 1946—47. Research fellow Found. Econ. Edn., 1970 Mem. Am. Econ. Assn., Eastern Econ. Assn., Nat. Assn. Bus. Economists, Acad. Internat. Bus., World Future Soc., Fin. Mgmt. Assn. Home: 19 Lorraine Dr Eastchester NY 10709-2008 Office: Fairleigh Dickinson U Economics Dept Teaneck NJ 07666

CASSINELLI, JOSEPH PATRICK, astronomy educator; b. Cin., Aug. 23, 1940; s. Herbert John and Louise Margaret (Schlottman) C.; m. Mary LeFever; children: Joseph Michael, Carolyn Marie, Mary Kathleen. BS in Physics, Xavier U., 1962; MS in Physics, U. Ariz., 1965; PhD in Astronomy, U. Wash., 1970. Research asst. Kitt Peak Nat. Obs., Tucson, 1963-65; research engr. Boeing Co., Seattle, 1965-66; postdoctoral research assoc. Joint Inst. for Lab. Astrophysics, Boulder, Colo., 1970-72; postdoctoral fellow U. Wis., Madison, 1972-73, asst. prof., 1973-77, assoc. prof., 1977-81, prof., 1981—2005, emeritus prof., 2005—, chmn. astronomy dept., 1986-89. Vis. scientist Space Astronomy Lab., Utrecht, the Netherlands, 1975-76, Space Telescope Sci. Inst., 1991, High Altitude Obs., 1998; Donders chair U. Utrecht, 1985; sr. vis. fellow dept. physics and astronomy U. Glasgow, Scotland, 1998, 2000. Co-author: Introduction to Stellar Winds, 1999. Langley Abbot research fellow Harvard Smithsonian Ctr. for Astrophysics, 1981; Fulbright research fellow Sonnenborgh Obs., 1986. Mem. Am. Astron. Soc., Internat. Astron. Union. Roman Catholic. Home: 1520 Chandler St Madison WI 53711-2210 Office: U Wis Astronomy Dept 475 N Charter St Madison WI 53706-1582 Business E-Mail: cassinelli@astro.wisc.edu.

CASSITY, MICHAEL DAVID, music therapy educator; b. Alexandria, Va., Oct. 18, 1945; s. Dale Max and Lucile Bessie Cassity; m. Julia Ellen Cravey, July 1, 1989; children: Sharel, Christopher, Austin. BA in Psychology, S.W. Bapt. U., Bolivar, Mo., 1971; M in Music Therapy, Loyola U., New Orleans, 1975; PhD, U. Iowa, 1985. Cert. music therapist. Music therapy intern S.E. La. Hosp., Mandeville, 1974; supr. edn. Belle Chasse (La.) State Sch., 1975—77; grad. asst. music therapy U. Iowa, Iowa City, 1977—79; asst. prof. music therapy Slippery Rock (Pa.) State U., 1979—81; prof., dir. music therapy S.W. Okla. State U., Weatherford, 1981—2001; prof., dir. music therapy dept. Drury U., Springfield, Mo., 2001—. Pianist S.W. Playhouse Theater, Clinton, Okla., 1998—2001; prof. emeritus Bd. Regents of Okla. Colls., Oklahoma City, 2001. Author: Multimodal Psychiatric Music Therapy, 1998; contbr. articles to profl. jours. Grant writer Barry Count Bd. for Developmentally Disabled, 2004, Lawrence County Bd. for Developmentally Disabled, 2004. Served with N.G., 1966—71. Mem.: Am. Music Therapy Assn. (pres. S.W. Region 1985—87, assembly of dels. 1996—2001, editl. bd. Jour. Music Therapy 2001—07, Hon. award for outstanding contbns. to rsch. 1998). Republican. Baptist. Avocations: piloting private plane, playing jazz piano. Home: 4598 S Quail Creek Ave Springfield MO 65810 Office: Drury U 900 N Benton Ave Springfield MO 65802 Office Phone: 417-873-7370. Business E-Mail: mcassity@drury.edu.

CASSO, RAMIRO RAUL, physician, academic administrator; b. Laredo, Tex., Aug. 4, 1922; s. Francisco Margarito and Josefa (Villarreal) C.; m. Emma Laurel, July 18, 1949; children: Thelma Casso Morales, Lydia Casso Tummel, Sylvia Casso, Daniel, David BSME, Tex. A&M U., College Station, 1943; BA in Chemistry, Baylor U., Waco, Tex., 1952; MD, U. Tex., Dallas, 1956. Diplomate Am. Bd. Family Practice. Hydraulic engr. Internat. Boundary and Water Commn., Laredo, 1948-50; tchr. math. Martin HS, Laredo, 1946—48; med. intern Robert B. Green Hosp., San Antonio, 1956-57; pvt. family med. practice McAllen, Tex., 1957—95; v.p. instnl. advancement South Tex. CC Hidalgo-Starr County CC Dist., McAllen, 1995—2002. Adj. prof. Tex. A&M U. Health Sci. Ctr., 1999-2004; bd. dirs. McAllen Mcpl. Hosp./McAllen Med. Ctr. Hosp., 1975-85; founder, bd. dirs. Nuestra Clinica del Valle, 1975-85; mem. nat. adv. bd. health rsch. facilities NIH, Washington, 1964-67; participant White House Confs. on Food and Food Nutrition and Health, Washington, 1965-69; spkr. on pub. health and primary care issues pertaining to South Tex. and US-Mex. borderlands; presenter Hispanic health issues position Tex. Minority Health Conf., Houston, 1999 *On May 1, 2007, the University of Texas-Pan American of Edinburg, Texas held the Inaugural Texas-Mexico Borderlands Symposium to honor Dr. Ramiro R. Casso for having founded, during the past 50 years, 3 charity medical clinics to treat farm workers and other indigents who cannot afford to pay for medical care. He was also honored for helping to negotiate, as a member of a LULAC delegation in 1948 with Attorney General Price Daniels, the end to segregation of Latino children in Texas public schools.* Mem. McAllen Ind. Sch. Dist. Sch. Bd., 1959-65; mem., v.p. Tex. Bd. Health, Austin, 1977-81, 91-97; mem. Texas Human (Employment) Rights Commn., Austin, 1983-87; established charity clinic for farm workers United Farmworkers, McAllen, 1968; founded Nuestra Clin. Hidalgo County, Tex., 1974; bd. dirs. Area Health Edn. Ctr., 1997-98; pres., bd. dirs. El Milagro Clinic Bd., 1998—; founder El Milagro Charity Primary Care Clinic, McAllen, Tex., 1995. Capt. anti-aircraft arty. US Army, 1943-46 Named McAllen Man of Yr., McAllen C. of C., 1996, Notable Rio Grande Valley Hispanic, U. Tex.-PanAm., Edinburg, 1999, 100 Outstanding Hispanic-Ams. in Tex. in 20th Century Latino Monthly Mag., 2000, Star Supporter of Edn., South Tex. Coll., 2006; recipient Bishop Medeiros Golden Deeds award Tex. AFL-CIO and United Farmworkers, 1970, yearly award Hidalgo County Women's Polit. Caucus, 1991, Disting. Citizen award League United L.Am. Citizens, 1997, Living Legend award South Tex. C.C., 2002, Golden Trowel Masonic award City of Rio Grande and McAllen Tex. Lodges, 2003; Dr. Ramiro R. Casso S.T.C.C. Nursing and Allied Health Ctr. bldg. named in his honor, 2001. Fellow Am. Acad. Family Physicians; mem. AMA (life), Tex. Med. Assn. (life). Democrat. Baptist. Avocations: travel, reading, hunting, fishing. Office: El Milagro Clinic 901 E Vermont St Mcallen TX 78501 Home: 3400 West Pecan Mcallen TX 78501 Office Phone: 956-686-8012.

CASSON, ALAN GRAHAM, thoracic surgeon, researcher; b. Birmingham, Eng., Apr. 22, 1958; arrived in Can., 1981; m. Sharon Margaret Coffey; 1 child, Angela. MB ChB, Manchester U., Eng., 1981; MSc, Meml. U., St. John's, Nfld., Can., 1986. Asst. prof. surgery and oncology U. Western Ont., Canada, 1991-93; asst. prof. surgery, program dir. thoracic surgery U. Toronto, Canada, 1994-97; prof. thoracic surgery U. of Warwick, England, 1997-98; cons. thoracic surgery Heartlands Hosp., Birmingham, England, 1997-98; prof. surgery, head divsn. thoracic surgery Dalhousie U., Halifax, N.S., Canada, 1998—2006; F. H. Wigmore prof. and head dept. surgery Royal U. Hosp., U. Sask., Saskatoon, Canada, 2006—. Author: Oncogene Activation in Esophageal Cancer, 1992, Key Topics in Thoracic Surgery, 1999, Molecular Biology of Cancer, 2004; asst. editor Cancer Detection and Prevention; mem. editl. bd. Jour. Surg. Oncology, Diseases of the Esophagus; contbr. chpts. to surg. textbooks and articles to profl. jours. Fellow ACS, Royal Coll. Surgeons Can., Am. Coll. Chest Physicians (Young Investigator award 1993); mem. Internat. Soc. for Diseases of the Esophagus, Am. Assn. for Thoracic Surgery, Am. Assn. Cancer Rsch., Soc. Thoracic Surgeons, World Ortn. Specialized Studies Diseases Esophagus (mem. permanent sci. com.). Avocations: fly fishing, squash, sailing. Office: Royal Univ Hosp Univ Saskatchewan 103 Hosp Dr Rm 2646 Saskatoon S7N 0W8 Canada Home Phone: 902-479-7091; Office Phone: 306-966-8641.

CASSON, RICHARD FREDERICK, lawyer, hotel executive; b. Boston, Apr. 11, 1939; s. Louis H. and Beatrix S. C. AB, Colby Coll., 1960; JD, U. Chgo., 1963. Bar: Ill. 1963, Mass. 1964. Ptnr. Casson & Casson, Boston, 1967-68; assoc. counsel, corp. sec. Bankers Leasing Corp., 1968-75; asst. gen. counsel, corp. sec. Commonwealth Planning Corp., 1975-76; assoc. gen. counsel, asst. sec. Prudential Capital Corp., 1976-92; pres. Autumn Crest Corp., 1991-98; v.p. Casseden Corp. Asst. innkeeper Jackson House Inn, Woodstock, Vt. Capt. JAGC U.S. Army, 1964-67. Decorated Bronze Star. Jewish. Home and Office: 6648 John Smith Ln Hayes VA 23072 Office Phone: 804-642-6006. Personal E-mail: rfcasson@cox.net.

CASSOTTO, MARY LOU GRACE, counselor, educator, lawyer; b. Winsted, Conn., Feb. 12, 1949; d. Vito Anthony Cassotto and Grace Lucy Paxcia; m. Donald J. McCarthy, Jr., Oct. 17, 1977 (div. May 2001); 1 child, Gabriella McCarthy. BA in English, Coll. New Rochelle, 1974; JD, Seton Hall U., 1974; MEd, Trinity U., 1981; cert. in art, Ctrl. Conn. State U., 1991; cert. ednl. adminstr., U. Conn., 1993; MLS, So. Conn. State U., 2007. Assoc. lawyer Athanson & Webber, Hartford, Conn., 1974—81; tchr. art and English East Cath., Manchester, Conn., 1981—93; counselor Cath. Family Svcs., Hartford, 1995—97; tchr., counselor Gastonbury/Middletown/Windsor Sch. Sys., Middletown, Conn., 1997—. Adj. prof. Tunxis C.C., Farmington, Conn., Manchester C.C., Conn., Eastern Conn. C.C., Willimantic, Conn., U. Hartford. Mem.: AAUW (legis. chair 1972—73), Nat. Coun. Tchrs. English, Hartford Women's Polit. Caucus (chair 1972—74), Phi Delta Gamma (legis. chair 1982—84). Republican. Roman Catholic. Achievements include establishment of Permanent Com. on Status of Women of the Conn. bar, first Latchkey Day Care of Conn., first woman chair Rocky Hill Econ. Devel. Commn; aided in establishment of first Battered Wives' Shelter, chair/draftee Battered Wives' Bill; hiring of first woman lobbyist, obtaining of funds for first woman who ran for Senate, lobbying for women's rights. Home: 17 Adenas Walk Glastonbury CT 06033 Office Phone: 860-830-8805. Personal E-mail: mlcassotto@aol.com.

CASSTEVENS, CHARLES FRANKLIN, JR., music educator, minister; b. Elkin, NC, Jan. 25, 1964; s. Charles Franklin and Nonnie Etta Casstevens; m. Holly Anne Hykes, Sept. 26, 1998; 1 child, Trevor Jordan. BS in Music and Bus., Wingate U., NC, 1986; MAT, Winthrop U., 1993. Min. to music/youth Mineral Springs Bapt. Ch., Jonesville, NC, 1982; min. to youth South Florence (S.C.) Bapt. Ch., 1985; ch. accompanist Union Bapt. Ch., Monroe, NC, 1985; min. to music/youth New Salem Bapt. Ch., Monroe, 1985—; music specialist Benton Heights Elem. Sch., Monroe, 1986—. Accompanist Charlotte (N.C.) Children's Choir, 1998; chmn. youth com. Union Bapt. Assn., Monroe, 2001—; chmn. site base Benton Heights Elem. Sch., Monroe, 2002—, chmn. splty. areas, 2003—05. Named Tchr. of Yr., Benton Heights Elem. Sch., 1995. Mem.: Music Educators Nat. Conf. Republican. Baptist. Avocations: tennis, arts events, travel. Office: Benton Heights Elem Sch 1200 Concord Ave Monroe NC 28112 Home: 2805 Telefair Ln Monroe NC 28110 Office Phone: 704-296-3100. Office Fax: 704-296-3106. E-mail: fcasstevens@carolina.rr.com.

CASSULLO, JOANNE LEONHARDT, foundation administrator; b. Glen Cove, NY, Dec. 2, 1955; d. John Louis and Dorothea Louise (Leonhardt) C. BA in English, Elementary Ed., & Fine Arts, Roanoke Coll., Salem, Va., 1978; MFA, So. Meth. U., 1982. Cert. tchr. elem. edn., Va. Dir. counseling and edn. PCI, Inc., Ft. Worth, 1978-80; gallery asst. Washburn Gallery, Inc., NYC, 1983-86; pres. Dorothea L. Leonhardt Found., NYC, 1988—. Contbr. articles to profl. jours. Trustee Whitney Mus. Am. Art, NYC, 1985—, v.p.; bd. dirs. Phoenix House Found., Inc., NYC, 1982—, Bklyn. Acad. Music, 1989—, Children of Alcoholics Found., NYC, 1990—, RxART, Children's Advocacy Ctr. of Manhattan, Housing Enterprises for Less Privileged (HELP USA). Helena Rubinstein fellow in Mus. Studies, Whitney Mus. Am. Art, 1982-83. Mailing: c/o Whitney Mus Am Art 945 Madison Ave New York NY 10021

CAST, ANITA HURSH, retired small business owner; b. Columbus, Ohio, July 11, 1939; d. Charles Walter and Hulda Marie (Ramsey) Hursh; m. William R. Cast, Apr. 1, 1961; children: Jennifer, Carter, Meghan. BA, DePauw U., 1961. Ptnr. Cast Hursh and Assocs., Ft. Wayne, Ind., 1982—; pianist Words and Music, Ft. Wayne, 1983—; owner Anita Cast's Wearable Art, Ft. Wayne, 1986—. Bd. dirs. Fort Wayne Philharm., Indpls. Internat. Violin Competition; past pres. Ind. U. Friends of Music, Ind. Endowment for the Arts; mem. adv. bd. Leadership Ft. Wayne; mem. dean's nat. adv. bd. Jacobs Sch. Music Ind. U. Author: (arts chpt.) New History of Fort Wayne, New History of Fort Wayne/Allen County. Advisory bd., pres. Am. Symphony Orch. League, vol., v.p., 1985—86; commr. Ind. Gov.'s

Mansion Commn., 1987, Ind. Arts Commn., 1979—87; bd. dirs. Ft. Wayne Philharm., pres., 1977—79; mem. Mayor's Bicentennial Exec. Bd., 1989—94, Ind. Cultural Congress Hon. Com.; active Ft. Wayne's Celebrate 2000 Com.; pres. bd. of friends of music Jacobs Sch. Music, 2007—; pres. Ind. U. Friends of Music, 2007—; bd. dirs. WBNI Nat. Pub. Radio, Ft. Wayne; chmn. bd. dirs. Fine Arts Found., Ft. Wayne, 1988; pres. bd. dirs. Ind. Endowment Arts; chmn. bd. dirs. Arts United Greater Ft. Wayne, 1988—90; bd. dirs. Arts United; mem. nat. adv. coun. Ind. Jacobs Sch. Music; pres., bd. dirs. Ind. U. Friends Music, 1995—97, past pres. exec. com., pres., 2007—; v.p. adv. bd. Leadership Ft. Wayne; pres. Met. YMCA, Ft. Wayne, 1986—; bd. mem. Internat. Violin Competition, Ind.; chmn. search com. Ft. Wayne Philharmonic. Named Miss Ind.; recipient Sagamore of the Wabash awards (2); Lily Endowment Leadership fellow. Mem.: Quest Club, Duodecimo Club (hon.). Republican. Episcopalian. Avocations: music, cooking, golf, hiking, reading. Home and Office: Anita Cast Wearable Art 4401 Taylor St Fort Wayne IN 46804-1913 Personal E-mail: anitatune@yahoo.com.

CASTAGNA, VANESSA J., retail executive; b. Muncie, Ind., 1949; m. Neil Castagna. BS in psychology and speech comm., Purdue U., 1971. With Lazarus most recently as sr. v.p. and gen. mgr., 1972—85; v.p. merchandising - women's Target Stores, 1985—92; sr. v.p., gen. merchandising mgr. - women's and jr.'s Marshall's Stores, Mass., 1992—94; sr. v.p., gen. mdse. mgr. - home decor, furniture, crafts, children's apparel Wal-Mart Stores, Bentonville, Ark., 1994—96, sr. v.p., gen. mdse. mgr. - women's and children's accessories and apparel, 1996—99; exec. v.p. J.C. Penney Co., Inc., Plano, Tex., 1999—2004; COO JC Penney Stores, Merchandising, & Catalog, 1999—2001; pres., COO J.C. Penney Stores, Catalog, & Internet, Plano, Tex., 2001—03, chmn., CEO, 2003—04; exec. chmn. Mervyns, Hayward, Calif., 2005—07; sr. mem., ops. divsn. Cerberus Capital Mgmt., NYC, 2005—. Chair Women's Leadership Coun. United Way of Met. Dallas; bd. dirs. JC Penney Afterschool Fund, Nat. Minority Supplier Devel. Coun., Cox Sch. Bus. So. Methodist U. Named one of most powerful women, Forbes mag., 2001—05, Next 20 Female CEOs, Pink Mag. & Forté Found., 2006; recipient AMY award, Young Menswear Assn., 2006.*

CASTAGNA, WILLIAM JOHN, federal judge; Student, U. Pa., 1941-43; LLB, JD, U. Fla., 1949. Bar: Fla. 1949. Ptnr. MacKenzie, Castagna, Bennison & Gardner, 1970-79; judge U.S. Dist. Judge (mid. dist.) Fla., 1979—, now sr. judge. Democrat.

CASTAGNETTI, DAVID A., political strategist; BA, Lake Forest Coll.; MS in Pub. Adminstrn., U. Mass. Sr. staff mem. Congressman Ed Markey; chief of staff Congressman Norman Y. Mineta, Sen. Max Baucus; ptnr. Bergner, Bockorny, Castagnetti & Hawkins; dir. Congl. affairs John Kerry for US Senate campaign, 2004; ptnr. Mehlman Vogel Castagnetti Inc., Washington. Democrat. Office: Mehlman Vogel Castagnetti Ste 1100 1341 G St NW Washington DC 20005 Office Phone: 202-585-0258. Office Fax: 202-393-3031. E-mail: dcredsox@mvc-dc.com.*

CASTAGNOLA, GEORGE JOSEPH, JR., arbitrator, secondary school educator; b. Scotia, Calif., July 6, 1950; s. George Joseph and Olga Esther Castagnola; m. Sandra Annette Castagnola, June 7, 1975; children: George Joseph III, Laura, Joseph. Grad., U. San Francisco, 1974; JD, N.W. Calif. U., Sacramento, 1990, D Juridical Sci., 1992. BAr: Calif. 1990. Tchr. El Molino H.S., Forestville, Calif., 1977—; charter boat capt. Castagnola Fishing, Petaluma, Calif., 1971—; prof. law N.W. Calif. U., 1990—; atty., mediator Law and Mediation Office of George Castagnola, Petaluma, Calif., 1990—. Cpl. USMCR, 1968-74. Mem. Calif. Bar Assn., Sonoma County Bar Assn., Calif. Tchrs. Assn., Golden Gate Sport Fishing Assn. Roman Catholic. Avocations: weightlifting, fishing. Home and Office: 802 Wine Ct Petaluma CA 94954-7420

CASTALDI, DAVID LAWRENCE, health products executive; b. Logansport, Ind., Jan. 27, 1940; s. Lawrence J. and Ruth (Speitel) C.; m. Judith A. Pille, June 18, 1966; children: Valerie A., Maria C. BBA maxima cum laude, U. Notre Dame, 1962; MBA with high distinction, Harvard U., 1966. Sec., bd. dirs. Mid-West Spring Mfg. Co., Inc., Chgo., 1961-71; with Baxter-Travenol Labs., Inc., 1971-87, exec. v.p. Artificial Organs divsn. Deerfield, Ill., 1976-77, pres. hyland therapeutics divsn. Glendale, Calif., 1977-87; founder, pres., CEO, bd. dirs. BioSurface Tech., Inc., Cambridge, Mass., 1987-94; founder, pres. Synovex Corp., Cambridge, 2004—06, also bd. dirs. Bd. dirs. Biolink Corp., Middleboro, Mass., chmn. bd. dir., 1995-98, CEO, 1996-98; founder, chmn. Cadent Med. Corp., Bedford, Mass., 1996-2000, CEO, 1998-1999; chancellor, CFO Roman Cath. Archdiocese Boston, 2001; bd. dirs., Nabi Biopharms., Boca Raton, Fla., chmn. audit com., 1996—, Embrex Inc., Durham, NC, Biolex Inc., Pittsboro, NC, Serica Technologies, Inc., Medford, Mass., Harbus Investors, Inc., St. Petersburg, Fla. treas. Mass. Biotech. Coun., 1991-93. Bd. transplantation svcs. ARC, 1988-90, nat. skin adv. coun., 1990-92; gov.'s biotech. subcom., 1991; trustee St. John's Sem., Brighton, Mass.; founder, Voice of the Faithful Inc., Newton, Mass., trustee, 2002-07, chmn. bd. trustees, 2005-07. With US Army, 1962—64. Republican. Roman Catholic.

CASTAÑEDA, JAMES AGUSTÍN, language educator, golf coach; b. Bklyn., Apr. 2, 1933; s. Ciro Castañeda and Edna May Sincock; m. Terrill Lynn McCauley, Sept. 14, 1957; 1 child, Christopher James; m. Clara Luz Gutiérrez, Dec. 9, 1991. BA summa cum laude, Drew U., 1954; MA, Yale U., 1955, PhD, 1958; Certificat d'Aptitude à l'Enseignement du Français à l'Etranger, Université Paris, 1957; postgrad., Universidad de Madrid, 1957—; student summer inst. tchrs. fgn. langs., Purdue U., 1959. Asst. to assoc. prof. Spanish and French Hanover (Ind.) Coll., 1958-61; asst. prof. Spanish Rice U., Houston, 1961-63, assoc. prof. Spanish, 1963-67, prof. Spanish, 1967—. Vis. prof. Spanish U. So. Calif., 1959, U. N.C., 1962, 68, Western N.Mex. U., 1970; Florence Purington vis. prof. Mt. Holyoke Coll., 1976-77; prof. summer program Hispanic studies in Spain Rice U., 1979, 82, 83-90, head freshman baseball coach, 1962-67, asst. varsity coach, 1962-83, chmn. dept. Classics, Italian, Portuguese, Russian and Spanish, 1964-72, moderator television series, 1964-67, 68-69, head golf coach, 1983-98; lectr., dir., adviser and sponsor numerous acad. and other coms. in field. Author: A Critical Edition of Lope de Vega's Las paces de los reyes, y Judía de Toledo, 1962, introducción, edición, 1971, Agustín Moreto, 1974, Mira de Amescua, 1977, El esclavo del demonio, 1980; contbr. numerous articles to profl. jours. Chmn. interview team in Europe Kent Fellowship Program, 1968; active Internat. Good Neighbor Coun. Rose Meml. scholar Drew U., 1950-54, Varsity Club scholar, Alumni Assn. Meml. scholar, Fulbright scholar Université de Paris, 1956-57, scholar Instituto de Cultura Hispánica, 1971; Danforth fellow Yale U., 1954-58, teaching fellow 1958—; named Miembro Titular, Instituto de Cultura Hispánica de Madrid, 1972, Hon. Master Will Rice Coll., 1976, Spanish Tchr. of Yr. and Fgn. Lang. Tchr. of Yr., Tex. Fgn. Lang. Tchrs.' Assn., 1982; recipient Drew U. Alumni Achievement award in Humanities, 1973, Will Rice Coll. James St. Fulton Svc. award 1973, Bklyn. Cadets Alumni Assn. Achievement award, 1976, Spanish Heritage award 1982, Disting. Svc. award Assn. Rice Alumni, 2000; named to Drew U. Athletics Hall of Fame, 1997. Mem. Am. Assn. Spanish and Portugese (numerous coms. and offices), Am. Assn. Tchrs. French, Am. Coun. Tchrs. Fgn. Langs. (del. affiliate assembly, 1970-75), S. Ctrl. Modern Lang. Assn. (various coms. and offices), Houston Area Tchrs. Fgn. Langs. (various coms. and offices), Modern Lang. Assn. (various coms. and offices), Inst. Hispanic Culture Houston (founding mem. 1966, numerous other coms. and offices), Hispanic Soc. Am. (hon.), Sigma Delta Pi (hon. pres. 1998). Office: Rice Univ 6100 Main St Houston TX 77005-1892 Office Phone: 713-348-3248. Business E-Mail: spangolf@rice.edu.

CASTEEL, CAMILLE, school system administrator; m. Tom Casteel; children: Tawni, Cari. EdD, Nova Southeastern U. Fischler Grad. Sch. of Edn. and Human Svcs., 1991. 1st grade tchr. to supt. Chandler Unified Sch. Dist., Ariz., 1971—91, supt., 1991—. Bd. dirs. Chandler C. of C.; bd. mem. Chandler Regional Hosp., 1988—; chmn. Cath. Healthcare West Southwest Divisional Bd.; founding mem. Ariz. Bus. Edn. Coalition. Named Ariz. Nat. Supt. of Yr., 2002, Woman of Distinction, Soroptimist Internat., 2004; recipient Excellence award, Ariz. Sch. Pub. Rels. Assn., Achievement award, Ariz. Year Round Edn. Assn., Disting. Alumni award, Nova Southeastern U., 2000, Excellence in Leadership award, East Valley Partnership, 2001. Office: Chandler Unified Sch Dist 1525 W Frye Rd Chandler AZ 85224 Office Phone: 480-812-7000. E-mail: casteel.camille@chandler.k12.az.us.

CASTEEN, JOHN THOMAS, III, academic administrator; b. Portsmouth, Va., Dec. 11, 1943; s. John Thomas and Naomi Irene (Anderson) C.; children: John Thomas IV, Elizabeth, Lars. BA (hon.), U. Va., 1965, MA, 1966, PhD, 1970; LLD (hon.), Shenandoah Coll. Conservatory Music, 1984; DHL (hon.), Bentley Coll., 1992; degree (hon.), Piedmont CC, Va., 1992; DPA, Bridgewater Coll., 1993; degree (hon.), U. Athens, Greece, 1996; DHL (hon.), Transylvania U., 1999. Asst. prof. English U. Calif., Berkeley, 1970—75; assoc. prof., dean admissions U. Va., Charlottesville, 1975—82; adj. prof. Va. Commonwealth U., Richmond, 1982—85; pres., prof. English U. Conn., Storrs, 1985—90; George M. Kaufman presdl. prof. of English U. Va., 1990—, pres., 1990—. Bd. dirs. NCAA, Wachovia, Inc., Sallie Mae, Ctrl. Va.'s Pub. Broadcasting; mem. Assn. Acad. Health Ctrs.' Coun. Health Scis. and Univ.; mem. com. Nat. Inst. on Alcohol Abuse and Alcoholism and Misuse on Coll. Campuses; chair Coun. for Higher Edn. Accreditation, 2000—. Author: 16 Stories, 1981; contbr. articles to various publs.; mem. editl. adv. bd. The Presidency. Sec. edn. Commonwealth of Va., Richmond, 1982-85; trustee Mariner's Mus., 1990—, Coll. Entrance Exam Bd., N.Y.C., 1980-90, chmn. 1986-88; mem. So. Regional Edn. Bd., 1982-85. New Eng. Bd. of Higher Edn., 1986-90; mem. nat. adv. com. Nat. Domestic Violence Media Campaign, 1992—; dir. Am. Coun. on Edn., 1993-96. Recipient Outstanding Virginian award, 1993, Gold medal award Nat. Inst. Social Scis., 1998. Mem. Assn. Am. Univs. (exec. com.), So. Assn. Colls. and Schs. (chair commn. on colls. 1995-97, pres.-elect 1997, pres. 1998), Assn. Governing Bds. Colls. and Schs. (coun. of pres. 1992—), Keswick Club, Farmington County Club, Commonwealth Club (Richmond), Phi Beta Kappa. Episcopalian. Office: P O Box 400224 Charlottesville VA 22904 E-mail: jtc@virginia.edu.*

CASTEL, JEAN GABRIEL, lawyer, educator, international arbitrator; b. Nice, France, 1928; Lic., U. Paris, 1948; JD, U. Mich., 1953; SJD, Harvard U., 1957; LLD (hon.), Aix-Marseille, France, 1988. Created queen's counsel. From asst. prof. to assoc. prof. law McGill U., 1954-57; now prof. emeritus law Osgoode Hall Law Sch., York U., Toronto, Ont. Author: International Law as Interpreted and Applied in Canada, 1978, Canadian Criminal Law: International and Transnational Aspects, 1981, Extraterritoriality in International Trade, 1988, The Canadian Law and Practice of International Trade, 1991, 2d edit., 1997, Canadian Conflict of Laws, 5th edit., 2002; editor: Can. Bar Rev., 1957-83. Mem. spl. group for settlement of disputes under Can.-U.S. Free Trade Agreement, 1989-93. Served with French Resistance, 1943-45. Decorated officer Order of Can., officier Ordre Nat. du Merite, chevalier Légion d'Honneur, Order of Ont.; recipient medal Law Soc. Upper Can., John Read medal Internat. Law. Fellow Acad. Arts and Scis., Royal Soc. Can.; mem. Can. Bar Assn. (hon.), Internat. Acad. Comparative Law (assoc.). Home Phone: 519-940-9862; Office Phone: 519-940-9862. E-mail: jgcastel@sympatico.ca.

CASTEL, P. KEVIN, federal judge; b. NYC, Aug. 5, 1950; BS, St. John's U., Jamaica, NY, 1972, JD, 1975; LLD (hon.), St. John's U., 2004. Bar: N.Y. 1976, U.S. Dist. Ct. (so. and ea. dists.) N.Y. 1976, U.S. Ct. Appeals (2nd cir.) 1979, U.S. Supreme Ct. 1983, U.S. Ct. Appeals (fed. cir.), 1986, U.S. Ct. Appeals (10th cir.), 1988, U.S. Ct. Appeals (3rd cir.) 1989, U.S. Ct. Appeals (4th cir.) 1991, U.S. Ct. Appeals (7th cir.) 1995, U.S. Ct. Appeals (11th cir.) 1997. Law clk. to judge U.S. Dist. Ct. (so. dist.) N.Y., 1975-77; assoc. Cahill Gordon & Reindel, NYC, 1977-83, ptnr., 1983—2003; judge U.S. Dist. Judge (so dist.) N.Y., 2003—. Mem. departmental disciplinary com. appellate divsn. 1st dept., 1987—93, hearing panel chair, 1991—93, mem. policy com., 1997—2002. Articles editor St. John's Law Rev., 1974-75. Mayor's panel Martin Luther King Jr. Inst. for Law and Social Justice, 1987—89; nat. chmn. ann. giving campaign St. John's U., 1994—95; bd. dirs. Legal Aid Soc., 2000—03. Recipient Pres.'s medal St. John's U., 2000. Fellow: N.Y. Bar Found., Am. Bar Found.; mem.: Fed. Bar Coun. (sec. 1983—85, trustee 1985—93, v.p. 1988—90, trustee 1997—2002, pres. 2000—02), Assn. Bar City of N.Y. (com. profl. and jud. ethics 1994—97, com. on jud. adminstrn. 1997—2000), N.Y. State Bar Assn. (com. on cts. of appellate jurisdiction 1979—86, com. fed. cts. of appellate jurisdiction 1979—86, com. fed. cts. 1986—89, chmn. com. fed practice 1989—91, exec. vice chmn. comml. and fed. litig. sect. 1991—92, chmn. 1993—94, ho. of dels. 1994—95), St. John's U. Law Sch. Alumni Assn. (bd. dirs. 1991—, v.p. 1998—2006, pres. 2006—07), Supreme Ct. Hist. Soc. Office: US Dist Ct So Dist NY 500 Pearl St New York NY 10007-1790

CASTELE, THEODORE JOHN, radiologist; b. New Castle, Pa., Feb. 1, 1928; s. Theodore Robert and Anne Mercedes (McNavish) C.; m. Jean Marie Willse, Oct. 20, 1951; children: Robert, Ann Marie, Richard, Mary Kathryn, Thomas, Daniel, John. BS, Case Western Res. U., 1951, MD, 1957. Diplomate Am. Bd. Radiology, 1962. Intern then resident U. Hosps. Cleve., 1957-61, fellow, 1961-62; dir. of radiology Luth. Med. Ctr., Cleve., 1968-75, 77-89, chief of staff, 1975-81; pres. Med. Ctr. Radiologists, Inc., Cleve., 1978-95; v.p. med. and corp. devel. Health Cleve. Inc., 1989-91; chmn. Lakeshore Radiology Inc., Cleve., 1991-96, emeritus chmn., 1996—. Med. editor sta. WEWS-TV-ABC, Cleve., 1975-99; chmn. bd. Med. Cons. Imaging Co., Cleve., 1981-97; asst. clin. prof. radiology Case Western Res. U., chmn. dean's tech. coun. Sch. Medicine, 1996—, chmn. vis. com. Cleve. Health Scis. Libr., chmn. campaign for future of acad. medicine, 1998—. Exec. editor Prime mag., 2000—. Chmn. Southwestern dist. Greater Cleve. coun. Boy Scouts Am., 1969, 73; mem. bd. med. cons. Cleve. Police Dept., pres., 1988-90; trustee Comty. Dialysis Ctr., chmn. 1997-99, chmn. emeritus, 2000—; active Luth. Med. Ctr. Found., chmn. bd. trustees, 1969-75, pres., 1988-90; trustee Case Western Res. U., Blue Cross/Blue Shield Ohio, Greater Cleve. Hosp. Assn., Fairview Health, Luth. Med. Ctr., 1975-80, Fairview Hosp. Found.; bd. trustees Fairview Luth. Hosp. Found., 1999—, No. Ohio Lung Assn.; chmn. Health Mus. Cleve., 1996—, Humility of Mary Healthcare Sys., 1995-98; dir. Coun. Pub. Reps. for NIH, 1999-2001. With USN, 1946-47. Recipient Order of Merit award Boy Scouts Am., 1971, Silver Beaver award, 1972, Nat. Disting. Eagle Scout award, 1984, Frances Payne Bolton Sch. of Nursing Disting. Svc. award, 1990, Outstanding Philanthropist award Nat. Soc. of Fundraising Execs., 1991, Alumnus of the Yr. award Dept. Radiology of Case Western Res. U., 1996, LMC Found. Women's Bd. award, 1996, Luth. Hosp. award Fairview Health Sys. Bd., 1996, Midwest Nursing Rsch. Soc. Media award, 1998, Lamplighter Humanitarian award 2001; named Knight of the Equestrian, Order of the Holy Sepulchre of Jerusalem, 1993—; recipient Magis award St. Ignatius H.S.; named to Med. Hall of Fame, Case Western Res. U., Cleve. Mag., 1999, No. Ohio Italian-Am. Found., 1999. Fellow Am. Coll. Radiology; mem. AMA (Physician Spkr. Gold award 1978, 80, Silver 1979, Bronze 1978, Benjamin Rush award 1989, Golden Achievement award Golden Age Ctrs., 1996, chmn. Ohio del. 1987-96), Ohio State Med. Assn. (5th dist. councilor 1977-79, Spl. award 1979, Disting. Svc. award 1997), Cleve. Radiol. Soc. (pres. 1969-70), Cleve. Med. Libr. Assn. (pres. 1996, 97-98), Case Western Res. U. Med. Alumni Assn. (pres. 1971-72, 91-92, Disting. Svc. award 1987, Spl. Trustees award 1997, Univ. medal 1998), Cleve. Acad. Medicine (pres. 1974-75, Disting. Mem. award 1990, Disting. Svc. award 1984, Spl. Honor award and portrait 1998), Ohio State Radiol. Soc. (Silver award 1990). Home: 18869 Canyon Rd Cleveland OH 44126-1703 Office: Case Western Reserve Univ Sch Medicine Cleveland OH 44106

CASTELLANETA, DAN (DANIEL LOUIS), actor; b. Chgo., Sept. 10, 1958; m. Deb Lacusta, 1987. Grad., No. Ill. U. Actor, writer, originator (TV series) The Simpsons, 1987 (2 Emmys, 1992, 1993), voice Homer Simpson, Grampa Abe Simpson, Krusty the Klown, Barney Gumble, Groundskeeper Willie, Mayor Quimby, Hans Moleman, Sideshow Mel, The Simpsons, 1989—2006 (Primetime Emmy for voice-over performance, 2004), Tiny Toon Adventures, 1990, Chula The Tarantula, Fievel's American Tails, 1991, Dr. Emmett Lathrop Doc Brown, Back to the Future, 1991, Mister Thickley, Taz-Mania, 1991, Megavolt, Darkwing Duck, 1991—95, Mittens, Bill, Eek! The Cat!, 1992, Genie, Icafrak, Aladdin, 1993, Grandpa Steely Phil, Willie the Golly Olly Man, Early, Dr. Murray Steiglitz, Nick Vermicelli, Hey Arnold!, 1996, Charles' father, The Tick, 1994, (TV films) Comet and Blitzen, The Online Adventures of Ozzie the Elf, 1997, Postman, Olive, the Other Reindeer, 1999 (Annie award, 1993), (films) All Dogs Go to Heaven, 1996, Grandpa Steely Phil, Nick Vermicelli, Hey Arnold! The Movie, 2002, Thing One and Thing Two, The Cat in the Hat, 2003, The Simpsons Movie, 2007; actor: (TV series) Tracy Ulman Show, (guest appearance) Alf, 1986, LA Law, 1986, Married.with Children, 1987, Murphy Brown, 1988, Wings, 1990, Dream On, 1990, Bagdad Café, 1990, Dinosaurs, 1991, Rugrats, 1991, Mad About You, 1992, Grace Under Fire, 1993, Bakersfield, P.D., 1993, NYPD Blue, 1993, Frasier, 1993, Animaniacs, 1993, Duckman, 1994, Friends, 1994, George Carlin Show, 1994, The Critic, 1994, Drew Carey Show, 1995, Cybill, 1995, Nash Bridges, 1996, Everybody Loves Raymond, 1996, Johnny Bravo, 1997, That '70s Show, 1998, Hercules, 1998, Batman Beyond, 1999, Futurama, 1999, Yes, Dear, 2000, Jackie Chan Adventures, 2000, Buzz Lightyear of Star Command, 2000, Reba, 2001, Adventures of Jimmy Neutron: Boy Genius, 2002, Lucky, 2003, The Pitts, 2003; actor (TV films) Lady Against the Odds, 1999, Tracey Takes on New York, 1993, Related by Birth, 1994, The Computer Wore Tennis Shoes, 1995, My Giant, 1998, Rhapsody in Bloom, 1998, Laughter on the 23rd Floor, 2001, Behind the Camera: The Unauthorized Story of Charlie's Angels, 2004, (films) Nothing in Common, 1986, War of the Roses, 1989, Love Affair, 1994, The Client, 1994, The Settlement, 1999, Return to Neverland, 2002, Adventures in Homeschooling, 2004, I-See-You.Com, 2006, I Want Someone to Eat Cheese With, 2006, The Pursuit of Happyness, 2006. Mem. Chgo. Second City. Achievements include has a trademark phrase d'oh from the Simpsons added to the Oxford Dictionary. Office: The Simpsons c/o Twentieth TV Matt Groening's Office PO Box 900 Beverly Hills CA 90213*

CASTELLANI, FREDERICK C., insurance company executive; Sr. v.p. investment and retirement svcs. CIGNA, 1993—96; sr. v.p. MassMutual Fin. Group, Springfield, Mass., 1996—2001, exec. v.p. retirement svcs., 2001—. Pres., trustee MassMutual Select Funds, 2001—; bd. trustees MML Series Investment Fund, 2001—, v.p., 2006—, MassMutual Premier Funds, 2004—; trustee, vice chmn., v.p. MML Series Investment Fund II, 2006—. Office: MassMutual Fin Group 1295 State St Springfield MA 01111-0001 Office Phone: 800-767-1000.*

CASTELLANO, JOSEPHINE MASSARO, medical records specialist; d. Ignazio and Maria Massaro Castellano. BS in Med. Tech., Fla. State U., 1952; tchrs. cert., U. Tampa, 1955; MA, Columbia U., 1961. Med. technologist St. Joseph's Hosp., Tampa, Fla., 1952—55; tchr. Hillsborough County Sch. Bd., Tampa, 1955—85; med. records specialist Robert Martinez, M.D., Tampa, 1985—95, David L. Castellano, DDS, Tampa, 1996—, Domenic M. Castellano, DDS, Tampa, 1996—. Mem.: AAUW (mem. adv. bd. 1999—2002), Christian Med. Found. (mem. adv. bd. 1996—2003), Kappa Delta Pi (mem. adv. bd. 2000—02). Roman Catholic. Avocations: reading, horseback riding, tennis, gardening, bowling. Home: 305 N Hesperides St Tampa FL 33609-2020 Office: David L and Domenic M Castellano DDS 8365 W Hillsborough Ave Tampa FL 33615-3899

CASTELLANO, MARK JOSEPH, music educator; b. Oceanside, NY, Aug. 5, 1957; s. Salvatore Francis and Carmela Cecelia Castellano. MusB in edn., La. State U., 1975—79; MusM in edn., U. of Southwestern La., 1983—85. Profl. Educator's Certificate Fla. Dir. of bands Acadia Parish Pub. Schools, Rayne, La., 1980—82; asst. to the dir. of bands U. of Southwestern La., Lafayette, La., 1985—87; dir. of bands Mariner H.S., Cape Coral, Fla., 1987—93; Three Oaks Mid. Sch., Ft. Myers, Fla., 1993—; adj. instr. of music Barry U., Ft. Myers, Fla. Instr., summer music camps Music Found. of SW Fla., Ft. Myers, Fla., 1994—; v.p. Teachers Assn. of Lee County, Ft. Myers, Fla.; instr., summer staff devel. inst. Sch. Dist. of Lee County, Ft. Myers, Fla., lee county core curriculum writing team for music, Ft. Myers, Fla. Mem. Music Program Exploration Task Force, Fla. Gulf Coast U., Ft. Myers, Fla., 2000—01; chmn. and founding mem. Unified Arts Coun., Sch. Dist. of Lee County, Ft. Myers, 1995—98; mem. Bargaining Team, Teachers Assn. of Lee County, Ft. Myers, 1998—2004; chmn., crisis com. Teachers Assn. of Lee County, Ft. Myers, 1997—99; founding mem. Lee County Arts for a Complete Edn., Ft. Myers; mem. Polit. Action Com., Teachers Assn. of Lee County, Ft. Myers, Fla., 1999—2004. Named Tchr. of Distinction, Golden Apple Tchr. Recognition Program, Found. for Pub. Edn., Lee County, 1997, 1998, 2000, 2003; recipient Outstanding Grad. Student, Music Dept., Music Dept., U. of Soutwestern La., 1984, Finalist, Golden Apple Tchr. Recognition Program, Found. for Pub. Edn., Lee County, 1999 and 2001; Music scholarship, La. State U., 1975—79, Grad. Tchg. Assistantship, U. of Southwestern La., 1983—85. Mem.: NEA, Island Coast Educators (mem. polit. action com. 2000—), Internat. Horn Soc., Am. Sch. Band Directors Assn., Am. Fedn. of Teachers, Fla. Edn. Assn., Tchrs. Assn. Lee County (v.p. 2002—04, mem. membership devel. team 2003—), Music Educators Nat. Conf., Fla. Music Educators Assn., Fla. Bandmasters Assn., Pi Kappa Lambda, Phi Mu Alpha Sinfonia. Avocations: fishing, writing, reading. Office Phone: 239-267-9272.

CASTELLANO, MICHAEL JOHN, investment company executive; b. Bklyn., May 17, 1946; s. Wilbur Paul and Mary Ellen (Quigley) C.; m. Kathleen Suzanne Nitka, Aug. 5, 1967; children: Susan Kathleen, Karen Lizabeth. BBA, Baruch Coll., 1967. CPA, N.Y. Sr. acct. Deloitte & Touche, NYC, 1980—91; with Merrill Lynch & Co. Inc., NYC, 1991—2001, sr. v.p., 1980—2001, chief control officer capital markets bus., sr. v.p., corp. controller, chmn. Merrill Lynch Internat. Bank; mng. dir., CFO Lazard Ltd., NYC, 2001—. Mem. Cherry Valley Country Club (Skillman, N.J.). Office: Lazard Ltd 30 Rockefeller Plz New York NY 10112 Business E-Mail: michael.castellano@lazard.com.

CASTELLI, ALEXANDER GERARD, accountant; b. NYC, May 3, 1929; s. Gerard and Carmela (Canzoneri) C.; m. Michelina Castelli, Jan. 8, 1961; children— Gerard, Alexander, JoAnn. BS, N.Y. U., 1958. C.P.A., N.Y., Md., 1970. Chief accountant Daitch Crystal Dairies, Inc., Bronx, NY, 1965-68; asst. controller Alexander's, Inc., NYC, 1968-70; v.p., treas. Bond Stores, Inc., NYC, 1970-73; v.p. fin. McBrides, Inc., Washington, 1973-77; mng. ptnr. Castelli & Catudal, P.A., 1977—. Bd. advisers Nat. Bank of Washington. Served with CIC AUS, 1951-53. Recipient Founder's Day award NYU, 1958 Mem. Am. Inst. CPA's, N.Y. State Soc. CPA's, Beta Gamma Sigma. Roman Catholic. Home: 10009 Gainsborough Rd Rockville MD 20854-4276 Office: 7925 Glenbrook Rd Bethesda MD 20814-2441 E-mail: agcast2@msn.com.

CASTELLINI, ROBERT H. (BOB CASTELLINI), food products executive, professional sports team executive; BS in Econ., Georgetown

Univ.; MBA, Wharton Grad. Sch., 1967. Exec. v.p. Castellini Group of Cos., 1967—70, pres., 1970—92, chmn., 1992—; ptnr. Tex. Rangers, 1989, Balt. Orioles, 1993; investor St. Louis Cardinals; CEO Cin. Reds, 2006—, also owner, 2006—. Office: Castellini Group of Cos PO Box 721610 Newport KY 41072-1610

CASTELLINO, RONALD AUGUSTUS DIETRICH, radiologist, educator; b. NYC, Feb. 18, 1938; s. Leonard Vincent and Henrietta Wilhelmina (Geffken) C.; m. Joyce Cuneo, Jan. 26, 1963; children: Jeffrey Charles, Robin Leonard, Anthony James. Student, Creighton U., Omaha, 1955-58, MD, 1962. Diplomate: Am. Bd. Radiology. Rotating intern Highland Alameda County Hosp., Oakland, Calif., 1962-63; USPHS/Peace Corps physician Brazil, 1963-65; resident in diagnostic radiology Stanford U. Hosp., 1965-68, chief resident, 1967-68; asst. prof. radiology Stanford U. Med. Sch., 1968-74, assoc. prof., 1974-81, prof., 1981-93, chief diagnostic oncologic radiology, 1970-89, chief CT body scanning, 1979-89, dir. div. diagnostic radiology and assoc. chmn. dept. radiology, 1981-86, acting chmn. dept. diagnostic radiology and nuclear medicine, 1986-89, prof. emeritus NYC, 1993—; chair dept. radiology, Carroll and Milton Petrie chair Meml. Sloan Kettering Cancer Ctr., NYC, 1990-98; prof. radiology Cornell Med. Sch., 1994-98, chief med. officer R-2 tech., 1998—. Mem. U.S. Cancer del., People's Republic China, 1977 Co-editor: Pediatric Oncologic Radiology, 1977; assoc. editor; Lymphology, 1973-97, Investigative Radiology, 1985-94, Academic Radiology, 1994-97, Radiology, 1986-94, Postgrad. Radiology, 1986-98; contbr. numerous rsch. papers to profl. jours., chpts. to books. Recipient T.F. Eckstrom Fund award, 1978; Guggenheim fellow, 1974-75 Mem.: N.Y. Acad. Medicine, N.Y. Roentgen Soc., Calif. Acad. Medicine, N.Am. Soc. Lymphology (charter), Soc. Cancer Imaging (charter), Soc. Thoracic Radiology (charter), Calif. Radiol. Soc., Calif. Med. Assn. (adv. panel sect. radiology 1972—89), Western Angiography Soc. (charter), Internat. Cancer Imaging Soc. (charter), Am. Roentgen Ray Soc., Soc. Cardiovascular and Interventional Radiology (charter), Radiol. Soc. N.Am., Assn. Univ. Radiologists (exec. com. 1981—85), Am. Coll. Radiology, Internat. Soc. Lymphology (exec. com. 1975—85), Am. Soc. Therapeutic Radiation Oncologists (hon.), Alpha Omega Alpha. Office: Chief Med Officer R-2 Tech 2585 Augustine Dr Santa Clara CA 95054 Office Phone: 408-352-0100. Personal E-mail: rcastellino@sbcglobal.net. Business E-Mail: rcastellino@r2tech.com.

CASTEN, RICHARD FRANCIS, physicist, educator; b. NYC, Nov. 1, 1941; s. Daniel F. and Constance Mary (Bell) C.; m. Jo Ann Daly, June 6, 1964. BS magna cum laude, Coll. of the Holy Cross, 1963; PhD, Yale U., 1967; D (hon.), U. Bucharest, Romania, 2005. Postdoctoral fellow Niels Bohr Inst., Copenhagen, 1967-69, Los Alamos Sci. Lab., N.Mex., 1969-71; asst. scientist Brookhaven Nat. Lab., Upton, NY, 1971-73, assoc. scientist, 1973-76, scientist, 1977-81, sr. scientist, 1981-96, group leader nuclear structure group, 1981-96; prof. physics, dir. A.W. Wright Nuclear Structure Lab. Yale U., New Haven, 1995—, D. Allan Bromley prof. physics, 2006—. Chmn. N.Am. steering com. for Isospin Lab. Radioactive Beam Facility, 1989-2002; co-chmn. steering com., Rare Isotope Accelerator, 2002-03, chair, 2002-03, 06-07; mem. panel on basic nuc. data, Nat. Acad. Scis., 1990-92; guest prof. U. Cologne, Germany, 1985—; long-range plan working group Nuc. Sci. Adv. Com., 1989, 95, 2001, 07; mem. Nuc. Sci. Adv. Com., 1998-2000, chmn. 2003-05; mem. subcom. on implementation of long range plan, 1991; spl. emphasis panel NSF, 1993; US rep. Megasci. Forum for Nuc. Physics, Subpanel on Intense Beams and Target Sys., 1997-98; co-chair writing panel for Columbus White Paper on sci. opportunities with an advanced ISOL facility, 1997; chair ISAC/TRIUMF rev. com., 1997; mem. Can. NSERC com. on subatomic physics, 1999-2001; mem. panels internat. rev. of standing and potential of physics rsch. in UK, 2001, 05; co-convenor 1995 TUNL Town Meeting on Nuc. Structure and 2000 Rare Isotope Accelerator Workshop; chair adv. com. Nustar Pac for GSI-Fair Project, 2004-05; mem. Internat. Union of Pure and Applied Physics working group on internat. coop. in nuc. physics, 2004-; mem. Nat. Rsch. Council Rare Isotope Assessment Com., Nat. Acad. Sci., 2006; Mercator guest prof. German Phys. Soc., 2007-; mem. numerous other nat. and internat. coms.; co-organizer 8 internat. confs. on nuclear physics; adv. com. for many internat. confs.; spkr. in field. Author: Nuclear Structure from a Simple Perspective, 1990, rev. edit., 2000; co-author, co-editor: Algebraic Approaches to Nuclear Structure, 1993; mem. editl. bd. (Jours.) Nuclear Physics News Internat., Internat. Jour. Modern Physics, Modern Physics Letters, assoc. editor Phys. Rev. C, 2001—; contbr. over 500 articles to profl. jours. Pres. Jo Ann and Richard Casten, Ltd., 1973—. Danforth fellow, 1963-67; recipient Sr. Alexander von Humboldt prize, 1983; honoree Internat. Nuc. Structure Conf., Jackson, Wyo., 2002. Fellow AAAS, Am. Phys. Soc. (exec. com. divsn. nuc. physics 1991-93, vice chmn. Divsn. Nuc. Physics 2006, chair-elect 2007, chmn. task force to rev. jour. Phys. Rev. C 1995, fellow Inst. Physics), Inst. Physics; mem. NAS (rare isotope sci. asseesment com. 2006), Sigma Xi. Achievements include discovery of O(6) symmetry of IBA model and other experimental verifications of the IBA including extensive study of 168-Er and 196-Pt; invention of symmetry triangle of the IBA known as the Casten Triangle; co-inventor of consistent Q formalism; evolution of nuclear structure with nucleon number, valence p-n interaction, NpNn scheme and P-factor, quenching of the N=20 and Z=64 shell gaps, fragility of magicity; empirical extraction of p-n interaction, strengths, and relation to collectivity and shell structure; research in generalization of the Federman-Pittel mechanism for the onset of deformation in nuclei; radioactive nuclear beams, Q-invariants, application of Landau theory to equilibrium structure of nuclei; development of signatures of nuclear structure, ARC method of complete spectroscopy; first to use the GRID technique for nuclear structure studies, evidence for large hexadecapole deformations in odd-A nuclei, extensive tests of Coriolis mixing in nuclei; test Bose-Fermi Symmetry E(5/4); discovery of empirical examples of E (5) and X (5) critical point symmetries for nuclear quantum phase transitional regions; co-discovery of evidence for multi-phonon states in nuclei, global correlations of nuclear observables; co-discovery of tripartite correlations of nuclear observables; co-discovery of nuclei in the internal arc of regularity of symmetry triangle; new interpretation of E0 transitions; first intermediate energy Coulomb excitation experiment in inverse kinematics; mapping of structural evolution in nuclei; discovery of direct empirical link between proton-neutron interaction strengths and growth rates of collectivity in nuclei. Avocations: tennis, golf, baseball, hiking, travel. Office: Yale Univ Wright Nuc Structure PO Box 208124 New Haven CT 06520-8124 Office Phone: 203-432-6174. Business E-Mail: rick@riviera.physics.yale.edu.

CASTENELL, LOUIS ANTHONY, academic administrator; b. NYC, Oct. 2, 1947; s. Louis Anthony Sr. and Marguerite (Barzon) C.; m. Mae Beckett, May 3, 1975; children: Louis Calvin, Elizabeth M. BA, Xavier U., 1968; MS, U. Wis., Milw., 1973; PhD, U. Ill., 1980. Cert. counselor and tchr. Elem. tchr. Orleans Parish Schs., New Orleans, 1968; academic advisor U. Wis., Milw., 1970-74; alumni dir. Xavier U., New Orleans, 1974-77, dean Grad Sch., 1980-89; dean Coll. Edn. U. Cin., 1990-99, U. Ga., 1999—. Cons. in field. Contbr. chpts. to books and articles to profl. jours. Mem. edn. commn. Nativity Sch., Cin., 1990, NAACP, 1990; mem. steering com. Cin. Youth Collabarative, 1990; bd. dirs. Tri-State Edn. and Tech. Found., Cin., 1990. Sgt. U.S. Army, 1968-69, Korea. Recipient Presdl. Citation, Assn. Multicultural Counseling, Washington, 1983. HEW fellow, 1978-80, Outstanding Faculty, Kappa Delta Epsilon, 2000, Disting. Alumni in Higher Edn., U. Ill., 2002, Pedro Zamora award Contbns. to Diversity, 2003, Am. Coun. Edn. Bd. Svc. award, 2003, U. Ga. Diversity Leadership award, 2003, NBPTS Svc. award, 2006. Mem. AACD, Am. Edn. Rsch. Assn., Am. Assn. Colls. Tchrs. Edn. (chmn. bd. dirs. 2001—), Nat. Bd. Profl. Tchg. Stds., Assn. Tchr. Educators, State U. Deans Edn., Kappa Delta Pi, Phi Delta Kappa. Democrat. Roman Catholic. Avocations: reading, travel, photography. Home: 1320 Beverly Dr Athens GA 30606-7610 Office: U Ga Coll Edn Aderhold Hall G-3 Athens GA 30602 Business E-Mail: lcastene@uga.edu.

CASTER, ANDREW IAN, ophthalmologist; b. Coral Gables, Fla., Oct. 30, 1954; s. Milton and Carolyn (Teperson) C.; m. Jacqueline Jacobs, Oct. 15, 1989; children: Bryce, Jocelyn. AB, Harvard Coll., 1976; MD, Harvard Med. Sch., 1980. Diplomate Am. Bd. Ophthalmology; cert. Coun. Refractive Surgery Quality Assurance, 2000. Resident UCLA Jules Stein Eye Inst., LA, 1981-84; intern Wadsworth VA Hosp., Los Angeles, 1980-81; resident UCLA Jules Stein Eye Inst., Los Angeles, 1981-84; med. dir. Caster Eye Ctr., Beverly Hills, Calif., 1986—. Refractive surgery clin. adv. bd. Alcon Lab., 2003—; clin. instr. ophthalmology UCLA Sch. Medicine; mem. med. staff Cedars-Sinai Med. Ctr. Author: The Eye Laser Miracle: The Complete Guide to Better Vision, 1997, 5th edit.; contbr. articles to profl. jour. Spl. advisor Everychild Found.; bd. dirs. Wonder or Reading. Named Best Laser Eye Surgeon in LA, LA Mag., 1999; recipient Alumni Rsch. award, Jules Stein Eye Inst. UCLA, 1994, Visx Star Surgeon award, 1998, 1999, 2000, 2001, Best Doctors in Am., 2005—06, Excellence Laser Vision Correction, Alcon Centurion, 2005. Fellow ACS, Am. Acad. Ophthalmology, Calif. Assn. Ophthalmology (asst. v.p. 1992); mem. Am. Soc. Cataract and Refractive Surgeons, Internat. Soc Refractive Surgeons. Achievements include performing over 15,000 laser vision correction treatments and participation in clinical trials in laser vision correction; patents for apparatus to induce relaxation and sleep in infants. Avocations: skiing, travel, photography, golf. Office: Caster Eye Ctr 9100 Wilshire Blvd Ste 265E Beverly Hills CA 90212-3482 Office Phone: 310-274-1221. Business E-Mail: acaster@castervision.com.

CASTER, JACQUELINE JACOBS, not-for-profit executive; d. Walter Harvey Jacobs and Dorothy Jacobs Duncan; m. Andrew Ian Caster, Oct. 15, 1989; children: Bryce William, Jocelyn Lily. BA, Pomona Coll., 1979; M in City and Regional Planning, Harvard U., John Fitzgerald Kennedy Sch. Govt., 1983; JD, Boston U. Sch. Law, 1983. Bar: Calif. 1984. Atty. Loeb and Loeb, Los Angeles, Calif., 1983—86; mgr. market rsch. Disney Devel. Co., Burbank, 1987—90; pres. Jacqueline Caster Consulting, Pacific Palisades, 1990—2000; pres., founder Everychild Found., Pacific Palisades, 2000—. Mem. adv. bd. Alternative Living for the Aging, Los Angeles, 2004—, Blue Heron Found., Los Angeles, 2004—. Named Woman Yr., Santa Monica-Westside YWCA, 2005; recipient Humanitarian award, First Star Found., 2004, Optimist Youth Home, 2005, Shane's Inspiration, 2005. Mem.: Calif. State Bar (licentiate). Office: Everychild Found PO Box 1808 Pacific Palisades CA 90272 Home Phone: 310-573-2153; Office Phone: 310-573-2153.

CASTIGLIA, PATRICIA ANNE THORSON, dean, nursing educator; b. Johnson City, NY; d. Theodore William and Isabelle Alice (Lane) Thorson; children: Karen, Patricia, Joseph. Diploma in Nursing, St. Vincent's Hosp., NYC, 1955; BSN, U. Buffalo, 1962; MSN, SUNY, Buffalo, 1965; PhD, SUNY, 1976. RN, N.Y.; cert. sch. nurse tchr., N.Y. Staff nurse Our Lady of Lourdes Hosp., Binghamton, NY, 1955-56; asst. head nurse Hosp. of the Good Shepherd, Syracuse, NY, 1956; sch. nurse tchr. North Collins Cen. Sch., North Collins, NY, 1956-62; clin. instr. SUNY, Buffalo, 1965-73; asst. prof. Niagara U., NY, 1976-77; from asst. prof. dir. ind. study to assoc. prof. SUNY, Buffalo, 1977-89, assoc. dean, 1983-89; acting dean, assoc. prof. SUNY at Buffalo Sch. Nursing, 1989; dean, prof. Coll. Nursing and Health Scis. U. Tex., El Paso, 1990—2002, asst. to pres. for health affairs, 2001—02, prof. emeritus, 2002—, SUNY, Buffalo, 1991—, cons. for higher edn. issues; interim assoc. dean U. Tex. Med. Br., Galveston, 2004—. Stockholder, treas. Profl. Nurse Consultants P.C., Buffalo; pediatric nurse practitioner Erie County Health Dept., Buffalo, 1982-89; vis. prof. SUNY Buffalo, 2003, 05, 06; dean emeritus Am. Assn. Colls. Nursing, 2003. Author chpts. to books; chair book of yr. awards Pediatric Nursing, 1986-88; manuscript reviewer Pediatric Nursing, Clin. Nurse Specialist, 1985—; editor: Jour. of Pediatric Health Care; co-editor: Child Health Care: Process and Practice, 1992; contbr. articles to MCN, Pediatric Nursing, Jour. Pediatric Health Care. Recipient Reach award YWCA, 1995, Charles and Shirley Leavell Endowed chair; named Nurse of Yr., Tex. Nurse Assn. 1996, Woman of the Yr. in Edn., El Paso Commn. for Women, 1996; grantee P.I. Kellogg Cmty. Partnership; SUNY Faculty Exch. scholar, Albany, 1985. Fellow Am. Acad. Nursing; mem. NAPNAP, N.Y. State Nurses Assn., Coalition of Nurse Practitioners, U. Buffalo Alumni Assn., St. Vincent's Alumni Assn., Rotary Internat., Sigma Theta Tau. Roman Catholic. Avocations: travel, piano, theater, reading, knitting. Personal E-mail: pcastiglia@adelphia.net.

CASTILE, RAND (JESSE RANDOLPH III), retired museum director; b. NC, 1938; s. Jesse Randolph II and Pauline Virginia (Simmons) C.; m. Sondra Meadow Myers, 1960; children: Leath Willow, Heather Rain. BA, Drew U., Madison, NJ, 1960; diploma, Urasenke Tea Ceremony, Kyoto, Japan, 1967; LHD (hon.), Drew U., 1992. With ARTnews, NYC, 1963-65; dir. edn. Japan Soc., NYC, 1967-71, dir. performing arts, 1981-86, dir. Japan House Gallery, 1971-86; dir. Asian Art Mus., San Francisco, 1986-94, dir. emeritus, 1994—. Vis. com. Met. Mus. Art, 1974-99; sec., mem. US-Japan Cultural and Ednl. Conf., 1972-86; mem. Maine Art Commn., 1997-2001, vis. com. Asian Art, Mus. Fine Arts, Boston, 2000-2004; sr. adv. Sherman E. Lee Inst. Japanese Art, 2000-2002; mem. North Atlantic Cultural Coun., 2002-; mem. Can.-Am. Cultural Bd., 2003-. Author: The Way of Tea, 1971, 79; (exhbn. catalogue) Japanese Art Now: Tadaaki Kuwayama & Rikuro Okamoto, 1980, other catalogues; editor: Japanese Art Exhibitions with Catalogue in US, 1980; contbr. articles to profl. jour. Panelist Calif. Arts Coun., 1986-91; bd. dir. West-East Coun. Cathedral Ch. of St. John the Devine, 1977-86, AAM/ICOM, 1982-85, Japan Soc. No. Calif., 1986-95, San Francisco Bay Area Dance Coalition, 1986-88, Rock and Roll Mus., San Francisco, 1988-89, U. San Francisco Ctr. for Pacific Rim, 1989-95, Seoul-San Francisco Sister City Com., 1987-93, Nat. Maritime Mus., San Francisco, 1989-93; mem. internat. adv. com. Ctr. for Internat. Contemporary Arts, 1989-95; chair co-chair gov. State Calif. awards for Art and Philanthropy, 1990-94, others; chmn. Eastport Area Millenium Festival, 1997-2000; mem. vis. com. Mus. Fine Arts, Boston. Fulbright-Hayes fellow, 1966-67; recipient Mayor's award of Honor for Arts and Culture, NYC, 1982, Plowshares Humanitarian award, 1990, Harry Mattin award Eastport Area C. of C., 2000, award Global Heritage Fund, 2004. Mem. Assn. Art Mus. Dirs. (emeritus), Am. Assn. Mus. (bd. dirs. Internat. coun. 1982-86), Mus. Trustee Assn. (adv. coun. of dirs. 1989-95), Am. Fedn. Arts (nat. exhbn. com. 1980-95), Acad. Lacquer Rsch. Tokyo (Am. sec. 1977-86), Japan Soc. No. Calif. (bd. dir. 1986-95, mem. collections com. Farnsworth Mus. 2000-), Century Assn., St. Croix Country Club (bd. dirs. 2001—05), Herring Cove Golf Club. E-mail: rcastile@bellsouth.net.

CASTILLE, RONALD D., state supreme court justice; b. Miami, Fla., Mar. 16, 1944; s. Henry and Marie Nash Castille. BS in Econs., Auburn U., 1966; JD, U. Va., 1971. Asst. dist. atty., 1971-81; chief asst. dist. atty. Career Criminal Unit, 1982-84; dep. dist. atty. Pre-Trial Unit, 1984-85; dist. atty. Phila., 1986-91; with litigation dept. Reed Smith Shaw & McClay, Phila., 1991-93; justice Pa. Supreme Ct., 1993—. Mem. Appellate Ct. Procedural Rules Com., 1994-96; liaison justice Ad Hoc Com. on Evidence, 1994-, Criminal Procedural Rules Com., 1994-. Minor Ct. Rules Com., 1994-. Co-chmn. Pa. Anti-Crime Coalition for George Bush for Pres., 1988, 92; commr. Presidents' Commn. on Model State Drug Laws, 1992; mem. Pa. Advisory Com. of U.S. Commn. on Civil Rights, 1992-; bd. dirs. mem. Nat. Alliance for Model State Drug Laws, 1993-, Pa. Ctr. for Adapted Sports, 1996-. Lieutenant USMC, 1966—68. Decorated Bronze Star with Combat V, Purple Heart (2), Combat Infantry badge; recipient Disting. Pub. Svc. award Pa. County and State Detectives Assn., 1987, Layman award Pa. Chiefs of Police Assn., 1987, Spirit of Am. award Inst. for Study of Am. Wars, 1988, Pres.'s award for Outstanding Svc., Nat. Dist. Attys. Assn., 1991; named Man of Yr., Fraternal Order of Police Lodge #5, 1988, Outstanding Disabled Vet. of Yr., Nat. Disabled Am. Vets., 1988. Mem. Nat. Dist. Attys. Assn. (v.p. 1986-91), Pa. Dist. Attys. Assn. (legis. chmn. 1986-91). Office: 1818 Market St Ste 3730 Philadelphia PA 19103-3639

CASTILLO, CHRISTINE LYNN, pediatric neuropsychologist; d. James Robert and Sharon Joy French. BA summa cum laude, Pacific Christian Coll. of Hope Internat. U., Fullerton, Calif., 1998; PhD, Tex. A&M U., College Station, 2003. Cert. in sch. psychology NASP, 2003, sch. psychologist Md. State Dept. Edn., 2004, lic. psychologist Tex., specialist in sch. psychology Tex. Predoctoral neuropsychology intern Lewisville Ind. Sch. Dist., Tex., 2002—03; pediat. neuropsychology postdoctoral fellow Mt. Washington Pediat. Hosp., Balt., 2003—05; pediat. neuropsychologist Children's Med. Ctr., Dallas, 2005—. Clin. supr. Loyola Coll. in Md., Balt., 2005; lectr. Mt. Washington Pediatric Hosp., Balt., 2003—05; guest lectr. U. Md. Sch. Medicine, Balt., 2004—05; mem ADHD adv. coun. Md. State Dept. Edn., Balt., 2004—05; guest lectr. Tex. A&M U., College Station, 2001; tchg. asst. Pacific Christian Coll. of Hope Internat. U., Fullerton, Calif., 1998; adj. prof. Hope Internat. U., Fullerton, Calif., 2005, 07. Contbr. articles and revs. to profl. jours., chapters to books. HEEP fellow, Tex. A&M U., 1998—2001, Alumni Assn. scholar, Pacific Christian Coll. of Hope Internat. U., 1997, Christian Svc. and Leadership scholar, 1994—98, Presdl. scholar, 1994—98, Calif. Scholarship Fedn. scholar, 1994. Mem.: APA, Nat. Assn. Sch. Psychologists, Nat. Acad. Neuropsychology, Internat. Neuropsychol. Soc. Office: Childrens Med Ctr Dallas 1935 Motor St Dallas TX 75235 Business E-Mail: christine.castillo@childrens.com.

CASTILLO, KATHERINE LYNN, secondary school educator, writer, translator, business owner; b. Columbus, Ohio, Aug. 30, 1970; d. Dana Leslie and Judith Lynn Jordan; m. Pedro Castillo, Dec. 28, 1999; children: Dana Pedro, Andrew Patrick. BS in Edn., Kent State U., 1994; MA in Distance Edn., 2003, PhD in Distance Edn., 2004. Cert. tchr. K-12 Spanish Ohio, 1994, ATA translations Ohio, 1995. Translator, interpreter Spanish, English pvt. practice, Stow, Ohio, 1991—2005; lead tchr. Spanish Kent State U. Upward Bounds Program, 1998—2002; tchr., translator Berlitz Lang. Sch., Akron, 1998—2003; tchr. K-8 Spanish, music St. Matthew's Parish Sch., 1999—2002; activity coord. Alzheimer's patients Maison Aine, Stow, 1999—2002; online fgn. lang. tchr. Ohio Distance and Electronic Learning Acad., Akron, 2002—05; fgn. lang. tchr. Euclid HS, 2006—07; tchr. Electronic Classroom of Tomorrow, 2007—. Author: (children's novel) Say Hello to the World; translator: Go Get Benjamin. Precious parent mem. Akron Children's Hosp., 2001—05; hand bell choir Stow United Meth. Ch., Stow, 2002—05, sec., 2002—03, mission team, 2003—04, sec. United Meth. women, 2002—04, mission team mem., translator, 2003—04. Recipient Outstanding Am. Tchr. award, 2006; scholar, Ravenna Profl. Bus. Women, 1989, Stow Teachers, 1989. Mem.: Am. Translators Assn. Democrat. Methodist. Achievements include research in Research in Foreign Language Online Education; development of Online Spanish for Law Enforcement Program; first to Online Education K-12. Avocations: travel, reading, computers, course design, crafts. Home: 3421 Sanford Ave Stow OH 44224 Home Phone: 330-688-3710. Personal E-mail: kathycastillo830@yahoo.com.

CASTILLO, LUIS ANTONIO DONATO, professional baseball player; b. San Pedro de Macoris, Dominican Republic, Sept. 12, 1975; Infielder Fla. Marlins, Miami, 1996—2005, Minn. Twins, 2005—07, NY Mets, 2007—. Named to Nat. League All-Star Team, 2002—03, 2005; recipient Nat. League Gold Glove award, 2003—05. Achievements include being a member of World Series Champion Florida Marlins, 1997, 2003; led National League in stolen bases, 2000 (62) and 2002 (48). Mailing: NY Mets Shea Stadium 123-01 Roosevelt Ave Flushing NY 11368-1699 Fax: 305-626-7428.*

CASTILLO, MARIO ENRIQUE, artist, educator; came to U.S., 1955, naturalized, 1965; s. Manuel Castillo and Maria Enriquez de Allen. Cert., Ill. Inst. Design, 1964; BFA, Sch. of Art Inst. Chgo., 1969; MFA, Calif. Inst. Arts, 1972; postgrad., U. So. Calif., 1969—70, Pasadena City Coll., 1977, Calif. State U. L.A., 1980—81, Calif. State U., Dominguez Hills, 1986—88, East L.A. City Coll., 1982, Nat. U., Inglewood, Calif., 1990, Columbia Coll., Chgo., 1996. Designer J.M. Pateros Studios, Inc., Chgo., 1965, Lukas & Assocs., Chgo., 1966; instr. Pilsen Settlement House, Chgo., 1967; comml. artist Chgo. Bd. Edn., 1968; instr. United Christian Cmty. Svc., Chgo., 1968—69; mural dir. Halsted Urban Progress Ctr., 1968, Dept. Human Resources, Chgo., 1969, McHenry Coll., Crystal Lake, Ill., 1992, No. Ill. U., DeKalb, 1993, Joliet Jr. Coll., Ill., 1994, Coll. of Lake County, Grayslake, Ill., 1994, U. Guadalajara, Ocotian, Mexico, 1995, SAIC & Lincoln Park Cultural Ctr., Chgo., 1996, Bemis Found., Omaha, 1996, Triton Coll., River Grove, Ill., 1997; tchg. asst. Calif. Inst. Arts, Valencia, 1970—72, instr., 1972—73, Santa Monica City Coll., Calif., 1973; mem. faculty dept. art U. Ill., Champaign, 1973—76; comml. artist LA, 1977; instr. art Immaculate Heart Coll., Hollywood, Calif., 1979—80, Pacific Asian Consortium in Edn., 1980—81, E.C.F. Art Ctr., LA, 1986—90, L.A. Unified Sch. Dist., 1986—90, Instituto Comercial Artistico, Maywood, Calif., 1987, Lexicon Sch. Langs., 1987—88, Plaza de la Raza, 1989—90; mem. faculty art dept. Columbia Coll., Chgo., 1990—. Panelist at Northeastern Ill. U., Chgo., 1974, Coll. Art Assn., Chgo., 1975, Columbia Coll., Chgo., 1992, 94, 96, Chgo. Artist Coalition, 1993, Nat. Assn. Chicano Studies, Chgo., 1994, 96, Suburban Fine Arts Ctr., Highland Park, Ill., 1995, U. Guadalajara, Jalisco, 1995; presenter workshop Human Rights Portfolio, Chgo., 1994, Chgo., 1995; guest lectr. Galeria J.M. Velazco, Mexico City, 1975, Centro de la Causa, Chgo., 1975, Latino Cultural House, Champaign, 1975, U. Ill., Champaign, 1975, 76, Corpus Christi (Tex.) State U., 1978, McHenry County Coll., 1991, 92, Northwestern U., 1991, Columbia Coll., Montebello Sch. Dist., 1990, No. Ill. U., DeKalb, 1993, Triton Coll., River Grove, Ill., 1993, 94, Prospectus Gallery, Chgo., 1993, Joliet (Ill.) Jr. Coll., 1994, St. Cloud (Minn.) State U., 1994, MacMurry Coll., Jacksonville, Ill., 1994, Coll. of Lake County, 1994, Nat.-Louis U., Chgo., 1995, Melrose Park (Ill.) Pub. Libr., 1995, Mobil Art Gallery, Jacksonville, Ill., 1994, Northeastern U., Chgo., 1995, Harold Washington Libr., Chgo., 1995, Munster Ind. Cultural Ctr., 1995, U. Guadalajara, Ocotlan, Jalisco, 1995, 96, CCC Art Gallery, Chgo., 1995, Winnetka (Ill.) Cultural House, 1995, No. Ill. U., DeKalb, 1995, U. Guadalajara, La Barranca Campus, 1996, Lincoln Park Cultural Ctr., Chgo., 1996, Triton Coll., River Grove, 1996, 97; art juror Weisman Scholarship CCC, Chgo., 1993, Old Town Art Fair, Chgo., 1994, Hokin Gallery CCC, Chgo., 1995, Weisman Best of Show, Chgo., 1996; curator art exhibitions U. Ill., Champaign, 1975, Columbia Coll., Chgo., 1994, 95, Triton Coll., 1995, No. Ind. Arts Assn., Munster, 1995, 11th Street Art Gallery CCC, 1995, Hokin Ctr. Gallery, Columbia Coll., 1996; interior designer El Mercado Co., L.A. 1981-83; regular performer musical program Noches Rancheras, East L.A., Calif., 1981-83; cons. in field. One-man shows include Scholarship and Guidance Assn., Chgo., 1968, Calif. Inst. of the Arts, Burbank, 1971, Valencia, Calif., 1972, Latino Cultural House, U. Ill., Champaign, 1976, Inst. for Hispanic Cultural Studies, Santa Monica, Calif., 1989, Orlando Gallery, Sherman Oaks, Calif., 1989, Sangre De Cristo Arts and Conf. Ctr., Pueblo, Colo., 1991, Prospectus Gallery, Chgo., 1991, 93, McHenry County Art Gallery, 1991, No. Ill. U. Art Gallery, DeKalb, 1993, Atwood Art Ctr., St. Cloud U., 1994, MacMurry Coll., Jacksonville, Ill., 1994; numerous group shows including Fresno Art Mus., Calif., 1991, San Francisco Art Mus., 1991, San Francisco Mus. of Modern Art, 1991, Albuquerque Mus., 1991, Denver Art

Mus., 1991, 93, Expo, 1993, San Antonio Mus. of Art, 1993, Nat. Mus. of Am. Art, 1993, Chgo., 1993, 94, Chgo. Latino Film Festival, 1994, Las Artes Galeria, Omaha, 1994, Open Windows Gallery, Chgo., 1994, S. Suburban Coll., South Holland, Ill., 1994, Columbia Coll., Chgo., 1994, 95, J.R. Shapiro Gallery, Oak Park, 1994, Cath. Theol. Union, Chgo., 1995, John Linsey Dallery, Oak Park, 1995, Hokin Gallery CCC, Chgo., 1995, Oak Park Art League, 1995, Pilsen Artist to Artist, Chgo., 1996, Prospecturs Gallery, Chgo., 1998, CCC Faculty Exhbn., Chgo., 1996, Richard Love Gallery, Chgo., 1996, La Llorona Gallery, Chgo., 1997, Prospectus Art Gallery, Chgo., 1997, Mexican Fine Arts Ctr. Mus., 1997, Chgo. Hist. Soc., 1996, 97, Mus. Contemporary Art, Chgo., 1996, 97, numerous others film screenings U.S., Europe, and Mexico; commd. muralist in public locations and pvt. residences; represented in permannet collections: Sara Lee Corp., Chgo., Mexican Mus. of Fine Arts, Chgo., San Francisco Mus. of Art, San Francisco Mus. of Contempory Art, Tucson Mus. of Art, Latino Inst., Chgo., Columbia Coll., Chgo., Bell Telephone Co., Chgo., Lake Meadows Assn., Chgo., Scholarship and Guidance Assn., Chgo., City of Chgo., San Antonio Art Mus., Guadalupe Cultural Arts Ctr., Denver, Evergreen State Coll., Olympia, Wash., Chgo. Humanities and Art Coun., Denver, Ariztlan, Inc., Phoenix, Mira, Chgo., Centro Cultural de La Raza, San Diego, San Diego Art Mus, Albuquerque Mus., San Francisco Art Mus., San Diego Mus. Contemporary Art, Denver Art Mus., Mex. Mus., San Francisco, Portland Art Mus., Nat. Mus. Am. Art, Washington, numerous group exhibitions include: Norris Gallery Cultural Arts Ctr., 1997, Instituto Cultural Puertoriqueno, 1998, Chgo. Athenaeum, Schaumburg, 1998, Ill. State Museum, 1999, Guadalupe Cultural Ctr., 2000; also numerous pvt. collections. Contbr. articles to numerous publications. Active contributor to cultural organizations. Recipient numerous awards including nat. gold medal, gold keys and certs. Scholastic Mag., 1963-65, cert. of merit N.Y. Times, 1965, 1st Prize award, Chgo. Police Dept., 1964, 1st Prize award Chgo. Assn. Commerce & Industry, 1965, 1st Pl. award U. Ill. Chgo. LASP design competition, 1st prize Maldef Art Competition, 1989, 1st pl. ESDC's Archtl. Relief Design Competition for New Homes in Chgo., 1992; artist to represent Midwest in nat. workshop, UCLA, 1988, artist to represent Latino culture in Spanish TV comml., 1989, 1st prize Homewood (Ill.) C. of C., 1967, 1st prize Fiesta del Quinto Sol, Chgo., 1974, 1st prize Mus. Sci. and Industry, Chgo., 1975, 1st prize for 18th St. banner design, Chgo., 1994; Am. Film Inst. grantee, 1972; Oakley fellow U. So. Calif., 1969-70; Scholarship and Guidance Assn. grantee, 1965-68, Ford Found. grantee, 1975; named Artist of Yr., Latino Inst., 1991. Achievements include rsch. in Perceptualism (the phenomena of after-images and optical illusions in paintings to create the feeling of the 4th dimension and alterations in color perception, visual investigations into discovering peculiar ways of presenting the human condition on this planet using superimposed layers of different states of realities and warping images and space so as to turn them "up-side-down"; composing numerous songs. Home: 10101 S Avenue M Chicago IL 60617-5925 Office: Columbia Coll Dept Art & Design 600 S Michigan Ave Chicago IL 60605-1900 Office Phone: 312-344-7590. Business E-Mail: mcastillo@colum.edu. E-mail: mario@mariocastillo.com.

CASTILLO, NELSON A., lawyer; BS cum laude, St. John's U., Jamaica, NY, 1993, JD, 1998. Bar: NY, US Dist. Ct. (so. dist.) NY, US Dist. Ct. (ea. dist.) NY. Legal intern US SEC, NYSE, NY Mercantile Exchange; Hon. Deborah A. Batts US Dist. Ct. (so. dist.), NY, 1996—98; dean's fellow St. John's U. Sch. Law, NY, 1998—99; legal cons. Sullivan & Cromwell, Davis Polk & Wardwell, Morgan Stanley Dean Witter & Co, Lehman Brothers Inc., Young & Rubicam Inc., NY, 1999—2002; prin. Castillo Law Firm PLLC, Roslyn Heights, NY, 2002—. Exec. coun. Network of Bar Leaders, Inc., NY, 2003—05; mem. presdl. adv. coun. on diversity in the profession ABA, 2005—06; spkr. in immigration law and diversity field. Named to 100 Influentials List, Hispanic Bus. Mag., 2006; recipient Recent Graduate Svc. award, St. John's Univ. Law Sch., 2005, Builders of the New NY award, NY Immigration Coalition, 2006, Disting. Latino in Law award, Latin Am. Law Students Assn., Benjamin N. Cardozo Sch. Law, 2006. Mem.: Hispanic Nat. Bar Assn. (NY region pres. 2002—04, nat. pres. 2005—06, immigration com. chair 2005—06, mem. Founders' Cir.), NY State Bar Assn. (exec. com. real property law sect. 2005—07, mem. house of delegates, internat. law and practice sect. com. on immigration and nationality, com. on leadership devel. and diversity), Nat. Assn. Hispanic Journalists (life), Golden Key Hon. Soc., Omicron Delta Epsilon, Beta Gamma Sigma. Office: Castillo Law Firm PLLC Ste 205 99 Powerhouse Rd Roslyn Heights NY 11577 Office Phone: 516-621-8646. Office Fax: 516-620-3051. Business E-Mail: nelson.castillo@caslawfirm.com.

CASTILLO, RUBEN, federal judge; b. Chgo., 1954; BA, Loyola U., 1976; JD, Northwestern U., 1979. Bar: Ill. 1979. Assoc. Jenner & Block, Chgo., 1979—84; asst. US atty. (No. dist.) Ill. US Dept. Justice, 1984—88; regional counsel Mexican Am. Legal Def. & Edn. Fund, Chgo., 1988—91; ptnr. Kirkland & Ellis, Chgo., 1991-93; judge US Dist. Ct. (no. dist.) Ill., 1994—. Adj. prof. Northwestern U., 1988—; vice chair, US Sentencing Commn., 1999-. Mem. ABA, Latin Am. Bar Assn., Chgo. Bar Found., Chgo. Coun. Lawyers (v.p. 1991-93). Office: U S Courthouse 2378 Dirksen Bldg 219 S Dearborn St Chicago IL 60604-1702*

CASTILLO, SUSAN, school system administrator; b. LA, Aug. 14, 1951; m. Paul Machu. BA in Comm., Oreg. State U., 1981. Mem. staff Oreg. Pub. Broadcasting Radio, 1979-82; journalist, reporter legis. sessions Sta. KVAL-TV, Salem, 1991, 93, 95, journalist, reporter Eugene, 1982-97; mem., Dist. 20 Oreg. State Senate, Salem, 1997—2002, vice chair edn. com., mem. health and human svcs. com., mem. transp. com., asst. Dem. leader legis. sessions, 1999, 2001; supt. pub. instrn. State of Oreg., Salem, 2003—. Leader Oreg. Women's Health & Wellness Alliance. Mem. Gov.'s Task Force on DUII, 1997, Gov.'s Task Force on Cmty. Right to Know; bd. dirs. Oreg. Commn. on Hispanic Affairs, 1997, Birth to Three, Oreg. Environ. Coun.; mem. adv. com. Oreg. Passenger Rail Adv. Coun.; mem. Labor Comm.'s Adv. Com. on Agrl. Labor; vice-chair Farm Worker Housing Task Force. Democrat. Achievements include being the first Hispanic woman to serve in Oregon legislature. Office: Oregon Dept Education 255 Capitol St NE Salem OR 97310-0203 Office Phone: 503-947-5740. E-mail: superintendent.castillo@state.or.us.*

CASTLE, ALFRED, administrator; b. Washington, Dec. 22, 1948; m. Mary Ann Slagle (div. 1979); m. Lilia Kruglova, 1992. BA, Colo. State U., 1971, MA, 1972; postgrad., U. N.Mex., Columbia U., 1980, U. N.Mex. Chmn., div. humanities Sunset Hill Sch., Kansas City, 1973-75; teaching asst. U. N.Mex., Alburquerque, 1975; prof., history N.Mex. Mil. Inst., Roswell, 1976-83, exec. dir. NMMI Fedn., 1983-87; v.p. devel. Hawaii Pacific U., Honolulu, 1987-95; v.p. univ. advancement Calif. State U., San Marcos, 1995-98; CEO Castle Found., 1998—. Trustee Samuel N. and Mary Castle Found., Honolulu, 1987—, pres.-elect, 1992-96; trustee Acad. Pacific, Honolulu, 1987-94, Hawaiian Hist. Soc., Honolulu, 1988-95; grants mgr., Pettus Found., Honolulu, 2001-. Author: Century of Philanthropy, 1992, Diplomatic Realism, U.S. Foreign Policy 1919-1953, 1998; contbr. over 60 articles to profl. jours., chpts. to books. Trustee Hawaii Food Bank, Honolulu, 1987-92, Hawaii Sch. Girls, Honolulu, 1987-92, Henry Dorothy Castle Fund, Trimble Charitable Trust, Grantmakers for Children, Youth & Families, Md., 1997-2006, mem. coun. on founds. com. on family philanthropy, Wash., DC, 1998-2006; trustee, pres. Samuel N. and Mary Castle Found. NEH fellow, 1978, 79-80, 81, 86, 91, Hoover fellow, 1983, 86, 90, 93, 96, Coolidge fellow, 1988. Mem. Assn. Grantmakers Hawaii, Govrs. Coun. Children Youth, Coun. Founds., San Diego Coun. Grantmakers, Phi Beta Kappa. Episcopalian. Avocation: writing. Home: 733 Bishop St Ste 1275 Honolulu HI 96813-4019 Office Phone: 808-522-1101. E-mail: acastle@aloha.net.

CASTLE, CAREY WILLIAM, dean; s. Allan B. and Patricia A. Castle; m. Sheila A. Bundy, Apr. 3, 1978; children: Ronald Gary Martin, Nathan Lee. BS in Edn., Valdosta State Coll., Ga., 1988; MPA, Valdosta State U., Ga., 1995. Cert. airframe & powerplant technician FAA, 1983. Advanced through grades to chief master sgt. USAF, 1975—2001, ret., 2001; aircraft maintenance tech. dept. head Greenville Tech. Col., SC, 2001—04; dean indsl. tech. Greenville Tech. Coll., 2004—. Home: 713 Sugar Maple Ct Fountain Inn SC 29644-2144 Office: Greenville Tech Coll PO Box 5616 Greenville SC 29608 Personal E-mail: cwcastle@charter.net. Business E-Mail: carey.castle@gvltec.edu.

CASTLE, EMERY NEAL, economist, educator; b. Eureka, Kans., Apr. 13, 1923; s. Sidney James and Josie May (Tucker) C.; m. Merab Eunice Weber (dec.), Jan. 20, 1946; 1 child, Cheryl Diana Delozier; m. Betty Thompson, Mar. 18, 2000. BS, Kans. State U., 1948, MS, 1950; PhD, Iowa State U., 1952, LHD (hon.), 1997, Oreg. State U., 2006. Economist Fed. Res. Bank of Kansas City, 1952—54; from asst. prof. to prof. dept. agrl. econs. Oreg. State U., Corvallis, 1954—65, dean faculty, 1965—66, prof., head dept. agrl. econs., 1966—72, dean Grad. Sch., 1972—76, Alumni disting. prof., 1970, prof. grad. faculty econs., 1986—93; v.p., sr. fellow Resources for the Future, Washington, 1976—79, pres., 1979—86. Vice-chmn. Environ. Quality Commn. Oreg., 1988-95. Editor: The Changing American Countryside: Rural People and Places, 1995. Recipient Alumni Disting. Service award Kans. State U., 1976; Disting. Service award Oreg. State U., 1984. Fellow AAAS, Am. Assn. Agrl. Economists (pres. 1972-73), Am. Acad. Arts and Scis. Home: 4649 SW Hollyhock Cir Corvallis OR 97333 Home Phone: 541-752-3755. Personal E-mail: emerycastle@comcast.net.

CASTLE, HOWARD BLAINE, retired religious organization administrator; b. Toledo, July 15, 1935; s. Russell Wesley and Letha Belle (Hobbs) C.; m. Patricia Ann Haverty, Aug. 12, 1957; 1 child Kevin Blaine. AB, Marion Coll., 1958; postgrad., Valparaiso U., 1960. Pastor The Wesleyan Ch., Valparaiso, Ind., 1958-60, Toronto, Ohio, 1963-69; assoc. pastor Northridge Wesleyan Ch., Dayton, Ohio, 1960-63; exec. dir. gen. dept. youth Wesleyan Ch. Hdqrs., Marion, Ind., 1968-72, dir. field ministries gen. dept. Sunday schs., 1972-74, exec. dir. curriculum, 1980-81; mng. editor WIN Mag., Marion, Ind., 1969-72; asst. gen. sec. Gen. Dept. of Local Ch. Edn., Marion, Ind., 1974-80; gen. dir. estate planning Wesleyan Ch. Internat Ctr., Indpls., 1982—2002, ret., 2002. Editor Ohio dist. The Wesleyan Ch., Columbus, 1961-69; gen. conf. del. The Wesleyan Ch., Anderson, Ind., 1968, Greensboro, N.C., 2000. Writer: Curriculum-Religious Adult Student/Teacher, 1982—, Light from the Word, 1982—. Mem. Christian Holiness Partnership, Christian Stewardship Assn., Christian Mgmt. Assn. Mem. Wesleyan Ch. Avocations: music, reading. Personal E-mail: castlehb@aol.com. *Life's choices impact more than any other factor the measure of our success and achievements. Circumstances cannot defeat one who chooses to rise above them by acting in accord with his choice.*

CASTLE, JAMES CAMERON, information technology executive; b. Peoria, Ill., Nov. 4, 1936; s. Charles Cameron and Betty Evelyn (Shaw) C.; m. Dorothy Patricia Gorbandt, June 7, 1958; children: James Charles, Patricia Elizabeth. BS, U.S. Mil. Acad., 1958; MSEE, U. Pa., Phila., 1963, PhD, 1966. Pres., chief exec. officer Honeywell Bull Network Info. Svcs., S.A., Paris, 1975-78; gen. mgr. GE, Daytona Beach, Fla., 1978-80; v.p. ops. Honeywell, Inc., Billerica, Mass., 1980-82; exec. v.p. Memorex Corp., Santa Clara, Calif., 1982-84; pres. TGB Info. Systems, Inc., NYC, 1984-87; chmn., pres., CEO Infotron Systems Corp., Cherry Hill, NJ, 1987—91; CEO Teradata Corp., El Segundo, Calif., 1991-92; chmn., CEO USCS Internat., Sacramento, 1992—2002; pres., CEO Castle Info. Techs., Manhattan Beach, 2000—. Bd. dirs. PMI Group, Inc., San Francisco, VeriFone, Inc., San Jose; pres. Chief Exec. Orgn., Bethesda, Md., 2001-02; trustee emeritus West Point (NY) Assn. Grads. 1st lt. US Army, 1958-61. Mem. World Presidents Orgn.

CASTLE, JOHN KROB, merchant banker; b. Cedar Rapids, Iowa, Dec. 22, 1940; s. Clyo F. and Emma (Krob) C.; m. Marianne Sherman, Sept. 20, 1969; children: William Sherman, John Sherman, James Sherman, David Alexander. SB, MIT, 1963; MBA with high distinction, Harvard U., 1965; LHD (hon.), NY Med. Coll., 1988, Canisius Coll. Assoc. Donaldson, Lufkin & Jenrette, Inc., NYC, 1965-68, v.p., 1968-71, exec. v.p., 1971-73, mng. dir., 1973-80, chief operating officer, 1979-84, pres., 1980-86, chief exec. officer, 1985-86; pres., chief exec. officer Branford Castle, Inc., NYC, 1986—; also founder, chmn., CEO Castle Harlan, Inc., NYC, 1987—, also founder, chmn., chief exec. officer, 1987; chmn., gen. ptnr. Castle Harlan Ptnrs. II, III and IV. Bd. dirs. Morton's Restaurant Group, Inc., Perkins & Marie Callender's, AdobeAir, Inc., Advanced Accessory Sys., LLC, Horizon Lines, Inc., Ames True Temper, Inc. Author: Financial Executives Handbook: Dividend Policy and Equity Financing, 1970, The Strategy of Corporate Financing: Packaging a Merger of Acquisition, 1971, Acquisition and Merger Negotiation Strategy, 1971; co-pub. Castle Connolly Guide, 1994, 1995, 1997—2006, Parent's Helper, 1996. With NY Med. Coll., chmn. bd., 1979-90; life mem. corp. MIT, 1987-; mem. vis. com. dept. econs., dept. physics; trustee The Whitehead Inst. for Biomed. Rsch., NY Presbyn. Hosp.; chmn. Rhodes Scholar Selection Com., NY State, 1986-90, Columbia-Presbyn. Health Sci. Adv. Coun.; endowed Castle Krob Fellowship for grad. study in econs. MIT, Castle Krob Fund for rsch. support at NY Med. Coll., Castle Krob Devel. Chair in econs. MIT, John K. Castle Publs. Fund on Ethics, Politics and Econs., Yale U. Mem. Links Club, Met. Club, Harvard Club, NY Yacht Club, Palm Beach Polo Club, Doubles Ltd., Club Collette, Sailfish Club. Home: 1095 N Ocean Blvd Palm Beach FL 33480-3230 Office: Castle Harlan Inc 150 E 58th St New York NY 10155-0002 Business E-Mail: jcastle@castleharlan.com.

CASTLE, MAURICE EMMETT, orthopedist, surgeon; s. Robert Emmett and Sylvia Mae (Johnson) Castle; m. Helen Philips; children: Robert, Adriane. BS, U. Detroit, 1941; MD, Wayne State U., Detroit, 1944. Diplomate Am. Bd. Orthop. Surgery. Intern City of Detroit Receiving Hosp., 1944—45; resident in gen. surgery Mt. Carmel Mercy Hosp., Detroit, 1945—46; resident in orthop. surgery Ind. U. Med. Ctr., Indpls., 1948—51; pvt. practice Detroit; chmn. dept. orthop. surgery Grace Hosp., Detroit, 1970—96; clin. assoc. prof. Wayne State U. Sch. Medicine, Detroit; orthop. cons. Midwest Health Ctr., Dearborn, Mich. Adj. assoc. asst. prof. Wayne State U. Sch. Medicine; past co-dir. orthop. physicians assistants program Marygroove Coll., Detroit; cons., presenter in field. Mem. editl. bd.: Phys. and Occupl. Therapy in Pediat.; contbr. articles to profl. jours. Adv. bd. Assn. Operating Rm. Technicians. Capt. M.C. US Army. Fellow: ACS; mem.: Detroit Acad. Orthop. Surgeons (past pres., past sec.-treas.), Wayne County Med. Soc., Mich. State Med. Soc., Am. Med. Soc., Mich. Orthop. Soc., Am. Acad. Cerebral Palsy and Devel. Medicine, Lamplighters Orthop. Assn., Clin. Orthop. Soc., Am. Acad. Orthop. Surgeons. Achievements include research in prevention of pulmonary embolic phenomena in trauma, leg length discrepancy in growing children; development of the Interposition Arthroplasty (Castle Procedure) which has become the operation of choice for difficult, severe and painful dislocation of the hip in the Cerebral Palsy patient. Avocations: golf, walking, music. Home: 19966 Old Pond Ct Beverly Hills MI 48025-2910

CASTLE, MICHAEL N., congressman, lawyer; b. Wilmington, Del., July 2, 1939; s. J. Manderson and Louisa B. Castle. BA, Hamilton Coll., 1961; JD, Georgetown U., 1964. Bar: Del. 1964, D.C. 1964. Assoc. Connolly Bove and Lodge, Wilmington, 1964-73, ptnr., 1973-75; dept. atty. gen. Del., 1965-66; mem. Del. Ho. of Reps., 1967-69, Del. State Senate, 1969-77; ptnr. Schnee and Castle P.A., 1975-80; lt. gov. State of Del., Wilmington, 1981-85, gov., 1985-93; prin. Michael N. Castle P.A., 1981—; mem. US Congress from Del., 1993—, mem. edn. and workforce com., intelligence com., chmn. subcom. edn. reform, chmn. tech. and tactical intelligence. Mem. Del. Ho. of Reps., 1966-67, Del. State Senate, 1968-76, minority leader, 1976 Bd. dirs. Boys Club of Wilmington. Mem. Del. State Bar Assn., ABA, Council State Govts., Nat. Gov.'s Assn., Rep. Gov.'s Assn., Southern Gov.'s Assn. Republican. Roman Catholic. Office: US Ho Reps 1233 Longworth Bldg Washington DC 20515-0801*

CASTLE, WILLIAM EUGENE, retired academic administrator; b. Thomas, SD, Sept. 5, 1929; s. Eugene Albert and Kathryn E. (Barkley) C.; m. Diane Lee Sklar, Aug. 8, 1963. BS, No. State Tchrs. Coll., 1951; MA, U. Iowa, 1958; PhD, Stanford U., 1963. Tchr. Faulkton HS, SD, 1951; instr. St. Cloud Tchrs. Coll., Minn., 1958-60, Central Wash. Tchrs. Coll., Ellensburg, 1961; asst. prof. U. Va., 1963-65; asso. sec. for research and sci. affairs Am. Speech, Lang. and Hearing Assn., Washington, 1965-68; dean Nat. Tech. Inst. for Deaf, Rochester Inst. Tech., NY, 1968-79, v.p., 1979-95, dir., 1977-95. Author: The Effect of Narrow Band Filtering on the Perception of Certain English Vowels, 1964. Served with USAF, 1952-56. Named Outstanding Alumnus, No. State Coll., 1984 Mem. Am. Speech Lang. and Hearing Assn., Alexander Graham Bell Assn. for Deaf (pres. 1982-84, 90-92). Home: Cypress Landing 104 Roanoke Ln Chocowinity NC 27817-8809 *Though it took more than one-third of the years I have thus far spent, a great sense of relief from skepticism and cynicism occurred for me when I reasoned within myself that life is the only absolute and that the greatest component of feeling and the finest advocacy are that of love, not just for fellow human beings but for all parts of life that reflect beauty. Without these two prime thoughts and without lifegiven talents, integrity, and flexibility for living cooperatively with others, I would have no sense of success.*

CASTLEBERRY, JAMES NEWTON, JR., retired law educator, dean; b. Chatom, Ala., Dec. 28, 1921; s. James Newton and Nellie (Robbins) C.; m. Mary Ann Blocker, Feb. 12, 1944 (dec.); children: Jean, Nancy, James III (dec.), Elizabeth, Cynthia, Robert, Mary Ann. JD magna cum laude, St. Mary's U., 1952; diploma in comparative law, Nat. U. Mex., 1960; diploma in tchg. of comparative law, Strasburg, 1963. Bar: Tex. 1952. Asst. atty. gen. State of Tex., 1953-55; prof. law St. Mary's U., San Antonio, 1955-92, dean, 1978-89, dean emeritus, 1989—, ret., 1992. Dir. St. Mary's U. Summer Program in Internat. and Comparative Law, Innsbruck, Austria, 1986-89; exec. dir. Tex. Ctr. for Legal Ethics and Professionalism, 1990-92; lectr. comparative law fgn. legal study tours Corp. for Profl. Confs., 1990-2003. Co-author: Water & Water Rights, 1970; contbr. articles to law jours. Bd. dirs. San Antonio Conservation Soc., 2002-06; trustee Tex. Supreme Ct. Hist. Soc. Mem. ABA, Am. Bar Found. (life), San Antonio Bar Assn., Tex. Bar Found. (life), San Antonio Bar Found. (life), Tex. State Bar, Phi Delta Phi (internat. pres. 1977-79). Home: 680 East Basse Rd 425 San Antonio TX 78209

CASTLE-HUGHES, KEISHA, actress; b. Donnybrook, WA, Australia, Mar. 24, 1990; d. Tim Castle and Desrae Hughes; 1 child, Felicity-Amore. Actor: (films) Whale Rider, 2002 (New Zealand Film and TV award for best actress, 2003, Acad. award nomination for best actress, 2004), Star Wars: Episode III-Revenge of the Sith, 2005, The Nativity Story, 2006. Mailing: Creative Artists Agy c/o Kim Hodgert 9830 Wilshire Blvd Beverly Hills CA 90212-1825*

CASTLEMAN, ALBERT WELFORD, JR., physical chemist, educator; b. Richmond, Va., Jan. 7, 1936; s. Albert W. and Mildred L. Castleman; m. Heide Gisela Engel, Mar. 10, 1976; children: Sharon Beth, Robert Gill, Clifton Carl. BChemE, Rensselaer Poly. Inst., 1957; MS, Poly. Inst. Bklyn., 1963, PhD, 1969; PhD (hon.), U. Innsbruck, Austria, 1987. Leader chemistry rsch. group Brookhaven Nat. Lab., 1958-75; adj. prof. atmospheric chemistry depts. earth and space sci. and mechanics SUNY, Stony Brook, 1973-75; prof. chemistry, CIRES fellow U. Colo., Boulder, 1975-82; prof. chemistry Pa. State U., University Park, 1982—, Evan Pugh prof. chemistry, 1986—, adv. bd. Particulate Materials Ctr., 1987-94, mem. Ctr. for Materials Physics, 1993—, Eberly disting. chair in sci., 1999—, prof. physics, 1999; adv. bd. Ctr. for Nanoscale Sys. Materials Va. Commonwealth U., 1992—. Vis. prof. Physics Inst., Leopold-Franzens U., Innsbruck, Austria, 1981, 84, 99; rev. com. chem. physics programs, Oak Ridge Nat. Lab., 1979, adv. com. to lab. dir. chem. physics programs, Health and Safety Divsn., 1987-90, chmn., 1990, mem. Dept. Energy rev. com. for chem. physics and radiol. physics program, 1985, Fulbright guest prof., 1990; adv. to Dept. Energy on chem. physics pertaining to energy related environ. programs, 1980; mem. ad hoc. panel on atmospheric chemistry Com. on Atmospheric Scis., NRC, NAD, 1980; rev. com. for radiol. and environ. rsch. divsn. Argonne Univs. Assn. Argonne Nat. Lab., 1977-81, chemistry divsn., Argonne, 1988; mem. various rev. and adv. coms. Nat. Ctr. for Atmospheric Rsch., US Dept. Energy US Nuc. Regulatory Commn.; cons. Mfg. Chemists Assn., 1975-80, nuc. divsn. Oak Ridge Nat. Lab., 1976-86, E.I. Dupont de Nemours, 1989—2000; chmn. subcom. on ions, aerosols and radioactivity Internat. Commn. Atmospheric Electricity, 1976-80; sr. scientist von Humboldt awardee Tech. Hochschule Darmstadt, 1987, Philipps U., Marburg, Germany, 1988, U. Wuerzburg, 1998; bd. dirs. chem. sci. and tech. NRC-NAS Mem. editl. bd. Jour. Phys. Chemistry, 1985-88, 2000—, sr. editor, 1988-98; mem. editl. bd. Jour. Am. Chem. Soc., 2002—, Chem. Phys. Letters, 1995—, Jour. Cluster Sci., Internat. Jour. Mass Spectrometry and Ion Proc., 1987-90, Jour. Chem. Physics, 1985-87, Jour. Atmospheric Chemistry, 1982-94, Aerosol Sci. and Tech., 1982-86, Advances in Chem. Physics, 1995—, Nano Letters, 2000—, Springer Series in Chem. Physics, 2003—, Chem. Physics, 2003—; co-editor, mem. editl. bd. Zeitschrift fer Physick D., 1987-90; mem. chem. physics editl. adv. bd. Rsch. Trends; contbr. articles to profl. jours. Recipient Sr. Scientist Alexander von Humboldt award, 1986, Sr. Scientist Fulbright award, 1990, Wilhelm-Jost-Meml. Lecture award, 2000; Sherman Fairchild Disting. scholar, Calif. Inst. Tech., 1977; NSF Creativity Award grantee, 1985-87; Japanese Soc. for Promotion Sci. fellow, 1983, 97, Fellow AAAS, Am. Acad. Arts and Scis., Am. Phys. Soc., NY Acad. Scis.; mem. Nat. Acad. Scis., Am. Chem. Soc. (Creative Advances in Environ. Sci. and Tech. award 1988), Am. Geophys. Union, Am. Assn. Aerosol Rsch., Materials Rsch. Soc., Sigma Xi; Phi Lambda Upsilon. Home: 425 Hillcrest Ave State College PA 16803-3419 Office: Pa State U Dept Chemistry 152 Davey Lab University Park PA 16802-6300 Business E-Mail: awc@psu.edu.

CASTLEMAN, BREAUX BALLARD, health management company executive; b. Louisville, Aug. 19, 1940; s. John Pryor and Mary Jane (Ballard) Castleman; m. Sue Ann Foreman (div. 1995); children: Matthew B., Shea B.; m. Patricia Templin, 2002. BA in Econs., Yale U., 1962; postgrad., NYU, 1963. Mgmt. trainee Bankers Trust Co., NYC, 1963-65; mng. dir. Castleman and Co., Houston, 1965-71; dir. program planning, econ. U.S. Dept. HUD, Ft. Worth, Dallas, 1971-73; v.p., office mgr. Booz Allen and Hamilton, Dallas, Houston, 1973-85; mng. dir. Castleman Group, Houston, 1985-87; CEO Kelsey-Seybold Clinic, P.A., Houston, 1987-95; pres. physician resources divsn. Caremark Internat., Inc., 1994-96; pres. Scripps Clinic, La Jolla, Calif., 1996-99; CEO Physia Corp., Houston, 2000—; pres., CEO Syntiro Healthcare Svcs., Inc., Irvine, Calif., 2001—; chmn. Electro-Optical Scis., Inc., Irvington, NY, 2003—. Contbr. articles to profl. jours. Candidate state legislature, Houston, 1968. Mem. Am. Med. Group Assn. (bd. dirs. 1996-99), Planning Forum (chmn. 1985-86), Yale Club NY. Office: 591 Redwood Hwy #2320 Mill Valley CA 94941 Personal E-mail: xcastleman@aol.com.

CASTLEMAN, LOUIS SAMUEL, retired metallurgist, educator; b. St. Johnsbury, Vt., Nov. 24, 1918; s. Max and Fannie (Svetkey) C.; m. Mildred Blanche Rubin, Jan. 25, 1948; children— Michael Z., David A., Steven J.,

Daniel J. BS, MIT, 1939, DSc, 1950. Plant metallurgist Sunbeam Electric Mfg. Co., Evansville, Ind., 1939-41; sr. scientist, supr., acting sect. mgr. Westinghouse Atomic Power Div., Pitts., 1950-54; metall. specialist Gen. Telephone & Electronics Labs., Inc., Bayside, NY, 1954-64; prof. phys. metallurgy Poly. U., NY, 1964-89, prof. emeritus NY, 1989—. Cons. phys. metallurgy. With AUS, 1941-46; lt. col. Ret. Recipient Distinguished Tchr. award Poly. Inst. N.Y., 1975 Fellow AAAS; mem. Am. Soc. Metals (chpt. chmn. 1963-64), Am. Inst. Mining, Metall. and Petroleum Engrs., Am. Phys. Soc., Metal Sci. Club N.Y. (pres. 1973-74), Sigma Xi. Democrat. Jewish religion. Home: 120 Morris Ave Apt C5 Rockville Centre NY 11570-4240 Personal E-mail: lcastlem@optonline.net.

CASTON, J(ESSE) DOUGLAS, retired medical educator; b. Ellenboro, NC, June 16, 1932; s. Lemuel Joseph and Myrtice Elizabeth (Vassey) C.; m. Mary Ann Keeter, June 1, 1958; children: John Andrew, Elizabeth Anne, Mary Susan. AB, Lenoir Rhyne Coll., 1954; MA, U. N.C., 1958; PhD, Brown U., 1961. Fellow Carnegie Instn., Washington, Balt., 1961-62; asst. prof. anatomy Case Western Res. U., Cleve., 1962-71, assoc. prof., 1971-76, prof., 1976-98, co-dir. Devel. Biology Ctr., 1971-77, prof. emeritus, 1999—. Cons. Diamond Shamrock Corp., Cleve., 1975-77; coordinator Core Acad. Program, Sch. Medicine, 1985-94. Patentee folate assay, methotrexate assay; contbr. numerous articles to sci. jours., 1962—. With AUS, 1954—56. Fellow H.W. Wilson, 1956; grantee USPHS, 1963—, Cancer Soc., 1963— Mem. Am. Chem. Soc., AAAS, Am. Soc. Zoologists and Developmental Biologists, Biophys. Soc., Soc. Cell Biology, Am. Assn. Anatomists Episcopalian.

CASTOR, JON STUART, electronics executive; b. Lynchburg, Va., Dec. 15, 1951; s. William Stuart and Marilyn (Hughes) Castor; m. Stephanie Lum, Jan. 7, 1989; 1 child, David Jon. BA, Northwestern U., Evanston, Ill., 1973; MBA, Stanford U., Calif., 1975. Mgmt. cons., Menlo Park, Calif., 1981-96; pres., CFO TeraLogic, Inc., 1996—2000, CEO, 2000—02; sr. v.p., gen. mgr. Oak Tech. Inc., Sunnyvale, 2002—03, Zoran Corp., Sunnyvale, 2003—04; bd. dir. Genesis Microchip, Alviso, Calif., 2004—. Bd. dirs. Artimi, Cambridge, England, chmn., 2006—; bd. dirs. Adaptec, Inc., Milpitas, Calif.; chmn. bd. dirs. Omneon Video Networks, Sunnyvale, Calif., 2007—. Dir. midwest consumer adv. bd. FTC, 1971—73; v.p., bd. dir. San Mateo coun. Boy Scouts Am., 1991—93, bd. dir. Pacific Skyline coun., 1994—2003; trustee Coyote Point Mus. Environ. Edn., San Mateo, 1992—95. Achievements include patents in field.

CASTOR, KATHY, congresswoman; b. Miami, Aug. 20, 1966; d. Don Castor and Betty Bowe; m. William Lewis; 2 children. BA, Emory U., 1988; JD, Fla. State U., 1991. Atty., Fla.; mem. Hillsborough County Commn., Fla., 2002—06, US Congress from 11th Fla. dist., 2007—, mem. Armed Svcs. and Rules Coms. Democrat. Office: 4144 N Armenia Ave, Ste 300 Tampa FL 33607 also: 317 Cannon House Office Bldg Washington DC 20515 Office Phone: 813-871-2817, 202-225-3376. Office Fax: 813-871-2864, 202-225-5652.*

CASTORINO, SUE, communications executive; b. Columbus, Ohio, May 5, 1953; m. Randy Minkoff, Oct. 23, 1983. BS in Speech, Northwestern U., Evanston, Ill., 1975. Producer, community affairs Sta. WBBM-TV, Chgo., 1975; news anchor, reporter Sta. WBBM, Chgo., 1981—86; news reporter Sta. WHTH-AM/FM, Newark, Ohio, 1975; news anchor, reporter Sta. WERE, Cleve., 1975—78, Sta. WWWE, Cleve., 1978—81; founder, pres. Sue Castorino: The Speaking Specialists, Chgo., 1986—. Pvt. voice coach; active internat. exec. comm. tng. in media, crisis and issue mgmt.; presenter, lectr. in field. Author: North Shore Mag., 1987—92; active voice-over and on-camera talent, 1986—. Recipient Golden Gavel award, Chgo. Soc. Assn. Execs., 1991, various news reporting awards, AP, UPI, Chgo., 1981—86. Avocations: sports, films, piano. Office: The Speaking Specialists Ste 2602 435 N Michigan Ave Fl 2602 Chicago IL 60611-4001 Office Phone: 312-527-2252.

CASTORO, ROSEMARIE, sculptor; b. Bklyn., Mar. 1, 1939; d. Michael Peter and Camille C. Student in painting, Mus. Modern Art, NYC, 1955-56; BFA cum laude, Pratt Inst., Bklyn., 1963. Tchr. Sch. Visual Arts, NYC, 1971, Hunter Coll., NYC, 1972, Calif. State U., Fresno, 1973, Syracuse (N.Y.) U., 1975, U. Colo., Boulder, 1977, Stockton State U., NJ, 1983, Boston Mus. Sch., 1983, Am. U., Corciano, Italy, 2000. Lectr. art Boston Mus. Sch. Art, 1971, 80, New Sch. Social Rsch., N.Y.C., 1972, 73, Phila. Coll. Art, 1974, Atlanta Coll. Art, 1974, Rome Art Assn., N.Y. State, 1975, Syracuse (N.Y.) U., 1975, U. Calif., Berkeley, 1976, Suzuki-Walker, Sausalito, Calif., 1976, Art Inst. Sch., Chgo., 1980, Pratt Inst., N.Y.C., 1982, 95, C.W. Post, L.I., N.Y., 1984, San Jose (Calif.) U., 1984, 85, N.J. Ctr. for Visual Arts, Summit, 1989, Ecole Nat. Superieure des Beaux-Arts, Paris, 1995. One-woman shows include Tibor de Nagy Gallery, N.Y.C., 1971, 1972, 1973, 1975, 1976, 1978, 1981, 1983, 1985, 1989, Hal Bromm Gallery, 1976, 1978, 1979, 1980, 1983, 1987, 1991—92, 1997, 2002, 2006—07, Julian Pretto, 1978, 1979, Marion Deson, Chgo., 1981, Am. Ctr., Paris, 1983, Eaton/Shoen Gallery, San Francisco, 1984, 1986, Newark Mus., 1991, Arnaud Lefebvre Gallery, Paris, 1993, 1995, 1997, 1998, 1999, 2003, 2004, Stella R Graphics, Paris, 1993, Eaton Fine Arts, West Palm Beach, Fla., 2000, 2004, exhibited in group shows at Bklyn. Mus., 1963, Tibor de Nagy Gallery, 1966, Stable Gallery, 1966, Dwan Gallery, N.Y.C., 1968, 1969, Richard Feigen Gallery, 1968, Paula Cooper Gallery, 1969, 1971, Vancouver (B.C., Can.) Art Gallery, 1970, Stadtische Kunsthalle, Dusseldorf, Germany, 1970, Allen Art Mus., Oberlin, Ohio, 1970, Hundred Acres Gallery, N.Y.C., 1970, 112 Greene St Gallery, 1971, 1972, Richard Gray Gallery, Chgo., 1972, Storm King Art Gallery, Mountainville, N.Y., 1972, 1974, 1975, Grapestake Gallery, San Francisco, 1975—76, Moore Coll. Art, Phila., 1977, John Weber Gallery, N.Y.C., 1977, Hal Bromm Gallery, 1977, 1981—82, 1985—87, 2006, Indpls. Mus. Art, 1978, Whitney Mus. Am. Art, N.Y.C., 1978, Nancy Lurie Gallery, Chgo., 1978, Smithsonian Instn., Washington, 1980, Hunter Mus. Art, Chattanooga, Tenn., 1980, Banco Gallery, Brescia, Italy, 1980, Hirshhorn Mus. and Sculpture Garden, Washington, 1981, Pratt Inst. Art Gallery, Bklyn., 1981, Eaton/Shoen Gallery, 1982, 2003, 2006, Maier Mus. Art, Lynchburgh, Va., 1983, 1990, Laguna Gloria Art Mus., Austin, Tex., 1985, Mus. Modern Art, N.Y.C., 1985, Newark Mus., 1987, Marvin Seline Gallery, Houston, 1990, Jan Baum Gallery, LA, 1990, Stellar Graphics, Paris, 1992, Galerie Arnaud Lefebvre, 1993, 1995—96, 2001, 2003, 2004, 2006, 2007, Henry St. Settlement, N.Y.C., 1993, Atheneum Music & Arts Libr., La Jolla, Calif., 1995, Beaumanoir, Le Leslay, France, 1995, 2004, PS #1, N.Y.C., 2004, many others, commns. include, Battery Park City, N.Y.C., 1978, GSA, Topeka, Kans., 1979, Am. Ctr., Paris, 1983, Athena Found., L.I., N.Y., 1986, Woodstock '94, Saugerties, N.Y., 1994, Millbrook, N.Y., 2005, Represented in permanent collections Allen Art Mus., Oberlin, Ohio, Boca Raton (Fla.) Mus., Bank of Am., Calif., Chase Manhattan Bank, N.A., GSA, Washington, Mus. Modern Art, N.Y.C., Newark Mus., Fonds Nat. d'Art Contemporain, Paris, Univ. Art Mus., U. Calif., Berkeley, U. Mass., Woodward Found., Washington. Treas. HIV-Arts, NYC, 1994—2006. Guggenheim fellow, 1971; grantee Woodward Found., 1970, CAPS, 1972, 74, NEA, 1974-75, 84-85, Tiffany Found., 1977, Pollock-Krasner Found., 1989-90, 97-98. Home: 151 Spring St # 6 New York NY 10012-3850 Office Phone: 212-966-4637. E-mail: rcastoro@earthlink.net.

CASTRALE, NICOLE, professional golfer; b. Glendale, Calif., Mar. 24, 1979; d. Anthony and Patricia Dalkas; m. Craig Castrale, Jan. 8, 2005. Grad. in Social Sci., U. So. Calif., LA, 2001. Mem. Futures Tour, 2001, 2004—05, LPGA, 2002—03, 2006—. Named a Rolex First-Team All-Am., Am. Jr. Golf Assn., 1996. Achievements include winning the 2007 Ginn Tribute on the LPGA Tour; winner, Northwest Indiana FUTURES Golf Classic, 2005, and Quality Concepts Kankakee FUTURES Golf Classic, 2005, on the Futures Tour. Avocation: cooking. Mailing: c/o LPGA 100 International Golf Dr Daytona Beach FL 32124-1092*

CASTRATARO, BARBARA ANN, lawyer; b. Bethpage, NY, Apr. 25, 1958; d. Vincent James and Theresa (Chiarini) C. BA in Music, L.I. U., 1984; JD, N.Y. Law Sch., 1989. Bar: N.Y. 1990, U.S. Dist. Ct. (so. dist.) N.Y. 1990. Music dir. CBS Network, NYC, 1979-81, exec. ops., 1985-88; music dir. NBC Network/Score Prodns., NYC and L.A., 1983-84, Score Prodns./ABC Network, NYC and L.A., 1980-84; assoc. Donald Frank Esq., NYC, 1989-93, Law Offices of Joel C. Bender, White Plains, N.Y., 1993-99, Bender, Jenson, Silverstein & Castrataro, LLP, White Plains, 1999-2000; pvt. practice Law Offices of Barbara A. Castrataro, Chappaqua, N.Y., 2000—. Lectr. on divorce and separation parenting; founder Castrataro Artist Mgmt., 1997-99; adj. faculty mem. Berkeley Coll., White Plains, N.Y. Mem. New Castle Dem. Com., Chappaqua, NY, dist. leader; mem. voting protection rights com. Westchester Dem. Lawyers. Recipient 3 Emmy nominations N.Y. Acad. TV Arts and Sci., 1979, 82-83. Mem.: New Castle Dem., N.Y. Dem. Lawyers, N.Y. State Bar Assn. Avocations: gourmet cooking, gardening, swimming. Office: PO Box 132 Chappaqua NY 10514 Office Phone: 914-666-2574. Business E-Mail: bacesq800@aol.com.

CASTRO, ALEXANDRO C., commonwealth supreme court justice; b. Tinian, Northern Marianas, Apr. 23, 1952; m. Carmen Moses; children: Patrick, Eric, Yvonne, Alex Jr., Rodney, Ariel. BL, U. Papua New Guinea, 1979. Bar: U.S. Ct. Appeals (9th cir.), U.S. Dist. Ct. No. Mariana Islands. Mem. Rota Mcpl. Coun., 1972; asst. prosecutor Atty. Gen.'s Office, 1979—86, atty. gen., 1986—89; assoc. judge Northern Mariana Islands Superior Ct., 1989—93, presiding judge, 1993—98; assoc. judge Northern Mariana Islands Supreme Ct., 1998—. Office: House of Justice Guma Hustisia, Imwaal Aweewe PO Box 502165 Saipan MP 96950 Business E-Mail: cnmilaw@itecnmi.com.*

CASTRO, JAN GARDEN, writer, art educator, consultant; b. St. Louis, June 8, 1945; d. Harold and Estelle (Fischer) Garden; 1 child, Jomo Jemal. Student, Cornell U., Ithaca, NY, 1963—65; BA, U. Wis., 1967; pub. cert., Radcliffe Coll., 1967; MA in Tchg., Washington U., St. Louis, 1974, MA, 1994. Life cert. tchr. secondary English, speech, drama and social studies, Mo. Tchr., writer, St. Louis, 1970—80; dir. Big River Assn., St. Louis, 1975-85; adj. prof. humanities Lindenwood Coll., 1980—2005, Touro Coll., NYC, 2006—. Co-founder, dir. Duff's Poetry Series, St. Louis, 1975-81; founder, dir. River Styx P.M. Series, St. Louis, 1981-83; arts cons. Harris-Stowe State Coll., 1986-87; vis. scholar Am. Acad. in Rome, summer 2000. Contbg. author: rev. books San Francisco Rev. Books, 1982—85, Am. Book Rev., 1990—93, Mo. Rev., 1991, New Letters, 1993, 1996, Tampa Rev., 1994—2000, The Nation, Am. Poetry Rev., Sculpture Mag., 1997—; author: (poetry) Mandala of the Five Senses, 1975, The Art and Life of Georgia O'Keeffe, 1985, 1995, Memories and Memoirs.Contemporary Missouri Authors, 2000, (poetry) The Last Frontier, 2001—, Sonia DeLaunay: La Moderne, 2002—, (online pub.) Notebooks of My Other Selves, 2007 (finalist Fulton award); contbg. editor: (jours.) Sculpture Mag. Seeking St. Louis, Voices from a River City, 1670—2000; editor: River Styx mag., 1975—86; co-editor: (essays) Margaret Atwood: Vision and Forms, 1988; co-prodr.(TV host, co-prodr.): (shows) The Writers Cir., Double Helix, 1987—89. Mem. University City Arts and Letters Commn., Mo., 1983-84. NEH fellow UCLA, 1988, Johns Hopkins U., 1991, Camargo Found. fellow (Cassis, France), 1996; recipient Arts and Letters award St. Louis Mag., 1985, Editor's award and editor during G.E. Younger Writers award to River Styx Mag., Coord. Coun. for Lit. Mags., 1986, Arts award Mandrake Soc. Charity Ball, 1988, Leadership award YWCA St. Louis, 1988. Mem. MLA, CAA, PEN Am. Ctr., Nat. Coalition Ind. Scholars (bd. 2006), Margaret Atwood Soc. (founder), Art Table. Home: PO Box 486 New York NY 10159-0486 Personal E-mail: jancastro7@gmail.com.

CASTRO, LEONARD EDWARD, lawyer; b. LA, Mar. 18, 1934; s. Emil Galvez and Lily (Meyerholtz) Castro; 1 child, Stephen Paul. AB, UCLA, 1959, JD, 1962. Bar: Calif. 1963, US Supreme Ct. 1970. Assoc. Musick, Peeler & Garrett, LA, 1962—68, ptnr., 1968—. Mem. bd. editors, note and comment editor UCLA Law Rev., 1961—62; panelist, spkr. legal edn. programs. Contbr. chapters to books. Mem.: ABA, LA County Bar Assn. Office: Musick Peeler & Garrett 1 Wilshire Blvd Ste 2000 Los Angeles CA 90017-3876

CASTRO, MARIA GRACIELA, medical educator, geneticist, researcher; b. Buenos Aires, Mar. 2, 1955; d. Nestor Antonio Castro and Maria Esther Rodriquez; m. Pedro Ricardo Lowenstein, Jan. 12, 1988; 1 child, Elijah David Lowenstein. BSc 1st class in Chemistry, Nat. U. La Plata, Argentina, 1979, MSc in Biochemistry, 1981, PhD in Biochemistry, 1986. Fogarty postdoctoral fellow Lab. Neurochemistry and Neuroimmunology NICHHD/NIH, Bethesda, Md., 1986—88; sr. rsch. fellow Lab. Molecular Endocrinology, dept. biochemistry and physiology U. Reading, England, 1988—90; lectr. neurosci., dept. physiology U. Wales Coll., Cardiff, 1991—95; sr. lectr. medicine Sch. Medicine U. Manchester, England, 1995—98, prof. molecular medicine, 1998—. Lectr. dept. molecular and life scis. U. Abertay, Dundee, Scotland, 1991—92; dir. molecular medicine and gene therapy U. Manchester, England, 1996—; expert Women in Sci. Tech., Sheffield, 1996—; mem. neurosci. panel Wellcome Trust, 1999—; co-dir. dept. molecular medicine Cedars-Sinai Med. Ctr., 2001—, co-dir. bd. govs. Gene Therapeutics Rsch. Inst., 2001—; prof. medicine UCLA, 2002—, prof. molecular and med. pharmacology, 2004—. Mem. editl. bd.: Jour. Endocrinology, Jour. Molecular Endocrinology, Current Gene Therapy, Gene Therapy, Pituitary, 2000, Neuro Molecular Medicine, 2001—; contbr. articles to profl. jours. Rsch. grantee, Brit. Heart Found., 1997, Med. Rsch. Coun., 1998, Biotech. and Biol. Rsch. Coun., 1999—2000, Wellcome Trust, 1999, NIH, 2003—. Mem.: Nat. Inst. Neurol. Disorders and Stroke, Internat. Soc. Nerovirology (founding mem.), Soc. Neurosci., Endocrine Soc., Am. Gene Therapy Assn. Achievements include patents in field; research in program development of gene therapy for chronic neurological diseases and brain cancer. Business E-Mail: castromg@cshs.org.

CASTRO, MARY MCDERMOTT, language educator; b. East Liverpool, Ohio, Apr. 13, 1952; d. Robert James and Elizabeth Costello McDermott; 1 child, Sarah Elizabeth. BA, Seton Hill, 1974; MA, Ohio U., 1976. Tchr. Spanish, Mercyhurst Prep. Sch., Erie, Pa., 1976—78; lectr. in Spanish, U. Minn., Duluth, 1979; tchg. asst. in English, U. Pitts., 1979; tchg. asst. in Spanish, U. N.C., Chapel Hill, 1980—83; lectr. in Spanish, N.C. State U., Raleigh, 1984—90, U. N.C., Charlotte, 1990—. Dir. of Spanish lang. & culture in Costa Rica program U. N.C., Charlotte, 1993—, Sigma Delta Pi advisor, 1995—2005; instr. English, Inst. Anglo-Mexicano, Jalapa, Mexico, 1982. Named Outstanding Tchr., N.C. Gen. Assembly, 1994, 1996. Mem.: Southeastern Coun. Latin Am. Studies, Fgn. Lang. Assn. N.C., Am. Coun. on Tchg. of Fgn. Langs., N.C. State U. Acad. Outstanding Tchrs. (life). Avocation: dog breeding. Home: 2520 Savannah Hills Dr Matthews NC 28105 Office: University of North Carolina-Charlotte 9201 University City Blvd Charlotte NC 28223-0001 Office Phone: 704-687-8775. Personal E-mail: marysec88@aol.com. Business E-Mail: mfcastro@email.uncc.edu.

CASTRO, RAUL HECTOR, lawyer, retired government, ambassador; b. Cananea, Mexico, June 12, 1916; arrived in US, 1926, naturalized, 1939; s. Francisco D. and Rosario (Acosta) C.; m. Patricia M. Norris, Nov. 13, 1954; children— Mary Pat, Beth. BA, Ariz. State Coll., 1939; JD, U. Ariz., 1949; LL.D. (hon.), No. Ariz. U., 1966, Ariz. State U., 1972, U. Autonoma de Guadalajara, Mex. Bar: Ariz. 1949. Fgn. service clk. Dept. State, Agua Prieta, Mexico, 1941-46; instr. Spanish U. Ariz., 1946-49; practiced in Tucson, 1949-51; dep. county atty. Pima County, Ariz., 1951-54; county atty., 1954-58; judge Superior Ct., Tucson, 1958-64, Juvenile Ct., Tucson, 1961-64; U.S. ambassador to El Salvador, San Salvador, 1964-68, to Bolivia, La Paz, 1968-69; practice internat. law Tucson, 1969-74, Phoenix, 1980—; gov. Ariz., 1975-77; U.S. ambassador to Argentina, 1977-80; operator Castro Pony Farm, 1954-64. Pres. Pima County Tb and Health Assn., Tucson Youth Bd., Ariz. Horseman's Assn.; Bd. dirs. Tucson chpt. A.R.C., Tucson council Boy Scouts Am., Tucson YMCA, Nat. Council Christians and Jews, YWCA Camp; Bd. Mem. Ariz. N.G., 1935-39. Recipient Outstanding Naturalized Citizen award Pima County Bar Assn., 1964, Outstanding Am. Citizen award D.A.R., 1964; Pub. Service award U. Ariz., 1966; John F. Kennedy medal Kennedy U., Buenos Aires. Mem. Am. Fgn. Service Assn., Am. Judicature Soc., Inter-Am. Bar Assn., Ariz. Bar Assn., Pima County Bar Assn., Nat. Council Crime and Deliquency (bd. dirs.), Assn. Trial Lawyers Am., Council Am. Ambassadors, Nat. Assn. Trial Judges, Nat. Council Juvenile Ct. Judges, Fed. Bar Assn., Nat. Lawyers Club, Phi Alpha Delta. Clubs: Rotarian. Democrat. Roman Catholic.

CASTRO, TERESA JACIRA, small business owner; b. Chgo., July 18, 1956; d. Jene Paul and June Edith (Aleff) Harper; m. Oscar Armando Rodriguez (div. 1981); 1 child, Avelina; m. Jorge Castro (div. 1993); 1 child, Pablo. AA in Opera, Fleming Coll., Florence, Italy, 1975; BA in Spanish and Portuguese cum laude, U. N.Mex., Albuquerque, 1979; MS in Info. Tech., Am. Intercontinental U., Ft. Lauderdale, 2001. Pers. banker Chase Manhattan Bank, Santiago, 1993-94; pres. SalsaPower.com, Inc., 2000—; freelance computer and systems analyst. Tech. translator and simultaneous interpreter specializing in engring., fin., legal and med. matters, Ft. Lauderdale, Fla., 1995—; owner, Accent Translations, 1995—; founder/dir. Absolute Salsa Dance Studio, 1999—. Vol. notary pub. People With AIDS/ARC, 1985-91, The AIDS Found./Shanti Project, San Francisco, 1986-90; vol. working on reunification searches for adoptees and birth parents, Calif., N.Y., Latin Am. Mem. NAFE, Nat. Assn. Photoshop Profls., Toastmasters Internat. Avocations: dancing samba, salsa, teaching dance classes.

CASTRO, VALENTINO, psychologist, counseling administrator; b. Humacao, PR, Oct. 6, 1950; s. Vale and Dolores (Mulero) Castro; m. Angelica Alba, Sept. 13, 2001; children: Daniel, Raoul, Jorge, Deborah, Ariana. M in Planning, U. PR, Rio Piedras, 1976; EdD, Interamerican U., PR, 1987; specialist in sch. psychology, Govs. State U., University Park, Ill., 1998; resp. clin. psychology, Ill. Sch. Profl. Psychology, Rolling Meadows, 2000. Cert. sch. psychologist, lic. Fla., profl. planner PR Dept. of State. Rehab. counselor Dept. Social Svcs., Humacao, PR, 1971—76; profl. planner V&C Planning Assocs., San Juan, Miami, 1976—83; prof. Interam. U., San Juan, 1983—87; dir. evaluation Met. U., San Juan, 1984—85; prof. Phoenix U., San Juan, 1984—89; dir. evaluation Regional Colls. Adminstrn. U. PR, Rio Piedras, 1986—87; h.s. advanced math and stats. tchr. Chgo. Pub. Schs., 1991—96; sch. psychologist Cicero (Ill.) Pub. Schs., 1998—99, Dist. 141, Elgin, Ill., 1999—2000, Manatee County Sch. Bd., Bradenton, Fla., 2000—, Spl. Edn. Coop., Woodstock, Ill., 2000—01, Duval County Pub. Schs., Jacksonville, Fla., 2001—02; sr. psychologist Fla. State Prison, Starke, Fla., 2002—03. Cons. McNeill Labs., Las Piedras, 1983—87, PR Med. Bd., San Juan, 1987—91; com. mem. Manatee County Sch. Evaluation Com., Bradenton, Fla., 2004—; crisis specialist Nat. Orgn. For Victims Assistance, Fla., 2000—, NASP, Bethesda, Md., 2001—; social security reform commn. Office of Gov., San Juan, 1976—77; cons. Office of Gov., San Juan, 1983—91, PR Legislature (Senate) Edn. Reform Commn., San Juan, 1987—89, Johnson & Johnson, PR, 1987—90; cons., trainer Ponce Mcpl. Govt., 1990—91; cons. Dept. Children and Families, Chgo., 1996—97; testing cons., examiner Harcourt Pub., Dallas, 2003—. Contbr. articles to profl. jours., scientific papers. Troop chmn. Boys Scouts, Humacao, PR, 1976—80; mem. Catholic Charities, Chgo., Woodstock, 2000—01; chmn. bd. dirs. Comm. and Social Svcs. Org., Chgo., 1992—2001; mem. Govs. Commn. on Child Welfare, Springfield, Ill., 1998—2000. Recipient Scholastic Achievement award, Interam. U., 1987; fellow, Nat. Edn. Acad., 1998; scholar, Nat. Mental Health Inst., 1974. Mem.: NASP, APA, Am. Planning Assn. (assoc.). Office: Manatee County Sch Bd 215 Manatee Ave W Bradenton FL 34221 Home Phone: 941-723-3917; Office Phone: 941-708-8540. Personal E-mail: valetoben@yahoo.com. Business E-Mail: castrov@fc.manatee.k12.fl.us.

CASTRO-BLANCO, JAMES, law educator; b. Bronx, NY, 1959; Bachelor, SUNY, Albany, 1988; JD, Bklyn. Law Sch., 1991. Litigation assoc. Winthrop Stimson Putnam & Roberts; asst. U.S. atty. Ea. Dist. N.Y.; asst. dean, adj. prof. law St. John's U. Sch. Law; mgr. assoc. devel. Shearman & Sterling. Mem. faculty N.Y.C. Corp. Counsel Trial Program, 1999—; coach mock trial teams Bklyn. Law Sch. and St. Johns U. Sch. Law. Mem. Mayor's adv. com. on judiciary, NYC; exec. coun. Network of Bar Leaders. Mem.: N.Y. State Bar Assn. (com. on legal edn. and admission to bar), Assn. of Bar of City of N.Y. (com. on recruitment and retention of lawyers). Office: St Johns U 8000 Utopia Pkwy Jamaica NY 11439

CASTRO-KLAREN, SARA, Latin American literature professor; b. Arequipa, Sabandia, Peru, June 9, 1942; d. José Andrés and Zoila Rosa (Rivas) Castro-Valdivia; m. Peter F. Klaren, Sept. 3, 1962; 1 child, Alexandra. BA, UCLA, 1962, MA, 1965, PhD, 1968. Asst. prof. Dartmouth Coll., No. Hampshire, NH, 1970-84; chief Hispanic div. Lib. of Congress Fed. Govt., Washington, 1984-86; prof. Latin Am. lit. Johns Hopkins U., Balt., 1986—. Dir. program Latin Am. Studies, JHU. Author: El Mundo Magico de J.M. Arquedas, Lima, 1973, Mario Vargas Llosa, Analisis Introductorio, Lima, 1988, Escritura Sujeto y Transgresión, Mex., 1989, Understanding Mario Vargas Llosa, U.S.C., 1990; editor: Women's Writing in Latin America, 1991, Latin American Women's Narrative: Practices and Theoretical Perspectives, 2003, Beyond Imagined Communities: Reading and Writing the Nation in Nineteenth Century Latin America, 2003. Fellow Woodrow Wilson Ctr. for Scholars, Washington, 1977-78. Mem. MLA, AAUP, Latin Am. Studies Assn. Avocation: gardening. Home: 9438 Rabbit Hill Road Great Falls VA 22066

CASTRONEVES, HÉLIO, race car driver; b. Sao Paulo, Brazil, May 10, 1975; Amateur race car driver (domestic and internat. races), 1992—98; race car driver Bettenhausen Motorsports & Hogan Racing, 1998—99, Penske Racing, 2000—; owner NasrCastroneves Racing. Performer: Dancing with the Stars, 2007; featured in People, Cosmopolitan, Esquire and Sports Illustrated, interviewed by David Letterman and Regis and Kelly. Amb. Smile Found., 2004—. Named Next Hottest Race Car Driver, ESPN Mag., 2000, winner, Indpls. 500, 2001, 2002, 2nd Pl., 2003; recipient Key of Miami, Mayor Manual Diaz. Achievements include becoming the fifth race car driver in history to win the Indianapolis 500 for two consecutive years. Avocations: tennis, running. Mailing: Penske Racing 200 Penske Way Mooresville NC 28115 Office Phone: 704-664-2300.*

CASTRONOVA, JOHN, special education educator; b. Bklyn., Mar. 3, 1959; MS in Edn., Bklyn Coll., 1985, Advanced Degree in Sch. Psychology, 1985, Advanced Degree in Supervision, 1993; D in Psychology, Yeshiva U., Bronx, NY, 1997. Cert. supervision and adminstrn. NY, 1993, sch. psycholgy NY, 1985, spl. edn. NY, 1981, lic. mental health counselor NY, 2005. Undergrad. prof. Sch. Visual Arts, NYC, 1997—2005; individual needs dept. leader Locust Valley Ctrl. Sch. Dist., NY, 2004—; grad. prof. Coll. New Rochelle, NY, 2004—. Individual, family, marriage counselor Ctr. for Optimal Living, Seaford, NY, 1998—; ordained min. New Sem., NYC, 2004—. Contbr. chapters to books. , Arnold and Marie Schwartz Sch. Pharmacy scholar, 1981. Mem.: LI Assn. Spl. Edn.

Adminstrs. (assoc.), Nat. Assn. Sch. Psychologists (assoc.), Imago Relationship Internat. (assoc.). Home Phone: 516-679-3328; Office Phone: 516-674-6388. Personal E-mail: john@centerforoptimalliving.com.

CASTRONOVO, THOMAS PAUL, architect, consultant; b. Chgo., Apr. 7, 1932; s. Paul Thomas and Nancy (Racina) C. Student, U. Akron, 1949-51; BArch, Ohio State U., 1955. Registered architect, Ohio, Calif., Colo. Intern architect E.J. Guran, Architect, Akron, Ohio, 1957-58, A.W. Petersen, Architect, Akron, 1958-60; pres., owner Thomas P. Castronovo, Architect, Akron, 1960—. Chmn. Akron Urban Design and Fine Arts Commn.; mem. Akron Civic Design Awards Com., 1972, Akron Regional Devel. Bd., 1983-87. 1st lt. USAF, 1955-57. Mem. AIA (bd. dirs. Akron chpt. 1987-90), Architects Soc. Ohio, Pi Kappa Epsilon (Akron U. chpt., pres. alumni 1982-84, mem. Hall of Fame 1982). Avocations: tennis, skiing, gardening, cooking, boating. Office: 1175 N Main St Akron OH 44310-1047 Office Phone: 330-928-1080.

CASTRO-WRIGHT, EDUARDO, retail executive; b. Ecuador, 1956; BS in Mech. Engring., Tex. A&M Univ. Pres., Venezuela, Mexico divsn. Nabisco, 1991—94, pres., Asia-Pacific; pres. Honeywell Transp., Power Sys., Torrance, Calif., 2000, Wal-Mart Mex., 2001—05, COO, 2001—03, CEO, 2003—05; exec. v.p., COO Wal-Mart Stores USA, Bentonville, Ark., 2005, pres., CEO, 2005—. Bd. dirs. Dow Jones & Co., 2006—. Office: Wal-Mart Stores Inc 702 SW 8th St Bentonville AR 72716

CASWELL, DOROTHY ANN COTTRELL, performing arts association administrator; b. NYC, Dec. 18, 1938; d. Donald Peery and Eleanor Hildaborg (Westberg) Cottrell; m. Allen Edward Caswell, Oct. 24, 1959; children: David Alan, Bruce Leland. Student, Carleton Coll., Northfield, MN., 1956-59; AB in Psych., George Wash. U., 1960-61; postgrad. in vocal performance, SUNY, Oneonta, 1971-76. Sec. U.S. Fgn. Service, Tunis, Tunisia, 1959-61; mng. dir. Glimmerglass Opera, Inc., Cooperstown, NY, 1975-78; exec. dir. Upper Catskill Community Council on the Arts, Oneonta, NY, 1978-80; devel. officer Catskill Arts Consortium, Oneonta, 1981-83; devel. cons. Otsego Urban Rural Self-Devel. Assocs., Inc., Oneonta, 1982-83; co-founder, pres. Catskill Choral Soc., 1970-76, 81-84; assoc. producer Orpheus Theatre, Inc., Oneonta, 1984-91; voice tchr. Oneonta, 1984—; ptnr., co-owner OnStage Prodn. Svcs., 1991—. Cons., arts adminstrv. Dorothy Caswell Assocs., Oneonta, 1981—; past pres., mem. sub-area coun. Health Sys. Agy. NE, NY, mem. planning adv. group, rev. adv. Singer/actress: Orpheus Theatre, 1984—; actor(film series Susquehanna Stories): WSKG-TV Pub. TV, 1990—. Mem. chorus Glimmerglass Opera, Cooperstown, 1974—; mem. mil. acad. selection com. Congressman Sherwood Boehlert, NY, 1993—2006; mem. Otsego County Health Planning Adv. Coun. Otsego Publ Health Partnership; bd. dirs. Otsego County Tourism Bur., 1987—90, Oneonta Downtown Coalition, 1982—84; mem. vet.'s affairs and mil. acad. selection com. Michael Arcuri, NY, 2007—. Recipient Honored for Outstanding Performance and Svcs. to Cmty., SUNY, 1975. Democrat. Avocations: painting, performing arts, gardening, swimming.

CASWELL, JAMES L., government agency administrator; b. Mich. m. Susan Caswell; 3 children. BS in Forestry, Mich. State U., 1967. Various positions Bur. of Land Mgmt., Bonneville Power Adminstrn., US Forest Svc.; head Idaho Governor's Office, Office of Species Conservation, 2000—07; dir. Bur. of Land Mgmt., 2007—. 2nd lt. US Army, 1967—73. Office: US Bureau of Land Mgmt 1849 C St Rm 406-LS Washington DC 20240 Office Phone: 202-452-5125. Office Fax: 202-452-5124.*

CASWELL, RANDALL SMITH, physicist; b. Eugene, Oreg., Feb. 7, 1924; s. Albert Edward and M. Constance (Edwards) C.; m. Jean M. Miller, June 14, 1945; children: William Edward (dec.), Virginia Lee, Anne Marden, Ellen Sue, Wendy Jean (dec.), Julia Constance. SB, MIT, 1947, PhD in Physics, 1951. Assoc. prof. physics U. Ky., 1950-52; rschr. particle solid state physics Oak Ridge Nat. Lab., 1952; physicist neutron physics Nat. Bur. Standards, 1952-69; dep. dir. Ctr. Radiation Rsch., 1969-78, chief nuclear radiation divsn., 1978-85; chief ionizing radiation divsn. Nat. Inst. Standards & Tech., Gaithersburg, Md., 1985-94, ret., 1994. Adj. prof. physics Am. U. 1957-71; mem. Nat. Coun. Radiation Protection & Measurements, 1967-91; chmn. neutron measurements sect. Adv. Com. Standards Ionizing Radiation Measurement, Bur. Internat. des Poids et Measures, 1969-89; mem. Internat. Commn. Radiation Units & Measurement, 1975-2002, sec., 1979-2002; chmn. sci. panel Com. Interagy. Radiation Rsch. and Policy Coord. Office Sci. and Tech. Policy, 1984-94. Assoc. editor Radiation Rsch., 1977-80. Recipient Silver medal, US Dept. Commerce, 1961, Gold medal, 1979, Rosa award, Nat. Inst. Stds. and Tech., 1991, Disting. Svc. award, Coun. Ionizing Radiation Measurements and Stds., 2000. Fellow: Am. Physics Soc.; mem.: Radiation Rsch. Soc. Office: Nat Inst of Stds Tech Physics Rm C229 Radiation Physics Bldg 245 Gaithersburg MD 20899-0001 Office Phone: 301-975-5525. Business E-Mail: randall.caswell@nist.gov.

CATALANI, RICHARD WILLIAM, forensic specialist, writer; b. Worcester, Mass., Dec. 14, 1955; s. Armand Richard and Carolyn Tierney Catalani; m. Donna Marie DeMaio, Feb. 13, 1988. BA, Calif. State U., Northridge, 1981. Cert. med. toxicologist technologist Calif., 1983, profl. competency, criminalistics Calif. Assn. Criminalistics, 1989. Sr. criminalist LA County Sheriff's Dept., 1987—98; supervising criminalist, 1998—2001; sr. tech. cons. CSI: Crime Scene Investigation, Universal City, Calif., 2002—, story editor, 2005—06, exec. story editor, 2006—. Author: (TV series) CSI: Crime Scene Investigation. Mem.: AAAS, NRA (life), Writers Guild, Acad. TV Arts and Scis., Assn. Firearm and Toolmark Assn., Am. Acad. Forensic Scis. (assoc.), Heritage Found., Am. Conservative Union, Calif. Rifle and Pistol Assn. (life). Conservative. Office: Richard Catalani Firearms Consultant 18565 Soledad Canyon Rd #178 Canyon Country CA 91351-3700 Office Phone: 661-252-1512. Office Fax: 661 252-1512. Business E-Mail: rcatalani@socal.rr.com.

CATALANO, CARL PHILIP, small business owner; b. Chgo., May 13, 1953; s. Philip Thomas and Arlene Margret (Hora) C.; m. Maria Rosa Diaz, Feb. 14, 1983. AS, Miami Dade Community Coll., Fla., 1984, AA, 1985; student, Am. Inst. Med. Law, 1986; BS in Audio Engring., Kennedy-Western U., 1993, PhD in Mgmt. Info. Sys., 2002. Cert. TV and radio broadcaster FCC, Nat. Radio Inst. (NRI), 1993. Drummer Queens Kidds, Miami and Ft. Lauderdale, Fla., 1970—74; show drummer Kickin, Fla., 1974—76; producer I.J.E. Distbrs. Inc., Hollywood, Fla., 1976—79; coord. internet tech., v.p., case mgr., computer engr. Catalano Registry Inc., Hialeah, Fla., 1979—2006; owner, prodr. Soundtrack Rec., Hialeah, 1986—96; computer programmer, arranger Final Chpt. Inc., Hialeah, 1988—89; owner, MIS engr., prodn. specialist Studio-K Prodns., Miramar, Fla., 1996—. Stage and location gripper Channels 1 and 2, Miami, 1984-85; free-lance programmer drum computer, photographer, Miami and Hialeah, 1983—; musician various studios, Fla., 1983—; mem. rsch. panel Microsoft, Network World Tech. Appeared in (TV series) Miami Vice, 1985, (TV films) Mean Season, 1985; contbr. articles pub. to profl. jour. Mem. NYU Navi Quest Group, Marsh Affinity Group, NOP World/CMP Profl. Developers Panel, Eweek Advisory Panel, Tech. Rsch. Advisory Bd., Decision Analyst Inc.; regional alumni dir. Kennedy-Western U., 2005—; mem. Rep. Nat. Com., Rep. Presdl. Task Force, Presdl. Victory Team. Mem. IEEE Computer Soc., Computer Security Inst., Nat. Drum Assn., Am. Bd. Risk Mgmt. Profls. (diplomate), Assn. Computing Machinery (adv. bd.), Internat. Photographers Soc. (founding mem., Outstanding Achievement award 2003), South Fla. Musicians Assn. Berklee Music Coll. (prodn. specialist, adv. panel eweek), Nat. Fedn. Ind. Bus., Microsoft Ptnrs., Microsoft Bus. Solutions, Network Solutions, Sun Developer Panel, Trump U. Real Estate Alliance. Home: 2522 SW 180th Ave Miramar FL 33029-5191 Office Phone: 954-292-3744. Business E-Mail: c.catalano@computer.org. E-mail: c.catalano@ieee.org.

CATALANO, DOMINIC, art educator, illustrator; b. Syracuse, NY, Jan. 9, 1956; s. Dominic Catalano and Virginia Mae Mayer; m. Oksana Anatoly Chaban, July 27, 2001; children: Sara, Oleksiy, Peter, Cristian. BS in Art Edn., Buffalo State U., 1978; MA in Fine Art, Oswego State U., NY, 1984; MFA in Illustration, Syracuse U., 1991; PhD in Art Edn., Ohio State U., 2005. Cert. tchr. NY. Various art tchg. positions, NY, 1978—89; art dir. Syracuse Newspapers, 1981—86; asst. prof. art dept. Oswego State U., 1992—95, Broome C.C., Binghamton, NY, 1998—2000; asst. prof. Columbus (Ohio) Coll. Art and Design, 2002—04; asst. prof. art dept. Ashland (Ohio) U., 2004—05; asst. prof. Sch. Art Bowling Green (Ohio) U., 2005—. Presenter workshops and seminars in field. Author, illustrator: Wolf Plays Alone, 1992, Frog Went A-Courting, 1998, Santa & the Three Bears, 2000, Mr. Basset Plays, 2003, Hush: A Fantasy in Verse, 2003; illustrator The Bear Who Loved Puccini, 1992, Rabbit Surprise, 1993, Rise and Shine, 1993, That Extraordinary Pig of Paris, 1994, Bernard series, 1996—2004, Sleeping Beauty (Retold), Merry Christmas Old Armadillo, 1995, Basil Bear series, 1998—99, A Tree for Christmas, 2004, numerous other textbooks, children's publs.; one-man shows include Limestone Gallery, Fayetteville, NY, Tyler Gallery of SUNY Oswego, exhibited in group shows at Soc. Illustrators, 1992, 1996, 1998, 2001, 2004, Tyler Gallery, SUNY Oswego, Represented in permanent collections Mazza Gallery Original Picturebook Art, murals, Oswego C. of C., Hilliard Elem. Sch. Recipient 1st prize in graphic arts, NY State Fair, 2d prize, Everson Art Invitational, Syracuse. Mem.: Nat. Art Edn. Assn., Coll. Art Assn., Illustrators' Partnership of Am., Soc. Children's Book Writers and Illustrators. Democrat. Lutheran. Avocations: camping, cooking, travel. Home: 803 Cherry St Perrysburg OH 43551 Personal E-mail: dcatalano@buckeye-express.com.

CATALANO, JANE DONNA, lawyer; b. Schenectady, NY, Feb. 21, 1957; d. Alfred and Joan (Futscher) Martini; m. Peter Catalano, June 18, 1988. BA, SUNY, Plattsburgh, 1979; JD, Albany Law Sch., 1982. Bar: N.Y. 1983, U.S. Dist. Ct. 1983. Atty. Pentak, Brown & Tobin, Albany, NY, 1982-87, Niagara Mohawk Power Corp., Albany, 1987—. Mem. N.Y. State Bar Assn., Albany County Bar Assn. Home: 7 Blackburn Way Latham NY 12110-1943 Office Phone: 518-433-5257. Business E-Mail: jane.catalano@us.ngrid.com.

CATALANO, LOUIS WILLIAM, JR., neurologist; b. Bklyn., Apr. 20, 1942; s. Louis William and Aileen (Bobb) C.; m. Diana Catalano; children: Louis William III, Jamea Elizabeth, Adriana Louise. BS cum laude, U. Pitts., 1963, MD, 1967. Diplomate Am. Bd. Psychiatry and Neurology, Am. Bd. Electroencephalography, Am. Bd. Pain Medicine, Am. Bd. Med. Examiners. Intern Presbyn.-St. Luke's Hosp., Chgo., 1967-68; rsch. assoc. NIH, Bethesda, Md., 1968-70; fellow neurology The Neurol. Inst., NYC, 1970-73; clin. asst., prof. neurology U. Pitts. Sch. Med., 1973—; pvt. practice Greensburg, Pa., 1973—. Staff Latrobe (Pa.) Area Hosp., 1973—, Westmoreland Regional Hosp., Greensburg, 1973—, Indiana (Pa.) Hosp., 1983—; cons. Jeannette (Pa.) Mercy Hosp., 1984—, Frick Hosp., Mt. Pleasant, Pa., 1991—, Torrance (Pa.) State Hosp., 2000—; lectr. in field. Contbr. articles to profl. jours. Pres. Neurol. Inst. We. Pa.; bd. dirs. Epilepsy Found. Western/Cen. Pa., 2000— Spl. fellow Columbia U., NIH, 1970-73, epilepsy minifellow, Bowman Gray Sch. Medicine, Winston-Salem, N.C., 1988. Fellow: Am. Acad. Neurology, Royal Soc. Medicine; mem.: AMA, Pa. Nuerological Soc. (v.p.), European Fedn. Neurol. Socs., Pitts. Neurosci. Soc., Latrobe Acad. Medicine, Westmoreland County Med. Soc., World Fedn. Neurology, Pa. Med. Soc., Am. Sleep Disorders Assn., Am. Acad. Clin. Neurphysiology, Am. Soc. Neuroimaging, Am. Med. Electroencephalographic Assn., Am. Acad. Pain Mgmt., Alpha Omega Alpha, Sigma Xi. Avocations: sport fishing, scuba diving, skiing, travel. Office Phone: 724-537-0885.

CATALANO, ROBERT ANTHONY, ophthalmologist, hospital administrator, writer; b. Albany, NY, Nov. 24, 1956; s. Anthony Joseph and Ida Santa (Muscolino) C.; m. Madeline Faye Kalmer, Aug. 6, 1978; children: Christopher, Ruth, Thomas, Matthew. BS, Union Coll., Schenectady, 1978; MD, U. Va., 1982; MBA, Rensselaer Poly. Inst., 1992. Resident in ophthalmology Albany Med. Coll., 1983-86, vice-chmn. dept. ophthalmology, 1989-90, acting chmn., 1990-91; fellow in pediatric ophthalmology Wills Eye Hosp., Phila., 1986-87; v.p. med. affairs Olean (N.Y.) Gen. Hosp., 1991-93, COO, 1994-95, pres., CEO, 1995—2001; med. dir. Albany Med. Ctr. Hosp., 2001—05, 2006—, interim chief med. officer, 2005—06, chief med. officer, 2006—. Bd. dirs. Westlink Corp. Author: Atlas of Ocular Motility, 1989, Ocular Emergencies, 1992, Pediatric Ophthalmology: A Text/Atlas, 1994, When Autism Strikes, 1998; contbr. articles to profl. jours. Recipient Nat. Found. award March of Dimes Found., 1978, Robert D. Reinecke award Albany Med. Coll., 1985, Shannon award U. Va., 1982; Heed Found. fellow, 1986, Forty Under Forty award, 1993. Mem.: So. Tier Healthcare Network (bd. dirs. 1994—2001, chmn. 2001), Western N.Y. Hosp. Assn. (bd. dirs. 1992—95, 1999—2001, treas. 2001), Am. Coll. Healthcare Execs., Am. Coll. Physician Execs., Acad. Ophthalmology, Alpha Omega Alpha. Roman Catholic. Office: Albany Med Ctr S Clin Campus Mail Code 201 Albany NY 12208-3499 Office Phone: 518-262-8062.

CATALANOTTO, FRANK A., dentist; DMD, U. Medicine and Dentistry NJ, 1968. Fellow in pediat. dentistry Harvard U. and Children's Hosp. Med. Ctr., Boston, 1968—71; faculty mem. Harvard U., 1971—72; assoc. epidemiologist US Navy Great Lakes Dental Rsch. Inst., 1972—74; asst. prof. pediat. dentistry Dept. Pediat. Dentisty, U. Conn. Health Ctr., 1974—85, founding dir. sch. faculty practice, dir. predoctoral program and postdoctoral residency in pediat. dentistry; chair pediat. dentistry U. Tex. Health Sci. Ctr., San Antonio, 1985—88; assoc. dean acad. planning faculty devel. U. Medicine and Dentistry, NJ Dental Sch., 1988—89, assoc. dean rsch., indsl. rels. and profl. devel., 1989—95; dean U. Fla. Coll. Dentistry, 1995—2002; prof. pediat. dentistry U. Fla., 2002—. Co-founder, prin. investigator NIH-supported Conn. Chemosensory Clinical Rsch. Ctr., 1980—85, Northeastern Minority Oral Health Rsch. Ctr., NJ, 1992—95; cons. basic sci. curriculum Commn. Dental Accreditation, ADA, 1989—97; mem. adminstrv. bd. ADEA Coun. Deans, 1996—2000; pres.-elect Am. Dental Edn. Assn., 2003, pres., 2004—05; edit. bd. Pediat. Dentistry jour., Am. Dental Acad.; mem. nat. affairs com. Am. Assn. Dental Rsch., 1989—95; mem. adv. com. on training in primary care medicine and dentistry US Dept. Health's Health Resources and Svc. Adminstrn. Co-author more than 60 sci. publ. Recipient Rsch. Career Devel. award, Nat. Inst. Health. Office: Univ Fla Coll Dentistry PO Box 103628 Gainesville FL 32610-0426 Office Phone: 352-273-5970. Office Fax: 352-273-5985. Business E-Mail: fcatalanotto@dental.ufl.edu.

CATALDI-MAY, LAUREN MICHELLE, head of religious order, music director; d. Alan Barry and Rebecca Elaine Cataldi; m. Jeffrey Ben May, June 12, 2004. MusB in Vocal Performance, U. Del., 2004. Dir. music ministries Bethesda United Meth. Ch., Middletown, Del., 2002—. Mem.: Music Educators Nat. Conf., Am. Choral Dirs. Assn., Am. Guild Organists, No. Del. Alumnae Assn. of Sigma Alpha Iota (treas. 2006). Democrat-Npl. United Methodist. Office: Bethesda United Methodist Church 116 East Main St Middletown DE 19709 Home Phone: 302-653-6580; Office Phone: 302-378-2313. Personal E-mail: lcataldimay@yahoo.com. Business E-Mail: music@bethesda-middletown.org.

CATALFO, ALFRED, JR., (ALFIO CATALFO), lawyer; b. Lawrence, Mass., Jan. 31, 1920; s. Alfio and Vincenza (Amato) C.; m. Caroline Joanne Mosca (dec. Apr. 1968); children: Alfred Thomas, Carol Joanne, Gina Marie; m. Gail Varney, 1988. BA, U. N.H., 1945, MA in History, 1952; LLB, Boston U., 1947, JD (hon.), 1969; postgrad., Suffolk U. Sch. Law, 1955-56, Am. Law Inst., NYC, 1959. Bar: N.H. 1947, U.S. Dist. Ct. 1948, U.S. Ct. Appeals 1978, U.S. Supreme Ct. 1979. Pvt. practice, Dover, NH, 1948—; ptnr. Catalfo Law Firm, Dover, 1980—; county atty. Strafford County, Dover, NH, 1949-50, 55-56; bd. immigration appeals U.S. Dept. Justice, 1953—; football coach Berwick Acad., South Berwick, Maine, 1944, Mission Catholic H.S., Roxbury, Mass., 1945-46. Author: Laws of Divorces, Marriages, and Separations in New Hampshire, 1962, History of the Town of Rollinsford, 1623-1973, 1973. Pres. Young Dems. of Dover, 1953-55; 1st vice-chmn. Young Dems., N.H., 1954-56; mem. Strafford County Dem. Com., 1948-75; vice-chmn. N.H. Dem. Com., 1954-56, 1st chmn., 1956-58, chmn. spl. activities, 1958-60; del. Dem. Nat. Conv., 1956-60, 76; chmn. N.H. Dem. Conv., 1958, conv. dir., 1960; mem. Dem. state exec. com., 1960-70; Dem. nominee for U.S. Senate, 1962; vice-chmn. Dover Cath. Sch. Com., 1969-71; mem. Dover Bd. Adjustment, 1960-65; apptd. lt. commdr. N.H. Govs. Mil. Staff. Pilot U.S. Naval Air Corp., lt. commdr. USNR, 1942-44. Recipient keys to cities of Dover, Somersworth, Concord, Berlin, Manchester and Rochester N.H., 6 nat. plaques DAV, 3 disting. svc. awards Am. Legion, Am. Legion Life Membership award, spl. recognition award Berwick Acad., 1985. Mem. ABA, N.H. Bar Assn., Strafford County Bar Assn. (v.p. 1966-67, pres. 1968-69), Assn. Trial Lawyers Am., N.Y. State Trial Lawyers Assn., Mass. Trial Lawyers Assn., N.H. Trial Lawyers Assn., Tex. Trial Lawyers Assn., Nat. Assn. Criminal Def. Lawyers, N.H. Assn. Criminal Def. Lawyers, Am. Judicature Soc., Phi Delta Phi, DAV (judge adv. N.H. dept. 1950-68, 72—; comdr. chpt. 1953-54, comdr. N.H. 1956-57), Am. Legion (life, chmn. state conv. 1967, 77, 84), Navy League, N.H. Hist. Soc., Dover Hist. Soc., Rollinsford Hist. Soc., Eagles Club, Sons of Italy, Lions, Elks, K.C. (grand knight 1975-77), Moose, Lebanese Club. Clubs: Eagles (Somersworth, N.H.), Sons of Italy (Portsmouth, N.H.). Lodges: Lions, Elks, K.C. (grand knight 1975-77), Moose, Lebanese (Dover). Home: 20 Arch St Dover NH 03820-3602 Office: 450 Central Ave Dover NH 03820-3451

CATALFOMO, PHILIP, retired university dean; b. Providence, Dec. 27, 1931; s. Antonio and Frances (Di Giuseppe) C.; m. Magdalena Wettstein, Jan. 8, 1962; children— Kristina, Anthony Werner. BS, Providence Coll., 1953, U. Conn., 1958; MS, U. Wash., Seattle, 1960, PhD, 1962. Mem. faculty Oreg. State U., 1963-75, prof. pharmacognosy, 1966-75, head dept., 1966-75; prof. pharmacognosy, dean Sch. Pharmacy, U. Mont., Missoula, 1975-86; dean coll. health scis. U. Wyo., Laramie, 1986-91; ret., 1991. Author research articles fungal metabolism. Served with AUS, 1953-55. Gustavus A. Pfeiffer Meml. research fellow, 1969-70 Home: 24502 Old Hwy # 93 Dayton MT 59914

CATANESE, ANTHONY JAMES, academic administrator; b. New Brunswick, NJ, Oct. 18, 1942; s. Anthony James and Josephine Marlene (Barone) C.; m. Sara Jean Phillips, Oct. 23, 1968; children: Mark Anthony, Michael Scott, Mark Alexander. BA, Rutgers U., 1963; M in Urban Planning, NYU, 1965; PhD, U. Wis., 1968. Asst. prof. city planning Ga. Inst. Tech., Atlanta, 1967-78, assoc. prof., 1968-73, chmn. doctoral studies com., 1970-73; James A. Ryder prof. transp. and planning, dir. Ryder program in transp. U. Miami, Coral Gables, Fla., 1973-75; dean Sch. Architecture and Urban Planning U. Wis., Milw., 1975-82; prof. architecture and urban planning, provost Pratt Inst., NYC, 1982-84; dean Coll. Architecture, U. Fla., Gainesville, 1984-89; pres. Fla. Atlantic U., Boca Raton, 1989—2002, pres., prof., 1990—2002; pres. Fla. Inst. Tech., Melbourne, 2002—. Sr. Fulbright prof., Colombia, 1971-72; sr. cons. State of Wis., 1965-67, sr. planner State of N.J., 1963-67; pres. A. J. Catanese & Assocs., Inc., 1967—; mem. pres. commn. NCAA, 1991-93. Author: Scientific Methods of Urban Analysis, 1972, New Perspectives on Urban Transportatio Research, 1972, Systematic Planning-Theory and Applications, 1970, Planners and Local Politics: Impossible Dreams, 1973, Urban Transportation in South Florida, 1974, Personality, Politics and Planning, 1978, Introduction to Urban Planning, 1979, Introduction to Architecture, 1979, The Politics of Planning and Development, 1984, Uban Planning, 1988; contbr. articles to profl. jours. Chmn. Mid. DeKalb County Dem. Party, 1969-71, mem. 5th Congl. Dist. Dem. caucus, 1971; aide-de-camp Gov.'s Office, State of Ga., 1971-72; mem. Ga. Dunes Studies Commn., 1972-73; bd. dirs. Archtl. Rsch. Ctrs. Consortium, 1976—; mem. Urban Policy Task Force, Carter presdl. campaign, 1976, 80; pres. Park West Redevel. Corp., 1976-78; chmn. Milw. City Plan Commn., 1978-82; bd. dirs. Goals for Milw. 2000, 1978-82, Environ. Edn. Found. Fla.; chmn. Gainesville (Fla.) Planning Bd., 1986-89. With USAR, 1961-63. Recipient fellowships State of N.J. Act of 1927, 1962-63, Werner Hegemann Found., 1963-65, Wis. Alumni Rsch. Found., 1965-68, Richard King Mellon Trust, 1966-67, Ford Found., 1967, Nat. Endowment Arts, 1980. Mem. Am. Inst. Planners (bd. govs., v.p. 1971-74), Am. Inst. Cert. Planners (mem. exec. com. 1971-74), Am. Planning Assn., Transp. Rsch. Bd., Regional Sci. Assn., Am. Acad. Polit. and Social Scis., Assn. Coll. Schs. Planning, Heritage Club, Wycliff Club, Tower Club. Office: Fla Inst Tech 150 W University Blvd Melbourne FL 32901 Office Phone: 321-674-7232. Business E-Mail: catanese@fit.edu.

CATANIA, A(NTHONY) CHARLES, psychologist, educator; b. NYC, June 22, 1936; s. Charles John and Elizabeth (Lattarulo) C.; m. Constance J. Britt, Feb. 10, 1962; children: William John, Kenneth Charles BA Psychology highest honors, Columbia U., 1957, MA, 1959. Postdoctoral rsch. fellow Harvard U., 1961—62; sr. pharmacologist Smith, Kline & French Labs., Phila., 1962—64; asst. prof. NYU, 1964—66, asso. prof., 1966—69, prof., chmn. dept. psychology, 1969—73; prof. dept. psychology U. Md. Baltimore County, Catonsville, 1973—2004, program co-dir. master's track in applied behavior analysis, 2004—. Vis. prof. Keio U., Tokyo, 1992; mem. psychobiology com. NSF, 1982-85 Author: Learning, 1979, 4th edit., 1998; co-author: (with E. Shimoff and B.A. Matthews) Behavior on a Disk, 1989; editor: Contemporary Research in Operant Behavior, 1968; co-editor: (with T.A. Brigham) Handbook of Applied Behavior Analysis, 1978, (with S. Harnad) The Selection of Behavior: The Operant Behaviorism of B.F. Skinner, 1988, (with P.N. Hineline) Variations and Selections, 1996, (with V.G. Laties) B.F. Skinner's Cumulative Record, definitive edit., 1999; editor: Jour. Exptl. Analysis Behavior, 1966-69, rev. editor, 1969-76, 83-91; assoc. editor: Behavioral and Brain Scis., 1980—; mem. bd. editors various jours.; contbr. articles to profl. jours.; contbr. chpts. to textbooks. Recipient James McKeen Cattell Sabbatical award, 1986-87, Outstanding Sci. Contbns. to Psychology award Md. Psychol. Assn., 1993, Outstanding Contbr. Behavior Analysis award No. Calif. Assn. Behavior Analysis, 1990; NSF grantee, 1965-67, 74-79, 82-88, USPHS grantee, 1967-73, 79-83; Fulbright sr. rsch. fellow, Wales, Bangor, 1986-87 Fellow APA (pres. divsn. 25 1976-79, 96-98, Don Hake award divsn. 25), Assn. Behavior Analysis (pres. 1982-83, chair publ. bd. 1992-95, pres. Md. chpt. 2001-02); mem. Ea. Psychol. Assn. (dir. 1979-82), Soc. Exptl. Analysis of Behavior (pres. 1966-67, 81-83, v.p. 2003-04), Lang. Origins Soc. (program chair 1996), Md. Assn. Behavior Analysis (pres. 2001-02), Icelandic Assn. Behavior Analysis (hon. founder 2004) Home: 10545 Rivulet Row Columbia MD 21044-2420 Office: U Md Baltimore County Dept Psychology Baltimore MD 21250-0001 Office Phone: 410-455-3002. Business E-Mail: catania@umbc.edu.

CATANIA, KENNETH C., neuroscientist, educator; BS in Zoology, U. Md., College Park, 1991; PhD in Neuroscience, U. Calif., San Diego, 1997. Postdoctoral fellow Vanderbilt U., Nashville, 1997—98, asst. prof., dept. biol. sciences, 1997—98, assoc. prof., dept. biol. sciences, 2006—. Contbr. articles to Nature, Proceedings of NAS USA, Nature Neuroscience, and others. MacArthur Fellow, John D. and Catherine T. MacArthur Found., 2006, Searle Scholar, 2001. Office: Vanderbilt U VU Station B Box

35-1634 Nashville TN 37235 Address: Vanderbilt U 8270B MRBIII 465 21st Ave S Nashville TN 37235 Office Phone: 615-343-1079. Office Fax: 615-343-0336. Business E-Mail: kenneth.catania@vanderbilt.edu.

CATCHINGS, TAMIKA DEVONNE, professional basketball player; b. Stratford, NJ, July 21, 1979; d. Harvey Catchings and Wanda Cathings. Grad., U. Tenn., 2001, M in Sports Studies, 2005. Player Ind. Fever, 2001—. Mem. USA Basketball Women's Sr. Nat. Team, 2004; pres. WNBA Players Assn. Host Catch the Fever basketball camp, 2002, 2003, Catch the Fitness clinic, 2003. Named Naismith Player of Yr., 2000, AP Player of Yr., 2000, US Basketball Writers Assn. Player of Yr., 2000, Kodak/Women's Basketball Coaches Assn. Player of Yr., 2000, Coll. Women's Basketball Player of Yr., ESPY Awards, 2001, WNBA Rookie of Yr., 2002, WNBA Defensive Player of Yr., 2005, 2006; named to WNBA Ea. Conf. All-Star Team, 2002—07, All-WNBA First Team, 2002, 2003, 2006, WNBA All-Defensive First Team, 2005, 2007; recipient Reynolds Soc. Achievement Award, Mass. Eye and Ear Infirmary, Off-Season WNBA Cmty. Assist award, 2002, 2003. Achievements include winning a Gold medal as a member of the US Women's Basketball FIBA Jr. World Championship Team, 1997; winner, Gold medal, US Women's Basketball FIBA World Championship Team, 2002, US Women's Olympic Team, Athens, 2004. Office: Ind Fever Conseco Fieldhouse 125 S Pennsylvania St Indianapolis IN 46204*

CATE, JAN HARRIS, lawyer; b. NYC, Jan. 9, 1964; BA with honors, Univ. Calif., San Diego, 1986; JD, Boston Univ., 1989. Bar: Calif. 1989. Ptnr., leader Bank Fin. practice Pillsbury Winthrop Shaw Pittman, LA. Contbr. articles to profl. jours. Mem.: LA County Bar Assn. Office: Pillsbury Winthrop Shaw Pittman Suite 2800 725 S Figueroa St Los Angeles CA 90017 Office Phone: 213-488-7539. Office Fax: 213-629-1033. Business E-Mail: jan.cate@pillsburylaw.com.

CATE, RICHARD H., school system administrator; BS in Civil Engring., U. Vt.; MPA in Pub. Adminstrn., U. Albany. CFO NY State Dept. Edn., exec. dep. commr., COO, commr. edn., 2003—. City mgr. Barre City, Vt.; past mem. Barre City Coun.; exec. dir. Vt. Supt. Assn. Office: Vt Dept Edn 120 State St Montpelier VT 05620-2501 Office Phone: 802-828-3135. Office Fax: 802-828-3140. Business E-Mail: richard.cate@state.vt.us.*

CATELL, ROBERT BARRY, gas industry executive; b. Bklyn., Feb. 1, 1937; s. Joseph Daniel and Belle (Mishkind) Cicatelli; m. Joan Kathryn Weigand, June 25, 1971; children: Laura Anne, Erica Anne; children by previous marriage: Robert Edward, Carla Ann, Donna Theresa. BME, CCNY, 1958, MME, 1964. Registered profl. engr. Asst. v.p. Bklyn. Union Gas Co., 1974-78, v.p., 1978-82, sr. v.p., 1982-84, exec. v.p., 1984-86, exec. v.p., COO, 1986-90, pres., COO, 1990-91, pres., CEO, 1991-96; chmn., CEO Key Span Energy Corp. (formerly Bklyn. Union Gas Co.), 1996—. Trustee Independence Savs. Bank, Bklyn., 1984—, Gas. Rsch. Inst., 1992; mem. regional adv. com. Chase Bank; chmn. N.Y. State Energy Assn., L.I. Assn. Mem. N.Y. Serda Bd.; chmn. N.Y.C. Partnership; mem. N.Y. State Bus. Coun., vice chmn. Mem. Am. Gas Assn., Soc. Gas Lighting. Avocations: swimming, golf, tennis. Office: Key Span Corp One Metrotech Ctr Brooklyn NY 11201*

CATES, CHRISTOPHER UPTON, cardiologist; b. Atlanta, Dec. 25, 1956; s. Hugh Gordon and Lois Bizzell Cates; m. Joy Johnston, Aug. 17, 1979; children: Nathaniel, Andrew, Caroline. BS in Biology summa cum laude, The Citadel, Charleston, SC, 1978; MD, Med. Coll. Ga., Augusta, 1982. Lic. physician Ga., diplomate Am. Bd. Internal Medicine with subspecialties in cardiovascular diseases and interventional cardiology; lic. ltd. nuclear license. Intern in medicine Vanderbilt U. Med. Ctr., Nashville, 1982—83, resident in medicine, 1983—85, fellow in angioplasty, 1987—88, fellow in cardiology, 1985—87; instr. medicine divsn. cardiology Vanderbilt U., 1987—88; cardiologist St. Joseph's Hosp., Atlanta, 1988—98; med. dir. Emory Heart Ctr., Hiawassee, Ga., 1998—; assoc. prof. Emory U. Hosp., Atlanta, 1998—; dir. vascular intervention Emory Hosps., Atlanta, 2002—; dir. Emory Angiography Simulation Tng. Ctr., 2005—. Med. staff Emory U. Hosp., Atlanta, Chatuge Regional Hosp., Hiawassee, Union Gen. Hosp., Blairsville, Ga., Crawford Long Hosp., Atlanta, Dunwoody Med. Ctr., Atlanta, Ga. Bapt. Hosp., Atlanta, Lanier Park Hosp., Atlanta, Piedmont Hosp., Atlanta; med. adv. bd. numerous corps., instns.; reviewer various jours. including Jour. of AMA, Chest; cons. in field; lectr. in field; conf. dir. various nat. and internat. confs. Editor: Ga. Health Law Update, 1996, Am. Coll. Cardiology Guide to CPT, 1999—2004; contbr. articles and abstracts to profl. jours. Grantee numerous grants; scholar, Joseph Collins Found., 1979—82, Ty Cobb Ednl. scholar, 1979—82. Fellow: ACP, Soc. for Cardiovascular Angiography and Intervention (bd. trustees 2006—, chair bd. govs. 2005—), Am. Coll. Cardiology; mem.: AMA, Internat. Andreas Gruentzig Soc., Med. Assn. Ga., Soc./Coun. of Nuclear Medicine, Soc. for Med. Simulation (bd. dirs. 2005—), Internat. Soc. Med. Simulation, Alpha Omega Alpha. Achievements include patents for percutaneous puncture sealing system; blood vessel sealing system; invention of Cates curve, coronary guidewire. Office: Emory University Hospital 1364 Clifton Rd NE Ste C430 Atlanta GA 30322

CATES, DENNIS LYNN, minister; b. Dallas, Nov. 25, 1946; s. Robert N. and Wanda June (Boyd) C.; m. Sue Anne Sadler, Aug. 9, 1975. BA, Tex. Tech U., 1968, MEd, 1976, EdD, 1986; MA, Sul Ross State U., 1981. Cert. secondary edn. tchr., deficient vision, learning disabilities, mental retardation, supervision, mid-mgmt., orientation and mobility instr. Tchr. Eagle Pass (Tex.) Ind. Sch. Dist., Beeville (Tex.) Ind. Sch. Dist., Levelland (Tex.) Ind. Sch. Dist.; tchg. asst. Tex. Tech. U., Lubbock; asst. prof. West Tex. State U., Canyon, 1986-89, U. S.C., Columbia, 1989-95, dir. Ctr. for Excellence in Spl. Edn. Tech., 1992-93; assoc. prof. Cameron U., Lawton, Okla., 1995-2000, prof., 2000—04; cons., 2004—06; pastor United Meth. Ch., 2006—. Presenter numerous profl. confs.; field reviewer edn. jours. and pubs. Contbr. articles to profl. jours. Sgt. USAF, 1969-73. Grantee Consultation Tchrs. grant, 1981—82. Mem.: AAUP, ASCD, Assn. Tchr. Edn., Assn. Edn. and Rehab. for Blind and Visually Impaired (chmn. Divsn. 3 1998—2000, past chmn. 2000—02, newsletter editor Divsn. 3 1998—2004), Am. Coun. for Rural Spl. Edn. (bd. dirs. 1998—2004, chmn.-elect 2000—02, chmn. 2002—03, past chmn. 2003—04), Coun. for Exceptional Children (pres. Okla. chpt. 2001—02, treas. Okla. subdivsn. devel. disabilities divsn. 2001—04, past pres. Okla. chpt. 2002—03), Am. Ednl. Rsch. Assn., Internat. Assn. Spl. Edn., Am. Assn. Mental Retardation, Nat. Coun. Geog. Edn., Nat. Coun. for Social Studies, Phi Delta Kappa. Office Phone: 903-674-4455. Personal E-mail: dcnb@prodigy.net.

CATES, GILBERT, television and film producer, theater director; b. NYC, June 6, 1934; s. Nathan and Nina (Peltzman) Katz; m. Jane Betty Dubin, Feb. 9, 1957 (div.); children: Melissa Beth, Jonathan Michael, David Sawyer, Gilbert Lewis; m. Judith Reichman, Jan. 25, 1987; stepchildren: Ronit Reichman, Anat Reichman. BS, Syracuse U., 1955, MA, 1965. Prof. theatre, film and TV UCLA, 1990—, dean, 1990-99; with Cates-Doty Prodns., Inc.; prodr. dir. Geffen Playhouse, LA, 1995—. Com. mem. 1 drama dept. Syracuse U., 1969-73. TV prodr., dir. Haggis Baggis, 1959, Camouflage, 1961-62, Internat. Showtime, 1962-64, Hootenanny, 1962, To All My Friends on Shore, 1972, The Affair, 1974, After the Fall, 1974, Johnny, We Hardly Knew Ye, 1977, The Kid From Nowhere, 1982, Country Gold, 1982, Faerie Tale Theatre, 1982, Hobson's Choice, 1983, Consenting Adult, 1984, Child's Cry?, 1986, Fatal Judgement, 1988, One More Time, 1988, Muffin Man, 1989, Call Me Anna, 1990, Absolute Strangers, 1991, Overruled, 1992, Confessions-Two Faces of Evil, 1994, Innocent Victims, 1995, A Death in the Family - Masterpice Theatre, 2001, Collected Stories-PBS, 2002; film prodr., dir.: The Painting, 1962, Rings Aroung the World, 1967, I Never Sang for My Father, 1970, Summer Wishes, Winter Dreams, 1973, Dragonfly, 1976, The Promise, 1978, The Last Married Couple in America, 1979, O God, Book II, 1980, Backfire, 1986; theatrical prodr.: You Know I Can't Hear You When the Water's Running, 1967, I Never Sang for My Father, 1968, The Chinese and Doctor Fish, 1970, Solitaire-Double Solitaire, 1971; dir.: Voices, 1972, Tricks of the Trade, 1980, Collected Stories, 1999, Under the Blue Sky, 2002, Paint Your Wagon, 2004, Cat on a Hot Tin Roof, 2005, A Picasso, 2007; prodr.: Ann. Acad. Awards, 1990-1995, 97-99, 2001, 03-06, To Life, America Celebrates Israel's 50th (CBS-TV), 1998, America Celebrates Ford's Theater (ABC-TV), 1999, 2000, 02, 03, 04, 05, CBS at 75, 2003. Bd. dirs. Israeli Cancer Rsch. Fund, 1992-94. Recipient Best Short Film award Internat. Film Importers and Distbrs., 1962, Chancellor's medal Syracuse U., 1974, Emmy award, 1991, Star on Hollywood Walk of Fame, 1994, Jimmy Doolittle award L.A. Theater, 1998, Best Prodn. Ovation award, 1999, Lifetime Dirs. Achievement award Caucus of Prodrs., Writers and Dirs., 1998, Arents award Syracuse U., 2003, Career Achievement award Am. Soc. Cinematographers, 2004, Cinema Audio Soc., 2007. Mem. Dirs. Guild Am. (hon. life award 1990, v.p. Ea. region 1965, Western region 1980—, pres. 1983-87, Robert B. Aldrich award 1989, nat. sec.-tras. 1997—, Pres.'s award 2005), Acad. Motion Picture Arts and Scis. (bd. govs., chmn. bd. dirs. 1985-94, 2003—), Women in Film (bd. dirs. 1993-94. v.p. 2003), League N.Y. Theatres. Office: 10920 Wilshire Blvd Ste 1840 Los Angeles CA 90024-6510 E-mail: gil@geffenplayhouse.com. *Craft is freedom.*

CATES, JO ANN, library director; b. Ft. Worth, June 25, 1958; d. Charles Kimbrough and Lydia Joe (Sachse) C.; children: Jacob Abraham Frank, Mabel Rose Frank. BS in Journalism, Boston U., 1980; MLS, Simmons Coll., 1984. Advt. asst. Boston Phoenix, 1978-79; med. serials asst. Mass. Gen. Hosp., Boston, 1979-80; editorial asst. Exceptional Parent Mag., Boston, 1980-81; libr. reference asst. Lesley Coll., Cambridge, Mass., 1981-84; head reference libr. Lamont Libr., Harvard U., Cambridge, Mass., 1984-85; chief libr. Poynter Inst. for Media Studies, St. Petersburg, Fla., 1985-91; head transp. libr. Northwestern U., Evanston, Ill., 1991-94; regional rsch. mgr. Ctr. for Bus. Knowledge Ernst & Young, 1997—2001; libr. dir. Columbia Coll., Chgo., 2001—04, dean of the libr., 2004—, assoc. v.p. acad. rsch., 2005—. Tchr. News Libr. and Newsroom Seminars Poynter Inst., 1990-91; mem. Harvard Com. on Instrn. Libr. Use, 1984, mem. adv. com. on book and serial budgets, 1991-94; mem. Acad. Affairs Commn., 2001—; book reviewer Libr. Jour., Choice, 1985-2000, Am. Reference Book Annual, 1993-2000; knowledge mgmt. column editor B&F Divsn. Bull., 1999-2000. Author: Journalism: A Guide to the Reference Literature, 1990, 3d edit., 2004; editor Transp. Divsn. Bull., 1992-94; mem. editorial bd. Footnotes, 1991-94; contbr. articles to profl. jours. Mem. Transp. Rsch. Bd. Info. Svcs. Com., 1991-94; media intern Dem. Nat. Com., Boston, 1979-80. Scholar Women in Comm., 1976-78; Trustee scholar Boston U., 1978-80; Simmons Coll. grantee, 1982-84. Mem. Spl. Librs. Assn., Assn. for Edn. in Journalism and Mass Comm., Suncoast Info. Specialists (pres. 1990-91). Am. Libr. Assoc. Home: 540 Hinman Ave Apt 4 Evanston IL 60202-3081

CATES, MARSHALL E., pharmacist, medical educator; b. Ripley, Tenn., Oct. 16, 1962; s. Franklin E. Cates and Geneva S Palmer; m. Deborah L. Bailey, Dec. 16, 1988; children: Dalton M., Bailey P. BS in Biology, Rhodes Coll., Memphis, 1984; PharmD, U. Tenn., Memphis, 1991. Registered pharmacist Tenn., 1991, Ala., 1996, cert. psychiat. pharmacist Bd. Pharm. Specialties, 1996. Psychiat. pharmacy practice resident U. Tenn., Memphis, 1991—92; clin. pharmacy specialist in psychiatry VA Med. Ctr., Salt Lake City, 1992—95; asst. prof. pharmacy practice Samford U. McWhorter Sch. of Pharmacy, Birmingham, Ala., 1995—2001, assoc. prof. pharmacy practice, 2001—06, prof., 2006—. Program dir. psychiat. pharmacy practice residency VA Med. Ctr., Tuscaloosa, Ala., 1997—2003. Editl. bd. psychiatry panel (biomed. jour.) Annals of Pharmacotherapy, reviewer, Pharmacotherapy, American Journal of Health-System Pharmacy. Recipient Excellence in Pharmacy award, Mylan Pharms. Inc., 1991, Pharmacy Leadership award, Bristol-Myers Squibb, 2005. Fellow: Am. Soc. Health-Sys. Pharmacists; mem.: Am. Assn. Coll. Pharmacy (faculty del. 2001—02, acad. leadership fellow 2004—05, nominating com. 2006—), Coll. Psychiat. and Neurologic Pharmacists (chair membership com. 1999—2000, membership com. 2000—03, pub. and profl. rels. com. 2003—05, rsch. com. 2006—), Ala. Soc. Health-Sys. Pharmacists (bd. dirs. 2002—04, pres. 2004—05, Health-Sys. Pharmacist of Yr. award 2006), Rho Chi Pharm. Honor Soc., Phi Lambda Sigma Pharmacy Leadership Soc. Office: Samford Univ Sch Pharmacy 800 Lakeshore Dr Birmingham AL 35229 Office Phone: 205-726-2457. Business E-Mail: mecates@samford.edu.

CATES, MATT, actor, writer; b. St. Joseph, Mo., Sept. 18, 1951; s. Joseph Cates and Laura Bray; m. Johanna Harris, June 30, 1991; children: Sara, Thom, Steve Harris. Attended, Mo. We. State Coll., St. Joseph, 1969—81. Program/news dir. KUSN, St. Joseph, 1979—80; announcer, talk-show host KKJO, St. Joseph, 1980—82; prodn. dir. KWUN, Concord, Calif., 1982—88, KKIS-FM, Concord, 1989—92, news dir., 1993. Conservatory bd. mem. SAG, San Francisco, 2006—; conv. del. AFTRA, Phila., 2007—. Actor: (TV series) The Evidence; narrator (films) Saint Agnes' Eve, voice-actor (various radio & television commls.). Adult leader Cub Scouts, BSA, Concord, 1987—96; adult literacy tutor Project Second Chance, Pleasant Hill, Calif., 1995—98; vol. coord. Loaves and Fishes, Concord, 1998—2006; lectr. KC, Concord, 2004—. Recipient Addy Advt. award, Ad Coun., 1981, Jumbo Prawn Prodn. award, No. Calif. Broadcasting Assn., 1990. Mem.: SAG (vol. BookPALS 1995—98), Forum Prodns. (founding mem. 1980), Am. Fedn. TV & Radio Artists, Broadcast Legends, Mensa (archivist 2006—). Roman Cath. Avocations: music, travel, languages.

CATES, SUE SADLER, special education counselor; b. Ft. Worth, Aug. 7, 1947; d. Randall and Mary Jo (Merkt) Sadler; m. Dennis Lynn Cates, Aug. 9, 1975. BA, Baylor U., 1970; MEd, Sul Ross State U., 1977. Cert. tchr., counselor, ednl. diagnostician, Tex. Tchr. spl. edn. Eagle Pass (Tex.) Ind. Sch. Dist., 1974-76, Beeville (Tex.) Ind. Sch. Dist., 1976-80; supr., ednl. diagnostician Sinton (Tex.) Ind. Sch. Dist., 1980-81; counselor, diagnostician Snyder (Tex.) Ind. Sch. Dist., 1981-86; ednl. diagnostician Pampa (Tex.) Ind. Sch. Dist., 1987-89; elem. counselor Richland County Sch. Dist., Columbia, SC, 1989-95; ednl. diagnostician Wichita Falls (Tex.) Ind. Sch. Dist., 1995-97, Graham (Tex.) Ind. Sch. Dist., 1997-98, Carrollton-Farmers Branch (Tex.) Ind. Sch. Dist., 1998-2000, Cedar Hill Ind. Sch. Dist., 2000-01, Arlington (Tex.) Ind. Sch. Dist., 2001—02, Ft. Worth (Tex.) Can! Acad. Charter Sch., 2002—, Ft. Worth Can! Acad. Charter Sch., 2002, Van Zandt/Rains County SSA-Edgewood Ind. Sch. Dist., 2003—04, Rains Ind. Sch. Dist., Emory, 2004—06, Pittsburg Ind. Sch. Dist., Tex., 2006—. Bd. dir. Scurry County Sheltered Workshop, 1981-85, Tex. Assn. Children with Learning Disabilities, 1976-77, 81-83; coach Tex. Spl. Olympics, Beeville, amd Sinton, 1978-81; mem. sanctuary choir Floral Heights United Meth. Ch., Wichita Falls, 1995—, Stephen Ministry, 1992-2005, Stephen Ministry L.T.C., 2005—, tchr. Sunday sch., youth coord. Mem. NEA, AAUW, Tex. Ednl. Diagnosticians' Assn., Coun. Exceptional Children, Coun. Ednl. Diagnosticians, Assn. Supervision and Devel., Nat. Assn. Workshop Dirs., Tex. State Tchrs. Assn., Tex. Classroom Tchrs. Assn., Am. Assn. Counseling and Devel., Tex. Assn. Counseling and Devel., Tex. Ednl. Diagnosticians Assn., Phi Delta Kappa, Zeta Phi Eta. Avocations: swimming, coin collecting/numismatics, travel, singing, jewelry. Home: PO Box 234 Detroit TX 75436 Home Phone: 903-674-4455; Office Phone: 903-856-1142. Personal E-mail: bu70@prodigy.net.

CATHELL, DALE ROBERTS, judge; b. Berlin, Md., July 30, 1937; s. Dale Parsons Cathell and Charlotte Robert (Hocker) Terrell; m. Charlotte M. Kerbin; children: Kelly Ann, Dale Kerbin, William Howard. Student, U. Md., 1962-64; LLB, U. Balt., 1967; cert., Nat. Jud. Coll., 1983. Bar: Md. 1967. Atty. City of Ocean City, Md., 1970-76; assoc. judge Md. Dist. Ct., Worcester County, 1980-81; judge Md. Cir. Ct., Worcester County, 1981-89, Ct. Spl. Appeals, 1st Appellate Cir., 1989-97, Md. Ct. Appeals, 1998—. Instr. WOR-WIC C.C., 1973, Salisbury State U., 1978; adj. prof. law U. Balt., 1997—; mem. family and domestic rels. law com. Md. Jud. Conf., 1995-97, past mem. exec. com.; chair Commn. on Racial & Ethnic Fairness in Jud. Process, 2002-04. Author: From Lands Over, 2003, Scent of Lilacs, 2005. Mem. Pub. Service Commn. Adv. Panel, Md., 1970, charity revision com. Mayor City Council, Ocean City, 1970; mem. Worcester County Shoreline Com., Md., 1971; mem. charter revision com. City of Ocean City, 1973, mem. utility consumer adv. panel, 1978; creator Alt. Com. Service Program, Md., 1980—; organizer Legal Intern Program Pub. Schs., Worcester County, 1981—. Served in USAF, 1955—59. Mem. Md. Bar Assn. (jud. appointment com. 1970), Worcester County Bar Assn. (pres. 1970), Balt. City Bar Assn. Democrat. Episcopalian. Office: Md Ct Appeals PO Box 4306 Salisbury MD 21803-4306 Office Phone: 410-543-6014.*

CATHEY, CHRISTOPHER D., lawyer; b. Nov. 2, 1973; BA, U. Fla., 1994; JD, U. Cin., 1999. Bar: Ohio 1999, Fla. 2003, Ky. 2003, US Ct. of Appeals Sixth Cir., US Dist. Ct. Southern Dist. Ohio. Assoc. Ulmer & Berne LLP, Cin. Named one of Ohio's Rising Stars, Super Lawyers, 2006. Fellow: Cin. Acad. of Leadership for Lawyers; mem.: Ohio State Bar Assn. (Banking, Comml., Bankruptcy Com.), ABA (Litig., Bus. Sections). Office: Ulmer & Berne LLP 600 Vine St Ste 2800 Cincinnati OH 45202 Office Phone: 513-698-5000. Office Fax: 513-698-5001.

CATHEY, GERTRUDE BROWN, retired medical/surgical nurse; b. NYC, Sept. 1, 1933; d. William Robert Brown and Helen Elizabeth Dobrovich-Brown; m. Delter Dalton Cathey, Apr. 20, 1960; children: William, Colleen, Eileen, Christopher. Diploma in nursing, Bellevue Hosp., 1954; BS in Edn., Hunter Coll., 1961; MPA, John Jay Coll., 1984. Staff nurse, head nurst Bellevue Hosp., NYC, 1954—58, supr., 1965—88, asst. dir. nursing, 1988—92; staff nurse, head nurse St. Mary's Hosp., Passaic, NJ, 1958—59; office nurse Dr. Harold Cole, Rutherford, NJ, 1959—65. Facilitator support group Alzheimer's Assn., Rutherford, 1995—. Vol. Kip Ctr., Rutherford, 1992—, Star Fish, Rutherford; mem. social concerns com. St. Mary Ch., Rutherford, 1992—, extraordinary min. of Holy Communion, 2002—. Named Vol. of Yr., Kip Ctr., 2002. Mem.: AARP (sec. Rutherford chpt. 1995—2000), ANA. Home: 35 Union Ave East Rutherford NJ 07073 Personal E-mail: trudybcathey@verizon.net.

CATHEY, WADE THOMAS, electrical engineering educator; b. Greer, SC, Nov. 26, 1937; s. Wade Thomas Sr. and Ruby Evelyn (Waters) C.; children: Susan Elaine, Cheryl Ann. BS, U. S.C., 1959, MS, 1961; PhD, Yale U., 1963. Group scientist Rockwell Internat., Anaheim, Calif., 1962-68; from assoc. prof. to prof. elec. engring. U. Colo., Denver, 1968-85, chmn. dept. elec. engring. and computer sci., 1984-85, chmn. faculty senate, 1982-83, prof. Boulder, 1985-97, rsch. prof., 1997—2003, prof. emeritus elec. engring., 2003—; chief tech. officer CDM Optics, 2005—06. Pres. CDM Optics, 1996-2005; dir. NSF Ctr. Optoelectronic Computing Sys., Boulder, 1987-93; cons. in field, 1968—. Author: Optical Information Processing and Holography, 1978; contbr. articles to profl. jours.; inventor in field. Croft fellow, U. Colo., 1982, Faculty fellow, U. Colo., 1972-73. Fellow IEEE, Optical Soc. Am. (topical editor 1977-79, 87-90), Soc. Photo-Optic Instrumentation Engrs. Achievements include extend focal depth and passive ranging in imaging systems, research on matching image acquisiton and signal processing systems. Home: 360 Alpine Way Boulder CO 80304 Office: U Colo Dept Elec and Computer Engring Boulder CO 80309-0425 Office Phone: 303-492-1888. Business E-Mail: cathey@colorado.edu.

CATHEY-GIBSON, SHARON SUE RINN, principal, academic administrator; b. Reed City, Mich., June 11, 1940; d. Sherwood and Ellen (Hutson) Rinn.; children: Joel A. Cathey, Julie A. Maez, Sharon Sue Rinn Cathey-Gibson, Aug. 27, 1996; m. Warren Gibson. BA in Edn., San Francisco State U., 1962; postgrad., U. Mich., 1972-74, U. Calif., 1975-77; MA in Edn., U. Nev., 1988, EdD in Curriculum and Instrn., 1991. Tchr. Laguna Salada Union Sch. Dist., Pacifica, Calif., 1962-64, Redwood City (Calif.) Sch. Dist., 1964-66, Lapeer (Mich.) Sch. Dist., 1970-74; tchr., choral dir. Pine Middle Sch., Reno, 1978-84; tchr. Washoe County Sch. Dist., Reno, 1985—, adminstrv. elem. edn. cons., 1991-92; adminstrv. cons. Nev. State Dept. Elem. Edn., Carson City, 1990—; prin. Anderson Elem. Sch., Reno, 1992—, Elizabeth Lenz Elem. Sch., 1994, Libby Booth Sch., Reno, 1994-97; prof., adminstr. Sierra Nev. Coll., 1994—2002, adminstr., 1997—2002, ret., 2002; asst. prof. U. Nev., Reno, 2002—, cons. for literacy, 2001—05; cons., ptnr., editl. staff Superior Edn. and Leadership Inc.; interim dir. Ctr. Learning & Literacy, U. Nev., Reno, 2004—05. Statewide exec. dir. tchr. edn. Thompson Learning Ctr., Reno, 1987—89, diagnostician, 1987—89; asst. U. Nev., Reno, 1988—90; adminstr., prof. and coord. sch. based programs, dir. tchr. edn. dept. Sierra Nev. Coll.; ct. apptd. spl. adv. worker; cons., editor Superior Learning & Leadership Corp.; ptnr. Superior Learning Co.; cons., presenter in field. Adminstr., founder, and pres. Sierra Advocates for Family Equity. Recipient Celebrate Literacy award, Internat. Reading Assn., 2003; grantee, Nev. ESSA, 1977. Mem.: AAUW (pres. 1976—2005), Nev. Assn. Coll. Tchrs. Edn., Nat. Coun. Tchrs. English, Nat. Reading Assn., Internat. Reading Assn. (state pres. 1992, local pres. 1993—94, Literacy award 1995, Celebrate Literacy award 2003), Washoe County Tchrs. Assn., Kiwanis (Reno Sunrisers chpt. sec. 1995—98, pres. 2001—02, Kiwanian of Yr. 2003, Disting. Club Pres. 2003), Kappa Delta Epsilon (adviser), Delta Kappa Gamma (state pres. 1989—91, chptr. pres. 2004—, chair nominating com.), Phi Kappa Phi, Golden Key (hon.; ct. appted spl. advocate 2002—05). Republican. Episcopalian. Avocations: music, art, swimming. Home: 2550 Comstock Dr Reno NV 89512-1347 E-mail: sharons@gbis.com.

CATHOU, RENATA EGONE, chemist, consultant; b. Milan, June 21, 1935; d. Egon and Stella Mary Egone; m. Pierre-Yves Cathou, June 21, 1959. BS, MIT, Cambridge, 1957; PhD, MIT, 1963. Fellow, rsch. assoc. in chemistry MIT, Cambridge, 1962-65; rsch. assoc. Harvard U. Med. Sch., Cambridge, 1965-69, instr., 1969-70; rsch. assoc. Mass. Gen. Hosp., 1965-69, instr., 1969-70; asst. prof. dept. biochemistry Sch. Medicine, Tufts U., 1970-73, assoc. prof., 1973-78, prof., 1978-81; pres. Tech. Evaluations, Lexington, Mass., 1983-2000; sr. cons. SRC Assocs., Park Ridge, NJ, 1984-93. Sr. investigator Arthritis Found., 1970-75; vis. prof. dept. chemistry UCLA, 1976-77; mem. adv. panel NSF, 1974-75; mem. bd. sci. counselors Nat. Cancer Inst., 1979-83; ind. cons. and writer. Mem. editl. bd. Immunochemistry, 1972-75; contbr. chpts. to books and articles to profl. jours. MIT Company Founders citation, 1989; NIH predoctoral fellow, 1958-62; grantee Am. Heart Assn., 1969-81, USPHS, 1970-81. Mem. AAAS, Am. Soc. for Biochemistry and Molecular Biology, Am. Assn. Immunologists, Circumnavigators Club. Avocations: photography, opera, fine arts. Personal E-mail: rcathou@aol.com.

CATHY, S. TRUETT, food products executive; m. Jeannette Cathy; children: Dan, Don, Trudy. Owner The Dwarf House, Atlanta, 1946; founder, chmn. Chick-fil-A, Inc., 1967—. Founder WinShape Ctr. Found., 1984—, WinShape Homes prog., WinShape Camps, 1985—. Author: It's Easier to Succeed Than to Fail, 1989, Eat Mor Chikin: Inspire More People, 2002, It's Better to Build Boys Than Mend Men, 2004; co-author: The Generosity Factor, 2002. Named one of Forbes' Richest Americans, 2006; recipient Horatio Alger award, Horatio Alger Assn., 1989, Entrepreneur of Yr. - Lifetime Achievement award, Ernst & Young, 2000, Chmn. award, Georgia Sports Hall of Fame, 2003, Catalyst Lifetime Achievement award, Injoy/John Maxwell, 2003, Humanitarian award, Norman Vincent & Ruth Stafford Peale, 2003, Lifetime Achievement award, Nat. Poultry & Food Distributors Assn., 2005. Office: Chick-fil-A Inc 5200 Buffington Rd Atlanta GA 30349-2998

CATLETT, RICHARD H., JR., retired lawyer; b. Boston, May 1, 1921; s. Richard Henry and Martha Barton (Taylor) Catlett; m. Marion Frances Buckey, Apr. 3, 1948 (dec. Sept. 1967); children: Ross C. Rose, Richard H. III, Thomas Y., Maria C. Eldredge; m. Barbara Ann L'Orange, May 1, 1969. BSEE, Va. Mil. Inst., 1943; LLB, U. Richmond, 1952. Engr. C&P Tel. Co., Richmond, Va., 1946-47, Catlett-Johnson Corp., Richmond, Va., 1947-50; assoc., ptnr. Christian & Barton, Richmond, Va., 1952-76; ptnr. McGuire Woods LLP, Richmond, Va., 1976-91; ret., 1991. Bd. dirs. James River Corp., gen. counsel, sec., 1969—90; gen. counsel Signet Banking Corp., Richmond, 1985—89; adj. asst. prof. law U. Richmond, 1990—93. Chmn. City of Richmond Personnel Bd., 1971—80; dir. Westminster-Canterbury Corp., Richmond, 1985—89, chmn., 1987—89; mem. vestry St. James Episc. Ch., Richmond, 1954—75. 1st lt. US Army, 1943—46, ETO. Mem.: ABA, Va. State Bar Assn. (chmn. bus. law sect. 1972—73), Va. State Bar (chmn. bus. law sect. 1971—72), Commonwealth Club (Richmond), Country Club Va. (dir. 1966—69, 1971—74). Home: 300 N Ridge Rd #26 Richmond VA 23229 Office Phone: 804-775-4308. E-mail: rcatlett@mcguirewoods.com.

CATLETT, ROBERT BISHOP, economics professor; b. Grand Junction, Colo., Aug. 29, 1952; s. Charles William and Hellen Kathrine (Bishop) C.; m. Lorraine Elizabeth (Arsenault), Sept. 9, 1977; children: Mariah Elizabeth, Johanna Kathrine, Emma Christine. BA, U. Nebr., 1974, MA, 1975, postgrad., 1980—81. Lectr. econ. Emporia State U., Kans., 1976—78, asst. prof., 1978—, dir. ctr. econ. edn., 1988—. Econ. model developer USDA, Emporia, Kans., 1982-88; program evaluator Assn. Collegiate Bus. Sch. and Programs, 1991-93, Chgo. Bd. Trade Judge of 1992 Commodity Challenge; participant NSF program exptl. econ. U. Ariz., 1991; bd. dir. FCI; judge NASDAQ Ednl. Found. Nat. Tchg. Awards, 1999, 2002-03, InvestWrite, 2006; chief judge Fed. Challenge Fed. Res. Bank Kansas City, 2005; coord., judge Goldman Sachs Economics Challenge, Kans., 2001-02; founding mem. econ. edn. adv. coun. Fed. Reserve Bank Kans. City., 2005-, cons. in field. Author: Microeconomics, Principles and Applications Test Bank, 1998, Macroeconomics, Principles and Applications Test Bank, 1998, Microeconomics: A Contemporary Introduction-Test Bank, 1997, Economics: A Contemporary Introduction-Test Bank, 1997; contbg. author: Strategies for the Future, 1990, Human Energy Facing the Future, 1991, others; manuscript, book reviewer: Southwestern Pub. Co., 1991—; manuscript reviewer: Harper Collins Coll. Pub., 1994, West Pub. Co., 1995, Blackwell Pub. Co., 1997, Simon and Schuster, 1998-99, Prentice Hall, 1999, McGraw Hill, 2003, 06, Addison Wesley Lang., 2003, Thompson Bus. and Profl. Publ., 2005; reviewer, item writer: National Assessment of Educational Progress Economics, 2003; referee: Jour. Risk and Ins., 1998-2002; contbr. over 20 articles to profl. jours. Named an Outstanding Prof., Phi Delta Theta, Emporia, Kans., 1987. Mem. AAUP (Emporia State U. chpt. exec. com., pres. 2004-07, exec. com. Kans. conf. 2004—, pres. Kans. conf. 2007—), Nat. Assn. Econ. Educators (chair legal and legis. com. 2002-04), Kans. Econ. Assn. (pres. 1986-87), Kans. Coun. Econ. Edn. (exec. com. 1990, bd. dirs. 1999-2002), Mo. Valley Econ. Assn., Healthy Cmty. Alliance (steering com. 2005—). Avocations: victorian house restoration, sports. Home: 405 Exchange St Emporia KS 66801-3817 Office: Emporia State Univ 1200 Commercial St Emporia KS 66801-5087 Office Phone: 620-341-5678. Business E-Mail: rcatlett@emporia.edu.

CATLEY, ANDREW PAUL, veterinarian, researcher; b. Birmingham, Eng., July 22, 1964; s. Joe William and Pauline Mary Catley; m. Susan Clare Bishop, Aug. 25, 2005; children: Fred, Joe. BVM, U. London, 1988; MS, U. Edinburgh, Scotland, 1991, PhD, 2004. Program mgr. Actionaid, Erigavo, Somalia, 1993—94; livestock specialist Christian Aid/Oxfam, Asmara, Eritrea; vet. advisor Save the Children UK, Addis Ababa, Ethiopia, 1995—96, Vetwork UK, Edinburgh, 1996—98; assoc. rschr. Internat. Inst., London, 1998—2000; policy and rsch. advisor Tufts U., Medford, Mass., 2000—05, rsch. dir., 2005—. Cons. Vetwork UK, 1996—. Author, editor: Community-Based Animal Health, 2002; contbr. articles to profl. jours., chpts. to books. Recipient Dunsheath Expedition award, U. London, 1987, David Moore Meml. award, Arkleton Trust, Oxford, 1987. Mem.: Brit. Vet. Assn., Royal Coll. Vet. Surgeons. Achievements include first to novel approaches to epidemiological research and deliver of basic services in marginalized conflict zones in the Horn of Africa. Avocations: photography, music. Office: Tufts U 200 Boston Ave Medford MA 02155

CATLEY-CARLSON, MARGARET, not-for-profit executive; b. Nelson, BC, Oct. 6, 1942; d. George Lorne and Helen Margaret Catley; m. Stanley F. Carlson, Oct. 30, 1970. BA with honors, U. B.C., 1966, LLD (hon.), 1994; postgrad., Inst. Internat. Rels., U. W.I., St. Augustine, Trinidad and Tobago, 1970; LLD (hon.), U. Regina, 1985; LittD (hon.), St. Mary's U., 1985; LLD (hon.), Concordia U., 1989, Mt. St. Vincent U., 1990, Carleton U., 1994, U. Calgary, 1994. Joined Dept. External Affairs, Canada, 1966, with, 1970-74, asst. under-sec., 1981-82; 2d sec. Can. High Commn., Colombo, Sri Lanka, 1968, econ. counsellor London, 1975-77; v.p. Can. Internat. Devel. Agy., 1978, sr. v.p., acting pres., 1979-80, pres., 1983-89; asst. sec. gen. UN; dep. exec. dir. ops. UNICEF, 1981—83; fellow Ryerson Poly. U., 1986; dep. min. Health and Welfare Country Can., 1989—92; pres. Population Coun., NYC, 1993—99. Chmn. Global Water Partnership; chmn. water resource adv. com. Group Suez, Paris; chmn. change devel. and mgmt. team CGIAR, Washington, 2001; vice-chair Internat. Devel. Rsch. Ctr., Ottawa; chmn. Ctr. Agr. Rsch. Dry Areas, Syria; mem. 2020 vision policy, global food policy Internat. Food Policy Rsch. Inst., Washington; with Libr. Alexandria, Egypt, Inter-Am. Dialogue, Washington; clin. prof. Tulane U., New Orleans. Home: 249 E 48th St Apt 8A New York NY 10017

CATLIN, DON H., molecular pharmacologist, educator; With UCLA Sch. Medicine, 1972—; pharmacologist, dir. Olympic Analytical Laboratory, UCLA, 1982—. Prof. molecular and med. pharmacology UCLA. Contbr. articles to profl. jours. Led the effort to isolate and analyze tetrahydrogestrinone (THG). Office: UCLA Sch Medicine UCLA Olympic Analytical Lab 2122 Granville Ave Los Angeles CA 90025 Office Phone: 310-825-2635. Office Fax: 310-206-9077. Business E-Mail: dcatlin@ucla.edu.

CATLIN, FRANCIS IRVING, physician; b. Hartford, Conn., Dec. 6, 1925; s. Robert Irving and Frances Rose (Maleski) C.; m. Rebecca Vaughan Graham, June 11, 1948; children: Robert, Andrew, Martha. AA, Princeton U., 1949; MD, Johns Hopkins U., 1948, DSc, 1959. Diplomate: Am. Bd. Otolaryngology. Intern Union Meml. Hosp., Balt., 1948-49; resident in otolaryngology Johns Hopkins Hosp., Balt., 1950, 52-54; from instr. to assoc. prof. Johns Hopkins U. Med. Sch., Balt., 1956-72; prof. otorhinolaryngology and communicative scis. Baylor U. Med. Sch., Houston, 1972-91, prof. emeritus, 1991—. Chief otolaryngology svc. Tex. Children's Hosp., 1972-91, emeritus staff, 1991—, mem. credentials com., 1989—. Contbr. articles to med. jours. Capt. M.C. USAF, 1950-52. Fellow Am. Otol. Soc.; mem. AMA, ASTM (F29 com. on anesthesia and respiratory equipment 1989-2004), Tex. Med. Soc., Am. Acad. Otolaryngology, Am. Coun. Otolaryngology, Am. Laryngological, Rhinological and Otol. Soc., Am. Speech and Hearing Assn. (life), Houston Philos. Soc., Am. Soc. Pediat. Otolaryngology (charter mem. 1985—, v.p. 1985-86, pres. 1986-87, guest hon. 2000, 07). Republican. Episcopalian. Home: 13307 Queensbury Ln Houston TX 77079-6013

CATMULL, EDWIN E., film company executive, computer graphics engineer; b. Parkersburg, W.Va., Mar. 31, 1945; married; 5 children. BS in Computer Sci. and Physics, U. Utah, PhD in Computer Sci., 1974. V.p. computer divsn. Lucasfilm, Ltd., 1979—86; co-founder, pres. Pixar Animation Studios, Emeryville, Calif., 1986, pres., 1986—88, chmn., chief tech. officer, 1988—91, pres., 1991—. Named to High-Tech Hall of Fame, Utah Info. Tech. Assn., 2001; recipient Coons award, 1993, Academy award of Merit, 2001, John von Neumann medal, IEEE, 2006. Mem. NAE, Acad. Motion Picture Arts and Scis. (Sci. and Tech. engrng. award, sci. and tech. awards com.). Achievements include research in computer graphics, video editing, video games, digital video, digital computer graphics and animation. Office: Pixar Animation Studios 1200 Park Ave Emeryville CA 94608

CATOE, BETTE LORRINA, pediatrician, educator; b. Apr. 7, 1926; d. John Booker and Laura Beola (Adams) C.; m. Warren J. Strudwick, Sept. 17, 1949; children: Laura Christina, Warren J., William J. BS cum laude, Howard U., 1948, MD, 1951. Intern Freedmen's Hosp., Washington, 1951-52; pediat. resident Howard U./Freedman's Hosp., 1952-55, practice medicine specializing in pediatrics Washington, 1956—2003; cons. Govt. of DC Income Maintenance Adminstrn., Washington, 2003—; instr. bacteriology Howard U., 1955-57; mem. staff Providence Hosp., Columbia Hosp., Howard U. Hosp., Wash., Hosp. Ctr.; sch. health officer Dept. Health, Washington, 1960-64; clin. instr. Howard U., 1956-58; health cons., 2003—; cons. income maint. admin. Govt. DC, 2003—. Mem. DC Health Planning Adv. Coun., 1967-77, chmn. 1973-77; chmn. DC Devel. Disabilities Adv. Coun., 1970-74; mem. DC Mayor's Commn. on Food and Nutrition, 1971-72, Mayor's Commn. on Maternal and Child Health, 1978-84, appt. vice chmn. Pub. Benefit Corp., 1997-2001; mem. DC Commn. Jud. Tenure and Disabilities, 1977-2001, chmn. Bd. Public Benefit Corp. of DC, 1998-2001; bd. govs. St. Alban's Sch., 1978-84; bd. dirs. DC Health and Welfare Coun., 1968-73, pres., 1973-74; del. Democratic Nat. Conv., 1976; bd. dirs. Met. Washington Health and Welfare Coun., 1970-72, Parent Coun. of Washington, 1974-75, Met. Med. Founds., Inc., Silver Spring YMCA, 1977-80, Kingsburg Ctr., 1997-99; mem., chair emergency med. com. Mayor's Health Policy Coun., 1998-2001; cons. income maintenance adminstrn. Govt. of DC Dept. Human Svcs., 2003—. Mem.: NAACP, AMA, Women's Aux. Medico-Chirurg. Soc., Assn. Comprehensive Health Planners (dir. 1975—77), Urban League, Am. Med. Women's Assn., Nat. Med. Assn. (chmn. pediat. sect. 1981—83), D.C. Chirurg. Soc. (trustee 1996—99, nominating com. 2000—03, jud. legis. com. 2001—03), Women's Nat. Dem., Jack and Jill Am., Carrousels Club (nat. v.p. 1986—88, nat. pres. 1988—90), Links Club, Century Club of Nat. Assn. Negro Bus. and Profl. Women's Clubs (pres. 1985—89), Alpha Kappa Alpha. Home and Office: 1748 Sycamore St NW Washington DC 20012-1031 Office Phone: 202-882-2406.

CATOLINE-ACKERMAN, PAULINE DESSIE, small business owner; b. Ft. Worth, Dec. 17, 1937; d. Byron Hillis and Dessie Elizabeth (Plumlee) Doggett; children: Sherry Lou, Brenda Lynn; m. Donald Ralph Ackerman, Feb. 19, 1993. BA in Bus. Mgmt. (labor rels. specialty), Hiram Coll., 1989. Sec. Gen. Am. Life Ins. Co., Ft. Worth, 1956—57, Kelly Girl Svcs., Youngstown, Ohio, 1965—69; legal sec. Burgstaller, Schwartz & Moore, Youngstown, 1962—65, Green, Schiavoni, Murphy & Haines, Youngstown, 1969—71, Flask & Policy, Youngstown, 1971—83; sec. We. Res. Care Sys., Youngstown, 1983—87, exec. sec., 1987—90; owner, mgr. Pauline's Place, Youngstown, 1990—; legal sec. Henderson, Covington, Stein, Donchess & Messenger Law Firm, 1993—94; exec. adminstrv. asst. to pres. CEO, sr. v.p. Internat. Renaissance Developers, Youngstown, 1994—96; adminstrv. asst. to v.p. and client svc. mgr. Bank One Investment Mgmt. & Trust Group, Youngstown, 1996—2000; admin. assoc. regional divsn. Am. Heart Assn., Youngstown, 2000—01; owner, mgr. Paulines Pl., 2001—; staff Kelly Svcs., Youngstown, 2001—. Sub. tchr. K-12 Austintown Sch. Sys., 2001. Pres. PTA, Cottage Hills, Ill., 1968-69, brownie and scout leader Girl Scouts U.S.A., 1968-69 Mem. Mahoning County Legal Secs. Assn. (v.p. 1973-74, editor monthly booklet 1974-75), Exec. Link, Missionary Group Club. Democrat. Methodist. Avocations: painting, reading, tennis, swimming, horseback riding. Home: 3961 Cannon Rd Youngstown OH 44515-4604 Office Phone: 330-793-4265.

CATON, SCOTT BRENON, history professor; b. Brockport, NY, July 22, 1960; s. Brenon Phelps and Bonnie (Rohr) Caton; m. Bonnie Lee Marshall, Aug. 21, 1982; children: Emily, Elizabeth, Brooke, Catherine, Victoria, Alexander. BA in Religion and Philosophy, Roberts Wesleyan Coll., Rochester, NY, 1986; MAR, Westminster Theol. Seminary, Phila., 1988; PhD in History, U. Rochester, NY, 1998. History prof. Roberts Wesleyan Coll., Rochester, NY, 1990—; prof., founding faculty mem. Northeastern Seminary, Rochester, NY, 1998—. Cons. Adept Gifted and Talented Program, BOCES, Rochester, NY, 1998—; curriculum writer Barnes & Noble U., 2002—03. Author: The Compleat Minister: The De Profundis Sermons of Jonathan Mitchel, 1998. Mem.: Am. Chesterton Soc. (founding mem., Rochester, N.Y. chpt.), Am. Soc. Church History, Am. Hist. Assn. Roman Catholic. Avocations: camping, classical music, hiking, travel. Home: Branches 223 Lyell Ave Spencerport NY 14559 Office: Roberts Wesleyan Coll 2301 Westside Dr Rochester NY 14624 Office Phone: 585-594-6336. Business E-Mail: catons@roberts.edu.

CATON-JONES, MICHAEL, film director, film producer; b. Broxburn, Scotland, 1958; m. Laura Viederman, 2000; 1 child. Student, Nat. Film Sch., London. Dir. (films) Scandal, 1989, Memphis Belle, 1990, Doc Hollywood, 1991, This Boy's Life, 1993, Shooting Dogs, 2005, Basic Instinct 2, 2006, (TV series) Trinity, 1998; dir., prodr. Rob Roy, 1995, The Jackal, 1997, City by the Sea, 2002. Office: Creative Artists Agency 9830 Wilshire Blvd Beverly Hills CA 90212-1825

CATRAKIS, HARIS JOHN, science educator; b. Athens, Greece, Sept. 3, 1970; s. John H. and Ioanna C. Catrakis. BS, MS, Calif. Inst. Tech., Pasadena, 1991, PhD, 1996. Assoc. prof. mech. and aerospace engrng. U. Calif., Irvine, 1998—. Mem. AAAS, Am. Phys. Soc. Achievements include theoretical, computational and experiemental discoveries in turbulence, fluid dynamics and multiscale phenomena. Office: Mech & Aerospace Engring Gateway 4200 Univ Calif Irvine Irvine CA 92697-0001 E-mail: catrakis@uci.edu.

CATRON, STEPHEN BARNARD, lawyer, real estate developer, director; b. Bowling Green, Ky., Feb. 4, 1949; s. Eugene and Gladys (Bell) C.; m. Deborah Faye Grigsby, Nov. 28, 1981. BA, Western Ky. U., Bowling Green, 1971; JD, U. Miss., 1974. Bar: Ky. 1974, Miss. 1974, Tenn. 1988, U.S. Dist. Ct. (we. dist.) Ky, 1974, U.S. Dist. Ct. (no. dist.) Miss. 1974, U.S. Supreme Ct. 1982, U.S. Ct. Appeals (6th cir.) 1983. Atty. Ky. Dept. Human Resources, Bowling Green, Ky., 1974-75; atty., ptnr. Reynolds, Catron, Johnson & Hinton, Bowling Green, Ky., 1975-95, Lewis, King, Kreig, Waldrop and Catron, P.C., Bowling Green, Ky., 1995-2001; ptnr. Wyatt, Tarrant & Combs, LLP, Bowling Green, Ky., 2001—04; dir. real estate devel. Bridgemont Devel. Group, LLC, 2004—05; cons. Pinnacle View Consulting, LLC, 2005—. Pres. Bowling Green-Warren County Bar, 1989-90; chair., bd. trustees Ky. IOLTA Fund, Frankfort, Ky., 1990-94; bd. dirs. Nat. Assn. IOLTA Programs, Chgo., 1991-92. Author: Kentucky Corporations Law, 1989. Bd. dirs. Bowling Green (Ky.) Human Rights Commn., 1976-78; vice chair Ky. Ednl. TV Auth., Lexington, Ky., 1988-92; bd. regents Western Ky. U., Bowling Green., 1991-92; chairperson Bowling Green-Warren County Indsl. Authority; trustee Western Ky. U. Found. Fellow Am. Bar Found.; mem. Ky. Bar Assn. (bd. govs. 1992-2000, v.p. 2000-01, pres.-elect 2001-02, pres. 2002-03). Democrat. Episcopalian. Avocations: reading, jogging, golf, computers. Home: 509 Saint Charles Ln Knoxville TN 37922 Office: Pinnacle View Consulting LLC 2732 Florence Dr Pigeon Forge TN 37863 Home Phone: 865-675-5515; Office Phone: 865-453-9983. Business E-Mail: scatron@pinnacleviewconsulting.com.

CATSIMATIDIS, JOHN ANDREAS, retail executive; b. Nissiros, Greece, Sept. 7, 1948; came to U.S., 1949, naturalized, 1950; s. Andreas John and Despina (Emmanulides) C. BS in Engring., NYU, 1970. Chmn., CEO Gristedes Foods, 1969—, Red Apple Cos. (Gristedes, Red Apple stores), NYC, 1970—, United Refining Inc., Warren, Pa., 1986—. Chmn., CEO Sloan's Supermarket, NYC. Pres. Greek Orthodox Ch. of Am., 2001—02. Recipient Humanitarian award NCCJ, 1978, Am. Jewish Com., 1982, Nat. Kidney Assn., 1986; Entrepreneurship award NYU Bus. Sch., 1987. Mem.: Young Men Philanthrapic League, Westside C. of C., N.Y. Athletic Club, Wings, N.Y. U. Club. Office: Red Apple Group 823 11th Ave New York NY 10019-3557

CATTANACH, ROBERT EDWARD, JR., lawyer; b. Thorp, Wis., Jan. 14, 1949; s. Robert Edmund Sr. and Irene Louise (Papierniak) C.; m. Terry Theirl, June 9, 1972; children: Philip, Sarah, Katherine. BS, U.S. Naval Acad., 1972; JD, U. Wis., 1975. Bar: Wis. 1975, U.S. Supreme Ct. 1980, Minn. 1983, U.S. Dist. Ct. (8th cir.) 1989. Spl. counsel to Sec. of Navy, Washington, 1976-78; trial atty. U.S. Dept. of Justice, Washington, 1978-80; ptnr., chair litigation dept. Oppenheimer Wolff & Donnelly, St. Paul, 1983-94; ptnr., co-chmn., telecom. Dorsey & Whitney LLP, Mpls., 1994—. Articles editor U. Wis. Law Rev., 1974-75. Mem. St. Paul Heritage Preservation Commn., 1993-98. Mem. ABA, Wis. Bar Assn. (pres. non-resident divsn. 1990-92), Minn. Bar Assn., Fellow, Am. Bar Found. Avocations: cross-country skiing, bicycling. Office: Dorsey & Whitney LLP 50 S 6th St Ste 1500 Minneapolis MN 55402-1553 Office Phone: 612-340-2873. Office Fax: 612-340-8800. Business E-Mail: cattanach.robert@dorsey.com.

CATTANEO, JACQUELYN ANNETTE KAMMERER, artist, educator; b. Gallup, N.Mex., June 1, 1944; d. Ralph John and Gladys Agnes (O'Sullivan) Kammer; m. John Leo Cattaneo, Apr. 25, 1964; children: John Auro, Paul Anthony. Student, Tex. Woman's U., 1962-64. Portrait artist, tchr., Gallup, N.Mex., 1972. Coord. Works Progress Adminstrn. art project renovation McKinley County, Gallup, Octavia Fellin Performing Arts wing dedication, Gallup Pub. Libr.; formation com. mem. Multi-Modal/Multi-Cultural Ctr. for Gallup; exch. with Soviet Women's Com. USSR Women Artists del., Moscow, Kiev, Leningrad, 1990; Women Artists del. and exch., Jerusalem, Tel Aviv, Cairo, Israel; mem. Artists Del. to Prague, Vienna and Budapest; mem. Women Artists Del. to Egypt, Israel and Italy, 1992, artist del., Brazil, 1994, Greece, Crete, Turkey, Spain, 1996, N.S. and Ont., N.B., PEI, Can., 2000. One-woman shows include Gallup Pub. Libr., 1963, 66, 77-78, 81, 87, Gallup Lovelace Med. Clinic, Santa Fe Sta. Open House, 1981, Gallery 20, Farmington, N.Mex., 1985—, Red Mesa Art Gallery, 1989, Soviet Retrospect Carol's Art & Antiques Gallery, Liverpool, N.Y., 1992, 97, N.Mex. State Capitol Bldg., Santa Fe, 1992, Lt. Govt. Casey Luna-Office Complex, Women Artists N.Mex. Mus. Fine Arts, Carlsbad, 1992, Rio Rancho Country Club, N.Mex., 1995; exhibited in group shows at Navajo Nation Libr., 1978, Santa Fe Festival of the Arts, 1979, N.Mex. State Fair, 1978-80, Catharine Lorrilard Wolfe, NYC, 1980-81, 84-92, 2004-05, Salmagundi Club, 1984, 90, 98, Palm Beach Internat., New Orleans, 1984, Fine Arts Ctr., Taos, 1984, O'Brien's Art Emporium, Scottsdale, Ariz., 1986, Gov.'s Gallery, 1989, N.Mex. State Capitol, Santa Fe, 1987, Pastel Soc. West Coast, Sacramento Ctr. for Arts, Calif., 1986-90, Magnifico Fest. of the Arts, Albuquerque, 1991, Assn. pour la Promotion du Patrimone Artistique Française, Paris Nat. Mus. of the Arts for Women, Washington, 1991, Artists of N.Mex., Internat., Trammell Corw Pavillion, Dallas, Carlsbad (N.Mex.) Mus. Fine Art; represented in permanent collections Zuni Arts and Crafts Ednl. Bldg., U. N.Mex., C.J. Wiemar Collection, McKinley Manor, Gov.'s Office, State Capitol Bldg., Santa Fe, Hist. El Rancho Hotel, Gallup, Sunwest Bank, Fine Arts Ctr., Taos, Armand Hammer Pvt. Collection, Wilcox Canyon Collections, Sadona, Ariz., Galaria Impi, Netherlands, Woods Art and Antiques, Liverpool, NY, Stewarts Fine Art, Taos, N.Mex., Rehoboth McKinley Christian Hosp. & Sacred Heart Cathedral, Gallup, NM, 2005. Mem. Dora Cox del. to Soviet Union-U.S. Exch., 1990. Recipient Cert. of Recognition for Contbn. and Participation Assn. pour la Patrinome du Artistique Français, 1991, N.Mex. State Senate 14th Legislature Session Meml. # 101 for Artistic Achievements award, 1992, Award of Merit, Pastel Soc. West Coast Ann. Membership Exhbn., 1998, Disting. Mem. Juried Exhbn., 2006, award N.Mex. State Ho. Reps. for Artistic Achievement, 2001, Holbein award for excellence in painting Pastel Soc. West Coast Internat. Juried Exhbn., Award of Merit Pastel Soc. S.W. Ann. Signature and Disting. Pastelists Juried Exhbns., 2006, others; 2 paintings named Top 100 Best Paintings in Am., Paint Am., 2006; honored for preservation of WPA Dept. Edn. N.Mex. State Ho. of Reps., 2001. Mem. Internat. Fine Arts Guild, Am. Portrait Soc. (cert.), Internat. Landscape Artists, Oil Painters Am., Pastel Soc. Am. (signature, Award of Merit 2004), Pastel Soc. West Coast (cert., signature, Holbein award, award of excellence mem.'s show 1999), Landscape ARtists Internat., Mus. N.Mex. Found., N.Mex. Archtl. Found., Mus. Women in the Arts, Fechin Inst., Artists' Co-op (co-chair), Gallup C. of C., Gallup Area Arts and Crafts Coun. (nat. and internat. artist of distinction award 1997), Catharine Lorillard Wolfe Art Club of N.Y.C. (Pastel Soc. of Am. award for Excellence, 2004, oil and pastel juried membership, 1st Pl. Pastel Membership Exhbn. award 2004, 2d Pl. Pastel Membership Exhbn. award 2005), Pastel Soc. N.Mex. (participant artist's presentation Australia chpt. 2006), Soroptomists (Internat. Woman of Distinction 1990), Salmagundi Art Club. Address: 210 E Green St Gallup NM 87301-6130 Office Phone: 505-722-4090. Business E-Mail: cattaneo@cnetco.com.

CATTELAN, MAURIZIO, artist; b. Padua, Italy, 1960; Co-curator 4th Berlin Biennale, Germany, 2006; co-founder The Wrong Gallery, NYC. Projects 65, Mus. Modern Art, NY, 1998, 48th Venice Biennale, La Biennale di Venezia, Venice, 1999, Apr. 1999, Galleria Massimo De Carlo, Milano, 1999, Au-delà du spectacle, Centre Pompidou, Musée National d'Art Moderne, Paris, 2000, Over the Edges, Stedelijk Mus. voor Acutuele Kunst, 2000, 49th Venice Biennale, La Biennale Di Venezia, Venice, 2001, Irony, Fundación Joan Miró, Barcelona, 2001, Recaptured Nature, Marian Goodman Gallery, NY, 2002, Accrochage I: Photographs, Van de Weghe Fine Art, NY, 2002, Hollywood is a Verb, Gagosian Gallery, London, 2002, Felix, Mus. Contemporary Art, Chgo., 2002, It happened tomorrow, La biennale d'art contemporain de Lyon, 2002, Dreams & Conflicts: Dictatorship of the Viewer, La Biennale di Venezia, Venice, 2003, Whitney Biennial Exhbn., Whitney Mus. Am. Art, 2004, Bodily Space: New Obsessions in Figurative Sculpture, Albright-Knox Art Gallery, Buffalo, NY, 2004, The Big Nothing, Inst. Contemporary Art, Phila., 2004, None of the above, Swiss Inst., NY, 2004, Speaking With Hands: Photographs from the Buhl Collection, Guggenheim NY, 2004, Monument to now, Deste Found. Ctr. Contemporary Art, 2005, 20045 Carnegie International, Carnegie Mus. Art, 2005, Contrepoint, Musee du Louvre, 2005, Universal Experience: Art, Life and the Tourist's Eye, Hayward Gallery, Eng., 2005; co-editor: Charley mag. Mailing: c/o Marian Goodman Gallery 24 West 57th St New York NY 10019

CATTERALL, WILLIAM A., pharmacology, neurobiology educator; b. Providence, Oct. 12, 1946; s. William V. and Alice C.; children: W. Douglas, Elizabeth R.; m. Christine E. BA in Chemistry, Brown U., 1968; PhD in Physiol. Chemistry, Johns Hopkins U., 1972. Postdoctoral research fellow Lab. of Biochem. Genetics NIH, Bethesda, Md., 1972-76, staff scientist, 1976-77; assoc. prof. dept. pharmacology U. Wash., Seattle, 1977-82, prof., 1982—, chmn. dept. pharmacology, 1984—, chmn. interdisciplinary com. on neurobiology, 1986—. Editor: Molecular Pharmacology, 1986—90; contbr. chapters to books, articles to profl. jours. Recipient Young Scientist award Passano Found., 1981, Jacob Javits Neurosci award, NIH, 1984, 91, Basic Sci. prize Am. Heart Assn., 1992, Bristol Myers Squibb award, 2003; numerous grants. Mem. Nat. Acad. Sci., Inst. of Medicine, Am. Acad. Arts and Sci., Am. Soc. Pharmacology and Exptl. Therapeutics, Soc. for Neurosci., Am. Soc. Biol. Chemists. Avocations: sailing, skiing. Office: Univ Wash Dept Pharmacology PO Box 357280 Seattle WA 98195-7280 E-mail: wcatt@u.washington.edu.

CATTO, HENRY EDWARD, former government official, retired ambassador; b. Dallas, Dec. 6, 1930; s. Henry Edward and Maurine (Halsell) C.; m. Jessica Oveta Hobby, Feb. 15, 1958; children: Heather, John, William, Elizabeth. BA, Williams Coll., 1952; JD (hon.), U. Aberdeen, 1990. Ptnr. Catto & Catto, San Antonio, 1955—2003, ret., 2003; dep. rep. Orgn. Am. States, Washington, 1969-71; ambassador to El Salvador, 1971-73; U.S. chief protocol White House, Washington, 1974-76; ambassador to UN, Geneva, 1976-77; asst. sec. def. Pentagon, Washington, 1981-83; vice chmn. H & C Communications, 1983-89; amb. to U.K., 1989-91; dir. U.S. Info. Agy., Washington, 1991-93; adj. prof. U. Tex., San Antonio, 1993—. Mem. Coun. on Fgn. Rels., NYC, 1973; vice chmn. The Aspen Inst., 1993—; chmn. Atlantic Coun. U.S., 1999—2007, chmn. emeritus, 2007—. Mem.: Alibi Club (Washington), Metro Club (Washington). Office: 4028 Fawnridge San Antonio TX 78229

CATTRALL, KIM, actress; b. Liverpool, Eng., Aug. 21, 1956; d. Dennis and Shane Cattrall; m. Larry Davis, 1975 (div.); m. Andre J. Lyson, 1982 (div. 1989); m. Mark Levinson, Sept. 4, 1998. Student, London Acad. Music and Dramatic Art, Banff Sch. Fine Arts, Alta., Can.; grad., Am. Acad. Dramatic Arts, NYC. Actor: (films) Rosebud, 1975, Tribute, 1980, Ticket to Heaven, 1981, Porky's, 1982, Police Academy, 1984, Turk 182!, 1985, City Limits, 1985, Hold-Up, 1985, Big Trouble in Little China, 1986, Mannequin, 1987, Masquerade, 1988, Palais Royale, 1988, Midnight Crossing, 1988, The Return of the Musketeers, 1989, La Famiglia Buonanotte, 1989, Honeymoon Academy, 1990, Bonfire of the Vanities, 1990, Star Trek VI: The Undiscovered Country, 1991, Split Second, 1992, Breaking Point, 1993, Live Nude Girls, 1995, Above Suspicion, 1995, Where Truth Lies, 1996, Unforgettable, 1996, Exception to the Rule, 1997, Modern Vampires, 1998, Baby Geniuses, 1999, The Devil and Daniel Webster, 2001, 15 Minutes, 2001, Crossroads, 2002, Ice Princess, 2005, others; (TV films) Sins of the Past, 1984, Miracle in the Wilderness, 1992, Double Vision, 1992, Two Golden Balls, 1994, Running Delilah, 1994, OP Center, 1995, The Heidi Chronicles, 1995, Every Woman's Dream, 1996, Invasion, 1997, Creature, 1998, 36 Hours to Die, 1999, Sex and the Matrix, 2000; (TV series) Angel Falls, 1993, Sex and the City, 1998—2004 (SAG award, 2001, Golden Globe award, 2002, Women in Film Lucy award, 1999), Him and Us, 2006—; (TV miniseries) Wild Palms, 1993, (various TV guest appearances); (plays) Whose Life Is It Anyway?, 2005; co-author (with Mark Levinson): Satisfaction, 2002; author: Sexual Intelligence, 2005. Office: c/o Jeffrey Witjas William Morris Agy 151 El Camino Dr Beverly Hills CA 90212

CATZ, BORIS, endocrinologist, educator; b. Troyanov, Russia, Feb. 15, 1923; came to U.S., 1950, naturalized, 1955; s. Jacobo and Esther (Galbmilion) C.; m. Rebecca Schechter; children: Judith, Dinah, Sarah Lea, Robert. BS, Nat. U. Mex., 1941, MD, 1947; MS in Medicine, U. So. Calif., 1951. Intern Gen. Hosp., Mexico City, Mex., 1945-46; prof. sch. medicine U. Mex., 1947-48; instr. medicine U. So. Calif., 1952-54, asst. clin. prof., 1954-59, 1959-83, clin. prof., 1983—; pvt. practice LA, 1951-55, Beverly Hills, Calif., 1957—. Chief Thyroid Clinic L.A. County Gen. Hosp., 1955-70; sr. cons. thyroid clin. U. So. Calif., L.A. Med. Ctr., 1970—; clin. chief endocrinology Cedars-Sinai Med. Ctr., 1983-87. Author: Thyroid Case Studies, 1975, 2d edit., 1981; contbr. numerous articles on thyroidology to med. jours. Capt. U.S. Army, 1955-57. Rsch. fellow medicine U. So. Calif., 1949-51; Boris Catz lectureship in his honor Thyroid Rsch. Endowment Fund, Cedars Sinai Med. Ctr., 1985. Fellow ACP, Am. Coll. Nuclear Medicine (pres. elect 1982), Royal Soc. Medicine, Am. Thyroid Assn. (Disting. Svc. award 2001); mem. AMA, AAAS, Cedars Sinai Med. Ctr. Soc. History of Medicine (chmn.), L.A. County Med. Assn., Calif. Med. Assn., Endocrine Soc., Am. Thyroid Assn., Soc. Exptl. Biology and Medicine, Western Soc. Clin. Rsch., Am. Fedn. Clin. Rsch., Soc. Nuclear Medicine, So. Calif. Soc. Nuclear Medicine, N.Y. Acad. Scis., L.A. Soc. Internal Medicine, Collegium Salerni, Cedar Sinai Soc. History Medicine, B'nai B'rith Club, The Profl. Man's Club (past pres.), Phi Lambda Kappa. Home: 300 S El Camino Dr Beverly Hills CA 90212-4212 Office: 435 N Roxbury Dr Beverly Hills CA 90210-5027 Office Phone: 310-273-3166.

CATZ, SAFRA A., computer software company executive; b. Israel, 1961; married; 2 children. BA, U. Pa., Phila., 1983, JD, 1986. Various investment banking positions Donaldson, Lufkin & Jenrette, 1986—94, sr. v.p., 1994—97, mng. dir., 1997—99; sr. v.p. Oracle Corp., Redwood City, Calif., 1999, exec. v.p., 1999—2004, co-pres., 2004—, interim CFO, 2005—. Bd. dirs. Oracle Corp., 2001—. Named one of 100 Most Powerful Women, Forbes mag., 2005—06, 50 Women to Watch, Wall St. Jour., 2005. Office: Oracle Corp 500 Oracle Pky Redwood City CA 94085 Address: PeopleSoft Inc 4460 Hacienda Dr Pleasanton CA 94588-8618 Office Phone: 650-506-7000. Office Fax: 650-506-7200.*

CAUCIA, LOUISA B., retired elementary school educator; b. San Francisco, Aug. 9, 1946; d. Louis and Blanca Caucia. BA in Journalism, Calstate U., Hayward, 1969. Cert. Elem. Calif, English secondary tchr. Calif. Elem. tchr. San Francisco Unified Sch. Dist., 1970—77; mid. sch. tchr. Berryessa Unified Sch. Dist., San Jose, 1976—87, LA Unified Sch. Dist., 1987—2006; ret., 2006. Mid. sch. commr. Nat. Journalism Edn. Assn., 1999—2000. Mem. Latino Children's Action Coun., LA, 1995, Glendale Dem. Club, 2001—06. Mem.: Hispanic Ams. for Fairness in Media. Democrat. Avocations: films, hiking, travel, reading.

CAUDILL, WILLIAM HOWARD, lawyer; b. Memphis, Mar. 18, 1951; s. John W. Caudill and Elizabeth (Rivers) Stayton; m. Chris Looney, Sept. 2, 1978; children: Lucy L., W. Christopher. BSBA, U. Ark., 1973; M in Pub. Acctg., U. Tex., 1977, JD, 1978. Bar: Tex. 1978, U.S. Dist. Ct. (so. dist.) Tex. 1978, U.S. Tax Ct. 1978, U.S. Claims Ct. 1978, U.S. Ct. Appeals (5th cir.) 1978; CPA. Ptnr. Fulbright & Jaworski, LLP, Houston, 1986—. Mem. Tex. Quarter Dollar Coin Design Com., 2002-04; mem. vestry St. John the Divine Episc. Ch., Houston, 1982-86, 89-93; coun. del. Episcopal Diocese of Tex., 2003-06; bd. dirs., pres. St. John the Divine Meml. Endowment Fund, 1995-2007; bd. dirs. Sam Houston Area coun. Boy Scouts Am., 2004—. Mem.: ABA (chair CLE subcom. 1994—2000, chair spl. projects subcom., vice chair, chair partnership com. 1994—2006, tax sect.), Am. Coll. Tax Counsel, State Bar Tex. (dir. tax course 1986—87, bd. dirs. taxation sect. 1987—92, chair-elect 1990, chair 1991—92). Avocations: fishing, music, golf. Office: Fulbright & Jaworski LLP 1301 Mckinney St Ste 5100 Houston TX 77010-3031 Office Phone: 713-651-5292. E-mail: wcaudill@fulbright.com.

CAUDLE, FAIRFID MONSALVATGE, psychology professor; d. Theron Lamar and Fairfid Monsalvatge Caudle. BA, Duke U., Durham, NC, 1963; MA, New Sch. Social Rsch., NYC, 1966, PhD, 1975. Lic. psychologist NY, 1979. Rsch. asst. Inst. Devel. Studies, NYC, 1963—64; asst. rsch. scientist Inst. Devel. Studies, NYU, NYC, 1964—66; dir. ednl. svcs. Responsive Environments Corp., Englewood Cliffs, NJ, 1966—68, dir. early childhood programs, 1968—72; instr. Richmond Coll., SI, NY, 1972—75; asst. prof. psychology CUNY, SI, 1975—81, assoc. prof. psychology, 1982—92, prof. psychology, 1993—. Exec. com. Instn. Engring. & Tech., New Eng. Network, London, 2003—. Contbr. chapters to books, articles to profl. jours. Recipient Dolphin award for outstanding svc., CUNY, 1981, Presdl. award for excellence in tchg., 2007. Fellow: Instn. Elec. Engrs. (Companion award 1995), Royal Soc. Arts; mem.: APA, Phi Beta Kappa. Democrat. Avocations: singing, art. Office: CUNY 2800 Victory Blvd Staten Island NY 10314

CAUDLE, LETHA GRACE, secondary school educator; b. Bristow, Okla., June 21, 1949; d. William Frederick and Effie Dorothy Caudle. BS, Okla. State U., Stillwater, 1971; MA, Okla. State U., 1977. Tchr. Bristow Pub. Schs., 1973—. Contbr. articles to publs. Pres. Faculty Club, Bristow, 1985—86, Bus. Profl. Women's Club, Bristow, 1989—90, Am. Legion Aux., Bristow, 1991—93, Okla. State History Day Tchrs. Adv. Coun., Oklahoma City, 1996—, Bristow Edn. Assn., 1999—2003; mem. Tulsa (Okla.) Oratorio Chorus, Tulsa Vocal Arts Ensemble. Named Tchr. of Yr., Dist. 6 History Day, Okla., 1999, 2000, 2002; recipient cert. of appreciation Voice of Democracy, Bristow VFW and Aux., annually, 1973—85, cert. of appreciation, Nat. Geog. Soc., 1993, 1994, 1995. Mem.: Okla. Hist. Soc., Okla. Coun. Tchrs. Social Studies, Okla. Coun. History Tchrs. (bd. dirs. 2005—, sec. 2006), Nat. Coun. Social Studies. Baptist. Avocations: reading, piano, singing, writing. Home: PO Box 177 Bristow OK 74010 Office: Bristow Mid Sch Bristow Pub Schs 10 Weatherwood Way Bristow OK 74010 Office Phone: 918-367-3551. Office Fax: 918-367-1362. Business E-Mail: lcaudle@bristow.k12.ok.us.

CAUGHMAN, PATRICIA ANN, mathematics educator; Tchr. math. and algebra Coquille HS, Coquille, Oreg., 1970—72; tchr. math. grade 9-12, earth sci grade 8, dept. chair Dept. Def. Overseas Tchg., Guantanamo Bay, Cuba, 1972—73, tchr. math. grade 7, 8, dept. chair Naha AFB, Okinawa, 1973—74. Presenter at confs., workshops. Nominee Presdl. award of Excellence Sci., 1988, Presdl. award of Excellence Math., 1988; named Palm Beach County Tchr. of Yr. Math., 1986—87, Tchr. of Month, Conniston Mid. Sch., 1987. Mem.: NEA, Nat. Coun. Tchrs. Math., Palm Beach County Coun. Tchrs. Math. (mid. dir. 1987—90, math tournament com. 1988—, co-chair registration Fall math conf. 1988—, treas. 1990—), Fla. Coun. Tchrs. Math. (com. chair fall conf. 1995, 2005, PROMISE cert. chair 2005—), Classroom Tchrs. Assn., Asphalt Angels Antique Car Club, Eastern Star (Grand Cross of Color award). Office: Santaluces HS 6880 Lawrence Rd Lantana FL 33462 Office Phone: 561-642-6257.

CAUGHMAN, RICHARD BANKSTON, retired manufacturing executive; b. Columbia, SC, Jan. 17, 1921; s. Frederick Porter and Emmie Hawley Caughman; m. Elaine Florence Robinson, Nov. 2, 1946; children: Christine Caughman Hodde, Julie Caughman Fazlollah. B Mech. Engring., Clemson Coll., SC, 1946; LLB, John Marshall Law Sch., Atlanta, 1954, LLM, 1955. Registered profl. engr., SC, Ga.; bar: (Ga.). Sales engr. Chrysler Airtemp, Detroit, 1946—48; sales and constrn. specialist Dominican Republic, 1948—49; sales engr. Advanced Refrigeration, Atlanta, 1950—51; R&D officer USAF, Patrick AFB, Fla., 1951—52; sales engr. John A. Dodd Co., Atlanta, 1952—71; owner Richard B. Caughman Co., Atlanta, 1971—99; ret., 1999. Mem. Commn. on Future Clemson U., 1997; past club and dist. pres. Kiwanis, Atlanta. Capt. USAF, 1962—64. Mem.: State Bar Ga. (ret.), NSPE (ret.). Republican. Episcopalian. Avocations: photography, walking. Home: 225 Brickleberry Dr Roswell GA 30075

CAULEY, JAMES ROBERT, lawyer; b. Milw., Apr. 9, 1952; m. Brenda Andrews; children: Anne, Thomas. BA with highest honors, U. Notre Dame, 1974; MA, Brown U., 1977; JD magna cum laude, U. Minn., 1980. Bar: Wis. 1980, U.S. Dist. Ct. (ea. dist.) Wis. 1980, U.S. Dist. Ct. (we. dist.) Wis. 1985, U.S. Ct. Appeals (7th cir.) 1986. Assoc. Foley & Lardner, Milw., 1980-86; div. counsel Johnson Controls, Inc., Milw., 1986-89, group counsel, 1989-93; corp. counsel Best Power Technology, Inc., 1993-95, gen. counsel, 1995; gen. counsel Best Power unit Gen. Signal Power Systems, Inc., Waukesha, Wis., 1995—98; asst. gen. counsel Gen. Signal Corp., Waukesha, Wis., 1997-98; group gen. counsel SPX Corp., Waukesha, Wis., 1998—2005, segment gen. counsel, 2005—. Editor U. Minn. Law Rev., 1979-80. Brown U. Fellow, 1976. Mem. ABA, Wis. Bar Assn., Milw. Bar Assn., St. Thomas More Lawyers Soc. (bd. govs. 1986-93, pres. 1988), Order of Coif, Phi Beta Kappa. Office: SPX Corp 400 S Prairie Ave Waukesha WI 53186-5969 Home: 5020 N Woodruff Ave Whitefish Bay WI 53217 Office Phone: 262-513-0600.

CAULEY, PATRICK C., lawyer; BS, JD, U. Mich. CPA. Ptnr. Bodman, Longley & Dahling, LLP, Detroit; asst. gen. counsel Hayes Lemmerz Internat., Inc., Northville, Mich., 1999—2004, v.p., gen. counsel, sec., 2004—. Office: Hayes Lemmerz Internat 15300 Centennial Dr Northville MI 48167 Office Phone: 734-737-5000.*

CAULFIELD, JAMES BENJAMIN, pathologist, educator; b. Mpls., Jan. 1, 1927; s. Linus Joseph and Olive Bell (Curtis) C.; m. Virginia Walsh, Jan. 28, 1950; children: Ann, John, Clare. BA, Miami U., Oxford, Ohio, 1947; BS, U. Ill., 1948, MD, 1950. Intern Henrotin Hosp., Chgo., 1950-51; resident U. N.C., Chapel Hill, 1951-52, U. Kans. Med. Ctr., Kansas City, 1954-55; vis. investigator Rockefeller Inst., NYC, 1955-56; instr. pathology Harvard U., 1959-64, asst. prof., 1964-70, assoc. prof., 1970-75; asst. pathologist Mass. Gen. Hosp., Boston, 1960-64, assoc. pathologist, 1964-75; prof., chmn. dept. pathology U. S.C., 1975-85; prof. pathology U. Ala., Birmingham, 1985—. Adj. prof. Med. U. S.C., Charleston, 1981-85; rsch. on collagen network of heart and changes associated with alterations in the network. Contbr. articles to profl. jours. Served with USN, 1944-46, 52-54. Mem. Am. Soc. Cell Biology, Am. Soc. Pathology, Internat. Acad. Pathology, Fedn. Exptl. Pathology, Electron Microscopy Soc., Internat. Study Group for Heart Research (treas. Am. sect. 1972-85), N.Y. Acad. Scis., Harvard Club, Boston Athenaeum Club, Sigma Xi, Phi Eta Sigma. Office: U Ala Dept Pathology 506 Kracke Bldg 619 19th St S Birmingham AL 35233-0001 Home Phone: 205-870-6640; Office Phone: 205-954-4220. Business E-Mail: jcaufield@pattvab.edu.

CAULFIELD, JEROME JOSEPH, lawyer; b. Phila., Aug. 9, 1949; s. Charles Patrick and Pauline Gertrude (Riley) C.; m. Rosita Noyes Murray, Aug. 4, 1973; children: Andrew, Alexandra. BS in Fgn. Svc., Georgetown U., 1971; JD, Am. U., 1974; LLM, NYU, 1977. Bar: N.Y. 1976, U.S. Tax Ct. 1980, U.S. Dist. Ct. (so. dist.) N.Y. 1986. Assoc. Carter, Ledyard & Milburn, NYC, 1978-83, ptnr., 1984-99, mng. ptnr., 1999—2003, mem. exec. com., 2003—. Contbr. articles to profl. jours. Bd. dirs. Impact on Hunger Inc., 1984-86. Mem. ABA, N.Y. State Bar Assn., Assn. of Bar of City of N.Y. Roman Catholic. Home: 35 Stanwich Rd Greenwich CT 06830-4842 Office: Carter Ledyard & Milburn LLP 2 Wall St Fl 13 New York NY 10005-2072 Home Phone: 203-869-7780; Office Phone: 212-732-3200. Business E-Mail: caulfield@clm.com.

CAULFIELD, JOAN, director, educator; b. St. Joseph, Mo., July 17, 1943; d. Joseph A. and Jane (Lisenby) Caulfield; m. Alan Warne, Sept. 7, 1996. BS in Edn. cum laude, U. Mo., 1963, MA in Spanish, 1965, PhD, 1978; postgrad. (Mexican Govt. scholar), Nat. U. Mexico, 1962-63. TV tchr. Spanish Kansas City (Mo.) pub. schs., 1963-68; tchr. Spanish, French Bingham Jr. High Schs., Kansas City, 1968-78; asst. prin. S.E. High Sch., Kansas City, 1984; prin. Nowlin Jr. High Sch., Independence, Mo., 1984-86, Lincoln Coll. Preparatory Acad., Kansas City, Mo., 1986-88; asst. supt. Kansas City, 1988-89; part-time instr. U. Mo.-Kansas City; dir. English Inst. Rockhurst Coll., summers 1972-75; coord. sch. coll. rels. Rockhurst U., 1989-2001, chmn. edn. dept.; adj. prof. St. Louis U., 1997—2001; pres., CEO The Brain Inc., 2001—. Mem. nat. steering com. Brain-Based Learning Network, facilitator; assessor dept. elem. and secondary edn. State Mo.; mem. women's coun. bd. U. Mo.-Kansas City, 1994-98, pres. 1998-; pres., vis. social scientist Midwest Rsch. Inst., 2000; adj. prof. Baker U.; bd. dirs. Kipp Sch., Kans. City, Mo.; regent Rockhurst U., 2007. Co-author: Inciting Learning: a Guide to Brain Compatible Instr., Bridging the Learning/Assessment Gap: Showcase Teaching, The Adolescent Brain, 2006 (Hon. Alumni award U. Mo. Coll. Edn., 2006); contbr. articles to profl. jours. Active Sister City Commn., Kansas City, 1980—, Kans.' Quality Performance Assessment Team, Metro-Vision Task Force; ofcl. translator to mayor on trip to Seville, Spain, 1969; bd. dirs. Kansas City chpt. NCCJ, Expo '92 World's Fair, Seville, transl., 1992, St. Theresa's Acad., 1991-94, Kansas City Acad. of Learning, KIPP Sch., Wonderscope Children's Mus.; selected leadership training Greater Mo.; trainer Harmony in a World of Difference, 1989-93; task force C. of C. bd. dirs.; edn. alumni bd. U. Mo., Kansas City; del. leader Spain People to People Internat., 1997; trustee Kansas City Pub. Libr., treas. bd.; mem. mayor's commn. on race, Kansas City; mem. adv. bd. NCCJ, 2002—; mem. humanitarian project to Ukraine Rotary Club, 2006. Named Outstanding Secondary Educator, 1973, Disting. Alumnus, U. Mo.-Columbia, 2006. Mem.: MLA (contbr. jour.), ASCD, Mo. Mid. Sch. Assn. (contbr. jour.), Am. Assn. Tchrs. Spanish and Portuguese, Nat. Assn. Secondary Sch. Prins., Magnet Schs. Am. (contbr. jour.), Friends of Art, Friends of Seville, Sigma Delta Pi, Phi Kappa Phi, Delta Kappa Gamma (state scholar 1977—78, contbr. jour. Bull.), Phi Delta Kappa, Phi Sigma Iota, Kappa Delta Pi. Presbyterian. Home: 431 W 70th St Kansas City MO 64113-2022 Office Phone: 816-361-6192. Personal E-mail: joancaulfield@prodigy.net.

CAULKINS, ANN, publishing executive; b. Shreveport, La., 1962; m. Kelley Anderson; 2 children. BA, Baylor U., 1984. Retail advt. dir. Ft. Worth Star-Telegram, 1984—98; advt. dir., sr. v.p. sales & mktg. Lexington (Ky.) Herald-Leader, 1998—2002; pub. The State, Columbia, SC, 2002—05; pres. & pub. Charlotte (NC) Observer, 2006—. Meth. Office: Charlotte Observer 600 S Tryon St Charlotte NC 28202-1880 Office Phone: 704-358-5000. E-mail: acaulkins@charlotteobserver.com.*

CAUSEY, ROBERT CRAWFORD, veterinarian, researcher; b. Harrogate, UK, Oct. 12, 1961; s. Earl Dewey and Heather Fleming Causey. BS, U. Minn., St Paul, 1985, DVM, 1989; PhD, La. State U., Baton Rouge, 1998. Diplomate Am. Coll. Theriogenologists, 1996. Clin. instr. U. Fla., Gainesville, 1996—98; assoc. prof. U. Maine, Orono, 1998—. Dir. equine program U. Maine, 1998—. Contbr. articles to profl. jours. Mem.: Royal Coll. Vet. Surgeons. Avocation: guitar. Home: PO Box 1235 Bangor ME 04402 Office: U Maine Animal and Vet Scis 5735 Hitchner Hall Orono ME 04469-5735 Office Phone: 207-581-2782.

CAUSEY, ROBERT LOUIS, philosopher, educator, consultant; b. LA, Apr. 13, 1941; s. Robert Vester and Gertrude (Bloom) C.; m. Sandra Lee Shliff, Jan. 25, 1964; children— Britt Ann, Diane Sue. BS, Calif. Inst. Tech., 1963; PhD, U. Calif., Berkeley, 1967. Asst. prof. dept. philosophy U. Tex., Austin, 1967-73, asso. prof., 1973-79, prof., 1979—2006, chmn. dept. philosophy, 1980-88; co-founder, assoc. dir. U. Tex. Artificial Intelligence Lab., 1984-97; prof. emeritus U. Tex., Austin, 2006—. Cons. NSF, 1979-81; spkr. numerous confs., univs., broadcasts; cons. to U.S. Army and various pvt. corps. and univs. Author: Supplement to Logic, Sets, and Recursion, 2002, Logic, Sets, and Recursion, 1994, rev. edit., 2001, 2d edit., 2006, Unity of Science, 1977; co-author: Introduction to Artificial Intelligence and Expert Systems, Video-Course, 1988; contbr. articles and revs. to philos. and sci. jours.; author various ednl. and exptl. computer programs. NSF fellow, NSF grantee, 1973-74, 79-81; U. Tex. Rsch. Inst. grantee, 1979; rsch. scientist, U.S. Army Rsch. Office grantee, 1984-89; U. Tex. Dean's fellow, 1997. Mem.: Assn. Computing Machinery, Am. Assn. Artificial Intelligence, Philosophy of Sci. Assn. (bd. govs. 1980—81), Am. Philos. Assn. (mem. com. on computer use in philosophy 1994—97, rev. editor electronic newsletter on philosophy and computers 1996—2001). Achievements include development of new system for automated defeasible reasoning. Office: Univ Tex Dept of Philosophy Waggener Hall # 316 Austin TX 78712 Business E-Mail: rlc@cs.utexas.edu.

CAUTHEN, CHARLES EDWARD, JR., retired retail executive, management consultant; b. Columbia, SC, Oct. 26, 1931; s. Charles Edward and Rachel (Macaulay) C.; m. Hazel Electa Peery, June 13, 1959; children: Portia Cauthen White, Rachel Cauthen Rohrer, Sara Cauthen Landfear, Sidney Cauthen Bullard. BA, Wofford Coll., Spartanburg, SC, 1952; cert. Charlotte Meml. Hosp., Sch. Hosp. Adminstrn., 1956; MS in Bus. Adminstrn. and Labor Mgmt., Kennedy-Western U., Aguoro Hills, Calif., 1986, PhD in Bus. Adminstrn., 1986; LLD, Montreat-Anderson Coll., NC, 1991. Asst. adminstr. Union Meml. Hosp., Monroe, NC, 1956-58; adminstr. Lowrance Hosp., Inc., Mooresville, NC, 1958-61; v.p., mgr. Va. Acme Market, Bluefield, W.Va., 1961-68; v.p. Acme Markets and A-Mart Stores (now Acme Markets of Tazewell, Va., Inc.), North Tazewell, Va., 1965-87; adminstr. Lowrance Hosp., Inc., Mooresville, NC, 1958-61; v.p., mgr. Va. Acme Market, Bluefield, W.Va., 1961-68; v.p. Acme Markets and A-Mart Stores (now Acme Markets of Tazewell, Va., Inc.), North Tazewell, Va., 1965-87, exec. v.p., 1968-71, pres., 1971-87; provost, pres. King Coll., Bristol, Tenn., 1987—92; pres. Doran Devel. Corp., 1971-87, Big A Market, Inc., 1981-87. Cons. in field, 1992—2000. Author: Evaluation of the Small Company for Strategic Planning, Merger or Acquisition, 1987. Elder Westminster Presbyn. Ch., Bluefield, W.Va., deacon, trustee; bd. dir. Internat. Inst. Christian Studies, 1993—97, Tenn. Inst. Pub. Policy, 1994—2001. To 1st lt. US Army, 1952—54. Mem. W.Va. Assn. Retail Grocers (v.p., dir. 1968-82), Va. Food Dealers Assn. (dir. 1978), Bluefield Sales Exec. Club (dir. 1965-67), Rotary (bd. dirs. 1966). Republican. Home and Office: 100 Muirfield Williamsburg VA 23188

CAUTHORNE-BURNETTE, TAMERA DIANNE, family practice nurse practitioner, consultant; b. Richmond, Va., Apr. 13, 1961; d. Robert Francis Cauthorne and Lois Avery (Lloyd) Cumashot; m. William Nichols Burnette, Dec. 3, 1983. BSN, U. Va., 1983; postgrad., Med. U. S.C., 1988; MSN, Old Dominion U., 1993, grad. cert. in women's studies, 1994; postgrad., Oxford U., Eng., 1996. RN, Va.; family nurse practitioner. Staff nurse, charge nurse gynecology-oncology unit U. Va. Med. Ctr., Charlottesville, 1983, staff nurse, charge nurse high-risk labor and delivery, ICU, 1984-85; staff nurse, charge nurse, preceptor med. ICU Med. U. S.C., 1985-87, staff nurse ICU, 1988; staff nurse, charge nurse med.-surg. ICU, progressive care Stuart Cir. Hosp., Richmond, Va., 1988-90; staff nurse pediat. and neonatal ICU Childrens' Hosp. of the King's Dau., Norfolk, Va., 1990, staff nurse, team leader neonatal ICU, 1990-91; pvt. health care cons., 1993—; with Delmar Pub., 1994—; pres. The Foxmont Co., LLC, 1995—; with Sussex Ctrl. Health Ctr., 1995; men's responsibility clinic coord. Planned Parenthood, 1996; chief nurse practitioner med. svcs. Va. League Planned Parenthood, 1997-99; pvt. practice Air Park Med., Ashland, Va., 1999-2001; with James Jones and Assocs. Ob-gyn., 2001. Cons. Old Dominion U. Coll. Health Sci., Sch. Nursing, 1993—, undergrad. clin. facility, 1994—; condr. analysis of Russian and Ukrainian health care system; breast self-exam instr. Am. Cancer Soc., 1982—; presenter at profl. confs.; mng. mem. The Foxmont Co., L.L.C.; mem. adj. faculty Sch. Nursing U. Va., 1996; primary med. provider Va. League Planned Parenthood, 1997; mem. clin. faculty sch. of nursing Va. Commonwealth U., 1999, assoc. prof., 2001. Contbg. author A Quick Reference for Health Assessment, 1997, Clin. Companion to Health Assessment and Physical Examination, 1998; contbr. articles to profl. jours. Vol. Ronald McDonald House, 1980-83; docent Spoleto Festival USA, 1984-92, MacArthur Meml. Mus., 1991; vol. receptionist info. ctr. Gibbes Art Gallery, 1987-89; vol. ARC Blood Donation Ctr., 1986-92; mem. coun. U. Va. Coll. of Health Scis.; mem. adv. coun. U. Va. Sch. Nursing, 1997—; chmn. Va. Nurses PAC, 2002. Named Vol. of Yr., U. Va. Sch. Nursing; recipient Outstanding

Preceptor award, Va. Commonwealth U., 2006—07. Fellow Internat. Pedagogical Acad./Moswoc. Order of Omega Nat. Honor Soc., Raven Honor Soc. U. Va., Sorenson Inst. Polit. Leadership U. Va.; mem. AACN, DAR, AAUW, Va. Coalition for Nurse Practitioners, U. Va. Sch. Nursing Alumnae Assn. (pres., CEO 1994—, adv. coun. 1997—), Jr. League Va. (chair state pub. affairs com.), Virginians Patient Choice Coalition, Jr. League Norfolk and Virginia Beach (state pub. affairs vice chmn./lobbyist 1995), Daus. of Confederacy, Carolina Art Assn., S.C. Hist. Soc., Confederate Meml. Lit. Soc., U. Va. Coll. Health Scis. Coun., Alpha Delta Pi (chmn. nat. panhellenic rels. com., nat. by-laws and resolutions com.), Sigma Theta Tau. Avocations: riding, raising and showing thoroughbred racing horses, collecting sporting art, foxhunting.

CAUTHRON, ROBIN J., federal judge; b. Edmond, Okla., July 14, 1950; d. Austin W. and Mary Louise (Adamson) Johnson. BA, U. Okla., 1970, JD, 1977; MEd, Cen. State U., Edmond, Okla., 1974. Bar: Okla. 1977. Law clk to Hon. Ralph G. Thompson US Dist. Ct. (We. Dist.) Okla., 1977-81; staff atty. Legal Svcs. Ea. Okla., 1981-82; pvt. practice law, 1982-83; spl. judge 17th Jud. Dist. State Okla., 1983-86; magistrate US Dist. Ct. (We. Dist.) Okla., Oklahoma City, 1986-91, judge, 1991—, chief judge. Editor Okla. Law Rev. Bd. dirs. Juvenile Diabetes Found. Internat., 1989-92; mem. nominating com. Frontier Coun. Boy Scouts Am., 1987, Edmond Ednl. Endowment; trustee, sec. First United Meth. Ch., 1988-90. Mem. ABA, Okla. Bar Assn., Okla. County Bar Assn. (bd. dirs. 1990— bench and bar com.), McCurtain County Bar Assn. (pres. 1986), Am. Judicature Soc., Nat. Assn. Women Judges, Fed. Bar Assn., Nat. Coun. Women Magistrates (bd. dirs. 1990-91), Okla. Jud. Conf. (v.p. 1985), Am. Inns of Ct. (pres. 1991-92), Order of Coif, Phi Delta Phi. Office: US Courthouse 200 NW 4th St Ste 3108 Oklahoma City OK 73102-3029

CAVA, ROBERT J., chemistry professor; BS, MS in Materials Sci. and Engring., MIT, 1974, PhD in Ceramics, 1977. Temp. mem. tech. staff Lincoln Lab., 1977; NRC postdoctoral fellow Nat. Inst. Standards and Tech., 1978; mem. tech. staff Bell Labs., 1979-85, disting. mem. tech. staff., 1985-96; prof. chemistry Princeton U., 1996—, chair dept. chemistry, 2004—; prof. Princeton Materials Inst., 1996—, assoc. dir., 1999—2001, acting dir., 2001—02. Vis. scientist Brookhaven Nat. Lab., Nat. Inst. Standards and Tech., Riso Nat. Lab., Denmark, Lab. Crystallography CNRS, Grenoble, France, Inst. Chem. Rsch., Kyoto U., Japan; chair NSF workshop on Future of Solid State Chemistry, 2001. Contbr. articles to profl. publs. Recipient Honor Scroll Award, Am. Inst. Chemists, 1990, Bernd Matthias Prize for new superconducting materials, 1996, Prize in the Chemistry of Materials, Am. Chem. Soc., 1997, Wulff Award in Materials Sci., 2000, Excellence in Tchg. Award, Princeton Engring. Coun., 2003. Fellow Am. Phys. Soc., Am. Ceramic Soc.; mem. NAS (John J. Carty Award for the Advancement of Sci., 2005), Materials Rsch. Soc. Achievements include 30 patent applications; research on solid state chemistry, synthesis, crystallography and phase equilibria of new transition metal oxide, chalcogenide, intermetallic and pnictide compounds with interesting magnetic and electronic properties. Office: Princeton Materials Inst Bowen Hall 70 Prospect Ave Princeton NJ 08540 Fax: (609) 258-6878.

CAVALCANTI, DAVE ALBERTO TAVARES, electrical engineer; b. Vicencia, Brazil, Aug. 18, 1976; s. Jose Alberto and Maria da Salete Tavares Cavalcanti; m. Andrea Carla Fragoso, Aug. 16, 2003. BSEE, Fed. U. Pernambuco, 1999, MS in Computer Sci., 2001; D in Computer Sci. and Engring., U. Cin., 2006. Engr. Companhia Hidroeletrica do Sao Francisco, Recife, Brazil, 1997—98; rsch. assoc. Fed. U. of Pernambuco, Recife, 1999—2003; computer sci. lectr. U. Salgado de Oliveira, Recife, 2001—03; rsch. asst. U. Cin., 2003—; intern Philips Rsch. USA, Briarcliff Manor, NY, 2005; sr. mem. rsch. staff Philips Rsch. North Am., Briarcliff Manor, NY, 2005. Contbr. articles to profl. jours. Recipient laurels, Fed. U. of Pernambuco, 1999; scholar, U. Cin., 2003—05. Mem.: IEEE. Achievements include development of simulation tools for wireless networks, such as cellular systems and WLAN's. Office: Philips 345 Scarborough Rd Briarcliff Manor NY 10510 Office Phone: 914-945-6083. Personal E-mail: dave_cavalcanti@hotmail.com.

CAVALIER, GINA M., lawyer; b. Long Beach, Calif., Jan. 19, 1971; BA in Internat. Rels., summa cum laude, Boston U., 1993; JD cum laude, Georgetown U., 1996. Bar: NY 1997, DC 2000. Atty. Atty. Gen.'s Honors Program, US Dept. Justice; law clk. to Hon. Mary Ellen Bittner Drug Enforcement Adminstrn.; assoc., health care group Reed Smith; assoc., health law group Shaw Pittman; assoc., health care practice group Sonnenschein Nath & Rosenthal LLP, Washington, 2003—04, ptnr., 2004—. Mem.: Health Care Compliance Assn., Healthcare Businesswomen's Assn., DC Bar Assn., Am. Health Lawyers Assn. Office: Sonnenschein Nath & Rosenthal LLP Ste 600, E Tower 1301 K St NW Washington DC 20005 Office Phone: 202-408-9156. Office Fax: 202-408-6399. Business E-Mail: gcavalier@sonnenschein.com.

CAVALLARO, JOSEPH JOHN, retired microbiologist; b. Lawrence, Mass., Mar. 18, 1932; s. John and Salvatrice (Zappala) C.; m. Margaret Hare, Aug. 24, 1964; children: Theresa Margaret, Sandra Marie; m. Kathleen Frances Kraus, Dec. 2, 1972; children: Elizabeth Camille, Danielle Kay, Gina Kathleen. BS, Tufts U., 1952; MS, U. Mass., 1954; PhD, U. Mich., 1966. Pub. health sanitarian Hartford (Conn.) Health Dept., 1954-55, 57-61; tchg. asssoc. dept. microbiology U. Mass., Amherst, 1961-62; rsch. virologist Med. Rsch. Labs. Charles Pfizer & Co., Groton, Conn., 1966-67; rsch. assoc. dept. epidemiology Sch. Pub. Health U. Mich., Ann Arbor, 1967-70; microbiologist, diagnostic immunology tng. br. Ctrs. for Disease Control, Atlanta, 1971-86, rsch. microbiologist anaerobic bacteria br., 1986-2000; ret., 2000. Lectr. resident pathologists Grady Meml. Hosp., Atlanta, 1975; asst. prof. pathology Morehouse Sch. Medicine, 1982-85, clin. assoc. prof., 1986-97; adj. asst. prof. pathology and lab. medicine Emory U. Sch. of Medicine, 1985-2000; cons. Pan Am. Health Orgn., Colombia and Brazil, 1976-77, WHO, 2003. Prin. author: lab. manuals; contbr. articles to profl. jours., chapters to books. Served with M.C., AUS, 1955-57. Registered specialist microbiologist Nat. Registry Microbiologist, Am. Acad. Microbiologist. Fellow Am. Acad. Microbiology; mem. Am. Soc. Microbiology, Sigma Xi. Democrat. Home: 1325 Balsam Dr Decatur GA 30033-2905 Personal E-mail: cavallaro@mindspring.com.

CAVALLARO, MARY CAROLINE, retired physics professor; b. Everett, Mass., Feb. 2, 1932; d. Joseph and Domenica Cavallaro. BS, Simmons Coll., 1954, MS, 1956; EdD, Ind. U., 1972; postgrad., Tufts U., 1980-81. Inst. math. and physics Sweet Briar (Va.) Coll., 1955-56; instr. physics Simmons Coll., Boston, 1956-58, Randolph-Macon Woman's Coll., Lynchburg, Va., 1958-59; lectr. Boston U., 1960-61; asst. prof. physics Framingham (Mass.) State Coll., 1961-63; prof. physics Salem (Mass.) State Coll., 1963-94; ret., 1994. Cons. Introductory Phys. Scis. group Edn. Devel. Ctr., Newton, 1966; asst. to dean grad. studies Salem State Coll., 1971-78, coord. pre-engring. program, 1980-89, coord. secondary edn. program, 1989-91; vis. scholar Harvard U. Grad. Sch. Edn., Cambridge, Mass., 1989-90. Grantee, NSF, 1962. Mem.: MTA, NEA, AAUW, Am. Inst. Physics, Am. Assn. Physics Tchrs., Am. Phys. Soc., Ind. U. Alumnae Assn., Simmons Coll. Alumnae Assn., Pi Lambda Theta. Avocations: travel, reading, swimming. Home: 14 Winford Way Medford MA 02155-1526 Personal E-mail: mary46@comcast.net.

CAVALLERI, SILVIA, professional golfer; Grad. in Architecture, Politecnico of Milan, Italy, 1998. Profl. golfer, 1997; mem. European LPGA, 1998, LPGA, 1999—. Achievements include winning Corona Morelia Championship, 2007, on the LPGA tour; winner, Royal Marie Claire Open, 1999, on the Ladies European Tour; first Italian to win on the LPGA tour. Avocations: skiing, movies. Mailing: LPGA 100 International Golf Dr Daytona Beach FL 32124-1092*

CAVALLI, ROBERTO, fashion designer; b. Florence, Italy, Nov. 15, 1940; m. Eva Duringer. Attended, Acad. Art. Owner Roberto Cavalli Co., Florence, Italy. Showed his first collection in the historic White Room of Palazzo Pitti in Florence in 1972; designer of the following product lines: Just Cavalli, Freedom, Class, CASA (china, textiles, table tops, and gifts), Roberto Cavalli Angels (clothes for girls), Devils (clothes for boys), Roberto Cavalli Devils (clothes for newborns), accessories (men's and women's shoes, scarves, and ties), underwear, eyewear, timewear (watches); released signature men's fragrance, Man, 2003. Named Grand Marshal, guest of honour, 59th Annual Columbus Day Parade, NYC, 2003. Achievements include presenting his fall/winter 2004-2005 collection during the Annual Mercedes Benz DesignCure Benefit, raised funds for Parkinson's Disease in 2004. Office: Roberto Cavalli Co 8 Via Sento 20121 Milan Italy Address: C&M Media 307 7th Ave Ste 1801 New York NY 10001 Office Phone: 39 02 7630371, 646-336-1398. Office Fax: 39 0276303739, 646-336-1401.*

CAVALLINI, DONNA FRANCESCA, law librarian; b. St. Louis, Nov. 3, 1962; d. Giovanni Iader and Yolanda Marie (Boveri) Cavallini; m. Jeffrey Alan Mills, Jan. 13, 1986 (div. Nov. 1991); m. Gregory Joseph Kern, Aug. 31, 2000. BA, Washington U., St. Louis, 1983; JD, St. Louis U., 1990. Ref. libr. Huey, Guilday, Kuersteiner & Tucker, P.A., Tallahassee, 1988-91; libr. program adminstr. Office of the Atty. Gen., Tallahassee, 1991-96; ref. libr. Kilpatrick Stockton, LLP, Atlanta, 1996-99, mgr. competitive knowledge, 1999—. Fla. State Ct. and County Law Librs. scholar, 1992; recipient Davis Productivity award Fla. Taxwatch Inc., 1994. Mem. Am. Assn. Law Librs., Soc. Competitive Intelligence Profls.

CAVALLI-SFORZA, LUIGI LUCA, geneticist, educator; b. Genoa, Italy, Jan. 25, 1922; arrived in U.S., 1970; s. Pio and Attilia (Manacorda) Cavalli-Sforza; m. Albamaria Ramazzotti, Jan. 12, 1946; children: Matteo, Francesco, Tommaso, Violetta. MD, U. Pavia, 1944; MA, Cambridge U., Eng., 1950, DSc (hon.), 1994, Columbia U., 1980. Asst. rsch. Istituto Sieroterapico Milanese, Milan, 1945—48, dir. rsch., 1950—57; asst. rschr. dept. genetics Cambridge U., 1948—50; prof. genetics U. Parma, Italy, 1951—62; prof. genetics, dir. Istituto di Genetica U. Pavia, Italy, 1962—70; prof. genetics Stanford (Calif.) U., 1970—92, chmn., 1986—90, prof. emeritus, 1992—. V.p. Internat. Congress Genetics, Tokyo, 1968. Author: Genes Peoples and Languages, 2000; co-author (with W. Bodmer): The Genetics of Human Populations, 1971, Genetics, Evolution and Man, 1976; co-author: (with M. Feldman) Cultural Transmission and Evolution, 1981; co-author: (with A. Ammerman) The Neolithic Transition in Europe, 1984; co-author: (with Francesco Cavalli-Sforza) The Great Human Diasporas, A History of Human Diversity, 1996; co-author: (with A. Moroni) Consanguinity, Inbreeding and Drift in Italy, 2004; editor: African Pygmies, 1986; co-editor (with P. Menozzi and A. Piazza): History and Geography of Human Genes, 1994. Med. officer Italian Army, 1947—48. Recipient T.H. Huxley lecture in anthropology, 1972, Weldon award in biometry, 1975, Allen award, Human Genetics Premio Acad., Lincei, 1982, prize, Fyssem Found., 1992, Catalonia award, 1993, prize, Balzan Found., 1999, Kistler hon. prize, Found. for Future, 2004; fellow, Gonville and Caius Coll. Cambrige U. Mem.: AAAS, French Acad. Scis., U.S. Nat. Acad. Sci., Royal Soc. London, Japanese Soc. Human Genetics, Acad. dei Lincei, Am. Soc. Human Genetics (pres. 1989). Office: Stanford U Dept Genetics Stanford CA 94305 Business E-Mail: cavalli@stanford.edu.

CAVALLO, JO ANN, language educator; b. Summit, NJ, May 21, 1959; d. Joseph Anthony and Jacqueline Amelia (Toth) C.; children: Maria Cristina, Alberto Joseph. Student, U. Florence, Italy, 1979-80, U. Valencia, Spain, 1980; BA, Rutgers U., 1981; student, Inst. French Studies, Avignon, 1982; MA, Yale U., 1984, PhD, 1987. Instr. dept. Italian Yale U., New Haven, 1983-86, instr. dept. Spanish, 1986-87, instr. Sch. Music, 1986-87; asst. prof. U. Wash., Seattle, 1987-88; assoc. prof. of Italian Columbia U., NYC, 1988—. Mem. sci. com. Boiardo Quincentennial Celebration, Italy, 1993-94; founder and program dir. Columbia U. Summer Program in Scandiano, Italy, 1995-2001. Author: Boiardo's Orlando Innamorato: An Ethics of Desire, 1993; co-editor: Fortune and Romance: Boiardo in America, 1998; adapter: Orlando Innamorato for young readers, 2001; author: Il Maggio Epico Emiliano: ricordi, riflessioni, brani, 2003, The Romance Epics of Boiardo, Aristo, and Tasso: From Public Duty to Private Pleasure, 2004. Recipient scholarship Nat. Italian Am. Found., Washington, 1986, fellowship grant Columbia U. Coun. for Rsch. in the Humanities, 1989, 90. Mem. Am. Assn. for Tchrs. of Italian, Am. Assn. of Italian Studies, Renaissance Soc. Am., Am Folklore Soc., Phi Beta Kappa. Roman Catholic. Home: 733 Buchanan St Toms River NJ 08753-7207 Office: Columbia Univ Italian Dept 1130 Amsterdam Ave Hamilton Hall Rm 514 New York NY 10027 Office Phone: 212-854-4982. Business E-Mail: jac3@columbia.edu.

CAVALLO, ROB, recording industry executive; b. Washington; With A&R dept. Reprise Records, 1992, sr. v.p. Prodr.: albums by BBMAK, Michelle Branch, Butthole Surfers, Eric Clapton, Phil Collins, Fleetwood Mac, Chris Isaak, Jawbreaker, Kara's Flowers, L7, Less Than Jake, Alanis Morissette, The Muffs, Prince & The Revolution, Sixpence None the Richer, others, (Green Day) Longview, 1994, Dookie, 1994, Insomniac, 1995, Nimrod, 1997, Warning, 2000, International Superhits!, 2001, Shenanigans, 2002, American Idiot, 2004 (Grammy award for Record of Yr., 2006), Bullet in a Bible, 2005, (Goo Goo Dolls) Dizzy up the Girl, 1998, Ego, Opinion, Art & Commerce, 2001, Iris/Slide, 2001, Gutterflower, 2002, Live in Buffalo, 2004, (soundtracks) Angus, 1995, Clueless, 1995, Tommy Boy, 1995, Private Parts, 1997, City of Angels, 1998, Godzilla, 1998, Detroit Rock City, 1999, The Other Sister, 1999, Runaway Bride, 1999, Tarzan, 1999, Varsity Blues, 1999, Driven, 2001, The Princess Diaries, 2001, The Wedding Planner, 2001, Treasure Planet, 2002, Laurel Canyon, 2003, Rent, 2005. Recipient Prodr. of Yr., Grammy Awards, 1998. Office: Reprise Records 75 Rockefeller Plz New York NY 10019 also: Warner Bros Records 3300 Warner Blvd Burbank CA 91505 Office Phone: 212-275-4500.

CAVALLUCCI, EUGENE S. (GENE CAVALLUCCI), lawyer; B in Labor Mgmt. Relations, Pa. State U., 1969; JD, Pa. State U. Dickinson Sch. of Law, 1972; M in Govt. Procurement Law, George Wash. U. Law Ctr., 1977. Bar: Fla., Pa. Chief of contracts Eastern Space & Missile Ctr., Patrick Air Force Base, Fla.; atty. priv. practice, Fla., 1980; v.p., gen. counsel, sec. DBA Systems, Inc., Melbourne, Fla.; v.p., gen. counsel Harris Govt. Comm. Systems & Harris RF Comm. (div. of Harris Corp.), 1990—2004, Harris Corp., 2004—. Chair S. Brevard County Bar Grievance Comm., 2003—04; adjunct prof. govt. contract admin. & negotiations Fla. Inst. of Tech., Melbourne, Fla.; chair govt. contracts council Mfr. Alliance; mem. Defense Industry Initiative Working Group. Served in USAF, 1973—80. Mem.: ABA, Aerospace Industries Assn. (mem. legal comm.), Nat. Contract Mgmt. Assn. (Fellow 1992—), Fla. State Bar Assn. Office: Harris Corp 1025 W NASA Blvd Melbourne FL 32919

CAVANAGH, DENIS, gynecologist, obstetrician, educator, gynecological oncologist; MB, ChB, U. Glasgow, Scotland, 1952. Diplomate Am. Bd. Ob-Gyn. Former prof. gynecology and obstetrics, chmn. dept. St. Louis U. Sch. Medicine, 1966-77; prof. obstetrics, gynecology, dir. gynecologic oncology U. South Fla. Coll. Medicine, 1977—. Fellow ACS, ACOG, Am. Gyn-Ob Soc., Royal Coll. Obstetricians and Gynecologists; mem. South Atlantic Assn. Obstetricians and Gynecologists, Soc. Gynecol. Oncologists, Soc. Pelvic Surgeons. Home and Office: 8701 Midnight Pass Rd #206A Sarasota FL 34242 Office Phone: 941-346-2480.

CAVANAGH, HARRISON DWIGHT, ophthalmologist, educator; s. William Edwards and Marie Corrine (Logue) C.; m. Lynn Ayres Gantt, Dec. 27, 1964; 1 dau., Catherine DuVal. AB, Johns Hopkins U., 1962, MD (Joseph Collins scholar 1963-65), 1965; PhD in Biology, Harvard U., 1972. Life diplomate Am. Bd. Ophthalmology. Intern Johns Hopkins Hosp., 1965-66, resident in ophthalmology, 1969-73; fellow corneal surgery Mass. Eye and Ear Infirmary, Boston, 1973-75; instr. ophthalmology Johns Hopkins Med. Sch., 1969-73; asst. prof. Harvard U. Med. Sch., 1975-76; mem. faculty Emory U., 1976-87, F. Phinizy Calhoun prof. ophthalmology, chmn. dept., 1978-87; prof. Georgetown U., Washington, 1987-91; Disting. Univ. prof., vice chmn. dept. ophthalmology U. Tex. Southwestern Med. Ctr., Dallas, 1991-95, W. Maxwell Thomas chair prof., 1995—; med. dir., assoc. dean clin. svcs. Zale Lipsky U. Hosp./U. Tex. Southwestern Med. Ctr. Vis. prof. Georgetown U., 1986-87; cons., chmn. visual scis. study sect A NIH, 1980-84; Heed Found. scholar, 1973-74; sci. adv. panel Nat. Soc. Prevention Blindness, Knights Templar Found.; civilian cons. USAF, 1983-86, USN, Bethesda Naval Hosp., 1989-91; mem. neurosci. behavior study sect. NIH, 1989-93; organizing com. 3rd-4th Internat. Conf. on Confocal Microscopy and 4th-5th Internat. Conf. on 3D Image Processing in Microscopy, 1991—. Editor-in-chief Jour. Cornea, 1989-96, Eye and Contact Lens Jour., 2002-2007; mem. editorial bd. Jour. Scanning, Bioimaging Jour.; contbr. articles to profl. jours. Named 2d Joseph Koplowitz lectr., Georgetown U., 1983, 14th Waldert lectr., U. Rochester, 1987, 5th Morton B. Server lectr., U. Calif., Berkeley, 1991, George Nissal lectr., Brit. Contact Lens Assn., 1997, 21st James McDonald lectr, Loyola U. Chgo., 1998, 3d Maxwell Boschner lectr., U. Toronto; recipient Heed Found. award, 1981, Gold medal for lifetime achievement, Brit. Contact Lens Assn., Sr. Sci. Investigators award, Rsch. to Prevent Blindness, Inc., 1996. Fellow: ACS, Internat. Coll. Surgeons, Royal Microscopy Soc., Am. Acad. Optometry (lectr. 2005, Max Shapiro award 2001, Hon. Fellowship award), Royal Soc. Medicine, Am. Acad. Ophthalmology (hon.; assoc. sect. govt. rels. and rsch. 1979—83, Honor Recognition award 1982, Whitney Sampson lectr. 1997, Sr. Achievement award 1999); mem.: Eye Bank Assn. Am. (bd. dirs. 1997—99, R. Townley Paton, M.D. award 2000, Bausch and Lomb Visionaries award 2005), South-Ctrl. Eyebank Assn. (pres. 1997), Assn. Rsch. in Vision and Opthalmology (exec. sec.-treas. 1981—86, Honor Recognition award 1987), New Eng. Ophthal. Soc., Internat. Soc. Contact Lens Rsch. (Montague Ruben medal 2005, Brit. Contact Lens Assn. medal 2007), Internat. Eye Found. Eye Surgeons, Keratorefractive Soc. (bd. dirs.), Castroviejo Soc. Corneal Surgeons (pres. 1988—90, Honor Recognition award 1987, 1996), Contact Lens Assn. Ophthlamologists Am. (pres. 1987, Honor Recognition award 1988, 20th Conrad Behrens medal lectr. 1989), Harvard Club (Dallas, N.Y.), Park Cities Club, Johns Hopkins Club, Order of St. John (U.S., U.K.), Phi Beta Kappa. Republican. Episcopalian. Home: 27 Lakeside Park Dallas TX 75225-8110 Office: U Tex Southwestern Med Ctr Dept Ophthalmology 5323 Harry Hines Blvd Dallas TX 75390-9057 Office Phone: 214-648-8074. Business E-Mail: dwight.cavanagh@utsouthwestern.edu.

CAVANAGH, JOHN HENRY, political economist; b. Boston, Aug. 20, 1955; s. James Ellsworth and Elizabeth (Brady) C.; m. Robin Broad, Apr. 26, 1982. BA, Dartmouth Coll., 1977; MPA, Princeton U., 1980. Asst officer econ. affairs UN Conf. on Trade and Devel., Geneva, 1977-78, 80-81; tech. officer World Health Orgn., Geneva, 1981-82; fellow Inst. for Policy Studies, Washington, 1983-95; co-dir. Inst. Policy Studies, Washington, 1996-97, dir., 1998—. Co-author: The World in Their Web, 1983, Alcoholic Beverages, 1985, From Debt to Development, 1986, Trade's Hidden Costs, 1988, Merchants of Drink, 1988, Trading Freedom, 1992, Plundering Paradise, 1993, Global Dreams: Imperial Corporations and the New World Order, 1994, Beyond Bretton Woods, 1994, Alternatives to Economic Globalization, 2004, Field Guide to the Global Economy, 2005. Co-coord. Debt Crisis Network, Washington, 1984-89; advisor World Coun. Chs., Geneva, 1984-85; bd. dirs. Internat. Labor Rights Fund, Washington, 1987—, Philippine Devel. Forum, 1989-95, Inter-Hemispheric Resource Ctr., 1993—; mem. Civil Soc. Com., UN Devel. Program, 2001—. Harbison fellow Princeton U., 1979. Democrat. Home: 214 Tulip Ave Silver Spring MD 20912-4202 Office: Inst for Policy Studies 733 15th St NW Ste 1020 Washington DC 20005

CAVANAGH, MATTHEW JOHN, lawyer; b. Cleve., May 19, 1975; s. John Anthony and Sonia Cavanagh; m. Amanda Marie Campagna, Apr. 22, 2006. BSME, Boston U., 1998; JD magna cum laude, Case Western Res. U., Cleve., 2005. Bar: Ohio 2005, US Dist. Ct. (no. dist.) Ohio 2005. Project engr. LTV Steel Co., Inc., Cleve., 1998—2001; assoc. atty. Baker and Hostetler LLP, Cleve., 2005—. Mem. leadership cir. United Way of Greater Cleve., 2005—; mem., pro bono atty. St. Thomas More Law Ctr., Ann Arbor, Mich., 2005—. Mem.: ABA, Cleve. Bar Assn., Ohio Bar Assn., Mensa, Order of Coif. Roman Catholic. Avocations: baseball, computers, home repair, movies, politics. Office: Baker and Hostetler LLP 3200 National City Ctr 1900 E 9th St Cleveland OH 44114

CAVANAGH, MICHAEL FRANCIS, state supreme court justice; b. Detroit, Oct. 21, 1940; s. Sylvester J. and Mary Irene (Timmins) C.; m. Patricia E. Ferriss, Apr. 30, 1966; children: Jane Elizabeth, Michael F., Megan Kathleen BA. U. Detroit, 1962, JD, 1966. Bar: Mich. 1966. Law clk. to judge Ct. Appeals, Detroit, 1966-67; atty. City of Lansing, Mich., 1967-69; ptnr. Farhat, Story, et al., Lansing, Mich., 1969-73; judge 54-A Dist. Ct., Lansing, 1973-75, Mich. Ct. Appeals, Lansing, 1975-82; justice Mich. Supreme Ct., Lansing, 1983—, chief justice, 1991—95. Supervising justice Sentencing Guidelines Com., Lansing, 1983-94, Mich. Jud. Inst., Lansing, 1986-94, 2001—; bd. dirs. Thomas M. Cooley Law Sch., 1979-88; chair Mich. Justice Project, 1994-95, Nat. Interbranch Conf., Mpls., 1994-95; supreme ct. liaison Mich. Indian Tribal Cts., Mich. State Cts. Bd. dirs. Am. Heart Assn. Mich., 1982—, chmn. bd. Am. Heart Assn. Mich., Lathrup Village, 1984-85; bd. dirs. YMCA, Lansing, 1978. Mem. ABA, Fed. Bar Assn., Ingham County Bar Assn., Inst. Jud. Adminstrn., Soc. of Irish/Am. Lawyers (pres. 1987-88). Democrat. Roman Catholic. Avocations: jogging, racquetball, fishing. Office: Mich Supreme Ct PO Box 30052 925 W Ottawa St Lansing MI 48933-1067 Office Phone: 517-373-8683.*

CAVANAGH, MICHAEL J., bank executive; CFO Citibank Consumer in Europe, the Mid. East and Africa; chief adminstrv. officer Salomon Smith Barney, Europe; sr. v.p. strategy & planning Bank One Corp., 2000—01, treas., 2001—03, chief adminstrv. officer comml. bank, 2003; head mid. market banking JP Morgan Chase, NYC, 2003—04, CFO, mem. exec. com., 2004—. Office: JP Morgan Chase 270 Park Ave New York NY 10017-2070 E-mail: mike.cavanagh@jpmchase.com.*

CAVANAGH, RICHARD EDWARD, corporate executive director; b. Buffalo, June 15, 1946; s. Joseph John and Mary Celeste (Stack) C.; m. Patricia Sypher, 1995; 1 child. BA, Wesleyan U., Middletown, Conn., 1968; MBA, Harvard U., 1970. Assoc. McKinsey & Co. Inc., Washington, 1970-77, ptnr., 1980-88; exec. dir. fed. cash mgmt. U.S. Office Mgmt. and Budget, Washington, 1977-79; exec. dean Kennedy Sch. Govt. Harvard U., Cambridge, Mass., 1988-95; pres., CEO The Conf. Bd., Inc., NYC, 1995—2007. Domestic coord. Pres.' Reorgn. Project, The White House, Washington, 1978-79; mem. exec. com. Pres.' Pvt. Sector Survey on Cost Control, Grace Commn., 1982-83. Co-author: (with Donald K. Clifford Jr.) The Winning Performance: How America's High-Growth Midsize Companies Succeed, 1985, 2d edit., 1988 (pub. in 11 fgn. langs.). Trustee Ctr. for Excellence in Govt., 1985, 96—, Ednl. Testing Svc., 1997—, vice chmn., 2002-05, chmn. 2005—; trustee, dir. Black Rock Mut. Funds, 1994—, chmn., 2007—; dir. Fremont Group, 1997—, The Guardian Ins., 1998—, Arch Chems., Inc., 1996—, Aircraft Fin. Trust, 1999—. Recipient Presdl. commendation, 1979, 80, 83. Mem. Coun. on Fgn. Rels., Wesleyan U. (trustee emeritus), Met. Club (DC), Harvard Club (NYC, Boston), Siwanoy Country Club (Bronxville, NY), The Links (NYC), Beta Theta Pi. Democrat. Roman Catholic.

CAVANAGH, WILLIAM G., lawyer; b. Ctrl. Valley, NY, Apr. 22, 1950; BA, Syracuse U., 1972; JD, George Washington U., 1975; LLM, NYU, 1979. Bar: DC 1975, NY 1980, US Tax Ct. Law clk. to Judge Arthur L. Nims III US Tax Ct., 1979—80; ptnr., tax dept. Chadbourne & Parke LLP, NYC. Adj. asst. prof. Fordham U. Sch. Law, 1985; bd. adv. NYU Inst. Fed. Taxation. Contbr. articles to profl. jour. Mem.: Internat. Bar Assn., DC Bar, ABA, NY Bar Assn. Office: Chadbourne & Parke LLP 30 Rockefeller Plz New York NY 10112 Office Phone: 212-408-5388. Office Fax: 212-541-5369. Business E-Mail: wcavanagh@chadbourne.com.

CAVANAUGH, JAMES HENRY, health products executive, retired federal official; b. Orange, NJ, Mar. 3, 1937; s. James H. and Madeline Rachel (McFerren) C.; m. Esther Sally Musselman, Jan. 20, 1962; children: Elizabeth Anne, Michael Patrick. BS, Fairleigh Dickinson U., 1959; MA, U. Iowa, 1961, PhD, 1964. Asst. adminstr. Princeton Hosp., NJ, 1961-62; asst. prof. hosp. and health care adminstrn. U. Iowa, 1964-66; spl. asst. to surgeon gen. USPHS, 1966-67, dir. office comprehensive health planning, 1967-68; dep. asst. sec. health and sci. affairs HEW, 1969-71; staff asst. for health affairs Pres. Nixon, The White House, 1971-73, asst. dir. domestic council, 1973-74, dep. dir., 1974-75; dep. chief White House staff for Pres. Ford, 1975-76; v.p. corp. devel. Allergan Pharms., Irvine, Calif., 1977-78, sr. v.p. sci. and planning, 1978-81; spl. cons. to Pres. Reagan, 1981; pres. Allergan Internat., 1981-82, SmithKline BioSci. Labs., 1983-85, Smith Kline & French Labs. US, Phila., 1985-01; gen. ptnr. HealthCare Ventures, LLC. Founding bd. dirs. Marine Nat. Bank, Santa Ana Calif.; bd. dirs. Middlebrook Pharms., Shire Pharms. Group, PLC, Verenium Corp., chmn. bd. Mem. Pres.'s Export Council, 1981-85; bd. dirs. Proprietary Assn., 1980-82; trustee Nat. Com. for Quality Health Care, nat. chmn. 1988; trustee emeritus Calif. Coll. Medicine; mem. nat. adv. com. Am. Refugee Com. Recipient Disting. Alumnus award U. Iowa Coll. Medicine, Disting. Alumni Achievement award U. Iowa. Mem. Am. Hosp. Assn. (hon.), Pharm. Mfrs. Assn. (bd. dirs. 1986-88), Union League Club (Phila.), Union League Club. Episcopalian (vestryman). Home: 554 Dorset Rd Devon PA 19333-1845 Office: HealthCare Ventures LLC 44 Nassau St Princeton NJ 08542-4506 Office Phone: 609-430-3930.

CAVANAUGH, JAMES MICHAEL, lawyer; b. Columbus, Ohio, Mar. 19, 1949; s. James Francis and Virginia (Allen) C.; m. Susan Boulineaux, Sept. 4, 1977; children: James, Thomas, Matthew, Daniel. BS, Ohio State U., 1971; JD, Stanford U., 1974. Bar: Ohio 1974, D.C. 1977, U.S. Dist. Ct. D.C. 1978, U.S. Claims Ct. 1981, U.S. Ct. Appeals (D.C. cir.) 1978, U.S. Ct. Appeals (fed. cir.) 1984. Atty.-advisor, Office of Gen. Counsel U.S. Dept. Commerce/Maritime Adminstrn., Washington, 1974-77, counsel Great Lakes region, 1976-77; assoc. Graham & James, Washington, 1977-80, ptnr., 1980—, mng. ptnr., chmn., 1987-92; ptnr. Holland & Knight LLP, Washington, mem. dir. com. Chmn. water transp. law com. Fed. Bar Assn., Washington, 1979-80; adj. prof. George Mason U. Sch. Law 1997-. Contbr. articles to profl. jours. Trustee Ctr. for Law and Social Policy, Washington, 1973-74. Mem. Maritime Law Assn. (assoc.), Maritime Adminstrv. Bar Assn., ABA, Phi Beta Kappa. Office: Holland & Knight LLP 2099 Pennsylvania Ave NW Ste 100 Washington DC 20006 Office Phone: 202-828-5084.

CAVANAUGH, JAMES W., lawyer; b. Ft. Dodge, Iowa, 1948; m. Annie Cavanaugh; children: Bridget, James, Matthew, Kevin, Michael, Mark. BA, U. Notre Dame, 1971; JD, St. Louis U., 1974; MA, Georgetown U., 1978. Bar: Iowa 1972, Ga. 1974, Minn. 1982. With Hormel Foods Corp., Austin, Minn., 1982—, sr. v.p. external affairs, corp. sec., 2001—, sr. v.p., gen. counsel, 2005—. With USAF, Vietnam. Mem.: ABA, State Bar of Ga, Minn. State Bar Assn., Iowa State Bar Assn. Avocations: bicycling, skiing, basketball. Office: Hormel Foods Corp 1 Hormel Pl Austin MN 55912 Office Phone: 507-437-5901.*

CAVANAUGH, JANIS LYNN, protective services official, educator; b. Montebello, Calif., Feb. 15, 1952; d. William Franklin Cavanaugh and Anne Mildred Dederick; life ptnr. Jeanne Lynn Renner, Aug. 14, 1992. AS in Police Sci., Rio Hondo Coll., Whittier, Calif., 1973; BS in Criminal Justice, Calif. State U., LA, 1995; MPA, U. of La Verne, Calif., 2000. Police officer El Monte Police Dept., Calif., 1972—77, Amtrak R.R. Police, LA, 1977—84; asst. rangemaster Rio Hondo Police Acad., Whittier, 1977—96; prof. adminstrn. of justice and forensic sci. Rio Hondo C.C., Whittier, 1996—; coord. forensic sci. program & acad. La Puente Valley Regional Occupl. Program, City of Industry, Calif., 2003—, pub. safety coord., 1992—2000, instr., 2002—, supr., coord., 2000—02, supr., 2002—. Cons. Tri-Cities Regional Occupl. Program, Whittier, 2000—, East San Gabriel Valley Regional Occupl. Program, West Covina, Calif., 2002—, SE Regional Occupl. Program, Cerritos, Calif., 1995. Mem. Whittier Conservancy, 1984—; vol. ARC, Whittier, 1984—. Recipient Women of Yr. award, Soroptomist Orgn., 1996; Vocat. Ednl. Equipment grantee, State of Calif., 2001, Vocat. Ednl. grantee, 2003. Mem.: Am. Acad. Forensic Sci., Crim. Justice Educators, Forensic Sci. Club (advisor 2000—), Nat. Assn. Pub. Adminstrn. (assoc.), Rio Hondo Faculty Assn. (assoc.; sec. 1996—98), Calif. Assn. Criminal Justice Educators (assoc.; sec. 1994—96), Internat. Assn. Identification (assoc.), So. Calif. Assn. Fingerprint Officers (assoc.), Kiwanis Greater Whittier, NRA (life), Calif. Police Pistol Assn. (life), Alpha Gamma Sigma (assoc.; advisor 1996—2003, v.p. 2002—03). Presbyterian. Achievements include patents pending for forensic identification logo; forensic science curriculum. Avocations: combat shooting, hiking, photography. Home: 11743 North Circle Dr Whittier CA 90601 Office: La Puente Valley ROP 18501 E Gale Ave City Of Industry CA 91748 Home Phone: 562-699-1168; Office Phone: 562-699-6704. Personal E-mail: cavarenn@aol.com. E-mail: msforensics@janiscavanaugh.com.

CAVANAUGH, KENNETH CLINTON, retired real estate consultant; b. Fremont, Mich., Apr. 30, 1916; s. Frank Michael and Buryll Marie (Preston) C.; m. Barbara Blythe Boling, Feb. 24, 1979; children from previous marriage: Patricia Ann, James Lee, John Thomas. BS in Forestry, Mich. State U., 1939. County supr. Farm Security Adminstrn., USDA, Kalamazoo, 1939-43; community mgr. PHA, Willow Run, Mich., 1946-49, dir. fiscal mgmt. Washington, 1949-55, dir. elderly housing Housing & Home Fin. Agy., 1955-57, reg. dir. San Juan, 1957-58; dir. housing programs HUD, Washington, 1958-73; controller/dep. dir. San Francisco Housing Authority, 1973-78; pres. Ken C. Cavanaugh & Assocs., pvt. internat. housing and community devel. cons., Vista, Calif., 1978—; fin. finder Merrill Lynch-Hunton Paige Co., San Francisco, 1979-81, Western Pacific Fin. Co., Newport Beach, Calif., 1981-83; gen. ptnr. The Knolls, Rogers, Ark., 1980-89. Exec. dir. Arlington (Va.) Youth Found., 1950-58; advisor Salvation Army adv. bd., Honolulu, 1985-88. Served to capt. USN, 1943-46, USNR, 1946-73. Recipient Superior Svc. award, Pub. Housing Adminstrn., 1956. Mem. Nat. Assn. Housing & Redevel. Ofcls., Ret. Officers Assn., Res. Officers Assn., Naval Res. Assn., Shadowridge Golf Club (Vista), Elks, Masons. Avocations: golf, travel. Home and Office: PO Box 749 Vista CA 92085-0749 Personal E-mail: blythecav@aol.com.

CAVANAUGH, LUCILLE J., oil industry executive; b. Phila. Bachelor's, Immaculata Coll. With Exxon Mobil Corp., 1977—; former head Asia Divsn.; gen. mgr. supply and engring. Exxon Mobil Corp., pres. credit corp., gen. mgr. west coast refining and mktg., v.p. global supply and distbn., v.p. human resources, 2002—. Bd. dirs. United Way Met. Dallas. Office: Exxon Mobil Corp 5959 Las Colinas Blvd Irving TX 75039-2298 Office Phone: 972-444-1000. Office Fax: 972-444-1198.

CAVANAUGH, MICHAEL EVERETT, lawyer, arbitrator, mediator; b. Seattle, Dec. 23, 1946; s. Wilbur R. Cavanaugh and Gladys E. (Herring) Barber; m. Susan P. Heckman, Sept. 7, 1968. AB, U. Calif., Berkeley, 1973; JD, U. Wash., 1976. Bar: Wash. 1976, U.S. Dist. Ct. (we. dist.) Wash. 1977, U.S. Ct. Appeals (9th cir.) 1977, U.S. Dist. Ct. (ea. dist.) Wash. 1978. Staff atty. U.S. Ct. of Appeals (9th crct.) Calif., San Francisco, 1976-77; from assoc. to ptnr. Preston & Thorgrimson, Seattle, 1981-85; ptnr. Bogle & Gates, Seattle, 1985-97, assoc., 1977-81, ptnr., 1985-97; propr. Michael E. Cavanaugh, J.D., Arbitration and Mediation, Seattle, 1997—. Contbg. author: Employment Discrimination Law, 3d edit., 1995. Mem.: Nat. Acad. Arbitrators. Avocations: sailing, creative writing, music. Office: 1004 Commercial Ave #369 Anacortes WA 98221 E-mail: mec@cavanaugh-adr.com.

CAVANAUGH, ROBERT B., department store executive; BA in Econ., Providence Coll., 1973; MBA in Corp. Fin., U. Pa. Wharton Bus. Sch. Treas. J.C. Penney, mgr. of planning; v.p., treas. J.C. Penney Holding Co., 1996—99, CFO Eckerd subs., 1999—2001, exec. v.p., CFO, 2001—. Bd. dir. J.C. Penney Holding Co., 2002—. Office: J C Penny Co 6501 Legacy Dr Plano TX 75024*

CAVANAUGH, STEVEN M., healthcare company executive; BA magna cum laude, U. Toledo; MA in Fin., U. Mich. Joined Manor Care, Inc., Toledo, 1993, gen. mgr. impatient and outpatient rehab. ops., v.p., dir. corp. devel., 1999—2006, CFO, 2006—. Mem. Bus. Adv. Coun., U. Toledo. Office: Manor Care Inc 333 N Summit St Toledo OH 43604 Office Phone: 419-252-5554.

CAVANEY, RED, trade association administrator; b. Kansas City, Mo., Feb. 26, 1943; m. Victoria West, Jan. 14, 1967 (dec.); children: Thomas Scott, Kristin. AB in History and Econs., U. So. Calif., 1964. Asst. v.p., mgr. Security Pacific Nat. Bank, Irvine, Calif., 1969-73; spl. asst. to Pres. The White House, Washington, 1973-77, dep. asst. to Pres., 1981-83; pres., CEO Ericson Yachts, Inc., Irvine, Calif., 1977-81, Am. Forest and Paper Assn., Washington, 1985—97, Am. Plastics Coun., 1994—97, Am. Petroleum Inst., 1997—. Bd. dirs. Buckeye Techs., Inc., 1996- Mem. adv. bd. USCG, New London, Conn., 1986-91; mem. Pres.'s Commn. Exec. Interchange, Washington, 1977-80; chmn. Trade Assn. Liaison Coun., 1990; trustee Gerald R. Ford Found.; bd. dirs. Rebuilding Together, 2005—. Lt. USN, 1964-69, Vietnam. Named Assn. Exec. of the Yr., Assn. Trends, 1997; recipient Bryce Harlow Found. Bus. Industry award, 2005. Mem. Nat. Assn. Engine and Boat Mfrs. (bd. dirs. 1978-81), Nat. Assn. Mfrs. (bd. dirs. 1990-93), U.S. C. of C. (bd. dirs. 1994—97, chmn. com. of 100, 1994—2002), U.S. Energy Assn., Capitol Hill Club, Old Dominion BC Club. Republican. Roman Catholic. Avocations: skiing, jogging, sailing. Office: Am Petroleum Inst 1220 L St NW Washington DC 20005-4018

CAVANNA, DINO FRANCESCO, chemicals executive; b. Arona, Novara, Italy, Oct. 5, 1939; came to U.S., 1967; s. Carlo and Carla (Gelada) C.; m. Barbara Dziewulska, Nov. 30, 1946; children: Robert, Danielle. Degree in polit. and social scis., U. Milan, 1964; degree in internat. policy and indsl. diplomacy, Inst. Study Internat. Policy, Milan, 1965; degree in law, economy of European cmtys, Internat. Ctr. Studies and Documentation European Cmtys., Milan, 1966; postgrad., NYU, 1974. Exec. v.p. Indesit, Inc., NYC, 1967-69, pres., 1969-82, Indesit Mfg., Harrison, N.Y., 1982-89, Domestic Appliances Trading of Am., Inc., NYC, 1989-91; exec. v.p. The Tartaric Chems. Co., NYC, 1991—2001, GC Chems. Corp., Larchmont, NY, 2001—. Mem. Italy-Am. C. of C. (N.Y.C. chpt., bd. dirs. 1996—, mem. adv. com. 1997-2005, v.p.), Larchmont (N.Y.), Shore Club (bd. dirs. 1994-2001), Famija Piemonteisa Cultural Found. (bd. dirs. 1991, mem. exec. com. 1996—), European-am. C. of C. U.S., Inc. (N.Y.C. chpt. bd. dirs. 1998-2001). Avocations: tennis, historical social studies. Home: 38 Howell Ave Larchmont NY 10538-3249 Office: GC Chems Co 1890 Palmer Ave Larchmont NY 10538 E-mail: info@gcchemicals.com.

CAVARNOS, CONSTANTINE PETER, philosopher, writer; b. Boston, Oct. 19, 1918; s. Peter (Panagiotes) John and Irene (Maistrou) C. AB magna cum laude, Harvard U., 1942, AM, 1947, PhD, 1948. Tchg. asst. in philosophy Harvard U., Radcliffe Coll., 1945-46; teaching fellow in philosophy Harvard U., Cambridge, Mass., 1946-47; teaching asst. in philosophy Tufts U., Wellesley (Mass.) Coll., 1948-49; asst. prof. philosophy U. N.C., Chapel Hill, 1949-54; assoc. prof., prof. philosophy and Byzantine art Greek Orthodox Sch. Theology, Brookline, Mass., 1954-56; vis. assoc. prof. philosophy Wheaton Coll., Norton, Mass., 1965-67, Clark U., Worcester, Mass., 1967-68; pres. Inst. for Byzantine and Modern Greek Studies, Belmont, Mass., 1969—. Adj. prof. philosophy and Byzantine art Hellenic Coll., Brookline, 1978-82. Author: A Dialogue Between Bergson, Aristotle and Philologos, 1949, Byzantine Sacred Art, 1957, Anchored in God, 1959, Romanian edit., 2005, Man and the Universe in American Philosophy, 1959, Symbols and Proofs of Immortality, 1964, Modern Greek Philosophers on the Human Soul, 1967, 2d edit., 1987, Byzantine Thought and Art, 1968, Modern Greek Thought, 1969, The Holy Mountain, 1973, Plato's Theory of Fine Art, 1973, 2d edit., 1998, The Classical Theory of Relations, 1975, Plato's View of Man, 1975, Orthodox Iconography, 1977, Japanese edit., 1999, A Dialogue on G.E. Moore's Ethical Philosophy, 1979, Paths and Means to Holiness, 1980, Finnish edit., 1988, Romanian edit., 2002, Modern Orthodox Saints, Vols. I-XV, 1971-2006, vol. 10 Romanian edit., 2003, St. Nectarios of Aegina, 1981, 2d edit., 1988, 95, The Future Life According to Orthodox Teaching, 1984, The Educational Theory of Benjamin Lesvos, 1984, Meetings with Kontoglou, 1985, Bysanttilainen Taide, 1987, The Goodness of God and the Self-Willed Wickedness of Man, 1987, St. Methodia of Kimolos, 1987, Smoking and the Orthodox Christian, 1988, Fasting and Science, 1988, The Hellenic-Christian Philosophical Tradition, 1989, New Library, Vol. 1, 1989, Vol. 2, 1992, Vol. 3, 1995, Vol. 4, 2002, Immortality of the Soul, 1993, Guide to Byzantine Iconography, Vol. I, 1993, Vol. II, 2001, Romanian edit. vols. I and II, 2005, Pythagoras on the Fine Arts as Therapy, 1994, Biological Evolutionism, 1994, 2d edit., 1997, Orthodox Christian Terminology, 1994, Cultural and Educational Continuity of Greece, 1995, To Haigion Oros (Greek version of The Holy Mountain 1973), 2000; editor: Greek Language and Culture: Their Vitality and Importance Today, 1995, Byzantine Churches of Thessaloniki, 1995, He Hiera Byzantine Techne, 1995, Spiritual Beauty, 1996, The Concept of Christian Love, 1996, The Seven Sages of Ancient Greece, 1996, Ecumenism Examined, 1996, Victories of Orthodoxy, 1997, Nikai tes Orthodoxias (Greek version of Victories of Orthodoxy), 2005, St. Nectarios' Study on Holy Icons, 1997, Byzantine Chant, 1998, Fine Arts as Therapy, 1998, St. Photios The Great: Philosopher and Theologian, 1998, Dostoievsky's Philosophy of Man, 1998, Koncepti i Dashurise Kristiane, 1998, The Hellenic Heritage, 1999, St. Gregory of Nyssa on the Human Soul, 2000, Plutarch's Advice on Keeping Well, 2001, Photios Kontoglou peri Byzantines Eikonographias kai Mousikes, 2001, Aristotle's Theory of the Fine Arts, 2001, Holiness: Man's Supreme Destiny, 2001, The Priest as Spiritual Father, 2002, Psychopheleis Didachai tou Photiou Kontoglou, 2003, Orthodoxy and Philosophy, 2003, Sacred Catechism of the Orthodox Church, 2003, Greek Letters and Orthodoxy, 2004, Fine Arts and Tradition, 2004, Philosophical Dictionary, English-Greek, Greek-English, 2006, Man's Spiritual Evolution, 2006, St. Athan. Sheldon Traveling fellow in philosophy, Harvard/Athens-Paris-Cambridge (Eng.)-Oxford, 1947-48, Fulbright Rsch. scholar U. Athens, 1957-59; recipient Archon of the Oecumenical Patriarchate, Constantinople, 1979, Ann. Faculty award Hellenic Coll., 1986, The Florovsky Theol. prize Ctr. for Traditionalist Orthodox Studies, 1992, Lifetime Achiev. award, Societe Internat. De Psychopathologie et D'Art-Therapie, Am. Soc. Psychopathology of Expression, 2004. Mem. Am. Philos. Assn., Metaphysical Soc. Am. (past treas. 1949), Am. Soc. Aesthetics, Internat. Inst. Arts & Letters, Revista Soc. Argentina Philosophy, Plomaritan Soc. Boston (past pres.), Ctr. Estudios Bizantinos Neohelénicos Fotios Malleros U. Chile (hon.). Greek Orthodox. Avocations: music, restoration of icons, walking. Office: Inst Byzantine & Greek Studies 115 Gilbert Rd Belmont MA 02478-2200 Office Phone: 617-485-6595.

CAVAZOS, LAURO FRED, medical educator, former secretary of education; b. King Ranch, Tex., Jan. 4, 1927; s. Lauro Fred and Tomasa (Quintanilla) C.; m. Peggy Ann Murdock, Dec. 28, 1954; children: Lauro III, Sarita, Ricardo, Alicia, Victoria, Roberto, Rachel, Veronica, Tomas, Daniel. BA, Tex. Tech U., 1949, MA, 1951; PhD, Iowa State U., 1954; numerous hon. degrees, various univs. and colls. Teaching asst. Tex. Tech U., Lubbock, 1949-51; pres. Tex. Tech. U., Lubbock, 1980-88, pres. Health Scis. Ctr., 1980-88; prof. biol. sci. Tex. Tech U., Lubbock, 1980-88, prof. anatomy Health Scis. Ctr., 1980-88; instr. anatomy Med. Coll. Va., 1954-56, asst. prof. anatomy, 1956-60, assoc. prof., 1960-64; prof. anatomy Tufts U. Sch. Medicine, Boston, 1964-80, chmn. dept., 1964-72, assoc. dean, 1972-73, acting dean, 1973-75, dean, 1975-80, prof. pub. health & family medicine, 1991—; spl. and sci. staff New Eng. Med. Ctr. Hosp., Boston, 1974-80; sec. US Dept. Edn., Washington, 1988-90. Cons. edn. and mgmt.; fellow program adv. com. Nat. Bd. Med. Examiners, 1978; project site vis. Nat. Libr. Medicine, 1978-80, mem. biomed. libr. rev. com., 1981-85; cons. coun. med. edn. Tex. Med. Assn., 1980-87; active Pan Am. Health Orgn.; bd. regents Uniformed Svcs. U. Health Scis., 1980-85; bd. dirs. Diamond Shamrock, Inc., Luby's Cafeterias, Inc., 1993-2001, Nellie Mae, Caritas Christi. Mem. editorial bds. Anat. Record, 1970-73, Med. Coll. Va. Quar., 1964—, Tufts Health Sci. Rev., 1972-80, Jour. Med. Edn., 1980-85; contbr. articles to profl. jours., chpts. to books. Bd. dirs. campaign chmn. Tex. Tech U. United Way, 1980-88; mem. Tex. Gov.'s Task Force on Higher Edn., 1980-82; mem. Tex. Gov.'s Higher Edn. Mgmt. Effectiveness Coun., 1980-81, chmn., 1981-82; trustee S.W. Rsch. Inst.; chmn. Lubbock Boy Scoouts Am. Campaign, 1981, S.W. Athletic Conf. Coun. Pres., 1987-88. Served with U.S. Army, 1945-46. Named Disting. Alumnus Tex. Tech U., 1977; recipient edn. and teaching awards from graduating med. class, 5 yrs., Alumni Achievement award Iowa State U., 1979, Lauro F. Cavazos award Tex. Tech U., 1987, LULAC Nat. Hispanic Leadership award, 1988, medal of Merit Pan Am U., 1988, pres. medal A for Disting. Achievement CCNY, 1989, medal of Honor U. Calif., 1989, Midby-Byron Disting. Leader award U. Nev., 1989, Disting Alumni award, Iowa State U., 2006; named to Hispanic Hall of Fame League of United Latin Am. Citizens Hispanic Bus. Mag., 1987; named Most Influential Hispanic in US, Hispanic Bus. Mag., 1990. Mem. AAAS, Am. Assn. Anatomists, Endocrine Soc., Histochem. Soc., Assn. Am. Med. Colls., Pan Am. Assn. Anatomy (founding, councilor from U.S., rep. Am. Assn. Anatomy 1974), Philos. Soc. Tex., Tex. Sci. and Tech. Coun. (chmn. edn. com. 1984-85), Lubbock C. of C. (bd. dirs. 1980-88), Tufts Med. Alumni Assn. (hon. 1976), Sigma Xi. Roman Catholic. Office: Tufts U Sch Med 136 Harrison Ave Boston MA 02111

CAVE, DAMIEN, journalist; BA in English, Boston Coll.; MS in Journalism, Columbia Univ. Staff writer Keene Sentinel, NH; sr. writer Salon.com; ed. Rolling Stone Mag.; reporter NY Times. Author: (articles) For Recruiters, a Hard Toll From a Hard Sell, 2005, Why Netizens Can't Learn to Stop Worrying and Love ICANN, 2000. Grantee Phillips Fell., 2002. Office: NY Times Newark Bur 11 Mulberry St Newark NJ 07102 Office Phone: 973-802-1877. Office Fax: 973-623-1461. Business E-Mail: damienc@nytimes.com.

CAVE, ELLIS, information technology executive; V.p. engring. Teknekron Infoswitch, Telephone Broadcasting Sys., 1979—89; dir. R&D Intervoice, Inc., 1989—2005, chief scientist, 2005—. Address: Intervoice Inc 17811 Waterview Pkwy Dallas TX 75252-8016

CAVE, KENT R., parks director; b. Elkin, NC, Oct. 6, 1952; s. John Marvin and Bessie Irene (Dezern) C.; m. Annette Gail Pruitt, May 28, 1983; children: John Carlton, Jacob Reuben, Benjamin Pruitt. BA, Appalachian State U., 1974, student, 1974—76, U. Tenn., 1976—80. Editl. asst. Papers of Andrew Johnson, Knoxville, 1976-80; Pk. ranger Blue Ridge Pky., Asheville, NC, 1975-77, Gt. Smoky Mountains Nat. Pk., Gatlinburg, Tenn., 1980-83, Andrew Johnson Nat. Hist. Site, Greeneville, Tenn., 1984-87, chief Pk. ranger, 1987-88, Ft. Pulaski Nat. Monument, Savannah, Ga., 1988-97; info. officer NPS E. Region Incident Mgmt. Team, 1994—; interpretive media br. chief, resource edn. Gt. Smoky Mountains Nat. Pk., Gatlinburg, 1997—. Active Bull St. Bapt. Ch., Savannah, 1992-97, dir. Royal Amb. youth group, 1993-97; active 1st Bapt. Ch., Gatlinburg, 1997—, mem. missions com., 1998-2000, bd. mem. Smoky Mountain Heritage Ctr., 2002-. Hilton Smith fellow U. Tenn., 1980. Mem. Nat. Park Svc. Employees and Alumni Assn. (life), Savannah Fed. Exec. Assn. (pres. 1991), Appalachian Studies Assn., Great Smoky Mountains Assn. (life). Avocations: woodworking, hiking, photography, history. Office: Gt Smoky Mountains Nat Park Resource Edn 107 Park Headquarters Rd Gatlinburg TN 37738-4102 Home Phone: 865-429-6470; Office Phone: 865-436-1262. E-mail: kent_cave@nps.gov.

CAVENAUGH, MATT, actor; b. Jonosboro, Ark., May 31, 1978; BFA, Ithaca Coll., 2001. Actor: (Broadway plays) Urban Cowboy, 2003, Grey Gardens, 2006; (plays, nat. tours) Ragtime, 2001, Strike Up the Band, 2003, Thoroughly Modern Millie, 2003; (plays) Pirates of Penzance, 1997, Babes in Arms, 1999, A Little Night Music, 2000, Footloose, 2002, Dorian, 2002, Princesses, 2004, Anything Goes, 2005; (TV series) One Life to Live, 2004, As the World Turns, 2006; (films) Little Monster, 1989, Sexual Dependency, 2003. Mailing: c/o ABC-TV 77 W 66th St New York NY 10023*

CAVENDISH, KIM L. MAHER, museum administrator; b. Washington, Feb. 25, 1946; d. Joseph Wilson and Helen Elizabeth (Bell) Leverton; m. William Fredrick Maher, June 12, 1965 (div. 1980); 1 child, Lauren Robinson; m. Daryl Kent Cavendish, Feb. 26, 2000. Student, Duke U., 1963-65, George Washington U., 1966; BA in English, U. Fla., 1969. Social worker Fla. Health and Rehab. Svc., Gainesville, 1969-71, Delray Beach, 1972-74, fraud unit supr. West Palm Beach, 1974-76, direct svc. supr., 1977-78; ctr. dir. Palm Beach County Employment and Tng. Adminstrn., West Palm Beach, 1979-81; exec. dir. Discovery Ctyr., Inc., Ft. Lauderdale, Fla., 1981-92, Mus. Discovery & Sci., Ft. Lauderdale, 1992-94; CEO Va. Air and Space Ctr., Hampton, 1995-99; pres. Orlando Sci. Ctr., 2000—02, Mus. Discovery & Sci., Ft. Lauderdale, 2002—. Bd. dirs. Singing Pines Mus., Boca Raton, Fla., 1984-88, Broward Art Guild, Ft. Lauderdale, 1985-91, Va. Space Grant Consortium, Va. Aerospace Bus. Roundtable, Hampton, 1995—2000, Assn. Sci./Tech. Ctrs., 2002—, Giant Screen Cinema Assn., 2005-, South East Coastal Ocean Observing Refined Assn., 2007-; mem. Leaderhip Broward II, Ft. Lauderdale, 1983-84, faculty Inst. New Sci. Ctrs., 1992, Cultural Execs. Coun. Broward County. Recipient Cultural Arts award Broward Cultural Arts Found., 1985, Woman of Yr. award Women in Comm., 1990, Woman of Distinction award So. Fla. Mag., 1993; namedOutstanding Fundraiser, Fla. Assn. Nonprofit Orgns., 1994. Mem. Am. Assn. Mus., Assn. Sci. and Tech. Ctrs., Southeastern Mus. Conf., Va. Assn. Mus. (bd. dirs. 1999—), Fla. Sci. Tchrs. Assn. (bd. dirs.), Fla. Assn. Mus. (bd. dirs. 1989—, pres. 1993-95), Leadership Broward Alumnae (curriculum com. 1984—), Ft. Lauderdale Downtown Coun. (bd. dirs. 1992—95), Women's Exec. Club, Phi Kappa

Phi. Democrat. Methodist. Avocations: scuba diving, piano, creative writing, collecting art and antiques, painting. Office: Mus Discovery & Sci 401 SW 2nd St Fort Lauderdale FL 33311

CAVENDISH, MICHAEL ROBERT, lawyer; b. Hollywood, Fla., Mar. 4, 1972; s. Thomas Hamilton and Cheryl Anne Cavendish; m. Michele Lynne Cavendish, June 5, 1994. BS, Fla. State U., Tallahassee, 1993; MA, U. Fla., Gainesville, 1995, JD, 1998. Bar: Fla. 1998. Assoc. McGuire Woods, LLP, Jacksonville, Fla., 1998—2003; shareholder Boyd & Jenerette, PA, Jacksonville, 2004—. Contbr. articles to profl. jours. Mem. Million Dollar Advocates Forum, 2006—; bd. dirs. Cmty. Connections Jacksonville, Inc., 2002—05; co-chmn. Challenge Capital Campaign, 2005; co-chmn. campaign Charlie Crist for Gov., Jacksonville, 2006; elder Riverside Presbyn. Ch., Jacksonville, 2002—. Named one of Legal Elite, Fla, Trend Mag., 2006; named to, Law Deacon 3000, 2006; Ralph R. Bailey scholar, U. Fla., 1996—98. Fellow: Fla. Bar Found.; mem.: ABA (chair ethics subcom. 2007, chair trial evidence com. 2007), Fla. Bar (mem. rules of civil procedure com. 2003—, Excellence in Legal Writing award 2000), Chester Bedell Am. Inn of Ct. Presbyterian. Office: Boyd & Jenerette PA 201 N Hogan St Ste 400 Jacksonville FL 32202

CAVENEE, WEBSTER K., director; b. Sept. 12, 1951; BS in Biology, Kansas State U., 1973. Vis. rsch. scientist Ctr. Cancer Rsch. MIT, 1979—81; assoc. Howard Hughes Med. Inst., U. Utah, 1981—83; assist. then assoc. prof. microbiology & molecular genetics U. Cincinnati, 1983—86; vis. prof. Karolinska Inst., Stockholm, 1985; dir. Ludwig Inst. Cancer Rsch., prof. medicine, neurology, pathology, & human genetics McGill U., 1986—91; sokolow vis. prof. U. Calif., San Francisco, 1988, dir., prof. Ludwig Inst. for Cancer Rsch. LaJolla, 1991—. Mem. GM Adv. Council, Cancer Rsch. Found.; chair exec. com. World Alliance Cancer Rsch. Organizations, 2002; fellow Nat. Found. Cancer Rsch., 2003. Fellow: Am. Acad. Microbiology, Internat. Union Against Cancer, Am. Assn. Cancer Rsch.; mem.: NAS, Am. Soc. Clinical Investigation (hon.), Am. Soc. Microbiology, Am. Assn. for Advancement of Sci., Am. Soc. Human Genetics. Office: Ludwig Inst 9500 Gilman Dr La Jolla CA 92093-0660 E-mail: wcavenee@ucsd.edu.

CAVENY, LEONARD HUGH, mechanical engineer, aerospace scientist, consultant; b. Atlanta, Oct. 30, 1934; s. Elmer Leonard and Dorothy (Franklin) C.; m. Joyce Rodal, Apr. 10, 1957; children: Polly J., Rebecca R., Teresa L., Leslie Y., Susan C. BME, Ga. Inst. Tech., 1956, MSME, 1960; PhD in Mech. Engring., U. Ala., 1969. Registered profl. engr. Ala., 1965. Supr. aerothermodynamics Thiokol Chem. Corp., Huntsville, Ala., 1960-67; sr. tech. staff Princeton (N.J.) U., 1969-80; program mgr. Air Force Office Sci. Rsch., Washington, 1980-85; dep. dir. sci. and tech. Strategic Defense Initiative Orgn., Washington, 1985-93; dir. sci. & tech. Ballistic Missile Defense Orgn., Washington, 1993-97. Mem. Com. on Thermionic Rsch. and Tech. NRC, 2000—01, mem. com. to review NASA's pioneering revolutionary tech., 2002—, chair Air Force propulsiton proposal rev. panel, 2004—; cons. in field; nat. rsch. coun. Air Force Propulsion Proposal Review Panel, 2003—. Editor: Orbit-Raising and Maneuvering Propulsion, 1984; inventor in field. Lt. (j.g.) USN, 1956-59. Recipient Yuri Gagarin medal, Moscow, 1993. Fellow AIAA (chair elec. propulsion tech. com. 1984-86, chair Princeton sect. 1974-75, tech. chair internat. elec. propulsion conf. 1985, editorial adv. bd. 1988—, Wyld Propulsion medal 1997); mem. The Combustion Inst. Avocations: photography, construction, tennis. Home: 13715 Piscataway Dr Fort Washington MD 20744-6635

CAVERT, HENRY MEAD, retired physician, educator; b. Mpls., Mar. 30, 1922; s. William Lane and Mary (Mead) C.; m. June Lorraine Sederstrom, Jan. 27, 1946; children: John Mead (dec.), Harlan McCrea, Winston Peter. BS in Agrl. Biochemistry, U. Minn., 1942, MD, 1951, PhD in Physiology, 1952. Postdoctoral research fellow Am. Heart Assn., 1951-54; faculty U. Minn. Med. Sch., 1953-92, assoc. dean, 1964-92, prof. physiology, 1967-92, prin. investigator Gen. Clin. Rsch. Ctr., 1978-92, prof. emeritus, 1992—. Nat. Heart Inst. spl. rsch. fellow, vis. prof. biochemistry U. Edinburgh, Scotland, 1961-62; established investigator Am. Heart Assn., 1954-57; mem. program project com. B, Nat. Heart Inst., 1966-69; cons. Nat. Heart and Lung Inst., 1969-92. Author (with A.J. Carlson and V. Johnson): Machinery of the Body, 5th edit., 1961; author: also numerous articles. Met. bd. dirs. YMCA, Mpls., 1968-70, endowment com., 1988-2000, bd. mgmt. U. Minn. br., 1955-57, 77-90, chmn., 1968-70, chmn. capital campaign endowment, 1992-95, chmn. capital bldg. campaign, 1998-99, capital campaign steering com., 2004—; bd. parish edn. Am. Luth. Ch., 1958-72, Luth. Health Care Bangladesh, 1994-2005; trustee Minn. Med. Found., 1958-92, chmn. scholarship and loan com., 1960-68, chmn. honors and awards com., 1970-76, spl. grants com., 1981-2005, chmn. student fin. aid com., 1984-92, active 1992-95, planned giving com., 1991-2001, heritage soc. com., 2001— Recipient Harold S. Diehl award, 2001. Mem. AMA, Assn. Am. Med. Coll. (chmn. com. student aspects internat. med. edn. 1966-68, steering com. group on student affairs 1967-68, com. internat. rels. med. edn. 1968-75), Am. Physiol. Soc., Minn. Acad. Medicine (pres.-elect 1989-90, pres. 1990-91), Minn. Med. Alumni Soc. (bd. dir. 1992-98), Minn. Med. Assn. (pres. award 1988, mem. various coms.), Sigma Xi, Phi Lambda Upsilon, Alpha Omega Alpha, Gamma Sigma Delta, Alpha Zeta. Home: 2250 Luther Pl Condo #106 Saint Paul MN 55108

CAVETT, DEBORAH J., federal agency administrator; b. Fairfax, Mo. married; 1 child. BA, U. No. Iowa, 1973, MA in Spanish, 1974. With Soil Conservation Svc. (now Natural Resources Conservation Svc.) USDA, Mills County, Iowa, 1974, head employee orientation program Des Moines, 1978, mgmt. analyst Washington, dir. interagency initiatives Cooperative State Rsch., Edn. and Extension Svc., 1997—2006; exec. dir. White House Initiative on Tribal Colls. and Univs. US Dept. Edn., Washington, 2006—. Office: US Dept Edn 400 Maryland Ave, SW Washington DC 20202 Office Phone: 202-208-3545.*

CAVIEZEL, JAMES PATRICK, actor; b. Mt. Vernon, Wash., Sept. 26, 1968; s. James and Maggie; m. Kerri Browitt, 1997. Student, Bellevue CC, Wash., U. Wash.; student in Acting, U. So. Calif.; degree (hon.), King's Coll., 2003. Actor: (films) My Own Private Idaho, 1991, Diggstown, 1992, Wyatt Earp, 1994, Ed, 1996, The Rock, 1996, G.I. Jane, 1997, The Thin Red Line, 1998, Ride with the Devil, 1999, Frequency, 2000, Pay It Forward, 2000, Madison, 2001, Angel Eyes, 2001, The Count of Monte Cristo, 2002, High Crimes, 2002, I Am David, 2003, Highwaymen, 2003, The Final Cut, 2004, The Passion of the Christ, 2004, Bobby Jones, Stroke of Genius, 2004, Unknown, 2006, Deja Vu, 2006; (TV films) Children of the Dust, 1995; (TV series) The Wonder Years, 1992, Murder She Wrote, 1995. Office: c/o Pamela Cole United Talent Agency 9560 Wilshire Blvd Beverly Hills CA 90212-2400*

CAVILL, RONALD WILLIAM, financial planner; b. Escanaba, Mich., July 8, 1944; s. Robert Hugh and Lorraine (Kondory) Cavill. BA, U. Md., 1971. Cert. financial planner. Regional v.p. Am. Gen. Corp., Houston, 1973-75; pres. Corp. Benefit Cons., Inc., Denver, 1975-80, Cavill and Co., Washington, Denver, 1980—; dir. Internat. Downshifters Inst., Golden, Colo., 1996—. Bd. advisors Tax Mgmt. Fin. Planning (BNA), Washington, 1985—88; mem. faculty Am. Inst. Fin. Gerontology, 2003. Pres. Jefferson County Assn. Retarded Citizens, Denver, 1977; bd. dirs. Celebrate Colo. Artists, 1999—2004, treas., 2003—04; bd. dirs. Inst. Sci. and Pub. Policy, Washington, 1997—99, Good Shepherd Life Care Ctr., Silver Spring, Md., 1985, Ronald McDonald Ho., Washington, 1989—96; chmn. Nat. Inst. Fin. Issues and Svcs. Elders, 1991—96; chair audit com. Wireless Tech. Rsch., LLC, Washington, 1995—2000; bd. dirs. Panorama Orthopedic Found., 2007, Nat. Coun. Aging, 1991—99, treas., 1995—99. Mem.: Internat. Assn. Fin. Planning (v.p. nat. capital chpt. 1984—86). Office Phone: 303-572-0370. E-mail: RWCavill@msn.com.

CAVIN, SUSAN ELIZABETH, sociologist, writer; b. Trion, Ga., Mar. 18, 1948; d. John Charles and Mary (Risk) C.; 1 child, Julian Samuel Cavin-Zeidenstein. BA, Vanderbilt U., 1970; MA, Rutgers U., 1973, PhD, 1978. Teaching asst., sociology Rutgers U., Newark, N.J., 1970-75; typesetter SoHo News, NYC, 1976; asst. prof. sociology Green Mountain Coll., Poultney, Vt., 1979-83; lectr. women's studies Rutger's U., New Brunswick, 1984-91, asst. dir. women's studies, 1988-91; adj. asst. prof. sociology NYU, 1990—97, assoc. prof., 1998—2006, adj. prof. sociology, 2007—; project dir. women in engring. sci. tech. program, 1991-97; rsch. scientist N.Y.C. Dept. Health, 1999; lectr. women's studies Rutgers U., Newark, 1999—2000; dir. evaluation Annenberg Grant, 2002—05. Cons. Gov.'s Study Commn. on Discrimination, Trenton, NJ, 1992; regional technician N.Y. Regional Census Ctr., Census 2000, 2000; adj. asst. prof. sociology NYU, 1990—97, assoc. prof., 1998—2007, prof., 2007—. Author: Lesbian Origins, 1985, poetry book, 1973, (cd-rom) Alice in Techiland, 1997; founding editor: (newspapers) Radical Chick, 1992-95, Big Apple Dyke News (B.A.D. News), 1981-88, Green Mountain Dyke News, 1980, (jour.) Tribad, 1977-79. Declamation award Ga. High Sch. Assn., 1965, 66, Fiction prize N.Y.C. Gay Ctr. Ann. Writing Contest, 2002-03, Tchg. Excellence award NYU, 2005-06; named Outstanding Tchr. of Yr., Green Mountain Coll., Poultney, 1982-83; N.Y.C. Tchg. fellow Bd. Edn., 2000-07. Mem. Nat. Writers Union, Am. Sociol. Assn., Nat. Women's Studies Assn., N.Y. Acad. Scis. Democrat. Avocations: writing, poetry. Business E-Mail: susan.cavin@nyu.edu.

CAVINESS, KIMBERLY SWEAT, environmental engineer; b. Booneville, Miss., Jan. 31, 1977; d. Dennis E. and Wanda A. Sweat; m. Don Caviness, Sept. 18, 1999; 1 child, Sophia Louise. AA in Gen. Engring., NE Miss. C.C., Booneville, 1997; BS in Biol. Engring., Miss. State U., Starkville, 1999; MS in Civil/Environ. Engring., U. Miss., Oxford, 2004. Registered profl. engr., Miss. State Bd. Profl. Engrs. and Land Surveyors, 2004. Environ. engr. Miss. Dept. Environ. Quality, Jackson, Miss., 1999—. Home: 310 Park Ridge Dr Brandon MS 39042 Office: MS Dept Environmental Quality 2380 Highway 80 West Jackson MS 39204 Home Phone: 601-824-3074; Office Phone: 601-961-5390. Business E-Mail: kim_caviness@deq.state.ms.us.

CAVINESS, MADELINE HARRISON, art history educator, researcher; b. London, Mar. 27, 1938; d. Eric Vernon and Gwendoline (Rigden) Harrison; m. Verne Strudwick Caviness Jr.; children: Gwendoline Angela, Alison Chantal. BA, Cambridge U., Eng., 1959; PhD, Harvard U., 1970. Program organizer Brit. Council, London, 1959-60; asst. prof., art dept. Tufts U., Medford, Mass., 1972-76, assoc. prof., 1976-81, chmn. dept., 1975-81, 88-90, prof. art history, 1981—, Mary Richardson prof., 1987—2007, mem. women's programs bd., 1989—. Sr. advisor Internat. Ctr. Medieval Art, 1987—, pres., 1984-87. Author: The Early Stained Glass of Canterbury Cathedral c. 1180-1220, 1977 (J.N. Brown prize 1981), The Windows of Christ Church Cathedral, Canterbury, 1981, Stained Glass Before 1540: An Annotated Bibliography, 1983, Sumptuous Arts at the Royal Abbeys in Reims and Braine, 1991 (Haskins medal 1993); co-editor: Studies in Medieval Glass, 1985, 94, Checklist of Stained Glass in American Collections I-IV, 1985-91. Rsch. grantee NEH, 1977-78, Am. Coun. Learned Socs., 1980, NEH, 1985-93, Getty grantee, 1987-90; fellow Radcliffe Inst., 1970-71, Am. Coun. Learned Socs., 1980. Fellow Am. Acad. Arts & Scis., Medieval Acad. Am. (pres. 1993-94), Soc. Antiquaries of London; mem. Corpus Vitrearum Medii Aevi (pres. 1987-95), Phi Beta Kappa. Home: 60 Elm St Charlestown MA 02129-2450 Office: Tufts U Dept Art 11 Talbot Ave Medford MA 02155-5812

CAVUTO, NEIL, newscaster, business journalist, television host; s. Pat and Kathleen Cavuto; m. Mary Cavuto; children: Tara, Jeremy, Bradley. BA in Journalism, St. Bonaventure U., 1980. Journalist Investment Age mag., Wash., DC; weekend anchor WCAX, Burlington, Vt., 1982—85; reporter Nightly Bus. Report, PBS, 1985—89; host, Market Wrap, Power Lunch, Business Insiders CNBC, 1989—96; contributor Today Show, NBC, 1989—96; anchor, mng. ed. of bus. news FOX News Channel, 1996—2000, v.p. bus. news, 2000—, host, Your World With Neil Cavuto, 1996—, host, Cavuto on Business, 1999—. Author: More Than Money: True Stories of People Who Learned Life's Ultimate Lesson, 2004. Named one of most influential bus. journalists in Am., The Journalist and Financial Reporter; recipient 5 Cable ACE award nom. Office: FOX News Channel 1211 Ave Of Am New York NY 10036 Office Phone: 212-301-3000.

CAWLEY, JOSEPH DOUGLAS, retired reading professor; b. Savannah, Ga., Dec. 12, 1929; s. Henry Hughes and Bertha (Platt) C.; m. Grace Ashliman, June 21, 1951; children: Lorraine Cawley Gaufin, Carolyn Nielsen; m. Jacqueline Boss, May 22, 1987. BS, Brigham Young U., 1954; MS, U. Utah, 1961, PhD, 1970. Cert. elem. tchr., Utah, Ga. Tchr. Dekalb County Sch. Dist., Atlanta, Salt Lake City Sch. Dist.; asst. prof. edn. Adams State Coll., Alamosa, Colo.; prof., chmn. reading dept. Met. State Coll., Denver, prof. emeritus, 2001—. Author: Handbook for Experiential Education, 1988, From Alsace to South Carolina Jonas Beard, 1730-1796, Patriot, Statesman, 2002, From Herrstein to South Carolina Reverend John Nicholas Martin 1724-1795, Pastor, Patriot, 2003, From Lampertheim to South Carolina Captain Daniel Strobel, 1775-1806, Patriot and Civic Leader, 2004, From Mounthill to Georgia Lieutenant Colonel Matthew Lyle 1748-1831, Loyalist, Militiaman, 2005, From Virginia to Georgia Captain Henry Hughes 1756-1814, Patriot of the Continental Line, 2006, From Ballymoran to South Carolina Col. Robert Stewart 1755-1820 British Officer and Merchant, 2007. Mem. CCIRA (past pres., Pres. award), Kappa Delta Pi (Outstanding Counselor award), Phi Delta Kappa. Personal E-mail: cawleyjd@msc.com.

CAWLEY, MICHAEL A., foundation administrator, lawyer; b. Wichita, Kans., Apr. 15, 1947; BA in Econ., U. Okla., 1969, JD, 1972. Bar: Okla. 1972. Atty., Ardmore, Okla., 1972—85; atty., pres. Thompson & Cawley, 1985—91; of counsel Thompson, Cawley, Veazey & Burns, 1991—; exec. v.p. Noble Found., 1991, pres., CEO, 1992—. Bd. dirs. Noble Energy, Inc. Mem.: Order of the Coif. Office: Thompson Cawley Veazey & Burns 422 2nd Ave NW Ardmore OK 73401 also: Noble Found 2510 Sam Noble Pky Ardmore OK 73401

CAWLEY, THOMAS J., lawyer; b. Carbondale, Pa., Oct. 7, 1943; BS, U. Scranton, 1966; LLB, U. Va., 1969. Bar: Va. 1969. Mem. Hunton & Williams LLP, Fairfax, Va., mng. ptnr., litig., intellectual property, antitrust McLean, Va. Mem. Am. Coll. Trial Lawyers. Office: Hunton & Williams PO Box 1147 1751 Pinnacle Dr Ste 1700 Mc Lean VA 22102-3836 Office Fax: 703-714-7410. Business E-Mail: tcawley@hunton.com.

CAWOOD, ALBERT MCLAURIN (HAP CAWOOD), retired newspaper editor; b. Harlan, Ky., Nov. 10, 1939; s. Frank Finley and C. Eugene (Barwick) C.; m. Sonia Barreiro, July 3, 1965; children: Romy Lanier, Shuly Xochitl. BA in English, Union Coll., 1962; MA in Journalism, Ohio State U., 1966. Asst. city editor Dayton (Ohio) Daily News, 1966, editorial writer, 1966-82, editorial page editor, 1982-99; ret., 1999. Author: The Miler, 2003. Vol. Peace Corps., Sierra Leone, 1962-64; chmn. Ohio Com. on Crime and Delinquency, 1969-70; bd. dirs. Engring. Sci. Found., Dayton, Ohio, 2003—04. Recipient Disting. Svc. award Nat. Soc. Profl. Journalists, 1968, Walker Stone award Scripps-Howard Found., 1984; named to Union Coll. Bus. and Profl. Hall of Fame. Mem. Am. Soc. Newspaper Editors, Nat. Conf. Editl. Writers, Engrs. Club Dayton (pres. 2003-04). Democrat. Home: 211 S Winter St Yellow Springs OH 45387-1730

CAWOOD, ELIZABETH JEAN, public relations executive; b. Santa Maria, Calif., Jan. 6, 1947; d. John Stephen and Gertrude Margaret (Shelton) Dille; m. Neil F. Cawood, Jan. 4, 1975; 1 child, Nathan Patrick. BA, Whitworth Coll., 1964-68. Dir. pub. info. Inland Empire Goodwill, Spokane, Wash., 1967-72; adminstrv. asst. N.W. Assn. Rehab. Industries, Seattle, 1973-74; pres., counselor Cawood , Eugene, Oreg., 1974—. Pres. Women in Comm., Inc., 1981-83; stragegy bd. Benton Lane Lincoln Linn Region, 1993-99, chair, 1993-94; bd. dirs. AAA Oreg./Idaho, 1999—. Editor: Dictionary of Rehabilitation Acronyms, (newsletters) INTERCOM, Family Communicator, Oreg. Focus, (dictionary) Work-Oriented Rehabilitation Dictionary and Synonyms, 1st and 2nd edits. Bd. dirs. Laurel Hill Ctr., 1993—, v.p., 2001, pres. 2002-2004; bd. dirs. Lane County Boy Scouts Am., 1986-2001, Eugene Action Forum, 1981-86, Birth-to-Three, 1982-85, Lane County chpt. ARC, 1982-83, 84-89, Lane County chpt. Am. Cancer Soc., 1984-87, Eugene Opera, 1985-88, Joint Com. Econ. Diversification, 1985-89, 91-93, Lane County United Way, 1987-93, campaign cabinet, 2002-04, chair leadership, 2001-2003, Lane Econ. Com., vice chmn., 1990-95, chair, 1996-2001; bd. dirs. So. Willamette Pvt. Industry Coun., 1985-88, pres., 1988; chmn. Eugene Pvt. Industries Coun., 1981-83, vice chmn., 1983-84; chmn. Bus. Owners Network, Eugene, 1980-81; advisor Eugene Jr. League; trustee Nature Conservancy, Oreg., 1999—, exec. com., 2005—; advisor Sustainable Advantage Conf., U. Oreg., 2004—; mem. educator quality task force Chalkboard Project, 2005-06. Recipient Hunger Buster award, Oreg. Food Bank, 2006. Mem. LWV (bd. dirs. 1979), Pub Rels. Soc. Am. (bd. dirs. Columbia River chpt. 1987-88, advisor U. Oreg. chpt. 1987-91, pres. Greater Oreg. chpt. 1991-92, bd. dirs. 1991-93), Oreg. Nat. Rehab. Assn. (pres. 1980-81), Profl. Women's Network (bd. dirs. Oreg. chpt. 1982), Eugene C. of C. (bd. dirs. 1980-87, 92-97, local govt. affairs coun. 1999-2002, econs. devel. coun. 2002-2004, chmn. econ. devel. 1982-83, bd. dirs. exec. com. 1984-87, v.p. 1987, 93, chmn. edn. com., pres.-elect 1994, pres. 1995), Mid-Oreg. Advt. Club (bd. dirs. 1985-87), Oreg. Sales and Mktg. Execs. (bd. dirs. 1985-87), Eugene/Springfield Assn. Quality and Performance (chmn. 1991-93, bd. dirs. 1991-94), Internat. Assn. Sports and Human Performance (bd. dirs. 1993), Rotary (Eugene pub. rels. chair 2000-2004), Eugene City Club (bd. dirs. 1992-98, pres.-elect 1995, pres. 1996) Office: Cawood 1200 High St Ste 200 Eugene OR 97401-3266 Home Phone: 541-746-4894; Office Phone: 541-484-7052. Business E-Mail: liz@cawood.com.

CAWOOD, GARY KENNETH, photography educator; b. Chattanooga, Jan. 17, 1947; s. Kenneth Garnett and Minnie Christine (Malos) C.; m. Teresa Louise Taft, Feb. 1,1 986 (div. Apr. 1988). BArch, Auburn U., Ala., 1970; MFA, East Tenn. State U., Johnson City, 1976. Designer Hayes B. Fleming, Architect, Johnson City, 1970-75; asst. prof. photography La. Tech. U., Ruston, 1976-80, assoc. prof. photography, 1980-85, U. Ark., Little Rock, 1985-97, prof. photography, 1997—. Summer workshop faculty The Sch. for Photographic Studies in Prague, 1995—. Author: Scenes Unseen, 1990. Recipient Eugene Feldman award Print Club, 1986, Publ. award Soc. for Contemporary Photography, 1988; Nat. Endowment for Arts fellow, 1982, Ark. Arts Coun. fellow, 1991—, Mid-Am. Arts Alliance fellow, 1995; U. Ark. Rsch. grantee, 1986. Mem. Soc. for Photographic Edn. (regional chair 1983-84), Phi Kappa Phi. Democrat. Home: 1703 Fair Park Blvd Little Rock AR 72204-2719 Office: U Little Rock Dept of Art 2801 S University Ave Little Rock AR 72204-1000 Home Phone: 501-666-8731; Office Phone: 501-569-3128. Business E-Mail: gkcawood@ualr.edu.

CAWOOD, JAMES M., III, lawyer; b. Ft. Thomas, Ky., Apr. 28, 1972; BA, U. Ky., 1995; JD, Salmon P. Chase Coll. Law, 1999. Bar: Ky. 1999, US Dist. Ct. Eastern Dist. Ky. 2000, US Dist. Ct. Western Dist. Ky. 2001, Ohio 2004. Atty. def. firm, Ky.; ptnr. Freund, Freeze & Arnold, Cin. Named one of Ohio's Rising Stars, Super Lawyers, 2006. Mem.: ABA, Northern Ky. Bar Assn., Ky. Bar Assn., Ohio State Bar Assn., Cin. Bar Assn., Ky. Acad. Trial Lawyers, Salmon P. Chase Inn of Ct., Def. Inst. Rsch., Ohio Assn. Civil Trial Attorneys. Office: Freund Freeze & Arnold Ste 1400 Fourth and Walnut Ctr 105 E Fourth St Cincinnati OH 45202-4035 Office Phone: 513-665-3500. Office Fax: 513-665-3503.

CAWS, MARY ANN, literature and language professor; b. Wilmington, NC, Sept. 10, 1933; d. Harmon Chadbourn and Margaret Devereux (Lippitt) Rorison; m. Peter Caws, June 2, 1956 (div. 1987); children: Hilary, Matthew; m. Boyce Bennett, Nov. 3, 2007. BA, Bryn Mawr Coll., 1954; MA, Yale U., 1956; PhD, U. Kans., 1962; DHL (hon.), Union Coll., 1983. Asst. instr. Romance langs. U. Kans., Lawrence, 1957-62, asst. editor Univ. press, 1957-58, vis. asst. prof., spring 1963; lectr. Barnard Coll. Columbia U., NYC, 1962-63; mem. faculty Sarah Lawrence Coll., Bronxville, NY, 1963-64, Hunter Coll. CUNY, NYC, 1966-88; prof. Grad. Sch. CUNY, NYC, 1969-88, exec. officer comparative lit. program Grad. Sch., 1977-79, exec. officer French program Grad. Sch., 1979-86, Disting. prof. French and comparative lit. Grad. Sch., 1983—, prof. English, 1985—, Disting. prof. French, comparative lit., English Grad. Sch., 1987—. Phi Beta Kappa vis. scholar, 1982-83; dir. NIH summer seminars for coll. tchrs., 1978, 85; faculty Sch. of Criticism and Theory, Dartmouth U., 1988, Sch. Visual Arts, 1993; assoc. prof. U. Paris VII, 1993-94; co-chair Henri Peyre Inst. for the Humanities, 1980-1996, French Inst., 1997-2002; lectr. NY Coun. for Humanities, 1992-96. Author: Surrealism and the Literary Imagination, 1966, The Poetry of Dada and Surrealism, 1970, The Inner Theatre of Recent French Poetry, 1972, The Presence of René Char, 1976, René Char, 1977, The Surrealist Voice of Robert Desnos, 1977, La Main de Pierre Reverdy, 1979, The Eye in the Text, Essays on Perception, Mannerist to Modern, 1981, André Breton, 1982, 96, The Metapoetics of the Passage, Architextures in Surrealism and After, 1982, Yves Bonnefoy, 1984, Reading Frames in Modern Fiction, 1988, Edmond Jabès, 1988, The Art of Interference: Stressed Readings in Visual and Verbal Texts, 1989, Women of Bloomsbury, 1991, Robert Motherwell: What Art Holds, 1996, Carrington and Lytton: Alone Together, 1996, The Surrealist Look: An Erotics of Encounter, 1997, Picasso's Weeping Woman: The Life and Art of Dora Maar, 2000, Virginia Woolf: Illustrated Life, 2002, Robert Motherwell with Pen and Brush, 2003, Marcel Proust: Illustrated Life, 2003, To the Boathouse: A Memoir, 2004, Pablo Picasso, 2005, Henry James, 2006, Surprised in Translation, 2006, Glorious Eccentrics: Modernist Women Painting and Writing, 2006; co-author: Bloomsbury and France: Art and Friends, 1999; editor: Dada-Surrealism, 1972, co-editor, 1980-2002, Le Siècle éclaté, 1974-78, About French Poetry from Dada to Tel Quel, 1974, Selected Poetry Prose of Stéphane Mallarmé, 1982, Selected Poems of St.-John Perse, 1983, Writing in a Modern Temper, 1984, Textual Analysis, 1986, Perspectives on Perception: Philosophy, Art, and Literature, 1989, City Images, 1992, Joseph Cornell's Theater of the Mind: Selected Diaries, Letters and Files, 1994, Manifesto: A Century of Isms, 2001, Mallarme in Prose, 2001, Surrealist Painters and Poets, 2001, Surrealist Love Poems, 2002, Vita Sackville-West: Selected Writings, 2002, Surrealism, 2004, Yale Anthology of Twentieth-Century French Poetry, 2004, Maria Jolas: Woman of Action, 2004; co-editor: Selected Poems of René Char, 1992, Contre-Courants: Les femmes s'écrivent à travers les siècles, 1994, Écritures de femmes: Nouvelles Cartographies, 1996; translator: Poems of René Char, 1976, Approximate Man and other Writings of Tristan Tzara, 1975, Mad Love, 1987, The Secret Art of Antonin Artaud, 1998, Ostinato, 2002; co-translator: Poems of André Breton, 1984, Communicating Vessels, 1990, Break of Day, 1999; chief editor Harper Collins World Reader, 1994, Manifesto: A Century of isms, 2001, Surrealist Painters and Poets, 2001, Mallarmé in Prose, 2001, Yale

Anthology of Twentieth-Century French Poetry, 2004; contbr. articles to profl. jours. Decorated officier Palmes Académiques, France; fellow Guggenheim Found., 1972-73 NEH, 1979-80, Fulbright traveling fellow, 1972-73, Rockefeller Found. fellow at Bellagio, 1994, 2005; Getty scholar, 1990. Mem. MLA (exec. coun. 1973-77, v.p. 1982-83, pres. 1983-84), Am. Assn. Tchrs. French, Assn. for Study Dada and Surrealism (pres. 1982-86), Internat. Assn. Philosophy and Lit. (exec. bd. 1982—, chmn. 1984), Acad. Lit. Studies (pres. 1985), Am. Comparative Lit. Assn. (exec. com. 1981, v.p. 1986—, pres. 1989-91). Home: 140 E 81st St New York NY 10028-1805 Office: CUNY Grad Ctr 365 Fifth Ave New York NY 10016 Personal E-mail: cawsma@aol.com.

CAWTHON, FRANK H., retired construction company executive; b. Kissimmee, Fla., Apr. 3, 1930; s. Benjamin Hill and Eva Elizabeth (Mullins) C.; m. Mary Elizabeth Dickert, July 10, 1959; 1 child, Frank H. Grad. high sch. Asst. sec.-treas. Orange Belt Truck & Tractor, Orlando, Fla., 1948-52, Murdock Constrn. Co., Inc., Orlando, 1954-59; sec.-treas. Amick Constrn. Co., Inc., Orlando, 1959-90; ret., 1990. Bd. dirs. Amick Constrn. Co., Inc. Bd. dirs. Conway Little League, Orlando, 1977. With U.S. Army, 1952-54. Mem. Cen. Fla. Rd. Bldrs. Assn. Democrat. Lutheran. Avocations: painting, gardening, fishing. Home: 391 Brushwood Ln Casselberry FL 32708-4955 Office: Amick Constrn Co 401 Ferguson Dr Orlando FL 32805-1009

CAWVEY, CLARENCE EUGENE, retired physician; b. Du Quoin, Ill., May 16, 1929; s. Clarence Eli and Lois Jane (Matheny) C.; m. Paulina Isabel Hincke, Sept. 12, 1953 (dec. Apr. 1973); children: Janet Edna, William Clarence, Paulina Ann, Jean Hincke; 1 stepchild, Douglas Lance Hester; m. Linda Mae Rice, Jan. 26, 1974. BA, Yale U., 1951; MD, U. Chgo., 1955. Diplomate Am. Bd. Family Practice. Intern Cook County Hosp., 1955-56; resident in psychiatry Brook Army Hosp., 1956-57; ptnr. Pinckneyville (Ill.) Med. Group, 1958—98; ret., 1998. Clin. asst. prof. Med. Sch. So. Ill. U., Springfield, 1976-2000, adv. com. continuing med. edn., 1977-2000; exec. com. Ctrl. Ill. Profl. Rev. Orgn., Champaign, 1988-2002; bd. dirs., chmn. First Nat. Bank, Pinckneyville. Founding mem., pres. Perry County Health Dept., Pinckneyville, 1970. Capt. U.S. Army, 1956-58. Fellow Am. Acad. Family Physicians; mem. AMA, Ill. State Med. Soc. (del. 1960-70), Perry County Med. Soc. Republican. Methodist. Avocations: skiing, photography, travel, gardening. Home: 204 W Laurel St Pinckneyville IL 62274-1019 Office Phone: 618-357-9393.

CAYARI, CHRISTOPHER, music educator; b. Oak Lawn, Ill., Aug. 6, 1981; s. Nathaniel Cayari and Pamela Hickey. MusB in Edn., Trinity Christian Coll., 2003. Dir. music Westlake Christian Acad., Grayslake, Ill., 2004—, worship coord., 2004—. Worship leader The Chapel, Grayslake, Ill., 2005—. Composer: (albums) A Mountaintop Experience, Meditations on the Lord, 2005. Mem.: ASCAP, Guitar Found. Am., Music Educators Nat. Conf., Guitar Found. Am., Am. Choral Music Educators Nat. Conf., Am. Choral Dirs. Assn. Office: Westlake Christian Academy 275 S Lake St Grayslake IL 60030 Home Phone: 847-543-4967; Office Phone: 847-548-6209. Personal E-mail: lfulord@yahoo.com. Business E-Mail: ccayari@westlakechristian.org.

CAYNE, BERNARD STANLEY, editor; b. NYC, Nov. 8, 1924; m. Helen M. Burgard, Apr. 11, 1953; children— Claudia Elizabeth, Douglas Andrew. Student, Cornell U., 1940-42; BS, Moravian Coll., 1945; postgrad., U. Pa., 1945-46; research fellow, Harvard U., 1953-55; MA, Columbia U., 1947. Head sci. dept. Adelphi Acad., 1946-47; instr. Bklyn. Coll., 1947-49; tchr. N.Y.C. Pub. Schs., 1948-49; head sci. sect., test devel. dept. Ednl. Testing Service, Princeton, NJ, 1949-53; dir. research Boston U. Coll. Basic Studies, 1953-54; sr. sci. editor Ginn & Co., Boston, 1955-61; v.p. Crowell-Collier Ednl. Corp., NYC, 1961-68; exec. editor Collier's Ency., 1963-68, Collier's Ency. Yearbook, 1963-68; editor-in-chief Merit Students Ency., 1961-69, asst. editorial dir. corp., 1963-68; mng. editor, sch. div. Macmillan Co., 1968-69; editor-in-chief Ency. Americana, Danbury, Conn., 1969-90; v.p., editorial dir. Grolier, Inc., Danbury, 1980-90; creative dir. Readfern Group, Durham, NC, 1990—. Chmn. bd. editors: Harvard Edn. Rev, 1954. Fellow AAAS, Am. Psychol. Soc.; mem. N.Y. Acad. Scis., Am. Ednl. Rsch. Assn., Phi Delta Kappa. Home and Office: 2701 Pickett Rd #2044 Durham NC 27705

CAYNE, JAMES E. (JIMMY), diversified financial services company executive; b. Evanston, Ill., Feb. 14, 1934; m. Patricia Cayne; 2 children. Student, Purdue U., West Lafayette, Ind. With Bonn Bush Mach, 1954-66, Lebenthal and Co., 1966-69; retail salesman Bear Stearns and Co. Inc., 1969, gen. ptnr. retail dept., 1973, mem. Office of the Pres., 1985—88, sr. mng. dir., 1985, pres., 1988—2001, CEO, 1993—, chmn., 2001—. Bd. dirs. Bear Stearns & Co. Inc., 1995—. Served in US Army, Japan. Named one of Forbes' Richest Ams., 2006. Achievements include being a world-ranked bridge player; represented the US in multiple internat. competitions, including the 1990 championship. Avocation: bridge. Office: Bear Stearns & Co Inc 383 Madison Ave New York NY 10179*

CAYTAS, IVO GEORGE, lawyer; b. Plovdiv, Bulgaria, Feb. 3, 1958; s. George I. and Hilda (Plankl) Kaitasow. MA in Diplomacy, U. St Gallen, Switzerland, 1982, PhD in Law, 1984, PhD in Fin., 1986; LLM, Yale U., 1986. Bar: D.C. 1997, U.S. Ct. Internat. Trade, U.S. Claims Ct., U.S. Tax Ct., U.S. Dist. Ct. (so. and ea. dists.) N.Y. 1992, (no. and ctrl. dists.) Calif. 1992, U.S. Ct. Appeals (1st-11th cirs., fed. and D.C. cir.), U.S. Supreme Ct. 1996. Asst. to chmn. IMAG Corp., Vienna, Austria, 1979-80; ptnr. Caytas & Cie, St. Gallen, 1984-89, CCCC, St. Gallen, 1989-91; mng. dir. Swissconsult Corp., NYC, 1990-91; pres., gen. counsel Swiss Am. Group Inc., NYC, 1991-95; ptnr. Caytas & Assocs., 1996—. Bd. dirs. The London Ct. of Internat. Abritration. Author: Investment Banking, 1988, Global Political Risk, Modern Financial Instruments, 1992, Transnational Legal Practice, 1992; contbr. articles to profl. publs. Fellow Swiss Nat. Sci. Found., 1985, 88, Max Planck Inst., 1987; recipient Walther-Hug Found. award, 1984. Mem. ABA (sect. of internat. law and practice, internat. investment com., internat. taxation com.), Assn. of Bar of City of N.Y. (com. on govt. ethics), Calif. Bar Assn. (internat. law com., task force on internat. legal svcs.), Yale Club. Roman Catholic. Office: 146 W 57th St New York NY 10019-3301 Business E-Mail: icaytas@caytas.com.

CAZALAS, MARY REBECCA WILLIAMS, lawyer, nurse; b. Atlanta, Nov. 11, 1927; d. George Edgar and Mary Annie (Slappey) Williams; m. Albert Joseph Cazalas (dec.). *Mary Cazalas' great-great-grandfather, General John Coffee, fought in the Battle of New Orleans. His son, Peter Coffee married Mary Donelson, who was niece of Mrs. Andrew Jackson. Their son, Major John A. Coffee, served in the Civil War. His daughter, Mary Stevens Coffee, married Dr. John George Slappey, a prominent physician at Jeffersonville, Georgia. His grandfather was Hans (John) George Slappey, who fought in the Revolution, and his father was Robert Rutherford Slappey. His daughter, Mary Annie Slappey, married George Edgar Wiliams. His mother was Sarah Cobb of Kosiesco, Mississippi. He graduated from Mercer University and was Chief Dispatcher of Central of Georgia Railroad.* BS in Pre-medicine, Oglethorpe U., Atlanta, 1954; MS in Anatomy, Emory U., 1960; JD, Loyola U., 1967, Loyola U., New Orleans, 1967. RN, Ga.; Bar: La. 1967, U.S. Dist. Ct. (ea. dist.) La. 1967, U.S. Ct. Appeals (5th cir.) 1972, U.S. Supreme Ct. 1975, U.S. Ct. Appeals (fed. cir.) 1999. Gen. duty nurse, 1948-68; instr. maternity nursing St. Josephs Infirmary Sch. Nursing, Atlanta, 1954-59; med. rschr. in urology Tulane U. Sch. Medicine, New Orleans, 1961-65; legal rschr. for presiding judge La. Ct. Appeals (4th cir.), New Orleans, 1965-71; pvt. practice New Orleans, 1967-71; asst. U.S. atty., 1971-79; sr. trial atty. Equal Employment Opportunity Commn., New Orleans, 1979-84; owner Cazalas Apts., New Orleans, 1962—. Lectr. in field. Contbr. articles to profl. jours. Bd. advisors Loyola U. Sch. Law, New Orleans, 1974, v.p. adv. bd., 1975; active New Orleans Drug Abuse Adv. Com., 1976-80; task force Area Agy. on Aging, 1976-80, pres. coun. Loyola U., 1978—; adv. bd. Odyssey House, Inc., New Orleans, 1973; chmn. womens com. Fed. Exec. Bd., 1974; bd. dirs. Bethlehem House of Bread, 1975-79. Named Hon. La. State Senator, 1974; recipient Superior Performance award U.S. Dept. Justice, 1974, Cert. Appreciation Fed. Exec. Bd., 1975-78, Rev. E.A. Doyle award, 1976, Commendation for tchg. Guam Legislature, 1977, Career Achievement award Mt. de Sales Acad., 1995. Mem. Am. Judicature Soc., La. Sate Bar Assn., Fed. Bus. Assn. (v.p. 1976—, pres. 1976-78, bd. dirs. 1972-75), Fed. Bar Assn. (1st v.p. 1973, pres. New Orleans chpt. 1974-75, nat. coun. 1974-79), Assn. Women Lawyers, Nat. Health Lawyers Assn., DAR, Bus. and Profl. Womens Club, Am. Heart Assn., Emory Alumni Assn., Oglethorpe U. Alumni Assn., Loyola U. Alumni Assn. (bd. dirs. 1974-75, 77, v.p. 1976), Jefferson Parish Hist. Soc., Sierra Club, Zonta, Leconte Hon. Sci. Soc., Phi Delta Delta (merged with Phi Alpha Delta pres. 1970-72, bd. dirs., vice justice 1974-75), Alpha Epsilon Delta, Phi Sigma. Democrat.

CAZALOT, CLARENCE P., JR., oil industry executive; BS in Geology, La. State. U. Various positions with Texaco, 1972—2000, v.p., 1999—2000; pres., CEO Marathon Oil, 2000—. Mem. bd. advisors Maguire Energy Inst.; bd. dirs. Baker Hughes, US-Saudi Arabian Bus. Coun.; mem bd. mgrs. Marathon Ashland Petroleum LLC. Trustee Spindletop Charities; bd. dirs. Sam Houston Area Coun. Boy Scouts Am. Mem.: NAM (bd. dirs.), Am. Petroleum Inst. (bd. dirs.), All-American Wildcatters, Nat. Petroleum Coun., Am. Assn. Petroleum Geologists. Achievements include Member 25 Yr. Club, Petroleum Industry. Office: Marathon Oil 5555 San Felipe Rd Houston TX 77056*

CAZAN, SYLVIA MARIE BUDAY (MRS. MATTHEW JOHN CAZAN), retired real estate company executive; b. Youngstown, Ohio, Nov. 17, 1915; d. John J. and Sylvia (Grama) Buday; m. Matthew John Cazan, July 14, 1935; 1 child, Matthew John G. Student, U. Bucharest, Romania, 1933—35, Youngstown Coll., 1936—38, Georgetown U. Inst. Langs. and Linguistics, 1950. Adminstrv. asst. statistics US Dept. Def., 1941—52; spl employee Dept. Justice, 1956—58; mgr. James L. Dixon & Co. Realtors, Falls Church, Va., 1959—70, Lewis & Silverman, Inc., Chevy Chase, Md., 1970—2006; ret., 2006. Mem. bd. examiners Georgetown U., 1950. Bd. dirs. Magnolia Internat. Debutante Ball; mem. Rumanian Orthodox Ch. Recipient Commendation and Meritorious award, Dept. Justice, 1958. Mem.: Washington No. Va. Real Estate Bds., Md. Bd. Realtors, Interscholastic Debating Soc., Gen. Fedn. Women's Clubs (pres. 1955—56). Home: 6369 Lakeview Dr Lake Barcroft Estates Falls Church VA 22041

CAZEAUX, ISABELLE ANNE MARIE, retired music educator; b. NYC, Feb. 24, 1926; d. François and Marie-Anne (Fort) C. BA magna cum laude, Hunter Coll., 1945; MA in Musicology, Smith Coll., 1946; MS in Libr. Sci., Columbia U., 1959, PhD in Musicology, 1961. Licence d'Enseignement, Ecole Normale de Musique, Paris, 1950; Première Médaille, Conservatoire Nat. de Musique, Paris, 1950. Sr. music cataloguer, head sect. music and phonorecords cataloguing N.Y. Pub. Libr., NYC, 1957-63; mem. faculty Manhattan Sch. Music, NYC, 1969-82, Bryn Mawr Coll., Pa., 1963-92, chmn. dept., 1978-92, prof., 1972-92, Alice Carter Dickerman prof. emeritus music, 1992—. Vis. prof. Douglass Coll. Rutgers U., New Brunswick, N.J., 1978. Author: French Music in the 15th and 16th Centuries, 1975; editor: The Chansons of Claudin de Sermisy, 1974; translator: The Memoirs of Philippe de Commynes, 1969, 2d vol., 1973; contbr. articles to profl. jours. Recipient Libby van Arsdale prize Hunter Coll., 1945; fellow Smith Coll., 1945-46, Inst. Internat. Edn., 1948-50; Martha Baird Rockefeller Fund grantee, 1971-72, Herman Goldman Found. grantee, 1980. Mem. Am. Musicol. Soc. (coun. 1968-70, com. on status of women 1974-76), Music Libr. Assn., Soc. Française de Musicologie, Internat. Musicol. Soc. Roman Catholic. Avocations: opera, concerts. Home: 415 E 72nd St Apt 5FE New York NY 10021-4412

CAZEL, FRED A., JR., history professor; b. Asheville, NC, Feb. 25, 1921; s. Fred Augustus Cazel and Agnes Miller Petrie; m. Annarie Jane Peters, 1946 (dec. 1983). AB, U. N.C., 1941; MA, Johns Hopkins U., 1943, PhD, 1948. Instr. Johns Hopkins U., Balt., 1947—48; asst. prof. U. Conn., Storrs, 1948—54, assoc. prof., 1954—62, prof., 1962—88, prof. emeritus, 1988—. Vis. asst. prof. U. Minn., Mpls., 1950; vis. prof. U. Calif., Berkeley, 1965—66; presenter in field. Editor: Feudalism and Liberty: Articles and Addresses of Sidney Painter, 1961, Foreign Accounts, 1982; co-editor (with Annarie P. Cazel): Early Subsidy Rolls, 1983; contbr. articles to profl. jours. Mayor Town of Mansfield, Conn., 1991—97, justice of peace, 1968—. John Martin Vincent fellow, Johns Hopkins U., 1941—43, 1946—47, Gustav Bissing fellow, 1951—52, Fulbright fellow, King's Coll., London, 1955—56. Fellow: Royal Hist. Soc.; mem.: AAUP, Conn. Acad. Arts and Scis., Conn. Hist. Soc., New Eng. History Tchrs. Assn., New England Medieval Conf. (past exec. sec.), New Eng. Hist. Assn. (past pres.), Ecclesiastical Hist. Soc., Pipe Roll Soc., Conf. Brit. Studies, Medieval Acad. Am., Am. Hist. Assn., Phi Beta Kappa. Democrat. Avocations: gardening, travel, reading, local history. Home: 309 Gurleyville Rd Storrs Mansfield CT 06268-1439

CAZENAVE, ANITA WASHINGTON, secondary school educator; b. Austin, Tex., Nov. 9, 1948; d. Willis Hunt and Henry Etta Washington Littleton; m. Noël Anthony Cazenave, July 20, 1971; 1 child, Anika Tené. BA in Early Childhood/Elem. Edn., Dillard U., New Orleans, 1971; MEd in Reading Edn., Loyola U. of New Orleans, 1976; PhD in Psychology of Reading Edn., Temple U., 1993. Cert. tchr., La., Pa.; cert. reading tchr., adminstr., Conn. Dir. Second Bapt. Day Nursery, Ann Arbor, Mich., 1971-72; reading cons. New Orleans Pub. Schs., 1972-78; reading instr. Temple U., Phila., 1979-80; reading specialist Operation Re-Entry Career Svcs., Inc., Phila., 1980-81; coord. ednl. svcs. Phila. O.I.C. Project new Pride, 1981; reading and math. tchr. Reading Edn. and Diagnostic Svcs. Inc., Phila., 1981-84; lang. arts/reading tchr. FitzSimons Middle Sch., Phila., 1985-91; reading tchr. Putnam Middle Sch., Conn., 1991-92; reading cons. Bloomfield HS, Conn., 1992-98, Carmen Arace Mid. Sch., Bloomfield, 1998—2002, Manchester HS, Conn., 2002—04, Carmen Arace Mid. Sch., Conn., 2004—. Presenter workshops Bloomfield Bd. Edn., 1993-94, others; reader SAT II writing tests Ednl. Testing Svcs.; adj. prof. English Manchester Cmty. Tech. Coll., 1997. Leader Girl Scouts US, New Orleans, 1977-78, Brownie troop leader, 1983-90; Sunday sch. supt. Mt. Airy United Meth. Ch., Phila., 1980-82; campaign worker Wilson Goode for Mayor, Phila., 1982; dir. ministry Acolyte Min. met. A.M.C. Zion Ch., Hartford, Conn.; asst. supt. of youth Met. A.M.E. Zion Ch., 2000. Named Outstanding Leader, Troop Parents Girl Scouts, Phila., 1985. Mem. ASCD, Internat. Reading Assn., Phila. Coun. of Internat. Reading Assn. (com. chair 1983-85), Greater Hartford Coun. Internat. Reading Assn. (recording sec. 1994—), Delta Sigma Theta (Hartford Alumnae chpt. chaplain and collegiate advisor 1994—, parliamentarian 1996—, chair state coun. chpts. heritage & archives 1994—, chair SAT tng. com. 1995—). Democrat. Avocations: reading, sewing, travel, camping, old movies. Home: 8526 Scenic Green Dr Houston TX 77088 Personal E-mail: anitacazenave@hotmail.com.

CEASOR, AUGUSTA CASEY, medical technician, microbiologist, clinical laboratory scientist; b. Birmingham, Ala., Feb. 22, 1943; d. Augustus and Willie Mae (Stubbs) C. AS, SUNY, 1981; BS, So. Ill. U., 1981. Cert. clin. lab. scientist Nat. Cert. Agy. Lab. asst. Mt. Sinai Hosp., Miami Beach, Fla., 1967—68; lab. technician Coordinated Lab. Svcs., Jamaica, NY, 1969—71; med. technician Andrew Radar U.S. Army Health Clinic, Ft. Myer, Va., 1972—76; med. technologist Armed Forces Inst. Pathology, Washington, 1976—91, Dept. Army, Mil. Dist. Wash., Ft. Myer, 1991—97; ret. Dept. of Army, 1997; cons. clin. lab. sci., 1997—. Dept. asst. Webster U., Ocala, Fla., 1999; sci. fair judge Am. Soc. Microbiology, Washington, 1988—97; high sch. sci. mentor Minority Women in Sci., 1989—; spkr. to profl. groups; records mgr. Marion County Govt., 2000—01. Mem. editl. bd. Metroscope Newsletter, 1985-98, editor, 1989-98; tech. asst. Mycobacteriology Rsch., 1985-90. Active minority alumni scholarship com. So. Ill. U., Carbondale, 1981—; mem. Montgomery Knolls Cmty. Assn., Silver Spring, Md., 1983-96, v.p., chmn. safety and environ. com., 1984-85. Recipient Cert. of Meritorious Svc., 1991, Performance award, 1987, 89, 93, 95-97. Fellow: Alpha Mu Tau (scholarship com. 1995—97, program/social chair 2001—02, newsletter editor 2003—05, program/social chair 2004—05); mem.: Fla. Soc. for Clin. Lab. Sci. (dir. Dist. II 2000—05, chair membership devel. com., bd. dirs. 2000—), Capital Area Soc. for Clin. Lab. Sci. (pres.-elect 1995—96, pres. 1996—97, past pres. 1997—98), D.C. Soc. Med. Tech. (chair profl. and pub. rels. 1985—86, chair program com. 1986—87, pres. 1987—88, chair microbiology 1988—89, chair awards 1988—98, chair profl. and pub. rels. 1992—93, Past Pres. award 1988, Svc. award 1989, Mem. of Yr. 1989—90, Disting. Svc. award 1991, Profl. Achievement award in Microbiology 1994), Am. Bd. Bioanalysis, Internat. Soc. Clin. Lab. Tech. (cert. gen. supr.), Am. Soc. Med. Tech. (Region II Coun. 1986—93, Region II microbiology chair 1988—89, chair Region II 1990—93, coun. Region II 1996—97, Cert. of Recognition 1990), Am. Soc. Clin. Lab. Sci. (minority forum sec. 1994—96, forum scholarship com. 1996—2005, chair forum scholarship com. 1997—2004, editor The Forum newsletter 2002—, forum for the concerns of minorities scholarship liaison 2004—, Omicron Sigma award 1987—97, 2001, 2002, 2003, 2004, 2005). Roman Catholic. Achievements include research in unique toxin of mycobacterium ulcerans.

CEBULA, RICHARD JOHN, economist, educator; b. Bklyn., Mar. 24, 1944; s. Jerome Matthew and Miriam (Lyons) C.; m. Louise E. Bedrossian, June 2, 1965 (div. Dec. 1981); children: David, Christina. BA, Fordham Coll., 1966; MA, U. Ga., 1968; PhD, Ga. State U., 1971. Asst. prof. Ohio U., Athens, 1971-73; from assoc. to full prof. Emory U., Atlanta, 1973-92; prof. econs. Ga. Inst. Tech., Atlanta, 1992-99; Shirley and Philip Solomons Eminent Scholar Chair in Econs. Armstrong Atlantic State U., 1999—. Author: Determinants of Human Migration, 1979, The Deficit Problem in Perspective, 1987, Crisis in Commercial Banking, 1993, Geographic Living Cost Differentials, 1983, Economics of the Sports Industry, 1995, Savings and Loan Crisis, 1992, Microeconomics Alive!, 1997, Macroeconomics Alive!, 1997, Financial Economics, 1999; editor Jour. Econs. and Fin., 1995-98; assoc. editor Annals of Regional Sci., 1998—; co-editor Jour. Econs. and Fin. Edn.; regional editor Internat. Advances in Econ. Rsch., 1996—; mem. editl. bd. Am. Jour. Econs.; mem. editl. bd., adv. editor Pub. Fin. Rev., East Econ. Jour., Rev. Fin. Econ., Rev. Reg. Stud., Global Bus. Econ. Rev., Internat. Migration Rev., others; contbr. more than 2050 articles to profl. jours. Econ. advisor U.S. Congressman Levitas, Washington, 1974-84, Fed. Res. Bank Atlanta, 1984, U.S. Senator Sam Nunn, Washington, 1995. Recipient citation of excellence Anbar Electronic Intelligence, U.K., 1996. Mem. Am. Econs. and Fin., Am. Econ. Assn., Acad. of Econs. and Fin. (v.p. 1999-2001, pres. 2001-03, rsch. fellow 2000, service fellow 2003). Achievements include research on effects of welfare on migration, determinants of geographic living-cost differentials, effects of budget deficits on interest rates, economic growth, causes of bank and thrift failures. Home: 11935 Abercorn St Savannah GA 31419 E-mail: cebulari@mail.armstrong.edu.

CECALA, TED THOMAS, JR., banker, accountant; b. Trenton, NJ, Jan. 26, 1949; s. Ted Thomas and Kathrine Rose (Danito) C.; m. Janice Redfield, Sept. 13, 1980. AA, Miami-Dade Jr. Coll., 1969; BS, Fla. State U., 1971. CPA, Fla., Del. Asst. treas. S.E. Banking Corp., Miami, Fla., 1972-77; treas. Am. Bankshares, Miami, 1977-79; controller Wilmington Trust Co., Del., 1979-84, sr. v.p. corp. devel. Del., 1985-88, exec. v.p., CFO Del., 1988—96, vice chmn., COO Del., 1996, chmn., CEO Del., 1996—. Mem. Fed. Advisory Coun., 2006—. Mem. AICPA, Fin. Execs. Inst., Del. Inst. CPAs, Fla. Inst. CPAs, Wilmington Country Club, Pike Creek Country Club (Newark, Del.). Republican. Presbyterian. Office: Wilmington Trust Co Rodney Sq N 1100 N Market St Wilmington DE 19890-0001

CECCHINI, LEO, entrepreneur; b. Washington, June 13, 1940; s. Leo Francis and Ruth Elizabeth Cecchini; m. Sandra Jean Cecchini, Feb. 4, 1978; children: Chiara, Sabrina. BS in Econs., U. Md., 1962; MA in Bus., Schiller Internat., 1985. Vol. Peace Corps, Asmara, Eritrea, 1962-64; diplomat U.S. Dept. State, Washington, 1965-90; mng. dir. Hill & Knowlton, Ankara, Turkey, 1990-91; owner NK Internat., Windhoek, Namibia, 1991-94; gen. mgr. South African Trade Ctr., Orlando, Fla., 1994-95; dir. Gemmex Intertrade Am., McLean, Va., 1996—. Assoc. Global Bus. Access, Washington, 1995—; bd. dirs. N'FETN Co., Asmara. Bd. dirs. E&E Returned Peace Corps Vols., Pittsford, N.Y., 1994—, Balkan Forum, Washington, 1999—, Nat. Peace Corps Assn., Washington, 1999—. Recipient Outstanding Svc. award City of Saigon, Vietnam, 1969, Spl. Achievement award Union C. of C., Ankara, 1980, Outstanding Am. award Am. Club, Madrid, 1984. Mem. Mensa Internat., Order of St. George. Republican. Roman Catholic. Avocations: travel, writing, motorcycles. Home: PM1-D4 Paseo Arta E07579 Betlem Mallorea Spain E-mail: leo@cecchini.org.

CECERE, ANDREW, bank executive; b. 1960; m. Kathy M. Cecere; 1 child. B, U. St. Thomas, 1982; MBA, U. Minn., 1991. Sr. v.p. fin. U.S. Bancorp, Mpls., 1992—96, sr. v.p. acquisition integration and process mgmt., 1996-99, sr. v.p. ops. and adminstrn. wholesale banking, 1999, vice chmn. comml. svcs., 1999—2001, CFO, 2000—01, vice-chmn. wealth mgmt., 2001—07, vice-chmn., CFO, 2007—. Bd. dir. Fair Isaac Corp., DeCare Internat. Bd. dir. Greater Twin Cities United Way, Capital City Partnership; mem. bd. overseers Carlson Sch. Mgmt., U. Minn. Office: US Bancorp US Bancorp Ctr 800 Nicollet Mall Minneapolis MN 55402*

CECERE, DOMENICO, homebuilding company executive; b. June 10, 1949; BA in Fin. and Acctg., U. Okla. V.p. fin. indsl. controls Honeywell, Inc., v.p. fin. home and bldg. controlling bus., v.p. fin. European bus. Brussels; v.p., contr. Owens Corning, Toledo, 1993-95, pres. roofing sys. bus., 1995-98, sr. v.p., CFO, 1998-2000, exec. v.p., COO, 2000-01; cons. Gryphon Investors; sr. v.p., CFO KB Home, LA, 2002—. Office: 7th Fl 10990 Wilshire Blvd Los Angeles CA 90024*

CECH, THOMAS ROBERT, medical association administrator, chemistry professor; b. Chgo., Dec. 8, 1947; m. Carol Lynn Martinson; children: Allison E., Jennifer N. BA in Chemistry, Grinnell Coll., 1970; PhD in Chem., U. Calif., Berkeley, 1975; DSc (hon.), Grinnell Coll., 1987, U. Chgo., 1991, Drury Coll., 1994, Colo. Coll., 1999, U. Md., Baltimore County, 2000, Williams Coll., 2000, Charles U., Prague, 2002, Ohio State U., 2003, Moscow State U., 2004, U. Vt., 2005. Postdoctoral fellow dept. biology MIT, Cambridge, Mass., 1975—77; from asst. prof. to assoc. prof. chemistry U. Colo., Boulder, 1978—83, prof. chemistry and biochemistry also molecular cellular and devel. biology, 1983—, disting. prof., 1990—; rsch. prof. Am. Cancer Soc., 1987—; investigator Howard Hughes Med. Inst., 1988—99, pres., 2000—. Co-chmn. Nucleic Acids Gordon Conf., 1984; Phillips disting. visitor Haverford Coll., 1984; Vivian Ernst meml. lectr. Brandeis U., 1984; Cynthia Chan meml. lectr. U. Calif., Berkeley; mem. Welch Found. Symposium, 1985; Danforth lectr. Grinnell Coll., 1986; Pfizer lectr. Harvard U., 1986; Hastings lectr., 92; Verna and Marrs McLean lectr. Baylor Coll. Medicine, 1987; Harvey lectr., 87; Mayer lectr. MIT, 1987; HHMI lectr., 89; T.Y. Shen lectr., 94; Martin D. Kamen disting. lectureship U. Calif., San Diego, 1988; Alfred Burger lectr. U. Va., 1988; Berzelius lectr. Karolinska Inst., 1988; Osamu Hayaishi lectr. Internat. Union Biochemistry, Prague, 1988; Beckman lectr. U. Utah, 1989; Max Tishler lectr. Merck, 1989; Abbott vis. scholar U. Chgo., 1989; Herriott lectr. Johns Hopkins U., 1990; J.T. Baker lectr., 90; G.N. Lewis lectr. U. Calif. , Berkeley, 1990; Sonneborn lectr. Ind. U., 1991; Sternbach lectr. Yale U., 1991; W. Pauli lectr., Zurich, 92; Carter-Wallace lectr. Princeton U., 1992; Stetten lectr. NIH, 1992; Dauben lectr. U. Wash., 1992; Marker lectr. U. Md., 1993; Hirschmann lectr. Oberlin Coll., 1993; Beach lectr. Purdue U., 1993; Abe White lectr. Syntex, 1993; Robbins lectr. Pomona Coll., 1994; Bren lectr. U. Calif., Irvine, 1994; Wawzonek lectr. U. Iowa, 1994; Sumner lectr. Cornell U., 1994; Steenbock lectr. U. Wis., 1995; Murachi lectr. FAOB Congress, Sydney, 1995; Streck award lectr. U. Nebr., 1996; Gardner-Davern lectr. U. Utah, 1996; Priestley lectr. Pa. State U., 1996; Beckman lectr. Calif. Inst. Tech., 1996; Lemieux lectr. U. Alta., Canada, 1997; Hogg Award lectr. M.D. Anderson Cancer Ctr., 1997; DeCoursey Nobel lectr. Trinity U., 1998; Tschirgi lectr. U. Calif., San Diego, 1998; Boxer Meml. lectr. Robert Wood Johnson Med. Sch., 1998; Thomas lectr. U. Mo., 1999; Bachmann Meml. lectr. U. Mich., 1999; DuPont-Marshall lectr. U. Pa., 1999; Feodor Lynen lectr. Mosbach Germany, 2001; The Morgenthaler lectureship Case Wetern Res. U., 2001; Tercentenary Silliman lectr. Yale U., 2001; Nathans lectr. Johns Hopkins U., 2002; Tishler Prize lectr. Harvard U., 2002; Furlaud Disting. lectr. The Rockefeller U., 2002; non-resident fellow Salk Inst., 1999. Assoc. editor Cell, 1986—87, RNA Jour., mem. editl. bd. Genes and Devel.; contbg. editor: Sci. mag., 1999. Trustee Grinnell Coll. Named Westerner of Yr., Denver Post, 1986; named to Esquire Mag. Register, 1985; recipient medal, Am. Inst. Chemists, 1970, Rsch. Career Devel. award, Nat. Cancer Inst., 1980—85, Young Sci. award, Passano Found., 1984, Harrison Howe award, 1984, Pfizer award, 1985, U.S. Steel award, NAS, 1987, V.D. Mattia award, 1987, Louisa Gross Horowitz prize, Columbia U., 1988, Newcombe-Cleveland award, AAAS, 1988, Heineken prize, Royal Netherlands Acad. Arts and Scis., 1988, Gairdner Found. Internat. award, 1988, Lasker Basic Med. Rsch. award, 1988, Rosenstiel award, Brandeis U., 1989, Warren Triennial prize, 1989, Nobel Prize in Chemistry, 1989, Hopkins medal, Brit. Biochem. Soc., 1992, Feodor Lynen medal, 1995, Nat. Sci. medal, 1995, Mike Hogg award, M.D. Anderson, 1997, Wright prize, Harvey Mudd Coll., 1998, Gregor Mendel medal, Acad. Sci. Czech Republic, 2002; fellow, NSF, 1970—75, Pub. Health Svc.; rsch. fellow, Nat. Cancer Inst., 1975—77, Guggenheim fellow, 1985—86. Mem.: NAS, AAAS, RNA Soc. (v.p. 1993—96), European Molecular Biology Orgn., Am. Philos. Soc., Am. Acad. Arts and Scis., Am. Soc. Biochem. Molecular Biology, Inst. Medicine. Office: Howard Hughes Med Inst 4000 Jones Bridge Rd Chevy Chase MD 20815-6789 Office Phone: 301-215-8550. Office Fax: 301-215-8558. Business E-Mail: president@hhmi.org.*

CECIL, ALEX THOMSON, travel executive; b. Birmingham, Ala., May 5, 1930; s. Alex Thomson and Martha (Lamar) C.; m. Jennifer Brown, Dec. 2, 1962 (div. 1976); children: Thurston, Lila; m. Jacqueline Bottger, May 10, 1980 (div. 1997); children: Julia, Caroline; m. E. Ritter, May 5, 1997; 1 child, Henry. Student, Ohio State U., 1950-52. Chmn., CEO, owner Auto-Europe, Inc., NYC, 1953—97; chmn. Cognoscenti Health Inst., Orlando, Fla., 1999—2006. Home Phone: 617-492-4710; Office Phone: 617-492-4710. E-mail: acecil@europe.com.

CECIL, ALLAN, corporate communications executive; s. Laymond Bud and Mary Eleanor (Vaughn) C.; m. Ellen Kay Jones, Feb. 1, 1964 (dec. 1969); m. Patricia B. Wilcox, Oct. 22, 2000; children: Jill Maureen, Sarah Ellen, Molly Kate. BA in Journalism, U. Okla., 1963, postgrad., 1963-64, West Tex. State U., 1979. Dir. corp. comm. Mesa Petroleum Co., 1976—85; v.p. corp. comm., investor rels. National Gypsum, 1985—96; v.p. investor rels. and corp. affairs Sonoco Products, Hartsville, SC, 1996—2006, mem. exec. com. Capt. USAF, 1964-69. Mem. Nat. Investor Rels. Inst. Republican. Presbyterian. Office: Sonoco Products One N 2d St Hartsville SC 29550

CECIL, BONNIE SUSAN, elementary school educator; b. Louisville, Sept. 29, 1951; d. Robert Lawrence and Mary Hedwig (Kluesner) C. BA in Edn., U. Ky., 1973; MS in Edn., Ind. U., 1978; postgrad., U. Louisville, 1988—. Tchr. grades 1-4 Roosevelt Cmty. Sch., Jefferson County, Ky., 1972-80; tchr. ages 6 and 7 Wandle Primary Sch., London, 1980-81; tchr. 1st grade Foster Elem. Sch., Jefferson County, 1981-82; tchr. ages 5-8 Brown Sch. Primary, Jefferson County, 1982—. Co-dir., instr. writing process for tchrs. Ky. Writing Insts. I and II, Boone County, 1986-88; instr. writing process insvc. Jefferson County Pub. Schs., 1988-89, workshop presenter on environ. edn., 1990, 92, supr. student tchrs., 1989-90, 92, 94, 95, 97; instr. lang. arts U. Louisville, 1990-91; participant Fulbright Tchr. Exch. Program, London, 1980-81, Brown Sch. Dream Team, 1992; presenter ann. conf. Ky. Assn. Edn. Young Children-Louisville Assn. for Children Under Seven, 1990; presenter Cmty. Learning Resource Conf., 1992; participant Louisville Writing Project, 1984-85, premier class Leadership Edn., 1986-87. Tchr. rep. J. Graham Brown Sch. PTSA, 1983-90, 92-97; tchr. rep. site-based decision making coun., 1996—; bd. dirs. Roosevelt Cmty. Sch., Inc., 1973-76; creator, dir. summer reading and writing program Portland Mus., Louisville, 1985; treas. Louisville Homefront Performances, Inc., 1986-87, sec., 1988-90, bd. dirs. 1984-96; state bd. dirs. Cmty. Farm Alliance, 2001-2002, v.p. Henry County chpt., 2001-. Recipient Golden Apple Achievement award Ashland Oil Co., 1989, Individual Tchr. Achievement award, 1992, Nat. Educator award Milken Family Found., 1994, ExCel award WHAS-TV and PNC Bank, 1995; named Jefferson County Elem. Tchr. of Yr., 1992, Ky. Elem. Tchr. of Yr., 1993, Ky. Tchr. of Yr., 1993, Milken Family Nat. Educator Project Mentor, 1998; grantee Ky. Arts Coun., 1986-87, Jefferson County Pub. Schs.-U. Louisville, 1989-91, U. Louisville, 1991, Rosenbaum Found., 1998; named Milken Virtual Workspace Mentor, 1998; inducted into The Commonwealth Inst. for Tchrs., 1998. Mem. ASCD, NEA, Assn. Childhood Edn. Internat., Nat. Coun. Tchrs. English (conf. presenter 1988, chmn., presenter nat. conf. 1992), Ky. Edn. Assn., Jefferson County Tchrs. Assn., Leadership Edn. Alumni Assn. Avocations: music, gardening, pets. Office: J Graham Brown Sch 546 S 1st St Louisville KY 40202-1816 E-mail: bcecil2@jefferson.K12.ky.us.

CECIL, CHARLES HARKLESS, artist, educator; b. Kansas City, Mo., May 12, 1945; s. Charles F. and Alice (Harkless) C.; m. Isabelle Claude Jeanne Touren, Dec. 30, 1982; 1 dau., Charlotte Alice Marcelle. BA, Haverford Coll., 1967; postgrad., Yale U., 1967-69. Co-dir. Studio Cecil-Graves, Florence, Italy, 1983-91; dir. Charles H. Cecil Studios, Florence, 1991—; instr. Villa Schifanoia, Grad. Studio Fine Arts, Florence, 1983-87. Exhibited in group shows at N.A.D., N.Y.C., 1979, 80, Dallas, 1983; represented in permanent collections at: Portrait Gallery, Haverford Coll., Pa., West Bend Gallery Fine Arts, Wis; executed: portrait Dr. Jonathon Rhodes for Am. Philos. Soc.; 10th Anniversary Exhibit of Charles H. Cecil Studios, London, 2001. NDEA grantee, 1967-69; Elizabeth Greenshields Found. grantee, 1970-73; John F. Stacey Found. grantee, 1980; R.H. Ives Gammell Studios Trust grantee, 1986-2001; recipient Julius T. Hallgarten First prize for oil painting, 1979, Benjamin Altman Second prize for landscape 155 Ann. Exhbn. Nat. Acad. Design, 1980 Home: Via Pandolfini 21 50122 Florence Italy Office: Charles H Cecil Studios Borgo San Frediano 68 50124 Florence Italy Home Phone: 0039-055290907; Office Phone: 0039-055285102. E-mail: cecilstudios@dada.it.

CECIL, DAVID ROLF, mathematician, educator; b. Tulsa, July 12, 1935; s. Neil McKinley and Ola Ethel (Turner) C.; m. Betty Lou Poe, June 14, 1958; 1 child, Eric Alan. Student (Pitts. Plate Glass Co. scholar), Carnegie Inst. Tech., 1954-55; BA, U. Tulsa, 1958; postgrad (fellow), Tulane U., 1958-59; MS, Okla. State U., 1960, PhD, 1962. Grad. teaching asst. Okla. State U., 1959-62; sr. research mathematician Atlantic Refining Co., 1962; asst. prof., then assoc. prof. math. North Tex. State U., Denton, 1962-69; prof. math. Butler U., Indpls., 1969-70, Tex. A&M U., Kingsville, 1970—2006, chmn. dept., 1980-85, asst. dean coll. arts and scis., 2000—04; pres. Tex. Acad. Sci., 2001—02. Cons. Edn. Service Ctr. Region II, 1979-80, Air Force Office Sci. Rsch., Wilford Hall Med. Ctr., Tex., 1988-90; organizer Kingsville Computer Club, 1980; mem. credit com. Kingsville Area Educators Fed. Credit Union, 1979—. Author Debugging BASIC Programs, 1984, (in Spanish) Depuracion de Programas en BASIC, 1989, (with Stan Albert) Probability, 1993; contbr. articles to math. jours. Founder Kingsville Computer Club, 1980; mem. credit com. Kingsville Area Educators Fed. Credit Union, 1979-2006, bd. dirs., 2006-. Faculty fellow North Tex. State U., 1968-69; Faculty fellow Tex. A&I U., 1971-73; presidential grant, Tex. A&M U., 2005. Fellow Tex. Acad. Scis. (v.p. 1999, pres. 2001-2002); Sigma Xi. Methodist. Avocation: woodworking. Office Phone: 361-592-1839. Business E-Mail: d-cecil@tamuk.edu.

CECIL, DONALD, retired investment company executive; b. NYC, Jan. 3, 1927; s. Leopold and Viola C.; m. Jane Grossman, Mar. 5, 1953; children: Alec, Leslie (twins). BS in Applied Econ., Yale U., 1947. V.p. Cecil Mfg. Co., 1947—58; securities analyst Ira Haupt & Co., 1958—61; sr. instl. rsch. analyst Eastman Dillon Union Securities, NYC, 1961—63; from dir. instl. rsch. to sr. v.p. Shearson Hamill, Inc., NYC, 1963—70; pres. Shearson Hamill Mgmt. Co., 1966—70; founding ptnr. Cumberland Assocs., NYC, 1970—82; ret., 1982. Trustee 45 Merrill Lynch domestic, global and offshore mutual funds and trusts, 1977-99; bd. dirs. Rycote Adv. Panel, Geneva, Switzerland; chmn. valuation bd. Biotech. Investments, Ltd., London, 1986-99; dep. chmn. Internat. Biotech. Trust Ltd., London, 1994-2001; chmn. dirs. svc. com., Investment Com. Inst., Washington, 1996-2000. Chmn. Bd. Transp., Westchester County, White Plains, N.Y., 1978—; vice-chmn. bd. trustees SUNY Purchase Coll. Found., 1987—; sponsor I Have a Dream Found., Mt. Vernon, N.Y., 1987—; chmn. bd. Friends of Neuberger Mus., Purchase, 1989-91; sponsor, writing thru The Arts Program, Neuberger Mus., 1993—, sponsor Jandon Scholars Program Westchester County, 1999—; dir., treas. Ctr. for Ednl. Innovation/Pub. Edn. Assn.; apptd. bd. dirs. Met. Transp. Authority N.Y.C., 2005—. Mem. Chartered Fin. Analysts (cert.), N.Y. Econ. Club, N.Y. Soc. Security Analysts. Avocations: theater, travel, tennis. Office: Cumberland Assocs Rm 3803 1114 Avenue Of The Americas New York NY 10036-7703 Office Phone: 212-536-9727.

CECIL, ELIZABETH JEAN, writer; b. Biloxi, Miss., Apr. 13, 1938; d. Dudley Charles and Margaret Jean (Gilchrist) Andrews; m. Anthony Francis Cieslewicz (Cecil), Nov. 22, 1962; children: Stephen Charles, Sarah Jean. BA, Colo. State Coll., 1959; MA, Stanford U., 1963. Cert. speech and lang. pathologist, Wis. Speech-lang. pathologist Racine Unified Sch. Dist., Wis., 1985—95, ret., 1995. Author: (essays) Jean's Stuff, 1993. Office Vocat. Rehab. fellow Stanford U. Mem.: ASCD. Presbyterian. Personal E-mail: writeshop@wi-net.com.

CECIL, J. ROBB, lawyer; b. 1960; BS, Mt. St. Mary's Coll., Emmitsburg, Md.; JD, U. Balt. Asst. state atty. Anne Arundel County, Md.; ptnr. McGowan, Cecil & Smathers, Laurel, Md. Named one of The Top Lawyers: The Next Generation, Balt. Mag., 2003. Mem.: Assn. Trial Lawyers Am., Md. Trial Lawyers Assn. Office: McGowan Cecil & Smathers 317 Main St Laurel MD 20707-4129 Office Phone: 301-483-9960. Office Fax: 301-483-9970.*

CEDARBAUM, MIRIAM GOLDMAN, federal judge; b. NYC, 1929; d. Louis Albert and Sarah (Shapiro) Goldman; married; 2 children. BA, Barnard Coll., 1950; LLB, Columbia U., 1953. Bar: N.Y. 1954, U.S. Dist. Ct. (so. dist.) N.Y. 1956, U.S. Ct. Appeals (2d cir.) 1956, U.S. Ct. Claims 1958, U.S. Supreme Ct. 1958, U.S. Dist. Ct. (ea. dist.) N.Y. 1980, U.S. Ct. Appeals (5th and 11th cirs.) 1981. Law clk. to judge Edward Jordan Dimock U.S. Dist. Ct. (so. dist.) N.Y., 1953-54, asst. U.S. atty., 1954-57; atty. Dept. Justice, Washington, 1958-59; part-time cons. to law firms in litig. matters, 1959-62; 1st asst. counsel N.Y. State Moreland Act Commn., 1963-64; assoc. counsel Mus. Modern Art, NYC, 1965-79; assoc. litig. dept. Davis Polk & Wardwell, NYC, 1979-83, sr. atty., 1983-86; acting village justice Village of Scarsdale, NY, 1978—82, village justice, 1982-86; judge U.S. Dist. Ct. (so. dist.) N.Y., 1986-98, sr. judge, 1998—. Trustee emerita Barnard Coll.; com. defender svcs. Jud. Conf. U.S., 1993—99; mem. emerita bd. visitors Columbia Law Sch., chmn. NY state selection com. for Rhodes scholar, 2003, 04. Mem. bd. revising editors Columbia Law Rev.; contbr. articles to profl. jours. James Kent scholar; recipient Medal of Distinction Barnard Coll., 1991, Jane Marx Murphy prize Columbia Law Sch. Mem. ABA (chmn. com. on pictorial graphic sculptural and choreographic works 1979-81, copyright com. fed. practice and procedure 1983-84), Am. Law Inst., Fed. Bar Coun., Copyright Soc. U.S.A. (trustee, exec. com. 1979-82), Supreme Ct. Hist. Soc., Am. Judicature Soc. Jewish. Office: US Dist Ct US Courthouse 500 Pearl St Rm 1330 New York NY 10007-1312

CEDDIA, ANTHONY FRANCIS, university administrator; b. Boston, Mar. 4, 1944; s. Antonio John and Marie (Loungo) C.; m. Valerie Ann Mulkern, Apr. 15, 1966; children: Ann-Marie, Michael. BS in Edn., Northeastern U., 1965, MEd, 1968; EdD, U. Mass., 1980; postgrad. John F. Kennedy Sch. Govt., Harvard U., 1990; LLD (hon.), North Adams State Coll., 1990; cert. sr. exec. program in local govt., Harvard U., 1990; LLD (hon.), North Adams State Coll., 1990. Cert. counselor, secondary sch. tchr., Mass. Tchr. social studies, counselor Melrose High Sch., Mass., 1965-70; fin. aid and admissions ofcl. North Adams State Coll., Mass., 1970-73, dean of adminstrn Mass., 1973-78, exec. v.p. Mass., 1978-81; acting pres. North Adams State Coll., Mass., 1979; pres. Shippensburg U., Pa., 1981—. Chmn. bd. Univ. Ctr., State System Higher Edn., Harrisburg, 1987-90; chmn. Commn. Univs. of Pa., 1986-88; mem. Sico Found., Sico Oil Corp., 1983—; mem. adv. bd. Orrstown Bank, Shippenburg, 1984-87. Mem. Cumberland County Transp. Bd., 1990; trustee Chambersburg Hosp. Bd., 1989—; mem. exec. com. South Ctrl. Pa. coun. Boy Scouts Am., 1982—, adv. panel Nat. Army ROTC, 1984—, chair, 1990-92; bd. dirs. Ams. for the Competitive System, 1981-87; chair divsn. II steering com. NCAA, 1990-92. Recipient Disting. Alumni Northeastern U., 1979 Mem. Am. Assn. State Colls. and Univs. (editor 1982-86, chmn. com. rsch. and liaison, com. on policy and purpose 1987-90), Am. Assn. Higher Edn., Mid. States Assn. Colls. and Schs. (commn. on higher edn. 1986-92), Nat. Intercollegiate Athletic Assn. (coun.). Home: PO Box 606 Shippensburg PA 17257-0606 Office: Shippensburg U Office of Pres 1871 Old Main Dr Shippensburg PA 17257-2299

CEDERBERG, JAMES, retired physics professor; b. Oberlin, Kans., Mar. 16, 1939; s. J. Walter and Edith E. (Glad) C.; m. Judith Ness, June 10, 1967; children: Anna Sook, Rachel Eun. BA, U. Kans., 1959; MA, Harvard U., 1960, PhD, 1963. Lectr., rsch. assoc. Harvard U., Cambridge, Mass., 1963-64; from asst. prof. to prof. St. Olaf Coll., Northfield, Minn., 1964—80, prof., 1980—92, Grace A. Whittier prof. sci., 1992—2005; prof. emeritus, 2006—. Councilor Coun. on Undergrad. Rsch., 1985-91, 92-95, pres. physics coun., 1985-88; summer rsch. assoc. U. Mich., 1967, Harvard U., 1980; fellow Duke U., 1969-70, Harvard U., 1976-77; vis. prof. U. Washington, 1991-92, U. Canterbury, Christchurch, New Zealand, 1998-99. Recipient Distinguished Svc. Citation awd., Am. Assn. Physics Tchrs., 1993; fellow NSF, Woodrow Wilson; grantee NSF, RUI Fellow: Am. Phys. Soc. (Undergraduate Rsch. prize 2002); mem.: Am. Assn. Physics Tchrs., Sigma Xi, Pi Mu Epsilon, Sigma Pi Sigma, Phi Beta Kappa. Lutheran. Office: St Olaf Coll 1520 Saint Olaf Ave Northfield MN 55057-1098 Office Fax: 507-646-3968. Business E-Mail: ceder@stolaf.edu.

CEDERING, SIV, poet, writer; b. Overkalix, Sweden, Feb. 5, 1939; came to U.S., 1953, naturalized, 1958; d. Hilding and Elvy (Wikstrom) C.; children: Lisa, Lora, Kelly. Artist Elaine Benson Gallery, Bridgehampton, NY, 1991—98, Loveland Mus., Loveland, Colo., 1992, East End Arts Coun. Gallery, Riverhead, NY, 1992, Clayton-Liberatori Gallery, Bridgehampton, NY, 1991, Guild Hall Mus., East Hampton, NY, 2001, Hutchin Gallery, Green Vale, NY, 1993, Peconic Gallery, Riverhead, NY, 1993, East. New Mex. Univ., Portales, N.Mex., 1992, Nordic History Mus., 1998. Lectr. U. Mass., Amherst, 1973; cons. Coordinating Council Lit. Mags., 1972-75 Author: (poems and photographs) Cup of Cold Water, 1973, Letters from the Island, 1973; (poems) Letters from Helge, 1974, Two Swedish Poets, Gost Friberg and Goran Palm (transl. from Swedish), 1974, Mother Is, 1975, The Juggler, 1977, How to Eat a Fortune Cookie, 1977, Color Poems, 1978, Letters From the Floating World: New and Selected Poems, 1984, The Blue Horse, 1979; (children's poems) Leken i Grishuset, 1980 (books transl. into Japanese, Swedish); Oxen, 1981, Letters From an Observatory, 1998, Poetry Paintings, 2003, Adirondack Notebook, 2004; editor, translator: Det Blommande Trädet (The Flowering Tree, collection Am. Indian and Eskimo lyrics), 1973, You and I and the World, Poems by Werner Aspenström, 1980, Letters From The Observatory New and Selected Poem 1973-1998, 1998, Painting Poems, 2003, Adirondack Notebook, 2004; poems and prose published in several periodicals, including, Harper's, New Republic, Partisan Rev., Paris Rev., Quar. Rev. Lit., others, exhibited photography, Modernage Galleries, NYC, 1973. Recipient William Marion Reedy award Poetry Soc. Am., 1970, John Masefield Narrative Poetry award, 1969; Annapolis Fine Arts Festival poetry prize Md. Fine Arts Council, 1968; Photography prize Sat. Rev., 1970; Borestone Mountain Poetry award, 1974; Pushcart prize, 1977; Emily Dickinson award, 1978; NY State Council on Arts fellow, 1974; Swedish Writers Union stipend, 1979; grantee Swedish Writers Found., 1995-2000. Mem. Poetry Soc. Am. Home: 93 Merchants Path PO Box 1300 Sagaponack NY 11962-1300 Office Phone: 631-537-7525. Personal E-mail: siv@hamptons.com.

CEDOLINI, ANTHONY JOHN, psychologist; b. Rochester, NY, Sept. 19, 1942; s. Peter Ross and Mary J. (Anthony) C.; m. Clare Marie De Rose, Aug. 16, 1964; children: Maria A., Antonia C., Peter E. Student, U. San Francisco, 1960-62; BA, San Jose State U., 1965, MS, 1968; PhD in Ednl. Pscyhology, Columbia Pacific U., 1983. Lic. ednl. psychologist, sch. adminstr., marriage, family child counselor, sch psychologist, sch. counselor, social worker, real estate broker, Calif. Ptnr., founder Cienega Valley Vineyards and DeRose Winery (formerly Almaden Vineyards) and Comml. Shopping Ctrs., 1968—; coord. psychol. svcs. Oak Grove Sch. Dist., San Jose, Calif., 1968-81, asst. dir. pupil svcs., 1977-81, dir. pupil svcs., 1981-83; pvt. practice, ednl. psychologist Ednl. Assocs., San Jose, 1983—. Co-dir. Biofeedback Inst. of Santa Clara County, San Jose, 1976-83; ptnr. in Cypress Ctr.-Ednl. Psychologists and Consultancy, 1978-84; cons., program auditor for Calif. State Dept. Edn.; instr. U. Calif., Santa Cruz and LaVerne Coll. Ext. courses; guest spkr. San Jose State U.; lectr., workshop presenter in field. Author: Occupational Stress and Job Burnout, 1982, A Parents Guide to School Readiness, 1971, The Effect of Affect, 1975; contbr. articles to profl. jours. and newspapers. Co-founder, bd. dirs. Lyceum of Santa Clara County, 1971—, Graham Owners Club of Calif. Avocations: coin collecting/numismatics, antiques, winemaking, classic cars, woodcarving. Home and Office: 1183 Nikulina Ct San Jose CA 95120-5441 Office Phone: 408-997-2700. Personal E-mail: tonyced@pacbell.net.

CEDRASCHI, TULLIO, investment company executive; b. Zurich, Switzerland, Oct. 4, 1938; s. Guido and Ida (Colombara) C. Degree in Civil Engring., Coll. Tech., Zurich, 1960; MBA, McGill U., 1968. Civil engr., project mgr. Conrad Zschokke, Zurich, 1960-61, Bur. D'Etudes Quoniam, Paris, 1961-63, BBR Switzerland and Can., 1963-65, R. R. Nicolet and Assocs., Montreal, 1968—, gen. mgr. CN investment divsn., 1973-77, pres., CEO, 1977—. Bd. dirs. Toronto Stock Exch., Freehold Resources Ltd., Helix Investments. Bd. govs. emeritus McGill U.; bd. govs. Nat. Theatre Sch. Mem. Montreal Soc. Fin. Analysts, Hillside Tennis Club. Avocations: tennis, skiing. Home: # 605 2600 ave Pierre-Dupuy Habitat 67 Cite du Havre Montreal PQ Canada H3C 3R6 Office: CN Investment Divsn Fl 11 PO Box 11002 5 Pl Ville Marie Montreal PQ Canada H3C 4T2 also: CN 935 de la Gauchetiere St W Montreal PQ Canada H3C 3N4

CEDRONE, LOUIS ROBERT, JR., retired critic; b. Balt., Md., June 25, 1923; s. Louis and Lucia (Mazzola) C.; m. Nancy Nelson, Sept. 11, 1954; children— Linda, David. BS, U. Md., 1951. With Balt. Evening Sun, 1951-92, drama-film critic, 1963-92, ret., 1992; corr. Variety, 1957-77, 82-85; TV show cablevision Critics Corner, 1982-85. Swimming instr. ARC, 1961-68. Served with inf. AUS, 1943-45. Decorated Purple Heart with oak leaf cluster, Bronze Star. Mem. Sigma Nu, Omicron Delta Kappa, Pi Delta Epsilon. Home: 9 Muirfield Ct Lutherville Timonium MD 21093-3905

CEE-LO, (THOMAS DECARLO CALLAWAY), singer; b. Atlanta, May 30, 1974; m. Christina Johnson, 2000 (div. 2005); 1 child, Kingston. Mem. Goodie Mob, 1995—, Gnarls Barkley, 2004—. Singer: (albums) Cee-Lo Green & His Perfect Imperfections, 2002, Cee-Lo Green.Is the Soul Machine, 2004, Art of Noise: The Best of Cee-Lo, 2006, Closet Freak: The Best of Cee-Lo Green the Soul Machine, 2006, (with Goodie Mob) Soul Food, 1995, Still Standing, 1998, World Party, 1999, (with Gnarls Barkley) St. Elsewhere, 2006 (Grammy award for Best Alternative Music Album, 2007), (songs) Crazy, 2006 (2 MTV Video Music awards for Best Direction & Best Editing, MTV Europe Music award for Best Song, 2006, Grammy award for Best Alternative Performance, 2007, Soul Train award for Soul Single, 2007); actor: (films) Mystery Men, 1999. Recipient Left Field Woodie award, mtvU, 2006, Best Group award (as Gnarls Barkley), Black Entertainment TV (BET) Awards, 2007. Office: Waxploitation Inc 11601 Wilshire Blvd Los Angeles CA 90025

CEFALO, ROBERT CHARLES, obstetrician, gynecologist; b. Boston, 1933; MD, Tufts U., 1959. Diplomate Am. Bd. Ob-Gyn. Intern Chelsea Naval Hosp., Boston, 1959—60; resident in ob.-gyn. U.S. Naval Hosp., Oakland, Calif., 1961—64; now prof. dept. ob-gyn. Med. Sch. U. N.C., Chapel Hill, and asst. dean, head of office grad. med. edn. Mem.: SGI, AMA, ACOG.

CEHELSKY, MARTA, scientific organization executive; BA, Barnard Coll., 1964; MA in Polit. Sci., Columbia U., 1968, PhD in Polit. Sci., 1974. News editor Latin Am. Rsch. Rev., 1970-71; vis. sr. rsch. assoc. U. Houston Inst. Urban Studies, 1974; asst. prof. dept. polit. sci. Bklyn. Coll., CUNY, 1971-76; pub. policy cons., 1967-68, 77-79; policy analyst Lyndon B. Johnson Space Ctr., 1977-79, NASA Hdqrs., 1979-80; spl. asst. Senator Ernest F. Hollings, Washington, 1983-84; from polit. analyst to exec. officer Nat. Sci. Bd. NSF, Washington, 1980—2002; sr. adv. sci. and tech., dept. sustainable devel. InterAm. Devel. Bank, 2002—06; sr. advisor Office. of Dirs., NSF, 2006—. Author: Land Reform in Brazil: The Management of Social Change, 1979, Guatamala Election Factbook, 1966; contbr. chpts. to books, articles to profl. jours.; presenter in field. Charter mem. The Washington Group (bd. dirs.). Fulbright fellow, 1964, Fulbright Hays fellow, 1965, Ford Fgn. Area fellowp, LEGIS Exec. fellow, Nat. Def. Fgn. Lang. fellow Barnard Soc. Proctors. Fellow AAAS; mem. AIAA, Exec. Women in Govt., Sr. Execs. Assn., Ukranian Phys. Soc., Am. Astronautical Soc., Am. Polit. Sci. Assn. Office: NSF 4201 Wilson Blvd Arlington VA 22230 Office Phone: 703-292-8003. Business E-Mail: mcehelsk@nsf.gov.

CEJAS, PAUL L., diplomat, executive; b. Havana, Cuba, Jan. 4, 1943; BBA in Acctg., U. Miami, 1969; PhD (hon.), Fla. Internat. U., 1988. CPA. Amb. to Belgium U.S. Dept. of State, 1998—; chmn., CEO PLC Investments, Inc. Founder, chmn., CEO CareFlorida Health Systems, Inc. Former chmn. Dade County Sch. Bd.; apptd. by Gov. Chiles to bd. regents

State of Fla. U., 1994; chmn. Post-Summit Com. for the 1994 Hemispheric Summit of the Americas; chmn. Fla. Partnership of the Americas, 1994-97; rep. to U.S. Delegation to the Gen. Assembly of the Orgn. of Am. States, 1996, others. Office: 27 Blvd de Regent Box 002 Psc 82 APO AE 09710-0082

ČEJKA, JIŘÍ, retired chemist, researcher; b. Roudnice, N.L., Czech Republic, Sept. 2, 1929; s. Josef and Božena (Roudnická) C.; m. Marie Sedláčková, July 26, 1958; children: Jiří, Jan. MSc, Inst. Chem. Tech., Prague, Czechoslovakia, 1961, PhD, 1970; DSc, Acad. of Scis. of Czech Republic, 1994. Rsch. chemist Reagencia, Kralupy, Czechoslovakia, 1954-59, Glazura, Roudnice, 1959-72; head rsch. chem. divsn. Nat. Mus.-Natural History Mus., Prague, 1972-93, scientist, 1972-88, sr. rsch. scientist, 1988—, dir., 1991-2001, dir. emeritus, 2001—. Author: Secondary Uranium Minerals, 1990; editor Acta Mus. Nat. Prague, Hist. Natur., 1974-93; regional editor Czech Republic Art and Archaeology Tech. Abstracts, The Getty Conservation Inst., Marina del Rey, Calif., 1988-94; contbr. articles to profl. jours. Fellow: Scout History Assn.; mem.: Nat. Geog. Soc., Internat. Mineral. Assn., Commn. on New Minerals and Mineral Names (a new mineral named cejkaite to honor contributions to uranium mineralogy 1999), European Crystallographic Assn., Junák Assn. of Scouts and Guides of Czech Republic (award 1947, 1987, 1990, 1992, 1999, 2002, award A 2003, award B 2003, 2004, 2007), Crystallographic Soc., Slovak Chem. Soc., Czech Chem. Soc., Confederation Polit. Prisoners Czech Republic (award 1998), Dr. Milada Horakova Club, Scouts' Velen Fanderlik Troop (troop leader 1999—2001, 2005—06, award 1999, 2006). Achievements include patents in field. Avocations: classical music, jazz, fine arts, philosophy of the world scout movement. Home: Michálkova 1672 413 01 Roudnice N.L. Czech Republic Office: Nat Scis Mus of Nat Mus Václavské náměstí 68 115 79 Prague 1 Czech Republic Business E-Mail: jiri_.cejka@tiscali.cz.

CEKO, THERESA C., lawyer, educator; BA, U. Chgo., 1981; JD, DePaul U., 1984. Clin. prof. Loyola U., Chgo., 1987—, dir. Cmty. Law Ctr., 1999—. Contbr. articles to Ill. Ct. publ. Office: Loyola U Chgo Sch of Law 25 E Pearson Ste 1400 Chicago IL 60611 Office Phone: 312-915-7836. Business E-Mail: tceko@luc.edu.*

CELAIRE, JAUNELLE ROBERTA, music educator; d. Jones Anthony and Grace Elenora Celaire. MusD, U. Mich., Ann Arbor, 2003. Dir. worship music Zion Luth. Ch., Fairbanks, Alaska, 2003—06. Mem.: Natinal Assn. Tchrs. Singing (life), Phi Kappa Phi. Office: Univ Alaska Fairbanks 312 Tanana Loop PO Box 755660 Fairbanks AK 99775-5660 Home Phone: 907-451-0740; Office Phone: 907-474-5291. Business E-Mail: ffjrc@uaf.edu.

CELENTANO, FRANCIS MICHAEL, artist, educator; b. NYC, May 25, 1928; s. Michael Anthony and Rafaela (Valentino) C. BA, NYU, 1951, MA in Art History, 1957. Lectr. C.W. Post Coll., LI, NY, 1961-63, N.Y. Inst. Tech., Old Westbury, NY, 1965-66; from assoc. prof. to prof. Sch. Art, U. Wash., Seattle, 1966-93. One-man shows include Howard Wise Gallery, N.Y.C., 1963, Foster/White Gallery, Seattle, 1971, 73, 75, 78, Diane Gilson Gallery, Seattle, 1981, 82, Fountain Gallery, Portland, Oreg., 1983, Greg Kucera Gallery, Seattle, 1986, 89, 91, Safeco Plaza, Seattle, 1990, 95, Laura Russo Gallery, Portland, 1990, 2004, 07, Woodside/Braseth Gallery, 1993, 95, 97, Bryan Ohno Gallery, Seattle, 2005; retrospective exhbn. Portland Ctr. for the Visual Arts, 1986, Whatcom County Mus., Bellingham, Wash., 1992; represented in permanent collections at Mus. Modern Art, N.Y.C., Whitney Mus. Am. Art, NYC, Albright-Knox Mus., Buffalo, Seattle Art Mus., Fed. Res. Bank of San Francisco, Wash. State Arts Commn., King County Arts Commn., U. Wash. Hosp., Seattle, Whitney Mus., NYC. Fulbright scholar Rome, 1958; fed. regional fellow in painting Western States Arts Fedn. Nat. Endowment for the Arts, 1990. E-mail: fcelent@u.washington.edu.

CELENTANO, JOHN E., pharmaceutical executive; BA, U. Del., 1982; MBA, Drexel U., Phila., 1989. With Bristol-Myers Squibb, 1982—94, 1996—, sales rep., 1982, sr. dir. Anti-Infectives, 1996, gen. mgr. Puerto Rico and the Caribbean, v.p., gen. mgr. No. Europe, 1999—2002, pres. Can., Mex. and the Caribbean, 2002, pres. Can. and L.Am., pres. Health Care Group, 2005—. Office: Bristol Myers Squibb 345 Park Ave New York NY 10154-0037*

CELENTANO, SUZANNE, movement educator; b. Pitts., Nov. 4, 1967; d. Patrick Earl and Dixie Lea Carmack; m. Ronald Joseph Celentano, June 19, 1993; children: Christopher, Brandon, Sophia. BA in Comm. Arts and Theater, Allegheny Coll., Meadville, Pa., 1989; MFA in Theater, U. Ala., Tuscaloosa, 1991. Cert. instr. group fitness ACE, pilates instr. Pilates Method Alliance, yoga instr. Yoga Alliance RYT. Actor, dir., choreographer, 1992—; master trainer pilates and yoga, 2006—. Adj. instr. theater Coll. Charleston, SC, 1992—95, St. Louis U., 1996—99; arts mgmt. cons., 1992—; spkr., presenter in field, 1992—; profl. lectr., dept performing art Am. U., Washington, 2003. Dancer Am. Coll. Dance Festival Nat. Gala and Southeastern Gala, 1990, company mem. Kathy Harty Gray Dance Theatre, 2003—; actor: (films, TV and theater) April Is My Religion, 2001 (award), Wilma Theatre, Ala. Shakespeare Festival, Walt Disney World; co-author: (book) Theatre Management: A Successful Guide to Producing Plays on Commercial and Nonprofit Stages, 1998; author: (plays) Phoenix Theatre, 2004; choreographer South County Secondary Sch. (Regional award Cappies, 07). Theater coord. Piccolo Spoleto Festival, Charleston, 1994; 1st v.p. Lorton Sta. Elem. Sch. PTA, 2003—04; bd. dirs. Lorton Arts Found., Va., 2002—05. Scholar, Internat. Thespian Soc., 1985, Bolling AFB and Ft. Belvoir Officer's Wives Club, 2006. Mem.: Dance Critics Assn., Yoga Alliance, Pilates Method Alliance (cert. instr. and master trainer of mat and apparatus), Southeastern Theatre Conf., Officers Wives Clubs (scholarship coord. 1994—95, 2000—01), Officers Spouses Club (pres. 2001—02), Alpha Chi Omega Found. Democrat. Roman Catholic. Avocations: distance running, community activist, yoga. Home: 8710 Bittersweet Ct Lorton VA 22079 Office Phone: 703-298-6934. Personal E-mail: scelentano@aol.com.

CELENTINO, CHRISTOPHER, lawyer; b. Tarrytown, NY, July 2, 1962; BS, Northwestern U., 1984; JD cum laude, Georgetown U., 1987. Bar: Calif. 1987, US Dist. Ct. So., No., Ctrl. & Ea. Districts Calif. Assoc. Luce, Forward, Hamilton & Scripps LLP, San Diego, 1987—94, ptnr., 1994—2003, Duane Morris LLP, San Diego, 2003—, mng. ptnr. San Diego office, 2004—. Bd. dirs., mem. exec. com. Calif. Bankruptcy Forum; bd. dirs. San Diego Bankruptcy Forum, pres., 2002. Head coach & team mgr. Presidio Little League. Recipient Wiley M. Manual Award for Pro Bono Legal Svc., State Bar Calif., 1992, Frank Curran Humanitarian Award, San Diego Downtown Partnership, 1993. Mem.: Louis M. Welch Inn of Am. Inns Ct., San Diego Fin. Lawyers Group, San Diego County Bar Assn. (Annual Award for Outstanding Svc. to the Cmty. 1994), Northwestern U. Alumni Club San Diego, Georgetown U. Alumni Club San Diego. Office: Duane Morris LLP Ste 900 101 W Broadway San Diego CA 92101-8285 Office Phone: 619-744-2246. Office Fax: 619-744-2201. Business E-Mail: ccelentino@duanemorris.com.

CELENTO, FLORENCE M., librarian; b. Phila., May 2, 1934; d. Dennis and Dorothy Rose Haggerty; m. Joseph Stephen Celento, Jr., Dec. 17, 1953 (dec. Dec. 1996); children: Christine, Elizabeth, Dennis, Marysusan, Stephanie, Joseph, Emily. BA, Washington & Jefferson Coll., 1983. Cert. libr., Pa. Asst. libr. Chartiers Houston Libr., Houston, Pa., 1980-89; customer svc. rep. United Airlines, Dulles, Va., 1989-90; sec., treas. Celento Assoc. Archs., Houston, Pa., 1990-96; mem. staff Canonsburg (Pa.) Libr., 1999—2001, Peters Twp. Pub. Libr., McMurray, Pa., 2001—. Vol. Rep. Councilman, McMurray, Pa., 1996. Avocations: reading, walking, travel, needlecrafts. Home: 403 Scott Ln Venetia PA 15367-1121 Office: Peters Twp Pub Libr 616 E McMurray Mc Murray PA 15317-1312

CELESIA, GASTONE GUGLIELMO, neurologist; b. Genoa, Italy, Nov. 22, 1933; came to U.S., 1959, naturalized, 1970; s. Raffaele Amadeo and Ottavia (Tortrino) C.; m. Linda Irene Pike, Aug. 1, 1964; children: Gloria, Laura. MD, U. Genoa, 1959; MS, McGill U., Montreal, 1965. Diplomate Am. Bd. Psychiatry and Neurology in Neurology, Am. Bd. Psychiatry and Neurology in Clin. Neurophysiology. Intern Madison Gen. Hosp., Wis., 1960; fellow neurophysiology U. Wis., Madison, 1960-62, asst. prof. neurology, 1966-69, assoc. prof., 1970-73, prof., 1974-79, 1979-83; resident in neurology Montreal Neurol. Inst./McGill U., Montreal, Que., Canada, 1962-66; chief neurology svc. VA Hosp., Madison, 1979-83; prof. neurology Loyola U., Chgo., 1983—99, chmn. dept. neurology, 1983-99, prof. neurology, 2000—03; cons. Exec. Svc. Chgo., 2003—. Cons. Exec. Svc. Core of Chgo. Editor in chief: Electroenceph. Clin. Neurophysiol., 1988-99; contbr. articles to profl. jours. Fellow Am. Acad. Neurology; mem. AMA, Am. Acad. Clin. Neurophysiology (pres. 1993-95), Am. Neurol. Assn., Wis. Neurol. Soc. Wis. Med. Alumni Assn., Wis. Neurol. Soc. (pres. 1975-76), Soc. Neurosci., Am. Epilepsy Soc., AAAS, Am. Soc. Office: 25 E Washington St Ste 1500 Chicago IL 60602-1804 Personal E-mail: g.celesia@comcast.net.

CELESTE, RICHARD F., academic administrator, retired ambassador, governor; b. Cleve., Nov. 11, 1937; s. Frank C.; m. Dagmar Braun, 1962; children: Eric, Christopher, Gabriella, Noelle, Natalie, Stephen; m. Jacqueline Lundquist; 1 child, Sam; 6 stepchildren. BA in History magna cum laude, Yale U., 1959; Ph.B. in Politics, Oxford U., 1962. Staff liaison officer Peace Corps, 1963, dir. Washington, 1979-81; spl. asst. to U.S. amb. to India, 1963-67; mem. Ohio Ho. of Reps., Columbus, 1970-74, majority whip, 1972-74; lt. gov. State of Ohio, Columbus, 1974-79, gov., 1983-91; mng. ptnr. Celeste & Sabety, Ltd., Columbus, Ohio, 1991—97; US amb. to India US Dept. State, New Delhi, 1997—2001; co-chair, Homeland Security Proj. The Century Found., 2002—; pres. Colorado Coll., 2002—. Mem. Ohio Dem. Exec. Com. Rhodes scholar Oxford U., Eng. Mem. Am. Soc. Pub. Adminstrn., Italian Sons and Daus. Am. Methodist. Office: Office Pres Colorado Coll 14 E Cache La Poudre St Colorado Springs CO 80903*

CELIA, GEORGE, composer, writer; b. Ragusa, Italy, Mar. 17, 1921; came to U.S., 1923; s. Giorgio Giuseppe and Lucia Giovanna (Sola) C.; m. Rosemary Fern Walker, Apr. 26, 1958; 1 child, Georgene Fern. Student, Northwestern U., 1944-48, U. Chgo., 1968. Personnel mgr., asst. contr. Consolidated Radio Products Co., Chgo., 1949-55; office mgr., chief acct., contr., treas. Gulbransen Piano & Organ Co., Melrose Park, Ill., 1955-70; owner George Celia U. & Libr., 1971, Life Mgr. Co., Richardson, Tex., 1971-73, Get Organized Co., Richardson, 1973-97, Ultimate You, George Celia Creative Enterprises, Richardson, 1986-97, Midland, Tex., 1998—, Celia Ingram Comm. Spl. feature writer Chgo. (Ill.) Tribune, 1954. Composer (processional): The Triumph of Ideals, 1945; composer: March of the Nations-UN song, 1945, Fight Boys Fight Sport Song, 1945, Song of the Returning Soldier, 1945, Rispetto, 1989, Student's Prosection on the Shoulder's of Giants, 2000, The Gladness, 2001, AnniMETsary Song, 2003, New Day Symphony, 2005; author: Focus Books, 1971, Ultimate You, 1989, Personal Magna Carta, 1989, The Triumph of Ideals, 1997, Love Affair with Every Day, 1997, Musikgarten & Art, 2000, Incredible Galleries, 2000, The Unstilled Quills, 2001, Keyboard Extravaganza, 2002, Historic Letter to Louisa, 2003, 6 Generations, 2004, Grafa Park, 2005, Dancing with Words, 2006; author: (travel and autobiog. drama scenes) Roman Britain, 1992, Columbus 500th, Genoa Maternal Relatives Reunion, 1992, Rome, Paternal Relatives Reunion, 1992, Scafati (bordering Pompeii) Maternal Roots, 1992, Awed by Ragusa, Beautiful Sicilian City Scene, 1992, Ode to the Statue of Liberty and to the Marseillaise, 1992. Treas. City Coun. Campaign, Richardson, 1987. Mem.: Alpha Kappa Psi. Republican. Methodist. Avocations: composer, author, photographer, sports. Home: 3208 Whitney Dr Midland TX 79705-6246

CELL, GILLIAN TOWNSEND, retired historian, educator; b. Birkenhead, Cheshire, Eng., June 5, 1937; arrived in US, 1962; d. Thomas Edmund and Doris Abigail (Clark) Townsend; m. John Whitson Cell, Oct. 19, 1962 (dec.); children: Thomas K., Katherine A., John D. BA, U. Liverpool, Eng., 1959, PhD, 1964; DLitt, Meml. U., Newfoundland, 1988. Instr. U. N.C., Chapel Hill, 1965-66, asst. prof., 1966-70, assoc. prof., 1970-78, prof., 1978-91, affirmative action officer, 1981-83, chmn. dept. history, 1983-85, dean Coll. Arts and Scis., 1985-91; provost Lafayette Coll., 1991-93, Coll. of William and Mary, 1993—2003; ret., 2003. Author: English Enterprise in Newfoundland; 1577-1660, 1969; editor: Newfoundland Discovered, 1982. Home: 1152 Fearrington Post Fearrington Village NC 27312-5014 E-mail: gtcell@wm.edu.

CELLARIUS, RICHARD ANDREW, biology professor; b. Oakland, Calif., July 28, 1937; s. Herman Gerhard and Florence Gillies Cellarius; m. Doris Ruth Scheuchenpflug, June 10, 1959; children: Barbara Ann, Karen Lynn. BA in Physics, Reed Coll., Portland, Oreg., 1958; PhD in Bio. Sci., Rockefeller U., NYC, 1965. NIH, USPHS postdoctoral rsch. fellow in biophysics U. Mich., Ann Arbor, 1965—66, asst. prof. botany, 1966—72; mem. faculty plant biology, biophysics, environ. policy Evergreen State Coll., Olympia, Wash., 1972—99, dir. grad. program environ. studies, 1995—99, emeritus mem. faculty, 1999—; assoc. faculty mem. Prescott Coll., Ariz., 2006—. Author: (textbook) Introduction to Bioenergetics: Thermodynamics for the Biologist. Trustee, pres. NW Sci. Assn., 1987—99. Mem.: Am. Inst. Biol. Scis., Sierra Club (life; bd. dirs., chmn. com. 1968—, pres., v.p., sec. 1974—95, trustee, treas. 1988—2003, Walter Starr award 1996, Raymond Sherwin award 2006, hon. v.p. 2001), Sigma Xi, Phi Beta Kappa. Home Phone: 928-778-6724. Personal E-mail: richard@cellarius.net.

CELLUCCI, (ARGEO) PAUL, former ambassador, governor; b. Marlboro, Mass., Apr. 24, 1948; s. Argeo R. and Prisicilla Rose C.; m. Janet Garnett, 1971; children: Kate, Anne. BS, Boston Coll., 1970, JD, 1973. Atty. Kittredge, Cellucci and Moreira, Hudson, Mass., 1973-90; mem. Hudson charter commn. Hudson, 1970-71; selectman, 1971-77; state rep. Third Middlesex Dist., Mass., 1977-84; state senator Middlesex and Worcester Dists., Mass., 1985-90; lt. gov. State of Mass., 1991-97, gov., 1997—2001; U.S. amb. to Canada U.S. Dept. State, Ottawa, 2001—05; exec. v.p. corp. devel. Magna Entertainment Corp, 2005—. Capt. USAR, served in USAR 1970-1978. Recipient Haskins and Fells Found. award, 1969. Mem. ABA, Mass. Bar Assn., Elks, Sons of Italy. Republican. Roman Catholic. Office: Magna Entertainment Corp 337 Magna Dr L4G 7K1 Aurora ON Canada

CELLURA, A(NGELE) RAYMOND, psychologist; b. Rochester, NY, Dec. 22, 1932; s. Raymond Anthony and Helen (Balistrere) Cellura; children: Jon, Jane, Todd. BA, St. Francis Coll., 1957; MS, L.I. U., 1960, SUNY, New Paltz, 1960; EdD, U. Rochester, 1965. Lic. psychologist Mass., Ga. Psychologist City Sch. Dist., Rochester, 1961-63; sr. clin. psychologist N.Y. State Dept. Mental Hygeine, 1964-65; asst. dir. cmty. mental health rsch. tng. program Washington U., St. Louis, 1964-65, asst. prof. Grad. Inst. Edn., 1964-65; head dept. human devel. U. Mass., Amherst, 1965-68; assoc. prof. psychology R.I. Coll., Providence, 1968-70; pres. EDPSI, Inc., Sharon, Mass., 1970-89; psychologist IV, S.C. Dept. Mental Health, Columbia, 1989-91; med. cons. disability determination S.C. Divsn. Voc. Rehab., 1991-93; prin. Behavior Consults, Hartwell Ga., 1993—, Abbeville, S.C., 1993—. Mental health cons. Head Start program Ctrl. Savannah River Area-Econ. Opportunity Authority, Augusta, Ga., 1998—2000; trainee postdoctoral program in psychopharmacology U. Ga.-Ga. State U., 1999—2000; chief psychology svcs. Ga. Regional Hosp. Augusta, 2002—; dir. Psychosocial Treatment Svcs. E. Ctr. Regional Hosp., Augusta, 2003—. Author: Cellura's Cento, 1987, The Genomic Environment and Niche-Experience, 2005; contbr. articles to profl. jours. Mem.: AAAS, N.Y. Acad. Scis., Am. Psychol. Assn. Office: Behavior Consults 2418 Cedar Springs Rd Abbeville SC 29620-9803 E-mail: arcellura@wctel.net.

CELOTTA, ROBERT JAMES, physicist; s. Bart and Agnes Margaret (Comerford) C.; m. Beverly Kay Lauter, Nov. 20, 1966; children: Jennifer Ann, Daniel Wayne. BS in Physics, CCNY, 1964; PhD in Physics, NYU, 1969. Rsch. asst. IBM Watson Lab., NYC, 1963-64; rsch. asst. dept. physics NYU, NYC, 1964-69, instr., 1966-69; postdoctoral rsch. assoc. Joint Inst. Lab. Astrophysics, Boulder, Colo., 1969-71; physicist Nat. Inst. Standards and Tech., Gaithersburg, Md., 1971-86, fellow, 1987—. Mem. gen. com. Internat. Conf. on Physics of Electron and Atom Collisions, 1985—89; participant NSF-Nat. Coun. for Sci. and Tech. U.S.-L.Am. Coop. Sci. Program, 1984—86, U.S.-Spain Sci. Program, 1985—88, U.S.-Yugoslav Coop. Rsch. Program, 1978—87; vice chair Gordon Conf. on Magnetic Nanostructures, 1997—99, chair, 2000—02; mem. com. on emerging micro and nano technologies NRC, 2002—03. Series editor Methods of Exptl. Physics, 1981-95, Exptl. Methods in Phys. Scis., 1995—; mem. editl. bd. Rev. Sci. Instruments, 1982-85, vice chair Davisson-Germer Prize Com., 1990-91, chair, 1992-93, adv. com. Conf. on Magnetics and Magnetic Materials, 1996-97; contbr. articles to Phys. Rev. Letters, Science, Phys. Rev., Jour. Vaccum Sci. Tech., Jour. Applied Physics, Applied Physics Letters, Revs. Sci. Instruments, Sci., Jour. Physics, Jour. Magnetism and Magnetic Materials, Jour. Chem. Physics, numerous others; contbr. to conf. procs. Recipient Disting. Young Scientist award Md. Acad. Scis., 1978, Edward V. Condon award U.S. Dept. Commerce, 1980, IR-100 award R & D Mag., 1980, 85, Fed. Lab. Consortium award Excellence in Tech. Transfer, 1988, William P. Slichter award Nat. Inst. Stds. and Tech., 1992, Alumni Achievement award NYU, 1997. Fellow: AAAS (Centennial spkr. 1998—99), Washington Acad. Sci. (Outstanding and Disting. Career in Sci. award 1994), Am. Vacuum Soc. (Gaede-Langmuir prize 1994), Am. Phys. Soc. (exec. com. topical group on instrumentation and measurement scis. 2000—, mem. McGrody prize com. 2000—02). Achievements include patents for Absorbed Current Electron Polarization Detectors; Apparatus and Methods for Electron Spin Polarization Detection; Laser Controlled Nanolithography; developed photodetachment spectroscopy method for electron affinity measurement; pioneering measurements in polarized electron scattering from atoms and surfaces, scanning tunneling microscopy, surface magnetism and laser controlled atom deposition; developed the GaAs polarized electron source, the diffuse low energy polarization detector, the technique of scanning electron microscopy with polarization analysis (SEMPA), and autonomous atom assembly. Office: NIST 100 Bureau Dr Gaithersburg MD 20899-8412 Home Phone: 301-330-4229; Office Phone: 301-975-3710. Business E-Mail: Robert.Celotta@nist.gov.

CEMBALEST, ROBIN, arts editor, critic; b. NYC, 1960; B in Art Hist., Yale Univ. Asst. editor Art Forum, 1982—86; arts editor Forward Newspaper, 1994—98; assoc. editor ARTnews Mag., NYC, 1988—94, exec. editor, 1998—. Contbg. writer NY Times, Wall St. Jour. Lectr. in field. Recipient Nat. Headliner award, Silurians award for arts/cultural reporting. Office: ARTnews Magazine 48 W 38th St New York NY 10018-0042 Office Phone: 212-398-1690. Office Fax: 212-819-0394. E-mail: rcembalest@artnews.com.

CENDALI, DALE MARGARET, lawyer; b. NYC, Feb. 11, 1959; d. John Amos and Eleanor M. (Avocato) C.; m. John Francis Fitzpatrick, Sept. 12, 1987. BA summa cum laude, Yale U., 1981; JD, Harvard U., 1984. Bar: N.Y. 1985, U.S. Dist. Ct. (so. and ea. dists.) N.Y. 1985, U.S. Dist. Ct. (ea. dist.) Mich. 1988, U.S. Dist. Ct. (no. dist.) Calif. 2001, U.S. Ct. Appeals (2d cir.) 1989, U.S. Ct. Appeals (Fed. cir.) 1990, U.S. Ct. Appeals (9th cir.) 2001, U.S. Supreme Ct. 2002. Assoc. Fried, Frank, Harris Shriver & Jacobson, NYC, 1984-91, O'Melveny & Myers, NYC, 1991—. Editor-in-chief Harvard Jour. Legis. 1983-84; contbr. numerous articles to profl. jours. Named one of Am. Top 50 Women Litigators, Nat. Law Jour., The 50 Most Influential Women Lawyers in Am., 2007, The Magnificent 7 - IP's Best Young Trial Lawyers, IP Worldwide Mag., Nifty 50 - Harvard Law Sch. Women Alumnae, Harvard Law Bulletin. Mem. ABA (chair intellectual property com. litig. sect., programming co-chair 1993 litig. sect. ann. meeting), N.Y. State Bar Assn. (chair work for hire subcom. intellectual properties com. fed. and comml. sects.), Assn. of Bar of City of N.Y. (copyright and literary property com., media law com., chair trademark com.); Phi Beta Kappa. Avocations: theater, books collector, sailing, comic book collecting. Office: O'Melveny & Myers LLP Times Sq Tower 7 Times Sq New York NY 10036 Office Phone: 212-326-2051. Business E-Mail: dcendali@omm.com.*

CENNAME, AUGUST, investment advisor; Sr. v.p., fin. advisor Merrill Lynch, Columbus, Ohio. Named one of Top 100 Fin. Advisers, Barron's Mag. Office: Merrill Lynch Ste 2600 65 E State St Columbus OH 43215 Office Phone: 614-225-3070.*

CENSULLO, MICHAEL, radiologist; BA, Wesleyan U., Middletown, Conn., MA, 1990; MD, Georgetown U., Washington, 1997. Diplomate Am. Bd. Radiology, Am. Bd. Nuc. Cardiology, Am. Bd. Vascular and Interventional Radiology, lic. Tex., N.J., Md., Va. Intern Riverside Regional Medical Ctr., Newport News, Va., 1997—98; resident U. Tex. (health sci. ctr.), Houston, 1998—2002, interventional fellow, 2002—03, asst. prof., 2004—; med. dir. interventional radiology LBJ Hosp., Houston, 2004—. Mem. cancer com. Meml. Hermann Hosp., Houston, 2004—06, mem. liver tumor com., 2007—; med. sch. faculty senate rep. dept. diagnostic U. Tex. Health Sci. Ctr., Houston, 2005—, coord. vascular and interventional radiology, interviewer Med. Sch., 2005—; presenter in field. Reviewer: Am. Jour. Roentgenology, 2004—; contbr. scientific papers to profl. jours. Vol. mem. First Aid and Rescue Squad, Matawan, NJ, 1986—90; hon. mem. Honor Legion of Police Depts. State of N.J., 2000—; donor YMCA Greater Houston Area, 2002—; mem. Houston Zoo, 2004—, Houston Mus. Natural Sci., 2004—; donor Houston Pub. Radio, 2006. Recipient Vol. award, Meml. Sloan Kettering Cancer Ctr., 1988, Hawk award, Wesleyan U., 1990, Excellence in Design, Sci. Exhibit Category, Radiology Soc. N.Am., 2000, Dean's Tchg. Excellence award, U. Tex. Health Sci. Ctr. Houston, 2006; fellow Howard Hughes Found. Rsch. fellow, 1989—90; scholar, Georgetown U., 1992—95; Ford Found. Undergraduate Rsch. fellow, 1988. Mem.: Interventional Radiology Soc. Houston (moderator 2004—, dir. 2007—), Tex. Radiology Soc., Houston Radiologic Soc., Am. Roentgen Ray Soc., Soc. Interventional Radiology, Radiology Soc. N.Am. (Cert. of Merit Sci. Exhibit Category 2000, Excellence in Design Sci. Exhibit Category 2000, Roentgen Resident/Fellow Rsch. award 2000, Magna Cum Laude award Sci. Exhibit category 1998). Achievements include research in molecular pharmacology of HIV Integrase; value of catheter aortography for blunt trauma in the Multi-detector CT era; anterograde needle tract seeding in a biopsy model; portal vein embolization in a patient with Renal Cell Carcinoma with direct extension into the Right Hepatic Lobe; comparisons of endovascular pulmonary embolism options; CAT scan venography in detection of deep vein thrombosis; nuclear venography and lung perfusion scans in detection of venous thromboembolic disease; fine structure and bending of DNA oligonucleotides; endovascular and interventional procedures in obese patients; interventional radiology's role in renal transplantation; stratification of nuclear medicine GI bleeding studies for angiography; influence of body habitus and age on inferior vena cave size. Avocations: bicycling, photography, computers. Home Phone: 713-721-8532.

CENTAFONT, LUCY ANN ALEXANDER, occupational therapist, consultant; b. Anchorage, Alaska, Apr. 6, 1953; d. Robert C. and Lucy Ann (Morgan) Alexander; m. Richard A. Centafont, May 13, 1978; children: Ryan Alan, Jeffrey Richard, Lauren Ann. BS in Occupational Therapy, Temple U., 1977, MS, 1987; BS in Health Edn., Slippery Rock U., 1975. Occupational therapy cons. Bucks County Assn. for Retarded Citizens, Doylestown, Pa.; dir. occupational therapy Community Found. for Human Devel., Sellersville, Pa.; chief occupational therapy Rolling Hill Hosp., Elkins Park, Pa.; pvt. practice occupational therapy cons. Southampton, Pa. Mem. Am. Occupational Therapy Assn., Pa. Occupational Therapy Assn. (developmental disabilities spl. interest group, adminstrv. spl. interest group).

CENTANNI, ROSS J., engineering executive; b. 1946; BS, La. State UNiv.; MBA, La. State Univ. With B.F. Goodrich Co., Hooker Chem. divsn. Occidental Petroleum; mgr. corp. planning Cooper Industries, Quincy, Ill., 1981, dir. mktg. Gardner-Denver Indsl. Machinery divsn., 1985-90, v.p., gen. mgr. Gardner-Denver Indsl. Machinery divsn., 1990-93; pres., CEO Gardner Denver, Inc., Quincy, 1993—, chmn. bd., 1998—. Bd. dir. Esterline Technologies, Denman Services, Petroleum Equip. Suppliers Assn.; mem. exec. com. Internat. Compressed Air & Allied Machinery Com. Office: 1800 Gardner Expy Quincy IL 62305-9364 Office Fax: 217-228-8247.*

CENTANNI, STEVE, national news correspondent; Attended, U. Colo.; Bachelor's Degree in Broadcasting, San Francisco State U. Anchor, reporter for radio stations, San Francisco, Oakland, Calif.; wrote and produced news segments KRON-TV, San Francisco; with FOX News Channel, 1996—, nat. correspondent, Washington Bur. Abducted from TV van in Gaza City on Aug. 14, 2006 and released on Aug. 27, 2006. Recipient Alaska Press Club award for producing a weekly new mag. for KTUU-TV (NBC), 1989. Achievements include being the first TV reporter to provide on-site reports from the building where Uday and Qusay Hussein were killed after a gun battle with 101st Airbourne Division in 2003; was the first to report the fall of the Taliban in Kandahar; served as an embedded journalist with the Navy Seals during operation Iraqi Freedom. Office: Fox News Channel 400 N Capitol St Ste 550 Washington DC 20001

CENTNER, CHARLES WILLIAM, lawyer, educator; b. Battle Creek, Mich., July 4, 1915; s. Charles William and Lucy Irene (Patterson) C.; m. Evi Rohr, Dec. 22, 1956; children: Charles Patterson, David William, Geoffrey Christopher. AB, U. Chgo., 1936, AM, 1939, PhD, 1941; LLB, LaSalle Extension U., 1965; JD, Mich. State U., 1970. Bar: Mich. 1970. Asst. prof. U. N.D., 1940-41, Tulane U., New Orleans, 1941-42; liaison officer for Latin Am., Dept. State at Lend-Lease Adminstrn., 1942; assoc. dir. Western Hemisphere divsn. Nat. Fgn. Trade Coun., N.Y., 1946-52; exec. Ford Motor Co., Detroit, 1952-57, Chrysler Corp. and Chrysler Internat. S.A., Detroit and Geneva, Switzerland, 1957-70. Adj. prof. Pace U., N.Y.C., 1950-52, Wayne State U., Detroit, 1971-78, U. Detroit, 1970-72, Wayne County C.C., 1970-2001. Author: Great Britian and Chile, 1810-1914, 1941. Lt. comdr. USNR, 1942-45, Res., 1945-75. Mem. ABA, State Bar Mich., Oakland County Bar Assn., Masons. Republican. Episcopalian. Home: 936 Harcourt Rd Grosse Pointe Park MI 48230-1874

CENTO, JUAN N., delivery service executive; b. Cuba; Student, Miami Dade Cmty. Coll., Fla. Internat. Univ. Bus. Sch. With Flying Tiger Line Inc. (merged with FedEx), 1962—89; mng. dir. S., Ctrl. Am. and v.p. Mexico, Ctrl. Am., and FedEx Global Svcs. Provider Network FedEx, 1989, now pres., Latin Am & Caribbean Divsn. Miami. Bd. dirs. World Trade Ctr., Miami, Beacon Coun., Assurant, Inc.; v.p. Chile-US C. of C., Miami; chmn. Latin Am. Assn. Express Cos., 2002—04; pres. Mexican Assn. Express Couriers. Named one of 50 Most Influential Hispanics in Tech. & Bus., Hispanic Engr. & Info. Tech. mag., 2005. Office: FedEx Latin Am & Caribbean Divsn Ste 1000 701 Waterford Way Miami FL 33126 Office Phone: 786-388-2628. Office Fax: 786-388-0114.

CENTO, WILLIAM FRANCIS, retired newspaper editor; b. St. Louis, Mar. 20, 1932; s. Frank and Augusta (Albietz) C.; m. Vera Ann Shaide, May 16, 1964 (dec. Dec. 3, 2006). BS, St. Louis U., 1954. Gen. assignment reporter East St. Louis (Ill.) Jour., 1954-56; suburban editor Globe-Democrat, St. Louis, 1956-61; copyeditor Post-Dispatch, St. Louis, 1961-62; make-up editor Pioneer Press, St. Paul, 1962-65, wire editor, 1965-67, Sunday editor, 1967-73; graphics editor Pioneer Press & Dispatch, St. Paul, 1974-77; mng. editor St. Paul Dispatch, 1977-84; assoc. editor Pioneer Press, St. Paul, 1984-90. Owner Give Me Rewrite, West St. Paul, 1990—; editor, pub. Letter from Minn., West St. Paul, 1995—. Editor: Fifty and Feisty APME: 1933 to 1983, 1983. Recipient numerous awards including Twin Cities Newspaper Guild Page 1 award Makeup 1st pl. award, 1969, 71, 74, 2d pl., 1971, 72, Award of Appreciation, AP Mng. Editors Assn., 1983. Mem. Soc. Profl. Journalists, AP Mng. Editors Assn. (bd. dirs. 1982-88). Roman Catholic. Avocations: painting, graphic design. Home and Office: 111 Imperial Dr W Apt 103 West Saint Paul MN 55118-2249 Home Phone: 651-451-8565; Office Phone: 651-451-8565. E-mail: mnletter@aol.com.

CENTOFANTI, JOSEPH, accountant; b. Watervliet, NY, Oct. 2, 1965; s. Anthony Joseph and Mary Ann (Sutton) C. AS in Mgmt., Bentley Coll., 1987, BS in Acctg., 1987. CPA, Conn.; cert. govt. fin. mgr.; cert. fraud examiner; cert. forensic CPA. Staff acct. Pannell Kerr Forster, Hartford, Conn., 1987—88, sr. acct., 1988—91, Kostin, Ruffkess and Co., Farmington, Conn., 1991—92, supr., 1992—95, mgr., 1995—99, dir. govt. svcs., 2000—01; prin. Kostin Ruffkess & Co. LLC, Farmington, 2001—. Author: Audit Manual; contbr. articles to profl. jours. Treas. Greater New Britain Art Alliance, 2001-03, 05-07, bd. dirs. 2007—; treas. Middlesex County Substance Abuse Action Coun., 2005—. Mem.: AICPA, Forensic CPA Soc., Info. Sys. Audit and Control Assn., High Tech. Crime Investigation Assn. (membership chair Conn. chpt. 2004—05, treas. 2005—), Conn. Soc. CPA (chair govtl. acctg. and auditing com. 2002—03), Assn. Govt. Accts., Assn. Cert. Fraud Examiners (v.p. 2002—03, tng. dir. 2002—, pres. 2003—, Conn. chpt.), Govt. Fin. Officers Assn. (spl. rev. com.). Office: Kostin Ruffkess & Co LLC Pond View Corp Ctr 76 Batterson Park Rd Farmington CT 06032-2515 Home: 527 Killingworth Rd Higganum CT 06441-4309 Office Phone: 860-678-6002. E-mail: jcentofanti@kostin.com.

CENTRELLO, GINA, publishing executive; Joined as copy editor Pocket Books, Simon & Schuster, 1981, exec. v.p. pub., 1993—94, pres. pub., 1994—99, Ballantine Books, 1999—2003, Random House Pub. Group, 2003—. Office: Random House Pub Group 1745 Broadway New York NY 10019

CENZIPER, DEBBIE, journalist; Reporter Charlotte Observer, NC, Miami Herald. Co-recipient National awards for Edn. Reporting, 1st prize, Breaking or Hard News, Edn. Writers Assn., 1999, Green Eyeshade Excellence in Journalism award, Best of Print, Soc. Profl. Journalists, 2002, Grand prize for Investigative Reporting, Fla. Bar Media Awards, 2005, Gold Medal for Pub. Svc., Fla. Soc. Newspaper Editors, 2005; recipient Nat. Headliner award, Health/Med. Sci. Writing, 2006, George Polk award for Met. Reporting, 2006, Sigma Delta Chi award for Investigative Reporting, Soc. Profl. Journalists, 2007, Pulitzer Prize for Local Reporting, 2007. Office: Miami Herald 1 Herald Plz Miami FL 33132 E-mail: dcenziper@herald.com.*

CEP, CASEY NICOLE, writer, theology scholar; b. Cordova, Md., 1985; d. W.C. and Sandy C. BA in English, Am. Lit., Harvard Coll., 2007; MPhil student in theology, Oxford Univ., 2007—. Intern New Republic mag. Pres. Harvard Advocate lit mag., an editor Harvard Crimson, Harvard Book Rev. Rhodes Scholar. Avocations: crabbing, fishing.*

CEPEDA, ORLANDO, retired professional baseball player; b. Ponce, PR, Sept. 17, 1937; m. Miriam Cepeda; children: Orlando Jr., Hector, Malcolm, Ali Manuel. 1st baseman San Francisco Giants, 1958—66, St. Louis Cardinals, 1966—69, Atlanta Braves, 1969—72, Oakland Athletics, Calif., 1972, Boston Red Sox, 1973, Kansas City Royals, 1974; cmty. rep. San Francisco Giants, 1990—. Named Rookie of Yr. San Francisco Giants, 1958, Comeback Player of Yr., St. Louis Cardinals, 1966, Nat. League Most Valuable Player, 1967; named to Sports Hall of Fame, P.R., 1993, Baseball Hall of Fame, 1999; recipient Designated Hitter of Yr. award, 1973. Achievements include being lifetime .297 hitter with 379 home runs; making 1,364 RBIs; appearing in 3 World Series games; being an 11-time All-Star; hitting over .300 9 times in career. Office: c/o San Francisco Giants 3 Com Park San Francisco CA 94124-3904

CEPERLEY, DAVID MATTHEW, physics professor; BS in Physics and Maths., U. Mich., 1971; PhD in Physics, Cornell U., 1976. Postdoct. fellow Lab. Physique Theorique, Orsay, France, 1976-77, Rutgers U., NJ, 1977-78; staff scientist Nat Resource for Computation in Chemistry Lawrence Berkeley Lab., 1978-81; staff scientist Lawrence Livermore Nat. Lab., 1981-87; assoc. prof. physics U. Ill., 1987-91, prof. physics Champaign-Urbana, 1991—. Staff scientist Nat. Ctr. for Supercomputing Applications, 1987—, assoc. dir. applications, 1997-98; on sabbatical U. Trento, Italy, 1985-86 IRRMA Ecole Poly. Lausanne, Switzerland, 1993; coord. workshop Inst. Theoretical Physics U. Calif., Santa Barbara, 1994; rschr. Beckman Inst. Advanced Sci. and Tech, Frederick Seitz Materials Research Laboratory; co-organizer numerous workshops Contbr. numerous articles to profl. jours. Grad. fellow NSF, 1971-74, Joliot-Curie fellow, 1976-77; recipient Eugene Feenberg meml. award for many-body physics, 1994. Fellow Am. Phys. Soc. (Aneesur Rahman prize for computational physics 1998); mem. AAAS, Am. Acad. Arts & Scis., NAS Achievements include development and contributions to fermion quantum Monte Carlo methods, contributions to understanding of physical or formal understanding of quantum many-body systems, mainly his calculation of the energy of electron gas; pioneer in the development and application of Path Integral Monte Carlo methods for quantum systems at finite temperatures. Office: 4141 Beckman Inst 405 N Mathews Urbana IL 61801-2325 Fax: (217) 244-2909.

CEPHAS, DERRICK D., bank executive, lawyer; b. Cambridge, Md., Jan. 22, 1952; AB, Harvard Univ., 1975, JD, 1979, Counsel & dep. supt. of banks NY State Banking Dept., 1983—85; gen. counsel Urban Develop. Corp., NY, 1985—86; adj. prof. Bklyn. Law Sch., 1986—89; ptnr. banking Breed, Abbott & Morgan, NYC, 1986—91; chmn. NY State Legislature Spec. Com. on Interstate Banking, 1987; supt. banks State of NY, 1991—94; ptnr. banking & fin. dept. & mem. mgmt. com. Cadwalader Wickersham & Taft LLP, NYC, 1994—2005; pres., CEO Amalgamated Bank, 2006—. Bd. dir. Dime Savings Bank, NY, D.E. Shaw & Co. Office: Amalgamated Bank 275 Seventh Ave New York NY 10001

CEPPOS, JEROME MERLE (JERRY CEPPOS), newspaper editor; b. Wash., Oct. 14, 1946; s. Harry and Florence (Epstein) C.; m. Karen E. Feingold, Mar. 7, 1982; children: Matthew, Robin. BS in Journalism, U. Md., 1969; postgrad., Knight-Ridder Exec. Leadership Program, 1989-90. Reporter, asst. city editor, night city editor Rochester (N.Y.) Democrat & Chronicle, 1969-72; from asst. city editor, to nat. editor, to asst. mng. editor The Miami (Fla.) Herald, 1972-81; various editl. positions, including assoc. editor San Jose (Calif.) Mercury News, 1981—83, mng. editor, 1983—85, exec. editor, sr. v.p., 1995-99; v.p. news Knight Ridder, 1999—. Bd. visitors Coll. Journalism, U. Md., 1999-; pres. Accrediting Coun. on Edn. in Journalism and Mass Comm. 2003-04. Recipient Journalism award, Soc. Profl. Journalists' Nat Ethics, 1997, Disting. Journalism Alumnus award, U. Md., 2001. Mem. AP Mng. Editors (immediate past pres.), Am. Soc. Newspaper Editors, Calif. Soc. Newspaper Editors (former mem. bd. dirs., past pres.), Soc. Profl. Journalists, Assn. for Edn. in Journalism and Mass Comm., No. Calif. Cancer Ctr. (bd. trustees), Silicon Valley Capital Club Office: Knight Ridder 50 W San Fernando St San Jose CA 95113-2429 E-mail: jceppos@knightridder.com.

CERAN, JENNIFER ELLEN, treasurer; b. NYC, July 30, 1963; BA in Comm. and French, Vanderbilt U., 1985; MBA in Fin. and Acctg., U. Chgo., 1989. Fin. asst. Merrill Lynch, NYC, 1985-86, mktg. assoc., 1986-87; sr. bus. analyst corp. devel. Sara Lee Corp., Chgo., 1989-90, mgr. internat. treas., 1992-94, sr. mgr. internat. treas., 1994-96, asst. treas. Utrecht, Netherlands, 1996—2003; head treasury ops. Cisco Systems Inc., Dublin, 2000—01, head global treasury ops. San Jose, Calif., 2001—02, asst. treas., 2002—03; v.p., treas. eBay Inc., 2003—. Treas. Elmhurst Hist. Soc., 1991—96. Mem.: Dutch Assn. Corp. Treas. Office: eBay Inc 2145 Hamilton Ave San Jose CA 95125*

CERASUOLO, JENNIFER LYN, preservationist; b. Trenton, Mich., July 19, 1975; d. Pamela Fay Slomers and Albert E. Nichol Jr.; m. Pasquale Enzo Cerasuolo, July 17, 1999; children: Pasquale Enzo II, Lorenzo Giuseppe. AS, Monroe County CC, Mich., 2003; BA in Psychology, U. Mich., 2006. Prin., founder Huron Crusaders, Inc., Flat Rock, Mich., 2004—. Recipient Restoration of Old Burial Ground award, City of Trenton, Mich., 2006. Mem.: Soc. for Am. Archaeology, Nat. Trust Hist. Preservation (corr.), Assn. Gravestone Studies (corr. Oakley Merit cert. 2006), Am. Assn. State and Local History (assoc.), Partners Sacred Places (assoc.), Heritage Conservation Network (assoc.), Hist. Soc. Mich. (assoc.), Phi Theta Kappa (life scholarship 2003). Democrat. Roman Catholic. Avocations: reading, history, travel, art, trivia. Home and Office: Huron Crusader INC 29535 Tamarack Dr Flat Rock MI 48134 Home Phone: 734-782-0811; Office Phone: 734-341-1147. Personal E-mail: dr_flash1975@yahoo.com. Business E-Mail: lapresidente75@msn.com.

CERE, RONALD CARL, languages educator, consultant, researcher; b. NYC, Oct. 22, 1947; s. Mindie Anthony and Edvige Clelia (Ruggero) C. BA, CUNY, 1968; MA, Queens Coll., 1969; PhD, NYU, 1974. Asst. prof. SUNY, Old Westbury, 1974-77, U. Ill., Urbana, 1977-80, U. Nebr., Lincoln, 1980-83, Gettysburg (Pa.) Coll., 1983-85; prof. Ea. Mich. U., Ypsilanti, 1985-90, 1990—. Cons. Trinity Dynamics, N.J., Harper & Collins, D.C. Heath, Prentice-Hall, Random House, Scott Foresman Pub. Cos., Thomson Learning, 1985—; spkr., presenter in field. Author: Los Fabulistas, 1969, Exito Comercial, 4th edit., 2006; contbr. articles to profl. jours. Recipient James C. Healy award NYU, 1974. Mem. MLA, ASTD, Am. Assn. Tchrs. Spanish and Portuguese (dir. career svcs.), Am.Coun. Teaching Fgn. Langs., Soc. for Intercultural Edn., Tng. and Rsch., Southern Conf. Lang. Teaching (bd. advisors). Home: 2281 Glencoe Hills Dr Apt 7 Ann Arbor MI 48108-3017 Office: Ea Mich U Dept Fgn Langs 219 Alexander Hall Ypsilanti MI 48197-2255 Business E-Mail: rcere@emich.edu.

CEREZO, CARMEN CONSUELO, judge; b. 1940; BA, U. P.R., 1963, LLB, 1966. Pvt. practice, 1966-67; law clk. U.S. Dist. Ct., San Juan, 1967-72; judge Superior Ct., P.R., 1972-76, Ct. Intermediate Appeals, 1976-80, U.S. Dist. Ct., P.R., 1980-93, chief judge P.R., 1993—; dist. judge. Office: Federico Degetau Fed Bldg Rm CH-131 150 Carlos Chardon Ave Hato Rey PR 00918-1761

CERF, VINTON GRAY, information technology executive; b. New Haven, June 23, 1943; s. Vinton Thruston and Muriel (Gray) C.; m. Sigrid L. Thorstenberg, Sept. 10, 1966; children: David, Bennett. BS, Stanford U., 1965; MS in Computer Sci., UCLA, 1970, PhD in Computer Sci., 1972; PhD (hon.), Capitol Coll., Gettysburg Coll., U. Balearic Islands, U. Lulea, Swiss Fed. Inst. Tech.; PhD (hon.), George Mason U., U. Twente, U. Rovira and Virgili, U. Pisa, Tschingua U., U. Beijing, U. Poets and Telecomm., Rensselaer Polytech. Inst. Sys. engr. IBM Corp., 1965-67; prin. programmer UCLA, 1967-72; asst. prof. elec. engring. and computer sci. Stanford U., Calif., 1972-76; sr. programmer Jacobi Sys. Corp., Santa Monica, Calif., 1968-70; program mgr. info. processing techniques office Def. Advanced Rsch. Projects Agy., U.S. Dept. Def., Arlington, Va., 1976-81, prin. scientist, 1981-82; dir. sys. devel. MCI Comm. Corp., 1982-83; v.p. engring. MCI Digital Info. Svcs. Co., Washington, 1983-86; v.p. Corp. for Nat. Rsch. Initiatives, Reston, Va., 1986-94; sr. v.p. technology strategy MCI, Ashburn, Va., 1994—2005; v.p., chief internet evangelist Google Inc., Mountain View, Calif., 2005—. Author: A Practical View of Communication Protocols, 1979. Named to Datamation Hall of Fame, 1989, Nat. Inventors Hall of Fame, 2006; recipient Kilby award, 1995, Silver medal Internat. Telecomms. Union, 1995, Industry Legend award Computer and Comms. Industries Assn., 1996, NEC Computer and Comm. prize, 1996, Computer Networks and Smithsonian Leadership award, 1996, Nat. Medal of Tech., 1997, Fellow award, Computer History Mus., 2000, Prince of Asturias award, 2002, Presdl. Medal of Freedom, The White House, 2005; Marconi fellow, 1998. Fellow IEEE (Kobayashi award 1992, Alexander Graham Bell award 1997), AAAS, Assn. Computing Machinery (chmn. SIG Comm. 1987-91, coun. 1990-92, Software award), Internat. Fedn. Info. Processing, Internet Activities Bd. (chmn. 1979-82, 89-91), Internet Soc. (pioneer mem., trustee 1992-2002, pres. 1992-95, v.p. chpts. 1996-97, chmn. 1998-99); mem. NAE (Charles Stark Draper award, 2001), Sigma Xi. Office: Google Inc 1600 Amphitheatre Pkwy Mountain View CA 94043 Home Phone: 703-448-0965; Office Phone: 703-234-1823. E-mail: vint@google.com. *My entire working career has been focused on science and technology, in many forms—teaching, research, engineering management. The trait I have come to admire most among technical colleagues is absolute honesty in reporting or assessing results—blemishes and failures as well as successes.*

CERFOLIO, NINA ESTELLE, psychiatrist, educator; b. Paterson, NJ, Feb. 15, 1960; d. Robert David and LaVerne Estelle Cerfolio. BA, Grinnell Coll., 1986; MD, Chgo. Med. Sch./U. Health Scis., 1991. Cons., liaison fellow Meml. Sloan Kettering, NYC, 1991—94; human sexuality fellow Cornell U. Med. Ctr., NYC, 1992—93; cons. liaison attending psychiatrist NYU, NYC, 1993—94; chief psychiat. emergency room and walk-in clinic St. Vincent's Hosp., NYC, 1995—98; attending psychiatrist NYU Med. Ctr., NYC, 1998—, clin. asst. prof. psychiatry, 1999—; clin. asst. prof. ob/gyn. NYU Downtown Hosp., NYC, 1998—. Contbr. articles to profl. publs. Founding mem. Grief Relief Network, 2001; pregnancy expert E Pregnancy Mag., 2002; bd. advisors Achilles Track Club, Disabled Iraqi Vets., 2004—; bd. dirs. Tri-State Cmty. Adv. Bd. Edn. Broadcasting, 2003—. Oncology fellow, Am. Cancer Soc., 1992—93. Fellow: Am. Psychiat. Assn. (founding mem. early career psychiatry exec. coun. 1996—98, corr. mem. com. on women, coun. on nat. affairs 1998—99, chmn. com. on women NY County dist. br. 2002—03, mem. exec. coun. NY County dist. br. 2002—06, disting., Woman of Yr. 2006); mem.: Morgagni Med. Soc. (mem. exec. com. 1997—99). Avocations: ironman competitions, tennis, ultra-marathons, triathlons. Home: 20 E 9th St 4J New York NY 10003 Office: 2 Fifth Ave # 5 New York NY 10011 Office Phone: 212-414-0531. Business E-Mail: ninacerf@nyc.rr.com.

CERJAN, MARTIN, law librarian, educator, dean; BA, U. Mich.; JD, MSLS, U. NC, Chapel Hill. Staff mem. law libr. U. Wash., U. NC, Chapel Hill; dep. dir. Garbrecht Law Libr. U. Maine Sch. Law; assoc. dir. Alyne Queener Massey Law Libr., Vanderbilt U. Law Sch., Nashville, 1999—2003, dir., asst. dean for libr. and info. tech., asst. prof. law, 2003—. Contbr. articles to profl. jours. Office: Vanderbilt U Law Sch 131 21st Ave South Nashville TN 37203-2615 Office Phone: 615-322-0020. Office Fax: 615-343-1265. E-mail: martin.cerjan@law.vanderbilt.edu.

CERMAK, JOHN FRANK, JR., lawyer; b. New Bedford, Mass., Nov. 27, 1956; s. John Frank Cermak Sr. and Barbara Jane (Cardoza) Savage. BA summa cum laude, Boston U., 1979; JD magna cum laude, Am. U., 1982. Bar: DC 1982, US Ct. Appeals DC Cir. 1982, US Ct. Appeals 9th Cir.& 4th Cir. 1984, US Ct. Appeals 5th Cir., 10th Cir. & 6th Cir. 1985, US Ct. Appeals 7th Cir. 1987, US Supreme Ct. 1988, Pa. 1989, Calif. 1990. Law clk. US Dist. Ct. Conn., New Haven, 1982-83, US Ct. Appeals 9th Cir., Phoenix, Seattle, 1983-84; trial atty. US Dept. Justice, Land Natural Resources Div., Washington, 1984-87; sr. assoc. Jones, Day, Reavis & Pogue, LA; atty. Rodi Pollock Pettker Galbraith & Cahill, LA; now shareholder, environ. & adminstrv. advocacy practice group Jenkens & Gilchrist, P.C., LA, mng. shareholder LA & Pasadena offices, firm v.p. bd. dirs. Settlement officer US Dist. Ct. Ctrl. Dist. Calif., 1998—. Mem.: ABA, Environ. Law Inst., Assn. Trial Lawyers of Am., Fed. Bar Assn., LA County Bar Assn., Valley Industry & Commerce Assn., LA Hdqs. Assn., Swiss Am. C. of C., German Am. C. of C., LA County C. of C. Avocations: travel, scuba diving, racquetball, photography. Office: Jenkens & Gilchrist PC 15th Fl 12100 Wilshire Blvd Los Angeles CA 90025-7120 Office Phone: 310-442-8885. Office Fax: 310-820-8859. Business E-Mail: jcermak@jenkens.com.

CERMAK, JOSEF RUDOLF CENEK, lawyer, director; b. Skury, Czech Republic, Nov. 15, 1924; s. Rudolf and Rosalie (Zahalkova) C. JUC, Charles U., Prague, 1945; JD, U. Toronto, Ont., Can., 1958. Called to Ont. bar, 1960, created Queen's counsel, 1975. Mem. firm Borden, Elliot, Kelley & Palmer, Toronto, 1960-61, Wahn, Mayer, Smith, Creber, Lyons, Torrance & Stevenson, Toronto, 1962-92; ptnr. Smith, Lyons, Torrance, Stevenson & Mayer (and predecessors), Toronto, 1967-92. Bd. dirs. pvt. Can. corps. Author: Pokorne Navraty, 1955, Going Home, 1963, My Toronto, 1984, Fragmenty ze zivota Cechu a Slovaku v Kanade, 2000, Winston Churchill, Nástin zivota, 2000, Buh se tu zastavil, 2001, It All Started with Prince Rupert, 2003; editor: Zpravy News, 1965-67; chmn. editl. bd. Nase Hlasy, Toronto Czech Weekly, 1960-68; host (Czechoslovak TV show) The Window, Can.; contbr. articles to Czechoslovakian newspapers in Can. and U.S. Actor, New Theatre, Toronto, Snizek Theatre, N.Y.C., CBC Radio, others; mem. Exec. Pro Arte Orch. Assn., 1963-66; bd. dirs. Can. Ethnic Heritage Found., Pro Arte Orch. Soc. Recipient Panhellenic prize, Epstein award Univ. Coll., U. Toronto, Masarykova cena CSSK, Arbor award U. Toronto, Commemorative Medal of Pres. of Czech Republic. Mem. Can. Bar Assn., Ont. Bar Assn., Czechoslovak Soc. Arts and Scis. Am. (pres. Toronto chpt. 1970-79), Czechoslovak Nat. Assn. Can. (mem. exec. com. 1958-70, pres. 1999-2003), Pres.'s Cir. U. Toronto, Group of 175 U. Toronto. Clubs: Sokol Gymnastic Assn., Lawyers.

CERNICA, JOHN N., engineering educator, civil engineer, consultant; b. Calvaser, Romania, May 14, 1932; arrived in U.S., 1945; s. John and Mary Cernica; m. Mary Patricia Marinelli, June 25, 1959; children: Kathy, Jude, Alice, Johanna, Patricia, Sarah. BE, Youngstown State U., Ohio, 1954; MS in Engring., Carnegie Mellon U., Pitts., 1955, PhD in Engring., 1957. Registered Ohio, Tex., Fla., Ga., Ind., Iowa, DC, Ky., Md., Mich., NY, NJ,

Miss., Pa., SC, Tenn., Va., W. Va., Nat. Cert. Prof. civil engring. Youngstown State U., 1958—, dept. head civil engring.; owner J.N. Cernica & Assoc., Cons. Engrs., Youngstown, Ohio, 1962. Panelist Nat. Sci. Found.; examiner Ohio Bd. Registration Profl. Engrs. and Surveyors. Author: (textbooks) Fundamentals of Reinforced Concrete, 1964, Strength of Materials, 1 edit., 1966, (Textbooks) Strength of Materials, Spanish edit., 1968, (textbooks) Strength of Materials, 2 edit., 1977, Strength of Materials, Chinese edit., 1982, Geotech. Engring., 1982, Soil Mechanics, 1994, Found. Design, 1994; contbr. scientific papers, articles to profl. jours. Recipient Ohio's Outstanding Engr., 1964, Man of the Yr. award, 1970, Outstanding Civil Engr., 1981, Disting. Prof. award, Youngstown State U. Mem.: Mahoning County Soc. of Profl. Engrs., Nat. Soc. of Profl. Engrs., Am. Soc. of Engring. Edn., Am. Concrete Inst., Am. Soc. of Civil Engrs., Sigma Tau, Sigma Xi, Phi Kappa Phi, Tau Beta Pi. Mailing: 611 Plymouth Dr Youngstown OH 44512

CERNUGEL, WILLIAM JOHN, consumer products company executive, distributor; b. Joliet, Ill., Nov. 19, 1942; m. Laurie M. Kusnik, Apr. 22, 1967; children: Debra, James, David. BS, No. Ill. U., 1964. CPA, Ill. Sr. supr. KPMG LLP, Chgo., 1964-70; asst. corp. contr. Alberto-Culver Co., Melrose Park, Ill., 1970-71, corp. contr., 1972—74, v.p., contr., 1974-82, v.p. fin., 1982-93, sr. v.p. fin., 1993-2000, sr. v.p., CFO, 2000—. Mem. bd. govs., treas. Gottlieb Meml. Hosp., Melrose Park; assoc. mem. bd. advisors Coll. Bus., No. Ill. U. Mem. AICPA, Am. Mgmt. Assn. (fin. coun.), Inst. Mgmt. Accts., Ill. Soc. CPAs, Fin. Exec. Internat., Lions. Home: 8111 Lake Ridge Dr Burr Ridge IL 60527-5977 Office: Alberto-Culver Co 2525 Armitage Ave Melrose Park IL 60160-1163

CERNY, CHARLENE ANN, director; b. Jamaica, NY, Jan. 12, 1947; d. Albert Joseph and Charlotte Ann (Novy) Cerny; children: Elizabeth Brett Cerny-Chipman, Kathryn Rose Cerny-Chipman. BA, SUNY, Binghamton, 1969. Cert. Fundraising Exec. Curator Latin-Am. folk art Mus. Internat. Folk Art, Santa Fe, 1972-84, mus. dir., 1984-99; dir. advancement Santa Fe Prep. Sch., 1999—; founder Santa Fe Internat. Folk Art Market. Adv. bd. C.G. Jung Inst., Santa Fe, 1990-98. Mem. Mayor's Commn. on Children and Youth, Santa Fe, 1990-93, adv. bd. Recipient Exemplary Performance award State of N.Mex., 1982, Internat. Ptnr. Among Mus. award, Mayor's Recognition award, 1999, Mus. N.Mex. Regents award, 1999; Smithsonian Instn. travel grantee, 1976; Florence Dibell Bartlett Meml. scholar, 1979, 91; Kellogg fellow, 1983. Mem. Am. Assn. Mus. Internat. Coun. Mus. (bd. dirs. 1991—, exec. bd. 1991-95), Am. Folklore Soc., Mountain-Plains Mus. Assn., N.Mex. Assn. Mus. (chair membership com. 1975-77). Office: 1101 Camino De Cruz Blanca Santa Fe NM 87505-0349 Office Phone: 505-982-1829 x232.

CERNY, JOSEPH, III, chemistry professor, retired dean, director; b. Montgomery, Ala., Apr. 24, 1936; s. Joseph and Olaette Genette (Jury) C.; m. Barbara Ann Nedelka, June 13, 1959 (div. Nov. 1982); children: Keith Joseph, Mark Evan; m. 2d Susan Dinkelspiel Stern, Nov. 12, 1983. BS in Chem. Engring., U. Miss.-Oxford, 1957; postgrad. Fulbright scholar, U. Manchester, Eng., 1957-58; PhD in Nuclear Chemistry, U. Calif.-Berkeley, 1961; PhD in Physics (hon.), U. Jyväskylä, Finland, 1990. Asst. prof. chemistry U. Calif., Berkeley, 1961-67, assoc. prof., 1967-71, prof., 1971—, chmn. dept. chemistry, 1975-79, head nuclear sci. div., 1979-84, assoc. dir. Lawrence Berkeley Lab., 1979-84, dean grad. div., 1985-2000, provost for research, 1986-94, vice chancellor for rsch., 1994-2000. Mem. Nat. Acad. Scis. Physics Commn., chair nuclear physics panel, 1983-86; mem. NASA Adv. Coun., Univ. Rels. Task Force, 1991-93, NRC Study of Rsch. Doctorates, 1992-95, chmn. nuc. sci. adv. subcom. edn., 2003-04. Editor: Nuclear Reactions and Spectroscopy, 4 vols., 1974; contbr. numerous articles to field to profl. jours. Served with U.S. Army, 1962-63. Recipient E.O. Lawrence award AEC, 1974, A. von Humboldt sr. scientist award, 1985; named to U. Miss. Alumni Hall of Fame, 1988. Fellow AAAS, Am. Phys. Soc.; mem. Am. Chem. Soc. (Nuclear Chemistry award 1984), Assn. Grad. Schs. (v.p., pres. 1992-94). Democrat. Home: 860 Keeler Ave Berkeley CA 94708-1324 Office: Lawrence Berkeley Nat Lab Univ Calif Bldg 88 Berkeley CA 94720 Office Phone: 510-486-7852. E-mail: jcerny@berkeley.edu.

CERNY, JOSEPH CHARLES, urologist, educator; b. Apr. 20, 1930; s. Joseph James and Mary (Turek) Cerny; m. Patti Bobette Pickens, Nov. 10, 1962; children: Joseph Charles, Rebecca Anne. BA, Knox Coll., 1952; MD, Yale U., 1956. Diplomate Am. Bd. Urology. Intern U. Mich. Hosp., Ann Arbor, 1956—57, resident, 1957—62; pvt. practice Ann Arbor, Detroit, 1962. Pres. Resistors, Inc., Chgo., 1960—; from instr. to assoc. prof. urology U. Mich., Ann Arbor, 1962—77, clin. prof., 1971—, mem. instl. rev. bd. rsch. Med. Sch., 2001; chmn. dept. urology Henry Ford Hosp., Detroit, 1971—98, chmn. emeritus urology, 1998; cons. St. Joseph Hosp., Ann Arbor, 1973—; chief urology sect. dept. surgery Ann Arbor VA Hosp., 1999—. Mem. editl. bd. Am. Jour. Kidney Diseases, 1988—; contbr. articles to profl. jours., chapters to books. Bd. dirs. Ann Arbor Amateur Hockey Assn., 1980—83; pres. PTO Ann Arbor Pub. Schs., 1980; chmn. urology coun., mem. exec. com. Nat. Kidney Found. Mich., Ann Arbor, 1987—, bd. dirs., trustee, pres., 1988—, emeritus trustee, 1997, chmn. capital campaign, 2002. Lt. USNR, 1956—76. Recipient Disting. Svc. award, Nat. Kidney Found. Mich., 1993, Champion of Hope award, 1997, Disting. Career award, Henry Ford Hosp. Alumni, 2000. Fellow: ACS (pres-elect Mich. br. 1984—85, pres. 1985—); mem.: S.W. Oncology Group, Am. Fertility Soc., Am. Assn. Urologic Oncology, Soc. Univ. Urologists, Endocrine Surgeons, Am. Assn. Transplant Surgeons, Transplantation Soc. Mich. (pres. Mich. 1983—85, Disting. Svc. award 1982), Am. Urol. Assn. (pres. Mich. br. 1980—81, pres. N. Ctrl. sect. 1985—86, mem. fiscal affairs rev. commn. 1985—89, mem. manpower com. 1987—88, mem. tech. exhibits 1987—88, mem. jud. rev. com. 1987—91, mem. manpower com. 1990—92, mem. audit commn. 1992—96, mem. exec. commn. 1993—, bd. dirs., mem. audio-visual com., mem. program rev. com. 1994—, chmn., mem. work force com., mem. publs. com. 1995, chmn. publs. com. 1999, mem. jud. and ethics com. 1997—, Best Sci. Exhibit award 1978, Best Sci. Films award 1980, 1982), Internat. Soc. Urology, Am. Coll. Physician Execs., Am. Acad. Med. Dirs., Ann Arbor Racquet Club, Barton Hills Country Club. Avocations: tennis, fishing, civil war. Office: U Mich Health Sys Sect Urology Dept Surgery 1500 E Medical Center Dr Ann Arbor MI 48109-0005 Home Phone: 734-971-7163; Office Phone: 734-615-3039. Business E-Mail: jocerny@umich.edu.

CERNY, LOUIS THOMAS, civil and transportation engineer, consultant; b. Berwyn, Ill., Mar. 7, 1942; s. Thomas Alois and Rosalia Patricia (Havranek) C.; m. Lana Sally Taylor, June 6, 1964; children— Leonard, David BSCE, U. Ill., 1964, MS, 1965. Registered profl. engr., Ill., Miss. Rsch. asst. U. Ill., Urbana, 1964-65; various engring. positions Elgin, Joliet & Eastern Ry., Joliet, Ill., 1965-75; v.p., chief engr. Columbus & Greenville Ry., Miss., 1975-78; v.p. ops. Erie Western Ry., Huntington, Ind., 1978-79; exec. dir. Am. Ry Engring. Assn., Washington, 1979-94. Exec. dir. engring. divsn. Assn. Am. Railroads, 1979-97, cons., 1997—; leader engring. dels. to China, 1983, 84. Contbr. articles to profl. jours.; patentee in field Mem. Am. Railway Engring. and Maint.-of-Way Assn. Unitarian Universalist. Avocations: travel, photography, hiking, astronomy.

CERNY, WILLIAM, retired education educator, musician; b. NYC, Dec. 27, 1928; s. Karl Otto Cerny and Martha Rosseler; m. Mary Ann Cunningham, June 26, 1954; children: Elaine, Jean, Mary, Carol. BA magna cum laude, Yale Univ., New Haven, Conn., 1951; MusB, Yale Sch. of Music, New Haven, Conn., 1952, MusM, 1954. Profl. accompanist freelance, NYC, 1954—59; assoc. prof. Eastman Sch. of Music, Rochester, NY, 1959—72; prof. Univ. Notre Dame, South Bend, Ind., 1972—2000. Chmn., music dept. Notre Dame Univ., South Bend, Ind., 1972—81; evaluator Nat Assoc. of Sch. of Music, Washington, 1980—95; founder Wilmarc Rec., Inc. Musician (concert pianist and chamber musician): coll. and univ., 1965—96. Seaman USNR, 1948—57. Mem.: Phi Beta Kappa. Independent. Roman Catholic. Avocations: carpentry, sailing, fishing.

CERONE, DAVID, academic administrator; m. Linda Sharon Cerone. Dir. and mem. summer faculty Meadowmount Sch. Music; prof. violin Oberlin Conservatory, 1962—71; chmn. string dept. and Kulas prof. Cleve. Inst. Music, 1971—81, pres., 1985—, Mary Elizabeth Callahan pres. chair; mem. violin faculty Curtis Inst. Music, 1975—85, head violin dept., 1981—85. Founder Cleve. Chamber Music Seminar, 1974; co-founder and dir. ENCORE Sch. Strings; bd. advisors Astral Artistic Svcs.; juror various violin competitions; bd. dirs. Univ. Cir., Inc., Avery Fisher Artist Program. Cleve. Orch. debut, 1987, former mem. Cleve. Chamber Players; musician: (violin and chamber ensemble) Donald Erb's View of Space and Time, 1987, Canterbury Trio, 1984—89. Mem. Leadership Cleve. Class of 1989. Named Person of Yr., Am. Italian Heritage, 1994; recipient No. Ohio Live Award of Achievement, 1986. Mem.: Suzuki Assn. (aux. dir. internat. bd.). Office: Cleve Inst Music 11021 East Blvd Cleveland OH 44106-1705 Office Phone: 216-791-5000. E-mail: ceroned@cs.com.*

CERQUEIRA, MANUEL DECASTRO, nuclear medicine physician; b. Minho, Portugal, Nov. 25, 1948; AB, Franklin and Marshall Coll., Lancaster, Pa.; MD, NYU, 1976. Diplomate Am. Bd. Nuclear Medicine, Am. Bd. Internal Medicine, Am. Bd. Cardiovascular Diseases. Intern, resident Bellevue Hosp. Ctr., NYC, 1976-80; resident cardiology, fellow nuclear medicine Yale-New Haven Hosp., 1980-83; sr. staff Veteran's Affairs Med. Ctr., Seattle; prof. Georgetown U., Washington, 1983—; chmn., dept. molecular, functional imaging Cleve. Clin. Found., 2004—. Dir. nuclear cardiology and labs, assoc. dir. cardiology Georgetown U. Hosp., Washington, 1983—, chmn. Nuc. Regulatory Commn. Adv. Com. on Med. Uses of Isotopes, 1999. Mem. ASNC, Am. Coll. Cardiology, Am. Heart Assn., Soc. Nuclear Medicine. Office: Cleve Clin Found Gb3 9500 Euclid Ave Cleveland OH 44195 Office Phone: 216-444-2665.*

CERRI, ROBERT NOEL, photographer; b. Boston, Dec. 25, 1947; s. Lawrence Alfred and Angelina (Arena) C. BA, Georgetown Coll., 1972. Dir., head counselor The Open Door, Boca Raton, Fla., 1972-77; actor, model Miami, 1977-79; photojournalist Newsweek/Nat. Geographic, Miami, 1979-85; comml. advt. photographer Miami, 1985-98; pres. RC Photo and Video Prodns., Miami, NY, LA, Orlando, The Caribbean, 1985—, Dream Light Prodns., 1994—, Robert Cerri Group, 2000—. Cons. in field. Mem. USGA, Acad. Model Aeronautics, Tasters Guild, U.S. Golf Assn., Meeting Profl. Internat., Nat. Trust for Historic Preservation, Williamsburg Preservation Soc., PGA Ptnrs. Club. Republican. Avocations: golf, rollerblading, horseback riding, travel, bicycling. Office: Robert Cerri Group Inc 12846 Langstaff Dr Windermere FL 34786 Office Phone: 321-206-9363. Business E-Mail: rcerri@robertcerrigroup.com.

CERVANTES LAUREAN, DANIEL, biochemist; b. Sahuayo, Michoacan, Mex., July 4, 1963; s. Daniel Cervantes Marin and Maria Concepcion Cervantes; m. Yelidsa Maria Bejarano, July 31, 1970. BS, U. Michoacan, Movelia, Mexico, 1985; PhD, U. N.Tex., Denton, 1992. Intramural rsch. fellow NIH, 1992—99; sr. rsch. scientist Ariz. Cancer Ctr. U. Ariz., Tucson, 1999—2004; asst. prof. SD State U., Brookings, 2004—; cons. Clin. Advisors, LLC, NYC, 2007—. Contbr. chapters to books. Vol. Cath. Ch., Brookings, SD, 2004—07. Grantee, State of SD, 2006—07. Mem.: Am. Soc. Biochemistry and Molecular Biology (assoc.). Achievements include patents for method and use of penicillamines and other a-Amino-b-Mercapt. Home: 1060 Western Ave Brookings SD 57006 Office: SD State Univ 121 SH Box 2202 Brookings SD 57007 Home Phone: 714-442-7601; Office Phone: 605-688-6732. Office Fax: 605-688-6364. Business E-Mail: daniel.cervantes@sdstate.edu. E-mail: dcervanteslaurean@yahoo.com.

CERVENY, DAVID JOHN, lawyer; s. John William and Mary Christine Cerveny; m. Laurie Aurelia Cerveny, Oct. 3, 1997; children: Sydney Elizabeth, Brady John. BS in Biomed. Engring., Marquette U., Milw., 1988; JD, Boston Coll. Law Sch., Newton, Mass., 1997. Bar: Mass. 1997, U.S. Patent and Trademark Office 1999. Engr. McDonnell Douglas Corp., Long Beach, Calif., 1988—94; atty. Fish & Richardson, P.C., Boston, 1997—99, Hale and Dorr LLP, Boston, 1999—2004, Proskauer Rose LLP, Boston, 2004—06; intellectual property counsel Palomar Med. Techs., Burlington, Mass., 2006—. Author: (chpt. to continuing edn. manual) Trying the Case; contbr. articles to profl. jours. Named Mass. Super Lawyer Rising Star, Law and Politics Mag., 2006, 2007. Mem.: IEEE, Boston Patent Law Assn. (co-chair corp. practice com.), Am. Intellectual Property Law Assn., Tau Beta Pi, Alpha Eta Mu Beta. Achievements include research in Self-Contained Artificial Heart Project. Avocation: sailing. Mailing: Palomar Med Techs Inc 82 Cambridge St Burlington MA 01803 Office Phone: 781-993-2300. Business E-Mail: dcerveny@palomarmedical.com.

CERVERIS, MICHAEL, actor; b. Bethesda, Md., Nov. 6, 1960; Ed., Phillips Exeter Acad., 1979, Yale U., 1983. Actor: (Broadway plays) The Who's Tommy, 1993 (Theatre World Award, 1993), Titanic, 1997, Assassins, 2004 (Tony award best featured actor in a musical, 2004), Passion, 2004, Children and Art, 2005, Sweeney Todd, 2005, Lovemusik, 2007, (Off-Broadway) MacBeth, 1983, Life is a Dream, 1984, The Games, 1984, Green Fields, 1985, Total Eclipse, 1985, Blood Sports, 1986, Abingdon Square, 1986, Hedwig and the Angry Inch, 2000, Fifth of July, 2003, The Apple Tree, 2005, King Lear, 2007; (TV series) Fame, 1986; (films) Tokyo Pop, 1988, Rock 'n' Roll High School Forever, 1990, Steel and Lace, 1991, A Woman, Her Men, and Her Futon, 1992, Lulu on the Bridge, 1998, The Mexican, 2001, The Temptation, 2004, Brief Interviews with Hideous Men, 2007; performer: (albums) Dog Eared, 2004. Mailing: c/o Good Cop Public Relations 111-25 75th Rd Forest Hills NY 11375*

CESAR, KAMALA, dancer, educator; b. Bklyn., Dec. 9, 1948; d. Bruno Gonzales Cesar and Mary Kariwahawe Papnieau; m. Thomas Watson Buckner, Mar. 16, 1992; children: Robin, Paul, Tuy, Rana, Meera, Kiran. BA in Conservation of Natural Resources, U. Calif., Berkeley, 1976. Exec. dir., bd. dirs. The Balasaraswati Sch. of Music and Dance, NYC, 1985—89; founder, artistic and exec. dir. Lotus Fine Arts Prodns. Inc., NYC, 1989—, also bd. dirs. Artistic dir., performer (videotape) Bharata Natyam, The Sacred Dance of India, 1991. Named Am. Indian of Yr., Thunderbird Am. Indian Dancers, N.Y.C., 2002; recipient Ethnic Dance award, Dance Giant Steps, Inc., Bklyn., 1996; Folk Arts Apprentice, Nat. Endowment for the Arts, 1986. Democrat. Buddhist. Avocation: carnatic vocals. Office: Lotus Music and Dance Studios 109 W 27th St 8th Fl New York NY 10001 Business E-Mail: info@lotusarts.com.

CESARE, CHRISTINE B., lawyer; BA magna cum laude, Conn. Coll., 1981; JD, Fordham U., 1984. Bar: NY 1985, Conn. 1986. Ptnr. comml. litig., mem. oper. group Bryan Cave LLP, NYC. Office: Bryan Cave LLP 1290 Ave of the Americas New York NY 10104 Office Phone: 212-541-1228. E-mail: cbcesare@bryancave.com.

CESAREO, FRANCESCO, academic administrator, historian, educator; m. Filomena Cesareo; 3 children. Grad. summa cum laude, Cathedral Coll. of Immaculate Conception; MA, PhD, Fordham U. Mem. History Dept. John Carroll U., University Heights, Ohio, 1989—2004, founding dir. Inst. Cath. Studies, 1997—2004, John J. and Mary Jane Breen chair Cath. studies; dean McAnulty Coll. and Grad. Sch. Liberal Arts Duquesne U., Pitts., 2004—07; pres. Assumption Coll., Worcester, Mass., 2007—. Author: Humanism and Catholic Reform: The Life and Work of Gregorio Cortese, A Shepherd in Their Midst: The Episcopacy of Girolamo Seripando (1554-1563), 1999; mng. editor Archivum Historicum Societatis Iesu; contbr. articles to profl. jours. Fellow Mandel Found.; Fulbright Scholar, U. Rome, Pontifical Gregorian U. Office: Assumption Coll Office of Pres 500 Salisbury St Worcester MA 01609*

CESARIO, ROBERT CHARLES, marketing executive; b. Chgo., Apr. 6, 1941; s. Valentino A. and Mary Ethel (Kenny) C.; m. Susan Kay DePoutee; children: Jeffrey, Bradley. BS in Gen. Edn., Northwestern U., 1975; postgrad., DePaul U., 1975. Mgr. fin. ops. Midas Internat. Corp., Chgo., 1968-73; dir. staff ops. Am. Hosp. Supply Corp., McGaw Park, Ill., 1973-76; v.p. Car X Svc. Sys. Inc., Chgo., 1976-78, v.p. oil svcs., 1983-84; v.p. Chicken Unltd. Enterprises Inc., Chgo., 1978-83; pres. Growth Strategies, Inc., 1984-87; pres., CEO Lube Pro's Internat., Inc., 1987—2004; CEO Franchise Strategies, Inc., Chgo., 2005—. With USMC, 1960-62. Office: Franchise Strategies Inc 360 East Randolph St Ste 2103 Chicago IL 60601

CESARSKY, CATHERINE, astrophysicist; b. Ambazac, France, 1943; married; 2 children. Grad. in Phys. Sci., U. Buenos Aires, Argentina; PhD in Astronomy, Harvard U., 1971. Postdoctoral rschr. Calif. Inst. Tech.; staff mem. Commissariat a l'Energie Atomique, France, 1974—94, dir. direction des sciences de la matiere, 1994—99; dir. gen. European So. Obs., Munich, 1999—2007. Pres. sci. program com. Ctr. Nat. d'Etudes Spatiales, 2005—; pres. Internat. Astronomical Union, 2006—. Recipient Space Sci. award, Com. on Space Research (COSPAR), 1998. Mem.: Internat. Astron. Union (pres. 2006—), Swedish Acad. Sci. (fgn. mem.), Royal Soc. of London (fgn. mem.), Internat. Acad. Astronautics, Academia Europaea, French. Soc. Profl. Astronomers (pres. 1994—96), NAS (fgn. assoc.), Am. Astron. Soc. (hon.). Office: European Southern Obs Karl-Schwarzchild-Strasse 2 D-85748 Garching Germany Business E-Mail: ccesarsk@eso.org.

CESNIK, JAMES MICHAEL, retired labor union administrator, publishing executive; b. Marshfield, Wis., Oct. 6, 1935; s. Ignatius Anthony and Mary Catherine (Bayuk) C.; m. Elizabeth Louise Havlik, Aug. 1, 1959 (div. 1987); children: Margaret Mary, Sarah Elizabeth, Michael Ignatius; m. Barbara E. Nelson, Jan. 1, 1990. BA, St. John's U., Collegeville, Minn., 1958. Reporter, Rice Lake (Wis.) Chronotype, 1958; reporter, copy, makeup and layout editor Mpls. Star & Tribune, 1958-64; internat. rep., asso. dir. rsch. and info., dir. rsch. and info. Newspaper Guild, CWA,AFL-CIO/CLC, Washington, 1965-75; editor Guild Reporter, 1973-93; v.p. Internat. Labor Press Assn., Washington, 1973-79, pres., 1980-82; sec.-treas. Internat. Labor Comm. Assn., Washington, 1984-87; editor Internat. Labor Comm. Assn. Reporter, Washington, 1983-84; sec.-treas. JBTM Enterprises Inc., Winchester, Va., 1989-91, 2002, pres., 1991—2001, Signet Screen Printing and Embroidery, Winchester, Va., 1993—2007; ptnr. TJC LLC, Winchester, Va., 1999—. Elijah P. Lovejoy lectr. So. Ill. U., Carbondale, 1970; cons. in field. Mem. Falls Church (Va.) Democratic Com., 1970-84; founding mem. Falls Church Com. on Status of Women, 1975-76; pres. Montessori Sch. No. Va., 1970. Mem. Slovenian Heritage Com. Washington, Slovenian Choral Soc. Washington, Am. Slovenian Cath. Union, Soc. for Slovene Studies. Roman Catholic. Business E-Mail: jim@cesnik.com.

CESTNICK, LAURIE L., neuropsychologist, educator, scientist; PhD, Maquarie U., Australia, 2000. Cert. neuropsychologist Mass. Scientist Med. Sch. Harvard U., Cambridge, Mass., 2001—, adj. prof., 2001—; neuropsychologist Weaver Clinic, Weston, Mass., 2005—. Contbr. articles to profl. publs. Wildlife rescuer Wildlife Info. and Rescue Emergency Svcs., NSW, Australia, 1995—2000. Recipient Postdoctoral Fellow award, CIHR, Henry Jackman award, Ont. Lt. Gov., G. Allan Rsch. award, Scottish Rite Charitable Found. Can.; rsch. fellow, Harvard Med. Sch., Overseas Postgrad. Rsch. scholar, Australia. Mem.: Soc. Neuroscience (assoc.). Office: Harvard Med Sch Cambridge MA Home Phone: 617-413-2065; Office Phone: 781-894-4561. Personal E-mail: laurie@nmr.mgh.harvard.edu.

CETÍN, ANTON, artist; b. Bojana, Croatia, Sept. 18, 1936; arrived in Can., 1968, naturalized, 1973; s. Tomo and Terezija (Grcic) C.; m. Milka Katalenic, Dec. 16, 1962; 1 child, Dawn Antonia. Diploma, Sch. Applied Arts, Zagreb, 1959; masters diploma, Acad. Fine Arts, Zagreb, 1964. One-man shows include Art Gallery Hamilton, 1978, Galeria Juan Martin, Mexico City, 1979, Gilman Galleries, Chgo., 1983, Mus. Arts and Crafts, Zagreb, 1986, Beverly Gordon Gallery, Dallas, 1987, Nat. and Univ. Libr., Zagreb, 1988, Oberhausmuseum, Passau, Germany, 1990, Sony Plaza Art Gallery, Tokyo, 1991, Gallery 7, Hong Kong, 1993, Museo del Chopo, Mexico City, 1993, Salas Nacionales de Cultura-Palais de Glace, Buenos Aires, Argentina, 1994, Museo Mcpl. de Arte J.C. Castagnino, Mar del Plata, Argentina, 1995, Mus. and Gallery Ctr., Zagreb, 1996, City Mus. Varazdin, Croatia, 1998, Art Gallery, Split, Croatia, 1998, Gallery Fine Arts & Waldinger Gallery, Osijek, Croatia, 2000, Herman Hesse Mus., Calw, Germany, 2000, Mercedes Zentrum, Stuttgart, Germany, 2000-01, Gallery Anton Cetín, Cazma, Croatia, 2001, State Archives and Gallery Kortil, Rijeka, Croatia, 2002, Gallery HKZ-Hrvatsko slovo, Zagreb, Croatia, 2003, Multicultural Gallery, Halifax, Can., 2003, Gallery Ministry of Fin., Zagreb, Croatia, 2003, Mus. Mimara, Zagreb, 2004, City Mus. Vukovar, Croatia, 2005, Kamern Theatre, Sarajevo, 2005, Gallery Kula, Split, Croatia, 2005, Mus. Mimara, Zagreb, 2005, Canadian Embassy, Zagreb, Croatia, 2006, 07, Gallery Murska Sobota, Slovenia, 2007; group exhbns. include Mus. Modern Art, Crakow, Poland, 1972, Brockton Art Ctr., 1974, Nat. Libr. France, 1978, 2d Cabo Frio Internat. Print Biennial, Brazil, 1985, Del Bello Gallery, Toronto, 1986, 87, 89, 90, Crespano del Grappa, Italy, 1988, Nat. Libr. Can., 1990, Art Asia, 1993, Olympic Games, Atlanta, 1996, Shenzhen Fine Art Inst., Shenzhen Mus. Modern Art, Shanghai, 2000, Point K Galerie, Nice, France, 2001, Círculo del Arte, Barcelona, Spain, 2002, Six Stories, Multicultural Gallery, Halifax, Can., 2003, Centro Hist., Mexico City, 2004, CODA Mus., Apeldoorn, Holland, 2005, Galería del Centro Universitario , Ciudad del Carmen, Mex., 2005, others; represented in permanent collections at nat. librs. France, Croatia, Can., U.N., Japan and Salas Nacionales-Palais de Glace, Buenos Aires, Museo del Chopo, Mexico City, Vatican, Italy, Mus. Arts and Crafts, Gallery Klovicevi dvori, Zagreb, Croatia, Can. Cultural Ctr., France, Circulo del Arte, Barcelona, Spain, Gallery Anton Cetin, Cazma, Croatia, others; author: Eve and the Moon, 1975; co-author: Amerika Croatan America, 1988. Named Artist of Yr., Can. Croatian Artists Soc., 1986; honored for outstanding merits in the field of culture, govt. of Croatia, 1995 Home: PH3 5 Greystone Walk Dr Scarborough ON Canada M1K 5J5 Studio: 916-5 Greystone Walk Dr Scarborough ON Canada M1K 5J5 Personal E-mail: acetineve@sympatico.ca.

CETRULO, JERRY, artist, sculptor; b. Jersey City, Sept. 10, 1941; s. Gerardo Cetrulo and Eva Augustine; m. Renate Cetrulo, 1961 (div.); children: Michael, Mark, Heidi; m. Barbara Cetrulo, Aug. 2, 1998. Customer engr. IBM, Cranford, NJ, 1967-99; ret., 1999; instr. Am. Woodcarving Sch., Wayne, NJ, 1992—, owner, 2006—. With U.S. Army, 1959-62. Avocations: woodcarving, painting. Home: 18 Cayuga Ave Rockaway NJ 07866-1012 Office: Am Woodcarving Sch 21 Pompton Plains Xrd Wayne NJ 07470-6326 Office Phone: 973-835-8555. E-mail: njcarver@optonline.net.

CEYER, SYLVIA T., chemistry professor; Grad. summa cum laude, Hope Coll., Holland, Mich.; PhD, U. Calif., Berkeley. Postdoctoral fellow Nat. Bur. Standards; faculty mem. dept. chemistry MIT, Cambridge, Mass., 1981—, J.C. Sheehan prof. chemistry, assoc. dept. chmn. Recipient Recognition award, AAUW Ednl. Found., 1988, Nobel Laureate Signature award Grad. Edn. in Chemistry, Am. Chem. Soc., 1993, Gibbs medal,

2007. Fellow AAAS, NAS (past chmn. chemistry sect., class sec.), Am. Phys. Soc., Am. Acad. Arts and Scis. Office: MIT 6-217 Dept Chemistry 77 Mass Ave Dept Cambridge MA 02139-4307 Business E-Mail: stceyer@mit.edu.

CEZAR, GABRIELA, research scientist, entrepreneur; d. Ivo and Sonia Gebrin Cezar; m. Frederico Moreira. MS, U. de Brasilia, Brazil, 1994, U. Edinburgh, Scotland, 1998; PhD, U. Wis., Madison, 2002; DVM, U. Fed. de Mato Grosso do Sul, Brazil. Prin. sr. scientist Pfizer Inc., Groton, Conn., 2002—05; asst. prof. U. Wis., Madison, 2005—, head stem cell safety scis. lab., 2006—; co-founder Stemina Biomarker Discovery Inc., Madison, Wis. Cons. in field; spkr. in field. Contbr. articles to profl. jours. and mags. Recipient 40 Under 40 award, In Bus. Mag., 2006; scholar, Rotary Internat., 1997. Mem.: Pfizer Womens Leadership Network (assoc.), Internat. Soc. Stem Cell Rsch. (assoc.), Internat. Womens Forum. Achievements include patents pending for stem cell models to predict toxicity of chemicals; methods for in vitro differentiation of dopaminergic neurons from embryonic stem Cells; research in stem cell research for childhood and neurodevelopmental disorders; first to application of stem cells in drug discovery and development; research in metabolomics and discovery of cancer biomarkers. Avocations: travel, languages, reading. Home Phone: 608-831-2157; Office Phone: 608-263-4307. Business E-Mail: ggcezar@wisc.edu.

CHA, CHARLES, surgical oncologist, hepatobiliary surgeon; b. Chgo. m. Seema Sanghavi; children: Alexia, Jacob. BA, Northwestern U., 1990, MD, 1995. Diplomate Am. Bd. Surgery. Resident in surgery U. Wis. Hosp. and Clinics, Madison, 1995—2000, chief resident in surgery, 2000—01; fellow in surg. oncology Meml. Sloan-Kettering Cancer Ctr., NYC, 2001—03; asst. prof. surgery Yale Sch. Medicine, New Haven, 2003—. Recipient Benjamin Layton award for outstanding tchg., U. Wis. Dept. Surgery, 2001, Dennis Jahnigen Career Devel. award, Am. Geriat. Soc., 2004—, Ohse Surg. Rsch. award, Yale Dept. Surgery, 2005; NIH/NCI Rsch. fellow, 1993, David and Monica Gorin Sarcoma fellow, 2002—03. Fellow: Am. Coll. Surgeons (Faculty Fellowship Rsch. award 2004—); mem.: New Eng. Surgical Soc., Assn. VA Surgeons (chmn. awards com. 2005—), Assn. Acad. Surgery (membership com. 2005—), Pancreas Club, Am. Assn. Cancer Rsch. (assoc.), Soc. Am. Gastrointestinal Endoscopic Surgeons, Am. Soc. Clin. Oncology, Soc. Surg. Oncology, Soc. Surgery of Alimentary Tract. Achievements include research in SiRNA inhibition of angiogenesis in GI malignancy. Office: Yale U Sch Medicine 330 Cedar St LH 118 New Haven CT 06520 Office Phone: 203-785-2380. Personal E-mail: chk_cha@hotmail.com.

CHA, JUNHO, medical researcher; b. Seoul, Republic of Korea, July 18, 1969; s. Sook il Cha and Eun Seung Jeong; m. Hyunkyung Park, Mar. 31, 2002. BSEE, Kwangwoon U., Seoul, 1996; MSEE, U. Wash., Seattle, 1998, PhD, 2006. Rsch. asst. U. Wash., 1997—2006, postdoctoral rsch. assoc., 2006—; co-op. engr. Intel Corp., Sacramento, 2000—01. Contbr. articles to profl. jours. Mem.: IEEE, Korean-Am. Scientist & Engrs. Assn. (v.p. 2004—06, staff 2001—03). Home: 1344 Bellevue Way NE #2 Bellevue WA 98004 Office: Univ Wash 211 Electrical Engring Seattle WA 98195

CHA, SE DO, internist; b. Seoul, Korea, Dec. 17, 1942; came to U.S., 1966, naturalized, 1977; s. Young Sun and Hee Joo (Chang) C.; m. Elsa Jane Greene, Dec. 21, 1974; 1 child, Elizabeth. MD, Yon Sei U., 1966. Diplomate Am. Bd. Internal Medicine. Intern Presbyn.-U. Pa. Med. Ctr., Phila., 1966-67; resident in medicine Harrisburg (Pa.) Hosp., 1967-70; chief resident in medicine Roger Williams Gen. Hosp., Providence, 1970-71, cardiologist, 1973-75; fellow in cardiology Deborah Heart and Lung Center, Browns Mills, N.J., 1971-73, cardiologist, 1975—; from asst. dir. adult cardiac catheterization lab. to dir. Deborah Heart and Lung Ctr., Browns Mills, NJ, 1975—2003. Instr. Brown U., Providence, 1973-75. Contbr. articles to profl. jours. Fellow ACP, Soc. for Cardiac Angiography; mem. AMA, Fedn. Clin. Rsch., Am. Heart Assn. Office: Deborah Heart and Lung Ctr Trenton Rd Browns Mills NJ 08015 Office Phone: 609-893-6611. Business E-Mail: sdcha@msn.com.

CHA, SOYOUNG STEPHEN, mechanical engineer, educator; b. Inchon, Republic of Korea, June 25, 1944; arrived in US, 1974; s. Sang O. and Sook S. (Lee) C.; m. Young W. Park, Sept. 4, 1974. BS, Seoul U., Republic of, 1969; MS, Mich. State U., East Lansing, 1976; PhD, U. Mich., 1980. Project rsch. engr. Northrop Corp., Research Triangle Park, NC, 1979-84; prof., dir. opto-mech. lab. U. Ill., Chgo., 1984—. Co-chair Beijing Optical Diagnostics Symposium, 2002; spkr. in field. Editor: Optics Lasers in Engineering, numerous procs. vols.; contbr. more than 145 articles to profl. jours. Dept. of Energy fellow, 1987, NASA fellow, 1994, USAF fellow, 1996. Fellow Internat. Soc. Optical Engring. (conf. chair, co-chair 1991—), ASME (tech. com. 1983-87), Am. Soc. Aeronautics and Astronautics (tech. com. 1994-97, 1998—), Visualization Soc. Japan (conf. co-chair 1998, 2002). Methodist. Achievements include patent for holographic velocimetry. Office Phone: 312-996-9612. Business E-Mail: sscha@uic.edu.

CHA, STEPHEN S., emergency physician; b. Wilmette, Ill., Nov. 6, 1972; s. Eung Man and Sue Ok Cha; m. Jennifer Megan Telfair, Aug. 15, 2004; 1 child, Gabriel S. Telfair-Cha. AB, Brown U., Providence, 1994; MD, Brown U., 2000; MHS, Yale U., New Haven, Conn., 2006. Diplomate Am. Bd. Internal Medicine, 2003. Robert Wood Johnson clin. scholar Yale U., 2004—06; profl. staff Com. Oversight, US Ho. Reps., DC, 2006—.

CHA, SUK WON, engineering educator, researcher; b. Seoul, Republic of Korea, Oct. 1, 1971; m. Unjung Nam; 1 child, William. PhD, Stanford U., 2004. Rsch. assoc. Stanford (Calif.) U., 2003—05; asst. prof. Seoul Nat. U., 2005—. Author: Fuel Cell Fundamentals. Served with Republic of Korea Army, 1994—96. Achievements include research in micro fuel cells. Office: Seoul Nat U Dept Mech and Aero Engring Shinlim 9 Gwanak 151-744 Seoul Republic of Korea Office Phone: 82-2-880-1700.

CHAAR, BASSEM T., hematologist, oncologist; arrived in US, 1999; s. Tarek and Baria M. Chaar. BS, Am. U., Beirut, 1994, MD, 1998. Cert. Am. Bd. Internal Medicine, Am. Bd. Hematology, Am. Bd. Oncology. Rotating intern Am. U., Beirut, 1998—99; intern, internal medicine St. Louis U. Sch. Medicine, 1999—2000, resident in internal medicine, 2000—02, med. chief resident, 2002—03, hematology/oncology fellow, 2003—06; hematology/oncology staff Bothwell Regional Health Ctr., Sedalia, Mo., 2006—. Contbr. articles to profl. jours. Mem.: AMA (assoc.), Am. Soc. Clin. Oncology (assoc.), Am. Soc. Hematology (assoc.), Am. Soc. Internal Medicine (assoc.). Avocations: jogging, swimming, Web surfing. Office: Bothwell Regional Health Ctr 601 E 14th St Sedalia MO 65301 Home Phone: 660-827-9889; Office Phone: 660-829-7792. Office Fax: 660-826-7698. Personal E-mail: chaarbt@iland.net.

CHABNER, BRUCE A., oncologist, researcher; b. Shelbyville, Ill., June 3, 1940; married; 2 children. BA summa cum laude, Yale Coll., 1961; MD cum laude, Harvard Med. Sch., 1965; DPhil (hon.), U. Nebr., 2001. Diplomate Am. Bd. Internal Medicine. Intern, jr. resident, internal medicine Peter Bent Brigham Hosp., Boston, 1965-67; sr. resident Yale-New Haven Med. Ctr., Conn., 1969-70; rsch. assoc. dept. medicine and pharmacology Yale U., New Haven; sr. staff fellow, sr. investigator lab. clin. pharmacology and med. oncology svc. Nat. Cancer Inst., NIH, Bethesda, Md., 1971-72, sr. surgeon divsn. cancer treatment, 1972-75, head biochem. pharmacology sect., lab. clin. pharmacology, 1973-75, chief clin. pharmacology br., clin. oncology program, 1976-80, assoc. dir. clin. oncology program, divsn. cancer treatment, dep. clin. dir., 1980-82, dir. divsn. cancer treatment, 1982-95; clin. dir. Mass. Gen. Hosp. Cancer Ctr., 1995—, chief hematology/oncology, 1995—; prof. medicine Harvard Med. Sch., 1995—. Mem. com. revision U.S. Pharmacopeia, chmn. subcom. on hematologic and neoplastic disease therapy, 1974-79; mem. study sect. experimental therapeutics, NIH, 1974-79; mem. molecular biology adv. bd. NCI, Bethesda, 1977; with U.S./France Agreement in Clin. Trials and Treatment Rsch., 1977-80; with U.S./Italy AGreement in Clin. Cancer Rsch., 1980—; program chmn. Conf. on Folate and Antifolate Polyglutamates Airlie Ho., Warrenton, Va., 1981; assoc. mem. com. med. oncology Am. Bd. Internal Medicine, 1981-83, chmn., 1981-87, mem. parent bd., 1985-87; Pfizer lectr. in Clin. Pharmacology U. Vt., 1980, Yale U., 1981, Brown U., 1987; vis. prof. U. Capetown, South Africa, 1981; Terry Fox Meml. lectr. Princess Margaret Hosp., Toronto, Ont., 1982; program chmn. Keystone (Colo.)/UCLA Conf. Rational Design of Cancer Treatment, 1982; mem. protocol review com. EORTC, 1982—; William Dameschek Meml. lectr. Tufts U., 1985; program chmn. conf. new biology Inst. Medicine NAS, 1988, mem. roundtable for devel. drugs and vaccines against AIDS, 1988—; Centennial vis. prof. medicine, U. Toronto, 1989; William N. Creasy vis. prof. in Clin. Pharmacology, U. So. Calif., 1989; Gertrude Victorson Ratner Meml. lectr., Evanston Hosp., 1989; asst. surgeon gen. USPHS, ret. Editor-in-chief Cancer Treatment Reports, 1976-79, The Oncologist, 1996- (also founding editor); assoc. editor Blood, 1979-88, Cancer Rsch., 1982-84, 90—, Jour. Nat. Cancer Inst., 1988—; mem. editl. com. Jour. Clin. Investigation, 1984-89; mem. editl. bd. Internat. Medicine for the Specialist, 1990—; co-author (with Dan Longo), Principles and Practices of Cancer Chemotherapy and Biological Response Modifiers; contbr. articles to profl. jours. With USPHS, 1972—. Recipient Melville Jacobs award Am. Radium Soc., 1986, Steven Beering award for Advancement of Biomed. Sci. Ind. U., 1993, Bob Pinedo prize, Med. Knowledge Inst.(MKI), The Netherlands, 2007; named Disting. Oncologist Dayton Oncology Soc., 1986. Mem. ACP (med. knowledge self-assessment program com. 1980—), Am. Assn. Cancer Rsch. (program com. 1979-81, Bruce F. Kane award for Drug Develop., 1998), Am. Soc. Clin. Oncology (program com. 1982, David A. Karnofsky Meml. lectr. 1985), Am. Soc. Clin. Investigation, Am. Soc. Hematology, Am. Assn. Physicians, Phi Beta Kappa, Alpha Omega Alpha. Home: 29 Beacon Heights Dr Newton MA 02459-2022 Office: Mass Gen Hosp 55 Fruit St Cox-640 LH 2nd Fl Boston MA 02114-2696*

CHABON, MICHAEL, writer; b. Washington, May 24, 1963; m. Ayelet Waldman, 1993; children: Sophie, Ezekiel Napoleon, Ida-Rose, Abraham. BA, Univ. Pitts.; MFA in Creative Writing, Univ. Calif., Irvine. Author: (novels) The Mysteries of Pittsburgh, 1988, Wonder Boys, 1995 (made into feature film), The Amazing Adventures of Kavalier & Clay, 2000 (Pulitzer Prize for Fiction, 2001, Notable Book of Yr. Am. Libr. Assn., 2000), Summerland, 2002 (Mythopoeic Fantasy award for children's lit., 2003), The Yiddish Policemen's Union, 2007, (novella) The Final Solution, 2004 (Nat. Jewish Book award, 2005, Aga Khan prize for fiction Paris Rev., 2004), (short stories) Son of the Wolfman (O. Henry Prize collection, 1999, Nat. Magazine award), (collections) A Model World and Other Stories, Werewolves in Their Youth; columnist Details mag., 2005—. Home: Berkeley CA Mailing: Author Mail HarperCollins 10 E 53rd New York NY 10022

CHABOT, ELLIOT CHARLES, lawyer; b. Anniston, Ala., Mar. 29, 1955; s. Herbert L. and Aleen (Kerwin) C.; m. Christine H. Swan, July 3, 1998. BA with honors, U. Md., 1977; JD, George Washington U., 1980. Bar: D.C. 1980, U.S. Dist. Ct. D.C. 1981, U.S. Ct. Fed. Claims 1981, U.S. Ct. Internat. Trade 1981, U.S. Tax Ct. 1981, U.S. Ct. Appeals Armed Forces 1981, U.S. Temporary Emergency Ct. Appeals 1981, U.S. Ct. Appeals (D.C. cir.) 1981, U.S. Ct. Appeals (4th, 5th, 8th, 9th, 10th, 11th, fed. cirs.) 1982, U.S. Ct. Appeals (7th cir.) 1983. Applications analyst, atty., House Info. Systems U.S. Ho. of Reps., Washington, 1980-81, project leader integrated law revision and retrieval project, 1981-89, legal support project leader House Info. Sys., 1989-95, webmaster internet law libr., 1994-99, sr. sys. analyst, 1995—. Bd. dirs. Am. Revenue Assn., Rockford, Iowa, 1983—87, Threshold Services, Inc., Silver Spring, Md., 1984—89; v.p. Banor Housing Inc., Kensington, Md., 1987—88, dir., 1987—, v.p., 1990—2001, 2006—. Columnist Aspen Hill Gazette, 1987-96. Pres. Aspen Hill Civic Assn., Md., 1985—95, dir. Md., 1995—2000; adv. com. Aspen Hill Libr., Md., 1972, Md., 1986—2001, Md., 2006—; sec. Friends Aspen Hill Libr., 1994—96, dir., 1996—; chmn. Political Forum Com., 2005—; mem. exec. com. Allied Civic Group, Silver Spring, 1987—89, corr. sec., 1992—94; mem. Sta. 21 com. Kensington Vol. Fire Dept., 1989; mem. Greater Layhill Community Night Com., 1989, Aspen Hill Master Plan Citizens Adv. com., 1990—94, Wheaton Action Group, 1990—95; chmn. Wheaton Woods Recreation Ctr. Adv. Com., 1990; mem. Bauer Drive Community Ctr. Adv. Com., 1992—2002; bd. dirs. Strathmore-Bel Pre Civic Assn., 2003—; chmn. governing documents com. Bel Pre Recreational Assn., 2006—; rec. sec. Dist. 19 Dem. Club, Montgomery County, 1983—86, 2d v.p., 1986—89, 1st v.p., 1989—92; sec. Montgomery County Dem. Party, 1994—, chmn. rules com., 1994—, chmn. Internet Svcs. com., 1995—2002, mem. ballot questions adv. com., 1988—90, 1998—2004, chmn., 2006—; vice chmn. precint orgn. com. of the party opers. task force, 1991—92; area coord. Dist. 19, 1992—94, chmn. Precinct 13-43, 1987—92, treas. Precinct 13-45, 1978—85; campaign chmn. Dist. 19 Democratic Team, 1989—90, 2006—; dir. dist. 3 Montgomery Citizens Polit. Action Com., 1991—92; sec. Montgomery County United Democrats, 1997—2002; mem. Md. State Dem. Ctrl. Com., 1994—, alt. mem. exec. com., 2002—04, mem. rules com., 2003—, mem. exec. com., 2004—; vice chmn. homeless com. Temple Shalom, Chevy Chase, Md., 1992—93; pres. Parkland Community Sch. Coun., Aspen Hill, 1983—87, 1994—96, v.p., 1971—73, mem. coun., 1970—74, 1982—96; chmn. community svcs. com. Greater Wheaton (Md.) Citizens Adv. Bd., 1986—92; chmn. Ga. Ave. Men's Shelter Adv. Bd., Aspen Hill, 1989—96, Community Edn. Devel. subcom. of Citizens Adv. com. to the Interagency Coordinating Bd. for Community Use of Ednl. Facilities and Svcs., 1985—88; dist. 3 v.p. Montgomery County Civic Fedn., 1990—91; exec. com. Robert E. Peary High Sch. PTA, Aspen Hill, 1972—73, Montgomery County Coun. com. on re-use of Peary High Sch., 1986, task force to examine the regional dist. act, 1991; corr. sec. Area 2 adv. coun. Montgomery County Pub. Schs., 1972—74, adv. com. spl. edn. programs, 1974; commr. Gov.'s Commn. on Student Affairs, Md., 1976—77; legal and acctg. div. steering com. Washington Israel Bonds, 1984—86; chmn. Kensington/Wheaton Human Svcs. Area Plan Adv. Group, 1988; sec. Robert E. Peary H.S. Alumni Assn., Aspen Hill, Md., 2001—. Recipient George Washington award, George Washington U., 1980, Donald R. Spivak award Montgomery County Interagency Coordinating Bd. Community Use of Edn. Facilities and Services, 1987, Total Quality Team award Chief Adminstrv. Officer of U.S. Ho. of Reps., 1996; named One of Outstanding Young Men, U.S. C. of C., 1982, Ky. Col. Hon. Order Ky. Cols., 1967, Citizen of Yr. Greater Wheaton Citizen's Adv. Bd., 1990, One of the Federal 100 Federal Computer Week, 1994. Mem. ABA, FBA, Internat. Law Inst. (mem. faculty legis. drafting 2000—), George Washington U. Law Alumni Assn. (pres. Capitol Hill chpt. 1987-89, sec. 1985-87), Phi Alpha Delta (clk. Jay chpt. 1979-80), Omicron Delta Kappa. Home: 3501 Beret Ln Aspen Hill MD 20906-3029 Office: US Congress House Info Resources H2-646 Ford Ho Office Bldg Washington DC 20515-6165 Office Phone: 202-226-6456.

CHABOT, HERBERT L., federal judge; b. NYC, July 17, 1931; s. Meyer and Esther (Mogilansky) C.; m. Aleen Carol Kerwin, June 16, 1951; children: Elliot C., Donald J., Lewis A., Nancy Jo. BA, CCNY, 1952; LLB, Columbia U., 1957; LLM, Georgetown U., 1964. Bar: NY 1958. Staff counsel Am. Jewish Congress, 1957-60; law clk. US Tax Ct., Washington, 1961-65, judge, 1978—2001, sr. judge, 2001—. Atty. Joint Congl. Com. Taxation, 1965—78. Del. Md. Constl. Conv., 1967-68. With US Army, 1953—55. Mem. ABA, Fed. Bar Assn. Office: US Tax Ct 400 2nd St NW Washington DC 20217-0002 Office Phone: 202-521-0644.

CHABOT, STEVEN JOSEPH, congressman, lawyer; b. Cin., Jan. 22, 1953; s. Gerard Joseph and Doris Leona (Tilly) Chabot; m. Donna Daly, June 22; children: Erica, Randy. BA in Hist., Coll. William & Mary, Williamsburg, Va., 1975; JD, Salmon P. Chase Coll. Law, Highland Heights, Ky., 1978. Bar: Ohio; cert. tchr., Ohio. Tchr. St. Joseph Sch., Cin., 1975-76; atty. pvt. practice, Cin., 1978-95; mem. City Coun., Cin., 1985-90, Hamilton County Commn., Ohio, 1990-94, US Congress from 1st Ohio dist., 1995—, mem. judiciary com., mem. fgn. affairs com., ranking mem. small bus. com. Republican. Roman Catholic. Avocations: reading, spending time with family. Office: US House Reps 129 Cannon House Office Bldg Washington DC 20515-3501 Office Phone: 202-225-2216. Office Fax: 202-225-3012.

CHABRA, ANAND, public health physician, epidemiologist; b. Bukit Mertajam, Malaysia, May 16, 1966; s. Harbans L. and Lilly Chabra; m. Michelle E.D. Chabra, Mar. 25, 1995; children: Isaac, David. BA, Stanford U., 1988; MD, U. Wash., 1993; MPH, U. Calif., Berkeley, 1995. Diplomate Am. Bd. Pub. Health and Gen. Preventive Medicine. Pediatric intern U. Calif., San Francisco, 1993-94, resident preventive medicine Berkeley, 1994-96; med. epidemiologist Calif. Maternal and Child Health, Berkeley, 1996-99; maternal, child and adolescent health dir. San Mateo County, Calif., 1999—. Mem. preventive medicine resident adv. com. U. Calif. Berkeley, U. Calif. San Francisco, 1994-96, resident mem., 1998-; mem. exec. com., Calif. Perinatal Quality Care Collaborative, 1997-99; mem. Adolescent Health Collaborative, 1999-; treas. exec. com. MCAH Action, 2000-03, chair, integrated child health program com., 2002-03, pres. exec. com., 2003-04, past pres. exec. com., 2004-06; mem. communicable disease control and environ. health com., Calif. Conf. Local Health Officers, 1999-2003; mem. teen pregnancy prevention program work group Calif. Dept. Health Svcs., 2001, mem. CDC, Heasources Svcs. Adminstrn. joint adv. com. bioterrorism preparedness, 2003-04, mem. caring for Calif.'s children adv. workgroup, 2005; maternal and child health bur. Title V grant reviewer, Health Resources and Svcs. Adminstrn., Dept. HHS, 2002, mem. oral health initiative adv. com., San Francisco Found., 2006-. Mem. editl. bd., Wellness Newsletter, U. Calif., Berkeley, 1994-95; contbr. articles to profl. jours. Program svcs. com. mem., No. Calif. chpt. March of Dimes, San Francisco, 1999—2004, co-chmn. firearm safety com., 2000—03. Named a Super Star, Maternal, Child and Adolescent Health Action, 2004; recipient Outstanding Resident, Student Presentation award, Prevention 96, 1996, Celebrating Excellence in Pub. Health award, March of Dimes, 2004, SAFE KIDS Coalition award, Most Innovative award, CityMatCH, 2004; fellowship, James S. Westra Meml. Endowment, 1993, scholarship, King County Med. Soc. Aux., 1990. Fellow: Am. Coll. Preventive Medicine (mem. adolescent health com. 2002—, cons. preventative practice com. 2002—); mem.: APHA, Calif. Pub. Health Assn., Calif. Med. Assn., Am. Assn. Pub. Health Physicians (mem. adv.com. 2005—), Christian Med. Assn., Calif. Acad. Preventive Medicine (bd. dirs. 1997—2000), CityMatch, Stanford Alumni Assn. Office: San Mateo County Health Dept 225 37th Ave Rm 300 San Mateo CA 94403-4324 E-mail: achabra@co.sanmateo.ca.us.

CHABRAJA, NICHOLAS D., equipment manufacturing executive, lawyer; b. Gary, Ind., Nov. 6, 1942; BA, Northwestern U., 1964, JD, 1967. Bar: Ind. 1967, Ill. 1968. Ptnr. Jenner & Block, Chgo., 1968-97; sr. v.p., gen. counsel Gen. Dynamics Corp., 1993-94, exec. v.p., bd. dirs., 1994-97, vice chair, 1996—97, chmn., CEO, 1997—. Spl. counsel to Ho. of Reps. re-Impeachment Trial of Judge Harry E. Claiborne before U.S. Senate, 1986. Fellow Am. Coll. Trial Lawyers; mem. ABA, Ill. Bar Assn., Chgo. Bar Assn. Office: General Dynamics Corp Ste 100 2941 Fairview Park Dr Falls Church VA 22042 Office Phone: 703-876-3000.*

CHABRIA, SHIVEN B., physician, educator; s. Bansilal L. and Shobha Chabria. MD, NDMVP Med. Coll., India, 1997. Diplomate Am. Bd. Internal Medicine, 2004, Am. Bd. Geriatric Specialists, 2006, Am. Bd. Hosp. Physicians, 2006, Am. Bd. Bariatric Physicians, 2006, Am. Bd. Ethical Physicians. Resident, internal medicine Lincoln Med. and Mental Ctr., Bronx, NY, 2001—04; academic hospitalist Waterbury Hosp., Conn., 2005—; pvt. practice physician Trumbull. Clin. instr. Yale U. Sch. Medicine, New Haven. Clin. cons., appearing role (documentary) Tobacco and death: perfect together; news media clin. info. provider: Waterbury Rep. Am. Newspaper, 2006; contbr. papers in field. Active Adopt a Classroom Program, Greater Waterbury Region. Named Internal Medicine Educator of Yr., America's Registry of Outstanding Profls., 2006. Mem.: Soc. Hosp. Medicine, ACP (corr.), AMA (assoc.). Avocations: guitar, piano, calligraphy, computers. Office: Waterbury Hosp 64 Robbins St Waterbury CT Home: 46 Mill Hill Rd Southport CT 06890 Home Phone: 646-594-4828. Personal E-mail: shivenchabria@yahoo.com.

CHABROW, PENN BENJAMIN, lawyer; b. Phila., Feb. 16, 1939; s. Benjamin Penn and Annette (Shapiro) Chabrow; m. Sheila Sue Steinberg, June 18, 1961; children: Michael Penn, Carolyn Debra, Frederick Penn. BS, Muhlenberg Coll., 1959; JD, George Washington U., 1962, LLM in Taxation, 1968; postgrad. in econs., Harvard U. Bar: Va. 1963, D.C. 1964, U.S. Ct. Appeals (D.C. cir.) 1964, U.S. Tax Ct. 1964, U.S. Supreme Ct. 1966, Fla. 1972, U.S. Ct. Claims 1974, U.S. Ct. Appeals (5th and 11th cirs.) 1981, bd. cert. tax atty. Fla. tax law specialist IRS, Washington, 1961—67; tax counsel C. of C. U.S., Washington, 1967—74; pvt. practice Miami, 1974—; shareholder Wampler, Buchanan, Walker, Chabrow, Banciella, & Stanley, PA, Miami, 1993—. Pres. Forum Realty Co., Phila., Pure Poultry Enterprises, Inc., Miami, Heartland Farms of Fla., Inc.; lectr. fed. taxation Barry U. Grad. Schl. of Bus., 1977—81. Contbr. articles to profl. jours. Founding dir. The Dan Marino Found., Inc., The Melissa Inst. for Violence Prevention and Treatment, Inc., The Elier Dacal Found., Inc. Fellow: Am. Coll. Tax Counsel; mem.: ABA, D.C. Bar Assn., Va. Bar Assn., Fed. Bar Assn., Fla Bar Assn., George Washington Alumni Assn. (bd. dirs.), Muhlenberg Coll. Internat. Vis. Com., Phi Sigma Tau, Phi Alpha Delta. Office: SunTrust Internat Ctr 1 SE Third Ave Ste 1700 Miami FL 33131 Home Phone: 305-665-7800; Office Phone: 305-577-0044. Business E-Mail: pchabrow@wbwcb.com.

CHACE, JAMESON FALES, ecologist, educator; b. Fall River, Mass., Apr. 22, 1967; s. N. Jameson Chace and Eleanor Fales Hibbert, James J. Hibbert (Stepfather); m. Tara W. Prince, Aug. 13, 1994; children: Wyndom Sage, Tori Jackson. BS in Biology, Ea. Conn. State U., Willimantic, 1987—89; MA in Biol. Scis., U. Colo., Boulder, 1993—95, PhD in Biol. Scis., 1996—2001. Post-doctoral fellow Villanova U., Pa., 2001—05; asst. prof. Salve Regina U., Newport, RI, 2005—. Pres. Ctr. No. Forest Rsch., Island Pond, Vt., 2003—. Contbr. articles to profl. jours. and pubs. Mem.: Wilson Ornithol. Soc., Soc. Conservative Biology, Am. Assn. Advancement Sci., Am. Ornithologists' Union. Independent. Office: Salve Regina Univ 100 Ochre Point Ave Newport RI 02840 Home Phone: 401-294-1420; Office Phone: 401-341-3204. Business E-Mail: jameson.chace@salve.edu.

CHACE, WILLIAM MURDOUGH, former university administrator, literature educator; b. Newport News, Va., Sept. 3, 1938; s. William Emerson and Grace Elizabeth (Murdough) Chace; m. JoAn Elizabeth Johnstone, Sept. 5, 1964; children: William Johnstone, Katherine Elizabeth. BA in English, Haverford Coll., 1961; MA in English, U. Calif., Berkeley, 1963; PhD in English, U. Calif., 1968; LLD (hon.), Amherst Coll., 1990, William Coll., 1992. Instr. Stillman Coll., Tuscaloosa, Ala., 1963—64; teaching asst. U. Calif., Berkeley, 1964—66, acting instr., 1967—68; asst. prof. English Stanford U., 1968—74, assoc. prof.,

1974—80, prof., 1980, assoc. dean Sch. Humanities and Scis., 1981—85, vice provost for acad. planning and devel., 1985—88; pres. Wesleyan U., Middletown, Conn., 1988—94, Emory U., Atlanta, 1994—2003. Dir. Sun Trust Banks; cons. Hewlett-Packard, Hallmark Cards, Inc., Hawaiian Ednl. Fund, Midwestern Mgmt. Assn.; vis. prof. The Coll. Aboard the Delta Queen, 1979, 80, 82, The Coll. in Western Europe and Brit. Isles, 1985; lectr. to libr. assocs. Stanford U., 1976; lectr. 6th Internat. James Joyce Symposium, Dublin, 1977, MLAL Ann. Conv., 1977, 78, Tufts Symposium, 1978, English Conf. U. Calif., Berkeley, 1979, Eighth Internat. James Joyce Symposium, Dublin, 1982, IBM Internat. Bus. and Acad. Conf., Monte Carlo, 1984, Ezra Pound Centennial Colloquium, San Jose State U., 1985, Ann. Meeting of Assn. of Grad. Liberal Studies Programs, St. Louis, 1986, Chico State U., La. State U., 1987, U. Utah Sch. Medicine Pub. Lecture series, 1987, No. Calif. Sci. Meeting Am. Coll. Physicians, Monterey, Calif., 1987, 13th Internat. James Joyce Symposium, 1992; presenter Joyce and History conf. Yale U., 1990; spkr. Fleur Cowles Flair Symposium, U. Tex., Austin, 2000. Author: James Joyce: A Collection of Critical Essays, 1973, The Political Identities of Ezra Pound and T.S. Eliot, 1973, Lionel Trilling: Criticism and Politics, 1980, 100 Semesters: My Adventures as Student, Professor and University President and What I Learned along the Way, 2006; co-author: Graham Greene: A Revaluation, 1990; co-editor: Justice Denied: The Black Man in White America, 1970, An Introduction to Literature, 1985; co-editor: (with JoAn E. Chace) Making It New, 1972; contbr. articles to profl. jours. Home: 1325 Cowper St Palo Alto CA 94301 Office Phone: 650-329-1962. Personal E-mail: billchace@yahoo.com.

CHACKO, GEORGE KUTTICKAL, management science educator, consultant; b. Trivandrum, Kerala, India, July 1, 1930; arrived in US, 1953, naturalized, 1967; s. Geevarghese Kuttickal and Thankamma (Matthew) C.; m. Yo Yee, Aug. 10, 1957; children: Rajah Yee, Ashia Yo Chacko Lance. MA in Econs. and Polit. Philosophy, Madras U., Chennai, India, 1950; B in Commerce, St. Xavier's Coll., Calcutta, India, 1952; cert. postgrad. tng., Indian Stat. Inst., Calcutta, 1951; postgrad., Princeton U., NJ, 1953—56; PhD in Econometrics, New Sch. for Social Rsch./New School U., NYC, 1959; postdoctoral, UCLA, 1961. Asst. editor Indian Fin., Calcutta, 1951-53; comml. corr. Times of India, 1953; asst. rsch. econ. faculty Princeton U., 1953—54; cons. def. sys., computer, space, tech. sys., internat. devel. sys., assoc. math. test devel. Ednl. Testing Svc., Princeton, NJ, 1955-57; dir. mktg., mgmt. rsch. Royal Metal Mfg. Co., NYC, 1958-60; mgr. dept. ops. rsch. Hughes Semicondr. Div., Newport Beach, Calif., 1960-61; asst. prof. bus. adminstrn. UCLA, 1961-62; ops. research staff cons. Union Carbide Corp., NYC, 1962-63; mem. tech. staff Rsch. Analysis Corp., McLean, Va., 1963-65, MITRE Corp., Arlington, Va., 1965-67; lectr. Dept. Agr. Grad. Sch., 1965-67; asst. profl. lectr. George Washington U., 1965-68; sr. staff scientist TRW Sys. Group, Washington, 1967-70; profl. lectr. Am. U., 1967-70, adj. prof., 1970; vis. prof. U. So. Calif., 1970-71, prof. sys. mgmt., 1971-83, prof. sys. sci., 1983-94, prof. emeritus, 1994—; vis. prof. def. sys. Mgmt. Coll., Ft. Belvoir, Va., 1972-73; prof. mgmt. U. Pertanian/U. Putra, Selangor, Malaysia, 1996—97; prof. tech. mgmt. Malaysian Grad. Sch. Mgmt., U. Putra, 1997—2000; founder chmn. Joint MIT-MGSM Pan-Asian Program Mgmt. Tech., U. Putra, 1997—2000; chmn. to sr. adv. Ctr. Excellence Mgmt. Tech., Multimedia U. Cyberjava, Selangor, Malaysia, 2001—05; prof. mgmt. tech. Multimedia U., 2001—05; sr. cons. Profitera Corp. Malaysian Govt. Multimedia Devel. Corp. R&D Project: Electronic Enhancement Receivables Realization, Kuala Lumpur, Malaysia, 2002—03; cons. ptnr. Natl. Info. Tech. Coun., Govt. Malaysia, Kuala Lumpur, 2003—05; chmn., CEO George Chacko Mgmt. Ltd., Kuala Lumpur, Washington DC, 2003—. Cons. Hughes Semiconductor Divsn., 1961-62, Med. Svcs. Corp. Internat., vector biology and control project US Agy. Internat. Devel., 1991; prin. investigator US Nat. Sci. Found. Project: Use of Scientific and Tech. Info. in the Electronic Alternative to Paper-based Communication, 1975-76; sr. Fulbright prof., 1983-84, sr. Fulbright rsch. prof., 1984-85, Nat. Chengchi U., Taipei; prin. investigator, program dir. Tech. Transfer Project, Taiwan Nat. Sci. Coun., 1984-85; disting. fgn. expert lectr. Taiwan Ministry Econ. Affairs, 1986; sr. vis. rsch. prof. Taiwan Nat. Sci. Coun. & Nat. Chengchi U., Taipei, 1988-89, Dah-Yeh Inst. Tech., Dah-Tsuen, Chang-Hwa, Taiwan, 1993-94; vis. prof. Nat. Chengchi U., Taipei, 1993-94; v.p. program devel. Sys. and Telecom. Corp., Potomac, Md., 1987-90; chief sci. cons. RJO Enterprises, Lanham, Md., 1988-89; guest lectr. 36 Tech. Univs. throughout Asia, Europe, South America, and Africa, 1992-2006; USIA sponsored US sci. emissary Egypt, Burma, India, Singapore, 1987; USIA sponsored US expert tech. transfer and mil. conversion 1st Internat. Conf. Reconstrn. of Soviet Republics, Hanover, Germany, 1992; keynote speaker 2d Ann. Conf. Mgmt. Edn. in China, Taipei, Taiwan, 1989, World Conf. Transition to Advanced Market Economies, Warsaw, Poland, 1992, Ann. Conv. Indian Inst. Indsl. Engring., Hyderabad, India, 1993, First Sino-South Africa Bilateral Symposium Tech. Devel., Taipei, 1994, First Asia-Pacific Convention Bus. mgmt. Edn., Kuala Lumpur, 1996, Ann. Conf. Malaysian Soc. of Ops. Rsch. and Mgmt. Scis, 1997, Ann. Conf. Malaysian Inst. Accts., 2001, Biannual Regional Conf. CPA, Australia, 2001, Portland Intl. Conf. Mgmt. of Engring. and Tech., 2003; mem. internat. adv. com. restructuring strategies for electronics info. industry Asian Inst. Tech. Workshop, 1994, Technological Forecasting and Social Change, 1996—; mem. First Conv. Bus. and Mgmt. Edn., Kuala Lumpur, 1996, Asian-Pacific Conf. Mgmt. Sci., Malaysia, 1997; charter mem. Ind. US Entrepreneurs (Malaysian chpt.), 2002-05; mem. internat. adv. coun. Portland Internat. Conf. Mgmt., Engring. & Tech., 2003-; first disting. prof. Indian Inst. Mgmt., Ahmedabad, vis. 2004; prof. mgmt. tech. Multimedia U., Cyberjaya, 2001-05; pres., CEO Sanan Biotech Internat., Beijing, 2006-; spkr. in field. Columnist: The Sunday Star, Kuala Lumpur, 1998-2003, Bus. Times, Kuala Lumpur, 2003, Asian Beacon, Kuala Lumpur, 2003; translator: Mar Thoma Syrian Church Order of Holy Communion, 1956, Mar Thoma Syrian Church Order of Holy Matrimony, 1957; editor, contbr. 25 books including Management Science: Models and Techniques, 1961, Long-Range Forecasting Methodology, 1968, The Recognition of Systems in Health Services, 1969, Reducing the Cost of Space Transportation, 1969, Systems Technology Applied to Social and Community Problems, 1969, Planning Challenges of the 70s in the Public Domain, 1970, Congressional Recognition of Goddard Rockets and Space Museum, 1970, Systems Approach to Environmental Pollution, 1971, Hope for the Cities-Systems Approach to Human Needs, 1971, The Use of Modern Management Methods in the Public Administration of Developing Countries, 1972, Alternative Approaches to the National Delivery of Health Care, 1972, Health Handbook: VOL. I: Environmental Management for Improved Health Services: US, UK, Europe, 1979, VOL. II: National Organization of Health Services-U.S., USSR, China, Europe, 1979, VOL. III: Computer Augmentation of HealthService Operations: Diagnosis to Decision Making: US, Europe, Africa, Asia, Asutralia, 1979, VOL. IV: Educational Innovation in Health Services-U.S., Europe, Middle East, Africa, 1979, VOL. V: Health Indicators and Health Services Utilization-US, Europe, Middle East, Africa, 1979, Systems Approach to Strokes and Heart Diseases, 1980, Management Education in the Republic of China: Second Annual Conference, 1989, Expert Systems: 3rd Annual World Congress Proceedings, 1991, Transition to Advanced Market Economies: Strategic Options-International Federation of Operations Research Socieites Internat. Conf. Proceedings, 1992, Industrial Engineering Interfaces: Indian Nat. Conf. Proceedings, 1993, Technological Development: 1st Sino-South Africa Bilateral Symposium Proceedings, 1994, Lenten Daily Devotions, 1996, Asia Pacific Convention on Dynamism and Invention in Management Education Procs., 1996, Foundations of Game Theory, 1997; mng. editor: Jour. Astronautical Scis., 1969-75; guest editor Jour. Rsch. Comm. Studies, 1978-79; assoc. editor: Internat. Jour. Forecasting, 1982-85; mem. internat. editl. bd. Malaysian Jour. Mgmt. Scis., 1996-98, Tech. Forecasting & Social Change: An Internat. Jour., 1996-; creator: (DVD) Authentic Hatha Yoga: Discourse & Demonstration, 2006; lyricist: Crown them with Joy, O Lord their life with Peace, 1997, Country of Mine, 2000; contbr. over 410 jour. and rsch. papers and conf. presentations in field. Sole Official Youth Representative of Mar Thoma Syrian Church of India to the World Council of Churches Assembly, Evanston, IL., 1954; mem. chancel choir, 1957-59, Madison Avenue Presbyterian Ch., New York, Active Nat. Presbyn. Ch., Washington, 1967-84, mem. ch. coun., 1969-71, mem. chancel choir, 1967-84, co-dean, ch. family camp, 1977, coord. life abundant discovery groups, 1979; occasional soloist, Eighth US Army Chapel, Yongsan, Korea, 1983-84; chmn. worship com. Taipei Internat. Ch., 1984, founding dir. Intercessory Prayer Power Partnership, 1984, mem. adult choir, occasional solosit, 1983-85, 88-89, 93-96, chmn. membership com., 1985, chmn. stewardship and fin. com., 1985, chmn. com. Christian edn., 1988, Sunday Sch. supt., 1989, adult Sunday sch. leader, 1993,; adult Sunday Sch. leader 4th Presbyn. Ch., Bethesda, Md., 1986-87, mem. sanctuary choir, 1985—96; participant 9th Internat. Ch. Mus. Festival, Coventry Cathedral, 1992; mem. Men's Ensemble, 1986-93; mem. Ministry Com. Men of 4th Rep. to Session, 1990-96; founding dir. Prayer Power Partnership, 1990-96; adult Sunday sch. leader, 1996-98, Kuala Lumpur Internat. Ch.,occasional soloist, 1996-98; sr. advisor Acacia Home Fellowship, Full Gospel Assembly, Kuala Lumpur, 1998-2005; mem. chancel choir Interfaith Chapel, Leisure World, Silver Spring, Md., 2006-, Men's Chorale, 2006, occasional soloist, 2006-; charter mem. IndUS Entrepreneurs, Malaysian chpt. 2002—05; mem. internat. adv. coun. Portland Internat. Conf. on Mgmt. & Engring. & Tech., 2003-. Commendation by Princeton U. prof. Oskar Morgensternsn for Theory of Games exposition, 1950, Leonard Bernstein for review of his musical "Mass", 1971, MIT prof. Edward Roberts for superior ability tchg. mgmt. of tech.; recipient NSF Nat. Competitive Contract award on what became the Internet, 1975, Tchg. Ability award., Prof. Edward Roberts, 1997, Internat. Sci. Lectures award, NSF, 1982, Pioneer Premier Project Internat. Presdl. award Kiwanis Internat. Asia-Pacific Conf., 1986, USIA Scientific Lectures Program Award, 1987, 92, USIA citation for invaluable contbr. to America's pub. diplomacy, 1992, Commendation for 2 books US-Taiwan Technology Transfer by Presdl. Palace, Taipei, 1993; sr. Fulbright prof., Taiwan, 1983-84; sr. Fulbright rsch. prof., Taiwan, 1984-85, Taiwan Nat. Sci. Coun. Rsch. Fellowship, 1988-89; named First Disting. Prof. Indian Inst. Mgmt., Ahmedabad, 2004-, Postgrad. scholar, Indian Stat. Inst., Calcutta, 1950-1951, John A. Machkay Ecumenical fellow, Princeton Theol. Sem., 1953-1956, fellow, UCLA, 1961. Fellow AAAS (nat. coun. 1968-73, chmn. or co-chmn. symposia 1971, 72, 74, 76, 77, 78), Am. Astronautical Soc. (v.p. publs. 1969-71, editor Tech. Newsletter 1968-72, mng. editor Jour. Astronautical Scis. 1969-75), Ops. Rsch. Soc. Am. (vice-chmn. com. of representation on AAAS 1972-78, nat. coun. tech. sect. on health 1966-68, editor Tech. Newsletter on Health 1966-73); mem. Washington Ops. Rsch. Coun. (trustee 1967-69, chmn. tech. colloquia 1967-68, editor Tech. Newsletter 1967-68, Banquet chmn. 1992-93), Inst. Mgmt. Scis. (rep. to Internat. Inst. for Applied Systems Analysis in Vienna, Austria 1976-77, session chmn. Athens, Greece 1977, Atlanta 1977), World Future Soc. (editl. bd. publs. 1970-71), N.Y. Acad. Scis., Soc. Scientific Mgmt. and Ops. Rsch. (Egypt, 1st hon. fgn. mem.), Inst. for Ops. Rsch. and the Mgmt. Scis. (founding, INFORMS 1994); Kiwanis (charter 1st v.p., Life-time Hickson fellow 1995, 2003), Costa Mesa North Club (charter 1st v.p., dir.), NYC Club (chmn., internat. relations, 1962-63), Friendship Heights Club (charter pres., dir., Outstanding Svc. award 1972-73, Life award), Bethesda Club (disting. divsn. one svc. award, 1968, 70, capital dist. chmn. 1967, 69-70, 71-72, inter divsn. chmn. Green Candle of Hope Dinner, 1965-82), Capital Dist. Found. (life) 1982, Capital Dist. Founders' Soc., 2003, Taipei-Yang Ming Shan Club (charter pres., disting. dir., spl. rep. of internat. pres. and counselor to dist. of Republic of China 1983-86, Legion of Honor 1985), Bethesda Club (dir. 1967-69, 95, chmn. internat. rels. 1991-2003, chmn. hon. com.1992-2003, numerous coms. 1966—2003, nat. anthem soloist capital dist. conv. 2003), Leisure World Kiwanis Club (chmn. internat. liaision sibling rels. with Kiwanis Club of Kuala Lumpur, 2003-, 46-Year Perfect Attendance Pin, 2006), Kiwanis Club Kuala Lumpur (permanent vis. kiwanian 1996-, US nat. anthem soloist, US ambs. visit to Kuala Lumpur disvn. 2001, US nat. anthem soloist, Kiwanis Internat. (pres. visit to Malaysia dist. 2003, soloist-composer Malaysian nat. anthem in English to First Lady Malaysia 2002, Internat. Presdl. award, 1986), Kuala Lumpur Kiwanis Cir. K Club (co-founder 2004), Chinese Club of Leisure World (sec. 2004-). Republican. Presbyterian. Author: 42 books in field including India-Toward an Understanding: A de novo inquiry into the mind of India in search of an answer to the question: Will India go Communist?, 1959, International Trade Aspects of Indian Burlap-An Econometric Study, 1961, Today's Information for Tomorrow's Products-An Operations Research Approach, 1966, Studies for Public Men: Daily Reflections on the Bible and Topics for Intercessory Prayer, 1969, Applied Statistics in Decision Making, 1971, Computer Aided Decision Making, 1972, Technological Forecontrol: Prospects, Problems, and Policy, 1975, Systems Approach to Public and Private Sector Problems, 1976, Applied Operations Research/Systems Analysis in Hierarchical Decision-Making: VOL. I:Systems Approach to Public and Private Sector Problems, 1976, VOL. II: Operations Research Approach to Problem Formation and Solution, 1976, Management Information Systems, 1979, Trade Drain Imperatives of Technology Transfer: U.S.-Taiwan Concomitant Coalitions, 1985, Life Abundant: Day by Day: Daily Reflections on the Bible, and Topics for Your Intercessory Prayer, 1985, Interceding with the Infinite: Practicing Prayer Power, 1985, Robotics/Artificial Intelligence/Productivity: U.S.-Japan Concomitant Coalitions, 1986, Technology Management: Applications to Corporate Markets and Military Missions, 1988, The Systems Approach to Problem-Solving: From Corporate Markets to National Missions, 1989, Toward Expanding Exports Through Technology Transfer: IBM-Taiwan Concomitant Coalitions, 1989, Dynamic Program Management: From Defense Experience to Commercial Application, 1989, Decision-Making Under Uncertainty: An Applied Statistics Approach, 1991, Operations Research/Management Science: Case Studies in Decision Making Under Structured Uncertainty, 1993, Invoking Intercessory Prayer Power: Mediating Modern-day Miracles, 1997, Targeting Strategies for Continuous Competitiveness-Information Technology (IT) Industry in Malaysia: Operational Protocol Developed and Demonstrated in 33 Case Studies, 1998, Half-Indian, Half-Chinese, and All American, 1998, Synergizing Invention and Innovation for Missions and Markets: Operational Protocol Developed and Demonstrated in 31 Case Studies Integrating Technology and Territory within and Between Corporations and Countries, 2000, Survival Strategies of Hitech Corporations: Operational Protocol Developed and Demonstrated in 71 Case Studies Drawn from 285 years of Executive Experience in 20th Century Autobiographical Narratives, 2000, Comprehensive Strategy + TQM=Continuous Competitiveness: Operational Protocol Developed and Demonstrated in 64 Case Studies Integrating Operational Concepts of Quintet of Quality with Survival Strategies, 2001, Chief Technology Officer (CTO) Decisions to Dare for Corporate/Country Survival: Operational Protocol Developed and Demonstrated in 51 Case Studies in Anticipating, Acquiring, Adapting and Applying Unproven High Technology to Enhance Survival Chances, 2002, Chief 'Ntrepreneur Officer (CNO) Decisions to Dare for Corporate/Country Survival: Operational Protocol Developed and Demonstrated in 44 Case Studies of Forming, Dissolving, and Re-forming Coalitions to Compete and Cooperate Simultaneously on the next "New, New" Thing, 2005, Pre-PhD Proposal Preparation: Problem Formation & Formulation: 39 Real-Life Applications (14 in Physical and Bilogical Sciences and 25 in Social and Behavioral Sciences), 2004, Pre-PhD Proposal Preparation: Problem Formation & Formulation Study Guide, 2004, Internet Economy Imperatives-:VOL. I:Initiative Imperatives in the Internet Economy: US, India, Malaysia (Macro Issues): Operational Protocol Developed and Demonstrated in 22 Case Studies in Averting Structural Unemployment and in moving from Coding to Consulting, 2005, VOL. II: Integrating Imperatives in the Internet Economy (Micro Issues): Operational Protocol Developed and Demonstrated in 20 Case Studies of Forward and Backward Integration through Morphing and Supply Chain Management, 2005, Managing Unproven Technology: Concepts & Applications: 51 Case Studies of Anticipating, Acquiring, Adopting and Applying Emerging Hitech to improve the Probability of Corporate/Country Survival/Success, 2006, Managing Unproven Technology Study Guide, 2006, Disequilibria Entrepreneurship: Concepts & Applications: Operational Protocol Developed and Demonstrated in 50 Case Studies of Investing in Opportunities of Disequilibria in Emerging Hitech, 2006, Disequilibria Entrepreneurship Study Guide, 2006, Memory Management in Survival Decisions of Corporations, 1948-2003: VOL. I: Multi-Product, Multi-Service, Multi-Billion Dollar Multinationals: Operational Protocol Developed and Demonstrated in 7 Case studies of Chief Technology Officer/Chief 'Ntrepreneur Officer Decisions to Dare, 2006, VOL. II: Three Billion Dollar Success of Startups and One Failure: Operational Protocol Developed and Demonstrated in 4 Case Studies of Chief Technology Officer/Chief 'Ntrepreneur Officer Decisions to Dare, 2006; Combating Internet Obsolescence: VOL. I: Global Alliances to Acquire Unproven Technology for R&D and Co-Development: Operational Protocol Developed and Demonstrated in 8 Case Studies of Chief Technology Officer/Chief 'Ntrepreneur Officer Decisions to Dare, 2007, VOL. II: Collaborative Imagining of Non-Existent Technology for Markets and Missions: Operational Protocol Developed and Demonstrated in 6 Case Studies of Chief Technology Officer/Chief 'Ntrepreneur Officer Decisions to Dare, 2007. Originator of Game-theoretic concept (Concomitant Coalitions), 1961, Forecasting computer algorithm (Modified Exponential Smoothing-Growth Stage: MESGRO), 1982 (NSF award for international lectures on MESGRO, 1982), definition of new professions: Chief Tech. Officer, 1999, Chief Etrepreneur Officer, 2002, definition of new field: Pre-Ph.D. Proposal Preparation in Physical & Biological, Social & Behavioral Sciences, 2004. Avocations: yoga, singing, writing. *As one who was privileged to be born into a Christian family tracing itself to the founding in the year 52 of the Mar Thoma Syrian Church in Southwest India by Thomas the Doubting Disciple of Jesus Christ, I look upon the exciting encounters I have had with new ideas (such as Theory of Games) and new professions (such as Operations Research) as precious talents over which I exercise stewardship by enjoying excellence of effort and exposition toward a better tomorrow at home and abroad, as an Indian-American blest with a most supportive family.*

CHACKO, SAMUEL, association official; came to U.S., 1970; s. Chanda Pillai and Sosamma (Cheriyan) C.; m. Omana Chellimalayil George, May 21, 1979; children: Roshen Samuel, Renee Susan. BA in Econs., U. Kerala, 1963, MA in History, 1966, MA in Polit. Sci., 1968; BA in Social Sci., Olivet Nazarene U., Kankakee, Ill., 1971; MA in Comm., Govs. State U., 1974; postgrad., U. Ill., Chgo., 1981—86. Cert. in gerontology, cmty. nutrition. Dir. dept. aging Kankakee Land Community Action Agy., 1972—76; head sr. citizens dept. Oakland-Livingston Human Svcs. Agy., Pontiac, Mich., 1976—78; dir. Benton Harbor (Mich.) Area Parks and Recreation Bd., 1978—79; program analyst Ill. Migrant Coun., Chgo., 1980—84; dir. energy svcs. Community and Econ. Devel. Assn. Cook County, Inc., Chgo., 1985—2001; v.p. Cmty. and Econ. Devel. Assn. Cook County, Inc., Chgo., 2001—04. Mem. Ill. State Commerce Commn. Task Force on Rewriting Utility Svc. Rules, 1995—, Ill. State Energy Assistance Program Working Group, 1991-93. Bd. dirs. NAACP, 1973-76; bd. dirs., Ea. Ill. U. Parents Club, 2000-. Mem.: Lions Club Internat. Office: Cmty and Econ Devel Assn Cook Cty Inc 208 S Lasalle St Ste 850 Chicago IL 60604-1000

CHADEN, LEE A., apparel and former food products executive; BS in Indsl. Engring., Purdue U.; MBA, U. Calif., Berkeley. Brand mgr. Procter & Gamble, 1966—70; sr. product mgr. Playtex Apparel, Inc., 1970—74, pres., Playtex Can., 1974—76, area v.p., internat. divsn., 1976—77, v.p., gen. mgr., family products divsn., 1977—79; ptnr. Mktg. Corp. of Am., 1979—81; prin. Gen. Consumer Elecs., 1981—83; CEO Interac Corp., 1983—85; gen. ptnr. Marketcorp Ventures, 1985—91; pres., U.S. and Westfar divsns. of Playtex Sara Lee Corp., 1991—94, pres., CEO, Sara Lee Intimates, 1994—95, v.p., 1995—98, sr. v.p., 1998—99, CEO, Sara Lee Branded Apparel, 1999—2001, sr. v.p., human resources, 2001—03, exec. v.p., 2003—06, CEO, branded apparel unit, 2004—06, exec. chmn. branded apparel, 2006; exec. chmn. Hanesbrands Inc., Winston Salem, NC, 2006—. Office: Hanesbrands Inc 1000 E Hanes Mill Rd Winston Salem NC 27105

CHADICK, GARY ROBERT, lawyer; b. Manhasset, NY, June 19, 1961; s. Howard and Norma (Cohen) C.; m. Lori J. Branson, Sept. 22, 1990, children: Jonathan, Jennifer BA cum laude, Union Coll., Schenectady, 1983; JD, George Washington U., 1986. Bar: Calif. 1987, U.S. Dist. Ct. (cen. dist.) Calif. 1987, D.C. 1988, U.S. Ct. Appeals (fed. cir.) 1988, Iowa, 2002. Research and writing asst. George Washington U., Washington, 1984-85; summer assoc. Epstein, Becker, Borsody and Green, Washington, 1985; assoc. McKenna & Cuneo, LA, 1986-92; asst. gen. counsel, group counsel & divsn. counsel Litton Industries, Woodland Hills, 1992—2001; sr. v.p., gen. counsel, sec. Rockwell Collins, Inc., Cedar Rapids, 2002—. Lectr. SBA, Washington, 1985, Nat. Contracts Mgmt. Assn., Orange County chpt., L.A., 1987, Pepperdine Law Sch., 1988; in-house lectr. Terminations and Claims, 1990-91. Fed. Publs. Truth in Negotiation Act, San Jose, Calif., 1990; co-author: Cost Acctg. Standards: New Developments, 1989. Active Big Bros.-Big Sisters Program, Schenectady, 1982, United Way contbr. Mem. ABA (bus.law sec.), Nat. Contracts Mgmt. Assn., Am. Soc. Corp. Sec., Am. Corp. Counsel Assn., Nat. Assn.Stockplan Profls., Aerospace Industries Assn. (chmn. legal com. 1999-2000) Avocations: soccer referee, golf. Office: Rockwell Collins Inc 400 Collins Rd NE Cedar Rapids IA 52498*

CHADSEY, HAROLD A., astronomer, physicist; s. Harold E. and Delores G. Chadsey; m. Carol Ellen Cooper, Nov. 9, 1991. BS, Centenary Coll., 1982; MS, Am. U., 1995; PhD, Kennedy-Western U., 2001. Astronomer U.S. Naval Obs., Miami, Fla., 1985—89, Washington, 1989—2004; physicist U.S. Dept. Navy, 2004—. GPS timing Precise Time & Time Interval, 1993—2004; timing and clock adviser USCG, Alexandria, Va., 1989—2004; atomic frequency stds., 1995—2004. Author: An Automated Quality Control System for Cesium Frequency Standards, 2001. Judge HS sci. fairs DC Pub. Schs., Washington, 1991—2002, Fairfax County Pub. Schs., 1998—; mentor HS students Dept. of the Navy, U.S. Naval Obs., 2002; chmn. HSSCI Fair Grand Prize Judges, 2004—07. Named Safety Rep., Naval Dist. Washington, 2002. Mem.: No. Va. Radio Control (pres. 1997), Quantico Flying Club, El Karubah Shrine. Avocations: building and flying remote control airplanes, private pilot.

CHADWICK, CHRISTOPHER MICHAEL, military officer; b. Waco, Tex., July 20, 1981; s. Danny Paul and Linda Kathern Schonerstedt. Diploma, La Vega HS, Bellmead, Tex., 2000. Commd. lt. USMC, 2000, advanced through grades to sgt. Camp Lejeune, NC, with security L3 comm. Waco, Tex., 2006—. Decorated Sept. 11th Achievement medal US Army. Home: 508 Penton Ln Bellmead TX 76705 Office: US Marine Corps Bldg H1 2F South Camp Lejeune NC 28542 Home Phone: 254-214-0955; Office Phone: 910-451-8086. Personal E-mail: christopher.m.chadwi@usmc.mil.

CHADWICK, DEREK JAMES, foundation administrator; b. Carshalton, Surrey, Eng., Feb. 9, 1948; s. Dennis Edmund and Ida (Kay) Chadwick; m. Susan Reid, Dec. 20, 1980 (dec. May 15, 2002); children: Andrew John, Frederick Mark. BA in Chemistry, Oxford U., 1969, BSc, 1970, MA, 1972, D Philosophy, 1972. ICI fellow Cambridge U., 1972-73; Prize fellow Magdalen Coll., Oxford U., 1973-77; Royal Soc. European exch. fellow

Eidgenössische Technische Hochschule, Zurich, Switzerland, 1975-77; lectr., sr. lectr., reader Liverpool U., 1977-88; vis. prof. U. Alsace, Mulhouse, France, 1988; dir. The Ciba Found. (now named The Novartis Found.), London, 1988—. Coun. mem. Louis Jeantet Found., Geneva, 1988-98, Assn. Med. Rsch. Charities, London, 1991-2000; vice-chmn., 1994-2000; coun. mem. Coun. Ctrl. Lab. of Rsch. Couns., 2002-07; mem. steering com. Scientists Inst. for Pub. Info., N.Y.C., 1989-96; vis. prof. U. Trondheim, Norway, 1996—. Editor 60 books; author 100 papers and chpts. in sci. jours. and books. Fellow Royal Soc. Chemistry; mem. Am. Chem. Soc., Worshipful Soc. Apothecaries London, Hague Club Dirs. European Founds. (sec. 1993-97). Avocations: music, gardening, skiing. Office: The Novartis Found 41 Portland Pl London W1B 1BN England Office Phone: 44207-636-9456. E-mail: dchadwick@novartisfound.org.uk.

CHADWICK, ERIC HUGH, lawyer; b. 1968; BS, Iowa State U., 1991; JD with honors, William Mitchell Coll. Law, 1994. Bar: Minn. 1994, US Dist. Ct. (dist. Minn.), US Ct. Appeals (8th cir.), US Ct. Appeals (Fed. cir.). Law clk. to Hon. Peder B. Hong Minn. 1st Jud. Dist.; atty. trial dept. Dorsey & Whitney, L.L.P., 1996; ptnr. Patterson, Thuente, Skaar & Christensen, P.A., Mpls., 1997—. Editor: William Mitchell Law Rev. Named a Rising Star, Minn. Super Lawyers mag., 2006. Office: Patterson Thuente Skaar & Christensen PA 4800 IDS Ctr 80 S 8th St Minneapolis MN 55402 Office Phone: 612-349-5778. E-mail: chadwick@ptslaw.com.*

CHADWICK, ROBERT, lawyer, judge; b. Jackson, Miss., Apr. 5, 1924; s. Hudson and Annie (Eley) C.; m. Helen Faye Josey, Apr. 5, 1953; children: Robert Hudson, Celia, Dan, Lea Ann, Robin. BA, Auburn U., Ala., 1950; JD, Miss. Coll., Clinton, 1957; postgrad., U. So. Calif., LA, 1973, 75-76. Bar: Miss. 1963, U.S. Supreme Ct. 1970, U.S. Ct. Mil. Appeals 1975, Ky. 1980, U.S. Dist Ct. (ea. dist.) Ky. 1987. Chief regulation staff div. pesticide regulation USDA, Washington, 1965-70; atty., ecologist div. enforcement EPA, Washington, 1970-75, chmn. com. pesticide misuse rev., 1975-79; asst. gen. counsel Presdl. Clemency Bd. White House Dept. Justice, Washington, 1975; pvt. practice law Frankfort, Ky., 1980-82, 83—; law judge parole bd. Corrections Cabinet, Frankfort, 1982-83; asst. dir. div. hazardous materials Ky. Dept. Natural Resources and Environ. Protection, Frankfort, 1983—. Chmn. bd. Exis, Inc.; staff atty., gen. counsel Ky. Cabinet for Human Resources, 1989—90. Pres. PTA Oxon Hill (Md.) Jr. High Sch., 1974, Frankfort Audubon Soc., 1981-83. Cpl. U.S. Army, 1943-45. Mem. ABA, Nat. Assn. Adminstrv. Law Judges, Miss. State Bar Assn., Ky. State Bar Assn., Franklin County Bar Assn., VFW, Masons. Home and Office: 16 Ryswick Ln Frankfort KY 40601-3848

CHADWICK, SIMON, management consultant; b. Matatiele, Transkei, South Africa, Oct. 13, 1956; s. Graham Charles and Jeanne Suzanne Chadwick; m. Johnnie Crosby, Oct. 16, 1994; children: Rudi Kersten, Elizabeth, Kahren Kersten, Robert. MA, PPE, Oxford U., Eng., 1977. Mng. dir. Rsch. Internat. Specialist Units, London, 1982—85; chmn., CEO Rsch. Internat. Italia, Milan, 1986—88; vice chmn. Rsch. Internat. UK, London, 1989—90; chmn., CEO Rsch. Internat. USA, NYC, 1991—95, Winona Group, Phoenix, 1994—99; global CEO NOP World, NYC, 2000—04; mng. ptnr. Cambiar LLC, Phoenix, 2004—. Dir. MSMR program U. Tex., Arlington, 1997—2000; trustee Mktg. Sciences Inst., Cambridge, Mass., 2001—04; dir. Coun. for Am. Survey Rsch. Orgns., Port Jefferson, NY, 2001—06, chmn., 2004; presenter in field. V.p. Pointe Squaw Peak HOA, Phoenix, 2006. Fellow: Market Rsch. Soc. (bd. dirs., editl. bd. 1998—); mem.: Am. Mktg. Assn., ESOMAR, Market Rsch. Coun. Avocations: classic cars, travel, cooking. Office: Cambiar LLC 2375 E Camelback Rd Ste 500 Phoenix AZ 85016 Office Phone: 602-387-5109. Business E-Mail: simon@consultcambiar.com.

CHAE, SEUNG-HYUN, research scientist; s. Seok-Joon Chae and Oe-Soon Choi. BS cum laude, Seoul Nat. U., 2003; MS, U. Tex., Austin, 2003. Grad. level coop. IBM T.J. Watson Rsch. Ctr., Yorktown Heights, NY, 2007; grad. rsch. asst. U. Tex., Austin, 2003—. Recipient Profl. Devel. award, U. Tex., Austin, 2006; scholar, Seoul Nat. U., Republic Korea, 1996—97, 2001—02. Office: Univ Tex 10100 Burnet Rd Bldg 160 R8650 Austin TX 78758-4445 Office Phone: 512-471-8995.

CHAFE, WALLACE LESEUR, linguist, educator; b. Cambridge, Mass., Sept. 3, 1927; s. Albert J. and Nathalie (Amback) C.; m. Mary Elizabeth Butterworth, June 23, 1951 (div. 1980); children— Christopher, Douglas, Stephen; m. Marianne Mithun, Jan. 25, 1985 BA, Yale U., 1950, MA, 1956, PhD, 1958. Asst. prof. U. Buffalo, 1958-59; linguist Bur. Am. Ethnology, Smithsonian Instn., 1959-62; mem. faculty U. Calif.-Berkeley, 1962-86, prof. linguistics, 1967-86, U. Calif., Santa Barbara, 1986-91, prof. emeritus, 1991—, rsch. prof., 2003—. Author: Seneca Thanksgiving Rituals, 1961, Seneca Morphology and Dictionary, 1967, Meaning and the Structure of Language, 1970, The Pear Stories, 1980, Evidentiality, 1986, Discourse, Consciousness, and Time, 1994, The Importance of Not Being Earnest, 2007. Served with USNR, 1945-46. Mem. Linguistic Soc. Am., Am. Psychol. Assn., Am. Psychol. Soc. Office: Univ Calif Dept Linguistics Santa Barbara CA 93106 Business E-Mail: chafe@linguistics.ucsb.edu.

CHAFE, WILLIAM HENRY, history professor; b. Boston, Jan. 28, 1942; s. William Robinson and Elsie (Crabtree) C.; m. Lorna Jane Waterhouse, July 12, 1964; children: Christopher Robert, Jennifer Elizabeth. AB, Harvard U., 1962; AM, Columbia U., 1966, PhD, 1971. Instr. Columbia Grammar Sch., NYC, 1963-65, Vassar Coll., Poughkeepsie, NY, 1970-71; from asst. prof. to prof. Duke U., Durham, NC, 1971—79, prof., 1979—, Alice Mary Baldwin Disting. prof., 1988—, dean Faculty Arts and Scis., 1995—2004, vice provost undergrad. edn., 1999—2004. Author: The American Woman, 1972, Women and Equality, 1977, Civilities and Civil Rights, 1980 (R.F. Kennedy book award 1981), The Unfinished Journey, 1986, A History of Our Time, 1986, The Paradox of Change, 1991, Never Stop Running, 1993 (Sidney Hillman Found. book award 1994), The Road to Equality, 1994, Remembering Jim Crow, 2002 (Lillian Smith award, 2003), Private Lives/Public Consequences, 2005. NEH fellow, 1974-75, 84-85, Rockefeller Found. fellow, 1978, Guggenheim fellow, 1989-90; grantee Nat. Humanities Ctr., Rsch. Triangle Pk., N.C., 1981-82, Ctr. for Advanced Study, Palo Alto, Calif., 1989-90. Fellow Soc. Am. Historians; mem. Am. Hist. Assn. (chmn. nominating com., 1987-88), Orgn. Am. Historians (co-chmn. program com. 1981-82, chair nominating com. 1991, exec. bd. 1993-96, pres. 1998-99), Am. Studies Assn., So. Hist. Assn. Avocations: sailing, tennis. Office: Duke U 224 Carr Building Box 90719 Durham NC 27706 Business E-Mail: william.chafe@duke.edu.

CHAFEE, INGRID ROBERTA HOOVER COLEMAN, retired language educator; b. Evanston, Ill., Dec. 12, 1934; d. Richard Thomas and Ingrid (Krogvig) Hoover; m. Samuel Henry Coleman III, Sept. 10, 1958 (wid. Oct. 1974); children: Robert D., Charles E.; m. Nathaniel Chafee, July 8, 1989. AB, Western Coll. of Miami, Oxford, 1956; MA, U. Va., Charlottesville, 1959; PhD, Emory U., Atlanta, 1980. Part-time instr. Ga. State U., Atlanta, 1976—81; asst. prof. Morehouse Coll., Atlanta, 1981—83, 1990—95, assoc. prof., 1995—2004, acting chair dept. modern fgn. langs., 2000; ret., 2004. Tech. writer, trainer Am. Software, Inc., Atlanta, 1984-90; coord. European Program, Morehouse Ctr. for Internat. Studies, Atlanta, 1994-96; jour. referee Jour. of Assn. for W. Ga. Coll., 1996—. Contbr. articles to profl. jours. Coord. prisoner of conscience coms., Amnesty Internat., Atlanta, 1983-87. Mem. MLA, South Atlantic Modern Lang. Assn., Am. Assn. Tchrs. of French, Phi Beta Kappa. Democrat. Avocations: writing, history, films, theater, swimming. Home: 476 Princeton Way NE Atlanta GA 30307-1131 Home Phone: 404-633-0596. Personal E-mail: ingridcc@aol.com.

CHAFEE, LINCOLN DAVENPORT, political science professor, former senator; b. Warwick, RI, Mar. 26, 1953; s. John Chafee; m. Stephanie Danforth; children: Louisa, Caleb, Thea BA in Classics, Brown U., 1975; postgrad., Mont. State U. Farrier various harness racktracks; planner Gen. Dynamics, Quonset Point, RI, 1983; exec. dir. N.E. Corridor Initiative; del. RI Constnl. Conv., 1985; mem. Warwick City Coun., 1986—93; mayor City of Warwick, 1993—99; US Senator from RI, 1999—2007; disting. vis. fellow Thomas J. Watson Jr. Inst. Internat. Studies, Brown U., Providence, 2007—. Mem. com. environment and public works US Senate, com. fgn. relations, com. homeland security and govt. affairs. Recipient Fiscal Responsibility award, Concord Coalition, 2003, Congressional award, Nat. Breast Cancer Coalition, 2004. Republican. Episcopalian. Office: Watson Inst for Internat Studies 111 Thayer St Box 1970 Providence RI 02912 Office Phone: 202-224-2921, 401-453-5294.*

CHAFEL, JUDITH ANN, education educator; b. Rochester, NY, Apr. 8, 1945; d. James Arthur and Florence Joan (Santangelo) Chafel. AB, Vassar Coll., 1967; MSEd, Wheelock Coll, 1971; PhD, U. Ill., 1979. Cert. elem. tchr., Mass., N.J., N.Y. Tchr. Spruce St. Sch., Lakewood, NJ, 1972-74, Sodus (N.Y.) Primary Sch., 1974-76; grad. research and teaching asst. U. Ill., Urbana, 1976-79; vis. asst. prof. U. Tex., Austin, 1979-80; asst. prof. dept. curriculum and instrn. Ind. U., Bloomington, 1980-86, assoc. prof., 1986—2001, prof., 2001—; mem. profl. staff U.S. Ho. Reps., Washington, 1989-90. Adj. assoc. prof. philanthropic studies Ctr. on Philanthropy, 1991-2001; reviewer Hist. Publs. and Records Commn., Nat. Archives, Washington, 1979, Little, Brown and Co., Boston, 1982-84, Office for Ednl. Rsch. and Improvement, US Dept. Edn., 1991, 93. Mem. editl. adv. bd. Early Child Devel. and Care, 1985—, Youth and Soc., 1995-2005, Jour. of Poverty: Innovations on Social, Political and Economic Inequalities, 1998—; cons. editor Early Childhood Rsch. Quar., 1988-91, 92-95, 2005—; contbr. editor Am. Jour. of Orthopsychiatry, 2000—; reviewer, book editor; contbr. articles to profl. jours.; contbr. chapts. to books. Proffitt Endowment grantee, Ind. U., 1982, 88, 1998, Ctr. on Philanthropy grantee, 1991, Spencer Found. grantee, 1985, 98; Congl. Sci. fellow Soc. Rsch. in Child Devel., 1989. Mem. Soc. Rsch. in Child Devel. (program com. 1986, 92), Am. Ednl. Rsch. Assn. (program com. various yrs., nominations com. 1986, 88, chair 1993-95, mem.-at-large spl. interest group on early edn. and child devel. 1991-93), Nat. Assn. Edn. Young Children, Assn. Childhood Edn. Internat. (pub. com. 1982-84, bull. and pamphlets rev. editor jour. 1982-84, rsch. com. 1984-88), Nat. Soc. for the Study of Edn.

CHAFETZ, BARRY RICHARD, lawyer; b. Chgo., Dec. 16, 1946; s. David and Mildred (Dick) C.; m. Frances Therese Gawel, Apr. 2, 1968; children: Rochelle, Robyn, Ronald. BS, U. Ill., 1969, JD, 1972. Bar: Ill. 1972, U.S. Dist. Ct. (no. and cen. dists.) Ill. Asst. state atty., Mt. Vernon, Ill., 1972-74; assoc. Delano Law Offices, Springfield, Ill., 1975-80, Heller & Morris, Chgo., 1980, Leonard M. Ring & Assocs., Chgo., 1981-94; ptnr. Corboy & Demetrio, Chgo., 1994—. Mem. ABA, Ill. Bar Assn., Assn. Trial Lawyers Am., Ill. Trial Lawyers Assn. Office: 21st Fl 33 N Dearborn St Fl 21 Chicago IL 60602-3102 Home: 6338 Clarendon Hills Rd Willowbrook IL 60527-2133 Office Phone: 312-346-3191. E-mail: brc@corboydemetrio.com.

CHAFFEE, PAUL CHARLES, newspaper editor, publisher; b. Racine, Wis., Aug. 10, 1947; s. Raymond Russell and Ellen Mary (Tiles) C.; m. Bonnie Louise Burmeister, Aug. 9, 1969. BA in Journalism, U. Minn., 1969. Reporter Grand Rapids (Mich.) Press, 1969-79, asst. met. editor, 1979-81; met. editor Saginaw (Mich.) News, 1981-88, editor, 1988—, pub., 2006—. Founding mem. adv. bd. dept. journalism Ctrl. Mich. U., Mt. Pleasant, 1987—, pres. bd. publs., 2004—; past mem. Hispanic adv. bd. dept. journalism Mich. State U.; past pres. bd. dirs. Mich. AP Editl. Assn.; past bd. dirs. Mid Am. Press Inst. Bd. dirs. Salvation Army, Saginaw, 1986—, St. Charles Cmty. Schs. Found., Mich., 1994—, Westlund Child Guidance Clinic, 1995-99, Saginaw Bay Symphony, 1996—, Saginaw Cmty. Found.; steering bd. Leadership Saginaw; adv. bd. Saginaw County Jr. League; past steering com. Bridge Ctr. Racial Harmony; bd. fellows Saginaw Valley State U. Mem.: Nat. Assn. Hispanic Journalists, Soc. Profl. Journalists, Am. Soc. Newspaper Editors, Saginaw Country Club. Avocation: gardening. Office: Saginaw News 203 S Washington Ave Saginaw MI 48607-1283

CHAFFEE, PHILIP, retired military officer, retired small business owner; b. Erie, Pa., Dec. 18, 1933; s. Frank and Nora Chaffee; m. Reva Irene Grover, Nov. 5, 1955; children: Linda Karen, Carol Reneé. BA in Natural Sci., Colgate U., Hamilton, NY, 1955; MS in Engring. Adminstrn., Syracuse U., NY, 1966. Commd. 2d lt. USAF, 1955, advanced through grades to col., 1977, pilot Goldsboro, NC, 1957—58, instr. pilot Greenville, Miss., 1958—65, Chandler, Ariz., 1958—65, aircraft commdr. Vietnam, 1967, configuration mgr. F-4 program Washington, 1967—72, chief F-4 program office Bonn, Germany, 1972—76, dir. engring. E-3A program Burlington, Mass., 1976—79; owner, operator Ye Old eBook Shoppe, Corry, Pa., 1980—91; ret. Dir. small bus. divsn. Corry C. of C., 1982—85; chmn. adv. bd. Salvation Army, Corry, 1988—2006; chmn. zoning variance bd. Corry City Govt., 1992—2006. Decorated DFC with oak leaf cluster USAF, Air medal with 14 oak leaf clusters, Rep. of Vietnam Armed Forces Honor medal, Vietnam Svc. medal, Joint Svc. Commendation medal, Legion of Merit. Avocations: golf, bowling, model building, caneing furniture. Home: 1267 N Center St Corry PA 16407

CHAFFERS, JAMES A., architect, educator; b. Nov. 1941; BArch magna cum laude, So. U., 1964; MArch, U. Mich, Ann Arbor, 1969; DArch, U. Mich., Ann Arbor, 1971; postdoctoral student in Design Mgmt., Stanford U. Terman Engring. Ctr., Calif., 1980—81. Lic. arch., Mich., La., Nat. Coun. Archtl. Registration Bds. Prof. architecture U. Mich., Ann Arbor, 1979—; pres., design prin. J. Chaffers - Arch., Ann Arbor. Dir. Villa Corsi-Salviati Design Studio, Florence, Italy, Taubman Coll. West African Studio, Accra and Kumasi, Ghana. Founder Detroit - Ann Arbor Workshop, 1973—98. Capt. Corps of Engrs. US Army, 1964—68, Europe and Vietnam. Named Educator of Yr., Mich. Colls. and Univs., Archtl. Studies Found., Lansing, Mich., 1995. Fellow: AIA (mem. environ. edn. and urban design coms., AIA Mich. Pres.'s award 2006); mem.: Mich. Acad. Sci., Arts & Letters, Assn. Collegiate Schs. Architecture, Mich. Soc. Archs. Office: A Alfred Taubman Coll Architecture + Urban Planning 2000 Bonisteel Blvd Ann Arbor MI 48109-2069 Office Phone: 734-936-0213. E-mail: chaffers@umich.edu.*

CHAFFIN, CEÁN, producer; b. June 26, 1957; Prodr.: (films, with Steve Golia) The Game, 1997, Fight Club, 1999; (films) Panic Room, 2002, Zodiac, 2007; actor: Lords of Dogtown, 2005. Recipient Grammy award Best Music Video-Short Form, 1995, 1996. Office: Anonymous Content 8522 National Blvd Ste 101 Culver City CA 90232-2454*

CHAFFIN, DON BRIAN, industrial engineering educator, research director; b. Sandusky, Ohio, Apr. 17, 1939; m. 1966; 3 children. B of Indsl. Engring., Gen. Motors Inst., 1962; MS in Indsl. Engring., U. Toledo, 1964; PhD in Engring., U. Mich., 1967. Registered profl. engr., Ohio; cert. prof. ergonomist. Quality ctrl. engr. New Departure Divsn. GM Corp., Ohio, 1960-62, inspection foreman Ohio, 1962-63; project engr. Micrometrical Divsn. Bendix Corp., Mich., 1963-64; asst. prof. phys. medicine U. Kans., 1967-68, asst. prof. indsl. engring., 1968-70, assoc. prof. indsl. engring., 1970-77; prof. indsl. and ops. engring. U. Mich., Ann Arbor, 1977-93, dir. Ctr. for Ergonomics, 1980-97, Disting. Univ. prof. and Johnson prof. indsl. engring. and biomed. engring., 1993—. Fellow AAAS, Human Factors Soc. (Paul Fitts award 1992), Am. Indsl. Hygiene Assn. (Edward Baier award 1994), Ergonomics Soc., Am. Inst. Med. and Biol. Engring.; mem. NSPE, NAE, Am. Inst. Indsl. Engrs. (Baker Disting. Rschr. award 1991), Am. Soc. Biomechanics (Borrelli award), Sigma Xi. Achievements include research on effects and applications of electromyography for measuring human performance, concepts of biomechanics for injury prevention in skeletal-muscle system; expanding the teaching of physiological, neurological and anatomical concepts related to the simulation of human motions and exertions in the design of operated systems in manufacturing and service organizations, and in vehicle operation and maintenance. Office: U Mich Ctr Ergonomics 1656 IOE Bldg Ann Arbor MI 48109-2117

CHAFKIN, RITA M., retired dermatologist; b. NYC, Apr. 11, 1929; d. Joseph and Dora (Winslow) Melnick; m. Samuel Chafkin, June 29, 1952; children: Elise Ceil Perkins, Marc David Chafkin (dec.). BA, NYU, 1949; MD, NYU Med. Sch., 1953; cert. in dermatology, NYU Postgrad. Med. Sch., 1957. Diplomate Am. Acad. Dermatology, 1959. Intern in internal medicine Kings County Hosp., Bklyn., 1953-54; dermatology resident Bellevue Hosp., NYC, 1954-55; postgrad. trainee NYU Postgrad. Med. Sch., 1955-56, fellow in dermatology, 1956-57; precepteeship with Dr. Marion Sulzberger; pvt. practice dermatology Modesto, Calif., 1958—94; ret., 1994; assoc. clin. prof. dermatology U. Calif., Davis, 1975-97. Clinic dir. dermatology Stanislavs County Med. Ctr., Modesto, 1958-97. Artist in mixed media. Bd. dirs. Stanislaus County Med. Ctr. Found., 1982-97, pres. 1984-85. Recipient Tchr. of the Yr. award Stanislaus County Med. Ctr., Modesto, 1988, Founder's Dinner honoree, 1992. Fellow Am. Acad. Dermatology; mem. AMA, Calif. Med. Soc., San Francisco Dermatology Soc., Stanislaus County Med. Soc. (pres. 1983-84), Pacific Dermatology Assn. (fin. com. 1959—). Jewish.

CHAGANTI, RAJU S., geneticist, educator, researcher; b. Samalkot, Andhra, India, Mar. 12, 1933; came to U.S., 1960. s. Sanyasi Raju and Seetasiromani (Vallury) C.; m. Seeta Ramam Kurada, Aug. 20, 1966; children: Seeta, Sara. BS with honors, Andhra U., 1954, MS, 1955; PhD, Harvard U., 1964. Diplomate Am. Bd. Med. Genetics. Mem. Med. Rsch. Coun. Radiobiology Unit, Harwell, Berkshire, England, 1967—71; rsch. assoc. N.Y. Blood Ctr., NYC, 1971—73, assoc. investigator, 1973—76; asst. prof. Meml. Sloan-Kettering Cancer Ctr., NYC, 1976—83, assoc. prof., 1983—87, prof., 1987—, William E. Snee chair NYC, 1995—. Profl. assoc. N.Y. Hosp., N.Y.C., 1979—; founder, bd. dirs. Cancer Genetics, Inc., Hackensack, N.J. Editor: Genetics in Clinical Oncology, 1985; contbr. articles to profl. jours. Recipient research awards NIH, Nat. Cancer Inst., 1979—. Fellow AAAS, Am. Coll. Med. Genetics; mem. Am. Soc. Human Genetics, Harvey Soc. Achievements include research in the genetic basis of cancer development. Home: 235 Pascack Rd Hillsdale NJ 07642 Office: Meml Sloan-Kettering Cancer Ctr 1275 York Ave New York NY 10021-6094 Office Phone: 212-639-8121. Business E-Mail: chagantr@mskcc.org.

CHAGARES, MICHAEL ARTHUR, federal judge; b. Pitts., May 1, 1962; m. Margaret M. Chagares; 4 children. BA, Gettysburg Coll., 1984; JD, Seton Hall U., 1987. Bar: NJ 1987. Law clk. to Hon. Morton I. Greenberg US Ct. Appeals (3rd Cir.), 1987—88, judge, 2006—; atty. McCarter & English, 1988—90; asst. US atty. Dist NJ US Dept. Justice, 1990—2004, dir. affirmative civil enforcement unit, 1996—99, chief civil divsn., 1999—2004; ptnr. Cole, Schotz, Meisel, Forman & Leonard, P.A., Hackensack, NJ, 2004—06. Adj. prof. law Seton Hall U., 1991—; hearing officer 9/11 Compensation Fund. Trustee Fed. Bar State NJ. Mem.: Lawyers Adv. Com., US Dist. Ct., NJ, NJ State Bar Assn. (chair, Fed. Practice & Procedure Sect. 1998—2000). Office: US Ct Appeals 601 Market St Philadelphia PA 19106 also: US Courthouse 50 Walnut St Newark NJ 07101*

CHAGNON, KATHLEEN, lawyer; BA with honors, Stanford U., 1981; JD, Columbia U., 1985. Assoc. O'Melveny & Myers, Washington, 1985—89, Hogan & Harlson, Balt., 1989—94; asst. v.p., assoc. group counsel USF&G Corp., 1996—98; v.p., corp. group gen. counsel St. Paul Cos., Inc., 1999—2003; v.p., gen. counsel, corp. sec. Constellation Energy, Balt., 2002—05; with Saul Ewing LLP; ptnr. DLA Piper, Balt., 2006—. Office: DLA Piper 6225 Smith Ave Baltimore MD 21209-3600 Office Phone: 410-580-4109. Office Fax: 410-580-3001. E-mail: kathleen.chagnon@dlapiper.com.*

CHAGPAR, ANEES BAHADURALI, surgeon; b. Toronto, Ont., Can., Dec. 8, 1971; MS; MD, U. Alberta, 1996. Intern U. Saskatchewan, Saskatoon, Canada, 1996—97, resident, 1997—2002; fellow U. Tex. MD Anderson, Houston, 2002—03; surgeon U. Louisville Hosp., Louisville, Norton Health Care, Louisville, Jewish Hosp., Louisville; asst. prof. surg. oncology U. Louisville, Louisville; dir. Multidisciplinary Breast Clin. James Graham Brown Cancer Ctr. Recipient Leadership award (Young Physician), AMA Found., 2006. Mem.: Surgeons Can., Royal Coll. Physicians, Soc. Surg. Oncology, Am. Soc. Breast Surgeons, Am. Soc. Clin. Oncology, Am. Assn. Cancer Rsch., Am. Coll. Surgeons (Oncology Group). Office: Univ Louisville Ste 312 315 East Broadway Louisville KY 40202 Office Phone: 502-629-6950. Office Fax: 502-629-3183. E-mail: abchag01@louisville.edu.

CHAGULA, PAUL MACHIYA, information technology executive, consultant; b. Dar es Salaam, Tanzania, July 16, 1969; s. Wilbert Kumalija and Jane (Ubwe) C.; m. Aug. 1, 1993; 1 child, James M. Student, Westchester Bus. Inst., White Plains, NY, 1988—90. Troubleshooting asst., operational mgr. Bloomingdale's Inc., White Plains, 1990-91; pres. PC Courier Svc., Mt. Vernon, N.Y., 1991—; co-founder, v.p. J&P Cleaning Svc., Mt. Vernon, 1994—; founder, chmn., CEO, Tangible Techs. Internat. Inc., Bronx, N.Y., 1997—. Cons. Tanzania C. of C., Dar es Salaam, 1994-96; copy cons. Kinko's Inc., Mt. Kisco, N.Y. Advisor Tanzania Am. Assocs., N.Y.C., 1992-93, Chama Cha Mapinduzi, revolutionary party, Dar es Salaam, 1994, Govt. of Tanzania, N.Y.C., 1996. Avocation: writing. Home: 56 Sheridan Ave Apt 4C Mount Vernon NY 10552-2525 Personal E-mail: chagula@hotmail.com.

CHAHINE, MOUSTAFA TOUFIC, atmospheric scientist; b. Beirut, Jan. 1, 1935; s. Toufic M. and Hind S. (Tabbara) C.; m. Marina Bandak, Dec. 9, 1960; children: Tony T., Steve S. BS, U. Wash., 1956, MS, 1957; PhD, U. Calif., Berkeley, 1960. With Jet Propulsion Lab., Calif. Inst. Tech., Pasadena, 1960—, mgr. planetary atmospheres sect., 1975—, sr. research scientist, mgr. earth and space scis. div., 1978-84, chief scientist, 1984—2001. Vis. scientist MIT, 1969-70; vis. prof. Am. U., Beirut, 1971-72; regent's lectr. UCLA, 1989-90; mem. NASA Space and Earth Sci. Adv. Com., 1982-85; mem. climate rsch. com. Nat. Acad. Scis., 1985-88, bd. dirs. atmospheric scis. and climate, 1988—; chmn. sci. steering group Global Energy and Water Cycle Experiment World Meteorol. Orgn., 1988-99; cons. U.S. Navy, 1972-76 Contbr. articles to profl. jours. Recipient medal for exceptional sci. achievements NASA, 1969, NASA Outstanding Leadership medal, 1984, William T. Pecora award, 1989, Jule G. Charney award, 1991, Losey Atmospheric Scis. award AIAA, 1993, NASA Exceptional Achievement medal, 2000, William Nordberg medal Com. on Space Rsch., 2002, NASA Exceptional Achievement medal, 2007. Fellow AAAS, Am. Geophys. Union, Am. Phys. Soc., Royal Soc., Am. Meteorol. Soc.; mem. Internat. Acad. Astronautics, Sigma Xi. Office: 4800 Oak Grove Dr Pasadena CA 91109-8001 Office Phone: 818-354-6057. Business E-Mail: chahine@jpl.nasa.gov.

CHAHINIAN, A(RAM) PHILIPPE, oncologist; b. Paris, June 21, 1942; came to U.S., 1974; m. Marjorie Ellen; 1 child, Michael J. B., Buffon Coll., Paris, 1960; MD, Paris U., 1969. Diplomate Am. Bd. Internal Medicine, Am. Bd. Med. Oncology. Intern, resident Paris Univ. Hosps., France, 1968-74; fellow noeplastic diseases Mt. Sinai Sch. Medicine, NYC, 1974-76, asst. prof., 1976-79, assoc. prof., 1980-88; prof. clin. medicine

Coll. Physicians and Surgeons Columbia U., NYC, 1990-92; prof. dept. medicine Mt. Sinai Sch. Medicine, NYC, 1995—, prof., 1995—. Adj. prof. dept. neoplastic diseases Mt. Sinai Sch. Medicine, N.Y.C., 1992-95. Author: Lung Cancer, 1976; author (with others) of books; contbr. articles to profl. jours. Lt. Med. Corps, French Army, 1970. Rsch. grantee Nat. Cancer Inst., 1984. Fellow Am. Coll. Physicians; mem. Am. Soc. Clin. Oncology, Am. Assn. Cancer Rsch., Am. Fedn. Clin. Rsch., N.Y. Acad. Scis. Achievements include research in treatment of various cancers including lung cancer, asbestos related cancers, and mesothelioma by transplantation of human cancers into mice. Office: Mt Sinai Sch Medicine Dept NeoPlastic 1 Gustave L Levy Pl New York NY 10029-6500 Office Phone: 212-241-0484.

CHAHOUD, GEORGES, medical educator, preventive medicine physician; b. Aleppo, Syria, Mar. 17, 1973; s. Elias Chahoud and Madelaine Moussalli; m. Rime Azrak, May 30, 1999; children: Elias Georges, Marc Cesar. BS, St. Gregory's Secondary Sch., Aleppo, Syria, 1990; MD, Aleppo U. Sch. Medicine, Syria, 1996. Diplomate Internal Medicine Am. Bd. Internal Medicine, 2002, Cardiovascular Medicine Am. Bd. Internal Medicine, 2005, Certification Bd. Nuc. Cardiology, 2005, cert. Comprehensive Adult Echocardiography Nat. Bd. Echocardiography, 2005. Asst. prof. internal medicine U. Ark. for Med. Scis., Little Rock, 2005—. Co-dir. heart failure and transplantation program U. Ark. for Med. Scis., 2005—; dir. non-invasive cardiology Ctrl. Ark. Vets. Health Care Sys., 2006—. Recipient Superior/Outstanding Performance in Clin. Medicine award, St. Louis U. Hosp., 2000, Physician's Recognition award, AMA, 2002—05, 3d Ann. Profl. Recognition award, Cardiology Fellows Forum of Excellence, 2003. Mem.: Internat. Soc. Heart and Lung Transplantation, Nat. Arab-Am. Med. Assn. (Ark. Chpt.) (sec., treas. 2006—), Am. Soc. Echocardiography, Am. Heart Assn. (mem., coun. on clin. cardiology), Am. Coll. Cardiology. Roman Catholic. Achievements include research in sleep disorders and depression in patients with heart failure; statin use in patients with non-ischemic cardiomyopathy. Office: U Ark 4301 W Markham St Little Rock AR 72205 Home Phone: 501-247-8126; Office Phone: 501-603-1267. Office Fax: 501-686-8319.

CHAI, NELSON J., stock exchange executive; b. June 16, 1965; married; 2 children. BA, U. Pa.; MBA, Harvard U. Various fin. and strategy positions Pepsi-Cola Co., Philip Morris Cos., Inc.; gen. mgmt. and sr. fin. positions AlliedSignal Inc., 1995—97; corp. v.p. worldwide field fin. to sr. v.p. bus. devel., mem. exec. com. Dade Behring, Inc., 1997—2000; CFO Archipelago Holdings, Inc., Chgo., 2000—06, NYSE Group, Inc., NYC, 2006—07, NYSE Euronext, NYC, 2007—. Bd. dirs. UNICEF, Chgo. Office: NYSE Euronext 11 Wall St New York NY 10005*

CHAI, WINBERG, political science professor, foundation administrator; b. Shanghai, Oct. 16, 1932; came to U.S., 1951, naturalized, 1973; s. Ch'u and Mei-en (Tsao) C.; m. Carolyn Everett, Mar. 17, 1966 (dec. 1996); children: Maria May-lee, Jeffrey Tien-yu. Student, Hartwick Coll., 1951-53, LittD, 2002; BA, Wittenberg U., 1955; MA, New Sch. Social Rsch., 1958; PhD, NYU, 1968; DHL, Wittenberg U., 1997; DL, Hartwick Coll., 2002. Lectr. New Sch. Social Rsch., 1957-61; vis. asst. prof. Drew U., 1961-62; asst. prof. Fairleigh Dickinson U., 1962-65, U. Redlands, 1965-68, assoc. prof., 1969-73, chmn. dept., 1970-73; prof., chmn. Asian studies CCNY, 1973-79; disting. prof. polit. sci., v.p. acad. affairs, spl. asst. to pres. U. S.D., Vermillion, 1979-82; prof. polit. sci., dir. internat. programs U. Wyo., Laramie, 1988—. Chmn. Third World Conf. Found., Inc., Chgo., 1982—; pres. Wang Yu-fa Found., Taiwan, 1989—; exec. editor Asian Affairs, 1997-. Author: (with Ch'u Chai) The Story of Chinese Philosophy, 1961, The Changing Society of China, 1962, rev. edit., 1969, The New Politics of Communist China, 1972, The Search for a New China, 1975; editor: Essential Works of Chinese Communism, 1969; (with James C. Hsiung) Asia in the U.S. Foreign Policy, 1981; (with James C. Hsiung) U.S. Asian Relations: The National Security Paradox, 1983; (with Carolyn Chai) Beyond China's Crisis, 1989, In Search of Peace in the Middle East, 1991; (with Cal Clark) Political Stability and Economic Growth, 1994, China Mainland and Taiwan, 1994, rev. edit. 1996, Hong Kong Under China, 1998; editor: Saudi Arabia: A Modern Reader, 2005; co-editor: (with May-lee Cai) China = A to Z, 2007; co-translator: (with Ch'u Chai) A Treasury of Chinese Literature, 1965; co-author (with May-Lee-Chai) The Girl from Purple Mountain, 2001, China A to Z, 2007. Haynes Found. fellow, 1967, 68; Ford Found. humanities grantee, 1968, 69, Pacific Cultural Found. grantee, 1978, 86, NSF grantee, 1970, Hubert Eaton Meml. Fund grantee, 1972-73, Field Found. grantee, 1973, 75, Henry Luce Found. grantee, 1978, 80, S.D. Humanities Com. grantee, 1980, Pacific Culture Fund grantee, 1987, 90-91. Mem. AAAS, AAUP, NAACP, Am. Polit. Sci. Assn., Am. Assn. Chinese Studies (pres.1978-80), N.Y. Acad. Scis., Internat. Studies Assn. Democrat. Home: 1071 Granito Dr Laramie WY 82072-5045 Office: Univ Wyoming Dept 3197 1000 E University Ave Laramie WY 82071-4098 Office Phone: 307-766-6771. Personal E-mail: winbergchai@aol.com. *Born in China and educated in the United States, I feel privileged to have experienced two rich cultures. My goals include promoting better understanding of all cultures and peoples.*

CHAIDARUN, SUSHELA SONGTANIN, endocrinologist, researcher; b. Sawankaloke, Sukhothai, Thailand, Apr. 13, 1963; arrived in U.S., 1994; d. Kittisak and Kanitha Songtanin; m. Sumet Chaidarun; children: Arthur Nachapon, Leo Pirapon, Tricia Tanyawan. MD, Chulalongkorn U., 1988; PhD, U. Birmingham, Eng., 1994; postgrad., Harvard U., 1994—98. Bd. certified internal medicine Am. Bd. Internat. Medicine, bd. certified endocrinology & metabolism. Postdoctoral rsch. fellow Mass. Gen. Hosp./ Harvard Med. Sch., Boston, 1994—98; med. resident internal medicine St. Vincent Hosp./Worcester Med. Ctr., U Mass. Med. Sch., Worcester, 1998—2001; endocrine clin. fellow U. Va. Health Sys., Charlottesville, 2001—03. Rsch. fellow /assoc. Harvard Med. Sch., Boston, 1994—98. Contbr. articles to profl. jours. Grantee Travel grant, Am. Endocrine Soc./Women in Endocrinology, 1996. Mem.: AMA, ACP (Med. Jeopardy Championship award Mass. chpt. 2000), Am. Assn. Clin. Endocrinologists, Am. Diabetes Assn., Am. Endocrine Soc. Avocations: travel, swimming, cooking, piano, music. Office: Walla Walla Clin 55 W Tietan St Walla Walla WA 99362 Office Phone: 509-525-3720. Personal E-mail: schaidarun@hotmail.com. Business E-Mail: sushelac@wallawallaclinic.com.

CHAIFETZ, DAVID HARVEY, lawyer; b. Worcester, Mass., Nov. 6, 1942; s. Harry and Gertrude (Katz) C.; m. Edith Jakubs; children: Rosalyn, Pamela, Matthew. BS in Bus. Adminstrn., Clark U., 1965; JD, Boston Coll., 1968. Bar: Mich. 1968, U.S. Dist. Ct. (ea. dist.) Mich. 1968, U.S. Supreme Ct., 1995. Staff atty. Chrysler Corp., Highland Park, Mich., 1968-75; div. atty. Union Carbide Corp., NYC, 1975-77, sr. div. atty., 1978-81, group counsel Danbury, Conn., 1981-85, asst. gen. counsel, 1985-92; gen. counsel Union Carbide Indsl. Gases Inc., Danbury, 1988-92; v.p., gen. counsel, sec. Praxair, Inc., Danbury, 1992—2004; mem. Town of Fairfield (Conn.) Police and Fire Retirement Bd., 2000—05. Bd. dirs. Conn. Legal Svcs., Middlebury, Bridgeport Jewish Com. Found., Movo Mobile LLC, Sarasota, Fla., 2006; mem. Am. Israel Pub. Affairs Com., 2002—; trustee Clark U., 2006- Trustee US China Legal Coop. Fund, 1998—2002, Sarasota Opera Assn., 2007—. Mem. ABA, Mich. State Bar, Conn. Bus. and Industry Assn. (bd. dirs. 1999-2003), Corp. Bar Assn. (chmn. pro bono com. 1990-93), Westchester-Fairfield Corp. Counsel Assn. (pres. 1988-89, bd. dirs. 1984-90), Coun. Chief Legal Officers (conf. bd. 1997-2004). Avocations: golf, travel.

CHAIFETZ, MARSHAL LAWRENCE, educational consultant, educator; b. Stamford, Conn., Jan. 29, 1973; s. Alan Marvin Chaifetz, Rose Janet Aschkanozy and Kenneth Blitz (Stepfather). BA, Ind. U., 1994, JD, 1997. Regional rep. Law Sch. Admission Coun., Newtown, Pa., 1997—99; dir. upward bound project Ind. U., Bloomington, 1999—; lectr., 2001—. Freelance computer cons., Bloomington, 1991—; grant reader US Dept. Edn., Washington, 2000—; ednl. cons., Bloomington, 2004—. Editor (reviewer): Grant Writing: Strategies for Developing Winning Proposals, 2002, Test Development: Guidelines, Practical Suggestions and Examples, 2001, Body Language: An Illustrated Introduction for Teachers, 2005, Body Language on the Job, 2006. Panel mem. consumer adv. panel Delta Airlines, Atlanta, 2003. Louis Stokes Alliance Minority Participation Program grant, US Dept. Edn., 2002—, Upward Bound Expansion Initiative grant, 2003—, Upward Bound grant, 2004—. Independent. Jewish. Home: 3209 E 10th St Apt I 2 Bloomington IN 47408 Office: Indiana Univ Upward Bound Project Smith Rsch Ctr Ste 100 Bloomington IN 47408 Home Phone: 812-330-1246. Personal E-mail: marshalchaifetz@gmail.com. Business E-Mail: mchaifet@indiana.edu.

CHAIKEN, BERNARD HENRY, internist, gastroenterologist; b. Bklyn., Oct. 14, 1927; s. Max and Esther (Golland) C.; m. Mildred Gilbert, Dec. 5, 1950; children: Barry Glenn, Caryl Joy Gordon. Student, NYU, 1944-45; MD, U. Tex., Dallas, 1949. Diplomate Am. Bd. Internal Medicine, subspecialty Bd. Gastroenterology. Intern Boston City Hosp., 1949-50; resident physician Cushing VA Hosp., Framingham, Mass., 1950-51, Phila. VA Hosp., 1953-54; staff physician VA Hosp. Dallas, 1954-55, VA Hosp., East Orange, NJ, 1955-56; attending physician Overlook Hosp., Summit, NJ, 1956—, St. Barnabas Med. Ctr., Livingston, NJ, 1956—. Vis. fellow Hosp. of U. Pa., Phila., 1954; clin. instr. Southwestern Med. Sch., U. Tex., Dallas, 1954-55; clin. asst. prof. medicine Seton Hall Coll. Medicine, Jersey City, 1956-58. Contbr. articles to med. jours. Capt. U.S. Army M.C., 1951-53. Fellow ACP, Am. Coll. Gastroenterology (Best Clin. Vignette Paper and Poster Presentation 1995); mem. Am. Soc. Internal Medicine, Am. Gastroenterol. Assn., Med. Soc. N.J., N.J. Gastroenterol. Soc. (pres. 1964-65). Avocation: collecting early american folk art. Home: 12 Taylor Rd Short Hills NJ 07078-2226 Office: 58 Chatham Rd Short Hills NJ 07078-2321 Office Phone: 973-376-5750.

CHAIKIN, PAUL M., physicist; PhD in Physics, U. Pa. Henry DeWolf Smyth prof. physics Princeton U. Mem. sci. advisory bd. Arryx, Inc. Co-author: Principles of Condensed Matter Physics, 1995. Fellow, A.P. Sloan Found., Guggenheim. Fellow: Am. Physical Soc.; mem.: Am. Acad. Arts and Scis., NAS. Office: Princeton U Dept Physics PO Box 708 Princeton NJ 08544 Business E-Mail: chaikin@pupgg-princeton.edu.

CHAIN, BOBBY LEE, electrical contractor, former mayor; b. Hattiesburg, Miss., Sept. 19, 1929; s. Zollie Lee and Grace (Sellers) Chain; m. Betty Sue Green, June 30, 1967; children: Robin Ann, Laura Grace, Bobby Lee, John Webster. BS, U. So. Miss., Hattiesburg, 1957; DBA (hon.), William Carey U., Hattiesburg, 1983. Chief electrician Miss. Power & Light Co., Natchez, 1950—53; asst. to gen. supt. atomic energy plant Allegany Electric Co., Oak Ridge, 1954—55; owner, chmn. bd. Chain Electric Co., Hattiesburg, 1955; owner, pres. Chainco, Two LLC, oil properties, Hattiesburg, 1974—2003; dir. Deposit Guaranty Nat. Bank, Jackson, Miss., 1965—2000; adv. dir. Am. South Bank, 2000—01; ret., 2003. Mem. Interstate Oil Compact Commn., 1972—; mem. nat. adv. coun. SBA, 1966—67; bd. dirs. Miss. Econ. Coun., 1991—93; dir. Fed. Home Loan Bank Dallas; past mem., past pres. Miss. Trustees Instns. Higher Learning. Nat. coord. Trent Lott Nat. Ctr. Excellence Con. Devel. and Entrepreneurship; past mem., pres. So. Regional Edn. Bd., Mississipians Quality Edn.; past chmn. Commn. Efficiency Govt., Miss. Econ. Coun.; mem. Miss. State Workforce Devel. Coun.; chmn. Pearl River County Dist. Workforce Coun.; past bd. dirs. Pub. Edn. Forum Miss.; mem. commissioning com. USS John C. Stennis CVN-74 Aircraft Carrier, 1995; bd. dirs., v.p. Armed Forces Mus., Camp Shelby, Miss.; mem. Friend of West Point Assn. Grads.; mayor City of Hattiesburg, 1980—85; chmn. Advanced Tech. Ctr. Pearl River Coll. With US Army, 1950—51, Korea. Named Noble Patron, Hon. Order St. George 155th Separate Armored Brigade, Bobby L. Chain Tech. Ctr. in his honor, Bobby L. Chain Hattiesburg Mcpl. Airport in his honor; named to Miss. Bus. Hall of Fame, U. So. Miss., 1994; recipient Disting. Svc. award, 1976, Hub award, 1979, Continuous Outstanding Svc. award, 1980, Liberty Bell award, Forrest County Bar Assn., 1980, Svc. to Edn. award, Phi Delta Kappa, 1980, Disting. Citizen award, Pine Burr Area Coun. Boy Scouts Am., 1995; Paul Harris fellow, Rotary Internat., 1990. Mem.: Miss. Bus. Roundtable, Newcomen Soc. N.Am., Hattiesburg C. of C., U. So. Miss. Alumni Assn. (Outstanding Svc. award 1972, Sales and Mktg. Man of the Yr. award 1981), U. So. Miss. Century Club, Hattiesburg Country Club (past bd. dirs.), Shriners, Kiwanis, Beta Gamma Sigma, Omicron Delta Kappa. Presbyterian. Home: 312 6th Ave Hattiesburg MS 39401-4294 Office: PO Box 2058 Hattiesburg MS 39403-2058 E-mail: blc@bchain.com.

CHAIT, MAXWELL MANI, physician; b. Linz, Austria, Nov. 7, 1947; came to the U.S., 1953; s. Morris and Eva (Lederman) C.; m. Lynne Robin Milstein C.; children: Alanna Rose, Daniel Lawrence, Michael Paul. BA magna cum laude, U. Utah, Salt Lake City, 1969; BS cum laude, U. Calif., San Francisco, 1969, MD, 1972. Diplomate Am. Bd. Internal Medicine, 1975, Am. Bd. Gastroenterology, 1977; lic. N.Y., Utah. Med. intern U. So. Calif. Med. Ctr., L.A. County, 1972-73; resident in medicine Cornell Coop. Hosps., North Shore U. Hosp., Manhasset, NY, 1973-75; fellow GI Cornell Coop. Hosps., Meml. Sloan-Kettering Cancer Ctr., NYC, 1975-77; attending physician White Plains (NY) Hosp., 1977—. Trustee Crohn's & Colitis Found., 2000—02; lectr. in field. Pres. Westchester Assn. of Hebrew Schs., 1992-94; former mem. bd. trustees Temple Israel of White Plains; former coach baseball, softball, basketball Scarsdale Recreation Dept. Fellow Am. Coll. Gastroenterology, Am. Coll. Physicians, Am. Gastroenterological Assn.; mem. Am. Soc. Gastrointestinal Endoscopy, N.Y. Acad. Gastroenterology, N.Y. Soc. Gastrointestinal Endoscopy, Westchester Acad. Medicine, Crohn and Colitis Found. of Am. (CMAC com.). Office: Hartsdale Med Group 180 E Hartsdale Ave Hartsdale NY 10530-3544 Home Phone: 914-472-5250; Office Phone: 914-725-2010. Personal E-mail: mdgi77@aol.com.

CHAITMAN, HELEN DAVIS, lawyer; b. NYC, July 5, 1941; d. Philip and Miriam (Pfeffer) D.; m. Edmund Chaitman, Feb. 29, 1964 (div. 1978); children: Jennifer, Alison; m. George B. Gelman, Oct. 21, 1979. AB cum laude, Bryn Mawr Coll., 1963; JD, Rutgers U., 1976. Bar: NJ, 1976, NY 1978, US Dist. Ct. NJ 1976, US Dist. Ct. (so. and ea. dists.) 1978, US Supreme Ct. 1981, Ct. Fed. Claims 2001, US Ct. Appeals (8th cir.) 2002. Assoc. Paul, Weiss, Rifkind, Wharton & Garrison, NYC, 1977-82; ptnr. Wilentz, Goldman & Spitzer, Woodbridge, NJ, 1983-87, Ross & Hardies, Somerset, NJ, 1987-99, Wolf Haldenstein Adler Freeman & Herz LLP, NYC, 1999—2002, Phillips Nizer LLP, NYC, 2002—. Author: The Law of Lender Liability, 1990; contbg. author: Commercial Damages, 1985; editor Emerging Theories of Lender Liability, 1985-87, Lender Liability Law Report, 1987— Mem.: ABA (chmn. comml. fin. svcs. com. 1994—97, sect. bus. law), Am. Law Inst. (sustaining mem. 1992—2007). Home: The Farm 115 Fairview Rd Frenchtown NJ 08825-3013 Office: Phillips Nizer LLP 666 Fifth Ave New York NY 10103-0084 Address: 25 Main St Hackensack NJ 07601 Office Phone: 212-841-1320. Business E-Mail: hchaitman@phillipsnizer.com.

CHAJET, CLIVE, brand and corporate image consultant; b. London, Feb. 27, 1937; came to U.S., 1950, naturalized, 1964; s. Henry W. and Anne (Kravis) C.; m. Bonnie Sue Loeb, Mar. 20, 1966; children: Lisa Ellen, Lori Menschell. BA, Columbia U., N.Y.C., 1959. Acct. exec. Fuller, Smith & Rose, NYC, 1960-63; designer Milprint, NYC, 1963-65; exec. Gould Assocs., NYC, 1965-72; founder Chajet Design Group, NYC, 1972-83; chmn. Lippincott & Margulies, Inc., NYC, 1983-96, Chajet Consultancy, 1997—. Bd. dirs. Triac Cos., Inc., Sr. Bridge Family Co., Inc. Author: Image by Design, 1991, From Corporate Vision to Corporate Reality, 1991, 2d edit., 1997. Trustee Town Sch., NYC, 1980—83; bd. dirs. 92d St. YMHA, 1997—, Jewish Communal Fund, Am. Jewish Congress. Mem. Package Designers Coun. (pres. 1980-82), University Club. Jewish. Home: 1035 Fifth Ave New York NY 10028-0135 Office: Chajet Consultancy LLC 575 Madison Ave Fl 10 New York NY 10022-2511 Office Phone: 212-605-0414. Personal E-mail: thechaj@aol.com.

CHAK, AMITABH, gastroenterologist, researcher; b. Lucknow, India, June 11, 1959; arrived in U.S., 1966; s. Anand Mohan and Kusum Chak; m. Anjani Kaul, Dec. 18, 1988; children: Avinash, Ashwin. BS, Yale U., 1978, MS, 1979; MD, Columbia U., 1984. Asst. prof. Case Sch. Medicine, Cleve., 1991—99, assoc. prof., 1999—2005, prof. medicine and oncology, 2005—. Fellow: Am. Soc. Gastrointestinal Endoscopy, Am. Gastroenterological Assn., Am. Coll. Gastroent., Am. Coll. Physicians. Office: U Hosps Case Med Ctr 11100 Euclid Ave Cleveland OH 44106-5066 Office Phone: 216-844-5386.

CHAKRABARTI, SUBRATA KUMAR, marine research engineer; b. Calcutta, India, Feb. 3, 1941; came to U.S., 1964, naturalized, 1981; s. Asutosh and Shefali C.; m. Prakriti Bhaduri, July 23, 1967; children: Sumita, Prabal. BSME, Jadavpur U., 1963; MSME, U. Colo., 1965, PhD, 1968. Registered profl. engr., Ill. Asst. engr. Kuljian Corp., Calcutta, 1963—64, Simon Carves Ltd., Calcutta, 1964; instr. engring. U. Colo., Boulder, 1965—66; hydrodynamicist CB&I Tech. Svcs. Co. (formerly Chgo. Bridge and Iron Co.), Plainfield, Ill., 1968—70; head analytical group CB&I Tech. Svcs. Co., 1970—79, dir. marine rsch., 1979—95, dir. structural devel., 1995—96; pres. Offshore Structure Analysis, Inc., Plainfield, 1996—; prof. CME/MIE U. Ill., Chgo., 2005—. Vis. prof. U.S. Naval Acad., Annapolis, Md., 1986, 88, Indian Inst. Tech., Madras, 1996; presenter in field. Author: Hydrodynamics of Offshore Structures, 1987, Nonlinear Methods in Offshore Engineering, 1990, Offshore Structure Modeling, 1994, Theory and Practice of Hydrodynamics and Vibration, 2002; editor: Fluid Structure Interaction in Offshore Engineering, 1994, Fluid Structure Interaction, 2001, Fluid Structure Interaction II, 2003, Fluid Structure Interaction III, 2005; tech. editor Applied Ocean Rsch., 1998—, Numerical Modelling in Fluid-Structure Interactions, 2005;: Fluid Structure Interaction IV, 2007; tech. editor: Handbook of Offshore Engineering, 2005; mem. editl. bd. Applied Ocean Rsch., Marine Structures, Topics in Engring., Advances in Fluid Mechanics series, assoc. editor Energy Resources Tech., 1983—86; contbr. articles to profl. jours., chapters to books. Recipient Gold medal Jadavpur U., 1963, Eminent Scientist medal Wessex Inst., 2005, Disting. Engring. Alumni award U. Colo., 2006; named Outstanding New Citizen, 1981; U. Colo. fellow, 1968. Fellow AAAS, ASCE (publ. com. waterway divsn., James R. Croes Gold medal 1974, Freeman scholar 1979), ASME (exec. com., editor jour. offshore mechanics and arctic engring. divsn. 1986-96, chmn. divsn., 1987-88, awards com. 1983-2004, tech. session devloper, chmn. 1983—, chmn. tech. program com. 1988-89, tech. program chair, 2004, Ralph James award 1984, co-editor proc. internat. symposium, Offshore Mechanics and Arctic Engring. achievement award 1990, Ten Paper award 1991, Disting. Svcs. award 1998, Lifetime Achievement award 2005), NAS (com., design group, marine structures group 1989-91, chmn. 1992-95), Nat. Acad. Engring., Sigma Xi. Achievements include patents in field. Office: Offshore Structure Analysis Inc 13613 Capista Dr Plainfield IL 60544-7966 Home Phone: 815-436-4863; Office Phone: 815-436-4863. Personal E-mail: chakrab@aol.com. Business E-Mail: chakrab@uic.edu.

CHAKRABARTI, SUPRIYA, space astrophysicist; b. Howrah, India, June 22, 1953; came to U.S., 1975; s. Chiraranjan and Ranu Chakrabarti; m. Joanne Soljack, Dec. 17, 1983; children: Misha, Robin. BE, U. Calcutta, India, 1975; MS, U. Calif., Berkeley, 1980, PhD, 1982. Sr. fellow U. Calif., Berkeley, 1983-92; assoc. prof. astron. dept. Boston U., 1992-96, prof., 1996—, dir. Ctr. for Space Physics, 1997—, prof. dept. elec. and computer engring., 2001—. Mem. Ultraviolet/Visible and Gravitational Astrophysics Mgmt. Ops. Working Group, NASA, 1992-95, Universe Working Group, 2005-. Author: (ency.) Remote Sensing of the Upper Atmosphere, 1991; guest editor Optical Engring., 1993; editor conf. procs. in field. Mem. Am. Geophys. Union (life), Am. Inst. Physics, Am. Astron. Soc. Achievements include research in space instrumentation, planetary atmosphere and ionosphere, astrophysical plasma. Office: Boston U Ctr for Space Physics 725 Commonwealth Ave Boston MA 02215-1401 Office Phone: 617-353-5990. Business E-Mail: supc@bu.edu.

CHAKRABARTY, ANANDA MOHAN, microbiologist; b. Sainthia, India, Apr. 4, 1938; arrived in U.S., 1965; s. Satya Dos and Sasthi Bala (Mukherjee) Chakrabarty; m. Krishna Chakraverty, May 26, 1965; children: Kaberi, Asit. BSc, St. Xavier's Coll., 1958; MSc, U. Calcutta, India, 1960, PhD, 1965. Sr. rsch. officer U. Calcutta, 1964-65; rsch. assoc. biochemistry U. Ill., Urbana, 1965-71, prof. dept. microbiology Med. Ctr., 1979-89, disting. prof., 1989—; mem. staff GE R&D Ctr., Schenectady, NY, 1971-79. Editor: (book) Genetic Engineering, 1977, Biodegradation and Detoxification of Environmental Pollutants, 1982. Named Scientist of Yr., Indsl. Rsch. Mag., 1975; recipient Inventor of the Yr. award, Patent Lawyers' Assn., 1982, Pub. Affairs award, Am. Chem. Soc., 1984, Disting. Scientist award, EPA, 1985, Merit award, NIH, 1986, Pasteur award, 1991, Proctor & Gamble award, 1995; scholar, U. Ill., 1989. Mem.: Am. Soc. Biol. Chemists, Am. Soc. Microbiology. Home: 206 E Julia Dr Villa Park IL 60181-3340 Office: U Ill Med Ctr Dept Microbiology M/C 790 835 S Wolcott Ave Chicago IL 60612-7340 Home Phone: 630-834-4388; Office Phone: 312-996-4586. Business E-Mail: pseudomo@uic.edu.

CHAKRABORTY, ARUP K., chemical engineering educator; b. Calcutta, India, Nov. 26, 1961; s. Ajit K. and Meena C.; m. Shanmila Chatterjee; 1 child, Meenakshi. BTech in Chem. Engring., Indian Inst. Tech., Kanpur, 1983; PhD in Chem. Engring., U. Del., 1988. Rsch. assoc. dept. chem. engring. and material sci. U. Minn., 1987-88; asst. prof. to assoc. prof. dept. chem. engring. U. Calif., Berkeley, 1988-97, prof. chem. engring., chemistry, 1997—2005, Warren and Katherine Schlinger Disting. prof., chair dept. chem. engring., 2001—05; Robert T. Haslam prof. chem. engring., prof. chemistry, prof. biol. engring. MIT, Cambridge, 2005—. Vis. prof. dept. chem. engring. MIT, 1996; Allan P. Colburn Meml. lectr. U. Del., 1993. Contbr. articles to sci. jours. Shell Young Faculty fellow, 1989-92, ICI fellow Royal Acad. Engring. (UK), 1993-98; recipient Ernest Orlando Lawrence award in Life Scis. Dept. Energy, 2007. Fellow Am. Acad. Arts & Scis.; mem. AIChE (Allan P. Colburn award 1996), NAE, Am. Chem. Soc., Am. Phys. Soc., Alpha Chi Sigma. Avocations: history of science, squash, professional sports. Office: Dept Chem Engring MIT Rm E19-502C 77 Massachusetts Ave Cambridge MA 02139 Office Phone: 617-253-3890. Office Fax: 617-258-5766. E-mail: arupc@mit.edu.*

CHAKRABORTY, GOUTAM, marketing educator; BME, Indian Inst. Tech., Kharagpur, 1980; postgrad., Indian Inst. Mgmt., Calcutta, 1982-84; MS in Stats., U. Iowa, 1989, PhD of Mktg., 1991. Engr. Union Carbide Corp., 1980-82; asst. mgr. mktg. Tribeni Tissues Ltd., 1982-86; teaching asst. U. Iowa, Iowa City, 1986—91; prof. Okla. State U., Stillwater, 1991—. Contbr. articles to profl. jours. Mem. Am. Mktg. Assn., Assn. for Consumer Rsch., Direct Mktg. Ednl. Found., Acad. Mktg. Sci. Office: 419A SBA Okla State Univ Stillwater OK 74078-0555

CHAKRABORTY, JOANA, physiologist, educator, science administrator; b. Calcutta, India, June 1, 1934; arrived in U.S., 1962; d. Mohadev and Nilima Mukherjee; m. Ajit Chakraborty; 1 child, Mellary. BS, Sci. Coll., Calcutta, 1954, MS, 1956; PhD, Inst. of Nuclear Physics, Calcutta, 1962. Rsch. asst. Inst. Nuc. Physics, Calcutta, 1960-62, lectr., 1963—69; postdoctoral asst. Iowa State U., Ames, 1962-63; Ford Found. fellow Harbor Gen. UCLA Med. Ctr., 1969-70; dir. Electron Microscopy Lab. Med. Coll., Toledo, 1970-89; from asst. prof. to assoc. prof. Med. Coll. Ohio, Toledo, 1972—82, prof., 1982—, interim chmn., 1991-94. Spkr. in field. Author: Chemical Exposure and Toxic Responses, 1997; contbr. chapters to books, articles to profl. jours. Recipient World AIDS Found. award; Rsch. grantee, NIH, others. Mem.: AAAS, Am. Soc. Microbiology, Internat. AIDS Soc., N.Y. Acad. Scis., Am. Soc. Cell Biology. Office: Med Coll Ohio 3035 Arlington Ave Toledo OH 43614-2570 Business E-Mail: jchakraborty@meduohio.edu.

CHALASANI, VENKAT, management consultant; s. Venkateshwara Rao and Marudhwati Chalasani; m. Sujata Chalasani; 1 child, Shekhar. PhD, U. Va., Charlottesville, 2000. Mgr. Eicher Goodearth, Ltd., New Delhi, 1990—94; data mining cons. SRA Internat., Fairfax, Va., 2000—; cons. Office Pers. Mgmt., DC, 2006—07. Cons. Office Pers. Mgmt., DC, 2006—. Contbr. articles to profl. jours. Achievements include development of new tools and techniques to discover healthcare fraud. Home: 2517 Congreve Ct Herndon VA 20171 Office: SRA Internat 4300 Fairlakes Ct Fairfax VA 22033 Personal E-mail: vsc4d@yahoo.com.

CHALCRAFT, ELENA MARIE, actress, singer; b. Bklyn., Oct. 14, 1959; d. James Abdou and Vivian (Trovato) Edwards; m. Rory Charles Chalcraft, Aug. 1, 1992; 1 child, Christopher Aston. BA in Speech, English and Theater Arts, Shippensburg State Coll., 1981; MFA in Acting, Va. Commonwealth U., 1984. Human resources analyst APA, Washington, 1985-98; music dir. Our Lady Queen of Peace Ch., Arlington, Va., 1992-98; soprano Philomusica Chamber Choir, 1999—2006; ind. kitchen cons. The Pampered Chef, 1999—; soprano St. Bartholomew Choir, 2000—01, 2006—; substitute tchr. South River Elem. Sch. and Corpus Christi Sch., South River, NJ, 2005—; lector and eucharistic minister St. Bartholomew's Ch., 2006—. Substute tchr. South River Elem. Sch., 2005—, Corpus Christi Sch., 2005—07. Actor, singer (plays): Man of La Mancha, 1988, Ben, 1989-90, Maryland Renaissance Festival, 1987-91, Ziggy, 1992, The Snow Queen, 1994; actor: (play) Broadway Bound, 1993, (tng. film) GAO, 1990; dramaturg (play) Ballets Russes and Drood, 1993. Mem. liturgy com. Our Lady Queen of Peace Ch., 1995—98. Roman Catholic. Avocations: reading, writing children's books, piano, cross-stitch, crosswords. Personal E-mail: emcrcc@verizon.net.

CHALEFF, CARL THOMAS, investment company executive; b. Indpls., Nov. 21, 1945; s. Boris Carl and Betty J. (Miller) C.; m. Carolyn F. Heath, Apr. 26, 1970 (div. Apr. 1985); children: Fritz. Eric; m. Darlene Finkel, Dec. 13, 1987. BS in Econs., Purdue U., 1969; MBA in Fin., Xavier U., 1976. Asst. v.p. Am. Can Corp., NYC, 1969-70, sales mgr. Cin., 1970-73; account exec. Merrill Lynch, Cin., 1973-76; v.p. Oppenheimer, Chgo., 1976-81; assoc. dir. Bear Stearns & Co., Chgo., 1981-88; ptnr., mng. dir. CIBC Oppenheimer, 1988—2004; pres. Polaris Capital Ptnrs., 2004—. Former pres. bd. dirs. Nat. Kidney Found. Ill.; exec. coun. U. Chgo. Childrens Hosp., Boy Scouts Am., 1992-94; former pres. bd. dirs. AIDS Care, 1992-98, bd. dir. Adler Planetarium & Mus., Chgo., 1998-2005; treas., bd. dir., Jobs for Youth; bd. dirs. Nat. Kidney Found. Mem. Chgo. Bond Club, Am. Arbitration Assn., Nat. Bd. Arbitrators, East Bank Club, Rainbows (bd. dirs. 1984-96), Met. Club, Chgo. Mercantile Exch. Club, Chgo. Yacht Club, Ctr. for Excellence in Edn. (bd. dirs. 1990-92), Chgo. Filmmakers (bd. dirs. 1986-98). Avocations: sailing, skiing, tennis. Home: 55 W Goethe St Chicago IL 60610-7406 Office Phone: 312-327-5280. Business E-Mail: chaleff@polarischicago.com.

CHALFIE, MARTIN, biology professor; m. Tulle Hazelrigg. William R. Kenan, Jr. prof. bio. scis. Columbia U. Editl. bd. Genome Biology, Molecular Biology of the Cell; co-editor (with Steven Kain): Green Fluorescent Protein: Properties, Applications and Protocols, 1998. Mem.: NAS. Achievements include being credited (with others) with popularization of green fluorescent protein (GFP) found in jellyfish as a genetic marker. Office: Columbia U Dept Bio Sci 1012 Fairchild Ctr MC 2446 New York NY 10027 Office Phone: 212-854-8870. Office Fax: 212-856-8246. Business E-Mail: mc21@columbia.edu.

CHALIF, RONNIE, medical association administrator, artist; d. Norman and Ruth London Stern; m. Seymour Chalif, June 13, 1954; children: John Lewis, Peter Adley. Grad. with honors, Parson Sch. Design, 1953; BS in Art Edn., NYU, 1954. Buyer I. Magnin & Co., NYC, 1954—59; artist, sculptor, painter, 1968—; founder, dir. Neuropathy Assn., NYC, 1995—2007, pres., 2005—. Author, illustrator: Exercising with Neuropathy, 2001; one-woman shows include Guild Hall Mus., East Hampton, NY, Benson Gallery, Bridghampton, NY, 1972, 1975, Fed. Court House, NYC, 1984—85, Marymount Manhattan Coll. Gallery, 1986, Jackb K. Javits Fed. Bldg., 1986, Gayle Willson Gallery, 2000, 2003, Garrison Arts Ctr., NY, 1989, Benton Gallery, Southampton, NY, 1989, Arlene Bujese Gallery, 1996, 2006, exhibited in group shows at GE Co., Fairfield, Conn., 1983, Benson Gallery, 2000—02, Atelier 14, NYC, 2000, Ashwagh Hall, East Hampton, NY, 1987—2007, Guild Hall Mus., 1992—93, Arlene Bujese Gallery, 1995—2006, others, Represented in permanent collections Guild Hall Mus., Continental Telephone Co., Washington, McGraw-Hill, Inc., Cadillac-Fairview, Dallas, GE Internat. Hdprs., Fairfield, Grey Advt. Inc., NYC, US Home Corp., Houston, Zimmerli Art Mus., New Brunswick, NJ, World Trade Ctr. Mem.: Women's Caucus for Art, Women in Arts Found., Nat. Assn. Women Artists, Artists Craftsmen NY, NY Soc. Women Artists. Business E-Mail: schalif@kayescholer.com, rchalif@neuropathy.org.

CHALIKIAN, ALICE BEATRICE, chiropractor; b. Bucharest, Romania, Dec. 7, 1974; arrived in U.S., 1984; d. Nubar and Mary Anahid Chalikian. BA in Biology, Calif. State U., Northridge, 1997; DC, So. Calif. U. Health Scis., 2001. Mem.: Armenian Med. Assn., Am. Chiropractic Assn. (lobbyist student assn. 1998—), Calif. Chiropractic Assn. (lobbyist student assn. 1998—2002), Armenian Young Profl. Assn. So. Calif., Hyeties, Armenian Gen. Benevolent Union. Ea. Orthodox Gregorian. Avocations: painting, poetry, beach volleyball, skiing, dance. Office Phone: 188-837-2542. E-mail: chiroalice@yahoo.com.

CHALIL, JOSEPH MATHEW, sales executive, consultant, liver disease specialist, medical products executive; b. Pala, Kerala State, India, June 30, 1973; arrived in US, 1999; s. Joseph Mathew Chalil and Claramma A. Scaria; m. Sumy T. Chalil, June 15, 1998; children: Mathew Joseph, Thomas Mathew. MB, BChir, J.J.M. Med. Coll., Davangere, India, 1999; MBA, Davenport U., Warren, Mich., 2004; cert., Cert. Med. Rep. Inst., Roanoke, Va., 2006. Lic. physician India. Adminstrv. fellow Henry Ford Health Sys., Detroit, 2002—03; profl. sales exec. TAP Pharm. Products, Inc., Lake Forest, Ill., 2003—06, sr. sales exec., 2006; liver disease specialist Roche Labs., Inc., Nutley, NJ, 2006—; pres. Clin. Cons. Internat., LLC, Mich., 2006—. Founder and dir. KTC Healthcare Inc., Union, NJ, 2002—. With med. corps USN, 1999—. Named to Excalibur Guild, TAP Pharm. Products, Inc, 2004; recipient Will Hall Sayishu, TAP Pharm. Products, Inc., 2003, 2004. Achievements include research in multiple myeloma. Home: 7285 Millrock Ave Shelby Township MI 48317 Office: 101 W Big Beaver Rd Ste 1400 Troy MI 48084 Home Phone: 586-427-4442; Office Phone: 586-872-7370. Personal E-mail: drchalil@aol.com.

CHALK, DAVID, lawyer; b. Balt., May 18, 1967; BS summa cum laude, Univ. Baltimore, 1989; JD with honors, Univ. Md., 1992. Bar: Md. 1992, DC 1993. Atty. div. corp. fin., SEC; ptnr., co-chmn. Capital Markets practice group DLA Piper Rudnick Gray Cary, Balt. Adj. prof. Univ. Md. Sch. Law. Editor (assoc.): The Bus. Lawyer, 1991—92. Mem.: ABA, Md. State Bar Assn., Order of the Coif. Office: DLA Piper Rudnick Gray Cary 6225 Smith Ave Baltimore MD 21209-3600 Office Phone: 410-580-4120. Office Fax: 410-580-3120. Business E-Mail: david.chalk@dlapiper.com.

CHALK, JOHN ALLEN, SR., lawyer; b. Lexington, Tenn., Jan. 16, 1937; AA, Freed-Hardeman Coll., 1956; BS, Tenn. Tech. U., 1962, MA, 1967; JD, U. Tex., 1973. Bar: Tex. 1973, DC 1977; ordained to ministry Ch. of Christ, 1956; credentialed advanced mediatior Tex. Mediator Credentialing Assn. Pastor chs., Dayton, Ohio, 1956-60, Cookeville, Tenn., 1960-66, Abilene, Tex., 1966-71; assoc. Rhodes and Seamster, Abilene, 1973-74, Rhodes and Doscher, Abilene, 1974; ptnr. Rhodes, Doscher, Chalk and Heatherly, Abilene, 1975-78; gen. counsel La Jet, Inc., Abilene, 1978-84, also v.p., sec; exec. v.p. Dabney Corp., Dallas, 1984-86; pres. Dabney Capital, Dallas, 1984-86; assoc. Gandy, Michener, Swindle, Whitaker & Pratt, Ft. Worth, 1986, ptnr., 1987-93, Michener Larimore Swindle Whitaker Flowers Sawyer Reynolds & Chalk, Ft. Worth, 1993-2000, Whitaker Chalk Swindle & Sawyer LLP, Ft. Worth, 2000—. Pres. Equity, Inc., 1982-90; mem. strategic alliances edn. com. Nat. Ct. Reporters Assn., 1994-95; sec.-treas. Tarrant County Bar Assn., 2006-; cert. master mediator Dispute Resolution Svcs. Tarrant County, Tex.; Tex. court-approved mediator; mem. panel of neutrals Am. Arbitration Assn., 1992—; mem. CPR Internat. Inst. Dispute Resolution Panel of Neutrals, 2005—; contract mediator EEOC, Dallas, 1999-2001; mem. neutrals panel Internat. Ctr. Dispute Resolution, Dublin, 2003—; mem London Ct. Internat. Arbitration, 2003—. Author: The Praying Christ, 1964, Three American Revolutions, 1970, Jesus' Church, 1970, The Christian Family, 1973, Great Biblical Doctrines, 1973, The Devil, You Say!, 1974; editor The Arbitration Newsletter, 2006—; contbr. numerous articles on U.S. Dept. Edn. fed. student fin. assistance, domestic and internat. arbitration and mediation, also articles on religion; presenter in fields. Trustee Osteo. Health Care Found., Inc., Ft. Worth, 1987—96, sec.-treas., 1990—91, sr. v.p., pres.-elect, 1991—92, pres., 1992—93; mem. nat. adv. coun. Am. United Separation of Ch. and State, 1979—82, pres. bd. trustees, 1981—82; mem. Strategy for 2000, City of Ft. Worth, 1995—2000; featured spkr. radio and TV programs Herald of Truth, 1966—69; trustee Christian Scholarship Found., Inc., Atlanta, 1980; co-chair capital gifts campaign All Church Home Children, Inc., 2004—06; trustee Abilene Regional Mental Health Retardation Ctr., 1978—80; chmn. Abilene Bicentennial Com., 1975—76; dir. Health Care of Tex., Inc., 1987—2003; chmn. bd. Christian Scholarship Found., Inc., Atlanta, 1992—93; bd. dir. Ft. Worth Symphony Orch. Assn., 2005—, mem. exec. com. Named Atty. of Excellence, Ft. Worth Bus. Press, 2003—06. Fellow Tex. Bar Found. (life), Chartered Inst. Arbitrators London (chartered arbitrator), Tarrant County Bar Found. (founding, life); mem. ABA (acting assoc. editor, mem. editl. bd. Family Adv. 1977-78), Fed. Bar Assn., Coll. State Bar Tex. (maintaining fellow, mem. Tex. alternative dispute resolution sect. coun. 2006—, treas. 2007—), Am. Health Lawyers Assn. (dispute resolution svc. panel of neutrals, mem. task force), Am. Arbitration Assn. (panel arbitrators and mediators), Internat. Ctrs. Arbitration (panel arbitrators and mediators), CPR Internat. Inst. for Conflict Resolution (Tex. at large panel of neutrals; S.W. region employment panel of neutrals), Internat. Ctr. Dispute Resolution (mem. panel arbitrators), Tex. Assn. Mediators, Tarrant County Assn. Mediators, State Bar Tex., Tarrant County Bar Assn. (officer), Nat. Arbitration Forum (panel of neutrals), Tex. Mediator Credentialing Assn. Home: 3601 Verde Vista Ct W Aledo TX 76008-3679 Office: Whitaker Chalk Swindle & Sawyer 3500 DR Horton Tower Fort Worth TX 76102-4186 Office Phone: 817-878-0575. Office Fax: 817-878-0501. Business E-Mail: jchalk@whitakerchalk.com.

CHALK, ROSEMARY ANNE, health science association administrator; b. Cin., May 25, 1948; d. John Henry and Virginia R. (Kamphaus) Chalk; m. Michael Anthony Stoto, June 28, 1986; children: Anna Murilius, Benjamin John. BA, U. Cin., 1970; postgrad., George Washington U., 1970-72. Policy analyst Libr. of Congress, Washington, 1972-75; rsch. fellow MIT, Cambridge, Mass., 1982-83; program dir. AAAS, Washington, 1976-86; cons. Harvard Sch. Pub. Health, Boston, 1986-87; study dir. Inst. of Med., Washington, 1987-89, Nat. Acad. Sci., Washington, 1989—; dir. Bd. on Children, Youth, and Families, Inst. of Med., Washington, 2000—. Cons. The Field Found., N.Y.C., 1986-87, The Acadia Inst., Bar Harbor, Maine, 1988-91; adv. com. on ethics and values studies NSF, 1984-87. Editor: Science, Technology and Society: Emerging Relationships, 1988; contbr. articles to profl. jours. Fellow AAAS (coun. and section officer 1987—), Fedn. Am. Scientists (coun. mem. 1982-90), Student Pugwash USA (bd. dirs. 1988—). Roman Catholic. Office: Inst Medicine NAS 500 Fifth Street NW Washington DC 20001

CHALKLEY, JACQUELINE ANN, retail company executive; b. Benson, Minn., Jan. 3, 1946; d. Vincent Otto and Dorothy Mildred (Alsaker) Kaehler; m. C. Wayne Callaway. BA in Art History cum laude, Brown U., 1967; MA, Columbia U., 1968; postgrad. in Contemporary Art, New Sch. for Social Rsch., NYC, 1968—70; postgrad. in Ceramics, U. Md., 1970—72. Art tchr. Summit (NJ) HS, 1968-70, Rockville (Md.) HS, 1970-74; adj. prof. ceramics Montgomery Coll., Rockville, 1974-78; owner Jackie Chalkley at Foxhall Sq., Washington, 1978-99, Jackie Chalkley at Willard Collection, Washington, 1986-99, Jackie Chalkley at Chevy Chase Plz., Washington, 1989-99; retail and product devel. cons., 1999—. Juror Rhinebeck Craft Fair, 1981, New Eng. Buyers Market, Boston, 1982, Craft Art 1982, Richmond, Va. Craft Show, 1983, Smithsonian Crafts Exhbn. 1983, Smithsonian Instn. Women's Com. Craft Show, 1984, Annie Albers fashion show at Renwick Gallery, 1984, Morristown Craft Fair, 1984, Washington Craft Show, 1986, Potomac Craftsmen's Guild Show, 1987, Harrisburg Arts Festival, 1987, Ceramic Guild Washington, 1987, Washington Guild Goldsmiths, 1987, 18th Bienniel Exhbn. Creative Crafts Coun., 1988, Art Balt., 2003-04, Torpedo Factory Art Ctr., 2006, others; appointee screening com. Piedmont Craftsman's Guild, Winston-Salem, NC, 1983-86, DC Commn. Arts, 1983-85; hon. com. Brandeis Art Exhbn., 1984, Textile Mus., 1984-86. Featured in Ceramics Monthly, 1994, Women's Wear Daily, 1995. Hon. com. 34th St. Art Fair, John Eaton Sch., 1985; benefit com. Washington Charitable Fund, 1989; hon. bd. trustees DC chpt. Design Industries Found. for AIDS, 1989-90; auction benefit com. Washington Project for Arts, 1989, 90; benefit com. Source Theater, 1993, Corcoran Mus. Jazz Evening, 1993, Living Stage & Arena Theatre, 1997-99; hon. com. Lab Sch. Wash., 1992, Aid to Artisans DC, Cambodian Embassy, 2003; hon. benefit com. Arena Stage Living Theater, 1997-98; sponsor Wearable Art Fashion Show, Renwick Mus., 1993; juried Smithsonian Craft Show, 1994; hon. chair Friends of the Corcoran Mus. Benefit, 1999-2000, exec. com., 2001-02; chair Craft Leaders Caucus Day 2000; nat. resource bd. James Renwick Alliance of Renwick Mus., 2000-03, gala exec, com. Rincones Dance Theater, 2001—; fundraising chair Aid to Artisans Benefit, DC, 2005 Appeared on cover of Forecast Mag., 1978; recipient Best Taste in Washington award Washingtonian Mag., 1982, 1st Ann. Outstanding Accessories Merchandising award Accessories Mag., 1985; named one of 23 People to Watch in 1983, Washingtonian Mag., 1982; her apt. chosen as Residential Interior of Yr., Am. Soc. Interior Designers, 1985, 92; her store named 1986 Comml. Interior of Yr., Am. Soc. Interior Designers; nat. award for logo Am. Corp. Identity, 1988, 91 Mem. Am. Craft Coun., Washington Fashion Group, James Renwick Craft Leaders Caucus, Chmns. Guild of the Corcoran Gallery of Art, Washington Performing Arts Soc. (impresario coun. 2001-), Nat. Gallery Art and Hishorn Mus. (cir. mem.). Avocations: travel, dance, visual arts, swimming. Office: Jackie Chalkley 2130 Cathedral Ave NW Washington DC 20008-1502

CHALKLEY, ROGER, mathematics professor; b. Cin., June 21, 1931; s. Curtis Rathbone and Dorothy Alice Chalkley. ChE, U. Cin., 1954, AM in Math., 1956, PhD in Math., 1958. Mathematician Oak Ridge Nat. Lab., Tenn., 1958—59; asst. prof. math. Knox Coll., Galesburg, Ill., 1960—62, U. Cin., 1962—63, assoc. prof. math., 1963—80, prof. math., 1980—. Author: Basic Global Relative Invariants for Homogeneous Linear Differential Equations, 2002. Mem.: Math. Assn. Am. (life), Am. Math. Soc. (life), Sigma Xi (life). Office: Univ Cin Rm 822A Old Chemistry Bldg Cincinnati OH 45221-0025

CHALLENGER, VICKI LEE, elementary school educator; b. Parkersburg, W.Va., Jan. 5, 1962; d. Harold Leroy and Lois Jeanette Rush; 1 child, Vincent Lance. M in Adminstrn., Cleve. State U., 1993. Cert. tchr. Ohio, 1993. Tchr. art Sunbeam Elem. Sch., Cleve., 1993—94; tchr. Monticello Mid. Sch., 1994—. Dem. precinct ward capt., Olmsted Township, Ohio, 2006, 2006. Avocation: golf. Home: 27012 Oakwood Dr Apt#102 Olmsted Falls OH 44138 Office: Monticello Middle School 3665 Monticello Blvd Cleveland Heights OH 44118 Home Phone: 440-427-2283; Office Phone: 216-320-4999. Personal E-mail: vlcgolf@yahoo.com.

CHALLINOR, DAVID, retired biologist; b. NYC, July 11, 1920; s. David and Mercedes (Crimmins) C.; m. Joan Ridder, Nov. 22, 1952; children: Julia M., Mary E., Sarah L., D. Thompson. BA, Harvard U., 1943; MF, Yale U., 1959, PhD, 1966. With Offerman-Anderson, Clayton & Co., Houston, 1947-51; cotton farmer Culberson County, Tex., 1951-53; asst. sec. First Mortgage Co., Houston, 1953-57; research asst. Conn. Agr. Expt. Sta., New Haven, 1959-60; dep. dir. Yale Peabody Mus., New Haven, 1960-65, acting dir., 1965-66; spl. asst. in tropical biology Smithsonian Instn., Washington, 1966-67, dep. dir. office internat. activities, 1967-68, dir. office internat. activities, 1968-70, asst. sec. sci., 1971-87, sci. advisor, 1988-95, scientist emeritus, 1996—; v.p. for No. Am. Charles Darwin Found., 1971-92. Contbr. articles to sci. jours. Trustee Manhattanville Coll., 1964-70, Environ. Law Inst., 1975-84, 86-92; bd. dirs. Environ. Def. Fund, 1982-94, African Wildlife Found., 1980-2004, chmn. bd. N Fixing Tree Assn., 1988-94, Ctr. for Marine Conservation, 1992-99. With USNR, 1943-46. Fellow AAAS; mem. Sigma Xi. Home: 3117 Hawthorne St NW Washington DC 20008-3540 Office: Smithsonian Inst Nat Zoo 3000 Connecticut Ave NW Washington DC 20008-2509 Office Phone: 202-633-4187.

CHALLIS, DIANE LESLIE, theater director; b. Newport Beach, Calif., Sept. 3, 1957; d. Richard Bracebridge and Carlene Joanne Challis; m. Stephen Richard Davy, May 3, 1987; 1 child, Thomas Stevenson Davy. BFA, Calif. Inst. Arts, Valencia, 1979. Asst. Challis Galleries, Laguna Beach, Calif., 1972—76; prop maker Chichester Fetival Theatre, England, 1978—79; asst. dir. Pageant of the Masters, Laguna Beach, 1980—95, dir., 1995—. Avocation: painting. Address: Laguna Beach Festival of Arts 650 Laguna Canyon Rd Laguna Beach CA 92651-1837

CHALLIS, RICHARD BRACEBRIDGE, art dealer, educator; b. Aug. 12, 1920; Student, King's Coll. Sch., London, 1934—37, Chelsea Coll., 1938—39. Founder, dir. Challis Galleries, Laguna Beach, Calif., 1950—; art dir. LA Home Show, 1965—67. Cons. Esther Wells Collection, 1983—; lectr. on fine art U. Calif., Irvine, and Orange County Dept. Edn.; moderator Ruth Stover Fleming Collection, Newport Beach, Calif.; coord. Roger Kuntz Retrospective, Laguna Beach. Mem.: Orange County Mus. Art, Laguna Beach Festival Art, Laguna Mus. Art (life).

CHALLONER, DAVID REYNOLDS, academic administrator, endocrinologist; b. Appleton, Wis., Jan. 31, 1935; s. Reynolds Ray and Marion (Below) C.; m. Jacklyn Davnes Anderson, Aug. 30, 1958; children: David Harvey, Laura Reynolds, Britt-Davnes. BS cum laude, Lawrence Coll., Appleton, 1956; postgrad., Cambridge U., Eng., 1958; MD cum laude, Harvard, 1961. Resident in internal medicine Columbia Presbyn. Hosp., NYC, 1961—63; research assoc. Nat. Heart Inst., Bethesda, Md., 1963—65; chief med. resident and endocrinology research fellow U. Wash., Seattle, 1965—67; prof. medicine, asst. chmn. dept. Ind. U. Sch. Medicine, Indpls., 1967—75; vis. scholar Inst. Medicine, Nat. Acad. Sci., 1974; dean St. Louis U. Sch. Medicine, 1975—82; v.p. health affairs U. Fla., Gainesville, 1982—98; dir. Inst. for Sci. and Health Policy U. Fla., Gainesville, Fla., 1998—2002. Chmn. pres.'s com. on nat. med. sci. NIH, 1988-91, mem. dirs. adv. com., 1990-96; mem. com. sci., engring. pub. policy NAS, 1993-97; cons. Eli Lilly & Co., NIH; mem. NAS Nat. Rsch. Coun. governing bd., 1997-2006; foreign sec. NAS, Inst. Med., 1998-2006. Served to lt. cdr. USPHS, 1963—65. Recipient Harvard Med. Alumni award, 1961, Dr. William Beaumont award AMA, 1982, Disting. Alumnus award Lawrence U., 1987. Fellow AAAS; mem. Inst. of Medicine (fgn. sec. 1998-2006), Am. Fedn. Clin. Rsch.pres. 1975), Inst. Medicine, Nat. Acad. Sci., Am. Soc. Clin. Investigation, Endocrine Soc., Am. Diabetes Assn., Assn. Am. Physicians, Boylston Soc., Am. Clin. and Climatol. Assn., Phi Beta Kappa, Alpha Omega Alpha, Beta Theta Pi. Clubs: Racquet (St. Louis); Cosmos (Washington). Home: 2715 NW 22nd Dr Gainesville FL 32605-2975

CHALMERS, DAVID B., petroleum executive; b. Denver, Nov. 17, 1924; s. David Twiggs and Dorrit (Bay) C.; 1 child, David B. BA, Dartmouth Coll., Hanover, NH, 1947; A.M.P., Harvard U., Cambridge, Mass., 1966. Various positions Bay Petroleum Co., Denver, 1951-55; various positions Tenneco Oil Co., Houston, 1955-67; v.p. Occidental Petroleum Corp., Houston, 1967-68; pres. Can. Occidental Petroleum Ltd., 1968-73; pres., CEO Petrogas Processing Ltd., 1968-73; officer Cansulex Ltd., 1968-73; chmn., CEO, dir. Coral Petroleum, Inc. and subs., Houston, 1973—. Served to lt. USMC, 1943-45, 49-50, Korea Mem. Am. Petroleum Inst., Petroleum Club of Houston, Lochinvar Golf Club, Houston Racquet Club, Denver Country Club, Houston Club. Republican. Episcopalian. Home: 5600 San Felipe St Unit 4 Houston TX 77056 Home Phone: 713-968-7357. Personal E-mail: coraloil@aol.com.

CHALPIN-FLEITAS, SUSAN GAIL, environmental health specialist, forester; b. Berwyn, Pa., June 14, 1954; d. William and Irena Chalpin; m. Gene Fleitas, Sept. 26, 2004; 1 child, Alexandra. BS, Mich. State U., 1977. Registered environ. health specialist. Forester U.S. Forest Svc., Challenge, Calif., 1980—86, timber mgmt. officer Georgetown, Calif., 1988—90, Redding, Calif., 1988—90; environ. health specialist Placer County, Auburn, Calif., 1986—88; owner, designer Chalpin Environ. Svcs. Inc., Nevada City, Calif., 1990—. Mem. wastewater adv. bd. Nevada County, Nevada City, dir. resource conservation dist.; advisor Nevada County Wastewater Code, Nevada City. Author criteria for soil evaluation. Mem. choir Music in the Mountains, Grass Valley, Calif.; bd. mem. Nev. County Land Trust. Recipient Cert. of Merit, U.S. Forest Svc., 1986, 1989. Mem.: Soc. Agrl. Engrs., Nevada City Rotary Club. Avocations: beekeeping, hiking, piano, bicycling, swimming. Office: Chalpin Environ Inc PO Box 2223 Nevada City CA 95959 Office Phone: 530-265-2422. Personal E-mail: sgchalpin@saber.net.

CHALSTY, JOHN STEELE, investment banker; b. Port Elizabeth, Republic of South Africa, Nov. 7, 1933; came to U.S., 1955, naturalized, 1964; s. Frederick H. and Sarah S. (Lamprecht) C.; m. Jill Siegal, June 11, 2005; children from previous marriage: Susan Chalsty Neely, Deborah Ann. B.Sc. in Chemistry and Physics, U. Witwatersrand, 1952, B.Sc. with honors in Chemistry, 1953, M.Sc., 1954; MBA (Baker scholar), Harvard U., 1957. With Exxon Corp. (formerly Standard Oil Co.), NYC, 1957-69; dir. Donaldson, Lufkin & Jenrette, Inc., NYC, 1969-2000, pres., CEO, 1986—98, chmn., 1996—2000; prin., chmn. Muirfield Capital Mgmt. LLC, 2003—. Bd. dirs. NY Stock Exch. 1988-94, Occidental Petroleum Corp., 1996-, Metromedia Internat. Group Inc.; vice chmn., NY Stock Exch., 1990-94, N.Y. Econ. Devel. Corp. Bd. dirs. Teagle Found. Inc.,

1974—, chmn., 1997—; trustee Columbia U.; pres. Lincoln Ctr. Theater. Home: 151 E 58th St Apt 49A New York NY 10022 Home Phone: 646-416-6462; Office Phone: 212-332-2502. E-mail: jchalsty@muirfieldcap.com.

CHALUPSKY, MARY ETTA GRIFFITH, health products executive; d. Edgar Griffith and Viola Berdina Brown Griffith; m. LaVerne Leo Chalupsky, Sept. 17, 1953; children: Catherine Mary Abbey, Teresa Ann Kaplan, David Alan, Patricia Lee, Andrew LaVerne, Edward George. Degree in liberal arts, Kirkwood Coll., Cedar Rapids, Iowa. Cert. podiatric medical asst. Doctors Hosp., Tucker, GA, 1985, podiatry Am. Soc. Podiatric Assts., 1985, surgical asepsis-sterile technique Iowa Med. Assn., 1985, med. terminology/risk mgmt. Iowa Med. Assn., 1985, med. coding profls. Iowa Med. Assn., 1987, osteopathic medicine Iowa Med. Assn., 1995, office mgmt./surgery/insurance Coding Iowa Med. Assn., 1998, local anesthesia administer Iowa Med. Assn. Surg. asst. Podiatry Assocs., Cedar Rapids, Iowa, 1983—96; CEO Med. Claims Billing, Cedar Rapids, 1990—98; co. ptnr. North Ctrl. Svcs., Horseshoe Bend, Ark., 2006—. Mem. State Ins. Network Podiatry, Des Moines, 1985—94, Linn County Cert. Med. Assts., Cedar Rapids, 1988—94, Cert. Am. Podiatric Med. Assts., Iowa. Athletic trainer advisor State Iowa, Des Moines; v.p., sec., women's chmn. Linn County Farm Bur., Marion, Iowa; mem. State Jud. Compensation Commn., Des Moines; tax study commn. State Iowa, Des Moines; sec. St. Mary of Mt., 1999—2002, parish coun. pres., 2002—07; mem. Coll. Cmty. Bd. Edn., Cedar Rapids, 1980—83, Baxter County Med. Bd., Horseshoe Bend, Ark., 2005—07. Recipient Silver Poet award, 1990, Editor's Choice award, 2003, 2005—06, Family of Yr. award, Knight's of Columbus, 2005—06, Outstanding Vol. award, St. Mary of Mt., 2007. Mem.: DAR. Catholic. Avocations: writing, painting.

CHALWELL-BREWLEY, LAVON PATRICIA, biology educator; d. Kenneth Chalwell and Dinis George-Chalwell; m. Ray Moore Brewley. BA in Biology, U. V.I., St. Thomas, 1987, MA in Edn., 1992. Biology lab asst. U. V.I., St. Thomas, British Virgin Islands, 1986—87; tchr. sci. Brit. V.I. H.S., Road Town, Tortola, British Virgin Islands, 1988—, head dept. sci., 1995—. Adj. lectr. H. Lavity Stoutt C.C., Paraquita Bay, Tortola, 1995—2005. Mem.: ASCD, Nat. Assn. Biology Tchrs., Internat. Reading Assn. Avocations: reading, travel, flute, piano, guitar. Office: British Virgin High School Road Town Tortola British Virgin Islands Home Phone: 284-494-6131; Office Phone: 284-494-3701 6703.

CHAMBERLAIN, ADRIAN RAMOND, transportation engineer; b. Detroit, Nov. 11, 1929; s. Adrian and Leila (Swisher) C.; m. Melanie F. Stevens, May 19, 1979; children: Curtis (dec.), Tracy, Thomas (dec.). BS, Mich. State U., 1951, D Engring., 1971; MS, Wash. State U., 1952; PhD, Colo. State U., 1955; LittD, Denver U., 1974. Registered profl. engr., Colo. lic. real estate broker, Colo., 1981-91. Rsch. engr. Phillips Petroleum Co., 1955; rsch. coord., civil engr. Colo. State U., 1956-57, chief civil engr. sect., 1957-61, acting dean engring., 1959-61, v.p., 1960-66, exec. v.p., treas., governing bd., 1966-69, pres., 1969-80; chmn. bd. dirs. Univ. Nat. Bank, 1964-69, dir., 1964-74; pres., dir. Mitchell & Co., Inc., 1981-85; exec. v.p. Simons, Li & Assocs., Inc., 1985-87; pres., CEO, Chemagnetics, Inc., Ft. Collins, Colo., 1987-89; exec. dir. Colo. Dept. Hwys., Denver, 1987-91, Colo. Dept. Transp., 1991-94; v.p. engring. cons. firm Parsons Brinckerhoff, Denver, 1998—. Chmn. NSF Commn. Weather Modification, 1964-66; mem. Nat. Air Quality Criteria Adv. Com., 1967-70; vice chmn. rsch. and tech. coord. com. Fed. Hwy Adminstrn. of Transp. Rsch. Bd., NRC, 1991-94. Colo. commr. Western Interstate Commn. on Higher Edn., 1974-78; pres. State Bd. Agr. Sys., 1978-80; trustee Cystic Fibrosis Found., 1971-84; bd. trustees Univ. Corp. for Atmospheric Rsch., 1967-72, 74-81, chmn. bd. trustees, 1977-79; pres. Black Mountain Ranch, Inc., 1969-85; bd. dirs. Nat. Ctr. for Higher Edn. Mgmt. Sys., 1975-80, chmn. bd. dirs., 1977-78; bd. visitors Air U., USAF, 1973-76, chmn., 1975-76; exec. com. Nat. Assn. State Univs. and Land Grant Colls., 1976-80, pres.-elect, 1978-79, chmn., 1979-80; mem. adv. coun. to dir. NSF, 1978-81; chmn. Ft. Collins-Loveland Airport Authority, 1983-86; bd. dirs. Synergetics Internat. Inc., 1987-90; mem. exec. com. strategic hwy. rsch. commn. Transp. Rsch. Bd. NRC, 1989-93, chmn. strategic transp. rsch. study hwy. safety, 1989-90, exec. com., 1991-96, vice-chmn., 1992, chmn., 1993; mem. Gov.'s Cabinet, State of Colo., 1987-94; mem. Info. Mgmt. Commn., 1988-93. Fulbright student U. Grenoble, 1955-56 Mem. ASCE, NAE, Am. Assn. State Hwy. and Transp. Ofcls. (policy com. 1987-92, v.p. 1990-91, pres. 1991-92, bd. dirs. 1992-94, chmn. standing com. on adminstrn. 1993-94), Am. Trucking Assn. (v.p. for freight policy 1994-98, mng. dir. found. 1998), Order of Aztec Eagle, Mex., Nat. Assoc. Nat. Acads., Western Stock Show Assn., Sigma Xi, Tau Beta Pi, Phi Kappa Phi, Chi Epsilon. Office: Parsons Brinckerhoff 1660 Lincoln St Ste 2100 Denver CO 80264-2001 Office Phone: 303-832-9091. Business E-Mail: chamberlain@pbworld.com.

CHAMBERLAIN, BARBARA KAYE, communications executive; b. Lewiston, Idaho, Nov. 6, 1962; d. William Arthur and Gladys Marie (Humphrey) Greene; m. Dean Andrew Chamberlain, Sept. 13, 1986 (div.); children: Kathleen Marie, Laura Kaye; m. Daniel Eric Pocklington, Apr. 11, 1998 (div.); m. Eric Lee Abbott, July 7, 2007. BA in English cum laude, BA in Linguistics cum laude, Wash. State U., 1984; MPA, Ea. Wash. U., 2002. Temp. sec. various svcs., Spokane, Wash., 1984-86; office mgr. Futurepast, Spokane, 1986-87; dir. mktg. and prodn. Futurepast: The History Co., Melior Publs., Spokane, 1987-88, v.p., 1988-89; founder, owner PageWorksInk, 1989—2006; mem. dist. 2 Idaho State Ho. of Reps., 1990-92; mem. Idaho State Senate, 1992-94; dir. comm. and pub. affairs Wash. State U., Spokane, 1998—. Adj. faculty North Idaho Coll., 1995, trustee, 1996-2001, bd. chair, 1999-2001. Author North Idaho's Centennial, 1990; editor Washington Songs and Lore, 1988. Bd. dirs. Mus. North Idaho Coeur d'Alene, 1990-91, Ct. Apptd. Spl. advocates, 1993-96; bd. dirs. Spokane Pub. Rels. Coun., 1999-2004, pres., 2002-03; bd. dirs. Friends of the Falls, 2005—, pres., 2007; co-chair Citizens for Spokane Schs., 2005-; bd. dirs. Deaconess/Valley Healthcare Found., 2007-. Named Child Advocate Legislator of Yr., Idaho Alliance for Children, Youth and Families, 1993. Democrat. Office: Academic Ctr PO Box 1495 Spokane WA 99210-1495

CHAMBERLAIN, CHARLES JAMES, railroad labor union executive; b. Ashton, Ill., Aug. 7, 1921; s. Charles Hubert and Katherine (Reitz) C.; m. Joyce Lois Swanson, June 27, 1942; children— Richard B., Charles M. Student pub. schs. With signal dept. C. & N.-W. Ry., 1938-57; grand lodge rep. Brotherhood of R.R. Signalmen, 1957-61, sec.-treas., 1961-67, pres., 1967—. Appointed Labor mem. by Pres. Carter to U.S. R.R. Retirement Bd., Chgo., 1977, reappointed, 1979-84, reappointed by Pres. Reagan, 1986-89, reappointed by Pres. Bush, 1989-92, ret. 1992; arbitrator Nat. Mediation Bd., 1996. Alderman DeKalb (Ill.) City Coun., 1949-57; pres. 4 Colonies Condo Assn., Crystal Lake, Ill., 1987—; chmn. St. John's Luth. Ch., Algonquin, Ill., 1990-91, 94—. Mem. Ry. Labor Execs. Assn. (chmn. 1970—) Home and Office: 740 St Andrews Ln Apt 33 Crystal Lake IL 60014-7043 Personal E-mail: brsrrb@aol.com.

CHAMBERLAIN, DANIEL ROBERT, retired college president; b. Mexico, Mo., Aug. 22, 1932; s. Ray Willis and Marianne Elizabeth (Horine) C.; m. Joyce F. Books, June 22, 1952; children: Rodney, Mark, Anthony, Priscilla, Aletha, Cynthia, Marianne. BA, Upland Coll., 1953; MA, Calif. State U., Los Angeles, 1957; postgrad., UCLA, 1958-59; D.Ed., U. So. Calif., 1967; DHL (hon.), Huntington Coll., 2000, Houghton Coll., 2001. Tchr., adminstr. Western Pilgrim Schs., El Monte, Calif., 1953-59; tchr. English and history Pasadena (Calif.) City Schs., 1959-63; chmn. div. profl. studies, acting pres. Upland Coll., 1963-65; asst. univ. dean for univ. wide activities SUNY, Albany, 1965-68; dean of coll. Messiah Coll., Grantham, Pa., 1968-76; pres. Houghton Coll., NY, 1976—2006; ret. Lectr. on higher edn. and social scis. in People's Republic of China, 1984, 87-89. Chmn. Ind. Coll. Fund, NY, Western NY Consortium Higher Edn., 1976—2006, 1991—93; pres. Calif. youth Wesleyan Ch., 1954—64, mem. gen. bd. adminstrn., 1988—92, 2000—06; pres. men's commn. Christian Holiness Assn., 1975—80; chmn. bd. dirs. Mile High Camp, Barton Flats, Calif., 1959—65; bd. dirs. Commn. Ind. Colls. and Univs., NY State Commn. on Ind. Colls. and Univs., 1994—97. Named One of 50 Most Outstanding Alumni, Calif. State U., L.A., 1997; recipient Lifetime Christian Svc. award Messiah Coll., 2007. Mem. Christian Coll. Consortium (chmn.), Council of Mennonite Coll. Deans (chmn.), Am. Assn. Higher Edn., Middle States Assn. Schs. and Colls. (evaluator, team chmn.), Wesleyan Edn. Council (chmn.), Lions, Phi Delta Kappa. Republican. Home: 8051 Peter Ct Brooksville FL 34601 Business E-Mail: daniel.chamberlain@houghton.edu.

CHAMBERLAIN, DAVID M., retail executive; b. Ft. Benning, Ga., 1943; m. Karin Chamberlain; children: Pamela, Katheryn. BS, U. Pa., 1965; MBA, Harvard U., 1969. With Quaker Oats Co., Chgo., 1969-74, v.p., gen. mgr., 1974-77, pres. frozen foods divsn., 1977-80; pres. margarine & desserts divsn. Nabisco Brands, Inc., NYC, 1980-82, sr. v.p. Toronto, Can., 1982-83; pres., COO Shaklee Corp., San Francisco, 1983-85, pres., CEO, 1985—93, chmn., 1989—94; pres. Genesco Inc., Nashville, 1994—96, CEO, 1994—97, chmn., 1994—99; chmn., CEO The Stride Rite Corp., Lexington, Mass., 1999—. Bd. dirs. The Stride Rite Corp., 1999—. Bd. dirs. San Francisco Boys and Girls Club, San Francisco Opera, U.S. C. of C., Washington, Calif. Roundtable; pres. San Francisco C. of C. Served to 1st lt. U.S. Army, 1965-67 Mem. St. Francis Yacht Club, University Club, Apawamin Club, Larchmont (N.Y.) Yacht Club, Royal Canadian Yacht Club. Republican. Office: The Stride Rite Corp 191 Spring St Lexington MA 02420*

CHAMBERLAIN, JOHN ANGUS, sculptor; b. Rochester, Ind., Apr. 16, 1927; s. Claude Chester and Mary Francis (Waller) Chamberlain; m. Elaine Grulkowski, 1956 (dec.); children: Angus, Jesse, Duncan; m. Lorraine Belcher, Dec. 31, 1977 (div.). Student, Art Inst. Chgo., 1951—52, Black Mountain Coll., NC, 1955-56. Artist-in-residence Skowhegan Sch. Painting & Sculpture, 1985. One-man shows include Cleve. Mus. Art, 1967, New HemisFair, 1968, York U., Toronto, Ont., Can., 1969, Guggenheim Mus., 1971, Indpls. Mus. Art, 1972, Pratt Inst., 1974, Josechoff Gallery U. Hartford, 1977, Flint Inst. Art, Mich., 1978, Whitney Mus. Am. Art, 1979, Leo Castelli Gallery, 1982, U. Calif. Santa Barbara, Xavier Fourcade, 1984, Pace Gallery, 1988, Pace Wildenstein, NYC, 2004, numerous others; two-man shows include Taft Mus., Cin., 1972, Newport Art Festival, 1976, U. Calif. Art Mus., Santa Barbara, 1984, Mus. Contemporary Art, LA, Galerie Pierre Huber, Geneva, 1987, 88, Galerie Heiner Friedrich, Cologne, 1979, Galerie Karsten Greve, Cologne, 1992, 93, 94, 95, Paris, 1993, 95, 97, Milan, 1999, Cheim & Read, NYC, 1997, Pace Wildenstein, LA, 1997, Mus. für Lackkunst, Münster, 1997, Pace Wildenstein, NYC, 1998, Dan Flavin & John Chamberlain: Sculptures, Gagosian Gallery Madison, NYC, 2003; group shows include Galerie Rive Droit, Paris, 1960, Sao Paolo Mus. Modern Art, Brazil, Art Inst. Chgo., 1961, Tate Gallery, 1964, Carnegie Inst., 1967, Nova Scotia Coll. Art, Palais de Beaux-Arts, Brussels, 1970, La. Mus., Copenhagen, 1972, Inst. Contemporary Art, Phila., 1975, Fitzwilliam Mus., Cambridge, Eng., 1977, Grace Borgenicht Gallery, 1982, Nat. Gallery Art, Washington, Ecole Nat. Superior des Beaux-Arts, Paris, 1985, Weatherspoon Art Gallery, 1984, Retrospective Staatliche Kunsthalle Baden-Baden, Germany & Staatliche Kunstsammlungen Dresden, 1991, Crossroads of Am. Sculpture, Indpls. Mus. Art, 2000, Lenore and Burton Gold Collection of 20th-Century Art, High Mus. Art, Atlanta, 2001, Art Downtown: NY Painting and Sculpture, Wall Street Rising, 2002, Design is not Art, AAM Aspen Art Mus., Aspen, Colo., 2005, Bilderwechsel III - Amerikanische Malerei, Mus. Frieder Burda, Baden-Baden, 2006, numerous others; films include Wedding Night, 1967, The Secret Life of Hernando Cortez, 1968, Wide Point, 1968, Thumbsuck, 1971. Served in USN, 1943—46. Recipient Brandeis award, Creative Arts award, 1984, Lifetime Achievement award Internat. Sculpture Ctr., Washington, 1993, Skowhegan medal for Sculpture Skowhegan Sch. Painting & Sculpture, Skowhegan, Maine, 1993; Guggenheim fellow, 1966, 77. Mem. Am. Acad. and Inst. of Arts and Letters. Republican. Taoist. Mailing: c/o Pace Gallery 32 E 57th St New York NY 10022

CHAMBERLAIN, JOHN LOOMIS, III, retired pediatrician, educator; b. Balt., July 18, 1930; s. John Loomis Jr. and Marie (Brosius) C.; m. Eleanor Fulton, 1956 (div. Apr. 1976); m. Amelie Marie Chamberlain, Apr. 29, 1977; children: Carolyn, Allison, John Loomis IV. BA, Amherst Coll., Mass., 1953; MD, U. Va., Charlottesville, 1957. Pediatrician Lexington Clinic, Ky., 1962-66; asst. prof. pediat. U. Ky. Sch. Medicine, Lexington, 1962-66; clin. prof. child health and devel. George Washington Sch. Medicine, Washington, 1966—; pediatrician Office of Drs. Howard, Daisley and Ong, Washington, 1966-70; pvt. practice, 1970—89; ret., 1992. Chmn. med. staff Children's Hosp., 1976—79. Editor-in-chief Clin. Proceedings, 1979-84; mem. editl. rev. bd. Contemporary Pediat., 1984-87, Pediat. in Review, 1985-88. Col. U.S. Army, 1991-93. Decorated Army Commendation medal US Army, Meritorious Svc. medal. Fellow Am. Acad. Pediat. (v.p. Washington chpt. 1985-88); mem. Vis. Nurse Assn. (med. adv. bd. 1972-89), D.C. Med. Soc. (exec. bd. 1988-89), U. Va. Med. Alumni Assn. (pres. 1992-93), Cosmos Club. Republican. Episcopalian. Avocation: self education. Home: 4321 Westover Pl NW Washington DC 20016-5553

CHAMBERLAIN, JOSEPH MILES, retired astronomer, educator; b. Peoria, Ill., July 26, 1923; s. Maurice Silloway and Roberta (Miles) C.; m. Paula Bruninga, Dec. 12, 1945; children: Janet Ann, Susan Louise, Barbara Jean. BS, U.S. Mcht. Marine Acad., 1944; BA, Bradley U., 1947; AM, Tchrs. Coll. Columbia, 1950, EdD, 1962. Instr. Columbia Jr. High Sch., Peoria, 1943; instr. nav. War Shipping Adminstrn., 1944-45; boys sec. YMCA, Peoria, 1946-47; instr. U.S. Mcht. Marine Acad., Kings Point, NY, 1947-50, asst. prof., 1950-52; asst. curator Am. Museum-Hayden Planetarium, NYC, 1952-53, gen. mgr., chief astronomer, 1953-56, chmn., 1956-64; asst. dir. Am. Mus. Natural History, 1964-68; dir. Adler Planetarium, Chgo., 1968-91, pres., 1977-91, ret., 1991. Prof. astronomy Northwestern U., 1968-78; professorial lectr. U. Chgo., 1968-71; led eclipse expdns. to Atlantic Ocean, 1972, 73, 94, Mexico, 1970, Can., 1954, 79, Ceylon, 1955, Pacific Ocean, 1977, 91, astro-geodetic expdns. to Can., 1956, 57, Greenland, 1958; dean coun. of sci. staff Am. Mus. Nat. History, 1960-62. Co-author: Planets, Stars and Space, 1957; author: Time and the Stars, 1964, also articles on popular astronomy. Active Boy Scouts Am., Met. Chgo. YMCA; trustee Lakeview Mus. Arts and Scis., Peoria, 1993—2003; bd. dirs. Heartland Water Resources Coun., 1995-98. Lt. USNR, 1945-46; staff Naval Res. Officers Sch. 1953-54, N.Y.C. Mem. Am. Astron. Soc., Internat. Astron. Union, Internat. Planetarium Dirs. Conf. (vice chmn. 1968-77, chmn. 1977-87), Am. Polar Soc., Am. Assn. Museums (mem. council 1965-77, v.p. 1971-74, pres. 1974-75), Mus. Trustee Assn. (bd. dirs. 1996-98), Peoria Hist. Soc. (trustee 1993-96), Ill. Valley Yacht Club, Univ. Club (Chgo.). Republican. Presbyterian. Home: 5424 W Flagstone Dr Peoria IL 61615-9466

CHAMBERLAIN, ROBERT GLENN, retired tool manufacturing executive; b. Cedar Rapids, Iowa, Feb. 17, 1926; s. Glenn Arlie and Ora Margarite (Castle) C.; m. Jane Helen Newlin, June 13, 1946; children: Carole, James, Sue, Patricia, Tracey. BSM.E., Iowa State U., 1949; postgrad., U. Wis.Milw. With Link-Belt Speeder, Cedar Rapids, 1949-54, Giddings & Lewis, Fond du Lac, Wis., 1954-83, group v.p. indsl. products, 1980-82, exec. v.p. machine tools, 1982-83, ret., 1983. Pioneer numerical control programmer, 1954-59. Mem. PTO; v.p. Bay Lakes coun. Boy Scouts Am., Menasha, Wis., 1982-89, exploring chmn. in sch., Dallas, 1981, exploring chmn. Area 1 NC region, Oak Brook, Ill., 1977; bd. dirs. Evergreen Retirement Cmty., 1989-94. With USNR, 1944-46. Recipient Silver Beaver award Boy Scouts Am., 1974, Silver Antelope award, 1983. Mem. Masons. Home: W2728 Oakwood Beach Rd Markesan WI 53946-8904

CHAMBERLAIN, SONJA KAY, music educator; d. Clarence Samuel and Hilda Elzona Peterson; m. Ronald George Chamberlain, June 6, 1970; children: Benjamin Andrew, Lucas Samuel. BA, Luther Coll., Decorah, Iowa, 1970; M of Music Edn., U. of Minn., Mpls., 1981. Elem. music educator Anoka-Hennepin Sch. Dist., Coon Rapids, Minn., 1972—82; dir. of choirs Anoka-Hennpin Dist., Coon Rapids, 1982—. Choral festival dir.; participant, Minn. Humanities Commn. Named Tchr. Outstanding Performance, Anoka-Hennpin Edn. Found., 2005; recipient Proff. Opportunity grant, Minn. Ctr. for the Arts. Mem.: VoiceCare Network (assoc.), Minn. Music Educators Assn. (assoc. Choral Dir. of the Yr. 1994), Am. Choral Dirs. Assn. (assoc.; mem.-at-large, exec. bd.). Avocations: hiking, kayaking, bicycling, singing, interior design. Home: 1707 Levee Anoka MN 55303 Office: Fred Moore MS Ctr for Arts 1523 5th Ave S Anoka MN 55303 Home Phone: 763-421-5392; Office Phone: 763-506-5043.

CHAMBERLAIN, WILLARD THOMAS, retired metal products executive; b. New Haven, Nov. 22, 1928; s. Thomas Huntington and Alice Irene (Daley) C.; m. Harriet Halbert Keck, Nov. 20, 1965; children: Huntington Wilson, Amy Thatcher. B.E., Yale U., 1950; postgrad., Ill. Inst. Tech., 1951-53. With Armour Research Found., Chgo., 1951-53; asst. to tech. mgr. Anaconda Brass div. Anaconda Corp., Waterbury, Conn., 1953-56, tech. supr., 1956-60, metall. mgr. Torrington, Conn., 1960-61, mgr. devel. Waterbury, 1961-62, lab. mgr., 1962-64, mgr. research-tech. ctr., 1964-67, mgr. Valley Mills, 1967, Ansonia, 1967-70, mgr. prodn. planning, 1970-71, v.p. mfg., 1971-72, exec. v.p. Brass div., 1972-74, pres., 1974-80, Anaconda Industries, 1980; sr. v.p. Atlantic Richfield Co., 1980-82; pres. Arco Metals Co., 1982-85; sr. v.p. corp. affairs Atlantic Richfield Co., 1985-87; sr. v.p. govt. and pub. affairs ARCO, 1987-89. Mem. So. Calif. bus. com. Econ. Literacy Council Adv. of Calif. Mem. exec. bd. Waterbury Republican Town Com., 1964-70; commr. Waterbury Bd. Fin., 1966-67, chmn. charter revision com., 1966-67; mem. exec. bd. Mattatuck council Boy Scouts Am., 1965-72, Waterbury Assn. for Retarded Children, 1965-66; co-chmn. Clergy-Industry Conf., 1965-66; campaign chmn. Valley United Fund, 1970-71; bd. dirs. United Way, Central Naugatuck Valley, 1974, The Banking Ctr., 1974-81, Western Conn. Indsl. Council, 1974-81, Calif. State U. Found., Found. for Am. Communications, Los Angeles Arts Council; trustee Calif. Mus. Found., Harvey Mudd Coll.; bd. trustees Greater Los Angeles Partnership for the Homeless; bd. dirs. L.A. Habitat for Humanity. Recipient Outstanding Civic Leader award, 1967. Mem. Copper Devel. Assn., Aluminum Assn. (dir.), Am. Soc. Metals, Yale Engring. Assn., Greater Waterbury C. of C. (bd. dirs. 1974), Alliance Aging Rsch. (bd. dirs.), Am. Petroleum Inst. (emerging issues task force), Brookings Instn. (coun. mem.), Calif. State U. Found. (bd. dirs., compensation planning com., chmn. investment com.), Calif. State U. Bus. Assocs., Constl. Rights Found. (bus. adv. coun.), Econ. Literacy Coun. Adv. Calif. (so. Calif. bus. com.), Found. Am. Communications (dir.), Hugh O'Brian Youth Found., Math. Engring. and Sci. Achievement (industry adv. bd.), Nat. Action Coun. for Minorities in Engring., Nat. Minority Supplier Devel. Coun. (bd. dirs.), Nat. Wetlands Policy Forum, Nat. Wildlife Fedn. (vice chmn. corp. conservation coun.), Vols. of Am., L.A., Town Hall, U.S. C. of C., World Affairs Coun., Univ. Club L.A., Yale Club, So. Calif. Presbyterian. Home: 7115 Hawarden Dr Riverside CA 92506 Personal E-mail: wtc91107@yahoo.com.

CHAMBERLAIN, WILLIAM EDWIN, JR., management consultant; b. St. Louis, June 8, 1951; s. William Edwin Sr. and Grace (Salisbury) C. AA in Bus. Mgmt., Mesa C.C., Arz., 1983; BBA, U. Phoenix, 1988; MBA, Almeda U., 2005. Tng. and human resources devel. specialist Motorola, Inc., Phoenix, 1979-87; pres., seminar spkr. Chamberlain Cons. Svcs., Reno, 1987—. Curator, dir. ops. U.S. Wolf Refuge. Mem. Network for Profl. Devel. Avocations: wildlife preservation and management, hiking, backpacking, tennis, basketball, racquetball. Office Phone: 775-475-0510. Business E-Mail: bill@uswolfrefuge.org. *Personal philosophy: Better people make better workers and better workers make better people. A company's workforce is often its biggest investment, therefore efforts to develop its workers will often bring the biggest returns.*

CHAMBERLIN, JOHN STEPHEN, investor, consumer products company executive; b. Boston, July 29, 1928; s. Stephen Henry and Olive Helen (McGrath) C.; m. Mary Katherine Leahy, Oct. 9, 1954; children—Mary Katherine, Patricia Ann, Carol Lynn, John Stephen Jr., Liane Helen, Mark Joseph. AB cum laude, Harvard U., Cambridge, Mass., 1950, MBA, 1953. Lamp salesman Gen. Electric Co., NYC, 1954-57, mgmt. cons., 1957-60, mgr. product planning TV receiver dept. Syracuse, NY, 1960-63, mgr. mktg., gen. mgr. radio receiver dept. Utica, NY, 1963-70; exec. v.p., dir. Lenox Inc., Trenton, NJ, 1970-71; v.p., gen. mgr. housewares div. Gen. Electric Co., Bridgeport, Conn., 1971-74, v.p., gen. mgr. housewares and audio div., 1974-76; pres., chief exec. officer, dir. Lenox Inc., Lawrenceville, NJ, 1976-81, chmn., chief exec. officer, 1981-85; pres., chief operating officer Avon Products, Inc., NYC, 1985-88; pvt. investor Princeton, NJ, 1988—. Sr. advisor Mancuso & Co., 1992—98. Trustee Univ. Med. Ctr. at Princeton, vice chmn. 1995, chmn., 2002; chmn. Princeton Health Care Sys., 2003-2007. Mem. Bedens Brook Club, Harvard Club N.Y.C., Nassau Club. Home: 182 Fairway Dr Princeton NJ 08540-2410 Office Phone: 609-497-9117.

CHAMBERLIN, MARY ELLEN, music educator; b. Rockmart, Ga., July 7, 1945; d. Benjamin Cuttino Scarborough and Ellen Mizell; m. Leonard Martin, Jr. Chamberlin (dec.); children: Leonard III, Heather King, Clay. Student, U. So. Miss., U. Miss. Music educator Bruce (Miss.) HS, 1966, River Forest Acad., Covington, La., 1967—69; dir. enrichment Parklane Academy, McComb, Miss., 1988—; organist, choir dir. Ch. of Mediator/Redeemer, McComb, Miss., 1997—. Mem.: Red Hat Soc., Cameo Soc. of Miss., DAR, Am. Choral Dirs. Assn. Republican. So. Baptist. Avocation: music. Home: 6512 Bates School Rd Magnolia MS 39652 Office: Parklane Acad 1115 Parklane Rd Mccomb MS 39648

CHAMBERLIN, MICHAEL JOHN, retired biochemistry professor; b. Chgo., June 7, 1937; s. John Windsor and Marian (McMichael) C.; m. Caroline Marie Kane, Jan. 31, 1981. AB, Harvard U., 1959; PhD, Stanford U., 1963. Asst. prof. virology U. Calif., Berkeley, 1963—67, assoc. prof. molecular biology, 1967—71, assoc. prof. biochemistry, 1971—73; prof., 1973—99, U. Calif., Berkeley, 1973, vice chmn. dept. biochemistry, 1983—88, prof. biochemistry and molecular biology, 1989; emeritus prof., 1999. Mem. physiol. chemistry study sect. NIH, 1970-74, molecular biology study sect., 1980-84; mem. study sect. Am. Heart Assn., 1983-86. Mem. editorial bd. Jour. Biol. Chemistry, 1975-78, Biochemistry, 1993—; contbr. articles to profl. jours. Recipient Charles Pfizer award Am. Chem. Soc., 1974. Mem. NAS, AAAS, Am. Acad. Arts and Scis., Am. Soc. Biochemistry and Molecular Biology, Am. Soc. Microbiology, Am. Acad. Microbiology, Phi Beta Kappa, Sigma Xi. Office: U Calif Dept Molecular/Cell Biology 401 Barker Hall Berkeley CA 94720-3208 E-mail: profmjc@berkeley.edu.

CHAMBERLIN, MICHAEL MEADE, lawyer; b. Omaha; s. Cecil Meade and Helen Gail (Russell) C. AB in Econs., Princeton U., NJ, 1972; JD, George Washington U., Washington, DC, 1975. Bar: N.Y. 1976. Assoc.

Shearman & Sterling, NYC, 1975-83, ptnr., 1984-93; CEO, exec. dir. EMTA, 1994—. Avocations: running, choral music, skiing, flying. Office Phone: 646-637-9100. Business E-Mail: mchamberlin@emta.org.

CHAMBERS, ANNE COX, publishing executive, former diplomat; b. Dayton, Ohio; 3 children. Student, Finch Coll., NYC; D in Pub. Svc. (hon.), Wesleyan Coll., 1982; DHL (hon.), Spelman Coll., 1983; LLD (hon.), Oglethorpe U., 1983; DHL (hon.), Brenau Coll., 1989; LLD (hon.), Clark Atlanta U., 1989. Bd. dirs. Cox Enterprises, Inc.; Am. amb. to Belgium, 1977-81; dir. Bank of the South, 1977—82, Coca-Cola Co., 1981—91; chmn. bd. Atlanta Jour.-Constn. Bd. mem. Fulton National Bank, 1973, Ctrl. Atlanta Progress, 1973; mem. Atlanta C. of C., 1973; dir. Am. Soc. of Fr. Leg. of Honor, Am. Adv. Bd. of Pasteur Found. Bd. dirs. Atlanta Arts Alliance, High Mus. Art, Cmtys. in Schs., MacDowell Colony, Forward Arts Found., Emory Mus. Art and Archaeology, NY Bot. Garden, Coun. Am. Ambs., Chmn.'s Coun., Met. Mus. Art, Fr.-Am. Found.; trustee Mus. Modern Art, Carter Ctr.; mem. internat. coun. Mus. Modern Art; mem. nat. com. Whitney Mus. Am. Art; mem. Coun. Fgn. Rels. Decorated Legion of Hon. France, l'Order de la Couronne Belgium; named one of Forbes Richest Ams., 2006, World's Richest People, Forbes mag., 2007; recipient Women of Achvmt. award, YMCA, 1985. Office: 6205 Peachtree Dunwoody Rd Atlanta GA 30328*

CHAMBERS, CHARLES MACKAY, academic administrator, lawyer, consultant; b. Hampton, Va., June 22, 1941; s. Charles McKay and Ruth Ellanora (Wallach) C.; m. Barbara Mae Fromm, June 9, 1962; children: Charles M., Catherine M., Christina M., Carleton M. BS, U. Ala., 1962, MS, 1963, PhD, 1964; JD, George Washington U., 1976; DSc (hon.), Lawrence Tech. U., Southfield, Mich., 2006. Bar: Va. 1977, DC 1978, US Patent and Trademark Office, 1978, US Supreme Ct. 1980, US Dist. Ct. DC 1985, US Ct. Appeals (DC cir.) 1987, US Dist. Ct. (ea. dist.) Va. 1988, US Ct. Appeals DC, 1987, US Ct. Appeals (4th cir.) 1990, Mich. 1994; cert. comml. pilot, multiengine, land and instrument. Aerospace engr. NASA, Huntsville, Ala., 1962-63; rsch., teaching asst. U. Ala. Rsch. Inst., Huntsville, Ala., 1963-64; research fellow NASA, Cambridge, Mass., 1964-65; assoc. prof. U. Ala., Tuscaloosa, 1965-69; mng. dir. Univ. Assocs., Washington, 1969-72; prof., assoc. dean George Washington U., Washington, 1972-77; v.p., gen. counsel Council on Postsecondary Accreditation, Washington, 1977-83; exec. dir. Am. Inst. Biol. Sci., Washington, 1983-87; pres. Am. Found. Biol. Scis., Washington, 1987-93, Lawrence Tech. U., 1993—2006, chancellor, 2006—. Cons., evaluator, accreditation rev. coun. commn. on instns. of higher edn. Noth Ctrl. Assn. Colls. and Schs., Chgo.; bd. dirs. Automation Alley, Mich. Sci. and Math. Alliance, Mich. Small Aircraft Transp. Sys. Author: (with others) Understanding Accreditation, 1983; pub. BioScience; contbr. chpts. to books. Mem. Diocesan Adv. Coun., Arlington, Va., 1978-84, Fairfax County Dem. Com., Va., 1979-95; judge No. Va. Sci. Fair, 1976—; trustee, sec. Southeastern U., Washington, 1983-87; trustee BIOSIS, Inc., Phila. and London, 1991-93; mem. Oakland County Workforce Devel. Bd., Mich., 1996—; bd. dirs. Automation Alley, 1999—, Detroit area coun. Boy Scouts Am., 2003-. Recipient Citizenship award Am. Legion, 1959, Olive Branch award Editors and Writers Com., NYC, 1986, Horace H. Rackham award Engring. Soc. Detroit, 2004; fellow NSF, 1964. Fellow AAAS; mem. ABA, AAUP, Am. Assn. Univ. Adminstrs. (pres. 1984-85), Engring. and Sci. Devel. Found. (bd. dirs., pres. 1996-2000, fellow Engring. Soc. 1997), Am. Coun. Edn. (bus. and higher edn. forum), Soc. Automotive Engrs., Nat. Soc. Black Engrs. (hon.), The Engring. Soc. Detroit (bd. dirs. 1999—), Assn. Ind. Colls. and Univs. Mich., Mich. Small Aircraft Transp. Program, Detroit Regional C. of C. (bd. dirs.), Circumnavigators Club, Detroit Econ. Club (bd. dirs.), Detroit Athletic Club, Cosmos Club, Capitol Hill Club, Phi Beta Kappa, Sigma Xi, Tau Beta Pi. Roman Catholic. Avocations: flying, history, sailing. Office: Lawrence Tech U 21000 W 10 Mile Rd Ste M351 Southfield MI 48075-1058 Personal E-mail: mail@charleschambers.com.

CHAMBERS, CURTIS ALLEN, clergyman, church administrator; b. Damascus, Ohio, Sept. 24, 1924; s. Binford Vincent and Margaret Esther (Patterson) C.; m. Anna June Winn, Aug. 26, 1946; children: David Lloyd, Curtis Allen II, Deborah Ann, Charles Cloyde. Th.B., Malone Coll., 1946; AB, Ind. Wesleyan U., 1947; B.D., Asbury Theol. Sem., 1950; postgrad., Oberlin Grad. Sch. Theology, 1951-53; S.T.M., Temple U., 1955, S.T.D., 1960; D.D. (hon.), Lebanon Valley Coll., 1967. Ordained to ministry Evang. United Brethren Ch., 1954. Pastor 1st Ch., Cleve., 1951-53, Rockville Ch., Harrisburg, Pa., 1953-59; editor adult publs. Evang. United Brethren Ch., 1959-65; assoc. editor Ch. and Home mag., Dayton, Ohio, 1963-66, editor, 1967-69; asst. editorial dir. Together and Christian Advocate, Meth. Pub. House, Park Ridge, Ill., 1969; editor Together mag., 1969-73; acting editorial dir. gen. periodicals United Meth. Ch., 1971-72, editorial dir., 1972-73; gen. sec. United Meth. Communications, 1973-84; gen. mgr. Alternate View Network, 1984-85; minister edn. and communication First United Meth. Ch., Shreveport, La., 1985-87, minister pastoral care and communication, 1987-88; minister program and communication St. Paul's United Meth. Ch., Monroe, La., 1988-90; religious communication cons. Nashville, 1990—; assoc. pastor Andrew Price United Meth. Ch., Nashville, 1991-94. Book editor Evang. United Brethren Ch., 1965-68; co-editor Plan of Union, United Meth. Ch., 1965-68, Plan of Union, United Meth. Ch. (Book of Discipline), 1968, chmn. staff com. long range planning, 1969-72, mem. commn. on ch. union, 1965-68; dir. radio-TV relations gen. confs. Evang. United Brethren Ch., 1958, 62, 66, United Meth. Ch., 1966, 68; Chmn. commn. on ednl. media Nat. Council Chs., 1965-66, chmn. com. on audio visual and broadcast edn., 1962-65, exec. com. broadcasting and film commn., chmn. communications commn., 1975-78, v.p., 1975-78; chmn. Religious Communications Congress, 1980; named 1 of 12 editors sent to Middle East on fact-finding trip, 1969 Contbr. articles to religious lit. Served as capt. (chaplain) CAP, 1960-65. Recipient Distinguished Alumni award Malone Coll., 1967, 92, Alumni of Year, 1978, Distinguished Alumni award Goshen High Sch. Alumni Assn., 1992; named to Communicators Hall of Fame United Meth. Assn. Communicators, 1992. Mem. Aircraft Owners and Pilots Assn., United Meth. Assn. Communicators (v.p. 1968-72, Communicators' Hall of Fame 1992), World Assn. Christian Communications (central com., chmn. Jour. editorial bd. 1975-82, chmn. periodical devel. com., exec. com., sec. 1978-82), Asso. Ch. Press (hon. life), Religious Pub. Relations Council. Clubs: Chgo. Press (Dayton), Torch (Dayton). Home: Westminster Village 1120 E Davis Dr Apt 423 Terre Haute IN 47802-4067 Office Phone: 812-238-8516. Personal E-mail: curtisa@joimail.com. E-mail: curtisa3@verizon.net. *When I was young I thought that anything was possible for me and that I had a long, long time to achieve it. With maturity I have come to a recognition of mortality, finitude, a limitation of time and opportunity. Thus my life has taught me three things: 1) Choose the best. Life is too precious to squander it on the second rate. 2) Live for others. The quality of one's life is enhanced rather than diminished as one shares himself/herself with others. 3) Fulfill your dreams. Tomorrow may never come; act now so that life's opportunities may not be lost forever.*

CHAMBERS, DENNING JESSYCA, middle school educator; b. Westport, Conn., Feb. 15, 1952; d. James Peter and Iva Fay (Owens) McCleery; m. Thomas Neil Chambers (div.); 1 child, Melanie. BS in Mus. Edn. cum laude, U. Bridgeport, Conn., 1992; M in Mus. Edn., SUNY, Fredonia, 1998. Cert. tchr. NY. Vocal and music tchr. various elem. schs. and East Mid. Sch., West Seneca, NY, 1993—. Panelist Arts in Edn. Inst.; presenter, lectr. in field. Musician (soloist): Orchard Park Symphony. Pianist, vocalist Our Lady of Sacred Heart Ch., Colden, NY, 2002—04. Named Best Performer of Music Sch., U. Bridgeport, 1990; Dana scholar, 1990. Mem.: NY State Music Educators Assn., Erie County Music Educators Assn. Independent. Avocation: horseback riding. Home: 60 Tarn Tr Glenwood NY 14069

CHAMBERS, DONALD ARTHUR, biochemistry and molecular medicine educator; b. NYC, Sept. 24, 1936; AB, Columbia U., 1959, PhD, 1972. Rsch. biochemist dept. surgery Harvard Med. Sch./Mass. Gen. Hosp., Boston, 1961-66; rsch. fellow in hematology dept. surgery Harvard Med. Sch./Beth Israel Hosp., Boston, 1967-68; faculty fellow in chem. biology Columbia U., NYC, 1969-71; asst. rsch. biochemist Ctr. for Med. Genetics dept. medicine U. Calif. Med. Ctr., San Francisco, 1972-74, lectr. in biochemistry and biophysics, 1972-74, asst. prof. molecular biology and biochemistry, 1974-75; asst. prof. biol. chemistry and dermatology U. Mich., Ann Arbor, 1975-79, assoc. prof. biol. chemistry, 1979; prof. molecular biology U. Ill., Chgo., 1979—, prof. biol. chemistry, 1980—, rsch. prof. dermatology, 1981—, prof. biol. psychiatry, 1996. Assoc. mem. Dental Rsch. Inst. U. Mich., 1978-79, adj. rsch. investigator Dept. Biol. Chemistry, 1979—; dir. Ctr. for Molecular Biology of Oral Disease, U. Ill., Chgo., 1979—, interim head dept. biochemistry, 1985, head dept. biochemistry, 1986—; vis. scholar Green Coll., Oxford U., 1989-93, hon. vis. fellow, 1993—; sr. rsch. assoc. Wellcome Unit History of Medicine, Oxford. 2000-; fellow Honors Coll., 1985—, Phi Kappa Phi lectr., 1991, Sigma Xi lectr., 2001; nat. action com. Am. Assn. Dental Rsch., 1981—; study sect. rev. NIH, 1983-86, 92, 98—. Mem. editl. bd.: Perspectives in Biology and Medicine. Recipient James Howard McGregor prize Columbia U., 1971; named Inventor of Yr., U. Ill., 1990; fellow in hematology NIH, 1967-68, fellow in chem. biology, 1969-71; Rsch. grantee NIH, Am. Cancer Soc., Office of Naval Rsch.,1986—, Helene Curtis, Inc., 1988—, Tng. grantee NIH-NIGMS, 1975-79, NIH-NIAMDD, 1976-79, 77-80, NIH-NIDR-NIAMDD, 1980—, NIH-NCI, 1982-88, NIH-NIDCR, 2003-, NIH-NIAID, 2003-. Mem. AAAS, Am. Assn. Med. Colls., Am. Assn. Immunology, Am. Chem. Soc., Am. Fedn. Clin. Rsch., Am. Soc. Biol. Chemistry, Am. Soc. Cell Biology, Am. Soc. Microbiology, Internat. Assn. Dental Rsch. (com. on rsch. progress 1982-85, chmn. 1984-85, chmn. grad. tng. forum com. exptl. pathology sect. 1983), Assn. Dept. Chmn. Biol. Chemistry, Chgo. Assn. Immunologists, N.Y. Acad. Scis. (organizer meeting The Double Helix, 40 Yrs. 1993), Royal Soc. Medicine, Soc. Investigative Dermatology, Oxford Med. Alumni Assn. (N.Am. rep. 2000—), Green Coll. Oxford Soc. (N.Am. rep. 2000—), Athenaeum Club London, Phi Kappa Phi, Sigma Xi (NIDCR 1998, spl. emphisii panel), Sigma Xi (pres.-elect 2000, pres. 2001), Oxford Med. Alumni (N.Am Sec. 2001-). Achievements include patents (U.S., Can.) for method of determining periodontal disease, (with other) method of quantifying aspartate amino transferase in periodontal disease; research in role of cyclic nucleotides, prostaglandins, hormones and other regulatory factors in the regulation of cell function, proliferation and differentiation, in molecular medicine in neural-immune interactions, the regulatory mechanisms of host-microbial interactions, in the history and devel. of concepts in the bio-med. scis. Office: U Ill Coll Med Dept Biochemistry 1819 W Polk St # C 536 Chicago IL 60612-7331 also: Ctr Molecular Biol Oral Diseases 801 S Paulina St # C 860 Chicago IL 60612-7210 Office Phone: 312-996-1294. Business E-Mail: donc@uic.edu.

CHAMBERS, DUSTIN LEE, economics professor; b. Fresno, Calif., Nov. 15, 1976; s. Dwaine Lee and Linda Faye Chambers; m. Silvana Stojmenovska, May 30, 1997; children: Sarah J., Devin L. BA in Econs., Calif. State U., Fresno, 1997; MA in Econs., U. Calif., LA, 1998; PhD in Econs., U. Calif., Riverside, 2004. Asst. prof. econs. Salisbury U., Md., 2004—. Mem.: Econometric Soc., Am. Econ. Assn., Omicron Delta Epsilon. Office: Salisbury U 1101 Camden Ave Salisbury MD 21801-6860 Office Phone: 410-543-6320. E-mail: dlchambers@salisbury.edu.

CHAMBERS, ELENORA STRASEL, artist; b. Strassel, Oreg. d. Augustine George and Frieda Rose (Westermann) Strasel; m. Edward Lucas Chambers, Oct. 9, 1954; children: Robert, Margaret L. BA, Marylhurst Coll., Oreg., 1942; student, Portland Art Mus. Sch., U. Miami, Fla., Fla. Internat. U. One person shows include Mirell Gallery, Coconut grove, Fla., 1961, Miami Mus. Modern Art, 1965, 80 Washington Sq. E., N.Y.C., 1983; Kendall Campus Art Gall., Miami, 1992, group exhbns. include Ringling Mus. Sarasota, Fla., 1956, Norton Gallery, West Palm Beach, 1956, Lowe Art Mus., Miami (award winner), 1957, 1976, Soc. of Four Arts, Palm Beach, 1958, 61, 62, 65, 67, 72, 74, 77, 81, Ft. Lauderdale Mus. Arts (award winner), 1964, 65, Profl. Women Artists, Lowe Art Mus., Miami, 1976, Mus. of Arts and Scis., Daytona Beach, Fla., 1979, Met. Dade County Coun. of Arts and scis., Miami, 1979, Lowe Levinson Gallery, Miami Beach, 1981, North Miami Mus. and Art Ctr., 1987, Metro-Dade Cultural Ctr., Miami, 1990, Mus. Contemporary Art, 1995, House Art Gallery, N.Y., 1996, Ambrosino Gallery, Miami, 1997, Ambrosino Gallery, Miami, 1998, Robert Hittel, Ft. Lauderdale, 1998, Dorsch Gallery, Miami, 1999, Kendall Campus Art Gallery, Miami, 2000, Snitzer Gallery, Miami, 2002; works in permanent collections Miami Mus. Modern Art, Hopkins-Easton Assocs., Omni Internat., many pvt. collections. Recipient Beaux Art award Lowe Art Mus., 1957, Hortt Meml. award Ft. Lauderdale Mus. Arts, 1964, Atwater Kent award 29th Ann. Exhbn. Contemporary Am. Paintings, Soc. Four Arts, 1967, 39th Ann. exhbn., 1977.

CHAMBERS, GUY WAYNE, lawyer; b. Harvey, Ill., Feb. 18, 1956; s. Robert Rood and Martha (Wayne) C. BS in Chem. Engring. with highest honors, U. Calif., Santa Barbara, 1978; JD, Columbia U., 1981. Bar: Calif. 1981, U.S. Ct. Appeals (fed. cir.) 1982, U.S. Patent and Trademark Office 1982, U.S. Ct. Appeals (9th cir.) 1992, U.S. Supreme Ct. 1995. Trial atty. civil div. U.S. Dept. Justice, Washington, 1981-84; assoc. Townsend and Townsend and Crew, San Fransisco, 1984-91, ptnr., 1991—. Project mgr. patent svcs. contract NIH; spkr. in field. Contbr. articles to profl. publs. Mem. San Francisco Intellectual Property Law Assn. Office: Townsend & Townsend & Crew 8th flr 2 Embarcadero Ctr San Francisco CA 94111 Office Phone: 415-576-0200. Office Fax: 415-576-0300. E-mail: gwchambers@townsend.com.

CHAMBERS, HENRY GEORGE, orthopedic surgeon; b. Portsmouth, Va., June 22, 1956; s. Walter Charles and Teresa Frances (Fernandez) C.; m. Jill Annette Swanson, June 10, 1978; children: Sean Michael, Reid Christopher. BA summa cum laude in Biochemistry, U. Colo., 1978; MD, Tulane U. Sch. Medicine, New Orleans, 1982. Diplomate Am. Bd. Orthop. Surgery. Commd. 2d lt. US Army, 1978, advanced through grades to maj., 1988; intern Fitzsimmons Army Med. Ctr., Aurora, Colo., 1982—83; resident orthop. surgery Brooke Army Med. Ctr., Ft. Sam Houston, Tex., 1983—87, chief resident, 1986—87, staff orthop. surgeon to asst. dir. residency program, 1987—89, asst. chief surgeon orthop. surgery svc., 1990—92; staff orthop. surgeon DeWitt Army Hosp., Ft. Belvoir, Va., 1987; pediat. orthop. fellow San Diego Children's Hosp., 1989—90; asst. prof. surgery Uniformed Svcs. U. Health Scis., Bethesda, Md., 1987—; asst. program dir. Brooke Army Med. Ctr. Orthop. Surgery, 1987—92; assoc. prof. U. Calif.-San Diego Med. Ctr., 1989—; pvt. practice San Diego, 1992—; chmn. dept. orthop. surgery San Diego Children's Hosp., 1997—2001, chief of staff, 2004—06; med. dir. Motion Analysis Lab.; med. affairs officer, David Sutherland dir. cerebral palsy Rady Children's Hosp., San Diego. Co-author: Long Distance Runner's Guide to Training, 1983, The Pediatric Spine—Principles and Practice, 2000, Fractures in Children, 2001; contbr. over 70 articles to profl. jours. Physician, St. Vincent de Paul Clinic for Homeless, San Diego, 1989—; v.p. United Cerebral Palsy. Recipient Comdrs. award for outstanding rsch., Brooke Army Med. Ctr., 1987. Fellow: Am. Orthop. Assn., We. Orthop. Assn. (pres. San Diego Chpt.), Am. Acad. Orthop. Surgeons, Acad. Orthop. Soc., Pediat. Orthop. Soc. N.Am., Acad. Cerebral Palsy Devel. Medicine (v.p.), Am. Acad. Pediats., Orthop. Rsch. Soc.; mem.: Physicians for Social Responsibility, Phi Beta Kappa. Democrat. Unitarian Universalist. Avocations: weightlifting, golf. Home: 5458 Sandburg Ave San Diego CA 92122-4128 Office Phone: 858-966-6798. Business E-Mail: hchambers@rchsd.org.

CHAMBERS, JACK ALLEN, application developer, educator; b. Hamilton, Ohio; s. Glen S. and H. Edna C.; m. Ruth Coe; children: Melissa Ann, Wendy Colleen AB, U. Miami, 1954; MA, U. Cin., 1955; PhD in Indsl. and Orgnl. Psychology, Mich. State U., 1964. Dir. computer ctr. Mansfield (Pa.) U., 1972-74; dir. computing and comms. Calif. State U., Fresno, 1974-86, Duquesne U., Pitts., 1986-89; exec. dir. computing and comms. Loyola Coll., Balt., 1989-90; planning and info. rsch. ctr. mgr. Fla. C.C., Jacksonville, 1990-99, interim dir. Assessment and Cert. Ctrs., 1999—2000, dir. program devel. for instrnl. tech., 2000—04, dir. learning technologies and profl. devel., 2004—05; exec. dir. Orgnl. Learning Svcs., 2005—. Co-author: (with others) (book) Computer Assisted Instruction: Its Use in the Classroom, 1983; (chpt.) Motivating Students for Lifetime Learning in New Directions in Education and Training Technology, 1985; author: chpt. in Facilitating Academic Software Development, 1988; editor: (books) Selected Papers Fifth InternatConf. on College Teaching and Learning, 1994, Sixth Conf., 1995, Seventh Conf., 1996, Eighth Conf., 1997, Ninth Conf., 1998, Tenth Conf., 1999, Eleventh Conf., 2000, Twelfth Conf., 2001, Thirteenth Conf., 2002, Fourteenth Conf., 2003, Fifteenth Conf., 2004, Sixteenth Conf., 2005, Seventeenth Conf., 2006, Eighteenth Conf., 2007. Grantee: James McKeen Cattell Fund, Calif. State Dept. Edn., Calif. State Univ. System, NSF, FIPSE. Office: Fla CC at Jacksonville 501 W State St Jacksonville FL 32202-4086 Office Phone: 904-632-3231. Business E-Mail: jchamber@fccj.edu.

CHAMBERS, JERRY RAY, school system administrator, consultant; b. St. Joseph, Mo., Oct. 1, 1947; s. Ray Linden and Betty Allene (Roach) C.; m. Jacqueline Kaye Thomas, Feb. 11, 1967; children: Sandra Kaye, Jennifer Lynn. AS, Mo. Western State Coll., 1967; BA, U. Mo., Kansas City, 1969, MA in Edn. Adminstrn. and History, 1971; postgrad., U. Madras, India, 1974; PhD in Edn. Adminstrn., U. Mo., Kansas City, 1986. Tchr. Lillis High Sch., Kansas City, Mo., 1969; high sch. tchr. Sch. Dist. St. Joseph, Mo., 1969-80, dir. media svcs. Mo., 1980-90; prof. Mo. We. State Coll., 1986, U. Mo. Kansas City, 1984—85; supt. schs. Sch. Dist. Washington, Mo., 1990-2001; prof. St. Louis U., 1998; supt. schs. Wolf Br. Sch. Dist., Swansea, Ill., 2001—04, Mehlville Sch. Dist., St. Louis, 2006—. Coun. pres. ITV Kansas City Pub. TV, 1988-90; assessor Mo. Prin. Assess Ctr., DESE, Jefferson City, Mo., 1987-90; bd. dirs. 353 Econ. Devel. Corp. Washington, 1991-2000, Network Ednl. Devel., St. Louis, 1993-96; exec. com. Coop. Sch. Dists. St. Louis, chmn., 1999-2000. Author: Missouri Students Tune IN, 1987, History of Missouri Instructional Television, 1986, Beyond the Bullet Hole, 1988. Bd. dirs. Regional Bluffs Libr., St. Joseph, 1989, United Fund, Washington, 1992-95; campaign co-chmn. Earnings Tax Com., St. Joseph, 1988; chmn. edn. divsn. United Way, St. Joseph, 1986-89, bd. dirs. 1992; bd. dirs. Tri-County Fine Arts Ctr., 1992-97. Recipient Alumni Achievement award U. Mo., Kansas City, 1988, Disting. Alumni award Mo. Western State Coll., 1990, Disting. Leadership award Nat. Assn. Com. Leadership, 1988, Key to City award City of St. Joseph Mayor, 1990, Mo. Outstanding Supt. award, 1999, Pearce award 1999; Fulbright scholar, 1974. Mem. Am. Assn. Sch. Adminstrs., Ill. Assn. Sch. Adminstrs., Lions Club (Washington chpt., 1990-2003, St. Joseph Host Club pres. 1989-90, chmn., exec. com. Cooperating Sch. Dists. Greater St Louis, 1996-98, pres. CSD 1999-2000), Mo. Assn. Sch. Adminstrs. Avocations: basketball, tennis, reading, model railroading, nostalgia, baseball. Home and Office: 2 Winchester Ct Washington MO 63090-5314 Office Phone: 314-302-6902. E-mail: jjchambers@charter.net.

CHAMBERS, JOAN LOUISE, retired librarian, dean; b. Denver, Mar. 22, 1937; d. Joseph Harvey and Clara Elizabeth (Carleton) Baker; m. Donald Ray Chambers, Aug. 17, 1958 BA in English Lit., U. No. Colo., Greeley, 1958; MS in L.S., U. Calif.-Berkeley, 1970; MS in Systems Mgmt., U. So. Calif., 1985; cert., Coll. for Fin. Planning, 1989. Libr. U. Nev., Reno, 1970-79; asst. univ. libr. U. Calif., San Diego, 1979-81, univ. libr. Riverside, 1981—85; dean librs., prof. Colo. State U., Ft. Collins, 1985-97, emeritus dean and prof., 1997—. Mgmt. intern Duke U. Libr., Durham, N.C., 1978-79; sr. fellow UCLA Summer, 1982; cons. tng. program Assn. of Rsch. Libraries, Washington, 1981; libr. cons. Calif. State U., Sacramento, 1982-83, U. Wyo., 1985-86, 94-95, U. Nebr., 1991-92, Calif. State U. System, 1993-94, Univ. No. Ariz., 1994-95. Contbr. articles to profl. jours., chpts. to books. Bd. dir. Consumers Union, 1996-2006. U. Calif. instl. improvement grantee, 1980-81; State of Nev. grantee, 1976, ARL grantee, 1983-84. Mem.: PEO, Colo. Mountain Club, Phi Kappa Phi, Kappa Delta Phi, Phi Lambda Theta, Beta Phi Mu. Avocations: hiking, snow shoeing, skiing, bicycling, tennis. Home and Office: PO Box 1477 Edwards CO 81632-1477 E-mail: chambers@vail.net.

CHAMBERS, JOHN THOMAS, computer systems network executive; b. Cleve., Aug. 23, 1949; s. June and John Chambers; m. Elaine Prater, 1974; 2 children. BS, BA, W.Va. U., 1971, JD, 1974; MBA, Ind. U., 1975. Mktg. mgr. IBM, 1976—82; v.p. central U.S. ops. Wang Laboratories, 1983—87, sr. v.p., Americas/Asia/Pacific ops., 1987—89, sr. v.p., U.S. ops., 1989—90; sr. v.p. worldwide ops. Cisco Systems, Inc., San Jose, Calif., 1991-94, exec. v.p., 1994-95, pres., CEO, 1995—2006, chmn., CEO, 2006—. Vice chmn. Nat. Infrastructure adv. coun., 2002—; Served on Bill Clinton Trade Policy com.; bd. dirs. Cisco Sys. Inc., 1993—, Clarify, Inc., San Jose, 1995—96, Arbor Software, Sunnyvale, Calif., 1995—96. Named one of 50 Who Matter Now, Business 2.0, 2007; recipient Woodrow Wilson Award for Corp. Citizenship, Woodrow Wilson Center for internat. ctr. for Scholars of the Smithsonian Inst., Lifetime Achievement award, Smithsonian Inst., Presdl. award, Ron Brown award for Corp. Leadership, Bus. Coun., Frederick D. Patterson Award, United Negro Coll. Fund. Office: Cisco Sys Inc 170 W Tasman Dr Bldg 10 San Jose CA 95134-1706 E-mail: jochambe@cisco.com.*

CHAMBERS, JOHN WHITECLAY, II, history professor; b. West Chester, Pa., Aug. 6, 1936; s. John McCausland and Le-Arie P. Chambers; m. Dorothy Roman, 1958; children: John Bret, Jeffrey Mark, Michael Adam; m. Amy Russo Piro, 1982; 1 child, Tacy Elizabeth. Reporter Pasadena (Calif.) Ind. Star-News, 1958-60, San Rafael (Calif.) Ind.-Jour., 1960-61; news and documentary writer/prodr. KRON-TV, San Francisco, 1961-65; asst. prof. history Barnard Coll., Columbia U., NYC, 1972-82, Rutgers U., New Brunswick, NJ, 1982-87, assoc. prof., 1987-93, prof., 1993—2002, disting. prof., 2002—, dept. chair, 1997-98. Fulbright lectr. U. Rome, spring 1982; project dir. Rutgers Ctr. Hist. Analysis, 1993-95; vis. lectr. U. Tokyo, 1997. Author: Three Generals on War, 1973, Draftees or Volunteers, 1975, The Eagle and the Dove: The Peace Movement and U.S. Foreign Policy, 1900-1922, 1976, 2d edit., 1991, The Tyranny of Change: America in the Progressive Era, 1890-1920, 1980, 3d edit., 2000; author: (with Warren Susman) American History Reading Lists, 3 vols., 1983; author: To Raise an Army: The Draft Comes to Modern America, 1987 (Best Book award Soc. Mil. History, 1988, Best Book on Mil. History, 1987); author: (with Charles C. Moskos) The New Conscientious Objection: From Sacred to Secular Resistance, 1993; author: (with David Culbert) World War II Film and History, 1996; author: (with G. Kurt Piehler) Major Problems in American Military History, 1998; author: George Washington in Cranbury: The Road to the Battle of Monmouth, 2003 (Dist. Pub. award N.J. League Hist. Soc., 2004); author: (with Arlene Gardner) Conflict Resolution and United States History, 2007; editor in chief Oxford Co. to Am. Mil. History, 1999 (Disting. Ref. Book award Soc. Mil. History, 2001). NEH grantee, 1974; humanities fellow Rockefeller Found., 1981-82, vis. fellow Inst. Advanced Study, Princeton, 1995-96; recipient Outstanding Tchrs. award Rutgers U., 2005, Outstanding Tchr. award, 1995. Mem.: Soc. Mil. History, Orgn. Am. Historians, Am. Hist. Assn., Peace History Soc. (pres. 1975—77). Office: Rutgers U 16 Seminary Pl New Brunswick NJ 08901-1108 E-mail: chamber@rci.rutgers.edu.

CHAMBERS, JULIUS LEVONNE, lawyer; b. Montgomery County, NC, Oct. 6, 1936; BA, N.C. Cen. U., 1958; MA, U. Mich., 1959; LLB, U. N.C., 1962; LLM, Columbia U., 1963. Bar: N.C. 1962, N.Y. 1986. Ptnr. Chambers, Ferguson, Stein, Chambers, Adkins, Gresham & Sumter, Charlotte, NC, 1964-84; dir., counsel NAACP Legal Def. and Ednl. Fund, NYC, 1984-92; chancellor N.C. Ctrl. U., Durham, 1993-2000; with Ferguson, Stein, Gresham & Sumter, Charlotte, 2000—. Former trustee N.J. State Bd. Higher Edn.; former bd. visitors Harvard U., Columbia U. Law Sch.; former trustee U. Pa., mem. bd. overseers Law Sch.; former bd. dirs. Children's Def. Fund, Legal Aid Soc. N.Y. Mem. ABA (bd. editors ABA jour.), N.C. Bar Assn., Mecklenburg County Bar Assn., N.Y. State Bar Assn., Assn. of Bar of City of N.Y., Nat. Bar Assn., Assn. Black Lawyers N.C., Order of Coif, Order of Golden Fleece, Phi Alpha Theta. Office: Ferguson Stein Gresham & Sumter 741 Kenilworth Ave Ste 300 Charlotte NC 28204 Office Phone: 704-375-8461. Personal E-mail: jchamb1230@aol.com. Business E-Mail: jchambers@fergusonstein.com.

CHAMBERS, JUSTIN, actor; b. Springfield, Ohio, July 11, 1970; m. Keisha Chambers, 1993; children: Isabella, Maya, Kaila, Eva, Jackson. Actor: (TV films) Harvest of Fire, 1996, Rose Hill, 1997, Seasons of Love, 1999, Hysterical Blindness, 2002, The Secret Service, 2004; (TV series) Four Corners, 1998, Cold Case, 2003, Grey's Anatomy, 2005— (Outstanding Performance by an Ensemble in a Drama Series, SAG, 2007); (films) Liberty Heights, 1999, The Wedding Planner, 2001, The Musketeer, 2001, Leo, 2002, For Which It Stands, 2003, Southern Belles, 2005, The Zodiac, 2005. Office: c/o Grey's Anatomy Los Feliz Tower 4th Fl 4151 Prospect Ave Los Angeles CA 90027 also: c/o The Gersh Agency 232 N Canon Dr Beverly Hills CA 90210*

CHAMBERS, KENTON LEE, botany educator; b. LA, Sept. 27, 1929; s. Maynard Macy and Edna Georgia (Miller) C.; m. Henrietta Laing, June 21, 1958; children: Elaine Patricia, David Macy. AB with highest honors, Whittier Coll., 1950; PhD (NSF fellow), Stanford U., 1955. Instr. biol. scis. Stanford (Calif.) U., 1954-55; instr. botany, asst. prof. Yale U., New Haven, Conn., 1956-60; assoc. prof., prof. botany Oreg. State U., Corvallis, 1960-90, prof. emeritus, 1991—. Curator Herbarium, 1960-90; program dir. systematic biology NSF, Washington, 1967-68. Contbr. articles in field to profl. jours. Fellow AAAS; mem. Bot. Soc. Am. (Merit award 1990), Am. Soc. Plant Taxonomists, Am. Inst. Biol. Scis., Calif. Bot. Soc. Home: 4761 SW Hollyhock Cir Corvallis OR 97333-1385 Office: Oreg State U Herbarium Botany Dept Corvallis OR 97331-2902 E-mail: chamberk@science.oregonstate.edu.

CHAMBERS, LETITIA PEARL CAROLINE, consulting firm executive; b. Alva, Okla., Feb. 1, 1943; d. E. Wade and Anita (Sims) Chambers; m. Stephen Morelock, Mar. 1964 (div. 1970); 1 child, Melissa. BA, U. Okla., 1965; MS, Okla. State U., 1971, EdD, 1973. Tchr. Oklahoma City Pub. Schs., 1965-70, adminstr., 1973-74; dir. fed. programs N.Mex. State Edn. Agy., Santa Fe, 1974-75; sr. analyst US Senate Budget Com., Washington, 1976-77; minority staff dir. US Senate Spl. Com. on Aging, Washington, 1978; staff dir. US Senate Com. on Labor & Human Resources, Washington, 1979-81; pres. Chambers Assocs., Inc., Washington, 1982—2003; U.S. rep. to the UN gen. assembly 51st Session, NYC, 1996; exec. dir. N.Mex. Commn. on Higher Edn., Santa Fe, 2004—05; mng. dir. Navigant Cons., Washington, 2005—. Pres. Coalition of Publicly Traded Partnerships, Washington, 1987-2004; dir. Adams Nat. Bank, Washington, 1989-94; dir. Stratego Investments, Prague, Cech Republic, 1997-2000; commr. Western Interstate Commn. on Higher Edn., 2004-05. Author various senate reports, policy studies. Chief budget adv. Clinton/Gore Transition, 1992—93; trustee Inst. Am. Indian Arts and Culture, Santa Fe, 1997—2006; dir. nature youth program Wings, 2006—; elder Chevy Chase (Md.) Presbyn. Ch., 1986—89; bd. visitors U. Okla., 1995—2002; bd. dirs., chair IAIA Found., 1997—2000; bd. dirs. Internat. Shakespeare Guild, 1998—, Ctr. for Nat. Policy, 1993—2002. Recipient Disting. Alumni award U. Okla., 1998. Mem. Coun. for Excellence in Govt. (bd. dirs. 1990-2003), Cosmos Club. Avocation: gardening. Office: Navigant Consulting 1801 K St NW Washington DC 20006 Home: 2022 Foothills Rd Santa Fe NM 87505 Business E-Mail: lchambers@navigantconsulting.com.

CHAMBERS, MILTON WARREN, retired architect; b. LA, Aug. 5, 1928; s. Joe S. and Barbara N. (Harris) C.; m. Elizabeth M. Smith, Nov. 27, 1949; children: Mark, Michael, Daniel, Matthew. Student, Coll. of Sequoias, 1948-49, Harvard U., 1990. Lic. architect, Calif., Nev., Colo., Hawaii, Mont.; cert. Nat. Coun. Archtl. Registration Bds. Apprentice architect Kastner & Kastner Architects, Visalia, Calif., 1950-57; project architect Wurster, Bernardi & Emmons, Architects, San Francisco, 1958-63, Claude Oakland, Architect, 1964-65; chief architect Bank of Am., 1965-68; pres., owner Milton W. Chambers, Architect, San Rafael, 1969-82, The Chambers Group, Architects, Rancho Mirage, 1983—99. Architect, designer St. Margaret's Episcopal Church, 1988. Foreman Marin County Grand Jury, San Rafael, 1976; mem. Archtl. Design Rev. Bd., Rancho Mirage, 1986-99; trustee Marywood Sch., Rancho Mirage, 1990-99; trustee, pres. Rep. Pub. Devel. Authority, 2003-06, Friends of Stonerose Eocene Era Fossil Site, Rep., 2004-06. Cpl. U.S. Army, 1946-48, PTO, 50-51. Mem. AIA (pres. Calif. Desert chpt. 1986-87, 96&, dir. Calif. coun. 1989-90, 96-98), Rotary Internat., Terra Linda Rotary Club (pres. 1975-76, dist. gov. 1993-94), Rancho Mirage Rotary Club (pres. 1986-87). Republican. Episcopalian. Avocation: playing the banjo and guitar. Mailing: PO Box 1235 Republic WA 99166 Personal E-mail: mwcaia@aol.com.

CHAMBERS, NORMAN C., manufacturing executive; B, Springfield Coll.; MBA, Boston Coll., 1982. Mgmt. positions through sr. v.p. Halliburton Co., 1985—2000; pres., CEO Petrocosm Corp., 2000—01; COO Capstone Turbine Corp., 2001—02; pres. Comfort Systems USA, 2002—03, pres., COO, 2003—04, NCI Bldg. Systems Inc., Houston, 2004—06, pres., CEO, 2007—. Office: NCI Bldg Systems 10943 N Sam Houston Pkwy Houston TX 77064*

CHAMBERS, ROBERT HUNTER, III, academic administrator, consultant, historian, educator; b. Winston-Salem, NC, Oct. 24, 1939; s. Robert Hunter and Hildred (MacDonald) C.; m. Alice Louise Grant, Aug. 18, 1962 (div. 1995); children: Lisa, Grant. AB, Duke U., 1962; B.D., Yale U., 1965; PhD, Brown U., 1969. Asst. prof., dean Davenport Coll. Yale U., New Haven, 1969-74; vis. fellow Clare Coll., Cambridge U., Eng., 1972-73; prof., dean Coll. Arts and Scis. Bucknell U., Lewisburg, Pa., 1975-84; vis. scholar Doshisha U., Kyoto, 1982; pres., prof. English Western Md. Coll., Westminster, 1984—2000; sr. cons. Marts & Lundy, Inc., Gainesville, Fla., 2001—; provost, dean Trinity Coll., U. Melbourne, Australia, 2004—05. Founding dir. Wellway Ctrs., Inc., Ft. Worth, 1984—88, WMC Devel. Corp., 1985—88; presdl. chmn. Centennial Conf., Md. and Pa., 1986, 1998—99; mem. segmental adv. com. State Bd. Higher Edn., Annapolis, Md., 1985—88; mem. internat. adv. coun. U. Buckingham, England; mem. cmty. bd. Carroll Co. Health Svcs., Inc., 1988—2000; assoc. fellow Davenport Coll., Yale U. Author, editor: Twentieth Century Interpretations of All the King's Men, 1977. Contbr. articles to profl. jours. Bd. dirs. Ind. Coll. Fund of Md., Balt.,1984—; mem. coun. on grad. edn. Brown U., 1989; mem. City of Westminster Mayoral Task Force, 1990; co-chair spl. gifts Am. Heart Assn.; mem. task force on assessment Nat. Assn. Ind. Colls. and Univs., 1991-92, mem. commn. on state rels., 1992-95; mem. Gov.'s Edn. Policy Transition Team, 1994-95; mem. Md. Citizens for Arts; bd. dir. Coun. of Ind. Colls., 1997-2000. Rockefeller Brothers fellow, 1962-63; Nat. Endowment for the Humanities grantee, 1978, U.S.-Japan Friendship Commn. grantee, 1982; recipient Balt. Regional Coun. Govts. award, 1989. Mem.: NCAA (pres. coun. 1999—2000), MLA, Internat. Assn. Univ. Presidents, Coun. on Econ. Edn. in Md. (trustee 1), Am. Studies Assn., Md. Ind. Coll. and Univ. Assn. (bd. dirs. 1984—2000, exec. com. 1985—88, 1991—2000, budget com. 1985—89, 1991, chair 1994—98), Mid. States Assn. Colls. and Schs. (commr. 1985—91, exec. com. 1986—91, vice chair 1987—89, chair 1990), Higher Edn. Commn., The Japan Soc., Nat. Assn. Ind. Colls. and Univs. (policy com. 1998—2000), Melbourne Club, Center Club, Yale Club, Rotary (hon. 1990), Phi Beta Kappa Assocs., Phi Beta Kappa. Avocations: running, reading, travel. Office: Marts & Lundy Inc 10040 SW 52d Rd Gainesville FL 32608 Home Phone: 352-505-6097. Personal E-mail: rchambers22@cox.net.

CHAMBERS, SUSAN (M. SUSAN CHAMBERS), retail executive; B. in systems and data processing, William Jewell Coll., Liberty, Mo. With Amoco Oil Corp.; dir. applications devel. Hallmark Cards Inc.; joined Wal-Mart Stores Inc., 1999, store, club mgr., 1999, v.p. applications devel. merchandising, Info. Systems Divsn., sr. v.p. CMI benefits and ins. adminstrn., 2002—03, exec. v.p. risk mgmt. benefits adminstrn., 2004—06, exec. v.p. Human Resources Divsn., 2006—. Mem. bus. advisory bd. Kansas State U.; advisory coun. Women Impacting Public Policy Advisory Coun. Office: Wal-Mart Stores Inc Bentonville AR 72716-8611

CHAMBERS, THOMAS EDWARD, academic administrator, psychologist; b. Cleve., Aug. 1, 1934; s. James Clyde and Mary Celestine (Malone) C. BA, U. Notre Dame, 1956, MA, 1962, PhD, 1976; MA, Holy Cross Coll., 1961; DHL (hon.), U. Portland, 2003, King's Coll., 2004, Our Lady Holy Cross Coll., New Orleans, 2006. Lic. counselor, Ohio, La. Dir. student residences U. Notre Dame, Ind., 1969-73, dir. student activities Ind., 1973-74, asst. v.p. student affairs Ind., 1974-76; v.p. acad. affiars Ursuline Coll., Cleve., 1976-87; pres. Our Lady of Holy Cross Coll., New Orleans, 1987—2003; provincial adminstrn.-provincial counselor Congregation of Holy Cross Ind. Province, 2003—. Founder Internat. Student Leadership Inst., 1968; mem. exec. com. Sta. WLAE-TV, New Orleans, 1987—; pres. Willwoods Cmty., 2003—. Editor: For Leaders Only, 1975. Mem. exec. com. Met. Area Com., New Orleans, 1987—; trustee Gilmour Acad., Cleve., 1978—, United Way, Boy Scouts Am.; bd. dirs. King's Coll., Wilkes-Barre, Pa., 1989—, St. Joseph Sem. Coll., Will Woods Cmty., New Orleans, 1998—. Recipient Nat. League Nursing award of Ohio Nat. League Nursing, 1986, Trustee award Cathedral High Sch., 1987. Mem. Am. Psychol. Assn., Am. Cath. Colls. and Univs., Plimsoll Club, Internat. House Club. Roman Catholic. Office: Willwoods Cmty 3330 N Causeway Blvd Ste 345 Metairie LA 70002 Home Phone: 504-884-7260; Office Phone: 504-830-3701. Business E-Mail: tchambers@willwood.org.

CHAMBERS, THOMAS JEFFERSON, state supreme court justice; b. Yakima, Wash., Oct. 11, 1943; s. Thomas J. and Doris May (Ellyson) C.; m. Judy Larene Cable, June 11, 1967; children: Jolie, Jana, Tommy. BA in Polit. Sci., Wash. State U., 1966; JD, U. Wash., 1969. Bar: Wash., U.S. Dist. Ct. (we. and ea. dists.) Wash. 1969. Assoc. Lycette, Diamond & Sylvester, Seattle, 1969-71, Barokas & Martin, Seattle, 1972; sole practice Seattle, 1972—2001; justice Wash. Supreme Ct., 2001—. Mem. congestion com. Wash. State Cts., 1984, King County Mandatory Arbitration Council, 1981-86, Damages Atty. Roundtable, 1983-86. Editorial adv. bd. Everday Law mag.; contbr. articles to profl. jours. Mem. jud. evaluation com. Mcpl. League, 1982; volunteer Internat. Smile Power Found.; hon. bd. mem. Rise n' Shine Found. Mem. Wash. State Trial Lawyers Assn. (pres. 1985-86, pres.-elect 1984-85, bd. govs. 1976—, various coms.), Am. Bd. Trial Advs. (past. pres. Wash. chpt.), Am. Trial Lawyers Assn. (past mem. bd. govs.), Wash. State Bar Assn. (pres. 1996-97). Avocation: flying. Office: PO Box 40929 Olympia WA 98504-0929*

CHAMBERS, VIRGINIA ANNE, music educator; b. Middlesboro, Ky., Jan. 28, 1931; d. Jason C. and Virginia Claire (Dobyns) C. MusB, U. Louisville, 1952; MusM, Eastman Sch. Music, 1964; PhD, U. Mich., 1970. Gen. elem. music tchr. Oak Ridge Pub. Schs., 1952-63, Rochester (N.Y.) Sch. Dist., 1963-64; prof. music SUNY-Geneso, 1964-66, Ea. Mich. U., Ypsilanti, 1966-68, U. Wis., Madison, 1968-75, U. Toledo, 1975—; ret., 1997. V.p., cons. Tometic Assocs., Ltd., Buffalo, 1980—. Author: Words and Music: An Introduction to Music Literacy, 1976; Tometics: Reading Rhythm Patterns, 1979; Piano Accompaniments for A Nichol's Worth, Vols. 3 and 4, 1982; editor: A Nichol's Worth, Vols. 3 and 4, Reading Tonal Patterns, 1984, Basic Keyboard Accompaniments, 1986, Tometics: Music for the Classroom Teacher, 1988, Tometics: Source Book for Music Theory and Aural Perception, 1988. Mem. Music Educators Nat. Conf., Ohio Music Educators Assn., Sonneck Soc., University Club. Avocations: needlepoint, travel. Home: 2129 Brookdale Rd Toledo OH 43606-3323 E-mail: veecee@buckeye-express.com.

CHAMBERS, WILL EARL, retired freelance writer; b. South Fulton, Tenn., Nov. 23, 1938; s. Hall and Sallie Louise Hunter Chambers; m. Judith Tilghman Chambers; 1 child, Carissa. BS in Sociology and English, Pane Coll., Augusta, Ga., 1961; BD in Theology and Sociology, Phillips Sch. Theology, Atlanta, 1965; MST in Christian Edn., Boston Sch. Theology, 1971. Editor CME Bd. Christian Edn., Memphis, 1965—69; pastor Parkwood Ch., Charlotte, NC, 1969—70; prof. Miles Coll., Birmingham, Ala., 1971—72, Livingstone Coll., Salisbury, NC, 1972—85; presiding elder Christian Meth. Ch., Carolina region, 1985—2002; freelance writer, 2002—07. Author: CME Membership Manual, 1986, The Ministry of Stewardess, 1997; contg. author: Book of Rituals CME Ch., 2006; author: The Nitty-Gritty of Giving Talks, 2007; creator CME denominational logo, 1970, CME denominational flag, 1997. Recipient citation for outstanding svc., CME Denomination, 2006. Avocations: writing, photography, teaching. Home: 29875 Dutchman's Ln Easton MD 21601-4713 Personal E-mail: wchamber@goeaston.net.

CHAMBERS, WILLIAM EDMOND, writer; b. Bklyn., Oct. 9, 1943; s. William Robert and Julia Mary (Lynch) Chambers; m. Marie Antoinette Kaczanowska, Aug. 29, 1964. Cert. merit United Way of Tri-State, 1980. Dir. MWA, NYC, 1970—74; owner Chambers Pub, 1983—89. Author: (novels) Death Toll, 1976, The Redemption Factor, 1980, The Tormentress, 2005; author, editor (columns) Vital Signs; Bloodlines; contbr. short stories and poems to various jours. Nominee Brooke Russell Astor award, 2002; recipient leadership CWA, City of Hope, 1986, Couple of Yr., Seneca Club/ Dem. Party, 1998, Seneca Club/ Dem., 2001, 2002, 2003, 2004, 2005, 2006, 2007. Mem.: Internat. Thriller Writers, Inc., Sisters in Crime, Pvt. Eye Writers Am., Mystery Writers Am. (hon.; N.Y. chpt. pres. 1995—97, exec. v.p. 2000—02). Democrat. Roman Catholic. Avocations: history, reading, weight training, collecting books, politics and community activism. Home: 65 Meserole Ave Brooklyn NY 11222 Office Phone: 718-383-4265. Personal E-mail: billchambers@verizon.net.

CHAMBERS, WILLIAM MCWILLIE, artist, art dealer; b. Baton Rouge, La., Aug. 6, 1951; s. William McWillie and Bessie Opal Chambers. BFA, Kansas City Art Inst., 1973. Art dealer, v.p. Grace Borgenicht Gallery, NYC, 1973—95; artist, pvt. dealer William McWillie Chambers Fine Art, NYC, 1995—. Represented by John Davis Gallery, Hudson, NY. 17 one-man shows, numerous group exhbns. Avocations: tennis, piano, guitar. Home and Studio: 319 E 50th St New York NY 10022 Office: John Davis Gallery 362 1/2 Warren St Hudson NY 12534

CHAMBERS-BELIDA, CANDACE R., radio personality, writer, television producer, educator; b. Dayton, Ohio, May 25, 1958; d. James A and Sondra B Elmore; m. David P Belida, Aug. 26, 1995 (dec. Aug. 5, 1999); m. Freeman Chambers -First Husband 1979; 1 child, Elisha Anne Verity Chambers. Studied Acting/Pschology, U. of Cin., 1976—79; Assoc. Degree, Rancho Santiago Coll., Santa Ana, Calif., 1986—89. Lifestyles writer Pacific News and Rev., Anaheim, 1986—98; radio talk show host KHPY-Radio, Moreno Valley, Calif., 2002, KTYM-Radio, LA, 2005—06. Exec. prodr. KYOU-TV, Santa Ana, 1986—98; tv prodn. ABC-Network, 1991—92, CBS-Network. Author: Dare To Stand, The Secret Codes of Conduct for Marriage, Are You Ready Now?; prodr.: (TV series) Puttin' On the Ritz (Video Award, 1986); author: (screenplays) Hosea, Counterfeit Alliance, True Covenant. Founder, CEO Holy Hwy. Ministries, Internat.; spkr. Spkr. Platform, San Francisco, 2001—06. Recipient Leadership Awards, Video Awards. Achievements include appearing as guest on television shows, KCBS, KNBC, OCN, KOCE-TV, KDOC-TV, KPAX-TV, and at numerous book signings. Avocations: travel, reading, volunteer work. Office: Ewe Babe Productions Inc 73 Quiet Hills Rd Phillips Ranch CA 91766 Office Phone: 909-629-9522. Personal E-mail: cchamb7545@aol.com.

CHAMBERS TUCKER, JOHNNIE L., elementary school educator, rancher; b. Crocket County, Tex., Sept. 28, 1929; d. Robert Leo and Lois K. (Slaughter) Tucker; m. R. Boyd Chambers; children: Theresa A., Glyn Robert, Boyd James, John Trox. EdB, Sul Ross State U., Alpine, Tex., 1971. Tchr. 1st and 2d grades Candelaria Elem. Sch., Tex., 1971-73; head tchr. K-8 Ruidosa Elem. Sch., Tex., 1973-77, Candelaria Elem. Sch., 1977—91, tchr. 2d and 3d grades, 1991—93, tchr. pre-kindergarten, kindergarten and 1st grade, 1993—98; acting prin. Candelaria Elem. and Jr. High, 1995—98, head tchr. pre-K to 8th grades, 1996—98, tchr. pre-K, kindergarten, 1st and 2d grades, 1996—99; tchr. pre-K-6 Redford Elem. Sch., Tex., 2001, tchr., 2001—. Mem. sight-base decision making, Presidio, 1991-94; mem. Chihuahuan Desert Rsch. Inst., Alpine, 1982-94. Leader Boy Scouts Am., Ruidosa and Candelaria, 1973-91, Cub Scout leader, 1973-91; chpt. mem. Sheriffs Assn. Tex., Austin, 1980; bd. dirs. Big Bend Regional Hosp. Dist., 2001—, Family Crisis Ctr. Big Bend Inc., 2006; mem. Ctr. for Big Bend Studies. Recipient awards Boy Scouts Am., 1969, 83, Litter Gitter award, 1994-95. Mem. Tex. State Tchrs. Assn., Tex. Fedn. Rep. Women, The Archaeol. Conservancy, Phi Alpha Theta. Avocations: hiking, camping, anthropology, cave exploring, cooking. Home: PO Box 187 707 E Hancock Alpine TX 79830 Office Phone: 432-229-4707. Personal E-mail: johnnieltchambers@yahoo.com. Business E-Mail: johnnieltc@rionet.coop.

CHAMBLISS, CARROLL CHRISTOPHER, professional baseball coach; b. Dayton, Ohio, Dec. 26, 1948; m. Audra Garvin; children: Russell, Denair. Student, Mira Costa Jr. Coll., UCLA; B.Phys. Edn. and Recreation, Montclair State Coll. Baseball player Wichita Class AAA, 1970, N.Y. Yankees, 1974-79, Cleve. Indians, Atlanta Braves; batting coach N.Y. Yankees, Cardinals, 1993-95, NY Yankees, 1995—99; mgr. Class AA London/Tigers, 1989-91, Class AA Greenville, 1991, Class AAA Richmond/Internat. League, 1992, Class AAA Calgary Cannons, 2000; batting coach Cin. Reds, 2006. Named Am. League Rookie of the Yr., 1971; winner Gold Glove award, 1st base, 1978; named So. League Mgr. of the Yr., 1991, Internat. League Mgr. of Yr., 1990. Office: Cin Reds Great Am Ballpark 201 E Pete Rose Way Cincinnati OH 45202

CHAMBLISS, LINDA R., obstetrician, consultant; b. Summit, NJ, Feb. 13, 1951; d. Robert E. and Alice (Dunne) C.; children: Alice, Kevin, Christopher, Daniel Patrick. BSN, Duke U., Durham, NC, 1973; MD, Mich. State U., East Lansing, 1980; MPH, Johns Hopkins U., Balt., 2004. Diplomate with spl. certification in maternal-fetal medicine Am. Bd. Ob-Gyn. Pediat. intern U. Chgo., 1980—81; resident in ob-gyn. Cook County Hosp., Chgo., 1981—85; fellow in maternal-fetal medicine U. So. Calif.-LA County Hosp., LA, 1988—90; chief obstetrics Indian Health Svcs., Tuba City, Ariz., 1985-88; clin. prof. ob-gyn. U. Ariz., 2001—06; prof. ob-gyn. St. Louis U., 2006—, med. dir. labor and delivery, 2006—. Comdr. USPHS, 1985—. Named Tchr. of Yr., Dept. Ob-Gyn., Maricopa Med. Ctr., 1991, Alumni of Yr., Mich. State U., Coll. Human Medicine, 2000; recipient Nat. Edn. award, Coun. on Resident Edn. in Ob-Gyn., 1995, 2007, Nat. Faculty Excellence award, 1995, Alumna Excellence award, Mich. State U., 1996, Alumni award, 2001. Fellow ACOG; mem. AMA (cons.), AAUW, Soc. Maternal Fetal Medicine, Am. Women's Med. Assn., Am. Inst. Ultrasound Medicine. Democrat. Office: St Louis Univ 6420 Clayton Rd Saint Louis MO 63117 Office Phone: 314-768-8154. Personal E-mail: LRChambliss@yahoo.com.

CHAMBLISS, SAXBY (C. SAXBY CHAMBLISS), senator; b. Warrenton, NC, Nov. 10, 1943; m. Julianne (Frohbert) Chambliss; 2 children. BA in Bus. Adminstrn., U. Ga., 1966; JD, U. Tenn., 1968. Bar: Ga. 1969, US Supreme Ct. 1974, US Ct. Appeals (5th circuit) 1976. Atty. Moore, Chambliss and Warfel, Moultie, Ga.; state atty. Colquitt County, Ga., 1970—76; mem. US Congress from 8th Ga. dist., 1995—2002; US Senator from Ga., 2003—. Mem. Colquitt County Econ. Devel. Corp., Ga., Moultrie-Colquitt Econ. Devel. Authority, Ga.; mem. com. security and coop. in Europe US Senate, chmn. com. agr., nutrition and forestry, mem. com. armed svc., com. rules and adminstrn., joint com. printing, select com. intelligence. Vol. basketball and baseball coach YMCA, Recreation Dept., Moultrie, Ga.; bd. managers U. Ga. Alumni Assn. Recipient Friend of Farmer award, Ga. Farm Bur., 1995, Disting. Svc. award, Ga. Peanut Commn., 1997, W. Stuart Symington award, Air Force Assn., 1998, Fed. Legis. of Yr., Safari Club Internat., 1999, Lucite award, Rep. Nat. Lawyers Assn., 2003, Disting. Alumni award, Terry Coll. Bus. U. Ga., 2004, Cmty. Health Defender award, Nat. Assn. Cmty. Health Centers, Inc., 2005, Legis. of Yr., Biotechnology Industry Orgn., 2005, Taxpayer Hero award, Coun. Citizens Against Govt. Waste, 2005. Mem.: Southern Judicial Bar Assn., Moultrie Bar Assn., ABA. Republican. Episcopalian. Office: US Senate 416 Russell Senate Office Building Washington DC 20510 also: District Office Ste 1340 100 Galleria Parkway SE Atlanta GA 30339-3179 Office Phone: 202-224-3521, 770-763-9090. Office Fax: 202-224-0103, 770-226-8633.

CHAMEAU, JEAN-LOU, academic administrator; b. 1953; m. Carol Carmichael. M in Civil Engring., Stanford U., 1977, PhD in Civil Engring., 1980. Joined Purdue U., 1980, prof. civil engring., head geotechnical engring. program; dir. Sch. Civil and Environ. Engring. Ga. Inst. Tech., 1991, dean Coll. Engring., provost, v.p. academic affairs, 2001—06, Ga. Rsch. Alliance Eminent Scholar; pres. Calif. Inst. Tech., 2006—. Pres. Golder Assocs., Inc., 1994—95; bd. dirs. MTS Sys. Corp. Recipient Presdl. Young Investigator Award, NSF, Casagrande Award, ASCE, Rodney D. Chipp Meml. Award, Soc. of Women Engrs., 2004. Office: Calif Inst Tech Office of Pres 1200 E California Blvd Pasadena CA 91125 Business E-Mail: chameau@caltech.edu.*

CHAMILLIONAIRE, (HAKEEM SERIKI), rap artist, recording industry executive; b. Houston, Nov. 28, 1979; Co-founder Chamillitary Entertainment/Universal Records, 2005—; musician & prodr. mixtapes, 2004—; major record label debut, 2005. Musician: (albums) The Sound of Revenge, 2005, Ultimate Victory, 2007, (songs) Ridin', 2005 (MTV Video Music award, Best Rap Video, 2006, Grammy award, Best Group Rap Performance, 2007). Recipient Rookie of Yr. award, BET (Black Entertainment TV) Hip Hop Awards, 2006, People's Champ award, 2006. Office: PMB 309 5380 W 34th St Houston TX 77092*

CHAMIS, CHRISTOS CONSTANTINOS, aerospace scientist, educator; b. Sotira, Greece, May 16, 1930; arrived in U.S., 1948; s. Constantinos and Anastasia (Kyriakos) C.; m. Alice Yanosko, Aug. 20, 1966; children: Chrysanthie, Anna-Lisa, Constantinos. BS in Civil Engring., Cleve. State U., 1960; MS, Case Western Res. U., 1962, PhD, 1967. Draftsman, designer Cons. Engring., Cleve., 1955-60; rsch. asst. Case Western Res. U., Cleve., 1960-62, rsch. assoc., 1964-68; rsch. mathematician B.F. Goodrich, Brecksville, Ohio, 1962-64; aerospace engr. Glenn Rsch. Ctr. NASA, Cleve., 1968-78, sr. rsch. engr., 1978-86, sr. aerospace scientist, 1986—.

Cons. Lawrence Livermore Labs., Calif., 1974-79; adj. prof. Cleve. State U., 1968—, Akron U., 1980—, Case Western Res. U., 1984—. Editor: Composites Analysis/Design, 1975, Test Methods and Design Allowables for Composites, 1979, 89; mem. editl. bd. Jour. Composites Rsch. and Tech., Reinforced Plastics and Composites, Internat. Jour. Damage Mechanics, Theoretical and Applied Fracture Mechanics; contbr. numerous articles to sci. jours.; patentee in field for Intraply Hybrid Composites and Exoskeletal Engine Concepts; rschr. in hygrothermal composite micromechanics, computational composite mechanics-computer codes, high-temperature composite structures, structural tailoring of engine structures, computational simulation of progressive fracture, engine structures computational simulations, computational simulation/tailoring of coupled multi-discipline problems, and probabilistic structural analysis. Served with USMC, 1952-53. Recipient Softward of Yr. award on computational multi-disciplinary simulator, NASA, 1999, IR-100 award, 2001, Dist. award for life time contbn., NASA, 2004. Fellow ASME (Engine Structures award 1992), AIAA (assoc. editor 1986-88, Structures, Dynamics and Material award 1998), ASCE, ASTM, Soc. Advancement Materials and Process Engring., Soc. Automotive Engrs. (Probabilistic Structural Analysis award 1997); mem. Soc. Exptl. Mechanics, Am. Soc. Metals, Am. Soc. Composites, Soc. Engring. Sci., Am. Ceramic Soc., Sigma Xi. Home: 24534 Framingham Dr Cleveland OH 44145-4902 Office Phone: 216-433-3252. Business E-Mail: christos.c.chamis@nasa.gov.

CHAMMAH, WALID A., investment banker; b. Beirut, Apr. 12, 1954; s. Atef A. and Salma (Achour) C.; m. Laura Roosevel. B in Bus., Am. U. of Beirut, 1976; M in Internat. Mgmt., Am. Sch. of Internat. Mgmt., 1977. Assoc. First Boston, NYC, 1978-79, v.p., 1985—; sr. v.p. Paine Webber (predecessor firm), NYC, 1979-85; head, US debt capital markets Morgan Stanley, NYC, 1993—96, head, worldwide debt capital markets svcs., 1996—2005, head, worldwide leveraged fin., 2001—05, head, investment banking, 2005—. Mem. mgmt. com. Morgan Stanley, NYC, 2006—. Avocations: skiing, running, reading. Office: Morgan Stanley 1585 Broadway New York NY 10036 Office Phone: 212-761-1900.

CHAMOT, DENNIS, science policy executive; b. Bklyn., June 5, 1943; s. Joe and Sarah C.; m. Judith Chamot; 2 children. BS in Chemistry, MS in Chemistry, Poly. Inst. Bklyn., 1964; PhD in Chemistry, U. Ill., 1969; MBA, U. Pa., 1974. Rsch. chemist E.I. duPont de Nemours and Co., Wilmington, Del., 1969-73; asst. to exec. sec. coun. unions for profl. employees AFL-CIO, Washington, 1974-77, asst. dir. dept. for profl. employees, 1977-84, assoc. dir. dept., 1984-90, exec. asst. to pres. dept., 1990-94; assoc. exec. dir. Commn. on Engring. and Tech. Sys., NRC, Washington, 1994—2000, Divsn. on Engring. and Phys. Sciences, NRC, 2001—. Com. mem. NRC, acting dir. bd. on infrastructure and constructed environment, 1994-95, acting dir. bd. on engring. edn., 1995, acting dir. Nat. materials adv. bd., 2004-05; adv. coun. NSF, 1984-89; adj. faculty George Mason U., Fairfax, Va., 1983, 84; adj. asst. prof. U. Coll. U. Md., College Park, 1993-96; external rev. com. Nat. Inst. Occupl. Safety and Health; adv. panel on info. tech., automation and the workplace Office Tech. Assessment, U.S. Congress, 1982-84; nat. adv. com. for tng. in new tech. Work in Am. Inst., 1985-87; rev. panel Ctr. on Edn. Quality of Workforce, U.S. Dept. Edn., 1990; presenter in field. Contbr. numerous articles to profl. publs. Recipient Charles Gordon award Chem. Soc. Washington, 1986; travel grantee Swedish Inst., 1984; Mary E. Switzer meml. scholar Nat. Rehab. Assn., 1989. Fellow AAAS; mem. Am. Chem. Soc. (councilor 1975—, com. on profl. rels. 1988-89, chmn. subcom. on career support and mem. assistance 1990-91, chmn. subcom. on career support 1989, cons. 1992-93, chmn. com. on Project Seed 1992-94, chmn. divsn. profl. rels. 1982, chmn. mem. adv. bd. 1973, com. on econ. status 1978-86, mem. task force on occupl. health and safety 1987-94, Henry Hill award 1992, chmn. coun. com. on econ. and profl. affairs, 2001-02, coun. policy com., 2001-02, bd. dirs. 2002—, trustee group ins. plans, 2004—, exec. com. 2004-06, chmn. com. on budget and fin. 2007—), Soc. for Occupl. and Environ. Health (sec.-treas. 1978-82, plaque 1982), Sigma Xi, Phi Kappa Phi, Phi Lambda Upsilon. Office: NRC 500 Fifth St, NW Washington DC 20001

CHAMOT, JOSHUA ANDREW, science administrator; s. Dennis I. and Judith M. Chamot. BS in Geology, Coll. William and Mary, Williamsburg, Va., 1998; MS in Geology, U. Tenn., Knoxville, 2000. Contbg. writer Geotimes, Alexandria, 1998—2004; comm. cons. Temple U. Inst. Survey Rsch., Washington, 2000—02; pub. affairs asst. Smithsonian Instn. Nat. Mus. of Natural History, Washington, 2001—01; pub. affairs specialist NSF, Arlington, Va., 2004—. Trombonist Fairfax Wind Symphony, Braddock Brass Quintet; bd. mem. Beth El Ho., Alexandria, 2006—07. Fellow Acad. fellow, NASA, 2000; Monroe scholar, Coll. William and Mary, 1994—98, Carol Woody scholar, 1998, Rsch. Tng. Program SEED grantee, NSF, Smithsonian, Nat. Mus. Natural History, Rsch. Tng. Program, 1997. Mem.: Nat. Assn. Sci. Writers, Meteoritical Soc., Paleontol. Soc. Wash. (sec. 2002—07), D.C. Sci. Writers Assn. (treas. 2003—05). Office: NSF 4201 Wilson Blvd Arlington VA 22230 Office Phone: 703-292-7730. Business E-Mail: jchamot@nsf.gov.

CHAMPAGNE, DUANE WILLARD, sociology educator; b. Belcourt, ND, May 18, 1951; m. Carole Goldberg; children: Talya, Gabe, Demelza. BA in Math., N.D. State U., 1973, MA in Sociology, 1975; PhD in Sociology, Harvard U., 1982. Teaching fellow Harvard U., Cambridge, Mass., 1981-82, rsch. fellow, 1982-83; asst. prof. U. Wis., Milw., 1983-84, UCLA, 1984-91, assoc. prof., 1991-97, prof., 1997—. Publs. dir. Am. Indian Studies Ctr., UCLA, 1986-87, assoc. dir., 1990, acting dir., 1991, dir., 1991-02, affiliate faculty UCLA Native Nations Law and Policy Ctr., 2003-, acting dir. Tribal Learning Cmty. and Edn. Exch., 2004-05; adminstrv. co-head interdepartmental program for Am. Indian studies UCLA, 1992-93; vis. prof. Harvard U., 2006—. Author: American Indian Societies, 1989, Social Order and Political Change, 1992, Service Delivery for Native American Children in Los Angeles County, 1996, The ACCIP Community Service Report: A Second Century of Dishonor-Federal Inequities and California Indians, 2002, Social Change and Cultural Continuity Among Native Nations, 2007; editor: Native Am. Studies Assn. Newsletter, 1991—92, Native North American Almanac, 1994, 2d edit., 2001, Chronology of Native North American, 1994, Native America: Portrait of the Peoples, 1994, Native American Activism: Alcatraz to the Longest Walk, 1997, Contemporary Native American Issues, 1999, Contemporary Native American Cultural Issues, 1999, Special Issue on Indigenous Issues: Hagar, International Social Science Review, 2001, Native American Studies in Higher Education: Models for Collaboration Between Indigenous Nations, 2002, The Future of Indigenous Peoples' Strategies for Survival and Development, 2003, Education, Equity and Empowerment Among Indigenous Peoples: The Case of the Palestinians, 2005, Indigenous and Minority Education: International Perspectives on Empowerment, 2005, Indigenous Peoples and the Modern State, 2005, Indigenous Education and Empowerment: International Perspectives, 2006, American Indian Nations: Yesterday, Today and Tomorrow, 2007; book rev. editor: Am. Indian Culture and Rsch. Jour., 1984—86; editor, 1986—2002; series editor: Contemporary American Indian Issues, 1998—, sr. editor: Indian Country Today, 2006—07; contbr. articles to profl. jours. Mem. City of L.A. Cmty. Action Bd., 1993, L.A. County/City Am. Indian Commn., 1992—, chair, 1993, 1995—97, 2000—02, 2004, 2005—, sec., 2002, vice chair, 1997—2000; mem. subcom. for cultural and econ. devel. L.A. City/County Native Am. Commn., 1992—93, 2004; bd. dirs. Ctr. for Improvement of Child Caring, 1993—, Greater L.A. Am. Indian Culture Ctr., Inc., 1993, incorporator, 1993; trustee Southwest Mus., 1994—97, Nat. Mus. Am. Indian, 1998—2003; master Coll. Humanities and Social Sci., N.D. State U., 1996. Recipient LA Sr. Health Peer Counseling Cmty. Vol. Cert. of Recognition, 1996; Writer of Yr. award Cir. Native Writers and Storytellers, 1999; honoree Nat. Ctr. Am. Indian Enterprise, 1999; grantee Rockefeller Found., 1982-83, U. Wis. Grad Sch. Rsch. Com., 1984-85, Wis. Dept. Edn., 1984-85, 87-88, 88-89, NSF, 1985-88, 88-89, Nat. Endowment for Arts, 1987-88, 91-92, NRC, 1988-89, Nat. Sci. Coun., 1989-90, John D. and Catherine T. MacArthur Found., 1990-91, Hayes Found., 1990-93, Calif. Coun. for Humanities, 1991-92, Ford Found., 1990-92, Gale Rsch. Inc., 1991-93, 93-95, Rockwell Corp., 1991-93, GTE, 1992-93, Kellog Found., 1997-2000, Pequot Mus. and Rsch. Ctr., 1997-2002, So. Calif. Indian Ctr., 1998; Fund for the Improvement of Post Secondary Edn., 1998-2003, NEH, 2002—, Dept. Justice, 2001-05, NEH, 2003-05, San Manuel Band of Serrano Indians Endowment, 2004—, Dept. Justice, 2006—; Am. Indian scholar, 1973-75, 80-82, Minority fellow Am. Sociol. Assn., 1975-78, RIAS Seminar fellow, 1976-77; Rockefeller Postdoctoral fellow, 1982-83, NSF fellow, 1985-88, Postdoctoral fellow Ford Found., 1988-89. Avocations: chess, jogging. Home: 2152 Balsam Ave Los Angeles CA 90025 Office: UCLA Native Nations Law and Policy Ctr Dept Sociology 264 Haines Hall Los Angeles CA 90095-1551 Office Phone: 310-475-6475. Business E-Mail: champagn@ucla.edu.

CHAMPION, HALE (CHARLES HALE CHAMPION), academic administrator, lecturer, government official, consultant; b. Coldwater, Mich., Aug. 27, 1922; s. Paul Upham and Ruth Emma (Hungerford) C.; m. Marie Ozine Tifft, Aug. 21, 1952; children: Thomas Paul, Katherine Marie. BA, Stanford U., 1952. Journalist UPI, Milw. Jour., Sacramento Bee, San Francisco Chronicle, Reporter mag., 1946-49, 52-58; legis. asst. to Congressman Andrew J. Biemiller of Wis., 1950; press and exec. sec. to Gov. Edmund G. Brown of Calif., 1958-60; dir. fin. State of Calif., 1961-66; dir. Boston Redevel. Authority, 1968-69; v.p. fin., planning and ops. U. Minn., Mpls., 1969-71; v.p. fin. Harvard U., Cambridge, Mass., 1971-76, exec. dean John F. Kennedy Sch. Govt., 1980-87; undersec. HEW, Washington, 1977-79; chief of staff to Gov. Michael S. Dukakis of Mass., Boston, 1987-88; lectr. John F. Kennedy Sch. Govt. Harvard U., 1989-91; chmn. Champion-Murphy Assocs., 2004—. Mem. Presdl. Task Force Reorgn. Fed. Govt., 1966-67, Presdl. Task Force Role of Univ. in Urban Affairs, 1967-68; chmn. Mass. Joint Legis.-Exec. Com. Fed. Base Conversion, 1973-74; chmn. Presdl. Commn. on Nat. Health Ins., 1977-78. Bd. dirs. Kaiser Family Found., 1984-92, chmn., 1989-92; bd. dirs. Ctr. for Study of Social Policy, 1986—, chmn., 1998-2002. Served with AUS, 1942-46. Nieman fellow Harvard U., 1956-57; fellow John F. Kennedy Inst. Politics, 1967 Mem. Nat. Acad. Pub. Adminstrn. (trustee 1980-86). Democrat. Office: Harvard Univ John F Kennedy Sch Govt 79 Jfk St Cambridge MA 02138-5801 Office Phone: 617-495-1339. E-mail: hale@championmurphy.com.

CHAMPION, KATHLEEN ANN, mathematics professor; d. Richard J and Patricia A Schreier. BA, Coll. of St. Catherine, St. Paul; MS in edn., U. Minn., Mpls., 1994; PhD, U. ND, Grand Forks, 2004. Cert. Math. Tchg. grades 7-12 Edn. Standards & Practice Bd., 2002, Sci. Tchg., grades 5-12 MN Dept. of Edn., 1990, Math Tchg., grades 7-12 MN Dept. of Edn., 1990. Sci., math. tchr. Anoka-Hennepin Sch. Dist. ISD 11, Coon Rapids, Minn., 1990—97; assoc. prof. math. edn. Mayville State U., ND, 2000—. Presenter From Euclid to Einstein in Fiber Optic Speed, Elem. Tchg. of Geometry, 2005. Sch. bd. mem. Finley- Sharon Sch., ND, 2001—04. Mem.: Mathematical Assn. Am. (corr.), Am. Chem. Soc. (corr.), Nat. Coun. Tchrs. Math. (corr.), ND Coun. Tchrs. Math. (corr.). Avocations: sewing, swimming, gardening. Office: Mayville State U 330 Third St NE Mayville ND 58257 Office Phone: 800-437-4104. Business E-Mail: k_champion@mayvillestate.edu.

CHAMPION, MARGRÉT GUNNARSDÓTTIR, literature and language educator; b. Reykjavik, Iceland, Jan. 30, 1953; arrived in Sweden, 1995, naturalized; d. Gunnar Ragnarsson and Þórdis Hilmarsdóttir; m. Scott Champion, Dec. 1, 1979 (div. Mar. 1984). Student, Trinity Coll., 1975—77; BA magna cum laude, U. Ga., 1980, MA, 1985, PhD, 1991. Tchg. asst. U. Ga., Athens, 1985—90; lectr. dept. comparative lit. U. Iceland, 1992—94; rsch. fellow dept. English U. Uppsala, Sweden, 1995—98; lectr. dept. English U. Stockholm, Sweden, 1999—2000; sr. lectr. U. Gothenburg, Sweden, 2000—. Guest lectr. U. Uppsala, 2006—. Recipient Exch. scholarship, Irish Govt., Trinity Coll., 1975—76; Rsch. grant, Swedish Coun. of Sci., 2000. Mem.: MLA, Medieval Acad., Soc. for the Study of Narrative, U. of Ohio. Avocations: art, theater, travel. Home: Geijersgatan 50A 75231 Uppsala Sweden Office Phone: 0046(0)31 786-1783. Business E-Mail: margret.gunnarsdottir@eng.gu.se.

CHAMPION, NORMA JEAN, communications educator, state legislator; b. Oklahoma City, Jan. 21, 1933; d. Aubra Dell and Beuleah Beatrice (Flanagan) Black; m. Richard Gordon Champion, Oct. 3, 1953 (dec.); children: Jeffrey Bruce, Ashley Brooke. BA in Religious Edn., Cen. Bible Coll., Springfield, Mo., 1971; MA in Comm., Mo. State U., 1978; PhD in Tech., U. Okla., 1986. Producer, hostess The Children's Hour, Sta. KYTV-TV, NBC, Springfield, 1957-86; asst. prof. Cen. Bible Coll., 1968-84; prof. broadcasting Evangel U., Springfield, 1978—; mem. Springfield City Coun., 1987-92, Mo. Ho. of Reps., Jefferson City, 1993—2002, Mo. Senate, 2003—, chair aging and health com., appropriations, edn. Adj. faculty Assemblies of God Theol. Sem., Springfield, 1987—, pres. coun.; bd. dirs. Global U.; mem. Commn. on Higher Edn., Assemblies of God, 1998—; spkr. Internat. Pentecostal Press Assn. World Conf., Singapore, 1989. Mem. bd. Mo. Access to Higher Edn. Trust, 2003-, pain mgmt. bd., 2004-, Boys & Girls Town of Mo.; adv. coun. pain mgmt.; judge Springfield (Mo.) City Schs. Recipient commendation resolution Mo. Ho. of Reps., 1988; numerous awards for The Children's Hour; Aunt Norma Day named in her honor City of Springfield, 1976; named 20 Most Influential Women in Ozarks, Springfield Bus. Jour., 2005. Mem. Nat. Broadcast Edn. Assn., Mo. Broadcast Edn. Assn., Nat. League Cities, Mo. Mcpl. League (human resource com. 1989, intergovtl. rels. com. 1990), Nat. Assn. Telecom. Officers and Advisors, PTA (life). Republican. Mem. Assemblies of God Ch. Avocations: gardening, reading, yoga. Home: 3609 S Broadway Ave Springfield MO 65807-4505 Office: Evangel Univ 1111 N Glenstone Ave Springfield MO 65802-2125 Office Phone: 573-751-2583. Business E-Mail: normachampion@senate.mo.gov.

CHAMPION, SUSAN MICHELE, music educator; d. William Liles and Phyllis Brown Champion. BA in Music, Miss. Coll., Clinton, 1993; cert. in Tchg., U. Ala., 1998; MusM, Miss. Coll., Clinton, 2002; D in Music, U. Miss., 2006. Cert. level one Am. Orff Schulwerk Assn., 2001, level two Am. Orff Schulwerk Assn., 2003. Specialist elem. music Jefferson County Pub. Schs., Birmingham, Ala., 1999—2000, Jackson Pub. Schs., Miss., 2000—03; doctoral tchg. asst. U. Miss., Univ., 2003—06; asst. prof. music Augusta State U., Ga., 2006—. Asst. to dir. Birmingham Children's Choir, Ala., 1998—2000; asst. dir. Oxford Children's Choir, Miss., 2003—06. Contbr. articles to profl. jours. Nominee Tchr. of Yr., Ptnrs. Edn.; named Outstanding Young Music Educator, Miss. Mem.: OAKE (corr.), ACDA (corr.), Ga. Music Educators Assn. (corr.), Music Educators Nat. Conf. (corr.; faculty advisor 2006—), Ala.Orff Schulwerk Assn. (corr.), Kappa Delta Epsilon (corr.), Pi Kappa Lambda (corr.), Sigma Alpha Iota (corr.). Republican. Baptist. Office: Augusta State Univ 2500 Walton Way Augusta GA 30904 Home Phone: 706-729-2338; Office Phone: 706-729-2338. Business E-Mail: schampi1@aug.edu.

CHAMPION, WILL, musician; b. Hampshire, England, July 31, 1978; Student in Anthropology, U. Coll. London. Drummer Coldplay, 1998—. Musician: (albums) Parachutes, 2000 (Grammy award: Best Alternative Music Album, 2001), A Rush of Blood to the Head, 2002 (Grammy awards: Best Alternative Music Album, 2002, Best Rock Performance By A Duo Or Group With Vocal for song "In My Place", 2002, Record Of The Yr. for song "Clocks", 2003), Live 2003, 2003, X&Y, 2005, Love, Actually, 2006. Recipient Favorite Alternative Artist (Coldplay), Am. Music Awards, 2005. Office: Capital Records 1750 North Vine Street 10th Floor Hollywood CA 90028

CHAMPLIN, CHARLES DAVENPORT, television personality, critic, writer; b. Hammondsport, NY, Mar. 23, 1926; s. Francis Malburn and Katherine Marietta (Masson) C.; m. Margaret Frances Derby, Sept. 11, 1948; children: Charles Jr., Katherine, John, Judith, Susan, Nancy. AB cum laude, Harvard U., 1947. Reporter Life mag., NYC, 1948-49, corr. Chgo., 1949-52, Denver, 1952-54; asst. editor Life mag., NYC, 1954—59; corr. Time mag., LA, 1959-62, London, 1962-65; arts editor, columnist L.A. Times, 1965-91, prin. film critic, 1967-80, book critic, 1981-82. Host-commentator Ste. KCET-TV, L.A., ETV Network, Z Channel Cable TV, Bravo Channel, 1969-96; adj. prof. Loyola-Marymount U., L.A., 1969-86; adj. prof. U. So. Calif., 1986-96. Author: (with C. Sava) How to Swim Well, 1960, The Flicks, 1977, The Movies Grow Up, 1981, Back There Where the Past Was, 1989, George Lucas: The Creative Impulse, 1992, enlarged, 1997, John Frankenheimer: A Conversation, 1995, Woody Allen at Work, 1995, Hollywood's Revolutionary Decade, 1998, Tony's World, 1999, My Friend, You Are Legally Blind, 2001, A Life in Writing, 2006; contbr. numerous articles to mags. and publs. Trustee L.A. Film Tchrs. Assn. With U.S. Army, 1944-46, ETO. Decorated Purple Heart; recipient Order Arts and Letters, France, 1977 Mem. PEN, L.A. Film Critics Assn., Authors Guild. Democrat. Home: 2169 Linda Flora Dr Los Angeles CA 90077-1408 Personal E-mail: champc@aol.com.

CHAMPLIN, STEVEN KIRK, lawyer; b. Omaha, July 6, 1944; m. Marjorie Eckenberg, Mar. 15, 1969; children: Anne, Paul, Jane. BA, Vanderbilt U., 1966; JD cum laude, U. Minn., 1969. Bar: Minn. 1969, U.S. Dist. Ct. Minn., U.S. Ct. Appeals (8th cir.). Pub. defender Hennepin County, Mpls., 1972-73; assoc. Dorsey & Whitney, Mpls., 1969-70, 71-72, 73-75, ptnr., comml. litig., 1976—, and co- chmn., construction & design law. Capt. U.S. Army, 1970-71. Mem. USTA. Office: Dorsey & Whitney LLP 50 S 6th St Ste 1500 Minneapolis MN 55402-1553 Office Phone: 612-340-2913. Office Fax: 612-340-2868. Business E-Mail: champlin.steve@dorsey.com.

CHAN, CARLYLE HUNG-LUN, psychiatrist, educator; b. Clarksdale, Miss., July 4, 1949; s. Henry Howe and Jennie (Wong) C.; m. Patricia Meyer, June 18, 1977; children: Christopher, Diana. BS, U. Wis., 1971; MD, Med. Coll. Wis., 1975. Diplomate Am. Bd. Psychiatry and Neurology. Resident in psychiatry U. Chgo., 1975-78; postdoctoral fellow R.W. Johnson clin. scholar Yale U. Sch. Medicine, 1978-80; asst. prof. Med. Coll. Wis., Milw., 1980-86, assoc. prof., 1986-98; prof. Med. Coll. Wis., Milw., 1998—; dir. residency edn. Med. Coll. Wis., Milw., 1987—2005, prof., 1998—2005, vice chair edn. and informatics, 1997—, dir. continuing med. edn., 1990—, vice chair, prof. devel. and edn. outreach, 2005—, med. dir. continuing med. edn., 2007—; dir. catchment area Milw. County Mental Health Complex, 1981-82; chief psychiatrist Psychiatrist Ctr., Columbia Hosp., Milw., 1982-87; dir. continuing med. edn. Soc. Tchg. Scholars, 1994. Dir. course annual psychiat. conf., 1982—, Door County Summer Inst., Wis., 1987—. Asst. editor Asian-Am. Psychiatry Newsletter, Washington, 1983-84; assoc. editor Acad. Psychiatry Newsletter, 1991-94; contbr. articles to profl. jours. Bd. dirs. Planning Coun. Mental Health and Social Svc., 1983—. Jr. Faculty Devel. award NIMH, 1983-85; Community Devel. award Apple Computer Co., Milw., 1984, Parker Palmer award, 2004. Fellow Am. Psychiat. Assn (disting.); mem. Am. Coll. Psychiatrists (pres.-elect 2005—), Wis. Psychiat. Assn. (pres. Milw. chpt. 1990-91, chair edn. com. 1995—, pres. 2007—), Assn. Acad. Psychiatry (regional coord. 1987-, regional coord. dir. 1993-96, treas. 1996—), Am. Assn. Dirs. Psychiat. Residency Tng. (sec. 1994-95, pres.-elect 1995, pres. 1996, treas. 1990-92, program com. chair 1993-94), Orgn. Program Dirs. Assns. (sec.-treas., chair 2004—), Wis. State Med. Soc., Milw. County Med. Soc. Med. Coll. of Wis., Soc. Teaching Scholars. Avocations: tennis, golf, running. Office: Med Coll Wis Dept Psychiatry 8701 W Watertown Plank Rd Milwaukee WI 53226-3548 Office Phone: 414-456-7250. Business E-Mail: cchan@mcw.edu.

CHAN, DAVID RONALD, tax specialist, lawyer; b. LA, Aug. 3, 1948; s. David Yew and Anna May (Wong) Chan; m. Mary Anne Chan, June 21, 1980; children: Eric, Christina. AB in Econs., UCLA, 1969, MS in Bus. Adminstrn., 1970, JD, 1973. Bar: Calif. 1973, U.S. Tax Ct. 1974, U.S. Ct. Appeals (9th cir.) 1974, U.S. Dist. Ct. (ctrl. dist.) Calif. 1980. Acct. Oxnard Celery Distbrs., LA, 1968-73, Touche Ross & Co., LA, 1970; tax prin. Kenneth Leventhal & Co. (name now E&Y Kenneth Leventhal Real Estate Group of Ernst & Young LLP), LA, 1973—. Contbr. chpts. to books and articles to profl. jours. Founder, dir. Chinese Hist. Soc. So. Calif., L.A., 1975—; mem. spkrs. bur. L.A. 200 Bicentennial, L.A., 1981; spkr. Project Follow Through, L.A., 1981, EY Tax Forum, UCLA Real Estate Forecast, Merril Lynch Symposium, Calif. CPA Soc. Recipient Forbes Gold medal Calif. Soc. CPAs, L.A., 1970, Elijah Watt Sells cert. AICPA, L.A., 1970, cert. recognition Chinese Hist. Soc. So. Calif., L.A., 1985. Mem. So. Calif. Chinese Lawyers Assn., L.A. County Bar Assn., Chinese Am. CPAs So. Calif., Asian Bus. League, Chinese For Affirmative Action. Republican. Avocations: Chinese cuisine, sports memorabilia, stamp collecting/philately. Office: E&Y Kenneth Leventhal Real Estate Group 725 S Figueroa St 5th Fl Los Angeles CA 90017-5418 Home Phone: 213-706-4367; Office Phone: 213-977-3310. E-mail: david.chan02@ey.com.

CHAN, JACKIE, actor, film director; b. Hong Kong, Apr. 7, 1954; s. Chi-Ping and Lee-Lee Chan; m. Lin Fong Chiao; 1 child: J.C. Trained, Peking Opera Sch. Films include: Little Tiger of Guangdong, Little Tiger from Canton, Hand of Death, 1975, New Fist of Fury, 1976, Shaolin Wooden Men, 1976, To Kill with Intrigue, 1977, Snake in the Eagle's Shadow, Snake and Crane Arts of Shaolin, Magnificent Bodyguards, 1978, Drunken Master, 1978, Spiritual Kung Fu, 1978, The Fearless Hyena, Dragon Fist, 1979, The Young Master, 1980, Half a Loaf of King Fu, Battle Creek Brawl, 1980, The Cannonball Run, 1981, The Dragon Lord, 1982, Marvelous Fists, 1982, Winners and Sinners, 1983, The Fearless Hyena Part 2, Project A, 1983, Cannonball Run II, 1984, Wheels on Meals, 1984, My Lucky Stars, 1985, The Protector, 1985, Twinkle Twinkle Lucky Stars, 1985, Heart of the Dragon, 1985, Police Story, 1986, Armour of God, 1987, Project A Part 2, 1987, Dragons Forever, 1987, Police Story II, 1987, Mr. Canton and Lady Rose, 1989, Amour of God II: Operation Condor, 1991, Island of Fire, 1991, Twin Dragons, 1992, Police Story III: Super Cop, 1992, City Hunter, 1993, Crime Story, 1993, Drunken Master II, 1994, Rumble in the Bronx, 1994, Thunderbolt, 1994, Police Story IV: First Strike, 1996, Mr. Nice Guy, 1997, Rush Hour, 1998, Who Am I?, 1998, Gorgeous, 1999, The King of Comedy, 1999, Gen-X Cops, 1999, Shanghai Noon, 2000, The Accidental Spy, 2001, Rush Hour 2, 2001, The Tuxedo, 2002, Shanghai Knights, 2003, The Medallion, 2003, Around the World in 80 Days, 2004, Fa dou daai jin, 2004, San gin chaat goo si, 2004, San Wa, 2005, Rush Hour 3, 2007. Recipient Lifetime Achievement award MTV, 1995, Best Picture award Hong Kong Film, 1989, Best Action Choreography Hong Kong Film, 1996, 99, 2002, Maverick Tribute award Cinequest San Jose Film Festival, 1998, PETA Humanitarian award, 1999, Internat. Lifetime Achievement award, Internat. Leadership Found., 2000, Taurus Hon. award, Outstanding Achievement for Acting in Actions Film, World Stunt awards, 2002. Named Goodwill Amb., 2004.*

CHAN, JANET, editor-in-chief; children: Jack, Laura. Sr. editor Glamour Mag., NYC; exec. editor Redbook, NYC, 1991—94, Good Housekeeping, NYC, 1994—96; editor-in-chief Parenting Mag., NYC, 1996—; and editl. dir. The Parenting Group, NYC, 1996—. Editl. dir. Time Inc.'s Parenting

Group including Mom-to-Be Babytalk, and Parenting mags. Office: The Parenting Group 3d Fl 135 W 50th St New York NY 10020 Office Phone: 212-522-9808. Office Fax: 212-522-8750.*

CHAN, KATHLEEN ANN, writer, social worker; d. Edwin Quong Chan and Doris Gok; m. Donald Edison Bragg. BA, U. Calif., Berkeley, 1968. LCSW Ariz. Bd. Behavioral Health Examiners, 1998. Author: (poetry) Ancient Tapestry, (collection of poetry) The Journey To Fatima. Democrat. Achievements include established new paradigm for psychotherapy. Avocations: creative writing, poetry reading. Home: 12802 W Windsor Ave Avondale AZ 85323-7101 Home Phone: 623-536-8118; Office Phone: 602-997-6105. Personal E-mail: abraggdon@netzero.net.

CHAN, KITYU EVAN, civil engineer; s. Hing Yuen Chan and Lin Ying Ko; m. Mei Yee Billie Ho; 1 child, Ka Chai Jesse. BSCE, Lakehead U., Ont., Can., 1981. Registered profl. engr., Can., US. Chief engr. Sang Lee Contrn. Co. Ltd., Hong Kong, 1981—86; asst. airport mgr. Hong Kong Civil Aviation Dept., 1986—87; contract adminstr. Dawn Enterprises, Thornhill, 1987—88; soil engr. Chih S. Huang & Assocs., Markham, 1988—91; geotech. engr. Walter H. Gibson & Assocs., Bowmanville, 1991—93; mgr. Dragages Hong Kong Ltd., 1993—2006; non-exec. dir. Fine Wealthy Ltd., 2006—. Bd. dirs. Planning Adv. Com., Toronto, Canada, 1993. Named Internat. Scientist of Yr., Cambridge, Eng., 2004; Entrance scholar, Lakehead U., 1977. Fellow: ASCE; mem.: Profl. Engrs. USA, Ont. Soc. Profl. Engrs., Profl. Engrs. Ont. Avocations: swimming, lawn bowling.

CHAN, LAWRENCE SIU-YUNG, dermatologist, educator; b. Hong Kong, Dec. 10, 1949; came to U.S., 1975; s. Cheong-Yin Chan and Chun-Fun Wu. AA, Montgomery Coll., Takoma Park, Md., 1978; student, Messiah Coll., Grantham, Pa., 1978-79; BS, BS, MIT, 1981; MD, U. Pa., 1985. Diplomate Am. Bd. Dermatology, Nat. Bd. Med. Examiners. Intern Rutgers Med. Sch., Camden, NJ, 1986-87; resident U. Mich., Ann Arbor, 1987-91; asst. prof. Wayne State U., Detroit, 1991-93, Northwestern U., Chgo., 1993—2002, dir. immunodermatology divsn., 1993—2002; assoc. prof. U. Ill., 2002—05, dir. immunology rsch., 2002—, prof., 2005—, head dept. dermatology, 2005—. Adj. lectr. U. Mich., 1991-93. Author: (med. textbook) Blistering Skin Diseases, 2007; editor: (sci. textbook) Animal Models of Human Inflammatory Skin Disease, 2003. Recipient Clin. Investigator award, NIH, Bethesda, 1996; grantee Merit Rev., VA Rsch. Com., 1996; Small Project, High-risk Project and Rsch. Project grantee, NIH, 2001. Fellow Am. Acad. Dermatology; mem. Soc. Investigative Dermatology, Ctrl. Soc. Investigative Dermatology (chmn. 1995), Dermatology Found. (Career Devel. award 1993), Am. Assn. Immunologists, Am. Soc. Investigative Pathology, Microcirculatory Soc., Alpha Omega Alpha. Achievements include identification of a novel skin basement membrane component, generation of an animal model of atopic dermatitis, generation of an animal model of an autoimmune hairless disorder alopecia areata. Office: U Ill Dept Dermatology 808 S Wood Chicago IL 60612-3010 Office Phone: 312-996-6966. Business E-Mail: larrycha@uic.edu.

CHAN, LO-YI CHEUNG YUEN, architect; b. Canton, China, Dec. 1, 1932; came to U.S., 1942, naturalized, 1954; s. Wing tsit and Wai hing (Lei) C.; m. Mildred Wu, Sept. 1, 1957; children: Christopher, Leighton, Leicia. BA, Dartmouth Coll., 1954, DArts (hon.), 2004; MArch, Harvard U., 1959, postgrad. (Appleton fellow), 1959-60. Asso. firm I. M. Pei & Partners, NYC, 1960-65; practiced architecture NYC, 1965—2002. Adj. asst. prof. architecture Columbia, 1963-67; vis. critic Coll. Architecture, Cornell U., 1965-68, Harvard U., 1976, 78, 80, Mass. Inst. Tech., 1977; panelist Am. Arbitration Assn., 1972-80. Exhibitions include, The Museum of Modern Art, The Whitney Museum, Columbia U., Nat. Academy of Design, Boston Architectural Center. Bd. dirs. Parks Coun., N.Y.C., 1971-85, pres., 1974; trustee Cmty. Svc. Soc., N.Y.C., 1977-86, Henry St. Settlement, 1980-99, Lingnan Found., 1986—, chmn., 1990—, mem. N.Y.C. Art Commn., 1992-97, Berkshire Sch., 1992— trusteeColby-Sawyer Coll., 2003-06; active N.Y. State Coun. Arts, 1993-96; bd. dirs. Berkshire Taconic Cmty. Found., 2000—. With AUS, 1955-57. Nat. Endowment for Arts Design fellow, 1975-76 Fellow AIA (corp.); mem. Phi Beta Kappa. Home and Office: 270 Riverside Dr New York NY 10025

CHAN, MOSES HUNG WAI, physics educator, researcher; b. Xi-an, Shensi, China, Nov. 23, 1946; came to U.S., 1964, naturalized, 1984. BA magna cum laude, Bridgwater Coll., Va., 1967; MS, Cornell U., 1970, PhD, 1974. Asst. lectr. U. Hong Kong, 1969-70; asst. prof. U. Toledo, Ohio, 1976-79; asst. prof. Pa. State U., University Park, 1979-84, assoc. prof., 1984-86, prof. 1986-90, disting. prof., 1990—. Contbr. articles to profl. jours. Sr. rsch. fellow Inst. for Solid State Physics, U. Tokyo, summer 1982; NSF grantee; Fellow Am. Phys. Soc., Am. Acad. Arts & Sci.; mem. NAS; recipient Senior Rsch. Fellowship Japan Soc. for Promotion Sci., 1982, John Simon Guggenheim Fellowship, 1986, Fritz London Memorial prize in low temperature physics, 1996. Office: Pa State U Dept of Physics 104 Davey Lab University Park PA 16802

CHAN, PHILIP, retired dermatologist, retired military officer; b. Oceanside, NY, Oct. 14, 1946; s. Walter O. and Ann (Yee) C. BA, Harvard U., 1968; MD, Columbia U., 1972. Diplomate Am. Bd. Dermatology. Commd. capt. U.S. Army, 1973, advanced through grades to col., 1997; dermatologist Martin Army Cmty. Hosp., Ft. Benning, Ga., 1995-98; ret. U.S. Army, 1998; tchr. Tai Chi, Reiki, blues harmonica Columbus, Ga., 1999—. Adj. asst. prof. Uniformed Svcs. U. Health Scis., 1995—97; part-time instr. Rankin Arts Ctr., Columbus State U. Editor (govt. pub.) Procs. of Vesicant Workshop, 1987; conbtr. articles to profl. jours. Fellow: Am. Acad. Dermatology; mem.: AMA, Tai Chi for Health Cmty., Internat. Assn. Reiki Profls., Assn. Mil. Dermatologists, Mensa. Home: 6300 Milgen Rd #1285 Columbus GA 31907-0962

CHAN, PHILIP J., medical educator; married; 3 children. BA cum laude in biology, Kalamazoo Coll., 0979; MS in Physiology, Mich. State U., 1981, PhD in Physiology, 1983. Diplomate Am. Bd. Bioanalysis. Dir. sperm processing & IVF and embryo transfer lab. Kennedy Meml. Hosps./U. Med. Ctr., Cherry Hill, NJ, 1983—87; dir. labs. Hillcrest Fertility Ctr., Tulsa, 1987—89; dir. andrology/male reproduction and molecular biology labs. Loma Linda U. Obstetrics Med. Group, Calif., 1989—. Mgr. info. sys. lab. computers and network Loma Linda U. Ob-Gyn. Med. Group, Inc., 1991—; from instr. to asst. prof. U. Medicine and Dentistry of N.J. Sch. Osteopathic Medicine, 1983-87; assoc. prof. Oral Roberts U. Sch. Medicine, 1987-89; from assoc. prof. to prof. Loma Linda U. Sch. Medicine, 1989—; mem. comparative medicine study sect. NIH, 1994-98, chmn. site visit Nat. Ctr. for Rsch. Resources, 1999; insp. Coll. Am. Pathologists, 1993—. Contbr. articles to profl. jours. Recipient Walter-MacPherson First Pl. Rsch. award The Walter E. Macpherson Soc., 1997, Outstanding Attending Staff Physician award WYETH, 2003, Nat. Faculty award Coun. on Resident Edn. in Ob-Gyn., 2006. Mem. Am. Soc. Reproductive Medicine, Soc. Assisted Reproductive Tech., Am. Assn. Bioanalysts. Avocations: computers, stamp collecting/philately, coin collecting/numismatics, piano. Office: Loma Linda U Fac Med Office Dept Ob-Gyn Ste 3950 11370 Anderson St Loma Linda CA 92354-3450 Personal E-mail: pchann@yahoo.com.

CHAN, SHU-PARK, electrical engineering educator; b. Canton, China, Oct. 10, 1929; came to U.S., 1951, naturalized, 1965; s. Chi-Tong and Shui-Ying (Mok) C.; m. Stella Yok-Sing Lam, Dec. 28, 1956; children: Charlene Li-Hsiang, Yau-Gene. BEE, Va. Mil. Inst., Lexington, 1955; MEE, U. Ill., 1957, PhD, 1963. Instr. elec. engring. and math. Va. Mil. Inst., 1957-59; instr. elec. engring. U. Ill., 1960-61, rsch. assoc., 1961-62, asst. prof. math., 1962-63; assoc. prof. elec. engring. U. Santa Clara, 1963-68, prof., 1968-92, chmn. elec. engring. and computer sci. dept., 1969-84; Nicholson Family Chair prof. Santa Clara U., 1987-92, prof. emeritus, 1992—, acting dean Sch. Engring., 1987-88; founder, pres. Internat. Technol. U., Santa Clara, 1994—; pres. Chu Hai Coll., Hong Kong, 1995-96. Prin. investigator NSF, NASA; Univ. fellow U. Ill., 1959-60; vis. spl. chair prof. elec. engring. dept. Nat. Taiwan U., 1973-74; spl. lectr. Acad. Sci., Peking, China, summer 1980; hon. prof. elec. engring. dept. U. Hong Kong, 1980-81; hon. prof. Anhuei U., China, 1982; spl. chair Tamkang U., Taipei, Taiwan, 1981; apptd. mem. J. William Fulbright Fgn. Scholarship Bd., 1991-93; founder, pres. Internat. Tech. U. Found., 1994—. Author: introductory Topological Analysis of Electrical Networks, 1969, (with others) Analysis of Linear Networks and Systems—A Matrix-Oriented Approach with Computer Applications, 1972, (with E. Moustakas) Introduction to the Applications of the Operational Amplifier, 1974; editor: Network Topology and Its Engineering Applications, 1975, Graph Theory and Applications, 1982. Chmn. bd., pres. Acad. Cultural Co., Santa Clara; founder, pres. China Exptl. U. Found., 1985—; chmn. Santa Clara County Bicentennial Chinese Festival Com.; pres. Chinese Arts and Culture Inst., 1976—; trustee Inst. Sino-Am. Studies, San Jose, Calif., 1971-76, West Valley-Mission C.C. Dist., Calif., 1988. Recipient Disting. Elec. Engring. Alumnus award U. Ill., 1983, 1991 Rschr. of Yr. award Sch. Engring., Santa Clara U., 1992, Courvoisier Leadership award in Edn., 1994; named Engr. of Yr. in Engring. Edn. San Francisco session AIAA, 1994, Chinese Am. Pioneer award Orgn. Chinese Ams., San Francisco, 1996; Hon. Prof. award S. China Normal U., Guangzhou, China, 1997—, Educator of Yr. award Chinese Consol. Benevolent Assn. and Chinese Consol. Women's Assn., 1999, Mayor's awrd City of San Francisco, 1999. Fellow IEEE (past chmn. circuit theory group San Francisco sect., chmn. asilomar conf. circuits and sys. 1970); mem. Am. Soc. Engring. Edn., Chineses Alumni Assn. U. Santa Clara (pres.), U. Santa Clara Faculty Club (pres. 1971-72), Sigma Xi, Tau Beta Pi, Eta Kappa Nu, Pi Mu Epsilon, Phi Kappa Phi. Home: 2085 Denise Dr Santa Clara CA 95050-4557 Office Phone: 408-331-1014. Business E-Mail: spchan@itu.edu. *I would like to attribute my personal success to the teaching of my father, the late General of the Army Chi-Tong Chan, who taught me the Four Principles of Goodness: Set a good goal in mind; acquire a good wealth of knowledge; exercise good self-discipline; and perform only good deeds.*

CHAN, SIU-WAI, materials science educator; m. Kung Yip Cheung; children: L.Y., K.Y. BS, Columbia U., 1980; ScD, MIT, 1985. Mem. tech. staff Bellcore, Murray Hill, NJ, 1985-86, Red Bank, NJ, 1986-90; assoc. prof. materials sci. Columbia U., NYC, 1990—2002, prof., 2002—. Presdl. Faculty fellow, NSF, 1993, Guggenheim fellow, 2003—04. Office: Columbia U Sch Engring & Applied Sci 200 Mudd Bldg MC 4701 500 W 120th St New York NY 10027-8031 Business E-Mail: sc174@columbia.edu.

CHAN, SUNNEY IGNATIUS, retired chemistry educator; b. San Francisco, Oct. 5, 1936; s. Sun and Hip-For (Lai) C.; m. Irene Yuk-Hing Tam, July 11, 1964; 1 son, Michael Kenneth. BSChemE, U. Calif., Berkeley, 1957, PhD in Chemistry, 1960; DSc honoris causa, Hong Kong Bapt. U., 2003. Asst. prof. chemistry U. Calif., Riverside, 1961—63; mem. faculty Calif. Inst. Tech., Pasadena, 1963—2006, prof. chem. physics, 1968—92, prof. biophys. chemistry, 1976—92, George Grant Hoag prof. biophys. chemistry, 1992—2001, exec. officer for chemistry, 1977—80, 1989—94, master student houses, 1980—83, chmn. faculty, 1987—89, George Grant Hoag prof. biophys. chemistry emeritus, 2002—06; dir. Inst. of Chemistry Academia Sinica, Taipei, Taiwan, 1997—99; disting. rsch. fellow Academia Sinica, Taipei, 1997—2006, v.p., 1999—2003, chair disting. rsch. fellow, 2006—. Trustee, Croucher Found., Hong Kong, 1999-2006, R.T. Major lectr. U. Conn., 1998; Wilson T.S. Wang Disting. Internat. prof. Chinese U. Hong Kong, 1993; Reilly lectr. U. Notre Dame, 1973-74; Chan Meml. lectr. U. Calif., Berkeley, 1984; Lee Wee Nam vis. prof. Nanyang Tech. U., Singapore, 2006; cons. in field. Author numerous articles in field. Recipient CB Net award in biophysics, 2005; Guggenheim fellow, 1968-69; Sloan fellow, 1965-67; NSF Postdoctoral fellow, 1960-61; Fogarty fellow NIH, 1986. Fellow AAAS, Biophys. Soc., Am. Phys. Soc.; mem. Academia Sinica, Am. Chem. Soc., Chinese Am. Chem. Soc. (chmn. bd. 1988-97), Am. Soc. Biochemistry and Molecular Biology (William C. Rose award 2004), Biophys. Soc. Taiwan (pres. 1998-2001), So. Calif. Chinese Engrs. and Scientists Assn. (Progress award 1971), Chinese Collegiate Colleagues So. Calif. (v.p. 1970-71, pres. 1971-72), Chinese Am. Faculty Assn. (pres. 1988, Achievement award 1991, Disting. Svc. award 2000), Third World Acad. Scis., Phi Beta Kappa, Sigma Xi, Tau Beta Pi, Alpha Chi Sigma, Phi Tau Phi (pres. 1981-83, nat. pres. 2004-) Home: 327 Camino Del Sol South Pasadena CA 91030-4107 Office: Calif Inst Tech Chem Dept Pasadena CA 91125-0001 Office Phone: 626-395-6508. Personal E-mail: sunneychan@yahoo.com. Business E-Mail: chans@its.caltech.edu.

CHAN, THOMAS TAK-WAH, lawyer; b. Kowloon, Hong Kong, 1950; BA magna cum laude, U. Wis., Whitewater, 1973; JD, U. Wis., 1979. Bar: Wis. 1979, Minn. 1983, Calif. 1987. Judicial intern Wis. Supreme Ct., 1978; atty. Wausau (Wis.) Ins., 1979-82; staff atty. CPT Corp., Eden Prairie, Minn., 1982-84; gen. counsel Lee Data Corp., Eden Prairie, 1984-85; dep. gen. counsel Ashton-Tate Corp., Torrance, Calif., 1985-87; mng. ptnr. Chan Law Group LLP, LA, 1987—. Mem. adv. bd. SBA Export Devel. Ctr., 1992-2000; founder Bus. Software Alliance, Washington, 1987; mem. industry sector adv. com. and U.S. trade rep., U.S. Dept. Commerce, 1988-91; bd. dirs. Asian Pacific Am. Legal Ctr., 2002-05. Bd. dirs. Torrance Meml. Med. Ctr. Found., 2000-07. Mem. Asian Pacific Am. Bar Assn. (founder, dir. 1998-00), Wis. Bar Assn., Calif. Bar Assn. (lectr. 1988) Computer Law Assn., So. Calif. Chinese Lawyers Assn. (gov. 1990-92) Export Mgrs. Assn. So. Calif. (dir. 1990-92), South Bay Chinese Am. C. of C. (founder, dir. 1997-2004, pres. 2003-04), South Bay Chinese Culture Ctr. (dir. 1998-01), Cause (dir. 1994-97, chmn. 1995-96), Phi Kappa Phi. Avocations: hiking, tai chi. Office: Chan Law Group LLP 1055 W Seventh St Ste 1880 Los Angeles CA 90017 Office Phone: 213-624-6560. Business E-Mail: thelaw@chanlaw.com.

CHAN, WING-CHI, cultural consultant and organization administrator, musicologist; b. Hong Kong, Aug. 10, 1952; came to U.S., 1979; s. Hing and Mui-Fung (Leung) C.; m. Mina Chan, Jan. 1, 1979; children: Tidings, Leona, Dexter. BA, Chinese U., Hong Kong, 1978; MMus, No. Ill. U., DeKalb, 1981; postgrad., U. Amsterdam, 1991. Pres. Chinese U. Student Union, Hong Kong, 1977; rsch. asst. U. S.W. La., Lafayette, 1979; mgr. Charm's Trading Co., Houston, 1982; asst. to dir. coll. honors program U. Md., Catonsville, 1974—85; dir. devel. Washington Youth Orch., 1985—96; broadcaster Voice of Am. Radio, 1989—90, Fairchild Radio, Canada, 2001; exec. dir. Nat. Chamber Orch., Washington, 1992; DC commr. Nat. and Cmty. Svcs., Washington, 1994—97; v.p. Washington Symphony Orch., 1997—99; pres. Washington Cultural Internat. Inc., 1996—. Lectr., spkr. U. Md., College Park, 1983, 84, Tenri (Japan) U., 1986, Kingston Poly., London, 1988, Hong Kong U., 1990, 2003, Macao U. Sci. Tech., 2003, Columbia U., 2004; instr. multi-cultural, 2003—; tour coord. Washington Youth Orch. to China, Hong Kong, Taiwan, Korea, Spain, France, Netherlands, and Russia, 1986-94; cons. NEA, Washington, 1989—, N.J. State Arts Coun., 1995, 97, S.C. Arts Commn., 1993; vis. assoc. prof. ShenYang Conservatory, China, 1992—; adj. prof. Green Mountain Coll., Vt. 2002—; artistic adv. China Nat. Symphony Orch., Bejing, 2001—; organizer conf. Asia 4th Pacific Life Underwriters Assns. Conf., Hong Kong, 1997; organizer seminar Aetna Sales Congr., Hong Kong, 1998; organizer Hong Kong New Youth Forum's 2004 U.S. Election observation tour. Recipient Supr. Svc. award Mayor of Washington, 1987. Mem. Assn. Asian Studies, Am. Symphony Orch. League, Cultural Alliance Greater Washington. Office: Ste 201 419 7th St NW Washington DC 20004 Office Phone: 202-489-8383. Personal E-mail: wcichan@aol.com.

CHAN, YIUMO, biochemist; b. Hong Kong, June 25, 1967; s. Man and Kwok-ying Chan; m. Mei-hua Chen, Dec. 19, 2001. BS in Chemistry, U. Chgo., 1989, PhD of Devel. Biology, 1995. Postdoctoral fellow Harvard Med. Sch., Boston, 1995—2001; staff scientist Geisinger Hosp., Danville, Pa., 2001—. Adv. Coun. Healthcare Gerson Lehrman Group, NYC, 2001—; mem. Sci. Adv. Bd., Arlington, Va., 2002—. Co-author: Principles of Molecular Medicine, 1998; contbr. articles to profl. jours. Mem.: ACLU, AAAS, NY Acad. Scis., Am. Soc. Human Genetics (mentorship program), Amnesty Internat. Democrat. Achievements include discovery of genetic basis of an inherited skin blistering disease, Weber-Cockayne Epidermolysis Bullose Simplex; research in understanding neuromuscular diseases. Avocations: reading, travel, art, coin collecting/numismatics, stamp collecting/philately. Office: Geisinger Hosp Weis Ctr for Rsch 100 N Academy Ave MC 26-11 Danville PA 17822 Home Phone: 570-275-3137; Office Phone: 570-271-6851. E-mail: ymchan@geisinger.edu.

CHANCE, JANE, English literature educator; b. Neosho, Mo., Oct. 26, 1945; d. Donald William and Julia (Mile) C.; m. Dennis Carl Nitzsche, June, 1966 (div. Mar. 1969); 1 child, Therese; m. Paolo Passaro, Apr. 30, 1981,(div. May 2002); children: Antony Damian, Joseph Sebastian. BA in English with honors and highest distinction, Purdue U., West Lafayette, Ind., 1967; AM in English, U. Ill., Urbana, 1968, PhD in English, 1971. Lectr. U. Sask., Canada, 1971—72, asst. prof., 1972—73; asst. prof. English, Rice U., Houston, 1973—77, assoc. prof., 1977—80, prof., 1980—, dir. medieval studies program, 2005—; hon. rsch. fellow U. Coll. U. London, 1977—78. Dir. NEH Summer Seminar for Coll. Tchrs. on Chaucer and Mythography, 1985, NEH Inst. for Coll. Tchrs. on Medieval Women, 1997; pres., founder TEAMS, 1986-89; founder, dir. medieval studies program Rice U., 1986-92, 2005—; founding mem. Rice U. Commn. on Women, 1986-88; resident Rockefeller Found., Bellagio, Italy, 1988; mem. Sch. Hist. Studies, Inst. for Advanced Study, Princeton, 1988-89; vis. rsch. fellow Inst. for Advanced Studies in Humanities, U. Edinburgh, 1994; Eccles fellow Humanities Ctr., U. Utah, 1994-95; spkr., lectr. in field. Author: The Genius Figure in Antiquity and the Mid. Ages, 1975, Tolkien's Art: A Mythology for Eng., 1979; author: (rev. edit.), 2001; author: Woman as Hero in Old English Literature, 1986, 2d edit., 2005, The Lord of the Rings: The Mythology of Power, 1992, rev. edit., 2001, Japanese trans., 2003, Medieval Mythography: From Roman North Africa to the Sch. of Chartres, AD 433-1177 (South Ctrl. MLA book prize, 1994), The Mythographic Chaucer: The Fabulation of Sexual Politics, 1995, Medieval Mythography, vol. 2: From the Sch. of Chartres to the Ct. at Avignon, 1177-1350, 2000, The Literary Subversions of Medieval Women, 2007; translator: Christine de Pizan's Letter of Othea to Hector, 1990; editor: The Mythographic Art: Classical Fable and the Rise of the Vernacular in Early France and Eng., 1990, Medievalism in the Twentieth Century, Studies in Medievalism, vol. 2:2, 1983, The Inklings and Others, vol. 3:3, 1990, Gender and Text in the Later Mid. Ages, 1986, The Assembly of Gods, 1999, Listening to Heloise, 2000 (Best Essay prize Soc. Medieval Feminist Scholarship, 2005), Tolkien the Medievalist, 2002, Tolkien and the Invention of Myth: A Reader, 2004, Women Medievalists and the Academy, 2005; co-editor: Approaches to Teaching Sir Gawain, 1986, Mapping the Cosmos, 1985, Tolkien's Modern Middle Ages, 2005; gen. editor: Focus Libr. of Medieval Women, 1988—, Boydell & Brewer Libr. of Medieval Women, 1997—, series editor: Greenwood Guides to Hist. Events in the Medieval World, 2001—, Praeger Series on the Mid. Ages, 2003—, mem. editl. bd.: Coll. Lit., 2002—; contbr. numerous essays, reviews, poems. Bd. dirs. Rice U. Press, 1981-88, Internat. Chaucer Studio, 2003—. NEH fellow, 1977-78, Guggenheim fellow, 1980-81, Mellon leave Rice U., 1988, Disting. Faculty Tchg. fellow, 1995, Ctr. for Study Cultures fellow, 1998, NEH fellow St. Louis U. Ctr. for Med. Studies, 2003, Mellon fellow, Pope Pius Vatican Film Libr., 2003; Travel grant ACLS, 1982; recipient Women's Ctr. IMPACT award Rice U., 1998. Mem. AAUP (Rice U. chpt. sec., treas. 1975-76), MLA, SC MLA, Scientia (acting dir. 1983-84, sec. 1982-83), Tex. Faculty Assn. (exec. com. 1995-99, v.p. 1998-2000, Achievement award 1998), New Chaucer Soc., Medieval Acad. Am., Internat. Arthurian Soc. Avocations: book collecting, photography, travel. Office: Rice U Dept English MS 30 PO Box 1892 Houston TX 77251-1892 Home Phone: 713-524-3282; Office Phone: 713-348-2625. Business E-Mail: jchance@rice.edu.

CHANCE, KENNETH BERNARD, SR., endodontist educator, academic administrator; b. NYC, Dec. 8, 1953; s. George E. and Janie L. (Bolles) Chance; m. Sharon Lee Lewis, July 11, 1981 (div.); children: Kenneth Bernard, Dana Marie, Christopher, Jaquelyn. BS, Fordham U., Bronx, NY, 1975; DDS, Case Western Res. U., Cleve., 1979; Cert. in Endodontics, U. Medicine and Dentistry NJ, 1982. Asst. attending Jamaica Hosp., Queens, NY, 1981-87; chief endodontics Kings County Med. Ctr., Bklyn., 1982-91; assoc. prof. endodontics U. Medicine and Dentistry NJ, 1987; also dir. external affairs NJ Dental Sch.; asst. attending North Ctrl. Bronx Hosp., NY, 1983-91, Kingsbrook Jewish Med. Ctr., 1986-92; asst. dean external affairs and urban resource devel. NJ Dental Sch., 1989-97; cons. Harlem Hosp., NYC, 1982-90; health policy advisor to US Senator Frank Lautenberg of NJ, 1991—99; dir. health policy program The Joint Ctr. Polit. and Econ. Studies, 1993-94; acting chmn. dept. endodontics NJ Dental Sch., 1994-97; fed. rels. adv. com. U. Medicine and Dentistry NJ, 1994-97; dean, prof. endodontics Meharry Med. Coll. Sch. Dentistry, 1997-2000; prof., dir. divsn. endodontics U. Ky., Lexington, 2000—. Spkr., presdl. leadership lecture series Megar Evers Coll., 2006. Mem. healthcare task force Congl. Black Caucus, 1994—2001; trustee Case Western Res. U., 2005—, mem. alumni and univ. rels. com., 2005—06, mem. presdl. search com., 2006, vice chmn. academic affairs and student life com., 2006, mem. audit com., 2006; mem. nat. adv. com. Robert Wood Johnson Summer Med. and Dental Edn. Program, 2006; min. music, sr. organist Sharon Bapt. Ch., Bronx, 1983—91. Recipient Dr. Paul P. Sherwood award for excellence in endodontics Case Western Res. U. Dental Sch., 1979, Cmty. Svc. award U. Medicine and Dentistry NJ, 1997, Tenn. Outstanding Achievement award, 1998, Outstanding Academician award U. Medicine and Dentistry NJ, 1999, Disting. Alumnus of Yr. award, Case Western Res. U., 2004, Found. grant award U. Medicine and Dentistry NJ, 1984, Exceptional Merit award, 1985, Excellence award, 1990, Disting. Practioner award Nat. Acad. Practice Dentistry, 2001, Faculty award U. Ky., Sch. Dentistry, 2005, award Megar Evers Coll., 2006; fellow Nat. Dental Leadership Devel. PEW, 1991, Robert Wood Johnson Health Policy, 1991, Pierre Fauchard Acad., 1996; named to The Best Dentists in America Woodward/White, Inc., 2004. Fellow Am. Coll. Dentists, Internat. Coll. Dentists; mem. ADA, Internat. Assn. Dental Rsch., Am. Dental Edn. Assn. (chair minority affairs sect. 2003), Am. Assn. Dental Schs., Nat. Dental Assn., Am. Assn. Endodontists, Greater Met. Dental Soc. NY (pres.-elect 1986-87, v.p. 1984-86), Ky. Assn. Endodontists, Omicron Kappa Upsilon (pres.-elect 2006, pres. 2007). Home: 2140 Mangrove Dr Lexington KY 40513 Office Phone: 859-323-5891. Business E-Mail: kbchan2@uky.edu.

CHANCE, STEVEN KENT, lawyer; b. Bryn Mawr, Pa., July 9, 1945; s. Henry Martyn and Elisabeth (Reese) C.; m. Colleen Benson Meyle; 1 child, Anna Benson. BA, Wesleyan U., 1967; MS, London Sch. Econs., 1968; JD, U. Pa., 1973. Assoc. Dechert Price & Rhoads, Phila., 1973-82, ptnr., 1982-84; dir. legal services Teleflex Inc., Limerick, Pa., 1984-86, v.p., dir. legal services, 1986—92, v.p., gen. counsel, sec., 1992—2003. Mem. Corinthian Yacht Club (Phila.) (trustee 1986-), Cruising Am. Club. Episcopalian. Home Phone: 610-525-3934; Office Phone: 484-431-2328. Personal E-mail: schance10@comcast.net.

CHANCELLOR, VAN, women's college basketball coach; b. Louisville, Miss., Sept. 27, 1943; m. Betty Chancellor; children: John, Renee. Student, East Ctrl. Jr. Coll., Decatur, Miss.; B Math. and Phys. Edn., Miss. State U., 1965, MEd, 1974. Head coach boys' basketball Noxapater HS, Miss.; head coach women's basketball U. Miss., Oxford, 1978—97; head coach, gen. mgr. Houston Comets, 1997—2007; head coach women's basketball La. State U., 2007—. Head coach West Team WNBA All-Star Game, 1999, 2000, 01; head coach USA Basketball Women's World Championship Team, 2002, US Women's Olympic Basketball Team (gold medal), Athens, Greece, 2004, Named Southeastern Conf. Coach of Yr., 1987, 90, 92, Nat. Coach of Yr., Women's Basketball News Svc., 1992, WNBA Coach of Yr., 1997, 98, 99, USA Basketball Nat. Coach of Year, 2002; named to Women's Basketball Hall of Fame, 2001, Naismith Meml. Basketball Hall of Fame, 2007. Achievements include winning 4 WNBA Championships as head coach of the Comets, 1997-2000. Office: La State U Womens Basketball Athletics Dept PO Box 25095 Baton Rouge LA 70894-5095 Office Phone: 225-578-6643.*

CHANCELLOR, WILLIAM JOSEPH, agricultural engineering educator; b. Alexandria, Va., Aug. 25, 1931; s. John Miller and Caroline (Sedlacek) C.; m. Nongkarn Bodhiprasart, Dec. 13, 1960; 1 child, Marisa Kuakul BS in Agr., BSME, U. Wis., 1954; MS in Agrl. Engring., Cornell U., 1956, PhD, 1957. Registered profl. agrl. engr., Calif. Prof. agrl. engring. U. California.-Davis, 1957-94; prof. emeritus. Vis. prof. agrl. engring. U. Malaya, Kuala Lumpur, Malaysia, 1962-63; UNESCO cons. Punjab Agrl. U., 1976 Contbr. articles to profl. jours.; patentee transmission, planters, dryer, 1961-73 East/West Ctr. sr. Fellow, Honolulu, 1976 Fellow Am. Soc. Agrl. Engrs. (Kishida Internat. award 1984, John Deere Gold Medal award 2004); mem. NAE, Soc. Automotive Engrs., Sigma Xi: found. mem. Asian Assoc. for Agrl. Office: Univ of California Dept Biol & Agrl Engineering Davis CA 95616 Business E-Mail: wjchancellor@ucdavis.edu.

CHANCY, MARK A., bank executive; BBA in Fin., So. Meth. U., Dallas; MBA, Northwestern U. With First Boston Corp., 1986; with corp. fin. dept. Robinson-Humphrey Co., 1989, CFO, 1997—2001, bd. dirs., 1998—2001; sr. v.p., treas. SunTrust Banks, Inc., Atlanta, 2001—04, corp. exec. v.p., CFO, mem. policy com., 2004—. Office: SunTrust Banks Inc PO Box 4418 Atlanta GA 30302-4418 Office Phone: 404-588-7711. Office Fax: 404-827-6173.*

CHANDIWAL, AMITO, research scientist; s. Mahendra and Saroj Chandiwal. MB, B.J. Med. Coll., India, 1999; MS in Biomedical Engring., U. Memphis, 2003; M in Clin. Trials Mgmt., U. Chgo., 2005. Intern Civil Hosp., Jalgaon, Maharashtra, India, 1998—99; clin. asst. Inlaks and Budhrani Hosp., Pune, Maharastra, 2000; rsch. asst. U. Memphis, 2000—03; rsch. engr. U. Chgo., 2004—. Recipient Rsch. award, Lifeline Found., 2004, Charles C. Guthrie award, 2006. Achievements include research in model of neointimal thickening; odulation of vascular remodeling induced by a brief intraluminal exposure to the recombinant r7020 strain of herpes simplex-1; balloon injury with low shear stress augments neointimal thickening in carotid arteries. Office Phone: 718-579-5000. Personal E-mail: amitochandiwal@hotmail.com.

CHANDLER, ALICE, retired academic administrator, educational consultant; b. Bklyn., May 29, 1931; d. Samuel and Jenny (Meller) Kogan; m. Horace Chandler, June 10, 1954; children: Seth, Donald, Barnard C. AB, Columbia U., 1951, MA, 1953, PhD, 1960; LHD, Kean U., 1997, Ramapo Coll., 2001. Instr. Skidmore Coll., 1953-54; lectr. Columbia U. Barnard Coll., 1954-55, Hunter Coll., CUNY, 1956-57; from instr. to prof. CCNY, 1961-76, v.p. instl. advancement, 1974-76, v.p. acad. affairs, 1974-76, provost, 1976-79, acting pres., 1979-80; pres. SUNY, New Paltz, 1980-96; interim pres. Ramapo Coll., 2000-2001; ret., 2001. Cons. in higher edn., 1996—. Author: The Prose Spectrum: A Rhetoric and Reader, 1968, The Theme of War, 1969, A Dream of Order, 1970, The Rationale of Rhetoric, 1970, The Rationale of the Essay, 1971, From Smollett to James, 1980, Foreign Student Policy: England, France, and West Germany, 1985, Obligation or Opportunity: Foreign Student Policy in Six Major Receiving Countries, 1989, Access, Inclusion and Equity: Imperatives for America's Campuses, 1997, Public Higher Education and the Public Good: Public Policy at the Crossroads, 1998, Paying the Bill for International Education: Programs, Purposes and Possibilities at the Millenium, 1999. Bd. dir. Mohonk Mountain House, NJ Coun. Humanities, chair, 2006—07. Lizette Fisher fellow. Mem.: Lotos, Phi Beta Kappa. Personal E-mail: hchand5066@aol.com.

CHANDLER, AUSTIN GRACE, psychologist; BA in Psychology with honors, Columbia U., 1970, MA, 1972; PhD, Fordham U., 1982; postgrad. in Bus., U. N.C., Greensboro, 1990. Lic., clin. psychologist. Corp. cons. Farr Assocs., 1983-85; mem. adj. faculty, founder, dir. coll. counseling ctr. Greensboro Coll., 1985-92; founder, pres. Allied Counseling and Consulting Enterprises, 1992—; chief psychologist Evergreens Sr. Health Care Facilities, NC, 1997—2001; psychology cons. Therapeutic Alternatives, Inc., NC, 2002—03; dir. psychology Guilford Child Health, Inc., NC, 2003—. Mem. adj. faculty U. N.C., Greensboro; bd. dirs. Ashley Industries. Author: (with Jack Bornstein) Food is Killing You, 1997; contbr. articles to profl. jours. Bd. dirs. N.C. Aging and Mental Health Coalition. Recipient Psychologist of Yr. award N.C. Chiropractic Assn. Mem. APA, N.C. Psychol. Assn., Prescription Privileges for Psychologists Register (charter), Sigma Xi. Avocations: painting, writing, following the stock market, skiing. Office: Allied Counseling & Consulting Enterprises 8200 Crows Nest Ln Greensboro NC 27455-9294 Office Phone: 336-272-1050. Office Fax: 336-643-6850. Business E-Mail: austin_chandler@bellsouth.net.

CHANDLER, BEN (ALBERT BENJAMIN CHANDLER III), congressman, former state attorney general; b. Lexington, Ky., Sept. 12, 1959; m. Jennifer Chandler; children: Lucie Brasher, Albert Benjamin IV, Russell Branham. BA in History with distinction, U. Ky., 1983, JD, 1986. Bar: Ky. 1986. Assoc. Brown, Todd & Heyburn, Lexington, Ky., Reeves & Graddy, Versailles, Ky.; auditor State of Ky., 1992—95, atty. gen., 1996—2003; mem. US Congress from 6th Ky dist., 2004—. Recipient Achievement of Yr. award, Assn. Govt. Accts., 1993—94. Mem.: ABA, Woodford County Bar Assn., Ky. Bar Assn. (named Outstanding Young Lawyer 1993). Democrat. Presbyterian. Office: US Ho Reps 1504 Longworth Ho Office Bldg Washington DC 20515-1706 Office Phone: 202-225-4706. Office Fax: 202-225-2122.*

CHANDLER, EDWARD WILLIAM, communication systems engineer, electrical engineer, electrical engineering educator; b. Milw., Oct. 10, 1953; s. Donald Harold and Helen Aleidia (Wonders) C.; m. Christine Anne Wohl, June 13, 1987; children: Rebecca Marie, Marcella Anne, Mary Elizabeth, Andrew Donald. BS, U. Wis., Milw., 1975; MSEE, Ill. Inst. Tech., 1978; PhD, Purdue U., 1985. Registered profl. engr., Wis. Electronics engr. Comms. and Electronics divsn. Motorola Inc., Schaumburg, Ill., 1976-77; instr. elec. engring. Milw. Sch. Engring., 1977-79, asst. prof., 1979-80, assoc. prof., 1982-84, prof., 1992—, acting head electronic comms. engring. tech. program, 1978-79, head, 1979-80, dir. elec. engring. program, 1982-84, dir. MS in Engring. program, 1992-2001, dir. elec. engring. tech. program, 2003—; asst. prof. elec. engring. Marquette U., Milw., 1984-86; sr. engr. L-3 Comm. (formerly Titan Corp.), San Diego, 1986-88, mem. tech. staff, 1988-92, engring. cons. Linkabit Divsn., 1992—2005, engring. cons., 2005—. Lectr. U. Wis., Milw., 1979-83; invited lectr. Czech Tech. U., 1997-98, Tech. U. Budapest, 1998, Fachhoschchule, Lübeck, Germany, 2000; grad. instr. rsch. Purdue U., West Lafayette, Ind., 1980-82; rsch. cons. Naval Ocean Systems Ctr., San Diego, 1986. Contbr. articles to profl. jours. David Ross summer grantee, 1981, Faculty Rsch. grantee Milw. Sch. Engring., 1983; recipient Karl O. Werwath Engring. Rsch. award Milw. Sch. Engring., 2004. Mem. IEEE (sr., newsletter editor Milw. sect. 1985-86), Am. Soc. Engring. Edn., Armed Forces Comms. and Electronics Assn., Air Force Assn., Triangle, Tau Beta Pi, Eta Kappa Nu. Home: 7030 N Range Line Rd Glendale WI 53209-2621 Office: Milw Sch Engring 1025 N Broadway Milwaukee WI 53202-3109 Office Phone: 414-277-7337. Business E-Mail: chandler@msoe.edu.

CHANDLER, EDWIN RUSSELL, clergyman, writer; b. LA, Sept. 9, 1932; s. Edwin Russell Sr. and Mary Elizabeth (Smith) C.; m. Sandra Lynn Swisher, Aug. 24, 1957 (div. 1977); children— Heather, Holly, Timothy John; m. Marjorie Lee Moore, Dec. 21, 1978; 3 stepchildren Student, Stanford U., 1950-52; BS in Bus. Adminstrn., UCLA, 1952-55; postgrad., U. So. Calif. Grad. Sch. Religion, 1955, New Coll., Edinburgh, Scotland, 1955-56; M.Div., Princeton Theol. Sem., 1958; grad., Washington Journalism Ctr., 1967. Ordained to ministry Presbyterian Ch., 1958. Asst. pastor 1st Presbyn. Ch., Concord, Calif., 1958-61; pastor Escalon Presbyn. Ch., Calif., 1961-66; reporter Modesto Bee, Calif., 1966-67; religion editor Washington Star, 1968-69; news editor Christianity Today, Washington, 1969-72; reporter Sonora Daily Union Dem., Calif., 1972-73; religion writer L.A. Times, 1974-92; interim pastor 1st Presbyn. Ch., Columbia, Calif., 1995-96. Author: The Kennedy Explosion, 1972, Budgets, Bedrooms and Boredom, 1976; co-author: Your Family--Frenzy or Fun?, 1977, The Overcomers, 1978, Understanding the New Age, 1988 (Silver Angel award 1989, Wilbur award 1989), Racing Toward 2001, 1992, Doomsday, 1993, Feeding the Flock, 1998; contbr. articles to profl. jours. Recipient Arthur West award United Methodist Communications Council, 1978, Faith and Freedom award Religious Heritage of Am., 1993; co-recipient Silver Angel award, Religion in Media, 1985 Mem. Religion Newswriters Assn. (pres. 1982-84, co-founder ann. Chandler award 2003, James O. Supple Meml. award, 1976, 1984, 86, John M. Templeton Reporter of Yr. award 1984, 87, 89), Religion Newswriters Assn. (Lifetime Achievement award, 2007), Phi Delta Theta Republican. Avocations: travel, beekeeping, birdwatching, theater. Home and Office: 14493 Kebra Ln Sonora CA 95370-9477 Personal E-mail: erchandler@aol.com.

CHANDLER, ELIZABETH B., lawyer; BBA magna cum laude, JD magna cum laude, Univ. Ga. Bar: Ga. Former ptnr., corp. atty. Troutman Sanders LLP; asst. gen. counsel Mirant Corp., v.p., corp. sec.; city atty. Legal Dept., Atlanta, 2006—. Mem.: ABA, Ga. State Bar Assn. (mem. bd. govs.). Office: City Dept Law Ste 4100 68 Mitchell Street Atlanta GA 30303

CHANDLER, FAY MARTIN, artist; b. Norfolk, Va., Sept. 15, 1922; d. Howard Gresham and Alpine Douglas (Gatling) Martin; m. Alfred Dupont Chandler Jr., Jan. 8, 1944; children: Alpine C. Bird, Mary C. Watt, Alfred D. III, Howard Martin. BA, Sweetbriar Coll., Va., 1943; MFA, Md. Inst. Coll. Art, Balt., 1967. Coord., dir. Fell's Point Gallery Md. Inst. Coll. Art, 1968-73; fellow Va. Ctr. Creative Arts, Sweetbriar, 1993. Hon. bd. dirs. Mass. Vol. Lawyers Arts; founder, bd. dirs. The Art Connection, Boston; arts in edn. adv. coun. Harvard Grad. Sch. Edn.; mem. Coun. Arts at MIT; adv. bd. Boston Landmarks Orch. One-woman shows include Kenneth Taylor Little Gallery, Nantucket, 1973, 76, Fells Point Gallery, Balt., 1974, 76, Mills Gallery, Boston, 1974-88, Main St. Gallery, Nantucket, 1977, Ensign-Sibley Gallery, Nantuckett, 1978, Sibley Gallery, Nantucket, 1980-85, Billiard Room Gallery, Cambridge, Mass., 1980, Helen Shlien Gallery, Boston, 1980, Bodley Gallery, NYC, 1980, St. Botolph Club, Boston, 1982, Stebbins Gallery, Cambridge, Mass., 1987, Bentley Coll., Waltham, Mass., 1987, Columbia (Md.) Ctr. for the Arts, 1987, Babcock Gallery Sweet Briar Coll., Va., 1993, Wenham (Mass.) Mus., 1993, Nantucket Island Sch. Design Gallery, 1994, Boston Ctr. For the Arts, 1995, Children's Mus., Boston, 1996, Decker Gallery/Md. Inst. Art, 1997, Steinbaum Krauss Gallery, NYC, 1997, Sacramento St. Gallery, Cambridge, Mass., 2002, Revolving Mus., Lowell, Mass., 2003, Boston Ctr. for the Arts, 2005; exhibited in group shows. Papers and slides chosen to be preserved Schlesinger Libr., Radcliffe Coll., Cambridge, Mass.; honoree Boston Landmarks Orch., 2007. Mem. Cambridge Art Assn Avocations: mystery books, philosophy. Home: 1010 Memorial Dr Apt 17E Cambridge MA 02138-4857 Studio: Engine House Studios 444 Western Ave Boston MA 02135-1016 Business E-Mail: fay@dougwatt.com.

CHANDLER, HARRIETTE LEVY, state legislator, management consultant, educator; b. Balt., Dec. 20, 1937; d. S. Lester and Reba K. Levy; m. Burton Chandler, July 12, 1959; children: Frank Levy, Victoria Jane, Edward Lee. BA, Wellesley Coll., 1959; MA, Clark U., 1963, PhD, 1973; MBA, Simmons Coll., 1983; PhD in Pub. Adminstrn. (hon.), Worcester State Coll., 1998. HS history tchr. Worcester (Mass.) Pub. Schs., 1959-61; polit. sci. prof. Clark U., Worcester, 1973-77; prof. polit. sci. Tufts U., Medford, Mass., 1977-78; exec. dir. nat women's com. Brandeis U., Waltham, Mass., 1978-81; cons. Prime Computer, Natick, Mass., 1983-84; mgr. documentation tng. Adelie Corp., Cambridge, Mass., 1984-85, mgr. mktg. svcs., 1985-87, prin., 1987-89; dir. communication Open Software Found., Cambridge, 1989; mgmt. cons. Chandler Assocs., 1990—. Author: U.S. Soviet Relations During World War II, 1982. Chmn. com. on shareholder responsibility Clark U., 1982—86; founding mem. Worcester Women's Polit. Caucus, 1985; chmn. bd. trustees Worcester Meml. Auditorium, 1987—89; com. mem. Worcester Sch., 1992—94, vice-chmn., 1994, Mass. Comm. on Common Core of Learning, 1994, Transp. Com., Worcester Com. Fgn. Rels.; incorporator YWCA, Greater Worcester Cmty. Found., Worcester Art Mus.; past pres. Jewish Healthcare Ctr.; chair Joint Com. Cmty. Devel. and Small Bus.; state rep. 13th Worcester Dist., Mass. Legislature, 1995—2000; mem. Dem. State Com., 1999—; state sen. 13th Worcester Dist., Mass. Legislature, 2001—; mem. steering com. Reforming States Group, 1996—; various coms. Ctrl. Mass. Legis. Caucus, 1991—, co-chair, 2001—02, co-chair women's legis. caucus, 2006, co-chair oral health com. Mem.: Worcester Econs. Club. Jewish. Avocations: walking, swimming, cooking, reading. Home: 97 Aylesbury Rd Worcester MA 01609-1314 Office: State House Rm 312D Boston MA 02133 Business E-Mail: hchandle@senate.state.ma.us.

CHANDLER, HUBERT THOMAS, former army officer; b. Charleston, W.Va., Dec. 8, 1933; s. Hubert Paris and Eleanor Lee (Gay) C.; m. Mary Frances Ritter, June 4, 1955; 1 son, Thomas Ritter. Student, Morris Harvey Coll., Charleston, 1951-52, U. Louisville, 1952-53; D.D.S., Balt. Coll. Dental Surgery, 1957; grad., Army War Coll., 1974. Diplomate: Am. Bd. Prosthodontics. Commd. Dental Corps U.S. Army, 1957, advanced through grades to maj. gen., dep. to chief Dental Corps, 1975-78, dep. comdr. Med. Command, dental surgeon Europe, 1979-82, asst. surgeon gen., chief Dental Corps, 1982-86, dir. personnel Med. Dept., 1983-85; assoc. dean for profl. devel. Dental Sch., U. Md., Balt., 1988-92. Exec. com. Transatlantic council Boy Scouts Am., 1980-82; chmn. trust fund Girl Scouts Europe, 1981-82; pres. European Assn. Rod and Gun Clubs, 1981-82, Am. German Friendship Club, Heidelberg, W. Ger., 1981-82. Decorated D.S.M., Bronze Star, Meritorious Service medal, Army Commendation medal Fellow Am. Coll. Prosthodontists; mem. ADA. Office: 1714 Besley Rd Vienna VA 22182-2004 Personal E-mail: htchandler@earthlink.net.

CHANDLER, JAMES BARTON, international education consultant; b. Conway Springs, Kans., May 27, 1922; s. James Perry and Bessie May (Stone) C.; m. Madeleine Racoux, July 27, 1946; children: Paul A., Peter R., Michele A. Chandler. AB, U. Kans., 1947, MA, 1949; postgrad., U. Mich., 1950—54. Asst. prof., fgn. student advisor Ea. Mich. U., 1953-55, 57-58; lang. edn. advisor Okla. A&M/Ethiopia, 1955-57, U. Mich./Laos, 1958-60; tchr. edn., advisor U.S. AID-Laos, Vientiane, Laos, 1960-61, edn. div. chief, 1961-63, asst. dir. manpower, industry, pub. adminstrn., 1965-69, deputy mission dir., 1969-73; higher edn. advisor U.S. AID-Tunisia, Tunis, Tunisia, 1963-65; dir. Office of Edn. AID, Washington, 1973-76, assoc. asst. adminstr., 1976-77; dir. Internat. Bur. Edn. UNESCO, Geneva, 1977-83; pvt. practice Ann Arbor, 1983—88, St. Louis, 1989—. With Rotary, Vientiane, Laos, 1966-73, sec. 1968-69. Capt. U.S. Army, 1943-47, ETO. Decorated Bronze Star; recipient Meritorious Honor award AID, 1973, Disting. Career Svc. award, 1977, Cert. Appreciation Pres. Gerald Ford, 1975, Letter Appreciation Dir. Gen. UNESCO, Geneva, 1983, Cold War Recognition cert. Sec. Def., 1998; S.L. Whitcomb fellow U. Kansas, 1948-49, Ford Found. fellow, 1951-52, WWII medal, State of Mo. Mem.: VFW, AARP, NRA, AAUP, Assn. Former Internat. Civil Servants, Nat. Assn. Ret. Fed. Employees (pres. Ann Arbor chpt. 1986—89, v.p. St. Louis chpt. 1989—90, pres. 1991—93, bd. dirs. 1992—93), Diplomatic and Ret. Consular Officers Ret. (regional corr.), Comparative and Internat. Edn. Soc., Nat. Assn. Scholars, Nat. Icarian Soc., Am. Fgn. Svc. Assn., Am. Acad. Social and Polit. Sci., UN Assn. USA, Ctr. for Internat. Understanding, Soc. Francaise St. Louis (bd. dirs., v.p., pres., sec., sgt.-at-arms), Alliance Francaise, St. Louis-Lyon Sister Cities Com., Austrian Soc. St. Louis, Nature Conservancy, Nat. Pks. and Conservation Assn., Nat. Wildlife Fedn., Archaeol. Inst. Am., Ind. Rights Found., Mo. Hist. Soc., Richmond Heights Srs. (v.p., pres.), Smithsonian Assocs., World Affairs Coun., Wilson Ctr. Assn., 4th Cavalry Assn., St. Louis Discussion Club, Rotary (bd. dirs., officer 1992—2001, Mid-County chpt. 2001—, sec. 2004—), Am. Legion, Phi Kappa Phi, Pi Delta Phi, Phi Beta Kappa. Roman Catholic. Avocations: bowling, bridge, billiards, painting, writing memoirs, stamps and coins. Home and Office: 7449 Rupert Ave Richmond Heights MO 63117 Office Phone: 314-781-7727. E-mail: jchandlr@aol.com.

CHANDLER, JAMES JOHN, surgeon, educator; b. Dayton, Ohio, Nov. 13, 1932; s. James Kapp and Margaret Bertha (Paulson) Chandler; m. Fleur Elizabeth Varney, July 23, 1955; 1 child, Jennifer Hauge. AB, Dartmouth Coll., 1954, diploma in medicine, 1955; MD cum laude, U. Mich., 1957. Diplomate Am. Bd. Surgery. Intern Harvard Surg. Svc., Boston City Hosp., 1957-58, jr. asst. resident, 1958; resident, chief resident in surgery, clin. fellow Am. Cancer Soc. U. Oreg. Hosps., Portland, 1961-64, instr. surgery, 1964; hon. staff, chmn. surgery Med. Ctr. at Princeton, NJ, 1972—92, pres. med. and dental staff, 1993-94; clin. prof. surgery U. Medicine and Dentistry N.J.-Robert Wood Johnson Med. Sch., Piscataway, 1976—; active staff Robert Wood Johnson U. Hosp., New Brunswick, NJ, 2000—. Cons. in surgery Princeton U.; trustee Med. Ctr. Princeton, 1993—94. Contbr. chapters to books, articles to profl. jours. Bd. dirs. Trinity Counseling Svc., 1968—, chmn., 1968—72; pres. Princeton Day Sch. PTA, 1976—78, trustee, 1976—81; mem. alumni coun. Dartmouth Med. Sch., 1981—86, Dartmouth Coll., 1983—86; mem. Govs. Task Force on Cancer in NJ, 2000—; active All Sts. Episcopal Ch., Princeton, 1965—. Lt. USN, 1958—60, served to lt. comdr. USNR, 1960—61. Fellow: ACS (pres. N.J. chpt. 1976—77, gov. 1981—87), Soc. Surg. Oncology, Am. Coll. Chest Physicians; mem.: AMA, Soc. Internat. Surgery, Soc. Surg. Alimentary Tract, Collegium Internationale Chirurgiae Digestivae, Med. Soc. N.J. (sec., chmn. surgery sect. 1967—69), Soc. Surgeons N.J., Am. Soc. Clin. Oncology, Gatineau Fish and Game Club, Bedens Brook Club, Nassau Gun Club (pres. 2001—02), Alpha Omega Alpha. Office: 1 Robert Wood Johnson Pl Box 19 New Brunswick NJ 08903-0019 Office Phone: 732-235-7920.

CHANDLER, JAMES PHILLIP, III, law educator; b. Bakersfield, Calif., Aug. 15, 1938; s. Isaac and Lillie Mae Chandler; m. Elizabeth Thompson (div.); children: James P. IV, Elizabeth Lynne, Dennis Augustine, Ruth Rebekah, Isaac II, Aaron Daniel Pushkin, David Martin Thompson. BA, U. Calif., Berkeley, 1962; JD, U. Calif., Davis, 1970; LLM, Harvard U., 1971; LLD (hon.), La Academia Mexicana de Derecho Internacional, 1988. Bar: DC 1979, Pa. 1978, U.S. Dist. Ct. D.C., U.S. Dist. Ct. Md., U.S. Dist. Ct. (ea. dist.) Pa., U.S. Ct. Appeals (1st, 3d, 4th and 7th cirs.), U.S. Supreme Ct. Grad. fellow Harvard U., Cambridge, Mass., 1970—71; fellow Acad. Engring. of the NAS, Washington, 1971; faculty fellow engring. dept. Stanford U., Calif., 1972; disting. vis. prof. law U. Miss., Oxford, 1975; prof. law and dir. Computers in Law Inst. George Washington U. Nat. Law Ctr., Washington, 1977—93; mng. prin. The Chandler Law Firm, Chartered, Washington, 1979—; pres., bd. dirs. Nat. Intellectual Property Law Inst., Washington, 1993—. Vis. scholar Harvard U., Cambridge, 1984; cons. U.S. Gen. Acctg. Office, Washington, 1973—82, Computer Application in the Cts., Md. Ct. of Appeals, Adminstrv. Office of the Cts., Annapolis, 1974—76; mem. White House Nat. Infrastructure Assurance Coun., Washington, 1999. Contbr. articles to profl. jours. Mem.: Army-Navy Club DC. Avocation: racquetball. Office: 2020 Pennsylvania Ave NW Washington DC 20006 Office Phone: 202-842-4800. Business E-Mail: chandler@nipli.org, professorchandler@chandlerlawfirm.com.

CHANDLER, JEFFREY, family trust and agricultural products executive; s. Philip Chandler. Attended, Woodbury Coll., USC. Trustee, beneficiary Chandler Trusts; pres., CEO Chandler Ranch Co., 1984—, Western Telecommunications, Inc. Bd. dirs. Tribune Co., 2000—, Construction Bidboard, Inc.*

CHANDLER, JOHN WESLEY, educational consultant; b. Mars Hill, NC, Sept. 5, 1923; s. Baxter Harrison and Mamie (McIntosh) C.; m. Florence Gordon, Aug. 25, 1948; children: Alison, John, Jennifer, Patricia. Student, Mars Hill Coll., 1941-43; AB, Wake Forest Coll., 1945, LHD (hon.); BD, Duke U., 1952, PhD, 1954; LLD, Hamilton Coll., 1968, Colgate U., 1968, Williams Coll., 1973, Amherst Coll., 1974, Wesleyan U., 1978, North Adams State Coll., 1983; LHD, Wake Forest U., 1968, Trinity Coll., 1982, Middlebury Coll., 1983, Bates Coll., 1983, Beaver Coll., Duke U., 2002. Instr. philosophy Wake Forest Coll., 1948-51, asst. prof., 1954-55; asst. prof. religion Williams Coll., 1955-60, assoc. prof., chmn. dept., 1960-65, Cluett prof. religion, 1965-68, acting provost, 1965-66, dean faculty, 1966-68; pres. Hamilton Coll., Clinton, NY, 1968-73, Williams Coll., Williamstown, Mass., 1973-85, Assn. Am. Colls., Washington, 1985-90; ednl. cons. Korn/Ferry Internat., Washington, 1990-91, Acad. Search Cons. Svc., Washington, 1992—2003. Contbg. author: Miscellany of American Religion, 1963, Masterpieces of Religious Literature, 1963, also jour. articles and revs. Trustee Williams Coll., 1969-73; bd. visitors Wake Forest Coll., 1971-77, 79-91; bd. dirs. Williamstown Theatre Festival, 1973-85, Sterling and Francine Clark Art Inst., 1973-85; pres. New Eng. Assn. Schs. and Colls., 1977-78, Assn. Ind. Colls. and Univs. Mass., 1977-79; chmn. New Eng. Colls. Fund, 1978; trustee Duke U., 1985-94, chmn., 1993-94; trustee Randolph-Macon Woman's Coll., 1985-88, Phillips Collection, 1997-2001; dir. Value Line Funds, 1991—. Fulbright fellow India, 1963; Kent fellow. Mem. Phi Beta Kappa. Mem. United Ch. of Christ. Clubs: Williams; Cosmos (Washington). Office: Williams Coll Oakley Ctr Williamstown MA 01267 Home Phone: 413-458-3502. Business E-Mail: john.w.chandler@williams.edu.

CHANDLER, JULIE LIGHT, secondary school educator; b. Indpls., Dec. 8, 1949; d. Edward Carl and Genneve Elder Light; m. Felix Chandler Jr. (dec. Dec. 30, 1991); 1 child, Scott Andrew. BS in Edn., Ind. U., Bloomington/Indpls., 1984, MS, 1984. Tchr. Cathedral HS, Indpls., 1981—84; h.s. tchr. Indpls. Pub. Schs., 1984—. Recipient Scholastic Achievement award, Sigma Pi Alpha, 1981. Home: 353 E Clear Lake Ln Westfield IN 46074 Office: Broad Ripple HS 1115 Broad Ripple Ave Indianapolis IN 46220 Home Phone: 317-896-5560; Office Phone: 317-693-5700. Personal E-mail: chandlerj@insightbb.com.

CHANDLER, KENT, JR., lawyer; b. Chgo., Jan. 10, 1920; s. Kent and Grace Emeret (Tuttle) C.; m. Frances Robertson, June 19, 1948; children: Gail, Robertson Kent. BA, Yale U., 1942; JD, U. Mich., 1949. Bar: Ill.

1949, U.S. Dist. Ct. (no. dist.) Ill. 1949, U.S. Ct. Appeals (7th cir.) 1955, U.S. Ct. Claims 1958. Assoc. Wilson & McIlvaine, Chgo., 1949-56, ptnr., 1957-94, spl. counsel to firm, 1994-98; of counsel Bell Jones & Quinlsk, Chgo., 1998—2007, Jones & Quinlsk LLC, Chgo., 2007—. Bd. dirs. Internat. Crane Found. Mem. zoning bd. appeals City of Lake Forest, Ill., 1953-63, chmn., 1963-67, mem. plan commn., 1955-69, chmn., 1969-70, pres. bd. local improvements, 1970-73, mayor, 1970-73, mem. bd. fire and police commn., 1975-82, chmn., 1982-84. Served to maj. USMCR, 1941-46. Mem. ABA, Ill. State Bar Assn., Chgo. Bar Assn., Lake County Bar Assn., Lawyers Club Chgo. (pres. 1985-86), Univ. Club, Onwentsia Club (Lake Forest), Old Elm Club (Highland Park, Ill.). Republican. Presbyterian. Office: 205 N Michigan Ave Ste 2500 Chicago IL 60601 Office Phone: 312-606-8797.

CHANDLER, KIMBERLEY LYNN, educational association administrator; b. Waynesboro, Va., Sept. 28, 1961; d. Alden Hugh and Cecille Frances (Brooks) C. BA in Elem. Edn., Coll. William and Mary, 1984, MA in Gifted Edn., 1992, PhD in Ednl. Policy, Planning and Leadership, 2004. Lic. educator, Va. Tchr. Fredericksburg (Va.) Pub. Schs., 1984-87, Henrico County Pub. Schs., Richmond, Va., 1987-98; gifted edn. resource specialist Hanover County Pub. Schs., Richmond, Va., 1998-2000; supr. enrichment programs, coord. of sci. K-12 Amherst County Pub. Schs., Va., 2000—03; cert. curriculum cons. Ctr. for Gifted Edn., 2002—; panel reviewer Jacob K. Javits Grant Program, U.S. Dept. Edn., 2002; postdoctoral fellow Ctr. for Gifted Edn. Coll. of William and Mary, Williamsburg, Va., 2003, curriculum dir., 2003—; acad. rev. team leader Va. Dept. Edn., 2004—. Summer sch. coord. Henrico County Pub. Schs., 1996, 97, staff devel. presenter, 1996, 97; curriculum cons. Coll. of William and Mary, Williamsburg, Va., 1996; presenter in field.; mem. gifted edn. staff devel. talent bank, mem. tchr. stds. com. Va. Dept. Edn.; mem. peer coaching program, Prin.'s Acad.; sch. renewal planning team facilitator Hanover County Pub. Schs.; mem. adj. faculty U. Va. Sch. Continuing and Profl. Studies, 2001—; instr. Casenex, Inc.; participant David L. Clark Grad. Student Seminar, 2003. Author: (curriculum unit) Literary Reflections, 1992; author: (with others) Aiming for Excellence-Gifted Program Standards: Annotations to the NAGC Pre-K-Grade 12 Gifted Program Standards, ERIC Research Report, 2002, (book review) Gifted and Talented International; editor (newsletter): Va. Assn. for the Gifted, 1999—. Vol. Hanover Humane Soc., 1994—, Habitat for Humanity Global Village Program, Nicaragua Disaster Relief Mission Team, 1999, Brazil VBS Mission Team, 2000; mem. Habitat for Humanity Global Village Team to South Africa, 2001. Recipient Doctoral Student award Nat. Assn. for Gifted Children, 2002, Hollingworth Rsch. award, 2003; grantee Henrico Edn. Found., 1997, Henrico Gifted Adv. Coun., 1997, Pntrs. in Arts grantee Richmond Arts Coun., 1996, Hanover Edn. Found., 1999, Coll. William and Mary, 2003; postdoctoral fellow Ctr. Gifted Edn., Coll. William and Mary, 2003—. Mem.: Va. Assn. for the Gifted (ex officio bd. dirs.), Va. Soc. for Tech. in Edn., Hanover County Prins. Acad., Nat. Assn. for Gifted Children (sec./treas. technol. divsn. 1997—99, sec./treas. profl. devel. divsn. 1997—99, chair profl. devel. divsn. 2003—, Harry Passow Classroom Tchr. scholarship 1997, Outstanding Curriculum award 2000, Doctoral Student award 2002, Hollingworth award 2003), Delta Kappa Gamma, Kappa Delta Pi (chpt. sec.). Home: 11444 New Farrington Ct Glen Allen VA 23059-1629 Office: Coll William and Mary Ctr for Gifted Edn PO Box 8795 Williamsburg VA 23187-8795 Personal E-mail: kchan11444@aol.com. Business E-Mail: klchan@wm.edu.

CHANDLER, LAWRENCE BRADFORD, JR., lawyer; b. New Bedford, Mass., June 20, 1942; s. Lawrence Bradford and Anne (Crane) C.; m. Madeleine Bibeau, Sept. 7, 1963 (div. June 1984); children: Dawn, Colleen, Brad. BS in Bus. Adminstrn., Boston Coll., 1963; LLB, U. Va., 1966, JD, 1970. Bar: Mass. 1966, U.S. Supreme Ct. 1967, Va. 1970, W.Va. 1993, adv.: Am. Bd. Trial Advs. Ptnr. Chandler, Franklin & O'Bryan, Charlottesville, Va., 1971—. Pres. Western Va. Chpt., 1992-93. Capt. U.S. Army, 1967-71. Mem.: ATLA (chair state dels. 1993—94, exec. com. 1993—94, bd. govs. 1995—2001), ABA, Am. Assn. Profl. Liability Attys., Am. Soc. on Law, Medicine and Ethics, Am. Coll. Legal Medicine, Charlottesville Bar Assn., Am. Bd. Trial Advs. (pres. Va. chpt.), Va. Trial Lawyers Assn. (pres. 1985—86), Assn. U.S. Army (pres. 1971—73). Roman Catholic. Office: Chandler Law Group PO Box 6747 Charlottesville VA 22906-6747 Home: 2200 Ballad Ridge Dr Charlottesville VA 22906 Office Phone: 434-971-7273. Personal E-mail: goofyc@mindspring.com.

CHANDLER, MARGUERITE NELLA, real estate company executive; b. New Brunswick, NJ, May 16, 1943; d. Edward A. and Marguerite (Moore) Chandler; m. Ronald Wilson, May 30, 1964 (div. Nov. 1973); children: Mark Wilson, Adam Wilson; m. Richmond Shreve, Nov. 22, 1979; 1 child, Laura Shreve. BS in Acctg., Syracuse U., 1964; MS in Polit. Mgmt., George Washington U., 1968. Tax acct. Peat Marwick Mitchell, Providence, 1964; grant adminstr., psychology dept. Brown U., Providence, 1965; intern in devel. cons. Washington, 1973-75; prin., tng. cons. M. Chandler Assocs., 1975-76; mgmt. cons. Edmar Corp., Bound Brook, NJ, 1976-78, pres., chief exec. officer, 1978-90, pres., 1991—. Vol. Peace Corps, 1966—68, Somerset Cmty. Action Program, 1969—71; treas. Somerset County Day Care Assn., 1969—71; established Food Bank Network Somerset County, 1982, pres., 1982—85; established Worldworks Found., Inc., 1983; founder PeopleCare Ctr., 1984, pres., 1984—86; bd. dirs. United Way Somerset Valley, 1984—91, gen. campaign mgr., 1985—86; recorder Blue Ribbon Com. Ending Hunger in N.J., 1984—86; bd. dirs. N.J. Coun. Arts, 1986—87; mem. N.J. Gov.'s Task Force Pub./Pvt. Sector Initiatives, NJ, 1986—91; mem. adv. bd. US-USSR Youth Exch., Ptnrs. in Peacemaking, Giraffe Project; chmn. bd. dirs. Friends Retirement Inc., 1996—2002; Dem. candidate U.S. Congress Dist. 12, 1990; vol. Missionaries Charity, Calcutta, India, 1981; pres. bd. trustees N.J. Coun. Chs., 1985—90. Named Woman of Yr., Women's Resource Ctr. Somerset County, 1983, Citizen of Yr., NJ chpt. Nat. Assn. Soc. Workers, 1986, Bus. and Profl. Women's Club, 1987, Person of the Decade, Courier-News, 1989, Bus. Person of the Yr., Bus. Ctrl. NJ mag., 1993; recipient People's Champaion award, Somerset Family Planning Svc., 1985, Brotherhood award, Ctrl. Jersey chpt. Nat. Conf. Christians and Jews, 1986, Disting. Svc. award, NJ Speech-Lang.-Hearing Assn., 1986, N.J. Women of Achievement award, Douglass Coll. and N.J. Fedn. Women's Clubs, 1986, Presdl. End Hunger award, 1987, Somerset Alliance for the Future Quality of Life award, 1996, Women of Inspiration award, Nat. Assn. Women Bus. Owners, 2007. Mem.: Celebrate N.J. (founder, coord. 2005—), World Bus. Acad. (bd. dirs. 1988—89), Assn. N.J. Recyclers (pres. 1991—93), Regional Plan Assn. (bd. dirs. 1994—96), Somerset C. of C. (chmn. bd. dirs. 1989—90, chmn. strategic planning cultural and heritage com., tourism coun., Citizen of the Yr. 1985), Crossroads Am. Revolution Assn. (founder, pres. 2001—05), Heritage Trail Assn. Somerset County (founder, pres. 1994—99), Rotary (pres. Bound Brook-Middlesex 1993—94). Mem. Soc. Of Friends. Avocation: quilting. Home: PO Box 250 Cape May Point NJ 08212 Office: PO Box 246 Cape May Point NJ 08212

CHANDLER, MARK D., computer systems network executive, lawyer; b. 1956; m. Chris Kenrick; 3 children. AB, Harvard U., 1978; JD, Stanford U., 1981. Bar: Calif. 1982. Law clk. to Spl. Master J. Keith Mann, 1981—83; atty. Law Office of James E. Baer, Palo Alto, Calif., 1983—85; fellow Robert Bosch Found., 1985—86; with mktg. dept. Sienna Capital Corp., 1986—88; v.p., corp. devel., gen. counsel Maxtor Corp., 1988—94; gen. counsel Stratacom, Inc., 1994—96; mng. atty., Europe, the Middle East, Africa Cisco Systems, Inc., 1996—2001, v.p., worldwide legal services, 2001, gen. counsel San Jose, Calif., 2001—, v.p. legal services, 2001—06, sec., 2003—, sr. v.p. legal services, gen. counsel, 2006—. Office: Cisco Sys Inc 255 W Tasman Dr San Jose CA 95134-1705 Office Phone: 408-527-0238. E-mail: mark.chandler@cisco.com.*

CHANDLER, MARSHA, academic administrator, educator; BA, CCNY, 1965; PhD, UNC Chapel Hill, 1972; grad. in advanced Mgmt. Program, Harvard Bus. Sch., 2004. Prof. political econ. Univ. Toronto, 1977-96, dean arts and sci., 1990-97; sr. vice chancellor U. Calif., San Diego, 1996—. Vis. scholar Harvard U., 1995-96, 2004-05. Co-author: Trade and Transmissions, 1990, The Political Economy of Business Bailouts, 2 vols., 1986, The Politics of Canadian Public Policy, 1983, Public Policy and Provincial Politics, 1979, Adjusting to Trade: A Comparative Perspective, 1988; contbr. articles to profl. jours. Fellow, Royal Soc. of Canada, mem.dirs. San Diego Opera, Mingei Mus. Internatl. Folk Art (bd. dir.), UCSD Found. Bd. and the Charter 100, adv. com. on Fed. Judicial Appts., Canadian Inst. for Adv. Rsch.; trustee (bd. mem.), Art Gall. of Ontario, Mt. SInai Hosp., Huntsman Marine Sci. Ctr., Ontario Lightwave, Laser Rsch. Ctr. Office: U Calif 9500 Gilman Dr La Jolla CA 92093-5004

CHANDLER, MICHAEL JONATHAN, allergist, physician; b. Detroit, May 9, 1955; BS, U. Mich., 1977; MD, Wayne State U., 1981. Diplomate Am. Bd. Allergy & Immunology, Am. Bd. Internal Medicine. Resident in medicine Northwestern U., Chgo., 1981-84, fellow allergy & immunology, 1984-86; allergist Mt. Sinai Hosp., NYC, 1986—, clin. instr. medicine, 1986—. Fellow Am. Assn. Allergy, Asthma & Immunology; mem. Am. Coll. Physicians. Office: 115 E 61st St New York NY 10021-8183

CHANDLER, NETTIE JOHNSON, artist; b. Christian County, Ky., Nov. 15, 1912; d. Sol James and Georgia Bell (Davis) Johnson; m. Percy Scott Chandler, Oct. 14, 1944. Student, Watkins Inst., Nashville, 1937—45, Watkins Inst., 1953—56, Harris Sch. Art, Nashville, 1937, Oklahoma City U., 1952, Coll. William and Mary, 1957—58; AS cum laude, Thomas Nelson C.C., 1983. Bookkeeper Keach Furniture Co., Hopkinsville, Ky., 1929—32; office sec., bookkeeper Baus Mfg. Co., Hopkinsville, 1933—35; bookkeeper Castner Knott Co., Nashville, 1936—39; sec., artist, editor Young South page' Baptist & Reflector, Nashville, 1939—45; real estate saleswoman Grinnell Realty, Nashville, 1950—51; typist Griffiss AFB, Rome, NY, 1952—53; sec., artist Tenn. State Libr., Nashville, 1953—56; tech. illustrator NASA, Hampton, 1956—72. Comml. artist to 1972, fine arts painter, 1973—. Represented in permanent collections Va. Air and Space Mus., Bapt. and Reflector, Nashville. Vol. ARC, Nashville, 1985—86. Recipient awards for art including 2d pl. Watkins Inst., 1955, 1st place Parthenon, Nashville, 1956, 1st place Watkins Inst., 1956, 1st place (3 times) Tenn. State Fair, 1985-96, Best of Show, Watkins Inst., 1986, 3d pl. Watkins Inst., 1987, 2d pl. for miniatures Tenn. Art League (3 times), 1988-92, 3d pl. Tenn. Art League, 1989, Best of Show, 1990, 2d pl. for graphics, 1996, 2d pl. oils, 2005, Best of Show, Gallery Eight WDCN TV, 1997, Daily Press Newport News, Va. Snapshot award, 1983. Mem. Tenn. Art League (leader Monday Painters 1984-98). Republican. Baptist. Avocations: writing, reading, painting, computer designing and printing, knitting. Home and Office: 404 Deer Lake Dr Nashville TN 37221-2108 Office Phone: 615-646-7163. Personal E-mail: nettie.chandler@comcast.net.

CHANDLER, RICHARD E., JR., lawyer; b. 1956; Grad., Loyola U. New Orleans Sch. Law. Bar: Tex. 1982. Gen. counsel, sec. M-I SWACO, Houston, 1986—2005, v.p., 1986—2004, sr. v.p. adminstrn., 2004—05; gen. counsel Smith Internat., Inc., Houston, 2005—, sr. v.p., sec., 2006—. Office: Smith Internat Inc PO Box 60068 Houston TX 77205-0068*

CHANDLER, RICHARD GATES, lawyer; b. Stockton, Calif., July 6, 1952; s. Kensal Roberts and Barbara (Gates) Chandler; m. Heidi Pankoke, Oct. 22, 1994. BA, Lawrence U., 1974; JD, U. Chgo., 1977. Bar: Wis. 1977. Assoc. Minahan & Peterson SC, Milw., 1979—84; legis. counsel to State Rep. Tommy G. Thompson, Wis. Assembly, Madison, 1985—86; legis. asst. Congressman Robert W. Kasten, Jr., Washington, 1977—78; budget dir. State of Wis., 1987—2001; sec. Dept. Revenue, Madison, Wis., 2001—03; public policy cons. Chandler Cons. LLC, Madison, 2003—. Mem.: Phi Beta Kappa. Republican. Methodist. Home: 810 Ottawa Trail Madison WI 53711-2941 Office Phone: 608-628-0433.

CHANDLER, ROBERT CHARLES, healthcare consultant; b. Birmingham, Ala., Apr. 15, 1945; s. Coleman Duke and Myrtle (Cleveland) C.; m. Anne; children: Jason Charles, Jonathan Robert. BS in Pharmacy, Samford U., 1968; MS in Hosp. and Health Adminstrn., U. Ala.-Birmingham, 1972. Registered pharmacist. Pharmacy intern Carraway Meth. Hosp., Birmingham, 1968-69; chief pharmacist Holy Family Hosp., Birmingham, 1969-70; v.p. Ft. Sanders Med. Ctr., Knoxville, Tenn., 1971-78; sr. v.p. Bapt. Med. Ctrs., Birmingham, 1978-79; exec. v.p. Princeton, 1979-85; pres. E. Tenn. Bapt. Hosp., Knoxville, 1985-90, The Bapt. Health Sys. East Tenn., Knoxville, 1986-90; ptnr. Ward Howell Internat., Atlanta, 1991-98, TMP Worldwide, Atlanta, 1998-99; sr. v.p., global practice leader Healthcare and Pharms., Stratford Group, Atlanta, 2000—01; exec. v.p., nat. practice leader for healthcare and life scis. DHR Internat., Atlanta, 2002—. Bd. dirs. Am. Healthcare Sys. San Diego, 1988-90; chmn. bd. dirs. SunHealth Care Plans Tenn., 1986-88; bd. dirs. Ala. Quality Assurance Found., Birmingham, 1984-85, Ala. Med. Rev., Birmingham, 1980-84; mem. adv. bd. Blue Cross/Blue Shield, Birmingham, 1983-85; mem. liaison com. Jefferson County Med. Soc., Birmingham, 1984-85; various faculty appts. U. Ala., Birmingham, Emory U. Sch. Medicine, Atlanta; divsn. chmn. United Way, Birmingham, 1984; bd. dirs. United Way Greater Knoxville, 1987-88, Knoxville Opera Co., 1988; Sunday sch. tchr. Dawson Bapt. Ch., Birmingham; deacon chmn. 1st Bapt. Ch., Knoxville, 1988-90. Recipient Cert. Appreciation, Tenn. Gov. Ray Blanton, 1978, Disting. Svc. award Tenn. Com. on Employment of Handicapped, 1978, Award of Excellence Ala. Pub. Rels. Coun., 1979. Fellow Am. Coll. Hosp. Adminstrs.; mem. Birmingham Regional Hosp. Coun. (pres.-elect 1985), Hosp. Alliance Tenn. (pres. 1987-88), Ala. Hosp. Assn. (trustee 1984-85), Birmingham C. of C. (chmn. health svcs. com. 1980), The Club (Birmingham), Rotary (mem. group study exch. 1977). Office: DHR Internat 100 Galleria Pkwy Ste 1150 Atlanta GA 30339 Business E-Mail: rchandler@dhrinternational.com.

CHANDLER, ROBERT LESLIE, public relations executive; b. Phila., Mar. 3, 1948; s. Joel Leslie and Evelyn Laney (DeLaney) C.; m. Pamela Lin Gemmel, Sept. 22, 2002. AS, Atlantic C.C., 1969; BS, Bowling Green State U., 1971; MS, Ohio U., 1972; MBA in Hosp. Adminstrn., Wagner Coll., 1980. Dir. pub. rels. Athens Mental Health Ctr., Ohio, 1972; internal comms. editor, pub. affairs dept. Owens-Corning Fiberglas Corp., Toledo, 1972-74; dir. cmty. rels. Wyandotte Gen. Hosp., Mich., 1974-76; v.p. asst. adminstr. mktg., pub. affairs Meth. Hosp., Bklyn., 1976-82; exec. v.p. Burson-Marsteller Pub. Rels., NYC, 1982-95; pres. Chandler Chicco Agy., 1995. Spl. cons. Am. Soc. Hosp. Mktg. and Pub. Rels./Am. Hosp. Assn., 1989—90; spkr. at numerous comms. confs. Contbr. articles to profl. jours. Mem. budget com. United Way Mich., 1975—76; bd. dirs. NY chpt. Am. Heart Assn. Recipient Healthcare Agy. of Yr. award Holmes Report, 2002-04, numerous other awards; named 7th in PR Week's Agy. rankings Top Pub. Rels. firms, 2004; Am. Heart Assn. NJ/NY State scholar, 1969. Mem. Pub. Rels. Soc. Am. (Silver Anvil awards), Am. Soc. Health Care Mktg. and Planning, Am. Coll. Healthcare Execs. (assoc.), Sigma Delta Chi, Kappa Tau Alpha.

CHANDLER, TERRY WINFORD, insurance company executive, real estate developer, small business owner; b. Cullman, Ala., July 10, 1936; s. Grady Howard and Dona Naioma Chandler; m. Julie Pratt Chandler, Dec. 17, 1994; 1 child, Terrence Winford II;children from previous marriage: Jennifer, Laurie. BS in Edn., Auburn U., Ala., 1958. Basketball, baseball and football coach Lanett HS, Ala., 1958—59; gen. agt. Vulcan Life Ins. Co., Birmingham, Ala., 1959—62, regional mgr., 1962—64, v.p., 1964—98; owner Express Oil Change, Cullman, 1998—, Athens, Ala., 1998—, Express Storage, Albertville, Ala., 1998—. Developer Marina Bay Resort, Ft. Walton Beach, Fla., Casa Blanca Resort, Panama City, Fla. Pres. SE AAU of US, 1970—74, Shoot N Bragg Club, Ala., 1982. Avocations: golf, hunting, fishing, travel. Office: Express Storage LLC 902 Rose Rd PO Box 1953 Albertville AL 35950 Office Phone: 256-891-4500.

CHANDLER, THEODORE LINDY, JR., title insurance company executive, lawyer; b. South Boston, Va., May 13, 1952; s. Theodore Lindy and Jacqueline Anne (Hodnett) C.; m. Laura Lee Hankins, June 22, 1974; children: Katherine Anne, Rebecca Lee. BS in Commerce, U. Va., 1974; JD, U. Richmond, 1977. Bar: Va. 1977. Attorney, bd. dir., head corp. & securities team Williams, Mullen, Christian & Dobbins, Richmond, Va., 1977—2000; bd. dir. LandAmerica Fin. Group, Richmond, Va., 1991—, sr. exec. v.p., 2000—02, COO, 2002—04, pres., COO, 2004, pres., CEO, 2005—. Bd. dir. Hilb, Rogal & Hobbs, Richmond Va., Mutual Assurance Soc. Va., SunTrust Ctrl. Va.; bd. mem. Am. Land Title Assn. Bd. dirs. Reeds Landing Community Assn., Richmond, 1988—, Theatre IV, Richmond, 1988—; bd. mem. Mid-Atlantic Am. Heart Assn., Greater Richmond C. of C., Richmond Region 2007, Mariners Mus. Mem. Richmond Estate Planning Coun., Country Club Va., Capital Club, Commonwealth Club. Republican. Baptist. Avocations: golf, skiing, sailing, squash. Office: Williams Mullen Christian D 1021 E Cary St 17th Fl Richmond VA 23219*

CHANDLER-MUNSON, CYNTHIA, elementary school educator; b. Houston, Oct. 12, 1961; d. Richard and Jewel Chandler; m. Kenneth D. Munson, Feb. 14, 1991; children: William Chandler, Kamika Chandler children: Jewel Munson. BA in Social Work, Tex. So. U., Houston, 1993. Cert. tchr. Tex. Edn. Agy., 2000. Clin. social worker Mental Health Mental Retardation Authority Harris County, Houston, 1993—99; tchr. East Houston Intermediate Sch. North Forest Ind. Sch. Dist., Houston, 1999—2003; instr. Houston CC, 2003—05; tchr. Meyer Elem. Sch. Spring Ind. Sch. Dist., Houston, 2004—. Program coord., parent liaison Assn. Retarded Citizens, Houston, 1997—. Mem.: Tex. State Tchrs. Assn. (assoc.), Houston Area Urban League. Baptist. Home: 3010 Oklahoma St Houston TX 77093 Office: Meyer Elem Sch Spring ISD 16330 Forest Way Dr Houston TX 77090 Home Phone: 832-293-1651; Office Phone: 281-586-2680. Personal E-mail: reneemchandler@aol.com. Business E-Mail: cmunson@springisd.org.

CHANDONNET, ANN FOX, journalist, poet; b. Lowell, Mass., Feb. 7, 1943; d. Leighton Dinsmore Fox and Barbara Amelia (Cloutman) Curran; m. Fernand Leonce Chandonnet, June 11, 1966; children: Yves, Alexandre BS in Edn. magna cum laude, Lowell Coll., Mass., 1964; MS in Eng. Lit., U. Wis., 1965. Cert. in secondary edn., Mass., Calif. Tchr. Kodiak (Alaska) High Sch., 1965-66; instr. Lowell (Mass.) State Coll., 1966-69; sec. First Enterprise Bank, Oakland, Calif., 1972-73; freelance writer Calif. and Alaska, 1972—. Instr. Eagle River CC, Alaska, 1976-82; feature writer Anchorage Times newspaper, 1982-92, Juneau Empire, 1999-2002. Author: (poems) Ptarmigan Valley, 1980, Auras, Tendrils, 1984, Canoeing in the Rain, 1990, (history) On the Trail of Eklutna, 1985, Anchorage: Early Photographs of the Great Land, 2001, Gold Rush Grub, 2005; (children's book) Chief Stephen's Parky, 1989. Recipient Wis. Union award, 1965, Excellence in Edn. Writing award Phi Delta Kappa, 1989, Utah Wilderness Soc. Poetry award, 1990. Mem. Niagara-Erie Writers, Literary Artist Guild of Alaska (founder 1980-82). Avocations: hiking, canoeing, beadwork, gourmet cooking, reading. Home: 6415 Tarheel Dr Vale NC 28168-8988

CHANDOR, STEBBINS BRYANT, pathologist; b. Boston, Dec. 18, 1933; s. Kendall Stebbins Bryant and Dorothy (Burrage) C.; m. Mary Carolyn White, May 30, 1959; children: Stebbins Bryant Jr., Charlotte White. BA, Princeton U., 1955; MD, Cornell U., 1960. Diplomate Am. Bd. Pathology. Intern Bellevue Hosp., NYC, 1960-61, resident, 1965-66, Stanford U. Med. Ctr., Palo Alto, Calif., 1962-65; pathologist Tripler Army Med Ctr, Honolulu, 1966—69; instr. Cornell U., Ithaca, NY, 1966; asst. prof. U. So. Calif. Med. Ctr., LA, 1969-73, assoc. prof., 1974-76, SUNY, Stony Brook, 1976-80; dir. clin. lab. Univ. Hosp., Stony Brook, 1978-80; dir. JMMS Labs., Huntington, 1981-91; prof., chmn. dept. pathology Marshall U. Sch. Medicine, Huntington, W.Va., 1981—91, assoc. dean for clin. affairs, 1990-91; prof., vice chmn. Sch. Medicine U. So. Calif., 1991—2004, dir. labs. U. Hosp., 1991—2004, prof. emeritus, 2004—. Bd. dirs. Immunopathology Med. Ctr., 1969—76; mem. provosts oversight com. U. So. Calif., 2005—. Contbr. articles to profl. jours. Pres. San Marino Tennis Found., 1975; governing bd. U. Path. Consortium, 1999-2004. Served to maj. USAR, 1966-69. Decorated Army Commendation medal; recipient Physicians Recognition award AMA, 1983, 86, 89, 93, 99, 04. Fellow Am. Assn. Med. Colls., Am. Soc. Clin. Pathologists (dep. commn. 1993-98, continuing edn. bd. dirs. 1990-96, chair by-law com., 1993-96, chmn. pathology group, 1993-98, v.p. 1997-98, pres. 1999-2000, awards com. 2001-), Coll. Am. Pathologists (state commr. I&A program 1987-91, dist. commr. 1991-99); mem. Calif. Soc. Pathologists (sec.-treas. 1974-75, pres.-elect 1975-76), Assn. Am. Pathologists, W.Va. Assn. Pathologists (pres. 1985-86), Assoc. Path. Chmn. Acad. Clin. Lab. Physicians and Scientists (rep. CAS 1991-2003, adminstrv. bd. 1997-2003), Am. Assn. Med. Colls. (exec. coun. 1998-2000), LA Acad. Medicine, Rt. Faculty Assn. (bd. dirs. 2005—), U. So. Calif. Ret. Faculty Assn. (bd. dirs. 2005—, v.p. 2006-07, pres.-elect 2006-07, pres. 2007—), Princeton Club, Valley Club (v.p. 1975, bd. dirs. 1993), City Club (v.p. 1988-89, pres. 1989-90), San Gabriel Country Club, Valley Hunt Club, The Valley Club of Montecito. Republican. Episcopalian. Home: 2170 East Valley Dr Santa Barbara CA 93108 Office: 2011 Zonal Ave Los Angeles CA 90033-1034 Office Phone: 323-442-8591. Personal E-mail: sbchandor@verizon.net. Business E-Mail: chandor@usc.edu. *Have fun and make life enjoyable for those around you.*

CHANDRA, ABHIJIT, engineering educator; b. Kolkata, West Bengal, India, Jan. 4, 1957; arrived in US, 1980, naturalized, 1990; s. Ramesh Kumar and Sandhya (Dey) C.; m. Dolly Day, June 4, 1984; children: Koushik, Shoma. B of Tech. with honors, Indian Inst. Tech., 1978; MS, U. N.B., 1980; PhD, Cornell U., 1983. Sr. rsch. engr. GM Rsch. Labs., Warren, Mich., 1983—85; asst. prof. U. Ariz., Tucson, 1985—89, assoc. prof. engring., 1989—95; prof. Mich. Tech. U., Houghton, 1995—99; Engel prof., dir. Engel lab. Iowa State U., Ames, 1999—2004, prof., 1999—. Cons. Goodyear Tire and Rubber Co., Akron, Ohio, 1988-89, Advanced Ceramic Rsch., Tucson, 1990-95, ALCOA, Pitts., 1990-95, Thermoanalytics Inc., 1999-2001; chief tech. officer, bd. dirs. Actus Potentia, Inc. Author: Boundary Element Methods in Manufacturing, 1997; guest editor: Internat. Jour. Solid Structures, 1994; assoc. editor: IEEE Trans Electronic Pkg. and Mfg., 2006-; contbr. over 90 articles to profl. jours. Alexander von Humboldt fellow, 1991; recipient Presdl. Young Investigator award NSF, 1987, Arc Welding Achievement award J. F. Lincoln Arc Welding Found., 1989. Fellow ASME (sec. So. Ariz. sect. 1988-89); mem. SME (Outstanding Paper award 1999), IEEE, Sigma Xi. Avocations: swimming, skiing, tennis, gardening, fiction writing. Business E-Mail: achandra@iastate.edu.

CHANDRA, RANJIT KUMAR, research scientist, educator, physician; b. Mailsi, Punjab, India, Feb. 2, 1938; s. Hukam Chandra and Kaushalya Devi-Khurana; children: Sujata Chandra-Pike, Amrita, Tarang Chandra-Faeh, Rahul. MBBS, Panjab U., Amritsar, India, 1960; MD, All India Inst. Med. Scis., New Delhi, 1963; Doctorate (hon.), Pontificial Cath. U., Santiago, Chile, 1981; PhD (hon.), Beijing Med. U., 1987; DM (hon.), Universite di Chile, Santiago, 1993; DrMedChir (hon.), Universite di

Napoli, Italy, 1994; DSc (hon.), Panjab U., Chandigarh, India, 2003. Lic. Med. Coun. of India, 1960, Med. Coun. of Can., 1977, diplomate Am. Acad. of Pediat., 1982. Lectr. Postgrad. Inst. Med. Edn. and Rsch., Chandigarh, India, 1964—65; asst. prof. All-India Inst. Med. Scis., New Delhi, 1966—74; rsch. prof. Meml. U. of Nfld., St. John's, Canada, 1975—2001; pres., vice-chancellor Université Internationale des Sciences de la Santé, Crans-sur-Sierre, Switzerland, 2002—04. Cons. WHO, Geneva, 1966—2000, Indian Coun. of Med. Rsch., New Delhi, 1966—75, NAS, Washington, 1979—94, Health Can., Ottawa, Ontario, 1979—99; editor-in-chief Nutrition Rsch., New York, 1980—2003; pres. Internat. Congress of Nutrition, Montreal, Quebec, Canada, 1993—97; editor Reviews of Biomed. Books and Jours., Toronto, Ontario, Canada, 2004—, Survey Nutritional Immunology, Toronto, Ontario, Canada, 2006—. Author: (book) Nutrition, Immunity and Infection, 1977; editor: Nutrition and Immunology, 1992; author: over 20 books. Pres. Friends of India Assn., St. John's, Newfoundland, Canada, 1996—97. Named Officer of Order of Can., Queen Elizabeth II, 1990; recipient Medal in Medicine, Royal Coll. of Physicians of Can., 1982, prize, Hermes GmbH, 1988, Queen's Jubilee medal, Queen Elizabeth II, 2002. Master: Am. Coll. Physicians; fellow: Royal Coll. Pediatrics and Child Health, Royal Coll. Physicians Can.; mem.: NAS, Am. Acad. Allergy. Achievements include patents for nutritional supplement for the elderly; nutritional supplement for children; nutritional supplement for adolescents; patents pending for nutritional supplement for adults; nutritional supplement for infants, iron (III) hydroxide polymaltose; discovery of Chandra-Khetarpal syndrome; first to establish nutritional immunology; research in food allergy and allergic disease. Home: Y-182 Regency Pk 2 DLF Phase 4 Gurgaon Haryana 122002 India Office: TSAR Health 3044 Bloor St W Ste 316 Toronto ON Canada M8X 2Y8 Home Phone: -91-124-2386653; Office Phone: -91-124-4103830. Office Fax: 91-124-405-1832. Personal E-mail: rkchandra2004@yahoo.com.

CHANDRA, SATISH, psychologist; b. Dankaur, India, Dec. 22, 1944; arrived in U.S.A., 1966, permanent resident; s. Murari Lal and Yashoda Devi. BSc in Physics, Chemistry and Math., U. Allahabad, 1961; BSEE with hons., Indian Inst. Tech., 1966; MA in Psychology, SUNY, 1975; postgrad., U. Rochester, 1969—71; postgrad. in Clin. Psychology, SUNY, 1971—77. Engr. electronics divsn. Gen. Dynamics, 1968—69; rsch. Dept. Psychology Harvard U., Cambridge, Mass., 1977—78; pvt. practice psychotherapy Cambridge, 1978—. Contbr. articles to profl. jours. Fellow, U. Rochester, 1969—70. Mem.: APS, Am. Chem. Soc., Soc. Philosophy and Psychology, N.Y. Acad. Scis. Achievements include research in psychology leading to end of B.F. Skinner's school of psychology; economics: multiplying finance resources available to government for research and development and other purposes; chemicals leading to more effective and economical treatments with fewer side effects for various medical conditions. Office: PO Box 381629 Cambridge MA 02238 Office Phone: 617-407-0071.

CHANDRA, SUBODH, lawyer; b. Oklahoma City, July 17, 1967; s. Suresh and Shanta Chandra; m. Meena Morey; 3 children. AB with honors and distinction, Stanford U., 1989; JD, Yale U., 1994. Bar: N.Mex. 1995, Calif. 1997, Ohio 1998. Asst. dir. internat. affairs Participation 2000, Columbus, Ohio, 1990-91; aide to Gov. David Walters, State of Okla., Oklahoma City, 1991; spl. counsel to pres.-elect ABA, Albuquerque, 1994-95; litigation assoc. Christensen, Miller, Fink, Jacobs, Glaser, Weil & Shapiro, LA, 1996-97; litigator Thompson Hine & Flory LLP, Cleve., 1997-99; asst. U.S. atty. criminal divsn. U.S. Dept. Justice, Cleve., 1999—2002; law dir. and prosecuting atty. City of Cleveland, 2002—05; disting. practitioner in residence Case Western Reserve U. Sch. of Law, 2005; candidate for Ohio Atty. Gen., 2005—06; principal The Chandra Law Firm LLC, 2005—. Mem. Calif. Dem. Ctrl. Com., 1989—90. Recipient award from FBI Dir. Robert Mueller for demonstrated excellence in prosecution, 2002; Named to 40 under 40 leaders Crain's Cleveland Bus. 2002; named Outstanding Lawyer, N.Mex. Bar Found./Albuquerque Bar Assn., 1995; John Gardner fellow Haas Ctr. for Pub. Svc., Stanford U., 1989-90. Mem. ABA, State Bar N.Mex., State Bar Calif., Cleveland Bar Assn. (bd. trustees, 2005-). Democrat. Hindu.

CHANDRAMOULI, SRINIVASAN (CHANDRA CHANDRAMOULI), management and systems consultant; came to U.S., 1978; BS in Math. and Physics, Ferguson Coll., Pune, India, 1973; postgrad., Indian Inst. Tech., New Delhi, 1973-74; MBA in Mktg. and Gen. Mgmt., Indian Inst. Mgmt., Ahmedabad, 1976; MBA in Fin. and Acctg., U. Chgo., 1980. CPA, Ill. Cons. Hindustan Petroleum Corp. Ltd., Bombay, 1975; fin. mgr. prodn. Associated Cement Cos., Bombay, 1976-77; cons., researcher The World Bank, Washington, 1979-80; v.p. CGI Inc., Chgo. and Denver, 1980—98, Denver, 2003—06, head india ops., 2006—; ptnr. Deloitte Cons., Sacramento, 1999—2003. Vis. faculty mem. K.C. Coll. Mgmt. U. Bombay, 1976-77. Gen. sec. Jawahar Mitra Mandal, Pune, 1970-74. Fellow Inst. Profl. Acctg. U. Chgo., 1979-80; Open Merit and Nat. Merit scholar Govt. of India U. Poona, 1969-73. Mem. Am. Inst. CPA's, Ill. CPA Soc., Beta Gamma Sigma. Republican. Hindu. Avocations: bridge, chess, tennis. Home: 16118 E Prentice Pl Centennial CO 80015-4172 Office Phone: 303-215-3636. E-mail: s.chandramouli@cgi.com.

CHANDRASEKARAN, BALAKRISHNAN, computer scientist, educator; b. Lalgudi, Tamil Nadu, India, June 20, 1942; came to U.S., 1963; s. Srinivasan and Nagamani Balakrishnan; m. Sandra Mamrak, Oct. 21, 1978; 1 child, Mallika. B in Engring., Madras U., Karaikudi, India, 1963; PhD, U. Pa., 1967. Devel. engr. Smith Kline Instruments, Phila., 1964-65; rsch. specialist Philco-Ford Corp., Blue Bell, Pa., 1967-69; asst. prof. computer and info. sci. Ohio State U., Columbus, 1969-71, assoc. prof., 1971-77, prof., 1977-95; sr. rsch. scientist, 1995—; dir. Lab. for Artificial Intelligence Rsch., Columbus, 1983—. Co-chmn. Symposium on Potentials and Limitations of Mech. Intelligence, Anaheim, Calif., 1971; chmn. Norbert Wiener Symposium, Boston, 1974; sci. dir. Summer Sch. on Computer Program Testing, SOGESTA, Urbino, Italy, 1981; vis. scientist Lawrence Livermore Nat. Lab., Livermore, Calif., summer 1981, cons. fall 1981; vis. scientist MIT Computer Sci. Lab., 1983; dir. NIH Artificial Intelligence in Medicine Workshop, 1984; organizer panel discussion on artificial intelligence and engring. ASME, 1985; vis. scholar Stanford U., 1990-91; keynote spkr. World Congress on Expert Sys., Mexico City, 1998, Internat. Conf. on Diagrammic Reasoning, Callaway Gardens, Ga., 2002; tech. area leader US Army Rsch. Labs. Tech. Alliance on Decision Architectures, 2001—. Editor: Diagrammatic Reasoning, 1995; co-editor Computer Program Testing, 1981; editor ACM Sigart Spl. Issue on Structure, Function, and Behavior, 1985; assoc. editor Artificial Intelligence in Engring., 1986—; mem. bd. editors Internat. Jour. Pattern Recognition & Artificial Intelligence, Med. Expert Systems, Artificial Intelligence in Engring.; assoc. editor Internat. Jour. Human-Computer Interactions, 1996—. Recipient Outstanding Paper award Pattern Recognition Soc., 1976; Moore fellow U. Pa., 1964-67. Fellow IEEE (editor-in-chief Expert Jour. 1990-94), Am. Assn. for Artificial Intelligence (chmn. workshops on diagrammatic reasoning 1992), Assn. for Computing Machinery; mem. Sys. Man and Cybernetics Soc. IEEE (v.p. 1974-75, pattern recognition com. 1969-72, assoc. editor Trans. 1973—, guest editor spl. issue on distributed program solving 1981). Democrat. Avocation: travel. Home: 2053 Iuka Ave Columbus OH 43201-1415 Office: Ohio State U Dept Computer and Info Sci 2015 Neil Ave Columbus OH 43210-1210 Office Phone: 614-292-0923. Business E-Mail: chandra@cse.ohio-state.edu.

CHANDRASEKARAN, RAJIV, editor, writer; b. Calif., 1973; BA, Stanford U. Editor in chief Stanford (Calif.) Daily; with Washington Post, 1994—, met. reporter, nat. tech. corr., S.E. Asia corr. Jakarta, Indonesia, bur. chief Cairo, Baghdad, Iraq, 2003—04, asst. mng. editor continuous news Washington, 2006—. Journalist in residence Internat. Reporting Project, Johns Hopkins Sch. for Advanced Internat. Studies, Washington, 2005; pub. policy scholar Woodrow Wilson Internat. Ctr., Washington, 2005. Author: Imperial Life in the Emerald City: Inside Iraq's Green Zone, 2006 (Samuel Johnson prize for Non-Fiction, BBC 4, 2007). Recipient Cornelius Ryan award, Overseas Press Club Am., 2007. Office: Washington Post 1150 15 St NW Washington DC 20071 also: c/o Knopf Publishing 1745 Broadway New York NY 10019*

CHANDRASEKHAR, SUJANA S., otologist, educator, neurotologist; 4 children. BS cum laude, City Coll. N.Y., 1984; MD, Mt. Sinai Sch. Medicine, NYC, 1986. Intern, residency otolaryngology NYU Med. Ctr., 1986—92; fellow in otology/neurology House Ear Inst., LA, 1993; from asst. to assoc. prof. UMDNJ-N.J. Med. Sch., Newark, 1994—2001, dir. otology/neurotology, 1996—2001; assoc. prof. otolaryngology Mt. Sinai Sch. Medicine, NYC, 2001—04, clin. assoc. prof. otolaryngology, 2004—. Dir. otology/neurotology Mt. Sinai Med. Ctr., NYC, 2001—04, dir. cochlear implant program, 2001—04. Recipient Honor award, AMA, 2000, Am. Acad. Otolaryngology-Head and Neck Surgery, 2002. Office: 364 E 69th St New York NY 10021 Office Phone: 212-249-3232. Personal E-mail: ssc@verizon.net.

CHANDROSS, EDWIN ARTHUR, chemist, consultant; b. NYC, Oct. 13, 1934; BS, MIT, 1955; MA, Harvard U., 1957, PhD, 1960. Mem. tech. staff Bell Labs., Murray Hill, NJ, 1959—2001; head dept. organic chemistry R & D Bell Labs./Lucent Techs., Murray Hill, 1980-94, dir. materials rsch. dept., 1994—2001; prin. materials rsch. dept. to cons. Materials Chemistry, LLC, Murray Hill, 2001—. Mem. editl. bd. Chem. Revs., 1978, Jour. Am. Chem. Soc., 1995-2000, Jour. Organic Chemistry, 2002-04, Chemistry of Materials, 2004, Nanoletters, 2005. Recipient Life Achievement award North Jersey sect. Am. Chem. Soc., 1997, Bloch medal U. Chgo., 2001, Award Indsl. Innovation Am. Chem. Soc., 2001, Award Indsl. Chemistry Am. Chem. Soc., 2005. Fellow AAAS, Internat. Union Pure and Applied Chemistry; mem. NAE. Achievements include over 60 US patents in optical properties of polymers, and photosensitive materials; development of a process to remove impurities in materials used to make optical fibers; discovery of the chemiluminescent system that is the basis of the lightstick. Office: Materials Chemistry LLC 14 Hunterdon Blvd New Providence NJ 07974 E-mail: eac@materialschemistry.com.*

CHANEY, ROBIN WHITE, secondary school educator, consultant; m. Alan Chaney; children: Ric Forbes, Kate Forbes, Odana. AB in Edn., Glenville State Coll., W.Va., 1974; MS in Edn., Walden U., Minn., 2006. Tchr. Hurricane H.S., W.Va., 1981—. Exec. coun. GSC Alumni Coun., Glenville, W.Va. Home: 2051 Main St Culloden WV 25510 Office: Hurricane HS 3350 Teays Valley Rd Hurricane WV 25526 Home Phone: 304-743-5868.

CHANEY, WILLIAM ALBERT, retired history professor; b. Arcadia, Calif., Dec. 23, 1922; s. Horace Pierce and Esther (Bowen) Chaney. AB, U. Calif., Berkeley, 1943, PhD, 1961. Mem. faculty Lawrence U., Appleton, Wis., 1952-99, George McKendree Steele prof. western culture, 1966-99, Steele prof. emeritus, 1999—, chmn. dept. history, 1968-71, 95-96. Vis. prof. Mich. State U., 1958. Author: The Cult of Kingship in Anglo-Saxon England: The Transformation from Paganism to Christianity, 1970, reprinted, 1999; contbr. articles to profl. jours. and encys. Grantee, Am. Coun. Learned Socs., 1966—67; Jr. fellow, Harvard Soc. Fellows, 1949—52. Fellow: Royal Soc. Arts; mem.: AAUP, MLA, Archeol. Inst. Am., Conf. Brit. Studies, Am. Soc. Ch. History, Medieval Acad. Am., Am. Hist. Assn. Episcopalian. Home: 215 E Kimball St Appleton WI 54911-5720 Office: Lawrence Univ Dept History Appleton WI 54912 Office Phone: 920-832-6676.

CHANG, BARBARA KAREN, medical educator, director; b. Milltown, Ind., Jan. 6, 1946; m. M.F. Joseph Chang-Wai-Ling, Oct. 6, 1967; children: Carla Marie Yvonnette, Nolanne Arlette. BA, Ind. U., 1968; MA, Brandeis U., 1970; MD, Albert Einstein Coll. Medicine, 1973. Diplomate Am. Bd. Internal Medicine, Am. Bd. Med. Oncology, Am. Bd. Hematology. Resident in internal medicine Montefiore Med. Ctr., Bronx, NY, 1973-75; fellow in hematology/oncology Duke U. Med. Ctr., Durham, NC, 1975-78; staff physician VA Med. Ctr., Augusta, Ga., 1978-95, chief hematology/oncology, 1980-89, assoc. chief of staff edn., 1990-95, chief of staff, chief med. officer Albuquerque, 1995—2002; prof. medicine Med. Coll. Ga., Augusta, 1978-95; assoc. dean U. N.Mex. Sch. Medicine, Albuquerque, 1995—2002; cons. Capital Assets Realignment for Enhanced Svcs. Program VA Ctrl. Office, Washington, 2002—03, dir. program evaluation Office Academic Affiliations, 2003—, acting dir. grad. med. edn., 2006—. Mem. Sci. Adv. Bd., Washington, 1983-88; mem. expert panels computer applications Dept. Vets. Affairs, Washington, 1988-95; Va. liasion to steering com. group on resident affairs Assn. Am. Med. Colls., 2000-06; Va. rep. Coun. Grad. Med. Edn., 2006-, Accreditation Coun. Grad. Med. Edn., 2006-; presenter in field. Contbr. numerous articles on cancer rsch. to profl. jours. Youth coord. Am. Hemerocallis Soc., Augusta, 1993-95, pres. local chpt. 1997, Albuquerque, garden judge 1997-03, region 6 youth liaison, 2000-01, exhbn. judge, 2001—, nat. youth liaison com., 2003-. Grantee Nat. Cancer Inst., Am. Cancer Soc., 1978-93; David M. Worthen award Acad. Excellence Dept. Vet. Affairs, 2000. Fellow ACP, Am. Soc. Clin. Oncology, Bioelectromagnetic Soc. (bd. dirs. 1983-86). Office: Dept Vets Affairs Med Ctr 1501 San Pedro Dr SE Albuquerque NM 87108-5153 Business E-Mail: barbara.chang@va.gov.

CHANG, CARMEN, lawyer; b. Nanjing, China, 1948; BA, Sarah Lawrence Coll., 1970; MA, Stanford U., 1973, JD with distinction, 1993. Bar: Calif. 1994, U.S. Ct. Appeals (9th cir.) 1994. Ptnr. Shearman & Sterling, LLP, Menlo Park, Calif., 2003—05; ptnr., leader China practice Wilson Sonsini Goodrich Rosati, Palo Alto, Calif., 2005—. Spkr. in field; mem. adv. bd. Stanford Project Regions of Innovation and Entrepreneurship Asia-Pacific Rsch. Ctr. Stanford U., Stanford, Calif. Contbr. articles to profl. jours. Fluent in English, Mandarin, Cantonese, Japanese. Office: Wilson Sonsini Goodrich & Rosati 650 Page Mill Rd Palo Alto CA 94304 Business E-Mail: cchang@wsgr.com.

CHANG, CHING MING (CARL), engineering executive, mechanical engineer, educator, writer; b. Nanking, China; came to U.S., 1967; m. Birdie S.C. Chang, Dec. 18, 1964; children: Andrew L.P., Nelson L.A., Michele Chang. Dipl. Ing., Technol. U. Aachen, Germany, 1962; PhD, Technol. U. Aachen, 1967; MBA, SUNY, Buffalo, 1985. Registered profl. engr., N.Y., Va. Asst. prof. N.C. State U., Raleigh, 1968-73; sr. engr. to sr. devel. assoc. Praxair, Inc. (formerly Union Carbide Indsl. Gases), Tonawanda, NY, 1973-95, bus. devel. mgr., 1995-98; pres. CarlChang LLC Bus. Cons., Amherst, NY, 1998—; dir. analytical engring. O'Mara Cons. Engrs., Buffalo, 2001—02. Adj. prof. engring. SUNY, Buffalo, 1979-2007, dir. svc. sys. engring. program dept. indsl. and sys. engring., 2007—; cons. Great Am. Ins., Dresser-Rand, AccMed Tech., Harper Internat., BOC Edwards Pharm. Sys., Tonawanda NY; mem. indsl. applications program com. Portland Conf. Mgmt. Engring. and Tech., 2007—. Author: Engineering Management: Challenges in the New Millennium, 2005 (Best Book award, Internat. Assn. Mgmt. Tech., 2007); mem. editl. bd.: Internat. Jour. Innovation and Tech. Mgmt., 2005—; contbr. articles to profl. jours. Named Person of Yr. Tech. Soc. Coun., Buffalo, 1986. Mem. NSPE (pres. Erie-Niagara chpt. 1980-81, Disting. Svc. award 1981, Basinsky award 1984, Engring. Educator of Yr. award 1990, Praxair Special Recognition award for Technol. Leadership, 1992, Basinski-Wohler award 1994). Achievements include invention of holder of five U.S. patents, in the fields of electrostatic precipitation, turbomachinery, and artificial intelligence. Avocations: tennis, travel, computer games, writing, reading. also: SUNY Buffalo Dept Indsl and Sys Engring 323 Bell Hall Buffalo NY 14260 Personal E-mail: CChangLLC@aol.com.

CHANG, CHING-JER, medicinal chemistry educator; b. Hsinchu, Taiwan, China, Oct. 17, 1942; came to the U.S., 1968; s. Tin-lian and Awei (Lai) C.; m. Shu-fang Kuo, Dec. 25, 1978; children: Philip, Sylvia. BS, Nat. Taiwan Cheng Kung U., 1965; PhD, Ind. U., 1972. Asst. prof. Purdue U., West Lafayette, Ind., 1973-78, assoc. prof., 1978-84, prof., 1984—. Mem. bioorganic and natural products chemistry study sect., NIH, Bethesda, Md., 1986-90, spl. study sect.,1985, 1991—; editl. adv. bd. Jour. Natural Products, 1989-99; reviewer Human Frontier Sci. Program, Strassbourg, France, 1992—, Hong Kong Govt. Rsch. Grant Coun., 1997—; mem. breast cancer rsch. study sect. Dept. Def., 1997-2002; N.Am. regional editor Jour. Asian Natural Products Rsch., 2002—. Contbr. articles to profl. jours. Mem. Am. Soc. Pharmacognosy (exec. com. 1993-97, 2004—), Am. Chem. Soc., Am. Assn. for Cancer Rsch., Phytochem. Soc. N.Am., Argentinian Soc. Organic Chemistry (hon. mem.). Achievements include patents in field. Office: Dept Medicinal Chemistry Purdue Univ West Lafayette IN 47907-2091 E-mail: cjchang@pharmacy.purdue.edu.

CHANG, CHONG HYUCK, engineer; BS, Seoul Nat. U., Korea, 1977—81; MS, U. Ill., Chgo., 1981—83; PhD, U. Minn., 1989. Adv. engr. Idaho Nat. Lab., Idaho Falls, 1989—97; sr. rsch. scientist Thermosciences Inst., Moffett Field, Calif., 1997—99; tech. staff mem. Los Alamos Nat. Lab., N.Mex., 1999—. Prin. investigator Idaho Nat. Engring. Lab., 1993—97; task mgr. Thermosciences Inst., Moffett Field, 1997—99; project leader Los Alamos Nat. Lab., 2005—06. Contbr. papers to profl. jours. and pubs. Grantee, U.S. Dept. Energy, 1991—97. Achievements include research in theory development of multicomponent ambipolar diffusion; development of comprehensive computer code (LAVA) for modeling plasma spraying processes; research in high temperature reactive fluid dynamics.

CHANG, CHRIS C.N., pediatric surgeon; b. Taiwan, China, June 20, 1943; s. Shu-Ming and Yu-Bow (Chow) C.; m. Rose Lee Chang, Mar. 4, 1972; children: Lynda, Steven. MD, Nat. Taiwan U., 1969. Intern Nat. Taiwan Univ. Hosp., 1968-69, resident in surgery, 1970-72, Albert Einstein Med. Ctr., Phila., 1972-76; resident in pediat. surgery St. Christopher's Hosp. for Children, Phila., 1976-78; dir. pediat. surgery Lehigh Valley Hosp., Allentown, Pa., 1993—. Fellow ACS, Internat. Coll. Surgeons, Am. Acad. Pediats.; mem. Am. Pediat. Surg. Assn. Office: 1259 S Cedar Crest Blvd Ste 210 Allentown PA 18103 Office Phone: 610-402-7999. Business E-Mail: chris.chang@lvh.com.

CHANG, CHUNG-CHE, hematopatholgist, medical researcher, medical educator; b. Tainan, Taiwan, July 25, 1958; s. Chu-Chang and Yeh-Ing Chang; m. Horng-Wen Hsieh, Aug. 18, 1970; children: Edwin, Ellen, Ayei Elizabeth. MD, Nat. Yang-Ming U., Taipei, Taiwan, 1983; PhD, Case Western Res. U., Cleve., 1990. Diplomate Am. Bd. Pathology, 1997. Asst. prof., dir. hematopathology fellowship Med. Coll. Wis., Milw., 1999—2003; assoc. prof. Baylor Coll. Medicine, Houston, 2003—, Weil Med. Coll. of Cornell Univ., 2003—. Dir. Chenn-Kung Town Group Med. Ctr., Taiwan, 1991—93; dir. hematopathology and flow cytometry lab The Meth. Hosp., Houston, 2003—. Pricipical investigator (novel research) Clonotypic B-cell In Myeloma; author: (manuscript) MUM1 In CLL; pricipal investigator (research) MDR1 In Childhood Leukemia. Grantee, NIH, 2003. Fellow: ASCP, Coll. Am. Pathologists (com. 1998—2003, scholar 1998, Tng. in Tech. award 1997). Achievements include development of computer software to diagnose Anemia; Quality Control System For Hematologic Analyzers. Office: The Meth Hosp 6565 Fannin Ms205 Houston TX 77030 Business E-Mail: jeffchang@pol.net.

CHANG, CHUN-SHU, historian, educator, writer; b. Shandong, China, Apr. 25, 1934; arrived in U.S.A, 1957; s. Yun-an Chang and Ming-fang Kuo; m. Shelley Hsueh-lun Chang, Sept. 26, 1959; children: Chien-ju Jean, I-ju Deborah, Wei-chung Victor. BA in History, Nat. Taiwan U., Taipei, China, 1956; PhD., Harvard U., 1964. Richard Hudon prof. history U. Mich., Ann Arbor, 1966—83; from chair history to dept. head and dir. grad. studies The Chinese U. of Hong Kong, China, 1983—85; hon. prof. Chinese history The Peoples Republic of China, 1985—; vis. prof. Chinese history, dept. history Lanzhou U., Gansu, China, 1983, 1985, 1990; disting. vis. prof. Chinese History Taiwan, 1992; 29th Carl Becker lectr., 2002. Chair Internat. Conf. on Sung China, 1994; dir. Archeol. Expeditions, Gansu, China, 1982, 83, 85, 90, Summer Inst. of Han Studies, 1985. Author: The God of Soil in Ancient China, 1956, 1957, The Han Colonists and Their Settlements on the Chu-yen Frontier, 1966, Pre Modern China: A Bibliographical Introduction, 1971, revised edition, 1977, Studies in Han Frontier History, 1975, War and Peace with the Hsiungnu in Early Han China: The Hsiungnu Challenge and the Origins of Han Wu-ti's Military Expansion, 200-133 B.C., 1979, South China in the Twelfth Century, 1982, Essays on the History of Northwest China, 1982, A New Critical Biography of the First Emperor, 260-210 B.C., 1985, (collection of Chinese poetry) Wei-ch'ing shih-chi, 1985—2003, Redefining History, 1998, State and Theatre in Seventeenth-Century China: Drama and Politics during the Ming-Ch'ing Transition, 2003, Nation, State, and Imperialism in Early China, ca. 1600 B.C. - 8 A.D., 2004, Frontier, Immigration and Empire in Han China, 129 B.C. -A.D.107, 2004; co-author (with Shelley Hsueh-lun Chang): Crisis and Transformation in Seventeenth-Century China: Society, Culture, and Modernity, 1998; editor: Two Studies in Chinese Literature, 1968, The Making of China, 1975, 2d edit., 2000, Sung-Yuan Studies, The Continent Magazine; contbr. articles to profl. jours and magazines; exhibitions include An Exhibition of Chinese Calligraphy The Language of Art, Ann Arbor, Mich, 2003. Nominee Pulitzer Prize, 1991; recipient The Warner G. Rice award for Outstanding Acheivements in Humanities, 1977, Sino-Am. Culture award, 1956; grantee The Am. Council of Learned Soc., Social Sci. Rsch. Coun., Ford Found., Harvard U., The Chinese U. of Hong Kong; Cultural Reconstruction Foundation. Mem.: The Am. Acad. of the Polit. and Social Sci. (delegate 1960s-2000), Assn. for Asian Studies (panel chair), Soc. of Xu Xiake Studies (Council mem.), Soc. of Sung-Yuan Studies (exec. editl. bd.), Am. Historical Assn. (chair). Avocations: basketball, Peking Opera. Office: U Mich Dept History 1029 Tisch Hall Ann Arbor MI 48109

CHANG, CLARENCE DAYTON, retired chemist; b. Tianjin, China, Mar. 8, 1933; came to U.S., 1939; s. Hsueh Tseng and Lucy Chang; m. Cheryl Schucker, June 28, 1958 (div. 1987); 1 child, Christopher E.; m. Elizabeth C. O'Donoghue, June 28, 1987; 1 child, Stephen D. AB, Harvard U., 1954. Project chemist Weyerhaeuser Co., Longview, Wash., 1954-55, Sugar Rsch. Found., NYC, 1955-61; supr. M.W. Kellogg Co., Piscataway, NJ, 1961-70; sr. rsch. chemist Mobil R & D Corp., Princeton, NJ, 1970-74, rsch. assoc., 1974-81, rsch. scientist, 1981-84, sr. scientist, 1984-95, Mobil Tech. Co., Paulsboro, NJ, 1995-2000. Author: Hydrocarbons from Methanol, 1983; editor: Methane Conversion, 1988; also articles; over 200 U.S. patents in field. Recipient Hall of Fame, NJ Inventor's, 2005. Pem. Catalysis Soc. (excellence in catalysis award 1984), Am. Chem. Soc. (E.V. Murphree award 1992), Chinese-Am. Chem. Soc. (bd. dirs. 1993), N.Am. Catalysis Soc. (E.J. Houdry award 1999).

CHANG, DAVID, chef; b. Arlington, Va., 1977; Grad., Trinity Coll., Hartford, Conn., French Culinary Inst., NYC. Chef Mercer Kitchen, NYC, Craft Restaurant, NYC, soba-ya Fuyu-Rin, Tokyo, Restaurant New York Grill and Kozue, Tokyo, Cafe Boulud, NYC, 2003; owner, chef Momofuku Noodle Bar, NYC, 2004—, Momofuku Ssäm Bar, NYC, 2006—. Named Rising Star Chef of Yr., James Beard Found., 2007; recipient Am. Best New Chef award, Food and Wine Mag., 2006. Office: Momofuku c/o David Chang 163 First Ave New York NY 10003 Office Phone: 212-254-3500.

CHANG, DAVID Z., oncologist; MB, Taishan Med. Coll., 1989; PhD, Dartmouth Med. Sch., Hanover, NH, 1997, MD, 1998. Lic. Am. Bd. Internal Medicine, 2001, oncologist Am. Bd. Internal Medicine, 2004. Intern, resident Cleve. Clin. Found., 1998—2001; fellow Meml. Sloan-Kettering Cancer Ctr., 2001—04; physician UT MD Anderson Cancer Ctr., Houston, 2004—. Recipient Clin. Cancer Rsch. award, Cancer and Leukemia Group B, 2003—04. Mem.: Am. Soc. Clin. Oncology (Young Investigator award 2003—04, Career Devel. award 2006—), Am. Assn. Cancer Rsch. (Clin. Rsch. fellow 2003—04). Office Phone: 713-792-2828. Business E-Mail: dzchang@mdanderson.org.

CHANG, DEBBIE I-JU, health programs and research executive, director; BS in Chem. Engring., MIT, 1984; MPH, U. Mich., 1987. Presdl. mgmt. intern Health Care Fin. Adminstrn. Office Legislation and Policy, 1987-89; sr. health policy advisor Senator Donald W. Riegle Jr., 1989-94; dir. office legis. and intergovt. affairs Health Care Fin. Adminstrn., Washington, 1994-98; dir. State Children's Health Ins. Program Health Care Fin. Adminstrn., Dept. HHS, 1997-99; dir. Medicaid coverage benefits and payments Health Care Fin. Adminstrn., Balt., 1998; dep. sec. health care financing Medicaid Md. Dept. Health and Mental Hygiene, Balt., 1999—2003; sr. v.p., exec. dir. Nemours Divsn. Child Health and Prevention Svcs., Del., 2004—. Contbr. articles to profl. jours. Office Phone: 302-444-9127. Personal E-mail: dchang@nemours.org.

CHANG, HELEN CHUNG-HUNG HSIANG, music educator; b. Shanghai, July 20, 1937; d. Shou-Tsu Edward and Chen-Tze Kiang Hsiang; m. Nai Lin Chang; children: Tai Deborah, Huan Justina, Lan Samantha, Ling Patricia. BA cum laude, Mt. Mercy Coll., Cedar Rapids, Iowa, 1960; BMus cum laude, Lawrence U., 1980; postgrad. in pedagogical study, Am. Suzuki Inst., Stevens Point, Wis., 1972, 83, 88-89. Cert. tchr. Music Tchrs. Nat. Assn., Wis. Music Tchr. Assn., Suzuki Assn. of the Ams. Co-chair Fox Valley Keyboard Tchrs., Appleton, Wis., 1981-82, chair, 1982-83, treas., 1996-97; recital chair Suzuki Edn. Assn. of the Fox Valley, Appleton, 1984-96. Judge regional competitions Wis. Music Tchrs. Assn., 1988-97, state competition, 1994, 95, others, coach numerous students. Mem. Northeast Wis. Chinese Assn. (Chinese lang. instr. 1972-76), Wis. Music Tchrs. Assn. (award of excellence 1981, 94, 99, 2003), Music Tchr. Nat. Assn., Suzuki Assn. of the Ams., Suzuki Assn. of Wis.

CHANG, HEMMIE, lawyer; b. Mar. 19, 1960; AB, Princeton Univ., 1981; JD, Harvard Univ., 1984. Bar: Mass. 1985. Law clk. Judge David S. Nelson, US Dist Ct. (Mass.); assoc. Ropes & Gray, Boston, 1985—93, ptnr. corp. dept., 1993—, head energy & utilities practice group. Bd. mem. South Cove Nursing Home; bd. mem. Cambridge Ctr for Adult Edn.; bd. mem. Commonwealth Sch. Mem.: Women's Corp. Counsel Network, Boston Law Firm Group. Office: Ropes & Gray 1 International Pl Boston MA 02110-2624 Office Phone: 617-951-7317. Office Fax: 617-951-7050. Business E-Mail: h.chang@ropesgray.com.

CHANG, HENRY C., library administrator; b. Canton, China, Sept. 15, 1941; came to U.S., 1964, naturalized, 1973; s. Ih-ming and Lily (Lin) C.; m. Marjorie Li, Oct. 29, 1966; 1 dau., Michelle. LLB, Nat. Chengchi U., 1962; MA, U. Mo., 1966; MA in Libr. Sci., U. Minn., 1968, PhD, 1974. Reader advisor Braille Inst. Am., LA, 1965-67, dir. libr. svcs., 1990—; reference libr. U. Minn., Mpls., 1968-70, instr., libr., 1970-72, asst. head govt. document divsn., 1972-74; libr. dir., lectr. in social scis. U. of the V.I., St. Croix, 1974-75, dir. divsn. librs., museums and archeol. svcs., 1975-88; dir. V.I. Libr. Tng. Inst., 1975-76; coord., chmn. V.I. State Hist. Records Adv. Bd., 1976-88, pres., libr. cons., 1988-89; project dir. Calif. Telephone Reader Program, 2000—. Chmn. microfilm com. ACURIL, 1977-88; mem. V.I. Bicentennial Commn., 1975-77, Ft. Frederik Commn., 1975-76; adv. com. on rsch. tng. Caribbean Rsch. Inst., 1974-75; coord. Libr. Conf., 1977-87; project dir. cultural heritage project NEH, 1979-83; chmn. nat. collection devel. com. nat. libr. svcs. Libr. of Congress, 1998, chmn. western conf. group, 2001-04; commr. Accreditation Commn. for Acupuncture and Oriental Medicine, 2004-, chair stds. and criteria com., 2006-. Author: A Bibliography of Presidential Commissions, Committees, Councils, Panels and Task Forces, 1961-72, 1973, Taiwan Democraphy, 1964-71: A Selected Annotated Bibliography of Government Documents, 1973, A Selected Annotated Bibliography of Caribbean Bibliographies in English, 1975, A Survey of the Use of Microfilms in the Caribbean, 1978, Long-Range Program for Library Development, 1978, Institute for Training in Library Management and Communications Skill, 1979; contbr. numerous articles and book revs. on libr. sci. to profl. jours. Chmn. bd. dirs. Eden Found. for People with Disabilities, 1995—96; mem. adv. com. Nat. Std. and Guideline Svcs., Libr. Congress Network Librs., 2002—05. 2d lt. Taiwan Army, 1962—63. Named Mem. Staff of Yr., Coll. V.I., 1974—75; recipient Libr. Adminstrs. Devel. Program fellowship award, 1972, Cert. of Appreciation, Govt. V.I., 1985, Eden Found., 1999, L.A. Internat. Lions Club award, 1992, 1995, Driver Safety award, 1993, Cert. of Achievement, Braille Inst., 2001, Network Libr. of Yr. award, Libr. of Congress, 2004—05, 2005, Libr. Award, Am. Libr. Assn., 2007; grantee, Nat. Commn. on Librs. and Info. Sci. Mem. ALA (counselor 1980-84), AAUP, Asian Pacific ALA (chmn. fin. com. 1993-96), Population Assn. Am., Am. Sociol. Assn., Chinese Am. Profl. Soc. Home: 3713 Lowry Rd Los Angeles CA 90027-1437 Office: Braille Inst Am 741 N Vermont Ave Los Angeles CA 90029-3594 Office Phone: 323-906-3185, 323-660-3880. Business E-Mail: dls@braillelibrary.org.

CHANG, HERNAN ROBERT, infectious disease consultant; s. Hector Chang and Julia Pinares. MD, San Marcos U., Lima, Peru, 1982, U. Geneva, Switzerland, 1988. Diplomate Am. Bd. Internal Medicine, 2000, Infectious Diseases Am. Bd. Infectious Diseases, 2002. Rsch. fellow Dept. Microbiology Inst. Tropical Medicine, Antwerp, Belgium, 1984—85; rsch. fellow Dept. Genetics and Microbiology U. Geneva Med. Sch., 1986—92; sr. lectr. Dept. Microbiology, Nat. U. Singapore, 1992—95; rsch. fellow Deaconess Hosp., Harvard Med. Sch., Boston, 1996—97; resident Salem Hosp., Mass., 1997—2000; fellow New Eng. Med. Ctr., Boston, 2000—01, Boston U. Med. Ctr., 2001—02; cons. Salem Hosp., Mass., 2002—04, Infectious Disease Cons., Jacksonville, Fla., 2004—. Chief resident Salem Hosp., Mass., 1999—2000. Author: Elysium: A Collection of Haiku and Senryu, 2005, MRSA-Spider Bites: The Flesh-Eating Epidemic that Threatens America, 2006, MRSA and Staphylococcal Infections, 2006; contbr. articles to profl. jours. Recipient Maxwell Finland Award, Mass. Infectious Diseases Soc., 2002; grantee Rsch., Swiss NSF, 1993—95, Finanz-Pool 3R Found., Switzerland, 1988—91. Mem.: AMA, ACP, Dictionary Soc. N.Am., The Mind Soc., Epimetheus Soc., Sigma Xi Rsch. Soc., Mass. Med. Soc., Swiss Soc. for Cell Biology, Molecular Biology and Genetics, Swiss Soc. for Microbiology, European Soc. Clin. Microbiology and Infectious Diseases, Infectious Diseases Soc. Am., Am. Soc. for Microbiology, Mass. Med. Soc. (com. pubs. 2001—02), Am. Acad. HIV Medicine, Internat. Soc. Travel Medicine (cert. travel health 2003), Boston Med. Libr. (life; bd. trustees 2003—04), Omega Soc., Genius Soc., Intertel, Cerebrals, Top-One-Percent Soc., One-in-a-Thousand Soc., Glia Soc., Internat. Soc. for Philos. Enquiry, Triple Nine Soc., Mensa, Shriners, Scottish Rite, Grand Lodge of Mass. Home Phone: 904-327-6860; Office Phone: 904-646-9839. Business E-Mail: hrc@massmed.org.

CHANG, HSUEH-LUN SHELLEY, historian, researcher, writer; b. Nanning, China, Sept. 18, 1934; d. Chun-su Loh and Chien-Yun Huang; m. Chun-shu Chang, Sept. 26, 1959; children: Chien-ju Jean, I-Ju Deborah, Wei-chung Victor. BA in History, Nat. Taiwan U., 1956; MA in History, Boston U., 1961. Rsch. assoc. Ctr. Chinese Study, Ann Arbor, Mich., 1984—. Vis. lectr. Chinese U. Hong Kong, 1983—85, U. Lan-chou China, 1984; vis. assoc. prof. U. Mich., Ann Arbor, 1987, 94, v.p. women's rsch. club, 91. Author: Windmills: A Collection of Essays, 1970, History and Legend, 1990; co-author: Crisis and Transformation in 17th-Century China, 1992, Redefining History, 1998. Mem.: Assn. Asian Studies, Am. Hist. Assn. Home: 3236 Bluett Dr Ann Arbor MI 48105

CHANG, JAE CHAN, hematologist, oncologist, educator; b. Aug. 29, 1941; arrived in US, 1965; s. Tae Whan and Kap Hee (Lee) Chang; m. Sue Young Chung, Dec. 4, 1965; children: Sung-Jin, Sung-Ju, Sung-Hoon. MD, Seoul Nat. U., 1965. Diplomate Am. Bd. Internal Medicine, Hematology, Med. Oncology, Am. Bd. Pathology (Hematology). Intern Ellis Hosp., Schenectady, NY, 1965—66; resident Harrisburg Hosp., Pa., 1966—69, fellow in nuc. medicine, 1969—70; fellow in hematology and oncology, instr. U. Rochester, 1970—72; chief hematology sect. VA Hosp., Dayton, Ohio, 1972—75; hematopathologist, co-dir. hematology lab. Good Samaritan Hosp., Dayton, 1975—2002, dir. oncology unit, 1976—2001, chief hematology and oncology sect., 1976—2003; clin. prof. medicine U. Calif., Irvine, Calif., 2003—, dir. hematology and oncology fellowship program, 2003—05; mem. Chao Family Comprehensive Cancer Ctr., U. Calif., Irvine, 2003—. Asst. clin. prof. Ohio State U., Columbus, 1972—75; assoc. clin. prof. Wright State U., Dayton, 1975—80, clin. prof., 1980—99, prof., 1999—2003, co-dir. hematology and med. oncology fellowship program, 1993—98; cons. hematology VA Hosp.; adv. com. Greater Dayton Area chpt. Leukemia Soc. Am., 1977; trustee Montgomery County Soc. Cancer Control, Dayton, 1976—85, Dayton Area Cancer Assn., 1985—88, Cmty. Blood Ctr., 1982—86, Hipple Cancer Rsch. Crt., 1999—2003. Contbr. articles to profl. jours., columns in newspapers. Recipient Med. Econ. Essay Competition award, 1990, Wright State U. Acad. of Medicine award, 1985, Laureate award, ACP-ASIM Ohio Chpt., 2001, Spl. Commendation, Ohio Senate, 2002, Orange County Physician of Excellence award, Orange County Soc. Calif., Orange Coast Mag., 2007. Fellow: ACP; mem.: Montgomery Med. Soc. (dir. 1990—93), Dayton Soc. Internal Medicine (pres. 1989), Am. Soc. Clin. Oncologists, Am. Soc. Hematology. Office: UCI Med Ctr Div Hematology/ Oncology Chao Family Comp Cancer Ctr 101 The City Dr Orange CA 92868 Office Phone: 714-456-5153, 714-456-6578. Business E-Mail: jaec@uci.edu.

CHANG, JANE P., chemical engineering educator; BS, Nat. Taiwan U., 1993; MS, MIT, 1995, PhD, 1998. Engring. intern Merck and Co., Inc., Lansdale, Pa., 1994, Dow Chem. Co., Midland, Mich., 1994; postdoctoral mem. tech. staff Bell Labs, Lucent Technologies, Murray Hill, NJ, 1998—99; asst. prof. chem. engring. UCLA, 1999—2003, assoc. prof. chem. engring., 2003—05, prof. chem. engring, 2005—. Chair com. undergrad. admission and rels. with schs. UCLA, 2005—06. Contbr. articles to profl. jours. Named Prof. of Yr., UCLA, 2003—04; recipient Chancellor's Career Devel. award, 2000—02, Career award, Nat. Sci. Found., 2002, Excellence in Tchg. award, TRW, 2002, Young Investigator award, Office of Naval Rsch., 2003, Hugo Schuck Best Paper award, Am. Automatic Control Coun., 2004. Mem.: Material Rsch. Soc., Am. Vacuum Soc. (Coburn and Winters award 1996, Peter Mark award 2005), Am. Inst. Chem. Engrs., Am. Physics Soc., Electrochem. Soc., Am. Chem. Soc., Phi Tau Phi. Office: UCLA Chem and Biomolecular Engring Dept BH 5532-D 420 Westwood Plz Los Angeles CA 90095

CHANG, JASON, artist, educator; b. Ear-Shui, Taiwan, Sept. 9, 1940; arrived in US, 1980; s. Sion-Chu and Yuan Chang; m. Li-Jen Chang, Jan. 18, 1968; children: E-May, Fon Shebg. M Studio Art, Coll. New Rochelle, NY, 1992. Instr. Sch. Pastel, Golden Eagle Inst., NY, 1999—. Mem. awards jury, organizer Taiwan Ctr. Internat. Pastel Open Juried Exhbn., NY, 2005—; juror numerous nat. and internat. art competitions. Author: Pastel World of Jason Chang, 1999. Mem.: Am. Artists Profl. League (Top award 2001, 2002), Pastel Soc. Am. (master pastelist 2005, instr. Sch. Pastel 1998—, signature mem., award of excellence 2001, 2005), Golden Eagle Inst. (v.p. 2003—), N.Am. Pastel Artists Assn. (pres. 1997—). Avocations: singing, antiques, writing, art demonstrating, travel. Home: 151-56 21st Ave Whitestone NY 11357 Office: NAm Pastel Artists Assn 133-03 41st Ave Flushing NY 11355

CHANG, JE-YOUNG, electronics engineer; s. Ki-Sung Chang and Hak-Jeo Kim; m. Sung-Yun Kim, May 30, 1992; children: Alena H., Paul A. BS in Mech. Engring., Seoul Nat. U., 1988, MS in Mech. Engring., 1990; PhD in Mech. Engring., U. Tex., Arlington, 1997. Project mgr. KIA Motors Co., Seoul, 1989—92; tchg. and rsch. asst. U. Tex., Arlington, 1992—97; rsch. assoc. Pa. State U., University Park, 1997—2000; staff packaging engr. Intel Corp., Chandler, Ariz., 2000—. Contbr. articles to profl. jours. Condr. ch. choir Korean Cath. Ch., Ft. Worth, 1992—97, chmn. ch. com. State College, Pa., 1998—99, mem. ch. com. Phoenix, 2005—07. Mem.: ASME. Achievements include 5 US patents issued; 9 US patents pending. Office: Intel Corporation 5000 W Chandler Blvd M/S# CH5-157 Chandler AZ 85226-3699 Home Phone: 480-699-0269; Office Phone: 480-554-2411. Personal E-mail: jxc433@dreamwiz.com. Business E-Mail: je-young.chang@intel.com.

CHANG, KATHY KUHL, computer programmer, analyst; b. Olney, Ill., Oct. 26, 1956; d. John Joseph and Jeanette Catherine (Ochs) Kuhl; m. Michael Anthony DiSalvo, Aug. 31, 1985 (div. Dec. 1988). BS in Bus., Ea. Ill. U., 1977. Systems programmer, systems analyst, programmer/analyst Western Ill. U., Macomb, 1980-85; cons. Mattoon, Ill., 1985-86; programmer analyst St. Lucie County Sch. Bd., Ft. Pierce, Fla., 1986-88; rsch. programmer U. Ill., Urbana, 1989—99, sr. rsch. programmer, 1999—. Mem.: IEEE, NAFE. Home: 1619 Sangamon Dr Champaign IL 61821-4936 Business E-Mail: katzemutter@yahoo.com.

CHANG, KUK WON, theology educator, researcher, pastor; b. Yesan, Chungnam, Korea, Apr. 15, 1938; arrived in U.S., 1999; parents Hyun Tae Chang and Dae Jae Lee; m. Yeon Sook Lee, May 15, 1982; children: Sang Eun, Sang Young. BA, Seoul Nat. U., 1961, MA, 1967; AM, Duke U., 1971; PhD, Dr. Habil, Muenster U., 1980. Dir. Aram Inst. for Ancient Studies, Anyang, Republic of Korea, 1981—2001; pres. Korean Soc. for Ancient Near Ea. Studies, Seoul, 1983—2001; prof. Hansei U., Kunpo, 1990—2001. Vis. scholar Cornell U., Ithaca, NY, 1985—87; rsch. scholar Duke U., Durham, NC, 1999—2002; sec. gen. United Cultural Conv., Raleigh, NC, 2001—; sr. fellow Inst. for Interdisciplinary Studies, Pasadena, Calif., 1997—; advisor to dir. gen. Internat. Biog. Ctr., Cambridge, England, 2001—; dir. Inst. for Rschs. on Metatheology, Chapel Hill, NC, 2003—. Contbr. articles to profl. jours. 1st lt. Korean Army, 1963—67. Office: 223 Forbush Mountain Dr Chapel Hill NC 27514-1909 Office Phone: 919-960-2565. Personal E-mail: kwpchang@hotmail.com.

CHANG, LAURA, editor; Studied journalism and psychology, U. Washington. Nat. desk editor to assignment editor Seattle Times, spl. projects editor; dep. sci. editor NY Times, science editor, 2004—. Mem.: Asian Am. Journalists (grad. exec. leadership program, NY 1996). Office: NY Times 229 W 43rd St New York NY 10036 Office Phone: 212-556-3634. Office Fax: 212-556-7306.

CHANG, LYDIA LIANG-HWA, social worker, educator; b. Wuhan, Hubei, China, Sept. 25, 1929; came to US, 1960; d. Shu-Tze Yu-Rou and Jian-Bung (Young) C.; m. Norman Stock, Aug. 20, 1998; children: Elizabeth Shu-Mei L. Ip, George Shu-Ang Lee. Diploma in Spanish and Lit., U. Sorbonne, Paris, 1959; MSW, NYU, 1963; cert. in advanced social work, Columbia U., NYC, 1977, PhD in Social Work, 1980. Cert. social worker, cert. sch. bilingual social worker, NY; LCSW; LMSW. Supr. Cath. Charities, NYC, 1969-71; dir. mental health cons. ctr. Univ. Settlement, NYC, 1971-73; psychotherapist Luth. Med. Ctr., Bklyn., 1974-78; assoc. prof. U. Cin., 1978-80; asst. prof. Borough of Manhattan C.C., NYC, 1983-86; bilingual sch. social worker NYC Bd. Edn., 1987-98, instr. for staff devel. program, 1991-98; psychotherapist Western Queens Consultation Ctr., NY, 1998—2004; pvt. practice psychotherapy, 2005—; psychotherapist Family Support Sys. Unlimited, Inc., Bronx, 2007—. Govt. of cl.; mem. mty. sch. bd. Dist. 30 NYC Bd. Edn., 1999-2007; cons. Cath. Social Svc. Bur., Cin., 1978-80; faculty advisor Borough of Manhattan C.C., 1983-86. Author: numerous poems; contbr. articles to profl. jours. Adv. bd. Pub. Sys. of Schs., Cin., 1978-80, Orange County Asian Am. orgn., Goshen, NY, 1980-82; founder of the Shu-Tze Chang and Jian-Bung Young Chang Ednl. scholarship fund, China, 1996. Mem. NASW, Nat. Assn. Sch. Social Workers, Columbia Alumni Assn., Nankai Alumni Assn. (v.p. 1991-94), Am. Voters Assn., Asian-Am. Dem. Assn. Episcopalian. Avocations: flute, tai chi, swimming, reading. Home: 77-11 35th Ave Apt 2P Jackson Heights NY 11372 Personal E-mail: stockchang@mac.com.

CHANG, MARIAN S., filmmaker, composer; b. Atlanta, Aug. 19, 1958; d. C. H. Joseph and C. S. (Chun) Chang. MusB, Harvard U., Cambridge, Mass., 1981; MFA in Film Making, Columbia U., NYC, 1994. Composer, dir., choreographer Exptl. Theatre, Dance, Boston, 1981-88; composer for modern dance co. Performing Arts Ensemble, Boston, 1986-88; co-dir., choreographer, performer Theatre S., Boston, 1987-88; prodr., dir., writer, sound designer, composer NYC, 1991—. Founder, prodr. Shy Artists Prodns., Boston, NYC, 1988—94. Recipient 1st prize, Kansas City Music Scholarship Competition, 1976, Nino Cerruti Film award, 1995; fellow, Mass. Artists' Fellowship Program in Choreography, 1987, Mass. Artists' Fellowship Program in Music Composition, 1988; grantee, N.Y. Coun. Humanities, 1998. Achievements include first artist in Mass. Artists' Fellowship Program to receive awards in both music and choreography. Home: 220 E 27th St Apt 7 New York NY 10016-9234

CHANG, MICHAEL, professional tennis player; b. Hoboken, NJ, Feb. 22, 1972; s. Joe and Betty Chang. Round of 16 U.S. Open, NYC, 1988, 89, 91, 94, Wimbledon, London, 1989, 90, quarterfinalist, 1994; champion French Open, Paris, 1989, quarterfinalist, 1990, 91, finalist, 1995; semifinalist Australian Open, Melbourne, 1995, finalist, 1996, U.S. Open, NYC, 1996. Other tournaments include: semifinalist WCT Scottsdale (Ariz.) Open, 1987; champion Transamerica Open, San Francisco, 1988; semifinalist Volvo Tennis Indoor, Memphis, 1989, semifinalist, 1991; finalist Volvo Tennis L.A., 1989, 90, 93; champion Silk Cuts Championships, Wembley, Eng., 1989; semifinalist Sovran Bank Classic, Washington, 1990; champion Player's Ltd. Internat. Can. Open, Toronto, 1990; semifinalist Suntory Japan Open, Tokyo, 1991, 92; semifinalist Open de la Ville de Paris, 1991, 94; finalist Compaq Grand Slam Cup, Munich, 1991, 92; champion Diet Pepsi Indoor Challenge, Birmingham, Eng., 1991; semifinalist Thriftway ATP Championships, Cin., 1992, champion, 1993, 94, finalist, 1995; semifinalist Waldbaum's Hamlet Cup, L.I., N.Y., 1992; semifinalist Seiko Super Tennis, Tokyo, 1992, finalist, 1994, champion, 1995; semifinalist European Cmty. Championships, Antwerp, Belgium, 1992; finalist Salem Open, Hong Kong, 1992, champion, 1994, 95, champion, Osaka, 1993, champion, Kuala Lumpur, 1993, champion, Beijing, 1993, 94, 95; champion Volvo Tennis/San Francisco, 1992; champion Newsweek Champions Cup, Indian Wells, Calif., 1992, semifinalist, 1993; champion Lipton Internat. Players Championships, Key Biscayne, Fla., 1992; semifinalist Kroger St. Jude Internat., Memphis, 1993, finalist, 1998; Ford Australian Open, Melbourne, 1997, U.S. Open, N.Y.C., 1997; champion Indonesian Open, Jakarta, 1993; finalist Japan Open, Tokyo, 1994, semifinalist, 1995; champion Indonesian Men's Open, Jakarta, 1994; champion Comcast U.S. Indoor, Phila., 1994, finalist, 1995; champion AT&T Challenge, Atlanta, 1994, 95, Infiniti Open, L.A., 1996, U.S. Men's Clay Ct. Championships, 1997, Salem Open, Hong Kong, 1997, Legg Mason Tennis Classic, Washington, 1996, 97, Kroger St. Jude, 1997, Newsweek Champions Cup, Indian Wells, Calif., 1996, 97; finalist Sybase Open, San Jose, Calif., 1995, semifinalist, 1996, 1998; finalist ATP World Tour Championships, Frankfurt, Germany, 1995; mem. U.S. Davis Cup Squad, 1989-91; semifinalist du Maurier Open, Montreal, Canada, 1997; semifinalist Great Amer. Insurance ATP Championship, Cincinnati, Oh., 1997; semifinalist Heineken Open, Rosmalen, The Netherlands, 1997. Achievements include being the youngest player to win USTA Boys' Nat. Championships, 1987; youngest male to advance to semifinals of Super Series tournament, 1987; youngest male to win match at U.S. Open, 1987; youngest male to win match at Wimbledon, 1988; youngest player to win Super Series tournament, 1988; youngest player to be named to U.S. Davis Cup Squad, 1989; youngest male Grand Slam Champion in Open Era, 1989; youngest ever French Open Champion, 1989; first Am. since Tony Trabert to win French Open, 1989. Address: Advantage Internat 1751 Pinnacle Dr Ste 1500 Mc Lean VA 22102-3833

CHANG, NANCY T., pharmaceutical executive; b. Taiwan; PhD in Biological Chemistry, Harvard Med. Sch. Dir. rsch. Molecular Biology Group Centocor Inc., 1981—86; founder Tanox Inc., 1986, pres., 1986—, CEO, 1990—, chmn. bd. dir., 1986—2003; with Roche Inst. of Molecular Biology, 1980—81. Assoc. prof. molecular virology Baylor Coll. Medicine; bd. dir. Biotechnology Industry Orgn., Houston Tech. Ctr., BioHouston, Greater Houston Partnership. Contbr. articles to profl. jour. Named Houston Entrepreneur of Yr.; named one of Top 20 Houston Women in Tech.; named to Tex. Sci. Hall of Fame, 2001. Office: Tanox Inc 10555 Stella Link Houston TX 77025-5631

CHANG, PETER M.J., musicologist, educator; arrived in US, 1981; s. Kuo Wei Chang and Jiali Chou; m. Jean Liu, Dec. 18, 1991; children: Philip, Julia. BA in Music, Ctrl. Wash. U., 1986; MA in Music History, Calif. State U., Fresno, 1988; PhD in Musicology, U. Ill., 1995. Tchg. and rsch. asst. Calif. State U., Fresno, 1986—88, U. Ill., Urbana, 1988—92; asst. specialist Ctr. U.S.-China Arts Exch., Columbia U., NYC, 1993—94; instr. El Paso (Tex.) CC, 1994—95; assoc. prof. Northeastern Ill. U., Chgo., 1995—2007, prof., 2007—. Author: Chou Wen-Chung: The Life and Work of a Contemporary Chinese-born American Composer, 2006. Mem.: Am. Musicol. Soc., Soc. Asian Music, U. Chgo. Ctr. for East Asian Studies. Home: 29630 N Birch Ave Lake Bluff IL 60044 Office: Music Dept Northea Ill U 5500 N St Louis Ave Chicago IL 60625 Office Phone: 773-442-5914. Office Fax: 773-442-5910. E-mail: p-chang1@neiu.edu.

CHANG, R. P. H., materials science educator; b. Chung King, Peoples Republic China, Dec. 22, 1941; s. Joseph K. Cho; m. Bennie Chang; children: Vivian, Samuel. BS in Physics, MIT, 1965; PhD in Plasma Physics, Princeton U., 1970. Postdoctoral fellowship Princeton Plasma Physics Lab., 1970-71; mem. tech. staff AT&T Bell Labs., Murray Hill, N.J., 1971-86; prof. Material Sci. & Engring. Northwestern U., 1986—. Dir. Materials Rsch. Ctr., 1989—. 7 original inventions 1977—; author over 170 sci. publs.; co-author chpts. in Plasma Diagnostics and Material Sci. & Engring.; co-editor: Plasma Synthesis & Etching of Electronic Materials, 1985. Fellow Am. Vacuum Soc.; mem. Am. Physics Soc., Materials Rsch. Soc. (pres. 1989), Internat. Union of Materials Rsch. Socs. (pres. 1991-92). Office: Northwestern U Dept Materials Sci Engring 2225 N Campus Dr Evanston IL 60208-0876

CHANG, RUNZI, electrical engineer; s. Xuejing Chang and Shuge Li; m. Jinghua Hao; 1 child, Michael Hao-Pujie. B of Engring., Tsinghua U., Beijing, 1999; MSEE, U. Calif., Berkeley, 2001, PhD, 2004. Rsch. intern Intel Corp., Santa Clara, Calif., 2002—03; mem. integrated circuits process integration staff Applied Materials, Santa Clara, Calif., 2004—. Jiang Nanxiang scholar, Tsinghua U., 1994. Mem.: IEEE (corr.). Achievements include invention of method for single-pass solvent cleaning.

CHANG, SAM HSIEN-CHENG, lawyer; b. Nanking, Peoples Republic of China, Sept. 6, 1946; came to US, 1973; s. Tien-Yi and Ju-Jen (Wang) C.; m. Susie Hsi-Ling, July 12, 1970; children: Richard, Edward. LLB,

Taiwan U., 1968; M of Comparative Laws, Howard U., 1975. Bar: DC 1981. Assoc. Wasserman, Orlow, Washington, 1981-83; ptnr. Wasserman, Mancini & Chang, Washington, 1983—. Gen. counsel Chinese Restaurant Owner's Assn., 1988-; host Cable TV Legal Advice Program, Fairfax, Va., 1989-92, Cable TV Free Immigration Advice Program, Montgomery County, Md., 1994-; panelist in field. Contbr. articles to profl. jours. Gen. counsel Asian Am. Voters' Coalition, Washington, 1986-2000; prin. Gaithersburg Chinese Sch., Md., 1983-84; sec. gen. Monte Jade Sci. and Tech. Assn., Washington, DC. Mem. ABA, DC Bar, Bar Assn. of DC, Am. Immigration Lawyers Assn. Avocations: swimming, golf. Office: Wasserman Mancini & Chang 1915 I St NW Ste 400 Washington DC 20006-2112 Office Phone: 202-783-8905. Business E-Mail: wmclawfirm@aol.com.

CHANG, SAM S., urologist, surgeon, educator; b. Seoul, Republic of Korea, Feb. 19, 1966; m. Michelle Chang; children: Grace, Rachel, Julia. AB, Princeton U., NJ, 1988; MD, Vanderbilt U., Nashville, 1992. Asst. prof. urol. surgery Vanderbilt U. Med. Ctr., 2000—05, assoc. prof. urol. surgery, 2005—. Com. chair Am. Joint Com. Cancer, Chgo., 2003—; urology rep. VUMC Alumni Assoc. Bd., 2004—; faculty advisor-med. students I & II Vanderbilt U., 2001—; sec., treas. Rhamy-Shelley Vanderbilt Urology Soc., 2002—04. Recipient CaPCURE Young Investigator award, Prostate Cancer Found., 2001—04, Disting. Svc. award, Soc. Urol. Oncology, 2005; fellow, Meml. Sloan-Kettering Cancer Ctr., NYC, 1999—2000, Am. Urol. Assn./European Assn. Urology, 2006. Mem.: AMA (assoc.), Tenn. Med. Assn. (alt. ho. of dels. 2003—05), Am. Urol. Assn. (assoc.; guidelines panel-treatment superficial bladder cancer 2004—, mem. prostate adv. coun. 2004—). Office: Vanderbilt University Medical Center A-1302 Medical Center North Nashville TN 37232-2765 Home Phone: 615-665-0721; Office Phone: 615-322-2101. Office Fax: 615-322-8990. E-mail: sam.chang@vanderbilt.edu.

CHANG, SAMUEL HENRY, computer scientist, educator; s. Zonba Chang and Suying Wang; m. Xiaoyuan Yu, Jan. 1, 1979; 1 child, Yu. Diploma, Xiamen U., China, 1978; MSEE, Cath. U. Am., 1991; PhD, George Mason U., 1997. Asst. rschr. Chinese Acad. Scis., Beijing, 1978—82; vice dir. Traffic Control Rsch. Inst., Guangzhou, China, 1983—87; rsch. asst. Cath. U. Am., Washington, 1990—91; rsch./tchg. asst. George Mason U., Va., 1992—94; cons. NIH, Md., 1995—97, U.S. Naval Rsch. Lab, Washington, 1998—99; program tech. leader Crown Comm., Md., 1999—2000; sr. software engr. Cambridge Rsch. Assocs., Va., 2000—01; sr. scientist, mgr. Spatial Integrated Systems, Rockville, Md., 2002—. Part-time prof. Southea. U., Washington, 1998—; guest prof. Xiamen U., 2005—; disting. vis. prof. Chung-Ang U., 2006. Contbr. articles to profl. jours. in computer vision imaging. Mem.: IEEE. Home Phone: 301-424-6738; Office Phone: 301-610-7965 ext. 108. Personal E-mail: changsamue@hotmail.com. Business E-Mail: sam.chang@sisinc.org.

CHANG, SARAH, violinist; b. Phila., Dec. 10, 1980; Attended, Julliard Sch. of Music. Featured artist in The Art of Time global advertising campaign Movado. Performances with Bavarian State Orch., Munich, Danish Nat. Symphony Orch., Helsinki Philharmonic, NY Philharmonic, Los Angeles Philharmonic, Phila. Orch., Boston Symphony, Vienna Philharmonic, Berlin Philharmonic, Philharmonia, Royal Concertgebouw Orch., Leipzig Gewandhaus Orch., Orchestre Nat. de France, numerous others, albums include Debut, 1992, subsequent releases Tchaikovsky Concerto with the London Symphony Orch., Paganini Concerto No. 1, works of Saint-Saens with Wolfgang Sawallisch, Vieuxtemps' Violin Concerto No. 5 with Chalres Dutoit, Simply Sarah, 1997, Sibelius and Mendelssohn Violin Concertos with Berlin Philharmonic, 1998, Fire and Ice, numerous others. Named Young Artist of Year, Gramophone mag., 1993, Newcomer of Yr., Internat. Classical Music Awards, 1994; recipient Avery Fisher Career Grant, 1992, Avery Fisher Prize, 1999, Hollywood Bowl Hall of Fame award, 2004, Accademia Musicale Chigiana Prize, Italy, 2004. Office: c/o EMI Group plc 27 Wrights Ln London W8 5SW England*

CHANG, SEUNGHYUK, physicist, electrical engineer; b. Seoul, Republic of Korea, Jan. 23, 1971; s. Sang-Hyon Chang and Jeong-Hye Yoon. PhD, U. So. Calif., LA, 2001. Rsch. assoc. U. So. Calif., LA, 2001—03; sr. rschr. Samsung Advanced Inst. Tech., Suwon, Republic of Korea, 2004—. Contbr. articles to profl. jours. Achievements include research in aberrations of off-axis reflective optical systems. Office: Samsung Advanced Inst Tech PO Box 111 Suwon 440-600 Republic of Korea Office Phone: 82 31 280 9169. Office Fax: 82 31 280 8368. Business E-Mail: chang@offaxis.co.kr.

CHANG, SHAN NAN, education educator, academic administrator; b. Hualien, Taiwan, Jan. 17, 1957; s. Liang Song and Lin Chuang Chang; m. Mei Tze Huang, Oct. 10, 1981; children: Eddie, Evan, Yi Chi. PhD, Pa. State U., 1993. Dean acad. affairs Nat. Taitung Tchrs. Coll., Taiwan, 2000—01; vis. prof. Ctr. Studies on Higher Edn., State College, Pa., 2001; dir. cultural divsn. Taipei Econ. and Cultural Office, Boston, 2003—. Reviewer, reader Nat. Sci. Coun., Taipei, Taiwan; editor in chief Ministry of Edn., Taiwan, 1999—2001. Pres. Youth Corp ROC, Taitung chpt. Friend Assn., Taiwan; mem. Nat. Assn. of Curing Down Syndrome, Taipei, Taiwan; pres. Mind Farm Mental Devel. Ctr., Taitung, Taiwan. Recipient Rsch. award, Nat. Sci. Coun.; Terminal Degree Study Abroad grant, Ministry of Edn., Taiwan Govt., 1990—93, Vis. fellow, Sinica Academia, Taiwan ROC, 1998—99. Mem.: NAFSA, AERA. Achievements include development of a framework for a national longitudinal study in education, published by the Proceedings of Humanities of National Science Council; proposed a project to advocate the establishment of a teaching center and student learning center three years before the Taiwan Ministry of Education adopted it as an important higher edn. policy. Office: Taipei Econ and Cultrual Office 99 Summer St Ste 801 Boston MA 02110 Home Phone: 617-484-7662; Office Phone: 617-737-2055. Business E-Mail: sxc135@tecoboston.org.

CHANG, SHIRLEY LIN (HSIU-CHU CHANG), librarian, educator; b. Chia-yi, Taiwan, June 22, 1937; came to U.S., 1962; naturalized, 1977. d. Tzu-kun and Ying (Chang) Lin; m. Parris H. Chang, Aug. 3, 1963; children: Yvette Y., Elaine Y., Bohdan P. BA, Nat. Taiwan U., Taipei, 1960; postgrad., U. Wash., 1962-63; MLS, Columbia U., 1967; MA, Pa. State U., 1988. Libr. asst. Yale U., New Haven, 1964-67; asst. ref. libr. Pa. State U., University Park, 1971-75; cataloguer Australian Nat. U., Canberra, 1978; catalog/ref. libr. Lock Haven U., 1979—, asst. prof., 1982-88, assoc. prof., 1988—, chair and acting chair libr. dept., 1991—2000. Catalog/reference libr., reference desk coord. Lock Haven U., Pa. Author: Taiwan's Brain Drain and Its Reversal, 1999. Mem. ALA, Chinese-Am. Librs. Assn. (chmn. awards com. 1982-83), Asian/Pacific Am. Librs. Assn., Assn. for Asian Studies, Pa. Libr. Assn., Phi Beta Delta Honor Soc. Office: Lock Haven U Stevenson Libr Lock Haven PA 17745 Office Phone: 570-893-2312. E-mail: schang@lhup.edu.

CHANG, STANLEY, ophthalmologist; BEE, MIT, 1964—68; MS in Biomedical Electronic Engring., U. Pa., 1968—70; MD, Columbia U., 1970—74. Lic. NY, Conn., diplomate Nat. Bd. Med. Examiners, 1975, Am. Bd. Ophthalmology. Vis. clin. fellow med. Columbia U. Coll. Physicians and Surgeons, NYC, 1974—75; intern Dept. Medicine Columbia-Presbyterian Med. Ctr., NYC, 1974—75; resident in ophthalmology Mass. Eye and Ear Infirmary, Boston, 1976—78; clin. fellow ophthalmology Harvard Med. Sch., Boston, 1977—78; fellow vitreoretinal diseases Bascom Palmer Eye Inst. Univ. Miami, 1978—79; asst. prof. clin. ophthalmology Cornell U. Med. Coll., NYC, 1979—81, asst. prof. ophthalmology, 1981—84, assoc. prof. clin. ophthalmology, 1984—87, assoc. prof. clin. ophthalmology (with tenure), 1987—92, prof. ophthalmology, 1993—94; Edward S. Harkness prof. and chmn. ophthalmology Columbia U., NYC, 1995—; asst. attending in ophthalmology The NY Hosp., 1979—84, assoc. attending in ophthalmology, 1984—92, attending in ophthalmology, 1993—94; cons. in ophthalmology Meml. Sloan Kettering Cancer Ctr., NYC, 1991—94; sr. attending in ophthalmology St. Luke's Roosevelt Hosp. Ctr., NYC, 1994—; dir. and chief of svc. ophthalmology NY Presbyterian Hosp. - Columbia Campus, 1996—. Named one of Medical Marvels, New York Mag., 2006; recipient Alvin M. Behrens award ophthalmology, Columbia U., 1997, John Milton McLean medal, Cornell U. Med. Coll., 1993, G.B. Bietti Internat. Found. award, Rome, 1993, Scientific Achievement award, Escalon, Inc., NJ, 1993. Fellow: Am. Acad. Ophthalmology (Sr. Honor award 1998); mem.: The Macula Soc., The Vitreous Soc. (W.H. Helmerich III award 1998), Club Jules Gonin (Hermann Wacker prize 1992), The Retina Soc., Pan Am. Assn. Ophthalmology, Assn. Rsch. Vision and Ophthalmology, Rsch. to Prevent Blindness (assoc.), Am. Eye Study Club, Am. Soc. Ophthalmic Ultrasound, Chinese Am. Ophthalmology Soc., NY Soc. Clin. Ophthalmology, NY State Med. Soc., Chinese Am. Med. Soc. (Scientific Achievement award 1999), Bascom Palmer Alumni Assn., Mass. Eye & Ear Alumni Assn., Columbia P & S Alumni Assn., Alpha Omega Alpha. Achievements include patents for method and apparatus for treatment of complicated retinal detachments, patent number 5,037,384 issued 1991. Office: Dept Ophthalmology Edward S Harkness Eye Inst 635 West 165th St New York NY 10032 Office Phone: 212-305-2725. Office Fax: 212-305-5962.

CHANG, STEVE, internet security company executive; BS in Applied Math., Fu-Zen Cath. Univ., Taiwan; MS in Computer Sci., Lehigh U. Engr. Hewlett Packard; founder Asia Tek, Inc., Taiwan; founder, chmn. Trend Micro, Calif., 1988—, CEO Calif., 1988—2004. Named in FORTUNE Mag., 1996, Asia Innovator of the Yr., Asia Bus. Leader awards, 2004; named one of 25 Movers and Shakers, ZDNet Asia, 2001; recipient Innovator of Yr. award, EDN Asia Mag., 1996, Stars of Asia award, Bus. Week Mag., 1997, 1998. Office: Trend Micro Inc Odakyy So Tower 10th Fl 2-2-1 Yoyogi Shibuya-ku Tokyo 1S1-8583 Japan also: Trend Micro Inc 10101 N De Anza Blvd Cupertino CA 95014

CHANG, SUN-YUNG ALICE, mathematics professor; b. Ci-an, China, Mar. 24, 1948; came to U.S., 1970; d. Fann Chang and Li-Ching Chen; m. Paul Chien-Ping Yang, Mar. 24, 1973; children: Ray Yang, Lusann Yang. BS, Nat. Taiwan U., 1970; PhD, U. Calif., Berkeley, 1974. Asst. prof. math. U. Md., College Park, 1977-79; prof. UCLA, 1981—, Princeton U., 1998—. Speaker Internat. Congress of Math., 1986, 2002. Sloan Found. fellow, 1977, 78; Guggenheim fellow, 1999. Mem. Am. Math. Soc. (v.p. 1989, 90, Ruth Lyttle Satter prize 1995), Am. Women in Math. Office: Princeton Univ/Dept Math Fine Hall Washington Rd Princeton NJ 08544-1000 Home Phone: 609-688-0895; Office Phone: 609-258-5114. Business E-Mail: chang@math.princeton.edu.

CHANG, SUSAN MARINA, neuroscientist; d. Charmaine Zelia and Kenneth Winston Chang; m. Douglas George Wilkinson, June 11, 1983; children: Marina Margaret Wilkinson, Sean Robert Wilkinson. MD, U. BC, Can., 1985. Attending physician U. Calif., San Francisco, 1993—, prof., 2004—, dir. divsn. neuro-oncology, 2005—. Achievements include research in neuro-oncology. Office Phone: 415-353-2966.

CHANG, SYLVIA TAN, health facility administrator, educator; b. Bandung, Indonesia, Dec. 18, 1940; came to U.S., 1963. d. Philip Harry and Lydia Shui-Yu (Ou) Tan; m. Belden Shiu-Wah Chang, Aug. 30, 1964 (dec. Aug. 1997); children: Donald Steven, Janice May. Diploma in nursing, Rumah Sakit Advent Indonesia, 1960; BS, Philippine Union Coll., 1962; MS, Loma Linda U., 1967; PhD, Columbia Pacific U., 1987. Cert. RN, PHN, ACLS, BLS instr., cmty. first aid instr., IV, TPN, blood withdrawal. Head nurse Rumah Sakit Advent, Bandung, Indonesia, 1960—61; critical care, spl. duty and medicine nurse, team leader White Meml. Med. Ctr., LA, 1963—64; nursing coord. Loma Linda U. Med. Ctr., 1964—68; team leader, critical care nurse, relief head nurse Pomona Valley Hosp. Med. Ctr., Calif., 1966—67; evening supr. Loma Linda U. Med. Ctr., 1967—69, night supr., 1969—79, adminstrv. supr., 1979—94; sr. faculty Columbia Pacific U., San Rafael, Calif., 1986—94; dir. health svc. La Sierra U., Riverside, Calif., 1988—. Site coord. Health Fair Expo La Sierra U., 1988-89; adv. coun. Family Planning Clinic, Riverside, 1988-94; blood and bone marrow drive coord. La Sierra U., 1988—. Counselor Pathfinder Club Campus Hill Ch., Loma Linda, 1979-85, crafts instr., 1979-85, music dir., 1979-85; asst. organist U. Ch., 1982-88. Named one of Women of Achievement YWCA, Greater Riverside C. of C., The Press Enterprise, 1991, 2000, Safety Coord. of Yr. La Sierra U., 1995. Mem. Am. Coll. Health Assn., Pacific Coast Coll. Health Assn., Adventist Student Pers. Assn., Sigma Theta Tau. Republican. Seventh-day Adventist. Avocations: music, travel, collecting coins, shells and jade carvings. Home: 1025 Crestbrook Dr Riverside CA 92506-5662 Office: 4500 Riverwalk Pkwy Riverside CA 92515-8247 Home Phone: 951-780-6958; Office Phone: 951-785-2200. Business E-Mail: schang@lasierra.edu.

CHANG, TED T., chemist; b. Tainan, Taiwan, Oct. 6, 1935; arrived in U.S., 1961; s. Shei-huei and Ou-chiu Chang; m. Kay H. Hsu, Jan. 10, 1960; children: Grace, Susan, Diana. BS, Nat. Taiwan U., Taipei, 1957; MS, U. Va., 1963, PhD, 1965; postgrad., Calif. Inst. Tech., 1965—66. Lectr. Nat. Cheng-Kung U., Tainan, 1959—61; rsch. chemist Am. Cyanamid, Stamford, Conn., 1966—71, prin. rsch. scientist, 1979—86; group leader Wyeth Labs., Radnor, Pa., 1971—79; assoc. rsch. fellow Am. Cyanamid/Cytec, Stamford, 1986—92; rsch. fellow Cytec Industries, Stamford, 1992—. Tech. expert to China UN, 1984. Contbr. more than 50 articles to profl. publs. Mem.: Chinese Am. Soc. Mass Spectrometry (pres. 1981—98, hon. permanent pres. 1998), Am. Soc. Mass Spectrometry, Am. Chem. Soc. (mem. U.S. delegation to Sino-Japan conf. 1987). Achievements include research in mass spectrometry, polymer analysis, ionic liquids analysis, electrochemistry, colorimetry and atomic absorption spectroscopy; introduced tandem analytical techniques of TGA-GC-MS and TLC-FAB-MS. Home: 157 Dogwood Ln Stamford CT 06903 Office: Cytec Industries 1937 W Main St Stamford CT 06904 Office Phone: 203-321-2341. E-mail: ted.chang@cytec.com.

CHANG, THOMAS MING SWI, research scientist, biotechnologist, educator; b. Swatow, Kwantang, China, Apr. 8, 1933; arrived in Can., 1952; m. Lancy Yuk Lan Jin, June 21, 1958; children: Harvey, Victor, Christine, Sandra. BSc, McGill U., Montreal, Que., Can., 1957, MD, CM, 1961, PhD, 1965. Intern Montreal Gen. Hosp., 1961-62; rsch. fellow depts. physiology and chemistry McGill U., 1962-65, asst. prof. physiology, 1966-69, assoc. prof., 1969-72, prof. physiology, 1972—, dir. artificial organs rsch. unit, 1975-79, prof. medicine, 1975—, dir. Artificial Cells and Organs Rsch. Ctr., 1979—, assoc. Dept. Chem. Engring., 1985—2002, assoc. Dept. Chemistry, 1986—2001, prof. biomed. engring., 1990—, dir. MSSS-FRSQ Rsch. Group (d'equipe) on Blood Sub. in Transfusion Medicine, 2002—; lab. and clin. rschr. med. scis., biotech., biomed. engring. Montreal, 1962—. Mem. staff Royal Victoria Hosp.; hon. staff Montreal Chinese Hosp., 1970-, cons., 1970-; fellow Med. Rsch. Coun., 1962-65, scholar, 1965-68, career investigator, 1968-99; hon. prof. Nankai U., 1983—. Author: Artificial Cells, 1972, Biomedical Application of Immobilized Enzymes and Proteins, Vols. I and II, 1977, Artificial Kidney, Artificial Liver and Artificial Cells, 1978, Hemoperfusion-Kidney and Liver Supports and Detoxification, 1980, Hemoperfusion, 1981, Past, Present and Future of Artificial Organs, 1983, Microencapsulation and Artificial Cells, 1984, Hemoperfusion and Artificial Organs, 1985, Blood Substitutes, 1988, Blood Substitutes and Oxygen Carriers, 1993, Blood Substitutes: Principles, Methods, Products & Clinical Trials, Vol. I, 1997, II, 1998, Artificial Cells, 2007; editor-in-chief: Artificial Cells, Blood Substitutes and Biotechnology; serial editor: Regenerative Medicine, Artificial Cells & Nanomedicine, 2006-; sect. editor: Internat. Jour. Artificial Organs, 1977—, Trans. Am. Soc. Artificial Organs, 1977-2001; assoc. editor: Biotechnology Ann. Rev., 1995—; mem. editl. bd. Jour. Biomaterial Med. Devel. and Orgn., 1972-87, Jour. Membrane Sci., 1975-92, Jour. Bioengring., 1975-79, Jour. Enzyme and Microbial Tech., 1978-86. Recipient Decorated officer, Order of Can., 1992—, Can. 125th Confereration medal, 1993, Queen Elizabeth Jubilee medal, 2002. Fellow Royal Coll. Physicians Can., Royal Soc. Can.; mem. Internat. Soc. Artificial Organs (trustee 1982-87, 89-92, congress pres. 1991, pres. 1994-96, immediate past pres. 1996-98), Can. Soc. Artificial Organs (pres. 1980-82), Internat. Soc. Artificial Cells, Blood Substitutes and Biotech. (hon. pres. 1990—, hon. congress pres. 1994, 97, 2001), Internat. Symposium Blood Substitutes (hon. pres. 2003—), Internat. Soc. Microencapsulations (hon.). Achievements include invention of artificial cells and blood substitutes. Office: McGill U Artificial Cells and Organs Rsch Ctr 3655 Drummond St Rm 1004 Montreal PQ Canada H3G 1Y6 Business E-Mail: artcell.med@mcgill.ca.

CHANG, VICTOR TSU-SHIH, oncologist, researcher, educator; b. Queens, NY, Nov. 28, 1956; s. M.H. and C.H. (Chu) C. SB/SM in Chem. Engring., MIT, 1979; MD in Physiology with honors, NYU, 1983. Diplomate Nat. Bd. Med. Examiners, Am. Bd. Internal Medicine, Am. Bd. Hospice Palliative Medicine. Faculty scholar Project Death in Am.; intern Johns Hopkins Hosp., Balt., 1983—84; rsch. assoc. Howard Hughes Med. Inst., Balt., 1984—85; intern, resident Good Samaritan Hosp., Balt., 1985—87, chief resident, 1987—88; fellow hematology-oncology Cornell U. Med. Coll., NYC, 1988—91, fellow clin. pharmacology, 1991—92; fellow cancer pain Meml. Sloan Kettering Cancer Ctr., NYC, 1992—93; asst. profl. clin. medicine U. Medicine and Dentistry N.J., N.J. Med. Sch., Newark, 1993—2001, assoc. prof., 2001—; staff physician East Orange VA Med. Ctr., NJ, 1993—; faculty scholar Project Death in Am. Open Soc. Inst., 2000. Mem. Am. Soc. Clin. Oncology, Am. Pain Soc., Am. Soc. Hematology, Eastern Coop. Oncology Group (pain and symptom subcom. 1994—), Chinese Am. Med. Soc. (bd. dirs. 1992-96), Radiation Therapy Oncology Group, Chinese Alumni MIT (bd. dirs. 1989-91, newsletter contbr. 1990-92). Avocations: music, history.

CHANG, WALTER TUCK, SR., draftsman, real estate agent, religious studies educator; b. Honolulu, Feb. 16, 1920; s. Awai Abner and Clara Pa'a auao (Fairman) C.; m. Rita AnaMarie Yee Chang, Aug. 16, 1950 (div. June 1959); children: Walter Tuck Jr., Nani; m. Mercedes Arroyo Chang, June 15, 1961 (div. June 1973); m. Evelyn Show Chiao Huang, Aug. 25, 1973. BA in Indsl. Arts with honors, Tchr.'s credential, San Jose State U., 1945; postgrad. in trade and industry edn. and adminstrn., U. Calif., Berkeley, 1949—55; MA in Edn. and Adminstrn., San Francisco State U., 1959; postgrad. in elem. sch. adminstrn. and supv. of practice tchrs., U. Hawaii, 1959-64; postgrad. in indsl. arts and vocat. edn., U. Md., 1967-68. Gen. secondary credential, Calif., spl. subject supervision vocat. class A, spl. subject supervision vocat. class C1, spl. secondary life diploma in indsl. arts, secondary sch. adminstrn., supervision secondary sch. tchrs., Calif., spl. secondary life diploma in trade industry; profl. secondary cert. in indsl. arts, Hawaii. Drafting apprenticeship engring. and estimation dept. Hawaiian Elec. Co., Honolulu, 1937-39; journeyman machinist, leadman, nat. war manpower job instr. Joshua Hendy Iron Works, Sunnyvale, Calif., 1942-45; vocat. instr. San Jose State U., 1942-45; automotive machinist Garden City Sales and Svc. Co., San Jose, Calif., 1945-46; journeyman machinist Oliver M. Johnson Machine Shop, San Jose, Calif., 1946; machinist Food Machine Corp., San Jose, Calif., 1946; machinist, tool maker Ames Aero. Lab., NASA, Moffet Field, Calif., 1946-51; adult evening vocat. instr. Leland Evening H.S., San Jose, 1951; vocat. inst., supr., driver edn., tng. John Swett Union H.S., Crockett, Calif., 1951-59; journeyman machinist Oliver United Filters Inc., Oakland, Calif., 1952-53; vocat. dir., night prin. John Swett Union H.S., Crockett, Calif., 1952-59; indsl. arts, English, World Hist. instr. McKinley H.S., Honolulu, 1959-62; indsl. arts metal works instr. Kailua H.S., Oahu, 1962; indsl. arts tchr. edn. instr., supr. indsl. arts student tchrs. U. Hawaii Coll. Edn. Manoa Campus, Honolulu, 1962-64; drafting instr. archtl. engring., electronics and metals tech., auto-cad, supr. driver edn. tng. Kamehameha Schs., Honolulu, 1964-90. Built over 1,000 engines for liberty, cargo steam ships, minesweepers during WWII, 1942-45. Author: Getting Started With the Calipro, 1965, The Kidjel Ratio Concept in Designing and Drafting. Hawaiian musician entertainer ARC, Vet. Hosps. San Francisco Bay Area, 1942-49; Sunday Sch. tchr. Hayward (Calif.) Missionary Bapt. Ch., 1958-59, Missionary Bapt. Chs. on Oahu, Hawaii, 1960—; v.p. PTA of New Keolu Elem. Sch., 1961-62, v.p. monthly meetings; designed and built 3 chs. and 2 parsonages, Calif. and Hawaii; support Missionary Bapt. Chs. and Missions, U.S., Can., South Am., The Philippines, Japan, China, India, Africa, Russia, Jerusalem, 1958—. Recipient Nat. Merit Honor Soc. award, 1938, Best Auto-CAD Architecture in Hawaii award Sausilito Software, 1985, Nat. Hon. Edn. Fraternity Pin award Phi Delta Kappa, 1962, award Solid Wood Poi Pounder, Best Designed 4 Million Dollar Indsl. Arts Complex in Hawaii award Kamehameha Schs.; named Most Outstanding Alumni in field of edn., Kamahameha Alumni Assn., Honolulu, 1984. Mem. Oahu Indsl. Arts Tchrs. Assn. (exec. bd. 1959, v.p. in charge of monthly workshops 1960, pres. 1961), Epsilon Pi Tau, Kappa Delta Pi. Achievements include aiding in perfection of first working guided missile; implemented Unified Phonics into Keola Pub. Elem. Sch. curriculum. Avocations: photography, raising gold fish, travel, reading books, sports. Home: 94-1015 Uke'e Pl Waipahu HI 96797-4272

CHANG, WEI TSUN, music educator; s. Joel and Suzana Chang; m. Seanad Dunigan. MusB Violin Performance, Ind. U. Bloomington, 1988; MusM Chamber Music, N.C. Sch. Arts, 1991; D Music Arts in Violin Performance, Mich. State U., 2006. Artist-in-residence Alma Coll., Mich., 1995—2002; assoc. prof. violin Tenn. Technol. U., Cookeville, 2002—. Concertmaster Bryan Symphony Orch., Cookeville, Tenn., 2002—, Midland Symphony Orch., Mich., 1998—2002, West Shore Symphony, Muskegon, Mich., 1997—99, Alma Symphony, 1995—2002; soloist L'Orchestre de Chambre Antonio Vivaldi, Paris, 1997—2002, L'Orchestra de Chambre Francais Alberic Magnard, Spain. Author: (textbook) Music Appreciation: A Shared Experience; musician: (performance) French Chamber Orch., Mozart Bicentennial, Accueil Musical, 2006. Recipient Tchg. Innovation award, Bd. Regents Distance Edn. Tenn., 2005. Mem.: Am. Fedn. Musicians. Achievements include being fluent in five languages: Chinese, Portuguese, Spanish, French, and English; first to premier an American Composition at Fondation Danoise in Paris, France; develop of a hybrid course in music using multiple intelligence; teach music appreciation course using tablet PC; research in developing a humanities course using multiple intelligence. Avocations: painting, chess, travel, language, philosophy. Office: Tenn Tech U Box 5045 Cookeville TN 38505 Home Phone: 931-528-7482; Office Phone: 931-372-3714. Office Fax: 931-372-6279; Home Fax: 931-528-7482. Personal E-mail: chang1wt@gmail.com. E-mail: wtchang@tntech.edu.

CHANG, WILLIAM SHEN CHIE, electrical engineering educator; b. Nantung, Jiangsu, China, Apr. 4, 1931; s. Tung Wu and Phoebe Y.S. (Chow) C.; m. Margaret Huachen Kwei, Nov. 26, 1955; children: Helen Nai-yee, Hugh Nai-hun, Hedy Nai-lin. BSE, U. Mich., 1952, MSE, 1953; PhD, Brown U., 1957. Lectr., rsch. assoc. in elec. engring. Stanford (Calif.) U., 1957-59; asst. prof. elec. engring. Ohio State U., 1959-62, assoc. prof., 1962-65; prof. dept. elec. engring. Washington U., St. Louis, 1965—79, chmn. dept., 1965-71, dir. Applied Electronic Scis. Lab., 1971-79, Samuel Sachs prof. elec. engring., 1976-79; prof. dept. elec. and computer engring. U. Calif., San Diego, 1979—, chmn. dept., 1993-96. Author: Principles of

Quantum Electronics, 1969, RF Photonic Technology in Optical Fiber Links, 2002, Principles of Lasers and Optics, 2005; Contbr. articles to profl. jours. Named Samuel Sachs Prof., Washington U., St. Louis; recipient Disting. Prof. Achievement award, U. Mich., Ann Arbor. Fellow: IEEE, Am. Optical Soc.; mem.: Am. Phys. Soc. Achievements include research in quantum electronics and guided wave optics. Home: 12676 Caminito Radiante San Diego CA 92130 Office: U Calif San Diego MS-0407 Dept Elec/Computer Engring La Jolla CA 92093-0407 Office Phone: 858-534-2737. Business E-Mail: wchang@ucsd.edu.

CHANG, WILLIAM ZHI-MING, research scientist; b. Shanghai, June 6, 1955; s. Yinfang Chang and Shanlin Chen; m. Sandra Schlachter, Aug., 1987; 1 child, Caroline Dagmar. BS, U. So. Calif., 1984, MS, 1985, PhD, 1992. Rsch. assoc. U. So. Calif., LA, 1992-93; rsch. scientist Max Planck Soc. x-ray optics group Friedrich-Schiller U., Jena, Germany, 1993-96; sr. scientist advanced rsch. and applications corp. Aracor, Sunnyvale, Calif., 1996—. Contbr. articles to profl. jours. and books. Disting. scholar Microbeam Analysis Soc., San Jose, Calif., 1991, Boston, 1992. Mem. Optical Soc. Am. Achievements include patents in field. Avocations: opera, calligraphy. Home: 8592 Peachtree Ave Newark CA 94560-3342 Office: Rapiscan Sys HEIC 520 Almanor Ave Sunnyvale CA 94085-3533 Office Phone: 408-961-9722. Personal E-mail: wchang@rapiscansystems.com.

CHANG, WON, economist; b. Seoul, Republic of Korea, Jan. 7, 1969; s. Charlie H.J. Chang and Moon Sook Uhm. BA, NYU, 1992; PhD, Columbia U., 1999. Cons. The World Bank, Washington, 1997—2000; internat. economist U.S. Dept. Treasury, Washington, 2000—. Contbr. articles to profl. jours. Achievements include research in Regional Integration Impact and Analysis. Personal E-mail: wchang_264@msn.com. E-mail: won.chang@do.treas.gov.

CHANG, WUNG, academic administrator, investment advisor, educator; b. Kangke Pyongbuk, Republic of Korea, Apr. 24, 1942; came to US, 1973; s. Jae Sun and Key Bok (Yoo) C.; m. Han Jin Yung, Nov. 14, 1970; children: Min, Won. *Wife, Han Jin Chang, is an RN and nurse manager at Temple Community Hospital, Los Angeles. Son, Min Chang, is an attorney at law, with an LLM and JD from Duke Law School. Min's wife, June (Kim) Chang, is a pharmacist with a PharmD from University of the Pacific, School of Pharmacy. Son, Won Chang, is an attorney at law, with a JD from Cornell Law School. Won's wife, Jenny (Ko) Chang, is also an attorney at law, with a JD from University of California Berkeley Law School.* MPA, Yon-Sei U., 1971; PhD in Bus. Mgmt., Union U., 1983; PhD in Theology, Yuin U., 2006. Editor-in-chief Korea Photo Times, Seoul, 1970—73; sec.-gen. Wum Found., LA, 1986—87; sr. analyst Pacific Rsch. Inst., LA, 1988—92; advisor Korea Travel News, Seoul, 1988—93; contr. US Top Capital Corp., LA, 1991—2000; sr. adv., chmn. Hypnosis Career Coll., 2002—05; chancellor Lordland U., 2005—06; chmn. NeoWorld Found. and NeoWorld Rsch. Inst., 2006—. Vice chmn. Mid-Wilshire Tng. Ctr. divsn. Adult and Career Edn., LA Unified Sch. Dist. Adv. Coun., 1994—96; vol. lectr. The Korean Sr. Citizens Assn. of San Fernando Valley Coll., 1995—96; co-chmn. Internat. Rsch. Inst. Govt. and Pub. Adminstrn., LA, 1995—99; commentator Radio Korea, USA, 1997—2000; sr. advisor So. Calif.-Korean Fedn. Coun. of No. Korea, 1998—2001; adv. mem. So. Calif.-Korean Assn. of Pyung-An-Book-Do Province, 1999—. Mem. Rep. Presdl. Adv. Commn., Washington, 1991; active Rep. Senatorial Com., Washington, 1991; nat. campaign advisor Rep. Senatorial Inner Circle, Washington, 1995—; chmn. bd. dirs. Kang I. Lee Found., Inc., 2002-05. Capt. Korean Army, 1966-70. Recipient Presdl. Order of Merit, 1991, Rep. Presdl. Task Force Wall of Honor, 1992, Rep. Senatorial medal of freedom, 2002. Avocations: fishing, swimming, music, baseball. Home: 7625 Radford Ave North Hollywood CA 91605-2858 Personal E-mail: changwung@gmail.com, ushanchang@yahoo.com, drchangonlive@gmail.com.

CHANG, YING CHIH, engineering educator, researcher; d. Chau-Ting and Li-Yen Chang. PhD, Stanford U., 1998. Sr. engr. Maxmedia Calif. (Maxtor) Corp., San Jose, Calif., 1998; postdoctor Stanford (Calif.) U./ Affymetric Corp., 1998—99; prof. U. Calif., Irvine, 1999—2003; scientist Palo Alto Rsch. Ctr., Calif.; rsch. fellow Genomics Rsch. Ctr., Academia Sinica, Taipei, Taiwan, 2004—. Contbr. articles to profl. jours. (Engr. award, 1998). Fellow, Max Planck Inst., 1997; grantee, U. Calif., 2000—02, 2002—03. Mem.: AIChE, Materials Rsch. Soc., No. Am. Taiwanese Engineers Assn. (corr.; biotech. group leader 2002—03), Stanford Alumni Assn. (life). Achievements include patents for biochip and materials design.

CHANG, YING-LAN, technologist; b. ChangHua, Taiwan, Dec. 20, 1963; d. Ching-Shu Chang; m. I-Hsing Tan, July 29, 1990; children: Whitney Tan, Kevin Tan. BS, Nat. Tsing-Hua U., Shin-Chu, Taiwan, 1986; MS, Princeton U., NJ, 1991; PhD, U. Calif., Santa Barbara, 1995. Project scientist Hewlett Packard Co., Palo Alto, Calif., 1995—99, Agilent Techs. Co., Palo Alto, 1999—2005; v.p. platform devel. Nanomix, Inc., Emeryville, Calif., 2005—. Com. mem. Electrochem. Soc., Pennington, NJ, 2004—, Elec. Material Symposium, Sunnyvale, Calif., 2001—04. Contbr. articles to profl. jours. Achievements include patents in field. Office: Nanomix Inc 5980 Horton St Ste 600 Emeryville CA 94608 Home Phone: 408-996-8771; Office Phone: 510-428-5332. Office Fax: 510-658-0425. Personal E-mail: yinglan.chang@gmail.com. E-mail: ylchang@nano.com.

CHANG, YOON IL, nuclear engineer; b. Seoul, Korea, Apr. 12, 1942; came to U.S., 1965; s. Paul Kun and In Sil (Hahn) C.; m. Ok Ja Kim, Dec. 19, 1966; children: Alice, Dennis, Eugene. BS in Nuclear Engring., Seoul Nat. U., 1964; ME, Tex. A & M U., 1967; PhD, U. Mich., 1971; MBA, U. Chgo., 1983. Mgr. spl. projects Nuclear Assurance Corp., Atlanta, 1971-74; asst. nuclear engr. Argonne (Ill.) Nat. Lab., 1974-76, group leader, 1976-77, sect. head, 1977-78, assoc. divsn. dir., 1978-84, gen. mgr. IFR program, 1984-94, dep. assoc. lab. dir. for engring. rsch., 1994—98, assoc. lab. dir. for engring. rsch., 1998—2002, interim lab. dir., 1999—2001, assoc. lab. dir. at large, 2002—. Recipient E. O. Lawrence award U.S. Dept. Energy, 1994. Fellow Am. Nuclear Soc. (Walker Cisler award 1997—). Home: 2020 Palmer Dr Naperville IL 60564-5664 Office: Argonne Nat Lab 9700 Cass Ave Argonne IL 60439-4803 Home Phone: 630-305-8792; Office Phone: 630-252-4856. E-mail: ychang@anl.gov.

CHANGERI, MICHAEL DENNIS, contractor, protective services official; b. Lakewood, Ohio, June 9, 1967; s. Louis and Francis Mary; m. Traci Lynn Johnson, Sept. 27, 1997; children: Michael, Hannah. Grad. in Bldg. Engring., Westside Inst. Tech., Cleve., 2003. Cert. pipefitter Ohio State Apprenticeship Coun., police officer Ohio Peace Officer Tng. Commn. V.p. sales ETC Cards and Gifts Airworks Balloons, Brooklyn, 1977—99; customer svc. rep. Key Bank, Brooklyn, 1994—97; pipefitter GM, Parma, Ohio, 1997—. Spl. officer City Bklyn. Police Dept., 2005—. Dist. res. mem. Boy Scouts Am., 2000—; asst. security officer Cmty. Emergency Response Team, Brooklyn, Ohio, 2005—. Named Eagle Scout, Boy Scouts Am., 1985. Mem.: Nat. Rifle Assn.

CHANG-MOTA, ROBERTO, electrical engineer; b. Caracas, Venezuela, Dec. 28, 1935; arrived in US, 1948; s. Roberto W. and Mary C. (Mota) Chang; m. Alicia Santamaria-Gonzales, May 4, 1968; children: Roberto Ignacio, Roxana Ivette, Ricardo Ignacio. D Elec. Engring., U. Ctrl. Venezuela, 1960; MS, U. Ill., 1962; AR, Harvard U., 1970; PhD, UCLA, 1983. Dir. sch. engring., prof. Ctrl. U., Caracas, 1964—69; prof., dean Simon Bolivar U., Caracas, 1971—77; pres. Colegio de Ingenieros de Venezuela, Caracas, 1974—79; dir. Venezuelan Power Co., Caracas, 1974—79; pres. L.Am. Orgn. Engring., Quito, Ecuador, 1977—79, Corporoil, Caracas, 1981—85, Audio Interface Corp., Caracas, 1983—96; v.p. ESCA Corp., Caracas, 1991—95; pres. 3R Corp., Caracas, 1995—; CEO, pres. Cositel Corp., 2002—, SSS Corp., 2002—; pres. 35 Corp., 2002, Inti Corp., Caracas. Spl. cons. Venezuelan Navy and Army, 1971-75, Venezuelan Congress, 1989-96; mem. tech. com. Venezuelan Supreme Election Coun., 1971-81, exec. dir., 1981-82, gen. dir., 1982-97; gen. dir. Consejo Nacional Electoral, 1991-98; cons. Ministry of Interior, 1990; v.p. Electronic Cir. Corp., 1991-2000; trustee Simon Bolivar U., 1985-98; bd. dirs. Sistemas y Procesos Automatizados, SEPAI Corp. Gen. dir. Nat. Election Coun., 1985-99; pres. Sistemas Electorales y Procesos Automatizados, 2001. Mem. IEEE, Am. Soc. Engring. Edn., Venezuelan Soc. Elec. and Mech. Engring. (pres. 1972-73), Instn. Elec. Engrs., Puerto Azul Club, Playa Pintada Club, Caracas Racquet Club. Roman Catholic. Home: 7861 SW 180th St Miami FL 33157-6216 Office: Prados del Este Calle Colon Quinta Cumana Caracas 1080 Venezuela Personal E-mail: yasifu@gmail.com.

CHANG-ROBBINS, JOYCE, diversified financial services company executive; b. Peoria, Ill., May 22, 1965; m. David I. Robbins; children: Matthew, Isabel. Degree, Columbia U., 1986; M in Pub. Affairs, Princeton U., Woodrow Wilson Sch. Pub. and Internat. Affairs, 1990. Intern Ms. Magazine; cons. US AID, Manila, Philippines, Amman, Jordan, New Delhi; emerging mktg. strategist Saloman Brothers, 1990—96; mng. dir., global head of internat. emerging markets rsch. Merrill Lynch, 1996—99; mng. dir., global head fgn. exchange, emerging markets and commodities rsch. group JP Morgan Chase & Co., NY, 1999—. Named Number One Emerging Markets Strategist, Institutional Investor, 2007; named one of 50 Women to Watch, Wall Street Journal, 2005, 20 Most Influential Women, Newsweek, 2006. Office: JP Morgan Chase & Co 270 Park Ave New York NY 10017-2014

CHANG-YONG, NAM, engineer, researcher; BE in Metall. Engring., Korea U., Seoul, 1999; MS in Materials Sci. & Engring., Korea Advanced Inst. Sci. & Tech., Daejon, 2001; PhD in Materials Sci. & Engring. with distinction, U. Pa., Phila., 2007. Vis. rsch. asst., divsn. engring. Brown U., Providence, 2001; commd. rschr. Korea Inst. Sci. & Tech., Seoul, 2001—02; rsch. assoc. Brookhaven Nat. Lab., Upton, NY, 2007—. Contbr. articles to profl. jours. Sgt. Republic of Korea Army, 1995—97, Kangwon Province. Mem.: Minerals, Metals and Materials Soc., Internat. Soc. Optical Engring., Am. Phys. Soc., Materials Rsch. Soc. Achievements include research in th growth mechanism in GaN nanowires; focused ion beam contact patterning to GaN nanowires; NEMS properties in GaN nanowires. Avocations: basketball, golf.

CHANIN, BERNARD, lawyer; b. Phila., Oct. 12, 1942; s. Benjamin and Irene (Holutin) C. BA, U. Pa., 1962, LLB cum laude, 1965. Bar: Pa. 1965, U.S. Supreme Ct. 1976. Law clk. to Samuel J. Roberts, Assoc. Justice Supreme Ct. Pa., Phila., 1965-66; ptnr. Wolf, Block, Schorr & Solis-Cohen, Phila., 1966—. Judge pro tem Phila. Ct. Common Pleas; mem. comml., constrn. and complex case panels Am. Arbitration Assn. Mem. ABA, Pa. Bar Assn., Phila. Bar Assn., Order of the Coif. Office: Wolf Block Schorr & Solis-Cohen 1650 Arch St Fl 22 Philadelphia PA 19103-2097 Office Phone: 215-977-2396. Business E-Mail: bchanin@wolfblock.com.

CHANIN, MICHAEL HENRY, lawyer; b. Atlanta, Nov. 11, 1943; s. Henry and Herma Irene (Blumenthal) C.; m. Margaret L. Jennings, June 15, 1968; children: Herma Louise, Richard Henry, Patrick Jennings. AB, U. N.C., 1965; JD, Emory U., 1968. Bar: Ga. 1968, D.C. 1981. Dir. So. Ctr. for Studies in Pub. Policy, Atlanta, 1968-69; asst. and acting legal officer 1st Coast Guard Dist., Boston, 1969-72; atty. Powell, Goldstein Frazer & Murphy, Atlanta, 1972-77; spl. asst. to sec. U.S. Dept. Commerce, Washington, 1977-78; dep. asst. to pres. The White House, Washington, 1978-81; ptnr. Powell, Goldstein LLP, Washington, 1981—. Served to lt. USCGR, 1969-72. Mem. ABA, D.C. Bar Assn., State Bar Ga. Democrat. Office: Powell Goldstein LLP 901 New York Ave NW Fl 3 Washington DC 20001-4432 Business E-Mail: mchanin@pogolaw.com.

CHANNING, CAROL, actress; b. Seattle, Jan. 31, 1921; d. George Channing and Adelaide (Glaser) C.; m. Charles F. Lowe, Sept. 5, 1956 (div.); 1 son, Channing George. Student, Bennington Coll. Actress: (Broadway prodns.) No for an Answer, 1941, Let's Face It, 1941, Proof Through the Night, 1942, So Proudly We Hail, Lend an Ear, 1948 (Theatre World award, Critic's Circle award), Gentlemen Prefer Blondes, 1949, 51-53, Wonderful Town, 1953, Pygmalian, 1953, The Vamp, 1955, Show Business, 1959, Show Girl, 1961, George Burns-Carol Channing Musical Revue, 1962, The Millionairess, 1963, Hello Dolly, 1964-67, also 3 revivals (Tony award for Best Actress, N.Y. Drama Critics Cir. award for Best Actress), Carol Channing and Her Ten Stout-Hearted Men, 1970 (London Critics award), Four on a Garden, 1971, In Cabarets, 1972, Festival at Ford's, 1972, Carol Channing and Her Gentlemen Who Prefer Blondes Revue, 1972, Jerry's Girls, 1984-85, Legends, 1986, (theatre tours) Lorelei, 1973-75, Carol's Broadway Revue, The First Eighty Years Are The Hardest, 2005; (films) First Travelling Saleslady, 1956, Thoroughly Modern Millie, 1967 (Golden Globe award as Best Supporting Actress 1967), Skidoo, 1968, Shinbone Alley (voice), 1971, Sgt. Peppers Lonely Hearts Club Band, 1978, Happily Ever After (voice), 1990, Hans Christian Andersen's Thumbelina (voice), 1994, The Line King: Al Hirschfeld, 1996, Edie & Pen, 1996, others; (TV prodns.) Svengali and the Blonde, Three Men on a Horse, Crescendo; (TV appearances) The Love Boat, 1977, Alice in Wonderland, 1985, Where's Waldo? (voice), 1991, Addams Family (voice), 1992, The Magic School Bus (voice), 1994, The Brave Little Toaster Goes to Mars (voice), 1998, Martha, 2005; host Broadway's Lost Treasures III: The Best of the Tony Awards, 2005; autobiography: Just Lucky I Guess, 2002 Recipient Best Night Club Act award, 1957, 64, Spl. Tony award, 1968, Theatre World award for Bronze medallion City of N.Y., 1978, Lifetime Achievement Tony award, 1995. Christian Scientist. Office: William Morris Agy 1 William Morris Pl Beverly Hills CA 90212

CHANNING, STOCKARD (SUSAN ANTONIA WILLIAMS STOCKARD), actress; b. NYC, Feb. 13, 1944; d. Lester Napier and Mary Alice Stockard; m. Walter Channing, Jr., 1963 (div. 1967); m. Paul Schmidt, 1970 (div. 1976); m. David Debin, 1976 (div. 1980); m. David Rawle, 1982 (div. 1988). Attended, Radcliffe Coll.; BA in History and Lit., Harvard U. Actress movies include Up the Sandbox, 1972, The Fortune, 1975, The Big Bus, 1976, Sweet Revenge, 1977, The Cheap Detective, 1978, Grease, 1978, A Different Approach, 1978, The Fish That Saved Pittsburgh, 1979, Safari 3000, 1982, Without a Trace, 1983, The Men's Club, 1986, Heartburn, 1986, A Time of Destiny, 1988, Staying Together, 1989, Meet the Applegates, 1991, Married To It, 1991, Lunes de Fiel, 1992, Six Degrees of Separation (Acad. award nomination Best Actress), 1993, To Wong Foo, Thanks for Everything! Julie Newmar, 1995, Smoke, 1995, The First Wives Club, 1996, Up Close and Personal, 1996, Moll Flanders, 1996, Edie and Pen, 1997, Twilight, 1998, Lulu on the Bridge (voice), 1998, Practical Magic, 1998, The Venice Project, 1999, Other Voices, 2000, Isn't She Great, 2000, Where the Heart Is, 2000, The Business of Strangers, 2001, Life or Something Like It, 2002, Behind the Red Door, 2002, Bright Young Things, 2003, Le Divorce, 2003, Anything Else, 2003, Must Love Dogs, 2005; TV movies include Girl Most Likely to., 1973, Lucan, 1977, Silent Victory: The Kitty O'Neill Story, 1979, Table Settings, 1984, Not My Kid, 1985, The Room Upstairs, 1987, Echoes in the Darkness, 1987, Tidy Endings, 1988, Perfect Witness, 1989, Lincoln, 1992, David's Mother, 1994, Mr. Willowby's Christmas Tree, 1995, An Unexpected Family, 1996, Lily Dale, 1996, The Prosecutors, 1996, An Unexpected Family, 1996, An Unexpected Life, 1998, The Baby Dance, 1998, The Truth About Jane, 2000, Confessions of an Ugly Stepsister, 2002, The Matthew Shepard Story, 2002 (Emmy Outstanding Supporting Actress in a Miniseries or a Movie, SAG award), Hitler: The Rise of Evil, 2003, The Piano Man's Daughter, 2003, Jack, 2004 (Outstadning Performer in a Children's Spl., Daytime Emmy award, Acad. TV Arts & Scis., 2005); TV series include Sesame Street, 1969, The Stockard Channing Show, 1980, Road to Avonlea, King of the Hill (voice), Batman Beyond (voice), 1999, The West Wing, 2001-06 (Emmy Outstanding Supporting Actress in a Drama Series 2002), Out of Practice, 2005-; actress (plays) A Day in the Death of Joe Egg, 1985 (Tony Actress in a Play, 1985), House of Blue Leaves, Four Baboons Adoring the Sun, The Little Foxes, Hapgood, Women In Mind, The Rink, The Golden Age, The Lion in Winter, They're Playing Our Song, Love Letters; TV mini series A Girl Thing, 2001. Office: ICM c/o Andrea Eastman 40 W 57th St Fl 16 New York NY 10019-4098

CHANNON, CHRISTOPHER T., ophthalmologist; m. Kathy Channon; children: Terence, Brian, Courtney. BA, Queens Coll., Flushing, NY, 1966—71; MD, NY Med. Coll., 1973—76. Diplomate Am. Acad. Ophthalmology, 1982, lic. ophthalmologist Fla. Ophthalmologist St. Lucie Eye Assocs., Ft. Pierce, Fla., 1981—. Grantee Mosby scholar, NY Med. Coll. Fellow: ACS; mem.: Fla. Soc. Ophthalmology, Alpha Omega Alpha. Avocations: travel, exercise. Office: St Lucie Eye Assocs 2201 S 10th St Fort Pierce FL 34950 Office Phone: 772-461-2020. Business E-Mail: info@stlucieeye.com.

CHANOCK, ROBERT MERRITT, pediatrician; b. Chgo., July 8, 1924; married; two children. BS, U. Chgo., 1945, MD, 1947, DSc (hon.), 1977. NRC fellow Children's Hosp., Cin., 1950—52; asst. prof. rsch. pediat. Coll. Medicine, U. Cin., 1954—56; asst. prof. epidemiology Sch. Hygiene and Pub. Health, Johns Hopkins U., 1956—57; surgeon USPHS, 1957—59, head respiratory viruses sect., 1959—61; chief lab. infectious diseases Nat. Inst. Allergy and Infectious Diseases, NIH, Bethesda, Md., 1968—. Nat. Found. Infantile Paralysis fellow, 1951—52; sr. rsch. fellow USPHS, 1956—57; virologist Children's Hosp. D.C., 1957—; mem. Internat. Nomenclature Com. Myxoviruses, 7th and 8th Internat. Microbiol. Congress, Armed Forces Epidemiology Bd., Com. Acute Respiratory Disease, 1960—62; assoc. mem. Com. Influenza, 1963—74; dir. Internat. Ref. Ctr. Lab. Mycroplasms, WHO, 1962; mem. Internat. Com. Nomenclature Bacteria, 1966; clin. prof. Georgetown U., 1970—71; mem. nominating com. NAS, 1979—80; mem. sci. rev. com. Scripps Clin. and Rsch. Found., 1986—89. Recipient E. Mead Johnson award pediatric rsch., 1964, Squibb Gorgas medal, Assn. Mil. Surgeons, 1972, Robert Koch medal, Fed. Republic of Germany, 1981, Virol prize, ICT Internat., 1990, Bristol-Myers Squibb award, Albert B. Sabin Gold medal. Mem. NAS, Soc. Pediat. Rsch., Am. Soc. Microbiology, Am. Epidemiol. Soc., Am. Epidemiology, Am. Pediat. Soc., Am. Soc. Clin. Investigation, Soc. Exptl. Biology and Medicine, Assn. Am. Physicians, Royal Danish Acad. Scis. (fgn. mem.). Office: NIH Inst Allergy Infectious Diseases Lab Infectious Diseases 7 Center Dr Rm 100 Bethesda MD 20817

CHANOS, GEORGE J., former state attorney general; b. Wauwatosa, Wis., Aug. 1958; m. Adriana Escobar Chanos; 1 child, Alexandra. BA in Psychology, UNLV, 1981; JD, U. San Diego, 1985. Assoc. Finley, Kumble, Wagner, Heine, Underberg, Manley, Myerson and Casey, San Diego; ptnr. Chanos, Escobar, Chanos, Las Vegas, 1995—2005; atty. gen. State of Nev., Carson City, 2005—07. Chmn. Nev. Policy Rsch. Inst., 1998. Chmn. bd. dirs. Jr. Achievement of So. Nev., 1997. Republican.*

CHANOS, JAMES S., investment company executive; b. Milwaukee, 1958; BA, Yale U., 1980. Analyst Paine Webber, Gilford Securities, Deutsche Bank; founder Kynikos Associates LP, NYC, 1985—. Office: Kynikos Associates LP 20 W 55th St New York NY 10019 Office Phone: 212-649-0200. Office Fax: 212-649-0269.

CHANSLEY, DEBORAH LYNN, education educator; BSEd, U. Ariz., Tucson, 1975, MEd, 1982. Cert. standard secondary edn. Ariz., cmty. coll. edn. Ariz., 1994. Tchr. Douglas Pub. Schs., Ariz., 1975—77, Tucson Unified Sch. Dist., 1977—80, substitute tchr., tchr., elem. sch. monitor, 1989—92; mem. adj. faculty Pima C.C., Tucson, 1981, 1992—. Temp. scorer NCS Pearson, Tucson, 2002—06. Co-treas. San Rafael Neighborhood Orgn., Tucson, 1988—; election poll worker City of Tucson, Pima County, 2001—; Sunday sch. tchr. Tucson Bapt. Temple, 1983—91. Recipient Faculty Standards Tchg. award, Pima C.C., 2005, Apple award, 2002—03.

CHANYUNGCO, DELLY YANGCO, dean; b. Sept. 25, 1945; BS in Elem. Edn., Philippine Normal Coll., MA in Guidance and Counseling, 1982; PhD in Counseling Psychology, De La Salle U., U. Philippines, 1986. Vocat. placement coord./chief career guidance & placement svcs. Dept. Edn., Culture & Sports, Manila, 1979-86; student svcs. divsn. supr. Marikina Inst. Sci. and Tech., Philippines, 1986—90; internat. student advisor/coord. Truman Coll., Chgo., 1991—96; chief non-immigrant sect. Azulay & Azulay, P.C., 1996—2000; admin. and human resource dir. Azulay, Horn & Seiden, LLC, 2003—05; dean student affairs and employment Northwestern Inst. Health and Tech., Chgo., 2005—. Cons. in field. Vol. leader self-help programs Ravenswood Hosp. and Med. Ctr., Chgo.; vol. counselor APNA GHAR Inc., Chgo.; intake counselor DARE Found. Philippines; vol. cons. ASEAN Regional and Nat. Coun. Welfare and Disabled Persons. Named Outstanding Trainer, Tarlaac Divsn. Pub. Schs., Outstanding SNLP Coord., Dept. Edn., Culture and Sports; recipient Plaque of Recognition, Malaysia Vocational Guidance Assn., Kuala Lumpur, 1982, Plaque of Appreciation, Commonwealth Schs. Commn., Canberra, Australia, 1986, President's award of Recognition, Truman Coll., 1996, Pub. Svc. Merit award, Marikina Dist. Teacher's Club. Mem.: Assn. Am. Women Cmty. Colls., Nat. Notary Assn., Assn. Internat. Educators. Office: Northwestern Inst Health and Tech 4641 N Ashland Chicago IL 60640 E-mail: dchanyungco@sbcglobla.net.

CHAO, ALBERT, chemicals executive; B, Brandeis U., Waltham, Mass.; MBA, Columbia U., NYC. Dep. mng. dir. plastics fabrication bus., Singapore; asst. to chmn. China Gen. Plastics Group; with plastics group Gulf Oil Corp.; with tech. dept. Hercules Inc.; with contr.'s group Mobil Oil Corp.; co-founder Westlake Chem. Corp., 1985, exec. v.p., 1985—96, pres., 1996—, bd. dirs., 2003—, CEO. Bd. dirs. Titan Group. Office: Westlake Chem Corp 2801 Post Oak Blvd Ste 600 Houston TX 77056 Office Phone: 713-960-9111.*

CHAO, ALLEN Y., pharmaceutical executive; m. Lee Hwa-Chao. PhD in Indsl., Physical Pharmacy, Purdue Univ., 1973, DSc (hon.), 2000. Founder Watson Pharm., Inc., Corona, Calif., 1984, CEO, 1985—, chmn., 1996—. Office: Watson Pharm, Inc 311 Bonnie Cir Corona CA 92880 also: Watson Pharm, Inc 360 Mt Kemble Ave PO Box 1953 Morristown NJ 07962*

CHAO, BEI TSE, mechanical engineering educator; b. Soochow, China, Dec. 18, 1918; arrived in U.S., 1948, naturalized, 1962; s. Tse Yu and Yin T. (Yao) C.; m. May Kiang, Feb. 7, 1948; children: Clara, Fred Roberto. BS in Elec. Engring. with highest honor, Nat. Chiao-Tung U., China, 1939; PhD (Boxer Indemnity scholar), Victoria U., Manchester, Eng., 1947. Asst. engr. tool and gage div. Central Machine Works, Kunming, China, 1939-41, asso. engr., 1941-43, mgr. tool and gage div., 1943-45; research asst. U. Ill., Urbana, 1948-50, asst. prof. dept. mech. engring., 1951-53, assoc. prof., 1953-55, prof., 1955-87, prof. emeritus, 1987—, head thermal sci. div., 1971-75, head dept. mech. and indsl. engring., 1975-87; assoc. mem. U. Ill. (Center for Advanced Study), 1963-64. Cons. to industry and govt. agys., 1950-94; vis. Russell S. Springer prof. mech. engring. U. Calif., Berkeley, 1973; mem. reviewing staff Zentralblatt für Mathematik,

Berlin, 1970-82; mem. U.S. Engring. Edn. Del. to Visit People's Republic of China, 1978; mem. adv. screening com. in engring. Fulbright-Hays Awards Program, 1979-81, chmn., 1980, 81; mem. com. U.S. Army basic sci. rsch. NRC, 1980-83; Prince disting. lectr. Ariz. State U., 1984; bd. dirs. Aircraft Gear Corp., 1989-94. Author: Advanced Heat Transfer, 1969; tech. editor Jour. Heat Transfer, 1975-81; mem. adv. editl. bd. Numerical Heat Transfer, 1977-95; mem. hon. edit. bd. Internat. Jour. Heat and Mass Transfer, 1987-97, Internat. Comm. in Heat and Mass Transfer, 1987-97; contbr. numerous articles on mech. engring. to profl. jours. Recipient Outstanding Tchr. award, Ill. Mech. Engring. Alumni, 1978, Max Jakob Meml. award, ASME/Am. Inst. Chem. Engrs., 1983, Tau Beta Pi Daniel C. Drucker eminent faculty award, 1985; Univ. scholar, 1985. Fellow AAAS, ASME (hon.; Blackall award 1957, Heat Transfer award 1971, William T. Ennor Mfg. Tech. award 1992), Am. Soc. Engring. Edn. (Outstanding Tchr. award 1975, Western Electric Fund award 1973, Ralph Coats Roe award 1975, Benjamin Garver Lamme award 1984, Centennial Medallion 1993); mem. Nat. Acad. Engring., Academia Sinica, Chiao-Tung U. Alumni Assn. (pres. Midwest sect. 1975-76), Tau Beta Pi, Pi Tau Sigma (hon.). Home: 101 W Windsor Rd Apt 6103 Urbana IL 61802-6663 Office: Univ Ill 264 Mech Engring Bldg 1206 W Green St Urbana IL 61801-2906 Personal E-mail: btmchao@hotmail.com.

CHAO, CEDRIC C., lawyer; b. Cambridge, Mass., Apr. 9, 1950; BA, Stanford U., 1972; JD, Harvard U., 1977. Bar: Calif. 1977, U.S. Dist. Ct. (no. dist.) Calif. 1977, U.S. Ct. Appeals (9th cir.) 1979, U.S. Supreme Ct. 1988. Law clk.to Hon. William H. Orrick U.S. Dist. Ct. (no. dist.) Calif., San Francisco, 1977-78; asst. U.S. atty. U.S. Atty.'s Office, San Francisco, 1978-81; assoc. Morrison & Foerster, San Francisco, 1981-83, ptnr., 1983—. Lawyer del. 9th cir. judicial conf., 1990-92; chair magistrate judge selection com. No. Dist. Calif., 1996. Author: Creating Your Discovery Plan, 1999. Named One of Calif.'s Top 25 Lawyers Under Age 45, Calif. Law Bus., 1994. Fellow Am. Bar Found.; mem. ABA (standing com. fed. judiciary, 1991-94), State Bar Calif. (com. profl. responsibility and conduct 1980-84, exec. com. litigation sect. 1986-91, vice chair 1989-90, chair 1990-91), San Francisco Bar Assn. (bd. dirs. 1988-90), Am. Law Inst., Asian Am. Bar Assn. Greater Bay Area (bd. dirs. 1977-82, pres. 1982), 9th Judicial Cir. Hist. Soc. (trustee 2000—), San Francisco C. of C. (bd. dirs. 1996-99), Singapore Am. Bus. Assn. (bd. dirs. 1999—, pres. 2001), World Affairs Coun. No. Calif. (trustee 1994-99), Commonwealth Club Calif. (quar. chair 1989). Office: Morrison & Foerster 425 Market St San Francisco CA 94105-2482 E-mail: cchao@mofo.com.

CHAO, EDWARD C., internist; b. LA, June 13, 1972; s. Hung-Ju and Martha Chao. BS in Biology, UCLA, 1994; MA in Med. Scis., Boston U., 1996; Dr. of Osteo. Medicine, U. New Eng. Coll. Osteo. Medicine, Biddeford, Maine, 2002. Rsch. coord. radiology Brigham and Women's Hosp., Boston, 1996—97, rsch. coord. thrombolysis in myocardial infarction study, 1997—98; resident internal medicine Loma Linda U. Med. Ctr., Calif., 2002—05; physician internal medicine Kaiser Permanente, San Diego, 2005—; fellow endocrinology U. Calif. San Diego Med. Ctr., 2007—. Author: (abstract) 72nd Annual Postgraduate Conf., Loma Linda University; author: (co-investigator) (sci. abstract) Annual Sci. Sessions, Am. Diabetes Assn.; author: (jour. article) Brain Research. Vol. Make-A-Wish Found., San Diego, 2005. Recipient Scholastic Rsch. award, Am. Diabetes Assn., 2003, scholarship, C.V. Starr Found., 1990—94. Mem.: San Diego Osteo. Med. Assn. (assoc.), San Diego County Med. Soc. (assoc.), ACP (assoc.), Sigma Sigma Phi (life). Achievements include research in the effect of pioglitazone on peripheral edema in patients with Type II diabetes mellitus on insulin; the impact of rosiglitazone on the microvascular and macrovascular circulation. Avocations: running, travel, dance, classical music, volunteering. Office: Univ Calif San Diego Med Ctr 9500 Gilman Dr La Jolla CA 92093-0673 Office Phone: 858-534-6651. Personal E-mail: edwardcchao@yahoo.com. Business E-Mail: ecchao@ucsd.edu.

CHAO, ELAINE LAN (HSIAO), secretary of labor; b. Taipei, Taiwan, Mar. 26, 1953; d. James S.C. and Ruth M.L. (Chu) C.; m. Mitch McConnell, Feb. 6, 1993. AB, Mt. Holyoke Coll., 1975; MBA, Harvard U., 1979; LLD (hon.), Villanova U., 1989, St. John's U., 1991, Sacred Heart U., 1991, U. Notre Dame, 1998, St. Marys Coll., 2002, Fu-Jen Cath. U., 2003, Cath. U. Am., 2004; DHL (hon.), Niagara U., 1992, Bellarmine Coll., 1995, U. Toledo, 1995, Goucher Coll., 1996, U. Louisville, 1996, U. S.C., 2001, No. Ala. U., 2003, Centre Coll., 2003, Wingate U., 2004; DHum (hon.), Drexel U., 1992, Thomas More Coll., 1994, Ky. Wesleyan Coll., 1998; D Arts and Letters (hon.), Miami-Dade C.C., 2001; DPA (hon.), Campbellsville U., 2002, No. Ky. U., 2004; D Pub. Svcs. (hon.), DePauw U., 2002; D in Orgnl. Leadership (hon.), Regent U., 2003. Assoc. Gulf Oil Corp., Pitts., summer 1978; sr. lending officer Citicorp, NA, NYC, 1979-83; v.p. capital markets group BankAmerica, San Francisco, 1984-86; dep. maritime adminstr. US Dept. Transp., Washington, 1986-88; chmn. Fed. Maritime Commn., Washington, 1988; dep. sec. US Dept. Transp., Washington, 1989-91; dir. Peace Corps., Washington, 1991—92; pres. United Way Am., Alexandria, Va., 1992-96; sr. editor, disting. fellow The Heritage Found., Washington, 1996—2001; sec. US Dept. Labor, Washington, 2001—. White House fellow, 1983-84; adj. asst. prof. Grad. Sch. Bus. Adminstrn., St. John's U., 1984; dir. Peace Corps., 1991-92. Recipient Young Achiever award Nat. Coun. Women U.S., Inc., 1986; Eisenhower Fellow Assn. fellow, 1984; named. one of 10 Outstanding Women of Am., 1988. Mem. Coun. on Fgn. Rels., Inc., Am. Coun. Young Polit. Leaders (bd. dirs. 1989), Harvard Bus. Sch. (vis. com. 1989, Outstanding Alumni award 1993), Harvard Club. Republican. Office: US Dept Labor Frances Perkins Bldg 200 Constitution Ave NW Washington DC 20210*

CHAO, HOWARD H., lawyer; b. Taipei, Republic of China, June 13, 1954; came to U.S., 1958; s. Kuang-Chu and Jun-Jing (Su) C. BS in Math. with highest distinction, Purdue U., 1976; JD, U. Calif. Boalt Hall Sch. Law, Berkeley, 1980. Bar: Calif. 1980, U.S. Dist. Ct. (No. Dist. Calif.) 1980, Hong Kong, 1997. Assoc. O'Melveny & Myers LLP, Los Angeles, 1980—, ptnr. Menlo Park, Calif., partner-in-charge, Shanghai, chair, internat. practice group. Exec. sec. Los Angeles Com. Fgn. Relations, 1984-85; vis. prof. Fudan U., Shanghai, Republic of China, 1985, Beijing (Republic of China) U. of Internat. Bus., 1985. Assoc. editor Calif. Law Review, 1977—80. Rotary Internat. fellow, Geneva, 1979-80. Mem. Law Soc. Hong Kong, Phi Beta Kappa, Order of Coif. Office: O'Melveny & Myers LLP 2765 Sand Hill Rd Menlo Park CA 94025-7019 Address: O'Melveny & Myers LLP Kerry Centre 20F 1515 Nanjing Rd West Shanghai 200040 China also: O'Melveny & Myers LLP Suite 1905 Tower Two Lippo Ctr 89 Queensway Central Hong Kong Office Phone: 650-473-2628. Fax: 8621 5298 5500, 852 2522 1760; Office Fax: 650-473-2601. Business E-Mail: hchao@omm.com.

CHAO, JAMES MIN-TZU, architect; b. Dairen, China, Feb. 27, 1940; came to U.S., 1949; naturalized, 1962; m. Kirsti Helena Lehtonen, May 15, 1968. BArch, U. Calif., Berkeley, 1965. Cert. arch. Nat. Coun. Archtl. Registration Bds.; registered arch. Calif., Ariz., Colo., Ill., N.Mex., Nev.; cert. real estate instr. Calif. Intermediate draftsman Spencer, Lee & Busse, Archs., San Francisco, 1966-67; asst. to pres. Import Plus Inc., Santa Clara, Calif., 1967-69; job capt. Hammaberg and Herman, Archs., Oakland, Calif., 1969-71; project mgr. B A Premises Corp., San Francisco, 1971-79; constrn. mgr. The Straw Hat Restaurant Corp., San Francisco, 1979-81, mem. sr. mgmt., dir. real estate and constrn., 1981-87; mem. mktg. com. Straw Hat Coop. Corp., San Francisco, 1988-91; pvt. practice Berkeley, 1987—; dir. real estate Papillon Devel. Inc., 1998—. Pres. Food Svc. Cons. Inc., 1987-89; pres., CEO Stratsac, Inc., 1987-92; prin. arch. Alpha Cons. Group Inc., 1991-98; v.p. Intersyn Industries Calif., 1993-99; nat. tng. dir. Excel Telecom., Inc., 1995-99; CEO Nuts and Bolts Books, 1997—; lectr. comml. real estate site analysis and selection for profl. real estate seminars; coord. minority vending program, solar application program Bank of Am.; guest faculty mem. NW Ctr. for Profl. Edn.; cert. mem. Nat. Coun. Archtl. Registration Bds., 1998—. Author: The Street-Smart Restaurant Development Handbook, 1996; patentee tidal electric generating system; author 1st comprehensive consumer orientated performance specification for remote banking transaction. Patron charter mem. Asian Art Mus., San Francisco, 2002—. Mem. Encinal Yacht Club (bd. dirs. 1977-78), Asian Pacific Islander Am. Pub. Affairs Assn. (life; gold sponsor). Republican.

CHAO, JAMES SI-CHENG, maritime executive; b. Shanghai, Dec. 29, 1927; came to the U.S., 1959; s. Yi Jen and Yu Chin (Hsu) C.; m. Ruth Mu-Lan Chu, Nov. 12, 1951. BS, Nat. Maritime Coll., China, 1949; MBA, St. John's U., NYC, 1964, DCS, 1979; LLD, Niagara U., NYC, 1992. Cert. marine master certificate license. Marine officer, master port capt., Taiwan, 1949-59; asst. to dir. China Merchant Nav. Corp, NYC, 1960-64; gen. mgr. exec. v.p. Foremost Maritime Corp., NYC, 1964-69, pres., dir., 1969—; chmn. Foremost Group, NYC, 1986—. Adj. prof. St. John's U., N.Y.C., 1977-83, trustee; hon. prof. Dalian Maritime U., Dalian, China, 1987—; hon. prof., pres. Shanghai Maritime Coll., China. Author: (monograph) International Shipping: Prospects and Opportunities, 1982; co-author: (monograph) Rise and Decline of the U.S. Shipping and Shipbuilding Industries, 1993. Bd. advisors St. John's U. Coll. of Bus. Adminstrn., N.Y., 1971—; hon. trustee Shanghai Jiao Tong U., China.; trustee St. John's U., 1995-2005, trustee emeritus, 2005—. Recipient medal of honor St. John's U., 1981, Ellis Island medal of honor, 2005; named Bus. Cmty. Leader Fed. Res. Bank of N.Y., 1976, 1981; named to Internat. Maritime Hall of Fame at UN, 2004. Mem. Chinese Maritime Assn. (pres. 1974—), Soc. Maritime Arbitrators, Chinese Opera (hon. mem., bd. dir. 1969—), Chiao Tung U. Alumni Assn. in Am. (chmn. 1989-99, 2001), Beta Gamma Sigma, Omicron Delta Epsilon (hon. mem.). Office: Foremost Group 60 E 42nd St 2212 New York NY 10165

CHAO, KWANG-CHU, chemical engineer, educator; b. Chongqing, China, June 7, 1925; came to U.S., 1954, naturalized, 1969; s. Chung-Pu and Jui-Pu (Chou) C.; m. Jiun-Ying Su, May 2, 1953; children: Howard Honshuen, Albert Honchi, Bernard Honwei. BS, Zhejiang U., China, 1948; MS, U. Wis., 1952, PhD, 1956. Chem. engr. Taiwan Alkali Co., 1948-51, 52-54; research engr. Chevron Research Co., Richmond, Calif., 1957-63; asso. prof. Ill. Inst. Tech., Chgo., 1963-64, Okla. State U., 1964-68; prof. Purdue U., West Lafayette, Ind., 1968-93, Harry C. Peffer Disting. prof. chem. engring., 1989-93, Harry C. Peffer disting. prof. emeritus chem. engring., 1994—. Cons. to industry, 1964—; lectr., internat. scientist Nat. Sci. Coun., Taiwan, 1989; hon. prof. Beijing U. Chem. Tech., 1984—, Zhejiang U., 1988—. Author: (with R.A. Greenkorn) Thermodynamics of Fluids, 1975; Editor: Applied Thermodynamics, 1968, Equations of State in Engineering and Research, 1979; Equations of State-Theories and Applications, 1986. Co-founder, chmn., sec. bd.dirs. Am. Zhu Kezhen Edn. Found., 1995-2005. Recipient Donald Katz award Gas Processors Assn., 1994. Fellow Am. Inst. Chem. Engrs. (editorial bd. jour., also Ind. Engring. Chem. Ann. Revs.); mem. Am. Chem. Soc., AAUP, Sigma Xi, Omega Chi Epsilon. Home: 36281 Fremont Blvd Fremont CA 94536 Personal E-mail: chuchao@aol.com.

CHAO, MARSHALL, chemist; b. Changsha, Hunan, China, Nov. 20, 1924; came to U.S., 1955; s. Heng-ti and Hwei-yng C.; m. Patricia Hu, July 20, 1968; 1 dau., Anita A. BS, Nat. Central U., Nanking, China, 1947; MS, U. Ill., 1958, PhD, 1961. Tech. asst. Taiwan Fertilizer Co., Taipei, 1949-55; research chemist Dow Chem. Co., Midland, Mich., 1960-72, research specialist, 1973-80; research leader Dow chem. Co., Midland, Mich., 1980-86; sr. assoc. Omni Tech Internat., Ltd., Midland, 1986—. Author: Taiwan Fertilizers, 1951; editor newsletter Midland Chinese Christian Fellowship, 1987-94; contbr. articles to profl. jours.; patentee in field. Mem. Ch. Council Grace Bapt. Ch., Taipei, 1951-55; deacon 1st Baptist Ch., Midland, 1974-76. Univ. fellow U. Ill., 1957-60 Fellow Am. Inst. Chemists; mem. Am. Chem. Soc., Electrochem. Soc. (sect. chmn. 1973-74, 83-84, councilor 1974-76, 85—, vice chmn. 1964-65), Soc. Electronanalytical chemistry (charter), N.Y. Acad. Scis., Mensa, Sigma Xi, Phi Lambda Upsilon Clubs: Midland Chinese (chmn. 1975-76), Tittabawassee Toastmasters (sec.-treas. 1976-77). Home: 1206 Evamar Dr Midland MI 48640-7213 Office: Omni Tech Internat Ltd 2715 Ashman St Midland MI 48640-4449 E-mail: mschao@aol.com. *A man's intrinsic worth is measured by the good he has done his fellow men. As for outward signs of success, such as recognition or rewards, he should much rather have people wondering why he didn't get them than have people wondering why he got them at all.*

CHAO, RUTH, psychologist, researcher; b. Keelung, Taiwan, Apr. 1, 1967; arrived in U.S., 1996; d. Shi-yi Chao and Chin Chang. BS, Nat. Taiwan U., 1989; postgrad., U. Mo., 2000—. Clin. psychologist Samaritan Psychology Clinic, Chia-yi, Taiwan, 1994—96; rschr. U. Mo., Columbia, 2002—03, clin. supr., 2001—03; doctoral counselor Mich. State U., East Lansing, 2003—04. Cons. Mich. State U., East Lansing, 2003—04, coord., 2003—04. Author: (exhbn.) Listening to Clients' Voices (Winter Roundtable Scholarship, 2004), (vistas) Non-traditional Students on Counseling Needs, 2004, Clients' Perceptions of Mental Health Services, 2005, (book chpt.) Going through Cultural Barriers in Counseling, 2004, Integrating Taoism and Western Therapeutic Approaches in the Treatment of Anxiety, 2005, Integrating Holland's Theory with Tao-te Ching for Career Counseling, 2005; translator: (book) Abnormal Psychology, 1995, Social Psychology, 1995, Teaching and Learning, 1997; author: Historical Review of Multiculturalism, How Ethical is Contemporary Multicultural Training?, 2003, (exhbn.) Adult Students' Perspectives on Counseling and Education (ACCA Grant Award, 2004), Re-thinking Non-traditional College Students' Counseling Needs, 2004, Toward a Successful Experience at Graduate School, 2003, Gender and Smoking: A Qualitative Study, 2004, Minority Clients' Perspectives on Multicultural Competence, 2004, Counselors' Multicultural Self-awareness: A Way to Client Advocacy, 2004, A Qualitative Analysis of College Students' Smoking, 2003, (exhbn.) Creating a Hoslitic Environment for Clients (Rsch. and Profl. Devel. Award, 2003), College Smokers' Perspectives on Smoking (Rsch. Award, Sch. of Medicine, U. of Kans., 2003), Racial Identity Development in Minority Counselors (Winter Roundtable Schoolarship, Columbia U., 2002); contbr. articles to profl. jours. Christian student leader, Taipei, 1988—89. Recipient Multicultural Rsch. award, 2002, Outstanding Acad. Achievements award, 2002, Walter Scott Monroe Rsch. fellowship, 2002—03, Superior Rsch. award, 2004, Rsch. scholarship, Profl. R&D Support award, 2004, faculty rsch. award, Tenn. State U. Mem.: APA, Am. Counseling Assn., Psi Chi (life). Home Phone: 573-462-0318; Office Phone: 615-963-2177. Personal E-mail: ruth_chao2000@yahoo.com. Business E-Mail: rchao@tnstate.edu.

CHAO, TSAI CHUNG, physician, medical association administrator; b. Hangzhou, Zhejiang, China, Oct. 13, 1944; came to U.S., 1981; s. Chi Chang and Chi Hsiao (Sun) C.; m. Hsian Fang Hsiang; children: Charlene, James. Diploma, Zhejiang U. Sch. Medicine, 1969; MD, SUNY, NYC, 1993. Diplomate Am. Bd. Phys. Medicine and Rehab. Ind. Med. Examiners, Am. Acad. Pain Mgmt. Surg. intern Xiaoshan County Hosp., Xiaoshan City, China, 1969-70; gen. practitioner Xiaoshan Coal & Iron Mining, 1970-72; surg. ho. physician Linpu People's Hosp., Xiaoshan City, 1972-74; surg. resident Zhejiang Med. U., Hangzhou City, 1974-80; surg. oncology fellow Hangzhou Cancer Inst., 1980; asst. prof., staff surgeon Zhejiang Med. U., Hangzhou City, 1980-81; instr. S. Baylo U., Garden Grove, Calif., 1984-86, SAMRA U. Oriental Medicine, LA, 1985-86; surg. resident Interfaith Med. Ctr., Bklyn., 1986-88; rehab. medicine resident SUNY Downstate Med. Ctr., Bklyn., 1988-91, clinic asst. prof., attending physician, 1991-97, dir. rehab. med. residency program, 1996—2004, assoc. dir. rehab. med. residency program, 2004—. Course dir. continuing med. edn. program in med. acupuncture, rehab. medicine SUNY Downstate Med. Ctr., dir. Low Back Pain Ctr.; med. dir. Naturo-Med. Health Care, PC. Contbr. articles to profl. jours. Fellow Am. Acad. Phys. Med. and Rehab.; mem. AMA, Am. Congress Rehab. Medicine, Am. Acad. Med. Acupunture, Am. Coll. Occupl. and Environ. Medicine, N.Y. Acad. Scis. Home: 330 E 38th St Apt 37N New York NY 10016-2782 Office: SUNY Health Sci Ctr PO Box 30 Brooklyn NY 11203-0030 Office Phone: 212-473-9155. Business E-Mail: tsai.chao@downstate.edu.

CHAPDELAINE, PERRY ANTHONY, JR., public health service officer, preventive medicine physician, educator; b. Mason City, Iowa, Feb. 23, 1950; s. Perry Anthony Sr. and Ruby Elizabeth (McCurley) Chapdelaine; 1 child, Rachel Maria. BA in Sociology, St. Ambrose U., Davenport, Iowa, 1972; MD, Meharry Med. Coll., Nashville, 1989, MSPH, 1992. Diplomate Am. Bd. Preventive Medicine. CEO, pres. AC Projects Inc., Franklin, Tenn., 1974-86; epidemiologist Meharry Med. Coll., Nashville, 1992-95, asst. prof., 1993-95, 2001—03, dir. preventive medicine residency program, 1995; chief med. physician City of Nashville, Metro Health Dept., 1995-2000; pvt. cons. practice, 2000—. Cons. St. Thomas Hosp. Clin. Ethics Ctr., Nashville, 1993-98, Nashville Prevention Mktg. Initiative, 1994-96; med. dir. Samaritan Recovery Cmty., Nashville, 1993-95; mem. Access Med Plus Peer Rev. Com., Nashville, 1996-2000. Co-editor: The John W. Campbell Letters, 1985 (Hugo award nominee 1986). Mem. Alpha Chi, Alpha Omega Alpha. Avocations: writing, photography, dulcimer, hiking. Home: 5384 Village Way Nashville TN 37211 Office: Gen and Alternative Medicine 229 Ward Cir Ste B-12 Brentwood TN 37027 Office Phone: 615-377-6767. Business E-Mail: genalt.staff@gmail.com.

CHAPEL, ROBERT CLYDE, theater director, educator; b. June 25, 1945; married. BA in TV, U. Mich., 1967, MA in Theatre, 1968, PhD in Theatre, 1974. Asst. prof. dept. theatre U. Ala., Ala., 1974-75; profl. actor LA, 1975-77; dir. devel. Force Ten Prod., LA, 1977-78; v.p. prodn. Trans-Atlantic Enterprises, LA, 1978-81; actor, dir. LA, 1981-83; dir. BFA mus. theatre program U. Mich., Mich., 1983-84; coordinating dir. MFA mus. theatre program Tisch Sch. of Arts NYU, NYC, 1984—86; co-prodr. Shubert Archives Series Lyceum Theatre, NYC, 1984-86; artistic dir. Music Theatre North, Potsdam, NY, 1986; freelance dir. NYC, 1986—88; dir. mus. theatre program San Diego State U., 1988-90; prof., chair dept. drama U. Va., 1990—2005; mng. dir. Heritage Repertory Theatre, Charlottesville, Va., 1990-94, prodr., artistic dir., 1995—; exec. dir. Va. Film Festival, Va., 1996—2000; prof. drama U. Va., 2005—. Chmn. pres. commn. on fine arts and performing arts U. Va., 1998-2001; guest dir. U. Mich., 2005, U. Tasmania, 2006, Sweeney Todd, Gitis, Moscow, 2006, Arthur Miller Theatre, U. Mich., 2007; guest tchr., Moscow, Russia, 2005. Mem. SAG, AFTRA, Assn. for Theatre in Higher Edn., Nat. Assn. Schs. of Theatre, Actors Equity Assn., Soc. Stage Dirs. and Choreographers. Home: 1029 Hazel St Charlottesville VA 22902-4904 Office Phone: 434-924-8961. E-mail: rcc2u@virginia.edu.

CHAPELA, IGNACIO H., biologist, researcher; b. Mex. City, Mex., Sept. 12, 1959; s. Gonzalo Chapela Montañéz and Maria De La Luz Mendoza; m. Laura García-Moreno, July 23, 1987; 1 child: Inés. Biologo, Nat. U. Mex., Mex. City, 1984; PhD, U. Wales, Cardiff, 1987. Scientist Sandoz, Ltd, Basel, Switzerland, 1989-91. Vis. prof. Cornell U., Ithaca, N.Y., 1987-88, 92-93; founder, scientific dir. Mycological Facility: Oaxaca (Mex.), 1994—; cons. World Bank Group, Washington, 1994, Pan-Am. Health Orgn., Washington, 1994; adv. bd. Andes Pharmaceuticals, Washington, 1995—; asst. prof. U. Calif., Berkeley. Contbr. articles to profl. jours. Fellow Instituto Nacional de Cardiologia, Mex. City, Mex., 1981-84; grantee Am. Philos. Soc., Phila., 1988, MacArthur Fdn., 1993, Vice Chancellors & Prins. of Brit. U., Wales, 1985-87. Mem. Brit. Mycological Soc. Ecology Com., 1985—, Mycological Soc. of Am., 1995—. Achievements include elucidation of symbiotic relationships of fungi and other organisms conservation through revaluation of biodiversity in Latin Am. Home: 3144 O St NW Washington DC 20007-3116 Office: U Calif Environ Sci Policy & Mgmt Berkeley CA 94720-0001

CHAPELLE, SUZANNE ELLERY GREENE, history professor; b. Phila., Sept. 21, 1942; d. John Channing and Jessie Horn (Myers) Ellery; m. Michael Thomas Greene, Sept. 15, 1972 (dec. 1973); 1 child, Jennifer; m. Francis Oberlin Chapelle, Apr. 14, 1984 (dec. 1999). BA, Harvard U., 1964; MA, Johns Hopkins U., 1966, PhD, 1970. Asst. prof. Am. history Towson State U., Balt., 1969-71; assoc. prof. Am. history Morgan State U., Balt., 1971-75, prof., 1975—2006, coord., environ. studies program. Author: Books for Pleasure, 1976, Baltimore: An Illustrated History, 1980, 2d rev. edit., 2000; sr. author: Maryland: A History of its People, 1986; revisions author: A Child's History of the World, 1994, African American Leaders of Maryland, 2000, The Maryland Adventure, 2001; mem. publs. bd. Md. Hist. Soc. Bd. dir. Md. Interfaith Coalition for the Environment, 1997-2001, v.p., 1999-2001; bd. dirs. Md. Conservation Coun., 1999-2000; bd. trustees Irvine Nature Ctr., 2001—; mem. water quality adv. coun. Md., 2004-06; mem. Md. State Dept. Edn. Social Studies Task Force, 2004—. Mem. Am. Hist. Assn., Am. Studies Assn. (mem. exec. bd. Chesapeake chpt. 1988-90), Popular Culture Assn. (bd. dirs. 1980-82), Orgn. Am. Historians, Md. Hist. Soc. (publs. com. 1998—), Mid-Atlantic Assn. (pres. 1977-80), Balt. County League Environ. Voters (exec. bd. 1992-96), Episcopal Diocese of Md. Com. on the Environ. (sec. 1994-2003), Ruxton-Riderwood Assn. (bd. govs. 1987-91), The Johns Hopkins Club, The Harvard-Radcliffe Club Md. Episcopalian. Home: 6021 Lakeview Rd Baltimore MD 21210-1033 Office: Morgan State U Hist Dept Baltimore MD 21251-0001 Office Phone: 443-885-3190. Personal E-mail: suechapelle@yahoo.com.

CHAPIN, DAVID CHESTER, lawyer; b. Holyoke, Mass., Apr. 14, 1954; s. Hugh A. and Judith Anne (Kinne) C.; m. Sheeran Phelps Howard, May 30, 1981. BA summa cum laude, Lafayette Coll., 1972-76; JD cum laude, Harvard Law Sch., 1980. Bar: Mass. 1980. Assoc. Ropes & Gray LLP, Boston, 1980—89, ptnr., 1989—. Named a Dealmaker of Yr., Am. Lawyer mag., 2007; named one of New Stars, New Worlds, Lawdragon 500, 2006, Leading Lawyers in Am., Lawdragon 3000, 2006. Mem. Mass. Bar Assn. (bus. law sect.), Phi Beta Kappa. Democrat. Episcopalian. Avocations: tennis, golf, skiing. Office: Ropes & Gray 1 International Pl Boston MA 02110-2624 Office Phone: 617-423-7371. Office Fax: 617-235-0015. E-mail: david.chapin@ropesgray.com.*

CHAPIN, F. STUART, III, ecologist; BA in biology, Swarthmore Coll., 1966; PhD in bio. scis., Stanford U., 1973. Asst. and assoc. prof. U. Alaska, Fairbanks, 1973—84, prof. ecology, 1984—86, 1996—; asst. dir. Inst. Arctic Biology, 1981—83; prof. biology U. Calif., Berkeley, 1989—98. Vis. instr. biology Peace Corps U. Javeriana, Colombia, 1966—68. Co-author: Principles of Terrestrial Ecosystem Ecology, 2002; editl. bd. mem. Physiological Ecology Series, Ecology and Soc. Recipient Kempe award, 1996; fellow, Guggenheim, 1979. Mem.: Ecol. Soc. Am., Ecology Inst., Swedish Royal Acad. Agriculture and Forestry, Am. Acad. Arts and Scis., NAS. Office: U Alaska Inst Arctic Biology Dept Biology and Wildlife Fairbanks AK 99775 Business E-Mail: terry.chapin@uaf.edu.

CHAPIN, JULIE KURTZ, lawyer; b. Phila., Mar. 25, 1951; d. Louis Kurtz and Adele (Gersh) Greenfield; m. Thomas J. Chapin, May 18, 1986; children: Alexis Kate, Stephanie Lynn, Benjamin Thomas, Madeline Charlotte. Student, Vassar Coll., 1968-69; BA, BS summa cum laude, U. Pa., 1971, JD, 1974. Bar: Pa. 1974, US Ct. Appeals (2d cir.) 1975, NY 1976, US Dist. Ct. (so. dist.) NY 1976, US Dist. Ct. (ea. dist.) NY 1977, US

Ct. Appeals (DC cir.) 1978, DC 1978, US Supreme Ct. 1979; cert. primary edn., NASD arbitrator 2006. Law clk. to Chief Justice Benjamin R. Jones Pa. Supreme Ct., Phila., 1974-75; assoc. Hughes Hubbard & Reed, NYC and Washington, 1975-82; dep. gen. counsel Celanese Corp., NYC, 1982-87; asst. sec. assoc. gen. counsel, unit mgr. Hoechst Celanese Corp., 1987-99; v.p., corp. sec., assoc. gen. counsel Celanese Ams. Corp., 1999—2006; chair Celanese Ams. Polit. Action Com., 1999—2006; prin. exec. officer Celanese Ams., 2002—06; dep. gen. counsel, chief compliance officer Celanese Corp., Dallas, 2004—06; exec. cons. AE Feldman Assocs., NYC, 2007—. Trustee Casa of NJ; dir. Eagleville Found., chair compliance com. Mem. ABA (sect. corp., banking and bus. law), Twin Mgmt. Forum (hon. 1989), Am. Soc. Corp. Secs. & Govt. Profls. (NYC), SCCE, NJCCA, Phi Beta Kappa, Pi Lambda Theta. Home: 418 Sked St Pennington NJ 08534-2725 Office: 708 Third Ave New York NY 10017 Office Phone: 212-324-7900. Personal E-mail: jul.chap@comcast.net.

CHAPIN, LLOYD WALTER, academic administrator; b. Atlanta, Jan. 7, 1937; s. Lloyd Walter and Carolina (McCall) C.; m. Louise Williams, June 21, 1958; children: Laura, Caroline, Lloyd, Anne. BA cum laude, Davidson Coll., 1958; MDiv cum laude, N.Y., 1961; PhD, Union Theol. Sem., NYC, 1967. Ordained to ministry, Meth. Ch., 1961. Asst. prof. Philosophy & Religion Colgate U., Hamilton, N.Y., 1965-70, asst. dean of faculty, 1968-70; assoc. dean Emory U., Atlanta, 1970—79; v.p., dean of faculty, prof. philosophy and religion Eckerd Coll., St. Petersburg, Fla., 1979—. Bd. dirs. Presbyn. Counseling Ctr., St. Petersburg, Fla., 1986-93. Editor symposium proceedings Future of Church Related Coll., 1986; contbr. articles to profl. jours. Pres. Sch. PTA, Atlanta, 1974; trustee St. Paul Sch., 1992-96, Canterbury Sch., 2005-; bd. dirs. Fla. Humanities Coun., 1993-2000. Recipient Rockefeller and Kent fellow, 1962-65; U.S. Dept. Edn. grantee Eckerd Coll., 1983, Ford Found., 1986, 91, Knight Found., 1989, Coun. for the Advancement of Pvt. Higher Edn., 1989, Nat. Endowment for the Humanities, 1989, 91, Howard Hughes Med. Inst., 1991. Mem. Am. Conference of Acad. Deans (bd. dirs.), Soc. for Values in Higher Edn., Omicron Delta Kappa, Phi Beta Kappa. Democrat. Avocations: reading, classical music. Home: 4737 Dolphin Cay Ln S Apt 207 Saint Petersburg FL 33711-4671 Office: Eckerd Coll PO Box 12560 Saint Petersburg FL 33733-2560 Office Phone: 813-864-8212. Business E-Mail: chapinlw@eckerd.edu.

CHAPIN, MARY Q., arbitrator, director, mediator, writer; b. Shepherdstown, W.VA., May 5, 1933; d. Guy Estil and Anne Mildred (Jones) Quisenberry; m. Edward John Chapin Jr.; children: John Edward, Susan Q. (dec.). SUNY Regent's Degree, 1985; AAS, SUNY, Binghamton, BS, 1991. Pers. adminstr. Mohawk Valley Psychiatric Ctr., Utica, NY, 1976-89; arbitrator Am. Arbitration Assn., NYC, 1989-99; pres. Dispute Resolution Internat., New Hartford, NY, 1993—; neutral chair NYSDOL Office of Labor Mgmt., Albany, NY, 1993—. Mem. adv. coun. on safety and security in N.Y. State schs. N.Y. State Dept. Edn., Albany, 1995-97; founder, mem., bd. dirs. Forum on Conflict and Concensus, 1993-94l chair Mohawk Valley Women's History Project, 1998—; host weekly TV show, Mohawk Valley Srs., Sta. WUTR, 2002—. Author: Woman's Suffrage: A Dream of Full Citizenship. Pres. Utica/Rome Metro League of Women Voters, 1992-97; coord. Com. on Met. Orgn., 1995-97; coord. of multicultural commn. League of Women Voters Edn. Fund, 1997; trustee amerita Mohawk Valley Cmty. Coll., 1996-2002; Utica C. of C., 1995-98. Recipient Found. award The Found. of SUNY at Binghamton, 1992, Recognition award NYS League of Women Voters, 1995, 97, Recognition award U.S. LWV Edn. Fund, 1998, Labor Mgmt. award Office of Mental Health, 1988, Conservator of Women's History award NOW, 2002. Mem. AAUW, Central N.Y. Futurist, Bd. Neighborhood Ctr. Home and Office: 56 Woodbrooke Rd New Hartford NY 13413-4805

CHAPIN, RICHARD, trustee, director; b. Boston, Dec. 25, 1923; s. Vinton and Elizabeth (Higgins) C.; m. Maryan Gainor Fox, Nov. 3, 1956; children: Aldus Higgins II, Margery Rodman Carr, Marya Chapin Lundgren, Richard Dickinson. SB, Harvard U., 1944, MBA, 1949; LLD (hon.), Emerson Coll., 1972. Asst. to treas. Anderson, Davis & Platt, Inc., 1946; journeyman machinist Yale & Towne Co., 1947; various adminstrn. and instnl. positions Harvard Grad. Sch. Bus. Adminstrn., 1949-67; pres. Emerson Coll., Boston, 1967-75. Exec. dir. Cheswick Ctr., 1976-84; bd. dirs. Alden Yachts, Inc.; hon. dir. Nickerson Lumber Co. Trustee, chmn. Bigelow Found.; chmn. Riggs Cove Found.; trustee Bigelow Lab. Ocean Sci. With USNR, 1942—46. Mem.: St. Botolph Club, NY Yacht Club. Home and Office: 13 Knubble Rd Georgetown ME 04548-9410 Personal E-mail: rchapin440@aol.com.

CHAPIN, RICHARD EARL, retired librarian; b. Danville, Ill., Apr. 29, 1925; s. Harry W. and Lula May (Briggs) C.; m. Eleanor Jane Lang, Aug. 15, 1949; children: Robert Lang, David Brian, Rebecca Anne. AB, Wabash Coll., 1948; MS, U. Ill., 1949, PhD, 1954; LHD (hon.), Wabash Coll., 1991. Reference asst. Fla. State U., 1949-50; libr. asst. U. Ill., 1950-53, vis. prof., 1957; asst. dir., asst. prof. Sch. Libr. Sci., U. Okla., 1953-55; assoc. libr., assoc. prof. Mich. State U., East Lansing, 1955-59, dir. librs., prof. journalism, 1959-89, dir. librs. emeritus, prof. emeritus, 1989—; libr. advisor United Arab Emirates U., 1989-92. Dir. Mich. State U. Press, 1986-90; cons. to govts., founds., colls., and univs.; bd. dirs. Ctr. for Rsch. Librs., 1978-83; bd. dirs. OCLC Users' Coun., 1980-83, pres., 1983. Contbr. articles to libr. periodicals and encys. Mem. East Lansing Human Relations Commn., 1966-69, chmn., 1969; mem. East Lansing Bd. Edn., 1970-74, 75, pres., 1973-74; bd. dirs. W.B. and Candace Thoman Found., 1991—. Served to lt. (j.g.) USNR, 1943-46. Mem. ALA, Mich. Library Assn. (pres. 1967), Assn. Research Libraries (bd. dirs. 1984-87), Blue Key, Sigma Chi, Phi Kappa Phi Home: 2539 Koala Dr East Lansing MI 48823-7211 E-mail: chapinR@msu.edu.

CHAPIN, SAMUEL R., investment company executive; BA, Lafayette Coll.; MBA, U. Pa. Wharton Sch. Bus. With Chase Manhattan Bank; mem. mergers and acquisitions grp. Merrill Lynch & Co., 1984—, mng. dir. corp. banking grp., 1993, co-head global industries investment banking grp., head global investment banking divsn., 2001—03, vice chmn. exec. client coverage grp., 2003—. Office: Merrill Lynch 4 World Fin Ctr 250 Vesey St New York NY 10080*

CHAPIN, SCHUYLER GARRISON, retired cultural organization administrator, retired dean; b. NYC, Feb. 13, 1923; s. L.H. Paul and Leila H. (Burden) C.; m. Elizabeth Steinway, Mar. 15, 1947 (dec. 1993); children: Henry Burden, Theodore Steinway, Samuel Garrison, Miles Whitworth; m. Catia Zoullas Mortimer, Sept. 15, 1995. Student, Longy Sch. Music, 1940-41; LHD (hon.), NYU, 1974, Hobart/William Smith Coll., 1974, Hofstra Coll., 1999; DLitt (hon.), Emerson Coll., 1976; MusD (hon.), Mannes Coll., New Sch., 1990, Curtis Inst. Music, 2000. Spot salesman NBC-TV, NYC, 1947-51; gen. mgr. Tex and Jinx McCary Enterprises, NYC, 1951-53; booking dir. Judson, O'Neill & Judd divsn. Columbia Artists Mgmt., 1953-59; dir. masterworks to v.p. creative svcs. Columbia Records divsn. CBS, 1959-63; v.p. programming Lincoln Center for the Performing Arts, 1964-69; exec. producer Amberson Enterprises, NYC, 1969-71; acting gen. mgr. Met. Opera, NYC, 1972-73, gen. mgr., 1973-75; dean faculty arts Columbia U., 1976-87, dean emeritus, 1987—; v.p. worldwide concert and artist activities Steinway & Sons, NYC, 1990-92; commr. of cultural affairs City of N.Y., 1994—2002; ret., 2002. Cons. Carnegie Hall Corp., 1979-87. Author: (autobiography) Musical Chairs, 1977, Leonard Bernstein: Notes from a Friend, 1992, Sopranos, Mezzos, Tenors, Bassos and Other Friends, 1995. Past chmn. Bagby Music Lovers Found.; past chmn., trustee Am. Symphony Orch. League, 1985-92; trustee Naumburg Found., 1949, Richard Tucker Found., 1975-92, Am. Inst. for Verdi Studies, 1975, Bklyn. Philharm., 1978-92, Lenox Music Theatre Group, 1984, Lincoln Ctr. Theatre, 1985-94, 2001—, Carnegie Hall Soc., 1987-94, 2001—, Curtis Inst. Music, 1986-92, Pres.'s Com. on Arts and Humanities, 1982-90, Redwood Libr. and Athenaeum, 1990-96; chmn., exec. com. Franklin and Eleanor Roosevelt Inst., 1982-2004, co-chair bd. govs., 2004—. 1st lt. Air Corps US Army, 1942—46, China, Burma, India. Decorated chevalier Legion of Honor (France); recipient N.Y. State Conspicuous service cross, 1951, Christopher award, 1971, Emmy awards 1972, 76, 80, Gold Medal Nat. Arts Club, 1983. Fellow Am. Acad. Arts & Scis. Clubs: Century Assn. (N.Y.C.), Knickerbocker. Home: 655 Park Ave New York NY 10021-5937 Office Phone: 212-734-5553. Personal E-mail: SGC655@aol.com. *Throughout my career, and indeed my life, I have been fortunate to make my avocation my vocation. I've worked in, around, about and for the arts in a variety of ways. That, I hope, has brought as much happiness to others as it has to me. I have been privileged to be part of what a poet once called the Arts: the Signature of Man.*

CHAPLIN, ANSEL BURT, lawyer; b. Deerfield, Ill., June 12, 1931; s. Robert Tappan and Ruth (Burt) C.; m. Maud Denise Hazeltine, 1959 (div. 1993); children: Rawson, Margaret, Jane; m. Anne Carol Kenney, 1995. BA magna cum laude, Princeton U., 1953; postgrad., Inst. Polit. Sci., Paris, U. Algiers; JD, Harvard U., 1959. Bar: Mass. 1959. Law clk. to chief justice Mass. Supreme Ct., 1959-60; ptnr. Chaplin & Chaplin, Boston; practice Boston, 1960-99, Cape Cod, Mass., 1981—. Owner Cape Cod Fishnet Industries, North Truro, Mass., 1980-96; chmn. com. legal edn. Mass. Supreme Ct., 1979-90, mem. com. lawyer advt., 1979-82; vice chmn. commn. on legal profession and the economy of New Eng., New Eng. Bd. Higher Edn., 1991; mem. U.S. Dist. Ct. Ad. Practice Com., 1981-85; chmn. vis. com. So. New England Sch. Law, 1992-93; bd. dir. Housing Land Trust for Cape Cod, Outer Cape Health Svcs., v.p. 2007—. Author papers in field. Pres. Truro Neighborhood Assn., 1979—83, Compact of Cape Cod Conservation Trusts, 1986—2001, Friends of the Pamet, Inc., 1994—96; mem. corp. Perkins Sch. for Blind, Watertown, Mass., 1973—, Winsor Sch., Boston, 1980—83; sec., adminstrv. trustee Truro Conservation Trust, 1981—2005; trustee Payomet Performing Arts Charitable Trust, 1998—2000, Dexter Keezer Cmty. Fund, 1998—2005, Truro Parks Preservation Trust, 2003—; mem. Truro Planning Bd., 2001—, vice chair, 2007—; mem. Truro Local Comprehensive Plan Implementation Com., 2004—06; chmn. Truro Shellfish Adv. Com., 2000—04, 2007—; bd. dirs. Mass. Appleseed Ctr. for Law and Justice, 1994—96. Recipient Thoreau award Cape Cod Mus. Natural History, 1987, Environmental Merit award EPA, 2000; Fulbright fellow, 1953-54 Fellow Am. Bar Found., Mass. Bar Found., Boston Bar Found.; Mem. ABA, Am. Law Inst., Mass. Bar Assn. (chmn. law practice sect. 1978-80), Boston Bar Assn. (co-chair peer support com. 1997—), Harvard Law Sch. Assn. Mass. (pub. interest coord. 1994-2006), Harvard Law Sch. Assn. (mem. coun. 1997-2000), Wellesley Boat Club, Harvard Club (Boston). Democrat. Unitarian Universalist. Office: 8 High Pamet Rd PO Box 867 Truro MA 02666-0867 E-mail: abchaplin@cs.com.

CHAPLIN, C. EDWARD (CHUCK), diversified financial services company executive; married; 2 children. B, Rutgers U.; M in City and Regional Planning, Harvard U. CFA. Secured investment mgr., Prudential Realty Group Prudential Fin., Inc., 1983—89, regional v.p., Prudential Mortgage Capital Co., 1989—92, v.p., asst. treas., 1992—93, mng. dir., asst. treas., 1993—95, treas., 1995—, sr. v.p. and treas., 2000—, chmn., Fin. Controls Coun. Bd. trustees Newark Sch. of the Arts; bd. mem., treas. Exec. Leadership Coun. Office: Prudential Financial Inc 751 Broad St Newark NJ 07102-3777*

CHAPLIN, DAVID DUNBAR, medical research specialist, educator; b. London, Aug. 28, 1952; came to U.S., 1952; s. Hugh Jr. and Alice Elizabeth (Dougherty) C.; m. Jane Ellen Bryant; children: Vernon H., Rosalind K., Daniel B. AB, Harvard U., 1973; MD, PhD, Washington U., St. Louis, 1980. Intern, then resident Parkland Meml. Hosp., Dallas, 1980-82; post-doctoral fellow dept. genetics Harvard U. Med. Sch., Boston, 1982-84; asst. prof. medicine Washington U. Sch. Medicine, St. Louis, 1984-91, prof. medicine, 1995—; assoc. investigator Howard Hughes Med. Inst., St. Louis, 1984—. Assoc. editor: The New Biologist, 1990-92, Diabetes, 1992-96; contbr. articles to profl. jours. Mem. grants com. Arthritis Found., Atlanta, 1989-92, NIAID AITR, 1998—. Scholar Harvard U., 1972, 73; Jane Coffin Childs Fund for Med. Rsch. fellow, 1982-84. Mem. Am. Soc. Clin. Investigation, Am. Fedn. Clin. Rsch., Am. Assn. Immunologists, Am. Soc. Human Genetics, Assn., Assn. Am. Physicians, Alpha Omega Alpha. Democrat. Roman Catholic. Office: Howard Hughes Med Inst 10050 Clin Scis Res Bldg 660 S Euclid Ave # 8022 Saint Louis MO 63110-1010 E-mail: cahplin@im.wustl.edu.

CHAPLIN, HARVEY R., wine and liquor wholesale executive; b. Bklyn., 1929; Chmn., CEO So. Wine Spirits of Am., Miami, 1994—. Named to Sky Ranch Found. Hall of Fame, 2006. Office: Southern Wine & Spirits 1600 NW 163rd St Miami FL 33169-5672*

CHAPLIN, HUGH, JR., preventive medicine physician, educator; b. NYC, Feb. 4, 1923; m. Alice Dougherty, June 16, 1945; 4 children; m. Lee Nelken Robins, Aug. 5, 1998. AB, Princeton U., 1943; MD, Columbia U., 1947. Diplomate Am. Bd. Internal Medicine, Nat. Bd. Med. Examiners. Intern Mass. Gen. Hosp., Boston, 1947-48, resident, 1948-50; fellow in hematology Brit. Postgrad. Med. Sch., London, 1951-53; physician in charge Clin. Center Blood Bank, NIH, Bethesda, Md., 1953-55; Commonwealth Fund fellow Wright Fleming Inst. Microbiology, London, 1962-63, Josiah Macy Faculty scholar, 1975-76. Instr. in medicine Washington U. Sch. Medicine, St. Louis, 1955-56, asst. prof. medicine and preventive medicine, 1956-62, asso. dean, chmn. admissions com., 1957-62, asso. prof., 1963-65, prof., 1965, William B. Kountz prof. preventive medicine, 1965-83; dir. IWJ Inst. of Rehab., St. Louis, 1964-72; prof. pathology, dir. Barnes Hosp. Blood Bank, St. Louis, 1983-91; emeritus prof. pathology and medicine, 1991—; mem. Am. Standards Com. for Blood Transfusion Equipment; mem. subcom. on transfusion problems NRC, 1959-62, mem. com. on blood and transfusion problems, 1963-67; chmn. ad hoc blood program research com. ARC, 1967-73, bd. govs., 1978-84 Assoc. editor Transfusion, 1960-98; contbg. editor Vox Sanguinis, 1960-79. Served with USNR, 1942-45. Mem. Am. Fedn. Clin. Research, Central Soc. Clin. Research, Am. Soc. Clin. Investigation, Assn. Am. Physicians, Am., Internat. socs. hematology, Brit. Med. Research Soc., Brit. Royal Soc. Medicine, Am. Assn. Blood Banks (sci. program com. 1959-60, Emily Cooley award 1968, Morton Grove-Rasmussen award 1985), Phi Beta Kappa, Alpha Omega Alpha, Sigma Xi. Office: Washington U Sch Medicine Box 8118 4949 Barnes Hospital Plz Saint Louis MO 63110-1003 E-mail: hughchapln@yahoo.com.

CHAPLIN, PEGGY LOUIE, lawyer; b. Guantanamo Bay Naval Base, Cuba, Nov. 22, 1940; d. Raymond Gerard Fannon and Joan Marie (Carguil) Boyce. BS, Johns Hopkins U., 1971; JD, U. Md., 1973; LLM in Internat. Comml. Law, Georgetown U., 1983. Bar: Md. 1973, U.S. Dist. Ct. Md. 1973, U.S. Ct. Internat. Trade 1975, U.S. Ct. Appeals (fed. cir.) 1986, (D.C. cir.) 1988, U.S. Supreme Ct. 2003. V.p. Vanguard Shipping & Import, Balt., 1972-77, F.W. Myers & Co., Inc., Balt., 1977-84; assoc. Ober, Kaler, Grimes & Shriver, Balt., 1984-91, ptnr., 1992-97, Sandler, Travis & Rosenberg, P.A., Balt., 1997—. Chair Johns Hopkins U. Inst. of Policy Studies com. Logistics and the Economy, 1996-99. Contbr. articles to bar jours. Mem. Gov.'s Commn. World Trade Efforts, 1984, Balt. City Wage Commn., 1986-90, Md. Trade Policy Com., 1986; chair 2d Ann. Md. Internat. Trade Conf.; chair air cargo devel. com. BWI Econ. Devel. Coun., 1993-96. Mem.: NAFTA (chpt. 19 roster), Assn. Transp. Law Profls. (newsletter editor Import/Export Regulation), Am. Assn. Exporters and Importers, Am. Arbitration Assn. (panelist), Md. Internat. Trade Assn. (pres. 1984—86), Women's Bar Assn. Md. (pres. 1977—78), Md. State Bar Assn. (chair internat. comml. law sect. 1991—92), Md. C. of C. (chmn. internat. trade com. 1984—97). Office: Sandler Travis & Rosenberg PA 111 S Calvert St Ste 2700 Baltimore MD 21202-6143 Office Phone: 410-385-5208. Business E-Mail: pchaplin@strtrade.com.

CHAPMAN, ALAN JESSE, engineering educator; b. LA, June 22, 1925; s. Wallace Webster and Isabel (Smith) C.; m. Marjorie Bray, June 8, 1950; children: Alan Jesse, Katherine Lynn. BS in Mech. Engring, Rice U., 1945; MS, U. Colo., 1949; PhD, U. Ill., 1953. Registered profl. engr., Tex. Faculty Rice U., Houston, 1946—, prof. mech. engring., 1954-69, chmn. dept. mech. and aerospace engring. and materials sci., 1954-69, v.p., 1968—70, prof. emeritus, 1996—; dean G.R. Brown Sch. Engring., 1975-80, Harry S. Cameron prof. mech. engring., 1980—95. Cons. to Manned Spacecraft Ctr., NASA, Houston, 1961—95. Author: Introductory Gas Dynamics, 1970. Heat Transfer, 4th edit, 1984, Fundamentals of Heath Transfer, 1987. Pres. S.W. Athletic Conf., 1965-67; mem. coun. NCAA, 1968-73, pres., 1973-74. Served with USNR, 1942-45. Fellow AIAA (assoc.) ASME (hon.); mem. ASHRAE, Am. Soc. Engring. Edn., Sigma Xi, Tau Beta Pi. Home: 10031 Doliver Dr Houston TX 77042-2015 Office: Rice Univ PO Box 1892 6100 South Main Houston TX 77251 Office Phone: 713-348-4908. Business E-Mail: chapman@rice.edu.

CHAPMAN, ALGER BALDWIN, financial services company executive, lawyer; b. Portland, Maine, Sept. 28, 1931; s. Alger Baldwin, Sr. and Elizabeth (Ives) Chapman; m. Beatrice Bishop, Oct. 30, 1983; children: Alger III, Samuel P., Andrew I., Henry H. BA, Williams Coll., 1953; JD, Columbia U., 1956. Bar: N.Y. 1957. Pres. Shearson, Hammill & Co., 1970-74; co-chmn. Shearson & Co., 1974-81; vice chmn. Am. Express Bank, 1982—86; chmn., CEO Chgo. Bd. Options Exch., 1986-97; vice chmn. ABN Amro, Inc., 1997—2001; chmn. ABN Amro Fin. Svcs, 1998—2004; dir. The Cambridge Group, Chgo., 2005—. Bd. dirs. HDO; chmn. Prime Ins. Mem.: Econ. Club, Country Club Little Rock, Glenview Club, Comml. Club, Met. Club (NYC), Racquet Club Chgo., Chgo. Club. Avocations: golf, reading. Home: 33 Hickory Hills Cir Little Rock AR 72212 Office: 227 W Monroe St Ste 3200 Chicago IL 60606 Office Phone: 312-961-9914.

CHAPMAN, ALVAH HERMAN, JR., retired newspaper executive; b. Columbus, Ga., Mar. 21, 1921; s. Alvah Herman and Wyline (Page) Chapman; m. Betty Bateman, Mar. 22, 1943; children: Dale Page Chapman Webb, Chris Ann Chapman Hilton. BS, The Citadel, 1942, degree (hon.), 1971, Barry U., 1985, Fla. Internat. U., 1988, U. Miami, Coral Gables, Fla., 1989, U. Notre Dame, 1991. Bus. mgr. Columbus Ledger, 1945-53; exec. v.p., gen. mgr. St. Petersburg (Fla.) Times, 1953-57; pres., pub. Morning News and Evening Press, Savannah, Ga., 1957-60; exec. Knight-Ridder Newspapers, Inc., Miami, Fla., 1960-89, exec. com., 1960-2000; dir. Knight Ridder, 1962-2000; exec. v.p. Knight-Ridder Newspapers, Inc., 1967-73, pres., 1973-82, CEO, 1976-88, chmn., 1982-89, dir., chmn. exec. com., 1984-95; v.p., gen. mgr. Miami Herald, 1962-70, pres., 1970-82. Lectr. Am. Press Insts., Columbia; vice chmn., exec. com. Miami Coalition for Safe & Drug-Free Cmty.; mem. Pres.'s Drug Adv. Coun., 1989-92; chmn. emeritus Fla. Internat. U. Found.; bd. trustees Fla. Internat. U., 2001-2002; trustee John S. and James L. Knight Found., 1971-2002. Founder, chmn. emeritus Cmty. Anti-Drug Coalitions Am.; chmn. We Will Rebuild, 1992—93, Gov.'s Commn. on Homeless, 1992—94; founding chmn. Cmty. Partnership for Homeless, Inc., 1993—; mem. State's Commn. on the Homeless, 2000; bd. dirs. ARC Greater Miami and the Keys, 2001—04. Maj. USAAF, World War II. Decorated Croix de Guerre, D.F.C. with 2 oak leaf clusters, Air medal with 5 clusters U.S.; named Outstanding Young Man, Columbus Jr. C. of C., 1952, Dade County's Outstanding Citizen of 1968-69, Brigham Young U. Internat. Businessman of Yr., 1984, Hon. Dir., Fla. C. of C., 1997, Grad. Sch. Bus. Fla. Internat. U. in honor of Alvah H. Chapman, Jr., 2001, Alvah H. Chapman, Jr. and Betty B. Chapman Ctr. in honor of Betty and Alvah Chapman, Cmty. Partnership Homeless, 2002; named one of 22 Who Make a City Magic, Jr. League, 2003, Legends South Fla., South Fla. CEO mag., 2004; named to South Fla. Bus. Hall of Fame, 2000, Arland D. Williams Soc. at The Citadel, 2002, Builders Assn. South Fla. Housing Hall of Fame, 2003, Fla. Newspaper Hall of Fame, 2004; recipient Citadel Palmetto award, 1985, Isaiah Thomas award, Rochester Inst. Tech., 1986, Joseph Wharton Statesman award, 1988, United Negro Coll. Fund's Disting. Svc. award, 1988, The Miami Herald Spirit of Excellence Lifetime Achievement award, 1989, Anne Ackerman Disting. Floridian award, 1991, LeRoy Collins Lifetime Achievement award, Leadership Fla., 1992, United Way Dorothy Shula award for Volunteerism, 1994, Salvation Army Red Shield award, 1994, ARC Humanitarian of Yr. award, 1994, Health Found. of South Fla. Concern award, 1995, Drum Maj. of Justice award, Miami-Dade C. C., 1996, Spirit of Martin Luther King Jr. Parade & Festivities Dinner Com. award, 1996, Citizen of Yr. award, Gray Panthers North Dade, 1996, Resolution State Fla., 1996, Lifetime Achievement award, Cmty. Anti-Drug Coalitions Am., 1999, Ellis Island medals of honor, 2000, Pontifical medal Benemerenti, 2000, Fla. Meml. Coll. Cmty. Leadership award, 2001, Pillar award, Fla. Internat. U., 2001, 1st recipient Cmty. Partnership for Homeless's Alvah H. Chapman, Jr. Humanitarian award, 2002, Corp. Citizenship award, Nat. Coalition for Homeless, 2002, Disting. Svc. award, Cmty. Anti-Drug Coalitions Am., 2004, Mayor's Lifetime Achievement award, 2004, Advocacy award, Homeless/Formerly Homeless Forum Inc., 2004, Peace and Unity award, St. Martin de Porres Assn., 2005, Cornerstone award, Broward Partnership Homeless, 2007, Lifetime Achievement award, Miami Coalition Christian and Jews, 2007. Mem. Newspaper Assn. Am., Am. Newspaper Pub. Assn. (chmn., pres. 1986-87), So. Newspapers Pubs. Assn. (pres. 1976). Methodist. Home: Grove Harbour 1690 S Bayshore Ln 10ab Miami FL 33133-4073 Office: One Herald Plz Miami FL 33132-1693 Home Phone: 305-859-9191; Office Phone: 305-376-3870.

CHAPMAN, ANGELA MARIE, science educator; b. Wayne, Mich., Aug. 7, 1964; d. Hugh Richard and Sarah Treva Norris; m. Joseph Alfred Chapman, Jan. 5, 1985. BS in Zoology, Mich. State U., 1990; MS in Biology, U. Ky., 1994. Cert. profl. educator Fla. Tchg. asst. U. Ky., Lexington, 1991—93; adj. faculty Midway (Ky.) Coll., 1993; instr. Baker Coll., Flint, Mich., 1994—99; rsch. asst. Mich. State U., East Lansing, 1994—2000; prof., instr. Lansing (Mich.) C.C., 1999—2002, Polk C.C., Lakeland, Fla., 2003—; tchr. Polk County Schs., Lakeland, 2004—. Pres. C & S Works, Holt, Mich., 1995—2001; grad. student coun. Mich. State U., 1995—99, dean's student adv. coun., 1996—97; chairperson metric olympics com. Sleepy Hill Mid. Sch., Lakeland, 2003—, curriculum com. mem., 2005—; chairperson, textbook adoption, curriculum devel. Polk County Schs., Bartow, Fla., 2005—; co-director Polk Regional Sci. Fair, Bartow, 2005—; exec. dir., founder Sci. Explores Examines Discovers, Lakeland, 2006—. Author: Fundamentals of Neuroanatomy; contbr. articles various profl. jours. Named Tchr. of Yr., Sleepy Hill Mid. Sch., 2005; recipient Tchr. Hon., Disney, 2006; Summer fellowship, U. Ky., 1992, 1993, Rsch. fellowship, Mich. State U., 1995, Tchr. to Tchr. Developer grant, Polk Edn. Found., 2005, Classroom grant, Fla. Assn. Sci. Tchrs., 2005. Mem.: AAAS, AAUW, NEA, NSTA (point of light rep. 2004—06), Fla. Assn. Sci. Tchrs. Avocations: reading, travel, bicycling, photography. Office: Sleepy Hill Mid Sch 2215 Sleepy Hill Rd Lakeland FL 33810 Home Phone: 863-838-2001; Office Phone: 863-815-6577.

CHAPMAN, ANTHONY BRADLEY, psychiatrist; b. Salem, Mass., June 22, 1938; s. Anthony Bredick and Gladys Gwendolyn (Poole) C.; m. Ella Mueller, Aug. 30, 1963; children: Bradley, Jeffrey. BS with honors, Northeastern U., 1961; MD, Stanford U., 1966. Diplomate Am. Bd. Psychiatry and Neurology. Rsch. asst. Harvard Med. Sch., Boston, 1957-61; intern Case-Western Res. U., Cleve., 1966-67; resident Johns Hopkins

Hosp., Balt., 1967-69, fellow in behavioral medicine, 1967-69; fellow in child psychiatry U. Pa., Phila., 1969-71; pvt. practice Alexandria, Va., 1973—. Dir. Attention Disorder Ctr. No. Va., Alexandria, 1991—; guest lectr. Children and Adults with Attention Deficit Disorder, Arlington, Va., 1990-96. Editor Hyperactive Child Newsletter, 1974-78. Maj. US Army, 1971—73. Recipient Outstanding Tchr. award Am. Acad. Family Practice, 1976-81. Mem. Am. Med. Soc., Am. Psychiat. Electrophysiology Assn., Va. Med. Soc., Alexandria Med. Soc., Attention Deficit Disorders Profls. No. Va. (pres. 1990-92). Avocations: jazz, Brazilian music, tennis, skiing. Office: 2059 Huntington Ave Ste 108 Alexandria VA 22303-1602 Home Phone: 703-916-0972; Office Phone: 703-960-4900. E-mail: brad_chapman@att.net.

CHAPMAN, BETH KILLOUGH, state official; b. Greenville, Ala., Apr. 4, 1962; m. James Chapman, 1988; children: Winston Taylor, William Thatcher. BS, U. Montevallo, Ala., 1984; M magna cum laude, U. Ala., Birmingham. Founder, owner Beth Chapman & Assocs., L.L.C., 1996—; state exec. dir. Cystic Fibrosis Found., Ala.; appointments sec. to Gov. State of Ala., Montgomery, 1995—96, press sec. to Gov., 2000—01, auditor, 2002—06, sec. state, 2007—. Author: The Power of Patriotism: The Speech Heard Around the World (George Washington Honor Medal). Mem. Shelby County Child Advocacy Ctr., Shelby County Ct. Appointed Spl. Advocates Prog.; George W. Bush del. Rep. Nat. Conv., 2000, 2004; mem. Rep. Women's Leadership Coun., Lakeside Baptist Ch., Ala. Electoral Coll., 2004—. Republican. Baptist. Office: Office Sec State PO Box 5616 Montgomery AL 36103-5616 E-mail: beth.chapman@auditor.state.al.us.*

CHAPMAN, CONRAD DANIEL, lawyer; b. Detroit, July 31, 1933; s. Conrad F. and Alexandrine C. (Baranski) C.; m. Carol Lynn DeBash, Sept. 1, 1956; children: Stephen Daniel, Richard Thomas, Suzanne Marie. BA, U. Detroit, 1954, JD summa cum laude, 1957; LLM in Taxation, Wayne State U., 1964. Bar: Mich. 1957, U.S. Dist. Ct. (so. dist.) Mich. 1957. Former pres. chmn. of bd. Powers, Chapman, DeAgostino, Meyers & Milia, 1990—2003, of counsel Troy, Mich., 2004—. Mem. ABA, Detroit Bar Assn., Oakland Bar Assn., Met. Detroit Estate Planning Coun., Nat. Assn. Estate Planning Coun., Detroit Athletic Club, Detroit Golf Club. Office: Powers Chapman DeAgostino Meyers & Milia 3001 W Big Beaver Rd Ste 704 Troy MI 48084-3108

CHAPMAN, CRAIG E., lawyer; b. 1954; BA, Conn. Coll, 1977; JD, Case Western Reserve Univ., 1980. Bar: NY 1981. Atty. corp. fin., Sydney, Australia, 1981—83; assoc. Sidley Austin Brown & Wood LLP, NYC, 1983—92, ptnr., 1992—, resident ptnr. Tokyo, 1992—95, also now co-chmn. internat operations and practice devel. com. NYC. Mem.: ABA. Office: Sidley Austin Brown & Wood LLP 787 Seventh Ave New York NY 10019 Office Phone: 212-839-5564. Office Fax: 212-839-5599. Business E-Mail: cchapman@sidley.com.

CHAPMAN, CYNTHIA B., lawyer; b. Bronxville, New York, July 7, 1965; BA in Art History, U. of Calif., San Diego, 1988; JD, U. of San Diego Law School, 1992. Bar: Texas, California. Assoc. English & Gloven, LLP, Seltzer, Caplan, Wilkens, and McMahon; partner Caddell & Chapman. Named one of top 50 Litigators, Nat. Law Journal, 2001, top 40 under 40 most successful litigators, 2002, Houston's 200 Best Lawyers, H Tex. Mag., 2005. Mem.: Houston Bar Assoc., Assoc. of Trial Lawyers of Am., Trial Lawyers for Public Justice. Office: Caddell & Chapman The Park in Houston Center 1331 Lamar Houston TX 77010

CHAPMAN, DREW GORDON LEE, lawyer; b. Sydney, NSW, Australia, Dec. 12, 1974; arrived in US, 1997; s. Vaughn Lee and Kerry Patricia Chapman; m. Katharine Fuhrmann, Jan. 11, 2002; children: Sydney Livanos, Gordon Lee. LLB, Bond U., Queensland, Australia, 1995; LLM, Fordham U., NYC, 1998. Solicitor Hardings Solicitors, Sydney, 1996—97; assoc. Greenberg Taurig, NYC, 1998—99, Fox Horan & Camerini LLP, NYC, 1999—2004, ptnr., 2005—06; ptnr., chmn. fund svcs. group Sonnenschein Nath & Rosenthal LLP, NYC, 2006—. Mem.: ABA, Managed Funds Assn, Leash Club. Office: Sonnenschein Nath & Rosenthal LLP 1221 Ave of Americas New York NY 10020

CHAPMAN, DUANE LEE (DOG), bail enforcement agent, television personality; b. Denver, Feb. 1, 1953; s. Wesley and Barbara Chapman; m. Beth Smith, May 20, 2006; children: Duane Lee, Leland, Lyssa, Tucker, Christopher, Barbara(dec.) , Wesley, Cecily, Bonnie Jo, Gary. Owner Da Kine Bail Bonds, Honolulu. Actor: (films) Aussie Park Boyz, 2004; (TV series) Dog the Bounty Hunter, 2005—, (TV appearances) The Osbournes, 2005, George Lopez, 2005; co-author (with Kent Black): You Can Run But You Can't Hide: The Life and Times of Dog the Bounty Hunter, 2007. Achievements include the apprehension of over 6,000 fugitives, including most notably Andrew Luster in Mexico, June 18, 2003. Office: Da Kine Bail Bonds 1383 Queen Emma St Honolulu HI 96813*

CHAPMAN, FAY L., lawyer, bank executive; b. San Jose, Calif., Dec. 17, 1946; BA, UCLA, 1968; JD, NYU, 1972. Bar: NY 1973, Wash. 1975. Atty. Foster Pepper & Shefelman, Seattle, 1979—97; exec. v.p., gen. counsel Washington Mutual, Inc., Seattle, 1997—99; sr. exec. v.p., gen. counsel Washington Mutual Inc, Seattle, 1999—. Mem. ABA, Wash. Bankers Assn., Wash. Savs. League. Office: Washington Mutual Inc 1301 2nd Ave Ste 3301 Seattle WA 98101*

CHAPMAN, GENEVA JOYCE, entrepreneur, educator, writer; b. Calvert, Tex., Sept. 23, 1951; d. John Henry and Deborah Betty Chapman. BA, Cameron U., 1973; MEd, Wichita State U., 1976; EdSp in early intervention edn., U. Toledo, 1997. Cert. tchr., Ohio. Tchr.'s aide Newton Pub. Schs., Kans., 1973—74; classroom tchr. Wichita Pub. Schs., 1976—83; ednl. cons. Ginn and Co., Columbus, Ohio, 1984—86; vol. coord. Friends of Homeless Shelter, Columbus, 1986—88; family life educator Pilot Program, Toledo, 1988—89; journalist Toledo Jour., 1989—91; behavior mgmt. specialist Lucas County Bd. Mental Retardation/Devel. Disabilities, Toledo, 1991—98, tchr. spl. edn., 1998—99, habilitation specialist, 1999—; CEO TALMAR, Toledo, 1993—. Dir. Showcase Prodns. divsn. TALMAR. Newspaper columnist Chit-Chat, 1989-1995; reporter The Sojourner's Truth Newspaper, 2002; editor The Holland Herald, 2002; author (musical comedy) The Race, 1975, (musical): A Marvel, A Miracle, America, 1982, (drama) B.R.AIDS, 1990; founder a Capella duo Two Voices Only, 1991; mem. Spectrum, women's music group, 1989-95; creator Ms. Hipps comic strip, 1984; featured playwright Chgo. Dramatist Workshops, 1993-94; writer, dir., prodr. original musical drama: Juneteenth, 1990. Founder Toledo Blackstage Theatre Co., 1990, playwright-in-residence; founder For Colored Girls Repertory Co., 1994; mem. Da' Coloured Gurlz Collective, 1995—; U.S. del. World AIDS Conf., Paris, 1990 Recipient Community Svc. Fine Arts award Save Our Children, 1993. Mem. NEA (bldg. supr. 1974-79), NAFE, Am. Fedn. Tchrs., Nat. Assn. to Advance Fat Acceptance (Toledo kwanzaa com. 1992—, bd. trustees 2004—) Avocations: acting, writing and directing plays, singing. Office Phone: 419-243-0007. E-mail: gjcinc@yahoo.com.

CHAPMAN, GILBERT BRYANT, physicist; b. Uniontown, Ala., July 8, 1935; s. Gilbert Bryant and Annie Lillie (Stallworth) Chapman; m. Loretta Woodward, June 5, 1960 (dec. Sept. 1994); children: Annie L., Bernice M., Cedric N., David O., Ernest P., Frances Q. H., Gilbert Bryant III; m. Betty J. Ellis, June 27, 1999; stepchildren: Michael, Lorri, Marc. BS in Math. and Chemistry, Baldwin Wallace Coll., Berea, Ohio, 1968; MS in Physics, Cleve. State U., 1973; MBA, Mich. State U., 1990; postgrad., Kent State U., Ohio, 1974—76; PhD in Physics, U. Windsor, Ont., Can., 2007. Phys. sci. technician NASA-Lewis Rsch. Ctr., Cleve., 1953—68, emission spectroscopist, 1968—75, materials engr., 1975—77; sr. rsch. engr. Ford Motor Co., Redford Twp., Mich., 1977—83, project engr., 1983—86; adv. materials testing specialist Chrysler Corp., Highland Park, Mich., 1986—89, adv. materials specialist Madison Heights, Mich., 1989—91, advanced materials and product exec., 1991—95, advanced materials cons., 1995—98; sr. mgr. advanced materials and product devel. Daimler-Chrylser Corp., Rochester Hills, Mich., 1998—2003, dir. advanced transp. tech., 2003—. Chmn. auto com. '87 Soc. Mfg. Engrs. Composites Group, Dearborn, Mich., 1987, chair bd. dirs., 96; chmn. ind. adv. bd. NDE/Ctr., Iowa State U., Ames, 1989, Ames, 90; mem. indsl. adv. bd. Inst. Mfg. Rsch., Wayne State U., Ctrl. State U., U. Tex.-Pan Am., U. Mich., Dearborn, Oakland U., Rochester, Mich.; chair Internat. Symposium Automotive Tech. and Automation Materials Conf., 1996, 98, Automotive Composites Consortium, 1996; MLK prof. physics Wayne State U., 2001. Contbr. articles to profl. jours., chapters to books. Trustee Mt. Vernon Acad. Ohio, Ohio, 1972—76; lay adv. coun. Ohio Conf. SDA, 1974—77; lay leader, elder SDA Ch., Southfield, Mich., 1983—95, elder Farmington Hills, Mich., 2000—. With USAF, 1959—61. Named Black Engr. of the Yr., U.S. Black Engr. and Info. Tech. Mag., 1999; named one of Best and Brightest Profls., Dollars and Sense Mag., 1993; recipient Apollo Achievement award, NASA Lewis Rsch. Ctr., 1968, NASA Group Achievement award, 1970, Mayor Archer's proclamation, Motor City Youth Fedn., 1994, Spirit of Detroit award, Detroit City Coun., 1994, Career Achievement award, U.S. Black Engr. and Info. Tech. Mag., 1999. Fellow: Am. Soc. Nondestructive Testing (cert. level III 6 NDT methods); mem.: SAE (award for excellence in oral presentation), ASTM, IEEE, ASM (mem. polymer composites program com. 1986), Soc. Mfg. Engrs. (chaired CMA adv. bd.), Soc. Applied Spectroscopy (Cleve. vice chair, sec.), Nat. Tech. Assn. (mem. Cleve. program com.), Fedn. Analytical Chemists, Engring. Soc. Detroit (mem. sci. com., ASM/ESD Best Paper award 1993), Can. Assn. Physicists, Am. Soc. Composites, Am. Phys. Soc., Am. Chem. Soc., Soc. Physics Students, Sigma Pi Sigma. Achievements include patents for infrared inspection method for friction welds in thermoplastics and advanced vehicle concepts; development of low-frequency ultrasonic inspection methods for polymer composites and adhesive bond joints; co-development of D.C. arc method of determining work functions of refractory alloys, spectrochemical analysis of microgram-size samples. Home and Office: Advanced Transp Techs 38671 Greenbrook Ct Farmington Hills MI 48331-2979 Personal E-mail: gbchapman2@aol.com. *The persistant pursuit of moral and ethical values, faith and the concomitant virtues while seeking to serve more effectively, can lead to a successful and satisfying life.*

CHAPMAN, GILBERT WHIPPLE, JR., publishing executive; b. NYC, July 1, 1933; s. Gilbert W. and Katherin (Bright) C.; m. Judith Coste, June 14, 1956; 1 child, Gilbert W. III BA, Yale U., 1956. Pub. McGraw-Hill, Inc., N.Y.C., 1958-72; exec. v.p., dir. Morgan Grampain, Inc., NYC, 1971-75; pres. Pub. Group Esquire Inc., NYC, 1975-78; pres., dir. Diversion Communications, Inc., NYC, 1978-85, Kalo Communications, Inc., NYC, 1985-91; chmn., CEO Cemark, Inc., 1991—. Trustee Village of Mill Neck, 1993—2000, Choate Sch., Wallingford, Conn., 1986—91, Pomfret Sch., 1980—86; bd. dirs. Planned Parenthood of Nassau County, 1985—2002, Planned Parenthood of Nassau County Found., 2000—, Cmty. Hosp. of Glen Cove, 1986—90, North Shore U. Hosp., 1990—94. Mem.: Piping Rock Club (pres. 2000—06), Racquet and Tennis Club. Republican. Episcopalian. Home: Factory Pond Rd Locust Valley NY 11560-1405 Office: 13531 E Boundary Rd Midlothian VA 23112-3953 Office Phone: 516-676-0277.

CHAPMAN, HUGH MCMASTER, banker; b. Spartanburg, SC, Sept. 11, 1932; s. James Alfred and Martha (Marshall) Chapman; m. Anne Allston Morrison, Dec. 27, 1958 (dec. Mar. 1993); children: Anne Allston, Rachel Buchanan, Mary Morrison; m. Janis Felkel, Aug. 17, 2001. BSBA, U. N.C., 1955. With Citizens & So. Nat. Bank S.C., 1958-91, pres., 1971-74, chmn. bd., 1974-91; pres. Citizens & So. Corp., Atlanta, 1986-91; vice chmn. C&S/Sovran Corp., 1990-91; chmn. Nations Bank S., 1992-97; ret., 1997. Bd. dirs. Inman Mills. Trustee East Lake Fedn., Duke Endowment. 1st lt. USAF, 1955-57. Office: Bank of Am Plz 600 Peachtree St Fl 16 Atlanta GA 30308-2265

CHAPMAN, JAMIE L., pharmacist; d. Noel and Anita Cotton; m. Patrick Chapman, Aug. 7, 1999. BA in Chemistry, Maryville Coll., Tenn., 1995—99; PharmD, U. Tenn., Memphis, 2000—04. Lic. immunization APhA, 2001, diabetes patient care ACPE, 2003, pharmacist Ohio, 2004. Gen. practice resident Veterans Affairs Puget Sound, Seattle, 2004—05; critical care pharmacist Swedish Med. Ctr., Seattle, 2005—06; critical care clin. pharmacist Ft. Hamilton Hosp., Ohio, 2006—. Pharmacy preceptor, Seattle, 2004—06, Ft. Hamilton Hosp., 2006—. Vol. Union Gospel Mission, Seattle, 2004. Recipient Leadership award, Am. Soc. Health Sys. Pharmacy, 2004, Tom C. Sharp Leadership award, U. Tenn., 2004. Mem.: Am. Coll. Clin. Pharmacy, Am. Soc. Health Systems Pharmacist, Phi Lambda Sigma (pres. 2002—03), Student Govt. Assn. (pres. 2003—04), Phi Delta Chi (worthy corr. 2001—02, social chair 2002—03). Avocations: running, hiking, camping, kickboxing. Office: Ft Hamilton Hosp 630 Eaton Ave Cincinnati OH 45013 Home Phone: 513-867-2891.

CHAPMAN, JOHN ANDREW, retired chamber of commerce executive; b. Evanston, Ill., Oct. 12, 1928; s. Roger Edington and Margaret Holloway (Morgan) Chapman; m. Betsy Miller, June 23, 1951; children: Andrew K., Jean M., Margaret(dec.) , Peter S. BS, Northwestern U., 1950. Cert. Nat. Inst. Orgn. Mgmt., C. of C. exec. Asst. dir. pub. rels. Northwestern U., Evanston, 1950-54; asst. mgr. Joliet Assn. Commerce, 1954-57; mgr. Twin Cities Area C. of C., Benton Harbor/St. Joseph, Mich., 1957-67; pres. Muskegon Area Devel. Coun. and C. of C., Mich., 1967-74, Charleston C. of C., 1974-94; mng. dir. Kanawha Pastoral Counseling Ctr., 1994-98; ret., 1998. Former chmn. Berrien County (Mich.) Planning Commn.; past treas. Tri-Cap, Inc.; mem. emeritus Salvation Army, Charleston; dir., past pres. Kanawha County Pub. Safety Coun.; bd. dirs., treas. Good News Mountaineer Garage; former mem. Cmty. Coun. Charleston Job Corps; past chmn., dir. Charleston Police Civilian Rev. Bd.; co-chair Coun. Historic Orgns.; past sec. Bishop Whittemore Found.; past treas. W.Va. Taxpayers Assn.; past pres. Charleston Leadership Coun. Pub. Safety; past vice-chair, dir. W.Va. Regional Cmty. Policing Inst.; vice-chair Eisenhower Math.-Sci. Consortium; past dir. Craik-Patton House, Inc.; past exec. dir. Craik-Patton House Found., past treas.; past vestryman St. John's, St. Edward's and St. Gregory's Episcopal Ch.; past warden St. Augustine's Episcopal Ch.; former bd. dirs. Charleston Symphony; bd. dirs. Charleston Renaissance Corp.; past v.p. Southwestern br. Mich. Children's Aid Soc. Mem.: So. Assn. C. of C. Execs. (past pres., sec.), Am. C. of C. Execs. (bd. dirs.), Mich. C. of C. Execs. (past pres.), W.Va. C. of C. Execs. (past pres.), Anvil Club (sec.), Rotary. Republican. Home: 209 Ashby Ave Charleston WV 25314-1009 E-mail: johnandbetsy51@yahoo.com.

CHAPMAN, LAVONYA KELLEY, lawyer, director; b. Troy, Ala., Dec. 16, 1952; d. Roscoe Douglas and Sara Southerland Kelley; m. William Reynolds Chapman, III (div.); 1 child, Kelley Chapman Larkin. ADN, Jefferson State CC, 1973; BSN, Samford U., 1981; JD, Birmingham Sch. Law, 1995. Bar: Ala. 1996, U.S. Dist. Ct. 1996. Nurse emergency dept. Edge Regional Med. Ctr., Troy, 1973, UAB Hosp., Birmingham, 1974—76; med. case mgr. USF& G Ins. Co., 1991—96; atty. McFerrin & Assocs., 1996—99, Gaines, Wolter, & Kinney, 1999—2000; dir. claims/litigation Robinson Adams Ins. Co., 2000—. Instr. U. Ala., 1976—81; chmn. State Com. on Emergency Med. Svc. Edn., 1982—83; cons. Ala. Hosp. Assn., 1983—83. Mem. missions com. Presbyn. Ch. of the Hills, 2000—. Mem.: Def. Rsch. Inst., Am. Health Lawyers Assn., Ala. Def. Lawyers Assn., Sigma Delta Kappa, Sigma Theta Tau, Phi Kappa Phi. Republican. Presbyn. Avocation: music. Home: 5141 Chicksaw Cir Birmingham AL 35242 Office: Robinson Adams Insurance Co 2200 Woodcrest Pl Birmingham AL 35209

CHAPMAN, LENORA ROSAMOND, day care provider, social service organization director; b. Bklyn., Feb. 22, 1922; d. William Leon and Rosamond Cecile (Walker) C.; m. Thomas Leftwich, Oct. 12, 1968 (div. 1972). BA, Brooklyn Coll., 1944; MEd, NYU, 1957; cert. in mgmt. of non-profit orgns., Hofstra U. Cert. tchr., N.Y. Tchr. N.Y.C. Pub. Schs., 1944-67, Hempstead (N.Y.) Pub. Schs., 1967-79, tchr. adult basic edn., 1980—96; tchr., tutor Hofstra U., Hempstead, 1982-89; tchr. NOAH program comm. arts and math Hofstra Univ., Hempstead, 1982-84, tchr., Upward Bound Program Comm. Arts, 1984-89, tutor psychology and basic study skills New Coll., 1987-88; directress Jackson Meml. Day Care Ctr., Hempstead, 1983-84, 88-94, Rosamond's Day Care, Hempstead, 1996—2002. Tchr., tutor Hempstead Homebound Students, 1977-83, Catholic Guardian Soc.-Foster Care Children, 1979-89. Den mother Girl Scouts, 1978-79; chairperson Nassan County Dept. Sr. Citizens Foster Grandparent program, 1988-2002; chairperson Sr. Citizens Foster Grandparent Program Village of Hempstead, 1992; choir mem. United Meth. Ch. Sun City Ctr. Recipient 60 Yrs. As Educator award, Bklyn. Coll., 2004. Mem. NAACP (50 Yr. Educator award, 1994), ASCD, Assn. Childhood Edn. Internat., Nat. Assn. Edn. Young Children, Smithsonian Inst. Nat. Mus. Am. Indian (charter), Ctrl. Nassau Negro Bus. and Profl. Women's Clubs Inc., Phi Beta Kappa, Phi Delta Kappa (NYU chpt. membership award 1988, Svc. award for membership Beta Omicron chpt. 1990), Kappa Delta Pi. Methodist. Avocations: singing, dance, sewing, operas, arts and crafts. Home and Office: 1125 Jameson Greens Dr Unit 55 Sun City Center FL 33573 Office Phone: 813-634-8062.

CHAPMAN, LEWIS DUANE, economist; b. Sept. 3, 1940; s. Lewis Ray and Alice Louise (Fullerton) Chapman; m. Mary Jane Angelacos, Aug. 16, 1961 (div. 1986); children: Erin Marie, Amy Nicole; m. Josephine Carol Crossley, Feb. 22, 1991 (div. 1998). BA, Mich. State U., East Lansing, 1961; PhD, U. Calif., Berkeley, 1969. Economist Oak Ridge (Tenn.) Nat. Lab., 1969—71; asst. prof. dept. applied econs. and mgmt. Cornell U., Ithaca, NY, 1971—76, assoc. prof., 1976—82, prof., 1982—, coord. Climate Change Rsch. Program, 1993—97. Leader, industry and the urban environ. U.S. AID, 1991—95. Author: Energy Resources and Energy Corporations, 1983, Environmental Economics, Theory, Application and Policy, 2000; mem. editl. bd.: Contemporary Econ. Policy, Internat. Jour. Environ. Sci. and Tech.; contbr. more than 185 articles to profl. jours. and publs. Task force on regional transmission Nat. Gov.'s Assn., 2001—02. Scholar, Fulbright Found., U. Natal, South Africa and U. Zimbabwe, 1991. Mem.: NAS (mem. nuc. power panel 1976—80, mem. electric power panel 1986, mem. U.S.-Czechoslovakia agr. and environ. panel 1986—87), Internat. Soc. Ecol. Econs., Western Econ. Assn. Internat., Assn. Environ. and Resource Economists, Internat. Assn. Energy Economists, Am. Econ. Assn. Avocations: hiking, tennis, travel, snow shoeing. Office: Cornell U 246 Warren Hall Ithaca NY 14853-7801 Home Phone: 607-564-7003.

CHAPMAN, LINDA LEE, computer company executive, consultant; b. Omaha, Apr. 27, 1965; d. Olin Parks Chapman and Phyllis May Chapman-Wakefield; m. Chris Barkley; children: Lea Lee Noell, Phillip Wayne Noell, Cameron David Barkley, Jasmine Lauren Barkley. Grad., Centennial H.S., Utica, Nebr., 1983. MCSE, MCP Microsoft, cert. product specialist NT 4.0 Enterprise Microsoft, product Ssecialist NT 4.0 Workstation Microsoft, product specialist NT 4.0 Server Microsoft, product specialist IIS 3.0 and Index Server Microsoft. LAN mgr. and programmer Wiig-Codr Underwriters, Omaha, 1986—93; sr. IT engr. MCI Consumer Markets, Austin, Tex., 1993—94; sr. migration cons. Levi-Strauss & Co., San Fransisco, 1994—95, Advanced Micro Devices (AMD), Austin, 1995—96; sr. migration cons., tech. project mgr. Continental Airlines, Houston, 1996—97; sr. migration cons., global arch. Dell Computer Corp., Round Rock, Tex., 1997—99, sr. product mgr., 1999—2000; pres., CEO, founder Migration Specialists Inc., Round Rock, 2001—. Recipient Outstanding Tech. Article award, 2000. E-mail: linda@migrationspecialists.com.

CHAPMAN, LOREN J., psychology professor; b. Muncie, Ind., Jan. 5, 1927; s. Herbert L. and Lurana Gertrude (Treff) C.; m. Jean Marilyn Paulsen, June 6, 1953; children: Nancy, Laurence. AB cum laude, Harvard U., Cambridge, Mass., 1948; MS, Northwestern U., Evanston, Ill., 1952, PhD, 1954. USPHS postdoctorate research fellow U. Chgo., 1954-56, instr., asst. prof., 1956-59; assoc. prof. U. Ky., Lexington, 1959-62; from assoc. prof. to prof. Southern Ill. U., Carbondale, 1962-67; prof. U. Wis., Madison, 1966-93, NIMH rsch. scientist, 1988-93; prof. emeritus, 1994—. Author: Disordered Thought in Schizophrenia, 1973; contbr. articles to profl. jours. Recipient Disting. Scientist award Soc. for Sci. Clin. Psychology, 1992; NIMH research grantee, 1952-97. Fellow AAAS, APA (Disting. Sci. award for application of psychology 1999); mem. Am. Psychopathol. Assn., Soc. Rsch. Psychopathology (pres. 1989, Joseph Zubin award 1992), Am. Psychol. Soc. (William James fellow 1995). Home: 129 Richland Ln Madison WI 53705-4834 Office: Univ Wis Dept Psychology 1202 W Johnson St Madison WI 53706-1611 Office Phone: 608-238-8426. Business E-Mail: lorenchapman@mindspring.com.

CHAPMAN, MARGARET ELIZABETH, elementary school educator; b. Haverstraw, NY, Aug. 12, 1946; d. William David Sr. and Pauline Ann (Newell) C.; divorced June 1978; 1 child, Jennifer. Student, Rockland Community Coll., 1964-67; BS in Edn., St. Thomas Aquinas Coll., 1975; postgrad., Fairfield U., 1977. Cert. elem. tchr., counselor, N.Y. Elem. tchr. Immaculate Conception Sch., Stony Point, NY, 1967-72; elem. tchr. Haverstraw-Stony Point Sch. Dist., Garnerville, NY, 1975—. Counselor Haverstraw-Stony Point Sch. Dist., Garnerville, 1988—; tchr. liason, PTA, 1999—; student coun. advisor, 2000—; mem. health adv. coun., mid. sch. adv. coun; bd. dirs. Rockland Tchrs. Ctr. Bd. dirs. Rockland Coun. on Alcoholism, Nyack, N.Y., 1989—; developer Impact II, 1987, adaptor, 1989; com. mem. Am. Cancer Soc. Relay for Life Kids Walk. AIDS Mini grantee Regional Health Ctr., Yorktown Heights, N.Y., 1989, Bus. Week grantee Bus. Week Mag., 1990. Mem. Rockland Tchrs.' Ctr. (bldg. rep., co-chairperson 1986-88), Assn. for Supervision and Curriculum Devel. Roman Catholic. Avocations: travel, tutoring, counseling, curriculum writing. Home: 44 Blauvelt Ave West Haverstraw NY 10993-1307 Office: Haverstraw Stony Point Cen Sch Dist 65 Chapel St Garnerville NY 10923-1238 Home Phone: 845-429-2380; Office Phone: 845-942-3200. Personal E-mail: mchap2@aol.com.

CHAPMAN, MAX C., JR., investment company executive; b. June 1943; MBA, Columbia Bus. Sch., 1969. Pres., COO Kidder, Peabody & Co; former co-chmn. of bd., CEO Nomura Securities Internat., NYC; former chmn. bd. Nomura Holding Am. Inc., 1996; former chmn. Gardner Capital Management Corp., NYC. Chmn. bd. Nat. Fish & Wildlife Found.; bd. overseers Columbia Bus. Sch., NYC; bd. trustees Intrepid Sea, Air, Space Mus. Office: Max C Chapman Jr 575 Madison Ave New York NY 10022-2511

CHAPMAN, MICHAEL WILLIAM, orthopedist, educator; b. Newberry, Mich., Nov. 29, 1937; m. Elizabeth Casady; adopted sons: Mark, Craig. AA, Am. River Coll., Sacramento, Calif., 1957; BA, U. Calif., Davis, 1958; BS, U. Calif., San Francisco, 1959, MD, 1962. Diplomate Am. Bd. Orthopaedic Surgery (ad hoc appeal com. 1986, site visitor 1986, certification renewal com. 1985-88, certification renewal com. chmn. 1986-88). Intern San Francisco Gen. Hosp., 1962-63, asst. chief orthopaedic surgery svc., 1971-79, acting chief orthopaedic surgery svc., 1972-73; resident in orthopaedic surgery U. Calif., San Francisco, 1963-67, asst. prof. dept. orthopaedic surgery, Sch. Medicine, 1971-76, assoc. prof. dept. orthopaedic surgery, Sch. Medicine, 1976-79; resident in orthopaedic surgery U. Calif. Hosps., San Francisco, 1963-64, Samuel Merritt Hosp., Oakland, Calif., 1964, Highland-Alameda County Hosp., Oakland, 1965, Children's Hosp. of the East Bay, Oakland, 1966, Shriners Hosp., Honolulu, 1966-67; fellow Nat. Orthopaedic Hosp., London, 1967-68; chmn. dept. orthopaedic surgery U. Calif., Davis, Sacramento, 1979-99, prof. dept. orthopaedic surgery, 1981-2000, David Linn chair orthopaedic surgery, 1998-2001, prof. emeritus, 2000—. Panelist Calif. Crippled Children Svcs. Panel in Orthopaedic Surgery; cons. VA Hospital, Martinez, Calif.; co-chmn. Zimmer Trauma Panel, 1983-84; vis. prof. Fresno Valley Med. Ctr., 1975, Dept. Orthopaedics, U. Calif., Davis, 1976, U. Hawaii, Honolulu, 1977; vis. prof., cons. to Surgeon Gen. U.S. Army, Europe, 1978; vis. prof. U. Basel, Switzerland, 1979, Phoenix Orthopaedic Residency Program, 1979, Stanford U., 1981, U. Hawaii, 1982, U. So. Calif., L.A., 1984, SUNY, Buffalo, 1985, U. Utah, 1985, U. Iowa Coll. Medicine, 1987, Duke U. Sch. Medicine, 1988, U. Calif. Irvine, Div. Orthopaedics, 1990, U. S.C., 1990, Mass. Gen. Hosp., Harvard U., 1990, Boston U., 1994, Stanford U., 1995, Med. Coll. Pa., 1996, numerous others; also guest lectr. numerous instns.; insp. for residency rev. com. ad hoc appeal com. Accreditation coun. for Grad. Med. Specialist Site, 1983-86. Editor: (with M. Madison) Operative Orthopaedics, 1988 (Best New Book in Clin. Medicine Assn. Am. Pubs.); contbr. numerous articles and numerous abstracts to profl. jours.; presenter exhibits, audiovisual programs, some 500 other presentations; cons. editor Skiing Mag., 1973-77; mem. bd. assoc. editors Clin. Orthopaedics and Related Rsch., 1982-85, Internat. Med. Soc. Paraplegia, 1972-80; reviewer Jour. Bone and Joint Surgery, 1980-85, trustee, 1995-03, sec. to bd. trustees, 1999, chmn. bd. trustees, 2000; past reviewer New Eng. Jour. Medicine; patentee in field. With U.S. Army, 1968-70. Decorated Army Commendation medal; recipient Outstanding Tchg. award U. Calif., San Francisco, 1972, Outstanding Tchr. award U. Calif., Davis, 1984, 93; named One of Best 100 Doctors Am., Good Housekeeping Mag.; Fogarty Sr. Internat. fellow NIH, 1978-79, 80-81; grantee Johnson & Johnson, 1983-84, Zimmer Inc., 1983-85, 85-86, 87-90, Interpore Internat., 1985-86, 89-90, Collagen Inc., 1985-86, 88-89, Upjohn Inc., 1985-86, Orthopaedic Rsch. and Edn. Found., 1988-89. Mem. AMA (Physicians Recognition award 1989-96), ACS, Am. Acad. Orthopaedic Surgeons (bd. dirs. 1982-83, numerous coms., Zimmer award for Disting. Contbn. to Orthop. Surgery, 2002), Am. Orthopaedic Assn. (bd. dirs. 1985-86, pres. 1990-91, various coms.), Internat. Orthopaedic Assn., Assn. for Study of Internal Fixation (N.Am. chpt.), Internat. Soc. Orthopaedic Surgery and Traumatology, Internat. Soc. for Fracture Repair, Brit. Orthopaedic Assn., South African Orthopaedic Assn. (hon.), Am. Acad. Orthopaedic Surgeons, Am. Assn. for Surgery of Trauma, Am. Bd. Med. Spltys., Assn. Am. Med. Colls., Leroy C. Abbott Orthopaedic Soc., Austrian Trauma Assn., Paul R. Lipscomb Soc., Northwestern Med. Assn., Orthopaedic Rsch. Soc., Orthopaedic Trauma Assn., Sierra Club, U. Calif. San Francisco Alumni Assn., Western Orthopaedic Assn., Houston Orthopaedic Assn. (hon.), Calif. Med. Assn., Calif. Orthopaedic Assn., Sacramento-El Dorado Med. Soc., Wilson Interurban Orthopaedic Soc., Alpha Omega Alpha. Avocations: skiing, mountain climbing, backpacking, tennis, bicycling. Office: U Calif-Davis Sch Med Dept Orthopedics 4860 Y St Ste 3800 Sacramento CA 95817-2307

CHAPMAN, MORRIS HINES, denominational executive; b. Kosciusko, Miss. m. Jodi Francis; 2 children. Grad., Miss. Coll.; MDiv of Ministry, Southwestern Bapt. Theol. Sem.; doctorate (hon.), SW Bapt. U., Miss. Coll. Pastor 1st Bapt. Ch., Albuquerque, 1974-79, Wichita Falls, Tex., 1979-92; pres. So. Bapt. Conv., 1990-92, pres., CEO, exec. com., 1992—. Pres. pastor's conf. So. Bapt. Conv., 1986, preacher Conv. Sermon, Las Vegas, 1989. Author: Faith: Taking God at His Word, The Wedding Collection. Office: Executive Committee Southern Baptist Convention 901 Commerce St Nashville TN 37203-3620

CHAPMAN, PAUL B., oncologist; b. Chgo., 1955; MD, Cornell U., Ithaca, NY, 1981. Diplomate Am. Bd. Internal Medicine, Am. Bd. Med. Oncology. Intern U. Chgo. Hosp., 1981—82, resident, 1982—84; fellow Meml. Sloan-Kettering Cancer Ctr., NYC, 1982—88, clin. asst., 1988—91, asst. attending physician, 1991—97, assoc attending physician, 1997—2005, attending physician, 2005—06. Assoc. prof. medicine Cornell U. Med. Coll., NYC, 2005—06, prof. medicine, 2006—. Office: 1275 York Ave New York NY 10021-6007

CHAPMAN, PAULETTE ELAINE, lawyer; JD with honors, George Washington U., 1988; BA, George Mason U., 1976. Bar: US Dist. Ct. (Dist. DC), US Ct. Appeals (DC Cir.), US Dist. Ct. (Dist. Md.). Ptnr. Koonz McKenney Johnson DePaolis & Lightfoot, Washington. Mediator and arbitrator Superior Ct. DC; adj. prof. fed. civil procedure Catholic U. Sch. Law, 1995—96; instr. Nat. Inst. Trial Adv. Skills Program and Deposition Program Georgetown U. Law Sch., 2001. Mem.: DC Bar (co-chair tort law sect. steering com. 2001—02), Trial Lawyers of DC (bd. gov. 1999—2003), Women's Bar Assn. DC (co-chair Litig. Forum 2000—01, pres.-elect 2002—03, pres. 2003—04), Bar Assn. DC (pres.-elect 2006—07, bd. dirs. 2002—03). Achievements include patents for air conditioning cord warning label, April 1998. Office: Koonz McKenney Johnson DePaolis & Lightfoot Ste 450 2001 Pennsylvania Ave NW Washington DC 20006 Office Phone: 202-659-5500. E-mail: pchapman@koonz.com.

CHAPMAN, REX, professional sports team executive and retired basketball player; b. Bowling Green, Ky., Oct. 5, 1967; s. Wayne Chapman; m. Bridget Chapman; children: Caley Michelle, Zeke Everett. Student, U. Ky., 1986—88. Player Charlotte Hornets, 1988—91, Washington Bullets, 1992—95, Miami Heat, 1995—96, Phoenix Suns, 1996—2000, basketball ops. position, 2002—05; scout Minn. Timberwolves, 2005—06; v.p. player pers. Denver Nuggets, 2006—. Named to NBA All-Rookie Second Team, 1989. Avocations: golf, swimming, music. Office: Denver Nuggets 1000 Chopper Cir Denver CO 80204*

CHAPMAN, ROBERT FOSTER, federal judge; b. Inman, SC, Apr. 24, 1926; s. James Alfred and Martha (Marshall) Chapman; m. Mary Winston Gwathmey, Dec. 21, 1951 (dec. Sept. 1998); children: Edward, Foster, Winston; m. Mary Vail St. Georges, Sept. 30, 2000. BS, U. SC, 1945, LLB, 1949, LLD (hon.), 1986, Coll. Charleston, 1999. Bar: S.C. 1949. Assoc. firm Butler & Moore, Spartanburg, 1949—51; partner firm Butler, Chapman & Morgan, Spartanburg, 1953—71; judge US Dist. Ct. S.C., 1971—81, US Ct. Appeals (4th Cir.), 1981—91, sr. judge, 1991—. Chmn. S.C. Rep. Party, 1961—63. Lt. USNR, 1943—46, lt. USNR, 1951—53. Recipient Nat. Patriot's award, Congl. Medal of Honor Soc., 1985. Fellow: Am. Coll. Trial Lawyers; mem.: Order of Palmetto. Presbyterian.

CHAPMAN, ROBERT GALBRAITH, retired hematologist, administrator; b. Colorado Springs, Colo., Sept. 29, 1926; s. Edward Northrop and Janet Galbraith (Johnson) Chapman; m. Virginia Irene Potts, July 6, 1956; children: Lucia Tully, Sarah Northrop Bohrer, Robert Bostwick. Student, Westminster Coll., 1944-45; BA, Yale U., 1947; MD, Harvard U., 1951; MS, U. Colo., 1958. Diplomate Am. Bd. Internal Medicine and Pathology; lic. physician, Colo., Calif. Intern Hartford (Conn.) Hosp., 1951-52; resident in medicine U. Colo. Med. Ctr., Denver, 1955-58; fellow in hematology U. Wash., Seattle, 1958-60; chief resident in medicine U. Colo., Denver, 1957-58, instr. medicine, 1960-62, asst. prof. medicine, 1962-68, assoc. prof., 1968-91; chief staff VA Hosp., Denver, 1968-70; dir. Belle Bonfils Meml. Blood Ctr., Denver, 1977-91, retired, 1991. Regionalization com. Am. Blood Commn., Washington, 1985-87, Colo. sickle cell com., Denver, 1978-91, gov.'s AIDS Coun., 1987-88; trustee Coun. Cmty. Blood Ctrs., v.p., 1979-81, pres., 1989-91, Rsch. Inst. bd. Palo Alto Med. Found., 1991-97. Contbr. articles to profl. jours. Treas. Carmel Valley Village Improvement Com., 1995—. Capt. USAF, 1953-55. USPHS fellow, 1958-60. Fellow ACP; mem. Am. Assn. Blood Banks, Mayflower Soc., Denver Med. Soc., Colo. Med. Soc., Western Soc. Clin. Rsch., Am. Radio Relay League, Alpha Omega Alpha. Mem. United Ch. Christ. Avocations: amateur radio, computers, investments, genealogy. Home: 47 La Rancheria Carmel Valley CA 93924-9424 Personal E-mail: drrobc@comcast.net.

CHAPMAN, ROBERT JAMES, psychiatrist, educator; b. Delaware, Ohio, July 10, 1936; s. Edward Samuel and Frances Mae (Stephenson) Chapman; m. Janice Holmes, June 18, 1960; children: Steven Holmes, Scott Edward, Erik Wellington. AB, Oberlin Coll., 1958; MD, Ohio State U., 1963. Diplomate Am. Bd. Psychiatry and Neurology. Instr., fellow, USPHS U. Rochester Sch. Med., NY, 1968—69; asst. prof. clin. psychiatry Dartmouth Med. Sch., Hanover, NH, 1869—1979, asst. prof. cmty. and family med., 1976—79, assoc. prof. clin. psychiatry, 1980—94, adj. assoc. prof. psychiatry, 1994—2002, adj. assoc. prof. psychiatry emeritus, 2003—. Dir. comprehensive alcoholism svcs. program Dartmouth Med. Sch., Hanover, 1973—75, dir. Robert Wood Johnson Primary Care/Physician Mgr. residency program, 1977—79, dir. fellowship program rural cmty. psychiatry, 1979—81; dir. Mt. Ascutney Psychiat. Assocs., Windsor, Vt., 1984—94, Choate Psychiat. Assocs., New London, NH, 1995—99. Contbr. chapters to books, articles to profl. jours. Physician Peace Corps, Nigeria, 1964—66; mem. Area Planning Coun., NH, 1977—80; bd. dirs. Planned Parenthood Assn. Upper Valley, Lebanon, 1970—78; chmn. profl. adv. com. Hanover Vis. Nurse Svc., 1979—80; bd. dirs. Hanover Conservation Coun., 2003—; mem. Handel Soc. Dartmouth Coll., 1983—88; mem. steering com. Upper Valley Health Care Coalition, White River Junction, Vt., Lebanon, NH, 1984—86. Sr. asst. surgeon USPHS, 1964—66. Fellow: Am. Psychiat. Assn. (disting. life); mem.: AAAS, AMA, Global Health Coun., Physicians for Social Responsibility, N.H. Psychiat. Soc. (pres. 1983—84, chmn. ethics com. 1985—86), Union Concerned Scientists, Amnesty Internat., Human Rights Watch, Internat. Physicians for Prevention Nuc. War, Physicians for Human Rights. Avocations: camping, canoeing, photography, wilderness travel. Home: 33 Rip Rd Hanover NH 03755-1616

CHAPMAN, ROBERT LEE, III, real estate developer; b. Jacksonville, Fla., Dec. 14, 1946; s. Robert Lee Jr. and Elisabeth (Trotter) C.; m. Vicky Lee Patton, July 19, 1945; children: Margaret Patton, Robert Lee IV, Anna Elisabeth, Charlotte Elisabeth. BA, Duke U., 1971. Gen. mgr. Sta. WDBS-FM, Durham, N.C., 1971; dir. media ctr. Duke U., Durham, 1972-73; pres. Chapman Patton & Assocs., Durham, 1974-75, Learning Resources Network, Durham, 1975-90, Southlake Devel. Group, Clermont, Fla., 1990—2002, Southlake Utilities, Inc., Clermont, 1990—2002; mng. dir. Traditional Neighborhood Devel. Ptnrs., LLC, Durham, 1999—. Bd. dirs. Broadcasting Found. Am., N.Y.C., 1980-82, Coun. Entrepreneurial Devel., Research Triangle Park, N.C., 1982-86; cons. interactive tech., Burroughs Wellcome Co. and Glaxo, Inc., Research Triangle Park, 1982-86; coord. USA-USSR Summer Arts Festival; juror, Kammerer Meml. Filmmaking prize, Duke U., 1984-89. Editor: Arts Festival Planning Guide, 1974; exec. producer over 100 films and videos. Coord., Durham Bicentennial Commn., 1975-76; bd. dirs. Ctrl. Park Sch. for Children, 2001—, Historic Preservation Soc. of Durham, 2002-06, Carolina Cinema Corp., Durham, 1978-82, Friends of Duke U. Arts Mus., Durham, 1986-89, Nat. Town Builders Assn.; chmn. N.C. Smart Growth Alliance, Chapel Hill, 2000-05; trustee, Duke Sch. for Children, Durham, 1986-90. Mem. Samuel Cook Soc. (Duke U.), Order of Red Friars, Sigma Nu. Avocations: travel, jogging, backpacking, skin diving. Home: 2525 Lanier Pl Durham NC 27705-5005 Home Phone: 919-489-1884.

CHAPMAN, ROGER EUGENE, historian, educator; b. Washington, Feb. 25, 1960; s. Herbert Lee and Lois Jean Chapman; m. Deborah Reece, Aug. 4, 1990; children: Christine, Elizabeth. BS, U. Md., 1986; MA, Wheaton Coll., Ill., 1992; PhD, Bowling Green State U., 2004. Newspaper reporter Suburban Record, Silver Spring, Md., 1982—83; legis. aide Mongtomery County Coun., Rockville, Md., 1983—88; social studies tchr. Inter-Am. Sch., Quetzaltenango, Guatemala, 1989—90; missionary Ch. of Christ, St Petersburg, Volgograd, Russia, 1992—97; history instr. Lincoln Trail Coll., Robinson, Ill., 2002—07; asst. prof. Palm Beach Atlantic U., West Palm Beach, Fla., 2007—. Asst. editor N.W. Ohio Quar., Bowling Green, 1999—2000; mem. faculty adv. bd. Ill. Bd. of Higher Edn., Springfield, 2004—05. Author: (historical work) It Started with Doctors on Horseback (Henry Howe Book award, 2002). With US Army, 1978—81. Decorated Humanitarian Svc. medal U.S. Army; recipient Faculty Excellence award, U. of Tex. at Austin, 2005, Local History Publ. award, Ctr. for Archival Collections, 2002. Mem.: Am. Hist. Assn. Democrat. Church Of Christ. Office: Palm Beach Atlantic U Sch Arts & Scis PO Box 24708 West Palm Beach FL 33416 Office Phone: 618-544-8657.

CHAPMAN, ROGER STEVENS, JR., construction company executive; b. Hartford, Conn., Dec. 3, 1927; s. Roger Stevens Chapman, Katherine Marie (Willetts) Chapman; m. Viola Mohl, Feb. 7, 1959; children: David, Ellen. BCE, Cornell U., 1949; MS in Mgmt., Rensselaer Poly. Inst., 1970. Registered Profl. engr. Field engr. A.S. Wikstrom, Inc., Skaneateles, NY, 1949—54; project engr. Savin Constrn. Co., East Hartford, Conn., 1954—58; project mgr. Merritt-Chapman & Scott Corp., NYC, 1958—62; supt., chief estimator, v.p. C.W. Blakeslee & Sons, Inc., New Haven, 1962—76; v.p., dir. Blakeslee Arpaia Chapman, Inc., Branford, Conn., 1976—86, pres., 1986—. V.p., dir. BAC Marine, Inc., Branford, 1977—. Bd. dirs. Sou;theastern Conn. Better Bus. Bur., 1980—86. With US Army, 1951—53. Fellow: ASCE (Benjamin Wright award 2005); mem.: Conn. Constrn. Industries (chmn. 1991—94, bd. dirs.), Conn. Rd. Builders Assn. (v.p. 1985—88, pres. 1988—91), Am. Rd. and Transp. Builders Assn. (bd. dirs. 1988—99, pres. contractors divsn. 1993—94), Am. Arbitration Assn. Republican. Episcopalian. Achievements include patents in field. Office: Blakeslee Arpaia Chapman Inc 200 N Branford Rd Branford CT 06405-2846

CHAPMAN, RONALD THOMAS, musician, educator; b. Bklyn., Dec. 16, 1933; s. William Leon and Rosamond (Walker) C.; m. Joyce Elaine Chase, Dec. 1966 (dec. May 1973); adopted child, Debra Anne (dec. July 1992); m. Virginia Marie Knochenhauer, Feb. 14, 1975 (dec. July 1989); stepchildren: Suzanne, Michael. BS cum laude, CUNY, 1982; MAT, Lehman Coll., 1983; PhD in Music in Higher Edn., NYU, 1989. Cert. tchr. music, NY, tchr. Spanish, NY. Toured with Leonard dePaur Infantry Chorus, 1953—55; mem. trio The Versatones, US and Can., 1955—59; vocalist, 1978—; asst. dir. men's choir Kingsborough CC, 1980—82; asst. to dir. mixed chorus Lehman Coll. CUNY, 1982—83; instr. voice NYU, 1986—; instr. computer music for music tchrs. NY Inst. Tech., 1987; tchr. music Hempstead Sch. Dist., 2002—. Pvt. instr. voice, piano, guitar, computerized music, music theory, sight singing and music lit., 1980—; substitute tchr. Hempstead Sch. Dist., NY, 1983-85, faculty, 1988-89, tchr. adult edn., ESL, 1993—, tchr. group piano, group voice in continuing adult edn. program, 1993—, substitute music tchr., 2002—; bd. dirs. Cultural Environ, Queens, NY. Singer (TV shows) Johnny Carson Show, Arthur Godfrey Talent Scouts, Gary Moore Show, Tex and Jinx Falkenburg Show, others, (albums) Island in the Sun, (Broadway plays) Kwamina, (films) Rueda de Sospechosos, 1963, The Ronnie Chapman Show, 1968-69; singer Fox Hollow, 1978-93, Caterer/Restaurant, Woodbury, NY, 1978—; starred in Playboy Club and Hotel Chain, 1960-67; singer, musician Broadway Show Tunes and Internat. Art Songs; singer Hilton Hotels, 1967-71, Vietnam tour for U.S. Troops, 1968, Carnegie Hall, 1991-96, Cafe Trilussa, 1996-97, J. DeCarlos Restaurant, Huntington, NY, 1998—, Merkin Hall, NYC, 2004-05. Bd. dirs. Cultural Environment, Queens, NY, 1978—; apptd. dep. gov. Am. Biog. Inst. Rsch. Assn., 1992; dir. adult choir Amez Ch., Westbury, NY, 2005—. Mem. Internat. Assn. for Rsch. in Singing (rsch. assoc. Found. for Rsch. Singing), Nat. Assn. Tchrs. Singing, NY Singing Tchrs. Assn., NY State Sch. Music Assn. (cert. adjucator voice), Internat. Assn. Jazz Educators, Chopin Found. NY, Am. Assn. Choral Dirs., Music Educators Nat. Conf., Music Tchrs. Nat. Assn., Assoc. Music Tchrs. League NY, Internat. Platform Assn., Am. Choral Dirs. Assn., Phi Delta Kappa (v.p. programs NYU chpt. 1988-89), Pi Kappa Lambda, Kappa Delta Pi (chpt. 3d v.p. 1994—) Achievements patent for portable back rest/supporter. Home and Office: Roncha Inc 103 Commons Way Deer Park NY 11729 Office Phone: 631-392-0023. Personal E-mail: ronchamusic@aol.com.

CHAPMAN, SAMUEL GREELEY, political science professor, criminologist; b. Atlanta, Sept. 29, 1929; s. Calvin C. and Jane (Greeley) C.; m. Patricia Hepfer, June 19, 1949 (dec. Dec. 1978); children: Lynn Randall, Deborah Jane; m. Carolyn Hughes, June 1, 1991. AB, U. Calif.-Berkeley, 1951, MA, 1959. Officer Police Dept., Berkeley, 1951-56; police cons. Pub. Adminstrn. Service, Chgo., 1956-59; asst. prof. Sch. Police Adminstrn., Mich. State U., East Lansing, 1959-63; police chief Multnomah County, Portland, Oreg., 1963-66; asst. dir. Pres.'s Commn. on Law Enforcement and Adminstrn. of Justice, Nat. Crime Commn., Washington, 1966-67; prof. dept. polit. sci. U. Okla., Norman, 1967-91; prof. emeritus, 1991—; chmn. athletic council U. Okla., 1971-72, 79-80. Adj. prof. criminal justice U. Nev., Reno, 1995—; assoc.'s disting. lectr., 1985-86. Author: Dogs in Police Work, 1960, The Police Heritage in England and America, 1962, Police Patrol Readings, 1964, rev. edit., 1970, Perspectives on Police Assaults in the South Central United States, 1974, Short of Merger, 1976, Police Murders and Effective Countermeasures, 1976, Police Dogs in North America, 1979, 2d. edit., 1990, Cops, Killers and Staying Alive: The Murder of Police Officers in America, 1986; Murdered On Duty: The Killing of Police Officers in America, 1998; contbr. chpts. to books, articles to profl. jours. Mem. Norman City Council, 1972-83, mayor pro-tem, 1975-76, 79-80, 81-83. Recipient Amoco Found. award, 1986. Mem. Nev. Hist. Soc. (docent), Alpha Delta Phi. Republican. Home and Office: 680 Kane Ct Reno NV 89512-1354 Office Phone: 775-786-9011.

CHAPMAN, SILAS STACY, III, lawyer; b. Milford, Mass., June 27, 1954; s. Silas Stacy Jr. and June F. (Wilde) C.; m. Lorraine M. Lipsett, Aug. 7, 1976; children: Kristen A., Jessica L. BA cum laude, Stonehill Coll., 1976; JD cum laude, Vt. Law Sch., 1979. Bar: Vt. 1979, U.S. Dist. Ct. Vt. 1980, U.S. Dist. Ct. Mass. 1980. Law clk. to judge State of Vt., Burlington, 1979-80; assoc. Webber & Costello, Rutland, Vt., 1980-82; ptnr. Webber Costello and Chapman, Ltd., Rutland, 1982, Webber, Chapman & Kupferer Ltd., Rutland, Vt. Mem. ch. coun. Grace Congl. Ch., Rutland, 1987—. Mem. ABA, Vt. Bar Assn. (treas. young lawyers 1987, pres.-elect, 2006-07, pres. 2007-08), Am. Trial Lawyers Assn., Def. Rsch. Inst., Lions Club (pres. 1988). Avocations: boating, fishing, tennis. Office: Webber Chapman & Kupferer Ltd PO Box 807 Rutland VT 05702 Office Phone: 802-773-9109. Office Fax: 802-773-5966. E-mail: schapman@sover.net.

CHAPMAN, STEPHANIE LYNN, education educator; d. Frank Harold and Barbara Selma Kruck; m. David G. Chapman, July 21, 1979; children: Jonathan David, Rebecca Lynn. BS in Spl. Edn. (hon.), U. Wis. Whitewater, 1980, MEd (hon.), 1983. Cert. spl. edn. tchr., K-12 Wis., 1980, elem. edn. tchr. Wis., 1980, child dev. and elem sch. tchr. Waukesha County Tech. Coll., 1990. Academic staff. U. Wis., Whitewater, 1989—92, 2003—; faculty Carroll Coll., Waukesha, Wis., 1999—2004. Learning disabilities tchr. Waukesha Pub. Sch., Wis., 1981—89, West Allis-West Milw. Pub. Sch., Wis., 2002—03; student tchr. supr. Cardinal Stritch, Milw., 1990—91; presenter in field. Office: U Wis Whitewater 4047 Winther Hall 800 W Main St Whitewater WI 53190 Home Phone: 262-472-1225; Office Phone: 262-472-1225. Business E-Mail: chapmans@uww.edu.

CHAPMAN, STEPHEN JAMES, columnist; b. Brady, Tex., Feb. 25, 1954; s. Thurman James and Betty Dee (Sell) C.; m. Fern Brenda Schumer, Sept. 10, 1983, (div.); 3 children AB cum laude, Harvard Coll., 1976; student, U. Chgo. Sch. Bus., 1982-84. Assoc. editor The New Republic, Washington, 1978-81; editorial writer, columnist The Chicago Tribune, 1981—. Office: Chgo Tribune 435 N Michigan Ave Chicago IL 60611-4041 Business E-Mail: schapman@tribune.com.

CHAPMAN, THOMAS B., air transportation executive; m. Mary Scott O'Connell; 1 child, Patrick. Grad., Long Island U., 1978; JD, Am. U., 1982. Sr. v.p. govt. and tech. affairs Aircraft Owners and Pilots Assn., Washington; legis. counsel Southwest Airlines, 1998—2006; v.p. congl. & fed. affairs US Airways Group, Inc., 2006—. Office: US Airways Group Ste 1075 1401 H St, NW Washington DC 20005 Office Phone: 202-326-5150.

CHAPMAN, THOMAS WILLIAM, hospital executive; b. May 17, 1945; s. Alice Chapman; m. Cheryl Edmonds. BA, St. Anselm's Coll., 1968; postgrad., Boston Coll., 1968-69; MPH, Yale U., 1971. Adminstrv. resident Children's Hosp. Med. Ctr., Boston, 1970-71; sr. staff cons. Arthur D. Little, Inc., Cambridge, Mass., 1971-76, sr. cons. Washington, 1982-84; asst. exec. dir. Group Health Assn., Washington, 1976-78; pres. Provident Hosp., Balt., 1978-82, Greater Southeast Community Hosp., Washington, 1984-91, Greater Southeast Healthcare System, Washington, 1991-94; sr assoc. v.p. network dev., ceo The Univ. Hosp., Geo Wash. Univ. Med Ctr, Washington, 1994—. Lectr., Johns Hopkins U., Balt., Howard U., Washington, 1986—; guest lectr., Harvard U. Contbr. articles to profl. publs. Fellow Am. Coll. Healthcare Execs.; mem. AHA (mem. nominating com., governing coun. Met. Hosp. sect., mem. conv. adv. panel), D.C. Hosp. Assn. (chmn. bd. dirs. 1988-90), Am. Pub. Health Assn., Assn. Yale Alumni, Nat. Assn. Health Svc. Execs.

CHAPMAN, WILLIAM, baritone; b. LA; s. William Cloud and Augusta Jane (Kiel) C.; m. Irene Veronica Meyer, Sept. 15, 1957; children— Alexa Maria, Teren Cloud. BA in Drama, U. So. Calif. Propr. vocal studio, Los Angeles, 1967—. Mem. faculty U.S. Internat. U. Performing Arts Sch., San Diego, 1971-86; mem. extension faculty UCLA. Leading baritone N.Y.C. Opera, 1956—, also other opera houses, U.S. and Europe; opened Spoleto Festival as Macbeth in Macbeth, 1957; leading performer: Menotti's Maria Golovin as produced by David Merrick, Broadway, Frank Loesser's Greenwillow, Alvin Theater, (original prodn.) Candide, Martin Beck Theater; Broadway appearances as Charlie in Shenandoah, 1978-79, also in N.Y.C. Center revival of South Pacific; appeared as Frank Maurrant for N.Y.C. Opera, also PBS-TV; TV appearances on Wonderful World of Disney; Columnist: Notes for the Singing Actor, Voice Mag.; appearing as Cecil B. DeMille in 1996-97 Nat. Touring Co. of Sunset Blvd. Rockefeller grantee; recipient DramaLogue award for performance, 1992, various certs. of appreciation. Mem. Screen Actors Guild, Actors Equity, Am. Guild Variety Artists, AFTRA. Personal E-mail: icy1@roadrunner.com.

CHAPMAN, WILLIAM B., lawyer; b. NYC, Feb. 7, 1935; s. Bruce Woodallen and Edna Mae (Coleman) C.; m. Judith B. Skillman, Sept. 22, 1956 (div. 1970); children: William, David; m. Mary L. Hudson, May 29, 1971. *Mr. Chapman is a direct descendant of Mayflower Pilgrim leader William Brewster. His father, born in Rhode Island, was a graduate of Brown University and a broadcast pioneer. He was one of the creators of the popular radio program "The Answer Man," on which he answered questions from listeners for some twenty-five years. Mr. Chapman's mother was born in Indian Territory and later moved to New York where she graduated from Columbia University and became a journalist. She was a chief script-writer for "The Answer Man" and the author of a long-running* *syndicated newspaper feature, "Here's Howe."* BS, Swarthmore Coll., 1956; JD, Stanford U., 1979. Bar: Calif. 1979, U.S. Dist. Ct. (ctrl. and no. dists.) Calif. 1979, U.S. Dist. Ct. (so. and ea. dists.) Calif. 1983, U.S. Ct. Appeals (9th cir.) 1982, U.S. Supreme Ct. 1984. Engr. Bell Tel. Co. Pa., Phila., 1958-59; creative dir. The Ullman Orgn., Phila., 1960-64; exec. dir. Am. Inst. Archs., Phila., 1965-69; v.p., dir. planning U. Hawaii, Honolulu, 1970-76; atty. Pettit & Martin, San Francisco, 1979; ptnr. Rogers, Joseph, O'Donnell & Quinn, San Francisco, 1980-93; founding ptnr. Chapman, Popik & White, San Francisco, 1993—. Adj. prof. Hastings Coll. Law, San Francisco, 1992-2000. Co-author: Our Man-made Environment, 1969. Fellow: Am. Bar Found.; mem.: ABA, Am. Bd. Trial Advs. Avocations: reading, skiing, trout fishing, squash, golf. Home: 100 South St Apt 209 Sausalito CA 94965-2566 Office: Chapman Popik & White 650 California St Ste 1900 San Francisco CA 94108-2723 Home Phone: 415-331-8229; Office Phone: 415-352-3000. Business E-Mail: chapman@chapop.com.

CHAPMAN COLLINS, JANICE, school system administrator; b. LA; d. William and Milrene Hooks; m. Michael Dean Collins; children: Arshaun, Ashley. BA in Liberal Arts, Pepperdine U., 1979, EdM, 1985, MS in Sch. Mgmt. & Adminstrn., 1989, MA in Edn., 1985. Ryan Multiple Subject Credential Calif. Commn. Tchr. Credentialing, 1979, Sylvan Program Instr. Sylan Learning Ctr., 1998, Adminstrv. Svcs. Credential Calif Commn. Tchr. Credentialing, 2000, Cert. Profl. Devel. Trainer L.A. Unified Sch. Dist.- Calif., 2002. Elem. tchr. L.A. Unified Sch. Dist., 1979—92, instrnl. coord., 1992—94, advisor, 1994—96, mid. sch. tchr., 1996—99, adminstr., mentor tchr. program, 1999—2000, adminstr., mid. sch. programs, 2000—. Mentor tchr. L.A. Unified Sch. Dist., 1986—92, drop out prevention coord., Seventy-Fifth St. Sch., 1986—88, adult sch. tchr., 1987—89, program quality rev. team mem., 1990, ldpass/aemp facilitator, 1996—99, sylvan program instr., 1998—99, adminstrv. facilitator, phys. edn. focus group, 2000—, social studies adv. bd. mem., 2001—, mem.- secondary redesign com., 2003—, mem. Calif. phys. edn. content standards devel. com., 2004; cons. USC: Calif. writing project Calif. Subject Matter Projects, LA, 1987—; mem. social studies adv. bd. Pearson Prentice Hall Pub., LA, 2003—; mem. phys. content standards devel. com. Calif. Dept. Edn., mem. com. phys. edn. model content standards. Contbr. ednl. handbook, Successful Strategies Handbook, curriculum guide, History-Social Sci. Guidelines for Instrn.; co-author: America History For Our Nation, 2005. Founding mem. Nat. Campaign for Tolerance, Montgomery, Ala., 2005—; adminstrv. liasion L.A. Unified Sch. Dist. Nat. Campaign To Stop Violence, Washington, 2000—. Recipient Do the Write Thing Challenge 2003, Nat. Campaign to Stop Violence, 2003, 2004. Mem.: ASCD, Associated Adminstrs. L.A., Calif. Assn. Health Phys. Edn., Recreation and Dance, Orgn. Mgmt. Adminstrs., Calif. League Mid. Schools, Coun. Black Adminstrs. (profl. devel. com. 1998), Nat. Women's History Mus. (charter mem.), Pepperdine Alumni Assn., Phi Delta Kappa. Baptist. Avocations: travel, art collector, creative writing, theater. Office: LA Unified Sch Dist 333 S Beaudry Ave 25th Floor Los Angeles CA 90017 Office Phone: 213-241-4134. Business E-Mail: janice.collins@lausd.net.

CHAPMAN HOLLEY, SHAWN SNIDER, lawyer; b. LA, Apr. 11, 1962; d. Henry Stewart and Freddi (Snider) King; m. Michael J. Chapman, Sept. 12, 1992; m. Dorian Holley; 1 child, Olivia Rose BA in English, UCLA, 1984; JD, Southwestern U., 1988. Bar: Calif. 1988, U.S. Dist. Ct. (ctrl. dist.) Calif. 1989. Deputy pub. defender L.A. County Pub. Defenders Office, 1988-94; mng. ptnr. The Cochran Firm (formerly Law Offices of Johnnie L. Cochran Jr.), LA, 1994—2006; ptnr. Kinsella Weitzman Iser Kump & Aldisert LLP, Santa Monica, Calif., 2006—. Chief legal corr. E! Network. Commr. of community affairs Southwestern U. Sch. Law, L.A., 1987. Mem. Black Pub. Defenders Assn., Black Women Lawyers, Langston Bar Assn. Democrat. Office: Kinsella Weitzman Iser Kump & Aldisert LLP 808 Wilshire Blvd 3rd Fl Santa Monica CA 90401*

CHAPNICK, DAVID B., lawyer; b. NYC, Apr. 24, 1939; s. H.M. and G. (Kraft) C.; m. Elaine Schlozman, Dec. 25, 1966; children: Adam Lawrence, Melissa Rachel. AB with honors, Union Coll., 1959; LLB, NYU, 1962. Bar: N.Y. 1963. Law clk. to Hon. Warren E. Burger U.S. Ct. Appeals (D.C. cir.), Washington, 1962-63; pvt. practice NYC, 1963-67; assoc. Simpson Thacher & Bartlett, NYC, 1967-69, ptnr., 1970—2000, of counsel, 2001—. Trustee Union Coll., Schenectady, N.Y., 1991—, vice chmn., 1995-96, chmn., 1998-02; trustee Hunter Coll. Found., N.Y.C., 2005—; bd. govs. Wurzweiler Sch. Social Work, 2004—. Office: Simpson Thacher & Bartlett 425 Lexington Ave New York NY 10017-3954

CHAPPARS, TIMOTHY STEPHEN, lawyer; b. Cin., July 23, 1952; s. Gregory S. and Helen (Maragos) C.; m. Laurie A. Kress, Dec. 24, 1986 (div. Sept. 1987); m. Laurie A. Kress, Apr. 18, 1990; children: Alexander T., Jake A., Madeline Claire. BS, Duke U., 1974; JD, U. Cin., 1978. Propr. Chappars Law Office. Mem. ATLA, Ohio Bar Assn., Ohio Acad. Trial Lawyers. Methodist. Avocations: tennis, piano, hiking, bicycling, skiing. Home: 2025 Winding Brook Way Xenia OH 45385-9382 Office: PO Box 280 Xenia OH 45385-0280 Office Phone: 937-374-0077.

CHAPPEL, DONALD R., petroleum pipeline company executive; b. Oct. 19, 1951; m. Erin Chappel. Grad., U. Ill. CPA, Ill. With Arthur Andersen & Co., Chgo., 1973—82, Beatrice Cos., Inc./Esmark, Inc., 1982—87, dir. N.Am. ops. analysis, dir. fin./ops. analysis and audit; joined Waste Mgmt., Inc., 1987, v.p., contr. chem. waste mgmt. divsn., v.p., contr. West and Mountain groups, v.p., contr. N.Am. solid waste ops., 1995-97, v.p., acting CFO, 1997-2000; sr. v.p., CFO The Williams Cos., Inc., Tulsa, 2003—. Office: One Williams Ctr Tulsa OK 74172*

CHAPPELEAR, STEPHEN ERIC, lawyer; b. Columbus, Ohio, Dec. 25, 1952; s. Thornton White and Phyllis Evelyn (Williams) C.; m. Sharon Sue Starr, June 8, 1974; children: Katherine Sue, Christopher Charles. BA, Ohio State U., 1974, JD, 1977. Bar: Ohio 1977, U.S. Dist. Ct. (so. dist.) Ohio, U.S. Dist. Ct. (no. dist.) Ohio, U.S. Dist. Ct. (ea. dist.) Wis., U.S. Tax Ct., U.S. Ct. Appeals (6th cir.). Assoc. Emens, Hurd, Kegler & Ritter, Columbus, 1977—82, prin., 1983—2001, Kegler Brown Hill & Ritter, Columbus; ptnr. Hahn, Loeser & Parks, Columbus, 2001—. Mem. exec. coun. Nat. Conf. Bar Pres., 1997-2000; pres. Met. Bar Caucus, 2001-02. Author: The Complete Book of Jury Verdicts II, Franklin County, Ohio, 1985-91, The Complete Book of Franklin County Jury Verdicts, 1990, So What's Your Case Realy Worth?: A Decade of Jury Trial Verdicts, 1995; editor jour. Bar Briefs, 1986-88; contbr. articles to profl. jour. Fellow Am. Bar Found. (co-chair), Ohio State Bar Found. (trustee), Columbus Bar Found.; mem. ABA (ho. dels., litig. sect., chmn. real estate litig. com., trial and ins. practice sect. ethics and professionalism com.) Ohio State Bar Assn. (bd. gov., coun. dels., former chair fed. cts. and practice com., litig. sect., bd. gov., pres. 2002-03), Columbus Bar Assn. (bd. govs., pres. 1995-96), Am. Inns of Ct. (Franklin chpt. pres. 1994-95, 2005-06), Million Dollar Adv. Forum, New Albany Country Club. Avocations: sports, movies, theater, writing. Office: Hahn Loeser & Parks 65 E State St Ste 1400 Columbus OH 43215-4213 Office Phone: 614-233-5148. Office Fax: 614-233-5149.

CHAPPELL, ANNETTE M., educational consultant, minister; b. Washington, Oct. 31, 1939; d. Joseph John and Annette B. (Harley) C.; m. Brian Thomas Flower, Sept. 3, 1960 (div. Mar. 1983); m. Frank Joseph Sanders, Apr. 8, 1985 (dec. Dec. 1995). BA in English, U. Md., 1962, MA, 1964, PhD, 1970; MDiv, Gen. Theol. Sem., 2003. Lectr. European div. U. Md., Eng., 1965-66, instr. English College Park, 1966-69; asst. prof. English Towson (Md.) U., 1969-72, assoc. prof., 1972-79, prof., 1979—99, spl. asst. to pres., affirmative action officer, 1974-77; dean humanistic, social and managerial studies Towson (Md.) State U., 1977-82, dean Coll. Liberal Arts, 1982-95, assoc. v.p. acad. affairs, 1995-99; ind. cons., 1999—; rector Ch. of the Redemption, Balt., 2003—. Contbr. articles to profl. jours. and book revs. to Ms Mag., Balt. Sun. Lay reader, chalicist All Saints Episcopal Ch., Reisterstown, Md., 1973-2003; pres. Baltimore County Commn. for Women, 1977-79; bd. dirs. Baltimore County Sexual Assault and Domestic Violence Center, 1978-83, pres., 1980-82. Mem. AAUP, MLA, Am. Assn. Higher Edn., Council Colls. Arts and Scis. (bd. dirs. 1984-86), Exec. Women's Council Md. (1st v.p. 1980, pres. 1981) Business E-Mail: achappell@towson.edu.

CHAPPELL, CHARLES FRANKLIN, meteorologist, consultant; b. St. Louis, Dec. 7, 1927; s. Hubert Guy and Wilma Halle (Lindsey) C.; m. Doris Mae Kennedy, Aug. 4, 1951; children— Christa Ann, Susan Lynne, Deborah Louise BS, Washington U., St. Louis, 1949; postgrad., St. Louis U., 1952-54; MS, Colo. State U., 1967, PhD, 1971. Flight data engr. McDonnell Aircraft Co., St. Louis, 1950-55; weather forecaster U.S. Weather Bur., Kansas City, Mo., 1956-67; research assoc. Colo. State U., Ft. Collins, 1967-70; assoc. prof. Utah State U., Logan, 1970-72; research meteorologist NOAA, Boulder, Colo., 1972-79, research dir., 1979-87; head applied sci. group Nat. Ctr. for Atmospheric Research, Boulder, 1988-89, sr. scientist coop. program for operational meteorology edn. and tng., 1989-94; meteolologist cons., Boulder, 1995—. Cons. meteorologist Midwest Weather Service, Kansas City, Mo., 1958-60 Assoc. editor Jour. Atmospheric Sci., 1984-87; contbr. articles to prof. jours. (Best Sci. Paper award in NOAA-Environ. Research Labs. 1981). Served as seaman 1st class USN, 1945-46 Recipient silver medal Dept. Commerce, 1957 Fellow Am. Meteorol. Soc.; mem. Nat. Weather Assn., Weather Modification Assn., Am. Geophys. Union, Phi Kappa Phi. Avocations: hiking, painting, gardening, piano. Home and Office: 3110 Heidelberg Dr Boulder CO 80305-7010 E-mail: chapmo@msn.com. *You can always accomplish more than you think, so do it.*

CHAPPELL, CHARLES RICHARD, space scientist; b. Greenville, SC, June 2, 1943; s. Gordon Thomas and Mabel Winn (Ownbey) Chappell; m. Brenda Kay Taylor; 1 child, Christopher Richard. BA magna cum laude, Vanderbilt U., 1965; PhD in Space Sci., Rice U., 1968. Assoc. research scientist Lockheed Palo Alto (Calif.) Research Lab., 1968-70, research scientist, 1970-72, staff scientist, 1972-74; chief magnetospheric physics br. NASA-Marshall Space Flight Ctr., Huntsville, Ala., 1974-80, chief solar terrestrial physics div., 1980-87, assoc. dir. for sci., 1987-97; rsch. prof. physics, dir. sci. and rsch. comm. Vanderbilt U., Nashville, 1997—2002; rsch. prof. physics, dir. Vanderbilt Dyer Obs., Nashville, 2002—. Trainee NASA, 1966—68; selected as alternate payload specialist for the ATLAS-1 mission of the Space Shuttle, 1985; spl. asst. for environ. outreach to NASA adminstr., 1994—95; dep. dir. Global Learning and Observations to Benefit the Environment (GLOBE), 1994—95; vis. profl. scholar Freedom Forum First Amendment Ctr. Vanderbilt U., 1996—97; dir. Dyer Obs., 2003—. Author: (ency.) Plasmasphere, 1970, Spacelab Mission, 1985; contbr. articles to profl. jours. Recipient medal for Exceptional Sci. Achievement, NASA, 1981, 1984, Exceptional Svc. medal, 1998. Mem.: Congress of Space Rsch., Am. Geophys. Union, Internat. Acad. Astronautics, Phi Eta Sigma, Phi Beta Kappa. Methodist. Avocations: distance running, sailing. Home: 569 Midway Cir Brentwood TN 37027-5178 Office: Vanderbilt U Dyer Obs 1000 Oman Dr Brentwood TN 37027 Office Phone: 615-373-4897.

CHAPPELL, FRED DAVIS, language educator, poet; b. Canton, NC, May 28, 1936; s. James Taylor and Anne Mae (Davis) C.; m. Susan Nicholls, Aug. 2, 1959; 1 son, Christopher Heath. BA, Duke U., 1961, MA, 1964; LittD, U. NC, Asheville, 1989, Spring Hill Coll., 1991. Prof. English U. NC, Greensboro, 1964—2004, emeritus prof. English, 2004—. Adv. editor Skyhook, 1958-59, Red Clay Reader, 1964-65, Greensboro Rev., 1964—, Ga. Rev., 1990—. Author: It Is Time, Lord, 1963, The Inkling, 1965, Dagon, 1968, The World Between the Eyes, 1971, The Gaudy Place, 1972, Midquest, 1981, Moments of Light, 1982, Castle Tzingal, 1984, I Am One of You Forever, 1985, Source, 1985, The Fred Chappell Reader, 1988, First and Last Words, 1989, Brighten the Corner Where You Are, 1989, More Shapes Than One, 1992, C, 1993, Plow Naked, 1993, Spring Garden: New and Selected Poems, 1995, Farewell, I'm Bound To Leave You, 1996, A Way of Happening, 1998, Look Back All the Green Valley, 1999, Family Gathering, 2000, Backsass, 2004. Named NC Poet Laureate, 1997—2002; named to NC Lit. Hall of Fame, 2006; recipient Roanoke-Chowan Poetry prize, NC Lit. Assn., 1979, Prix de Meilleur des Lettres Etrangers, 1973, NC award in lit., State of NC, 1987, Bollingen prize for poetry, 1985, World Fantasy award, World Fantasy Assn., 1992, 1994, T.S. Eliot prize, Ingersoll Found., 1993, Aiken Taylor Poetry award, 1996, Irene Lenore Heasley prize, 1999, SEBA Novel award, 2000, Eminescu medal for poetry, 2001, Appalachian Heritage Writers award, 2004, Thomas Wolfe award, 2005, Caroliniana award, 2007; grantee Nat. Acad. Arts and Letters, 1968; NDEA fellow, 1961—63, Rockefeller grantee, 1967—68. Mem.: Order of the Longleaf Pine. Democrat. Avocations: books, wine. Office Phone: 386-275-8851.

CHAPPELL, JOHN CHARLES, lawyer; b. Minden, Nebr., Jan. 28, 1935; s. Charles Arthur and Eletta Hope (Pattison) C.; m. Joyce Joan Dawson, Sept. 1, 1957; children: Laura, Pamela, James, Allegra. BS in Edn., U. Nebr., 1956; JD, NYU, 1960. Bar: N.Y. 1960. Summer assoc. firm Dewey Ballantine, NYC, 1959, assoc., 1960-68; ptnr. Dewey Ballantine LLP, NYC, 1968-00, ret. ptnr., 2000. Served to 1st lt. U.S. Army, 1957. Root-Tilden scholar NYU, 1956 Mem.: Assn. Bar City N.Y. Office: Dewey Ballantine LLP 1301 Ave Of The Americas New York NY 10019-6022

CHAPPELL, MILES LINWOOD, JR., art historian, educator; b. Norfolk, Va., June 6, 1939; s. Miles Linwood Sr. and Melrose Clarice (Debnam) C.; m. Marcial Cassada, July 23, 1966; children: Ashley, Oliver, Picot. BS in Chemistry, Coll. William and Mary, 1960; PhD in Art History, U. N.C., 1971. Prof. art history Coll. William and Mary, Williamsburg, Va., 1971—2005, chair dept., Chancellor prof. art history, 1987, prof. emeritus, 2005—; elected to Accademia delle Arti del Disegno Florence, Italy, 2006. Mem. artistic adv. bd. Interlochen Ctr. for Arts. Author: Cristofano Allori, 1984, Lodovico Cigoli, Disegni, 1992, The Fine Art of Drawing, 1993; co-author: Disegni dei Toscani, 1979, Lodovico Cigoli, tra maniersmo e barocco, 1992, Renascence of the Florentine Baroque in "Dialoghi di storia dell'arte", 1998, The Artistic Education of Maria de'Medici, 2003, Cigoli's Treatise on Perspective in The Perspective Treatise, 2002; contbg. author: The Medici. Michelangelo and Late Renaissance Art, 2002; formulator and co-author: Form, Function and Finesse: Drawings from the Herman Found., 1983; co-editor L'Arte, Collezionismo, Conservazione: scritti in onore di Marco Chiarini, 2004; asst. editor: Studies in Iconography, 1978-80; mem. adv. bd. Eighteenth-Century Life, 1980-84, 85—; contbr. more than 100 articles on Renaissance and Baroque art to profl. jours. Mem. internat. survey of Jewish monuments, U. Ill., 1978. Harvard U. Ctr. for Italian Renaissance Studies fellow, Florence, 1980; Cité Internat. des Arts, 1995; recipient numerous rsch. grants. Mem. Kunsthistorisches Institut Florence, Phi Beta Kappa (Alpha chpt. award for scholarship 1987, v.p. 1992-93, 2003-05, Thomas Ashley Graves, Jr. award for excellence in tchg. 2005). Avocations: drawing, painting, music. Home: 139 Ridings Cv Williamsburg VA 23185-3903 Office: Coll William and Mary Dept Art History Williamsburg VA 23187 Office Phone: 757-220-1433. E-mail: mlchap@wm.edu.

CHAPPELL, RICHARD LEE, biology educator, neuroscientist; b. Buffalo, Mar. 9, 1938; s. G. Howard and Gertrude Lyth (Myers) C.; m. Alice Carol Merckens, Sept. 6, 1968; children: Carol, Dreux. BS in Engring., Princeton U., 1962; PhD, Johns Hopkins U., 1970. Asst. prof. biology Hunter Coll., CUNY, NYC, 1970-74, assoc. prof., 1975-79, prof., 1980—, chmn. dept., 1987-90; exec. officer PhD program in biology Grad. Ctr. CUNY, NYC, 1993—, chmn. coun. exec. officers, 2001—. Cons. Bell Lab., Murray Hill, N.J., 1982-83, chmn. Physiology and Neuroscience Subprogram CUNY, N.Y.C., 1986-88. Author: Antarctic Scout, 1959; contbr. articles to profl. jours. Chmn. Sci. Devel. Program, Inc., N.Y.C., 1980—; Lt. USN, 1962-66. Recipient Antarctic medal U.S. Congress, 1959; Chappell Peak, Antarctica, named in his honor; grantee Nat. Eye Inst., NIH, 1971-2004, NSF, 2006—. Fellow The Explorers Club (bd. dirs. 1972-75); mem. Assn. for Rsch. in Vision and Opthalmology, Am. Polar Soc. (v.p. 1989-97, pres. 1997-2000), IEEE, Marine Biol. Lab. Corp., Sigma Xi. Office: Hunter Coll Dept Biol Scis 695 Park Ave New York NY 10021-5024 Business E-Mail: rchappell@gc.cuny.edu.

CHAPPELL, WALLACE, performing company executive; b. Dallas, Aug. 8, 1941; BA, Dartmouth Coll., 1963; MFA, U. Hawaii, 1965; postgrad., U. Minn. Staff dir. L.A. Music Ctr. Mark Taper Forum, 1969—75; assoc. artistic dir. Alliance Theatre, Atlanta, 1975—78; artistic dir. Repertory Theatre of St. Louis, 1980—83; dir. Hancher Auditorium, U. Iowa, 1986—2001; exec. dir. Am. Ballet Theatre, NYC, 2001—04, Paul Taylor Dance Co., NYC, 2004—. Cons., spkr., panelist, advisor, site visitor various orgns., including Nat. Endowment for Arts, Wallace Found., Assn. Performing Arts Presenters; bd. dirs. Iowa State Bank and Trust, Inc. Bd. dirs. Dance/USA, Iowa City C. of C. Mem.: Stage Soc. Dirs. and Choreographers, Internat. Soc. Performing Arts (pres. 1993—95).

CHAPPELLE, DAVE (DAVID CHAPPELLE), actor, comedian; b. Washington, Aug. 24, 1973; m. Elaine Chappelle; 2 children. Actor: (films) Robin Hood: Men in Tights, 1993, Undercover Blues, 1993, Getting In, 1994, The Nutty Professor, 1996, Joe's Apartment, 1996, Con Air, 1997, The Real Blonde, 1997, Bowl of Pork, 1997, Woo, 1998, You've Got Mail, 1998, 200 Cigarettes, 1999, Blue Streak, 1999, Screwed, 2000, Undercover Brother, 2002; (TV series) Buddies, 1996, Comedy: Coast to Coast, 1994, (voice) Crank Yankers, 2002; actor, writer, exec. prodr. (TV series) Chappelle's Show, 2003—, actor, co-writer, and prodr. (films) Half Baked, 1998, writer and exec. prodr. (TV special) The Dave Chappelle Project, 1997, Dave Chappelle: Killin' Them Softly, 2000, writer, prodr. (films) Dave Chappelle's Block Party, 2006. Mailing: Gersh Agy 232 N Canon Dr Beverly Hills CA 90210

CHAPPELLE, EMMETT W., physical scientist; b. Phoenix, Oct. 24, 1925; s. I.C. and Viola Chappelle; m. Rosemary Phillips, 1947; children: Emmett, Carlotta, Deborah, Marc. AA in Elec. Engring., Phoenix Coll., 1947; BS in Biochemistry, U. Calif., Berkeley, 1950; MS in Biochemistry, U. Wash., 1954; postgrad., Stanford U., 1954-56. Instr. biochemistry Meharry Med. Coll., Nashville, 1950-52; rsch. assoc. dept. chemistry Stanford U., 1956-58; staff scientist Rsch. Inst. for Advanced Studies Martin Marrietta Corp., Balt., 1958-63; sr. biochemist Hazelton Labs., Falls Church, Va., 1963-66; exobiologist NASA/Goddard Space Flight Ctr., Greenbelt, Md., 1966-70, astrochemist, 1970-72, tech. utilization specialist, 1972-75, phys. scientist remote sensing Lab. for Terrestrial Physics, 1977—; NASA rsch. sabbatical Johns Hopkins U., 1975-77. Spl. adj. prof. dept. geography U. Md.; presenter in field. Contbr. chpts. to books and articles to profl. jours. Mentors talented minority HS and coll. students. Cpl. US Army, 1943—46. Decorated Purple Heart with cluster; named to the Nat. Inventors Hall of Fame, 2007. Mem. AAAS, Am. Chem. Soc., Am. Soc. Microbiology, Am. Soc. Photobiology, Am. Soc. Biochemistry and Molecular Biology, Am. Soc. Black Chemists, Can. Laser Soc., Md. Assn. Biology Tchrs., N.Y. Acad. Sci., Sigma Xi. Achievements include patents for Lyophylized Reaction Mixtures, Use of Enzyme Hexokinase for the Reduction of Inherent Light Levels, Light Detection Instrument, Method for the Detection of Cancer, Method for the Detection of Viruses, Flavin Coenzyme Assay, Protein Sterilization Method, Method of Detecting and Counting Bacteria in Body Fluids, Automatic Instrument for Chemical Processing to Detect Microorganisms in Biological Samples by Measuring Light Reactions, Method of Detecting and Counting Bacteria, Application of Luciferase ATP Assay to Antimicrobial Drug Susceptibility, Determination of Antimicrobial Susceptibilities of Infected Urines Without Isolation, Rapid Quantitative Determination of Bacteria in Water, Crop Residue Meter; research in biochemistry, photobiology, astrochemistry, remote sensing vegetation.*

CHAPPELLE, RICHARD ALLEN, SR., bishop; b. Feb. 25, 1934; s. M. Peter Chappelle and Mabel Juanita Chappelle-Wright; m. Barbara Jeanne Wooten; children: Richard Allen, Beverly Joyce, Kristen Nicole. BS, Bethune-Cookman Coll., 1955; DD (hon.), B. F. Lee Theol. Seminary, 1975, Payne Theol. Seminary, 1990. Pastor, Fellsmere, Fla., 1964—66, Gifford, Fla., 1966—68, Hurst Chapel, Riviera Beach, Fla., 1968—72, Allen Chapel, Melbourne, Fla., 1972—75, Mt. Olive, Orlando, Fla., 1975—76, Asbury Chapel, Louisville, 1978—79, Ward Chapel, Kinlohck, Mo., 1980—81; bishop Eighteenth Episcopal Dist. African M.E.Ch., 1992—96, bishop Eighth Episcopal Dist., 1996—2000, bishop Twelfth Episcopal Dist., 2000—04, presiding prelate, pres. gen. bd. Little Rock, 2004—. Exec. bd. World Meth. Coun.; mem. La. Interfaith Coun.; tchr. Broward County, 1960—74. Named one of Most Influential Black Americans, 2006. Mem.: NAACP, Religious Conf. Mgmt. Assn., Prince Hall Mason, Alphi Phi Alphia. Office: African MECh PO Box 147 Little Rock AR 72203 Office Phone: 501-375-4310. Office Fax: 501-375-0306. E-mail: RAChappelle@worldnet.att.net.

CHAPPLE, JOHN H., telecommunications industry and former professional sports team executive; b. Syracuse, NY, Apr. 8, 1953; Grad., Syracuse U.; postgrad., Harvard U. Sr. mgmt. positions Rogers Cablesystems, 1978—83; sr. v.p. ops. Am Cablesystems, 1983—88; exec. v.p. ops. McCaw Cellular Comms., Inc. (became AT&T Wireless Svcs.), 1988—95; former exec. v.p. AT&T Wireless Svcs. (acquired McCaw); past chmn. Cellular One Group; pres., COO Orca Bay Sports and Entertainment parent co. of Vancouver Grizzlies (NBA), Vancouver Canucks (NHL), 1995—97; pres., CEO, chmn. Nextel Ptnrs., Kirkland, Wash., 1998—. Former chmn. Personal Comm. Industry Assn.; former vice chmn. Cellular Telecomm. Industry Assn.; former bd. of governors NHL and NBA; bd. of governors Fred Hutchinson Cancer Rsch. Bus. Alliance Bd. of Governors; adv. bd., Maxwell Sch. Syracuse U.; bd. dir. Cbeyond Comm., Atlanta, 2004—. Office: Chmn & CEO Nextel Partners 4500 Carillon Pt Kirkland WA 98033

CHAPPLE, THOMAS LESLIE, lawyer; b. Canandaigua, NY, Nov. 28, 1947; s. Howard Leslie and Elizabeth Chapple; m. Shelly Smith, July 17, 1982; children: Adam Roger, Hannah Elizabeth. BA, Cornell U., 1970; JD, Albany Law Sch., 1973. Bar: N.Y. 1974, U.S. Supreme Ct. 1981, Va. 1992. Atty. assoc. Nixon, Hargrave, Devans & Doyle, Rochester, NY, 1973-76; sec., asst. gen. counsel Gannett Co., Inc., Rochester, NY, 1977-79, assoc. gen. counsel., sec., 1979-81, v.p., assoc. gen. counsel, sec., 1981-91, gen. counsel, sec. McLean, Va., 1991-95, sr. v.p., gen. counsel, sec., 1995—2003, sr. v.p., chief adminstrv. officer, gen. counsel, 2003—06. Sec. The Gannett Found., 1983-89. Mem. ABA, Assn. Corp. Counsel, N.Y. State Bar Assn., Sigma Pi Republican. Methodist.

CHAPUT, CHARLES J., archbishop; b. Concordia, Kans., Sept. 26, 1944; Student, St. Fidelis Coll., Capuchin Coll., Cath. U., U. San Francisco. Ordained priest Roman Cath. Ch., 1970, consecrated bishop 1988. Bishop, Rapid City, SD, 1988—97; archbishop Denver, 1997—. Office: Cath Pastoral Ctr 1300 S Steele St Denver CO 80210-2526

CHAPUT, EUGENE MICHAEL, advertising executive; b. San Francisco, July 5, 1941; s. Eugene Rene and Lucille Marie (Longuy) C.; m. Susan Mary Oliphant, Dec. 18, 1965; children: J. Michael, E. John, Thomas Patrick. BS, U. So. Calif., 1963, MBA, 1965. Sr. media planner

Young & Rubicam, San Francisco, 1965-69; v.p., dir. mktg. svcs. Grey Advertising, San Francisco, 1969-78; v.p., mgmt. supr. Hoefer, Dieterich & Brown, San Francisco, 1978-79; v.p. Young & Rubicam, San Francisco, 1979-2000; founder, pres., CEO One-Off Products Group (OOPGROOP), 2000. Patentee; inflatable portable sofa, 1996, electronic self defense weapon disguised as personal accessory, 1999; copyright holder parent-child bonding exercise program; contbr. to numerous creative advertising concepts. Coach Little League Baseball, Youth Soccer, Portola Valley, Calif., 1973-86; chmn. Portola Valley Parks and Recreation, 1978-83. Recipient numerous advt. awards, 1985—; named first honoree Top of the Dial award, No. Calif. Broadcasters Assn., 1995. Mem. San Francisco Olympic Club (physical fitness commr. 1982-87, Weight Lifting record 1998, 2000, 03), Montgomery St. Motorcycle Club. Avocations: physical fitness, skiing, tennis, motorcycling. Personal E-mail: genechaput@sbcglobal.net.

CHAR, PATRICIA HELEN, lawyer; b. Honolulu, Mar. 23, 1952; d. Lincoln S. and Daisy Char; m. Thomas W. Bingham, Mar. 20, 1982; children: Matthew Thomas Bingham, James Nathan Bingham. BA, Northwestern U., 1974; JD, Georgetown U., 1977. Bar: Wash. 1977, U.S. Dist. Ct. (we. dist.) Wash. 1977, U.S. Dist. Ct. (ea. dist.) Wash. 1982, U.S. Ct. Appeals (9th cir.) 1981, U.S. Supreme Ct. 1984. Assoc. Bogle & Gates, Seattle, 1977-84; ptnr., mem. Bogle & Gates PLLC, Seattle, 1984-99; of counsel Garvey, Schubert & Barer, Seattle, 1999-2000; ptnr. Kirk Preston Gates Ellis LLP, Seattle, 2000—06, Kirkpatrick Lockhart Preston Gates Ellis LLP, Seattle, 2007—. Author: Ownership By a Fiduciary, 1997. Trustee YWCA, Seattle-King County-Snohomish County, 1997-2006, United Way King County, 2004-06, Childrens Hosp. and Regional Med. Ctr., Seattle, 2006—; vol. King County Big Sisters, United Way of King County, Seattle, 1987-90, Guardian Ad Litem Program, Seattle, 1987-93 Fellow Am. Coll. Trust and Estate Counsel; mem. ABA, Wash. State Bar Assn. (co-author chpts. 3 and 4 Wash. Civil Procedure Deskbook 1992). Office: Kirkpatrick Lockhart Preston Gates Ellis LLP 925 4th Ave #2900 Seattle WA 98104-1158 Office Phone: 206-623-7580. Business E-Mail: pat.char@klgates.com.

CHAR, VERNON FOOK LEONG, lawyer; b. Honolulu, Dec. 15, 1934; s. Charles A. and Annie (Ching) C.; m. Evelyn Lau, June 14, 1958; children: Richard, Daniel, Douglas, Charles, Elizabeth. BA, U. Hawaii, 1956; LLB, Harvard U., 1959. Bar: Hawaii 1959. Dep. atty. gen. Office of Atty. Gen., Honolulu, 1959-60, 62-65; ptnr. Damon Key Char & Bocken, Honolulu, 1965-89, Char, Sakamoto, Ishii, Lum & Ching, Honolulu, 1989—. Chmn. Hawaii Ethics Commn., Honolulu, 1968-75, Hawaii Bicentennial Com., 1986-91; mem. Hawaii Tourism Authority, 2003—. Mem. ABA (bd. govs. 1991-94), Hawaii Bar Assn. (pres. 1985), U. Hawaii Alumni Assn. (pres. 1989-90). Home: 351 Anonia St Honolulu HI 96821-2052 Office: Char Sakamoto Ishii Lum & Ching Davies Pacific Ctr 841 Bishop St Ste 850 Honolulu HI 96813-3957 Office Phone: 808-522-5133. Business E-Mail: vflchar@lawcsilc.com.

CHARA, ZDENO, professional hockey player; b. Trencin, Slovakia, Mar. 18, 1977; Defenseman NY Islanders, 1997—2001, Ottawa Senators, 2001—06, Boston Bruins, 2006—, capt., 2006—. Player NHL All-Star Game, 2003. Named to First All-Star Team, 2004, Second All-Star Team, 2006. Office: Boston Bruins TD Banknorth Garden 100 Legends Way Boston MA 02114*

CHARANIA, BARKAT, real estate consultant; b. Ahmedabad, Gujrat, India, June 27, 1941; came to U.S., 1961; s. Ismail and Zenabai Charania; m. Jerilyn Lee Scott, Apr. 10, 1962 (div. May 1970); children: Sultana, Ramzan, Kalvin, Kevin, Stephen; m. Maher Kurani, Oct. 11, 1970; children: Munira, Rahim, Munira Moon. Student, Alpena CC, Mich., 1961-62, U. Calif., LA, 1962-63, U. Pa., 1965-68, Lincoln Tech. Sch., 1983. Cert. comml. investment mem.; cert. hotel adminstr. Pres. Eurindus, Inc., Cherry Hill, NJ, 1965-83, Airline Inn, Inc., Atlanta, 1980-83; owner B.C. Investments & Realty Co., Atlanta, 1985—; pres. Southern Inn, Inc., Chattanooga, 1987—; owner B.C. Hospitality Mgmt. Co., Atlanta, 1987—; pres. Trident Devel. Corp., Charleston, SC, 1989—, BJM Hospitality, Inc., 1993—, ICI Long Distance Inc., 1995—, Universal Connect Corp., 1995—; CEO CRM Ventures, LLC, 1997—, RBM Properties, LLC, 2000—; sr. assocs. Marcus & Millichap, Atlanta, 1996-97; CEO Charania Bros., LLC, 1999—, 786 Investments, LLC, 2003—, Small Axe, Inc., 2003—; ptnr., CEO CQ Capital, 2005—; CEO Creative Capital Inc., 2004—, CQ Capital Ptnrs., 2006—, CQ Constrns. LLC, 2006—, Camp Geek Villas, LLC, 2007—. Cons. Pattni Holdings, Atlanta, 1984—, Esmail Internat., Inc., Atlanta, 1986—, Harbour Enterprise, Chattanooga, 1987—, Shin Inc., Chattanooga, 1987—, ABC Inc., Chattanooga, 1988—. Ga. coord. Agakhan Found. U.S.A., Atlanta, 1988; chmn. Southeastern Enterprising People's Assn., 1990, 91. Mem. Atlanta Bd. Realtors, Nat. Assn. Realtors, Realtor Nat. Mktg. Inst., Comml. Investment Real Estate Coun., Edn. Inst., Internat. Real Estate Inst., Ismaili Commerce Club (v.p. Atlanta chpt. 1982), S.E. Region (chmn. Agakhan econ. planning bd. for U.S.A.), Internat. Real Estate Fedn. Republican. Avocations: reading, travel, swimming, tennis. Home: 3000 Edmonton Green Ct Alpharetta GA 30022 Office: 3700 Market St Bldg E Clarkston GA 30021 Office Phone: 404-499-2247. Business E-Mail: bc@bcirealty.com. *People don't care how much you know until they know how much you care.about them. How far you go in life depends on your being tender with the young, compassionate with the aged, sympathetic with the striving, and tolerant of the weak and the strong. Because someday in life you will have all of these.*

CHARAP, STANLEY HARVEY, electrical engineering educator; b. NYC, Apr. 21, 1932; s. William and Esther Charap; m. Marilyn Novick, Aug. 7, 1955; children: Joshua David, Lawrence Gordon. BS in Physics, Bklyn. Coll., 1953; PhD in Physics, Rutgers U., 1959. Mem. rsch. staff IBM T.J. Watson Rsch. Ctr., Yorktown Heights, NY, 1958-64; rsch. scientist Rsch. div. Am.-Standard Inc., Piscataway, NJ, 1964, supr. solid state physics, 1965-66, mgr. physics and electronics, 1966-68; assoc. prof. elec. and computer engring. Carnegie Mellon U., Pitts., 1968-71, prof., 1971-96; prof. emeritus, 1997—; assoc. head dept. Carnegie Mellon U., Pitts., 1980-85, acting head dept., 1981-82, vice chmn. faculty senate, 1972-73, chmn. faculty senate, 1986-87, assoc. dir. Data Storage Systems Ctr., 1990-96. Cons. Westinghouse Rsch. Ctr., Pitts., 1969-84; mem. tech. staff Bell Labs., Whippany, NJ, summer 1973; sr. vis. fellow U. Wales, Cardiff, spring 1976; vis. scientist Control Data Corp., Mpls., summer 1987. Editor: Physics of Magnetism, 1964; contbr. to Magnetism & Metallurgy, 1969; contbr. over 60 tech. articles to profl. jours. V.p. Sch. Advanced Jewish Studies, Pitts., 1989—91. Recipient Tech. Achievement award, Nat. Storage Industry Consortium, 1998, Outstanding Rsch. award, Carnegie Mellon U., 2006. Fellow IEEE (fellow com. 1997-2005, Millennium medal 2000); mem. IEEE Magnetics Soc. (sec.-treas. 1987-88, v.p. 1989-90, pres. 1991-92, editor-in-chief IEEE Trans. on Magnetics 1982-86, editl. bd. IEEE Press 1989-91, IEEE Tech. activities bd., liaison coun. 1993, gen. chmn. Joint INTERMAG-MMM conf. 1994, Disting. Lectr. 1996, Achievement award 1998, chair Disting. Lectr. Program 2003-04), Am. Inst. Physics, Conf. on Magnetism and Magnetic Materials (treas. 1981-83, gen. chmn. 1986). Office: Carnegie Mellon Univ Dept Electrical Computer Engineering 5000 Forbes Ave Pittsburgh PA 15213-3890 Business E-Mail: s.charap@ieee.org.

CHARASH, BRUCE D., cardiologist, educator; b. NYC, Apr. 8, 1956; BA in Chemistry, Cornell U., 1977; MD, Cornell U. Med. Coll., 1981. Lic. NY State, 1982, cert. Am. Bd. Internal Medicine, 1984, Cardiovascular Disease subspecialty 1987. Intern, internal medicine Mt. Sinai Med. Ctr., dept. of medicine, 1982, resident, internal medicine, 1982—84; instr. Cornell Med. Sch., 1986—87, asst. prof. medicine, 1987—93; fellow, divsn. cardiology NY Hosp.-Cornell Med. Ctr., 1984—86, asst. attending physician, 1986—91; sr. attending physician Lenox Hill Hosp., 1991—2005, chief cardiac care unit, 1991—2005; clin. assoc. prof. medicine NYU Med. Sch., 1993—2005; vis. assoc. prof. medicine SUNY Health Ctr., Bklyn., 1998—2005; assoc. prof. clinical medicine Columbia U., 2005—; attending physician New York-Presbyterian Hospital. Investigator in field. Contbr. to profl. publs., jours., abstracts, and chap. in books; author: Heart Myths, 1991. Daniel and Elaine Sargent Cardiology Fellow, 1985. Fellow: Am. Coll. of Cardiology; mem.: AMA, ACP, Am. Red. Cross-NY Chap. (med. dir. AED program), Alpha Omega Alpha, Phi Kappa Phi, Phi Beta Kappa. Office: 16 E 60th St Ste 330 New York NY 10022 Home Phone: 212-832-2686; Office Phone: 212-606-0006. Business E-Mail: bdc2104@gmail.com.

CHARBONEAU-MCINNIS, JANINE JOYCE, veterinary animal behaviorist; b. Detroit, Nov. 19, 1954; d. Ernest Russel and Shirley Ann (Mistele) Charboneau; m. William Andrew McInnis Oct. 5, 1985; children: Brandon Christopher McInnis, Madison Mae McInnis, Jonathan Martin McInnis. BS in Poultry Sci., Mich. State U., Lansing, DVM, 1981. Past owner Cameo Kennels, Mich., Cameo Vet. Clin., Mich., 1982-84; owner, dir., instr. Cameo canine courses City of Dallas, 1983-87; svc. rep. Hill's Pet Products, Inc., 1987-89; owner, vet. animal behaviorist Behavioral Vet. Cons. Dallas, Dallas, 1989—. Past prodr., trainer, handler Lhasa Apso and Chihuahuas; guest spkr. Nat. Basset Hound Futurity, 1982; guest lectr. Terrant County Vet. Med. Assn., Tex., 1992. Appearances (video) The Standard of the English Mastiff in the United States; contbr. articles to profl. jours., chpt. to book. Fred Waring scholar: recipient Prodr.'s award producing 5 or more champion get, Best of Breed award Madison Sq. Gardens, Best in Show Brace Houston Astrodome Dog Show Series, 1998, 100th Ann. Tex. Kennel Club Dog Show, 1998, 75th Chihuahua Nat. Specialty , 1998, Lapeer's Most Outstanding Young Career Woman's award. Mem. Am. Vet. Assn., Tex. Vet. Med. Assn. (guest spkr. 1997, moderator), Dallas County Med. Assn. Avocations: photography, painting. Office: Behavioral Vet Cons PO Box 796473 Dallas TX 75379-6473 Fax: 972-250-0444.

CHARDKOFF, JOAN CORB, language educator; arrived in US, 1963; d. Henry and Midlred (Wolfe) Corb; m. Richard Bruce Chardkoff, Aug. 25, 1963; children: Deena Chardkoff Shapiro, Leslie Chardkoff Scarlett. BA, Fla. STate U., Tallahassee, 1965, MA, 1966; EdD, U. La., Monroe, 1978. Cert. supr. instrn. La., prin. La. Tchr. English Balboa HS, Panama, 1968—69; tchr. French River Oaks Sch., Monroe, 1976—80, Jack Hayes Elem. Sch., Monroe, 1980—84, Lakeshore Elem. Sch., Monroe, 1984—87, Ouachita Parish HS, Monroe, 1987—. Part-time instr. New River CC, Dublin, 1970—71; part-time tchr. River Oaks Sch., Monroe, 1971—73; cons., presenter McDougal Littell, Boston, 1996—2006. Editor: Sol's Story, 2002; co-author: The Navigators, 2007. Patron, bd. dirs. Monroe Little Theater, 1980—2006; mem., chairperson Shaekspeare competition English-Spkg. Union, Monroe, 1990—2006. Named Tchr. of the Yr., Ouachita Parish HS, 2001—02; grantee, Jr. League, 1996—99, 2003; CODOFIL scholar, 1981, 1987. Mem.: La. Fgn. Lang. Tchrs. Assn. (pres. 1991—93), Am. Assn. Tchr. French (pres. La. chpt. 1998—2000), Am. Coun. Tchg. Fgn. Langs., Phi Delta Kappa. Avocations: travel, reading, aerobics. Office: Ouachita Parish HS 681 Hwy 594 Monroe LA 71203

CHARDON, MARC D'ESTOURNELLES, software company executive; b. Concord, NH, Nov. 1, 1955; s. Alain Jean and Phoebe Warren (Ashley) C.; m. Sallie Garrett Shepherd, May 24, 1986; 1 child, Robert d'Estournelles. BA magna cum laude, Harvard U., 1976. Secretaire-generale Groupe Dumay, Geneva, 1977-82; prin. Chardon Energy Systems, Westport, Mass., 1982-83; various internat. mktg., bus., and operational roles, including head of corp. strategy and gen. mgr. Digital France Digital Equipment Corp., Maynard, Mass., 1983—98; gen. mgr. Microsoft France, 1998; CFO, Info. Bus. Worker Microsoft Corp., 2003—05; pres., CEO Blackbaud, Inc., 2005—. Office: Blackbaud Inc 2000 Daniel Island Dr Charleston SC 29492

CHAREN, MONA, columnist; b. NYC, Feb. 25, 1957; d. George and Claire (Rosenfeld) C.; m. Robert P. Parker. BA, Columbia U., 1979; JD, George Wash. U., 1984. Editorial assoc. Nat. Review Mag., NYC, 1979-81; speechwriter White House, Washington, 1984, assoc. dir., office of pub. liaison, 1985-86; speechwriter Jack Kemp for Pres., Washington, 1986; syndicated columnist Creators Syndicate, LA, 1987—. Panelist The Capital Gang CNN, Washington. Contbr. articles profl. mags. and publs.; author: Useful Idiots, 2003, Do-Gooders, 2005. Republican. Jewish. Office: Creators Syndicate 5777 W Century Blvd Ste 700 Los Angeles CA 90045-5675 Home Phone: 703-759-5919. Personal E-mail: charenmail@cox.net.

CHARFOOS, LAWRENCE SELIG, lawyer; b. Detroit, Dec. 7, 1935; s. Samuel and Charlotte (Salkin) C.; m. Jane Emerson. Student, U. Mich., 1953-56; LLB, Wayne State U., 1959. Bar: Mich. 1959, Ill. 1965. Pvt. practice, Detroit, 1960-63; pres., ptnr. Charfoos & Christensen PC, Detroit, 1967—; theatrical producer, legitimate theater mgr. Chgo., 1963-67. Cons. med.-legal problems Mich. Med. Soc., Mich. Hosp. Coun., ATLA; US cts. com. State Bar Mich. Author: The Medical Malpractice Case: A Complete Handbook, 1974, Daughters at Risk, 1981, Personal Injury Practice, Technique and Technology, 1986; contbr. articles to profl. jours. Trustee Lawrence S. Charfoos Found. Elected to Inner Circle of Advocates, 1973, named one of Best Lawyers in Am., 2006. Mem. ABA, Mich. Bar Assn. (com. U.S. cts. 1999-2003), Detroit Bar Assn. (past dir.), Am. Bd. Profl. Liability Attys. (founder, past pres.), Internat. Acad. Trial Lawyers. Office: 5510 Woodward Ave Detroit MI 48202-3804 Office Phone: 313-875-8080. Business E-Mail: lcharfoos@c2law.com.

CHARGOIS, DEBORAH MAJEAU, psychology professor, researcher; b. New Orleans, Nov. 8, 1940; d. John Ashton and Marie Barbot Majeau; m. Ashton Joseph Chargois, Sept. 6, 1969. BA, U. Notre Dame, South Bend, Ind., 1963; MS, La. State U., New Orleans, 1967; PhD, La. State U., 1969, MD, 1983. Lic. physician Calif., Fla. Rsch. assoc. in otorhinolaryngology La. State U. Med. Ctr., New Orleans, 1965—67, instr. in otorhinolaryngology and physiology, 1967—70, liason officer to NASA, 1967—74, asst. prof. otorhinolaryngology and physiology, assoc. mem. grad. faculty, 1970—74, asst. prof. physiology, mem. grad. faculty, 1974—77, dir. dental physiology programs, 1975—79; postdoctoral fellow in clin. chemistry and toxicology La. State U. Med. Ctr. and VA Hosp., New Orleans, 1979—81, resident in psychiatry, 1983—87; sr. rschr. sonic boom studies Miss. Test Facility, 1967—69; sr. rschr. high voltage elec. field studies Hebert Rsch. Facility, 1980—84; rsch. assoc. in elec. engring. Tulane U., New Orleans, 1980—82, adj. asst. prof. elec. engring., mem. grad. faculty, 1982—84; clin. toxicologist River Oaks Hosp., New Orleans, 1987—91; adj. prof. psychology, mem. grad. faculty Jacksonville (Ala.) State U., 1998—. Spl. lectr. divsn. engring. rsch. La. State U., Baton Rouge, 1969—71; vis. scientist Charity Hosp. of La. at New Orleans, 1969—71, 1981—83; moderator panel on schizophrenia Am. Psychiat. Assn. Ann. Conv., Dallas, 1985; advisor Inst. Rev. Bd. Jacksonville State U., 2005—. Contbr. articles to profl. jours. Contbr. Am. Nat. Red Cross, Washington, 2001—, Magen David Adom, Jerusalem, 2001—; mem. Dem. Nat. Com., Washington, 2000—, Ala. Dem. Party, Birmingham, 2002—. Lt. comdr. USN, 1982. Recipient 1st pl. award for presentation, Am. Speech and Hearing Assn., 1969, 2d pl. award for sci. merit, 1969; fellow Medicine in the Tropics, Bur. Medicine and Surgery, USN and Gorgas Meml. Lab., Panama, 1982; predoctoral fellow in physiology, NIH, 1966—67, postdoctoral fellow in tropical medicine, 1973, Bio-Space Tech. Tng. Program fellow, 1969, postdoctoral fellow in clin. chemistry and toxicology, 1979—81. Mem.: AMA, APA, So. Med. Assn., Am. Psychol. Soc., Am. Psychiat. Assn., Mensa, Psi Chi, Sigma Xi. Jewish. Avocations: stamp collecting/philately, coin collecting/numismatics, amateur radio, history, sailing. Home: 2040 Highland Ave # 804 Birmingham AL 35205 Office: Jacksonville State U 700 Pelham Rd N Jacksonville AL 36265 Office Phone: 256-782-5402. Office Fax: 256-782-5637. Personal E-mail: chargois2@aol.com.

CHARI, RAVI S., surgeon; s. Ranga S. and Rajiswari B. Chari; m. Sharon Elizabeth Albers, Mar. 20, 1993; children: Tristan Albers, Danielle Jean. MD, U. of Saskatoon, 1989. Asst. prof. of surgery and cell biology U. Mass med. Ctr., Worcester, 1998—2001; prof. of surgery and cancer biology Vanderbilt U. Med. Ctr., Nashville, 2001—. Mem. sci. com. Internat. Hepato-Pancreaitoc-Biliary Assn., Germany, 2004—06; sec. Soc. of U. Surgeons, Winter Park, Fla., 2006—; counselor Am. Hepato-Pancreatico-Biliary Assn., Winter Park, Fla., 2006—. Grant, NIH, 2005—. Fellow: ACS (ACS Faculty Fellowship award 1999—2001). Office: Vanderbilt Univ 1313 21st Avenue South Nashville TN 37232-4753 Office Phone: 615-936-2573. Business E-Mail: ravi.chari@vanderbilt.edu.

CHARISSE, CYD (TULA ELLICE FINKLEA), actress, dancer; b. Amarillo, Tex., Mar. 8, 1921; d. Ernest E. and Lela (Norwood) Finklea; m. Nico Charisse, Aug. 12, 1939 (div. 1947); 1 child, Nicholas; m. Tony Martin, May 9, 1948; 1 child, Tony. Toured with Ballet Russe, U.S. and Europe; stage, Broadway debut: Grand Hotel, 1992; appeared in films including Mission to Moscow, 1943, Something to Shout About, 1943, Ziegfield Follies, 1945, The Harvey Girls, 1946, Three Wise Fools, 1946, Till the Clouds Roll by, 1946, Fiesta, 1947, The Unfinished Dance, 1947, On an Island with You, 1948, Words and Music, 1948, The Kissing Bandit, 1949, East Side West Side, 1949, Tension, 1949, Mark of the Renegade, 1951, The Wild North, 1952, Singin' in the Rain, 1952, Sombrero, 1953, East to Love, 1953, The Band Wagon, 1953, Brigadoon, 1954, Deep in My Heart, 1954, It's Always Fair Weather, 1955, Meet Me in Las Vegas, 1956, Invitation to the Dance, 1957, Silk Stockings, 1957, Twilight for the Gods, 1958, Party Girl, 1958, Five Golden Hours, 1961, Black Tights, 1961, Two Weeks in Another Town, 1962, The Silencers, 1967, Maroc 7, 1967, Assassination in Rome, 1967, Warlords of Atlantis, 1978, Vision Privati, 1990, That's Entertainment! III, 1994, Satin and Silk, 2003; TV film: Portrait of an Escort, 1980, Swimsuit, 1989; author (with Tony Martin) The Two of Us, 1976. Elected Star of Tomorrow, 1948; named to Hollywood Walk of Fame, 1960, Tex. Film Hall of Fame, 2002; recipient Nijinsky award, 2000, Movado Dance award, 2003, Nat. Medal Arts, Nat. Endowment Arts, 2006. Office: Ste 1406 10724 Wilshire Blvd Apt 1406 Los Angeles CA 90024-4473*

CHARLA, LEONARD FRANCIS, lawyer, publishing executive; b. New Rochelle, NY, May 4, 1940; s. Leonard A. and Mary L. Charla; m. Kathleen Gerace, Feb. 3, 1968 (div. Dec. 1988); children: Larisa, Christopher; m. Elizabeth A. Du Mouchelle, Aug. 27, 1993. BA, Iona Coll., New Rochelle, NY, 1962; JD, Cath. U., Washington, DC, 1965; LLM, George Wash. U., Washington, DC, 1971. Bar: DC 1967, NJ 1970, Mich. 1971. Tech. writer IRS, Washington, 1966-67; atty. adv. ICC, 1967, atty., 1968-69; mgmt. intern HEW, 1967-68; atty. Bowes & Millner, Transp. Cons., Newark, 1969-71; atty. legal staff GM, Detroit, 1971-85, sr. counsel, 1985-87, asst. gen. counsel, 1987-89; sr. v.p. Clean Sites Inc., Alexandria, Va., 1989-90; atty. Butzel Long, Detroit, 1990—2005; pres. Countinghouse Press, Inc., Bloomfield, Mich., 1997—. Mem. faculty Coll. Creative Studies, Detroit, 1978—89, adj. asst. prof., 1988—89; faculty art U. Mich., 1980, 1984—89, adj. asst. prof., 1988—89; disting. vis. prof. U. Detroit Mercy Law Sch., 2004; instr. Henry Ford Cmty. Coll., Dearborn, Mich., 2004—; pres. 38 Huguenot Corp., 2000—. Author: Never Cooked Before/Gotta Cook Now!, 1999; pub.: A Letter from Marty (Mary O'Herron), 2004, The Freya Project (Phil Rosette), 2004, The Better Bottom Line, 2005. Bd. dirs. Gt. Lakes Performing Artists Assocs., 1983—85, Mich. Assn. Cmty. Arts Agys., 1983—89, 1992—93, vice chair, 1986—88, chair, 1988—89; active Info. Network Superfund Settlements, 1988—2004; bd. dirs. Friends Modern Art, Detroit Inst. Arts, 1996—2003, v.p., 1998—2003; bd. dirs. Art Ctr. Mt. Clemens, Mich., 1997—2005, chair facilities com., v.p. Mich., 2001—04; bd. govs. Cath. U. Am. Alumni, 1982—2002, v.p., 1993—98, Cranbrook Writers Guild, Birmingham, Mich., 2005—07; bd. regents Cath. U. Am., 1992—2002, Birmingham Bloomfield Art Assn., 1987—88, 1994—95; sec. Green Acres Condo Assn., 2005—. Mem.: ABA, State Bar Assn. (mem. arts com. entertainment and sports sect. 1979—, chmn. 1980—81, mem. coun. 1992—2004). Office: Countinghouse Press 6632 Telegraph Rd 311 Bloomfield Hills MI 48301 Home Phone: 248-642-7191; Office Phone: 248-642-7191. Office Fax: 248-642-7192. Personal E-mail: nuhuguenot@aol.com, lcharla@comcast.net.

CHARLES, ALLAN G., obstetrician, educator; b. NYC, Nov. 15, 1928; s. Harry G. and Alice (Grotzky) C.; m. Phyllis V. J. Vail, June 28, 1957; children: Della Marie, Aaron Joseph, David Jonathan. AB cum laude, NYU, 1948, MD, 1952. Diplomate: Am. Bd. Ob-gyn. Intern Phila. Gen. Hosp., 1952-53; resident in ob-gyn. Mt. Sinai Hosp., NYC, 1955-57, Michael Reese Hosp., Chgo., 1957-60, clin. asst., 1960-61, assoc. attending physician, 1961-69, attending physician, 1969—; co-dir. Michael Reese Hosp. (Rh-Investigative Clinic), 1963—, vice-chmn. dept. ob-gyn., 1971, pres. staff, 1978, bd. dirs., 1981-84; chief ob-gyn. Michael Reese Hosp., 1990-99; chmn. rsch. and edn. found. Michael Reese Hosp. Med. Staff, 1996-2000; pvt. practice specializing in office gynecology Chgo., 1960—. Courtesy staff Chgo. Lying-In-Hosp.; clin. asst. prof. ob-gyn. U. Ill. Coll. Medicine, Chgo., 1960-64, Chgo. Med. Sch., 1964-72; clin. prof. Pritzker Sch. Medicine, U. Chgo., 1972-84; attending physician Northwestern Meml. Hosp., 1984-90; prof. clin. ob-gyn. Northwestern U., 1983; clin. prof. ob-gyn. U. Ill. Coll. Medicine, 1991. Author: Rh Iso Immunization and Erythroblastosis Fetalis, 1969; Contbr. articles to profl. jours. Fellow Am. Coll. Obstetricians and Gynecologists, Internat. Coll. Surgeons (chmn. Am. sect. ob-gyn. 1979-83, sec., asst. treas. Am. sect.), Ctrl. Assn. Obstetricians and Gynecologists; mem. AMA, Ill., Chgo. med. socs., Chgo. Gynecol. Soc. (v.p. 1980—, sec. 1988-90, pres.-elect, 1992, pres. 1993-94). Achievements include developing substitute for uterine tube, Rh-sensitization. Home: 1150 N Lake Shore Dr Apt 22GH Chicago IL 60611 Office: 55 E Washington St Fl 37 Chicago IL 60602-2103 Office Phone: 312-263-5517. Personal E-mail: charles0920@sbcglobal.net.

CHARLES, GERARD, performing company executive, choreographer; b. Folkstone, Eng. m. Catherine Yoshimura; 1 child, Max. Student, Royal Ballet Sch. Ballet master BalletMet, Les Grands Ballets Canadiens; profl. dancer Ballet Internat., London, Milw. Ballet; assoc. artistic dir. BalletMet Columbus, artistic dir., 2001—. Choreographer, tchr., restager of works internationally in field. Choreographer The Sleeping Beauty, Coppelia; artistic dir.: Cinderella. Choreographic fellow, Nat. Endowment for Arts. Office: BalletMet Columbus 322 Mount Vernon Ave Columbus OH 43215 E-mail: gcharles@balletmet.org.*

CHARLES, JOEL, forensic audio and video recording analyst, voice identification consultant; b. Phila., Jan. 12, 1914; s. Samuel William and Minnie (Fink) Blumenstein; m. Lillian DuBowe, May 31, 1938 (div. 1964); children: Mark Blumenstein, Richard Blumenstein; m. Nancy Sher, Oct. 24, 1988. BSChemE, Drexel U., 1938. Pres. The Charles Agy., Phila., 1938-42, 45-64; physicist Naval Air Exptl. Station, Phila., 1942-45; pres. The Dento-Med. Tapes, Upper Darby, Pa., 1957-73, Associated TV Prodns., Inc., Phila., 1948-52, Computerized Electronic Edn., Upper Darby, Pa., 1969-73; dir. continuing edn., media instructional methodology Pa. Coll. of Podiatric Medicine, Phila., 1973-77; pvt. practice Plantation, Fla., 1977-96, Coral Springs, Fla., 1996—2001, Boynton Beach, Fla., 2001—. Expert witness on tape recordings; lectr. Tex. Criminal Def.

Lawyers Inst., La. Pub. Def. Criminal Lit. Seminar, Broward Criminal Def. Lawyers Assn., Dade Criminal Def. Lawyers Assn., Phoenix Pub. Defenders, Dade Fed. Pub. Defenders, Fla. Investigators Assn. Contbr. articles to profl. and law jours. Mem. NACDL (assoc.), Am. Fedn. Musicians, Am. Dialect Soc., Audio Engring. Soc. (chmn. forensic tape com.) Achievements include development of early rapid form of computerized voice identification, designed first high-speed portable audio cassette duplicator. Home and Office: 1505 Siena Ln Boynton Beach FL 33436 Office Phone: 561-740-2142. Fax: 561-740-2143. Personal E-mail: jayceco@aol.com.

CHARLES, LUENDA E., public health service officer, researcher; arrived in US, 1991; d. Eric and Princess Charles. BSc in Clin. Lab. Sci., Union Coll., Lincoln, Nebr., 1984; MPH, Emory U., Atlanta, 1993; PhD, U. NC, Chapel Hill, 2000. Clin. lab. scientist out-patient clinic KennMed Shallowford, Marietta, Ga., 1991—95; rsch. epidemiologist Ctr. Disease Control, Morgantown, W.Va., 2003—. Mem.: APHA (assoc.), Delta Omega. Avocations: reading, music, piano, travel. Home Phone: 304-692-2559; Office Phone: 304-285-5922.

CHARLES, MARILYN KAY, secondary school educator; b. Rock Springs, Wyo., Oct. 16, 1947; d. Walter Harvey and Mariam Louise (Tanner) Banks; m. Clinton Robert Charles, Jan. 30, 1975; stepchildren: Coralynn, Shane. AA, Western Wyo. Coll., Rock Springs, 1967; BA, Brigham Young U., Provo, Utah, 1971. Cert. secondary edn. tchr. Wyo. Typist/sec. dept. med. records Wyo. State Hosp., Evanston, 1972—73; instr. English, phys. edn. Evanston Jr. H.S., 1973—75; sec. Lyman H.S., 1978—86, instr. English, health, 1986—88, instr. English, 1988—2006. Drill team advisor Evanston H.S., Wyo., 1974—75; class advisor Lyman H.S., Wyo., 1986—, drill team advisor, 1987—89, yearbook advisor, 1992—98. Author: Roadshow Prodn. (LDS Ch. Stake award). Mem.: Wyo. Edn. Assn., Lyman Edn. Assn. Avocations: rock-hound, creative writing, crocheting, gardening, art work.

CHARLES, MICHAEL RAY, artist; b. Lafayette, La., 1967; BA, McNeese State U., Lake Charles, La., 1985; MFA, U. Houston, 1993. Drawing workshop instr. Blaffer Gallery U. Houston, intermediate painting instr.; painting workshop instr. Mus. Fine Arts, Houston, drawing instr., sculpture workshop instr.; art instr. 5th Ward Enrichment Prog., Houston, Mental Retardation Authority, Houston; lectr. to prof. studio art and painting U. Tex., Austin, 1993—. Exhibitions include Barnes-Blackman Galleries, Houston, 1991, Tony Shafrazi Gallery, NYC, 1994, Now is the Time, 1995, Bamboozled, 2000, Michael Ray Charles, Albright Knox Gallery, Buffalo, 1997, exhibited in group shows at Houston Internat. Festival: The Case for Art, Lawndale Art and Performance Ctr., Houston, 1992, Tex. Contemporary: Acquisitions of the 90's, Mus. Fine Arts, Houston, 1993, Looking Forward Looking Black, Balt. Mus. Art, 2002. Office: U Tex Austin Fine Arts 1 Univ Sta D1400 Austin TX 78712-0340

CHARLES, ROBERT BRUCE, lawyer, former federal agency administrator; b. Portsmouth, Va., Aug. 23, 1960; s. Roland Wilbur Charles Jr. and Doris Anne (Hassell) Holman; m. Marina Timasheff, Oct. 16, 1988; children: Nicholas Westcote, Sophia Anne. AB, Dartmouth Coll., 1982; MA, Oxford U., 1984; JD, Columbia U., 1987. Bar: N.Y. 1989, Conn. 1989, Maine 1990. Law clk. to judge U.S. Ct. Appeals (9th cir.), Seattle, 1987-88; assoc. Kramer, Levin et al, NYC, 1988-91, Weil, Gotshal & Manges, NYC, 1991-92, Washington, 1993-95; dep. assoc. dir. office of policy devel The White House, Washington, 1992-93; chief staff, chief counsel nat. security, internat. affairs and criminal justice subcommittee U.S. Ho. of Reps., Washington, 1995-99; chief staffer Speaker's Task Force on Drug Free Am., 1997-99; prof. govt. and cyberlaw Harvard U. Extension Sch., 1998—2001; pres. The Charles Group, 1999—2003, 2005—; asst. sec. of state, internat. narcotics & law enforcement US Dept. State, Washington, 2003—05. Summer assoc. The White House, Washington, 1982-84, Supreme Ct. India, 1985. Author: Narcots and Terrorism: Logic, Links, and Looking Forward, 2003; contbr. articles to profl. jours., chpts. to books. Mem. coun. fgn. rels., bd. dirs. Theodore Roosevelt Assn., bd. dirs.; bd. dirs. George C. Marshall Found., Nat. Eagle Scout Assn. Officer USNR, 1998—. Keasbey scholar, Phila. 1982, Tony Patino fellow Columbia U., 1984; recipient Petra T. Shattuck Disting. Tchg. award Harvard U., 2000. Republican. Avocations: running, hiking, writing. Office Phone: 202-546-2262. Office Fax: 202-546-2265. Personal E-mail: RCharlesZZ@aol.com.

CHARLES, SHARON PATRICIA, elementary school educator; b. Antigua, Oct. 26, 1958; d. David and Muriel Charles; 1 child, Soneil. B of Elem. Edn. cum laude, U. VI, St. Croix, 1990, M of Elem. Edn., 1993. Tchr. All Sts. Primary Sch., Antigua and Barbuda, 1976—78, 1980—83, St. Croix Moravian Sch., 1983—85, Caribbean Cmty. Sch., 1986—91, Lew Muckle Elem. Sch., 1991—. Chair Lew Muckle Elem. Sch., 1995—. Mem. ARC, St. Croix, 2000—. Mem.: VI Writing Project, Internat. Reading Assn., Nat. Coun. Tchrs. English. Avocations: writing, reading, poetry. Home: 9014 Little Princess Hill Christiansted VI 00820 Office: Lew Muckle Elem Sch 317 Estate Sion Farm St Croix VI 00820

CHARLES, WALTER, actor; b. East Stroudsburg, Pa., Apr. 4, 1945; s. Theodore Edmund and Catherine Alexandra (Carstensen) Jacobsen. MusB, Boston U., 1968. Appeared in Broadway shows La Cage Aux Folles, Aspects of Love, Me & My Girl, Cats, Sweeney Todd, Grease, Knickerbocker Holiday, Call Me Madam, A Christmas Carol, Sunset Boulevard (Can. co.), Kiss Me Kate, Boys from Syracuse, Big River, The Woman in White, 2005, The Apple Tree, 2006; off Broadway, Wit, The Immigrant; films: A Fine Mess, Weeds, Fletch Lives, Prancer, TV programs Cagney & Lacey, Kate & Allie, Law & Order: Criminal Intent, The Street, 1981 Tony Awards, PBS Great Performances, 1983 Grammy awards, All My Children, others, also various nat. tours, regional and stock theatrical prodns., commls. and voice-overs. Recipient Best Actor in Musical award Bay Area Drama Critics, 1984; nominee Helen Hayes award, 2007.

CHARLESWORTH, ARTHUR THOMAS, mathematics professor; b. Gainesville, Fla., Nov. 8, 1944; s. Arthur Riggs and Martha Jean (Hamilton) C.; m. Josephine Ann Owenby, Sept. 10, 1966; 1 child, Jonathan David. BS in Math., Stetson U., 1966; AM in Math., Duke U., 1968, PhD in Math., 1974; MS in Computer Sci., U. Va., 1983. Trajectory analysis engr. Apollo support dept. GE, Daytona Bch., Fla., 1966-67; instr. Jacksonville (Fla.) U., 1968-69, Randolph-Macon Coll., Ashland, Va., 1969-71; asst. prof. Queens Coll., Charlotte, NC, 1974-76, U. Richmond, Va., 1976-82, assoc. prof. Va., 1982-89, prof. Va., 1989—. Sec. astronomy, math., physics sect. Va. Acad. Sci., 1977-78, chmn., 1978-79; treas. Md., D.C., Va. sect. Math. Assn. Am., 1980-82. Contbr. articles to maj. computer sci. jours. Chmn. Trinity Meth. Comsn. on Missions, Richmond, 1981. Research grantee NASA Langley Rsch. Ctr., Hampton, Va., 1987, 88, 89, 90, 91, 92. Mem. IEEE, Assn. Computing Machinery (sr.), Omicron Delta Kappa, Sigma Xi. Avocations: hiking, rock collecting. Office: U Richmond Dept Math/Computer Sci Richmond VA 23173 Business E-Mail: charlesworth@richmond.edu.

CHARLETON, MARGARET ANN, child care administrator, consultant; b. Orange, Calif., Aug. 3, 1947; d. Arthur Mitchell and Isabelle Margaret (Esser) Charleton; m. Terrence Joseph Marecic, July 21, 2001. AA in Liberal Arts, Orange Coast Coll., 1968; BA in Psychology, Chapman U., 1984. Head tchr. Presbyn. Ch. of the Master, Mission Viejo, Calif., 1977-81; child care program adminstr. Crystal Stairs, Inc., LA, 1981—2001; pvt. practice counseling and consulting. Mem. adv. bd. Children's Home Soc., Santa Ana, Calif., 1982-83; cons. Calif. Sch. Age Consortium, Costa Mesa, 1987, Calif. State Dept. of Edn., 1988; trainer preschool edn. program Sesame Street PBS, 1994-96; lectr. in field; presenter Western Regional Child Care Food Program Conf., San Francisco, 1997, Save the Children Conf., Atlanta, Ga., 1998, 10th Ann. Child Care Food Program Sponsor's Conf., 2001. Contbr. articles to profl. jours. Mem. South Orange County Community Svc., Mission Viejo, 1983—; liaison Family Svcs.-Marine Base, El Toro, Calif., 1989—; mem. adv. bd. Dept. Social Svc., 1997—. Recipient Plaque of Recognition, Vietnamese Community of Orange County, 1984. Mem. NAFE. Roman Catholic. Avocations: sailing, skiing, travel, wine.

CHARLIP, RALPH BLAIR, military officer, health facility administrator; b. Detroit, July 16, 1952; s. Jack Edward and Dorothea (Steinman) Charlip; m. Cynthia Lanell Sallas, May 23, 1987. BA, U. Ariz., 1976, MPA, 1977. Commd. 2nd lt. USAF, 1978, advanced through grades to lt. col., 1994; squadron comdr. USAF Regional Hosp., Langley AFB, Va., 1978-79, dir. patient adminstrn., 1979-80, plant mgr., 1980-81; dir. med. resource mgmt. USAF Clinic Andersen, Andersen AFB, Guam, 1981-82; dir. patient adminstrn. Malcolm Grow USAF Med. Ctr., Andrews AFB, Md., 1983-84; intern Data Systems Design Ctr., Gunter AFB, Ala., 1984-85; health policy devel. officer USAF Hdqs., Bolling AFB, DC, 1985-89; dir. patient adminstrn. USAF Med. Ctr., Wright-Patterson AFB, Ohio, 1989-92; assoc. dir. med. svcs. Air Nat. Guard Hqrs., Andrews AFB, 1992-94; dir. plans integration and mktg. Dept. Def. Health Svcs. Region VII, Ft. Bliss, Tex., 1994-96; comdr. 423 Clinic, Upwood, England, 1996-97; adminstr. aerospace med. Armstrong Lab., Brooks AFB, Tex., 1997; dep. comdr. 59 Med. Support Group, Lackland AFB, Tex., 1997-99; assoc. adminstr. 59 Med. Wing, Lackland AFB, 1999-2000; dir. health adminstrn. ctr. VA, Denver, 2000—. Chair U.S. Air Force Med. Svc. Corps. Career Devel. Com., 1995—2000; adj. faculty U. Md., St. Leo Coll., Air Nat. Guard Quality Ctr., Met. State Coll., Denver, Denver Fed. Exec. Bd., 2000—; mem. Civil Air Patrol Nat. Health Svc. Group, 2005—06. Author: (book) Your Health Benefits, 1989. Recipient Ray Brown award, AMSUS, 2004. Fellow: Am. Acad. Med. Adminstrs. (state chairperson 2005—), Am. Coll. Healthcare Execs. (regent's adv. coun. 1994—, credentials com. 1999, awards com. 2004—05, editl. bd. 2005—); mem.: Air Force Assn., Air Force Med. Svc. Corps. Assn. (sec., v.p.). Office: VA HAC 3773 Cherry Creek Dr N Denver CO 80209

CHARLOT, JOSEPH LEONCE, JR., preventive medicine physician; b. Bklyn., Oct. 19, 1967; s. Joseph Leonce and Marie Andree Charlot; m. Denise Michelle Johnson, July 11, 1967. BA, Rutgers U., 1986—90; MD, U. Medicine & Dentristry NJ, 1990—95, MPH, 1991—93. Med. Rev. Officer Med. Rev. Officer Certification Coun., Ill. State, 2001, Advanced Cardiac Life Support Am. Heart Assn., Ill. State, 2004, Basic Life Support Am. Heart Assn., Ill. State, 2004, Preventive Medicine Am. Bd. of Preventive Medicine, Ill. State, 2003, Am. Bd. of Preventive Medicine, Ill. State, 2004; Prison Religious Vol. Prison Fellowship, Va. State, 1999. Resident physician U. of Md. Med. Sys., Balt., 1995—97, Trover Clinic, Madisonville, Ky., 1997—98; locum tenens occupl. medicine physician Concentra Med. Centers, Richmond, Va., 1999—2000; resident physician Ft. Wayne Med. Found., Ft. Wayne, Ind., 2000—00; med. dir. Cmty. Occupl. Medicine, Elkhart, Ind., 2001—02; 2004plant occupl. medicine physician Daimler Chrysler Kokomo Transmission Plant, Kokomo, Ind., 2002; med. dir. US Health Works, Branford, Conn., 2004—. Prison religious vol. Prison Fellowship, Richmond, Va., 1999—2000; religious vol. Kokomo Rescue Mission, Kokomo, Ind., 2003—03; physician vol. Kokomo Cmty. Health Initative, 2002—03. Fellow Rsch. Fellowship, Robert Wood Johnson Med. Sch., 1991. Mem.: APHA (assoc.), AMA (assoc.), Am. Coll. of Preventive Medicine (assoc.), Christian Med. and Dental Associations (assoc.). Avocations: basketball, reading, computer programming, bicycling, weightlifting. Office: Naval Health Clinic Occupational Medicine Dept 47149 Base Rd Patuxent River MD 20670 Office Phone: 301-342-1490. Personal E-mail: jcharlot@earthlink.net.

CHARLSON, ROBERT JAY, atmospheric sciences educator; b. San Jose, Calif., Sept. 30, 1936; s. Rolland Walter and Harriet Adele (Stucky) C.; m. Patricia Elaine Allison, Mar. 16, 1964; children: Daniel Owen, Amanda Marcella. BS in Chemistry, Stanford U., 1958, MS in Chemistry, 1959; PhD in Atmospheric Scis., U. Wash., 1964; postgrad. (Fulbright scholar), London U., 1964-65; PhD (hon.), Stockholm U., 1993. Rsch. engr. Boeing Co., Seattle, 1959-62; rsch. asst. prof. dept. civil engring. U. Wash., Seattle, 1965-69, assoc. prof. atmospheric chemistry, 1969-71, assoc. prof. civil engring. and geophysics, 1971-74, prof. atmospheric chemistry in civil engring. geophysics and environ. studies, 1974-94, prof. atmospheric scis., 1985-98, adj. prof. chemistry, 1985-96, prof., 1996-98, prof. emeritus, 1998—; King Carl XVI Gustaf prof. environ. sci. Sweden, 1999-2000. Author: (with S.S. Butcher) An Introduction to Air Chemistry, 1972; assoc. editor: Jour. Applied Meteorology, 1971-73; co-editor: Global Biogeochemical Cycles, 1992; Earth System Science: From Biogeochemical Cycles to Global Change, 2000; mem. editorial bd. Jour. Boundary Layer Meteorology, 1971-86, Water, Air and Soil Pollution, 1971-85; contbr. articles on atmosphere chemistry to profl. jours.; patentee in field. Co-recipient Gerbier/Mumm award World Meteorol. Orgn., 1988; grantee USPHS, EPA, NSF, NASA, NOAA. Fellow Am. Meteorol. Soc., Am. Geophys. Union; mem. AAAS, Am. Chem. Soc., Sigma Xi, Phi Lambda Upson (hon.). Office: U Wash Dept Atmospheric Scis PO Box 351640 Seattle WA 98195-0001

CHARLTON, JESSE MELVIN, JR., retired management educator, lawyer; b. Livonia, La., May 12, 1916; s. Jesse Melvin and Anna Lela (Medlin) C.; m. Mary Camp, Oct. 4, 1941; children: Jesse Melvin, Frances Anne. BS, La. State U., 1937, MBA, 1938; JD, Harvard U., 1951. Bar: US Ct. Mil. Appeals 1952, US Supreme Ct 1963, DC 1951. Instr. U. Ala., 1938-40; commd. 2d lt., inf. U.S. Army, 1940; advanced through grades to col. U.S. Army (Judge Adv. Gen.'s Corps), 1962; dep. comdr. Judge Adv. Gen. Sch., Charlottesville, Va., 1962-64; ret., 1964; mem. faculty U. New Orleans Coll. Bus., 1964-81, prof. mgmt., 1971-81, prof. emeritus, 1981—; asst. dean coll. bus. U. New Orleans, 1967-71, dean grad. sch., 1978-80. Author handbook; co-editor: Statistical Abstract of Louisiana, 5th edit, 1974. Decorated Bronze Star. Mem. DC Bar Assn. Republican.

CHARLTON, JOHN KIPP, pediatrician; b. Omaha, Jan. 26, 1937; s. George Paul and Mildred (Kipp) C.; m. Susan S. Young, Aug. 15, 1959 (dec. June, 2003); children: Paul, Cynthia, Daphne, Gregory. AB, Amherst Coll., 1958; MD, Cornell U., 1962. Intern Ohio State U. Hosp., Columbus, 1962-63; resident in pediatrics Children's Hosp., Dallas, 1966-68, chief resident in pediatrics, 1968-69; fellow in nephrology U. Tex. Southwestern Med. Sch., Dallas, 1969-70; pvt. practice medicine specializing in pediatrics, Phoenix, from 1970; chmn. dept. pediatrics Maricopa Med. Ctr., Phoenix, 1971-78, 84-93, pres. med. staff, 1991; med. dir., bd. dirs. Crisis Nursery, Inc., 1977—. Clin. assoc. prof. pediat. U. Ariz. Coll Medicine, asst. dean for student affairs, 2000—. Author articles and book revs. in field. Pres. Maricopa County Child Abuse Coun., 1977-81; bd. dirs. Florence Crittenton Svcs., 1980-83, Ariz. Children's Found., 1987-91; mem. Gov.'s Coun. on Children, Youth and Families, 1984-86. Officer M.C., USAF, 1963-65. Recipient Hon. Kachina award for volunteerism, 1980, Jefferson award for volunteerism, 1980, Horace Steel Child Advocacy award, 1993, Cmty. Quarterback award, 2003; named Clin. Sci. Educator of Yr., U. Ariz., 1997, 99, 2000, 2001, Best Doctor in Am., 1976-2006, Miss. Found. Phoenix award, 2006. Mem. Am. Acad. Pediatrics, Ariz. Pediatric Soc., Maricopa County Pediatric Soc. (past pres.). Home: 6230 E Exeter Blvd Scottsdale AZ 85251-3060 Office: Maricopa Med Ctr 2601 E Roosevelt St Phoenix AZ 85008-4973 Office Phone: 602-344-5404. Business E-Mail: kipp_charlton@medprodoctors.com.

CHARLTON, MICHAEL THOMAS, surgeon; BS in Biology, USAF Acad., Colo. Springs, 1990—94; MD, Uniformed Svcs. U. Health Scis., Bethesda, Md., 1994—98. Chief orthopaedic surgery 51st Med. Grp., Osan, Republic of Korea, 2005—06; orthopaedic trauma fellow U. Tex. Southwestern Med. Ctr., Dallas, 2006—. Flight comdr. surg. svcs. 51st Med. Group, 2005—06. Maj. USAF, 1989—2006. Decorated Meritorious Svc. medal with one oak leaf cluster 51st Med. Wing; recipient Best Pediatric Poster award, Am. Acad. Orthopaedic Surgeons, 2005. Mem.: Soc. Mil. Orthopaedic Surgeons, Am. Acad. Orthopaedic Surgeons, Orthopaedic Trauma Assn. (assoc.), USAF Acad. Assn. Graduates (life), Assn. Mil. Surgeons of US (life). R-Consevative. Lutheran. Achievements include research in orthopaedic fracture surgery. Avocations: tennis, travel, cooking. Office: Dept Orthopaedic Surgery 5323 Harry Hines Blvd Dallas TX 75390-8882 Personal E-mail: mtcharlton2000@yahoo.com.

CHARLTON, PAUL K., former prosecutor, lawyer; b. 1960; m. Susan Charlton; 2 children. BA in Spanish, U. Ariz., 1983; JD, Ariz. State U., 1988. Law clk. to Thomas Kleinschmidt Ariz. Ct. Appeals; law clk. to Atty. Gen. Bob Corbin State of Ariz., Phoenix, asst. atty. gen.; asst. US atty. Dist. Ariz. US Dept. Justice, Phoenix, 1991—2001, US atty., 2001—07. Recipient Prosecutor of Yr., Fed. law Enforcement Officer's Assn., 1997.*

CHARNAS, CHARLES N., lawyer, computer company executive; BA, Stanford U.; JD, U. Calif., Berkeley. Joined Hewlett-Packard Co., Palo Alto, Calif., 1989, asst. sec., 1999, head corp., securities and mergers and acquisitions sect., 1999, v.p., dep. gen. counsel, 2002—, acting gen. counsel, 2006—07. Office: Hewlett-Packard Co 3000 Hanover St Palo Alto CA 94304 E-mail: charles.charnas@hp.com.*

CHARNAS, MICHAEL (MANNIE), investment company executive; b. Cleve., Sept. 24, 1947; s. Max and Eleanor (Gross) Charnas; m. Mimi F. Stein, June 10, 1990; 1 child from previous marriage, Matthew. BBA, Ohio State U., 1969, MBA in Fin., 1971. Page Ohio Ho. of Reps., 1969; mem. Ohio Staters, Inc., 1969; fin. analyst Addressograph-Multigraph, Inc., Cleve., 1971-73; asst. to pres., dir. planning and budget 1st Nat. Supermarkets, Inc. (Pick-N-Pay), Cleve., 1975-78, asst. to pres., v.p. planning and budgets, 1978-79, sr. v.p. fin., adminstr., 1979-81, sr. v.p., CFO, adminstrv. officer Hartford, Conn., 1981-86; founder Charnas Mktg. and Investment Co., 1986—; pres., owner Indsl. Pallet and Packaging Co., Beachwood, Ohio, 1986-94; regional v.p. Pallet Pallet, Inc. (formerly Indsl. Pallet and Packaging Co.), Toronto, 1995-97; co-owner Samm Properties and Samm Mgmt. Svcs., Ltd., 1998—; owner, operator Self Storage Facilities, Ohio, Fla.; owner, CEO Pallet Distbrs., Inc., 1999—2001; v.p., owner PMC Investment Group, 2003—. Co-owner Fat Burrito, Inc., a Qdoba Mexican Grill Restaurants franchise; franchisee Qdoba Mexican Grill Restaurants, Ill., Iowa. Recipient Weatherhead 100 award, Weatherhead Sch. Bus. Case Western Res. U., 2006. Jewish. Avocations: tennis, reading, collecting modern classic cars. Office: 3659 Green Rd Ste 105 Cleveland OH 44122 Office Phone: 216-378-3306. E-mail: bizwiz924@cs.com.

CHARNEY, DOV, apparel executive; b. Montreal, Jan. 31, 1969; Attended, Tufts U. Founder, CEO Am. Apparel, 1997—. Named Man of Yr., GQ, 2003, Man of Yr., Grand All-Star Award, Apparel Mag., 2004, Man of Yr., LA Apparel Industry, Fashion Industries Guild, 2004, Most Beautiful People, Paper Mag.; named one of 100 Most Powerful People of So. Calif., LA Times Mag., 2006; named to Power 50, Details mag., 2006; recipient Ernst & Young Entrepreneur of Yr. Award, 2004, Man of Yr., Counselor award, Advertising Specialty Inst. Office: Am Apparel Inc 747 Warehouse St Los Angeles CA 90021 Office Phone: 213-448-0226. Office Fax: 213-448-0334.*

CHARNEY, MARC D., editor; BA in Polit. Sci., Williams Coll., 1965. Reporter Providence Jour., 1965—68; reporter, editor, fgn. corr. Associated Press, 1969—84; fgn. desk editor NY Times, 1984—88, Week in Review editor, 1988—. Office: NY Times 229 W 43rd St New York NY 10036 Office Phone: 212-556-1748. Office Fax: 212-556-3738. E-mail: charney@nytimes.org.

CHARNEY, MELVIN, artist, architect, educator; b. Montreal, Que., Can., Aug. 28, 1935; s. H. and F. (Cassack) C.; m. Ann Korsower, May 29, 1960; 1 child, Dara Alexandra. BArch, McGill U., Montreal, 1958; MArch, Yale U., 1959. Prin. Melvin Charney, Architect, Montreal, 1964—; prof. U. Montreal, 1964-95. Mem. architects com. Am. Acad. Arts and Scis., Boston, 1968-69; co-dir. task force on housing Govt. of Can., Ottawa, 1970-71; mem. adv. com. Can. Centre for Architecture, Montreal, 1983-89; exec. founding bd. dirs. Conseil des Arts et des Lettres, Quebec, 1994-97; invited prof. to numerous univs. One-man shows include Harvard U., 1977, Art Gallery of Ont., Toronto, 1978, Musee d'Art Contemporain, Montreal, 1979, P.S.1, N.Y.C., 1979, Can. Cultural Ctrs., Paris and Brussels, 1980, Mus. Contemporary Art, Chgo., 1982, Richard Gray Gallery, Chgo., 1982, 49th Parallel, Centre for Can. Contemporary Art, N.Y.C., 1982, 87, Agnes Etherington Art Centre, Kingston, Ont., 1983, represented Can. at the 42nd Venice Biennale of Art, 1986, Renè Blouin Gallery, Montreal, 1987, 88, Ctr. for Can. Art, N.Y., 1987, Sable-Castelli Gallery, Toronto, 1988, 91, 92, 93, 95, 97, 99, 2001, 03, maj. retrospective Can. Centre for Architecture, Montreal, 1991-92, de Beyrie Gallery, Paris, 1994, Israel Mus., Jerusalem, 1996, Power Plant Gallery Contemporary Art, Toronto, 1995, Franc Basse-Normandie, Caen, France, 1997, Fondation pour l'architecture, Brussels, 1997; represented Can., 7th Venice Biennale of Architecture, 2000, major retrospective Musée d'art Contemporain de Montréal, 2002, Can. Mus. Contemporary Photography, Nat. Gallery, Ottawa, 2003-04; exhibited in group shows at Montreal Mus. Fine Arts, 1972, 83, Musee d'Art Moderne de la Ville de Paris, 1973, Institut d'Art Contemporain, Montreal, 1975, 76, XXI Olympic Games, Montreal, 1976, John Weber Gallery, N.Y., 1979, Max Protetch Gallery, Washington, 1979, L.A. Inst. Contemporary Art, 1980, Vancouver Art Gallery, 1980, Centre George Pompidou, 1980, Musee du Que., 1981, 83, 85, 89, 91, 98, Akademie der Kunst, Berlin, 1983, Kunstverein, Stuttgart, 1983, Mus. Contemporary Art, Chgo., 1984, Internationalen Bauasstellung, Berlin, 1984, 17th Trianale di Milano, 1985, Centre internat. d'art contemporain, Montreal, 1985, 96, Musee d'art Contemporain de Montreal, 1987, 92, 99, 2000, Power Plant, Contemporary Art at Harbourfront, Toronto, 1988, The Canadian Ctr. Architecture, Montreal, 1989, 99, 00, Musee du Quebec, 1989, 91, Nat. Mus. Contemporary Art, Seoul, South Korea, 1990, Canadian Pavilion, V Biennale di Architettura, Venice, 1991, Passages, Ctr. d'art contemporain, Troyes, France, 1992, Musèe nat. d'art moderne, Paris, 1994, Ctr. Cultura Contemporania, Barcelona, 1994, Royal Festival Hall Galleries, London, 1995, Manchester City Art Gallery, 1995, Marlborough-Chelsea Gallery, N.Y., 1998, Espaid'art Contemporani de Castello, Spain, 2000, Bibliotheque Nat. de France, Paris, 2000, Concordia U. Art Gallery, Montreal, 2001, Centre nationale de la photographie, Paris, 2002, others; sculpture commns. The Can. Tribute to Human Rights, Ottawa, 1986, Urban Sculpture Garden for Can. Ctr. Architecture, Montreal, 1987, Place Berri, Montreal, 1991, Esplanade Frontenac, Sherbrooke, Que., 2003-04; represented in permanent collections Nat. Gallery Can., Ottawa, Can. Coun. Art Bank, Ottawa, Art Gallery Ont., Toronto, Musee d'art contemporain, Montreal, Can. Ctr. Architecture, Montreal, Mus. Contemporary Art, Chgo., IBM Collection, Chgo., Fonds Nat. d'Art Contemporain, Paris, Musee du Quebec, Montreal Mus. Fine Arts, Frac Basse Normandie, France, Art Gallery Hamilton, Israel Mus., Jerusalem, others; contbr. articles to profl. jours. Decorated Order of Que., comdr. Order Arts and Letters (France), Ordre Architects du Que.; recipient Arts award Minister des Affaires Culturelles, 1967, research award Humanities and Social Scis. Coun., 1971, Berlin Arts award Deutcher Akademischer Austanschdienst, 1982, Sr. Arts award Can. Coun., 1983, 87, 96, Prix du Que. in visual arts,

1996, Lynch-Stanton award to disting. artists Can. Coun., 1997, Arts award Couseil Arts et Letters du Que., 2000. Mem. Royal Can. Acad., Ras. des Artists du Que, Royal Archtl. Inst. Can., Ordre Archs. du Québec. Home: 3620 Marlowe Ave Montreal PQ Canada H4A 3L7 Office Phone: 514-489-9501. Personal E-mail: mcharney@aei.ca.

CHARNEY, NATALIE J., mental health services professional, educator, researcher; d. Frances E. and Leon A. Seidman; m. David Charney (dec.); 1 child, Melissa D Jonassen. BA in Psychology cum laude, U. Pa., 1988, MA in Social Gerontology, 1991, MSEd in Counseling Psychology, 1991; PhD in Health Care Adminstrn., Suffield U., 2005. Bd. cert. med. psychotherapist/psychodiagnostician, cert. cognitive behavioral therapist; co-occurring disorders profl. diplomate. Rsch. and adminstrv. assoc./acting dir. psychoendocrinology in psychiatry Hosp. U. Pa., Phila., 1972—82; pvt. practice Phila., 1991—; asst. adminstr. Phila. Mental Health Clinic, Phila., 1983—85; adminstr. sect. geriatric psychiatry Hosp. U. Pa., Phila., 1985—93; dir. family-based mental health svcs. Dr. Warren E. Smith CMH/MR/SA Ctrs., Phila., 1993—95, dir. mental health svcs. divsn., 1995—96; mgr. mental health svcs. divsn., vocat. rehab. programs Phila. OIC, 1998; dir. admissions, adult outpatient behavioral health svcs. and rsch. Cmty. Coun. for MH/MR, Inc., Phila., 1998—2004; clin. assoc. in psychiatry U. Pa. Med. Sch., Phila., 1992—, staff therapist Ctr. for Cognitive Therapy, 1992—; exec. dir. Treatment and Recovery Partnership, Phila., 2006—. Project dir. Sobriety Through Out Patient Inc., Phila., 2004—; mem. Am. Bd. Psychotherapists and Psychodiagnosticians; presenter in field. Mem. editl. bd. The Med. Psychotherapist; contbr. articles to profl. jours. Recipient Cert. of Gratitude, Sled Toys for Tots, 1994. Mem.: APA (assoc.), Nat. Assn. Cognitive-Behavioral Therapists, Gerontol. Soc. Am. (rsch. edn. and practice com., pvt. sector task force 1989—92), Phila. Coalition of Cmty. Care Providers (mental health dirs. com., children's mental health com.), Pa. Cmty. Providers Assn. (family-home based subcom., mental health com. 1993—96). Office: Med Tower 255 S 17th St Ste 1907 Philadelphia PA 19103 Home Phone: 215-292-2881; Office Phone: 215-725-6080. Personal E-mail: ncharney@bellatlantic.net.

CHARNIGO, RICHARD JOHN, JR., statistician, educator; s. Richard John, Sr. and Barbara Ann Charnigo. BS in Math., Case Western Res. U., Cleve., 1997, MS in Math., 1999, PhD in Stats., 2003. Instr. Case Western Res. U., Cleve., 1997—99, 2001, 2002; asst. prof. U. Ky., Lexington, 2003—. Mem. acad. affairs com. U. Ky. Coll. Pub. Health, Lexington, 2004—06, vice chair faculty coun., 2005—06; cons. Accumetrics, Inc., 2005, Naval Postgrad. Sch., 2006—07. Contbr. articles to profl. jours. Grantee, NIH, 2004—, NSF, 2007—. Mem.: Interface Found. N.Am., Am. Statis. Assn., Phi Beta Kappa. Independent. Roman Catholic. Office: U Ky Dept Statis 851 Patterson Office Tower Lexington KY 40506-0027

CHARNVEJA, PAT S., civic leader, former oil and gas industry executive; b. Bangkok; came to US, 1961; m. Kitipot Charnveja; 3 children. Attended, W. Tex. A&M, Canyon, Tex., U. Houston. Various positions in oil and gas industry, 1976—98; mng. dir. PSKC Internat. LLC. Liaison Royal Thai Embassy & Royal Thai Consulate Gen. Founder & pres. Thai Am. Chamber of Commerce; pres. Thai Arts and Culture of Houston; former pres. Thai Assn. of Greater Houston; mem. bd. dirs. & former pres. Asian/Pacific Am. Heritage Assn.; mem. Focus Group for Leadership Ed. for Asian Pacifics, Inc.; mem. cultural diversity com. Holocaust Museum Houston; treasurer Asian Am. Voters' Coalition; adv. bd. mem. Asia Soc. Tex. Ctr.; mem. Chinese Cmty. Ctr., VN Teamwork.

CHARO, ROBIN ALTA, law educator; b. Bklyn., June 6, 1958; d. Jon and Ethel (Munach) C. AB in Biology (cum laude), Harvard-Radcliffe Coll., 1979; JD, Columbia U. Sch. Law, 1982. Bar: N.Y. 1983. Asst. dir. Legis. Drafting Rsch. Fund, Columbia U., NYC, 1982—83, assoc. dir., 1983—85; lectr. Columbia Law Sch., NYC, 1983-85; Fulbright Jr. lectr. in Am. Law, assoc. prof. U. Paris, Pantheon-Sorbonne, 1985-86; legal analyst, biol. applications program Congl. Office of Tech. Assessment, Washington, 1986-88; AAAS Diplomacy fellow, policy develop. divsn. of office of population U.S. Agy. for Internat. Devel., Washington, 1988-89; asst. prof., law & bioethics, dept. med. history & bioethics U. Wis. Law Sch., U. Wis. Med. Sch., Madison, 1989—95; assoc. prof. law U. Wis. Law Sch., Madison, 1995—98, Warren P. Knowles prof. law & bioethics, 1998—2003, Elisabeth S. Wilson prof., 2003—. Cons. N.J. Bioethics Comm., Draft Legsi. on Living Wills, 1988, Congl. Office of Tech. Assessment, 1988-92, U.S. AID, Office of Population 1988-91, Can. Law Reform Commn., Ottawa, Can., 1989-90, Comm. on Uniform Laws, Draft Legislation on Surrogacy, 1989, NIH office Protection from Rsch. Risks; mem. NIH Human Embryo Rsch. Panel, 1993-94, Presdl. Nat. Bioethics Adv. Comm., 1996-2001, ethics standard working group, Calif. Inst. for Regenerative Medicine, 2005-; vis. lectr. and professorships Fachbereich Rechtswissenschaft, Justus-Liebig-Univ., Giessen, Germany, 1992, Centre de Droit de la Famille, Université de Lyon, France, 1992, Escuela Latinoamericana de la Bioetica, La Plata, Argentina, 1992, Instituto Superior de la Medicina, Santiago, Cuba, 1996, Nova Law Sch., Ft. Lauderdale, Fla., 2001, Facultad Latinoamericana de Ciencias Sociales, Buenos Aires, Argentina, 2003, U. Va. Law Sch., Charlottesville, Virginia), 2004, vis. prof. law, U. Calif. Berkeley Law Sch., 2006-; mem. bioethics adv. bd., Howard Hughes Med. Inst., 2004-, Internat. Soc. for Stem Cell Rsch., 2004-; mem. adv. bd., project on reproductive genetics, Ctr. for Genetics and Pub. Policy, John Hopkins U., 2004-; current mem. com. to review the FDA and U.S. nat. system for assurance of drug safety. Contbr. articles to profl. jours.; mem. editl. bd. Cloning: Science and Policy, 98-, Monash Bioethics Review, 99-, Am. Jour. Bioethics, 2000-01, Public Library of Science, 2003-; policy review editor Journal of Law, Medicine, Healthcare, and Ethics, 1993-. Active U. Wis. Human Subjects Com., Madison, U. Wis. Hosp. Ethics Com., Madison, Abortion Strategy Group, Madison; cons. Rural South Cen. Wis. Perinatal Substance Abuse Project, 1989-; mem. Univ. Bioethics Adv. Com., U. Wis., 1998-, mem. stem cell rsch. program, 2003-; bd. dir. Alan Guttmacher Inst., 1991-96, 98-2000, 2002-,Found. for Genetic Medicine, 1997-Nat. Med. Com. Planned Parenthood Fedn. Am., 2004-; mem. scientific adv. bd. CuresNow, 2002-, Juvenile Diabetes Rsch. Found., WiCell, 2002-, Wis. Stem Cell Rsch. Program, 2004-. Fulbright grantee, 1985-86. Fellow AAAS, Wis. Acad. Sciences, Arts and Letters, Inst. Soc., Ethics & Life Sciences; mem. Internat. Bioethics Assn., Am. Soc. Law and Medicine, NAS(cons.; mem. bd, on life sciences, 2001-, mem.comm. on preventing destructive applications of biotechnology, 2002-03), Inst. Medicine (cons.; mem. com. on smallpox vaccination program implementation, 2002-05, mem. comm. on HIVNET 012 HIV Perinatal Transmission Trials, 2004-, mem. assess the drug safety system in the US, 2005-; (in conjunction with NRC) BLS liasion, comm. on embryonic stem cell rsch guidelines, 2004-, mem. adv. com. human embryonic stem cell rsch., 2006-), Soc. for the Advancement of Women's Health, 1998-2000, Am. Assn. Bioethics (bd. dir.), Open Soc. Inst. Program on Reproductive Health & Rights, 1999-. Democrat. Jewish. Avocations: travel, folk and salsa music, foreign languages, poker, reading, rollercoaster riding, home renovation. Office: U Wis Law Sch Law Bldg 975 Bascom Mall Rm 5211C Madison WI 53706-1399 Office Phone: 608-262-5015. Office Fax: 608-262-5485. Business E-Mail: racharo@wisc.edu.

CHARON, RITA, internist, medical educator, writer; b. Providence, 1949; BA in Biology and Child Edn., Fordham U., 1970; MD, Harvard U., 1978; MA in English, Columbia U., 1990, MPhil in English, 1992, PhD in English, 1999. Resident, internal medicine Montefiore Hosp. and Med. Ctr., Bronx, NY, 1978; fellow, gen. internal medicine, Coll. Physicians and Surgeons Columbia U., 1982, practiced gen. internal medicine, 1981—, instr. in medicine Coll. of Physicians and Surgeons, 1982—88, asst. prof. medicine, 1983—88, asst. prof. clinical medicine, 1988—93, assoc. prof. clinical medicine, 1993—2001, prof. clinical medicine Coll. Physicians and Surgeons, 2001—, dir. program in narrative medicine and clinical skills assessment program, 1996—; asst. attending physician Presbyn. Hosp., NYC, 1982—93, assoc. attending physician, 1993—. Editor-in-chief: Lit. and Medicine jour.; co-editor: (anthology) Stories Matter: The Role of Narrative in Medical Ethics, 2002. Named Outstanding Woman Physician of Yr., 1996; recipient Nat. award for innovation in med. edn., Soc. Gen. Internal Medicine, 1997; grantee Guggenheim fellowship, 2002; 1st recipient of Virginia Kneeland Frantz award for Outstanding Woman Dr. of Yr., 1987. Achievements include development of innovative new teaching method called the parallel chart systems which brings together literature and medicine. Office: Presbyn Hosp 9 E 105 Gen Medicine 622 W 168th St New York NY 10032*

CHARPAK, GEORGES, physicist, nuclear scientist; b. Dabrovica, Poland, Aug. 1, 1924; naturalized, France, 1946; s. Maurice and Anna (Szapiro) C.; m. Dominique Vidal, 1953; children: Yves, Nathalie, Serge. BSc in Engring., Ecole des Mines de Paris, 1948; PhD in Physics, Collège de France, 1954; doctorate (hon.), U. Geneva, 1977, U. Thessalonica, Greece, 1993, Vrije Univ. Brussels, 1994, U. Coimbra, Portugal, 1994, U. Ottawa, Can., 1995, U. Rio de Janeiro, 1996. Lic. civil mining engr. Prof. Centre Nation de la Recherche Scientifique, 1948-59, Centre Européen pour la Recherche Nucléaire, Geneva, 1959—; rschr. Cern Lab. for Particle Physics, Geneva. Joliot-Curie prof. Ecole Supérieure de Physique et Chimie de la Ville de Paris, 1984—. Contbr. articles to profl. jours. With French Army, prisoner of war, Dachau. Decorated chevalier Legion of Honor, Mil. Cross 39-45, Croix de Guerre (France), Officer Nat. Order of Merit; recipient Paul Ricard prize French Soc. Physics, 1980, High Energy and Particle Physics prize, 1989, Nobel prize for physics, 1992. Mem. NAS (fgn. assoc.), French Acad. Scis. (Commissariat prize of Atomic Energy 1984), Austrian Acad. Scis. (hon.), Russian Acad. Scis. (fgn.), Lisboa Acad. Scis. (corr.), French Acad. Medicine (nat. corr. mem.). Achievements include invention of multiwire proportional chambers, drift chambers, diverse types of flash chambers without photography; development of particle detectors in high energy physics, installations for biological research using Beta-ray imagery; new fast gaseous detector adapted to accelerators to be constructed; research in nuclear structure by reactions. Home: 22 rue Pierre et Marie Curie 75005 Paris France Office: CERN Lab for Particle Physics CH-1211 Geneva Switzerland Office Phone: +41-227672144.

CHARPIE, ROBERT ALAN, physicist, researcher; b. Cleve., Sept. 9, 1925; s. Leonard Asbury and Dorothy (McLean) C.; m. Elizabeth Downs, July 12, 1947; children: Richard Alan, Carol Elizabeth, David Wayne, John Robert. BS with honors, Carnegie Inst. Tech., 1948, MS, 1949, D.Sc. in Theoretical Physics, 1950; D.H.L., Denison U., 1965; D.Sc., Alderson-Broaddus Coll., 1967; LL.D., Marietta Coll., 1975; D.Sc., Boston Coll., 1982. With Westinghouse Electric Corp., 1947-50; with Oak Ridge Nat. Lab., 1950-51, tech. asst. to research dir., 1952-54, asst. research dir., 1954-58, dir. reactor divsn., 1958-61; mgr. adv. devel. Union Carbide Corp., 1961-63, gen. mgr. devel. dept., 1963-64, dir. tech., 1964-66, pres. electronics divsn., 1966-68; pres. Bell & Howell Co., Chgo., 1968-69, Cabot Corp., Boston, 1969-86, also. bd. dirs., chmn. Waltham, Mass., 1986-88, Ampersand Ventures, Wellesley, Mass., 1988—. Trustee Mitre Corp., Boston, 1966-82, chmn., 1972-82; sec. gen. adv. com. AEC, 1959-63; mem. Nat. Sci. Bd., 1969-76; sci. sec., editor-in-chief proc., also asst. U.S. mem. 7 nation adv. com. 1st Internat. Conf. Peaceful Uses Atomic Energy, 1955; coordinator U.S. fusion research exhibit, 2d Conf., 1958; chmn. invention and innovation panel U.S. Dept. Commerce, 1965-67. Gen. editor: Internat. Monograph Series on Nuclear Energy, 1955-60; editor: Progress Series in Nuclear Energy, 1955-60, Jour. Nuclear Energy, 1955-60. Mem. Oak Ridge Bd. Edn., 1957-61; pres. Byram Hills Central Sch. Dist., 1966-68; trustee Carnegie Inst. Tech., 1962—. Recipient Alumni Merit award Carnegie Inst. Tech., 1957 Fellow Am. Phys. Soc., Am. Nuclear Soc. (dir.); mem. N.Y. Acad. Sci., Nat. Acad. Engring., Sigma Xi, Tau Beta Pi, Phi Mu Epsilon. Office: Ampersand Ventures 55 William St Ste 240 Wellesley MA 02481-4003 Office Phone: 781-235-1282.

CHARRON, JOSEPH L., bishop; b. Redfield, SD, Dec. 30, 1939; Ordained priest Roman Cath. Ch. 1967. Asst. theology prof. St. John's U., Collegeville, Minn., 1970—76; asst. gen. sec. U.S. Catholic Conf., 1976—79; assoc. gen. sec. Nat. Conf. Cath. Bishops, 1976—79; Kansas City Provincial dir. CPPS, 1979—87; aux. bishop Diocese of St. Paul/Mpls., 1990—93; bishop Diocese of Des Moines, 1994—. Admin. comm. Nat. Conf. Cath. Bishops/U.S. Cath. Conf. Mem.: Cath. Theol. Soc. Am., Soc. Precious Blood. Roman Catholic. Office: Chancery 601 Grand Ave Des Moines IA 50309

CHARRON, PAUL RICHARD, retail executive; b. Schenectady, NY, Aug. 24, 1942; s. Richard Armand and Helen Marie (Barringer) C.; m. Kathy Lyn Herdt, June 29, 1974; children: Bradley, Ashley. BA, U. Notre Dame, 1964; MBA, Harvard U., 1971. Brand mgr. Procter & Gamble Corp., Cin., 1971-78; category mgr. Gen. Foods Corp., White Plains, NY, 1978-81; sr. v.p. sales, mktg. Cannon Mills Co., N.Y. and N.C., 1981-83; pres., COO Atwater Group, Inc., St. Paul, 1983-87, Brown & Bigelow, St. Paul, 1983-87; exec. v.p. VF Corp., Wyomissing, Pa., 1988-94; CEO Liz Claiborne Inc., NYC, 1994—2006, chmn., 1994—2006, chmn. emeritus, 2006—. Bd. dirs. Campbell Soup Co., 2003—. Lt. USN, 1964-69, Vietnam. Decorated Meritorious Service medal.*

CHARROW, JOEL, pediatrician, geneticist, educator, director; b. NYC, May 24, 1951; s. Saul David and Doris Elaine (Yates) C.; m. Martha K. McClintock, Oct. 23, 1982; children: Benjamin Whitmore, Julia Rachel. BS in Chemistry and Psychology, Antioch Coll., 1972; MD, Mt. Sinai Sch. Medicine, 1976. Diplomate Nat. Bd. Med. Examiners, Am. Bd. Pediatrics; diplomate in clin. genetics and biocehem. genetics. Am. Bd. Med. Genetics. Pediatric intern Children's Meml. Hosp./Northwestern U. Med. Sch., Chgo., 1976-77, resident in pediatrics, 1977-79, fellow in clin. and biochem. genetics, 1979-81; attending physician Children's Meml. Hosp., Chgo., 1981; from asst. prof. to assoc. prof. pediatrics Northwestern U. Med. Ctr., Chgo., 1981-94, prof. pediatrics, 2002—; dir. Genetics Lab., head sect. clin. genetics Children's Meml. Hosp., Chgo., 1991—, head, divsn. genetics, birth defects, metabolism, 2006—. Mem. adv. bd. Fabry Disease Registry, 2001—. Contbr. chpts. to books, more than 50 articles to profl. jours. Regional coord. Internat. Collaborative Gaucher Group, 1994—; mem. health profl. adv. com. March of Dimes, Chgo., 1986-2004; mem. sci. adv. com. Nat. Tay-Sachs and Allied Diseases Assn., 1984—; mem. State of Ill. Genetic and Metabolic Diseases Adv. Com., 1989-97; mem. Genetics Task Force of Ill., 1982—, v.p., 1990-91, pres., 1991-93. Recipient Bela Schick Pediatric Soc. award Mt. Sinai Sch. Medicine, 1976. Fellow Am. Coll. Med. Genetics (founding), Am. Acad. Pediatrics; mem. Midwest Soc. for Pediatric Rsch., Soc. for Inherited Metabolic Disorders, Bone Dysplasia Soc., Internat. Neurofibromatosis Assn., Alpha Omega Alpha. Office: Children's Meml Hosp Sect Clin Genetics 2300 N Childrens Plz Chicago IL 60614-3394 Office Phone: 773-880-4462.

CHARTERIS, FRANCES I.A., art educator, artist; b. Paris, Oct. 16, 1950; arrived in U.S., 1977; d. Hugo Guy Francis Charteris and Virginia Mary Forbes Adam; m. Albert Chong (div.); children: Ayinde Netifnet, Chinwe Amelia Chances. BA, U. York, Heslington, Eng., 1970; BFA with honors, Sch. Visual Arts, NYC, 1979; MFA, U. San Diego, Calif., 1992. Freelance photographer, 1969—72; with Inroads Performance Troupe, 1970—72; photographer Sotheby and Parke Bernet, London, 1973—75; tchr. Kingston Coll., Jamaica, 1975—77; with Bettman Archives, NYC, 1980—83; photo printer UN, NYC, 1984—87; tchg. asst. U. Calif., San Diego, 1988—92; sr. instr. U. Colo., Boulder, 1993—, dir. Paris study abroad, 2005—. Dir., founder Farouche Performance Troop, 2006—, Denver Art Mus., 2007; prof. art history NYU, Paris, 1999—2001. Exhibitions include Tucuman, Argentina, 2006, Bahia, Blanca, Argentina, 2007, Colo. U. Art Mus., 2007. Builder, vol. Habitat for Humanity, Boulder, 1995—96; vol. homeless shelter, Boulder, 1995—97. Mem.: Women's Caucus for Art, Jung Study Group, Coll. Art Assn., Boulder Faculty Assembly. Democrat. Avocations: dance, hiking, travel, African and Jungian studies, healing. Office: Univ Colo Dept Art and Art History Boulder CO 80304 Office Phone: 303-492-3580. Business E-Mail: frances.charteris@colorado.edu.

CHARTERS, ANN, literature educator; b. Bridgeport, Conn., Nov. 10, 1936; d. Nathan and Kate Danberg; m. Samuel B. Charters, Mar. 14, 1959; children: Mallay, Nora Lili. AB, U. Calif.-Berkeley, 1957; MA, Columbia U., 1960, PhD, 1965. Mem. faculty Colby Jr. Coll., New London, NH, 1961—63; lectr. Columbia U., 1965—66; asst. prof. Am. lit. N.Y.C. Community Coll., 1967-70; assoc. dean of the coll. Brown U., 1989-90; prof. Am. lit. U. Conn., Storrs, 1974—. Author: Nobody-Life and Times of Bert Williams, 1967, Kerouac, 1973, 2d edit., 1986, I Love—Story of Vladimir Mayakovsky and Lili Brik, 1979, The Story and Its Writer, 7th edit., 2007, The Beats: Literary Bohemians in Post-War America, 1983, Beats and Company: A Portrait of a Literary Generation, 1986, The Viking Portable Beat Reader, 1992, Major Writers of Short Fiction, 1993, The Viking Portable Jack Kerouac Reader, 1995, Selected Letters of Jack Kerouac, 1995, (with Samuel Charters) Literature and Its Writers, 1997, 4th edit., 2007; author intro. Penguin Classic edit. Three Lives and Q.E.D. (Gertrude Stein), On the Road (Jack Kerouac), Selected Letters of Jack Kerouac, vol. 2, 1999, The American Short Story and Its Writer, 1999, (with Samuel Charters) Blues Faces, 2000, Beat Down to Your Soul, 2000, The Portable Sixties Reader, 2003. Office: U Conn Dept English PO Box U-25 Storrs Mansfield CT 06269-0001 Office Phone: 860-486-2141. Business E-Mail: acharters@uconn.edu.

CHARTERS, KAREN ANN ELLIOTT, critical care nurse, health facility administrator; b. Chelsea, Mass., Apr. 3, 1946; d. Albert Charles and Hazelle Marie (Kraus) Elliott; m. Byron James Charters, Feb. 4, 1972. Diploma, Grace New Haven Sch. Nursing, New Haven, Conn., 1967; student, So. Conn. State Coll., 1968, U. New Haven, 1974; BS in Healthcare Adminstrn., St. Leo Coll., 1999. CCRN. Asst. head nurse Yale New Haven (Conn.) Hosp., 1972-76; staff nurse critical care unit Hosp. Corp. Am., 1982—; relief clin. coord. Cmty. Hosp. of New Port Richey, Fla., 1987—, nursing supr. Fla., 1997—. Mem. AACN (bd. dirs. Gulf Coast chpt. 1990-91, 96-97, treas. 1991-93), Am. Heart Assn. (past bd. dirs.). Home: 7519 Clanton Trail Hudson FL 34667 Office: Cmty Hosp New Port Richey 5637 Marine Pkwy New Port Richey FL 34652

CHARTIER, VERNON LEE, electrical engineer; b. Feb. 14, 1939; s. Raymond Earl and Margaret Clara (Winegar) C.; m. Lois Marie Schwartz, May 20, 1967; 1 child, Neal Raymond. BSEE, BS in Bus., U. Colo., 1963. Registered profl. engr., Pa.; cert. electromagnetic compatibility engr. Rsch. engr., cons. Westinghouse Electric Co., East Pitts., Pa., 1963-75; prin. engr. high voltage phenomena Bonneville Power Adminstrn., Vancouver, Wash., 1975-95; power sys. EMC cons. Portland, 1995—. Co-author 5 chpts. in reference books; contbr. over 50 articles to profl. jours. Fellow IEEE (fellow com. 1993-96, 2004-06, Herman Halperin Transmission and Distbn. award 1995, 3d Millennium medal 2000, chmn. Herman Halperin Transmission and Distbn. Award com. 2002-04); mem. NAE, Power Engring. Soc. of IEEE (chmn. transmission and distbn. com. 1987-88, chmn. fellows com. 1990-92), Internat. Conf. Large High Voltage Electric Sys. (Attwood Assoc. award 1999), Chartier Family Assn. Baptist. Home and Office: 13095 SW Glenn Ct Beaverton OR 97008-5664 Office Phone: 503-646-8186. Business E-Mail: vlchartier@ieee.org.

CHARTOFF, ROBERT IRWIN, film producer; b. NYC; s. William and Bessie Chartoff; children: Jenifer, William, Julie, Charley, Miranda. AB, Union Coll., 1955; LLB, Columbia U., 1958. Producer: numerous films including Double Trouble, 1967, Point Blank, 1967, The Split, 1968, Leo the Last, 1969, They Shoot Horses Don't They, 1969, The Strawberry Statement, 1970, The Gang That Couldn't Shoot Straight, 1971, The New Centurions, 1972, The Mechanic, 1972, Up the Sandbox, 1972, Busting, 1974, Peeper, 1975, The Gambler, 1975, Rocky, 1976 (Acad. award for best picture), Nickelodeon, 1976, New York, New York, 1977, Valentino, 1977, Comes A Horseman, 1978, Uncle Joe Shannon, 1978, Rocky II, 1979, Raging Bull, 1980, True Confessions, 1981, Rocky III, 1982, The Right Stuff, 1983, Rocky IV, 1985, Beer, 1986, Rocky V, 1990, Straight Talk, 1992, In My Country, 2005, Rocky Balboa, 2006. Home: 457 Howland Canal Venice CA 90291-4619 E-mail: chartoffprod@cs.com.

CHARTON, MARVIN, chemist, educator; b. Bklyn., May 1, 1931; s. William and Elsie (Halpern) C.; m. Barbara Israel, Aug. 28, 1955; children— Michael, Sarah, Deborah. BS, CCNY, 1953; MA, Bklyn. Coll., 1956; PhD, Stevens Inst. Tech., 1962. Instr. chemistry Pratt Inst., Bklyn., 1956-61, asst. prof., 1961-64, asso. prof., 1964-67, prof., 1967—, chmn. dept., 1969—. Vis. prof. Polymer Rsch. Inst., Poly. U., Bklyn., 1985—. Editor: Advances in Quantitative Structure Property Relationships Vol. 1, 1996, Vol. 2, 1999, Vol. 3, 2002; co-editor: Topics in Current Chemistry, vol. 114, 1983; contbr. articles to profl. jours.; mem. editl. bd.: Quantitative Structure Activity Relationships, Activity Relationships, Arkivoc, Drug Design Reviews, Current Computer-Aided Molecular Design. Fellow AAAS, Intrasci. Rsch. Found.; mem. Am. Chem. Soc., Internat. Group for Correlation and Modeling in Chemistry (formerly Internat. Group for Correlation Analysis in Chemistry), Internat. QSAR Soc., Royal Chem. Soc. London, N.Y. Acad. Scis., Sigma Xi. Avocation: collecting antiquarian chemistry books. Home: 1 Grace Ct Brooklyn NY 11201-4195 Home Phone: 718-875-5908; Office Phone: 718-636-3763. Business E-Mail: mcharton@pratt.edu.

CHARWAT, ANDREW FRANCISZEK, engineering educator; b. Poland, Feb. 10, 1925; came to U.S., 1945; s. Franciszek and Wanda (Niec) C.; m. Halina M. Stieglitz, Aug. 18, 1948 (dec.); 1 child, Danuta K. Charwat McCall. M Engring., Stevens Inst. Tech., 1948; PhD, U. Calif., Berkeley, 1952. Aerodynamicist Propulsion Research Corp., Los Angeles, 1952-53; designer Northrup Aircraft Corp., Los Angeles, 1953-55; prof., dept. mech. and aerospace engring. UCLA, 1955-92, prof. emeritus, 1992—. Cons. to numerous industry and govt. agys., 1955—; expert witness various legal cases; dir. Univ. Study Ctr., Lyon and Grenoble, France, 1986-88. Contbr. over 80 articles and research papers. Guggenheim fellow, 1962. E-mail: acharwat@ucla.edu.

CHARYK, JOSEPH VINCENT, retired satellite telecommunications executive; b. Canmore, Alta., Can., Sept. 9, 1920; came to U.S., 1942, naturalized, 1948; s. John and Anna (Dorosh) C.; m. Edwina Elizabeth Rhodes, Aug. 18, 1945; children: William R., J. John, Christopher E., Diane E. B.Sc., U. Alta., 1942, LL.D., 1964; MS, Calif. Inst. Tech., 1943, PhD, 1946; D.Engring. (hon.), U. Bologna, 1974. Sect. chief Jet Propulsion Lab., Calif. Inst. Tech., 1945-46, instr. aeros., 1945-46, asst. prof. aeros. Princeton U., NJ, 1946-49, assoc. prof., 1949-55; dir. aerophysics and chemistry lab., missile systems div. Lockheed Aircraft Corp., 1955-56; dir. aero. lab. Aeronutronic Systems, Inc. subs. Ford Motor Co., 1956-58, gen. mgr. space tech. div., 1958-59; asst. sec. for research and devel. USAF, 1959, under sec., 1960-63, dir. nat. reconnaissance office, 1961—63; pres. Communications Satellite Corp., 1963-79, chief exec. officer, 1979-85, chmn., 1983-85, Draper Labs., 1987-90. Recipient Lloyd V. Berkner Space Utilization award, 1967, Disting. Aviation Aerospace Svc. award, 1973, Gugliemo Marconi Internat. award, 1974, TV Arts and Scis. Directorate award, 1974, Theodore Von Karman award, 1977, Goddard Astronautics award, 1978, award Computer and Comm. Found., 1985, Nat. Medal of Tech., 1987, Arthur C. Clarke award, 1992, Disting. Alumni award U. Alta., 1993. Fellow AIAA, IEEE; mem. Nat. Acad. Engring., Internat. Acad. Astronautics, Nat. Space Club, Chevy Chase Country Club, Gulf Stream Golf Club, Gulf Stream Bath and Tennis Club, Sigma Xi. Home: 790 Andrews Ave Apt A302 Delray Beach FL 33483-7257 Personal E-mail: chjv@comcast.com.

CHARYTAN, LYNN R., lawyer; b. Oct. 29, 1965; BA summa cum laude, Columbia Univ.; JD magna cum laude, Harvard Univ., 1990. Bar: DC 1991, NY 1991. Law clk. Judge Stanley Sporkin, US Dist Ct. (DC dist.), 1990—91; in-house counsel Washington Post, 1991—93; ptnr., vice chmn. Comm. & E-Commerce dept. Wilmer Cutler Pickering Hale & Dorr, Washington. Mem.: ABA, Fed. Comm. Bar Assn., Phi Beta Kappa. Office: Wilmer Cutler Pickering Hale & Dorr 1801 Pennsylvania Ave NW Washington DC 20006 Mailing: Wilmer Cutler Pickering Hale & Dorr 2445 M St NW Washington DC 20037 Office Phone: 202-663-6455. Office Fax: 202-663-6363. Business E-Mail: lynn.charytan@wilmerhale.com.

CHASANOW, HOWARD STUART, retired judge, mediator; b. Washington, Apr. 3, 1937; 1 child from previous marriage, Andrea; m. Deborah Hovis Koss, May 15, 11983. BA, U. Md., 1959, JD, 1961; LLM, Harvard U., 1962. Bar: Md. 1961, U.S. Supreme Ct. 1965. Asst. states atty. Prince George County, Upper Marlboro, Md., 1963-64, dep. states atty., 1964-67; judge Dist. Ct., Upper Marlboro, 1971-77, 7th Jud. Cir., 1977-90, Ct. Appeals of Md., 1990-99, ret., 1999. Lectr. Sch. Law U. Md., Balt., 1973—, Nat. Jud. Coll., Reno, 1980—, Am. Acad. Jud. Edn., 1984—; chmn. adv. bd. Sentencing Guidelines, Md., 1982-90, chmn. jud. adminstrn. sect., 1982-84; mem. Md. Commn. on Criminal Sentencing Policy, 1996—; mem. standing com. on rules of practice and procedure Ct. Appeals, 1985-90; mem. govs. task force to Revise Criminal Code, 1992—. Contbr. law rev. articles. Served with USAF, 1968-69. Address: 7849 Belle Point Dr Greenbelt MD 20770 Office Phone: 301-441-3366.

CHASE, ALEXANDRA NIN, psychologist, writer; b. Panama City, Panama, June 19, 1958; arrived in U.S., 1963; d. Paul Thorvald and Derith Alexander Chase; life ptnr. Richard Allen Frustere. BA in Sociology, San Francisco State U., 1981; MA in Creative Writing, San Francisco State U., 1985; PhD in Psychology, Calif. Inst. Integral Studies, 2001. Lic. psychologist Calif. Bd. Psychology, 2002. Instr. creative writing San Francisco (Calif.) State U., 1985—91, City Coll. San Francisco, 1989—94; rsch. assoc. Kaiser Permanente, Oakland, Calif., 1996—2000; counselor mental health Pyramid Alternatives, Pacifica, Calif., 2000—01; clin. psychologist Westside Cmty. Mental Health, San Francisco, 2001—; geriatric psychologist Vericare Sr. Svcs., San Diego, 2003—05; pvt. practice Pacifica, Calif., 2005—. Editor: Five Fingers Rev., 1987—91; author: The Beginning of Difficulty, 1989 (nomination L.A. Times Book prize, 1989); contbr. poetry to jours. Vol. instr. sr. writing workshop Raphael House Sr. Program, San Francisco, 1986—87; v.p. Light Up the Sky Fourth of July Fireworks Prodn., Half Moon Bay, Calif., 2005. Mem.: APA. Avocations: dogs, dance, dream work, collage. Office: Westside Community Mental Health 1663 Mission 310 San Francisco CA 94103 Address: 80 Eureka Sq 213 Pacifica CA 94044 Personal E-mail: alekac@comcast.net.

CHASE, BARBARA LANDIS, headmaster; b. Hershey, Pa., May 6, 1945; d. Floyd and Ruth Landis; m. David William Chase; children: Ashley Lawrence, Katherine Landis Chase. AB in History, Brown U., 1967; MLA, Johns Hopkins U., 1990. Tchr. 3rd grade Moses Brown Sch., Providence, 1967-68; tchr./dir. admissions Wheeler Sch., Providence, 1973-80; headmistress Bryn Mawr, Baltimore, Md., 1980-94; head of sch. Phillips Acad., Andover, Mass., 1994—. Contbr. articles to profl. jours.; presentations in field. Trustee Pike Sch., 1996-99, Sch. Yr. Abroad, 1994—, Tower Hill Sch., 1990-94, Brown U. 1995-00; mem. Baltimore Ednl. Scholarship Trust, 1987-94, Baltimore Consortium Tchg. Am. History, 1987-90; bd. govs. Boys and Girls Club Lawrence, 2006-. Mem. Nat. Assn. Independent Schs. (bd. dirs. 1989-93, cons. 1988-89, chair sch. heads adv. com. 1986-88), Assn. Independent Md. Schs. (pres. bd. trustees 1986-88), The Headmasters Assn., Nat. Assn. Principals Schs. Girls, Headmistresses Assn. East.

CHASE, CAROL JOHNSON, mathematics educator; b. New London, Conn., Nov. 21, 1954; m. Graham R. Chase, June 5, 1976; children: Molly C.W., Samuel J.V. BS in Math., Ctrl. Conn. State U., New Britain, 1976, MS in Supr. and Adminstrn., 1980, cert. in Supr. and Adminstrn., 1988. Lic. Conn., 1976. Math. tchr. West Hartford (Conn.) Bd. Edn., 1976—. Named Tchr. of Yr., West Hartford, 1997—98. Mem.: West Hartford Edn. Assn. (mem. exec. bd. 1979—). Home: 1596 Boulevard West Hartford CT 06107-2501 Office: Sedgwick Mid Sch 128 Sedgwick Rd West Hartford CT 06107 Home Phone: 860-521-7676; Office Phone: 860-570-6500.

CHASE, CHEVY (CORNELIUS CRANE CHASE), comedian, actor, writer; b. Woodstock, NY, Oct. 8, 1943; s. Edward Tinsley and Cathalene Crane (Widdoes) C.; m. Jacqueline carlin Dec. 4, 1976 (div. 1980); m. Jayni Chase, Jen 19, 1982; children: Cydney Cathalene, Caley Leigh, Emily Evelyn. BA in English, Bard Coll., 1967; CCS, Inst. Audio Rsch., 1970. Artist MGM Records, 1968; writer, Mad mag., 1969; dir., writer, actor, Nat. Lampoon Theatre Co., 1972-74, performing in Nat. Lampoon's Lemmings, off Broadway and on nat. tour, 1973; writer, actor (TV series) writer, actor, The Great American Dream Machine, 1971, Saturday Night Live, 1975-76; actor: (films) Walk. Don't Walk, 1968, The Groove Tube, 1974, Foul Play, 1978, Oh Heavenly Dog, 1980, Caddyshack, 1980, Seems Like Old Times, 1981, Under the Rainbow, 1981, Modern Problems, 1981, National Lampoon's Vacation, 1983, Deal of the Century, 1983, Fletch, 1984, National Lampoon's European Vacation, 1985, Spies Like Us, 1985, Sesame Street Presents:Follow That Bird, 1985, Three Amigos, 1986, Funny Farm, 1988, The Couch Trip, 1988, Caddyshack II, 1988, Fletch Lives, 1989, National Lampoon's Christmas Vacation, 1989, Nothing But Trouble, 1991, L.A. Story, 1991, Memoirs of an Invisible Man, 1992, Hero, 1992, Last Action Hero, 1993, Cops and Robbersons, 1994, Man of the House, 1995, National Lampoon's Vegas Vacation, 1997, Dirty Work, 1998, The One Armed Bandit, 2000, Snow Day, 2000, (narrator) Pete's a Pizza, 2001, Vacuums, 2002, Orange County, 2002, Bad Meat, 2003, Our Italian Husband, 2004, (voice only) The Karate Dog, 2004, Ellie Parker, 2004, Goose on the Loose, 2006, (voice only) Doogal, 2006, Funny Money, 2006, Zoom, 2006; (TV movies) America's Most Terrible Things, 2002, The Secret Policeman's Ball, 2006; (TV appearances) Will Rogers: Look Back in Laughter, 1987, The Dave Thomas Comedy Show, 1990, Law & Order, 2006; host, The Chevy Chase Show, 1993 Recipient award for best script in comedy variety spl. Writers Guild, award best supporting actor in comedy variety series Nat. Acad. TV Arts and Sci.; won two Emmy Awards for Saturday Night Live and a third Emmy for co-writing The Paul Simon Special, Harvard Lampoon Lifetime Achievement award, 1996; hon. by Harvard U. Hasty Pudding Theatrical Group, 1992. Mem. Am. Fedn. Musicians, Stage Actors Guild, Actors Equity, AFTRA. Democrat. Office: Cornelius Prods PO Box 257 Bedford NY 10506-0257*

CHASE, COCHRANE, advertising agency executive; b. Berwyn, Ill., Feb. 6, 1932; s. Henry Cochrane and Roselyn (Scott) C.; m. Janis Valeria Kueber, June 19, 1954; children— Katherine Ann, Anthony Scott, Lisa Marie. BA, Wesleyan U., 1954. With steel warehousing div. Jessop Steel Co., Broadview, Ill., 1956-62, mgr. sales, 1961-62; with Jessop Steel Calif., Santa Fe Springs, 1963-64; asst. mgr. market rsch. Ducommun Metals & Supply Co., LA, 1964—65; v.p. Newport Advt. Inc., Newport Beach, Calif., 1965; pres. Cochrane Chase, Livingston & Co., Inc., Irvine, Calif., 1966, chmn. bd., CEO, 1966—88; chmn. emeritus AC&R/CCL, Irvine, Calif., 1988-89. Co-author: Marketing Problem Solver, 1973, Newport Financial Planner, 1985. Served with USNR, 1954-56. Home: 2162 Papaya Dr La Habra CA 90631-7917

CHASE, DAVID (DAVID DECAESARE), scriptwriter, television director and producer; b. Mt. Vernon, NY, Aug. 22, 1945; Student in Filmmaking, Sch. Visual Arts, NY; degree, NYU; MA in Film, Stanford U., Calif. Dir.: (TV series) Alfred Hitchcock Presents, 1985; writer, dir. (TV series) Almost Grown, 1988, writer Kolchak: The Night Stalker, 1974, (TV films) Grave of the Vampire, 1972, Moonlight, 1982, writer, prodr. (TV series) The Rockford Files, 1976—80 (Emmy award, 1977), writer, exec. prodr. I'll Fly Away, 1991 (Norman Felton award Prodrs. Guild Am., 1993), Northern Exposure, 1990, writer, prodr. (TV films) Off the Minnesota Strip, 1980 (Writers Guild Am. award, 1980, Emmy award, 1979), writer, prodr., dir. (TV series) The Sopranos, 1999—2007 (Emmy award for College episode, 1998, Golden Globe award, 1999, Norman Felton award Prodrs. Guild Am., 2000, Outstanding Directorial Achievement award Dirs. Guild Am., 1999, Peabody award, 2000, Drama Series of Yr. award Am. Film Inst., 2001), prodr. (TV films) The Rockford Files: A Blessing in Disguise, 1995, writer, prodr., dir. The Rockford Files: The Punishment and Crime, 1996. Office: David Harbert United Talent Agency 9560 Wilshire Blvd Ste 500 Beverly Hills CA 90212

CHASE, ERIC LEWIS, lawyer; b. Princeton, NJ, Sept. 21, 1946; s. Harold William and Bernice Mae (Fadden) C.; m. Jamie Campbell, Dec. 29, 1979; children: Eric Campbell, Kathryn Dianne, John Harold. BA, Princeton U., 1968; JD cum laude, U. Minn., 1974. Bar: NJ 1974, DC 1975, US Ct. Appeals (3d cir.) 1979, US Supreme Ct. 1981, US Claims Ct. 1982, US Tax Ct. 1982, NY 1983, US Ct. Appeals (2d cir.) 1988, US Ct. Appeals (6th cir.) 2003. Trial atty. FCC, 1974-78; asst. US atty. Dist. NJ, Newark, 1978-80; ptnr. Margolis Chase, Verona, NJ, 1980-90, Hannoch Weisman, Roseland, NJ, 1990-93, Bressler, Amery & Ross, Florham Park, NJ, 1993—. Prof. law of war Marine Corps Command and Staff Coll., Quantico, Va., 1990—99. Author: Automobile Dealers and the Law, 1994, 7th edit., 2000; contbr. articles on law and mil. to profl. publs., including NY Times, Washington Post, Newsweek mag. With USMC, 1968-71; col. Res., ret. Named N.J. Super Lawyer, 2005, 2006, 2007. Mem. ABA (mem. task force on internat. criminal ct.), NJ State Bar Assn. (franchise com 1997—, co-chair franchise com. 1999-2001). Office: Bressler Amery & Ross 325 Columbia Tpke Ste 8 Florham Park NJ 07932-1212 Home Phone: 973-744-3533; Office Phone: 973-514-1200. Business E-Mail: echase@bressler.com.

CHASE, ERNEST FRANK, JR., retired federal agency administrator; b. Oct. 3, 1919; CPA, Bentley Inst. Acctg., Boston, 1939; BA, Harvard U., Cambridge, Mass., 1950, MA, 1951. Dir. Westinghouse, Pitts., 1939—40; lt. US Army 8th Air Force, 1940—43; capt. US Army Strategic Bombing Survey, 1943—45; with Atomic Energy Commn. Secretariat, 1952—53, US State Dept., Washington, 1953—54, 1958—63, CIA, Washington, 1954—58, US Econ. Commn. to UN, Geneva, 1958—63; dir. energy policy, office asst. sec. internat. affairs US Treasury Dept., Washington, 1963—86. Home: 1507 Oakview Dr Mc Lean VA 22101

CHASE, FRANCIS MARVIN, SR., education educator, consultant; b. Waldorf, Md., Feb. 2, 1957; s. Francis Leo and Agnes Blondell Chase; m. Belinda Ann Briscoe, July 23, 1983; children: Francis Marvin, LaToya Belinda. B in Fine Art and Edn., U.Md., 1988; M in Ednl. Rsch., George Mason U., Virginia, 1998. Art tchr. Alexandria Pub. Schools, Alexandria, Va., 1990—. Sch. sys. cons. DC, Md. and Va. schools; motivational spkr. DC, Md. and Va. Chmn. Tchrs. Bargaining Com., Alexandria, Va.; mem. Tchrs. Evaluating Com., Alexandria, Va., Gov. of Va., 2002; pres. Edn. Assn. of Alexandria, Va., 2004—06. Recipient Outstanding Artist, U. Md., 1988, Nat. Edn. Hall of Fame, NAESP, 2002, Cmty. Svc. award, Alpha Kappa Alpha Sorority, 2003, Inductee, Alexandria Edn. Hall of Fame, 1999, Outstanding Tchr., C. of C., 1995, ARCH award for work with the disabled, City of Alexandria, Va., 1995, Outstanding Tchr., George Mason Elem. Sch., 1998, Charles Barrett Elem. Sch., 1998, George Mason Elem. Sch., 1999, Charles Barrett Elem. Sch., 1999, Agnes Meyer Outstanding Tchr., Wash. Post newspaper, 1999, Achievement award, Md. State Dept. Edn., 2006. Mem.: Phi Delta Kappa (life). Achievements include design of a logo for the Department of Defense Armed services; co-developed a workshop for developing cultural awareness in the classroom; development of a pilot program for using fine art to teach the core curriculum of math and reading. Avocations: running, music, art. Office Phone: 703-706-4440. Business E-Mail: fchase@acps.k12.va.us.

CHASE, J. VINCENT, property manager; b. NYC, Nov. 5, 1949; m. Addie Lee Pickus, Sept. 3, 1983. BS, U. Bridgeport, 1972. Pers. adminstr. Ins. Svcs. Office, NYC, 1972-77; gen. mgr. pers. John Wiley & Sons, NYC, 1977-79; pers. dir. CitiCorp, NYC, 1979-83; pres., owner Colonial Square Shopping Ctr., Stratford, Conn., 1983—; mem. Conn. Ho. of Reps., Hartford, 1980-96, dep. minority leader, 1990-96; asst. treas. Conn. Office of the State Treasurer, Hartford, 1997-98, justice of the peace, 1996—2004; chief investigator U.S. Ho. of Reps., Washington, 1998—2006. Bd. dirs. Union Cemetery Assn; bd. trustees Stratford Libr. Assn.; candidate for U.S. Ho. or Reps. from 3d Dist. Conn., 1990; bd. mem. Stratford Red Cross, Stratford Vis. Nurse Assn., U. Bridgeport Alumni Assn., Kennedy Ctr., Sacred Heart U. Adv. Bd. Recipient Outstanding Svc. award Stratford Tenants' Coun., 1982, Man of Yr. award Stratford Civitan Club, 1983, Alumnus of Yr. award U. Bridgeport, 1990, Legislator of Yr. award Conn. Profl. Ins. Agts. Assn., 1991, Legislator of Yr. award Conn. Assn. Optometrists, 1993, Legislator of Yr. award Conn. Chiropractic Assn., 1994, Legislator of Yr. award Conn. Adoption Coun., 1996, Legislator of Yr. award U.S. Humane Soc., 1997. Mem. U. Bridgeport Alumni Assn. (bd. dirs.), Washington D.C.-Conn. Soc., Masons, Scottish Rite. Congregationalist.

CHASE, JACQUELYN VERONICA, marketing professional; b. Balt., Jan. 25, 1965; AA in Applied Sci. & Bus. Mktg., Balt. City CC, 1997; BSBA in Mktg., Towson U., 2005. Sales mgr. Ann Taylor, Inc., Balt., 1990—2004; rsch. analyst Towson U., Md., 2001—. Amb. Towson U., 2000—02; pres. Am. Mktg. Assn., Towson, 2002—03. Evangelist missionary Friendship Bapt. Ch., Balt., 1998—2005. Office: Towson U 8000 York Rd Towson MD 21252-0001 Home Phone: 410-935-3460; Office Phone: 410-935-3460. Business E-Mail: jchase2@towson.edu.

CHASE, JAMES RICHARD, retired college president; b. Oxnard, Calif., Oct. 7, 1930; s. James Warren and Nina Marie (Fiscus) C.; m. Mary Corinne Sutherland, Dec. 16, 1950; children: Kenneth Richard, Jennifer Corinne. B. Theology, Biola Coll., 1951; BA, Pepperdine U., 1953, MA, 1954; PhD, Cornell U., 1961. Instr. Biola Coll., La Mirada, Calif., 1953-57, prof., chmn. dept. humanities, 1959-65, v.p. acad. affairs, 1965-70, pres., 1970-82, Wheaton (Ill.) Coll., 1982-93, pres. emeritus, 1993—. Teaching asst. Cornell Univ., Ithaca, N.Y., 1957-59; bd. dirs. World Christian Tng. Ctr., 1970-82; bd. dirs. Christian Coll. Coalition, 1977-79, chmn. bd., 1977-79; bd. dirs. Mission Aviation Fellowship, 1975-81, chmn. bd., 1978-81; bd. dirs. Western Coll. Assn., 1980-82 Mem. Nat. Assn. Ind. Colls. and Univs. (dir. 1980), Assn. Ind. Calif. Colls. and Univs. (mem. exec. com. 1978-82), Am. Assn. Bible Colls. (dir. 1974-80), Nat. Assn. Intercollegiate Athletics (pres. adv. com. 1976-82), Nat. Assn. Evangelicals (exec. com. 1984-92), We. Assn. Schs. and Colls. (sr. commn. 1981-82), Am. Assn. Pres. Ind. Colls. and Univs. (dir. 1980-85, v.p. 1982-85), Speech Communication Assn., Christian Coll. Consortium (chmn. 1986), Coalition (chmn. 1976), Fedn. Ind. Ill. Colls. and Univs. (exec. com., chmn. bd. 1989-91). Baptist.

CHASE, JEANETTE KNAPP, music educator; b. New Orleans, Jan. 27, 1938; d. Roger Seaman Knapp and Jean Louise Sinclair; m. William Raymond Chase, Aug. 3, 1957; children: William Edward II, Beverly Ann. AA in Vocal Performance, San Jacinto Coll. Ctrl., Pasadena, Tex., 1972; MusB in Vocal Performance, U. Houston, 1976; MA in Fine Arts Edn., U. Houston Clear Lake, 1982. RN Tex. Staff nurse Meth. Hosp., Houston, 1957—59, Columbia Hopsital, Pitts., 1959—60, St Agnus Hosp., Balt., 1960—61, Gulfway Gen. Hosp., Houston, 1962—63, SE Bapt. Hosp., Houston, 1963—64, Pasadena Bayshore Hosp., Tex., 1965—69; office nurse, lab tech. Office of Dr. Terry Vincent, Houston, 1958—59; dir. music Webster Presbyn. Ch., Tex., 1972—2001; voice tchr., choral dir. San Jacinto Coll. Ctrl., Pasadena, 1977—93; pvt. voice tchr. El Lago, Tex., 1977—; voice tchr. Lee Coll., Baytown, Tex., 1992—. Dir. music emerita Webster Presbyn. Ch., 2001—; vocalist Temple Beth Israel, Houston, 1975—81. Pres. Westinghouse Wives Club, Pitts., 1959—60; youth choral dir. Presbyn. Ch. of Covenant, Houston, 1969—72; deacon, elder Webster Presbyn. Ch., 1972—2006; bd. govs., fin. com. US Synchronized Swimming, Indpls., 1977—2006; coach, dir. Corkettes/KTRK Kittens/Aquanauts, Houston, 1962—2006. Named Outstanding HS Voice Tchr., Baylor U., 1990; named to Outstanding Young Women of Am., 1973; recipient Tex. All State Choir award, Tex. Music Educators Assn., 1954. Mem.: AAU (licentiate; sec.-treas., synchro adminstrn. chmn. Gulf chpt. 1962—77, nat. bd. govs., fin. com. 1977—), Tex. Choral Dirs. Assn. (corr.), Am. Choral Dirs. Assn. (corr.), Nat. Assn. Tchrs. of Singing Houston (corr.; pres. 1993—2004), Bay Area Chorus (corr.; publicity chmn., pres., historian 1973—2006, Continuing Musical Excellence award 1992). Republican. Presbyterian. Avocations: synchronized swimming, singing, travel. Home and Office: 418 Bayou View Dr El Lago TX 77586-6106 Home Phone: 281-326-1286; Office Phone: 281-326-1286. Personal E-mail: wchase2@houston.rr.com.

CHASE, JENNY WEI-LANG KAO, singer, music educator; b. Quan Ming, China, June 15, 1941; arrived in U.S., 1964; d. Pun-Fei and Shu Kao; m. Robert Chase, June 28, 1969; 1 child, Wayne Hwa. BA, Judson Coll., 1966; MusM cum laude, U. Miss, 1968; studied with Dolf Swing, Juilliard Sch., 1969—72; cert. adminstr., U. Bridgeport, 1986. Music tchr. Yonkers Bd. Edn., 1969—99; voice tchr. Music Conservatory of Westchester, White Plains, NY, 1982—2002; prin., founder Chinese Sch. So. Westchester, Scarsdale, NY, 1981—95, pres. bd. dirs., 1981—99, hon. pres., prin., 1998—. Soprano soloist Mt. Vernon Cmty. Ch., 1974—79, Ch. in the Highlands, 1979—92, Carnegie Hall, NYC, 1981; concert (soprano) recitalist Lincoln Ctr., NYC, 1983—85. Soprano: CD Memory, 1997, Phoenix Rising, 2004; one-woman shows include Spring Hill Br., Merchants Nat. Bank, 1965, U. Miss., 1966, Mus. Oxford, Miss., 1967, Pen Women's Assn., Bronxville Pub. Libr., NY, 1984. Founder Evergreen Club Westchester, 2000; pres. Westchester Chinese Assn., 1997—99. Named Outstanding Alumna, Nat. Taiwan Coll. Arts, 2000; recipient Outstanding Leadership award, Westchester Chinese Assn., 1996, Dynamic Achiever award, Orgn. Chinese Americans, 1989, Art Achievement award, Chinese Am. Arts Coun., 1999. Mem.: Yonkers Fedn. Tchrs., Westchester Musicians Guild, Delta Omicron (life Cert. of Honor 1982). Mem. United Ch. Of Christ. Home: 17 Morgan Pl White Plains NY 10605 Personal E-mail: rac02rac@yahoo.com.

CHASE, JOHN DAVID, retired dean, internist; b. Detroit, Sept. 24, 1920; s. Clyde Harrison and Bonnie Lucille (Fogas) Chase; 1 child, Robert Winslow. AB, Wabash Coll., Ind., 1942; MD, Western Res. U., 1945. Diplomate Am. Bd. Internal Medicine. Intern Detroit Receiving Hosp., 1945—46; resident in internal medicine Wayne State U. Hosp., 1948—52; teaching fellow Nat. Heart Inst., 1952; with VA, 1952—78, dep. asso. chief med. dir. academic affairs Washington, 1970—73; chief med. service VA Hosp., Tacoma, 1973—74; chief med. dir. VA Central Office, Washington, 1974—78; assoc. dean clin. affairs U. Wash. Sch. Med., Seattle, 1978—81, dean Sch. Medicine, 1981—82, dean emeritus, 1983—. Mem. nat. adv. coun. Heart and Lung Inst., 1968—70, Regional Med. Programs, 1970—73, Nat. Libr. Medicine, 1972—73; mem. Nat. Adv. Coun. VA Edn., 1973, Nat. Adv. Coun. Health Svcs. Planning and Resources, 1976, Fed. Coordinating Coun. Sci., Engring. and Tech., 1976—78, Nat. Adv. Coun. Health Planning and Devel., 1976—; bd. govs. Armed Forces Inst. Pathology, 1976—78. With M.C. USNR, 1946—48. Recipient Disting. Svc. award, Wayne State U. Med. Sch., 1976. Fellow: ACP, Am. Coll. Chest Physicians; mem.: AMA (ho. dels.), Nat. Inst. Med., Am. Hosp. Assn. (trustee 1976—78), Assn. Mil. Surgeons U.S., Inst. Medicine. Home; Apt 409 96 Frederick Rd Fredericksburg TX 78624 Personal E-mail: j.chase2@austin.rr.com.

CHASE, MARTIN LESLIE, literature and language educator, priest; b. Bay City, Mich., May 18, 1953; s. Harold Frank and Virginia Chase. BA, Oberlin Coll., Ohio, 1975; MA, PhD, U. Toronto, Can., 1981; MDiv, Weston Sch. Theology, Cambridge, Mass., 1990. Cert. Danish Ministry of Edn., 1996. Asst. prof. John Carroll U., Clev., 1985—87; adj. Niels Steensens Gymnasium, Copenhagen, 1992—99; assoc. prof. Fordham U., Bronx, NY, 1999—. Priest Roman Cath. Ch., NYC, 1991. Fellow, Am. Coun. of Learned Soc., 1984—85, Pontifical Inst. Mediaeval Studies, 1984—85; grantee, Am. Philos. Soc., 1985, American-Scandinavian Found., 1985; Fulbright grant, Inst. Internat. Edn., 1979—80, Franklin Rsch. grant, Am. Philos. Soc., 2006—07. Mem.: Viking Soc. for No. Rsch., Internation Soc. Anglo-Saxonists, Soc. for Advancement of Scandinavian Studies, Medieval Acad. Am., New Eng. Hist. Geneal. Soc., NY Geneal. and Biog. Soc., St. Nicholas Soc. of the City of NY, Appalachian Trail Conservancy, NY-NJ Trail Conf., Holland Soc. (assoc.), Sons of the Revolution (life), Jamestowne Soc. (life), Soc. Mayflower Desdendants (life). Office: Fordham Univ 441 E Fordham Rd Bronx NY 10458

CHASE, PETER, library director; V.p. Libr. Connection, Inc., Windsor, Conn.; dir. Plainville Pub. Libr., Conn. Co-recipient ProQuest-SIRS State & Regional Achievement award, ALA Intellectual Freedom Roundtable, 2007; recipient Paul Howard award for Courage, ALA, 2007. Mem.: Conn. Libr. Assn. (chmn. intellectual freedom com., Outstanding Libr. award 2006). Achievements include challenging the constitutionality of FBI National Security Letters and gag orders imposed under the USA PATRIOT Act, as one of four Connecticut "John Does". Office: Plainville Pub Libr 56 E Main St Plainville CT 06062 also: Libr Connection 599 Matianuck Ave Windsor CT 06095 Office Phone: 860-793-1446, 860-298-5322. Office Fax: 860-793-2241. E-mail: pchase@libraryconnection.info.

CHASE, ROBERT ARTHUR, surgeon, educator; b. Keene, NH, Jan. 6, 1923; s. Albert Henry and Georgia Beulah (Bump) Chase; m. Ann Crosby Parker, Feb. 3, 1946; children: Deborah Lee, Nancy Jo, Robert N. BS cum laude, U. N.H., 1945, DSc (hon.), 1993; MD, Yale, 1947. Diplomate Am. Bd. Surgery, Am. Bd. Plastic Surgery. Intern New Haven Hosp., 1947—48, asst. resident, 1949—50, sr. resident surgery, 1952—53, chief resident surgeon, 1953—54; mem. faculty Yale Sch. Medicine, 1948—54, 1959—62, asst. prof. surgery, 1959—62; mem. faculty U. Pitts., 1957—59, resident plastic surgeon, also teaching fellow, 1957—59; attending surgeon VA Hosp., W. Haven, Conn., 1959—62, Grace New Haven Community Hosp., 1959—63; prof., chmn. dept. surgery Stanford Sch. Medicine, 1963—74, Emile Holman prof. surgery, 1972—; prof. surgery U. Pa., 1974—77; attending surgeon Pa. Hosp., Hosp. U. Pa., Grad. Hosp., Phila., 1974—77; pres., dir. Nat. Bd. Med. Examiners, Phila., 1974—77; prof. anatomy Stanford (Calif.) U., 1977—. Cons. plastic surgery Christian Med. Coll. and Hosp., Vellore, India, 1962; cons. to surgeon gen. USAF, 1970—; Benjamin K. Rank prof. Australasian Coll. Surgeons, 1974. Author: Atlas of Hand Surgey; editor: Videosurgery, 1974—; mem. editl. bd.: Med. Alert Communication, —; contbr. articles to profl. jours. Mem. bd. overseers Dartmouth Med. Sch., 1998-; mem. found. bd. U. N.H., 1998-. Maj. M.C.

AUS, 1949—57. Named an Hand Ctr. in his name, Stanford U., 2004; recipient Francis Gilman Blake award, Yale Sch. Medicine, 1962, Henry J. Kaiser award, Stanford U. Sch. Medicine, 1978, 1979, 1984, 1986, 1990, 1993, Calif. Golden Apple award, 1991, Albion William Hewlett award, 1992, Pettee award, U. N.H., 1998. Fellow: ACS, Australasian Coll. Surgeons (hon.); mem.: AMA, NAS, Halsted Soc., Am. Soc. Most Venerable Order Hosp., St. John of Jerusalem, Inst. Medicine (exec. com. 1976, coun. 1986—), Soc. Univ. Surgeons, Found. Am. Soc. Plastic and Reconstructive Surgery (dir.), Am. Cancer Soc. (clin. fellowship com.), James IV Assn. Surgeons, Pacific Coast Surg. Soc., Western Surg. Assn., Soc. Clin. Surgery, Plastic Surgery Rsch. Coun., Am. Assn. Surgery Trauma, Am. Soc. Cleft Palate Rehab., Am. Soc. Surgery Hand (pres.), Conn. Med. Soc., Santa Clara County Med. Soc., Am. Surg. Assn., San Francisco Surg. Soc., Calif. Acad. Medicine (pres.), Am. Soc. Clin. Anatomists (hon.; pres.), South African Soc. Plastic and Reconstructive Surgery (hon.), South African Soc. Surgery Hand (hon.), Am. Assn. Plastic Surgery (hon.), Am. Assn. Clin. Anatomists (hon.; pres.), Am. Assn. Plastic Surgeons (hon.), Sigma Xi, Phi Beta Kappa. Home: 69 Pearce Mitchell Pl Stanford CA 94305 Office: Stanford U Div Anatomy 269 Campus Dr Stanford CA 94305-5102 Home Phone: 650-473-9049; Office Phone: 650-725-6618. E-mail: rchase6880@aol.com.

CHASE, THOMAS NEWELL, neurologist, researcher, educator; b. Westfield, NJ, May 23, 1932; s. Newell Adams and Gudrun Margarethe (Eskesen) C.; 1 child, Thomas Newell. BS, MIT, 1954; postgrad., Columbia U., 1957-58; MD, Yale U., 1962; postgrad., Harvard U., 1963-66. Engr. Singer Mfg. Co., Bridgeport, Conn., 1954-55; technician Columbia U. Coll. Phys. and Surgs., 1957-58; intern in internal medicine Yale-New Haven Med. Center, 1962-63; asst. resident in neurology Mass. Gen. Hosp., Boston, 1963-64, resident, 1965-66; fellow in neuropathology Harvard U. Med. Sch., 1964-65; guest worker NIMH, Bethesda, Md., 1966-68, chief unit on neurology, 1968-70, chief sect. exptl. therapeutics, 1970-74; chief lab. of neuropharmacology Nat. Inst. Neurol. and Communicative Disorders and Stroke, Bethesda, 1974-76, dir. intramural research, 1974-83, chief pharmacology sect., 1976—2005, chief exptl. therapeutics br., 1983—2005; CEO Hamilton Pharms., Inc., 2005—07, Chase Pharms. Corp., 2007—. Mem. sci. adv. bd. Nat. Parkinson Found.; mem. adv. bd. Nat. Ataxia Found., Astra-Zenica. Assoc. editor Jour. Psychiatry and Neurosci.; mem. editl. bd. Progress in Neuro-Psychopharmacology, Movement Disorders, Drug Devel. Rsch., Parkinsonian and Related Disorders, Contemporary Neurology, Current Treatment Options in Neurology, Jour. Neural Transmission, Neurotoxicology Rsch., Neurodegenerative Diseases; contbr. articles to med. jours. Served with Signal Corps U.S. Army, 1955-57. Recipient Winternitz prize in pathology, 1960, Ramsay prize for clin. medicine, 1961, diploma of recognition of merit for humanitarian svcs. Govt. of Bolivia, 1974, USPHS Meritorious Svc. medal, 1978, 96, USPHS Outstanding Svc. medal, 1991, Springer prize for Parkinson's disease rsch., 1994; summer fellow, 1960; USPHS summer fellow, 1961; Nat. Inst. Neurol. Diseases and Blindness spl. fellow, 1966-68. Fellow Am. Coll. Neuro-Psychopharmacology; mem. Am. Neurol. Assn., Am. Acad. Neurology, Am. Soc. Exptl. Neurotherapeutics (pres. 1997-2001), Soc. Neurosci., Internat. Soc. Neurochemistry, Am. Soc. Neurochemistry, Assn. for Rsch. in Nervous and Mental Disease, Internat. Brain Rsch. Orgn., Internat. Basal Ganglia Soc., World Fedn. Neurology, Movement Disorder Soc. Office: Chase Pharms Inc Ste 520 1825 K St NW Washington DC 20006 Office Phone: 202-223-7001. E-mail: tchase@hamiltonpharma.com.

CHASE, THOMAS STANHOPE, language educator, department chairman; s. Oliver Stuart and Edmonia Johnson Chase; m. Sarah Alexander; children: Harrision Weld, Alexander Stark, Davis Henry. BA in History and Classics, Williams Coll., Williamstown, Mass., 1982; JD, Suffolk U., Boston, 1985; MA in Classical Civilizations, Harvard U., Cambridge, Mass., 2000. Bar: Mass. 1985. Assoc. atty. Vaughn and Dale, Nantucket, Mass., 1985—86; law clk. US Fed. Dist. Ct., Boston, 1986—88; litig. assoc. Choate, Hall & Stewart, Boston, 1988—91; tchr. Latin Pomfret Sch., Conn., 1992—, chmn. dept. fgn. lang., 2005—. Coach boys varsity squash Pomfret Sch., 1992—, coach boys varsity tennis, 1998—. Coach N.E. Conn. Youth Soccer, Pomfret, 2005—07. Recipient Tchg. Excellence prize, Pomfret Sch., 2000; grantee, Fulbright Commn., 2002. Office: Pomfret Sch 398 Pomfret St PO Box 128 Pomfret CT 06258-0128

CHASE, WILL, actor; b. Frankfurt, Ky., Sept. 12, 1970; s. Jerry and Betty Chase; m. Lori Chase; children: Daisy, Gracie. Grad. in Percussion and Conducting, Oberlin Conservatory of Music, 1992. Actor: (plays) Trask & Fenn, 1992, Electra, 1993, Son of Fire, 1993, Assassins, 1993, Mame, 1994, Black Patent Leather Shoes., 1994, The Pajama Game, 2007; (Broadway plays) Rent, 1998, 2005—06, Miss Saigon, 1998, Aida, 2001, The Full Monty, 2001, Lennon, 2005, High Fidelity, 2006, (TV guest appearances) Third Watch, 2002, Law & Order, 2003, 2004, (films) Shaft, 2000.*

CHASE, WILLIAM ROBERT, television executive; b. Mt. Vernon, NY, Mar. 8, 1951; s. Irving Warren and Muriel Ada Chase. BA, Queens Coll., 1974; MS, Bklyn. Coll., 1976. Scenic and lighting dir. Bklyn. Coll. of CUNY, 1974-76; freelance lighting dir. NYC, 1974—; unit prodn. mgr. various TV prodn. cos., 1983-87; prodn. mgr. Sta. WNET-TV/PBS, NYC, 1979-87; dir. prodn. mgmt. Sta. WNET-TV, NYC, 1987-88; dir. east coast prodn. HBO, Inc., NYC, 1988-90, v.p. prodn., east coast, 1990—. Instr. Bklyn. Coll., 1976-85, assoc. prof., 2006; instr. N.Y. Inst. Tech., 1982-85. Assoc. producer Roanoak, 1985; unit prodn. mgr: (TV shows, mini-series, spls.) Kennedy, 1983, Finnegan Begin Again, 1984, Murder of Mary Phagan, 1987; line producer (TV series) Pee-Wee's Playhouse, 1986. Mem. Dirs. Guild Am., Nat. Acad. TV Arts and Scis. Avocations: photography, computers.

CHASEMAN, JOEL, communications consultant; b. Feb. 18, 1926; m. Marlene Meyerson, Sept. 11, 1955; children: Martha Hope, Joanne Amy. BA, Cornell U., 1948. CEO Post-Newsweek Stas., Washington, 1973-90; chmn. NATAS, 1980-82; dir. Advt. Coun., 1986-90; prin. Chaseman Enterprises Internat., 1990—. Chmn. Advanced TV Test Ctr., 1987—93; CEO NevadaVision, Inc., 1990—2001, Hobby Craft Interactive Network, 1999—2002; chmn. adv. bd. Nearware Networks, 2001—; advisor Ctr. for Pub. Integrity, 2003—. Trustee Mus. Broadcasting, 1988. Mem. Assn. Maximum Svc. Telecasters (chmn. 1988-91), Nat. Assn. Broadcasters (bd. dirs. 1988-90), TV Operators Caucus (co-founder). E-mail: joechase@wdn.com.

CHASEN, JERRY SIMON, lawyer; BA summa cum laude, Tufts U., 1973; JD cum laude, NYU, 1976; LLM in Estate Planning, U. Miami Law Sch., 1994. Bar: NY 1976, Fla. 1977, N.Mex. 1987, Calif. 1988. Law clk. to Hon. Edward Weinfeld US Dist. Ct. (so. dist. NY), 1977—78; ptnr. Chasen & Assocs., P.A., Miami, Fla. Contbr. articles to profl. publs. Mem. friends bd. Bass Mus. Art, 2003—; chair gay and lesbian cmty. project fun adv. com. Dade Cmty. Found., 2005—; mem. steering com. Greater Miami Leave a Legacy Campaign; vice chair bd. dirs. Mus. Contemporary Art, North Miami, Fla., 1995—99; nat. bd. dirs. Lambda Legal Def. & Edn. Fund, 1998—2002. Named one of Top 100 Attys., Worth mag., 2005—06. Mem.: Planned Giving Coun. Miami-Dade County (past pres. bd. dirs. 1995—). Office: Chasen & Assocs PA 1000 Venetian Way #801 Miami FL 33139 Office Phone: 305-377-0718. Office Fax: 305-377-1427. E-mail: jchasen@chasenlaw.com.

CHASEN, SYLVAN HERBERT, data processing executive, financial planner; b. Richmond, Va., May 19, 1926; s. Nathan and Hanna (Pass) C.; m. Catherine Hudlow, Mar. 25, 1946; children: Deborah Wyatt, Dianne Lipsey, Jane Morrison, Susan Mazur. Student, Va. Poly. Inst., 1943-44; BS in Engring, Ga. Inst. Tech., 1946, B. Chem. Engring., 1946; MS, Emory U., 1951. Registered investment advisor 1993. Math. instr. Ga. Inst. Tech., Atlanta, 1946-50; head computer facility Naval Air Test Ctr., Patuxent, Md., 1951-58; dir. advanced computing CAD and interactive graphics Lockheed-Ga. Co., Marietta, 1958-87; pres. Center CAD/CAM Tech., Inc. Adj. instr. Emory U., 1993-2005; disting. vis. prof. NJ Inst. Tech. Grad. Sch., 1983; lectr., cons. in field. Author: Geometric Principles and Procedures for Computer Graphics Applications, 1978, The Guide for the Evaluation and Implementation of CAD/CAM Systems, 1980, 2d edit., 1983. Served as ensign USN, 1944-46. Recipient Outstanding Contbns. award Gov. Md., 1957; recipient Disting. Contbns. award Soc. Mfg. Engrs., 1982 Mem. ASME (charter), AIAA (charter), Soc. Mfg. Engrs., SIGGRAPH, NCGA, Emory U. Srs. Investment Club. Home: 760 Starlight Ct NE Atlanta GA 30342-2826

CHASNOFF, BARRY A., lawyer; b. Houston, July 22, 1949; BA, Trinity U., 1971; JD with honors, U. Tex., 1974. Bar: Tex. 1974, US Dist. Ct. (we., no.and so. dists.) Tex. 1981, US Ct. Appeals (5th cir.) 1982, US Supreme Ct. 1983. Trial atty. office gen. counsel Dept. Transp., 1974-77; ptnr., head litig. practice and mem. mgmt. com. Akin, Gump, Strauss, Hauer & Feld LLP, San Antonio. Teaching quizmaster U. Tex. Sch. Law, 1973-74. Mem. ABA, State Bar of Tex. San Antonio Bar Assn., Tex. Bar Found., San Antonio Bar Found., Internat. Assn. Def. Counsel, Order of Coif. Office: Akin Gump Strauss Hauer & Feld LLP Ste 1500 300 Convent St San Antonio TX 78205-3732 Office Phone: 210-281-7001. Office Fax: 210-281-2035. Business E-Mail: bchasnoff@akingump.com.

CHASSE, EMILY SCHUDER, librarian, educator; b. Paducah, Ky., June 10, 1953; d. Charles Bernard and Ann (Sidwell) Schuder; m. William Chasse, Aug. 30, 1980; 1 child, Sarah Ann Schuder Chasse. Student, Iowa State U., 1972-74; BA in Elem. Edn., Antioch Coll., 1976; MLS, U. R.I., 1979. Cert. tchr., Conn. Child care worker Walker Home & Sch., Needham, Mass., 1975-78; children's libr. Plainville (Conn.) Pub. Libr., 1979-82; part-time instr. in children's lit. Manchester (Conn.) Community Coll., 1981-83; asst. curriculum lab. libr. Cen. Conn. State U., New Britain, 1982-89, libr. on-line search svcs., 1989—. Prodr. West Hartford Pub. Access TV, 2004—; freelance storyteller, 1980—. Contbr. articles to profl. jours. Mem. ALA, Conn. Libr. Assn., Conn. Storytelling Assn., Hither & Yon Storytellers. Democrat. Mem. Soc. Of Friends. Office: Cen Conn State U Burritt Libr 1615 Stanley St New Britain CT 06053-2439 Home Phone: 860-521-9033; Office Phone: 860-832-2063. Business E-Mail: chasse@ccsu.edu.

CHASSIN, JAMESON LEWIS, retired surgeon; b. Maspeth, NY, Mar. 12, 1922; s. Isaac and Esther Chassin; m. Charlotte Eunice Cowan, Nov. 6, 1945; children: Mark Russell Gray, Pamela Sue, Robert Glenn, Richard Niles. BA, Harvard U., Cambridge, Mass., 1941; MD, Johns Hopkins U., Balt., 1945. Chmn. dept. of surgery N.Y. Hosp. of Queens, Flushing, 1960—93; prof. of clin. surgery NYU Med. Ctr., NYC, 1965—. Author: (textbook) Operative Strategy in General Surgery, (author) Chassin's Operative Strategy in General Surgery. Capt. med. unit, 1949—52. Home Phone: 212-223-0940. Personal E-mail: jchassin@nyc.rr.com.

CHASSMAN, KAREN MOSS, educational association administrator; b. Bklyn., Aug. 18, 1946; d. Bernard and Esther (Steier) Kahn; m. Robert Moss (div. 1973); 1 child, Jeff; m. Richard Chassman, Oct. 31, 1992 (dec. Feb. 1994). BA, Hunter Coll., 1967; MS in Edn., Bklyn. Coll., 1969, advanced cert. in lang. arts, 1978. Tchr. nursery, kindergarten and grades 1-6 Common Branches, 1967-78; sales rep., real estate broker various cos., 1978-91; dir., owner The Reading Improvement Ctr., East Islip, N.Y., 1991—. Mem. Islip C. of C., Islip Rotary (ednl. scholar 1992—). Avocations: antiques, travel, exercise. Office: Reading Improvement Ctr 2545 Middle Country Rd Centereach NY 11720 also: Reading Improvement Ctr 268 East Main St East Islip NY 11730 also: Reading Improvement Ctr 2907 Milburn Ave Baldwin NY 11510 Home Phone: 516-431-1446; Office Phone: 631-581-0500, 631-467-3590. Personal E-mail: readingcenter@aol.com, prinitch@aol.com.

CHASSMAN, LEONARD FREDRIC, retired labor union administrator; b. Detroit, Sept. 30, 1935; s. Joachim and Lillian (Abrams) C.; m. Phyllis Perlman, Aug. 25, 1957; children: Mark, Cheryl, Gregory. BA, UCLA, 1957. Rep. AFTRA, LA, 1959-63, SAG, LA, 1963-65; staff exec. Writers Guild Am., West, Inc., LA, 1965-77, exec. dir., 1978-82; nat. exec. sec. Screen Extras Guild Inc., 1982-84; Hollywood exec. dir. SAG Inc., 1984—2001, trustee SAG prodrs. pension and health funds; bd. dirs. Entertainment Industry Found. Pres. Hollywood Entertainment Labor Coun. Bd. dirs. L.A. Pvt. Industry Coun.

CHAST, ROZ, cartoonist; b. Bklyn., Nov. 26, 1954; d. George and Elizabeth (Buchman) C.; m. William Franzen, Sept. 22, 1984; children: Ian, Nina. BFA, RISD, 1977. Contract artist The New Yorker Mag., NYC, 1979—; cartoonist The Scis. Mag. Author: (cartoon collections) Unscientific Americans, 1982, Parallel Universes, 1984, Mondo Boxo: Cartoon Stories, 1987, The Four Elements, 1988, Proof of Life on Earth, 1991, The Party, After You Left: Collected Cartoons 1995-2003, 2004; illustrator of various books including The Joy of Being Single, 1992, Meet My Staff, 1998, Now I Will Never Leave the Dinner Table, 1999, Rationalizations to Live By, 2000, The New Yorker Book of Kids Cartoons, 2001, Weird and Wonderful Words, 2002, You're an Animal, Viskovitz!, 2003; work has been featured in Scientific American, N.Y. Times Mag., Rolling Stone, Nat. Lampoon.

CHASTAIN, BRANDI DENISE, professional soccer player; b. San Jose, Calif., July 21, 1968; m. Jerry Smith; 1 stepchild. Student, U. Calif., Berkeley, 1986—88; BA in TV Comm., Santa Clara U., 1991. Mem. U.S. Women's Soccer Team, 1996—; asst. coach women's soccer team Santa Clara U.; profl. soccer player San Jose CyberRays, 2001—03. Mem. Shiroke Serena, Japan, 1993, U.S. Olympic Soccer Team, Athens, 2004. Named World Cup Champion, 1999; recipient Gold medal, Atlanta Olympic Games, 1996, Gold Medal, Athens Olympic Games, 2004, Silver medal, Sydney Olympic Games, 2000. Achievements include mem. championship team U.S. Olympic Festival; CONCACAF Championship, N.Y., 1993. Office: c/o Santa Clara U Athletics Dept 500 El Camino Real Santa Clara CA 95050-4345 also: US Soccer Fedn 1801 S Prairie Ave # 1811 Chicago IL 60616-1319

CHASTAIN, KENNETH DUANE, retired foreign language educator, writer; b. Salem, Ind., July 20, 1934; s. Lloyd Lionel and Cristal Louise (Hoke) C.; m. Mary Janice McFadden, June 14, 1959; children: Kevin Duane, Brian Duane, Michael Allen. BS, Ind. U., 1956; MA, Ball State U., 1962; PhD, Purdue U., 1968. Tchr. Seymour HS, Ind., 1956-62, Columbus HS, Ind., 1962-64; grad. instr., prof. Purdue U., Lafayette, Ind., 1964-72; prof. Asbury Coll., Wilmore, Ky., 1972-73, U. Va., Charlottesville, Va., 1973-95, prof. emeritus, 1995—. Author: Developing S-L Skills, 1988, Spanish Grammar in Review, 1993, Exploraciones en la Literatura Hispanica, 1993, The Money Chase: Counting the Cost, 2000, Social Security and More: Comments on Government, 2001, English as a Communication System, 2001, Omri and the Boy, 2001, Imaginate, 2004. With U.S. Army, 1957-58. Recipient Florence Steiner Leadership in Fgn. Lang. Edn. award Am. Coun. Teaching Fgn. Langs., 1989. Avocations: exercise, gardening, nature, travel. Home: 2674 Bakers Chapel Church Rd Big Sandy TN 38221-5318 Personal E-mail: jkc373@compu.net.

CHASTEEN, BEVERLY JOAN, parochial school educator, retired secondary school educator; d. Donald Arthur and Elizabeth May Bennett; m. Donald Lee Chasteen, June 1, 1962; 1 child, Stephanie Elizabeth Brimmer. BA, U. Louisville, 1961. Tchr. Jefferson County Bd. Edn., Louisville, 1961—69, 1976—84; lang. arts., history tchr. St. Clement's Sch., 1984—2004; ind. living skills specialist Ctr. Accessible Living, Louisville, 2005—. Advocate rsch. mem. Arthritis Found., 1999—2006; mem. Susan G. Koman Breast Cancer Found., 2000—06, Nat. Humane Edn. Soc., Charlestown, W.Va., 2006; nat. assoc. The Smithsonian Instn., Washington, 2004—; PCA asst. Ctr. for Accessible Living, Louisville, 2005—; chair call com., mem. ch. coun. St. Mark Ch. Recipient Prin.'s award, Wilkerson Elem. Sch., Louisville, 1980. Mem.: Nat. Women's History Mus., Ky. Congress of Parents and Tchrs. (life). Lutheran. Avocation: reading. E-mail: bjchasteen@igloo.com.

CHATARD, PETER RALPH NOEL, JR., aesthetic plastic surgeon; b. New Orleans, June 25, 1936; s. Peter Ralph Sr. and Alberta Chatard; m. Patricia Myrl White, Jan. 31, 1963; children: Andrea Michelle, Faedra Noelle, Tahra Deonne. BS in Biology, Morehouse Coll., 1956; MD, U. Rochester, 1960. Diplomate Am. Bd. Plastic Surgery, Am. Bd. Otolaryngology. Intern Colo. Gen. Hosp., 1960-61; asst. resident in gen. surgery Highland Gen. Hosp., Rochester, NY, 1963-64; resident in otolaryngology Strong Meml. Hosp., Rochester, 1964-67; resident in plastic and reconstructive surgery U. Fla., 1980-82; staff otolaryngologist Group Health Corp. of Puget Sound, Seattle, 1967-68; practice medicine specializing in otolaryngology Seattle, 1968-80; practice medicine specializing in plastic surgery, 1982—; clin. asst. prof. otolaryngology, head and neck surgery U. Wash., Seattle, 1975—. Plastic surgery cons. western sec. Maxillofacial Rev. Bd. State of Wash., 1982-90, cons. Conservation of Hearing Program, 1968-80; trustee Physicians and Dentist Credit Bur., 1974-80, 84-87, pres. 1976-77, 84-85; active staff mem. Northwest Hosp., Seattle; courtesy staff Swedish Hosp., Overlake Hosp., Bellevue, Stevens Meml. Hosp., Edmond, Wash., Seattle, others. Capt. USAF, 1961-63. Fellow ACS, Am. Rhinologic Soc., Seattle Surg. Soc., Am. Acad. Facial Plastic and Reconstructive Surgery, Am. Acad. Otolaryngology-Head and Neck Surgery, Northwest Acad. Otolaryngology and Head and Neck Surgery, Soc. for Ear, Nose and Throat Advances in Children, Pacific Oto-Ophthalmological Soc.; mem. Am. Soc. Plastic Surgery, Am. Soc. for Aesthetic Plastic Surgery, Inc., Lipoplasty Soc. N. Am., Wash. Soc. Plastic Surgeons, Nat. Med. Assn., King County Med. Soc., Wash. State Med. Assn., N.W. Soc. of Plastic Surgeons. Avocations: photography, cynology, microcomputing, architecture. Home: 13211 Frazier Pl NW Seattle WA 98177-4132 Office: AEsteem Aesthetic Plastic Surgery Inc 1200 N Northgate Way Seattle WA 98133-8916 Office Phone: 206-522-0200. Business E-Mail: aesteempsc@aol.com. E-mail: chatard@aol.com.

CHATELIER, PAUL RICHARD, aviation psychologist; s. Paul and Mary Chatelier; m. Mary Lu Moss; children: Michael, Suzanne. BS in Biology, Chemistry, Psychology, U. Fla., 1960; MA in Psychology, U. Miss., 1962; postgrad., U. N.Mex., 1967-69. Joined USN, 1962, advanced through grades to capt., 1986; sr. v.p. strategic planning Perceptronics, Inc., Washington, 1986—93; with Office Sci. and Tech. Policy Exec. Office of Pres. U.S., Washington, 1993—96; dir. for edn. tech. edn. activity Dept. Def., Washington, 1996—. U.S. rep. on human factors NATO, Brussels, 1978—86; mem. task force tng. and wargaming Def. Sci. Bd., 1986—88, task force edn. and tng., 1999; U.S. rep. on tng. Tech. Coop. Panel, Washington, 1986—87; mem. indsl. adv. com. U. Ctrl. Fla. Inst. for Simulation and Tng.; edn. and tng. cons. Office Sci. and Tech. White Ho., 1993—96; workshop dir. internat. tng. and human factors; del. at large human factors and medicine panel NATO, 1999; dep. dir. Advanced Distributed Learning Co-Lab., Alexandria, Va., 1999—2001; cons. Potomac Inst. for Policy Studies, 2002—. Co-author: (book) Psychology of Reality, 1985; editor: Manprint & System Integ. 1988, International Human Factors, 1991, Advanced Technology for Training Design, NATO, 1993, Opening the Classroom Doors.Distance Learning, 1995, Virtual Reality Trainings Future?, 1997. Career advisor Fairfax County Pub. Sch., 1982—88. Mem.: Nat. Security Indsl. Assn. (chmn. manpower pers. tng. 1986—89), Va. Human Factors Soc. (pres. 1982—83), Nat. Human Factors Soc. (mem. exec. coun. 1982—85). Avocations: tennis, community activities. Home: 8021 W Point Dr Springfield VA 22153-3023 Personal E-mail: pchat@mindspring.com.

CHATFIELD, DEAN CHARLES, business professor; b. Rochester, NY, 1967; m. Lynn Chatfield. BS in Mgmt. Sys., Rensselaer Poly. Inst., Troy, NY, 1989; MBA in Fin., Penn State U., University Park, 1991; MS in Mgmt. Info. Sys., Penn State U., 1993, PhD in Mgmt. Sci. & Info. Sys., 2000. Bus. rsch. analyst Xerox Corp., Rochester. 1994—95; asst. prof. mgmt. sci. & info tech. Va. Tech, Blacksburg, Va., 2001—07; prof. decision scis. & info. tech. Old Dominion U., Norfolk, Va., 2007—. Contbr. articles to profl. jours. Recipient Best Applied Rsch. paper award, Decision Scis. Inst. Nat. Meeting, 2005. Mem.: Prodn. and Ops. Mgmt. Soc., Inst. Ops. Rsch. and Mgmt. Scis., Decision Scis. Inst., Assn. Info. Sys. Achievements include development of advanced supply chain simulation software; research in factors impacting the bullwhip effect in supply chains; inventory system performance in supply chains; application of genetic algorithms to production and inventory problems. Home: 117 Huntington Ln Blacksburg VA 24060 Personal E-mail: deanchat@aol.com.

CHATFIELD, MARY VAN ABSHOVEN, retired librarian; d. Cornelius and Elma Elizabeth (Sumner) van Abshoven; m. Robert W. Chatfield, June 22, 1963 (div. 1981); 1 child, Robert Warner Jr.; m. Alexander Watts, Jan. 6, 1996 (div. 2000). AB, Radcliffe Coll., 1958; SM, Columbia U., 1961; MBA, Harvard U., 1972. With library system Harvard U., Cambridge, Mass., 1961-92, librarian Bus. Sch., 1963-78, head libr., 1978-92; acting head libr. Countway Libr. Harvard Med. Sch., 1988-89; head libr. Angelo State U., San Angelo, Tex., 1992-95; collections care mgr. Fosterfields, Morristown, NJ, 1996-97; mgr. libr. svcs. Montclair (N.J.) Art Mus., 1997; exec. dir. Mendham (N.J.) Free Pub. Libr., 1997-99; coord. pub. and tech. svcs. Tom Green County Libr., San Angelo, Tex., 1999—2004; Concho Valley Master Gardener, docent, rschr. San Angelo Mus. Fine Arts, 2004—; ind rschr.; v.p. mktg. rsch. Xurex Nano-Coatings Corp., 2005—. Rschr., tutor Adult Literacy Coun.; bd. dirs. Historic San Angelo; pres. Friends Tom Green County Libr. Democrat. Episcopalian. Avocations: reading, embroidery, collecting, museum studies, public art. Home: 115 N Jackson St San Angelo TX 76901-3215 Personal E-mail: marychat@wcc.net.

CHATFIELD, WILLIAM AUSTIN, federal agency administrator; b. 1951; Attended, Union Coll., Am. U. Doorkeeper US Ho. of Reps., Washington, 1978—79; with Reagan Admnstrn., 1980—87; mem. staff of dep. under sec. for policy US Dept. Def.; regional dir. Civil Aeronautics Bd.; spl. asst. to dir. Office of Pers.l Mgmt.; asst. to chmn. Consumer Product Safety Commn.; spl. asst. to Congl. liaison US Dept. Interior; staff advisor to commr. Interstate Commerce Commn.; co-founder, govt. rels. cons. Kindness & Chatfield Assocs., 1989—2004; dir. Selective Svc. Sys., Arlington, Va., 2004—. Office: US Selective Svc Sys 1515 Wilson Blvd Arlington VA 22209 Office Phone: 703-605-4100. Office Fax: 703-605-4106.*

CHATI, MANDAR KALIDAS, operations research specialist; arrived in U.S., 1993; s. Kalidas Madhav and Pratibha Kalidas Chati; m. Prachi Mandar Chati, Dec. 27, 1997; children: Prathamesh, Pranav. B in Tech., Indian Inst. Tech., Mumbai, 1993; MS, Iowa State U., 1995; PhD, Cornell U., 1999. Rschr. Gen. Electric, Niskayuna, NY, 1999—. Recipient Whitney award, Gen. Electric, 2000. Mem.: Am. Soc. Quality (cert.). Avocations: keyboards, languages, formula one cars.

CHATILLON, DEVEREUX, lawyer, publishing executive; BA cum laude, Harvard U.; JD, NYU. With Cahill Gordon & Reindel; sr. gen. atty. litig. and law-journalism ABC Inc.; v.p., gen. counsel, editl. counsel The New Yorker; exec. v.p., gen. counsel Talk Mag. and Talk Miramax Books; exec. v.p. Miramax Books & Miramax Film Corp.; ptnr. Sonnenschein Nath & Rosenthal LLP; sr. v.p., gen. counsel, sec. Scholastic Corp., NYC, 2006—. Office: Scholastic Corp 557 Broadway New York NY 10012*

CHATILOVICZ, PETER, lawyer; b. Kenosha, Wis., Dec. 11, 1946; BA, Beloit Coll., 1969; JD magna cum laude, U. Miami, 1974. Bar: Fla. 1974, DC 1975. Mem. Seyfarth Shaw LLP, Washington, ptnr., mem. exec. com., mng. ptnr. Washington DC Office. Adj. prof. Georgetown U. Sch. Law, Washington, 1988—94. Editor-in-chief U. Miami Law Rev., 1973—74. Named Labor Lawyer of Yr., Washington Bus. Jour., 2005. Mem.: DC Bar Assn., Fla. Bar Assn. Office: Seyfarth Shaw LLP 815 Connecticut Ave NW Washington DC 20006-4004 Office Phone: 202-828-5330. Office Fax: 202-828-5393.

CHATLOS, WILLIAM EDWARD, management consultant; b. Turtle Creek, Pa., Aug. 28, 1927; s. Rudolph and Elizabeth (Mraz) C.; m. Margaret Eileen Jackson. Student, U. Pitts., 1946-47, Ursinus Coll., 1948-49; BS magna cum laude, Boston U., 1951; postgrad., N.Y. Inst. Fin., 1955-56. With Georgeson & Co., NYC, 1952-81, prin. in charge mgmt. cons. for investor rels., 1957-81; prin. Chatlos & Co. Inc., North Caldwell, N.J., 1981—. Bd. dirs. Kelso Inst.; cons. state govts.; lectr. in field. Editor Trends in Mgmt.-Investor Rels., 1957-81; contbr. articles to profl. publs. Mem. Soc. Profl. Mgmt. Cons., Pub. Rels. Soc. Am., Am. Mgmt. Assn., Assn. Corp. Growth, Investor Rels. Assn. (pres. 1966-67), Nat. Investor Rels. Inst. (co-founder, pres. 1974-75). Office: Chatlos & Co Inc 302 Milanville Rd Beach Lake PA 18405 Home Phone: 570-729-7698.

CHATO, JOHN CLARK, mechanical and bioengineering educator; b. Budapest, Hungary, Dec. 28, 1929; s. Joseph Alexander and Elsie (Wasserman) C.; m. Elizabeth Janet Owens, Aug. 1954; children: Christine B., David J., Susan E. ME, U. Cin., 1954; MS, U. Ill., 1955; PhD, MIT, 1960. Co-op student, trainee Frigidaire div. GMC, Dayton, Ohio, 1950—54; grad. fellow U. Ill., Urbana, 1954—55; grad. fellow, inst. MIT, Cambridge, 1955—58, asst. prof., 1958—64; assoc. prof. U. Ill., Urbana, 1964—69, prof., 1969—96, prof. emeritus, 1996—, chmn. exec. com. bioengring. faculty, 1972—78, 1982—83, 1984—85, asst. dean of engring., 1997—98. Cons. Industry and Govt., 1958—; dir., founder Biomed. Engring. Systems Team, Urbana, Ill, 1974-78; assoc. editor Jour. Biomech. Engring., 1976-82. Patentee in field; contbr. articles to profl. jours., chpts. to books on heat transfer, bio-heat transfer, refrigeration, air conditioning, cryogenics, and thermal systems. Com. mem. troop 6 Boy Scouts Am., Urbana, 1984—86; com. mem. Urbana Plan Commn., 1973—78; mem. adv. com. Urbana Park Dist., 1981—84; 2nd v.p. Champaign County Izaak Walton League, 1986, 1st v.p., 1987, pres., 1988—92, bd. dirs., state dir., 1992—; mem. Urbana Postal Customer Adv. Coun., 2002—; trustee 1st Presbyn. Ch., Urbana, 1976—78, 1999—2001, elder, 1982—85, 2004—07; bd. dirs. Univ. YMCA, Champaign, Ill., 1976—78, 1987—90, Champaign-Urbana Mass Transit Dist., 2005—. Recipient Tobin award Champaign County Izaak Walton League, 1992, Cmty. Svc. award Urbana Park Dist., 1996, Russell Scott Meml. award, Cryogenic Engring. Conf., 1979; named Disting. Engring. Alumnus, U. Cin., 1972, U. Ill., 2005; NSF fellow 1961, Fogarty Sr. Internat. fellow 1978-79; Japan Soc. Promotion of Sci. fellow, 1997. Fellow: ASHRAE (treas. East Ctrl. Ill. chpt. 1984, sec. 1985, 1987, 1st v.p. 1988, pres. 1989), ASME (exec. com. bioengring. divsn. 1992—96, sec. 1993—94, chmn. 1994—95, Charles Russ Richards Meml. award 1978, H.R. Lissner award 1992, Dedicated Svc. award 2000), Am. Inst. Med. and Biol. Engrs.; mem.: IEEE (sr.), Am. Soc. Engring. Edn., Internat. Inst. Refrigeration (assoc.), Audubon Soc. Champaign County (bd. dirs. 1988—89, v.p. 1990, treas. 1991—93, v.p. 1995—96, treas. 1998—99, pres. 2000—02, bd. dirs. 2002, pres. 2005—06), Exch. Club Urbana (bd. dirs. 1989—91, 1995—96, pres.-elect 1996—97, pres. 1997—98, dist. dir. 2001—05). Presbyterian. Achievements include research in fields of heat transfer, bio-heat transfer, refrigeration, air conditioning, cryogenics, and thermal systems. Avocations: tennis, photography, birdwatching, hiking, kayaking. Office: U Ill Dept Mech Sci and Engring 1206 W Green St Urbana IL 61801-2906 Business E-Mail: jbchato@uiuc.edu.

CHATOFF, MICHAEL ALAN, lawyer; b. NYC, Aug. 18, 1946; s. Alexander Zelig and Leona Rhoda (Weiss) C. BA, CUNY, 1967; JD, Bklyn. Law Sch., 1971; LLM, NYU, 1978. Bar: N.Y. 1971, U.S. Dist. Ct. (so. and ea. dists.) N.Y. 1978, U.S. Ct. Appeals (2d cir.) 1980, U.S. Supreme Ct. 1980. Reader Chgo. Title Ins. Co., NYC, 1972; chief U.S. Code Congl. and Adminstrv. News West Pub. Co., Westbury, N.Y., 1972-97. Cons. N.Y. Sch. for Deaf, N.Y.C. Mayor's Office for Disabled, Westchester County Legis.; lectr. N.Y. State Dept. of Edn. Vocat. Ednl. Svcs. for Individuals with Disabilities, N.Y. Sch. Deaf, Lexington Sch. for Deaf, Parents for Deaf Awareness, Am. Profl. Soc. for Deaf, N.Y. Ctr. for Law and the Deaf, Coun. on Jewish Deaf Edn. and Rehab., Nat. Coun. on Deaf People and Deafness, NYU. Assoc. law editor Ency. on Deaf People and Deafness; contbr. articles to Nat. Law Jour., N.Y. Law Jour., Able Adv., Communication Outlook, Deaf Spectrum. Bd. dirs. Westchester Cmty. Svcs. for Hearing Impaired; counsel Conn. African-Am. Deaf Advocate; mem. Supreme Ct. Hist. Soc.; del. nominee Dem. Nat. Conv., 1992. Mem. ABA, Queens County Bar Assn., Assn. of Bar of City of N.Y., Nat. Assn. Deaf, Am. Contract Bridge League, Nassau Bar Assn. Avocations: bridge, jogging, weight-lifting. Home: 26909T Grand Central Pkwy Floral Park NY 11005-1010 Personal E-mail: mchatoff@aol.com.

CHATROO, ARTHUR JAY, lawyer; b. NYC, July 1, 1946; s. George and Lillian (Leibowitz) C.; m. Christina Daly, Aug. 6, 1994; 1 child, Alexander. BChemE, CCNY, 1968; JD cum laude, New York Law Sch., 1979; MBA with distinction, NYU, 1982. Bar: NY 1980, Calif. 1993, US Patent Office 1998. Process engr. Std. Oil Co. of Ohio, various locations, 1968-73; process specialist BP Oil, Inc., Marcus Hook, Pa., 1974-75; sr. process engr. Sci. Design Co., Inc., NYC, 1975-78; mgr. spl. projects The Halcon SD Group, NYC, 1978-82; corp. counsel, tax and fin. The Lubrizol Corp., Wickliffe, Ohio, 1982-85, sr. counsel spl. investment projects, 1989-90; gen. counsel Lubrizol Enterprises, Inc., Wickliffe, 1985-89; chmn. Correlation Genetics Corp., San Jose, Calif., 1990-91; gen. counsel Agrigenetics Co., Eastlake, Ohio, 1990-92; gen. counsel, dir. comml. contracting Agrigenetics, L.P., San Diego, 1992-93; counsel Agrigenetics, Inc. dba Mycogen Seeds, Mycogen Corp., San Diego, 1994-97; dir. legal affairs Mycogen Corp., San Diego, 1997-98; exec. v.p. bus. devel., legal and regulatory affairs Global Agro, Inc., Encinitas, Calif., 1998-99; exec. v.p., gen. counsel Akkadix Corp., San Diego, 1999—2001; atty., bus. cons. San Diego, 2001—. Mem. Met. Parks Adv. com., Allen County, Ohio, 1973. Mem. ABA, Am. Chem. Soc., San Deigo County Bar Assn., Am. Corp. Counsel Assn., Jaycees (pers. dir. Lima, Ohio chpt. 1972-73), Licensing Execs. Soc., Omega Chi Epsilon, Beta Gamma Sigma. Avocations: sailing, photography, skiing. Home and Office: 3525 Del Mar Hts Rd 285 San Diego CA 92130-2122 Office Phone: 858-775-0098. Business E-Mail: achatroo@san.rr.com.

CHATT-ELLIS, ALLEN BARRETT, psychologist, neuroscientist; b. Phoenix, July 17, 1949; s. Arthur Beecher Ellis and Helen (Scheidt) Chatt; m. Gail Nancy Anguish, Aug. 21, 1971. *Dr. Chatt is a descendant of Lyman Beecher, Henry Ward Beecher and Harriet Beecher Stowe, clergy, novelists and abolitionists of the 19th century. He credits his mother and surrogates Bernice Cole of Batavia, New York, Bill Redmond and Matthew and Doris Kalicki of Stafford, New York with providing the values necessary to pursue a productive life. Finally, his wife, Gail has provided strength when it was most needed.* BS in Psychology with honors, SUNY, Buffalo, 1971; MS in Psychology, Fla. State U., 1974, PhD in Psychology and Neuroscience, 1978. Rsch. asst. Fla. State U., Tallahassee, 1971-76; predoctoral fellow in neuroanatomy U. Tex. Med. Br., Galveston, 1977; postdoctoral fellow in neurology sch. medicine Yale U., New Haven, 1978-80, rsch. asst. prof. neurology Sch. Medicine, 1981-87, rsch. assoc. prof., 1988—91, retirement scholars chair, 1991; rsch. psychologist VA Med. Ctr., West Haven, Conn., 1978-84, sr. rsch. psychologist, 1985-90, sr. rsch. psychologist disability retirement pension, 1991—; founder, exec. dir., consulting psychologist Phoenix Fund for Neurologically Challenged, New Haven, Tallahassee, 1991—. Grant reviewer NSF, 1982—, NIH, 1982—, VA, 1982—; vis. prof. neuroscience Beijing Normal U., 1987, U. Glasgow, 1994—95; neuroscience reviewer Am. Psychol. Soc. Convs., 1991—; psychol. cons., case mgr. neurologically impaired; pvt. funding neurol. rsch.; courtesy prof. movement scis. Fla. State U., 1999—. *Before injuries from an automobile accident forced his disability retirement in 1991, Dr. Chatt was engaged in biomedical research at Yale University which revealed insights into the neuronal circuitry involved in the onset, spread and potential pharmacologic and surgical control of epilepsy. For this body of work, he was nominated (with J.S. Ebersole, M.D.)for the Nobel Prize for Physiology and Medicine in 1988 and 1989.Currently, he is founder and executive director of The Phoenix Fund, a privately endowed philanthropic organization committed to the support of neuroscience research, training, education, financial assistance to individuals with special needs and community outreach. He is also a consulting psychologist for the Fund. He was recently re-appointed Courtesy Professor of Movement Science at Florida State University after serving as Courtesy Eminent scholar since 2003.* Contbr. chapters to books, articles articles to profl. jours.; mem. editl. rev. bd. Brain Rsch., 1983—86, Exptl. Neurology, 1982—86, mem. editl. bd. Exptl. Brain Rsch., 1984—88, Quar. Jour. Exptl. Physiology, 1986. Sponsor Bobby Bowden Classic Fellowship Christian Athletes, 1992—, Bill Campbell Challenge Children's Miracle Network, 1996—99; mem. devel. bd. Sandels Fund Excellence Coll. Human Scis., Fla. State U., 1999—; bd. dirs. Wal-Mart/Children's Miracle Network, No. Fla., 1996—99, Jennifer Harrison Fund, 1995—; judge Sam Walton Cmty. Leadership Scholarship Program, 1998—99, Phoenix Fund Grad. Fellowship Human Scis., 2003—; sponsor Jennifer Harrison Meml. Golf Tournament, 1991—2000, Freedom Scholarship Batavia HS Class 1965, 1992—, Camp Sunshine, 1992—, Goodspeed Opera Ho., 1995—, Fla. State U. Seminole Classic, 1998—2000, Boy's Town Invitational N. Fla., 1998—2000, Phoenix Fund Scholarship Applied Biomedical Undergraduate Study, 1999—; mem. Rep. Senatorial Inner Cir., Washington, 1985, Eisenhower Commn., 1995; life mem. Rep. Nat. Com., 1993—; mem. adv. bd. Ellingsworth Press, 1998—. Recipient Most Sr. Benefactor award, Children's Miracle Network, 1996—99, Gold Miracle Maker award, 1998, Platinum Miracle Maker award, 1999; Regents scholar, N.Y. State, 1965—69, VoReHab scholar, 1965—71, Rsch. grantee, VA, 1978—91, NIH, 1982—87. Mem.: AAAS, Soc. Pain Practice Mgmt., Am. Epilepsy Soc., Soc. Neuroscience, Epilepsy Found. Am., Am. Psychol. Soc., Yale Neurology Alumni Assn. (charter), Fla. State U.'s Pres.'s Club. Republican. Achievements include development of neurosurgical procedure increasing the effectiveness of stellate ganglion blocks for the treatment of relfex sympathetic dystrophy in humans; discovery of differential neuronal circuits involved in focal and secondarily generalized seizure activity in neocortical model of epilepsy; brain cells that become abnormal initially in focal and secondarily generalized seizure activity; mid brain neuronal circuits modulating pain; thermal evoked potential in humans and the localization of cortical cells responsive to pain. Home: 699 Goose Ln PO Box 1449 Guilford CT 06437-0549 also: 2949 Golden Eagle Dr E Tallahassee FL 32312-4008

CHATTERJEE, ANINDYA, economist, researcher; b. Uttarpara, West Bengal, India, June 25, 1969; s. Kedar Nath and Sulekha Chatterjee; m. Tahiti Roy; 1 child, Aahana. MA, Delhi Sch. Econ., India, 1992, Tulane U., 1994; MS, Claremont Grad. U., 2001. Economist Smith New Ct. Securities (IIT InvesTrust), Bombay, Maharashtra, 1994—95, HSBC James Capel B&K, Bombay, 1995—96, NatWest Markets, Singapore, 1996—98; head rsch. ANZ Investment Bank, Bombay, 1998—2000; market strategist, Asia IDEAGlobal, NYC, 2001—04; economist, strategist Bear Stearns, Hong Kong, 2004—06; ptnr. Boutique Investment Bank, InSite Equity, 2006; head, Asia equity rsch. Jefferies & Co., 2006—. Adv. bd. mem. Flowering Tree Inc. Hindu. Avocations: painting, swimming, tennis.

CHATTERJEE, JAYANTA, architecture and planning educator; b. Calcutta, India, Mar. 19, 1936; arrived in US, 1959; s. Hari Charan and Asha (Mukherjee) Chatterjee; m. Janet Ley Smith, Aug. 31, 1968; children: Eric, Brinda. BArch, Indian Inst. Tech., 1958; AA, Arch. Assn. Sch. Arch., 1959; M in Regional Planning, U. NC, 1962; MArch in Urban Design, Harvard U., 1965. Asst. prof. U. of Cin., 1967-72, assoc. prof., 1972-77, assoc. dean, 1975-77, prof., 1977—, dir. sch. planning, 1977-82, acting dean, 1982-83, dean, 1982-2001, prof. arch. and planning, 2001—. Regional designer Met. Area Planning Commn., Boston, 1965—67; urban scholar Cities Recovery Program, Cleve., 1981—82. Co-author: The Partnership Planning, 1982, Rebuilding American Cities, 1983, Breaking the Boundaries, 1989; co-editor/founder: Jour. Planning, Education and Research, 1981-84. Mem. Ohio Eminent Scholar Rev. Panel, 1985, Urban Design Rev. Bd., Cin., 1988—; chmn. design review bd. U. Cin., 1987—; mem. historic conservation bd. City of Cin., 2004—; bd. dirs. Arts Consortium, Cin., 1983—87, Contemporary Arts Ctr., Cin., 1983—, Hillside Trust, Cin., 1983—84, Bethesda Hosp., Inc., Cin., 1982—95, Total Living Concept, Inc., Cin., 1976—88, Ctr. Mediation of Disputes, Cin., 1989—92, The Emery Ctr., Cin., 1988—90, Better Housing League, Cin., 1989—92, Archtl. Found., Cin., 1990—, pres., 2003—05; bd. dirs. Season Found. for Good Govt., 2003—, pres., 2004—06. Recipient Apple award Archtl. Fedn. Cin., 1996, Disting. Alumnus award U. N.C., 1996, Disting. Svc. award Assn. Coll. Schs. of Planning, 1991. Fellow Am. Inst. Cert. Planners (editl. bd. AICP Casebook 1991-93, tech. adv. bd. 1993-96); mem. AIA (assoc.; Thomas Jefferson award pub. arch. 2000), Am. Planning Assn. (pres. Ohio chpt. 1970-72, editorial adv. bd. Jour. APA), Ptnrs. of Ams. (Ohio-Parana), Assn. Collegiate Schs. of Planning (pres. 1983-85, Jay Chatterjee award 1998), Internat. Coun. Fine Arts Deans, Cin. Post/Corbett Found. (Lifetime achievement award in Arts 1999). Office: U Cin Coll of Design Architecture Art and Planning PO Box 210016 Cincinnati OH 45221-0016 Office Phone: 513-556-1204. Office Fax: 513-556-3288. Business E-Mail: jay.chatterjee@uc.edu.

CHATTERJEE, SHARMILA, marketing educator; arrived in US, 1986, naturalized; d. Sunil N. and Pronoti Chatterjee; m. Arup K. Chakraborty, July 8, 1992; 1 child, Meenakshi. PhD in Mktg., U. Pa., 1994. Asst. prof. Fairfield U., Conn., 1995—98, Golden Gate U., San Francisco, 1998—2000, assoc. prof., chair dept. mktg., 2000—, Nagel T. Miner prof. bus., 2004—, prof., 2005—. Vis. prof. MIT Sloan Sch. Mgmt., 2006—. Contbr. articles to profl. jours. Mem.: Informs, Am. Mktg. Assn. (mgr. collegiate activities San Francisco chpt. 1998—). Avocations: reading, music. Office: 1 Amherst St E40-166 A Cambridge MA 02142 Office Phone: 617-253-8214. Business E-Mail: schatterjee@mit.edu.

CHATTERJI, DEBAJYOTI, retired manufacturing executive; b. Puri, India, Aug. 4, 1944; came to U.S., 1967, naturalized, 1980; s. Kumud Chandra and Mrinmoyee (Mukherji) C.; m. Smee Banerjee, July 11, 1968; children: Ananya, Kooheli, Miabi. BS with honors, Utkal U., India, 1963; B in Metall. Engring., Indian Inst. Tech., Kharagpur, India, 1966; MS, Purdue U., 1968, PhD, 1971. Vis. scientist Wright-Patterson AFB, Ohio, 1971-73; with R & D Ctr., Gen. Electric Co., Schenectady, 1973-83, mgr. electrochemistry br., 1975-79; mgr. Chem. Systems and Tech. Lab., 1979-80, Inorganic Materials and Structures Lab., 1980-83; v.p. tech. affairs The BOC Group, Inc., Murray Hill, NJ, 1983-89, chef exec. tech. activities, 1990, mng. dir. tech., 1990-99. Bd. dirs. The BOC Group, plc., Indsl. Rsch. Inst.; vis. prof. Lehigh U., 1999-2000; pres. Far Hills Group Inc. Chmn. editl. bd. Rsch. and Tech. Mgmt.; mem. editl. bd. R & D Mgmt.; contbr. articles to profl. jours.; patentee in field. Bd. dirs. BOC Found. for Environment, Imperial Coll., London; trustee Ananda Mandir, Inc. Recipient Disting. Engring. Alumnus award Purdue U., 1987, Maurice Holland award Ind. Rsch. Inst.; Disting. fellow Indian Inst. Mgmt., Calcutta; indsl. fellow Ctr. for Innovation Mgmt. Studies, NC State U. Mem. Internat. Assn. Mgmt. of Tech. (adv. bd.). Office: The BOC Group 100 Mountain Ave New Providence NJ 07974-2069

CHATTERTON, RAYMOND EDWARD, economics educator; b. Springfield, Mo., July 27, 1946; s. David Paul and Fern Katherine (Stotts) C.; children: Paul Allen, Robert Emerson, Douglas Howard. BA, SW Mo. State Coll., 1968; PhD, Washington State U., 1980. Lic. comml. pilot. Asst. prof. econs. Randolph-Macon Woman's Coll., Lynchburg, Va., 1975-80; assoc. prof. Lock Haven (Pa.) U., 1982-88, prof., 1988—. Vis. prof. Marie-Curie Sklodowska U., Lublin, Poland, 1988, Chernitsvi (USSR) State U., 1990, Kemerovo (Russia) State U., 1994. Capt. AUS, 1968-71, Vietnam. H.L. Mednick Found. grantee, Lynchburg, Va., 1976. Mem. Am. Econs. Assn. Avocations: tennis, chess, flying, scuba diving.

CHATTERTON, ROBERT TREAT, JR., reproductive endocrinology educator; b. Catskill, NY, Aug. 9, 1935; s. Robert Treat and Irene (Spoor) Chatterton; m. Patricia A. Holland, June 24, 1956 (div. 1965); children: Ruth Ellen, William Matthew, James Daniel; m. Astrida J. Vanags, June 4, 1966 (div. 1977); 1 child, Derek Scott; m. Carol J. Lewis, May 24, 1985. BS, Cornell U., 1958, PhD, 1963; MS, U. Conn., 1959. Postdoctoral fellow Med. Sch. Harvard U., 1963-65; rsch. assoc. div. oncology Inst. Steroid Rsch. Montefiore Hosp. and Med. Ctr., NYC, 1965-70; asst. prof. Coll. Medicine U. Ill., 1970-72, assoc. prof. Coll. Medicine, 1972-79; prof. Med. Sch. Northwestern U., Chgo., 1979—. Mem. sci. adv. com. AID, chairperson Instnl. Rev. Bd. Northwestern U., 1982—83, mem. intellectual properties com., 1987—95, chairperson radiation safety com., 2000—02; dir. Immunoassay Facility, R. H. Lurie Cancer Ctr. Northwestern U. Med. Sch., 1997—; dir. clin. labs., dept. ob-gyn. Northwestern Med. Facutly Found., 1996—99, dir. shared clin. labs., 1999—. Contbr. articles to profl. jours. Grantee, NIH, 1972—90, 1995—2006, NSF, 1975, 1995—98, AID, 1971—86, Army Office Rsch., 1987—94. Mem.: AAAS, Am. Assn. Clin. Rsch., Am. Assn. Cancer Rsch., Chgo. Assn. Reproductive Endocrinologists (pres. 1987—88), Soc. Study Reproduction, Soc. Gynecologic Investigation, Endocrine Soc., Am. Chem. Soc., N.Y. Acad. Scis., Phi Kappa Phi, Sigma Xi. Presbyterian. Achievements include patents for method of totally suppressing ovarian follicular devel. and method of ovulation detection. Home: 6001 N Knox Ave Chicago IL 60646-5821 Office: Northwestern U Olson 8408 710 N Fairbanks Ct Chicago IL 60611-3015 Home Phone: 773-777-1311; Office Phone: 312-503-5272. Business E-Mail: chat@northwestern.edu.

CHATTMAN, RAYMOND CHRISTOPHER, association executive; b. San Rafael, Calif., Apr. 11, 1956; s. Raymond Rene Chattman and Virginia Mae (Kirkland) Robinson; m. Patti Lyn Barnard Chattman, Feb. 14, 1975 (div. 1977); m. Dawn Irene Russell Kilpatrick, Aug. 21, 1993 (div. 1998); children: Christian Paige, Bradley Charles Kilpatrick. BS, SUNY, Albany, 1988; MBA, Averett Coll., Danville, Va., 1995. Dir. planning, ops. Comms. Media Group Inc., Alexandria, Va., 1981; comms. mgr. ANPA Found., Reston, Va., 1982-84; graphics editor Times-Herald Record, Middletown, NY, 1984-85; editor employee comms. Washington Gas Light Co., 1985-86; exec. dir., CEO Soc. Newspaper Design, Reston, 1986-96; dir. comm. and outreach AIAA, Reston, 1996—2005; v.p. Am. Chiropractic Assn., Arlington, Va., 2005—06. Asst. coach Herndon Optimist Youth Football, Va., 1994, Herndon Youth Soccer, 1992. Served in US Army, 1974-81, Korea, Germany, USAR, 1981-90. Recipient Thomas Jefferson award Dept. Def., 1979, Keith L. Ware award Dept. Army, 1978, 83, 86, 87. Mem.: Am. Mgmt. Assn., Nat. Assn. Govt. Communicators (blue pencil award 1978), Am. Soc. Assn. Execs. (cert. assn. exec. 2005). Avocations: travel, reading, golf.

CHATZINOFF, HOWARD, lawyer; b. Bklyn., Feb. 25, 1952; m. Leslie Chatzinoff. BSE with honors, Princeton U., 1974; JD, U. Va., 1977. Bar: NY 1978. Mem. Weil, Gotshal & Manges, NYC, ptnr. Lawyers com. NYC2012. Planning com. Ray Garrett Jr. Corp. and Securities Law Inst. Northwestern U. Sch. Law; exec. com. bd. dirs. Pub. Edn. Needs Civic Involvement in Learning (PENCIL); exec. com. NYC Adv. Bd. Enterprise Found. Mem. ABA (corp., banking and bus. law sect., comm. law com. 1985—). Office: Weil Gotshal & Manges 767 5th Ave 10th Fl New York NY 10153-0119

CHAU, PIN PIN, bank executive; b. Hong Kong; d. Waihing Wong; m. Raymond Chau; 1 child, Christine. BA, Coe Coll., 1965; MA in Asian hist., Yale U., 1967; grad., Rutgers U. With Nat. Westminster Bank (now Fleet), 1970—87; chief lending officer United Orient Bank, NYC, 1987—88, COO, 1988—89, pres., CEO, 1989—93, The Summit Nat. Bank, Atlanta, 1993—; CEO Summit Bank Corp., Atlanta, 1999—. Bd. dirs. Consumer Credit Counseling Service; exec. com. Ga. Dept. Industry, Trade and Tourism, 1999—. Bd. dirs. Atlanta Coll. Arts; bd. councilors Carter Ctr. Mem.: Internat. Women's Forum, Soc. Internat. Bus. Fellows (assoc.). Avocation: painting. Office: Summit Bank Corp 4360 Chamblee-Dunwoody Rd Atlanta GA 30341

CHAU, WAI YIP, surgeon; b. Hong Kong, Aug. 19, 1970; m. Jessica Moncada, May 29, 1998; children: Jade Marie, Ariel Jessica. MD, St George's U. Sch. Medicine, Genada, West Indies, 1998. Cert. Am. Bd. Surgery, 2004. Bariatric fellow Hackensack U. Med. Ctr., NJ, 2003—04; bariatric surgeon U. Med. Ctr. Princeton, 2004—. Presenter in field. Contbr. articles to profl. jours. Recipient Glenn A Sanford Meml. award, North Oakland Med. Ctrs., 2003. Mem.: Am. Soc. Bariatric Surgeons. Home: 1 Eldridge Dr Robbinsville NJ 08691 Office: NJ Bariatrics Ste 1 4250 US Hwy 1 North Monmouth Junction NJ 08852 Home Phone: 609-223-0267; Office Phone: 732-274-3434. Office Fax: 732-274-3435.

CHAUDERLOT, FABIENNE-SOPHIE, foreign language educator; b. Marseilles, France, Aug. 11, 1960; came to U.S., 1985; d. Michel Hubert and Georgia Kalafatides. Maitrise English Lit., U. Scis. Humaines, Aix-en-Provence, France, 1982; MBA in Internat. Adminstrn., Puyricard, France, 1985; PhD, U. Calif., San Diego, 1995. Lectr. U. Calif., Riverside, 1995-96; asst. prof. U. P.R., Mayaguez, 1996-97, Wayne State U., Detroit, 1997-2000; with Veritas Software Internat. Strategies, 2000—. V.p. Alliance Francaise, San Diego, 1990-93; founder, pres. Femmes Francaises du Sud Calif., San Diego, 1989-93. Rsch. grantee Humanities Ctr., Detroit, 1997-98. Avocations: painting, piano, cats, aerobics, photography. Office: Wayne State U 487 Manoogian Hall Detroit MI 48202 E-mail: f.chauderlot@Wayne.edu.

CHAUDHARI, PRAVEEN, science administrator, materials physicist; b. Ludhiana, Punjab, India, Nov. 30, 1937; came to U.S., 1961; s. Hans Raj and Ved (Kumari) C.; m. Karin Romhild, June 13, 1964; children: Ashok, Pia. BS with honors, Indian Inst. Tech., Kharagpur, 1961; MS in Phys. Metallurgy, MIT, 1963, ScD in Phys. Metallurgy, 1966. Rsch. assoc. MIT, Cambridge, Mass., 1966; rsch. staff mem. IBM T.J. Watson Rsch. Ctr., Yorktown Heights, NY, 1966-70, mgr., 1970-80, dir. phys. scis., 1981-82, v.p. sci., dir. phys. scis., 1982-91, v.p. sci., tech. com., 1988-91, rsch. staff, 1991—2003; dir. Brookhaven Nat. Lab., Upton, NY, 2003—06. Exec. sec. Presdl. Com. on Super Conductivity, 1988; mem. Presdl. Commn. on Super Conductivity, 1989; chmn. U.S. Liaison Commn. to Internat. Union of Pure and Applied Physics; mem. com. on Physics for the Next Decade, sponsored by NRC/NAS, Nat. Critical Tech. panel; chmn. sci. coun. Internat. Ctr. for Theoretical Physics, Trieste, Italy; chmn. adv. coun. math. and phys. scis. NSF; mem. governing bd. NY State Inst. Superconductivity. Author of papers on mechanical properties and defects in crystalline solids, amorphous solids, quantum transport, superconductivity and magnetic monopoles and neutrino mass experiments. Recipient Harry C. Gatos prize MIT, 1994, Nat. Medal Tech., 1995, Excellence award US Pan Asian Amer. C. of C., Liebmann prize IEEE, 1992, George Pake award Am. Phys. Soc., 1987. Mem.: NAS (mem. governing bd. physics and astronomy), Am. Acad. Arts and Sci., Nat. Acad. Engring., Am. Inst. Physics (mem.-at-large governing bd.), NY Acad. Scis. (mem. governing bd.). Office: Brookhaven Nat Lab PO Box 5000 Upton NY 11973

CHAUDHARY, MOHAMMAD ASHRAF, biostatistician, researcher; b. Sialkot, Punjab, Pakistan, Dec. 20, 1955; PhD, U. NC, Chapel Hill, 1996. Asst. prof. Punjab U., Lahore, Pakistan, 1986—99; scientist, biostatistician King Faisal Specialist Hosp. and Rsch. Ctr., Riyadh, Saudi Arabia, 1999—2003; assoc. scientist, biostatistician Johns Hopkins Sch. Pub. Health, Balt., 2004—. Mem.: Internat. Biometric Soc., Am. Statis. Assn. Home: 6028 Signal Flame Ln Clarksville MD 21029-1299 Office: Johns Hopkins Sch Pub Health 615 N Wolfe St Baltimore MD 21205 Home Phone: 410-531-3295; Office Phone: 410-502-0741. Office Fax: 410-502-6733; Home Fax: 410-502-6733. Personal E-mail: chaudhary_ashraf@hotmail.com. Business E-Mail: mchaudha@jhsph.edu.

CHAUDHARY, SATVEER, state senator; b. June 12, 1969; BA, St. Olaf Coll., 1991; JD, U. Minn., 1995. Mem. Minn. Ho. Reps., 1996-2000, Minn. State Senate, 2000—, vice chair finance com., mem. capital investement, mem. judiciary environ. natural resources, transp., and state govt. budget divsn.; owner Chaudhary Cons. Law clk., intern Hennepin County Atty.'s Office, Minn.; aide Minn. Atty. Gen. Hubert H. Humphrey III. Co-chair Anoka County Legis. Delegation; hon. adv. coun. Asian-Pacific Endowment for Cmty. Devel.; mem. Coalition of Labor Union Women, Minn. Outdoor Heritage Alliance; hon. chair Minn. Cricket Assn.; mem. Minn. Welcome Com. for The Dalai Lama, U. Minn. Indsl. Rels. Adv. Coun., Twin Cities Internat. Citizen Award Com.; Fridley Human Resources Commn.; vol. Mounds View Festival in the Park; mem. New Brighton Hist. Soc., New Brighton Sportsmen's Club, Minn. Pheasants Forever Soc.; state affirmative action officer Minn. DFL Party; co-founder, chair Minn. Asian-Indian Dem. Assn.; bd. dirs. World Trade Ctr., St. Paul, A Blanket of Hope. Named Legislator of the Yr., Coll. Dems. of Minn., 1999; recipient Cert. of Commendation, Legal Aid Soc. of Minn., Cert. of Appreciation, DFL Party, 1995, Achievement award, Indian Assn. Minn. Mem.: New Brighton Eagles, Bass Anglers Soc. Am., Columbia Hts. Lions. Dfl. First Asian Indian sen. in Am. history and first Asian-Am. mem. of Minn. legis. Office: Minn Senate 75 Rev Dr Martin Luther King Jr Blvd Saint Paul MN 55155 E-mail: sen.satveer.chaudhary@senate.mn.

CHAUDHRI, JAVADE, lawyer, utilities executive; b. Nairobi, Kenya, Apr. 30, 1952; BS, Yale U., 1975, MS, 1977; JD, Georgetown U., 1980. Bar: DC 1980, Calif. 2000. Atty. Surrey & Morse, Washington, 1980—86; ptnr. Jones, Day, Reavis & Pogue (merger with Surrey & Morse), Washington, 1986—93; sr. ptnr. Winston & Strawn, Washington, 1993—99; v.p. law, dep. gen. counsel Gateway, Poway, Calif., 1999—2001, sr. v.p., gen. counsel, 2001—03; exec. v.p., gen. counsel Sempra Energy, San Diego, 2003—. Vis. faculty mem. Internat. Devel. Law Inst., Rome, Internat. Law Inst., Washington. Mem.: ABA, Internat. Bar Assn., DC Bar. Office: Sempra Energy 101 Ash St San Diego CA 92101-3017*

CHAUHAN, ASHOK KUMAR, medical educator; b. Village-Lath, Haryana, India, May 7, 1962; s. Shyam Chand and Chand Kaur; m. Pushpa Dahiya; children: Mallika, Malini Singh. MBBS, Postgraduate Inst. Med. Scis., Rohtak, Haryana, India, 1986; MD, Postgraduate Inst. Med. Scis., 1992. Prof. dept. radiotherapy, Postgrad. Inst. Med. Scis., 2006—07, sr. prof., head radiotherapy II, 2007—. Recipient Best Article award, Postgrad. Inst. Med. Scis., 1998. Achievements include research in radiations in the benign conditions of musculoseketal diseases. Home: 4 / 8 J Haryana Rohtak 124001 India Office: Postgrad Inst Med Sci Haryana Rohtak 124001 India Office Fax: 911262213432; Home Fax: 911262213432. Personal E-mail: drchauhanashok@yahoo.co.in.

CHAULET, (FRÉDÉRIQUE) EMMANUELLE, performing company executive, actress, educator, writer; b. La Rochelle, France, Mar. 4, 1962; d. Lucien Chaulet and Nanou Chaulet-Rigolage; m. Jean-Pierre Jacques Rousset, July 9, 2005; 1 child, Lukas Jefferson Willoughby. Degree, Paris Grad. Sch. of Bus./ESCP, 1983; student, Lee Strasberg Inst., NYC, 1988—89. Cert. RYSE III practitioner, energy awareness counselor Spa Tech Inst./Polarity Realization Inst., Ipswich, Mass. and Portland, Maine. Rsch. cons. Ministry of Culture, Paris, 1984; asst. to exec. dir. Celebration Barn Theatre, South Paris, Maine, 1993—94; exec. and artistic dir. Deertrees Theatre and Cultural Ctr., Harrison, Maine, 1993—96; arts events dir. U. So. Maine, Theatre and Sch. of Music, Gorham, 1994—; artistic dir., founder, pres. Two Lights Theatre Ensemble, Portland, Maine, 2001—05; dir., owner, founder Starlight Acting Inst., Gorham, 2003—; founder Energize! a holistic approach to acting. Pres. of jury Que. Film Festival, Quebec City, Canada, 1990; mem. jury Dunkerque Film Festival, France. Actor: (films) Boyfriends and Girlfriends, Chocolat, Je T'ai Dans La Peau, Multiple Futures, All the Vermeers in New York, I Want to Go Home, The Girl Who Would be Russian, Sundowning; (plays) A Little Cut (Une petite Entaille), A Rose Under The Skin, Bal Trap; dir.: The Marriage Proposal and The Brute, Miss Julie, The Maids, A Taste of Killing on the Tip of The Tongue, Rest Stop, Endurance, Phaedra, El Cid au Flamenco, (theatre play) Africa/Portland; transl., dir.: plays La Promise (Xavier Durringer), Music Hall (Jean-Luc Lagarce). Bd. dirs. Maine Performing Arts Network, Portland, 2003—05. Named Guest of Honor, Venice Film Festival, 1988, New Caledonia Film Festival, 1989, London Film Festival; Fulbright scholar, Franco Am. Commn., Paris, 1988—89. Office: U So Maine-Theatre Dept 37 College Ave Gorham ME 04038 Home Phone: 207-671-7890; Office Phone: 207-780-5146. Fax: 207-780-5005. Business E-Mail: chaulet@usm.maine.edu. E-mail: energize@starlightacting.org.

CHAVARRIA, ADAM, federal agency administrator; BA, MPA, U. Minn. V.p. SER-Jobs for Progress, Dallas; exec. dir. Hispanic Coll. Fund (HCF), Washington; assoc. dir. White House Initiative on Ednl. Excellence for Hispanic Americans, US Dept. Edn., Washington, 2001—03, exec. dir., 2003—. Mem. US Senate Rep. Conf. Task Force on Hispanic Affairs Adv. Com., 1991—. Mem.: Dallas Assn. Mexican Am. Profls., Dallas Hispanic C. of C. Office: US Dept Edn 400 Maryland Ave, SW Washington DC 20202 Office Phone: 202-401-8377.*

CHAVE, CAROL, arbitrator, retired lawyer; b. Chgo., Jan. 30, 1948; d. Grant Carruthers and Priscilla Morrison (Shaw) C.; m. Robert Edmund Hand; children: Joshua, Chloe, Robert, Grant. BA, U. Chgo., 1970; MAT, Oakland U., 1971; JD, Loyola U., Chgo., 1976. Bar: Ill. 1976, N.Y. 1980. Tchr. corps intern Pontiac (Mich.) Pub. Schs., 1970-71; sec., receptionist Grad. Sch. Bus., U. Chgo., 1971; counselor Sonia Shankman Orthogenic Sch., Chgo., 1972; pvt. practice Chgo., 1976-78; asst. v.p., assoc. counsel Bank of Tokyo, NYC, 1978-85; substitute tchr. N.Y.C. Pub. Schs., 1986-88; with Breckenridge Law Offices, 1986-88; sr. v.p., counsel, mgr. human resources Tokai Bank, NYC, 1988-97; dir., counsel Deutsche Bank, NYC, 1997-99; arbitrator Internat. Ctr. for Dispute Resolution, NYC, 2001—. Arbitrator Am. Arbitration Assn., NYC, 1986—. Vol. lawyer Chgo. Vol. Legal Svcs., 1977-78; designer playground PS 41 Parent Assn., Greenwich Village, N.Y., 1987. Avocations: weaving, dance. Personal E-mail: chavec@gmail.com.

CHAVERS, BLANCHE MARIE, pediatrician, educator, researcher; b. Clarksdale, Miss., Aug. 2, 1949; d. Andrew and Mildred Louise C.; m. Gubare Mpambara, May 21, 1982; 1 child, Kaita. BS in Zoology, U. Wash., 1971, MD, 1975. Diplomate Am. Bd. Pediats. Intern U. Wash., Seattle, 1975-76, resident in pediatrics, 1976-78; instr. U. Minn., Mpls., 1982, asst. prof. pediatrics, 1983-90, assoc. prof. pediatrics, 1990-99, prof. pediatrics, 1999—. Attending physician dept. pediatrics, U. Minn. Sch. Medicine, Mpls., 1982. Co-editor: Am. Jour. Kidney Diseases, 2001—; contbr. articles to profl. jours. Recipient Clin. Investigator award NIH, 1982; Pediatric Nephrology fellow U. Minn., 1978-81. Mem. Am. Soc. Nephrology, Am. Soc. Pediatric Nephrology, Internat. Soc. Nephrology, Internat. Soc. Pediatric Nephrology, Am. Soc. Transplantation, Internat. Pediatric Transplant Assn. Democrat. Methodist. Avocations: tennis, reading, collecting African artifacts, art. Office: Univ Minn MMC 491 420 Delaware St SE Minneapolis MN 55455-0348

CHAVES, JOSE MARIA, diplomat, lawyer, foundation administrator, educator; b. Bogotá, Colombia, Aug. 19, 1922; s. Carlos Chaves and María García de C.; m. Elena Gómez y Samperio; children: Cristina María, Tomás José. Bachiller, Bogotá, 1939, cert. in anthropology, 1942, JD, 1945; DSc (hon.), U. Antióquia, 1948; MA, Columbia U., NYC, 1951, PhD, 1953; LLD, U. Popayán, Colombia, 1957, Mercy Coll., Dobbs Ferry, NY, 1991. Bar: Columbia 1944, InterAmerican 1953. Editor in chief Revista Colegio del Rosario (arts and letters mag.), Colombia, 1944; gen. legal duties specializing in public adminstrn. Bogotá, 1942-45; instr. Romance langs. Columbia U., NYC, 1945-48, 50-51; founder, 1st dean faculty U. Andes, Bogotá, 1948-49; head area studies Queens Coll. NYU, 1951-53; counselor Colombian Embassy, Washington, 1953-55; prof. internat. law U. Colombia, 1955-58, U. Paris, 1957; guest prof. internat. law and relations Brit. Council, various univs. Eng., Scotland, 1957; dir., chief exec. Am. Found. for Cultural Popular Action, Inc. (pvt. internat. orgn. for mass edn. by radio), NYC, 1958—; amb. of Kyrgyzstan to UN, 1992—. Dir. Center Latin Am. Studies, CUNY; chmn. Hispanic Am. editorial bd. Grolier, Inc., 1971—; ambassador extraordinary, permanent del. Iberoam. Bur. Edn. to UN; A.E. and P., permanent rep. Grenada to OAS; permanent rep. orgn. Iberoam. Countries to UN and OAS, 1986—; alt. gov. World Bank and Internat. Monetary Fund, 1974-77, 94; chmn. C.I.P., 1972—; organizer, dir. tech. assistance mission Unitarian Service Com. in Latin Am.; dir. gen. Nat. Univ. Fund, Colombia, 1955-58; amb. extraordinary Spl. Mission to Brazil, 1995. Editor-in-chief: Grolier Spanish Universal Ency; author: Chaves Plan for settlement religious conflict between Caths. and Protestants in Latin Am; Author: Francisco de Vitoria. Founder International Law, 1945, Intergroup relations in the Spain of Cervantes, 1953, University Reform in Colombia, 1957. Pres. Assn. Latin Am. Unity, 1984; chmn. Summit Coun. World Peace, 1985-92; ambassador extraordinary and plenipotentiary of Kyrgyztan to the UN, 1992-93; ambassador to Brasilia, 1995. Decorated Legion of Honor (France); gran cruz Order of St. Constantine the Great; comdr., knight comdr. Grand Order Isabel La Católica (Spain); knight comdr. Alfonso El Sabio; grand cross Vasco N'nez de Balboa Panama, 1970; grand cross Juan P. Duarte Sanchez y Mella Dominican Republic, 1970, Medal of Jerusalem Israel, 1972; grand cross Order of Malta, 1976; grand cross Order Justice Law and Peace of Mex., 1977, grand cross Order Latin Am. Unity 1986, grand cross Order of St. Michael (Portugal), 1990; grand cross Order of Holy Cross of Jerusalem, 1991, grand cross of Saint Dennis of Zanthe, 1991; recipient medaglia universitaria U. Po Deo, Rome, 1957, medalla de los Andes U., 1958, medaille de Versailles, France, 1990, medalla Universidad, Lima, 1990, Lord Perry World prize for Edn., 1993, Order of Manas of Kyrgyzstan 1995. Mem. Internat. Law Assn., Inter-Am. Bar. Assn., Acad. Polit. Sci., MLA, Academia Hispano Americana, Assn. for Latin Am. Unity (founder, pres. 1984), Summit Coun. for World Peace (dir. 1987), Met. Club, Columbia U. Club (NYC), Quill Club USA (pres.), Brook Club, Phi Delta Kappa (v.p. Univ. World). Clubs: Metropolitan, Brook, Columbia U. (NYC), Quill of U.S.A. (pres.). Home: 118 E 60th St New York NY 10022-1103 Office: 401 5th Ave New York NY 10016-3317 *Faith in God is also faith in man. Service of man is also service of God. As we enter a new period of peace in the world, our faith can sustain our peace building efforts and help create a better life for all mankind.*

CHAVES-CARBALLO, ENRIQUE, neuropediatrician; b. San Jose, Costa Rica, Dec. 2, 1936; arrived in U.S., 1955, arrived in Saudi Arabia, 1996; s. Enrique Chaves and Celina Carballo; m. Vilma Irene Peralta, Aug. 26, 1961; children: Antonio, Maria, Miguel, Karen. MD, U. Okla., 1963. Diplomate Am. Bd. Psychiatry and Neurology, Am. Bd. Pediatrics. Prof. pediatrics and neurology Ea. Va. Med. Sch., Norfolk, 1979-89, U. Kans., Kansas City, 1990-94; chief pediatric neurology King Faisal Specialist Hosp. and Rsch. Ctr., Riyadh, Saudi Arabia, 1996—2002; fellow pediatrics Mayo Clinic, 1964—67, fellow neurology, 1972—75; clin. prof. pediatrics U. of Kans., Kans. City, 2003; clin. prof. hist. medicine U. Kans., Kans. City, Kans., 2004. Author: The Tropical World of Samuel Taylor Darling, 2007; contbr. articles to profl. jours., chapters to books; reviewer numerous jours. Recipient award Am. Neurol. Assn.; fgn. scholar Wesleyan U., 1955; grantee Rockefeller Archives, 1979. Fellow Am. Acad. Neurology; mem. Am. Assn. Hist. Medicine, Costa Rica Assn. Neuroscis. (hon.), Child Neurology Soc., Internat. Child Neurology Soc., Iberoam. Acad. Pediat. Neurology, Profs. Child Neurology, Soc. for Study of Inborn Errors of Metabolism, Soc. for Inherited Metabolic Disorders. Achievements include research in Reye syndrome, history of medicine and inborn errors of metabolism. E-mail: echaves17@hotmail.com.

CHAVEZ, BRENDA G., construction executive, real estate agent; d. Walter Samuel and Edythe Carleen (Campbell) Todd; children: Regena Bean, Tamara Keeton, Lacey. BS in Bus. Mgmt. cum laude, Northwood U., 1992; MBA, U. Tex., 1994. Lic. real estate agt. Pres. Lone Star Model and Talent Agy., Inc., Houston, 1979—81, Total Rep Inc., Houston, 1982—85; sales mgr. MCN Constrn., Houston, 1982—90; pres., CEO Chavez Constrn. Co., Houston, 1991—. Owner, founder, dir. NBA Houston Rockets Cheerleaders, 1980—82, Second Bapt. H.S. Drill Team, Houston, 1984—86; bd. dirs. Houston Minority Bus. Coun., Hispanic Contractor's Assn., Houston Texans Hispanic Adv. Coun. Named Ms. Tex., 2004, Ms. Tex. UN, 2005. Mem.: Mexican Am. Contractors Assn. (founder, exec. dir. 2002—), Profl. Cheerleaders Alumni Assn. (founder, exec. dir. 1995—). Avocations: weight training, ballroom dancing, jogging, decorating. Home: 11215 Marseilles Ln Houston TX 77082 Office: Chavez Service Cos 11201 Richmond Ave Ste 111-A Houston TX 77802 Office Phone: 281-493-3900. Office Fax: 281-493-3902. Personal E-mail: xprocheerldr@yahoo.com. Business E-Mail: bchavez@chavezservicecompanies.com.

CHAVEZ, EDWARD L., state supreme court justice; b. Santa Fe, Oct. 15, 1957; BA in Pers. Mgmt. with honors, Eastern New Mexico U., 1978; JD, New Mexico Sch. of Law, 1981. Bar: N.Mex 1981. Ptnr. Carpenter & Chavez, Ltd.; assoc. justice N. Mex. Supreme Ct., Santa Fe, 2003—07, chief justice, 2007—. Spl. counsel N.Mex Disciplinary Bd., 1987—95; lectr. Nat. Inst. Trial Advocacy, 1998—99; adj. prof. U. N.Mex; chmn. disciplinary bd. Supreme Ct. N.Mex. Mem. Ctr. Civic Values; trustee U. N.Mex Mental Health Ctr., 1989; mem. Task Force Regulation Lawyer Advt., 1990. Fellow: Internat. Acad. Trial Lawyers, Am. Coll. Trial Lawyers; mem.: ATLA (minority del.), Hispanic Nat. Bar Assn., N.Mex. Hispanic Bar Assn., Am. Inns Ct., Trial Lawyers Pub. Justice, State Bar N.Mex, N.Mex Trial Lawyers Assn. (feature editor newsletter 1987—90, bd. dirs. 1990—, pres. 1997—98), Nat. Spinal Cord Injury Assn. Office: NMex Supreme Ct Box 848 Santa Fe NM 87504

CHAVEZ, ERIC, professional baseball player; b. LA, Dec. 7, 1977; Third base Oakland Athletics, 1998—. Recipient Am. League Gold Glove Award, 2001—05. Office: Oakland Athletics Net Assoc Coliseum 7000 Coliseum Way Oakland CA 94621

CHAVEZ, J. ANTHONY, lawyer; b. Auburn, Calif., Oct. 5, 1955; s. Marco Antonio and Barbara Ann (Lawrence) Chavez-Rivas; m. Terry Leavitt-Chavez. BA, U. Calif., Santa Barbara, 1977; JD, Stanford U., 1981. Bar: Calif. 1981, Tex. 1982, US Dist. Ct. (so. and no. dists.) Calif. 1982, (cen. dist.) Calif. 1983, US Dist. Ct. (so. dist.) Tex. 1982, (we. dist.) Tex. 1983, (no. dist.) Tex. 1991, NY 1986, US Dist. Ct. (ea. and so. dists.) NY 1986, US Supreme Ct. 1986. With legal dept. Exxon Co. U.S.A., Houston, 1981-85, NYC, 1985-86; assoc. gen. counsel Sybron Corp., Saddlebrook, NJ, 1986-88, Crown Equipment Corp., New Bremen, Ohio, 1989-90; trial atty. Exxon Co. U.S.A., Houston, 1990-92; counsel complex litigation Exxon Chem. Co., Houston, 1992-95; counsel internat. oil and gas exploration Exxon Exploration Co., Houston, 1995-96; counsel antitrust, mergers and acquisitions Exxon Chem. Co., Houston, 1996-2000; counsel intellectual property licensing ExxonMobil Chem. Co., Baytown, Tex., 2000—04, Univation Technologies, 2004—. Presenter numerous legal edn. seminars and programs. Contbr. articles to profl. jours. Mentor Ft. Bend Ind. Sch. Dist., 1998, Houston Bar Assn., 1998. Chancellor's scholar U. Calif., 1976; Univ. Svc. award for dist. svc. to campus cmty. U. Calif., Santa Barbara, 1977. Fellow Houston Bar Found.; mem. ABA (antitrust sect., vice chair corp. counseling com. 1998-2000, vice chair intellectual property com. 2000-03, vice chair Sherman Act sect. 2 com. 2003-06, vice-chair Listserve 2006-, mem. long range planning com. 2006—), Houston Bar Assn. (chair antitrust and trade regulation sect., 1997-98, vice-chair 1996-97, sec.-treas. 1995-96, coun. 1993-95). Republican. Avocations: hiking, theater, travel. Home: 4908 Cedar St Bellaire TX 77401 Office: Univation Technologies LLC 5555 San Felipe Rd Houston TX 77056-2723 Office Phone: 713-892-3779. Business E-Mail: achavez@univation.com.

CHAVEZ, JEANETTE, editor; BS in Journalism, U. Colo., 1973. Mem. staff Office of U.S. Rep. Spark Matsunaga, Washington; reporter Colorado Springs (Colo.) Sun, 1973—74; reporter, copy desk chief, city editor, news editor Ft. Collins (Colo.) Coloradoan, 1974—81; copy editor Daily Herald, Arlington Heights, Ill., 1981—82; copy editor, then news editor bus. sect. Chgo. Sun Times, 1982—84; dep. news editor Denver Post, 1984—86, news editor, 1987—88, asst. mng. editor, 1988—91, assoc. editor features, 1991—97, mng. editor, 1997—. Office: Denver Post 101 W Colfax Ave Denver CO 80202

CHAVEZ, JOHN RICHARD, historian, educator; b. Pasadena, Calif., Jan. 12, 1949; s. Manuel and Andrea (Quiroz) Chavez; m. Lorena Jeanne Poirier, Aug. 11, 1984; children: Monica Antonia, David Mario. BA in English, Calif. State U., LA, 1971, MA in English, 1972, BA in Spanish, 1975; MA in Am. Culture, U. Mich., Ann Arbor, 1978, PhD in Am. Culture, 1980. Lectr. Calif. State U., LA, 1980-81, Long Beach, 1981-84; vis. asst. prof. program in Am. culture U. Mich., Ann Arbor, 1984-86; asst. prof. dept. history Tex. A&M U., College Station, 1986-89; assoc. prof. history So. Meth. U., Dallas, 1989-97, prof., 1997—. Fulbright lectr., Spain, 2001. Author: The Lost Land: The Chicano Image of the Southwest, 1984 (nominated Pulitzer prize, 1984), Eastside Landmark: A History fo the East LA Community Union, 1998; contbr. articles to profl. jours. Mem.: Tex. State Hist. Assn., Orgn. Am. Historians, Western History Assn., Nat. Assn. Chicano Studies, Am. Studies Assn. Democrat. Roman Catholic. Office: So Meth U Dept History Dallas TX 75275-0176 Business E-Mail: jchavez@smu.edu.

CHAVEZ, LINDA, civil rights organization executive; b. Albuquerque, June 17, 1947; m. Christopher Gersten Chavez; 3 children. BA, U. Colo., 1970; postgrad., UCLA, 1970-72, U. Md., 1974-75. Mem. staff House Judiciary Subcom. on Civil and Constl. Rights, Washington, 1972-74; asst. dir. legis. Am. Fedn. Tchrs., 1975—77; cons. civil rights sect. Office Mgmt. and Budget, Washington, 1977; editor Am. Educator mag., 1977-83; asst. to pres. Am. Fedn. Teachers, 1982—83; staff dir. U.S. Commn. on Civil Rights, 1983-85; dep. asst. to pres. and dir. Office Pub. Liaison Exec. Office of Pres., 1985-86; US Senate candidate Md., 1986; chmn. Nat. Commn. Migrant Edn., 1988—92; mem. UN Subcommission on prevention of discrimination and protection of minorities, 1992—96; founder, pres. Ctr. for Equal Opportunity, Washington, 1995—, Stop Union Polit. Abuse, 2001—; founder, chmn. Rep. Issues Campaign, 2003—. Bd. dirs. ABM Industries, Inc.; polit. analyst FOX News Channel; Pres. George Bush's nominee for Sec. Labor until she withdrew her name from consideration, 2001. Author: Out of the Barrio: Toward a New Politics of Hispanic Assimilation, 1991, An Unlikely Conservative: The Transformation of an Ex-Liberal, 2002; syndicated weekly columnist Chgo. Tribune; freelance columnist Wall St. Jour., Washington Post, The New Republic, Commentary, Crisis; appeared on To the Contrary, CNN & Co., Equal Time, The McNeil-Lehrer News Hour; host (radio show) Linda Chavez Show. Bd. dirs. Campaign to Prevent Teen Pregnancy. Recipient Living Legend award, Libr. of Congress, 2000. Mem.: Coun. Fgn. Rels. (co-chair com. on diversity 1998—2000). Office: Ctr for Equal Opportunity 14 Pidgeon Hill Dr Ste 500 Sterling VA 20165-6151

CHAVEZ, MARTIN JOSEPH, mayor, lawyer; b. Albuquerque, Mar. 2, 1952; s. Lorenzo Armijo and Sara (Baca) C.; m. Margaret Aragon de Chavez, July 29, 1988; children: Martinique, Ezequiel Lorenzo. BS, U. N.Mex., 1975; JD, Georgetown U., 1978. Staff asst. U.S. Senate, Washington, 1976-77; dep. dir. LULAC Nat. Scholarship Fund, Washington, 1977-78; law clk. N.Mex. Atty. Gen., 1978-79; pvt. practice, 1979-86, 87-93, 98—; first and founding dir. N.Mex. Workers Compensation Adminstrn., 1986-87; mem. N.Mex. Senate, 1988-93; mayor City of Albuquerque, 1993-97, 2001—. Mem. Med. Rev. Commn., 1990—; bd. dirs. Senior Arts Project, 1987—, Tree New Mex., 1991-92. Mem. Citizens Rev. Bd., 1988—; bd. dirs. N.Mex. First, Sr. Arts; founding mem., bd. dirs. Tree N.Mex.; mem. Citizens Adv. Bd., N.Mex. Med. Rev. Commn., U.S. Conf. Mayors (adv. coun., urban water coun., homeland security comm.), Nat. Conf. Dem. Mayors (vice chair fin., 2003), Albuquerque/Bernalillo Water Utility Authority (chmn. 2003); Dem. candidate for Gov., 1998. Recipient Outstanding Young Men of Am. award, 1984, Appreciation award Friends of Albuquerque Petroglyphs, 1989, Cert. Appreciation, Am. Merchant Marines, 1989, Disting. Svc. award N.Mex. Dietetic Assn., 1989, Appreciation award West Mesa Little League, 1989, Excellence in Edn. award Friend of Edn., 1990, Appreciation award FHP N.Mex., Inc., 1990, Devoted and Invaluable Svc. award Indian Pueblo Cultural Ctr., 1990, Recognition award Ind. Ins. Agts. N.Mex., 1991, Accomplishment, Dedication and Performance award West Mesa High Sch., 1991, N.Mex. State Meml. award, 1991, Exemplary Dedication and Svc. award Sec. of State, 1991, Cert. Spl. Appreciation, MADD, 1991, Disting. Svc. award Hispanic Bar Assn., 1992, Legis. Recognition award Dem. Party N.Mex., 1992, Commitment to Edn. award Alamosa Elem. Sch., 1992, Recognition and Appreciation award N.Mex. First, 1992, Dedication award Albuquerque Hispano C. of C., 1993, Pride of N.Mex. award Hispanic Round Table, 1993; named Outstanding Youth Advocate, Youth Devel., Inc., 1993. Mem. N.Mex. State Bar Assn. (Pub. Svc. Recognition award 1989). Avocation: fly fishing. Office: Office of the Mayor PO Box 1293 Albuquerque NM 87103 Fax: 505-768-3019.*

CHAVEZ, MARY ANN, osteopathic family physician; b. York, Pa., Dec. 6, 1942; d. Henry David Gross and Mary Ellen (Ness) Rhoads; m. Richard L. Ziegler, Dec. 24, 1965 (div. Jan. 1983); children: Richard L. Ziegler Jr., Mara L. Tammaro, Brian L. Ziegler. BS, Alvernia Coll., 1983; DO, Coll. Osteo. Medicine, Phila., 1992. Legal sec. Louis Sager, Esquire, Pottstown, Pa., 1962-67; homemaker, tailor in pvt. practice Pottstown, 1967-85; intern Riverside Hosp., Wilmington, Del., 1992-93, resident in family practice, 1993-95; pvt. practice Spring Grove, Pa., 1995-97, Lancaster, Pa., 1997-999, Chillicothe, Ohio, 1999-2000, Sullivan, Ind., 2001—. Pell grantee, Beog grantee Alvernia Coll., 1979-83. Mem. AMA, Am. Osteo. Assn., Am. Coll. Osteo. Family Physicians, Ind. State Med. Assn., Ind. Osteopathic Assn., Sullivan Rotary Club, Sullivan Bus. and Profl. Women's Club. Avocations: painting, piano, tailoring, gardening. Home: 204 W Giles St PO Box 450 Sullivan IN 47882-0450 Office: Sullivan Med Clinic 222 W Beech St Sullivan IN 47882 Personal E-mail: maryannchavez@verizon.net.

CHAVEZ, MARY ROSE, counselor, educator; b. Agujita, Coahuila, Mexico, Oct. 7, 1954; arrived in U.S., 1959; d. Ignacio Chavez and Josefina Villa; m. Pedro Pablo Tijerina, Mar. 18, 1978; children: Pablo Esteban Tijerina, Daniel Ignacio Tijerina. MD, U. Monterrey, Mexico, 1984; MA, Tex. A&M Internat. U., Laredo, 2004. Med. license Mex., 1984. Physician Plan Integral de Salud, Monterrey, 1984—99; qualified mental health profl. Border Region Mental Health and Mental Retardation, Laredo, 2000—01; adj. faculty Tex. A&M Internat. U., Laredo, 2001—, counselor, 2005—, assoc. dir. career svcs., 2001—04. Dir. edn. Tex. Careers, Laredo, 2004—05. Scholar, Dominican Coll., 1972. Mem.: APA (assoc.), Neuvo Laredo Assn. Female Physicians, Am. Coll. Counseling Assn. Democrat. Roman Catholic. Avocations: reading, dance, swimming, knitting, painting. Home: 9903 Crystal Ct #117 Laredo TX 78045 Home Phone: 956-791-6090; Office Phone: 956-326-2762. Office Fax: 956-326-2231. Personal E-mail: chavezmd2000@yahoo.com. Business E-Mail: mchavez@tamiu.edu.

CHAVEZ, NELBA R., state and former federal agency administrator; b. Mar. 9, 1940; BA in Sociology and Psychology, U. Ariz.; MSW, UCLA; PhD in Philosophy, U. Denver; student sr. exec. program in state and local govt., Harvard U. From therapist to exec. dir., CEO, COO La Frontera Ctr., Tuscon, 1971-89; prin. Chavez and Assocs., 1989-91; dir. juvenile probation svcs. City and County of San Francisco, 1991-94; adminstr. Substance Abuse and Mental Health Svcs. Adminstrn., U.S. Dept. Health and Human Svcs., Washington, 1994-2000; dep. dir. Ariz. Rehab. Svcs. Dept. Econ. Security, Phoenix, 2003—. Bd. dirs. nat. coalition of Hispanic Health and Human Svc. Organs,; mem. U.S. Senate Hispanic Adv. Com., Pres. Nat. Coun. on Handicapped, White House Prevention Com. on Drug-Free Am. Mem. Tucson Mayor's Task Force on Children. Recipient Outstanding Leadership award Ariz. State U., 1985, Dedication and Commitment award Tenth Ann. Chicano Conf., 1989, Disting. Svc. award Nat. Assn. Profl. Asian Am. Women, 1995, Mujer 95 award League United L.Am. Citizens, 1995, Rafael Tavares, MD, Meml. award Assn. Hispanic Mental Health Profls., 1995, Nat. Health Leadership award Nat. Coalition Hispanic Health and Human Svcs., 1997, Leadership award Fedn. Families for Children's Mental Health, 1997, Nat. Coun. on Aging award for Leadership in Health Promotion, 2000; named to Honor Roll Latino Behavioral Health Inst., 1998. Office: Ariz Rehab Svcs Dept Econ Security 1789 W Jefferson 2NW PO Box 6123 Phoenix AZ 85007

CHAVEZ, VICTOR EDWIN, judge; b. LA, Aug. 28, 1930; s. Raymond C. and Sarah (Baca) C.; m. Marlene Schell Chavez; children: Victoria, Catherine, Stephanie, Christopher, Robert, Elizabeth. BS, Loyola U., LA, 1953, JD, 1959. Bar: Calif. 1960. Mem. firm Early, Maslach, Foran and Williams, LA, 1960-69, Pomerantz and Chavez, LA, 1969-90; judge L.A. Superior Ct., 1990—, asst. presiding judge, 1997, 98, presiding judge, 1999—2000. Mem. exec. com. L.A. Superior Ct., 1996, 2003—04. Mem. com. State Bar Examiners, 1972-76; del. to State Bar, 1971-75; bd. regents Loyola Marymount U., 1973-78. 1st lt. USAF, 1953-55. Mem. ABA (standing com. on fed. judiciary 1979-86), L.A. County Bar Assn., Mex.-Am. Bar Assn. of L.A.(pres. 1971), Am. Bd. Trial Advocates (pres. L.A. chpt. 1979), Law Soc., Internat. Acad. Trial Judges, Nat. Conf. Met. Cts. (bd. dirs. 2000—, exec. com. 2000—). Office: Dept 96 111 N Hill St Los Angeles CA 90012-3117 Office Phone: 213-893-1021.

CHAVEZ, VIRGINIA, counselor; b. Fontana, Calif., June 22, 1958; d. Jose Frausto Chavez, Jr. and Ruth Saldaña. AA, Chafty Coll., Altaloma, Calif., 1978; BA, U. LaVerne, Calif., 1983; MA, Calif. State U., San Bernardino, 2003. Cert. nursing asst.; counseling credential U. Redlands, Calif. Rschr. Ariz. State U., Tempe, 1991—97; job coach Cole Vocational, Moreno Valley, Calif., 1997—98; counselor intern Moreno Valley Unified Sch. Dist., 2005—06; employment program rep. Employment Devel. Dept., Riverside; counselor Fresh Start Ministries, Ontario, 2006—. Vol. D.D. Men's Group Home, Moreno Valley, Calif., 2001—. Contbr. chapters to books, scientific papers to profl. meetings and seminars, articles to profl. jours. Sgt. USAR, 1986—, sgt. nat. guard US Army, 1978—2006. Fellow, Baylor Coll., 1992. Mem.: ACA, Am. Rehab. Assn., Am. Sociol. Assn., Calif. Assn. Sch. Counselors. Office: Fresh Start Ministry and Cmty Svcs Inc 610 A N Euclid Ave Ontario CA 91762 Home: 12952 Douglas St Yucaipa CA 92399

CHAVIN, WALTER, biological sciences educator, researcher; b. NYC, Dec. 6, 1925; s. Isidor and Fanny (Kesch) C. BS, CCNY, 1946; MS, NYU, 1949, PhD, 1954. Rsch. asst. N.Y. Aquarium, NYC, 1947-48; instr. dept. zoology U. Ariz., Tucson, 1949-51; rsch. specialist dept. fishes Am. Mus. Natural History, NYC, 1951-53; prof. biol. scis. Wayne State U., Detroit, 1953-90, prof. emeritus, 1990—; prof. radiology Wayne State U. Med. Sch., Detroit, 1975-80; dir. Radiation Biology Inst. Wayne State U., Detroit, 1959-71; pres. Chavin Design and Fine Arts, Inc., 2007—. Research assoc. Argonne (Ill.) Nat. Lab., 1955-58. Contbr. 225 articles to profl. jours. NSF Sr. Postdoctoral fellow, 1960-61; Rsch. grantee NSF, AEC, NIH. Fellow AAAS (sec. 1978-85), N.Y. Acad. Scis.; mem. Nat. Assn. Photoshop Profls., Am. Physiol. Soc., Am. Soc. Zoologists (treas., sec.), Soc. Exptl. Biology and Medicine (com. 1986-90), Endocrine Soc., Am. Orchid Soc., South Fla. Orchid Soc., Pan Am Orchid Soc., Am. Bonsai Soc., Gold Coast Bonsai Soc., Lighthouse Bonsai Soc., Palm Beach Bonsai Soc., Sigma Xi (chpt. pres. 1974), Palm Beach Digital Imaging Group, Boca Raton Mus. Art, Art League. Independent. Home: 16484 Bridlewood Cir Delray Beach FL 33445-6678 E-mail: raja25@bellsouth.net.

CHAVIRA, RICARDO ANTONIO, actor; b. San Antonio, Sept. 1, 1971; MFA, U. Calif., San Diego. Actor: (films) Barstow 2008, 2001, Boris, 2002, The Alamo, 2004; (TV series, guest appearances) NYPD Blue, 2001, Philly, 2001, JAG, 2001, 2003, The Grubbs, 2002, 24, 2002, Six Feet Under, 2002, The Division, 2002, Joan of Arcadia, 2003, George Lopez, 2005; (TV series) Desperate Housewives, 2004— (Screen Actors Guild Award for outstanding performance by an ensemble in a comedy series, 2005, 2006). Office: Desperate Housewives Touchtone Television 100 Universal City Plaza Bldg 2128 Ste G Universal City CA 91608

CHAVIRA-SLIVA, CLARICE F. See SILVA, CLARICE F.

CHAVIS, GLENN ROMERO, retired historian, writer; b. High Point, NC, Dec. 3, 1940; s. Roy Lloyd and Ruth Elmira Chavis; m. Gladys Faye McBee, Oct. 10, 1958; children: Rory Keith, Trey Emilliano. BA in English, Johnson C. Smith U., Charlotte, NC, 1963. Profl. hosp. rep. Abbott Labs., N. Chgo., 1969—70, profl. pharm. rep., 1971—73, minority recruiter, profl. pharm. rep, 1973—74, nat. recruiting cons., 1974—88, vision specialist, 1988—90, account exec., 1991—95, dist. sys. specialist, 1995—2000; ret., 2000. Cardiovasc. cons. panel Abbott Labs., 1970—72, antibotic cons. panel, 1971—73, abbott diagnostics diverstity task force, 1998—2000. Contbg. rschr., writer: African American Heritage Guide, 2005; rschr.: African Am. Exhibit, High Point Mus. & Hist. Pk., 2006; featured article appeared in: Editor and Pub. Mag. Mem. Undo Racism Task Force, High Point, 2001, High Point Racial Healing, 2002, Kivett Dr. Gateway Com., High Point, NC, 2003, High Point 311 Bypass Gateway Com., 2003, Southside Revitalization Steering Com., High Point, 2004, High Point Sesquicentennial Commn., 2007; mem., chmn. City High Point Citizens Adv. Com., 2002—06; trustee High Point Regional Hosp., 1986—94, High Point Mus., 2003—05, United Way Greater High Point, 2003—07; rschr., column writer News-Record, Greensboro, NC, 2002. Recipient Chairman's award, High Point Visitor's Bur., 2005, Walsh award, 2006. D-Conservative. Methodist. Home: 137 Orville Dr High Point NC 27260 Home Fax: 336-884-8623. Personal E-mail: grchavis40@aol.com.

CHAVKIN, JEFFREY S., lawyer; BA, Tufts U., 1972; JD, Boston U., 1975; LLM, NYU, 1981. Bar: NY 1976. Ptnr., group leader Banking, Bus. and Pub. Fin. Bryan Cave LLP, NYC. Office: Bryan Cave LLP 1290 Ave of the Americas New York NY 10104 Office Fax: 212-541-1261. E-mail: jschavkin@bryancave.com.

CHAVOUS, KEVIN P., lawyer; b. Indpls., May 17, 1956; s. Harold and Betty Chavous; m. Beverly Bass; children: Kevin, Eric. BA in Polit. Sci., Wabash Coll., 1978; JD, Howard U., 1981. Bar: Colo. 1983, DC 1983, Md. 1990, Va. 1990, US Dist. Ct. Dist Colo. 1983, US Dist. Ct. DC 1984, US Dist. Ct. Ea. Dist Va. 1990, US Dist. Ct. Dist. Md. 1990, US Ct. Appeals 10th Cir. 1983, US Ct. Appeals DC Cir. 1985. Atty. DC Pub. Defender Svc., Cadeaux & Taglieri, Washington; city councilman Ward 7 Washington City Coun., 1993—2004, past chair Com. on Edn., Libraries and Recreation; of counsel Arent Fox Kinter Plotkin & Kahn, Washington, 1998—99, 2001—02; v.p. legis. affairs Covad Comm., 1999—2001; of counsel Sonnenschein Nath & Rosenthal LLP, Washington, 2002—. Adj. prof. law Am. U., 2001—. Mem.: ABA, Trial Lawyers Assn. of Met. Washington (bd. governors 1991—93), Assn. Trial Lawyers of Am., Md. State Bar Assn., Colo. Bar Assn., Washington Bar Assn. (bd. dirs. 1990—96), Denver Bar Assn. Democrat. Episcopalian. Office: Sonnenschein Nath & Rosenthal LLP Ste 600, E Tower 1301 K St NW Washington DC 20005 Office Phone: 202-408-6381. Office Fax: 202-408-6399. Business E-Mail: kchavous@sonnenschein.com.

CHAWNER, LUCIA MARTHA, language educator; b. Ithaca, NY, Dec. 2, 1933; d. Lowell Jenkins and Lucia Mary (Soule) Chawner; m. Movses Guichen Andreassian, Mar. 18, 1967 (div. June 1971). Student, Earlham Coll., 1951-53; BA, U. Colo., 1956; MA, So. Meth. U., 1975. Provisional cert. elem., secondary and talented and gifted Tex., profl. cert. reading specialist Tex. Tchr. grade 7 lang. arts and social studies Stonewall Jackson, Dallas Ind. Sch. Dist., 1959-63; reading clinician Reinhardt, Dallas Ind. Sch. Dist., 1963-66; Reading Resource Pilot Project Lakewood, Dallas Ind. Sch. Dist., 1972-74; devel. curriculum specialist El Centro Coll., Dallas County C.C. Dist., Dallas, 1977-78; English tchr. Health Magnet, Dallas Ind. Sch. Dist., 1979-95; univ. supervising tchr. U. Tex. Dallas, Richardson, 1996—. Part-time instr. El Centro & Richland Colls., Dallas, 1978—88, Brookhaven Coll., Farmers Branch, Tex., 1996—98; mem. English lit. textbook adoption com. Dallas Ind. Sch. Dist., 1988—89, chmn. English dept. Health Magnet, 1989—94, mgr. innovative grant, 1994—95. Region 7 chmn., nat. bd. dirs. English-Speaking Union, 1996—2000; co-leader child and youth study U. Md., Dallas, 1967—69; pres. English-Speaking Union, Dallas, 1992—96, mem. nat. edn. com., 1996—; mem. Leadership Arts Dallas Bus. Com. Arts, 1994—95; mem. World Affairs Coun. Greater Dallas. Named Tchr. of the Yr., Health Magnet, 1991, Rotary Tchr. of the Yr., 1993; recipient Nat. Merit award, English-Speaking Union, 2000; Advanced Study grantee, Dallas Ind. Sch. Dist., 1973, Instrnl. grantee, Richland Coll., 1980. Mem.: Brit. Am. Bus. Coun., Assemblage (pres. 1987—88), Friends SMU Librs. (bd. dirs. 1995—98), Dallas Mus. Art League (bd. dirs. 1997—2004), New Conservatory Dallas (bd. dirs. 1999—, sec. 2002—), Dallas Knife and Fork Club (bd. dirs. 2003—), Soc. Mayflower Descs., Dau. Brit. Empire (sec. 2003—06), Pi Lambda Theta (chpt. pres. 2002—), Phi Delta Kappa, Delta Delta Delta. Avocations: sculpture, needlepoint, fitness exercise, travel. Office: PO Box 141179 Dallas TX 75214-1179 Office Phone: 972-883-2730.

CHAYET, ARTURO S., ophthalmologist, surgeon, consultant; b. Monterrey, Mexico, Dec. 23, 1959; s. Jose and Dora Chayet; m. Silvia Chayet, Aug. 14, 1982; children: Daniel D., Leon R., Jose B. MD, U. La Salle, Mexico City, 1983. Cert. Mexican Bd. Ophthalmology, 1989. Dir. Codet Eye Inst., Tijuana, Mexico, 1988—; founder, dir. Banco De Ojos Del Noroeste, Tijuana, Mexico, 1988—92; pres. Colegio De Oftalmologos De Baja Calif., Tijuana, Mexico, 1994—95, Centro Mexicano De Cornea, Mexico City, 1997—98. Named Hon. Prof. Yr., U. Calif. San Diego Dept. Ophthalmology, 2001. Mem.: Sociedad Mexicana De Oftalmologia, Internat. Soc. Refractive Surgery (Lans award 2000, Caseebeer award 2005), Am. Soc. Cataract and Refractive Surgery, Am. Acad. Ophthalmology (Achievement award 2001). Achievements include development of Intralasik; invention of Bitoric Excimer Laser Treatments; design of Chayet Lasik Drain; development of Nidek Mk 2000 Microkeratome. Office: Codet Eye Institute Padre Kino 10159 Bc Tijuana 22320 Mexico Home Phone: 858-454-8161; Office Phone: 619-662-4999. Business E-mail: arturo.chayet@arisvision.com.mx, arturo.chayet@codetvision.com.

CHAYET, SERGIO, finance educator; s. Ruben and Yolanda Chayet; m. Nancy Lisker; children: Natalie, Daniel Moises. BS in Math., Nat. U., Mexico City, 1988, BS in Physics; MS in Physics, U. Chgo., 1993; PhD, MS in Indsl. Engring. & Mgmt. Scis., Northwestern U., Evanston, Ill., 1999. Asst prof. of ops. mgmt. U. Chgo. Grad. Sch. Bus., 1999—2005; asst prof. of ops. and mfg. mgmt. Olin Sch. Bus. Wash. U., Saint Louis, Mo., 2005—. Recipient Gabino Barreda medal, Nat. U., Mex., 1988, Reid Tchg. award, Olin Sch. Bus., 2006, 2007. Mem.: Inst. Ops. Rsch. Mgmt. Sci. Office: Olin Sch Bus One Brookings Dr Saint Louis MO 63130-4899 Office Phone: 314-935-6769.

CHAYKIN, ROBERT LEROY, manufacturing and marketing executive; b. Miami, Fla., May 2, 1944; s. Allan Leroy and Ruth Chaykin; m. Patty Jean Patton, Feb. 1971 (div. May 1975); children: Stephanie Lee, Michele Alee; m. Evalyn Marcy Slodzina, Sept. 3, 1989; children: Catrina Celia, Ally Sue. BA in Polit. Sci., U. Miami, Fla., 1965, LLB, 1969. Owner, operator Serrating Svcs. Miami, 1969-71, Serrating Svcs. Las Vegas, Nev., 1971-84; pres. Ser-Sharp Mfg., Inc., Las Vegas, 1984—; nat. mktg. dir. Coserco Corp., Las Vegas, 1987—2006; owner, agt. AAABA Bail Bonds, Las Vegas, Nev., 2006—. Patentee in mfg. field. With US Army, 1962. Recipient 2d degree black belt Tae Kwon Do, Profl. Karate Assn., 1954—61. Avocations: travel, camping. Office Phone: 702-643-3333. Personal E-mail: sersharp1@hotmail.com.

CHAZEN, HARTLEY JAMES, lawyer; b. NYC, Feb. 14, 1932; s. Joseph and Helen (Jacobson) C.; m. Lois Audrey, Dec. 12, 1967; 1 child, Nicole Joanna. AB, CCNY, 1953; LLB, Harvard U., 1958; LLM, NYU, 1959. Bar: N.Y. 1959. Assoc. Hays, St. John, Abramson & Heilbron, NYC, 1959-65, Shea & Gould, NYC, 1965-68, Rosenman & Colin, NYC, 1968-70; ptnr. Monasch Chazen & Stream, NYC, 1970-82; pvt. practice NYC, 1982-88; ptnr. Chazen & Fox, NYC, 1988—; of counsel McLaughlin & Stern, NYC, 1992-2000. Lectr. in field. Capt. USAR, 1958-68. Mem. Assn. Bar City N.Y., ABA (subcom. corp. taxation 1987—), Harvard Club. Home: 75 Perkins Rd Greenwich CT 06830-3510 Office: Chazen & Fox 767 Third Ave Fl 35 New York NY 10017 Home Phone: 203-869-4091; Office Phone: 212-588-1818. E-mail: hchazen@chazenfox.com.

CHAZEN, STEPHEN I., oil industry executive; b. Buffalo, Aug. 26, 1946; s. Michael M. and Marcia Chazen; m. Patricia L. Orr, Dec. 18, 1971. AB, Rutgers U., 1968; PhD, Mich. State U., 1973; MS, U. Houston, 1977. Lab. mgr. Northrop Svcs., Inc., Houston, 1973-77; dir. project evaluation Columbia Gas Devel. Corp., Houston, 1977-81; v.p. Merrill Lynch, Houston, 1982-86, mng. dir. NYC, 1987-93; exec. v.p. Occidental Petroleum Corp., LA, 1994—2004, sr. exec. v.p, 2004—, CFO, 1999—. Dir. Lyondell Chem. Corp., Houston. Mem. L.A. C. of C. (dir. 1996—). Home: PO Box 427 Pacific Palisades CA 90272-0427 Office: Occidental Petroleum Corp 10889 Wilshire Blvd Los Angeles CA 90024-4201

CHE, MAGGIE, endocrinologist, researcher; b. NYC, Sept. 1, 1958; MD, Boston U. Sch. Medicine, 1987. Cert. endocrinology, diabetes, and metabolism Am. Bd. Internal Medicine, 2005. Osteoporosis/ menopause champion Kaiser Permanente, Vacaville, Calif., 2001—, chair No. Calif. bone density adv. com. Oakland, 2005—. Mem.: Endocrine Soc. Achievements include research in osteoporosis. Office: Kaiser Permanente Vacaville 3600 Vacavalley Pkwy Vacaville CA Home Phone: 707-453-5516; Office Phone: 707-453-5516. Office Fax: 707-453-2911. Business E-Mail: maggie.che@kp.org.

CHEADLE, DON, actor; b. Kansas City, Mo., Nov. 29, 1964; 2 children. Actor: (films) 3 Days, 1984, Moving Violations, 1985, Punk, 1986, Hamburger Hill, 1987, Colors, 1988, Roadside Prophets, 1992, The Meteor Man, 1993, Things to Do in Denver When You're Dead, 1995, Devil in a Blue Dress, 1995, Rosewood, 1997, Volcano, 1997, Boogie Nights, 1997, Bulworth, 1998, Out of Sight, 1998, Mission to Mars, 2000, The Family Man, 2000, Traffic, 2000, Things Behind the Sun, 2000, Manic, 2001, Swordfish, 2001, Rush Hour 2, 2001, Ocean's Eleven, 2001, The Hire: Ticker, 2002, The United States of Leland, 2003, The Assassination of Richard Nixon, 2004, Hotel Rwanda, 2004, Ocean's Twelve, 2004, The Other Side of Simple, 2006, The Dog Problem, 2006, Reign Over Me, 2007, Ocean's Thirteen, 2007; actor, prodr. (films) Crash, 2004 (winner, Outstanding Performance by a Cast in Motion Picture, SAG awards, 2006, Best First Feature, Independent Spirit award, 2006); actor: (TV films) Lush Life, 1993, Rebound: The Legend of Earl The Goat Manigault, 1996, The Rat Pack, 1998 (Golden Globe award for Best Performance in a Supporting Role, 1999), A Lesson Before Dying, 1999, Fail Safe, 2000, (TV appearances) Hill Street Blues, 1981, Fame, 1982, L.A. Law, 1986, The Bronx Zoo, 1987, Hooperman, 1988, Night Court, 1984, Booker, 1989, China Beach, 1988, The Simpsons, 1989, The Fresh Prince of Bel-Air, 1990, Picket Fences, 1992, The Golden Palace, 1992, Hangin' with Mr. Cooper, 1992, The Bernie Mac Show, 2001, ER, 2002.*

CHEALANDER, STEVEN RUSSELL, federal agency administrator; b. 1946; married; 2 children. BS, U. So. Calif.; postgrad., U. Utah. Advanced through grades to lt. col. USAF, 1964—91, mem. air demonstration squadron, the Thunderbirds, 1981—85, comdr. tactical fighter squadron Williams AFB, Ariz., 1988—89, comdr. F-16 squadron Luke AFB, Ariz., 1989—91, ret., 1991; various positions including pilot, capt., chief pilot, flight safety mgr., mgr. flight ops. efficiency Am. Airlines, DC and LA, 1991—2007; mem. Nat. Transp. Safety Bd. (NTSB), 2007—. Office: Nat Transp Safety Bd 490 L'Enfant Plz SW Washington DC 20594*

CHEAP, RICHARD A., lawyer, bank executive; b. 1951; BA, John Carroll U.; JD, Northwestern U.; M in Taxation, Georgetown U. Bar: 1977. Atty. Porter, Wright, Morris & Arthur, Columbus, Ohio, 1981—87, ptnr., 1987—98; exec. v.p., gen. counsel, sec. Huntington Nat. Bank, 1998—; gen. counsel, sec. Huntington Bancshares, Inc., 1998—, v.p., dir. sec., 2001—. Mem.: ABA. Office: Huntington Bancshares Inc 41 S High St Huntington Ctr Columbus OH 43287

CHEATHAM, JOHN BANE, JR., retired mechanical engineering educator; b. Houston, June 29, 1924; s. John Bane and Winnie (Carr) C.; m. Juanita Faye Burns, July 19, 1947; children— Preston, Curtis. BME, So. Methodist U., 1948, MS, 1953; ME, M.I.T., 1954; PhD, Rice U., 1960. Registered profl. engr. Design engr. Linkbelt Co., Dallas and Houston, 1949-50; rsch. engr. Atlantic Refining Co., Dallas, 1950-53; rsch. assoc., head drilling rschr. Shell Devel. Co., Houston, 1954-63; prof. mech. engring. Rice U., 1963-96; chmn. dept. mech. engring. and materials sci., 1994-96; pres. Cheatham Engring. Inc., Houston, 1977-94, Techaid Corp., Houston, 1978-88. Cons. in field. Contbr. to profl. jours.; tech. editor: Jour. Energy Resources Tech, 1979-81. Served to 2d lt. USAAF, 1943-45. Fellow ASME; mem. Am. Inst. Mining and Petroleum Engrs., Sigma Xi. Address: 5671 Longmont Dr Houston TX 77056-2344 Personal E-mail: john_cheatham@hotmail.com.

CHEATHAM, ROBERT WILLIAM, retired lawyer; b. St. Paul, June 4, 1938; s. Robert William and Hildegard Frances Cheatham; m. Kay C. Sarnecki, Mar. 20, 1964; children: Ann Marie, Lynn Marie, Paul William. BCE, U. Minn., 1961, JD, 1966. Bar: Calif. 1967, U.S. Dist. Ct. (no. dist.) Calif. 1967. Assoc. Brobeck, Phleger & Harrison, San Francisco, 1967-74, ptnr., 1974-88, Cheatham & Skovronski, San Francisco, 1988-96, Cheatham & Tomlinson, San Francisco, 1996-97, Cassidy, Cheatham, Shimko & Dawson, San Francisco, 1997-2000, Foley & Lardner, San Francisco, 2000—04; ret., 2004. Speaker on continuing legal edn., San Francisco. Co-author: Calif. Attorneys Guide to Real Estate Syndicates, 1970, Cheatham and Merritt California Real Estate Forms and Commentaries, 1984-90. Mem. ABA, Calif. Bar Assn. Business E-Mail: rwcheatham@sbcglobal.net.

CHEATHAM, SHARIF, lawyer; b. Phila. BS cum laude, Ga. Coll., 1996; JD, Mercer Univ., 1999. Bar: State of Ga. 1996. Insurance, corp. atty. Goodman McGuffey Lindsey & Johnson, LLP, Atlanta, also ptnr. Spkr. in field. Mem.: ABA, Atlanta Bar Assn., State Bar Assn. Ga. Office: GMLJ Attorneys 2100 Tower Pl 3340 Peachtree Rd NE Atlanta GA 30326-1084

CHEATHAM, WALLACE MCCLAIN, music educator; b. Cleveland, Tenn., Oct. 3, 1945; s. Martin Luther and Ollie Frances (Simpson) Cheatham; m. Willie Faye Watson, May 22, 1971; children: Tosca Carmé, Kimberly Ann. BS, Knoxville Coll., 1967; MS, U. Wis., Milw., 1972, DFA, 2002; PhD, Columbia Pacific U., 1982. Music tchr. Knoxville (Tenn.) City Sch. Sys., 1967—68, Unified Sch. Dist., Racine, Wis., 1968—71, Milw. Pub. Schs., 1971—2003. Presenter, cons. in field; composer in residence Menasha (Wis.) H.S., 2004; dir. music Brookfield (Wis.) Presbyn. Ch.; music dir. African Am. Children's Theatre, Milw.; panelist NEA, 2005; mus. dir., adj. prof. Cardinal Stritch U., 2006; artistic dir. New Jubilee Choral Ensembles, Milw.; scholar Am.'s Art Form Milw. Pub. Libr., 2007; pianist, featured composer, panelist African Am. Art Song Alliance Conf. U. Calif., Irvine, 2007, Intercultural Music, vol. 6. Contbg. author: Challenges in Music Education, 1976, Just Tell The Story-Troubled Island, 2006, contbg. composer: Art Songs by African American Composers, 2004, Piano Music of Africa and the African Diaspora, 2007; editor: Dialogues on Opera and the African American Experience, 1997; composer: U. Maine Singers, 1992, Spiritual Fantasy, 2001, Beginnings, 2001, Towards An African Pianism, 2005, My Soul is a Witness, Dese Bones Gonna Rise Again, I Belong To That Band, You Must Come In Through The Door, Sinner, Please Don't Let This Harvest Pass, When the Roll is Called Up Yonder, Glory Hallelujah, My Hope Is Built, On Our Knees, Kwanzaa Songs, Anthology of Art Songs, I Am A Soldier, Praise, Thanksgiving, Missa, Portraits, O Holy Yahweh, Hymn Suite, Ode To An Organism, Children Go Where I Send Thee, For Unto Us A Child is Born, Symphony

No. 1, String Quartet No. 1, Over My Head, Passacaglia and Fugue, Drinking Of The Wine, Dies Irae, Theme and Variations on Austria, Charge From A Pauline Epistle, Statements From The Light, Do Not Press Me To Leave You, Yonder Comes Mary, He Shall Purify The Sons of Levi, The Glory of The Lord, Fanfare and Tocatta, Tone Poem, Three Preludes, Ode to a Destiny, Done Made My Vow, Stone in the Road, Pied Piper of Hamelin, Walk About Elders, Umukoro Songs, The inaugural anthem for the investiture of Coppin State Coll. Pres. Stanley Battle, 2003, Fanfare, Cannon and Postlude, Blessed Richard, Psalm 117, (fortieth biennial music fetival cd) Milw. Pub. Schs., 2004; musician (pianist): (world premiere) Sonata for Basson and Piano by Ulysses Kay, Internat. Double Reed Soc. Conv., 2006; composer, condr.: Train Up A Child, Series II, 2005, condr.: Let God Arise, 2003; contbr. articles to profl. jours. Participant Operation Crossroads Africa, 1966. Named Milw. Pub. Schs. Disting. Music Tchr., 2002, profiled on Milw. Pub. TV, 2005, David Nunley's Film Documentary subject, 2006; recipient Sullivan-Spaights Prof. Leadership award, U. Wis., Milw., 1999, Lifetime Achievement award, Civic Music Assn. Milw., 2000, Morris D. Hayes award, Wis. Choral Dirs. Assn., 2003, Achievement award, Unity Grand chpt. Order of Ea. Star State of Wis., Prince Hall Affiliation, 2003, Knoxville Coll. Outstanding Alumni of Nat. Prominence award, 2004. Mem.: Lyrica Soc., Nat. Assn. Negro Musicians, Internat. Consortium for the Music of Africa and its Diaspora (bd. dirs.), Wis. Alliance Composers, Am. Choral Dirs. Assn., Music Educators Nat. Conf., Am. Guild Organists (svc. playing cert.), Milw. MacDowell Club (bd. dirs.), Phi Beta Sigma. Mem. African Methodist Episcopal Ch. Achievements include being one of seventeen composers from around the world celebrated at the annual Festival of New Organ Music in London 2006. Home: 2961 N Fifth St Milwaukee WI 53212 Office Phone: 414-374-4215. Personal E-mail: FChea44172@aol.com.

CHEATUM, DON ELWOOD, rheumatologist; b. Dallas, Aug. 11, 1939; s. Elmer Phillip and Edith (Deck) Cheatum; m. Carolyn Clayton, Feb. 2, 1985; children: Kathleen Miller, Melissa Borelli, Christopher, Don Jr., Timothy. BA, So. Meth. U., Dallas, 1960; MD, Washington U., St. Louis, 1964. Lic. Am. Bd. Internal Medicine, 1974, Am. Bd. Internal Medicine and Rheumatology, 1974. Intern internal medicine Dallas Vets. Adminstrv. Hosp., 1965—65, resident internal medicine, 1965—68; fellow rheumatology U. Tex. S.W. Med. Sch., Dallas, 1971—73; rheumatologist Tex. Med. and Surg. Assocs., Dallas, 1993—. V.p. Tex. Med. and Surg. Assn., Dallas, 1994—2006, bd. dird., 1994—. Major donor Washington U., St. Louis, 2006. Maj. med. corp US Army, 1968—91, Germany. Fellow: Am. Coll. Chest Physicians, Am. Coll. Rheumatology, Am. Coll. Physicians. Avocations: travel, reading. Office: Tex Med and Surg Assocs 8440 Walnut Hill Ste400 Dallas TX 75231

CHEATWOOD, ROY CLIFTON, lawyer; b. Rome, Ga., Aug. 27, 1946; s. Herman Arthur and Dorothy Mary (Griffin) C.; m. Cynthia Morrison, June 27, 1969; children: Clifton, Scott, Dancy. BA, U. South Fla., 1968; JD, Tulane U., 1974. Bar: La. 1974, U.S. Dist. Ct. (ea. dist.) La. 1974, U.S. Dist. Ct. (mid. dist.) La. 1975, U.S. Ct. Appeals (5th cir.) 1975, U.S. Dist. Ct. (we. dist.) La. 1977, U.S. Supreme Ct. 1977, U.S. Ct. Appeals (11th cir.) 1981, U.S. Dist. Ct. (no. dist.) Tex. 1990. Assoc. Jones, Walker, Waechter, Poitevent, Carrere & Denegre, New Orleans, 1974-78, ptnr., 1978-91, Phelps Dunbar, New Orleans, 1991—2004, practice coord., comml. litigation practice group, 1992—2004, mem. mgmt. com., 1995—2002; shareholder Baker, Donelson, Bearman, Caldwell & Berkowitz, New Orleans, 2004—, office mgn. ptnr., 2004—, bd. dirs., 2005—. Adj. prof. La. State U., Baton Rouge, 1980, Loyola U., New Orleans, 1981, 84-86; faculty mem. Nat. Inst. Trial Advocacy, 1986-2003; master barrister Tulane Inn of Ct. Co-author: Louisiana Courtroom Evidence, 1993. Firm campaign rep. United Way, New Orleans, 1982, 98, recruiter, 1983-86, 88, acct. exec. area lawyers, 1989; bd. dirs. Children's Bur., New Orleans, 1988, 1st v.p., 1991, pres., 1993-95; mem. session St. Charles Presbyn. Ch., 1988-91, session New Covenant Presbyn. Ch., 2000—03, clk. of session, chair pastor-nominating com., 2000—02. 1st lt. U.S. Army, 1968-71, Vietnam. Mem. ABA (litigation sect./vice chmn. 5th cir. trial practice com. 1975-76, co-chmn. 1976-78, judge regional nat. appellate adv. com. 1978, co-chmn. ann. litigation meeting 1981, judge nat. appellate adv. competition 1978, membership chmn. litigation sect. 1983-86), La. State Bar Assn. (bd. legal specialization 1998-2004, chmn. 2000-02, cont. legal edu. comm., 2005-). Office: 201 St Charles Ave Ste 3600 New Orleans LA 70170 Office Phone: 504-566-5200. Business E-Mail: rcheatwood@bakerdonelson.com.

CHEAVENS, JOSEPH D., lawyer; b. Dallas, Aug. 27, 1940; s. David A. and Alice (Dawson) C.; m. Georgine Roberts, Aug. 15, 1964; children: Mark, Joseph, Elizabeth, Sarah. BA magna cum laude, Baylor U., 1962; JD cum laude, Harvard U., 1965. Bar: Tex. 1965, US Dist. Ct. No. So. Ea. dist. Tex., US Ct. Appeals Fifth Sixth Eleventh Cir., US Supreme Ct. Assoc. Baker Botts LLP, Houston, 1965-72, ptnr., chmn. trial dept. & mem. exec. com., 1973—. Adj. prof. So. Tex. Coll. Law, 1967-68. Gen. counsel Concert Chorale Houston, bd. dirs.; pres. Houston Internat. Seaman's Ctr., bd. dirs. Named a Texas Super Lawyer, Texas Monthly mag. & Law & Politics Mag., 2003—04; named one of Top 100 Houston Region Super Lawyers, Texas Monthly mag. Law & Politics mag., 2003—04. Fellow Am. Coll. Trial Lawyers; mem. ABA, Tex. Bar Assn., Houston Bar Assn., Maritime Law Assn. (chmn. com. on maritime legislation, bd. dirs. 1992-95). Office: Baker Botts LLP One Shell Plz 910 Louisiana St Houston TX 77002-4995 Office Phone: 713-229-1250. Office Fax: 713-229-2850. Business E-Mail: joseph.cheavens@bakerbotts.com.

CHEBAANE, MOHAMED, water management specialist, consultant; s. Mohamed Ben Ahmed and Nessria Chebaane; m. Sallouha Ayari; children: Ahmed Karim, Mohamed Amine, Wafa, Maher. Diploma in Advanced Studies, Faculte des Sciences de Tunis, Tunisia, 1977; BSc in Agr. Engring., Institut Nat. Agronomique de Tunis, Tunisia, 1979; MSc in Water Sci., U. Paris VI, France, 1980; MSc in Hydrology, O.R.S.T.O.M, France, 1981; PhD, Colo. State U., 1988. Sefl-employed internat. cons., Fairfax, Va., 1997—; prin. devel. specialist Devel. Alternatives Inc., Bethesda, Md., 2003—. Lectr. Institut Nat. Agronomique de Tunis, Tunisia, 1981—; sr. water mgmt. specialist Ministry of Water Resources, Muscat, Oman, 1988—; chief tech. advisor FAO, UN, Entebbe, Uganda, 2001—; cons. in field. Author: (book) Springs in the Sultanate of Oman (Ministerial award, 1995); contbr. articles to profl. jours. Regional pres. Tunisian Sci. Soc., Ft. Collins, Colo., 1986—88. Mem.: Internat. Water Resources Assn. Achievements include development of a new concept of horizontal precipitation for measurement of fog precipitation; developed a new gauge that measures both rain (vertical component) and mist (horizontal component); a new stochastic model for intermittent processes such as seasonal rainfall and flows in intermittent rivers; invited by ASCE as one of four world panelists on water utilities and environmental management, special international session on Water Management, ASCE Annual Meeting, Salt Lake City, 2004; played a key role, when he served in FAO and the World Bank, in promoting the Nile Basin Initiative and building capacity in Transboundary Water Resources Management in the 10 Nile Basin countries; development of a participatory approach for groundwater management. Office: Development Alternatives Inc (DAI) 7250 Woodmont Ave Ste 200 Bethesda MD 20814 Home Phone: 703-255-3558. Office Fax: 301-718-7968. Personal E-mail: m_chebaane@yahoo.com.

CHECCHI, ALFRED A., air transportation executive, financial consultant; b. 1948; BA, Amherst Coll., 1970; MBA, Harvard Univ., 1974. V.p. Marriott Corp., 1975-82; with Bass Bros., 1982-86; pres. Alfred Checchi Assocs., Inc., 1986—; co-chmn., bd. dirs. Wings Holdings Inc., 1997—; bd. dirs. Northwest Airlines, Inc., St. Paul, 1997—, co-chmn., 1991—97; pres. Washington Strategic Ptnrs., 2002—. Exec. and adv. bd. mem. J.E. Robert Cos., 2002—; exec. adv. bd. mem. Elizabeth Glaser Pediat. AIDS Founds. Office: Washington Strategic Ptnrs c/o JE Robert Cos 1650 Tysons Blvd Ste 1600 Mc Lean VA 22102

CHECHOPOULOS, PETER, photographer, educator; b. Chgo., Oct. 28, 1947; s. James and Helen Economu Chechopoulos; m. Cynthia Mary Keane, July 29, 1979. BA in Design with honors, U. Ill., Chgo., 1970; MS in Photography, Ill. Inst. Tech., Chgo., 1974; MA in Film/Video, Columbia Coll. Chgo., 1993. Staff photographer Crocus Prodn., Inc., Evanston, Ill., 1973—74, Allied Van Lines, Broadview, Ill., 1974—75, W. Suburban Assn. For Hearing Orthopedically & Visually Impaired, Lombard, Ill., 1975—76; dir. sch. arts, asst. dir./mgr. art ctr., curator art exhibitions, chmn annual art fair Beverly Art Ctr., 1977—81; staff photographer Chgo. Jour. Newspaper, 1978—79; film dir., freelance editor Lithuanian Photo Libr., Chgo., 1980—81; adj. art faculty in photo, film and graphic design Chgo. State U., 1982—2000; lectr. photo history Richard J. Daley Coll., Chgo., 1987; photography instr., Dept. Art McHenry County Coll., Crystal Lake, Ill., 1987—90; staff photographer, office pub. affairs Chgo. State U., 1993—94; head camera testing area Helix Camera & Video, Chgo., 1994—96; adj. photography faculty Moraine Valley C.C., Palos Hills, Ill., 1995—96; art, photo and computer technician, Art & Design Dept. Chgo. State U., 1996—2000; adj. digital video faculty, Graphic Comm. Dept. Prairie State Coll., Chgo. Hts., 2000; computer graphic design instr. Latino Youth Alternative HS, Chgo., 2000—01; computer specialist, computer graphic design instr. Harvey/Dixmoor Sch. Dist., Harvey, 2001—02; dir. art ctr., photo and computer instr., glalery curator, photographer/designer Jane Addams Hull Ho. Assoc. Ctr. Arts & Culture, Chgo., 2003—05, photo instr., 2005—06; digital photography & photoshop tchr. City Chgo.-After Sch. Matters Gallery 37, 2006—07. Represented in permanent collections Libr. Congress, Nat. Film Collection, DC, Libr. Health Scis., U. Ill., Midwest Photographer' Project, Chgo., primary photographer, Excellence Mag., Vol. 1, Chgo. State U., 1994, exhibitions include digital photographic image Elec. Immersions Exhibition Catalog, Ill. Art AGallery, Chgo., 1997, Third Photography & Digital Image Biennnial Exhibition, E.Carolina U., Greenville, 2003, Represented in permanent collections, Ill. Photographers Exhibition Catalog, Ill. State Mus., Chgo. Jour. Newspaper, Camera Arts Mag., Ziff-Davis Pub. Co., NYC, Midway Review Mag., Chgo., Photo Review, Langhorne, Pa., Maine Photographic Workshops, Annual Awards Catalog, Rockport, The Goose Creek Gazette, Vol. VII, No. I, Maine Photographic Workshops, Rockland Register Newspaper, Entertainment Sect., Invitational Cmty. Coll. Art Faculty Show Catalog, Rockford Coll., U. Chgo. Mag., Chgo. Defender Newspaper, Calumet Coll. St. Joseph, Hammond, Ill., Inst. Design Archives, IIT Chgo., Chgo. State U., McDonald's Corp., Oak Brook, Ill., Maine Photographic Workshops, Rockport, Maine, Mus. Contemporary Photography, Columbia Coll., Chgo., Ill. State Mus., Springfield, Ill. Named one of Top 10 New Photographers for Maine Photographic Workshops annual awards, Profl. Photography Divsn. Eastman Kodak Co., 1987; recipient Cert. Distinction award, 19th Chgo. Internat Film Festival, 1974, Purchase award, Ill. Photographers, Ill. State Mus., 1978, Honorable Mention award, Dittmar Gallery, Northwestern U., 1979, 1st Place Purchase award for summer show, Maine Photographic Workshops, 1981, 4th Place Purchase award for McDonald's Fine Art Competition, McDonald's Corp., 1983, 2d Place award for E.Tex. Internat. Photography contest, E.Tex State U., 1984, 2d Place award for Little Sister Awards, Midway Review Mag. & SW Area Cultural Arts, 1984, 3d Place award in photography, Ill. State Fair Profl. Art Exhibition, Ill. State Fair, 1984, Excellence award for outstanding film of yr., Documentary Resource Ctr., 1991, Honorable Mention award, Film Coun. Greater Columbus, 1993. Mem.: Coll. Art Assn., Hellenic Mus. & Cultural Ctr., Soc. Photographic Edn. Democrat. Avocations: reading, collecting sci-fi literature and art. Home: PO Box 593 Crystal Lake IL 60039-0593

CHECKETTS, DAVE (DAVID WAYNE CHECKETTS), professional sports team executive; b, Salt Lake City, Sept. 16, 1955; s. Clyde Alvin and Edith (Jones) C.; m. Deb Leishman, June 2, 1977; children: Spencer, Katie, Nathaniel, Andrew, Benjamin, Elizabeth. BS, U. Utah, 1979; MBA, Brigham Young U., 1981. Mgmt. cons. Bain and Co., Boston, 1980-83; exec. v.p. Utah Jazz, NBA, Salt Lake City, 1983-84, pres., 1984-87, pres., gen. mgr., 1987-88, gen. mgr., 1988-89; v.p. devel. NBA, NYC, 1990—91; pres. NY Knickerbockers, NBA, 1991—94; pres., CEO Madison Sq. Gardens, 1994—2001; founder, chmn. Sports Capital Partners, 2001—; chmn. SportsWest Comm., 2002—; prin. owner, operator Real Salt Lake (MLS franchise), Salt Lake City, 2004—. Bd. dirs. JetBlue Airways Corp., 2000—, Citadel Broadcasting Corp., 2002—, McLeodUSA Inc., 2004—. Trustee Salt Lake Visitor and Conv. Bur., 1986. Mem. LDS Ch. Lodge: Rotary. Avocations: basketball, golf, water sports, photography.

CHEDDIE, DENVER FARON, engineering educator, researcher; b. San Fernando, Trinidad and Tobago, Feb. 7, 1974; s. Ray and Phyllis Cheddie. PhD, Fla. Internat. U., Miami, 2006. Asst. lectr. U. WI, St. Augustine, Trinidad and Tobago, 1999—2000; rsch. asst. Fla. Internat. U., Miami, 2002—06, rsch. scientist, 2006—. Founder Controversial Bible Issues. UWI Open scholar, U. WI, 1992—95. Mem.: Delta Epsilon Iota (life; webmaster 2005—06). Home Phone: 786-877-9235; Office Phone: 305-348-2377.

CHEDEKEL, LISA, journalist; Staff reporter Hartford (Conn.) Courant. Co-recipient Worth Bingham prize, Nat. Press Found., 2007, George Polk award for Mil. Reporting, 2007. Office: Hartford Courant 285 Broad St Hartford CT 06155 Office Phone: 860-241-6200. E-mail: lchedekel@courant.com.*

CHEDID, ANTONIO, pathologist, educator, researcher; b. Barranquilla, Colombia, May 5, 1939; came to U.S., 1966; s. Aziz Antonio and Maria (Turbay) C.; m. Hoda Abi-Rached; children: Anthony John, Marie-Claude, Erica Houda. BS, Coll. of Barranquilla, 1954; MD, U. Madrid, 1962. Diplomate Am. Bd. Pathology. Intern Columbus Hosp., Chgo., 1967-68; resident in pathology Michael Reese Hosp., Chgo., 1968-72; instr. pathology Pritzker Sch. Medicine U. Chgo., 1972-73; asst. prof. pathology U. Cin. Coll. Medicine, 1973-76; assoc. prof. pathology Chgo. Med. Sch., North Chicago, Ill., 1976-84, prof. pathology, 1985—, prof. microbiology and immunology, 1995—, prof. medicine, 1997—. Author: (pen name Anthony Strong) The Phoenicians in History and Legend, 2002, The Idea of God, 2007; current work: immunology of alcoholic liver disease and hepatitis C; specialties include pathology, medicine, hepatology and immunology. Mem. Am. Assn. Pathology, Internat. Assn. for Study of the Liver, Am. Assn. for Study Liver Diseases, Am. Soc. for Cell Biology, Fedn. Am. Socs. Exptl. Biology, Internat. Acad. Pathology. Home: 650 Rockefeller Rd Lake Forest IL 60045-3142 Office: Rosalind Franklin U Chgo Med Sch 3333 Green Bay Rd North Chicago IL 60064-3037 Office Phone: 847-578-3409. Business E-Mail: antonio.chedid@rosalindfranklin.edu.

CHEECHOO, JONATHAN, professional hockey player; b. Moose Factory, Ont, Can., July 15, 1980; Right wing Cleve. Barons, 2001—02, San Jose Sharks, 2002—. Recipient Maurice Richard Trophy, 2006. Avocations: fishing, hunting. Office: San Jose Sharks 525 W Santa Clara St San Jose CA 95113

CHEEGER, JEFF, mathematics educator; b. Bklyn., Dec. 1, 1943; BA in Math., Harvard U., 1964; MS in Math., Princeton U., 1966, PhD in Math., 1967. Tchg., rsch. asst. Princeton U., 1966—67; NSF postdoctoral fellow and instructor U. Calif. Berkeley, 1967—68; asst. prof. U. Mich., 1968—69; assoc. prof. SUNY at Stony Brook, 1969—71, prof., 1971—85, leading prof., 1985—92, disting. prof., 1990—92; prof. math. Courant Inst. of Math. Sciences NYU, 1989—, Silver prof., Courant Inst. of Math. Sciences, 2003—. Marston Morse lectr. Inst. Advanced Study, 1992, Blyth lectr. U. Toronto, 1997, Andrejewski lectr. U. Göettingen, 1997, Rado lectr. Ohio State U., 1998, Roever lectr., Washington U., 1999, Yamabe lectr., U. Minn., 2000, DeLong lectr., U. Colo., 2001, Fermi lectr., Scuola Normale Superiore, Pisa, 2001, Landau lectr., Hebrew U. Jerusalem, 2004, NSF fellow, summer support, 1969-; vis. position IMPA, Rio de Janeiro, Brazil, 1971, Harvard, 1972, Institut des Hautes Études Scientifiques, 1984-85, Math. Sciences Rsch. Inst., 1985; invited spkr. in field. Editor Journal Geometric and Functional Analysis, 1990-2000, mem. editl. bd. 2000-; assoc. editor Journal Differential Geometry, 1980-83, editor 1994-98; mem. editl. bd. Communications on Pure and Applied Mathematics 1997-; contbr. articles to profl. jours. Recipient Max Planck Rsch. award Alexander von Humboldt Soc., 1992-94; Alfred P. Sloan fellow, 1971-73, Guggenheim fellow, 1984-85. Mem. NAS, Am. Math. Soc. (Oswald Veblen prize in Geometry, 2001), Finnish Acad. Letter and Sci.; fellow Am. Acad. Arts & Sciences Office Phone: 212-998-3282. Office Fax: 212-995-4121. Business E-Mail: cheeger@cims.nyu.edu.

CHEEK, JAMES RICHARD, ambassador; b. Decatur, Ga., Apr. 27, 1936; s. Woodrow Wilson and Dorothy (Webb) C.; m. Carol Ruth Rozzell, Sept. 1, 1957; children— Leesa Lynn, Forrest Craig, Surya Tamang BA, Ark. State Tchrs. Coll., 1959; M. Internat. Service, Am. U., 1961. Dep. chief mission Am. Embassy, Montevideo, Uruguay, 1977—79; dep. asst. sec. state U.S. Dept. State, Washington, 1979—81; dep. chief mission Am. Embassy, Kathmandu, Nepal, 1982—85, charge d'affaires, chief mission Addis Ababa, Ethiopia, 1985—88; diplomat-in-residence Howard U., Washington, 1988—89; U.S. amb. to Sudan Am. Embassy, Khartoum, 1989—92, U.S. amb. to Argentina Buenos Aires, 1993—96; global cons., amb. in residence U. Ark., Little Rock, 1997—; pres. Am. Internat. Airports, LLC, 2002—. Served to capt. U.S. Army, 1954-56 Recipient spl. commendation Women's Orgn., Dept. State, 1979, Disting. Alumnus award U. Ark., 1992, U. Ctrl. Ark., 1997. Mem. Am. Fgn. Service Assn. (William R. Rivkin award 1974) Avocations: antique clocks, fishing, trekking, playing squash. Home: 31 Saint Andrews Dr Little Rock AR 72212-2908 Office Phone: 501-225-8452. E-mail: arkiecheek@aol.com.

CHEEK, JIMMY GEARY, academic administrator, agricultural studies educator; b. Gorman, Tex., Sept. 7, 1946; s. Geary B. and Mayme (Wright) C.; m. Ileen Griffin, Aug. 23, 1969; children: Jennifer Leigh, Jeffrey Stewart. BS with high honors, Tex. A&M U., 1969, PhD, 1975; MEd, Lamar U., 1972. Agrl. edn. instr. Beaumont (Tex.) High Sch., 1969-73; supr. manpower tng. Beaumont Ind. Sch. Dist., 1971-73; grad. fellow Tex. A&M U., College Station, 1973-74, instr., 1974-75; asst. prof. U. Fla., Gainesville, 1975-80, assoc. prof., 1980-85, prof., 1985—, asst. dean for acad. programs Coll. Agr., 1992-99, dean Coll. Agrl. and Life Scis., 1999—2004, sr. v.p. for agr. and natural resources, 2005—. Cons., seminar leader Pa. Coop. Extension Svc., 1985, Dept. Agrl. and Extension Edn., Pa. State U., 1985; cons. Gainesville (Fla.) Bd. Realty, Inc., 1988, 89, 90, 91, 92; review team mem. So. Assn. Colls. and Schs., 1977, 78; reviewer various books. Sr. author: (with others) Effective Oral Communication, 2d edit., 2000. Chair Rawlings Elem. Sch. Adv. Com., 1982-83, 85-86; pres. Rawlings Elem. Sch. PTA, 1985, v.p., 1984; mem. Ft. Clarke Sch. Adv. Com., 1987—; mem. Hidden Oak Elem. Sch. Adv. Com., 1988-90. Recipient Hon. Tex. State Future Farmers Am. degree, 1972, Hon. Fla. State Future Farmers Am. degree, 1978, Hon. Am. Future Farmers Am. degree, 1984, Outstanding Rsch. Paper award So. Agrl. Edn. Rsch. Conf., 1984, 88, 92; Merit award scholar Tex. A&M U., 1967-69; named of the 30 Notable Grads. Coll. Edn., Tex A&M U., 1999. Fellow N.Am. Colls. and Tchrs. Agr. (Ensminger-Interstate Disting. Teaching award 1990, Disting. Educator award 2005), Am. Assn. Agrl. Edn.(v.p. 1991-92, Disting. Svc. award 1998); mem. Am. Vocat. Ednl. Rsch. Assn. (pres. 1986), Fla. Vocat. Assn. (pres. 1992), Am. Vocat. Assn., Nat. Vocat. Agr. Tchrs. Assn. (Outstanding Svc. award so. region 1987), Fla. Vocat. Agr. Tchrs. Assn., Fla. Assn. Vocat. and Adult Tchr. Educators, Nat. Future Farmers Am. Alumni Assn., Assn. Internat. Agrl. Edn., U. Fla. Agrl. Alumni and Friends, Sigma Xi, Phi Kappa Phi (pres. 2003—), Gamma Sigma Delta, Alpha Zeta, Phi Delta Kappa, Iota Lambda Sigma, Alpha Gamma Rho (hon.). Office: Sr Vice Pres Agriculture Natural Resources U Fla PO Box 110180 Gainesville FL 32611-0180 Business E-Mail: jgcheek@ufl.edu.

CHEEK, JOEY, Olympic athlete; b. Park City, Utah, June 22, 1979; Mem. U.S. Olympic Speedskating Team, 2002, 2006. Named one of 100 Most Influential People, Time Mag., 2006; recipient Bronze Medal, Men's 500 Meter Speed Skating, Winter Olympics Games, 2002, Gold Medal, Men's 500 Meter Speed Skating, 2006, Silver Medal, Men's 1000 Meter Speed Skating, 2006. Achievements include first place finish, Men's American Cup Junior Speedskating Championship, 1997; finished first overall, U.S. Junior Speedskating, 1998; finished first men's all-around, America's Cup, 1999, first men short all-around, 2000; winner, 1 sillver medal and 2 bronze medals men's world cup, 2003; winner, World Championship's men's 500 m Speedskating, 2006. Office: c/o US Olympic Training Ctr One Olympic Plz Colorado Springs CO 80909

CHEEK, MICHAEL CARROLL, lawyer; b. Fostoria, Ohio, Aug. 28, 1948; s. Carroll Wright and Mabel A. (Smith) C. BA, Hanover Coll., 1970; JD, U. Cin., 1974. Bar: Ohio 1974, Fla. 1974, U.S. Dist. Ct. (mid. dist.) Fla. 1975. Pub. defender, Clearwater, Fla., 1974-77; lawyer sole practice, 1977—. Vice chmn. bar grievance Clearwater, 1990—94; trustee Pinellas County Law Libr., Clearwater, 1977—92; chmn. Ct. Law Libr., 1982—89. Pres. 1st Step Corp., Clearwater, 1986-93; vice chmn. Long Ctr. Found., Clearwater, 1994-95; founder Head Start Learn-to-Swim Program, 1994. With Ohio NG, 1970—74, with Fla. NG, 1974—76. Mem.: Pinellas Criminal Def. Assn. (v.p. 1987), Nat. Assn. Criminal Def. Lawyers.

CHEEK, NORMA JEAN, retired elementary school educator; b. Ada, Okla., Feb. 7, 1928; d. John Herbert and Jewell Esther (Hobbs) Winters; m. George A. Cheek, Dec. 5, 1947; children: George Allen III, Michael Kirby. AA, Conners Jr. Coll., 1948; BS, Ctrl. State Coll., Edmond, Okla., 1961, MEd, 1964. Tchr. Mid-Del Schs., Midwest City, Okla., 1961-89, coach, 1978-87. Salesman vol. YMCA, 1970—; bldg. rep. Midwest City Assn. Classroom Tchrs., 1980. Mem. AAUW, Alpha Delta Kappa (various positions including v.p. 1980). Democrat. Baptist. Home: 604 Traub Pl Midwest City OK 73110-2738 Personal E-mail: normacheek@yahoo.com.

CHEEK, WILLIAM SHIELDS, JR., protective services official; b. Nashville, Oct. 25, 1942; s. William Shields and Josephine Elizabeth (Womack) C.; m. Kathleen Glynneth Brisby, June 22, 1969; children: Heather Elizabeth, Rebecca Caroline. AA, Daytona Beach CC, Fla., 1965; BS, Fla. State U., 1968; MS, U. Louisville, 1980. Dist. supr. Daytona Beach News-Jour., 1963-65; res. patrolman Daytona Beach Police Dept., 1964-65; patrolman police dept. Fla. State U., Tallahassee, 1965-67; patrolman Tallahassee Police Dept., 1967-68; spl. agent Naval Investigative Svc., Alexandria, Va., 1968-71, Health Edn. & Welfare, Washington, 1971; spl. agt. FBI, Phila., 1971-72, Ashland, Ky., 1972-74, Louisville, 1974-95, Jacksonville, Fla., 1996—. Adj. prof. Ea. Ky. U., Richmond, 1984-95; adj faculty mem. med. sch. U. Louisville, 1987-95. Bd. dirs. Area-Wide Alcohol/Drug Rehab. Edn. & Enforcement Coun., 1990-95. Lt. (j.g.) USN, 1968-70. Recipient Law Enforcement Commendation medal SAR, 1991; named Alumnus of Month Daytona Beach Jr. Coll., 1972, 75, Ky. Col., Commonwealth of Ky., 1974, Hon. Chief of Police, Shively, Ky. Police Dept., 1986, Col. Aide De Camp, Ky. State Police, 1992; Rsch. grantee U. Louisville, 1986-90. Mem. Ky. Chiefs Police (officers sect., mem. publs. com. 1986-88), Ky. Peace Officers Assn. (bd. dirs. 1984-95),

Ky. Crime Prevention Assn. (bd. dirs. 1984-95, pres. 1990-95), Internat. Assn. Chiefs Police (vice chmn., chmn. pub. info. 1987—), Jaycees (Daytona Beach), Elks, Pi Kappa Alpha (silver chpt. 1986). Republican. Presbyterian.

CHEEKS, GEORGE, lawyer, broadcast executive; b. 1965; BA Polit. Sci., Yale U., 1987; JD, Harvard Law Sch., 1992. Entertainment assoc. Loeb & Loeb, 1992—94; v.p., bus. affairs Castle Rock Entertainment Inc., 1994—96; entertainment atty. Hansen, Jacobson, Teller, Hoberman, Newman, Warren & Richman, Beverly Hills, 1996—98; sr. counsel Nickelodeon, 1998—2003; gen. counsel MTV, 2003—05; exec v.p., gen. counsel MTVN Music, Logo and Films Grp., 2005—07; co- gen. counsel, exec. v.p. MTV Networks Co., 2007—. Avocations: yoga, exercise, movies, reading magazines. Office: MTV Networks Co 1515 Broadway 14th Fl New York NY 10036 Office Phone: 212-258-8000. Office Fax: 212-846-1804.*

CHEEKS, MAURICE EDWARD, professional basketball coach, retired professional basketball player; b. Chgo., Sept. 8, 1956; Grad., West Tex. State U., 1978. Guard Phila. 76ers, 1978-89, asst. coach, 1994—2001, head coach, 2005—; guard San Antonio Spurs, 1989-90, NY Knicks, 1990—91, Atlanta Hawks, 1991—92, NJ Nets, 1992—93; head coach Continental Basketball Assn. Quad City Thunder, 1993—94, Portland Trial Blazers, 2001—05. Named to NBA All-Star Team, 1983, 1986—88, NBA All-Defensive First Team, 1983—86, NBA All-Defensive Second Team, 1987. Achievements include winning the NBA Championship as a member of the Philadelphia 76ers, 1983. Office: Phila 76ers 3601 S Broad St Philadelphia PA 19148*

CHEELY, DANIEL JOSEPH, lawyer; b. Melrose Park, Ill., Oct. 24, 1949; s. Walter Hubbard and Edith Arlene (Orlandino) C.; m. Patricia Elizabeth Dorsey, May 14, 1977; children: Mary Elizabeth, Daniel, Katherine, Laura, Anne-Marie, Thomas, Susan, Michael, William. AB, Princeton U., 1971; JD, Harvard U., 1974. Bar: Ill. 1974, U.S. Dist. Ct (no. dist.) Ill. 1975, U.S. Ct. Appeals (7th cir.) 1975. Ptnr. Baker & McKenzie, Chgo., 1974-81, ptnr. litigation, 1981-85, capital ptnr. litigation, 1985-94; ptnr. Mauck, Bellande & Cheely, Chgo., 1994-2000, Bellande, Cheely & O'Flaherty, Chgo., 2000—05, Cheely, O'Flaherty & Ayres, Chgo., 2005—. Liaison counsel Asbestos Claims Facility, Chgo., 1985-88, bus. devel. com., 1987-90, Chgo. assoc. train com., 1988-91, chmn. Chgo. assoc. evaluation; liaison coun. Com. for Claims Resolution, 1988-89; cons. Midwest Theol. Forum, 2003—. Advisor Midtown Sports and Cultural Ctr., Chgo., 1974—; mem. River Forest Regular Reps., Ill., 1980-88, Ill. Rep. Assembly, Chgo., 1984—; pres. Cath. Evidence Forum, 1984—; pres. Ch. History Forum, 1994—; dir. Cath. Citizens of Ill., 1997—; bd. dirs. Cath. Lawyers Guild, 2000—; cons. Midwest Theological Forum, 2003-. Mem. ABA (vice chmn. environ. law sect. 1989-97), Ill. Bar Assn., Appellate Lawyers Soc. Ill., Chgo. Bar Assn., Trial Lawyers Club. Chgo., Serra Club (v.p. Chgo. chpt. 1988-89, 92-94, 96—, treas. 1989-92), United Rep. Fund, Phi Beta Kappa. Roman Catholic. Avocations: history, christian apologetics, travel. Office: Cheely O'Flaherty & Ayres 19 S La Salle St Ste 1203 Chicago IL 60603-1406 Office Phone: 312-853-8714. Personal E-mail: dcheely@aol.com. Business E-Mail: dcheely@lawchicago.net.

CHEEMA, FAISAL HABIB, surgeon, researcher; b. Hafizabad, Punjab, Pakistan, Mar. 26, 1977; s. Habib Ullah and Safia Begum Cheema; m. Ayesha Faisal Shaukat, Aug. 11, 2001. MBBS, The Aga Khan U., Karachi, Pakistan, 2000. Extern in histopathology Shaukat Khanum Meml. Cancer Hosp. and Rsch. Ctr., Lahore, 1996; extern in gen. surgery and urology Mansoorah Hosp., Lahore, 1997; extern in gen. surgery King Edward Med. Coll. and Mayo Hosp., Lahore, 1997; extern in cardiac surgery Punjab Inst. Cardiology, Lahore, 1999; extern in cardiothoracic surgery St. Joseph Med. Ctr. and Loyola U., Chgo., 2000; extern in pediatric trauma surgery Johns Hopkins U. Hosp., Balt., 2000; rsch. assoc. in heart transplantation Dept. Thoracic and Cardiovasc. Surgery and Robert Van Kampen Heart Transplant Resource Ctr. Loyola U. Med. Ctr., Chgo., 2001; postdoctoral rsch. fellow in surgery Divsn. Cardiothoracic Surgery Dept. Surgery Coll. Physicians and Surgeons Columbia U. - NY Presbyn. Hosp., NYC, 2002—05, asst. surg. fellow Cardiopulmonary Procurement Team Heart and Lung Transplant Program, 2002—, preceptor gross anatomy Dept. Anatomy, 2004—, assoc. rsch. scientist Divsn. Cardiothoracic Surgery Dept. Surgery, 2005—. Reviewer Annals of Thoracic Surgery, Blackwell Synergy Pubs., Jour. Heart and Lung Transplantation; mem. organizing com. 14th Biennial Asian Congress on Cardiothoracic Surgery; founder Young Pakistani Physicians Resource Ctr., 2004. Contbr. articles to abstracts, book chpts. and manuscripts, scientific papers, articles to profl. jours. Coord. Sponsor A Child's Mind Project, Karachi, Pakistan, 1998—2000. Sci. fellow, Govt. Coll. Lahore, Pakistan, 1994—95, Start-up Rsch. grantee, Columbia U., 2002—05, 2003—04, 2004—05, 2005—06, Clin. Rsch. Indsl. grantee, Edwards Lifescis. Corp., 2004—05, NIH grantee, 2004—, New Era Cardiac Care scholar, 2006. Mem.: AMA, Islamic Med. Assn. N.Am., Assn. Physicians Pakistani Descent of N.Am. (taskforce visa and licensure issues 2003, young physicians task force 2004, mem. com. young physicians 2005, best sci. poster presentation 2005, disting. oral presentation 2005), Doctors Worldwide, Heart Net, Academic Rsch. Coun., Am. Soc. Artificial Internal Organs, Internat. Soc. Heart & Lung Transplantation, N.Y. Acad. Scis. (future entrepreneur 2005), Pakistan Med. & Dental Coun., Am. Heart Assn. (coun. on cardio-thoracic and vascular surgery 2003), Khwarzimic Sci. Soc. (life), Aga Khan U. Alumni Assn. Islam. Achievements include discovery of renal papilla as a niche for adult kidney stem cells; patents pending for Casein Hydrolysate as additive for Dialysate in Hemodialysis. Avocations: skydiving, travel, squash, horseback riding. Home: 106 Haven Ave Apt 20 New York NY 10032 Office: Coll Physicians and Surgeons Columbia U NY Presbyn Hosp MHB 7 GN 435 177 Fort Washington Ave New York NY 10032 Home Phone: 917-499-5115; Office Phone: 212-305-5108. Office Fax: 212-342-5309; Home Fax: 212-342-5309. Business E-Mail: fc2020@columbia.edu.

CHEESEBORO, MARGRIT, retired economics educator; b. Zurich, Switzerland; BA of Bus. Mgmt., U. Redlands, 1980; MSEd, U. So. Calif., 1981; MA in Ednl. Adminstrn., Calif. State U., LA, 1982; postgrad, UCLA, 1990. Cert. tchr. and adminstr. Sch. office adminstr. Mid-City Alternative Sch., LA, 1973—80; tchr. econ., govt., US and world history Crenshaw HS, LA, 1982—2006; ret., 2006. Bd. dirs. Baldwin Village Cmty. in Action, 1998—; sec., treas. Baldwin Village Apt. Owners Assn., 2004—. Mem. United Tchrs. L.A. (chpt. chmn. 1991-98), Kappa Delta Pi. Home: 3525 S Bronson Ave Los Angeles CA 90018-3636

CHEESMAN, JOHN MICHAEL, corporate financial executive; b. Wichita, Kans., Feb. 4, 1943; s. Norman Carlyle and Anne Lucille (Norris) C.; m. Sharon Lindsey, Feb. 8, 1964 (div. 1968); children: Mary Kathleen, Deborah Kristine; m. Oksun Elledge, Aug. 29, 2000; children: James Richard, Anthony Wayne Elledge. AA in Math., Social Scis., Wichita State U., BBA, 1986, MA in Social Scis., 1987; MBA, W. Frank Barton Sch. Bus., Wichita, 1997; diploma, Inst. Lit., West Redding, Conn., 1994, grad. diploma, 1996; MS summa cum laude, Newman U., 2000. Cert. quality engr., Kans.; cert. in supervision mgmt. Wichita State U. Ctr. Mgmt. Devel., 2001. Mgr. Guardian Industries, Wichita, 1966-72; supr. Cessna Aircraft Corp., Wichita, 1972-78; stats. analyst Boeing Airplane Co., Wichita, 1978-85; lead engr. Boeing Mil. Airplanes, Wichita, 1985-89; coord. prodn. conformance Boeing Comml. A/P Group, Wichita, 1994—2002; pres., CEO Portfolio Fin. Group, Inc., Wichita, 2004—. Founder, funder Mike Cheesman Endowed Bus. Scholar, Wichita State U. Found. Endowment Fund, 1997. Vol. United Meth. Urban Ministries Wichita, 1984—; numerous positions local and regional chpts. Boy Scouts Am., including commr. of scouting Quivira coun., Wichita; nat. staff mem. Boy Scouts Am., Fort A.P. Hill, Va., phys. arrangements group 1985, 89, 93, 97; leader United Meth. Men and Boys Retreat Youth Ministries, 1984—; chmn. United Meth. Neighborhood Outreach, 1988—; institutional rep. United Meth. Coun. on Ministries, Wichita; active Wichita-Sedgwick County Hist. Mus. Assn., 1985—, Rep. Nat. Com., 1981—, Nat. Rep. Congl. Com., 1986—, Wichita Children's Home, 1989—, Big Bros./Big Sisters, Wichita/Sedgwick County, 1989—; vol. leader Wichita Spl. Olympics, 1985—, chmn.; chmn. adv. bd. Rep. Nat. Com., 1994—; grad. Citizens Acad., 2005, Citizen Police Acad., 2006; bd. dirs. Dept. Human Svcs., City of Wichita, 1991—, Citizens Participation Orgn., City of Wichita, 1998—; mem. state bd. examiners Kans. Award for Excellence Found., 2002—; commd. col. Conf. Air Force, 1985, Commemorative Air Force, 2000. Recipient Campaign Victory cert., 1983, Presdl. Achievement award Rep. Nat. Com., 1986, cert. of merit, 1990, Congl. cert. of appreciation, 1991; Presdl. cert. of recognition, 1991; Presdl. cert. of appreciation, 1992; Vice presdl. cert. of commendation, 1992; Congl. cert. of merit, 1992, Eisenhower Commn., 1995; George Meany award Nat. Fedn. Unions, 1986, God and Svc. award United Meth. Ch., 1986, Torch award Kans. West conf. United Meth. Ch., 1986, 88, Community Vol. of Yr. awards Boeing Co., 1987-89, Cross and Flame award United Meth. Ch., 1988, 91, Award of Merit Boy Scouts Am., 1988, God and Svc. award Presbyn. Ch. U.S.A., 1991, William M. Allen award Boeing Corp., 1989, Cert. of Appreciation Nat. Rep. congl. Com., 1990, 91, Wichita's First Citizen award First Nat. Bank, 1992, Disting. Commr. award Boy Scouts Am., 1993, Silver Beaver award Boy Scouts Am., 1993, Eagle Scout award Boy Scouts Am.; James E. West fellow, 1994; inducted as air and space leader NASA Exploration Wall of Honor/Smithsonian Air and Space Mus.; named Ky. col. Hon. Order of Ky. Cols., 1994. Mem. AIAA (sr.), Am. Computer Scientists Assn., Am. Mgmt. Assn., Adminstrv. Mgmt. Soc., Am. Soc. for Quality Control, Am. Assn. Family Counselors (cert. profl. counselor, nat. adv. bd. 1995—), Wichita State U. Alumni Assn. (life), Wichita State U. Soc. of 1895 (life), Wichita State U. Endowment Assn. (life), The Royal Aero. Soc., The Am. Air Mus. in Britain, Wichita Aero. Hist. Assn./Kans. Aviation Mus., U.S. Hist. Soc., United Meth. Men (past pres.), Nat. Assn. United Meth. Scouters (charter life, coord./chartered orgnl. rep.), Nat. Assn. Presbyn. Scouters (life), Nat. United Ch. of Christ Assn. Scouters (charter life Nat. Adv. Coun. 1984—), Orders and Medals Soc. Am., Medal of Honor Hist. Soc., Token and Medal Soc. Am., New Life Club (charter), The Augustan Soc. (charter), Masons (32 degree), Ky. Cols., Scottish Rite, York Rite, Shriners. Achievements include founded Mike Cheesman Endowed Bus. Scholarship Fund, Wichita State U. Found. Endowment Fund, 1997. Avocations: collecting, travel, reading. Personal E-mail: trbleagle@yahoo.com.

CHEESMAN, KERRY LEE, biology educator, researcher; b. Santa Barbara, Calif., Sept. 28, 1954; s. Theodore Richard and Barbara Jean (Wyckoff) C.; m. Sara Day Cheesman, June 17, 1978; children: Ian Walling, Nathan Elisha. BA, U. Calif., Santa Barbara, 1976; PhD, U. Ill., 1981; MS, Ind. U., 1987. Rsch. asst. U. Ill. Med. Ctr., Chgo., 1977—80; rsch. assoc. Med. Sch. Northwestern U., Chgo., 1981—82, asst. prof., 1983—86, St. Francis Coll., Ft. Wayne, Ind., 1987—90, assoc. prof., 1991—92, Capital U., Columbus, Ohio, 1993—96, prof., 1996—, chair biology dept., 1994—2001. Assoc. dir. endocrine labs. Northwestern U. Med. Sch., Chgo., 1983-86; dir. med. tech. program St. Francis Coll., 1989-92; health prof. dir. Capital U., 1993-. Author: Scientific Terminology, 1997, Medical Terminology, 1999, Photographic Guide to Species and Ecology of Camp Lazarus, 2006; editor: Ohio Jour. Sci., 2004—. Bd. dirs. Habitat for Humanity, Ft. Wayne, 1985-92, Boy Scouts Am., Ft. Wayne, 1985-92, Columbus, Ohio, 1994—, Boy Scouts Am. Nat. Coun., 1999—, Native Am. Indian Ctr., Columbus, 1996—, Ohio Sci. & Ednl. Rsch. Assn., 1997—, Ctrl. Assn. Adv. in Health Professions, 2002—, Nat. Assn. Adv. in Health Professions, 2004—, Bldg. a Presence for Sci. in Ohio, 2004—. U. Calif. scholar, 1972. Mem. AAAS, NSTA (mem. coll. sci. tchg. com.), Endocrine Soc., Soc. for Study Reprodn., Soc. Coll. Sci. Tchrs. (bd. dirs., mem. chair), N.Am. Assn. Environ. Edn., NY Acad. Scis., Ohio Acad. Scis. (bd. dirs.), Nat. Assn. Biology Tchrs (mem. coll. and univ. com.), Ohio Sci. Ednl. and Rsch. Assn. (bd. dirs., edn. com.). Achievements include being a nationally known speaker on college science education reforms. Avocations: camping, backpacking, working with youth. Office: Capital U Biol Scis Dept 1 College and Main Columbus OH 43209-2394 Office Phone: 614-236-6951.

CHEETHAM, ALAN HERBERT, paleontologist; b. El Paso, Tex., Jan. 30, 1928; s. Herbert and Hildegard Marguerite (Moreton) C.; m. Marjorie Rogers, Apr. 20, 1951; children: Alan Christopher, Jan Alison, Susan Hilarie, Hilary Taber. BS, N.Mex. Inst. Mining & Tech., 1950; MS, La. State U., 1952; PhD, Columbia U., 1959. Instr. paleontology La. State U., Baton Rouge, 1954-60, asst. prof., 1960-63, assoc. prof., 1963-66, cons. prof., 1966-72; assoc. curator Smithsonian Instn., Washington, 1966-69, curator, 1969-87, sr. invertebrate paleontologist, 1987-2001, sr. scientist emeritus, 2001—. Guest prof. U. Stockholm, 1964—65; adj. prof. U. N.Mex., 1994—97. Author: Geological Society of America, Memoir 91, 1963; editor: Animal Colonies, 1973, Fossil Invertebrates, 1987; contbr. articles to profl. jours. Recipient Raymond C. Moore medal for paleontol., 1997, Disting. Achievement Alumni award, N.Mex. Inst. Mining and Tech., 1990; fellow Humble Oil Co., 1951, NSF, 1952, 1961. Fellow: Paleontol. Soc. (medal 2001), AAAS; mem.: Paleontol. Rsch. Instn., Soc. Sedimentary Geology, Internat. Bryozoology Assn. Home and Office: 3101 Old Pecos Trail 647 Santa Fe NM 87505 Office Phone: 505-955-1840. Business E-Mail: cheetham@si.edu.

CHEEVER, GEORGE MARTIN, lawyer; b. Boston, Jan. 13, 1947; s. Francis Sargent and Julia Whitney (Martin) C.; m. Mary Margaret Duplain, Feb. 10, 1979; children: Charles Duplain, Frances Sargent, Mary Conner. AB, Harvard U., 1969; JD, U. Pa., 1973. Bar: Pa. 1973, U.S. Dist. Ct. (we. dist.) Pa. 1973, U.S. Ct. Appeals (3d cir.) 1978, U.S. Ct. Appeals (4th cir.) 1985, U.S. Ct. Appeals (7th cir.) 2004, U.S. Supreme Ct. 1992. Law clk. to assoc. justice Pa. Supreme Ct., Pitts., 1973—74; assoc. Kirkpatrick & Lockhart, LLP, Pitts., 1974—82; ptnr. Kirkpatrick & Lockhart Nicholson Graham, LLP, Pitts., 1982—. Mem. ABA, Am. Bankruptcy Inst., Pa. Bar Assn., Allegheny County Bar Assn. Office: Kirkpatrick & Lockhart Preston Gates Ellis LLP Henry W Oliver Bldg 535 Smithfield St Pittsburgh PA 15222-2312 Office Phone: 412-355-6544. E-mail: george.cheever@klgates.com.

CHEEVER, JAMES JEFFERSON, counselor; b. Newport, RI, Sept. 16, 1941; s. Horace Jefferson and Daisy Gabriella Cheever; m. Diane Marie Gagnon (div.); children: Jeffrey William, Amy Ellen. BA, Brown U., Providence, 1963; EdM, RI Coll., Providence, 1972. Cert. tchr. Mass., 1963. History tchr. Bellingham HS, Mass., 1963—97; residential counselor Challenges Group Home, Pawtucket, RI, 1998—. Tennis coach Bellingham HS, Mass., 1965—84, chess team dir., 1966—85, summer sch. co-dir., 1992—97; tennis coach Woonsocket Jr. HS, RI, 1984—92. Baseball coach Little League, Woodsocket, 1978—82. Mem.: Mensa, Phi Delta Theta. Democrat. Episcopalian. Avocations: sports memorabillia collector, wrist watch collector, swimming, tennis. Home: 20 Chaplain St Pawtucket RI 02861

CHEEVER, SUSAN, writer; b. N.Y.C., July 31, 1943; d. John and Mary Watson (Winternitz) C.; m. Robert Cowley, May, 1967 (div. 1975); m. Calvin Tomkins, II, Oct. 1, 1982; m. Warren James Hinckle III, June 10, 1989; children: Sarah Liley Cheever Tomkins, Warren James Hinckle IV. BA, Brown U., 1965. Tchr., Colo. Rocky Mountain Sch., Colo., 1965-67, Scarborough Sch., N.Y., 1968-69; writer Westchester-Rockland Newspapers, N.Y., 1970-72; editor, writer Newsweek Mag., N.Y., 1974-78; free lance writer, N.Y., 1978—; council mem. Authors Guild. Author: Looking for Work, 1980, A Handsome Man, 1981, The Cage, 1982, Home Before Dark, 1984, Doctors and Women, 1987, Elizabeth Cole, 1989, Treetops: A Famiy Memoir, 1991, A Woman's Life, 1994, Note Found In A Bottle, 1999, As Good As I Could Be, 2001, My Name is Bill, Bill Wilson's Life, 2004, American Bloomsbury, 2007. Recipient Associated Press award, 1970; Guggenheim Found. fellow, 1984, nominee Nat. Book Critics Circle, 1984. Mem. Pen/Am. Ctr., Authors League. Democrat. Episcopalian E-mail: susancheever@aol.com.

CHEH, HUK YUK, electrochemist; b. Shanghai, Oct. 27, 1939; s. Tze Sang and Sue Lan (Che) C.; m. An-li, July 26, 1969; children: Emily, Evelyn. BASc in Chem. Engring., U. Ottawa, Can., 1962; PhD in Chem. Engring., U. Calif., Berkeley, 1967. Mem. tech. staff AT&T Bell Labs., NJ, 1967-70; asst. prof. chem. engring. Columbia U., NYC, 1970-73, assoc. prof., 1973-79, prof., 1979-82, Ruben-Viele prof., 1982—2001, Ruben-Viele prof. emeritus, 2001—, chmn. dept., 1980-86; v.p. tech. Duracell, Inc., 1999—2005. Program dir. NSF, 1978-79; vis. rsch. prof. Nat. Tsinghua U., Taiwan, 1977 Vice editor Chinese Battery Industry Jour.; contbr. articles to sci. jours.; patentee in biomaterials and in electrophoresis. Recipient Harold C. Urey award, 1980, sci. achievement award Am. Electroplaters and Surface Finishers Soc., 1989. Fellow Electrochem. Soc. (Electrodeposition Rsch. award 1988, Battery Tech. award 2000). Office: Columbia U Dept Chem Engring New York NY 10027 Office Phone: 212-854-4453. Business E-Mail: hyc1@columbia.edu.

CHEIT, EARL FRANK, economist, educator; b. Mpls., Aug. 5, 1926; s. Morris and Etta (Warshausky) C.; m. June Doris Andrews, Aug. 28, 1950; children: Wendy, David, Ross, Julie. BS, U. Minn., 1947, LLB, 1949, PhD, 1954. Rsch. economist, prof. Sch. Bus. Adminstrn. U. Calif., Berkeley, 1960—, exec. vice chancellor, 1965-69, dean Sch. Bus. Adminstrn., 1976-82, 90-91, dean emeritus Sch. Bus. Adminstrn., 1995; dir. Inst. Indsl. Rels. Program officer in charge higher edn. and rsch. Ford Found., 1972-73; assoc. dir., sr. rsch. fellow Carnegie Coun. on Policy Studies in Higher Edn., 1973-75; sr. adv. con. Asian-Pacific econ. affairs Asia Found.; dir. CNF Transp., Inc., Shaklee Corp., 1976-2001, Simpson Mfg. Corp. Author: The Useful Arts and the Liberal Tradition, 1975, The New Depression in Higher Education, 1971, Foundations and Higher Education, 1979; editor: The Business Establishment, 1964. Trustee Richmond (Calif.) Unified Sch. Dist., 1961-65, Russell Sage Found., NYC, 1979-89, Mills Coll., 1991-; chmn. State of Calif. Wage Bd. for Agrl. Occupations, 1980-81. Office: U Calif Haas Sch Bus Berkeley CA 94720-1900 Office Phone: 510-642-2448. Business E-Mail: cheit@haas.berkeley.edu.

CHEITEN, MARVIN HAROLD, playwright, manufacturing executive; b. New Brunswick, NJ, Apr. 24, 1943; s. Samuel and Sarah (Peretzman) Cheiten. AB, Princeton U., 1965, MA, 1967, PhD, 1971. Ptnr. The Water Master Co., Highland Park, NJ, 1971-76, v.p., 1976-86, pres., 1986—. Author: (plays) Trial by Fire, 1972, Queen Jane, 1976, The Vault, 1978, The Golden Spy, 1996, Chowder, She Wrote, 1996, Le Coq d'Or, 2000, Zenobia, 2004, Miss Connections, 2005, Whizzer's Island, 2007, (novella) The Long Hello, 1995, (essays) The fate of Princeton Graduate School, 1991, Touching a Goddess, 1996, Two Voices in the Darkness, 1997, To the Millstone, 1997, Escape from Raritan Prep, 1998, Songs for My Love, 2000, Return of the Plymouth, 2004, A Portrait of Winter, 2006, (lyrics) The Inn Cabaret, 1978—80, Deborah, 1996, A Princess in Death, 1998, Dorothea, 2000, Terry Catherine, 2001, Ballade to 911, 2002, The Hunting of the Deer, 2002, Some Gave All, 2003, Go On, 2004, A Little English Girl, 2005; contbr. short stories; mem. editl. bd.: Princeton Alumni Weekly, 1983—87. Trustee Princeton Symphony Orch., 1993—, Friends of Theatre Intime, 1996—, Princeton Summer Theatre, 2005—; mem. coun. Princeton U. Libr., 2002—05; bd. dirs. Princeton Rep. Assn., 1972—74. Mem.: Alliance LA Playwrights, Dramatists Guild, Assn. Princeton Grad. Alumni (gov. bd. 1973—88), Campus Club, Nassau Club. Jewish. Office: Princeton NJ 08540

CHELAPATI, CHUNDURI VENKATA, civil engineering educator; b. Eluru, India, Mar. 11, 1933; came to U.S., 1957, naturalized, 1971; s. Lakshminarayana and Anjamma (Kanumuri) Chunduri. B.E. with honors, Andhra U., India, 1954; diploma in civil and hydraulics, Indian Inst. Sci., Bangalore, India, 1956; MS, U. Ill., 1959, PhD, 1962. Jr. engr. Office of Chief Engr., State of Andhra, India, 1954-55; asst. prof. structural engring. Birla Coll. Engring., Pilani, India, 1956-57; research asst. dept. civil engring. U. Ill., 1957-62; asst. prof. engring. Calif. State U., Los Angeles, 1962-65, assoc. prof. Long Beach, 1965-70, prof. civil engring., 1970—96, vice chmn. dept., 1971-73, chmn. dept., 1973-79, coordinator profl. engring. rev. programs, 1972-81, dir. continuing engring. edn., 1982—96, dir. CADDS Research Ctr., 1986—96; pres. C.V. Chelapati & Assos., Inc., Huntington Beach, Calif., 1979—2001. Cons. USN Civil Engring. Lab., 1962—68, 1975—94, Holmes & Narver, Inc., Anaheim, Calif., 1968—73; pres. Profl. Engring. Devel. Publs., 1988—, Continuing Profl. Edn. Inst., 2000—, Irvine Institute of Technology, 2002—. Contbr. articles to profl. jours. Mem. ASCE, Am. Soc. Engring. Edn., Structural Engrs. Assn. So. Calif., Earthquake Engring. Research Inst., Seismol. Soc. Am., Am. Concrete Inst., Am. Inst. Steel Constrn., Sigma Xi, Chi Epsilon, Tau Beta Pi, Phi Kappa Phi. Office: 8659 Research Dr Ste 200 Irvine CA 92618 Home: 21 Shadowcast Newport Coast CA 92657-1647 Office Phone: 949-585-9137. *When a person is indeed fortunate enough to reach a position of responsibility, that person should even more zealously follow the path of truth and justice, keeping in mind the good of humanity. One should look for long range objectives and not be deterred by minor setbacks.*

CHELARIU, ANA RADU, library director; b. Bucharest, Romania, Nov. 19, 1946; m. Serban H. Chelariu; 1 child, Andrea. MA, U. Bucharest, 1972; MLS, Rutgers U., 1981. Indexer H. W. Wilson Co., NYC, 1981-85; dir. Palisades Pk. (N.J.) Pub. Libr., 1981—99, Cliffside Park (N.J.) Pub. Libr., 1999—. Mem. Soc. Romanian Studies, N.J. Libr. Assn. Christian Orthodox. Office: Cliffside Park Pub Libr 505 Palisade Ave Cliffside Park NJ 07010 Office Phone: 201-945-2867. E-mail: chelariu@bccls.org.

CHELBERG, ROBERT DOUGLAS, military officer; b. Ironwood, Mich., Sept. 1, 1938; s. Raymond Rodahl and Marion Dora (Watson) C.; children: Robert, Kathryn. BS, U.S. Mil. Acad., West Point, NY, 1961; MBA, N.Mex. State U., 1973. Commd. 2d lt. U.S. Army, 1961, advanced through grades to lt. gen., 1991, ret., 1993; various assignments in U.S., Europe, Vietnam, 1961-78; student Nat. War Coll., Ft. McNair, Washington, 1978-79; asst. dir. pers. adminstrn. and svcs. Office Asst. Sec. Def. for Mil. Pers. Policy, Washington, 1979-80, staff dir., dep. to dep. asst. sec. def., 1980-81; comdr. 528th Arty. Group, U.S. Army So. Europe Task Force, 1981-83; chief of staff, dep. comdg. gen. Ft. Jackson, SC, 1983-86; asst. chief of staff, plans and policy Allied Forces So. Europe, 1986; exec. to supreme allied comdr. Europe, 1986-87; chief policy and programs br., policy div. Supreme Hdqrs., 1987-90; spl. asst. to supreme allied comdr. Europe for harmonization and verification Supreme Hdqrs., 1990; spl. advisor to sec.-gen. NATO, 1990-91; chief of staff U.S. European Command, Stuttgart, Germany, 1991-93; dep. dir. George C. Marshall European Ctr. for Security Studies, Garmisch, Germany, 1994-95; mng. dir. European region CUBIC Applications Inc., Stuttgart, Germany, 1995-98; sr. cons. European region Cubic Applications, Inc., 1998—2003; sr. advisor European affairs Econ. Devel. Partnership, Aiken, SC, 1999—; sr. fellow Joint Forces Staff Coll., 2001—; program mgr. Def. Threat Reduction Agy, European Field Office, 2003—06; cons. Northrop Grumman, 2006—. Dist. commr. Transatlantic coun. Boy Scouts Am., Brussels, Belgium, 1987-90, v.p. membership, 2004—. Decorated DSM, Def. Superior Svc. medal with oak leaf cluster, Army DSM, Legion of Merit, Bronze Star with four oak leaf clusters, 10 Air medals, Meritorious Svc. medal with oak leaf cluster;

recipient Vet. of Yr. award VFW Post 3676, 1985, Outstanding Alumnus Svc. award Lake Superior State U., 1986, Army Exceptional Civilian Svc. award, 1995, Disting. Eagle Scout award, 1990; named to N.Mex. State U. Bus. Sch. Hall of Fame, 2001. Mem. Fedn. German-Am. Clubs (pres. 1994-96), S.C. Coun. Ret. Officers Assn. (v.p. 1999-2003), Rotary, Phi Eta Sigma, Phi Kappa Phi. Avocations: swimming, trap shooting. Home and Office: 262 East Gate Dr #225 Aiken SC 29803

CHELIOS, CHRIS (CHRISTOS K. CHELIOS), professional hockey player; b. Chgo., Jan. 25, 1962; Student, U. Wis. Defenseman Montreal Canadiens, Que., 1981—90, Chgo. Blackhawks, 1990—99, Detroit Red Wings, 1999—. Mem. Team USA, World Cup of Hockey, 1996, 2004, USA Olympic Hockey Team, Nagano, 1998, Salt Lake City, 2002; player NHL All-Star Game, 1985, 1990—94, 1996—98, 2000, 02. Founder Cheli's Children's Found., 1992. Named All Star Tournament Team, NCAA, 1983; named to All-Rookie Team, NHL, 1985, First All-Star Team, 1989, 1993, 1995, 1996, 2002, Second All-Star Team, 1991, 1997; recipient James Norris Meml. Trophy, 1989, 1993, 1996, Bud Light Plus/Minus Award, 2002, Mark Messier Leader of Yr. Award, 2007. Achievements include being a member of Stanley Cup Champion Montreal Canadiens, 1986, Detroit Red Wings, 2002; being a member of silver medal winning USA Hockey Team, Salt Lake City Olympics, 2002; served as Captain to Team USA, Salt Lake City Olympic Games, 2002, World Cup of Hockey, 2004. Office: Detroit Red Wings 600 Civic Center Dr Detroit MI 48226-4419*

CHELL, BEVERLY C., retired media company executive, lawyer; b. Phila., Aug. 12, 1942; d. Max M. and Cecelia (Portney) C.; m. Robert M. Chell, June 21, 1964. BA, U. Pa., 1964; JD, N.Y. Law Sch., 1967; LLM, NYU, 1973. Bar: N.Y. 1967. Assoc. Polur & Polur, NYC, 1967-68, Thomas V. Kingham Esq., NYC, 1968-69; v.p., sec., asst. gen. counsel, dir. Athlone Industries Inc., Parsippany, N.J., 1969-81; asst. v.p., asst. sec., assoc. gen. counsel Macmillan Inc., NYC, 1981-85, v.p., sec., gen. counsel, 1985-90; vice chmn., gen. counsel K-III Holdings, NYC, 1990-92; vice chmn. Primedia Inc. (formerly K-III Comm. Corp.), NYC, 1991—2006, gen. counsel, sec., 1992—2005, CFO, 2005—06, cons., 2006—. Bd. dirs. Penton Media Inc., 2007—. Adv. bd. U. Pa. Athletic Dept. Mem. Assn. of Bar of City of N.Y., Am. Soc. Corp. Secs. Office: Primedia Inc 745 5th Ave Fl 23 New York NY 10151-0099*

CHELLARAJ, RAJKUMAR, federal agency administrator; married; 1 child. B in Chem. Engring., Madras U.; MS in Chem. Engring., Clarkson U., Potsdam, NY, 1978; MBA in Fin., NYU; MPA, Harvard U., Cambridge, Mass.; attended, London Bus. Sch. Internat. Mgmt. Exchange Program, Sorbonne, Paris. Dir. corp. devel. Celanese Corp.; v.p. Strategic Analysis Inc.; with Office Asst. Adminstr. Internat Activities EPA; counselor to asst. adminstr. of Asia US Dept. State AID; various mgmt. positions Exxon Corp., 1994—98; chief info officer US Mint, sr. exec. officer, 2001—05; asst. sec. for adminstrn. US Dept. State, 2006—. Office: US Dept State Harry S Truman Bldg 2201 C St NW Rm 6330 Washington DC 20520 Office Phone: 202-647-1492. Office Fax: 202-647-1558.

CHELLE, ROBERT FREDERICK, electric power industry executive, educator; b. New Brunswick, NJ, July 18, 1948; s. Robert and Frances (Brown) C.; m. Karen Ann Cederburg, Aug. 7, 1971; children: Robert, Pamela. BA, Bethany Coll., 1970; MBA, U. Dayton, 1972. Asst. contr. Tait Mfg. Co., Dayton, Ohio, 1972-73; pres. High Voltage Maintenance Corp., Dayton, 1973-99; dir. Crotty Ctr. for Entrepreneurial Leadership, U. Dayton, 1999—. Bd. dirs. The Siebenthaler Co., Dayton; adv. bd. U. Dayton Sch. Bus., 1994—. Contbr. articles to profl. jours. Chmn. Dayton C. of C., 1993, County Corp., Dayton, 1995. Recipient Cert. Appreciation Montgomery County Commn., Dayton, 1984-85, Up and Comer award for engring. City of Dayton, 1988. Mem. Nat. Elect. Testing Assn., Ohio Bar Assn. (mem. profl. ethics com. 2001—), Rotary (pres. 1984-85). Presbyterian. Avocations: yachting, fishing.

CHELLGREN, PAUL WILBUR, energy industry executive; b. Tullahoma, Tenn., Jan. 18, 1943; s. Wilbur E. Chellgren and Kathryn L. (Berquist) Chellgren; children: Sarah, Matthew, Jane; m. Deborah Ann Cole, May 12, 2007. BS, U. Ky., 1964; MBA, Harvard U., 1966; diploma in devel. econ., Univ. Coll., Oxford, Eng., 1967. Assoc. McKinsey & Co., Washington and London, 1967—68; ops. analyst Office Sec. Def., Washington, 1968—70; adminstrv. asst. Boise Cascade Corp., Idaho, 1970—71, divsn. gen. mgr. LA, 1971—72; gen. mgr. Universal Capital Corp., Kansas City, Mo., 1972—74; exec. asst. to chmn. Ashland (Ky.) Inc., 1974—77; adminstrv. v.p. Ashland Chem. Co., Columbus, Ohio, 1977—78, group v.p., 1978—80; sr. v.p., group oper. officer Ashland Inc., Covington, Ky., 1980—88, sr. v.p., CFO, 1988—92, pres., COO, 1992—96, pres., CEO, 1996—97, chmn., CEO, 1997—2002; operating ptnr. Snow, Phipps and Guggenheim LLC, NYC, 2005—. Bd. dirs. PNC Bank Corp., Centre Coll., The Conf. Bd.; adj. prof. No. Ky. U. Dir. Am. Friends of Univ. Coll. Oxford, Inc.; dir., chmn. Taft Mus., Cin.; trustee Cin. Mus. Art; bd. dirs., vice chmn. Greater Cin. Found.; trustee No. Ky. U. Found., Ea. Ky. U. Found. 1st lt. US Army, 1968—70. Fellow: Univ. Coll. (Oxford, Eng.) (hon.); mem.: U. Ky. Fellows, Queen City Club (Cin.), Comml. Club, Met. Club. Home: 817 Squire Lake Dr Villa Hills KY 41017-1337 Office: 541 Buttermilk Pike # 207 Crescent Springs KY 41017 Home Phone: 859-426-8381.

CHELLY, JACQUES E., anesthesiologist; b. Paris; s. David and Mirielle; m. Lorelee Chelly; children: Marjorie, Brice, Thomas, David. BS, Monte-Rouge Coll., Paris, 1970; MD, Necker-Enfants Malades Med. Sch., Paris, 1976; MS in Pharm., Lariboistiere-St. Louis Med. Sch., Paris, 1979; PhD in Pharm., U. Houston, 1985, MBA, 1992. Resident Broussais Hosp., Paris, 1976—79; attache asst. dept. biochem. Necker-Enfants Malades Med. Sch., 1975—76; attache asst. dept. pharm. Broussais-Hotel-Dieu Med. Sch., 1976—77, asst. dept. pharm., 1977—80, chief dept. pharm., 1980—2001; lectr. dept. anesthesiology Baylor Coll. Medicine, Houston, 1981, rsch. instr. dept. anesthesiology, 1982, rsch. asst. prof. dept. anesthesiology, 1982—86, assoc. prof. dept. anesthesiology, 1986; prof., dir. divsn. clin. pharm. U. Tex. Health Sci. Ctr., 1989—92, prof., dir. clin. rsch. dept. anesthesiology, 1992—97; prof., dir. clin. rsch. orthopedic anesthesia U. Tex. Med. Sch., 1997—2002; prof., vice chmn. clin. rsch. U. Pitts. Sch. Medicine, 2002—, prof. orthopaedic surgery, 2002—. Vis. assoc. prof. dept. pharm. U. Houston, 1980—81; vis. prof. U. Pitts., 2002—03, dir. orthopaedic anesthesia, 2002; staff anesthesiologist Broussais Hosp., 1977—80; attending physician Hermann Hosp., Houston, 1992—2002, dir. dept. clin. rsch., 1991—93; dir. orthopaedic anesthesia Meml. Hermann Hosp., 1998—2002; attending anesthesiologist U. Pitts. Med. Ctr. South Side, U. Pitts. Med. Ctr. Presbyn., Magee Hosp.; dir. cardiovascular anesthesia rsch. lab. Baylor Coll. Medicine, 1980—87; dir. clin. rsch. U. Tex. Med. Sch., Houston, 1992—2002; vice chmn. clin. rsch. U. Pitts. Sch. Medicine, 2002—; presenter, lectr. in field. Editor: Peripheral Nerve Block Technique, 1999, Continious Peripheral Nerve Block Techniques: An Illustrated Guide, 2001, Peripheral Nerve Block Technique, 2d edit., 2003; contbr. articles to profl. jours., chapters to books. Recipient Flouthane prize, France, 1980, Outstanding Rsch. Facilitator award, U. Tex. Med. Sch., Houston, 1996, Excellence Surg. Pain Mgmt. award, 2000. Mem.: Am. Soc. Regional Anesthesia and Pain Medicine, Am. Soc. Pharm. and Exptl. Therapeutics, Western Pharm. Soc., Coun. High Blood Pressure, Coun. Basic Sci., Am. Heart Assn., Tex. Gulf Coast Anesthesia Soc., Soc. Cardiovascular Anesthesiologists, Tex. Soc. Anesthesiologists (alt. del. 2002), Internat. Anesthesia Rsch. Soc., Am. Soc. Anesthesiologists, French Soc. Pharm., French Soc. Anesthesiology. Office: UPMC Presbyn-Shadyside Hosp Dept Anesthesiology 5230 Centre Ave Ste M-104 Pittsburgh PA 15232

CHELSTROM, MARILYN ANN, political science educator, consultant; b. Mpls., Dec. 05; d. Arthur Rudolph and Signe (Johnson) Chelstrom. BA, U. Minn., 1950; LHD, Oklahoma City U., 1981. Staff asst. Mpls. Citizens Com. Pub. Edn., 1950—57; coord. policies and procedures Lithium Corp. Am., Inc., Mpls. and NYC, 1957—62; dir. The Robert A. Taft Inst. Govt., NYC, 1962—77, exec. v.p., 1977—78, pres., 1978—89, pres. emeritus, 1990—; polit. edn. cons., 1990—; pres. Chelstrom Connection, 1992—. Compiler (book) Tribute to Outstanding Minnesota Women, 2001. Home: 9600 Portland Ave Minneapolis MN 55420-4564 Office: 155 E 38th St New York NY 10016-2660

CHEM, WIDHYA, ambassador; b. Phnom Penh, Cambodia, Dec. 6, 1958; married; 3 children. Student Study of internat. relations (diplomatic course) at the Inst. of Internat. Relations, Potsdam-Babelsberg, 1984; Masters (hon.), Polit. Sci., 1986; Doctor rerum politicarum (hon.), Inst. of Internat. Relations, Potsdam-Babelsberg, 1989. Private sec. Prime Minister H.E. Hun Sen, 1990—91; official mem. Secretariat of the Supreme Nat. Coun., 1991—93; dep. gen.-sec. Constituent Assembly, 1993; under sec. of state Permanent Sec. of the Ministry of Foreign Affairs and Internat. Cooperation of the Kingdom of Cambodia, 1996—97, sec. of state, 1997—2004; amb. Canada; permanent rep. of Cambodia to the UN NYC, 2004—. Mem. Bd. of Dir. Royal Sch. of Admin., 1995—, Bd. of Dir. Cambodia Devel. Resource Inst. (CDRI), 2000. Recipient Commandeur of the Royal Order of Mony Saraphoan, Cambodia, 2003, Chevalier of the Royal Order of Mony Saraphoan, 2003. Buddhism.

CHEMA, THOMAS V., government official, lawyer, academic administrator; b. East Liverpool, Ohio, Oct. 31, 1946; s. Stephen T. and Dorothy Grace (McCormack) C.; m. Barbara Burke Orr, Aug. 15, 1970; children: Christine, Stephen. AB, U. Notre Dame, 1968; JD, Harvard U., 1971. Bar: Ohio 1971, U.S. Supreme Ct. 1977. Assoc. Arter and Hadden, Cleve., 1971-79, ptnr. 1979-85, 1989-2003; of counsel Tucker, Ellis and West, 2003--; co-founder, pres. Gateway Cons. Group, Inc., 1994-; pres.Hiram Coll., Ohio, 2003--; exec. dir. Ohio Lottery Commn., Cleve., 1983-85, Gateway Econ. Devel. Corp. Greater Cleveland, 1990-95; chmn. Pub. Utilities Commn. Ohio, Columbus, 1985-89; chmn. Ohio Bldg. Authority, 1990-96. Candidate for Ohio Senate, 1980; campaign mgr., Senator Howard M. Metzenbaum, 1976; co-chmn. task force on violent crime, Cleve., 1981-83; trustee Hiram Coll., 1994—2003, Cleve. Works, Inc., 1995-98, Cleve. City Club, 1993-96, Sisters of Charity of St. Augustine Health Sys., 1994—, Hist. Gateway Neighborhood, Inc., 1995—; dir. Transtechnology, Inc., Fairport Funds. Mem. ABA (adv. coun.), Nat. Assn. Regulatory Utility Commrs., Nat. Assn. State Lotteries (bd. dirs.), Greater Cleve. Bar Assn., Ohio State Bar Assn., Cleve. Legal Aid Soc., Ohio Legal Assistance Found. (chmn. 1996-99), Electric Power Rsch. Inst., Sr. Citizens Resources Inc. (trustee), Hospice Coun. No. Ohio (sec., trustee, legal counsel), Citizens League, NAACP, League Women Voters, Am. Soc. Pub. Adminstrs. Trustee, St. Ignatius High Sch., Prospect Vision, Inc., Downtown Devel. Coords. Cleve. Found. Arch. Democrat. Roman Catholic. Club: City (Cleve., trustee 1993—). Avocation: skiing. Home: 18580 Parkland Dr Cleveland OH 44122-3469 Office: Office of President Hiram College Hiram OH 44234 Home Phone: 330-569-5120; Office Phone: 330-569-6112. Business E-Mail: chematv@hiram.edu.

CHEMBERLIN, PEG, minister, religious organization administrator; b. York, Nebr., Sept. 27, 1949; d. Charles Norman and Donna May (Chemberlin) Bean. BA with distinction, U. Wis., Parkside, 1973; grad., United Theol. Sem. Twin Cities, 1982. Ordained deacon Moravian Ch. Am., 1982, consecrated presbyter Moravian Ch. Am., 1986. Formerly dir. campus ministries, tchr., youth min.; also outreach min., parish intern pastor; exec. dir. Minn. Coun. Chs., 1995—. Former pres., former program chmn. Nat. Assn. Ecumenical and Interfaith Staff, 1992, 97; hon. campaign chair Minn. Food Share, 2003. Recipient Women of Excellence award Minn. Gov., 1994, NOVA Peace and Justice award, 1985; Angel of Reconciliation award, 2003. Mem.: Nat. Coun. of Ch. (mem. governing bd. 2003—07). Office: Minn Coun Chs 122 W Franklin Ave Minneapolis MN 55404-2447

CHEMERINSKY, ERWIN, law educator; b. Chgo., May 14, 1953; s. Arthur and Raeda Chemerinsky; m. Catherine Fisk, 1993; 4 children. BS, Northwestern U., 1975; JD cum laude, Harvard U., 1978. Bar: Ill. 1978, D.C. 1979. Atty. civil divsn. US Dept. Justice, Washington, 1978—79; assoc. Dobrovir, Oates & Gebhardt, Washington, 1979—80; asst.prof.law De Paul U., Chgo., 1980—83, assoc. prof., 1983—84, U. So. Calif., LA, 1984—87, prof., 1987—2004; Alston & Bird prof. law Duke U., Durham, NC, 2004—. Vis. assoc. prof. U. So. Calif., 1983—84; mem. task force Diversity State Govt. Gov., 1999—2000; lectr. in field. Author: Interpreting the Constitution, 1987, 1990 Supplement to Federal Jurisdiction, 1990, 1992 Supplement to Federal Jurisdiction, 1992, Federal Jurisdiction, 1989, 4th edit., 2003, Constitutional Law: Principles and Policies, 1997, Constitutional Law, 2001, Supreme Ct. Rev.: October 2000 Term, 2001, 17th Annual Section 1983 Civil Rights Litigation, 2001, Fourth Annual Supreme Court Review: October 2001 Term, 2003; mem. editl. adv. bd.: Calif. Lawyer, 1994, Aspen (Colo.) Law & Bus., 2001—. Bd. dirs. Progressive Jewish Alliance, 2000—; bd. dirs., regional coun. Am. Jewish Congress, 1993—98; chmn. LA (Calif.) Charter Reform Commn., 1997—99. Mem.: AAUP (litigation com. 1991—95), ABA (tech. asst. constn. drafting), ACLU (bd. dirs. 1987—98, exec. com. 1991—98), Am. Assn. Law Schs. (planning com. mini workshop 1989, steering com. profl. responsibility 1987—90, task force profl. responsibility 1987). Office: Duke Law Box 90360 Durham NC 27708-0360

CHEMERS, MARTIN M., psychologist, educator; m. Barbara Goza Chemers; children: Michael, Holden. BS, U. Ill., 1964, MS, 1966, PhD, 1968. Asst. prof. psychology U. Del., 1968—70; prof., chmn. dept. psychology U. Utah, Salt Lake City, 1970—87; Henry R. Kravis prof. leadership and orgnl. psychology Claremont McKenna Coll., dir. Kravis Leadership Inst.; dean social scis. U. Calif., Santa Cruz, 1995—2003, interim provost, exec. vice chancellor, 2003—04, acting chancellor, 2004—05, prof. psychology. Cons. in field. Author: An Integrative Theory of Leadership, 1997, 1999; co-author (with Fred Fiedler): Improving Leadership Effectiveness; contbr. articles to profl. jours. Recipient Sears-Roebuck Found. Tchg. Excellence and Campus Leadership award, 1991. Fellow: APA, Am. Psychol. Soc.; mem.: Soc. Exptl. Social Psychology (pres.-elect). Office: Univ Calif 1156 High St Santa Cruz CA 95064-1077 Office Phone: 831-459-4516.

CHEMERS, ROBERT MARC, lawyer; b. Chgo., July 24, 1951; s. Donald and Florence (Weinberg) C.; m. Lenore Ziemann, Aug. 16, 1975; children: Brandon J., Derek M. BA, U. So. Calif., 1973; JD, Ind. U.-Indpls., 1976. Bar: Ind. 1976, Ill. 1976, U.S. Dist. Ct. (so. dist.) Ind. 1976, U.S. Dist. Ct. (no. and so. dists.) Ill. 1977, U.S. Ct. Appeals 7th cir.) 1977, U.S. Ct. Appeals (5th cir.) 1985. Assoc. Pretzel & Stouffer, Chgo., 1976-79, officer, 1979-81, dir., 1981—. Author: IICLE - Civil Practice, 1978, rev. edit. 1982, 87; IICLE Settlements, 1984. Mem. ABA, Ill. State Bar Assn., Chgo. Bar Assn., Def. Rsch. Inst., Ill. Def. Counsel, Appellate Lawyers Assn. Office: Pretzel & Stouffer One S Wacker Dr Chicago IL 60606 Business E-Mail: rchemers@pretzel-staouffer.com.

CHEMIDLIN, MICHELE LYNN, athletic trainer, consultant; b. Vineland, NJ, Jan. 31, 1975; d. Dennis Joey and Joyce Ann Swawola; m. Andrew Chemidlin. BA in Phys. Edn., Kean U., Union, NJ, 2000, BA in psychology, 2000. Cert. instr. ARC. Asst. athletic trainer NJ City U., Kessler Inst., Jersey City, 2000—02; athletic trainer Montclair H.S., 2002—. Athletic trainer USA Field Hockey Assn.- Futures Program, Montclair, NJ, 2002—; cons. Essex County Coll. Police Acad., Cedar Grove, 2006—. Active ARC, NJ, 1993, Am. Inst. Cancer Rsch., 1993, Mar. Dimes, 2000, Susan G. Komen Breast Cancer Fund, 1999. Recipient Acad. All-Am., Ea. Collegiate Athletic Assn., 1994, 1996, Field Hockey Defensive Player Yr., 1996. Mem.: NJ Edn. Assn., Athletic Trainer's Soc. NJ, Nat. Athletic Trainer's Assn. Avocations: travel, scrapbooks, camping, canoeing, athletic activities. Office: Montclair High School 100 Chestnut Street Montclair NJ 07042 Home Phone: 908-468-0517; Office Phone: 973-509-4100 3920. E-mail: mchemidlin@montclair.k12.nj.us.

CHEMTOB, NANCY NADEL, lawyer; b. Lawrence, NY, Apr. 2, 1965; BA, Syracuse U., 1987; JD, U. Miami Sch. Law, 1990. Bar: NY 1992. Ptnr. Chemtob, Moss, Forman & Talbert, LLP, NYC. Lectr. Practicing Law Inst. Co-founder Friends of Newborn Medicine. Named one of Top 100 Attys., Worth mag., 2006. Mem.: Am. Assn. Justice, NY County Lawyers Assn., ABA (family law sect.), NY State Bar Assn. (family law sect.). Office: Chemtob Moss Forman & Talbert LLP 3 E 54th St 16th Fl New York NY 10022 Office Phone: 212-317-1717. Office Fax: 212-317-1555. E-mail: nancy@cmftlaw.com.*

CHEN, BIN, materials scientist; b. Shanghai, Oct. 11, 1963; d. Zhaowei and Yiling Chen; m. Shoudan Liang, July 7, 1988; children: Philip Chijui Liang, Benjamin Kaishiang Liang. PhD, Pa. State U., 1997. Rsch. scientist NASA Ames Rsch. Ctr., Moffett Field, Calif., 1997—2000, sr. scientist, 2000—. Grantee, NASA, 2005—. Achievements include research in multifunctional nanomaterials. Home: 280 Parkside Dr Palo Alto CA 94306 Office: NASA Ames Rsch Ctr MS 245-3 Moffett Field CA 94035 Home Phone: 650-856-9122; Office Phone: 650-604-0310. Office Fax: 650-604-6778. E-mail: bchen@mail.arc.nasa.gov.

CHEN, CHAU-CHYUN, chemical engineer; BS, Nat. Taiwan U., 1973; MS, MIT, 1977, ScD in Chem. Engring., 1980. V.p. tech. Aspen Tech. Inc., Cambridge, Mass. Mem. editl. bd. Internat. Jour. of Fluid Phase Equilibria. Mem.: NAE, AAAS, Chinese Am. Chem. Soc., Am. Inst. of Chem. Engrs. (Computing Practice Award 2001), Am. Chem. Soc. Office: Aspen Tech. Inc Ten Canal Park Cambridge MA 02141-2201 Business E-Mail: chauchyun.chen@aspentech.com.

CHEN, CHIEN-HSING, Chinese traditional health practices educator; b. Taipei, Taiwan, Mar. 18, 1957; came to U.S., 1990; s. Chin-tui and Man (Yu) C.; m. Deborah Lucille Brody, Nov. 13, 1986. Grad. H.S., Taiwan, 1975. Cert. master tchr., acad. dir. Kuoshu excercise and med. practices, Taiwan Kuosho Assn. Founder, dir. Kien Hing Chinese Health Practices Inst., Taipei, 1982—; founder, dir. Hsimgado Ctr. for Health and Enlightenment, Taipei, 1992—, Brookfield, Conn., 1994—, Bethel, Conn., 1997—. Dir., head instr. Pan Chiao Sr. H.S. Kuoshu Rsch. Soc., Pan Chiao, Taiwan, 1977—, Chung Yuan Christian U. Kuoshu Rsch. Soc., Chung Li, Taiwan, 1981—, Fu Jen Cath. U. Kuoshu Rsch. Soc., Hsin Chuang, Taiwan, 1988—; instr. Nat. Taiwan U., Taipai, 2002—. Author: Advanced Eight-Character Matrix Divination (3 vols.), 1987. Rsch. fellow Republic of China Hsing Hsiang Assn., Republic of China I Ching Learning Soc. Office: PO Box 6805 Kamuela HI 96743-6805 also: Hsimgado Hu Fa Hui 150 Chi Lin Rd Ste 5-1 Taipai Taiwan Office Fax: 2-2581-5850. Business E-Mail: dharmahelpers@hsimgado.org.

CHEN, CHING-CHIH, information science educator, consultant; b. Foochow, Fukien, China, Sept. 3, 1937; came to U.S., 1959; d. Han-chia and May-ying (Liu) Liu; m. Sow-Hsin Chen, Aug. 19, 1961; children: Anne, Catherine, John. BA, Nat. Taiwan U., Taipei, 1959; MLS, U. Mich., 1961; PhD, Case Western Res. U., 1974. Asst. Sch. Libr. Sci. U. Mich., Ann Arbor, 1960-61, svc. libr., 1961-62; sci. reference libr. McMaster U., Hamilton, Ont., Canada, 1962-63, head sci. libr., 1963-64; sr. sci. libr. U. Waterloo, Ont., Canada, 1964-65, head engring., math. and sci. libr., 1965-68; assoc. sci. libr. MIT, Cambridge, Mass., 1968-71; asst. prof. Grad. Sch. Libr. and Info. Sci. Simmons Coll., Boston, 1971-76, asst. dean for acad. affairs, 1977-79, assoc. dean, prof., 1979-96, prof., 1979—; exec. dir. UNESCO/WHC World Heritage Ctr., 2007—. Cons. Am. Soc. Info. Sci./Cath. U. Am., 1976-77, Chung-Shan Inst. Sci. Rsch., Taiwan, 1977-87, Abt Assocs., Inc., 1980-82, Sci. and Tech. Info. Ctr. Nat. Sci. Coun., Taiwan, 1973-77, S.E. Asia Region WHO, 1980, 81, Engring. Info. Inc., 1982, UNESCO, Paris, 1984, Nat. Geog. Soc., 1985, Norman Bethuen U. Med. Scis. Libr., 1986, Getty Trust, 1988, USIA, 1988, Ont. Coun. Gradual Studies, 1989, FID, 1989, World Bank, 1990, UNESCO, 1991, DataConsult, Mex., 1991, Soros Found., 1992-93, USIA, 1993-95, UN Devel. Program, 1997, Tsinghua U., Taiwan, 1997, Nat. Sci. Coun., Taiwan, 1998—2001, OCLC Global Digital Initiative, 2005—; mem. US President's Info. Tech. Adv. Com., 1997-2002; guest prof. Tsinghua U., Beijing, 1999-2002; U. prof. U. Hainan, China, 2004, cons. Chinese Acad. Sci. Libr., 2002—; evaluator Nat. Digital Archives Program, Taiwan, 2007. Author, editor 36 books including Biomedical, Scientific and Technical Book Reviewing, 1976, Sourcebook on Health Sciences Librarianship, 1977, Quantitative Measurement and Dynamic Library Service, 1978, Scientific & Technical Information Sources, 2nd edit., 1987, (with others) Numeric Databases, 1984, HyperSource on Hypermdia/Multimedia Technologies, 1989, HyperSource on Optical Technologies, 1989, Optical Technologies in Libraries; Use & Trends, 1991, Planning Global Information Infrastructure, 1995, Consortium of Electronic Resources, 1999, IT and Global Digital Library Development, 1999, Global Digital Library Development in the New Millennium, 2001; editor-in-chief: Microcomputers for Information Management, 1983-96; mem. editl. bd.: Electronic Library, 1990-; also editor numerous conf. procs.; contbr. over 150 articles to profl. jours. Barbour scholar U. Mich., 1959-61, Case Western Res. U. fellow, 1973-74, NATO fellow, 1975, AAAS fellow, 1985; Emily Hollowell Rsch. grantee, 1972—, Simmons Coll. Fund Rsch. grantee, 1972-81, co-principal investigator NSF US-China Million Book Digital Libr. Grant Project, 2001-; recipient Disting. Svc. award Chinese-Am. Librs. Assn., 1982, Cert. of Appreciation Asian-Pacific-Am. Librs. Assn., 1983, Disting. Alumni award U. Mich., 1983, Outstanding Svc. award Nat. Cen. Libr., 1986, Disting. Svc. award Asian-Am. Libr. Assn, 1992, Cindy award Assn. Visual Comm., 1992, Grazella Shepherd Meml. award for Excellence in Edn. Case Western Reserve U. Educator's Forum, 1999, NSF Internat. Digital Libr. Program award Chinese Memory Net: US-Sino Collaborative Rsch., 1999-2003, NSF Internat. Digital Libr. Program award, 2000—, Ernest A. Lynton award Am. Assn. Higher Edn., 2001, NSF Internat. Digital Libr. Program Project Global Memory Net, 2002—, Peace prize US United Cultural Convention's Internat., 2006. Fellow AAAS; mem. ALA (disting. svc. award 1989, Humphrey award 1996), AAUP, Am. Soc. Info. Sci. (best Info. Sci. Tchr. award 1983), Assn. Am. Libr. Schs., Assn. Coll. and Rsch. Librs., Libr. Info. Tech. Assn. (Gaylord Libr. and Info. Tech. Achievement award 1990, Outstanding Achievement Libr. Hi Tech. award 1994, Frederick Kilgous award 2006), New Eng. Libr. Assn. (Emerson Greenaway award 1994), Assn. Libr. and Info. Sci. Edn. (1st ALISE Pratt-Severn Nat. Faculty award 1997). Avocations: travel, stamp collecting/philately. Home: 1400 Commonwealth Ave Newton MA 02465-2830 Office: Simmons Coll 300 Fenway Boston MA 02115-5820 Business E-Mail: chen@simmons.edu.

CHEN, CHUN-HUNG, engineering educator; b. Kaohsiung, Taiwan, Oct. 27, 1964; came to U.S., 1991; s. Ping-Ho and Pao-Yu Chen; m. Mei-Mei Liu, June 15, 1991; 1 child, Valerie. PhD, Harvard U., 1994. Asst. prof. U. Pa., Phila., 1994-2000, acting grad. group chair, 1999-2000; prof. George Mason U., Fairfax, Va., 2000—. Cons. Computer Command and Control Co., Phila., 1997—. Recipient Grad. Assistance in Areas of Nat. Need award U.S. Dept. Edn., 1998; recipient Motion Planning and Simulation award U.S. Army Rsch. Office, 1997, Engring. Design award NSF, 1998, Robust Design Optimization award Sandia Nat. Labs., N.Mex., 1998, Small Aircraft Sys. Transportation Devel. award NASA, 2002, Info. Tech. Rsch. award NSF, 2003. Mem. IEEE (sr.; Best Paper in Automation award

2003), Inst. Ops. Rsch. and Mgmt. Scis. Achievements include development of simulation tool, 1992 (MasPar award); patents for optimal computing allocation, 1999 (Eliahu Jury award 1994). Avocations: trains, aircraft, weather forecasting. Office: George Mason U Dept Sys Engring & Ops Rsch 4400 University Dr MS 4A6 Fairfax VA 22030 Office Phone: 703-993-3572. Business E-Mail: cchen9@gmu.edu.

CHEN, CHUN-JEN, lawyer, educator; BA, LLB, Chinese Culture U., Taipei, Taiwan, 1990—95; LLM in Corp. Law and Fin., Widener U. Sch. Law, Wilmington, Del., 1996—97; LLM in Securities & Fin. Regulation, Georgetown U. Law Sch., DC, 1997—98, PhD in Judicial Sci., 1998—2003. Asst. prof. law Feng Chia U., Taichung, Taiwan, 2003—06, Nat. Cheng Kung U., Tainan, Taiwan, 2006—. Editor Republic China Constl. Ct. Reporter for Judicial Yuan, Taipei, 2004—. Editor: (translation of interpretations) The Republic of China Constitutional Court Reporter; contbr. articles. Grantee, Nat. Sci. Coun., 2004-2005, 2006—. Mem.: Chinese Soc. Internat. Law. Office: Nat Cheng Kung Univ Dept Law No 1 Ta-Hsueh Rd 701 Tainan Taiwan Office Fax: 8866-276-6492. Business E-Mail: chenc4@mail.ncku.edu.tw.

CHEN, DAVID, spinal cord injury physician; b. Mpls., Minn., Dec. 16, 1960; BA summa cum laude in Fin., Univ. Ill., 1983; MD, U. Ill. Coll. Medincine, 1987. Cert. physical medicine and rehab. Intern Northwestern U. Med. Sch., Chgo., 1987—88, resident, 1988—91; dir., spinal cord injury program Rehab. Inst. of Chgo., 1994—, med. dir., spinal cord injury, 1996—. Named one of 40 Under 40, Crain's Bus. mag., 1997; recipient Bronze Tablet award, U. Ill., 1979—83, Alumni Recognition award, Naperville (Ill.) Central High Sch., 1999. Mem.: Am. Spinal Injury Assn., Midwest Reg. Spinal Cord Injury Care System (dir. data acquisition unit 1993—), Khi Kappa Phi, Alpha Lambda Delta, Phi Beta Kappa. Office: Rehab Inst Chgo 345 E Superior St Chicago IL 60611 Business E-Mail: d-chen@northwestern.edu.*

CHEN, DAVID, reporter; b. Providence; Grad., Yale U. With AP, Hong Kong, NY Times, 1995—, bur. chief Upstate NY, reporter Trenton Bur. Recipient Dr. Suzanne Ahn Award for Civil Rights and Social Justice for Asian Ams., 2004. Office: NY Times Trenton Bur PO Box 021 Trenton NJ 08625-0021 also: NJ State House 125 W0 State St Trenton NJ 08625 Office Phone: 212-556-5284. E-mail: dachen@nytimes.com.

CHEN, DEL-MIN AMY, lawyer; b. Balt. d. Chung-Hsien and Show-Fen Chen. BA, U. Tex., Austin, 1993; MPA, JD, Rutgers U., Camden, NJ, 1998. Law clk. Superior Ct. NJ, 1998—99; presdl. mgmt. intern, 1998—2000; with US Dept. Labor, Washington, 1999—. Pro bono atty., guardian ad litem Lawyers for Children Am., 2003—07. Cmty. affairs com. chair Labor's Effective Advocates Devel. (L.E.A.D.), 2005—07. Mem.: DC Bar. Avocations: reading, volunteering, baking, entertaining, floor hockey. Personal E-mail: demiamch@yahoo.com.

CHEN, DI, electronics executive, optical engineer, consultant; b. Chekiang, China, Mar. 15, 1929; came to U.S., 1954, naturalized, 1972; s. Hsun Yu and chien (Wang) C.; m. Lynn C. Wang, June 14, 1958; children: Andrew A.J., Daniel T.Y. BS, Nat. Taiwan U., 1953; MS, U. Minn., 1956; PhD, Stanford U., 1959. Asst. prof. U. Minn., Mpls., 1959-62; rsch. fellow Honeywell Co., Bloomington, Minn., 1962-80; tech. dir. Optical Peripherals Lab., Colorado Springs, Colo., 1980-84; co-founder, exec. v.p. tech. Optotech, Inc., 1984-89; pres. Chen and Assocs. Cons., 1989—. V.p. tech. and engring. Literal Corp., Colorado Springs, 1990-91; chmn., then co-chmn., advisor, sr. advisor Optical Data Storage, 1983-98. Topical editor Applied Optics Jour., 1991-97; contbr. articles to profl. jours, chpts. to ref. books; patentee in field. Founder, chair bd. dirs. Chinese Am. Assn. Minn., 1965—79. Recipient Honeywell Sweatt Scientists and Engrs. award, 1972. Fellow IEEE (life, chmn. IEEE-MAG Twin Cities chpt. 1974); mem. SPIE, Optical Soc. Am., Sigma Xi, Eta Kappa Nu. Office Phone: 952-472-1036. E-mail: dichen2127@frontiernet.net.

CHEN, DING-SHINN, gastroenterologist, educator; MD, Nat. Taiwan U. Assoc. prof. NIH, Bethesda, Md., 1979—80; lectr. Nat. Cancer Ctr. Rsch. Inst., 1975; lectr. Dept. Internal Medicine Nat. Taiwan U. Coll. Med., 1975, assoc. prof. Dept. Internal Medicine, 1978, prof., 1983—, dean, 2001—. Chmn. hepatitis control com. Govt. Taiwan; assoc. editor Hepatology Jour. Biomedical Sci. Recipient Trieste Sci. prize in Med. Sciences, Third World Acad. Scis., 2006. Mem.: Internat. Assn. for Study of Liver (v.p. 2000), Gastroenterological Soc. Taiwan (pres. 1997—2003), Formosan Med. Assn. (pres. 2001—), Taiwan Assn. for Study of Liver (pres. 1996—98), Academia Sinica, NAS (fgn. assoc. 2005—). Office: National Taiwan University No 1 Jen Ai Sec 1 Taipei Taiwan

CHEN, ERIC YEN-PO, accountant, consultant; b. Kaohsiung City, Taiwan, Nov. 7, 1971; came to the U.S., 1994; s. Jeng-Quey and Hsiu-Chuan C.; m. Irene Hsiao-pu Jao, May 22, 1997. BS in Atmospheric Sci., Nat. Taiwan U., 1994; MBA in Accountancy, CUNY, 1996. CPA, N.Y., N.J. Account analyst Dean Witter Trust Co., Jersey City, 1994-95; contr. APWM, Inc. (Roven Dino), Pine Brook, NJ, 1995-96; assoc., tax specialist Kuan C. Tsai & Assocs., P.C., CPA's, Metuchen, NJ, 1996-98; assoc. Rothstein, Kass & Co., P.C., CPA's, Roseland, NJ, 1998-99; bus. analyst mgr. Formosa Plastics Corp., Livingston, NJ, 1999—. Cons. Keydata Internat., Inc., South Plainfield, N.J., 1996-98, Aaeon Electronics, Inc., Hazlet, N.J., 1997-98, New Bay Corp., N.Y.C., 1997-98, Pine Tech. USA, Edison, N.J., 1997-98. Supporter Nutley (N.J.) Fire Dept., 1994-98, Nutley Police Dept., 1994-98. Mem. AICPA, N.J. Soc. CPAs (mem. polit. action com., internat. taxation, young CPAs com.), Beta Gamma Sigma. E-mail: ecij_cpaotr@yahoo.com.

CHEN, FEN, mathematician, educator, researcher; b. Lutsao Village, Chia-Yi Shien, Taiwan, Nov. 28, 1939; arrived in U.S., 1979; s. Shin-Ting Chen and Susan Liaw; m. Ann-Hua Shieh, Aug. 10, 1966; children: Chu-Yi, Chu-Win. BS, Nat. Taiwan Normal U., Taipei, 1968; MEd, Tokyo U, 1977; postgrad., U. Mich., 1978—79, U. Wis., 1979—80; AGS, U Md., 1984. Tchr. math. Tailin Jr. HS, Tailin, Chia-Yi, Taiwan, 1961—63, Pekung Sr. HS, Pekung, Iling Shien, Taiwan, 1963—66, Taichung 1st Sr. HS, Taichung City, Taiwan, 1966—70; instr. math. Tainan Pharmacy U., Tainan Shien, Taiwan, 1970—74; tchg. asst. U. Md., College Park, 1981—83, vol. instr., 1982—86; substitute tchr. math. Prince George's and Montgomery County Pub. Schs., 1984—90; pvt. instr. Montgomery Coll., Md., 1985; substitute tchr. math. Fairfax County Pub. Schs., Md., 1990—98, Arlington Pub. Sch. Sys., Va., 1999—2002. Author: Elem. Calculus, 1972, New Theory of Trisection, 1999, Regular Polygons Vol. I, 2001, Regular Polygons Vol. II. Del. People to People Amb. Program, Egypt, 2007. Fellow Kyo-Dai-Ken Math. Study Group, 1975—78. Mem.: Math. Edn. Rsch. Group (Tokyo), Nat. Coun. Tchrs. of Math., Am. Math. Soc., Math. Assn. Am. (assoc.). Achievements include development of the New Theory of Trisection to solve the most controversial trisection-problem in over 2500 years in the history of mathematics; a regular P-gon (P is no less than 3 natural number); research in theory of trisection from a regular triangle, tetragon, pentagon, hexagon, heptagon, octagon, nonagon, decagon, undecagon, dodecagon, tridecagon, tetradecagon, pentadecagon. Home: 4520 King St No 902 Alexandria VA 22302 Office: Internat Sch Math & Scis Inst PO Box 16707 Alexandria VA 22302 Office Phone: 703-671-6176. Personal E-mail: f.chen@earthlink.net.

CHEN, FENG, adult education educator, researcher; s. Guanghui Chen and Shuhua Liu; m. Ju Guan, July 30, 1996; children: Kevin, Iris. PhD, U. Calif., Davis, 2000. Postdoctoral fellow U. Mich., Ann Arbor, 2001—04; asst. prof. U. Tenn., Knoxville, 2004—. Scholar, Max Planck Soc., 2001. Achievements include discovery of genes for important agricultural traits. Home Phone: 865-766-0726; Office Phone: 865-974-8521.

CHEN, GENSHE, research scientist; s. Dongming Chen and Juxia Xu; m. Yingqi Wu; children: Sherry, Kylie. PhD, Northwestern Poly. U., Xi'an, China, 1991—94. Postdoctoral rschr. Wright State U., Dayton, Ohio, 1996—97; Alexander Von Humboldt rsch. fellow Tech. U. Braunschweig, Germany, 1997—99; rsch. fellow Nat. Aerospace Lab., Mitaka, Tokyo, 1999—2001; postdoctoral rschr. Ohio State U., Columbus, 2001—04; program mgr. Intelligent Automation, Inc., Rockville, Md., 2004—. Home: 14163 Furlong Way Germantown MD 20874 Office: Intelligent Automation Inc 15400 Calhoun Dr Ste 400 Rockville MD 20855 Home Phone: 301-916-6805.

CHEN, HO-HONG H.H., industrial engineering executive, educator; b. Taiwan, Apr. 11, 1933; s. Shui-Cheng and Mei (Lin) C.; m. Yuki-Lihua Jenny, Mar. 10, 1959; children: Benjamin Kuen-Tsai, Carl Joseph Chao-Kuang, Charles Chao-Yu, Eric Chao-Ying, Charmine Tsuey-Ling, Dolly Hsiao-Ying, Edith Yi-Wen, Yvonne Yi-Fang, Grace Yi-Sing, Julia Yi-Jiun. Owner Tai Chang Indsl. Supplies Co., Ltd., 1967—; pres. Pan Pacific Indsl. Supplies, Inc., Ont., Canada, 1975—, Maker Group Inc., Md., 1986—, Wako Internat. Co., Ltd., Md., 1986—; CEO, pres. Nitor Co., Ltd., Taipei, Taiwan, 2000—. Prof. First Econ. U., Japan; commr. Overseas Chinese Affairs Commn., Taiwan; chmn. supervisory bd. Global Alliance for Democracy and Peace, Taiwan. Author: 500 Creative Designs for Future Business, 1961; A Summary of Suggestions for the Economic Development in Central America Countries, 1979; Access and Utilize the Potential Fund in Asia, 1980. Mem. Univ. Club (Washington), Kenwood Golf & Country Club (Bethesda, Md.). Personal E-mail: hohongchen@comcast.net.

CHEN, JAMES PAI-FUN, biology professor, researcher; b. Fungyuan, Taichung, Taiwan, May 1, 1929; came to U.S., 1952; s. Chuan and Su-wuo (Lin) C.; m. Metis Hsiu-chun Lin, Dec. 19, 1964; children: Mark Hsin-tzu, Eunice Hsin-yi, Jeremy Hsin-tao. BS, Houghton Coll., NY, 1955; MS, St. Lawrence U., 1957; PhD, Pa. State U., 1961. From instr. to assoc. prof. Houghton Coll., 1960-64; rsch. assoc. Coll. of Medicine U. Vt., Burlington, 1964-65; rsch. assoc. Sch. of Medicine SUNY, Buffalo, 1965-68; asst. prof. U. Tex. Med. Br., Galveston, 1968-75; sr. rsch. assoc. NASA/Johnson Space Ctr., Houston, 1975-76; rsch. assoc. prof. U. Tenn. Meml. Rsch. Ctr., Knoxville, 1976-78; assoc. prof. Coll. of Medicine U. Tenn., Knoxville, 1978-84, prof. Grad. Sch. of Medicine, 1984—2003, prof. emeritus Grad. Sch. of Medicine, 2005—. Rsch. rev. com. Tex. affiliate Am. Heart Assn., Austin, 1974-76; co-investigator Spacelab I project, Johnson Space Ctr., Houston, 1976-83; vis. prof. Trnovo Hosp. Internal Medicine, Ljubljana, Yugoslavia, 1985. Grantee Robert Welch Found., 1970-74, Ortho Rsch. Found., 1971-75, NIH, 1975-82, Am. Heart Assn. Tex. affiliate, 1969-72, 74-75, Am. Heart Assn. Tenn. affiliate, 1984-85, 89-90, U.S. Army Med. Rsch., 1988-91. Fellow Internat. Soc. Hematology; mem. Am. Assn. Immunologists, Am. Soc. Biochemistry and Molecular Biology, Internat. Soc. Thrombosis and Haemostasis, Internat. Fibrinogen Rsch. Soc., Internat. Soc. Fibrinolysis Proteolysis, Am. Bd. Bioanalysis (clin. lab. dir.). Achievements include research in thrombosis and hemostasis; discovery of additional proteolytic fragmentation in the high temperature trypsin cleavage of human IgM; development of a radioimmunoassay for fragment E-neoantigen and applied it to the clinical assay of hypercoagulable state; discovered evidence of the coagulopathy in Pichinde virus-infected guinea pigs; establishment of blood tests to monitor trauma patients for thromboembolism; recognized that hypercoagulability in preterm infants with intraventricular hemorrhage is associated with fibrinolytic shutdown; ascertained that complement and cytokines are responsible for antibody-mediated hypercoagulability in the anti-T-cell therapy of transplantation. Office: U Tenn Med Ctr Grad Sch Medicine Box 2 1924 Alcoa Hwy Knoxville TN 37920-1511 Home Phone: 865-690-7003. Business E-Mail: jchen@utk.edu.

CHEN, JAMES TSING-FANG, art association administrator, cultural organization administrator; b. Tainan, Taiwan, June 2, 1936; came to U.S., 1975; m. Lucia Hou, Dec. 20, 1975; children: Ted, Julie. BA, Nat. Taiwan U., Taipei, 1959; cert., Beaux Arts, Paris, 1972; MA in Contemporary French Lit., U. Paris, 1965; PhD in Art History, La Sorbonne, Paris, 1972. Editor-in-chief Formosan Report, Paris, 1973-80; founder T.F. Chen Cultural Ctr., NYC, 1996—, New World Art Ctr., NYC, 1996—. Chmn. fine arts sect. Internat. Conf. Arts, Paris, 1987, N.Y.C., 1988. Author of 18 books: Ten Year's of My Pictorial Voyages, 1974, The Spirit of Liberty, 1986, The Art of Dr. T.F. Chen: Neo-Iconography, 1990, Dreaming Towards A New Renaissance, 1990, My Days in Paris, 1996, Towards the 21st Century, 1999, others; over 100 one-man shows in Europe, N.Am. and Asia, including Phila. Art Alliance 1978, State World Forum, 1998, 2000; retrospective show New World Art Ctr., 1996, Taipei Fine Arts Mus., 1996-97; exhibited in numerous group shows in Europe, N.Am., Asia; prodr. series The Statue of Liberty, Post-Van Gogh, East-West, Space Age, Humanity, Princess Diana, others; represented in permanent collections Mus. Modern Art, Paris, Smithsonian Instn., Washington, Pacific Asia Mus., Taipei Fine Arts Mus., also pvt. collections; appeared on cable TV program Art for Humanity World Tour. Organizer, sec.-gen. Fedn. World Formosan Assns., Paris and N.Y.C., 1974-80. Recipient Achievement award in arts and humanities Taiwanese-Am. Found., L.A., 1983, Disting. Alumnus award Tainan 1st H.S., 1995, Global Tolerance award UN, 2001; scholar Govt. of France, 1963. Avocations: music, cooking, chess, reading. Home and Office: TF Chen Museum Bldg 250 Lafayette St New York NY 10012-4040 Office Phone: 212-966-4363. Business E-Mail: chen@tfchen.org.

CHEN, JIQUAN, ecologist, educator; b. Xiaoyi, China, Aug. 24, 1962; s. Guisheng Li; m. Xiang Jiang, May 1, 1998; children: Sylvia, Erika Sequoia. BS, Inner Mongolia U., Huhehot, 1983; M, Chinese Acad. Scis., Beijing, 1986; D, U. Wash., Seattle, 1991. Postdoctoral rschr. U. Wash., Seattle, 1992—93; mem. faculty Mich. Tech U., Houghton, 1993—2001, U. Toledo, 2001—. Vis. fellow Harvard U., Boston, 1999—2000. Named Fgn. Expert, Korean Acad. Forest Rsch., 2003, Japanese Forest Rsch. Inst., 2004; Bullet fellow, Harvard U., 1999. Mem.: IUFRO (group co-chair 2005—), Am. Geophys. Union, Sino-Eco Assn. (pres. 1992—93), Soc. Conservation Biology, Ecol. Soc. Am. (sect. chair, com. chair 1993—99). Office: U Toledo 2801 W Bancroft St Toledo OH 43606 Home Phone: 419-882-2912; Office Phone: 419-530-2664. Office Fax: 419-530-4421. Business E-Mail: jiquan.chen@utoledo.edu.

CHEN, JIUHUA, physicist, geophysicist, educator, materials scientist; b. Shenyang, Liaoning, China, Dec. 2, 1962; arrived in U.S., 1994; s. Xixue Chen and Yukun Li; m. Hongyu Lu, Dec. 28, 1986; 1 child, Jeddy Chang. PhD, Nat. Lab. High Energy Physics, Tsukuba, Japan, 1994. Postdoctoral rsch. assoc. Ctr. High Pressure Rsch., Stony Brook, NY, 1994—96, rsch. asst. prof., 1996—2001; rsch. assoc. prof. SUNY, Stony Brook, 2001—07, rsch. prof., 2007; assoc. prof. mech. and material engring. Fla. Internat. U., Miami, 2007—. Mem. dissertation com. SUNY, Stony Brook, 1996—97, assoc. dir. Mineral Physics Inst., 2002—06, acting dir. Mineral Physics Inst., 2004—05, asst. dean admissions, 2005—06, assoc. dean admissions, 2006—07; organizer workshop high pressure tech., ann. user's meeting Nat. Synchrotoron Light Source, Upton, NY, 1998; organizer workshop High Pressure X-ray Rsch., Upton, 2006. Editor: Advances in High Pressure Technology for Geophysical Applications, 2005. Grantee, NSF, 1999—, Dept. Energy, 2002—, Dept. Def., 2004—; Rsch. fellow, Japan Soc. Promotion Sci., 1998. Mem.: Japan Soc. High Pressure Sci. Tech., Am. Geophys. Union, Internat. Union Crystallography. Achievements include inventor in field. Office: Fla Internat U Ctr Study Matter Extreme Condtiions Mech and Material Engring Miami FL 33199 Office Phone: 631-632-8058. Office Fax: 631-632-8140. E-mail: jiuhua.chen@sunysb.edu.

CHEN, JOHN CALVIN, retired psychiatrist, educator; b. Augusta, Ga., Apr. 30, 1949; s. Calvin H. Chen and Lora L. Liu. BA in History, Pacific Union Coll., 1971; MD, Loma Linda U., 1974; PhD in Philosophy, Claremont Grad. U., 1984; JD, UCLA, 1987. Bar: Calif. 1987, US Dist. Ct. (ctrl. dist.) Calif. 1988; diplomate Am. Bd. Psychiatry and Neurology, Child and Adolescent Psychiatry. Resident in psychiatry Loma Linda U. Med. Ctr., 1975-77; fellow in child and family psychiatry Cedars-Sinai Med. Ctr., LA, 1977-78; psychiat. cons. San Bernardino County Mental Health Dept., Calif., 1979-83; pvt. practice Claremont, Calif., 1980-84; fellow in child and adolescent psychiatry U. So. Calif., LA, 1983-84; law clk. to Hon. William P. Gray US Dist. Ct., LA, 1987-88; mental health psychiatrist LA County Dept. Mental Health, LA, 1988-94, Alameda County Health Care Svcs. Agy., Fremont, Calif., 1994-97; physician specialist LA County Dept. Health Svcs., 1997—99; sr. physician, 1999—2003; attending physician Martin Luther King Jr. Hosp., LA, 1997—2004; child and adolescent psychiatrist Augustus F. Hawkins Mental Health Ctr., LA, 1997—2004, chief child/adolescent svc., 1998—2003; staff Behavioral Neuroscience Rsch. Ctr., Charles Drew Univ., 2003—05; ret., 2005. Adj. instr. social scis., philosophy, Fullerton Coll., Calif., 1989-90; adj. asst. prof. psychiatry Charles Drew U., 1998-2004, asst. clin. prof., 2004-; asst. clin. prof. psychiatry UCLA Sch. Medicine, 1998-2004; faculty Trinity Coll. Grad. Studies, 2004- Contbr. chapters to books Calif. hist., articles to profl. jours. Univ. fellow, Claremont Grad. Sch., 1980—81. Office: 745 E Valley Blvd PMB 120 San Gabriel CA 91776-3549

CHEN, JOHN S., computer company executive; b. Hong Kong, July 1, 1955; came to U.S., 1974; s. Peter and Harmie (Lee) C.; m. Sherry Hai, Nov. 5, 1980; children: Jacqueline, Stephanie. BSEE, Brown U., 1978; MSEE, Calif. Inst. Tech., 1979. V.p. pres., gen. mgr. Unisys, Blue Bell, Pa., 1979-91; exec. v.p. Pyramid Tech., San Jose, Calif., 1991—92, COO, 1992—95, pres., 1993—95, CEO, 1995—97; pres. Sybase, Inc., Dublin, Calif., 1997—, chmn., CEO, 1998—. Mem., bd. dirs., Sybase, Inc., 1997-, Walt Disney Co., 2003- Republican. Roman Catholic. Office: Sybase Inc One Sybase Dr Dublin CA 94568

CHEN, JONATHAN, pediatric surgeon; BS cum laude, Yale U., New Haven, 1990; MD, Columbia U. Coll. Physicians and Surgeons, NYC, 1994. Intern, resident gen. surgery NY Presbyn. Hosp./Columbia U. Med. Ctr., NYC, 1994—99, rsch. fellow, cardiac surgery, 1997—98, chief resident gen. surgery, 1999—2000, fellow cardiothoracic surgery, 2000—02, advanced fellow, mechanical cardiac assistance, 2002, advanced fellow in congenital cardiac surgery, 2003—04, asst. attending surgeon, 2002—. Asst. prof. surgery Columbia U. Coll. Physicians and Surgeons, 2004—; site chief, pediatric surgery NY Weill Cornell Med. Ctr., 2004; asst. prof. cardiothoracic surgery Weill Cornell Med. Coll., NYC. Named Physician of Yr., NY Presbyn. Hosp., 2002; named one of 40 Under 40, Crain's NY Bus. Mag., 2006; named to, Best Drs. NY, 2007; recipient Best Sr. Resident Tchg. award, Columbia U., dept. surgery, 2000, Blakemore Rsch. award, 2000. Mem.: ACS, Am. Acad. Pediatrics, Am. Coll. Cardiology, Soc. Thoracic Surgeons, Internat. Soc. Heart and Lung Transplantation, Soc. Alum. NY Presbyterian, Am. Soc. Transplantation, NY Soc. for Thoracic Surgery. Office: Morgan Stanley Childresn Hosp NY Presbyterian CHN Rm 270 3959 Broadway New York NY 10032 Office Phone: 212-305-5975. Business E-Mail: jmc23@columbia.edu.

CHEN, KENICHI, chef; b. Tokyo, 1956; s. Kenmin and Yoko. Grad., Tamagawa U. Apprenticeship Shisen Hanton Grp., mgr. Chef (TV series) Iron Chef. Achievements include last remaining original chef on Iron Chef; redefined Japanese-Szechwan cooking.

CHEN, KEVIN GANG, oncologist, researcher, molecular pharmacologist; b. Nanbu County, Sichuan Province, China, Aug. 3, 1962; s. Ze-yi Chen and Ying-bi Lai; m. Xiao-yu Jing, June 6, 1963; children: Lawrence (Larry) Xichuan, Richard J. MD, Sichuan U., Chengdu, China, 1983; PhD, Stanford U., 2002. Resident in oral and maxillofacial surgery Xian Jiao-Tong U., Shannxi Province, China, 1983—85; acting chief divsn. oral and maxillofacial surgery Shantou U. Med. Coll., Guangdong Province, China, 1988—91; rsch. fellow in lab. cell biology Nat. Cancer Inst., Bethesda, Md., 2002—05; rsch. scientist Nat. Inst. Neurol. Disorders and Stroke, Bethesda, 2005—. Co-investigator multidrug resistance in human cancers Stanford U. Sch. Medicine, Calif., 1995—2002. Contbr. articles to profl. jours. Mem.: Am. Assn. Cancer Rsch. (assoc.). Achievements include research in identification and characterization of the deletion of phenylalanine at position 335 (Phe335) of P-glycoprotein; regulation of the multidrug resistance gene MDR1; origins of the multidrug resistant cancer cells; first to identify isforms of the multidrug transporter ABCB5; melanosomal sequestration of cytotoxic drugs contributes to multidrug resistance in malignant melanomas; patents for P-glycoprotein mutant resistant to cyclosproin modulation; patents in field. Office: NIH Rm 1000 Bldg 37 37 Convent Dr Bethesda MD 20892 Office Phone: 301-402-8118. Office Fax: 301-480-1022. Business E-Mail: cheng@mail.nih.gov.

CHEN, KEVIN S., management executive, consultant, educator; b. Dover, NJ, Aug. 17, 1960; s. Irving S. and Judy Chen. BS, Stevens Inst. Tech., Hoboken, NJ, 1984, MS, 1988. Purchase parts planning mgr. Rowe Internat. Inc., Whippany, N.J., 1984-86; materials mgr. KDI/Triangle Electronics, Whippany, 1986-90; prodn. control supr. Micron Powder Systems, Summit, N.J., 1990-93; pres., CEO, Bus. Methods Corp., Randolph, NJ, 1995—. Registered and cert. profl. cons. to mgmt. Nat. Bur. Cert. Cons., 1993—2005, adv. coun., 1993—97, regional dir. (N.J.), 2001—05, nat. com. for continuing edn. in consultancy, 1999—2001; pres., CEO Logo In Motion, Randolph, NJ, 1999—; supr. Ctr. Assessment and Learning, County Coll. of Morris, 2000—. Mem. coll. coun. County Coll. of Morris, 2002—04; mem. acad. std. com. County Coll. Morris, 2002—06; mem. Small Bus. and Entrepreneurship Coun.; mem. Presdl. Bus. Commn., Nat. Rep. Com., 2005, hon. chair State of N.J. bus. adv. coun., 2002—06; walk chair ADA, 1993—96, bd. dirs., 1995—97, mem. N.W. regional coun., 1993—97; mem. steering com. United Way's Mentoring Tng. and Cons. Ctr., 2001—02; vice chmn., chmn. spl. events., chmn. survey subcom. Randolph Township Environ. Com., 1985—89; dir. Custom Scholarship Search Program, 1991—94; instr. bus. County Coll. of Morris, 1996—98, instr., 2001—; racquetball events coord. Stevens Alumni Assn., 1994—2000; racquetball coord. Madison Area YMCA, 1999—2001; N.J. state dir. Cons. Inst., 1999—2001; bd. dirs. Better Bus. Bur., NJ, 2001—02, NJ, 2005—; coun. CEO Small Bus. and Entrepreneurship Coun. Recipient Nat. Leadership award, Nat. Rep. Congl. Com., Businessman of Yr., 2003—04, Ronald Reagan Gold medal, 2004, Tchg. Excellence award, Nat. Inst. for Staff and Orgnl. Devel., 2006; grantee, Ednl. Opportunity Fund, 2006. Mem.: NJ Bus. Tech. Edn. Assn. (bd. dirs.), Nat. Bus. Edn. Assn., NJ Regional Cons. Assn. (founder, regional dir., bd. dirs.), Delta Pi Epsilon. Avocations: racquetball, coaching, team sports. Home: PO Box 520 Mount Freedom NJ 07970-0520 Office: Business Methods Corp 503 State Route 10 E Randolph NJ 07869-2152 Home Phone: 973-703-2022; Office Phone: 973-328-0086. Personal E-mail: businessabc@aol.com.

CHEN, KUEN HAI, physician; b. Tachia, Taiwan, May 23, 1937; arrived in U.S., 1966, naturalized, 1976; s. John Bei and Yeh (Liang) Chen; m. Fu Mei Lai, Jan. 1, 1966; children: Richard, Humphrey, Christopher. BS, Nat. Taiwan U., Taipei, 1959, MD, 1964. Diplomate Am. Bd. Family Practice.

Intern Ill. Ctrl. Hosp., Chgo., 1966—67; resident gen. surgery Sister's Hosp., Buffalo, 1967—69; resident gen. surgery C and O Hosp., Huntington, W.Va., 1970—71; fellow spinal cord injury svc. VA Hosp., East Orange, NJ, 1971—72; chief Veteran's Hosp., East Orange, NJ, 1972—76; staff mem. First Ave. Med. Ctr., NYC, 1976—. Adv. bd. Dupont, 1999—, Mc Neil Health Network, 1999—, Agouron, 2000—, Bristol Myers Roche, 2000—; cons. Schering/Key Glaxo Wellcome Inc. Nat. Irritable Bowel Syndrome Awareness Registry, 2000—; mem. physicians coun. Heritage Found., 1994—; dir. K.F.C. Corp.; analyst Am. Bd. Disability, 1999. Author: Am. Spoken English; founding prodr. GOP TV, 1994—. Mem. Presdl. Adv. Commn., 1992, Presdl. Commn. Am. Agenda, 1992; del. Presdl. Trust, 1992; pres. Parents' Assn., 1980—84; hon. chmn. Physician's Adv. Bd.; adv. mem. Rep. Nat. Commn. Am. Agenda, 1992—; chmn. adv. bd. Rep. Nat. Com., 1994—, hon. co-chmn. bus. adv. coun., 1998, mem. adv. coun., 1998, hon. co-chmn., 1999—; founding mem. Rep. Campaign Coun., 1994—, nat. campaign advisor, 1995—; founding mem. Eisenhower Commn., 1995—96; mem. Rep. Senator Adv. Coun., 1997—; chmn. adv. coun. Rep. Nat. Com., 1999; mem. Rep. Senator Inner Cir., 1998—; hon. co-chair inaugural com. 43d Pres. of U.S., 2001; del. N.J. Rep. Presdl. Task Force, 1994—98; co-chmn. Election Adv. Bd., 2000—; chmn. joint session, bd. deaconess mtgs. Taiwan Union Presbyn. Ch., NY, 1983, active NY; elder Taiwan Presbyn. Ch. No. Jersey, 2007—. With Taiwan Air Force, 1965. Named Mem. of the Yr., Rep. Presdl. Task Force, 1996, Physician of Yr., 2001—03, Rep. of the Yr., 2002, Bus. Man of the Yr., 2004—07, Patriot of Yr., 2007; recipient Disting. Svc. and Leadership Award, Nat. Taiwan U., Patriotic Award Medal, Pres. of U.S., Congl. Medal of Distinction, 2001, Rep. of the Yr. award, Presdl. Bus. Commn., 2002—03, Rep. Senatorial Medal of Freedom Award, 2002. Fellow: Am. Geriat. Soc., Am. Acad. Family Physician; mem.: AMA (Physician Recognition award 1969, 1972, 1975, 1978, 1981, 1984, 1987, 1990, 1993), Presdl. Bus. Commn., Nat. Irritable Syndrome Awareness Registry, N.Am. Taiwanese Med. Assn. (bd. dir. greater N.Y. chpt. 1985—, pres. 1987—89, chmn. edn. com. 1989—95), W.Va. Med. Inst., Nat. Bd. Addiction Examiners (Dr. addiction counselor), Am. Spinal Injury Assn., Taita Jing-Fu Med. Found. (hon. dir.), Internat. Soc. Paraplegia, NY County Med. Soc. (mem. com. health care agy.), Am. Coll. Emergency Physicians, NY Acad. Sci., Am. Bd. Disability Analysis, Nat. Taiwan U. Alumni Assn. (bd. dir. 1981—, chmn. edn. com. 1984—94, treas. 1991—94, chmn. by-law com. 1994—96, pres. 1999—2001), Nat. Taiwan U. Med. Coll. Alumni Assn. (exec. dir. 1979—81, pres. 1981—83, permanent bd. dir. 1984, trustee 1985—88, chmn. edn. com. 1987—95, chmn. fund campaign com. 1988—94, N.Y. chpt. bd. dir. 1994, chmn. by-law com. 1994—), Heritage Found., Alpha Omega Alpha. Presbyterian.

CHEN, KUN-MU, electrical engineering educator; b. Taiwan, China, Feb. 3, 1933; came to U.S., 1957, naturalized, 1969; s. Tsa-Mao and Che (Wu) C.; m. Shun-Shun Chen, Feb. 22, 1962; children: Margaret, Katherine, Kenneth, George. BS, Nat. Taiwan U., 1955; MS, Harvard, 1958, PhD, 1960. Research assoc. U. Mich., 1960-64; vis. prof. Chao-Tung U., Taiwan, 1962; asso. prof. elec. engring. Mich. State U., 1964-67, prof., 1967-95, Richard M. Hong Endowed prof. elec. engring. Lansing, 1995—99, dir. elec. engring. grad. program, 1967-70, Richard M. Hong prof. emeritus, 1999—. Vis. prof. Tohoku U., Japan, 1989, Nat. Taiwan U., 1989. Author articles on electromagnetic radiation, plasma physics, electromagnetic bioeffects. Recipient Disting. Faculty award Mich. State U., 1976, Outstanding Achievement award in sci. and engring. Taiwanese Am. Found., 1984; Withrow Disting. scholar Coll. Engring., Mich. State U., 1993; C.T. Loo fellow, 1957; Gordon McKay fellow, 1958-60. Fellow IEEE, AAAS; mem. Internat. Union Radio Sci. (commn. A, B and C), AAUP, Sigma Xi, Phi Kappa Phi, Tau Beta Pi. Home: 7585 Mona Ln San Diego CA 92130 Office: Mich State U Dept Elec Engring East Lansing MI 48824 Business E-Mail: chen@msu.edu.

CHEN, LAN X., physician, educator; arrived in U.S., 1989; d. B. K. Xuan and R. L. Young; m. Tao Chen, Mar. 12, 1990; children: Sophia, Gavin. MD, Shanghai Med. U., China, 1987; PhD, Temple U., Phila., 1996. Diplomate in internal medicine and rheumatology Am. Bd. Internal Medicine. Intern Drexel U., 1996—97; resident Hahnemann/Drexel, 1997—99; attending physician Presbyn. Med. Ctr., UPHS, Phila., 2002—; asst. clin. prof. U. Pa., Phila., 2003—. Co-leader del. to China People to People, Pa. Named Intern of Yr., Temple U. Med. Sch., 1996; grantee, 1995. Mem.: ACP, Am. Coll. Rheumatology. Office: U Pa 3701 Market St Ste 741 Philadelphia PA 19104 Home Phone: 215-283-9488; Office Phone: 215-662-4333. Office Fax: 215-823-6032.

CHEN, LINCOLN CHIN-HO, medical educator; b. Peoples Republic China, Feb. 12, 1942; came to U.S., 1949; s. Samuel S.T. and Winifred (Wan) C.; m. Martha Alter, July 1, 1967; children: Gregory, Alexis. BA magna cum laude, Princeton U., 1964; MD cum laude, Harvard U., 1968; MPH, Johns Hopkins U., 1973. Lic. doctor, Mass. Intern in internal medicine Mass Gen. Hosp., Boston, 1968-69, asst. resident in internal medicine, 1969-70; clin. fellow Harvard Med. Sch. Harvard U., Boston, 1969-70; chmn. population svcs. dept. Harvard Sch. Pub. Health Harvard U., Boston, 1987, Takemi prof. internat. health, 1987—97, study dir. Commn. on Health Rsch., 1987—97; clin. rsch. assoc. Nat. Inst. Allergy and Infectious Diseases NIH, D.C., Bangladesh, England, 1970-72; staff assoc. Population Coun., Washington, 1972-77; officer program for population Ford Found., Bangladesh, 1973-75, acting rep., 1976, project specialist devel. Internat. Ctr. for Health Rsch., 1977, rep. India, Sri Lanka, Nepal, 1981-86; mem. White House Task Force on Internat. Health, 1977; sci. dir. IC Diarrhoeal Disease Rsch., B, Bangladesh, 1977-80; exec. v.p. strategy Rockefeller Found., 1997—2002, dir., global equity initiative, JFK Sch. Govt. Harvard U., 2002—. Vis. prof. nutrition U. Dhaka, Bangladesh, 1970-80; vis. assoc. prof. population sci. and internat. health Harvard U., Boston, 1980-81; vis. lectr. MIT, Cambridge, 1976-81; vis. scholar Bangladesh Inst. Devel. Studies, 1977-78; mem. U.S. panel U.S.-Japan Malnutrition Panel NIH, 1979-80; mem. global adv. com. UN Univ., 1980-83; mem. adv. com. on child survival revolution UNICEF, 1984—, chmn. CARE, 2001-. Editor, author (with others): Disaster in Bangladesh: Health Crisis in a Developing Nation, 1973; contbr. articles to profl. jours., chpts. to books. Recipient award NSF, 1964. Mem. Am. Pub. Health Assn., Population Assn. Am., AAAS, Internat. Union Nutritional Scis., Internat. Epidemiol. Assn., Nat. Coun. Internat. Health (bd. dirs. 1982-83), NAS (com. internat nutrition programs 1982-84, 86, subcom. on vitamin A), Internat. Ctr. Rsch. Women (bd. dirs. 1987), Phi Beta Kappa, Alpha Omega Alpha, Inst. Medicine, 2004. Office: JFK Sch Govt 79 John F Kennedy St Cambridge MA 02138

CHEN, LU, neurobiologist, biology professor; BS, U. Sci. and Tech., China, 1993; PhD, U. So. Calif., 1998. Postdoctoral fellow U. So. Calif., 1998—99, U. Calif., San Francisco, 1999—2002, asst. prof. neurobiology Berkeley, 2003—, mem., Helen Wills Neuroscience Inst. Author: (articles) published in journals such as Nature, Jour. of Neuroscience, and Proceedings of the Nat. Acad. of Sciences USA. Named an Disting. Young Scholars in Med. Rsch., W.M. Keck Found., 2005; MacArthur Fellow, John D. and Catherine T. MacArthur Found., 2005. Office: Univ Calif Berkeley Dept Molecular & Cell Biology 124 Life Sciences Addition # 3200 Berkeley CA 94720-3200 Office Phone: 510-643-8163. Office Fax: 510-643-6791. E-mail: luchen@berkeley.edu.

CHEN, MING, quality assurance professional; b. Taikang, Henan Province, China, Mar. 5, 1966; s. Dongqing Chen and Qiying Zhao, adopted s. Dongying Chen and Chaozhen Qin; m. Donghui Shi; children: Catherine Rock, Jacqueline Stone. BSc, Shenyang Agrl. Coll., China, 1981; MSc, Beijing Agrl. U., 1985—88; PhD, Chinese Acad. Agrl. Scis., Beijing, 1988—91. Post-doctoral rsch. scientist Inst. Geography Chinese Acad. Scis., Beijing, 1991—93, assoc. prof. Com. Integrated Survey Natural Resources, 1993—95; vis. prof. Soil Survey & Land Rsch. Ctr. Cranfield U., Silsoe, England, 1995—96; rsch. assoc. Soil & Water Sci. U. Fla., Gainesville, 1996—2001; quality assurance officer Everglades REC, Belle Glade, Fla., 2001—07; quality assurance adminstr. South Fla. Water Mgmt. Dist., West Palm Beach, 2007—. Contbr. articles to profl. jours. Mem.: Soil & Crop Sci. Soc. Fla., Soil Sci. Soc. Am. Achievements include research in baseline concentration of arsenic in Florida surface soils; specific conductance in farm canal water in the Everglades agricultural arena. Office: South Fla Water Mgmt Dist 3301 Gun Club Rd MSC 4610 West Palm Beach FL 33406 Home Phone: 561-383-6823. Business E-Mail: mchen@sfwmd.gov.

CHEN, PETER PIN-SHAN, engineering, computer science and Internet/web educator, data processing executive; b. Taishan, Kwangtung, China, Jan. 3, 1947; came to U.S., 1969; s. Man-See and T.T. Chen; m. Li-Chuang Ho; children: Victoria, Angela, Gloria Lily. BSEE, Nat. Taiwan U., Republic of China, 1968; MS, Harvard U., 1970, PhD, 1973. Student assoc. IBM, Yorktown Heights, NY, 1970; teaching fellow Harvard U., Cambridge, Mass., 1970-71; prin. engr. Honeywell, Waltham, Mass., 1973-74; vis. researcher Digital Equipment Corp., Maynard, Mass., 1974; asst. prof. MIT, Cambridge, Mass., 1974-78; assoc. prof. UCLA, 1978-82; Sinclair vis. prof. MIT, 1986-87; Foster Disting. Chair prof. La. State U., Baton Rouge, 1983—. Vis. prof. Harvard U., Cambridge, 1990, MIT, Cambridge, 1990-92; chmn. Chen & Assocs. Inc., Baton Rouge, 1978—; pres. ER Inst., Baton Rouge, 1980—. Author: Entity-Relationship Approach to Logical DB Design, 1978, ER to Systems Analysis, 1980, ER to Information Modeling, 1983; patentee in field. Tech. officer with Republic of China mil. svcs., 1968-69. Named to Data Mgmt. Hall of Fame, 2000; recipient Faculty Career award, UCLA, 1979, Info. Tech. award, Data Adminstrn. Mgmt. Assn., 1990, Gt. Paper in Computer Sci. Achievement award, Data Adminstrn. Mgmt. Assn. Internat., 2000, Stevens award, 2001, Allen Newell award, ACM/AAAI, 2002, Pan Wen-Yuan Outstanding Rsch. award, 2004, Disting. Faculty award, La. State U., 2005; Rsch. grantee, NSF, NIST, NIH, Dept. Def., Air Force, Air Force Office Sci. Rsch., Navy, others, 1978—. Fellow: AAAS, IEEE (Harry Goode award 2003), Assn. Computing Machines; mem.: European Acad. Scis. Office: La State Univ Computer Sci Dept Baton Rouge LA 70803-0001 E-mail: pchen@lsu.edu.

CHEN, PHILIP MINKANG, strategic consultant; b. Chungking, Szechuan, China, Oct. 20, 1944; s. Yin Ching and Wansu (Wu) C.; m. Deborah Lynn Carlson, May 7, 1971; children: Martin, Emily. BME with distinction, U. Va., 1968; MS, Stanford U., 1969; JD, U. Minn., 1979. Bar: Minn. 1979, U.S. Dist. Ct. Minn. 1979, N.Y. 1982; registered profl. engr. Va., 1972, N.Y.; diplomate Am. Acad. Environ. Engrs., 1994. Copy boy Washington Star Newspaper, 1962-65; mech. engr. Pope, Evans & Robbins, Alex., Va., 1967-68; engr. Westinghouse Orec, Annapolis, Md., 1969-71; sr. environ. engr. Stone & Webster Engring. Corp., Boston, Denver, 1971-78; sr. engr. Dames & Moore, Denver, 1978; assoc. Dorsey & Whitney, Mpls., 1979-82, Mudge, Rose, Guthrie & Alexander, NYC, 1982; mng. dir. Lehman Bros., NYC, 1982-92; pres. Weston Internat., 1992-94; exec. v.p. Roy F. Weston, Inc., West Chester, Pa., 1992-94; investment banker The Chase Manhattan Bank, N.A., NYC, 1995-96; mng. dir. South Africa Infrastructure Fund, Johannesburg, 1996-2000, PNC Capital Markets, Inc., Phila., 2003—05, ABN AMRO Inc., NYC, 2005—06; exec. dir. UBS Investment Bank, 2006—07; strategic cons. Eight East Lawn Strategic Consulting, LLC, 2007—. Editl. adv. bd. American City and County Mag., 1986-87, Project Finance Monthly, 1989-92; mem. environ. technologies trade adv. com., Dept. Commerce, 1995-96, co-chmn. fin. subcom. Patentee for mooring system. Mem. Town Mtg. Winchester, Mass., 1973; past bd. dirs. U.S. Environ. Tech. Export Coun., Greater Phila. Internat. Network, Greater Phila. First Ptnrship. for Econ. Devel.; mem. The Union League of Phila., 1994—; participant Presdl. Bus. Devel. mission to Brazil, Argentina, and Chile, 1994. Mem. ABA (vice chmn. elec. power com. natural resources law sect. 1982-85, chmn. spl. com. on energy fin. 1988-89), ASME, Nat. Resource Recovery Assn. (adv. bd. U.S. conf. of mayors 1989), U. Va. Alumni Assn., Phi Sigma Kappa. Avocations: art, writing, fishing. Personal E-mail: chenpm@aol.com. Business E-Mail: philip.chen@eighteastlawn.com.

CHEN, QIANG, engineer; BS in Engring., Saint-Petersburg State Electrotech. U., Russia, 1994, MS in Engring., 1996; MS in Elec. and Computer Engring., Ga. Inst. Tech., 2000, PhD in Elec. and Computer Engring., 2003. Lead engr. Korona Semiconductor Co., Zelenograd, Moscow, 1996—98; postdoctoral fellow Ga. Inst. of Tech., Atlanta, 2003; mem. tech. staff Advanced Micro Devices, Sunnyvale, Calif., 2003—. Author: articles in profl. jours. Recipient Mem. of Phase I Winning Team at Copper Design Contest, Semiconductor Rsch. Corp., 2000, Outstanding Student award, Saint-Petersburg Electrotech. U., 1992, 1st Pl. award, U. Physics Olympiad of Saint-Petersburg, 1992, 3rd Pl. award, U. Math. Olympiad of Saint-Petersburg, 1991. Office Phone: 408-749-6586. Business E-Mail: qchen.ece03@gtalumni.org.

CHEN, QIMING, engineer; s. Jiaqing Chen and Yunmei Zhang; m. Li Rong, Apr. 28, 1999; 1 child, Roger. BS, Huazhong U. Sci. and Tech., Wuhan, China, 1995, MS, 1998; PhD, Iowa State U., Ames, 2004. Sr. engr. PJM Interconnection, LLC, Norristown, Pa., 2003—. Sr. engr. PJM Interconnection, LLC, Norristown, Pa., 2003—. Contbr. scientific papers to profl. jours. Recipient Rsch. Excellence award, Iowa State U., 2004. Mem.: IEEE, Inst. Ops. Rsch. and the Mgmt. Scis. Achievements include research in electric power systems cascading outage mechanism and prevention. Office Fax: 610-666-2296.

CHEN, QINGHUA, engineering educator; s. Dengyuan Chen and Guiying Lin; m. Gezhou Qian; 1 child, Yisha. MS in Engring., Chongqing U., 1994, PhD, 2000. Cert. tchr. Chongqing U., 2000. Lectr. Chongqing U., 1990—98, assoc. prof., 1999—2002, prof., 2003—. Dir. Inst. Shudong Refrigeration & Air-conditioning R&D, Chongqing, 1999—2000; cons. Yantai Zhentai Ancillary Equipment of Refrigeration Machine Corp., China, 2001—03; project asst. U. Wis., 2002—03, vis. scholar, 2002—. Contbr. chapters to books, scientific papers in field. Recipient Excellent Tchg. award, Edn. Commn., Sichuan Province, 1993, Excellent Tchr. award, Chongqing U., 2001; Rsch. grant, Nat. Natural Sci. Found. China, 2002. Mem.: Am. Soc. Mechanics & Engring., Chinese Soc. Engring. Thermophysics. Achievements include patents for high efficient tube-in-tube evaperative condenser. Avocations: travel, cooking, reading, movies, music. Office: U Wis 3200 N Cramer Ave Milwaukee WI 53201 Home: 4110 N Bartlett Ave Milwaukee WI 53211 Home Phone: 414-967-5058; Office Phone: 414-229-6895. Office Fax: 414-229-6958. Business E-Mail: qhchen@cqu.edu.cn.

CHEN, RAY GOW HWEI, artist, educator, department chair; b. Taipei, Taiwan, Jan. 9, 1962; s. Chi Wen Chen and Chang Wuo Kuo; m. Ann Mei Hui Huang, June 28, 2003. BFA in Music, Nat. Taiwan Ednl. U., 1986; BFA in Ceramics, Ohio U., 1995; MFA in Ceramics & Ceramics Sculpture, Rochester Inst. Tech., 1997. Prof., ceramics dept. chair U. So. Maine, Gorham, Maine, 2001—; exhbn. dir. The Internat. Ceramics Group, Portland, Maine, 2005—. Symposium chmn. U. So. Maine, 2002, faculty senate, 2003—, symposium chmn., Maine, 2004—, 2006, 07; vis. artist U. Mass., Dartmouth, Mass., 2004, Watershed Ctr. Ceramic Art, U. Maine, 2004, Ctrl. Mich. U., Mt. Pleasant; vis. artist 4th East-West ceramics collaboration internat. U. Hawaii; vis. artist Balt. Inst. Coll. Art, NH Inst. Art, Manchester, Ind. State U., Terre Haute; guest curator Highland Art Gallery, 2005; curator Nat. Coun. on Edn. for Ceramic Arts, Louisville, 2006, U. So. Maine; spkr. in field; juror in field; presenter in field. Ceramic sculpture, Mother and Child (Emerging Talant Artist award, Nat. Coun. Edn. Ceramics Arts, 2001), Life (The 3rd Cheongju Internat. Biennale, Korea, 2003), Relationship (Sidney Myer Internat. award, Australia, 1999), Mother and Child (Altech Ceramics Triennial, South Africa, 2003), In Between (54 Concorso Internat. Della Mus. award, France, 2004), Tradition, Galerie Handwerk, Koblenz, Germany, 2006, Cheongin Internat. Biennele, Taipei County Hingge Ceramics Mus., Mus. Tex. Tech U., 2005, exhibitions include Sir Mashiko Ceramics Exhbn., Mashiko Mus. Fine Arts, Japan, Yingge Ceramics Mus., Taiwan, 2006, 4th World Ceramic Biennale, Republic of Korea, Icheon World Ceramic Ctr., exhibitions include Chinese Am. Friendship Assn., Portland, Maine, 2007, Warren Meml. Libr., Maine, 2007, Springfield Mus. Art, Ohio, 2007, NE Upstream Gallery, 2007. Deacon Portland Chinese Gospel Ch., Portland, 2004—. Soldier Mil. Police, 1982—86, Taiwan. Recipient Silver award, Forte Cup 20th Century Asian Pacific Art Internat., 1999, First Place, Internat. Art Vision 2.0, 2002, Elizabeth R. Raphael Founder's prize, Soc. Contemporary Craft Mus., 2003, Hon. Mention award, St. Petersburg Clay Nat., 2003, Gallery Internat., 2005, Cheonju Internat. Craft Biennale, 2005, 4th World Ceramic Biennale, 2007; fellow Lormina Salter Fellowship, Balt. Clayworks, 1997, U. So. Maine, 2006—08, Provost, U. So. Maine, 2007; grantee Sculpture Excellence award, The Va. A. Groot Found., 2001, Faculty Profl. Devel. grant, U. So. Maine, 2001-2005, Internat. Exch. & Rsch. Found, 2004, Jingdezhen 1000 Yrs. Porcelain Internat. Rsch. grant, Jingdezhen Mcpl. People's Govt., Chian, 2004, Coll. Arts & Scis. Rsch. Creative award, U. So. Maine, 2004, 2005, Berkshire Taconic Cmty. Found.; scholar Nat. Coun. Edn. for Ceramic Arts, SHIMPO Co., Japan, 1993, Alfred L. & Ruby C. Davis Internat., Rochester Inst. Tech., 1997. Baptist. Avocations: travel, music, art collection, reading, exercise. Office: U So Maine 37 College Ave Gorham ME 04038-1032 Home Phone: 207-878-5728; Office Phone: 207-780-5464. Office Fax: 207-780-5759. Personal E-mail: raychenclay@msn.com. Business E-Mail: gowhwei.chen@maine.edu.

CHEN, SANDRA YI-TING, political organization worker; BA in Polit. Sci. & Chinese Lit., U. Calif., Riverside; student, UCLA. Exec. dir. Ctr. for Asian Am. United for Self Empowerment, Pasadena. Dir. of mentorship Asian Professional Exchange. Adv. bd. mem. San Gabriel Valley YMCA, Make A Wish Found. of San Gabriel Valley; mem. League of Women Voters-Greater Pasadena. Office: Ctr for Asian Am United for Self Empowerment 260 S Los Robles Ave 118 Pasadena CA 91101

CHEN, SHOEI-SHENG, retired mechanical engineer; b. Taiwan, Jan. 26, 1940; s. Yung-cheng and A-shu Chen; m. Ruth C. Lee, June 28, 1969; children: Lyrice, Lisa, Steve. BS, Nat. Taiwan U., 1963; MS, Princeton U., 1966, MA, 1967, PhD, 1968. Rsch. asst. Princeton U., 1965—68; asst. mech. engr. Argonne Nat. Lab., Ill., 1968—71, mech. engr., 1971—80, sr. mech. engr., 1980—2001; ret., 2001. Cons. to Internat. Atomic Energy Agy. to assist developing countries in R & D of nuc. reator sys. components, 1977, 79, 80, 94; cons. NASA, NRC, Rockwell Internat., others. Author: Flow-Induced Vibration of Circular Cylinderical Structures, 1987; mem. internat. adv. editl. bd. Acta Mechanica Solida; adv. bd. JSME Internat. Jour.; assoc. editor Applied Mechs. Rev., Jour. of Pressure Vessels Tech.; contbr. articles to profl. jours. Recipient Disting. Performance award U. Chgo., 1986, ASME pressure vessel and piping medal, 2001. Fellow ASME (chmn. tech. subcom. on fluid and structure interactions pressure vessels and piping divsn. 1987-90, honors chmn. 1990-94, exec. com. 1990-96, organizer symposia, tech. program chmn. 1994, conf. chair ASME/JSME pressure vessels and piping conf. 1995, pressure vessels and piping divsn., chmn. 1995-96, senate pres. 1997-98, honors and awards chair of materials and structures tech. group 1996-99), Instn. Diagnostic Engrs.; mem. Am. Acad. Mechanics, Acoustical Soc. Am., Sigma Xi. E-mail: sschen88@gmail.com.

CHEN, SHUANG, computer science professional; b. China, Jan. 29, 1958; m. Hongwen Yan, Aug. 3, 1987; children: Jessica Y., Julia Y. BSEE, Nanjing Aeronautical U., 1982; MSEE, South China U. Tech., Guangzhou, China, 1985; MPH in Computer Engring., Rutgers U., 1990, PhD in Computer Engring., 1991. Mem. faculty South China U. Tech., Guangzhou, 1985-86; rsch. asst. Rutgers U., New Brunswick, 1986-91; sr. rsch. engr. Comm. Intelligence Corp., Redwood Shores, Calif., 1991-95; rsch. staff mem. IBM Thomas J. Watson Rsch. Ctr., Yorktown Heights, NY, 1995-98; pres., CEO, chmn. bd. Internat. Interactive Commerce, Ltd., Armonk, NY, 1999—2001; chmn. bd., pres. Op40, Inc., White Plains, NY, 2002—. Author: (with others) Studies in Pattern Recognition, 1997; reviewer profl. jours. Mem. IEEE, Sigma Xi.

CHEN, SOW-HSIN, nuclear science and engineering educator, researcher; b. Chia-Yi, Taiwan, Mar. 5, 1935; came to U.S., 1958, naturalized, 1974; s. Pi-Yu Chen and Liang Hsu; m. Ching-Chih Liu, Aug. 19, 1961; children: Anne, Catherine, John. BS in Physics, Nat. Taiwan U., 1956; MS in Physics, Nat. Tsinghua U., 1958; MS in Nuc. Sci., U. Mich., 1962; PhD in Physics, McMaster U., 1964. Postdoctoral fellow AERE Harwell, Berkshire, England, 1965; asst. prof. physics U. Waterloo, Ont., Canada, 1964-67; rsch. fellow Harvard U., Cambridge, Mass., 1967; asst. prof., then assoc. prof. nuclear engring. MIT, Cambridge, 1968-74, prof. nuclear engring., 1974—. Vis. prof. Tsinghua U., Peking, China, 1982, Ecole Superieure de Physique et Chemie, Paris, 1981, Univ. Konstanz, Germany, 1988, Univ. Bayreuth, Germany, 1988, Univ. Brodeaux I, France, 1991, 93; chmn. Gordon Conf., 1986; co-organizer ACS Conf., Conf. Colloid and Interface Sci.: Trends and Applications, 1985; dir. NATO ASI on Scattering Techniques Applied to Supramolecular and Non-Equilibrium Systems, 1980, Structure and Dynamics of Supramolecular Aggregates and Strongly Interacting Colloids, 1991; hon. prof. U. Hainan, China, 2004—; chmn. workshop, NSF, 2006; academician Academia Sinica, 2007. Author: Spectroscopy in Biology, Chemistry and Physics-Neutron, X-Ray and Laser, 1975, Scattering Techniques Applied to Supramolecular and Non-Equilibrium Systems, 1981, Micellar Solutions and Microemulsions: Structure: Dynamics and Statistical Thermodynamics, 1990, Structure and Dynamics on Strongly Interacting Colloids and Supramolecular Aggregates in Solution, 1992, Interaction of Photons and Neutrons with Matter-An Introduction, 1997; contbr. 350 articles to sci. jours. Alexander von Humboldt US sr. scientist award Govt. of Germany, 1987-88, 95, Career Achievement award, MIT, 2004, Cozzavelli prize, Nat. Acad. Sci., 2007. Fellow AAAS, Am. Phys. Soc., Japan Soc. for the Promotion of Sci. (Rsch. fellow 1995); mem. Sigma Xi. Home: 1400 Commonwealth Ave Newton MA 02465-2830 Office: MIT 24-209 77 Mass Ave Cambridge MA 02139-4307 Office Phone: 617-253-3810. Business E-Mail: sowhsin@mit.edu.

CHEN, STEPHEN SHI-HUA, pathologist, biochemist; b. Taipei, Taiwan, Republic of China, Dec. 25, 1939; came to U.S., 1965; s. Ah-wen and Shun (Pan) C.; m. Hsin-Hsin Yii, July 5, 1969; children: Peter T., Margaret T. MD, Nat. Taiwan U., 1964; PhD, U. Pitts, 1972. Diplomate Am. Bd. of Pathology. Asst. prof. pathology U. Pitts., 1972-76; staff pathologist Presbyn. Hosp., Pitts., 1973-76; asst. prof. pathology dept. Stanford U., Palo Alto, Calif., 1976-80, clin. assoc. prof. pathology dept., 1980-96, clin. prof., 1996—; staff pathologist Veterans Affairs Med. Ctr., Palo Alto, 1976—. Contbr. articles to Jour. Cellular Physiology, Jour. Chromatography, Clinica Chimca Acta. Fellow Coll. Am. Pathologists; mem. Am. Soc. Investigative Pathology, U.S. and Can. Acad. Pathology Inc., Am. Soc. Clin. Pathologists, Am. Soc. Cytopathology. Achievements include chromatography of phospholipids. Office: Vets Affairs Med Ctr 113 3801 Miranda Ave Palo Alto CA 94304-1207

CHEN, STEVE SHIH, Internet company executive; b. Aug. 1978; Student in Computer Sci., U. of Ill. at Urbana-Champaign. With PayPal, 1999—2005; co-founder, CTO YouTube Inc. (sold to Google in 2006), San

Mateo, Calif., 2005—. Named (with Chad Hurley) Webby Person of the Yr., 2007; named one of 50 Who Matter Now, CNNMoney.com Bus. 2.0, 2006, The World's Most Influential People, TIME mag., 2007, 25 Most Influential People in Web Music, Powergeek 25, 2007.*

CHEN, TAK-MING, retired civil engineer, consultant; b. Changning, Hunan, China, July 29, 1936; came to U.S., 1970; s. Jenn-Chiu and Yin (Peng) C.; m. Taining Chou, July 1, 1973; children: Merry, Terry. BS in River/Harbor Engring., Taiwan Provincial Coll. of Marine Sci. and Tech., 1966; MSCE, U. Mo., 1971. Registered profl. engr., N.Y., Md., D.C. Project engr. Chinese Petroleum Corp., Taipei, Taiwan, 1973; structural designer Bellante, Clauss, Miller & Nolan, inc., Scranton, Pa., 1974-76; structural engr. Wayman C. Wings, Cons. Engrs., NYC, 1978-80, Gibbs & Hills, Inc., NYC, 1980-81; civil/structural engr. Bechtel Power Corp., Gaithersburg, Md., 1981-84; structural engr. Hazen & Sawyer, P.C., NYC, 1984-85; civil/structural engr. N.Y.C. Dept. Sanitation, 1985-87; civil engr. N.Y.C. Dept. Bldgs., 1987-94, N.Y.C. Comptroller's Office, 1994—2005; ret., 2005; pres. Chen's Cons. Engrs., Queens, NY, 1985-87. Bd. dirs. RFK Dem. Assn., Inc., Forest Hills, N.Y., 1994—. Recipient Cert. of Honor for leadership Dem. Nat. Com. Mem. NSPE, N.Y. State Soc. Profl. Engrs., Chinese Am. Assn. City of N.Y., MSM-UMR Alumni Assn., Comptr. Engrs. Assn. Home: 82-28 255th St Floral Park NY 11004 Office: New York City Comptrollers Office Bur of Engring 1 Centre St Rm 650 New York NY 10007 Personal E-mail: takchen@aol.com.

CHEN, THOMAS, mathematical physicist, researcher, educator; s. Yian Nian Chen and Shu Xia Chao; m. Isabelle Angliker, June 21, 2001; 1 child, Leonard Li-De. PhD in Mech. Engring., ETH Zurich, Switzerland, 1999, PhD in Theoretical Physics, 2001. Instr. Courant Inst., NYU, NYC, 2001—04; asst. prof. math. Princeton U., NJ, 2004. Contbr. articles to various sci. jours. Recipient Rsch. Challenge award, NYU, 2003-2004; grantee, NSF, 2004—. Office: Dept Math Washington Rd Princeton NJ 08544 Home Phone: 609-924-8993; Office Phone: 609-258-6466.

CHEN, TONY F., mathematics professor, dean; BS in Engring., Calif. Inst. Tech., 1973, MS in Aeronautics, 1973; PhD in Computer Sci., Stanford U., 1978. Rsch. fellow, applied math dept. Calif. Inst. Tech., 1978—79; asst. prof., computer sci. dept. Yale U., 1979—84, assoc. prof., computer sci. dept., 1984—86; prof., dept. math. UCLA, 1986—, grad. vice chair, math. dept., 1996—97, chair, math dept., 1997—2000, dean, phys. sciences, 2001—. Prin. investigator, bd. trustee Inst. for Pure and Applied Math., UCLA, 1999—, dir., 2000—01; mem., Nat. Com. on Math. Nat. Acad.; mem. adv. com. Lawrence Livermore Nat. Lab. Computation Directorate, 2000—04; mem. U. Space Rsch. Assn. Sci. Coun. for Applied Math. and Computer Sci.; one of five delegates representing the US at the Gen. Assembly at the Internat. Math. union, Santiago de Compostela, Spain, 2006; co-dir. UCLA, NIH Ctr. for Computational Biology. Mem. editl. bd. Soc. Indsl. and Applied Math. Jour. Scientific Computing, Asian Jour. Math.; contbr. articles to rsch. publs. Mem.: Assn. for Computing Machinery, IEEE (won two best paper award), NSF (mem. adv. com., math. and phys. sci. 1999—2002, chair, search com. for dir. NSF divsn. math. sciences 2002, mem. com. visitors, divsn. math. sci., asst. dir., math and phys. sciences 2006—), Am. Math. Soc. (chair., com. on committees 1999—, mem. editl. bd.), Soc. Indsl. and Applied Math. (chair, com. on sci. policy, bd. trustee 2000—, former mem. com. human rights). Office: UCLA Math Dept MS 7519E Box 951555 Los Angeles CA 90095-1555 Address: UCLA Math Dept 520 Portola Plz Math Sciences Bldg 6363 Mailcode 155505 Los Angeles CA 90095 also: Dept Math UCLA Inst Pure and Applied Math 1158A IPAM Bldg Box 957121 Los Angeles CA 90095-7121 Office Phone: 310-825-2601. Office Fax: 310-206-6673. Business E-Mail: chan@math.ucla.edu.

CHEN, WAI-FAH, civil engineering educator; b. Chekiang, China, Dec. 23, 1936; m. Lily Chen; children: Eric, Arnold, Brian. BS, Cheng-Kung U., 1959; MS, Lehigh U., 1963; PhD, Brown U., 1966. From asst. prof. to prof. civil engring. Lehigh U., 1966-76; prof. civil engring. Purdue U., Lafayette, Ind., 1976-92, head structural engring., 1980-99, George E. Goodwin disting. prof., 1992-99; dean engring. U. Hawaii, Honolulu, 1999—2006. Cons. Exxon Products, 1979, Karagozian & Case Structural Engrs., 1985, Ga. Tech., 1987, Skidmore, Owings & Merrill, 1987, World Bank, 1988—. Editor-in-chief The Handbook of Structural Engineering, 1997, Bridge Engineering Handbook, 1999, Earthquake Engineering Handbook, 2002, The Civil Engring. Handbook, 2d edit., 2002. Mem.: ASCE (hon.), Academia Sinica, Nat. Acad. Engring., Am. Inst. Steel Constrn., Am. Concrete Inst., Am. Acad. Mech., Structural Stability Rsch. Coun., Internat. Assn. Bridge & Structural Engring. Office: U Hawaii Dept Civil and Environ Engring 2540 Dole St Holmes Hall 383 Honolulu HI 96822-2303 Office Phone: 808-956-9618. Personal E-mail: chenwilfred@hotmail.com. Business E-Mail: chenwf@eng.hawaii.edu.

CHEN, WAI-KAI, electrical engineering and computer science educator, consultant; b. Nanking, China, Dec. 23, 1936; came to U.S., 1959; s. You-Chao and Shui-Tan (Shen) C.; m. Shirley Shiao-Ling, Jan. 13, 1939; children— Jerome, Melissa BS in Elec. Engring., Ohio U., 1960, MS in Elec. Engring., 1961; PhD in Elec. Engring., U. Ill., Urbana, 1964. Asst. prof. Ohio U., 1964-67, assoc. prof., 1967-71, prof., 1971-78, disting. prof., 1978-81; prof., head dept. elec. engring. and computer sci. U. Ill., Chgo., 1981-2001, prof. emeritus, 2001—; vis. assoc. prof. Purdue U., 1970-71; v.p. internat. tech. U. Santa Clara, Calif., 1999—2005. Hon. prof. Tianjing U., Peoples Republic of China, 1990, Beijing U. of Posts and Telecomms., Beijing U. of Aeronautics and Astronautics, 1992. Author: Applied Graph Theory, 1970, Theory and Design of Broadband Matching Networks, 1976, Applied Graph Theory: Graphs and Electrical Networks, 1976, Active Network and Feedback Amplifier Theory, 1980, Linear Networks and Systems, 1983, Passive and Active Filters: Theory and Implementations, 1986, The Collected Papers of Professor Wai-Kai Chen, 1987, Broadband Matching: Theory and Implementations, 1988, Theory of Nets, 1990, Linear Networks and Systems: Computer-Aided Solutions and Implementations, 1990, Active Network Analysis, 1991, Modern Network Analysis, 1992, Computer-Aided Design of Comm. Networks World Scientific, 2000, Circuit Analysis and Feedback Amplifier Theory, 2005, Nonlinear and Distribution Circuits, 2005, Passive, Active and Digital Filters, 2005, Feedback Networks: Theory and Circuit Applications, 2007; editor: Brooks/Cole Series in Electrical Engineering, 1982-84; editor in chief Advanced Series in Elec. and Computer Engring., 1986—, Jour. Circuits, Sys. and Computers, 1989—, The Circuits and Filters Handbook, 1995, 3d edit., 2007, The VLSI Handbook, 2000, 2nd edit., 2006, Design Automation, Languages and Simulations, 2003, VLSI Technology, 2003, Memory, Microprocessor and ASIC, 2003, Analog Circuits and Devices, 2003, Logic Design, 2003; editor The VLSI Series, 2000—; assoc. editor Jour. Circuits, Systems and Signal Processing, 1981-04; editor in charge Advanced Series in Circuits and Systems, World Scientific Publ. Co., 1991—; sect. editor Encyclopedia of Physical Science & Technology, 1998-01. Recipient Lester R. Ford award Math. Assn. Am., 1967, Baker Fund award Ohio U., 1974, 78, Disting. Accomplishment award Chinese Acad. & Profl. Assn. in Mid-Am. , 1985, Disting. Guest Prof. award Chuo U., Tokyo, 1987, Outstanding Svc. award Chinese Acad. & Profl. Assn. in Mid-Am., 1988, Outstanding Achievement award Mid-Am. Chinese Sci. & Tech. Assn, 1988, Disting. Alumnus award Elec. and Computer Engring. Dept. Alumni Assn. U. Ill. Urbana-Champaign, 1988, Alexander von Humboldt award Alexander von Humboldt Stiftung, Fed. Republic of Germany, 1985, Rsch. award U. Ill. Chgo. Coll. Engring., 2000, hon. prof. award Nanjing Inst. of Technology and Zhejing U., Peoples Republic of China, 1985, The Northeast U. Tech., East. China Inst. Tech., Nanjing Inst. of Posts & Telecommunications, AnHui U., Chengdu Inst. Radio Engring., Wuhan Univ.; Rsch. Inst. fellow Ohio U., 1972, Japan Soc. for Promotion of Sci., 1986, Sr. U. Scholar award U. Ill., 1986, Ohio U. Alumni Medal Merit for Disting. Achievement in Engring. Edn., 1987, Hon. Prof. award Hangzhan U. of Electronic Tech., China, 1990, Disting. Prof. award Internat. Technol. U., 1995, Hon. Prof. award Taichung U. Healthcare and Mgmt., Taiwan, 2002, Disting. Alumnus award Taipei U. Sci. and Tech., Taiwan, 2002, Certificate of Spl. Congl. Recognition, 2004. Fellow IEEE (Circuits and Sys. Soc. Meritorious Svc. award 1977, Edn. award 1998, Golden Jubilee medal 2000, Third Millennium medal 2000), AAAS; mem. NSPE, IEEE Cirs. and Sys. Soc. (adminstrv. com. 1985-87, exec. v.p. 1987, assoc. editor Trans. on Cirs. and Sys. 1977-79, editor 1991-93, pres.-elect 1993, pres. 1994), Md.-Am. Chinese Sci. and Tech. Assn. (bd. dirs. 1984-86, 89-93, pres. 1991-92), Chinese Acad. and Profl. Assn. Mid-Am. (advisor to bd. dirs. 1984-89, pres. 1986-87), Soc. Indsl. and Applied Math., Assn. Computing Machinery, Tensor Soc. Gt. Britain, Sigma Xi (sec.-treas. Ohio U. chpt. 1981), Phi Kappa Phi, Eta Kappa Nu. Office: Internat Technol U 3802 Belmont Ter Fremont CA 94539-8358 Office Phone: 408-556-9031. Business E-Mail: wkchen@ece.uic.edu.

CHEN, WESLEY, lawyer; b. NYC, Nov. 29, 1954; s. Tom Y.M. and Mary (Don) C.; m. Vivien Wong, Dec. 10, 1983; 2 children: Marissa, Jocelyn. BA, N.Y. U., 1976, JD, 1980. Bar: NY 1981, US Dist. Ct. (so. and ea. dists.) NY 1981. Lawyer Meissner, Tisch & Kleinberg, NYC, 1980-81; pvt. practice NYC, 1982—85, 2003—, 1989—90; of counsel Serchuk, Wolfe & Zelermyer, White Plains, NY, 1985-88, ptnr. NYC, 1995—2003, Cantwell & Chen, NYC, 1988, Kimmelman, Sexter, Warmflash & Leitner, NYC, 1990-91, Krasner & Chen, NYC, 1992-94; pvt. practice, 2003—. Mem. NY State Banking Bd., 1992—. Mem. ABA, NY State Bar Assn. (banking law com.), NY County Lawyers Assn. (banking law com.), Chinese C. of C. (legal adviser 1982—). Office: 425 Park Ave 5th Fl New York NY 10022 Office Phone: 212-751-7100.

CHEN, XI, research scientist; arrived in US, 1997; BS, Xi'an Jiaotong U., China, 1994; PhD, Harvard U., Cambridge, Mass., 2001. Asst. prof. Columbia U., NY, 2003—06, assoc. prof., 2006—. Office: Columbia U Dept Civil Eng 500 W 120th St New York NY 10027 Office Phone: 212-854-3787.

CHEN, XIAO, process engineer; s. Mengcheng Chen and Huimei Xiao. Bs, Tsinghua U., Beijing, 1996; MS, U. Tex., Austin, 1998, PhD, 2003. Key account technologist Applied Materials, Inc., Sunnyvale, Calif., 2003—. Contbr. articles to profl. jours. Mem.: IEEE. Achievements include research in the manufacturing of MOS capacitors on epitaxial Ge/Si1-xGex with high-k dielectrics using remote plasma chemical vapor deposition; high-resolution transmission electron microscopy of silicide formation and stability of Ni/Si and Ni/SiGe. Home: 5230 Birkdale Way San Jose CA 95138 Office: Applied Materials Inc 974 E Arques Ave Sunnyvale CA 94085 Home Phone: 408-481-9261; Office Phone: 408-584-7802. Business E-Mail: xiao_chen@amat.com.

CHEN, YOUNG-KAI, electronics engineer, researcher; PhD in Elec. Engring., Cornell U. With GE Corp.; dir. high-speed electronics rsch. Bell Labs., Lucent Technologies, Murray Hill, NJ. Contbr. articles to profl. jours. Fellow: IEEE (David Sarnoff Award); mem.: NAE. Office: Lucent Technologies 600 Mountain Ave New Providence NJ 07974-0636

CHEN, YU, acupuncturist, Chinese herbologist; b. Beijing, Sept. 10, 1942; arrived in U.S., 1985; d. Hai Chen and Xiu (Wang) C.; m. Paul L. Munson, Feb. 27, 1987; 1 child by previous marriage: Ming An. MD, Capital Med. Coll., Beijing, 1965; D in Traditional Chinese Medicine, Chinese Traditional Med. Sch., Beijing, 1977; MS, Chinese Acad. Med. Sci., Beijing, 1981. Diplomate in acupuncture Nat. Commn. Cert. Acupuncture; cert. Chinese herbologist; lic. acupuncturist, Md. Physician Govt. China, Ching Yang, Gan Su, 1968-73; resident physician dept. ob-gyn. Worker's Hosp., Yen Shan Oil Factory, Beijing, 1974-78; attending physician dept. genetics Nat. Rsch. Inst. Family Planning, Beijing, 1982-83; WHO postdoctoral fellow Karolinska Inst., Stockholm, 1983-85; postdoctoral fellow dept. physiology U. Tex., Houston, 1985-87; postdoctoral fellow dept. pharmacology U. N.C., Chapel Hill, 1987-90; pvt. practice acupuncture and herbology Cmty. Wholistic Health Ctr., Carrboro, NC, 1989-93; pvt. practice acupuncture, Chinese herbology, magnet therapy Pikesville and Parkville, Md., 1993—. Author The Voice of Medicine--Integration of Traditional Chinese Medicine and Western Medicine, 2007; contbr. articles to profl. jours.; patentee in field; inventor of way to treat panic attack by acupuncture and tiny hammer, ear magnet therapy to treat diabetes mellitus and control appetite, scalp magnet therapy to treat attention deficit disorder, herbal suppository for treatment of vaginal yeast infection, herbal treatment of AIDS meningitis. Recipient Best Essay award 1st Internat. Conf. Micro-Acupuncture Therapy, San Francisco, 1995. Democrat. Lutheran. Avocations: painting, photography, travel, classical music, gardening. Office: Beijing Acupuncture Chinese Herb & Magnetic Ctr 1401 Reisterstown Rd Baltimore MD 21208-6502 Office Phone: 410-484-4892. Personal E-mail: dryuchen@hotmail.com.

CHEN, ZONG, computer scientist, educator; b. Nanjing, Jiangsu, China, Apr. 17, 1971; s. Xin Chen and Manli Dong; m. Li Zhang, June 22, 1973. B, Nanjing U. Sci. and Tech., 1992; M, SE U., 1997; D, N.J. Inst. Tech., 2002. Rschr. N.J. Inst. Tech., Newark, 2003—04; asst. prof. Fairleigh Dickinson U., Teaneck, 2004—. Mem.: Upsilon Pi Epsilon (fairleigh dickinson u.), Sigma Xi (nj. inst. of tech.). Achievements include research in Pioneering research on dynamic handgrip recognition for biometric authentication. Home: 27 Jernee Dr East Brunswick NJ 08816 Office: Fairleigh Dickinson U 1000 River Rd T-BE2-01 Teaneck NJ 07666 Home Phone: 732-390-3342; Office Phone: 201-692-2721. Office Fax: 201-692-2773. Personal E-mail: zong71@yahoo.com. E-mail: zchen@fdu.edu.

CHENAULT, JAMES STOUFFER, judge; b. Richmond, Ky., May 1, 1923; s. Joe Prewitt and Russell (Stouffer) C.; m. Dorothy Neff, Apr. 21, 1960; children: Jean Russell. AB, Ea. Ky. U., 1949, LLD (hon.), 1975; LLB, U. Ky., 1949. Bar: Ky. 1949, U.S. Ct. Mil. Appeals 1956, U.S. Supreme Ct. 1960. Prosecuting atty. City of Richmond, Ky., 1950-57; commonwealth's atty. 25th Jud. Ct. of Ky., Clark, Jessamine and Madison Counties, 1964-66, cir. judge, 1966-80, chief cir. judge Clark and Madison Counties, 1980-93; chief regional judge Bluegrass Region of Ky., 1978-93; spl. judge Ky. Ct. of Appeals, 1973, Ky. Supreme Ct., 1984. Ky. rep. Nat. Ctr. State Cts., 1972-78; mem. Ky. Commn. on Corrections and Community Svc., 1973-77, Ky. Crime Commn. Cts. Sect., 1972-80, chmn., 1976-80, Task Force on Office for Pub. Advocacy, 1981-82, Gov.'s Jud. Adv. Coun., 1972-75, Ky. Jud. Coun., 1977-81, State and Fed. Jud. Coun., 1979-84; vol. faculty intensive trial seminar U. Ky., 1983, 85, 87, 90; lectr. So. Police Inst., 1970-80, Nat. Conf. Appellate Ctr. Clks., 1985, Nat. Conf. U.S. Dist. Ct. Clks., 1988, Nat. Conf. on Tech. and the Cts., Chgo., 1984, Denver, 1988, 3rd Fed. Jud. Conf, 1987, Ala. Appellate Judges Conf., 1990; adj. faculty Sch. Law Enforcement Ea. Ky. U., 1967-73; lectr. numerous state jud. confs.; presenter 1st Nat. Jud. State of the Art Conf., Phoenix, 1987. Councilman City of Richmond, 1949-50. Lt. (j.g.) USN, 1943-46, PTO. Recipient Outstanding Contbn. award Ky. Coun. Crime and Delinquency, 1974, Outstanding Contbn. award City of Richmond, 1977, Disting. Svc. award Dept. Mass Comm. Ea. Ky. U., 1993, Outstanding Trial Judge award Ky. Acad. Trial Attys., 1993, Ky. Chief Justice Spl. award, 1994; named Outstanding Alumnus Ea. Ky. U., Richmond, 1982; inducted into U. Ky. Law Sch. Hall of Fame, 2000. Mem. ABA (lectr., presenter ann. meeting San Francisco chpt. 1987), Am. Judicature Soc., Internat. Acad. Trial Judges, Ky. Bar Assn. (pres. younger lawyers conf. 1956-57), Ky. Assn. Cir. Judges (pres. 1970-75, editor newsletter 1976-93, Outstanding Contbn. award 1978), Ky. Commonwealth's Attys. Assn. (pres. 1965-66), Richmond C. of C. (Outstanding Svc. award 1983, Outstanding Achievement award 1989), Exch. Club (pres. Richmond chpt. 1955, Outstanding Lifetime Achievement award 2003), Elks. Avocations: Kentucky history, gardening. Home and Office: 302 High St Richmond KY 40475-1344

CHENAULT, KENNETH IRVINE, finance company executive; b. NYC, June 2, 1951; s. Hortenius and Anne N. (Quick) C.; m. Kathryn Cassell, Aug. 20, 1977; children: Kenneth I. Jr., Kevin A. BA, Bowdoin Coll., 1973; JD, Harvard U., 1977; PhD (hon.), Morgan State U., 1990, Stony Brook U., 1996, Adelphi U., 1995, Bowdoin Coll., 1996, Xavier U., 1997, S.C. State U., 1997, Howard U., 1998, U. Notre Dame, 1998; LLD, Iona Coll., 1996. Bar: Mass. 1981. Assoc. Rogers & Wells, NYC, 1977-79; cons. Bain & Co., Boston, 1979-81; dir. strategic planning Am. Express Co., NYC, 1981-83; from v.p. to sr. v.p. Am. Express Travel Related Svcs. Co., Inc., NYC, 1983-96, exec. v.p. platinum card/gold, 1986-88, exec. v.p. personal card divsn., 1988-89, pres. consumer card and fin. svcs. group, 1990-93, pres. U.S.A., 1993-95; vice-chmn. Am. Express Co., NYC, 1995-97, pres., COO, 1997-2000, chmn., CEO, 2001—. Bd. dirs. IBM, Am. Express Co., NYU Hosp.'s Ctr./NYU Sch. Medicine. Dean's adv. bd. Harvard Law Sch.; mem. Coun. Fgn. Rels., N.Y.C., 1988. Recipient Most Influential Black Americans, Ebony mag., 2006. Mem. ABA; fellow Am. Acad. Arts and Sciences Congregationalist. Office: Am Express Co Am Express Tower World Fin Ctr 200 Vesey St New York NY 10285-5104

CHÊNEVERT, LOUIS, manufacturing executive; b. June 25, 1957; B. in Prodn. Mgmt., U. of Montreal. Prodn. gen. mgr. Canada's St. Therese operation GM; with Pratt & Whitney Canada, 1993—96, v.p. operations; exec. v.p. operations Pratt & Whitney, East Hartford, Conn., 1997, exec. v.p. operations, worldwide purchasing, and after market bus., 1998, pres., 1999—2006; pres., COO, dir. United Technologies Corp., East Hartford, Conn., 2006—. Spkr. in tech. field. Bd. overseers Bushnell Ctr. Performing Arts, Hartford, Conn.; dir.'s advisory bd. Yale Cancer Ctr. Office: UTC United Technologies Bldg Hartford CT 06101*

CHENEY, BRIGHAM VERNON, physical chemist, consultant; b. Salt Lake City, June 11, 1936; s. Silas Lavell and Klara (Young) C.; m. Marsali McAllister, Aug. 20, 1964; children: Jill, Mark Vernon, Heather, Karin, Brigham McAllister, John David. BA, U. Utah, 1961, PhD, 1966. Rsch. asst. U. Utah, 1964-66; rsch. scientist Upjohn Co., Kalamazoo, 1966-71, scientist, 1971-75, sr. rsch. scientist, 1975-98; cons. Vis. scientist Oxford (Eng.) U., 1986-87. Contbr. articles to profl. jours. Missionary LDS Ch., Germany, 1956-59, high councilor, Lansing, Mich., 1969-75, Grand Rapids, Mich., 1975-78, bishop, Kalamazoo, 1978-84; leader Boy Scouts Am., 1972-98. With U.S. Army NG, 1959-67. Mem. Am. Chem. Soc., Sigma Xi, Phi Eta Sigma, Sigma Pi Sigma. Home: 1765 N 2000 W Provo UT 84604-1128 Personal E-mail: bvcheney@iprovo.net.

CHENEY, DICK (RICHARD BRUCE CHENEY), Vice President of the United States; b. Lincoln, Nebr., Jan. 30, 1941; s. Richard Hebert and Marjorie Lauraine (Dickey) C.; m. Lynne Anne Vincent, Aug. 29, 1964; children: Elizabeth, Mary Claire. Student, Yale U., 1959—62, Casper C.C., 1963; BA in Polit. Sci., U. Wyo., 1965, MA in Polit. Sci., 1966; student, U. Wis., 1966—68. Staff aide to Gov. Warren Knowles State of Wis., 1966; congl. fellow, staff mem. to Rep. William A. Steiger US Congress, Washington, 1968—69; spl. asst. to dir. Office of Econ. Opportunity The White House, Washington, 1969—70, dep. to presdl. counselor, 1970—71, asst. dir. for ops. Cost of Living Coun., 1971—73; ptnr. Bradley, Woods & Co., 1973—74, 1977—78; dep. asst. to Pres. for White House ops. The White House, Washington, 1974—75, chief of staff to Pres., 1975-77; mem. US Congress from Wyo., Washington, 1979—89, chmn. Republican Ho. Policy Comm., 1981—88, minority whip, 1988—89; sec. U.S Dept. Def., Washington, 1989-93; sr. fellow Am. Enterprise Inst., Washington, 1993-95; chmn., CEO Halliburton Co., Dallas, 1995-2000; v.p. U.S., Washington, 2001—. Co-author (with Lynne V. Cheney): Kings of the Hill: Power and Personality in the House of Representatives, 1983. Recipient J.E. Davies Congl Fellowship award, 1968, Presdl. Medal of Freedom, The White House, 1991. Republican. Methodist. Office: The White House 1600 Pennsylvania Ave NW Washington DC 20501*

CHENEY, ELEANORA LOUISE, retired secondary school educator; b. Seneca Falls, NY, June 3, 1923; d. Guy Darrell and Alice Augusta (McCoy) Stevenson; m. John C. Dinsmore, Jan. 13, 1941 (dec.); children: Patricia Walter, Nancy Dinsmore, Jon Dinsmore (dec.); m. Daniel Lavern Cheney, Aug. 8, 1959. BA, Rutgers U., 1966; MA, U. Glassboro, 1971. Account clk. GE, Auburn, N.Y., 1953-58; supr. accounts payable Sylvania Electric, Camillus, N.Y., 1958-60; cost acctg. clk. RCA, Cherry Hill, N.J., 1960-64; honors English tchr. Lenape Regional High Sch., Medford, N.J., 1966-74; guidance counselor Shawnee High Sch., 1974—84; owner Another World of Travel, Marlton, N.J., 1984-86; co-founder, trustee, sec. Danellie Found., 1991—. Travel agt., 1986-89. Counselor Contact Ministries, Moorestown, NJ, 1976-99; fin. com., nominating com. Haddonfield (NJ) United Meth. Ch., 1987-92, supr. ch. sch., 1980-82; bd. dirs. Fellowship House, Camden, NJ, 1994—, Robins' Nest, Glassboro, NJ, 1995-2000; adminstrv. coun. Haddonfield United Meth. Ch., 1996-99, leader small group, 1990—, adminstrv. coun., 2003—; established Jon W. Dinsmore Meml. Math. Scholarship Cherry Hill West, NJ, 1997—,vol. Interfaith Caregivers, Haddonfield, NJ, 2006-. Named to Nat. Woman's Hall of Fame, 1994. Mem. AAUW. Republican. Methodist. Avocations: reading, knitting, gardening. Home: 5 Periwinkle Pl Marlton NJ 08053-5556

CHENEY, JAMES ADDISON, civil engineering educator; b. LA, Feb. 2, 1927; s. Burton Howard and Esther Jesse (Dumaresq) C.; m. Frankyee Jane Jackson, June, 23, 1951 (dec. Oct. 1966); children: John Addison, Linanne Dando, Matthew Jackson, Sarah Allan, Sharla Ryan, Jennifer Dumaresq; m. Barbara Louise Chadwick, June 1967 (div. Feb. 1987); children: Michael Chadwick, David Grant; m. Elaine Disbrow Barratt, Apr. 1988. BS, UCLA, 1951, MS, 1953; PhD, Stanford U., 1963. Registered profl. civil engr., Calif. Assoc. engr. L.T. Evans, Foundation Engrs., Los Angeles, 1953-55; staff engr. Lockheed Missile and Space Co., Sunnyvale, Calif., 1955-65; prof. civil engring. U. Calif., Davis, 1962-91, prof. emeritus civil engring., 1991—. Contbr. over 50 articles to scientific jours. Served with USN, 1944-45. Recipient Silver Beaver award, Golden Empire coun. Boy Scouts Am., 2002. Fellow ASCE; mem. Alpha Sigma Phi. Republican. Episcopalian. Home: 418 Anza Ave Davis CA 95616-0404 Office: U Calif Dept Civil Engring Davis CA 95616 E-mail: jacheney@ucdavis.edu.

CHENEY, LYNNE VINCENT, humanities educator, writer; b. Casper, Wyo., Aug. 14, 1941; d. Wayne and Edna (Lybyer) Vincent; m. Richard Bruce Cheney, Aug. 29, 1964; children: Elizabeth, Mary. BA with highest honors, Colo. Coll., 1963; MA, U. Colo., 1964; PhD in 19th century Brit. lit., U. Wis., 1970. Freelance writer, 1970-83; lectr. No. Va. CC, 1968—71, George Washington U., Washington, 1972-77, U. Wyo., Casper, 1977-78; researcher, writer Md. Pub. Broadcasting, Owings Mills, 1982-83; sr. editor Washingtonian mag., Washington, 1983-86; chmn. NEH, Washington, 1986-93; W.J. Brady Jr. fellow Am. Enterprise Inst., Washington, 1993-95, sr. fellow, 1996—. Commr. U.S. Constitution Bicentennial Commn., Washington, 1985-87. Author: Executive Privilege, 1978, Sisters, 1981, Telling the Truth, 1995; (with others) Kings of the Hill, 1983, 96, (with Victor Gold) The Body Politic, 1988, (report) American Memory: A Report on the Humanities in the Nation's Public Schools, 1988, (essay) Academic Freedom, 1992; (children's books) America: A Patriotic Primer, 2002, A Is for Abigail: An Almanac of Amazing American Women, 2003, When Washington Crossed the Delaware: A Wintertime Story for Young Patriots, 2004, A Time For Freedom: What Happened When in America, 2005;

contbr. articles to profl. jours. Mem. Women's Forum, Washington. Mem.: Congl. Club, Kappa Alpha Theta, Phi Beta Kappa. Republican. Methodist. Office: Am Enterprise Inst 1150 17th St NW Ste 1100 Washington DC 20036-4603

CHENEY, MARGARET, writer, retired editor; b. Eugene, Oreg., Apr. 5, 1921; d. George and Josie Goughnour Swisher; m. Robert Millius (dec.); m. Michael S. Cheney, May 29, 1952 (dec.); 1 child, Victoria Cheney Summers. Student, Cornish Sch. Arts, Seattle, 1940. Reporter Aberdeen (Wash.) Daily World, 1940—42; editor AP, Seattle, 1943—46; pers. sec. Bechtel Corp., Dhahron, Saudi Arabia, 1946—48; pub. rels. writer Arabian Am. Oil Co., Dhahron, 1948—52, U. Calif., Berkeley, 1960—69; editor Carnegie Commn. on Higher Edn., Berkeley, 1970—71. Author: Tesla-Man Out of Time (Tesla Gold medal); author: (with Robert Uth) Tesla-Master of Lightning; contbr. articles to profl. jours. Environ. coord. DeAnza Nat. Hist. Trail; mem. exec. bd. Tesla Meml. Soc. Mem.: Authors Guild. Democrat. Avocations: painting, gardening, travel. Home: 10168 Adam Ave Grass Valley CA 95945 Office Phone: 530-477-0753. Fax: 530-272-4099. Personal E-mail: mcheney@nccn.net.

CHENEY, MARY CLAIRE, Internet company executive; b. June 14, 1969; d. Dick and Lynne Cheney; life ptnr. Heather Poe; 1 child, Samuel David. BA in History, Colo. Coll., Colo. Springs, 1991; MBA, U. Denver, 2002. With promotions dept. Colo. Rockies baseball team, 1993—94; pub. relations mgr. Coors Brewing Co., 1994—2000; position with audience bus. dept. Am. Online, Inc., Dulles, Va., 2005—06, chief of staff, 2006—. Author: Now It's My Turn: A Daughter's Chronicle of a Political Life, 2006. Mem. Bush-Cheney Campaign, 2000; mem. adv. bd. Rep. Unity Coalition, 2002—03; dir. v.p. ops. Bush-Cheney 2004 Presdl. re-election campaign, 2003.*

CHENEY, RICHARD EUGENE, public relations executive, psychoanalyst; b. Pana, Ill., Aug. 30, 1921; s. Royal F. and Nelle E. (Henke) C.; m. Betty L. McCray, Oct. 17, 1943; children: R. Christopher, Elyn G. Cheney MacInnis; m. 2d, Virginia B. Burns, Jan. 23, 1966; children: Benjamin, Anne. AB, Knox Coll., Galesburg, Ill., 1943; MA, Columbia U., 1960; postgrad., Ctr. Modern Psychoa. Studies, 1995. Assoc. editor Tide Mag., 1953; dir. pub. relations Tri Continental Corp., 1953-55; asst. mgr. pub. relations dept. Mobil Corp., 1955-60; chmn. bd., emeritus chmn. Hill & Knowlton, Inc., NYC, 1987-91, 91—, chmn. bd., 1987-91, chmn. emeritus, 1991-93. Bd. dirs. Chattem Inc., Chattanooga, Stoneridge, Inc., Warren, Ohio, Rowe Furniture, Salem, Va. Served to lt. (j.g.) USNR, 1943-47, PTO. Mem. Soc. for Modern Psychoanalysis (trustee), Edgewood Club (Tivoli, N.Y.), Century Assn. Home: 108 E 86th St New York NY 10028-1024 Office: 108 E 86th St, 14 N New York NY 10028 Home Phone: 212-860-2582; Office Phone: 212-860-2451. Personal E-mail: dcheney212@earthlink.net.

CHENG, ALBERT, communications executive; b. Hawaii, 1971; married. BS, Mass. Inst. Tech.; MBA, Harvard U. Grad. Sch. Bus. Adminstrn. Bus. strategy cons. Boston Consulting Grp.; dir., Bus. Devel. Fox/Liberty Networks; dir., Distbn. Strategy Fox Cable Networks Grp.; v.p., Nat. Accounts and Distbn. Strategy ABC Cable Networks, 2000, sr. v.p., Distbn. Strategy and Ops., 2002—04; sr. v.p., Bus. Strategy and Devel. Disney and ESPN Networks Affiliate Sales and Mktg.; exec. v.p., Digital Media Disney-ABC TV Grp., Burbank, Calif., 2005—. Named one of 40 Executives Under 40, Multichannel News, 2006. Mem.: Nat. Assn. for Multi-Ethnicity in Comm. (treasurer). Office: Disney ABC Television Group 500 S Buena Vista St Burbank CA 91521

CHENG, ALEXANDER HUNG-DARH, engineering educator, consultant; b. Taipei, Taiwan, May 25, 1952; came to U.S., 1976; s. Chia-hua and Yu-Chuen (Chwang) C.; m. Daisy T. Cheng, Nov. 23, 1979; children: Jacqueline, Julia. BS, Nat. Taiwan U., Taipei, 1974; MS, U. Mo., 1978; PhD, Cornell U., 1981. Asst. prof. Cornell U., Ithaca, 1981-82, Columbia U., NYC, 1982-85; assoc. prof. U. Del., Newark, 1985-93, prof., 1993—2001; dept. chair, prof. U. Miss., Oxford, 2001—. Author: Multi-layered Aquifer Systems, 2000; editor: Engineering Analysis with Boundary Elements, 1996—; editor 9 books; editor-in-chief Progress in Water Resources Series, 1998—; assoc. editor Jour. Engring. Mech., 1998—2004; contbr. over 100 articles to profl. jours. Recipient Basic Rsch. award U.S. Nat. Com. Rock Mechanics NRC, 1994, 99, Eminent Scientist award WIT. Mem. ASCE (chair, exec. com. engring. mech. divsn., W.L. Huber Civil Engring. prize 1994), Am. Geophys. Union, Am. Inst. Hydrology (v.p. acad. affairs). Office: U Miss Dept Civil Engring University MS 38677 Office Phone: 662-915-5362. E-mail: acheng@olemiss.edu.

CHENG, CHU YUAN, economics professor; b. Kwangtung Province, China, Apr. 8, 1927; arrived in U.S., 1959, naturalized, 1964; s. Hung Shan and Shu Cheng (Yang) C.; m. Alice Hua Liang, Aug. 15, 1964; children: Anita tung I, Andrew Y.S. BA in Econs., Nat. Chengchi U., Nanking, China, 1947; MA, Georgetown U., 1962, PhD, 1964. Rsch. prof. Seton Hall U., 1960-64; sr. rsch. economist U. Mich., Ann Arbor, 1964-69; assoc. prof. Lawrence U., Appleton, Wis., 1970-71; assoc. prof. econs., chmn. Asian studies com. Ball State U., Muncie, Ind., 1971-73, prof. econs., 1974—. Vis. prof. George Washington U., Washington, 1963; cons. NSF, Washington, 1964—; rsch. mem. presdl. Coun. for Nat. Unification, China, 1992-98. Author: Scientific and Engineering Manpower in Communist China, 1966, The Machine-Building Industry in Communist China, 1971, China's Petroleum Industry: Output Growth and Export Potential, 1976, China's Economic Development: Growth and Structural Change, 1981, The Demand and Supply of Primary Energy in Mainland China, 1984, Taiwan as a Model for China's Modernization, 1986, Sun Yat-sen's Doctrine in Modern World, 1988, Taiwan Experience and China's Reconstruction, 1989, Behind the Tiananmen Massacre, Social, Political and Economic Ferment in China, 1990, Economic Development and Interaction between Two Sides of the Taiwan Straits, 1993, The Transformation of Social, Political and Economic Structure in China, 1994, China's Transition From A Planned to A Market Economy, 1994, Township-Village Enterprises: China's New Route to Industrialization, 1995, China's Economic Reform: Programs, Effects and Prospects, 1997, China's Economic Reform and Cross-Strait Economic Relations, 2000, Economies on the Two Sides of the Taiwan Straits: Reforms and Development, 1950-2000, 2002, Development of Contemporary Economic Thought in East and West, 2004, China's Quiet Revolution: Process and Consequences, 2005, China's New Development Plan: Strategy, Agenda and Prospects, 2007. Bd. dirs., pres. Dr. Sun Yat-sen Inst., Chgo., 1978—. Grantee NSF, 1960-64, Social Sci. Rsch. Coun., 1965-67, 74, Chiang ching-Kuo Found., 1996. Mem. Am. Econ. Assn., Assn. Asian Studies, Assn. Comparative Econ. Studies, Am. Acad. Polit. and Social Sci., Assn. Chinese Social Scientists in N.Am. (bd. dirs., pres. 1994-96), Am. Assn. Chinese Studies (bd. dirs., pres. 1996-98), Chinese-Am. Soc. (pres. Washington 1989-92), Chinese Acad. and Profl. Assn. Mid-Am. (pres. 1983-84), Ind. Acad. Social Sci., Omicron Delta Epsilon. Home: 1211 N Greenbriar Rd Muncie IN 47304-2934 Office: Ball State U Coll Bus Rm 123 Muncie IN 47306-0340 Office Phone: 765-285-5366. Business E-Mail: ccheng@bsu.edu.

CHENG, DAVID KEUN, engineering educator; b. Kiangsu, China, Jan. 10, 1918; came to U.S., 1943, naturalized, 1955; s. Han J. and Ying H.C.; m. Enid Kwok, Mar. 27, 1948; 1 child, Eugene. BS in Elec. Engring., Nat. Chiao Tung U., 1938; S.M., Harvard U., 1944, Sc.D., 1946; D.Engr. (hon.), Nat. Chiao Tung U., Taiwan, 1985; PhD (hon.), Xidian U., China, 1998. Electronics and project engr., rsch. labs. U.S. Air Force, Cambridge, Mass., 1946-48; asst. prof. elec. and computer engring. Syracuse U., 1948-51, assoc. prof., 1951-55, prof., 1955—, Centennial prof., 1970—. Hon. prof. Beijing Univ. Posts and Telecomm., 1982—, N.W. Inst. Telecomm. Engring., 1982—, Shanghai Jiao Tong U., 1985—, China; exch. scientist NAS, Hungary, 1972, Yugoslavia, 1974, Poland and Romania, 1978; liaison scientist Office of Naval Rsch., London, 1975-76; disting. European lectr. IEEE, 1975-76; pres., chmn., bd. trustees Li Instn. Sci. & Tech., 1992-98; cons. IBM, GE, TRW. Author: Analysis of Linear Systems, 1959, Field and Wave Electromagnetics, 1983, 2d edit., 1989, Fundamentals of Engineering Electromagnetics, 1993, transl. Chinese, Spanish, Korean, and Turkish; cons. editor elec. sci. Addison-Wesley, 1961-78, elec. engring. monographs Intext Edn. Pubs., 1969-72; contbr. numerous articles to profl. jours. Recipient Disting. Achievement award Chinese Inst. Engrs., 1962, Disting. Engr. award Li Inst. Sci. and Tech., 1979; Guggenheim fellow, 1960-61; Chancellor's citation, 1981. Fellow IEEE, AAAS, Inst. Elec. Engrs. (U.K.); mem. AAUP, Am. Soc. Engring. Edn., N.Y. Acad. Scis., Sigma Xi (7 Best Paper prizes), Eta Kappa Nu, Phi Tau Phi (Disting. Svc. award 1975). Home: 4620 N Park Ave Apt 104E Chevy Chase MD 20815-4550 Personal E-mail: chengkeun@aol.com.

CHENG, H. H., soil scientist, agronomic and environmental science educator emeritus; b. Shanghai, Aug. 13, 1932; arrived in U.S., 1951, naturalized, 1961; s. Chi-Pao and Anna (Lan) Cheng; m. Jo Yuan, Dec. 15, 1962; children: Edwin, Antony. BA, Berea Coll., 1956; MS, U. Ill., 1958, PhD, 1961; LLD (hon.), U. Minn., 2004. Lic. profl. soil scientist Minn. Rsch. assoc. Iowa State U., Ames, 1962-64, asst. prof. agronomy, 1964-65; asst. prof. dept. agronomy and soils Wash. State U., Pullman, 1965-71, assoc. prof., 1971-77, prof., 1977-89, interim chmn., 1986-87, chmn. program environ. sci. and regional planning, 1977-79, 88-89, assoc. dean Grad. Sch., 1982-86; prof., head dept. soil, water, and climate U. Minn., St. Paul, 1989—2002, prof. emeritus, 2002—. Vis. scientist Juelich Nuc. Rsch. Ctr., Germany, 1971-73, 79-80, Academia Sinica, Taipei, China, 1978, Fed. Agrl. Rsch. Ctr., Braunschweig, Germany, 1980; mem. acad. adv. coun. Inst. Soil Sci., Academia Sinica, Nanjing, China, 1987-2000; mem. adv. bd. Inst. Botany, Academia Sinica, Taipei, 1991-2000; mem. first sci. adv. bd. Dept. Ecology State of Wash., 1988-89; chief tech. advisor project on water-saving agr. N.W. China, UNDP, 2001-04; mem. agr. and natural resources bd., Nat. Acad., 2003—, mem. NRC Com. Miss. River and Clean Water Act, 2005—. Editor: Pesticides in the Soil Environment: Processes, Impacts, and Modeling, 1990; assoc. editor Jour. Environ. Quality, 1983-89; mem. editl. bd. Bot. Studies (formerly Bot. Bull. Academia Sinica), 1988—, Jour. Environ. Sci. and Health, Part B-Pesticides, Food Contaminants, and Agrl. Wastes, 2000-03; cons. editor: Pedosphere, 1991—; contbr. articles to profl. jours. Tech. adv. Mekong-Miss. River Partnership, 2003—. Recipient U. Minn. Coll. Agrl., Food and Environ. Scis. Internat. Achievement award, 2004, Berea Coll. Disting. Alumnus award, 2006; Fulbright rsch. scholar State Agrl. U., Ghent, Belgium, 1963-64. Fellow AAAS, Am. Soc. Agronomy (bd. dir. 1990-2000, exec. com. 1994-2000, pres. 1998-99), Soil Sci. Soc. Am. (divsn. chair 1985-86, bd. dir. 1990-93, exec. com. 1994-97, pres. 1995-96, co-chair Smithsonian soils exhibit com. 2002—); mem. Am. Chem. Soc., Soc. Environ. Toxicology and Chemistry, Internat. Soc. Chem. Ecology, Internat. Humic Substances Soc., Coun. Agrl. Sci. and Tech., Soil and Water Conservation Soc., Minn. Assn. Profl. Soil Scientists (Soil Scientist of Yr. 2003), Inst. Internat. Devel. in Edn. and Agrl. and Life Scis. (chair bd. dir. 2000—), Miss. River Basin Inst. Internat. Coop. (chair, bd. dir. 2004—), Sigma Xi (pres. U. Minn. chpt. 1995-96), Phi Kappa Phi, Gamma Sigma Delta (pres. Wash. State chpt. 1988-89, Award of Merit U. Minn. chpt. 2000). Methodist. Office: U Minn Dept Soil Water and Climate 1991 Upper Buford Cir Saint Paul MN 55108-0010 Office Phone: 612-625-1244. Business E-Mail: hcheng@umn.edu.

CHENG, HONG, library and information scientist; s. Yizhi Cheng and Yueqin Wang; m. Diane Lu. MA, UCLA, 1988, PhD, 1990, MLS, 1994. Libr. dir. Art Inst. Calif., Los Angeles, 1997—2005; libr. U. Calif., Los Angeles, 2005—. Pub. Ednl. Publications, San Marino, Calif., 2004—. Author: Jian zheng er zhan = Eyewitness WWII, 2005 (10 Best Books of Shanghai Book Exhbn., 2005). Mem.: Assn. for Asian Studies, Am. Libr. Assn. (com. mem. 2005—). Avocations: writing and publishing, travel, web design. Office: U Calif Los Angeles 21617 YRL Box 951575 Los Angeles CA 90095 Office Phone: 310-206-9606. Business E-Mail: chengh@ucla.edu.

CHENG, JIAN-YU, mechanical engineer, researcher, application developer; b. Shanghai, Aug. 2, 1960; arrived in U.S., 1996; s. Dewu Cheng and Fan Shen; m. Xiaolin Lu; children: Jennifer, Bridget. BS, U. Sci. and Tech. of China, 1982; PhD, U. of Sci. and Tech. of China, 1989. Asst. prof. U. of Sci. and Tech. of China, Hefei, Anhui, China, 1988—91; postdoctoral fellow Inst. de Mecanique de Grenoble, Grenoble, France, 1991; Alexander von Humboldt fellow U. of Saarlandes, Saarbruecken, Saarlandes, Germany, 1991—93; rsch. staff U. of Leeds, Leeds, England, 1993; fellow St. Francis Xavier U., Antigonish, Nova Scotia, Canada, 1994—96; sr. mech. project engr. Smith Internat., Inc, Houston, 1996—97; fellow U. of Del., Newark, Del., 1997—99; sr. rsch. scientist Dynaflow, Inc, Jessup, Md., 1999—2002; sr. software engr. Westover Cons., Inc., Silver Spring, Md., 2002—05; configuration mgmt. engr. Convera Corp., Vienna, Va., 2005—07; sr. computer scientist Computer Sci. Corp., Lanham, Md., 2005, application arch. prin. leader, 2007—. Cons. computer sci. NOAA, Nat. Environmental Satellite Data and Info. Svc., Comprehensive Large Array-Data Stewardship Sys. Contbr. articles to profl. jours. (Natural Sci. prize of Academia Sinica, China, 1993). Fellow, Alexander von Humboldt Found., Germany, 1991—93, Natural Sci. & Engring. Rsch. Coun. of Can., 1994—96; grantee, NOAA, 2001. Mem.: ASME. Avocation: travel. Home: 8538 Eastern Morning Rd Laurel MD 20723 Office: CSC MTC 7900 Harkins Rd Lanham MD 20706 Personal E-mail: cheng_jj@hotmail.com. Business E-Mail: jceng7@csc.com.

CHENG, JOSEPHINE, computer scientist, educator; IBM Fellow, v.p. IBM China Devel. Labs., Beijing, 2000—. Mem. Nat. Rsch. Coun. Info. Panel, 1998—2000; hon. prof. Shanghai U., 2002—03. Recipient Tribute to Women and Industry Award, YWCA, 1996, Women of Color 2001 Tech. Innovation Awards, Asian Am. Engr. of Yr. Award, 2003. Mem.: NAE. Office: IBM China Rsch Lab Building 19, Zhouguancun Software Park 8 Dongbeiwang W Rd, Haidian Dist Beijing 100094 China

CHENG, KUANG LU, chemist, educator; b. Yangchow, China, Sept. 14, 1915; came to U.S., 1947, naturalized, 1955; s. Fong Wu and Yi Ming (Chiang) C.; children: Meiling, Chiling, Hans Christian. PhD, U. Ill., 1951. Microchemist Comml. Solvents Corp., Terre Haute, Ind., 1952-53; instr. U. Conn., Storrs, 1953-55; engr. Westinghouse Electric Corp., Pitts., 1955-57; assoc. dir. research metals div. Kelsey Hayes Co., Utica, NY, 1957-59; mem. tech. staff RCA Labs., Princeton, NJ, 1959-66; prof. chemistry U. Mo., Kansas City, 1966-90, prof. emeritus, 1990—. Recipient Achievement award RCA, 1963, Benedetti-Pichler award Am. Microchem. Soc., 1989; N.T. Veatch award for Disting. rsch. and creative activity U. Mo., 1979; cert. of recognition U.S. Office of Naval Rsch., 1979, cert. of recognition Coll. Engring., Tex. A&M U., 1981; bd. trustees fellow U. Kansas City, 1984. Fellow AAAS, Chem. Soc. London; mem. Am. Chem. Soc. (Longtime Achievement award 2004), Electrochem. Soc., Soc. Applied Spectroscopy, Am. Inst. Physics. Achievements include development of ISE double capacitor theory, 1983; discovery of interfacial triple layer, 2001. Office: U Mo Dept Physics Kansas City MO 64110 Business E-Mail: chengk@umkc.edu. *Part of the art of research is to simplify complex phenomena and to elaborate the simple observations. Scientific research resembles gold prospecting — staying away from the spots crowded by people, exploring new territories.*

CHENG, LIANG, pathologist; b. Zhejiang, China, Nov. 9, 1965; came to U.S., 1988; MD, Beijing Med. U., 1987; MS, U. Ill., 1990. Diplomate Am. Bd. Pathology. Resident Case We. Res. U., Cleve., 1993—97, instr. pathology, 1994—97; fellow Mayo Clinic, Rochester, Minn., 1997—98; assoc. prof. pathology Ind. U. Sch. Medicine, Indpls., 1998—, asst. prof. urology, 1999—. Spkr., cons. in field. Co-author: (chpts.) Therapeutics: Methods and Applications of Direct Gene Transfer, 1994, Immunotherapeutics Approaches for the Treatment of Cancer, 1995; editor: Essentials of Anatomic Pathology 2d edit., 2005; contbr. articles to profl. jours. Recipient Resident Competition award Cleve. Soc. Pathologists, 1997, Young Investigator Travel award, 1998, Eminent Scientist of Yr. Gold award, Internat. Rsch. Promotino Coun., 2000; Am. Cancer Inst. grantee, Clarian Value Fund grantee, Biomed. Rsch. Fund grantee, Dept. Def. grantee; Molecular Biology Lab. fellow U. Ill., 1990. Mem. AAAS, Am. Assn. Cancer Rsch., Am. Urologic Assn., U.S. and Can. Acad. Pathology (Stowell-Orbison award 1996), Coll. Am. Pathologists (cert. recognition), Am. Soc. Clin. Pathologists (cert. recognition), Internat. Soc. Urologic Pathology, Assn. Molecular Pathology. Office: Ind U Sch Medicine 350 W 11th St CPL 4010 Indianapolis IN 46202-5149 Office Phone: 317-491-6442. Personal E-mail: liang_cheng@yahoo.com. Business E-Mail: lcheng@iupui.edu.

CHENG, LIANG, video architect, researcher; s. Deqing Cheng and Jiatong Yan; m. Chen Zhang. BSEE, Beijing U. Posts and Telecom., 1997, MSEE, 2000; MS, U. Calif., 2004, PhD, 2005. Rsch. asst. U. Calif., Irvine, 2000—05; sr. architect NVIDIA Corp., Santa Clara, Calif., 2005—. Contbg. author Adaptation Techniques in Wireless Multimedia Networks. Recipient Best Paper award, IEEE Consumer Comm. and Networking Confs., Las Vegas; fellow Calif. Inst. Telecomm. and Info. Tech.; scholar U. Calif. Sch. Info. and Computer Sci., 2002, U. Calif. Ctr. Pervasive Comm. and Computing, 2002, 2004. Mem.: ACM, IEEE (Best Paper award 2006). Achievements include patents pending for Systems And Methods For Video Compression For Low Bit Rate And Low Latency Video Communications. Personal E-mail: liang.cheng@gmail.com.

CHENG, THERESA, neurosurgeon; d. Wayne and Florence Cheng. Degree in Biomed. Engring., Marquette U., 1982; MD, PhD, Med. Coll. Wis., Milw., 1989. Diplomate Am. Bd. Neurol. Surgeons, cert. Advanced Trauma Life Support ACS, 1996, Advanced Cardiac Life Support Am. Heart Assn., 1989; Eucharistic Ministry Cath. Ch., 1980. Tchg. asst. engring. level math. and physics Marquette U., Milw., 1979—82; tchg. asst. med. gross anatomy dept. anatomy and cellular biology Med. Coll. Wis., Milw., 1983—84, rsch. asst. dept. medicine, endocrinology, 1984, rsch. asst. dept. neurology, 1984, tchg. asst. med. neuroanatomy dept. anatomy and cellular biology, 1984—87, adj. instr. med. neuroanatomy dept. anatomy and cellular biology, 1987—89; neurosurgery resident Mayo Clinic, Rochester, Minn., 1989—95, post-doctoral fellow molecular genetics, 1992—93, spl. fellow neurosurgery, 1998—99; cons. neurosurgery Luther Midelfort, Mayo Health Sys., Eau Claire, Wis., 1995—2002, chmn. dept. neurosurgery, 2000—02; chief neurosurgery Affinity Health Systems, Oshkosh, Wis., 2002—. Contbr. articles to profl. jours. Med. dir. Think First Found., Eau Claire, Wis., 2000—02; co-director of neuro-peds-trauma icu Luther Midelfort, Mayo Health Sys., Eau Claire, Wis., 2001—02; eucharistic min. Cath. Ch., 1980—2003; bd. of directors Gold Cross Ambulance Svc., Fox Valley area, Wis., 2002—; elected to the med. exec. committe Luther Midelfort, Mayo Health Sys., Eau Claire, Wis., 2001—; pres. elect, bd. of directors, profl. adv. bd. Epilepsy Found. of Western Wis., Eau Claire, Wis., 1999—2002; bd. dirs. Dunn-Eau Claire-Pepin County Med. Soc., 1999—2002. Recipient 2nd Pl. award, Wis. State Fair, 1985; grantee, Mayo Clinic, 1992; scholar, Nicolet Clinic, 1979, 1980; Coll. scholar, AAUW, 1979, Med. Coll. of Wis. Summer Rsch. fellow, Med. Coll. Wis., 1983. Master: Epilepsy Found. Western Wis. (hon.); mem.: AAAS, Am. Assn. for Cancer RSch., Wis. State Med. Soc., Am. Assn. Neurol. Surgeons, Caduceus Soc., Samaritan Club, Alpha Epsilon Delta, Tau Beta Pi (life). Avocations: outdoor activities, sports and recreation, music, writing, community volunteering. Office: Affinity Health Systems Ste 203 2700 W Ninth Ave Oshkosh WI 54904 E-mail: tcheng@affinityhealth.org.

CHENG, TSEN-CHUNG, electrical engineering educator; b. Shanghai, Dec. 24, 1944; s. Yik Yu and Shun Lan (Tsui) C.; m. Doris Tin Gen Lee, Aug. 25, 1974; 1 child, Jason. BS, MIT, 1969, MSEE, 1970, ScD, 1974. Asst. prof. U. So. Calif., Los Angeles, 1974-80, assoc. prof., 1980-84, Lloyd F. Hunt prof., dir. electric power program, 1984—. Pres. T.C. Cheng ScD Inc., San Marino, Calif., 1981—; cons. Los Angeles Dept. Water and Power, 1984—, So. Calif. Edison Co., 1982—, Pacific Gas & Electric Co., San Francisco, 1982—, and numerous other pub. utilities and elec. and electronic mfrs. worldwide. Patentee in field; author over 120 pubs. Recipient Outstanding Elec. Engring. faculty award U. So. Calif., 1976, Engring. Service award U. So. Calif., 1981. Fellow IEEE (relay com. award 1986, Best Paper award 1988), Sigma Xi, Eta Kappa Nu, Tau Beta Pi. Office: Univ of So Calif Phe 634 Dept Ee Ep # 634 Los Angeles CA 90089-0001 Office Phone: 213-740-4712. Personal E-mail: tccheng@socal.rr.com. Business E-Mail: tcheng@usc.edu.

CHENG, TSUNG O., cardiologist, educator; b. Shanghai, Mar. 30, 1925; came to U.S., 1950, naturalized, 1960; s. Keith S. and Fanny (Wang) C.; m. Marie Ellen Roe, June 18, 1955; children: Mark Dudley, Yvonne Joyce. BS, St. John's U., China, 1945; MD, U. Pa., 1950, MS in Medicine, 1956. Diplomate Am. Bd. Internal Medicine (subsplty. cardiovasc. disease), Nat. Bd. Med. Examiners. Intern St. Barnabas Hosp., Newark, 1950-51; resident in medicine Cook County Hosp., Chgo., 1952-55; fellow in cardiovasc. disease George Washington U., Washington, 1955-56; instr. cardiology Harvard Med. Sch. Mass. Gen. Hosp., Boston, 1956-57; fellow in cardiorespiratory physiology Johns Hopkins U. Sch. Medicine and Hosp., 1957-59, staff cardiac cath. lab., 1957—59; asst. prof. medicine SUNY Downstate, 1959-70; practice medicine specializing in cardiology Washington, 1970—; assoc. prof. medicine George Washington U., 1970-72; chief cardiology D.C. Gen. Hosp., 1971-72; prof. George Washington U., 1972—. Dir. cardiac catheterization lab. George Washington U. Med. Ctr., 1972—78, assoc. dir. cardiology, 1972—75; asst. physician Cardiac Clinic Johns Hopkins Hosp., 1957—59; dir. cardiopulmonary lab. Bklyn. Hosp., 1959—66, co-chief Pediat. Cardiac Clinic, 1959—66, chief Adolescent Cardiac Clinic, 1961—66, attending physician Adult Cardiac Clinic, 1959—66; chief Pediat. Cardiac Clinic Cumberland Hosp., Bklyn., 1963—66; asst. chief cardiology VA Hosp., Bklyn., 1966—69, chief cardiovasc. lab., 1966—70, chief cardiology, 1969—70; asst. vis. physician Kings County Hosp. Med. Ctr., Bklyn., 1964—70; attending physician U. Hosp., SUNY, Bklyn., 1967—70; guest lectr. Chinese Med. Assn., 1972—73, 1975, 77, 79, 83, 86, 89, 92, Chinese Ministry Health, 1990; hon. prof. Shanghai 2nd Med. U., 1986—, Qingdao Med. Coll., 1989—, Binzhou Med. Coll., 1992—, Taishan Med. Coll., 1992—, Tongji Med. U., Wuhan, China, 1994—, U. Cape Town, South Africa, 1995—, U. Natal, Durban, South Africa, 1995—, U. Morón, Buenos Aires, 2003—, Beijing Hosp. and Med. Coll. Peking U., 2007—, U. Cordoba, Spain, 2007; hon. dir. Quingdao Cardiovascular Rsch. Inst., 1990—, Inst. Invasive Therapy PLA 150th Ctrl. Hosp., Luoyang, China, 1994—; hon. pres. Dandong 1st Hosp., Liaoning Province, China, 1988—, Shanghai St. Luke's Hosp., 1990—, Binzhou Med. Coll. Affil. Hosp., 1992—, Taishan Med. Coll. Affil. Hosp., 1992—, Jujiang Med. Coll. Affil. Hosp., Jiangxi, China, 1994—, 2nd People's Hosp., Jin De Zhen, Jiangxi, 1994—, China Heart Failure Assn., 2001—; vis. prof. Peking Union Med. Coll., 1986—, Sun Yatsen Med. U., Canton, 1992—, Cairo U., Egypt, 1994—, U. Oxford, 1995—, U. Witwatersrand Med. Sch., Johannesburg, 1995—, U. Paris Hosp., Tenon, France, 1995—, Cath. U. Inst. Cardiology, Rome, 1996—, Inst. Clin. Physiology, Nat. Rsch. Coun., U. Pisa, Italy, 1996—, Inst. Clin. Physiology, Nat. Rsch. Coun., U. Milan, Inst. Pathol. Anatomy, Med. Sch. U. Milan, 1996—, U. Dusseldorf, Germany, 1997—, U. Hamburg, Germany, 1997—, U. Hannover, Germany, 1997—, U. Melbourne, Australia, 1997—, U. NSW, Sydney, 1997—, U. Istanbul, Turkey, 1999—, U. Athens, Greece, 1999—, U. Córdoba, Spain, 2000—, U. Las Palmas, Spain, 2000—, U. Complutense, Madrid, 2000—, Chinese U. Hong Kong, 2002—, Capital U. Med. Scis., Beijing, 2002—, U. Geneva, 2003—, U. Zurich, 2003—, U. Bern, Switzerland, 2003—, U. Tex., Houston, 2003—, McMaster U., Hamilton, Ont., Canada, 2004—; vis. prof. Med. Faculty Charite Humboldt U. Berlin, 2001—; v.p. Am. Ctr. Chinese Med. Sci., 1982—91; pres. Friends of St. Luke's Hosp., Shanghai, 1991—, chmn. bd., 1992—; disting. sr. visitor Royal Brompton Hosp./Nat. Heart and Lung Inst. London, 1995—; hon. advisor Guangdong Soc. Interventional Cardiology, Guangzhou, China, 1996—; cons. in field. Sr. editor: Vascular Medicine, 1983—88, Angiology, 1986—97; editor: The International Textbook of Cardiology, 1986—87, Percutaneous Balloon Valvuloplasty, 1992; mem. editl. bd.: Catheterization and Cardiovasc. Diagnosis, 1991—99, Catheterization and Cardiovasc. Interventions, 1999—2003, Jour. Noninvasive Cardiology, 1997—, Chinese Jour. Misdiagnostics, 1999—; mem. editl. bd. Internat. Jour. Cardiology, 2006—; co-editor: Congestive Heart Failure, 1991, 2d edit., 1997, Modern Cardiology, 1994, 2d edit., 2002, Genetics of Cardiovasc. Diseases, 1995, Textbook of Congestive Heart Failure, 2003; editl. cons.-in-chief: Internat. Jour. Cardiovascular Medicine, 2003—, contbg. med. editor: Cortlandt Forum, 1997—98, roving amb. Chinese cardiovascular sci.: Internat. Jour. Cardiology, 2007—; contbr. articles to profl. jours. and textbooks, chapters to books. Recipient Lifetime Achievement Disting. Rschr award, George Washington U. Sch. Medicine, 2007. Fellow ACP, Am. Coll. Chest Physicians, Am. Coll. Cardiology (ofcl. rep. to stds. com. on catheters Assn. Advancement Med. Instrumentation 1971—), Am. Heart Assn., Coun. Clin. Cardiology, Soc. Cardiac Angiography and Interventions, Internat. Coll. Angiology, Am. Coll. Angiology, Soc. Geriat. Cardiology (founding), Royal Soc. Medicine; mem. AAAS, Am. Fedn. Clin. Rsch., Am. Heart Assn., Washington Heart Assn. Home: 7508 Cayuga Ave Bethesda MD 20817-4822 Office: George Washington U Med Ctr 2150 Pennsylvania Ave NW Washington DC 20037-3201 Office Fax: 202-741-2324. Business E-Mail: tcheng@mfa.gwu.edu. *My goal in life is to serve the people the best way that I know, that is, through medicine which knows no international boundary. Perseverance, patience, hard work and selflessness will always be rewarded by the satisfaction of a job well done.*

CHENG, WAN-LEE, mechanical engineer, educator; b. Yi-Hsin, Chiang-Su, China, Dec. 28, 1945; arrived in U.S., 1971; s. Teh-Chih and Mei-Nung (Shih) Cheng; m. Viki Shu-Whei Lu, Dec. 16, 1972; children: Julie Wheichung, Paul Yichung, Lisa Yenchung. BS, Chung Yuan U., Taiwan, 1969; MEd, Sul Ross State U., 1972; PhD, Iowa State U., 1976. Mech. engr. Taiwan Power Co., Taipei, 1970-71; instr. Iowa State U., Ames, 1974-76; asst. prof., then prof. U. N.D., Grand Forks, 1976-85; prof., chmn. dept. design and industry San Francisco State U., 1985-2000, assoc. dean Coll. Creative Arts, 2000—05, acting dean Coll. Creative Arts, 2005—. Cons. High-Tech Mobile Lab., N.D. Vocat. Edn. Dept., Bismarck, 1984—85; vis. prof. Nat. Sci. Coun. and Chung Yuan U., Taiwan, 1990—91; dean Coll. Design Chung Yuan Christian U., Taiwan, 1994—95. Author: computer software; mem. rev. bd. Jour. Indsl. Tech., 1986—89, Jour. Tech. Studies, 2002—, mem. editl. bd. Jour. Design Sci., 2001—; contbr. articles to profl. jours. Session elder 1st Presbyn. Ch., Grand Forks, 1984—85, Lakeside Presbyn. Ch., 1989—91. Recipient Indsl. Arts Profl. Devel. award, N.D. Indsl. Arts Assn., 1985, Outstanding Tchg. and Faculty Devel. award, Burlington No. Found., 1985, Outstanding Profl. Indsl Tech. award, Nat. Assn. Indsl. Tech., 1992; 10 grants, U. N.D., 1979—85. Mem.: Chinese Am. Econ. and Tech. Devel. Assn. (pres. 1997—99), Chinese Inst. Engrs. (v.p. 1993), Soc. Mfg. Engrs. (sr.), Joint Alumni Assn. Chinese Univs. and Colls. No. Calif. (pres. San Francisco 1988—89), Chung Yuan Alumni Assn. No. Calif. (pres. San Francisco 1987—88), Epsilon Pi Tau (trustee Gamma Gamma chpt. Grand Forks 1984—85, Laureate award Beta Beta chpt. San Francisco 1991, Disting. Svc. award 2000), Phi Kappa Phi. Home Phone: 415-285-1779. Business E-Mail: wlcheng@sfsu.edu.

CHENG, YUE, molecular geneticist, pathologist; arrived in U.S., 2003; s. Renbin Cheng and Benzhao Zhou; m. Yuxing Xiong, Mar. 16, 1988; 1 child, Jasmine S. Cheng MBBS in medicine, Anhui Med. Coll., Hefei, China, 1982; MS in oncology, Sun Yatsen U. Med. Sci., Guangzhou, China, 1987; PhD in biology, Hong Kong U. Sci. and Tech., 2002. Asst. prof. Sun Yatsen U. Med. Sci., Guangzhou, 1989-93; vis. asst. rschr. U. Calif., Irvine, 1993-95; vis. scholar Hong Kong U. Sci. and Tech., 1995—2002; vis. fellow Nat. Cancer Inst., Bethesda, Md., 2003—. Dir. grad. course Sun Yatsen U. Med. Sci., Guangzhou, 1991-93. Contbr. articles to profl. jours. Grantee Sun Yatsen U. Med. Sci., 1991, scholar Am. Chinese Med. Bd., NY, 1993; NIH fellow, 2003—. Mem.: AAAS, Internat. Union Against Cancer, Am. Soc. Hematology, Am. Assn. Cancer Rsch., Chinese Med. Assn. Hong Kong. Achievements include first identification of tumor suppressor gene activities in nasopharyngeal carcinoma; detection of tumor suppressive region at chromosome 3p21.3 in human cells which has led to identification of critical genes associated with development of various sporadic cancers; establishment of a theoretical basis: multiple genes may be used in gene therapy for the treatment of nasopharyngeal carcinoma. Avocations: music, travel, swimming, hiking, photography. Personal E-mail: yuecheng@hotmail.com.

CHEN-MAXHAM, LI-CHAN, soprano; BA, Nat. Taiwan Normal U., China, 1980; MusM, Manhattan Sch. Music, NY, 1984. Participant Merola Opera Program, San Francisco, 1984; adj. faculty Rutgers U., Newark. Singer: (Operas) (roles include) Pamina, Lauretta, Musetta, Nannetta, Adina, Fiorilla, Monica, Juliette, Micaela, Despinaq, Zerlina, Susanna, Eurydice, Gilda, Blanch, 1979—, (concert repertoire) Bach, b-minor Mass, St. John Passion, Mendelssohn, A Midsummer Night's Dream, Franck, A-major Mass, Mozart, Coronation Mass, Handel, Messiah, Orff, Carmina Burana, Haydn, Mass in Time of War, others. Recipient 2d prize, Internat. Concours de Chant de Paris, 1990; fellow Adler fellow, San Francisco Opera, 1985—87; scholar, Ravel Academie, France. Mem.: Nat. Assn. Tchrs. Singing, Nat. Music Tchrs. Assn. Home: 31 Woodbury Rd Edison NJ 08820 Office Phone: 732-603-0302.

CHENOWETH, KRISTIN, actress; b. Broken Arrow, Okla., July 24, 1968; MA in Opera, Oklahoma City U. Actor: (Broadway plays) Steel Pier, 1999 (Theatre World award), You're a Good Man, Charlie Brown, 1999 (Tony award Best Featured Actress, 1999, Drama Desk award, 1999, Clarence Derwent award, 1999, Outer Critics Circle award, 1999), Epic Proportions, 1999—2000, Funny Girl, 2002, Wicked, 2003—04 (Tony award nominee, Best Actress in a Musical, 2004); (plays) A New Brain, Scapin, The Fantasticks, Dames at Sea, Strike Up the Band, 1998, The Apple Tree, 2005, Stairway to Paradise, 2007; (TV series) LateLine, 1998, Frasier, 1993, Kristin, 2001, Baby Bob, 2002, Sesame Street, 2003, The West Wing, 2004—06; (TV miniseries) Paramour, 1999; (TV films) Annie, 1999, The Music Man, 2003; (films) Topa Topa Bluffs, 2002, Bewitched, 2005, The Pink Panther, 2006, RV, 2006, Stranger than Fiction, 2006, Running with Scissors, 2006, Deck the Halls, 2006, (guest appearance) Ugly Betty, 2007; guest soloist: West Side Story Suite of Dances; singer: (albums) Let Yourself Go, 2001, As I Am, 2005. Metropolitan Opera award. Performed leading roles at Goodspeed Opera House, Guthrie Theatre, Paper Mill Playhouse, North Shore Music Theatre; guest soloist with National Symphony Orchestra, New York Philharmonic, London's Divas at Donmar series, Carnegie Hall, Lincoln Center and the Kennedy Center, and has performed with Placido Domingo, Paul Newman, Joshua Bell and Harvey Fierstein. Office: c/o SAG 360 Madison Ave #12 New York NY 10017-7111*

CHENOWETH, TIM, information scientist, educator; m. Heather Chenoweth, Mar. 27, 2000; children: Holly, Jacob. BS in Math., Coast Guard Acad., 1981; MBA in Fin., Wash. State U., 1991, MS in Computer Sci., 1996, PhD, 1996. Asst. prof. Boise State U., Idaho, 2003—06, assoc. prof., 2006—. Contbr. articles to profl. jours. Office: Boise State Univ COBE 1910 University Dr Boise ID 83725-1615 Office Phone: 208-426-1181.

CHEPIGA, MICHAEL JOSEPH, lawyer; b. NYC, Jan. 14, 1948; s. Michael Andrew and Frances (Karasek) C.; m. Pamela Rogers, Nov. 21, 1970; children: Geoffrey Rogers, Emily Rogers. BA in English Lit., cum laude, Fordham U., 1970; PhD in English Lang. and Lit., NYU, 1975; JD, Yale U., 1979. Bar: N.Y. 1980, U.S. Ct. Appeals (2d cir.) 1986, U.S. Ct. Appeals (11th cir.) 1988, U.S. Dist. Ct. (so. dist.) N.Y. 1981, U.S. Dist. Ct. (ea. dist.) N.Y. 1983, U.S. Ct. Claims 1988. Tchr. English Washington Irving High Sch., NYC, 1970-76; law clk. Hon. Milton Pollack, NYC, 1979-80, Hon. Amalya Kearse, NYC, 1980-81; assoc. Simpson, Thacher & Bartlett, NYC, 1981-86, ptnr., mem. exec. com., 1986—. Bd. dirs. Legal Aid Soc. N.Y., exec. com., 1992—, v.p., 1994-96, pres., 1996—; adj. instr. English, writing skills LaGuardia C.C., L.I., N.Y., 1973-76; mem. bd. advisors Bank and Corp. Governance Law Reporter, 1988—. Mem. ABA (fellow), N.Y. State Bar Assn. (fed. cts. com. 1987-89), Assn. of Bar of City of N.Y. (fed. cts. com. 1992-95). Office: Simpson Thacher & Bartlett 425 Lexington Ave Fl 8 New York NY 10017-3954 Office Phone: 212-455-2598. Office Fax: 212-455-2502. Business E-Mail: mchepiga@stblaw.com.

CHERCOVER, MURRAY, television executive; b. Montreal, Que., Can., Aug. 18, 1929; s. Max M. and Betty (Pomerance) (dec.) C.; m. Barbara Ann Holleran, Aug. 8, 1953; children: Hollis Denny, Sean Peter. Grad., Acad. Radio TV Arts, Toronto, Ont., Can., Neighborhood Playhouse Sch. Theatre, NYC. With Radio Sta. CFPA, Port Arthur, Ont., 1944-46, New Play Soc. Jupiter Theater, Toronto, 1946-48; exec. dir. Equity Library Theatre, NYC, 1948-52; producer, dir. network TV drama Louis G. Cowan Agy., NYC, 1948-52; with Canadian Broadcasting Co., 1952-60; exec. producer all prodn. Sta. CFTO-TV, Toronto, 1960, dir. programming, 1961; exec. v.p., gen. mgr. CTV TV Network Ltd., Toronto, 1966, pres., chief operating officer, 1968, pres., mng. dir., 1969—, pres., chief exec. officer, 1987-90, 1990—; pres. Chercover Comm., 1990—. Pres., dir. Avanti Mgmt. Ltd.; founding dir., fellow Internat. Coun. Nat. Acat. TV Arts and Scis.; past mem. adv. com. theatre arts George Brown Coll. Applied Arts and Tech.; past mem. adv. coun. film/TV prodn. program Humber Coll. Bd. dirs. Found. for Ocean Rsch. (founding), Can. Satellite Learning Svcs., Inc.; founding, past trustee Ruth Hancock Scholarship Found. Recipient Gold medal Can. Film and TV Assn., 1988, Rockie award for Lifetime Achievement Banff TV Festival, 1990, Excellence in Broadcasting Lifetime Achievement award Conestoga Coll., 1990, Achievement award for outstanding contbn. to broadcasting Broadcast Exec. Soc., 1991; named to Can. Broadcasting Hall of Fame, 1994. Fellow NATAS (founding dir. internat. coun., spl. citation 1989); mem. Acad. Can. Cinema and TV, Internat. Press Inst., Can. Assn. Broadcasters (Disting. Svc. gold ribbon medal 1986), Ctrl. Can. Broadcasters Assn. (past bd. dirs., Broadcaster of Yr. award 1990), Toronto Radio Control Club, Model Aeros. Assn. Can., Giant Scale Club (Oshawa), 400 RC Club, Seaton Valley R/C Flying Club. Personal E-mail: chercover@sympatico.ca.

CHERDUNOLO, STEVE, professional soccer player; b. Rockford, Ill., Feb. 19, 1979; Attended, Univ. Portland. Defender Hannover 96, Germany, 1998—. 34 caps, 1 goal U.S. Nat. Soccer team, 1999—; mem. U.S. World Cup team, 2006. Mailing: US Soccer Fedn 1801 S Prairie Ave Chicago IL 60616

CHEREWKA, MICHAEL, lawyer; b. Taylor, Pa., July 3, 1955; s. Michael Jr. and Anne (Regan) C.; m. Michele Mary Robinson, Aug. 2, 1980; children: Michael Colin, Matthew Bryan, Meaghan Kelly. Student, U. Bristol, Eng., 1976-77; BSBA cum laude, Bucknell U., 1978; JD cum laude, Dickinson Sch. Law, 1981. Bar: Pa. 1981, U.S. Dist. Ct. (mid. dist.) Pa. 1983, U.S. Tax Ct. 1983, U.S. Ct. Appeals (3d cir.) 1983, U.S. Supreme Ct. 1985. Sr. mem. tax staff Ernst & Whinney, Harrisburg, Pa., 1981-83; assoc. Ball, Skelly, Murren & Connell (formerly Ball & Skelly), Harrisburg, 1983-89; pvt. practice Harrisburg, 1989—96, Wormleysburg, Pa., 2002—; mng. ptnr. Cherewka & Radcliff, LLP, 1996—2002; pvt. practice, 2002—. Mem. Keystone Family Bus. Ctr., LLC, 2000—; bd. dirs. Keystone Partnership, chair planned giving com., 2005—; mem. Wealth Counsel, LLC, 1996—. Co-author: Pennsylvania Tax Service, 1987; contbg. editor (legal column) Cen. Penn Bus. Jour., 1985-88, Strictly Business, 2002; advisor Dauphin County Law Explorers Post, 1982-88. Mem. Country Club Park Civic Assn., 1983-98, pres., 1987-88; mem. Hist. Harrisburg Assn., 1982-84; active Tri-County United Way, 1985-90, cons. planning giving, mem. adv. com., 1988-90; bd. dirs. Capital divsn. Am. Heart Assn., chmn. 1989-91, bd. dirs. Pa. affiliate, 1989-98 , exec. com., 1989-90, 93, treas., 1994-95, incoming chmn. bd., 1995-96, chmn. 1996-97; chmn., bd. dirs. Concertante Chamber Ensemble, 1996-97; bd. dirs. Pa. Assn. Nonprofit Orgns., 1996-; mem. planned giving com. Keystone Svc. Sys. Found., 1995-2000; mem. adv. bd. Found. Caths. United in Svc., Cath. Diocese of Harrisburg, 1991-97; mem. devel. bd. Trinity H.S., 2003—; coach HMMS Youth Soccer Assn., 1994—. Named Outstanding Young Man Am., U.S. Jaycees, 1983. Mem. Nat. Network Estate Planning Attys., Pa. Bar Assn. (tax sect. 1981—, real estate, probate and trust law sect. 1981—, com. state taxation 1984-99, chmn. subcom. on compromise tax 1986-97), Dauphin County Bar Assn. (interprofl. rels. com. 1984-89, estate planning sect. 1992—), Estate Planning Coun. Cen. Pa. (chmn. CPA subcom. 1982-83, bd. dirs. 1988-96, treas. 1989-90, v.p. 1990-91, pres. 1991-92), Polit. Info. Com. CPAs Pa. (treas. 1982-83), Greater Harrisburg C. of C. (bus. liaison com. 1984-87, econ. devel. com. 1988-89, 92-93, reaccreditation task force 1996), Pa. Chamber Bus. and Industry (bus. subcom. 1989), Harrisburg Assn. Ins. and Fin. Advs., Greater West Shore Area C. of C. (comml.-indsl. devel. com. 1987-89), Alzheimer's Assn. of So. Ctrl. Pa. (bd. dirs. 1998-2001), Pa. Assn. Nonprofit Orgns. (bd. dirs. 2000—), Delta Mu Delta, Omicron Delta Kappa. Republican. Roman Catholic. Avocations: coin collecting/numismatics, golf, basketball. Home: 125 Pelham Rd Camp Hill PA 17011-1353 Office: 624 N Front St Wormleysburg PA 17043-1022 Office Phone: 717-232-4701. Business E-Mail: mcestateplanlaw@earthlink.net.

CHERKAOUI, MOHAMED, sociologist; b. Boujad, Morocco, Apr. 22, 1945; s. Abdelaziz and Saadia (Moutawakil) C.; m. Khadija Sadif, Feb. 17, 1985; children: Youssef, Selma, Anas MA Philosophy, Sorbonne, Paris, 1967, MA Sociology, 1972, BSc Stats., 1972, PhD Sociology, 1975, PhD Scis., 1981. Asst. prof. Sorbonne, Paris, 1972—73; cons. Paris, 1974—75; rsch. officer Nat. Ctr. for Sci. Rsch., Paris, 1976—85, rsch. dir., 1986—; prof. U. Lausanne, 1989-94, Sorbonne, 1995—. Prof. U. Lausanne, 1989-94, Sorbonne, 1995—, U. Geneva, 1995—; cons. French Min. Planning, Paris, 1976-85, UNESCO, Paris, 1975; expert, cons. Nat. Com., CNRS, 1995—; expert Min. Planning Morocco, Min. Higher Edn. and Rsch., Morocco, 2005- Author: Les Paradoxes de la Réussite Scolaire, 1979, Les Changements du Système Éducatif en France, 1982, Sociologie de l'education, 1986, Naissance d'une Science Sociale, 1998, European Tradition in Qualitative Research, 2003, Histoire et Theorie des Sciences Sociales, 2003, Invisible Codes, 2004, Le Paradoxe des Conséquences, 2006, Good Intentions, 2006, Le Sahara, liens sociaux et enjeux stratégiques, 2007, Morocco and the Sahara: Social Bonds and Geopolitical Issues, 2007; co-author: The Classical Tradition in Sociology, 1997, Central Currents in Social Theory, 1999, Dictionnaire de Sociologie, 1999, Le Suicide: Un Siécle aprés Durkheim, 2000, Ecole et société, Les paradoxes de la démocratie, 2001, Dictionnaire de la Pensée Sociologique, 2005; editor: French Jour. Soc., GEMAS Studies in Social Analysis Series. Mem.: Coll. European Sociology (pres.), Internat. Sociol. Assn., Academia Europaea, European Acad. Sociology, French Sociol. Soc., Le Cercle. Avocation: collecting 19th century English and French silver. Office: 54 Blvd Raspail Maison des Scis de l'Homme 75006 Paris France Personal E-mail: mcherkaoui@yahoo.fr. Business E-Mail: cherkaoui@msh-paris.fr.

CHERKASKY, MICHAEL G., insurance company executive; b. White Plains, NY, Mar. 2, 1950; m. Betsy Cherkasky; 4 children. BA, Case Western Reserve U., JD, 1975. Law clk. US Dist. Ct. (no. dist) Ohio; asst. dist. atty. NY County Dist. Atty. Office, 1978—85; mgr. Robert Morgenthau re-election campaign, 1985; asst. dist. atty. NY County Dist. Atty. Office, 1985—93, dep. bureau chief, trial bureau 40, 1983—84, bureau chief, trial bureau 40, 1984—85, head, Rackets Bureau, 1986—90, head, investigations divsn., 1990—94; chief NY office Kroll Associates, 1994—96, chief, N. Am. region, 1996—97, pres., COO, 1997—2001; pres., CEO Kroll Inc. (formerly The Kroll-O'Gara Co.), NYC, 2001—04; CEO Marsh Kroll, 2004; pres., CEO Marsh & McLennan Inc., NYC, 2004—. Supr. to the state prosecutors assigned to the Joint Terrorist Task Force investigating the World Trade Ctr. bombing NYC, 1993; compliance officer LI carting industry, 1994; election officer Internat. Brotherhood of Teamsters, 1997; ind. monitor LA Police Dept., 2001. Author: Forewarned: Why the Government is Failing to Protect Us and What We Must Do to Protect Ourselves, 2002. Office: Marsh & McLennan Inc 1166 Ave Americas New York NY 10036-2774*

CHERKEN, HARRY SARKIS, JR., lawyer; b. Phila., Dec. 8, 1949; s. Harry Sarkis and Lorna G. (Demurjian) Cherken. BA, Lafayette Coll., 1971; JD, Villanova U., 1976. Bar: Pa. 1976, U.S. Dist. Ct. (ea. dist.) Pa. 1976, U.S. Supreme Ct. 1983. Assoc. counsel Albert M. Greenfield & Co., Inc., Phila., 1976-79; assoc. Drinker, Biddle & Reath LLP, Phila., 1979—84, ptnr., 1984—, co-chmn. real estate group, 1991—2007, mng. ptnr., 1996—2000. Assoc. Wharton Real Estate Rsch. Ctr., U. Pa., 1996—; adv. bd. Advanced Comml. Leasing Inst., Georgetown U. Law Ctr.; bd. dirs. Urban Outfitters, Inc., Mikronite Techs. Group, Inc., Law Dept. Am. U. Armenia. Trustee Kulicke Fund, Phila., 1985—, Balch Inst., 1992—2000, Woodmere Art Mus., 2002—; fellow trustee Armenian Assembly Am., 1986—, bd. dirs., 1988—2000, vice-chmn. bd. dirs., 1988—91, 1994—95; bd. dirs. Howard Karagheusian Commemorative Corp., 2003—; sec., bd. dirs. Reading Terminal Market Preservation Fund, 1991—. Mem.: ABA, Am. Coll. Real Estate Lawyers, Pa. Land Title Assn. (affiliate), Phila. Bar Assn., Pa. Bar Assn., Internat. Coun. Shopping Ctrs. (assoc.). Armenian Apostolic. Office: Drinker Biddle & Reath LLP One Logan Sq 18th & Cherry Sts Philadelphia PA 19103-6996 Office Phone: 215-988-2721. Office Fax: 215-988-2757. Business E-Mail: harry.cherken@dbr.com.

CHER-KILLIGM, BEATRICE M., history professor, art educator; d. Alfred and Katherine Cherkezian. BFA in painting and art history magna cum laude, Fla. Internat. U., Miami; MFA in Visual Arts cum laude, U. Miami, Coral Gables, 1997. Tchr. drawing and two-dimensional design U. Miami Coral Gables, 1996—97; tchr. arts and philosophy dept. Miami Dade Coll., 1997—2001; adj. prof. New World Sch. Arts, Miami, 1998—2000, Barry U., Miami, 1999—2001; adj. instr. U. Phoenix, Plantation, Fla., 1999—2001; prof. Am. Intercontinental U., Weston, Fla., 2001—. Dir. Sch. Ballet Dance Experience Coral Gables, 1978—82, Gables Art Gallery, 1978—82. Exhibitions include The New Gallery, Coral Gables, 1996, Lowe Mus., 1997, Arte Contemporaneo, Miami, 2000, Cornell Mus. Art, Fla., 2000, M-DCC Kendall Campus Art Gallery, Miami, 2000, Union Planters Bank, Coral Gables, 2001, Miura Mus. Art, Tokyo, 2003, R. Martin Gallery, Buenos Aires, 2005, Promo Arte Gallery, Tokyo, 2006. Apptd. vice chairperson City Coral Gables Cultural Affairs Bd., 1995—2001; mem. Coral Gables Cultural Coun., 1999—2001, vice chairperson, 2001—, Mozart Festival Coral Gables, 2001—, Bach Soc. Coral Gables, 2001—.

CHERLA, GAUTAM V., physician, nephrologist, researcher; s. Sastri B.N. and Kamala Sastri Cherla; m. Aparna Vadlamani, Nov. 24, 1999. MD, Andhra Med. Coll., Visakhapatnam, India, 1997. Diplomate Am. Bd. Internal Medicine. Ho. staff internal medicine Mt. Vernon Hosp./ NY Med. Coll., 1999—2002, chief ho. staff, 2001—02; postdoctoral rsch. fellow NY Med. Coll., Valhalla, 2002—03; clin. fellow in nephrology and hypertension U. Miami/ Jackson Meml. Hosp., Fla., 2003—, clin. fellow in interventional nephrology, 2004—. Contbr. articles to profl. jours. Mem.: Am. Soc. Diagnostic and Interventional Nephrology, Nat. Kidney found., Renal Physicians Assn., Am. Soc. Nephrology, AMA. Home: 13189 Sw 23rd St Miramar FL 33027 Office: 8130 Royal Palm Blvd Ste 102 Pompano Beach FL 33065 Home Phone: 954-442-7924; Office Phone: 305-243-3583, 954-345-4333.

CHERMAYEFF, IVAN, graphics designer; b. London, Eng., June 6, 1932; s. Serge Ivan and Barbara Maitland (May) C.; m. Sara Anne Duffy, July 15, 1956; children: Catherine, Alexandra, Maro; m. Jane Clark, Sept. 24, 1978; 1 son, Sam. Grad., Phillips Acad., Andover, Mass., 1950; student, Harvard, 1950-52, Ill. Inst. Tech., 1952-54; BFA, Yale, 1955; LLD (hon.), Maine Sch. Art, 1981; BFA (hon.), Corcoran Sch. Art, 1991, U. of Arts, Phila., 1991. Asst. to Alvin Lustig (designer), 1955; asst. art dir. Columbia Records, 1956; ptnr. Brownjohn, Chermayeff & Geismar Assoc., 1956-59, Chermayeff & Geismar Inc., NYC, 1959—2005, Chermayeff & Geismar Studio LLC, 2005—, Cambridge Seven Assoc., 1965-96. Bd. dir. Internat. Design Conf., Aspen, Colo., 1968-99; bd. dir. Mcpl. Art Soc. NY, 1972-76, Smithsonian Instn., 1988-96; trustee Mus. Modern Art, NYC, 1966-86, Archives of Am. Art, 1987-90, New Sch. Univ., 1988-2002; bd. overseers Parson's Sch. Design, 1988-2002; disting. vis. prof. UCLA, 1998; vis. prof. Kansas City Art Inst., Cooper Union; co-chmn. First Fed. Design Assembly, Nat. Endowment for the Arts and Humanities, 1973. Author: Observations on American Architecture, 1972, Ellis Island, 1987. Mem. com. on art and arch. Yale U.; mem. bd. overseers com. on visual and environ. studies Harvard U. Recipient Awards Art Dir. Club, NY, awards Am. Inst. Graphic Arts, awards Type Dirs. Club, Indsl. Arts, medal AIA, 1967, Gold medal Phila. Coll. Art, 1971, Claude M. Fuess medal Phillips Acad., 1980, Pres.'s award RISD, 1981, Yale Arts medal 1985, Grand Prix Biennale Brno, 1992; named to NY Art Dir. Club Hall of Fame, 1981, Soc. of Illustrators, gold medal, 2002. Mem. SPEE, Am. Inst. Graphic Arts (pres. 1963-66, Gold medal 1979), Nat. Soc. Indsl. Designers, Alliance Graphique Internat., Royal Soc. Arts and Commerce (Benjamin Franklin fellow), Royal Designer for Industry (RDI hon.), Century Assn., Yale Arts Assn. (past v.p.). Home: 140 E 81st St New York NY 10028-1805 also: Sheep's Hill North Salem NY 10560 Office: Chermayeff & Geismar Studio 137 E 25th St New York NY 10010-1505 Home Phone: 212-744-3970; Office Phone: 212-532-4595. Personal E-mail: ic@cgnyc.com.

CHERN, SHYH-SHI RICHARD, radiologist; PhD in Physics, U. Pitts., 2001. Diplomate Am. Bd. Radiology, 2006. Postdoctoral fellow U. Pitts. Med. Ctr., 2001—03; clin. asst. prof. U. Utah, Salt Lake City, 2003—07; chief med. physicist St. Vincent Hosp., Worcester, Mass., 2007—. Mem.: AAPM (rocky mountain chpt. sec. 2003—06), ASTRO (assoc.). Office: Saint Vincent Hosp 123 Summer St Worcester MA 01608 Office Phone: 508-363-7124.

CHERNAVSKY, GEORGE Y., composer, producer, song writer; b. Tambov, Russia, Mar. 17, 1947; s. Alexander and Alexandra Chernavsky; m. Tatiana Dolgova, July 14, 1977; children: Damon, Alex. Degree, Rachmaninov State Acad. Music, Tambov, 1968. Artist, composer Rosconcert, Moscow, 1969—91; composer, prodr. How's That Music Gmbh, Berlin, 1991—94, La3D Motion Gbr, Beverly Hills, Calif., 1994—. Creator music group DINAMIC; musical dir., composer Worldwide Festival of Youths and Students, Moscow, 1985, Good Will Games, 1986,

Russian-Indian Festivals, 1987—88; founder, pres. Record, Russia, 1986; founder How's that Music, 1990—. Songwriter Belaya Panama, White Door, Superman, Zurbagan, Tango, Margarita, Ostrova, I Know the Last Words, Snow Queen, Only You, numerous others. Soldier Arty., 1968—69, Russia. Recipient Hon. Artist medal, Russian Fedn., 1987. Mem.: GEMA (assoc.). Office Phone: 310-854-9770. Office Fax: 818-541-1779. Business E-Mail: info@mir-united.com.

CHERNESKY, RICHARD JOHN, lawyer; b. Scranton, Pa., July 27, 1939; s. Frank Peter and Mary C.; m. Alice Faye Nyfenger, Aug. 1, 1959; children: Christopher John, Joshua James. BA, Ohio St. U., 1963, JD, 1966. Bar: Ohio 1966. Ptnr. Smith & Schnacke, Dayton, Ohio, 1966-88; mng. ptnr. Chernesky, Heyman & Kress P.L.L., Dayton, 1988—. Pres. Ohio Sports Ctr., Miamisburg, Ohio, 1991—; trustee Hipple Cancer Rsch. Ctr., Kettering, Ohio, 1994-96, Dayton Internat. Aviation Corp., Inc., 1990-92; sec. Iams Co., 1997-99; bd. dirs. Internat. Display Systems, Inc. Bd. dirs. Dolly Inc., Tipp City, Ohio, 1989-93, Chapel of the Air, Wheaton, Ill., 1985-91, 94-95, Miami Valley Hosp. Found., Dayton, 1987-88, Am. Indoor Soccer Assn., Inc., 1992-96, Mike-sell's, Inc., 1994—, US Soccer Fedn. Found., Inc., 1996—; trustee Luth. Sch. Dayton, 1988-91, The Waynesville Area Friends of the Parks, 1992—, Sinclair C.C., 2006—; mem. Luth. Social Svcs. Devel. Com., Dayton, 1987-93; chmn. Wayne Twp. Zoning Bd., Waynesville, 1987-95. Mem. Nat. Lawyers AssnOhio State Bar Assn., Dayton Bar Assn., Dayton Better Bus. Bur. (bd. dirs. 1989-94). Home: 8027 New Burlington Rd Waynesville OH 45068-9705 Office: Chernesky Heyman & Kress PLL PO Box 3808 Ste 1100 10 Courthouse Plz SW Dayton OH 45401-3808

CHERNEV, MELVIN, retired beverage company executive; b. Bklyn., Nov. 29, 1928; s. Irving and Selma (Kulik) C.; m. Noemi Dohnert, May 29, 1955 (dec. July 1, 1985); 1 child, Celia Ann; m. Marlene G. Tonkin, Sept. 4, 1988. AB, Cornell U., 1950. Chief statistician Eversharp, Inc., NYC, 1951-52, sales adminstr., 1952-55, asst. gen. sales mgr., 1955-58; sales promotion mgr. Internat. Latex Corp. (Playtex), NYC, 1959-64, product mgr., 1964-66; pres. Snow White Corp., San Jose, Calif., 1966-67; dir. planning and research Fromm and Sichel, Inc., distbrs. Christian Bros. wines and brandy, San Francisco, 1967-70, dir. mktg. services, 1970-73, v.p. mktg. services, 1973-76, sr. v.p. mktg., 1976-77, exec. v.p., 1977-78, pres., chief operating officer, 1978-83, bd. dirs. Mem. Sacramento County Grand Jury, 2000—01; bd. dirs., trustee Cogswell Coll., San Francisco, 1976—86, chmn., 1983—85; bd. govs. City U., Seattle, 1985—99; bd. dirs., treas. The Lakes at Northridge Homeowners Assn.; pres. bd. dirs. Albert Einstein Residence Ctr., 1997—2000. Mem. Cornell Club No. Calif., Cornell Club (N.Y.C.), North Ridge Country Club (Fair Oaks, Calif.). Home: 7529 Pineridge Ln Fair Oaks CA 95628-4858 Personal E-mail: mchernev@aol.com.

CHERNEY, EUGENE JOSEPH, plastic surgeon, director; b. Chgo., Mar. 16, 1956; married; 3 children. BA in English magna cum laude, Windham Coll., Putney, Vt., 1977; MD, Rush Med. Coll., Chgo., 1983. Cert. Am. Bd. Plastic Surgery, Nat. Bd. Med. Examiners, lic. Iowa. Resident gen. surgery U. Medicine and Dentistry NJ, 1983—87, resident plastic and reconstructive surgery, 1987—89; participating physician Iowa Luth. Hosp. Residency Program, Met. Med. Ctr. Residency Program, Broadlawns Med. Ctr. Residency Program; breast implant adj. study coord. Health South Surgery Ctr., 1993; med. dir. Iowa Hand Rehab. Ctr.; founder, surgeon, med. dir. Heartland Plastic and Reconstructive Surgery, P.C., Des Moines. Adj. prof. Des Moines U. Med. Sch.; faculty Coll. Osteopathic Medicine and Health Scis., Des Moines; assoc. faculty Iowa Meth. Med. Ctr. Resident Program, 1994; mem. trauma com. Mercy Hosp., mem. quality assurance com.; mem. peer review com. Iowa Found. for Med. Care; mem. utilization review com. Met. Med. Ctr.; staff appointments include Iowa Meth. Med. Ctr., Mercy Hosp. Med. Ctr., Health Surgery South Ctr., Iowa Luth. Hosp., Met. Med. Ctr., Walter Reed Army Med. Ctr. Maj. med. corps USAR. Decorated Army Svc. ribbon, Overseas Svc. ribbon, Army Achievement medal, Nat. Def. medal; named one of Am.'s Top Surgeons, Consumer Rsch. Coun. Am., 2002—03, 2004—05, 2006—07. Fellow: ACS; mem.: Midwest Soc. Plastic Surgeons, Internat. Microsurgery of Hand Surgery, Christian Med. Dental Soc., Am. Cleft Palate - Craniofacial Assn., Iowa State Med. Soc., Polk County Med. Soc., Am. Soc. Aesthetic Plastic Surgeons, Am. Soc. Plastic and Reconstructive Surgeons. Office: Heartland Plastic and Reconstructive Surgery 10611 Hickman Rd Des Moines IA 50322 Office Phone: 515-254-2265. Office Fax: 515-254-2272.*

CHERNIACK, NEIL STANLEY, pulmonologist, educator; b. Bklyn., May 28, 1931; s. Max and Rebecca (Roulnick) C.; m. Sandra Lebowitz, Dec. 31, 1954; children: Evan, Andrew, Emily. AB (hon.), Columbia U., 1952; MD, SUNY, 1956; MD (hon.), Karolinska Inst., Stockholm, Sweden, 1990; MA, U. Pa., 1972; degree (hon.), Karolinska U., 1991. Cert. Am. Bd. Internal Medicine, 1956. Intern U. Ill., Chgo., 1956-57, resident, 1957-58, 60-62; resident, fellow Columbia Presbyn. Hosp., NYC, 1962-64; practice medicine specializing in pulmonary disease Chgo., 1964-69, Phila., 1969-77, Cleve., 1977—95; asst. prof. medicine U. Ill., Chgo., 1964-68, assoc. prof., 1968-69, U. Pa., Phila., 1969-73, prof., 1973-77, Case Western Res. U., 1977—, chief pulmonary svc., 1977-89, prof. physiology, 1982—, assoc. dean, 1983-90, dean sch. medicine, v.p. med. affairs, 1990-95, vice chmn. div. gen. med. sci., 1986-90, vice chmn. dept. medicine, 1987-90; chief pulmonary svc., sr. attending physician Phila. Gen. Hosp., 1969-77; assoc. dir. pulmonary svc., attending physician U. Pa. Hosp., 1973-77, U. Hosps. of Cleve., Cleve. VA Med. Ctr.; vis. prof. Karolinska U., Stockholm, 1976-77, dir. clin. svc., 1995—2000; dir. of clin. svcs., acting chmn. dept. physiology & pharmacology U. Medicine & Dentistry N.J., Newark, 1995—97. External vis. com. Aga Khan U., Karachi, 1980—85; chmn. vis. com. neurosci. program Howard U., 1998—. Mem. editl. bd.: Circulation Rsch., Am. Rev. Respiratory Disease, Chest; editor: Jour. Applied Physiology, Handbook of Physiology; assoc. editor: Jour. Lab. Clin. Medicine, Respiration Handbooks of Physiology, Respiration and Respiratory Medicine Revs. Capt. USAF, 1958—60, with USAF, 1960—62. Mem.: N.Y. Clin. Soc., Neurosci. Soc., Ctrl. Soc. Clin. Rsch., Biomed. Engring. Soc. (bd. dirs. 1984—87, councilor 1986), Biogengring. Soc., Am. Physiol. Soc., Am. Lung Assn., Am. Thoracic Soc. (councilor 1982), Am. Soc. Clin. Investigation, Am. Assn. Physicians, Morris County Art Assn., Soc. Columbia Grads., Beta Sigma Rho, Alpha Omega Alpha, Phi Beta Kappa. Jewish. Avocation: digital art. Home: 11 Wood Dr Morris Plains NJ 07950-1509 Office: Univ Med Dental NJ Newark NJ 07103-2714 Business E-Mail: cherniack@umdnj.edu.

CHERNICHAW, MARK, broadcast, cable television, corporate communications and advertising executive, television producer, director, media consultant, educator; s. Nathan H. and Irma (Walker) C.; m. Pauline Papernik; children: Adam, Ian. BA, U. Miami, Fla., 1969; MS, Bklyn. Coll., 1972. Assoc. prof., tv dept. head NYU, 1972-82; ind. TV prodr., dir., 1973-82; exec. prodr. TV commls., video, film prodns., exec.-in-charge of prodn. Avon Products, Inc., NYC, 1982-92; pres. Entertainment Enterprises Inc., 1991-96; exec. v.p. creative svcs. and prodn. SLP & Co., NYC and L.A., 1995—97; v.p. advt., promotion, prodn. The Home Shopping Network, USA Network, 1997—99; v.p. global comms. and TV prodn. Prudential Fin., 1999—. Writer, prodr., dir. commls. ABC-TV Sweeps; exec. prodr., shows featuring celebrities including Ricki Lake, Cindy Crawford, Mary Hart, John Glenn, George Burns, Henry Fonda, Bob Hope, Frank Sinatra, Martin Sheen, Whoopie Goldberg, Colin Powell; consultant for MTV, Action for Children's Television, Sesame Street, SNL, cons. NJ Coalition for Fair Broadcasting, Trenton; guest spkr. Directing TV seminars Video Comms. Congress, Academy of TV Arts and Sciences; lectr. Video Expo, NY; judge Emmy, Clio awards. Dir. One Person Too Late, ABC-TV (Internat. Film and TV award), syndicated TV series The Road to the White House (represented in permanent collection Smithsonian Instn. and The Peabody Award Archives), CBS Sports, Script Consultant for Edward Scissorhands, Executive Producer for "Shape Up With Mary Hart" exercise video, Cable TV series The Home Shopping Show, various network, nat. and regional TV commls. (Clio Award); mem. editl. adv. board. Video Mgr. Mag.; contbr. articles to profl. jours. Polit. media cons. Recipient Clio award, Peabody Archives award, Top Ten Picks by People Magazine and Video Review Magazine for exercise video "Shape Up With Mary Hart", 1 Grand, 2 Gold, 4 Silver and 3 Bronze awards Internat. Film and TV Awards, Grand award, Gold award Internat. Assn. Bus. Communicators, Telly award. Mem. NIMA Internat., NATAS, Am. Film Inst., Internat. TV Assn. Avocations: music, sports, travel, art.

CHERNIN, PETER F., multimedia company executive; b. May 29, 1951; Pres. Lorimar Film Entertainment, 1988—89; pres. entertainment group Fox Broadcasting Co., LA, 1989—92; chmn. Twentieth Century Fox Film Corp., now Fox Filmed Entertainment, Beverly Hills, Calif., 1992—; chmn., CEO Fox Entertainment Group, Beverly Hills, Calif., 1992—; pres., COO News Corp., 1996—. Bd. dirs. News Corp., E Trade, Am. Express Corp. Office: Fox Inc Rm 5080 10201 W Pico Blvd Bldg 100 Los Angeles CA 90064-2606*

CHERNIS, MARK, educational organization executive; BA, Vassar Coll. Sys. analyst, 1984—89; joined The Princeton Review, NYC, 1984, v.p. ops., 1989—95, COO, sec., 1995—, pres., 2000—. Bd. mem. SchoolNet, Inc. Office: Princeton Review 2315 Broadway New York NY 10024 Office Phone: 212-874-8282. Office Fax: 212-874-0775.*

CHERNO, MELVIN, humanities educator; b. El Paso, Feb. 24, 1929; s. Sol and Deborah (Andes) C.; m. Dolores Ellen Himelstein, Dec. 25, 1950; children— Steven Philip, Paige Elise, Julie Rosanne AB, Stanford U., 1950; AM, U. Chgo., 1952; PhD, Stanford U., 1955. Instr. Bakersfield Coll., Calif., 1955-60; successively asst. prof., assoc. prof., prof. Oakland U., Rochester, Mich., 1960-80; Vaughan prof. tech., culture and comm. U. Va., Charlottesville, 1980-2000, Vaughan prof. emeritus humanities, 2001—, prin. second residential coll., 1991-95, 2000-01, co-prin., 1995-96. Co-editor: (4-vol. anthology) Western Society., 1967; editor, translator: (essay) Feuerbach on Luther, 1968; contbr. articles on historical topics to profl. jours. Former mem. Am. Hist. Assn., Am. Soc. Engring. Edn., So. Hist. Assn., Soc. for History of Tech., Soc. for Lit. & /Sci., Soc. for 19th Century Studies. Fellow Ford Found., 1953-55, Deutscher Akademische Austauschdienst, 1966, Inst. für Europäische Geschichte, 1966 Mem. Phi Beta Kappa. Home: 360 Forest Ave Apt 103 Palo Alto CA 94301 Personal E-mail: melanddee@sbcglobal.net.

CHERNOCK, MICHELLE LEIGH, medical researcher; b. San Jose, Calif., June 25, 1970; d. Michael Martin and Virginia Ann Chernock; 1 child, Emily Virginia. BS, U. Calif., Riverside, 1996; PhD, U. Calif., Berkeley, 2003. Med. sci. liaison Boehringer Ingelheim Pharmaceuticals, Ridgefield, Conn., 2004—07, Allergan, Inc., Irvine, Calif., 2007—. Founder Bay Area MSL Networking Group, San Francisco, 2007—. Rsch. scholar, NIH, 1999—2003. Mem.: Soc. Neurosci. (assoc.), Am. Urol. Assn. (assoc.), U Calif. Riverside Bay Area Alumni Assn. (chmn. 1998—2000), Mensa (life). Achievements include research in elucidating function of inhibitory neurotransmitters in multi-sensory integration in the inferior colliculus. Avocations: reading, photography, fine art, travel. Office: Allergan Inc 2525 Dupont Ave Irvine CA 92612 Home Phone: 415-563-1751; Office Phone: 415-205-9466. Home Fax: 415-563-3734.

CHERNOFF, HERMAN, statistics educator; b. NYC, July 1, 1923; s. Max and Pauline (Markowitz) C.; m. Judith Ullman, Sept. 7, 1947; children— Ellen Sue, Miriam Cheryl. BS, CCNY, 1943; MSc, Brown U., Providence, RI, 1945, PhD, 1948; DSc (hon.), Ohio State U., Columbus, 1983, Technion, Israel, 1984; AM (hon.), Harvard U., Cambridge, Mass., 1985; laurea (hon.), U. Rome, Sapienza, 1996; PhD (hon.), U. Athens, Greece, 1999. Rsch. assoc. U. Chgo., 1948-49; asst. prof. U. Ill., Urbana, 1949-51, assoc. prof., 1951-52, Stanford (Calif.) U., 1952-56, prof. stats., 1956-74; prof. applied math. MIT, Cambridge, 1974-85, prof. emeritus, 1985—; prof. stats. Harvard U., Cambridge, 1985-97, prof. emeritus, 1997—. Researcher in large sample theory, optimal design of expts., sequential analysis, pattern recognition. Author: (with L.E. Moses) Elementary Decision Theory, 1959, Sequential Analysis and Optimal Design, 1972. Recipient Townsend Harris medal CCNY Alumni Soc., 1981. Mem. NAS, Internat. Statis. Inst., Am. Acad. Arts and Scis., Inst. Math. Stats. (pres. 1967-68), Am. Statis. Assn. (Wilks medal 1987, Statistician of Yr. award Boston chpt. 1991). Home: 75 Crowninshield Rd Brookline MA 02446-6777 Office: Harvard U Dept Statistics Cambridge MA 02138 Business E-Mail: chernoff@stat.harvard.edu.

CHERNOV, YURIY D., engineering executive; b. Sizran, Kuibyshev, Russia, Dec. 6, 1945; s. David Y. Chernov and Bella I. Shekhel; m. Liliya A. Orlovskaya, Jan. 18, 1975; 1 child, Alla Y. Chernova. BSEE, Inst. Automated Control Sys. and Radio Elecs., Tomsk, Russia, MSEE, 1967; PhD in Mech. Engring., Poly. U., Tashkent, Uzbekistan, 1986. Sr. project engr. State Bur. Elecs., Tashkent, Uzbekistan, 1968—73, State Bur. Cotton Machinery, Tashkent, 1973—86. Dir. state rsch. and testing ctr. State Bur. Cotton Machinery, Tashkent, 1986—94; maintenance mgr. Corrugated Box Co., NYC, 1995—98; rsch. dir. Chocolate Printing Co., Inwood, NY, 1998—2007; pres. Integrated Design and Engring. Klecher LLC, NYC, 1996—2007; presenter in field. Contbr. articles to profl. jours. Achievements include patents pending in field. Avocation: yoga. Home: 2337 East 22 St Brooklyn NY 11229 Office: Chocolate Printing Co 600 Bayview Ave Inwood NY 11096 Home Phone: 718-332-9184. Home Fax: 718-332-9184. Personal E-mail: yuriychernov@gmail.com.

CHERNOW, ANN LEVY, artist, educator; b. NYC, Feb. 1, 1936; d. Edward P. and Mollie (Citrin) Levy; m. Philip Chenok, Aug. 11, 1957 (div. Jan. 1969); children: David Charles Chenok, Daniel Joshua Chenok; m. Burt Chernow, Dec. 11, 1970. MA, NYU, 1969. Instr. Mus. Modern Art, NYC, 1966-71; prof., head art dept. Norwalk (Conn.) Cmty. Tech. Coll., 1974-96. Guest lectr., instr. studio and art history Silvermine Sch. Arts Silvermine Coll., 1968—2006; vis. artist, lectr. Housatonic CC, Conn., 1975—80; guest lectr. Am. Coll. in Paris, 1985, Salem State Coll., 1993, 94, Yale U., 1995, Westport Hist. Soc., 1994, Fairfield U., 1993, 2006; vis. artist CAP program Wesleyan U., 1979; coord. Bicentennial Exhbn. Norwalk CC, 1976, Yale U. Art Gallery, 1996; master drawing class The Nat. Acad., NYC, 2000—, NYC, 2001; vis. artist and lectr. Bryn Mawr U., 2003, Ind. U., 2003; vis. artist Pa. Acad. Fine Arts, 2004, U. Ind., 2002. One-woman shows include Queens Coll., N.Y.C., 2000, Erlich Gallery, Marblehead, Mass., 2002, Uptown Gallery, N.Y.C., 2002, 2004, Raclin Gallery Ind. U., 2003, Print Ctr., Phila., 2003, Silvermine Guild, Conn., 2005, Uptown Gallery, N.Y.C., 2006, Amity Art Found., Conn., 2006, Dorothy Rogers Fine Art, Santa Fe, N.Mex., 2007, P.M.W. Gallery, Stamford, Conn., 2007, numerous others, exhibited in group shows at Millennium Portfolio of Time and Place, 1999—2001, Americas, 2000, Bklyn. Mus., 2001, Nat. Acad., 2001, NY Soc. Etchers, 2002, Nat Arts Club, NYC, 2002, Mus. City of NY, 2002, Salle des Fetes, Paris, 2003, Trois Rivieres, Can., 2003, Lessedra Gallery, Sophia, Bulgaria, 2004, Black Ch. Gallery, Dublin, 2004, Westport Arts Ctr., Conn., 2004, Housatonic Mus. Art, 2005, NAD, N.Y.C., 2005, numerous others, Nat. Arts Club, NYC, 2005, Uptown Gallery, 2006, 2007, Represented in permanent collections Met. Mus. Art, Rose Art Mus., Brandeis U., Nat. Mus. Women in Arts, Washington, William Benton Mus. Art, Storrs, Conn., Mus. of City of N.Y., UN, Westport, Achenbach Found., San Francisco, New Britain Mus. Am. Art, Conn., Neuberger Mus., Purchase, N.Y., Housatonic Mus. Art Yale U., Mattatauk Mus., Lehigh U. Art Collection, Pa., Utah Mus. Fine Arts, U. Ariz. Art Collection, Lyman Allyn Mus., Conn., Bruce Mus., Butler Inst. Am. Art, Ohio, Rutgers U., Hofstra U., Elvejhem Mus., Wis., N.Y. Pub. Libr., Duxbury Mus. Mass., USO of Met. N.Y., Amity Art Found., Conn., Reading (Pa.) Pub. Mus., Portland (Oreg.) Art Mus., De Cordova Mus., Lincoln, Mass., Yale U. Art Gallery, Utah Mus. Fine Arts, Ohio Wesleyan U., Worcester Mus. Art, Mass., Oakland Mus., Calif., U.S.O. Greater Met. N.Y., Reading Pub. Mus., Pa., Transit Mus., N.Y.C., Bklyn. Mus., Libr. Congress, Nat. U. Coalition Taiwan, San Diego Mus. Art, Nat. Acad. N.Y.C., San Diego (Calif.) Mus., Sacred Heart U., Conn., Fairfield U., Toledo Mus. Art; author poetry, short stories; contbr. articles to profl. jours.; artistic dir.: (documentaries) A Gathering of Glory, 2005; Years in the Making, 2007. Active Westport Arts Adv. Com., Westport Schs. Permanent Art Collection Com. Named Conn. Woman of Decade in Arts, UN Assn., 1987, U.S.A. rep., Agart World Print Festival, Ljubljana, Slovenia, 1999, UN Artist of Yr., 2002; recipient Purchase award, Delta Internat. Prints, 1996, Etching award, L.A. Printmaking Soc., 1997, Painting award, Manhattan Arts Internat., 1997, Etching award, Audubon artists, 1997, Print Biennial Silvermine Guild of Art, Conn., 1998, Four winners award, Stamford Mus. & Nature Ctr., Conn., 1998, Eisner Found. award, 1998, Richard Florsheim award, 1998, Exhbn. award/Boston Printmakers and Delta Internat. awards, Print Club, 2001, Purchase award, Delta Internat. Prints, 2001, Trustees Merit award, Housantonic C.C., 2003, Legion of Honor award, Achenbach Found., San Francisco, Catalog Raisonée Graphics award, Amity Art Found., 2003, Lifetime Honors award, Silvermine Guild, Conn., 2004; fellow Yale Mellon, 1993—94; grantee Yale/Mellon, 1995; scholar Conn. Humanities Coun., 1980—. Mem.: N.Y. Etchers Soc., Print Club Albany, Print Club Phila., L.A. Print Soc., Boston Printmakers, Calif. Soc. Printmakers, Nat. Acad. Art, Nat. Acad. Art (elected Academician Graphics), Soc. Am. Graphic Artists (past coun.). Studio: 2 Gorham Ave Westport CT 06880-2531 Office Phone: 203-227-8016. Personal E-mail: ctfinearts@sbcglobal.net.

CHERNOW, BART, critical care physician; b. NYC, June 26, 1947; BA, Queens Coll., 1968; MD, SUNY, NYC, 1976. Internal medicine intern Nat. Naval Med. Ctr., Bethesda, Md., 1976-77, internal medicine resident, 1977-79, endocrine fellow, 1979-81; dir. rsch. dept. critical care medicine Bethesda Naval Hosp., 1981-85, head acad. affairs, 1985-86; assoc. prof. anesthesia Harvard Med. Sch., Boston, 1986-90; assoc. dir. surg. ICU Mass. Gen. Hosp., 1986-90; prof. medicine, anesthesia and critical care Johns Hopkins U. Sch. Medicine, Balt., 1990-99; physician-in-chief Sinai Hosp., 1990-97; program dir. John Hopkins U./Sinai Hosp. Program in Internal Medicine, 1990-97; vice dean for rsch. and tech. Sch. Medicine Johns Hopkins U. Sch. Medicine, 1997-99; pres., CEO GMP Cos., Inc., Ft. Lauderdale, Fla., 1999—2004, chief tech. officer, 2004—07; v.p. spl. programs and resource strategy Miller sch. medicine U. Miami, Fla., 2007—, vice provost tech. advancement, 2007—. Adj. prof. medicine Johns Hopkins U. Sch. Medicine, 1999—2007. Editor: Pharmacologic Approach to the Critically Ill Patient, 1983, 88, 94; editor-in-chief: Critical Care Medicine, 1990-97. Comdr. med. corps USNR, 1969-86. Recipient Achievement award Am. Coll. Nutrition, 1995. Fellow ACP (master), Am. Coll. Critical Care Medicine; mem. Soc. Critical Care Medicine (Presdl. citation 1997), Am. Coll. Chest Physicians (regent 1990-98, pres. 1996-97, master fellow, chair CHEST found.1996-2002). Office: Deans Office Univ Miami Miller Sch Medicine PO Box 016099 R-690 Fort Lauderdale FL 33101 Home: 215 Aqua Terr Miami Beach FL 33141

CHERNOW, JEFFREY SCOTT, lawyer, educator, writer; b. Phila., Mar. 8, 1951; s. William and Sylvia Ann (Rosenberg) C.; m. Debra Sharon Shapiro, Dec. 29, 1974; children: William Ross, Stephanie Lynne. BS, Pa. State U., 1972; JD, U. Balt., 1976. Bar: Md. 1976, U.S. Dist. Ct. Md. 1977, U.S. Supreme Ct. 1980, U.S. Ct. Claims 1991. Assoc. Goodman, Meagher & Enoch, Balt., 1977-79; asst. atty. gen. State of Md., Balt., 1980-85; assoc. Cardin & Cardin, P.A., Balt., 1985-86; pvt. practice law Balt., 1986-89; ptnr. Kandel, Klitenic, Kotz, Betten & Chernow LLP, Owings Mills, Md., 1990—2002; pvt. practice law, 2002—. Asst. prof. Towson (Md.) State U., 1978-83, assoc. prof., 1983-86; panel chmn. Md. Health Claims Arbitration Office, 1983-84; lectr. Md. Inst. for Continuing Profl. Edn. of Lawyers, Inc., 1986; bd. dirs. Altex Industries, Inc. Contbr. chpt. to book. Sec., trustee Basic Cancer Rsch. Found., Inc., 1986—; chmn. bldg. com. Congregation Adat Chaim, 1985-86, trustee, 1986-90. Mem. ABA, Md. Bar Assn., Bar Assn. Balt. City, N.Am. Securities Adminstrs. Assn. (mem. various coms. 1980-85, chmn. franchise and bus. opportunities com. 1984-85), Md. State Bar Assn. (sec. bus. law, franchise law com. 1991). Office: 10995 Owings Mills Blvd Ste 208 Owings Mills MD 21117 Home: 2331 Old Court Rd Unit 414 Baltimore MD 21208 Office Phone: 410-363-7120.

CHERNOW, RON, writer, journalist; b. Bklyn., Mar. 3, 1949; s. Israel and Ruth (Goldspinner) C.; m. Valerie Stearn, Oct. 22, 1979 (dec. Jan. 2006). BA in English summa cum laude, Yale U., 1970; MA in English, Cambridge U., Eng., 1972; LHD, Marymount Manhattan Coll., 2005, Hamilton Coll., 2005. Free-lance writer, NYC, 1973-82; program officer for fin. policy studies The Twentieth Century Fund, NYC, 1983-86; writer, essayist, lectr., book reviewer NYC, 1988—; occasional columnist The Wall St. Jour., 1990-91; commentator Nat. Pub. Radio, 1994-97. Frum Meml. lectr., 1997; guest curator Mus. Am. Fin. History, 1998-99; hist. cons. WGBH Boston. Author: The House of Morgan: An American Banking Dynasty and the Rise of Modern Finance, 1990, The Warburgs: The Twentieth-Century Odyssey of a Remarkable Jewish Family, 1993, The Death of the Banker: The Decline and Fall of the Great Financial Dynasties and the Triumph of the Small Investor, 1997, Titan: The Life of John D. Rockefeller, Sr., 1998, Alexander Hamilton, 2004; also 13 cover stories; contbr. articles to N.Y. Times, N.Y. Mag., Time mag., Bus. Week, Saturday Rev., Vanity Fair, Am. Heritage, Smithsonian and 30 other publs. Vice chmn. Cambridge U. Assn. of N.Y., 1986-87. Recipient Jack London award United Steelworkers, 1980, Nat. Book award Nat. Book Found., 1990, Books to Remember award N.Y. Pub. Libr., 1990, Ambassador Book award English Speaking Union, 1991, George S. Eccles prize Columbia Bus. Sch., 1993, Notable Book citation ALA, 1993, Annual Book award Colonial Dames Am., 1998, Scholar of Yr. award N.Y. Coun. Humanities, 1999, Ohiana Book award Ohiana Libr., 1999, Abraham Lincoln Lit. award The Union League Club, 2000, Notable Book citation ALA, 2004, George Washington Book prize, 2005, Book award Yale Club of Boston, 2005, Washington Irving medal St. Nicholas Soc., 2005, Alexander Hamilton award Manhattan Inst., 2005, Ann. Book award Colonial Dames Am., 2005; named honoree Bklyn. Pub. Libr. Found., 2005. Mem. PEN (chmn. readers and writers com. 1994-98, trustee 1997-2003, sec. 1999, v.p. 2000-03, co-chmn. planning com. 2004, pres. 2006-07), Authors Guild, Leo Baeck Inst., Wildlife Conservation Soc., The Nature Conservancy, Alexander Hamilton Hist. Soc. (mem. adv. bd. 2003—), N.Y. Hist. Soc., Century Assn., Orgn. Am. Historians, Internat. Vocal Arts Inst., Alexander Hamilton Friends Assn., Soc. Am. Historians, Phi Beta Kappa (Couper lectr. 2004). Democrat. Jewish.

CHERNY, ROBERT WALLACE, historian, educator; b. Marysville, Kans., Apr. 4, 1943; s. Clarence L. and Lena M. (Hobbs) C.; m. Rebecca Ellen Marshall, June 11, 1967; 1 child, Sarah Catherine. BA with distinction, U. Nebr., 1965; MA, Columbia U., 1967, PhD, 1972. From instr. history to prof. San Francisco (Calif.) State U., 1971—81, prof., 1981—, assoc. dean behavioral and social scis., 1984, acting dean behavioral and social scis., 1985, chmn. history dept., 1987-92; interim dean undergrad. studies San Francisco State U., 2005—. Disting. Fulbright lectr. Moscow State U., 1996; vis. rsch. scholar U. Melbourne, 1997; mem. academic senate San Francisco (Calif.) State U., 1981-84, 95-2005, chmn.

academic senate, 2002-04; cons. in field. Author: A Righteous Cause: The Life of William Jennings Bryan, 1985, rev. edit., 1994, Populism, Progressivism and the Transformation of Nebraska Politics, 1981, American Politics in the Gilded Age, 1869-1868, 1997; co-author (with William Issel): San Francisco, 1865-1932, 1986; co-author: San Francisco: Presidio, Port and Pacific Metropolis, 1981; co-author: (with Carol Berkin, Christopher L. Miller, James L. Gormly) Making America: A History of the United States, 1995, 4th edit., 2006; co-author: (with R. Griswold del Castillo and G. Lemke-Santangelo) Competing Visions: A History of California, 2005; co-editor (with William Issel and Keiran Taylor): American Labor and the Cold War: Unions, Politics and Postware Political Culture, 2004. Mem. San Francisco Landmarks Preservation Adv. Bd., 2003—, v.p., 2006—. Woodrow Wilson fellow, 1965-66, Woodrow Wilson dissertation fellow, 1969, NEH fellow, 1992-93. Mem. Am. Hist. Assn., Orgn. Am. Historians (treas. 2003-), S.W. Labor Studies Assn. (pres. 1982-86), Calif. Hist. Soc., Soc. Historians of Gilded Age and Progressive Era (pres. 1995), Nebr. State Hist. Soc., HNet--Humanities and Social Studies Online (pres. 2003, v.p. tchg. 2005-06). Democrat. Office: San Francisco State U Dept of History 1600 Holloway Ave San Francisco CA 94132-4155

CHEROUTES, MICHAEL LOUIS, lawyer; b. Chgo., Apr. 27, 1940; s. Louis Samuel Cheroutes and Maria Jane (Zimmerman) Dodd; m. Trisha Flynn, Oct. 30, 1965; children: Michael Louis Jr., Trisha Francesca, Matthew Dodd. BA, Harvard U., 1962; LLB, Stanford U., 1965. Bar: Colo. 1965. Assoc., then ptnr. Sherman & Howard, Denver, 1965-85; chief of staff to Rep. Patricia A. Shroeder U.S. Ho. of Reps., Washington, 1972-74; ptnr. Davis, Graham & Stubbs, Denver, 1985-93, Hogan & Hartson LLP, London, Moscow, Denver, 1993—2005, of counsel Denver, 2005—, dir. pub. fin. practice group. Contbr. articles to profl. jours. Mem. Colo. Commn. on Higher Edn., 1988-91, chmn., 1989-91; mem. state bd. Gt. Outdoors Colo. Trust Fund, 1996-97. Mem. ABA, Colo. Bar Assn., Nat. Assn. Bond Lawyers. Avocation: sailing. Office: Hogan & Hartson LLP One Tabor Ctr 1200 17th St Ste 1500 Denver CO 80202-5840 Home Phone: 303-871-9730; Office Phone: 303-899-7310. Business E-Mail: mlcheroutes@hhlaw.com.

CHEROVSKY, ERWIN LOUIS, lawyer, writer; b. Dover, NJ, Dec. 31, 1933; s. Sam and Ida (Bluestein) C.; m. Edith Mayer, June 26, 1966; children: Kim, Karen; children by previous marriage: Debra, Jill. AB, U. Rochester, 1955; LLB, Harvard U., 1958. Bar: N.Y. 1958, U.S. Dist. Ct. (so. dist.) N.Y. 1964, U.S. Ct. Appeals (2d cir.) 1964. Assoc. Stamer & Haft, NYC, 1958-63, Summit Rovins & Feldesman, NYC, 1963-68, ptnr., 1968-88, Proskauer Rose LLC, 1988-89; chmn., legal cost containment cons. WIK Cons. Inc., NYC, 1992-97; pres. Old Quarry Devel., Englewood, NJ, 1996—. Sec. Space & Leisure Time, Ltd., N.Y.C., 1972-80, Ghiordian Knot, Ltd., N.Y.C., 1978-88, ORS Automation, Inc., Princeton, N.J., 1983-86, Cook United, Inc., Cleve., 1986; lit. agt. for Random House Russian-English Dictionary of Idioms, Sophia Lubensky, 1995, From Central Park to Sinai, Roy S. Neuberger, 2000. Author: The Guide to New York Law Firms, 1991, Competent Counsel: The Business Guide to Selecting, Hiring Lawyers and Monitoring Their Work, 1992; contbr. articles to profl. jours. Fellow Phi Beta Kappa Soc.; mem. N.Y.State Bar Assn., Assn. Bar City of N.Y., Fed. Bar Coun. (chmn. winter meeting 1980, mem. alternative dispute resolution com. 1984), Can. Club (N.Y.C.) (bd. govs. 1988-89, editor Maple Leaf 1984-89), Met. Club (N.Y.C.). Office Phone: 201-567-4505. Personal E-mail: cherovsky@aol.com.

CHEROWITZO, WILLIAM EDWARD, mathematics professor; b. Bklyn., June 16, 1947; s. Louis and Saraphine Cherowitzo; m. Anne Suiter, Aug. 6, 1994. BS, CUNY, 1969; MA, Columbia U., NYC, 1973, PhD, MPhil, Columbia U., NYC, 1983. Asst. prof. math. Mich. State U., E. Lansing, 1977—79, Allegheny Coll., Meadville, Pa., 1979—81; prof. math. U. Colo., Denver, 1983—. Fellow: Inst. Combinatorics & Applications; mem.: Math. Assn. Am., Am. Math. Soc. Achievements include discovery of various hyperovals in projective planes. Avocations: racquetball, travel. Home: 1752 W Barberry Cir Louisville CO 80027 Office: Univ Colo Campus Box 170 PO Box 173364 Denver CO 80217-3364 Office Fax: 303-556-8550. Personal E-mail: william.cherowitzo@cudenver.edu.

CHERPAS, CHRISTOPHER THEODORE, lawyer; b. Toledo, Mar. 23, 1924; s. Theodore C. and Mary (Veronie) C.; m. Ortha N. Mollis, June 23, 1946; children— Maria, Patricia, Christopher T. BS in Polit. Sci., Akron U., 1949; postgrad. Akron Law Sch., 1949-50, Western Res. U., 1951; JD, Cleveland Marshall U., 1951. Bar: Ohio 1952, US Dist. Ct. (7th dist.) Ohio 1954, US Ct. Appeals (6th cir.) 1966. Counsel United Rubber Workers, Akron, Ohio, 1954-57; ptnr. Cherpas, Manos & Syracopoulos, Akron, 1957-74, Cherpas and Manos, Akron, 1974-79, Teodosio, Cherpas and Manos, Akron, 1979—98. Served to capt. US Army, ETO, PTO, Korea, 1942-46, 51-53. Mem. ABA, Ohio Bar Assn., Akron Bar Assn., VFW, Am. Legion, Disabled Am. Vets, 37th Div. Assn. Democrat. Greek Orthodox. Clubs: Pan Arcadian Fedn. (Chgo.) (supreme pres. 1957-58); Fairlawn Country, Am. Hellenic Edn. Progressive Assn. (chpt. pres. 1979-80). Lodges: Masons, Shriners, K.T. Home: 80 Mackinaw Ave Fairlawn OH 44333 Office: Quality Mold Inc 2200 Massilon Rd Akron OH 44312 Home Phone: 330-836-2621; Office Phone: 330-645-4907. Business E-Mail: ccherpas@qualitymold.com.

CHERRI, MONA Y., computer scientist, educator, computer scientist, consultant; d. Mitri Abo-Chedid and Yvonne Madi; m. Youssef Cherri; children: Mike, John, David, Jacob. MS in Math., Okla. State U., Stillwater, 1982, PhD in Math., 1985; PhD in Computer Sci., U. North Tex., Denton, 1996. Assoc. prof. computer sci. Tex. Woman's U., Denton, 1989—98; info. specialist EDS, Plano, Tex., 1998—99; cons. Excel Comm., Carrolton, Tex., 1999; data translation staff engr. Ericsson Inc., Richardson, Tex., 1999—2001, EXI Parsons, Richardson, 2001—03; cons. Plexon, Inc, Richardson, Tex., 2003—04; mem. computer info. sci. faculty North Lake Coll., Irving, Tex., 2004—. Contbr. articles to profl. jours. Recipient Maclachlan award, Okla. Sate U.; grantee, NIH, 1994—98. Mem.: IEEE (assoc.), Upsilon Pi Upsilon (life), Pi Mu Epsilon (life). Mem. Lds Ch. Home: 4437 Avebury Dr Plano TX 75024 Office: North Lake College 5001 N Mac Arthur Blvd Irving TX 75038 Home Phone: 972-712-7465; Office Phone: 972-273-3472. Office Fax: 972-273-3471. Personal E-mail: jcherri@flash.net. Business E-Mail: mcherri@dcccd.edu.

CHERRINGTON, PAMELA JO, special education educator; b. Binghamton, NY, Mar. 15, 1957; d. William and Marian Baldwin Timson; m. James W. Cherrington, July 7, 1979; children: Ian James, Kellie Marie. AA, Broome CC, 1976; BA in Edn., SUNY, Cortland, 1978; MA in Edn., Nat. U., 1986; student, Azusa Pacific U. Cert. Resource Specialist U. Calif., Riverside, Elem. Edn. Tchr. SUNY, Cortland, in Spl. Edn. Nat. U. Elem. tchr. St. Thomas Aquinas, Binghamton, NY, 1978—79, Broward County Sch. Dist., Coral Springs, Fla., 1979—80; pvt. tutor Broward County, 1980—82; pre-sch. dir., kindergarten tchr. Country Day Sch., Coral Springs, 1982—84; substitute tchr. Escondido Elem. Sch. Dist., Calif., 1984—86; spl. day class tchr. Temecula Valley, Calif., 1986—93; resource specialist United Sch. Dist., Temecula, 1993—. Mem.: Calif. Assn. Resource Specialists, Calif. Assn. Sch. Psychologists (student mem.). Republican. Presbyterian. Avocations: travel, gardening, interior decorating. Home: 34105 Milat St Temecula CA 92592

CHERRY, ANDREW LAWRENCE, JR., social work educator, researcher; b. Dothan, Ala., Nov. 11, 1943; s. Andrew L. Cherry and Wyalene Cain; m. Mary Elizabeth Dillon, July 16, 1988. MSW, U. Ala., Tuscaloosa, 1974; D Social Work, Columbia U., 1986. Child welfare worker Escambia County Dept. Pensions and Securities, Brewton, Ala., 1968-72; psychiat. social worker Bryce State Hosp., Tuscaloosa, 1974-79; instr. Salisbury (Md.) State Coll., 1981-85; asst. prof. Marywood Coll. Sch. Social Work, Scranton, Pa., 1986-87; prof. Barry U. Sch. Social Work, Miami, Fla., 1987—2003; prof. mental health Sch. Social Work U. Okla., Tulsa, 2003—, endowed prof. mental health sch. social work, 2003—. Cons. Informed Families Dade County, Miami, 1990—98, Miami Coalition for Care to Homeless, 1991—93, NAACP Minority Media and Telecomm. Coun., 1992—2000; with drug abuse prevention program Cath. Charities, Miami, 1991—2000, Broward Children's Svc., Ft. Lauderdale, 1992—94, The Biscayne Inst., 1994—2004, St. Luke's Addiction Recovery Ctr., 1995—2000; interim dir. child welfare divsn. Cath. Charities, 1998—2000; project evaluator Substance Abuse and Mental Health Svcs. Adminstrn., Okla., 2004—. Author: The Socializating Instinct: Individual, Family and Social Bonds, 1994, A Research Primer for the Helping Professions: Methods, Statistics, and Writing, 2000, Examining Global Social Welfare Issues Using MicroCase, 2002, 2d edit., 2004; co-author: Social Bonds and Teen Pregnancy, 1992; co-editor: Teenage Pregnancy: A Global View, 2001, Substance Abuse: A Global View, 2002; series advisor Greenwood Press World View of Social Issues, 1999; contbr. articles to profl. jours. Scholar, NIMH, 1979. Fellow: Am. Orthopsychiat. Assn.; mem.: NASW, N.Y. Acad. Scis., Conf. Social Work Edn. Achievements include research in and devel. of the social bond theory; extensive work and rsch. among the mentally disabled, homeless, at-risk children and the addicted. Office: U Okla Tulsa Campus 4502 E 41st St Ste 2J02 Tulsa OK 74135-2512 Office Phone: 918-660-3363. Business E-Mail: alcherry@ou.edu.

CHERRY, BARBARA WATERMAN, speech and language pathologist, physical therapist; b. Norfolk, Va., June 25, 1949; d. Robert Bullock and Dorothy Estelle (Walsh) Waterman; m. Albert Glen Cherry, Sept. 17, 1977; 1 child, Dorothy Louise. BS in Phys. Therapy, U. Fla., 1972, MA in Speech-Lang. Pathology, 1982. Lic. phys. therapist, speech and lang. pathologist, Fla.; cert. tchr., Fla. Staff phys. therapist Retreat for the Sick Hosp., Richmond, Va., 1973-75; clin. instr. in phys. therapy Sch. of Rehab. Scis., Tehran, Iran, 1975-76; staff phys. therapist Sulmaniya Hosp., Manama, Bahrain, 1976-77, Cathedral Rehab. Ctr., Jacksonville, Fla., 1978-80; staff speech-lang. pathologist S. Allen Smith Clinic, Jacksonville, 1982-87, Mt. Herman Exceptional Child Ctr., Jacksonville, 1987-91, Duval County Sch. System, Jacksonville, 1991-98, Mt. Herman Exceptional Student Ctr., Jacksonville, 1998—, Brooks Rehab. Hosp., Jacksonville, 2003—. Mem. Am. Speech, Lang., and Hearing Assn., Am. Phys. Therapy Assn., Phi Kappa Phi. Episcopalian. Avocation: Karate (black belt). Home: 8821 Ivey Rd Jacksonville FL 32216-3369 Office: Mt Herman Exceptional Student Ctr 1741 Francis St Jacksonville FL 32209 also: Brooks Rehab Hosp 3599 University Blvd S Jacksonville FL Office Phone: 904-630-6740. E-mail: cherrybw@bellsouth.net.

CHERRY, DANIEL RONALD, lawyer; b. Mpls., Dec. 31, 1948; s. Clifford D. and Ruby E. (Norman) C.; m. Dianne Brown, Jan. 24, 1971 (dec.); children: Matthew A., Kathryn E.; m. Q. Rhea Walker, Oct. 25, 1998. SB, MIT, 1970; JD cum laude, Harvard U., 1976. Bar: Ohio 1976, U.S. Dist. Ct. (no. dist.) Ohio 1976, U.S. Patent and Trademark Office 1978, U.S. Ct. Appeals (6th and Fed. cirs.) 1982, Ill. 1987, U.S. Dist. Ct. (no. dist.) Ill. 1987. Assoc. Squire, Sanders & Dempsey, Cleve., 1976-85, ptnr., 1985-87; ptnr., prin. Welsh & Katz, Ltd., Chgo., 1987—. Co-author: Patent Practice, 1997. With USCG, 1970-73. Mem. ABA, Ohio State Bar Assn., Ill. State Bar Assn., Chgo. Bar Assn., Am. Intellectual Property Law Assn., Intellectual Property Law Assn. Chgo., Licensing Execs. Soc. Home: 1046 Vine St Winnetka IL 60093-1834 Office: Welsh & Katz Ltd 120 S Riverside Plz # 22 Chicago IL 60606-3913 Office Phone: 312-526-1526. E-mail: drcherry@welshkatz.com.

CHERRY, HAROLD, actuary, consultant; b. Bronx, NY, June 20, 1931; s. Isidor and Esther C.; m. Maida Weit, Aug. 12, 1961; children— Gina, Joshua. BS cum laude, CCNY, 1953. With N.Y. Life Ins. Co., NYC, 1956-89, 2d v.p., actuary, 1972-78, v.p., actuary, 1978-89; pres. Actuarial Study Materials, Merrick, NY, 1983—. Cons. in field. Served with U.S. Army, 1954-56. Fellow Soc. Actuaries; mem. Am. Acad. Actuaries, Nat. Assn. Watch and Clock Collectors (past pres. L.I. chpt.) Jewish. Office: Actuarial Study Materials 3217 Wynsum Ave Merrick NY 11566-5549 also: Actuarial Study Materials 276 Roosevelt Way Westbury NY 11590-6672

CHERRY, JAMES DONALD, pediatrician; b. Summit, NJ, June 10, 1930; s. Robert Newton and Beatrice (Wheeler) C.; m. Jeanne M. Fischer, June 19, 1954; children: James S., Jeffrey D., Susan J., Kenneth C. BS, Springfield Coll., Mass., 1953; MD, U. Vt., 1957; MSc in Epidemiology, London Sch. Hygiene and Tropical Medicine, 1983. Diplomate Am. Bd. Pediat., Am. Bd. Pediat. Infectious Diseases. Intern, then resident in pediat. Boston City Hosp., 1957-59; resident in pediat. Kings County Hosp., Bklyn., 1959-60; rsch. fellow in medicine Harvard U. Med. Sch.-Thorndike Meml. Lab., Boston City Hosp., 1961-62; instr. pediatrics U. Vt. Coll. Medicine, also asst. attending physician Mary Fletcher DeGoesbriand Meml. hosps., Burlington, Vt., 1960-61; asst. prof., then assoc. prof. pediat. U. Wis. Med. Sch., Madison, 1963-66; assoc. attending physician Madison Gen., U. Wis. hosps., 1963-66; dir. John A. Hartford Rsch. Lab., Madison Gen. Hosp., 1963-66. Mem. faculty St. Louis U. Med. Sch., 1966-73, prof. pediatrics, 1969-73, vice chmn. dept., 1970-73; mem. staff Cardinal Glennon Meml. Hosp. Children, St. Louis U. Hosp., 1966-73; chief divsn. infectious diseases UCLA Med. Ctr. UCLA Sch. Medicine, 1973-2000, prof. pediat., 1973--; acting chmn. dept. pediatrics UCLA Med. Ctr., 1977-79; attending physician, chmn. infection control com. UCLA Med. Ctr., 1975-93; cons. Project Head Start; vis. worker dept. cmty. medicine Middlesex Hosp. and Med. Sch., London, 1982-83; vis. worker Common Cold Rsch. Unit, 1969-70; acad. visitor U. Cambridge, Eng., 2000-01. Co-editor: (Textbook) Pediatric Infectious Diseases, 1981, 5th edit., 2003; assoc. editor Clin. Infectious Diseases, 1990—99, Am. regional editor Vaccine, 1991—2000, cons. editor Pediatric Research, 2004—; contbr. scientific papers numerous in field; editl. reviewer (profl. jours). Bd. govs. Alexander Graham Bell Internat. Parents Orgn., 1967-69. With USAR, 1958-64. Recipient Disting. Academic Achievement award, U. Vt., 1984, Med. Sci. award, Med. Alumni UCLA, 2005; John and Mary R. Markle scholar acad. medicine, 1964. Mem. AAAS, APHA, Am. Acad. Pediat. (mem. exec. com. Calif. chpt. 2 1975-77, mem. com. infectious diseases 1977-83, assoc. editor 19th Red Book 1982), Am. Soc. Microbiology,Soc. Pediat. Rsch., Infectious Diseases Soc. Am., Am. Epidemiol. Soc., Am. Pediat. Soc., L.A. Pediat. Soc., Internat. Orgn. Mycoplasmologists, Am. Soc. Virology, Soc. Hosp. Epidemiologists Am., Pediat. Infectious Diseases Soc. (pres. 1989-91, Disting. Physician award 2003), Alpha Omega Alpha. Office: UCLA David Geffen Sch Medicine and Mattel Children's Hosp Dept Pediatrics Rm 22-442 10833 Le Conte Ave Los Angeles CA 90095-1752 Home Phone: 310-395-3915; Office Phone: 310-825-5226. Business E-Mail: jcherry@mednet.ucla.edu.

CHERRY, JOHN D., JR., lieutenant governor, former state senator; b. Sulphur Springs, Tex., May 5, 1951; s. John D. Sr. and Margaret L. (Roark) C.; m. Pamela M. Faris, 1979; children: Meghan M., John D. BA, U. Mich., 1973, MA, 1984. Chmn. 7th Cong. Dist. Dem. Com., Mich., 1973-75; adminstrv. asst. Mich. State Sen. Gary Corbin, 1975-81; Mich. polit. dir. Am. Fedn. State, County & Munic Employees AFL-CIO, 1981-82; mem. Mich. Ho. Reps. from 79th dist., Lansing, 1983-86, Mich. State Senate from 28th dist. (formerly 29th dist.), Lansing, 1987—2002, minority leader, mem. legis. coun.; lt. gov. State of Mich., Lansing, 2003—. Mem. Genesee County Dem. Exec. Bd., 1983-2002; mem. Mich. Jobs Commn. Bd., 1996-2000; del. Dem. Nat. Conv., 1996, 2000, 04; treas. Nat. Lt. Govs. Assn., 2004-05; vice chair Great Lakes Commn., 2005-. Named Conservationist of Yr., Mich. United Conservation Club, 2005. Democrat. Mailing: Office Lt Governor PO Box 30013 Lansing MI 48909 Office Phone: 517-373-6800. Office Fax: 517-241-3956.

CHERRY, KENNETH JEROME, JR., surgeon; b. Richmond, Va., Oct. 22, 1947; s. Kenneth Jerome and Alice (Cottingham) Cherry; m. Robin Wheeler, Sept. 10, 1983; children: Katherine, Sarah, Kenneth III. Undergrad., Duke U., Durham, NC, 1970; MD, U. Va., Charlottesville, 1974. Diplomate Am. Bd. Surgery, Gen. Vascular Surgery. Intern, resident surgery U. Va., Charlottesville, 1974-80; resident vascular surgery U. Calif. San Francisco, 1980-81; instr. surgery Mayo Med. Sch., Rochester, Minn., 1981—84, asst. prof. of surgery, 1988—95, assoc. prof. of surgery, 1995—, prof. of surgery, 1995—2004; prof. of surgery, head divsn. vascular surgery U. Va. Health Sys., 2004—. Surgeon Rochester Meth. Hosp., St. Mary's Hosps., Rochester. Contbr. articles to profl. jour. Mem. ACS, Am. Surg. Assn, Midwestern Vascular Surg. Soc., Soc. Vascular Surgery (Disting. Fellow), Peripheral Vascular Soc., Soc. for Vascular Surgeons. Avocations: reading, history, outdoor activites. Home: 1010 Tanglewood Rd Charlottesville VA 22901 Office: Divsn Vascular Surgery Univ Va Health System PO Box 800679 Charlottesville VA 22908-0679 Office Phone: 434-243-7052. Business E-Mail: kjc5kh@virginia.edu.

CHERRY, MICHAEL A., state supreme court justice; b. St. Louis; 2 children. BA, U. Mo., 1966; JD, Washington U. Sch. Law, 1969. Ptnr. Manos & Cherry, Cherry, Bailus & Kelesis; dep. pub. defender Clark County, Nev., justice of the peace pro tem & small claims referee Nev.; alt. mcpl. judge Cities of Las Vegas and Henderson, Nev.; chief Clark County Spl. Pub. Defender's Office, 1997—98; judge 8th Jud. Dist. Ct., Dept. 17, 1998—2006; assoc. justice Nev. Supreme Ct., 2006—. Spl. master MGM Grand Hotel Fire Litig., Nev., 1981, Las Vegas Hilton Fire Litig., 1983; instr. U. Phoenix, 1994. Office: Nev Supreme Ct 201 S Carson St Carson City NV 89701-4702*

CHERRY, PETER BALLARD, electrical products corporation executive; b. Evanston, Ill., May 25, 1947; s. Walter Lorain and Virginia Ames (Ballard) C.; m. Crissy Hazard, Sept. 6, 1969; children: Serena Ames, Spencer Ballard. BA, Yale U., 1969; MBA, Stanford U., 1972. Analyst Cherry Elec. Products Corp., Waukegan, Ill., 1972-74, data processing and systems mgr., 1974, treas., 1974-77; v.p. fin. and bus. devel. Cherry Elec. Products Corps., Waukegan, Ill., 1977-80; exec. v.p. Cherry Elec. Products Corp., Waukegan, Ill., 1980-82, pres., chief oper. officer, 1982-86; pres., chief exec. officer Cherry Corp., Waukegan, 1986-92, chmn., pres., 1992—. Trustee Lake Forest Coll., Ill., 1982-90; trustee Lake Forest Hosp., 1982—, chmn., 1989-92. Mem.Onwentsia Club. Office: Cherry Corp 10411 Corporate Dr Pleasant Prairie WI 53158

CHERRY, ROBERT A., surgeon; BA, Columbia U., NYC, 1987, MD, 1987—91. Lic. gen. surgery & surgical critical care ACS, 1997. Internship North Shore U. Hosp., NY, 1991—92, resident gen. surgery, 1992—96; fellowship trauma and critical care R. Adams Coulley Shock Trauma Ctr., U. Md., 1996—97; trauma program med. dir. Penn State Shock Trauma Ctr., Hershey, Pa., 2002—; chief sect. trauma & critical care Penn State Milton S. Hershey Med. Ctr., 2004—. Program chair, master homeland security degree in pub. health preparedness Penn State Coll. Medicine, 2005. Office: Penn State Milton S Hershey Medical Ctr 500 University Dr MC H075 Hershey PA 17033 Home Phone: 717-533-4137.

CHERRY, ROBERT STEVEN, III, municipal official; b. Chgo., Aug. 13, 1951; s. Robert Lee and Jean Louise (Curry) C. BA, Kensington U., 1988. Exec. dir. Nu Skin Enterprises (Photomax Divsn.); with Chgo. Pk. Dist., 1968—2004, supr. beaches and swimming pool lifeguards south side, 2003, aquatic supr., 1983—2004; ret., 2004. Asst. capt. 37th precinct, 7th ward, City of Chgo., 1979-80, precinct capt., 1980-83, asst. precinct capt. 2d precinct, 42d ward, 1984-92, capt., 1992-2002. 1st lt. U.S. Army/Ill. Nat. Guard, 1970-82. Named one of Outstanding Young Men of Am., 1985. Mem. Am. Legion (Post 1976), Young Dems. Am. (Ill. del. 1985), Young Dems. Ill., Young Dems. Cook County, U.S. Water Polo, U.S. Lifesaving Assn., Res. Officers Assn. U.S., Pub. Svc. Employees Union, Lambda Alpha Epsilon. Roman Catholic. Avocations: reading, backgammon, ping pong/table tennis, swimming. Home Phone: 773-343-1282; Office Phone: 866-460-8609. Personal E-mail: r.cherryiii@comcast.net.

CHERRY, SABRINA, psychiatrist; b. NYC, Mar. 20, 1959; d. Sheldon H. and Gloria B. Cherry; m. Marc N. Gourevitch, Sept. 10, 1988; children: Rebecca, Ruth. BA, Brown U., 1981; MD, Harvard U, 1987. Diplomate in psychiatry Am. Bd. Psychiatry and Neurology. Attending psychiatrist N.Y. Presbyn. Hosp., NYC, 1991; asst. clin. prof. psychiatry Columbia U., NYC, 1993; pvt. practice psychiatry, NYC, 1991. Faculty Columbia Ctr. for Psychoanalytic Tng., 1998.

CHERRY, SCHROEDER, federal agency administrator; BFA summa cum laude, U. Mich., 1976; M in Tchg. in Mus. Edn., George Washington U., 1978; EdD in Mus. Edn., Columbia U., 1988. Mus. educator Anacostia Mus., Smithsonian Inst., Washington; dir. edn. The Studio Mus. in Harlem; chief edn. N.Y.C. Transit Exhibit; mus. educator J. Paul Getty Mus., 1988—90; dir. edn. and cmty. Balt. Mus. Art, 1990—96; program officer Wallace-Reader's Digest Funds, 1996—2000; dep. dir. for edn. and pub. programs Md. Hist. Soc., 2000—02; dep. dir. mus. svcs. Inst. Mus. and Libr. Svcs., Washington, 2002—. V.p. African Am. Mus. Assn., 1984; commr. Balt. Coun. for Historic and Archtl. Preservation, 1992—95; ea. regional dir. mus. edn. divsn. Nat. Art Edn. Assn., 1993—95; tchr. trainer Nat. Gallery Art, 1994, Balt. County Pub. Schs., 1998; cons. proposals for humanities project Nat. Endowment for the Humanities, 1999; presenter, project dir., scriptwriter ednl. media prodns. Contbr. articles to profl. jours. Achievements include coordinated the Joshua Johnson Council, the oldest African-American support group established by a major museum. Office: Inst Mus and Libr Svcs 1800 M St NW 9th Fl Washington DC 20036-5802 Office Phone: 202-653-4670.

CHERRY, WILLIAM ASHLEY, surgeon, state health official, educator; b. Halls, Tenn., Oct. 25, 1924; s. and Bessie R. C.; m. Jacqueline Guidry, June 2, 1989; children by previous marriage: Neal, Darrell, Philip, Susan. BS, Tulane U., 1946, MD, 1949. Diplomate Am. Bd. Surgery. Rotating intern Phila. Gen. Hosp., 1949-51; resident gen. surgery La. State U. div. Charity Hosp., New Orleans, 1953-56, resident thoracic surgery, 1956-57, asst. chief fracture service, 1963-65; practice medicine specializing in gen. and thoracic surgery New Iberia, La., 1957-63; commd. med. officer USPHS, 1963; mem. surg. staff USPHS Hosp., New Orleans, 1963-66, dir., 1966-71, asst. chief surgery dept., 1963-65, dep. chief, 1965-66, dir., 1966-71; regional health dir. Health Services and Mental Health Adminstrn., HEW, USPHS, Region VI, Dallas, 1971-74; sec., state health officer La. Dept. Health and Human Resources, Baton Rouge, 1977-80; commd. ensign USN, 1946, advanced through grades to comdr., 1963; sr. surgeon, comdr. USPHS, 1963; advanced through grades to asst. surgeon gen., admiral; comdg. officer Naval Res. Med. Co. 8-32, 1953-55; ret., 1963; chief med. officer USCG, Washington, 1974-77; pres., CEO, S. La. Health Svcs. Inc., 1987; med. dir. Lallie Kemp Regional Med. Ctr., Independence, La., Div. Mental Retardation and Developmental Disabilities, State of La., Baton Rouge, 1992-93, La. Dept. Health and Hosps., 1992-93; CEO, La. Health Care Authority, 1993-96; staff Met. Health Group, 1996—. Asst. clin. dir. surgery Charity Hosp., 1956-57, vis. surgeon, 1963—; chief of surgery Iberia Parish Hosp., 1959-61; chief of staff Dauterive Hosp., New Iberia, 1962-63; clin. asso. instr., surgery dept. La. State U. Sch. Medicine, 1953-57, clin. instr., 1963-66, clin. asst. prof. surgery, 1966-67; clin. asso. prof. surgery Tulane U. Sch. Medicine, 1967-70; adj. asso. prof. health services adminstrn. Tulane U. Sch. Medicine (Sch. Pub. Health and Tropical Medicine), 1969-70, adj. prof., 1970-73, clin. prof. surgery, 1970— Contbr. articles to med. jours. Chmn. ofcl. bd. First Methodist Ch., New Iberia, 1960-62; mem. ofcl. bd. Carrollton Meth. Ch., New Orleans, 1964-66; chmn. La. Inter-Agy. Council for Tb, 1966-70; mem. exec. com. New Orleans Poison Control Center, 1966-71; mem. Health Goals Task Force, State of La., 1969-70; mem. Fed. Exec. Bd., New Orleans, 1970-71, Dallas, 1972-73; med. adv. to sec. Dept. Transp., 1974-77; pres. So. Inst. Human Resources, Atlanta, 1979-80; mem. La. Gov.'s Adv. Com. on Edn. of Handicapped Children, 1977-80. Recipient Querens-Rives-Shore award Tulane U. Sch. Medicine, 1949; USPHS Commendation medal, 1969; USPHS Meritorious Service medal, 1974; USPHS Disting. Service award, 1980; USCG Meritorious Service award, 1977; cert. of merit State of La., 1980; Grace A. Goldsmith Disting. Alumnus lectr. Tulane U. Med. Alumni Assn., 1974 Fellow ACS; mem. USPHS Clin. Soc., Nat. Tb Assn., James D. Rives Surg. Soc., Commd. Officers Assn., Mil. Order World Wars, La. Heart Assn., La. Tb and Respiratory Disease Assn. (dir. 1964—), La. Thoracic Soc., La. Pub. Health Assn., Assn. Mil. Surgeons of U.S., Phi Beta Kappa, Alpha Omega Alpha, Delta Omega. Home: 12674 S Highmeadow Ct Baton Rouge LA 70816-2528 Office: 4550 North Blvd Ste 100 Baton Rouge LA 70806-4013 Office Phone: 225-926-3343.

CHERRY, WILLIAM SPEAKMAN, real estate consultant; b. Galveston, Tex., June 20, 1940; s. William Wallace and Naomi Speakman Cherry; m. Patricia Ann Bowers, Aug. 24, 1995. BS, U. North Tex., Denton, 1965, MA, 1966, PhD, 1967; grad., Rice U., Houston, 1984. Lic. 1st class radio telephone engr., Fed. Comm. Commn., 1957; real estate broker Tex., 1964, registered fin. prin. Nat. Assn. Securities Dealers, 1968, cert. tchr. secondary edn. Tex., 1967, registered tax appraisal arbitrator Tex., 2005. Exec. v.p., dir. Columbia Cmtys., Inc., Houston, 1975—80; prin., owner Bill Cherry Realtor, Dallas, 1980—. Dir. Guaranty Fed. Savings & Loan Assn., 1980. Author: Bill Cherry's Galveston Memories, 2000; columnist: Galveston County Daily News, 1994—2005; radio and TV personality, 1954—. Mem. All Saints Episcopal Ch. Named to Tex. Radio Hall of Fame, 2005. Mem.: Rotary Club. Episcopalian. Avocation: jazz piano. Home and Office: Bill Cherry Realtor 9936 WIndlake Circle Dallas TX 75238 Office Phone: 972-380-7347. Personal E-mail: wscandco@aol.com.

CHERRYH, C. J., writer; b. St. Louis, Sept. 1, 1942; d. Basil L. and Lois Ruth (Van Deventer) C. BA in Latin, U. Okla., 1964; MA in Classics, Johns Hopkins U., 1965. Cert. tchr., Okla. Tchr. Oklahoma City Pub. Schs., 1965-77. Lectr. in field Author: (novels) Gate of Ivrel, 1976, Well of Shiuan, 1978, Brothers of Earth, 1976, Hunter of Worlds, 1976, The Faded Sun: Kesrith, 1977, The Faded Sun: Shon'Jir, 1978, Fires of Azeroth, 1979, The Faded Sun: Kutath, 1979, Hestia, 1979, Sunfall, 1981, Downbelow Station, 1981 (Hugo award for best novel 1982), Wave Without a Shore, 1981, The Pride of Chanur, 1982, Merchanter's Luck, 1982, Port Eternity, 1982, Forty Thousand in Gehenna, 1983, The Dreamstone, 1983, The Tree of Swords and Jewels, 1983, Chanur's Venture, 1984, Cuckoo's Egg, 1985, Visible Light, 1985, The Kif Strike Back, 1985, Angel with the Sword, 1985, Chanur's Homecoming, 1986, Exile's Gate, 1988, Cyteen, 1988 (Hugo award 1988, 89), Smuggler's Gold, 1988, Rimrunners, 1989, Rusalka, 1989, Chernevog, 1990, Yvgenie, 1991, Heavy Time, 1991, Rumrunners, 1991, Hellburner, 1992, Chanur's Legacy, 1992, Goblin Mirror, 1993, Faery in Shadow, 1993, Tripoint, 1994, Foreigner, 1994, Rider at the Gate, 1995, Invader, 1995, Fortress in the Eye of Time, 1995, Inheritor, 1996, Cloud's Rider, 1996, Lois & Clark, 1996, Finity's End, 1997, Fortress of Eagles, 1998, Precursor, 1999, Hammerfall, 2001, Forge of Heaven, 2004, Collected Short Fiction of C.J. Cherryh, 2004, Destroyer, 2005; editor: Flood Tide, 1990; translator: Stellar Crusade by Pierre Barbet, 1980, The Green Gods by Nathalie & Charles Henneberg, 1980, The Book of Shai by Daniel Walther, 1982; contbr. short stories to numerous mags. Woodrow Wilson fellow, 1965; recipient John W. Campbell award for best new writer, 1977, Hugo award for short story, 1979, for novel, 1982, 89, Locus award for best sci. fiction novel, 1988. Mem. Sci. Fiction Writers Assn., Alpha Lambda Delta, Phi beta Kappa. Avocations: galactic mapping, guitar and music composition, travel. Office: c/o Matt Bialer Sanford J Greenburger Assoc 55 Fifth Ave New York NY 10003

CHERTAVIAN, GERALD, nonprofit organization executive; b. Lowell, Mass., 1966; BA in Economics, Bowdoin Coll., Maine; MBA, Harvard Bus. Sch. Officer Chem. Banking Corp.; head mktg. Transitional Fin. Services, London; co-founder Conduit Comm., 1993—99; founder, CEO Year Up, Boston, 2000—. Featured in Boston Globe, Boston Herald, Bus. Week, Fortune Small Bus., Christian Sci. Monitor, Time Mag. Vol. Bog Brother prog., 1985—; trustee Cambridge Coll., Bowdoin Coll.; mem. bd. advisors Harvard Bus. Sch. Social Enterprise Club, New Sector Alliance. Named one of NY's outstanding Big Brothers, 1989; recipient 2003 Social Entrepreneurship award, Manhattan Inst., Archie R. Williams, Jr. Tech. award, Freedom House, 2005. Office: Year Up 93 Summer St Boston MA 02110 Office Phone: 617-542-1533. Office Fax: 617-542-1539.*

CHERTOFF, MICHAEL, secretary of homeland security, former federal judge; b. Elizabeth, NJ, Nov. 28, 1953; s. Gershon and Livia Chertoff; m. Meryl Justin; 2 children. AB magna cum laude, Harvard U., 1975, JD magna cum laude, 1978. Bar: D.C. 1980, N.Y. 1987, N.J. 1990. Editor Harvard Law Review, 1978; summer assoc. Miller, Cassidy, Larroca & Lewin, 1978; law clk. to Hon. Murray I. Gurfein U.S. Ct. Appeals (2nd Cir.), NYC, 1978-79; law clk. to Justice William J. Brennan Jr. U.S. Supreme Ct., Washington, 1979-80; assoc. Latham & Watkins LLP, Washington, 1980-83, ptnr., 1994—2001; asst. U.S. atty. (So. dist.) NY US Dept. Justice, NYC, 1983-87, 1st asst. U.S. atty. dist. NJ Newark, 1987-90, U.S. atty. dist. NJ, 1990—94, asst. atty. gen. criminal div. Washington, 2001—03; spl. counsel for Whitewater com. US Senate, Washington, 1994—96; judge US Ct. Appeals (3rd Cir.), Newark, 2003—05; sec. US Dept. Homeland Security, Washington, 2005—. Mem. lawyer's adv. com. U.S. Dist. Ct. N.J., Newark, 1990-94, U.S. Atty. Gen.'s Adv. com. of U.S. Atty.'s, Washington, 1991-94. Recipient John Marshall award U.S. Dept. Justice, Washington, 1987. Office: US Dept Homeland Security 3801 Nebraska Ave NW Washington DC 20528

CHERY, REGINALD, minister; b. Bklyn., July 12, 1968; s. Pierre Charlot and Viviane Chery; m. Bernadette L. Armstrong, Sept. 16, 2001. BBA in Computer Info. Sys., Baruch Coll., 1993; MDiv, Andrews U., 1997. Ordained min. Seventh-day Adventist Ch., 2004. Sales person Superior Computer Svcs., NYC, 1988; sys. analyst Rsch. Found. Mental Hygiene, NYC, 1992—93; bible worker assoc. evangelist Grand Concourse Seventh Day Adventist Ch., Bronx, NY, 1998; min. Gen. Conf. Seventh Day Adventist Chs., Silver Springs, Md., 1999—. Computer cons. Northeastern Conf. Seventh Day Adventists, Queens, NY, 1997; sch. chaplain Oakview Prep. Sch., Yonkers, NY, 1999—2002. Author: (manual) Straight Talk Youth Ministry. Recipient Police Athletic Leagues award, 1984. Mem.: Black Ministers Assn. Greater NY (assoc.). Seventh-Day Adventist. Achievements include design of Hotel Software. Avocations: basketball, reading, football, travel, weightlifting. Office: Gen Conf Seventh-day Adventists 12501 Old Columbia Pike Silver Spring MD 20904 E-mail: ministerchery@aol.com.

CHESANOW, CHARLES, psychiatrist; BA, Case Western Res. U., Cleve., 1974; DO, Coll. Osteopathic Medicine and Surgery, Des Moines, 1977. Diplomate Am. Bd. Psychiatry and Neurology, cert. in psychiatry 1982, in addiction psychiatry 1994, 2002, in forensic psychiatry 1998. Sys. chief clin. officer Alcohol Drug and Mental Health Bd., Franklin County, 1995—2002; chief psychiatrist Fed. Aviation Adminstrn., Washington, 2003—. Mem.: Animal and Soc. Inst. (bd. mem. 2005—), Aerospace Med. Assn. Office: Fed Aviation Adminstrn 800 Independence Ave SW Washington DC 20591 Home Phone: 301-476-7848; Office Phone: 202-267-3767.

CHESLER, DORIS ADELLE, real estate broker; b. Lincoln, Ill., Sept. 23, 1924; d. Harry and Esther Pearl (Campbell) Schoth; m. Eugene Albert Aughenbaugh, May 23, 1943 (div. Sept. 1970); children: Judith C., Rodney E., Paula Sue; m. Arthur Bernard Chesler, Oct. 16, 1972 (dec. Oct. 1998). Lic. real estate broker Fla. Realtor, assoc. Kilgore Real Estate, Brandon, Fla., 1969—76; broker Doris A. Chesler, Brandon, 1976—. Den mother Cub Scouts Am., Tampa, 1961—62; leader 4-H Club, Decatur, Ill., 1956. Republican. Presbyterian. Avocations: interior decorating, sewing, gardening, music, painting.

CHESLER, EVAN ROBERT, lawyer; b. NYC, July 17, 1949; s. Philip and Doris (Sims) C.; m. Diane Lynn Ackerman, May 30, 1970 (div. 1983); children: David Andrew, Matthew Lawrence, Rebecca Faye; m. Barbara Jean Gloven, Sept. 10, 1983. BA, NYU, 1970, JD, 1975; MA, Hunter Coll., 1973. Bar: NY 1976, US Dist. Ct. (so. dist. NY) 1976, US Supreme Ct. 1982, US Ct. Appeals (2nd cir.) 1982, US Dist. Ct. (no. dist. Calif.) 1982. Tchr. NYC Bd. Edn., 1970-72; law clk. US Dist. Ct. (so. dist. NY), NYC, 1975-76; assoc. Cravath, Swaine & Moore, NYC, 1976-82, ptnr., 1982—, dep. presiding ptnr., 2005-06, presiding ptnr., 2007-; head of litig. Pres., Inst. Jud. Adminstrn., NYC Sch. Law. Mem. bd. overseers Faculty Arts & Scis, NYC; trustee NYS League Women Voteres Edn. Found.; mem. exec. com. Ctr. Pub. Resources. Author: The Russian Jewry Reader, 1973. Topics editor NYU Law Rev., 1974-75. Contbr. articles to legal jours., chpts. to books. NY Regents scholar, 1966-70, 72-75; Ctr. for Internat. Studies jr. fellow, 1974-75. Fellow Am. Coll. Trial Lawyers; mem. Assn. of Bar of City of NY, State Bar Assn., ABA, Order of Coif. Democrat. Jewish. Office: Cravath Swaine & Moore Worldwide Plz Fl 38 825 8th Ave New York NY 10019-7475*

CHESLEY, STANLEY MORRIS, lawyer; b. Cin., Mar. 26, 1936; s. Frank and Rachel (Kinsburg) C.; children: Richard A., Lauren B. BA, U. Cin., 1958, LLB, 1960. Bar: Ohio 1960, Ky. 1978, W.Va. 1981, Tex. 1981, Nev. 1981. Ptnr. Waite, Schneider, Bayless & Chesley Co., Cin., 1960—. Contbr. articles to profl. jours. Past chmn. bd. commrs. on grievances and discipline Supreme Ct. Ohio; past pres. Jewish Fedn. Cin.; nat. vice chair, bd. govs., United Jewish Coms.; exec. bd., nat. bd. govs. Am. Jewish Com.; nat. bd. govs. Hebrew Uninon Coll.; exec. com. U.S. Holocaust Meml. Mus. Mem. bd. of dirs. Am. Jewish Joint Distbn ABA, ATLA, FBA, Am. Judicature Soc., Melvin M. Belli Soc., Ohio Bar Assn., Ky. Bar Assn., W.Va. Bar Assn., Tex. Bar Assn., Nev. Bar Assn., Cin. Bar Assn. Office: Waite Schneider Bayless & Chesley 1513 4th and Vine Tower Cincinnati OH 45202 Office Phone: 513-621-0267. Personal E-mail: wsbclaw@aol.com.

CHESNE, EDWARD LEONARD, physician; b. Chgo., June 11, 1931; m. Carol Chesne; children: Lauren, Christopher, Greig. BA, U. Chgo., 1950; MD, Northwestern U. Med. Sch., Chgo., 1955. Lic. phys., Ill., Hawaii. Capt. U.S. Army, 1957. Fellow Am. Coll. Physicians, Am. Coll. Cardiology, Coun. Clin. Cardiology, Am. Heart Assn. Office: 1380 Lusitana St Ste 1002 Honolulu HI 96813-2461 Home Phone: 805-524-2575; Office Phone: 808-521-7402.

CHESNEY, KENNY, country singer, songwriter; b. Knoxville, Tenn., Mar. 26, 1968; m. Renee Zellweger, May 9, 2005 (annulled Dec. 20, 2005). Degree in advt., E. Tenn. State U., 1991. Performer Chuckie's Trading Post and Quarterback's Barbecue, Johnson City, Tenn.; resident performer The Turf, Nashville; publ. deal with Acuff-Rose, 1992; record contract with Capricorn, Tenn., 1993; with RCA, Subsidiary BNA, Tenn. Translator: (albums) In My Wildest Dreams, 1993; singer All I Need To Know, 1995, Me & You, 1996, I Will Stand, 1997, Everywhere We Go, 1999, Greatest Hits, 2000, No Shirt, No Shoes, No Problem, 2002, All I Want For Christmas is a Real Good Tan, 2003, When the Sun Goes Down, 2004 (Album of Yr. Country Music. Assn., 2004), The Road & the Radio, 2005, Live: Live Those Songs Again, 2006, (songs) The Good Stuff, 2002 (Single of Yr., Acad. Country Music, 2003), You Save Me, 2005 (Male Video of Yr., Country Music TV, 2007), I Go Back, 2004 (Male Video of Yr., Country Music TV, 2005); singer: (guest appearance with Willie Nelson and Leon Russell) Last Thing I Needed First Thing This Morning, 2003. Named Top New Male Vocalist, Acad. Country Music Awards, 1997, Top Male Vocalist, 2002, Entertainer of Yr., 2005—07, Country Music Assn., 2004, 2006, Favorite Male Singer, People's Choice Awards, 2007; recipient Country Songs Artist of Yr. award, Billboard Music Awards, 2006. Office: Kenny Chesney Fan Club PO Box 128529 Nashville TN 37212-8529*

CHESNEY, LEE ROY, JR., artist; b. Washington, June 1, 1920; s. Lee Roy and Rena Ruth (Beach) C.; m. Betty J. Lamb, Jan. 28, 1943; children: Lee Roy III, Terril Ann Bauer. B.F.A., U. Colo., 1946; M.F.A., U. Iowa, 1948; postgrad., U. Michoacan, Mex., 1950-51. Instr. drawing U. Iowa, 1947-50; prof. art, dir. printmaking, head grad. printmaking and painting U. Ill., Urbana, 1950-67; assoc. dean fine arts U. So. Calif., Los Angeles, 1967-72; prof. art, chmn. grad. art programs U. Hawaii, Honolulu, 1972-84, prof. emeritus, 1984—; Louis D. Beaumont vis. disting. prof. Washington U. Vis. artist Otis Art Inst., L.A., U. Colo., U. Wash., Mich. State U., Honolulu Acad. Arts Sch., Visual Arts Center, Anchorage, Portland (Oreg.,) State U., 1988, U. Fla., 1989, Lacoste Sch. Arts, France, 1989, UCLA, 1989-90; mem. com., nat. juror Sr. Fulbright Research Awards, 1968-71, com. chmn., 1969-71; mem. visual arts selection com., Calif. Arts Coun., 1990; juror Hawaii Print Exhbn., 1991, 10th Internat. Pacific Rim Exhbn. Hilo, Hawaii; mem. Pacific Rim Lectrs. and Workshops, 1992; artist-in-residence U. Tex., 1993, Pacific Rim Series, 1994. Symposium Amon Carter Mus., Ft. Worth, 1990, Archer M. Huntington Art Gallery, 1993; one-man shows include Newman Brown Gallery, Chgo. , U. Fla. , U. Louisville , U. Mich. , U. Wis., Madison , Ohio State U. , Ill. State U. , Yoseido Gallery, Tokyo , Atrium Gallery, Seattle , Visual Arts Center, Anchorage , Washington U., St. Louis , U. Utah , U. Alaska , Am. Cultural Ctr., Paris, 1964 , Fisher Galleries, U. So. Calif., 1968 , State Fedn. Culture and Art, 1967—87 , Honolulu Acad. Arts, 1973 , Comsky Gallery, Beverly Hills, Calif., 1970—76 , Downtown Gallery, Honolulu, 1975 , BIMC Galerie, Paris, 1979 , 1981 , 1983 , Galerie Sandoz, 1979 , Cité Internat. des Arts, 1979 , Honolulu Acad. of Arts, Focus Gallery, 1985 , Contemporary Arts Center, Honolulu, 1980 , 25-yr. retrospective exhbn. of prints circulated by U. Fla., 1977—80 , retrospective exhbn. Portland State U., 1988 , U. Fla., 1989 , Printmaking 1985, Tallahassee , So. Graphics Coun. Emeritus Printmaker Exhbn. Knoxville Mus. Art, 1992 , Williams Lamb Gallery, Long Beach, Calif., 1990 , 1992 , West Tex. A&M U., 1993 , Oracle (Ariz.) Art Ctr., 1995 , State Founds. and Arts, Hawaii, 1997 , Parsons Sch. Design, Paris, 1998 , solo exhbn. of paintings, Davis Dominguez Gall., Tucson, Ariz., 1999—2000 , Hawaii State Mus. Art Inaugural Exhbn., 2003 , exhibited in group shows at Am. Fedn. Arts traveling exhbn. , Mus. Modern Art traveling exhbn. , USIS traveling exhbn. , Soc. Am. Graphic artists traveling exhbns., 1973—77 , Nihon Sosaku Hanga Kyokai, 1957—84 , Contemporary Am. Painting, Bucharest, 1977 , Hawaii Nat. Biennial Print Exhbn., Honolulu Acad. Arts, 1971 , 1973 , 1975 , 1977 , 1978 , 1980 , 1983 , BIMC Galerie, 1978 , 1979 , 1980 , 1981 , 1982 , 1983 , 70th Nat. Invitational Drawing Exhbn., Emporia, Kans., 1986 , U. West Fla., 1986 , Neville-Sargent Gallery, 1986 , Northwest Printmakers, 1986 , U. Calif., Davis, 1985 , Calif. Artists exhbn. at Thomas Ctr. Gallery, Gainesville, Fla., 1987 , 25th Anniversary Exhbn. State Found. for Culture and the Arts (reproduction), Honolulu, 1988 , 50th Anniversary Exhbn. of Commd. Prints, Honolulu Printmakers, Honolulu Acad. of Arts, 1988 , N.W. Print Coun. Exhbn., Australia, 1988 , Overreact Gallery, Long Beach, 1989 , U. Hawaii, Hilo, 1989 , Williams Lamb Gallery, 1990 , 1991 , 1992 , Worcester (Mass.) Art Mus., 1991 , Amon Carter Mus., 1990 , Ft. Worth, 1990 , Artists Who Teach Exhbn., Champaign, Ill., 1990 , Nelson Atkins Mus., Kansas City, 1990 , Mona Bismark Found., Paris, 1991 , Soc. Am. Graphic Artists (prize) Nat. Exhbn., N.Y.C. , Internat. Exhbn. Artists of Lacoste, France, Paris, 1991 , San Diego Art Inst. Invitational, 1991 , Williams Lamb Gallery, Long Beach, Calif., 1991 , 1992 , 12th U. Dallas Nat. Print Exhbn., 1991 , 1992 , Nat. Exhbn. Copper Engraving, Portand, Oreg., 1992 , Pacific States Biennial Exhbn., Hilo, 1992—94 , Northwest Print Coun., Eugene, Oreg., 1993 , Indpls. Mus. Art, 1993 , Pacific Rim Internat., 1993 , 1997 (award) , Works on Paper, L.A., 1995 , 1996 , 1997 , 1998 , Southern Graphics Exhib. of Disting. Print Makers, Tampa, Fla., 1997 , L.A. Print Soc. Exhbn., 1997 , Portland Art Mus. Intern. Pr. Exhib., 1997 , Davis Dominguez Gallery, Tucson, 1997 , "Exclusively Etchings" Lankersheim Arts, Pacific Rim Internat. Monoprint Exhibition, Hilo, Hawaii, 1998 , State Fedn. 30 yr. anniv. exhbn., Hofstra Univ. Mus. N.Y. Exhbn. "Abstract Expressionism: Then and Now", 2001 , Tradition of Excellence, U. Hawaii Art Gallery, 2002 , Hawaii State Art Mus. Grand Opening, Honolulu, 2002—03 , 2005 , Davis Domingus Gallery, Tucson, 2005—07 , Cleve. Mus. Art, 2003 , Cinema Gallery, Urbana, Ill., 2006 , others , Represented in permanent collections Nat. Gallery Art, Washington , Biblioteque Nationale, Paris , Victoria and Albert Mus., London , Tokyo U. Fine Art , Tokyo Mus. Modern Art , Nat. Gallery Art, Stockholm , Tate Gallery, London , USIS, State Dept., Washington , Library of Congress , Bklyn. Mus. , Mus. Modern Art, N.Y.C. , Phila. Mus. , Denver Mus. , Dallas Mus. , Pasadena Mus. , Honolulu Acad. Arts , Hawaii Council for Arts , Art Inst. Chgo. , Oakland Mus. , L.A. County Mus. , Seattle Mus. , Worcester Art Mus. , Am. Embassy, Bonn , Bank of Am. , United Calif. Bank , U. Hawaii , IBM , Litton Industries Corp. , Hartford Ins. Co. , Fuji Bank Calif. , Northrop Corp. , 1st Hawaii Trust Bank , Mus. Contemporary Art, Honolulu , Portland (Oreg.) Mus. Art , Univ. Hawaii, Hilo , Indpls. Mus. Art , Elvehjem Mus. Art, Wis. , West Tex. A&M U. , Wycross Press, Auburn, Ala., 1994. Mem. Commn. for Founders' Portfolio for N.W. Printmakers, Portland, 1977. Served to capt. AUS, 1942-45. Recipient Francis G. Logan medal Art Inst. Chgo., 1962, Pauline Palmer award, 1966; Concora Found. prize, 1963; Vera List award Soc. Am. Graphic Artists, Am. Acad., Rome, 1964; appointee Cité Internat. des Arts, Paris, 1970, 78-83; Fondation Gardilanne-Moffat Studio award, 1978-80; purchase award Epinal (France) Biennial Invitational Exhbn., Pacific Rim Internat., 1993, 97; awards Hawaii State Found. for Culture and Arts, 1972, 74, 75, 78, 80; awards Honolulu Acad. Arts, 1973, 78; award San Diego Art Inst., 1991, Fulbright sr. rsch. award, 1956-57; U. Ill. rsch. grantee, 1963-64; Ford Found. faculty enrichment award, 1978, 82, Printmaker Emeritus award So. Graphics Coun., 1992. Mem. Coll. Art Assn. Am., Calif. Soc. Printmakers, N.W. Print Coun. (bd. dirs.), Japan Print Assn., Soc. Am. Graphic Artists, Color Print Soc., World Print Coun., L.A. Printmaking Soc. (hon. dir.), Honolulu Printmakers (past v.p., pres.), Painters and Sculptors League Hawaii, Hawaii Artists League, So. Graphics Coun., Fulbright Assn. Address: 14601 Whitfield Ave Pacific Palisades CA 90272-2645 Office Phone: 323-939-6212.

CHESNEY, ROBERT HENRY, management consultant, director; b. Rockville Centre, NY, Aug. 12, 1950; s. Robert Lewis and Maureen C. (Oates) C.; m. Donna Marie Mazian, May 1, 1976; 1 child, Alexis Mary. BA in Indsl. Psychology, Hofstra U., 1972, MBA in Qualitative & Quantitative Analysis, 1979. Internal auditor Grumman Aerospace, Bethpage, NY, 1974—77, sr. ops. specialist, 1978; sr. sys. analyst Sta. WNET, NYC, 1978—79, mgr. mgmt. info. sys. and procedures, 1979—81, asst. dir. mgmt. info. sys. and procedures, 1981—82; sr. tech. cons. N.Y. Tel., Melville, 1982—83, AT&T Info. Sys., Melville, 1983—89; from sr. exec. data sales to mgr. territory AT&T Computer Sys., Melville, 1990—94; from sr. client cons. to mng. client cons. AT&T Ops. Consulting Group, Manhasset, NY, 1994—95; ptnr. AT&T Bus. Consulting, Manhasset, 1995, dist. mgr. Atlanta, 1996—97; dist. mgr. CFO SAP Lucent Techs. Inc., Warren, NJ, 1997—99, dist. mgr. GSP IPS, 1999—2000, sr. mgr. SPN NNS CFO sys. and procedures, 2000—01; mgmt. cons. strategic planning and process re-engring. UN Joint Staff Pension Fund, NYC, 2002—05; pres. Bus. Ops. Blueprinting Corp., 2003—; v.p. Anti Money Laundering Compliance, Deutsche Bank Trust Co Ams, NYC, 2006—. Mem.: IEEE, Project Mgmt. Inst., N.Y. Acad. Scis., Assn. Computing Machinery, IEEE Computer Soc., Hostra U. Alumni Assn. Republican. Roman Catholic. Office: Deutsche Bank Trust Co Ams Anti Money Laundering Compliance 60 Wall St New York NY 10005 Office Phone: 516-398-1413. Personal E-mail: bobcorp@optonline.net, chez01@optonline.net.

CHESNEY, RUSSELL WALLACE, pediatrician; b. Knoxville, Tenn., Aug. 25, 1941; s. Jack and Helen Wallace (McColl) C.; m. Patricia Joan Cook, June 8, 1968; children: Karen, Christopher, Gillian. AB, Harvard U., Cambridge, Mass., 1963; MD, U. Rochester, NYC, 1968. Diplomate Am. Bd. Pediatrics. Intern then resident Johns Hopkins U. Hosp., Balt., 1968-70, 72-73; renal fellow NIH, Balt., 1970-72, Montreal Childrens Hosp., Montreal, Que., Canada, 1973-75; asst. then prof. U. Wis., Madison, 1975-85; prof., vice chmn. U. Calif., Davis, 1985-88; prof., chmn. pediatrics U. Tenn., Memphis, 1988—. Mem. Rsch. Study Sect. NIH, Washington, 1983—88, mem. Nat. Kidney and Urology Diseases Adv. Bd., 1988—91; sec.-treas., pediat. dept. chmn. Am. Med. Schs., 1993—99, pres., 2001—03; mem. coun. Am. Pediat. Soc., 1995—2004, v.p., 2001—02, pres., 2002—03; chmn. Fed. Pediat. Orgn., 1995—96; Birdsong lectr. U. Va., 1995; vice chair Task Force on Pediat. Edn., 1996—99; chair Am. Bd. Pediats., 2000—02; bd. trustees Assn. Children's Hosps., 2002—. Contbr. articles to profl. jours., chpts. to text and med. books. Lt. comdr. USPHS, 1970-72, Balt. Recipient Founders award in Pediatric Rsch., So. Soc. Pediatric Rsch., 1993; Jour. Pediatrics lectr. U. Rochester, 1985, Paul Gaffney lectr. U. Pitts., 1988. Mem. Am. Pediat. Soc. (mem. coun. 1995-, v.p. 2001-02, pres. 2002-03), Am. Acad. Pediats. (pres. Tenn. state chpt. 1995-98, E. Meade Johnson award 1985, Nutrition award 1996, St. Geme award 2001, Henry Barnett award 2004, Founders award 2005), Soc. for Pediat. Rsch. (pres. 1986-87), Midwest Soc. for Pediat. Rsch. (pres. 1984-85), Am. Soc. for Pediat. Nephrology (pres. 1986-87), VA Merit Rev. Bd. (chmn. 1988-90). Office: U Tenn Dept Pediats 50 S Dunlap St Memphis TN 38103-4909 Business E-Mail: rchesney@utmem.edu.

CHESNOFF, DAVID ZELTNER, lawyer; b. Paterson, NJ, May 13, 1955; BA cum laude, Alfred U., 1976; JD, Suffolk U., 1979. Bar: Tex. 1979, US Dist. Ct. (so. dist. Tex.) 1979, Nev. 1981, US Dist. Ct. (dist. Nev.) 1981, US Dist. Ct. (ea. dist. Mich.) 1988, US Dist. Ct. (dist. Mont.) 1989, US Dist. Ct. (dist. Ariz.) 1997, US Dist Ct. (so., ctrl. and no. dists. Calif.), US Dist. Ct. (dist. Ala.), US Dist. Ct. (dist. Mass.), US Dist. Ct. (dist. NJ), US Dist. Ct. (dist. N.Mex.), US Dist. Ct. (dist. Utah), US Dist. Ct. (dist. Vt.), US Ct. Appeals (1st, 2nd, 3rd, 5th, 6th, 8th, 9th, 10th & 11th cirs.), US Supreme Ct. 1988. Ptnr. Goodman & Chesnoff, Las Vegas, Nev., Chesnoff & Schonfeld, Las Vegas. Legal cons. ABC; prof. Mercer Law Sch., Macon, Ga.; spkr. in field. Guest appearances American Justice, City Confidential, CNBC TV, Charlie Rose Show. Mem.: Am. Inns of Ct., Am. Bd. Criminal Lawyers, Assn. Trial Lawyers Am., Nat. Assn. Criminal Def. Lawyers (vice chmn. continuing legal edn. com. 1991—92, mem. lawyers assistance strike force 1993, bd. dirs.), Nev. Trial Lawyers Assn., State Bar Tex., State Bar Nev., Clark County Bar Assn. Office: Chesnoff & Schonfeld PC 520 S Fourth St Las Vegas NV 89101-6593 Office Phone: 702-384-5563. Office Fax: 702-598-1425.*

CHESNUT, NONDIS LORINE (ANGEL LOVE), education educator, writer, learning specialist, scriptwriter; b. South Daytona, Fla., June 29, 1941; d. Anthony Valentine and Myrtle Marie (Allen) Campbell; m. Raymond Otho Chesnut, Aug. 25, 1962; 1 child, Starlina Mintina Chesnut

Kladler. BS in English and Speech, Concord U., Athens, W.Va., 1962; postgrad. in Linguistics, Frostburg U., Md., 1967; postgrad., W.Va. U., Morgantown, 1973; AGS in Reading, U. Md., Coll. Park, 1974; postgrad., Md. State Dept. Edn., Balt., 1981—95, Inst. Children's Lit., 1996—98; postgrad. in Screenwriting, Screenwriters Unlimited, Orlando, Fla., 1998; writing coursework, Charter Oak State Coll., 2000. Cert. adminstr., secondary prin., elem. prin., reading splist., tchr. English and speech, drama. Tchr. English and speech Harpers Ferry (W.Va.) H.S., 1962-64; with Sears Roebuck, summer 1965; libr. Great Mills (Md.) H.S., 1968-69; tchr. English and reading North Hagerstown H.S., Hagerstown, Md., 1964-73; tchr. South Hagerstown H.S., Hagerstown, 1974-77; reading resource tchr. Woodland Way Elem. Sch., Hagerstown, 1977-83; adj. instr. grad. sch. Hood Coll., Frederick, Md., 1982-83; reading specialist Fountain Rock Elem. Sch., Hagerstown, 1983-85; tchr. Williamsport (Md.) H.S., 1985-95. Reading and lang. arts cons., Md., 1973-95, Fla., 1996-2007; adj. reading instr. Daytona Comm. Coll., 1996-97, Galaxy Middle Sch., 1997-98, drama, lang. arts, reading tchr., 1997-98, Key Source, 1999; instr. English and writing Bethune-Cookman Coll., fall 2000, adj. instr. reading, writing and English Daytona Beach C.C., 2001—, Learning Ctr. specialist, 2004-; spkr., presenter local, nat. and internat. workshops, 1973-2007; speech and debate coach. Writer for radio programs and advertisements for reading, 1986—, TV programs, 1974-78, 90-91; appeared on TV programs, 1974-78; co-editor column Beckley Post Herald, 1957-59; contbr. articles to newspapers and mags., 1964—; appeared in film Guarding Tess, 1993; screenwriter Heaven on Planet Earth, 2000; author (nonfiction) A Touch of Love From God, 2003, A Touch of Love From Heaven, 2005. Mem. debating team Concord Coll., 1961-62, mem. newspaper staff, 1959-61; mem. Washington County Network of Orgns., 1984-88; co-dir. Billy Bud, 1962; v.p. Women's Ind. Club, 1962, treas., 1961; sec.-treas. Fgn. lang. Club, 1961, Debate Club, 1961-62; treas. Meth. Youth Fellowship, 1961; pres. Tri-Hi-Y, 1959; legis. chairperson State of Md. Reading Coun., 1977-78; active Emmanuel Meth. Ch., White Sul, 1953-84, Life in Spirit Group, 1994-95, St. Ann's Roman Cath. Ch., 1994-95, Grace United Meth. Ch., 1984-95, Lady of Hope Cath. Ch., 1996—; mem. Fla. State Reading Coun., 1996-. Recipient Pres.'s award State of Md. Reading Coun., 1981, Pres.'s award Washington County Reading Coun., 1981, Guidance Helping award, 1987, Voice of Democracy award VFW/Ladies Aux., 1992, Am. Heritage Writing award Williamsport Lions Club, 1995, Recognition of Valuble Contrbn. award, Acad. Support Ctr., Daytona Beach CC Intercollegiate Athletic Dept. 2007, numerous others; W.Va. Legislature scholar, 1959-62. Mem. AAUW (ednl. chairperson 1983-85, legis. v.p. 1986-87, cmty. chairperson 1987-89), NEA (publicity and scholarship coms., bldg. rep. 1989-95, del.), ASCD, VFW (chairperson Voice of Democracy 1989-95, VFW award 1989-95), Md. Dist. Am. Heritage Lions (Region II Lions award, Williamsport Am. Heritage Lions award 1995), State of Md. Internat. Reading Assn. Coun. (sec. 1975-79, v.p. elect 1979-80, v.p. 1980-81, pres. 1981-82, nominating chairperson 1982-83), Washington County Tchrs. Assn. (rep., scholarship chair, publicity), Internat. Reading Assn. (sec.-treas. sex differences in reading group 1976-77, 83-85, mem. gender differences in reading group 1985-86, mem. readability interest group, mastery learning interest group, del. convs., internat. rsch. com. 1976-77, 84-85, disabled learners interest group 1975-82), Washington County Reading Assn. (pres. 1981-82), Am. Legion (chairperson oratorial contest 1989-95, speech coach), Fla. Devel. Edn. Assn. (mem. com. registration 1996, 1997-), Assn. Rsch. and Enlightenment. Democrat. Avocations: writing, swimming, dance, travel, psychology. Home: Box 291523 Port Orange FL 32129 Personal E-mail: AngelLove4peace@aol.com.

CHESNUTT, JANE, editor-in-chief; b. Kenedy, Tex., Oct. 10, 1950; m. W. Mallory Rintoul. BJ, U. Tex., 1973. With Environment Information Ctr., NY, 1973; editorial asst. Am. Jour. Nursing, NYC, 1975-78; asst. editor Woman's Day mag., NYC, 1978—83, health editor, 1983—89, beauty, health, fashion editor, 1989-91, editor-in-chief, 1991—, sr. v.p., group editl. dir., 2002—. Sr. v.p. & group editl. dir. Transplant Am. Nat. Kidney Found. Mem. bus. adv. coun. Washington Irving H.S., N.Y.C. Named one of Editor of Yrl, Adweek, 1992, Top Players, Min Mag., 2000; recipient Editor of Yr., Adweek, 1992. Mem. Am. Soc. Mag. Editors, Women in Comms., Inc. (Clarion award 1985, Headliner award 1996), YWCA Acad. of Achievers. Office: Woman's Day Mag Hachette Filipacchi Mags Inc 1633 Broadway New York NY 10019-6708 Office Phone: 212-767-6250. Office Fax: 212-767-5610.*

CHESNUTT, ROD MARTIN, music educator; s. Clarence and Natalie Brown Chesnutt; m. Jennifer Kathleene Wright, Oct. 22, 1970. BS in Music Edn., Tenn. Technol. U., 1981; MusM in Trombone Performance, Ark. State U., 1983; PhD in Music Edn., Fla. State U., 1995. Grad. tchg. asst. Ark. State U., Jonesboro, 1981—83; h.s. band dir. Trumann Pub. Schs., Trumann, 1983—87; dir. bands, supr. instrumental music Blytheville Pub. Schs.; tchg. asst. Fla. State U., Tallahassee, 1992—95; assoc. dir. bands U. Nebr., Lincoln, 1995—98; dir. bands State U. West Ga., Carrollton, 1998—99, Miss. State U., Starkville, 1999—2002; dir. symphonic, marching bands U. No. Iowa, Cedar Falls, 2002—. Condr, music dir. Starkville Symphony, 2001—03; adjudicator Parade of Bands, Moanalua, Hawaii, 2004—04, Ky. State Marching Championships, Bowling Green, 2000—03, SW Mo. Classic, Springfield, 2002—02, La. Showcase, Lafayette, 2000—00, Windfest, Syracuse, NY, 1997—2000; vis. prof. Charleston So. U. Grad. Symposium, SC, 1998—98, U. Mont. Grad. Music Edn. Program, Missoula, 1997—97; guest condr. Oahu All-District Band, Honolulu, 2004—04, SW Iowa All-District Band, Gilbertville, 2004—04, NE Iowa All-District Band, Oelwein, 2003—03, NE Miss. All-District Band, Fulton, 2001—01, Western Ky. Honor Band, Bowling Green, 2001—01, Mont. AA All-State Band, Kalispell, 2000—00; dir. U. No. Iowa Jr. Band Camp, Cedar Falls, 2003—; adjudicator Ill. State Concert Contest, Bloomington. Conductor (premiere) Bandancing; contbr. performance analyses; arranger (musical arrangement) American Quadrille, La Prima Donna, (musical arrangment) Trombone concerto; prodr.: (compact disc) Hear the Roar, Out of the Storm; conductor (premier) Danzante. Named Outstanding Young Men Am., 1988; recipient award of Merit, Nat. Music Clubs, 1991, Sudler trophy, Outstanding Collegiate Marching Band, John Phillip Sousa Found., 1996. Mem.: World Assn. Bands and Ensembles, Nat. Band Assn., Music Educators Nat. Conf., Iowa Music Educators Assn., Coll. Music Soc., Coll. Band Dirs. Nat. Assn. (state chair 2000—02), Iowa Alliance Arts, Phi Beta Mu, Pi Kappa Lambda (chpt. sec. 2003—05), Phi Mu Alpha, Kappa Kappa Psi (life; nat. vice pres., pres.-elect 2003—05). Achievements include research in International Conference of the World Association for Symphonic Bands and Ensembles, Schladming, Austria, July 5 - 12 1997; poster session, Biennial National Conference, College Band Director's National Association, Athens, GA, February-March 1997; Southern Division meeting of the College Band Director's National Association, Williamsburg, VA, February 1994. Avocations: gardening, cooking, fishing. Office: UNI Bands 48 GBPAC Cedar Falls IA 50614 Home Phone: 319-277-3670; Office Phone: 319-273-2025. Office Fax: 319-273-7306. E-mail: chesnutt@uni.edu.

CHESS, PATRICIA R., pediatrician, medical educator, researcher; d. Edward G. and Rosemary A. Batchelor; m. Mitchell A. Chess, June 28, 1987; children: Rachel R., Laura H., Daniel E., Stephen A. BA in Math., Chemistry with honors, cum laude, Colgate U., Hamilton. NY, 1983; MD, Columbia U., NYC, 1988. Cert. pediatrics Am. Acad. Pediat., 1991, neonatology Am. Acad. Pediat., 1995. Asst. prof. U. Rochester, 1996—2003, assoc. prof., 2003—. Contbr. articles to profl. jours. and book revs. in field. Oversee clinic for individuals with disabilities Easter Seals, Rochester, 2001—. Grantee, NIH, 1999-2004. Mem.: Perinatal Rsch. Soc., Soc. Pediatric Rsch., Am. Acad. Pediat., Am. Thoracic Soc. Office: Univ Rochester 601 Elmwood Ave Box 651 Rochester NY 14642 Home Phone: 585-244-5116; Office Phone: 585-275-6198. Office Fax: 585-461-3614. Business E-Mail: patricia_chess@urmc.rochester.edu.

CHESSA, LUCIANO, composer, musicologist, educator; b. Sassari, Italy, Jan. 12, 1971; arrived in US, 1998; s. Antonio Natale Chessa and Angela Demelas. Diploma in Piano, G. B. Martini Conservatory Music, Bologna, Italy, 1995; MA in Composition, G. B. Martini Conservatory of Music, Bologna, Italy, 1998; MA in History of Medieval and Renaissance Music magna cum laude, U. Bologna, 1997; PhD in Musicology and Music Criticism, U. Calif., Davis, 2004. Music program coord. Italian Cultural Inst., San Francisco, 1999—; assoc. instr. U. Calif., Davis, 2002—05; mem. collegiate faculty San Francisco Conservatory Music, 2006—. Concert prodr. Link Project, Bologna, 1995—98. Author: (record) Humus, 1997 (Best Record of Yr. - Rockerilla, 1997); author text: CD ensemble piece Peppa, 1997, author text: Il pedone dell'aria, 2006, score for string orchestra and baritone Strelitzie, 2006, score for quintet Polinesiano, 2006; composer: (score for piano and three turntables) Cinque quadri da una città fantasma, 2006. Recipient Travel award, Kunsthistorisches Institut in Florenz. Max-Planck Institut, Transl. award, Italian Govt., 2006, Award, 14th Suzuki Method World Conv., 2006; Grad. fellow and Chandler fellow, U. Calif., Davis, 1998—99, Karl Schwarze Chandler fellow, 1999—2002, William E. Valente Karl Schwarze fellow, 2001—02, Grad. fellow, 2002—04. Mem.: Am. Musicological Soc. (travel award 2006). Office Phone: 510-841-2005. Business E-Mail: lchessa@sfiic.org.

CHESSER, MICHAEL J., gas and electric power industry executive; BS, Ga. Tech. Univ.; MBA, Loyola Coll., Balt. With Balt. Gas & Electric; pres., COO Atlantic Energy Inc., 1994—98; pres., CEO Itron Inc., Spokane, Wash., 1999—2000, GPU Energy, Morristown, NJ, 2000—02; chmn., CEO United Water Resources, Harrington Park, NJ, 2002—03, Great Plains Energy, Kansas City, Mo., 2003—. Bd. mem. Edison Elec. Inst., Elec. Power Rsch. Inst. Trustee Univ. Mo., Kansas City, Midwest Rsch. Inst.; bd. mem. Heart of Am. United Way, Partnership for Children; mem. leadership bd. Mid-Am. Regional Council; mem. Civic Council Greater Kansas City, Kans. Bus. Edn. Partnership. Office: Great Plains Energy 1201 Walnut St Kansas City MO 64106 Mailing: Great Plains Energy PO Box 418679 Kansas City MO 64141-9679*

CHESSLER, RICHARD KENNETH, gastroenterologist, endocrinologist; b. NYC, Apr. 6, 1944; BS, Fairleigh Dickinson U., Rutherford, NJ, 1965; MD, Chgo. Med. Sch., 1969. Diplomate Am. Bd. Internal Medicine and Gastroenterology. Asst. chief gastroenterology Englewood Hosp., NJ, 1982—, chief endoscopy NJ, 1992-99; asst. prof. medicine Mt. Sinai Hosp., NYC, 1994-97. Author: Chemical Technicians Ready Reference Book, 1996; mem. editl. bd. Practical Gastroenterology, 1977—. Fellow ACP, Am. Coll. Gastroenterology (bd. govs. 1989). Avocations: ski, racquetball, golf. Office: 1555 Center Ave Fort Lee NJ 07024-4612 Office Phone: 201-945-6564.

CHESSON, EUGENE, retired civil engineering educator, consultant, volunteer; b. São Paulo, Brazil, Dec. 1, 1928; s. Eugene and Mary Josie (Foy) C.; m. Marilyn Ryder Hershey, Aug. 21, 1954; children: Christopher Eugene, David Anson. BSc in Civil Engring., Duke U., 1950; MS, U. Ill.-Urbana, 1956, PhD, 1959. Registered profl. engr., Ill., Del., Ariz. Refinery engr. Standard Oil Ind., Whiting, 1953; research asst., research assoc. civil engring. dept. U. Ill.-Urbana, 1953-59, asst. prof., 1959-62, assoc. prof., 1962-66; prof. civil engring. U. Del., Newark, 1966-86, dept. chmn., 1966-75, prof. emeritus, 1986—; pres. Chesson Engring., Inc., Newark, 1981-85; treas., project mgr. HPR Investors, L.C., Prescott, Ariz., 1992—2004, Sedona Pinon Woods Partnership, Prescott, 1992—2000; treas. Hershey Partnership, Prescott, 1993—. Contbr. articles in field to profl. jours. Mem. Nat. Def. Exec. Res., U.S. Dept. Transp., 1973-84; vol. Sharlot Hall Mus., Prescott, 2001—. Lt. (j.g.) Civil Engr. Corps, USN, 1950-53. Named Outstanding Young Faculty Mem., Dept. Civil Engring., U. Ill., 1962; Del. Outstanding Engr. Del. Soc. Profl. Engrs., 1981; recipient Teaching award AT&T Found., 1986 Fellow ASCE (pres. local sect. 1982-83); mem. Am. Soc. Engring. Edn. (W.E. Wickenden award 1981), No. Ariz. Geneal. Soc. (v.p., pres. 1989-91). Republican. Presbyterian. Home: 640 Cosmos Way Prescott AZ 86303-5049

CHESSON, MICHAEL BEDOUT, history professor, writer; b. Richmond, Va., Sept. 5, 1947; s. Wesley Earle and Virginia Winborne (Ramsey) Chesson; m. Jane B. Sherwin, July 2, 1988; children: Mark Allyn, Virginia Woodward. AB with high honors in History, Coll. William and Mary, Williamsburg, Va., 1969; postgrad. Gilman fellow, Johns Hopkins U., Balt., 1972-73; PhD in History, Harvard U., Cambridge, Mass., 1978. Clk. R.F. & P. R.R., Richmond, 1966-69; park ranger-historian Colonial Nat. Hist. Park, Nat. Park Svc., Yorktown and Jamestown, Va., 1969-70, 72, 73; tchg. fellow Harvard U., 1975-78; asst. prof. history U. Mass., Boston, 1978-82, assoc. prof. history, 1982-96, prof. history, 1996—. Author: Richmond After the War, 1865-1890, 1981, Exile in Richmond: The Confederate Journal of Henri Garidel, 2001, The Journal of a Civil War Surgeon, 2003; co-author: Effective State Standards for U.S. History, 2003. Served to capt. USNR, 1969-2005, ret. Fellow Mass. Hist. Soc.; mem. Am. Hist. Assn., So. Hist. Assn., Va. Hist. Assn., Orgn. Am. Historians, Mil. Hist. Soc. Mass., Naval Res. Assn., Res. Officer Assn., Fleet Res. Assn., Navy League. Clubs: Wardroom Club (Boston). Democrat. Office Phone: 617-287-6887. Business E-Mail: michael.chesson@umb.edu.

CHESTER, ALEXANDER CAMPBELL, III, physician; b. NYC, Dec. 21, 1947; s. Alexander C. II and Gladys (Edelhauser) C.; m. Kimberly Robinson Chester, Dec. 20, 1970; children: Kristin Elizabeth, Alexander C. IV. BS cum laude, Georgetown U., 1969; MD, Columbia U., 1973. Diplomate Am. Bd. Internal Medicine, Nat. Bd. Med. Examiners; advanced achievement in internal medicine; voluntary recert., 1998. Intern Georgetown U., Washington, 1973-74, resident in medicine, 1974-76, clin. fellow in nephrology, 1976-77, rsch. fellow in nephrology, 1977-78, clin. instr. medicine, 1978-80, clin. asst. prof. medicine, 1980-84, clin. assoc. prof. medicine, 1985-89, clin. prof. medicine, 1990—. Govs. com. for coll. affairs ACP, 1980-90; clin. prof. medicine Georgetown U. Med. Ctr.; reviewer Annals of Internal Medicine. Contbr. articles to profl. jours. and publs. Named one of Top Doctors, Washingtonian Mag., 1999, 2002, 05, Area Outstanding Specialists, Checkbook mag., 1998, 2005, Area Outstanding Specialists Checkbook mag., 2002, 05; featured in Consumers' Guide to Top Doctors, editors of Checkbook Mag., 2002, 03. Mem. AAAS, AMA, ACP (gov.'s nominating com.), Am. Soc. Internal Medicine (alt. del. Nat. Meeting 1980), Am. Fedn. Clin. Rsch., Hippocrates-Galen Med. Soc. (sec., treas. 1991-92, pres. 1993-94), Osler Soc. (sec., treas. 1986-88, pres. 1989-90), Nat. Kidney Found. (coun. clin. nephrology, dialysis and tranplantation, profl. adv. bd. 1983-86, program com. ann. kidney symposium 1983-86), N.Y. Acad. Scis., Am. Heart Assn. (coun. kidney 1988-90), Clinico-Pathol. Soc. (pres. 2003—), Am. Rhinologic Soc., Soc. for Study Human Behavior and Evolution, Pavlovian Soc. N.Am., Assn. Medicine and Psychiary, Am. Assn. Chronic Fatigue Syndrome, European Rhinologic Soc., Myalgic Encephalomyelitis Assn. (U.K.), Cosmos Club, Phi Beta Kappa. Achievements include research in nasal reflexes, sick building syndrome and chronic fatigue syndrome. Home: 4618 Laverock Pl NW Washington DC 20007-2544 Office: 3301 New Mexico Ave NW Ste 348 Washington DC 20016-3622 Office Phone: 202-362-4467. Office Fax: 202-362-2303.

CHESTER, JOHN JONAS, lawyer, educator; b. Columbus, Ohio, July 13, 1920; s. John J. and Harriet Bonnadine (Rice) C.; m. Cynthia Johnson, Apr. 18, 1959; children: John, James, Joel, Cecily. AB cum laude, Amherst Coll., Mass., 1942; JD, Yale U., New Haven, Conn., 1948. Bar: Ohio 1948. Ptnr. Chester & Chester, Columbus, 1948-57, Chester & Rose, Columbus, 1958-70, Chester Willcox and Saxbe and predecessor firm, Columbus, 1971—. Spl. counsel Pres. of US, 1974. adj. prof. Ohio State U. Coll. Law. Past bd. dirs. Grant Riverside Meth. Hosps.; past chmn. Doctor's Hosp.; past chmn., bd. dirs. Ohio Health, 2001—; past trustee Doctor's Hosp., Columbus Sch. for Girls, Columbus Acad., Shepherd Hill Hosp., Ohio Hist. Found., Ohio Hist. Soc.; active Ohio Gen. Assembly, 1953-58; dir. emeritus Ohio Health, 2005—; dir. Navy Meml. Found., 2006—. Lt. USNR, 1942-46. Mem. ABA, Ohio State Bar Assn., Columbus Bar Assn., Am. Coll. Trial Lawyers, Columbus Club, Columbus Athletic Club, Rocky Fork Hunt and Country Club. Republican. Episcopalian. Home: 4906 Riverside Dr Columbus OH 43220-2876 Office: Chester Willcox & Saxbe 65 E State St Ste 1000 Columbus OH 43215-3442 Office Phone: 614-221-4000. Business E-Mail: jackchester@cwslaw.com.

CHESTER, ROBERT SIMON GEORGE, lawyer; b. Chelmsford, Essex, Eng., Feb. 11, 1949; arrived in Can., 1971. s. Robert John and Elizabeth Poyitt (Forteath) C.; m. Anna Tharyan, Sept. 18, 1975; 1 child, Rahael Elizabeth Anna. BA, Oxford U., England, 1971, MA, 1979; LLM, Osgoode Hall Law Sch., Toronto, 2003. Bar: Ontario 1982, England and Wales 1988. Vis. lectr. Osgoode Hall Law Sch., Toronto, 1972-74; rsch. staff Ontario Law Reform Commn., Toronto, 1974-77; exec. counsel Dep. Atty. Gen. Ontario, Toronto, 1977-82; counsel policy devel. Ministry Atty. Gen., Ontario, 1982-85; ptnr., dir. rsch. McMillan Binch, Toronto, 1985—2004, ptnr., 1988—2004, Heenan Blaikie LLP, 2004—. Counsel Study on Access to Legal Svcs. by Disabled, Ontario, 1982-83; cons. Royal Commn. on Employment Equity, 1983-84, Royal Commn. on Electoral Reform, 1990-91, Royal Commn. on Aboriginal Peoples, 1992. Author: (with others) Environmental Rights in Canada, 1981, The Quality Pursuit, 1988, ABA Guide to Legal Marketing, 1995, Barristers and Solicitors in Practice, 1998; co-editor: Winning with Computers, 1991, 2d vol., 1993; contbr. articles to profl. jours. V.p., trustee Coll. Law Practice Mgmt.; bd. dirs. Can. Rhodes Scholars Found. Can. Rhodes Found. scholar, 1972; fellow Coll. Law Practice Mgmt. Mem. ABA (chmn. mag. editl. bd., law practice mgmt. sect., chmn. Techshow 1992-93), Can. Bar Assn. (com. legal opinions), Oxford Univ. Soc. (pres. Toronto). Anglican. Home: 41 Walmsley Blvd Toronto ON Canada M4V 1X7 Office: Heenan Blaikie LLP Ste 2600 Royal Bank Plz S Tower 200 Bay St Toronto ON Canada M5J 2J4 Office Phone: 416-643-6905. Office Fax: 866-252-6067. Business E-Mail: schester@heenan.ca.

CHESTER, THOMAS WAYNE, state agency administrator; b. Clarksville, Tenn., July 19, 1950; s. Douglas Bell and Ida Mae Chester; m. Betty Ruth Davis, Feb. 14, 1990; 1 child, Andrew Douglas. BSBA, Austin Peay State U., 1973; MPA, Tenn. State U., 1999. Cert. govt. fin. mgr. Acct. I dept. fin. and adminstrn. State of Tenn., Nashville, 1973-76, acct. II dept. fin. and adminstrn., 1976-79, asst. dir. fiscal affairs dept. gen. svcs., 1979-81, asst. chief fiscal svcs. dept. gen. svcs., 1981-84, dir. of fin. I dept. gen. svcs., 1984-93, dir. fin. III dept. gen. svcs., 1993—. Notary pub. at large, Tenn., 1996—. Treas. Cub Scout Pack #753, Mt. Juliet, Tenn., 1999—; coach Mt. Juliet (Tenn.) Little League Baseball, 1999-2000, 2000—. Mem. Am. Soc. Pub. Adminstrn. (bd. dirs., treas. 1995-97, pres.-elect 1998-2000, pres. 1999-2000), Assn. Records Mgrs. and Adminstrs. (audit com. 1995-96). Presbyterian. Avocation: team sports. Home: 803 Ridgetop Dr Mount Juliet TN 37122-4136

CHESTNUT, COLETTE, broadcast executive; BS, Bucknell U. CPA. Sr. mgr. Price Waterhouse; controller Chiat/Day/Mojo (merger TWBA), NYC, 1992—95; Americas CFO TBWA Worldwide, NYC, 1995—2000; N.Am. CFO J. Walter Thompson Co. (JWT), NYC, 2000—06; exec. v.p., CFO MTV Networks, NYC, 2006—. Office: MTV Networks 1260 Ave of the Americas New York NY 10020 Office Phone: 212-397-6030.

CHESTON, SHEILA CAROL, lawyer; b. Washington, Nov. 5, 1958; d. Theodore C. and Gabrielle Joan (Hellings) C. BA, Dartmouth Coll., 1980; JD, Columbia U., 1984. Bar: N.Y. 1986, D.C. 1986, U.S. Dist. Ct. D.C. 1987, U.S. Ct. Appeals (D.C. cir.) 1987, U.S. Dist. Ct. (so. and ea. dists.) N.Y. 1989, U.S. Ct. Appeals (2d cir.), U.S. Supreme Ct. 1989. Law clk. to judge U.S. Ct. Appeals for 9th Cir., LA, 1984-85; assoc. Wilmer, Cutler & Pickering, Washington, 1985-92, ptnr., 1992-93; gen. counsel Def. Base Closure and Realignment Commn., 1993; spl. assoc. counsel to Pres. of U.S., 1994; dep. gen. counsel Dept. Air Force, 1993-95, gen. counsel, 1995-98; ptnr. Wilmer, Cutler & Pickering, Washington, 1998—2002; sr. v.p., gen. counsel, sec. BAE Systems, Inc., Rockville, Md., 2002—. Adj. prof. in internat. litig. Georgetown Law Sch., 1991—2003. Mem. ABA, D.C. Bar Assn., Women's Bar Assn., Am. Bar Found., Am. Soc. Internat. Law, Coun. on Fgn. Rels. Democrat. Episcopalian. Office: BAE Systems Inc 1601 Research Blvd Rockville MD 20850-3173 E-mail: sheila.cheston@baesystems.com.

CHETIN, HELEN CAMPBELL, writer; b. Chgo., July 6, 1922; d. Guy Edward Campbell and Helen May Collins; m. Adnan K. Chetin, May 1945 (div. 1980); children: Timur Claude, Sara Ruth. BS, U. Tex., Austin, 1945. Author: Tales From an African Drum, 1970, Perihan's Promise, 1973, 1992, How Far is Berkeley?, 1977, Lady of Strawberries, 1978, Angel Island Prisoner, 1982, Chambers of the Heart, 1990, Handles to an Ax, 1999; editor: New Seed Press, 1972—97, The Wild Iris, 1973—79. Mem.: Calif. Writers Assn., U. Calif. Berkeley Alumni, Turkish Edn. Found. Independent. Home: 1663 Euclid Ave Berkeley CA 94709-1213

CHEUNG, MIN REX, medical educator; BS in Biology, Columbia U., NYC, 1992, MD, 1996, PhD, 1997. Diplomate Am. Bd. of Radiology, 2003. Asst. prof. U. Tex. MD Anderson Cancer Ctr., Houston, 2002—07, reviewer instnl. rev. bd. Mem. exam writing task force Am. Bd. Radiology, 2005—07. Reviewer Internat. Jour. Radiation Oncology, Biology and Physics, Jour. Applied Clin. Med. Physics; contbr. articles to profl. jours. Recipient Drs. William Nastuk, Beatrice Seegal, and Conrad Hsu award, Coll. Physicians and Surgeons, Columbia U., 1997, Holman Rsch. Pathway award, Am. Bd. Radiology, 2000, Resident/Fellow Rsch. award, RSNA, 2001, Merit award, Am. Soc. Clin. Oncology, 2001. Mem.: AMA, Am. Assn. Cancer Rsch., Am. Soc. Therapeutic Radiology and Oncology. Office: U Tex MD Anderson Cancer Ctr 1515 Holcombe Blvd Houston TX 77030 Office Phone: 713-563-2329. Office Fax: 713-563-6940. Business E-Mail: mrcheung@mdanderson.org.

CHEUNG, SHERI T., lawyer; b. Gardena, Calif., Jan. 28, 1973; BA, Smith Coll., 1994; JD, Univ. So. Calif., 1997. Bar: Calif. 1997, US Dist. Ct. Ctrl. Calif., US Dist. Ct. So. Calif., US Ct. Appeals Ninth Cir. Assoc., intellectual property, labor & employment litigation Hogan & Hartson LLP, LA. Named a Rising Star, So. Calif. Super Lawyers, 2005—06. Office: Hogan & Hartson LLP Ste 1400 1199 Ave of the Stars Los Angeles CA 90067 Office Phone: 310-785-4600. Office Fax: 310-785-4601. Business E-Mail: stcheung@hhlaw.com.

CHEUNG, YIN-WONG, economics professor; b. Macao, June 11, 1957; s. Kai-Ming Cheung and Oi Chan; m. TikLing D. Wong, Oct. 31, 1956; children: Ivy N., Vincent W. B of Social Scis., U. Hong Kong, 1980; MA in Econs. with distinction, U. Essex, Eng., 1984; PhD, U. Pa., Phila., 1990. Fgn. exch. dealer Bank Tokyo, Hong Kong, 1980—83; prof. econs. U. Calif., Santa Cruz, 1990—. Guest prof. Shandong U., Jinan, China, 2004—. Co-author (with Y.H. Liu and W.C. Lo): An Introduction to Financial Options (in Chinese); contbr. articles to profl. jours.; editor: Multinational Fin. Jour., 2001—, Pacific Econ. Rev., 2003—, Internat. Jour. Applied Econs., 2004—; assoc. editor: Applied Fin. Econs., 1999—, Internat. Econ. Jour., 2005—, Economie Internat., 2006—; Jour. Econs.

and Mgmt., 2006—; assoc. editor Pacific Basin Fin. Jour., 2006—. Recipient Lawrence Robbin's Econs. prize, U. Pa., 1986; fellow, 1985—86, 1986—87, 1988—89; Hiram C. Haney fellow, 1989. Mem.: Chinese Econ. Assn. N.Am. (life; v.p. 2001—02, pres. 2007). Office: Economics Dept University of California 1156 High Street Santa Cruz CA 95064 Home Phone: 831-459-4247; Office Phone: 831-459-4247. Business E-Mail: cheung@ucsc.edu.

CHEVALIER, DENISE ANN, director; b. Houston, May 4, 1978; d. James Donald and Adline Ann Chevalier. BA in Acctg., U. Miss., University, 2000; BBA in Mgmt., U. Houston Downtown, 2003; MS in Edn., Capella U., Mpls., 2004, post grad. in Edn., 2005—. Fin. aid advisor, Houston, 2001—03, C.C., Kingwood, 2003—04; dir. of fin. aid Proprietary Sch., Houston, 2004—05, tchr., 2005—. Mem.: NAACP, Am. Women In Univs., Tex. Assn. Fin. Aid Adminstrs., So. Poverty Law Ctr., Delta Sigma Theta. Roman Catholic. Home Phone: 281-852-8478. Personal E-mail: denise1913@hotmail.com.

CHEVALIER, JUDITH A., economics professor, finance professor; BA Distinction in the major Economics (summa cum laude), Yale U., 1989; PhD in Economics, MIT, 1993. Asst. prof. economics, dept. economics Harvard U., 1993—94; asst. prof. economics, grad. sch. bus. U. Chgo., 1994—97, assoc. prof. economics, grad. sch. bus., 1997—99, prof. economics, grad. sch. bus., 1999—2001; prof. economics and finance Yale Sch. Mgmt., 2001—. Faculty rsch. fellow Nat. Bur. Econ. Rsch., 1993—99, rsch. assoc., 1999—; bd. mem., com. on the Status of Women in Economics Profession Am. Econ. Assn., 2002—04; fellow, Davenport Coll. Yale U., 2002—. Assoc. editor Rand Journal of Economics, 1996—2004, Journal of Industrial Economics, 1997—2004, Review of Financial Studies, 1999—2002, Quarterly Journal of Economics, 1999—2003, Journal of Economic Perspectives, 1999—2003, Journal Finance, 2000—04 (Smith Breeden Disting. Paper prize, 1995, nominated paper, Smith Breeden prize, 1999), Review of Financial Studies, 1999—2002, adv. bd. Quantitative Marketing and Economics, 2002—, adv. editor, 2003—; editor: The B.E. Journals in Econ. Analysis and Policy, 2003—04; assoc. editor American Economic Review, 2001—02, co-editor, 2004—; contbr. articles to profl. jours. Recipient Elaine Bennett prize, Am. Econ. Assn., 1999; Sloan Rsch. Fellow, Alfred P. Sloan Found., 1997—99, NSF Grad. Fellowship, 1989—92, NSF rsch. grant, 1994—96. Fellow: Am. Acad. Arts & Sciences. Office: Yale Sch Mgmt 135 Prospect St New Haven CT 06520 also: Horchow Hall 55 Hillhouse Ave New Haven CT 06520 Office Phone: 203-432-3122. Business E-Mail: judith.chevalier@yale.edu.

CHEVALIER, PAUL EDWARD, retired retail executive, lawyer; b. NYC, Jan. 30, 1939; s. Arthur and Grace (Eaton) C.; 1 child, Marc. BA, Columbia U., 1960, LLB, MBA, Columbia U., 1966; AMP, Harvard U., 1979. Bar: Ill. 1968, U.S. Supreme Ct. 1974. Dir. labor rels. Carter Hawley Hale Stores, Inc., LA, 1972-74, v.p. employee rels., 1974-86, sr. v.p. employee rels., 1986-93; pres. Chevalier Cons. Group, 1993-98. Vice chmn. We. Fed. Credit Union, 1989-93; bd. dirs., exec. com. Sedona Cultural Park, 2000—04; chmn. emeritus Jonathan Art Found. Past pres., bd. dirs. Calif. Employment Law Coun.; chmn. Art and Culture Commn., City of Sedona, 1999-2003; bd. dirs. Ariz. Humanities Coun., 2002-04; mem. Harvard Bus. Sch. Alumni Coun., 1989-92; mem. adv. coun. Verde Valley United Way, 2006—. Lt. USN, 1960-66. Mem. Nat. Retail Fedn. (chmn. employee rels. com. 1979-82), Calif. Retail Assn., Harvard Bus. Sch. Assn. (bd. dirs. 1980-90, pres. 1984-85). Personal E-mail: westwinds3@aol.com.

CHEVALIER, ROGER ALAN, astronomy educator, consultant; b. Rome, Sept. 26, 1949; came to US, 1962; s. Frank Charles and Marion Helen (Janhke) C.; m. Margaret Mary With, July 27, 1974.; children: Chase Arthur, Max Toussaint. BS in Astronomy, Calif. Inst. Tech., 1970; PhD in Astronomy (Woodrow Wilson and NSF fellow), Princeton U., 1973. Asst. astronomer Kitt Peak Nat. Obs., Tucson, 1973-76, assoc. astronomer, 1976-79; assoc. prof. astronomy U. Va., Charlottesville, 1979-85, prof. astronomy, chmn. dept., 1985-92, W.H. Vanderbilt prof. astronomy, 1990—; dir. Leander McCormick Obs., 1985-92. Cons. Lawrence Livermore Nat. Lab., Livermore, Calif., 1981-90; bd. trustees U. Space Rsch. Assn., 2000-06. Contbr. numerous rsch. articles to Astrophys. Jour., other astronomy and physics jours. Recipient Heineman prize for astrophysics Am. Astron. Soc./Am. Inst. Physics, 1996; named Va. Outstanding Scientist, Sci. Mus. Va., 1991; Woodrow Wilson Found. fellow Princeton U., 1970-71, NSF fellow, 1970-73; elected to Nat. Acad. Scis., 1996. Mem. NAS, Am. Astron. Soc. (councilor 1988-91), Internat. Astron. Union, Ill. Sci. Lectr. Assn. (v.p. 1975-85), US Nat. Com. for Internat. Astron. Union (vice chair 2005-). Home: 1891 Westview Rd Charlottesville VA 22903-1632 Office: U Va Dept Astronomy PO Box 400325 Charlottesville VA 22904-4325

CHEVALIER, TRACY ROSE, writer; b. Washington, Oct. 1962; BA, Oberlin Coll., 1984; MA, U. East Anglia, 1994. Reference book editor, London, 1988—93; freelance editor, 1994—97. Author: The Virgin Blue, 1997, Girl with a Pearl Earring, 1999, Falling Angels, 2001, The Lady and the Unicorn, 2003; editor: Twentieth-Century Children's Writers, 3d edit., 1989, Contemporary Poets, 5th edit., 1991, Contemporary World Writers, 1993, Encyclopedia of the Essay, 1997. Office: c/o Jonny Geller Curtis Brown Haymarket House 28/29 Haymarket London SW1Y 4SP England

CHEVIGNY, PAUL GRAVES, law educator; b. Seattle, July 12, 1935; s. Hector and Claire (Graves) C.; m. Bell Gale, July 24, 1964; children: Katy, Blue. BA magna cum laude, Yale U., 1957; LLB, Harvard U., 1960. Bar: NY 1961, US Dist. Ct. So. Dist. NY 1963, US Ct. Appeals 5th Cir. 1964, US Ct. Appeals 2nd Cir. 1969, US Supreme Ct. 1972. Assoc. Hughes Hubbard & Reed, NYC, 1961—64; dir. Harlem Neighborhood Legal Assistance, 1965-66; mem. legal staff NY Civil Liberties Union, 1966-77; assoc. prof. NYU Sch. Law, 1977—81, prof., 1981—, Joel S. and Anne B. Ehrenkranz prof. law. Author: Police Power: Police Abuses in New York City, 1969, Cops & Rebels, 1972, Criminal Mischief, 1977, More Speech: Dialogue Rights & Modern Liberty, 1988, Gigs: Jazz and the Cabaret Laws in New York City, 1991, Edge of the Knife: Police Violence in the Americas, 1995. Served US Army, 1960—61. Mem. ABA, Assn. Am. Law Schools. Avocation: jazz music. Office: NYU Sch Law Vanderbilt Hall Rm 419 40 Washington Sq S New York NY 10012-1099 Office Phone: 212-998-6249. E-mail: chevigny@turing.law.nyu.edu.

CHEVINS, ANTHONY CHARLES, retired advertising agency executive; b. Frackville, Pa., Apr. 1, 1921; s. Charles A. and Mary (Swade) C.; m. Margaret Macy, Sept. 18, 1948; children: Cheryl L., Christopher M., Cynthia M. AB in Eng. and Advt. magna cum laude, Syracuse U., 1947; postgrad., Columbia U., 1948-49. Writer Batten, Barton, Durstine & Osborn (advt.), 1948-51; with Cunningham & Walsh, 1951-87, sr. v.p., 1959-61, creative dir., 1958-61, exec. v.p., 1961-68, pres., chief operating officer, 1968-84, chmn., chief exec. officer, 1984-87, The C&W Group Inc., 1985-87; vice chmn. N.W Ayer Inc., 1987-90, also bd. dirs. Contbr. articles to mags. Mem. Nat. Advt. Rev. Bd.; mem. dean's adv. coun. Newhouse Sch.; bd. dirs. Medic Alert Found. Internat. Served to lt. USNR, 1941-45. Mem. Phi Beta Kappa, Alpha Delta Sigma. Clubs: Sky, Union League (N.Y.C.); Woodway Country (Darien, Conn.); Nat. Golf Links Am. (Southampton, L.I.); Ocean Reef, Card Sound (Key Largo, Fla.).

CHEVIS, CHERYL ANN, lawyer; b. Ann Arbor, Mich., Nov. 9, 1947; d. Peter Paul and Antoinette (Slapinski) C.; m. Edwin Mahaffey Gerow, Nov. 18, 1976. BA, U. Wash., 1969, MA, 1974; postgrad. in Sanskrit, U. Chgo., 1974-77, JD, 1980. Bar: Ill. 1980, U.S. Dist. Ct. (no. dist.) Ill. 1980, U.S. Ct. Appeals (7th cir.) 1982, U.S. Tax Ct. 1982, Oreg. 1986. Tax assoc. Sidley and Austin, Chgo., 1979-80, Mayer Brown and Platt, Chgo., 1981-85; sr. tax atty. Perkins Coie, Portland, 1985-87, tax ptnr., 1987-99; assoc. gen. counsel Portland Gen. Electric, 1999—. Mem. faculty Ill. Continuing Legal Edn., Chgo., 1982; vis. lectr. U. B.C., Vancouver, Can., 1983; lectr. Chgo. Tax Club, 1983, Oreg. Securities Lawyers Bar, Bend, 1986, Internat. Employers Seminar, Portland, 1991. Contbr. articles to Jour. Taxation. Vol. atty. Com. Civil Rights Under Law, Chgo., 1982-85; exec. com., chair devel. com. Portland State U. Found.; exec. com., treas. Friends of Chamber Music; coun. mem. Oreg. Coun. for the Humanities. Grantee, Smithsonian Inst., 1981. Mem. ABA (tax sect., com. capital recovery and leasing), Oreg. State Bar (sister-bar com. with Lithuanian Lawyers Assn. 1997—). Avocations: music, theater, outdoor sports. Office: Portland Gen Electric 121 SW Salmon St Portland OR 97204-3713 Home: Apt 2504 1414 SW 3rd Ave Portland OR 97201-6625 Office Phone: 503-464-7193.

CHEVLI, LYN, writer; b. New Haven, Dec. 24, 1931; d. Arthur Reginald Keith and Elizabeth Weston MacBrayne; m. Narendrakumar Aditram Chevli (div.); children: Neela, Shanta. BS in Art, Skidmore Coll., 1953. Designer, colorist Seneca Textiles, NYC, 1953—54; former mag. columnist Orange County Blade, Calif.; silversmith, sculptor Festival of Arts, Laguna Beach, Calif., 1964—72; bookstore owner Farhenheit 451, Laguna Beach, 1968—72; pub., writer, artist Nannygoat Publs., Laguna Beach, 1971—79; pub., writer, owner Parkhurst Press, Laguna Beach, 1980—90; freelance writer. Spkr. various colls. and univs. Author: Alida: An Erotic Novel, 1981; co-artist, writer, pub. (comics) Pandora's Box, Abortion Eve, 1972—80; Exhibited in group shows at Internat. Mus. Erotic Art, San Francisco. Co-founder, organizer, birth control, abortion counselor Laguna Beach Free Clinic, 1970—71; mem. Alliance for Survival. Green Party. Avocations: gardening, walking, cooking, recycling. Home and Office: PO Box 143 Laguna Beach CA 92652 Office Phone: 949-499-1032.

CHEVLI, RENATE NAREN, gynecologist, obstetrician; b. Hannover, Germany, 1937; d. Johann and Martha (Bruns) Schmidt; m. Naren A. Chevli, Sept. 18, 1965. MD, SUNY, Syracuse, 1971. Diplomate Am. Bd. Ob-Gyn. Intern St. Joseph's Hosp., Syracuse, 1971-72; resident in ob-gyn. SUNY Upstate Med. Ctr., Syracuse, 1972-76; pvt. practice Syracuse, 1976—. Fellow: ACOG; mem.: AMA, Onondaga County Med. Soc., N.Am. Menopause Soc., Med. Soc. NY State. Office: The Womens Place 4117 Medical Center Drive Fayetteville NY 13066 Office Phone: 315-329-4968.

CHEVRAY, PIERRE M., medical educator; s. René and Keiko Chevray; m. Keiko Yamaguchi, 1992; children: Kenji, Yukiko. BS, Mass. Inst. Tech., 1987; MD, PhD, Johns Hopkins U. Sch. Medicine, 1994. Cert. Am. Bd. Plastic Surgery, MD Tex., Md. Resident gen. surgery John Hopkins Hosp., 1994—98, resident plastic surgery, 1998—2000; asst. to assoc. prof. U. Tex. M.D. Anderson Cancer Ctr., Houston, 2000—; clin. asst. to clin. assoc. prof. Baylor Coll. Medicine, Houston, 2000—. Mem.: AMA, AAAS, Am. Assn. Plastic Surgeons, Am. Soc. Reconstructive Microsurgery, Am. Soc. Plastic Surgeons. Office: U Tex MD Anderson Cancer Ctr 1515 Holcombe Blvd Unit 443 Houston TX 77030 Office Phone: 713-794-1247. Office Fax: 713-794-5492. Business E-Mail: pchevray@mdanderson.org.

CHEVRAY, RENE, engineering educator; b. Paris, Feb. 6, 1937; came to the U.S., 1962; naturalized U.S. citizen, 1989; s. Robert and Marie-Louise (Fracher) C.; m. Keiko Uesawa, Aug. 9, 1964; children: Pierre-Yves Masaki, Veronique Mie. BS, U. Toulouse, France, 1962; Dipl. Ing. (French Govt. Highest scholar), Ecole Nationale Supérieure d'Electronique, d'Electrotechnique et d'Hydraulique de Toulouse, 1962; MS (Alliance Française of N.Y. fellow), U. Iowa, 1963, PhD, 1967; D.Sc., U. Claude Bernard, Lyon, France, 1978. Product and mfg. engr. Centrifugal Pumps Worthington, Paris, 1963-64; research assoc. Iowa Inst. Hydraulic Research, Iowa City, 1964-67; postdoctoral fellow, lectr. aeronautics Johns Hopkins U., 1967-69; asst. prof. SUNY, Stony Brook, 1969-72, assoc. prof., 1972-79, prof., 1979-82; prof. dept. mech. engring. Columbia U., NYC, 1982-87, chmn. dept. mech. engring., 1987-90. Cons. physics of fluids and instrumentation; vis. prof. Japan Soc. for Promotion Sci., 1975; vis. prof., von. Humboldt fellow U. Karlsruhe, 1975-76 Author: Topics in Fluid Mechanics, 1993; contbr. articles to profl. jours.; rschr. in transport processes in fluids. Recipient Great Tchr. award Soc. Columbia Grads., 1993; Fulbright scholar, 1962-63; grantee NSF, 1970-73, 73-91, Dept. Energy, 1979-89, Office Naval Rsch., 1985-90, Whitaker Found., 1995—; Rsch. Found. SUNY Faculty Rsch. fellow, 1970-71. Mem. Internat. Assn. Hydraulic Rsch., Am. Phys. Soc., N.Y. Acad. Scis., Sigma Xi Home: 300 Riverside Dr Apt 10A New York NY 10025-5239 Office: Columbia U Mech Enging New York NY 10027

CHEW, GEOFFREY FOUCAR, physicist; b. Wash., June 5, 1924; s. Arthur Percy and Pauline Lisette (Foucar) C.; m. Ruth Wright, June 10, 1945 (dec. Apr. 1971); children— Berkeley, Beverly; m. Denyse Odette Mettel, Dec. 30, 1971; children— Pierre-Yves, Jean-Francois, Pauline BS in Physics, George Washington U., 1944; PhD in Physics, U. Chgo., 1948. Research physicist Los Alamos Sci. Lab., N.Mex., 1944-46; research physicist Lawrence Berkeley Lab., Calif., 1948-49; asst. prof. physics U. Calif., Berkeley, 1949-50; asst. prof., assoc. prof. physics U. Ill., Urbana, 1950-56; prof. physics U. Calif., Berkeley, 1957—, chmn. dept. physics, 1974-78, Miller prof., 1981-82, dean physical scis., 1986-92. Group leader theoretical physics Lawrence Berkeley Lab., Calif., 1964-83; vis. prof. Princeton U., N.J., 1970-71; sci. assoc. CERN, Geneva, 1978-79; vis. prof. U. Paris, 1983. Author: S-Matrix Theory of Strong Interactions, 1961; Analytic S Matrix, 1966; contbr. articles to profl. jours. Chmn. passport com. Fedn. Am. Scientists, Washington, 1951-56 Recipient E.O. Lawrence award AEC, 1969, Disting. Alumni award George Washington U., 1974, Berkeley citation U. Calif., 1991; Churchill Coll. overseas fellow, 1962 Fellow Am. Phys. Soc. (Hughes prize 1962); mem. Nat. Acad. Scis., Am. Acad. Arts and Scis. Home: 10 Maybeck Twin Dr Berkeley CA 94708-2037 Business E-Mail: gfchew@sbcglobal.net.

CHEW, KEITH ELVIN, health facility administrator; b. Webb City, Mo., Jan. 1, 1957; s. David Elvin and Melinda Lou (Barker) C. BS in Physiology with distinction, U. Ill., 1979, MS in Biol. Sci., 1981, postgrad., 1981-83; MA in Health Svc. Adminstrn., Sangamon State U., Springfield, Ill., 1986. Instr. Sangamon State U., 1985-86; program dir. So. Ill. U. Sch. Medicine, Springfield, 1984-86; dir. bus. and clin. affairs Tex. Tech Health Sci. Ctr., Lubbock, 1986-88; cons. Profl. Cons. Svcs., Long Grove, Ill., 1988-90; adminstr. Primary Care Family Ctr., Libertyville, Ill., 1988-90; instr. Coll. St. Francis, Joliet, Ill., 1991; adminstr. North Suburban Clinic, Skokie, Ill., 1990-91; cons. KEC Healthcare Mgmt. Cons., Forest Lake, Ill., 1991-92; dir. practice mgmt. Contemporary Mgmt. Assocs., Inc., Portsmouth, NH, 1992-95; exec. dir. Network, Health Mgmt. Ltd. Partnership-Drs. Hosp., Springfield, 1995-96, v.p., 1996-97; CEO Imaging Radiologists, MSO, Inc., Springfield and Chgo, 1998—2006, Imaging Radiologists, LLC, Springfield and Chgo., 2000—02; prin. Vinculum Cons., LLC, 1998—2006; sr. cons. McKesson Corp. (formerly Per-Se Technologies), 2006—. Author: reports and articles. Mem. Am. Coll. Med. Group Adminstrs. (cert. med. practice exec. 1994), Med. Group Mgmt. Assn., Healthcare Fin. Mgmt. Assn., Chgo. Health Exec. Forum. Avocations: music (aural and vocal), golf, fishing, aviation, gardening. Home: 18 Hawks Nest Chatham IL 62629-2016 Home Phone: 217-483-6467; Office Phone: 217-483-6467. E-mail: kechew@springnet1.com, kchew@vinculumconsulting.com.

CHEW, RON ALPHA, museum director; b. Seattle, May 17, 1953; s. Soo Hong and Gam Har (Wee) C.; m. Loan Thi Nguyen. Attended, U. Wash., 1971—75, degree, 2002. Editor Internat. Examiner, Seattle, 1977-80, 81-88; exec. dir. McKenzie River Gathering Found., Seattle, 1980-81; multicultural program coord. Seattle Cen. C.C., 1988-89; confidential sec. Commn. in Asian Am. Affairs, Seattle, 1989-91; exec. dir. Wing Luke Asian Mus., Seattle, 1991—. Coord. Chinese Oral History Project, Seattle, 1990; pres. Nat Coun. on Humanities, 2001. Bd. dirs. Chinese Info. and Svc. Ctr., Seattle, 1991, Inter-Im Cmty. Devel. Assn., Seattle, 1979; adv. bd. Northwest Nikkei Newspaper, 1989; pub. com. Kin On Chinese Nursing Home, 1987; publ. bd. Seattle Cen. C.C., 1990; cmty. media adv. coun. Amerasia Jour., 1988-89; publ. adv. com. Neighborhood House, Seattle, 1988. David Douglas fellow Wash. Hist. Soc., 1993; named to Hall of Fame, Dept. Communication, U. Wash.; recipient Leadership for a Changing World award, Ford Found., 2004. Mem. Internat. Dist. Econ. Assn. (cmty. svc. award 1988), Western Mus. Assn. (Dirs. Chair award 2004), Wash. Mus. Assn. (instnl. excellence award 1993), Assn. King County Hist. Orgns. (outstanding exhibit award 1993), Asian Am. Journalist Assn. (co-founder Seattle chpt., treas. 1985-89), Northwest Minority Publishers Assn. (co-founder, sec. 1987-88). Avocations: research of chinese american history, seattle's chinatown. Office: Wing Luke Asian Mus 407 7th Ave S Seattle WA 98104-2948*

CHEW, RUSSELL G. (RUSS), air transportation executive; b. LA; Attended, Stanford U.; doctorate, U. So. Calif. Various positions including mng. dir. Am. Airlines, 1986—2003; COO Fed. Aviation Adminstrn., 2003—07, JetBlue Airways Corp., 2007—. Served as chmn. air traffic control steering com., Air Transp. Assn., flight ops. com., Internat. Air Transp. Assn. Office: JetBlue Airways Corp 118-29 Queens Blvd Forest Hills NY 11375 Office Phone: 718-286-7900. Office Fax: 718-709-3621.*

CHEWNING, THOMAS N., energy executive; m. Nancy Jones; 2 children. B in History, U. NC, 1967; MBA, U. Pa., 1969. CEO Air Van Lines, Inc., Seattle; v.p. adminstrn. Dominion Capital, v.p. and treas. Dominion Lands Dominion (formerly Dominion Resources, Inc.), Richmond, Va., 1987—88, asst. treas., 1988—91, v.p., treas. Va. Power, 1991—92, v.p., 1992—94, treas. Dominion Energy, 1992—94, pres., CEO Dominion Energy subs., 1994—99, exec. v.p., CFO, 1999—, Consol. Natural Gas Co., 2000—. Bd. dirs. U. NC Gen. Alumni Assn. Named Co-Richmonder of Yr., Richmond's Style Mag. Office: Dominion PO Box 26532 Richmond VA 23261-6532 Office Phone: 804-771-3884. Office Fax: 804-273-4271.*

CHEY, WILLIAM D, physician, researcher; s. Fan and William Y Chey; m. Janine Zwiren, Nov. 26, 1960; children: Samuel William, Russell David, Josephine Julianna. MD, Emory U. Sch. Medicine, 1986. Intern and resident in internal medicine Emory U. Sch. Medicine, Atlanta, 1986—89; fellow in gastroenterology U. Mich., Ann Arbor, 1990—93, faculty mem., 1993—; dir. gi physiology lab. U. Mich. Health Sys., Ann Arbor, 1993—. Mem. Rome Found. Functional Gi Disorders, 2004—. Named one of The Best Doctors in Am., 2001—. Fellow: Am. Gastroent. Assn. (chair clin. practice sect. 2006—), Am. Coll. Gastroenterology, Am. Coll. Physicians; mem.: Am. Soc. Gastrointestinal Endoscopy (corr.), Internat. Found. Functional GI Disorders (corr.; adv. bd. mem. 2005—06). Office: U Mich Health System 3912 Taubman Ctr Ann Arbor MI 48109-0362 Home Phone: 734-936-4775; Office Phone: 734-936-4775. Business E-Mail: wchey@umich.edu.

CHEY, WILLIAM YOON, physician; b. Ki Jang, Korea, Jan. 21, 1930; s. Kee Bok and Myungkwon (Lee) C.; m. Fan K. Tang, May 21, 1959; children: William D., Donna C., Richard D., Laura C. MD, Seoul Nat. U., Korea, 1953; MSc, U. Pa., 1962, DSc, 1966. Intern NYC Hosp., 1954-55, resident, 1955-56; resident in pathology Mount Sinai Hosp., NYC, 1956-57; fellow in hepatology Seton Hall Med Coll., Jersey City, 1957-58; practice medicine specializing in gastroenterology Phila., 1967-71; attending physician Temple U. Med Center, Phila., 1963—; rsch. fellow in gastroenterology Samuel S. Fels Rsch. Inst., 1959-60; rsch. assoc. Samuel S. Fells Rsch. Inst., 1961, instr. medicine, 1961, assoc., 1963, asst. prof., 1965-68, assoc. prof., 1968-71; prof. medicine U. Rochester, NY, 1971-77, NY, 1988—2000, clin. prof. NY, 1977-88; sr. attending physician, founding dir. Isaac Gordon Ctr. for Digestive Diseases and Nutrition, The Genesee Hosp., 1971-91; dir. divsn. gastroenterology and hepatology U. Rochester Sch. Medicine and Dentistry, 1992-2000; physician Strong Meml. Hosp., Rochester, 1992-2000; founding dir. William B. and Sheila Konar Ctr. for Digestive Liver Disease, Rochester, 1995—2000. Dir. Rochester Inst. Digestive Diseases and Scis., NY, 2000—; cons. gastroenterologist Canadaigua VA Hosp., Canadagiua, 1977—; emeritus prof. Cath. U. Med. Coll., Seoul, Republic of Korea, 1983—86; clin. prof. medicine Yunsei U. Sch. Medicine, 1984—86; vis. prof. Peking Union Med. Coll., Chinese Acad. Med. Scis., Beijing, 1985—, Hallym U. Coll. Medicine, Choonchun, Republic of Korea, 1986—, Shanghai Med. U., 1987, Korea U. Coll. Medicine, Seoul, 1991—; mem. surgery and bioengring. study sect. Nat. Inst. Diaetes, Digestive and Kidney Diseases, NIH, Bethesda, Md., 1982—86. Contbr. articles to profl. and sci. jours and textbooks; mem. editorial bd. The Pancreas, Am. Jour. Physiology. Fellow Am. Coll. Gastroent., Am. Gastroent. Assn. (Disting. Clinician award 2004, Mentors Rsch. award 2007); mem. AAAS, Am. Fedn. Clin. Rsch., Am. Physiol. Soc., Am. Assn. Study Liver Disease, Am. Pancreatic Assn. (pres. 1999-2000), Internat. Assn. Pancreatology, Am. Motility Soc., Am. Soc. Gastrointestinal Endoscopy, Am. Soc. Acupuncture, Am. Coll. Acupuncture, Sigma Xi. Home: 133 Crescent Hill Rd Pittsford NY 14534-2406 Office: 222 Alexander St Ste 3100 Rochester NY 14607 Office Phone: 585-325-2390. Business E-Mail: williamchey@ridds.org.

CHI, DAVID H., otolaryngologist; b. Seoul, Republic of Korea, Mar. 9, 1971; s. Young and Kyung Chi; m. Catherine Chi, Sept. 25, 1999; children: Ethan, Connor. BS, U. Mich., Ann Arbor, 1993, MD, 1997. Resident U. Va., Charlottesville, 1997—2002; fellow Chilren's Hosp. Pitts., 2002—04; asst. prof. U. Pitts. Med. Sch., 2004—. Adv. bd. mem. DePaul Sch. Hearing and Speech, Pitts., 2005—. Mem.: Am Acad. Otolaryngology, Phi Beta Kappa. Office: Children's Hosp Pitts 3705 Fifth Ave Pittsburgh PA 15213 Office Phone: 412-692-5466. Business E-Mail: david.chi@chp.edu.

CHI, JE GEUN, retired pathologist; b. Seoul, Republic of Korea, Feb. 25, 1938; Kyu Hyock and Chung Wha (Lee) C.; m. Mina Lee, May 8, 1965; children: Yong-suk, Yong-seung. MD, Seoul Nat. U., 1962, MS, 1964, PhD, 1968. Lic. physician, Korea, U.S.A.; anatomical pathology specialist diplomat, Korea, U.S.A., neuropathology specialist diplomat, U.S.A. Resident Seoul Nat. U. Hosp., 1962-67; instr. pathology Seoul Nat. U., 1969-70; resident Boston Children's Hosp., Boston, 1970-71, 73-75, Beth Israel Hosp., Boston, 1971-73; instr. pathology Seoul Nat. U., 1969-70; lectr. neuropathology Harvard Med. Sch., Boston, 1975-76; head pathology dept. Seoul Nat. U. Children's Hosp., 1985—2003; prof., chmn. dept. pathology Seoul Nat. U. Coll. Medicine, 1992-96; prof. emeritus, 2003—; v.p. Korean Acad. Sci. and Tech., 2000—04. Author: Diagnostic Ultrastructural Neuropathology, 1991, Sequential Atlas of Human Development, 1992, Diagnostic Ultrastructural Pathology, 1992, Color Atlas of Pathology, 1998, Atlas of Human Embryo and Fetus, 2001; editor Jour. Korean Med. Sci., 1987-93, Seoul Jour. Medicine, 1994-95. Recipient Best Paper award, Dongshin-Smith Kline, Seoul, 1985, Med. Achievement award, Nat. Acad. Scis., Korea, 1992. Fellow: Third World Acad. Sci.; mem.: Nat. Acad. Medicine Korea (pres. 2004—06), Korean Soc. Teratology (pres. 1998—), Korean Soc. Med. Genetics (pres. 1997—99), N.Y. Acad. Scis., Korean Acad. Med. Scis. (pres. 1999—2003), Korean Acad. Sci. and Tech. (v.p. 2001—04), Korean Soc. Pathologists (pres. 1996—97). Home: Hanyang Apt 22-203 Apkujong-dong Kangnam-gu Seoul 135 906 Republic of Korea Office: Seoul Nat U Coll Med 28 Yongon-dong Chongno-gu Seoul 110-744 Republic of Korea Personal E-mail: chi3802@hotmail.com.

CHI, KEON SOO, editor, educator, researcher; b. Taegu, Korea, Nov. 26, 1936; came to U.S., 1965; s. Chong-Yun Chi and Pun-Sun Kim; m. Insoon Chi; children: Ronald, John. BA, Yonsei U., 1959; MA, Claremont U., Calif., 1968, PhD, 1970. Prof. polit. sci. Georgetown (Ky.) Coll., 1970—; sr. fellow Coun. of State Govts., Lexington, 1981—, academic dean, 1999—2001, editor jour. of state govt., 2000—; editor-in-chief The book of the State, 2001—. Contbr. chpts. to books and articles to profl. jours. Recipient Ky. Prof. of Yr. Carnegie Found., 1999; recipient James E. Webb award Am. Soc. for Pub. Adminstrn., 1996. Democrat. Presbyterian. Avocations: reading, travel, painting. Home: 3641 Gloucester Dr Lexington KY 40510 Office: Coun State Govts PO Box 11910 Lexington KY 40578

CHIA, DAVID THIEN-SHING, internist, gastroenterologist; b. Sandakan, Malaysia, Mar. 24, 1942; came to U.S., 1966; s. Kiam Vun Chia and Su Lan Lo; m. Gloria Chia; children: Timothy Than-Han, Catherine Loo Ling. MD, Nat. Def. Med. Ctr., Taipei, Taiwan, 1996. Diplomate Am. Bd. Internal Medicine, Am. Bd. Gastroenterology. Rotating intern Resurrection Hosp., Chgo., 1966-67; resident in internal medicine and gastroenterology Bklyn. VA Hosp. and Downstate Med. Ctr., 1967-71; chief divsn. gastroenterology Phelps Meml. Hosp., Sleepy Hollow, N.Y., 1989-99; pvt. practice Sleepy Hollow, N.Y. Asst. prof. medicine N.Y. Med. Coll., N.Y.C., 1975. Fellow ACP, Am. Coll. Gastroenterology. Lutheran. Avocations: asian antiques, mountain bicycling. Office: 777 N Broadway Ste 305 Sleepy Hollow NY 10591-1040

CHIANG, ALBERT CHINFA, polymer chemist; b. Pai-ho, Tainan, Taiwan, Jan. 3, 1946; came to U.S., 1973; s. Long and Ping (Su) C.; m. Geraldine Chin, June 4, 1978; 1 child, Scott Jinlong. BS, Nat. Chung-Hsing U., Taichung, Taiwan, 1970; MS, Georgetown U., DC, 1977; PhD, Am. U., DC, 1980. Teaching asst. Georgetown U., Washington, 1974-77, Am. U., Washington, 1977-80; assoc. chemist Pitney Bowes, Stamford, Conn., 1980-81, chemist, 1982-83, staff chemist, 1984-86, sr. chemist, 1987-89, tech. advisor, 1989-92; v.p. R&D Mearthane Products, Cranston, RI, 1992—. Mem. Chinese Oversea Scholar, Taipei, Taiwan, 1980—. Mem. adv. bd. Am. Security Coun., Washington, 1984. Dissertation fellow Am. U., 1979. Mem. Am. Chem. Soc. (rubber divsn. 1987—), Soc. Plastics Engring. (sr.), Photography of Sci. and Engring. Achievements include development of thermostat urethanes for pneumatic nail bumper application; medical grade urethane and silicone for medical applications; toner for office machine application; in-line skate, hockey wheels, skate board wheel, indoor and outdoor speed wheels; live action skate wheels having a breaking mechanism; multiple-layer skate wheels and various track hockey wheels; processes for preparation of polypheynlacetylene and desulphurization of coal; invention of materials for electrophotographic toners, high solid content emulsion formation, fluorescent thermal transfer ribbon formation, and new dual-step thermal transfer printing; development and production of laser printer rollers including charge roller, developer roller, toner pick-up roller, and paper transport roller; research in rubber, photopolymers, thermal printing, silicone casting, and polyurethane manufacturing; conducting polymers including conductive urethane, conductive silicone, acrylate, highly conjugated rubber and plastics, and high temperature superconducting material formation; non-impact printing technology and printing materials for postage meter and other mailing system machines; patents in field. Home: 10 Fox Hollow Ledyard CT 06339 Office Phone: 401-946-4400. Business E-Mail: achiang@mearthane.com.

CHIANG, CHIA-CHU, computer scientist, educator; b. Nan-Tou, Taiwan, Apr. 11, 1959; s. Yi-Ting Chiang and Chin-Nun Liao; m. Jung-Yung Wang; children: Robert, Michael, Jennifer. BBA, Soochow U., Taipei, Taiwan, 1981; MS, Ea. Mich. U., 1988; PhD, Ariz. State U., 1995. Software engr. ASG Co. (formerly Viasoft), Phoenix, 1996—2001; asst. prof. U. Ark., Little Rock, 2001—. Spkr. in field. Contbr. articles to profl. jours. 2d lt. Taiwanese Army, 1981—83, Taiwan. Recipient Outrageous Contbr. award, Viasoft Co., 1998, Excellence in Tchg. award, 16th Ann. Cyber Coll. Faculty, 2004. Mem.: ACM, IEEE, Upsilon Pi Epsilon, Tau Beta Pi, Phi Kappa Phi. Avocations: jogging, swimming, reading, travel. Office: University of Arkansas at Little Rock 2801 South University Ave Little Rock AR 72204-1099 Office Phone: 501-569-8142. Business E-Mail: cxchiang@ualr.edu.

CHIANG, FU-PEN, mechanical engineering educator, researcher; b. Oct. 10, 1936; s. Chien-lo and Lien-yin C.; m. Jin-lin Li; children: Ted, Michelle, Winston, Peter. BSCE, Nat. Taiwan U., 1953-57; MS, U. Fla., 1963, PhD in Engring. Sci. and Mechanics, 1966. Civil engr., 1958-62; asst. prof. mech. engring. SUNY, Stony Brook, NY, 1967-70, assoc. prof., 1970—74, prof., 1970—87, lead prof., 1987—2003, dir. Lab. for Exptl. Mechanics Rsch., 1984—, chmn., 1994—, SUNY Disting. prof., 2003—. Vis. prof. Swiss Fed. Inst. Tech., Lausanne, 1973-74; sr. vis. fellow dept. physics Cavendish Lab., U. Cambridge, Eng., 1980-81, Nat. Taiwan U., 1990-91; cons. Army Material and Mechanics Research Ctr., Army Missile Command, Grumann Aerospace Corp., Electric Boat Corp., and others. Editor: Internat. Jour. Optics and Lasers in Engring., 1987-93; assoc. editor Jour. Exptl. Mechs., 1972-74, Jour. Engring. Materials and Tech., 1997-99; guest editor Jour. Optical Engring, 1982, 88; contbr. articles to profl. jours. Recipient B. J. Lazan award, 1993; postdoctoral fellow Cath. U. Am.; NSF grantee, 1968-73, 76-87, 96—, Office of Naval Rsch. grantee, 1982-99, 2003—, Army Rsch. Office grantee, 1988-91, 95-96, Air Force of Sci. Rsch. grantee, 1993-98, 2003-06, NIH, 2002-04. Fellow Soc. Exptl. Mechanics, Optical Soc. Am.; mem. AAAS, ASME, Soc. Photo-Optical Instrumentation Engrs., Am. Acad. Mechanics, Soc. Mfg. Engring., Am. Soc. Engring. Edn. Research on development of optical experimental mechanics technique such as laser speckles techniques, holographic interferometry, white light speckle techniques, moire methods, photoelasticity, electron speckle photography and their applications to solid mechanics, nondestructuve evalutaion and biomechanics problems. Office: SUNY Dept Mech Stony Brook NY 11794-0001 Office Phone: 631-632-8311. Business E-Mail: fu-pen.chiang@stonybrook.edu.

CHIANG, I-TING, engineering educator; US, 2002; s. Hong-Chang Chiang. BSEE, Nat. Taiwan U., Taipei, 1996, PhD, 2002. Elec. engring., Nat. Taiwan U. Postdoctoral rsch. assoc. U. Ill., Urbana, 2002—06; r&d engr. Lorentz Solutions, Inc., Silicon Valley, Calif., 2006—. Mem.: IEEE (assoc.). Achievements include research in computational electromagnetics and fast convolution algorithm. Avocations: major league baseball, aviation technology, travel. Home Phone: 217-721-4317.

CHIANG, JOHN YOUNG LING, biochemistry professor, researcher; b. Hangchew, CheKiang, China, July 29, 1947; came to U.S., 1970, naturalized, 1980; s. Ming-ming and Ya-Jung (Huang) C.; m. Lisa H. Kang, Aug. 3, 1973; children— Eric, David. B.S., Chung-Hsing U., Taichung, Taiwan, 1969; M.S., SUNY-Albany, 1973, Ph.D., 1976. Postdoctoral scholar U. Mich. Med. Sch., Ann Arbor, 1976-78; asst. prof. biochemistry and molecular pathology Northeastern Ohio U. Coll. Medicine, Rootstown, 1978-83, assoc. prof., 1983-88, prof., 1988—. Contbr. articles to profl. jours. NIH fellow, 1977-78; Pharm. Mfrs. Assn. Found. grantee, 1982-83; Am. Heart Assn. grantee, 1980-82; NIH grantee, 1983—. Mem. AAAS, Am. Soc. Biol. Chemists, Am. Assn. for Study Liver Disease, Am. Soc. Pharmacology and Experimental Therapeutics, Endocrine Soc. Subspecialty: Biochemistry (medicine), Molecular biology. Current work: Biochemical research in studying the induction and regulation of enzymes involved in cholesterol and bile acid metabolism and liver detoxication enzymes. Home: 3020 Fox Burrow Dr Stow OH 44224-4778 Office: Northeastern Ohio U Coll of Medicine 4209 State Route 44 Rootstown OH 44272 Office Phone: 330-325-6694. Business E-Mail: jchiang@neoucom.edu.

CHIANG, MICHAEL FRED, physician; b. Pitts., Aug. 6, 1970; BS, Stanford U., 1991; MD, Harvard U., 1996. Resident in ophthalmology Johns Hopkins Hosp., 1997—2000, fellow pediat. ophthalmology, 2000—01; asst. prof., ophthalmology and biomed. informatics Columbia U., NYC, 2003—. Office Phone: 212-305-9535.

CHIANG, MUNG, engineering educator, consultant; b. Tianjin, China, Feb. 2, 1977; arrived in US, 1996, naturalized, 2002; s. Chi Tung Chiang and Man Ching Lau; m. Ying Kei Hui. PhD, Stanford U., Calif., 2003. Prof. Princeton U., Princeton, NJ, 2003—. Lead guest editor of spl. issue on nonlinear optimization of communication systems IEEE Jour. of Selected Areas in Comm., NJ. Co-editor: Control and Optimization of Com. Sys.; contbr. articles to profl. jours. Recipient CAREER award, NSF, 2004, Howard B. Wentz Jr. Faculty award, Princeton U., 2005, Young Investigator award, ONR, 2007, TR35 award, Tech. Review Mag.; fellow Grad. fellow, Hertz Found., 1999—2003. Mem.: IEEE (assoc. editor of Trans. Wireless Commn., spkr., guest editor Trans. Info. Theory and Trans. Networking). Achievements include invention of optimization algorithms for communication networks; patents for evolable network design tool; research in FAST Copper Project on fiber and DSL broadband access networks; generalized network utility maximization, network architectures, and 'Layering as Optimization Decomposition'decomposition'; Network X-ities Project; algorithms in Internet traffic engineering and wireless network power control; geometric programming for communication systems. Office Phone: 609-258-5071.

CHIANG, TOM, medical educator, researcher; b. Taipei, Taiwan, Dec. 30, 1970; BS, Boston U., MD, 2002. Asst. prof. medicine NJ Med. Sch., Newark, 2005—. Achievements include research in mechanisms of antibiotic resistance in gram negative bacteria. Home: 10 Depot Sq #1F Montclair NJ 07042 Office: Va Njhcs 385 Tremont Ave 111-ID East Orange NJ 07018 Home Phone: 973-744-3375; Office Phone: 973-676-1000 1383. Personal E-mail: tchiang@pol.net.

CHIANG, TZE I., economist, researcher, consultant; b. Fuzhou, Fujian, China, Feb. 4, 1922; arrived in U.S., 1953; s. Swe-hwa and Wan-lun Chiang; m. Wei-chih Chou Chiang, Feb. 4, 1952 (dec. 1999); children: Chi, Ling, Ding. BA in Agrl. Econs., Fujian Christin U., Fuzhou, 1946; MS in Agrl. Econs., Okla. State U., 1955; PhD in Agrl. Econs., U. Fla., 1958. Tchr. Sin-Ding H.S., Fuzhou, 1946—47; asst. to gen. mgr. China Textile Industries, Inc., Shanghai, 1947—53; grad. asst. Okla. State U., Stillwater, 1954—55; rsch. asst. U. Fla., Gainesville, 1955—58; prin. rsch. scientist Ga. Inst. Tech., Atlanta, 1958—86. Advisor Qingdao (China) Spl. Econ. Zone, China, 1986; vis. scholar to scholar Ga. Inst. Tech., Atlanta, 1986; cons. tech. transfer China Tech., Atlanta, 1986—87. Contbr. articles to profl. jours. Mem.: Gamma Sigma Delta. Achievements include research in economic feasibility; market analysis; economic and industrial development; international trade. Avocations: reading, music, gardening. Home: 3165 Frontenac Ct NE Atlanta GA 30319

CHIANG, WEN-CHYUAN, operations management educator; s. Zong-Chung and Chen-Lun Chiang. Grad., Nat. Taiwan Normal U.; PhD, U. Tex., Austin. Prof. U. Tulsa. Editor: Internat. Jour. Revenue Mgmt.; sr. editor: Prodn. Ops. Mgmt. E-mail: wen-chiang@utulsa.edu.

CHIANG, YUNG FRANK, law educator; b. Taichung, Taiwan, Jan. 2, 1936; came to U.S., 1961; s. Ruey-ting and Yueh-yin (Ho) C.; m. Quay-yin Lin, Nov. 1, 1969; children: Amy P., David H. LLB, Nat. Taiwan U., 1958; LLM, Northwestern U., 1962; JD, U. Chgo., 1965. Bar: Taiwan 1960, N.Y. 1974. Assoc. Yen & Lai Law Office, Taipei, Taiwan, 1960-61; editor The Lawyers Co-op Pub. Co., Rochester, NY, 1965; rsch. assoc. Harvard Law Sch., Cambridge, Mass., 1965-67; asst. prof. U. Ga. Sch. Law, Athens, 1967-72; assoc. prof. Fordham U. Sch. Law, NYC, 1972-76, prof., 1976—. Vis. prof. Chuo U., Tokyo, 2005; bd. dirs. Taiwan Ctr., N.Y.C.; legal cons., vice-chmn. Asia Bank, N.A., Flushing, N.Y., 1983-88, also bd. dirs.; leader N.Y. judge and lawyers del. to China and Hong Kong, People to People Internat., 1994; organizer, moderator 5 Russian delegations to U.S., People to People Amb. Program, 1994-95; pres. Fordham U. Law Faculty Union, 2000—. Contbr. articles to profl. jours. Organizer, bd. dirs. The Taiwan Mcht. Assn. N.Y., Flushing, 1976-96, pres., 1980-84; pres. N.Y. chpt. Formosan Assn. for Pub. Affairs, Washington, 1991-92. Recipient 20th Century Achievement award, Internat. Biographical Ctr., Eng., 1995. Mem. N.Y. State Bar Assn., N.Am. Taiwanese Profs. Assn. (bd. dirs. 1994-2000, v.p. 1997-98, pres. 1998-99), Nat. Assn. of Securities Dealers (arbitrator 1976-98), Order of Coif. Avocations: reading, skiing, archery, swimming. Office: Fordham U Sch Law 140 W 62nd St New York NY 10023-7407 Office Phone: 212-636-6835. Business E-Mail: fchiang@law.fordham.edu.

CHIAO, LEROY, astronaut; b. Milw., Wis., Aug. 28, 1960; s. Tsu Tao and Cherry (Chu) Chiao; m. Karen Chiao, 2003. BS in Chemical Engring., U. Calif., Berkeley, 1983; MS, U. Calif., Santa Barbara, 1985, PhD in Chemical Engring., 1987. Postdoctoral researcher U. Calif., Santa Barbara, 1987; materials engr. Hexcel Corp., Dublin, Calif., 1987-89, Lawrence Livermore (Calif.) Nat. Lab., 1989-90; astronaut NASA, Houston, 1990—. Keynote commencement spkr. Dept. Engring., U. Calif., Berkeley, 1996, Santa Barbara, 96; lectr. Beijing Inst. Aeronautical Materials, 1988, Changsha Inst. Tech., 5th Dept., Peoples Republic of China, 1988; mission specialist STS-65, 1994, STS-72, 1996, STS-92, 2000. Contbr. Internat. Encyclopedia Composite Materials, 1989. Recipient NASA Space Flight medal, 1994, 1996, 2000, NASA Exceptional Svc. award, 1996, 2000, NASA Individual Achievement award, 2001, 2002, 2003, 2004, NASA Group Achievement award, 1995, 1997, NASA Going the Extra Mile award, 2004, Komarov Diploma, Fedn. Aeronautique Internationale, 1996, De La Vaulx medal, 1994, Korolev Diploma, 2002, Excellence award in Sci. and Tech., US Pan Asian Am. C. of C., 2003, 100 Most Influential Asian Americans in the 1990's award, A-Magazine, 2000. Mem. ASTM, AIAA, Soc. Advancement Material and Process Engring. Broke a nearly 30 year tradition of having at least one crewman with previous experience in piloting the capsule. Comdr. and NASA Sci. Officer of Expedition-10 headed for the International Space Station with Russian-US crew (with Salizhan Sharipov and Yuri Shargin) in the Soyuz TMA-5 on October, 2004, landed in April, 2005 (with Salizhan Sharipov and Roberto Vittori). First Asian-Am. to perform a spacewalk. First Am. to vote in presidential election while in space, 2004. Office: NASA-JSC 2101 NASA Rd 1 Houston TX 77058-3691

CHIARA, MARGARET MARY, former prosecutor, lawyer; b. 1943; BA, Fordham U.; MA in Edn. Adminstrn., Pace U.; JD, Rutgers U., 1979. Assoc. French and Lawrence, Cassopolis, Mich., 1979—82; prosecuting atty. Cass County Prosecutor's Office, 1982—96; adminstr. Trial Ct. Assessment Commn., 1997—98; policy and planning dir. Office of Chief Justice of Mich. Supreme Ct., 1999—2001; US atty. (we. dist.) Mich. US Dept. Justice, 2001—07.*

CHIARAMIDA, SALVATORE, cardiologist, educator, health facility administrator; b. NYC, Sept. 15, 1948; s. Joseph and Dina (DiBlasi) C.; m. Susan Postula, June 14, 1970; children: Todd, Tory. BS in Chemistry, Fordham Coll., 1970; MD, N.Y. Med. Coll., 1974. Diplomate Am. Bd. Internal Medicine, Am. Bd. Cardiovasc. Diseases. Intern North Shore U. Meml. Hosp., 1974-75, asst. resident in internal medicine, 1975-76, sr. resident in internal medicine, 1976-77, fellow in cardiology, 1977-79; fellow in medicine Cornell U. Med. Coll., 1975-77; chief cardiology Raritan Bay Med. Ctr., 1979-89, Our Lady of Mercy Med. Ctr., Bronx, NY, 1989—2000, assoc. dir. medicine, 1999—2000, COO, 1999, exec. v.p. clin. ops., 1999; dir. coronary care unit Med. Univ. S.C., Charleston, 2000—, prof. medicine, 2000—. Instr. cardiology North Shore U. Hosp., 1977-79; clin. instr. medicine U. Medicine and Dentistry N.J., 1981-83, clin. asst. prof., 1983; clin. assoc. prof. N.Y. Med. Coll., 1990—99, prof. clin. medicine, 1999-2002; cons. Woodbridge (N.J.) Devel. Ctr., 1989; v.p., trustee Mercy Care PHO, 1994-2000; bd. dirs. Cath. Health Care Network, Cath. Health Care Network Physicians Orgn., Servitas IPA, Cath. Health-care Resources LLC, Benefice Health LLC, Cath. Health Care Sys.; prof. medicine Med. U. S.C., 2000—, dir. CCU, 2001—. Contbr. articles to profl. jours. Fellow: ACP, Am. Coll. Cardiology. Office: Med Univ SC Heart Ctr Divsn Cardiology 135 Rutledge Ave Ste 1201 PO Box 250592 Charleston SC 29464 Office Phone: 843-792-4457. Business E-Mail: chiara@musc.edu.

CHIARAMONTE, CHRISTINE LOREN, elementary school educator; b. Westwood, NJ, Sept. 26, 1979; d. Paul Thomas and Lois Gloria Chiaramonte. BS, Seton Hall U., 2001; MA, Montclair State U., 2005. Teacher of Handicapped Elementary, Reading Specialist. After sch. tchr. Elmwood Pk. Recreation, Elmwood Pk., NJ, 2001—; tchr. handicapped Hasbrough Heights Bd. Edn., NJ, 2001—05; tchr. Paramus Bd. Edn., NJ, 2005—, Elmwood Park Summer Day Camp, 2001—. Tutor Hasbrouck Heights and Paramus Bd. Edn., 2001—; adv. Student Coun., Hasbrough Heights, 2004—05, Respect Com., Paramus, 2005—. Sunday sch. tchr. Grace Luth. Ch., River Edge, NJ, 2001—, lector, usher, 2001—. Mem.: Internat. Reading Assn., NJ Edn. Assn., Alpha Epilson Lambda, Kappa Delta Pi. Avocations: softball, exercise, antiques, running.

CHIARCHIARO, FRANK JOHN, lawyer; b. Sept. 11, 1945; s. Joseph Russell and Mary Catherine (Salmieri) C.; m. Judith Ann Penna, July 5, 1970; 1 child, Peter. BEE, Manhattan Coll., 1967; MSEE, NYU, 1970; JD, Bklyn. Law Sch., 1976. Bar: N.Y. 1977, U.S. Dist. Ct. (ea. and so. dists.) N.Y. 1977, U.S. Ct. Appeals (11th cir.) 1985, U.S. Ct. Appeals (4th cir.) 1989, U.S. Ct. Appeals (5th cir.) 1991, U.S. Supreme Ct. 1987. Engr. USN, Bklyn., 1968-72, USCG, NYC, 1972-77; ptnr. Mendes & Mount, LLP., NYC, 1977—. Contbr. articles to profl. jours. Decorated knight comdr. with star Order of Holy Sepulchre of Jerusalem. Mem. N.Y. State Bar Assn., Def. Rsch. Inst. Roman Catholic. Office: Mendes & Mount 750 7th Ave New York NY 10019-6834 Office Phone: 212-261-8278. Business E-Mail: frank.chiarchiaro@mendes.com.

CHIARELLA, PETER RALPH, vintner; b. Bklyn., Dec. 6, 1932; s. C. Ralph and Catherine (Zinzi) C.; m. Frances M. Crane, Oct. 10, 1953; children: Ralph, Thomas, John, Karen. BBA, St. John's U., 1957. C.P.A., N.Y. Sr. accountant Peat, Marwick, Mitchell & Co., NYC, 1957—61; asst. controller Bonwit Teller, NYC, 1961—62; accounting mgr. plastics div. Celanese Corp., Newark, 1963—67; v.p., controller Clairol, Inc., NYC, 1967—72; pres., dir. Kleinert's, Inc., Kutztown, Pa., 1972—77; v.p., corp. controller United Brands Co., NYC, 1977—79; sr. v.p., chief fin. officer Max Factor & Co., Hollywood, Calif., 1979—83; sr. v.p. fin. and adminstrn. Syncor Internat., Sylmar, Calif., 1983—85; exec. v.p. Doctors' Co., Napa, Calif., 1985—92; pres. Cakebread Cellars, Inc., Rutherford, Calif., 1992—97; pres., CEO Crane Family Vineyards, Napa, 1999—. Mem. budget com. United Fund, Stamford, Conn., 1970; bd. dirs. Vis. Nurse Assn., L.A., 1983-90, Napa Valley Opera House, 1991-96, Napa Valley Coll. Found., 1991-99, Cakebread Cellars, Inc., Rutherford, 1992-2004; Napa Valley Fair Bd., 1994-2000, Napa Physicians IPA Bd., 1999-2001, Pacific Vision Found., 2001—06. With USN, 1952-54. Mem. AICPA, Fin. Execs. Inst., Delta Mu Delta. Home: 1051 Borrette Ln Napa CA 94558-9702 Office Phone: 707-259-0175. E-mail: peter@cranefamilyvineyards.com.

CHIARELLI, PETER, professional sports team executive; m. Alicia Chiarelli; children: Talia, Cameron. BA, Harvard U., 1987; LLB, U. Ottawa. Bar: Ontario, Can. 1993. Atty., player agent Kelly Mgmt. Group Inc., 1995—99; dir. legal rels. Ottawa Senators, 1999—2004, asst. gen. mgr., 2004—06; gen. mgr. Boston Bruins, 2006—. Office: Boston Bruins TD Banknorth Garden 100 Legends Way Boston MA 02114 Office Phone: 617-624-1900.

CHIARELLI, PETER W., career military officer; b. Seattle, Mar. 23, 1950; m. Beth Kirby; children: Peter, Erin, Patrick. BSc, Seattle U., 1972; MPA, U. Wash.; MA in Nat. Security Studies, Salv U.; graduate, Nat. War Coll. Commd. 2d. lt. U.S. Army, 1972, advanced through grades to lt. gen., 2005; various assignments Fort Lewis, Wash., 1972-75, 89-90, A Troop 3d. Squadron 5th Cavalry, 1975-80; assoc. prof. U.S. Military Acad., West Point, NY, 1980-84; stationed at Fed. Rep. Germany, 1985-89; comdr. 2d. Battalion 1st Infantry Regiment, 1990-92; stationed at Fort Hood, Tex., 1993-95; various assignments III Corps, 1995-96; comdr. 3d. Brigade 2d. Infantry Divsn., 1996-98; exec. officer Supreme Allied Comdr. Europe, 1998—; dir. ops., readiness, & mobilization, Office Dep. Chief of Staff, G-3 U.S. Army, Washington; commdg. gen. 1st Cavalry Divsn., Ft. Hood, Tex., 2003—06; comdr. Multi-Nat. Corps-Operation Iraqi Freedom, Baghdad, Iraq, 2006; spl. asst. to comdr. US Ctrl. Command, 2006—07; sr. mil. asst. to sec. US Dept. Def., Washington, 2007—. Decorated Legion of Merit with one oak leaf cluster, Meritorious Svc. medal with four oak leaf clusters. Office: US Dept Def 1000 Defense Pentagon Washington DC 20301*

CHIARELLI, ROBERT CHARLES, audio engineer; b. Mass., Jan. 13, 1963; s. Carmello Charles C.; m. Theresa Pauline; children: Robert Michael, Angela Maria. Student, U. Miami. CEO 3.6 Music, LA. Mixer albums for Will Smith, Christina Aguilera, Madonna, Ricky Martin, Temptations, Michael Bolton, Janet Jackson. Bd. dirs. Great Leap, Santa Monica, Calif. Mem. Am. Fedn. Musicians, Nat. Acad. Arts & Scis. Office: Final Mix Inc 2219 W Olive Ave Ste 102 Burbank CA 91506-2625

CHIARELLO, MICHAEL, chef; b. Red Bluff, Calif., 1962; Grad., Culinary Inst. Am., 1982; BA in Hospitality Mgmt., Fla. Internat. U., 1984. Founder The Grand Bay Hotel, Coconut Grove, Fla., 1985; owner, exec. chef Toby's Bar and Grill; founder, exec. chef Tra Vigne restaurant, Napa Valley, Tomatina, Napa Valley, Caffe Museo, San Francisco, Ajax Tavern, Aspen, Bump's, Aspen, Bistecca, Scottsdale, Ariz. Founder NapaStyle products, Consorzio product line. Host (TV series) Season by Season, PBS, 2000, Michael Chiarello's Napa, 2001, Michael Chiarello's Napa: Casual Cooking, 2002, NapaStyle, Easy Entertaining with Michael Chiarello, Food Network; author: Flavored Oils and Flavored Vinegars, 1995, Tra Vigne Cookbook, 1999, Napa Stories, 2001, Michael Chiarello's Casual Cooking, 2002. Named Chef of Yr., Food and Wine Mag., 1985, Culinary Inst. of Am., 1995. Office: NapaStyle 574 Gateway Dr Napa CA 94558

CHIARENZA, CARL, art historian, critic, artist, educator; b. Rochester, NY, Sept. 5, 1935; s. Charles and Mary Rose (Russo) C.; m. Heidi Faith Katz, Aug. 13, 1978; children: Suzanne Mari, Jonah Katz, Gabriella Christine. B.F.A., Rochester Inst. Tech., 1957; MS, Boston U., 1959; MA, 1964; PhD, Harvard U., 1972. Lectr. Boston U., 1963-64, instr. dept. fine arts, 1964-68, asst. prof., 1968-72, univ. prof., 1972-73, assoc. prof., 1973-80, prof. dept. art history, 1980-86, acting chmn. dept. art history, 1973-74, chmn. dept. art history, 1976-81; Fanny Knapp Allen prof. U. Rochester, NY, 1986-98, acting chmn. dept. art history NY, 1986-87, prof. emeritus, artist-in-residence, 1998—. Adj. vis. prof. Visual Studies Workshop, SUNY, 1972-73; vis. prof. Cornell U., 1991; Harnish vis. artist Smith Coll., 1983-84; vis. artist/scholar, U. Ga., Athens, 2002; artists adv. panel Artists Found., Boston, 1977-81; guest curator Inst. Contemporary Art, Boston, 1980-81; cons. Nat. Endowment for Arts, 1978-80, mem. Artists' Fellowships panel, 1982; bd. dirs. Photographic Resource Ctr.; trustee Visual Studies Workshop; lectr. in field. One-man shows include George

Eastman House, 1995, Southeast Mus. of Photography, 1995, Rochester (NY) Inst. Tech., 1996, The Witkin Gallery, NYC, 1996, Kennedy Ctr. Gallery, Hiram Coll., 1997, High Mus. Art, Atlanta, 1997, U. Iowa Mus. Art, 1997, Stephen Cohen Gallery, LA, 1999, Robert Klein Gallery, Boston, 1999, Spectrum Gallery, Rochester, 1999, 2002, Troyer Gallery, Washington, 1999, Alan Klotz/Photocollect, NYC, 2000, U. RI, 2003, U. Rochester, 2003, Carl Solway Gallery, Cin., Ohio, 2004—05, Ctr. Photographic Arts, Carmel, Calif., 2005, Ryerson Gallery, Toronto, C an., 2006, Studio Hart, Buffalo, 2007, others, numerous group shows including most recently, exhibited in group shows at Fitchburg Art Mus., 2001, DeCordova Mus. and Sculpture Pk., Lincoln, Mass., 2001, Boise (Idaho) Art Mus., 2001, Kiyosato (Japan) Mus. Photographic Arts, 2001, Adirondack C.C., 2001, Amon Carter Mus., Ft. Worth, Tex., 2002, Visual Studies Workshop Gallery, 2002, others, Represented in permanent collections LA County Mus. Art, Nat. Mus. Am. Art, Washington, Phila. Mus. Art, Mus. Modern Art, NYC, J. Paul Getty Mus., LA, Art Inst. Chgo., Cleve. Mus. Art, Mpls. Inst. Arts, Mus. Fine Arts, Boston, Houston, San Francisco Mus. Modern Art, Amon Carter Mus., Ft. Worth, others; author: Aaron Siskind: Pleasures and Terrors, 1982, Landscapes of the Mind, 1988, Evocations, 2002, The Peace Warriors of 2003, 2005, Solitudes, 2005, Interaction: Verbal/Visual, 2006; contbr. more than 185 articles to profl. jours. Served with U.S. Army, 1960-62. Mass. Art and Humanities Found. fellow, 1975-76; Nat. Endowment for Arts fellow, 1977-78, 90-91; recipient Artist award Arts and Cultural Coun. for Greater Rochester, 1996, Artist-in-Residence award Hiram Coll., 1997, Spl. Opportunity Stipend award N.Y. Found. for the Arts, 1997, Disting. Alumnus of Yr., Rochester Inst. Tech., 1997, Honored Educator award Soc. for Photographic Edn., 1999, Lillian Fairchild Artist award, 1999, Best of Show award Nazareth Coll., 2000, 02, 04 Mem. Soc. Photographic Edn., Assn. Historians Am. Art. Office: U Rochester Morey # 424 Rochester NY 14627 Office Phone: 585-275-9249. Business E-Mail: ccrz@mail.rochester.edu. *I am a switch-hitter. I have always made, written about, or lectured about pictures. Because I seem to do each best when working in a concentrated spurt, I am often torn between these modes of communication. I work intuitively and in a state of agitation until things find their rightful place on a page or in a picture. It is as if I am reaching for a place of equilibrium or understanding as I move through the world from a position of essential ignorance about the meaning of life.*

CHIARENZA, FRANK JOHN, language educator; b. New Britain, Conn., Dec. 10, 1926; s. Sebastian X. and Josephine C. AB, Yale, 1949, PhD in Medieval Lit, 1956; MA in English, Rutgers U., 1950; certificate, Inst. for Ednl. Mgmt.; Sloan Found. grantee, Harvard, 1970. Lectr. English U. Conn., 1954-55; instr. English Hillyer Coll., Hartford, Conn., 1955-57; from asst. prof. to prof. Coll. Arts and Scis., U. Hartford, 1958-67, prof. English, 1978-89, emeritus, 1989, chmn. dept., 1958-67, acad. dean Coll. Arts and Scis., 1967-78. Cons., reader English Coll. Entrance Exam. Bd., 1959—; reader advanced placement tests Ednl. Testing Service, Princeton, N.J., 1961—; chmn. for Conn., Nat. Council Coll. Publs. Advisers, 1966-67; adv. council Career Opportunity Program, 1970—; resource cons. Conn. Commn. for Higher Edn., 1972-73; chief reader Coll. Level Exam. Program, Ednl. Testing Service, N.J., 1978— Author: The Milk Glass Book, 1998; contbr. articles to profl. jours. Corporator Watkinson Sch., West Hartford, Conn.; bd. dirs. Nat. Milk Glass Collectors Soc., 1991—, pres., 1997-99; founder Frank Chiarenza Mus. of Glass, Meriden, Conn. Served with USNR, 1944—46. Fulbright grantee U. Rome, 1953-54. AAUP (pres. Hartford 1962-64), NEA, Am. Assn. Higher Edn., Am. Conf. Acad. Deans, Am. Coun. Edn., Conn. Acad. Arts and Scis., Nat. Milk Glass Collectors Soc. (bd. dirs. 1991—, v.p. 1994—, v.p., chmn. publs. com. 1994—, pres. 1997—), Yale Club. Home: 80 Crestview Dr Newington CT 06111-2405 E-mail: mgmfrank@aol.com.

CHIASSON, WILLIAM B., electronic games executive; BA in Anthropology and Polit. Sci., U. Ariz., 1974; MBA, U. So. Calif., 1976. Various positions to v.p., contr. hospital group Baxter Healthcare, 1979—88; various positions to sr. v.p. fin. and info. sys. Kraft Foods, 1988—98; sr. v.p., CFO Levi Strauss & Co., San Francisco, 1998—2003; CFO LeapFrog Enterprises, 2004—. Mem. AICPA. Office: LeapFrog Enterprises 6401 Hollis St Ste 100 Emeryville CA 94608-1071

CHIATE, KENNETH REED, lawyer; b. Phoenix, June 24, 1941; s. Mac Arthur and Lillian (Lavin) C.; m. Jeannette Jensen, Aug. 21, 1965; children: Gregory Jensen, Carley MaKay. BA with honors, Claremont Men's Coll., 1963; JD, Columbia U., 1966; postgrad., U. So. Calif. Law Sch., 1967. Bar: Calif. 1967, U.S. Dist. Ct. (cen. dist.) Calif. 1967, Ariz. 1971, U.S. Dist. Ct. Ariz. 1971, U.S. Dist. Ct. (no. Dist.) Calif. 1982. Law clk. presiding justice U.S. Dist. Ariz., 1971; ptnr. Lillick McHose & Charles, LA, 1971-91, Pillsbury Winthrop, LLP (formerly Pillsbury Madison), LA, 1991—. Arbitrator Los Angeles Superior Ct. Arbitration Panel, 1979-82; mcpl. ct. judge protem Los Angeles, 1979-81; vice chmn. Los Angeles Open Com., 1969-71. Named among Calif. Lawyers of Yr. 2000, Calif. Mag.; named one of So. Calif. Superlawyers, L.A. Mag., 2004. Mem. ABA, L.A. County Bar Assn., Calif. State Bar Assn., Ariz. State Bar Assn., Maricopa County Bar Assn., Am. Trial Lawyers Assn., L.A. Bus. Trial Lawyers Assn. Office: Quinn Emanuel Urquhart Oliver & Hedges LLP 865 Figueroa St 10th Fl Los Angeles CA 90017 Office Phone: 213-443-3000. E-mail: kenchiate@quinnemanuel.com.

CHIAVERINI, JOHN EDWARD, construction company executive; b. Providence, Feb. 6, 1924; s. John and Sadie (Ginsberg) C.; m. Cecile Corey, Mar. 31, 1951; children: Caryl Marie, John Michael. Cert. in advanced san. engring., U. Ill., 1945; BS in Civil Engring., U. RI, Kingston, 1947. Registered profl. engr., Mass., RI. Project engr. Perini Corp., Hartford, Conn., 1950-51, project mgr., 1951-55, asst. project mgr. Pitts. and Que., 1955-61, v.p. Framingham, Mass., 1965-84, sr. v.p. San Francisco, 1984—; pres., dir. Compania Perini S.A., Colombia, 1961—; v.p., exec. mgr. Perini Yuba Assocs., Marysville, Calif., 1966-70, v.p. Western ops., 1970-78, 79-84, group v.p., 1978-79; sr. v.p. spl. projects Perini Corp., 1984-90, dir., asst. to chmn., 1991—. Mem. U.S. com. Internat. Commn. on Large Dams; bd. dirs. Bldg. Futures Coun., 1990—, vice chmn., 1993, chmn., 1994—; active Civil Engring. Rsch. Found., 1990—, mem. corp. adv. bd., 1992—; mem. Cons. Constructors Coun. Am. Served to 2d lt. USAAF, 1944-46. Recipient Golden Beaver Supervision award San Francisco Bay Area Coun. Boy Scouts Am., 1989, Good Scout award, 1989; named to RI Engring. Hall of Fame, 1997. Fellow ASCE (mem. exec. com. constrn. divsn., vice chmn. 1994-95, chmn. 1995—), Soc. Am. Mil. Engrs. (Acad. of Fellows 1997, pres. San Francisco post 1991-92, bd. dirs.); mem. NSPE (life), Am. Arbitration Assn., Calif. Soc. Profl. Engrs., Dispute Resolution Bd. Found., Beavers (bd. dirs.), Moles, Commonwealth Club of Calif., KC, Rotary (mem. dispute resolution bd. found.), Consulting Constructor's Coun. Am. Republican. Roman Catholic. Home and Office: Perini Corp 37 Dutch Valley Ln San Anselmo CA 94960-1045 Office Phone: 415-454-8251. Personal E-mail: ceejayIII3@comcast.net.

CHIAZZE, LEONARD, JR., biostatistician, epidemiologist, educator; b. Falconer, NY, June 19, 1934; s. Leonard and Jennie (Bondi) C.; m. Ellen Anne Bergman, June 12, 1954; children: Kathleen, Caroline, Michael, Ellen. AA, SUNY, Jamestown, 1953; BS, U. Buffalo, 1955, MBA, 1957; ScD, U. Pitts., 1964. Instr. stats. U. Buffalo, 1955—57; biostatistician Nat. Cancer Inst., Bethesda, Md., 1957—66, acting chief biometry br., 1975—76; asst. prof. Georgetown U. Sch. Medicine, Washington, 1966—69, assoc. prof., 1969—77, prof., 1977—2005, prof. emeritus, 2005—, founder, dir. grad. program in biostats., 1970—94, dir. biostats. and epidemiology divsn., 1966—94, dir. occupl. health studies divsn., 1994—2005. Mem. com. toxicology NAS/NRC, 2000—04; vice chair Georgetown U. Instl. Rev. Bd., Washington; mem. data and safety monitoring bd. Nat. Inst. on Drug Abuse. Contbr. articles to profl. jours. Served with USPHS, 1957-66. Fellow: APHA, Am. Coll. Epidemiology; mem.: Soc. Occupl. and Environ. Health (past pres. governing coun.), Soc. Epidemiologic Rsch., Am. Statis. Assn., Sigma Xi, Beta Gamma Sigma. Home: 11237 Waycross Way Kensington MD 20895-1034 Home Phone: 301-946-4658. E-mail: lchiazze@att.net.

CHIBA, MACHIKO, cooking advisor; Founder Machiko Chiba Cooking Studio, Tokyo, 1988—; tchr., cooking Nippon Club Culture Ctr., NYC; cons. Machiko Cooking USA Inc., NYC. Originator Kikurage Essence Dietary Supplement. Author: (book) Japanese Dishes for Wine Lovers, 2005; author of seven additional cookbooks. Achievements include designer of microwavable dishware. Office: Machiko Chiba Cooking Studio 1 12 1 Nishitutujigaoka Cyofu shi Tokyo 182 0006 Japan also: Machiko Cooking USA Inc 160 W 66th St 22c New York NY 10023 Office Phone: 81 424-40-2311, 212-875-0950. Office Fax: 81 424-40-2315.

CHICCO, GIANFRANCO, healthcare communications executive; b. Maracay, Venezuela, Apr. 9, 1958; came to U.S., 1979; s. Giuseppe and Maria C.; 1 child, Marco Alesandro. BA in Health Scis., Kalamazoo Coll., 1980; MS in Comm., Boston U., 1982. Med. rschr. Biomechanics Lab. of Brigham and Women's Hosp. Harvard Med. Sch., Boston, 1980-82; sr. account supr. Edelman Pub. Rels. Worldwide, NYC, 1982-86; v.p. Ruder-Finn, NYC, 1986-88; sr. v.p., founder health and sci. comm. div. Rowland Worldwide, NYC, 1988-90; exec. v.p., co-dir. healthcare group Burston-Marsteller, NYC, 1990—95; prin., owner Chandler Chicco Agy., NYC, 1995—. Recipient Big Apple award Pub. Rels. Soc. Am., 1988, Creativity in Pub. Rels. award, 1991. Office: 450 W 15th St New York NY 10011-7097 Fax: 212-229-8496.

CHICHILNISKY, GRACIELA, mathematician, economist, educator, writer; b. Buenos Aires, Mar. 27, 1946; arrived in U.S., 1968, naturalized, 1992; d. Salomon Chichilnisky and Raquel Gavensky; children: Eduardo Jose, Natasha Sable. Student, MIT, 1967—68; MA, U. Calif., Berkeley, 1970, PhD in Math., 1971, PhD in Econs., 1976. Postdoctoral fellow Harvard U., 1974, lectr. dept. econs., 1975, fellow Harvard Inst. Internat. Devel., 1978; assoc. prof. Columbia U., NYC, 1977—79, prof., 1980—, dir. Program on Info. and Resources, 1994—, prof. stats., 1996—, dir. Columbia Ctr. for Risk Mgmt., 1998—, UNESCO prof. math. and econs., 1995—. CEO Cross Border Exch. Corp., 1999-2003, chmn. 2003-05; co-chmn. UN Latin Am. Econ. Forum, NY, 2006, 07; advisor UN Assn., 2006; spl. advisor to Pres. Oscar Arias, Costa Rica, 2007; sr. adviser to pres., U. Ariz., 2004—; architect carbon market The Kyoto Protocol of the UN, 1997; mem. presdl. cabinet Banco Ctrl. Republica Argentina, 1971-74; co-prin. investigator Urban Inst., Washington, 1975-77; vis. scholar Internat. Inst. Applied Sys, Analysis Laxenburg, Austria, 1975-77; prin. investigator U.S. Dept. Labor, 1977-78, Rockefeller Found. Project Internat. Rels., 1981-83; project dir. UN Inst. Tng. and Rsch., N.Y., 1979-83; chaired prof. econs. U. Essex, 1980-81; vis. prof. inst. math and its applications U. Minn., 1983-84, U. Siena, Italy, summers, 1991-93, 2002; vis. prof. Stanford Inst. Theoretical Econs., Stanford U., 1991-93, dept. econs., Inst. Internat. Studies, 1993—, vis. prof. depts., econ. and ops. rsch. Stanford U., 1993-94; prof. missionaire U. des Antilles et de la Guyane, 1984-85; NSF prof. dept. math. U. Calif., Berkeley, 1985-86; CEO, chmn. FITEL Ltd., 1985-89; exec. dir. Sci. Internat. Ltd., 1989-90; vis. prof. U. Cath. Buenos Aires, 1993; cons. in field; UNESCO chair in math. and econs., Columbia U., 1995—; Salinbemi chair U. Siena, Italy, 1994-95; spl. adv. World Fedn. UN Assns., 2006; mng. dir. Bizmakers, NY, 2006; sr. adviser Pres. U. Ariz., 2004—, Pres. Costa Rica, 2006-07; sr. rsch. fellow Internat. Monetary Fund, Washington, 2007. Co-author: Catastrophe or New Society? A Latin American World Model, 1976; author: (with G. Heal) The Evolving International Economy, 1986, Oil in the International Economy, 1991, Sustainability: Dynamics and Uncertainty, 1998, Mathematical Economics, 1998, Topology and Markets, 1998, Markets, Information and Uncertainty, 1998, Environmental Markets: Equity and Efficiency, 1999; assoc. editor Jour. Devel. Econs., 1976-86, Advances in Mathematics, 1985, Risk Decision and Policy; mem. various editl. bds.; contbr. articles to profl. jours. Mem. coun. Social Health and Welfare Soc.; bd. trustees Nat. Resources Def. Coun., 1994—. Recipient Internat. Rels. award Rockefeller Found., 1983-84; named Most Disting. Woman Economist, Newcombe Found. and Omega Delta Epsilon, 1991, Leif Johansen award U. Oslo, Norway, 1995, St. Charles, Ill., 2007; named on of 10 Most Influential Latinos in US, Hispanic Bus., 2006—; grantee NSF, 1974—; fellow Ford Found., 1967-69, Banco Ctrl. Republica Argentina, 1972-74, spl. fellow UN Inst. Tng. and Rsch., 1977-76. Mem.: Nat. Women's Studies Assn. (Speaking Out prize 2007). Office: Columbia U Stats Dept 1255 Amsterdam Ave 10th Fl New York NY 10027 Mailing: 335 Riverside Dr New York NY 10025 Office Phone: 212-678-1148. Business E-Mail: chichilisky1@gmail.com.

CHICKERING, HOWARD ALLEN, insurance company executive, lawyer; b. San Francisco, Mar. 21, 1942; s. Allen Lawrence and Caroline Cranford (Rogers) C.; m. Elizabeth Douglas Dalton, June 29, 1968; children: Philip Dalton, Caroline Howe. BS in Econs., U. Pa., 1966; JD, Stanford U., 1971. Bar: Calif. 1972. Assoc. Chickering & Gregory, San Francisco, 1971-76; sr. counsel Itel Corp., San Francisco, 1976-79; v.p., gen. counsel, bd. dirs. Clarendon Ins. Co. (Bermuda) Ltd., NYC, 1979-81; pres. Clarendon Group Svcs. Inc., NYC, 1981-85; exec. v.p., bd. dirs. Clarendon Ins. Group, NYC, 1985-88; founder, pres., chief underwriting officer R.V.I. Guaranty Co., Ltd., Hamilton, Bermuda, 1989—; founder, pres. R.V.I. Am. Ins. Co., Stamford, Conn., 1994—. Spkr. in field. Contbr. articles to profl. publs. Co-author, acting campaign chmn. San Francisco Proposition C (Open Space), 1974; campaign sec. Proposition J (Open Space and Park Renovation), 1974; mem. San Francisco Open Space Citizens Adv. Commn., 1976-78; deacon Stanwich Congregational Ch.; leader, adminstr. Alpha Course on Basic Christianity. Lt. (j.g.) USNR, 1966-68, Vietnam. Mem. State Bar Calif., Soc. Colonial Wars, Soc. Mayflower Descs., Mil. Order Fgn. Wars, Order Founders and Patriots, Racquet and Tennis Club, N.Y. Yacht Club, Belle Haven Club (commodore 1996). Republican. Home: 80 Otter Rock Dr Greenwich CT 06830-7029 Office: RVI Am Ins Co 177 Broad St Ste 9 Stamford CT 06901-5003

CHICO, BEVERLY ANN, history professor, humanities educator; b. Boston, May 14, 1931; d. Theodore Francis and Genevieve Valentine (Mahoney) Berghaus; m. Raymundo J. Chico, July 25, 1959; children: Christian James, Gregory John, Raymund Matthew, Marta Vida. BA, Boston Coll., 1962; MLA, Johns Hopkins U., Balt., 1965, CASLA, 1973; DA, U. No. Colo., Greeley, 1979. Cert. mus. adminstrn. Windale, U. Tex. Assoc. prof. history C.C. Balt., 1965—75; adj. prof. history U. Colo., Denver, 1976—77, 1990—92; adj. history prof. Met. State Coll., Denver, 1976—; program coord. Belmar Mus., Lakewood, Colo., 1983—85; dir. outreach Mizel Mus. Judaica, Denver, 1985—90; adj. history prof. Columbia Coll., Aurora, Colo., 1991—; affiliate/lead history prof. Regis U., Denver, 1991—. Ofcl. observer UN Com. Status Women, Buenos Aires, 1960, Nat. Conf. Women, Houston, 1977; cons. Can. Mus./Civilization, Ottawa, 1994; lectr. in field. Contbr. articles to profl. jours.; exhibitions include Headwear Symbolism in Judaism, Christianity & Islam, Mizel Mus. Judaica, 1986—87. Mem. bd. advisors Mizel Mus., Denver, 2004—. Recipient Foremother award, Colo. Women's Agenda, 1994; grantee, Folger Inst., Washington, 1998; 11 Faculty grants, Regis U., Denver, 1992—2005, vis. profl., Smithsonian Instn., Washington, 1986, inaugural vis. scholar, Columbia Coll., 2000. Mem.: Costume Soc. Am. (bd. dirs. 1999—), Nat. League/Am. Pen Women (pres. Denver 1986—87), Denver Woman's Press Club (pres. Denver 1992—93). Home: 9600 E Grand Ct Greenwood Village CO 80111 E-mail: beverlychico@chicogroup.com.

CHICO, DARLENE EHRICH, elementary school educator; d. Jacques Rene and Denise Anita Richer; m. Leonard Chico, Dec. 21, 2002; children: Rocky James Ehrich, Jason Paul Ehrich, Holly Richer Ehrich. BA in Liberal Arts, Cal Poly U., Pomona, Calif., 1999. Cert. tchr. Calif. State Dept. Edn., 1997. Instrnl. aide Azusa USD, Calif., 1989—97; tchr. St. Mary of Assumption, Whittier, Calif., 1997—99, Don Julian Elem., La Puente, Calif., 1999—. Beginning tchr. support and assessment mentor tchr. Grantee Rsch. grant, Civic Connection, 2005. Mem.: Calif. Assn. for the Gifted (assoc.), Golden Key. Roman Catholic. Avocations: camping, travel. Office: Don Julian Elem Sch 13855 Don Julian Rd La Puente CA 91746 Business E-Mail: dchico@bassett.k12.ca.us.

CHICOINE, DAVID LYLE, academic administrator; b. Elk Point, SD, June 17, 1947; s. Roland and Evelyn (Lyle) C.; m. Marcia Kay Elgie, Mar. 8, 1969; children: Jason, Joshua. BS, S.D. State U., 1969; MS, U. Del., 1971; MA, Western U., 1978; PhD, U. Ill., 1979. Area extension adv. Coop. Extension Service, Urbana, Ill., 1971-77; prof. Inst. Govt. and Pub. Affairs U. Ill., Urbana-Champaign, 1984—, asst. prof. dept. agr. econs., 1979-84, assoc. prof., 1984-87, prof., head Dept. Agrl. Econs., 1988—95, dean Coll. Agrl., Consumer and Environ. Sci., 1995—2001, v.p. tech. and econ. devel., 2001—06, interim v.p. academic affairs, 2006; pres. SD State U., Brookings, 2007—. Mem. Bd. Govs. for Argonne Nat. Lab., U. Chgo. Co-author: Government Structure and Local Public Finance, 1985; co-editor: Financing Rural Infrastructure, 1987, Financing Economic Development, 1987; contbr. more than 100 articles to profl. jours. Recipient Legis. leadership award, Ill. Farm Bur., 1981, research awards/grants several founds. and govt. agys., 1982-88. Mem. Am. Agriculture Econs. Assn., Am. Econs. Assn., Midwest Econs. Assn., Nat. Tax Assn. Office: Office of Pres SD State U Adminstrn Bldg 201 Brookings SD 57007*

CHICOINE, NICOLE, lawyer; b. Portland, Ore., Mar. 7, 1972; BS cum laude, Univ. Ore., 1996; JD, Univ. Wash., 1999. Bar: Wash. 1999. White collar criminal defense atty. Chicoine & Hallett, P.S., Seattle, 1999—. Contbr. articles to numerous profl. jours. Named Seattle Rising Star, SuperLawyer Mag., 2006. Mem.: ABA, Legis. Com. Tax Coun. (chmn. 2005—), Wash. State Bar Assn. Office: Chicoine and Hallett Waterfronmt Pl One Ste 803 1011 Western Ave Seattle WA 98104

CHICOREL, RALPH, librettist, composer, playwright; b. Detroit, Dec. 4, 1930; s. Jacob and Judith (Louza) C.; m. Phyllis Philko, Feb. 3, 1957 (div. 1979); children: Steven Mitchell, Daniel Adam, Jacob; m. Debra Anne Lisch, Jan. 10, 1981; children: Matthew Aaron, Tyler William, Allison Anne. Grad., Am. Acad. Dramatic Arts, 1955. Performer various groups, Detroit, 1948-51; salesman Stein Ellbogen, Detroit, 1953-57; co-owner, entertainer Kenwood Restaurant and Lounge, Detroit, 1957-66; salesman Music Merchants, Detroit, 1966-67; co-owner Weight Watchers of Wis., Inc., Milw., 1968-92, also advt. spokesperson; pres. Chicorel Music Corp., Milw., 1970-92; co-owner Weight Watchers in Hawaii, Honolulu, 1989-91. Pres. Civic Music Assn., Milw., 1990-91. Producer, composer, lyricist 5 albums on Pleasure Records label, 1970-79; composer, lyricist (stage mus., album) Jean, 1973, 85, (CDs) C. Dickens' Great Expectations, 1995, Anna Karenina, 2002; co-composer: (TV) The Engagement Ring, 2005; composer: (song) Milwaukee (premiere performance Milw. Symphony Orch. Feb. 1988); producer Lynn Redgrave and the World of Weight Watchers, The Milw. Auditorium, 1989; contbg. author: Milwaukee: The Best of All Worlds, 1991. Bd. dirs. Congregation Emanuel Bne Jeshurun Brotherhood, Milw., 1984—86, Comedy Sportz Bd., Milw., 1992—, Jazz Unltd., 2005—06. Served with USMC, 1951—53, Korea. Mem. Dramatists Guild, Song Writers Guild Am., ASCAP, Milw. Broadcasters Club. Sephardic. Avocation: collecting recordings of musical shows. Office: N64w14660 Poplar Dr Menomonee Falls WI 53051-5197

CHIDA, JUNAID HASAN, lawyer; b. Lahore, Punjab, Pakistan, June 23, 1956; came to U.S., 1974; s. Noorul Hasan and Nazneen (Mohajir) C.; m. Rakhshan Mahmood, Jan. 16, 1986. BBA cum laude, U. Wis., Eau Claire, 1978, JD cum laude, 1983. Bar: Wis. 1983, N.Y. 1984, U.S. Dist. Ct. (so. dist.) N.Y. 1984, Calif. 1986. Ptnr., chmn. leasing fin. practice group Dewey Ballantine, NYC, 1983—. Mem. Klanwatch project So. Poverty Law Ctr., Montgomery, Ala., 1987. Mem.: Calif. Bar Assn. Muslim. Office: Dewey Ballantine LLP 1301 Ave Of The Americas New York NY 10019-6092 Office Phone: 212-259-6308. Office Fax: 212-259-6333. Business E-Mail: jchida@dbllp.com.

CHIDGEY, GUY CLEMENT, marketing executive; b. Gary, Ind., Dec. 15, 1956; s. Francis Joseph and Isabelle Marie Chidgey; m. Susan Mary Scaffidi, 1987 (div. 1994); children: Guy, Nicholas, Mary Katherine. BSBA, MBA in Mktg. Lic. realtor 1994. CEO Chedzoy Schmit Internat. (formerly ChiDCo Inc. & ChiDCO Broker Internat.), Bakerfield, Calif., 2000—. Prodr. jazz radio show KIWI FM, Bakersfield; prodr. jazz radio show, host KMCL, McCall, Idaho. Prodr.: (flood aid concert) Red River Valley, Come Hell or High Water, (concert) CSUB's 2d annual jazz festival; author: Daddy, I Can't Wanna Do That/ Tangents of a Mad Man; prodr.: (promotion) Travel the Californias. Corp. sponsorship chmn. Kern County Scottish Soc., Bakersfield, 2003—04. Republican. Roman Catholic. Avocations: travel, reading, swimming. Office: Chedzoy Schmit Internat PO Box 43262 Bakersfield CA 93384 Home Phone: 661-831-7693. Personal E-mail: gcchidgey@yahoo.com.

CHIDNESE, PATRICK NICHOLAS, retired lawyer; b. Neptune, NJ, May 26, 1940; s. Louis and Helen Chidnese; 1 child, Krista; m. Kathy J. Chidnese, Feb. 16, 1985; children: Patrick, Nicole. BA, U. Miami, 1964, JD, 1968. Assoc. Sinclair, Louis & Huttoe, Miami, 1968-69, Stephens, Demos, Magil & Thornton, Miami, 1969-70, Howell, Kirby, Montgomery, D'Aiuto, Dean & Hallowes, Ft. Lauderdale, Fla., 1970-71; sole practice Ft. Lauderdale, 1971-88; ret., 1988. County atty. Broward County Juvenile Ct., 1971—72. Mem. Fla. Bar Assn. (chmn. auto ins. com. 1977-78, chmn. 17th jud. circuit legis. com. 1977-80), Broward County Bar Assn., Acad. Fla. Trial Lawyers, Broward County Trial Lawyers Assn. (bd. dirs. 1974-80). Home: PO Box 18419 Asheville NC 28814-0419 Office Phone: 828-252-4239. Personal E-mail: pchid@aol.com.

CHIDSEY, JOHN W., food service executive; married; 2 children. B in Adminstrn., Davidson Coll., NC, 1983; MBA in Fin. and Acctg., Emory U., Atlanta, Ga., JD. CPA. CFO, Pepsi-Cola Eastern Europe PepsiCo., Inc.; CFO PepsiCo World Trading Co., Inc.; joined HFS, Inc. (merger HFS, Inc. and CUC Internat. Inc., formed Cendant Corp. in 1997), 1995; chmn., CEO, vehicle svc. divsn. Cendant Corp., chmn., CEO, financial services divsn., chmn. CEO, direct mktg. divsn., 2000—04; pres. Americas Burger King Corp., Miami, Fla., 2003—04, pres., N.Am., 2004, CFO, adminstrv. officer, 2004—06, CEO, 2006—. Former chmn. bd. dirs. Avis Europe, plc, non-exec. bd. dir. Mem.: Ga. Bar Assn. Office: Burger King Corp 5505 Blue Lagoon Dr Miami FL 33126 Office Fax: 305-378-3000.*

CHIECHI, CAROLYN PHYLLIS, federal judge; b. Newark, Dec. 6, 1943; BS magna cum laude, Georgetown U., 1965, JD, 1969, LLM in Taxation, 1971, LLD (hon.) honoris causa, 2000. Bar: DC 1969, US Dist. Ct. DC, US Ct. Fed. Claims, US Tax Ct., US Ct. Appeals (5th, 6th, 9th, DC, and fed. cirs.), US Supreme Ct. Atty. adv. to Hon. Leo H. Irwin US Tax Ct., Washington, 1969-71, judge, 1992—; assoc. Sutherland, Asbill & Brennan, Washington, 1971—76, ptnr., 1976—92. Mem. bd. regents Georgetown U., Washington, 1988—2001, mem. nat. law alumni bd., 1986—93; mem. bd. govs. Georgetown U. Alumni Assn., 1994—2000; bd. dirs. Stuart Stiller Meml. Found., 1986—99; prin. Coun. for Excellence in Govt., 1990—92. Dept. editor: Jour. Taxation, 1986—92; contbr. articles to profl. jours. Recipient Law Alumni award, Georgetown U., 1994, Alumnae Achievement award, Georgetown U. Law Ctr., 1998. Fellow: Am. Coll. Tax Counsel, Am. Bar Found.; mem.: Am. Judicature Soc., Women's Bar Assn., DC Bar Assn., Fed. Bar Assn. Office: US Tax Ct 400 2nd St NW Washington DC 20217-0002

CHIEGER, KATHRYN JEAN, consumer products company executive; b. Detroit, July 13, 1948; BA, Purdue U., 1970; MA, U. Mich., 1974; MBA, U. Denver, 1983. Libr. U. Mich., Ann Arbor, 1970-74; staff aide U.S. Sen. Gary Hart, Denver, 1974-79; dir. fin. rels. Petro-Lewis Corp., Denver, 1979-86; dir. investor rels. Kraft Inc., Glenview, Ill., 1987-89; v.p. corp. affairs Gaylor Container Corp., Deerfield, Ill., 1989-96; v.p. corp. and investor rels. Brunswick Corp., Lake Forest, Ill., 1996—. Mem. Nat. Investor Rels. Inst. (chpt. bd. dirs. 1979-84, v.p. mem. 1982-83, pres. 1983-84, nat. bd. dirs. 1984-88), Investor Rels. Assn., Chgo. Coun. Fgn. Rels., Sr. Investor Rels. Roundtable. Office: Brunswick Corp 1 N Field Ct Lake Forest IL 60045-4811 Office Phone: 847-735-4612. Business E-Mail: kathryn.chieger@brunswick.com.

CHIEGO, WILLIAM J., museum director; b. Newark, Sept. 17, 1943; s. William Joseph and Rose Marie (Del Guercio) C.; m. Elizabeth Kimball Lee, July 3, 1971; children: Ruth Katharine, Rose Monica. BA in History with distinction, U. Va., 1965; MA in Art History, Case Western Reserve U., 1968, PhD in Art History, 1974. Asst. curator Toledo (Ohio) Mus. Art, 1973-74, assoc. curator European Paintings, 1974-76; curator Portland Art Mus., 1976-79, chief curator, 1979-82, N.C. Mus. Art, Raleigh, 1982-86; dir. Allen Meml. Art Mus. Oberlin (Ohio) Coll., 1986-91; dir. Marion Koogler McNay Art Mus., San Antonio, 1991—. Trustee Intermuseum Conservation Assn., Oberlin, 1986-91; mem., co-chmn. mus. liaison com. Midwest Art History Soc., 1987-91; mem. exhbn. adv. com. Am. Fedn. Arts, 1988-94; mem. conservation grant panel Inst. Mus. Svcs., 1991-93; chair membership com. Assn. Art Mus. Dirs., 1997-99, trustee, 2000-02; lectr. in field. Co-author, editor exhbn. catalog Sir David Wilkie of Scotland, 1987, An Eye for the Stage The Tobin Collection of Theatre Arts at McNay Art Mus., 2004; co-organizer, author intro. to French Paintings from The Chrysler Museum, 1986; coord. rsch. The N.C. Mus. Art Intro. to the Collections, 1983; author: Master Prints from the Gilkey Collection, 1980, From Oregon Private Collections, 1977; organizer, author: (with others) Oberlin Alumni Collect Modern and Contemporary Art, 1989, Reginald Rowe: A Retrospective, 1996, Carl Rice Embrey: A Retrospective, 1997, O'Keeffe and Texas, 1998, César A. Martinez: A Retrospective, 1999; author/editor: Modern Art at The McNay, 2001; contbr. articles to profl. jours. Resident fellow Yale Ctr. for British Art, New Haven, Conn., 1982, Bingham Travel fellow Art History Case Western Reserve U., 1970-71, Univ. fellow Art History, 1969-70, Nat. Defense Edn. Act fellow Latin Am. History, 1965; Mus. Mgmt. Inst. scholar, 1981. Mem. Phi Beta Kappa. Office: McNay Art Museum PO Box 6069 San Antonio TX 78209-0069 E-mail: william.chiego@mcnayart.org.

CHIEN, JENNIE, sculptor; d. Linsan and Helen Ling Chien. AA Graphic Design, City Coll., San Francisco, Calif., 1972; BA Econ., Columbia U., NYC, 1983; MBA, Stanford U., Palo Alto, Calif., 1985. Graphic designer Hisata Design, Steven Jacobs Design, Palo Alto, Calif.; art dir. Am. Express, CBS, Hakuhodo Advt., Leber Katz Ptnrs., Muir Cornelius Moore, NYC, 1973—79; Fortune circulation mktg. mgr. Time Inc., 1985—87, Fortune Internat. subscription dir. Amsterdam, Netherlands, 1987—89; gen. mgr. Time Warner Inc., Editl. Svcs., NYC, 1990—93; mktg. project mgr. Luna Inc., Nyack, 1994—2000; artist Luna A+D, 2000—. Treas., bd. dir. Asian Am. Arts Alliance, New York, 1992—97; panel mem., cmty. art grants Arts Coun. of Rockland County, Spring Valley, NY, 2003—06. Prin. works include Chien Noir: The Black Dog, The Guardian Angels, Open Heads, exhibitions include A. Houberbocken Old Ch. Cultural Ctr., Chgo., 2002—05, Demerest, N.J., 2001—05, one-woman shows include Flat Iron Gallery, Peekskill, N.Y., 2006, in publ., 500 Animals in Clay, Lark Books, 2007. Com. mem. Rockland County Art in Pub. Places, 2003—05. Recipient Gold Medal, Silver Medal, Merit Award for Design Excellence, Western Art Dir. Club, 1975—77, Design Excellence award, San Francisco Art Directors Club, 1975—77, AIGA, 1979, Print Mag., 1980, Gold award, Folio Mag., 1986, Art and Industry award, Rockland Kitchen, Gamerville, N.Y., 2004, Mamaroneck Artists Guild award, Assocs. Show, 2005, Spel Opportunity Stipend award, NY Found. Arts, 2007. Mem.: Hudson River Potters Assn., Phi Beta Kappa. Democrat. Office: Luna A+D 42 Village Gate Nyack NY 10960 Personal E-mail: chiennoir@verizon.net.

CHIEN, NGUYEN TAM, ambassador; b. Nghe An Province, Vietnam, Jan. 20, 1948; married; 3 children. B in Elec. and Mech. Engring., Engring. U., former Soviet Union, 1972; M in Internat. Rels., Moscow Diplomacy Acad., 1984. With Vietnamese Embassy, Moscow, 1972—73; desk officer Dept. Min. Fgn. Affairs, Moscow, 1973—75, 1980—82; attache Vietnam Embassy, Moscow, 1975—80; policy planning dept. Min. Fgn. Affairs, 1984—92, dep. dir. gen., 1988—90, dir. gen., 1990—92; amb. Extraordinary and Plenipotentiary Republic of Vietnam to Japan, 1992—96; asst. min. Fgn. Affairs Vietnam, 1996—97; vice min. Fgn. Affairs, 1997—2000; amb. Socialist Republic of Vietnam, 2000—; amb. Extraordinary and Plenipotentiary Socialist Republic of Vietnam to US, 2001—. Home: Embassy of Vietnam Ste 400 1233 20th St NW Washington DC 20036

CHIEN, SHU, physiology and bioengineering educator; b. Beijing, June 23, 1931; arrived in US, 1954, naturalized, 1971; s. Shih-liang and Wan-tu (Chang) Chien; m. Kuang-Chung Hu, Apr. 7, 1957; children: May Chien Busch, Ann Chien Guidera. MD, Nat. Taiwan U., Taipei, 1953; PhD in Physiology, Columbia U., 1957. Instr. physiology Columbia U. Coll. Physicians & Surgeons, NYC, 1956-58, asst. prof., 1958-64, assoc. prof., 1964-69, prof., 1969-88, dir. divsn. circulatory physiology and biophysics, 1974-88; dir. Inst. Biomedical Scis. Academia Sinica, Taipei, 1987-88; prof. bioengineering and medicine U. Calif. San Diego, La Jolla, 1988—, bioengineering group coord., 1989-94, dir. Whitaker Inst. Biomedical Engring., 1991—, chmn. dept. bioengineering, 1994-99, 2002—05, univ. prof., 2002—, Y.C. Fung prof., 2006—. Chmn. adv. com. Am. Bur. Med. Advancement in China, NYC, 1991-03, Inst. Biomedical Scis., Academia Sinica, Taipei, 1991-2004, Nat. Health Rsch. Inst., Taipei, 1991-2004. Editor: Vascular Endothelium in Health and Disease, 1988, Molecular Biology in Physiology, 1989, Molecular Biology of Cardiovascular System, 1990; co-editor: Nuclear Magnetic Resonance in Biology and Medicine, 1986, Handbook of Bioengineering, 1986, Clinical Hemorheology, Applications in Cardiovascular and Hematological Disease, Diabetes, Surgery and Gynecology, 1987, Fibrinogen, Thrombosis, Coagulation and Fibrinolysis, 1990, Biochemical and Structural Dynamics of the Cell Nucleus, 1990, others; contbr. more than 400 sci. articles on physiology, bioengineering and related biomedical rsch. to profl. jours. Recipient Fahraeus award European Soc. Clin. Haemorheology, London, 1981, Melville award ASME, 1990, 96, Zweifach award World Congress of Microcirculation, Louisville, 1991, Spl. Creativity Grant award NSF, 1985-88, Merit Grant award NIH, 1989-99, Nat. Health medal, Taiwan, 1998, Poiseuille Gold Medal Internat. Congress Biorheology, 2002, Asian Am. Engr. of Yr. for Disting. Life Time Achievement Chinese Inst. Learning, 2005, Lifetime Achievement award Soc. Chinese Bioscientists in Am. Fellow Biomedical Engring. Soc. (pres. 2006-, ALZA award 1993, Disting. Svc. award 2001), Am. Acad. Arts and Scis. (Founders award 2006); mem. NAE (Founders award 2006), Academia Sinica, Taipei, Am. Physiol. Soc. (pres. 1990-91, Ray Daggs award 1999, Walter B. Cannon Lecture award, 2003), Internat. Soc. Biorheology (v.p. 1983-89, pres. 2005-), Microcirculatory Soc. (pres. 1980-81, Landis award 1983), N.Am. Soc. Biorheology (chmn. steering com. 1985-86), Fedn. Am. Socs. for Exptl. Biology (pres. 1992-93), Am. Inst. Med. and Biol. Engring. (pres. 2000-01, Pierre Galletti award 2004), Inst. Medicine, NAS Internat. Union Physiol. Sci. (treas. 1997-01, chair Internat. Congress 2005), Chinese Acad. Scis. (fgn.). Achievements include elucidation of the mechanism of red cell aggregation in terms of energy balance at cell surface; demonstration of the role of endothelial cell turnover in the transport of protein molecules into the artery wall; research on the molecular basis and physiological implications of blood cell deformability; studies on the effects of mechanical forces on endothelial cell gene expression, signal transduction, and remodeling. Office: U Calif San Diego Dept Bio Engring 9500 Gilman Dr La Jolla CA 92093-0412 Home Phone: 858-622-0888; Office Phone: 858-534-5195. Business E-Mail: shuchien@ucsd.edu.

CHIEN, SUFAN, surgeon, educator; b. Zhejiang Province, China, July 20, 1938; came to U.S., 1982; s. Jiaxing and Julian (You) C.; m. Lorrain Wilson; children: Samson, Lynn. MD, Shanghai 1st Med. Coll., 1962. Resident dept. gen. surgery Zhongshan Hosp. Shanghai 1st Med. Coll., 1962—66, attending gen. surgeon, 1975—79; supr. cardiopulmonary bypass Shanghai Inst. Cardiovasc. Diseases, 1975—82, attending surgeon cardiovasc. surgery, 1979—82; vis. scientist cardiovasc. divsn. Mayo Clinic, Rochester, Minn., 1982—84; vis. scientist physiology and biophysics La. State U. Med. Ctr., Shreveport, 1984—85; vis. scientist surgery, physiology and biophysics U. Ky. Med. Ctr., Lexington, 1985—87, asst. prof. divsn. cardio-thoracic surgery, 1987—93, assoc. prof., 1993—96; assoc. prof. surgery U. Louisville, 1996—2004, prof. surgery, 2004—. Invited lectr., presenter in field; mem. sci. rev. com. study sect. NIH. Author: Hibernation Induction Trigger for Organ Preservation, 1993; mem. editl. bd. Internat. Medicine Rev., 1979-84; contbr. articles and abstracts to med. jours., chpts. to books. Grantee NIH, VA, U.S. Army, AHA, Univ. Fellow Am. Coll. Angiology; mem. AHA, N.Y. Acad. Scis., Chinese Med. Assn., Chinese Surg. Assn., Chinese Soc. Thoracic Surgeons, Shanghai Med. Soc., Internat. Soc. Heart and Lung Transplantation. Office: U Louisville Sch Medicine Rudd Heart-Lung Ctr 1200 201 Abraham Flexner Way Louisville KY 40202-3841 Office Phone: 502-852-4418. Personal E-mail: sufanc@netscape.net.

CHIEN-HALE, ELIZABETH, lawyer; d. Tony Tze-Chu Chien and Ni-Teh Ou; m. Roger Hale, May 19, 1985; children: Miranda, Morgan Lloyd. BS, U. Calif., Berkeley, 1983, MA, 1989; JD, U. Hawaii, 1994; LLM, Georgetown U., 1997. Bar: Hawaii 1994, DC 1996, Calif. 1998, US Patent and Trademark Office 1998, US Supreme Ct. 2006, registered: Hong Kong Law Soc. (fgn. lawyer) 2000; non-resident patent agt. Can. Intellectual Property Office. Assoc. Wilson Sonsini Goodrich & Rosati, Palo Alto, Calif., 1997—99, Fish & Richardson, Menlo Park, Calif., 1999—2000; sr. assoc. Baker & McKenzie, Hong Kong, 2000—01; pvt. practice Fremont, Calif., 2001—; dir. Inst. for Intellectual Property in Asia, Fremont, 2002—. Rsch. scholar Peking U. Coll. Law, 1995; adj. prof. Northwestern Poly. U., Fremont, 2003—05. Contbr. articles to profl. jours.; corr. editor: Internat. Legal Materials. Elected mem. Neighborhood Bd., Honolulu, 1994; bd. dirs. Sunnyvale Ctr. for Innovations, Inventions and Ideas, Sunnyvale, Calif., 2004—05; environ. com. mem. City of Los Altos, Calif., 2007—; mem. com. bar examiners State Bar Calif., 2007—. Fellow: Am. Bar. Found.; mem.: ABA (assoc.; com. chair 2002—, co-chmn. joint task force on amendments), Silicon Valley-China Wireless Tech. Assn. (dir. programs 2004—05, legal counselor 2006—), Internat. Assn. for Protection of Intellectual Property, Am. Intellectual Property Law Assn. (assoc.), Am. Soc. Internat. Law (co-chair Intellectual Property Law Interest Group, vice chair Pacific Rim Interest Group, corr. editor internat. legal materials). Office: Inst for Intellectual Property in Asia 40087 Mission Blvd #367 Fremont CA 94539 Office Phone: 408-776-8719. Business E-Mail: ech@institute-ip-asia.org, echienhale@echlaw.com.

CHIGBU, PAULINUS, fisheries biologist, educator, research scientist; s. Peter A. and Sussana A. Chigbu. BSc in Zoology/Hydrobiology with honors, U. Benin, Nigeria, 1984, MSc in Zoology/Hydrobiology, 1987; PhD in Fisheries, U. Wash., Seattle, 1993. Vis. faculty Elizabeth City State U., NC, 1996—97; from asst. prof. to assoc. prof. Jackson State U., Miss., 1998—2005; assoc. prof., dir. U. Md. Ea. Shore, Princess Anne, 2006—. Dir. marine sci. program Jackson (Miss.) State U., 1998—2005; dir., noaa living marine resources coop. sci. ctr. U. Md. Ea. Shore, Princess Anne, 2006—. Contbr. articles to profl. jours. Recipient Rsch. Innovation award, Jackson State U., 2004—05; fellow, Fulbright Found., 1987—93, Electric Power Rsch. Inst., 1989—92; Chapman Meml. scholar, U. Wash. Sch. Fisheries, 1990, Mason Keeler Endowment for Excellence fellow, 1992—93. Mem.: Am. Soc. of Limnology and Oceanography, Miss. Acad. Sci. (chair, marine and atmospheric sciences divsn. 2005—06), Am. Fisheries Soc. (sec.-treas. Miss. chpt. 2000—01, Svc. award 2001). Avocations: soccer, tennis. Office: Univ Md Eastern Shore Carver Hall Princess Anne MD 21853 Home: 163 Nina Ln Fruitland MD 21826 Office Phone: 410-621-3034. Office Fax: 410-651-7869. Business E-Mail: pchigbu@umes.edu.

CHIH, LUKE, music educator, conductor; b. Taichung, Taiwan, July 2, 1957; s. Bob Chih and Mary Shau; m. Fanny Chen, Apr. 28, 1955; children: Grace, Samuel. MusM, Chinese Ch. Music Inst., 1987; MBA, Internat. Concordia U., 1994, Concordia U., M of Ch. Music, 1997. Mem. Glory Ministries, Taipei, Taiwan, 1981—; gen. editor Glory Music, Hayward, Calif., 1981—; assoc. pastor worship and music Taipei Internat. Ch., 1984—88; music dir. Grace Bapt. Ch., 1991—94; assoc. pastor worship and music Taipei Tabernacle Ch., 1996—97; CFO Media Group, Inc., Fremont, Calif., 1997—98; dir. outreach First United Presbyn. Ch., San Francisco, 2001—04; asst. prof. ch. music Truth Theol. Sem., Arcadia, 2004—, dir. ch. music dept., 2004—. Lecture Christ Coll., Taipei, 1994—96. Author: (book) Church Music Ministries, Today's High Tech and Church Administration; composer: (music) Concerto for Violin and Two Pianos (PCMC, 1985). Recipient Voting Mem. Grammy award, NARAS, 1988—. Fellow: NARAS; mem.: Choral Music Dir. Assn., Christian Music Pub. Assn., Chinese Composor League, Gospel Music Assn. Home: 21112 E Rimpath Dr Covina CA 91724 Office: Truth Theol Sem 141 E Durate Rd Arcadia CA 91006 Home Phone: 626-331-3598; Office Phone: 626-574-0770 x20. Office Fax: 626-574-0497; Home Fax: 626-331-3598. Personal E-mail: lukechih@verizon.net. E-mail: lukechih@truthseminary.com.

CHIHARA, CHARLES SEIYO, philosophy educator; b. July 19, 1932; s. George I. and Mary N. (Fushiki) C.; m. Carol J. Rosen, June 14, 1964; 1 child, Michelle N. BS, Seattle U., 1954; MS, Purdue U., 1956; PhD, U. Wash., 1960. Instr. U. Wash., Seattle, 1961-62; asst. prof. U. Ill., Urbana, 1962-63, U. Calif., Berkeley, 1963-68, assoc. prof., 1968-74, prof. philosophy dept., 1974—2000, emeritus prof., 2000—. Author: Ontology and the Vicious-Circle Principle, 1973, Constructibility and Mathematical Existence, 1990, The Worlds of Possibility, 1998, A Structural Account of Mathematics, 2004. NEH fellow for ind. rsch., Paris, 1985-86, U. Calif., 1994-95; postdoctoral fellow Mellon Found., 1964-65, Humanities Rsch. fellow U. Calif., 1967-68; U. Calif. Pres.'s rsch. fellow in humanities, 1996-97. Office: Univ Calif Dept Philosophy Berkeley CA 94720-0001 Office Phone: 510-642-2722. Business E-Mail: charles1@socrates.berkeley.edu.

CHIHOREK, JOHN PAUL, electronics company executive; b. Wilkes-Barre, Pa., June 22, 1943; s. Stanley Joseph and Caroline Mary C.; m. Cristina Maria Marroquin, Dec. 28, 1968; children: Jonathan, David, Crista, Daniel. BSEE, Pa. State U., 1965; postgrad., Calif. State U., San Diego, 1970-71; MBA, Calif. State U., Sacramento, 1972. Program officer Hdqrs. Air Force Logistic Command, Dayton, Ohio, 1972-75; sr. engr. Hdqrs. Air Force Space Div., LA, 1975-78; mgr. software systems dept. Logicon Inc., San Pedro, Calif., 1978; mgr. software product assurance dept. Loral Aeronutronics, Rancho Santa Margarita, Calif., 1978-85, mgr. software engring., 1985—. Pres. CMC Sys. Inc. Mem. Congl. Adv. Bd., 1980; active Republican Nat. Com. Served with USN, 1965-70, Vietnam. Decorated Bronze Star. Mem. IEEE (mgmt. bd. Computer Soc., exec. com. on standard), AAAS, Engring. Mgmt. Soc. (v.p. publs.), Air Force Assn., Internat. Platform Assn. Clubs: Lions, Odd Fellows. Roman Catholic. E-mail: john@cmcsystemsinc.com.

CHIHULY, DALE PATRICK, artist; b. Tacoma, Wash., Sept. 20, 1941; s. George and Viola C.; m. Silvia Peto (div.); 1 son with Leslie Jackson. BA in Interior Design, U. Wash., 1965; MS in Sculpture, U. Wis., 1967; MFA in Ceramics, RISD, 1968; Doctorate (hon.), Brandeis U., 2000. Apprentice Venini Glass Factory, Murano, Venice, Italy, 1968; instr., head glass program RISD; instr. Haystack Mtn. Sch., Maine; founder, Pilchuk Sch., 1971. Mem. various juries and panels Nat. Endowment for Arts One-man exhbns. include U. Minn., 1976, Handler Galleries, Houston, 1977, Crocker Art Mus., Sacamento, Calif., 1984, Bellevue (Wash.) Art Mus., 1984-87, Israel Museum, Jerusalem 1990, Hudson River Museum, Yonkers 1990, Contemporary Museum Honolulu 1990, Azabu Museum, Tokyo Japan 1990, Museum of Arts and Crafts, Hamburg 1992, Marlborough Gallery, NY, 2006, Franklin Park Conservatory, Columbus, Ohio, 2006, and others; group shows include Charles Cowles Gallery, N.Y. 1981-83, "World glass Now" Hokkaido Museum of Modern Art, Sapporo, Japan, 1982, Columbus Coll. Art and Design, Ohio, 1983; installation exhbns.: Chihuly Over Venice, 1995-96, Chihuly in the Light of Jerusalem 2000, Tower of David Mus. of the History of Jerusalem, 2000, Crystal Tree of Light, White House Millennium Celebration, 2000 (permanently installed at the Clinton Presdl. Ctr., Little Rock 2004), Chihuly in the Park: A Garden of Glass, Garfield Park Conservatory, Chgo., 2001-02, Chihuly at the Victoria & Albert, London, 2001, Chihuly Bridge of Glass, Tacoma, 2002, Salt Lake Art Ctr., Olympics, 2002, Mille Fiori, Tacoma Art Mus., 2003, A Transparent Legacy, Seattle Art Mus., Washington, 2006, Niijima Float Installation, Tacoma Art Mus., Washington, 2006, Material Matters, LA County Mus. Art, Calif., 2006; represented in permanent collections including Seattle Art Mus., Met. Mus. Art, N.Y.C., Wadsworth Atheneum, Hartford, Conn., Phila. Mus. Art, Corning Mus. Glass, N.Y., Lannan Found., Palm Beach, Fla., Mus. Art of RISD, Providence, Victoria and Albert Mus., London, Mus. Contemporary Crafts of Am., Crafts Council, N.Y.C.; dir. Pilchuk Glass Ctr., Stanwood, Wash.; author: Chihuly: Glass, 1982, Chihuly: Color Glass and Form, 1986. Recipient Louis F. Tiffany Found. award, 1967; named First Nat. Living Treasure, Inst. for Human Potential, U. N.C., Wilmington, 1992; Nat. Endowment for Arts grantee, 1975, 77, Governor's Art Award (Washington State) 1984, 85; Fulbright fellow, Murano, Italy, 1968 Mem.: Providence Art.*

CHIKLIS, MICHAEL, actor; b. Lowell, Mass., Aug. 30, 1963; m. Michelle Moran, June 21, 1992; children: Autumn, Odessa. BFA in acting, Boston U., 1986. Actor: (TV series) The Commish, 1991—95, St. Michael's Crossing, 1999, Daddio, 2000, Heavy Gear: The Animated Series (voice), 2001—02, The Shield (also prodr., 2003), 2002— (Emmy award for outstanding lead actor in a drama series, 2002, Golden Globe award for best performance by an actor in a TV series - drama, 2003); (TV films) The Commish: In the Shadow of the Gallows, 1995, The Three Stooges, 2000; (films) Wired, 1989, The Rain Killer, 1990, Nixon, 1995, The Taxman, 1998, Soldier, 1998, Body and Soul, 1998, Carlo's Wake, 1999, Last Request, 1999, Do Not Disturb, 1999, (voice only) Sen to Chihiro no Kamikakushi, 2001, Fantastic Four, 2005; (Broadway plays) Defending the Caveman, (off-Broadway plays) Tracks, Return to Sender, The Fester and Rot Raw View, Ersatz Life, (regional theater) As You Like It, Romeo and Juliet, Streetcar Named Desire, You Can't Take It With You, The Rivals.

CHILCOTE, GARY M., museum director, reporter; b. St. Joseph, Mo., Nov. 2, 1934; s. Merrill and Mary Thelma C.; m. Mary Carolyn Abmeyer, April 2, 1958; children: Douglas A., Carolyn D. BA, Northwest Mo. State U., Maryville, 1956. News-press spl. corr. St. Joseph News-Press/Gazette, 1954—2002; mus. dir. Patee House Mus. and Jesse James Home Mus., St. Joseph, 1963—. Vocat. tchr. Hillyard Tech. Sch., St. Joseph, 1964-91. Author, editor Pony Express Mail, 1972—. Staff sgt. Mo. Air Guard, 1957-63. Mem. Nat. Pony Express Assn. (nat. dir., nat. v.p. 1990—), Pony Express Hist. Assn. (bd. dirs., co-founder 1963), James-Younger Gang (nat. pres. 1997—, 98-99). Republican. Home: 1910 N 32nd St Saint Joseph MO 64506-2313 Office: Patee Ho Mus/Jesse James Ho Mus 1202 Penn St Saint Joseph MO 64503-2560 Office Phone: 816-232-8206. Personal E-mail: patee@ponyexpress.net.

CHILCOTE, LEE A., lawyer; b. Cleve., May 5, 1942; BA, Dartmouth Coll., 1964; BE, Thayer Sch. Engring., 1965; JD, U. Calif., San Francisco, 1972. Bar: Ohio 1972. Ptnr. Chiloote Law Firm, Cleve. Bd. dirs., The Chilcote Co., sec., 1972—. Trustee Hough Housing Corp. 1972-88; bd. dirs. Cleve. Warehouse Dist. Local Devel. Corp., 1986—. Mem. ABA (real property and corp. sects.), Am. Coll. Real Estate Lawyers, Cleve. Bar Assn., Order of Coif, Thurston Soc. Office: The Chilcote Law Firm The Cedar Grandview Bldg 12434 Cedar Rd Ste No 3 Cleveland Heights OH 44106 Office Phone: 216-795-4117. Business E-Mail: lee.chilcote@chilcotelaw.com.

CHILCOTE, LUGEAN LESTER, retired architect, researcher; b. Oklahoma City, Jan. 14, 1929; s. Mark H. and Myrita A.J. (Lugeanbeal) C.; m. Clara Bernice Dudis, Dec. 18, 1953; children: Martin L., Frederick M., David L.(dec.), Bradley R. BArch, U. Ark., 1951. Registered architect, Ark.; cert. Nat. Coun. Archtl. Registration Bds. Designer, draftsman Ken Cole, Jr., Architect, Little Rock, 1953—54; architect Swaim & Allen Architects, Little Rock, 1954—58; architect, prin. Blass Chilcote Carter Gaskin Bogart Norcross (and predeccessor firms), Little Rock, 1958—99. Gen. chmn. Gulf States Regional Conf., 1966; judge City Beautiful Commn., 1967-68; pres. Ark. State Bd. Architects, 1991-96; apptd. mem. bldg. code bd. of appeals, City of Little Rock, 1986-94. Co-author: 50 Years of Design, 1980; prin. works include First Christian Ch., 1962, Main Toll and Dial bldg. Southwestern Bell Telephone Co., 1968, Bapt. Med. Center Complex, 1971-73, U. Ark. Med. Sci. Campus, 1973-99 , US Postal Svc. Gen. Mail Facility, Conv./Exhibit/Excelsior-Trust Hotel Complex, 1978-96, Ark. Children's Hosp., 1983-98, all Little Rock, US Post Office and Courthouse, Pine Bluff, Ark., 1967, Nat. Center for Toxicological Research, Pine Bluff, 1973-90, Jefferson Reg. med. Ctr., Pine Bluff, 1985-96, White River Med. Ctr., Batesville, Ark., 1992-95, Drew Meml. Med. Ctr., Monticello, Ark., 1990-. Mem. com. Ark. Art Festival, 1968, West Little Rock YMCA, 1969; mem. Ark. Arts Ctr., 1965—99; bd. dirs., treas., mem. exec. com. Ark. Cmty. Found., 1972-85; bd. dirs. Ark. Hall of Fame, Quapaw coun. Boy Scouts Am., Pulaski County, Ark.; dist. chmn., mem. exec. bd. coun. Boy Scouts Am.; mem. Little Rock Bldg. Codes Bd. Appeals, 1986-96; v.p. Ark. Christian Men's Orgn.; mem. exec. com., chmn. bd., elder Ark. Christian Ch.; compliance review and cons. City of Little Rock, 1997-99. Served to capt. USAF, 1951-53. Recipient Woodbadge Tng. award Boy Scouts Am., Little Rock, 1974, Dist. Award of Merit, 1981, Silver Beaver award, Pulaski County, 1976, Meritorious Svc. award Ark. Cmty. Found., 1985. Fellow AIA (pres. Ark. chpt. 1966-67, trustee ednl. endowment fund 1970-72, 83-95, gen. chmn. gulf states regional conf. 1966, nat. del. 1967, chmn. nat. profl. interest com. 1982-83, bd. dirs. nat. polit. action com. 1983-85, chmn. legis. affairs, chmn. Nat. Risk Mgmt. Com., chair 1997, profl. adv. bd. U. Ark. 1997, E. Fay Jones Gold Medal award Ark. chpt. 1996, bd. dir. 2000-2002); mem. Pleasant Valley Country Club Little Rock (bd. dirs., bd. govs.) Mem. Christian Ch. (Disciples Of Christ). Avocations: golf, fishing, hunting. Home: 806 Carywood Ln Little Rock AR 72205-2802 Personal E-mail: lchilcote@aristotle.net.

CHILCOTE, SAMUEL DAY, JR., trade association administrator; b. Casper, Wyo., Aug. 24, 1937; s. Sam D. and Juanita C. (Cornelison) C.; m. Ellen Sheridan Spear, Nov. 11, 1966. BS, Idaho State U., 1959. Adminstrv. asst. Continental Oil Co., Glenrock, Wyo., 1960-63; asst. supt. public instrn., dir. Wyo. Surplus Property Agy., Wyo. Sch. Lunch Program, Cheyenne Wyo. Dept. Edn., Wyo., 1963-67; supr. North Ctrl. region Distilled Spirits Inst., Denver, 1967-71, exec. dir., COO North Ctrl. region Washington, 1971-73; exec. v.p., COO, Distilled Spirits Coun., Inc., Washington, 1973-77, pres., CEO, 1978-81; pres. Tobacco Inst., Washington, 1981-99; chmn. Chilcote Enterprises, Potomac, Md., 1999—; mng. ptnr. Tubac (Ariz.) Golf Resort and Spa, 2003. Adv. council consumer goods industry sect. Dept. Commerce. Pres. Sky Ranch Found. for Boys, 1975-81, pres. emeritus, 1981—; treas. Ford's Theatre, 1984-88, vice chmn., trustee, 1988-96, chmn., 1997-99; treas. Santa Cruz County Tourism Coun., 2004-07; bd. dirs. St. Andrew's Children's Clinic, 2005-07, Art Barn, exec. com.; chmn. Awards Dinner Com., 1989-2000, USO Met. Washington, past pres. Capt. U.S. Army, 1959-60. Recipient Profl. Achievement award Idaho State U. Coll. Bus., 1986, Man of Yr. award Anti-Defamation league, 1986, Humanitarian of the Yr. award Tobacco and Confectionery Div. Dinner for the UJA-Fedn. 1991 campaign, Good Scout award Greater N.Y. Coun. Boy Scouts Am., 1996. Mem. Santa Cruz County Citizens Assn. (v.p. 2000-2005), Tubac Hist. Soc. (bd. dirs., exec. com. 2004—), Tubac Hist. Soc. (bd. dirs. 2005—), Georgetown Club, Congl. Country Club (past pres., exec. com., bd. govs.), Burning Tree Club, Nat. Press Club, Capitol Hill Club, City Club, F St. Club, TPC Avenel (Washington), Jefferson Islands Club (bd. govs.), Masons, Elks, Shriners. Mailing: PO Box 1235 Tubac AZ 85646-1235 Personal E-mail: s.chilcote@aol.com.

CHILDEARS, LINDA, foundation administrator; b. Council Bluffs, Iowa, Jan. 25, 1950; d. Nolan Glen and Mary Lucile (Dunken) Jackson. Grad., U. Wis., Am. Inst. Banking; student, U. Colo., U. Denver. Various positions First Nat. Bank Bear Valley (formerly Norwest Bank Bear Valley), Colo., 1969-79; v.p. adminstrn. First Nat. Bancorp., 1979-83; pres., CEO, Equitable Bank of Littleton, 1983—87; founder The Fin. Consortium; pres., CEO, Young Ams. Bank, Denver, 1987—2005; pres., CEO Daniels Fund, 2005—. Bd. dirs., First State Bancorporation, 2007- Contbr. articles to Time and Newsweek. Bd. dirs. Cherry Creek Art Festival, Denver, 1989-96, Jr. Achievement, Mile High United Way, Cherry Creek Bus. Improvement Dist., U. Denver Bridge Project; mem. adv. bd., nat. past pres. Camp Fire Coun. Colo., Daniels Coll. of Bus.; bd. mem. Cableland Home Found. Named hon. life mem. Nat. CampFire, past chmn., numerous other awards Camp Fire Inc. Mem. Am. Bankers Assn. (past chmn. Edn. Found.), Found. Tchg. Econs. (trustee), Colo. Bankers Assn., Metro C. of C. Republican. Office: Daniels Fund 101 Monroe St Denver CO 80206*

CHILDERS, BOB EUGENE, educational association executive; b. Cleveland, Miss., Sept. 16, 1930; s. William Nick and Allie Jeanette (Doty) C.; m. Jo Ann Roberts, May 1, 1953; children: William Frank, Robert Clayton, John Murry, Julia Ann. BA, Union U., 1953; MA, Memphis State U., 1958; EdD, U. Tenn., 1964. Cert. tchr., adminstr., Tenn. Field engr. RCA, El Paso, Tex., 1955-57; instr. USN, Memphis, 1957-60; prin. Halls H.S., Knoxville, Tenn., 1960-61, McMinn County H.S., Athens, Tenn., 1961-64; asst. commr. Tenn. State Dept. Edn., Nashville, 1964-66; regional dir. USOE, Vocat.-Tech. and Adult Edn., Atlanta, 1966-69; exec. dir. Commn. Occupl. Edn., Atlanta, 1969-82, So. Assn. Colls. and Schs., Atlanta, 1982-92. Cons. U.S. Dept. Edn., Washington, 1963-79, Fla. State Legislature, Tallahassee, 1979, Md. Values Edn. Commn., Annapolis, 1979-80; founder, pres. Childers-Childress Family Assn., 1982-88, 90-96. Editor SACS Procs., 1982-92. Bd. dirs. Boy Scouts Am., Atlanta, 1980-87, Ctr. for Citizenship Edn., Washington, 1978-81; bd. trustees YMCA, Nashville, 1964-66; v.p. Religious Heritage of Am., St. Louis, 1979-86; active Rotary, Atlanta, 1981-92. With U.S. Army, 1953-55. Mem. Am. Vocat. Assn. (life 1966, cons.), Am. Tech. Edn. Assn. (life 1978, pres.1984, v.p. 1983), Am. Vocat. Rsch. Assn., Am. Soc. Assn. Execs., Phi Delta Kappa (past treas. 1960-61, sec. 1960-61), Iota Lambda Sigma, Sigma Alpha Epsilon (pres. 1952). Democrat. Baptist. Avocations: genealogy, vitaculture, gardening. Home and Office: 960 River Rd Woodruff SC 29388-9110

CHILDERS, CHARLES EUGENE, mining company executive; b. West Frankfort, Ill., Oct. 29, 1932; s. Joel Marion and Cora E. (Choate) C.; m. Norma A. Casper, June 8, 1952; children: Joel M., Katrina K. BS, U. Ill., 1955; LLD (hon.), U. Saskatchewan, 1994. With Duval Corp., Carlsbad, N.Mex., 1955-62, Internat. Minerals Corp. (IMC), 1963-77; v.p. Esterhazy oper. IMC, 1977-79; pres. IMC Coal, Lexington, 1979-81; v.p. potash oper. IMC, 1981-82, v.p. expansion and devel., 1982-87; pres., chief exec. officer Potash Corp. of Sask., Inc., Saskatoon, Can., 1987-90, chmn., pres., chief exec. officer, 1990-98, chmn., chief exec. officer, 1998-99, chmn., 1999—. Bd. dirs., past chmn. bd. Canpotex Ltd., Sask., Found. for Agronomic Rsch.; past chmn. bd. The Fertilizer Inst.; bd. dirs. Conf. Bd. Can., Battle Mountain Gold Corp.; past chmn. Potash and Phosphate Inst.; mem. fertilizer industry adv. com. to FAO. Dir. at large Jr. Achievement of Can. 1st lt. U.S. Army, 1955-57. Mem. AIME, Can. Inst. Mining and Metallurgy, Sask. Potash Producers Assn. (past. chmn.), Internat. Fertilizer Industry Assn. (past pres.). Republican. Baptist.

CHILDERS, SUSAN LYNN BOHN, special education educator, school system administrator, human resources and transition specialist, consultant; m. Lawrence J. Childers; 1 child. AA, Ohio U., 1978, BS in Edn. cum laude, 1982; MEd in Supervision, Ashland U., 1991. Profl. cert. 1-8 elem. tchr., K-12 edn. handicapped; spl. edn. tchr., Ohio. Educator learning disabilities, developmentally handicapped Maysville Local Sch. Dist., South Zanesville, Ohio, 1982-89; work-study supr. Holmes County Office Edn., Millersburg, 1990, editor spl. edn. newsletter, 1990—93, cons., supervisor work-study programming, 1991—93; spl. edn. supr. Wayne County Bd. Edn., Wooster, 1993—94; adminstr. severe behavior handicapped program, supr. special edn. Ashland-Wayne County Bd. Edn., Wooster, 1994—95; cons. Tri-County Ednl. Svc. Ctr., Wooster, 1996—99; supr. spl. edn., supr. instrn. support Zanesville City Sch., 1999—2000; dir. spl. edn. Licking County Ednl. Svc. Ctr., Newark, 2000—01; supr. spl. edn. Lancaster City Sch., 2001—06, Canal Winchester Local Sch., 2006—. Mem. Holmes County Spl. Edn. Adv. Coun., 1990—93, E. Holmes Local Sch. Dist. Strategic Planning Action Team Job/Life Skills, 1993; rep. Ohio Devel. Handicapped Issues Forum; mem. steering com. Ohio Speaks, 1991—94; mem. strategic planning com. Ashland-Wayne County Bd. Edn., 1994—95; mem. Chippewa Local Sch. Dist. Child Care Bd., 1995—96; chmn. Direct Student Svcs. Strategic Planning Com., 1995—96; mem. safety com. Ashland-Wayne Ednl. Svc. Ctr., 1994—96; mem. svc. coordination com. Wayne County Children and Family First Initiative, 1995, 96, Edn. Rep. Safety Com., Tri-County Ednl. Svc. Ctr., Wooster, 1997—99; mem. exec. com. Licking County Children and Family First Initiative, 2000—01; mem. Licking County Mental Health and Recovery Bd., Newark, 2001, Licking County Behavioral Health Assessment Team, 2000—01, Newark Cmty. Corps Adv. Com., 2001, Fairfield County Children and Family First Clin. Cluster, 2001—02; pres.-elect Ohio Assn. Suprs. and Coords. of Exceptional Students, 2002; pres. Ohio Assn. Supr. and Coord. of Exceptional Students, 2003; spkr. in field. Editor Spl. Edn. Newsletter Holmes County Office Edn., 1990-93. Mem. adv. bd. Holmes County Job Placement, Holmes County Litter Prevention Cmty. Action Plan Com., 1993; vol. Ohio Buckeye Book Fair, 1991—93, 1999, Holmes County Spl. Olympics, 1990—93, chairperson vols., 1993; mem. jr. assembly Bethesda Hosp., 1970—78; mem. Beaux Arts Zanesville Art Ctr., 1972—78; mem. spl. needs adv. bd. Ashland-West Holmes Career Ctr., 1990—93; mem. Transition and Comm. Consortium on Learning Disabilities, Ohio U. Alumni Career Resource Network, Holmes County Abuse Prevention Cmty. Action Plan Com., 1993, Ohio Staff Devel. Coun., Wayne County Family and Children First Coun. (Clin. Cluster), 1994—96; co-chairperson fundraising com. Creating Connections Symposium, Akron, Ohio, 1994; mem. Ashland-Wayne-Holmes Counties Adv. Com. for Tech. and Tng. Subcom., Ohio, 1996—97; adv. com. for tech. 3-county rep. Ashland, Wayne, Holmes, Ohio, 1996—98; A-site tech. tng. com., 1996—97; mem., regional rep. School/Net Communities of Practice, 1996; mem. Licking County Behavioral Health Assessment Team, 2000—01, Licking County Spl. Edn. Collaborative Com., 2000—01, Cmty. Corps Adv. Com., Newark, Ohio, 2001, Licking County Mental Health and Recovery Bd, Newark, 2001, Licking County Fostercare Collaborative Coun., Newark, 2000—01; mem. asst. tech. com., chair speech-lang. dept. Lancaster City Sch., 2002—03; mem. Lancaster City Schs. Career Adv. Bd., 2003—06. Recipient award Muskingum County Office Litter Prevention, 1988, Kids Care Project, 1989, Maysville Bd. Edn. commendation, 1989, Merit award Keep Ohio Beautiful program, 1991, Ohio Future Forum's Exemplary Transition from Sch.-to-Work Model award, 1993, Model Program designation Ohio's Employability Skills Project, 1987, Franklin B. Walter Outstanding Educator award, 1996, 98. Mem. ASCD, Career Edn. Assn., Coun. Exceptional Children, Ohio Rural Edn. Assn., Ohio Sch. Supr. Assn., Ohio Assn. Vocat. Edn. Spl. Needs Pers., Wayne-Holmes Elem. Adminstr. Assn., Ohio Pupil Pers. Assn., Ohio Assn. Supervision and Coordination for Exceptional Students (regional pres. 2003), Phi Delta Kappa. Office: Crooksville EVS Dist 4065 School Dr Crooksville OH 43731

CHILD-OLMSTED, GISÈLE ALEXANDRA, retired language educator; b. Port-au-Prince, Haiti, Dec. 27, 1946; (parents Am. citizens); d. Daniel McGuire Child and Alice Dejean Child; m. Hans George Bickel, Sept. 1967 (div. Apr. 1984); children: Anna Kristina Villemez, Maia Selena Deubert; m. Jerauld Lockwood Olmsted, June 17, 1988. BA in French with honors, U. Md., 1970; MA in French, Johns Hopkins U., 1978, PhD in Romance Langs., 1981; cert. in translation, Georgetown U. Vis. instr. U. Md., College Park, 1980-81; instr. Johns Hopkins U., Balt., 1981-82; lang. instr. Holton-Arms Sch., Bethesda, Md., 1982-83; asst. prof. dept. modern langs. and lit. Loyola Coll., Balt., 1983-89, assoc. prof., 1989-98, chair dept. modern lang. langs. and lit., 1989-94, prof., 1998—2003; ret., 2003. V.p. faculty coun. Loyola Coll., 1998—2000, mem. steering com. Ctr. for Humanities, 1989—94; organizer, dir. Colloquia on Lang., Lit. and Soc., Balt., 1990, Balt., 95, Balt., 99, Balt., 2002. Author: Jean Genet: Criminalité et Transcendance, 1987; contbr. articles to profl. jours. Faculty Rsch. grant Loyola Coll., 1984, 89, Study grant French Embassy, 1986, 89; Gillman fellow, 1970-73, 79-80; visitor's scholar U. Cape Town, South Africa, 1995. Mem. MLA (del. Mid-Atlantic region 1992-94, 96-98), Am. Assn. Tchrs. French, Soc. Prof. Français et Francophones d'Amérique, Les Amis de Stendhal, Phi Beta Kappa. Avocations: painting, golf, antiques, classical music, flamenco dancing. Home: 7735 Arrowood Ct Bethesda MD 20817-2821 Office Phone: 301-365-6230.

CHILDRE, AMY, education educator; PhD in Spl. Edn., Vanderbilt U., Nashville, Tenn. Assoc. prof. Ga. Coll. and State U., Milledgeville, 1999—. Contbr. articles to profl. jours. Pers. Preparation grantee, US Dept. Edn., Office Spl. Edn. and Rehabilitative Svcs., 2006—. Mem.: Baldwin Assn. for Persons with Developmental Disabilities, Am. Assn. Intellectual and Devel. Disabilities, Coun. Exceptional Children (Susan Phillips Gorin award 2007). Office: Georgia Coll and State U CBX 072 Milledgeville GA 31061 Office Phone: 478-445-0506. Business E-Mail: amy.childre@gcsu.edu.

CHILDRESS, BRAD, professional football coach; b. Aurora, Ill., June 27, 1956; m. Dru-Ann Childress; children: Kyle, Andrew, Christopher, Cara. Graduate, Ea. Ill. U. Wide receivers coach Illinois U., 1978—84; quarterbacks coach Indianapolis Colts, 1985; offensive coord. No. Ariz. U., 1986—89, Utah U., 1990—92; quarterback coach, offensive coord. Univ. Wisconsin, 1992—98; quarterback coach Phila. Eagles, 1999—2001, offensive coord., 2002—06; head coach Minn. Vikings, 2006—. Office: Minnesota Vikings 9520 Viking Dr Eden Prairie MN 55344

CHILDRESS, JOEL M., music educator; b. Monroe, La., Mar. 18, 1955; s. Wilbur Theron and Monteal Finley Childress; m. Dee R. Robinson, Oct. 19, 1996; 1 child, Keely C. B in music edn., U. La., 1978, M in music edn., 1979; MA+30, various, 1981. Cert. Class A La., 1982. Assoc. dir. of bands West Monroe H.S., West Monroe, La., 1984—98; dir. of bands Pearl River Jr. High, Pearl River, La., 1998—2000, Mandeville Jr. High/Tchefuncte Mid. Sch., Mandeville, La., 2000—03, Tchefuncte Mid. Sch., Mandeville, 2003—. Coord. of instrumental music St. Timothy United Meth. Ch., Mandeville, La., 2003—. Author (presenter): (classroom tchr. workshop) The Planets Music Across the Curriculum; author: (article) Field Preparation Suggestions for the Young Director. Vice pres. greens chmn. Covington Country Club, Mandeville, La., 2000—03; pres. Versailles Property Owners Assn., Covington, La., 1999—2002. Recipient Commendation of Excellence, Ouachita Parish Sch. Bd., 1991, 1994. Mem.: Music Educators Nat. Conf., La. Music Educators Assn., Nat. Band Assn., Phi Beta Mu, Kappa Kappa Psi (life). R-Consevative. Meth. Avocations: golf, travel, biking. Home: 308 Ave Palais Royal Covington LA 70433 Office: St Tammany Parish Schs 1530 W Causeway Approach Mandeville LA 70471 Home Phone: 985-892-7377; Office Phone: 985-626-7118. E-mail: joel.childress@stpsb.org.

CHILDRESS, RICHARD THOMAS, international business consultant; b. Huntington, W.Va., Nov. 22, 1942; s. Grover Burgess and Zenna Belle C.; m. Elli Lisbeth, June 13, 1962; 1 child, Tyrone Richard. BA in Psychology, U. Cin., 1964; MA in Asian Studies, U. Ariz., 1976. Commd. 2d lt. U.S. Army, 1964, advanced through grades to col., 1984; gen. staff officer Asian affairs, exec. officer Dept. of Army, 1978—81; dir. Asian and polit. mil. affairs White House, Nat. Security Coun., 1981—89; pres. Asian Investment Strategies, 1989—; pres., co-founder Asian Energy Corp., Tulsa, Okla., 1992—. Sr. adv. Sec. of State, 1982-88; US del. Assn. Southeast Asian Nations, 1982-88; leader, participant US Policy Del., Vietnam, Laos, 1982-89; designated White House Surrogate Spkr. Pres. US; NSC advisor to two presdl. envoys; Rep. Nat. Comm., adv. bd. US-ASEAN Bus. Coun., Inc.; policy adv. Nat. League Prisoners of War, Missing in Action families, mem. U.S.-Philippine Bus. Com.; exec. com. US-Thailand Bus. Coun.; co-chair adv. com. Nat. Ctr. S.E. Asian Studies, Georgetown U.; Indochina forum Aspen Inst.; spkr. in field. Contbr. articles to profl. jours. Decorated Def. Disting. Svc. medal, Legion of Merit with Oak Leaf, Bronze Star, Vietnamese Cross of Gallantry, others; recipient Humanitarian awards Fgn. Govts., Nat. League Prisoners of War/Missing in Action Families, Svc. to Mankind, Pace award Dept. Army. Mem. Asia Soc., Thai-Am. Assn. Mailing: PO Box 104 Flat Rock NC 28731

CHILDRESS, SCOTT JULIUS, medicinal chemist; b. Greenville, SC, Apr. 6, 1926; s. Julius Dunford and Ola Irene (Scott) C.; m. Nelly Araxy Medzadour, Dec. 20, 1975 BS, Furman U., 1947; PhD, U. N.C., 1951. Research chemist Tenn. Eastman, Kingsport, 1951-52; research chemist Wallace & Tiernan, Belleville, N.J., 1952-58, Wyeth Labs., Radnor, Pa., 1959-62, mgr. medicinal chemistry, 1962-68, asst. to v.p. research and devel., 1968-73, asst. v.p. research and devel., 1973-85. Patentee in field; contbr. articles to profl. jours. Served with AUS, 1944-46 Fellow NY Acad. Scis.; mem. Am. Chem. Soc. (treas. med. divsn. 1969-71, chmn. nat. med. chem. symposium 1968), Sigma Xi Home: 604 S Washington Sq Philadelphia PA 19106-4152

CHILDS, ALEX JOSEPH, gynecologist; b. Athens, Ga., Dec. 5, 1975; s. Larry and Gayle Childs; m. Julie Ann Johnson, May 22, 2001; children: Abigael, Emma, Andrew. BS, Mercer U., 1997; MD, Med. Coll. Ga., 2001. Lic. Practice Medicine Ga., 2002, Ala., 2004. Clin. fellow pelvic pain and advanced gynecologic laparoscopy C. Paul Perry Pelvic Pain Ctr. U. Ala. Birmingham, 2005; resident ob-gyn Meml. Health U. Med. Ctr., Savannah, Ga., 2001—05. Chmn. Jr. fellow state sect. Am. Coll. Ob-Gyn, Savannah, 2004—05, vice-chmn. jr. fellow state sect., 2003—04; v.p. acad. affairs Med. Coll. Ga., Augusta, 1999—2001. Contbr. articles to profl. jours. Vol. educator Boot Camp for New Dads, Savannah, 2004—05; vol. healthcare provider Beulah Grove Indigent Health Cmty. Clinic, Augusta, 1999—2001; vol. Habitat for Humanity, Macon, Ga., 1995—2001; educator Southside Bapt. Ch., Savannah, 2001—05. Recipient Physician's Physician Award, Med. Coll. Ga., 2001; Ednl. Grant for Hysteroscopic Rsch., ACMI, Inc., 2003, Acad. and Cmty. Svc. Scholarship, Ty Cobb Found., 1997—2001, Ednl. Scholarship, Jacques Found., 1997—2001, Freshman Scholar, AMA, 1997—98, Penfield Scholar, Mercer U., 1994—97. Mem.: Christian Med. And Dental Assn. (corr.), Internat. Pelvic Pain Soc. (assoc.), Am. Assn. Gynecologic Laparoscopic Surgeons (assoc.), Am. Coll. Ob-Gyn (assoc.; chmn. of state jr. sect. 2004—05), Phi Beta Sigma (corr.), Phi Kappa Phi (corr.), Alpha Omega Alpha (corr.). R-Consevative. Baptist. Avocations: tennis, travel, music. Office: C Paul Perry Pelvic Pain Ctr Ste 402 2006 Brookwood Medical Ctr Dr Birmingham AL 35209 Home Phone: 205-978-1625; Office Phone: 205-397-9000. Personal E-mail: alex_j_childs@yahoo.com.

CHILDS, DAVID M., architectural firm executive; Grad., Yale U., Yale Sch. Art and Architecture. Sr. designer Pennsylvania Ave. Commn., Washington, 1968—71; with Skidmore, Owings & Merrill LLP, Washington, 1971—84, consulting design ptnr. NYC, 1984—. Chmn. Nat. Capital Planning Commn., 1975—81, Commn. Fine Arts, 2002—; bd. dir., trustee Mus. Modern Art; bd. dir. Am. Acad. in Rome, Mcpl. Art Soc., Nat. Bldg. Mus.; served as juror at local and nat. design awards programs; vis. critic or studio head at profl. schools of architecture; lectr. and panelist at numerous conferences and symposia. Prin. works include Washington Mall Master Plan and Constitution Gardens, Nat. Geographic Hdqs. Bldg., 1300 Park Ave, Metro Ctr., U.S. News and World Report Hdqrs., Evening Star renovation and addition on Pennsylvania Ave, Four Seasons, Park Hyatt and Regent Hotels, Bertelsman Tower at Time Square, AOL Time Warner Hdqrs. at Columbus Cir., expansion of Dulles Internat. Airport main terminal, Washington, DC, U.S. Embassy, Ottawa, Can., T-3 Terminal, Changi Internat. Airport, Singapore, The Freedom Tower at the World Trade Center Site, Worldwide Plz. on Eighth Ave, NY Mercantile Exch., JFK Internat. Arrivals Bldg., Bear Sterns Hdqs., master plan for Riverside So., Stuyvesant Sch. Bridge, Tribeca, 450 Lexington Ave over the main post office at Grand Central Station, Swiss Bank Ctr., Stamford, Conn., Deerfield Acad. Natatorium, US Courthouse, Charleston, W.Va.; architect preparing plans for two new office towers in NYC financial district; new NY Stock Exchange, new Pennsylvania Station at the historic Farley Post Office Bldg., the Con Ed properties adjacent to the UN, a science bldg. for Deerfield Acad., Deerfield, Mass.; under construction are designs for new 7 World Trade Ctr., 50 Story Tower for Boston Properties at the head of Time Square, the renovation and preservation of Lever House, has completed or has under construction internat. projects Lester B. Pearson Internat. Airport, Toronto, Can., Ben Gurion Internat. Airport, Tel Aviv, Israel, West Ferry Circus at Canary Wharf, London, US Embassy, Ottawa. Can. Bd. mem. NYC Partnership. Fellow: AIA. Office: Skidmore Owings & Merrill LLP 24th Fl 14 Wall St New York NY 10005

CHILDS, ERIN C., lawyer; b. Chgo., 1977; BA, St. Louis U., 1998; JD, U. Cin., 2002. Bar: Ohio 2002, US Dist. Ct. Southern Dist. Ohio 2002, US Ct. of Appeals Sixth Cir. 2004. Assoc. Thompson Hine LLP, Cin. Ct. apptd. special adv. ProKids. Named one of Ohio's Rising Stars, Super Lawyers, 2006. Mem.: Ohio State Assn., ABA, Cin. Bar Assn. (sec., Young Lawyers Divsn.). Office: Thompson Hine LLP 312 Walnut St 14th Fl Cincinnati OH 45202-4089 Office Phone: 513-352-6756. Office Fax: 513-241-4771.

CHILDS, ERIN THERESE, psychotherapist; b. Redlands, Calif., Apr. 2, 1958; d. C. Russell and Maryann (Carpenter) C. BA in Psychology cum laude, Loyola Marymount U., LA, 1979, MA magna cum laude in Counseling Psychology, 1980; postgrad. in behavioral medicine, Calif. Grad. Inst., 1982-84. Lic. marriage, family and child therapist, 1982, Calif. Youth counselor II, Chino Youth Svcs., Calif., 1979-80; counselor chem. dependency Behavioral Health Svcs., Gardena, Calif., 1981-83; pvt. practice psychotherapy, LA, 1986—; vis., adjunct faculty Phillips Grad. Inst., Grad. Sch. Psychology, 1997-2000; instr. Human Svcs. program U. Phoenix, 2000-; psychotherapist, cons. Thomas Aquinas Psychotherapy Clinic, Encino, Calif., 1981-83; clin. dir. Emergency Crisis Counseling, West LA, 1983; counselor, unit supr. Southbay Outpatient Unit, Behavioral Health Svcs., Gardena, Calif., 1980-82, dir. driving under the influence program, 1984-86; clin. treatment coord. New Beginnings, Century City Hosp., LA, 1985-86, staff psychotherapist, cons. immune supressed unit, 1987-93; instr. cmty. svcs. Pierce Jr. Coll., Woodland Hills, Calif., 1983, Santa Monica City Coll., Calif., 1984, West LA CC., Culver City, Calif., 1984, mental health clinician, Addiction Medicine Dept. Cedar Sinai Med. Ctr., LA, 1997-2000; facilitator Cancer Support Group H.O.P.E. Found., 2001-05; oral examiner Calif. State Bd. Behavioral Sci. Examiners for Marriage Family Therapists; presenter in field. Mem., bd. dirs. Wilton House, 2002-; pres. St. Matthews Luth. Ch., North Hollywood, Calif., 2002-03, coun. mem. 2003-04, v.p. 2005-06; participant Honolulu Marathon, 2001, Vancouver Marathon, 2003, San Francisco Marathon, 2005, as fundraising for the Nat. AIDS marathon. Mem. Calif. Assn. Marriage and Family Therapists, Psi Chi, Alpha Sigma Nu. Democrat. Lutheran. Office: 11650 Riverside Dr Ste 7 Studio City CA 91602 Office Phone: 818-985-4200. E-mail: etchilds@sbcglobal.net.

CHILDS, JOHN DAVID, retired computer company executive; b. Washington, Apr. 26, 1939; s. Edwin Carlton and Catherine Dorothea (Angerman) C.; m. Margaret Rae Olsen, Mar. 4, 1966 (div.); 1 child, John-David. Student, Principia Coll., 1957—60; BA, Am. U., 1963. Jr. adminstr. Page Comms., Washington, 1962-65; account rep. Friden Inc., Washington, 1965-67; Western sales dir. Data Inc., Arlington, Va., 1967-70; v.p. mktg. Rayda, Inc., LA, 1970-73, pres., 1973-76, chmn. bd., 1976-84; v.p. sales Exec. Bus. Systems, Encino, Calif., 1981—87, sr. v.p. sales and mktg., 1987—2001, ret., 2001; sr. assoc. World Trade Assn., Inc., 1976—2001. Pres. Coll. Youth for Nixon-Lodge, 1959-60, dir. state fedn.; mem. OSHA policy formulation com. Dept. Labor, 1967; polit. dir. Coun. 76, AFSCME, 2003--. Served with USAFR, 1960-66. Mem. Assn. Data Ctr. Owners and Mgrs. (chmn. privacy com. 1975, sec. 1972-74, v.p. 1974, sec. supr. com.). Democrat. Christian Scientist.

CHILDS, JOHN FARNSWORTH, retired bank executive; b. NYC, Nov. 24, 1909; s. Albert Ewing and Amelia (McGraw) C.; m. Mary Elizabeth Cardozo, Apr. 21, 1950; 1 dau., Susan Elizabeth. BS, Trinity Coll., Hartford, Conn., 1931, MS, 1932; MBA, Harvard, 1933; LLB, Fordham U., 1946. Bar: N.Y. 1946. Analyst Dick & Merle-Smith, NYC, 1935-40; sr. v.p., head corporate services div. Irving Trust Co., NYC, 1941-74; sr. v.p. Kidder-Peabody Inc., 1974-94, Paine Webber Inc., NYC, 1994-97. Mem. tech. adv. com. on fin. Fed. Power Commn., 1973-74; adj. prof. Columbia Grad. Bus. Sch.; cons. in field. Author: Long-Term Financing, 1961, Profit Goals and Capital Management, 1968, Earnings Per Share and Management Decisions, 1971, Encyclopedia of Long Term Financing and Capital Management, 1976, Corporate Finance and Capital Management for the Chief Executive Officer and Directors, 1979; Contbr. articles to profl. publs. Past treas., trustee Lenox Sch.; bd. dirs. N.Y. Council on Econ. Edn.; past bd. dirs. Sch. Book Fair Inc., Fla. Power Corp. Served as lt. comdr.

USNR, World War II. Mem. Am. Mgmt. Assn. (pres. coun., past dir.), Atomic-Indsl. Forum (past dir.), N.Y. Soc. Security Analysts, Pine Valley Golf Club (Clementin, N.J.). Home: 15 Washington Pl New York NY 10003-6641

CHILDS, MARILYN CARLSON, journalist, educator; b. Springfield, Mass., Aug. 26, 1923; d. Carl Oscar and Dorothy M. (Davis) Carlson; m. Harold Lofton Childs, Febr. 2, 1952; children: David Loring, Robert Stuart, Carl Albert. AA, Vermont Jr. Coll., 1942; BA, Am. Internat., Springfield, 1945. Cert. tchr., Vt. Reporter Montpelier (Vt.) Argus, 1942, Springfield Union, 1943-45; assoc. editor Am. Horseman, Lexington, Ky., 1945-47; mng. editor Popular Horsemen, Harrisburg, Pa., 1948-52; freelance writer various publs., 1953-90; tchr. Chelsea (Vt.) H.S., 1966-88, debate coach, 1970-99, asst. prin., 1975-85. Author: Riding Show Horses, 1963, Mandate For A Morgan Horse, 1967, Training Your Colt to Ride and Drive, 1969, Men Behind the Morgan Horse, 1979; co-author: Training Your Colt to Ride and Drive, revised edit., 1994. Del. Vt. State Rep. Party, Montpelier, 1982-07; chmn. Rep. Fun Days, Chelsea, 1986-92; justice of the peace, Chelsea, 1986-94; mem. Orange County Reparative Bd., 1997—; founding charter mem. Morgan Horse Heritage Found., Inc., 2005-. Named Outstanding Speech Educator Nat. Fedn. State H.S. Assns., 1989, Debate Coach of the Yr. Vt. Debate/Forensics League, Burlington, 1995, VFW's Vt. Citizenship Tchr., 2000. Mem. Am. Horse Shows Assn., Am. Morgan Horse Assn. (life), Am. Saddlebred Horse Assn., Nat. Fedn. Interscholastic Speech/Debate (zone rep. 1986-89), New England Horseman's Coun. (past pres. 1990-95, judge), Delta Kappa Gamma Internat. (pres. 1994-96). Republican. Christian Scientist. Avocations: horses, travel. Home: 48 Harolyn Hill Rd Tunbridge VT 05077-9660

CHILES, MARY JANE, secondary school educator; b. Hampton, Iowa, Apr. 26, 1950; d. Thomas Donald and Grace Hermina (Bouvink) Stark; m. Stephen Eugene Chiles, July 8, 1972; 1 child, Samantha Kathryn Chiles Graef. BA, U. Iowa, Iowa City, 1972; postgrad., Morningside Coll., Sioux City, Iowa, 1974, Okla. State U., Stillwater, 1979—82. Tchr. 7th and 8th grade English Woodbury Ctrl. Sch., Moville, Iowa, 1974—75; tchr. 5-8th grade English Anderson Mid. Sch., Sand Springs, Okla., 1979—80; tchr. 6th grade Anderson Elem. Sch., Sand Springs, 1980—81; tchr. 9th and 10th grade English Moore West Mid. H.S., Okla., 1981—88; tchr. 9th grade English Moore West Jr. H.S., 1988—2005, Moore Ctrl. Jr. H.S., 2005—. Mem. Supt.'s Adv. Coun., Moore, 1997—, Supt.'s Patron Adv. Coun., Moore, 1997—, chair profl. devel. com., 1998-2000; field tester book Elements of Writing, 1993 Mem. steering com. Educators Moore PAC, 1983—90. Mem.: NEA (del. assembly 1985—, Western regional conf. 1990—, mem. elections com. 2003, 2005, 2006, 2007), Moore Assn. Classroom Tchrs. (profl. negotiations team 1982—2004, exec. com. 1985—86, sec. 1986—88, exec. com. 1988—2007, chair constn. com. 1989—90, chair resolutions com. 1992—94, v.p. 1996—98, chair constn. com. 1998—99, treas. 1999—2005, chmn. constn. com. 2005—06, treas. 2006—07), Okla. Edn. Assn. (del. assembly 1983—, sec. resolutions com. 1984—97, standing rules com. 1997—98, resolutions com. 1998—2002, mem. ESP com. 2003—06, bd. dirs. 2003—06), Moore C. of C. (edn. com. 1997—). Democrat. Avocations: travel, swimming. Home: 3201 Willow Lane Moore OK 73170-7912 Office: Moore Ctrl 400 N Broadway Moore OK 73160 Business E-Mail: maryjanechiles@mooreschools.com.

CHILES, STEPHEN MICHAEL, lawyer; b. July 15, 1942; s. Daniel Duncan and Helen Virginia (Hayes) C.; m. Deborah E. Nash, June 13, 1964; children: Stephen, Abigail. BA, Davidson Coll., 1964; JD, Duke U., 1967. Bar: N.Y. 1970, Pa. 1978, Wis. 1981, Ill. 1986, U.S. Dist. Ct. (ea. dist.) Pa. 1978, U.S. Tax Ct. 1978, U.S. Supreme Ct. 1978. Officer trust dept. Irving Trust Co., NYC, 1970-75, v.p., 1975-77; assoc. atty. Stassen Kostos & Mason, Phila., 1978-79, mem., shareholder, 1979-85; ptnr. McDermott, Will & Emery LLP, Chgo., 1986—2004, of counsel, 2005—06. Contbr. articles to profl. jours. Served to capt. U.S. Army, 1967-69. Decorated Bronze Star, Army Commendation medal. Mem.: State Bar Wis., Landings Club, (Savannah, Ga.). Republican. Episcopalian. Office: McDermott Will & Emery 227 W Monroe St Ste 4700 Chicago IL 60606-5096 Personal E-mail: smchiles@comcast.net.

CHILIVIS, NICKOLAS PETER, retired lawyer; b. Athens, Ga., Jan. 12, 1931; s. Peter Nickolas and Wessie Mae (Tanner) C.; m. Patricia Kay Tumlin, June 3, 1967; children— Taryn Tumlin, Nicole Tumlin, Nickolas Peter Tumlin. LL.B., U. Ga., Athens, 1953; LL.M., Atlanta Law Sch., Ga., 1955. Bar: Ga. 1952, U.S. Supreme Ct. 1965. Ptnr. Lester & Chilivis, Athens, Ga., 1953-58; ptnr. Erwin, Epting, Gibson & Chilivis, Athens, Ga., 1958-75; commr. of revenue State of Ga., Atlanta, 1975-77; ptnr. Powell, Goldstein, Frazer & Murphy, Atlanta, 1977-84, Chilivis & Grindler, Atlanta, 1984-95, Chilivis, Cochran, Larkins & Bever, Atlanta, 1995—2003. Adj. prof. U. Ga. Sch. Law, Athens, 1964-74. Author: Termination Settlement, 1955. Contbr. chpts. to books, articles to profl. jours. Bd. visitors U. Ga., Athens, 1983-85; trustee Skandalakis Found., Atlanta, 1984, Found. of the Holy Apostles; former trustee U. Ga. Found.; former mem. U. Ga. Rsch. Found. Bd.; pres. and sr. warden Ch. of Apostles. With USAFR, 1953-55. Recipient Archdiocesan medal Archbishop of North and South Am., 1980. Fellow Internat. Soc. Barristers, Am. Coll. Trial Lawyers, Am. Acad. Appellate Lawyers; mem. Am. Inns. of Ct. (emeritus, master), Old War Horse Lawyers Club, Lawyers Club Atlanta, Heritage Club (Atlanta), Pres.'s Club (U. Ga.), Elks. Avocations: handball, tennis, writing, lecturing. Office: Chilivis Cochran Larkins & Bever Chilivis Bldg 3127 Maple Dr NE Atlanta GA 30305-2503 Home: 2293 Ivy Crest Ln Smyrna GA 30080-6648 Home Phone: 404-231-5355; Office Phone: 404-233-4171. E-mail: fdorfman@cclblaw.com.

CHILLINGWORTH, LORI, bank executive; Grad., Pacific Coast Banking Sch., U. Wash. Sr. v.p., mgr. women's financial group Zions Bank (subsidiary of Zions Bancorporation), Salt Lake City, 1997—. Bd. mem. Family Counseling Ctr., Pete Sauzo Bus. Ctr., Salt Lake Community Coll. Found., Utah Micro-Enterprise Loan Fund; mem., credit com. Salt Lake County Revolving Loan Fund. Named one of 25 Women to Watch, US Banker, 2005, 2006. Office: Zions Bank One S Main St Salt Lake City UT 84111

CHILSON, JOHN A., lawyer, military officer; s. Kenneth N. and Jean Kay Chilson; m. Donna Carol Mays, May 2, 1992; children: Matthew A., Cara N. BS, US Naval Acad., 1991; JD, U. Mich., 1999; grad., Naval War Coll., Newport, RI, 2007. Bar: Mich. 1999, U.S. Ct. Appeals for the Armed Forces 1999, N.C. 2003, U.S. Dist. Ct. (ea. dist.) N.C. 2003, U.S. Dist. Ct. (mid. dist.) N.C. 2003, U.S. Dist. Ct. (we. dist.) N.C. 2003, U.S. Ct. Appeals (4th cir.) 2003. Commd. ensign USN, 1991, advanced through grades to lt. comdr., 2002, surface warfare officer, engr. Charleston, SC, 1992—95, instr. leadership Newport, RI, 1995—97, atty. JAG Corps Pensacola, Fla., 1999—2003; atty. Womble Carlyle Sandridge & Rice PLLC, Winston-Salem, NC, 2003—04; lt. comdr. USNR, 2003—; atty. Ellis & Winters LLP, Greensboro, NC, 2004—06, Comerford Britt, LLP, Winston-Salem, NC, 2006—. Editor: Mich. Jour. Law Reform (Louis Honigman Meml. award, 1999, Dykema Meml. award, 1998), Adelphia Law Jour. Naval acad. info. officer Naval Acad. Admissions Office, Clemmons, NC, 2003—; youth soccer coach YMCA, Clemmons, NC, 2003—; baseball coach Little League, Clemmons, NC, 2005—; at large bd. mem. S.W. Forsyth Little League, Clemmons, NC, 2006—; nonresident dir. Navy Mut. Aid Assn., Arlington, Md., 1999—2003. Named one of NC's Best Lawyer's Under 40, Bus. NC Mag., 2007. Mem.: ABA, Assn. Am. Justice, NC Acad. Trial Lawyers, NC Bar Assn. (young lawyer's divsn. mil. liaison com. 2003—04, lawyer effectiveness and quality life com. 2005—07, professionalism com. 2007—). Avocations: sports, teaching, coaching, studying. Office: Comerford & Britt LLP Ste 200 250 W First St Winston Salem NC 27101 Home Phone: 336-414-8711; Office Phone: 336-631-8510. Office Fax: 336-631-8228. Personal E-mail: chilsonj@comerfordbritt.com.

CHILTON, BART (BARTHOLOMEW HAMILTON CHILTON), commissioner; b. Wilmington, Del., May 1, 1960; BA, Purdue U., 1982. Field dir. Fithian for U.S. Senate, Ind., 1982; adminstrv. asst. Hon. Win Moses, Ft. Wayne, Ind., 1983; regional field dir. Mondale for Pres., Chgo., 1983-84; legis. asst. Hon. Terry Bruce, Washington, 1985-86; legis. dir. Hon. Jim Jontz, Washington, 1987-88, Hon. Jill Long, Washington, 1989-95; exec. dir. House Rural Caucus, Washington, 1993-95; legis. dir. Hon. Earl Pomeroy, Washington, 1995; sr. policy dir. for rural devel. USDA, Washington, 1995-98, dep. chief staff, 1999—2001; sr. v.p. Bio Environ. Technologies, Inc., 2001; sr. adv. to Senator Tom Daschle US Senate, 2001—05; sr. adv. US Farm Credit Adminstrn., Washington, 2005—06; v.p. strategic devel. & govt. rels. & chief of staff to pres. Nat. Farmers Union, 2006—07; commr. Commodity Futures Trading Commn., Washington, 2007—. Mem. Phi Delta Theta. Office: CFTC Three Lafayette Ctr 1155 21st St NW Washington DC 20581*

CHILTON, ELIZABETH EASLEY EARLY, newspaper executive; b. Williamson, W.Va., Dec. 9, 1928; d. Carl Brooks and Susie Mason (Easley) Early; m. William Edwin Chilton III, Apr. 5, 1952 (dec. Feb. 1987); 1 child, Susan Carroll Chilton Shumate Student, Hollins Coll., Va., 1946—48; AA Primary Edn., Marjorie Webster Coll., Washington, 1950; LLD (hon.), W.Va. State U., 2004; D (hon.), U. W.Va., 2004. Pub. rels. staff Charleston Gazette, W.Va., 1952—87; v.p., treas. Daily Gazette Co., Charleston, 1987—91, pres., 1991—, pub., 2004—, also dir., chmn. bd. dirs., 1994—. Mgmt. com. The Charleston Newspapers, 1991-99; adv. bd. Eberly Coll. Arts and Scis., 1996 Mem. editl. bd. The Charleston Gazette, 1987— Chmn. W.Va. Gov.'s Mansion Preservation Found., Charleston, 1989—; bd. trustees U. Charleston, 1989-98, Marshall U.-Yeager Scholars, Huntington, W.Va., 1990-96, W.Va. State Coll. Found., 1988-96, WSWP-TV Pub. Broadcasting, 1980-94, Faculty Merit Scholars, 1991—, W.Va. Humanities Coun., 1994-00; bd. dirs. BIDCO, 1996-98, Advantage Valley, Charleston, 1996-98, Greater Kanawha Valley Found., 1980-86, adv. bd., 1986—; bd. dirs. W.Va. U., Sulgrave Manor Found., 2001, Childrens Express, Charleston Renaissance, Washington, Gunston Hall Plantation, 1977-92, pres., 1989-92; bd. dirs. Clay Ctr. Arts and Scis., Nat. Youth Sci. Found., 1998, Kid's Count; bd. dirs. Worth Bingham Prize Found., exec. com. 1987—; sec. bd. govs. W.Va. U., 2004—. Recipient John Marshall medal for civic responsibility, Marshall U., 1997, Pres. Disting. Svc. award, W.Va. U., 2000, Second Century award for excellence in leadership, W.Va. State Coll., 2003. Mem. So. Newspaper Pubs. (journalism edn. com. 1992-94, minority affairs com. 1994—), Nat. Soc. Colonial Dames W.Va. (pres.), Internat. Press Inst. (dir. Am. com. 1994—), Newspaper Assn. Am. (com. 1987—), Nat. Trust for Historic Preservation, Garden Club Am. (chmn. libr., bd. dirs. 1989-92); Jr. League Charleston, Edgewood Country Club Charleston, Yale Club N.Y.C., Sulgrave Club Washington, Briar Hills Garden Club, Kanawha Garden Club, Sea Pines Country Club Hilton Head Democrat. Presbyterian. Avocations: travel, reading, gardening. Home: 806 Cedar Rd Charleston WV 25314-1206 Office: The Charleston Gazette 1001 Virginia St E Charleston WV 25301-2895

CHILTON, LANCE ALIX, pediatrician; b. Akron, Ohio, Nov. 2, 1944; BA in Human Scis., Johns Hopkins U., 1966, MD, 1969. Diplomate American Board of Pediatrics. Intern U. Wash., Seattle, 1969—70; resident pediat. U. Pitts., 1972—74; faculty mem., dept. pediatrics U. N.Mex., 1975—82, prof. pediatrics, 2005—; former pediatrician Gallup Indian Med. Ctr.; pediatrician U. N.Mex. Hosp., N.Mex., 1975—82; former pediatrician Lovelace Pediat., Albuquerque, 1982—2005; pediatrician Lovelace Med. Ctr., N.Mex., 1982—2005, St. Vincent Hosp., N.Mex., 1995—, Holy Cross Hosp., Taos, 2005—, U. N.Mex. Hosp., 2005—. Prof. pediatrics U. N.Mex., 1975—81, 2005—. Columnist: Albuquerque Jour. Recipient Cmty. Svc. award, N.Mex. Med. Soc., 2006. Mem.: N.Mex. Med. Soc., N.Mex. Pub. Health Assn., N.Mex. Pediat. Soc., Am. Acad. Pediat. (mem. first Indian child project adv. com., former chmn. com. on Native Am. child health, vice chair Dist. VIII, Native Am. Child Health Adv. award 2002). Office: 306A San Pablo SE Albuquerque NM 87108 Office Phone: 505-272-9242.

CHILTON, RONALD HANLEY, broadcasting executive, actor; b. Harrodsburg, Ky., Oct. 15, 1935; s. Hanley Ernest and Dorothy Pearl (Purvis) C.; m. Mary Lee Yates, Feb. 10, 1963; children: Mark Hanley, Brandi Lee. Student, Transylvania U., 1953-54, Miami U., Fla., 1955-56; BA, U. Ky., 1957; postgrad., U. Tenn., Chatanooga, 1971-72; MS, U. Louisville, 1974. Lic. FCC. Staff announcer Sta. WVLK, Lexington, Ky., 1962-66; announcer, sport dir. Sta. WLAP, Lexington, 1966-69; deputy dir. Fed. Model Cities Program, Washington, 1969-72; sta. mgr. Great Trails Broadcasting, Louisville, 1972-76; gen. mgr. Sta. WUOL, Louisville, 1976-77; instr. communications dept. U. Louisville, 1976-77; advt. dir. Gen. Foods Mgrs., Inc., Chattanooga, 1977-81; dir. ops. Sunnyside Broadcasting, Jeffersonville, Ind., 1981—. Appeared in (feature films) Raintree County, 1958, The Great Race, 1965, Stripes, 1981, The Act, 1983, Eight Men Out, 1987, (NBC mini-series) Bluegrass, 1987. Mem. Jaycees, Louisville, 1977. Named Showtime Screen Test regional winner The Movie Channel, N.Y.C., 1986. Mem. Ky. Broadcasters Assn. (Golden Mike award 1976), Louisville Area Radio Execs. Democrat. Mem. Christian Ch. Clubs: Douglas Hills Raquet and Swim, Am. Turners. Lodge: Kiwanis. Avocations: photography, chess, tennis, jogging. Home: 803 Moser Rd Louisville KY 40223-3713 Office: Sta WXVW and WAKG 213 Magnolia Ave Jeffersonville IN 47130-6446

CHILTON, WILLIAM DAVID, architect; b. Tulsa, Jan. 4, 1954; s. Horace Thomas Jr. and Betty Jane (Gray) C. BA in Architecture, Iowa State U., 1976; MArch, U. Minn., 1980. Registered arch., Minn., Conn., Calif., Va., Tex., Okla., Wash., Oreg., D.C., Mass. Designer CDG, Tulsa, 1976; assoc. architect Olson-Coffey Architects, Tulsa, 1977-78, The Leonard Parker Assocs., Mpls., 1980-81; sr. architect Conoco, Inc., Ponca City, Okla., 1981-89; v.p., project mgr. Ellerbe Becket, Inc., Mpls., 1989, v.p., sr. project mgr., 1990, v.p., project dir., 1991-93, sr. v.p., project dir., 1994-98; dir. The Ellerbe Becket Co., Mpls., 1995-99, pres. arch., mng. prin., 1998-99, mem. mgmt. com., 1997-99; mng. prin. Pickard Chilton, New Haven, 1999—. Bd. dirs. Rainier Tech., Mpls., 1998-2001; mem. architecture adv. coun. Iowa State U., 1994-99, chair, 1997-98. Prin. works include as project designer Milne Point (Alaska) Ops. Complex (award Best of Engrng. News Record, 1986, Excellence in Arch. award North Ctrl. Okla. chpt. AIA, 1987, Honorable Mention Builder mag., 1985), Conoco Corp. Offices, Wilmington, Del. (Excellence in Arch. award North Ctrl. Okla. chpt. AIA, 1987), Conoco Office/Housing Facilities, Luanda, Angola, 1985—88, prin. works include as mng. prin. Dow Chem. Corp. Hdqrs. Master Plan, Midland, Mich., 1991, Dow Chem. Global Data Ctr., 1992, Sci. Mus. Minn., St. Paul, 1991—99, Kingdom Centre, Riyadh, Saudi Arabia, 1996—2002, CalPERS Hdqrs., Sacramento, 1999—2005. Bd. dirs. Children's HeartLink, Mpls., 1997-99; mem. nat. adv. bd. U. Minn. Coll. Architecture, 2004-06. Recipient Design Achievement award Iowa State U., 1995. Mem. Conn. Soc. AIA (sec. North Ctrl. Okla. chpt. 1986, v.p. 1987, pres. 1988, bd. dirs. 1986-88, bd. dirs. Okla. Coun. 1987-88), Leadership Mpls., Inst. Dirs. (London), Interlachen Country Club (Edina, Minn.), Mpls. Club. Lutheran. Avocations: fly fishing, golf, reading, music. Home: 452 E River Rd Guilford CT 06437-2289 Office: Pickard Chilton 980 Chapel St New Haven CT 06510-2045 E-mail: wchilton@pickardchilton.com.

CHILVERS, DEREK, insurance company executive; b. Torquay, Eng., Feb. 7, 1940; came to U.S., 1962; s. Reginald Charles and Selina Adelaide (Adamson) C.; m. Elizabeth Anne Locke, Aug. 25, 1968 (div. 1983); m. Cheryl Baker, Apr. 14, 1984; children: Justine, Derek Jr. BA, MA, Cambridge U., 1962. With John Hancock Life Ins. Co., Boston, 1962—, v.p. internat., 1980-85, sr. v.p. internat., 1985-2000, exec. v.p., 2001—04; chmn., CEO John Hancock Internat. Inc., 2006—; dir. Tianan Ins. Co., Shanghai.

CHILVERS, ROBERT MERRITT, lawyer; b. Long Beach, Calif., Oct. 23, 1942; s. James Merritt and Elizabeth Louise (Blackburn) C.; m. Sandra Lee Rigg, Sept. 5, 1969; children: Jeremy Merritt, Jessica Rigg. AB, U. Calif., Berkeley, 1972; JD, Harvard U., 1975. Bar: Calif. 1975, U.S. Dist. Ct. (no. dist.) Calif. 1975, U.S. Ct. Appeals (9th cir.) 1980, U.S. Supreme Ct. 1980, U.S. Dist. Ct. (ctrl. dist.) Calif. 1981, U.S. Ct. Fed. Claims, 1984, U.S. Dist. Ct. (ea. dist.) Calif. 1987, U.S. Ct. Appeals (fed. cir.) 1987. Assoc. Brobeck, Phleger & Harrison, San Francisco, 1975-82, ptnr., 1982-93; spl. master U.S. Dist. Ct. (no. dist.) Calif., 1994-99; pres. Chilvers & Taylor, San Rafael, Calif., 1996—. Neutral evaluator and mediator U.S. Dist. Ct. (no. dist.) Calif., 2001—; faculty U. Calif. Hastings Sch. Law, San Francisco, 1983-89, Emory U., Atlanta, 1984-90, fed. practice program U.S. Dist. Ct. (no. dist.) Calif., 1984-86, Nat. Inst. for Trial Advocacy, 1986—, Cardozo Law Sch., Yeshiva U., N.Y.C., 1993-99, Stanford U. Law Sch., 1994—, Widener U. Sch. Law, Wilmington, 1994-96, U. San Francisco Sch. Law, 1994—. Mem. Calif. Sch. Bds. Assn., 1985—89; trustee Mill Valley Sch. Dist., Calif., 1985—89, chmn. Calif., 1987—89; bd. dirs. Marin County Sch. Bds. Assn., Calif., 1985—86, Artisans, Mill Valley, Calif., 1999—2001. With USMC, 1964—71. Mem. Calif. Bar Assn. (commendation for Outstanding Contbns. to the delivery of vol. legal svcs. 1984), Marin County Bar Assn., Tau Beta Pi, Sigma Tau. Office: Chilvers & Taylor 83 Vista Marin San Rafael CA 94903-5228 Office Phone: 415-444-0875.

CHIMENTI, DALE E., engineering educator; b. Chgo., July 26, 1946; s. Cyro and Lola Chimenti; m. Linda M. Ott, July 15, 1947; children: Michael S., Peter C. BA, Cornell Coll., Mt. Vernon, Iowa, 1968; PhD, Cornell U., Ithaca, NY, 1974. Rsch. assoc. Argonne (Ill.) Nat. Lab., 1974—76; sci. asst. U. of Tuebingen, Baden-Wuertemberg, Germany, 1976—78; rsch. materials engr. Air Force Materials Lab., Dayton, Ohio, 1978—89; rsch. prof. of materials sci. and engrng. Johns Hopkins U., Balt., 1989—93; prof. of aerospace engrng. Iowa State U., Ames, 1993—. Invited prof. U. of Bordeaux, Talence, Gironde, France (incl. Monaco), 1999—2000; Alexander von Humbolt fellow U. of Stuttgart, Baden-Wuertemberg, Germany, 2000—01. Editor: (jour.) NDT&E Internat., (conf. procs.) Rev. of Progress in Quantitative Nondestructive Evaluation. Recipient TTCP Achievement award, U.S. Dept of Def., 1989, Air Force Sci. Achievement award, Air Force Materials Lab., 1982, 1986. Fellow: Acoustical Soc. of Am. (assoc. editor 1998—2004). Achievements include research in Elastic waves in layered heterogeneous materials; patents pending for Spherically focused membrane air-coupled ultrasonic transducer; Leak location on board manned spacecraft using structure-borne leak noise. Office: Iowa State U Dept Aerospace Engrng 1200 Howe Hall Ames IA 50011-2271 Business E-Mail: chimenti@iastate.edu.

CHIMNEY, MICHAEL JOHN, aquatic biologist/limnologist, consultant; b. Cleve., Dec. 19, 1951; s. Florian Frank and Lucille Colleta (Moenich) C. MS in Zoology, Miami U., Oxford, Ohio, 1976; PhD in Zoology, So. Ill. U., 1981. Grad. teaching asst. dept. zoology Miami U., Oxford, 1974-76; grad. rsch. asst. dept. zoology So. Ill. U., Carbondale, 1976-77, grad. teaching asst. dept. zoology, 1977-80, rsch. project dir., 1980-83; project mgr., limnologist Normandeau Assocs. Inc. (formerly Environ. and Chem. Scis. Inc.), New Ellenton, S.C., 1984-93, mgr. div. ecol. scis., 1990-93; adj. prof. dept. biology U. S.C., Aiken, 1985-89; sr. supervising environ. scientist South Fla. Water Mgmt. Dist., West Palm Beach, 1993—. Adj. prof. dept. biol. sci. Fla. Atlantic U., 1997-2004; vis. asst. prof. dept. zoology So. Ill. U., Carbondale, 1981-82. Contbr. articles to profl. jours. Dissertation Rsch. fellow So. Ill. U., 1979; grantee Ill. Mining and Mineral Resources Inst., 1981. Mem. AAAS, Am. Soc. Limnology and Oceanography, Ecol. Soc. Am. (cert. ecologist 1985, sr. ecologist 1989), N.Am. Benthological Soc., N.Am. Lake Mgmt. Soc. (cert. lake mgr., mem. profl. certificate rev. bd.), Internat. Assn. Theoretical and Applied Limnology, Sigma Xi (rsch. grantee 1979), Soc. Wetland Scientists (prof.). Achievements include research in applied limnology of lakes, reservoirs, and wetlands; lake and wetland management/restoration strategies; ecology of aquatic invertebrates. Office: South Fla Water Mgmt Dis 3301 Gun Club Rd West Palm Beach FL 33406-3007 E-mail: mchimney@sfwmd.gov.

CHIMPLES, GEORGE, lawyer; b. Canton, Ohio, Oct. 8, 1924; s. Mark and Katherine (Hines) C.; m. Eileen Mary Grumm, July 14, 2003; children: Alicia Candace, Mark II, John Hines, Katherine Hines. AB, Princeton U., 1951; LLB, Harvard Coll., 1954. Bar: Pa. 1955, U.S. Dist. Ct. (ea. dist.) Pa. 1955, U.S. Ct. Appeals (3d cir.) 1955, U.S. Ct. Claims, 1965, U.S. Tax Ct., 1965. Assoc. Stradley, Ronon, Stevens & Young, Phila., 1954-61, gen. ptnr., 1961-92; pvt. practice Wayne, Pa., 1993—. Adj. prof. law U. Pa., Drexel U. Grad. Sch. Bus.; co-authored establishment of overseas infrastructure for securities mktg. in Europe and the Antilles. Trustee Christ Ch. Preservation Trust; permament assoc. Phila. Mus. Art.; founding mem. Duxford (Eng.) Air Mus. Capt. USAAF, 1942-46, ETO. Decorated D.F.C., Air medal with four oak leaf clusters, Air Force Commendation medal, Victory medal, four Battle Stars; recipient Royal Air Force plaque, 1994. Mem. ABA (chmn. subcom. regulated investment cos.), Phila. Bar Assn. (tax sect.), Internat. Bar Assn., Internat. Fiscal Assn. (tax treaty sect.), Mid-Atlantic Coun., Newcomen Soc. U.S. (trustee emeritus, life mem.) Army and Navy Club (Washington chpt.), Penn Club (life, bd. dirs., historian) Athenaeum of Phila. (life), Libr. Co. of Phila. (life), Phila. Mus. Art (permanent assoc.), Phila. Club, Cannon Club (Princeton chpt.), Torresdale-Frankford Country Club. Home and Office: 1522 Overington St Philadelphia PA 19124-5808 Home Phone: 215-288-5080; Office Phone: 215-743-4070. E-mail: gchimples@aol.com.

CHIMSKY-LUSTIG, MARK EVAN, editor, consultant; b. Cin., Jan. 24, 1955; s. Matthew and Jean (Berger) C.; life ptnr. Robert Ira Chimsky-Lustig; 1 child, AJ BA, Carnegie-Mellon U., 1976. Editor Anderson Pub. Co., Cin., 1977-79; copy editor Book-of-the-Month Club, Quality Paperback Book Club, NYC, 1979-85; mng. editor Quality Paperback Book Club, NYC, 1985-89, exec. editor, 1989-91; editor in chief Collier Books Macmillan Co., NYC, 1991-94; dir. trade paperbacks Little, Brown and Co., NYC, 1994-96; from exec. editor to edit. dir. Harper, San Francisco, 1996-98, exec. editor, 1998-99; editl. cons. Mark Chimsky Editl. Plus, Riverdale, NY, 1999—. Adj. instr. NYU, NYC, 1999—; dir. NYU Summer Pub. Inst., NYC, 2000, NYC, 03, NYC, 04. Contbr. essays and poetry to lit. jours. including Jour. AMA Recipient New-Emerging Poet/Anna Davidson Rosenberg award, 1997 Mailing: PO Box 6760 Portland ME 04103-6760 Office Phone: 207-775-1885.

CHIN, ALBERT KAE, research physician; b. Spokane, Wash., May 5, 1953; s. Ting H. and Beatrice Y. Chin; m. Jeanne Yee, Aug. 6, 1977; children: Jennifer, Lisa, Stephanie. BSME, MIT, 1975; MSME, Stanford U., 1976; MD, U. Calif., San Francisco, 1983. Resident in gen. surgery U. Tex. Southwestern, Dallas, 1983-85; dir. rsch. Fogarty Rsch., Portola Valley, Calif., 1985-89; founder, v.p. rsch. Origin Medsystems, Inc., Menlo Park, Calif., 1989—2006; v.p. rsch. divsn. cardiac surgery Boston Sci. Corp., Santa Clara, Calif., 1994—. Cardiovasc. cons. Baxter Edwards LIS Divsn., Irvine, Calif., 1988; expert witness Advanced Cardiovascular Systems, Santa Clara, Calif., 1989; mem. adv. bd. dept. biomed. engrng.

Ga. Tech. U. Contbr. articles to profl. publs.; holder more than 150 patents in field. Bd. dirs. YMCA, Palo Alto, Calif., 1987-89. Mem. AMA, Soc. Laparoendoscopic Surgeons, Internat. Soc. Endovascular Surgery, FF Fraternity (chmn. San Francisco lodge 1986). Avocations: piano, violin, organ, guitar, weightlifting. Office: Boston Sci Corp Cardiac Surgery Divsn 3200 Lakeside Dr Santa Clara CA 95054-2807

CHIN, AUGUSTUS G., lawyer; Bar: Utah 1997. Pros. atty. Criminal Divsn. Summit County Atty.'s Office, Park City, Utah. Mem.: Utah State Bar (pres. 2006—07). Office: Criminal Divsn Summit County Courts Facilty 6300 N Silver Creek Dr #4 Park City UT 84098 Office Phone: 435-615-3828. Office Fax: 435-615-3833. E-mail: gchin@co.summit.ut.us.

CHIN, CHENG, physicist, educator; BS in Physics, Nat. Taiwan U., 1993; PhD in Physics, Stanford U., Calif., 2001. Postdoctoral fellow physics dept. Stanford U., 2001—03; vis. prof. U. Innsbruck Inst. Exptl. Physics, Austria, 2003, vis. scientist, 2003—05; vis. prof. Swiss Fed. Inst. Tech. (ETH), Zurich, 2005; asst. prof. dept. physics and James Franck Inst. U. Chgo., 2005—. Contbr. articles to sci. jours. Recipient Young Rschr. award, Overseas Chinese Physics Assn., 2006; Alfred P. Sloan fellow, 2006—, Packard fellow, 2006—. Office: Dept Physics U Chgo 929 E 57th St Chicago IL 60637 Office Phone: 773-702-7192. Office Fax: 773-834-5250. E-mail: cchin@uchicago.edu.*

CHIN, DAVIS, lawyer; b. Evansville, Ind., Dec. 13, 1947; s. Frank S. M. and Mamie (Shu) C.; m. Pauline C., Aug. 3, 1974; 1 child, Davis M. BS, Rose-Hulman Inst. Tech., Terre Haute, Ind., 1969; JD, U. Balt., 1974; LLM in Taxation, John Marshall Law Sch., 1981. Bar: Ill. 1974, U.S. Dist. Ct. (no. dist.) 1974, U.S. Ct. Appeals (7th cir.) 1974, U.S. Patent and Trademark Office 1974, U.S. Claims Ct. 1977, U. S. Tax Ct. 1977, U.S. Supreme Ct. 1977, U.S. Ct. Appeals (fed. cir.) 1982. Staff atty. CTS Corp., Elkhart, Ind., 1974; assoc. Petherbridge, Lindgren & Gilhooly, Chtd., Chgo., 1974-78; staff atty. Borg-Warner Corp., Chgo., 1978-80, Container Corp. Am., Chgo., 1980-84; pvt. practice Chgo., 1984—. Instr. Prairie State Coll., Chgo. Heights, 1987-90, 94, South Suburban Coll., South Holland, Ill., 1989-91, Roosevelt U., Olympia Fields, Ill., 1990-93. Elder United Presbyn. Ch., South Holland, 1986—; panel program atty. Chgo. Vol. Legal Svcs., 1988—. Mem. Am. Intellectual Property Law Assn., Chgo. Bar Assn., Intellectual Property Law Assn. Chgo., Patent Law Assn. Chgo. (bd. mgrs. 1985-87, 94-96). Avocations: tennis, golf, travel. Home: 11428 Plattner Dr Mokena IL 60448-9228 Office: 10281 West Lincoln Highway Frankfort IL 60423 Office Phone: 815-806-8477. Personal E-mail: davischin@juno.com.

CHIN, DER-TAU, chemical engineer, educator; b. Zhejiang, China, Sept. 14, 1939; came to U.S., 1963, naturalized, 1977; s. Tsu-Kang and Shou-Chen (Chen) C.; m. Lorna Fe Gencianeo, July 17, 1971; children: Janet G., Lynn G. BSChemE, Chungyuan Coll. Sci. & Engring, 1962; MSChemE, Tufts U., 1965; PhD in Chem. Engring., U. Pa., 1969. Plant engr. Lungyen Sugar Factory, 1962-63; sci. programmer USAF Cambridge (Mass.) Rsch. Lab., Lexington, Mass., 1965; sr. rsch. engr. rsch. labs. GM Corp., Warren, Mich., 1969-75; prof. Clarkson U., Potsdam, NJ, 1975—2004, prof. emeritus, 2004—. Vis. scientist Brookhaven Nat. Lab., Upton, N.Y., summers 1977, 80, U.S. Army Belvoir Research Devel. Ctr., Ft. Belvoir, Va., summer 1985, U.S. Army Electronics Tech. and Devices Lab., Ft. Mammouth, N.J., summer, 1986, Armstrong Lab. Tyndall Air Force Base, Fla., summer 1995; vis. prof. U. Calif., Berkeley, 1981, Swiss Fed. Inst. Tech., Zurich, 1981, Nat. U. Singapore, 1982, 87, Nat. Tsing Hua UNI, 1989, King Fahd U. Petroleum and Minerals, Dhahran, Saudi Arabia, 2000-2001; cons. Centro de Pesquisas do Energia Electrica, Rio de Janiero, Brazil, summer 1979. Fellow Electrochem. Soc. (Young Authors award 1971); mem. AIChE, Am. Electroplaters Soc., Am. Chem. Soc. Office: Clarkson U PO Box 5705 Potsdam NY 13699-5705 Home Phone: 315-265-4300; Office Phone: 315-268-7930. Business E-Mail: chin@clarkson.edu.

CHIN, HONG WOO, oncologist, educator, researcher; b. Seoul, Korea, May 14, 1935; came to U.S., 1974; s. Jik H. and Woon K. (Park) C.; m. Soo J. Chung, Dec. 27, 1965; children: Richard Y., Helen H., KiSik. MD, Seoul Nat. U., 1962, PhD, 1974. Diplomate Am. Bd. Radiology; cert. Korean bd. internal medicine. Resident in radiation oncology Royal Victoria Hosp., Montreal (Que., Can.) Gen. Hosp., 1975-79; asst. prof. U. Ky., Lexington, 1979-86; assoc. dir. Radiarium Found., Overland Park, Kans., 1987-88; clin. prof. radiology U. Mo., Kansas City, 1987-91; chief radiation oncology Va. Med. Ctr., Shreveport, La., 1988; assoc. prof. La. State U., Shreveport, 1988; prof. and dir. radiation oncology Creighton U. Sch. Medicine, Omaha, 1988-90; dir. dept. radiation oncology Creighton U. Cancer Ctr., Omaha, 1988-90; chief radiation oncology Overton Brooks VA Med. Ctr., Shreveport, La., 1990—2003, Dayton (Ohio) VA Med. Ctr., 2003—. Prof. La. State U. Med. Ctr., Shreveport. Author monographs. Lt. comdr. USN, 1967-70. Mem. Pan Am. Med. Assn. (mem. coun. 1984—), AMA, Am. Coll. Radiology, Am. Soc. Therapeutic Radiology and Oncology, Radiation Rsch. Soc., Am. Biograph Assn. (rsch. bd. advisors 1988), Internat. Platform Assn. Roman Catholic. Home: 3860 Mesquite Dr Dayton OH 45440

CHIN, MEL, sculptor; b. Houston, 1951; BA, Peabody Coll., Nashville, 1975. Lamar Dodd profl. chair fine arts U. Ga., Athens, 1994—97; consulting prof. Stanford U., Calif., 1998; sculpture prof. Cooper Union, NYC, 1999. Exhibited in group shows at The Manila Palm, Contemporary Arts Mus., Houston, 1978, Fire, 1979, Out of This World, 1994, Landscape as Metaphor, Denver Art Mus., Colo. and Columbus Mus., Ohio, 1994, Equal Rights & Justice, High Mus., Atlanta, 1994, Refuse/Refuse, Honolulu Acad. Arts, 1994, Old Glory: The Am. Flag in Contemporary Art, Cleve. Ctr. Contemporary Art, 1994, Robert McClain & Co., Houston, 1994, Sculpting with the Environment: A Natural Dialogue, Pratt Inst., NY, 1994, Black Male, Whitney Mus. Am. Art, 1994, Murder, Bergamot Sta. Arts Ctr., Santa Monica, Calif., 1995, Grounder, ART/OMI, 1995, Tex. Myths & Realities, Mus. Fine Arts, Houston, 1995, commissioned works, Ecliptic Fence, Houston, 1986, Conditions for Memory, Ctrl. Pk., NYC, 1989, public works, Birmingham Mus. Art, Ala., Harold Washington Libr., Chgo., Menil Found., Houston, Mus. Fine Arts, Prudential Svc. Corpn., Newark, exhibitions include Frumkin/Adams Gallery, 1988, Hirshhorn Mus. & Sculpture Garden, Washington, 1989, Walker Art Ctr., 1990, Menil Collection, Houston, 1991, Storefront for Art & Architecture, NY, 1991, Fabric Workshop & Swarthmore Coll., Phila., 1992, Colo. State U., Ft. Collins, 1995, KNOWMAD, Fredericke Taylor Gallery, NYC, 2000, Render, 2003, Do Not Ask Me, Sta. Mus., Houston, 2006. Recipient Penny McCall Found. award, 1991, CalArts Alpert award, Visual Arts, 1995, Joan Mitchell Found. award, 1997, Nancy Graves Found. award, 2004; grantee, Nat. Endowment Arts, 1988, 1990, 1991, Creative Capital Grant, 2001. Mailing: c/o Frederieke Taylor Gallery 535 W 22nd St 6th Fl New York NY 10011

CHIN, MING W., state supreme court justice; b. Klamath Falls, Oreg., Aug. 31, 1942; m. Carol Lynn Joe, Dec. 19, 1971; children: Jennifer, Jason. BA in Polit. Sci., U. San Francisco, 1964, JD, 1967; LLD (hon.), Southwestern U. Sch. of Law, 1996, Golden Gate Un. Sch. of Law, 1997, U. San Diego Sch. of Law, 1998, Western State U. Sch. of Law, 1998. Bar: Calif. 1970, U.S. Fed. Ct., U.S. Tax Ct. Assoc., head trial dept. Aiken, Kramer & Cummings, Oakland, Calif., 1973—76, prin., 1976—88; dep. dist. atty. Alameda County, Calif., 1970—72; judge Alameda County Superior Ct., 1988—90; assoc. justice divsn. 3 Ct. Appeal 1st Dist., 1990—94; presiding justice 1st Dist. Ct. Appeal Divsn. 3, San Francisco, 1994—96; state supreme ct. assoc. justice Calif. Supreme Ct., San Francisco, 1996—. Author: California Practice Guide: Employment Litigation, 2005. Capt. US Army, 1967—69, Vietnam, Capt. USAR, 1969—71. Decorated US Army Commendation medal, Bronze Star; named Outstanding Judge of the Yr., So. Alameda County Bar Assn., 1989, Honoree for Service in Field of Law, Chinese Consolidated Benevolent Assn. & Chinese Women's Assn. of Am., 1997; recipient Learned Hand award, Am. Jewish Com., 1997, Legal Impact award, Asian Pacific Am. Legal Ctr. of So. Calif., 1997, Citizen of the Yr. award, Chinese Americans United for Self Empowerment, 1998, Public Service & Govt. Leadership award, Asian Bus. Assn., 1998, Trailblazer award, Nat. Asian Pacific Am. Bar Assn., 1999. Mem.: ABA, Asian Am. Bar Assn., San Francisco Dist. Atty.'s Commn. Hate Crimes, Alameda County Bar Assn., State Bar Calif., Calif. Judges Assn., Commonwealth Club of Calif. (pres. 1998), Alpha Sigma Nu. Office: Supreme Court Calif 350 McAllister St Fl 1 San Francisco CA 94102-4783 Office Phone: 415-865-7050. E-mail: ming.chin@jud.ca.gov.*

CHIN, SIMON H., plastic surgeon; b. Seoul, June 9, 1973; s. Paul and Jennifer Chin; m. Sooa Chung, June 4, 2000; 1 child, Angelina. BA summa cum laude, Harvard U., Cambridge, Mass., 1992—95; MD, Vanderbilt U., Nashville, Tenn., 1996—2000. Gen. surgery residency Yale U. Sch. Medicine, New Haven, 2003, plastic surgery resident, 2003—06; hand surgery fellow U. Wash., Seattle, 2006—07; aesthetic surgery fellow Manhattan Eye, Ear & Throat Hosp., NYC, 2007—. Cons. surgeon Heal Children, New Haven, 2004—06; presenter in field. Author: (scientific exhibitions) Guidelines for Simultaneous Bilateral Endoscopic Carpal Tunnel Release, Molecular Analysis of Dupuytren's Disease, (medical exhibition) A Meta-analysis of Endoscopic vs. Open Carpal Tunnel Release; contbr. articles to profl. jours., chapters to books. Vol. surgeon Healing Children, Pereira, Colombia, 2004—05. Mem.: AMA, Am. Soc. Maxillofacial Surgeons, Am. Soc. Surgery Hand. Achievements include patents pending for vacuum assisted closure of upper extremity wounds. Avocations: travel, writing, running, guitar, zen philosophy. Office: Univ Wash 4245 Roosevelt Way Seattle WA 98112 Home: 1161 York Ave #9L New York NY 10065-7973 Personal E-mail: simonhchin2000@yahoo.com.

CHIN, SUE SOONE MARIAN (SUCHIN CHIN), artist, photojournalist; b. San Francisco; d. William W. and Soo-Up (Swebe) C. Grad., Calif. Coll. Art, Mpls. Arts Inst.; scholar, Schaeffer Design Ctr.; student, Yasuo Kuniyoshi, Louis Hamon, Rico LeBrun. Photojournalist All Together Now Show, 1973, East-West News, Third World Newscasting, 1975-78, Sta. KNBC Sunday Show, LA, 1975, 76, Live on 4, 1981, Bay Area Scene, 1981. Chmn. Full Moon Products; pres., bd. dirs. Aumni Oracle Inc. Graphics printer, exhbns. include: Kaiser Ctr., Zellerbach Pla., Chinese Culture Ctr. Galleries, Capricorn Asunder Art Commn. Gallery (all San Francisco), Newspace Galleries, New Coll. of Calif., L.A. County Mus. Art, Peace Pla. Japan Ctr., Congress Arts Comm., Washington, 1989; SFWA Galleries, Inner Focus Show, 1989—, Calif. Mus. Sci. and Industry, Lucien Labaudt Gallery, Salon de Medici, Madrid, Salon Renacimento, Madrid, 1995, Life is a Circus, SFWA Gallery, 1991, 94, UN/50 Exhibit, Bayfront Galleries, 1995, Somar Galleries, 1997, 2003 (Merit award 2003), Sacramento State Fair, 2000, Star Child, Women thru the Ages - Somarts Gallery, 2000, Kings Gallery, San Francisco, 2004, AFL-CIO Labor Studies Ctr., Washington, Asian Women Artists (1st prize for conceptual painting, 1st prize photography), 1978, Yerba Buena Arts Ctr. for the Arts Festival, 1994; represented in permanent collections L.A. County Fedn. Labor, Calif. Mus. Sci. and Industry, AFL-CIO Labor Studies Ctr., Australian Trades Coun., Hazeland and Co., also pvt. collections; author: (poetry) Yuri and Malcolm, The Desert Sun, 1994 (Editors Choice award 1993-94). Del. nat., state convs. Nat. Women's Polit. Caucus, 1977-83, San Francisco chpt. affirmative action chairperson, 1978-82, nat. conv. del., 1978-81, Calif. del., 1976-81. Recipient Honorarium AFL-CIO Labor Studies Ctr., Washington, 1975-76, Bicentennial award 1976; award Centro Studi Ricerche delle Nazioni, Italy, 1985; bd. advisors Psycho Neurology Found. Bicentennial award LA County Mus. Art, 1976, 77, 78, Mandalay Merit award Som Arts Gallery, 2003. Mem. Asian Women Artists (founding v.p., award 1978-79, 1st award in photography of Orient 1978-79, Merit award 2003), Calif. Chinese Artists (sec.-treas. 1978-81), Japanese Am. Art Coun. (chairperson 1978-84, dir.), San Francisco Women Artists, San Francisco Graphics Guild, Pacific/Asian Women Coalition Bay Area, Chinatown Coun. Performing and Visual Arts. Address: PO Box 421415 San Francisco CA 94142-1415

CHIN, SYLVIA FUNG, lawyer; d. Thomas and Constance (Yao) Fung; m. Edward G.H. Chin, July 10, 1971; children: Arthur F., Benjamin F. BA, NYU, 1971; JD, Fordham U., 1977. Bar: NY 1978, US Dist. Ct. (so. and ea. dists.) NY 1979, US Supreme Ct. 1990. Law clk. to dist. judge US Dist. Ct. (so. dist.), NYC, 1977-79; assoc. White & Case, NYC, 1979-86, ptnr., 1986—. Adj. assoc. prof. law Fordham U., NYC, 1979-81. Mem. editl. bd.: Bus. Law Today, 1996—2002. Vol. Ch. of the Resurrection, Rye, NY, 1995—; pres. Nat. Asian Pacific Am. Law Found., 2005—06. Recipient Leonard Manning Achievement award, Fordham Law Rev., 1999, Women's Alumni award, Fordham Law, 1997, Pace Asian Law Student's award, 1996. Mem.: ABA, NY State Bar Assn. (mem. house of delegates 2006—), Am. Bar Found., Am. Law Inst., Am. Coll. Comml. Fin. Lawyers (bd. regents 2006—), Am. Coll. Investment Counsel (bd. dirs. 1999—2005, pres. 2002—03), Nat. Asian Pacific ABA (treas. 1997—98, Trailblazers award 1999), Women's World Banking (bd. dirs. 1990—), Asian Am. Bar Assn. (pres. 1994—96, bd. dirs. 1991—97), NY County Lawyers Assn. (bd. dirs. 2004—07), Assn. Bar City NY, Asian Am. Law Fund NY (bd. dir. 1993—, 1993—), Fordham Law Alumni Assn. (bd. dirs. 1995—). Office: White & Case LLP 1155 Ave of Americas New York NY 10036-2711 Office Phone: 212-819-8200. Business E-Mail: schin@whitecase.com.

CHINA, DANIEL WILLIAM, lawyer; b. Balt., Feb. 27, 1966; BA summa cum laude, Syracuse U., 1988; JD cum laude, U. Md., 1991. Bar: Ct. Appeals Md., US Ct. Fed. Claims, US Dist. Ct. (dist. Md.). Ptnr. constrn. dept. and comml. litig. dept. Venable LLP, Towson, Md. Lectr. in field. Contbr. articles to profl. jours. Chairperson Legis. Com. Cumberland Valley County, Assn. Builders and Contractors. Named one of Top Twenty Up-And-Coming Lawyers, Balt. Mag., 2003; recipient Am. Jurisprudence award. Mem.: ABA, Md. State Bar Assn., Bar Assn. Balt. City, Phi Beta Kappa, Pi Sigma Alpha. Fluent in French.*

CHINARD, FRANCIS PIERRE, physiologist, consultant physician, educator; b. Berkeley, Calif., June 30, 1918; s. Gilbert and Emma (Blanchard) C.; m. Josephine L. Wise, June 23, 1943; children: Suzanne F., Jeanne M., Marc F. AB, U. Calif., Berkeley, 1937; MD, Johns Hopkins U., 1941. Intern, jr. asst. resident in medicine Presbyn. Hosp., NYC, 1941-42; asst. physician Hosp. Rockefeller Inst., NYC, 1945-49; instr. to assoc. prof. medicine and physiol. chemistry Johns Hopkins Sch. Med., Balt., 1949-54; asst. prof. medicine U. Md., 1954-62, assoc. prof., 1962-63; physician Johns Hopkins Hosp., 1956-63; prof. exptl. medicine, dep. dir. med. clinic McGill U., Canada, 1963-64; prof. medicine NYU, 1964-68, adj. prof., 1968-70; career scientist N.Y.C. Health Rsch. Coun., 1964-68; prof. medicine, chmn. dept. U. Medicine and Dentistry N.J., Newark, 1968-75, prof. exptl. medicine, 1975-77, prof. rsch. medicine, 1977—, prof. physiology, 1978—, Disting. prof., 1989—, emeritus, 1996; physician-in-chief Balt. City Hosp., 1962-63; acting physician-in-chief Goldwater Meml. Hosp., NYC, 1965-67; dir. med. svc. Martland Hosp., Newark, 1970-71; cons. physician VA Hosp., East Orange, NJ, 1971-79, 93-95. Mem. staff Balt. City Hosps., 1953-63; cons. in field; pres. Faculty Practice Svc. Corp., N.J. Med. Sch., 1986-88; vis. scientist Med. Rsch. Coun. Can., McGill U., Montreal, 1989-90; lectr. in field. Author: (With J.W. Bauman Jr.) Renal Function, 1975; editorial com.: Jour. Clin. Investigation, 1954-59, Jour. Applied Physiology, 1959-65, Am. Jour. Physiology, 1959-65, Circulation Research, 1967-72, Microvascular Research, 1981-89, Revue française des Maladies respiratoires, 1979-93, clin. and investigative medicine, 1985-96; contbr. articles on indicator-dilution techniques, membrane permeability and transport, pulmonary, renal function, free radicals and history of medicine, physiology, and med. ethical issues to med. jours. Mem. profl. adv. com. Martha's Vineyard Guidance Ctr., 1968-75; mem. pulmonary disease adv. com. Nat. Heart and Lung Inst., 1971-75, chmn., 1974-75, mem. bd. sci. counselors, 1976-80, chmn., 1978-80. Served to maj. M.C. USAAF, 1942-45. Decorated Legion of Merit; recipient Lucian award McGill U., 1989, Sir William Osler Humanitarian award N.J. Thoracic Soc., 1991, Laureate award N.J. chpt. Am. Coll. Physicians, 1993, Charles L. Brown award Alumni Assn. N.J. Med. Sch. Fellow: ACP, AAAS, N.Y. Acad. Scis.; mem.: Am. Chem. Soc., Am. Soc. Biochemistry and Molecular Biology, Am., Can. Socs. Clin. Investigation, Soc. Exptl. Biology and Medicine, Assn. Am. Physicians, Am. Physiol. Soc., Peripatetic Soc., Acad. Medicine NJ (trustee 1972—78), Am. Heart Assn. (rsch. com. NJ affiliate 1975—81), Inst Français Washington (trustee 1994—2005), Microcirculatory Soc. (Landis award), Am. Thoracic Soc., Soc. Scholars (Johns Hopkins), N.Y. Clin. Soc., Med. History Soc. NJ (pres. 1984—86), Am. Assn. History of Medicine (councilor), Harvey Soc., Interurban Clin. Club, Century Assn. Club (N.Y.C.), Charaka Club, Sigma Xi, Alpha Omega Alpha. Democrat. Achievements include research in pulmonary diseases; kidney and lung physiology; transcapillary water movement. Office: 40 Warren Pl Montclair NJ 07042-2534 Home Phone: 973-746-7847; Office Phone: 973-746-7847.

CHIN-BING, STANLEY ARTHUR, physicist, educator; b. New Orleans, La., Nov. 3, 1942; s. Arthur Joseph Chin-Bing and Adele Viola Peavy; m. Hilda Faye Taylor, Aug. 12, 1995 (dec. Aug. 12, 1997). BS, Tulane U., 1964; MS, U. New Orleans, 1966, PhD, 1973. Spl. lectr. U. New Orleans, 1973, asst. prof. of engring., 1975—79, adj. prof. of physics, 1988—; sys. analyst Martin Marietta Corp., New Orleans, 1974—75; advanced systems sr. engr. space divsn. Chrysler Corp., New Orleans, 1976—77; rsch. physicist Naval Ocean R & D Activity, Bay St. Louis, Miss., 1978—88; supervisory rsch. physicist Naval Oceanog. and Atmospheric Rsch. Lab., Bay St. Louis, 1988—92; head, acoustic simulation, measurements and tactics br. Naval Rsch. Lab., Stennis Space Center, Miss., 1992—. Contbr. more than 40 articles to sci. jours.; author: Procs. of Parabolic Equation Workshop II. Fellow: Acoustical Soc. Am. (assoc. editor 1996—2003); mem.: AAAS, Soc. Indsl. and Applied Mathematicians, NY Acad. of Sciences, Math. Assn. of Am., IEEE Ocean Engring. Soc., Am. Assn. of Physics Teachers, Optical Soc. of Am., Am. Phys. Soc., Sigma Pi Sigma. Home: 3619 Bauvais St Metairie LA 70001-5005 Office: Naval Rsch Lab 1005 Balch Blvd Stennis Space Center MS 39529-5004 Office Phone: 228-688-4798. E-mail: chinbing@nrlssc.navy.mil.

CHING, BRIAN, professional soccer player; b. Haleiwa, Hawaii, May 24, 1978; Attended, Gonzaga Univ. Forward LA Galaxy, 2001, Seattle Sounders, 2002, San Jose Earthquakes, 2003—05, Houston Dynamo, 2006—. 20 caps, 4 goals U.S. Nat. Soccer Team, 2003—; mem. U.S. World Cup Team, 2006. Named Comeback Player of the Yr., Major League Soccer, 2004. Mailing: US Soccer Fedn 1801 S Prairie Ave Chicago IL 60616

CHING, CHAUNCEY TAI KIN, agricultural studies educator, economist; b. Honolulu, July 25, 1940; m. Theodora Lam, July 7, 1962; children: Donna, Cory. AB in Econs., U. Calif., Berkeley, 1962; MS in Agrl. Econs., U. Calif., Davis, 1965, PhD in Agrl. Econ., 1967. Asst. prof. U. N.H., Durham, 1968-72; assoc. prof. U. Nev., Reno, 1972-77, prof., head div. agrl. and resource econs., 1977-80; prof., chmn. dept. agrl. and resource econs. U. Hawaii, Honolulu, 1980-84, prof. agrl. econs., 1992—, dir. Hawaii Inst. Tropical Agr. and Human Resources, 1984-92. Recipient Charles H. Seurferle award, U. Nev., Reno, 1977. Office: Hawaii Inst Tropical Agr 3050 Maile Way # 202 Honolulu HI 96822-2231 Office Phone: 202-262-6619. E-mail: cc@cching.com.

CHING, DAVID T., food products executive; BSEE magna cum laude, U. Wis.; MS in Computer Scis., U. Calif., Berkeley; MS in Mgmt. Sci., Stanford U. Formerly with Bell Canada and Control Data Canada, Ltd., Toronto; sr. v.p. info. systems Lucky Stores, Inc., 1989-93; gen. mgr. in N. Am. Brit.-Am. Cons. Group, 1993-94; sr. v.p., chief info. officer Safeway, Inc., Pleasanton, Calif., 1994—. Bd. dir. Petco, 2005—, TJX Companies. Office: Safeway Inc PO Box 99 Pleasanton CA 94566-0009*

CHING, HO, surgeon; b. Kaoshung, Taiwan, Feb. 20, 1950; arrived in U.S., 1970; d. Feng Chih and Ai Hua Yin Ho; m. Stephen Jay Keller; children: Lisa, Michele. BS, Nat. U. Taiwan, Taipei, 1970; PhD, U. Cin., 1975, MD, 1984. Rsch. fellow Roche Molecular Biol. Inst., Nutley, NJ, 1975—76; Fogarty fellow Nat. Cancer Inst., NIH, Bethesda, Md., 1976—78; rsch. assoc. U. Cin., 1978—80; chief surg. resident Jewish Hosp., Cin., 1989, surgeon, 1989—91, Donna Stahl Assocs., Cin., 1991—2000; pvt. practice surgery Cin., 2000—. Assoc. dir. surg. resident program Jewish Hosp., 1992, mem. exec. com., 2001—03; chmn. women in medicine Acad. Medicine, Cin., 1998; co-chair dept. surg. Bethesda North Hosp., Cin., 2005—07. Named one of Top Drs., Cin. Mag., 2001, 2003, 2007. Fellow: ACS; mem.: Am. Soc. Micriobiology, Cama Cinti (pres. 2005—06), Am. Soc. Cell Biology. Avocations: yoga, travel. Office: Ching Ho MD Inc 4760 E Galbraith Rd Cincinnati OH 45236 E-mail: drho@fuse.net.

CHING, JAMES MICHAEL, performing company executive, composer, conductor; b. Honolulu, Hawaii, Sept. 29, 1958; BA summa cum laude, Duke U., 1980. Pianist, composer Houston Opera Studio, 1980-81; music adminstr. Fla. Grand Opera, 1981-85; mus. dir. Triangle Opera Theatre, 1987-88; asst. to gen. dir. Va. Opera, 1989-91, assoc. artistic dir., 1991-92; artistic dir. Opera Memphis, Tenn., 1992—. Mem. Phi Beta Kappa. Office: 6745 Wolf River Pkwy Memphis TN 38120 Office Phone: 901-257-3100. Business E-Mail: Michael@operamemphis.org.

CHINN, MARK ALLAN, lawyer; b. Jackson, Miss., June 9, 1953; s. Rollin J. and Ann M. (Heiberg) C.; m. Cathy Hawkinson, Aug. 6, 1978; children: Courtney, Casey, Carly, Conley. BA in Polit. Sci., Iowa State U., Ames, 1975; JD, U. Miss., 1978. Bar: US Dist. Ct. (no. dist.) Miss. 1978, US Dist. Ct. (so. dist.) Miss. 1980; US Ct. Appeals (5th and 11th cirs.) 1981; US Supreme Ct. 1980; cert. civil trial expert Nat. Bd. Trial Advocacy. Staff atty. Miss. Senate, Jackson, 1978-79; spl. asst. Atty. Gen. Office, Jackson, 1979-80; assoc. Louis Baine, Jackson, 1980-82, Law Office William Latham, Jackson, 1982-88; atty. pvt. practice, Jackson, 1988—. Adj. prof. law Miss. Coll. Sch. Law; vice chair Supreme Ct. Gender Fairness Task Force; v.p. Gov. Children's Justice Task Force, 2001-2003. Author: The Constructive Divorce, How to Build and Manage a Family Law Practice, 2006; co-author: How To Capture and Keep Clients, 101 Practical Solution for the Family Lawyer. Bd. dirs. Arts Alliance, Jackson, 1990-97, Miss. Children's Home, Jackson, 1990-95; pres. Jackson Urban League Bd., 1995-2000; bd. dirs. Jubilee Jam Found., 1995-97, chmn. Jubilee! Jam '96; chair Lamar Order U. Miss. Law Alumni, 2001-02. Named one of Best Lawyers in Am., Mid South Super Lawyers, Top Lawyers in Jackson, Jackson Free Press; named to Bar Register of Preeminent Lawyers. Mem. ABA (v.p., mem. family law sect. governing coun.), Miss. Bar Assn. (chmn. family law sect. 1995-96, 2000-01, chmn. small firm practice com. 1995-96, Award of Merit 1996), Hinds County Bar Assn. (dir. 1994-95, pres. 1998-99), Am. Inn of Ct. (master Charles Clark), Rotary, Jackson C. of C., Miss. Bar Found., Miss. Law Alumni Assn. (chmn. 2001-02). Avocations: golf, physical fitness, Karate, tae kwan do (black belt), private pilot. Office: Chinn Associates PLLC 4316 Old Canton Rd Ste 200 Post Office Box 13483 Jackson MS 39236 Office Phone: 601-366-4410. Business E-Mail: mark@chinnandassociates.com.

CHINN, YUEN YUEY, art educator, painter; b. Canton, China, Dec. 24, 1922; arrived in U.S., 1936; s. Ah Wing Chinn and See Eng; m. Theres Chow (div.); children: Tcheck Tchung, Li Tchung. BFA, Columbia U., 1953, MFA, 1954. Tchr. art Art Study Abroad, Paris, 1968—69; dir. recreation City of N.Y., 1974—93; tchr. art and tai-chi Bklyn. Coll., 1974—2003. One-man shows include Numero Gallery, Florence, 1955, Galleria d'arte, Ancona, 1955, Galerie Arnaud, Paris, 1955, Beno Gallery, Zurich, 1956, Galerie Numaga, La Chaux-de-Fonda, 1957, Franz Bader Gallery, Washington, 1957, 1971, Galerie Karl Flinker, Paris, 1964, 1973, Galerie Rene Andrieu, Toulouse, 1965, Byron Gallery, N.Y., 1965, 1966, Club 44, Chaux-de-Fonda, 1967, Bklyn. Coll., 1977, exhibited in group shows at Galerie Karl Flinker, 1978, 1962, Mi-Chou Gallery, N.Y., 1970, 1958, Galerie Rene Andriew, 1966. Grantee Brevoort Eickmeyer, Columbia U., 1952—53, Fulbright Italy, 1954—55, John Hay Whitney, 1956—57. Avocations: music, tai chi, collecting classical audio equipments and old cameras. Home: 80 N Moore St Apt 15J New York NY 10013-2731 Address: 54 rue ducouedic 73014 Paris France Personal E-mail: bbigyuen@yahoo.com.

CHINNIAH, NIM, academic administrator; m. Swapna Chinniah; 1 child, Kiran. BS summa cum laude, Lambuth U., 1989; MBA, Vanderbilt U., 1991. Mgr. fin. & info. sys. Vanderbilt U., 1991, dir. fin. & info sys., fin. sys. project lead, 1998—99, dep. vice-chancellor adminstrn. & acad. affairs, 1999—2007; v.p. adminstrn., CFO U. Chgo., 2007—. Adv. bd. mem. First Tenn. Bank Nashville. Mem. Human Rels. Commn., City of Nashville; bd. mem. Boys and Girls Clubs of Middle Tenn. Recipient Rising Star Award, Nat. Assn. Coll. and Univ. Bus. Officers, 2003. Office: U Chgo 5801 South Ellis Ave Chicago IL 60637

CHINNIS, C. CABELL, JR., lawyer; b. Washington, May 28, 1958; BA in Pub. Affairs, Princeton Univ.; Kennedy fellow, Harvard Univ., 1980—81; JD, Yale Univ., 1984. Bar: Pa. 1986, DC 1988, Calif. 2002, US Tax Ct. 1988. Law clk. Hon. John Minor Wisdom, US Ct. of Appeals (fifth cir.), 1984—85, Hon. Lewis F. Powell Jr., US Supreme Ct., 1985—86; atty. Latham & Watkins, Washington, 1986—93; pvt. practice, 1993—94; assoc. Mayer, Brown, Rowe & Maw LLP, Washington, 1994—97, ptnr., 1997—2001, Palo Alto, Calif., 2001—, now ptnr.-in-charge, Palo Alto office, 2003—. Mng. editor Yale Law Jour., 1984. Mem.: Phi Beta Kappa. Office: Mayer Brown Rowe & Maw LLP Ste 300 3000 El Camino Palo Alto CA 94306-2112 Office Phone: 650-331-2020. Office Fax: 650-331-2067. Business E-Mail: cchinnis@mayerbrownrowe.com.

CHIODO, ANTHONY, medical educator; MD, U. Conn., Farmington, 1984. Assoc. prof. U. Mich. Hosp., Ann Arbor, 1998—. Office: U Mich 325 Eisenhower Pky Ann Arbor MI 48108 Office Phone: 734-936-7379.

CHIOGIOJI, MELVIN HIROAKI, retired federal official, entrepreneur; b. Hiroshima, Japan, Aug. 21, 1939; came to U.S., 1939; s. Yutaka and Harumi (Yamasaki) C.; m. Pallas A. Chiogioji; children: Wendy A., Alan K. BS in Elec. Engring., Purdue U., 1961; MBA, U. Hawaii, 1968; DBA, George Washington U., 1972. Registered profl. engr., Hawaii. Head weapons gen. component div. Quality Evaluation Lab., Oahu, Hawaii, 1965-69; dir. weapons evaluation and engring. div. Naval Ordinance Systems Command, Washington, 1969-73; dir. Office Indsl. Analysis Fed. Energy Adminstrn., Washington, 1973-75; asst. dir., div. bldg. and community systems Dept. Energy, Washington, 1975-79, dir. fed. program div., 1980—, dep. asst. sec. state and local assistance program, 1980-85, dir. office of transp. systems, 1985-90; constrn. mgr. Office of New Prodn. Reactors, Washington, 1990-92; pres. EFC, Inc., 1980-99, Precision Auto Care, Inc., 1989-97, Intemco, 1993-96, Mele Assocs., Inc., 1999—. Prof. mgmt. sci. George Washington U., 1972—. Author: Industrial Energy Conservation, 1979, Energy Conservation in Commercial and Residental Buildings, 1982; contbr. articles to profl. jours. Mem. Md. State Adv. Com. on Civil Rights, 1976—; mem. Nat. Naval Res. Policy Bd., 1977—; vestryman Grace Episcopal Ch., Silver Spring, Md., 1982—; bd. dirs. Japanese Am. Nat. Mus., 1996—; chmn. Nat. Japanese Am. Meml. Found., 1995—. With USN, 1961-65; rear adm. USNR. Decorated Navy Commendation medal, Meritorious Svc. medal, Legion Merit medal. Mem. IEEE (sr.), NSPE, Acad. Mgmt., Naval Res. Assn., Assn. for Sci., Tech. and Innovation (pres. 1979-81), Soc. Am. Mil. Engrs., Armed Forces Mgmt. Assn., Seabee Meml. Scholarship Assn. (bd. dirs. 1973—), Triangle Fraternity Edn. Found. (bd. dirs. 1995—), Purdue U. Alumni Assn., Nat. Japanese Am. Meml. Found. (chmn.), Japanese Am. Nat. Mus. (bd. dirs.). Address: 15702 Thistlebridge Dr Rockville MD 20853-3226 Office: 14660 Rothgeb Dr Rockville MD 20850-5309 Home Phone: 301-924-0760; Office Phone: 240-453-6990. E-mail: mel@meleassociates.com.

CHIORAZZI, MICHAEL GERARD, law librarian, educator; b. Jersey City, Dec. 3, 1954; s. John Dominic and Dolores (Bonn) Chiorazzi; m. Vickie Bletso, May 30, 1982; 3 children. BA, U. Miami, 1976; JD, Gonzaga U., 1980; MLL, U. Wash., 1981. Legal rsch. instr., dep. dir. Law Libr. Boston Coll. Sch. Law, Newton, Mass., 1989—96; reference libr., sr. instr. legal rsch. Duke U. Sch. Law, 1981—89; faculty mem. James E. Rogers Coll. Law, U. Ariz., Tucson, 1996—, prof. law & info. resources and libr. sci., dir. Law Libr. Editor: Legal Reference Svcs. Quarterly, 1999—; contbr. articles to profl. jours. Democrat. Office: U Arizona Coll Law Law Libr 1201 E Speedway Blvd Tucson AZ 85721 Home: 3854 E Marble Peak Pl Tucson AZ 85718 Office Phone: 520-621-5477. Office Fax: 520-621-3138. Business E-Mail: michael.chiorazzi@law.arizona.edu.*

CHIOU, SHIUN-KWEI, medical researcher; d. Wen-Jau and Mei-Sa Chiou. Grad., U. Mich., Ann Arbor, 1990; PhD, Rutgers U., NJ, 1997. Postdoctoral fellow U. Calif., Berkeley, 1997—2000, health sciences specialist, 2000—01; assoc. scientist Abgenix, Inc., Fremont, Calif., 2001—02; jr. investigator VA Med. Ctr., Long Beach, Calif., 2002—05, rsch. scientist, 2005—. Contbr. articles to profl. jours. Leader Sierra Club, Calif., 2006—07. Merit Rev. grantee, VA Med. Ctr., 2005—. Fellow: Am. Gastroent. Assn.; mem.: Am. Assn. Cancer Rsch. (assoc.). Achievements include patents in field; research in molecular mechanisms of apoptosis in cancer cells and NSAID induced injury. Office: VA Med Ctr 5901 E 7th st Long Beach CA 90822 Office Phone: 562-826-8000 4910. Business E-Mail: shiun.chiou@va.gov.

CHIOU-TAN, FAYE, physician, educator; b. Hsin-Chu, Taiwan, Mar. 27, 1964; d. George and Tricia Chiou; m. Filemon Tan, Jr.; children: Filemon III, Michelle. AB, Princeton U., NJ, 1985; MD, Baylor Coll. of Med., Houston, 1990. Diplomate Am. Bd. Electrodiagnostic Medicine, Am. Bd. Phys. Med. Rehab. Asst. prof. Baylor Coll. Medicine, Houston, 1995—2002, assoc. prof., 2003—, residency program dir., 2007. Contbr. articles to profl. jours. Chief svc. phys. medicine and rehab. Harris County Hosp. Dist., Houston, 2000—, dir. electrodiagnosis, 1995—, bd. mem. at large, dir. Ctr. for Trauma Rehab. Rsch., 2000—; med. bd. mem. at large, Harris County Hospital. Recipient Excellence in Rsch. Writing award Assn. Acad. Physiatrists/Am. Jour. Phys. Medicine and Rehab., 1999, 2000, 2003; named one of Am's Top Physicians, Consumer's Rsch. Coun. Am., 2003, 04. Mem.: Am. Bd. Electrodiagnostic Medicine (examiner 2006—), Assn. Acad. Physiatrists (chair rsch. coun. 2005, chair rsch. 2006—07), Am. Assn. Neuromuscular Electrodiagnostic Medicine (chmn. 2005—, mem. rsch. com.). Avocations: cooking, hiking, antiques. Office: Baylor Coll Medicine Dept PM&R 3601 N MacGregor Way Ste 240 Houston TX 77004

CHIPKIN, FREDERICK, textile designer, consultant, artist, writer; b. NYC, Mar. 11, 1963; s. Sidney and Pearl Chipkin; m. Rimma Zilman Chipkin, Feb. 28, 1985; children: Alexandra Elizabeth, Rebecca Tatiana. AS in Culinary Arts, Johnson and Wales Coll., 1983; BFA, Parsons Sch. of Design, 1989. Owner/designer Design Soc., Inc., NYC, 1987—90; textile designer Liz Claiborne, NYC, 1990—92, Bernard Chause, Inc., NYC; mgr., CAD dept. I. Appel, Inc., NYC, 1995—99; owner/designer Origin Inc., Textile Design Studio, 1999—. Author: Adobe Photoshop for Textile Design, 2001—06; prodr.: Origin, Inc. Textile Design Collection. Home and Office: Origin Inc 117-14 Union Turnpike CD2 Kew Gardens NY 11415 Office Phone: 718-544-2754. Office Fax: 718-544-2754. Business E-Mail: design@origininc.com.

CHIPMAN, DENNIS CLARENCE, JR., forensic psychiatrist, consultant; b. Seattle, Jan. 7, 1934; s. Dennis Clarence and Esther (Ränghild) Chipman; m. Karen Antoinette Ekern, Mar. 17, 1968 (div. Oct. 1982); children: Judith, Kimberly, Jason, Carolyn; m. Sandra Kay Woodell, Feb. 6, 1983. *Wife, Sandra Kay Woodell Chipman is a registered nurse and an attorney, in private law practice, in Anderson, SC. Daughter, Judith, has a BA from Willamette University and operates a land development corporation with her husband, David, from Seattle, Washington. Daughter, Kimberly, has a BA from Knox College and also an M.S. in Journalism from Northwestern; she works for Bloomberg media services in Washington, DC. Son, Jason, has a BA from Mary Washington and a JD from the University of Virginia Law School; he is with the Department of Justice in Washington, DC. Daughter, Carolyn, is a sophomore in College; she plans on studying architecture.* MD, U. Wash. Diplomate Am. Bd. Psychiatry and Neurology, subspecialty forensic psychiatry, diplomate Am. Bd. Adolescent Psychiatry. Intern U. Nebr. Hosp., Omaha, 1959-60; resident U. Wash. Hosp. Sys., Seattle, 1960-63; pvt. practice Seattle, 1963-66; dir. Mental Health Ctr., Kingsport, Tenn., 1969-84; pvt. practice Kingsport, 1969-84, Hickory, NC, 1984-86; med. dir. Pinewood Hosp., Texarkana, Ark., 1986-89, Charter Hosp. Mobile, Ala., 1989-94; chief psychiatrist Patrick B. Harris Hosp., Anderson, SC, 1994—2001, sr. psychiatrist, 2001—; cons. forensic psychiatry, 1994—. Cons. Meth. Children's Home, Greenville, Tenn., 1969—75, Disability Determinations Divsn. Vocat. Rehab. Bd. dirs. Sheltered Workshop, Kingsport, 1973—80, Gateways Farm for Girls, New Boston, Tex., 1988—94, Home of Grace for Women, Mobile, 1990—94, New Haven Program, Mobile, 1990—94. Capt. US Army, 1966—68. Named to Guide to America's Top Psychiatrists, Consumer Rsch. Coun. Am., 2003—. Mem.: AMA, Internat. Soc. Philos. Enquiry, U.S. Chess Fedn., Am. Psychiat. Assn., Am. Mensa Ltd., Civtan Club, Rotary, Kappa Sigma. Libertarian. Baptist. Avocations: music, chess, reading, travel. Home: PO Box 5587 Anderson SC 29623-5587 Office Phone: 864-231-6868. Personal E-mail: c1219d@aol.com.

CHIPMAN, JOHN SOMERSET, retired economist, educator; b. Montreal, Que., Can., June 28, 1926; s. Warwick Fielding and Mary Somerset (Aikins) C.; m. Margaret Ann Ellefson, June 24, 1960; children: Thomas Noel, Timothy Warwick. Student, U. Chile, Santiago, 1943—44; BA, McGill U., Montreal, 1947, MA, 1948; PhD, Johns Hopkins U., 1951; postdoctoral, U. Chgo., 1950—51; Doctor rerum politicarum honoris causa, U. Konstanz, Germany, 1991, U. Würzburg, 1998; D in Social and Econ. Scis., U. Graz, Austria, 2001. Asst. prof. econs. Harvard U., Cambridge, Mass., 1951—55; assoc. prof. econs. U. Minn., Mpls., 1955—60, prof., 1961—81, Regents' prof., 1981—2007. Fellow Ctr. for Advanced Study in Behavioral Scis., Stanford, Calif., 1972-73; Guggenheim fellow, 1980-81; vis. prof. econs. various univs.; permanent guest prof. U. Konstanz, 1985-91; bd. dirs. Leuthold Funds, Inc., 1995-. Author: The Theory of Intersectoral Money Flows and Income Formation, 1951; editor: (with others) Preferences, Utility, and Demand, 1971, Preferences, Uncertainty and Optimality, 1990, (with C.P. Kindleberger) Flexible Exchange Rates and the Balance of Payments, 1980; co-editor Jour. Internat. Econs., 1971-76, editor, 1977-87; assoc. editor Econometrica, 1956-60, Can. Jour. Stats., 1980-82; adv. bd. Jour. Multivariate Analysis, 1988-92. Recipient Humboldt Rsch. award for Sr. U.S. Scientists, 1992, 2003. Fellow AAAS, Econometric Soc. (coun. 1971-76, 81-83), Am. Statis. Assn., Am. Acad. Arts and Scis., Am. Econ. Assn. (disting.); mem. NAS (nat. assoc. 2004, chair sect. econ. scis. 1997-2000, James Murray Luck award 1981), Internat. Statis. Inst., Am. Philos. Soc., Inst. Math. Stats., Can Econ. Assn., Royal Econ. Soc., History of Econs. Soc. Home: 2121 W 49th St Minneapolis MN 55419-5229 Office: U Minn Dept Econs 1035 Heller Hall 217 19th Ave S Minneapolis MN 55455-0400 Office Phone: 612-625-2816. Business E-Mail: jchipman@umn.edu.

CHIPMAN, SUSAN ELIZABETH, psychologist, researcher; b. St. Paul, Feb. 12, 1946; d. Robert Louis and Margaret Alice Fitzgerald; m. Eric George Chipman, Aug. 27, 1966. AB in Math., Harvard U., 1966, MBA, 1967, AM in Psychol., 1969, PhD in Exptl. Psychol., 1973. Asst. prof. U. Mich., Ann Arbor, 1974-75; assoc. Nat. Inst. Edn., Washington, 1976-78, asst. dir., 1979-84; sci. officer U.S. Office Naval Rsch., Arlington, Va., 1984-85, cognitive sci. program mgr., 1985—2006. Mem. adv. bd. James S. McDonnell Found., St. Louis, 1987-98; cons. in field. Editor, author: Thinking and Learning Skills, 1985, Women and Mathematics, 1985, Foundations of Knowledge Acquisition, 1993, Cognitively Diagnostic Assessment, 1995, Cognitive Task Analysis, 2000; contbr. articles to profl. jours. Fellow APA (meritorious rsch. svc. commendation 2005), APS; mem. Cognitive Sci. Soc. (hon. life). Avocation: photography. Home: 2606 S Joyce St Arlington VA 22202-2214

CHIRA, SUSAN, editor; married; 2 children. BA in History and East Asian Studies, Harvard U., 1980. Reporter The NY Times, 1982—84, Tokyo corr., 1984—89, dep. fgn. editor, 2004—. Author: A Mother's Place, 1998. Office: The New York Times 229 W 43rd St New York NY 10036-3959

CHIRIAC, VICTOR ADRIAN, aerospace engineer, researcher; b. Bucharest, Romania, Feb. 22, 1969; arrived in U.S., 1994, naturalized, 2006; s. Florea Nicolae and Michaela Cornelia Chiriac. BSc, Poly. U. Bucharest, 1992, MSc, 1993; PhD Aero. and Mech. Engring., U. Ariz., 1999. Rsch. and tchg. asst. U. Ariz., Tucson, 1994—97; intern Motorola Inc., Tempe, Ariz., 1996—98, intern ON semiconductor, 1998—99, sr. staff engr., 1999—2004; prin. staff scientist Freescale, 2004—. Awareness sub.-com. Motorola Inc., 2001—02; session chair internat. congress INTERPACK, Hawaii, 2003, chmn. tutorials internat. congress, mem. gen. com., Canada, 07; session chair internat. congress ITHERM, Las Vegas, 2004; session chair, organizer poster chair ITHERM Conf., San Diego, 2006; panel chmn. Internat. Congress Interpack, San Francisco, 2005; invited panelist reviewer NSF, Washington, 2006; spkr. in field. Contbr. over 70 articles to profl. jours. and confs. Recipient Sci. and Tech. Soc. award, Motorola, 2003. Mem.: AIAA, ASME (k-16 com. mem. thermal divsn. 2002—, session chair numerous IMECE confs. 2003—06), ASHRAE (corr.), Internat. Microelectronics & Packaging Soc. Greek Orthodox. Achievements include patents for system and method for cooling using an oscillatory impinging jet; airbag circuit driver optimization; defensive publication on novel cooling system for microelectronics using thermoelectric coolers; trade secret for RC networks creation for microelectronics systems; 5 patents pending. Avocations: tennis, swimming. Home: 15016 S 28th St Phoenix AZ 85048 Office: Freescale Semiconductor 2100 East Elliot Tempe AZ 85284 Office Phone: 480-413-6756. Personal E-mail: vchiriac@cox.net. Business E-Mail: victor.chiriac@freescale.com.

CHIRICO, ANTHONY (TONY), publishing executive; With Knopf Pub., NYC, 1986—, various mgmt. positions, 1988—2000, exec. v.p., COO, 2000—05, pres., 2005. Office: Knopf Publishing 1745 Broadway New York NY 10019-4305 Office Phone: 212-751-9600.

CHIRICO, DONNA M., psychologist, educator, researcher; b. NYC, Feb. 26, 1956; d. Francis M. and Angela Chirico; m. Sidney Rosenberg, May 11, 1983; children: Debra L. Rosenberg, Daniel Rosenberg, Sharon E., Lindsey Chirico-Rosenberg. EdD, Columbia U., NYC, 2000. Adminstr. Office of the Jewish Chaplain Columbia U., NYC, 1990—93; assoc. prof. of psychology York Coll. of CUNY, Jamaica, NY, 1993—; psychology program coord. Book reviewer Choice, Middletown, Conn., 2005—; cons. Learning in the Real World Project, Berkeley, Calif., 1996—97; mem. faculty staff adv. coun. Calandra Italian Am. Inst. Contbr. articles to profl. jours. Ednl. vol. Duryea Farm of the Fellowship Cmty., Chestnut Ridge, NY, 2004—05; literacy vol. Green Meadow Waldorf Sch., Chestnut Ridge, 2003—04. Recipient mini grant, NY. Coun. for the Humanities. Mem.: Am. Statis. Assn., Kappa Delta Pi, Phi Delta Kappa, Sigma Xi, York Coll. Honor Soc. for the Liberal Arts (pres. 2002—06). Green Party. Roman Catholic. Avocations: theater, mah jongg. Office: York Coll CUNY 9420 Guy R Brewer Blvd Jamaica NY 11451 Home Phone: 845-371-6597; Office Phone: 718-262-2687. Office Fax: 718-262-2675. Business E-Mail: chirico@york.cuny.edu.

CHIRICO, EMANUEL, apparel executive; Ptnr. Ernst & Young; v.p., controller Phillips-Van Heusen Corp., NYC, 1993—98, exec. v.p., CFO, 1998—2005, pres., COO, 2005—06, CEO, 2006—07, chmn., CEO, 2007—. Bd. dirs. Dick's Sporting Goods, Inc. Office: Phillips-Van Heusen Corp 200 Madison Ave New York NY 10016*

CHIRICO-ELKINS, URSULA, retired librarian; arrived in Canada, 1958, 1966; d. Friedrich Winter and Gertrud Naake; m. John H. Elkins (dec.); children: Amadeus(dec.) , Naomi, George, Tabitha; m. Francesco Chirico, 2003. Diploma, Inst. Children's Lit., 1980, diploma, 1991; A in applied sci. and libr. sci., Mercer County CC, NJ, 1982. Libr. asst. Princeton U., NJ, 1978—81, David Sarnoff Rsch. Ctr. Princeton U., 1981—87, sr. libr. asst., 1983—87; prin. asst. Rider U., Lawrenceville, NJ, 1987—89, 1990—93; ret., 1993. Author: A Celebration of Poets, 1998, Michelangelo's Creation of Adam, 1998, Falling Snow, 1998, Unending Love, 1999, Omnipotence, 1999, Universal Truth, 2000, Springtime, 2003, Freedom of Spirit, 2004, Let Not Your Heart Be Troubled, 2004, (anthology) Great Poems of the Western World, 2004, Vol., libr. establisher Calvary Ch., Pemberton, NJ, 2000; literacy vol. Toms River, NJ, 1993—; vol. Samaritan Hospice, Moorestown, NJ, 1995—; hon. mem. edn. coun. Am. Indian Edn. Found., Albuquerque, 2004. Mem.: Am. Indian Edn. Found. (bd. dirs., coun. 2003—), Internat. Soc. Poets (Disting. Mem.). Congregationalist. Avocations: painting, classical music, literature, embroidery. Personal E-mail: whiteswan@netzero.net.

CHIRINOS, JULIO ALONSO, physician, researcher; s. Julio Chirinos and Josefina Medina de Chirinos; m. Melissa Ryan. MD, Santa Maria Cath. U., Arequipa, 2000. Diplomate Am. Bd. Internal Medicine, 2005. Internal medicine specialist Jackson Meml. Med. Ctr./U. Miami Sch. Medicine, 2001—04. Contbr. articles to profl. jours. Recipient Chief Med. Resident award, ACP, 2004, Thrombosis Young Investigator award, European Soc. Cardiology, 2005, Sodi award for excellency in tchg. EKG interpretation, Interamerican Soc. Electrocardiography, 2005. Mem.: Am. Coll. Cardiology. Achievements include research in endothelial cell biology and cell-derived membrane microparticles in multiple conditions, including venous thrombosis, atrial fibrillation, sepsis and heart failure; assessing the important prognostic role of arterial stiffness and wave reflection in the prognosis of patients with coronary artery disease; large studies of cardiovascular disease in Hispanic populations in South America; the role of coexisting medical diseases in the prognosis of patients with coronary artery disease; Cardiovascular Disease such as Stroke and Heart Disease in Different Ethnic Groups; discovery of quality of high-density lipoprotein cholesterol particles is important in protection against atherosclerotic events; binding of endothelial microparticles to leukocytes is an important regulating white blood cell functions in different disease states. Avocations: scuba diving, travel. Home Phone: 305-993-5170. Office Fax: 305-575-3116. Personal E-mail: jchirinos@prevencionperu.org. Business E-Mail: jchirinos@med.miami.edu.

CHIRIVA INTERNATI, MAURIZIO, immunologist, researcher; PhD, U. Milan, Italy, 1996. Asst. prof. Tex. Tech U. Health Scis. Ctr., Lubbock, 2001—, leader bone marrow transplant rsch. and translational immunology program, 2003—, dir. exptl. clin. translational rsch. program, 2005—. Fellow, U. Ark. Med. Scis., 1996—99. Mem.: Internat. Soc. Biol. Therapy Cancer (assoc.), Am. Assn. Immunologists (assoc.), Am. Assn. Cancer Rsch. (assoc.). Democrat. Roman Catholic. Achievements include patents pending for AAV technology; discovery of antigen. Avocations: travel, scuba diving. Office: Texas Tech U Health Scis Ctr 3601 4th St MS 6591 Lubbock TX 79430 Home Phone: 806-796-1717. Business E-Mail: maurizio.chiriva@ttuhsc.edu.

CHIRLS, RICHARD, lawyer; b. Newark, 1950; BS cum laude, U. Pa., 1973, JD, 1976; LLM in Taxation, NYU, 1979. Ptnr. Orrick, Herrington & Sutcliffe LLP, NYC, ptnr. in charge-rates, billing & collection. Mem. ABA (chmn. tax exempt fin.com. 1989-91), Nat. Assn. Bond Lawyers (vice chmn. com. edn. 1985-86, bd. dirs. 1987-92, treasure & exec. com. 1988--1989, pres. 1990-91), N.Y. State Bar Assn. (co-chmn. tax exempt fin. com. tax 1984-86). Office: Orrick Herrington & Sutcliffe LLP 666 5th Ave New York NY 10103-1798 Office Phone: 212-506-5250. Business E-Mail: rchirls@orrick.com.

CHIRON, HARLAN S., orthopedic surgeon, educator; b. NYC, Oct. 24, 1941; d. Albert Edward and Rose L. Chiron; m. Judy G. Chiron, Feb. 15, 1990; children: Stewart, Pamela, Diana. BA, Lafayette Coll., Easton, Pa., 1962; MD, Chg. Med. Sch., 1966. Intern Hosp. for Joint Disease, 1966—67, resident, 1967—68, 1970—72, fellow, 1972—73; ptnr. S. Fla. Orthopedic Assn., Miami, 1974—85, pres., 1985—; prof. U. Miami, 1974—2006. Chief orthopedic surgery Victoria Hosp., Miami, 1978—80, S. Miami Hosp., 1993—96. Capt. USAF, 1970—72. Frauenthal fellowship, Hosp. for Joint Disease, NYC, 1972. Avocations: tennis, piano, reading, photography. Office: S Fla Orthopedic Assn Ste 203 4675 Ponce de Leon Blvd Miami FL 33146 Office Phone: 305-663-4649.

CHIRURG, JAMES THOMAS, financial holding company executive; b. Wellesley, Mass., May 21, 1944; s. James T. and Virginia B. (Low) C.; AB in Asian Studies, Cornell U., 1964; MBA in Internat. Business, Harvard U., 1969; BLitt, MLitt in Internat. Economics, U. of Oxford (Knox fellow), 1972; postgrad. U. Calif., Berkeley; m. Lynne Louise Robertson Day, Sept. 15, 1983. Asst. mktg. mgr. Gen. Mills Inc., Tokyo, 1968; mem. corp. fin. dept. First Boston Corp., N.Y.C., 1969-70; gen. mgr. Protasis Trust, Ltd., London, 1971-72, lead ptnr., Berkeley, 1973-93; dir. Protasis Holdings (S.a.r.l.), Luxembourg, 1980—; fellow Salzburg Seminar (Austria), 1980, participant, The Ditchley Found. Confs. (U.K.), 1986; lectr. internat. fin. U. Calif., 1977-97. Trustee, Adelphic Cornell Ednl. Fund, 1987—. Served to lt. (j.g.) USN, 1964-67; comdr. USNR, 1968-80. Decorated Bronze Star with combat V, Navy Commendation medal. Fellow Inst. Dirs. (U.K.), Royal Asiatic Soc. (U.K.); United Oxford and Cambridge Club. Home: 2115 Bush St San Francisco CA 94115-3103 Office: Protasis Holdings PO Box 5000 Berkeley CA 94705

CHISARI, FRANCIS V., pathologist; b. NYC, Apr. 5, 1942; m. Linda Kornet; 2 children. BA, Fordham U., 1963; MD, Cornell U., Ithaca, NY, 1968. Lic. Am. Bd. Internal Medicine with subspecialty in anatomic pathology. Fellow Cornell U. Med. Coll., NYC, 1966—67, Mayo Clinic, Rochester, NY, 1969—70; intern NY Hosp./Cornell U. Med. Ctr., NYC, 1968—69; staff assoc. NIH, Bethesda, Md., 1970—72; resident Mary Hitchcock Meml. Hosp., Dartmouth Med. Sch., Hanover, NH, 1972—73; rsch. fellow Scripps Clinic & Rsch. Found., 1973—75, asst. prof. LaJolla,

Calif., 1975—81; assoc. prof. Scripps Rsch. Inst., LaJolla, Calif., 1984—89, prof., head, Dept. Exptl. Pathology, 1988—, dir. Gen. Clin. Rsch. Ctr., 1989—; asst. adj. prof. U. Calif. San Diego (UCSF) Sch. Med., LaJolla, Calif., 1976—81, adj. prof., 1987—98. Mem. Hepatitis Panel US-Japan Coop. Med. Sci. Program, 1992—98; nominating com. Am. Soc. Investigative Pathology, 1999—2002; sci. adv. bd. Liver Rsch. Ctr., Albert Einstein Coll. Medicine, 1995—2001, Epimmune, 1998—, Rockefeller U. Ctr. for Study of HCV, 2000—, Brown U. Ctr. Genetics & Genomics, 2000—02, N.E. Biodefense Ctr., 2004—; scientific rev. bd. German Cancer Rsch. Ctr., Heidelburg, 1990—91; mem. internat. rsch. scholars program Howard Hughes Med. Inst., 2000—; disting. adv. com. U. Calif. San Francisco Cancer Ctr., 2000—; bd. scientific councilors NIH, 2001—, Blue Ribbon Panel on Bioterrorism Rsch., 2002—, Expert Panel on Immunity & Biodefense, 2002—. Contbr. articles to profl. jours.; editorial bd. Jour. Virology, PLoS Pathogens, Virology, Jour. Clin. Investigation, Microbial Pathogenesis. Recipient Rsch. Career Devel. award, NIH, 1976—81, Merit award, 1990—2000, Ernst Jung prize in medicine, 1997, 1st Disting. Scientific Achievement award, Am. Liver Found., 1997, Rous-Whipple award, Assn. for Investigative Pathology, 1999, Disting. Achievement award, Am. Assn. Study of Liver Diseases, 1999, Sheila Sherlock Liver Rsch. prize, U. Toronto; fellow Fogarty Sr. Internat. fellow, NIH, 1983—84; Fgn. scholar, Fondation pour la Recherche Medicale, France, 1984. Fellow: AAAS; mem.: Assn. Am. Physicians, Molecular Medicine Soc., Am. Assn. Cancer Rsch., Am. Assn. Immunologists, Am. Soc. Virology, Assn. of Am. Physicians, Am. Soc. Investigative Pathology, Am. Acad. Microbiology, Inst. Medicine (life), Henry Kunkel Soc. Office: Scripps Rsch Inst Dept Molecular/Exptl Medicine 10550 N Torrey Pines Rd La Jolla CA 92037

CHISHOLM, LIONEL DONALD JOHN, ophthalmologist; b. Montreal, Que., Can., July 9, 1935; s. Donald Munro and Isabelle Anne (Frizzell) C.; m. Ann Violet Webster, Feb. 12, 1960; children: Sarah Ann, John Webster. MD, U. Toronto, 1959. Intern Toronto Gen. Hosp., 1959—60, Shaughnessy Hosp., Vancouver, 1960—61; resident Toronto Tchg. Hosp., 1961—64; retina fellow Retina Found., Mass. Eye and Ear Infirmary, Boston, 1964-66; asst. to assoc. prof. opthalmology U. Toronto, 1966-79, prof., 1979-93; ophthalmologist in chief Toronto Western and Toronto Hosp., 1979-93; prof., dir. of retina vitreous unit dept. ophthalmologyy W.Va. U., 1993—. Fellow: Assn. for Rsch. in Vision and Ophthalmology, Schepens Internal Soc., Am. Acad. Ophthalmology, Royal Coll. Surgeons (Can.); mem.: Can. Med. Assn., Retina Soc. (founding mem.). Avocation: equestrian. Office: WVa U Eye Inst PO Box 9193 Morgantown WV 26506-9193

CHISHOLM, MALCOLM HAROLD, chemistry professor; b. Bombay, Oct. 15, 1945; arrived in U.S., 1972; s. Angus and Gweneth Robey Chisholm; m. Cynthia Ann Truax, May 1, 1982; children: Calun R.I., Selby Scott, Derek Adrian. BS in Chemistry, Queen Mary Coll., London, 1966, PhD in Chemistry, 1969; DSc (hon.), London U., 1981. Postdoctoral fellow U. Western Ont., London, 1969-72; asst. prof. Princeton U., NJ, 1972-78; assoc. prof. chemistry Ind. U., Bloomington, 1978-80, prof., 1980-85, disting. prof. chemistry, 1985-99; disting. univ. prof. Ohio State U., Columbus, 2000—. Vis. prof. Cambridge U., 1986, 94, Humboldt U., 1986—; cons. in field. Editor: Polyhedron, Chem. Comm., Dalton Transactions; mem. editl. bd. Inorganic Chemistry, Organometallics, Inorganic Chimica Acta, Inorganic Syn. Inc., Jour. Cluster Sci., Chem. European Jour., Can. Jour. Chemistry, Chem. Record; contbr. articles to profl. jours. Recipient Basolo medal, Northwestern U., 2004, Bailar medal, U. Ill., 2006. Fellow: NAS, AAAS, Am. Chem. Soc. (Akron sect. award 1982, Buck Whitney award 1987, Inorganic Chemistry award 1989, Disting. Svc. award 1999, Basolo medal 2004, Bailar medal 2006), Royal Soc. Chemistry (Corday Morgan medal 1981, award for Transition Metal Chemistry, Centenary Lectr. and medal, Mond Lectr. and medal), Duetche Accademie Leopoldina, Am. Acad. Arts and Scis., Royal Soc. London (Davy medal). Home: 100 Kenyon Brook Dr Worthington OH 43085-3629 also: 38 Norwich St Cambridge CB2 1NE England Office: Ohio State U Dept Chemistry 100 W 18th Ave Columbus OH 43210-1185 Office Phone: 614-292-7216. Business E-Mail: chisholm.4@osu.edu.

CHISHOLM, ROBERT E., architect; b. Havana, Cuba, Jan. 17, 1950; s. Robert L. and Martha C. (Latour) C.; m. Aug. 9, 1975; children: Robert M., Jacqueline A. BArch, U. Fla., Gainesville, 1973; M in Urban Design, U. Miami, Fla., 1977; postgraduate student, Ga. Inst. Tech., 1992. Arch./planner Metro-Dade County Housing & Urban Devel., Miami, 1974-76; lead prin. planner Metro-Dade County OCED, Miami, 1976-80; v.p. Ramos & Assocs., Inc., Miami, 1980-82; pres. R.E. Chisholm Archs., Inc., Miami, 1982—. Design critic UM/MDCC/FIU, Miami. Mem. archtl. adv. com. City of Miami Beach, 1988-89, ad-hoc advisor Dade County Assn. for Retarded Citizens, 1980-83; chmn. design and constrn. CPHI Homeless Assistance Ctr.; arch./planner Moss Plan Hurricane Recovery Master Plan, Fla.; chmn. design/constrn. Cmty. Partnership for Homeless, Inc., Miami, 1993—. Fellow AIA (pres. 1992, AIA Fla. Silver medal 2007); mem. Greater Miami C. of C., U. Fla. Alumni Assn. Office: R E Chisholm Archs Inc 7254 SW 48th St Miami FL 33155-5525 Office Phone: 305-661-2070. Office Fax: 305-661-6090.*

CHISHOLM, SALLIE WATSON, biological oceanography educator, researcher; b. Marquette, Mich., Nov. 5, 1947; BA, Skidmore Coll., 1969; PhD in biology, SUNY, 1974. Postdoctoral researcher biol. oceanography Scripps Instn. Oceanography, 1974-76; vis. scientist, biology dept. Woods Hole Oceanog. Instn., 1978—; prof., dept. civil and environ. engring. MIT, Cambridge, 1976—, Edgerton asst. prof., 1977—78, Doherty prof. ocean utilization, 1980—82, prof. dept. biology, 1993—, McAfee prof. engring. (endowed chair), 1995—2000, Lee & Geraldine Martin prof. environ. studies, co-dir., Earth Sys. Initiative, 2002—, co-dir., Terrascope, 2003—, Gordon and Betty Moore Found. investigator in marine sci., 2004—. MIT dir. MIT-Woods Hole Joint Program in Oceanography, 1988-95; steering com. U.S. Joint Global Flux Study, 1989-92; mem. ocean studies bd. NRC, 1990-93, com. on molecular biology, 1991-92; corp. mem. Bermuda Biological Station, 1992-96; vis. com. oceanography, Brookhaven Nat. Labs., 1995-98; mem. sci. adv. bd. Joint Genome Inst., Dept. Energy, 2000-, mem. policy bd., 2003; mem. adv. com. Carnegie Instn. Dept. Global Ecology, 2003-; mem. bd. trustees Inst. Ecosystem Studies, 2003-. Assoc. editor Jour. Phycology, 1983-87; mem. editorial bd. Jour. Marine Molecular Biology and Biotech., 1991—, Marine Ecology Progress Series, 1992—, Oceanus Mag., 1991-93, Environmental Microbiology, 1998-; subject editor Aquatic Microbiol Ecology, 1995-99; contbr. articles to profl. jours. Recipient Rosenstiel Award in Ocean Sciences, 1991; fellow, Am. Acad. of Arts and Sciences, 1992; Guggenheim fellow, 1997—98, Resident Scholar, Bellagio Ctr., Italy, 1998, elected, NAS, 2003. Mem.: Internat. Ecology Inst., Soc. of Analytical Cytology, AAAS, Ecological Soc. of Am., The Oceanography Soc., Am. Geophysical Union (fellow 1996), Phycological Soc. of Am., Am. Soc. Microbiology (fellow 1993), Am. Soc. Limnology and Oceanography, Sigma XI. Office: MIT 48-419 15 Vassar St Cambridge MA 02139

CHISHOLM, TOMMY, lawyer, utilities executive; b. Baldwyn, Miss., Apr. 14, 1941; s. Thomas Vandiver and Rubel (Duncan) C.; m. Janice McClanahan, June 20, 1964; children: Mark Alan (dec.), Andrea, Stephen Thomas, Patrick Ervin. BSCE, Tenn. Tech. U., 1963; JD, Samford U., 1969; MBA, Ga. State U., 1984. Registered profl. engr., Ala., Del., Ga., Ky., La., N.H., Miss., Pa., Tenn., S.C., Va., W.Va. Civil engr. TVA, Knoxville, Tenn., 1963-64; design engr. So. Co. Svcs., Birmingham, Ala., 1964-69, coord. spl. projects Atlanta, 1969-73, sec., house counsel, 1977-82, v.p., sec., house counsel, 1982-98; v.p., assoc. gen. counsel, sec. So. Co., Atlanta, 1998—, asst. to pres., 1973-75, sec., asst. treas., 1977—; mgr. adminstrv. svcs. Gulf Power Co., Pensacola, Fla., 1975-77; sec. So. Energy, Inc., Atlanta, 1981-82. Mem. ABA, State Bar Ala., Am. Soc. Corp. Secs., Am. Corp. Counsel Assn., Nat. Assn. Corp. Dirs., Phi Alpha Delta, Beta Gamma Sigma.

CHISHOLM, WILLIAM DEWAYNE, retired contractor; b. Everett, Wash., Mar. 1, 1924; s. James Adam and Evelyn May (Iles) C.; m. Esther Troehler, Mar. 10, 1956; children: James Scott, Larry Alan, Brian Duane. BSChemE, U. Wash., 1949, BS in Indsl. Engring., 1949; MBA, Harvard U., 1955. Cert. profl. contracts mgr. Chemist, unit leader, tech. rep. The Coca-Cola Co., Atlanta and L.A., 1949-59; contract adminstr. Honeywell Inc., LA, 1959-61, mktg. administr., 1961-64, contracts work dir., 1964-66, contracts mgr. Clearwater, Fla., 1966-73, contracts supr., 1973-75, sr. contract mgmt. rep., 1975-80, prin. contract mgmt. rep., work dir., 1980-82, contracts mgr., 1982-89; ret. Chmn. bd. Creative Attitudes, Inc., 1987-96; adj. faculty Fla. Inst. Tech., 1976-96. Contbr. articles to profl. jours. Trustee John Calvin Found., 1974-82; mem. budget adv. com. City of Clearwater, 1983-85; commr. to 196th gen. assembly Presbyn. Ch. (USA), 1984; sec. bd. trustees, treas. Presbytery of Tampa Bay, 1990-96, 99-03, sec. coun., 1996-98, mem. rev., evaluation and planning com., 1996-98, treas. 1999-03, elder session mem., 1964-65, 73-76, 77-80, 81-84, 86-90, 97-2000, 01-04, treas., 1994-96; Clearwater rep. on Long Ctr. bd. dirs. , 1991-97, mem. exec. com., 1992-97, treas., 1992-93, v.p., 1993-95. With USN, 1944-46. Recipient Award of Distinction Fla. Inst. Tech. Grad. Ctr., 1987. Fellow Nat. Contract Mgmt. Assn. (chmn. S.E. region fellows 1985-87, past nat. dir., pres., v.p. Suncoast chpt.). Home: 1364 S Hercules Ave Clearwater FL 33764-3748 *We can't be too generous in sharing understanding and words of comfort, encouragement, and support to those facing adversity and challenge at various times in their lives.*

CHISU, IOAN, artist; b. Cluj-Napoca, Romania, Jan. 28, 1939; arrived in U.S., 88, naturalized, 96; s. Gheorghe and Hermina Chisu; m. Rodica Chisu, Mar. 24, 1961; children: Ioana, Daniel. M of Painting, Ion Andreescu Fine Arts Inst., Cluj-Napoca, 1963. Pres. Union Bd. Artists of Sibiu County, Romania, 1968-70, 80-89; mem. coun. Leadership Fine Arts Union Romania, 1980-89, mem., 1964-89. One-person shows include Sirius Gallery, Sibiu, 1965, 67, Apollo Gallery, 1970, Brukenthal Mus., Sibiu, 1973; exhibited in group shows Art Gallery, Brasov, 1964, 65-67, Art Movie Theater Show, Sibiu, 1965, Brukenthal Mus., Sibiu, 1964, 67, 68-70, 72, 88, Simu Mus., Bucharest, Romania, 1965, Dalles Gallery, Bucharest, 1965, 67-70, 73-88, Casa Armatei, Sibiu, 1966, 74, Sirius Gallery, Sibiu, 1967, 73-88, Mus. Art, Bucharest, 1968, Art Gallery Casa Artelor, Sibiu, 1971, 73-88, Culture's House, Medias, 1971, 74, Big Gallery, Cluj-Napoca, 1973, Ateneul Roman Gallery, Bucharest, 1976, Nat. Theater, Bucharest, 1977; exhibited in mus. Brukenthal Mus., Sibiu, Art Mus., Brasov, Art Mus., Tirgu Mures, Romania, Anchorage Mus. History and Art, Alaska, 1997-98; designs for monumental mosaic works: Tradition and Contemporary Times, Blaj, 1973, Homage to Human Creativity, Resita, 1980, Archways, Sibiu, 1981 Recipient Nat. Order of Cultural Merit for spl. artistic merits, Bucharest, 1968, Nat. Prize for Romania at 3d Internat. Festival of Painting, Cagnes-sur-Mer, France, 1971, 1st prize for painting Nat. Festival Art, Bucharest, 1985, 87, Grant award Cmty. Arts Assistance Program from City of Chgo. Dept. Cultural Affairs and Ill. Arts Coun. Access Program, 1993, 95. Home: 2417 Alton Rd Mchenry IL 60050 Personal E-mail: ichisu2003@yahoo.com.

CHISUM, EMMETT DEWAIN, historian, researcher, archaeologist; b. Monroe, La., Mar. 19, 1922; BA in Social Sci., Northwestern State U., 1942; MA in Social Sci., La. State U., 1946; MA in History, U. Wyo., 1952, MA in Polit. Sci. an dAnthropology, 1961. Tchr. sci. Cameron (La.) Parish Sch. System, 1947-51; tchr. English Welsh (La.) High Sch., 1946-47; social sci. librarian U. Wyo., Laramie, 1954-77, prof. rsch. history, archeology, 1977—. Mem. faculty senate U. Wyo., 1986—. Author: (books) Guide to Library Research, 1969, Guide to Research in Political Science, 1970, Guide to Research in Education, 1974, Memories: University of Wyoming 1886-1986, 1987; contbr. articles to Ency. of Lir. and Info. Sci. (45 vols.), 1986—, profl. jours. Mem. AAAS, ALA, Am. Archeol. Soc., Western Pol. Sci. Assn., Am. Assn. for State and Local History for Wyo. Publs. (Agnes Milstead award for Outstanding Librarianship 1995). Home: 2032 Holliday Dr Laramie WY 82070-4803

CHITAMBAR, CHRISTOPHER RAJIV, internist, oncologist, hematologist; b. Allahabad, India, Apr. 16, 1950; BS, Ewing Christian Coll., 1971; MD, Christian Med. Coll./Punjab U., Ludhiana, India, 1977. Diplomate Am. Bd. Internal Medicine with subspecialties in hematology and oncology. Intern Brackenridge Hosp., Austin, Tex., 1977-78, resident in internal medicine, 1978-80; fellow in hematology and oncology U. Colo. Health Scis. Ctr., Denver, 1980-83; active staff Froedtert Meml. Luth. Hosp., Milw.; prof. medicine, divsn. hematology/oncology Med. Coll. Wis., Milw. Mem. AAAS; mem. Am. Fedn. Clin. Rsch., Am. Soc. Clin. Oncology, Am. Soc. Hematology. Office: Med Coll Wisconsin Divsn Hematology/Onc FMLH 9200 W Wisconsin Ave Milwaukee WI 53226 Office Phone: 414-805-4600. Office Fax: 414-805-4604. Business E-Mail: chitambr@mcw.edu.*

CHITNIS, ASHAY, research scientist; b. Pune, Maharashtra, India, May 16, 1977; s. Suhas Manohar and Sujata Suhas Chitnis; m. Anvita Ashay Chitnis. BS in Electronics Engring., U. Pune, 1998; PhD in Electrical Engring., U. SC, Columbia, 2002. Grad. rsch. asst. U. SC, 1998—2002, rsch. assoc., 2003—04, rsch. asst. prof., 2004; rsch. scientist Cree, Santa Barbara Tech. Ctr., Goleta, Calif., 2004—. Presenter in field. Author, co-author over 30 publs. in internat. sci. jours; contbr. internat. conf. presentaions and articles in profl. mags. Achievements include development of novel packaging technologies for deep ultra violet light emitting diodes; expertise in semiconductor technology particularly III-Nitrides: devices, processing, packaging; several patents in process. Avocations: poetry, soccer. Personal E-mail: anvishay@gmail.com.

CHITRE, SUBODH SUBHASH, computer company executive; b. Mumbai, India, May 30, 1970; arrived in US, 2003; s. Subhash Shivram and Suhas Subhash Chitre; m. Sanjukta Abhay Mallapur, Mar. 14, 1999; 1 child, Atharva Subodh. BS in Engring., U. Bombay, Mumbai, India, 1991; MSc, Okla. State U., Stillwater, 1993; diploma in Mgmt., Indian Inst. Mgmt., Ahmedabad, India, 1998. Cert. quality engr., Am. Soc. Quality, 1995. Sr. prodn. engr. A B Dick Co., Niles, Ill., 1993—96; sr. cons. PriceWaterhouseCoopers, Mumbai, 1998—2000; prin. cons. Bristlecone, Mumbai, 2000—02; asst. v.p. Satyam Computer Svcs., Richmond, Va., 2002—. Mem. panel examiners Lincoln Found., Ill., 1995, Ill., 2006. Contbr. articles to profl. jours. Mem.: Phi Kappa Phi, Mensa. Hindu. Avocations: reading, writing, golf, cricket. Office Phone: 860-593-6694. Personal E-mail: subodh.chitre@gmail.com.

CHITTUM, ANTHONY, chef; b. 1978; m. Heather Chittum. Cook Elite Café, San Francisco; garde mgr. Equinox, Washington, 1999, sous chef, chef de cuisine; chef Aria Trattoria, Washington, 2004; exec. chef Dish, Washington, 2005—, Notti Bianche, Washington, 2005—. Named one of Washington DC's Rising Stars, StarChefs.com, 2006.*

CHITTUM, HEATHER, chef; m. Anthony Chittum. B in Govt. and Internat. Rels., Clark U., 1994; attended Fundamental of Pastry Arts prog., L'Academie de Cuisine, 2001. Worked for former NY Senator Daniel Patrick Moynihan, Share Our Strength; cook Equinox restaurant; pastry chef Circle Bistro, 2004, Dish, 2004—, Notti Bianche, 2005—, Michel Richard Citronelle. Named one of Washington DC's Rising Stars, StarChefs.com, 2006.*

CHIU, ALEXANDER G., otolaryngologist, educator; s. Paul and Elizabeth Chiu; m. Michelle D. Chuong, Dec. 3, 2005. MD, Albany Med. Coll., NY, 1997. Cert. otolaryngology Am. Bd. Otolaryngology, 2003. Clin. instr. Stanford U., Calif., 2002—03; asst. prof. U. Pa., Phila., 2003—. Cons. BrainLAB Surg. Nav., Munich, 2003—. Fellow: Am. Acad. Otolaryngology, Am. Rhinologic Soc. (Young Investigator award 2006). Achievements include development of topical medications for chronic sinusitis. Office: U Pa 3400 Spruce St 5 Ravdin Philadelphia PA 19085 Office Phone: 215-662-2360. Office Fax: 215-614-0071. E-mail: alexchiu11@hotmail.com.

CHIU, BELLA CHAO, astrophysicist, writer; b. Beijing, May 24, 1931; came to U.S., 1938; d. Yuen Ren and Buwei (Yang) Chao; m. Hong-Yee Chiu, June 25, 1960 (div. 1966); 1 child, Lihu Mason Chiu. BA, U. Calif., Berkeley, 1953; MS, Cornell U., 1956. Rsch. staff MIT, Cambridge, 1971-81; tchr. ESL Ctrl. S. U. Tech., Changsha, China, 1982-83; fgn. expert Qinghua U., Beijing, 1986-87; writer Arlington, Mass., 1987-97; rschr., 1997—. English editor Nat. Assn. Chinese Ams., 1984-86. Grantee NSF, 1972, 75, 79. Mem. Am. Astron. Soc. (hist. divsn.), Archeol. Inst. Am., Women's Health Initiative. Achievements include research in the evidence that the main driving force behind El Nino/La Nina storms comes from the combining of solar gravity with that of the moon; some cases solar eclipse paths can be used to predict a storm. Personal E-mail: bellacchiu@aol.com.

CHIU, DAVID TAK WAI, surgeon; b. Kwangtung, China, Oct. 23, 1945; s. Bud Yick and Lai Kwai (Lum) C.; m. Lilian Wah-Ying Shen, June 19, 1973; children: Vincent, Edmund, Jerome, Miranda. BA, U. Mo., St. Louis, 1969; MD, Columbia U., 1973. Diplomate Am. Bd. Plastic Surgery. Intern Barnes Hosp., St. Louis, 1973—74, resident in gen. surgery, 1974—77; resident in plastic surgery Columbia-Presbyn. Med. Ctr., 1977—79; fellow NYU Med. Ctr., NYC, 1980, instr. surgery, 1981, asst. prof., 1981—89, dir. N.Y. Nerve Ctr., 2003—, dir. Hand Surgery Svc., 2006—; supervisory attending Bellevue Hosp. Hand Clinic, NYC, 1981—89; assoc. dir. plastic surgery, chief hand/microsurgery and replantation surgery divsn. plastic surgery Columbia Presbyn. Med. Ctr., NYC, 1989—94, dir. microsurgery ctr., 1993, chief plastic surgery divsn. dept. surgery, 1994—97, prof. clin. surgery, 1990—2001, Thomas S. Zimmer prof., 1994—2000, Calvin F. Barber prof., 2000—01, dir. ctr. restorative surgery, 2000—; prof. plastic surgery NYU, 2001—06, prof. surgery NYC, 2006—; chief hand svcs. NYU Med. Ctr., 2006—. Adj. prof. Coll. Physicians and Surgeons Columbia U., NYC, 2001—. Author: Introduction to Microsurgery: A Lab Manual, 1985; mem. editorial bd. Jour. Reconstructive Microsurgery, 1990—. Recipient Alumni Fedn. Columbia U. medal, 1995. Fellow: ACS; mem.: AMA, Fedn. Chinese Med. Soc. Found. (founding pres. 2002, founding trustee 2002—), World Soc. Reconstructive Microsurgery (founding mem.), Tissue Engring. Soc., Sunderland Soc., Am. Acad. Pediat. (splty. fellow 1992), Internat. Soc. of Reconstructive Microsurgery, Northeast Soc. Plastic Surgery, Royal Soc. Medicine, Am. Soc. Peripheral Nerve Surgery (pres. 1999—2001, founding mem.), Am. Assn. Hand Surgery, Am. Soc. Plastic and Reconstructive Surgeons, Am. Soc. Surgery of Hand, Am. Soc. Reconstructive Microsurgery (pres. 1998—99), N.Y. Regional Soc. Plastic and Reconstructive Plastic Surgery (pres. 1997—98), Coll. Physicians and Surgeons Alumni Assn. (dir. 1984, pres. 2001—02, Bronze medal 1973, Gold medal 1997), Plastic Surgery Rsch. Coun., N.Y. Soc. Surgery of Hand (pres. 1996—97), N.Y. State Med. Soc., N.Y. County Med. Soc., Am. Assn. Plastic Surgeons, Chinese Am. Med. Soc. (dir. 1983—, pres. 1985—87, Presdl. medal 1987, Disting. Svc. award 1988, Scientific award 2001), Fedn. Chinese Am. and Chinese Can. Med. Socs. (founder 1994, founding pres. 1994—96, chmn. bd. dirs., Outstanding Achievement award 1996). Office: 900 Park Ave New York NY 10021-0231 Home Phone: 914-779-3484; Office Phone: 212-879-8880. Business E-Mail: office@davidchiumd.com.

CHIU, DOROTHY, retired pediatrician; b. Hong Kong, Aug. 8, 1917; came to U.S., 1946; d. Yan Tse Chiu and Connie Kwai-Ching Wan; m. Kitman Au; children: Katherine, Margo, Doris, James, Richard. BS, Lingnan U., 1939; MD, Nat. Shanghai Med. Coll., 1945. Diplomate Am. Bd. Pediats. Sch. physician L.A. Sch. Dist., 1954-55; pvt. practice Burbank, Calif., 1955—56, San Fernando, Calif., 1956—2000. Staff pediatrician Holy Cross Med. Ctr., Mission Hills, Calif., 1961-2000. Bd. dirs. Burbank Cmty. Concert, 1970-80. Fellow Am. Acad. Pediats.; mem. Calif. Med. Assn., L.A. County Med. Assn. Republican. Avocations: handicrafts, music, travel, reading, photography.

CHIU, HUNGDAH, law educator; b. Shanghai, Mar. 23, 1936; came to U.S., 1960; s. Han-ping and Ming-non (Yang) C.; m. Yuan-yuan Hsieh, May 14, 1966; 1 son, Wei-hsueh. LLB, Nat. Taiwan U., 1958; MA with honors, L.I. U., 1962; LLM, Harvard U., 1962, SJD, 1965. Assoc. in rsch. East Asian Research Center, Harvard U., 1964-65; assoc. prof. internat. law Nat. Taiwan U., 1965-66; rsch. assoc. in law Harvard U., 1966-70, 72-74; vis. prof. law Nat. Chengchi U., Taipei, Taiwan, 1970-72; assoc. prof. law U. Md., Balt., 1974-77, prof., 1977—2002, prof. emeritus, 2002—. Chmn. bd. dirs. Modern China Studies Quar., 2000—, Ctr. for Modern China, Princeton, NJ, 2000—; min. of state Exec. Yuan (Cabinet), Republic of China, Taiwan, 1993-94; mem. Presdl. Com. on Nat. Unification, Taiwan, 1995-2000, amb.-at-large, 1998-2000. Author: The Capacity of International Organizations to Conclude Treaties, 1966, The People's Republic of China and the Law of Treaties, 1972, (with J.A. Cohen) People's China and International Law, 2 vols, 1974 (certificate of merit Am. Soc. Internat. Law 1976), Normalizing Relations with China: Problems, Analysis and Documents, 1978, China and the Taiwan Issue, 1979, Agreements of the People's Republic of China, 1966-80, A Calendar of Events, 1981; (with S.C. Leng) China: 70 years after the 1911 Hsin-Hai Revolution, 1984, Criminal Justice in Post-Mao China, 1985, (with Y.C. Jao and Y.L. Wu) The Future of Hong Kong, 1987, (with G. Knight) International Law of the Sea: Cases, Documents and Readings, 1991; Hsian-t'ai Kuo-chi-fa (Modern International Law), 1995, rev. edit., 2005; (with Chun-i Chen) Hsien-tai Kuo-chi-fa Ts'an-kao Wen-chien (Reference Documents of Modern International Law), 1996, rev. edit., 2005, 1996 Case and Documentary Supplement for Knight and Chiu's International Law of the Sea, 1997; (with Hsing-wei Lee and Chih-Yu Wu) Implentationat Taiwan Relations Act: An Examination after Twenty Years, 2001; contbr. articles to profl. jours., chpts. to books; gen. editor: Contemporary Asian Studies, 1976—; editor in chief Chinese Yearbook of Internat. Law and Affairs, 1981-2006, Wen ti Lun ji Collected Essays on Territorial Borders Concerning China, 2004. Del. UN Conf. Law of the Sea, 1976—82; chmn. of the bd. Ctr. for Modern China, 2000—. Served to 2d lt. Chinese Army, 1958—60. Named One of 10 Outstanding Young Men, Jr. c. of C. of Republic of China, 1971; Social Sci. Rsch. Coun. fellow, 1968; recipient Cultural award Inst. Chinese Culture, 1980, Toulmin medal Soc. Am. Mil. Engrs., 1982, Nat. Reconstrn. award Chinese Profl. Assn. Mid-Am., 1980, Outstanding Achievement award Mid-Am. Chinese Sci. and Tech. Assn., 1991, 1st class Merit Svc. medal Exec. Yuan (Cabinet), Republic of China, 1994. Mem. Am. Soc. Internat. Law (panel on China and internat. order 1969-74, chmn. interest group on law Pacific region 1987-93), Assn. for Asian Studies (com. on Asian law 1976-89), Am. Assn. for Chinese Studies (v.p. 1982-84, pres. 1985-87), Assn. Am. Law Schs. (chair internat. legal exch. sect. 1986-88), Assn. Chinese Social Scientists, N.A. (pres. 1984-86), Chinese Soc. Internat. Law (pres. 1993-2000), Internat. Law Assn. (pres. 1998-2000, perm. v.p. 2000—). Home: 6168 Devon Dr Columbia MD 21044-3821 Office: U Md Law Sch 500 W Baltimore St Baltimore MD 21201-1786 Office Phone: 410-706-3870. Business E-Mail: hchiu@law.edu.

CHIU, JOHN TANG, physician; b. Macao, Jan. 8, 1938; s. Lan Cheong and Yau Hoon C.; m. Bonnie Doolan, Aug. 28, 1965 (div. Apr. 1986); children: Lisa, Mark, Heather; m. Karin Adams, Jan. 3, 2000. Student, U. Vt., BA, 1960, MD, 1964. Diplomate Am. Bd. Allergy & Immunology. Pres. Allergy Med. Group, Inc., Newport Beach, Calif., 1969-72, 1972—. Clin. prof. medicine U. Calif., Irvine, 1975—. Contbr. articles to profl. jours. Active Santa Ana Heights Adv. Commn., 1982-83; life mem. Orange County Sheriff's Adv. coun., 1987—. Recipient Freshman Chem. Achievement award Am. Chem. Soc., 1958. Fellow Am. Acad. Allergy Asthma and Immunology, Am. Coll. Allergy and Immunology, Am. Coll. Chest Physicians (sec. steering com. allergy 1977-81), Orange County Med. Assn. (chmn. comm. com. 1985-88, comm. com., mem. bull. editl. bd. 1995-2001). Avocations: skiing, golf, aerobics, travels. Office: Allergy Med Group Inc 400 Newport Center Dr Newport Beach CA 92660-7601 Office Phone: 949-644-1422. Personal E-mail: allergymed@yahoo.com.

CHIU, PETER YEE-CHEW, physician; came to U.S., 1965; naturalized, 1973; s. Man Chee and Yiu Ying Chiu; m. Elisa; children: Emma, Clara. BS, U. Calif., Berkeley, 1969, MPH, 1970, DrPH, 1975; MD, Stanford U., 1983. Diplomate Am. Bd. Family Practice, Am. Bd. Preventive Medicine; registered profl. engr., Calif.; registered environ. health specialist, Calif. Asst. civil engr. City of Oakland, Calif., 1970-72; assoc. water quality engr. Bay Area Sewage Services Agy., Berkeley, 1974-76; prin. environ. engr. Assn. Bay Area Govts., Berkeley, 1976-79; intern San Jose (Calif.) Hosp., 1983-84, resident physician, 1984-86; ptnr. Chiu and Crawford, San Jose, 1986-89, Good Samaritan Med. Group, San Jose, 1989-90, The Permanente Med. Group, 1991—. Adj. prof. U. San Francisco, 1979-83; adj. clin. assoc. prof. Stanford U. Med. Sch., 1987—. Contbr. articles to profl. publs.; composer, pub. various popular songs Southeast Asia, US. Bd. mem. Calif. Regional Water Quality Control Bd.,Oakland, 1979-84, Bay Area Comprehensive Health Planning Coun., San Francisco, 1972-76; mem. Santa Clara County Ctrl. Dem. Com., 1987—; mem. exec. bd. Calif. State Dem. Ctrl. Com.; commr. U.S. Presdl. Commn. on Risk Assessment and Risk Mgmt., Washington, 1993-97; mem. U.S. Presdl. Rank Rev. Bd., Washington, 2000; hearing bd. mem. alt. Bay Area Air Quality Mgmt. Dist., San Francisco, 2002—. Recipient Resident Tchr. award Soc. Tchrs. Family Medicine, 1986, Resolution of Appreciation award Calif. Regional Water Quality Control Bd., 1985, Norman Mineta Lifetime Achievement award Silicon Valley Asian Pacific Am. Dem. Club, 2006. Fellow Am. Acad. Family Physicians; mem. Am. Pub. Health Assn., Chi Epsilon, Tau Beta Pi. Democrat. Achievements include co-authored one of the first comprehensive regional environmental management plans in US; pioneered a comprehensive framework for enviromental health risk management. Avocations: songwriting, recording. Office: The Permanente Med Group 770 E Calaveras Blvd Milpitas CA 95035-5491

CHIU, TZU-CHIEN, geologist, researcher; BS in Geology, Nat. Taiwan U., Taipei, 1998, MS in Geology, 2000; MPhil in Earth and Environ. Scis., PhD in Earth and Environ. Scis., Columbia U., NYC, 2005. Rsch., tchg. asst. Lamont-Doherty Earth Obs. Columbia U., Palisades, NY, 2001—05, postdoctoral rsch. scientist, 2005—, lectr. frontiers of sci. dept. earth and environ. scis., sci. fellow, 2005—06. Contbr. articles to profl. jours. Recipient Dept. Tchg. Asst. award, Dept. Earth and Environ. Sciences, Columbia U., 2003; Geol. scholar, Ministry of Econ. Affairs, Taiwan, 1995—96, Student Poster Competition scholar, Geol. Soc. China, Taiwan, 1999, Postdoctoral Sci. fellow, Columbia U., 2005, Faculty fellow, Dept. Earth and Environ. Scis. Columbia U., 2000—04, Abrupt Climate Change fellow, Comer Sci. and Edn. Found., 2006. Mem.: AAAS, Nat. Postdoctoral Assn., Am. Geophys. Union (Internat. Student Travel award 1999). Achievements include research in extend the radiocarbon calibration (coral data set) up to 50,000 years before present; reconstruct the record of atmospheric radiocarbon content spanning the past 50,000 years; improve the application of U-series dating (particularly protactinium-231/uranium-235 decay system) on fossil corals; improve the screening procedure for selecting well-preserved fossil corals. Avocations: classical music, museums, concerts, opera, piano. Office: Lamont-Doherty Earth Obs 61 Route 9W Palisades NY 10964 Office Phone: 845-365-8647. Business E-Mail: tcchiu@ldeo.columbia.edu.

CHIVERTON, PATRICIA ANN, dean, nursing educator; b. Rochester, NY, Nov. 21, 1947; d. Paul and Eleanor (Buyck) Gilmore; 1 child, Laura. BS, Ctrl. Mo. State U., 1970; MS, U. Rochester, 1980, EdD, 1990. Exec. dir. Alzheimer's Assn., Rochester, NY, 1987-89; clin. assoc. U. Rochester, 1987-89, clin. chief psychiat. mental health nursing, 1990-97, asst. prof. clin. nursing, 1994-95, interim chair health care sys. divsn., 1994-95, assoc. prof. clin. clin. nursing, 1996—99, CEO cmty. nursing ctr., 1996—, assoc. dean clin. affairs Sch. Nursing and Med. Ctr., 1998—99, interim dean Sch. Nursing and Med. Ctr., 1999—2000, dean Sch. Nursing and Med. Ctr., 2000—. Judge Book of the Yr., Am. Jour. Nursing, 1999, reviewer, 1998—; cons. F.f. Thompson Continuing Care Facility, Canadaiguia, N.Y., 1997-99. Contbr. chpts. to books. in field. Rep. N.Y. State Alzheimer's Assn., 1985-88; bd. dirs. Health and Wellness Ctr., Livingston County, N.Y., Monroe County Long Term Care Agy., Rochester, 1997—. Mem. Am. Psychiat. Nurses Assn. (pres. Northwestern chpt. 1995-97, Excellence in Leadership award 1994), Ea. Nursing Rsch. Soc., Nat. Acads. Practice (Disting. Practitioner), Sigma Theta Tau. Office: U Rochester Sch Nursing 601 Elmwood Ave Rochester NY 14642-0001 E-mail: patricia_chiverton@urmc.rochester.edu.

CHIVIAN, ERIC SETH, psychiatrist, environmental scientist, educator; b. Newark, June 10, 1942; children: Cybele, Dylan C., Judah B. AB, Harvard U., 1964, MD, 1968. Staff psychiatrist MIT, 1980—2000; asst. clin. prof. psychiatry Harvard Med. Sch., 1987—, dir. Ctr. for Health and the Global Environment, 1996—. Recipient Nobel Peace prize, 1985. Mem.: AAAS, Internat. Physicians Prevent Nuc. War (co-founder, treas. 1980—85), Physicians for Social Responsibility. Achievements include research in first large scale scientific survey of American and Soviet teenagers' attitudes about the future; US-USSR relations and nuclear war; health implications of species extinction and loss of biodiversity. Home: 136 Carter Pond Rd Petersham MA 01366-9728

CHIZEN, BRUCE R., computer company executive; BS, CUNY Bklyn Coll. Mgr. merchandising Mattel Electronics, 1980—83; dir. sales Ea. Region Microsoft Corp., 1983—87; founding sr. mgr. to v.p. sales and worldwide mktg. to v.p., gen. mgr. Claris Clear Choice Claris Corp., 1987—94; v.p., gen. mgr. profl. graphics divsn. and consumer divsn. Adobe Systems, Inc., San Jose, Calif., exec. v.p. worldwide products and mktg., 1994—99, pres., 1999—2005, CEO, 2000—. Bd. dirs. Synopsys, Inc. Bd. dirs. Children's Discovery Mus., San Jose. Named one of 50 Who Matter Now, Business 2.0, 2007. Office: Adobe Systems Inc 345 Park Ave San Jose CA 95110-2704*

CHIZEWER, DAVID J., lawyer; b. Chgo., Apr. 4, 1966; BA magna cum laude in Econs., Pomona Coll., 1988; JD, U. Chgo., 1991. Bar: Ill. 1991. Prin. Goldberg, Kohn, Bell, Black, Rosenbloom & Moritz, Chgo. Named one of The Nation's Top Litigators, Nat. Law Jour., 2007; recipient Child Adv. award, Am. Assn. Pediat., 2005, Excellence in Pro Bono award, US Dist. Ct. (no. dist. Ill.), 2006; Leadership Fellow, Leadership Greater Chgo. Prog. Mem.: Def. Rsch. Inst., Chgo. Bar Assn., ABA, Phi Beta Kappa. Office: Goldberg Kohn Suite 3700 55 E Monroe St Chicago IL 60603-5802 Office Phone: 312-201-3938. Office Fax: 312-863-7438. Business E-Mail: david.chizewer@goldbergkohn.com.*

CHLEBUS, ANDREW J., lawyer; b. New Bedford, Aug. 30, 1949; AB magna cum laude, Brown U., 1971; JD, Harvard U., 1974. Bar: RI 1974, Mass. 1976. Mem. Edwards & Angell, Providence; ptnr. Edwards Angell Palmer & Dodge, Providence. Instr. Cape Cod C.C., 1976-78, 79, 83-89, 91; spkr. in various fields. Founder Golf Tournament. Recipient Best Lawyers in Am., Chambers USA. Mem. ABA (bus. law sect.), RI Bar Assn. (fee arbitration com.). Office: Edwards Angell Palmer & Dodge 2800 Financial Plaza Providence RI 02903 Office Phone: 401-276-6473. Office Fax: 401-276-6611. Business E-Mail: achlebus@eapdlaw.com.

CHLOUBER, DALE EDWARD, curator; b. Kingfisher, Okla., July 28, 1936; s. Clyde E. and Helen A. Chlouber; m. Carla Sue Sweet, Sept. 3, 1959; children: Belinda Lee, Beth Ann Fulgenzi, Steven Edward. BS, Okla. State U., 1959, MS, 1961. Guidance counselor Bur. Indian Affairs, Leupp, Ariz., 1961—65; ednl. psychologist, dep. dir. corpsman supervision Winslow (Ariz.) Job Corps Ctr., 1965—68; dir. student programs, registrar, fin. aid Navajo C.C., Many Farms, Ariz., 1968—70; mgr. Head Start tng. Ea. Okla. State Coll., Wilburton, 1970—75, Chadron (Nebr.) State Coll., 1975—77; mus. curator Washington Irving Trail Mus., Ripley, Okla., 1993—. Editor: Child Development Associate Units of Instruction, 1970—77. Host Reenactment of Battle of Round Mountains, Ripley, 1995—99; mem. adv. bd. Stillwater (Okla.) News Press, 2001—05. Recipient Meritorious Svc. award, Payne County Hist. Soc., 1997, Merit award for outstanding publ., Washington Irving Trail Mus., 2004. Mem.: Am. Assn. State and Local History, Okla. Museums Assn. (Outstanding Interpretive Exhibit award 1998), Payne County Hist. Soc. (Meritorious Svc. award 1997), Nat. Cowboy and Western Heritage Mus., Okla. Hist. Soc. Avocations: discovering historical artifacts, reading. Office: Washington Irving Trail Museum 3918 S Mehan Rd Ripley OK 74062 Home Phone: 405-624-9130; Office Phone: 405-624-9130. Personal E-mail: cchlouber@aol.com. Business E-Mail: trailmuseum@aol.com.

CHMELL, SAMUEL JAY, orthopedic surgeon; b. Chgo., Aug. 21, 1952; s. Samuel and Elsie (Wauterlek) C.; m. Nancy Jean Aumiller, June 22, 1974; children: Jessica, Carson, Alexis, Lesley, Samuel Jayson. BS, U. Notre Dame, 1974; MD, Loyola U., 1977. Diplomate Am. Bd. Orthop. Surgery. Intern Loyola U. Med. Ctr., Maywood, Ill., 1977-78, resident in orthop. surgery, 1980-84; emergency rm. physician USPHS Indian Health Svc., Chinle, Ariz., 1978-80; attending orthop. surgeon Hines (Ill.) VA Hosp., 1984-88, Shriners Hosp. for Crippled Children, Chgo., 1985-89, Gallup (N.Mex.) Indian Hosp., 1988-89, Humana-Michael Reese Hosp. and Health Plan, Chgo., 1989—99; chmn. sect. orthopaedic surgery Humana-Michael Reese Med. Ctr., Chgo., 1991—99; assoc. prof. dept. orthop. surgery U. Ill., Chgo., 1991—. Clin. instr. in orthop. surgery Loyola U. Med. Ctr., Maywood, 1985-88; assoc. prof. dept. orthop. surgery U. Ill., Chgo.; adv. coun. Coll. of Sci. U. Notre Dame. Contbr. articles to profl. jours. Active Olmsted Hist. Soc. Riverside, Ill. Sofield Travelling fellow Orthop. Rsch. Soc. Gt. Britain, 1985. Master: Alpha Omega Alpha; fellow: Am. Acad. Orthop. Surgeons, ACS; mem.: Founders' Cir. of Sorin Soc. U. Notre Dame, Notre Dame Orthop. Soc. Office: U Ill 1801 West Taylor St Ste 2A MC 743 Chicago IL 60612 Office Phone: 312-996-7161. Personal E-mail: samchmell@yahoo.com. Business E-Mail: schmell@uic.edu.

CHMIELINSKI, EDWARD ALEXANDER, retired electronics company executive; b. Waterbury, Conn., Mar. 25, 1925; s. Stanley ahd Helen Chmielinski; m. Elizabeth Carew, May 30, 1946; children: Nancy, Elizabeth, Susan Jean. BS, Tulane U., 1950; postgrad., Colo. U., 1965. V.p., gen. mgr. Clifton Products, Litton Industries, Colorado Springs, Colo., 1965-67; pres. Memory Products divsn. Litton Industries, Beverly Hills, Calif., 1967-69, Bowmar Instruments Can., Ottawa, Ont., Canada, 1969-73; gen. mgr. Leigh Instruments, Carleton Place, Ont., 1973—75; pres., CEO, dir. Lewis Engring. Co., Naugatuck, Conn., 1975—85, Liquidometer Corp., Tampa, Fla., 1975-85; pres. Lewis divsn. Colt Industries, 1985-90; ret., 1990. Pres. Acad. Water Bd., 1963-65; bd. dirs. United Way, Colorado Springs, 1965-67; fellow Tulane U. Served with USN, 1943-46. Mem. Air Force Assn., Navy League.

CHO, ALFRED YI, electrical engineer; b. Beijing, July 10, 1937; arrived in U.S., 1955, naturalized, 1962; s. Edward I-Lai and Mildred (Chen) Cho; m. Mona Lee Willoughby, June 16, 1968; children: Derek Ming, Deidre Lin, Brynna Ying, Wendy Li. BSEE, U. Ill., 1960, MS, 1961, PhD, 1968, D (hon.) Engring., 1999; DSc (hon.), City U. Hong Kong, 2000, Hong Kong Bapt. U., 2001, Hong Kong U. Sci. and Tech., 2003. Rsch. physicist Ion Physics Corp., Burlington, Mass., 1961—62; mem. tech. staff TRW-Space Tech. Labs., Redondo Beach, Calif., 1962—65, Bell Labs., Murray Hill, NJ, 1968—84, dept. head, 1984—87; dir. Materials Processing Rsch. Lab. AT&T Bell Labs., Murray Hill, 1987—90; semicondr. rsch. lab. v.p. Bell Labs. Lucent Techs. (formerly AT&T Bell Labs.), Murray Hill, 1990—2002; fellow Bell Labs., Lucent Techs. (formerly AT&T Bell Labs.), 1992—; rsch. asst. U. Ill., Urbana, 1965—68. Vis. prof. dept. elec. engring., vic. rsch. prof. coordinated sci. lab. U. Ill., Urbana, 1977—78, adj. prof. dept. elec. engring., adj. rsch. prof. coordinated sci. lab., 1978—; bd. dirs. Riber, Edison, NJ; trustee Coll. of N.J., 1996—2000. Contbr. over 590 articles to profl. jours. Named to, N.J. Inventors Hall of Fame, 1997; recipient Elec. and Computer Engring. Disting. Alumnus award, U. Ill., 1985, Disting. Achievement award, Chinese Inst. Engrs., USA, 1985, Internat. Gallium Arsenide Symposium award, 1986, Heinrich Welker Gold medal, 1986, The Coll. Engring. Alumni Honor award, U. Ill., 1988, World Materials Congress award, ASM Internat., 1988, Achievement award, Indsl. Rsch. Inst., Inc., 1988, Thomas Alva Edison Sci. award, N.J. Gov., 1990, Internat. Crystal Growth award, Am. Assn. for Crystal Growth, 1990, Asian Am. Corp. Achievement award, 1992, Chinese Am. Engrs. and Scientists Assn. So. Achievement award, 1993, Nat. Medal of Sci., NSF, 1993, Elliott Cresson medal, The Franklin Inst., 1995, Computer and Comm. prize, Japan, 1995, W.E. Lamb medal for laser sci. and quantum optics, 2000, Nat. Medal Tech., Dept. Commerce, 2005. Fellow: IEEE (Morris N. Liebman award 1982, IEEE Medal of Honor 1994, Third Millennium medal 2000), Am. Phys. Soc. (Internat. prize for new materials 1982); mem.: Third World Acad. Scis., Nat. Acad. Engring., U.S. Nat. Acad. Scis., Am. Acad. Art and Scis., Am. Philos. Soc., Chinese Acad. Scis., Academia Sinica (Taiwan), Materials Rsch. Soc. (Von Hippel award 1994), Electrochem. Soc. (electronic divsn. award 1977, Solid State Sci. and Tech. medal 1987), Am. Vacuum Soc. (Gaede-Langmuir award 1988), Sigma Tau, Eta Kappa Nu, Tau Beta Pi, Sigma Xi. Achievements include development of molecular beam epitaxy; patents in field. Office Phone: 908-582-2093. Fax: 908-582-2043. Personal E-mail: alcho@aol.com. Business E-Mail: ayc@acatel-lucent.com. *I learned early in my life that hard work is a major ingredient for success. We can always do more than we think we are able to do. I drive myself to my utmost capacity so that I will not have regrets later that I did not try my best. My first love is art but I earn my living as an engineer. In my work as a research scientist, the secret for success is that I combine Oriental patience with Western technology. We should always try to enhance the best part of what we have and not be afraid to change.*

CHO, CHONGDU, mechanical engineer, educator; b. Hong-cheon, Kang-won Do, Republic of Korea, Dec. 22, 1960; s. Dae-won Cho and Byung-soon Min; m. Kwanghee Choi, June 17, 1989; children: Judy, Amy. PhD, U. Michigan, Ann Arbor, 1991. Asst. mgr.r Hyundai Precision Co. Ltd., Kyung-gi Do, Republic of Korea, 1985—88; rsch. fellow U. Mich., Ann Arbor, 1991—92; prof. Inha University, Nam Ku, Inchon, Republic of Korea, 1992—. Vis. scholar UCLA, 2000—01; vice dean. rsch. affairs Inha U. Contbr. articles to profl.jours., 1999. Recipient Best Quality Promotion Award, Ministry of Industry, Rep. of Korea, 1998. Mem.: ASME, Korean Soc. Composite Materials (editl. bd.), Korean Soc. Precision Engring., Korean Soc. Tribologists and Lubrication Engrs., Korean Soc. Mech. Engrs. (life; assoc. editor 1999). Office: Inha Univ 253 Yong-hyun Incheon 402-751 Republic of Korea Home Phone: +82-2-566-1087; Office Phone: +82-32-860-7321. Business E-Mail: cdcho@inha.ac.kr.

CHO, EUNG-RAE (BRIAN), bank executive; b. 1961; BS, Hong-Ik U., 1983; MS, Calif. State U., 1989. CPA. Sr. v.p., CFO Wilshire State Bank, LA, 1995—, Wilshire Bancorp, LA, 2004, exec. v.p., CFO, 2005—. Recipient Elijah Watt Sells Award Gold Medal, 1988. Office: Wilshire Bancorp Inc 3200 Wilshire Blvd Los Angeles CA 90010 Office Phone: 213-387-3200. Office Fax: 213-427-6562.*

CHO, HO SOON MICHELLE L., adult education educator; m. Kyung Ku Peter Cho, Mar. 30, 1942; children: Michelle children: Michael. BS, Tex. Woman's U., 1977, MS, 1981, PhD, 1996. RN Tex., 1974. Instr. ElCentro Coll., Dallas, 1981—96; assoc. prof. nursing Tex. Woman's U., Dallas, 1997—. Author: (novel) A Korean Dream. Mem. adv. coun. Dem. Unification of Korea, Seoul, 2003—. Named Mem. of Yr., Parkland and Tex. Woman's U. Alumni Assn., 2002; recipient Disting. Alumni award, Gyungsang Nat. U., 2001. Master: Korean ANA (assoc.; v.p. 1982—84, Achievement award 1984), Gyungsang Nat. U. Can. and U.S. Alumni Assn. (assoc.; pres. 2003—05); mem.: North Tex. Korean ANA (bd. dirs.), Sigma Theta Tau (archivist 2000—05, sholar 1996, 2000, 2005). Roman Catholic. Achievements include patents for Papilla Gown. Home: 5217 Northmoor Dr Dallas TX 75229 Office: Texas Woman's U 1810 inwood Rd Dallas TX 75235-7299 Home Phone: 214-739-3904; Office Phone: 214-689-6532. Personal E-mail: hcho@twu.edu.

CHO, IN-KOO, economist, educator; b. Seoul, Korea, Sept. 26, 1958; s. Dong-Sun Cho and Chan-Mo Chung; m. Jeong Eun Lee, Mar. 22, 1989; 1 child, Nicholas. BA, Seoul Nat. U., 1981; PhD, Princeton U., 1986. Asst. prof. U. Chgo., 1986-91, assoc. prof., 1991-95; assoc. prof., prof. Brown U., Providence, R.I., 1995-98; William Kinkead Prof. U. Ill., Champaign, 1998—. Alfred P. Sloan Found. fellow, 1991-93; NSF grantee, 1987—. Mem. Econometric Soc. Office: U Ill Dept Econs 1206 S 6th St Champaign IL 61820-6978

CHO, JANG-CHEON, microbiologist, researcher; b. Seoul, Dec. 26, 1969; m. Hoonshik Lee, Dec. 15, 1996; children: MinJoo, Jace M. PhD, Seoul Nat. U., 2000. Postdoctoral rschr. Seoul Nat. U.; faculty rsch. assoc. Oreg. State U., Corvallis, 2001—. Mem.: Am. Soc. for Microbiology (assoc.). Achievements include discovery of novel phylum in Kingdom Bacteria; uncultured Oligotrophic Marine Gammaproteobacteria in the ocean; at least 10 novel genus in Kingdom Bacteria; development of automated, continuous toxicity measuring system. Office: Oreg State Univ Dept Microbiology NASH 222 Corvallis OR 97331 Home Phone: 1-541-738-2682; Office Phone: 1-541-737-0717. Office Fax: 1-541-737-0496. Personal E-mail: skycho@gmail.com.

CHO, LEE-JAY, social scientist, demographer; b. Kyoto, July 5, 1936; came to U.S., 1959; s. Sam-Soo and Kyung-Doo (Park) C.; m. Eun-Ja Chun, May 20, 1973; children: Kaia Nuy, Sang-Mun Ray, Han-Jae Jeremy. BA, Kookmin Coll., Seoul, Korea, 1959; MA in Govt., George Washington U., 1962; MA in Sociology, U. Chgo., 1964, PhD in Sociology, 1965; D in Econs. (hon.), Dong-A U., 1982; DSc in Demography, Tokyo U., 1983; D in Econs., Keio U., Tokyo, 1989; D in Econs. (hon.), Russian Acad. Scis., 2000. Statistician Korean Census Coun., 1958-61; research assoc., asst. prof. sociology Population Rsch. and Tng. Ctr., U. Chgo., 1965-66; assoc. dir. Cmty. and Family Study Ctr., 1969-70; sr. demographic adv. to Malaysian Govt., 1967-69; assoc. prof. U. Hawaii, 1969-73, prof., 1973-78; asst. dir. East-West Population Inst., East-West Ctr., Honolulu, 1971-74, dir., 1974-92; pres. pro tem East-West Ctr., 1980-81, v.p., 1987-98, sr. advisor, 1988—2006. Cons. in field; mem. NAS Com. on Population and Demography; mem. U.S. 1980 Census Adv. Com., Dept. Commerce. Author: (with others) Differential Current Fertility in the United States, 1970; editor: (with others) Introduction to Censuses of Asia and the Pacific: 1970-74, 1976, (with Kazumasa Kobayashi) Fertility Transition in East Asian Populations, 1979, (with Suharto, McNicoll and Mamas) Population Growth of Indonesia, 1980, The Own-Children Method of Fertility Estimation, 1986, (with R. Retherford and M. Choe) Economic Development of Republic of Korea: A Policy Perspective, 1989, (with Y.H. Kim) Korea's Political Economy: An Institutional Perspective, 1994, (with Yada) Tradition and Change in the Asian Family, 1994, (with Y.H. Kim) Hedging Bets on Growth in a Globalizing Industrial Order, 1997, (with Y.H. Kim) Korea's Choices in Emerging Global Competition and Cooperation, 1998, (with Y.H. Kim) Ten Paradigms of Market Economies and Land Systems, 1998, (with Y.H. Kim) The Multi-Lateral Trading System in a Globalizing World, 2000, Restructuring the National Economy, 2001, Restructuring the Korean Financial Market in a Global Economy, 2002, (with C.N. Kim and C.S. Ahn) A Changing Korea in Regional and Global Contexts, 2004; contbr. numerous articles on population and econ. devel. to profl. jours. Bd. dirs. Planned Parenthood Assn., Hawaii, 1976-77. Population Coun. fellow U. Chgo., 1963-64; Ford Found. grantee, 1977-79; Population Coun. grantee, 1973-75; Dept. Commerce grantee, 1974-78; recipient Award of Mugunghwa-Jang, govt. Republic of Korea, 1992, 4th N.E. Asia Niigata prize, 1996. Mem. Internat. Statis. Inst. (tech. adv. com. World Fertility Survey), Internat. Union Sci. Study Population, Population Assn. Am., Am. Statis. Assn., Am. Sociol. Assn., N.E. Asia Econ. Forum (founding chmn.). Home: 1718 Halekoa Dr Honolulu HI 96821-1027 Office: 1601 E West Rd Honolulu HI 96848-1601 *The survival and welfare of the future generations will depend largely upon what we do today to plan and manage human population growth and sustainable development.*

CHO, SUNG K., education educator; arrived in US, 1999, permanent resident; s. Keon Hyung Cho and Wan Sook Jeong; m. Soo Jeong Lee, June 19, 1969; children: Jae Hee, Claire Yenah. BS in Mech. Engring., Seoul Nat. U., Korea, 1990, MS in Mech. Engring., 1992, PhD in Mech. Engring., 1998. Rsch. fellow U. Calif., LA, 1999—2003; asst. prof. U. Pitts., 2003—. Author: (articles) Jour. Microelectromechaical Systems; Jour. Lab on a Chip (Best Paper Finalist in IEEE ROBIO Conf., 2005), Jour. Physics Experiments in Fluids, FASEB Jour., AIAA Jour., Jour. Fluids Engring., Annals Biomedical Engring., Sensors & Actuators A. Grantee, Coremicrosolutions Inc., 2005—, NSF, 2006—; Overseas Postdoctoral fellowship, Korea Sci. and Engring. Found., 1998. Mem.: APS (life), IEEE (life), ASME (life). Achievements include development of Droplet Bubble-Based Microfluidics. Office: Univ Pitts 636 Benedum Hall 3700 O'Hara St Pittsburgh PA 15261 Home Phone: 412-559-7921; Office Phone: 412-624-9798. Business E-Mail: skc@engr.pitt.edu.

CHO, SUNGDAI, linguist, educator; b. Seoul, Republic of Korea, Jan. 25, 1958; s. Keun H. Cho and Moo S. Park; m. Hyekyung K. Cho, June 24, 1989; 1 child, Stellar K. PhD, U. Hawaii Manoa, Honolulu, 1995. Prof. SUNY, Binghamton, 2000—. Chmn. Korean SAT com. Ednl. Testing Svc., Princeton, NJ, 1995—. Recipient Chancellor's Tchg. Excellence award, SUNY, 2006. Office: SUNY Binghamton Dept German Russian and East Asian Binghamton NY 13902-6000 Office Phone: 607-777-3950. Office Fax: 607-777-2658.

CHO, TAI YONG, lawyer; b. Seoul, Republic of Korea, May 27, 1943; arrived in U.S., 1966; s. Nam Suck and Sun Yeo (Yoon) C; m. Hea Sun Cho, July 14, 1973; children: Robert, Richard, Susan. BS, Seoul U., 1965; MS, Cooper Union, 1971; CE, Columbia U., 1971; JD, Fordham U., 1981. Registered profl. engr., N.Y., 1973; bar: NY 1982. Engr. Ministry of Constrn., Seoul, 1965-66, Andrews & Clark, NYC, 1967-68, Parsons, Brinckerhoff, Quade & Douglas, NYC, 1969-71; v.p. John R. McCarthy Corp., NYC, 1972-80. Mem. ASCE, ABA, N.Y. State Bar Assn., Am. Arbitration Assn. (panel of arbitrators), Am.-Korean Lawyers Assn. of N.Y. (pres. 1988), Korean TV Broadcasters Assn., Am. (pres. 1990), Internat. Korean Lawyers Assn. (v.p. 1991). Home: 56 Tuttle Rd Briarcliff Manor NY 10510-2233 Office: 445 5th Ave New York NY 10016-6509 E-mail: taicho7@aol.com.

CHO, YONG HYO, education educator, consultant; b. Sachon, Republic of Korea, Dec. 14, 1934; arrived in U.S., 60; s. Deuk Kyu Cho and Sue Nahm Park; m. Chung Soon Kim, May 6, 1960; children: Miyun Fellerhoff, Hearn Jay. PhD, Syracuse U., 1964. Prof. U. Nev., Las Vegas, 1964—67, U. Akron, 1967—89, San Francisco State U., 1989—97; dean Grad. Sch. Internat. Studies Sogang U., Seoul, 1997—2000; expert U.S. Dept. Edn., Washington, 2000—; sr. advisor Ctr. for Pub. Policy Edn., The Brookings Instn., Washington, 2002—. Author: The White House and the Blue House, 1997, Public Policy and Urban Crime, 1974, others. Nat. Conv. del. Dem. Party, Akron, Ohio, 1980. Recipient Diplomatic Svc. medal Govt. of Republic of Korea, 1998. Fellow Nat. Acad. Public Adminstrn. (life); mem. Am. Soc. for Pub. Adminstrn. (pres. 1996-97). Roman Catholic. Avocations: travel, golf. Home: 424 E Pine Lake Cir Vernon Hills IL 60061 Home Fax: (847) 362-7417. E-mail: yongcho@prodigy.net.

CHOAY, PATRICK HENRI, pharmaceutical executive; Nat. pharmacist diploma, U. Paris, 1969, DSc, 1973, PharmD, 1977. Rsch. asst. Centre Nat. de la Recherche Scientifique, Paris, 1969-75; gen. mgr. Laboratoire Choay, Paris, 1982-83; dir. rsch. Inst. Choay, Paris, 1975-84; pres. Lab. CCD, Paris, 1986—, Lab. Bailly, 1995—, Prodimed S.A.S., 1992—, Lab. Creat, 2001—, Lab. Bioes, 2003—, Lab. Gomenol, 2004. Lectr. biochemist and biophysics U. San Francisco, 1977; lectr. organic chemistry Worcester Found., Shrewsbury, Mass., 1975. Col. French Army Med. Corps. Recipient chevalier de l'Ordre Nat. de la Legion d'Honneur, 2004. Mem. French Nat. Pharm. Acad. Office: Patrick Choay SA 48 rue Petites Ecuries 75010 Paris France Business E-Mail: patrick@choay.com.

CHOBANIAN, ARAM, medical educator, cardiologist, former academic administrator; b. Pawtucket, RI, Aug. 10, 1929; s. Van and Marina (Arsenian) C.; m. Jasmine Goorigian, June 5, 1955; children: Karin, Lisa, Aram. BA, Brown U., Providence, 1951; MD, Harvard U., Cambridge, Mass., 1955; LHD (hon.), Boston U., 2006. Intern, resident Univ. Hosp., Boston, 1955-59, cardiovasc. rsch. fellow, 1959-62; from asst. prof. Sch. Medicine to prof. Sch. Medicine Boston U., 1964—70, prof. medicine, 1970—, dean Sch. Medicine, 1988—2003, provost Med. Campus, 1996—2003, pres., 2003—05, pres. emeritus, 2005—. Dir. Nat. Rsch. and Demonstration Ctr. in Hypertension, 1985-90; chmn. FDA Cardiovasc. and Renal Adv. Com., 1978-80, NIH Hypertension and Arteriosclerosis adv. com., 1977-78; chmn. Cardiovasc. Study Sect. B. NIH, 1982-84; chmn. Joint Nat. Com. on Hypertension, NIH, 1988, 2003; Sandoz lectr. Royal Coll. Physicians and Surgeons Can., 1989; mem. NIH Nat. Heart, Lung and Blood Adv. Coun., 1993-96; mem. bd. extramural advisers Nat. Heart, Lung and Blood Inst., 1999-2002. Author: Heart Risk Book, 1982; mem. editl. bd. New England Jour. Medicine, Hypertension, Jour. Hypertension, Jour. Vascular Biology, Hypertension Rsch., Cardiovasc. Pharmacology. Pres. Am. Heart Assn., Boston, 1974-75; bd. dirs. Armenian Culture Soc.; chmn. bd. trustees Wolfson Found., Fund for Armenian Relief, Mass. Tech. Collaborative, New Eng. Healthcare Inst.; fellow trustee Armenian Assembly of Am. Capt. USAF, 1956-57. Recipient Cmty. Edn. and Disting. Svc. award Am. Heart Assn., Boston, 1975, 78, Eastman Kodak award Nat. Acad. Clin. Biochemistry, 1987, Abbott award Am. Soc. Hypertension. Fellow ACP, Am. Acad. Arts and Scis.; mem. Am. Heart Assn. (chmn. coun. high blood pressure rsch. 1984-86, Corcoran lectr. 1989, award of merit 1990, Modern Medicine award 1990, Lifetime Achievement award in hypertension Bristol-Myers Squibb), Nat. Heart, Lung and Blood Inst. (Freis award 1997, Ellis Island Medal of Honor, 2007), Am. Soc. Clin. Investigation, Assn. Am. Physicians, Am. Physiol. Soc., New England Cardiovasc. Soc. (pres. 1985-86), Mass. Med. Soc. (chmn. pub. com. 2003—), Phi Beta Kappa, Sigma Xi, Alpha Omega Alpha. Home: 5 Rathburn Rd Natick MA 01760-1011 Office: Boston U 650 Albany St Boston MA 02118 Office Phone: 617-638-0300. Business E-Mail: achob@bu.edu.

CHOBOTOV, VLADIMIR ALEXANDER, aerospace engineer, educator; b. Zagreb, Yugoslavia, Apr. 2, 1929; came to U.S., 1946; s. Alexander M. and Eugenia I. (Scherbak) C.; m. Lydia M. Kazanovich, June 22, 1957; children: Alexander, Michael. BSME, Pratt Inst., 1951; MSME, Bklyn. Poly. Inst., 1956; PhD, U. So. Calif., 1963. Dynamics engr. Sikorsky Aircraft, Bridgeport, Conn., 1951-53, Republic Aviation, Farmingdale, N.Y., 1953-57, Ramo-Wooldridge, Redondo Beach, Calif., 1957-62; mgr. The Aerospace Corp., El Segundo, Calif., 1962-93; adj. prof. Northrop U., LA, 1982-91; instr. UCLA, 1984—. Cons. Univ. Space Rsch. Assn., Washington, 1984-85; ad hoc advisor USAF Sci. Adv. Bd., Washington, 1985-87; cons. NASA Space Sta. Adv. Com., Washington, 1990-91; course leader Space Debris, Washington, 1990-91. Author: Spacecraft Attitude Dynamics and Control, 1991; author, editor: Orbital Mechanics, 1991, 3d edit., 2002; contbg. author: Space Based Radar Handbook, 1989, Earth, Sea and Solar System, 1987; contbr. numerous articles and reports to profl. publs. Fellow AIAA (assoc., Achievement award 1993); mem. Internat. Acad. of Astronautics. Achievements include research in analysis and modeling of space debris. Office: The Aerospace Corp PO Box 92957 Los Angeles CA 90009-2957 Personal E-mail: chobotov@cox.net. Business E-Mail: vladimir.chobotov@aero.org.

CHOCK, CLIFFORD YET-CHONG, family practice physician; b. Chgo., Oct. 15, 1951; s. Wah Tim and Leatrice (Wong) C. BS in Biology, Purdue U., 1973; MD, U. Hawaii, 1978. Intern in internal medicine Loma Linda (Calif.) Med. Ctr., 1978-79, resident in internal medicine, 1979, U. So. Calif.-L.A. County Med. Ctr., LA, 1980; physician Pettis VA Clinic, Loma Linda, Calif., 1980; pvt. practice Honolulu, 1981—2006. Chmn. dept. family practice St. Francis Med. Ctr., Liliha, Hawaii, 1990-98, chmn. utilization rev. com. 1991, 95, physician reviewer, 1985-2002, chmn. Quality Care for Family Practice, 1990-93, 95-98; chmn. credentials Family Practice, 1990-93, 95-96, acting chmn. credentials com., 1992, 2003-05; physician reviewer Peer Rev. Orgn. Hawaii, Honolulu, 1987-93 Active audio hospitality HELPS divsns. Pacific Revival Ctr. Fellow Am. Acad. Family Physicians, Internat. Platform Assn. Avocations: model collecting, toy collecting, bible study. Office Phone: 808-526-0181.

CHOCOLA, CHRIS (JOSEPH CHRISTOPHER CHOCOLA), former congressman, lawyer; b. Jackson, Mich., Feb. 24, 1962; m. Sarah Chocola; children: Caroline, Colin. BLS, Hillsdale Coll., 1984; JD magna cum laude, Thomas Cooley Law Sch., 1988. Mgmt. trainee Soc. Nat. Bank, Cleve., 1984, fgn. exch. trader; credit mgr. Chocola Cleaning Materials; corp. counsel CTB Internat. Corp., Milford, Ind., 1988—94, CEO, 1994—99, chmn. bd. dirs., 1999—2002; mem. US Congress from 2nd Ind. dist., 2003—07, asst. majority whip, 2003—04, mem. ways and means com., agrl. com., small bus. com., transp. & infrastructure com. Mem. coun. advisors South Bend Ctr. for the Homeless; bd. dirs. Oaklawn Psychiat. Ctr. Mem.: Rotary Club. Republican. Presbyterian.

CHODOROW, JEFFREY, restaurant owner; b. NYC, Mar. 2, 1950; married; two children. BS in Econ., U. Pa. Wharton Sch.; JD, U. Pa. Law Sch. Co-owner Braniff Airlines, 1988, pres., CEO, 1991—92; CEO China Grill Management Inc.; owner China Grill, Manhattan, NY, 1987—, Miami, Fla., 1995—, Blue Door, Delano Hotel, Miami Beach, Fla., 1995—; co-owner Asia de Cuba, NYC, 1997—, Red Square, Las Vegas, 1998—, Rock Lobster, Las Vegas, 1998, China Grill, Las Vegas, 1998—, Asia de Cuba, Mondrian Hotel, LA, 1999—, Seabar, Mondrian Hotel, LA, 1999, Asia de Cuba, St. Martins Lane, London, 2000—, Spoon + at Sanderson, London, 2000—, Hudson Cafeteria, NYC, 2001—, Tuscan Steak, Miami, 2001—, Asia de Cuba, Clift Hotel, San Francisco, 2001—, Tuscan Steak (re-launched in 2003 as Tuscan), NYC, 2000—, China Grill, Mexico City, N.Mex., Rumjungle, Mandalay Bay Hotel, Las Vegas, Red White Blue, Mandalay Bay Hotel, Las Vegas, Bleu Blanc Rouge, Mandalay Bay Hotel, Las Vegas, MIX, NYC, Kobe Club Restaurant, 2006—. Financer Rocco's on 22nd, TV Reality Series "The Restaurant", NYC. Avocation: family. Office: China Grill 60 W 53rd St New York NY 10019-6106*

CHODOROW, NANCY JULIA, psychotherapist, educator; b. NYC, Jan. 20, 1944; d. Marvin and Leah (Turitz) C.; children: Rachel Esther Chodorow-Reich, Gabriel Issac Chodorow-Reich. BA, Radcliffe Coll., 1966; PhD, Brandeis U., 1975; grad., San Francisco Psychoanalytic, 1993. Cert. in adult psychoanalysis Am. Psychoanalytic Assn., 1993. From lectr. to assoc. prof. U. Calif., Santa Cruz, 1974-86, from assoc. prof. sociology to prof. Berkeley, 1986—2005, clin. faculty dept. psychology, 1999—, prof. emeritus, 2005. Faculty Psychoanalytic Inst. New Eng., East, San Francisco Psychoanalytic Inst., 1994—, Psychoanalytic Inst. New England, East, 2005—, Boston Psychonalytic Inst., 2005—, Mass. Inst. Psychoanalysis; vis. prof. psychiatry Harvard Med. Sch., 2005-06. Author: The Reproduction of Mothering, 1978 (Jessie Bernard award Sociologists for Women in Soc. 1979, named one of Ten Most Influential Books of Past 25 Years, Contemporary Sociology 1996), 2nd edit., 1999, Feminism and Psychoanalytic Theory, 1989, Femininities, Masculinities, Sexualities, 1994, The Power of Feelings: Personal Meaning in Psychoanalysis, Gender, and Culture, 1999 (L. Bryce Boyer prize Soc. for Psychol. Anthropology 2000); contbr. articles to profl. jours. Fellow Russell Sage Found., NEH, Ctr. Advanced Study Behavioral Scis., ACLS, Guggenheim Found., Radcliffe Inst. for Advanced Study; recipient Contbn. to Women and Psychoanalysis award APA, L. Bryce Boyer prize Soc. for Psychol. Anthropology, 2000. Mem. Internat. Psychoanalytic Assn., Am. Psychoanalytic Assn., San Francisco Psychoanalytic Soc., Boston Psychoanalytic Inst., Psychoanalytic Inst. New Eng. East, Mass. Inst. Psychoanalysis. Office: 75 Richdale Ave #4 Cambridge MA 02140 Home Phone: 617-354-4891; Office Phone: 617-354-1200. Business E-Mail: nancy_chodorow@hms.harvard.edu.

CHODOSH, HIRAM, dean, law educator; BA, Wesleyan U., Middletown, Conn., 1985; JD, Yale U., 1990. Mgmt. cons. Orion Consultants, Inc., NY, NY, 1985—87; summer assoc. Weil, Gotshal & Manges, NY, NY, 1988, Coudert Bros., Paris, Beijing, Hong Kong, 1989; atty. Cleary, Gottlieb, Steen & Hamilton, NY, NY, 1990—93; asst. prof. Case Western Reserve U., Cleveland, Ohio, 1993—96, assoc. prof., 1996—99, prof., 1999—2004, dir. Frederick K. Cox Internat. Law Ctr., 1998—2003, assoc. dean academic affairs, 2003—06, Joseph C. Hostetler-Baker & Hostetler Prof. of Law, 2004—06; dean S.J. Quinney Coll. of Law, U. Utah, 2006—. Sr. rapporteur Inst. for Study & Devel. of Legal Systems, San Francisco, 1993—2003; cons. Internat. Monetary Fund, Washington, 1999—2002, World Bank Grp., Washington, 2005—06, UNDP, Asia, 2006—; Fulbright Sr. Scholar Indian Law Inst., New Delhi, 2003. Author: (book) Global Justice Reform: A Comparative Methodology, 2005. Mem.: Am. Bar Assn., Am. Assn. Law Schools. Office: SJ Quinney Coll Law Univ Utah Office of the Dean 332 South 1400 East Salt Lake City UT 84112-0730 Office Phone: 801-581-6571. Business E-Mail: hiram.chodosh@law.utah.edu.

CHOE, KYLE SEUNG, facial plastic surgeon; s. Jung B. and Sung W. Choe; m. Hee C. Yoo, Dec. 21, 1996; children: Caleb, Grace, Samuel. BA, Occidental Coll., 1994; MD, U. Rochester, 1998. Diplomate Am. Bd. Otolaryngology, 2004. Resident NY Eye & Ear Infirmary, NYC, 1999—2003; fellow facial plastic surgery U. Rochester, NY, 2003—04; pvt. practice Virginia Beach, 2004—. Contbr. articles to profl. jours. Mem.: AMA, Am. Acad. Otolaryngology (Humanitarian Efforts Travel award 2003), Am. Acad. Facial Plastic Surgery (Ben Shuster Meml. award 2004). Avocations: reading, tennis. Office: 4400 Corporation Ln 102 Virginia Beach VA 23462 Office Phone: 757-389-5850.

CHOHAN, MUHAMMAD OMAR, neuroscientist, neurologist; b. Rawalpindi, Punjab, Pakistan, Mar. 9, 1979; arrived in US, 2003; s. Abdur Rashid and Zahida Chohan; m. Annie Chohan, May 30, 2002; 1 child, Marwa O. MD, Aga Khan U., Karachi, Pakistan, 2002. Edml. Commn. Fgn. Med. Grads., Phila., 2006. Instr. Sch. Medicine Aga Khan U., Karachi, 2002—03; assoc. rsch. scientist Rsch. Found. Mental Hygiene, SI, NY, 2003—06, rsch. scientist, 2006—. Mem. editl. bd. Jour. Alzheimer Disease, 2006; contbr. articles to profl. jours. Recipient World Assn. Alzheimer Disease Scientists award, 2006; Neural Stem Cell Rsch. grantee, PSF, 2004—06, Rsch. grantee, NIH, 2007—. Mem.: Am. Soc. Investigative Pathology, Internat. Brain Rsch. Orgn., Soc. Neuroscience. Achievements include discovery of novel small molecules that can positively regulate the proliferation and differentiation of neural stem cells (neurogenesis) in the dentate gyrus of mouse brain and enhance memory; mechanism of action of the anti-dementia drug Memantine in preventing neurofibrillary degeneration of the type seen in Alzheimer's disease; molecular pathway through which Inhibitor-2 of Protein Phosphatase 2A (I2PP2A) is able to regulate the intracellular activity of PP2A; development of novel ex-vivo methodology to study the dynamics of neuronal cytoskeleton by confocal microscopy; research in proposed a mechanism by which NMDA receptors might contribute towards abnormal hyperphosphorylation and subsequent neurofibrillary degeneration in Alzheimer's disease; showing murine tau is equally susceptible to self assembly into PHF-like filaments as human tau; association between human interleukin 1 gene polymorphisms and essential hypertension in a genetically defined human population. Office: NYS Inst Basic Rsch 1050 Forest Hill Rd Staten Island NY 10314 Home Phone: 718-759-8653; Office Phone: 718-494-5269. Office Fax: 718-494-1080. Business E-Mail: muhammad.chohan@omr.state.ny.us.

CHOI, DENNIS W., pharmaceutical executive, neurologist, educator; b. Ann Arbor, Mich., Sept. 26, 1953; three children. AB, Harvard Coll., 1974; MD, Harvard Med. Sch., 1978; PhD, Harvard U., 1978. Diplomate Am. Bd. Psychiatry & Neurology, Am. Bd. Clin. Neurophysiology, Am. Bd. Electrodiagnostic Medicine. Clin. fellow in medicine Harvard U., Boston, 1978-79, fellow in neurology, 1979-83; from asst. prof. to assoc. prof. Stanford (Calif.) U., 1983-91; prof., head dept. Washington U. Med. Sch., St. Louis, 1991—2002, adj. prof., Neurology, 2002—; exec. v.p. Merck Research Laboratories, 2002—. Mem. Am. Neurol. Assn. (v.p. 1996-97), Inst. Medicine, Soc. Neurosci. (pres. 1999—). Office: Merck & Co Inc 770 Sumneytown Pike PO Box 4 WP 14-2500 West Point PA 19486

CHOI, HONGSEOK, mechanical engineer, researcher; b. Pohang, Republic Of Korea, Feb. 7, 1972; s. Jongbae Choi and Boksoon Kim; m. Eunju Park, Dec. 14, 1997; 1 child, Ashley Seoyoon. PhD, U. Wis., Madison, 2007. Rsch. asst., dept. mech. engring. U. Wis., 2001—. Contbr. articles to profl. jours. Mem.: ASME, Laser Inst. Am., Soc. Mfg. Engrs. Achievements include patents for UV pulsed laser machining apparatus and method; apparatus and method of dispensing small-scale powders; microelectronics grade metal substrate, related metal-embedded devices and methods for fabricating; apparatus and method of fabricating small-scale devices; food processing apparatus and method. Home: 201 S Yellowstone Dr #101 Madison WI 53705 Office: Univ Wis Dept Mech Engring ME 3164 1513 University Ave Madison WI 53705 Business E-Mail: hschoi@cae.wisc.edu.

CHOI, HOON, electrical engineer; b. Seoul, Aug. 14, 1970; parents Young Choi and Young-ae Yim; m. Jeong-won Hwang, June 19, 1996; children: Seung-Joon, Hannah. BSEE, Yonsei U., Seoul, 1993; MSEE, Korea Advanced Inst. Sci. and Tech., Taejon, Korea, 1995; PhD in Elec. Engring., Korea Advanced Inst. Sci. and, Taejon, Korea, 1999. Cert. in Very Large Scale Integration/Computer Aided Design/design engring. From engr. to sr. engr. Samsung Electronics, Kyungki-do, Republic of Korea, 1993—2001; sr. engr. NeoPace Telecom., San Diego, 2001—02; tech. staff Silicon Image, Sunnyvale, Calif., 2002—. Presenter in field. Contbr. articles to profl. jours. Recipient Employee of Yr. award, Silicon Image, 2004. Avocations: swimming, body building. Office: 1060 E Arques Ave Sunnyvale CA 94085 Home: #C455 49 Showers Dr Mountain View CA 94040-4741 Office Phone: 408-616-4076. E-mail: hchoi@ieee.org.

CHOI, IN DAL, music educator; b. Daegu, Korea, Sept. 5, 1936; U.S.1963; m. Kuhn S. DAk, Jan. 27, 1968; 1 child, Jay. MusB, Yonsei U., Seoul, Korea, 1962; Postgrad. diploma, Juilliard Sch., 1969; MusM, Manhattan Sch. Music, 1973; D of Music Arts, Ind. U., 1986. Violist Seoul Philharmonic Orch., Republic of Korea, 1961—63; prof. music James Madison U., Harrisonburg, Va., 1977—. Recipient Outstanding Cultural Diplomat award, Prime Min., Republic of Korea, 1972, Disting. Faculty award, James Madison U., 2004. Mem.: Nat. Assn. Tchrs. of Singing (Va. chpt. pres. 1989—91), Korean-Am. Musician's Assn. Greater Washington (pres. 2004—). Home: 8134 Old Plank Rd Fredericksburg VA 22407 Office: James Madison Univ Harrisonburg VA 22807 E-mail: choiid@jmu.edu.

CHOI, IN-SUP, radiologist; b. Pusan, Korea, July 22, 1947; came to U.S., 1975; s. Keun-Yoo and Jung-Sun (Han) C.; m. Hyung-kyung Cho, Nov. 14, 1974; children: Ellen, Philip. MD, Seoul Nat. U., 1972. Clin. asst. prof. NYU Sch. Medicine, 1981-82; asst. prof. radiology Mt. Sinai Sch. Medicine, NYC, 1982-83; asst. prof. radiology Sch. Medicine NYU, 1984-92; assoc. prof. radiology Med. Sch. Harvard U., 1992—2004; prof. radiology Tufts U., Sch. Medicine, 2004—. Mem. Am. Soc. Neuroradiology, Am. Coll. Radiology, Radiol. Soc. N.Am., Am. Soc. Interventional & Therapeutic Neuroradiology (v.p.). Avocations: tennis, golf. Office: Lahey Clinic Med Ctr 41 Mall Rd Burlington MA 01805-0002 Office Phone: 781-744-3330. E-mail: in.sup.choi@lahey.org.

CHOI, IN-YOUNG, science educator; PhD, U. Minn., 2000. Sr. rsch. scientist Nathan Kline Inst., Orangeburg, NY, 2001—05; asst. prof. U. Kans. Med. Ctr., Kansas City, 2005—. Recipient Young Scientist Travel award, Internat. Soc. Neurochemistry, 2001, Travel Grant award, 2003, Young Scientist Travel award, 2002, Travel Grant award, 2005, Young Investigator Travel award, Am. Soc. Neurochemistry, 2002; grantee Nat. Inst. Biomedical Imaging and Bioengineering, NIH, 1999—2005, Nat. Inst. on Aging, 2003—05, Alzheimer's Disease rsch. grant, Am. Health Assistance Found., 2005—07, Shared Biomedical Rsch. Instrument grant award, Kans. U. Med. Ctr. Rsch. Inst., 2007. Mem.: Internat. Soc. for Magnetic Resonance in Medicine, Internat. Soc. Cerebral Blood Flow and Metabolism, NY Acad. Sci., Neuroscience Soc., Internat. Soc. Neurochemistry (assoc.). Office: U Kans Med Ctr HBIC 3901 Rainbow Blvd Mail Stop 1052 Kansas City KS 66160 Office Phone: 913-588-0174.

CHOI, JOHN U., periodontist, educator; b. Seoul, Korea (South), Apr. 1, 1962; s. Chin Hang and Young Ja Choi; m. Hijae Kim; children: Christine A, Ashley J. DDS, U. So. Calif., 1990, PhD, 2001. Periodontist U. of So. Calif., 1994. Rsch. instr. U. So. Calif., Los Angeles, 1990—96; postdoctoral fellow Nat. Institutes of Health U. So. Calif., 1990—96; peridontist Pvt. practice, Fullerton, Calif., 1996—. Recipient Periodontology Award, U. of So. Calif., 1990; fellow Craniofacial Biology Grant, Nat. Institutes of Health U. So. Calif., 1990-1991; grantee Rsch. Grant, NIH, 1991-1996; scholar Dentist Scientist Award, 1991-1996. Mem.: ADA, Orange County Dental Soc., Calif. Dental Assn., Am. Acad. Periodontology, Sigma Xi. Office: 301 W Bastanchury Rd Suite 255 Fullerton CA 92835 Office Phone: 714-449-8650. Office Fax: 714-449-8653. Business E-Mail: jcperio@aol.com.

CHOI, K.J. (KYUNG-JU CHOI), professional golfer; b. Wando, South Korea, May 19, 1970; m. Hyunjung Kim; children: David, Amanda; 1 child, Daniel. Mem. PGA Tour, 1994—. Achievements include earning first PGA Tour Card for Korean Citizen, 1994; winner, PGA Tour events including Compaq Classic of New Orleans, Tampa Bay Classic presented by Buick, 2002, Chrysler Classic of Greensboro, 2005, Chrysler Championship, 2006, Meml. Tournament, 2007, AT&T Nat., 2007; winner, Kolon Cup Korean Open, 1999, SK Telecom Open, Korea, 2003, 05. Office: c/o PGA 100 Ave Champions Palm Beach Gardens FL 33410-9601*

CHOI, MICHAEL KAMWAH, aerospace and mechanical engineer, researcher; b. Aug. 16, 1952; arrived in US, 1972, naturalized, 1987; s. Ying-Loi and Kan-Hau (Yuen) C.; m. Sophia Cheng; 1 child, Natalie. BSc in Engring. magna cum laude, Brown U., Providence, 1976; MSME, MIT, Cambridge, 1978, engr.'s degree in mech. engring., 1979. Registered profl. engr., Va. Rsch. asst. dept. mech. engring. MIT, Cambridge, Mass., 1977-79; sr. rsch. engr. Sci. Applications Internat. Corp., McLean, Va., 1979-87; sr. engr. spacecraft thermal control sys. Fairchild Space and Defense Corp., Germantown, Md., 1987-90; project leader, mgr. NASA Goddard Space Flight Ctr., Greenbelt, Md., 1990—. Intrument thermal mgr. WIND and POLAR spacecraft Global Geospace Sci. Mission, 1990-92; thermal sys. mgr. Far Ultraviolet Spectroscopic Explorer Project, 1992-94; lead thermal engr. High Energy Solar Imager project, 1994-96; thermal sys. mgr. LANDSAT-7 mission, 1994-00; lead thermal engr. electron reflectometer and magnetometer instruments on Lunar Prospector spacecraft, 1995-97, Next Generation Space Telescope, 1996-97, low energy neutral atom instrument on MIDEX IMAGE spacecraft, 1996-00, Solar Probe Plasma Spectrometer Study, 1996-2006, Triana PlasMag instrument, 1999-2001, Swift Burst Alert Telescope instrument, optical bench and instrument module, 1999-05, Solar Probe Plasma Wave instrument antenna study, Internal Rsch. and Devel., 2005-06; thermal architect Space Solar Power Exploratory Rsch. and Tech., 1999-00, Instrument Synthesis & Analysis Lab. Thermal Lead, 2005-, Discovery Mission Vesper study and phase A, 2005-; cons. EO-1 Advanced Land Imager, 1997-00, EO-1 Star Tracker thermal design, 2000, EO-1 obs. thermal vacuum & thermal vacuum test, 2000, MAP Star Tracker thermal design, 1999-00, IRAC thermal cooldown, 2000, inFOCus Balloon instrument thermal design, 2001, STEOREO SEP instrument thermal design, 2000; reviewer flight assurance office; organizer, chmn. spacecraft and instrument thermal control sessions 32d Intersoc. Energy Conversion Engring. Conf., 1997, chmn. spacecraft and aircraft thermal mgmt. sessions, 1998-02, chmn. spacecraft and aircraft thermal mgmt. sessions, Internat. Energy Conversion Engring. Conf., 2003-04, thermal mgmt. topical area coord., Internat. Engergy Conversion Engring. Conf., 2005-; chmn. spacecraft thermal mgmt. sessions Internat. Energy Conversion Engring. Conf., 2005-; contbr. solar heating and cooling program US Dept. Energy; spkr. nat. and internat. confs. Contbr. articles to profl. jours.; reviewer Solar Energy Jour., ASME Solar Energy Divsn., 1983-87. Fellow AIAA (assoc., Cert. Merit Best Paper in Aerospace Power Sys. 1996, Internat. Energy Conversion Engring. Conf. Topical Area Coord. award 2005, 06, 07); mem. ASME, Soc. Automotive Engring., Sigma Xi, Tau Beta Pi. Home: 2237 Halter Ln Reston VA 20191-5824 Home Phone: 703-435-5635. Business E-Mail: michael.k.choi@nasa.gov.

CHOI, MYONG YONG, chemist, researcher; b. Jinju, Gyeongnam, Republic Of Korea, July 7, 1972; s. Kyu Sun Choi and Oak Jae Jung; m. Kyeong Soon Park, Dec. 30, 2000; 1 child, Sophia Minji. BS (hon.), Gyeongsang Nat. U., Jinju, 1998; MS, U. Idaho, Moscow, 2002; PhD, U. NC, Chapel Hill, 2006. Tchg. asst. U. Idaho, 2000—02, rsch. asst., 2002—03; tchg. asst. U NC, 2002—03, rsch. asst., 2003—06; postdoctoral rsch. fellow U. So. Calif., LA, 2006—. Contbr. articles to profl. jours. Renfrew scholar, Dept. Chemistry, U. Idaho, 2001—02, Venable fellow, Dept. Chemistry, U. NC, 2002. Mem.: Am. Chem. Soc. Achievements include research in unambiguous structural assignments of isolated biomolecules (nucleic acid bases and their hydrated complexes) using high resolution spectroscopy in helium nanodroplets. Office: U So Calif Chemistry Dept SSC 710 920 Bloom Walk Los Angeles CA 90089-0482 Home

Phone: 1-818-249-4703; Office Phone: 1-213-821-2847. Office Fax: 1-213-740-3972. E-mail: myongyong.choi@usc.edu.

CHOI, NAMOK, education educator; arrived in US, 1990; d. Chuntack and Bockran (Lee) Choi; m. Robert Roy Eagle, July 20, 2002. BA, Sungshin Womens U., Seoul, 1983; MS, Okla. State U., 1993, PhD, 1997. Tchr. Dept. Edn., Kwangwon, Republic of Korea, 1983—90; from rsch. asst. to tchg. asst. Okla. State U., Stillwater, 1991—97; asst. prof. Ga. So. U., Statesboro, 1997—2000, U. Louisville, 2000—04, assoc. prof., 2004—. Mem. editl. bd.: Jour. Social Psychology, 1999—, Jour. Counseling and Devel., 2004—, Genetic, Social, and General Psychology Monograph, 2006—, reviewer: Sex Roles: A Journal of Research, 2006—, Jour. Ednl. Psychology, 2007—; contbr. articles to profl. jours. Vol. St. John Homeless Ctr., Louisville, 2001—03; bd. dirs. Louisville Korean Sch., 2004—. Mem.: Am. Ednl. Rsch. Assn. (proposal reviewer 1998—, session chair 1999, newsletter editor 2001—03, session chair 2004, textbook reviewer 2004, co-chair jur. faculty mentoring 2005, newsletter editor 2005, program co-chair Divsn. E counseling sect. 2006—08). Democrat. Presbyterian. Avocations: literature, reading, gardening, tennis. Office: Univ Louisvile Coll Edn and Human Devel Louisville KY 40292 Business E-Mail: namok@louisville.edu.

CHOI, STEPHEN SUKJUN, physicist; b. Seoul, Jan. 8, 1973; arrived in New Zealand, 1984, naturalized, 1987; s. Sang-Hyun and Gil-Ja (Lee) Choi. BS, U. Auckland, 1994, MS with first class hons., 1996; PhD, U. Oxford, 2000. Rsch. fellow U. Oxford, 1999—2001; vis. scientist U. Rochester, NY, 2001—06; sr. rsch. fellow U. Mass., Boston, 2006—. Session chmn. Oxford BEC Discussion Meeting, England, 1999; vis. fellow Nat. Inst. Nuc. Theory, Seattle, 2005. Contbr. articles to profl. jours. and book chpts. in field; referee: Phys. Rev. Letters, Phys. Rev. A, New Jour. Physics, Jour. Physics A: Math. and Gen., Jour. Physics B: Atomic, Molecular, Optical Physics, Jour. Modern Optics. Recipient Recognition Excellence award, New Zealand Qualifications Authority, 1991, Sr. Physics and Pure Math. prize, U. Auckland, 1994, Overseas Rsch. Student award, UK, 1996—99; fellowship, Royal Commn. Exhbn. 1851, 1999—2001, Harold H. Wingate Found. scholarship, London, 1997, Domus Sr. scholarship, Merton Coll., U. Oxford, 1997—99. Achievements include research in theory of Bose-Einstein condensation in atomic gases, atom lasers, quantum atom optics, many-body physics, quantized vortices, and quantum engineering. Avocations: classical music, opera. Personal E-mail: schoi108@yahoo.com.

CHOI, SUKHWAN, engineer; s. Eul-Yong Choi and Kye-Ok Chun; m. Yun-Hee Jang, Apr. 2, 1996; 1 child, Andrew. BS, Hanyang U., S. Korea, 1991—95; MS, Brown U., Providence, 1995—96; PhD, Rensselaer Poly. Inst., Troy, NY, 1997—2001. Profl. engr. GE Energy, Greenville, SC, 2001—06, six sigma black belt Marietta, Ga., 2006—. Recipient Six Sigma award, GE Energy, 2001, Power award, 2001, 2003, 2005, Patent award, 2002—03, Six Sigma award, 2003, Engring. award, 2004, Global Employee awards & recognition, 2006. Mem.: ASME LIfe Cycle Engring. (assoc.), Sigma Xi (assoc.). Achievements include patents for turbine blade (bucket) health monitoring and prognosis using infrared camera; turbine blade (bucket) health monitoring and prognosis using neural network based diagnostic techniques in conjunction with pyrometer signals. Office: GE Energy 4200 Wildwood Pky 1-06C-01 Marietta GA 30339 Home Phone: 770-663-6113. Business E-Mail: sukhwan.choi@ge.com.

CHOI, WON IL, entomologist, researcher; b. Seoul, Republic of Korea, Mar. 24, 1971; s. Chun Tack and Jin Kyeong Choi; m. Soo Na Lim, May 17, 2003; 1 child, Gar-Eun. BS in Agr. Biology, Korea U., 1994, MS in Applied Entomology, 1996; PhD in Agronomy, Korea U., Seoul, 2001. Postdoctoral rsch. assoc. Seoul Nat. U., 2001—03, U. Toledo, 2003—04, U. Vt., Burlington, 2005—06; rschr. Korea Forest Rsch. Inst., Seoul, 2006—. Contbr. articles to profl. jours. Mem.: Entomological Soc. of Am., Korean Soc. Applied Entomology, Korean Soc. Entomology. Office: Korea Forest Rsch Inst 207 Cheongyangni-2 dong Dongdaemun-g Seoul 130-712 Republic of Korea Home Phone: 82-11-7132-6896; Office Phone: 82-2-961-2663. Office Fax: 82-2-961-2679. Personal E-mail: choiw71@empal.com. Business E-Mail: wchoi@foa.go.kr.

CHOI, YONG-SEOK, communications engineer, researcher; b. Kwangju, Korea, July 20, 1958; s. Eunyoung and Yunim Choi; m. Eunkyoung Choi; children: Junsung, Jinyoung. PhD, U. Tokyo, 1994. Prin. rschr. Electronics and Telecomm. Rsch. Inst., Taejon, Republic of Korea, 1989—. Rschr. Korean Advanced Inst. Sci. and Tech., Taejon, 1990, Nat. Radio Obs., Nobeyama, Japan, 1990—94; vis. scholar James Madison U., Harrisonburg, Va., 2005—. Deacon Ojeong Ch., Taejon, Korea (South), 2000—06. 1st lt. Korean Air Force, 1983—86. Recipient Excellent Engr. award, Prime Min., 2005. Mem.: Korea Electromagnetic Engring. Soc. (life). Office: Electronics and Telecomm Rsch Inst 161 Gajeong Yuseong Daejeon 305-700 Republic of Korea Office Phone: 82 42 860 5263. Business E-Mail: yschoi@etri.re.kr.

CHOI, YOUNGOK, information science educator; d. Seung-Chil Choi and Nam-Soo Lee; m. Sung-Ju Cho, Dec. 9, 1997; 1 child, Ashley Han-Hee Cho. BA magna cum laude, Ewha Woman's U., 1988, MA, 1990; PhD, U. Pitts., 2000. Asst. prof. SUNY, Oswego, 2001—06, Cath. U. Am., 2006—. Program com. Internat. Assn. Sci. and Tech. for Devel., Calgary, Canada, 2004—. Contbr. articles to profl. jours. Recipient Margaret Corbett award, Sch. Info. Sci., U. Pitts., 2000; Eugene Garfield Doctoral Dissertation fellow, Beta Phi Mu, 1999. Mem.: Assn. Libr. and Info. Sci. Edn. (grantee 2005), Am. Soc. Info. Sci. and Tech., Assn. Computing Machinery. Home Phone: 315-343-0207.

CHOICE, PRISCILLA KATHRYN MEANS (PENNY), retired educational association administrator; b. Rockford, Ill., Nov. 8, 1939; d. John Z. and Margaret A. (Haines) Means; m. Jack R. Choice, Nov. 14, 1964; children: William Kenneth, Margaret Meta. BA, U. Wis., 1963; MEd, Nat.-Louis U., 1990; MA, N.E. Ill. U., 1995. Field rsch. dir. Tatham-Laird and Kudner Advt., Chgo., 1964-69; drama specialist Children's Theatre Western Springs (Ill.), 1969-81; gifted teaching asst. Sch. Dist. 181, Hinsdale, Ill., 1980-84; tchr. Sch. Dist. 99, Cicero, Ill., 1984-85; gifted edn. program coord. Cmty. Consolidated Sch. Dist. 93, Carol Stream, Ill., 1985-99; coord. gifted edn. and fine arts Ednl. Svcs. Divsn., Lake County Regional Office Edn., Grayslake, Ill., 1999—2004; retired, 2004—. Drama specialist, cons. Choice Dramatics, Hinsdale and Clarendon Hills, Ill., 1976-2004; producing dir. Mirror Image Youth Theatre, Hinsdale, 1986-88; adj. prof. Coll. DuPage, Glen Ellyn, Ill., 1990-92, Nat.-Louis U., Evanston, Ill., 1991—, Aurora (Ill.) U., 1995—, Govs. State U., University Park, Ill., 1992-93; internat. cons. in gifted edn. and drama-in-edn., 1989—; co-chair advocacy com. Ill. Assn. Gifted Children, 2002-05, co-chair underserved populations, 05—; trustee Friends of the Lake Co. Discovery Mus., 2003—; chair arts divsn. Nat. Assn. for Gifted Children, 2003-05, sec., treas. global awareness divsn., 2005—; tchr. First Folio Shakespeare Festival, 2005— Contbg. author Gifted/Arts Resource Guide, 1990; contbg. editor Ill. Theatre Assn., Followspot News, 1992-95. 96-2002. Mem. gifted adv. com. Ednl. Svc. Ctr., Wheaton, Ill., 1987—90, 1992—95, Regional Office of Edn., Wheaton, 1995—99, Northeastern Ill. U.1993-95., Chgo., 1993—95; co-chair advocacy Com. Ill. Assn. for Gifted Children, 2002—05, ch-chair underserved populations com., 2005—; bd. dirs. Ill. Theatre Assn., Chgo., 1983—87. Recipient Ill. State Bd. Edn. gifted edn. fellowship, 1988, AAUW continuing edn. scholarship, 1986, 90, Excellence award Ill. Theatre Assn., 1991, Excellence award Ill. Math. and Sci. Acad., 1990, 98, Recognition of Excellence, No. Ill. Planning Commn. Gifted Edn., 1990, Award of Excellence Ill. and Math. Sci. Acad., 1998. Mem. ASCD, World Coun. on Gifted Edn., Nat. Assn. Gifted Children, Ill. Assn. Gifted Children (membership chmn. 1992-94, advocacy com. 1995—, co-chair advocacy com. 2002-05, co-chair underserved populations 2005—), Ill. Coun. Gifted, Am. Assn. Theatre in Edn., Ill. Theatre Assn. (bd. dirs. 1983-87, Outstanding Achievement award 1991), Inst. for Global Ethics, Ill. Alliance Arts Edn., Theatre Western Springs, Phi Delta Kappa. Avocations: swimming, walking, reading. Home and Office: 113 S Prospect Ave Clarendon Hills IL 60514-1422 Office Phone: 630-452-6675. E-mail: pennychoice@comcast.net.

CHOJNOWSKI, DONNA APPLEGATE, cardiac nursing administrator, heart failure nurse practitioner; m. John Chojnowski. BSN, Coll. of NJ, 1979; MSN, Drexel U., 2003. Cert. clin. transplant coord., provider ACLS; CCRN, cert. acute care nurse practitioner. Staff nurse ICU, asst. head nurse Albert Einstein Med. Ctr., Phila., 1981-84, 84-87, asst. head nurse, 1985-87; nurse mgr. cardiothoracic surg., trauma ICU Temple U. Hosp., Phila., 1987-90; cardiac transplant clin. nurse coord., adminstr. Allegheny U. Hahneman Hosp., Phila., 1990-98; clin. transplant nurse coord. Hosp. U. Pa., 1998—2003, clin. mgr., nurse practitioner heart failure, heart transplant, adult congenital heart programs, 2003—. Lectr., rschr. pubs. on cardiac transplantation and heart failure, 1990—. Mem.: AACN (S.E. Pa. chpt., cert., bd. dirs., coord. monthly edn. program, Mgr. of Yr. award 1989, Dorothy Botdorf Nursing Leadership award 2005), Am. Coll. Cardiology, Bux-mont Nurse Practitioners Assn., Am. Acad. Nurse Practitioners, Sigma Theta Tau. Office Phone: 215-614-0482. Business E-Mail: donna.chojnowski@uphs.upenn.edu.

CHOKSI, MARY CLAIRE, investment company executive; b. 1950; m. Armeane Choksi; children: Maaren, Tristen, Alexander Nicolas. BA in French, U. Minn.; MA in Internat. Rels., John Hopkins U.; MPA, U. Minn. With pension devel. divsn. World Bank, sr. program officer South and S.E. Asia; mng. dir. Strategic Investment Ptnrs. Inc. and Emerging Markets Investors Corp., Arlington, Va., 1987—. Bd. dirs. Emerging Markets South Asia Fund, Emerging Markets Quantitative Portfolio, HJ Heinz Co., Avis Budget Group Inc. Trustee Nat. Mus. Women in the Arts; bd. dirs. Beauvoir-The Nat. Cathedral Elem. Sch. Office: Strategic Investment Group 16th Fl 1001 19th St N Arlington VA 22209-1722*

CHOKSY, JAMSHEED KAIRSHASP, historian, religious scholar, humanities educator, language educator; b. Bombay, Jan. 8, 1962; arrived in Sri Lanka, 1962; permanent resident, U.S. 1995, naturalized, 1999. s. Kairshasp Nariman and Freny Kairshasp (Cooper) C.; m. Carol Emma Burnside, Sept. 12, 1993; 1 child, Darius Jamsheed. AB in Mid.-Ea. Langs. and Culture, Columbia U., 1985; PhD in History and Religions, Harvard U., 1991. Tchg. fellow dept. anthropology and archaeology Harvard U., 1988, jr. fellow, 1988-91; vis. asst. prof. depts. history and internat. rels. Stanford U., 1991-93; from asst. prof. to prof. Ind. U., Bloomington, 1993—2001, prof. ctrl. Eurasian and India studies, history and religion, 2001—. Mem. Sch. Hist. Studies, Inst. for Advanced Study-Princeton, 1993—94; fellow Ctr. Advanced Study in Behavioral Scis., 2001—02; presenter in field; cons. in field. Author: Purity and Pollution in Zoroastrianism, 1989, Conflict and Cooperation, 1997, Evil, Good and Gender, 2002, Archeological Surveys in Pakistan, 1988-90, 1999-2001, Iran, 2003; contbr. numerous articles to profl. publs. Rsch. fellow Govt. India, Bombay, 1998; John Simon Guggenheim Meml. Found. fellow, 1996-97; resident scholar Ind. U., 1996-97, grantee 1994—, grantee Am. Acad. Religion, 1995-96, 2005-06; Andrew W. Mellon fellow, 1991-93, 2001-02, Am. Philos. Soc. fellow, 2006—07. Fellow: Royal Asiatic Soc. (Great Britain, Ireland); mem.: Mensa, Cosmos Club (Wash.), Explorers Club (NY). Office: Ind U Dept Ctrl Eurasian Studies Goodbody Hall 157 1011 E 3rd St Bloomington IN 47405-7005 Office Phone: 812-855-8643. Business E-Mail: jchoksy@indiana.edu.

CHOLDIN, MARIANNA TAX, librarian, educator; b. Chgo., Feb. 26, 1942; d. Sol and Gertrude (Katz) Tax; m. Harvey Myron Choldin, Aug. 28, 1962; children: Kate and Mary (twins). BA, U. Chgo., 1962, MA, 1967, PhD, 1979. Slavic bibliographer Mich. State U., East Lansing, 1967—69; Slavic bibliographer, instr. U. Ill., Urbana, 1969—73, Slavic bibliographer, asst. prof., 1973—76, Slavic bibliographer, assoc. prof., 1976—84, head Slavic and East European Libr., 1982—89, head, prof., 1984—2002, dir. Russian and East European Ctr., 1987—89, C. Walter and Gerda B. Mortenson Disting. prof., 1989—2002, dir. Mortenson Ctr. for Internat. Libr. Programs, 1991—2002, prof. emerita, 2003—. Author: Fence Around the Empire: Russian Censorship, 1985; editor: Red Pencil: Artists, Scholars and Censors in the USSR, 1989, Books, Libraries and Information in Slavic and East European Studies, 1986. Chair Soros Found. Network Libr. Program Bd., 1997—2000; pres. Rudomino Libr. Coun., 2005—. Recipient Pushkin gold medal for contbns. to culture, Russian Presdl. Coun. on Culture, 2000. Mem. ALA (John Ames Humphry/OCLC/Forest Press award 2005, Internat. Librarianship award 2005), Am. Assn. for Advancement of Slavic Studies (pres. 1995), Phi Beta Kappa. Jewish. Home: 888 S Michigan Ave #403 Chicago IL 60605 Personal E-mail: mcholdin@ameritech.net.

CHOLE, RICHARD ARTHUR, otolaryngologist, department chairman; b. Madison, Wis., Oct. 12, 1944; s. Arthur Steven and Wendy Elveyn (Danielczyk) C.; m. Cynthia Beiseker, Dec. 27, 1969; children: Joseph Michael, Timothy Thomas, Katharine, Melinda. Student, U. Calif., Berkeley, 1962-65; MD, U. So. Calif., 1969; PhD in Otolaryngology, U. Minn., 1977. Diplomate Am. Bd. Otolaryngology. Rotating intern U. So. Calif. Med. Ctr., 1969-70; med. fellow dept. surgery Sch. Medicine U. Minn., 1972-73, med. fellow dept. otolaryngology Sch. Medicine, 1973-77; asst. prof. dept. otolaryngology-head and neck surgery Sch. Medicine U. Calif., Davis, 1977-81, assoc. prof., 1981-84, prof., 1984-98, acting chmn. dept., 1985, chmn., 1985—98; chmn. dept. otolaryngology Washington U., St. Louis, 1998—. Mem. sci. rev. com. Deafness Rsch. Found., 1986—; mem. communicative disorders rev. com. Nat. Inst. Deafness and Communication Disorders, 1989—94; staff cons. Dept. Air Force, David Grant USAF Med. Ctr., Travis AFB, Calif., 1981—98; keynote spkr. 92d Japan Oto-Rhino-Laryngol. Soc. Meeting, Fukuoka City, Japan, 1990—; faculty mem. 4th Internat. Cholesteatoma Conf., Niigata City, Japan, 1992; bd. dirs. Am. Bd. Otolaryngology, 2000—; adv. coun. Nat. Deafness and Other Communication Disorders, 2001—; lectr. in field; bd. sci. counselors NIDCD, NIH, 2004—; bd. dirs. Barnes Jewish Hosp., 2005—; mem. residence rev. com. ACGME, 2002—05. Mem. editorial bd. Laryngoscope, 1985-87; mem. exec. editorial bd. Otolaryngology-Head and Neck Surgery, 1990—; contbr. numerous articles to profl. jours., book chpts., revs.; patentee in field. Mem. profl. edn. com. Am. Cancer Soc., 1977-78, Sacramento Noise Control Hearing Bd., 1977—, Greater Sacramento Profl. Standards Rev. Orgn., 1978-79; deacon 1st Bapt. Ch., Davis, 1979-82, elder, 1983-88. Recipient 1st pl. award Am. Acad. Ophthalmology and Otolaryngology, 1977, care recognition awards U. Calif., Davis, 1988-91; rsch. grantee NIH, Nat. Inst. Aging, Nat. Inst. Neurol. and Communicative Disorders and Stroke, Nat. Inst. on Deafness and Other Communication Disorders, Deafness Rsch. Found., Am. Otol. Soc., U. Calif., 1978-91. Mem. Collegeum Otorhinolaryngologicum Amicitiae Sacrum (U.S. group), Am. Acad. Otolaryngology-Head and Neck Surgery (Honors award 1984, com. on rsch. 1987—, rsch. coordinating coun. 1987—, continuing edn. com. 1991—), Am. Otol. Soc. (trustee rsch. fund 1986—, sec.-treas. 1989—, pres. 2001—), Assn. for Rsch. in Otolaryngology (pres. 1999-2000, award of merit com. 1988—), Am. Laryngol., Rhinol. and Otol. Soc., Am. Soc. for Bone and Mineral Rsch., Assn. Acad. Depts. Otolaryngology-Head and Neck Surgery (coun. 1986—), Calif. Med. Assn. (sci. adv. panel, sect. on otolaryngology-head and neck surgery 1986-98), Sacramento Soc. Otolaryngology and Maxillofacial Surgery, Soc. Univ. Otolaryngologists-Head and Neck Surgeons. Achievements include research in in experimental cholesteatoma, experimental otosclerosis, the aging auditory system, osteoclast cell biology. Office: Washington U Sch Med CB8115 660 S Euclid Ave # 8115 Saint Louis MO 63110-1010 E-mail: choler@msnotes.wustl.edu.

CHOLEWKA, PATRICIA ANNE, nursing educator; m. Michael A. Cholewka; children: Maureen, Kathleen. Diploma in Nursing, Bellevue Sch. Nursing, NYC, 1967; BSN magna cum laude, Castleton State Coll., Vt., 1979; MPA in Pub. and Nonprofit Mgmt. Policy, NYU, NYC, 1987, MA in Healthcare Informatics, 2005; EdD in internat. Edn. Devel., Columbia U., NYC, 1999. RN; cert. nursing adminstrn. ANA; cert. Nat. Assn. Healthcare Quality. Mgr. med.-surg. clin. svcs. in acute and managed care orgns., 1967-95; asst. prof. dept. nursing NY Coll. Tech., CUNY, NYC, 1995—; rschr. healthcare policy and econ. mgmt., 1993—. Healthcare orgn. devel. cons. Razgrad Hosp., Bulgaria, 1993, Kaunas Med. Acad. Hosp., Lithuania, 1996-98, Lviv (Ukraine) Mcpl. Health Dept., 1998; reviewer curriculum med. quality mgmt., Am. Coll. Med. Quality, 2005; asst. prof. Dept. Nursing, Coll. Tech. CUNY, 2006—. Author: Comparative Analysis of Two Post-Soviet Healthcare Organizations in Lithuania and Ukraine: Implications for Continuous Quality Improvement, 1999, Factors Affecting Sustainable Health Care Management Programs in Post-Soviet Transitional Economics; editor Jour. Healthcare Quality; guest editor Internat. Jour. Econ. Devel.; mem editl. bd Nursing Outlook, Jour. Nursing Scholarship, Jour. Transcultural Nursing. Mem. citizen emergency response team, Bay Ridge, 2004—; mem. cmty. coun., 2003—. Recipient Disting. Rsch. award, Columbia U., 1999, Fed. Nurse Traineeship award, NYU, 2003, Fulbright award, 2007—. Mem. Am. Pub. Health Assn., Am. Nursing Informatics Assn., Phi Delta Kappa, Sigma Theta Tau Internat. Republican. Roman Catholic. Home Phone: 718-680-7478. Personal E-mail: pacholewka@verizon.net.

CHOMICZ, THOMAS E., lawyer, consultant; b. Chgo., Apr. 9, 1941; BA, U. St. Thomas, St. Paul, 1963; JD cum laude, U. Minn., Mpls., 1969. CPA; bar: Ill. 1969, US Tax Ct. 1970. Atty. Quarles and Brady LLP, Chgo. Planning and faculty mem. ITT-Chgo. Kent Coll. Law Ann. Not-for-Profit Conf., 1982—2003, chair, 1984—86, co-chair, 2000—03; profl. devel. com. mem. Donors Forum Chgo., 1984—93, legis. and regulatory com. mem., 1987—2000, mem. bd. dirs., 1992—96, chair, 1993—94, membership com. mem., 1993—2003, officer/sec., 1994—96, chair, 1995—96, pub. policy com. mem., 1999—2003; advisor non-profit orgns., pvt. founds., profl. med. and svc. corps. and Congl. reps. and govt. agys.; advisor to work fund Chgo. Jobs Coun., 1999—2002, rep. credit policies com. Non-Profit Fin. Ctr.; mem. charitable adv. coun. Ill. Atty. Gen., 2001—03; mem. Found. Lawyers Group, Washington, 1986—2003; cons., reviewer IRS, 1987; chair pension and pers. com. Washington and Jane Smith Home, 1989—93, trustee, mem. investment com., mem. exec. com., 1989—2003, chair bldg. and grounds com., 1993—95, v.p., 1997—2002, pres., 2002—03; mem. Gt. Lakes TE/GE Coun. (formerly known as Mid-States EP/EO Coun.), 1996—2003, program com. chair, 2000—03. Chair devel. com. St. Barnabas Ch., 1992—96, fin. com. mem., 1993—94; bd. trustees St. Xavier U., 2002—03, devel. com. mem., 2002, exec. com. mem., 2003, co-chair, 2003. Mem.: ABA (former chmn. pvt. found. subcom. 1985—93, former co-chair joint ventures subcom. 1993—97, co-chair forms subcom. 1998—2003, tax sect., co-chair forms, ruling and adminstrv. devels. com.), St. Xavier U., Chgo. Bar Assn. (tax-exempt orgn. com. 1987—2003). Home: 9955 S Seeley Ave Chicago IL 60643

CHOMSKY, (AVRAM) NOAM, linguistics and philosophy educator; b. Phila., Dec. 7, 1928; s. William and Elsie (Simonofsky) C.; m. Carol Doris Schatz, Dec. 24, 1949; children: Aviva, Diane, Harry Alan. BA, U. Pa., 1949, MA, 1951, PhD, 1955, DHL (hon.), 1984, U. Chgo., 1967, Loyola U., Chgo., 1970, Swarthmore Coll., 1970, Bard Coll., 1971, U. Mass., 1973, U. Maine, 1992, Gettysburg Coll., 1992, Amherst Coll., 1995, U. Rovira i Virgili, Catalonia, 1998; DHL (hon.), McGill U., 1998; DHL (hon.), U. Guelph, Can., 1999, Columbia U., 1999, U. Conn., 1999, U. Toronto, 2000, U. Western Ont., 2000; DHL (hon.), U. Nat. Comahue, Argentina, 2001; LittD (hon.), U. London, 1967; DHL (hon.), U. Nat. Bogota, Colombia, 2002, Vrije U., Brussels, 2003, Ctrl. Conn. State U., 2003, U. Florence, 2004, Ctrl. Conn. State U., 2004, U. Athens, 2004; LittD (hon.), Delhi U., India, 1972, Visva-Bharati U., Santiniketan, West Bengal, 1980, Cambridge U., Eng., 1995; LittD (hon.), U. Calcutta, 2001; LLD (hon.), U. Buenos Aires, 1996; LLD, Harvard U., 2000; Doctorate (hon.), Scuola Normale Superiore, Pisa, Italy, 1999, Ljubljana, 2005, Bologna, 2005, others; DHL (hon.), U. de Chile, 2006, U. de la Frontera, Temuco, Chila, 2006, Uppsala U., Sweden, 2007. Mem. faculty MIT, 1955—, prof. modern langs., 1961—76, Ferrari P. Ward prof. modern lang. and linguistics, 1966—76, Inst. prof., 1976—. Vis. prof. Columbia U., NYC, 1957-58; mem. Inst. Advanced Study Princeton U., 1958-59; Linguistic Soc. Am. prof. UCLA, summer 1966; Beckman prof. U. Calif.-Berkeley, 1966-67; John Locke lectr. Oxford U., 1969; Bertrand Russell Meml. lectr., Cambridge, 1971; Nehru Meml. lectr., New Delhi, 1972; Huizinga lectr. U. Leiden, 1977; Woodbridge lectr. Columbia U., 1978; Kant lectr. Stanford U., 1979; Jeanette K. Watson disting. vis. prof. Syracuse U., 1982; Pauling Meml. lectr. Oreg. State U., 1995. Author: Syntactic Structures, 1957, Current Issues in Linguistic Theory, 1964, Aspects of the Theory of Syntax, 1965, Cartesian Linguistics, 1966, Topics in the Theory of Generative Grammar, 1966, (with Morris Halle) Sound Pattern of English, 1968, Language and Mind, 1968, American Power and the New Mandarins, 1969, At War with Asia, 1970, Problems of Knowledge and Freedom, 1971, Studies on Semantics in Generative Grammar, 1972, For Reasons of State, 1973, (with Edward Herman) Counterrevolutionary Violence, 1973, Peace in the Middle East, 1974, Logical Structure of Linguistic Theory, 1975, Reflections on Language, 1975, Essays on Form and Interpretation, 1977, Human Rights and American Foreign Policy, 1978, (with Edward Herman) The Political Economy of Human Rights, 2 vols., 1979, Language and Responsibility, 1979, Rules and Representations, 1980, Lectures on Government and Binding, 1981, Concepts and Consequences of the Theory of Government and Binding, 1982, Towards a New Cold War, 1982, Radical Priorities, 1982, Fateful Triangle, 1983, Turning the Tide, 1985, Barriers, 1986, Knowledge of Language, 1986, Pirates and Emperors, 1986, On Power and Ideology, 1987, Language and Problems of Knowledge, 1987, Language in a Psychological Setting, 1987, Generative Grammar, 1987, Culture of Terrorism, 1988, (with Edward Herman) Manufacturing Consent, 1988, Language and Politics, 1988, Necessary Illusions, 1989, Deterring Democracy, 1991, Chronicles of Dissent, 1992, What Uncle Sam Really Wants, 1992, Year 501, 1993, Rethinking Camelot, 1993, Letters from Lexington, 1993, The Prosperous Few and the Restless Many, 1993, Language and Thought, 1994, World Orders, Old and New, 1994, The Minimalist Program, 1995, Powers and Prospects, 1996, The Common Good, 1998, Profits Over People, 1998, The New Military Humanism, 1999, New Horizons in the Study of Language and Mind, 2000, Rogue States, 2000, A New Generation Draws the Line, 2000, Architecture of Language, 2000, 9-11, 2001, Propaganda and the Public Mind, 2001, Understanding Power, 2002, On Nature and Language, 2002, Pirates and Emperors, Old and New, 2002, Middle East Illusions, 2003, Hegemony or Survival: America's Quest for Global Dominance (The American Empire Project), 2003, Imperial Ambitions: Conversations with Noam Chomsky on the Post-9/11 World, 2005, Failed States: The Abuse of Power and the Assault on Democracy, 2006, (with Gilbert Achcar) Perilous Power: The Middle East and U.S. Foreign Policy, 2006, Interventions, 2007. Recipient Disting. Sci. Contbn. award, APA, 1984, Kyoto prize, Kyocera Found., 1988, 2001, George Orwell award, Nat. Coun. Tchrs. English, 1987, 1989, James Killian Faculty award, MIT, 1992, Lannan Lit. award for nonfiction, 1992, Joel Seldin Peace award, Psychologists for Social Responsibility, 1993, Homer Smith award, NYU Sch. of Medicine, 1994, Loyola Mellon Humanities award, Loyola U. Chgo., 1994, Helmholtz medal, Berlin-

Brandenburgische Akad. Wissenschaften, 1996, Benjamin Franklin Inst. award, 1999, Rabindranath Tagore Centenary award, Asiatic Soc. Calcutta, 2000, Rising Sun of Mehgarh award, Dawn Islamabad, 2001, Adela Dwyer St. Thomas Villanova Peace award, Villanova U., Phila., 2002, Peace award, Turkish Publishers' Assn., Istanbul, 2002, award, Kurdish Human Rights Assn., Dyarbakir, 2002, Soc. Writers and Artists award, UN, 2004, Carl-von-Ossietzky prize, Oldenburg, Germany, 2004; jr. fellow Soc. Fellows Harvard U., 1951—55. Fellow AAAS, Brit. Acad. (corr.), Brit. Psychol. Soc. (hon.), Royal Anthrop. Inst. Gt. Britain, Royal Anthrop. Inst. Ireland, Utrecht Soc. Arts and Scis. (hon.), Gesellschaft für Sprachwissenschaft (hon.), Am. Acad. Scis., Am. Acad. Philosophy, Royal Soc. Can. (fgn.), Am. Philos. Soc.; mem. APA (William James fellow 1990), NAS, Am. Acad. Arts and Scis., Linguistic Soc. Am., Deutsche Akademie der Naturforscher Leopoldina, Assn. for Edn. in Journalism and Mass Comm. (Profl. Excellence award 1991). Achievements include development of theory of generative grammar. Office: 77 Massachusetts Ave Cambridge MA 02139-4301 Home Phone: 781-862-6160; Office Phone: 617-253-7819. Business E-Mail: chomsky@mit.edu.

CHONG, ARTHUR, lawyer; B, U. Calif., Berkeley; grad., Harvard Law Sch., 1978. Bar: Calif. 1978. Assoc. McCutchen, Doyle, Brown & Enersen, San Francisco; with McKesson Corp., 1981—2005, dep. gen. counsel, 1999—2005; exec. v.p., gen. counsel Safeco Corp., Seattle, 2005—. Office: Safeco Corp Safeco Plz 4333 Brooklyn Ave NE Seattle WA 98185 Office Phone: 206-545-5000. Office Fax: 206-545-5559.*

CHONG, BRUCE SIMON, dean, broadcast executive; b. Honolulu, Apr. 6, 1956; s. Bruce Donald and Mildred (Gossen) C.; m. Mary Prudence Eddy, Aug. 10, 1991. AA, Grossmont CC, 1977; BA in Journalism, San Diego State U., 1979. Reporter, anchor KOGO-AM/KPRI-FM, San Diego, 1978-81; prodr. CNN Headline News, Atlanta, 1981—83; sr. editor CNN Radio Network, Atlanta, 1983—85, gen. mgr., 1985-89; prodr. CNN, Atlanta, 1989—93, exec./supervising prodr., 1993—99; dean. comm. Savannah Coll. Art and Design, 1999—. Exec. dir. video prodn. svcs. D61/SCAD TV, Savannah Coll Art & Design, 1999. Bd. dirs., v.p. Frank Callen Boys & Girls Club. Mem.: Boys and Girls Club (bd. mem. 2003—). Home: 2 Pepper Bush Cir Savannah GA 31411 Office: PO Box 3146 Savannah GA 31402-3146 Home Phone: 912-598-4922; Office Phone: 912-525-5225. Business E-Mail: bchong@scad.edu.

CHONG, JAMES I., information technology executive; BS in Engring., Va. Poly. Inst. Dir., integrated comm. divsn., divsn. mgr., visual comm. Dynamic Tech. Sys. Inc.; co-founder, chief tech. officer VidSys Inc., Marlborough, Mass. Named one of Top 25 Chief Tech. Officers, InfoWorld mag., 2007. Office: VidSys 293 Boston Post Rd W Ste 310 Marlborough MA 01752 Office Phone: 508-485-2900. Office Fax: 508-485-2920.

CHONG, JAMES TZEH-MIN, finance educator, researcher; s. Tian Hoo Chong and Lay Leng Yeap; m. Sing-Kiat Ting, July 24, 2004. B Acctg., Nanyang Technol. U., Singapore, 1993; MS in Fin., Lancaster U., Eng., 1996; MS in Fin. Math., U. Chgo., 1998; PhD, U. Reading, Eng., 2002. Credit officer DBS Bank, Singapore, 1993—94; quantitative analyst UBS, Chgo., 1998—99; assoc. Cameron Global Investments, San Francisco, 2001—02; asst. prof. Calif. State U., Northridge, 2003—. Contbr. articles to profl. jours. Recipient Overseas Rsch. Students award, Univ. UK, 1999—2002, Creativity Activity award, Calif. State U., Northridge, 2005—; scholar, Internat. Securities Market Assn. Centre, U. Reading, 1999—2003; Rsch. scholar, Calif. State U., Northridge, 2005—. Mem.: Acad. Fin. Svcs., Fin. Mgmt. Assn. Business E-Mail: jchong@csun.edu.

CHONG, PING, performing company executive; b. Toronto, Ont., Can., Oct. 2, 1946; s. Jin and Bak Lin Chong. Student, Pratt Inst., NY, 1964—66, Sch. Visual Arts, 1967—69; DFA (hon.), Cornish Coll., 1999; LHD (hon.), Kent State U., 2004. Founder, artistic dir., dir., choreographer, playwright Ping Chong and Co., NYC. Wynton chair U. Minn., 1994. Author: Kind Ness, 1988, Snow, 1989, Nuit Blanche, 1989, Gaijin/Undesirable Elements/NYC, 1995, SlutForArt, 1999, Truth & Beauty, 2000, East-West Quartet, 2005, Cathay: Three Tales of China, 2006; co-dir.: (TV) Paris, 1972; dir.: Education of the Girl Child, 1973; collaborator with Meredith Monk (TV) Paris, 1982, Turtle Dreams, 1982, (performance works) Chacon, 1974, Venice/Milan, 1976, The Games, 1983, film and video prodns. include Plage Concrete, 1988, Tempus Fugit, 1990, I Will Not Be Sad in This World, 1992, performance works include Lazarus, 1972, I Flew to Fiji, You Went South, 1973, Fear and Loathing in Gotham, 1975, Humboldt's Current, 1977, Nuit Blanche, 1980, Rainer and the Knife, 1981, Anna Into Nightlight, 1982, A.M./A.M.-The Articulated Man, 1982, A Race, 1983, Astonishment and the Twins, 1984, Nosferatu, 1985, 1991, Kind Ness, 1986, Angels of Swedenborg, 1986, Without Law, Without Heaven, 1987, Snow, 1988, Quartetto, 1988, Maraya, 1988, Noiresque-The Fallen Angel, 1989, Skin-A State of Being, 1989, Brightness, 1989, Elephant Memories, 1990, Deshima, 1990, 4AM America, 1990, American Gothic, 1992, Undesirable Elements, Artist Space, 1992, Cleve., 1993, Twin Cities, 1994, Seattle, 1995, Rotterdam, 1997, Newark, 1998, Hamilton, 1999, Chgo., 1999 (After Dark award, 1999), Washington, 2000, Madison, Wis., 2001, Pioneer Valley, 2003, Berlin, 2003, Albuquerque, 2006, Lafayette, 2006, Undesirable Elements 10 Yrs. Later, 2005, Persuasion, 1994, Chinoiserie, 1995, Gaijin, 1995, 98.6:a convergence in 15 minutes, 1996, After Sorrow, 1997, Excerpts from the Diary of a Chinese Envoy, 1997, Kwaidan, 1998 (UNIMA-USA citation of excellence in the art of puppetry, 1998), Nocturne in 1200 Seconds, 1998, Truth & Beauty, 1999, Pojagi, 1999, Slutforart, 1999 (Bessie award, 1999), Secret History, NYC, 2000 (Top 10 Show, NY Theatre Wire, 2001), Charleston, 2001, Edda: Viking Tales of Lust, Revenge and Family, 2001, Children of War, 2002, UE 92/02, 2002, Reason, 2002, Obon: Tales of Rain and Moonlight, 2002, God Favors the Predator, 2004, Secret History/Seattle Youth, 2004, Secret History: Journeys Abroad, Journeys Within, 2004, 2005, Blind Ness: The Irresistible Light of Encounter, 2004, Cathay: Three Tales of China, 2005 (Top 10 Show, NY Theatre Wire, 2006), Secret History/Native Voices, 2005; exhibitions include MIT, Cambridge, Mass., 1985, Three Rivers Arts Festival, Pitts., 1988, Williams Ctr. for the Arts, Easton, Pa., 1989, 2006, Austin Ctr. for the Arts, Hartford, Conn., 1989, Aidekman Arts Ctr., Medford, Mass., 1989, Haggerty Mus., Milw., 1990, Artists Space, NYC, 1992, Venice Bienniale, 1995. Named one of 100 Most Influential Asian Ams. of the Decade, 1999; recipient Obie award, 1977, 2000, Villager award, 1982, Grand prize, Toronto Video Festival, 1983, Maharam Design award, 1985, Bronze Star, Sacramento Internat. Film and Video Festival, 1990, Bessie award, 1992, Yomiuri Theatrical award, 1995, TCG Absolut Stages award, NY State Coun. Arts Theatre Commn., 1997, Vita award for lifetime achievement, Stony Brook, NY, 1998, OUT100 award, Out Mag., 2002, award, Playwrights USA, Nat. Inst. Music Theatre; CAPS fellow, 1974, 1975, New Genre fellow, Nat. Endowment Arts, 1981, Visual Arts fellow, 1984, Choreographer fellow, 1989, 1990, 1991, Playwrights fellow, 1996, Guggenheim fellow, 1985, Artist's fellow in choreography, NYFA, 1988, McKnight fellow, NY State Coun. Arts Individual Artists Theatre Commn., 1988, 1992, TCG/Pew Charitable Trust Nat. Theatre Artist Residency Program fellow, 1993—95, Individual Artists fellow, NY State Coun. Arts, 1995, Bellagio fellow, 1998, Artist's fellow, NYFA, 1998, 2003, USA Prudential fellow, US Artists Found., 2006. Office: Ping Chong & Co 47 Great Jones St New York NY 10012 Office Phone: 212-529-1557.

CHONG, RICHARD DAVID, architect; b. LA, June 1, 1946; s. George and Mabel Dorothy (Chan) C.; m. Roze Gutierrez, July 5, 1969; children: David Gregory, Michelle Elizabeth. BArch, U. So. Calif., 1969; MArch, UCLA, 1974. Registered architect, Utah, Calif., Wyo., Wash. Assoc. Pulliam, Matthews & Assocs., Los Angeles, 1969-76; dir. Asst. Community Design Ctr., Salt Lake City, 1976-77; prin. Richard D. Chong & Assocs., Salt Lake City and L.A., 1977—. Planning cons. Los Angeles Harbor Dept., 1974-76; asst. instr. So. Calif. Inst. Architecture, Santa Monica, 1973-74; vis. design critic Calif. State Poly. U., Pamona, 1975, U. Utah, Salt Lake City, 1976-78; design instr. Calif. State Poly. U., 1975-76; adj. asst. prof. urban design, U. Utah, 1980-84; bd. dirs. Utah Housing Coalition, Salt Lake City; Salt Lake City Housing Adv. and Appeals Bd., 1976-80; presenter Rail-Volution Conf., Washington, 1996. Author: Design of Flexible Housing, 1974; prin. works include Airmen's Dining Hall, 1985 (1st Pl. Mil. Facility Air Force Logistics Command, 1986), Oddfellows Hall, 1984 (Heritage Found. award, 1986), Light Rail Sys. for Salt Lake City. Mem. Task Force for the Aged Housing Com. Salt Lake County, Salt Lake City, 1976-77; Salt Lake City Mortgage Loan Instns. Rev. Com., 1978; bd. dirs. Neighborhood Housing Svcs. of Fed. Home Loan Bank Bd., Salt Lake City, 1979-81, devel. com.; vice-chmn. Water Quality Adv. Coun., Salt Lake City, 1981-83; vice-chmn. Salt Lake City Pub. Utilities Bd., 1985-87; mem. adv. bd. Pub. Utilities Commn., Salt Lake City, 1985—; bd. dirs. Kier Mgmt. Corp.; bd. mem. Camp Kostopulos, Altro Nat. Risk Mgmt. Adv. Bd., 1996—, Ft. Douglas Social Adv. Bd., 1996—, Altro Nat. Safety Bd., 1996-01. Mem. AIA (jury mem. Am. Soc. Interior Designs Ann. awards 1981-82, treas. Salt Lake chpt. 1988-89, treas. Utah Soc. 1991, sec. 1992, pres.-elect AIA Utah 1993, pres. 1994-95), Am. Inst. Planning (juror Ann. Planning award 1984-85), Am. Planning Assn., Am. Arbitration Assn., Nat. Panel Arbitrators, Cottonwood Country Club. Democrat. Avocations: tennis, sailing, travel. Office: Richard D Chong & Assocs 244 Edison St Salt Lake City UT 84111-2307 also: 714 W Olympic Blvd Ste 732 Los Angeles CA 90015-1439

CHONG, STEPHEN CHU LING, lawyer; b. Lakewood, Ohio, Aug. 1, 1957; s. Richard Seng Hoon C. and Betty J. (Chong) Wamego; m. Sheryl Kay Horton, Nov. 23, 1984; children: Evan M. G., Erin M.L., Elena M.L., Eric M.K., Ethan M.L. BA, Calvin Coll., Grand Rapids, Mich., 1979; JD, Ohio State U., 1982. Bar: Fla. 1982, US Dist. Ct. (mid. dist.) Fla. 1983, US Ct. Appeals (11th cir.) 1982, US Tax Ct. 1985; bd. cert. real estate lawyer Fla. Bar Bd. Legal Specialization and Edn. Assoc. Caudill, Drage, de Beaubien, Orlando, Fla., 1982-83; shareholder Caudill, Chong & Migliaccio, Winter Garden, Fla., 1983-84; assoc. Thomas R. Rogers & Assocs., Longwood, Fla., 1984-90; of counsel Litchford, Christopher, Orlando, 1990-92; pres., shareholder Marks & Chong, Orlando, 1992-2001; ptnr. Arnold Matheny & Eagan PA, Orlando, 2001—04; shareholder Nardella Chong, PA, Altamonte Springs, Fla., 2004—. Mem. nominating bd. City of Orlando, 1993-98, chmn. 1996-97; mem. area bus. com. Naval Tng. Ctr. Reuse Com., Orlando, 1994-95; bd. trustees Minority/Women Bus. Enterprise Alliance, Orlando, 1994-99; chair Realtor Rels. Com., Orlando, 1992-93; presenter in field. Contbr. articles to profl. jours. Mem. cultural diversity com. Orlando Sci. Ctr., 1993-2000; mem. cmty. adv. bd. WMFE-TV/FM, Orlando, 1994-95; mem. adv. bd. Ctrl. Fla. Family, Orlando, 1994-2000; mem. 9th Jud. Cir. Grievance Com., 2002-06; pres. Asian Am. C. of C., Orlando, 1993-94; vol. Income Tax Assistance, 1996—; trustee Calvin Coll., Grand Rapids, Mich., 1999—; bd. dirs. Econ. Devel. Commn. of Mid-Fla., Inc., 2001-03, Orlando Citizen Corps Coun., 2002-06, Children's Home Soc., 2004—. Recipient Vision award-Small Bus. Downtown Orlando Partnership, 1994. Mem. ABA, Orange County Bar Assn., Christian Legal Soc. Ctr. Fla. (pres. 1999-2000), Childrens Home Soc. (mem. adv. bd. 2004—). Presbyterian. Office: Nardella Chong PA 234 N Westmonte Dr Ste 3000 Altamonte Springs FL 32714 Office Phone: 407-786-2700.

CHONG, VERNON, retired surgeon, military officer; b. Fresno, Calif., Nov. 13, 1933; s. Seu Ling and Ruth (Lee) C.; m. Ann Sumiko Kawana, Sept. 7, 1957; children: Christopher Lee, Gerald Scott, Douglas James. BA, Stanford U., 1955, MD, 1958. Diplomate Am. Bd. Surgery. Intern Gen. Hosp. of Fresno (Calif.) County, 1958-59, resident in gen. surgery, 1959-63; commd. capt. USAF, 1963, advanced through ranks to maj. gen., 1987; chief gen. surgery svc. USAF Hosp., Scott AFB, Ill., 1963-65, staff surgeon, dir. edn. Tachikawa AFB, Japan, 1965-68; staff surgeon, instr. surgery David Grant USAF Med. Ctr., Travis AFB, Calif., 1968-70, dep. comdr., dir. hosp. svcs., 1976—78, comdr., 1978—81; surgeon, chief surgery, dir. hosp. svcs. USAF Acad. Hosp., Colorado Springs, Colo., 1970-74; dep. comdr. USAF Regional Hosp., March AFB, Calif., 1974—76; comdr. Malcolm Grow USAF Med. Ctr., Andrews AFB, Md., 1981-85; command surgeon Hdqrs., Mil. Airlift Command, Scott AFB, 1985-87; comdr. Wilford Hall USAF Med. Ctr., Lackland AFB, Tex., 1987-90, Joint Mil. Med. Command, San Antonio; command surgeon Hdqrs. Air Tng. Command, Randolph AFB, Tex., 1990-91, Hdqrs. U.S. European Command, 1991-94; ret., 1994; network dir. Vets. Integrated Svc. Network VA, Grand Prairie, Tex., 1995-2000; spl. asst. to network dir. Vets. Integrated Svc. Network-21, McClellan Clinic, Sacramento, 2000—03, ret., 2003. Bd. dirs. Alamo chpt. ARC, San Antonio, 1987-88, No. Calif. Retired Officers Cmty. Law, 2004; trustee Air Force Village Found., 1987-90; bd. dirs. San Antonio chpt. ARC, 1995—, No. Calif. Ret. Officers Cmty., 2004—, Calif. Vets. Bd., 2004—. Decorated D.S.M., Legion of Merit with bronze oak leaf cluster; recipient Order of Sword award USAF, 1989. Fellow ACS (gov. 1985-90); mem. Assn. Mil. Surgeons U.S. (bd. mgrs. 1997—, chmn. 2002-04), Soc. Air Force Clin. Surgeons (bd. govs. 1971-73), Am. Coll. Physician Execs., Calif. Vets Bd. Methodist. Avocation: physical fitness. Home: 1820 Starview Ln Lincoln CA 95648

CHONMAITREE, TASNEE, pediatrician, educator, epidemiologist; b. Bangkok, Dec. 9, 1949; came to U.S., 1975; d. Surajit and Arporn (Maitong) C.; m. Somkiat Laungthaleong Pong, June 27, 1981; children: Ann L. Pong, Dan L. Pong. BS, Mahidol U., 1971; MD, Siriraj Med. Sch., 1973. Diplomate Am. Bd. Pediat., Am. Bd. Pediat. Infectious Diseases. Rotating intern Siriraj Hosp., Bangkok, 1973—74, resident in pediat., 1974—75, Lloyd Noland Hosp., U. Ala., Birmingham, 1975—78; fellow infectious disease U. Rochester, NY, 1978—81; asst. prof. pediat. U. Tex. Med. Br., Galveston, 1981—87, asst. prof. pathology, 1985—87, assoc. prof. pediat. and pathology, 1987—94; prof. pediat. and pathology, 1994—. Assoc. dir. clin. virology lab. U. Tex. Med. Br., Galveston, 1985-92, dir. divsn. pediat. infectious disease, 1985-92. Contbr. 65 articles to profl. jours. Grantee NIH, 1993—. Fellow Am. Acad. Pediat., Pediat. Infectious Diseases Soc., Infectious Diseases Soc. Am.; mem. Soc. Pediat. Rsch., European Soc. for Pediat. Rsch., Tex. Infectious Disease Soc. Buddhist. Avocation: classical music. Home: 1906 Cherrytree Park Cir Houston TX 77062-2327 Office: U Tex Dept Pediat Med Br Ninth St & Market Galveston TX 77555-0001 Office Phone: 409-772-2798. Business E-Mail: tchonmai@utmb.edu.

CHOO, KRISTY, chef; b. Singapore; m. Kim Oh. Grad., Calif. Culinary Acad., San Francisco. Flight attendant World Air Network; pastry chef Raffles Hotel, Singapore; exec. pastry chef, owner Jin Patisserie, LA, 2003—. Chocolatières Hotel Food Asia competition, 2001; participant Culinary World Cup, Luxembourg, 2002. Named one of LA's Rising Stars, StarChefs.com, 2006. Office: Jin Patisserie 1202 Abbot Kinny Blvd Venice CA 90291 Office Phone: 310-399-8801.*

CHOO, SIN H., neurosurgeon; b. Taiping, Perak, Malaysia, Oct. 16, 1941; arrived in US, 1972; s. Ah W. Choo and Koon N. Chang; m. Phalk See Tan, Dec. 28, 1971. MBBS, U. Singapore, 1967. Diplomate Am. Bd. Neurol. Surgery. Intern Lawrence Gen. Hosp., Mass.; resident gen. surgery Burlington County Meml. Hosp., Mt. Holly, NJ; resident neurosurgery U. Ottawa, Ont., Canada; neurosurgeon Monroe Clinic, Wis., 1982—84, St. Paul-Ramsey Med. Ctr., 1984, Boston Med. Ctr., 1985—, Good Samaritan Med. Ctr., Brockton, Mass., 1985—2006, Brockton Hosp., 1985—2006. Co-author: Cerebral Arterial Spasm, 1980; author: Coma, 1982; contbr. articles to profl. jours. Recipient Physician Svc. award, Good Samaritan Med. Ctr., 2006. Fellow: ACS, Internat. Coll. Surgeons, Surgeons Can., Royal Coll. Physicians; mem.: Congress Neurol. Surgeons, Am. Assn. Neurol. Surgeons, Mass. Med. Soc. Avocations: photography, travel. Office: Boston U Neurosurgical Assocs PC 720 Harrison Ave # 710 Boston MA 02118

CHOPER, JESSE HERBERT, law educator, dean; b. Wilkes-Barre, Pa., Sept. 19, 1935; s. Edward and Dorothy (Resnick) C.; m. Marilyn Smith; children: Marc Steven, Edward Nathaniel. BS, Wilkes U., 1957, DHL, 1967; LLB, U. Pa., 1960. Bar: D.C. 1961. Instr. Wharton Sch. U. Pa., 1957-60; law clk. to Chief Justice Earl Warren U.S. Supreme Ct., 1960-61; asst. prof. U. Minn. Law Sch., 1961-62, assoc. prof., 1962-65; prof. Law Sch. U. Calif., Berkeley, 1965—, dean, 1982-92, Earl Warren prof. Pub. Law, 1991—. Vis. prof. Harvard U., 1970—71, Milan U., 1992, Autonoma U., Barcelona, 1996, Vrije U., Amsterdam, 1999, Fordham U., 1999, New South Wales U., 2002. Author: Constitutional Law: Cases-Comments-Questions, 10th edit., 2006, The American Constitution, Cases and Materials, 9th edit., 2001, Constitutional Rights and Liberties, Cases and Materials, 9th edit., 2001, Corporations, Cases and Materials, 6th edit., 2004, The Supreme Court and Its Justices, 2d edit., 2001, Judicial Review and the National Political Process, 1980, Securing Religious Liberty, 1995; contbr. articles to profl. jours. Mem. AAUP, Am. Law Inst., Am. Acad. Arts and Scis., Order of Coif. Jewish. Office: U Calif Sch Law Berkeley CA 94720-0001 Office Phone: 510-642-0339. Business E-Mail: choperj@law.berkeley.edu.

CHOPEY, NICHOLAS P., editor; b. NYC, Dec. 22, 1932; s. Nicholas W. and Alice I. (Keshelak) C.; m. Katherine J. Heaney, Sept. 12, 1959; children: Nicholas, Michael, John, James. BChE, U. Va., 1955; MA in Econs., NYU, 1972. Process engr. Esso Standard Oil Co., Linden, NJ, 1955-56, 58-59; asst. assoc. editor McGraw-Hill, Inc., NYC, 1960-67, sr. assoc. editor, 1967-72, mng. editor, 1972-78, exec. editor, 1978-82, editor-in-chief, 1982-87, 2000—, exec. editor, 1987-99, Chem. Week Assocs., 1999-2000, editor-in-chief, 2000—. Adv. com. Indsl. Energy Tech. Conf., Houston, 1992—. Editor: Handbook of Chemical Engineering Calculations, 1984, 3d edit., 2003; (reprint books) Environmental Engineering in the Process Plant, 1992, Fluid Movers, 1994. 1st lt. USAF, 1956-58. Mem. AIChE (past chair com.), Am. Soc. Engring. Edn., Knights of Malta, Roselle Golf Club, Tau Beta Pi. Roman Catholic. Office: Access Intelligence 110 William St New York NY 10038-3901

CHOPIN, CHRISTOPHER ALLEN, lawyer; b. Miami, Fla., Mar. 21, 1976; s. L. Frank and Susan G. Chopin. BA, Emory U., Atlanta, Ga., 1998; JD, U. Miami Sch. Law, Coral Gables, Fla., 2001. Bar: Fla. 2002. Clk. Judge Mark King Leban, Miami, Fla., 1999—2000; assoc. Weiss & Handler, P.A., Boca Raton, Fla., 2002—02; atty. Christopher Chopin, P.A., West Palm Beach, Fla., 2002—. Mem. Fla. Family Law Rules Com., 2004—06. Mem.: Palm Beach County Bar Assn., Fla. Bar, Palm Beach C. of C. (assoc.).

CHOPIN, L. FRANK, lawyer; b. New Orleans, Apr. 29, 1942; s. Alton Francis and Floretta (Thensted) C.; children: Philip, Alexandra, Christopher. BBA, Loyola U., New Orleans, 1964, JD, 1966; diploma in mil. law, Judge Adv. Gen.'s Sch., U. Va. Sch. Law, 1966; postgrad., Nat. Law Ctr., George Wash. U., 1967-68; LLM in Taxation, U. Miami, Fla., 1976; PhD in Law, Cambridge U., Eng., 1986. Bar: La. 1966, Fla. 1968, Iowa 1980, U.S. Dist. Ct. (so. dist.) Fla. 1968, U.S. Ct. Appeals (5th cir.) 1968. Ptnr. Chopin & Chopin, Miami, 1969—77; assoc. prof. law Drake U., Des Moines, 1979—80; ptnr. Cadwalader, Wickersham & Taft, Palm Beach, Fla., 1980—94, Chopin, Miller & Yudenfreund, Palm Beach, Fla., 1994—98, Chopin & Miller, Palm Beach, Fla., 1998—2005, L. Frank Chopin, PLC, West Palm Beach, Fla., 2005—. Adj. prof. law U. Miami, 1982—96, U. Sherbrooke, Canada, 1982—94. Author: The New Residency Rules for Canadian Tax Considerations, 1985; also numerous articles in legal jours. Mem. Housing Fin. Authority; trustee Preservation Found., Palm Beach Community Chest, Inc. Served to capt. U.S. Army, 1966-68. Mem. ABA, Internat. Bar Assn., Fed. Bar Assn., Fla. Bar (tax sect.), Loyola U. Alumni Assn., U. Miami Alumni Assn., St. Thomas More Law Soc., Phi Alpha Delta (charter). Republican. Roman Catholic. Office: PO Box 4297 West Palm Beach FL 33402 Office Phone: 561-655-9500.

CHOPIN, SUSAN GARDINER, lawyer; b. Miami, Fla., Feb. 23, 1947; d. Maurice and Judith (Warden) Gardiner; children: Philip, Alexandra, Christopher BBA, Loyola U., New Orleans, 1966; JD cum laude, U. Miami, 1972; MLitt (Law), Oxford U., Eng., 1983. Bar: Fla. 1972, Iowa 1979. Sr. law clk. to judge U.S. Dist. Ct. (so. dist.) Fla., Miami, 1972-73; ptnr. Chopin & Chopin, Miami, 1973-77; assoc. prof. law sch. Drake U., Des Moines, 1979-80; pvt. practice law Palm Beach, Fla., 1981—; ptnr. Chopin & Chopin, 1999—2003, Chopin, Chopin & Chopin, 2003—, Chopin & Chopin, 2004—. Lectr. in family law Mem. editl. bd.: Fla. Bar Jour., 1975—2004, co-chair editl. bd.: Fla. Bar Family Law Commentator, 2000—01. Trustee Preservation Found. of Palm Beach, 1986-89 Mem.: Palm Beach County Bar Assn., Soc. Wig and Robe, Fla. Assn. Women Lawyers, Fed. Bar Assn., Iowa Bar Assn., Fla. Bar Assn., ABA, Wolfson Coll., Oxford Cambridge Club, Phi Alpha Delta, Phi Kappa Phi. Office: Phillips Point West Tower 777 S Flager Dr Ste 800 West Palm Beach FL 33401 Office Phone: 561-651-7800. Office Fax: 561-651-7822. Business E-Mail: chopinlaw@bellsouth.net.

CHOPKO, MARK E., lawyer; b. Kingston, Pa., Nov. 4, 1953; s. Michael E. and Rose Ann C. (Gavlick) C.; m. Jane K. Chopko; children: Michael, Jessica, Laura, Sarah. BS summa cum laude, U. Scranton, 1974; JD cum laude, Cornell U., 1977. Bar: Pa. 1977, U.S. Supreme Ct. 1984, D.C. 1987. Gen. counsel US Conf. Cath. Bishops, Washington, 1987—2007; ptnr. Stradley Ronon Stevens & Young LLP, Phila., 2007—. Adj. prof. law Georgetown U. Law Ctr., 2004-; mem. religious liberty com. Nat. Coun. Chs., N.Y.C., 1987—. Mem. bd. editors Religious Freedom Reporter, N.C., 1987-2000; contbr. articles to profl. jours. Bd. advisors program on philanthropy and the law Sch. of Law, NYU, 1995-98; bd. dirs. Blessed Sacrament Sch., Alexandria, Va., 1986-88; legal advisor Ams. United for Life, Chgo., 1987-94; mem. legal scholars bd. DePaul Inst. for Ch.-State Studies, Chgo., 1988-2003; asst. coach basketball Cath. Youth Orgn., Alexandria, 1989-94. Recipient High Quality award U.S. Nuclear Regulatory Commn., 1982. Mem. ABA (vice chmn. religious, charitable and non-profit orgns. tort sect. 1990-92), Cath. Health Assn. (legal affairs com. 1988-96), Am. Corp. Counsel Assn. (com. on non-profit and profl. assn. law). Office: Stradley Ronon Stevens & Young LLP 2600 One Commerce Sq Philadelphia PA 19103*

CHOPLIN, JOHN M., II, lawyer; b. Cedar Rapids, Iowa, Nov. 10, 1945; s. John M. and Joyce G. (Mickelsen) C.; m. Linda H. Kutchen, Feb. 14, 1969; children: Julie, John, James. BA, Drake U., 1967; JD, U. Mich., 1974. Bar: Ind. 1974, U.S. Dist. Ct. (so. dist.) Ind. 1974, U.S. Ct. Appeals (7th cir.) 1976, U.S. Supreme Ct. 1977, U.S. Ct. Appeals (6th cir.) 1983, U.S. Dist. Ct. (no. dist.) Ind. 1991. Assoc. Wilson, Tabor & Holland, Indpls., 1974—80; ptnr. Norris, Choplin & Schroeder LLP, Indpls., 1980—. Committeeman precinct Carmel Reps., Ind., 1982-84. Served to capt. USAF, 1969-73. Mem. ABA, Ind. Bar Assn., Indpls. Bar Assn., Lawyers-Pilots Bar Assn., Ind. Trial Lawyers Assn., Am. Assn. for Justice, Phi Beta Kappa, Omicron Delta Kappa. Baptist. Avocations: water sports, tennis, flying. Home: 8553 Twin Pointe Cir Indianapolis IN 46236-8903 Office: Norris Choplin & Schroeder 101 W Ohio St Ste 900 Indianapolis IN 46204-4213 Office Phone: 317-269-9330.

CHOPP, REBECCA S., academic administrator; m. Frederick H. Thibodeau; 3 children. BA, Kans. Wesleyan U., 1974; MDiv, St. Paul Sch. Theology, 1977; PhD, U. Chgo., 1983; DD (hon.), Lehigh U. Asst. prof. theology U. Chgo. Div. Sch., 1982—86; asst. prof. Candler Sch. and Grad. Divsn. Religion Emory U., Atlanta, 1986—89, assoc. faculty Inst. Liberal Arts, 1987, assoc. faculty Inst. for Women's Studies, 1987, dean of faculty and acad. affairs Candler Sch. of Theology, 1993—97, prof. theology Candler Sch. and Grad. Divsn. Religion, 1993, Charles Howard Chandler prof. theology Grad. Divsn., 1996, interim provost, v.p. acad. affairs, 1997—98, provost, exec. v.p. for acad. affairs, 1998—2001, dir. grad. studies Inst. for Women's Studies; dean, Titus Street prof. theology and culture Yale U. Div. Sch., 2001—02; pres., prof. philosophy and religion Colgate U., 2002—. Bd. dirs. Scholars Press; trustee Carnegie Found. Author: The Praxis of Suffering: An Interpretation of Liberation and Political Theologies, 1986, The Power to Speak: Feminism, Language, God, 1989, Saving Work: Feminist Practices of Theological Education, 1995; Co-editor: Differing Horizons: Feminist Theory and Theology, 1997, Reconstructing Christian Theology, 1999; theology editor Religious Studies Rev., 1989-93; editor-at-large Christian Century, 1989-95; editor Quar. Rev., 1998-; editl. bd. Emory Theol. Studies, Religion and Ideology, Jour. of Religion, Word and World, Internat. Jour. of Practical Theology; contbr. articles to profl. publs. Recipient Alumna Achievement award Kans. Wesleyan U., 1990, Disting. Alumna award St. Paul Sch. of Theology, 1991, Founder's Day award Baker U., 1995, Alumna of Yr. award U. Chgo. Divinity Sch., 1997. Mem. Am. Acad. of Religion (pres. southeastern divsn.), Am. Theol. Soc. (chair women in leadership project). Office: Colgate U 301 James B Colgate Hall Hamilton NY 13346 Office Phone: 315-228-7444. Office Fax: 315-228-6010. E-mail: rchopp@mail.colgate.edu.*

CHOPPIN, GREGORY ROBERT, chemistry professor; b. Eagle Lake, Tex., Nov. 9, 1927; s. Gilbert P. and Nellie M. (Guidroz) C.; m. Ann M. Warner; children: Denise, Suzanne, Paul, Nadine. BS in Chemistry, Loyola U., New Orleans, 1949, DSc (hon.), 1969; PhD in Chemistry, U. Tex, 1953; DSc Tech. (hon.), Chalmers U., Göteborg, Sweden, 1985. Rsch. scientist Lawrence Radiation Lab., Berkeley, Calif., 1953-56; faculty Fla. State U., Tallahassee, 1956—, R.O. Lawton Disting. prof. chemistry, 1968—2001, prof. emeritus, 2001—. Vis. scientist Centre d'Etude Nucleaire, Mol, Belgium, 1962-63; vis. prof. Sci. U. Tokyo, 1978; vis. scientist European Transuranium Inst., Karlsruhe, Germany, 1979-80, 95; cons. Argonne Nat. Lab., Ill., Los Alamos Nat. Lab., N.Mex., Lawrence Livermore Nat. Lab., Calif., Brookhaven Nat. Lab., N.Y., Sandia Nat. Lab., N.Mex., Kaiser-Hill Co.; served on panels and commns. including NRC Chem. Sci. and Tech. Bd., NRC Radioactive Waste Mgmt. Bd. Co-author: Nuclear Chemistry: Theory and Applications, 1980, 2d edit., 1995, 3d edit., 2002; editor: Plutonium Chemistry, 1983, Actinide-Lanthanide Separations, 1985, Lanthanide Probes in Life, Chemical and Earth Sciences, 1989, Principles and Practice of Solvent Extraction, 1992, 2d edit., 2004, Separations of f-Elements, 1995, Chemical Separation Technologies and Related Methods of Nuclear Waste Management, 1999; mem. editl. bd. sci. jours. including Handbook on Physics and Chemistry of Rare Earths; co-discoverer of chemical element 101 Mendelevium; contbr. over 500 articles to sci. jours. Served to cpl. U.S. Army, 1946-48. Recipient Alexander von Humboldt Stiftung award, 1979, Chem. Mfrs. Assn. Edn. award, 1979, Seaborg Actinide Separations Sci. award, 1989, Presdl. citation, Am. Nuclear Soc., 1991, Scientist of Yr. award, Fla. Acad. Sci., 1992, Spedding award, N.Am. Rare Earth Rsch. Conf., 1996, Chem. Pioneer award, Am. Inst. Chemistry, 1997, Becquerel medal, Brit. Royal Soc. Chem., 2000, George Hevesy medal, Jour. Radiology and Nuc. Chem., 2005. Fellow AAAS; mem. Am. Chem. Soc. (award Fla. sect. 1973, So. Chemist award 1971, award in Nuclear Chemistry 1985, OESPER award Cin. sect. 1995), Royal Soc. Arts and Sci. (hon. fgn. mem.) (Sweden), Rare Earth Rsch. Conf. (pres. bd. 1981-83, chmn. 16th conf. 1983), Sigma Xi, Phi Beta Kappa. Avocations: sailing, racquetball. Home: 3290 Longleaf Rd Tallahassee FL 32310-6406 Office: Fla State U Dept Chemistry and Biochemistry Dittmer Bldg Tallahassee FL 32306-4390 Business E-Mail: choppin@chem.fsu.edu.

CHOPPIN, PURNELL WHITTINGTON, science administrator; b. Baton Rouge, July 4, 1929; s. Arthur Richard and Eunice Dolores (Bolin) Choppin; m. Joan Harriet Macdonald, Oct. 17, 1959; 1 child, Kathleen Marie. MD, La. State U., 1953; DSc (hon.), Emory U., 1988, La. State U., 1988; MD, MD, U. Cologne, 1988, D (hon.) Medicine, 1988; DSc (hon.), Tulane U., 1989, Washington U., 1991, Med. U. S.C., 1995, U. Md., Baltimore County, 1995; DHL (hon.), Mt. Sinai Sch. Medicine, 1996; DSc (hon.), U. Mass., 1999, Northwestern U., 1999; LLD (hon.), St. Francis Xavier U., 2000; DSc (hon.), Rockefeller U., 2000, Johns Hopkins U., 2002. Diplomate Am. Bd. Internal Medicine. Intern Barnes Hosp., St. Louis, 1953—54, asst. resident, 1956—57; fellow, rsch. assoc. Rockefeller U., NYC, 1957—60, asst. prof., 1960—64, assoc. prof., 1957—60, prof., sr. physician, 1970—85, Leon Hess prof. virology, 1980—85, v.p. acad. programs, 1983—85, dean grad. studies, 1985; v.p., chief sci. officer Howard Hughes Med. Inst., Chevy Chase, Md., 1985—87, pres., 1987—99, pres. emeritus, 2000—; prin. Washington Adv. Group, 2000—. Chmn. sect. 43 microbiology and immunology NAS, 1989—92, chmn. class IV med. scis., 1983—86, mem. com. on reorganization structure, 1985—86, coun., 2000—, Inst. Medicine, 1987—92, exec. com., 1988—91; mem. virology study sect. NIH, 1968—72, chmn. virology study sect., 1975—78; bd. dirs. Royal Soc. Medicine Found. Inc., NYC, 1978—93; mem. adv. com. fundamental rsch. Nat. Multiple Sclerosis Soc., 1979—84, chmn. adv. com. fundamental rsch., 1983—84; mem. adv. coun. Nat. Inst. Allergy and Infectious Diseases, 1980—83; mem. bd. scis., cons. Meml. Sloan-Kettering Cancer Ctr., NYC, 1981—86, chmn. bd. scis., 1983—84; co-chair NRA Task Force Goals and Ops., 1999—2000; mem. commn. on life scis. NRC, Washington, 1982—87; mem. sci. rev. com. Scripps Clinic and Rsch. Found., La Jolla, Calif., 1983—85, chmn. sci. rev. com., 1984; mem. coun. for rsch. and clin. investigation Am. Cancer Soc., NYC, 1983—85; mem. com. priorities for vaccine devel. Inst. Medicine, Washington; mem. governing bd. NRC, 1990—92. Contbr. articles to profl. pubs., chapters to books on virology, cell biology, infectious diseases, 1958; editor: Procs. Soc. Exptl. Biology and Medicine, 1966—69; assoc. editor: Virology, 1969—72; editor, 1973—86; assoc. editor: Jour. Immunology, 1968—72, Jour. Supramolecular Structure, 1972—75, mem. editl. bd.: Jour. Virology, 1972—85, Comprehensive Virology, 1972, mem. overseas adv. panel: Biochem. Jour., 1973—77. Capt. USAF, 1954—56, Japan. Named to alumni Hall of Distinction, La. State U., Baton Rouge, 1983; recipient Howard Taylor Ricketts award, U. Chgo., 1978, Waksman award for Excellence in Microbiology, NAS, 1984, Alumni Achievement award, Washington U. Sch. Medicine, 1990, Dean's medal, Harvard Med. Sch., 1992, Meml. Sloan-Kettering medal for outstanding contbns. to biomed. rsch., 1998, Spl. Recognition award, Assn. Am. Med. Colls., 1999, medal, U. Calif. San Francisco, 2000. Fellow: AAAS; mem.: NAS, Am. Soc. Virology (pres. 1985—86), Am. Clin. and Climatological Assn., Practitioners Soc. N.Y., Infectious Diseases Soc. Am., Soc. Cell Biology, Am. Assn. Immunologists, Harvey Soc., Am. Soc. Microbiology (chmn. virology divsn. 1977—79, divsn. group councilor 1983—85), Am. Soc. Clin. Investigation, Assn. Am. Physicians, Am. Philos. Soc. (coun. 1998—, v.p. 2000—), Am. Acad. Arts and Scis., Alpha Omega Alpha, Sigma Xi (chpt. pres. 1980—81). Office: Howard Hughes Med Inst 4000 Jones Bridge Rd Chevy Chase MD 20815-6789

CHOPRA, ANIL, oil industry executive; B in Chem. Engring., Indian Inst. Tech., Kanpur, India; PhD in Chem. Engring., U. Houston. Rsch. engr. Amoco Prodn. Co. Rsch. Ctr., Tulsa, Okla., 1982; CEO, pres. PetroTel Inc., Plano, Tex. Chmn. SPE Devel. Geology Geophysics Com., 1994. Recipient Exceptional Contbn. award, Reservoir Characterization Planning Grp., 1989, Disting. Panel Mem., 1993—96, ARCO Corp. award of Outstanding Tech. Achievement, 1995, Disting. Lectr., 1997—98, ARCO Exceptional Contbn. award, 1999. Achievements include publishing many tech. reports; actively seeking major sources of hydrocarbon for India and other countries throughout the world. Office: PetroTel Inc 5240 Tennyson Pkwy Ste 207 Plano TX 75024 Office Phone: 972-473-2767. Office Fax: 972-473-2667.

CHOPRA, DEEPAK, preventive medicine physician, writer; Medical dir. of edn. prog., CEO, founder The Chopra Center, La Costa Resort and Spa, 1995—. Author: Return of the Rishi, 1989, Quantum Healing, 1990, Perfect Health, 1990, Unconditional Life, 1991, Creating Health, 1991, Creating Affluence, 1993, Ageless Body, Timeless Mind, 1993, Restful Sleep, 1994, Perfect Weight, 1994, Journey Into Healing, 1994, The Seven Spiritual Laws of Success, 1995, Return of Merlin, 1995, Como Crear Abundancia/How to Create Wealth, 1999, Everyday Immorality: A Concise Course in Spiritual Transformation, 1999, How to Know God: The Soul's Journey into the Mystery of Mysteries, 2000, The Daughters of Joy: An Adventure of the Heart, 2002, Book of Secrets: Unlocking the Hidden Dimensions of Your Life, 2004, Peace Is the Way: Bringing War and Violence to an End in Our Time, 2005 (Quills award-religion/spirituality, 2005); (with David Simons, Vicki Abrams) Magical Beginnings, Enchanted Lives, 2005. Office: Chopra Ctr for Well Being 2100 Costa del Mar Rd Carlsbad CA 92009*

CHOPRA, INDER JIT, endocrinologist; b. Gujranwala, India, Dec. 15, 1939; came to U.S., 1967; s. Kundan Lal and Labhwati (Bagga) C.; m. Usha Prakash, Oct. 16, 1966; children: Sangeeta, Rajesh, Madhu. B of Medicine and BS, All India Inst. Med. Scis., New Delhi, India, 1961, MD, 1965. Intern All India Inst. Med. Scis., New Delhi, 1961-62, clin. resident, 1962-65, registrar in medicine, 1966-67; resident Queens Med. Ctr., Honolulu, 1967-68; fellow in endocrinology Harbor Gen. Campus UCLA Sch. Medicine, 1968-71; asst. prof. of medicine UCLA, 1971-74, assoc. prof., 1974-78, prof., 1978—. Mem. VA Merit Rev. Bd. in Endocrinology, 1988-91. Contbr. more than 280 rsch. articles, revs. and book chpts. to profl. lit. Recipient Rsch. Career Devel. award, NIH, 1972. Master Am. Coll. Physicians; mem. Endocrine Soc. (Ernst Oppenheimer award 1980), Am. Thyroid Assn. (Van Meter-Armour award 1977, Parke-Davis award 1988, Disting. Svc. award 1995), Am. Soc. Clin. Investigation, Assn. of Am. Physicians, Western Assn. Physicians, Am. Fed. for Clin. Rsch. Achievements include patent for radioimmunoassay for measurement of thyroxine and triiodothyonine. Office: UCLA Sch Medicine Ctr for Health Scis 24-130 Warren Hall 900 Veteran Ave Los Angeles CA 90024-2703 Home Phone: 818-222-5683; Office Phone: 310-825-2346. Business E-Mail: ichopra@mednet.ucla.edu.

CHOPRA, NIKHIL, systems engineer, researcher; b. New Delhi, India, Oct. 9, 1979; arrived in U.S, 2001; s. Sudhir Kumar and Madhu Chopra. BTech in Mech. Engring., Indian Inst. Tech., Kharagpur, West Bengal, 2001; MSc in Engring., U. Ill., Urbana, 2003, PhD in Sys. Engring., 2006. Grad. tchg. asst. U. Ill., Urbana, 2001, grad. rsch. asst. coord. sci. lab., 2001—06, postdoctoral rsch. assoc. coord. scis. lab., 2006—07; asst. prof. dept. mech. engring., Inst. Sys. Rsch. U. Md., College Park, 2007—. Rsch. intern Xerox Corp., Webster, NY, 2004. Contbr. scientific papers to profl. jours. Recipient Blues in Cricket and Tennis, Lala Lajpat Rai Hostel Indian Inst. Tech., 2001, Best Outgoing Sportsman, 2001, William A. Chittenden award, U. Ill.- Urbana, 2004; grantee Conf. Travel Grant, Grad. Coll. U. Ill.- Urbana, 2004; scholar, 2001, 2002, 2003, 2005, 2006; Vodafone Grad. fellow, U. Ill.- Urbana, 2003. Achievements include development of technology for efficient bilateral teleoperation over unreliable communication networks; algorithms for synchronization of networked systems. Avocations: cricket, tennis. Office: Univ Md Dept Mech Engring 2149 Glenn Martin Hall College Park MD 20742

CHOPRA, PARVEEN CHANDER, management consultant, educator, researcher, community activist; b. Punjab, India, May 2, 1941; came to U.S., 1970, naturalized, 1981; s. Om Parkash and Sumitra C.; m. Usha Bhatt, Sept. 6, 1970; children: Samir, Sachin. MA in Sociology with cert. of merit, Punjab U., India, 1966; MA with hons. in Pers. Mgmt. and Indsl. Rels., Tata Inst. Social Scis., India, 1968; BL, Bombay U., India, 1970; MBA, Baruch Coll., 1979; MPhil, CUNY, 1993, PhD in Bus. Adminstrn., 1997. Instr. mgmt. Hofstra U., Hempstead, N.Y., 1978-85, Rutgers U., Newark, N.J., 1977-78; asst. prof. mgmt. L.I. U., NYC, 1985-86, Kean Coll., N.J., 1986-91. Adj. prof. Stevens Inst. Tech., NJ, 1981-84, Fordham U., 1985—; coord. LI Jewish Abbott House Project, 1973-75; cons. NY State Legis. Inst., 1978-81; cons. on cultural diversity Mgmt. to Nassau County Med. ctr., 1997, Police Acad. 1999; mgr. adminstrn. Franco-Indian Pharms., Bombay, 1970; manpower mgmt. officer New India Assurance Co., Bombay, 1968-70; pers. mgr. Bofan Indian Textile Corp., Bombay, 1967-68; commr. Human Rights Commn., Nassau County, NY, 1989—, acctg. chmn., 2004—; vice chmn., 1996—, commr. planning 1996-2002; pres. Sunshine Mgmt. Svcs. Inc., 1998—; dir. Civil Liberties Union, NY, 2006-; advisor New Yorkers for Choice in Edn., 2006-. Author: Surveys on New York City Civil Servants, 1977, Corporate Crimes and Executive Liability: Analysis, Trends and Policy Guidelines, 1991; co-author: Organizational Communications, 1981-85; contbr. articles to profl. jours. Bd. dirs. Fedn. Indian Assns., NY, NJ, Conn., 1983—, pres. 1987-88; bd. dirs. Indian Assn. L.I., 1983—, pres. 1989-90; v.p. Indian-Am. Forum for Polit. Edn., 1990-92 (chmn., 1993-94); bd. dirs. Nassau Arts Decentralization Consortium, 1991—; mem. exec. com. Martin Luther King Jr. Celebration Com., 1990—; convener World Conf. Internat. Punjabi Soc. NY, 1991; founding mem. Nassau County Diversity Seminar, 1995—; sec. Nargis Dutt Meml. Found., 1995-96, v.p. 1997—; apptd. mem. steering com. for Asian Am. for Bush-Quayle, 1992; at-large del. Nat. Rep. Party planning com., 1996—; co-chair Bus. Coun. Global Orgn. People of Indian Origin, 1999—, co-chmn. Internat. Human Rights Coun., 2005—. Recipient numerous honors, including Ellis Island Medal of Honor, 2005, Disting. Cmty. Svc. award One Hundred Blackmen Inc., 2003, US House Reps. and US Senate, 2005; Martin Luther King award NY State Martin Luther King Commn. and MLK Celebration Com. Nassau County, 2005. Mem. Nat. Fedn. Indian Am. Assns. (nat. sec. 1992-94, exec. bd.), Jackson Heights Merchants' Assn. (NY, founder 1989—), Flushing Merchants' Assn. (NY, founder 1990—), Kiwanis Internat. (treas.), Baldwin Rep. Club (exec. bd.), Nassau County Rep. Party (committeeman election dists. in Baldwin), Ea. Acad. Mgmt., Acad. Mgmt. U.S.A., Indsl. Rels. Rsch. Assn., Asian Am. Coalition USA Inc. (founder, 1989, pres. 2006-). Avocations: marathon running, mountain climbing, indian dances. Office: PO Box 0165 Baldwin NY 11510-0165 Business E-Mail: parveenchopra@yahoo.com.

CHOPRA, PRADEEP, physician, educator; m. Shalini Chopra, Dec. 12, 1994. MD, Harvard U., 2001. Diplomate Am. Bd. Anesthesiology, 2002, sub speciality cert. in pain mgmt. Am. Bd. Anesthesiology, 2002. Asst. prof. Boston U. Med. Sch., 2001—; dir. Pain Mgmt. Ctr., So. New Eng. Anesthesia and Pain Assocs., Providence, 2002—. Contbr. chapters to books, articles to profl. jours. Recipient John Hedley-Whyte prize in Critical Care Medicine, Harvard Med. Sch., 2000, Nancy E. Oriol prize in Obstetric Anesthesia, 2000. Mem.: Am. Soc. for Interventional Pain Physicians (dir. R.I. divsn. 2002—). Achievements include design of medical simulation model for a stuck expiratory valve. Office: Southern New England Anesthesia and Pain 102 Smithfield Ave Pawtucket RI 02860 Personal E-mail: painri@yahoo.com.

CHOPRA, SAMIR, pharmaceutical and real estate company executive; b. NYC, Sept. 5, 1974; s. Parveen and Usha Chopra. BS, SUNY, 1996; MPH, Emory U., 1998; grad. Exec. Leadership Program, INSEAD, France, 2005. Sr. assoc. Ctrs. for Disease Control, Atlanta, 1996—97; cons. Huff Barrington & Owen, Atlanta, 1998; prin. Price Waterhouse Corp., NYC, 1998—2000; sr. mgr. Deloitte & Touche, NYC, 2000—04; dir. Pfizer, NYC, 2004—. Dir., chmn. judiciary com. South Asian Bar Assn., 2006. Exec. cabinet mem. Rep. Govs. Assn., NYC, 2003; N.Y. State chmn. Indian Am. Rep. Com., NYC, 2005. Recipient Bronze medal, Nat. Math. Competition, 1997, Gold medal, Columbia U. Scholastic Press Assn., 1998, W.E. Upjohn award, 2006. Mem.: N.Y. State Bar, Hindu Ctr. (trustee 2005), Iota Nu Delta (nat. dir. 2003). E-mail: samirchopra@yahoo.com.

CHOQUETTE, PAUL JOSEPH, JR., construction company executive; b. Providence, July 24, 1938; s. Paul Joseph and Virginia Josephine (Gilbane) C.; m. Elizabeth Walsh, Aug. 18, 1962; children: Jeanne Marie, Denise Elizabeth, Suzanne, Christine Noell, Paul Joseph III. BA, Brown U., 1960; LL.B., Harvard U., 1963. Assoc. firm Edwards & Angell, Providence, 1963-65; gov.'s legal counsel State of RI, Providence, 1965-67; assoc. Edwards & Angell, 1967-69; gen. counsel Gilbane Bldg. Co., Providence, 1969-71, v.p., 1971-75, exec. v.p., 1975-81, dir., CEO, 1981—2004, now chmn. Bd. dirs. FleetBoston Fin. Group, Ea. Utilities Assn., Carbide Corp., Carlisle Co.; chmn. bd. Gilbane Properties Inc. Dir. Nat. Football Found. and Coll. Hall of Fame; co-chmn. RI Econ. Policy Coun.; bd. trustee emeritus Brown U. Nat. Football Found. scholar, 1959; recipient Silver Ann. award NCAA, 1985. Mem. Greater Providence C. of C. (past pres., dir.) Clubs: Dunes, Hope, University. Roman Catholic. Office: Gilbane Bldg Co 7 Jackson Walkway Providence RI 02903

CHORBA, TIMOTHY A., lawyer, former ambassador; b. Yonkers, NY, Sept. 23, 1946; BA magna cum laude, Georgetown U., 1968; JD, Harvard U., 1972. Bar: N.Y. 1973, D.C. 1977, US Dist. Ct. (so. & ea. NY dist.), US Ct. Appeals (2d cir.). Legis. counsel to Hon. Jonathan B. Bingham US Congress, 1972-73; ptnr. Patton & Boggs LLP (formerly Patton, Boggs & Blow LLP), Washington, 1977—94, 1998—; US amb. to Singapore US Dept. State, 1994-97. Bd. dir. Wolfcraft Inc. Fulbright scholar in Internat. Law and Internat. Rels., U. Heidelberg, West Germany, 1968-69. Mem. D.C. Bar, Phi Beta Kappa, Coun. Am. Ambs. Office: Patton Boggs LLP 2550 M St NW Washington DC 20037-1350 Office Phone: 202-457-6000. Office Fax: 202-457-6315. Business E-Mail: tchorba@pattonboggs.com.

CHORIN, ALEXANDRE JOEL, mathematician, educator; b. Warsaw, June 25, 1938; came to U.S., 1962, naturalized, 1971; s. Joseph and Hannah (Judowicz) C.; m. Alice Louise Jones, Aug. 11, 1965 (div. June 2006); 1 son, Ethan Daniel; m. Esther Brass, Mar. 23, 2007. Diploma in engring., Swiss Fed. Inst. Tech., Lausanne, 1961; MSc, NYU, 1964, PhD, 1966; DSc (hon.), Israel Inst. Tech., 2003, Swiss Fed. Inst. Tech., 2005. Rsch. scientist NYU, 1966-69, asst. prof. math., 1969-71; assoc. prof. U. Calif., Berkeley, 1972-73, prof., 1973—, Miller rsch. prof., 1971-72, 82-83, Chancellor's prof., 1997-2000, Univ. prof., 2002—; sr. staff scientist Lawrence Berkeley Lab., 1980—; dir. Ctr. Pure and Applied Math. U. Calif., Berkeley, 1980—82, 1995—2004. Disting. vis. prof. Inst. for Advanced Study, Princeton, N.J., 1991-92; faculty rsch. lectr. U. Calif., Berkeley, 1999-00; vis. prof. Coll. France, 1992. Author: (with J. Marsden) A Mathematical Introduction to Fluid Dynamics, 1979, Computational Fluid Mechanics, selected papers, 1989, Vorticity and Turbulence, 1994, (with O.H. Hald) Stochastic Tools for Mathematics and Science, 2005; contbr. articles to profl. jours. Recipient Nat. Acad. Scis. award in applied math. and numerical analysis, 1989, Norbert Wiener prize Am. Math. Soc. and Soc. for Indsl. and Applied Math., 2000; fellow Sloan Found., 1972-74, Guggenheim Found., 1987-88. Fellow Am. Acad. Arts and Scis.; mem. NAS. Office: U Calif Dept Math Berkeley CA 94720-0001 Home: 522 Colusa Ave Berkeley CA 94707 E-mail: chorin@math.berkeley.edu.

CHOROSINSKI, EUGENE CONRAD, writer, poet, author; b. Sienno, Poland, Jan. 1, 1930; came to the U.S., 1954, naturalized, 1961; s. Jozef Chorosinski and Weronika Religa; m. Anni Homeier, Mar. 23, 1959; children: Heidi Marie, Ramona Angela, Veronica Ann. LLB, Blackstone Sch. of Law, 1968; MLitt (hon.), World Acad. Letters, 2005. Chief field classification AMS, Ehiopia-U.S. Mapping Mission, Addis Ababa, 1965-67; intelligence analyst Combined Intelligence Ctr. Vietnam, 1968-69; sr. intelligence advisor DCAT 70, Lai Khe, South Vietnam, 1970-71; intelligence analyst 1st Armored Divsn., Support Command, Nuremberg, Germany, 1971-73; pvt. investigator Alexandria, Va., Md., Va., Washington, 1973-74; chief zoning review Dept. of Consumer and Regulatory Affairs, Govt. D.C., 1974-85; chmn. disaster damage assessment ARC, Ctrl. Fla. chpt., Orlando, Fla., 1995-96; freelance writer Eustis, Fla., 1996-99; ret., 1999. Author: (novels) Through the Years, 1995, Days Remembered, 1999, Eugene's Saga to Freedom, War and Poetry, 2001; co-author: (anthologies) The Nat. Libr. Poetry, Famous Poets Soc., Sparrowgrass Poetry Forum, Poetry Guild, Internat. Libr. Poetry, Dr. Krishna Srinivas World Poetry; contbr. articles to profl. jours. Mem. Rep. Nat. com., 1994-04; mem. Rep. Presdl. Trust; mem. City of Eustis Parks and Trees Commn., 1996—, chmn., 1998-99; vol. Orlando, Fla., VA Healthcare Ctr., 2001—, literacy tutor, Lake County Libr. Sys., 2003-04; bd. dirs., treas.,Crooked Lake Ridge Homeowners Assn., Inc., 2006-. Decorated Bronze star, Air medal, Joint Svc. Commendation medal, Army Commendation medal, Nat. DSM with bronze svc. star, Vietnam Svc. medal with silver star, others; recipient Editor's Choice award for Outstanding Achievement in Poetry Nat. Libr. of Poetry, Honor Award Spl. Citation for Exceptional Vol. Svc., ARC, 1994, Diamond Homer trophy, 1998, Shakespeare Trophy of Excellence award, Eugene Conrad Chorosinski Poet of Yr. Medallion award, 2002, Excellence in World Poetry award, 2002, Internat. Peace Prize award, United Cultural Conv. USA, 2002, Voluntary Svc. medal Dept. Vets. Affairs, USA, 2003, Pres.'s Vol. Svc. Gold award The White House, 2005; named Best Poet, 1995, 96; declared and selected as the Poet of the Millennium 2000, Internat. Poets Acad., Chennai-86, India; named to Famous Poets Soc., Internat. Poetry Hall of Fame. Mem. VFW, DAV, Internat. Soc. of Poets (life, Poet of Merit award 2001), Nat. Assn. Ret. Fed. Employees, Crooked Lake Ridge Home Owners Assn., Inc. (treas. bd. dirs. 2006—). Roman Catholic. Avocations: chess, travel, ping pong/table tennis. Home: 131 Madrona Dr Eustis FL 32726-2016

CHORPENNING, H. R., III, minister; b. Arlington Heights, Ill., Aug. 28, 1960; s. Harry R. and Margaret E. Chorpenning; children: Cameron Hayes, Christopher Eddy. Student, U. St. Andrews, Scotland, 1981—82; BA magna cum laude, U. Calif., Santa Barbara, 1983; MDiv with distinction, Iliff Sch. Theology, Denver, 1999. Ordained min. United Ch. of Christ. Dir. devel. comm. U. Calif., Santa Barbara, 1985—87; sr. writer Stanford (Calif.) U., 1987—89; owner Hal Chorpenning Comm., Boulder, Colo., 1989—99; assoc. conf. min. Conn. Conf. United Ch. of Christ, Hartford, 1999—2002; sr. min. Plymouth Congl. Ch., Fort Collins, Colo., 2002—. Bd. dirs. Elderly Housing Mgmt., Hamden, Conn., 1999-2002, Cmty. Housing Mgmt., 1999-2002, Iliff Religious Leadership Conf.; mem. Colo. Coun. Chs. Mem. The Coalition, Interfaith Alliance, Westar Inst., Clergy Leadership Network, Phi Beta Kappa. Avocations: sea kayaking, swimming, classical music. Office: Plymouth Congregational Church UCC 916 W Prospect Rd Fort Collins CO 80526

CHORY, JOHN H., lawyer; b. 1958; BS in Computer Sci. and Psychology with honors, US Mil. Acad., West Point, 1980; MBA with honors, Golden Gate U., 1984; JD cum laude, Harvard Law Sch., 1988. Bar: Mass. 1988. Joined Wilmer, Culter, Pickering, Hale & Dorr LLP, Boston, 1988, ptnr., mem. Corp. dept., office ptnr.-in-charge Waltham, mem. exec. com.; chmn. Hale & Dorr Venture Group, Waltham. Teaching asst. Harvard Negotiation Project. Contbr. articles to profl. jours. USAR, 1978—88, intelligence officer US Army. Named a Mass. Super Lawyer-securities & venture fin., Boston Mag., 2004, High Tech All Star, Mass High Tech, 2002; named one of Boston's top lawyers, Boston Mag., 2002. Mem.: MIT

Enterprise Forum (adv. bd.). Office: Hale & Dorr Venture Group Bay Colony Corporate Ctr 1100 Winter St Waltham MA 02451 Office Phone: 781-966-2001. Office Fax: 781-966-2100. Business E-Mail: john.chory@wilmerhale.com.

CHOSET, HOWIE, engineering educator, researcher; PhD in Mech. Engring., Calif. Inst. Tech., 1996. Assoc. prof., mech. engring. and robotics Carnegie Mellon U., dir., undergraduate robotics minor. Mem., urban search and rescue response team Ctr. for Robot Assisted Search and Rescue; spkr. in field. Contbr. articles to profl. jours.; co-author: Principles of Robot Motion: Theory, Algorithms, and Implementations, 2005. Named one of Top 100 Innovators in the World Under 35, MIT Tech. Review; recipient Career award, NSF, 1997. Office: Newell Simon Hall 3211 Carnegie Mellon U 5000 Forbes Ave Pittsburgh PA 15213 Office Phone: 412-268-2495. Office Fax: 412-268-3348. Business E-Mail: choset@ri.cmu.edu.

CHOSY, JAMES LOUIS, lawyer, brokerage house executive; b. Madison, Wis., Dec. 17, 1963; s. Louis W. and Shirley A. Chosy; m. Julie Knox, Sept. 16, 1995; children: Emma Joy, Annabel. BA, U. Wis., 1986; JD magna cum laude, U. Minn., 1989. Bar: Minn. 1989. Assoc. atty. Dorsey & Whitney, Mpls., 1989—95; corp. atty. Deluxe Corp., Shoreview, Minn., 1995; assoc. gen. counsel, asst. sec. U.S. Bancorp, Mpls., 1995—2000, v.p., assoc. gen. counsel, corp. sec., 2000—01; gen. counsel Piper Jaffray, Mpls., 2001—. Mem.: ACCA, SIA, ABA. Office: Piper Jaffray Ste 800 800 Nicollet Mall Minneapolis MN 55402 Business E-Mail: jchosy@pjc.com.

CHOU, CHARISSA J., staff scientist; d. Si-Ying and Chung Yi Kao. BA in Acctg., Nat. Taiwan U., 1966; PhD in Stats., Kans. State U., 1972. CPA Pa., 1981. Statistician Kans. State U., Manhattan, Kans., 1972—73; asst. prof. Villanova U., Pa., 1974—81, assoc. prof., 1981—85; sys. analyst Rockwell Hanford Operations, Richland, Wash., 1985—88; principal scientist Westinghouse Hanford Co., Richland, 1988—93, prin. scientist, 1993—96; staff scientist V PAcific Northwest Nat. Lab., Richland, 1996—. Edtl. bd. Jour. of Environ. Monitoring and Assessment, Dordrecht, Netherlands, 2004—. Contbr. articles various profl. jours. and cptrs. in books. Recipient Outstanding Performance Svc. award, Pacific Northwest Nat. Lab., 2000, 2001, 2003, 2004, Women's Hist. Month Cert. of Honor award, 1998. Mem.: Nat. Rep. Com., Tri-Cities Chinese/Am. Assn. Achievements include development of liquid effluent monitoring program at the U.S. Dept. of Energy Hanford site. Avocations: gardening, travel, hiking. Office: Pacific Northwest Nat Lab K6-75 PO Box 999 Battelle Blvd Richland WA 99354 Office Phone: 509-372-3804. Office Fax: 509-376-2210. Business E-Mail: charissa.chou@pnl.gov.

CHOU, CHUNG-KWANG, bio-engineer; b. Chung-King, China, May 11, 1947; came to the U.S., 1969, naturalized, 1979; s. Chin-Chi and Yu-Lien (Hsiao) C.; m. Grace Wong, June 9, 1973; children: Jeffrey, Angela. BSEE, Nat. Taiwan U., 1968; MSEE, Washington U., 1971; PhD, U. Wash., 1975. Postdoctoral fellow U. Wash., Seattle, 1976-77, asst. prof., 1977-81, rsch. assoc. prof., 1981-85; rsch. scientist, head biomed. engring. sect. City of Hope Nat. Med. Ctr., Duarte, Calif., 1985-98, dir. dept. radiation rsch. divsn. radiation oncology, 1985-98; dir. Corp. RF Dosimetry Lab. Motorola, Inc., Plantation, Fla., 1998-2000; chief EME scientist, dir. Corp. EME Rsch. Lab. Motorola Inc., 2000—. Sci. adv. Mobile Mfrs. Forum, 2001—; sci. advisory bd. assoc. Motorola, 2005. Mem. editl. bd. IEEE EMC, MTT, 1999—; assoc. editor Jour. Bioelectromagnetics, 1987-2003; contbr. more than 190 articles to profl. jours. and chpts. to books. 2d lt. Army of Taiwan, 1968-69. Fellow: IEEE (subcoms. 1979—, com. on man and radiation 1990—2000, ad hoc task force on health care reform 1993—97, vice chmn. 1994—95, mem. med. tech. policy com. 1995—98, chmn. 1996—98, std. coordinating com., chmn. internat. com. electromagnetic safety, Standards medallion 2005), Motorola Sci. Adv. Bd. Assn., Electromagnetic Acad., Am. Inst. for Med. and Biol. Engring.; mem.: Internat. Radio Sci. Union, Radiation Rsch. Soc., Bioelectromagnetics Soc. (bd. dirs. 1981—84, Curtis Carl Johnson Meml. award 1995, d'Arsonval medal 2006), N.Am. Hyperthermia Soc., Internat. Microwave Power Inst. (1st Spl. Decade award 1981, Outstanding Paper award 1985), Nat. Coun. Radiation Protection and Measurements (subcom. vice chmn. 1995—2000, IEEE liaison 1997—99, coun. mem. 1998—2004), Commn. K., Tau Beta Pi, Sigma Xi. Office Phone: 954-723-5387. Business E-Mail: ck.chou@motorola.com.

CHOU, CLIFFORD CHI FONG, research engineering executive; b. Taipei, Taiwan, Dec. 19, 1940; came to U.S., 1966, naturalized, 1978; s. Ching piao and Yueh li (Huang) C.; m. Chu hwei Lee, Mar. 23, 1968; children: Kelvin Lin yu, Renee Lincy. PhD, Mich. State U., 1972. Rsch. asst. Mich. State U., East Lansing, 1967-70, Wayne State U., Detroit, 1970-72, rsch. assoc., 1972-76; rsch. engr. Ford Motor Co., Dearborn, 1976-81, sr. rsch. engr., 1981-82, prin. rsch. engr. assoc., 1982-89, prin. staff engr., 1989-93, sr. engring. specialist, 1993-95, staff tech. specialist, 1995—2003, tech. leader, 2003—07; ret. Adj. prof. Mich. Technol. U., 1997-2002, 2003—, Wayne State U., 2007—; lectr. to China under UN Devel. Program, 1987, 93, 95, lectr. to Taiwan under Automotive Rsch. and Test Ctr., 1991, 97, 98, 2005; organizer Safety Test Methodology, SAE session chair, 1997-2007, SAE fellow nom. com., 2004-07, IBEC session chair 1999, 2000, 2004; coord. Detroit Automobile Tech. Conf., 1993, session chair, 1997; mem. safety and environ. systems planning com. IBEC '98, 1997-2000, 01-03; indsl. acad. adv. to PhD Coms., U. Mich., 1995-98, Mich. Tchrs. U., 1997-2000, Wayne State U., 2006—; tchr. in field; co-organizer 6th U.S. Nat. Conf. on Computational Mechs., crashworthiness session, Dearborn, 2001; mem. safety tech. com. China SAE, 2002—, mem. nomination com., 2004-07. US regional editor Internat. Jour. Vehicle Safety, 2005-; contbr. chpts. to books, articles to profl. jours. Recipient Safety Engring. Excellence award Nat. Hwy. Traffic Safety Adminstrn., 1980, Best Paper award IBEC, 2002; grantee Soc. Automotive Engrs. Fellow: ASME, Soc. Automotive Engrs. (Forest R. McFarland award 2000, 2007); mem.: AIAA, Detroit Chinese Am. Assn., Mich. Chinese Acad. Profl. Assn. (bd. dirs. 1992—93, pres. 1993—94, advisor 1994—, seminar spkr. 2000), Ford Chinese Club (pres. 1991—92), Sigma Xi. Achievements include 8 patents. Avocations: travel, karaoke, ballroom dancing. Home: 28970 Forest Hill Dr Farmington Hills MI 48331-2439 Office: Wayne State U Bioengring Ctr 818 Hancock Detroit MI 48201 Home Phone: 248-489-5926; Office Phone: 313-577-0703. Business E-Mail: chou@rrb.eng.wayne.edu.

CHOU, JOHN G., lawyer; BA, Harvard Univ.; JD, Univ. Pa. Sr. legal positions CIGNA Corp.; chief corp. counsel, chief European counsel ARCO Chem. Co.; ptnr. Eckert Seamans Cherin & Mellott; v.p., dep. gen. counsel, sec. AmerisourceBergen Corp., Chesterbrook, Pa., 2002—07, sr. v.p., gen. counsel, sec., 2007—. Office: AmeriscorceBergen Corp Ste 100 1300 Morris Dr Chesterbrook PA 19087*

CHOU, STEPHEN Y., electrical engineer, educator; PhD, MIT, 1986. Rsch. assoc., acting asst. prof. Stanford U., Calif., 1986—89; asst. prof. U. Minn., 1989—91, assoc. prof., 1991—94, prof., 1994—97; positions up to Joseph C. Elgin prof. engring., prof. elec. engring., head Nanostructure Lab. Princeton U., NJ, 1998—. Founder Nanonex, 1999; co-founder NanoOpto, 2000. Contbr. articles to sci. jours. Named to NJ High Tech. Hall of Fame, 2005; recipient Pioneer award of Nanoimprint and Nanoprint Tech.; Packard fellow, 1990. Fellow: IEEE (Cledo Brunetti award 2004); mem.: NAE. Achievements include invention of a revolutionary technique to create the ultra-small features on computer chips using a nanometer-scale mold; patents in field. Office: Princeton U Dept Elec Engring Engring Quadrangle Olden St Princeton NJ 08544 Office Phone: 609-258-4416. Office Fax: 609-258-6279. E-mail: chou@princeton.edu.*

CHOU, SUNLIN, retired computer company executive; BSEE, MIT, 1966, MSEE, 1967; PhD in Elec. Engring., Stanford U., 1971. Devel. engr. Intel Corp., 1971—80, dir. tech. devel., 1980—88, v.p. Tech. and Mfg. Group, 1988—92, corp. v.p., 1992—98, sr. v.p. and gen. mgr. Tech. and Mfg. Group, 1998—2005. Mem.: NAE.

CHOU, TING-CHAO, inventor, educator; b. Taiwan, Sept. 9, 1938; arrived in U.S., 1965, naturalized, 1976; s. Chao-Yun and Sheng-Mei (Chen) C.; m. Dorothy Tsui-chin Tseng, June 26, 1965; children: Joseph Hsin-I, Julia Hsin-Ya. BS, Kaohsiung Med. Coll., Taiwan, 1961; MS, Nat. Taiwan U., 1965; PhD, Yale U., 1970. Tchg. asst. pharmacology Nat. Taiwan U., 1964-65; rsch. asst. pharmacology Yale U., 1969; postdoctoral fellow Johns Hopkins U., Balt., 1969-72; assoc. Sloan-Kettering Inst. Cancer Rsch., NYC, 1972-78, assoc. mem., 1978—88, acting chmn. dept. pharmacology, 1984—88, mem., 1988-95, head lab. biochmn. pharmacology, 1988-98, dir. preclin. pharmacology core lab., 1995—. Asst. prof. Grad. Sch. Med. Sci. Cornell U., 1972—78, assoc. prof., 1978—88, prof. pharmacology, 1988—2000; vis. prof. Chinese Second Mil. Med. U., Shanghai, 1992—, Tonji Med. U., 1993—, Nanjing Med. U., China, 1994—; hon. prof. Chinese Acad. Med. Scis., Beijing, 1993—, Chinese Acad. Mil. Med. Scis., Beijing, 1995—; cons. in field. Author (with J. Chou): Dose Effect Analysis with Microcomputers, 1986; author: (with M. Hayball) CalcuSyn for Windows, Biosoft, 1996; author: (with N. Martin) CompuSyn for Drug Combinations, ComboSyn Inc., 2004; co-editor (with D. Rideout): Synergism and Antogonism in Chemotherapy, 1991; mem. editl. adv. bd.: Cancer Biochemistry Biophysics, 1984—2004, Jour. of the Nat. Cancer Inst., 1988—92, Kaohisung Jour. Med. Scis., 1992—, chmn. pub. bd.: Bio/Pharma Quar., 1995—2002; contbr. scientific papers over 275 articles on cancer, and AIDS chemotherapy and theoretical biology to profl. jours.; cited in over 9,800 sci. papers in bio-med. jours. Chmn. Lim-Wang Meml. Scholarship Fund, 1998—2003; mem. adv. bd. divsn. biotechnology and pharm. rsch. Nat. Health Rsch. Inst., Taiwan, 2001—02. Rsch. grantee Nat. Cancer Inst., Nat. Inst. of Allergy and Infectious Diseases, Elsa U. Pardee Found. and Am. Cancer Soc., 1975—. Mem. AAAS, Am. Assn. Cancer Rsch., Am. Soc. Pharmacology and Exptl. Therapeutics, Am. Soc. Preventive Oncology (founding mem.), Am. Soc. for Biochem. and Molecular Biol., Am. Bur. Med. Advancement in China (bd. dirs. 1991-2003, v.p. 1994-98), NY Acad. Sci., Kaohsiung Med. Coll. Alumni Assn. Am. (bd. dir. 1968-91, pres. 1972), Harvey Soc., Sigma Xi. Achievements include 24 US patents ranked among the top 99 percentile based on the US Patent and Trademark Office records; inventions mainly in anticancer agents including desoxyepothilones, ardeemins, ningalins, and iso-oxazolefludelone; creator of the unified theory of dose and effect, median-effect equation and plot, multiple drug effect equation, combination index theorem and plot, dose-reduction index and plot, and polygonogram; life-time theoretical work was published in a leading scientific journal, Pharmacological Reviews in 2006. Office: Sloan-Kettering Inst Cancer Rsch 1275 York Ave New York NY 10021-6007 Business E-Mail: chout@mskcc.org.

CHOU, WUSHOW, retired computer scientist; b. Shanghai, Kiangsu, China, Feb. 12, 1939; m. Lena Sun, Apr. 17, 1965; children: Warren, Wesley. BEE, Cheng Kung U., Tainan, Taiwan, 1961; MEE, U. N.Mex., 1965; PhD in Elec. Engring. and Computer Sci., U. Calif., Berkeley, 1968. Acting asst. prof. U. Calif., Berkeley, 1968-69; v.p. Network Analysis Corp., Glen Cove, NY, 1969-76; vis. prof. SUNY, Stony Brook, 1976; rsch. prof. George Washington U., Washington, 1975-76; prof. computer sci. dept. and elec. and computer engring. dept. NC State U., Raleigh, 1976—2003, prof. emeritus, 2003—, dir. computer studies, 1976-88; dep. asst. sec. for info. systems U.S. Dept. Treasury, Washington, 1994-97, chief info. officer, 1996-97; ret. Pres. ACK Computer Applications, Cary, NC, 1978—93; vis. prof. Poly. U., Bklyn., 1988—89; cons. AT&T, IBM, U.S. Govt., Singapore Govt., French Govt. Author, editor: Computer Communication, Vol. 1, 1984, Vol. 2, 1985, Advances in Telecommunications, 1985—86, editor-in-chief: Jour. Telecom., 1982—85, IT Profl., 1998—2001; chmn. adv. bd. IT Profl., 2002—; contbr. articles to profl. jours. Recipient award, GSA, Washington, 1988, Treasury Dept., 1997; Rsch. grantee, NSF, 1978, Army Rsch. Office, 1982, AT&T, 1987. Fellow: IEEE (award 2001, 2002), Assn. Computing Machines. Office: NC State U Dept Computer Sci PO Box 8206 Raleigh NC 27695-0001 Business E-Mail: chou@ncsu.edu.

CHOUDHARY, ABDUR RAHIM, physics professor; b. Hoshiarpur, India, Jan. 16, 1944; s. Ali Mohammad and Khadija Begum Choudhary; m. Yasmeen Sultana Choudhary, Feb. 25, 1977; children: Rehan, Saba, Farhan, Adnan. Assoc. degree, D. J. Sci. Coll., Karachi, Pakistan, 1964; B in Physics, U. Karachi, 1967, MS in Physics, 1968; PhD in Theoretical Physics, U. London, 1971. Math. tchr. Darussafaka Lisesi, Istanbul, Turkey, 1972; vis. prof. Cath. U. Louvain, Louvain-La-Neuve, Belgium, 1972—74; solvay found. fellow U. Libre De Bruxells, Brussels, 1974—75; vis. scientist Internat. Ctr. Theoretical Physics, Trieste, Italy, 1975, UNESCO/IAEA, ICTP, Trieste, 1975; asst. prof., physics dept. Al-Mustansiriyah U., Baghdad, Iraq, 1975—76; assoc. prof., math. dept. Bayero U., Kano, Nigeria, 1977—84; sr. analyst Sys. & Rsch. Corp., Landover, Md., 1984; sr. mem. tech. staff Computer Scis. Corp., Greenbelt, Md., 1986—89; engring. specialist Loral Corp., Lanham, Md., 1989—92; chief sys. engr. Hughes STX, Lanham, 1992—96; mem. tech. staff Bell Labs., Middletown, NJ, 1996—2003; scientist SI Internat., Reston, Va., 2004—07; prof., computer sci. dept. Internat. U., Kualampur, Malaysia, 2007—. Author: (book) Mental Hijrah: Towards a Unified Muslim World-View, 2003; contbr. articles to profl. jours. Mem. planning com. US Mil. Acad., Info. Assurance Workshop, Westpoint, NY, 2004—07; co-chair policy work grp. Transformational Satellites Analysis Workshop, 2005—06. Solvay Found. fellow, Free U. Brussells, 1974. Mem.: IEEE. Islam. Avocations: travel, poetry. Home: 6426 Grendel Pl Bowie MD 20720 Office: SI Internat 12012 Sunset Hills Rd Reston VA 20190 Personal E-mail: rahimchoudhary@yahoo.com. Business E-Mail: rahim.choudhary@si-intl.com.

CHOUDHARY, ADIL MUSHTAQ, gastroenterologist; b. Dec. 19, 1964; MB, BChir, U. Karachi, Pakistan, 1989. Diplomate in internal medicine and gastroenterology Am. Bd. Internal Medicine, in Gastroenterology Am. Bd. Internal Medicine. Intern medicine/gen. surgery Civil Hosp. and Dow Med. Coll., Karachi, 1990, resident internal medicine, 1991—93, NYU VA/Bellevue Hosp. Ctr., Manhattan, 1993—96; tchg. asst. medicine NYU Sch. Medicine, Manhattan, 1994—96; fellow gastroenterology Yale U. Gastroenterology Program at Bridgeport (Conn.) Hosp., 1996—99; advanced fellow therapeutic gastrointestinal endoscopy Tulane U. Med. Ctr., New Orleans, 1999; pvt. practice gastroenterology and internal medicine Rio Pecos Med. Assocs., Roswell, N.Mex., 1999—2000, Digestive Disease Inst., So. N.Mex. Med. Assocs., Roswell, 2001—; clin. asst. prof. medicine U. N. Mex. Sch. Medicine, 2003—. Vol. tchg. faculty family practice residency Ea. N.Mex. Med. Ctr., Roswell, mem. pharmacy and therapeutics com.; vol. pharmacy practice faculty U. N.Mex. Coll. Pharmacy, Albuquerque, 2001—02; mem. grad. med. edn. com. Ea. N.Mex. Family Practice Residency Program, 2001—; bd. dirs. Southeastern N.Mex. Physicians IPA, Inc.; presenter in field. Contbr. articles to profl. jours. Recipient Man of Yr., Am. Biographical Inst., 2005; Janssen Pharmaceutica USA scholar, World Congress Gastroenterology, Vienna, 1998. Fellow: ACP, Royal Soc. Medicine, Royal Inst. Pub. Health, Royal Soc. for Promotion of Health, Am. Soc. Gastrointestinal Endoscopy, Am. Gastroent. Assn., Am. Coll. Gastroenterology (Cert. for outstanding contbn. to the field of gastroenterology and hepatology 1999, 1997); mem.: AMA (Physician's Recognition award in continuing med. edn. 1998—2001, 1999—2002), Crohn's and Colitis Found. Am., Inc., Am. Assn. for Study Liver Diseases. Home: 5 Victoria Ct Roswell NM 88201 Office: 303 W Country Club Rd Roswell NM 88201 Office Phone: 505-623-1442.

CHOUDHURY, BIKRAM, yoga instructor, writer, entrepreneur; b. Calcutta, India, 1946; Founder Yoga Coll. India, LA. Author: Bikram's Beginning Yoga Class, 1978, Bikram Yoga: The Guru Behind Hot Yoga Shows the Way to Radiant Health and Personal Fulfillment, 2007, Bikram's Beginning Yoga Class, 2003. Office: Bikram Yoga Coll India 1862 S La Cienega Blvd Los Angeles CA 90035 Office Phone: 310-854-5800. Office Fax: 310-854-6200. E-mail: Bikram@BikramYoga.com.*

CHOUDHURY, DIPA, mathematician, educator; b. Dhaka, Bangladesh, Feb. 1, 1953; d. Sisir and Monorama Sarkar; m. Japobrata Choudhury, July 18, 1972; children: Progga-Paromita, Atish-Dipankar. PhD, Johns Hopkins U., 1986. Asst. prof. Loyola Coll., Balt., 1986—94, assoc. prof., 1994—, chair, math. scis., 2006—. Tchg. Fulbright scholar Kenyatta U., Kenya, 1995—96, Dhaka U., Bangladesh, 2004—05. Contbr. articles to profl. jours. Pres. Sanskriti, Washington, 1998—99. Mem.: Math. Assn. Am. (program chmn. Md./D.C./Va. sect. 2002—). Home: 13026 Broadmore Rd Silver Spring MD 20904 Office: Loyola Coll 4501 N Charles St Baltimore MD 21210 Office Phone: 410-617-2898. Business E-Mail: dchoudhury@loyola.edu.

CHOUDHURY, RAJ DEO, automotive executive; b. NYC, 1969; s. Deo Chand and Annette Patricia Choudhury; m. Margarete Haeusler, 2002; 1 child, Amalia. BA, Princeton U., 1990; MA, Stanford U., 1993. Evaluation analyst Arco Alaska Inc., Anchorage, 1993—96; sr. planning analyst Atlantic Richfield Co., LA, 1996—99; mgr. fuel infrastructure and bus. devel. fuel cell activities Gen. Motors Corp., Mainz Kastel, Germany, 1999—2003, mgr. pub. policy Pub. Policy Ctr. Washington, 2003—. Contractor U.S. Army Rsch., Devel. and Engring. Command, 2004—. Author: On the Theory of Repeated Games, 1990; co-author: Well-to-Wheel Energy Use and Greenhouse Gas Emissions of Advanced Fuel-Vehicle Systems for North Am., 2001, Well-to-Wheel Energy Use and Greenhouse Gas Emissions of Advanced Fuel-Vehicle Systems for Europe, 2002. Mentor US Dept. Def. Dep. Sch., Wiesbaden, Germany, 1999—2002. Mem.: Meridian Internat. Ctr., Am. Radio Relay League, Internat. Assn. for Energy Econs. (bd. dirs. Anchorage chpt. 1995—96), Nat. Hydrogen Assn. (bd. dirs. 2003—), Soc. Automotive Engrs., Princeton Club of Washington, Mountaineering Club Alaska, Sigma Xi. Avocations: photography, international travel, amateur radio, mountain climbing. Office: Gen Motors Corp 25 Massachusetts Ave NW Ste 400 Washington DC 20001 Home Phone: 202-722-1880; Office Phone: 202-775-5033. Business E-Mail: raj.choudhury@gm.com.

CHOUERY, FARID ALEXANDRE, electrical and structural engineer, consultant; b. Cairo, Feb. 2, 1951; arrived in U.S., 1969; s. Alexandre Choukri and Yvonne Emile Chouery; m. Bernice Joan Furdal Chouery, Aug. 18, 1978; 1 child, Alexis Kristina. BSEE, U. Wash., Seattle, 1974, MSEE, 1979, MSCE in Structural Engring., 1984. Registered profl. engr., Wash. Design electronics engr. Nortec Corp., Tri-Cities, Wash., 1975—76; design elec. engr. Kenworth Truck Co., Kirkland, Wash., 1976—79; mgmt. in tng. GTE of the NW, Everett, Wash., 1979—80; cons. engr. Matrix Engring./DBM Inc., Federal Way, Wash., 1980—87; spl. assignment engr. ABKJ Inc., Seattle, 1988—91; testing engr. and proof reader Microsoft Corp., Redmond, Wash., 1993; pres., CEO and engr. FAC Systems Inc., Seattle, 1988—. Math tutor Seattle Ctrl. C.C., 1971—72. Author: Visualize Jesus: Ten Ways to Christian Meditation, 2006; composer: (15 minute symphony) The 21st Century. Scholar, Electric League of the Pacific NW, 1973—74. Independent. Christian. Achievements include patents in field. Avocations: guitar, composing, poetry, photography, travel. Business E-Mail: farid@facsystems.com.

CHOUINARD, YVON, sportswear outfitter executive; b. Lewiston, Maine, Nov. 9, 1938; s. Gerard and Yvonne (Lizzotte) C.; m. Carol Lamb, 1962 (div. 1963); m. Malinda Pennoyer, Dec. 25, 1970; children: Fletcher, Claire. LHD (hon.), Yale U., 1995. Founder Chouinard Equipment, Burbank, Calif., 1957, Great Pacific Iron Works, Inc., Ventura, Calif., 1970, Lost Arrow Corp., Ventura, 1974—, Patagonia Inc., Ventura, 1976—. Author: Climbing Ice, 1978, Let My People Go Surfing, 2005. Active Surf Rider Orgn., various environ. orgns. worldwide. With U.S. Army, 1962-64, Korea. Mem. Am. Alpine Club. Democrat. Avocations: tennis, skiing, kayaking, sailing, surfing. Office: Lost Arrow Corp 259 W Santa Clara St Ventura CA 93001

CHOUKAS-BRADLEY, JAMES RICHARD, lawyer; b. Hartford, Conn., Sept. 11, 1950; s. William Lee and Paula Ann (Elliott) Bradley; m. Melanie Rose Choukas, June 21, 1975; children: Sophia Crane, Jesse Elliott. BA cum laude, U. Vt., 1974; JD cum laude, Georgetown U., 1980. Bar: D.C. 1980, U.S. Ct. Appeals (D.C. cir.) 1981, U.S. Ct. Appeals (11th cir.) 1984, U.S. Ct. Appeals (10th cir.) 1985, U.S. Ct. Appeals (4th cir.) 1990, U.S. Ct. Appeals (6th cir.) 1993. Reporter, editor The Berlin (N.H.) Reporter, The Groveton (N.H.) News, The Northland News, 1973—74; editor, pub., creative dir. Ad Lib, Gorham, NH, 1974—75; asst. to city mgr. City of Berlin, 1975—77; contbg. reporter The Lewiston (Maine) Sun, 1976; legal intern Congl. Budget Office, Washington, 1978; rsch. assoc. Schlossberg-Cassidy & Assocs., Washington, 1978—80; assoc. Miller, Balis & O'Neil, P.C., Washington, 1980—84, mem., v.p., 1985—, exec. com., 1993—97. Legal advisor, 1st v.p. Sugarloaf Citizens Assn., Dickerson, Md., 1987—2000; counsel Mcpl. Gas Authority of Ga., Lower Ala. Gas Dist., Pub. Gas Ptnrs., S.E. Ala. Gas Dist., Ala. Mcpl. Distbrs. Group, Tenn. Customer Group, Mcpl. Gas Authority of Miss., Ctrl. Plains Energy Project; gen. counsel Tenn. Energy Acquisition Corp.; spkr. in field; pioneer in joint action and pub. financing in deregulated natural gas industry. Author: The Early Days, 1975; co-author: Report on Dynamics of Natural Gas Markets and Projected Gas Prices for 2005 and Beyond, 2005. Pres. D.C. Dukes Athletic Club, Washington, 1978-81, Montgomery Dukes, 1987-92; com. chmn. Berlin Bicentennial Commn., Berlin, 1975-76; youth soccer and flag football coach Seneca Sports Assn., 1999-2005; youth soccer coach Montgomery Soccer, Inc., 2005-06. Regents scholar State of N.Y., 1968. Mem.: Hist. Medley Dist., Energy Bar Assn., For A Rural Montgomery, Nat. Youth Sports Coaches Assn., Sugarloaf Citizens Assn., Audubon Naturalist Soc., Am. Farmland Trust, Randolph Mountain Club, Phi Beta Kappa. Avocations: softball, guitar, hiking, piano, singing-songwriting. Office: 1140 19th St NW Ste 700 Washington DC 20036 Home: 7100 Oakridge Ave Chevy Chase MD 20815 Address: 24130 Old Hundred Rd Dickerson MD 20842 Home Phone: 301-652-8799; Office Phone: 202-296-2960. Business E-Mail: jchoukasbradley@mbolaw.com.

CHOUKAS-BRADLEY, MELANIE, writer, photographer; b. Jacksonville, NC, Aug. 20, 1952; d. Michael Jr. and Juanita May (Crosby) Choukas; m. James Richard Bradley, June 21, 1975; children: Sophia Crane, Jesse Elliott. BA in English, U. Vt., Burlington, 1974; student, Pierce Coll., Athens, 1971; postgrad., U.S. Dept. Agr. Grad. Sch., Chevy Chase, Md., 1995—. From reporter to news dir. Radio Sta. WBRL, Berlin, N.H., 1975-77; rsch. asst. subcom. on oversight and investigations Commerce Com., U.S. Ho. of Reps., Washington, 1978; writer, 1978—. Earth Day chmn. Sugarloaf Citizens Assn., Barnesville, Md., 1990-92, programs and edn. dir., Celebrate Rural Montgomery, 2005, instr. botany USDA Grad. Sch., 2006—. Author: City of Trees, 1987, Sugarloaf: The Mountain's History, Geology and Natural Lore, 2003, An Illustrated Guide to Eastern Woodland Wildflowers and Trees, 2004; contbr. articles to Washington Post, Audubon Naturalist News, others. Dir. programs and edn. Celebrate Rural Montgomery Campaign, 2005; mem. tree ordinance bd. Town of Chevy Chase, Md., tree ordinance bd.; bd. dirs. Md. Native Plant

Soc., 2005—; panel discussion moderator DC Environ. Film Festival, 2007. Grantee Am. Forest Inst., Nat. Forest Products Assn., Time Inc., Bendix, Union Camp Corp., 1978-81, naturalist lead field trips for Audubon Naturalist Soc., 2000—; grantee Sugarloaf Regional Trails, 1995, 2001. Mem. Md. Native Plant Soc. (bd. dirs.). Democrat. Achievements include member Capitol Steps adult synchronized skating team, participant National Championships 2001 and 2002; member Capital Classics synchronized skating team, 2003-04, 04-05. Avocations: botany, hiking, cross country skiing, synchronized figure skating, ice dancing. Personal E-mail: choukas@erols.com.

CHOUTEAU, KRISTIN N., engineer; d. Kim Chouteau; m. Brian Zapata, July 21, 2006. BSChemE, U. NC, Charlotte, 2000—03. Cert. Mbb, Six Sigma, 2006. Quality & productivity engr. Bank Am., Charlotte, 2003—. Com. mem. Jr. League, Charlotte, 2004—06. Grantee fellow, NSF, 2003. Home Phone: 704-904-1865.

CHOVANES, EUGENE, lawyer; b. Hazleton, Pa., Jan. 1, 1926; s. Michael and Anna (Watro) C.; m. Claire Amelia Puhak, Mar. 27, 1952; children: Michael, George, Nicholas, Joseph, John. BS in Engring., Lehigh U., 1950; JD, Villanova U., 1960. Bar: Pa. 1961. Assoc. William Steell Jackson & Sons, Phila., 1957-63; ptnr. Jackson & Chovanes, Phila. and Bala-Cynwyd, Pa., 1963—. Lectr. patent law Villanova U., 1957-80. Sgt. U.S. Army, 1943-46, to 1st lt. Ordnance Corps, 1951-52. Mem. ABA, Phila. Intellectual Property Law Assn., Phila. Bar Assn., Soc. Registered Profl. Engrs., Am. Intellectual Property Law Assn. Office: 1 Bala Plz Ste 319 Bala Cynwyd PA 19004-1405

CHOW, ANTHONY SHONG-YU, library sciences educator; b. Tallahassee, Fla., Feb. 7, 1969; s. Chak and Lynne Chow; m. Theresa Ann DeWert, June 16, 1993; children: Alex, Maegan, Emma. D Instrnl. Sys., Fla. State U., Tallahassee, Fla., 2007. Rsch. assoc. Fla. State U., Tallahassee, 2000—06; asst. prof. U. NC, Greensboro, 2006—. Comm. coord. AECT, Bloomington, Ind., 2006—. Fellow Coll. Tchg. award, Fla. State U. Coll. Edn., 1996. Mem.: ALA, ASIST, ALISE, Pi Lamda Theta. Office: Univ NC Greensboro 305 Curry Bldg Greensboro NC 27402 Office Phone: 336-334-3411. Office Fax: 336-334-5060. Business E-Mail: aschow@uncg.edu.

CHOW, CHI-MING, retired mathematics professor; b. Tai-Yuan, Shansi, Republic of China, Nov. 15, 1931; arrived in U.S., 1959; s. Wei-Han Chow and Lu-Tsen Hsu. Cert. tech. officer, Chinese Air Force Tech. Inst., 1954; BS in Math., Ch. Coll. Hawaii, 1962; MS in Math., Oreg. State U., 1965. Tech. officer Chinese Air Force, 1954—59; prof. math. Oakland (Mich.) CC, 1965—92; ret., 1992. Author: The sight area A of a moving body is inversely proportional to the square of the distance D between the body and observing point, i.e. A=C/(DxD), where C is a constant; contbr. articles to profl. jours. including The Math. Tchr., 1965. 1st lt. Air Force Republic of China, 1954—59. Mem.: Pi Mu Epsilon. Achievements include first to proof of A=C/(DxD), where C is a constant. Avocation: piloting aircraft. Home: PO Box 903 Novi MI 48376-0903

CHOW, HUMPHREY WAI, mechanical engineer; b. Hoi Ping, Guangzhou, China, Feb. 7, 1954; came to U.S., 1972; s. Lai and Ming-Kuen (Wong) C.; m. Joanna Qi Deng, Nov. 17, 1988; children: Genevieve Daisy, Daphne Jolie. BSME, U. Mass., Lowell, 1978; MS, Ga. Inst. Tech., 1984; PhD, Rensselaer Poly. Inst., 1993; MS in Engring. Mgmt., Tufts U., 2002. Product design engr. GE Medium Power Transformers, Rome, Ga., 1979-82; mech. design engr. GE Ordnance Sys., Pittsfield, Mass., 1984-85; rsch. asst. Rensselaer Poly. Inst., Troy, N.Y., 1985-87; sr. mech. design engr. GE Power Sys., Schenectady, NY, 1987—90; teaching asst. Rensselaer Poly. Inst., Troy, 1990-93; dynamic analysis engr. GE Naval & Drive Turbine Sys., Fitchburg, Mass., 1993-94; methods devel. engr. Knolls Atomic Power Lab., Schenectady, 1994-96; staff engr. GE Aircraft Engines, Lynn, Mass., 1996-98, 99—, GE Deutschland, Frankfurt, Germany, 1998-99. Contbr. articles to profl. jours. including European Jour. Mechanics. Mem.: AIAA, ASME, Am. Soc. for Engring. Mgmt. Achievements include patents for rotor coil connectors of turbine generators; design of propulsion turbine generator for the Navy integrated electric drive program; methods development for nuclear fuel and core design analysis in the Navy nuclear propulsion program; metal forming process modeling of compressor airfoils manufacturing for aircraft engines; qualification of high pressure compressor for USAF trainer aircraft. Office: GE Aviation 1000 Western Ave Lynn MA 01910-0001

CHOW, JOAN K., food products executive; b. 1960; BA in Linguistics, Cornell U., Ithaca, NY; MBA, U. Pa. Wharton Sch. Bus. Various mgmt. positions Johnson & Johnson Products Inc., 1986—91, Info. Resources Inc., 1991—98; various mgmt. positions through sr. v.p., chief mktg. officer Sears Roebuck & Co., 1998—2007; exec. v.p., chief mktg. officer ConAgra Foods, Inc., Omaha, 2007—. Office: ConAgra Foods Inc 1 ConAgra Dr Omaha NE 68102-5001 Office Phone: 402-595-4000.*

CHOW, POO, forester; b. Shanghai, Apr. 27, 1934; arrived in U.S., 1960, naturalized, 1971; s. Kai and Yung-Kwan (Hsieh) C.; m. Ai-Yu Kuo, July 17, 1965; children: Eugenia, Andrew E. MS in Forest Products, La. State U., 1961; PhD in Wood Sci. and Tech., Forestry, Mich. State U., 1969. Lab. dir. Pope and Talbot, Inc., Oakridge, Oreg., 1962-67; asst. prof. wood sci. U. Ill., Urbana, 1969-74, assoc. prof., 1974-80, prof., 1980—. Sr. Fulbright scholar, Fed. Republic Germany; cons. to industry; external examiner U. Ibadan, Nigeria; expert witness. Contbr. numerous articles to profl. jours.; patentee in field. Mem. ASTM, Forest Products Soc., Soc. Wood Sci. and Tech., Am. Railway Engrs. and Maintenance-of-Way Assn., Internat. Rsch. on Wood Preservation Group, German Wood Technology Soc., RR Tie Assn., Am. Wood Preservatives Assn., Xi Sigma Pi. Office: Univ Ill 1102 S Goodwin Ave Urbana IL 61801-4730

CHOW, RITA KATHLEEN, nursing consultant; b. San Francisco, Aug. 19, 1926; d. Peter and May (Chan) Chow. BS, Stanford U., 1950, nursing diploma, 1950; MS, Case Western Res. U., 1955; profl. diploma in nursing edn. adminstrn, Columbia U., 1961, EdD, 1968; B of Individualized Studies, George Mason U., 1983. Asst. in teaching Stanford U., Calif., 1951—52; instr., dir. student health Fresno Gen. Hosp. Sch. Nursing, Calif., 1952—54; instr. Wayne State U. Coll. Nursing, Detroit, 1957—58; rsch. assoc., project dir. cardiovasc. nursing rsch. Ohio State U., Columbus, 1965—68; commd. officer USPHS, 1968, advanced through grades to nurse dir. (capt.), 1974; spl. asst. to dep. dir. Nat. Ctr. Health Svcs. Rsch., Health Svcs. and Mental Health Adminstrn., HEW, Rockville, Md., 1969—73, dep. dir. manpower utilization br., 1970—73; dep. dir. Office Long Term Care; dep. chief nurse officer USPHS, Rockville, 1973—77; chief quality assurance br. div. long-term care Office Stds. and Certification, Health Standards and Quality Bur., Health Care Fin. Adminstrn., HHS, 1977—82; supervisory clin. nurse and spl. asst. to health systems adminstr. USPHS Indian Hosp., IHS, HHS, Rosebud, SD, 1982—83; dir. patient edn., asst. dir. nursing G. W. Long Hansen's Disease Ctr., USPHS, Carville, La., 1984—89; dir. nursing Fed. Med. Ctr., Ft. Worth, 1989—95; pvt. cons., 1995—98; dir. Nat. Interfaith Coalition on Aging, Natl. Coun. on Aging, Washington, 1998—. Author: (book) Identifying Nursing Action with the Care of Cardiovascular Patients, 1967, Cardiosurgical Nursing Care: Understandings, Concepts and Principles for Practice, 1975; mem. editl. bd. Nursing and Health Care, 1983—95; contbr. articles to profl. jours. With Nurse Corps US Army, 1954—57, with USAR, 1954—68. Recipient Nursing Svc. award, Assn. Mil. Surgeons U.S., 1969, Commendation medal, USPHS, 1972, Meritorious Svc. medal, 1977, DSM, 1987, citation for outstanding contbn. to cardiovascular nursing, Am. Heart Assn., 1972—79, award for disting. achievement in nursing rsch., Nursing Edn. Alumni Assn., Columbia U. Tchrs. Coll., 1973, Disting. Alumnus award, Case Western Res. U. Sch. Nursing, 1979, Women's Honors in Pub. Svcs. award, ANA, 1988, USPHS Commendable Svc. medal, U.S. Dept. Justice, Bur. Prisons, 1995, Holistic Nurse of the Yr. award, Am. Holistic Nurses Assn., 2001, Artist of Life First prize, Internat. Womens Writing Guild, 1987, Chief Nurse Officer award, USPHS, 2003; grantee, Sigma Theta Tau, 1966. Fellow: Am. Assn. Advancement Sci., Am. Acad. Nursing, Gerontological Soc. Am., Nat. Gerontological Nursing Assn., Am. Assn. of Integrative Medicine (diplomate Coll. of Nursing 2003).

CHOW, STEPHEN (SING-CHI CHOW), actor; b. Hong Kong, June 22, 1962; Actor: (TV series) Sou hat yi, 1982, The Legend of the Condor Heros, 1982, Wut lik sap jat, 1982, The Justice of Life, 1983, Joi geen sup gao sui, 1983, But dou san hung, 1983, Sung meng chi loi, 1987, Happy Encounter, 1987, Mo min kap sin fung, 1988, The Last Conflict, 1988, My Father's Son, 1988, Final Combat, 1989, (TV) Power Eleven, The Nuts, On the Brink, It Runs In the Family, The Vacation of Life, Angels and Devils, The Price of Growing Up, Back to the Beyond, The Tribulation of Life, and Behind Silk Curtain; (films) Ying ging boon sik, 1988, Final Justice, 1988 (Best Supporting Actor, Taiwanese Film Awards), He Who Chases After the Wind, 1988, Faithfully Yours, 1988, Dragon Fighter, 1988, Thunder Cops II, 1989, The Unmatchable Match, 1989, Just Heros, 1989, God of Gamblers II, 1990, When Fortune Smiles, 1990, My Hero, 1990, Love is Love, 1990, Look Out, Officer!, 1990, Lung Fung Restaurant, 1990, Triad Story, 1990, Curry and Pepper, 1990, Sleazy Dizzy, 1990, All for the Winner, 1990, Legend of Dragon, 1991, The Ultimate Trickster, 1991, Fight Back to School, 1991, Magnificent Scoundrels, 1991, Crazy Safari, 1991, Top Bet, 1991, God of Gamblers II: Back to Shanghai, 1991, Fist of Fury, 1991, The Banquet, 1991, Fight Back to School II, 1992, Justice, My Foot, 1992 (Best Actor, Pacific Film Festival), Fist of Fury II, 1992, Royal Tramp, 1992, Royal Tramp II, 1992, The Thief of Time, 1992, Family Happiness, 1992, King of Beggers, 1992, My Hero 2, 1993, Fight Back to School III, 1993, Flirting Scholar, 1993, Mad Monk, 1993, A Chinese Odyssey Part 1, 1995 (Best Actor and Film of Merit, Hong-Kong Film Critics Soc., 1995), A Chinese Odyssey Part 2, 1995, Hail the Judge, 1994, Out of Dark, 1995, Sixty Million Dollar Man, 1995, All's Well, Ends Well, 1997, Lawyer Lawyer, 1997, The Lucky Guy, 1998, The Tricky Master, 1999, Gorgeous, 1999; actor, dir. (films) Love On Delivery, 1994, actor, dir., writer From Beijing with Love, 1994, Forbidden City Cop, 1996 (Film Merit award, Hong-Kong Film Critics Soc., 1996), actor, dir., writer, prodr. God of Cookery, 1996, actor, dir., writer The King of Comedy, 1999, actor, dir., writer, prodr. Shaolin Soccer, 2001 (Best Dir., Best Actor, Hong-Kong Film Festival, 2002), actor, dir., writer, prodr., composer Kung Fu Hustle, 2004 (Outstanding Film Performance, Asian Excellence Awards, 2006).

CHOW, TIMOTHY YI-CHUNG, mathematician, systems engineer; s. Daniel Tin-Wo and Nancy Yuk Chun Chow. AB in Math., Princeton U., 1991; PhD in Math., MIT, 1995. Asst. prof. math. U. Mich., Ann Arbor, 1995—98; rsch. engr. Tellabs Ops., Inc., Cambridge, Mass., 1998—2002; mem. tech. staff MIT Lincoln Lab., Lexington, Mass., 2002—05; mem. rsch. staff Ctr. Comms. Rsch., Princeton, NJ, 2005—. Contbr. articles to profl. jours. Grad. fellow, NSF, 1991—95, Postdoctoral fellow, 1995—98. Mem.: Am. Math. Soc., Phi Beta Kappa. Achievements include patents for telecommunications network design. Avocations: composer and solver of puzzles and chess problems, Peanuts comic strip, Christian philosophy.

CHOW, WINSTON, engineering executive, researcher; b. San Francisco, Dec. 21, 1946; s. Raymond and Pearl Chow; m. Lilly Fah, Aug. 15, 1971; children: Stephen, Kathryn. BSChemE, U. Calif. Berkeley, 1968; MSChemE, Calif. State U., San Jose, 1972; MBA cum laude, Calif. State U., San Francisco, 1985. Registered profl. chem. and mech. engr.; instr. credential Calif. CC. Chem. engr. Sondell Sci. Instruments, Inc., Mountain View, Calif., 1971; mem. R & D staff Raychem Corp., Menlo Park, Calif., 1971-72; supervising engr. Bechtel Power Corp., San Francisco, 1972-79; sr. project mgr. water quality and toxic substances control program Electric Power Rsch. Inst., Palo Alto, Calif., 1979-89, program mgr., 1990-97, product line mgr. environ. market sector, 1997-99, indsl. and agrl. energy techs. and svcs. bus. area mgr., 1999—2001, exec. dir. Energy Ctrs. Network, 1999—2001, dept. mgr. energy utilization rsch. and devel., 2001—02. Mem. steering com. Indsl. Energy Tech. Conf., 1999—2002. Editor: Hazardous Air Pollutants: State-of-the-Art, 1993; co-editor: Clean Water: Factors that Influence Its Availability, Quality and Its Use, 1996; co-author: Water Chlorination, vols. 4, 6; co-editor: 1997 Internat. Clean Water Conf.-Today's Sci. for Tomorrows Policies, The Environ. Profl., 1997; contbr. articles to profl. jours. Mem. strategic long-range planning and restructuring com. Sequoia Union HS Dist., 1990—93, chmn. dist. ctrl. com., 1992—94; mem. industry com. Am. Power Conf., 1988—2002; bd. dirs. Directions, Inc., San Francisco, 1984—87, chmn. strategic planning com., 1984—85, pres., CEO, 1985—86. Recipient Grad. Disting. Achievement award, Calif. State U., San Francisco, 1985; Calif. Gov.'s Exec. fellow, 1982—83. Mem.: NSPE, AIChE (Profl. Devel. Recognition award), ASME, Air and Waste Mgmt. Assn. (mem. electric utility com. 1990—2000), Water Environ. Fedn., Calif. Soc. Profl. Engrs. (v.p. 1982—83, pres. Golden Gate chpt. 1983—84, state bd. dirs.), U. Calif. Alumni Assn., Calif. State U. Alumni Assn. (bd. dirs., treas. 1989—91), Beta Gamma Sigma. Avocation: ballroom dancing.

CHOW, YUN-FAT (CHOW YUN-FAT), actor; b. Nam Nga Island, Hong Kong, May 18, 1955; s. Jasmine Chow. Appeared in Two Times: Hong Kong 1941, 1985 (Best Actor award Won Taiwan Golden Horse, Best Actor award Won Asian Pacific Festival 1985), An Autumn's Tale, 1987 (Best Actor award Won Taiwan Golden Horse), Three Times: A Better Tomorrow, 1987 (Best Actor award Won Hong Kong Acad.), City On Fire, 1988 (Best Actor award Won Hong Kong Acad.), The Eighth Happiness, 1988, All About Ah Long, 1989 (Best Actor award Won Hong Kong Acad.), A Better Tomorrow III, 1989, Triad Savages, 1989, Triads: The Inside Story, 1989, The Fun, the Luck and the Tycoon, 1989, God of Gamblers, 1989, The Killer, 1989, Wild Search, 1989, Once a Thief, 1990, Black Vengeance, 1990, Prison on Fire II, 1991, Full Contact, 1992, Now You See Love, Now You Don't, 1992, Ruthless Super-Cop, 1992, Hot-Handed God of Cops, 1992, All for the Winner, 1992, Treasure Hunt, 1994, God of Gamblers' Return, 1994, The Peace Hotel, 1995, The Replacement Killers, 1998, King's Ransom, 1998, The Corruptor, 1999, Anna and the King, 1999, Wo ho kang long, 2000, Bulletproof Monk, 2003, Pirates of the Caribbean: At World's End, 2007 Named Star of the Decade, CineAsia-The Asian Theatre Owners Conv.*

CHOWDARY, RAJ P., plastic surgeon; b. Visakhapatnam, India, Aug. 7, 1947; m. Jhansi L. Chode; children: Krishna M, Ashwani. MD, Andhra Med. Sch., Visakhapatnam, India, 1969; MBA, U. Phoenix, Ariz., 1997. Resident plastic surgery Columbia Presbyn. Hosp., NY, 1983—84, chief resident plastic surgery, 1983—84; attending plastic surgeon Lehigh Valley Hosp. and Health Network, Allentown, Pa., 1984—. Trip chief Healing the Children Midlantic, Butler, NJ, 1991. Scholar, Govt. Andhra Pradesh, India, 1964—68. Mem.: Pa. and Lehigh County Med. Socs., Am. Soc. Aesthetic Plastic Suregry, Am. Soc. Plastic Surgery. Independent. Avocations: golf, travel, reading. Office: Allentown Ctr Plastic Surgery 1230 South Cedar Crest Blvd Allentown PA 18103 Office Phone: 610-434-1269. Office Fax: 610-434-4083. Business E-Mail: rajchowdary@msn.com.

CHOWDHURI, PRITINDRA, retired electrical engineer, educator; b. Calcutta, India, July 12, 1927; came to US, 1949, naturalized, 1962; s. Ahindra and Sudhira (Mitra) C.; m. Sharon Elsie Hackebeil, Dec. 28, 1962; children: Naomi, Leslie, Robindro, Rajendro. B.Sc. in Physics with honors, Calcutta U., 1945, M.Sc., 1948; MS, Ill. Inst. Tech., 1951; D.Eng., Rensselaer Poly. Inst., 1966. Jr. engr. lightning arresters sect. Westinghouse Electric Corp., East Pittsburgh, Pa., 1951-52; elec. engr. high voltage lab. Maschinenfabrik Oerlikon, Zurich, 1952-53; research engr. High Voltage Rsch. Commn., Daeniken, Switzerland, 1953-56; devel. engr. high voltage lab. GE, Pittsfield, Mass., 1956-59, elec. engr. research and devel. ctr. Schenectady, NY, 1959-62, engr. elec. investigations transp. systems div. Erie, Pa., 1962-75; staff mem. Los Alamos Nat. Lab., N.Mex., 1975-86; prof. elec. engring. Ctr. Elec. Power Tenn. Technol. U., Cookeville, 1986—2005, emeritus prof., 2005—. Lectr. Pa. State U. Behrend Grad. Ctr., Erie, 1969-75. Author: Electromagnetic Transients in Power Systems, 2d edit., 2004. Patentee in field. Fellow AAAS, IEEE, Instn. Elec. Engrs., UK, NY Acad. Scis. Democrat. Unitarian Universalist. Home: 690 Valley Forge Rd Cookeville TN 38501-1574 Personal E-mail: pchowdhuri@charter.net.

CHOWDHURY, ALI ASRAF, electrical engineer, researcher, director; b. Jaldi, Chittagong, Bangladesh, July 1, 1955; s. Hesamuddin Ahmed Chowdhury and Mahfuza Khatun Chowdhurani; m. Razia Khanam; 1 child, Fariha. MSEE with honors, Belarus Poly. Inst., 1980; MSEE, U. Sask., Can., 1983, PhD in Elec. Engring., 1988; MBA, St. Ambrose U., Davenport, Iowa, 2002. Lic. profl. engr., Tex., registered Alta., Can., N.B., Can., chartered engr., Gt. Britain. Design engr. GE Mfg. Co., Chittagong, Bangladesh, 1980—81; reliability engr. Atlantic Nuclear Svcs. Ltd., Fredericton, New Brunswick, Canada, 1987—90; sr. engr. Alta. (Can.) Power Ltd., Edmonton, 1990—99; sr. engring. reliability planning specialist MidAm. Energy Co., Davenport, Iowa, 1999—2006. Chmn. composite sys. reliability working group Mid-Continent Area Power Pool, St. Paul, 1999—2005; mem. MRO Resource Assessment Subcom., 2006—; chmn. MidAm. Engring. Conf. MidAmerican Energy Co., Davenport, 2002; mem. Coun. Energy Advisors, USA, Davenport, 2001—; tech. advisor Electric Power Rsch. Inst., CA, Davenport, 2001—; industry advisor Power Sys. Engring. Rsch. Ctr., Davenport, 2000—; chmn. reliability task force Alta. Electric Utility Planning Coun., Calgary, 1990—95; chmn. coord. of reliability info. group Grid Co. Alta., Calgary, 1996—99; mem. tech. program com. Internat. Assn. Sci. and Tech. Devel., Calgary, 1991—99; mem. exec. com. Quad City Expo-Tech Orgn., Davenport, 1999, Quad City Engring. and Sci. Coun., Davenport, 1999—2002; advisor Jr. Achievement of No. Alta., Edmonton, 1990; mem. fund raising com. United Way of City of Edmonton, 1995; mem. organizing com., internat. tech. adv. com. 8th Internat. Conf. on Probabilistic Methods Applied to Power Sys., 2004; mem. internat. tech. adv. com. 9th Internat. Conf. Probabilistic Methods Applied to Power Sys., 2006. Contbr. over 110 articles to profl. jours. Mem. scholarship award com. Quad City Engring. and Sci. Coun., Davenport, 1999—2002. Recipient Best Paper award, Probabilistic Methods Applied Power Sys., 2004; scholar Talent Scheme scholar (7), Govt. Bangladesh, U. Sask., Can., 1965—88. Fellow: IEEE (chmn. Iowa-Ill. sect. 2004, chmn. regional chpt. coordination 2007—, PES fellow evaluation com. 2007—, Best Paper award 1997, Region 4 Outstanding Engr. of Yr. 2003, Regional Activity Bd. Achievement award 2005, Best Working Group award for IEEE Std. 762 2005), Instn. Engring. and Tech. Eng. (membership examiner 1999). Achievements include development of and advancement of innovative theories and application methodologis for power system reliability and value-based probabilistic planning in power industry applications. Avocations: travel, music, reading, writing, gardening. Office: Planning & Infrastructure Devel California ISO 151 Blue Ravine Rd Folsom CA 95630 Office Phone: 916-608-1113. Office Fax: 916-351-2264. Business E-Mail: achowdhury@caiso.com.

CHOWDHURY, DHIMAN, physician, consultant; b. Chittagong, Bangladesh, Jan. 1, 1953; arrived in Can., 1996; s. Chitta Ranjan and Aruna Chowdhury; m. Smriti Chowdhury, Sept. 6, 1978; children: Muna, Chinmoy, Priyanka. MB, BS, Chittagong Med. Coll., 1975; Diploma in Child Health, U. Coll. Dublin, Ireland, 1983, Royal Coll. Surgeons, 1984. Intern Chittagong Med. Coll., 1975-76; med. officer Primary Health Care Ctrs., Chittagong, 1976-79; resident Arab Child Hosp., Baghdad, Iraq, 1979-80; gen. physician Suk Al-Shiukh Hosp., Thedar, Iraq, 1980-83; registrar Suleimania Children's Hosp., Riyadh, Saudi Arabia, 1984-90, cons. pediatrician, 1990-97, No. Regional Health Bd., Nova Scotia, Can., 1997; clin. assoc. IWK-Grace Health Ctr., Halifax, Novia Scotia, Can., 1997-99, cons. pediatrician, 1999—. Asst. prof. pediatrics Dalhousie U., 1999—; clin. asst. prof. King Saud U., Riyadh, 1993-97; program dir. Arab Bd. in Pediat. Residency Program, Riyadh, 1993-95, 96-97. Contbr. articles to profl. jours., chpt. to textbook. Fellow Royal Coll. Physicians (Edinburgh, U.K.); mem. Royal Coll. Physicians (Eng.), Saudi Pediat. Assn., N.Y. Acad. Sci., Bangladesh Med. Assn. Avocations: clinical photography, desert trips, travel, reading journals, fishing. Home: 967 Winwick Rd Halifax NS Canada B3H 4L5 Office: IWK Grace Health Ctr Dept Pediatric Medi PO Box 3070 Halifax NS Canada B3J 3G9 Home Phone: 902-492-4184; Office Phone: 902-428-8888. E-mail: d.chowdhury@dal.ca, dchowdhury@ns.sympatico.ca.

CHOWDHURY, MD SHOAIB, engineer; b. Dhaka, Bangladesh, Jan. 2, 1966; s. Moqbul Ahmad and Jahanara Begum Chowdhurany. BSCE, Bangladesh U. Engring. & Tech., 1991; MCE, CCNY, 1996; PhD in Transp., NJ Inst. Tech., 2000. Jr. engr., tech. asst. Surface Water Modelling Ctr., Dhaka, Bangladesh, 1992; rsch. asst. City Coll. NY, 1995, 1996, NJ Inst. Tech., Newark, 1996—2000; transp. engr. Parsons Brinckerhoff Quade & Douglas, Inc., NYC, 2000—04, sr. transp. engr., 2004—. Rsch. asst. CCNY, 1995—96. Contbr. articles to profl. jours. Mem. simulation subcom. AHB 25(3) Transp. Rsch. Bd. Scholar, Intelligent Transp. Soc. Am., Washington, 1997, The George Krambles Transit Found., Ill., 1998. Mem.: ASCE (intermodal com. Transp. Devel. Inst., reviewer Jour. Transp. Engring.), Simulation Subcom. of Transp. Rsch. Bd. Traffic Signal Sys. Com. (reviewer ann. meeting paper presentations), Am. Assn. Bangladeshi Engrs. & Archs., Inst. Transp. Engrs., Alpha Epsilon Lembda, Sigma Xi. Avocations: movies, tennis, cricket, travel. Address: Sha-89 N Badda Dhaka 1212 Bangladesh Office: One Penn Plz New York NY 10119 Personal E-mail: chowdhury99_1999@yahoo.com.

CHOWDHURY, SUBIR, management consultant; came to U.S., 1991; s. Sushil Kumar and Krishna Keshi C.; m. Malini Guha, Feb. 26, 1997. BTech. in Aerospace Engring. with honors, Indian Inst. Tech., Kharagpur, India, 1989; MA in Indsl. Mgmt., Ctrl. Mich. U., 1993; PhD in Engring. (hon.), Mich. Tech. U., 2004. Software and sys. mgr. Ciproco Computers Ltd., Dhaka, Bangladesh, 1989-91; quality mgmt. cons. Gen. Motors Corp., Saginaw, Mich., 1993-97; exec. v.p. ASI Consulting Group LLC, Livonia, Mich., 1997—2002, chmn., CEO, 2002—. Author: QS-9000 Pioneers, 1996, Robust Engineering, 1999, Management 21C, 2000, The Power of Six Sigma, 2001, Design for Six Sigma, 2002, The Talent Era, 2002, The Power of Design for Six Sigma, 2002, Organization 21C, 2002, Taguchi's Quality Engineering Handbook, 2004, Next Generation Business Handbook, 2004, The Ice Cream Maker: An Inspiring Tale About Making Quality The Key Ingredient in everything you do, 2005; editor-in-chief Automotive Excellence, 1997-99; founding editor Silicon mag., 1990. Fellow Royal Statis. Soc., UK, Quality Soc. Australia, Am. Soc. for Quality (chair automotive divsn. 1999-2000, Philip Crosby medal 2003), Soc. Automotive Engrs. (Henry Ford II award of Excellence, 1996), Soc. Mfg. Engrs. (sr., Gold medal 2002); mem: Inst. Indsl. Engrs. (sr.), World Innovative Found. (hon. 2003), Internat. Tech. Inst. (hon., inducted into the Hall of Fame for Engring., Sci. and Tech. 2004). Avocations: photography, music, writing, reading, surfing the internet. Office: ASI Cons Group LLC 38705 Seven Mile Rd Ste 345 Livonia MI 48152-3908

CHOWHAN, NAVEED MAHFOOZ, oncologist; b. Pakistan, Oct. 19, 1960; came to U.S., 1979; Student, Mao and Forman Christian Coll., Pakistan, 1979; MD cum laude, U Cetec, Dominican Republic, 1982. Bd. cert. internal medicine, 1986, hematology, 1992, oncology, 1993. Resident internal medicine Georgetown U. Svc., D.C. Gen. Hosp., Washington, 1983-86; fellowship oncology-hematology SUNY, Stony Brook, 1988-91, clin. asst. prof. dept. medicine divsn. oncology, 1992-94; pvt. practice New Albany, Ind., 1994—. Pvt. practice, South Bend, Ind., 1986—88; attending physician Meml. Hosp. and St. Joseph Med. Ctr., South Bend, 1987—88, Floyd Meml. Hosp., New Albany, 1994—, chair cancer conf., 1995—97, 2001, 03, dir. stem cell transplant unit, 1997—, chair cancer com., 1997—2000, sec. med. staff, 1998—2000, vice-chair staff, 2001, chair credentials com., 01, chmn. med. staff, 02; attending physician Clark Meml. Hosp., Jeffersonville, Ind., 1994—, mem. cancer com., 1995—, chair blood transfusion com., 1997, cancer liaison physician, 1999—2001; mem. Com. on Rsch. Involving Human Subjects, 1993—94; pioneer bone marrow transplant program SUNY, Stony Brook, 1994; investigator, rschr. and presenter in field. Contbr. articles to profl. jours. Named Physician of Yr., Nat. Rep. Congl. Com. Physician Adv. Bd., 2003; recipient Leadership award, 2002. Fellow ACP; mem. Am. Soc. Clin. Oncology, Am. Soc. Hematology, Am. Soc. Bone Marrow Transplantation. Office: 2210 Greenvalley Rd Ste 1 New Albany IN 47150-6809

CHOWITZ PLACZEK, GAIL LOUISE, school psychologist; b. Milw., Oct. 17, 1967; d. Robert and Judith Louise Citowitz; m. Donald Joseph Placzek, June 28, 1997; children: Matthew, Sydney. BA in Psychology, U. Milw., 1992, MS in Ednl. Psychology, 1996. Sch. psychologist West Allis-West Milw. Sch. Dist., Wis., 1996—. Co-author: (parent handout) NASP Communiqué, 1996. Mem. Holy Cross Luth. Ch., Menomonee Falls, Wis., 2005—. With US Army, 1987—93. Mem.: NASP, Transracial Families Milw. Lutheran. Avocations: reading, crossword puzzles, sheepshead, ballroom dancing, swimming.

CHOYKE, PHYLLIS MAY FORD (MRS. ARTHUR DAVIS CHOYKE JR.), management executive, editor, poet; b. Buffalo, Oct. 25, 1921; d. Thomas Cecil and Vera (Buchanan) Ford; m. Arthur Davis Choyke Jr., Aug. 18, 1945; children: Christopher Ford, Tyler Van. BS summa cum laude, Northwestern U., 1942. Reporter City News Bur., Chgo., 1942-43, Met. sect. Chgo. Tribune, Chgo., 1943-44; feature writer OWI, NYC, 1944-45; sec. corp. Artcrest Products Co., Inc., Chgo., 1958-88, v.p., 1964-88; pres. The Partford Corp., Chgo., 1988-90. Founder, dir. Harper Sq. Press div., 1966-90. Author: (under name Phyllis Ford) (with others) (poetry) Apertures to Anywhere, 1979; editor: Gallery Series One, Poets, 1967, Gallery Series Two, Poets—Poems of the Inner World, 1968, Gallery Series Three Poets: Levitations and Observations, 1970, Gallery Series Four, Poets, I am Talking About Revolution, 1973, Gallery Series Five/Poets—To An Aging Nation (with occult overtones), 1977; (manuscripts and papers in Brown U. Library). Bonbright scholar, 1942. Mem.: DAR (corr. sec. Gen. Henry Dearborn chpt. 1991—92, treas. 1992—2003, regent 2003—06), Acad. Am. Poets (NYC), Poetry Soc. Am. (NYC), Chgo. Press Vets. Assn., Soc. Midland Authors (bd. dirs. 1987—, treas. 1988—93, pres. 1993—95, membership dir. 1997—98, corr. sec. 1999—), Mystery Writers Am. (assoc.), John Evans Club (Northwestern U.), Arts Club Chgo. Home: 23 Windsor Dr Elmhurst IL 60126-3971

CHOYKE, WOLFGANG JUSTUS, physicist; b. Berlin, Ger., July 24, 1926; s. Frederick Samuel and Alice Sophia Amalia (Dessauer) C.; m. Helen Ruth Rubenfeld, June 19, 1949 (dec. May 2007); children: Alice Mathea, Peter Lyle. BSc, Ohio State U., 1948, PhD, 1952. Rsch. physicist Westinghouse Rsch. Labs., Pitts., 1952-60, fellow physicist, 1960-63, adv. physicist, 1963-78, cons. physicst, 1978-88; adj. prof. physics U. Pitts., 1974-88, rsch. prof. physics, 1988—. Cons. Northrup-Grumman and Westinghouse Sci. & Tech. Ctr., Pitts., 1988-98; vis. prof. U. Erlangen-Nuremberg, 1990—. Contbr. articles to profl. jours. With U.S. Army Signal Corps, 1944-46. Recipient Westinghouse Order of Merit, 1983, Humboldt Rsch. prize, Bonn, 1990. Fellow: Am. Phys. Soc. (mem. com. applications physic 1977—86), AAAS; mem.: NRC (chmn. com. large band gap semiconductor devices 1993—95), Material Rsch. Soc. Achievements include development of Silicon Carbide into what is presently the most promising high temperature semiconductor. Office: U Pitts Dept Of Physics Pittsburgh PA 15260 Office Phone: 412-624-9251. Business E-Mail: choyke@imap.pitt.edu.

CHRETIEN, JANE HENKEL, internist; b. Jersey City, Mar. 24, 1941; m. Paul B. Chretien, Apr. 11, 1970; children: Jean Paul, Yves. AB, Barnard Coll., 1962; MD, N.J. Coll. Medicine, 1966; MPH, Harvard U., 1970. Diplomate Am. Bd. Internal Medicine, Am. Bd. Infectious Disease. Intern Cornell U. Med. Divsn-Bellevue Hosp. Ctr., NYC, 1966-67; resident Meml. Hosp. Sloan Kettering Inst. Med. Ctr., NYC, 1967-69; fellow Georgetown U. Hosp., Washington, 1970-72, clin. instr., staff physician student health svc., 1972-75, asst. dir. student health svc., 1975-87, med. dir., 1987-94, clin. asst. prof., 1975-79, clin. assoc. prof., 1979-94; assoc. prof. George Washington U., 1994-98, clin. assoc. prof., 1998—. Fellow ACP; mem. Internat. Soc. Travel Medicine. Office Phone: 301-656-4010.

CHRETIEN, PAUL BERNARD, oncologist, medical researcher; b. San Angelo, Tex., May 13, 1931; s. Joseph Rodney and Celeste Regina Chretien; m. Jane Susan Henkel, Apr. 11, 1970; children: Jean Paul, Yves Rene. BS, St. Louis U., Coll. Arts and Sci., 1953; MD, St. Louis U., Sch. Medicine, 1957. Diplomate Am. Bd. Surgery, lic. State of Md. From intern to chief resident, dept. surgery N.Y. U. Bellevue Hosp. Ctr., 1957—62; nat. cancer inst. fellow, oncology Mem. Sloan-Kettering Cancer Cent., 1962—66; sr. investigator, asst. chief surgery br. Nat. Cancer Inst., 1966—72, chief, tumor immunology sect., surgery br., founding mem. immunotherapy contracts prog., 1972—80, coord., head, neck cancer contracts prog., div. cancer treatment, 1974—80; prof., dir. rsch., dept. surgery U. Md. Sch. of Medicine, 1983—93. Mem., sr. exec. svc. U.S. Civil Svc., 1976—80; co-originator, co-chmn. First Head and Neck Cancer Rsch. Workshop, 1980; cons., immunotherapy prog. Hoffmann-LaRoche Inc., 1980—92; v.p., med. affairs Alpha 1 Biomedicals Inc., 1982—94; originator, chmn. First Internat. Conf. Head and Neck Cancer, 1984. Contbr. over 225 sci. abstract papers, articles, book chpts. Capt. Med. Corps. USAR, 1959—69. Mem.: Soc. Surg. Oncology, Clin. Immunology Soc., Am. Soc. Clin. Oncology, Am. Radium Soc., Am. Head Neck Soc., Am. Coll. Surgeons, Am. Fedn. Med. Rsch., Am. Assoc. Immunologists, Am. Assoc. Cancer Rsch., Am. Assoc. Advancement Sci. Achievements include assigned FDA IND 14,738 for first clin. trial of Thymosin alpa 1 (1978); designed successful NCI sponsored trial for patients with small cell carcinoma of the lung in 1978 and patients with non small cell carcinoma of the lung in 1990.

CHRÉTIEN, RAYMOND A.J., retired ambassador; b. Shawinigan, Que., Can., May 20, 1942; s. Maurice and Cécile (Marcotte) C.; m. Kay Rousseau; children: Caroline, Louis-François. BA, Sém. de Joliette, 1962; LLL, U. Laval, 1965. Bar: Que. 1966. Mem. legal affairs div. Div. External Affairs Govt. of Can., 1966-67, policy dir. industry, investments and competition, asst. undersec. mfg., tech. and transp., insp. gen., assoc. undersec. state for external affairs, 1988-91, 3rd sec. permanent mission to UN NYC, 1967-68, asst. sec. fed. and provincial rels. com. Privy Coun. Office, 1968-70, exec. asst. to sec., mem. treasury bd. Privy Coun. Office, 1970-71; exec. asst. to pres. Can. Internat. Devel. Agy., 1971-72; 1st sec. Can. Embassy, Beirut, 1972-75, 1st sec., counsellor Paris, 1975-78; Can. amb. to Zaïre, 1978-81; Can. amb. to Mexico, 1985-88; Can. amb. to Belgium and Luxembourg Brussels, 1991-94; Can. amb. to U.S. Washington, 1994—2000. Awarded Order of Aztec Eagle, Mex.

CHRIS, HAIDET TODD, minister, event producer; b. Columbus, Ohio, Oct. 21, 1972; s. Glenn Holland and Teresa Lee Smith; m. Barbara Diane Tillman, Nov. 20, 1993; children: Kristine Elaine Haidet, Todd Mark Haidet, Chad Michael Haidet. Lic. First Bapt. Ch. Yucaipa, Calif., 1996. Youth pastor First Bapt. Ch., Yucaipa, 1994—99, Cornerstone Christian Fellowship, Chandler, Ariz., 1999—2005; event prodr./ spkr. Steve Russo Evangelistic Assn., Ontario, Calif., 1996—; assoc. pastor The Rock Eternal, Queen Creek, Ariz., 2005—. Concert promoter, 1994—; youth spkr., 1996—. Actor: (plays) Ben Hur; prodr., performer (television) JC TV; prodr.: (television) John Ahul TV, India. Recipient Various State and Nat. awards, Young Am. Bowling Alliance, 1988—93. Mem.: Mysterium Soc., Mensa, Internat. Conservative. Avocations: tennis, travel, speaking, concerts, bowling. Office: The Rock Eternal PO Box 1418 Higley AZ 85236 Home Phone: 480-988-1668; Office Phone: 480-226-7777. Business E-Mail: chris@therocketernal.com.

CHRISANTHOPOULOS, PETER, advertising executive; b. NYC; s. George and Marika Chrisanthopoulos. BBA, Baruch Coll., 1978; MBA, Fordham U., 1982. Media planner, broadcast account exec. Ogilvy & Mather, NYC, 1978—82; broadcast supr. primetime Young & Rubicam, NYC, 1983—84; sr. v.p., dir. broadcast Ohlmeyer Comms., NYC, 1984—86; pres., COO RJR Nabisco Broadcast, NYC, 1986—90; pres., CEO Network TV Assn., 1990—93; exec. v.p. rsch, mktg. and promotion ABC-TV Network Group, 1993—96; pres. broadcast and programming USA Ogilvy & Mather Advt., 1996—2000; pres., COO sales and mktg. Pappas Telecasting Cos., 2000—03, pres., COO, 2003; prin. Pyramid Comm., Inc., 2004—06; sr. v.p., dir. integrated media Katz TV Group, 2006—.

CHRISMAN, JAMES JOSEPH, management educator; b. Kansas City, Mo., Oct. 11, 1954; s. James John and Mildred Fay (Nelson) C.; m. Karen Waller, June 11, 1991. AA, Ill. Cen. Coll., 1977; BB, Western Ill. U., 1980; MBA, Bradley U., 1982; PhD, U. Ga., 1986. Machinist WABCO, Peoria, Ill., 1974-78; asst. prof. U. S.C., Columbia, 1986-91; assoc. prof. La. State U., 1991-93; prof. U. Calgary, Canada, 1993—2002, co-dir. venture devel. program, 1996, assoc. dean rsch. and PhD program, 1996-2001, endowed prof. family bus. entrepreneurship, 1999—2002, dir. Ctr. Family Bus. Mgmt. and Entrepreneurship, 1999—2002; prof. Miss. State U., Starkville, 2002—. Cons. UN Devel. Program, 1989-90, Internat. Civil Aviation Orgn., 1990, La. Lottery Corp., 1992, Assn. Small Bus. Devel. Ctrs., 1993—. Editor (assoc.): Case Rsch. Jour., 1984—87; mem. editl. bd.:, 1988—94; editor (assoc.): Strategic Planning Mgmt., 1987—88; editor: (case collection) McGraw Hill; editor: (advt. and circulation) Am. Jour. Small Bus., 1986—88; editor: (promotions) Entrpreneurship Theory and Practice, 1989; mem. editl. bd.:, 1990—94; editor, 1994—98, 2003—; guest editor Entrpreneurship Theory and Practice, 2003—; guest editor: Jour. Bus. Venturing, 2003; mem. editl. bd. Jour. Bus. Venturing, 1993—2003, Jour. Small Bus. Mgmt., 1986—87, Jour. Bus. Strategies, 1993—96, Acad. Mgmt. Jour., 1994—96, Jour. Mgmt., 1995—96, Family Bus. Rev., 1999—; guest editor: Jour. Bus. Rsch., 2007; ad hoc reviewer Jour. Mgmt. Studies, —, others, —; contbr. articles to profl. jours. Fellow, The Ctr. for Innovative Studies, 2002—. Fellow U.S. Assn. Small Bus. and Entrepreneurship (competitive papers chmn. 1988, v.p. corp. entrepreneurship 1989, bd. dirs. 1989-93, program chmn. 1991, v.p. rsch. 1992, pres. elect 1993, hon. pres. 1994); mem. N.Am. Case Rsch. Assn. (v.p. publs. 1987, proc. editor 1987, v.p. membership 1988-89, bd. dirs. 1987-89), Internat. Coun. Small Bus. (competitive papers chmn. 1988, v.p. programs 1989, dep. program chmn. 1990, bd. dirs. 1999-2001), Ea. Casewriters Assn. (bd. dirs. 1990), Acad. Mgmt. (exec. com. Entrepreneurship divsn. 1991-92). Republican. Roman Catholic. Avocations: collecting first edition books, chess, lacrosse, darts, bowling. Home: 1121 Edinburgh Dr Starkville MS 39759 Office: Miss State Univ Coll Bus and Industry Mississippi State MS 39762-9581 Office Phone: 662-325-1991.

CHRISMER, RONALD MICHAEL, federal agency administrator; b. Washington, May 4, 1954; s. Michael Joseph and Phyllis Ann (Long) Chrismer; m. Dorothea May Shifflett, Sept. 20, 1986; 1 child, Jeffrey Ronald. BS magna cum laude, Towson State U., 1976; M in Gen. Adminstrn. and MIS, U. Md., 1987. Cert. purchasing mgr., grad. IT ptnrs. program Industry Adv. Coun., Am. Coun. Tech., 2006. Sr. proofreader Am. Assn. Life Ins., Washington, 1976-77; asst. supr. Coopers & Lybrand, CPAs, Washington, 1978-83, supr., 1983-85; purchasing mgr. APA, Washington, 1985-87; buyer U. Md., Balt., 1988; contract specialist IRS, Washington, 1988-98, contracting officer, 1994—2004, supr. contract adminstr., 1998—2004; supr. contract specialist, contracting officer Dept. Homeland Security, Washington, 2004—, dir., 2006. Mem. telecom. adv. coun. Bell Atlantic, Washington, 1983—85. Mem. World Affairs Coun., Washington, 1983—85, Nat. Trust Hist. Preservation, Washington, 1983—85; block capt. Neighborhood Watch, Cardinal Forest Devel., 1987—; asst. den leader Cub pack Boy Scouts Am., 1996—98, scoutmaster troop, 1998—2003, asst. scoutmaster, 2003—06, com. mem. venture crew, 2003—, mem. Order of Arrow, 2000—, com. mem. Indian Creek Dist., 2004—, com. mem. advanced jr. leader tng. nat. capital area coun., 2003—05, commr. unit, 2006—; mem. sch. bd. St. Mary's Sch., Laurel, Md., 1990—96, chmn., 1992—93, mem. parish coun., 1991—92; coach Cath. Youth Orgn., 1994—2000, Laurel Boys and Girls Club, 2001; min. children's liturgy St. Mary's, 1993—2000. Mem.: Inst. Supply Mgmt. (lifetime cert. 2003), Purchasing Mgmt. Assn. Washington, Purchasing Mgmt. Assn. Md. (chmn. edn. com. 1988), Nat. Assn. Purchasing Mgmt., KC (bd. dirs. club # 2203 1996—99, mem. Patuxent coun. 1996—, sec. 1997—99), Nat. Honor Soc., Psi Chi. Roman Catholic. Avocations: history, music, art, literature. Home: 8810 Cardinal Ct Laurel MD 20723-1241

CHRISPEELS, MAARTEN JAN, biology professor; b. Kortenberg, Belgium, Feb. 10, 1938; married, 1966; 2 children. PhD in Agronomy, U. Ill., 1964. Rsch. asst. agronomy U. Ill., La Jolla, 1963-64; rsch. assoc. plant biochemistry Rsch. Inst. Advanced Studies, 1964-65, AEC, 1965-67; rsch. assoc. microbiology Perdue U., 1967, from asst. prof. to assoc. prof., 1967-79; prof. biology U. Calif., San Diego, 1979—. Program mgr. competitive rsch. grant office USDA, 1979. John. S. Guggenheim Found. fellow, 1973-74. Mem. AAAS, NAS, Am. Soc. Plant Physiologists (Stephen Hales prize 1996), Am. Soc. Cell Biologists. Office: U Calif at San Diego Div Biological Sci 9500 Gilman Dr La Jolla CA 92093-0116

CHRIST, CAROL TECLA, academic administrator; b. NYC, May 21, 1944; d. John George and Tecia (Bobrick) Christ; m. Larry Sklute, Aug. 15, 1975 (div. Dec. 1983); children: Jonathan Sklute, Elizabeth Sklute. BA, Douglas Coll., 1966; M.Ph., Yale U., 1969, PhD, 1970. Asst. prof. English U. Calif., Berkeley, 1970-76, assoc. prof., 1976-83, prof., 1983—89, dean dept. English, 1985-88, dean dept. humanities, 1988, acting provost, dean, 1989-90, provost, dean Coll. Letters & Sci., 1990-94, vice chancellor, provost, 1994-2000; pres. Smith Coll., Northampton, Mass., 2002—. Bd. dirs. Merrill Lynch & Co., Inc., 2007—; fomer dir. summer seminars secondary and coll. tchrs. NEH; former tchr. Bread Loaf Sch. English; invited lectr. Am. Assn. Univs., Am. Coun. Edn. Author: The Finer Optic: The Aesthetic of Particularity in Victorian Poetry, 1975, Victorian and Modern Poetics, 1984; mem. editl. bd. Victorian Literature, The Victorian Visual Imagination, The Norton Anthology of English Literature; contbr. articles to profl. jours. Fellow: Am. Acad. Arts & Sci.; mem.: MLA. Office: Smith Coll College Hall 20 Northampton MA 01063 Office Phone: 413-585-2100.*

CHRIST, DUANE MARLAND, retired computer systems engineer; b. Lakota, Iowa, Jan. 5, 1932; s. George Andrew and Esther Gertrude (Franke) C.; m. Lily Esther Shih, Sept. 14, 1963; 1 child, Wesley Anzo. BS, Iowa State U., 1953; MA, U. Minn., 1960; PhD, Rutgers U., 1998. Sci. programmer United Aircraft Corp., Hartford, Conn., 1960-63; computer sys. analyst IBM, NYC, 1963-68, staff instr., 1968-76, adv. sys. engr., 1976-82, sr. sys. engr., 1982-87, prin., 1987—2003; ret., 2003. 1st lt. USAF, 1953—56. Recipient Ea. Regional Dir. award, 1983; named Area Specialist of Yr., 1986; IBM Resident Study fellow, 1966-68. Mem.: Assn. Computing Machinery, Inst. Ops. Rsch. and Mgmt. Scis., Math. Assn. Am., Am. Math. Soc., Soc. Indsl. and Applied Math. Home: 15 Tilton Dr Freehold NJ 07728-3359 Personal E-mail: christdm@msn.com.

CHRIST, F. MICHAEL, mathematics professor; BS, Harvey Mudd Coll.; PhD, Univ. Chgo., 1982. Miller rsch. prof. Univ. Calif., Berkeley, 2000—01, prof., math. Grantee Alfred P. Sloan Fellowship. Fellow: Am. Acad. Arts & Scis. Office: Dept Math 809 Evans Hall Univ Calif Berkeley CA 94720-3840 Office Phone: 510-642-2143. Business E-Mail: christ@math.berkeley.edu.*

CHRIST, KARYN LYNN, apparel designer, poet; b. Balt., Aug. 16, 1956; d. Robert John and Lois Mae Requard; m. Dale Robert Christ, Nov. 1, 1996. Diploma, Belair (Md.) H.S. Clothing designer Dress-Ups, Balt., 1974-86; master cutting contract designer Costume World, Pompano, Fla., 1994—; master designer, owner Jita Swim and Island Wear, 1987—; owner Hemp Huggers, 2000—. Contract for swimwear designs and Spandex hemp textiles specialist; designer for theatrical prodns.; poet: A Journey Thru a Love, 1996. Fundraiser swim and fashion shows Cancer an Leukaemia in Childhood Trust, Bristol, Eng., 1993, Natural Resources Def. Coun. Home: 1883 Jamaica Dr Navarre FL 32566 Office: 30 Papaya St Clearwater FL 33767 Office Phone: 850-939-5881. E-mail: jita@attglobal.net, jita@jitawear.com.

CHRIST, LILY ESTHER SHIH, mathematics professor; b. Korea, Sept. 19, 1936; came to U.S., 1955; d. Whan-Chang and Shin-Tze (Lin) Shih; m. Duane M. Christ, Sept. 14, 1963; 1 child, Wesley Anzo. BS, U. Minn., 1960; MA, Western Res. U., 1962; EdD, Columbia U., 1967. Tchr. Cleve. Pub. Schs., 1960-62; stats. lab. asst. Tchrs. Coll., Columbia U., NYC, 1964-71; asst. prof. Coll. of Mt. St. Vincent, NYC, 1966-68, John Jay Coll. Criminal Justice, CUNY, NYC, 1969-73, assoc. prof., 1974—2005, HI-TECH PREP dir., 1993—, prof. emerita math., 2005—. Fulbright-Hays Sr. scholar, 1972. Mem. Math. Assn. Am. (gov. 1990-93, Cert. of Merit Svc. 1987, Disting. Coll. Tchg. Math award 2004), Am. Statis. Assn. (dist. 2 gov. 1990-91), Nat. Coun. Tchrs. Math. Office: CUNY John Jay Coll Criminal Justice 445 W 59th St New York NY 10019-1104 Business E-Mail: christle@jjay.cuny.edu.

CHRISTEN, ARDEN GALE, dental educator, researcher, consultant; b. Lemmon, SD, Jan. 25, 1932; s. Harold John Christen and Dorothy Elizabeth (Taylor) Deering; m. Joan Ardell Akre, Sept. 10, 1955; children: Barbara, Penny, Rebecca, Sarah. BS, U. Minn., 1954, DDS, 1956; MSD, Ind. U., 1965; MA, Ball State U., 1973. Lic. dentist, Ind. Commd. 1st lt. USAF, 1956, advanced through grades to col., 1972; base dental surgeon Zaragoza Air Base, Spain, 1970—73; dental surgeon, cons. preventive dentistry RAF Bentwaters, England, 1973—75; officer air force preventive dentistry Sch. Aerospace Medicine, Brooks AFB, Tex., 1978—80; prof., chmn. dept. preventive dentistry Ind. U., Indpls., 1981—93, dir. preventive/cmty. dentistry, 1993—2000, co-dir. nicotine dependence program, 1997—, acting chair oral biology, 2000—04, prof. emeritus oral biology, 2004—. Sr. med. svc. cons. Surgeon Gen., U.S. Air Force, U.S. and Eng., 1974-80; spl. cons. to asst. surgeon gen. for dental svcs., Washington, 1975-80. Co-author: Primary Preventive Dentistry, 4th edit., 1995; contbr. over 300 articles to profl. jours. Bd. dirs. Bexar County chpt. Am. Cancer Soc., San Antonio, 1976-80, Marion County chpt., Indpls., 1980—; mem. Ind. divsn. Pub. Edn. Standing Com., Indpls., 1980. Decorated Service medal with 2 oak leaf clusters, Legion of Merit. Fellow Am. Coll. Dentists; mem. ADA, Am. Acad. Oral Pathology, Internat. Assn. Dental Rsch., Am. Acad. History of Dentistry (v.p. 1984-85, pres. 1986-87). Presbyterian. Avocations: photography, classical music, travel, writing. Home: 7112 Sylvan Ridge Rd Indianapolis IN 46240-3541 Office: Ind U Sch Dentistry 1121 W Michigan St Indianapolis IN 46202-5186 Office Phone: 317-849-1152. Business E-Mail: achriste@iupui.edu.

CHRISTEN, CAROL A., principal; b. Apr. 15, 1946; Asst. prin. Benjamin Franklin HS, New Orleans, prin., CEO, 2002—. Democrat. Office: Benjamin Franklin HS 2001 Leon C Simon Dr New Orleans LA 70122 Office Phone: 504-286-2600. Office Fax: 504-286-2642. E-mail: carol_christen@benfranklinhighschool.org.*

CHRISTENBURY, T. DANIEL, lawyer; b. 1959; BS, Lehigh Univ., 1981; MBA, JD, Univ. Richmond, 1985. Bar: Va. 1985, Pa. 1987, US Patent & Trademark Office. Ptnr., chmn. Patent Prosecution practice group DLA Piper Rudnick Gray Cary, Phila. Mem.: Am. Intellectual Property Law Assn., Phila. Intellectual Property Law Assn. Office: DLA Piper Rudnick Gray Cary One Liberty Pl Suite 4900 1650 Market St Philadelphia PA 19103 Office Phone: 215-656-3381. Office Fax: 215-656-2499. Business E-Mail: dan.christenbury@dlapiper.com.

CHRISTENSEN, ALLAN ROBERT, electrical engineer, financial consultant, social services counselor; b. Newton, Kans., Jan. 5, 1953; s. John Clyde and Margaret Ann (Christensen) Simpson. BSEE cum laude, Wichita State U., Kans., 1976; MSEE, So. Meth. U., U. Park, Tex., 1981; grad., Reg. Rep. Sch., Montano Securities, 1995; postgrad., Coll. Fin. Planning, Denver, 1992—99; grad. emergency care attendant, Tex. Dept. Health, Dallas, 1995. Registered profl. engr., Tex.; enrolled agt. lic. by US Treasury; accredited tax preparer, accredited tax advisor, by Accreditation Coun. for Accountancy and Taxation, 1996—; notary public, Tex.; cert. emergency care attendant, 1995—, storm spotter Nat. Weather Svc., 2007—; lic. Tex. Dept. Health; chartered mutual fund counselor, accredited asset mgmt. specialist Investment Co. Inst. and Nat. Endowment for Fin. Edn., gen. radio-telephone commns. program, FCC, Dallas, 1977. Asst. draftsman, tchr. and arch. Wichita HS South, 1970—71; draftsman, civil engrng. asst. Wichita State U. State Architect's Office, 1971-72; chem. lab. asst. Wichita State U., 1973; clk. U.S. Postal Svc., Wichita, 1976; indsl. trainer Tex. Instruments, Inc., Dallas, 1983—84, from electrical engr. to lead engr., 1977—87, lead engr., 1987—; project liaison U.S. Naval Weapons Ctr., U.S. Naval Fleet Ballistic Missile ctrs., Dallas, 1991—96, McDonnell Douglas Astronautics and Gen. Dynamics; with spl. projects dept. Tex. Instruments, Inc., 1996-97; digital design engr. spl. equipment/projects Raytheon Systems Co., 1997—99; design engr. Raytheon TI Sys., Dallas, 1998-99; sr. test engr. divsn. Kone Elevators and Escalators Montgomery Kone, Inc., McKinney, Tex., 2000—; authorized rep. food stamp, state medicaid Tex. Dept. Health and Human Svcs., 2005—; authorized rep. US Social Security Adminstrn., 2005—, Dallas County Dept. Health and Human Svcs., Emergency Assistance Programs, Dallas, 2005—, Dept. Agrl. Commodities Supplement Food Program, 2005—, ATMOS Energy, Inc., Garland, Tex., 2005—, Emergency Cmty. Food Programs, 2005—, Lifeline Program Tex. Dept. Aging, Disability Svcs., Mesquite, 2005—, City of Garland Customer Assistance Program, 2004—, Urban League of Greater Dallas Cmty. Svcs. Block Grant Program, Garland, 2005—. Co-facilitator semiconductor focus group Tex. Instruments Def. Systems Electronics Group, Dallas, 1993-94; ind. contbr. sr. des. engr. adv. Analog Components QIT, Dallas, 1993-94, core mem. Engrng. Sys. Divsn. PWB Adv. Team, 1994-96; core mem. engrng. sys. divsn. PWB Adv. Team, 1994-96; cons. engr. to the Nat. Coun. Examiners for Engrng. and Surveying, 1996; core mem. Spl. Guidance A3 signal processor TIGER team, 1989-90; core mem. Spl. Guidance A3 Interconnect Concurrent Engring Team, 1993-94; mem. Spl. Guidance mgmt. cost reduction team, 1996; core mem. Spl. Guidance IF Receiver Quality Improvement Team, 1994. Inventor in field; cons. engr. and published elec. engrng. exam. problem author, 1997 Elec. Engring. Profl. Engrs. Exam, Nat. Coun. Examiners for Engrng. and Surveying; co-author Guide to Dallas County Emergency Service Agencies, 1999-2000; pub. reports in field. Instr., cook Mormon Relief Soc., Rockwall, Tex., 1986; Christmas program com. Tex. Instruments for Hope Cottage, Dallas, 1988—89; vol. tax preparer IRS, Mesquite, Tex., 1990; fundraiser United Way, Dallas, 1990; ct. apptd. spl. advocate Dallas CASA, 305th Dist. Ct., 1995—97; bd. dirs. Cmty. Restoration Svcs., Inc., Dallas, 1998—2000, officer, fin. com., 1999—2000; sponsor, vol. Kans. State Math. Tchrs. Conf., 1970; vol., fundraiser March-of-Dimes, 1972; coord. Arnold Air Soc. Gift; active blood donor dr. Wichita State U., 1971—73; plant-a-tree coord. Arnold Air Soc., 1972; numerous vol. positions with various orgns.; bd. dirs., founder, coord. Vol. Clearinghouse Family Alliance, Dallas, 2000, planner, coord., website designer, 2000; founder, fundraiser, regional coord. food bank program Dallas/Tarrant County Metroplex Food Bank, 1999; founder, coord. Job Tng. Partnership Act Summer Youth Jobs Program, 1999; storm spotter Nat. Weather Svc., 2007—; authorized rep. Leukemia and Lymphoma Soc., Wichita, 2006—, Wichita Sr. Svcs., Linwood Sr. Ctr., Wichita, 2006—, State of Kans. Homestead Claim Program, 2006—, Tex. Dept. Ins. Consumer and Fraud Protection Progams, Garland, 2006—, Crime Victim's Compensation Fund, Tex. State Atty. Gen.'s Office, Garland, 2007—, Medicare Programs, US HHS Ctr. for Medicare and Medicaid Svcs., Dallas, 2007—. Winner Regional art Competition winner State of Kans., 1968; recipient 1st place award Indsl. Arts Fair, Friends U., 1971, Hon. Scholar, Kans. State U. Alumni Assn., 1971, Achievement in Def. Studies award Res. Officer's Assn. USAF, 1973, Outstanding Elec. Engring. Project award IEEE, 1976, Site Selection Blue Ribbon, Site Mgmt. and People's Choice award Tex. Instruments for Hope Cottage, 1989, Outstanding Engring. Achievement award Tex. Instruments, 1989, Outstnding Vol. and Edn. programs award IRS, 1990, Stretch award Tex. Instruments Def. Systems and Electronics Group, 1995, 96, continuing edn. cert. of achievement Tex. Bd. Registration for Profl. Engrs., 1996, 97, 98, 99, 2000, Defense Superior Mgmt. award US Navy, 1997-98, People Assets and Effectiveness award Systems Grp., 1990, "Take-a-Shot" award Tex. Instruments, 1996, Group award, Dallas Ct. Appointed Spl. Advs., JC Penney Golden Rule award, 1996, Svc. honoree Dallas CASA, 1997; Am. Citizenship scholar, Friend's U., Wichita, 1970, State of Kans. Hon. scholar, Kans. Engring. Soc. Hungerford Meml. scholar, Martin K. Eby scholar, Western Electric scholar, Ahrens scholar, Nat. Elec. Contractors scholar, Walter H. Beech scholar, 1971, collegiate scholarship, Wichita State U., 1972-75; grantee in field, 1989-94, Urban League of Greater Dallas Cmty. Svcs. Block Grant Program, 2005, 07. Mem. NSPE, Nat. Assn. Tax Practitioners (Achievers Club 1992, 93, 94, 95, 96, 97, 99, Def. Superior Mgmt. award, 1997-98, Sunsetted Silver medal 1998, 99, Sunsetted Gold medal 2000), Tex. Soc. Profl. Engrs. (Cmty. Restoration Svcs. summer enrichment program award 1999), Accreditation Coun. Accountancy and Taxation, Am. Def. Preparedness Assn., Mensa, Mysterium Soc., High Potential Soc., Elatenous Group, IHIQ Soc., Eta Kappa Nu, Tau Beta Pi. Republican. Achievements include design of switched resistance bridge; linear power regulators for airborne radar systems; switching power supplies for antiship missile airborne radar; development of algorithms for automatic test equipment reliability; research in cross-talk characteristics of various laminates; development of car operating panel and shaft bundle platforms and fixtures for hydraulic elevator systems; various test platform software. Avocations: CAD, home remodeling, investing, wood working, weightlifting. Home: 2629 Emberwood Dr Garland TX 75043-6047 *There are no extraordinary men, there are only ordinary men accomplishing extraordinary deeds.*

CHRISTENSEN, ANNE, art director; Contbr. stylist NY Times mag., 1998—2001, fahion dir., 2001—, T: NY Times Style mag., 2004—; contbr. Am. Vogue, Italian Vogue, L'Uomo Vogue. Cons. Roberto Menechetti, Diane Von Furstenberg, Gianfranco Ferre, Tommy Hilfiger, Abercrombie & Fitch, Gap, Nike. Office: NY Times 229 W 43rd St New York NY 10036 Office Phone: 212-556-1551. Office Fax: 212-556-7382.

CHRISTENSEN, BECKY VANDERHOOF, lawyer; m. Raymond T. Sheehan, Jr., July 15, 2000; children: Todd Sheehan, Casey Sheehan, Tiffany Sheehan. BS in Econs., Va. Tech., Blacksburg, 1980; JD, U. Va., Charlottesville, 1983. Bar: Calif. 1990, Wash. 1983. Assoc. atty. Ferguson & Burdell, Seattle, 1983, Munns Kofford, Pasadena, Calif., 1983; ptnr. Chan & Christensen, LA, 1994—96; mng. atty. Law Offices Becky Christensen, Malibu, Calif., 1996—2004; ptnr. O'Connor Christensen & McLaughlin, Irvine, Calif., 2004—06, Eclipse Group LLP, Irvine, 2006—. Nat. adv. bd. Yes I Can, Canoga Park, Calif., 2002—; pres. Paradise Cove Home Owners Assn., Malibu, 2002. Mem.: Nat. Assn. Women Bus. Owners (legal counsel 2006—). Office: Eclipse Group LLP 1920 Main St # 150 Irvine CA 92614

CHRISTENSEN, C. LEWIS, real estate developer; b. Laramie, Wyo., June 3, 1936; s. Raymond H. and Elizabeth C. (Cady) C.; m. Sandra Stadheim, June 11, 1960 (dec.); children: Kim, Brett. BS in Indsl. Engring., U. Wyo., 1959. Mgmt. trainee Gen. Mills, Chgo., 1959, Mountain Bell, Helena, Mont., 1962—63, mgr. data comms. Phoenix, 1964—66, dist. mktg. mgr., so. Colo., 1970—73; seminar leader AT&T Co., Chgo., 1966—68, mktg. supr. NYC, 1968—70; land planner and developer Village Assocs., Colorado Springs, Colo., 1973, exec. v.p., 1975—77; v.p. Cimarron Corp., Colorado Springs, 1974—75; pres. Lew Christensen & Assocs., Inc., Colorado Springs. Ptnr., gen. mgr. Briargate Joint Venture, 1977-82; pres. Vintage Comtys., Inc., 1982-95; bd. dirs. Kirkpatrick Bank, Edmond, Okla. Bd. dirs. Pikes Peak coun. Boy Scouts Am., Citizens Goals, Colo. Coun. on Econ. Edn., Cheyenne Mountain Zoo, U. Wyo. Found., engring. adv. bd.; chmn. Colorado Springs Econ. Devel. Coun., 1978, 89; bd. dirs., chmn. bd. Penrose St. Francis Hosp., chmn. 1999-2001. Served with USAF, 1959-62. Mem. Colorado Springs Home Builders Assn. (bd. dirs.), Urban Land Inst., Colorado Springs C. of C. (bd. dirs., chmn. bd.), Colorado Springs Country Club (bd. dirs.), Garden of Gods Club. Republican. Presbyterian. Achievements include development of 1,000-acre Peregrine planned community, south of USAF Academy; the 7,000 acre planned community of Briargate, just east of the USAF Academy. Office: Lew Christensen & Assocs Inc 2520 Stagsleap Pt Colorado Springs CO 80904-1192

CHRISTENSEN, DAVID ALLEN, retired manufacturing executive; b. 1935; BS, S.D. State U., 1957. With John Morrell & Co., 1960-62, Raven Industries Inc., Sioux Falls, S.D., 1962—, product mgr., 1964-71, pres., chief exec. officer, 1971-2000; ret., 2000. Served with AUS, 1957-60. Office: Raven Industries Inc PO Box 5107 Sioux Falls SD 57117-5107

CHRISTENSEN, DIETER, ethnomusicologist; b. Berlin, Apr. 17, 1932; PhD, Free U., Berlin, 1957. Curator, dir. Berlin Phonogramm Archiv, 1958-72; prof. Columbia U., NYC, 1970—, dir. Ctr. for Ethnomusicology, 1971—2003; lectr. Free U., Berlin, 1962-70. Vis. prof. Wesleyan U., 1970, U. Hamburg, Germany, 1977, Hunter Coll.-CUNY, NYC, 1978—80, U. Nova de Lisboa, 1992; sec. gen. Internat. Coun. for Traditional Music, UNESCO, 1981—2001; dir. The Universe of Music-A History, UNESCO, 1985—93. Author: Die Musik der Kate, 1957, Die Musik der Ellice-Inseln, 1964; co-author: El Anillo del Tlalocan, 1975, 1990, Dictionary of Traditional Music in Oman, 1994; editor: Yearbook for Traditional Music, 1981—2001, (compact disc) UNESCO Collection of Traditional Music, 1995—2000. Office: Columbia U Music Dept MC 1815 New York NY 10027 Business E-Mail: dc22@columbia.edu.

CHRISTENSEN, DOUGLAS D., school system administrator; BA in Biology and Edn., Midland Luth. Coll., Fremont, Nebr., 1965; MA Edn. Administrn. and Curriculum Develop., U. Nebr.-Lincoln, 1970, PhD, 1978. Tchr. Holdrege Sr. H.S., Nebr., 1965-70; h.s. prin. Bloomfield Cmty. Schs., Nebr., 1970-74, supt. of schs. Nebr., 1974-76; county supt. of schs. Knox County Ctr., Nebr., 1975-76; supt. of schs. Colby Pub. Schs. Unified Sch. Dist. #315, Nebr., 1978-85, North Platte Pub. Schs., Nebr., 1985-90; assoc. commr. of edn. Nebr. Dept. of Edn., Lincoln, 1990-92, dep. commr. of edn., 1992-94, commr. edn., 1994—. Adj. prof., Emporia State U., Emporia, Kans, 1986-, for curriculum and instruction and ednl. adminstrn., U. Nebr.-Lincoln, 1990-;presenter, cons. in field. Contbr. articles to profl. jours. Chair North Platte Area Econ. Devel. Task Force, 1986-90, Coun. for Inter-Agy. Cooperation, 1986-90; liturgist First Luth. Ch., 1986-90, chair fin. com., 1988-90; bd. dirs. Mid-Nebr. Cmty. Found., 1989-90, Mari Sandoz Soc., 1990-, Universal Srv. Adminstrv. Co.; mem. Nebr. Commn. for the Protection of Children, 1994—; advanced planning com. Southwood Luth. Ch., 1994-; bd. trustee Nebr. State Coll.; mem. adv. coun. Natice Am. Edn.; mem. steering com., Edn. Commn. of the States Recipient Spirit of PTA award Nebr. PTA, 1997-98, Cornerstone award Future Farmers Am., 1998, Walter Turner award Am. Assn. Ednl. Svc. Agys., 1998, David Hutchinson award U. Nebr., 1998, Burnham Yates award Nebr. Coun. Econ. Edn., 1999, U. Nebr.-Lincoln Teachers Coll. Alumni Assn. award Excellence, 2002, Disting. Svc. award, Nebr. Coun. Sch. Administrators, 2004; named Pub. Ofcl. of Yr. Governing Mag., 2003 Mem. ASCD (pres. Kans. affiliate 1984-85), Am. Assn. of Sch. Adminstrs. (Nebr. Supt. of Yr. 1990), Coun. Chief State Sch. Officers (v.p., bd. dirs. 1997—), Nebr. Coun. of Sch. Adminstrs., Rotary Internat. (pres. 1981-82), Nebr. Ctr. for Ednl. Excellence (chair 1985-90, bd. dirs. 1989-90), Midland Luth. Coll. Alumni Assn. (pres. 1992-93), Nebr. Info. Tech. Commn., Nebr. Ednl. Telecommunications Comn., Mari Sandoz Soc. Office: Commrs Office Dept of Edn PO Box 94987 Lincoln NE 68509-4987 also: 301 Centennial Mall S 6th Fl Lincoln NE 68509*

CHRISTENSEN, HAYDEN, actor; b. Vancouver, BC, Canada, Apr. 19, 1981; s. David and Alie Christensen. Actor: (TV series) Family Passions, 1993; (films) Street Law, 1995, In the Mouth of Madness, 1995, Strike!, 1998, The Virgin Suicides, 1999, Life as a House, 2001, Star Wars: Episode II Attack of the Clones, 2002, Shattered Glass, 2003, Star Wars: Episode III Revenge of the Sith, 2005 (Best Villain, MTV Movie awards, 2006); (TV films) Love and Betrayal: The Mia Farrow Story, 1995, Harrison Bergeron, 1995, No Greater Love, 1996, Freefall, 1999, Trapped in a Purple Haze, 2000, R2-D2: Beneath the Dome, 2001, numerous TV guest appearances. Office: c/o The Gersh Agy 232 N Canon Dr Beverly Hills CA 90210

CHRISTENSEN, HENRY, III, lawyer; b. Jersey City, Nov. 8, 1944; s. Henry Jr. and M. Louise (Brooke) C.; m. Constance L. Cumpton, July 1, 1967; children: Alexander, Gustavus, Elizabeth, Katherine. BA, Yale U., 1966; JD, Harvard U., 1969. Bar: N.Y. 1970, U.S. Tax Ct. 1973, U.S. Ct. Appeals (2d. cir.) 1973, U.S. Supreme Ct. 1975. Assoc. Sullivan & Cromwell, NYC, 1969-77, ptnr., 1977—2007, McDermott Will and Emery, NYC, 2007—. Adj. assoc. prof. NYU, NYC, 1985-88, 06-, U. Miami Law Sch., 1997—. Author: International Estate Planning, 1999, ann. supplements, 1999—; contbr. articles to profl. jours. Chmn. Prospect Park Alliance, Bklyn., 1985-2007, chmn. emeritus, 2007—; trustee, Peddie Sch., Hightstown, N.J., 1986—; trustee Am. Fund for the Tate Gallery, 1987—, Bklyn. Acad. Music, 1992—, Vincent Astor Found., 1993—, Alex Hillman Family Found., 2000—, Friends of the Prince's Trust, 2001—; dir., sec. Freedom Inst., N.Y.C., 1980—; dir., v.p. Am. Friends of Whitechapel Art Gallery Found., 1991—; trustee, mem. exec. com. Am. Ctr. Oriental Rsch. in Amman, 1993—. Fellow Am. Coll. Trust and Estate Counsel (chmn. internat. estate planning com. 2003-06, regent 2005—); mem. N.Y. State Bar Assn. (chmn. estate and gift tax com. 1983-84, chmn. exempt orgn. com. 1986, chmn. income taxation of trusts com. 1984-85, 87-89, exec. com. tax sect. 1983-89), Internat. Acad. Estate and Trust Law (pres. elect 2006). Home: 35 Prospect Park W Apt 8/9B Brooklyn NY 11215-2370 Office: McDermott Will and Emery 340 Madison Ave New York NY 10017

CHRISTENSEN, KAREN KAY, lawyer; b. Ann Arbor, Mich., Mar. 9, 1947; d. Jack Edward and Evangeline (Pitsch) Christensen; m. Kenneth Robert Kay, Sept. 2, 1977; children: Jeffrey Smithson, Braden Kay, Bergen Kay. BS, U. Mich., 1969; JD, U. Denver, 1975. Bar: Colo. 1975, DC 1976, U.S. Supreme Ct. 1979. Atty., advisor office of dep. atty. gen. U.S. Dept. of Justice, Washington, 1975-76, trial atty. civil rights div., 1976-79; legis. counsel ACLU, Washington, 1979-80; staff atty. DC Pub. Defender Svc., Washington, 1980-85; asst. gen. counsel Nat. Pub. Radio, Washington, 1985-93; gen. counsel Nat. Endowment Arts, Washington, 1993-98, acting dep. chmn. for grants and partnership, 1997-98, dep. chmn. grants and awards, 1998—2001; arts cons., 2002—. Mem. DC Bd. Profl. Responsibility, 1990—98, chair, 1996—98. Bd. dirs. Corcoran Art Mus., 2001—03, Liz Lerman Dance Exch., 2002—05, Tucson Pima Arts Coun. Pub. Art Com., 2005—; vice chair bd. Mus. Contemporary Art, Tucson, 2005—; mem. pub. adv. com. KUAT-KUAZ (Pub. Radio/TV Com. Group), 2005—. Mem.: NCA/ACLU (mem. exec. bd. 1986—93, chair 1993), DC Bar Assn., Phi Beta Kappa. Personal E-mail: chriskk2@earthlink.net.

CHRISTENSEN, MARVIN NELSON, venture capitalist; b. W. Branch, Iowa, July 15, 1927; s. Peter Ancher and Martha Henrietta (Neilsen) C.; m. Mary Lou Miller, Dec. 17, 1949 (dec. June 1999); children: Stephen R., Barbara; m. Virginia Thompson, 2001. BS, U. Iowa, 1950. Pvt. practice ins. and real estate, Iowa City, 1955-69; asst. to pres. Gen. Growth Cos., Des Moines, 1970-72; acquisitions dir. Life Investors of Iowa, Cedar Rapids, 1972-80; chmn., CEO Bus. Comml. Realty, Denver, 1980—, Colo. Internat. Devel., Colorado Springs, 1984—; chmn. Byers (Colo.) State Bank, 1987-89, Farmer's State Bank, Waubun, Minn., 1988-96. Founder, adminstr. Waubun Area Devel. Enterprises, 1988—. Columnist: View from My Window (monthly newspaper); contbr. many articles to nat. pubs. Lt. (j.g.) USNR, 1944-46. Mem. Am. Bankers Assn., Minn. Bankers Assn., Masons, Elks, Eagles, VFW. Avocations: writing, cabinet making, fishing. Home: RR 2 Waubun MN 56589-9802 also: 246 E Bain Dr Tidewater OR 97390

CHRISTENSEN, NIKOLAS IVAN, geophysicist, educator; b. Madison, Wis., Apr. 11, 1937; s. Ivan Rudolph and Alice Evelyn (Ethen) C.; m. Karen Mary Luberg, June 18, 1960; children— Kirk Nathan, Signe Kay. BS, U. Wis., 1959, MS, 1961, PhD, 1963. Rsch. fellow in geophysics Harvard U., Cambridge, Mass., 1963-64; asst. prof. geol. scis. U. So. Calif., 1964-66; prof. U. Wash., Seattle, 1966-83, Purdue U., Lafayette, Ind., 1983-97; Weeks disting. prof. U. Wis., Madison, 1997—2004, emeritus prof., 2004—. Mem. Pacific adv. panel Joint Oceanographic Instns. for Deep Earth Sampling, Seattle, 1973-75, mem. igneous and metamorphic petrology panel, 1973-75, mem. ocean crust panel, 1974-77; mem. adv. panel on oceanography NSF, 1976-78, mem. adv. panel on earth scis. 1994-97; mem. adv. panel on continental lithosphere NRC, 1979-83; mem. adv. panel Internat. Assn. Geodesy, 1980-88. Contbg. author: Geodynamics of Iceland and the North Atlantic Area, 1974; Contbr. numerous articles to profl. jours. NSF grantee, 1968—. Fellow Geol. Soc. Am. (chmn. geophysics divsn. 1984-86, assoc. editor Geology 1985-89, George P. Woollard award 1996), Am. Geophys. Union (assoc. editor Jour. Geophys. Rsch. 1998-2001). Achievements include research on nature of Earth's interior. Home: 11310 Marine Ln Anacortes WA 98221 Office: Dept Geology and Geophys U Wisc Madison WI 53706

CHRISTENSEN, PAMELA KAREN, pediatric nurse; b. Mason City, Iowa, Aug. 5, 1957; d. Buford LeRoy and Violet Mae (Shepherd) C. AS, North Iowa Area Community Coll, Mason City, 1982. Cert. med. asst. Lakeland Med. Acad., Mpls., 1977. Staff nurse pediat. and med.-surg. unit Boone County Hosp., Boone, Iowa, 1982-84; traveling charge nurse, pediat. and adult Yuma (Ariz.) Med. Ctr., 1985-86, 89, 90-92, White Meml. Hosp., LA, 1985, City of Faith Hosp., Tulsa, Okla., 1985, charge nurse pediat., staff nurse pediat. ICU, 1986-89; traveling nurse charge pediat. Chinle (Ariz.) Navajo Hosp., 1985; traveling charge nurse pediat. Dallas Children's Med. Ctr., 1989; traveling nurse in pediat. Havasu Samaritan Hosp., Lake Havasu City, Ariz., 1990, 93; traveling pediatric nurse Univ. Med. Ctr., Lubbock, Tex., 1990; traveling pediatric and adult nurse Vanderbilt U. Med. Ctr., Nashville, 1991-92; adult charge nurse and NICU Audubon Humana Hosp., Louisville, 1991-92; traveling pediatric nurse City of Hope Med. Ctr., Duarte, Calif., 1993; traveling pediatric charge nurse St. Vincent Meml. Hosp., Taylorville, Ill., 1993-94; traveling pediatric nurse Jersey Shore Med. Ctr., Neptune, NJ, 1994; traveling pediatric charge nurse Ark. Children's Hosp., Little Rock, 1994; traveling nurse in pediat. Phoenix Children's Hosp., 1995; staff nurse in pediats. ICU Mayo Eugenio Litta Children's Hosp., Rochester, Minn., 1995-98; ASK, Mayo Med. Ctr., 1998—. Spkr. pediat. ICU conf. Mem. Am. Assn. Med. Assts. (past local pres. and state sec.). Home: 329 Chestnut St Osage IA 50461-1920

CHRISTENSEN, PATRICIA ANNE WATKINS, lawyer; b. Corpus Christi, Tex., June 24, 1947; d. Owen Milton Jr. and Margaret (McFarland) Watkins; m. Steven Ray Christensen, May 28, 1977 (dec. 1985); children: Geoffrey Holland, Jeremy Ladd. BS, U. North Tex., 1971; JD, U. Houston, 1977. Bar: Utah 1977, Tex. 1977, U.S. Dist. Ct. Utah 1977, U.S. Ct. Appeals (10th cir.) 1977, U.S. Supreme Ct. 1990. Assoc. Berman & Giauque, Salt Lake City, 1977-80; ptnr. Parr, Waddoups, Brown, Gee & Loveless, Salt Lake City, 1980—, pres., 1991-93, 2002—03. Adj. prof. law U. Utah Law Sch., Salt Lake City, 1979-81; judge pro tem Third Dist. Ct., 1995—. Legis. asst. U.S. Senate, 1970-74; bd. dirs. Comml. Law Affiliate, 1997-2001, co-chair litigation sect.; trustee Rowland Hall St. Mark's Sch., chair devel. com., 1987-90; mem. steering com., comprehensive capital campaign U. Utah Sch. Nursing; mem. steering com. Utah Electronic Law Project. Named Utah Woman Lawyer of Yr., 1992. Mem. ABA, Utah State Bar (Dorothy Merrill Brothers award 1996), State Bar of Tex., Salt Lake County Bar Assn. (exec. com. 1979-87, author editor Utah Lawyers Practice Manual 1986), Women Lawyers Utah (pres. 1988-89, bd. dirs. 1987-90), Phi Delta Phi, Delta Gamma, Alpha Lambda Delta. Office: Parr Waddoups Brown Gee & Loveless 185 S State St Ste 1300 Salt Lake City UT 84111-1537 E-mail: pwc@pwlaw.com.

CHRISTENSEN, PAUL WALTER, JR., retired gear manufacturing company executive; b. Cin., Jan. 31, 1925; s. Paul Walter and Lucy (Sickler) Christensen; m. Sarah Ernst, Nov. 22, 1947; children: Delle, Sarah, Lucy Davis; m. Marianne Orr Mercier, Nov. 3, 2006. BSME, Cornell U., 1945. With Cin. Gear Co., 1946—47, v.p., 1947—58, pres., 1958—78, chmn. bd., 1978—87; ret., 1987; chmn. bd. Cin. Steel Treating Co., 1961—68, 1987, pres., 1968—87; ret., 1987. Commr. Hamilton County Park Dist., 1980-93. Mem. Am. Gear Mfrs. Assn. (past pres.), Ohio Mfrs. Assn. (past pres.), Ocean Reef Club, Queen City Club, Commonwealth Club, Camargo Club, Comml. Club, Key Largo Anglers Club, Card Sound Golf Club. Home: 4660 Drake Rd Cincinnati OH 45243-4118

CHRISTENSEN, RAY RICHARDS, lawyer; b. Salt Lake City, July 7, 1922; s. E.R. and Carrie (Richards) C.; m. Carolyn Crawford, July 9, 1954 (dec. 1986); children: Carlie, Paul Ray, Joan, Eric.; m. Jeanne F. Pyke, June 24, 1989. LL.B., U. Utah, 1944. Bar: Utah 1944. Enforcement atty. OPA, 1946; law clk. to Utah Supreme Ct. Justice Wolfe, 1947-48; practice in Salt Lake City, 1949—; ptnr. Christensen & Jensen, P.C. (and predecessors), 1949—. Mem. Utah Bar Commn., 1963-66. Bd. dirs. Salt Lake City Jr. C. of C., 1949-53, v.p., 1950-52. Served with AUS, 1943-46. Recipient award, Fed. Bar Assn., 2005. Fellow Internat. Acad. Trial Lawyers (bd. dirs. 1987-88), Am. Coll. Trial Lawyers (state chmn. 1984-85); mem. ABA (mem. council jr. bar conf. 1952-56, ho. of dels. 1966-68, 73-79, mem. council bar activities sect. 1967-70), Utah State Bar (pres. 1965-66, Utah Lawyer of Yr. 1981, Utah Trial Lawyer of Yr. 1993, Lifetime Svc. to Bar award 2006), Salt Lake County Bar Assn., Western States Bar Conf. (pres. 1969-70), Phi Eta Sigma, Phi Kappa Phi. Home: 992 Oak Hills Way Salt Lake City UT 84108-2022 Office: Christensen & Jensen PC 15 W South Temple Ste 800 Salt Lake City UT 84101 Office Phone: 801-323-5000. Business E-Mail: ray.christensen@chrisjen.com.

CHRISTENSEN, RONALD E., physician; b. Seattle, Oct. 22, 1948; MD, U. Tenn., Coll. Medicine, 1975. Intern Riverside Gen. Co. Hosp., 1974—75; resident in family practice San Bernardino Co. Hosp., 1975—77; asst. assoc. clinical prof. U. Alaska, Coll. Nursing and Health Sci.; preceptor U. Wash.; physician, family practice Arrowhead Reg. Med. Ctr. Trustee Am. Bd. Family Practice, 1999—2004, treas., 2002—03, pres., 2003—04. Mem.: Am. Acad. Family Physicians (bd. dirs. 1995—98). Avocations: fishing, skiing. Office: Independence Park Med Svc 9500 Independence Dr #900 Anchorage AK 99507-4600 Office Fax: 907-522-1343.

CHRISTENSON, ALLEN CECIL, retired mathematics educator; b. Montrose, Calif., Aug. 25, 1931; s. Clarence and Cecil Edna (Wells) Christenson; children: Gary Allen, Teresa Ann Thompson. Student, Glendale Coll., Calif., 1949—52; BA in Secondary Edn., Ariz. State Coll., Tempe, 1956; MA in Secondary Edn., San Fernando Valley State Coll., Northridge, Calif., 1966. Gen. secondary life diploma credential. Engring. analyst Rockedyne, Canoga Park, Calif., 1956—62; math. tchr. LA Unified Sch. Dist., 1962—97; ret., 1997. Sgt. US Army, 1953—55. Mem.: Am. Mensa. Republican. Avocations: sports, camping, fishing, hiking. Home: 7309 Sausalito Ave West Hills CA 91307

CHRISTENSON, CHARLES JOHN, retired business educator; b. Chgo., Sept. 25, 1930; s. John Edward and Ethel Dagmar (Osterberg) C. BS, Cornell U., 1952; MBA, Harvard, 1954, D.BA, 1961. Mem. faculty Harvard Grad. Sch. Bus., 1957-58, lectr., 1959-61, asst. prof., 1961-63, assoc. prof., 1963-68, prof., 1968-74, Jesse Isidor Straus prof., 1974-79, Royal Little prof., 1980-96, prof. emeritus, 1996—. Prin. Auerbach Christenson Tagiuri, Inc., 1983-92; bd. dirs. Profile Techs., Inc. Author: Strategic Aspects of Competitive Bidding for Corporate Securities, 1965, (with J.L. Bower) Public Management: Cases and Readings, 1978, (with W.L. Berry and J.S. Hammond III) Management Decision Sciences: Cases and Readings, 1979. Bd. dirs. Boston Baroque, 1980—; trustee, chmn. Deep Springs Coll., 1986-94. With AUS, 1955-57. Mem. AAAS. Home: 1 Chauncy Ln Cambridge MA 02138-2401 Office: Harvard Bus Sch Soldiers Fld Boston MA 02163-1317 Office Phone: 617-495-6668. E-mail: cchristenson@hbs.edu.

CHRISTENSON, GORDON A., law educator; b. Salt Lake City, June 22, 1932; s. Gordon B. and Ruth Arzella (Anderson) C.; m. Katherine Joy deMik, Nov. 2, 1951 (div. 1977); children: Gordon Scott, Marjorie Lynne, Ruth Ann, Nanette; m. Fabienne Fadeley, Sept. 16, 1979. BS in Law, U. Utah, 1955, JD, 1956; SJD, George Washington U., 1961. Bar: Utah 1956, U.S. Supreme Ct. 1971, DC 1978. Law clk. to chief justice Utah Supreme Ct., 1956-57; assoc. firm Christenson & Callister, Salt Lake City, 1956-58; atty. Dept. of Army, N.G. Bur., Washington, 1957-58; atty., acting asst. legal adviser Office of Legal Adviser, U.S. Dept. State, Washington, 1958-62; asst. gen. counsel for sci. and tech. U.S. Dept. Commerce, 1962-67, spl. asst. to undersec. of commerce, 1967, counsel to commerce tech. adv. bd., 1962-67, chmn. task force on telecom. missions and orgn., 1967, counsel to panel on engring. and commodity stds., tech. adv. bd., 1963-65; assoc. prof. law U. Okla., Norman, 1967-70, exec. asst. to pres., 1967-70; univ. dean for ednl. devel., ctrl. adminstrn. SUNY, Albany, 1970-71; prof. law Am. U. Law Sch., Washington, 1971-79, dean, 1971-77; on leave, 1977-79; Charles H. Stockton prof. internat. law U.S. Naval War Coll., Newport, RI, 1977-79; dean, Nippert prof. law U. Cin. Coll. Law, 1979-85, univ. prof. law, 1985—98, prof. emeritus, dean emeritus, 1998—. Assoc. professorial lectr. in internat. affairs George Washington U., 1961-67; vis. scholar Harvard U. Law Sch., 1977-78, Yale Law Sch., 1985-86, Law Sch. U. Maine, Portland, 1997; Wallace S. Fujiyama vis. disting. prof. law Univ. Hawaii Law Sch., 1997; participant summer confs.

on internat. law Cornell Law Sch., Ithaca, NY, 1962, 64; cons. in internat. law U.S. Naval War Coll., Newport, 1969; faculty mem., reporter seminars for experienced fed. dist. judges Fed. Jud. Ctr., Washington, 1972-77. Author: (with Richard B. Lillich) International Claims: Their Preparation and Presentation, 1962, The Future of the University, 1969; contbr. articles to legal jours. Cons. Ctr. for Policy Alternatives MIT, Cambridge, 1970-81; mem. intergovtl. com. on Internat. Policy on Weather Modification, 1967; v.p. Procedural Aspects of Internat. Law Inst., NYC, 1962-2001, trustee, 1962-, Glenn Weaver Found. Law Psychiatry, Cinn., 2006-. With intelligence sect. USAF, 1951—52, Japan. Fellow Grad. Sch. U. Cin. Mem. Am. Soc. Internat. Law (mem. panel on state responsibility), Utah Bar Assn., Cin. Bar Assn., Order of Coif, Lit. Club (Cin.), Cosmos Club (Washington), Phi Delta Phi, Kappa Sigma. Home and Office: 3465 Principio Ave Cincinnati OH 45208-4242 Personal E-mail: christga@msn.com.

CHRISTENSON, GREGG ANDREW, bank executive; b. Kalamazoo, June 11, 1958; s. Elmer J. and Marie E. (Durrstein) C.; m. Karen Peterson. BA, Mich. State U., 1980. CPA. Auditor Price Waterhouse, NYC, 1980-82; with Bankers Trust Co., NYC, 1982-92, v.p., 1987-92; sr. v.p. Huntington Nat. Bank, Columbus, Ohio, 1992-2000, Troy, Mich., 2000—. Bd. dirs. Holy Family Regional Sch.; bd. trustees Mich. Interfaith Trust Fund, Venture, Inc., Oakland Livingston Human Svcs. Agy. Mem. Mich. State Alumni Assn., Mich. Bankers Assn. (bd. dirs.). Republican. Roman Catholic. Office Phone: 248-269-2034. Business E-Mail: gregg.christenson@huntington.com.

CHRISTENSON, LE ROY HOWARD, missions mobilizer; b. Rochester, NY, Oct. 28, 1948; s. Howard Le Roy and Sigrid (Anderson) Christenson; m. Pamala Jean Mattson, Jan. 26, 1974; children: Nathan Lee, David Wayne. BS, Valparaiso U., 1970; MS, Purdue U., 1972; MA in Religion, Trinity Evangelical Divinity Sch., Chgo., 2006. CLU. Corp. actuary Western Life Ins. Co., St. Paul, 1972-84; v.p., reins. actuary Am. United Life Ins. Co., Indpls., 1984—99, exec. v.p., 1999—2000; pvt. practice cons. Fishers, Ind., 2001—02; Great Lakes assoc. dir. Advancing Chs. in Missions Commitment (ACMC), 2002—06; with Pioneers, 2007—. Fin. cons. Mgmt. Assistance Program, Mpls., 1982. Bd. mem. Interserve, 1996—; mission conf. chmn. Faith Missionary Ch., Indpls., 1987—89, elder, 1991—93, 1999—2002, 2006—, elder chmn., 1993, 2000—02, mission com. chmn., 1995—2000, 2006—, vice chmn., 2003—06, sr. pastor search team, 2003—04; bd. dirs. Lake Wapogasset Bible Camp, Mpls., 1982—83, Christian Businessman's Com., Indpls., 1985—88, Interserve, 1996—2004, chmn. nominating com., 1999—2004, mem. exec. com., 1999—2001; age group leader Pioneer Club, Indpls., 1983, 1987. Fellow: Soc. Actuaries (chmn. audit working group reins. sect. 1985—88, vice chmn. reins. sect. 1988—89, 1995—96, chmn. 1989—90, 1996—97, sec.-treas. reins. sect. 1994—95); mem.: Indpls. Actuarial Club (pres. 1987—88), Tri-State Actuarial Club (Indpls. rep. 1984—90, chmn. 1989—90), Am. Acad. Actuaries. Avocations: bible study, bicycling, motorcycling, hiking. Office: ACMC PO Box 841 Fishers IN 46038-0841 Personal E-mail: LeeChristenson@sbcglobal.net.

CHRISTENSON, WILLIAM NEWCOME, retired occupational and internal medicine physician; b. Biltmore Forest, NC, Dec. 2, 1925; s. William Lambert and Beth (Newcome) Christenson; m. Elizabeth Chandler White, Aug. 9, 1957; children: Lisa Ann, Laurie E., Susan. MD, Johns Hopkins U., 1948; BS, U. N.C., 1949. Intern, asst. resident Mass. Gen. Hosp., Boston, 1948-50; asst. resident N.Y. Hosp., NYC, 1953-55, dir. personnel health svc., 1960-85, asst. attending physician, 1961-64, assoc. attending physician, 1964-85; attending physician Westchester County Med. Ctr., 1985-95, physician Employee Health Svc., 1985-95; ret., 1995. Postgrad. rsch. fellow USPHS; postgrad. Med. Sch. London, 1955—56; instr. medicine Cornell U. Med. Coll., NYC, 1956—59, asst. prof., 1959—65, clin. assoc. prof., 1965—79, assoc. prof. clin. medicine, 1979—85; dir. Office Grad. Med. Advising N.Y. Med. Coll., 1985—88, 1988—95, prof., 1986—95, assoc. dean, 1988—95; cons. N.Y. Blood Ctr., 1976—90; practice medicine specializing in internal medicine and occupl. medicine, NY, 1960—85; co-chair com. med. ctr. Am. Occupl. Med. Assn., 1980—90. With USNR, 1950—52. Fellow: ACP, Am. Coll. Occupl. and Environ. Medicine; mem.: Am. Soc. Hematology, Am. Fedn. Clin. Rsch., Phi Beta Kappa, Delta Kappa Epsilon, Alpha Omega Alpha. Achievements include research in in hematology and human ecology.

CHRISTESEN, JOHN D., business educator; b. NYC, July 16, 1936; s. Charles Nicholas and Mary Antoinette (Koza) Christesen. AB, CUNY, 1970; MBA with distinction, Pace U., 1975; postgrad., Columbia U., 1976—; D in Indsl. Mgmt. (hon.), U. Indsl. Mgmt. Credit mgr. Butler Lumber Co., 1961—62; fiscal comptroller, sales staff Lever Bros., 1962—67; contr., sales v.p. Cycle Circus, Inc., 1967—70; v.p. Putnam Bicycle Importers Co., 1970—73; curriculum chmn. bus adminstrn., prof. mgmt., dept. chmn. bus. adminstrn. & pub. svc. SUNY Westchester CC, Valhalla, NY, 1975—, dir. Mgmt. Inst., chmn. faculty devel. conf., v.p. Faculty-Student Assn., Joseph and Sophia Abeles Disting. chair of bus., 1994—. Vis. prof. econs. Mercy Coll., Dobbs Ferry, NY; adj. assoc. prof. mgmt. Iona Coll., New Rochelle, NY; adv. bd. U. Indsl. Mgmt.; cons. N.Y. State Bd. Regents, NY, N.Y. State Edn. Dept.; bd. dirs. Investment Properties Corp., Computweather Corp., Bio Med. Concepts, Inc. Author (with R. Wunsch): (book) The Complete Resume Handbook, 1967; author: Management Miscellany, 1978, 4th edit., 1990; author: (with Heinze Weirich) Instructor's Manual for Management, 1984; author: (films) Introduction to Business, 1980, Introduction to Finance, 1982; dir. editor: Honors Jour., 1995—. Chmn. Urban Devel. Corp., Lewisboro, NY, Town of Lewisboro Housing Com.; bd. dirs. Westchester Minority Devel. Corp., 1983—84. Recipient Medallion Edn. award, WCCF. Mem.: N.Y. State Assn. Two-Yr. Colls. (exec. bd. 1980—84), Assn. MBA Execs., Am. Acad. Polit. and Social Scis., Am. Inst. Higher Edn., Nat. Econs. Club, Am. Acad. Mgmt., Phi Theta Kappa, Nat. Bus. Honor Soc., Delta Mu Delta, Sigma Lambda, Alpha Beta Gamma (nat. chmn. 1978—79, nat. devel. chmn. 1980—81, CEO 1983—). Republican. Roman Catholic. Home: 1160 Midland Ave Apt 4C Bronxville NY 10708-6430 Office: Westchester CC 75 Grasslands Rd Valhalla NY 10595-1636 Office Phone: 914-606-6554. Business E-Mail: ceo@abg.org.

CHRISTESEN, PAUL C., classical studies educator; AB in Hist. and Classical Studies, Dartmouth Coll., Hanover, NH, 1988; postgraduate student in Latin and Greek, CUNY, 1988—91; PhD in Ancient Hist., Columbia U., 2001. Lectr. Dartmouth Coll., Hanover, NH, 1999—2001, asst. prof., 2001—. Margo Tytus vis. scholar U. Cin., 2005. Contbr. articles to profl. jours., chapters to books. Recipient US Prof. of Yr. award, Carnegie Found. for Advancement of Tchg. and Coun. for Advancement and Support of Edn., 2006. Office: Dept Classics Dartmouth Coll Hinman Box 6086 Hanover NH 03755 Office Phone: 603-646-2073. E-mail: paul.c.christesen@dartmouth.edu.*

CHRISTIAN, BETTY JO, lawyer; b. Temple, Tex., July 27, 1936; d. Joe and Mattie Manor (Brown) Wiest; m. Ernest S. Christian, Jr., Dec. 24, 1960. BA summa cum laude, U. Tex., 1957, LL.B. summa cum laude, 1960. Bar: Tex. 1961, U.S. Supreme Ct. 1964, D.C. 1980. Law clk. Supreme Ct. Tex., 1960-61; atty. ICC, 1961-68, asst. gen. counsel Washington, 1970-72, assoc. gen. counsel, 1972-76, commr., 1976-79; ptnr. Steptoe & Johnson, Washington, 1980—. Atty. Labor Dept., Dallas, 1968-70 Fellow Am. Bar Found., Tex. Bar Found.; mem. ABA, FBA (Younger Fed. Lawyer award 1964), Tex. Bar Assn., Am. Law Inst., Am. Acad Appellate Lawyers, Adminstrv. Conf. US. Office: 1330 Connecticut Ave NW Washington DC 20036-1704 Office Phone: 202-429-8113. Business E-Mail: bchristi@steptoe.com.

CHRISTIAN, CAROLE ANN, psychologist, academic administrator; d. James Clifford and Jean LaBoyteaux Christian; m. Christopher Henry Hayden, Oct. 17, 1999; children: Jennifer, Kimberly, John, Jeff. BA in Psychology, Gettysburg Coll., Pa., 1965; MEd in Edn., Goucher Coll., 1966; MA in Counseling, Rider U., 1984; D in Psychology, Rutgers U., 1992. Cert. sch. psychologist NJ, 1984, profl. mediator Lemmen Inst., 1987, hypnotherapist Rankin, 1998, Gatekeeper Instr. QPR Suicide Prevention, 2006. Tchr. Cheltenham Schs., Wyncote, Pa., 1966—68, Riverside Sch., Princeton, NJ, 1968—69; tchr. spl. edn. Princeton (N.J.) Regional Schs., 1969—73, 1977—90; counselor Rider U., Lawrenceville, NJ, 1987—92, dir. counseling Westminster Choir Coll., 1992—, dir. counseling svcs., 1994—. Mem. dean's multi-cultural coun. Rutgers U., Piscataway, NJ, 1995—2000, mem. focus on diversity group, 2001—, coord. ednl. program Prayers for Bobby, 1996; lectr. in field. Pres. bd. edn. Pennington (N.J.) Nursery Sch., 1980—83. Recipient Ednl. Opportunity Program award, Westminster Choir Coll., 1998. Mem.: NEA, APA, Assn. U. and Coll. Counseling Ctr. Dirs. Office: Rider Univ and Westminster Choir Coll 101 Walnut Lane Princeton NJ 08540

CHRISTIAN, CORA L.E, health facility administrator, physician; b. St. Thomas, VI, Sept. 11, 1947; d. Alphonso Augustine and Ruth Christian; m. Simon B. Jones-Hendrickson, Oct. 23, 1976; children: Nesha Christian-Hendrickson, Marcus Christian-Hendrickson. BS in Biology, Marquette U., 1967; MPH, Johns Hopkins U., 1975; MD, Jefferson Med. Coll., Phila., 1971. Diplomate Am. Coll. Forensic Examiners, Am. Bd. Quality Assurance and Utilization Rev., Am. Acad. Family Practice. Pvt. family-based practice, Frederiksted, VI, 1975—; asst. commr. Dept. Health, St. Croix, VI, 1977—91; educator, CEO, now med. dir. VI Med. Inst., Inc, St. Croix, 1978—; dir., prin. investigator US VI Household Survey, St. Croix, VI, 1988; chief med. cons., med. dir. Hovensa, LLC, St. Croix, 1990—; cons. VI AIDS Edn. and Tng., NYC, 1992—2005. Pres. Caribbean Studies Assn., 2000—01; pres., exec. sec., treas. VI Med. Soc., St. Croix, 1995—. Contbr. articles to profl. jours., chapters to books. Bd. dirs. Am. Cancer Soc., St. Croix, 1991—2005. Named to Trail Blazers for Women's History, Women's Bus. Ctr., 2000; Paul Harris fellow, Rotary, 1997. Mem.: AARP (nat. bd. dirs. 2004—), Am. Acad. Family Physicians (com. mem. 1996—2005, pres. VI chpt. 1976—). Sgi/Buddhist. Avocation: dance. Home: PO Box 1338 Frederiksted VI 00841 Office: VI Med Inst Inc PO Box 5989 Christiansted VI 00823-5989 Home Phone: 340-772-1011; Office Phone: 340-712-2400. Office Fax: 340-712-2449. Personal E-mail: cchrisitian@aarp.org. E-mail: cchristi@viqio.sdps.org.

CHRISTIAN, DAVID A., energy executive; B in Mech. Engring., Va. Poly. Inst. and State U. V.p. nuc. ops. Dominion, 1998—2000, sr. v.p. nuc., 2000, sr. v.p. Dominion Resources Svcs. and nuc. ops., chief nuc. officer. Mem. adv. bd. Ga. Inst. Tech. George W. Woodruff Sch. Mech. Engring. Office: Dominion PO Box 26532 Richmond VA 23261-6532*

CHRISTIAN, EDWARD KIEREN, broadcasting station executive; b. Detroit, June 26, 1944; s. William Edward and Dorothy Miriam (Kieren) C.; m. Judith Dallaire, Nov. 25, 1966; children: Eric, Dana. BA, Wayne State U., 1966, postgrad.; MA, Cen. Mich. U., 1980. Mgr. John C. Butler Co., Detroit, 1968-69; nat. sales mgr. WCAR Radio, Detroit, WSUN Radio, St. Petersburg, Fla., 1969-70; v.p., gen. mgr., ptnr. WCER Radio, Charlotte, Mich., 1970-74; pres. Josephson Internat. Broadcast, 1975-86; pres., CEO Saga Comm., Inc., Detroit, 1986—. Pres., CEO, bd. dirs. Stas. WSNY-FM, WODB-FM, WJZA, WJZK, Columbus, Ohio, Sta. WNOR-FM, Norfolk, Va., Sta. WAFX, Norfolk, WJOI AM Norfolk, Stas. WKLH-FM, WHQG-FM, WJYI-AM, WFMR-FM, WJMR-FM Milw., Stas. KRNT, KSTZ-FM, KIOA-AM/FM, KAZR FM, KLTI FM, KPSZ AM, Des Moines, Stas. WLRW-FM and WIXY-FM, WCFF FM/WXTT, Champaign, Ill., Stas. WYMG-FM, WQQL-FM, WDBR-FM, WABZ FM, WTAX-AM, Springfield, Ill., Stas. WGAN-AM/WMGX, WZAN-AM/WYNZ-FM, WPOR/FM, WBAE-AM, WVAE, Portland, Maine, Sta. WFEA-AM/WZID-FM, WQLL-FM, Manchester, N.H., Sta. WAQY-FM, WHNP-AM, Springfield, Mass., WHMP-AM, WLZX-FM, WSRI, Northampton, Mass., WHMQ-AM, WHAI-AM, WPVQ, Greenfield, Mass., KOAM TV, KFJX TV, Joplin, Mo., WNAX-AM/FM, Yankton, SD, KGMI, KISM-FM, Bellingham, Wash., KBAI-AM, KAFE FM, Bellingham, Wash., Victoria Tex., KUNU TV, KXTS TV, KAVU TV, KVCT TV, KMOL TV, Victoria, WXVT TV, Greenville, Miss., KICD AM-FM, KLLT, Spencer, Iowa, WKFN, WJQI, WZZP-FM, WCVQ-FM, WVVR-FM, Clarksville, Tenn., KDXY-FM, KDEZ-FM, KJBX-FM, Jonesboro A.K., WKNE-FM, WKBK-AM, WSNI-FM, WUQL-FM, WINQ-FM, Keene, N.H., WKVT-AM/FM, WRSY, Brattleboro, Vt., WHCU AM, WNYY AM, WQNY FM, WYXL/WIII, Ithaca, NY, WINA AM, WVAX-AM, WWWV FM, WQMZ FM, WCNR, Charlottesville, Va., Mich. Radio Network, Ill. Radio Network, others; Mich. Farm Radio Network, Minn. Radio News Network; Bd. dirs., Nat. Assn. Broadcasters, Broadcast Found., chmn. Arbitron Radio Adv. Coun., 1978-79; bd. dirs. All Industry Music Licensing Com.; adj. prof. Ctrl. Mich. U. Bd. dirs. Am. Auto Immune Related Disease Found., 1995—; bd. mem. St. John Hosp.; consul Republic of Iceland for Mich., Ohio and Ind., 1996—. Mem. Alpha Epsilon Rho (nat. adv. coun. 1980—). Home: 21 Newberry Pl Grosse Pointe Farms MI 48236-3749 also: 3310 Sabal Cove Dr Longboat Key FL 34228-4154 Office: Saga Communications Inc 73 Kercheval Ave Grosse Pointe Farms MI 48236-3603 E-mail: echristian@sagacommunications.com.

CHRISTIAN, ELIOT JORDAN, information technology manager, consultant; b. Springfield, Mo., Aug. 17, 1952; s. Robert Aspel and Clara Mae (Hess) Smith; m. Marcia Bernadette FitzSimons Christian, July 4, 1976; children: Sikandra, Theresa, Sheila. BA in English, U. Wis., Milw., 1973. Dep. dir. field mgmt. svc. Office Data Mgmt. and Telecomm., VA, Washington, 1975-86; chief office mgmt. svcs. info. sys. divsn. geo. info. office U.S. Geol. Survey, Reston, Va., 1986—, key developer common alerting protocol, 2002—05, sys. arch. global earth obs. sys. systems, 2003—05; cons. World Meteorological Orgn., Arlington, 2006—. Chmn. Spl. Interest Group on Wide Area Info. Servers, Washington, 1993—98; arch., leader Global Info. Locator Svc., 1995—. Author: fed. reports. Sci. vol. U.S. Geol. Survey, Reston, Va., 2006—. Recipient Best Windows Application award, Windows World, 1993, Federal 100 award, Fed. Computer Week, 1995, 1996, Madison award for pub. right to know, ALA and AAAS, 1998. Democrat. Roman Catholic. Avocations: hiking, reading. Home: 2002 Lakebreeze Way Reston VA 20191-4006

CHRISTIAN, GARY D., chemistry professor; b. Eugene, Oreg., Nov. 25, 1937; s. Roy C. and Edna Alberta (Trout) Gonier; m. Suanne Byrd Coulbourne, June 17, 1961; children: Dale Brian, Carol Jean, Fred, Tanya Danielle, Tabitha Star. BS, U. Oreg., 1959; MS, U. Md., 1962, PhD, 1964; PhD (hon.), Chiang Mai U., 2005. Rsch. analytical chemist Walter Reed Army Inst. Rsch., Washington, 1961-67; asst. prof. U. Md., College Park, 1965-66, U. Ky., Lexington, 1967-70, assoc. prof., 1970-72; prof. chemistry U. Wash., Seattle, 1972—2006, acting chmn. dept., 1990, assoc. chmn., 1991—92, divisional dean sci., 1993—2001, prof. emeritus, 2006—. Vis. prof. Free U. Brussels, 1978-79; invited prof. U. Geneva, 1979; cons. Ames Co., 1968-72, Beckman Instruments, Inc., 1972-84, 88, Westinghouse Hanford Co., 1977-83, Tech. Dynamics, 1983-85, Porton Diagnostics, 1990-91, Bend Rsch., 1992-93, E.I. DuPont de Nemours, Inc., 1993; examiner Grad. Record Exam., 1985-90. Author: Analytical Chemistry, 6th edit., 2003, Instrumental Analysis, 1978, 2d edit., 1986, Atomic Absorption Spectroscopy, 1970, Trace Analysis, 1986, Problem Solving in Analytical Chemistry, 1988, Calculations in Pharmaceutical Sciences, 1993; editl. bd. Analytical Letters, 1971-2004, Can. Jour. Spectroscopy, 1974-96, Analytical Instrumentation, 1974-93, Talanta, 1980-88 (spl. editor USA honor issue, 1989), Analytical Chemistry, 1985-89, Critical Revs. in Analytical Chemistry, 1985—, The Analyst, 1986-90, Jour. Saudi Chem. Soc., 1995—; editor in chief Talanta, 1989—, Electroanalysis, 1988— (65th Birthday Spl. Issue, 2002), Jour. Pharm. and Biochem. Analysis, 1990-97, Fresenius' Z. Analytical Chem., 1991-93, Laborator Automation, 1992—, Quimica Analitica, 1993-2001, Sensors, 2001-, Jordanian Jour. Chemistry, 2005-, Inertnat. Jour. Electro Sci., 2006-; contbr. articles to profl. jours. Recipient Medal of Honor, U. Libre, Brussels, 1978, Talanta medal, Elsevier Sci., 1995, Commemorative medal, Charles U., 1999, Geoff Wilson medal, Deakin U., 2003, Sr. Scholar Silver award, Thailand Rsch. Fund, 2004; Fulbright Hays scholar, 1978—79. Mem. Am. Chem. Soc. (sect. chmn. 1982-83, chmn. elect divsn. analytic chemistry 1988-89, chmn. 1989-90, divsn. Analytical Chemistry award for Excellence in Tchg. 1988, Fisher award in analytical chemistry 1996), Soc. Applied Spectroscopy (sect. chmn. 1982), Spectroscopy Soc. Can., Am. Inst. Chemists (cert.), Soc. Electroanalytical Chemistry (bd. dirs. 1993-98), Japan Soc. Analytical Chemistry (Sci. Honor medal 2003). Republican. Home: PO Box 26 Medina WA 98039-0026 Office: Univ Wash Dept Chemistry Box 351700 Seattle WA 98195-1700 Home Phone: 425-454-9361; Office Phone: 206-543-1635. Office Fax: 206-685-3478. Business E-Mail: christian@chem.washington.edu.

CHRISTIAN, GARY IRVIN, lawyer; b. Albany, Ga., July 7, 1951; s. Rupert Irvin and Alice Amelia (Smith) Christian; m. Dierdre G. Christian; children: Amy Margaret, Rachel, Sarah. BA in History, Polit. Sci., David Lipscomb Coll., 1973; MPA, U. Tenn., 1974; JD, Vanderbilt U., 1979. Bar: Fla. 1979, U.S. Dist. Ct. (no. and mid. dists.) Fla 1979. Rsch. dir. Ala. League of Mcpls., Montgomery, 1974-76; instr. in pub. adminstrn. David Lipscomb Coll., Nashville, 1977-79; assoc. Rogers, Towers, Bailey, Jones & Gay, Jacksonville, Fla., 1979-83, Foley & Lardner, Jacksonville, 1983-86; ptnr. Christian, Prom, Korn & Zehmer, Jacksonville, 1986-92, Rumph, Stoddard & Christian, Jacksonville, 1992—. Editor-in-chief Vanderbilt Jour. of Transnational Law, 1978-79. Bd. dirs. PACE Ctr. for Girls, Inc., Jacksonville, 1984-92, pres., 1984-86; mem. Leadership Jacksonville, 1986-87; chmn. site selection com. St. Johns County Sch. Bd., 1993-95; mem. site selection com., St. Johns County Sch. Bd., 1989-91. Mem. ABA (condominiums and planned devels. com.), Jacksonville Bar Assn. (coord. continuing edn. 1984-85, vice chmn. real property sect. 1986-87, chmn. 1987-88, chmn. corps., banking & bus. sect. 1991-92), Wavemasters Soc. (pres. 1986-87), Jacksonville C. of C. (com. 100 1986-94), Southpoint Bus. Assn. (bd. dirs. 1990-2001, pres. 1991-93), Oak Bridge Country Club, Seminole Club, Salt Creek Homeowners Assn. (bd. dirs. 1993-97, pres. 1994-96), Univ. Club, Deer Creek Country Club. Republican. Mem. Ch. of Christ. Avocations: golf, fishing, racquetball, hunting, stamp collecting/philately. Office: Rumph Stoddard & Christian 3100 University Blvd S Ste 101 Jacksonville FL 32216-2777 Home Phone: 904-221-0407; Office Phone: 904-724-5060. E-mail: rsclaw@bellsouth.net.

CHRISTIAN, GEORGE, library organization administrator; Exec. dir. Libr. Connection, Inc., Windsor, Conn. Recipient Outstanding Libr. award, Ct. Libr. Assn., 2006, Paul Howard award for Courage, ALA, 2007, Pro-Quest SIRS State and Regional Achievement award, Intellectual Freedom Roundtable, 2007. Achievements include challenging the constitutionality of FBI National Security Letters and gag orders imposed under the USA PATRIOT Act, as one of four Connecticut "John Does.". Office: Libr Connection Inc 559 Matianuck Ave Windsor CT 06095 Office Phone: 860-298-5322 ext. 1012. Office Fax: 860-298-5328. E-mail: gchristian@libraryconnection.info.

CHRISTIAN, JAMES WAYNE, economist; b. Ft. Worth, Oct. 7, 1934; s. Nap B. and Daphne (Wright) Christian; m. Jo June Maples, June 5, 1952; children: Amy Joella, Nicole Denise. BA, U. Tex., Austin, 1962, MA, 1964, PhD, 1965. Dir. internat. div. Fed. Home Loan Bank Bd., Washington, 1972—74; sr. v.p., chief economist Nat. Savs. and Loan League, Washington, 1974—80, U.S. League Savs. Inst., Chgo., 1980—91; pres. James Christian Assocs., Fair Oaks Ranch, Tex., 1991; dir. Real Estate Ctr. at Tex. A & M Univ., 1993—95. Prof. econs. Iowa State U., 1965—74; dir. Nat. Housing Conf., 1980—84; cons. 23 developing country govts., 1970. Contbr. articles to profl. jour. With USN, 1952—55, with USAF, 1955—59. Recipient Am. Legion award, 1949; univ. fellow, 1964, NSF fellow, 1965, Social Sci. Rsch. Coun. grant, 1968—69. Mem.: So. Econ. Assn., Am. Fin. Assn., Am. Econ. Assn., Cosmos, Phi Kappa Phi, Pi Sigma Alpha, Omicron Delta Epsilon, Phi Beta Kappa.

CHRISTIAN, JOHN CATLETT, JR., lawyer; b. Springfield, Mo., Sept. 12, 1929; s. John Catlett and Alice Odelle (Milling) C.; m. Peggy Jeanne Cain, Apr. 12, 1953; children: Cathleen Marie, John Catlett, Alice Cain. AB, Drury Coll., 1951; LLB, Tulane U., New Orleans, 1956. Bar: La. 1956, Mo. 1956, US Supreme Ct. 1975. Assoc. Porter & Stewart, Lake Charles, La., 1956-58, Wilkinson, Lewis, Wilkinson & Madison, Shreveport, La., 1958-62, ptnr., 1962-64, Milling, Benson, Woodward, Hillyer, Pierson & Miller, New Orleans, 1964-92, of counsel, 1993-94. Pres. Sherburne Land Co., 1974-83, Pointe-Martin Mgmt., Inc., 1990-2000; dir. Emerald Land Corp. Pres. Kathleen Elizabeth O'Brien Found., 1963—. Served with USMCR, 1951-53. Fellow Am. Coll. Trial Lawyers; mem. ABA, Fed. Bar Assn., Mo. Bar, La. Bar Assn., La. Landowners Assn. (bd. dirs. 1983-2001), Boston Club, Hickory Hills Country Club, Highlands Falls Country Club, Kappa Alpha Order, Omicron Delta Kappa, Phi Delta Phi. Home: 4588 E Spruce Dr Springfield MO 65809 Personal E-mail: jcchristiansr@aol.com.

CHRISTIAN, JOHN EDWARD, health science association administrator, educator; b. Indpls., July 12, 1917; s. George Edward and Okel Kandus (Waltz) C.; m. Catherine Ellen Spooner, July 23, 1948; 1 dau., Linda Kay. BS, Purdue U., 1939, PhD, 1944. Control chemist Upjohn Co., 1939-40; faculty Purdue U., Lafayette, Ind., 1940—, prof. pharm. chemistry, 1950-59, head dept. radiol. control, 1956-59, prof. bionucleonics, head dept., 1959-82; chmn. adminstrv. com. Trace Level Research Inst., 1960-88; dir. Inst. for Environmental Health, 1965-88; head Sch. Health Scis., 1979-82, Hovde Disting. prof., 1979-88, Hovde Disting. prof. bionucleonics and health scis. emeritus, 1988—. Vis. prof. radiation therapy Ind. U. Sch. Medicine, 1970-88; Harvey Washington Meml. lectr. Purdue U., 1955; Edward-Kremers Meml. lectr. U. Wis., 1956; vis. lectr. U. Tex., 1959, Taylor U. Ann. Sci. Lecture Series, Upton, Ind., 1960; Julius A. Koch Meml. lectr. U. Pitts., 1961 Assoc. editor Radiochem. Letters. Mem. revision com. U.S. Pharmacopeia, 1950-60, mem. adv. panel on radioactive drugs, 1960-70; adv. com. isotope distbn. AEC, 1952-58, mem. med. adv. com., 1967-75; mem. radiation and chem. def. sect. Ind. Dept. Civil Def., 1954—; vice chmn. Radiation Control Adv. Commn., Ind., 1958—; mem. exec. com. Ind. Comprehensive Health Planning Council, 1972-76; mem. adv. com. radiopharms. FDA, 1970-75; mem. Ind. Gov.'s Pesticide Council, 1970-73; Alumni research councilor Purdue Research Found., 1964-88; mem. Ind. Environmental Mgmt. Bd., 1972-87, Nat. Energy Policy Task Force, Dept. Energy, 1981-83; mem. Bd. Grants Am. Found. for Pharm. Edn., 1989—. Recipient award Chilean Iodine Ednl. Bur., 1956, Julius Sturmer award Phila. Coll. Pharmacy and Sci., 1958, Leather medal Purdue U., 1971, Hovde Faculty Purdue U. fellow, 1988. Fellow AAAS (past sec. and chmn. pharm. sci. sect., mem. council), Ind. Acad. Sci.; mem. AMA (spl. affiliate), AAUP, Am. Inst. Architecture (bd. dirs. 1998—, Gibson award 1999), Am. Assn. Colls. Pharmacy (past mem. exec. com., chmn. conf. tchrs., chmn. conf. grad. study and grad. tchrs., chmn. com. study grad. edn. in pharmacy), Am. Chem. Soc. (past chmn. Purdue sect.), Am. Pharm. Assn. (Ebert medal 1957, Justin L. Powers Research Achievement award 1963, past chmn. sci. sect.), Acad. Pharm. Sci. (past v.p.), Ind. Pharm. Assn., Am. Pub. Health Assn., Am. Nuclear Soc., Am. Soc. Bacteriology, Health Phys. Soc., Historic Landmarks Found. of Ind. (bd. dirs., exec. com. 1997—), Frank Lloyd Wright Bldg. Conservancy (Wright

Spirit award 1997), Sigma Xi (past pres. Purdue chpt., research award Purdue chpt. 1950), Rho Chi, Phi Lambda Upsilon, Sigma Pi Sigma., Eta Sigma Gamma, Gamma Sigma Delta. Home: 1301 Woodland Ave West Lafayette IN 47906-2371 Office: Purdue U Sch Health Scis Civil Engring Bldg West Lafayette IN 47907

CHRISTIAN, JOHN KENTON, publishing executive, marketing professional, consultant; b. Pana, Ill., Nov. 6, 1927; s. Ben Ross and Ruth (Stevenson) C.; m. Marjorie Adair Pollock, Nov. 28, 1958; children—Jefrey, Dwane, Kevin. Student, Westminster Coll., 1945, Colo. Coll., 1948, Emerson Coll., 1949; BS, Boston U., 1951; student, Am. U., 1954-55. Relief editor, rep., columnist St. Louis Daily Record, 1950-51; reporter Commerce Clearing House, Washington, 1952; with U.S. News and World Report, 1953-68, regional sales mgr. Los Angeles, 1960-63, mktg. mgr. Washington, 1964-68; pub. Nation's Cities Mag., Washington, 1968-76; mem. U.S. Fed. Preparedness Agy. mission to Iran, 1975-76; pres. Internat. Center for Emergency Preparedness, Washington, 1977-80; also pub. Emergency Preparedness News, 1977-79; v.p. Nat. Radio Broadcasters Assn., 1979-84; pres. Communications Brokers, Inc., 1984-88; author, pub. and mktg. cons., 1988-92; mktg. dir. Marine Corps Assn., 1992-2000. Media and mktg. devel. cons., 2000—. Served with USAAF, 1945-48. Presbyterian. Home: 10867 Deborah Dr Potomac MD 20854-2716 Personal E-mail: jackchristian@verizon.net.

CHRISTIAN, JOSEPH RALPH, physician; b. Chgo., June 15, 1920; s. Ralph F. and Anna M. (Across) Co; m. Marcia Pomeroy, Sept. 25, 1944; children— Patricia Ann, Joseph Ralph. AA, U. Chgo., 1941; MD, Loyola U., Chgo., 1944. Diplomate: Am. Bd. Pediatrics. Intern Cook County Hosp., Chgo., 1944-45, resident, 1945-46, 48-49; faculty Stritch Sch. Medicine, Loyola U., Chgo., 1948-61; prof. Stritch Sch. Medicine, Loyola U. (pediatrics), 1957-61, chmn. dept., 1960-61; attending pediatrician Loyola Service at La Rabida Sanitarium, 1948-61; chmn. dept. pediatrics Mercy Hosp., 1960-61; chief pediatrics Lewis Meml. Maternity Hosp., 1951-61; chmn. dept. pediatrics Rush Presbyn.-St. Luke's Med. Center, Chgo., 1961-85; prof. pediatrics U. Ill. Coll. Medicine, Chgo., 1961-70; prof. Rush Med. Coll., Chgo., 1970-85, prof. emeritus, 1985—, chmn. dept. pediatrics, 1970-85. Sr. attending pediatrician children's div. Cook County Hosp., 1959-65 Editor: Pediatrics Digest, 1962-78; Mem. editorial bd.: Childcraft, 1963-87; Contbr. articles to med. jours. Chmn. poison control com. Chgo. Bd. Health, 1961-69; chmn. med. com. Infant Welfare Soc., Chgo., 1958-61; chmn. 9th Ill. Congress Maternal and Infant Health, 1962; chmn. bd. trustees Holy Cross Chgo., 1970-75. Served to capt. M.C. AUS, 1946-47. Recipient Clin. Faculty award Stritch Sch. Medicine, 1954, 57 Fellow Am. Coll. Chest Physicians, Am. Acad. Pediatrics (chmn. film rev. com. 1963-73, chmn. com. residency fellowships 1964-67), Am. Pub. Health Assn., A.C.P.; mem. A.M.A., Am. Fedn. Clin. Research, Am. Pediatric Soc., Am. Heart Assn., Ambulatory Pediatric Assn., Am. Assn. Poison Control Centers, Am. Assn. Maternal and Infant Health, Ill. Assn. Maternal and Infant Health (pres. 1964), Am. Pediatric Soc., Chgo. Pediatric Soc. (pres. 1964-65), Midwest Soc. Pediatric Research, Assn. Med. Sch. Pediatric Dept. Chairmen. Home: 3 Oakbrook Club Dr Apt E107 Oak Brook IL 60523-1330 Office Phone: 630-832-7648.

CHRISTIAN, LESLIE KOJO, ambassador; b. London, 1951; married; 3 children. BA with honors, U. Ghana, Legon; grad. diploma in Internat. Affairs, U. Ghana. With Africa divsn. Govt. Ghana, 1975—76, with Internat. Orgns. and Confs. Bur., 1977—81, 1st sec. Permanent Mission to UN Geneva, 1981—86, with protocol divsn., 1986—89, with fin. and accounts divsn., 1989, desk officer Africa and Orgn. African Unity Bur., 1989—90, counselor, head of chancery to min. counselor Embassy Rome, 1990—94, dep. chief protocol, 1994—95, acting dir. fin. and accounts bur. Fgn. Ministry, 1995—97, counselor, head of chancery, dep. permanent rep. to UN NYC, 1997—2001, 2006—07, dir. Africa and Orgn. of African Unity Bur., 2001—02, supervising dir. polit. and econ. dept. Fgn. Ministry, 2003—06, amb., permanent rep. to UN NYC, 2007—. Office: Permanent Mission of Ghana to UN 19 E 47th St New York NY 10017 Office Phone: 212-832-1300. Office Fax: 212-751-6743. E-mail: ghanaperm@aol.com.

CHRISTIAN, MILDRED STOEHR, health products executive; b. Phila., July 7, 1942; d. Harvey Edward and Alice Emily Stoehr. BS, Pa. State U., 1963, MS, 1965; PhD, Thomas Jefferson U., 1979. Sr. scientist McNiel Laboratories, a J and J Co., Fort Washington, Pa., 1965—79; pres. Argus Rsch. Laboratories, Horsham, 1979—89, Argus Internat., Inc., 1980—; sr. advisor sci. and compliance CRL - Argus Rsch., 1989—2003; chmn. and CEO Argus Health Products, LLC, 2004—. Dir. Pro-Pharmaceuticals, Inc., Newton, Mass., 2003—. Founder, editor-in-chief: Jour. Am. Coll. Toxicology, 1981—91. Initiated hist. restoration of lamposts Franklin Lamposts, La., 2003—05; pres. Hist. Preservation Soc. - Restored 200 yr. old bldg., Phila., 2000—04; pres., bd. trustees Kensington M.E. Ch. (Old Brick), 1980—; donated children's libr. (Stoehr libr.) to Girard coll. Girard Coll., 2002—04. Recipient Outstanding Graduate award, Thomas Jefferson U., 1995, Disting. Scientist award, Genzyme Transgenics Corp., 2000, Lifetime Achievement award, ACT, 2004, Alumni award, Pa. State U., Coll. Sci., 2007. Mem.: Acad. Toxicologic Sci. (pres. 1999—2000), Teratology Soc. (pres. 1989—90), European Teratology Soc. (councilor 2002—05), Am. Coll. Toxicology (pres. 1992—93), Soc. Quality Assurance (hon.), Union League, Plimsoll Club, Patriotic Order Sons Am. (state sec. 2000—), Thomas Jefferson Alumni Soc. (pres. 1992—93). Conservative. Methodist. Avocations: piano, opera, travel. Office: Argus Health Products 933 Horsham Rd Horsham PA 19044 Office Phone: 215-672-8867.

CHRISTIAN, RICHARD CARLTON, dean, former advertising agency executive; b. Dayton, Ohio, Nov. 29, 1924; s. Raymond A. and Louise (Gamber) C.; m. Audrey Bongartz, Sept. 10, 1949; children: Ann Christian Carra, Richard Carlton Jr. BS in Bus. Adminstrn, Miami U., Oxford, Ohio, 1948; MBA, Northwestern U., 1949; LLD (hon.), Nat.-Louis U., 1986; postgrad., Denison U., The Citadel, Biarritz Am. U. Mktg. analyst Rockwell Mfg. Co., Pitts., 1949-50; exec. v.p. Marsteller Inc., Chgo., 1951-60, pres., 1960-75; bd. dirs., exec. com. Young and Rubicam, Inc., 1979-84; chmn. bd. Marsteller Inc., 1975-84, chmn. emeritus, 1984—; assoc. dean Kellogg Grad. Sch. Mgmt. Northwestern U., 1984-91, assoc. dean Medill Sch. Journalism, 1991-99. Dir., chmn. Bus. Publs. Audit Circulation, Inc., 1969-75; spkr. in field. Trustee Northwestern U., 1970-74, Nat.-Louis U., Evanston, Ill., 1970-92, James Webb Young Fund for Edn., U. Ill., 1962-95; pres. Nat. Advt. Rev. Coun., 1976-77; bd. adv. coun. mem. Miami U.; mem. adv. coun. J.L. Kellogg Grad. Sch. Mgmt., Northwestern U.; v.p., dir. Mus. Broadcast Comm.; dir. Can. U.S. Ednl. Exch. (Fulbright Found.), 1988-92. With inf. AUS, 1942-46, ETO. Decorated Purple Heart, 1945; recipient Ohio Gov.'s award 1977, Alumni medal, Alumni, Merit and Svc. awards Northwestern U.; named to the Advt. Hall of Fame, 1991. Mem. Am. Mktg. assn., Indsl. Mktg. Assn. (founder, chmn. 1951), Bus. Profl. Advt. Assn. (life mem. Chgo., pres. Chgo. 1954-55, nat. v.p. 1955-58, G. D. Crain award 1977), U. Ill. Found., Northwestern U. Bus. Sch. Alumni Assn. (founder, pres.), Am. Assn. Advt. Agys. (dir., chmn. 1976-77), Am. Acad. Advt. (1st disting. svc. award 1978), Northwestern U. Alumni Assn. (nat. pres. 1968-70), Mid-Am. Club, Comml. Club, Econ. Club Chgo., Kenilworth Club, Westmoreland Country Club, Alpha Delta Sigma, Beta Gamma Sigma, Delta Sigma Pi, Phi Gamma Delta. Baptist. Home: 2 Arbor Ln Apt 412 Evanston IL 60201

CHRISTIAN, SHIRLEY ANN, journalist, author; b. Jan. 16, 1938; d. Herbert Walsh and Minnie Lucille (Acker) C. BA, Pittsburg State U., Kans., 1960; MA, Ohio State U., 1966. UN corr. AP, 1970-73, copy editor fgn. desk NYC, 1974-77, chief of bur. Santiago, Chile, 1977-79; Latin Am. corr. Miami (Fla.) Herald, 1979-84; fgn. affairs reporter N.Y. Times, Washington, 1985-86, bur. chief Buenos Aires, 1986-91, bur. chief Ctrl. Am., 1991-93; pres. Hemisphere Bus. Books, 1994-97; publ. editor, sr. writer Stowers Inst. for Med. Rsch., Kansas City, Mo., 1998—2003. Adj. prof. journalism Columbia U., 1977. Author: Nicaragua: Revolution in the Family, 1985, Before Lewis and Clark: The Story of the Chouteaus, The French Dynasty that Ruled America's Frontier, 2004. Nieman fellow Harvard U., 1973-74; recipient Pulitzer prize for internat. reporting, 1981, George Polk Meml. award for fgn. reporting, 1981. Home and Office: 6836 Glenwood St Overland Park KS 66204-1453 Personal E-mail: schristian@everestkc.net.

CHRISTIAN, SUZANNE HALL, financial planner; b. Hollywood, Calif., Apr. 28, 1935; d. Peirson M. and Gertrude (Engel) Hall; children: Colleen, Carolyn, Claudia, Cynthia. BA, UCLA, 1956; MA, Redlands U., 1979. CFP. Instr. L.A. City Schs., 1958-59, Claremont (Calif.) Unified Schs., 1972-84, dept. chair, 1981-84; fin. planner Waddell & Reed, Upland, Calif., 1982-96, sr. acct. exec., 1986; br. mgr. Hornor, Townsend & Kent, Claremont, 1996—2002, Linsco Pvt. Ledger Fin. Svcs., 2002—. Past corp. mem. Pilgrim Place Found., Claremont; lectr. in field. Author: Strands in Composition, 1979; TV cable host Money Talks with Suzanne Christian, 1992—. Legal and estate planning com. Am. Cancer Soc., 1988-95; profl. adv. com. YWCA-Inland Empire, 1987; treas. Fine Arts Scripps Coll., 1993-94; bd. dirs. Casa Colina Hosp., 1994-2003; past bd. dirs. Galelio Soc. Harvey Mudd Coll. Recipient Athena Internat. Businesswoman of Yr. award, 1997. Mem. Fin. Planning Assn., Estate Planning Coun. Pomona Valley (pres. 2001-2002, bd. dirs. 2000-07), Claremont C. of C. (pres., bd. dirs. 1994-95), Curtain Raisers Club Garrison (pres. 1972-75), Circle of Champions (pres.'s coun. 1994-95, Silver Crest award 1985-87, 94-95, HTK top ten leader 1996-2003), Harvey Mudd Coll. Galileo Soc. (bd. dirs. 1997-98), Patriots Club (Chmns. award), Chairman's Club, Kappa Kappa Gamma (pres. 1970-74). Avocations: tennis, gardening, archaeology. Office: Linsco Pvt Ledger 419 Yale Ave Claremont CA 91711-4340 Office Fax: 909-625-3661.

CHRISTIAN, TERRY CLIFTON, lawyer; b. Welch, W.Va., Aug. 4, 1952; s. Samuel Clifton and Mary Jane Christian; m. Wendy Lee McCoy, Feb. 14, 1991. BA, U. Del., Newark, 1984; JD, Ind. U., Indpls., 1987. Bar: Fla. 1988, U.S. Dist. Ct. (mid. dist.) Fla. 1989, U.S. Ct. Appeals (11th cir.) 1990, U.S. Dist. Ct. (no. and so. dists.) Fla. 1996, U.S. Supreme Ct. 1996; cert. Bd. Legal Edn. and Specialization, Fla.; cert. Nat. Bd. Trial Advocacy. Asst. state atty. Office of State Atty., Ft. Myers, Fla., 1988-89; mng. ptnr. Christian & Assocs., P.A., Tampa, Fla., 1989—; U.S. Immigration Judge Detroit, 2003. Mem. criminal justice act panel U.S. Dist. Ct. for Mid. Dist. Fla., 1989—, for No. Dist., 1996—2000, for So. Dist., 1998—2005; spl. asst. pub. defender capital and RICO cases only, Tampa, 1989—. Author immigration and criminal law seminars. Bd. dirs. Humane Soc. Tampa Bay, 2002-03. Capt. U.S. Army Res., 1986-90. Mem.: FBA (exec. com. Tampa Bay chpt. 1996—2001, svc. award 1997—2001), Am. Inns of Ct. (exec. com. 2000—03, parliamentarian 2001, sec. 2002—03, svc. award 2002—03), Hillsborough County Assn. Criminal Def. Lawyers (sec. 1996—97, pres. 1997—98, bd. dirs. 1999—2002, svc. award 1998), Fla. Bar (named Fla. Super Lawyer 2006, 2007—), Am. Immigration Lawyers Assn. (sec. Ctrl. Fla. chpt. 1992—94, treas. 1994—95, v.p. 1995—97, exec. com. 2005, bd. govts. 2005, v.p. 2006—, svc. award 1995—97, exec. v.p. 2007—). Democrat. Roman Catholic. Avocations: reading, sports, exercise, weightlifting. Office: Christian & Assocs PA 620 E Twiggs St Ste 203 Tampa FL 33602

CHRISTIAN-BROUGHAM, RUBY ROSALIE, education educator; d. Frank and Sylvia Arangure Brougham; m. William Steptoe Christian, IV, Dec. 20, 1996. PhD, U. So. Calif., LA, 1998. Postdoctoral rschr. Nat. Inst. of Aging U. So. Calif., LA, 1998—2000; asst. prof. Chapman U., Orange, Calif., 2000—. Curriculum devel. for criminal justice com. Nat. Alliance for the Mentally ill, Pasadena, Calif., 2005—. Author: (jour. article) Current Psychology, Internat. Jour. Aging & Human Development. Mem. Latino Orgn., Orange, 2006—, Human Soc., Pasadena, 2002—. Fellow Ruth L. Kirschstein Nat. Rsch. Svc. award, Nat. Inst. Aging, 1992—95. Mem.: Gerontol. Soc. Am. (assoc.), Western Psychol. Assn. (assoc.), Assn. Psychol. Sci. (assoc.). Office: Chapman Univ One University Dr Orange CA 92866 Home Phone: 626-355-7992; Office Phone: 714-744-7640.

CHRISTIAN-CHRISTENSEN, DONNA MARIE, congresswoman; b. Teaneck, NJ, Sept. 19, 1945; d. Almeric L. Christian and Virginia Sterling; children: Rabiah Green, Karida Green; m. Chris Christensen; stepchildren: Lisa, Esther, Bryan, David. BS, St. Mary's Coll., Ind., 1966; MD, George Washington U., 1970; LLD (hon.), Moravian Coll. Pvt. medical practice, 1973—74; cmty. health physician U.S. V.I. Dept. Health; med. dir. Gov. Juan F. Luis Hosp., St. Croix; vice chairperson U.S. V.I. Dem. Territorial Com., 1980; mem. U.S. V.I. Bd. Edn., 1984; committeewoman Nat. Dem., 1984; apptd. U.S. V.I. Status Commn., 1988-92; del. Dem. Nat. Conv.; at large repr. US Congress from VI, 1997—; chair Congl. Black Caucus Health Braintrust, 1999—. Mem. Resources Com., Small Bus. Com.; mem. Select Com. Homeland Security; mem. Congl. Caucus Women's Issues; mem. Steering Com. Congl. Travel and Tourism Caucus; mem. Congl. Rural Caucus, Congl. Nat. Guard and Res. Caucus. Trustee, founding mem. Caribbean Youth Orgn. Named an Most Influential Black Americans, Ebony mag., 2006; recipient Disting. Alumni award, George Washington U., Disting. Svc. award, Howard U. Sch. Medicine. Mem. Nat. Med. Assn. (trustee), Caribbean Studies Assn., V.I. Med. Inst., V.I. Med. Soc. (pres., sec.), Women's Coalition St. Croix, St. Croix Environ. Assn. Democrat. Achievements include first to be the female delegate from U.S. Virgin Islands. Office: 1510 Longworth Ho Office Bldg Washington DC 20515-0001 also: Dist Office Nisky Ctr Ste 207 St Thomas VI 00802 Office Phone: 202-225-1790. Office Fax: 202-225-5517. E-mail: donna.christensen@mail.house.gov.*

CHRISTIANS, CLIFFORD GLENN, communications educator; b. Hull, Iowa, Dec. 22, 1939; s. Arnold and Verbena Janette (Geerdes) Christians; m. Priscilla Jean Kreun, June 13, 1961; children: Glenn Clifford, Ted Arnold, Paul Raymond. AB, Calvin Coll., 1961; ThM, Fuller Theol. Sem., 1965; MA, U. So. Calif., 1966; PhD, U. Ill., 1974. Dir. comm. Christian Ref. Home Ministries, Grand Rapids, Mich., 1966—70; rsch. asst. prof, comm. U. Ill., Urbana, 1974—80, rsch. assoc. prof. comm., 1980—87, rsch. prof. comm., 1987—, Charles H. Sandage Disting. prof., 2005—. Rsch. fellow Calvin Ctr. for Christian Scholarship, Grand Rapids, 1983-84; vis. scholar in ethics Princeton (N.J.) U., spring, 1979; inst. fellow U. Chgo., 1986-87, vis. scholar, 2006; Pew Evangel. scholar in ethics Oxford U., spring, 1995; dir. Inst. Rsch. Comms., Urbana, 1987—2001. Co-author: Jacques Ellul: Interpretive Essays, 1981, Good News: Social Ethics and The Press, 1993, Media Ethics: Cases and Moral Reasoning, 1998, Communication Ethics and Universal Values, 1997, Moral Engagement in Public Life: Theorists fro Contemporary Ethics, 2002; editor: Critical Studies in Mass Communication, 1992-95. Bd. dirs. Empty Tomb, Inc., Champaign, Ill., 1986—; elder Christian Ref. Ch., Champaign, 1974-82; bd. dirs. Univ. YMCA, Champaign, 1974-77, Judah Christian Sch., Champaign, 1984-90. Rsch. fellow, Program for Cultural Values and Ethics, 1990. Mem. Soc. for Philosophy and Tech., Assn. for Edn. in Journalism and Mass Comm. (chair qualitative studies divsn. 1980-81), Internat. Assn. Mass Comm. Rsch. (program co-chair 1991-94), Ellul Studies Forum, Nat. Comm. Assn. Democrat. Avocations: fishing, travel, reading. Home: U Ill Inst Comm Rsch 1002 W William St Champaign IL 61821 Office: U Ill Comm Dept 810 S Wright St Urbana IL 61801 Office Phone: 217-333-1549. Business E-Mail: cchrstns@uiuc.edu.

CHRISTIANSEN, ANDREW P., website designer, historic archives digitilizer; b. Barre City, Vt., July 9, 1953; s. Stanley Lee and Joyce (Rowland) C.; m. Jennifer Dow Zollner, 1987; 2 children. BA, BM, Lawrence U., 1976. Active Dem. Town Com., 1978-88; justice of peace East Montpelier, Vt., 1980-92; co-chmn. Vt. Rainbow Coalition, 1986-87; state rep. dist. 2 Vt. Ho. of Reps., 1987-97; owner Old Barn Vt. LLC, 1997—. Dairy farmer, East Montpelier, 1958-86; rschr. dept. psychology Lawrence U., Appleton, Wis., 1971-76; piano tchr., Ctrl. Vt., 1976—96; website designer. Mem. Danish Brotherhood Am., Am. Soc. Dowsers, Rural Vt., Vt. Hist. Soc. Address: 470 Hammett Hill Rd East Montpelier VT 05651-4034 Home Phone: 802-223-1342; Office Phone: 802-223-7858. E-mail: andy@oldbarnvt.com.

CHRISTIANSEN, DONALD DAVID, electrical engineer, editor, publishing executive, consultant; b. Plainfield, NJ, June 23, 1927; s. David Carsten and Rita (Holmes) C.; m. Joyce Ifill, Jan. 1, 1951; children: Jacqueline, Jill. BEE, Cornell U., Ithaca, NY, 1950; postgrad., Mass. Inst. Tech., 1951-54, U. Wis., Madison, 1966, 68, 71. Registered profl. engr., Mass. Engr. Philco Corp., Phila., 1948-50, CBS, Danvers, Lowell and Newburyport, Mass., 1950-62; solid-state editor Electronic Design, Hayden Pub. Co., NYC, 1962-63; sr. editor EEE-Circuit Design Engring. Mactier Pub. Co., NYC, 1963-66; sr. assoc. editor Electronics McGraw-Hill Pub. Co., NYC, 1966, sr. editor, 1966-67, assoc. mng. editor, 1967-68, editor-in-chief, 1968-70, mgr. planning, devel. electronics publs., 1970-71; gen. mgr. Electronics in Medicine, 1971; editor and pub. Spectrum jour. of IEEE, NYC, 1971-93, editor emeritus, 1993—, chmn. editorial bd., 1972-93; IEEE rep. to UN, 1974-87; pres. Informatica, Huntington, NY, 1993—. Lectr. Newark Coll. Engring., 1967, U. Mich., Ann Arbor, 1973, Walla Walla (Wash.) Coll., 1973, Ga. Inst. Tech., 1976, NASA Goddard Space Flight Ctr., 1981, Cornell U., 1982, Disting. lectr. Purdue U., 1986; cons. Bur. of Census, Dept. Commerce, NSF; mem. NRC Com. on Edn. and Utilization of the Engr.; elec. engring. adv. com. Worcester Poly. Inst.; mem. AIP mag. policy com., 1996-98; mem. AIP adv. com. on Indsl. Physicist, chmn., 2000-01; adv. bd. Encyclopedia Americana, 2000-; advisor Am. Inst. Physics Resources Ctr., 2000-01. Editor-in-chief: Electronics Engineers' Handbook, 4th edit., 1997; editor: Engineering Excellence, 1987, Standard Handbook of Electronic Engineering, 2005; publ. com. Cornell Alumni News mag., 1986-91; contbr. articles to profl. jours. Bd. dirs. YMCA, Newburyport, Mass., 1962, Broadband Info. Svcs., N.Y.C., 1970-87, L.I. Mus. Sci. and Tech., 1993-96, Audio History Libr., 2006-. With USN, WWII. Recipient medal and citation for advancement of culture Flanders Acad. Art, Sci. and Lit., 1980, citation Folio mag., 1991. Fellow IEEE (co-founder, charter exec. com. chpt. 1958, Centennial medal, Gruenwald award), World Acad. Art and Sci., Radio Club of Am., 1987; mem. Nat. Press Club, N.Y. Acad. Sci., Cornell Soc. Engrs., Coun. Engring. and Sci. Soc. Execs., Am. Soc. Assn. Execs., Am. Soc. Mag. Editors, Soc. Nat. Assn. Publs. (dir. 1976-79, chmn. editl. com. 1976-79, pres. 1981-83), NY Bus. Press Editors (dir. 1978-79), Cornell Engring. Alumni Coun., Delta Club, Union Internat. de la Presse Radiotechnique et Electronique, Deadline Club, Nat. Conf. Electronics in Medicine (chmn. 1971), Soc. for History Tech., Soc. for Indsl. Archeology, Jovians, Antique Wireless Assn., Franklin Inst., Royal Instn., Newcomen Soc., Eta Kappa Nu (eminent mem., chmn., Outstanding Elec. Engr. award 1976-78, dir. 1982-84, chmn. Vladimir Karapetoff award 1991-2004, chmn. eminent mem. com. 1998-2007, Disting. Svc. award 2001), U.S. Naval Inst., Navy League of U.S. (life), USS San Jacinto Assn., Mu Sigma Tau, Sigma Delta Chi. Office: Informatica 434 W Main St Huntington NY 11743-3247

CHRISTIANSEN, JAY DAVID, lawyer; b. Slayton, Minn., Mar. 22, 1952; s. Holger K. and Dagny (Fjelstad) C.; children: Tyler, Carrie, Jayne. BA, Luther Coll., 1974; JD, Vanderbilt U., 1977. Ptnr. Faegre & Benson, Mpls., 1977—. Mem. ABA (chmn. 1997-99, health law sect., mem. ho. dels. 1999-2002), Order of Coif. Office: Faegre & Benson 90 S 7th St Minneapolis MN 55402-3901 E-mail: jchristi@faegre.com.

CHRISTIANSEN, KEITH, curator; b. Jan. 6, 1947; BA in Hist. and French Lit., U. Calif., Santa Cruz, 1965—69; MA in Art Hist., U. Calif., LA, 1969—72; PhD in Art Hist., Harvard U., 1972—77. Asst. curator, European Paintings Met. Mus. of Art, NYC, 1977—80, assoc. curator, European Paintings, 1980—87, curator, European Paintings, 1987—89, Jayne Wrightsman curator, 1989—; Clarence and Ruth Wedgewood Kennedy prof., Renaissance Studies Smith Coll., 1999. Mem., Grants Com. Met. Mus. of Art, 1980—83; adj. assoc. prof., Art Hist. and Archeology Columbia U., NYC, 1985, NYC, 86, NYC, 88, NYC, 1992—94, NYC, 1990, NYC, 97; adj. prof. Inst. Fine Arts, NYU, 1991, 98, 2001; bd. mem. Ctr. for Adv. Study of Visual Arts, 1995—98; mem., Grants Bd., I Tatti Harvard Ctr. for Renaissance Studies, Florence, 2002—. Curator (exhibitions) The Age of Caravaggio, Met. Mus. Art, 1985, The Age of Correggio and the Carracci, 1986—87, Nat. Gallery, Washington, DC, 1986—87, Pinacoteca Nat., Bologna, 1986—87, Caravaggio's Cardsharps Rediscovered, Met. Mus. Art, 1987, Andrea Mantegna's Descent into Limbo, 1988, Painting in Renaissance Siena: 1420-1500, 1988—89 (Alfred H. Barr Jr. award, 1988), A Caravaggio Rediscovered: The Lute Player, 1990, Andrea Mantegna, 1992, Royal Acad., London, 1992, Jusepe de Ribera, Nat. Mus. Capodimonte, Naples, 1992, Prado Mus., Madrid, 1992, Met. Mus. Art, 1992, Giambattista Tiepolo, 1996—97, Donato Creti: Melancholy and Perfection, 1998, From Van Eyck to Bruegel: Early Netherlandish Painting at the Met. Mus. of Art, 1998—99, La Tour's Magdalenes, The Birth of Baroque: The Carracci at the Met., 2000, Orazio and Artemisia Gentileschi, 2001—02, Palazzo Venezia, Rome, 2001—02, El Greco, Nat. Gallery, London, 2003—04, Met. Mus. Art, 2003—04 (Internat. Assn. of Art Critics award, 2004), From Filippo Lippi to Piero della Francesca: Fra Carnevale and the Making of Renaissance Master, 2005 (Salimbeni prize, 2005); author: Gentile da Fabriano, 1982 (Mitchell prize, 1983), The Jack and Belle Linsky Collection in the Met. Mus. of Art, 1984, Lae Caravage et 'l' esempio davanti del naturale, 1986 (Arthur Kingsley Porter prize, 1986), Quattrocento, 1987, A Caravaggio Rediscovered: The Little Flute Player, 1990, Italian Painting, 1992, Andrea Mantegna: Padua and Mantua, 1994, Giambattista Tiepolo, 1997, From Van Eyck to Bruegel, 1998, Orazio and Artemisia Gentileschi, El Greco, 2003—04, From Filippo Lippi to Piero della Francesca: Fra Carnevale and the Making of a Renaissance Master, 2005. Recipient Excellency award for Italian Culture, Found. for Italian Art and Culutre, 2005; fellow NDEA Title IV, 1969—72; granter Harvard Travel grant, Italy, 1975, Fulbright grant, 1975—76; vis. scholar Am. Acad., Rome, 1998. Fellow: Am. Acad. Art. & Sciences; mem.: Acad. Clementina. Office: Metropolitan Museum of Art 1000 5th Ave New York NY 10028 Office Phone: 212-535-7710.

CHRISTIANSEN, KEITH ALLAN, lawyer; b. Madison, Wis., Dec. 14, 1943; s. Herman Louis and Faith Louise (Haase) C.; m. Sheila Irene Stangel, Apr. 11, 1966; children: Douglas, Jeffrey. BS, U. Wis., 1965, JD, 1968. Bar: Wis. 1968, Fla. 1973, U.S. Dist. Ct. (ea. dist.) Wis. 1968. Assoc. Foley & Lardner LLP, Milw., 1968-74, ptnr., 1975—. Co-author: Marital Property Law in Wisconsin, 1984, 3d edit., 2004. Active Potawatomi coun. Boy Scouts Am. 1975—, past pres.; v.p. Area 3 Ctrl. Region Boy Scouts. Am., 1992—. Fellow Am. Coll. Trust and Estate Counsel; mem. Midwinter Estate Planning Clinic, Estate Counselors Forum. Republican. Office: Foley & Lardner LLP 777 E Wisconsin Ave Ste 3800 Milwaukee WI 53202-5306 Office Phone: 414-297-5746. E-mail: kchristiansen@foley.com.

CHRISTIANSEN, MARGARET LOUISE, law librarian, lawyer; d. James Birch and Elizabeth P. Dempsey; m. Phillip Edward Christiansen, June 1, 1996. BSBA in Econs., William Woods Coll., 1980; JD, Regent U., 1994; MS in Info. Sci., Fla. State U., Tallahassee, Florida, 2005. Bar: Va. 1996. Lectr. internat. trade Jiangsu Poly. Inst., Zhenjiang, China, 1990, Qingdao U., Shangdong, China, 1991; dir. career svcs. Regent U. Sch. Law, Virginia Beach, Va., 1994—95; faculty liaison Regent U. Law Libr., 1995—98, asst. libr., 1998—99, asst. dir., 1999—. Contbr. articles to profl.

publs. Kids ch. leader Coastlands Cmty. Ch., Chesapeake, Va., 2004—05. Recipient Am. Jurisprudence award in Real Property, Lawyers Coop. Pub. Co. and Regent U., 1991. Mem.: Va. Assn. Law Librs. (co-editor newsletter 2002—04, chair membership com. 2005—), Southeastern Chpt. Am. Assn. Law Librs. (mem. scholarship com. 2005—), Am. Soc. for Info. Sci. and Tech., Focus on Christian Law Librarianship, Am. Assn. Law Librs. (centennial celebration com. 2004—), Va. Bar Assn. Conservative. Avocations: camping, backpacking, canoeing, travel. Office: Regent Univ Law Libr 1000 Regent Univ Dr Virginia Beach VA 23464 Home Phone: 757-482-3069. Office Fax: 757-226-4451. E-mail: margchr@regent.edu.

CHRISTIANSEN, MATTHEW LANE, mathematics educator; b. Grass Valley, Calif., Apr. 16, 1977; s. Sidney Lane and Carol Anne Christiansen; m. Julie Ann Hendrix, Aug. 14, 1999. BA, U. No. Colo., Greeley, 2001, MA, 2005. Lic. profl. tchr. Colo., 2004. Math. tchr. Washoe County Sch. Dist., Reno, 2002, Weld County Sch. Dist. 6, Greeley, Colo., 2002—04, math. dept. chair, tchr., 2004—05, math. curriculum coord., 2005—. Missionary LDS Ch., Perth, Australia, 1996—98. Mem.: Nat. Coun. Suprs. Math., Nat. Coun. Tchrs. Math., Colo. Coun. Tchrs. Math. (conf. co-chair 2006—). Conservative. Lds Ch. Office: Weld County School District 6 1025 9th Ave Greeley CO 80631 Home Phone: 970-330-0203. Personal E-mail: matt_christiansen@msn.com. Business E-Mail: mchristiansen@greeleyschools.org.

CHRISTIANSEN, PATRICK T., lawyer; b. Mpls., 1947; BSEE summa cum laude, U. Notre Dame, 1969; JD, Harvard U., 1972. Bar: Fla. 1972, Minn. 1974, U.S. Tax Ct. 1977, U.S. Supreme Ct. 1980. Mem. Akerman, Senterfitt & Eidson P.A., Orlando, Fla. Chmn. bd. Orlando Mus. Art; mem., bd. dirs. The Greater Orlando C. of C., Jobs and Edn. Partnership; chmn. Orange County Transp. Roundtable, BusinessForce, 2002--; mem. Orange County Blue Ribbon Commn., steering com., chmn. transp. com.; bd. dirs. United Arts Cen. Fla., Orlando Downtown Devel. Bd.; trustee, chmn. Orlando Repertory Theatre, 2002--, U. Ctrl. Fla. Found., 2001--; bd. trustees U. Ctrl. Fla.; mem. Orange County Arts & Cultural Affairs Adv. Com., chmn. advancement com., 2001--. Mem. ABA (sects. on bus. law, taxation, real property), Fla. Bar (trial lawyers sect., co-chmn. land trust com. real property, probate and trust law sect. 1978-82, dir. real property divsn. 1982-84, vice chmn. 1984-85, chmn. 1985-86, vice-chmn. UCC subcom. corp., banking and bus. law sect. 1979-84, bd. govs. young lawyers sect. 1981-83), Am. Coll. Real Estate Lawyers, Minn. State Bar Assn., Orange County Bar Assn. Office: Akerman Senterfitt & Eidson PA Citrus Ctr 17th Fl PO Box 231 255 S Orange Ave Orlando FL 32801-3445

CHRISTIANSEN, RICHARD DEAN, retired newspaper editor; b. Berwyn, Ill., Aug. 1, 1931; s. William Edward and Louise Christine (Dethlefs) C. BA, Carleton Coll., Northfield, Minn., 1953; postgrad., Harvard U., 1954; LHD (hon.), DePaul U., 1988. Reporter, critic, editor Chgo. Daily News, 1957-73, 74-78; editor Chicagoan mag., 1973-74; critic-at-large Chgo. Tribune, 1978-83, entertainment editor, 1983-91, chief critic, sr. writer, 1991—2002; ret., 2002. Author: A Theater of Our Own: A History and a Memoir of 1,001 Nights in Chicago, 2004. Served to cpl. U.S. Army, 1954-56. Recipient award Chgo. Newspaper Guild, 1969, 74, Joseph Jefferson award, 1996, Excellence in the Arts award DePaul U., 1998, Peter Lisagor award for criticism, 2002, Lifetime Achievement award Chgo. Headline Club, Soc. Profl. Journalists, 2005; named to Chgo. Journalism Hall of Fame, 1998. Mem. Am. Theatre Critics Assn., Chgo. Acad. TV Arts and Scis., Soc. Midland Authors, Headline Club Chgo. (Peter Lisagor award 2002), Arts Club Chgo. (dir.), Phi Beta Kappa, Sigma Delta Chi. Republican. Lutheran. Personal E-mail: rchris5568@aol.com.

CHRISTIANSEN, RICHARD LOUIS, orthodontist, educator, dean; b. Denison, Iowa, Apr. 1, 1935; s. John Cornelius and Rosa Katherine C.; m. Nancy Marie Norman, June 24, 1956; children: Mark Richard, David Norman, Laura Marie. DDS, U. Iowa, 1959; MSD, Ind. U., Indpls., 1964; PhD, U. Minn., 1970; PhD (hon.), Nippon Dental U., Tokyo, 2000. Prin. investigator Nat. Inst. Dental Research NIH, Bethesda, Md., 1970-73, chief craniofacial anomalies program br., 1973-81, dir. extramural Nat. Inst. Dental Research, 1981-82; prof. dept. orthodontics U. Mich., Ann Arbor, 1982—, dean, Sch. Dentistry and dir. W.K. Kellogg Found. Inst., 1982—2001, prof., dean emeritus, 2001—. Organizer state-of-the -art workshops in field of craniofacial anomalies and other aspects of oral health; founder Internat. Union Schs. Oral Health, 1985; organizer oral health conf. in Poland, 1989, Jordan, 1995. Contbr. chpts. to books and articles to profl. jours. Chmn. Region III United Way, U. Mich., Ann Arbor, 1984; chmn., v.p. Trinity Luth. Ch., Rockville, Md., 1975; v.p. and chmn. planning task force Trinity Luth. Ch., Ann Arbor, chmn. bd. Sequoia Sr. Housing; vice chmn., bd. dirs. Luth. Soc. Svcs. Mich., 1997—; with USPHS, 1959-82, mem. dental prof. adv. com., 2005. Recipient Commendation medal USPHS, 1980, Cert. of Recognition NIH, 1982, others; named Dental Alumnus of Yr., U. Iowa, 2005, Southeast Mich. Philanthropy award, 2006. Fellow Internat. Coll. Dentists, Am. Coll. Dentists, Pierre Fauchard Acad.; mem. Am. Assn. Orthodontists, Am. Assn. Dental Sch., ADA (rsch. coun.), Mich. Dental Assn., Am. Assn. Dental Rsch. (dir. craniofacial biology group 1975-79, v.p. 1979-80, pres. 1981-82), Omicron Kappa Upsilon (com. mem.). Achievements include research in craniofacial research and international oral health. Avocations: reading, jogging, tennis, sailing. Business E-Mail: vista@umich.edu.

CHRISTIANSON, GERYLD B., government agency administrator, consultant; b. Boyd, Minn., Dec. 31, 1934; m. Sue Singer, July 9, 1960; children: Stephen, Alexander. BA in Internat. Rels., U. Minn., 1957; postgrad., Johns Hopkins U., 1967-68. Fgn. svc. officer Dept. State, NATO Office, Bur. European Affairs, various fgn. locations, 1958-75; fgn. policy advisor Senator Claiborne Pell, Washington, 1975-81; minority staff dir. Senate Fgn. Rels. Com., Washington, 1981-87, staff dir., 1987-95; sr. counselor The Evans Group, Ltd., Washington, 1995, 97—; v.p. Jefferson Waterman Internat., Washington, 1995-97. With USAR, 1957—63. Mem. Coun. on Fgn. Rels., Internat. Inst. for Strategic Studies (London). Democrat. Episcopalian. Avocations: collecting political buttons, tennis. Home: 8716 Mary Lee Ln Annandale VA 22003-3659 Office Phone: 202-333-8777. Personal E-mail: geryld.christianson@verizon.net.

CHRISTIANSON, JON L., lawyer; BS, Brigham Young U., 1984; JD, Columbia U., 1989; MBA, Columbia U. Bus. Sch., 1989. Bar: NY 1989, Hong Kong. Ptnr. Skadden, Arps, Slate, Meagher & Flom LLP, NYC, Hong Kong, 1992—. Named a Leading Lawyer, AsiaLaw, 2003—05, Key Contact Ptnr., Internat. Fin. Law Review, 2004—07, Leading Lawyer, 2004—07, Legal 500, 2004—07, Dealmaker of the Yr., Am. Lawyer mag., 2006. Office: Skadden Arps Slate Meagher & Flom LLP E Wing Office Level 4 1 Jian Guo Men Wai Ave Beijing 100004 China Office Phone: 011 86 10 6505 5511, ext. 8800. Office Fax: 011 86 10 6505 5522. E-mail: jonchris@skadden.com.

CHRISTIANSON, ROGER GORDON, biology professor, department chairman; b. Santa Monica, Calif., Oct. 31, 1947; s. Kyle C. and Ruby K. (Parker) Christianson; m. Angela Diane Rey, Mar. 3, 1967; children: Lisa Marie, David Scott, Stephen Peter. BA in Cell and Organismal Biology, U. Calif., Santa Barbara, 1969, MA in Biology, 1971, PhD in Biology, 1976. Faculty assoc. U. Calif., Santa Barbara, 1973-79, staff rsch. assoc., 1979-80; asst. prof. So. Oreg. U., Ashland, 1980-85, assoc. prof., 1985-93, prof., 1993—, coord. gen. biology program, 1980—, chmn. biology dept., 1996, 1997—2003. Instr. U. Calif. Santa Barbara, 1976, 78, 80. Contbr. articles to sci. and ednl. jours. Active Oreg. Shakespeare Festival Assn., Ashland, 1983—87; mem. bikeway com. Ashland City Coun., 1986—88; organizer Bike Oreg., 1982—92, Frontline HS Staff, 1985—2003; short-term mission work Mex. Orphanage, 1986—; ofcl. photographer Ashland H.S. Booster Club, 1987—92; coord. youth program 1st Bapt. Ch., Ashland, 1981—85, mem. ch. life commn., 1982—88, 2004—, chair ch. life commn., 2004—, bd. deacons, 1993—95, 2004—, mem. outreach commn., 1994, 1995, mem. constitution and by-laws rev. com., 2004—06, moderator, 2006—; youth leader jr. and sr. H.S. students Grace Ch., Santa Barbara, 1973—80; bd. dirs. El Sauzal Found., 2004—, treas., 2004—. Mem.: AAAS (chair Pacific divsn. edn. sect 1985—2001, coun. Pacific divsn. 1985—, exec. com. Pacific divsn. 1998—, chair local organizing com. Pacific divsn. ann. meeting 2000, chair Pacific divsn. student awards com. 2001, exec. dir. Pacific divsn. 2002—, chair local organizing com. Pacific divsn. ann. meeting 2005), Oreg. Acad. Scis., Assn. for Biology Lab. Edn., Oreg. Sci. Tchrs. Assn., Am. Mus. Natural History, Beta Beta Beta, Sigma Xi (chpt. membership com. 1998—2000). Republican. Avocations: sports, photography, youth work, multimedia presentations, amateur radio operator. Office: Southern Oregon U Dept Biology 1250 Siskiyou Blvd Ashland OR 97520-5010 Office Phone: 541-552-6747. E-mail: rchristi@sou.edu.

CHRISTIANSON, STANLEY DAVID, finance company executive; b. Chgo., Dec. 8, 1931; s. Stanley Olai and Emma Josephine (Johnson) D.; m. Elin J. Ballantyne, July 25, 1959; children: Erica Joanna, David Ballantyne. BS, U. Ill., 1954; MBA, U. Chgo., 1960. Auditor Price Waterhouse & Co., Chgo., 1956-58; asst. to controller Miehle-Goss-Dexter, Inc., Chgo., 1960-67, v.p. adminstrn. Goss Div., 1967-69; dir. mgmt. systems MGD Graphics Systems-N.Am. Rockwell (formerly Miehle-Goss-Dexter), Chgo., 1969-70; v.p. fin. Duchossois/Thrall Group (formerly Thrall Car Mfg. Co.), Chicago Heights, Elmhurst, Ill., 1970-83; vice chmn., bd. dirs. Thrall Enterprises, Inc., Chgo., 1983—. Bd. dirs. Midwestern U., 1992-98, chmn., 1997-98. Bd. govs. Internat. House, U. Chgo., 1988-2000, chmn. 1997-2000; trustee Cmty. Theatre Guild, Valparaiso, Ind., 2001- , chmn., 2005-06; mem. Hobart (Ind.) Plan Commn., 1986-92, pres., 1988-92. Capt. U.S. Army, 1954-56. Home: 141 Beverly Blvd Hobart IN 46342-4346 Office: Thrall Enterprises Inc 180 N Stetson Ste 3020 Chicago IL 60601-6223

CHRISTIANSON, WEI SUN, diversified financial services company executive; b. Aug. 21, 1956; BA, Amherst Coll., 1985; JD with honors, Columbia U., 1989. Atty. Orrick, Herrington & Sutcliffe, NYC; assoc. dir. Hong Kong Securities and Fin. Commn.; exec. dir., chief Beijing rep. Morgan Stanley, 1998—2002, CEO China Beijing, 2006—, mng. dir., mem. Asia Pacific Exec. Com., 2006—; country mgr. Credit Suisse First Boston, China, 2002—04, chair women China, 2004, Citigroup Global Markets (Asia) Ltd., 2004—06. Named one of 50 Women to Watch, Wall St. Jour., 2006. Office: Morgan Stanley Rm 2706 China World Tower II No 1 Jiah Guo Mah Wai Dajie Beijing 100004 China

CHRISTIE, CHRISTOPHER JAMES, prosecutor, lawyer; b. Mendham, NJ, 1963; BA, U. Del., 1984; JD, Seton Hall U., 1987. Bar: NJ 1987, US Dist. Ct. NJ 1987. Atty. Dughi & Hewit, Cranford, NJ, 1987—93, ptnr., 1993—2002; US atty. dist. NJ US Dept. Justice, 2002—. Bd. trustees Daytop Village-N.J., Mendham, 1998—2002; officer Christie Family Found., 2001—; chmn. Morris County Ins. Commn.; bd. dirs. United way Morris County, Family Svcs. Morris County, Morris County Bd. Social Svcs.; dir. bd. Morris County Bd. Chosen Freeholders, 1997—. Mem.: ABA, NJ State Bar Assn. Office: US Attys Office Peter Rodino Fed Bldg 970 Broad St Ste 700 Newark NJ 07102*

CHRISTIE, GEORGE CUSTIS, lawyer, educator, writer; b. NYC, Mar. 3, 1934; s. Custis and Sophie (Velimahitis) C.; m. Susan D. Monserud, Apr. 20, 1965 (div. July 1974); 1 child, Constantine George; m. Deborah D. Carnes, Dec. 20, 1974; children: Rebecca Sophia, Nicholas George. AB, Columbia U., 1955, JD, 1957; diploma in internat. law (Fulbright scholar), Cambridge U., Eng., 1962; SJD, Harvard U., 1966; Doctorate (hon.), U. Athens, 2007. Bar: NY 1957, DC 1958. Assoc. Covington & Burling, Washington, 1958-60; Ford Found. fellow in law teaching Harvard U., 1960-61; assoc. prof. law U. Minn., Mpls., 1962-65, prof. law, 1965-66; asst. gen. counsel for Near E. and S. Asia, AID, Dept. State, 1966-67; prof. law Duke U., 1967-79, James B. Duke prof. law, 1979—. Vis. lectr. U. Witwatersrand, South Africa, 1980, Fudan U., China, U. Otago, New Zealand, 1985; fellow Nat. Humanities Center, 1980-81; scholar-in-residence McGuire, Woods & Battle, Richmond, Va., 1983, vis. Freda Alverson prof. law George Washington U., spring 1988; vis. prof. law Northwestern U., 1991-92, U. Athens, Greece, 2000; vis. fellow Rsch. Sch. Social Scis., Australian Nat. U., 2002. Author: Jurisprudence: Text and Readings on the Philosophy of Law, 1973, 2d edit. (with P. Martin), 1995, The Sum and Substance of the Law of Torts, 1980, Law, Norms & Authority, 1982, Cases and Materials on the Law of Torts, 1983, 2d edit. (with J. Meeks), 1990, 4th edit. (with others), 2004, The Notion of an Ideal Audience in Legal Argument, 2000, French edit., 2005, (with others) Cases and Materials on Advanced Torts, 2004. With US Army, 1957. Mem. ABA, Am. Law Inst., Am. Soc. Internat. Law, Phi Beta Kappa. Democrat. Greek Orthodox. Home: 5212 Twin Pines Ln Durham NC 27705-8599 Office: Duke U Sch Law PO Box 90360 Durham NC 27708-0360 Office Phone: 919-613-7052. Business E-Mail: gcc@law.duke.edu.

CHRISTIE, GEORGE NICHOLAS, economist, consultant; b. Wilmington, NC, Nov. 2, 1924; s. Nicholas and Helen (Lymberis) C.; m. Mary Danatos, July 22, 1951; children: Sultana Helen, Stephanie Hope, Susan Adrianne, Sandra Alicia, Gregory Nicholas. BBA, U. Miami, 1948; MBA, NYU, 1956; PhD, 1963. With Dun and Bradstreet, Inc., NYC, 1949-61; staff bus. writer, 1959-61; assoc. dir. Credit Rsch. Found.; asst. dir. edn. Nat. Assn. Credit Mgmt., NYC, 1961-63; asst. sec. credit policy com., small bus. credit com., 1964-67; v.p., dir. rsch. Credit Rsch. Found., 1967-80; sr. v.p., 1980-82; exec. v.p., 1983-89; assoc. dir. Grad. Sch. Credit and Fin. Mgmt., 1967-86; exec. dir., 1986-87; dir. Nat. Inst. Credit, 1967-84; prin. Four Seas Cons. Group, Great Neck, N.Y., 1989—; instr. N.Y. Inst. Credit. Lectr. Dartmouth, Stanford U.; assoc. prof. L.I. U.; adminstr. 2d year banking course Stonier Grad. Sch. Banking, Rutgers U. Contbr. articles to profl. jours. Mem. Am. Econ. Assn., Am. Fin. Assn., Fin Mgmt. Assn., Shriner (recorder emeritus, past potentate), Masons (past master). Office: 65 Nassau Rd Great Neck NY 11021-4047 Office Phone: 516-487-8382. Personal E-mail: gnchristie@aol.com.

CHRISTIE, HANS FREDERICK, retired utilities executive; b. Alhambra, Calif., July 10, 1933; s. Andreas B. and Sigrid (Falk-Jorgensen) C.; m. Susan Earley, June 14, 1957; children: Brenda Lynn, Laura Jean BS in Fin., U. So. Calif., 1957, MBA, 1964. Treas. So. Calif. Edison Co., Rosemead, 1970-75, v.p., 1975-76, sr. v.p., 1976-80, exec. v.p., 1980-84, pres., dir., 1984-87; pres., chief exec. officer The Mission Group (non-utility subs. SCE Corp.), Seal Beach, Calif., 1987-89, ret., 1989, cons., 1989—. Bd. dirs. L.A. Ducommun Inc., L.A., A.E. Com., L.A., Am. Mut. Fund, Inc., AMCAP, Am. Variable Ins., I.H.O.P. Corp., AECom Tech., L.A., Internat. House of Pancakes, Inc., Southwest Water Co., L.A., Smallcap World Fund, L.A., Bond Fund Am., Inc., L.A., Tax-Exempt Bond Fund Am., L.A., Ltd. Term Tax-Exempt Bond Fund Am., Am. High Income Mcpl. Bond Fund, Capital Income Builder, L.A., Capital World Bond Fund, L.A., Capital World Growth Fund, L.A., Capital World Growth and Income Fund, Intermediate Bond Fund Am., L.A., Intermediate Tax-Exempt Bond Fund Am., Capital World Growth 2d Income Fund, L.A.; trustee Cash Mgmt. Trust Am., New Economy Fund, L.A., Am. Funds Income Series, L.A., The Am. Funds Tax-Exempt Series II, Am. High Income Trust, L.A., Am. High-Inc Mun. Board Fund, Am. Variable Ins. Trust, U.S. Treasury Fund Am., L.A Bd. councillor sch. policy, planning and devel. U. So. Calif., 1981—2001; trustee Occidental Coll., 1984—96, Idlwild Sch. Arts, 1998—2002, Chadwick Sch., Natural History Mus. Los Angeles County, 1984—2002. With US Army, 1953—55. Named Outstanding mem. Arthritis Found., L.A., 1975, Outstanding Trustee, Multiple Sclerosis Soc. So. Calif., 1979 Mem. Pacific Coast Elec. Assn. (bd. dirs. 1981-87, treas. 1975-87), L.A. C. of C. (bd. dirs. 1983-87), Calif. Club. Republican. Avocations: swimming, horseback riding, bicycling. Home: 548 Paseo Del Mar Palos Verdes Estates CA 90274-1260 Office: PO Box 144 Palos Verdes Peninsula CA 90274-0144 Personal E-mail: hfc548@aol.com.

CHRISTIE, JACQUELINE ANN, nurse; d. Alexander Michael and Dorothy Agnes (Schneider) Hefter; m. Paul John Christie, Sept. 10, 1994; 1 child, Holly. Student, U. Wis., 1980—82; diploma in nursing, Moraine Park, 1985; diploma in writing, Inst. Children's Lit., 2004. LPN, Wis., 1985. CNA St. Francis Home, Fond du Lac, Wis., 1980—82; LPN Care Ctr., Fond du Lac, Wis., 1987—91, Fond du Lac (Wis.) County, 1991—2005. Author: The Shepherd's Bell Sheep, 2005, Roger's Big Adventure, 2005; prodr.: (CD) Sacrifice of Praise. Small group leader Taycheedah Correctional, Fond du lac, Wis., 1985—2003, praise and worship leader, 1985—2003; missions chair person Fond du lac Assembly of God, Fond du lac, Wis., 2003—05. Nominee Poet of Yr. award, Am. Poets Soc., 2005. Mem.: Fond du lac Assembly of God (missions chair 2003—), Gospel Music Assn. Republican. Avocations: singing, poetry, guitar, piano. Home and Office: 186 E 10th St Fond Du Lac WI 54935

CHRISTIE, LAURENCE GLENN, JR., surgeon, educator; b. Houston, May 13, 1930; s. Laurence Glenn and Tommie Katherine (Myers) C.; m. Constance Graham Kelsey, Sept. 15, 1973; 1 child, Susan Eilzabeth. BS, Washington and Lee U., 1953; MD, Med. Coll. Va., 1957. Diplomate Am. Bd. Surgery. Intern Med. Coll. Va., Richmond, 1957-58, resident in surgery, 1957-62, clin. instr., 1963—; practice medicine specializing in gen. and vascular surgery, Ft. Smith, Ark., 1962-63, Richmond, 1963—. Mem. active staff Henrico Doctors Hosp.; mem. courtesy staff Johnston-Willis Hosp., Stuart Circle Hosp., St. Mary's Hosp., Richmond Meml. Hosp., St. Luke's Hosp., Retreat Hosp.; chmn. dept. surgery chmn. med. exec. com., med. dir. Henrico Doctors Hosp., also vice chmn. bd. trustees, 1981—, chief staff, 1974, 75, 82; courtesy staff Richmond Met. Hosp., Johnston-Willis Hosp., Chippenham Hosp.; pres. Med. Planning Corp.; mem. sci. adv. bd. Richmond chpt. Nat. Found. for Ileitis and Colitis, Inc. Contbr. articles to profl. jours. Fellow ACS; mem. AMA, Southeastern Surg. Congress, So. Med. Assn., Richmond Acad. Medicine, Richmond Surg. and Gynecol. Soc., Med. Soc. Va., Humera Soc., Bull and Bear Club, Irish Setter Club of Greater Richmond, Irish Setter Club Am. Episcopalian. Home: 12433 Killigay Ln Maidens VA 23102-2812 Office: 7605 Forest Ave Ste 402 Richmond VA 23229-4936 Home Phone: 804-749-4318. Personal E-mail: lgcgals@aol.com.

CHRISTIE, NANCY GAIL, psychology professor, department chairman; d. Monte and Mary Christie. BA in Psychology, U. Ariz., 1984, MS in Family Studies, 1987, PhD in Ednl. Psychology, 1992. Asst. prof. U. Colo., Denver, 1991—93; psychology faculty Pima CC, Tucson, 1993—, psychology dept. chair, 2007—. Mem.: APA. Office: Pima Cmty Coll 2202 W Anklam Rd Tucson AZ 85749 Office Phone: 520-206-6794.

CHRISTIE, SCOTT S., lawyer; BA, Colgate U., Hamilton, NY, 1986; JD, Harvard U., Cambridge, Mass., 1989. Bar: NJ 1989, NY 1990. Law clk. Hon. Maryanne Trump Barry, Newark, 1989—91; asst. US atty. US Atty.'s Office, Newark, 1991—2004; ptnr. McCarter & English, LLP, Newark, 2004—. Bd. dirs. InfraGard, Newark. Mem.: ABA, Am. Intellectual Property Law Assn., NY/NJ Electronic Crimes Task Force, Newark Tech. Group, NJ Tech. Coun., Internat. Tech. Law Assn., High Tech. Crime Investigation Assn., ASIS Internat., NJ State Bar Assn. Office: McCarter & English LLP 4 Gateway Ctr 100 Mulberry St Newark NJ 07102 Office Phone: 973-848-5388. Office Fax: 973-297-3981. E-mail: schristie@mccarter.com.

CHRISTIE, WILLIAM GARY, finance educator; b. Toronto, Sept. 22, 1955; s. Robert Louis and Margaret Elsa (Sparling) C.; m. Kelly Maureen McNamara, July 25, 1980. B in commerce with honors, Queen's U., Kingston, Ont., Can., 1978; MBA in fin., U. Chgo., 1980, PhD in fin. and economics, 1989. Fin. analyst Hewlett-Packard (Canada) Ltd., 1980-81, Ford Motor Co. of Canada Ltd., 1981-82; rsch. asst. in statistics and fin. U. Chgo., 1983-88; asst. prof. mgmt. Owen Grad. Sch. Mgmt., Vanderbilt U., Nashville, 1989—96, assoc. prof., 1996—2000, prof., 2000—, assoc. dean faculty devel., 1999—2000, dean, Ralph Owen prof. mgmt., 2000—04, Frances Hampton Currey prof. mgmt., 2004—, prof. law, 2005—. Econ. adv. bd. Nasdaq, 2000—03; bd. dirs. Grad. Mgmt. Admission Coun., 2002—. Contbr. articles to profl. jours. Fellow U. Chgo., 1982-89, Social Scis. and Humanities Rsch. Coun. Can., 1982-86, Ctr. for Rsch. in Securities Prices, 1983-84; recipient Irwin Disting. Paper award, 1994, Smith-Breeden award, 1995. Mem. Am. Fin. Assn., Southwestern Fin. Assn., Western Fin. Assn., Am. Econs. Assn., European Fin. Assn, Assn. to Advance Collegiate Schs. of Bus. (bus. com.), Fin. Mgmt. Assn. (academic dir.). Avocations: jogging, tennis, travel. Office: Vanderbilt U Owen Grad Sch 401 21st Ave S Nashville TN 37203

CHRISTIN, NICOLAS, computer scientist, researcher; b. Annemasse, France, June 5, 1977; s. Pierre and Christiane Christin. Diploma in engring., École Centrale Lille, 1999; MA in Computer Sci., U. Va., 2000, PhD in Computer Sci., 2003. Rsch. scientist U. Calif., Berkeley, 2003—05; sys. scientist, faculty Carnegie Mellon U., Pitts., 2005—. Mem.: Assn. Computing Machinery, IEEE. Achievements include discovery of technological solutions that could efficiently protect against illegal distribution of copyrighted works in peer-to-peer file sharing networks.

CHRISTINA, THOMAS MICHAEL, lawyer; b. Endicott, NY, June 3, 1955; s. Louis Anthony and Emily Marie (Motichka) C. AB, Cornell U., 1977; JD cum laude, Harvard U., 1980. Bar: Mass. 1980, DC, SC, US Dist. Ct. Mass. 1981, US Ct. of Appeals (1st cir.) 1981, NY 1982, US Dist. Ct. (no. dist.) NY 1983, US Supreme Ct. 1986, US Ct. of Appeals (4th cir.) 1988, US Ct. of Appeals (6th cir.) 1989, US Ct. of Appeals (7th, 9th & 11th cir.) NY, US Tax Ct. Assoc. Goodwin, Procter & Hoar, Boston, 1980-81, Ball & McDonough, P.C., Binghamton, N.Y., 1982-86, ptnr., 1986-87; dep. asst. atty. gen. Office Legal Policy Dept. Justice, Washington, 1987-88; assoc. dep. atty. gen. Dept. Justice, Washington, 1988-89; assoc. Covington & Burling, Wash., 1989—94; shareholder Ogletree, Deakins, Nash, Smoak & Stewart, P.C., Greenville, SC. Trustee Telluride Assn., Ithaca, N.Y., 1974—. Named Best Lawyer Am., 2003—04. Mem.: So. Employee Benefits Conf. US C. of C. Republican. Roman Catholic. Avocations: golf, bridge, reading. Office: Ogletree Deakins Nash Smoak & Stewart PC Ogletree bldg Greenville SC 29601 Office Phone: 864-271-1300. Office Fax: 864-235-8806. Business E-Mail: thomas.christina@ogletreedeakins.com.

CHRISTINE, CHAN B., educational consultant, researcher; BA with honors, U. Oreg., Eugene, 1985—89; PhD, Mich. State U., E.Lansing, 1999—2005. Cert. advanced edn. tchr. Min. Edn., Singapore, 1983. Cons., rschr. Mich. State U., 1999—2005; measurement rsch. assoc. AAMC, DC, 2005—06; cons. Ednl. Rsch. & Evaluation Va. Tech. U., Blacksburg, 2006—. Webmaster Inst. Rsch., Tchg. & Learning, Mich. State U., 2004—. Grad. student rep. career award com. Nat. Coun. Measurement Edn., Madison, Wis.; co-pres. Grad. Asian Am. Partnership, E.Lansing, 1999—2001; corr. press sec. Coun. Grad. Students, Mich. State U., 2000—04; grant writer-rschr. Episcopal & Anglican Chaplaincy, Mich. State U., 2004—05. Co-recipient Best of State award, Mich. Assn. Fgn. Student Advisors, 1998; recipient Outstanding Svc. award, Asian Am. Pacific Student Orgn., 1999; LASC Rsch. grantee, 2005—07. Mem.: Usability Profls. Assn., Nat. Coun. Measurement Edn., Human Factors

Ergonomic Soc., Cognitive Sci. Soc. (reviewer 2006—), Mich. State U. Alumni Assn. (webmaster 2005), Phi Beta Kappa. Episcopal. Achievements include development of dual-coding item formats for computerized-adaptive test environments; national certification of school boards of nursing tutorial proto-type & innovative item types; proposed American college test (ACT) assessment tutorial interface prototype; design of proposed law school admissions test (LSAT) tutorial interface proto-type design; research in dual-coding item types for the computerized adaptive test environments. Avocation: Tae Kwon Do. Home Phone: 517-214-6767. Personal E-mail: digitalcortex@comcast.net.

CHRISTISON, MURIEL BRANHAM, retired museum director, art history educator; b. Mpls. d. Harold D. and Helen (Ferguson) Branham; children: Evelyn, Carolyn. BA, U. Minn., 1933, MA, 1940; diploma, U. Paris, 1936, U. Brussels, 1938. Grad. asst. dept. fine arts U. Minn., Mpls., 1933-36; curatorial rsch. asst. Mpls. Inst. Arts, Mpls., 1936-42, head edn., 1944-47; assoc. dir. Va. Mus. Fine Arts, Richmond, 1948-61; oper. and assoc. dir. Krannert Art Mus. U. Ill., Champaign, 1962-74, dir. Krannert Art Mus., 1975-82; ret., 1982; interim dir. Muscarelle Mus. Coll. William and Mary, Williamsburg, Va., 1984-85, 94-96, mem. vis. com., 1982-96, vis. prof. fine arts, 1983-98. Head grad. program mus. studies U. Ill., 1974—82; cons. U. Tex., Austin, Washington U., St. Louis, 1972, St. Louis, 78, Ill. Arts Coun., 1968—82; v.p. Midwest Mus. Conf. Am. Assn. Mus., regional rep., 1972—82; examiner S.C. Arts Coun., 1984, 86, Ohio Arts Coun., 1986, Nat. Endowment for the Arts, 1973, 83, NEH, 1980. Author: numerous exhbn. catalogs; contbr. articles to profl. jours. Carnegie scholar Inst. Internat. Edn., 1936; CRB fellow Beligan-Am. Edn. Found., 1938; recipient Disting. Svc. award Midwest Mus. Conf., 1982 Mem.: Colonial Williamsburg Fund, William and Mary Found., Coun. Va. Mus. Fine Arts, Assn. Preservation Va. Antiquities, Am. Assn. Museums (regional rep. 1972—82, bd. dirs. 1972—82, surveyor, examiner 1982—), Assn. Art Mus. Dirs. (emerita 1982, hon. 1982—). Home: Apt 125 5700 Williamsburg Landing Dr Williamsburg VA 23185-5555 Personal E-mail: mbchri@aol.com.

CHRISTMAN, ARTHUR CASTNER, JR., science advisor, consultant; b. North Wales, Pa., May 11, 1922; s. Arthur Castner and Hazel Ivy (Schirmer) C.; m. Marina Ilia Diterichs, Apr. 17, 1945; children: Candace Lee Canto, Tatiana Marina Harvey, Deborah Ann Clark, Arthur C. III, Keith Ilia, Cynthia Ellen Buckwalter. BS in Physics, Pa. State U., 1944, MS, 1950. Teaching asst. dept. physics Pa. State U., State College, 1943-44, grad. asst., 1946-48; instr. dept. physics George Washington U., Washington, 1948-51; cons. U.S. Navy, 1950-51; physicist ops. research office Johns Hopkins U., Chevy Chase, Md., 1951-58; sr. physicist SRI Internat., Menlo Park, Calif., 1958-62, head ops. research group, 1962-64, dept. mgr., 1965-67, dir. dept., 1968-71, dir. tactical weapons systems, 1971-75; sci. advisor to comdg. gen. and dep. chief staff combat devel. U.S. Army tng. and doctrine command Ft. Monroe, Va., 1975-87; cons. in field, 1988—. Author numerous publs. Pres. Valle Verde Continuing Care Retirement Cmty. Coun., 1991—93, 1994—95, Am. Bapt. Homes of West Assn. of CCRC Resident Presidents, 1991—92; bd. mgrs. fin. com. Valle Verde, 1988—97; mem. Valle Verde Adv. Bd., 1997—2006, fin. com., 1988—2006, chair environ. svcs. com., 1999—2006, exec. com., 2002—06; continuing care contracts statutes rev. task force State of Calif., 1999—2000; umpire Palo Alto Little League, Calif., 1962—72; bd. dirs. Am. Bapt. Homes of the West, 1997—, fin. and investment com., 1998—2006, audit com., 1999, 2001—03, 2006—07, chair investment com., 2002—06, compensation com., 2007—, Cornerstone bd. dirs., 2001—, fin. com., 2004—; bd. dirs. Ctrl. Coast Commn. for Sr. Citizens Area Agy. on Aging, 1993. Lt. USNR, 1944—46, PTO. Decorated Meritorious Civilian Service award Dept. Army, 1983, Exceptional Civilian Service award Dept. Army, 1987; recipient Presdl. Rank, 1985, Governance award Am. Bapt. Homes of the West, 2002, Trustee of Yr. award Calif. Assn. Homes and Svcs. for the Aging, 2004. Fellow AAAS; mem. Am. Phys. Soc., Inst. for Ops. Rsch. and the Mgmt. Scis. (U.S. del. internat. confs. Operational Rsch., France 1960, Norway 1963, U.S. 1966, Ireland 1972), Santa Barbara Lawn Bowls Club (bd. dirs. 1990-93), MacKenzie Park Lawn Bowls Club, Sigma Xi, Sigma Pi Sigma, Delta Chi (chpt. pres.). Republican. Baptist (deacon, trustee). Avocations: lawn bowling, photography. Home and Office: 1028 B Senda Verde Santa Barbara CA 93105-4407 Personal E-mail: achristman@abhow.com.

CHRISTMAN, BRUCE LEE, lawyer; b. Bethlehem, Pa., Apr. 1, 1955; s. Raymond J. Jr. and Irene May (Bowman) C.; m. Lynn Eloise Brodt, Oct. 11, 1980; children: Jennifer Lynn, Amy Nicole. BA, Coll. William and Mary, 1977; JD, U. Pa., 1980. Bar: Va. 1980, U.S. Ct. Appeals (4th cir.) 1980, U.S. Dist. Ct. (ea. dist.) Va. 1980. Assoc. Hunton & Williams, Richmond, Va., 1980-84; prin., ptnr. Reed Smith LLP, Fairfax, Va., 1984—. Adj. prof. George Mason Sch. Law. Mem. Leadership Fairfax Class of 1993, bd. dirs. 1997, 2000-02—. Mem. Va. State Bar Assn., Phi Beta Kappa, Omicron Delta Kappa, Kappa Sigma. Democrat. Avocations: tennis, basketball, swimming, bicycling, camping. Home: 13610 Flintwood Pl Herndon VA 20171-3331 Office: Reed Smith LLP 3110 Fairview Park Dr Falls Church VA 22042-4503 Office Phone: 703-641-4259.

CHRISTMAN, EDWARD ARTHUR, physicist; b. Lakewood, Ohio, Aug. 3, 1943; s. John N.H. and Mary Elizabeth (Fuller) Christman; m. Florence T. Cua, July 21, 1979. MS, Rutgers U., 1975, PhD, 1977. Cert. Am. Bd. Health Physics. Mech. engr. missile systems div. AVCO Corp., Wilmington, Mass., 1966-72; instr. Rutgers U., New Brunswick, NJ, 1975-77, radiol. physicist, 1977-89, assoc. dir., 1989-91; dir. environ. health and safety Columbia U., NYC, 1991-99; cons. Princeton, NJ, 1999—. Assoc. faculty Rutgers U., 1978—; faculty Columbia U., 1991—; cons. in field. Mem.: NJ Tech. Coun., Health Physics Soc., Health Physics Soc. NJ (pres. 1989—90), Soc. for Risk Analysis, Am. Assn. Physicists in Medicine. Office: 443 Sayre Dr Princeton NJ 08540-5845 Office Phone: 609-919-0275. Personal E-mail: eac8@comcast.net.

CHRISTODOULOU, MARILENA, investment banker, finance company executive; b. Athens, Greece, Feb. 7, 1951; arrived in U.S., 1972; d. Demere and Theodora (Kasapoglou) Lyratzakis; m. Aris Christodoulou, Aug. 23, 1975; 1 child, Peter. License es scis. economiques with honors, U. Lausanne, Switzerland, 1972; MBA, U. Pa., 1974. With lending dept. Am. Express Internat. Banking Corp., NYC, 1974—75; corp. fin. assoc. Kuhn Loeb & Co., NYC, 1975—78, Lehman Bros., NYC, 1978—79; v.p. Worms & Co., Inc., NYC, 1979—86; exec. v.p. W. R. Assocs., Inc., NYC, 1984—86; dir. Mayfair Ptnrs., Inc., NYC, 1986—2000; dir. fin. and devel. Rubin Mus. Art, NYC, 2003—. Dir. Woodway Realty Corp., NYC, 1982—86. Bd. dirs. Greek Archdiocesan Cathedral, NY, trustee, v.p. NY; bd. dirs. 9/11 Environ. Action, Healthy Schs. Network, Inc.; chmn. bd. dirs. The Cathedral Sch. Mem.: Am. Assn. Mus., Wharton Club (N.Y.C.). Home: 137 E 66th St New York NY 10021-6150 Office: Rubin Mus Art 150 W 17th St New York NY 10011 Office Phone: 212-620-5000. Personal E-mail: marilenach@yahoo.com. Business E-Mail: mchristodoulou@rmanyc.org.

CHRISTOFFEL, KATHERINE KAUFER, pediatrician, epidemiologist, educator; b. NYC, June 28, 1948; d. George and Sonya (Firstenberg) Kaufer; children: Kevin, Kimberly. BA, Radcliffe Coll., 1969; MD, Tufts U., 1973; MPH, Northwestern U., 1981. Diplomate Am. Bd. Pediat., Nat. Bd. Med. Examiners. Intern Columbus (Ohio) Children' Hosp., 1972-73; resident then fellow Children's Meml. Hosp., Chgo., 1973-76; asst. prof. Sch. Medicine U. Chgo., 1976-79; asst. prof., then assoc. prof. Northwestern U. Med. Sch., Chgo., 1979-91, prof., 1991—; dir. Nutrition Evaluation Clinic Children's Meml. Hosp., Chgo., 1982-2000; med. dir. violent injury prevention ctr. Children's Meml. Ctr., Chgo., 1993—2000, interim dir. Mary Ann and J. Milburn Smith Child Health Rsch. Program, 2000—03, interim co-dir. Children's Meml. Inst. for Edn. and Rsch., 2001—03, med. and rsch. dir. Consortium to Lower Obesity in Chgo. Children, 2003—, dir. Ctr. on Obesity Mgmt. and Prevention, 2004—. Dir. then assoc. dir. Pediatric Practice Rsch. Group, Chgo., 1984-97; dir. statis. scis. and epidemiology program Children's Meml. Inst. for Edn. and Rsch., 1994-2000; chmn. steering com. HELP Network, Chgo., 1993-99, pres. bd. dirs., 1999—2006. Contbr. numerous articles to med. jours. Named one of 10 Most Powerful Women in Medicine in Chgo., Chgo. Sun Times, 2004; recipient M. Fay Spencer Disting. Woman Physician Scientist award, Nat. Bd. Hahnemann Med. Sch., 1997. Fellow Am. Acad. Pediat. (spokesperson on firearms 1985—, injury com. 1985-93, coun. on pediatric rsch. 1996-2000, chair adolescent violence task force 1994, 1st Injury Control award 1992); mem. APHA (Disting. Career award 1991), Am. Coll. Epidemiology, Soc. for Pediatric Rsch., Am. Pediat. Soc., Ambulatory Pediatric Assn. (bd. dirs. 2000-2003, Rsch. award 2000). Avocations: hiking, walking, creative writing, photography. Office: Childrens Meml Hosp 2300 N Childrens Plz #157 Chicago IL 60614-3394

CHRISTOFFERS, LYNN BERYL, curator, artist; b. Rahway, NJ, Sept. 29, 1952; d. Alfred Leroy Christoffers and Priscilla Smith Christoffers. BA, Drew U., Madison, NJ, 1974; MA, NYU, NYC, 1994. V.p. Viart Corp., NYC, 1982—85; ind. art advisor NYC, 1985—; curator JP Morgan Inc., NYC, 1988—2002, The Waitzkin Meml. Libr. Trust, NYC, 2004—. Treas. and mem. 494 Gallery, NYC, 1991—95. Photography, video, installation, one-woman shows include 494 Gallery, NYC, 1991, 1992, 1993, 1994, Pulse Art, 1996, 1997, 80 Washington Sq., 1988, exhibited in group shows at Bernstein Studio, NY, 2001, AIR Gallery, NYC, 2004, Treehouse Gallery, West Tisbury, Mass., 2006, others, archive group show, Here Is New York, NYC, 2001—, Martha's Vineyard Times, 2006—07, Martha's Vineyard Mag., 2007. Bd. mem. Heaven on Earth, Pittsfield, Mass., 2000—06. Mem.: Internat. Documentary Assn., Coll. Art Assn., ArtTable, Inc. (membership com. 1999—2000). Home and Office: 25 Leroy St No 1 New York NY 10014 Office Phone: 212-691-0954, 508-696-4920. Personal E-mail: lynnberyl@aol.com.

CHRISTOFFERSEN, RALPH EARL, chemist, researcher, director; b. Elgin, Ill., Dec. 4, 1937; s. Arthur Henry and Mary C.; m. Barbara Hibbard, June 10, 1961; children: Kirk Alan, Rachel Anne. BS, Cornell Coll., 1959, LLD (hon.), 1983; PhD, Ind. U., 1963. Asst. prof. chemistry U. Kans., Lawrence, 1966-69, assoc. prof., 1969—72, prof., 1972-81, asst. vice chancellor for acad. affairs, 1974-75, assoc. vice chancellor for acad. affairs, 1976-79, vice chancellor for acad. affairs, 1979-81; pres. Colo. State U., Ft. Collins, 1981-83; exec. dir. Upjohn Co., 1983-85, v.p. biotech. and basic rsch. support, 1985-87, v.p. discovery rsch., 1987-89; v.p. rsch. SmithKline Beecham, King of Prussia, Pa., 1989-90, sr. v.p. rsch., 1990-92; CEO, pres. Ribozyme Pharms., Inc., Boulder, Colo., 1992-2001, chmn. bd., 2001; gen. ptnr. Morgenthaler Ventures, 2001—. Bd. dirs. GlobeImmune Corp., AllChemie Corp., Catalyst Bioscis., Galleon Pharm., Tragara Pharm. Contbr. articles to profl. jours. NIH fellow, 1962-63, 64-66. Fellow Sigma Xi, Phi Lambda Upsilon; mem. Colo. BioSci. Assn.

CHRISTOFIDES, FOTINE, parochial school educator; b. NYC, July 12, 1948; s. Sergios and Theodora C. BA, Queens Coll., Flushing, NY, 1970, MA, 1972; PhD, CUNY, 1978; BA in Theology, Ind. Bible Coll., Indpls., 1985. Tchr. Jamaica (N.Y.) Day Sch., 1972—; adminstrv. asst. Bethel United Pentecostal Ch., Old Westbury, NY, 1984—. Mem. Pi Delta Phi. Avocations: singing, songwriting. also: Jamaica Day Sch 84-35 152nd St Jamaica NY 11432-1972 Office: Bethel United Pentecostal Ch 357 Jericho Tpke Old Westbury NY 11568-1411

CHRISTOFORIDIS, A. JOHN, radiologist, educator; b. Greece, Dec. 24, 1924; s. John P. and Ada A. C.; m. Ann Dimitriadis, Nov. 11, 1961; children: John, Gregory, Alex, Jimmy. MD summa cum laude, Nat. U. Athens, Greece, 1949; M.M.Sc., Ohio State U., 1957; PhD, Aristotelian U., Greece, 1969. Instr. to prof. Ohio State U., Columbus, 1956-74, clin. prof., 1974—; chmn. dept. radiology Aristotelian U., Salonika, Greece, 1971; prof., chmn. dept. radiology Med. Coll. Ohio, Toledo, until 1982; prof., chmn. dept. Ohio State U., Columbus, 1982—. Researcher in chest and gastrointestinal radiology; cons. Greek Ministry Health, Batelle Meml. Inst., Columbus. Contbr. to textbook Atlas of Axial Sagittal and Coronal Anatomy with Computed Tomography and Magnetic Resonance; author: Radiology for Medical Students, 4th edit., 1988, Diagnostic Radiology-Thorax, 1989; contbr. articles to profl. jours., chpts. to books. Served to lt. M.C. Greek Army, 1950-52. Recipient Silver award Ohio Med. Assn., 1969, awards Heart Assn., 1960, awards Batelle Meml. Inst., 1965, awards Astra Co., 1967, awards Lung Assn., 1970-71; named Hon. Citizen City of Thessalonike, 1973; Ohio Geriatrics Med. grantee, 1980; NSF grantee, 1980 Fellow Am. Coll. Chest Physicians, Am. Coll. Radiology; mem. AAA, AMA, AAUP, Ohio Radiol. Soc., Assn. Univ. Radiologists, Radiol. Soc. N. Am., Soc. Chmn. Acad. Radiology Depts., Fleishner Soc. (charter), Am. Hellenic Ednl. Progressive Assn., Greek-Am. Progressive Assn., Acad. of Athens (corr. mem.). Greek Orthodox. Office: Ohio State U 410 W 10th Ave Columbus OH 43210-1240

CHRISTOL, CARL QUIMBY, lawyer, political science professor; b. Gallup, SD, June 28, 1913; s. Carl and Winifred (Quimby) C.; m. Jeannette Stearns, Dec. 18, 1949 (dec.); children: Susan Quimby Christol-Deacon, Richard Stearns (dec.). AB, U. S.D., 1934, LLD (hon.), 1977; AM, Fletcher Sch. Law and Diplomacy, 1936; postgrad., Institut Universitaire des Hautes Etudes Internationales, Geneva, 1937-38, U. Geneva, 1937-38; PhD, U. Chgo., 1941; LLB, Yale U., 1947; postgrad., Acad. Internat. Law, The Hague, 1950. Bar: S.D. 1948, Calif. 1949. Assoc. firm Guthrie, Darling and Shattuck, Los Angeles, 1948-49; of counsel Fizzolio, Fizzolio & McLeod, Sherman Oaks, Calif., 1949-94; assoc. prof. polit. sci. U. So. Calif., 1949-59, prof., 1959-87, prof. emeritus, 1987—, chmn. dept. polit. sci., 1960-64, 75-77. Stockton chair internat. law U.S. Naval War Coll., 1962-63, cons., 1963-70; cons. World Law Fund; mem. L.A. Mayor's Adv. Com. Human Rels., Commn. to Study Orgn. of Peace; mem. adv. panel on internat. law Dept. State, 1970-76; v.p. Ct. of Man Found., 1971-77; scholar-in-residence Rockefeller Found. Bellagio Conf. and Study Ctr., Italy, 1980. Author: Transit by Air in International Law, 1941, Introduction to Political Science, 1957, 4th edit., 1982, Readings in International Law, 1959, The International Law of Outer Space, 1966, The International Legal and Institutional Aspects of the Stratosphere Ozone Problem, 1975, The Modern International Law of Outer Space, 1982, Space Law: Past, Present and Future, 1991, International Law and U.S. Foreign Policy, 2004, 2d edit., 2006; bd. editors: Western Polit. Quar, 1970-75, Internat. Lawyer, 1975-84, Space Policy, 1985— , Internat. Legal Materials, 1985—, Australian Internat. Law Jour., 1998—; contbr. articles to profl. jours. Bd. dirs. Los Angeles County Heart Assn., 1956—61, Santa Barbara County chpt. UWA-UNESO, 2006—. Served to lt. col. AUS, 1941—46, col. Res. ret. Decorated Bronze Star medal; recipient Dart award U. So. Calif., 1970, Assos. award for excellence in teaching, 1977, Raubenheimer award, 1982, Disting. Emeritus award, 1990, Rockefeller Found. fellow, 1958-59; Borchard Found. lectr., 2002. Mem. ABA, AIAA, Am. Soc. Internat. Law (exec. coun. 1973-76), Internat. Studies Assn. (chmn. internat. law sect. 1977-78), Internat. Acad. Astronautics, State Bar Calif., UN Assn. LA (pres. 1961-63), Am. Polit. Sci. Assn., Internat. Inst. Space Law (pres. Am. br. 1973-75, Lifetime Achievement award 1998), Internat. Law Assn., UN Assn. U.S. (dir. 1967-69), Masons, Blue Key, Skull and Dagger, Phi Beta Kappa, Phi Kappa Phi (award 1987), Alpha Tau Omega. Presbyterian. Home: 327B W Figueroa St Santa Barbara CA 93101 Office: U So Calif Polit Sci Dept Los Angeles CA 90089-0044 Personal E-mail: carlqc@cox.net.

CHRISTOPH, PETER RICHARD, historical editor, archivist; b. Albany, NY, Apr. 25, 1938; s. Hajo and Matilda Bertha (Haage) Christoph; m. Florence Anna Weaver, June 6, 1959; children: Daniel William, Richard Peter, AnnaLise Hall. BA, Hartwick Coll., NYC, 1960; MA, SUNY, 1964, MLS, 1968. Secondary tchg. English N.Y. State Edn. Dept., 1960, Profl. Libr. N.Y. State Edn. Dept., 1968, Archival Adminstrn. U. of Denver, 1969. Asst. libr. cataloging N.Y. State Libr., Albany, 1967—68, sr. libr. manuscripts and history, 1968—72, assoc. libr., 1972—91; editor N.Y. Hist. Manuscripts, Albany, 1974—, sr. editor Selkirk, NY, 1991. Dir. New Netherland Project, Albany, NY, 1974—84, N.Y. Hist. Manuscripts, Selkirk, NY, 1988—. Editor: (document collection) The Kingston Papers, 1661-1775, 1976, Diary of Henry Edgar Whittelsey, Catskill Mountain Storekeeper, 1835-1836, 1999, (document collection) The Leisler Papers, 1689-1691, 2002, Administrative Papers of Governors Richard Nicolls and Francis Lovelace, 1664-1673, 1980, Books of General Entries of the Colony of New York, 1664-1688, 1982, Records of the People of the Town of Bethlehem, 1690-1880, 1982, Records of the Court of Assizes for the Colony of New York, 1665-1682, 1983, The Andros Papers, 1674-1680, 1989—91, The Dongan Papers,1683-1688, 1993—96; author: (biography) Albert Andriessen Bradt, 2004, (book) A Norwegian Family in Colonial America. Pres. Town of Bethlehem Hist. Assn., Cedar Hill, NY, 1980—82, trustee, 1989—92; mem. Bethlehem Rural Cemetery Assn., Selkirk, NY, 1995—2000; archivist First Luth. Ch., Albany, NY, 1983—2003, lay preacher, 1985—99; rep. Bd. of the Luth. Archives Ctr., Phila., 1988—2003; mem. com. on minutes and protocol Upstate N.Y. Synod, Syracuse, 1988—2003; mem., congl. coun. First Luth. Ch., Albany, NY, 1986—89, 2000—03; archivist Upstate N.Y. Synod, Evang. Luth. Ch. in Am., Syracuse, 1993—2003; mem. Friends of Schuyler Mansion, Albany, NY, 1988—96. Grantee, Nat. Endowment for the Humanities, 1992—94. Fellow: Holland Soc. of N.Y.; mem.: Luth. Hist. Conf., Tombstone Ter. Rendezvous, Friends of New Netherland, NY Geneal. and Biog. Soc. Lutheran. Avocation: travel. Home: 181 Maple Ave Selkirk NY 12158 Personal E-mail: pchrist1@nycap.rr.com.

CHRISTOPHER, IRENE, librarian, consultant; b. Greece, Nov. 17, 1922; arrived in US, 1923; d. George and Helen (Stephens) Christopher. AB, Boston U., 1944; BLS, Simmons Coll., 1945. Gen. asst. Robbins Pub. Libr., Arlington, Mass., 1945-46, Boston U. Chenery Libr., 1946-47, head circulation dept., 1947-48, head reference dept., 1948-62; dir. libr. Emerson Coll., Boston, 1962-68; dir. Gordon McKay libr. Harvard U., Cambridge, Mass., 1968-70; chief libr. Boston U. Med. Ctr., 1970-92. Mem. AAUW, ALA (various coms. 1962-82, coun. 1970-74), Spl. Librs. Assn. (various coms. Boston chpt. 1952-75), Am. Soc. Info. Sci., Women's Nat. Book Assn., North Atlantic Health Scis. Librs., Med. Libr. Assn., New Eng. Online Users Group, Inc., Mass. Libr. Assn., Boston U. Women's Coun. Home: 790 Boylston St Apt 11C Boston MA 02199-7911

CHRISTOPHER, JAMES WALKER, architect, educator; b. Phila., Nov. 5, 1930; s. Arthur Bailey and Cornelia (Slater) C.; m. Carolyn Kennard, July 9, 1955; children: William W., Kathryn A., Kimberley, James S., Pamela W. BA, Rice U., 1953, BS in Architecture, 1953; M.Arch., MIT, 1956. Registered architect, Utah, Colo., Nev., Idaho, Wyo. Asst. prof. architecture U. Utah, Salt Lake City, 1956-60, adj. prof. architecture, 1983; archtl. designer various firms, Salt Lake City, 1960-63; founding prin. Brixen & Christopher Architects, Salt Lake City, 1963—. Architect, Phase I, Snowbird, Alta Canyon, Utah (AIA Western Mountain Region award 1971), Numemaker Place Chapel, Salt Lake City (AIA Western Mountain Region award 1977), Congregation Kol Ami, Salt Lake City (AIA Western Mountain Region award 1977), Block 53 Master Plan, Salt Lake City (Utah chpt. AIA award 1979). Mem. Utah Environ. Transp. Coun., Salt Lake City, 1970-77, vice chmn., 1970-75; mem. Big Cottonwood Citizens Planning Com., Salt Lake County, Utah, 1975, Salt Lake City Downtown Planning Com., 1981, Utah Transit Authority Transplan, Salt Lake City, 1982; trustee Utah Heritage Found., 2004-07, v.p., 2006. Served to lt. (j.g.) USNR, 1953-55. Fellow AIA (pres. Utah Soc. 1970 12 Utah Soc. Design awards, 12 Western Mountain Region Design awards 1968-83, 8 nat. Design awards 1975-83, Presdl. citation 1982, nat. design and planning com. 1976-2005, chmn. R/UDAT task group 1987-91, 98-2002, we. mountain region Firm of the Yr. award 1987, Silver medal 1991, Utah Soc. Bronze medal 1999). Clubs: Alta (pres. 2007). Episcopalian. Home: 2954 Millcreek Rd Salt Lake City UT 84109-3108 Office: Brixen & Christopher Architects 252 S 2nd E Salt Lake City UT 84111-2487

CHRISTOPHER, JOHN E., lawyer; b. Charlottesville, Va., May 18, 1967; BA, U. Ky., 1990; JD, Salmon P. Chase Coll. Law, 1993; LLM in Taxation, U. Fla., 1994. Bar: Ky. 1994, US Tax Ct. 1994, Ohio 1995. Ptnr. Dinsmore & Shohl LLP, Cin. Named one of Ohio's Rising Stars, Super Lawyers, 2006. Mem.: Cin. Bar Assn., Ohio State Bar Assn., Ky. Bar Assn., ABA. Office: Dinsmore & Shohl LLP 255 E Fifth St Ste 1900 Cincinnati OH 45202-4700 Office Phone: 513-977-8481. Office Fax: 513-977-8141.

CHRISTOPHER, LIN, artist; b. Talladega, Ala., Dec. 23, 1948; d. Newman and Mary Anna (Stewart) White; m. William Jackson Christopher, July 16, 1975. BS, Auburn U., 1971. Artist, Roswell, Ga., 1975—. Bd. dirs. Roswell Artists' Studio Tour. Represented in permanent collections at IBM, Sunkist, Bell South, Citicorp, Norcom, Hyatt Hotels, Ball Stalker, Ridgeview Inst., United Va. Bank, Price Waterhouse, John Harland Co., Taiyo Elec. Co., Equitable Life Ins. Co., Coopers & Lybrand, Allen & Co., Kinder Care, Hilton Hotels, Crestar Bank, Ala. Power, Ven Der Groen, Sharp Industries, World Carpets, King & Spalding, Workman & Co., Bluff Park Art Assn., Ctrl. Ill. Light Co., SAFE, A.R.T. Sta., Trammel Crowe, Shaw Industries, Perimeter Mall Atlanta, The Landmark Group, Eastman Pharm., James Madison U., Meadows Meml. Hosp., Gainesville Arts Coun., USAF, Bus. Coun. Ga., Albany Mus. Art, Merrill Lynch, Bank of the South, Arthur Anderson, Creative Arts Guild, South Trust Bank, The Marcus Group, Fuqua Industries, North Ga. Coll., So. Engring. Co., Walt Disney World, Springfield (Ill.) Civic Assn., Universal Studios, M G M, Royal Caribbean Cruise Line. Recipient over 100 awards. Mem. Nat. Assn. Ind. Artists, Am. Crafts Coun. Avocation: gardening. Home: 1534 Jones Rd Roswell GA 30075-2726 Home Phone: 770-992-4821.

CHRISTOPHER, MAURINE BROOKS, foundation administrator, writer, editor; b. Three Springs, Tenn. d. John Davis and Zula (Pangle) Brooks; m. Milbourne Christopher, June 25, 1949. BA, Tusculum Coll., Greenville, Tenn., 1941; LittD (hon.), St. John's U., 1984. Reporter, feature writer Balt. Sun, 1943-45; TV radio editor Advt. Age, 1947-51, sr. editor, head broadcast dept., 1951-77, dep. exec. editor NYC, 1977-84; producer-moderator Adbeat, 1970-78; roving editor, mem. editorial bd. Advt. Age, 1984-91; chmn. Milbourne Christopher Found., 1991—. Author: America's Black Congressmen, 1971, Black Americans in Congress, 1976; co-author: The Milbourne Christopher Library, 1589-1900, The Illustrated History of Magic, 1996, 3d edit., 2006, The Milbourne Christopher Library II, 1901-1996, 1998; editor: Howard Thurston's Illusion Show Workbook II, 1992, Houdini's A Magician Among the Spirits-The Original Manuscript, 1996, Milbourne Christopher's Favorite Routines, 2000 Mem.: Internat. Brotherhood Magicians, Soc. Am. Magicians. Home: 333 Central Park W Apt 25 New York NY 10025-7104 Office Phone: 212-663-0200. Personal E-mail: mcfdtn@aol.com.

CHRISTOPHER, NICHOLAS, poet, writer; b. NYC, Feb. 28, 1951; m. Constance Barbara Davidson, Nov. 21, 1980. AB cum laude, Harvard Coll., 1973. Prof. Columbia U. Sch. Arts, Columbia U., 1988—. Author: On Tour with Rita, 1982, A Short History of the Island of Butterflies, 1986, The Soloist, 1986, Desperate Characters, 1988, In the Year of the Comet, 1992, 5 Degrees and Other Poems, 1995, Veronica, 1996, Somewhere in the Night: Film Noir and the American City, 1997, The Creation of the Night

Sky, 1998, A Trip to the Stars, 2000, Atomic Field: Two Poems, 2000, Franklin Flyer, 2002, Crossing the Equator: New and Selected Poems, 1972-2004, 2004; editor: Under 35: The New Generation of American Poets, 1989, Walk on the Wild Side: Urban American Poetry Since 1975, 1994. Recipient Lavan award Acad. Am. Poets, 1991, Melville Cane award Poetry Soc. Am., 1993; NEA fellow, 1987, Guggenheim fellow, 1993, Amy Lowell fellow. Mem. PEN, Poetry Soc. Am. Office: Janklow & Nesbit Assocs 445 Park Ave New York NY 10022-2606 Office Phone: 212-421-1700. E-mail: ncl1@nyu.edu.

CHRISTOPHER, ROBERT PAUL, retired physical medicine physician; b. Cleve., Apr. 27, 1932; s. Walter Matthews and Charity Marie (Roberts) C.; m. Doreen Mary O'Leary, Apr. 28, 1962; children: Robert Jr., Judith, Mark. BS, Northwestern U., 1954; MD, St. Louis U., 1959. Diplomate Am. Bd. Physical Medicine and Rehab. Chief rehab. medicine V.A. Hosp., Ann Arbor, Mich., 1963-67; asst. prof. rehab. medicine U. Mich., 1964-67; assoc. prof. rehab. medicine U. Tenn., Memphis, 1967-71, prof. rehab. medicine, 1971-2001, ret., 2001. Med. dirs. Les Passees Children's Rehab. Ctr., Memphis, 1976-98, Le Bonheur Hosp. Rehab. Svcs., Memphis, 1981-2001, Regional Med. Ctr. Rehab. Svcs., Memphis, 1967-2001, assoc. med. dir. St. Joseph Rehab. Ctr., Memphis, 1981-98. Contbg. author: Seating the Cerebral Palsey Child, 1983; author: sound/slide program Systems of Physical Therapy in Cerebral Palsy, 1971; contbr. articles to profl. jours. Pres. Mid-South Health Systems Agy., Memphis, 1980; mem. Mayor's Adv. Council for Disabled, Memphis, 1977-98. Recipient Disting. Svc. Commn. on Accredited Rehab. Facilities, 1982. Fellow Am. Acad. Phys. Medicine and Rehab. (sec. 1982-88, v.p. 1992—, pres. elect 1993, pres. 1994), Am. Acad. Cerebral Palsy (pres. 1987); mem. AMA, Am. Congress Rehab. Medicine, So. Soc. Phys. Medicine and Rehab. (sec. 1976-2000), Am. Bd. of Phys. Medicine and Rehab. (vice chmn. 1992-98), East Memphis Cath. Club (bd. dirs. 1969-80), K.C. (Grand Knight 1969-70). Avocations: travel, swimming. Home: 818 Island Club Sq Vero Beach FL 32963-5505 Personal E-mail: drbobchris1@bellsouth.net.

CHRISTOPHER, RUSSELL LEWIS, baritone; b. Grand Rapids, Mich., Mar. 12, 1930; s. Russell Stewart and Violet (Jurewicz) C.; m. Gail B. Eldredge, Aug. 24, 1963 (div. 1985); 1 son, Russell Frederick. AA, Grand Rapids Jr. Coll., 1950; MusB, U. Mich., 1953, MusM, 1954. Music librarian NBC, NYC, 1955-58. Elected U. Mich. Sch. Music Alumni Bd. Govs., 1997-2003. Prin. artist, N.Y.C. Opera Co., 1958-60, San Francisco Opera Co., 1962, 63, Met. Opera Assn., N.Y.C., 1963-91, soloist, L.A., Montreal, Chgo., Richmond symphony orchs., 1963—; sang role Maecenas in: world premiere Antony and Cleopatra at new, Met. Opera House, 1966; recs.: Carmen (Deutsche Grammophon), 1973, La Traviata (Electra Records), 1982, (CD) I'll Take Romance, 2002; numerous TV prodns. Live from the Met (Emmy award 1985); Miami Beach Symphony, Hollywood Bowl, Balt. Civic Opera, Central City Opera, Dayton Opera Assn., Phila. Lyric Opera Assn., Met. opera tour, Japan, 1975, 86; concert soloist, Spoleto (Italy) Festival, 1977. Mem. U. Mich. Sch. Music Alumni Bd., 1997. Recipient award Martha Baird Rockefeller Fund for Music, 1961; auditions winner Am. Opera, 1962; auditions winner Met. Opera, 1963; Mrs. Frederick K. Weyerhaeuser award, 1963; Disting. Alumni award Grand Rapids Jr. Coll., 1964, Alumnus of Yr. award U. Mich. Club of N.Y., 1978; recipient citation of merit award for outstanding contbns. to field of music, Alumni Bd., Sch. of Music, U. Mich., 1995. Mem. Am. Guild Musical Artists (nat. bd. govs. 1985-91, 94-99, exec. com. 1994-99).

CHRISTOPHER, SHARON A. BROWN, bishop; b. Corpus Christi, Tex., July 24, 1944; d. Fred L. and Mavis Lorraine (Krueger) Brown; m. Charles Edmond Logsdon Christopher, June 17, 1973. BA, Southwestern U., Georgetown, Tex., 1966; MDiv, Perkins Sch. Theology, 1969; DD, Southwestern U., 1990; DST, McMurray Coll., 1996. Ordained to ministry United Meth. Ch., 1970; elected bishop 1988. Dir. Christian Edn. First United Meth. Ch., Appleton, Wis., 1969-70, assoc. pastor, 1970-72; pastor Butler United Meth. Ch., Butler, Wis., 1972-76, Calvary United Meth. Ch., Germantown, Wis., 1972-76, Aldersgate United Meth. Ch., Milw., 1976-80; dist. supt. Ea. Dist. Wis. Conf. United Meth. Ch., 1980-85; asst. to bishop Wis. Conf. Wis. Conf. United Meth. Ch., Sun Prairie, Wis., 1986-88; bishop North Cen. jurisdiction United Meth. Ch., Minn., 1988-96, bishop Ill. area Ill. area, 1996—, resident bishop Ill. area Springfield, 1996—. Contbr. articles and papers to religious publs. Bd. dirs. Nat. Coun. Chs. of Christ, 1988—, United Meth. Ch. Bd. of Ch. & Soc., 1988-92, bd. discipleship, 1992—; trustee Hamline U., St. Paul, 1988-96; gen. and jurisdictional conf. del., 1976, 80, 84, 88; mem. N. Cen. Jurisdiction Com. on Episcopacy, 1984-88, Com. on Investigation, 1980-88, Gen. Bd. Global Ministries, 1980-88, chmn. Mission Pers. Resources Program Dept., 1984-88. Named one of Eighty for the Eighties, Milw. Jour., 1980.

CHRISTOPHER, WARREN MINOR, lawyer, former secretary of state; b. Scranton, ND, Oct. 27, 1925; s. Ernest W. and Catharine Anna (Lemen) Christopher; m. Marie Josephine Wyllis, Dec. 21, 1956; children: Lynn, Scott, Thomas, Kristen. Student, U. Redlands, 1942—43; BS magna cum laude, U. So. Calif., 1945; LLB, Stanford U., 1949; LLD (hon.), Occidental U., 1977, Bates Coll., 1981, Brown U., 1981, Claremont Coll., 1981. Bar: Calif. 1949, US Supreme Ct. 1953, DC 1972, NY 1984. Law clk. to Justice William O. Douglas US Supreme Ct., Washington, 1949—50; dep. atty. gen. US Dept. Justice, Washington, 1967—69; dep. sec. US Dept. State, Washington, 1977—81, sec., 1993—97; mem. firm O'Melveny & Myers, LLP, 1950—67, 1969, ptnr., 1958—67, 1969—76, 1981—93, chmn., 1982—92, sr. ptnr., 1997—. Spl. counsel to Gov. State of Calif., Sacramento, 1959; cons. Office Under Sec. State, 1961—65; mem. bd. bar examiners State Bar Calif., 1966—67; bd. dirs. So. Calif. Edison Co., First Interstate Bancorp, Lockheed Corp.; chmn. bd. trustee Carnegie Corp. NY; mem. Calif. Coordinating Coun. for Higher Edn., 1960—67, pres., 1963—65; vice chmn. Gov.'s Commn. on LA Riots, 1965—66; chmn. US dels. to US-Japan Cotton Textile Negotiations, 1961, Geneva Conf. on Cotton Textiles, 1961; spl. rep. sec. state for Wool Textile Meetings, London, Rome, Tokyo, 1964—64; mem. Trilateral Commn., 1975—77, 1981—88; mem. internat. adv. coun. Inst. Internat. Studies; chmn. Ind. Commn. on L.A. Police Dept., 1991; co-chmn. Pacific Coun. on Internat. Policy; headed search for Gov. Clinton's running mate (Sen. Al Gore); served as dir. presdl. transition process. Author: In the Stream of History: Shaping Foreign Policy for a New Era, 1998, Chances of a Lifetime, 2001; co-author: American Hostages in Iran: The Conduct of a Crisis, 1985; pres. Stanford Law Review, 1947—48. Dir., vice chmn. Coun. on Fgn. Rels., 1982—91; mem. US-Korea Wisemen Coun., 1991—93; trustee Stanford U., 1971—77, 1981—93, pres. bd. trustees, 1985—88; dir. LA World Affairs Coun.; mem. exec. com. Am. Agenda, 1988. Lt. (j.g.) USNR, 1943—46. Decorated Presdl. Medal of Freedom; recipient Harold Weill award, NYU, 1981, Louis Stein award, Fordham U., 1981, Jefferson award, Am. Inst. for Pub. Svc., UCLA medal, U. Va., Thomas Jefferson award in law, First Civic Medal of Honor, LA C. of C., 2003, Lifetime Achievement award, Am. Lawyer mag., 2006. Fellow: AAAS, Am. Coll. Trial Lawyers, Am. Bar Found.; mem.: ABA (ho. dels. 1975—77, chmn. standing com. fed. judiciary 1975—77), Am. Law Inst., LA County Bar Assn. (pres. 1974—75), Calif. Bar Assn. (gov. 1975—77), Chancery Club, Calif. Club, Order of Coif, Phi Kappa Phi. Achievements include negotiating the release of 52 American hostages in Iran, 1981. Office: O'Melveny & Meyers LLP 1999 Avenue of Stars 7th Fl Los Angeles CA 90067-6035 Address: O'Melveny & Meyers LLP 400 South Hope St Los Angeles CA 90071-2899 Office Phone: 310-246-6750. Office Fax: 310-246-6779. Business E-Mail: wchristopher@omm.com.

CHRISTOPHER, WILLIAM F., metal products executive; b. Ridley Park, Pa., Mar. 17, 1954; m. Cathy Christopher; children: Bryan, Tony, Megan. Grad. in Acctg., Pa. State U., Univ. Park, 1975; MBA, Clarkson U., Potsdam, NY, 1980. With fin. orgn. Alcoa, Inc., Pitts., 1975, various fin. mgmt. positions Massena, NY, Davenport, Iowa and Tenn., sheet mill mgr. Davenport, 1988—91, v.p. comml. products sales and mktg., 1991—96, pres. Forged Products Cleve., 1996—2001, v.p., 1999—2001, exec. v.p., 2001—, head global deployment of Alcoa Bus. Sys. and customer quality initiatives, 2001—02, group pres. Aerospace and Comml. Transp., 2002—03, group pres. Aerospace, Comml. Transp. and Automotive, 2003—06, group pres. Engineered Products and Solutions Cleve., 2006—, dir. Global Aerospace Market Sector. Mem. Mayor's Task Force for Econ. Devel., Cleve.; bd. dirs. Greater Cleve. Partnership. Office: Alcoa Inc 1600 Harvard Ave Cleveland OH 44105 Office Phone: 216-641-3600. Office Fax: 216-641-4375.*

CHRISTOPHER, WILLIAM GARTH, lawyer; b. Beaumont, Tex., Oct. 14, 1940; s. Garth Daugherty and Ollye Mittie (Harkness) C.; m. Kathleen S. Christopher; children: John William, David Noah, Michael O'Hara. BS in Engring., U.S. Mil. Acad., 1962; JD, U. Va., 1970. Bar: Va. 1970, D.C. 1970, U.S. Supreme Ct. 1975, Mich. 1977, Fla. 1988, Tex. 1989, bd. cert. Bus. Litigation Law and Construction Law. Atty. Steptoe & Johnson, Washington, 1970-77; ptnr. Honigman MIller Schwartz & Cohn, Detroit, 1977-94, Holland & Knight, Tampa, Fla., 1994-95, Brown Clark Christopher & DeMay, P.A., Sarasota, Fla., 1995—2003, Gurley Dramis Lazo, Sarasota, 2003—. Contbr. articles to legal publ. Pres. Birmingham (Mich.) Hockey Assn., 1982-84; mem. Epsc. Diocese of Mich. Commn. on Ministry, 1983-88, co-chmn., 1987-88, standing com., 1988. Capt. C.E. U.S. Army, 1962-67. Mem.: Tex. Bar Assn., The Fla. Bar, Nat. Bd. Trial Advocacy, Sarasota County Bar Assn., Va. Bar, Order of Coif, Phi Delta Phi. Episcopalian. Office Phone: 941-952-5242. Business E-Mail: wchristopher@sarasotalaw.com.

CHRISTOPHERSON, CHARLES RICHARD, JR., (CHUCK CHRISTOPHERSON), federal agency administrator; b. Twin Falls, ID, June 24, 1964; BS, Brigham Young U., 1989; MS, U. Oreg., 1996. With Pacific Telecom, Vancouver, Wash., 1991—96, Comshare, Portland, Oreg.; CFO ICG Fiber Optic Technologies, Englewood, Colo., 1998—2000; corp. v.p., ops. & fin. Encompass Services Corp., Houston, 2001—03; co-founder, pres. CB Solutions, LLC, Dallas, 2003—05; CFO USDA, Washington, 2005—. Bd. dirs. Commodity Credit Corp., 2006—. Office: USDA Rm 139-W 14th & Independence Ave SW Rm 143-W Washington DC 20250*

CHRISTOPHERSON, ELIZABETH GOOD, broadcast executive; b. Cin. d. Walter R. and Jean S. Good; m. Paul C. Christopherson; 1 child, Katherine. BA, Wellesley Coll. Chmn., CEO NJ State Coun. Arts, 1989—91; exec. dir. NJ Pub. TV and Radio, Trenton, 1994—; pres. NJN Found., 1994—. Bd. dirs. PNC Bank N.J., PBS, Liberty Sci. Ctr., Wellesley Coll. Bus. Leadership Coun., NJ State Coun. Arts. Pres., bd. dirs. Leadership Am. Assn., Alexandria, Va., 1991—92; bd. dirs. N.J. Tech. Coun.; trustee Assn. Pub. TV Stas., 2007. Mem.: Assn. Pub. TV Stas. (trustee 2007), Internat. Woman's Forum (past pres. N.J. chpt.). Office: NJ Network PO Box 777 Trenton NJ 08625-0777

CHRISTOPHERSON, MYRVIN FREDERICK, college president; b. Milltown, Wis., July 21, 1939; s. Fred J. and Inger J. (Haug) C.; m. Anne Christine Marking, June 10, 1967; children: Kirsten, Berit, Bjorn, Nisse. BA, Dana Coll., 1961; MS, Purdue U., 1963, PhD, 1965; DD (hon.), Wartburg Theol. Sem., 1998. Teaching asst., instr. Purdue U., West Lafayette, Ind., 1961-65; asst. prof. speech U. Wis., Madison, 1965-69, assoc. prof. communication Stevens Point, 1969-76, prof. communication, 1976-86, assoc. dean. fine arts and communication, 1970-86; pres. Dana Coll., Blair, Nebr., 1986—2005, pres. emeritus, 2005—; pres. Dana Coll. Found. Inc., 2006—. Cons. Wis. Telephone, Milw., 1968-78, AT&T, N.Y.C., 1969-71, 1st Fin. Corp., Stevens Point, 1980-86; commr. Nebr. Coordinating Commn. for Post Sec. Edn., 1989-91; mem. N.E. jud. nominating commn. Ct. Appeals No. 3 Steering Com.; mem. adv. bd. Thrivent Fin. For Lutherans, 2002-. Author: Speaker's Trainer's Guide, 1970, The Company Speaker, 1979; editor: Jour. of the Wis. Communication Assn., 1978—80. Mem. adv. bd. The Lutheran, 1987—94, chmn., 1992—94; bd. dirs. Blair Cmty. Found., 1999—, Planned Giving Svcs., Nebr., chmn., 1992—94; ann. fund appeal chmn. Meml. Cmty. Hosp., 1994; trustee Palmer Chirpractic U., 1998—2004; mem. coun. pres. Evangel. Luth. Ch. in Am., 1999—, vice chmn., 1999—2000, chmn., 2000—, memls. com. churchwide assembly, 2001; mem. pastoral call com. First Luth. Ch., 1995, mem. ch. coun., 1999; mem. Nebr. Ednl. Fin. Authority, 1991—, chmn., 1992—99, 2001, 2004—, vice chmn., 2002—03. Decorated Knight 1st Class Order of Dannebrog, Denmark; named A.T. Weaver Outstanding Comm. Tchr., 1979; recipient Cmty. Svc. award Blair Area Chamber, 2004, Acad. award, Great Plains Athletic Conf., 2005, NE Govs. Outstanding Pub. Svc. award, 2006; inducted into Wall of Honor, Unity High Sch., Polk County, Wis.; fellow Palmer Coll. Chiropractic, Palmer Coll. Chiropractic-West. Fellow: Found. for Ind. Higher Edn. (bd. dirs. 2005, sec. 2003—05); mem.: Coun. of Pres., Luth. Edn. Conf. N.Am. (vice chmn. 1994—95, chmn. 1995—96), Nebr. Ind. Coll. Found. (exec. com. 1990—92, vice chmn. 1992—93, chmn. 1994—95), Nebr. Bus. Higher Edn. Forum, Nat. Assn. Intercoll. Athletics (coun. of pres. 1999—2005), North Ctrl. Assn. Colls. and Schs. (cons.-evaluator 1997—2005, accreditation rev. coun. 2001—, team chair 2002—05), Nebr. Ednl. TV Coun. for higher Edn., Assn. Ind. Colls. Nebr. (chmn. 1992—93), Nat. Assn. Ind. Colls. and Univs. (bd. dirs. 1997—99, 2003—05, chmn-.Great Plains athletic conf. coun. pres. 2004—05), Danish Brotherhood. Avocations: travel, reading, writing, antiques. Business E-Mail: mchristo@dana.edu.

CHRISTOPHERSON, RON, mathematics educator; BA, Univ. N.Mex. Math tchr. Carlsbad (N.Mex.) H.S. Named N.Mex. Tchr. of Yr., 2006. Mem.: Knights of Columbus. Office: Carlsbad High Sch 3000 W Church St Carlsbad NM 88220 Business E-Mail: ron.christopherson@carlsbad.k12.nm.us.*

CHRISTY, ARTHUR HILL, lawyer; b. Bklyn., July 25, 1923; s. Francis Taggart and Catherine Virginia (Damon) C.; m. Gloria Garvin Osborne, Feb. 14, 1980; children by previous marriage: Duncan Hill, Alexandra. AB, Yale U., 1945; LL.B., Columbia U., 1949. Bar: N.Y. 1950. Assoc. firm Baldwin, Todd & Lefferts, NYC, 1950-52; spl. asst. atty. gen. Saratoga Investigation, NY, 1952-53; asst. U.S. atty. So. Dist. N.Y., 1953-54; chief prosecutor spl. asst. atty. gen. Saratoga and Columbia County Investigations, 1954-55; asst. atty. gen. NY, 1955; chief criminal div. U.S. atty.'s Office, So. Dist. N.Y., 1955-57; chief asst. U.S. atty., 1957-58; U.S. atty., 1958-59; partner firm Christy & Viener (and predecessors), NYC, 1959—. Spl. asst. to Gov. Rockefeller, 1959-61; apptd. 1st spl. prosecutor Under Ethics in Govt. Act of 1978 to investigate charges against White House Chief of Staff, 1979-80. Artist in scrimshaw. Trustee, vice chmn. Bklyn. Hosp., Cmty. Svc. Soc.; v.p., gen. counsel, mem. coun. N.Y. Heart Assn. Lt. USNR, 1944-46. Mem. ABA, N.Y. State Bar Assn., Fed. Bar Assn., Assn. Bar City N.Y. (chmn. exec. com. 1966-67, v.p. 1968-69), Am. Coll. Trial Lawyers, Century Assn., Rockefeller Luncheon Club, Univ. Club (N.Y.C.), Mastigouche Fish and Game Club (Que., Can.). Republican. Episcopalian. Home: 165 East 72nd St Apt 14N New York NY 10021 Office: 620 5th Ave New York NY 10020-2402 Office Phone: 212-632-5507. Business E-Mail: achristy@salans.com.

CHRISTY, JOHN GILRAY, diversified financial services company executive; b. Silver Creek, NY, Aug. 27, 1932; s. John Van Vlack and Ruth (Gilray) Christy; life ptnr. Helen Llewellyn Christy, 1991; children: Andrew, Jennifer. BA, Dartmouth Coll., 1954; MA in Asian Studies, U. Calif., Berkeley, 1960. Loan officer US Devel. Loan Fund, 1960-61; with AID, New Delhi and Washington, 1961-65, chief extended risk guaranty divsn., 1965; with ITT, NYC, 1965-72, treasury dept., 1965-68, v.p. internat. comm., 1968-69, asst. group exec. internat. comm., 1969-70; pres. ITT World Directories, Inc., NYC, 1970-72; group v.p. land transp. IU Internat., Inc., Phila., 1972-76, exec. v.p., 1976-78; pres., COO IU Internat. Corp., 1978-80, chmn., pres., CEO, 1982-85, chmn., CEO, 1985-88; chmn. Chestnut Capital Corp., Phila., 1988—, First Fidelity Bank, Phila., 1991. Bd. dirs. Revis Bond Fund, Phila. Contributionship. Chmn. emeritus Fgn. Policy Rsch. Inst.; former trustee Colby Coll.; pres. coun. Eisenhower Exch. Fellowships Inc. Lt. USNR, 1958. Recipient Disting. Svc. award AID, 1965 Office: Chestnut Capital Corp PO Box 22 Flourtown PA 19031-0022 Office Phone: 215-233-3001. E-mail: jchristy@chapline.net.

CHRISTY, JOHN HILL, III, journalist; s. John Hill Christy Jr and Mary Kay Vasilosky; m. Asami Mori (div.); m. Yasuko Inaba; 1 child, Daniel Kenji Pequignot. BA in Econ., Fordham U., Bronx. Cert. chartered fin. analyst CFA Inst., VA. Sr. editor Forbes Mag., N.Y.C., 1994—2003; asia fin. editor Bloomberg News, Tokyo, 2003—05; sr. analyst Thomas White Internat., Chgo., 2005; founder borderlessinvestor.com, N.Y.C., NY, 2006—; founding editor Forbes Newsletter Group, Internat. Investment Report, N.Y.C., 2006—. Nominee Bus. Journalist of Yr., World Leadership Forum, 1999—2000, 2002. Mem.: U. Club Chgo. Office: Forbes 60 Fifth Ave New York NY 10011 Home Phone: 347-529-5995. Business E-Mail: jchristy@forbes.com.

CHRISTY, LARRY TODD, publisher; b. Tarentum, Pa., July 2, 1946; s. Todd Rowley and Eleanor Fern Christy; m. Kathleen Bernadette Braun, Nov. 26, 1976 (div. Feb. 1987); m. Lynn Elwell Sparrow, July 2, 1996. BA in Polit. Sci., Thiel Coll., 1968. Dir. Transact Corp., Geneva, 1972—76, pres. Pitts., 1976—96, Trendvest Corp., Virginia Beach, Va., 1978—, Thirders Found., Shelocta, Pa., 1989—; mgr. Trendvest Founders Ltd. Partnership Hedge Fund, 2000—, Trendvest Assocs. Ltd. Partnership, 2003—. Seminar speaker on Hedge Funds, Charles Schwab, Chgo., Phoenix, San Francisco, Pitts. and Columbus, 1989; publisher Internet World Wide Web Svc. for Investors, 1994—. Editor electronic investment svc./Trendvest Ratings, 1983—; author: Tax Trimmer Manual for Pennsylvania Corporations, 1980. Capt. mil. intelligence U.S. Army, Vietnam, Germany. Decorated Bronze Star. Mem. Thiel Coll. Alumni Assn. (pres. 1992-94, v.p. 1988-92, dir. 1983-95). Libertarian. Office: Trendvest Corp Ste 1805 923 First Colonial Rd Virginia Beach VA 23454 E-mail: larry@trendvest.com.

CHRISTY, NICHOLAS PIERSON, physician; b. Morristown, NJ, June 18, 1923; s. Leroy and Elizabeth (Baker) C.; m. Beverly Vairin Morris, June 21, 1947 (dec. Mar. 1997); children: Nicholas Pierson, Martha Vairin; m. Caroline P. Adams, June 26, 1999. AB, Yale, 1945; MD, Columbia, 1951. Diplomate: Am. Bd. Internal Medicine. Intern, asst. resident medicine, 1951—54; asst. vis. physician Delafield Hosp., NYC, 1955-66, vis. physician, 1966-75; asst. vis. physician 1st med. div. Bellevue Hosp., NYC, 1958-66; assoc. attending physician Presbyn. Hosp., NYC, 1962-78, attending physician, 1978-93. Dir. med. svc. Roosevelt Hosp., N.Y.C., 1965-79; faculty Columbia Coll. Phys. and Surg., N.Y.C., 1956—, assoc. prof. medicine, 1962-65, assoc. clin. prof., 1965-67, clin. prof. medicine, 1967-71, prof. medicine, 1971-79, lectr. in medicine, 1979-88, sr. lectr. medicine, 1988-93, spl. lectr. in medicine, 1993—; mem. Columbia U. Health Scis. adv. coun., 1993—; prof. medicine, assoc. dean vets. affairs Health Sci. Ctr. at Bklyn., SUNY, 1979-88, prof. emeritus, 1988—; chief staff Bklyn. VA Med. Ctr., 1979-88; writer-in-residence, alumni writer Coll. Physicians and Surgeons, Columbia U., 1988—; assoc. Nat. Humanities Ctr., Research Triangle Park, N.C., 1979; cons. FDA, 1966, Bd. of Health, N.Y.C., 1965—, NIH Nat. Inst. Diabetes, Digestive and Kidney Diseases tng. grants divsn., 1969-72, endocrinology study sect., 1975-79; cons., bd. dirs. Royal Soc. Medicine Found., 1984-93. Editor, co-author: The Human Adrenal Cortex, 1971; editor-in-chief: Jour. Clin. Endocrinology and Metabolism, 1963-67; assoc. editor: Beeson-McDermott Textbook of Medicine, 1968-75; cons. editor, 1975-79; cons. Med. Dictionary (Dorland), 1988; adv. editor and contbr. Internat. Dictionary of Medicine and Biology (Endocrinology), 1986; mem. adv. bd.: Am. Jour. Medicine, 1971-88; contbr. numerous papers to profl. publs. Served to lt. (j.g.) USNR, 1943-46, PTO. Recipient Borden award, Joseph Mather Smith prize Columbia; John and Mary R. Markle scholar; NIH tng. grantee, 1959-65, endocrinology study sect. grantee, 1958-69; honoree St. Luke's Roosevelt Hosp. Alumni Assn., 2000. Fellow Am. Med. Writers Assn. (hon., Swanberg award 1989); mem. Harvey Soc., AAAS, Soc. Exptl. Biology and Medicine, Am. Soc. Clin. Investigation, Assn. Am. Physicians, Am. Fedn. Clin. Rsch., A.C.P., N.Y. Acad. Medicine, Laurentian Hormone Conf., Am. Physiol. Soc., N.Y. State Med. Soc., N.Y. County Med. Soc., Am. Clin. and Climatol. Assn. (recorder 1977-88, pres. 1990), Am. Assn. Study Liver Diseases, Endocrine Soc. (sec.-treas. 1978-89, Ayerst award 1986), N.Y. Clin. Soc., N.Y. Med. and Surg. Soc., Assn. Am. Physicians, Interurban Clin. Club, Hosp. Grads. Club, Peripatetic Soc., Practitioners Soc., Elizabethan (Yale), Colony (Yale), Century Assn. (pres. 1987-90, hon. 1995—). Office Phone: 401-322-7973. E-mail: calnick@earthlink.net.

CHRITTON, GEORGE A., theater producer; b. Chgo. s. George A. and Dorothea G. Chritton; m. Martha Gilman, Aug. 26, 1956; children: Stewart, Andrew, Douglas, Laura, Neil, Lyle. BA, Occidental Coll., 1955; postgrad., Princeton U., 1955-57. With CIA & various US govt. agys., 1960-89; gen. ptnr. Margeo Investment Co., LA, 1963-76; pres. Wildacre Prodns., Inc., LA, 1990—. Pres., CEO Fin. Svcs. Bancorp, Reno, 1990—; pres. Sycamore Prodns. Ltd., Nev., Calif., 1994—. Prodr.: (plays) Thornton Wilder's Youth, In Shakespeare and The Bible, A Ringing of Doorbells, The Rivers Under the Earth, 1999. Mem. Am. Fgn. Svc. Assn., Washington, 1960—; chmn. bd. dirs. Neighborhood Learning Ctr., Capitol Hill, Washington, 1985—87; vol. Options House, Hollywood, Calif.; vol. coord. Rebuild LA; spl. adv. Los Angeles County Juvenile Ct., 2000—. Maj. USAF, 1957—60. Princeton Nat. fellow, 1955—56, Vis. fellow, lectr., U. Calif., 1987—88. Mem.: SAG, AFTRA, Nat. Assn. Ind. Film & TV Prodrs., Am. Film Inst., LA World Affairs Coun., Princeton Club (So. Calif.), Phi Beta Kappa, Alpha Phi Gamma, Alpha Mu Gamma, Phi Gamma Delta. Office: Wildacre Prodns Inc PO Box 719 Beverly Hills CA 90213-0719 Business E-Mail: Chritton@alumni.Princeton.edu.

CHROMIZKY, WILLIAM RUDOLPH, accountant; b. Chgo., Jan. 21, 1955; s. Rudolph Joseph and Helen M. Chromizky; m. Laura Lee Lamoureux, Oct. 24, 1992. BS, No. Ill. U., 1977; M of Mgmt., Northwestern U., 1987. CPA, Ill. Sr. auditor Arthur Andersen & Co., Chgo., 1977-83; supr. internal audit AM Internat., Chgo., 1983-84, mgr. fin. reporting, 1984-85, dir. acctg., 1985; mgr. bus. analysis Premark Internat., Inc., Deerfield, Ill., 1985-87, dir. fin. reporting, 1987-2000; v.p. external reporting Aon Corp., Chgo., 2001—. Vol. CPAs for the Pub Interest, Chgo., 1990-92; mem. fin. com. Brother Rice H.S., 1995—, bd. dirs., 1999—. Mem.: AICPA, Fin. Execs. Inst. Avocations: skiing, tennis, bowling. Office: Aon Corp 200 E Randolph St Chicago IL 60601 Home Phone: 630-985-5421; Office Phone: 312-381-3489. Business E-Mail: william_chromizky@asc.aon.com.

CHROMOW, SHERI P., lawyer; b. NYC, Aug. 27, 1946; d. Abe and Sara L. Pinsky. BA, Barnard Coll., NYC, 1968; JD, NYU, 1971. Ptnr. Shearman & Sterling, NYC, 1979—2001, Katten, Muchin, Rosenman LLP, NYC, 2001—. Lectr. Practising Law Inst., N.Y. County Bar Assn., Urban Land Inst.; mem. exec. com. N.Y. dist. coun. U. L.I.; mem. adv. bd. Furman Real Estate Inst. NYU Law Sch.; mem. adv. bd. Ticor Title Ins. Co; award judge Real Estate Bd. N.Y., 2003, 04; bd. experts The Internat. Real Estate Trade Orgn. Bd. dirs. Bklyn. Philharm. Orch. Mem. Urban Land Inst. (former gen. counsel), Assn. Fgn. Investors in Real Estate. Office: Katten Muchin

Rosenman LLP 575 Madison Ave New York NY 10022 Home Phone: 212-427-3562, 212-755-0026; Office Phone: 212-940-8529. Business E-Mail: sheri.chromow@kattenlaw.com.

CHRONISTER, GREGORY MICHAEL, newspaper editor; b. York, Pa., Nov. 28, 1953; s. Francis Gilbert and Mary Jane (Hamberger) C. AB, Grove City Coll., Pa., 1975. Features editor The Ghent Press, Norfolk, Va., 1975, mng. editor, 1976; co-founder, editor Tidewater After Dark, Norfolk, 1977-79; asst. dir. New Va. Rev. Inc., Norfolk, 1979-80; editor univ. publs. Old Dominion U., Norfolk, 1980-85; assoc. editor Edn. Week, Washington, 1985-89, mng. editor, 1989—2006, exec. editor, 2006—. Mem.: Theodore Roosevelt Assn., Hist. Soc. Washington, Omicron Delta Kappa. Office: Edn Week 6935 Arlington Rd Ste 100 Bethesda MD 20814-5273 Home: 3001 Veazey Ter NW Apt 1434 Washington DC 20008-5409 Business E-Mail: gchron@epe.org.*

CHRONLEY, JAMES ANDREW, real estate executive; b. Springfield, Mass., July 31, 1930; s. Robert Emmett and Eleanor Andrus (Sullivan) C.; m. Monique Mary Delpech, July 29, 1955; children: Mary Elizabeth, James Michael, Jean Louise, Patricia, Joseph Patrick, John Peter, Robert Emmett. AB, Brown U., 1952; diploma in real estate, U. R.I., 1963; MBA, Pepperdine U., 1991. With Arco Co., 1954-74, Ea. area mgr., until 1972; nat. real estate dir. Atlantic Richfield Co., LA, 1972-74; v.p. restaurant real estate Marriott Corp., Washington, 1974-78; exec. v.p. Burger Chef Systems, Inc., Indpls., 1978—83, pres., 1983; sr. v.p. devel. Taco Bell, Irvine, 1983-94. Served with AUS, 1952-54. Mem. KC, Nat. Assn. Corp. Real Estate Execs. (chpt. pres. 1979, chmn. bd. 1985-87, elected trustee 1987-92), Am. Arbitration Assn., Internat. Exec. Svc. Corps, Orange County Assn. Investment Mgrs. Roman Catholic. Office: Taco Bell 14602 Bel Aire St Irvine CA 92604-2201 Personal E-mail: moniqueusa@cox.net.

CHRUSCIEL, SUSAN MARIE, research scientist, molecular biologist; b. Carbondale, Pa., May 7, 1980; d. Edward and Janet Ann Chrusciel. BS, U. Scranton, Pa., 2004. Unit sec. Cmty. Med. Ctr., Scranton, Pa., 2000—02; lab. technician Aventis Pasteur, Swiftwater, Pa., 2004—04; asst. scientist Schering-Plough, Union, NJ, 2004—. Recipient Shining Performance Excellence award, Schering-Plough, 2005; scholar, Manus-Langan Found., 1998—2004; Loyola scholar, U. Scranton, 1998—2002, Lackawanna Med. Group scholar, 1998—2000, J.F Lavis scholar, 2001, 2003, 2004, Betty Redington scholar, 2001, 2003, 2004. Liberal. Office: Schering-Plough Research Institute 1011 Morris Ave Union NJ 07083 Home Phone: 973-582-0026; Office Phone: 908-820-6579. Office Fax: 908-820-3530. E-mail: susan.chrusciel@spcorp.com.

CHRYSIKOU, EVANGELIA G., psychology professor; b. Athens, Greece, Oct. 20, 1978; d. George A. Chrysikos and Maria M. Chrysikou. BA in Psychology summa cum laude with honors, Panteion U. Athens, 2000; PhD in Cognitive, Exptl. Psychology, Temple U., Phila., 2005. Asst. prof. Temple U., 2005—06; postdoctoral rsch. fellow U. Pa., Phila., 2006—. Contbr. articles to profl. jours. Recipient Disting. Tchg. award, Temple U. Coll. Liberal Arts, 2005; Fulbright scholar, US Dept. of State, 2001—06. Mem.: APA, Cognitive Neurosci. Soc., Soc. for Neurosci., Cognitive Sci. Soc., Assn. for Psychol. Sci. Achievements include research in goal-directed use of tools, creative problem solving, neuropathology of object knowledge and use. Avocations: travel, cooking, running, art. Office: Univ Pennsylvania Dept Psychology 3720 Walnut St Rm B51 Philadelphia PA 19104-6241 also: Ctr Cognitive Neuroscience 3810 Walnut St Rm 307 Philadelphia PA 19104 Home Phone: 215-235-4180; Office Phone: 215-573-6726. Business E-Mail: evangelg@psych.upenn.edu.

CHRYSSAKIS, CHRISTOS, mechanical engineer; b. Athens, Greece, July 24, 1976; s. Anastasios Chryssakis and Dimitra Chryssaki. Diploma in Mech. Engring., Nat. Tech. U. Athens, 1994—2000; MSc in Mech. Engring., U. Mich., Ann Arbor, 2000—02, PhD in Mech. Engring., 2002—05. Internship Robert Bosch GmbH, Stuttgart, Germany, 1999—2000; grad. student rsch. scientist U. Mich., 2001—05; postdoctoral rsch. scientist Inst. Francais du Petrole, Rueil-Malmaison, 2005—06; rsch. scientist Nat. Tech. U. Athens, 2007—. Photographer (exhibitions) A PhD Around the World; contbr. scientific papers. Mem.: ASME, Inst. Liquid Atomization & Spray Sys. (Internat. Student Travel grant 2003), Soc. Automotive Engrs., UM Sailing Club, Soaring & Gliding Club (treas. 2005), U. Mich. Hellenic Student Assn. (v.p. 2004—05). Business E-Mail: cchryssa@naval.ntua.gr.

CHRYSSIKOS, ALEXANDRA GIANELOS, secondary school educator; b. Welch, W.Va., Jan. 22, 1924; d. James and Virginia (Farasly) G.; m. Paul Nicholas Chryssikos, Dec. 5, 1944; children: Telemac P., Virginia A. BS in Edn., Concord State Tchrs. Coll., 1953; Masters, W.Va. U., 1962. 6th grade tchr. Ramsey Elem. Sch., Bluefield, W.Va., 1953-56; 4th-6th grade tchr. Cumberland Heights Elem. Sch., Bluefield, W.Va., 1956-68, Whitethorn Elem. Sch., Bluefield, W.Va., 1968-83; jr. high-high sch. tchr. Windy Mountain Learning Ctr., Bluefield, W.Va., 1983—. Contbr. articles to profl. jours. Pres. Bluefield Jr. Woman's Club, 1959-60. Mem. AAUW (pres. 1966-68), Asnn. Tchr. Edn. (pres. 1971-72), Alpha Delta Kappa. Avocations: reading, exercising, baking, gardening. Home: 1236 College Ave Bluefield WV 24701-4404

CHRYSSIS, GEORGE CHRISTOPHER, entrepreneur; b. Crete, Greece, May 21, 1947; came to U.S., 1966; naturalized U.S. citizen; s. Christopher and Ourania (Kamisakis) C.; m. Margo Sayegh, May 21, 1978; children: Rania, Lilian, Alexander. ASEE, Wentworth Inst., 1969; BEE, Northeastern U., 1972, MEE, 1977. Electronic engr. Orion Rsch., Boston, 1977-78; sr. engr. Datel, Inc., Mansfield, Mass., 1978-79; co-founder, v.p. ops. and engring. Power Gen. Corp., Canton, Mass., 1979-85; pres., founder, CFO Intelco Corp., Acton, Mass., 1985-90; pres., treas. G & M Enterprises, Inc., 1989-92; co-founder, chmn. Collegescape, Inc., 1997-98; pres. Arcadian Capital Mgmt., LLC, 1999—2005; founder, pub. The Hellenic Voice, 2001—02; founder, chmn. CEO Intergon Corp., 2003—. Pvt. investor, 1992—97; trustee Hellenic Coll/Holy Cross, 1989—97, 1999—2004, vice chmn., 2001—04; trustee U. Crete Endowment Fund, 1992—97, Wentworth Inst., 1996—, corporator, 1990—96, chmn. fund campaign, 1989, trustee, 1996—, mem. investment com., 1996—, chair long range planning com., 1999—; trustee Anatolia Coll., 1999—2002; chmn. Northeasteren U. Nat. Coun., 2001—04; bd. dirs. Nat. Coun. Northeastern U., 1986—, Nat. Coun. Wentworth Inst., 1987—95; mem. Capital Campaign Cabinet, 1992—97; bd. dirs. Delphi Comm., Inc., Continuum Control Corp., EliteView Corp.; corporator Northeastern U., 1990, bd. overseers, 1995—2002, trustee, 2002—, mem. indsl. adv. bd., 1997—2005, mem. long-range planning com., 1995—, audit com., 2002—, devel. com., 2002—; founding dir. Gorbachev Found. of N.Am., 1999; mem. adv. bd. Northeastern U. Sch. of Entrepreneurship, 2000. Author: High Frequency Switching Power Supplies, 1984, 1989, (poetry) Echoes and Re-Echoes, 1993, Heliotropia, 1996, Short Poems of Homecoming, 1999, Medea, 2004; contbr. articles to newspapers, mags., profl. jours. Active numerous cmty. and civic orgns., friends Univs. of Crete, 1995, Greek Inst., 1989, bd. dirs., 1998; mem. Am. Hellenic Inst., 1985, Mass. High Tech. Coun., 1986—90; bd. dirs. St. Demetrios Ch., Weston, Mass., 1987—99, parish coun. pres., 1998—99, chmn. ways and means com., 1992—93, ch. svcs. com., 1989—90, stewardship com., 1994—2002; fellow Orthodox Steward of Boston Diocese, 1986—, Greek Orthodox Archdiocese Leadership One Hundred, 2000, Archon Order of St. Andrew Ecumenical Patriarchate, 2000. Finalist Entrepreneur of Yr., Arthur Young Inc. and Inc. Mag., 1989; named Parishioner of Yr., Greek Orthodox Diocese, Boston, 1993; recipient New Englander award, Smaller Bus. Assn. New Eng. (SBANE), 1989, Golden Leopard award, Wentworth Inst., 1991, Arete award, Greek Inst., 1996, Hellenic Leadership award, 1997, Ellis Island medal of honor award, 2000, Minoan award, 2002, Hellenic Heritage award, 2004, W. Erwin Story citation, Northwestern U. Alumni Assn., 2004, Philanthropy award, Fedn. Hellenic Soc. of New Eng., 2006. Mem.: Hellenic Scientists Assn., Internat. Soc. Poets (disting.), PanCretan Assn. Am. (pres. Boston chpt. 1987—89, co-chmn. 30th nat. conv. 1988, bd. govs. dist. I 1990—92, nat. pres. 1995—97, Minoan award 2002), Huntington Soc., President's Club, 500 Club of Northeastern U., Alpha Omega (coun. 1990—, treas. 1994—97). Greek Orthodox. Avocations: writing, travel. Home: 3 Carriage Hill Cir Southborough MA 01772

CHRYSTAL, WILLIAM GEORGE, retired minister; b. Seattle, May 22, 1947; s. Francis Homer and Marjorie Isabell (Daubert) C.; m. Janie Guill, Oct. 7, 2006; children: Shelley, Sarah, John, Philip. BA, U. Wash., Seattle, 1969, MEd, 1970; MDiv, Eden Theol. Sem., 1978; MA, Johns Hopkins U., Balt., 1984. Ordained to ministry, United Ch. of Christ, 1977. Learning resources specialist Seattle CC Dist., 1970-71; dir. learning resources ctr. Whatcom CC, Ferndale, Wash., 1971-73; minister St. Peter's United Ch. of Christ, Granite City, Ill., 1978-79; sr. minister 1st Congl. Ch., Stockton, Calif., 1979-83, Reno, 1991—2007, pastor emeritus, 2007; minister Trinity United Ch. of Christ, Adamstown, Md., 1983-85; sr. minister Edwards Congl. Ch., Northampton, Mass., 1985-86. Hosp. chaplain Washoe Med. Ctr., Reno, 1993-99; host Thomas Jefferson Hour, on Nat. pub. radio stas. Author: Young Reinhold Niebuhr: His Early Writings, 1911-1931, 1977, 2d edit., 1982, A Father's Mantle: The Legacy of Gustav Niebuhr, 1982, The Fellowship of Prayer, 1987; author monographs; contbr. articles to profl. jours. V.p. Reno-Sparks Met. Ministry, Reno, 1994-97; Chautauqua scholar Great Basin Chautauqua, Reno, 1993, 94, 98, 99; historical characterization of Pres. John Adams, 2003—, Alexander Hamilton, 2006—. Lt. comdr. USN, 1986-91, maj. Nev. Army N.G., 1992-96. Decorated (2) Meritorious Svc. medal. Mem. Am. Soc. Ch. History, Nev. Soc. Mayflower Descs. (past gov.), Am. Legion, Disabled Vets. (life), VFW (life), Rotary Club (Paul Harris fellow 1997). Home: 3820 Bluebird Cir Reno NV 89509-5601 Office: 1st Congl Ch 627 Sunnyside Dr Reno NV 89503-3515 Office Phone: 775-747-1414. Personal E-mail: williamgchrystal@yahoo.com.

CHRYSTIE, THOMAS LUDLOW, investor; b. NYC, May 24, 1933; s. Thomas Witter and Helen (Duell) C.; m. Eliza S. Balis, June 9, 1955; children: Alice B., Helen S., Adden B., James McD. BA, Columbia U., 1955; MBA, NYU, 1960. With Merrill Lynch, NYC, 1955; dir. investment banking divsn. Merrill Lynch, Pierce, Fenner & Smith, Inc., NYC, 1970-75; sr. v.p. Merrill Lynch & Co., 1975-78, CFO, 1976-78; chmn. Merrill Lynch White Weld Capital Markets Group, 1978-81, Merrill Lynch Capital Resources, 1981-83; adv. on strategy Merrill Lynch & Co. Inc., 1983-88; pvt. investor Jackson, Wyo., 1988—. Bd. dirs. Jackson State Bank, Eeonyx Corp Trustee emeritus Columbia U.; trustee Nat. Mus. Wildlife Art. Capt. USAF, 1955-58. Mem. N.Y. Athletic Club, Teton Pines Tennis Club, Columbia Club. Home and Office: PO Box 640 Wilson WY 83014-0640 *Whatever you are involved in, see it as part of a larger picture.*

CHU, BENJAMIN K., hospital administrator; BA, Yale U., 1974; MD, NYU, 1978; MPH, Columbia Mailman Sch. Pub. Health, 1985. Diplomate Am. Bd. Internal Medicine, 1982. Intern, resident Kings County Hosp., 1978; assoc. prof. of clinical med., assoc. dean for clinical affairs NYU, 1994—2000; sr. assoc. dean Harlem Hospital Center, NYC, 2000—02; sr. v.p. med. affairs N.Y.C. Health and Hosp. Corp., 2001—02, pres., CEO, 2002—05; pres. Kaiser Found. Health Plan, Inc. and Kaiser Found. Hosp., So. Calif. Region, 2005—. Office: Kaiser Found Health Plan and Hosp 7th Fl 393 E Walnut St Pasadena CA 91188

CHU, CHI-CHENG, research scientist; s. Yu-Chu Chu and Hsiu-Mei Wu; m. Er-Mei Fan, Dec. 20, 1998; 1 child, Kenneth. BS, Nat. Taiwan U., Taipei, 1990; MS, U. of Wis., Madison, 1995, PhD, 2001. Rsch. asst. U. of Wis., Madision, 1996—2000; prin. engr. Simplylook.com Inc., Los Altos, Calif., 2000—03; sr. rschr. UCLA, 2003—. Forum convener, industry liaison UCLA Wireless Internet for Mobile Enterprise Consortium, LA, 2003—. Contbr. scientific papers to profl. jours. (2d Best Paper award, 2004). 2d lt. Taiwanese Armed Forces, 1990—92. Mem.: ASME (corr.). Achievements include patents for Network-based Viewing of Images of Three-Dimensional Objects, US Patent 6525732; patents pending for Low cost RFID-based Positioning System For Inventory Management; first to Virtual Reality based Computer Aided Design System; research in Collaborative Computer Aided Design System via wire/wireless network; Mobile Digital Right Management. Office: UCLA 44-116S ENG IV 420 Westwood Pl Los Angeles CA 90095 Home: 3717 Vinton Ave # 105 Los Angeles CA 90034 Home Phone: 310-741-8383; Office Phone: 310-267-4979. Personal E-mail: chichengwi@gmail.com. Business E-Mail: cchu@winmec.ucla.edu.

CHU, CHUNG KWANG, medicinal chemistry professor; b. Seoul, Republic of Korea, May 18, 1941; s. Jee Young Huh; children: Susan, Jackie. BS, Seoul Nat. U., 1964; MS, Idaho State U., 1970; PhD, SUNY, Buffalo, 1974. Rsch. assoc. Sloan-Kettering Cancer Inst., NYC, 1974-80; asst. prof. Idaho State U., Pocatello, 1990-82; asst. prof. medicinal chemistry U. Ga., Athens, 1982-87, assoc. prof., 1987-89, prof., 1990-98, disting. rsch. prof., 1998—. Adv. bd. NIH, Pharmasset, Atlanta. Lt. (j.g.) Korean Navy. Mem. Am. Chem. Soc. (Rsch. grant 1988), Am. Assn. for Cancer Rsch., Am. Assn. Colls. Pharmacy, Internat. Soc. Antiviral Rsch. Achievements include patents for drug discovery field. Office: U Ga Coll Pharmacy Athens GA 30602 Office Phone: 706-542-5379. Office Fax: 706-542-5381. Business E-Mail: dchu@rx.uga.edu.

CHU, DAVID S.C., federal agency administrator, economist; b. NYC, May 28, 1944; s. H. T. and Esther Chu; m. Laura L. Tosi. BA in Economics and Mathematics magna cum laude, Yale U., 1964, PhD in Economics, 1972. Asst. dir. nat. security and internat. affairs Congl. Budget Office, Washington, 1978—81; dir. then asst. sec. def. for program analysis and evaluation Dept. Def., 1981—93; economist RAND, Santa Monica, Calif., 1970—78, sr. fellow Washington, 1993—94, dir. Washington rsch. dept., 1994—96, dir. Washington office, assoc. chmn. of rsch. staff, 1996—98; v.p. army rsch. divsn., dir. Arroyo Ctr., 1998—2001; under sec. defense for personnel and readiness US Dept. of Defense, 2001—. Capt. US Army, 1968—70, Vietnam. Decorated Bronze Star, Army commendation medal. Fellow: Nat. Acad. Pub. Adminstrn. (chmn., bd. trustees 1999—2001); mem.: Phi Beta Kappa. Office: 4000 Defense Pentagon Washington DC 20301-4000

CHU, ELLIN RESNICK, librarian, consultant; b. Bklyn., Nov. 23, 1932; d. David and Isobel (Janowitch) Resnick; m. Wallace Chu, Aug. 29, 1960 (div. Sept. 1979); children: Steven, Joshua, Amanda. BA in Modern European Hist. with honors, Ind. U., 1954, MA in Libr. Sci., 1956; postgrad., Columbia U., 1956-57. Young adult libr. Donnell br. N.Y. Pub. Libr., 1956-57; order libr. Nat. Indsl. Conf. Bd., 1957-58; reference libr. Columbia U. Reference Libr., 1958-59; libr. dir. Hillside Hosp., 1959-61, L.I. Jewish-Hillside Med. Ctr., 1972—; adult/young adult libr. Glen Cove (N.Y.) Pub. Libr., 1973-77; young adult cons. Rochester (N.Y.) Pub. Libr. Monroe County Libr. Sys., 1977-93, mgr. lit., religion and philosophy divsn., 1993-98, ret., 1998. Mem. nomination com. Glen Cove Interagy. Coun., 1976, chair youth recreation com., 1974-75, chair pre-screening com., info. and referral adv. bd. Nassau Libr. Sys., 1977; mem. libr. planning com. Rochester Sesquicentennial, 1984; mem. cen. libr. planning com. Rochester Pub. Libr., 1985-86; sec. Rochester Area Youth Dirs. Coun., 1980-81, mem. nominating com., 1987, profl. improvement com., 1987-89; presenter programming and svcs. for young adults Mid-Hudson Libr. Sys., Albany, N.Y., 1989-90; mem. On-line pub. catalog planning com. Monroe County Libr. Sys., 1986-92; libr. programming presenter and resource team mem. Learning Odyssey/SUNY Albany and New York State Divsn. Libr. Devel., 1989; active Brighton Cable Commn., 1980-93. Co-author: (chpt. to book) Our Family, Our Friends, Our World: An Annotated Guide to Significant Multicultural Books for Children and Teenagers, 1991; contbr. articles to profl. jours. Recipient 1st prize N.Y. Libr. Ad Hoc Com. on Women's Concerns, 1975; grantee Young Adult Libr. Instrn. Project, 1982-84; scholar Robert Flaherty Film Seminar, 1976, Lyman Langdon scholar Audubon Ecology Workshop, 1977. Mem. ALA (young adult svcs. divsn., chair high interest/low literacy level materials evaluation com. 1979-81, pub. liaison com. 1988-90, Margaret A. Edwards Author Award com. 1991-93), Ednl. Film Libr. Assn. (juror Am. Film Festival 1976-78, jury chair 1979-88), N.Y. Libr. Assn. (pres. youth svcs. sect. 1984, founding mem./sec. film/video roundtable 1977), Nassau County Libr. Assn. (founding mem. young adult sect. 1976).

CHU, FELIX T., school librarian; b. Taipei, Taiwan, Feb. 27, 1949; s. Hsin-min Chu; m. Nancy L. Perkins; 1 child, Jonathan. BA in Spanish, U. Iowa, Iowa City, MA, 1972—73, MLS, 1973—74; PhD, Ill. State U., Normal, 1988—93, PhD in Ednl. Adminstrn. Libr. U. Nebr., Lincoln, 1975—78, Mid Am. Ctr. Bilingual Materials Devel., Iowa City, 1979—80; computer analyst Nebr. Dept. Revenue, Lincoln, 1981—84; libr. We. Ill. U., Macomb, 1984—. Author: (book) There's Another Way to Do It, 2005; contbr. articles to profl. jours. Mem.: ALA. Office: We Ill Univ 1 University Cir Macomb IL 61455-1390 Home Phone: 309-833-1855. Business E-Mail: f-chu@wiu.edu.

CHU, HSIEN-KUN, chemist, researcher; b. Shanghai, People's Republic of China, Oct. 14, 1947; came to U.S., 1971; s. Hwei-Teh and Yun-Hsiang (Chang) C.; m. Winnie K.S. Wong, Dec. 23, 1976; children: James C., Jason C. BS, Nat. Taiwan U., Taipei, Republic of China, 1970; PhD, Vanderbilt U., 1976. Vis. instr. U. Tex., Arlington, 1976-77; rsch. assoc. Tex. Christian U., Ft. Worth, 1977-80; rsch. specialist Dow Corning Corp., Midland, Mich., 1980-88; sr. scientist Loctite Corp., Rocky Hill, Conn., 1988—. Contbr. articles to profl. jours. Mem. Am. Chem. Soc., Sigma Xi. Achievements include patents on silicone sealants; research into mechanistic studies of organic reactions, silicone research. Home: 6 Harvest Hl Wethersfield CT 06109-2422 Office: Henkel Tech 1001 Trout Brook Xing Rocky Hill CT 06067-3910 Business E-Mail: hkchu@yahoo.com.

CHU, JACK J. (JACK J. ZHU), electrical engineer; b. Shanghai, Jan. 26, 1938; arrived in U.S., 1980; s. Baoling Zhu(Chu) and Zhi Yin Mo; m. Shannon Chongshan Sun, 1966; 1 child, Ling Zhu. BS in Automatic Control Engring., Tsinghua U., Beijing, 1960, MS in Automatic Control Engring., 1962; MSEE, U. Minn., 1990. Sr. control sys. engr. Spectra Engring., Inc., Roseville, Minn., 1992—95, Innovex Engring., Inc., Hopkins, Minn., 1995—96, Quickie Design Inc., Fresno, Calif., 1996—97, Sunrise Med. Inc., Longmont, Colo., 1997—98, Kriton Med., Inc., Citrus Heights, Calif., 1998, Avery Dennison Inc., Ft. Wayne, Ind., 1999; sr. control sys., software engr. Balance Tech., Inc., Ann Arbor, Mich., 2000—01, Avionics Specialties Inc., Charlottesville, Va., 2001—. Contbr. articles to profl. jours. Recipient Nat. Merit Citation Class 2 in China, 1982. Achievements include development of microprocessor model reference adaptive control system; of adaptive thin-film sensor grinding system; of blood pump controller with indicator. Avocations: ping pong/table tennis, swimming, cooking, travel, chess. Personal E-mail: jackjchu@earthlink.net. E-mail: jackjchu@embarq.net.

CHU, JAMES, electronics executive; b. Taiwan; m. Lily Chu; children: Tina, Kevin. Various sales positions, Taiwan; pres. Taiwanese keyboard mfg. co., U.S., 1986; founder Keypoint Tech. Corp., 1987-90; reorganized Keypoint Tech. Corp. (now ViewSonic Corp.), 1990; chmn., CEO ViewSonic Corp., Walnut, Calif., 1990—. Avocations: reading, tennis, exploring internet.*

CHU, JOHNSON CHIN SHENG, retired physician; b. Peiping, China, Sept. 25, 1918; arrived in U.S., 1948, naturalized, 1957; s. Harry S.P. and Florence (Young) Chu; m. Sylvia Cheng, June 11, 1949; children: Stephen, Timothy. MD, St. John's U., 1945. Intern Univ. Hosp., Shanghai, 1944-45; resident, research fellow NYU Hosp., 1948-50; resident physician in charge State Hosp. and Med. Ctr., Weston, W.Va., 1951-56; chief services, clin. dir. State Hosp., Logansport, Ind., 1957-84, ret., 1998. Active mem. Meml. Hosp., Logansport, Ind., 1968—. Contbr. articles to profl. jours. Fellow: Am. Coll. Chest Physicians, Am. Psychiat. Assn.; mem.: AAAS, AMA, Cass County Med. Soc., Ind. Med. Assn. Achievements include research in cardiology and pharmacology. Office: Southeastern Med Ctr Walton IN 46994

CHU, JUDY MAY, assemblywoman; b. LA, July 7, 1955; d. Judson and May C.; m. Michael Eng, Aug. 8, 1978. BA in Math., UCLA, 1974; MA in Clin. Psychology, Calif. Sch. Profl. Psychology, 1977, PhD, 1979. Lectr. UCLA, 1980-86; assoc. prof. L.A. City Coll., 1981-88; prof. East L.A. Coll., Monterey Park, 1988—2001; mem. Monterey Park City Council, 1988—2001, Calif. State Assembly, 2001—. Chair, select com. on hate crimes Calif. State Assembly, mem. select com. on language access, mem. rules, labor and employment com., environ. safety and toxic materials com., human svcs. com. & transportation com. Author, editor: Linking Our Lives: Chinese American Women in Los Angeles, 1984; contbr. articles profl. jours. Mem. city coun. City of Monterey Park, 1988—, mayor, 1990-91, 94-95; bd. dirs. Garvey Sch. Dist., 1985-88; chair Commn. for Sex Equity, L.A. Unified Sch. Dist., 1984-85; bd. dirs. Rebuild L.A.; mem. adv. com. U.S. Census Bur., 1994—; Bd. dirs. Gabriel Valley chpt. ARC; bd. dirs. Asian Youth Ctr., San Gabriel Valley United Way, West San Gabriel Valley Juvenile Diversion Project. Named One of 88 Leaders for 1988, L.A. Times, 1988, Dem. of Yr., 59th Assembly Dist. Dem. Com., 1989, Vol. of Yr. San Gabriel Valley chpt. United Way, 1989, L.A. Outstanding Founder, 1995; recipient Achievement award Asian Pacific Family Ctr., 1980, Pub. Svc. award Asian Pacific Legal Ctr., 1989, award for Excellence in Pub. Svc., UCLA Alumni, 1991, Leadership award West San Gabriel Valley chpt. ARC. Mem. Soroptimists. Office: Calif State Assembly PO Box 942849 Sacramento CA 94249 Business E-Mail: assemblymember.chu@asm.ca.gov.

CHU, KATHERINE K., music educator; arrived in U.S., 1983; d. James M. Chu and Lillian S. Yang. BA in Piano, Beijing Ctrl. Conservatory, 1982; BA in Profl. Music, Berklee Coll. Music, Boston, 1989; MS in Info. Sys., Northeastern U., Boston, 1992. Piano accompanist Children's Art Theater of China Welfare Soc., Shanghai, 1973—74; piano tchr. performance dept. Shanghai Drama Acad., 1974—78, Beijing Dance Acad., 1978—83; piano accompanist Boston Ballet, 1984—90; piano tchr., accompanist Boston Conservatory, 1985—91; piano tchr. KCHU Piano Studio, Boston, Phila. and Cupertino, Calif., 1985—. Bd. dirs. Steinway Soc. of the Bay Area, San Jose, Calif., 2002—04; participant 1st China-US Dance Exch. Program, Boston Ballet, 1984. Mem.: Music Tchrs. Assn. Calif., Am. Coll. Musicians. Personal E-mail: kachu19390@yahoo.com.

CHU, MORGAN, lawyer; b. NYC, Dec. 27, 1950; s. Ju Chin and Ching (Chen) Chu; m. Helen M. Wong, Dec. 29, 1970. BA, UCLA, 1971, MA, 1972, PhD, 1973; MSL, Yale U., 1974; JD magna cum laude, Harvard U., 1976. Bar: Calif. 1976, US Dist. Ct. (ctrl. dist. Calif.) 1977, US Dist. Ct. (no. dist. Calif.) 1980, US Ct. Appeals (9th cir.) 1980, US Dist. Ct. (so. dist. Calif.) 1984, US Dist. Ct. (ea. dist. Calif.) 1986, US Ct. Appeals (fed. cir.) 1989, US Supreme Ct. 1991. Law clk. to Hon. Charles M. Merrill U.S. Ct. Appeals 9th Cir., San Francisco, 1976—77; assoc. Irell & Manella LLP, LA, 1977-82, ptnr., 1982—, co-mng. ptnr., 1997—2003, exec. com., 1984—. Adj. prof. UCLA Sch. Law, 1979—82; judge pro tem LA Mcpl. Ct., 1980. Mem. editl. bd. Litig. News, 1981—84. Named One of 10 New

Superstars, Legal Times Wash., 1983, Top Players in High-Tech Intellectual Property, Nat. Law Jour., 1991, 100 Most Influential Lawyers in Am., 1994—, Top 10 Trial Lawyers in Nation, Nat. Law. Jour., One of Top Intellectual Property Lawyers, Calif. Lawyer, 1992, Dream Team Law Firm, Calif. Law Bus., 1992, Top 20 Lawyers LA Firms, 1994, Top 10 Most Influential Lawyers Calif., 1999, Exec. of Year in Law, LA Bus. Jour., 1994, Top Most Influential People in LA Internet Industry Co., 1998, Top 45 Lawyers Under 45 US, Am. Lawyer, 1995, Best Intellectual Property Lawyer in Nation, Corp. Bd., 2001, Number One IP Lawyer Calif., Chambers Global, 2003—04, Number 1 Super Lawyer in So. Calif., LA Mag., 2004, Top Intellectual Property Lawyer US, First Chambers, 2006, One of 100 Most Influential Lawyers Calif., LA Daily Jour.; recipient Significant Achievement award Excellence and Innovation in Alternative Dispute Resolution, Ctr. Pub., 1987, UCLA medal, 2007; fellow, Am. Coll. Trial Lawyers. Mem.: ABA (chmn. high tech. intellectual property and patent trials subcommittee 1986—90, trial practice com., litig. sect.), LA Intellectual Property Law Assn. (bd. dirs. 1991—93, bd. dirs. pub. counsel 1993—, exec. com. bd. dirs. pub. counsel 1995—), LA County Bar Assn. (judiciary com. 1983—2001), Calif. Bar Assn. Office: Irell & Manella LLP Ste 900 1800 Ave of the Stars Los Angeles CA 90067-4276 Office Phone: 310-203-7000. Office Fax: 310-203-7199. Business E-Mail: mchu@irell.com.

CHU, PAUL CHING-WU, physicist, director, academic administrator, educator; b. Hunan, China, Dec. 2, 1941; arrived in U.S., 1963; m. May P. Chern; children: Claire, Albert. BS, Cheng-Kung U., Taiwan, 1962; MS, Fordham U., 1965; PhD, U. Calif., San Diego, 1968; PhD (hon.), Fordham U., 1988, Northwestern U., 1988, Chinese U. of Hong Kong, 1988, Fla. Internat. U., 1989, SUNY, 1989, Whittier Coll., 1991, Hong Kong Bapt. U., 1999, Providence U., 2005, U. Macau, 2006, U. Macon, 2006. 2d lt. Nationalist Chinese Air Forces, 1962—63; tchg. asst. Fordham U., Bronx, NY, 1963—65; rsch. asst. U. Calif., San Diego, 1965—68; tech. staff Bell Labs., Murray Hill, NJ, 1968—70; asst. prof. physics Cleve. State U., 1970—73, assoc. prof., 1973—75, prof., 1975—79; prof. physics U. Houston, 1979—, dir. magnetic info. rsch. lab., 1984—88, dir. Space Vacuum Epitaxy Ctr., 1986—88, dir. Tex. Ctr. for Superconductivity, 1987—2001, dir. NSF/materials rsch. sci. and engring. ctr., 1996—97; prin. investigator Lawrence Berkeley Nat. Lab., 1999—; convenor Heads of Univs. Com., Hong Kong, 2003—; pres. Hong Kong U. Sci. and Tech., 2001—; exec. dir. Tex. Ctr. Superconductivity, 2005—. Resident, rsch. assoc. Argonne Nat. Lab., Ill., 1972; vis. scientist Hansens Physics Lab., Stanford, 1973; mem. vis. staff Los Alamos Sci. Lab., 1975—80; hon. prof. Zhongshan U., 1988, Chinese Acad. Scis. Physics Inst., 1979, Nankai U., 1991, Chinese U. Sci. and Tech., 1991, Nanjing U., 1996, Dongnan U., 2003; bd. dirs. Coalition for the Comml. Application of Superconductors, 1989—; mem. White House ad hoc rev. panel on long-range plan for R & D of superconductivity, 1989; mem. rsch. adv. com. Inst. for Tech. and Strategic Rsch., 1989; vis. Miller rsch. prof. U. Calif., Berkeley, 1991; mem. adv. com. to redesign the space sta. The White House, Washington, 1993; mem. sch. adv. bd. Ctr. Nanoscale Sci. and Tech., Rice U., 1995—; internat. adv. com. Hong Kong Bapt. U., 1995—; internat. adv. bd. China-Am. Tech. Corp., 1995—; mem. adv. com. on rsch. planning Higher Edn. Coordinating Bd., State of Tex., 1997—2000; bd. dirs. S.S. Chern Found. Math. Rsch., 2000—, Applied Superconductivity Conf.; pres. Applied Superconductivity Corp., 2000—02; mem. inst. physics acad. adv. com. Academia Sinica, 2001—, mem. ctrl. adv. com., 2002—, mem. coun., 2002—; chmn. ad hoc Com. on Future Nat. Energy, 2002—; dir. search com. Academia Sinica Ctr. Applied Sci. Engineering Rsch., 2002—; mem. rsch. adv. bd. U. Tex., Dallas, 2004—; mem. adv. bd. Ctr. for Nanomagnetic Systems U. Houston, 2004—, mem. pres.'s exec. adv. coun., 2004—; mem. founding governing bd. Acad. Medicine, Engring. and Sci. Tex., 2004—; mem. program adv. com. Inst. Advanced Studies, Nanyang Tech. U., 2005—; hon. pres. Jiaxing U., 2006; founding dir. Inst. Advanced Study, Hong Kong U. Sci. and Tech., 2006—; mem. univ. adv. com. Nat. Tsing Hua U., 2006—; mem. bus. and sci. adv. bd. Britton Chance Ctr. for Biomed. Protonics, Hunzhong U. Sci. and Tech., Wuhun, China, 2006—; cons. in field; mem. exec. com. Commn. on Strategic Devel., Hong Kong SAR Govt., 2006—. Mem. editl. bd.: High Tech. Bus., 1988—, Modern Physics Letters B, 1988—, Applied Superconductivity, 1992—98, Indian Jour. Pure and Applied Physics, 1992—, News and Reviews of Physics in China Today, 1992—, Internat. Jour. Modern Physics, 1988—, Brazilian Jour. Physics, 1995—, Sci. in China, 1997—, Chinese Sci. Bull., 1997—, Applied Physics Rev. (Korea), 1998—2000; contbr. articles to profl. jours. Internat. adv. com. World Lab. Pan Am. Ctr. for Collaboration in Sci. and Tech., 1998—; bd. dirs. T.S. Chang Scholarship Found., 1999—. Named hon. citizen, State of Tex., 1987, City of Houston, 1987, Best Rschr. in U.S., U.S. News and World Report, 1990, one of 20th Century's 100 most intellectual people in gas and electric, Century of Power, Heat Energy, 2000, honoree, Alliance for Multicultural Cmty. Svcs., 2000; recipient Phys. and Math. Sci. award, NY Acad. Sci., 1987, Leroy Randle Grumman medal, Grumman Corp., 1987, Achievement award, Chinese Am. Acad. and Profl. Assn., 1987, Disting. Alumnus award, U. Calif., San Diego, 1987, Faculty Rsch. award, U. Houston, 1987, Sigma Xi Rsch. Excellence award, 1987, Achievement award, NASA, 1987, Nat. Medal Sci., Pres. of US, 1988, Disting. Alumnus award, Cheng-Kung U., 1988, Medal of Sci. Merit, World Cultural Coun., 1989, Founders' prize, Texas Instruments, 1990, St. Martin de Porres award, 1990, Superconductivity Excellence award in sci. accomplishments, World Congress on Superconductivity, 1994, Bernd Matthias prize, 4th Internat. Conf. on Materials and Mechanisms of Superconductivity, High Temperature Superconductors, 1994, Disting. Sci. Achievement award, Washington Met. Assn. Chinese Am. Profls., 1998, Houston Hall of Fame award, George Bush Internat. Airport, 1999, Sharif U., 1999, Esther Farfel award, U. Houston, 2000, Houston Hall of Fame award, Greater Houston Conv. and Vis. Bur., 1988, John Fritz medal, United Engring. Found., 2001, Achievement award, Chinese Profl. Club, 2006. Fellow: Chinese Acad. Scis., Tex. Acad. Scis., Am. Phys. Soc. (teller divsn. Solid State Physics 1976, internat. prize com. 1988—89, selection com. Oliver E. Buckley Prize in condensed matter physics 2006—, Internat. prize for new materials 1988); mem.: NAS (mem. panel on High Temperature Superconductivity 1987, sect. co-chair 1992—95, selection com., Comstock award 1988, John J. Carty award for advancement of sci. 2005), AAAS, Royal Acad. Engring. (fgn.), Russian Acad. Engring. (fgn. mem. 2005), State of Tex. Sci. and Tech. Coun., Electromagnetic Acad., Third World Acad. Scis., Academia Sinica (Taipei, mem. adv. com. Inst. Physics 1997—2000), Am. Acad. Arts and Scis., Royal Soc. Encouragement of Arts Mfrs. and Commerce. Office: U Houston Texas Ctr Superconductivity 202 Houston Science Center Houston TX 77204-5002 also: Hong Kong U Sci and Tech Clear Water Bay Kowloon Hong Kong Office Phone: 713-743-8222, 852-2358-6101. Office Fax: 852-2358-0029, 713-743-8201.

CHU, QUYEN DINH, surgeon, educator, oncologist; b. Saigon, Vietnam, May 11, 1968; s. Trinh Van and Nhan Thi Chu; m. Trina T. Dang, Mar. 18, 1997; children: Thuy-Tien, Yen. BA, Dartmouth Coll., Hanover, NH, 1990; MD, Brown U., Providence, 1994. Resident in surgery St. Elizabeth's Med. Ctr., Boston, 1995—2000; fellow in surg. oncology Roswell Pk. Cancer Inst., Buffalo, 2000—02; assoc. prof. surgery La. State U. Health Scis. Ctr., Shreveport, 2002—. Dir. peritoneal surface malignancies program Feist-Weiller Cancer Ctr., Shreveport, 2006—. Dist. enrollment dir. Dartmouth Coll., 2006. Mem.: ACS (Young Surgeon award 2004), Assn. Acad. Surgery (instnl. rep. 2006), Soc. Surg. Oncology, Sigma Xi. Avocations: Karate, carpentry. Office: La State U Health Scis Ctr 1501 Kings Hwy PO Box 33932 Shreveport LA 71130-3932

CHU, RICHARD CHAO-FAN, mechanical engineer; b. Beijing, Hopei, Peoples' Republic China, May 28, 1933; came to U.S., 1958, naturalized, 1968; s. Liang Hsi and Yun Hwa (Wang) C.; m. Theresa Sou-Chin Lee, Aug. 24, 1963; children: Banjamin, Benson, Benedict, Bonita. BSME, Nat. Cheng-Keng U., Tainan, Taiwan, 1958; MSME, Purdue U., 1960. Jr. assoc. engr. IBM Corp., Poughkeepsie, NY, 1960-64, sr. assoc. engr., 1964-65, project engr., mgr., 1965-67, devel. engr., mgr., 1967-69, sr. engr., mgr., 1969-75, program mgr., product technology, 1975-79, program mgr., engring. lab., 1979-83, fellow, 1983—; v.p. IBM Acad. Tech., 1990, pres., 1991. Author 2 books; patentee in field; contbr. articles to profl. jours. Pres. Mid-Hudson Chinese-Am. Civic Assn., Poughkeepsie, 1969. Recipient Disting. Alumnus award Purdue U., 1984, Outstanding Alumni award Nat. Cheng-Kung U., 1986. Fellow ASME (Heat Transfer Meml. award 1986), AAAS; mem. N.Y. Acad. Sci., Nat. Acad. Engring. Republican. Roman Catholic. Avocations: swimming, jogging, sailing, skiing, wind surfing. Home: 30 Saint Andrews Ln Hopewell Junction NY 12533 Office: IBM Corp P520/003 Poughkeepsie NY 12601 Office Phone: 845-433-5236. Business E-Mail: rcchu@us.ibm.com.

CHU, ROBERT LANCE, physician; b. Kowloon, Hong Kong, Nov. 18, 1950; came to U.S., 1953; s. Lamtin and jane (Leung) C. BS in Biology, Fordham U., 1972; MD, Creighton U., 1976. Diplomate Am. Bd. Ob-Gyn. Intern in internal medicine U. So. Calif., 1977; resident in ob-gyn. Kaiser Permanante Med. Ctr., San Francisco, 1980; staff ob-gyn. So. Calif. Permanente Med. Group, LA, 1984—. With USAF, 1980-84, comdr. USAF Res., 1984—. Fellow Am. Coll Ob-Gyn. Roman Catholic. Office: So Calif Permanent Med Ctr 4900 W Sunset Blvd Los Angeles CA 90027-5814

CHU, RODERICK GONG-WAH, educational association administrator; b. NYC, Jan. 17, 1949; s. Norton Yuen and Frances (Liang) C. BS in Math. and Physics, U. Mich., 1969; MBA with honors, Cornell U., 1971; D in Pub. Svc. (hon.), U. Rio Grande, 1999; LHD (hon.), Youngstown State U., 1999; ArtsD (hon.), Cin. State Tech. and CC, 2001; AS (hon.), Edison CC, 2001; D in Pub. Svc. (hon.), Otterbein U., 2003; HHD (hon.), Capital U., 2003; LHD (hon.), Shawnee State U., 2004; LLD (hon.), Marietta Coll., 2006. Staff analyst Arthur Andersen and Co., NYC, 1971—75, mgr., 1975—81, ptnr., 1981—83; commr. Taxation and Fin., pres. State Tax Commn. State of NY, Albany, 1983—88; ptnr. Andersen Cons., NYC, 1988—95, worldwide mng. ptnr. state and local govt. practice, 1989—91, worldwide mng. ptnr. govt. practice, 1991—92; chancellor Ohio Bd. Regents, Columbus, Ohio, 1998—2006, chancellor emeritus, 2006—; interim pres. Edn. Commn. of the States, Denver, 2006—. Bd. dir. Housing Fin. Agy., Med. Care Facilities Fin. Agy.; adv. bd. Coun. Excellence in Govt., 1991-93, trustee, 1993-95, NYC real property tax reform commn., 1993; mem. Ohio Workforce Devel. Bd., 1998-1999, Ohio Commn. on African Am. Males, 1998-2006. Bd. dir., bd. overseers Jacob's Pillow Dance Festival, Becket, Mass., 1984-97; mem. Cornell U. Coun., 1988-92, 94-98, 2001-05, dean's alumni exec. coun. Johnson Sch. Grad. Mgmt., 1988-90, adv. coun., 1991-98, outdoor edn. adv. coun., 1992-98, strategic planning adv. bd., 1992-96; trustee SUNY, 1990-98, chmn. exec. compensation com., 1993-98; pres.'s adv. coun. China Inst. Am., 1990-94; co-chair pres. circle The Asia Soc., 1994-97; adv. bd. Barnard-Columbia Ctr. Leadership in Urban Pub. Policy, 1994-98; mem. State Higher Edn. Exec. Officers, 1998-, treas., 2002, pres., 2003, Gov.'s Workforce Policy Bd., 1999-2006, MidWest Higher Edn. Commn., 2000-06, Edn. Commn. of States, 2001-06, exec. com., 2003-06, steering com., 2004-06, Nat. Commn. on Arts in Edn., 2004-05, Nat. Ctr. Learning and Citizenship, 2005-06, Ohio Third Frontier Commn., 2003-06, Gov.'s Commn. on Higher Edn. and the Econ., 2003-04, Educators Stds. Bd., 2004-06, SchoolNet Commn., 2004-05, eTech Ohio Commn., 2005-06; trustee The Coll. Bd., 2004-, chmn. audit com., 2005—, Ohio Hist. Soc., 1998-2006. Recipient Man of Yr. award Chinese-Am. Planning Coun., 1984, NYC Police Dept., Asian Jade Soc., 1984, Disting. Achievement award United Chinese Am. League, 1985, Spl. Recognition award Asian Ams. for Affirmative Action, 1986, Champion of Excellence award Orgn. Chinese Am., 1986, Outstanding Chinese Entrepreneur award Chinese Mgmt. Assn., 1991, Disting. Friend award, So. State CC, 2002; Paul Harris fellow Rotary Internat., 1988, 92. Mem. Am. Soc. Pub. Adminstrn. (hon.), Cornell Club (NYC), Capital Club (Columbus), New Albany Country Club, Met. Opera Club, Cornell Asian Alumni Assn., Phi Kappa Phi. Republican. Lutheran. Avocations: skiing, photography, golf, fly fishing. Office: Edn Commn of States 700 Broadway #1200 Denver CO 80203-3460 Office Phone: 303-299-3600. Office Fax: 303-296-8332. Personal E-mail: rgwchu@gmail.com.*

CHU, STEVEN, physics professor, director; b. St. Louis, Feb. 28, 1948; s. Ju Chin and Ching Chen (Li) C.; children: Geoffrey, Michael. BS in Physics, AB in Math., U. Rochester, 1970; PhD in Physics, U. Calif., Berkeley, 1976. Post doctoral fellow U. Calif., Berkeley, 1976-78; mem. tech. staff Bell Labs., Murray Hill, NJ, 1978-83; head quantum electronics rsch. dept. AT&T Bell Labs., Holmdel, NJ, 1983-87; Frances and Theodore Geballe prof. physics and applied physics Stanford U., Calif., 1987—2004, chmn. physics dept. Calif., 1990—93, Calif., 1999—2001; dir. Lawrence Berkeley Nat. Lab., Berkeley, Calif., 2004—. Morris Loeb lectr. Harvard U., Cambridge, Mass., 1987-88; vis. prof. Coll. de France, fall 1990; Richtmeyer Meml. lectr., 1990. Contbr. papers in laser spectroscopy and atomic physics, especially laser cooling and trapping, and precision spectroscopy of leptonic atoms, polymer and biophysics. Bd. dirs. William and Flora Hewlett Found. Recipient Humboldt sr. scientist award, Sci. for Art prize, 1995; co-recipient King Faisal prize for sci., 1993, Nobel prize for physics, 1997; Woodrow Wilson fellow 1970, doctoral fellow NSF, 1970-74, postdoctoral fellow 1977-78, Guggenheim fellow, 1996. Fellow Am. Phys. Soc. (Herbert P. Broida prize for laser spectroscopy 1987, chair laser sci. topical group 1989, A.L. Schawlow prize 1994), Optical Soc. Am. (hon. lifetime mem., William F. Meggars award 1994), Am. Acad. Arts and Scis.; mem. NAS, Academica Sinica, Am. Philos. Soc., Chinese Acad. Sci. (fgn.), Korean Acad. Sci. and Tech. (fgn.). Achievements include development of methods to cool and trap atoms with laser light. Office: Lawrence Bekeley Nat Lab 1 Cyclotron Rd Mail Stop 50A4133 Berkeley CA 94720 Office Phone: 510-486-5111. Business E-Mail: SChu@lbl.gov.

CHU, TSANN MING, immunochemist, educator; b. Kaohsiung, Taiwan, Apr. 18, 1938; came to U.S., 1963, naturalized, 1971; s. Tsi Fa and Su Lian (Sun) C.; m. Bonnie Diane Covert, Sept. 28, 1967; children: Nancy, Daniel. BS, Nat. Taiwan U., Taipei, 1961; MS, N.C. State U., Raleigh, 1965, DSc (hon.), 2001; PhD, Pa. State U., University Park, 1967. Fellow Med. Found. Buffalo, 1967-69, Buffalo Gen. Hosp., 1969-70; assoc. chief cancer rsch. scientist, dir. diagnostic immunology and clin. chemistry Roswell Park Meml. Inst., Buffalo, 1970-76, dir. cancer rsch. in diagnostic immunology research and biochemistry, 1976-98; asst. prof. exptl. pathology SUNY, Buffalo, 1970-74, assoc. prof., 1974-77, prof., 1977-98, prof. emeritus, 1999—. Cons. nat. prostatic cancer project Nat. Cancer Inst., NIH, 1973-84, mem. com. cancer immunodiagnosis, 1978-79, mem. tumor immunology com., 1979-81; mem. immunology and immunotherapy com. Am. Cancer Soc., 1979-81; rsch. cons. Nat. Sci. Coun., Taiwan, 1976-94, vis. prof., 1986; adv. coun. Internat. Soc. Oncodevel. Biology and Medicine, 1978-94; mem. sci. rev. panel N.J. Commn. on Cancer Rsch., 1983-85, 87-99; cons. Merit Rev. Bd., VA, 1980-85, 94-98; mem. cancer therapeutic program rev. com. Nat. Cancer Inst., 1985-88; reviewers reserve NIH, 1988-92, 94-98; mem. scientific adv. coun. Internat. Acad. Tumor Marker Oncology, 1986-1998; mem. sci. coun. Swedish Cancer Found., 1988-1998; adv. com. Nat. Def. Med. Ctr. Cancer Rsch. Group, 1993-97. Mem. editl. bd. Tumor Biology, 1983-92, Jour. Clin. Lab. Analysis, 1985—, Jour. Tumor Marker Oncology, 1988-2003, Cancer Investigation, 1989-2003; contbr. over 300 articles to profl. jours. Recipient Presdl. citation Am. Urol. Assn., 1993, Am. Found. for Urologic Disease, 1993, Dornier Innovative Rsch. award, 1993, Symposium award Roswell Park Cancer Inst. and Geritourinary Cancer, 1993, Disting. Alumni award Pa. State U., 1994, N.C. State U., 1995, Abbott award Internat. Soc. Oncodevel. Biology and Medicine, 1996, Achievement in Health Care award D'Youville Coll., 1998, Honors award Pres. U.S., 1999, Pioneers Sci. award Western N.Y., 2002, Humanitarian award Pa. State U., 2006; fellow United Health Found. Western N.Y., 1968-69, Pa. State U., 1997. Mem. Am. Chem. Soc. (Jacob F. Schoellkopf medal 1997), Am. Assn. Clin. Chemists (Van Slyke award 1997), Am. Assn. Cancer Rsch. (cancer rsch. cover legend 1998), Am. Assn. Immunologists, Am. Urol. Assn. (hon.), Am. Soc. Biochem. and Molecular Biology, Am. Assn. Investigative Pathology, Biochem. Soc. (London), Am. Urological Assn. (hon.), Buffalo Urol. Soc., Taiwan Urol. Assn. (hon.), Phi Lambda Upsilon. Achievements include development of PSA test for early detection of prostate cancer. Office: Roswell Park Cancer Inst Elm And Carlton St Buffalo NY 14263-0001

CHU, VALENTIN YUAN-LING, author; b. Shanghai, Republic of China, Feb. 14, 1919; came to U.S., 1956, naturalized, 1961; s. Thomas V.D. and Rowena S.N. (Zee) Tsu; m. Victoria Chao-yu Tsao, Sept. 25, 1954; 1 child, Douglas Chi-hua. BA, St. John's U, Shanghai, 1940. Asst. Shanghai Mcpl. Coun., 1940-42; asst. mgr., pub., printer Thomas Chu & Sons, Shanghai, 1943-45; chief reporter China Press, Shanghai, 1945-49; pub. rels. officer Cen. Air Transport Corp., Hong Kong, 1949; Hong Kong corr. Time & Life mags., Hong Kong, 1949-56; with Time, Inc., NYC, 1956-76; writer, asst. editor Time-Life Books, NYC, 1968-76; assoc. editor Reader's Digest Gen. Books, NYC, 1978-83. Lectr. on China. Author: Ta Ta, Tan Tan---Fight Fight, Talk Talk, 1963, Thailand Today, 1968, (with others) U.S.A., A Visitor's Handbook, 1969, The Yin-Yang Butterfly---Ancient Chinese Sexual Secrets for Western Lovers, 1993; contbr. articles to popular mags. Recipient spl. award UN Internat. Essay Contest, 1948. Mem. Authors League Am., Authors Guild, China Inst. in Am., Inst. Noetic Scis. Presbyterian. Home: 2934 Saklan Indian Dr Walnut Creek CA 94595-3911 Personal E-mail: valentinchu@aol.com.

CHU, WAI C., engineer, researcher; arrived in US, 1990; s. Suet Fung Chu and Suet King Lau; m. Le Quan Luong, Dec. 10, 2001. BS in electronics engring., Simon Bolivar U., Caracas, 1990; MSEE, Stevens Inst. Tech., Hoboken, NJ, 1992; PhD, Pa. State U., 1998. Field apps. engr. Tex. Instruments Hong Kong, 1993—94; R&D engr. Digital Video Express, Herndon, Va., 1998—99; mem. tech. staff Intervideo Inc., Fremont, Calif., 1999—2001; sr. rsch. engr. DoCoMo Comms. Labs. USA Inc., San Jose, Calif., 2001—06; prin. engr. Magnum Semicondr., Milpitas, Calif., 2006—07; sr. scientist Shotspotter, Inc., Mountain View, Calif., 2007—. Author: (engring. textbook) Speech Coding Algorithms: Foundation and Evolution of Standardized Coders, 2003; contbr. articles to profl. jours. Mem.: IEEE, Audio Engring. Soc. Achievements include research in window optimization in linear prediction analysis; DCT-based image watermarking using subsampling; vector quantization of harmonic magnitudes in speech coding applications survey and new technique; vector quantization of neural networks; multistage tree-structured vector quantization. Office: 1060 Terra Bella Ave Mountain View CA 94043 Office Phone: 408-329-9232. Business E-Mail: wcc2@ieee.org.

CHU, WEI-KAN, physicist, researcher; b. Kunming, China, Apr. 1, 1940; came to the U.S., 1963; s. Din Yuan and Y.C. (Wong) C.; m. Agnes Kuen, May 28, 1966; 1 child, Lawrence D. BS in Physics, Cheng-Kung U., 1962; MS, Baylor U., 1965, PhD, 1969. Postdoctoral fellow Baylor U., Waco, Tex., 1969-72; rsch. fellow, sr. rsch. fellow Calif. Inst. Tech., Pasadena, 1972-75; staff advisor, sr. engr. IBM, Hopewell Junction, NY, 1975-81; rsch. prof. physics U. N.C., Chapel Hill, 1981-88; disting. prof. physics U. Houston, 1989—2002, Robert A. Welsh prof. physics, 2002—. Panel mem. NSF, Washington, 1992, U.S. Dept. Energy, Washington, 1992, 93, 94, 97. Co-author: Backscattering Spectrometry, 1978; co-editor: HTS Materials, Bulk Processing and Bulk Applications, 1992, Procs. of the 6th U.S.-Japan Workshop on High Tc Superconductors, 1994, Procs. of the 10th Anniversary High Temperature Superconductors Workshop on Physics, Materials and Applications, 1996, Procs. of 6th Internat. Conf. Materials and Mechanisms of Superconductivity and High Temperature Superconductors, VI, 2000; contbr. chpts. to books and numerous articles to profl. jours.; holder 23 US patents in field. Recipient Disting. Achievement award Baylor U., Waco, 1991, Assn. Am.-Chinese Profls., 1994, Superconductivity award of excellence for outstanding individual accomplishment World Congress on Superconductivity, 1994, Outstanding Alumni of Yr. Nat. Cheng-Kung U., 1997, 98. Fellow Am. Phys. Soc.; mem. Materials Rsch. Soc. Office: U Houston Tex Ctr Superconductivity Houston TX 77204-5002 Office Phone: 713-743-8252. Business E-Mail: wkchu@uh.edu.

CHUANG, ALFRED S., information technology executive; BS in Computer Sci., U. San Francisco; MS in Computer Sci., U. Calif., Davis, Calif. Mgmt. positions in software product devel., network infrastructure, systems architecture & operations mgmt. Sun Microsystems, Inc., 1986—94; former founder, dir. Sun Intercontinental Operations; former corp. dir., chief scientist SunIntegration Svcs.; from founder (with Bill Coleman and Ed Scott) to pres., CEO BEA Sys., Inc., San Jose, Calif., 1995—2001, pres., 2001—, CEO, 2001—, chmn., 2002—. Bd. dir Tealeaf Tech. Trustee U. San Francisco. Office: BEA Systems Inc 2315 N First St San Jose CA 95131 Office Phone: 408-570-8000. Office Fax: 408-570-8901.

CHUANG, TSU-YI, dermatologist, epidemiologist, educator; b. Amoy, China, May 21, 1946; arrived in U.S., 1976, naturalized, 1988; s. Hsi and Kia-Ling (Huang) C.; m. Lydia Ling-Chuan Lee, Dec. 22, 1973; children: Chester, Nancy. MB, Nat. Taiwan U., Taipei, 1971; MPH in Epidemiology, U. Wash., 1978. Diplomate Am. Bd. Dermatology, Am. Bd. Preventive Medicine. From asst. prof. to assoc. prof. dermatology U. Wis., Madison, 1984-92; chief dermatology svc. Middleton VA Med. Ctr., Madison, 1984-90; assoc. prof. dermatology Wright State U., Dayton, Ohio, 1990-95, dir. immunopathology lab., 1994-95; dir. dermatology clinic Frederick A. White Health Ctr., Dayton, 1995; prof. dermatology Ind. U., Indpls., 1995—2003, med. dir. melanoma program, 1996—2003, Arthur L. Norins prof., dir. dermatology clinic, 1999—2001; clin. prof. dermatology U. South Fla. Coll. Medicine, Tampa, 2004—06, U. So. Calif., LA, 2007—. Vis. prof. Wright State U., Dayton, 1990, Nat. Taiwan U., Taipei, 1991-97; vis. scientist Mayo Clinic, Rochester, 1986-92, Moss lectr. Meriter Found., 2002; mem. guidelines/outcomes com., 1996-2001, melanoma guidelines task force, 1997-2001, melanoma/skin cancer com., 2004—. Co-author: Conn's Current Therapy, 1992, The Challenge of Dermato-Epidemiology, 1997, Sleisenger & Fordtran's Gastrointestinal and Liver Disease, 2002; ad hoc reviewer Arch Dermatol., Chgo., 1990-99, Jour. Am. Acad. Dermatology, 1986-2004, Internat. Jour. Dermatology, 2001-06; editor Dermatologica Sinica, Taipei, 1994-96; contbr. over 100 articles to profl. jours. Pres. Rochester (Minn.) Chinese Culture Assn., 1980-82; v.p. Orgn. of Chinese Ams., Madison, 1986-90; pres. Midwest Chinese Christian Assn., Dayton, 1993-94, Indpls., 1996-97, Indiana Chinese-Am. Profls. Assn., Indpls. 1998. Rsch. grantee U. Wis., 1985-89, Schering, Glaxo, Genentech, Amgen 1986-2004; VA merit rev. bd. grantee Dept. Vets. Affairs, 1986-88, 90-94; recipient Burdette-Kunkel award Mary Margaret Walther Program for Cancer Care Rsch., 1996-97, 21st Century Research & Technology Fund award, 2000-02, Fellow Am. Acad. Dermatology (editl. cons. Am. Acad. Dermatology jour. 1986-2004), Am. Soc. for Dermatol. Surgery; mem. Soc. for Investigative Dermatology, Am. Acad. Dermatology, Ind. Chinese Profls. Assn. (pres. 1998). Achievements include first historical cohort study of human papilloma virus infection in U.S. in a defined population, first historical cohort study of genital herpes virus infection in U.S. in a defined population, first incidence study of polymyalgia rheumatica in the U.S. in a defined population, first population-based incidence study of skin cancer in U.S. in two well-defined populations. Office: Dermatology Desert Splty Group 69-844 Hwy 111 Ste A Rancho Mirage CA 92270 Office Phone: 760-318-4869. Business E-Mail: chuang007@yahoo.com.

CHUANG, YII-DER, retired manufacturing executive, diplomat; b. Chekiang, China, July 1, 1934; came to U.S., 1964; s. W.C. Chuang and Y.F. Chang; m. Chung-hwa Lee, Jan. 6, 1968; children: David, Michael, Nancy. BS in Automotive Engring., Chung-Cheng Inst., 1957; MS in Metall. Engring., Mich. State U., 1966; PhD in Materials Sci., NYU, 1971. Dir. hot lab. Inst. Nuclear Energy Rsch. Atomic Energy Coun., Exec. Yuan, Taoyuan, Taiwan, 1972-82; sr. scientist sci and tech. adv. group Exec. Yuan, Taipei, Taiwan, 1980-84; dep. dir. prep. office materials rsch. lab. Indsl. Tech. Rsch. Inst., Hsinchu, Taiwan, 1981-82; dep. dir. materials rsch. and devel. ctr. Chung Shan Inst. Sci. and Tech., Taoyuan, Taiwan, 1982-84; dir. sci. divsn. Taipei Econ. and Cultural Office, Houston, 1984—86, San Francisco, 1986—92, Taipei Econ. and Cultural Rep. Office, Washington, 1992—2000; pres. H&Q Taiwan Co. Ltd., H&Q Asia Pacific, Taipei, 2000—02; ret., 2003. Exec. sec. materials steering com. Exec. Yuan, 1981-84; dir. Rep. Office Hsin-Chu Sci.-based Indsl. Park Adminstrn., Taiwan, 1986-92; patent reviewer Nat. Bur. Standards, Taiwan, 1973-83; exec. sec. Commn. Third Asian-Pacific Corrosion Control Conf., 1981-83. Editor: Nuclear Sci. Jour., 1978—79; contbr. over 38 articles to profl. jours. Disting. scholar NYU, 1972. Mem. Nuclear Energy Soc. of Rep. of China, Chinese Soc. Materials Sci. (editor Materials Sci. Quarterly 1972-78), Chinese Inst. Mining and Metall. Engrs., Chinese Soc. Mech. Engrs., Monte Jade Sci. and Tech. Assn., Alpha Sigma Mu. Home: 11F-5 No 70 Sec 2 An-He Rd Taipei 10680 Taiwan Personal E-mail: ydchuang@ms77.hinet.net.

CHUBB, CHARLES RAY, physicist, researcher; b. Springfield, Mo., Apr. 18, 1931; s. Prosser Sylvester and Harriet Elizabeth Chubb; m. Jeanne R. C. (div. 1978); children: Alan C., Paula J. Mello, Thomas J., Lisa C. Rottler. BS in Engring. Physics, U. Ill., 1953; MS in Physics, U. Mo., 1958, PhD in Physics, 1963. Rsch. engr. N.Am. Aviation, LA, 1953-54; mem. scientific and profl. pers. U.S. Army, Ft. Lee, Va., 1955-56; cons. McDonnell Douglas, St. Louis, 1957-62, group engr. to sr. tech. specialist, 1962-90; cons. Storz Instruments, St. Louis, 1990-91; rschr. C. Chubb Assocs., Ferguson, Mo., 1991—. Patentee in field of skin light exposure control methods. Recipient Optical Fiber Innovation award NASA, Houston, 1983. Mem.: AAAS. Avocations: hiking, skiing. Home and Office: 438 Marie Ave Ferguson MO 63135-1904 Personal E-mail: c.r.chubb@sbcglobal.net.

CHUBB, RICHARD MARSHALL, retired physician; b. Joplin, Mo., Oct. 21, 1929; s. Leonard Louis and Nadine Marshall Chubb; m. Johna Marie Ferneti; children: Jeffrey A., Charles, SallyAnn, Richard, Laura, Kathy. BS in Medicine, Northwestern U., Chgo., 1951, MD, 1954; MPH, John Hopkins Sch. Pub. Health & Hygiene, Balt., 1959. Cert. aviation medicine Am. Bd. Preventive Med., 1963. Cons. aviation medicine Civil Aero Bd., Washington, 1961—63; safety analysis Dept. Inspector Gen. Safety, Norton AFB, Calif., 1963—66; med. monitor, manual space flights USAF, NASA, 1963—66; dir. base med. svcs. 22nd CSF, Danang AB, Vietnam, 1966—67; chief, preventative medicine HgPacific Air Forces, Hickam, Hawaii, 1967—69; gen. practice Self Employed, Baxter Springs, Kans., 1969—90; chief, gen. practice svc. Claremore Indian Hosp., Okla., 1990—98; ret. Mem. nutritional coun. Am. Diabetes Assn., 1993—98. Contbr. articles various profl. jours. Lt. col. USAF, 1956—69, Vietnam. Recipient Moseley award, Aerospace Med. Assn., 1967. Cath. Avocations: golf, gardening. Home: 601 W Craig Rd Pittsburg KS 66762

CHUBB, STEPHEN DARROW, health products executive; b. Newton, Mass., Mar. 16, 1944; s. Phillip Darrow and Clarissa Stoddard (Nye) C.; m. Kathleen Alice Zimmerman, 1973. BS, U.S. Naval Acad., 1965; MBA, Northwestern U., 1974. CPA, Ill. With Am. Can Co., 1970—73, Baxter Labs., Deerfield, Ill., 1974—81; pres. Hyland Diagnostics, 1978—81; pres., chief exec. officer, dir. Cytogen Corp., 1981—84, T Cell Scis., Inc., 1984—86, Matritech Inc., 1987—; dir. Charles River Labs., 1994—, Compucyte, Cambridge, Mass., 1992—2001, I-Stat, Princeton, NJ, 1999—2002. Alumni adv. bd. Northwestern U., 1998. Bd. dir. Sherwood Cmty. Assn., 1978-79, v.p., 1979-80; trustee Huntington Theatre Co., Boston, 1991-95, treas., 1992-95; trustee Mt. Auburn Hosp., Cambridge, 1995—, vice chmn., 2001-06, chmn., 2007-. With USN, 1965-70; capt., USNR (ret.). Recipient Meritorious Svc. medal, Combat Action Ribbon, U.S. Navy. Mem. AICPA, John Evans Club Northwestern U., U.S. Naval Acad. Alumni Assn. Avocation: deep sea diving. Office: Matritech Inc 330 Nevada St Newton MA 02460

CHUBB, TALBOT ALBERT, physicist, consultant; b. Pitts., Nov. 5, 1923; s. Charles F. and Mary Clare (Albert) C.; m. Martha Capps, Oct. 24, 1947 (dec. June 1990); children: Mary Carroll, Nancy Henderson, Talbot Spence, Constance Lamont. AB, Princeton U., 1944; PhD, U. N.C., 1950. Physicist, U.S. Naval Rsch. Lab., 1950-58, head upper air physics br., 1958-82; pres. Rsch. Systems, Inc., Oxon Hill, Md., 1982—2003, physicist cons., 2003—. Recipient Elisha Mitchell Soc. award U. N.C., 1951, E.O. Hulbert award Naval Research Lab., 1963, Pure Sci. award Naval. Research Lab.-Research Soc. Am., 1970, Disting. Civilian Service award Dept. Navy, 1978 Fellow Am. Geophys. Union, Am. Phys. Soc.; mem. Am. Astron. Soc. Achievements include rsch. on solar flare x-rays, x-ray stars, UV aurora, cosmology, solar thermal power, cold fusion theory. Home and Office: 5023 38th St N Arlington VA 22207-2845 Personal E-mail: tchubb@aol.com.

CHUDNOVSKY, MARIA, mathematician, educator; b. Russia, Jan. 6, 1977; BA summa cum laude in Math., Technion - Israel Inst. Tech., 1996, MSc, 1999; MA, Princeton U., NJ, 2002, PhD in Math., 2003. Rsch. fellow Clay Math. Inst., 2003—; Veblen rsch. instr. Princeton U. and Inst. Advanced Study, NJ, 2003—05; asst. prof. Princeton U., 2005—06; assoc. prof. depts. indsl. engring. and ops. rsch. and math. Columbia U., NYC, 2006—. Contbr. articles to profl. jours. Served in Israel Def. Force, 1996—99. Named one of Brilliant 10, Popular Sci. mag., 2004. Office: Dept Indsl Engring and Ops Rsch Columbia U 500 W 120th St New York NY 10027 Office Phone: 212-854-5237. E-mail: mchudnov@columbia.edu.

CHUDOBIAK, WALTER JAMES, electronics executive; b. Gliechen, Alta., Can., Apr. 2, 1942; s. John and Clara (Suchy) C.; m. Mary Annetta Budarick, Oct. 11, 1969; children: Michael, Anne. BSc in Elec. Engring., U. Alta., Edmonton, 1964; MEng in Electronic Engring., Carleton U., Ottawa, Ont., Can., 1965, PhD in Electronic Engring., 1969. Rsch. officer Def. Rsch. Bd., Ottawa, 1965-69; group leader, rsch. scientist Comm. Rsch. Ctr., Dept. Comm., Ottawa, 1969-75; assoc. prof. Carleton U., 1975-81; pres., founder, dir. Avtech Electrosystems Ltd., Ottawa, 1975—. Contbr. numerous articles to profl. jours.; patentee in field. Mem. IEEE, Assn. Profl. Engrs. (Ont.). Home: 12 Timbercrest Ridge Nepean ON Canada K2R 1B4 Office: 55 Grenfell Cres Ste 205 Nepean ON Canada K2G 0G3 E-mail: info@avtechpulse.com, walter@avtechpulse.com.

CHUEH, CHUN FEI, import/export company executive; b. Chaozhou, China; s. Yung Hsing and Ruu Mei Chueh; m. Cecilia Shih-mei Hsing, Apr. 15, 1961; children: Angelina Mary Kitten, Daniel Francis. BSChE, Nat. Taiwan U., 1954; MSChE, Kans. State U., 1957; PhD in Chem. Engring., Ga. Inst. Tech., 1962. Chem. engr. Sci. Design Co., NYC, 1962—78; dir. devel. Halcon Internat., Inc., NYC, 1978—86; gen. mgr. Haarmann & Reimer Cosfra, Ltd., Shanghai, 1987—97; pres. Elan Trading (Shanghai) Co., 1998—, Elan (Shanghai) Flavors & Fragrances Co., 2000—. Patentee in field. Office: Elan (Shanghai) Flavors & Fragrances Co #92 Ln 1129 Nanjing Rd W Shanghai 200041 China Home: No 15 Lane 3233 Yi Xian Rd Shanghai 300439 China Office Phone: 86-21-56448224.

CHUGH, OM PARKASH, mathematics professor, researcher, forensics specialist; b. D.G. Khan, Punjab, India, Apr. 29, 1933; arrived in U.S., 1992; s. Uttam Chand and Chimni Devi Chugh; m. Sawraj Devi Chugh, May 5, 1955; children: Jitander, Kul, Kirti Sachdeva. BA in Math., Govt. Coll., Rohtak, Haryana, India, 1953; MA in Math., Govt. Coll., Ludhiana, Punjab, India, 1955; B in Tchg., Vaish Coll., Rohtak, 1956; PhD in Internal Ballistics of Guns and Rockets, Delhi U., India, 1968, BSc in Physics and Chemistry with merit, 1972; MA in Math. Edn., CCNY/CUNY, NYC, 1995. Cert. tchr. secondary and higher secondary India, 1956, tchr. permanent day secondary NY Dept. Edn., 1996, tchr. permanent jr. high sch. NY Dept. Edn., 1996, tchr. permanent pub. schs. SUNY and NY Dept. Edn., 2000. Lectr. math. and sci. Vaish Tng. Coll., Rohtak, India, 1957; postgrad. tchr. Govt. Higher Secondary Schs., Dehli, 1957—60; jr. sci. asst., sr. sci. asst., jr. sci. officer Def. Sci. Svc., Dehli, 1960—67; founder, asst. dir. ballistics divsn. Ctrl. Bur. Investigation, Dehli, 1967—73; founder, dir. Forensic Sci. Lab., Haryana, India, 1973—91; permanent math. tchr. NYC Bd. Edn., 1996—2003; adj. asst. prof. Queensborough CC CUNY, 1992—, John Jay Coll. Criminal Justice CUNY, 1993—. Editl. bd. Alcohol, Drug, Traffic Safety, Stockholm, 1981—89; judge Greater Met. Math. Fair Pace U., NYC, 1995; presenter Real World Math. Summer Inst. CCNY/CUNY, 1995; referee Def. Sci. Jour., Indian Jour. Pure and Applied Physics, Jour. Indian Acad. Forensic Sci.; examiner, rsch. guide U. Dehli, U. Punjab, U. Punjabi, U. Sagar. Contbr. 76 sci. rsch. papers, articles to profl. jours. Mem.: Am. Fedn. Tchrs., NY State Tchrs., United Fedn. Tchrs. Achievements include development of two forensic labs from scratch, and the creation of research facilities in Central Bureau Investigation and Forensic Science Lab in Haryana; creating extenisve crime investigation facilities in Haryana, which became the referral lab for central and other state governments and commissions of enquiries in complicated and important cases; research in factoring trinomials; Proof of Picks theorum; logic; divisability rules; connection between Pythagorean Triples and derivatives of basic trigometric functions. Office: Math and Computer Sci Dept Rm 245 Queensborough CC/CUNY 222-05 56th Ave Bayside NY 11364-1497 Home: 42-45 Colden St 4D Flushing NY 11355 Personal E-mail: opchugh@aol.com.

CHUI, CHI ON, electrical engineer, educator; b. New Territories, Hong Kong, Jan. 23, 1977; s. Yu Chi Chui and Hau Ming Cheung; m. Hoi Yan Yiu, June 3, 2004. BEng in Elec. Engring., Hong Kong U. Sci. and Tech., 1999; MS in Elec. Engring., Stanford U., 2001, PhD in Elec. Engring., 2004. Doctoral rsch. asst. Stanford U., Calif., 2000—04, grad. tchg. asst., 2001—03; rschr.-in-residence Intel Corp., Santa Clara, Calif., 2004—06; asst. prof. elec. engring. U. Calif., LA, 2007—. Cons. asst. prof. Stanford U., 2005—06, Reviewer Jour. of the Electrochem. Soc., 2002. , Intel Corp. fellow, 2003, Microsoft Corp. grantee, 2003, Hong Kong Soc. Accts. scholar, 1996, Hong Kong Telecom Inst. of Info. Tech. scholar, 1998, Chiap Hua Cheng's Found. scholar, 1999, Hong Kong & Kowloon Elec. Appliances Mchts. Assn. scholar, 1999. Mem.: IEEE (reviewer, IEEE Electron Device Letters 2003—06), Materials Rsch. Soc. Achievements include patents pending for High-k dielectric for thermodynamically-stable substrate-type materials; MOS interface with reactive metal overlayers; Germanium substrate-type materials and approach therefor; first to Seminal contribution to incorporate high-permittivity gate dielectrics for germanium MOS field-effect device application; invention of Two low-noise photodetector architectures in Group IV semiconductor; A novel self-aligned MOS field-effect transistor fabrication process; development of Various germanium MOS technologies including three generations of gate dielectric, two generations of dopant incorporation, and three generations of MOS field-effect transistors. Office: Elec Engring Dept Box 951594 7440D Boelter Hall Los Angeles CA 90095-1594 Home: 5781 Hesperia Ave Encino CA 91316

CHUKWU, ETHELBERT NWAKUCHE, mathematics professor; b. Mbano, Imo, Nigeria, Nov. 22, 1940; s. Nwachukwu Chukwu Uwaezuoke and Ihejere Theresa; m. Regina Chukwu Nyere, Dec. 26, 1966; children: Chika, Eze, Emeka, Uche, Obioma, Ndubuisi. BSc, Brown U., 1965; MSc, Nsukka U., Nigeria, 1973; PhD, Case Western Res. U., 1972. Asst. lectr. U. Nigeria, Nsukka, 1970; asst. prof. math. Cleve. State U., 1972-76, assoc. prof., 1976-78; prof. U. Jos, Nigeria, 1978-81, dean postgrad. studies, 1977-81; vice chancellor Fed. U. Tech., Yola, Nigeria, 1981-86; prof. math. N.C. State U., Raleigh, 1987—. Mem. Nat. UN Commn. on African Scholarship Program for Am. Univs. fellow, 1962-65. Author 6 books in field; assoc. editor Non-Linear Studies; contbr. 90 articles to profl. jours. Mem. AAAS, Nigerian Math. Soc. (v.p. 1980-82), Math. Assn. Nigeria (pres. 1981-82), Am. Math. Soc., Math Assn. Am., N.Y. Acad. Scis., Am. Assn. for Advancement of Sci., Internat. Fedn. Nonlinear Analysts (mem. global com.), Sigma Xi, Sigma Iota Rho. Roman Catholic. Address: NC State U Mathematics Dept Raleigh NC 27695-8205 Office Phone: 919-515-7442. E-mail: chukwu@ncsu.math.edu.

CHUKWULEBE, BERNARD OBIOMA, manufacturing executive, consultant; arrived in US, 1997, permanent resident; s. Albert and Florence Chukwulebe; m. Larisa Georgievna Chukwulebe, Oct. 14, 1988; children: Steve, Catherine, Helen, Elizabeth. BSc/MSc in Metall. Engring., Inst. Steel & Alloys, Moscow, 1987; PhD in Metall., Inst. Steel & Alloys, 1992. Asst. prof. U. Lagos, Nigeria, 1993—97; engr. Delta Steel Co., Aladja, Nigeria, 1997—98; rsch. tchg. asst. Morgan State U., Balt., 1998—99; project engr. Ispat Inland Rsch. & Devel., E. Chgo., 1999—2000, sr. engr., 2000—04; staff engr. Mittal USA Rsch. & Devel. Ctr., E. Chgo., 2004—07; mgr. steelmaking & refractories rsch. Arcelor-Mittal USA Rsch. & Devel. Ctr., E. Chgo., 2007—. Contbr. articles to profl. jours. Mem.: Assn. Iron and Steel Tech. Achievements include development of steelmaking technologies and practices. Office: Arcelor-Mittal USA Rsch & Devel Ctr 3001 E Columbus Dr East Chicago IN 46312 Office Fax: 219-399-3899. Business E-Mail: bernard.chukwulebe@mittalsteel.com.

CHULACK, CHRISTOPHER M., television director, television producer; Prodr.: (TV films) The Man Who Fell to Earth, 1987, Police Story: Cop Killer, Johnny Ryan, 1990, Island City, 1994; prodr., dir.: (TV series) Homefront, 1991-93, ER, 1994-2006; exec. prodr., dir: (TV series) Citizen Baines, 2001, Third Watch, 1999, Presidio Med, 2002-03, Smith, 2006.

CHUMLEY, PERRY RAY, veterinarian, military officer; s. Raymond Farrell and Ann Lee Chumley; 1 child, Maleah Rae. BS in Gen. Agr., U. Nebr., Lincoln, 1982; DVM, Ohio State U., Columbus, 1986; MPH, U. Tenn., Knoxville, 1992; M Strategic Studies, U.S. Army War Coll., Carlisle Barracks, Pa., 2003. Cert. Am. Coll. Vet. Preventive Medicine, 1993, lic. vet. Ky., 1986, Nebr., 1986. Commd. 1st lt. US Army, 1987; br. chief Misawa AFB, Japan, 1992—93, US Army Vet. Command, Fort Knox, Ky., 1995—99, dist. comdr. Fort Rucker, Ala., 1999—2001; comdr. 43rd med. detachment 1st Med. Brigade, 13th COSCOM, III Corps, Fort Hood, Tex., 2001—03; chief food safety and pub. health US Army Vet. Command, San Antonio, 2003—05; advanced through grades to col. US Army, 2005; dir. pub. health, safety and security Def. Commissary Agy., Fort Lee, Va., 2005—. Dir. svc. dog tng. ctr. US Army Vet. Command, Fort Knox, 1995—99. Pres. Am. Assn. Human Animal Bond Veterinarians, 1994—95. Decorated Bronze Star US Army, Meritorious Svc. medals US Army Vet. Command, Expert Field Med. badge US Army Med. Command; named Ky. Col., Gov. Commonwealth Ky., 1999; recipient Dr. Daniel E. Salmon award, Nat. Assn. Fed. Veterinarians, 2000, The Alumni Recognition award, Ohio State U. Vet. Medicine Alumni Soc., 2006; scholar, Prodn. Credit Assn., 1977. Mem.: Am. Coll. Vet. Preventive Medicine, AVMA, Omega Tau Sigma (life). Republican. Methodist. Avocations: fishing, hiking, chess, gardening. Home: 727 Cobbs Point Ln Chester VA 23836 Office: Defense Commissary Agency 1300 E Ave Fort Lee VA 23801 Home Phone: 804-530-3275; Office Phone: 804-734-8305. Office Fax: 804-734-8960; Home Fax: 804-734-8960. Personal E-mail: veterinarian66@yahoo.com. Business E-Mail: perry.chumley@deca.mil.

CHUN, ASAPH Y., research scientist; s. YoungHee and Joseph Tok-Kyun Chun, Byung-Soon Lee; m. Myung-Joo P. Hong, May 4, 1991. BA, U. Mich., 1987, MA, 1989; ABD, U. Md., 2003. Data archivist Inst. Social Rsch., Ann Arbor, Mich.; instr. U. Md., College Park, 1991—94; pres., CEO Inst. Strategies and Reconciliation, Brookeville, 1998—; behavioral scientist U.S. Bur. Labor Stats., Washington; survey statisticián U.S. Bur. Census, 1999—2000; sr. rsch. scientist Am. Insts. Rsch., 2000—. Dir. Inst. Strategies and Reconciliation, Brookeville, Md.; rschr. ednl. policy Am. Insts. Rsch.; rschr. survey methodology U.S. Bur. Labor Stats., 1991—2000. Founding mem. InterAction North Korea Working Com., Washington; chmn. Inst. Strategies and Reconciliation, Brookeville, Md., 1998—2005. Fellow, U. Mich., 1985—87; grantee, Inst. Social Rsch., Ann Arbor, 1987—89. Mem.: World Assn. Pub. Opinion Rsch., Am. Ednl. Rsch. Assn. Achievements include first to Led ISR to send over $25 million vaule of humanitarian aid to DPRK (North Korea) since 1998 with focus on helping people with disability, children, pregnant/nursing women; research in Have published scores of research papers in leading academic journals, and presented over 100 papers in national and int'l academic conferences; Provided research-based policy recommendations in American education, diplomacy and conflict resolution approaches to DPRK. Avocations: gardening, jogging, hiking, travel. E-mail: ychun@air.org.

CHUN, JACQUELINE CLIBBETT, artist, educator; d. Sydney H. and Hilda C. Moore; m. Edward W.C. Chun, Dec. 1967; children: Christine, Diana, David. Student, London Coll. Music, 1956—58; BA summa cum laude, U. Hawaii Manoa, 1992, MFA, 1997. Freelance musician, singer, songwriter, 1960—; pres. JCM Prodns., Honolulu, 1978—; lectr. painting Kapiolani C.C., Honolulu, 1999; faculty Kaimuki Cmty. Sch. Adults, Honolulu, 1988—; lectr. U. Hawaii Manoa, Honolulu, 1996—. Courtroom sketch artist Sta. KGMB, Honolulu, 2000—; founder, dir. Girl Scout Band and Choir, 1987; poetry editor Hawaii Rev., 1992—93, asst. mng. editor, 1993—94, nonfiction editor, 1994—95; vice chair publs. bd. U. Hawaii at Manoa, 1988—89; mem. art adv. bd. Kapiolani C.C., U. Hawaii. Author: (plays) By the Hand of a Woman, 1992; co-author, co-illustrator, co-editor: Moiliili, The Life of a Community, 2005; editor: The Touch of God, 1999, The Science of Happiness, 2000; composer: (songs) (ofcl. sch. song) Ala Wai Elem. Sch., 1978, (ofcl. theme song) Girl Scout Coun. 75th Anniversary, Girl Scouts, 1988; contbr. articles to profl. jours. Band dir., choir dir. Girl Scout Coun. Pacific, Honolulu. Recipient Acquisition award, State Found. Culture and Arts, 1994, All USA Coll. Acad. First Team, USA Today, 1990, House Reps Resolution Ednl. Contribution award, State of Hawaii, Spirit award, Hawaii Rev., 1992, Gold award, 16th Ann. Shizuoka Friendship Postcard Art Contest, Japan, 2004, 1st pl. award, Nat. Arts Program, Honolulu Hale, 2006. Mem.: ASCAP, Am. Fedn. Musicians, Acad. Am. Poets, Portrait Soc. Am., Nat. Music Pub. Assn., Musician's Assn. Hawaii, Phi Beta Kappa. Avocations: swimming, gardening, travel.

CHUN, JANG HO, science educator, researcher; b. Koyang, Republic of Korea, Nov. 23, 1948; s. Oak Bae Chun and Soon Im Min; m. Kyung Won Hong, June 28, 1980; children: Mi Jin, Jin Young. BS in Elec. Engring., Kwangwoon U., Seoul, Republic of Korea, 1975; MS in Elec. Engring., Yonsei U., Seoul, Republic of Korea, 1978; PhD in Electrophysics, Stevens Inst. Tech., NJ, 1984. Full prof. Kwangwoon U., Seoul, Republic of Korea, 1990—. Vis. scientist dept. chemistry Princeton U., NJ, 1988—89; vis. scientist dept. applied chemistry U. Tokyo, 1994; technical advisor Mission Telecom Co., Seoul, Republic of Korea, 2004—. Contbr. articles to profl. jours. Deacon Shinheung Presbyn. Ch., Seoul, 1993—. Lance cpl. Korea Air Force, 1968—71, Osan. Recipient First prize of Graduation, Kwangwoon U., 1975, Commendation for Excellent Tchg. and Rsch., Korea Govt., 1997, 2006, Excellent papers award, Korean Fed. Sci. Tech. Soc., 2006; May 16 scholar, 1972—74, Studying Abroad scholar, Korea Govt., 1980—84, fellowship, Korea Sci. and Engring. Found., 1988—89, 1994. Mem.: Electrochem. Soc., Internat. Assn. for Hydrogen Energy, Korean Electrochem. Soc. (life; mem. editl. bd. 2000—). Presbyterian. Achievements include research in the phase-shift method for determining the Langmuir, Frumkin, and Temkin adsorption isotherms of hydrogen and hydroxide at interfaces; invention of methods for estimating adsorption isotherms in electrochemical systems; discovery of correlation constants between adsorption isotherms in electrochemical systems; zeta potentials of semiconductor microparticles. Avocations: photography, ceramics. Home: 2-504 Lucky Apt 296 Seoksudong Manangu Kyunggido Anyang 431-042 Republic of Korea Office: Kwangwoon U Dept Electronic Engring 447-1 Wolgyedong Nowongu Seoul 139-701 Republic of Korea Home Phone: 82-31-472-5147; Office Phone: 82-2-940-5116. Office Fax: 82-2-942-5235. Personal E-mail: jhchun2504@hanmail.net. Business E-Mail: jhchun@kw.ac.kr.

CHUN, SHINAE, federal agency administrator; m. Kyong Chul Chun; 2 children. BA, Ewha Women's U., Seoul, Korea; MA in Edu. and Social Policy, Northwestern U.; fellowship, Harvard U. John F. Kennedy Sch. of Govt. Project dir. Title IX Multiethnic Training, Assistance and Dissemination Project; founding mem. Asian Am. Advisory Council to Gov. James R. Thompson State of Ill., 1982—84, special asst. on Asian Am. affairs to gov., 1984—87; dir. Dept. of Fin. Institutions, Chgo., 1988—90, Labor Dept., Chgo., 1991—99; dir. women's bur. US Dept. of Labor, Washington, 2001—. Author: From the Mountains of Masan to the Land of Lincoln, 1996, Korean Culture: A Passage Through Hermit Kingdom, 1980. Recipient Special Achievement for Leadership award, Bus. Women's Network, 2004. Office: US Dept Labor Women's Bur 200 Constitution Ave NW Washington DC 20210

CHUNG, ANITA, curator; b. Hong Kong, Mar. 9, 1967; arrived in US, 2001; d. Fong Chung and Wai Lin Cheung. B in Social Sci., Chinese U. Hong Kong, 1989, MPhil, 1991; PhD, U. Hong Kong, 1999. Lectr. U. Edinburgh, Scotland, 1997—2000; curator Chinese art Nat. Museums Scotland, Edinburgh, 1997—2000, Nat. U. Singapore, 2000—01, Cleve. Mus. Art, 2004—, Andrew Mellon fellow Chinese art, 2001—04. Traveling exhibit curator Chinese Painting Shanghai Mus., Edinburgh, 2000. Author: Drawing Boundaries: Architectural Images in Qing China, 2004; co-author: (exhibit catalogue) Chinese Painting from the Shanghai Museum, 2000. Office: Cleve Mus Art 11150 E Blvd Cleveland OH 44106-1797 Office Phone: 216-707-2662.

CHUNG, BENJAMIN INBEH, urologist; b. Buffalo, Dec. 21, 1973; BA, Amherst Coll., Mass., 1991—95; MD, Jefferson Med. Coll., Phila., 1995—99. Resident, urology Lahey Clinic, Burlington, Mass., 2001—05; resident, gen. surgery Mass. Gen. Hosp., Boston, 1999—2001; fellow, sect. laparoscopy and endourology Cleve. Clinic Found., 2005—06; asst. prof. urology Stanford U., Calif., 2006—. Recipient Max K. Willscher prize, New Eng. Sect. Am. Urol. Assn., 2002, First Pl., Resident Essay Contest, Phila. Urologic Soc., 2002. Mem.: Am. Urol. Assn. Office Phone: 650-725-5546. Office Fax: 650-723-4200. Personal E-mail: benjamin_chung@hotmail.com.

CHUNG, CALEB, inventor, toymaker, toy company executive; b. Watsonville, Calif., 1957; Inventor Mattel, 1985—90; ind. cons., 1990—; co-founder & inventor UGOBE Inc., Emeryville, Calif., 2006—. Achievements include invention of Furby, 1998; Pleo, 2007. Office: UGOBE Ste V 5900 Hollis St Emeryville CA 94608 Office Phone: 510-655-0515. Office Fax: 510-655-0519. E-mail: info@ugobe.com.*

CHUNG, CAROLINE, marketing professional; b. Washington, Apr. 27, 1970; d. Jae Wan and Soojun Chung; m. Christopher James Del Corso. BS, U. Wis., 1992; MBA, Vanderbilt U., 1997. Cert. Mad Dogg spinning instr., group exercise instr.; cert. Pilates instr. Mgr. ops. rsch. and statis. analysis Continental Airlines, 1997—99; mgr. product devel. US Airways, 1999—2001; ops. rsch. cons. Warden Assocs., 2001—03; fgn. svc. officer, 2d sec. U.S. Dept. State, 2003—05; sr. dir. mktg. MAXjet Airways, Inc., 2005—. Roman Catholic. Avocations: health and fitness, travel, reading, world maps, music. Personal E-mail: carolinechung@hotmail.com.

CHUNG, CHANJIN, economics professor, researcher; s. Jongju Chung and Juduck Park. PhD, U. Minn., Twin Cities, 1996. Mgr. purchasing Ralston Purina Internat., Seoul, Republic of Korea, 1983—90; assoc. dir. Cornell U., Ithaca, NY, 1996—2002; prof. econs. Okla. State U., Stillwater, 2006—. Home: 110 E Lakeview Rd Apt A1 Stillwater OK 74078 Office: Oklahoma State Univ 322 Agricultural Hall Stillwater OK 74075 Home Phone: 405-334-2999; Office Phone: 405-744-6164. Office Fax: 405-744-8210. Business E-Mail: chanjin.chung@okstate.edu.

CHUNG, CHIA MOU (CHARLES CHUNG), former Oriental art business owner; b. Jiao Ling Hsien, Guangdong, China, Feb. 21, 1918; came to U.S., 1946; s. Kiu-Sin and Yee-Mui (Lee) C.; m. Sylvia E.E. Tuck, Jan. 16, 1955 (div. Jan. 1970); children: Wilma, Cathie, Vivian, Calvin; m. Betty Lee Sung, July 22, 1972; stepchildren: Tina, Cynthia, Victor, Alan Sung Grad., Ctrl. Police Coll., Chungking, Sichuan, China, 1940, Nat. Cheng-Chi Coll., Chungking, 1943; BS, MS, Wash. State U., Pullman, 1948; postgrad., NYU, 1948—51. Editor Ctrl. Police U., 1941—43; profl. officer Exec. Yuan, Chungking, 1943—45; calligrapher, transl., reviser Secretariat UN, NYC, 1948—79; pres. Jade and Oriental Arts, Inc., NYC, 1961—99; ret., 1999. Author: The Road for ROC (Taiwan) to be Readmitted to UN (in Chinese), 1994; co-editor: China Anthology (in English), 1996, Chung's Selected Essays (in Chinese), 1998, 2d edit., 2007; contbr. articles to Chinese newspapers and profl. pubs. Advisor Chinese Chee-Yue Cmty. Assn., N.Y.C., 1996-2004, pres. 2004—; bd. mem. Chinese Consol. Benevolent Assn., N.Y., 2004—. Recipient first prize Nat. Essay Contest on Police Sci. and Adminstrn. by Examination Yuan, 1941, Excellent Svc. award, Exec. Yuan, 1945, Chinese Rsch. Project award Tai-ti Found., 1951, Svc. award Sec. Gen. UN, 1985, Excellent Svc. award Ctrl. Police U. Alumni Assn., N.Am., 1993, Svc. award Shanghai Tiffin Club, 1995 Mem. Ctrl. Police U. Alumni Assn. Ea. U.S. (chmn. 1991—, Excellent Svc. award 1996), Nat. Cheng-ta Alumni Assn. Ea. U.S. (exec. dir. 1991-94, hon. v.p. 1994-99, adviser 1999—, Excellent Svc. award 1995), World Hakka Fedn. (pres. Ea. U.S. chpt. 1991-93, advisor 1993—), World Kwongtung Cmty. Assn. (advisor 1991—), ROC Nat. Devel. Assn. (overseas com. 1991—), Taiwan Devel. Inst. (rsch. fellow 1993—), Chinese-Am. Jewelry Assn. (sr. adviser 1991—) Home (Winter): 3200 NE 36th St Apt 1520 Fort Lauderdale FL 33308 Home: 165 Park Row Apt 20F New York NY 10038

CHUNG, DOO-RI, apparel designer; Grad., Parsons School of Design, NYC, 1995. Apprentice Geoffrey Beene, 1995, lead designer; owner Doo.ri boutique, NYC, 2001—. Clothing line debut NY Fashion Week, 2003. Named one of 2007 People to Watch, Sunday Star Ledger; recipient Designer of Yr. award, Parsons School of Design, 1995, Ecco Domani Fashion Found. award, 2004, Swarovski's Perry Ellis award for Emerging Talent in Womenswear, Coun. of Fashion Designers of Am., 2006, Coun. Fashion Designers of Am./Vogue Fashion Fund award, 2006; grantee Woolite Fashion Future grant, 2003. Business E-Mail: chris@laforce-stevens.com.*

CHUNG, JEN, blog editor; b. NJ; Grad., Columbia Coll., 1998. Co-founder, editor Gothamist.com, 2003—; with advertising agy. Manhattan. Blog writer Vox.com. Nominee Best NY Blog for Gothamist.com, NY Mag., 2004; named Best NY Blog, Gothamist.com, NY Press, 2004; recipient Rave award-Blogs (Gothamist.com), WIRED Mag., 2007. Office: Gothamist LLC Prince Street Station PO Box 510 New York NY 10012 Business E-Mail: jen@gothamist.com.*

CHUNG, JOSEPH SANG-HOON, economics professor; b. Unmunmyon, Chongdo-kun, Kyongbuk, Korea, Oct. 11, 1929; came to U.S., 1953; s. Anthony Doseng and Martha (Cho) C.; m. Louise Carol Guenther, Aug. 17, 1957; children: Vincent, Sara, Melissa. Student, Seoul Nat. U., Korea, 1949-51; BS in Econs., Marquette U., 1956, MA, 1958; PhD, Wayne State U., 1964. Lectr. in econs. Marquette U., Milw., 1958-60; from instr. to asst. prof. Kalamazoo Coll., 1962-63, 63-64; asst. prof. Ill. Inst. Tech., Chgo., 1964-68, chmn. dept. econs., 1975-82, assoc. prof., 1968-73, prof. econs., 1973-95, prof. emeritus, 1996—. Fulbright prof. Seoul Nat. U. Korea, 1966-68; cons. Hoover Instn., 1964-66, Def. Dept., 1969; assoc. Asia Sci. Rsch. Assocs., Menlo Park, Calif., 1968-85. Author: Evolution of the Japanese Electronics Industry, 1980, The North Korean Economy: Structure and Development, 1974; editor: Patterns of Economic Development: Korea, 1966. Social Sci. Rsch. Coun. fellow, 1962; Stanford U. Hoover Instn. grantee, 1964-65; Fulbright lectr. Dept. State, 1966-68; Gen. Electric Found. grantee, 1975 Mem. Am. Econs. Assn. Roman Catholic. Home: 22 W County Line Rd Barrington IL 60010 Personal E-mail: j1chung@aol.com.

CHUNG, JUNG GIT, retired aerospace engineer; b. Sun Wai, Moy Kok, Canton, China, Apr. 12, 1922; s. Pak Wing and Yow Fun (Dong) C.; m. Fay Yung Ma, May 3, 1951; 1 child, John Gingkeong. BAE, NYU, 1949, MAE, 1951. With Fairchild Republic, Farmingdale, NY, 1951—86, airloads and performance engr., 1962—64, airloads and performance engr. Mach-30 Aerospace Plane, 1964—66; head transonic, supersonic and hypersonic wind tunnels Republic Aviation, 1963-65; design air loads engr. Boeing 757 Boeing Aircraft, Seattle, 1979; NATO fighter design specification team Fokker, Amsterdam, 1969-70; preliminary design and performance FRC/SAAB Transport, Swearingen Aviation, San Antonio, 1980; loads and dynamics engr. Grumman E-2C, Grumman Aircraft, Bethpage, 1981, preliminary design of aerial refueling tank, 1982; AMRAM missile ejection and separation dynamics Grumman F-14, Bethpage, 1983, with ASW-340 store carriage and separation, F-15 dispenser tech., 1984, with A-10 performance maintenance, capacity acctg., interface mgmt., aircraft accident analysis, 1985, T-46 aeroperformance, quality control flying surfaces, 1986, ret., 1986. Mem. faculty N.Y. Inst. Tech., 1969; instr., tax preparer Vol. Income Tax Assistance, 1986-92; instr. SeniorNet Forest Hills Learning Ctr., 1993-95; sr. connections adv. bd. Adelphi U. Sch. Social Work, 1991-95, Nassau Libr. Sys., 1995-2000. Coord. and instr. Tax Counseling for the Elderly, AARP ADC/Tax Assistance, 1985-2000, tech. specialist, 1996-98, instr. AARP 55-Alive Mature Driving, 1998-2000; vol. Am. Fedn. Arts; program and membership chair Fairchild Republic Retirees, 1986-91; mem. adv. coun. planning and priorities com. Nassau County Dept. Sr. Citizen Affairs, 1996—2000; tutor English for spkrs. of other langs. Lit. Vols. Am., Nassau County chpt., 1993-2000 (Tutor of Yr. 1998). Mem. CAP, AAAS, AAIA, AARP (1st v.p. Farmingdale chpt. 1988-89, pres. 1992-93, alt. del. biennial conv. 1994, legis. com. 1990-94, LI sect. coun. 1996-00), US Naval Inst., Math. Assn. Am., Met. Mus. Art, Mus. Natural History, US Coast Guard Aux., Air Force Assn., Am. Def. Preparedness Assn., NY Acad. Sci. Republican. Presbyterian. Home: 32 Mulberry St Apt 5 New York NY 10013-4393 Personal E-mail: junggitfay@yahoo.com.

CHUNG, KYUNG CHO, Korean history specialist, writer, educator; b. Seoul, Korea, Nov. 13, 1921; s. Yang Sun and Kyung Ok (Peng) C.; m. Yosi S. Chung, Oct. 10, 1958; children: In Kyung, In Ja. Student, Waseda U., Tokyo, 1941-43; BA, Seoul Nat. U., 1947; postgrad., Columbia U., 1948-49; MA, N.Y. U., 1951; LL.D., Pusan Nat. U., 1965; Litt.D., Sungkyunkwan U., 1968; MA, Monterey Inst. Fgn. Studies, 1974. Mem. faculty U.S. Def. Lang. Inst., Monterey, Calif., 1951-92, Monterey Inst. Fgn. Studies, 1973-74, Hartnell Coll., Salinas, Calif., 1974-93. Pres. Korean Rsch. Coun.; adviser Korean Assn., Monterey, 1974—, Am.-Korean Found., Crossroads, Inc., 1992, Asia Devel. Inc.; treas. Korean Rsch. Bull.; hon. prof. Kunkuk U.; pres. South Carmel Hills Assn., 1962-99; hon. chmn. Inst. Far Eastern Studies Joint Rsch. Program U.S.-Russia-Korea-Japan-China, 1993—; chmn. Korea-Am. Assn. Author: Korea Tomorrow, 1957, New Korea, 1962, Seoul (Ency. Americana), 1965, Naeil Hankuk, 1965, Sae Hankuk, 1968, Korea: The Third Republic, 1972, Korean Unification, 1973, Korea Reunion and Reunification, 1974, Kankuk Gaido, 1988, The Korea Guidebook: North and South Korea, 6th edit., 2002, Korea edit., 2002, Hankuk-chongran, 1999, East and West 1000 Munsun, 1995, Japanese Kangoku Gaizobuk, 2002. Recipient Superior Performance award, U.S. Govt., 1964, Recognition award of 40 Yrs. Svc., 1991, Excellency medal, 1992, Korean Prime Min. citation, 1965, cert. of achievement, U.S. Def. Lang. Inst., 1976, Outstanding Performance award, 1980, Commendation award, 1991, Olympic-Svc. Gold medal, Korean Pres., 1989, Spl. Commendation award, 1990, Fifa World Cup Svc. award, 2002, Spl. award medal, Korean Govt., 2002, Excellency Svc. award medal, Overseas Korean Found., 2003, Spl, Commendation plaque award, Mayor of Korea, 2006, Cmty. Svc. award, Pres. Korean Assn., 2007. Mem. AAUP, Am. Assn. Asian Studies, Am. Assn. Modern Langs., Am.-Korean Polit. Assn., Carmel Found., Korean Rsch. Coun. (pres. 2005-06). Democrat. Mem. Korean Ch. Home and Office: 25845 S Carmel Hills Dr Carmel CA 93923-8310 Office Phone: 831-624-4929. *Dedicate and contribute toward better relations among the nations and the lasting peace in the world, teaching other languages to meet the other nations half way by speaking the same language.*

CHUNG, PAUL MYUNGHA, mechanical engineer, educator; b. Seoul, Dec. 1, 1929; came to U.S., 1947, naturalized, 1956; s. Robert N. and Kyungssook (Kim) C.; m. E. Jean Judy, Mar. 8, 1952; children: Maurice W., Tamara P. BSME, U. Ky., 1952, MS, 1954; PhD, U. Minn., 1957. Asst. prof. mech. engring. U. Minn., 1957-58; aero. research scientist Ames Research Center, NASA, Calif., 1958-61; head fluid physics dept. Aerospace Corp., San Bernardino, Calif., 1961-66; prof. mech. engring. U. Ill., Chgo., 1966-95, head dept. energy engring., 1974-79, dean engring., 1979-94, prof., dean emeritus, 1995—. Mem. tech. adv. com. Ill. Inst. Environ. Quality, 1975-77; corp. mem. Underwriters Lab., 1983-95; cons. to industry, 1966—. Author: Electric Probes in Stationary and Flowing Plasmas, 1975, Russian edit., 1978, numerous papers in field; contbr. chpt. to Advances in Heat Transfer, 1965, Dynamics of Ionized Gasses, 1973. Bd. govs. YMCA, Redlands, Calif., 1965—67. Fellow AIAA (nat. tech. com. on plasmadynamics 1972-74, com. on propellants and combustion 1976-80); mem. AIChE (nat. com. on internat. activities 1992-94), Am. Soc. Engring. Edn. (exec. bd. engring. dean's coun. 1983-84), Sigma Xi, Tau Beta Pi, Pi Tau Sigma, Phi Kappa Phi. Home: 2003 E Lillian Ln Arlington Heights IL 60004-4215 Office: Univ Ill Off of Dean Chicago IL 60680 E-mail: jjpc2003@earthlink.net.

CHUNG, PING TSAI, education educator; b. Taipei, Taiwan, Republic of China; s. Tai-Der and Kun-Sen Lin Chung; m. Hsin-Hwa Hsiao Chung, Jan. 18, 1987; children: Rebecca, Timothy. PhD Computer Sci., Polytechnic U., 1998; MS Computer Sci., Stevens Instit. Tech., 1986. Mem. tech. staff. Lucent Tech. Bell Lab., 1998—2000; software devel. AT&T Lab., 1997—98; asst. prof. dept. computer sci. LI U., NY, 2000—07, assoc. prof. dept. computer sci., 2007—. Advisor computer sci. club L.I. U., Bklyn., 2001—04, chmn. computer sci. pers. com., 2002—04, chair computer sci. dept., 2004—; mem. program com. Internat. Multconf. in Computer Sci. and Engring., 2004—. Contbr. articles to profl. jours. Mem.: IEEE, Assn. for Computing Machinery. Office: Dept of Computer Sci Long Island U 1 University Plz Brooklyn NY 11201 Office Phone: 718-488-1073. Business E-Mail: pchung@liu.edu.

CHUNG, SOON-JO, engineer, researcher; b. Seoul, Republic of Korea, Apr. 20, 1976; s. Jongsuk Chung and YoungGoo Yoo; m. Sunhee Lee, June 5, 2005. MS, MIT, Cambridge, Mass., 2002, PhD, 2006. Rsch. engr. Nat. Optical Astron. Obs., Tucson, 2002—03; rsch. asst. MIT, 2000—06. Cons. Nightsky Systems, Raleigh, NC, 2003. Sgt. Korean Army, 2000—02. Recipient AT&T Asia/Pacific Leadership award, 2000. Mem.: IEEE, AIAA. Achievements include development of microsatellites, launched to the international space station. Home: 500 Broadway Malden MA 02148 Office: MIT 77 Mass Ave Cambridge MA 02139 Home Phone: 617-571-0910; Office Phone: 617-253-6685. Business E-Mail: sjchung@alum.mit.edu.

CHUNG, TONG SOO, lawyer; BA magna cum laude, Harvard U., 1977; MA in Public Affairs, Princeton U., 1980; JD, UCLA Sch. of Law, 1984. Financial analyst Exxon Corp., 1980—81; assoc. Whitman & Ransom, Los Angeles, Calif., 1984—86; co-founder, of counsel Lim, Ruger & Kim, LLP (formerly Kim, Chung & Lim), Los Angeles, Calif., 1986—; dir. export promotion & coord. Internat. Trade Administration, US Dept. Commerce, 1994, former dir. advocacy ctr., 1995—2000, former acting dep. asst. secy. for svc. industries & fin., 2000—01. Sr. advisor Sewon Telecom. Commr. Los Angeles County Private Industry Council, 1988—92; mem. Calif. Economic Develop. Advisory Com. on Asia, 1989—91; commr. Los Angeles Fire and Police Pension System, 1991—93, Calif. Postsecondary Ed. Commn., 1992—93; bd. dirs. Constitutional Rights Found.; founding mem. The Ethnic Coalition; founding pres. Korean Am. Coalition. Office: Lim, Ruger & Kim, LLP 1055 W Seventh St Ste 2800 Los Angeles CA 90017

CHUNG, WOO CHEOL, electrical engineer; s. Jong Sik Chung and Young Rhan Lee; m. Kyung Ah Roh, Oct. 30, 1993; children: Soo Young, Hye Sim. BS with honors, Hanyang U., Seoul, Republic of Korea, 1991, MS, 1993; PhD, Va. Poly. Inst. and State U., Blacksburg, Va., 2006. Sr. engr. Samsung Electronics, Suwon, 1993—99; staff engr. IBM, Seoul, 2000, Qualcomm, Inc., San Diego, 2005—. Contbr. articles to profl. jours. Pres. Korean Cath. Cmty. Blacksburg, Va., 2003—04. Recipient Travel Fund award, Grad. Students Assembly, Va. Poly. Inst. and State U., 2003; Baeknam fellowship, Hanyang U., 1987—91, Samsung Electronics fellowship, 1989—93. Mem.: IEEE (reviewer 2003—), Korean-American Scientists and Engineers Assn. (Korea-U.S. Sci. Coop. Ctr. scholar 2005). Roman Cath. Achievements include research in the dual use of power distribution networks for data communications in high speed integrated circuits; development of a 16bit fixed point digital signal processor; application specific integrated circuits based on a 32bit microcontroller; patents pending for dual purpose mobile device using ultra wide band communications; over 5 patents in field. Avocations: golf, jogging, swimming. Personal E-mail: cstpaul@gmail.com.

CHUNG, WOON-GYE, toxicologist, researcher; arrived in US, 2003; s. Kyoyang Chung and Jungwhan Kim; m. Hyemee Shon; 1 child, Pearl. BS, Seoul Nat. U., Republic of Korea, 1986, MS, 1988; PhD, Oreg. State U., 1994. Rsch. assoc. Inha U., Inchon, Republic of Korea, 1994—2000, asst. prof., 2001—03; vis. scholar Oreg. State U., Corvallis, 2004—05, rsch. assoc., 2006—. Sr. rsch. cons. Korea Med. Sci. Inst. Co. Ltd., Seoul, 2000—03. Contbr. articles to profl. jours. Scholar, Internat. Rotary Found., 1991—92. Mem.: Am. Soc. Mass Spectroscopy (corr.), Soc. Toxicology (corr. Grad. Student Travel award 1993). Achievements include patents for novel method and solvent system thereof for determination of all metabolites of 6 CYP enzymes; composition for enhancement and maintenance of erection comprising plant extract; composition for treating a constipation. Office: Oreg State U 153 Gilbert Hall Corvallis OR 97331 Office Phone: 541-737-1878. Business E-Mail: woongye@yahoo.com.

CHUNILAL, DAMIAN, investment company executive; Grad. in Econs., U. Cambridge, UK. With Merrill Lynch, 1989—, global head debt capital markets fin. instns. grp. NYC, head debt issuer client grp. Europe, 2002—04, sr. v.p., co-head Pacific rim global markets and investment banking, 2004—. Office: Merrill Lynch 4 World Fin Ctr 250 Vesey St New York NY 10080

CHUNPRAPAPH, BOONMEE, physician, educator; b. Songkhla, Thailand, Nov. 23, 1938; came to U.S., 1966; s. Yen Hua Tseng; m. Kaysorn Suttajit, July 29, 1944; children: Benj, Kabin. MD, U. Med. Sci., Bangkok, 1964. Diplomate Am. Bd. Orthopedic Surgery. Rotating intern Samaritan Hosp., Troy, N.Y., 1966-67; pvt. practice gen. surgery Youngstown (Ohio) Hosp. Assn., 1967-68; pvt. practice specializing in orthopedic surgery Univ. Hosp., Mobile, Ala., 1968-71; assoc. prof. U. Ill., Chgo., 1980—. Contbr. articles to profl. jours. Fellow ACS, Internat. Coll. Surgeons; mem. AMA, Acad Orthopedic Surgeons, Am. Soc. Surgery of the Hand. Avocations: photography, gardening, tennis. Office: U Ill Coll Medicine 835 S Wolcott Ave M/C 844 Chicago IL 60612-7307 Office Phone: 312-996-7161. Business E-Mail: boonc@uic.edu.

CHUONG, CHENG-MING, pathologist, educator; b. Taipei, Taiwan, Sept. 15, 1952; came to U.S., 1978; s. You-Cheng and Yu-Yn (Lee) C.; m. Violet Shen, August 25, 1979; 1 child: Edward. MD, Nation Taiwan Univ., 1978; PhD in Develop. and Molecular Biology, Rockefeller U., NYC, 1983. Asst. prof. devel., molecular biology Rockefeller U., NYC, 1983-87; asst. prof. pathology U. So. Calif., LA, 1987-92, assoc. prof. pathology, 1992-98, prof. pathology, 1998—, head, Tissue Develop. Engring. Lab. in Pathology; mem. staff L.A. County Hosp., Norris Cancer Ctr., LA. Spkr. in field. Editor Jour. Inv. Dermatology, Frontiers in Biosci., N.Am. Prof. Taiwanese Assn. Tribune; author Molecular Basis of Epithelial Appendage Morphogenesis; contbr. several articles to profl. jours. Mem. Sci. Alliance, Irvine Sch. Dist. R01 Rsch. grantee NIH, 1988—; grantee NSF, 1992—; Zumberg fellow USC, 1992-93, tchg. award R.S. Cleland, 1994. Mem. Am. Soc. Cell Biologists, Soc. Devel. Biologists, Hair Rsch. Soc. Office: Keck Sch Medicine Dept Pathology 2011 Zonal Ave # HMR313B Los Angeles CA 90033 Office Phone: 323-442-1296. Office Fax: 323-442-3049. Business E-Mail: chuong@pathfinder.usc.edu. E-mail: cmchuong@zygote.hsc.usc.edu.

CHUPKA, WILLIAM ANDREW, chemical physicist, educator; b. Pittston, Pa., Feb. 12, 1923; s. William and Antoinette C.; m. Olive Augusta Pirani, May 21, 1955; children: Jocelyn Terese, Marc William. BS, U. Scranton, 1943; MS, U. Chgo., 1949, PhD, 1951. Instr. Harvard U., 1951-54; asso. physicist Argonne (Ill.) Nat. Lab., 1954-67; sr. physicist, 1967-75; prof. chemistry Yale U., 1975-96, prof. emeritus, 1996—. Research, numerous publs. in chem. physics. Served with U.S. Army, 1943-46. Guggenheim fellow, 1961-62 Mem. Am. Chem. Soc. Office: PO Box 208107 New Haven CT 06520-8107 Home Phone: 203-387-7492; Office Phone: 203-432-3989. Business E-Mail: william.chupka@yale.edu.

CHUPP, TIMOTHY EDWARD, physicist, educator, academic administrator; b. Berkeley, Calif., Nov. 30, 1954; AB, Princeton U., 1977; PhD in Physics, U. Wash., 1983. Instr., asst. prof. physics Princeton U., 1983-85; from asst. prof. to assoc. prof. physics Harvard U., 1985-91; assoc. prof U. Mich., Ann Arbor, 1991-94, prof. physics, 1994—. Fellow Alfred P. Sloan Found., 1987. Recipient Presdl. Young Investor award NSF, 1987. Fellow Am. Phys. Soc. (I.I. Rabi prize 1993). Achievements include research in low energy particle physics particularly by study of symmetries accessible with polarization; weak interactions: CP violation and time reversal violation; fundamentals of quantum mechanics; structure of nucleons; biomedical and technological applications of lasers and optical pumping. Office: U Mich Dept Physics Ann Arbor MI 48109

CHURAY, DANIEL J., lawyer; b. Sewickley, Pa., Aug. 23, 1962; m. Lynn Churay; children: Ryan, Addison, John. BA in Economics, U. Tex., Austin, 1985; JD, U. Houston Law Ctr., 1989. Bar: Tex. 1989. Atty. Fulbright & Jaworski LLP, Houston, 1989—95; dep. gen. counsel, asst. sec. Baker Hughes Inc., 1995—2000, acting gen. counsel, corp. sec., 2000; sr. counsel Fulbright & Jaworski LLP, Houston, 2000—02; sr. v.p., gen. counsel, sec. YRC Worldwide Inc., Kans., 2002—. Mem.: ABA, Tex. Bus. Law Found., Tex. State Bar Assn., Am. Corp. Counsel Assn. Office: YRC Worldwide Inc 10990 Roe Ave Overland Park KS 66211*

CHURCH, DALE WALKER, lawyer; b. Portland, Oreg., Dec. 17, 1939; s. Floyd Walker and Lydia Belle (Barnette) C.; m. Mollie Ann Harper, Apr. 11, 1964; 1 child, Forrest Gregory. BS, Oreg. State U., 1961; JD, George Washington U., 1967. Bar: D.C. 1968, Calif. 1971. Contracting officer, exec. sec. contract rev. bd. CIA, Langley, Va., 1963-69; corp. gen. counsel, asst. sec. directory of contracts ESL, Inc., Sunnyvale, Calif., 1969-77; dep. under sec. rsch. and engring. U.S. Dept. Def., Washington, 1977-80; ptnr. Surrey and Morse, Washington, 1980-84, Seyfarth, Shaw, Fairweather & Geraldson, Washington, 1984-88, Pillsbury, Madison & Sutro, Washington, 1988-93, McDermott, Will & Emery, Washington, 1993-97; chmn., CEO Ventures & Solutions, LLC, Williamsburg, Va., 1998—, Alive Tech., Inc., 2006—, Mech. Tech., Inc., 2002—05; chmn. MTI Micro Fuel Cells, 2002. Counsel def. mgmt. to pres.'s Blue Ribbon Commn.; cons. Def. Sci. Bd., Washington, 1980—; lectr. profl. orgns. and colls. Task force on Industry-to-Industry Coop., AMC Commander's Exec. Round Table.; active Ctr. Strategic and Internat. Studies Def. Orgn. Project; co-founder, counsel, treas. Youth Engaged in Svc. Am. Mem. ABA, Am. Electronics Assn. (former gen. counsel, chmn. def. conversion com.), Nat. Def. Indsl. Assn. (bd. dirs., chmn. investments com.), Nat. Contracts Mgmt. Assn., Def. Sci. Bd. Acquisition Reform Task Force, Calif. Bar Assn., D.C. Bar Assn., Fed. Bar Assn., Soc. Logistics Engrs. (hon.), Delta Theta Phi, Sigma Phi Epsilon. Home: 9 Franklin St Alexandria VA 22314-3828 Office: Ventures & Solutions LLC 704 Fairfax Way Williamsburg VA 23185-8202 Office Phone: 703-519-0800. Personal E-mail: legaldale@aol.com.

CHURCH, DOUGLAS D., lawyer; b. Indpls., Jan. 22, 1944; AB in Govt. and Economics, Ind. U., 1966; JD, Ind. U., 1970. Bar: Ind. 1970. Law clk. to Hon. George B. Hoffman Jr. Ind. Ct. Appeals, 1968—70; assoc. Church Church Hittle & Antrim, Noblesville, Ind., 1970—71, ptnr., 1971—87, mng. ptnr., 1987—2005, sr. ptnr., 2005—. Town atty. Town of Fishers, 1980—; city atty. City of Noblesville, 1988—96. Named Man of Yr., Greater Indianapolis YMCA Hamilton County Br., 1997; recipient Irv Merritt award, Greater Ind. Masters Swim Assn., 1989, Josiah K. Durfee award, Noblesville Preservation Alliance, 2000. Mem.: Ind. Bar Found., Ind. Mcpl. Lawyers Assn. (pres. 1999—2000), Am. Bd. Trial Advocates, Ind. Trial Lawyers Assn., ABA (Gold Key award 1970), Ind. State Bar Assn. (bd. gov. 1980—81, chmn. young lawyers sect. 1981—82, local govt. law sect. 1981—82, bd. gov. 1998—2000, v.p. 2005—06, pres.-elect 2006—07, pres. 2007—08, Citation of Merit 1982, Cinch Strap award 2000, 2004), Hamilton County Bar Assn. (pres. 1980—81, Frank Campbell Svc. award 1997). Office: Church Church Hittle & Antrim PO Box 10 Noblesville IN 46061-0010

CHURCH, EUGENE LENT, physicist, consultant; b. Yonkers, NY, July 30, 1925; s. Wallace L. and Wilhelmina L. (Binger) C.; m. Anne Richardson Meirs, May 15, 1948; children— Rebecca Meirs, David Lent.

AB, Princeton U., 1948; PhD, Harvard U., 1953. With U.S. Dept. Def., 1952-94; sr. phys. scientist Picatinny Arsenal, Dover, NJ, 1977-94; sr. physicist Frankford Arsenal, Phila., 1971-77. Guest physicist Argonne (Ill.) Nat. Lab., 1952-55, Brookhaven Nat. Lab., 1955-59, 61-71, 81—; vis. scientist Niels Bohr Inst., Copenhagen, 1959-61. Contbr. numerous articles to profl. jours. With USN, 1944—46. Recipient R&D-100 award, U.S. Army Achievement awards. Fellow AAAS, Am. Phys. Soc., Am. Optical Soc., Soc. Photo-Optical Instrumentation Engrs.; mem. IEEE (life sr.), St. Nicholas Soc. N.Y.C., Soc. Colonial Wars NJ, Holland Soc. Republican. Presbyterian.

CHURCH, FRANK FORRESTER, minister, writer; b. Boise, Idaho, Sept. 23, 1948; s. Frank Forrester and Bethine (Clark) C.; m. Amy Furth, May 30, 1970 (div. 1991); children: Frank Forrester, Nina Wynne; m. Carolyn Buck Luce, July 25, 1992. AB, Stanford U., 1970; MDiv, Harvard U., 1974, PhD, 1978. Min. All Souls Unitarian Ch., NYC, 1978—. Columnist The Chicago Tribune, 1987-88, The New York Post, 1989; vis. prof. Dartmouth Coll., Hanover, N.H., 1989. Author: Father and Son: A Personal Biography of Senator Frank Church of Idaho, 1985, The Devil and Dr. Church, 1985, Entertaining Angels, 1987, The Seven Deadly Virtues, 1988, Everyday Miracles, 1988, Our Chosen Faith: An Introduction to Unitarian Universalism, 1989, God and Other Famous Liberals, 1991, Life Lines, 1996, A Chosen Faith, 1998, Lifecraft, 2000, Bringing God Home, 2002, The American Creed, 2002, Freedom from Fear, 2004, So Help Me God, 2007; translator: Greek Word-Building (Matthias Stehle), 1976; editor: Continuity and Discontinuity in Church History, 1978, The Essential Tillich, 1987, 2d edit., 1999, The Macmillan Book of Earliest Christian Prayers, 1988, The Macmillan Book of Earliest Christian Hymns, 1988, The Macmillan Book of Earliest Christian Meditations, 1989, One Prayer at a Time: A 12 Step Anthology, 1989, The Jefferson Bible, 1989, Without Apology: The Liberal Faith of A. Powell Davies, 1998, Restoring Faith: America's Religious Leaders Answer Terror With Hope, 2001, The Separation of Church and State: Writings on Religious Freedom by America's Founders, 2004; contbr. chapters to books; contbr. (articles) Harvard Theol. Rev., (speeches) Rep. Am. Speeches, 1983—84, 1986—87, 1987—88, 1989—90, 1992—93, 1995—96, 1997—98; contbr. articles to profl. publs. Bd. dir. Union Theol. Sem., NYC, 1992-98, 2007—, Internat. Bridges Toward Justice, 2002; mem. exec. com. Franklin and Eleanor Roosevelt Inst., NYC, 1990—; chmn. Coun. on Environment NYC, 1995-2006; mem. svc. com. Unitarian Universalist Ch., 1978—; founder Lifelines Ctr., 1999 Montgomery fellow Dartmouth Coll., 1989. Mem. Unitarian Universalist Mins. Assn. Democrat. Home: 201 E 80th St New York NY 10021-0511 Office: All Souls Unitarian Church 1157 Lexington Ave New York NY 10021-0440 Home Phone: 212-772-0331. Personal E-mail: revchurch@aol.com.

CHURCH, GEORGE MCDONALD, geneticist, educatior, researcher; b. MacDill AFB, Fla., Aug. 28, 1954; s. Henry Stewart III McDonald and Virginia Anne Strong; m. Chao-ting Wu, Dec. 14, 1990; 1 child, Marie Tai-lien. BA in Zoology & Chemistry, Duke U., Durham, NC, 1974; PhD in Biochemistry & Molecular Biology, Harvard U., Cambridge, Mass., 1984. Scientist Biogen Rsch. Corp., Cambridge, 1984; rsch. fellow anatomy U. Calif., San Francisco, 1985—86; asst. prof. to assoc. prof. genetics Harvard Med. Sch., 1986—98, prof. genetics, 1998—. With Howard Hughes Med. Inst., 1986—97; dir. Lipper Ctr. Computational Genetics, 1997—, Harvard/MIT DOE Genomes-to-Life Ctr., 2002—; sr. assoc. Broad Inst. Harvard & MIT, 2006—; mem. sci. adv. bd. Helicos, Genomatica, Codon Devices; med. advisor DNAdirect; sci. advisor PharmoRx. Mem. editl. bd.: Nature/European Molecular Biology Orgn.-MSB, Genome Biology, Omics, BioMedNet; contbr. articles to sci. jours. Achievements include developing, with Walter Gilbert, the first direct genomic sequencing method, 1984. Avocations: water-skiing, swimming, sailing, tennis, skiing, bicycling, scuba diving, camping, rock climbing. Office: Harvard Med Sch Genetics NRB Rm 238 77 Avenue Louis Pasteur Boston MA 02115 Office Phone: 617-432-7562. E-mail: g1m1c1@receptor.med.harvard.edu.

CHURCH, KATHY LYNN, education educator, consultant; d. Bill and Marjorie Luttrell; children: Ian, Kaitlin. EdD, Ball State U., 1986. Lic. psychologist Ind., cert. tchr. Ind. Assoc. prof. grad. sch. edn. and psychology Pepperdine U., West L.A., 2004—; asst. prof. elem. edn. Ball State U., Muncie, asst. prof. ednl. psychology; assoc. prof. edn. Anderson U. Cons. on strategic learning, Muncie; early start prof. (supported by Lilly Grant) Ball State U.; ednl. cons. Menominee Indian Sch. Dist., Keshena, Wis.; cons. sch. psychologist Elwood Cmty. Schs., Elwood, Ind.; reading diagnostician and tutor, Muncie; proposal reviewer Am. Ednl. Rsch. Assn., Am. Assn. for Coll. Tchrs.; jour. reviewer, guest Tchr. Educator. Presenter, Hawaii Edn. Conf. (internat. presentation) Professional Development in Action: A Professional Development School's Year Long Writing Project, Considering Social Cognition as an Avenue to Enhance Comprehension and Promote Prosocial Behavior, contbg. author (jour. article) Curriculum Based Assessment: Reading and Academic Standards, (ednl. jour.) A Conceptual Model for Incorporating Conflict Resolution into Teacher Education; author: (conf. proceeding) Considering Social Cognition as an Avenue to Enhance Comprehension and Promote Prosocial Behavior, (abstract) Professional Development in Action: A Professional Development School's Year Long Writing Project; nat. presenter (presentation) Building Academic Standard Based Outcomes for All Children, Building Healthy Schools, presenter, Soc. Educators/Scholar (internat. presentation) Professional Development Schools: A New Model for Embedded Leadership; author: (conf. abstracts) Reading Assessment Techniques for School Psychologists. Cmty. mem., performance assessment team Muncie Cmty. Schs.; cmty. mem. of the pl 221 com. Storer Elem. Sch.; cmty. mem. Text Adoption Com. for Math.; ednl. vol. Morrison Mock Elem. Sch.; ednl. svc. learning coord. Ball State U.; participant Pepperdine voyage Pepperdine U., Florence, Italy, 2004; attendee Ch. in the Canyon, PCA; mem. children svcs. Westminster Presbyn. Ch.; attendee Malibu Presbyn. Ch. Recipient Tchg. Professorship, Ball State U., 1993, Outstanding Prof., Delta Rho chpt. Alpha Phi, 2000, Academic Recognition for Encouraging Academic Excellence, Office of Residence Life and Student Affairs, 1991, Recognition for Excellence in Tchg., Ball State U., 1990, 1991, 1992, 1993, 1998, 1999, 2001; fellow, Dept. Ednl. Psychology, Ball State U., 1983, 1984, 1985; grantee Tchr. Voice in Profl. Devel. Implementation grant, Tchr. Quality in Edn. Grant, 2003—04, Profl. Devel. for Enhanced Tchr. Planning grant, 2002—03, Ind. Campus Compact, 1999. Mem.: Calif. Reading Assn., Assn. Ednl. Therapists, Internat. Reading Assn. Office: Pepperdine Univ 16830 Ventura Blvd Encino CA 91436 Home Phone: 310-506-8051; Office Phone: 818-501-1640. Office Fax: 818-501-1631. Business E-Mail: kathy.church@pepperdine.edu.

CHURCH, LILLIAN HAZEL See BROOKS, LILLIAN

CHURCH, MARTHA ELEANOR, retired academic administrator; b. Pitts., Nov. 17, 1930; d. Walter Seward and Eleanor (Boyer) Church. BA, Wellesley Coll., Mass., 1952; MA, U. Pitts., 1954; PhD, U. Chgo., 1960; DSc (hon.), Lake Erie Coll., Painesville, Ohio, 1975; LittD (hon.), Houghton Coll., NY, 1980; LHD (hon.), Queens Coll., 1981, Ursinus Coll., 1981, St. Joseph Coll., 1982, Towson State U., 1983, Dickinson Coll., 1987, Coll. Notre Dame Md., 1995; LLD (hon.), Hood Coll., 1995; LHD (hon.), Ill. Coll., 2003. Instr. geography Mt. Holyoke Coll., South Hadley, Mass., 1953-57; lectr. geography Ind. U. Gary Ctr., 1958; instr., then asst. prof. geography Wellesley Coll., 1958—65; dean coll., prof. geography Wilson Coll., 1965-71; assoc. exec. sec. Commn. Higher Edn., Mid. States Assn. Coll. and Secondary Sch., 1971-75; pres. Hood Coll., Frederick, Md., 1975-95, pres. emerita, 1995—, chair bd. trustees, 2006—; sr. scholar Carnegie Found. Advancement of Tchg., Princeton, 1995—97; interim pres. Ill. Coll., 2002—03; interim v.p. acad. affairs Holy Names U., Oakland, Calif., 2005—06. Vice chmn. bd. dirs. Am. Coun. on Edn., 1978—78, nat. identification panel, 1977—95; mem. Md. Humanities Coun., 1985—86; co-chmn. nat. adv. panel Nat. Ctr. Rsch. to Improve Postsecondary Tchg. and Learning U. Mich., 1985—90; trustee Carnegie Found. Advancement of Tchg., 1986—96, vice chair, 1990—92, chair, 1992—94; bd. visitors Def. Intelligence Coll., 1988—91; trustee Nat. Geog. Soc., 1989—2007, com. rsch. and exploration, 1998—2006, audit rev. com., 1993—98, chair membership, medals and awards com., 2000—07, exec., audit and compensation, mission programs com.; adv. bd. dirs. Automobile Club Md., 1991—2002; adv. bd. Boyer Ctr. Messiah Coll., Grantham, Pa., 1997—2005; trustee Internat. Partnership Svc. Learning, 1999—2002; dir. emerita Farmers and Mechanics Nat. Bank, 2000—; cons. Choice: Books Coll. Librs. Author: The Spatial Organization of Electric Power Territories in Massachusetts, 1960; Co-editor: A Basic Geographical Library: A Selected and Annotated Book List for Am. Colls, 1966; cons. editor, Change mag., 1980-01. Bd. dirs. Japan Internat. Christian U. Found., 1977-91, Nat. Rsch. Com., 1993-96; bd. advisors Fund Improvement of Postsecondary Edn., HEW, 1976-79; mem. Sec. of Navy's Adv. Bd. on Edn. and Tng., 1976-80; chmn. Md. Commn. on Civil Rights, 1981-82; trustee Bradford Coll., Mass., 1982-87, Peddie Sch., N.J., 1982-98, chair acad. affairs com., 1987, 96-97, adv. trustee, 1998—, trustee; trustee Nat. Geog. Soc. Edn. Found., 1989-07, 99—; chmn. bd. dir. Medici Found., Princeton, N.J., 1985-05; trustee United Bd. Christian Higher Edn. in Asia, 1995-04, sec. bd. trustees, 1998-2003, chmn. com. on trustees, 1997-04, chmn. East and Intra-Asia program subcom., 1996-97, exec. com., 1998-04; mem. Md. Jud. Disabilities Commn., 1985-94; commr. Edn. Commn. States, Md., 1981-99; exec. com. Campus Compact: Project Pub. and Cmty. Svc., 1986-89. Named Disting. fellow, Internat. Partnership for Svc.-Learning and Leadership, 2006—. Mem. AAUW, Am. Assn. Advancement of Humanities (bd. dir. 1979-81), Am. Assn. Higher Edn. (chmn. 1980-81, bd. dir. 1979-83), Assn. Am. Geographers, Nat. Assn. Ind. Colls. and Univs. (bd. dir. 1983-86), Md. Ind. Colls. and Univs. Assn. (pres. 1979-81, mem. exec. com. 1988-92), Assn. Am. Colls. and Univs. (mem. adv. com. project on status and edn. of women 1980-85), Women's Coll. Coalition (mem. exec. com. 1976-80, 87-89), Am. Conf. Acad. Deans (sec., editor 1969-71), Coun. Protestant Colls. and Univs. (bd. dirs. 1969-71), Soc. Coll. and Univ. Planning (mem. editl. bd. 1979-95), Cosmos Club (mem. jour. editl. bd. 1990-94), Inst. Ednl. Leadership (bd. dirs. 1982-87), Sigma Delta Epsilon, Delta Kappa Gamma (hon.). Home and Office: 3124 Chartwell Crescent Ln Adamstown MD 21710-9643 Office Phone: 301-696-3855. Personal E-mail: marthachurch@edurostream.com.

CHURCH, PAMELA T., lawyer; b. Columbia, SC, Sept. 5, 1956; BA cum laude, Yale Univ., 1978; postgraduate, Univ. Bonn, Germany, 1978—79; JD, NYU, 1982. Bar: NY 1983. Ptnr., Global Mergers & Acquisition practice Coudert Bros. LLP, NYC, former mem. exec. bd. Contbr. articles to profl. jours. Mem.: ABA, Assn. Bar City of NY. Office: Coudert Bros LLP 1114 Ave of the Americas New York NY 10036 Office Phone: 212-626-4976. Office Fax: 212-626-4120. Business E-Mail: churchp@coudert.com.

CHURCH, RANDOLPH WARNER, JR., lawyer; b. Richmond, Va., Nov. 6, 1934; s. Randolph Warner and Elizabeth Lewis (Gochnauer) C.; m. Lucy Ann Canary, July 4, 1970; children: Leslie R. Pennell, L. Weeks Kerr. BA with honors, U. Va., 1957, LLB, 1960. Bar: Va. 1960, US Dist. Ct. (ea. dist.) Va. 1962, US Ct. Appeals (4th cir.) 1981, US Supreme Ct. 1999. Assoc. McCandlish, Lillard & Marsh, Fairfax, Va., 1960-63; ptnr. McCandlish, Lillard & Church and successor partnerships., Fairfax, 1963-84; city atty. Fairfax, 1968-72; mng. ptnr. McCandlish, Lillard & Church and successor partnerships, Fairfax, 1975-83, Hunton & Williams, Fairfax, 1984-99, mem. exec. com., 1988-94, sr. counsel, 2000—. Bd. dirs. George Mason Bank, George Mason Bankshares, Inc., George Mason Mortgage Co., 1991-98, Va. Found. Rsch. and Econ. Edn., Inc., 1994-2000. Author: Appellate Civil Litigation, 1984; panelist: Lawyer Professionalism: Is Change in Order? 1988, Marketing Legal Services: What's Hot and What's Not, 1990, (with others) Equity Practice and Tips on Brief Writing. Active Fairfax Com. of 100, 1988—, bd. dirs., 1989-92; bd. visitors George Mason U., Fairfax, 1982-90, rector, 1983-86, chmn. adv. bd. Coll. Arts and Scis., 1999-2006, gen. counsel, 2007—; bd. dirs. Fairfax Symphony, 1991-02, 2007-, gen. counsel, exec. com., 1996-02; bd. dirs. Fairfax Symphony Orch. Found., Inc., 1999—, Va. Found. Humanities and Pub. Policy, 1993-99, vice chmn., 1997-99; mem. Va. Mus. Fine Arts Found., 2000-06, exec. com., 2005-06; pres. Fall Book, Inc., 2001-04, bd. dirs., 2001—. Fellow Va. Law Found., Am. Bar Found.; mem. Va. Bar Assn. (v.p. 1975), Country Club of Fairfax, U. Va. Club, Phi Beta Kappa. Home: 5114 Forsgate Pl Fairfax VA 22030-4507 Office: Hunton & Williams 1751 Pinnacle Dr Ste 1700 Mc Lean VA 22102-3836 Office Phone: 703-714-7420. E-mail: rchurch@hunton.com.

CHURCH, RICHARD DWIGHT, electrical engineer, scientist; b. Ogdensburg, NY, June 27, 1936; s. Dwight Perry and Carmeta Elizabeth (Walters) C.; m. Vernice Naomi Ives, Aug. 26, 1961; children: Joel, Benjamin. BEE, Clarkson Coll. Tech., 1963. Elec. design engr. IBM, Owego, NY, 1963-69; prin. engr., pres. ASL Systems, Inc., Afton, NY, 1969-94, chmn. bd. dirs.; sr. elec. design engr. Magnetic Labs., Inc., Apalachin, NY, 1980-82, power supply engring. cons., 1982—; scientist Two Forty-Eight Co., Afton, 1994—2002, Norwood, NY, 2002—. Guest lectr. Afton Sch., Clarkson U. Co-author: Career Oriented Problems for Secondary Mathematics, 1974; contbr. articles to profl. jours.; patentee in field. Treas., trustee Candor Congl. Ch., 1972-84; vice chmn. Town Planning Bd. Candor, 1975-82; rep., mem. Candor Fire Co., 1972-87; bd. dirs., treas. Candor Cmty. Club, 1970-72; initiator endowed fund for Clarkson Theatre Co., Clarkson U., 1999; initiator The Dick Church Challenge, Hosmer Pipe Organ Fund, SUNY, Potsdam, 2005; initiator Richard D. Church lectureship fund in neurosci., St. Lawrence U., 2006. With USAF, 1955-59. Recipient Dr. Carl Michel award Clarkson Coll. Tech., 1960. Mem. IEEE (sr.), Assn. Energy Engrs. (sr.), Afton Bd. Fire Commrs. (fin. com. 1991-2002), Candor Coin Club (pres. 1978-81), Union of Concerned Scientists, The Cousteau Soc., NY Forest Owners Assn. (dir. 2003-), Am. Soc. Dowsers, Nat. Warplane Mus. Achievements include design of 1/100 scale, 16-ton concrete model of the Great Pyramid with internal passageways; design and construction of an 18-ton concrete ceiling beam; initiation of the Richard D. Church Lectureship Fund in Neuroscience at St. Lawrence University. Avocations: maple syrup production, maple tree farm development, singing, pyramid geometry, motorcycling. Home: 516 Obrian Rd Norwood NY 13668 Office: PO Box 248 Norwood NY 13668 Business E-Mail: rchurch248@cs.com.

CHURCH, STEVE, electronics executive; BS, Calif. State Poly. U., Pomona. Gen. mgr. So. Calif. divsn. Schweber Electronics; Western area mgr. and dir. distbn. Signetics (now Philips Semiconductor); v.p., SW area dir. then v.p. corp. mktg. Hamilton Hallmark Avnet, Inc., 1991—2001, pres. Electronics Mktg./Ams., co-pres. Electronics Mktg./Global, 2001—03, sr. v.p. and dir. svcs. and strategic bus. devel., 2003—, sr. v.p., chief human resources devel. officer. Exec. in residence Tex. A&M U., College Station, 2000—. Bd. advisors Ctr. Svcs. Leadership Coll. Bus. Ariz. State U. Avocations: skiing, running, tennis, golf, reading. Office: Avnet Inc 2211 S 47th St Phoenix AZ 85034-6403 Office Phone: 480-643-2000.*

CHURCH, THOMAS HADEN, actor; b. El Paso, Tex., June 17, 1960; Actor: (TV series) Wings, 1990—95, Ned and Stacey, 1995—97; (TV films) Fugitive Nights: Danger in the Desert, 1993, Mr. Murder, 1998, Broken Trail, 2006; (films) Tombstone, 1993, Demon Knight, 1995, George of the Jungle, 1997, One Night Stand, 1997, Susan's Plan, 1998, Free Money, 1998, Goosed, 1999, The Specials, 2000, 3000 Miles to Graceland, 2001, Lone Star State of Mind, 2002, The Badge, 2002, Serial Killing 4 Dummys, 2004, Sideways, 2004 (Screen Actors Guild Award, outstanding performance by cast in motion picture, 2005), Spanglish, 2004, Idiocracy, 2006, Spider-Man 3, 2007, (voice only) Over the Hedge, 2006, Charlotte's Web, 2006; actor, dir., writer: Rolling Kansas, 2003; exec. prodr.: (films) Scotch and Milk, 1998; TV appearances include: 21 Jump Street, 1989; Cheers, 1989; China Beach, 1989; Booker, 1989; Flying Blind, 1992; Partners, 1995; Lucky, 2003; (voice) Teen Titans, 2004.*

CHURCH, TIMOTHY ROBERT, medical educator, researcher; b. Cin., Nov. 4, 1950; s. Bill Grant and Elizabeth Ellen Church; life ptnr. Ann Louise Fredrickson; children: Ellen Rachel, Elizabeth Gene. PhD, U. Minn., Mpls., 1984. Biostatistician Medtronic, Inc, Mpls., 1980—82, mgr. biometry, 1982—87, dir., tachyarrhythmia clin. studies dept., 1993—96; rsch. fellow U. Minn., Mpls., 1975—80, sr. rsch. assoc., 1987—93, assoc. prof., 1996—2006, prof., 2006—. Prin. investigator Minn. PLCO, Mpls., 1999—. Contbr. numerous peer-reviewed jours articles to profl. jours. including: New England Jour. Medicine, Am. Jour. Epidemiology, Biometrics, Circulation and Statistician. Mem. Virginia Piper Cancer Inst. at Abbott Northwestern Hosp., Mpls., 1999—2002, Humphrey Cancer Ctr. at North Meml. Hosp., Mpls., 2003—. Mem.: Am. Assn. for Cancer Rsch., Soc. Epidemiologic Rsch., East North Am. Region Biometric Soc., Soc. Clin. Trials, Am. Statis. Assn., Delta Omega Honor Soc. Achievements include research in screening for colorectal cancer reduced deaths, led to nationwide recommendation for screening; efficacy of first rate-adjusting cardiac pacemaker; lowered energy requirements of steroid eluting cardiac pacing leads; lower defibrillation energy of implantable cardioverter/defibrillators using active can electrodes; lead-time biased ascertainment in epidemiology studies of chronic disease. Home: 1405 Osceola Ave Saint Paul MN 55105 Office: Univ Minn Environ Health Scis Ste 350 200 Oak St SE Minneapolis MN 55455-2008 Home Phone: 651-699-9384; Office Phone: 612-625-9091. Business E-Mail: trc@cccs.umn.edu.

CHURCHEY, RANDY L., health facility administrator; BS, U. Ala. Ptnr. Health Care Practice Coopers & Lybrand, LLP, Memphis, chmn. Hospitality and Real Estate Practice; sr. v.p., CFO FelCor Lodging Trust Inc.; pres., COO RFS Hotel Investors, Inc., 1999—2003, dir., 2000—03; pres. The Encore Cos., 2003—06; pres., CEO Beverly Enterprises, Inc. (BEI), 2006—. Bd. dirs. Edn. Realty Trust, Great Wolf Resorts, Innkeepers USA Trust, 2004—. Office: Beverly Enterprises Inc 1000 Beverly Way Fort Smith AR 72919 Office Phone: 479-201-2000. Fax: 479-201-1101.

CHURCHILL, BRUCE B., broadcast executive; b. Riverside, Calif., Aug. 30, 1957; s. James G. and Nancy (Wilkers) C. BA, Stanford U., Calif., 1979; MBA, Harvard U., 1984. Corp. lending officer Crocker Bank, San Francisco, 1979-82; assoc. McKinsey & Co. Inc., LA, 1984-88; v.p. fin. planning Paramount Pictures, LA, 1989; sr. v.p. fin. Fox TV; dep. CEO STAR Group Ltd., 1996—2000, pres., COO, 2000—03; CFO DIRECTV Group, El Segundo, Calif., 2004—05, exec. v.p., pres. DIRECTV L.Am., LLC and New Ventures, 2005—. Office: DIRECTV Group 2230 E Imperial Hwy El Segundo CA 90245 Office Phone: 310-964-5000.*

CHURCHILL, JAMES GARTON, retired finance company executive; b. Bklyn., July 16, 1930; s. S. Garton and Mary Ellen (Peck) C.; m. Nancy Barrett Wickers, July 31, 1954 (dec. Jan. 1997); children: Glenn Garton, Bruce Barrett, Ellen Wickers; m. Ruth Mathews Leiter, Mar. 24, 2001. BA, Dartmouth Coll., 1952; MBA, Harvard U., 1954. Fin. analyst Mobil Oil Corp., NYC, 1958-62; treas. Mobil Inner Europe, Geneva, 1962-65, Mobil Europe, London, 1965-68; fin. dir. Mobil Sekiyu, Tokyo, 1968-70; treas. internat. ops. Kaiser Aluminum & Chem. Corp., Oakland, Calif., 1970-81, treas., 1981-87; pvt. practice fin. cons. San Francisco, 1987-90. Served to lt. USNR, 1954-57. Avocations: French language study, reading, history. Home (Winter): 6333 Kennett Pl Mission KS 66202 Home (Summer): 2001 Grassy Ln Woodstock VT 05091 Personal E-mail: bootsandjim@sbcglobal.net.

CHURCHILL, JOHN HUGH, college academic administrator; b. Hector, Ark., Apr. 1, 1949; s. Olen Raymond and Mary Josephine (Cheek) C.; m. Jean Ann Hill, Aug. 19, 1972; children: William Houston, Mary Katherine Salisbury, Hugh Olen Hill. BA, Rhodes Coll., 1971; BA, MA, Oxford U., 1973; MA, MPH, PhD, Yale U., 1978. Asst. prof. philosophy Hendrix Coll., Conway, Ark., 1977—82, assoc. prof., 1982—92, prof., 1992—, dean of students, 1983—84, v.p. for acad. affairs, coll. dean, 1984—2001. Asst. Am. sec. The Rhodes Scholarship Trust, Middletown, Conn., 1974-77. Contbr. numerous articles to profl. jours. Mem. Rhodes Scholarship Com. Gulf Dist, 1977—, sec. Ark., 1980—. Recipient Rhodes scholarship Rhodes Trust, Oxford, Eng., 1971, NCAA Postgrad. scholarship, 1971. Mem. Soc. for Philosophy of Religion, Nat. Humanities Alliance (pres. 2006—), Phi Beta Kappa (sec. 2001—), Omicron Delta Kappa. Democrat. Avocations: poetry, walking, cooking, canoeing, reading. Office: 1606 New Hampshire Ave NW Washington DC 20009 Home: Apt 214 3133 Connecticut Ave NW Washington DC 20008-5104

CHURCHILL, MAIR ELISA ANNABELLE, medical educator; b. Liverpool, Eng., Nov. 28, 1959; BA in Chemistry, Swathmore Coll., Pa., 1981; PhD in Chemistry, Johns Hopkins U., 1987. Lab. asst. Swarthmore Coll., 1979-81; teaching asst. Johns Hopkins U., Balt., 1981-83; non-clin. sci. staff grade I MRC Lab. Molecular Biology, Cambridge, Eng., 1987-93; asst. prof. biophysics U. Ill., Urbana, 1993-98; assoc. prof. biophysics U. Colo., Denver, 1998—. Contbr. numerous articles to profl. jours. Am. Cancer Soc. fellow, 1987-89, Cambridge U. fellow, 1988-91. Mem. Am. Chem. Soc., Sigma Xi (assoc.). Office: U Colo Health Scis Dept Pharm PO Box 6511 MS8303 Aurora CO 80045

CHURCHILL, MELVYN ROWEN, chemistry professor; b. London, June 2, 1940; arrived in US, 1964; s. Charles Rowen and Irene Lucy (Elms) Churchill; m. Charlotte Elizabeth Simmons, July 10, 1966; m. Gayle Frances Nason, July 12, 2003; children: Ronald Rowen, David George. BSc, U. London, 1961, PhD, 1964. Instr. chemistry Harvard U., Cambridge, Mass., 1964—67, asst. prof., 1967—70, assoc. prof., 1970—71; prof. U. Ill., Chgo., 1971—75, SUNY, Buffalo, 1975—. Acting dept. chmn. SUNY, Buffalo, 1981—82, Buffalo, 1991—92; assoc. prof. U. Louis Pasteur, Strasbourg, France, 1982. Assoc. editor: Inorganic Chemistry, 1970—82, mem. editl. bd.: Jour. Chem. Crystallography, 1988—; contbr. articles to profl. jours. Fellow, Alfred P. Sloan Found., 1968—70; grantee, NSF, 1965, 1968, 1970, 1972, 1974, 1976, 1977, 1979, 1980. Mem.: Royal Soc. Chemistry (Corday-Morgan medal 1976), NY Acad. Sci., Internat. Gilbert and Sullivan Assn. (sec.-treas. Opera-Lytes), Am. Crystallographic Assn., Am. Chem. Soc. (Schoellkopf medal 2000), Buffalo Choral Arts Soc. United Ch. Of Christ. Home: 670 Lebrun Rd Buffalo NY 14226-4221 Office: SUNY Chemistry Dept Buffalo NY 14260-3000 Office Phone: 716-645-6800 2155. Business E-Mail: chexray@buffalo.edu.

CHURCHILL, ROBERT WILSON, state legislator, lawyer; b. Waukegan, Ill., Apr. 10, 1947; s. George Oliver and Helga C. (Carlson) Churchill; children: Abigail Lee, Julia Aubrey, Christine Lizbeth. BA, Northwestern U., Evanston, Ill., 1969; JD, U. Iowa, 1972. Pres., sr. ptnr. Churchill, Quinn, Richtman & Hamilton Ltd., Grayslake, Ill., 1972—; trustee Lake Villa Twp., Ill., 1981-83; mem. Ill. Ho. Reps., 1983-99, 2003—07; minority whip Ill. Gen. Assembly, 1987-89, asst. minority leader, 1989-91, dep. minority leader, 1991-94, 97-99; majority leader, 1995-97; chmn. Rep. Ctrl. Com. Lake County, Ill., 1990-94. Co-chmn. Ill.

Econ. and Fiscal Commn., Springfield, 1991-95, Space Needs Commn., 1997-99; mem. Ill. Prisoner Review Bd., 1999-2001; chief counsel, dir. legis. Ill. Ho. Reps., 2001-02. Del. Rep. Nat. Conv., 1980, 1992, 1996, 2004, alt. del., 1984. Mem. ABA, Lake County Bar Assn., Lake Villa Lions. Republican.

CHURCHILL, STUART WINSTON, chemical engineering educator; b. Imlay City, Mich., June 13, 1920; s. Howard Heenan and Faye Erma (Shurte) C.; m. Donna Belle Lewis, Feb. 22, 1946 (div.); children: Stuart Lewis, Diana Gail, Cathy Marie, Emily Elizabeth; m. Renate Ursula Treibmann, Aug. 3, 1974. BS in Math, U. Mich., 1942, BSChemE, 1942, MS, 1948, PhD, 1952; MA (hon.), U. Pa., 1972. Technologist Shell Oil Co., 1942-46; tech. supr. Frontier Chem. Co., 1946-47; mem. faculty U. Mich., 1949-67, prof. chem. engring., 1957-67, chmn. dept. chem. and metall. engring., 1962-67; mem. faculty U. Pa., 1967—, Carl V.S. Patterson prof. chem. engring., 1967-90, Carl V.S. Patterson prof. emeritus, 1990—; chmn. region 2 edn. and accreditation com. Engrs. Council Profl. Devel., 1961-65, mem. nat. council, 1965-71, exec. com., 1968-71; mem. bd. trustees Chemical Heritage Found., 1983-99, mem. bd. dirs., 1999-2001, mem. fin. com., 1987-2001. Cons. heat transfer and combustion. Recipient S. Reid Warren, Jr. award for disting. tchg. U. Pa., 1976, Max Jakob Meml. award for heat transfer ASME/Am. Inst. Chem. Engrs., 1979, medal for disting. achievement U. Pa., 1993, Alumni Merit award U. MIch., 2002; Japan Soc. for Promotion of Sci. grantee, 1977. Fellow AIChE (nat. coun. 1962-64, pres. 1966, Profl. Progress award 1964, William H. Walker award 1969, Warren K. Lewis award 1978, Founders award 1980, eminent chmn. engr. Diamond Jubilee 1983, heat transfer and energy conversion divsn. award 1997, inst. lectr. 1998); mem. Nat. Acad. Engring. (Founders award 2002), Combustion Inst., Am. Chem. Soc., Am. Soc. for Engring. Edn. (Corcoran award for best paper 1993), Verein Deutscher Ingenieure (corr. mem.), Sigma Xi, Phi Kappa Phi, Phi Lambda Upsilon (award U. Mich. chpt. 1961), Tau Beta Pi. Unitarian Universalist. Home: 137 Pole Cat Rd Glen Mills PA 19342-1301 Office Phone: 215-898-5579. Business E-Mail: churchil@seas.upenn.edu.

CHURCHILL, WARD L., social sciences educator, advocate; b. Urbana, Ill., Oct. 2, 1947; s. Jack Churchill and Maralyn L. (Allen) Debo; m. Leah R. Kelly, Aug. 8, 1995; 1 child, Jasmine Ann; m. Natsu Saito AA, Ill. Ctrl. Coll., 1972; BA, Sangamon State U., 1974, MA, 1975; LHD (hon.), Alfred U., 1992. Program dir. Boulder Valley Sch. Dist., Boulder, 1977-78, U. Colo., Boulder, 1978-90, assoc. prof., 1991-97, full prof., 1997—, chmn., Dept. Ethnic Studies, 1997—2005. Vis. prof. Alfred U., N.Y., 1990-91. Author: Pacifism as Pathology: Reflections on the Role of Armed Struggle, 1986, Struggle for the Land: Indigenous Resistance to Genocide, Ecocide and Expropriation in Contemporary North America, 1993, Indians Are Us?: Culture and Genocide in Native North America, 1994, Since Predator Came: Notes on the Struggle for American Indian Liberation, 1995, From a Native Son: Selected Essays in Indigenism, 1985-1995, 1996, A Little Matter of Genocide: Holocaust and Denial in the Americas 1492 to the Present, 1997, Fantasies of the Master Race: Literature, Cinema and the Colonization of American Indians, 1998, Struggle for the Land: North American Resistance to Genocide, Ecocide, and Colonization, 2002, Acts of Rebellion: The Ward Churchill Reader, 2002, Life in Occupied America, 2003, On the Justice of Roosting Chickens: Reflections on the Consequences on U.S. Imperial Arrogance and Criminality, 2003, Kill the Indian, Save the Man: The Genocidal Impact of American Indian Residential Schools, 2004; co-author (with Jim VanderWall) Agents of Repression: The FBI's Secret Wars Against the Black Panther Party and the American Indian Movement, 1988, The COINTELPRO Papers: Documents from the FBI's Secret War Against Domestic Dissent, 1991; editor: New Studies on the Left, 1987-94; contbg. editor: Z Magazine, 1987—, Issues in Radical Therapy, 1982-87, Dark Night Field Notes, 1992—. Mem. governing coun. Colo. AIM, Denver, 1993—, co-dir., 1982-93; comms. dir. Am. Indian Anti-Defamation Coun., Denver, 1992-94; mem. steering com. Yellow Thunder Camp, Rapid City, S.D., 1981-85. Recipient Gustavus Myers award in writing Gustavus Myers Ctr., 1984. Avocation: films. Office: U Colo Dept Ethnic Studies Ketchum 30 Campus Pass 339 Boulder CO 80309

CHURCHMAN, MICHAEL STEELE BRIGHT, educational consultant, educator; b. Indpls., Mar. 9, 1929; s. M. Steele and Luita Curtis Churchman; m. Jean Virginia Wood, Apr. 28, 1951; children: Jean Wood, Julia Churchman McCue, Diana Churchman Mason. BA, Wesleyan U, 1950; MA, U Mo., 1958; EdM, Harvard U, 1964. Tchr. The Barstow Sch., Kansas City, Mo., 1955—64; headmaster The Kent Sch., Denver, 1964—74, St. Catherine's, Richmond, Va., 1974—79, The Barstow Sch., 1979—85; dir. external affairs The Nelson-Atkins Mus. of Art, Kansas City, Mo., 1985—96, cons., 1996—. Trustee The Barstow Sch., Kansas City, Mo., 1999—2005, St. Paul's Episcopal Sch., Kansas City, Mo., 1994—2000, Episcopal Social Svcs., Kansas City, Mo., 2000—04. Author: The Kent Sch. 1922-1972, 1972, High Ideals and Aspirations: The Nelson-Atkins Museum of Art, 1993. Democrat. Episcopalian. Office: The Nelson Gallery Found 4525 Oak St Kansas City MO 64111 Office Phone: 816-751-1283. Business E-Mail: mchurchman@nelson-atkins.org.

CHURCHWELL, EDWARD BRUCE, astronomer, educator; b. Sylva, NC, July 9, 1940; s. Doris L. Churchwell; m. Dorothy S. Churchwell, June 24, 1964; children: Steven T., Beth M. BS, Earlham Coll., 1963; PhD, Ind. U., 1970. NASA fellow Ind. U., Bloomington, 1963; postdoctoral fellow Nat. Radio Astronomy Obs., Charlottesville, Va., 1970; Heinrich Hertz postdoctoral fellow Max Planck Inst. Radioastronomie, Bonn, Germany, 1970-72, staff scientist, 1972-77; asst. prof. U. Wis., Madison, 1977-79, assoc. prof., 1979-83, prof., 1983—, Alfred E. Whitford prof. astronomy, 2002—. Fellow NASA, 1985, Fulbright Rsch., 1988—89. Mem.: Internat. Astron. Union, Am. Astron. Soc. Office: U Wis Washburn Observatory 475 N Charter St Madison WI 53706-1582 E-mail: churchwell@astro.wisc.edu.

CHURGIN, AMY, publishing executive; Assoc. pub. Seventeen Mag., 1992—94; Pub. K III Mag. Corp. (now Primedia Corp.-NY Mag.), NYC, 1994—99; group pub., NY, Chgo. Automobile Mag., 1999; v.p., pub. Archtl. Digest, Condé Nast, LA, 1999—. Organizer Architecture Days. Office: Architectural Digest Condé Nast 6300 Wilshire Blvd Ste 1100 Los Angeles CA 90048-9083

CHUSED, RICHARD HARRIS, law educator; b. St. Louis, Jan. 31, 1943; s. Joseph and Marie Irene (Steinberg) C.; m. Elizabeth Langer, May 11, 1974; children: Benjamin Langer Chused, Samuel Chused Langer. BA, Brown U., 1965; JD, U. Chgo., 1968. Asst. prof. Sch. of Law, Rutgers U., Newark, 1968-71, assoc. prof., 1971-73, Georgetown U. Law Ctr., Washington, 1973-85, prof., 1985—. Author: Modern Approach to Property, 1978, Cases, Materials and Problems in Property, 1988, 2d edit., 1999, A Property Anthology, 1993, 2nd edit., 1997, Private Acts in Public Places: A Social History of Divorce in the Formative Era of American Family Law, 1994, A Copyright Anthology: The Technology Frontier, 1998; topic and comments editor U. Chgo. Law Rev., 1967-68; contbr. numerous articles to profl. jours. Bowman C. Lingle fellow, 1966-67; Brown U. Nat. Honor scholar, 1965-68, Fulbright scholar Hebrew U. Jerusalem, 2004-05. Mem. Soc. Am. Law Tchrs. (bd. govs. 1983-94), Am. Soc. Legal History, Am. Hist. Assn. Democrat. Jewish. Home: 3712 Ingomar St NW Washington DC 20015-1820 Office: Georgetown U Law Ctr 600 New Jersey Ave NW Washington DC 20001-2022 E-mail: chused@law.georgetown.edu.

CHUSID, MARTIN, musicologist, educator; b. Bklyn., Aug. 19, 1925; s. Jacob Chusid and Florence (Bakst) Weinberg; m. Anita Beverly Feinglass, Apr. 30, 1952; 1 child, Jeffrey Mark. BA, U. Calif., Berkeley, 1950, MA, 1955, PhD, 1961; DHL (hon.), Centre Coll., Ky., 1977. Assoc. in music, U. Calif., Berkeley, 1955-57; instr. music U. So. Calif., LA, 1959-62, asst. prof., 1962-63; assoc. prof. NYU, 1963-68, prof., 1968—, dir. Am. Inst. for Verdi Studies, 1976—2007, acting chmn. dept. music, 1966-67, 81, 86-87, chmn., 1967-70, assoc. dean Grad. Sch. Arts and Scis., 1970-72; vis. prof. Boston U., 1975, U. BC, 1979, So. Meth. U., 1980, Princeton U., 1981, Brigham Young U., 1982. Author: A Catalog of Verdi's Operas, 1974; author, editor: Schubert's Unfinished Symphony, 1968, 2d edit., 1971, Franz Schubert's Schwanengesang, A Companion to Schubert's Schwanengesang, 2000; editor: (music) Schubert's String Quintets, 1971, String Quartets, I, 1978, Verdi's Rigoletto, 1983; (with William Weaver) The Verdi Companion, 1979, Verdi's Middle Period, 1997; assoc. editor Coll. Music Symposium, 1967-71; mem. edit. bd. Works of Giuseppe Verdi, 1979—; contbr. articles to profl. jours. Am. Council Learned Socs. fellow, 1966, 69, 72, 74; NEH grantee, 1977-81, Martha Baird Rockefeller Music Fund grantee, 1976-83, Ford Found. grantee, 1979-83. Mem. Am. Musicol. Soc. (chmn. So. Calif. chpt. 1961-63), Am. Inst. Verdi Studies, Am. Schubert Inst. Office: NYU Dept Music 24 Waverly Pl New York NY 10003-6757 Office Phone: 212-998-8305. Business E-Mail: mc4@nyu.edu.

CHUTE, MARY L., library director; BA in art history, U. Mich.; MA in art history, Boston U.; MLS, Simmons Coll. With Mass. Libr. Sys.; pub. libr. cons. divsn. of devel. Md. State Dept. Edn., 1997—99; dir. and state libr. Del. Divsn. Libr./State Libr., 1999—2002; dep. dir. libr. services The Inst. Mus. & Library Services, Washington, 2002—, acting dir., 2005—06. Office: Inst Mus & Library Services 1800 M St NW 9th Fl Washington DC 20036 Office Phone: 202-653-4774.

CHUTORIAN, ABE M., pediatrician, educator; b. Winnipeg, Man., Can., Feb. 8, 1929; s. Morris and Rose (Cohen) C.; m. Helen Carol Olasker, Sept. 2, 1951; children: Leslie, Sandra, Tracy. MA, U. Man., 1952, MD, BSc, U. Man., 1957. Diplomate Am. Bd. Pediatrics, Neurology. Intern Winnipeg Gen. Hosp., 1957-58; resident L.A. Children's Hosp., 1958-60; from fellow of neurology to prof. pediatrics and neurology Columbia U., NYC, 1960-90; prof. pediats. and neurology Cornell U. NY Presbyn. Hosp., 1990—, chief dept. pediatric neurology, 1990—2004. Adv. bd. Riverdale Mental Health, NY, 1985—. Mem. editl. bd. Pediatric Neurology Jour., 1992—; assoc. editor ACTA Neuropediatrica, 1996—; contbr. chpts. in books, articles and abstracts to profl. jours. Fellow Am. Acad. Pediatrics, Am. Acad. Neurology; mem. AMA, Am. Neurol. Assn., Internat. Chile Neurol. Soc., Child Neurology Soc., NY State Med. Soc., NY County Med. Soc. Avocations: chess, opera, ballet, cinema, travel. Office: 6th Fl 654 Madison Ave New York NY 10021 Office Phone: 212-750-2800. E-mail: chutorian@rcou.com.

CHVETSOV, ALEXEI V., medical physicist, educator; b. Tashkent, Uzbekistan, Apr. 9, 1961; arrived in U.S., 2002; MSc, Moscow Engring. Physics Inst., 1985, PhD, 1992. Cert. radiation expert Ohio, Am. Bd. Radiology. Assoc. med. physicist Tom Baker Cancer Ctr., Calgary, Alberta, Canada, 1998—2002; asst. prof. Case Western Res. U., Cleve, 2002—. Contbr. articles to profl. jours., chpts. to books. Fellow, German Acad. Exch. Svc., 1992—93. Mem.: Can. Orgn. Med. Physicists (cert.), Am. Assn. Physicists in Medicine. Achievements include research in adaptive numerical methods, stability of numerical algorithms; inverse problems in radiation therapy, inverse treatment planning. Office: Case Western Res U 11100 Euclid Ave Lerner Tower B-181 Cleveland OH 44106 Home Phone: 216-752-0399; Office Phone: 216-844-2520. Office Fax: 216-844-2005. Business E-Mail: alexei.chvetsov@case.edu.

CHWAST, SEYMOUR, graphic artist; b. NYC, Aug. 18, 1931; Student, Cooper Union Sch., NYC; PhD (hon.), Parsons Sch. Design, 1992. Co-founder Push Pin Studios, 1954; dir., pres. The Pushpin Group Inc. Instr. Parsons Sch. of Design. One-man exhbns. include Royal Palm Gallery, Palm Beach, Fla., 1982, Galerie Delpire, Paris, 1974, Gutenburg Mus., Mainz, Germany, 1984, 35 yr. retrospective exhibition Cooper Union, 1986, Jack Gallery, N.Y., 1987, Mus. of Art, Sao Paulo, Brazil, 1989, Lustrare Gallery, N.Y., 1991, Ginza Graphic Gallery, Tokyo, 1992, Kunstschalter Gallery, N.Y.C., 1994, Sch. of Visual Arts Master Series, 1997, Warsaw Poster Mus., 2000; various group shows; work in permanent collections Mus. Modern Art, N.Y.C., Library of Congress, Washington, Met. Mus. Art, N.Y.C., Whitney Mus. Am. Art, N.Y. Recipient numerous awards including Saint-Gaudens medal, 1972; named to Art Dir.'s Hall of Fame, 1984. Mem. Am. Inst. Graphic Artists (former v.p., medal 1986), Art Dirs.' Club (v.p.), Alliance Graphique Internationale. Office: Pushpin Group 55 E 9th St Ste 1G New York NY 10003-3111 Office Phone: 212-529-7590. E-mail: seymour@pushpininc.com.

CHYBA, MONIQUE, mathematics professor; b. Geneva, Oct. 31, 1969; d. Miroslav and Jana Chyba; m. Iskandar Rabeendran; children: Amandin Thin Chyba Rabeendran, Mandarine Thin Chyba Rabeendran. BA in Civil Engring., ETS Geneva, 1989; PhD, U. Geneva, 1997; postgrad., U. Princeton, NJ. Assoc. prof. U. Hawaii, 2002—. Vis. asst. prof. U. Santa Cruz, Calif., 2000—02; project head Robo-Nemo; head STOMP Hawaii. Co-author (with Bernard Bonnard): The Role of Singular Trajectories in Control Theory, 2003; contbr. articles to profl. jours. Grantee, NSF, divsn. math scis., 2003—06, 2006—. Mem.: Assn. Women in Math., Am. Math. Assn. Achievements include research in geometric control for mechanical systems, application to underwater vehicles; development of outreach education program for young children to promote sciences. Office: University of Hawaii 2565 Mc Carthy Mall Honolulu HI 96822 Office Phone: 808-956-8464.

CHYLINSKI-POLUBINSKI, ROGER, academic administrator; b. Fairfield County, Conn., Dec. 7, 1945; s. Reginald Hillary and Susan Marie (Constantino de Cicco) C.-P. AOS, Culinary Inst. Am., 1965; AS in Bus. Adminstrn., Johnson and Wales U., 1967; BS in Bus. Mgmt., U. Balt., 1968, MBA in Mgmt., 1976; MBA in Mktg., Morgan State U., 1978. Cert. exec. chef, culinary educator. Instr. bus. adminstrn. Harbor Campus CC Balt., 1969—72, dir. hospitality mgmt. programs, 1972—87; exec. dir. Balt. Internat. Culinary Arts Inst., 1975—85; pres. Balt. Internat. Culinary Coll., 1985—. Founder L'ecole Restaurant, L'ecole Foods, L'ecole Catering. Trustee Am. Culinary Fedn. Ednl. Inst., 1983, chmn. accreditation commn., 1985-88, vice chmn., 1987-89. Recipient Outstanding Leadership award Culinary Fedn. Ednl. Inst., 1987. Mem. Am. Culinary Fedn. (cert. exec. chef, cert. culinary educator), Nat. Restaurant Assn., Internat. Assn. Cooking Profls., Profl. Chef's Assn., Chesapeake and Potomac Assn. Pvt. Schs. (chmn. scholarship com. 1982). Home: 529 Dunkirk Rd Baltimore MD 21212-2014*

CHYNOWETH, ALAN GERALD, retired telecommunications industry executive; b. Harrow, Eng., Nov. 18, 1927; came to U.S. 1952; s. James Charles and Marjorie (Fairhurst) C.; m. Betty Freda Edith Boyce, Sept. 22, 1950; children: Trevor Alan, Kevin Ray. BS in physics, U. London Kings Coll., 1948, PhD, 1950. Demonstrator U. London Kings Coll., 1948-50; postdoctoral fellow NRC, Ottawa, 1950-52; mem. tech. staff Bell Labs., Murray Hill, NJ, 1953-60, dept. head, 1960-65, dir., 1965-76, exec. dir., 1976-83; v.p. applied rsch. Bellcore, Morristown, NJ, 1984-92; cons. R/D Strategy and Mgmt., 1993—. Mem. vis. com. Cornell U. Materials Sci. Ctr., 1973-76; cons. advanced study inst. and rsch. workshops com. NATO, Brussels, 1982-90; lectr. Electrochem. Soc., 1983; alt. dir. Microelectronics and Computer Tech. Corp., Austin, Tex., 1984-92; mem. The Conf. Bd. Internat. Coun. on Mgmt. of Innovation and Tech., 1990-97, mgr., 1995; dir. Optoelectronic Industry Devel. Assn., 1991-92; mem. adv. bd. dept. elec. engring. and computer sci. U. Calif., Berkeley, 1987-93; mem. natural sci. adv. bd. U. Pa., 1988-93; mem. adv. bd. dept. elec. engring. U. So. Calif., 1988-93; mem. Indsl. Rsch. Inst., 1980-92, dir., 1990-92, emeritus, 1993—; mem. indsl. and profl. adv. coun. elec. engring. dept. Pa. State U., 1993-98, chmn., 1995; mem. adv. task force on U.S. indsl. competitiveness U.S. Ho. of Reps., 1987; cons. European Commn. Telecom. Directorate, 1995; advisor to panel on high performance computing and comm. Office Sci. and Tech. Policy, The White House, 1991-92. Assoc. editor Solid State Communications, 1975-83; co-editor: Optical Fiber Telecommunications, 1979; contbr. articles to profl. jours.; patentee in field. Mem. Am. Mgmt. Assn. R&D Coun., 1989-93; chmn. tech. transfer merit program N.J. Commn. on Sci. and Tech., 1992-98. Fellow IEEE (chmn. device rsch. conf. 1963, com. on US competitiveness 1988-89, bd. adv. task force on new initiatives 1989-90, chmn. Marconi award com. 1987, Alexander Graham Bell prize com. 1990-94, chmn. 1992-94, Frederik Philips award com. 1998-02, W.R.G. Baker prize, 1967, Frederik Philips award 1992, engring. leadership recognition 1996, corp. recognition award com. 1999-2003, chmn. 2001-02, awards bd. and policies and planning com. 2003-05, chmn. corp. recognitions coun. 2005-07), Am. Phys. Soc. (indsl. affiliates com. 1984-87, editl. bd. Physics Today 1985-88, George E. Pake prize 1992), Inst. Physics and Phys. Soc. (London), Internat. Engring. Consortium; mem. NRC (survey dir. com. on survey of materials sci. and engring. 1970-74, panel chmn. com. on mineral resources and environ. 1973-75, panel chmn. materials sci. engring. study com. 1986-88, nat. materials adv. bd. 1976-80), Metall. Soc. AIME (chmn. John Bardeen prize com. 1993-95), Materials Rsch. Soc., NY Acad. Scis. Avocations: travel, boating. Home: 6 Londonderry Way Summit NJ 07901-2914 also: 17 Mill Close Fishbourne Chichester West Sussex PO19 3JW England Office: Telcordia Techs One Telcordia Dr Piscataway NJ 08854-4182 Personal E-mail: algchy@aol.com.

CHYTIL, FRANK, biochemist; b. Prague, Czechoslovakia, Aug. 28, 1924; came to U.S., 1965, naturalized, 1971; s. Frantisek and Ruzena (Vitouskova) C.; m. Lucie Scheinost, Nov. 26, 1949; children: Frank, Anna, Helena. MS, Sch. Chem. Tech., Prague, 1949, PhD, 1952; C.Sc., Czechoslovak Acad. Sci., Prague, 1956. Rsch. biochemist Charles U., Prague, 1949-51; rsch. fellow Inst. Human Rsch., Prague, 1952-63; sr. scientist Czechoslovak Acad. Sci., Prague, 1956-64; sr. rsch. fellow Brandeis U., Waltham, Mass., 1964, sr. rsch. assoc., 1965-66; head sect. enzymology S.W. Found. Rsch. and Edn., San Antonio, 1966-69; mem. faculty Vanderbilt U., 1969—2000, prof. biochemistry, 1975—2000, Gen. Foods Disting. prof. nutrition, 1984-89, Harvie Branscomb disting. prof., 1993-94, prof. emeritus, 2000—. Adj. assoc. prof. U. Tex., San Antonio, 1968—2000. Editor: Vitamins and Hormones, 1983; mem. editl. bd. Analytical Biochemistry, 1980-87, Jour. Biol. Chemistry, 1982-88, 96-99, Am. Jour. Clin. Nutrition, 1993-95; contbr. articles to profl. jours. Recipient Osborne-Mendel and Lederle awards; USPHS grantee, 1967-99. Fellow Am. Soc. Nutritional Scis.; mem. Am. Soc. Biochemistry and Molecular Biology, Endocrine Soc., Sigma Xi. Home: 914 Lynnwood Blvd Nashville TN 37205-4527 Office: Vanderbilt U Sch Medicine Dept Biochemistry Nashville TN 37232-0146 Personal E-mail: frank.chytil@comcast.net.

CI, LIJIE, materials scientist; s. Xingcheng Ci and Yulan Pan; m. He Kang, Nov. 31, 2000; 1 child, Caleb. BS, Shangdong U., China, 1994; PhD, Tsinghua U., Beijing, 2000. Rsch. assoc. Physics Inst., Chinese Acad. Sci., Beijing, 2001—03; K.C. Wong/CNRS rsch. assoc. Ecole Centrale Paris, Chatenay-Malabry, France, 2003—04; rsch. assoc. Max-Planck Inst. Metal Rsch., Stuttgart, Germany, 2004—05, Rensselaer Poly. Inst., Troy, NY, 2005—. Contbr. articles to profl. jours. Fellow, Alexander von Humboldt Found.,Germany, 2004. Mem.: Materials Rsch. Soc. (assoc.), Alexander von Humboldt Assn. Am. (assoc.), Sigma Xi (assoc.). Achievements include patents for carbon nanotubes. Office: Rensselaer Polytechnic Inst 110 8th St Troy NY 12180 Office Phone: 518-276-6541. Business E-Mail: cil@rpi.edu.

CIALKOWSKI, DAVID MICHAEL, lawyer; b. South Holland, Ill., Feb. 22, 1973; BA cum laude, U. Ill., 1995; JD, U. Ill. Coll. Law, 1998. Bar: Ill. 1998, Minn. 2000. Assoc. Zimmerman Reed, P.L.L.P., Mpls., 2001—. Contbr. articles to profl. publs. Named a Rising Star, Minn. Super Lawyers mag., 2006. Mem.: ABA, Minn. State Bar Assn., Hennepin County Bar Assn., Phi Beta Kappa. Office: Zimmerman Reed PLLP 651 Nicollet Mall Ste 501 Minneapolis MN 55402 Office Phone: 612-341-0440. E-mail: dmc@zimmreed.com.*

CIAMPAGLIO, JEFF WILLIAM, sculptor; b. NYC, July 6, 1968; s. Joseph Anthony and Pauline Elizabeth (Bartels) C. Diploma, Calvert Hall Coll., 1987; BA in Art and Comms., Towson State U., 1992; postgrad., U. Md. Balt. County, 1998—. Tchr. Great Bay Sch., Dover, N.H., 1992-93; counselor Jewish Family Svcs., Park Heights, Md., 1993-95; foreman Finishing Touch Painting, Balt., 1995-97. Tutor Towson State U., 1996—; tchr. painting, Balt., 1996—. Artist: (sculptures) Circle of Life, 1992 (grant 1992), untitled piece for Towson U. campus, 1992 (scholarship 1992), other untitled works, 92, 96, (painting) Light House, 1993, others. Grantee Towson State U., 1992; recipient Jack F. Tolbert scholarship Towson U., 1992, Wood Guild award Wood Guild Soc. of Md., 1992. Democrat. Roman Catholic. Avocations: tai chi, Kung Fu, drawing, exercising.

CIANCIMINO, JOSEPH ANDREW, data processing executive; b. Austin, June 30, 1965; s. Joseph Ciancimino and Helen Kay Barbier; m. Melissa Kay McMahan, Mar. 7, 1989. Student aid North Harris Coll., Houston, 1985—86; mgr. Comics & Cards, 1988—96; pvt. practice Spring, 1989—2001; with Altech Computers/Metals, Houston, 1996—97; telecomm. World Datacom, 1997—99; instr. North Harris Coll., 1999—2001; data comm. World Datacom, 2002—04; web server tech. EVIServers, 2004—06; sys. adminstr. hostgator, 2006—; pvt. practice, 2007—. Home: 22033 Jay Dr Spring TX 77373 Office Phone: 832-467-0307. E-mail: ciancimino@gmail.com.

CIANI, ALFRED JOSEPH, dean; b. NYC, June 29, 1946; s. Joseph Alfred and Aurora Smiles (VanOver) C.; m. Sharon Skolkey, Aug. 16, 1968 (div. 1979); children: Mieke Jo, Gabriel Wolf; m. Lesley Lockwood, Aug. 9, 1980; children: Joseph Alfred, Clinton Lockwood. BA, U. Albany, 1969; MA, Coll. of St. Rose, 1972; EdD, Ind. U., 1974. Tchr. Greater Amsterdam Schs., NY, 1969—72; rsch. asst. Ind. U., Bloomington, 1972—73, assoc. instr., 1973—74; vis. prof. U. Wis., Milw., 1980; asst. prof. U. Cin., 1974—79, assoc. prof., 1979—2002, assoc. dean, info. officer, 1988—2003, prof. emeritus, 2003—. Pres. Ohio Internat. Reading Assn., Columbus, 1981-82; outside cons. State of Miss., Jackson, 1982-84, State of Ky., 1996-99, State of W.Va., 1972-74, 97-98, City of N.Y. Pub. Schs.; cons., U. Oreg. Profl. Devel., Eugene, 1979-80, Nashville Schs., 1982-83, State of W.Va., N.Y.C. Pub. Schs.; mem. Dean's Cabinet; mem. Urban Schs. Task Force. Author: Motivating Reluctant Readers, 1981; editor: (book series) Reading in Content Areas, 1979-81; rev. editor: Rsch. in Mid. Level Edn., 1995—. Grantee Ford Found., 1990, IBM, 1990. Mem. AAUP, Internat. Reading Assn., Am. Ednl. Rsch. Assn. (nat. coms.), Assn. Tchr. Educators (nat. coms.), Nat. Coun. Tchrs. English (nat. coms.), , Nat. Mid. Sch. Assn. (nat. coms.), Nat. Reading Coun., Phi Delta Kappa, Kappa Delta Pi (counselor). Democrat. Roman Catholic. Avocations: reading, walking. Office: U Cin Mail Location 02 Cincinnati OH 45221-0001 E-mail: alfred.ciani@uc.edu.

CIANNELLA, JOEEN MOORE, small business owner; b. Warren, Ohio, Mar. 20, 1948; d. Joseph Alvie and Elizabeth Dorthea Moore; m. Christopher M. Ciannella, July 31, 1976 (div. Jan. 1987); children: Bryce C., Tara E. BA in French, Denison U., 1970. Profl. staff US Senate Rep. Policy Com., Washington, 1971-75; owner Jo Moore-Sophisticated Country, Park Ridge, NJ, 1984—; dist. dir. Congresswoman Marge Roukema US Ho. Reps., Ridgewood, NJ, 1985—2002; exec. dir. Hermitage Mus.,

Hohokus, NJ, 2003—04; dir. devel. Helen Hayes Theatre Co., Nyack, NY, 2004—05; dir. external affairs Greater North Jersey chpt. Nat. Multiple Sclerosis Soc., Paramus, NJ, 2005; pres. JTB Enterprises, LLC, Park Ridge, NJ. Mem. Nat. coun. Boy Scouts Am., 1995—98; trustee Greater Roles and Opportunities for Women NJ GOP, 1997—2002; mem. Park Ridge Bd. Health, 1984—86; founding mem. Pioneer Women Bergen County, 1992—; mem. exec. bd. Bergen coun. Boy Scouts Am., 1991—98, co-chair Pascak Valley Dist. Lunchoree, 1991—92, chair spl. events fin., 1993—94, mem. exec. com., 1993—98, vice chmn. fin., 1995—98, mem. exec. bd. No. NJ coun., 1999—, vice chair fin., 2000—02; mem. exec. bd. Ramapo Coll. Found., 1991—, theme chairperson fundraiser, 1991—94, disting. citizen dinner com., 1991—, mem. bus. network com., 1994—97, chmn. pub. rels. and mktg. com., 1996—2000, mem. exec. com., 1996—, chmn. mktg./instl. rels., 2000—; com. mem. NJ Network Found. Gala, 2000—02; bd. dirs. Helen Hayes Theater Co., Nyack, NY, 2001—, mem. devel. com. spl. events, 2002—, Day in the Garden, 2003; chairperson spl. effects West Bergen Mental Health 40th Anniversary Ruby Ball, 2003; founding mem. W. Bergen Mental Health Found., 2003—; active Bush for Pres. Campaign, 1988, 1992, Dole for Pres. Campaign, 1996; elected mem. Park Ridge County Com., 1983—, mcpl. chairperson, 1986—96; active Bergen County Rep. Com., 1983—, Park Ridge Rep. Orgn., 1983—, v.p., 1988—89; active NE Rep. Orgn. Dist. 39, NJ, 1984—, sec. NJ, 1990—91, treas. NJ, 1991—92, chairperson NJ, 1992—93; ofcl. com. mem. NJ GOP Conv., 1991; charter mem. Women Leadership Summit Rep. Network to Elect Women, 1996—97. Recipient Mission award, Ramapo Coll. Found., 1999, Silver Beaver award, Boy Scouts Am., 1999. Mem.: Jr. League Bergen County (com. mem. Festival of Trees 1988), Ridgewood Unit Rep. Women, Bergen County Women's Rep. Club, NJ Fedn. Rep. Women, Rep. Women of 90's State NJ, Rotary (mem. com. annual auction Park Ridge chpt. 1990—, chairperson holiday party 1991—). Avocations: gardening, antiques, sports, travel. Home: 34 Spring Valley Rd Park Ridge NJ 07656-1860 Office: JTB Enterprises LLC 34 Spring Valley Rd Park Ridge NJ 07656 Personal E-mail: jciannella@optonline.net.

CIANO-FEDEROFF, LYNDA, psychologist, educator; b. Cambridge, Mass., Oct. 16, 1954; d. John A. Ciano and Doris M. Thorp; m. George W. Federoff, Nov. 29, 1986; 1 child, Taralyn Elizabeth Federoff. BA in Psychology, San Jose State U., 1992, MA in Psychology, 1994; PhD in Psychology, W.Va. U., 1999. Lic. psychologist Pa. Asst. prof. Indiana U. Pa., 1999—2003, assoc. prof., 2003—. Mental health profl. Critical Incident Stress Mgmt., 1999—; mental health cons. Vis. Nurse Assoc.-Hospice Unit, Indiana, 1999—; mem. disaster team, mental health profl. ARC, Indiana, 2000—. Mem.: DAR, APA, Pa. Psychol. Assn., Ea. Psychol. Assn., Assn. Advancement Behavioral Therapy, Soc. Behavioral Medicine, Psi Chi (advisor 2000—). Office: Indiana U Pa 1020 Oakland Ave Indiana PA 15705

CIAO, FREDERICK J., school system administrator, educator; b. Phila. married; 3 children. BA, LaSalle U., 1962; MEd, Temple U., 1965; MA, Villanova U., 1972; PhD, Southwest U., 1990. From tchr. to counselor to dept. chmn. N.E. Cath. High Sch., Phila., 1962-73; vice prin. Archibishop Wood High Sch., Warminster, Pa., 1973-85; prin. Bishop McDevitt H.S., Wyncote, Pa., 1985-93, pres., 1993—2003, Archbishop Wood H.S., Warminster, Pa., 2003—. Mem. adj. faculty St. Agnes Hosp. Nursing Sch., Phila., 1963-71, Spring Garden Coll., Phila., 1971-73, Gwynedd Mercy Coll., Gwynedd Valley, Pa., 1976-84, LaSalle U., 1980—; presentor Nat. Diffusion Network, 1992—. Mem. edn. advisor Phila. Orch., 1993—, Italian Lang. Preservation Found., 1999—. Named Man of the Yr., N.E. Cath. Alumni Assn., 1972, Educator of the Yr., Millay Club, 1986; named to Legion of Honor, Chapel of Four Chaplains, 1980; recipient John Neumann medal St. John Neumann High Sch., 1985. Mem. Nat. Assn. Secondary Sch. Prins., Nat. Cath. Edn. Assn., Nat. Coun. Tchrs. of Maths., Maths. Assn. Am., Nat. Assn. Curriculum Devel., Nat. Coun. for Self Esteem, Mid. States Assn. of Colls. (chair). Office: Archbishop Wood HS 655 York Rd Warminster PA 18974

CIARA, (CIARA PRINCESS HARRIS), R&B performer; b. Austin, TX, Oct. 25, 1985; Singer: (albums) Goodies, 2004, The Evolution, 2006, (songs) 1,2 Step (feat. Missy Elliott), 2004 (BET award, Best Collaboration, Soul Train Lady of Soul award, Best Dance Cut, 2005), Oh feat. Ludacris, 2005 (Vibe award, Best Collaboration, 2005); contbr. vocalist (songs) Lose Control by Missy Elliot, 2005 (MTV Video Music award, Best Hip Hop & Dance Video, Soul Train Lady of Soul award, Best Video, 2005, Grammy award, Best Short Form Music Video, 2006); actor: (films) All You've Got, 2006. Named Sammy Davis Jr. Female Entertainer Yr., Soul Train Awards, 2005, Best New Artist, Soul Train Lady of Soul Awards, 2005; recipient Grammy award for Best Short Form Music Video, 2006. Office: c/o Zomba Label Group 137-139 W 25th St New York NY 10001

CIARKA, AGNIESZKA, internist, researcher; d. Maria and Andrzej Ciarka. MD, Med. U., Warsaw, 2001; MPH, Free U., Brussels, 2004. Rsch. fellow Erasme Hosp., Brussels, 2002—04; internal medicine, cardiology fellow Free U., 2004—. Sec. Assn. Med. Doctors of Polish Origin in Belgium, 2005—07. Contbr. articles to profl. jours. Recipient Young Cardiologist award, Belgian Soc. Cardiology, 2004, Best Poster award, French Soc. Arterial Hypertension, 2005, European Soc. Cardiology, 2006; grantee, Erasme Hosp., 2004. Office: Erasme Hosp 808 Route de Lennik Brussels 1070 Belgium Office Phone: 0032 2 555 31 11. Business E-Mail: aciarka@ulb.ac.be.

CIATTO, FRANK A., lawyer; b. Jersey City, July 25, 1966; BA cum laude, Georgetown U., 1988; JD, Georgetown U. Law Ctr., 1994. CPA NY, 1991; bar: NJ 1994, NY 1995, DC 1995. Auditor Coopers & Lybrand LLP (now PricewaterhouseCoopers LLP), NYC; ptnr., Bus. Trans. Dept. Venable LLP, Washington. Contbr. Bd. gov., Alumni Assn. Georgetown U., Washington, 2003—. Avocation: baseball. Office: Venable LLP 575 7th St NW Washington DC 20004 Office Phone: 202-344-8510. Office Fax: 202-344-8300. Business E-Mail: faciatto@venable.com.

CIBES, WILLIAM JOSEPH, JR., retired academic administrator; b. Newton, Kans., Aug. 25, 1943; s. William Joseph and Dorothy Beulah Cibes; m. Margaret Ann Collins, Sept. 2, 1967; 1 child, Julia Katherine. BA, U. Kans., 1965; PhD, Princeton U., NJ, 1975. Instr. to prof. Conn. Coll., New London, 1969-91; sec. Office of Policy and Mgmt., State of Conn., Hartford, 1991-94; chancellor Conn. State U. System, Hartford, 1994—2006, chancellor emeritus, 2006—. State rep. Conn. Gen. Assembly, Hartford, 1979—91; bd. dirs., treas. Conn.Ctr. for Sci. and Exploration; bd. dirs. Conn. Health and Ednl. Facilities Authority. Mem.: Antiquarian and Landmarks Soc. (bd. dirs.), Conn. Assn. for Human Svcs. (bd. dirs.). Democrat. Roman Catholic. Home Phone: 860-525-4902.

CIBULL, MICHAEL LEE, pathologist, educator; MD, U. Ill., Chgo., 1969—73. Diplomate Am. Bd. Pathology, 1978. Prof. Coll. Medicine U. Ky., Lexington, 1978—. Vice-chair dept. pathology U. Ky, 2004—. Contbr. articles to profl. jours. Fellow: Coll. Am. Pathologists. Home Phone: 859-273-1656.

CICCARONE, DANIEL, medical educator, researcher, physician; b. NYC, Nov. 30, 1961; s. Pat and Joan Ciccarone; life ptnr. Kim Koester; 1 child, Isabel Alaya Koester Ciccarone. MD, SUNY, 1987; MPH, U. Calif., Berkeley, 1998. Bd. cert. Am. Bd. Family Practice, 1992, Am. Bd. Preventive Medicine, 2003. Assoc. prof. dept. family and cmty. medicine, dept. anthropology, history and social medicine U. Calif., San Francisco, 2000—. Contbr. articles to profl. jours. Grantee Career Devel. award, NIH, 2004. Mem.: APHA, Am. Anthrop. Assn. Liberal. Avocation: bicycling. Office: Univ Calif San Francisco 500 Parnassus MU-3E Box 0900 San Francisco CA 94143 Home Phone: 415-285-4433; Office Phone: 415-514-0275. Business E-Mail: ciccaron@fcm.ucsf.edu.

CICCARONE, RICHARD ANTHONY, financial executive; b. Akron, Ohio, June 15, 1952; s. Andrew and Marie Ciccarone; m. Marilyn Douglas DeBorde, May 26, 1984. BA, Miami U., Oxford, Ohio, 1974; MA, U. Akron, 1978. Mcpl. bond analyst Harris Bank, Chgo., 1977-82, mcpl. rsch. mgr., 1982-83; v.p., dir. rsch., sr. analyst Van Kampen Merritt Investment Adv. Corp. (formerly Am. Portfolio), Lisle, Ill., 1983-89; sr. v.p., dir. fixed income rsch. Blunt Ellis & Loewi, Inc., Chgo., 1989-90; exec. v.p., dir. tax exempt fixed income rsch. Everen Securities Inc. (formerly Kemper Securities), Chgo., 1990-96; sr. v.p., co-dir. mcpl. investments, dir. mcpl. rsch., co-head fixed income dept. Van Kampen Inv. Adv. Corp. unit of Morgan Stanley, Oakbrook Terrace, Ill., 1996—2001; pres. Merritt Rsch. Svcs. LLC, Cedar Rapids, Iowa, 2001—; mng. dir. McDonnell Investment Mgmt. LLC, Oakbrook, Ill., 2001—. Publisher MuniNet Guide Review, 1996—. Contbr. articles to profl. jours. and fin. pubs. Mem. exec. com., bd. dirs. Civic Fedn. Chgo.; mem. Village of Hinsdale Plan Commn., 1995-99, Hinsdale Firefighters Pension Fund Bd., 2006—; bd. trustees Village Hinsdale, 1999-2003; co-chair Am. Heart Assn., DuPage County Walkathon, 2000; bd. dirs. Hinsdale Libr. Found., 2003— Named All-Am Mcpl. Analyst (2d team), Global Guaranty, 1990, 91, The Bond Buyer, 1993, All-Am. Mcpls. Analyst, Generalist (2d team), 1993, Institutional Investor Mag., 1992, 94, Mcpl. Analyst Generalist (1st team), Institutional Investor Mag., 1995, 1st Team All-Star Smith's Rsch. and Ratings as Mcpl. Generalist, 1995, 96, 97, 98, 99, 2005, 06, 1st Team All-Star Buyside Mcpl. Rsch. Dir., 1997, 98, 99, 2003, 04 Mem. Nat. Fedn. Mcpl. Analysts (co-founder, nat. chmn. 1984-85, Disting. Svc. award 1988, Standards and Practices chair 1991-92, Long Term Planning Chair 1993-94, govt. acctg. standards adv. coun. 1996-99), Soc. Mcpl. Analysts (pres. 2006), Chgo. Mcpl. Analysts Soc. (pres. 1984), So. Mcpl. Fin. Soc., Miami (Ohio) U. Alumni Assn. (pres. Chgo. chpt. 1988-89), Com. of One Hundred (Hinsdale, Ill., pres. 1998-99), Omicron Delta Kappa Roman Catholic. Home: 733 S Bodin St Hinsdale IL 60521-4316 Office: McDonnell Investment Mgmt LLC 1515 W 22d St 11th Fl Oak Brook IL 60523 Office Phone: 630-684-8697. Business E-Mail: ciccaroner@mcdmgmt.com.

CICCIA, ANGELA HEIN, speech educator, speech pathology/audiology services professional; d. Raymond G. Hein, Jr. and Virginia Flanagan; m. Joseph A. Ciccia, Jr., Sept. 1, 2000; 1 child, Joseph A. III. BA, Case We. Res. U., Cleve., 1996; MA, George Wash. U., Washington, 1998; PhD, Case We. Res. U., Cleve., 2003. Cert. clin. competence Am. Speech-Lang. Hearing Assn., 1999, speech-lang. pathologist Ohio Bd. Speech-Lang. Pathology and Audiology, 1999. Asst. prof. Case We. Res. U., 2003—; consulting speech-lang. pathologist Cleve. Hearing & Speech Ctr., 1999—, dir. program, 2003—. Grantee, Am. Speech-Lang. Hearing Found., 2003—05, 2006—. Mem.: Internal Neuropsychological Assn., Acad. Neurogenic Comm. Disorders (assoc.), Phi Beta Kappa. Democrat. Roman Catholic. Achievements include research in functional magnetic resonance imaging of social cognition in adolescents with and without traumatic brain injury. Avocations: hiking, travel, reading. Office: Case We Res Univ 11206 Euclid Ave Cleveland OH 44106-7154 Home Phone: 216-701-6037; Office Phone: 216-368-5385. Office Fax: 216-368-6078. Business E-Mail: angela.ciccia@case.edu.

CICCOELLA, CHARLES S. (CHICK), federal agency administrator; BS, Auburn U.; MS, Ctrl. Mich. U. Dir. info. tech. policy, senate rules com. U.S. Senate, Washington; dep. asst. sec. for veterans US Dept. of Labor, Washington, acting asst. sec. for veterans employment & training, asst. sec., 2005—. Office: US Dept Labor 200 Constitution Ave NW Rm S1325 Washington DC 20210 Office Phone: 202-693-4700. Office Fax: 202-693-4754. E-mail: ciccolella.charles@dol.gov.

CICCOLO, ANGELA, lawyer; b. Indpls., Aug. 12, 1961; BSFS, Georgetown U., 1983, JD, 1992. Bar: DC 1992, admitted to practice: US Dist. Ct. (DC) 1993. Asst. gen. counsel NAACP, interim gen. counsel, 2005—. Staff mem. Georgetown Internat. Environ. Law Rev., 1990—91, Writing Program Editor, 1991—92. Mem.: Women's Bar Assn., DC Trial Lawyers Assn., Bar Assn. DC. Democrat. Office: NAACP 4805 Mt Hope Dr Fifth Floor Baltimore MD 21215 Office Phone: 410-580-5792.

CICCONE, J. RICHARD, psychiatrist, educator; b. NYC, Mar. 21, 1943; s. Louis and Vilma Olga (Musacchio) C.; m. Natalie A. Caputo, Dec. 9, 1967; children: Regina, Louis, Robert. AB, Columbia U., 1963; MD, U. Pitts., 1968. Diplomate Am. Bd. Psychiatry and Neurology (additional qualifications in forensic psychiatry). Intern Montefiore Hosp., Pitts., 1968-69; USPHS fellow in psychiatry Strong Meml. Hosp., Rochester, NY, 1969-72, asst. resident in psychiatry, 1969-70, assoc. resident in psychiatry, 1970-71, chief resident in psychiatry, 1971-72; instr. U. Rochester, 1971-72, asst. prof. Sch. Medicine, 1974-79, assoc. prof. Sch. Medicine, 1979-89, prof., 1989—, dir. residency edn., 1979-85, dir. psychiatry and law program, 1985—, dir. psychiatry and law fellowship, 1987—, prof. Sch. of Medicine, 1989—. Mem. Gov.'s Task Force to Study Reporting of Crimes at Psychiat. Ctrs., 1985, N.Y. State Commn. Quality Care, 1985-93; chair N.Y. State Med. Records Access Rev. Com., 1987—; vis. prof. U. Siena, Italy, 1994, 95, 97, 98, 2000. Assoc. editor: Bull. Am. Acad. Psychiatry and the Law; contbr. articles to profl. jours.; co-author: The Mental Health Professional and the Legal System, 1991. Served to lt. cmmdr. USN, 1972-74. Fellow Am. Psychiat. Assn. (vice chair coun. on psychiatry and law 1988-93, chair, commn. on jud. action 1993-2000, chair com. pub. policy, litigation and advocacy 2000-02, cons. 2002-04); mem. Genesee Valley Psychiat. Assn. (pres. 1983-85, mem. Issac Ray award com. 2004-05, chmn. 2005—), Am. Acad. Psychiatry and Law (pres. 1986-87), Assn. of Dirs. of Forensic Fellowship Programs (pres. 1992-96). Home: 70 Edgemoor Rd Rochester NY 14618-1206 Office: Strong Meml Hosp 300 Crittenden Blvd Rochester NY 14642-0001

CICCONE, MADONNA LOUISE VERONICA See MADONNA

CICCONI, JAMES WILLIAM, lawyer, telecommunications industry executive; b. Elmira, NY, June 8, 1952; s. Raymond Joseph and Doris Arlene (Strong) Cicconi; m. Patricia Olivia Burgess, Aug. 10, 1974; children: Jill, Sara, Rachel. BA, U. Tex., Austin, 1974; JD, U. Tex. Sch. Law, 1977. Bar: Tex. 1977, DC 1985. Issues dir. Jim Baker for Atty. Gen. campaign, Austin, Tex., 1977-78; adminstrv. asst. to the gov. State of Tex., Austin, 1979-80, gen. counsel to the sec. of state, 1980-81; spl. asst. to the pres., to the chief of staff The White House, Washington, 1981-85; sr. issues adv. Bush-Quayle '88 campaign, Washington, 1987-88; asst. to the pres., dep. chief of staff The White House, Washington, 1989-90; atty. Akin, Gump, Strauss, Hauer & Feld, Washington, 1985—88, ptnr., 1991—98; gen. counsel, exec. v.p. law and govt. affairs AT&T Corp., Washington, 1998—2005; sr. exec. v.p. external & legis. affairs AT&T Inc. (merger of SBC Comm. & AT&T Corp.), San Antonio, 2005—. Issues dir. Bush-Quayle '92 Campaign; dep. dir. strategy Dole-Kemp '96 Campaign; dir. El Paso Electric Co., Am. Coun. Germany; cons. US State Dept.; adv. Bush-Cheney transition. V.p. George Bush Presdl. Libr. Found., Coll. Sta., Tex., 1991—; del. Conf. Security Cooperation Europe (CSCE); mem. Adminstrv. Conf. US, US Reform Observation Panel for UNESCO. Mem. DC Bar Assn., State Bar Tex. Republican. Roman Catholic. Avocations: baseball, tennis. Mailing: AT&T Inc 175 E Houston St PO Box 2933 San Antonio TX 78299-2933*

CICERCHI, ELEANOR ANN TOMB, not-for-profit fundraiser; b. Sayre, Pa., Dec. 11, 1944; d. William Horton and Brinton Elizabeth (Cauffiel) Tomb; m. Robert A. Weskerna, Nov. 19, 1966 (div. Feb. 1981); children: Amy Marie, Robert Campbell; m. Philip J. Cicerchi, July 1982. AB with great distinction, Mt. Holyoke Coll., 1966; MS, New Sch. Social Rsch., 1992. Cert. fundraising exec. Sr. mktg. rep. Group Health Plan, Guttenberg, NJ, 1976-79; dir. comty. rels. Burke Rehab. Ctr., White Plains, NY, 1979-84; exec. dir. Bergen comty. Coll. Fedn., Paramus, NJ, 1984-86; campaign counsel Brakeley John Price Jones, Inc., Stanford, Conn., 1986-88; v.p. instnl. advancement Marymount Coll., Tarrytown, NY, 1988-93; dir. maj. gifts Am. Found. for AIDS Rsch., NYC, 1993-95, chief devel. officer, 1995-96; v.p. devel. and external affairs ORBIS Internat., Inc., NYC, 1996-2000; assoc. v.p. devel. Save the Children, Westport, Conn., 2000—02; dir. devel. The Corning Mus. of Glass, 2002—. Faculty mem. Fundraising Sch., Ctr. Philanthropy, Ind. U., Indpls., 1989—; adj. grad. faculty mem. NYU, N.Y.C., 1990-97, New Sch. for Social Rsch., N.Y.C., 1995—, chmn. PR Group for Vision 2000: The Right to Sight, Geneva, 1998-99; bd. dirs. AMD Alliance, 1999-01; vice chair devel. and membership com. Am. Assn. Mus., 2005-07, chair, 2007—. Author: Raid!, 1978, Anonymous Giving, 1991; co-author: The Earth Shook and the Sky Was Red, 1976, The Flower of the Virginian, 1980; editor: The Architecture of Bergen County, 1991. Bd. dirs., past chmn. Philharmonia Virtuosi, Dobbs Ferry, NY, 1985—2002; v.p. Orch. of the Finger Lakes, 2003—05, pres., 2005—, Dem. Club, River Vale, NJ, 1978—81; bd. dirs., sec. Am. Anorexia-Bulimia Assn., NYC, 1984—99; bd. dirs. Planned Parenthood of the So. Finger Lakes, 2003—. Woodrow Wilson fellow, 1966; Sarah Williston scholar, 1964, Mt. Holyoke scholar, 1963. Mem. Am. Assn. Fundraising Profls. (Greater N.Y. chpt. v.p. 1993-95, Finger Lakes chpt. v.p. 2005—, Finger Lakes chpt. Philanthropist of Yr. 2004), Assn. of Fundraising Profls. (Profl. Fundraiser of Yr., Finger Lakes chpt. 2004), Assn. for Rsch. on Nonprofit Orgns. and Voluntary Action, Phi Beta Kappa. Office: The Corning Museum of Glass One Museum Way Corning NY 14830 Office Phone: 607-974-5683. Business E-Mail: cicerchiet@cmog.org.

CICERO, CARMEN LOUIS, artist, educator; b. Newark, Aug. 14, 1926; s. Carmen and Mae C. BS in Fine Arts Edn., Newark State Coll., 1951; postgrad., Hunter Coll., NYC, 1953; MFA, Montclair State College, 1991. Tchr. elem. sch., Paterson, NJ, 1951-54; tchr. secondary sch. Roselle Park, NJ, 1954-57; prof. Sarah Lawrence Coll., Bronxville, NY, 1959-68, Montclair Coll., NJ, 1969—. Participated in 34 solo exhbns. including various one-man shows New Orleans, 1969-71, N.Y.C., 1971-74, 1982, Los Angeles, 1978, Provincetown, Mass., 1979, 81, groups shows Rome-N.Y. Art Found., Premiere Bienale De Paris, France, Mus. des 20 Jahrunderts, Austria, Roosevelt House, New Delhi, N.Y. World's Fair; represented in permanent collections at 26 Mus., including Fogg Mus., Harvard U., Guggenheim Mus., N.Y.C., Mus. Modern Art, N.Y.C., N.J. State Mus., Trenton, Worcester Mus., Mass., Whitney Mus. Am. Art, N.Y.C., Art Gallery of Toronto, Can., Newark Mus., Larry Aldrich Mus., Conn., Mus. Boymaus Van Beuningen, Holland, Hirschhorn Mus., Washington, Neuberger Mus., Purchase, N.Y., Exeter Acad., N.H., Cornell U., Springfield Mus., Mass., Mint. Mus., Charlotte, N.C., Nat. Mus. Am. Art. Smithsonian Inst., Met. Mus., Long Point Gallery, Mass., June Kelly Gallery, N.Y.C., 6 anns., Whitney Mus. Am. Art. Guggenheim fellow, 1957, 63 Mem. Graham Gallery N.Y.C.

CICERO, FRANK, JR., lawyer; b. Nov. 30, 1935; s. Frank and Mary Cicero; m. Janice Pickett, July 11, 1959; children: Erica, Caroline. AB with hons., Wheaton Coll., 1957; M in Pub. Affairs, Woodrow Wilson Sch. of Pub. & Internat. Affairs, 1962; JD, U. Chgo., 1965. Bar: Ill., U.S. Supreme Ct. 1965, various U.S. Ct. of Appeals and Dist. Cts. Polit. sci. instr. Wheaton Coll., Ill., 1957—58; assoc. Kirkland & Ellis, LLP, Chgo., 1965—70, ptnr., 1970—. Mem. vis. com. U. Chgo. Law Sch., 1971—74, 1996—99, 2003—. lectr., 1989—90, 1991—92; del. 6th Ill. Constl. Conv., 1969—70; mem. Jud. Conf. Civil Rules Adv. Com., 2003—06. Bd. editors: law rev. U. Chgo. Law Rev.; contbr. articles to profl. jours. Recipient Joseph Henry Beale prize, U. Chgo., 1963, Outstanding Young Man award, Evanston Jaycees, 1970. Fellow: Am. Coll. Trial Lawyers; mem.: ABA, Bar Assn. 7th Fed. Cir., Ill. State Bar Assn., Internat. Bar Assn., Saddle and Cycle Club (bd. govs. 1984), Mid-Am. Club (gov. 1981—84), Ventana Canyon Golf Club, Glen View Club, Chgo. Club. Office: Kirkland & Ellis LLP 200 E Randolph Dr Ste 6000 Chicago IL 60601-6636 Office Phone: 312-861-2216.

CICERO, J. DEBORAH, management consultant; b. Pitts., Mar. 24, 1948; d. James Francis and Margaret V. (Wuillmier) H. Diploma, Columbia Sch. Nursing, Pitts., 1969; BSN, La Roche Coll., Pitts., 1987; M in Pub. Mgmt./Healthcare, Carnegie Mellon U., 1988. Cert. med. staff coord., profl. in healthcare quality; RN Pa. Clin. asst. to exec. v.p. Forbes Health System, Pitts., 1983-88; dir. med. staff svcs. Monongahela Valley Hosp., Pitts., 1988-90; quality tracking mgr. Humana, Louisville, 1990-91, regional quality mgmt. dir., 1991-92; sr. cons. MetriCor, Inc., Louisville, 1992-94, mgr. accreditation svcs., 1994-95, HCIA-Sachs, Louisville, 1995-96, sr. quality mgmt. cons., JCAHO liaison, 1996-98; mgr. accreditation svcs. Performance Improvement, 1998-99; dir. accreditation svcs. and performance improvement Soluciant, LLC, 2000—03, PQC Enterprises, LLC, 2003—06; clin. quality program mgr. Allegheny Med. Practice Network, 2006—. Author study guide and publ. newsletter. Mem. Nat. Assn. Med. Staff Svcs., Nat. Assn. for Health Care Quality (study guide task force 1996-99), Ky. Assn. for Healthcare Quality (treas. 1996-99, pres. 2000-02), Am. Hosp. Assn., Pa. Assn. for Healthcare Quality. Avocations: exercising, biking, reading, music. Office: AMPN 366 Grass St Pittsburgh PA 15224 Office Phone: 412-578-6844. Personal E-mail: dcicero@wpahs.org.

CICERONE, RALPH JOHN, foundation administrator, research scientist; b. New Castle, Pa., May 2, 1943; m. Carol Cicerone; 1 child, Sara. SB, MIT, 1965; MS in Elec. Engring. and Physics, U. Ill., Urbana-Champaign, 1967, PhD in Elec. Engring. and Physics, 1970. Physicist U.S. Dept. Commerce, 1967; rsch. asst. aeronomy U. Ill., 1967—70; assoc. rsch. scientist aeronomy space physics rsch. lab. U. Mich., Ann Arbor, 1970—78; assoc. rsch. chemist ocean rsch. divsn. U. Calif., San Diego, 1978—80, rsch. chemist Scripps inst. oceanography, 1980—81, Daniel G. Aldrich chair in earth system sci., prof. chemistry Irvine, 1989—94, dean Sch. Phys. Scis., 1994—98, chancellor, 1998—2005; sr. scientist, dir. atmospheric chemistry divsn. Nat. Ctr. Atmospheric Rsch., Boulder, Colo., 1980—89. Lectr., asst. prof. elec. engring. U. Mich., Ann Arbor, 1973—75. Assoc. editor: Jour. Geophysics Rsch., 1977—79; editor, 1979—83. Mem. adv. bd. Marian Koshland Sci. Mus. Recipient UN Environ. Program Ozone award, Revelle medal, Bower award for Achievement in Sci., Franklin Inst., 1999, Albert Einstein World award of Sci., World Cultural Coun., 2004. Fellow: AAAS, Am. Geophys. Union (Macelwane award 1979, Revelle medal 2002), Am. Meteorol. Soc., Am. Chem. Soc.; mem.: NAS (elected 1990, bd. sustainable devel. 1995—98, mem. coun. 1996—99, com. on a guide for recruiting & advancing women in sci. and engring. 2000—, chair com. on climate sci. 2001, pres. 2005—), Am. Philos. Soc., Am. Acad. Arts and Scis. Office: Nat Acad Scis 500 Fifth St NW Washington DC 20001

CICET, DONALD JAMES, lawyer; b. New Orleans, May 24, 1940; s. Arthur Alphonse and Myrtle (Ress) C.; m. Iona Perry. BA, Nicholls State U., 1963; JD, Loyola U., New Orleans, 1969. Bar: La. 1969, U.S. Dist. Ct. (ea. dist.) La. 1972, U.S. Dist. Ct. (mid. dist.) La. 1978, U.S. Dist. Ct. (we. dist.) La. 1979, U.S. Ct. Appeals (5th cir.) 1972, U.S. Supreme Ct. 1972. Pvt. practice, Reserve, La., 1969—88, LaPlace, La., 1988—; staff atty. La. Legis. Coun., 1972-73; legal counsel Nicholls State U. Alumni Fedn.,

1974-76, 78-80; spl. counsel Pontchartrain Levee Dist., 1976—2001. Adminstrv. law judge La. Dept. Civil Svc., 1981—2006. Pres. Boys' State of La. Inc., 1990-92, bd. dirs., 1988-2007. With AUS, 1964, USNG, 1964-70. Recipient Am. Jurisprudence award Loyola U., 1968. Fellow La. Bar Found.; mem. ABA, La. Bar Assn. (ho. dels. 1973-77, 79-85), 40th Jud. Dist. Bar Assn. (pres. 1985-87), Nicholls State U. Alumni Fedn. (exec. coun. 1972-76, 77-85, pres. 1982, James Lynn Powell award 1980), Am. Legion (post cmdr. 1976-77, dist. judge adv. 1975-95, judge adv. La. dept. 1990-92, 93-96, mem. La. dept. commn. on nat. security and govtl. affairs 1974-89, chmn. 1977-78, 79-81, 85-89, M.C. Gehr blue cap award 1983). Roman Catholic. Home: 263 Central Ave Reserve LA 70084-6003 Office: 197 Belle Terre Blvd La Place LA 70069-0461

CICHELLO, SAMUEL JOSEPH, architect; b. Syracuse, NY, June 19, 1931; s. Anthony John and Margaret (Stanziana) C.; m. Eileen Agnes O'Toole, Feb. 13, 1960; children: Mary, Teresa, Claire, Anthony, John, Michael, Paul. BArch, Syracuse U., 1954. Lic. architect, N.Y. Draftsman Pederson & Hueber, Syracuse, 1951-53, Hawley E. McAfee, Fayetteville, N.Y., 1954-55; project adminstr. Hueber Hares & Glavin, Syracuse, 1959-63; pvt. practice Weedsport, N.Y., 1963—. Editor: Environment of Educational Facilities, 1966. Town assessor Town of Brutus, 1972-95. With U.S. Army, 1955-56. Mem. AIA (award of merit 1967), N.Y. State Assn. Architects, Weedsport C. of C. (pres. 1965-68), Lions Club (pres. 1968-70). Republican. Roman Catholic. Avocation: woodworking. Office Phone: 315-689-7090.

CICILIONI, ORLANDO JOSEPH, plastic surgeon; b. Scranton, Pa., June 29, 1967; s. Orlando Joseph Cicilioni, Sr. and Carmella Maria Ciaglia; m. Lori Anne Vaughn, Oct. 19, 2002; children: Kelly, Kurt, Orlando III. BS, U. Scranton, 1988, MD, 1992; PhD, Thomas Jefferson U., Phila., 1992. Diplomate Am. Bd. Surgery, 1997, Am. Bd. Plastic Surgery, 2001. Intern U. Fla., 1992—93, resident surgery, 1992—97, fellow plastic surgery, 1997—99; surgeon Fla. Hosp. Shares Found., Orlando, 2002—. Fellow: ACS. Office: Orlando Cosmetic Surgery LLC 1000 N Maitland Ave Ste B Maitland FL 32751 Office Phone: 407-681-3223. Office Fax: 407-681-0976.

CICILLINE, J. CLEMENT, mental health services professional, state legislator; b. Providence, Feb. 7, 1940; 6 children. AB, Providence Coll., 1962; MS, U. R.I., 1967. Mem. Newport (R.I.) Sch. Com., 1979-91, 92—, R.I. Senate, Dist. 50, Providence, 1992—2002; pres., CEO, Newport County Cmty. Mental Health Ctr., 1986—. Mem. Vols. in Newport Edn.; chair Dr. M.L. King Jr. State Holiday Commn.; chair Spl. Legis. Commn. to Study Svcs. to Mentally Ill Persons in Criminal Justice Sys.; vice chair Select Commn. on Race and Police Cmty. Rels.; mem. Gov.'s Commn. on Bias and Prejudice, Gov.'s Coun. on Mental Health. Mem. R.I. Coun. of Cmty. Mental Health Orgns., R.I. State Senate, 1992—, Senate Majority Pol. Leader; Forum Lodge Sons of Italy, Newport County Psychol. Soc. Democrat. Home: 100 Rhode Island Ave Newport RI 02840-3346

CICIRELLI, VICTOR GEORGE, psychologist; b. Miami, Fla., Oct. 1, 1926; s. Felix and Rene (DeMaria) C.; m. Jean Alice Solveson, Aug. 9, 1953; children: Ann Victoria, Michael Felix, Gregory Sheldon. BS, Notre Dame U., 1947; MA, U. Ill., Urbana, 1950; M.Ed., U. Miami, 1956; PhD (Univ. fellow), U. Mich., 1964; PhD, Mich. State U., 1971. Asst. prof. ednl. psychology U. Mich., 1963-65; dir. student teaching for elem., secondary and M.A.T. programs U. Pa., 1965-67; assoc. prof. early childhood edn. Ohio U., 1967-68; dir. research Nat. Evaluation of Head Start Westinghouse Learning Corp. at Ohio U., 1968-69; Office Edn. postdoctoral fellow U. Wis. Inst. Cognitive Learning, 1969-70; prof. human devel. Purdue U., 1970-73, prof. devel./aging psychology, 1974—, dir. devel. psychology program, 1977-78, 80-81, 82-83, 92-93, 96, 99-2001. Vis. sci. fellow Max Planck Inst. for Human Devel. and Edn., Berlin, 1991; fellow Ctr. for Health Policy Rsch., J. Hillis Miller Health Sci. Ctr., Sch. Medicine, U. Fla., Gainesville, 1991; Petersen vis. scholar in gerontology and family studies Oreg. State U., 2004-05; rsch. adv. bd. Calif. Commn. for Tchr. Preparation and Licensing, 1973-78; scholar NSF Inst., Ohio U., 1956, Am. U., 1958, U. Fla., 1960; cons. in field. Author: Helping Elderly Parents: Role of Adult Children, 1981, Family Caregiving: Autonomous and Paternalistic Decision Making, 1992, Sibling Relationships Across the Life Span, 1995, Older Adults' Views on Death, 2002; mem. editl. bd.: Jour. Marriage and the Family, 1990—; contbr. articles to profl. publs. Bd. dirs. Nat. Com. on Prevention of Elder Abuse, 1988-91; mem. adv. com. Ind. Geriatric Edn. Ctr., U. Ind., 1991. Grantee OEO, 1968-69, 71-73, U.S. Office Edn., 1971-73; Nat. Inst. Edn., 1973-74, NIH, 1973-74, Office Child Devel., 1973-74, Nat. Ret. Tchrs. Assn./Am. Assn. Ret. Persons Andrus Found., 1978-82, 90-92, 95, Retirement Rsch. Found., 1984-85, 87-89; fellow Andrew Norman Inst. Advanced Study, Andrus Gerontology Ctr., U. So. Calif., 1984, Gerontology Soc., 1983-84. Fellow APA, Gerontol. Soc.; mem. Internat. Soc. Study Behavioral Deve., Am. Psychol. Soc., Am. Assn. Aging, Nat. Coun. on Family Rels., Soc. for Chaos Theory, Phi Kappa Phi. Roman Catholic. Home: 1221 N Salisbury St West Lafayette IN 47906-2415 Office: Purdue U Dept Psychol Sci West Lafayette IN 47907 Office Phone: 765-494-6925. Business E-Mail: victor@psych.purdue.edu.

CICOLANI, ANGELO GEORGE, research and development company executive, operating engineer; b. Norwood, Mass., Mar. 4, 1933; s. Luigi and Maria (Fossa) Cicolani; m. Marilyn Adell Griffith, June 4, 1955 (div. Jan. 1968); children: George, Susanne, Diana; m. Patricia Anne Kirsch, Nov. 1, 1979 (dec. July 1995); m. Christine Elizabeth Blair, Apr. 1, 2001. Student, Northeastern U., 1950; BS, U.S. Naval Acad., Annapolis, Md., 1955, Naval Postgrad. Sch., 1969. Commd. ensign U.S. Navy, 1955, advanced through grades to lt. comdr., 1975, chief reactor operator, 1958-62, exec. officer, 1963-67, sys. analyst for Strategic Sys. Project Office Arlington, Va., 1969-75; cons. Arlington, 1975-77; sr. rschr. R&D Assocs., Arlington, 1977-82, program mgr., sr. scientist, 1982-87, chief staff, tech. dir. Springfield Rsch. Facility, 1988—2003. Underwriter music commns., 1987—; mission vulnerability cons., 2003—. Author: The Role of Systems Analysis, 1974; author, editor Mineral Minutes Jour., 1972—74; contbr. numerous reports on command and control survivability rsch., 1978-86, numerous reports on underground mil. facilities rsch., 1987. Pres. emeritus bd. dirs. Dumbarton Concerts, Washington, 1982—. Mem.: Mineral Soc. DC (pres. 1972—77), Ops. Rsch. Soc. Am., Nature Conservancy, Mil. Officers Assn., Naval Submarine League, Naval Inst. Achievements include development of installation and underground facilities vulnerability assessment techniques and courses of instruction. Home Phone: 703-329-9595. Personal E-mail: deadletterbox@verizon.net.

CIELEC, GREG J., literature and language educator; b. Cleve., Feb. 14, 1958; s. Marlene Cielec. BA in Speech Comm. and Edn., Ohio Wesleyan U., Delaware, Ohio, 1980; M of Edn. in Counseling, Cleve. State U., Ohio, 1984. Cert. tchr. Ohio, 1980. Novelist and freelance writer Pink Flamingo Creative Endeavors, Cleve., 1986—; asst. varsity football coach John Carroll U., University Heights, Ohio, 1999—; adj. humanities prof. Bowling Green State U., Firelands Coll., Huron, Ohio, 2002—; adj. speech/, theater prof. Lakeland CC, Kirtland, Ohio, 2004—. Author: (novels) My Cleveland Story, 1998, Home and Away Games, 2006; author, reviewer (of freelance articles). Coord. Various Charity Events, Cleve., 1998—2006. Vis. scholar, NEH, 2004—06. Mem.: Am. Football Coaches Assn., Nat. Coun. Tchrs. of English. Home: 1528 Botany Ave Cleveland OH 44109 Office: Streetsboro HS 1900 Annalane Dr Streetsboro OH 44241 Home Phone: 216-496-8286; Office Phone: 330-626-4902. Office Fax: 330-626-8103; Home Fax: 216-749-7352. Personal E-mail: cielec@hotmail.com. E-mail: gcielec@rockets.sparcc.org.

CIENCIALA, ANNA MARIA, history educator; b. Gdansk, Poland, Nov. 8, 1929; d. Andrew M. and Wanda M. (Waissmann) C.; came to U.S., 1965, naturalized, 1970; B.A., U. Liverpool, 1952; M.A., McGill U., 1955; Ph.D., Ind. U., 1962. Lectr. European history U. Ottawa, 1960-61, U. Toronto (Ont., Can.), 1961-65; asst. prof. history U. Kans., Lawrence, 1965-67, assoc. prof., 1967-71, prof. history and Soviet and Eastern European area studies, 1971-2002, ret., 2002. Recipient prize Pilsudski Inst. Am., 1968; Ford Found. fellow, 1958-60; Can. Council grantee, 1963; Fulbright-Hays fellow, 1968-69; U. Kans. gen. research grantee, 1965-75, 80-81; Am. Council Learned Socs. grantee, 1980, 83; Irex fellow, Poland, 1979-80, Russia 1993-94; NFH Poland 1993. Mem. AAUP, AAUW, Am. Assn. Advancement Slavic Studies, Am. Hist. Assn., Kosciuszko Found., PAU, Pilsudski Inst. Am., Polish-Am. Inst. Arts and Scis., Polish-Am. Hist. Assn., Hist. Preservation. Author: Poland and the Western Powers, 1938-39, 1968; From Versailles to Locarno, Keys to Polish Foreign Policy, 1919-25; editor: (with A. Headlam-Morley and R. Bryant) A Memoir of the Paris Peace Conference 1919, 1972; Jozef Beck Polska Polityka Zagraniczna, 1926-39, 1990; contbr. chpts. to books; contbr. articles to profl. jours. Home: 3045 Steven Dr Lawrence KS 66049-3025 Office Phone: 910-997-9812. Personal E-mail: hanka@ku.edu.

CIEPLY, MICHAEL, editor, writer; Bus. reporter Forbes mag.; chief investigative reporter for film industry Wall Street Jour.; west coast editor Inside.com; asst. editor Bus. Desk, writer LA Times, 2001—04; movie editor NY Times, 2004—. Film project developer Sony Pictures. Contbr. The Hearsts: Family and Empire. Office: NY Times 229 W 43rd St New York NY 10036 Office Phone: 212-556-3842. Office Fax: 212-556-1516. E-mail: cieply@nytimes.com.

CIESLA, FRED JOHN, astrophysicist, meteoriticist, researcher; b. Southbridge, Mass., Nov. 24, 1976; s. Vincent Bernard and Wendy Lee Ciesla; m. Carolyn Henley, May 10, 2003. BA in Physics, Cornell U., 1998; PhD in Planetary Scis., U. Ariz., 2003. Post doctoral rschr. U. Ariz., Tucson, 2003; assoc. NRC, Moffett Field, Calif., 2004—05; post doctoral fellow, dept. terrestrial magnetism Carnegie Inst., Washington, 2006—. Recipient Group Achievement award, NASA, 2002, Kuiper Meml. award, Lunar and Planetary Lab., U. Ariz., 2003. Mem.: Am. Astron. Soc. (divsn. planetary scis.), Meteorol. Soc. Avocations: reading, sports. Office: Carnegie Inst Washington Dept Terrestrial Magnetism 5241 Broad Branch Rd NW Washington DC 20015 Home Phone: 650-940-9441; Office Phone: 650-604-0328. E-mail: ciesla@dtm.ciw.edu.

CIFELLI, JOHN LOUIS, lawyer; b. Chicago Heights, Ill., Aug. 19, 1923; s. Antonio and Domenica (Liberatore) C.; m. Irene Romandine, Jan. 4, 1948; children— Carla, David, John L., Bruce, Thomas, Carol. Student, Bowdoin Coll., 1943, Norwick Mil. Acad., 1943, Mt. Piliar Acad., 1943, U. Ill. Extension Ctr., 1946—47; LLB, DePaul U., 1950, JD (hon.), 1975. Bar: Ill. 1950, U.S. Supreme Ct. 1960. Ptnr. Piacenti, Cifelli & Sims, Chicago Heights, 1950—78; 1978pres. John L. Cifelli & Assocs., Chicago Heights, 1978—85; sr. ptnr. Cifelli Baczynski & Scrementi Ltd. (now Cifelli & Scrementi), Chicago Heights, 1985—; spl. counsel City of Chicago Heights, 1961—72; village atty. Village of Richton Park, Ill., 1962—77, Village of Ford Heights, Ill., 1984—89. Counsel Maj. League Umpires Assn., 1973-78, Ill. High Sch. Baseball Coaches Assn., 1975-89. Sec. Bd. Fire and Police, Chicago Heights, 1959-65; co-founder Small Fry Internat. Basketball, 1969, pres., 1969—; coach, baseball coordinator Chicago Heights Park Dist., 1970-75; coach Babe Ruth League Baseball, 1972, 74, 75, asst. Ill. dir., 1973; dir. Ill. tournament, 1973. Served to 2d lt. USAAF, 1942-45, ETO. Mem. ABA, Ill. Bar Assn., Ill. Trial Lawyers Assn., Asns. Trial Lawyers Am., Justinian Soc. Lawyers, Isaac Walton League, Italo Am. Vets. Group, VFW (judge adv. 1951-72), Cath. War Vets. (judge adv. 1951-70), Am. Legion. Clubs: Chicago Heights Country (bd. dirs. 1972-76), Mt. Carmel; Pike Lake Fishing (Wis.). Lodges: Moose, Amaseno. Republican. Avocations: hunting, fishing, golf. Home: 879 Amico Dr Chicago Heights IL 60411 Office: Cifelli & Scrementi Ste 212 1010 Dixie Hwy Chicago Heights IL 60411-3555 Office Phone: 708-754-6200. Business E-Mail: cifellilawfirm@msn.com.

CIFTJA, ORION, physicist, researcher; b. Shkoder, Albania, Nov. 27, 1967; s. Gjon and Friderika Ciftja; m. Irena Hysi; 1 child, Brent. Diploma, U. Tirana, Albania, 1991; diploma in condensed matter physics, Internat. Ctr. Theoretical Physics, Trieste, Italy, 1994; PhD, Internat. Sch. Advanced Studies, Trieste, Italy, 1997. Post-doctoral rschr. Ames Lab., Iowa State U., 1997—99; vis. asst. prof. Tex. A&M U., College Station, 1999—2000; post-doctoral rschr. U. Mo., Columbia, 2000—02; asst. prof. Prairie View A&M U., Tex., 2002—. Contbr. more than 30 articles to profl. jours. Rsch. grantee, Dept. of Energy, 2005—06, NSF, 2006—07, Kavli Inst. Theoretical Physics scholar, 2007—. Mem.: Am. Phys. Soc. Avocations: soccer, travel. Office: Prairie View A&M Univ Prairie View TX 77446

CIKOVSKY, NICOLAI, JR., retired curator, art historian, educator; b. NYC, Feb. 11, 1933; s. Nicolai and Hortense (Hilbert) C.; m. Sarah Eden Greenough, June 17, 1978; children— Emily Hilbert, Sophia Greenough. AB magna cum laude, Harvard Coll., Cambridge, Mass., 1955; AM, Harvard U., Cambridge, Mass., 1958, PhD, 1965. Asst. prof. Skidmore Coll., Saratoga Springs, NY, 1961-63; chmn., assoc. prof. Pomona Coll., Claremont, Calif., 1964-68; vis. assoc. prof. U. Tex., Austin, 1969-70; dir. art gallery, assoc. prof. Vassar Coll., Poughkeepsie, NY, 1971-74; prof., chmn. dept. art U. N.Mex., Albuquerque, 1974-83; curator Am. and Brit. painting Nat. Gallery Art, Washington, 1983—2003, sr. curator Am. and Brit. painting, 1998—2003; ret., 2003. Author: Sanford Robinson Gifford, exhbn. catalogue, 1970; editor: Lectures on the Affinity of Painting with the Other Fine Arts (Samuel F.B. Morse), 1983; George Inness, 1971, The Life and Work of George Inness, 1977, Winslow Homer, 1990, Winslow Homer Watercolors, 1991, George Inness, 1993; contbg. author: exhbn. catalogues George Inness, 1985, Ansel Adams: Classic Images, 1985, William Merritt Chase: Summers at Shinnecock, 1987, Raphaelle Peale Still Lifes, 1988, William M. Harnett, 1992, James McNeill Whistler, 1994, Winslow Homer, 1995; also articles on William Merritt Chase, George Inness, Winslow Homer, Thomas Eakins, Am. landscape painting, Am. impressionism. Am. Council Learned Socs.-Smithsonian Instn. postdoctoral research fellow, 1968-69; Guggenheim fellow, 1978-79; Kress sr. fellow Nat. Gallery Art, 1983 Mem. Harvard Club (N.Y.C.), Phi Beta Kappa. Personal E-mail: nicolai.cikovsky@verizon.net.

CILELLA, MARY WINIFRED, director; b. Oak Park, Ill., Aug. 24, 1943; d. Charles William Sr. and Theresa Mary (Gilligan) Broucek; m. Salvatore G. Cilella Jr., Aug. 29, 1970; children: Salvatore George III, Peter Dominic. BA, Dominican U., 1965; MAT, U. Notre Dame, 1966; grad. The Prin.'s Inst., Harvard U., 1993; postgrad., U. S.C., 1994-97. Tchr. Miner Jr. H.S., Arlington Heights, Ill., 1966-67; sec. White House, Washington, 1969-70; devel. officer Textile Mus., Washington, 1982-83; dir. meetings and continuing edn. Am. Assn. Mus., Washington, 1983-87; interim lower sch. head, lower sch. head Heathwood Hall Episc. Sch., Columbia, S.C., 1989-94, dir. acad. adminstrn., 1994-95, dir. fin. and adminstrn., 1995-96, asst. head, 1996-98, assoc. head fin. and ops., 1998—2001; cons. Park Tudor Sch., Indpls., 2001—02, dir. Russel and Mary Williams Learning Project, 2002—05; head The Howard Sch., Atlanta, 2005—. Mem. profl. edn. unit adv. com. U. S.C., 1996-2001; mem. U.S. Dept. of Edn.'s Blue Ribbon Schs. Planning Group, 1996; examiner Malcolm Baldrige Nat. Quality award bd. U.S. Dept. Commerce and Nat. Inst. Stds. and Tech., 1999, 2000; adv. coun. Office Ministry Persons with Disabilities, Archdiocese Atlanta, 2006—; sec. Atlanta Assn. Ind. Schs. Mem. ASCD, Internat. Dyslexia Assn. (bd. Ga. br. 2006—), Phi Delta Kappa. Roman Catholic. Avocations: gardening, antiques, music. Home: 767 Springlake Ln NW Atlanta GA 30318 Office: Howard Sch 1192 Foster St Atlanta GA 30318 Office Phone: 404-377-7436. Business E-Mail: mcilella@howardschool.org.

CILELLA, SALVATORE GEORGE, JR., museum director; b. Chgo., Oct. 19, 1941; s. Salvatore G. and Mary Genevieve (LaRocque) C.; m. Mary Winifred Broucek, Aug. 29, 1970; children: Salvatore G. III, Peter Dominic. BA, U. Notre Dame, 1963, MA in Am. History, 1966; MA in Museum Adminstrn., Univ. N.Y., Oneonta, 1971. Community amb. Experiment in Internat. Living, Iran, 1965; exec. dir. No. Ind. Hist. Soc., South Bend, 1970-72; registrar, asst. dir. N.Y. State Hist. Assn., Cooperstown, 1973-76; exec. dir. Historic Bethlehem (Pa.) Inc., 1976-79; dir. devel. and membership Old Sturbridge (Mass.) Village, 1979-81; devel. officer Smithsonian Instn., Washington, 1981-87; exec. dir. Columbia (S.C.) Mus. Art, 1987-2001; pres., CEO Ind. Hist. Soc., Indpls., 2001—. Cons. various mus., 1979—; overseer Old Sturbridge Village, 1982-89; lectr. Seminar for Hist. Adminstrn., Williamsburg, Va., 1983—, Mus. Mgmt. Program, Boulder, Colo., 1993. Contbr. articles to profl. jours. Co-chmn. United Black Fund, 1999; chmn. search com. Hist. Columbia; vice chair Gov.'s Commn. on Heritage; bd. dirs. Indpls. Conv. and Visitors Assn. Decorated Army commendation medal, 1969. Mem.: Am. Assn. for State and Local History, Am. Hist. Print Collections Assn., Am. Assn. Mus. (chmn. devel. and membership com. 1984—89, bd. dirs. 1989—92), Univ. Club, Columbia Club. Roman Catholic. Avocations: collecting maps, antiques, collecting Civil War artifacts, collecting tribal rugs. E-mail: scilella@indianahistory.org.

CIMENT, MELVYN, mathematician; b. Bronx, Sept. 23, 1941; s. Jack and Regina C.; m. Barbara Ann Kagan, July 3, 1966; children: Ethan J., Daniel I. BS, U. Miami, 1962; MS, NYU, 1964, PhD in Math., 1968; JD, Am. U., 1978. Mathematician Denver Rsch. Ctr., Marathon Oil Co., 1968-69; asst. prof. math. U. Mich., Tel-Aviv U. and NYU, 1967-72; applied mathematician Naval Surface Weapons Ctr., 1972-77; sr. applied mathematician Nat. Bur. Stds., Gaithersburg, Md., 1977-83, prog. analyst, 1981-82; Dept. Commerce, Sci. and Tech. congl. fellow U.S. Senate Com. on Commerce, Sci. and Transp., Washington, 1980-81; prog. dir. applied math. DMS, NSF, 1983-86, prog. dir. computational math., 1986; dep. dir. div. Adv. Sci. Computing, Computer, Info. Scis. NSF, Washington, 1986-90, coord. high performance computing and communications program, 1991, exec. officer Computer Info. Sci. and Engring., 1992-93, acting asst. dir., 1993-94, dep. asst. dir., 1993-99; cons., sr. staff cons. Wash. Adv. Group, 2000—03. Mem. FCCSET Working Group on High Performance Computing, 1986-92, exec. com. high performance computing and comm. info. tech. subcom., 1993-94; vice chmn. com. info. and comm. Nat. Sci. and Tech. Coun., 1994, co-chmn. fed. info. svcs. and applications coun., com. computing, info. and comm., 1996-98; acting chmn. Fed. Networking Coun., 1993-94; vis. scientist U. Md., 1994-95; cons. Coun. on Competitiveness, 1994-95; sr. advisor Implementation Group, 2001-03; science adv. NSF EPSCOR Ctrs. Devel. Initiative, 2002-05; mng. mem. CS Cubed Group, LLC, 2004—; dir. info. tech. Potomac Inst. for Policy Studies, Arlington, Va., 1999-2000. Courant Inst. Math. Scis. fellow, 1962-66, others. Mem. Assn. for Computing Machinery, Soc. for Indsl. and Applied Math. (mem. coun. 1988-90, sr. advisor Washington office 2000-), Soc. for. Indsl. Applied Math. (sci. adv. Wash. chpt. 2001—), D.C. Bar Assn., Fla. Bar Assn., Md. Bar Assn. Jewish. Avocations: reading, music, biking. Home: 12205 Kemp Mill Rd Silver Spring MD 20902-1720 Personal E-mail: mel@ciment.com.

CIMINELLA, CHRISTINA CLAIRE See JUDD, WYNONNA

CIMINO, RICHARD DENNIS, lawyer; b. Omaha, June 6, 1947; s. Lewis Raymond and Louise (Monaco) C.; m. Mary Scott Reins, Feb. 12, 1977; children: John Damon, Mary Drusilla, Robert Andrew, Ann Marie. BBA, U. Notre Dame, 1969; JD, St. Louis U., 1974. Bar: Nebr. 1975, Kans. 1989, Fla. 1994, U.S. Dist. Ct. Nebr. 1975, U.S. Dist. Ct. Kans. 1989, U.S. Dist. Ct. Fla. 1995. Assoc. Kutak, Rock & Campbell, Omaha, 1975-78, ptnr., 1979; v.p., gen. counsel Silvey Refrigerated Carriers, Omaha, 1980-86, pres., 1987; ptnr. Dwyer, Pohren, Wood, Heavey & Grimm, Omaha, 1988-89; pvt. practice St. Marys, Kans., 1989-93; ptnr. Cimino & McElrath, Naples, Fla., 1993—. Editor St. Louis U. Law Jour., 1972-74. Bd. dirs. Bergan Mercy Hosp. Found., Omaha, 1986-87. With U.S. Army, 1969-71, Vietnam. Mem. Fla. Bar Assn., Kans. Bar Assn., Nebr. Bar Assn., Collier County Bar Assn., Notre Dame Alumni Club (pres. Omaha chpt. 1980), Alpha Sigma Nu (Acad. award). Republican. Roman Catholic. Avocation: golf. Office: 4501 Tamiami Trl N Naples FL 34103 Office Phone: 239-262-1202. Personal E-mail: dick@rcimino.com, dome96@comcast.net.

CIMPOERU, PETRE, archivist, educator; b. Gostinu, Romania, Nov. 29, 1939; s. Ion and Elena Cimpoeru; m. Lydia Nicola, Sept. 5, 1947; 1 child, Ligia Schaffer. MA in Libr. Sci., San Jose State U., Calif., 1992; MA in Nat. Security, Calif. State U., San Bernardino, 1988; MA in History and Romanian Lang., U. Bucharest, Romania, 1963; PhD in Internat. Studies, Preston U., Cheyenne, Wyo., 2004. Diploma West Point Mil. Acad., 1989. Bibliographer Nat. Libr., Bucharest, Romania, 1968—69; insp. Nat. Mil. Libr., Bucharest, Romania, 1970—73; history tchr. H.S., Bucharest, Romania, 1973—79; asst. prof. of history Calif. State U., San Bernardino, 1989—90, La Sierra U., Riverside, Calif., 1992—96; assoc. libr./asst. archivist Loma Linda U., Loma Linda, Calif., 1992—. Author: (book) Manual for Military Libraries; contbr. articles to profl. jours. Bd. dirs. Romanian Ministries Internat., Loma Linda, Calif., 1990—95. With Romanian Army, 1968—69. Named Safety Coord. of the Yr., Loma Linda U., 1995. Mem.: Am.-Romanian Acad. of Arts and Sci. (life; full mem. 1998—2004), The Acad. of Polit. Sci. (assoc.; mem. 2003—04). R-Conservative. Seventh-Day Adventist. Achievements include development of Automation of Romanian SDA Seminary Library. Avocations: sports, classical music, archaeology, politics, theology. Home: 25522 Nicks Ave Loma Linda CA 92354 Office: Loma Linda University 11072 Anderson St Loma Linda CA 92354 Home Phone: 909-796-4355. Personal E-mail: pcimpoeru@adelphia.net.

CINDRICH, ROBERT JAMES, lawyer, retired federal judge; b. Avella, Pa., Sept. 22, 1943; s. Anthony Joseph and Stella Dolores Cindrich; m. Bonnie Alice Jones, June 25, 1966; children: Stephen, Scott, Amanda. AB in Polit. Sci., Wittenberg U., 1965; JD magna cum laude, U. Pitts., 1968. Bar: Pa. 1968, U.S. Supreme Ct. 1968, U.S. Dist. Ct. (we. dist.) Pa. 1968, U.S. Ct. Appeals (3d cir.) 1974, U.S. Supreme Ct. 1980, U.S. Tax Ct. 1982. Law clk. to presiding judge U.S. Ct. Appeals (3d cir.), Pitts., 1968-69; asst. trial defender Pub. Defender of Allegheny County, Pitts., 1969-70; asst. dist. atty. Allegheny County, Pitts., 1970-71; ptnr. McVerry, Baxter, Cindrich & Mansmann, Pitts., 1972-78; US atty. (we. dist.) Pa. US Dept. Justice, Pitts., 1978-81; ptnr. Gondelman, Baxter, Mansmann, McVerry & Cindrich, Pitts., 1981, Mansmann, Cindrich & Titus, Pitts., 1981-94; judge US Dist. Ct. (we. dist.) Pa., 1994—2004; chief legal officer, gen. counsel U. Pitts. Medical Ctr., 2004—. Mem. Pa. Supreme Ct. Procedural Rules Com., Pitts., 1987—. Author: (with others) Criminal Courts Manual, 1975; contbr. articles, revs. to profl. jours. Former chmn. South Side Hosp., Pitts.; bd. dirs. U. Pitts. Med. Ctr. Sgt. USAR, 1968-75. Named Man of Yr. in Law and Govt., Pitts. Jaycees, 1981. Fellow ABA; mem. Pa. Bar Assn., Allegheny County Bar Assn., Assn. Former U.S. Attys., Allegheny Acad. of Trial Lawyers, Order of Coif, U. Pitts. Law Sch. Alumni Assn. (pres. bd. govs. 1984). Democrat. Roman Catholic. Avocations: fishing, hunting. Office: Forbes Tower 200 Lothrop St Ste 11037 Pittsburgh PA 15213-2546

CINK, STEWART, professional golfer; b. Huntsville, Ala., May 21, 1973; m. Lisa Cink; children: Connor Stewart, Reagan Braswell. Degree in mgmt., Ga. Inst. Tech. Winner Mexican Open, 1996, 1999, Canon Greater Hartford Open, 1997, MCI Classic, 2000, MCI Heritage, 2004, WGC-NEC Invitational, 2004. Mem. Presidents Cup team, 2000, Ryder Cup team, 2002, 04. Avocations: roller hockey, hiking. Office: c/o PGA Tour 112 PGA Tour Blvd Ponte Vedra Beach FL 32082

CINO, MARIA, political organization administrator, former federal agency administrator; b. Buffalo, Apr. 19, 1957; d. Richard J. and Lucy M. (Tripi) C. BA in Polit. Sci., St. John Fisher Coll. Project supr. Rep. Nat. Com., 1981-82, dir. local programs, 1983-84, exec. asst. field dir., 1985-86; rsch. analyst Am. Viewpoint, Inc., 1986-88; adminstrv. asst. to Rep. L. William Paxon US Congress, 1989-93; exec. dir. Nat. Rep. Congl. Com., 1993—97; sr. adv. Wiley, Rein & Fielding LLP, 1997—99; nat. polit. dir. Bush for Pres., 1999—2000; asst. sec., dir. gen., US Comml. Svc. US Dept. Commerce, Washington, 2001—03; dep. chmn. polit. & cong. rels. Rep. Nat. Com., 2000—01, dep. chmn., 2003—05, CEO Com. on Arrangements for 2008 Rep. Nat. Convention, 2007—; dep. sec. US Dept. Transport., Washington, 2005—07, acting sec., 2006. Mem. Ho. Adminstrv. Assts. Assn. Republican. Avocations: antiques, travel, golf. Office: Rep Nat Com 310 First St SE Washington DC 20003*

CIOCHETTY, JOHN BRYAN, protective services official; b. Parkersburg, W.Va., June 17, 1955; s. John Joseph and Mary Ann Ciochetty. BA, Marshall U., W.Va., 1980, MS, 1988. Polit. sci. instr. Marshall U., Huntington, W.Va., 1976—86; dep. sheriff Wood County Sheriff's Dept., Parkersburg, 1986—88; jud. officer probation svcs. W.Va. Supreme Ct., Charleston, 1988—90; sociology, criminology instr. W.Va. U., Parkersburg, 1990—91; loss prevention investigator Meijer Corp., Columbus, Ohio, 1995—2000; pub. safety campus police Ohio Wesleyan U., Delaware, 2001—. Mgmt. devel. v.p. Jr. C. of C., Parkersburg, W.Va., 1986—92; chief probation officer Marysville Mcpl. Ct., Ohio, 1991—92; custom protection officer and investigator Wackenhut Corp., Columbus, Ohio, 1992—95; patrolman, investigator Statewide Bur. Investigations, Parkersburg, W.Va., 1975—. Author: Nuclear Biological and Chemical Defense, 1986, The Ghosts of Stuyvesant Hall and Beyond, 2007. Adv. bd. mem. Big Brothers/Big Sisters of Am., Parkersburg, W.Va., 1980—83; mem. Nat. Performance Rev. Office of U.S. V.P. Al Gore, 1993—2000. Lt. USAR, 1980—88. Avocations: horseback riding, writing, computers, travel, Karate, Aikido. Office: Ohio Weslyan Univ Pub Safety 61 S Sandusky St Delaware OH 43015 Home: 534 Taft Ct Delaware OH 43015 E-mail: darkknightjc_007@msn.com.

CIOFALO, LINDA, vocalist, educator; d. Thomas S. Abbate and Lena Nuzzo; m. Joseph Ciofalo, Oct. 6, 1974; children: Jessica, Joseph, Nicholas, David. Student, Juilliard Sch, 1996—97. Vocalist, 1990—; tchg. artist Lincoln Ctr./Tilles Ctr., NYC, 2004—; vocal tchr. LI H.S. Arts, Syosset, NY, 2005—; pres. Lucky Jazz. Composer: Darlin, 1990, Lost Ticket Blues, 2000; rec. artist (CDs) Take the High Road, 2000, Sun Set, 2007. Mem. Freeport (NY) Coun. of Arts, 1998—; Arts in Motion rep. Rockville Ctr. (NY) Schs., 1990—2003. Recipient Jenkins award for cmty. svc., Coun. of PTA; grantee, NY State Coun. on Arts, 1999, 2000, 2001, 2002; Artist grantee, NY Found. of the Arts, 2004, 2005. Mem.: NARAS, Universal Jazz Coalition, Nat. Assn. Tchrs. Singing, Internat. Assn. Jazz Educators, Soc. Singers. Avocations: cooking, kickboxing, nature walks, yoga. E-mail: lcul84@aol.com.

CIOFFI, MICHAEL LAWRENCE, lawyer; b. Cin., Feb. 2, 1953; s. Patrick Anthony and Patricia (Schroeder) C.; children: Michael A., David P., Gina M. BA magna cum laude, U. Notre Dame, 1975; JD, U. Cin., 1979. Bar: Ohio 1979, U.S. Dist. Ct. (so. dist.) Ohio 1980, U.S. Dist. Ct. (no. dist.) Ohio 1983, U.S. Ct. Appeals (6th cir.) 1985. Asst. atty. gen. Ohio Atty. Gen., Columbus, 1979-81; from assoc. to ptnr. Frost & Jacobs, Cin., 1981-87; staff v.p., asst. gen. counsel Penn Cen. Corp., Cin., 1988-93; v.p., asst. gen. counsel Am. Fin. Group, Cin., 1993-2000; ptnr. Blank Rome LLP, Cin., 2000—. Adj. prof. law U. Cin. Coll. Law, 1983—. Author: Ohio Pretrial Litigation, 1991, rev. ed., 2007; co-author: Sixth Circuit Federal Practice Manual, 1993, 3d edit., 2006. Bd. dirs. Charter Com. of Greater Cin., 1985—88. Recipient Goldman Prize for Tchg. Excellence U. Cin. Coll. Law, 1995, Nicholas Longworth Disting. Alumni award, 1996, Adj. Faculty Tchg. Excellence award, 2000. Mem. ABA, Fed. Bar Assn. (mem. exec. com., pres.1994), Ohio Bar Assn., Cin. Bar Assn. Avocations: tennis, travel. Office: Blank Rome LLP 201 E 5th St Cincinnati OH 45202

CIPARICK, CARMEN BEAUCHAMP, state appeals court judge; b. NYC, 1942; m. Joseph Damian Ciparick; 1 child. Grad., Hunter Coll., 1963; JD, St. John's U., 1967. Staff atty. Legal Aid Soc., NYC, 1967—69; asst. counsel Office of Jud. Conf. State of NY, 1969—72; chief law asst. NYC Criminal Ct., 1972—74; counsel Office of NYCAdminstrv. Judge, 1974—78; judge NYC Criminal Ct., 1978—82, NYC Supreme Ct, 1982—94; assoc. judge NY State Ct. Appeals, NYC, 1994—. Former mem. N.Y. State Commn. Jud. Conduct. Trustee Boricua Coll.; bd. dirs. St. John's U. Sch. of Law Alumni Assn. Named to Hunter Coll. Hall of Fame, 1991. Office: NY State Ct Appeals 122 E 42nd St New York NY 10168-0002 Address: State NY Court of Appeals 20 Eagle St Albany NY 12207-1095*

CIPLIJAUSKAITE, BIRUTE, humanities educator; b. Kaunas, Lithuania, Apr. 11, 1929; came to U.S., 1957; d. Juozas and Elena (Stelmokaite) C. BA, Lycée Lithuanien Tubingen, 1947; MA, U. Montreal, 1956; PhD, Bryn Mawr Coll., 1960. Permanent mem. Inst. Rsch. in Humanities U. Wis., Madison, 1974, asst. prof., 1961-65, assoc. prof., 1965-68, prof., 1968-73, John Bascom prof., 1973—. Author: Solitude and Spanish Contemporary Poetry, 1962, Poetry and the Poet, 1966, Baroja, a style, 1972, Plenitude as Commitment: The Poetry of Jorge Guillén, 1973, The Generation of 1898 and History, 1981, The Unsatisfied Woman: Adultery in Realist Novel, 1984, Contemporary Women's Novel (1970-85), 1988, Literary Sketches, 1992, Of Signs and Significations. I: Games of the Avant-Garde, 1999, Carmen Martín Gaite, 2000, Guilleniana, 2002, Construction of the Feminine I in Literature, 2004; editor: (Luis de Góngora), Complete Sonnets, 1969, 75, 79, 81, 85, 99, critical edit., 1989, faxsimile edit., 2007, Jorge Guillén, 1975, (with C. Maurer) The Will to Humanism. Homage to Juan Marichal, 1990, Novísimos, postnovísimos, clásicos: Poetry of the 80s in Spain, 1991; translator: (Juan Ramón Jiménez), Platero and I, 1982, (María Victoria Atencia), Trances of the Holy Virgin, 1989, Voices Within Silence: Contemporary Lithuanian Poetry, 1991, Birute Pukeleviciute, Lament, 1994, (with Nicole Laurent-Catrice) Twenty Lithuanian Poets of Today, 1997, (Vidmante Jasukaitytė), The Miraculous Grass Along the Fence, 2002, (J. Degutytė and B. Pukelevičiute) Between the Sun and Dispossession, 2002, (Mercè Rodoreda) The Girl of the Doves, 2002, (Nijole Miliauskaitė) Forbidden Room, 2003, (with Emilio Coco) That Rustle of Nordic Herbs. Anthology of Lithuanic Contemporary Poetry, 2006, others. Guggenheim fellow, 1968 Mem. Assn. For Advancement Baltic Studies (v.p. 1981), Asociación Internacional de Hispanistas, Order Alfonso X elSabio (named commdr. Spain, 2003) Office: U Wis Inst Rsch in Humanities 1401 Observatory Dr Madison WI 53706-1209

CIPOLLA, MARK, lawyer; b. Bklyn., Sept. 20, 1964; BS, St. John's U., 1986, JD, 1992. Bar: NY 1993. Asst. dist. atty., Kings County, NY, 1992—98; ptnr. Wilson, Elser, Moskowitz, Edelman & Dicker LLP, NYC. Mem.: Assn. Trial Lawyers of Am. Office: Wilson Elser Moskowitz Edelman & Dicker LLP 23rd Fl 150 E 42nd St New York NY 10017-5639 Office Phone: 212-490-3000 ext. 2526. Office Fax: 212-490-3038. Business E-Mail: cipollam@wemed.com.

CIPRICH, PAULA MARIE, lawyer, gas industry executive; m. Greg Ciprich; 1 child. BA, U. Dallas1982; JD, SUNY, Buffalo, 1985. Bar: NY 1986. Assoc. Jaeckle, Fleischmann & Mugel, 1985—88; atty. Nat. Fuel Gas Co., Williamsville, NY, 1988—91, sr. atty., 1991—92, asst. gen. mgr., 1992—94, gen. mgr., 1994—97, asst. gen. counsel, asst. sec., 1997—2005, gen. counsel, 2005—. Office: Nat Fuel Gas Co 6363 Main St Williamsville NY 14221 Office Phone: 716-857-7048. E-mail: ciprichp@natfuel.com.

CIRANDO, JOHN ANTHONY, lawyer; b. Syracuse, NY, June 25, 1942; s. Daniel John and Anne Marie (Farone) C.; m. Carolyn Joyce Lace, Sept. 17, 1966; children: Lisa Marie, Julie Lynn, Jennifer Mary. BA in History, St. Bonaventure U., NY, 1963; JD, SUNY, Buffalo, 1966. Bar: NY 1966, US Dist. Ct. (no. dist.) NY 1966, US Dist. Ct. (we. dist.) NY 1994, US Claims Ct. 1991, US Ct. Mil. Appeals 1967, US Ct. Appeals (2d cir.) 1985, US Supreme Ct. 1974. Chief asst. dist. atty. Onondaga County Dist. Atty.'s Office, Syracuse, NY, 1971-87; atty. D.J. & J.A. Cirando, Syracuse, 1966—. Treas. NY State Dist. Attys.' Assn., 1977—87; chair Govs. Jud. Screening Com. 4th Jud. Dept., 1997—2006, mem., 2007, Ind. Jud. Elections Qual. Com., 2007—. Pres. bd. dirs. Vera House, Shelter for Women and Children in Crisis, Syracuse, 1988-90, gen. counsel, 1991—; trustee Leukemia Soc. Am., 1995—, asst. sec., 1995-96, sec., 1996-2000, mem. adv. bd., 2000—; trustee Loretto Health and Rehab. Ctr., 2004—, sec., 2004—; mem. NYS Law Rev. Commn., 2006-. Capt. JAG US Army, 1967—71. Recipient Sister Mary Vera Recognition award, 2005. Mem. NY State Bar Assn. (chair com. on county cts. 1975-78, chair com. on pub. rels. 1979-83), Onondaga County Bar Assn. (bd. dirs. 1974-77, sec. 1979). Office: DJ & JA Cirando 101 S Salina St Ste 1010 Syracuse NY 13202-4303 Office Phone: 315-474-1285.

CIRAOLO, DEBRA, sign language interpreter, consultant; d. Dave and Marie Ciraolo. BA, Baruch Coll., NYC, 1977; Cert. Sign Lang. Interpreter, U. Ariz., 1980; MA, NYU, 1982. Cert. sign lang. interpreter 1980. Ednl. evaluator N.Y.C. Bd. Edn., 1988—90; self employeed sign lang. interpreter/ cons./contr. NYC, 1990—; asst. to dir. N.Y.C. Ct. for Law and the Deaf, 1990—2007. Asst. to the dir. N.Y.C. Ctr. for Law and the Deaf, 1990—2006. Contbr. curriculum guide (Tinker Grant, 1984). Home Phone: 212-242-4312; Office Phone: 212-242-4312. Personal E-mail: signhands@verizon.net.

CIRASUNDA, ESTHER BOND, librarian; b. Richmond, Va., July 10, 1950; d. Hobart Genues and Beulah Ann (Neal) Bond; m. Gary Lee Musser, June 3, 1977 (div. 1989); children: Laura Beth Musser, Jessica Lynn Musser; m. Francis Peter Cirasunda, July 4, 1990. BS, Madison Coll., Harrisonburg, Va., 1972; MS, Radford U., 1983. Sch. libr. Botetourt County Pub. Schs., Fincastle, Va., 1972-74, Roanoke (Va.) City Pub. Schs., 1974—2003; ret., 2003; pvt. tutor; owner Motivation Plus, 2005—. Del. Gov.'s Conf. on Libr. and Info. Svcs., Richmond, 1990; teaching homebound students and private tutoring, 2003; spkr. Motivation Plus, 2005—. Author poems. Mem. NEA (life; del. conv. 1993, vice-chair libr. info. tech. caucus), Va. Edn. Assn., Roanoke Edn. Assn. (v.p. instrn. 1992-93, Polit. Action Com chair 1994-95, pres. 1996-98, dist. 5 pres. 1998-2000), Roanoke City Ret. Tchrs. Assn. (v.p. 2005, pres., 2006—), Va. Ret. Tchrs. Assn. (life), Roanoke Valley Reading Coun., Va. Ednl. Media Assn. (workshop presenter 1986), Phi Kappa Phi. Avocations: continuing education, working with women on survival skills. Home and Office: 5066 Dan Robin Rd Salem VA 24153 Office Phone: 540-797-1798. Personal E-mail: ecirasun@yahoo.com.

CIRAULO, DOMENIC ANTHONY, psychiatrist, educator; 3 children. BA, U. Hartford, 1971; MD, Georgetown U., 1975. Diplomate in psychiatry with added qualification in addiction psychiatry Am. Bd. Psychiatry and Neurology. Med. resident Inst. Living, Hartford, 1975—77; chief resident psychiatry Mass. Mental Health Ctr., Boston, 1977—78; clin. fellow psychiatry Harvard Med. Sch., Boston, 1977—78, clin. instr., 1978—79, lectr. psychiatry, 2002—; asst. prof. psychiatry U. Conn. Sch. Medicine, Farmington, 1979—84; from asst. prof. to assoc. prof. psychiatry Tufts U. Sch. Medicine, 1984—92, prof. psychiatry, 1992—96, lectr. pharmacology, 1993—; chief psychiatry svc. VA Med. Ctr./Outpatient Clinics, Boston, 1995—2001; psychiatrist in chief Boston Med. Ctr., 1996—; prof., chmn. divsn. psychiatry Boston U. Sch. Medicine, 1996—. Chair R&D com. VA Outpatient Clinic, Boston, 1987—94; mem. exec. com. dept. psychiatry Tufts U. Sch. Medicine, Boston, 1989—93, mem. addiction medicine com., 1989—96; sr. cons. Norcap Addictions Program, Norfolk, Mass., 1990—96; mem. dean's com. VA Med. Ctr., Boston, 1996—; mem. exec. com. Boston U. Sch. Medicine, 1996—, com. mem., 2001—02; gen. clin. rsch. ctr. adv. com. Boston U. Med. Ctr., 1997—; sci. adv. com. Boston U. Cmty. Tech. Fund, 1997—2000. Author: (book) Drug Interactions In Psychiatry, Clinical Manual of Chemical Dependence; contbr. chapters to books. Grantee, Nat. Inst. On Drug Abuse, 1995—, Nat. Inst. On Alcoholism and Alcohol Abuse, 1997—, Nat. Inst. On Drug Abuse, 2002—, 2002—, 2002—. Fellow: Am. Psychiat. Assn. (disting. fellow); mem.: AMA (ad hoc com. on physicians health 1996), FDA Adv. Bd., Am. Bd. Psychiatry and Neurology (examiner), Mass. Med. Soc., Mass. Psychiatry Soc. (com. on alcohol and addiction 1984—). Office: Boston Univ Sch Medicine Ste 914 720 Harrison Ave Boston MA 02118

CIRCEO, LOUIS JOSEPH, JR., research scientist, civil engineer; b. Everett, Mass., Aug. 31, 1934; s. Louis Joseph and Matilda (Marotta) C.; m. Brigitta H. Rockstroh, Jan. 26, 1961 (dec. 1986); children: Renata B., Craig L. BS in Engring., U.S. Mil. Acad., West Point, 1957; MS in Soils Engring., 1961; PhD in Civil Engring., Iowa State U., 1963. Registered profl. civil engr., DC. Commd. 2d lt. U.S. Army, 1957, advanced through grades to col., 1987; rsch. assoc. Lawrence Radiation Lab., Livermore, Calif., 1962-64; civil engr. Bangkok Bypass Road, Thailand, 1965—66; instr. dept. engring. and mil. sci. U.S. Army Engr. Sch., Ft. Belvoir, Va., 1966—68; civil engr. advisor Vietnamese Nat. Mil. Acad., Dalat, Vietnam, 1968-69; rsch. tech. mgr. Def. Atomic Support Agy., Washington, 1969-72; comdr. 20th Engr. Bn., Ft. Campbell, Ky., 1973-75; ops. rsch. analyst nuclear activities br. SHAPE, NATO, Mons, Belgium, 1975-79; dir. U.S. Army Constrn. Engring. Rsch. Lab., Champaign, Ill., 1979-83; dir. Nuclear Survivability, Security and Safety Directorate, Hdqrs. Def. Nuclear Agy., Washington, 1983-87; ret., 1987; dir. Constrn. Rsch. Ctr., Ga. Inst. Tech., Atlanta, 1987—98; prin. rsch. scientist Ga. Tech Rsch. Inst., Atlanta, 1998—. Mem.: ASCE, Soc. Am. Mil. Engrs., Assn. U.S. Army, Sigma Xi. Roman Catholic. Achievements include patents for recovery of fuel products from carbonaceous matter using plasma arc; in-situ plasma soil stabilization method and apparatus; in-situ plasma remediation and vitrification of contaminated soils, deposits and buried materials. Avocations: reading, travel. Home: 4245 Navajo Trl NE Atlanta GA 30319-1532 Office: Ga Tech Rsch Inst Atlanta GA 30332-0837 Office Phone: 404-407-8070. Business E-Mail: lou.circeo@gtri.gatech.edu. *It is important that an individual does the most with his God-given talents for the betterment of mankind.*

CIRELLO, JOHN, utility and engineering company executive; b. Bound Brook, NJ, Apr. 17, 1943; s. Fiore Avanti and Assunta Cirello; m. Sherron Anne Thomas, July 31, 1965; children: Sueann, Elizabeth Rose, Sherron Marie. BS, Rutgers U., 1965, MS, 1971, PhD, 1975. Registered profl. engr., N.J., Pa. Engr. Calif. Dept. Water, LA, 1965-66, U.S. Army Corps of Engrs., Ft. Belvoir, Va., 1966-68, Balt. Gas and Elec., 1968-69; rschr. Rutgers Water Resources Inst., New Brunswick, NJ, 1969-71; asst. prof. Rutgers U., New Brunswick, 1971-80; pres. Princeton Aqua Sci., Edison, NJ, 1980-85; v.p. IT Corp., Edison, NJ, 1985-88; v.p. ea. region Chem. Waste Mgmt., Inc., Princeton, NJ, 1988-92; pres. Metcalf & Eddy Svcs., Inc., Branchburg, NJ, 1992-95; with Environ. Engring. Svcs. Inc., 1995-96; pres., CEO Fla. Water Svcs. Corp., 1995—2002; exec. v.p. Allete Corp., Duluth, Minn., 1995—2002; v.p. WRF Ga. LLC, 2002—; dir. Environ. Svcs. Dept., Seminole County, Fla., 2005—. Editor (tng. manuals) Land Application of Effluents & Sludges, 1976, Ultimate Disposal of Organic and Inorganic Sludges, 1976, Water and Wastewater Polishing and Rennovation Techniques, 1976; co-editor (tng. manual) Construction and Environmental Inspectors Training Manual, 1977; contbr. articles to profl. jours. Mem. Bd. Adjustment, Bound Brook, N.J., 1976-81; councilman, pres., Bound Brook Town Coun., 1981-87; chmn. Dem. com. Bound Brook, 1982-86; Grad. Leadership Fla. Class XVI. Capt. U.S. Army Engr. Corps, 1966-68. Recipient award NJ Water Pollution Control Assn., 1990, Sterm leadership award, 2006. Mem.: ASCE, Fla. Water Wks. Assn. (bd. dirs. 1997—2002), Am. Chem. Soc., Water Environ. Fedn., Fla. State C. of C. Roman Catholic. Avocations: antique and classic cars, golf. Home: 540 Winding Creek Pl Longwood FL 32779-6119 Office Phone: 407-665-2012. Personal E-mail: drh20@cfl.rr.com. Business E-Mail: jcirello@seminolecountyfl.gov.

CIRELLO, RICHARD, physician, director; b. Hackensack, NJ, Oct. 8, 1945; s. Dominick Cirello; m. Caryle Lee Stroosnyder, June 28, 1969; children: Christina Lorraine Dunn, James Richard, Kathleen Caryle. BA, Rutgers U., 1967, B in Pharmacy, 1969; MD, Universidad Autonoma De Guadalajara, Mex., 1975. Cert. Am. Bd. Family Medicine, 1979. Family physician Town Med. Assocs., Verona, NJ, 1996—; program dir. Mountainside Family Practice Residency, 2005—. Del. NJ Acad. Family Physicians, Trenton. Named NJ Family Physician Yr, NJ Assn Family Physicians, 2006. Fellow: Am. Acad. Family Physicians. Avocation: golf. Office: Town Med Assocs 271 Grove Ave Verona NJ 07044 Home Phone: 973-857-2070; Office Phone: 973-239-2600. Office Fax: 973-239-0482. Business E-Mail: rcirello@townmedical.org.

CIRESE, ROBERT CHARLES, economist, real estate consultant; b. Oak Park, Ill., Feb. 25, 1938; s. Ferd Louis and Ruth (Olson) Cirese; m. Sarah Jane Williams, Apr. 3, 1965 (div. 1973); children: Lesley Mesarchik, Jeffrey Robert. BS, DePaul U., 1961; MS, U. Ill., 1963; postgrad., U. Calif., Berkeley, 1964. Lic. real estate broker Calif., cert. coll. tchr. Calif. Instr. Monmouth Coll., Ill., 1962—63; economist State of Calif. Employment Divsn., San Francisco, 1965—67; assoc. prof. Golden Gate U., San Francisco, 1967—72; v.p. Larry Smith & Co., San Francisco, 1972—77; dir. PricewaterhouseCoopers, San Francisco, 1977—79; v.p. Rubloff Inc., San Francisco, 1979—85; pres. Cirese Assocs., Sausalito, Calif., 1985—; concession mgr. bus. mgmt. divsn. Nat. Pk. Svc. Dept. Interior, San Francisco, 1994—; adj. prof. U. Phoenix, San Francisco, 2006—. Guest lectr.; spkr. in field; econ., fin. and real estate investment counselor corps., govt. agys., pvt. insts. Contbr. articles to profl. jours. Active Stanford U. Buck Fund, U. Calif. Berkeley Bear Backer, Berkeley Repertory Theater, Calif. Shakespeare Festival; bd. dirs. San Francisco Camp Fire, Inc., 1988—92; mem. San Francisco Ballet Assn., Am. Conservatory Theater, San Francisco Opera, San Francisco Symphony, Friends of Filoli, Sierra Club, San Francisco. With Ill. N.G., 1956—63. Mem.: Urban Land Inst., San Francisco Planning and Urban Rsch. Assn., Counselors of Real Estate (past chmn. No. Calif. chpt. 1988—89, bd. dirs. 1986—), U. Calif. Berkeley Alumni Assn., Stanford Alumni Assn., San Francisco Commonwealth Club. Avocations: hiking, theater, sports, humor writing. Home: 54 Buckelew St Sausalito CA 94965-1120 Office: Fort Mason Bldg 201 San Francisco CA 94123 Office Phone: 415-561-4943. Personal E-mail: bob.cirese@sbcglobal.net. Business E-Mail: robert_cirese@nps.gov.

CIRESI, MICHAEL VINCENT, lawyer; b. St. Paul, Apr. 18, 1946; s. Samuel Vincent and Selena Marie (Bloom) Ciresi; m. Ann Ciresi; children: Caroline, Dominic, Adam. BBA, U. St. Thomas, 1968; JD, U. Minn., 1971; LLD (hon.), Southwestern U., 2001. Bar: Minn. 1971, U.S. Dist. Ct. Minn. 1974, U.S. Ct. Appeals (8th cir.) 1971, U.S. Supreme Ct. 1981, U.S. Ct. Appeals (2d cir.) 1986, U.S. Ct. Appeals (9th cir.) 1987, U.S. Ct. Appeals (10th cir.) 1990, NY 1995, Fed. Cir. 1998, U.S. Ct. Appeals (5th cir.) 1999. Assoc. Robins, Kaplan, Miller & Ciresi, Mpls., 1971—78, ptnr., 1978—, exec. bd., 1983—, chmn. exec. bd., 1995—2006. Trustee U. St. Thomas, Saint Thomas Acad. Performing Arts; bd. dirs. Minn. Early Learning Found.; candidate U.S. Senate, 2000; bd. govs. U. St. Thomas Sch. Law; bd. dirs. Inst. Jud. Adminstrn. Sch. Law NYU; bd. dirs. Lawyers' Com. Civil Rights Under Law, Regions Hosp. Found., Pub. Radio Internat. Named Product Liability Lawyer of Yr., Australian Nat. Consumer Law Assn., 1989, Trial Lawyer of Yr., Trial Lawyers for Pub. Justice Found., 1998; named one of Ten of the Nation's Top Trial Lawyers, Nat. Law Jour., 1989, 1993, 100 Most Influential Lawyers, 1997, 2000, 2006; recipient Lifetime Achievement Award, Minn. Trial Lawyers, 1998, Disting. Alumnus Award, U. St. Thomas, 1999, Outstanding Achievement Award, U. Minn., 1999, Ellis Island Medal of Honor, Nat. Ethnic Coalition of Orgns. Found., 2002. Mem.: ATLA, ABA, Am. Coll. Trial Lawyers, Internat. Acad. Trial Lawyers, Trial Lawyers for Pub. Justice, Inner Cir. of Advocates, Internat. Bar Assn., Am. Bd. Trial Advocates, Ramsey County Bar Assn., Hennepin County Bar Assn., Minn. State Bar Assn. Roman Catholic. Avocations: sports, U.S. history. Home: 1247 Culligan Ln Saint Paul MN 55118-4151 Office: Robins Kaplan Miller & Ciresi 2800 Lasalle Plz Minneapolis MN 55402 Office Phone: 612-349-8533. Business E-Mail: mvciresi@rkmc.com.

CIRINCIONE, ROSS JOSEPH, mathematician, educator; b. Cleve., Apr. 8, 1948; s. Charles Ignatius and Mary Italia Cirincione. BA, Dartmouth Coll., 1970; MS, Harvard U., 1972; PhD, U. Calif., Berkeley, 1979. Radar sys. analyst Hughes Aircraft Co., El Segundo, Calif., 1981—83, stats. quality control instr., 1983—86; instrnl. asst. El Camino CC, Torrance, Calif., 1996—98; math. lectr. Case Western Res. U., Cleve., 2000—. Author: (company manual) Concepts in Experimental Design, 1985. Mem.: Am. Math. Soc., Dartmouth Alumni Assn. Avocations: photography, travel, jazz. Office: Case Western Res Univ 10900 Euclid Ave Cleveland OH 44106 Business E-Mail: rjc13@case.edu.

CIRONE, WILLIAM JOSEPH, educational administrator; b. Bklyn., Dec. 27, 1937; s. Joseph Nicholas and Marie Ann (Basile) C.; m. Barbara Jane Skirkie, Dec. 22, 1962; 1 child, Peter Craig. BA, Providence Coll., 1959; MA, NYU, 1960; adminstrv. cert., U. Calif., Santa Barbara, 1977. Tchr. N.Y.C. Pub. Schs., 1960-68; dir. product devel. ednl. divsn. Mead Corp., Atlanta, 1968-70, dir. mktg., 1970-73; founder, dir. Ctr. Cmty. Edn. and Citizen Participation, Santa Barbara, Calif., 1973-82; supt. schs. Santa Barbara County, 1983—. Vis. fellow Chisholm Inst. Tech., Melbourne, Australia, 1986; vis. scholar Ctr. for Excellence Tenn. State U., 1986. Host (cable talk shows) Education On-Line-A Line to Learning, Cirone on Schools. Bd. dirs., chair student aide com. Santa Barbara Cmty. Found., bd. dirs., 1998—, bd. chmn., 2003—04; bd. dirs. Cmty. Action Commn., 1973—81, Cmty. Resource Info. Svc., 1978—82, Fin. Crisis Mgmt. Assistance Team, 1993—, Nat. Partnership in Edn., 1998—, S.B. Fightnig Balk, 1994—, chmn., 2002—, Calif. Alliance for Arts Edn., 1999—, Santa Barbara Anti-Defamation League, 2001—; bd. dirs., sec. Pvt. Industry Coun., Santa Barbara, 1999—; bd. dirs. Industry Edn. Coun., Santa Barbara, 1983—, pres., 1990, 1999; bd. dirs. Coun. of Alcoholism and Drug Abuse, 1998—, Santa Barbara Lung Assn., 1983—87, Philip Francis Siff Ednl. Found., 1986—, Impact II, 1989—, pres., 1993—99, 2005—06; bd. dirs. Nat. Comm. Edn. Assn., 1989—92, pres., 1990; regional chair Calif. County Supt. Assn., 1990—96, bd. dirs. media and values, 1989—92; hon. bd. dirs. So. Coast Spl. Olympics; mem. Gov.'s Commn. on Earthquake Hazards, 1981; mem. state bd. Common Cause, 1974—77; organizer and 1st state chmn. Ga., 1970—73; mem. voter accessibility adv. bd. Santa Barbara County, 1986—; mem. adv. bd. CALM, Peace Resource Ctr., Marymount Sch., Women's Cmty. Bldg., Jodi House, Girl Scouts U.S.; comdrs. cmty. liaison com. Vandenberg AFB; mem. Access Theatre, Hon. Commn. for Goleta Hosp.; mem. campaign cabinet Santa Barbara

United Way, 1991, 1998; co-chair State Supts. Statewide Arts Task Force, 1997; pres.-elect Nat. Ctr. for Learning and Citizenship, 2004, 2005; bd. chmn. Nat. Com. for Citizenship and Learning, 2007. Recipient Smallheiser award United Fedn. Tchrs., 1968, Hon. Svc. award 15th Dist. PTA, 1979, 81, Intercongregation Orgn. Project Action award, 1995, Anti-Defamation League Santa Barbara Disting. Svc. award, 1996, Meritorious Svc. award Cmty. Action Com., Santa Barbara, 1981, Ind. Living Resource Ctr., 1985, Hon. Svc. award Calif. State PTA, 1995, 99 for '99 award, Santa Barbara C. of C., 1993-99, Profl. Publ. award Calif. County Supts. Assn., Comm. Achievement award Toastmasters Internat., 1999, Santa Barbara Wildlife Care Network award, 2000, Excellence in Svc. award South Coast Bus. and Tech., 2000, Vanguard award, 2002, Calif. Outstanding Art Educators' award Calif. Art's Commn., Emmanus Disting. Cmty. Svc. award, 2002-, Easy Lift Van Guard award, 2002, Lifetime Achievement award Santa Barbara News Press, 2004, Cmty. Action Champion award 2006, Lifetime Achievement award Calif. Art's Commn., 2006; named Calif. Cmty. Educator of Yr., Calif. Cmty. Edn. Assn., 1984, Pub. Servant of Yr. Santa Barbara County, 1987, County Supt. of Yr., 2007. Mem. World Future Soc. (life), Am. Assn. Sch. Adminstrs., Assn. Calif. Sch. Adminstrs. (Region XIII Adminstr. of Yr. award 2002), So. Coast Coord. Coun. (past chmn., past exec. com.), Nat. Soc. Fundraising Execs., Automobile Assn. Am. (So. Calif. adv. bd.), Phi Delta Kappa. Democrat. Unitarian Universalist. Home: 218 Valhalla Dr Solvang CA 93463-9608 Office: PO Box 6307 Santa Barbara CA 93160-6307

CIRULNICK, ARTHUR E., lawyer; b. Bklyn., June 20, 1954; BA, U. Calif. Santa Barbara, 1975; JD magna cum laude, U. San Francisco, 1979. Bar: DC 1979. Ptnr., Corp. Fin. & Securities Dept. Venable LLP, Washington, DC. Adj. prof. George Washington U. Law Ctr., Washington, 1985—; lectr. in field. Contbr. Mem.: DC Bar. Office: Venable LLP 575 7th St NW Washington DC 20004 Office Phone: 202-344-8511. Office Fax: 202-344-8300. Business E-Mail: aecirulnick@venable.com.

CISCHKE, SUSAN MARY, automotive executive; b. Detroit, 1954; BS, Oakland U., 1979; MS in Mech. Engring. and Mgmt., U. Mich., Dearborn. Engr. DaimlerChrysler Corp. (formerly Chrysler Corp.), 1976, gen. mgr. sci. labs. and proving grounds, 1994—96, v.p. vehicle certification, compliance and safety affairs, 1996—99, sr. v.p. regulatory Affairs and passenger car ops., 1999—2001; v.p. environ. and safety engring., chief safety officer Ford Motor Co., Dearborn, Mich., 2001—07, sr. v.p. sustainability, environ. and safety engring., 2007—. Bd. mem. Chgo. Climate Exchange, Henry Ford Health Sys. Found., Detroit Sci. Ctr.; Ford Motor Co. liaison World Bus. Coun. for Sustainable Devel.; mem. nat. adv. com. U. Mich. Coll. Engring. Bd. dirs. Inforu, Ctr. for Leadership; chair Women's Initiative United Way of S.E. Mich. Named one of Most Influential Women, Crain's Detroit Bus. Mem.: Women's Econ. Club (mem. leadership bd.), Engring. Soc. Detroit (Horace H. Rackham Award 1997), Soc. Women Engineers (Upward Mobility Award 2000), Soc. Automotive Engrs. Office: Ford Motor Co 1 American Rd Dearborn MI 48126*

CISKE, KAREN LYSBETH, retired medical/surgical nurse; b. Chgo., Dec. 28, 1937; d. Harry and Cleo Atkinson; m. Donald Albert Ciske, Mar. 21, 1959. BSN, Northwestern U., Chgo., 1960; MSN, U. Minn., Mpls., 1967. RN Ill., 1960, Minn., 1962. Staff nurse Wesley Meml. Hosp., Chgo., 1960—61; instr. nursing Ill. Masonic Sch., Chgo., 1961—62, Mounds-Midway Sch. Nursing, St. Paul, 1962—65; clinician, supr. U. Minn. Hosp., Mpls., 1967—74; cons. Primary Nursing Devel., Arden Hills, Minn., 1974—83; asst. prof. Bethel Coll. Sch. Nursing, St. Paul, 1983—2002; ret., 2002. Creator, dir. Advanced Primary Nursing Conf., Mpls., 1978; co-creator primary nursing professionalizing nursing U. Minn. Hosp., Mpls., 1968—74. Contbr. articles to profl. jours.; editor: Nursing Dimensions, 1979. Organist Presbyn. Ch. of the Way, Shoreview, Minn., 1974—98, facilitator youth music, chmn. fundraising. Faculty rsch. grantee, Bethel Coll., 1990. Mem.: Minn. Nurses' Assn., Am. Guild Organists, Sigma Theta Tau. Avocations: travel, gardening, music, reading. Home: 1708 Lake Valentine Rd Arden Hills MN 55112

CISKOWSKI, MICHAEL S., energy executive; BBA in Fin., MBA in Fin., Ctrl. State U., Okla. Position in fin. and planning Williams Exploration Co., Getty Oil Co.; various positions including investor rels. dir., fin. planning dir., mgr. fin. planning Valero Energy Corp., San Antonio, exec. v.p., CFO, 2003—. Office: Valero Corp PO Box 696000 San Antonio TX 78269-6000*

CISNEROS, HENRY G., homebuilding and broadcast executive, retired federal official; b. San Antonio, June 11, 1947; s. J. George and Elvira (Munguia) C.; m. Mary Alice Perez; children: Teresa Angelica, Mercedes Christina, John Paul. BA, Tex. A&M U., 1969, M. Urban and Regional Planning, 1970; MPA, Harvard U., 1973; D. Public Adminstrn., George Washington U., 1975. Adminstrv. asst. to city mgr., San Antonio, 1968, Bryan, Tex., 1969-70; asst. dir. dept. model cities San Antonio, 1969-70; asst. to exec. v.p. Nat. League Cities, Washington, 1970-71; White House fellow asst. Sec. of HEW, Washington, 1971-72; teaching asst. dept. urban studies and planning M.I.T., 1972; mem. City Coun., San Antonio, 1975-81; mayor City of San Antonio, 1981-89; chmn. Cisneros Asset Mgmt., 1989-93; sec. U.S. Dept. HUD, Washington, 1993-97; pres., COO, Univision Comm., Inc., LA, 1997-2000; chmn. City View, San Antonio, 2005—. Chmn. Nat. Civic League; vice chair New Am. Alliance. Recipient Thomas Jefferson award for pub. architecture AIA, 1995. Office: City View 454 Soledad St Ste 300 San Antonio TX 78205-1555 Fax: 210-228-9906. E-mail: hcisneros@city-view.net.

CISSELL, JAMES CHARLES, lawyer; b. Cleve., May 29, 1940; s. Robert Francis and Helen Cecelia (Freeman) C; children: Denise, Helene-Marie, Suzanne, James. Student, Sophia U., Tokyo, 1961; AB, Xavier U., 1962; postgrad., Ohio State U., 1963—64; JD, U. Cin., 1966; D. Tech. Letters, Cin. Tech. Coll., 1979. Bar: Ohio 1966, U.S. Dist. Ct. (so. dist.) Ohio 1967, U.S. Ct. Appeals (6th cir.) 1978, U.S. Supreme Ct. 1980, U.S. Dist. Ct. (ea. dist.) Ky. 1981. Pvt. practice law, 1966—78, 1982—2003; asst. atty. gen. State of Ohio, 1971-74; first v.p. Cin. Bd. Park Commrs., 1973-74; vice mayor City of Cin., 1976-77; U.S. atty. So. Dist. Ohio, Cin., 1978-82. Adj. instr. law No. Ky. U., 1982-86; pres. Nat. Assn. Former U.S. attys., 2001-02; mem. Legis. Task Force to Study Eminent Domain and It's Use and Application in the State of Ohio, 2006—. Author: Oil and Gas Law in Ohio, 1964, Federal Criminal Trials, 6th edit., 2003; editor: Proving Federal Crimes. Gen. chmn. amateur pub. links championship U.S. Golf Assn., 1987; mem. coun. City of Cin., 1974-78, 85-87, 89-92; clk of cts., Hamilton County, 1992-2003; judge Hamilton County Probate Ct., 2003-; commr. Recreation Bd. Cin., 1974, Planning Bd. Cin., 1977; pres. Ohio Clk. of Cts. Assn., 1998; mem. Ohio Bicentennial Commn., 1998-2003; mem. Ohio Cts. Futures Commn., 1998-2000; mem. Ohio Supreme Ct. Adv. Com. on Tech. and the Cts., 2000—, privacy of access subcom. of Supreme Ct. adv. com. on tech. of the Cts. Recipient Econ. Opportunity award, Dr. Martin Luther King Jr. Holiday Commn., 2002; fellow, Ford Found., 1973—74. Mem. Ohio Bar Assn., Cin. Bar Assn., Fed. Bar Assn., Former U.S. Attys. Assn. (pres. 2002-03), Greater Cin. Golf Assn. (pres. 2003-). Avocations: golf, table tennis. Office: William Howard Taft Law Ctr 230 E 9th St 10th Fl Cincinnati OH 45202 Office Phone: 513-946-3535. Business E-Mail: jcissell@probatect.org.

CITERA, PETER M., mortgage company executive; b. Skokie, Ill., Feb. 10, 1975; s. Anthony J. and Marcia R. Citera. BA, Miami U., Oxford, Ohio, 1997. Lic. mortgage loan broker Wis., 2003, loan originator Ind., 2004, mortgage broker Fla., 2005, mortgage loan originator Ill., 2005. Dir. ParagonCo, Chgo., 1997—2002; sr. mortgage banker, warehouse lending mgr. Providential Bancorp, Ltd., Chgo., 2002—04; v.p. A Am. Fin. Group, Inc., Chgo., 2004—. Pres. Windy City Darters, Inc., Chgo., 2004—. Named to Nat. Darts Hall of Fame, 2005. Mem.: Ill. Assn. Mortgage Brokers, Nat. Assn. Mortgage Brokers (assoc.), Torists Internat. S.S., Windy City Darters (pres. 2004—06), Kappa Kappa Psi (life). Conservative. Cath. Avocations: English darts, travel, writing. Office: A Am FinGroup Inc 1239 W Madison 2d Floor Chicago IL 60607 Home Phone: 847-373-9176; Office Phone: 312-491-9911, Home Fax: 312-896-9032. Personal E-mail: citerap@sbcglobal.net. E-mail: peter@aafgi.com.

CITRANO-CUMMISKEY, DEBRA MOIRA, chemist, network technician; b. Glen Cove, NY, Feb. 23, 1957; d. Helen Marie and Roy Maurice Citrano; 1 child, Nikki Marie Cummiskey. Student, Hofstra U.; BS in Edn., Almeda U., 2004, BS in Chemistry, 2004. A+ Certification Computer Career Ctr., 2002. Raw materials auditor Hi-Tech Pharm., Amityville, NY, 2003—; qc raw materials chemist Kos Pharmaceuticals, Edison, NJ, 2003—03. Corp. reference std. coord. DuPont Pharmaceuticals, Garden City, NY, 1978—2001. Mem.: Am. Chem. Soc. American Independent. Roman Catholic. Avocations: dance, swimming. Office: Hi-Tech Pharmacal Co Inc 369 Bayview Avenue Amityville NY 11701 Personal E-mail: corporatewoman@msn.com.

CITRON, BEATRICE SALLY, law librarian, educator; b. Phila., May 19, 1929; d. Morris Meyer and Frances (Teplitsky) Levinson; m. Joel P. Citron, Aug. 7, 1955 (dec. Sept. 1977); children: Deborah Ann, Victor Ephraim. BA in Econs. with honors, U. Pa., 1950; MLS, Our Lady of the Lake U., 1978; JD, U. Tex., 1984. Bar: Tex. 1985; cert. sch. libr., tchr. Tex. Claims examiner Social Security Adminstrn., Pa., Fla. and N.C., 1951-59; head libr. St. Mary's Hall, San Antonio, 1979-80; media, reference and rare book libr., asst. and assoc. prof. St. Mary's U. Law Libr., San Antonio, 1984-89; asst. dir. St. Thomas U. Law Libr., Miami, Fla., 1989-96, assoc. dir./head pub. svc., 1996-99, acting dir., 1997-98. Law libr. cons., 2000—. Mem.: ABA, South Fla. Assn. Law Librs. (treas. 1992—94, v.p. 1994—95, pres. 1995—96), S.E. Assn. Law Librs. (newsletter, program and edn. coms. 1991—98), S.W. Assn. Law Librs. (continuing edn. com. 1986—88, chmn. local arrangements 1987—88), Am. Assn. Law Librs. (publs. com. 1987—88, com. on rels. with info. vendors 1991—93, bylaws com. 1994—96).

CITRON, DIANE, lawyer; b. Cin., Oct. 9, 1953; d. Carl and Georgia (Reid) C. BA, Franklin and Mareshall Coll., 1975; JD, Case Western Res. U., 1978. Bar: D.C. 1978, Calif. 1985. Assoc. Wasserman, Orlow, Ginsberg & Rubin, Washington, 1978-80; staff atty. SEC, Washington, 1980-83; sr. counsel Freddie Mac, Washington, 1983-84; assoc. Orrick, Herrington & Sutcliffe, San Francisco, 1984-85, Brown & Wood, San Francisco, 1985-87; spl. counsel Skadden, Arps, Slate, Meagher & Flom, San Francisco, 1987-92; ptnr. Mayer, Brown Rowe & Maw LLP, NYC, 1992—; gen. counsel, chief compliance officer Carrington Capital Mgmt. LLC, Greenwich, Conn. Adj. prof. law real estate LLM program John Marshall Law Sch. Real Estate, Chgo., 1995—. Mem. ABA (subcom. securitization real property sect.), FBA, Women's Art Assn. D.C., Bar Assn. D.C., Pi Gamma Mu. Democrat. Jewish.

CITRON, RICHARD IRA, management consultant; b. Chgo., Apr. 1, 1944; s. Irving I. and Ruth (Katz) C.; m. Phyllis Sarah Kalifey, Dec. 26, 1971; children: Brian Todd, Dana Ann. BS, Roosevelt U., Chgo., 1966; MS, Ill. Inst. Tech., 1968, PhD, 1972. Enrolled Actuary. Consulting prin. A.S. Hansen, Inc., Chgo., 1972-79, mng. prin. NYC, 1979-82; exec. v.p. Frank B. Hall Consulting Co., NYC, 1982-86; pres., CEO W F Corroon, Inc., Stamford, Conn., 1986-92; pres. Benefit Svcs. div., exec. v.p., dir. Hogg Robinson, Inc., NYC, 1992-95; CEO Penn Gen. Svcs. Corp., Inc., NYC, 1992-95; chmn. Hogg Robinson Consulting Group, Inc., NYC, 1992-95, Group Plan Cons., Inc., NYC, 1992-95; corp. dir. worldwide benefits Campbell Soup Co., Inc., Camden, NJ, 1996—2002; CEO Nortic Cons., LLC, 2002—. Chmn., CEO Citron & Assocs., Inc.; bd. dirs. Employee Benefit Rsch. Inst., Washington, HRI, Inc., N.A; adv. bd. mem. Am. Benefits Coun., 1998—. Author articles in profl. jours. Trustee Optometric Ctr. of N.Y., mem. Coll. Council of SUNY; cons. State of Ill. Pension Laws Commn. 1974-78 Recipient: Blum-Kolver Found. grant 1963-66, Nat. Sci. Found. grant 1968-70. Mem. Am. Acad. of Actuaries, Internat. Found. Employee Benefits (chmn actuaries com. 1981-82), Assn. of Private Pension and Welfare Plans, Am. Soc. for Advancement of Sci., Boardroom, Landmark, Elmwood Country Club. E-mail: mardino@aol.com.

CITRONELLE, MICHEL RICHARD, chef; Owner, pastry chef Michel Richard, LA, 1977; owner, exec. chef Citrus, Calif., 1987, Citronelle, Santa Barbara, Calif., 1989—98, Balt., Phila., Washington, 1994—, Bistro M, San Francisco. Contbr. articles Food & Wine mag., Food Arts, Saveur, Bon Appetit, Wine Spectator, Wind Advocate; featured on Gourmet mag. cover, 2004, appearances on (TV series) Martha Stewart, Julia Child, Good Morning Am., Food Network, Outdoor Living Channel, PBS, CBS Early Show, Washington DC TV9, French TV TFI, Colameco's Food Show; author: Home Cooking with a French Accent, 1993, Happy in the Kitchen, 2006. Named Outstanding Chef, James Beard Found., 2007, Best Chef of Yr., Restaurant Assn. Metro. Washington, 2002. Office: 3000 M St NW Washington DC 20007 Office Phone: 202-625-2150.

CIUBOTARU, DAN, mathematics professor; b. Romania; married. PhD, Cornell Univ., 2004. Moore instr. math MIT. Achievements include being one of 18 top mathematicians and computer scientists (Atlas of Lie Groups Project) from the US to successfully map E8, one of the largest and most complicated structures in mathematics. Office: Dept Math 2-179 22 Massachusetts Ave Cambridge MA 02139-4307 Office Phone: 617-253-4388. Business E-Mail: ciubo@math.mit.edu.

CIVGIN, DON, corporate financial executive; B fin., Univ. Ill.; MBA, Univ. Chgo. V.p., treas. Alliant Foodservice Inc.; sr. v.p., fin. & mdse. ops. Montgomery Ward; sr. v.p., CFO Gen. Binding Corp., 2002—05; exec. v.p., CFO OfficeMax Inc., Itasca, Ill., 2005—. Office: OfficeMax Inc 150 E Pierce Rd Itasca IL 60143-1291*

CIVILETTI, BENJAMIN RICHARD, lawyer, former United States attorney general; b. Peekskill, NY, July 17, 1935; s. Benjamin C. and Virginia I. Civiletti; m. Gaile Lundgren Civiletti, 1958; 3 children. AB, Johns Hopkins U., 1957; LLB, Columbia U. and U. Md., 1961; LLD (hon.), U. Balt., 1978, NY Law Sch., 1979, Tulane U., 1979, St. John's Coll., 1979, U. Notre Dame, 1980, U. Md., 1983; LHD (hon.), Towson State U. Bar: Md. 1961, US Supreme Ct. 1965, DC 1981. Law clk. to the Hon. W. Calvin Chesnut US Dist. Ct. for Md., 1961-62; asst. US atty. Dist. Md. US Dept. Justice, 1962-64; assoc. Venable, Baetjer & Howard, Balt., 1964—68, ptnr., 1969—77, head litig. dept., 1971—77; asst. atty. gen. criminal divsn. US Dept. Justice, Washington, 1977-78, dep. atty. gen., 1978-79, atty. gen., 1979-81; ptnr. Venable LLP, Balt., 1981—2006, chmn., 1996—2006, sr. ptnr., 2006—. Founding chair Md. Legal Services Corp., 1982—86; mem. legal adv. bd. Lexis-Nexis/Martindale-Hubbell, 1990—; mem. lawyers com. Nat. Ctr. for State Courts, 2004—; dir. MBNA Corp., MBNA Internat.; mem. Matthew Bender & Co., Inc. Mem. bd. editors Fed. Litig. Guide Reporter; contbr. articles to profl. jours. Trustee Johns Hopkins U., 1980—98. Named Knight-Comdr., Order of Merit of the Italian Republic; recipient Herbert H. Lehman Ethics Award, Am. Jewish Theol. Sem., Disting. Alumnus Award, Johns Hopkins Alumni Assn., Equal Justice Award, Balt. Urban League, 1997, Am. Judicature Society's Justice award, 2005. Fellow Am. Bar Found., Am. Law Inst., Am. Coll. Trial Lawyers; mem. ABA (mem. ho. dels. 1990-, Commn. on Am. Jury, chmn. Task Force on Internat. Criminal Ct., rep. to UN), FBA, Md. Bar Assn., DC Bar Assn., Bar Assn. Balt. City, Am. Judicature Soc., Omicron Delta Kappa, Phi Alpha Delta., Order of Coif. Office: Venable LLP 1800 Merc Bank & Trust Bldg 2 Hopkins Plz Ste 2100 Baltimore MD 21201-2982*

CLAAR, VICTOR, economist, educator; s. Herbert and Marcille Claar; m. Elizabeth Greer Oswalt, Aug. 29, 1992. BA in Bus. Adminstrn., Houghton Coll., NY, 1987; MA in Econs., W.Va. U., Morgantown, 1995, PhD in Econs., 2000. Asst prof. econs Hope Coll., Holland, Mich., 2000—06, assoc. prof. econs, 2006—. Author: (book) Economics in Christian Perspective: Theory, Policy and Life Choices, 2007; contbr. articles to profl. jours. Bd. dirs. Black River Pub. Sch., Holland, Mich., 2005—07. Fellow, Fulbright Found., 2006—07. Office: Hope Coll Dept Econs PO Box 9000 Holland MI 49422-9000 Office Phone: 616-395-7579. Office Fax: 616-395-7490.

CLAASSEN, W(ALTER) MARSHALL, employment company executive; b. St. Paul, Jan. 16, 1943; s. Walter Marshall and Marie Christine (Petersen) C.; m. Nancy Rector Alcock, Mar. 2, 1974; children: Katherine, Walter. BA, BJ, U. Mo., 1966. Sr. adminstr. Honeywell, Inc., Chgo., 1968-74; pers. dir. Lyon-Healy, div. of CBS, Inc., Chgo., 1974-78; mgr., corp. placement CF Industries, Long Grove, Ill., 1978-82; mgr. of recruiting Newark Electronics, Chgo., 1983-84; dir. human resources Swift, div. of Reichold Chem., Downers Grove, Ill., 1984-86, ECM, Inc., Schaumburg, Ill., 1986-87; pres. GBX, Inc., dba Express Personnel Svcs., Vernon Hills, 1988—. Bd. dirs. Elk Grove-Schaumburg Mental Health Ctr., 1975-77, Pvt. Industry Coun. of Lake County, Waukegan, Ill., 1990-96, chmn., 1994-96; bd. dirs. Pvt. Industry Coun. Found., 1992—, Lake County Workforce Investment Bd., 2000—. Lt.(j.g.) USNR, 1966-68. Recipient Circle of Excellence award, 1992—. Mem. Libertyville-Vernon Hills C. of C., Lake County C. of C., Lincolnshire C. of C., Arlington Heights C. of C., Univ. Mo. Alumni Assn., Phi Delta Theta. Republican. Mem. Soc. Of Friends. Avocations: fly fishing, scuba diving. Office: Express Personnel Svcs 977 Lakeview Pkwy Ste 190 Vernon Hills IL 60061-1429 Home Phone: 847-381-7731. Personal E-mail: marshall.claassen@comcast.net.

CLABBY, MICHAEL, computer graphics designer, educator; m. Cindy Clabby; 1 child, Casey. Computer graphics, multimedia tchr. Lake City H.S., Coeur d' Alene, Idaho. Named Idaho Tchr. of Yr., 2007. Office: Lake City High Sch , 3101 Ramsey Rd Coeur D' Alene ID 83815 Business E-Mail: mclabby@sd271.k12.id.us.*

CLACK, JERRY, classics educator; b. NYC, July 22, 1926; s. Christopher Thrower and Mildred Taylor (VanDyke) C. AB, Princeton U., 1946, MA, 1958; PhD, U. Pitts., 1962; MA, Duquesne U., Pitts., 1977. Documents officer U.S. Nat. Commn. for UNESCO, 1946-52; exec. dir. Allegheny County chpt. Nat. Found., Pitts., 1953-68; asst. prof. dept. classics Duquesne U., Pitts., 1968-71, assoc. prof., 1971-75, prof., 1975—, chmn. dept., 1973-75, 80-83, mem. preprofl. health com., 1970-76, mem. univ. library com., 1979-93, mem. univ. due process, core curriculum, arts and scis. curriculum coms., 1986-94, mem. univ. promotion and tenure com., 1988-90. Editor: The Classical World, 1977-93, Anthology of Hellenistic Poetry, 1982, Meleager: The Poems, 1992, Asclepiades of Samos and Leonidas of Tarentum: The Poems, 1999, Dioscorides and Antipater of Sidon: The Poems, 2001; mem. editl. bd. Duquesne Univ. Press, 1991-94; author books, articles, revs. in field. Pres. We. Pa. Pub. Health Conf., 1967; v.p. We. Pa. chpt. Citizens for Global Solutions, 1965—88, treas. We. Pa. chpt., 1987—; U.S. del. 3d UNESCO Gen. Conf., Florence, Italy, 4th UNESCO Gen. Conf., Paris; bd. dirs. Pitts. Opera Theater, treas., 2003—. Mem. Classical Assn. Pitts. and Vicinity (treas. 1970-78, 85-2006, sec. 1988-2006), Pa. Classical Assn. (treas. 1977-99, sec. 1983-2006), Classical Assn. Atlantic States (pres. 1987, exec. com. 1974—, 2d v.p. 1975, 1st v.p. 1976, exec. dir. 1993-2001, archivist 2001-05), Am. Philol. Assn. (chmn. working group editors classical jours. 1982-93, chmn. com. regional classical orgns. 1986-95), Vergilian Soc. Am. (trustee 1985-87), Phi Sigma Iota, Delta Phi Alpha, Alpha Epsilon Delta, Phi Alpha Theta. Home: Apt 512 5850 Centre Ave Pittsburgh PA 15206 Office: Duquesne U Dept Classics Pittsburgh PA 15282-0001 Office Phone: 412-396-6452. E-mail: clack@duq.edu.

CLAES, DANIEL JOHN, physician; s. John and Claribel Claes; m. Gayla Christine Claes, Jan. 19, 1974. AB magna cum laude, Harvard U., 1953, MD cum laude, 1957. Intern UCLA, 1957-58; Bowyer Found. fellow rsch. in medicine LA, 1958-61; pvt. practice specializing in diabetes, 1962—. V.p. Am. Eye Bank Found., 1978—83, dir. rsch., 1980—, pres., 1983—, chmn., CEO, 1995—; pres. Heuristic Group, 1981—, Cavendish Assocs., 2002—; biotech. cons. SIRA Techs., 1995—. Contbr. articles to profl. jours. Mem. LA Mus. Art, 1960—. Mem.: AAAS, AMA, Cell Transplantation Soc., Diabetes Tech. Soc., Am. Math. Soc., Internat. Pancreas and Islet Transplant Assn., Internat. Diabetes Fedn, Am. Diabetes Assn. (profl. coun. on immunology, immunogenetics and transplantation), Los Angeles County Med. Assn., Calif. Med. Assn., Royal Commonwealth Club (London), Harvard and Harvard Med. Sch. So. Calif. Club. Achievements include research in supercomputer bioinformatics in medicine, computational chemistry, molecular modeling, quantum chemistry, genomics, proteomics and preventive care. Office: Am Eyebank Found 15237 W Sunset Blvd Ste 108 Pacific Palisades CA 90272-3690

CLAES, GAYLA CHRISTINE, writer, editor, consultant; b. LA, Oct. 17, 1946; d. Henry George and Glorya Desiree Blasdel; m. Daniel John Claes, Jan. 19, 1974. AB magna cum laude, Harvard U., 1968; postgrad., Oxford U., Eng., 1971; MA, McGill U., Montreal, 1975. Adminstrv. asst. U. So. Calif., LA, 1968-70; teaching asst. English lit. McGill U., Montreal, 1970-71; editorial dir. Internat. Cons. Group, LA, 1972-78; v.p. Gaylee Corp., LA, 1978-81, CEO, 1981-88; writer, cons. L.A. and Paris, 1988—. Dir. pub. rels. Ctr. Internat. for the Performing Arts, Paris and L.A., 1991—2000. Author: (play) Berta of Hungary, 1972, (novel) Christopher Derring, 1990; contbr. articles to lit. and sci. jours. Co-founder White Swan Awards, ann. benefit for Crippled Children's Soc. dba AbilityFirst, 1999. Mem. Harvard-Radcliffe Club of So. Calif., Royal Commonwealth Soc. (London).

CLAEYS, JEROME JOSEPH, III, investment company executive; b. South Bend, Ind., Oct. 23, 1942; s. Jerry F. and Evadna (Shoemaker) Claeys; m. Barbara Lauman, May 4, 1974; children: Elizabeth Anne, Matthew Jerome, Andrew Francis, Katherine Ellen. BS, Georgetown U., 1965; MBA, U. Notre Dame, 1969. First v.p. White Weld & Co., NYC, 1969—76; exec. v.p. JMB Realty Corp., Chgo., 1977—89; chmn. JMB Instnl. Realty Corp. (JMB Instnl. Realty Corp. and JMB Properties Co. merged with Heitman Financial), Chgo., 1990—94; co-chmn. Heitman Capital Mgmt., 1995; chmn, CEO Heitman Financial LLC, 1999—2002, chmn., 2002—. With US Army, 1965—67. Decorated Bronze Star with oak leaf cluster. Mem.: PREA, Real Estate Roundtable. Roman Cath. Office: Heitman Financial 191 N Wacker Dr Ste 2500 Chicago IL 60606 Office Phone: 312-541-6740. Business E-Mail: jerry.claeys@heitman.com.

CLAFLIN, ARTHUR CARY, lawyer; b. Bowling Green, Ohio, July 7, 1950; s. Edward Scott and Mona Sophia (Cretney) C.; m. Gretchen Elaine Anders, May 31, 1975; children: Rachel Anders, Emily Anders. BA magna cum laude, Wesleyan U., 1972; JD, Yale U., 1975. Bar: Wash. 1975, U.S. Dist. Ct. (we. dist.) Wash. 1975, U.S. Dist. Ct. (ea. dist.) Wash. 1981, U.S. Ct. Appeals (9th cir.) 1979, U.S. Ct. Appeals (5th cir.) 1982. Assoc. Bogle & Gates, Seattle, 1975-81, ptnr., 1981-99, Claflin & Christensen, Seattle,

1999-2000; mem. Hall, Zanzig, Zulauf, Claflin, McEachern, Seattle, 2000—. Mem. Phi Beta Kappa. Presbyterian. Office: Hall Zanzig Zulauf Claflin McEachern 1200 5th Ave Ste 1414 Seattle WA 98101-3106 Office Phone: 206-292-5900.

CLAFLIN, BRUCE L., software company executive; BA in Polit. Sci., Pa. State U. Formerly with IBM Corp.; gen. mgr. IBM PC Co., 1989-93; pres. PC Co. Americas, 1993-94, gen. mgr. products and brand mgmt., 1994-97; former sr. v.p. and gen. mgr. sales and mktg. Digital Equipment Corp., 1997-98; pres., COO 3Com Corp., Santa Clara, Calif., 1998—2001, pres., CEO, 2001—06, sr. advisor to CEO, 2006—. Bd. dirs. Advanced Micro Devices, 2003—, Time Warner Telecom, 3Com Corp., 2001—. Mass. Bus. Roundtable. Alumni fellow Pa. State U., 1998.

CLAFLIN, JAMES ROBERT, pediatrician, allergist; b. Apr. 30, 1946; m. Marcee Claflin; children: James Sean (dec.), Brian Scott (dec.), Susan Nicole, Timothy Lynn. Student, Northwestern State Coll.; MD, U. Okla., 1971. Diplomate Am. Bd. Pediatrics, Am. Bd. Allergy Immunology. Intern U. Tex. Med. Br., Galveston, 1971-72; advanced through grades to lt. col. USAF, 1969-84, chief pediatric svcs. Goodfellow AFB, 1972-73, 75-77, chief pediatric svcs. and hosp. svcs. RAF Upper Heyford Eng., 1977-80, chief allergy and clin. immunology Carswell AFB, 1982-84; fellow allergy/immunology Willford Hall USAF Med. Ctr., Lackland AFB, Tex., 1980-82; ret. USAF, 1984. Clin. asst. prof. pediatrics, Oklahoma U.; presenter in field. Contbr. articles to profl. jours. Advisor child welfare com. Tom Green County, 1976-77; mem. child welfare com. RAF, Upper Heyford, Eng., 1978-80; mem. sch. and pub. health com. Tarrant County Med. Soc., 1984-85, chmn., 1986-87, publs. com., 1988-89, religion and meml. com., 1989; mem. quality assurance and infectious disease coms. Cook-Ft. Worth Children's Hosp., 1986-89; v.p. Brenham State Sch. Parent Assn., 1987-88; pres. Parents Assn. for the Retarded of Tex., 1987-88; chmn. cmty. conscience com. Wedgwood Bapt. Ch. Recipient Svc. award Am. Diabetes Assn., 1976. Fellow Am. Acad. Pediatrics, Am. Coll. Allergy (mem. com. on allergic rhinitis, mem. com. on adverse reactions to food 1991-96), Am. Acad. Allergy; mem. AMA (alt. del.), Am. Coll. Allergy, Asthma and Immunology (spkr. ho. of dels. 2001-03, bd.regents), Oklahoma County Med. Soc. (pres.-elect 2003-04, pres. 2004-05, v.p. 2005-06, pres.-elect 2006—), Okla. State Med. Assn. (sec.-treas. 2003-05, v.p., 2005—), Okla. Allergy and Asthma Soc. (pres. 1998-2000). Home: 750 NE 13th St Oklahoma City OK 73104-5051

CLAGETT, BRICE MCADOO, lawyer, writer, genealogist; b. Washington, July 6, 1933; s. Brice and Sarah Fleming (McAdoo) Clagett; m. Virginia Lawrence Parker, Sept. 18, 1965 (div.); children: John Brice, Ann Calvert Brooke; m. Diana Wharton Sinkler, July 26, 1987. AB summa cum laude, Princeton U., 1954; postgrad., U. Allahabad, India, 1954-55; JD magna cum laude, Harvard U., 1958. Bar: D.C. 1958, U.S. Supreme Ct. 1962. Assoc. Covington & Burling, Washington, 1958-67, ptnr., 1967-2000, sr. counsel, 2000—02. Jud. counsellor Cambodian del. Internat. Ct. Justice, 1960—62; legal advisor Transition Team U.S. Dept. State, 1980—81; mem. nat. steering com. U.S. Iran Claimants Com., 1982—99; adv. bd. Inst. Transt. Arbitration, 1989—2000; trustee Wentz Holdings, Inc., Charitable Remainder Unitrust, 2001—. Co-author: (book) The Valuation of Property in International Law, vol. 4, 1987, An Illustrated History of St. Albans School, 1981; bd. editors: Harvard Law Rev., 1956—58; contbr. articles to legal, geneal. and hist. jours. Trustee Md. Hist. Trust, 1971—78, chmn., 1972—78; trustee Md. State Ho. Trust, 1972—76, Md. Environ. Trust, 1978—, vice chmn., 1981—85, chmn., 1985—89; bd. dirs. Chester-Sassafras Found., 1985—89; trustee New Eng. Hist. Geneal. Soc., 1989—92, 1995—98, Tudor Place Found., 1992—96, Found. Preservation Hist. Georgetown, 2000—; bd. advisors Nat. Trust Hist. Preservation, 1978—81; Clagett family com. Chesapeake Bay Found., 1982—; mem. Human Rights Law Group del. to Romania, 1990; counselor to the Pres. Gen. Soc. Cin., 1988—98, solicitor, 1998—; mem. adv. coun. Accokeek Found., 1989—91, trustee, 1991—94; comdr. Royal Order Cambodia, 1962. Recipient Cert. Disting. Citizens, State of Md., 1978. Mem.: So. Md. Soc., Federalist Soc., Washington Inst. Fgn. Affairs, Internat. Law Assn., Am. Law Inst., Am. Soc. Internat. Law, Mil. Order Stars and Bars, City Tavern Club (D.C.), Radnor Hunt Club (Pa.), Marlborough Hunt Club (Upper Marlboro, Md.), Met. Club (D.C.), Soc. Cin. Md., SCV, Phi Beta Kappa. Republican. Episcopalian. Office: Covington & Burling PO Box 7566 1201 Pennsylvania Ave NW Washington DC 20044 Home: Holly Hill PO Box 86 Friendship MD 20758 Office Phone: 202-662-5316. Business E-Mail: bclagett@cov.com.

CLAGETT, DIANA WHARTON SINKLER, museum docent; b. Phila., Aug. 24, 1943; d. James Mauran Rhodes and Sarah Brinton (Wentz) Sinkler; m. Peter John Knop, Nov. 23, 1966 (div.); children: Alexandra Brinton, Peter Rhodes Quast, William James Wharton; m. Brice McAdoo Clagett, July 26, 1987. BA, George Wash. U., 1966. Rsch. asst. Nat. Investigations Com. on Aerial Phenomena, Washington, 1966—69; docent Asia Hall Smithsonian Instn., Washington, 1982—83, docent Sackler Gallery, 1989—, docent Freer Gallery, 1993—; propr. Georgian Antiques and Decorative Arts, Washington, 1983—; docent Anderson House, Washington, 2004—. Bd. dirs. Sinkler Corp., Wentz Corp.; mem. Smithsonian Ednl. Vol. Adv. Bd., 1990-93. Mem. bd. devel. Hosp. for Sick Children, Washington, 1980—, vice chmn. bd. devel., 1985-86, co-chmn. flower and garden festival, 1988-90; mem. bd. devel. Children's Hearing and Speech Ctr., Washington, 1988—; mem. women's com. Phila. Acad. Fine Arts, 1980—; mem. alumni bd. Foxcroft Sch., Middleburg, Va., 1983-86; trustee The McLean Sch., 1993-96; mem. Founders Washington Com. Historic Mt. Vernon, 2001—; trustee, Tudor Place Found., 2003—, chmn. collections com., 2004—; dir. Friends of Nat. Arboretum, 2007-. Mem. City Tavern Club (bd. govs. 1990-98), Radnor Hunt Club (racing com.), Acorn Club, Evermay Club Georgetown, New Scotland Garden Club (pres. 1993-94), Sulgrave Club. Avocations: gardening, Asian art. Home: Holly Hill PO Box 86 Friendship MD 20758 also: 3331 O St NW Washington DC 20007-2814

CLAGETT, VIRGINIA PARKER, state official; b. Washington, July 18, 1943; d. William Merrick and Virginia (Lawrence) Parker; m. Brice McAdoo, Sept. 18, 1965; children: John Brice, Ann Brooke. Student, U. Geneva, 1963-64; BA, Smith Coll., 1965. Asst. reporter Triangle Stas., Phila., 1966-68; county councilwoman County of Anne Arundel, Annapolis, Md., 1974-94, council chmn., 1984-91; mem. Md. Gen. Assembly Ho. of Dels., 1994—. Vice chmn. Balt. Regional Planning Coun., 1984—; trustee Hammond-Harwood Ho., 1978—, Chesapeake EPA, 1976—; mem. Alcohol and Drug Abuse Adv. Com., 1985—; mem. Anne Arundel County Agrl. Adv. Com., 1978—; bd. dirs. Historic Annapolis, Inc. Mem. Am. Bus. Womens Assn., Md. Assn. Counties (legis. com.). Democrat. Episcopalian. Avocations: tennis, gardening, horseback riding. Home: PO Box 1 West River MD 20778-0001 Office: Ho of Dels Md Gen Assembly 212 Lowe Office Bldg 84 College Ave Annapolis MD 21401 Office Phone: 410-841-3216. E-mail: virginia_clagett@house.state.md.us.

CLAGUE, DAVID A., geologist; b. Phila., Aug. 3, 1948; married; 1 child. PhD in Earth Sci., Scripps Inst. Oceanography, 1974. With nat. rsch. coun. U.S. Geol. Survey, 1974-75, rsch. geologist, 1979-96; asst. prof. geology Middlebury Coll., 1975—79; scientist-in-charge Hawaiian Volcano Obs., 1991-96; dir. rsch. an devel. Monetary Bay Aquarium Rsch. Inst., 1996-99, sr. scientist, 1999—. Fellow Geol. Soc. Am., Am. Geophys. Union, Calif. Acad. Sci. Office: Monterey Bay Aquarium Rsch Inst 7700 Sandholdt Rd Moss Landing CA 95039-9644 E-mail: clague@mbari.org.

CLAIBORNE, KENYA WYNETTE, secondary school educator; b. Baton Rouge, Mar. 2, 1980; d. Sam Jr. and Dorothy Ann (Turner) Claiborne. BS in Secondary Edn., So. U., Baton Rouge, 2002; MA in Edn., La. State U., Shreveport, 2005. Math. tchr. Caddo Parish Sch. Dist., Shreveport, 2002—. Youth dir. Pleasant Grove Bapt. Ch., Shreveport, 2006—. Named Educator of Week, Channel 12 News, Shreveport, 2004, Tchr. of Week, Shreveport Sun newspaper, 2004; scholar, Nat. Honor Roll., 2006. Avocations: Bible study, shopping, decorating, reading.

CLAIR, BERNARD E., lawyer; b. 1951; BA, Adelphi U.; JD, St. John's U., 1976. Bar: NY 1977. Ptnr. Clair & Daniele, 1977—97; ptnr., chmn. Family Law Dept. Rosenman & Colin LLP, 1998—2002, Katten Muchin Zavis, 2002—04; ptnr. Clair Greifer LLP, 2004—. Co-author (with Anthony Daniele): Love Pact; co-author: Consultation with a Divorce Lawyer, The Ex-Factor. Office: Clair Greifer LLP Floor 9 555 Madison Ave New York NY 10022 Office Phone: 212-300-1100. Office Fax: 212-300-1111.

CLAIR, JOHN J., JR., lawyer; BA, Brown Univ., 1968; JD, Univ. Pa., 1972. Bar: Calif. 1973. Various mgmt. positions Latham & Watkins, LA, 2000—04, mng. ptnr., 2004—, and mem. tax dept. Mem.: ABA, State of Calif. Bar Assn., LA County Bar Assn. Office: Latham & Watkins Ste 4000 633 W Fifth St Los Angeles CA 90071-2007 Business E-Mail: john.clair@lw.com.

CLAIRE, THOMAS ANDREW, financial executive, consultant, educator, writer; b. Cleve., Feb. 13, 1951; s. William Henry and Dorothy Helen (Taylor) C. BA, Kenyon Coll., 1973; MA, Brown U., 1977; MBA, Columbia U., 1978. Account adminstr. Irving Trust Co., NYC, 1978-80; dir. fin. planning and analysis W.R. Grace & Co., NYC, 1980-83; asst. treasurer Harper & Row Publishers, Inc., NYC, 1983-87; treas., asst. sec. Moët-Hennessy U.S. Corp., NYC, 1987—91; pres., CEO Clairefontaine, Inc., NYC, 1991—. Speaker in field. Author: numerous books in field; contbr. articles to various jours. Fulbright scholar Acad. Coms., Paris, 1973-75; Nat. Merit scholar Ohio, 1969-73. Mem. Phi Beta Kappa, Beta Gamma Sigma. Home and Office: Grand Ctrl Sta PO Box 1040 New York NY 10163-1040

CLAMAN, MATTHEW W., lawyer; b. Boston, May 26, 1959; BA, Colo. Coll., 1981; JD with honors, U. Tex., Austin, 1987. Bar: Alaska 1988, US Dist. Ct. (Dist. Alaska) 1989, US Supreme Ct. 1992, US Ct. Appeals (9th Cir.) 1992. Atty. Mendel & Associates, Anchorage. Mem.: Maritime Law Assn., Assn. Trial Lawyers Am. (admiralty sect.), ABA (litig. sect.), Alaska Bar Assn. (admiralty sect., pres.-elect 2006—07). Office: Mendel & Associates Ste 101 431 W 7th Ave Anchorage AK 99501 Office Phone: 907-279-5001. Office Fax: 907-279-5437. E-mail: mclaman-mendel@gci.net.

CLAMAR, APHRODITE J., psychologist; b. Hartford, Conn. d. James John and Georgia (Panas) Clamar; m. Richard Cohen, June 24, 1973. BA, CCNY, 1953; MA, Columbia U., 1955; PhD, NYU, 1978; student, S. Adler Conservatory Acting, 1987-91. Mgmt. cons., psychologist Milla Alihan Assocs., NYC, 1957-62; rsch. psychologist coord. Inst. Devel. Studies N.Y. Med. Coll., NYC, 1964; intern psychologist Bellevue Psychiat. Hosp., NYC, 1964-66; assoc. prof. Fashion Inst. Tech., NYC, 1966-69; supervising psychologist Lifeline Ctr. Child Devel., NYC, 1966-67; chief psychologist I Spy Health Program Beth Israel Med. Ctr., NYC, 1967-70; dir. community-sch. mental health programs Soundview Community Svcs., Albert Einstein Coll. Medicine Yeshiva U., NYC, 1970-73; dir. treatment program court-related children, dept. child psychiatry Harlem Hosp.; mem. faculty dept. psychiatry Coll. Physicians and Surgeons Columbia U., NYC, 1973-76; pvt. practice psychotherapy, NYC, 1976—; co-founder, pres. Richard Cohen Assocs. Pub. Rels. Agy., NYC, 1979—99; prof. John Jay Coll., CUNY, 2000—06. Cons. to pub. health and mental health agys., N.Y.C., 1976-91; mem. faculty Lenox Hill Hosp. Psychoanalytic Psychotherapy Tng. Program, 1982-88; theater producer, artistic dir. Tom Cat Cohen Prodns., Inc., 1990—. Author: (with Budd Hopkins) Missing Time, 1981; contbr. articles to profl. jours. Fellow: AAAS; mem.: APA, Authors Guild. Democrat. Greek Orthodox. Home: 155 W 68th St Apt 1618 New York NY 10023-5829 Office Phone: 212-724-1091.

CLANCY, CAROLYN M., internist, federal agency administrator; m. Bill Clancy. BS in Math. and Chemistry magna cum laude, Boston Coll., 1975; MD, U. Mass., 1979. Henry J. Kaiser Family Found. fellow U. Pa., 1982—84; asst. prof. medicine, dir. med. clinic Med. Coll. Va., 1984—90; with Agy. Healthcare Rsch. and Quality, HHS, 1990—, dir. Ctr. Primary Care Rsch., dir. Ctr. Outcomes and Effectiveness Rsch., 1997—2002, acting dir., 2002—03, dir., 2003—. Clin. assoc. prof. dept. medicine George Washington U.; sr. assoc. editor Health Services Rsch.; mem. editl. bd. Annals of Family Medicine, Am. Journal Med. Quality, Med. Care Rsch. and Rev. Recipient award, APHA Women's Caucus. Master: Am. Coll. Physicians; mem.: Inst. Medicine. Office: Agy Healthcare Rsch and Quality John M Eisenberg Bldg 540 Gaither Rd Rockville MD 20850 Office Phone: 301-427-1200. Office Fax: 301-427-1201. E-mail: cclancy@ahrq.gov.

CLANCY, DENYSE FINN, lawyer; BA magna cum laude, Yale U., 1989; MA in English, Columbia U., 1992; JD summa cum laude, So. Meth. U., 1999. Bar: Tex. 1999. Atty. Baron & Budd, P.C., Dallas. Editor: So. Meth. U. Sch. Law Rev. Named a Rising Star, Tex. Super Lawyers mag., 2006. Mem.: Tex. Trial Lawyers Assn., Assn. Trial Lawyers of Am. Office: Baron & Budd PC 3102 Oak Lawn Ave Ste 1100 Dallas TX 75219 Office Phone: 214-521-3605. E-mail: dclancy@baronbudd.com.*

CLANCY, MATHEW P., chemical engineer; b. Worchester, Mass., Dec. 26, 1977; s. Paul Patrick and Patricia Clancy. BS in Chem. Engring., U. Mass., Amherst, 1999. Chem. engr. Rizzo Assoc., Inc., Farmington, Mass., 1999—2000; process engr. Millipore Corp., Bedford, Mass., 2000—05; sr. application engr. Stellar Energy Sys., Jacksonville, Fla., 2005—. Mem.: ASHRAE, Turbin Inlet Cooling Assn. (sec. 2006).

CLANCY, PATRICK, artist, educator; b. Hornell, N.Y., Oct. 19, 1941; s. Gerald E. and Regina McKay Clancy; m. Gwen Widmer, Mar. 10, 1945; children: Raphael, August Estabrook. BS, Pratt Inst., Bklyn., N.Y., 1964; BFA, MFA, Yale U., Nw Haven, Conn., 1967. Lectr., rsch. assoc. Yale U., New Haven, 1967—72; vis. artist (spring semester) Calfornia Inst. of Arts, Burbank and Valencia, Calif., 1971—72; asst. prof. Colgate U., Hamilton, NY, 1974—80; vis. artist U. N.Mex, Albuquerque, 1984—85; prof., chair of photography and new media Kansas City Art Inst., Mo., 1986—; vis. scholar, artist (July, yearly) U. Tasmania Sch. of Art, Hobart, Australia, 2000—02. Workshop faculty and symposium participant Banff Ctr. Arts, Alberta, Canada, 1995—2005; participant, lectr. FutureFusion, 4th Internat. Conf. of Virtual Systems and Multimedia, Gifu, Japan, 1998; resident fellow Rockefeller Found. Study and Conf. Ctr., Bellagio, Italy, 2001; consortium mem. and participant Bridges Internat. Consortium on Collaboration in Art and Tech. (sponsored by USC Annenberg Ctr. for Communication and Banff Ctr. for Arts New Media Inst.), L.A., 2001; charrette leader for visualization of data flow Lewis Environ. Studies Ctr., Oberlin Coll., Ohio, 2002; adj. co-curator dept. modern and contemporary art Nelson-Atkins Mus. Art, Kansas City, Mo. Interactive new media art work, The Writing Machine (Individual Artist grant Creative Capital Found., 2000), photography, (Visual Artist's fellowship in photography Nat. Endowment for Arts, 1995); dir.: Cyber-Site BNew Media Rsch.Ctr. (Devel. grant Rockefeller Found. Creativity and Culture Divsn., 2000); interactive installation art, Pulsa Installation (grant NY State Coun. Arts, 1971), installation art, (grant for advanced study in fine arts Grahm Found., 1968). Curator, theoretician, fund-raiser and technician for video as attitude exhbn. Mus. Fine Arts, Santa Fe and U. Art Mus., U. N.Mex, Santa Fe and Albuquerque, N.Mex., 1982—83. Recipient Disting. Achievement award, Kans. City Art Inst., 2000, Individual Artist's award, Mo. Arts Coun., 2001; Photography fellowship, Mid-Am./Nat. Endowment for Arts, 1993, Individual Artist grant, Charlotte St. Fund, 1998, New Media Co-Prodn. grant, Banff Ctr. for Arts, 2002. Home: 6 E 62nd Ter Kansas City MO 64113-1622 Office: Kansas City Art Inst 4415 Warwick Blvd Kansas City MO 64111 Home Phone: 816-363-6699; Office Phone: 816-802-3324. Personal E-mail: pat@patrickclancy.org. Business E-Mail: pclancy@kcai.edu.

CLANCY, PATRICK L., lawyer; b. Washington, Mar. 17, 1958; BA, U. Md., 1982, JD with honors, 1987. Bar: Md. 1987, DC 1988, admitted to practice: US Dist. Ct. (Dist. Md.) 1988, US Dist. Ct. (DC) 1988, US Ct. Appeals (4th Cir.) 1994. Lectr. in field. Exec. editor Venable's Workplace Labor Upadate. Bd. dir. Our Lady of Good Counsel High Sch., Wheaton, Md. Mem.: Md. Ct. Appeals (character com.), Fed. Bar Assn., DC Bar Assn. (Labor Sect., Employment Law Sect.), Md. State Bar Assn., ABA, Montgomery County Bar Assn., Order of Coif.

CLANCY, THOMAS L., JR., novelist, producer; b. Balt., Apr. 12, 1947; m. Wanda Thomas, Aug. 1969 (div. 1998); children: Michelle, Christine, Tom, Kathleen; m. Alexandra Marie Llewellyn, July 26, 1999. BA, Loyola Coll., 1969. Ins. agent, Balt., Hartford, until 1973, O. F. Bowen Agy., Owings, Md., 1973-80, owner, from 1980; formed Red Storm Entertainment, Morrisville, NC, 1997; co-owner Baltimore Orioles, vice chmn. cmty. projects and pub. affairs. Author: (novels) The Hunt for Red October, 1984, Red Storm Rising, 1986, Patriot Games, 1987, The Cardinal of the Kremlin, 1988, Clear and Present Danger, 1989, The Sum of All Fears, 1991, Without Remorse, 1993, Debt of Honor, 1994, Executive Orders, 1996, Balance of Power, 1998, Rainbow Six, 1998, The Bear and the Dragon, 2000, Red Rabbit, 2002, The Teeth of the Tiger, 2003, (non-fiction) Submarine, 1993, Armored Cav, 1994, Fighter Wing, 1995, Marine, 1996, Airborne, 1997, Into the Storm, 1997, Every Man a Tiger, 1999; co-author: Battle Ready, 2004; co-creator Tom Clancy's OP Center, 1995—97, (video game series) Ghost Recon, 2001, Tom Clancy's Splinter Cell, 2002; exec. prodr.: (films) The Sum of All Fears, 2002; (TV miniseries) Tom Clancy's OP Center, 1995; exec. prodr., creator Tom Clancy's NetForce, ABC, 1999; author (screen adaptations): (films) The Hunt for Red October, 1990, Patriot Games, 1992, Clear and Present Danger, 1994, The Sum of All Fears, 2002, (TV miniseries) Tom Clancy's OP Center, 1995, Netforce, 1999. Roman Catholic.*

CLANCY, WENDELL WHITE, mediator, lawyer; b. Chgo., Mar. 27, 1938; s. Gates White and Mary Lucille Clancy; m. Kay Ellen Achenbach, Sept. 6, 1958; children: Michael White, William Scott, Timothy Gates, Susan Clancy Boles. BA, Duke U., Durham, NC, 1959; JD, U. Chgo., 1962. Lawyer Law Offices Gates W. Clancy, Chgo., 1962—78; founding ptnr., owner Clancy Law Offices, Ltd., St. Charles, Ill. Mem., chair person Ill. Supreme Ct. Com. Pattern Jury Instns., Springfield, Ill., 1995—2005. Pres. Am. Bd. Trial Advocates, Chgo., 2004—06. Scholar, U. Chgo. Law Sch., 1959—60, 1960—61, 1961—62. Office: Clancy Law Offices Ltd 7 South Second Av Saint Charles IL 60174 Office Phone: 630-584-7666. Business E-Mail: wclancy@clancylaw.com.

CLANIN, DOUGLAS EDWARD, editor, researcher; b. Anderson, Ind., May 5, 1940; s. Howard Paul and Sarah Elizabeth (Weatherford) C.; m. Rebecca Suzanne Flowers, Aug. 9, 1970 (div. Dec. 1974); children: Christopher Lee, David Matthew. BS, Purdue U., 1963; MA, Ind. U., 1964. Social studies tchr. Whitewater-Fountain City H.S., Ind., 1964—65; asst. editor history U. Wis., Madison, 1970—80; editor publs. divsn. Ind. Hist. Soc., Indpls., 1980—2005. Editor: Papers of William Henry Harrison 1800-1815, 1993, 1999, Papers of Lew and Susan Wallace, 2006; asst. editor: Documentary History First Federal Elections, 1976, Documentary History Ratification of Constitution, 1976—81. Staff sgt. USAF, 1965-69. Mem. Assn. for Documentary Editing, Ind. Assn. Historians, Soc. for Historians Early Am. Rep., Am. Legion, Svc. Club Indpls. Methodist. Avocations: conducting oral history interviews, travel, classical music. Home: 4121 Montana Way Anderson IN 46013-2483 Personal E-mail: dclanin@insightbb.com.

CLANTON, WENDY MCCARLEY, elementary school educator, assistant principal; b. Pascagoula, Miss., Mar. 9, 1970; d. Aubry Lee McCarley, Sr. and Linda Gail McCarley; m. Darrin Hayden Clanton, Feb. 25, 1998; children: Stephen Craig Henry, Ashlyn Brooke, Lauren Elizabeth. BS in Elem. Edn. summa cum laude, Auburn U., 1996; M in Ednl. Leadership, U. South Ala., 2002; D, Nova S.E. U., 2005. Tchr. grade 3 Calvary Christian Sch., Mobile, Ala., 1997—98, tchr. grade 5, 1999—2000; math./sci. tchr. grad 5 East Ctrl. Upper Elem., Hurley, Miss., 1998—99; tchr. grade 5 Indian Springs Elem., Mobile, 2000—01; tchr. grade 3 Eichold-Mertz Elem., Mobile, 2001—04, reading coach, 2004—; asst. prin. Lee Intermediate Sch., 2005—. Pub. rels. rep. Eichold-Mertz Elem., Mobile, 2003—05. Rep. Student Govt. Assn., Troy, Ala., 1999. Leadership scholar, Troy State U. Mem.: Alpha Gamma Delta. Home: 8550 Bay Leaf Dr Eight Mile AL 36613 Office: Nova Southeastern Univ 1750 NE 167th St North Miami Beach FL 33162-3017

CLAPHAM, DAVID E., pharmacology educator; MD, Emory U., Atlanta, 1979; PhD, Emory U., 1981. Residency internal medicine Brigham and Women's Hosp., Boston; postdoctoral fellowship Max Planck Inst. Biophysical Chemistry, Göttingen, Germany; prof. pharmacology Mayo Med. Sch., Rochester, Minn., 1989; Aldo R. Castañeda prof. cardiovasc. rsch. Children's Hosp., Boston; prof. neurobiology and pediat. Harvard Med. Sch., Boston. Investigator Howard Hughes Med. Inst., 1997—; co-founder Hydra Biosciences, Cambridge, 2001, mem. sci. adv. bd. Contbr. articles to profl. jours. Recipient Basic Sci. prize, Am. Heart Assn., 1997, Cole award, Biophysical Soc., Bristol-Myers Squibb award. Mem.: NAS, Am. Acad. Arts and Scis. Office: Children's Hospital HHMI CV Res Enders 1309 320 Longwood Ave Boston MA 02115

CLAPMAN, LEAH MEREDITH, public television editor; d. Peter C. and Barbar J. Clapman; m. Richard David Fisher, Aug. 19, 2000. BA magna cum laude, Princeton Univ. Mng. editor, Online NewsHour PBS, Arlington, Va. Co-recipient AAAS Sci. Journalism award for online reporting, 2006. Office: NewsHour with Jim Lehrer 2100 Crystal Dr Arlington VA 22202 Office Phone: 703-739-5000. Business E-Mail: Lclapman@newshour.org.

CLAPNER, KATHERINE, chef; Attended, U. Tex., Arlington; A in baking and pastry, Culinary Inst. Am., NY. Pantry chef Sam's Cafe, Dallas; pastry chef Charlie Trotter's, Chgo., Windsor Court Hotel, New Orleans, Hotel Cipriani, Venice, The Savoy Hotel, London, Mansion at Judges Hill, Austin, Tex., Ranch 616, Austin, Liberty Tavern, Austin, Finn & Porter, Austin, Star Canyon, AquaKnox, Taqueria Canonita, Hilton Hotel, Austin; exec. pastry chef Stephan Pyles Restaurant. Chair Stars Across Tex., Saveur Hill Country Wine and Food Festival. Featured in Bon Appetit mag., The Chgo. Tribune, Gambit Weekly, Times Picayune, Restaurants and Institutions, Sante Mag., Austin Monthly, Austin Women's Mag., Austin Chronicle. Named one of Dallas' Rising Stars, StarChefs.com, 2007. Office: Stephan Pyles Restaurant 1807 Ross Ave Ste 200 Dallas TX 75201 Office Phone: 214-580-7000.

CLAPP, ALLEN LINVILLE, electric supply and communications utility consultant, mediator/arbitrator; b. Raleigh, NC, Oct. 8, 1943; s. Byron Siler and Alene Linville (Hester) C.; m. Anne Stuart Calvert, Dec. 18, 1966. BS in Engrng. Ops., N.C. State U., 1967, M in Econs., 1973. Lic. profl. engr., N.C., N.J. Asst. engr. Booth-Jones and Assocs., Raleigh, 1965-67, assoc., 1969-71; chief ops. analysis N.C. Utilities Commn., Raleigh, 1971-77, engrng. and econs. advisor to commrs., hearing examiner, 1977-82; dir. tech. assessment N.C. Alterative Energy Corp., Rsch. Triangle Park, 1982-85; pres. Clapp Rsch. Assocs., P.C., Clapp Rch. Inc., Raleigh, N.C., 1985—, Utility Bookstore, 2000—05, Power & Comm. Utility Tng. Ctr., 2005—. Pvt. practice elec. safety cons., Raleigh, 1971—; mem. nat. Elec. Safety Code Com., 1971—, chmn., 1984—93; lectr. in field. Editor: National Electric Safety Code Handbook, 1984, 91, 92, 96, 2001, 06, Assembly and Testing of Aerial Mines, 1968, Practical Utility Safety, 1999; editor, pub. Danesc Update Newsletter; contbr. to McGraw-Hill Std. Handbook for Elec. Engrs.; contbr. articles to profl. jours. Past co-chmn. Brookhaven/Deblyn Park Action Com., Raleigh. With U.S. Army, 1968-69. Recipient Cert. of Recognition and Appreciation Aerial Mine Lab., 1969. Mem. NSPE (past bd. dirs.), IEEE (stds. bd. 1989, 90), Profl. Engrs. N.C. (pres. 1980, Disting. Svc. award ctrl. Carolina chpt. 1978), N.C. Assn. Professions (pres. 1981), Power Engrng. Soc., Nat. Safety Coun., Am. Soc. Safety Engrs., Soc. Cable TV Engrs., Indsl. Applications Soc., Am. Nat. Stds. Inst. (chair Z535.2 std. on environ. and facility safety signs). Republican. Baptist. Avocations: leather carving, golf, engraving, wood-carving. Office: Clapp Rsch Assocs 6112 Saint Giles St Raleigh NC 27612-7043

CLAPP, KENT W., insurance company executive; b. Montpelier, Ohio; BS in Acctg., Tri-State Univ., Angola, Ind.; graduate Advanced Mgmt. Program, Harvard Sch. Bus.Adminstrn., 1989. CPA 1972. Corp. controller Blue Cross, NW Ohio (merged into Medical Mutual), 1976—89; sr. v.p. Medical Mutual of Ohio, Cleve., 1989—92, COO, 1992—97, pres., 1992—, CEO, 1997—, chmn., 1997—. Graduate Leadership Cleve., 1992; bd. dir. Harvard Bus. Club, Cleve., United Way Greater Cleve. Named Bus. Exec. Yr., Sales & Mktg. Execs, Cleveland, 2002; named an honoree at NE Ohio Multiple Sclerosis Soc. Dinner of Champions, 2002; recipient Franklin Delano Roosevelt Humanitarian award, March of Dimes, 2000. Office: Medical Mutual Ohio 2060 E Ninth St Cleveland OH 44115 Office Phone: 216-687-6514. Office Fax: 216-687-7632.*

CLAPP, ROGER HOWLAND, retired publishing executive; b. Scarsdale, NY, May 11, 1928; s. Kenneth John and Louise (Allen) Clapp; m. Patricia Anne Townshend, June 26, 1954 (dec. Nov. 18, 1998); children: Roger Howland Jr., Georgia Louise, Sarah Townshend. BA cum laude, Amherst Coll., 1954. V.p. Benton & Bowles, Inc., NYC, 1954-67, Rumrill-Hoyt, Inc., NYC, 1967-72; v.p., advt. dir. Richmond (Va.) Newspapers, Inc., 1972-93. Counselor Svc. Corps of Ret. Execs.; bd. dirs. Richmond chpt. Better Bus. Bur., 1986—88, ARC, 1987—93. With USN, 1948—52, Korea. Recipient Silver medal, Am. Advt. Fedn., 1980. Mem.: Internat. Newspaper Advt. and Mktg. Execs. (pres. 1988). Home: 15470 Cedarwood Ln # 103 Naples FL 34110-8638

CLAPP, STEPHEN HENRY, dean, violinist; b. Nov. 27, 1939; MusB, Oberlin Conservatory Music, 1961; MusM, Juilliard Sch. Music, 1965. Mem. Beaux-Arts String Quartet, NYC, 1965-67; asst. assoc. prof. violin Peabody Coll., Nashville, 1967-72; concertmaster Nashville Symphony, 1968-69; 1st violinist Blair String Quartet, Nashville, 1968-72; concertmaster Aspen (Colo.) Chamber Symphony, 1971-79; violinist, faculty Aspen Music Festival, 1971—94; assoc. prof. U. Tex., Austin, 1972-79; prof. Oberlin (Ohio) Conservatory Music, 1978-90; assoc. dean The Juilliard Sch., NYC, 1991-94; faculty Julliard Sch. Music, NYC, 1987—, dean, 1994—. Master classes, recitals and concerts nationwide, 1970—; mem. The Oberlin Trio, 1982-05; trustee Aspen Music Festival, Aspen and N.Y.C., 1978-90; concertmaster Austin Symphony, 1972-77. Rec. artist Orion, Advance Amplitude labels. Sr. warden Christ Episcopal Ch., Oberlin, 1986-88; vestry mem. Christ Episcopal Ch., Greenwich, Conn., 1993-96; sr. warden St. John's Episc. Ch., Stamford, Conn., 2004— Recipient 1st Chamber Music award Walter W. Naumburg Found., 1965. Mem. Violin Soc. Am. (bd. dirs. 1987-91), Music Tchrs. Nat. Assn., Am. String Tchrs. Assn. (contbr. articles to assn. jour. 1978-81), Chamber Music Am. Democrat. Avocations: tennis, restoring old houses. Office: The Juilliard Sch 60 Lincoln Center Plz New York NY 10023-6588 Office Phone: 212-799-5000.

CLAPPER, JAMES R., JR., federal agency administrator, retired military officer; b. 1941; s. James R. and Anne (Wheatley) Clapper; m. Susan T. Clapper. BS, U. Md., 1963; MS in Polit Sci., St. Mary's U., San Antonio, 1970; Grad., Armed Forces Staff Coll., Norfolk, 1975; student, Nat. War Coll., 1978—79; PhD in Strategic Intelligence (hon.), Joint Mil. Intelligence Coll. Advanced through grades to lt. gen. USAF, 1991, ret., 1995; analytic branch chief Air Force Spl. Comm. Ctr., Kelly AFB, Tex., 1964—65; watch officer & air def. analyst 2nd Air Divsn., Son Nhut Air Base, South Vietnam, 1965—66; aide to the comdr. & command briefer Air Force Security Svc., Kelly AFB, Tex., 1966—70; comdr. Detachment 3 6994th Security Squadron, Nakhon Phanom Royal Thai AFB, Thailand, 1970—71; mil. asst. to dir. Nat. Security Agy., Ft. George G. Meade, Md., 1971—73; aide to the comdr. & intelligence staff officer Air Force Systems Command, Andrews AFB, Md., 1973—74; chief, signal intelligence branch, J-23 US Pacific Command, Camp H.M. Smith, Hawaii, 1975—76, chief signal intelligence branch , J-23, 1976—78; Wash. area rep. for electronic security command Ft. George G. Mead, Md., 1979—80; comdr. 6940th Electronic Security Wing, Ft. George G. Meade, Md., 1980—81; dir. intelligence plans & systems Office Asst. Chief of Staff for Intelligence, USAF, Washington, 1981—84; commdr., Air Force Technical Applications Ctr. USAF, Patrick AFB, Fla., 1984—85, asst. chief of staff intelligence U.S. Forces Korea, dep. asst. chief of staff intelligence Repubic of Korea & US Combined Forced Command Seoul, Republic of Korea, 1985—87, dir. intelligence US Pacific Command Camp H.M. Smith, Hawaii, 1987—89, dep. chief of staff intelligence Strategic Air Command Offutt AFB, Nebr., 1989—90, asst. chief of staff intelligence Washington, 1990—91; dir. Def. Intelligence Agy., Washington, 1991—95; exec. v.p. Vredenburg, Inc., Reston, Va., 1995—98; exec. dir. mil. intelligence programs Booz-Allen & Hamilton, 1995—98; v.p., dir. intelligence programs SRA Internat., Inc., 1998—2001; dir. Nat. Geospatial-Intelligence Agy. (formerly Nat. Imagery and Mapping Agy.) US Dept. Def., Bethesda, Md., 2001—06, under sec for intelligence Washington, 2007—; dir def. intelligence Office Nat. Intelligence, Washington, 2007—. Vice chair Adv. Panel to Assess Domestic Response Capabilities for Terrorism Involving Weapons of Mass Destruction, 2000. Recipient Def. Disting. Svc. medal, DSM, Def. Superior Svc. medal, Legion of Merit with two oak leaf clusters, Bronze Star medal with oak leaf cluster, Def. Meritorious Svc. medal, Air medal with oak leaf cluster, Joint Svc. Commendation medal, Air Force Commendation medal, French Order of Nat. Merit, ROK Order of Nat. Security of Merit, Nat. Intelligence Disting. Svc. medal. Office: US Dept Defense 5000 Defense Pentagon Rm 3E604 Washington DC 20310*

CLAPTON, ERIC, musician, singer; b. Ripley, Surrey, Eng., Mar. 30, 1945; s. Edward Fryer and Patricia Molly Clapton; m. Patricia Anne Boyd, March 27, 1979 (div. 1988); m. Melia McEnery, Jan. 1, 2002; children: Julie Rose, Ella May, Sophie 1 child (with Yvonne Kelly), Ruth; 1 child (with Lory Del Santo), Conor (dec. 1991) Student, Kingston Art Sch. Guitarist The Roosters, 1963, Casey Jones & the Engineers, 1963, The Yardbirds, 1963—65; guitarist, singer John Mayall's Bluesbreakers, 1965—66; guitarist Powerhouse, 1966; guitarist, singer Cream, 1966—68, Blind Faith, 1969; guitarist Delaney and Bonnie & Friends, 1969—70; guitarist, singer Derek and the Dominos, 1970—71; solo artist, 1970—. Musician: (albums with The Yardbirds) Five Live Yardbirds, 1964, For Your Love, 1965, Having A Rave Up, 1965, (albums with John Mayall's Bluesbreakers) Bluesbreakers with Eric Clapton, 1966, (albums with Cream) Fresh Cream, 1966, Disraeli Gears, 1967, Wheels of Fire, 1968, Goodbye, 1969, Live Cream, 1970, Live Cream Volume II, 1972, Strange Brew: The Very Best of Cream, 1983, Those Were the Days, 1997, BBC Sessions, 2003, Cream Gold, 2005, Royal Albert Hall London 2-6 May 2005, 2005, (albums with Blind Faith) Blind Faith, 1969, (albums with Delaney and Bonnie & Friends) On Tour with Eric Clapton, 1970, (albums with Derek and the Dominos) Layla And Other Assorted Love Songs, 1970, In Concert, 1973, The Layla Sessions: The 20th Anniversary Edition, 1990, Live at the Fillmore, 1994, (solo albums) Eric Clapton, 1970, 461 Ocean Boulevard, 1974, There's One in Every Crowd, 1975, E.C. Was Here, 1975, No Reason to Cry, 1976, Slowhand, 1977, Backless, 1978, Just One Night, 1980, Another Ticket, 1981, Time Pieces: Best of Eric Clapton, 1982, Money and Cigarettes, 1983, Behind the Sun, 1985, Time Pieces Vol. II 'Live' in the 70's, 1985, August, 1987, Crossroads, 1988, One Moment in Time, 1988, Journeyman, 1989, 24 Nights, 1991, Unplugged, 1992 (Winner of 6 Grammy awards including Album of Yr., Record of Yr.), From the Cradle, 1994 (Grammy award Best Traditional Blues Album), The Cream of Clapton, 1995, Crossroads II: Live in the Seventies, 1996, Retail Therapy, 1997, Pilgrim, 1998, Clapton Chronicles: The Best of Eric Clapton 1981-1999, 1999, The Blues, 1999, Reptile, 2001 (Grammy award Best Pop Instrumental Perf.), One More Car, One More Rider, 2002, Me and Mr. Johnson, 2004, Sessions for Robert J., 2004, Back Home, 2005, (sountracks) Rush, 1992, (albums with others) A Concert for Bangladesh, 1972 (Grammy award Album of Yr.), Rainbow Concert, 1973, The Last Waltz, 1976, (albums with B.B. King) Riding with the King, 2000 (Grammy award Best Trad. Blues Album), (albums with J.J. Cale) The Road to Escondido, 2006; prodr. (with Rod Stewart): (albums) Beginnings, 2004; wrote songs: BBC miniseries Edge of Darkness, 1986; composer film score Homeboy, 1988, Lethal Weapon, 1986, Lethal Weapon 2, 1989, The Van, 1996, Nil by Mouth, 1997; co-composer film score: Lethal Weapon 3, 1992. Founder Crossroads Centre, 1997—. Named one of The 100 Greatest Guitarists of All-Time, Rolling Stone mag.; named to The Rock & Roll Hall of Fame, (as mem. of Yardbirds), 1992, (as mem. of Cream), 1993, (as solo artist), 2000; recipient Silver Clef Award Outstanding Achievement in World of British Music, presented by Princess Michael of Kent, 1983, Lifetime Achievement Award, British Phonographic Inst., 1987, presented with silver model of a Fender Stratocaster by Prince Charles to commemorate 25th yr. in music industry, 1988, Best Guitarist Award, Internat. Rock Awards, 1989, Living Legend Award, 1990, W.C. Handy Award For Blues, 16th Annual Ceremony, 1995, Man of Yr. Award music: solo artist, GQ Mag., 1999, Stevie Ray Vaughan, Music Assistance Program, 1999, Commander of the British Empire, 2003. Achievements include minor planet named "(4305) Clapton" in his honor, 1990; first triple inductee into Rock & Roll Hall of Fame. Office: c/o Warner Bros Records 3300 Warner Blvd Burbank CA 91505-4632*

CLAREY, JOHN ROBERT, executive recruiter, consultant; b. Waterloo, Iowa, June 5, 1942; s. Robert J. and Norma (Knox) Clarey; m. Kathleen Ann Kingsley, June 5, 1965; children: Sharon Diane, Suzanne Marie. BSBA, Iowa State U., 1965; MBA, U. Pa., 1972. Fin. analyst Ford Motor Co., Dearborn, Mich., 1972-74; cons. Price Waterhouse, Chgo., 1974-75, mgr., 1975-76; assoc. Heidrick & Struggles, Chgo., 1976-81, v.p., ptnr., 1981-82; pres. Clarey, Andrews & Klein, Inc., Northbrook, Ill., 1982—. Served to lt. USN, 1965—70, Vietnam. Mem.: Assn. Exec. Search Cons., Lifeline Pilots, Sunset Ridge Country Club (Northbrook), Mid-Am. Club (Chgo.), Stick and Rudder. Republican. Roman Catholic. Avocations: flying, microcomputers, tennis. Home: 1347 Hillside Rd Northbrook IL 60062-4612 Office: Clarey Andrews & Klein Inc 1200 Shermer Rd Ste 108 Northbrook IL 60062-4563 Personal E-mail: jackclarey@ameritech.net. Business E-Mail: jack@clarey-a-klein.com.

CLAREY, PATRICIA T., health insurance company executive, former state official; BS, Union Coll., Schenectady, NY, 1975; MPA, Harvard U. John F. Kennedy Sch. of Govt., Cambridge, Mass., 1983. Govt. affairs rep. Chevron Corp., San Francisco; govt. rels. position Ashland Oil, Inc.; dep. dir. legis. affairs Nat. Park Svc., Washington; congl. liaison US Dept. Interior, Washington, 1986—89; dep. chief of staff to Gov. State of Calif., Sacramento; v.p. public affairs Transamerica Corp., San Francisco, 1999—2001; pres. Transamerica Found., San Francisco, 1998; v.p. govt. rels. Health Net, Inc. (formerly known as Foundation Health Sys., Inc.), LA, 2001—03; ran primary campaign for Gov.-elect Arnold Schwarzenegger; chief of staff to Gov. State of Calif., Sacramento, 2003—06; COO Health Net of Calif., Inc., Woodland Hills, 2006—. Former bd. dir. Calif. Found. on the Environ. and the Economy; mem. joint pub. adv. com. Commn. for Environ. Cooperation of N.Am., 2003—. Office: Health Net of Calif Inc 21281 Burbank Blvd Woodland Hills CA 91367

CLAREY, TIMOTHY LEE, geologist, educator; b. Midland, Mich., Oct. 9, 1960; s. Harlan Dale and Betty Lou Clarey; m. Renee Lynn Atwood, Sept. 4, 2004; children: Ryan, Ashley, Hailey, Erin. BS in Geology, Western Mich. U., 1982, MS in Geology, 1993, PhD, 1996; MS in Geology, U. Wyo., 1984. Cert. profl. geologist. Exploration geologist Chevron USA, Denver, 1984—92; prof. geology Delta Coll., University Center, Mich., 1995—. Author: Introduction to Dinosaurs, 2001, Physical Geology Lab Book, 2002; contbr. articles to profl. jours. Named Endowed Tchg. Chair, Delta Coll., 2000; recipient Bergstein Tchg. award, 1998, Scholarly Achievement award, 2002. Mem.: Geol. Soc. Am., Am. Assn. Petroleum Geologists, Sigma Xi (chpt. pres.). Avocations: paleontology, running. Office: Delta Coll 1961 Delta Rd University Center MI 48710 Office Phone: 989-686-9252. Business E-Mail: tlclarey@delta.edu.

CLARIDGE, ELMOND LOWELL, retired engineering educator; b. Delaplaine, Ark., June 5, 1917; s. Elmond Lee and Irene Cynthia Gates (Compton) Claridge; m. Zola Ruth McDowell, Jan. 1, 1939 (dec. Oct. 9, 1990); children: David Elmond, Jonathan McDowell; m. Mary Lasley Moore, Feb. 11, 1995 (dec. Feb. 16, 1999); m. Claire North Patterson, Apr. 29, 2006. BSChemE, U. Mo., Rolla, 1939, MSChemE, 1941; PhD in Chem. Engrng., U. Houston, 1979. Registered profl. engr., Tex. Rsch. chemist Shell Oil Co., Wood River, Ill., 1941—43, technologist, 1943—48, asst. chief rsch. Houston, 1948—55, 1957—60, sr. technologist head office NYC, 1960—64; group leader Royal Dutch Shell, Amsterdam, 1955—57; sr. rsch. assoc. Shell Devel. Co., Houston, 1964—79; assoc. prof. chem. engrng. dept. U. Houston, 1979—91, dir. petroleum engrng. grad. program, 1979—87; ret., 1991. Cons. Gulf Univs. Rsch. Consortium, Houston, 1979—85, TCA Reservoir Engrng. Svcs., Houston, 1979—2000. Author: PE 506, Miscible Processes, 1992; contbr. articles to profl. jours. Recipient Disting. Life award, St. Luke's United Meth. Ch., 1990. Mem.: AAAS, AIChE, Soc. Petroleum Engrs. (editor reprint book Surfactant/Polymer Chemical Flooding vols. I, II 1982, Enhanced Oil Recovery Pioneer 1980), Petroleum Soc./Can. Inst. Mining, Metallurgy and Petroleum, Am. Petroleum Inst. (rsch. adv. bd. prodn. divsn. 1978—81), Am. Chem. Soc., Sigma Xi, Alpha Chi Sigma. Achievements include patents in field. Personal E-mail: elmondclaridge@sbcglobal.net.

CLARINGBOULD, JOHN, lawyer; Sr. exec. Mars, Inc., Australia, sr. v.p., gen. counsel, & sec. McLean, Va., 2005—. Co-chmn. internat. cocoa initiative Mars, Inc. Office: Mars Inc 6885 Elm St Mc Lean VA 22101

CLARIZIO, JOSEPHINE DELORES, retired foundation administrator, manufacturing and engineering company executive; b. Montclair, NJ, Dec. 15, 1922; d. Thomas and Raffaela (Caruso) D'Andrea; m. N. Robert Clarizio, June 3, 1951. Cert., Katharine Gibbs Sch., 1942; BS, Seton Hall U., 1947; postgrad., Fordham U. Sch. Law, 1947-48, N.Y. Inst. Fin., 1964. Registered rep. Drexel, Burnham & Co., NYC, 1965-70; asst. to pres. Wheelabrator-Frye Inc., Hampton, NH, 1970-78, corp. sec., 1981-83. Pres. Wheelabrator Found. Inc., Hampton, 1978-83; cons. Signal Cos. Inc., N.Y.C., N.H., 1983-85. Mem. Am. Assn. Ret. Persons, Seton Hall U. Alumni Assn. Republican. Roman Catholic.

CLARIZIO, LYNDA M., advertising executive, lawyer; b. Newark, Aug. 19, 1960; d. Attavio and Yolanda Clarizio; m. Mark Foulon, July 8, 1988. AB summa cum laude, Princeton U., 1982; JD, Harvard U., 1985. Bar: D.C. 1985. Ptnr. Arnold & Porter LLP, Washington, 1992—99; exec. v.p. Audience Bus. Am. Online LLC, 1999—2006; pres. Advertising.com, Balt., 2006—. Bd. dirs. Network Live, Human Rights First. Articles editor Harvard Internat. Law Jour., 1984-85. Mem. Phi Beta Kappa. Office: Advertising com 1020 Hull St Ivory Bldg Baltimore MD 21230

CLARK, A. JAMES, real estate company executive; b. 1927; BCE, U. Md., 1950. CEO, chmn., founder Clark Enterprises, Bethesda, Md., 1951—. Mem. bd. dir. CarrAmerica Realty Corporation, Geico Corp., PEPCO, Martin Merietta (now Lockheed Martin). Named in his honor: A. James Clark Sch. Engrng., U. Md.; laureate, Washington Bus. Hall of Fame. Mem.: NAE. Office: Clark Enterprises Inc 7500 Old Georgetown Rd Bethesda MD 20814

CLARK, ALICIA GARCIA, political party official; b. Vera Cruz, Mex. arrived in US, 1970; d. Rafael Garcia Aully and Maria Luisa (Cobos) Garcia; m. Edward E. Clark, Oct. 20, 1970; 1 child, Edward E. MSChemE, Nat. U. Mex., Mexico City, 1951. Chemist Celanese Mexicana, Mexico City, 1951—53, lab. mgr., 1953—60, sales promotion mgr., 1960—65, sales promotion and advt. mgr., 1965—70; nat. chmn. Libertarian Party, Houston, 1981—83, coord. coun. state chairs, 1987—95. Pres. San Marino (Calif.) Guild of Huntington Hosps., 1981-82, chmn. Celebrity Series, 1989-91; mem. Mex. Olympic Com., 1968. Pres. bd. dirs. LA Opera League, 1990-96; founder, co-chair Hispanics for LA Opera, 1991-99; bd. dirs. Guild Opera Co., 1994-96, Club 100, 1996-99; mng. dir. L.A. Opera, 1995—2006, life trustee, 2006—; opera panel Nat. Endowment for Arts, 1997; active Redcat Theater Coun., 2002-06; mem. bd. advisors Pasadena Symphony Orch., 2006—. Recipient award La Mujer de Hoy mag., 1969, Heroes LA award Hispanic Traditions and Heritage Coun., 1995, Star of Our Culture award Mex. Cultural Inst. LA, 1998, Placido Domingo award, 2000, Zachary Soc. Ann. award, 2001, Life Achievement award Hispanics for L.A. Opera, 2006. Mem. Fashion Group (treas. 1969-70, award 1970). Home Fax: 626-796-3485. Personal E-mail: balticed@aol.com.

CLARK, ANN RORABAW, English professor, consultant, writer; b. Orlando, Okla., Feb. 19, 1927; d. Nathan August Rorabaw and Martha Leota Wallace; m. Jerome Leslie Clark (dec. 1997); children: Jerry, Alice, Danny. BA in English, So. Missionary Coll. (now So. Adventist U.), Collegedale, Tenn., 1961; MAT, U. Chattanooga (now U. Tenn. Chattanooga), 1966; PhD iin English, U. Tenn., Knoxville, 1986. Elem. sch. tchr. Okla. Conf. Seventh-Day Adventists, Oklahoma City, 1945—50; sec. R&D Jacobs Instrument Co., Bethesda, Md., 1950—51; elem. sch. tchr. Ohio Conf. Seventh-Day Adventists, Mt. Vernon, 1952—54; English prof. So. Missionary Coll. (now So. Adventist U.), Collegedale, 1965—. Rsch. cons., writing cons., Ga., Tenn.; supt. Spalding Sabbath Sch. divsn. Collegedale Seventh-Day Adventist Ch., ch. deaconess, 1970—. Author: Pietism in the Journal of John, 1986; author, editor: Leona Peak: Her Story, 1995, The Way of the Cross, 1996. Named Alumnus of Yr., So. Adventist U. Alumni Assn., 2004. Mem.: Nat. Coun. Tchrs. English, Adventist Ret. Workers (program com.). Republican. Avocations: reading, writing, hiking, swimming, travel. Home: PO Box 515-0515 Collegedale TN 37315-0515 Office: So Adventist U Collegedale TN 37315

CLARK, ARTHUR WATTS, insurance company executive; b. Seattle, Nov. 28, 1922; s. Irving Marshall and Nell (Watts) C.; m. Mary Dick Cannon, Nov. 21, 1942; children: Arthur Watts, Claiborne Marshall, Johnston Jewell. AB, U. N.C., 1943; MA, U. Calif., 1948. With Home Security Life Ins. Co., Durham, NC, 1948-50, 52-85, pres., 1967-75, chmn., chief exec. officer, 1975-85, also dir.; chmn., chief exec. officer Peoples Life Ins. Co. of Washington, D.C., 1983-85; chmn., pres., chief exec. officer Peoples Security Life Ins. Co., 1985-86, chmn. bd., 1986-88. Mem. Res. Forces Policy Bd., Office Sec. Def., 1975-78. Treas. Research Triangle Regional Planning Commn., 1959-63; mem. N.C. Health Ins. Adv. Bd., 1966-70; chmn. bd. dirs. N.C. Ctrl. U. Found., Zool. Coun., 1994-96, chmn., 1996-2002; vice-chmn. bd. dirs. N.C. Med. Found.; chmn. Greater Triangle Cmty. Found., 1992-94, The Explorer's Club, 1999—. With USAAF, 1942-46, USAF, 1952, maj. gen. USAF, ret. Decorated D.S.M., Legion of Merit with oak leaf cluster, Bronze Star. Mem. Am. Life Conv. (dir. 1972), Am. Life Ins. Assn. (dir. 1973-75), Life Office Mgmt. Assn. (dir. 1973-76), Am. Council Life Ins. (dir. 1976), Life Insurers Conf. (exec. com. 1972-75, 1983-86), Assn. N.C. Life Ins. Cos. (chmn. 1986-87), Phi Beta Kappa, Sigma Xi. Office: 194 Finley Golf Course Rd Ste 100 Chapel Hill NC 27517 Home: 100 Cedar Berry Ln Chapel Hill NC 27517 Personal E-mail: artwclark@aol.com.

CLARK, BASIL ALFRED, language educator; b. Prospect, Maine, July 19, 1939; s. Bernard Emery and Dorothy Madeline Clark; m. Margaret Ann Bengtson, June 18, 1966; children: Dorothy Elizabeth Mackendrick, Timothy Bengtson. AB in Englidh, Bowdoin Coll., Brunswick, Maine, 1956—60; MA in English, U. Maine, Orono, 1967—69; PhD in English, Ohio State U., Columbus, 1969—75. Prof. English Saginaw Valley State U., University Center, Mich., 1975—. Exch. prof. Shikoku Women's U., Tokushima, Japan, 1989; exch. lectr. U. Mysore, India, 2002—02. Author: Saginaw Valley State University:The Early and Formative Years, 1998. Moderator United Ch. Christ, Midland, Mich., 2005—. Spl. 4 US Army, 1960—63, Germany. Recipient Ho. Family award for tchr. impact, Saginaw Valley State U., 1991, Univ. Svc. award, Saginaw Valley State U. Faculty Assn., 2006. Mem.: MLA, Saginaw Valley State U. Faculty Assn. (pres. 1989—91), Nat. Coun. Tchrs. English, Mich. Coun. Tchrs. English (pres. 1990—91). Home: 1802 Eastman Ave Midland MI 48640 Office: Saginaw Valley State Univ 7400 Bay Rd University Center MI 48710 Home Phone: 989-636-7724. Personal E-mail: clarkbasil@hotmail.com. Business E-Mail: baclark@svsu.edu.

CLARK, BETH, retired minister; b. Bradford, NH, Apr. 15, 1914; d. John Scott and Bessie (Murdock) Pendleton; m. John Guill Clark, June 20, 1940 (dec. June 1955); children: John Guill Jr. (dec. 1999), Beverly Estelle Clark Daggett. BA, Colby Coll., 1935; BD, Andover Newton Theol. Sch., 1938; MDiv, Ea. Bapt. Theol. Sem., 1967; D Ministry, Lancaster Theol. Sem., 1981; postgrad., U. Athens, 1970, Jungian Inst., Zurich, 1980, Mansfield Coll., Oxford, Eng., 1982, Mansfield Coll., 1985, Caribbean Inst., 1989. Ordained to ministry United Ch. of Christ, 1967. Exec. dir. YWCA, Bristol, Tenn., 1955—59, Asheville, NC, 1959—60; dean women Anderson Coll., SC, 1960—61, Ea. Coll., St. Davids, Pa., 1961—65; coord. vol. rsch. Selinsgrove State Sch., Pa., 1965—78; interim min. various chs. Pa. Ctrl. Conf., United Ch. of Christ, Harrisburg, 1968—96; ret., 1996. Author: Grief in the Loss of a Pastor, 1981; editor: Meditations on the Lord's Supper (John G. Clark), 1958. Bd. mgr. Bethany Children's Home, Womelsdorf, Pa., 1982-88; mem. adv. com. Sun Home Nursing Svcs., Northumberland, Pa., 1982-95, sec. bd. dirs., 1989-96; mem. stewardship coun. United Ch. of Christ, 1997-99. Mem. Interim Network (steering com. 1978-80), Assn. Ret. State Employees, Alban Inst., Interagy. Club (pres. 1966-68), Triangle Club (v.p. 1970-74, pres. 1996-98), Phi Mu. Democrat. Home: 8 Pine St Augusta ME 04330 *Our world is crying out for honesty, for absolute truth. Communication is impossible without belief and trust in the sincerity of the other person. Better the bitter truth than favor catering deception.*

CLARK, BEVERLY ANN, retired lawyer; b. Davenport, Iowa, Dec. 9, 1944; d. F. Henry and Arlene F. (Meyer) C.; m. Richard Floss; children: Amy and Barry (twins); stepchildren: Heather, Gretchan. Student, Mich. State U., 1963—65; BA, Calif. State U., Fullerton, 1967; MSW, U. Iowa, 1975, JD, 1980; grad., Iowa Massage Inst., 1999. Bar: Iowa 1980; lic. social worker, Iowa; nat. cert. lic. massage therapist. Probation officer County of San Bernardino, San Bernardino, Calif., 1968, County of Riverside, Riverside, Calif., 1968-69; social worker Skiff Hosp., Newton, Iowa, 1971-73, State of Iowa, Mitchellville, 1973-74, planner Des Moines, 1976-77, law clk., 1980-81; corp. counsel Pioneer Hi-Bred Internat., Inc., Des Moines, 1981-2000; atty. Jasper County Legal Aid, 2002—03; pvt. practice, 2000—06; ret., 2006. Instr. Des Moines Area C.C., Ankeny, Iowa, 1974—75, 2000—; adj. prof. Drake Law Sch., 1993—96, Buena Vista U., 2002—; pub. Sweet Annie Press; past owner Annie's Place, The B&B Connection Gift Catalog. Editor: Proceedings: Bicentennial Symposium on New Directions in Juvenile Justice, 1975; author monthly column Wellfem-In-Law; contbr. articles to prof. jours. Founder Mother of Twins Club, Newton, 1971; co-chmn. Juvenile Justice Symposium, Des Moines, 1974-75; mem. Juvenile Justice Com., Des Moines, 1974-75; mem. Nat. Offender Based State Corrections Info. Sys. Com., Iowa rep., 1976-78; incorporator, dir. Iowa Dance Theatre, Des Moines, 1981; mem. Pesticide User's Adv. Com., Fort Collins, Colo., 1981-88; co-developer Iowa Migrant Ombudsmen Project, Pioneer, Inc. and Proteus, Inc. Recipient Disting. Alumni award U. Iowa, 1990, Nat. award Ctr. for Pub. Resources. Mem.: DAR, ABA (termination-at-will subcom. 1982—2000, subcom. on devel. individual rights in work place), Iowa Bar Assn. E-mail: clarklaw@pcpartner.net.

CLARK, BRUCE BUDGE, humanities educator; b. Georgetown, Idaho, Apr. 9, 1918; s. Marvin E. and Alice (Budge) C.; m. Ouida Raphiel, Nov. 7, 1946; children: Lorraine, Bradley, Robert, Jeffrey, Shawn, Sandra. BA, U. Utah, 1943, PhD, 1951; MA, Brigham Young U., 1948. Teaching fellow Brigham Young U., 1946-47, U. Utah, 1947-50; asst. prof. Brigham Young U., 1950-55, assoc. prof., 1955-58, prof., 1959—, dir. humanities program, 1958-60, chmn. dept. English, 1960-65; dean Coll. Humanities, 1965-81. Author: The Spectrum of Faith in Victorian Literature, 1966, The Challenge of Teaching, 1966, Romanticism through Modern Eyes, 1968, Oscar Wilde, A Study in Genius and Tragedy, 1970, Brigham Young on Education, 1970, Idealists in Revolt, 1975, History of the Brigham Young U. Coll. Humanities, 3 vols., 1984, Family History, 3 vols., 1998, Selected Essays and Other Writings, 1998; Editor: Richard Evans Quote Book, 1971; anthology (Out of the Best Books, vol. 1, 1964, vol. II, 1966, vol. III, 1967, vol. IV, 1968, vol. V, 1969, Great Short Stories for Discussion and Delight, 1979; Contbr. articles to profl. jours. Served with AUS, 1944-46. Recipient Karl G. Maeser Teaching Excellence award, 1972, David O. McKay Humanities award, 1983, Brigham Young U. Presdl. citation for disting. svc., 1994. Mem. MLA, Nat. Coun. Tchrs. English, Rocky Mountain Modern Lang. Assn., Coll. Conf. on Composition and Communications, Phi Kappa Phi. Mem. Lds Ch. Home: 365 E 1655 S Orem UT 84058-7903

CLARK, BRUCE E., lawyer; b. NYC, 1946; AB, Holy Cross, 1967; JD, Harvard U., 1970. Bar: NY 1971, US Supreme Ct., Court of Claims. Clk. to Hon. Edward C. McLean US Dist. Ct. So. Dist. NY, 1970—71; assoc. Sullivan & Cromwell, NYC, 1975—80, ptnr., 1980—. Capt. USAF, 1971—75. Mem.: Assn. of the Bar of the City of NY (former mem. bankruptcy com.), State Bar NY (mem. com. bankruptcy law), ABA (mem. subcom. on letters of credit, com. uniform comml. code). Office: Sullivan & Cromwell 125 Broad St New York NY 10004-2498

CLARK, BRUCE ROBERT, geologist, consultant; b. Pitts., June 17, 1941; s. Harold Thomas and Florence (Miller) Clark; m. Karen Pelton Heath, Dec. 30, 1967; children: Adam, Andrea. BS, Yale U., 1963; PhD, Stanford U., 1967. Asst. prof. U. Mich., Ann Arbor, 1968-73, assoc. prof., 1973-77; v.p. Leighton and Assocs., Inc., Irvine, Calif., 1977-85, pres., 1986—2002, CEO, 1988—2002, sr. cons., 2002—. Contbr. articles to profl. jours. Commr. Calif. Seismic Safety Commn., 2000—, chmn., 2001—03; chmn. bd. dirs. YMCA Orange County, Calif., 1999—2002. Fellow: Geol. Soc. Am.; mem.: Seismol. Soc. Am., Assn. Engring. Geologists, Am. Geophys. Union, Earthquake Engring. Rsch. Inst. (bd. dirs. 2002—06). Office: Leighton Group Inc 17781 Cowan Irvine CA 92614-6009 Home Phone: 949-644-2052. Personal E-mail: bruce-clark@cox.net.

CLARK, BURTON ROBERT, sociologist, educator; b. Pleasantville, NJ, Sept. 6, 1921; s, Burton H. and Cornelia (Amole) C.; m. Adele Halitsky, Aug. 31, 1949; children: Philip Neil (dec.), Adrienne. BA, UCLA, 1949, PhD, 1954; Doctorate (hon.), U. Strathclyde, 1998, U. Turku, Finland, 2000. Asst. prof. sociology Stanford (Calif.) U., 1953-56; rsch. assoc., asst. prof. edn. Harvard U., 1956-58; assoc. prof., then prof. edn. and assoc. rsch. sociologist, then rsch. sociologist U. Calif., Berkeley, 1958-66; prof. sociology Yale U., 1966-80, chmn. dept., 1969-72, chmn. higher edn. rsch. group, 1973-80; Allan M. Cartter prof. higher edn. UCLA, 1980-91, prof. emeritus, 1991—. Author: Adult Education in Transition, 1956, The Open Door College, 1960, Educating the Expert Society, 1962, The Distinctive College, 1970, The Problems of American Education, 1975, Academic Power in Italy, 1977, The Higher Education System, 1983, The Academic Life, 1987, Places of Inquiry, 1995, Creating Entrepreneurial Universities, 1998, Sustaining Change in Universities, 2004; co-author: Students and Colleges, 1972, Youth: Transition to Adulthood, 1973, Academic Power in the United States, 1976, Academic Power: Patterns of Authority in Seven National Systems of Higher Education, 1978; editor: Perspectives on Higher Education, 1984, The School and The University, 1985, The Academic Profession, 1987, The Research Foundations of Graduate education, 1993; co-senior editor: Encyclopedia of Higher Education, 1992. Served with AUS, 1942-46. Recipient Comenius medal UNESCO, 1998. Fellow Brit. Soc. for Rsch. in Higher Edn.; mem. Am. Sociol. Assn., Am. Ednl. Rsch. Assn. (Am. Coll. Testing award 1979, Divsn. J. Disting. Rsch. award 1988, Outstanding Book award 1989), Assn. Study Higher Edn. (pres. 1979-80, Rsch. Achievement award 1985, Howard Bowen Disting. Svc. award 1997), Nat. Acad. Edn. (v.p. 1989-93), Consortium Higher Edn. Rschrs., European Assn. for Instnl. Rsch. (disting. mem.) Home: 201 Ocean Ave 1710B Santa Monica CA 90402 Office: UCLA Grad Sch Edn and Info Studies Los Angeles CA 90095-1521 Office Phone: 310-458-1640. Business E-Mail: clark@qseis.ucla.edu.

CLARK, CALEB MORGAN, political scientist, educator; b. Washington, June 6, 1945; s. Tanner Morgan and Grace Amanda (Kautzman) C.; m. Janet Morrissey Sentz, Sept. 28, 1968; children: Emily Claire, Grace Ellen, Evelyn Adair. BA, Beloit Coll., Wis., 1966; PhD, U. Ill., 1973. Lectr. N.Mex. State U., Las Cruces, 1972-75, asst. prof., 1975-78, assoc. prof. govt., 1978-81; assoc. prof. polit. sci. U. Wyo., Laramie, 1981-84, prof., 1984-92, U. Auburn, 1992—, prof., head polit. sci. Co-author: Comparative Patterns of Foreign Policy and Trade, 1976, Development's Influence on Yugoslav Political Values, 1976, Taiwan's Development, 1989, Women in Taiwan Politics, 1990, Foresight, Flexibility and Fortuna in Taiwan's Devel., 1992; mng. editor IS Notes, 1984-92; co-editor: North/South Relations, 1983, State and Development, 1988, Polit. Stability and Economic Development, 1988, Polit. Stability and Economic Development, 1991, The Evolving Pacific Basin, 1992, Technological Change and Rurdal Development in Poor Countries, 1994, Beyond the Developmental State, 1998, The ROC on the Threshold of the 21st Century, 1999, Democracy and the Status of Women in East Asia; cons., assoc. editor Soviet Union, 1974-77, World Affairs, 1975-84, Social Sci. Jour., 1978-80; contbr. articles to profl. jours. NDEA fellow, 1966-69; Woodrow Wilson dissertation fellow, 1969-70; grantee N.Mex. Humanities Coun., 1975, Wyo. Coun. for Humanities, 1982, U.S. Dept. Edn., 1983-85, Pacific Cultural Found., 1984-86, Am. Coun. Learned Socs., 1976, Met. Life Edn., 1978-80, NEH, 1978, NSF, 1981, Chiang Ching-Kuo Found., 1993-95. Mem. Am. Polit. Sci. Assn., Am. Assn. Chinese Studies (exec. coun. 1995-97), Western Polit. Sci. Assn., Assn. Asian Studies, Southern Polit. Sci. Assn., Internat. Studies Assn. (exec. dir. West 1981-84), Ala. Polit. Sci. Assn. (v.p. 1993-94, pres. 1994-95), Phi Beta Kappa (treas. 1983-91), Pi Eta Sigma, Phi Kappa Phi, Phi Beta Delta. Office Phone: 334-844-6460. Business E-Mail: clarkcm@auburn.edu.

CLARK, CANDY, actress; b. Norman, Okla., June 20, 1947; d. Thomas Prest and Ella Lee C.; m. Marjoe Gortner, 1978 (div. 1979); m. Jeff Wald, 1987 (div. 1988). Student public schs., Ft. Worth. Appeared in movies Fat City, 1971, American Graffiti, 1973 (nominated for best supporting actress), The Man Who Fell to Earth, 1975, I Will, I Will.for Now, 1976, Citizens Band, 1976, The Big Sleep, 1977, When Ya' Coming Back Red Ryder, 1978, More American Graffiti, 1978, National Lampoon Goes to the Movies, 1981, Q, 1982, Blue Thunder, 1983, Amityville 3-D, 1983, Stephen King's Cat's Eye, 1984, Hambone and Hillie, 1984, At Close Range, 1986, The Blob, 1988, Blind Curve, 1988, Cool-As-Ice, 1991, Buffy the Vampire Slayer, 1992, Original Intent, 1992, Deuce Coupe, 1992, Radioland Murders, 1994, Niagara, Niagara, 1996, Cherry Falls, 1999, The Month of August, 2002, The Big Empty, 2005, Zodiac, 2007, appeared in TV movies James Dean, 1976, Amateur Night at the Dixie Bar and Grill, 1978, Circus of the Stars #4, 1979, Where The Ladies Go, 1980, Rodeo Girl, 1980, Cocaine and Blue Eyes, 1983, Popeye Doyle, 1986, Plan of Attack, 1992, Mystery Woman: Redemption, 2006; TV appearances: Banacek, 1973, Faerie Tale Theatre, 1982, Magnum P.I., 1985, Simon & Simon, 1986, Starman, 1986, Hunter, 1986, The Hitchhiker, 1987, Matlock, 1987, St. Elsewhere, 1988, Father Dowling Mysteries, 1989, Baywatch Nights, 1995. appeared in off-Broadway show A Coupla White Chicks Sitting Around Talking, 1981, (play) It's Raining on Hope Street, 1988, Loose Lips, 1995.

CLARK, CAROLYN COCHRAN, lawyer; b. Kansas City, Mo., Oct. 30, 1941; d. John Rogers and Betty Charleton (Holmes) Cochran; m. L. David Clark, Jr., Dec. 29, 1967; children: Gregory David, Timothy Rogers. BA, U. Mo., 1963; LLB, Harvard U., 1968. Bar: N.Y. 1968, Fla. 1979. Assoc. Milbank, Tweed, Hadley & McCloy, NYC, 1968-76, ptnr., 1977—2001, cons. ptnr., 2002—. Mem. deferred giving com., former regional chmn. major gifts com. Harvard Law Sch. Fund; mem. vis. com. Harvard Law Sch., 1982-88; mem. com. on trust and estate gift plans Rockefeller U.; trustee Madison Ave. Presbyn. Ch., 1984-86, N.Y. Bot. Garden, 1993-96, Vis. Nurse Assn. N.Y. and Vis. Nurse Health Care, 1991-96, Riverdale Country Sch., 1994-98, Milbank Meml. Fund, 1996—, The Woodlawn Cemetery, 1999—; del. John D. Rockefeller Conf. Philanthropy in the 21st Century, N.Y., 1989; bd. advisors NYU program Philanthropy and the Law; chmn. program taxation exempt orgns. NYU Tax Inst. Recipient Disting. Alumna award U. Mo., 1989. Fellow Am. Coll. Trust and Estate Counsel (ind. regent, chmn. com. on charitable giving and exempt orgns.), N.Y. Bar Found., Am. Bar Found.; mem. ABA (chmn. subcom. income taxation of charitable trusts 1976-78, chmn. com. charitable instns. 1989-94), Assn. Bar City of N.Y. (chmn. com. on non-profit orgns. 1986-89, sec. com. philanthropic orgns. 1976-82, mem. com. trusts, estates and surrogates cts. 1977-80, 85-86), N.Y. State Bar Assn. (com. estate planning, trusts and estates sect. 1978-89), Am. Law Inst., Practising Law Inst. (lectr.), Harvard U. Law Sch., Assn. Greater N.Y. (trustee 1978-80, v.p. 1980-81, pres. 1981-82), NYU Tax Inst. (chmn. conf. tax planning charitable orgns. 1993-95), Nat. Harvard Law Sch. Alumni Assn. (exec. com. 1978-80, v.p. 1986-90, pres. 1990-92), Soc. Colonial Dames Am. in Mo., Maidstone Club. Home: 161 E 79th St New York NY 10021-0480 Office: Milbank Tweed Hadley Et Al 46th Fl 1 Chase Manhattan Plz New York NY 10005-1401 E-mail: cclark@milbank.com.

CLARK, CECIL LEE, military officer; b. Shreveport, La., Mar. 29, 1961; s. Brider Leroy (Stepfather) and Bobbye Cecile Ferguson; m. Laura Suzanne Brewer, Aug. 28, 2004. AA in Broadcasting, U. La., Monroe, 1984, BA in Radio, TV and Film Mgmt., 1986; MS in Strategic Studies, US Army Command and Gen. Staff Coll., Fort Leavenworth, Kans., 2004; MA in Mil. Studies, Spl. Ops and Low Insensity Conflict, Am. Mil. U., Charles Town, W.Va., 2006. Cert. combat lifesaver US Army Surgeon Gen., 1993; scuba diver Nat. Assn. Underwater Intrs., 1985. Inf. ranger airborne US Army, Fort Lewis, Wash., 1987—93, scout platoon leader, UN command security battalion Camp Bonifas (Pan Mun Jom), Republic of Korea, 1993—94, scout platoon leader, bfv platoon leader, asst. s3 Fort Carson, Colo., 1994—97, bn. s2 intelligence officer, UN command security battalion Camp Bonifas (Pan Mun Jom), 1997—99, bn. s2 intelligence officer, spl. ops. airborne Hunter Army Airfield, Savannah, Ga., 1999—2000, co. comdr., 2000—02, group s2 intelligence officer Fort Bragg, NC, 2002—03, task force s2 intelligence officer, spl. ops. airborne Fort Campbell, 2003—04, regtl. s2 intelligence officer, 2004—06, analysis and control element chief, 2006—. Guest columnist Shreveport Times. Charity vol. Salvation Army, Hopkinsville, Ky., 2004. Decorated Airborne Wings medal US Army, Pathfinder Badge medal, Combat Inf. Badge medal, Meritorius Svc. medal Comdr., US Forces Korea, Global War on Terror Expeditionary medal Sec. Def., Global War on Terror Svc. medal, Iraq Campaign medal, Afghanistan Campaign medal, Joint Achievement medal Joint Spl. Ops. Command, Expert Inf. Badge medal Sec. of Army, Armed Forces Expeditionary medal, Army Comendation medal, Bronze Star Pres. US. Mem.: NRA, M.I. Corps Assn., US Parachute Assn., Assn. Intelligence Officers (assoc.). R-Conservative. Baptist. Avocations: flying, skydiving, scuba diving, competitive shooting, skiing. Office: US Army 101st Airborne Divsn Air Assault Bldg 95 Fort Campbell KY 42223 Personal E-mail: cecil.clark@us.army.mil.

CLARK, CELIA RUE, lawyer; b. NYC, Aug. 16, 1951; d. Edward Frank and Rosemary (Reddick) Clark, Jr.; m. Edgar Crawford Gentry, Jr., Aug. 11, 1979; children: Diana Marron, Carl Edgar. BA with distinction, U. Wis., 1974; JD, U. Chgo., 1979; LLM, NYU, 1988. Bar: N.Y. 1980. Mng. editor Heldref Publs., Washington, 1974-78; assoc. Rogers & Wells, NYC, 1979-84; adj. asst. prof. law Yeshiva U., 1985; assoc. Weitzner, Levine & Hamburg, NYC, 1988-92; counsel Pirro, Collier, Cohen, Crystal & Block, White Plains, NY, 1992—96; ptnr. Smith, Buss & Jacobs, L.L.P., NYC, 1996—2002; pvt. practice NYC, 2002—. Co-author: Wealth Protection M.D., 2004; contbg. author: Asset-Based Financing, 1984; contbr. articles to profl. jours. Mem. planned giving coun. Am. Cancer Soc.; chair NY chpt. Arthritis Found., bd. govs.; bd. dirs. Louis R. Cappelli Found. Mem. ABA (tax sect.). Democrat. Office Phone: 212-370-4220. Business E-Mail: cclark@cclarklaw.com.

CLARK, CHARLES M., JR., medical school administrator; b. Greensburg, Ind., Mar. 12, 1938; s. Charles Malcolm and Mary Louise (Christian) C.; m. Julia Berg Freeman, Jan 27, 1963 (div. 1982); children: Margaret Louise, Brian Alexander; m. Eleanor DeArman Kinney, June 25, 1983; 1 child, Janet Marie Clark. BA, Ind. U., 1960, MD, 1963. From asst. prof. to prof. medicine Ind. U., Indpls., 1969—, from asst. prof. to prof. pharmacology, 1970—; assoc. chief staff rsch. and devel. VA Hosp., Indpls., 1988—2002; dir. Diabetes Rsch. and Tng. Ctr., Indpls., 1977—2002; co-dir. Regenstrief Inst., Indpls., 1993-97; assoc. dean Ind. U. Sch. Medicine, Indpls., 2002—. Chmn. Safety and Quality com. DCCT, 1982-93, Nat. Diabetes adv. bd., 1987-88; chair Nat. Diabetes Edn. Program, 1995-2002; vis. prof. Facultad de Ciencias Medicas, U. Nacional de la Plata, Argentina, 1999-2000. Editor Diabetes Care, 1996-2001; contbr. numerous articles to profl. jours. Lt comdr. USPHS, 1967-69. Fulbright scholar, 2004—05. Mem. ACP, Am. Soc. Clin. Investigation, Internat. Diabetes Fedn., Am. Diabetes Assn. (Banting award 1989, J.K. Lilly award 2003). Office: 714 N Senate Ave EF 200 Indianapolis IN 46202 Home Phone: 317-466-7858; Office Phone: 317-274-0104. E-mail: chclark@iupui.edu.

CLARK, CHARLES T(ALIFERRO), retired statistician; b. Danville, Ill., Mar. 18, 1917; s. Charles A. and Kathryn S. (Gentry) C.; m. Pearl W. DuBose, Oct. 6, 1943; children: Charles A., Mary D., Robert S. BBA, U. Tex., 1938, MBA, 1939, PhD, 1956. Asst. mgr. Austin C. of C., Tex., 1940-41; dir. personnel U. Tex., Austin, 1946-59, asst. prof. bus. stats., 1959-60, assoc. prof., 1961-79, prof., 1979-91, Mary Lee Harkins Sweeney Centennial prof. emeritus in bus., 1991—. Bd. dirs. Tex. Student Publs., Austin, 1964-69, Tex. Union, Austin, 1969-83, Univ. Fed. Credit Union, Austin, 1976-84 , Univ. Coop. Soc., Austin, 1980-84. Author numerous text books; (with L.L. Schkade) textbooks Statistical Analysis for Adminstrative Decision, 1969, 4th edit., 1983, (with John R. Stockton) Introduction to Business and Economic Statistics, 1971, 3d edit., 1980; contbr. articles to profl. jours. Served to 2d lt. USAAC, 1941-46, PTO. Recipient 11 teaching awards U. Tex., 1960-80 Mem. Coll. and Univ. Personnel Assn. (pres. 1959), Austin Personnel Assn. (pres. 1950), Austin Stat. Assn. (pres. 1975) Home: 4106 Farhills Dr Austin TX 78731-2812 Office: U Tex Dept Mgmt Sci & Info Systems Austin TX 78712 Personal E-mail: ctclark@austin.rr.com.

CLARK, CHARLES WINTHROP, physicist; b. Mpls., Sept. 30, 1952; s. Robert Newhall and Mary Quiatt C.; m. Deborah Jabon, Aug. 24, 1974. BA, Western Wash. State Coll., Bellingham, 1974; SM, U. Chgo., 1976, PhD, 1979. Rsch. assoc. U. Chgo., 1979; jr. rsch. assoc. Daresbury Lab., Warrington, Eng., 1979-81; NRC postdoctoral rsch. assoc. Nat. Bur. Standards, Gaithersburg, Md., 1981-83; pvt. practice physicist Gaithersburg, 1983-84; physicist Nat. Inst. Standards and Tech., Gaithersburg, 1984-89; acting chief Electron and Optical Physics div. Nat. Inst. Stds. and Tech., Gaithersburg, 1989-90, chief, 1990—. Cons. Princeton Plasma Physics Lab., NJ, 1984-90; vis. fellow Australian Nat. U., Canberra, 1986; mem. NAS/NRC Com. on Line Spectra of Elements, 1987-89, chmn., 1989-91; adj. prof. Inst. Phys. Sci. and Tech., U. Md., 1990—; program mgr. atomic and molecular physics Office Naval Rsch., 2003—; fellow Joint Quantum Inst., U. Md., 2006—; vis. prof. Nat. U. Singapore, 2006—. Editl. positions Jour. Physics B, Optics Express, Jour. Optical Soc. Am., NIST Digital Libr. Math. Functions; contbr. articles to physics, optics and chemistry jours. Sr. exec. svc. U.S. Dept. Commerce, 1998. Recipient NBS Excellence in Rsch. award Sigma Xi, 1987, Silver medal U.S. Dept. Commerce, 1994, Edward U. Condon award, NIST, 2002, Gold medal U.S. Dept. Commerce, 2004; Dr. Lee vis. fellow Christ Church, Oxford, 1999. Fellow: AAAS (mem. annual meeting program com. 2000—06), Joint Quantum Inst., Inst. Physics, Optical Soc. Am. (Archie Mahan prize 2002), Wash. Acad. Scis. (Phys. Scis. award 2003), Am. Phys. Soc. (chair divsn. atomic molecular and optical physics 2005). Office: Nat Inst Standards & Tech 100 Bureau Dr Stop 8410 Gaithersburg MD 20899-8410 Office Phone: 301-975-3709. E-mail: charles.clark@nist.gov.

CLARK, CLIFFORD EDWARD, JR., history professor; b. BayShore, NY, July 13, 1941; s. Clifford Edward and Helen C.; m. Grace Williams, Aug. 20, 1966; children: Cynthia Williams, Christopher Allen, Susan McGrath. BA, Yale U., 1963; MA, Harvard U., 1964, PhD in Am. Civilization, 1968. History tutor Harvard U., Cambridge, Mass., 1966-67; instr. Amherst (Mass.) Coll., 1968-69, asst. prof., 1969-70; from asst. to assoc. prof. Carleton Coll., Northfield, Minn., 1970-80, prof. history, 1980—, M.A. and A.D. Hulings prof. Am. studies, 1982—, dir. summer acad. programs, 1984—2002, chmn. history dept., 1986-89. Cons. Minn. Humanities Commn., Mpls., 1976—, Minn. Hist. Soc., Mpls., 1982—; Northfield Sch. Bd., 1978-87; editl. cons. Winterthur Portfolio, Del., 1983-92. Author: Henry Ward Beecher, Spokesman for a Middle-Class America, 1978, The American Family Home, 1800-1960, 1986; (with others) The Enduring Tradition, 6th edit. 2006; editor: Minnesota in a Century of Change: The State and Its People Since 1900, 1989 Mem. Northfield Heritage Preservation Commn., 1986—. Fellow Woodrow Wilson Found., 1964, 67; Demonstration grantee NEH, 1978, sr. fellow NEH, 1980; recipient Younger Humanist Summer Stipend, NEH, 1973. Mem. Am. Studies Assn., Am. Hist. Assn., Orgn. Am. Historians, Northfield Hist. Soc. Episcopalian. Avocations: woodworking, squash. Home: 718 4th St E Northfield MN 55057-2316 Office: Carleton Coll Dept History One N College St Northfield MN 55057 Office Phone: 507-646-4208. Business E-Mail: cclark@carleton.edu.

CLARK, CLIFTON BOB, physicist; b. nr. Fort Smith, Ark., July 8, 1927; s. Clifton Breckenridge and Coly (Stroud) C.; m. Sue Magruder, Sept. 1, 1950; children— Carol Jane, Charles Brian, Richard Thomas. BA, U. Ark., Fayetteville, 1949, MA, 1950; PhD, U. Md., College Park, 1957. Asst. prof. sci. Florence State Tchrs. Coll., 1950-51; asst. prof. physics U.S. Naval Acad., 1951-55; asso. prof., 1956-57; physicist U.S. Naval Research Lab., 1955-56; asso. prof. physics So. Meth. U., Dallas, 1957-61, prof., 1961-65, head dept., 1962-65; physicist, head dept. U. N.C., Greensboro, 1965-75, prof., 1965-94, prof. emeritus, 1994—. Vis. prof. physics Fla. State U., 1975-76 Served with USNR, 1945-46. Mem. Am. Assn. Physics Tchrs. (pres. South Atlantic Coast sect. 1974-75, 77-78, pres. N.C. sect. 1996-97), Am. Phys. Soc. (treas. S.E. sect. 1973-91), N.C. Acad. Sci., Phi Beta Kappa, Sigma Xi, Sigma Pi Sigma, Pi Mu Epsilon, Kappa Mu Epsilon, Omicron Delta Kappa. Home: Apt 3208 6100 W Friendly Ave Greensboro NC 27410-4085 Office: U NC Dept Physics and Astronomy PO Box 26170 Greensboro NC 27402-6170 Office Phone: 336-334-5844. Business E-Mail: cbclark@uncg.edu. *I believe people who are happy are those who accept doing things they do not enjoy as the price they pay for getting to do the things they enjoy. The most pleasant of experiences is the completion of a task which demanded extremely hard work. The most unhappy people I have known are those who cheated themselves of this satisfaction, because they tired of hard work and quit before they completed an endeavor.*

CLARK, COLIN WHITCOMB, mathematics professor; b. Vancouver, BC, Can., June 18, 1931; s. George Savage and Irene (Stewart) C.; m. Janet Arlene Davidson, Sept. 17, 1955; children: Jennifer Kathleen, Karen Elizabeth, Graeme David. BA, U. B.C., 1953; PhD, U. Wash., 1958; DSc (hon.), U. Victoria, 2000. Instr. math. U. Calif., Berkeley, 1958-60; asst. prof. math. U. B.C., 1960-65, assoc. prof., 1965-68, prof., 1968-94, acting dir. Inst. Applied Math., 1983-86, prof. emeritus, 1994—. Vis. prof. math. N.Mex. State U., 1970-71; vis. scientist Fisheries and Oceanography div. C.S.I.R.O., Cronulla, Australia, 1975-76, Ecology and Evolutionary Biology, U. Ariz., 1992; Regents lectr. U. Calif., Davis, 1986; vis. prof. Biol. Scis. Cornell U., 1987; vis. prof. Princeton U., 1997. Author: The Theoretical Side of Calculus, 1972, Mathematical Bioeconomics, 1976, 2d edit., 1990, Elementary Mathematical Analysis, 1982, Bioeconomic Modelling and Fisheries Management, 1985; (with J. Conrad) Resource Economics: Notes and Problems, 1987; (with J. Yoshimura, eds.) Adaption in Stochastic Environments, 1993; (with M. Mangel) Dynamic Modeling in Behavorial Ecology, 1988, Dynamic State Variable Models in Ecology, 2000, The Worldwide Crisis in Fisheries, 2007; contbr. articles to profl. jours. Fellow Royal Soc. Can., Royal Soc. (U.K.); mem. Can. Applied Math. Soc. (pres. 1981-83), Resource Modeling Assn. (pres. 1988-90). Office: Univ BC Dept Math Vancouver BC Canada V6T 1Z2 Personal E-mail: colin_clark@shaw.ca.

CLARK, CORNELIA A., state supreme court justice; b. Franklin, Tenn., Sept. 15, 1950; BA, Vanderbilt U., 1971; MA, Harvard U., 1972; JD, Vanderbilt Sch. of Law, 1979. Atty. Farris, Warfield & Kanaday (now Stites & Harbison PLLC), 1979—89; judge 21st Judicial Dist., Tenn., 1989—99;

dir. Tenn. Administrative Office of Ct., 1999—2005; justice Tenn. Supreme Ct., 2005—. Former adjunct prof. Vanderbilt U. Sch. of Law; faculty Nat. Judicial Coll.; former faculty mem. Am. Academy of Judicial Ed.; former mem. Supreme Ct. Commissions on Rules of Civil Procedure and Tech. Mem.: ABA, Am. Judicature Soc., Tenn. Bar Assn., Williamson County Bar Assn. (Liberty Bell award 2005), Nashville Bar Assn. (second v.p.), Lawyers Assn. for Women (bd. dirs. Marion Griffin chapter). Office: Tenn Supreme Ct 318 Supreme Ct Bldg 401 7th Ave N Nashville TN 37219

CLARK, CYNTHIA ZANG FACER, federal agency administrator; b. Sterling, Colo., Apr. 1, 1942; d. Joseph Elmer and Flora Burnell Zang; m. Glenn Willett Clark, Aug. 20, 1963; children: Randall, Drew, Ariel Silver, Allison, Timothy, Emily BA in Math., Mills Coll., Oakland, Calif., 1963; MS in Math., U. Denver, 1964; MS in Stats., Iowa State U., 1973, PhD in Stats., 1977. Instr. dept. maths. U. Denver, 1963-66, Drake U., Des Moines, 1971-72; mathematical statistician Statistical Rsch. Divsn. Bur. Census, 1977-79; econ. statistician Office Fed. Statistical Policy and Standards Dept. Commerce, 1979-81; statistical policy analyst Statistical Policy Office Office Info. and Regulatory Affairs Office Mgmt. & Budget, 1981-83; asst. divsn. chief for rsch. & methodology Agriculture Divsn Bur. Census, 1983-90, dir. rsch. and applications divsn., 1990-92; dir. survey mgmt. divsn. Nat. Agrl. Statistics Svc. Dept. Agriculture, 1992-96; assoc. dir. methodology and standards Bur. Census Dept. Commerce, Washington, 1996—2004; dir. methodology Office of Nat. Stats. U.K., London, 2004—. Contbr. articles to profl. jours. Recipient Sr. Exec. Svc. bonus award, 1994, 1995, 1997—2003. Fellow Am. Statis. Assn. (mem. InterCASIC 1996 conf. planning com., past pres. sect. govt. statistics, bd. dir.); mem. Am. Assn. Pub. Opinion Rsch., Washington Statis. Soc. (past pres.), Internat. Assn. Survey Stats., Sr. Exec. Assn. (Dept. Agr. chpt. pres. 1993-95), Caucus for Women in Stats. (past pres.), Natural Resource Conservation Svc. (blue ribbon panel on info. and data mgmt. 1996), Internat. Stats. Inst. (chair com. on women in stats. 2003—), Internat. Assn. Survey Statisticians (former bd. mem.). Mem. Ch. of Jesus Christ of Latter Day Saints. Avocations: genealogy, ice skating, cultural activities, travel. Office: Office for National Statistics 1 Drummond Gate London SW1V 2QQ England Home: Hugh St 32 Royal Belgrave House London SW1V 1RR England Office Phone: 4420 7533 6151. Business E-Mail: cynthia.clark@ons.gov.uk.

CLARK, DAVID JOSEPH, pharmacist; s. Edward Paul Clark and Mary Elizabeth Wheelock; children: Genevieve, Ryan, Patricia. BA in Am. Studies summa cum laude, Moorhead State U., Minn., 1977; BS in Pharmacy, ND State U., Fargo, 1991, PharmD, 1994. Registered pharmacist ND. Pharmacy resident ND State U., Hankinson, 1994—95, VA Med. Ctr., Fargo, ND, 1995—96, pharmacist, 1993—. Relief pharmacist Medicine Shoppe, Fargo, 1996—, Med. Pharmacy West, Fargo, 2006—. Mem.: ND PHarm. Assn., High IQ Soc., Mensa, Rho Chi, Phi Kappa Phi. Roman Catholic. Avocations: weight training, skiing, jogging, reading.

CLARK, DAVID MCKENZIE, lawyer; b. Greenville, NC, Sept. 1, 1929; s. David McKenzie and Myrtle Estelle (Brogdon) C.; m. Martha McKellar Early; children: David, Martha Dockery, Marietta Brogdon, Carolyn Elizabeth; m. Susan Summers Mullally; 1 child, McKenzie Lawrence. BA, Wake Forest Coll., 1951; LLD, NYU, 1957. Law clerk Chambers of Justice Black U.S. Supreme Court, Washington, 1957-59; assoc. Smith, Moore, Smith, Schell & Hunter, Greensboro, NC, 1959-63; ptnr. Stern Rendleman & Clark, Greensboro, NC, 1964-68, Clark & Wharton, Greensboro, NC, 1968-98, Clark Bloss & Wall, Greensboro, 1999—. Mem. bd. dirs. Legal Svcs. of N.C., Raleigh, 1976-82; pres. Summit Rotary Club, Greensboro, 1967; mem. bd. trustees W. Market Street Methodist Ch., Greensboro; chmn., co-founder Greensboro Legal Aid Found., 1965-68. Mem. ABA, ATLA, Am. Bd. Trial Advocates, N.C. Bar Assn. (bd. govs. 1982-85), N.C. Acad. Trial Lawyers, Greensboro Bar Assn. (bd. dirs.). Avocations: golf, tennis. Home: 21-C Fountain Manor Dr Greensboro NC 27405 Office: Clark Bloss & Wall 125 S Elm St Ste 600 Greensboro NC 27401-2644

CLARK, DAVID SCOTT, law educator, consultant; b. San Diego, Nov. 24, 1944; s. Homer Granville and Edna Susan (Maunus) C.; m. Marilee Oakes Wilson, Mar. 29, 1970; children: Richard, Susanna, Eliina, Liisa, David Scott II. AB, Stanford U., 1966, JD, 1969, JSM, 1972. Bar: Calif. 1972. Vis. prof. law U. Costa Rica, San Jose, 1969-71; asst. dir. studies in law and devel. Stanford Law Sch., Calif., 1973-75; asst. prof. law La. State U., Baton Rouge, 1976-78; assoc. prof. law U. Tulsa, 1978-81, prof., 1981—2002, dir. comparative and internat. law ctr., 1993—2001; Wilson prof. law Willamette U., Salem, Oreg., 2002—. Vis. scholar Max Planck Inst., Hamburg, Germany, 1984-85, 92; disting. vis. prof. So. Ill. U., Carbondale, 1987; vis. prof. law U. Colo., 1989; disting. vis. prof. Loyola U., Chgo., 1996; Fulbright sr. chair in comparative law, U. Trento, Italy, 1999; vis. prof. law U. Houston, 1999; vis. scholar, Inst. Advanced Legal Studies, London, 2000-01; disting. vis. prof. law, Bucerius Law Sch., Hamburg, Germany, 2002. Author: Comparative Law, 1978, Law and Social Change, 1979, The Civil Law Tradition, 1994, Oklahoma Civil Pretrial Procedure, 1995, The Organization of Lawyers and Judges, 2003; editor: Comparative and Pvt. Internat. Law, 1990, Introduction to the Law of the United States, 1992, 2d edit., 2002, Oxford Companion to American Law, 2002, American Law in the 21st Century, 2006, Encyclopedia of Law and Society: American and Global Perspectives, 2007, (jours.) Am. Jour. Comparative Law; contbr. articles to profl. jours. NEH grantee, 1981; von Humboldt Stiftung sr. research fellow, 1984-87. Mem.: ABA (internat. law and practice sect.), Am. Coun. Learned Socs. (exec. com. 1996—99, chair 1997—99, bd. dirs. 1997—99), Law and Soc. Assn., Internat. Acad. Comparative Law, Inns of Ct. (Inner Temple, London) (rsch. fellow 2000), Am. Soc. Comparative Law (exec. com. 1986—88, treas. 1989—95, v.p. 1998—2002, pres. 2002—06, hon. pres. 2006—). Democrat. Unitarian Universalist. Avocations: running, bicycling. Office: Willamette U Coll Law 245 Winter St SE Salem OR 97301 Home Phone: 503-373-3703; Office Phone: 503-370-6403. Office Fax: 503-370-6375. Business E-Mail: dsclark@willamette.edu.

CLARK, DAVID WILLIAM, lawyer, councilman; b. Manchester, Eng., Jan. 27, 1954; s. Chandler Kinney and May Clark; m. Sally Catherine Clark, June 27, 1987; children: Hilary Alexandra, Gillian Noelle. AB in History, Princeton U., 1975; JD, Duke U., 1978. Bar: Calif. 1978, Colo. 1990, Fla. 1992. Assoc. Thelen, Marrin, Johnson & Bridges, LA, 1978-84; counsel Ultrasys. Inc. (later Hadson Corp.), Irvine, Calif., 1984-89, Oxbow Corp., West Palm Beach, Fla., 1989—2003, 2004—, FPL Energy, LLC, Juno Beach, Fla., 2003—04. Councilman City of Palm Beach Gardens, Fla., 1993—2004, mayor, 1994-95; bd. dirs. Palm Beach County chpt. ARC, West Palm Beach, 1998-2001. Mem. State Bar Calif., Colo. Bar Assn., Fla. Bar Assn. Republican. Avocations: reading, history, ships and the sea. Office: Oxbow Corp 1601 Forum Pl Ste 1202 West Palm Beach FL 33401 Home: 14689 Crazy Horse Ln Palm Beach Gardens FL 33418 Home Phone: 561-694-2123; Office Phone: 561-640-8709. E-mail: Dave_Clark@oxbow.com.

CLARK, DAVID WRIGHT, lawyer; b. West Point, Miss., May 19, 1948; s. Douglas Earl and Sarah Evelyn (Wright) C.; m. Victoria Baugher, Oct. 16, 1976; children: Alexander, Nicholas, Peter. BA with high honors, Millsaps Coll., 1970; MA, Harvard U., 1971; JD, U. Mich., 1974. Bar: Ill. 1974, Miss. 1978, US Dist. Ct. (no. dist.) Ill. 1974, US Ct. Appeals (7th cir.) 1974, US Dist. Ct. (so. and no. dists.) Miss. 1978, US Ct. Appeals (5th cir.) 1978. Adj. prof. Miss. Coll. Sch. Law, Jackson, 1978-82; assoc. Wildman, Harrold, Allen & Dixon, Chgo., Friedman & Koven, Chgo., 1974-78; shareholder Wise Carter Child & Caraway, P.A., Jackson, 1978-96; ptnr. Lake Tindall, LLP, Jackson, 1996-2001, Bradley Arant Rose & White LLP, Jackson, 2001—. Pres. Miss. Bar Rev., 1979-2005. Mem. Miss. Constitution Study Commn., Jackson, 1985-87; bd. dirs. Miss. First, Inc., Jackson, 1983-87; pres. USA Internat. Ballet Competition, Jackson, 1990-98; mem. Leadership Jackson, 1989-90. Mem. ABA (ho. of dels. 1998—, sect. litigation, dir. divsn., com. chmn. and task force chmn. 1987-, chmn. gun violence coord. com. 1998-2002), Miss. Bar Assn. (chmn. litigation sect. 1994-95), Am. Law Inst., Charles Clark Am. Inn of Ct. Avocations: musicals, opera. Home: 110 Olympia Fields Jackson MS 39211-2509 Office: Bradley Arant Rose & White LLP One Jackson Pl Ste 450 Jackson MS 39201 Office Phone: 601-948-8000. E-mail: dclark@bradleyarant.com.

CLARK, DEANNA DEE, volunteer; b. Cedar Rapids, Iowa, June 1, 1944; d. Cyrus Dean and Isabelle Esther Hoge Thomas; m. Glen Edward Clark, July 16, 1966; children: Andrew Curtis, Carissa Jane. AA, Coll. of the Desert, 1964; BA, Coe Coll., 1966. Fund devel. chmn. Nat. Assistance League, 1992—94; resource devel. writer and trainer, 1992—2002; convenor U.S. Internat. Youth Exch. Initiative Cmty. Network, Utah, 1984—94; human svcs. subcom. child advocacy project, social justice and peacemaking min. unit Presbyn. Ch. U.S.A., 1992—93; sustaining mem. Jr. League Salt Lake City, 1976—, Assistance League Salt Lake City, 1986—; bd. dirs. Friends of Libr., U. Utah, 1991—94; numerous civic coms. and found. Utah, 1992—; pres. Provo-Jordan River Pkwy. Found., 1993—95; moderator, nominating com. Synod of the Rocky Mountains, 1999—2002; sec., vice-chmn. City of Holladay Interfaith Coun., 1999—2006; pres. bd. Neighborhood House Assn., 2006—; info practices com. Utah Legislature, 1990; exec. com. of Gen. Assembly Coun., Presbyn. Ch. (U.S.A.), 1993—97; elder Presbyn. Ch., 1983—; mem. coun. Presbytery of Utah, 1985—2001, moderator, 2000—01. Mem. LWV (Utah pres. 1981-83), P.E.O. (historian Utah chpt. 1992-95, chpt. H pres. 1995-97, Utah chmn. Gump and Ayers Scholarship Com. 1998-99). Home: PO Box 711098 Salt Lake City UT 84171-1098

CLARK, DICK, performer, producer; b. Mt. Vernon, NY, Nov. 30, 1929; m. Kari Wigton; children— Richard, Duane, Cindy. Grad., Syracuse U., 1951. Founder Dick Clark Corp. Prodns., Dick Clark Film Group, Dick Clark Communications, Inc., a group of casual dining restaurants, Dick Clark's American Bandstand Grill, Dick Clark's AB Grill, Dick Clark's Bandstand — Food, Spirits & Fun, and Dick Clark's AB Diner. Announcer, Sta. WRUN, summer 1950; then staff announcer, Sta. WOLF; rejoined, Sta. WRUN, then joined, Sta. WKTV, announcer, Sta. WFIL, Phila., 1952; host Am. Bandstand, 1956-89 (Outstanding Popular Music Program, Popular Music Mag. 1958, Daytime Emmy award 1981-82, 82-83), 32d Ann. Emmy Awards, 1981, Daytime Emmy Awards; formed, Dick Clark Prodns., 1956. Leading ind. T.V. producer with over 8500 hours of programming to credit, including The Savage Seven, 1968, Psych-Out, 1968, Killers Three, 1968, The Man in the Santa Claus Suit, 1979, The Birth of the Beatles, 1979, Elvis, 1979, The Dark, 1979, Murder in Texas, 1981, Demon Murder Case, 1983, Woman Who Willed a Miracle, 1983 (5 Emmmy awards, Peabody award), Remo Williams: The Adventure Begins, 1985, Copacabana, 1985, Liberace, 1988, Town Bully, 1988, Promised a Miracle, 1988, Death Dreams, 1991, Elvis and the Colonel: The Untold Story, 1993, Secret Sins of the Father, 1994, The Good Doctor: The Paul Fleiss Story, 1996, Deep Family Secrets, 1997; producer/host TV series: American Bandstand, The Dick Clark Show, Where the Action Is, The Rock'n Roll Years, others; host Dick Clark's Rock 'n Roll Revue, $ 20,000 Pyramid (Emmy award 1978-79), $25,000 Pyramid (Emmy award 1984-85, 85-86), $100,000 Pyramid, Miss USA, Miss Teen USA, Miss Universe; host/ exec. producer Super Bloopers and New Practical Jokes, New Years Rockin' Eve, 1972-, 40th Anniversary of American Bandstand; exec. producer Acad. of Country Music Awards, Am. Music awards, Golden Globe Awards, Soap Opera Awards, Daytime Emmy Awards, Cable Ace Awards; author: Your Happiest Years, 1959, To Goof or Not To Goof, 1963, Rock, Roll and Remember, 1976, Dick Clark & Richard Robinson, Looking Great, Staying Young, 1981, Dick Clark's The First 25 Years of Rock 'N Roll, 1981, The History of American Bandstand, 1985, Dick Clark's Guide to Good Grooming, 1985; producer VH1's Best fo American Bandstand, 1996, 97, Primetime Country, 1996, 97, Beyond Belief: Factor Fiction, 1997, The Weird Al Show, 1997, Dick Clarks's American Bandstand Collectors Edition, 1997; Donny & Marie, 1998-2000, Your Big Break, 1999, 2000, Greed, 1999, 2000; founder Dick Clark Media Archives. Recipient 6 Emmy awards as both prodr. and host, Grammy Nat. Trustees award, 1990, Am. Classic award ASCAP, 1990, Billboard Radio award Countdown Am., 1991, Disting. Svc. award Nat. Assn. Broadcasting, 1993, Daytime Emmys Lifetime Achievement award, 1994, Lifetime Achievement award Am. D.J. Assn., 1994, Lifetime Achievement award Syracuse U., 1994; named to Emerson Radio Hall of Fame, 1990, Broadcasting Mag. Hall of Fame, 1992, Rock 'N' Roll Hall of Fame, 1993, Internat. Person of Yr., NAPTE, 1990, Person of Yr., Phila. Advt. Club, 1995; inducted TV Hall of Fame, 1993. Achievements include honored with tribute at 2006 Emmy awards. Address: Dick Clark Productions Inc 3003 W Olive Ave Burbank CA 91505-7811

CLARK, DONALD MALIN, professional association executive; b. Buffalo, Feb. 11, 1929; s. Merritt Malin and Louise Mary C.; m. Joan Marie Coyle, Dec. 27, 1958; children— Kevin Malin, Michael John, Elizabeth Anne. BS magna cum laude, Canisius Coll., Buffalo, 1950, MA, 1952; Ed.D., SUNY, Buffalo, 1961; grad., U.S. Army Advanced Armor Sch., Ft. Knox, Ky., 1964, U.S. Army Command and Gen. Staff Coll., 1969, U.S. Army War Coll., 1975. Administrv. asst. Traveler's Ins. Co., Buffalo, 1950-57; mem. faculty Orchard Park (N.Y.) Sr. High Sch., 1957-66; dir. Ctr. Econ. Edn. SUNY, Buffalo, 1966-70; exec. dir. Industry-Edn. Coun., Niagara Falls, NY, 1970-79; pres., CEO, Nat. Assn. Industry-Edn. Cooperation, Buffalo, 1979—2004, pres. emeritus, 2005—. Radio and TV pub. info. news commentator, 1962-78; adj. prof. Canisius Coll. Grad. Sch., Buffalo, 1962-63, Lemoyne Coll. Sch. Mgmt., Syracuse, N.Y., 1973-79, Rochester Inst. Tech., 1983-84; adj. prof. Mt. Carmel Coll., Niagra Falls, Ont., Can., 1966; summer faculty Nat. War Coll., Washington, 1967-68; pres. Consumer Credit Counseling Svc., Buffalo, 1973, edn. chmn.; dir. Industry Edn. Coun. Calif., 1992-94; mem. Econ. Forum, Buffalo, 1994-2000; mem. editl. adv. bd. for Business Ethics, 1988-92; selected by People to People Internat.'s Citizen Amb. Program as del. leader for industry and edn. leaders in U.S. to visit Russia, Latvia, 1993, to China, 1995, South Africa, 1996, U.K., 1997, Australia/New Zealand, 1998, China, 1999; cons. (on site) to Ministry of Ed., Koror, Rep. of Palau, Micronesia, 1996; profl. pianist pvt. functions, spl. occasions for agencies and orgns., 1986—. Author: Meeting the Challenge of a Free Society, 1965; writer editls.: Buffalo News and Business First, also newsletters, handbooks, articles, guides for nat. publs.; prodr.: film on industry-edn. cooperation; mem. editl. bd.: Pro Education, 1987; contbr. articles over 100 articles to nat. and Can. publs. Apptd. by Pres. Reagan to Nat. Adv. Coun. on Ednl. Rsch. and Improvement, 1988-90; bd. dirs. N.Y. State Coun. Econ. Edn., 1980-84, Amherst (N.Y.) Symphony Orch., 1997-98; lectr. St. Michael's Roman Cath. Ch., Buffalo, 1976—; mem. cmty. adv. coun. SUNY, Buffalo, 1981—; mem. adv. com. ERIc Clearinghouse adult, career, and vocat. edn. Ohio State U., 1982-84; mem. adv. bd. Erie C.C., Williamsville, N.Y., 1995-97. With U.S. ANG, col. USAR, 1948-83; held position of chief of the Western/East European Divsn., Directorate of Fgn. Intelligence, Dept. Army, 1980-83, instr. U.S. Army Intelligence Sch., Ft. Holabird, Md., 1963-70; rev. panleist U.S. Dept. Edn.'s Nat. Elem. Sch. program, 1985-86, Secondary Sch. Recognition program, 1988-89. Recipient Kazanjian Found. Coll. Econs. Tchg. award, 1968, Inst Freedoms Found. medal, 1965, Presdl. Citation for Pvt. Sector Initiatives, 1985, Cert. of Recognition, U.S. Dept. Edn. for contbns. of time and talent toward adult literacy, 1984, Canisius Coll. Disting. Alumni award 1996; fellow NAM, 1965; fellow Am. Iron and Steel Inst., 1969 Mem. ASTD, Internat. Administrv. Mgmt. Soc. (chmn. econ. edn. com. 1968), Western N.Y. Export Coun. (assoc.), U.S. Dept. Commerce, Active Corps Execs., U.S. SBA, Mil. Officers Assn. of Am., Amherst Dance Club (pres. 1987-88), Am. Assn. Career Edn. (Disting. Mem. award 2005, Career Edn. Excellence and Innovation award 2006), Phi Delta Kappa (rsch. award 1996). Republican. Roman Catholic. Achievements include complete studies at the foriegn svc., Dept. of State, Washington, 1973, 1977 and 1982, and at the Naval amphibious warfare sch., Colo., Calif., 1974, 1983. Avocations: piano, writing, ballroom dancing, reading. Home: 235 Hendricks Blvd Amherst NY 14226-3304 Home Phone: 716-833-6346. Personal E-mail: dmalin@adelphia.net. *Being in the vanguard of change has been the most exciting aspect of my professional career. To participate in effecting change, particularly in education and human resources, economic development requires risk taking and the determination to gain support for one's ideas.*

CLARK, DONALD OTIS, lawyer; b. Charlotte, NC, May 30, 1934; s. Otis and Ruby Lee (Church) C.; m. Jo Ann Hager, June 15, 1957 (div. 1980); children: Deborah Elise, Stephen Merritt; m. Anja Maria Smith, Nov. 5, 1983. AB, U. S.C., 1956, JD cum laude, 1963; MA, U. Ill., 1957. Bar: S.C. 1963, Ga. 1964, D.C., 1999. Practice law, Atlanta, 1963-83; mem. Candler, Cox, McClain & Andrews, 1968-70, McClain, Mellen, Bowling & Hickman, 1970-75; ptnr. King & Spalding, 1975-78; sr. ptnr. Hurt, Richardson, Garner, Todd & Cadenhead, 1978-83; ptnr. Bishop, Liberman, Cook, Purcell & Reynolds, Washington, 1983-86, Kaplan Russin & Vecchi, Washington, 1986-92, Whitman & Ranson (merged with Breed Abbot & Morgan 1993), Washington, 1992-93; sr. ptnr. Whitman Breed Abbott & Morgan, Washington, 1993-95; ptnr. Keck, Mahin & Cate, Washington, 1995-97, Reed Smith LLP, Washington, 1997—2006; mediator U.S. Bankruptcy Ct. (so. dist.) NY, 2006—. Mem. dist. export council U.S. Dept Commerce, 1974—; adj. prof. law Emory U., 1970—, U.S.C., 1974; lectr. Ga. State U., 1972; mem. bd. vis. U. SC, 2006—; lectr. numerous internat. trade seminars and workshops Author: German govt. study on doing bus. in Southeastern U.S., 1974; editor-in-chief: S.C. Law Rev., 1963; contbr. articles to profl. jours. Served to capt. USAF, 1957-60. Decorated knight Order St. John of Jerusalem, Knights of Malta, knight Order St. Stanislas, knight and minister of justice Order of New Aragon, Sungrye medal Korea; recipient Nat. Leadership medal Air Force Assn., 1956, Coll. award Am. Legion, Outstanding Sr. award U. S.C., 1956, hon. consul Republic of Korea, 1972—. Mem. Atlanta Bar Assn., ABA, S.C. Bar Assn., Ga. Bar Assn., D.C. Bar Assn., Lawyers Club Atlanta, Am. Judicature Soc., Am. Soc. Internat. Law, Atlanta C. of C., Ga. C. of C. (exec. com. Internat. Councils), Inst. Internat. Edn. (chmn. Southeastern regional adv. bd. 1974—, nat. trustee), So. Consortium Internat. Edn. Inc. (dir.), Wig & Robe, Sigma Chi (pres. 1956 Province Balfour award), Omicron Delta Kappa, Kappa Sigma Kappa, Phi Delta Phi (pres. 1963 Province Grad. of Yr. award) Office Phone: 202-364-0111. E-mail: andon_6971@msn.com.

CLARK, DONNA M., retired elementary school educator; b. Roseville, Mich., Sept. 15, 1939; d. Granville Raymond Jewel and Evelyn Marie Steiger-Jewel; m. Buddy Lee Clark, Dec. 30, 1979; children: Thomas, Douglas Lee Jewel, Nancy Gruber, Barbara Merkle. BS in Elem. Edn., Olivet U., Kankakee, Ill., 1962; MS in Elem. Edn., St. Francis Coll., Ft. Wayne, Ind., 1970. First grade tchr. VanDyke Pub. Sch., Warren, Mich., 1962—69; upper elem. tchr. DeKalb County Ea. Cmty. Sch. Dist., Butler, Ind., 1969—2005; ret., 2005. Upper elem. dept. chair DeKalb County Ea., Riverdale Elem., Saint Joe, Ind., 1984—2005; summer sch. coord. DeKalb County Ea. Cmty. Sch. Dist., 1980—82. State field rep. Ind. Jr. Hist. Soc., Indpls., 1971—79; county pres. DeKalb County Hist. Soc., Auburn, Ind., 1977—78. Mem.: Delta Kappa Gamma (assoc.; assoc. v.p. 1980—82, v.p. 1980—82, corr. sec. 2006—), DAR (assoc.; state chmn. radio, tv and movie com. 1990—93, state libr. 1994—97, state chaplain 1997—2000, chpt. historian 2006—). Home: 7093 County Rd 59A Spencerville IN 46788 Home Phone: 260-238-4902.

CLARK, EARNEST HUBERT, JR., tool company executive; b. Birmingham, Ala., Sept. 8, 1926; s. Earnest Hubert and Grace May (Smith) C.; m. Patricia Margaret Hamilton, June 22, 1947; children: Stephen D., Kenneth A., Timothy R., Daniel S., Scott H., Rebecca G. BS in Mech. Engring, Calif. Inst. Tech., 1946, MS, 1947. Chmn., chief exec. officer Friendship Group, Baker Hughes, Inc. (formerly Baker Oil Tools, Inc.), LA, 1947-89, v.p., asst. gen. mgr., 1958-62, pres., chief exec. officer, 1962-69, 75-79, chmn. bd., 1969-75, 79-87, 87-89, ret., 1989; chmn. The Friendship Group, Newport Beach, Calif., 1989—. Bd. dirs. Regenesis Inc. Past chmn., bd. dirs. YMCA of U.S.A.; past chmn. bd. YMCA for Met. L.A.; mem. nat. coun. YMCA; trustee Harvey Mudd Coll. With USNR, 1944-46, 51-52. Mem. AIME, Am. Petroleum Inst., Petroleum Equipment Suppliers Assn. (bd. dirs.), Tau Beta Pi. Office: Friendship Group 3822 Calle Ariana San Clemente CA 92672-4502 Home Phone: 949-498-0866. Personal E-mail: ehclarkjr@cox.net.

CLARK, EDGAR SANDERFORD, insurance broker, consultant; b. Nov. 17, 1933; s. Edgar Edmund, Jr., and Katharine Lee (Jarman) C.; m. Nancy E. Hill, Sept. 13, 1975; 1 child, Schuyler; children by previous marriages: Colin, Alexandra, Pamela. Student, U. Pa., 1952-54; BS, Georgetown U., 1956; JD, 1958; postgrad., INSEAD, Fountainbleu, France, 1969, Golden Gate Coll., 1973, U. Calif. Berkeley, 1974. Staff asst. U.S. Senate, Washington, 1958-59; underwriter Ocean Marine Dept. Fireman's Fund Ins. Co., San Francisco, 1959-62; mgr. Am. Fgn. Ins. Assn., San Francisco, 1962-66; with Marsh & McLennan, 1966-72; mgr. for. Europe resident dir. Brussels Belgium, 1966-70; asst. v.p., mgr. captive and internat. div. San Francisco, 1970-72; v.p., dir. Risk Planning Group. Inc., San Francisco, 1972—75; v.p., dir. global constrn. group Alexander & Alexander Inc., San Francisco, 1975-94; exec. dir. The Surplus Line Assn. Calif., 1995-97. Lectr. in field.; guest lectr. U. Calif., Berkeley, 1973, Am. Grad. Sch. Internat. Mgmt., 1981-82, Golden Gate U., annually 1985-91; dir. Soc. Ins. Brokers, 1991-94; del. Calif. Agts. and Brokers Legis. Coun., 1992-95; pres. Ins. Forum of San Francisco. Mem. editl. bd. Risk Mgmt. Reports, 1973—76. With USAF, 1956—58. Mem. Am. Mgmt. Assn., Am. Risk and Ins. Assn., Internat. Insurance Soc., Chartered Ins. Inst., Am. Soc. Internat. Law, Soc. Calif. Pioneers San Francisco, Meadow Club, Fairfax, Calif. Republican. Episcopalian. Personal E-mail: snarkclark@yahoo.com.

CLARK, EDWARD EUGENE, academic administrator, educator, lawyer; b. Wichita, Kans., Apr. 15, 1948; came to Australia, 1975; s. Edward L. and Mary C. (Roets) C.; m. Patricia G. Sims, Dec. 26, 1970; children: Remy, Lisa. BA, St. Mary's U., Wichita, 1970, EdM, 1971; JD (hon.), Washburn U., 1978; postgrad., U. Tasmania, Australia, 1989, PhD, 1993. Bar: Kans. 1978, U.S. Dist. Ct. Kans. 1978, U.S. Supreme Ct. Atty. Foulston Siltkin, 1980-81; dep.-prin. St. Mary's Coll., Tasmania, Australia, 1988-92; lectr./sr. lectr. U. Tasmania, Tasmania, Australia, 1989-93; head Law Sch., prof. U. Canberra, Australia, 1994-97, dean mgmt. and law, 1998—, pro vice chancellor, 1998—2002, head Law Sch., 2003—. Fellow Ctr. for Enhancement of Learning, Tchg., and Scholarship. Author: New Ideas for Sch. Improvement, 1989; editor: Jour. Law and Info. Sci., 1991—; mem. editl. bd. Australian Bus. Law Rev., 1993—; author: Australian Comm. Law, 1993, Australian Market. Law, 1994, Australian Comm. Law, 2d edit., 1996, Managers and the Law, 1999; mem. editl. bd. Jour. Contemporary Issues on Bus. & Govt.; contbr. articles to profl. jour.; author: E-Bus. Law, 2000, Y2K: Avoiding the Legal Byte Marketers and the Law, 2000; mem. editl. bd. elaw Practice, 2001—; author: eMarketing@Internat, 2001, Privacy and the Internet, 2002, Managers and the Law, 2d edit., 2003, E-Law for Business and Government, 2004. Bd. dir. Australasian Inst. for Legal Info., 1994-99; dep.-chair consumer law com. Law Coun. Australia, 1994-98. Mem. Australian Legal Tchr. Assn., Australian Capital Territory Law Soc. Avocations: tennis, chess, guitar, jogging. E-mail: eugene.clark-@canberra.edu.au.

CLARK, ELOISE ELIZABETH, biologist, educator; b. Grundy, Va., Jan. 20, 1931; d. J. Francis Emmett and Ava Clayton (Harris) C. BA, Mary Washington Coll., 1951; PhD Zoology, U. N.C., 1958; DSc, King Coll., 1976; postdoctoral rsch., Washington U., St. Louis, 1957—58, U. Calif. Berkeley, 1958—59. Rsch. asst., then instr. U. N.C., 1952—55; from instr. to asst. prof. Columbia U., 1959—65, assoc. prof. biol. sci., 1966—69; with NSF, Washington, 1969—71, head molecular biology, 1971—73, divsn. dir. biol. and med. scis., 1973—75, dep. asst. dir. biol., behavioral and social scis., 1975—76, asst. dir. biol., behavioral and social scis., 1976-83; prof. biol. sci. to trustee prof. emeritus Bowling Green State U., Ohio, 1983—2002, trustee prof. emeritus, 2002—. Instr. Marine Biol. Lab., Woods Hole, Mass., 1958—62; v.p. acad. affairs Bowling Green State U., Ohio, 1983—96. Contbr. articles to profl. jours. and congl. hearings. Mem. alumnae bd. Mary Washington Coll., U. Va., 1967—70; bd. regents Nat. Libr. Medicine, 1973—83; mem. policy group competitive grants program U.S. Dept. Agr.; mem. White House Interdepartmental Task Force on Women, 1978—80, Task Force for Conf. on Families, 1980, Com. on Health and Medicine, 1976—80; vice chmn. Com. on Food and Renewable Resources, 1977—80; mem. selective excellence task force Ohio Bd. Regents, 1984—85; mem. Ohio Adv. Coun., Coll. Prep. Edn., 1983—84, Ohio Inter-Univ. Coun. for Provosts, 1983—96, chmn., 1984—85, 1995—96; nat. adv. rsch. resources coun. NIH, 1987—89; mem. informal sci. edn. panel NSF, 1986—88, adv. com., social, behavioral and econ. scis., 1997—2000; program adv. coun. sci., tech. and pub. policy Harvard U., 1988—90, mem. editl. bd. Forum, 1997—2001; mem. governing bd. OhioLink, 1990—96, vice chair, 1992, chair, 1993—94. Named Disting. Alumnus Mary Washington Coll., 1975; Wilson scholar, 1956; E.C. Drew scholar, 1956; USPHS postdoctoral fellow, 1957-59; recipient Disting. Svc. award NSF, 1978 Mem. AAAS (coun. 1969-71, bd. dirs. 1978-82, pres.-elect, 1992, pres., 1993, chmn. bd. 1994), Soc. Gen. Physiology (sec. 1965-67, coun. 1969-71), Biophys. Soc. (coun. 1975-76), Am. Soc. Cell Biology (coun. 1972-75), Marine Biol. Lab. (trustee 1993), Nat. Assn. State Univs. and Land Grant Colls. (higher edn. and tech. com. 1988-93, com. info. tech. 1994-96), Consortium Social Sci. Assn. (bd. dirs. 1993-96), Ohio Coun. Rsch. and Econ. Devel., Assn. Women Sci. (bd. dirs. 1998-2001), Phi Beta Kappa (com. qualifications 1985-2006, chair 1998-2004, senate 1996-2006, exec. com. 1997-2003), Sigma Xi, Omicron Delta Kappa Home: 1222 Brownwood Dr Bowling Green OH 43402-3503 also: 451 Crowfields Dr Asheville NC Office Phone: 419-372-9390. E-mail: eclark@bgsu.edu.

CLARK, EMORY EUGENE, diversified financial services company executive; b. Opelika, Ala., Jan. 24, 1931; s. Bunk Henry and Dorothy (Bolt) C.; m. Jean F. Reed, Sept. 30, 1951; children: Steven E., Michael E. Grad. pubs. schs. CLU, CFP. With Mgrs. Life Ins. Co., LA, 1956-74, agt. supr., 1956-60, mgr. Hawaii br., 1960-65, mgr. Pitts. br., 1965-68, mgr. Houston br., 1968-74; with Jefferson Std. Life Ins. Co., Fort Worth, 1974-82; fin. planner E.F. Hutton & Co., Inc., 1983-90; v.p. investments A.G. Edwards & Sons, Inc., Ft. Worth, 1990-99, sr. v.p. investments, 1999—. 1st lt. Inf. AUS, 1950-56. Named one of America's Best Fin. Planners, Consumers Rsch. Coun. Am., 2005—06. Mem. Fort Worth Life Underwriters Assn., Am. Soc. Life Underwriters, Fort Worth Soc. Life Underwriters, Ft. Worth Securities Dealers Assn., Inst. Cert. Fin. Planners (cert., registered practitioner). Home: 8109 Meadowbrook Dr Fort Worth TX 76120-5309 Office: AG Edwards & Sons Inc 420 Throckmorton Ste 1000 Fort Worth TX 76102 Personal E-mail: emoryclark@sbcglobal.net. Business E-Mail: emory.clark@agedwards.ca.

CLARK, ERIC C., state official; b. Smith County, Miss., 1951; s. John S. and Mame (Craft) Clark; m. Karan Killebrew; children: Charles, Catherine. BA, Millsaps Coll.; MA, U. Miss.; PhD in History, Miss. State U. Prof. history and govt. Miss. Coll., 1989-95; mgr. family tree farm Smith County; mem. Miss. Ho. Reps., 1980-96; sec. state State of Miss., Jackson, 1996—. Democrat. Baptist. Address: Office Sec of State PO Box 136 401 Mississippi St Jackson MS 39205-0136 Office Phone: 601-359-1350. Business E-Mail: administrator@sos.state.ms.us.*

CLARK, EUGENIE, zoologist, educator; b. NYC, May 4, 1922; m. Hideo Umaki, 1942; m. Ilias Konstantinou, 1949; 4 children; m. Chandler Brossard, 1966; m. Igor Klatzo, 1969; m. Henry Yoshinobu Kon, 1997. BA, Hunter Coll., 1942; MA, NYU, 1946, PhD, 1950; DSc (hon.), U. Mass., Dartmouth, 1990, U. Guelph, 1995, U. South Hampton, 1995. Rsch. asst. ichthyology Scripps Instn. Oceanography, 1946-47; with NY Zool. Soc., 1947-48; rsch. asst. animal behavior Am. Mus. Nat. Hist., NYC, 1948-49, rsch. assoc., 1950-80; instr. Hunter Coll., 1954; exec. dir. Cape Haze Marine Lab., Sarasota, Fla., 1955-67; assoc. prof. biology CUNY, 1966-67; assoc. prof. zoology U. Md., 1968-73, prof. zoology, 1973-92, prof. emerita, sr. rsch. scientist, 1992—. Vis. prof. Hebrew U., 1972; sr. rsch. scientist, trustee emerita Mote Marine Lab., Sarasota, Fla., 1999—. Author: Lady with a Spear, 1953, The Lady and the Sharks, 1969, Desert Beneath the Sea, 1991; subject of biographies Shark Lady (Ann McGovern), 1978, Adventures of the Shark Lady (Ann McGovern), 1998, Eugenie Clark, Adventures of a Shark Scientist (Ellen R. Butts, Joyce R. Schwartz), 2000, Fish Watching with Eugenie Clark (Michael E. Ross), 2000, America's Shark Lady (Ann McGovern), 2004, Eugenie Clark, Marine Biologist (Ronald A. Reis) 2005, Dr. Eugenie Clark Swimming with Sharks (Lisa Rao), 2006. Recipient Myrtle Wreath award in sci. Hadassah, 1964, Nogi award in art Underwater Soc. Am., 1965, Dugan award in aquatic sci. Am. Littoral Soc., 1969, Diver of Yr. award Boston Sea Rovers, 1978, David Stone medal, 1984, Stoneman Conservation award, 1982, Gov. of S. Sinai medal, 1985, Lowell Thomas award Explorers Club, 1986, Wild-screen Internat. Film Festival award, 1986, medal Gov. Red Sea, Egypt, 1988, Nogi award in Sci., 1988, Women's Hall of Fame award State of Md., 1989, Women Educators award, 1990, Alumnae award, Franklin Burr award Nat. Geog. Soc., 1993, Wyland Icon award, 2005, Henry Luce III Lifetime Achievement award, Wings WorldQuest Women of Discovery Awards, 2006; named to Hunter Coll. Hall of Fame, 1990, Diver's Equipment Mfg. Assn. Hall of Fame, 1993, Bermuda Underwater Explorers Inst. Hall of Fame, 2004, Hall of Fame Cmty. Video Archives, 2007; Fellow AEC, 1950; Saxton fellow, 1952; Breadloaf Writer's fellow; Fulbright scholar Egypt, 1951. Fellow: AAAS; mem.: Am. Elasmobranch Soc. (disting. fellow 1999), Am. Littoral Soc. (v.p. 1970—89), Nat. Pks. and Conservation Assn. (vice chmn. 1976), Internat. Soc. Profl. Diving Scientists, Soc. Woman Geographers (Gold medal 1975, U. Md. Pres.'s medal 1993), Israeli Zool. Soc. (hon.), Am. Soc. Ichthyology and Herpetology (life). Achievements include research in ecology and behavior of tropical sand and coral reef fishes; morphology and taxonomy marine fish; isolating mechanisms of poecillid fish; behavior of coral deep sea sharks. Office: Ctr Shark Rsch Mote Marine Lab 1600 Ken Thompson Pkwy Sarasota FL 34236 Office Phone: 941-388-4441. Business E-Mail: yoppe@mote.org.

CLARK, EVE VIVIENNE, linguist, educator; b. Camberley, U.K., July 26, 1942; arrived in U.S., 1967; d. Desmond Charles and Nancy (Aitken) Curme; m. Herbert H. Clark, July 21, 1967; 1 child, Damon Alistair. MA with honors, U. Edinburgh, Scotland, 1965, PhD, 1969. Rsch. assoc. Stanford (Calif.) U., 1969-71, from asst. prof. to assoc. prof., 1971-83, prof., 1983—. Author: Ontogenesis of Meaning, 1979, Acquisition of Romance, 1985, The Lexicon in Acquisition, 1993, First Language Acquisition, 2003; co-author: Psychology and Language, 1977. Fellow Ctr. for Advanced Study in the Behavioral Scis., 1979-80, Guggenheim Found., 1983-84. Mem. Dutch Acad. Scis. (fgn.). Business E-Mail: eclark@psych.stanford.edu.

CLARK, FRANK M., utilities executive; B in Bus. Adminstrn., DePaul Univ., JD, LLD (hon.), 2004; DHL (hon.), Governors State Univ., 2005. Mgmt. positions ComEd, Chgo., 1966—2000, exec. v.p., 2000—01, pres., 2001—05; exec. v.p., chief of staff Exelon Corp. (holding co. of ComEd), 2004—05; chmn., CEO ComEd, Chgo., 2005—. Bd. dir. Harris Fin. Corp., Waste Mgmt. Inc., 2002—, Aetna Inc., 2006—. Chmn. Metro. Family Services; trustee Adler Planetarium & Astronomy Mus., DePaul Univ., Chgo. Symphony Orch., Univ. Chgo. Hosp. & Health Sys.; bd. mem. Abraham Lincoln Presdl. Libr. Found., Governors State Univ. Found., Big Shoulders Fund, Ill. Council Econ. Edn., Ill. Mfr. Assn. Named one of 50 Most Powerful Black Executives in Am., Forbes mag.; recipient Nat. Humanitarian award, Nat. Conf. for Cmty. & Justice, Rerun Novarum award, Loyola Univ., HistoryMakers award, 2002. Mem.: Chgo. Bar Assn. Office: ComEd 37th Flr 10 S Dearborn St Chicago IL 60690

CLARK, FRED, writer, editor; b. Limón, Costa Rica, Dec. 12, 1930; came to US, 1968; s. Thomas and Irene (Penney) C.; m. Dorothy Hyacinth James, Aug. 4, 1956; children: Paul, Fred Jr., Lydia Ramona. Student, Ctrl. Am. Acad., San José, 1949; BLitt, U. Costa Rica, 1951; postgrad., Stafford Coll., London, 1957; barrister-at-law, Inner Temple, London, 1960. Bar: Eng. 1960, Jamaica 1960; cert. in law Coun. Legal Edn. Master of langs. Merl Grove Sch., 1951-55; trust officer Govt. of Jamaica, 1960-61; pvt. law practice Kingston, Jamaica, 1961-67; legal editor Corp. Trust Co., NYC, 1968-69; sr. legal editor Prentice-Hall, Inc., Englewood Cliffs, NJ, 1969-91. Cons. commonwealth law. Editor The Corp. Jour., 1968-69. Trustee United Ch. of Christ, 1970-78; spl. advisor U.S. Congl. Adv. Bd.; nat. adv. bd. Am. Security Coun. Recipient Disting. Leadership award, 1984, Presdl. medal of merit, 1986; inscription Hall of Tolerance Civil Rights Memorial Ctr. Ala. Mem. Am. Mgmt. Assn., Internat. Platform Assn., Internat. Commn. Jurists, Am. Mus. Natural History, Nat. Geog. Soc., NY Acad. Scis., Am. Ballet Theater, Met. Opera Guild, US Naval Inst., Freeport Bus. Promotion (bd. dirs.), US Power Squadron (asst. sec.), Inter-Am. Soc., Rosicrucians. Home: PO Box 291 Bergenfield NJ 07621-0291

CLARK, GARY CARL, lawyer; b. Flippin, Ark., Mar. 4, 1947; m. Jane W. Clark; children: Ross, Lauren. BS in Agrl. Edn., Okla. State U., 1969, MS, 1972; JD with honors, U. Tex., 1975. Bar: Okla. 1975, U.S. Dist. Ct. (no. dist.) Okla. 1975, U.S. Ct. Appeals (10th cir.) 1979. Tchr. Laverne H.S., Okla., 1969—70; assoc. Conner, Winters, Ballaine, Barry & McGowen, 1975—81, ptnr., 1981, Baker & Hoster, Tulsa, 1981—97; dir. Crowe & Dunlevy, PC, Tulsa, 1997—2004; v.p., gen. counsel Okla. State U. Found., Stillwater, 2004—. Lawyer-staffed Panel of Ct. Appeals, 1991; speaker in field. Vol. Legal Svcs. Ea. Okla., 1993—; trustee Okla. State Univ., Tulsa, 1999-2001; mem. bd. regents Okla. State Univ. and A&M Colls., 1993-2001, chmn., 1997-98; past v.p. Jane Addams Elem. Sch. PTA, sch. vol.; chair site adv.; mem. Okla. Jud. Evaluation Com., 1999. Recipient Silver Beaver award Boy Scouts Am., 1996. Fellow Am. Coll. Trust and Estate Coun., Am. Bar Found., Okla. Bar Found.; mem. Okla. Bar Assn. (pres. 2002, bd. govs. 1997-99, 2001-2003, John Shipp Ethics award 1999, chair estate planning and probate sect. 1988-89, vice chair probate code com. 1991, bd. dirs. young lawyers divsn., mem. real property sect., co-chair tech. strategic planning task force, 2000, Golden Gavel award, 2003, Golden Quill award, 2003, chair awards com., 2007), Tulsa County Bar Assn. (pres. 1993-94, Golden Rule award 1993, Outstanding Sr. Lawyer 1996), Tulsa County Bar Found. (pres. 1994-95, treas. 1995-99, charter fellow), Tulsa Title and Probate Lawyers Assn. (pres. 1989-90), Okla. State U. Alumni Assn. (life), FFA Alumni Assn. (life), Order of Coif, Alpha Gamma Rho Alumni Assn. (Okla. chpt. dir., past pres.), Phi Delta Phi. Office: OSU Found 400 S Monroe Stillwater OK 74076 Home: 2 Brentwood Dr Stillwater OK 74075 Office Phone: 405-385-5146. Business E-Mail: gclark@osuf.org.

CLARK, GARY M., statistician; b. Tacoma, June 15, 1945; s. Fred Alfred Clark; m. Carol A. Whitaker, Aug. 9, 1998; children: Michael Stephen, Jennifer Anne Weir, Jason Whitaker. BA, Wash. State U., Pullman, 1967; MS, U. Wash., Seattle, 1969, PhD, 1975. Asst. prof. U. Kans. Med. Ctr., Kansas City, 1975—78, assoc. prof., 1978—80; rsch. assoc. prof. U. Tex. Health Sci. Ctr., San Antonio, 1980—85, prof., 1985—99; prof., assoc. dir. Breast Ctr. Baylor Coll. Medicine, Houston, 1999—2002; v.p. biostatistics and data mgmt. OSI Pharmaceuticals, Inc., Boulder, Colo., 2002—. Contbr. articles to profl. jours. 1st lt. US Army, 1969—71, Vietnam. Named one of 100 Most Pub. Breast Cancer Rschrs., San Antonio Breast Cancer Symposium, 2000. Mem.: Biometric Soc., Internat. Assn. for the Study of Lung Cancer, Am. Assn. for Cancer Rsch., Am. Soc. Clin. Oncology, Am. Statis. Assn. Office: OSI Pharmaceuticals Inc 2860 Wilderness Pl Boulder CO 80301 Office Phone: 303-546-7633. Office Fax: 303-546-7889. Business E-Mail: gclark@osip.com.

CLARK, GARY R., newspaper editor; b. Cleve., June 27, 1946; s. Dale Francis and Mary Louise (Rozeski) C.; m. Caryn Elaine Helm, Dec. 18, 1976; children: Jessica Lynn, Brian Michael. BA, Ohio State U., 1973, MA, 1978. Reporter Chronicle-Telegram, Elyria, Ohio, 1973-77, The Plain Dealer, Cleve., 1978-88, state editor, 1988-89, nat. editor, 1989, city editor, 1989-90, mng. editor, 1990—2000; city editor The Columbus Dispatch, 2000—02; mng. editor for news The Denver Post, 2003—. Tchg. assoc. Ohio State U., Columbus, 1977-78; juror, Pulitzer Prize, 1996. Sgt. USMC, 1966-69, Vietnam. Recipient Best of Show award, Ohio Soc. Profl. Journalists, 1999. Mem. AP Mng. Editors, Am. Soc. Newspaper Editors, Investigative Reporters and Editors, Cleve. City Club. Office: Mng Ed Denver Post 1560 Broadway Denver CO 80202

CLARK, GERDA MARGARETE, special education educator; d. Rudolf Weiner and Anna Maria Bader; 1 child, John Thomas. Diploma, Moody Bible Inst., 1969; BA with honors, U. Ill., Chgo., 1975; MA, Northeastern Ill. U., 1992. Cert. learning and behavior specialist I Ill. State Bd. Edn., adminstrv. type 75 Ill. State Bd. Edn. German tchr. Gordon Tech. H.S., Chgo., 1975—89; learning disability tchr. and physically disabled facilitator Harvey (Ill.) Sch. Dist. 152, 1996—97; spl. edn. tchr. Chgo. Bd. of Edn., 1997—. Recipient Outstanding H.S. Tchr. award, U. Chgo., 1980, Tutoring award, Northeastern Ill. U., 1995; scholar Fortbildungskurs für Lehrer, Goethe Inst. of Chgo., 1980; Robert Bosch scholar, U. Ill. at Chgo., 1975, gifted fellow, Ill. State Bd. Edn., 1990—91. Mem.: ASCD, Am. Ednl. Rsch. Assn., Chgo. Bot. Garden. Home: 3716 N Richmond St Chicago IL 60618 Home Phone: 773-604-4748. Personal E-mail: clark6905@sbcglobal.net.

CLARK, GLEN EDWARD, judge; b. Cedar Rapids, Iowa, Nov. 23, 1943; s. Robert M. and Georgia L. (Welch) C.; m. Deanna D. Thomas, July 16, 1966; children: Andrew Curtis, Carissa Jane. BA, U. Iowa, 1966; JD, U. Utah, 1971. Bar: Utah 1971, U.S. Dist. Ct. Utah 1971, U.S. Ct. Appeals (10th cir.) 1972. Assoc. Fabian & Clendenin, 1971-74, ptnr., 1975-81, dir., chmn. banking and comml. law sect., 1981-82; judge U.S. Bankruptcy Ct. Dist. Utah, Salt Lake City, 1982-86, chief judge, 1986—. Bd. govs. nat. Conf. Bankruptcy Judges, 1988-94; mem. com. on bankruptcy edn. Fed. Jud. Ctr., 1989-92; vis. prof. U. Utah, Salt Lake City, 1977-79, 83; pres. Nat. Conf. Bankruptcy Judges, 1992-93; chair bd. trustees Nat. Conf. Bankruptcy Judges Endowment for Edn., 1990-92; vis. assoc. prof. law Univ. Utah; instr. adv. bus. law Univ. Utah. Articles editor: Utah Law Review. With U.S. Army, 1966-68. Finkbine fellow U. Iowa. Fellow Am. Coll. Bankruptcy (charter, mem. bd. regents 1995-2000, dir. found. 2002-03); mem. Jud. Conf. U.S. (mem. com. jud. br. 1992-99, 10th cir. bankruptcy appellate panel 1996—), Utah Bar Assn., Order of Coif. Presbyterian. Office: 365 US Courthouse 350 S Main St Salt Lake City UT 84101-2106

CLARK, GLORIA A., music educator; b. Indpls., Feb. 7, 1937; d. Franklin T. and Jean Agnes Gamage; m. Robert A. Mead, Dec. 5, 1957 (div. Dec. 1959); 1 child, Allison M. Szabo; m. William H. Clark, Jan. 25, 1981. BS in Sociology, Regents Coll., Albany, NY, 1989; MA in Philosophy, Calif. State U. Dominguez Hills, 1992. Svc. rep. United Telephone; prof. philosophy S. Fla. C.C.; tchr. Butte Ctrl. Cath. Schs. Performing musician; mural artist; organist, pianist Aldersgate United Meth. Ch., Butte, Mont.; pvt. piano tchr., Butte. Virginia City (Mont.) Art Festival, one-woman shows include Uptown Cafe, 2006. Bd. dirs. Cmty. Concerts, Butte; vol. cellist Butte Symphony, 1991—2001; pianist Grant Kohrs Nat. Park. Recipient Butte City Artist award, Butte Silver Bow County, 1991—97; grantee Music Edn. grant, Cmty. Concerts, Butte, 1996—2007. Mem.: Nat. Accredited Music Tchrs. Assn. Avocations: crocheting, theater, walking, cribbage, crossword puzzles. Home: 239 Mammoth Dr Butte MT 59701 Office Phone: 406-782-4500.

CLARK, GORDIE, professional sports team executive; b. Scotland; m. Carol Clark; children: Ashley, Brendan. Grad., U. NH. Former profl. hockey player; asst. coach Maine Mariners, Maine, 1987—89, Boston Bruins, 1989—92, mem. scouting dept., 1992—96; asst. gen. mgr., dir. player personnel NY Islanders, 1996—2002; dir. hockey ops. Bridgeport Sound Tigers; profl. scout NY Rangers, 2002, head armature scout, dir. player personnel, 2007—. Home: NY Rangers 2 Pennsylvania Plaza New York NY 10121*

CLARK, GORDON HOSTETTER, JR., physician; b. New Haven, Aug. 5, 1947; s. Gordon Hostetter and Elizabeth Master (Mapes) C.; m. Gail Marie Theroux, July 23, 1988; children: Emily Blakeslee Clark Ehl, Christopher Robert, Heather Mays Richmond, Adam Arthur. BA, Yale U., 1970; MDiv, Pacific Sch. Religion, 1973; MD, George Washington U., 1977. Diplomate Am. Bd. Psychiatry and Neurology, Am. Bd. Med. Mgmt., Am. Coll. Physician Execs.; cert. in adminstrv. psychiatry, APA, 1992; cert. physician exec. Commn. in Med. Mgmt., 1998. Intern, then resident, then fellow Dartmouth-Hitchcock Med. Ctr., Hanover, N.H., 1977-81; staff psychiatrist Lakes Region Med. Health Ctr., Laconia, N.H., 1981-82, med. dir., 1982-86; dir. psychiat. unit Lakes Region Gen. Hosp., Laconia, 1986-89; med. dir. behavioral svcs. St. Vincent Health Ctr., Erie, Pa., 1990-93; dir. med./profl. adminstrn. Deerfield Mgmt. Group, Erie, Pa., 1991-94; pres. Deerfield Profl. Assocs., 1992-94; med. advisor Deerfield Behavioral Health Network, 1994-95; sr. psychiat. cons. Med. Groups Divsn. Maine Harvard Cmty. Health Plan, Portland, Maine, 1995-96; pres., med. dir. Integrated Behavioral Healthcare, Portland, Maine, 1995—2007; med. dir. Behavioral Health Network of Maine, 1995-99, Augusta (Maine) Mental Health Inst., 1995-96; assoc. med. dir. Maine Dept. Mental Health and Mental Retardation, Augusta, 1995-96; med. dir. med.-psychiat. program Westbrook (Maine) Comty. Hosp., 1996-97; sr. physician advisor CMG Healthsource Maine, Maine, 1996-97; chief exec. and med. officer Integrated Behavioral Healthcare, Inc., Scarborough, Maine, 2007—. Adj. asst. prof. clin. psychiatry Dartmouth Med. Sch., Hanover, 1983-90; clin. asst. prof. psychiatry U. Pitts. Sch. Medicine, 1990-96; clin. assoc. prof. psychiatry U. Vt. Med. Sch., 1996-2004; chmn. com. psychiatrists in NH Cmty. Mental Health Ctrs., Concord, 1982-86; med. liaison to Pa. Office Mental Health and Mental Retardation and Erie County Office Mental Health and Mental Retardation, 1991-94; bd. dirs. Med. Network, Inc., credentials com. 1995-98, med. mgmt. com. 2002-07, med. dir. depression mgmt. program, 2002-07, mem. bylaws and nomating com., 2006, fin. com. 2007—, audit com., 2007—; New Eng. region adv. com. Cigna Behavioral Health Care, 2000-2001; New Eng. region pharmacy and therapeutics com. Cigna Health Care, 2000, nat. pharmacy and therapeutics com., 2001; depression work group MaineHealth, 2002-05; mem. provider adv. com., 2004—, quality mgmt. improvement com. Anthem Behavioral Health, 2004-06. Exec. v.p. Erie Phiharm., 1991—92. Recipient Exemplary Psychiatrist award Nat. Alliance for Mentally Ill, 1992; recipient Benjamin Manchester award George Washington U., 1977. Fellow: Am. Coll. Physician Execs. Vanguard, Am. Assn. Social Psychiatry (mem. coun. 1993—99), Am. Coll. Mental Health Adminstrn., Am. Psychiat. Assn. (disting.) (examiner oral part of exams. cert. adminstrn. psychiatry 1993—96, com. on stds. and survey procedures 1998—2001, APA/Bristol-Myers Squibb fellowship selection com. 1999—2002, task force develop guidlines psychiat. practice mental health ctrs., com. state and cmty. psychiatry sys., com. chronically mentally ill, Falk fellow 1979—81); mem.: Maine Psychiat. Assn. (chair program com. 1996—97), We. Pa. Psychiat. Soc. (pres. elect 1992—94), Psychiat. Physicians Pa. (fed. legis. rep. pbu. psychiatry com. 1993—94, treas. 1994, coun., govt. rels. com.), Nat. Psychiatric Alliance (chmn. med. staff com. 1992—94, exec. com. 1992—95), Am. Coll. Psychiatrists, Am. Assn. Psychiat. Adminstrs. (coun. 1996—97, pres.-elect 1997—99, pres. 1999—2001), Am. Assn. Cmty. Psychiatrists (founding pres. 1984—90, bd. dirs. 1984—92, com. psychiat. practice in cmty. mental health ctrs. guideline devel., Disting. Svc. award 1990). Avocations: skiing, biking, hiking, golf. Home: 10 Park St Yarmouth ME 04096-7757 Office: Integrated Behavioral Healthcare Inc 200 Professional Dr Scarborough ME 04074 Office Phone: 207-883-0711.

CLARK, GRANT LAWRENCE, corporate lawyer; b. Syracuse, NY, Apr. 15, 1954; s. Robert William and Linda (Grant) C.; m. Diana Christine Baker, Aug. 5, 1983. BA, Framingham State Coll., 1979; JD, Suffolk U., 1983. Bar: Mass. 1983, Calif. 1992. Judge advocate USAF, Washington, 1983-87; asst. gen. counsel GSA, Washington, 1987-88; assoc. Rivkin, Radler, Dunne & Bayh, Washington, 1988-91; assoc./ptnr. McKenna & Cuneo, Washington, 1991-94; asst. gen. counsel Sci. Applications Internat. Corp., San Diego, 1994-99; sr. v.p., gen. counsel Telcordia Tech., Inc., Morristown, NJ, 1999—2004; sr. v.p., chief dep. counsel Sci. Applications Internat. Corp., San Diego, 2004—07, sr. v.p., dir. contracts, chief dep. counsel, 2007—. Capt., USAF, 1983-87. Mem.: ABA. Avocations: running, latin dance, medieval history. Home: 1969 Zapo St Del Mar CA 92014 Office: Sci Applications Internat Corp 10260 Campus Point Dr San Diego CA 92121 Home Phone: 858-755-3571; Office Phone: 858-826-5068. E-mail: grant.l.clark@saic.com.

CLARK, HAROLD L., technology company executive, consultant; m. Joyce E. Lehmann; children: Elizabeth E. Olsen, Charles L., James, Harry L. BSBA, Bryant U., Smithfield, RI, 1959; MBA, Pepperdine U., Malibu, Calif., 1976; EdD, Nova U., Ft. Lauderdale, Fla., 1981. Pres., vice chmn. bd. Ingram Micro, Santa Ana, Calif., 1985—89; pres. Everex Systems, Fremont, Calif., 1990—92; CEO Ameriquest Techs., Santa Ana, 1992—95; chmn. XCD, Inc., 1995—98, Max Internet Comm., 1999—2001; dir. Jazz Techs. (formerly Acquicor Techs.), Newport Beach, Calif., 2006—. Chmn. bd. dirs. OpenPro, Fountain Valley, Calif., 2005—; cons. in field. With US Army, 1953—56. Home: 479 Garcia Hemet CA 92545 Office Phone: 951-325-8593.

CLARK, HARRY WESTLEY, federal agency administrator; BA in Chemistry, Wayne State U., 1969; MD, U. Mich., Ann Arbor, 1973, MPH, 1974; JD, Harvard U., 1981. Diplomate Am. Bd. Psychiatry and Neurology. Resident in psychiatry U. Mich. Hosp. Neuropsychiatric Inst., 1974—77; fellow in substance abuse VA Med. Ctr., San Francisco, 1984—86, chief associated substance abuse programs; dir. Ctr. Substance Abuse Treatment Substance Abuse and Mental Health Services Adminstrn., HHS, Rockville, Md., 1998—. Sr. program cons. Robert Wood Johnson Substance Abuse Policy Program; assoc. clin. prof. psychiatry U. Calif., San Francisco; adv. bd. Treatment-on-Demand Planning Coun., San Francisco. Recipient Vernelle Fox Award for Excellence in Addiction

Medicine, Edn., and Pub. Svc., Calif. Soc. Addiction Medicine, 2000, Leadership Award, Nat. Treatment Accountability for Safer Communities, 2001, Award for Disting. Svc., Sec. US HHS, 2001, 2003, Clifford R. Gross Award for Fed. Pub. Svc., Md. Chpt. of Am. Soc. Pub. Adminstrn., 2002, rank of Meritorious Exec. in Sr. Exec. Svc., Pres. of US, 2003. Fellow Am. Soc. Addiction Medicine; mem. Coll. on Problems of Drug Dependence. Office: Ctr Substance Abuse Treatment Rm 5-5015 1 Choke Cherry Rd Rockville MD 20857

CLARK, HOWARD LONGSTRETH, JR., finance company executive, director; b. NYC, Feb. 1, 1944; s. Howard Longstreth and Elsie (Dancaster) C.; m. Karen K. Burke, July 25, 1992; 1 child by previous marriage, Howard Longstreth III. BSBA, Boston U., 1967; MBA, Columbia U., 1968. Exec. v.p., chief fin. officer Am. Express Co., NYC, 1981-90; vice chmn. Lehman Bros., Inc. Bd. dirs. White Mountains Ins. Group, Ltd., Walter Industries, Inc., United Rentals, Inc., Mueller Water Products, Inc. Mem.: River, Racquet and Tennis, Round Hill, Blind Brook, Links, Seminole, Jupiter Island, Nantucket Golf. Episcopalian. Home: 404 Round Hill Rd Greenwich CT 06831-2637 Office: Lehman Bros Inc 745 7th Ave Fl 20 New York NY 10019 Office Phone: 212-526-6255. E-mail: hclark@lehman.com.

CLARK, I. E., publisher; b. Schulenburg, Tex., Dec. 9, 1919; s. Harvey Robert and Annie Ruby (Miekow) C.; m. Lila Rhea Norwood, Sept. 1, 1945; children: Candace Ann, Robin Rhea. BA, U. Tex., 1941, MA, 1945. Rancher, 1945-95; tchr., theatre dir., publs. dir., lang. arts coord. Schulenberg Pub. Schs., 1945-77; founder, owner I.E. Clark, Publs. pub. plays and books for theatre, 1959—. Tchr. Newspaper Fund seminars U. Tex. at Austin, summers, 1961-66; regional observer for Nat. Observer, 1961; mem. Tex. Edn. Agy. Commn. for Lang. Arts Curriculum Revision, 1958-59, State Com. Devel. of Speech-Drama Publ. of Tex. Edn. Agy., 1960-61. Author: (plays) Twelve Dancing Princesses, 1969, Hansel and Gretel, 1970, It's A Dungaree World, 1974, Once Upon a Texas, 1985; also several one-act plays including The Christmas Dream, transl. into Spanish, produced TV, Ecuador, 1973; (Tex. Sesquicentennial pageant) Fate of Fayette, 1986. Mem. Fayette County Hist. Survey Com., 1969—; founder, artistic dir., bd. dirs., officer Backstage, Inc., Fine Arts Coun. for South Ctrl. Tex., 1969—; adv. dir. 1st Nat. Bank of Schulenburg, 1974-80; Dem. precinct chmn. Fayette County Dem. Exec. Com., 1955-80; county campaign chmn. Lyndon B. Johnson, 1949, 55; area campaign chmn. Tex. Lt. Gov. Bill Hobby, 1972; bd. dirs. Schulenberg Hist. Soc. Recipient Finest Journalism Tchr. in Tex. award U. Tex. Interscholastic League, 1967, Outstanding Citizen award Colorado Valley Coun. on Drug and Alcohol Abuse, 1990; Order Golden Quill, 1977; named Hon. State Farmer, Future Farmers Am., 1956; Newspaper Fund fellow, 1959. Mem. Am. Theatre Assn. (nat. chmn. play publs. panel 1977, editor Secondary Sch. Theatre Jour. 1982-83), S.W. Theatre Assn. (hon., life), Dramatists Guild, Am. Alliance for Theatre and Edn., Tex. Secondary Theatre Conf. (dir., Newsletter editor 1966-69, mem. Interscholastic League adv. com.), Tex. Ednl. Theatre Assn. (Founders award 1985), Modern Music Masters (hon., life), Masons, Phi Beta Kappa, Delta Tau Delta, Sigma Delta Chi, Phi Eta Sigma. Methodist. Home and Office: PO Box 246 Schulenburg TX 78956-0246 Office Phone: 979-743-3232. E-mail: email@ieclark.com.

CLARK, IRENE L., literature and language professor; d. Nathaniel and Goldie Borah; m. William Av Clark, Mar. 25, 1978; children: Elisa, Louisa, Clifton, Justin. BA, Hunter Coll., NY, 1963; MA, Columbia U., NY, 1965; PhD, U. So. Calif., LA, 1979. Dir. writing ctr., dir. writing freshman program U. So. Calif.; prof. English Calif. State U., Northridge. Author: (book) The Genre of Argument, 1998, Concepts in Composition, 2002. Mem.: MLA, Nat. Coun. Tchrs. Home: 1314 Comstock Ave Los Angeles CA 90024

CLARK, JACK, retired health facility administrator; b. Munford, Ala., Feb. 23, 1932; s. Raymond E. and Ora (Camp) C.; m. Louise Omega Lackey, Jan. 30, 1951; 1 son, Terry Wayne. BS, Springhill Coll., Mobile, Ala., 1960. Staff acct. Max E. Miller, C.P.A., Mobile, 1960-62; comptr. Mobile Gen. Hosp., 1962-67; assoc. adminstr. fin. Univ. Med. Ctr., Mobile, 1967-74; regional mgr. Humana Inc., Mobile, 1974-75, v.p., 1975-80, sr. v.p., 1980-84, exec. v.p., 1984-93, Galen Health Care, Mobile, 1993-94; ret. Columbia-HCA Healthcare, 1994. Trustee Mid-South region Humana hosps., 1974-87, Southwestern region, 1987-89, region IV, 1989-91, region 2, 1991-93, Regional Hosps., Columbia/HCA, 1994—. Bd. dirs. Agape S. Ala., Mobile, 1983, Rainbow Omega, 2000—; trustee Faulkner U., Montgomery, Ala., 1993—. Served in USAF, 1952-56, Korea. Mem. Hosp. Fin. Mgmt. Assn. (assoc.), Am. Hosp. Assn., Ala. Hosp. Assn., Ala. Hosp. Assn. Accts. (pres. so. council, dir. 1967-68), Mobile C. of C. Democrat. Mem. Ch. of Christ. Home: 6449 Canebrake Rd Mobile AL 36695-3817

CLARK, JACK IVOR, civil engineer, researcher; BSc, Acadia U., 1955; B in Engring., Tech. U. NS, Can., 1957; PhD in Civil Engring., NS Tech. Coll., Can., 1970; MSc, U. Alta., Can., 1961; DEng honoris causa, Tech. U. NS, 1993; DSc (hon.), Laurentian U., 1998. With major civil engring. projects, 1957—; dir. Ctr. for Cold Ocean Resources Engring. Meml. U. Nfld., St. John's, Can, 1984-91, 1st pres., CEO, Ctr. for Cold Ocean Resources Engring., 1991-97, prin. cons. Ctr. for Cold Odean Resources Engring., 1997—. Past editor Can. Geotech. Jour. Decorated officer Order of Can.; recipient R.M. Hardy keynote address, 1996, Roger J.E. Brown award, 1996, Queen's Golden Jubilee Anniversary medal, 2002; Karl Terzaghi fellow Norwegian Tech. Inst., 1997, MMS Corp. Leadership award Minerals Mgmt. Svc., USDA, 1999, 25th Anniversary Achievement award Nfld. Ocean Industries Assn., 2002, Gold Medal award Can. Coun. Profl. Engrs., 2005. Fellow Engring. Inst. Can. (Julian C. Smith medal 1987), Can. Soc. Civil Engrs.; mem. Can. Acad. Engring., Nat. Scis. and Engring. Coun. (v.p., exec. com. for coun. 1988-94), Can. Geotech. Rsch. Bd. (chmn. 1991-94), Founds. for Offshore Structures (chmn. Can. Stds. Assn. Com. S472), Can. Geotech. Soc. (G. Geoffrey Meyerhof award 1995). Office: C-CORE Saint John's NL Canada A1B 3X5 E-mail: Jack.Clark@c-core.ca.

CLARK, JAMES ALLEN, lawyer, educator; b. Canton, Ill., Nov. 13, 1948; s. Howard R. and Helen (McElwain) C. BS in Edn., Miami U., Oxford, Ohio, 1971, BA in Polit. Sci., 1971; MS in Urban Studies, Cleve. State U., 1974; JD, Case Western Res. U., 1977. Bar: U.S. Dist. Ct. (no. dist.) Ohio 1977, U.S. Ct. Appeals (6th cir.) 1978, U.S. Dist. Ct. (no. dist.) Ill. 1979, U.S. Ct. Appeals (7th cir.) 1980, U.S. Supreme Ct. 1981, U.S. Ct. Appeals (D.C. cir.) 1985, U.S. Dist. Ct. (ea. dist.) Wis. 1986, U.S. Ct. Appeals (8th cir.) 1994. Law clk. U.S. Dist. Ct., Cleve., 1977-79; assoc. Schiff Hardin & Waite, Chgo., 1979-85, ptnr., 1985--; prof. De Paul U. Law Sch., Chgo., 1985—. Mem. Order of the Coif. Office: Schiff Hardin & Waite 7200 Sears Tower Chicago IL 60606 Business E-Mail: jclark@schiffhardin.com.

CLARK, JAMES COVINGTON, journalist, historian; b. Washington, May 22, 1947; s. William Edward and Louise (Covington) C.; children: Randall Healy, Kevin Healy. BA, Lenoir-Rhyne Coll., 1975; MA, Stetson U., 1986; PhD, U. Fla., 1998. Reporter UPI, Washington, 1967, Columbia (S.C.) Record, 1968, AP, Charlotte, NC, 1969-70, Phila., 1972-73, Hickory (N.C.) Daily Record, 1974-75; regional editor Tampa (Fla.) Tribune, 1976-77; asst. exec. editor The Orlando (Fla.) Sentinel, 1977-98; syndicated columnist UP Syndicate, 1997-99; editor, pub. Orlando mag., 2000—. Instr. U. Ctrl. Fla., Orlando, 1986—. Author: Last Train South, 1984, Faded Glory: Presidents Out of Power, 1985, The Murder of James Garfield, 1994, Trips Through Florida History, 2000. Recipient George Polk award L.I. U., 1983, Gerald Loeb award, L.A., 1983, Arthur Thompson prize Fla. Hist. Soc., Gainesville, 1989. Mem. Authors Guild, Orgn. Am. Historians, Am. Hist. Assn., Am. Soc. Mag. Editors, Fla. Mag. Assn. (pres.), Fla. Humanities Coun. (bd. dirs.). Personal E-mail: clarknews@aol.com.

CLARK, JAMES E., lawyer; b. Washington, Sept. 2, 1948; AB, Brown U., 1970; JD, U. Chgo., 1976. Bar: Ill. 1976. Ptnr. comml. law Sidley Austin Brown & Wood LLP (formerly Sidley & Austin), Chgo. Mem. faculty Practicing Law Inst., 1989. Lt. USN, 1970-72. Mem. ABA (chmn., subcom. acquisition fin. commercial fin. svcs. com. Bus law sect. 1990—94), Chgo. Bar Assn., Ill. State Bar Assn., Fellow Am. Coll. Comml. Fin. Lawyers, Phi Beta Kappa. Office: Sidley Austin Brown & Wood LLP Bank One Plz 10 S Dearborn St Chicago IL 60603 Office Phone: 312-853-7776. Office Fax: 312-853-7036. Business E-Mail: jclark@sidley.com.

CLARK, JAMES JOSEPH, lawyer; b. SI, Dec. 5, 1954; s. James J. and Patricia A. (Bruns) C.; m. Cynthia Ann Jorgensen, Aug. 29, 1980 (div.); 1 child, Caroline; m. Cristina Maria Arico, Nov. 29, 1997; 2 stepchildren, Joey and Mari. BS, Stonehill Coll., 1976; JD, Albany Law Sch., 1979. Bar: NY 1980, Calif. 1987. Assoc. Cahill Gordon & Reindel LLP, NYC, 1979—87, ptnr., 1987—. Editor-in-chief Albany Law Rev., 1978-79. Mem. ABA, NY State Bar Assn. Republican. Roman Catholic. Avocation: sports. Office: Cahill Gordon & Reindel LLP 80 Pine St New York NY 10005 Office Phone: . 212-701-3849. Office Fax: 212-378-2169. E-mail: JClark@cahill.com.

CLARK, JAMES KERMIT, JR., real estate executive; b. Atlanta, Nov. 17, 1942; s. George W. and Jean (Scutaro) K. BBA, U. Ga., 1965; grad., Realtor Inst. Ga., 1973. Lic. real estate broker, Ga. Chief appraiser First Fed. Savs. & Loan Assn., Atlanta, 1965-67; comml. appraiser Draper-Owens Co., Atlanta, 1967-69; pres. Tri-City Comml. Sales, Inc., College Park, Ga., 1969—2002; exec. v.p. Group VI Corp., Peachtree City, Ga., 1993—. Dir. Student Leadership Univ. Dir. Second Wind Ministries; advisor Bible Tng. Ctr. for Pastors; lead lay counselor First Bapt. Ch., Atlanta. Mem. Nat. Assn. Realtors, Ga. Assn. Realtors, Atlanta Bd. Realtors (comml. adv. coun., comml. dir. and ethics com., chmn. equal opportunity com. 1986-90), Million Dollar Club (active life; Phoenix award, Silver Phoenix award), Atlanta C. of C. (Southside devel. task force 1972), Phi Kappa Alpha, Rho Epsilon Real Estate Fraternity. Republican. Baptist. Office: 900 W Park Dr Ste 300 Peachtree City GA 30269-3521

CLARK, JAMES MILFORD, retired college president; b. Mich., Apr. 11, 1930; s. Roy Wesley and Florence (Grice) C.; m. Patricia Ann Haynes, Mar. 11, 1960; children— Pamela, Matthew, Timothy. BA, U. Mich., 1952, PhD (Horace H. Rackham fellow), 1962; MA, U. Philippines, 1955; Doctor (hon.), U. North London, 1993; Dr. (hon.), Capital Normal U., Beijing, 1994. Fulbright travel grantee, France, 1955-56; teaching fellow U. Mich., 1957-59; asst. prof. polit. sci. U. Maine, Orono, 1960-64, asso. prof., 1964-79, asst. to pres., 1966-68, v.p. for acad. affairs, 1968-79; pres. SUNY Coll., Cortland, 1979-95; ret., 1995. Fulbright lectr. U. Toulouse (France), 1965-66; mem. Com. on Internat. Exchange Scholars, 1988-92. Author: Teachers and Politics in France, 1967. Chmn. Maine Health Planning Coun., 1970-72, mem. exec. com., 1972-76; bd. dirs. Penobscot Valley United Fund, 1972-77, Cortland County United Way, 1979-85, Eden Alternative, Inc., 2002-05, Cortland Meml. Found., 2006—; bd. overseers Rockefeller Inst. Govt., 1988-91; mem. N.Y. State Citizens com. on Bicentennial of French Revolution, 1988-90; mem. Tioughnioga Waterfront Devel. Commn., 2000--, Cortland Rural Cemetary Found. (mem. bd. dirs 2002-); With U.S. Army, 1952-55. Mem. Nat. Assn. State Univs. and Land-Grant Colls. (exec. com. council for acad. affairs 1971-76, sec. council 1974-76), Am. Assn. State Colls. and Univs. (N.Y. rep. 1979-81), Phi Beta Kappa, Phi Kappa Phi, Phi Eta Sigma, Pi Sigma Alpha, Sigma Phi Epsilon.

CLARK, JAMES R., oil industry executive; B, MBA, Univ. Tex. Pres. Sperry-Sun subs., Halliburton Co., 1996—99, Consolidated Equipment Co., 2000—01; v.p., pres. Baker Petrolite Baker Hughes Inc., Houston, 2001—03, v.p. mktg. & tech., 2003—04, pres., COO, 2004—. Office: Bakes Hughes Inc 3900 Essex Ln Houston TX 77027-5177 Mailing: Baker Hughes Inc PO Box 4740 Houston TX 77210-4740*

CLARK, JAMES RICHARD, lawyer; b. Madison, Wis., Mar. 30, 1946; s. James F. and Gloria J. Clark; m. Martha C. Conrad, Mar. 18, 1950; children: Lindsey Kelley, Chad. BA, Ripon Coll., 1968; JD, U. Wis., 1971. Bar: Wis. 1971, U.S. Dist. Ct. (we. and ea. dists.) Wis. 1972, U.S. Ct. Appeals (7th cir.) 1973, U.S. Dist. Ct. (no. dist.) Ill. 1974, U.S. Supreme Ct. 1976. Assoc. Foley & Lardner, Milw., 1971-78, ptnr., 1978—. Editor-in-chief Wis. Law Rev., 1971. Trustee Ripon Coll., 1985—. 1st lt. U.S. Army, 1971. Mem. ABA, Am. Coll. Trial Lawyers, Am. Bd. Trial Advs., Def. Rsch. Inst., 7th Cir. Bar Assn., Wis. Bar Assn., Ripon Coll. Alumni Assn. (past pres.), Tripoli Country Club, Order of Coif, Phi Beta Kappa. Home: 9719 N Dalewood Ln Mequon WI 53092-6210 Office: Foley & Lardner Firstar Ctr 777 E Wisc Ave Milwaukee WI 53202 Office Phone: 414-297-5543. Business E-Mail: jclark@foley.com.

CLARK, JANET EILEEN, retired political science professor; b. Kansas City, Kans., June 5, 1940; d. Edward Francis and Mildred Lois (Mack) Morrissey; m. Caleb M. Clark, Sept. 28, 1968; children: Emily Claire, Grace Ellen, Evelyn Adair. AA, Kansas City Jr. Coll., 1960; AB, George Wash. U., Washington, DC, 1962, MA, 1964; PhD, U. Ill., 1973. Staff US Dept. Labor, Washington, 1962-64; instr. social sci. Kans. City Jr. Coll., Kans., 1964-67; instr. polit. sci. Parkland Coll., 1970-71; asst. prof. govt. N.Mex. State U., Las Cruces, 1971-77, assoc. prof., 1977-80; assoc. prof. polit. sci. U. Wyo., 1981-84, prof., 1984-94; prof. polit. sci., head dept. U. West Ga., Carrollton, 1994—2006; ret., 2006. Co-author: Women, Elections and Representation, 1987, The Equality State, 1988, Women in Taiwan Politics: Overcoming Barriers to Women's Participation in a Modernizing Society, 1990; editor Women and Politics, 1991-2000; contbr. articles to profl. jours. Wolcott fellow, 1963-64, NDEA Title IV fellow, 1967-69. Mem. Internat. Soc. Polit. Psychology (gov. coun., 1987-89), NEA (pres. chpt. 1978-79), Am. Polit. Sci. Assn., We. Polit. Sci. Assn. (exec. coun. 1984-87), Western Social Sci. Assn. (exec. coun. 1978-81, v.p. 1982, pres. 1985), Women's Caucus for Polit. Sci. (treas. 1982, pres. 1987), LWV (exec. bd. 1980-83, 2002-2003, treas. 1986-90, pres. 1991-93, 2004-06), Women's Polit. Caucus, Beta Sigma Phi (v.p. chpt. 1978-79, sec. 1987-88, treas. 1988-89, v.p. 1989-90, pres. 1990-91), Phi Beta Kappa, Chi Omega (prize 1962), Phi Kappa Phi. Home: 2507 Waterford Rd Auburn AL 36832-4113 Personal E-mail: jclark@westga.edu.

CLARK, JANET F., oil industry executive; b. New Orleans; BA, Harvard U., 1977; MBA, U. Pa., 1982. CFO Santa Fe Energy Resources, 1997—98, sr. v.p., CFO, 1998—99; exec. v.p. corp. develop. & adminstrn. Santa Fe Energy Resources / Snyder Oil, 1999—2001; sr. v.p., CFO Nuevo Energy, 2001—04, Marathon Oil, Houston, 2004—. Bd. dir. Universal Compression Holdings. Bd. dir. New Hope Housing; trustee Joy Sch. Office: Marathon Oil 5555 San Felipe Rd Houston TX 77056-2723*

CLARK, JEFFREY RAPHIEL, research and development company executive; b. Provo, Utah, Sept. 29, 1953; s. Bruce Budge and Ouida (Raphiel) C.; m. Anne Margaret Eberhardt, Mar. 15, 1985; children: Jeffrey Raphiel, Mary Anne Elizabeth, Edward William Eberhardt. BS, Brigham Young U., 1977, MBA, 1979. CPA, Tex. Fin. analyst Exxon Coal USA, Inc., Houston, 1979-83; constrn. mgr. Gen. Homes, Inc., Houston, 1983-84; controller Liberty Data Products, Houston, 1984-86; v.p. Tech. Rsch. Assocs., Inc., Salt Lake City, 1987—2001, also dir., 1987—2001; contr. Internat. Sports Broadcasting, LLC, 2001—03, Masterbuilt Cos., Inc., Fairfax, Va., 2003—04, Gen. Sci. Corp., 2004—06, 21st Century Sys., 2006—. Scoutmaster Boy Scouts Am., Salt Lake City, 1989-91. Mem. AICPA, Utah Inst. CPAs, Salt Lake C. of C. (legis. action com.), Salt Lake Country Club. Republican. Mem. Lds Ch. Avocations: skiing, golf, mountain climbing. Home: 12 Adams St NW Washington DC 20001-1026

CLARK, JIM (JAMES H.), entrepreneur, real estate company and former computer software company executive; b. Ft. Worth, Tex., 1944; BS in Physics, U. New Orleans, 1970; MS in Physics, Louisiana State U., 1971; PhD in Computer Sci., U. Utah, 1974, DSc (hon.), 1995. Asst. prof. U. Calif., Santa Cruz, 1974—78; assoc. prof. Stanford U., 1979—82; founder, chmn. bd. Silicon Graphics, Inc., 1981—94; co-founder (with Marc Andreessen), chmn. Netscape Communications (formerly Mosaic Comm. Corp.), 1994—2001; founder, chmn. myCFO, Inc., Mountain View, Calif., 1999—2002; co-chair WebMD (formerly Healtheon/WebMD), 1999—2000; chmn. Shutterfly Inc., Redwood City, Calif., 2000—07, Neoteris, 2001—02; with Hyperion Devel. Group, Fla., 2003—. Bd. dirs. Paracomp. Author: Netscape Time: The Making Of The Billion-Dollar Start-Up That Took On Microsoft. Named one of Forbes' Richest Americans, 2006. Fellow Am. Acad. Arts & Sci.; mem. NAE.

CLARK, JIM, labor union president; m. Carla Clark; 3 children. Studied bus. law, arbitration, labor studies, collective bargaining, grievances, Wright St. U.; studied, Sinclair Coll. Admin. Internat. Union Elec. Workers, Communications Workers of Am. (IUE-CWA), 1996—, committeeman, v.p., local 755 Dayton, Ohio, shop chmn.; pres. IUE-CWA, 2005—. Elected chmn. automotive conference bd. IUE-CWA, 2001. Office: IUE-CWA Headquarters Ste 600 1275 K St Nw Washington DC 20005-4064

CLARK, JOAN HARDY, retired journalist; b. Toronto, Ont., Can., Apr. 17, 1934; came to the U.S., 1960; d. Henry Robert Hardy and Irene Elsie Stevens; children: Lisa Anne Hanson, Anthony David Stuart Hanson. BA, Carleton U., Ottawa, Can., 1954; postgrad., Sarah Lawrence Coll., 1973-75. Co-chmn. internat. coun. World Monuments Fund, 2004—; bd. dirs. N.Y. Pub. Libr., NYC, 1996—, chmn. coun. conservators, 1986—2001, hon. chmn., 2001—; mem. exec. com. Whitney Nat. Com., 2003—; bd. dirs. Whitney Mus., NYC, 1984—2003. Mem. Cosmopolitan Club. Home: 1 Gracie Sq New York NY 10028-8001 also: Deer Meadow Farm Andover VT 05143

CLARK, JOHN B., academic administrator; BA cum laude, Providence Coll., 1972; MPA, John Jay Coll., 1977; MA in Econs., Fordham U., 1980; MA in Philosophy, NYU, 1984; EdD, Columbia U., 2001. Interim pres. SUNY Plattsburgh, 2003, SUNY Brockport, 2004; acting vice chancellor SUNY Sys., Albany, 2005—06, interim chancellor, 2007—; interim pres. Coll. Optometry, SUNY, 2006, State U. Coll. Tech., SUNY, Alfred, 2006—07. Mem. bus. adv. coun. Zicklin Sch. Bus., Baruch Coll., NYC; bd. dirs. St. Pius V HS. Office: SUNY Office of Chancellor State University Plaza Albany NY 12246*

CLARK, JOHN F., space systems engineering educator; b. Reading, Pa., Dec. 12, 1920; s. John F. Clark and Edith Dix (Long) Guenther; m. June Teubner Schweiger, July 14, 1974; children from previous marriage: Linda J. Marks, James C. BSEE with honors, Lehigh U., 1942, EE, 1947; MS in Math., George Washington U., 1946; PhD in Physics, U. Md., 1956. Registered profl. engr., N.J. Electronic engr. Naval Rsch. Lab., 1942-47, physicist, atmospheric electricity br. head, 1948-58; asst. prof. elec. engring. Lehigh U., 1947-48; dir. physics and astronomy programs NASA, 1958-63, dep. assoc. adminstr. space sci. and applications (scis.), 1963-65, chmn. space sci. steering com., 1963-65; dir. Goddard Space Flight Center, 1965-76; dir. space applications and tech. RCA Corp., Princeton, N.J., 1976-86; part-time cons. Gen. Electric Astro Space Div., 1987-88; NAVSPACE rsch. prof. U.S. Naval Acad. aerospace engring. dept., Annapolis, Md., 1988-90; dir. grad. studies, prof. space sytems Fla. Inst. Tech. Spaceport Grad. Ctr., 1990—. Part-time lectr. math. George Washington U., 1956-58; part-time cons. rsch. Grad. Coun., 1960-66; part-time lectr. physics U. Md., 1958; mem. indsl. and profl. adv. coun. Pa. State U., 1963-65; mem. vis. com. physics Lehigh U., 1966-74; mem. Com. on Fed. Labs., 1971-75, Md. Gov.'s Sci. Adv. Coun., 1972-76, N.J. Gov.'s Sci. Adv. Com., 1980-86, Am. Geophys. Union-URSI Bd. Radio Sci., 1974-78; mem. study panel Office Telecommunications, Nat. Assembly Engring., 1976-77; chmn. adv. com. FCC, 1981-83; mem. U.S. del. to Internat. Telecommunication Union Conf., Regional Adminstrv. Radio Conf., 1983, World Adminstrv. Radio Conf., 1985; chmn. Direct Broadcast Satellite Assn., 1986; mem. spectrum planning adv. com. U.S. Dept. Commerce, 1986-92; bd. dirs. ECON Inc.; mem. Calif. Inst. Tech. Jet Propulsion Lab.'s Mars Observer Program Rev. Bd., 1986-93. Contbr. numerous articles to profl. jours.; cons. editor space tech. McGraw-Hill Ency. Sci. and Tech, 1977—. Mem. Fla. Tech. Grad. Coun., Fla. Tech Promotion Com. Recipient NASA medals for Disting. Service, Outstanding Leadership, Exceptional Service, Collier trophy Nat. Aero. Assn. Fellow Am. Astron. Soc., AIAA (gen. chmn. Communications Satellite System Conf. 1984, v.p. pub. policy 1986-90), IEEE, Explorers Club; mem. Am. Geophys. Union, Am. Meterol. Soc., Satellite Broadcasting and Communications Assn. (chmn. 1987, chmn.'s coun. 1989-90, 1st Pres.'s award 1993), Internat. Soc. Satellite Profls. (bd. dirs. 1985-89), Internat. Acad. Astronautics, Phi Beta Kappa, Sigma Xi, Pi Mu Epsilon, Tau Beta Pi, Sigma Phi Epsilon, Sigma Pi Sigma. Achievements include patents in electronic circuits and systems. Home: 947 Loggerhead Island Dr Satellite Beach FL 32937-3863 Office Phone: 321-779-4295. Business E-Mail: jfclark@fit.edu.

CLARK, JOHN F., federal agency administrator; married. BS, Syracuse U. With US Border Patrol, US Capitol Police; chief Internat. Fugitive Investigations Div. US Marshals Svc., US Dept. Justice, chief Internal Affairs Divsn., acting marshal, chief dep. (Ea. Dist.) Va., marshal, 2002—05, acting dir., 2005—06, dir., 2006—.*

CLARK, JOHN J., economist, finance educator; b. NYC, June 21, 1924; s. John J. and Mary E. (Taylor) Clark; m. Margaret T. Norton, July 1, 1965; 1 child, Patricia Ann. BBA magna cum laude, St. John's U., 1948; MBA, CCNY, 1950; PhD, NYU, 1959. Prof. econs. Coll. Bus. Adminstrn., St. John's U., 1950-69, chmn. dept., 1959-62, dean, 1962-70; Royal H. Gibson Sr. prof. bus. adminstrn. Drexel U., Phila., 1971-90, prof. emeritus, 1990—, dir. doctoral studies LeBow Coll. Bus. Lectr. econs. Bklyn. Poly. Inst., 1954—58. Co-author: (book) The Impact of the Foundation Reports on Business Education, 1963, Business Fluctuations, Growth and Economic Stabilization, 1963, Professional Education for Business, 1964, The New Economics of National Defense, 1966, Financial Management: A Capital Market Approach, 1976, Management of Capital Expenditures, 1979, 3d rev. edit., 1989, Lease/Buy Decision, 1980, A Statistics Primer for Managers, 1980, Business Mergers and Acquisition Strategies, 1985, Restructuring Corporate America, 1996; contbr. articles to profl. jours.; editor: (book) Business and the Liberal Arts, 1962; contbg. editor: Fin. Mgmt. Jour., 1972—82. Mem. Borough Pres.'s Planning Com., Queens County, NYC, 1964—69; economist joint legis. com. banking law N.Y. State Legislature, 1965—68. Recipient Mil. Rev. award, U.S. Army Command and Gen. Staff Coll., 1964. Mem.: Royal United Svc. Inst. Def. Studies, Ea. Fin. Assn. (exec. dir. 1974—77), Am. Econ. Assn., Phila. Maritime Mus. (advisor), U.S. Naval Inst. (medal 1969), Omicron Delta Epsilon, Delta Mu Delta, Beta Gamma Sigma. Home: White Horse Village 535 Gradyville Rd # V101 Newtown Square PA 19073-2815 Office: Coll Bus Adminstrn Drexel U Philadelphia PA 19104 E-mail: casagrande13@yast.net.

CLARK, JOHN M., III, lawyer; b. Memphis, Feb. 27, 1950; BA, Rice U., 1972; JD, Stanford U., 1975. Bar: Calif. 1975. Law clk. U.S. Dist. Ct., LA, 1975-77; European counsel Nat. Semiconductor Corp., Santa Clara, Calif., 1979-82, corporate counsel, 1982-85, assoc. gen. counsel, 1985-86, v.p., assoc. gen. counsel, 1986-92, sr. v.p., gen. counsel, sec., 1992—. Office: Nat Semiconductor Corp 2900 Semiconductor Dr Santa Clara CA 95051-0606 Office Phone: 408-721-6529. Office Fax: 408-739-9803. E-mail: john.clark@nsc.com.

CLARK, JOHN PETER, III, engineer, consultant; b. Phila., May 6, 1942; s. John Peter Jr. and Victoria Mary (McQuaide) C.; m. Nancy Ann Lapin, June 22, 1968; children: Shannon John, Hannah Marie. BSChemE, Notre Dame U., 1964; PhD, U. Calif., Berkeley, 1968. Registered profl. engr., Va., Ill. Rsch. engr. Agrl. Rsch. Svc., USDA, Berkeley and Washington, 1968-72; from asst. to assoc. prof. Va. Poly. Inst. and State U., Blacksburg, 1972-78; dir. R & D, ITT Continental Baking, Rye, NY, 1978-81; pres. Epstein Process Engring. Inc., Chgo., 1981-94; pvt. practice, engring. cons., Oak Park, Ill., 1994-95; v.p. tech. Fluor Daniel, Inc., 1995-98. Co-author: Food Processing Operations and Scale-up, 1991; editor: Exercises in Process Simulation, 1977; contbg. editor Food Tech.; contbr. articles to profl. jours.; patentee (with C.J. King) in field for sys. for freeze drying. Fellow: AIChE (divns. chmn. 1982, award in chem engring. 1998); mem.: Inst. Food Technologists (divns. chmn. 1984). Roman Catholic. Avocations: reading, folk music, Indian art. Home and Office: 644 Linden Ave Oak Park IL 60302-1661 Office Phone: 708-848-2205. Personal E-mail: JPC3@worldnet.att.net.

CLARK, JOHN WALTER, physics professor; b. Lockhart, Tex., Apr. 7, 1935; s. John Preston and Gussie Walter Clark; m. Carolina Adrianna van den Berk, May 14, 1973;; children: Carissa Joanna, Mathilde Walter, Jessica Gussie, Sabrina Arabella, Eugene Preston, Marcel. BS, U. Tex., Austin, 1955, MA, 1957; PhD, Wash. U., St. Louis, 1959. NSF fellow Princeton U., NJ, 1959—61; assoc. rsch. scientist Martin Co., Denver, 1961; NATO fellow U. Birmingham, Birmingham, 1962, Centre d' Etudes Nucleaires de Saclay, Saclay, France, 1962—63; asst. to assoc. prof. Wash. U., 1963—72, prof., 1972—, Wayman Crow prof. physics, 1999—, chmn. dept. physics, 1996—97, 2002—07. Cons. Douglas Advanced Rsch. Lab., Huntington Beach, Calif., 1965—69; guest prof. U. Cologne, 1971, Abo Akademi, Turku, Finland, 1971—72; NATO sr. fellow Instituto di Cibernetica, Arco Felice, Italy, 1972; fellow McDonnell Ctr. Space Sci. Wash U., St. Louis, 1975—; mem. chair internat. adv. com. Conf. Series on Recent Progress in Many-Body Theories, 1981—; mem. internat. adv. com. Internat. Workshops on Condensed Matter Theories, 1981—; mem. Feenberg medal selection com. Internat. Conferences on Recent Progress in Many-Body Theories, 1987—94; lab. collaborator Los Alamos Nat. Lab., 1987; scientist in residence Argonne Nat. Lab., Ill., 1987; faculty Spring Coll. on Many-Body Techniques, Isfahan, Iran, 1991; co-dir. Workshop on Complex Dynamics in Neural Nets, Vietri, Italy, 1991; faculty Nathiagali Summer Coll. on Physics and Contemporary Needs, Pakistan, 1992; mem. internat. adv. bd. Inst. Advanced Studies in Basic Sci., Zanjan, Iran, 1996—; sci. co-dir. WE-Heraeus-Seminar on Theory of Spin Lattices and Lattice Gauge Models, Bad Honnef, Germany, 1996; vis. faculty Inst. Advanced Studies in Basic Scis., Zanjan, Iran, 1996; sci. co-dir. WE-Heraeus-Seminar on Sci. Applications of Neural Nets, Bad Honnef, Germany, 1998; assoc. European Ctr. for Theoretical Studies of Nuc. Physics and Related Areas, Trento, Italy, 1998—; docent Sommerakademi of the Studienstiftung des Deutschen Volkes, Alpbach, Austria, 2001; mem. Ctr. Materials Innovation, Wash. U., St. Louis, 2004—; mem. bd. gov. Inst. Complex Adaptive Matter, 2005—. Editor 9 books; contbr. over 250 articles to profl. jours. and topical vols. Recipient Eugene Feenberg medal for Many-Body Physics, Internat. Adv. Com. for Conf. Recent Progress in Many-Body Theories, 1987; fellow, Schlumberger Found., Wash. U., 1954, Von Barclomb Fund., 1958—59, Sloan Found., 1965—67; grantee, NSF, 1970—2004. Fellow: Am. Phys. Soc. (chmn. Wheatley prize selection com. 1998—2001); mem.: Acad. Sci. St. Louis, Neural Network Soc., Phi Beta Kappa. Achievements include method of correlated basis functions for strongly interacting quantum systems; mathematical foundations of quantum control; research in theories of superdense matter in neutron stars; models of neural information processing; fundamental research in complex systems. Office: Washington U Dept Physics 1 Brookings Dr Saint Louis MO 63130 Home Phone: 314-863-1791; Office Phone: 314-935-6276. Office Fax: 314-935-6219. Business E-Mail: jwc@wustl.edu.

CLARK, JON BRIAN, psychologist; s. Everett Milburn and Norma Nadine Clark; m. Debra Lin Striler, June 16, 1984; 1 child, Laura Elyse Striler. BA, Wayne State U., 1969; MA, The Merrill-Palmer Inst., 1980; PsyS, Ctr. Humanistic Studies, 1982; PhD, The Union Inst., 1987. Lic. psychologist Mich., 1989. Ct. counselor Wayne County Juvenile Ct., Detroit, 1969—80; psychologist Humanistic Resources, Farmington, Mich., 1980—82, Midwest Mental Health, Troy, Mich., 1982—87, North Metro Growth Ctr., Shelby Township, Mich., 1987—89; pvt. practice psychologist Rochester, Mich., 1989—. Presenter in field; cons. in field. Mem.: APA. Avocations: bicycling, jazz, boating. Office: 71 Walnut Blvd Ste 109 Rochester MI 48307

CLARK, JONATHAN MONTGOMERY, lawyer; b. Bklyn., Oct. 20, 1937; s. Russell Inslee and Lillian (Longmore) C.; m. Priscilla M. Jorgensen, Sept. 24, 1960; children: Jonathan M. Jr., Christopher D. BA, Yale U., New Haven, Conn., 1959; LLB, U. Va., Charlottesville, 1964. Bar: NY 1965. Assoc. Davis Polk & Wardwell, NYC, 1964-71, ptnr., 1971-93; gen. counsel, mng. dir. Morgan Stanley & Co., Inc., NYC, 1993—98; sr. counsel Davis Polk & Wardwell, NYC, 1999—. Advisor mission to Poland, Fin. Svcs. Vol. Corps, 1990, 92; cons. Warren Commn., Washington, 1965; bd. dirs. Greenwich Hosp. Assn., 1990-98, Prentice Cup Com. bd. dirs. Caramoor Ctr. Music & the Arts. 1st lt. USMC, 1959-61. Mem. ABA, NY State Bar Assn., Assn. Bar City NY, Securities Industry Assn. (bd. dirs., 1995-96), NY Stock Exchange Legal Adv. Com. Republican. Episcopalian. Avocations: golf, fly fishing, birding. Office: Davis Polk & Wardwell 450 Lexington Ave New York NY 10017 Business E-Mail: jonathan.clark@dpw.com.

CLARK, JOSEPH FRANCIS, JR., lawyer; b. Tulsa, Okla., Jan. 20, 1949; s. Joseph F. and Betty Sue C.; m. Carol J. Coleman, Nov. 2, 1974 (div. 1981); m. Cathy A. Baker, Jan. 6, 1989; children: Joseph F. Clark III, Thomas S. Clark, Joshua B. Baker. BA, Villanova U., 1971; JD, Tulsa U., 1973. Bar: Okla. 1974. Atty. Gibbon, Gladd, Clark et al, Tulsa, Okla., 1974-78; pvt. practice, 1979-80; atty. Williams, Clark et al, 1980-90; ptnr. Clark & Stainer, 1990-94, Layon, Cronin, Clark & Kaiser, P.L.L.C., 1994-99; pvt. practice, 1999—2003, Clark & Warzynski, 2003—. Mem.: Tulsa County Bar Assn. (fee dispute com. 1998—99, profl. responsibility com. 2001—), Am. Inns of Ct. (term master 1996—98, master 1999—2003, Council Oak chpt., master emeritus 2003—). Democrat. Roman Catholic. Home: 2922 E 39th St Tulsa OK 74105-3704 Office: 1622 S Denver Ave Tulsa OK 74119-4232 Office Phone: 918-583-5600. E-mail: jclarkatt@sbcglobal.net.

CLARK, KAREN HEATH, lawyer; b. Pasadena, Calif., Dec. 17, 1944; d. Wesley Pelton and Lois (Ellenberger) Heath; m. Bruce Robert Clark, Dec. 30, 1967; children: Adam Heath, Andrea Pelton. Student, Pomona Coll., Claremont, Calif., 1962—64; BA, Stanford U., 1966; MA in History, U. Wash., 1968; JD, U. Mich., 1977. Bar: Calif. 1978. Instr. Henry Ford C.C., Dearborn, Mich., 1968-72; assoc. Gibson, Dunn & Crutcher LLP, Irvine, Calif., 1977-86, ptnr., 1986—2003, adv. counsel, 2004—. Bd. dirs. Dem. Found. Orange County, 1989-91, 94—, Planned Parenthood Orange County, Santa Ana, Calif., 1979-82, New Directions for Women, Newport Beach, 1986-91, Human Options, 2001-03, Freedom Writers Found., 2004—, Women in Leadership, chair, 1995-99; trustee Newport Beach Pub. Libr., 2001—, vice chair, 2006-; mem. deans adv. coun. Sch. Humanities, U. Calif., Irvine, 2000—. Recipient Choice award Planned Parenthood of Orange & San Bernardino Counties, 1996. Mem. Women in Leadership (founder 1993). E-mail: kclark@gibsondunn.com.

CLARK, KIM BRYCE, academic administrator; b. Salt Lake City, Mar. 20, 1949; s. Merlin and Helen Mar (Hickman) C.; m. Sue Lorraine Hunt, June 14, 1971; children: Bryce, Erin, Jonathan, Andrew, Michael, Julia, Jennifer. BA in economics, Harvard U., 1974, MA in economics, 1977, PhD in economics, 1978. From asst. prof. to prof. Harvard Bus. Sch., Boston, 1978-89, Harry E. Figgie prof. bus. adminstrn., 1989-95, dean, 1995—2005, also George F. Baker prof. adminstrn.; pres. Brigham Young U.-Idaho, Rexburg, 2005—. Bd. dirs. Ceramics Process System Corp., Milford, Mass., Analysis Group, Belmont, Mass., Automotive Industries, Inc. Co-author: Industrial Renaissance, 1983, Dynamic Manufacturing, 1988, Product Development Performance, 1991, Revolutionizing Product Development, 1992, Leading Product Development, 1995, Design Rules: The Power of Modularity, 2000; editor: The Uneasy Alliance, 1985; co-editor: The Perpetual Enterprise Machine, 1994; contbr. articles to profl. jours. Coord. Belmont Youth Basketball, 1983—. Mem. IEEE (assoc. mem.), Am. Econ. Assn., Inst. Mgmt. Sci. Avocations: golf, jogging. Office: Brigham Young U 525 S Ctr St Rexburg ID 83460 Office Phone: 208-496-1111. Business E-Mail: clarkk@byui.edu.

CLARK, LAVERNE HARRELL, writer; b. Smithville, Tex., June 6, 1929; d. James Boyce and Belle Bunte Harrell; m. L.D. Clark, Sept. 15, 1951. BA, Tex. Woman's U., 1950; student, Columbia U., 1951-54; MA, U. Ariz., 1962, MFA, 1992. Reporter, libr., photographer Ft. Worth Press, 1950-51; with sales and advt. depts. Columbia U. Press, NYC, 1951-53; asst. promotion-news Episcopal Diocese Bull., NYC, 1958-59; founding dir. U. Ariz. Poetry Ctr., Tucson, 1962-66, photographer, 1966-99. Author, photographer: They Sang for Horses, 1966 (award U. Chgo. 1967), rev. edit., 2001, Revisiting the Plains Indian Country of Mari Sandoz, 1977, Focus 101, 1979, The Deadly Swarm and Other Stories, 1985, 87, Keepers of the Earth, 1997, 2d edit., 2002 (Best 1st Novel award Western Writers of Am. 1998), Mari Sandoz's Native Nebraska, 2000; editor, photographer: The Face of Poetry, 1976, 2d edit., 1979; photographer with 500 informal portraits of contemporary writers, 1962—. Recipient 19 awards Nat. League Am. Pen Women, 1967-96, Disting. Alumna award Tex. Woman's U., Denton, 1973; grantee Am. Philos. Soc., 1967, 69. Mem. PEN, Western Writers of Am., Westerners Internat., Women Writing the West, Sandoz Heritage Soc. (hon. mem. adv. bd. 1989-2002), Tex. Inst. Letters. Democrat. Episcopalian. Avocations: travel, bicycling, showing slides. Home: 604 Main St Smithville TX 78957 Office Phone: 512-237-2796. Personal E-mail: lhldclark@aol.com.

CLARK, LEROY D., law educator; b. 1934; BA, CCNY, 1956; LLB, Columbia U., 1961. Bar: N.Y. 1961. Staff atty. Office of N.Y. Atty. Gen., 1961-62; asst. counsel NAACP Legal Def. and Edn. Fund, Inc., NYC, 1962-68; prof. law NYU Law Sch., NYC, 1969-79, Cath. U., 1981—. Gen. counsel EEOC, 1979-81; arbitrator Am. Arbitration Assn., Fed. Mediation and Conciliation Svc. Author: The Grand Jury: The Use and Abuse of Political Power, 1975, Employment Discrimination Law--Cases and Materials, 5th edit., 2000. Office: Law School Catholic Univ Am 3600 John Mccormack Rd NE Washington DC 20064-0001 Home Phone: 202-244-7256; Office Phone: 202-319-5158. Business E-Mail: clarkl@law.cua.edu.

CLARK, LLOYD, historian, writer, educator; b. Belton, Tex., Aug. 4, 1923; s. Lloyd C. and Hattie May (Taylor) C.; m. Jean Reeves, June 17, 1950; children: Roger, Cynthia, Candyce. BSJ, So. Meth. U., 1948; B in Fgn. Trade, Am. Grad. Sch. Internat. Mgmt., Thunderbird, 1949; MPA, Ariz. State U., 1972. String corr. AP, Dallas, 1941-42; reporter Dallas Morning News, 1947; editor, pub. Ex-Press, Arlington, Tex., 1945-48; publicity mgr. Advt. Counselors Ariz., Phoenix, 1949; reporter Phoenix Gazette, 1949-65; asst. pub. Ariz. Weekly Gazette, 1965-66; founder Coun. on Abandoned Mil. Posts-USA, 1966, Papago Trackers, 1985, Once-Upon-a-Timers, 1986; project cons. City of Prescott, Ariz., 1971-72; dep. dir. adminstrv. svcs. No. Ariz. Coun. Govts., Flagstaff, 1972-73; regional adminstr. South Eastern Ariz. Govts. Orgn., Bisbee, 1973-75; local govt. assistance coord. Ariz. Dept. Transp., Phoenix, 1975-80, program adminstr., 1980-83; history instr. Rio Salado C.C., Phoenix, 1983-89, Ariz. State U.-West, Sun City, 1995-98; proprietor LC Enterprises, 1993—; columnist Daily News-Sun, Sun City, 1995—. Mem. spkrs bur. Ariz. Humanities Coun., 1998-99. Author: Lloyd Clark's Scrapbook, Vol. 1, 1958, Vol. 2, 1960, Here's Looking at You, 1997, The Usual Suspects, 1998, You Must Remember This, 1999; editor: Clark Biog. Reference Publ., 1956-62. Bd. dir. Friends of Channel 8, 1984-86; mem. transit planning com. Regional Pub. Transit Authority, 1988; bd. dir. Friends of Ariz. Hwys. Mag., 1989-92; mem. Ariz. State Geographic and Historic Names Bd., 1994—; condr. Annual Christmas Eve Sunrise Gathering, Phoenix Pks. and Recreation Dept., 1988-2004. Lt. AUS, 1942-46, maj., 1966-70, col. Res. Recipient Ariz. Press Club's exemplary gen. news coverage award, 1960, outstanding news reporting, 1961; Lloyd Clark Journalism scholarship named in honor U. Tex. at Arlington Alumni Assn., 1992. Mem. Ariz. Press Club (pres. 1962), Soc. Profl. Journalists (pres. Valley of Sun chpt. 1964), Am. Grad. Sch. Internat. Mgmt. Alumni Assn. Thunderbird (pres. Phoenix chpt. 1965), Ariz. Hist. Soc. (bd. dir. ctrl. Ariz. chpt. 1992-93, state bd. dir. 1993-95), Sharlot Hall Hist. Soc. (life), Res. Officers Assn. (life), Ex-Students Assn. No. Tex. Agrl. Coll. Arlington (pres. 1946-48), U. Tex. Arlington Alumni Assn. (life, bd. dir. 1994-98, Disting. Alumni Svc. award 1997, Mil. Sci. Dept. Hall of Honor 1998), The Westerners (sheriff Phoenix Corral 1986-88), Univ. Club (Phoenix). Address: PO Box 1537 Surprise AZ 85378-1537

CLARK, LUTHER THEOPOLIS, physician, educator, researcher; b. Bradenton, Fla., Oct. 21, 1949; m. Camille C. Jackson; children: Jason Myles, Monica Marie. AB, Harvard U., 1971, MD, 1975. Intern, resident, chief residency internal medicine Roosevelt Hosp., NYC, 1975-79, fellow cardiology, 1978-80; dir. preventive cardiology Health Sci. Ctr. SUNY, Bklyn., 1992-95, chief divsn. cardiovascular medicine Health Sci. Ctr., 1995—, prof. clin. medicine Health Sci. Ctr. Fellow ACP, Am. Coll. Cardiology; mem. Nat. Med. Assn. Avocations: tennis, jogging, golf. Office: SUNY Health Sci Ctr Box 1199 450 Clarkson Ave Brooklyn NY 11203-2056 Business E-Mail: ltclarke@downstate.edu.

CLARK, LYNN G., botanist, educator; BS in Botany & Horticulture, Mich. State Univ., 1979; PhD in Botany, Iowa State Univ., 1986. Temporary asst. prof., dept. botany Iowa State U., 1986—87, asst. to assoc. prof., dept. botany, 1987—2000, dir., Ada Hayden Herbarium, dept. Botany, 1989—, prof., dept. botany, 2000—, interim chair, dept. botany, 2001. Contbr. articles to profl. jours. Achievements include with colleagues discovering a new species of North American bamboo. Office: Dept Ecology Evolution & Organismal Biology Iowa State Univ 345 Bessey Hall Ames IA 50011-1020 Office Phone: 515-294-8218. Office Fax: 515-294-1337. Business E-Mail: lgclark@iastate.edu.

CLARK, MALCOLM GENE, SR., artist, consultant, historian, writer, conservator, researcher; b. Astoria, Ill., Mar. 8, 1930; s. Edward Ghlee Clark and Rebeca Marie Horton; m. Darline Pasewaldt; children: Malcolm Jr., Pamela. Student, Ill. Dept. Conservation, 1947—48; student in Art Edn., U. Wis., 1950; grad. in Writing, We. Tech. Coll., 1975—77. Line patrolman Ctrl. Ill. Pub. Svc. Co., Astoria, Ill., 1952—74; freelance artist Stoddard, Wis., 1975—. Cons. in field. Adv. com. Upper Miss. River Congressman Ron Kind, 1998—. Cpl. Nat. Guard, 1948—50, cpl. US Army, 1950—51. Mem.: Am. Inst. Conservation Hist. and Artistic Works (assoc.), Ky. Rifle Assn., Am. Legion (life). Avocations: antique rifle collecting, collecting Native American materials. Home: PO Box 1263 La Crosse WI 54602 Office: Am Inst for Conservation Box 1263 La Crosse WI 54602

CLARK, MARK JEFFREY, paralegal, researcher; b. Alton, Ill., Nov. 2, 1953; s. William Alfred and Winifred May (Young) C.; m. Patricia Ann Newell, July 29, 1989; children: Jason William, Brandi Leigh. AS in Bus. Adminstrn., Lewis & Clark Coll., 1978; cert. paralegal, Paralegal Inst., Atlanta, 1994, diploma in civil lit. and bus. law, 1994. Commd. spl. officer Lake Ozark (Mo.) Police Dept., 1975-78; ind. paralegal J & B Enterprises, Woodriver, Ill., 1994—; criminal rschr. Pinkerton Svcs. Group, Charlotte, N.C., 1998—, MPC Legal Rsch. Consulting Svcs., Battle Creek, Mich., 1999—. Cons., rschr. Nationwide Corps., 1994—. With USN, 1972-75, Vietnam. Mem. Nat. Paralegal Assn., KC (4th degree), Am. Legion. Democrat. Roman Catholic. Avocations: scuba diving, golf, bowling. Home and Office: 318 S Pence East Alton IL 62024 Home Phone: 618-334-4846; Office Phone: 618-406-0342. Personal E-mail: mjc356@netscape.net.

CLARK, MARTIN F(ILLMORE), JR., judge; b. Winston-Salem, NC, June 23, 1959; s. Martin Fillmore Sr. and Hazel Victoria (Young) C. BA cum laude, Davidson Coll., 1981; JD, U. Va., 1984. Bar: Va. 1984, U.S. Dist. Ct. (we. and ea. dists) Va. 1985. Judge 21st Jud. Cir., Stuart, Va., 1992—. Patrick County escheator, Stuart, 1984; commr. of accounts, 21st Jud. Cir., Patrick County, 1986. Author: The Many Aspects of Mobile Home Living, 2000 (N.Y. Times Notable Book, Book-of-the-Month Club selection, Stephen Crane Fiction award finalist), Plain Heathen Mischief, 2004. Bd. dirs. Patrick County Spl. Edn. Adv. Bd.; trustee Stuart Presbyn. Ch. Recipient Vereen Bell Creative Writing award Author's Panel, Davidson Coll., 1979, 81. Mem. ATLA, Patrick County C. of C. (bd. dirs.), Phi Beta Kappa. Avocations: writing fiction, horses, fishing. Office: PO Box 762 Stuart VA 24171-0762 E-mail: martinfclark@earthlink.net.

CLARK, MARY HIGGINS, writer, communications executive; b. NYC, Dec. 24, 1929; d. Luke J. and Nora C. (Durkin) Higgins; m. Warren Clark, Dec. 26, 1949 (dec. Sept. 1964); children: Marilyn, Warren, David, Carol, Patricia; m. John J. Coheeney, Nov. 3, 1996. BA, Fordham U., 1979; doctorate (hon.), Villanova U., 1983, Rider Coll., 1986, Stonehill Coll., 1992, Marymount Manhattan Coll., 1992, Chestnut Hill, 1993, Manhattan Coll., 1993, St. Peter's Coll., 1993. Advt. asst. Remington Rand, 1946; stewardess Pan Am., 1949-50; radio scriptwriter, prodr. Robert G. Jennings, 1965-70; v.p., ptnr., creative dir., prodr. radio programming Aerial Communications, NYC, 1970-80; chmn. bd., creative dir. D. J. Clark Enterprises, NYC, 1980—. Author: Silent Night, Aspire to the Heavens, A Biography of George Washington, 1969 (NJ Author award 1969), Where Are the Children?, 1976 (NJ Author award 1977), A Stranger Is Watching, 1978 (N.J. Author award 1978), The Cradle Will Fall, 1980, A Cry in the Night, 1982, Stillwatch, 1984, Weep No More, My Lady, 1987, While My Pretty One Sleeps, 1989, The Anastasia Syndrome and Other Stories, 1989, Loves Music, Loves to Dance, 1991, All Around the Town, 1992, I'll Be Seeing You, 1993, Remember Me, 1994, The Lottery Winner, 1994, Bad Behavior, 1995, Let Me Call You Sweetheart, 1995, Moonlight Becomes You, 1996, Pretend You Don't See Her, 1997, The Plot Thickens, 1997, You Belong to Me, 1998, All Through the Night, 1998, We'll Meet Again, 1999, Before I Say Good-Bye, 2000, Deck the Halls, 2000, Daddy's Little Girl, 2002, Silent Night/All Through the Night, 2002, On the Street Where You Live, 2002, Kitchen Privileges, 2002, The Second Time Around, 2003, Nighttime is My Time, 2004 (Publishers Weekly paperback bestseller list, 2005), No Place Like Home, 2005 (NY Times Bestseller list, Publishers Weekly Bestseller list), Two Little Girls in Blue, 2006; (with Thomas Chastain and others) Murder in Manhattan, 1986; editor: Murder on the Aisle: The 1987 Mystery Writers Anthology, 1987. Recipient Grand Prix de Litterature Policiere, France, 1980, Horatio Alger award, 1997, Gold Medal of Honor, Irish-Am. Hist. Soc., Spirit of Achievement award, Albert Einstein Coll. of Med., Yoshiva Univ., Nat. Arts Club Gold Medal in Edn., Grand Master award, Mystery Writers of Am., 2000. Mem. Mystery Writers Am. (pres. 1987, dir.), Authors League, Am. Soc. Journalists and Authors, Acad. Arts and Scis. Republican. Roman Catholic.

CLARK, MARYLIZ M., retired minister; b. Orange, NJ, Aug. 12, 1935; d. James Alexander Milling and Fernanda DeAngelis; m. Robert E. Hales (div.); m. Wendell J. Clark (div.); children: Teresa, Gregory, Lynn, Kristen, Amy, Robert. BA in English, Ind. U., 1957; MDiv, Andover-Newton Theol. Sch., 1979. Cert.: Harris Bus. Sch. (paralegal); tchr. N.J. Tchr. Indpls. Pub. Schs., 1957—59, Lenola Sch., Moorestown, NJ, 1962—64; bedside tchr. and substitute Mass. Hosp. Sch., Canton, 1974—76; assoc. pastor High St. Congl. Ch., Auburn, Maine, 1979—83, First Congl. United Ch. of Christ, East Hartford, Conn., 1983—86; interim and supply pastor United Ch. of Christ churches, Phila., 1988—98; ret., 1998. Pres. Hartford East Assn., East Hartford, Conn., 1984—86; mem. Lewiston-Auburn Ministerium, Maine, 1979—83, Phila. Ministerium, 1987—. Author: The Rainbow Bible Curriculum, 1976, Web of Love & Lies, 2005; contbr. meditations and articles to periodicals. Bd. mem. United Way, East Hartford, 1984—85. Avocations: writing, reading, gardening, crafts. Home: 18 Mindy Dr Moorestown NJ 08057-3024

CLARK, MATT, writer; b. Chgo., Feb. 3, 1930; s. Matthew and Kathryn Clark; m. Ellen Ann Mitchell, Aug. 23, 1952 (dec. 1978); children: Thomasin, Geoffrey Beach, Douglas Mitchell; m. Phyllis Malamud, Nov. 9, 1986. Grad., Hill Sch., 1947; AB, Wesleyan U., Middletown, Conn., 1951. Reporter Boston Traveler, 1953-56, sci. editor, 1956-58; writer Med. News, NYC, 1958- 61; medicine editor Newsweek mag., 1961-88; free-lance sci. writer, 1958—. Served with USNR, 1951-53. Recipient Albert Lasker Med. Journalism award, 1964, 67, Howard W. Blakeslee award Am. Heart Assn., 1965, 68, 73, 83, Penney-Mo. mag. award in health, 1967, 71, 75, med. journalism award AMA, 1969, Claude Bernard Sci. Journalism award Nat. Soc. Med. Rsch., 1971, Page One award Newspaper Guild N.Y., 1974, 83, Media award (mag.) Am. Cancer Soc., 1976, N.Y. Deadline Club award 1977, James T. Grady award Am. Chem. Soc., 1983, Am. Med. Writers Assn.-Searle Labs. journalism award, 1983. Fellow AAAS; mem. Nat. Assn. Sci. Writers, Century Assn., Coffee House Club (N.Y.C.).

CLARK, MATTHEW HARVEY, bishop; b. Troy, NY, July 15, 1937; s. M. Harvey and Grace (Bills) C. Student, Coll. Holy Cross, Worcester, Mass.; BA, St. Bernard's Sem., Rochester, NY; STL, N. Am. Coll., Rome; JCL, Gregorian U., Rome. Priest Roman Catholic Ch., 1962. Vice chancellor Diocese of Albany, NY; Cath. chaplain Albany Law Sch.; mem. faculty Vincentian Inst.; chmn. pers. bd. Diocese of Albany; spiritual dir. N. Am. Coll.; bishop Diocese of Rochester, Rochester, NY, 1979—. Office: Chancery Office 1150 Buffalo Rd Rochester NY 14624-1823

CLARK, MAURA J., oil and gas industry executive; CFO Clark Refining & Mktg. Inc.(now Premcor), Glen Ellyn, Ill., 1995—2000; v.p., fin. No. Am. Life Assurance Co.; sr. v.p., strategy and M&A Direct Energy, Toronto, Canada. Office: Direct Energy Atria III 4th Fl 2225 Sheppard Ave E Toronto ON M2J 5C2 Canada

CLARK, MELVILLE, JR., physicist, consultant, electrical engineer; b. Syracuse, NY, Dec. 19, 1921; s. Melville and Dorothy Drew (Speich) C. BS, MIT, 1943, postgrad., 1943-44, U. N.Mex., 1945-46, Princeton U., 1946; MA, Harvard U., 1947, PhD, 1949. Registered profl. engr., Mass. Mem. staff Radiation Lab. MIT, Cambridge, Mass., 1942-45; mem. staff Manhattan dist. U. Calif., Los Alamos, N.Mex., 1945-46; physicist

Brookhaven Nat. Lab., Upton, NY, 1949-53; dir. 416 South Salina St. Corp., Syracuse, NY, 1957—66, pres., 1965—66; mem. staff Radiation Lab. U. Calif., Livermore, 1953-55; dir. Clark Music Co., Syracuse, NY, 1948-60, v.p., 1957-60; pres. Meldor Corp., Cazenovia, NY, 1960-66; sr. engring. specialist Sylvania Electric Products, Waltham, Mass., 1962-64; sr. cons. scientist AVCO, Wilmington, Mass., 1964-67; sr. scientist NASA, Cambridge, 1967-70; sr. devel. engr. Thermo Electron, Waltham, 1970-73; sr. cons. engr., sr. tech. strategist Combustion Engring., Windsor, Conn., 1973-83; pres. Melville Clark Assocs., Wayland, Mass., 1949—. Cons. Raytheon Mfg. Co., Waltham, 1955-58, United Shoe Machinery Co., Beverly, Mass., 1956, Arthur D. Little, Cambridge, 1957-58, Aerodyne Rsch., Inc., Billerica, Mass., 1983-84; tech. expert witness Pennie and Edmonds, N.Y.C., 1984—; trustee Inst. Sci. Rsch. in Music, Wayland, Mass., 1990—; assoc. prof. nuclear engring. MIT, Cambridge, 1955-62; adviser Congressman Robert Drinan. Author: (with Rose) Plasmas and Controlled Fusion, 1961, (with Hansen) Numerical Methods of Reactor Analysis, 1964; translator, editor: (with B. Daniel) Introduction to the Theory of Ionized Gases, 1960; contbr. articles to profl. jours.; patentee in field. MIT scholar, 1939-43; NRC predoctoral fellow Harvard U., 1946-49, NRC predoctoral and Hercules Powder Co. fellow Princeton U., 1946. Mem. AAAS, IEEE, Am. Phys. Soc., Am. Inst. Physics, Fusion Power Assocs., Acoustical Soc. Am., Assn. Computing Machinery (Greater Boston chpt.), Soc. Music Perception and Cognition, Sigma Xi. Home and Office: 8 Richard Rd Wayland MA 01778-4099 Office Phone: 508-655-0906. Office Fax: 508-651-0602. Business E-Mail: mclarkjr@gis.net.

CLARK, MELVIN EUGENE, chemical company executive; b. Ord, Nebr., Oct. 2, 1916; s. Ansel B. and Ruth Joy (Bullock) C.; m. Virginia May Hiller, Sept. 16, 1938; children: John Robert, Walter Clayton, Dale Eugene, Merry Sue. BSChemE cum laude, U. Colo., 1937; grad. exec. program, Columbia U., 1952; grad. advanced mgmt. program, Harvard U., 1961. Asst. editor Chem. Engring., McGraw-Hill, NYC, 1937-41; mktg. staff Wyandotte Chem. Corp., Mich., 1941-53; chief program br. War Prodn. Bd., Washington, 1942-44; v.p. mktg. Frontier Chem. Co., Wichita, 1953-69; exec. v.p. chems. div. Vulcan Materials Co., Birmingham, Ala., 1969-81, v.p. planning, chems. and metals group, 1981-82; cons., 1982—. Pres. Chlorine Inst., 1977-80 Contbr. numerous articles to profl. jours. Recipient U. Colo. Alumni Recognition award, 1972; named Chem. Market Rsch. Assn. Man of Year, 1963, Disting. Engring. Alumnus, U. Colo., 1985, Centennial medalist Coll. of Engring., U. Colo., 1994, Geroge Norlin award U. Colo., 2005 Mem. AIChE, Comml. Devel. and Mktg. Assn., Am. Chem. Soc., Boulder Country Club, Tau Beta Pi, Pi Mu Epsilon. Republican. Mem. Christian Ch. Home and Office: 7145 Cedarwood Cir Boulder CO 80301-3716 E-mail: meclark1@aol.com.

CLARK, MERRELL EDWARD, JR., lawyer; b. Bklyn., Apr. 30, 1922; s. Merrell Edward and Eleanor Everest (Wild) C.; m. Hollis Logan, May 22, 1943; children: Julie Clark Goodyear, Kenyon Wild. BA, Yale U., 1943, LLB, 1948. Bar: N.Y. 1948, U.S. Dist. Ct. (so. dist.) 1949, U.S. Ct. Appeals (2d cir.) 1949, U.S. Tax Ct. 1951, Conn. 1952, U.S. Dist. Ct. (ea. dist.) N.Y. 1952, U.S. Dist. Ct. (ea. dist.) N.Y. 1952, U.S. Supreme Ct. 1956, U.S. Ct. Appeals (6th cir.) 1965, U.S. Ct. Appeals (8th cir.) 1973, U.S. Ct. Appeals (4th cir.) 1974, U.S. Dist. Ct. (no. dist.) N.Y. 1982, U.S. Dist. Ct. (we. dist.) N.Y. 1982. Assoc. Winthrop, Stimson, Putnam & Roberts, NYC, 1948—55, ptnr., 1956—91; sr. counsel Pillsbury Winthrop Shaw Pittman LLP, 1992—. Editor Yale Law Sch. Jour., 1947-48. Mem. Town Meeting, Greenwich, Conn., 1953-56, com. on jud. appointments (Appelate Divsn. 1st Dept.), 1978-82, 2d cir. jud. conf. evaluation com., 1980-87; dir., trustee Perrot Meml. Libr., Old Greenwich, Conn., 1956-63, Pomfret (Conn.) Sch., 1966-74, Richard Found., N.Y.C., 1965-2002, William Nelson Cromwell Found., N.Y.C., 1979—, Steep Rock Assn., Washinton, Conn., 1993-2004, Internat. Coll. Hospitality Mgmt., 1994-2002; adviser women's rights project ACLU, 1976-90; mem. N.Y.C. Bd. Ethics, 1987-89; chair N.Y.C. Conflicts of Interest Bd., 1989-90, N.Y.C. Hardship Appeals Bd., 1993-2001; bd. dirs. N.Y. Legal Aid Soc., 1985-88. Served to capt. AUS, 1943-46. Decorated Bronze Star with two battle stars. Mem. ABA (ho. of dels. 1985-89), Assn. of Bar of City of N.Y. (pres. 1978-80), Am. Law Inst., Am. Coll. Trial Lawyers, River Club (N.Y.C.), Washington Club (Conn.). Office: Pillsbury Winthrop Shaw Pittman LLP 1540 Broadway New York NY 10036 Personal E-mail: htgclark@aol.com. Business E-Mail: clarkm@law.com.

CLARK, MERRELL MAYS, management consultant; b. Clifton Springs, NY, Feb. 8, 1935; s. Arthur Tillotson and Ruthanna Frame (Anderson) C.; m. Lynne Ruth Butcher, June 14, 1957; children: Elisabeth Lynne Clark Jenks, Aimee Ruthanna Clark Peterson, Catherine Merrell Clark Seda. BA, Yale U., 1957, MA in Religion, 1970. Asst. to advt. mgr. Armstrong Rubber Co., West Haven, Conn., 1959—60; mktg. analyst SSC & B, NYC, 1960—62, account exec., 1962—64, v.p., account supr., 1964—68, v.p. mgmt. supr., 1968—70; prin. Knight, Gladieux & Smith, NYC, 1970—72; v.p. Edna McConnell Clark Found., NYC, 1972—77; exec. v.p. Acad. for Ednl. Devel., NYC, 1977—81; prin. Clark Co., Scarsdale, NY, 1981—. Contbr. articles to profl. jours. Bd. dirs. Westchester Cmty. Svcs. Coun., White Plains, 1965-72, Elderhostel, Boston, 1977-98, Scarsdale Cmty. Ctr., 2004—, Town ad Village Civic Club Edn Found., 2003—; pres. Elderworks, Scarsdale, 1978—, Nat. Sch. Vol. Program, Alexandria, Va., 1977-89, chmn. nat. adv. bd., 1977-1989, Scarsdale Adult Sch., 1988—, Coun. for Arts in Westchester, White Plains, 1978-83, Scarsdale Found., 1981-90; advisor Nat. Exec. Svc. Corps, N.Y.C., 1977-87, United Way Scarsdale-Edgemont, 1989-97; treas. Greenacres Assn. Scarsdale, Inc. 1993-97; active Scarsdale Arts Coun., 2002—. Mem. Fox Meadows Tennis Club, Yale Club (N.Y.C.), Yale Westchester Alumni Assn (treas. 1995-2001, pres. 1997-03, chmn. bd. dirs., chmn. scholarship com. 2003—). Republican. Presbyterian. Avocations: piano, organ, painting. Office: PO Box 1385 Scarsdale NY 10583-9385

CLARK, MICHAEL, artist; m. Felicity Hogan, Dec. 1995. BA, Corcoran Sch. Art. Founder & co-dir. Mus. Contemporary Art, Washington, 1991—. Represented in permanent collections, Nat. Gallery Art, DC, exhibitions include Clark & Hogan: Paintings & Collaborations, Barry Gallery, 2002—03, Clark in Context: Day of the Revolutionary, Mus. Contemporary Art, 2003. Office: Mus Contemporary Art 1054 31st St Washington DC 20007

CLARK, MICHAEL A., lawyer; b. Urbana, Ill., Sept. 23, 1954; BA summa cum laude, Ill. Wesleyan U., 1976; JD magna cum laude, Harvard U., 1979. Bar: Ill. 1979; CPA, Ill. 1976, US tax Ct. 1982, US Ct fed. claims 1983, US Ct. of Appeals (2nd cir.) 1983, US Dist. Ct. (no. dist.) Ill. 1982, US Ct. of Appeals (10th cir.) 1986, US Ct. of Appeals (9th cir.) 2000. Atty.-advisor to Hon. Arnold Raum U.S. Tax Ct., 1979-81; ptnr. Hopkins & Sutter, Chgo., Sidley Austin LLP, Chgo. Adj. prof. taxation of exempt organizations De Paul U. Coll. Law, 1984—, IIT Chgo.-Kent Coll. Law, 1987—. Mem. ABA (sect. taxation, com. exempt orgns. 1983—), Am. Acad. Hosp. Attys. (chair tax and fin. com.), Chgo. Bar Assn. (mem. fed. tax com. & past chair divsn. H, exempt orgn. subcom.), Phi Kappa Phi, Am. Health Lawyers Assn. (past chair, AAHA tax & fin. com. & former mem. planning com. Annual AAHA Healthcare tax law Inst.), Am. Bar Assn. Health Law Sect. (mem., health lawyer editl. bd. & vice chair, tax & fin. Interest Grp.), Great Lakes TE/GE Coun.(former eo coord.). Mem. bd. editors Harvard Law Review, 1978-79. Office: Sidley Austin LLP 1 S Dearborn Chicago IL 60603 Office Phone: 312-853-2173. Office Fax: 312-853-7036. Business E-Mail: mclark@Sidley.com.

CLARK, MICHAEL K., diversified financial services company executive; Grad., SUNY Maritime; MBA, NYU. Mem. staff Bankers Trust Co., J.P. Morgan Chase & Co., 1994—, head instl. trust svcs., 2000—, head investor svcs., 2005—, exec. v.p. Worldwide Securities Svcs. Capt. USMC, third mate USCG. Office: JP Morgan Chase & Co 270 Park Ave New York NY 10017-2070

CLARK, MICHAEL STEVEN, accountant; b. Marshfield, Mo., Dec. 5, 1960; s. Wanda Lee Taylor. BS, Humboldt State U., Arcata, Calif., 1983; MS, San Jose State U., Calif., 1995. CPA Calif. State Bd. Accountancy, 1985. Ptnr. Ernst & Young, San Jose, 1983—. Mem.: Am. Inst. CPAs (corr.). Liberal. Office: Ernst & Young 303 Almaden Blvd San Jose CA 95110 Home Phone: 408-723-2134; Office Phone: 408-947-5418.

CLARK, MICHELL C., federal agency administrator; married; 2 children. BS, West Point, 1978; MS, Purdue U., 1988; attended, Command & Gen. Staff Coll., 1990—91. Advanced through grades to lt. col. US Army, 1978—98; performance mgmt. and measurement chief, reserve components personnel adminstrn. ctr. US Dept. Def., with office of comptroller Yongsan Army Garrison, 1991—93, exec. asst., Office of Chmn. Joint Chiefs of Staff, 1993—95, with security and strategic planning, Office of Dir., 1995—96; budget coord. program analysis and evaluation directorate U.S. Dept. Def., 1997—98; gen. customer relationship mgmt. practice leader PricewaterhouseCoopers LLP, 1998—2003; sr. mgmt. cons. IBM Corp.; dir. security services US Dept. Edn., 2003—04, dep. asst. sec. for mgmt., 2003—05, acting chief human capital officer, 2005—06, acting chief info. officer, 2005—06, acting asst. sec. for mgmt., 2005—06, asst. sec. for mgmt., chief human capital officer, 2006—. Spkr. in field. Office: US Dept Edn 400 Maryland Ave SW Rm 2W311 Washington DC 20202-4500 Office Phone: 202-401-0485. Office Fax: 202-401-0485. E-mail: michell.clark@ed.gov.*

CLARK, MORTON HUTCHINSON, lawyer; b. Norfolk, Va., Apr. 21, 1933; s. David Henderson and Catharine Angelica (Hutchinson) C.; m. Lynn Harrison Adams, Aug. 12, 1961; children: Allison Adams, David Henderson, Susan West, Julia Dixon. BA in English, U. Va., 1954, LLB, 1960. Bar: Va. 1960, U.S. Dist. Ct. (ea. dist.) Va. 1960, U.S. Ct. Appeals (4th cir.) 1976, U.S. Ct. Appeals (1st cir.) 1993, U.S. Supreme Ct. 1993. Assoc. Vandeventer Black LLP, Norfolk, 1960-65, ptnr., 1965—. Co-editor: The Virginia Lawyer, 1991-93. Chmn. Va. Commn. for Children and Youth, Richmond. Fellow Am. Coll. Trial Lawyers, Va. Law Found.; mem. Maritime Law Assn. (exec. com. 1984-87), Hoffman l'Anson Am. Inns of Ct. (exec. com. 1993-95), The Harbor Club (pres.), Town Point Club. Episcopalian. Avocations: off shore racing, cruising. Home: 103 Rivers Edge Kingsmill Williamsburg VA 23185-8930 Office: 295 McLaws Cir Ste 1 Williamsburg VA 23185 Home Phone: 757-220-9557; Office Phone: 757-258-9515. E-mail: clarklaw2@verizon.net.

CLARK, NANCY LUCINDA BROWN, retired music educator; b. Akron, Ohio, Dec. 11, 1946; d. Gardner Lane Brown and Ruth Marie Thomas; m. Eugene Ernest Zielinski, Aug. 1968 (div. Mar. 1989); children: Ruth Karlotte Zielinski Hansen, Jennifer Jane Zielinski Webbler; m. Douglas Napier Clark, Mar. 11, 1989. Student, Kent State U., 1964-66; BS in Mus. Edn., U. Ill., 1968; postgrad., Nazareth Coll., 1981-82. Music tchr. pre-kindergarten and kindergarten Diocese of Rochester, NY, 1970s; tchr., supr. Muzak Cranford (N.J.) Mid. Sch., 1982-87; asst. music dir. First Presbyn. Ch., Maplewood, NJ, 1984-89; music min. Salem Bapt. Ch., Lexington, Ga., 1990-96, ret., 1996; mgr. Woods Hole Mus. Gift Shop, 2006—. Cons. Nat. Postal Mus., 2004—06. Host (internet radio program) APS Stamp Talk with Nancy Clark; contbr. articles to profl. jours., chapters to books. Pres. Olymphilex 96, Atlanta, 1992—96; mem. Barnstable County Hist. Pres. Commn., 2001—; juror, team leader Juvalux 98, Luxembourg, 1998, Bangkok, 2000, Olymphilex, Greece, 2004; chmn. 1st Nat. Youth in Philately Symposium, 2002; v.p. Barnstable County Hist. Pres. Commn., 2002—03, chair, 2003—; dir. edn. Stamp Camp USA, 2003—04, co-chair, 2003—04; bd. dirs. Oglethorpe County Libr., Lexington, 1989—98, Athens-Clarke County Regional Libr., 1992—98; bd. mem. Woods Hole Hist. Collection, 2006—. Recipient Internat. Gold award ROCPEX Taipei, China, 1981, Polska, 1997, Grand Stamporee award, Palm Beach, Fla., 1996, Rowland Hill award Southeastern Fed. Stamp Clubs, 2005, Clyde Jennings award for Svc., 2006. Mem.: Mass. Postal Rsch. Soc. (bd. dirs. 2003—, sec. 2006—), Mobile Post Office Soc. (bd. dirs. 2004—, treas. 2006—), Aux. Markings Club (pres. 2003—), Cape Cod Area Philatelic Group (bd. dirs. 2001—03, pres. 2004), Am. Assn. Philatelic Exhibitors, Boston Philatelic Group (sec.-treas. 2004—), Collectors Club N.Y., Am. Philatelic Soc. (Ernest Kehr award 2006). Personal E-mail: stampsintheclass@yahoo.com.

CLARK, NICHOLAS LELAND, contractor; b. Taylorville, Ill., Dec. 8, 1981; s. Phillip M. Clark and Karen J. Blethroade. AS in Mgmt., Lake Land Coll., Mattoon, Ill., 2003. Owner NL Constrn., Champaign, Ill., 2005—. Spl. full time min. Watchtower Farms, Wallkill, NY, 2003—05; vol. roofer Ill. Regional Bldg. Com. #2, 1997—2007; vol. drywaller NY Regional Bldg. Com. # 1, 2003—05. Scholar, Lake Land Coll., 2000. Mem.: Mensa. Jehovah'S Witness. Avocations: sports, travel, cooking, writing. Home: 4511 Gold Finch Rd Champaign IL 61822 Home Phone: 217-714-5454. Personal E-mail: nickelclark1@yahoo.com.

CLARK, NOEL A., physics professor; BS, John Carroll U., University Heights, Ohio, 1963, MS, 1965; PhD in Physics, MIT, Cambridge, 1970. Rsch. fellow to asst. prof. applied physics Harvard U.; faculty mem. to prof. physics dept., dir. Liquid Crystal Materials Rsch. Ctr. U. Colo., Boulder, 1977—. Co-founder Displaytech Inc., Longmont, Colo., 1984. Contbr. articles to sci. jours. Recipient IR100, Soc. Info. Display, Lab. Apparatus Competition First prize, Am. Assn. Physics Tchrs.; grantee Guggenheim Found. fellowship, 1985—86. Fellow: AAAS, Am. Phys. Soc. (Oliver E. Buckley Condensed Matter prize 2006); mem.: NAS. Office: Liquid Crystal Group U Colo Dept Physics 390 UCB Boulder CO 80309-0390 Office Phone: 303-492-6420. E-mail: clarkn@colorado.edu.

CLARK, NOREEN MORRISON, behavioral science educator, researcher; b. Glasgow, Scotland, Jan. 12, 1943; arrived in US, 1948; d. Angus Watt and Anne (Murphy) Morrison; m. George Robert Pitt, Dec. 3, 1982; 1 child, Alexander Robert. BS, U. Utah, 1965; MA, Columbia U., 1972, MPhil, 1975, PhD, 1976. Rsch. coord. World Edn. Inc., NYC, 1972-73; asst. prof. Sch. Pub. Health Columbia U., NYC, 1973-80, assoc. prof., 1980-81, Sch. Pub. Health U. Mich., Ann Arbor, 1981-85, prof., chmn. dept. health behavior and health edn., 1985-95; prof. pediat. and com. diseases, Marshall H. Becker prof. pub. health U. Mich. Med. Sch., Ann Arbor, 1995—2005, dean, 1995—2005, dir. ctr. mng. chronic disease, 2005—, Myron E. Wegman Disting. Univ. prof., 2006—. Adj. prof. health adminstrn. Sch. Pub. Health Columbia U., 1988—; prin. investigator NIH, 1977—; adv. com. pulmonary diseases Nat. Heart, Lung & Blood Inst., Rockville, Md., 1983-87, adv. com. for prevention, edn. and control, 1987-91, coord. com. Nat. Asthma Edn. Program, 1991—; assoc. Synergos Inst., NYC, 1987-99; nat. adv. environ. health scis. coun. NIH, 1999-2002; task force on preventive cmty. svc. CDC, 2002-05 Co-author: Evaluation of Health Promotion, 1984; editor Health Edn. and Behavior, 1985-97; assoc. editor Ann. Rev. of Pub. Health, 2002-05; mem. editl. bd. Women in Health, Advances in Health Edn. and Promotion, Home Health Care Services Quar.; contbr. articles to profl. jours. Bd. dirs., adv. Aaron Diamond Found., 1989-96, Family Care Internat., NYC, 1987—, Internat. Asthma Coun., 1996-2000, Am. Lung Assn., NYC, 1988—, World Edn., Inc., 1998-. Mem. Soc. Pub. Health Edn. (pres. 1985-86, Disting. Fellow award 1987), APHA (chair health edn. sect. 1982-83, Derryberry award in behavioral sci. 1985, Disting. Career award 1994), Am. Thoracic Soc. (Health Edn. Rsch. award Nat. Asthma Edn. Program 1992, Healthtrac Found. Health Edn. award, 1997), Internat. Union Health Edn., Soc. Behavioral Medicine, Coun. Fgn. Rels., Inst. Medicine of NAS, Pi Sigma Alpha. Office: U Mich Sch Pub Health 109 Observatory St Ann Arbor MI 48109-2029 Office Phone: 734-763-1457.

CLARK, PAT ENGLISH, lawyer; b. Austin, Tex., Feb. 26, 1940; s. Pat Wheeler and Jennie Bell (Lagrone) C.; m. Peggy Arnold Gray, March 16, 2002; 1 child, Susan Louise Beisert. BA, U. Tex., JD, 1963. Bar: Tex. 1963, U.S. Ct. Mil. Appeals 1964, U.S. Dist. Ct. (so. and no. dists.) Tex. Staff atty. Phillips Petroleum Co., Houston, 1967-69; atty. Amoco Production Co., Houston, 1969-75; ptnr. Vinson & Elkins, Houston, 1975-95, Borrego & Clark, 1996-99. Capt. JAGC, U.S. Army, 1964-67. Methodist. Office: 5725 Kempson Dr Austin TX 78735 Business E-Mail: pclark8@austin.rr.com.

CLARK, PAUL G., bank executive; B in History, Denison U., Granville, Ohio; MBA, Baldwin-Wallace Coll., Berea, Ohio; grad., Stonier Sch. Banking. Mgmt. trainee consumer fin. divsn. Nat. City Bank Nat. City Corp., 1976, v.p. Nat. City Bank, sr. v.p. corp. banking, 1989, exec. v.p. retail banking Nat. City Bank Pa., 1995—97, pres., CEO Nat. City Bank Mich./Ill., exec. v.p. Instl. Asset Mgmt., chmn. Nat. City Investment Mgmt. Co., 2000—04, corp. exec. v.p., pres. No. Ohio banking, 2004—. Chair bd. trustees Cath. Diocese of Cleve. Found., MetroHealth Found.; treas., bd. trustees Gt. Lakes Sci. Ctr.; bd. trustees Playhouse Sq. Found., The Union Club; bd. dirs. Cleve. Rock & Roll, Inc. Office: Nat City Corp Nat City Ctr 1900 E Ninth St Cleveland OH 44114-3484 Office Phone: 216-222-2000.*

CLARK, PAUL M., retired protective services official; b. Mason, W.Va., Oct. 6, 1960; s. Everett William Jr. and Freda Jean Clark; m. Cheryl Lynn Allman, Nov. 14, 1980; children: Jared Paul, Jessica Marie. Student, Marshall U., Huntington, W.Va. Cert. police offier W.Va., 1988, corrections officer W.Va., 1985. Emergency med. technician Jackson County Emergency Svcs., Ripley, W.Va., 1983—85; capt. Jackson County Sheriff's Dept., Ripley, 1985—2001. Dep. chief , pres. bd. dirs. Cottageville Vol. Fire Dept., W.Va., 1975—2001; scoutmaster Cub Scouts Am., Cottageville, 1992—94; asst. scoutmaster Boy Scouts Am., Ripley, 1994—96, 2007—. E-5/Master-at-arms 2d class USNR, 1992—2001. Decorated Navy Achiement medal, Naval Res. Meritorious Svc. award, , Nat. Def. medal USN, Expert Rifle medal, Expert Pistol medal, Outstanding Vol. Svc. medal; recipient Combat Cross, WV Dep. Sheriffs' Assn., 1995; Heroic Action award, Cottageville Vol. Fire Dept., W.Va., 1998, Award for Water Rescue, 1999. Mem.: NRA (police firearms instr. 1989—), Am. Fedn. Police (life Police Purple Heart 1986, 1995), Profl. Assn. Dive Instrs. (scuba diver 1998—), Masons. Democrat. Avocations: reading, woodworking, hunting. Home: Rt 1 Box 4 Cottageville WV 25239 Personal E-mail: p_m_clark@hotmail.com.

CLARK, PETER BRUCE, retired publishing executive; b. Detroit, Oct. 23, 1928; s. Rex Scripps and Marian (Peters) C.; m. Lianne Schroeder, Dec. 21, 1952 (dec. Jan. 1996); children: Ellen Clark Brown, James. BA, Pomona Coll., 1952, LL.D. (hon.), 1972; M.P.A., Syracuse U., 1953; PhD, U. Chgo., 1959; H.H.D., Mich. State U., 1973, Lawrence Inst. Tech., 1982; LL.D. (hon.), U. Mich., 1977. Research assoc., then instr. polit. sci. U. Chgo., 1957-59; asst. prof. polit. sci. Yale U., 1959-61; with Evening News Assn., Detroit, 1960-86, corp. sec., 1960-61, v.p., 1961-63, pres., 1963-86, chmn. bd., chief exec. officer, dir., 1969-86; pub. Detroit News, 1963-81, also dir.; dir. Gannett Co., Inc., 1986-99. Regent's prof. UCLA Grad. Sch. Mgmt., 1987; chmn. Fed. Res. Bank Chgo., 1975-77, former chmn. br. Fed. Res. Bank Detroit. Served with AUS, 1953-55. Mem.: Am. Soc. Newspaper Editors, Am. Newspaper Pub. Assn. (dir. 1966—74), Ironwood Country Club.

CLARK, PETER S., II, lawyer; b. Alexandria, Va., Feb. 13, 1957; s. Seymour Garland and Joan (Smith) Clark; m. Stacy Ellen West, June 19, 1988. BA in pub. policy & economics, Duke U., 1979; JD, Wash. U., 1982. Bar: Pa. 1982, NY 2004. Assoc. to ptnr. Duane Morris, Phila., 1982—2000; ptnr. Reed Smith LLP, Phila., 2000—, practice group leader corp. restructuring & bankruptcy group. Mem. editl. adv. bd. Jour. of Corp. Renewal. Mem. editl. bd.: Jour. Bankruptcy Law. Mem.: ABA (mem. com. on bus. bankruptcy, mem. com. on comml. fin. services), Comml. Law League of Am., Am. Bankruptcy Inst., Turnaround Mgmt. Assn. Office: Reed Smith LLP 2500 One Liberty Pl 1650 Market St Philadelphia PA 19103 Office Phone: 215-851-8142. Office Fax: 215-851-1420. Business E-Mail: pclark@reedsmith.com.

CLARK, PHILIP HART, retired urban and regional planner; b. Hartford, Conn., May 23, 1938; s. Raymond Gilbert and Phyllis Angeline (Hart) C. BArch, Cornell U., 1961, M in Regional Planning, 1968. Asst. project mgr. W.R. Grimshaw Co., Denver, 1964-65; project coord. U. Pa., 1968-69; sr. planner County of Fairfax, Va., 1969-72; urban planner Hellmuth, Obata & Kassabaum, Washington, 1972-73; chief air transp. planning Met. Washington Coun. Govts., Washington, 1973-77; urban planning cons. Reston, Va., 1977-78; with Gordian Assocs., Washington, 1978-79; program mgr. base comprehensive planning USAF Engring. and Svcs. Ctr., Tyndall AFB, Fla., 1979-81; program mgr. base comprehensive planning hdqrs. USAF Pentagon, Washington, 1981-92; environ. restoration program mgr. Sta. Hdqrs. USAF Pentagon, Washington, 1992-98; ret., 1998. Vis. lectr. George Washington U., 1975, Am. U. 1976-77, Air Force Inst. Tech., 1979-91, USAF Acad., 1989; spkr. Soc. Am. Mil. Engrs. Meetings, aviation assn. meetings. Mem. Paul Hill Chorale, 1970-76, Choral Arts Soc., 1977-79, 81-83, Reston Chorale, 1983-95, 1999-2002, Kaleidoscope Theatre, Panama City, Fla., 1980-81, Washington Men's Camerata, 1995-97. Capt. USAF, 1961-64. Fellow Am. Inst. Cert. Planners; mem. Am. Planning Assn. (Disting. Svc. and Leadership award fed. planning divsn. 2003), Theta Chi. Democrat. Avocations: music, reading, swimming, travel, photography. E-mail: fpdphil@aol.com, phc3@cornell.edu.

CLARK, PHILLIP R., lawyer; b. Indpls., Oct. 6, 1948; AB magna cum laude, Wabash Coll., 1970; JD cum laude, Harvard U., 1976. Bar: Colo. 1976. Ptnr. Holme, Roberts & Owen, LLC, Denver, 1976—. Exec. com. Rocky Mountain Mineral Law Found.; mem. IPAMS Royalties Com., Ind. Petroleum Assn. Mountain States. Recipient Best Lawyers in Am. Mem. Colo. Bar Assn., Denver Bar Assn., Phi Beta Kappa 1976, bd. dir. sec. & bd. coun Colo. Oil & Gas Assn. legal, Legis. & Regulatory Com. Office: Holme Roberts & Owen LLC 1700 Lincoln St Ste 4100 Denver CO 80203-4541 Office Phone: 303-861-7000. Office Fax: 303-866-0200. Business E-Mail: phillip.clark@hro.com.

CLARK, R. KERRY (KERRY CLARK), health products executive; b. Ottawa, Ont., Can., Apr. 29, 1952; B in Commerce, Queen's U., 1974. Brand asst. P&G Can. Procter & Gamble, 1974—75, asst. brand mgr. P&G Can., 1975—76, brand mgr. P&G Can., 1976—80, assoc. advt. mgr. P&G Can., 1980—84, assoc. advt. mgr. P&G Far East (Japan), 1984—85, advt. mgr. P&G Far East (Japan), 1985—87, gen. mgr. hard surface cleaners Cin., 1987—91, v.p., gen. mgr. laundry products Procter & Gamble USA, 1991—95, pres. laundry and cleaning products-U.S., Procter & Gamble N.Am., group v.p., 1995—97, pres. laundry and cleaning products-N.Am., Procter & Gamble N.Am., group v.p., 1997—98, exec. v.p. The Procter & Gamble Co., pres. Asia, Procter & Gamble Asia, 1998—99, pres.-Asia, 1999, pres. global feminine protection and Asia, 1999—2000, pres. global market devel. orgn., 2000—01, pres. global market devel. and bus. ops., 2001—02, vice chmn. bd. dirs., 2002—06, pres. global market devel. and bus. ops., 2002, vice chmn., pres. global health, baby and family care, 2004—06; pres., CEO, bd. dir. Cardinal Health Inc., Dublin, Ohio, 2006—. Mem. mgmt. bd. GS1; bd. dirs. EAN Internat.; past mem. Am. C. of C. in

Japan; past vice chairperson The Soap and Detergent Assn., NY; bd. dirs. Textron Inc. Chmn. bd. dirs. Cin. Zoo and Bot. Gardens; mem. Leadership Cin., Class XIX; past mem. Greater Cin. United Way Cabinet; chmn. Alexis de Tocqueville Soc., 2005. Mem.: Bacchus Soc. Am., Indian Hill Club, Queen City Club, Kenwood Country Club, The Commonwealth Club. Office: Cardinal Health Inc 7000 Cardinal Pl Dublin OH 43017*

CLARK, RAMSEY (WILLIAM RAMSEY CLARK), lawyer, former United States attorney general; b. Dallas, Dec. 18, 1927; s. Thomas Campbell and Mary (Ramsey) Clark; m. Georgia Welch, Apr. 16, 1949; children: Ronda Kathleen, Thomas Campbell III. BA, U. Tex., 1949; MA, JD, U. Chgo., 1950. Bar: Tex. 1951, US Supreme Ct. 1956, DC 1969, NY 1970. Assoc. to ptnr. Clark, Reed and Clark, Dallas, 1951-61; asst. atty. gen. lands divsn. US Dept. Justice, 1961-65, dep. atty. gen., 1965-67, atty. gen., 1967-69; atty. Paul, Weiss, NYC, 1969—73; pvt. practice lawyer, 1973—; founder Internat. Action Ctr., NYC, 1991, Internat. ANSWER (Act Now to Stop War and End Racism), Washington, 2001. Adj. prof. Howard U., 1969—72, Bklyn. Law Sch., 1973—81. Author: Crime in America, 1970, The Fire This Time: US War Crimes in the Gulf War, 1991. Served to cpl. USMC, 1945-46. Recipient Gandhi Peace award.*

CLARK, RANJANA B., bank executive; arrived in U.S., 1987; BA in Econs., MA in Mktg. and Sales. With Deutsche Bank, Bombay, 1982; product mgr. capital markets divsn. Wachovia Bank, Charlotte, NC, 1989, sr. v.p. - group exec. treas. services divsn., 1999—2001, exec. v.p., head treas. services divsn. Charlotte, NC, 2001—. Named one of Most Powerful Women in Banking, US Banker, 2003, 2006. Office: Wachovia Bank 301 South College St Charlotte NC 28288-0570*

CLARK, RICHARD EUGENE, music educator; b. Wenatchee, Wash., Apr. 16, 1930; s. Raymond Otto Clark and Maude Myrtle Bass. BA, We. Wash. U., 1952, MA, 1970; MDiv, Am. Bapt. Sem. of West, 1955; MA, Calif. State U., Carson, 1989; postgrad., Wycliffe Coll., 1960—61. Nat. cert. tchr. music. Instr. sociology Coll. of Ozarks, Point Lookout, Mo., 1970—71, S.W. Mo. State U., Springfield, 1971—72, Whatcom C.C., Bellingham, Wash., 1972—73; cmty. planner Whatcom County Opportunity Coun., Bellingham, 1973—76; itinerant prof. sociology and religion Chapman U., Orange, Calif., 1977—83; journalist, former editor Rec.-Jour. Newspaper, Ferndale, Wash., 1984—90; instr. piano Wash. State Music Tchrs. Assn.-Bellingham chpt., Blaine, 1990—. Editor The Clarion Wash. State Music Tchrs. Assn., 1994—97, pres. Bellingham chpt., 1997—99. Author: Point Roberts, USA: The History of a Canadian Enclave, 1980, Sam Hill's Peace Arch: Remembrance of Dreams Past, 2003; editor: The Last Diary of Andrew Jackson Loomis, 2005. Founder Pacific Arts Found.; vicar Ch. Holy Nativity, Calgary, Canada, 1961—67; pastor First Bapt. Ch., Pincher Creek, Alberta, Canada, 1955—59. Named to Wash. State Music Tchrs. Assn. Hall of Fame, 2004; recipient Dyson Hague Meml. Liturgics First prize, 1960, Bob Robbins Performing Arts award, Close Up Found. & No. Light Newspaper, 1999, Thomas L. George hon. lifetime achievement award, Record-Jour. Newspaper, 2004, Hon. Lifetime Achievement award, Internat. Peace Arch Assn., 2005. Mem.: Point Roberts Hist. Soc. (hon. life), Old Main Soc. Office Phone: 360-332-5175. Personal E-mail: dclark30@peoplepc.com.

CLARK, RICHARD T., pharmaceutical company executive; b. Johnstown, Pa., Mar. 7, 1946; married; 2 children. BA in Liberal Arts, Washington & Jefferson Coll., 1968; MBA, Am. Univ., 1970. Quality control insp., indsl. engr., quality control analyst, lead supr. pharm. prodn. MSD, 1972—78, sr. new products planner, 1978—81, prodn. mgr. Elkton Pharm. Labs., 1981—83, mgr. indsl. engring., 1983—84; sr. mgr. indsl. engring. MPMD, 1984—85, dir. ops. improvement, 1985—86; sr. dir. mgmt. engring. Merck Sharp & Dohme/MPMD, 1986—89; exec. dir. mgmt. engring. Merck Pharm. Mfg. Divsn., 1989—91; v.p. materials mgmt. and mgmt. engring. MMD, 1991—93, v.p. procurement and materials mgmt., 1993—94, v.p. N.Am. ops., 1994—96, sr. v.p. N.Am. ops., 1996—97; exec. v.p., COO Merck-Medco Managed Care, 1997—2000; chmn., pres., CEO Merck Medco Health Solutions, Inc. (formerly Merck-Medco Managed Care, L.L.C.), 2000—02; chmn. Merck Medco Health Solutions, Inc., 2002—03; sr. v.p. quality comml. affairs Merck Mfg. Divsn., 1997, pres., 2003—05; pres., CEO Merck & Co. Inc., 2005—07; chmn., pres., CEO Merck & Co., Inc., 2007—. Lt. US Army, 1970—72. Office: Merck & Co Inc One Merck Dr Whitehouse Station NJ 08889-0100*

CLARK, ROBERT ARTHUR, mathematician, educator; b. Melrose, Mass., May 3, 1923; s. Arthur Henry and Persis (Kidder) C.; m. Jane Burr Crofut Kinder, June 25, 1966. Student, Colo. Coll., 1940-42; BA, Duke, 1944; MA, MIT, 1946, PhD, 1949. Instr., research asso. MIT, 1946-50, vis. asst. prof., 1956-57; faculty Case Inst. Tech. (now Case Western Res. U.), Cleve., 1950—, prof. math., 1964-85, prof. emeritus, 1985—, acting head dept. math., 1960-61, assoc. chmn. dept. math., 1974-79, 82-84, exec. officer, 1981-82. Vis. mem. U.S. Army Math. Research Center, Madison, Wis., 1961-62 Mem. AAAS, Am. Math. Soc., Math. Assn. Am., Soc. Indsl. and Applied Math., Phi Beta Kappa, Sigma Xi. Achievements include spl. research asymptotic integration theory of differential equations and theory thin elastic shells. Home: 7469 Sherman Rd Gates Mills OH 44040-9769 Office: Case Western Res Univ Dept Math Cleveland OH 44106

CLARK, ROBERT CHARLES, law educator, former dean; b. New Orleans, Feb. 26, 1944; s. William Vernon and Edwina Ellen (Nuessly) Clark; m. Kathleen Margaret Tighe, June 1, 1968; children— Alexander Ian, Matthew Tighe. BA in Theology, Maryknoll Coll., 1966; PhD in Philosophy, Columbia U., 1971; JD, Harvard U., 1972. Bar: Mass. 1972. Assoc. Ropes & Gray, Boston, 1972-74; asst. prof. Yale Law Sch., New Haven, 1974-76, assoc. prof., 1976-77, prof., 1977-78; vis. prof. Harvard Law Sch., Cambridge, Mass., 1978—79, prof., 1979—, Royall prof. law, 1989—2003, Harvard U. disting. svc. prof., Austin Wakeman Scott prof. law, 2003—, dean, 1989—2003. Bd. dirs. Maybelline Inc., 1992—96, Collins & Aikman Corp., 1994—, Am. Lawyer Media Holdings, 1997—2003, Omnicon Group Inc., 2002—, Time Warner, Inc., 2004—, Lazard Ltd., 2005; trustee Teachers Ins. Annuity Assn., 1988—. Contbr. articles to profl. jours. Mem.: ABA. Office: Harvard Law Sch 1563 Massachusetts Ave Cambridge MA 02138

CLARK, ROBERT G., construction executive; m. Ellen Clark. Founder, chmn., CEO Clayco, 1984—; founder Clayco TiltUp, 1989; acting exec. dir. Ctrl. Inst. for the Deaf, 2002. Bd. dirs. LaBarge, Inc., 2001—. Bd. mem. Ctrl. Inst. for the Deaf, Regional Chamber and Growth Assn., St. Louis, Forest Pk. Forever, St. Louis U., Regional Bus. Coun. Co-recipient Lifetime Achievement award, March of Dimes; recipient John D. Levy Humanitarian award, Am. Jewish Coun., Cmty. Svc. award, Princeton Alumni Assn. Office: Clayco 2199 Innerbelt Business Center Dr Saint Louis MO 63114 Office Phone: 314-429-5100. Office Fax: 314-429-1890.*

CLARK, ROBERT HENRY, JR., finance company executive; b. Manchester, NH, Mar. 4, 1941; s. Robert Henry and Elva C. (Stearns) C.; m. Rosalie Foster Case, Dec. 21, 1963; children: Robert Henry III, Hilary Eagan, Hadley Case. BSBA, Boston U., 1964. Mcpl. bond underwriter Merrill Lynch, Pierce, Fenner & Smith, NYC, 1964-70; v.p. Case, Pomeroy & Co., Inc., NYC, 1971-75, exec. v.p., 1975-83, pres., 1983—, CEO, 1993—, chmn., 1999—; v.p. fin. Felmont Oil Corp., 1972-79, exec. v.p., 1979-84. Trustee Boston U., 1984-87. Mem. Sigma Alpha Epsilon Office: Case Pomeroy & Co Inc 521 5th Ave 36th Flr New York NY 10175

CLARK, ROBERT MUREL, JR., lawyer; b. Dallas, Mar. 7, 1948; s. Robert M. Sr. and Dorrace Helen (Schaerdel) C.; m. Kimberly Ann Kerss, Oct. 25, 1986; 1 child, Ashley Pendleton. BBA, U. Tex., 1972; MBA, So. Meth. U., 1978; JD, Oklahoma City U., 1982. Bar: Tex. 1982, US Dist. Ct. (no. dist.) Tex. 1982, US Ct. Appeals (5th cir.) 1982, US Supreme Ct. 1988; cert. in civil trial law Tex. Bd. Legal Specialization; cert. trial specialist Nat. Bd. Trial Advocacy. Ptnr. Eddleman & Clark, Dallas, 1989—. Author: The Evangelical Knights of Saint John, 2003; contbr. articles to profl. jours. Del. state conv. Tex. Rep. Party, 1970, 72, 74, 82, 90; bd. dirs. Haile Selassie Fund for Ethiopian Children in Need; sec., bd. dirs. Dallas Goethe Ctr., Tex. Conf. of Chs. Decorated grand officer Order of Ethiopian Lion, hon. Knight of Justice, Order of Vitez (Hungary), Knight Order of St. John (Brandenburg), Knight Order of Francis I, Knight Portquese Royal Order of St. Michael of the Wing, Knight Montenegro Royal Order Prince Danilo I; recipient Grand Cross, Rwandan Order of the Lion, 2000. Fellow Tex. Bar Found. (life), Soc. Antiquaries (Scotland); mem. State Bar Tex., Am. Bd. Trial Advs. (Dallas chpt.), Oak Cliff Bar Assn. (pres. 1990), Am. Soc. Legal History, Soc. of the Cin., Aztec Club, Sons Republic of Tex., Founders and Patriots Am. (atty. gen.), Nat. Huguenot Soc. (former coun. gen. and 3d v.p. gen.), St. Nicholas Soc., Johanniterorden-Bailiwick of Brandenburg, Johanniter Hilfsgemeinschaften (pres., bd. dirs., Tex.), Army and Navy Club (Washington), City Tavern Club (Washington), Phi Delta Phi, Phi Delta Theta. Episcopalian. Office: 4627 N Central Expy Dallas TX 75205-4022 Office Phone: 214-528-2400. Personal E-mail: rmkkclark@aol.com. Business E-Mail: rmc@robertmclark.net.

CLARK, ROBERT PHILLIPS, editor, consultant; b. Randolph, Vt, Dec. 3, 1921; s. James S. and Gladys M. (Phillips) C.; m. Jeanne Orr Rice, Dec. 14, 1949; children: Patricia Orr Clark Roy, Elizabeth Phillips Clark Christiansen. AB, Tufts U., 1942; MA, U. Mo., 1948. Reporter Owensboro Messenger & Inquirer, Ky., 1948-49; reporter, sci. writer Courier-Jour., Louisville, 1949-62, Washington corr., 1958; mng. editor Louisville Times, 1962-71; exec. editor Courier-Jour. and Louisville Times, 1971-79; editor Fla. Times-Union and Jacksonville Jour., 1979-82; v.p news Harte-Hanks Newspapers, 1983-86; co-chmn. rsch. com. Newspaper Readership Project, 1982-83; news, editorial cons., 1987—. Disting. vis. prof. Baylor U., 1990-92, Slippery Rock U., 1990; mem. accrediting com. Accrediting Coun. on Edn. in Journalism and Mass Comm., 1986-89. Author: Success Stories: What 28 Newspapers Are Doing to Gain and Retain Readers, 1988, Keys to Success: Strategies for Newspaper Marketing in the '90s, 1989; also numerous articles. Bd. dir. Louisville Presbyn. Theol. Sem., 1968-73, past sec.; trustee S.W. Sch. of Art and Craft, 1993-96; bd. dir. San Antonio Bot. Soc., 1996—2004; Pulitzer Prize juror, 1968, 69, 88, 89. Served to capt. US Army, WWII, PTO. Decorated Bronze Star, Purple Heart; Nieman fellow Harvard U., 1960-61; named Editor of Yr., Nat. Press Photographers Assn., 1967. Mem. Am. Soc. Newspaper Editors (pres. 1985-86, v.p. Found. 1980-81, 85-86, contbr. Am. Editor), Soc. Profl. Journalists (contbr. Quill Jour.), AP Mng. Editors Assn. (pres. 1974-75, chmn. regents 1979-80), Internat. Press Inst. (bd. dir. Am. com. 1981-87), Soc. Mayflower Descs. (capt. San Antonio colony 1999-2003, elder 2003—05), Torch Club (San Antonio, pres. 1997-98, contbr. The Torch), Delta Tau Delta. Democrat. Presbyterian. Home: 45 Laurel Lake Dr Hudson OH 44236-2159

CLARK, ROBERT THOMAS, ophthalmologist; b. Detroit, Sept. 21, 1951; s. Robert Charles and Mary Jane Clark; m. Deborah Ann Burcz, June 13, 1975; children: Robert Matthew, Kirstin Sarah. BS, U. Notre Dame, South Bend, Ind., 1973; MD, Wayne State U., Detroit, 1978. Ptnr. Met. Eye Surgeons, Detroit, 1982—84; pres. Clark Eye Ctr., Brighton, 1990—; dir. refractive surgery William Beaumont Hosp., Royal Oak, 1995—2004; chief ophthalmology Huron Valley Hosp., Detroit, 1986—. Fellow: Am. Coll. Surgeons, Am. Acad. Ophthalmology. Office: Clark Eye Ctr 7575 W Grand Ave Brighton MI 48114

CLARK, ROGER EARL, lawyer; b. New Orleans, Oct. 23, 1946; s. Earl B. and Erma Le (Chambers) C.; m. Barbara Jo Columbus, Dec. 23, 1971; 1 dau., Kelly Elizabeth. B.A., Rice U., 1968; J.D., Harvard U., 1971. Bar: Ill. 1971, Colo. 1973. Assoc. Pope, Ballard, Shepard and Fowle, Chgo., 1971-73, Hammond and Chilson, Loveland, Colo., 1973-76; assoc. Lynn A. Hammond Law Offices, Loveland, Colo., 1976-80, ptnr. Hammond, Clark and White, 1980-97, ptnr. Hammond and Clark, 1997, now ptnr. Clark Williams and Matsunaka LLC, Loveland; Bd. dirs. Loveland Econ. Devel. Coun., 1992-94; bd. dirs. Hospice of Larimer County, 1994—, pres. 1997-98; bd. dirs. Rocky Mountain Pub. Broadcasting Sys., Inc., 1999-2005, No. Colo. Econ. Devel. Corp., 2001-05. Mem. ABA, Colo. Bar Assn. (exec. council young lawyers sect. 1977-83, chmn. 1982-83, bd. of govs. 1985-87, 96-98, chmn. gen. practice sect. 1985-87, v.p. 1986-87, pres.-elect 2004, pres. 2005-06), Larimer County Bar Assn. (pres. 1984-85), Colo. Trial Lawyers Assn., Loveland C. of C. (bd. dirs. 1983-89, pres. 1988), Rocky Mt. Pub. Broadcasting Sys., Inc. (bd. dirs. 1999-2005). Democrat. Methodist. Club: Loveland Sertoma (pres. 1980-81). Home: 1220 W 6th St Loveland CO 80537-5347 Office: Clark Williams and Matsunaka LLC Suite 1-2881 N Monroe Ave PO Box 801 Loveland CO 80539*

CLARK, R(UFUS) BRADBURY, lawyer, director; b. Des Moines, May 11, 1924; s. Rufus Bradbury and Gertrude Martha (Burns) C.; m. Polly Ann King, Sept. 6, 1949; children: Cynthia Clark Maxwell, Rufus Bradbury, John Atherton. BA, Harvard U., 1948, JD, 1951; diploma in law, Oxford U., Eng., 1952; D.H.L., Ch. Div. Sch. Pacific, San Francisco, 1983. Bar: Calif. 1952. Assoc. O'Melveny & Myers, LA, 1952-62, sr. ptnr., 1961-93; mem. mgmt. com., 1983-90; of counsel O'Melveny & Myers LLP, LA, 1993—. Bd. dirs. Econ. Resources Corp., BIC Covina Corp., BCS Winter Haven Corp., Avoco Internat. Corp., John Tracy Clinic, also pres. 1982-88, Tracy Family Hearing Ctrs., Ch. Charitable Found. Episcopal Diocese L.A., 2000—. Editor: California Corporation Laws, 7 vols, 1976-2007. Chancellor Protetant Episcopal Ch. in the Diocese of L.A., 1967-2005, chancellor emeritus, hon. canon, 1983—. Capt. U.S. Army, 1943-46. Decorated Bronze Star with oak leaf cluster, Purple Heart with oak leaf cluster; Fulbright grantee, 1952. Mem.: ABA (com. law and acctg., task force on audit letters 1976—93, com. on opinions 1988—92), L.A. County Bar Assn., State Bar Calif. (chmn. drafting com. on gen. corp. law 1973—81, drafting com. on nonprofit corp. law 1980—84, exec. com. bus. law sect. 1977—78, 1984—87, sec. 1986—87, com. nonprofit orgns. 1991—, task force and standing com. on opinions 1999—), Alamitos Bay Yacht Club (Long Beach, Calif.), Chancery Club, Harvard Club. Republican. Office: O'Melveny & Myers LLP 400 S Hope St Los Angeles CA 90071-2899 Office Phone: 213-430-6123. Business E-Mail: bclark@omm.com.

CLARK, SANDRA MARIE, school administrator; b. Hanover, Pa., Feb. 17, 1942; d. Charles Raymond Clark and Mary Josephine (Snyder) Clark Wierman. BS in Elem. Edn., Chestnut Hill Coll., Phila., 1980; MS in Child Care Adminstrn., Nova U., Pa., 1985; MS in Ednl. Adminstrn., Western Md. Coll., Westminster, 1992. Cert. elem. tchr., elem. prin., Pa. Tchr. various elem. schs., Pa., 1962-75; asst. vocation directress Mt. St. Joseph Motherhouse, Chestnut Hill, Pa., 1975-76; tchr. St. Catharine's Sch., Spring Lake, NJ, 1976-77; asst. mgr. Jim's Truck Stop, New Oxford, Pa., 1977-81; adminstr. Little People Day Care Sch., Hanover, Pa., 1981-88, sec., treas. bd. dirs., 1985-86; coord. regional resource Magic Yrs. Child Care & Learning Ctrs., Inc., Hanover, 1987-88; prin. St. Vincent de Paul Sch., Hanover, 1988—. Presenter Hanover Area Seminar for Day Care Employees, 1983-86. Coord. sch. safety patrols St. Vincent's Sch., Hanover, 1969-75, vice-chmn. bd., 1982-84; multi-media instr. first aid ARC, Hanover, 1983-86, bd. dirs., 1984-88; exec. sec. of bd. of dirs. ARC, Hanover, 1988; 1st v.p. Hanover Area Coun. of Chs., 1988, pres., 1989; validator accredidation program Nat. Acad. Early Childhood Programs, Washington, 1987—; bd. dirs. Life Skills Unltd. Handicapped Adults, 1988—; facilitator Harrisburg Diocesan Synod, Hanover, 1985-88, parish del., 1988. Tng. grant, Pa. Dept. Pub. Welfare, 1986. Mem. NAFE, Nat. Cath. Ednl. Assn. Clubs: Internat. Assn. Turtles (London). Democrat. Roman Catholic. Avocations: swimming, reading, writing children's stories. Home: 348 Barberry Dr Hanover PA 17331-1302 Office: St Vincent De Paul Sch Hanover PA 17331 Office Phone: 717-637-5190. Personal E-mail: smclark@netrax.net.

CLARK, SHARON JACKSON, private school administrator; b. Istanbul, Turkey, Feb. 3, 1939; d. John Warren and Maxine Jett (Brient) Jackson; m. Ronald Eugene Clark, June 6, 1959 (dec.); children: Kristen Anne, Kevin Brooks, Jeffrey Kimball. BFA, Calif. Coll. Arts and Crafts, 1968; MS in Edn., Wheelock Coll., 1978; student, Moore Coll. Art. Co-founder Jowanio, Syracuse, NY, The Thoreau Sch., Salt Lake City, Glen Urquhart Sch., Beverly, Mass.; head, founder Clark Sch. for Creative Learning, Danvers, Mass. Mem. Gifted/Talented Educators North Shore (bd. dir.), Danvers Hist. Soc. (bd. dir.). Home: 502 Locust St Danvers MA 01923-1252 Office Phone: 978-777-4699. Business E-Mail: sharon@clarkschool.com.

CLARK, SHAUN C., lawyer; BBA, U. Tex., Arlington, 1992; JD, Loyola Marymount U., 1996. Bar: Calif. 1996, admitted to practice: US Dist. Ct. (Ctrl. Dist.) Calif. Fin. assoc. Buchalter Nemer Fields & Younger, LA; with Hill Wynne Troop & Meisinger, 1999; assoc. Katten Muchin Zavis Rosenman, ptnr., 2001—03; ptnr., Entertainment and Media Practice Group Sheppard, Mullin, Richter & Hampton LLP, Century City, Calif., 2003—. Named one of Top 35 Entertainment Exec. 35 yrs. old and under, Hollywood Reporter, 2004, Top 20 Lawyers under 40 in Calif., Daily Jour. Extra, 2005. Office: Sheppard Mullin Richter & Hampton 16th Floor 1901 Avenue of the Stars Century City CA 90067 Office Phone: 310-228-3707. Office Fax: 310-228-3907. E-mail: sclark@sheppardmullin.com.

CLARK, SHAWN L., psychologist, educator; b. Jackson, Miss., Aug. 23, 1971; d. Lawrence Hodges and Phoebe Jean Clark. BA, Purdue U., West Lafayette, Ind., 1992; MA, U. Miss., Oxford, 1999, PhD, 2003. Psychologist lic. Ga. State Bd. Examiners Psychology, 2004, Ark. Bd. Psychology, 2005. Postdoctoral fellow Emory U. Sch. Medicine, Grady Health Sys., Atlanta, 2003—04; instr. U. Ark. Med. Scis., Little Rock, 2004—06; program dir., clin. psychologist Ark. State Hosp., Little Rock, 2004—06. Dir. psychology predoctoral internship tng. Ark. Divsn. Behavioral Health Svcs., Little Rock, 2005—06, mem. cultural competency quality improvement com., 2005—06, mem. Ark. mental health rsch. and tng. inst., 2005—06, mem. Ark. mental health rsch. and tng. inst. smoking cessation com., 2005; staff psychologist Ctrl. Ala. Vets. Health Care Sys., Tuskagee, 2006—, mem.-at-large distruptive behavior com., 2007—. Mem.-at-large Task Force for the Homeless, Atlanta, 2004; facilitator Partners in Outreach Coalition, Little Rock, 2004. Mem.: APA. Avocations: cooking, singing, reading, travel. Office: 2400 Hosp Rd 123 Tuskegee AL 36083 Home Phone: 501-821-7731; Office Phone: 501-686-9821, 334-727-0550 5217. Office Fax: 501-686-9550. Business E-Mail: sclark@uams.edu.

CLARK, STEPHEN ROBERT, lawyer; b. Chgo., July 1, 1966; m. Laura Sliney. BA, U. Notre Dame, 1988; JD, St. Louis U., 1991. Bar: Mo. 1991, Ill. 1992, US Dist. Ct. (ea. dist.) Mo. 1991, US Dist. Ct. (cen. dist.) Ill. 1993, US Claims Ct. 1993, US Dist. Ct. (ea. dist.) Wis., 1998, US Dist. Ct. (we. dist.) Mo, 1999, US Dist. Ct. (so. dist.) Ill., 2003, US Dist. Ct. (no. dist.) Ill., 2003, US Dist. Ct. (so. dist.) Ind., 2004, US Dist. Ct. (dist. Kans.), 2005, US Ct. Appeals (8th cir.), 2003, US Ct. Appeals (5th cir.), 2003, US Ct. Appeals (10th cir.), 2004. Assoc. Greensfelder, Hemker & Gale, P.C., St. Louis, 1991—98, officer, 1998—99; ptnr. Polsinelli Shalton Welte Suelthaus PC, St. Louis, 1999—2006, Blackwell Sanders Peper Martin LLP, St. Louis, 2007—. Co-author: Death Penalty Resource Book of the US Ct. of Appeals for the 8th Circuit, 1991. Mem., econ. devel. campaign St. Louis Regional Chamber and Growth Assn.; pres., father's club Villa Duchesne/Oak Hill Sch. Devel. Com., 2005—06; mem., devel. bd. St. Patrick Ctr., 1992—97; mem., parish coun. Ch. of Annunziata, 2003—, chair, fin. com., 2005—; mem., adv. bd. Entrepreneurship Inst.; vol., lawyers prog. Legal Services Eastern Mo. Mem. ABA, Bar Assn. Met. St. Louis, Ill. State Bar Assn., Mo. Bar Assn., Psi Chi. Office: Blackwell Sanders Peper Martin LLP 720 Olive St Ste 2400 Saint Louis MO 63101 Office Phone: 314-345-6482. Office Fax: 314-345-6060.

CLARK, SUSAN (NORA GOULDING), actress; b. Sarnia, Ont., Can., Mar. 8, 1940; d. George Raymond and Eleanor Almond (McNaughton) Clark; m. Alex Karras; 1 child, Katie Karras. Student, Toronto Children's Players, Ont., 1956-59; student (Acad. scholar), Royal Acad. Dramatic Art, London. Ptnr. Georgian Bay Prodns. Actor: (stage prodn.) Appearances to the Contrary, 2000, Glass Menagerie, 2002, Sisters Rosensweig, 2002, BiCoastal Woman, 2003, Dancing at Lughnasa, 2003, Importance of Being Earnest, 2004, The Body, 2004, Triptych, 2006, (theatre) Retreat From Moscow, 2006; (TV series) Webster, 1983, Emily of New Moon, 1998; (films) Nobody's Perfekt, 1981, Porky's, 1981, Butterbox Babies, 1995; (TV films) Babe, 1975 (Emmy for oustanding lead actress in a drama, 1975), Sherlock Holmes: The Strange Case of Alice Faulkner, 1981, The Choice, 1981, Maid in America, 1982, Tonya & Nancy: The Inside Story, 1994, Snowbound: The Jim and Jennifer Stolpa Story, 1994. Mem. ACLU, Am. Film Inst. Office: Ste 308 13400 Riverside Dr Sherman Oaks CA 91423-2541

CLARK, SUZANNE, accountant; b. San Bernadino, Calif., Sept. 10, 1948; d. Richard Grant and Dorothy Jean Clark; children: Chelsea A. Clark-James, Graeme W. Clark-James. BS in Mktg. and Acctg., U. Colo., 1970, M in Urban Affairs, 1978. CPA 1983, cert. personal fin. specialist, 1995. Dir. adminstrv. svcs. Suburban Cmty. Tng. & Svc. Ctr., Englewood, 1973-78; staff adminstr. Solar Energy Rsch. Inst., Golden, Colo., 1979-80; rschr. Cmty. Coll. Denver, 1980-81; staff acct. R.E. Weise & Co., CPAs, Denver, 1982-83; owner Suzanne Clark, CPA, P.C., Denver, 1983—. Author: Providing Personal Financial Planning Services in Your CPA Practice, 1987, Providing Fiduciary Accounting and Tax Services, 1990, The Personal Financial Planning Process An Introduction, 1993, Personal Financial Planning in Crisis Situations, 1993, Estates and Trusts: A Guide to Fiduciary Advisors, 1996, Individual Tax Update, 1999-2004. Bd. dirs. Children's Ctr., Denver, 1982-84, Hospice of Peace, Denver, 1987-88. Mem. AICPA (personal fin. specialist edn. subcom. 1988-93), Colo. Soc. CPAs (specialization oversight bd. 1984-87, pers. fin. planning com. 1987-88, comms. com. 1994-97, bd. dirs. 1997-99, mem. fin. literacy task force 2005—). Office: Suzanne Clark CPA PC 495 Uinta Way # 100 Denver CO 80230 Home Phone: 303-363-1541; Office Phone: 303-364-2205. Personal E-mail: sclark2240@aol.com.

CLARK, SYLVIA DOLORES, business educator; b. NYC, June 5, 1959; d. Barna and Eva Anna (Beniczky-Gabriel) Csuros. BBA, Bernard Baruch Coll. CUNY, 1979, MPhil, 1993, PhD, 1994; MBA, NYU, 1982. Rsch. analyst Kornhauser and Calene and predecessor firm, NYC, 1979-80; project coord. Gen. Foods, Inc., White Plains, N.Y., 1980-82; rsch. assoc. Lord, Geller, Federico, Einstein, Inc., NYC, 1982-83; instr. Coll. of S.I. CUNY, 1984-93, asst. prof., 1994-97; instr. Wagner Coll., SI, 1993-94; asst. prof. Queensborough C.C. CUNY, 1997-98, St. John's U., Jamaica, NY, 1998—2004, assoc. prof., 2004—. Becker Family Fund scholar, 1978, Baruch Coll. Alumni Assn. scholar, 1979. Mem.: Am. Statis. Assn., Am. Mktg. Assn., Phi Beta Kappa, Beta Gamma Sigma (past exec. bd.). Home: 62 Renwick Ave Staten Island NY 10301-4216 Office: St John's U Spellman Hall TCB 300 Howard Ave Staten Island NY 10301-4496 Office Phone: 718-390-4552. E-mail: clark1094@aol.com.

CLARK, THOMAS B., SR., real estate broker; b. Ann Arbor, Mich., Jan. 21, 1943; s. Thomas W. and Helen (Sheldon) Clark; m. Dianne Stribley, Dec. 4, 1970; children: Thomas B. Jr., Andrea Lynn. BA, U. Mich., 1964. Dir. rec. U. Mich., Ann Arbor, 1965-70; sr. auditor Touche Ross (now Deloitte and Touche), Detroit, 1970-72; acctg. mgr. E.R.I.M., Ann Arbor, 1972-75; owner/developer Clark Apts., Ann Arbor, 1975—; owner Irish Hills Golf Club and Banquet Ctr., Onsted, Mich. Bd. dirs. Kenitis Corp. Mem.: Ann Arbor Apt. Assn. (bd. dirs.). Avocation: golf. Address: PO Box 7822 Ann Arbor MI 48107-7822 Office: 621 S Forest Ave Ann Arbor MI 48104-3123 Office Phone: 734-996-2836. Personal E-mail: tcapts@aol.com.

CLARK, THOMAS CARLYLE, retired banker; b. Barbourville, Ky., Dec. 1, 1947; s. Buford Thomas and Eleanor Randolph (Owens) C. AB, Duke U., 1969; MBA, Harvard U., 1971; LLD, Cumberland Coll., 1991, Union Coll., 2004. Officer Chem. Bank, NYC, 1975-78; divsn. pres., mng. dir. U.S. Trust Co. N.Y., NYC, 1978—2005. Pres. emeritus bd. dirs. Lubovitch Dance Co.; chmn. emeritus bd. trustees Union Coll., Ky.; trustee Duke U.; bd. dirs. Concert Artists Guild, past pres.; bd. dirs., treas. Svc. Mems. Legal Def. Network. With USN, 1971—75. Mem.: Am. Banking Assn. (past chair exec. com. for pvt. banking, alumni coun.), Lincoln's Inn Soc., Risk Mgmt. Assn. (past chmn. pvt. lending com.), Duke U. Alumni Assn. (bd. dirs., pres.), Met. Opera Club (past bd. dirs.), Kentuckians NY Club, Duke Club NY (past pres.). Republican. Methodist.

CLARK, THOMAS P., JR., lawyer; b. NYC, Sept. 16, 1943; AB, U. Notre Dame, 1965; JD, U. Mo., Kansas City, 1973. Bar: Calif. 1973. Shareholder Stradling, Yocca, Carlson & Rauth P.C., Newport Beach, Calif., 1978—. Editor-in-chief The Urban Lawyer, 1972-73; contbr. articles to profl. jours. Capt. USMC, 1966-70. Mem. State Bar Calif., Orange County Bar Assn., Phi Kappa Phi. Office: Stradling Yocca Carlson & Rauth PC 660 Newport Center Dr Ste 1600 Newport Beach CA 92660-6458 Business E-Mail: tclark@sycr.com.

CLARK, VICTORIA, actress; b. Dallas, Oct. 10, 1959; 1 child. B in Music, Yale Univ. Actor: (Broadway plays) Sunday in the Park With George, 1985, Guys and Dolls, 1992—93, A Grand Night for Singing, 1993—94, Titanic, 1997—99, Cabaret, 1999—2000, Urinetown, 2003, Bye Bye Birdie, 2004, The Light in the Piazza, 2005 (Tony award for best performance by a leading actress in a musical, 2005, Drama Desk award, outstanding actress in a musical, 2005, Outer Critics Circle award, outstanding actress in a musical, 2005, Joseph Jefferson award, 2005), (off Broadway) The Agony and the Agony, 2006; (films) Cradle Will Rock, 1999; (TV series) Law and Order, 1998, Law and Order: SVU, 2003, (TV spl.) Sweeney Todd: The Demon Barber of Fleet Street in Concert, 2002; dir.: (numerous operas); tchr. (voice). Mailing: c/o Vivian Beaumont Theatre Lincoln Ctr 150 W 65th St New York NY 10003*

CLARK, WENDY, advertising executive; b. England; m. Jeff Clark; 3 children. BA in English, Creative Writing, Fla. State U. Multiple field & corp. positions in mktg. & advt. BellSouth Mobility; sr. v.p., dir. client services GSD&M, Austin; sr. exec. v.p., advt. AT&T Inc., San Antonio, 2004—. Named a Woman to Watch, Advt. Age, 2007. Office: AT&T Inc 175 E Houston St San Antonio TX 78205 Office Phone: 210-223-7168.

CLARK, WESLEY KANNE, emergency management executive, educator, retired military officer; b. Little Rock, Dec. 23, 1944; m. Gertrude Kingston, 1966; 1 child, Wesley. Grad., U.S. Mil. Acad., West Point, 1966; BA, MA in philosophy, politics, and econ., Oxford U., 1968; grad., Nat. War Coll., Command and Gen. Staff Coll., Armor Officer Adv. and Basic Courses, Ranger and Airbourne Sch.; D Pub. Svc. (hon.), Drake Univ., 2002; DHL (hon.), Seton Hall Univ., 2002; LLD (hon.), Univ. Ark., 2002, Ripon Coll., 2005, Lyon Coll., 2005. Advanced through ranks to gen. US Army, 1997, ret., 2000; fellow White House, 1975—76; spl. asst. to dir., Office Mgmt. & Budget Exec. Office of the Pres., 1975—76; instr. to asst. prof. social sci. U.S. Mil. Acad.; comdr. 1st Battalion, 77th Armor, 4th Infantry Divsn. US Army, 1980—82; chief plans integration divsn. Office Deputy Chief of Staff Oper. and Plans, US Army, Washington, D.C., 1983; chief army's study group Office Chief of Staff of Army, Washington, D.C., 1983—84; comdr. oper. group US Army, 1984—86, comdr. 3rd Brigade, 4th Infantry Divsn., 1986—88, comdr. Nat. Tng. Ctr., 1989—91; deputy chief staff for concepts, doctrine, and developments US Army Tng. and Doctrine Command, Fort Monroe, Va., 1991—92; comdr. 1st Cavalry Divsn. US Army, Fort Hood, Tex., 1992—94, dir. strategic plans and policy, JR, the Joint Staff, 1994—96; comdr. US So. Command (USSOUTHCOM), Panama, 1996—97, US European Command (USEUCOM), Brussels, 1997—2000; supreme allied comdr. NATO, Europe (SACEUR), Brussels, 1997—2000; mng. dir. merchant banking Stephens Group Inc., Little Rock, 2000—03; chmn., CEO Wesley K. Clark & Associates, LLC, Little Rock; vice chair & sr. advisor James Lee Witt Assoc., LLC, Washington, 2004—; chmn. bd., head adv. bd. Rodman & Renshaw LLC, NYC, 2006—. Military analyst CNN, 2001—03; sr. fellow, lectr. Ronald W. Burkle Ctr. for Internat. Rels., UCLA, 2006—. Author: Waging Modern War: Bosnia, Kosovo and the Future of Combat, 2001, Winning Modern Wars: Iraq, Terrorism and the American Empire, 2003; co-author (with Tom Carhart): Time to Lead: For Duty, Honor and Country, 2007. Decorated Defense Disting. Svc. Medal (three awards), DSM, Silver Star, Legion Merit (four awards), Bronze Star Medal (two awards), Purple Heart, Meritorious Svc. Medal (two awards), Army Commendation Medal (two awards); named hon. Knight Comdr. OBE, United Kingdom, Comdr. Legion of Honor, France; recipient Presidl. Medal of Freedom, 2000, Knight Grand Cross, Order of Orange-Nassau, Netherlands; Rhodes scholar, Oxford U., 1966—68. Achievements include candidate for Dem. presdl. nomination, 2004; led mil. negotiations for the Bosnian Peace Accords at Dayton; commanded three companies to combat in Vietnam. Office Phone: 202-585-0780. Business E-Mail: wclark@wittassociates.com.*

CLARK, WESLEY M., manufacturing executive; b. 1952; BA magna cum laude in Philosophy, U. Calif., LA, Calif., 1974; MBA, Stanford U. With Cummins Engine Co.; mem. sr. mgmt. team Granite Rock, 1984—91; from mgr. to pres., COO W.W. Grainger, Inc., Lake Forest, Ill., 1992—2001, pres., 2001—04, COO, 2001—04. Bd. dir. W.W. Grainger, Inc. Bd. dir. Mex. Fine Arts Ctr. Mus.; bd. trustees The Lincoln Found. Bus. Excellence, Am. Second Harvest Nat. Food Bank Network, Preserve to Enjoy. Mem.: Econ. Club Chgo., Exec.'s Club Chgo.

CLARK, WILLIAM, JR., diplomat; b. Oakland, Calif., Oct. 12, 1930; s. William and Mary Edith (Coady) C.; m. Judith Lee Riley, Sept. 11, 1954; 1 child, Jared Riley. BA, San Jose State U., 1955; postgrad., Columbia U., 1967—68; diploma with distinction, Nat. War Coll., 1977; LittD (hon.), Calif. State U., 1992. Dir. liaison dept. U.S. Civil Adminstrn., Naha, Japan, 1970-72; U.S.-Japan Trade Officer Am. Embassy, Tokyo, 1972-74, minister, 1981-85, polit. counselor Seoul, Republic of Korea, 1977-80, minister Cairo, 1985-86, charge d'affaires, 1986; dir. spl. trade activities US Dept. State, Washington, 1974-76, dir. Japanese Affairs, 1980-81, dep. asst. sec., 1986-89, US amb. to India New Delhi, 1989-92, asst. sec. for E. Asian and Pacific affairs Washington, 1992-93; Japan chair, sr. advisor Ctr. for Strategic and Internat. Studies, Washington, 1993-95; pres. Japan Soc., NYC, 1996—2003, Chmn. Japan Am. Student Conf., 2003—05. Lt. (j.g.) USN, 1950-53. Recipient Superior Svc. award Dept. Army, 1971, Outstanding Svc. award Dept. Army, 1972, Disting. Svc. award Pres. U.S., 1985, Meritorious Svc. award Pres. U.S., 1987, 89, Disting. Honor award Dept. State, 1989, Charles E. Cobb award Dept. State, 1991, Disting. lectr. Fgn. Svc. Inst., 1995, Order of the Sacred Treasure, Gold and Silver Star, Emperor of Japan, 2000. Mem.: Coun. Fgn. Rels., Am. Japan Soc. (bd. dirs. 1981—85), Japan Am. Soc. (bd. dirs. 1994—2000), Asia Soc. (bd. adv.), Am. Fgn. Svc. Assn., Am. C. of C. (hon. mem. Tokyo 1981—85, Cairo 1985—86), COSMOS Club (Washington), Gizira Club (Cairo), Chevy Chase Club (Washington), Pres.'s Estate Polo Club (New Delhi), Tokyo Am. Club. Episcopalian. Avocations: tennis, riding, skiing, golf. Office Phone: 202-298-7160. Business E-Mail: jlnwclark@aol.com.

CLARK, WILLIAM ARTHUR V., geographer; b. Christchurch, N.Z., Mar. 21, 1938; arrived in U.S., 1961; s. Edward Arthur and Gertrude Rita (MacDonald) C.; m. Valmai Ruth Kirkham, July 1, 1961 (div. Oct. 1971); m. Irene Stephanee Borah, Mar. 25, 1978; children: Elisa, Louisa, Clifton, Justin. BA, U. N.Z., 1960; MA, U. Canterbury, New Zealand, 1961; PhD, U. Ill., 1964; Doctorem Honoris Causa, U. Utrecht, The Netherlands, 1992; DSc, U. Auckland, New Zealand, 1994. Lectr. U. Canterbury, 1964-66; asst./assoc. prof. U. Wis., Madison, 1966-70; prof. geography UCLA, 1970—, chmn. dept. geography, 1987-92, 95-97, assoc. dir. Inst. Social Sci. Rsch., 1984-87. Vis. prof. U. Amsterdam, 1981; Belle Van Zuylen prof. U. Utrecht, 1989; cons. state atty. gens. Mo., Calif., Wis., Minn. Author: Human Migration, 1986, Households and Housing, 1996, The California Cauldron: Immigration and the Fortunes of Local Communities, 1998, Immigrants and the American Dream: Remaking the Middle Class, 2003; author/editor: Residential Mobility and Public Policy, 1980, Rediscovering Geography: New Relevance for Science and Society, 1997. Recipient Decade of Behavior Rsch. award Nat. Adv Com. Decade of Behavior, 2005, 2006, Alumni Achievement award U. Ill.; fellow-in-residence Netherlands Inst. Advanced Studies, The Hague, 1993, Guggenheim fellow, 1994-95. Fellow Royal Soc. New Zealand (elected hon. 1997), Am. Acad. Arts and Scis.; mem. Assn. Am. Geographers (Honors award 1986), NAS, Population Assn. Am. Anglican Ch. Achievements include research in district and appellate court rulings on demographic change and school desegregation. Office Phone: 310-825-5856. Business E-Mail: wclark@geog.ucla.edu.

CLARK, WILLIAM H., JR., lawyer; b. Phila., Apr. 10, 1951; s. William H. and Alice Kimes (Metts) C.; m. Cristine D. Merkel, Aug. 18, 1973; children: Matthew, Alison, Daniel. BA summa cum laude, Amherst Coll., Mass., 1973; MA in Religion, Westminster Sem., Chestnut Hill, Pa., 1979; JD magna cum laude, Temple U., Phila., 1983. Bar: Pa. 1983. Assoc. Morgan, Lewis & Bockius, Phila., 1983-89; ptnr. Klett Lieber Rooney & Schorling, Pitts., 1989-98, Phila., 1998-99; ptnr., bus. fin. dept. Drinker Biddle & Reath LLP, Phila., 1999—. Chmn. corp. bur. adv. com. Pa. Dept of State, 1991—; cons. rules disciplinary bd. Supreme Ct. Pa., Harrisburg, 1983—; Pa. commr. Nat. Conf. Commrs. on Uniform State Laws, 2006—. Fellow Am. Bar Found.; mem. ABA (com. on corp. laws), Am. Law Inst., Pa. Bar Assn. (draftsman, lobbyist, corp. law com. 1984—, coun. sect. corp. banking and bus. law 1989-93, officer 1993-2001), Allegheny County Bar Assn. (coun. sect. corp. banking and bus. law 1991-97, officer 1997-98), Phila. Bar Assn. (coun. bus. law sect. 1998-2003, officer 2004—), Phi Beta Kappa. Republican. Presbyterian. Office: Drinker Biddle & Reath LLP One Logan Sq 18th & Cherry Sts Philadelphia PA 19103-6996 Office Phone: 215-988-2804. Office Fax: 267-402-4629. Business E-Mail: william.clark@dbr.com.

CLARK, WILLIAM HARTLEY, political science professor; b. Pitts., Apr. 29, 1930; s. Arthur Tillotson and Ruthanna Frame (Anderson) C.; m. Barbara Jean Rockne, June 27, 1953; children— Heather Anderson, Jill Eleanor, Robert Hartley, Edward Kirtland. BA, Carleton Coll., 1952; MA, N.Y. U., 1955, PhD, 1960. Researcher for Carnegie Endowment for Internat. Peace, Brookings Instn., N.Y. U., 1953-54; instr. polit. sci. Western Coll., Oxford, Ohio, 1954-55; instr. internat. relations Carleton Coll., 1955-60, asst. prof., 1960-66, assoc. prof., 1966-70, prof., 1970-92, prof. emeritus, 1992—, chmn. dept. polit. sci., 1972-76, Frank B. Kellogg prof. internat. rels., 1973-92. Lectr. U. Minn., 1970; dir. Geneva Seminar on Internat. Instns., 1975-91; pres. Clark Assocs., 1992—. Author: The Politics of the Common Market, 1967; contbr. articles and revs. to profl. publs. Fulbright research fellow, 1961-62; Ford Found. research fellow, 1967; NSF research fellow, 1970, 71, 79; von Humbolt-Stiftung fellow, 1961. Mem. Coun. Fgn. Rels. (St. Paul-Mpls. com. fgn. rels.), UN Assn. Home: 216 Nevada St Northfield MN 55057-2343 Personal E-mail: clark@carleton.edu.

CLARK, WILLIAM NORTHINGTON, lawyer, retired military officer; b. Meridian, Miss., Jan. 16, 1941; s. Oliver Watson and Mildred Catherine (Northington) C.; m. Faye Virginia Baker, Feb. 1, 1964; children: Helen Catherine Smith, William Northington Jr. BS, U.S. Mil. Acad., 1963; JD, U. Ala., 1971. Bar: Ala. 1971, U.S. Ct. Appeals (5th and 11th cirs.), U.S. Supreme Ct. Law clk. to Judge Walter P. Gewin U.S. Ct. Appeals (5th cir.), 1971—72; assoc. Rogers Howard Redden & Mills, Birmingham, Ala., 1972-74, ptnr., 1974-79, Redden Mills & Clark, Birmingham, 1979—. Adj. prof. evidence U. Ala. Sch. Law, 1979, adj. prof. criminal procedure, 2000, adj. prof. bus. fraud, 01; mem. Ala. Supreme Ct. Advisory Com. on Criminal Procedure, 1979—94. Bd. dirs. Boys and Girls Club of Cen. Ala., Birmingham, 1987—, Metro YMCA of Birmingham, 1989—, chmn., 1992-94. Capt. US Army, 1963—68, Vietnam, ret. maj. gen. AUS. Mem. Ala. State Bar Assn. (chmn. com. on indigent defense 1975-81, chmn. Fed. judiciary liaison com. 1983-85, pres.-elect 2002-03, pres. 2003-04) Birmingham Bar Assn. (sec., treas. 1987-88, pres.-elect 1992, pres. 1993), Ala. Law Inst. (chmn. children's code com. 1986-93), Nat. Assn. Criminal Def. Lawyers. Methodist. Office: Redden Mills & Clark 940 Financial Ctr 50520th St N Birmingham AL 35203-3288 Home Phone: 205-870-7050; Office Phone: 205-322-0457. Business E-Mail: wmc@rmclaw.com.

CLARK-BOURNE, KATHRYN ORPHA, retired consul; b. Ft. Collins, Colo., Oct. 15, 1924; d. Andrew Giles and Orpha Mae (Spielman) Clark; m. Kenneth Barnes Bourne, Jr. (div.). BA cum laude, U. Wash., 1947; MA, U. Minn., 1951; postgrad., George Wash. U., 1951—52. Draftsman Boeing Aircraft Co., Seattle, 1942—44; editor West Seattle Herald, 1947; intelligence analyst Dept. of Army, Tokyo, 1947—49; bookkeeper Panama Canal Co., Wash., 1951—52; editor, intelligence rsch. specialist Dept. State, Wash., 1952—56; polit. asst. U.S. Embassy, Teheran, Iran, 1956—58; consulate officer U.S. Consul Gen., Rotterdam, Netherlands, 1959—61, consulate & polit. officer Bombay, 1962—67; supr. comm. Coopers & Lybrand, NYC, 1969—74; comm. cons. George R. Block Actuaries, NYC, 1974—75; dep. dir. Office of Fisheries Affairs Dept. State, Wash., 1975—77; counselor for polit. affairs Am. Embassy, Lagos, Nigeria, 1977—80; dep. dir. Office of West Africa Dept. State, Wash., 1980—82; dep. chief of mission Am. Embassy, Conakey, Guinea, 1982—85; consulate officer Consul Gen., Douala, Cameroon, 1985—87; insp. Office Insp. Gen. Dept. State, Wash., 1988—89, sr. insp. Office Insp. Gen., 1990—93, hist. declassification Newington, Va., 1993—2007, ret., 2007. Lectr. Nat. War Coll., Georgetown U., Emory U.; alternate del. Conf. on Least-Developed Countries in Hague; chair North Pacific SEAL Negotiations with Can., Japan and U.S.S.R. Recipient Meritorious Honor award, Dept. of State, 1995. Mem.: World Affairs Coun., Am. Fgn. Svc. Assn. (bd. mem. 1993—97), Asia Soc., Diplomatic Consular Officers, Ret. (bd. mem. 2000—04). Home: 2230 Calif St NW Apt 6BE Washington DC 20008

CLARKE, SIR ARTHUR CHARLES, author; b. Minehead, Somerset, Eng., Dec. 16, 1917; s. Charles Wright and Norah (Willis) C.; m. Marilyn Mayfield, June 15, 1953 (div. 1964). B.Sc. in Physics and Math. with 1st class honors, King's Coll., London, 1948; D.Sc. (hon.), Beaver Coll., 1971, U. Moratuwa, 1979; D.Litt. (hon.), U. Bath, Eng., 1988, U. Liverpool, 1995, U. Hong Kong, Beijing, 1996. Auditor British Civil Service, His Majesty's Exchequer and Audit Dept., London, 1936-41; asst. editor Science Abstracts Inst. of Elec. Engineers, London, 1949-50; lectr., author, 1951—; chancellor U. Moratuwa, Sri Lanka, 1979—2002; Vikram Sarabhai prof. Phys. Rsch. Lab., Ahmedabad, India, 1980. Underwater explorer, photographer Great Barrier Reef of Australia and coast of Ceylon, 1954-64; commentator with Walter Cronkite Apollo missions, 1968-70; dir. Rocket Pub. Co., Underwater Safaris, Sri Lanka; founder Arthur C. Clarke Centre for Modern Technologies, Sri Lanka, 1984—; trustee Inst. Integral Edn.; fellow Franklin Inst., 1971, King's Coll., 1977, Inst. of Robotics, Carnegie-Mellon U., 1981; lectr. U.S. and Britain, 1957-74; bd. dirs. Nat. Space Soc., Space Generation Found., Internat. Astronomical Union, Planetary Soc., Rocket Pub. Co., Eng., Underwater Safaris, Sri Lanka; chmn. Second Internat. Astronautics Congress, London, 1951; moderator "Space Flight Report to the Nation", N.Y., 1961; fgn. assoc. Nat. Acad. Engring. (U.S.); mem. adv. coun. Internat. Sci. Policy Found., Fauna Internat., Sri Lanka, Earth Trust. Author: (non-fiction) Interplanetary Flight, 1950, The Exploration of Space, 1951 (Internat. Fantasy award 1952), The Young Traveller in Space, 1953 (pub. as Going Into Space, 1954), (with R.A. Smith) The Exploration of the Moon, 1955, The Coast of Coral, 1956, The Making of a Moon, 1957, The Reefs of Taprobane, 1957, The Scottie Book of Space Travel, 1957, (with Mike Wilson) Boy Beneath the Sea, 1958, Voice Across the Sea, 1958, The Challenge of the Spaceship, 1959, The Challenge of the Sea, 1960; (with Wilson) The First Five Fathoms, 1960, Indian Ocean Adventure, 1961, Profiles of the Future, 1962, The Treasure of the Great Reef, 1964, Indian Ocean Treasure, 1964; (with editors of Life mag.) Man and Space, 1964, Voices from the Sky, 1965, The Promise of Space, 1968; (with astronauts) First on the Moon, 1970, Report on Planet Three, 1972; (with Chesley Bonestell) Beyond Jupiter, 1972, The View from Serendip, 1977; (with Simon Welfare and John Fairley) Arthur C. Clarke's Mysterious World, 1980, Ascent to Orbit, 1984, 1984: Spring-A Choice of Futures, 1984, (with Welfare and Fairley) Arthur C. Clarke's World of Strange Powers, 1984, (with Peter Hyams) The Odyssey File, 1985, Arthur C. Clarke's July 20, 2019: Life in the 21st Century, 1986, Arthur C. Clarke's Chronicles of the Strange and Mysterious, 1987, Astounding Days, 1989, Opus 700, 1990, How the World Was One, 1992, (with Welfare and Fairley) Arthur C. Clarke's A-Z of Mysteries, 1993, By Space Possessed, 1993, The Snows of Olympus, 1994, Front Line of Discovery: Science on the Brink of Tomorrow, 1994, Greetings, Carbon-based Bipeds, 1999; (fiction) The Sands of Mars, 1951, Prelude to Space, 1951, Islands in the Sky, 1952, Against the Fall of Night, 1953, Childhood's End, 1953, Expedition to Earth, 1953, Earthlight, 1955, Reach For Tomorrow, 1956, The City and the Stars, 1956, Tales from the White Hart, 1957, The Deep Range, 1957, The Other Side of the Sky, 1958, Across the Sea of Stars, 1959, A Fall of Moondust, 1961, From the Oceans, from the Stars, 1962, Tales of Ten Worlds, 1962, Dolphin Island, 1963, Glide Path, 1963, Prelude to Mars, 1965, The Nine Billion Names of God, 1967, (with Stanley Kubrick) 2001: A Space Odyssey, 1968, The Lion of Comarre and Against the Fall of Night, 1968, The Wind from the Sun, 1972, Of Time and Stars, 1972, The Lost Worlds of 2001, 1972, Rendezvous with Rama, 1973 (Nebula award Sci. Fiction Writers Am. 1973, Hugo award World Sci. Fiction Conv. 1974, John W. Campbell Meml. award Sci. Fiction Rsch. Assn. 1974, Jupiter award Instructors of Sci. Fiction in Higher Edn. 1974), The Best of Arthur C. Clarke, 1973, Imperial Earth, 1975, The Fountains of Paradise, 1979 (Nebula award Sci. Fiction Writers Am. 1980, Hugo award World Sci. Fiction Conv. 1980), 2010: Odyssey Two, 1982, The Sentinel, 1983, Selected Works, 1985, The Songs of Distant Earth, 1986, 2061: Odyssey Three, 1988, (with Gentry Lee) Cradle, 1988, A Meeting with Medusa, 1988, (with Lee) Rama II, 1989, Tales from Planet Earth, 1989, (with Gregory Benford) Beyond the Fall of Night, 1990, Ghost from the Grand Banks, 1990, (with Lee) Garden of Rama, 1991, More Than One Universe, 1991, The Hammer of God, 1993, (with Lee) Rama Revealed: The Ultimate Encounter, 1994, (with Mike McQuay) Richter 10, 1996, 3001: The Final Odyssey, 1997, (with Mike-Kube-McDowell) Trigger, 1999, (with Stephen Baxter) The Light of Other Days, 2000, (with Stephen Baxter) Time's Eye, 2004, (with Stephen Baxter) Sunstorm, 2005; screenwriter: (films) (with Stanley Kubrick) 2001: A Space Odyssey, 1968 (Academy award nomination best original screenplay 1968, Second Internat. Film Festival Spl. award 1969); writer, host: (TV series) Arthur C. Clarke's Mysterious World, 1980, Arthur C. Clarke's World of Strange Powers, 1984, Mysterious Universe, 1994; actor: (films) Beddagama, 1979; editor: Time Probe: The Science in Science Fiction, 1966, The Coming of the Space Age, 1967, Three for Tomorrow, 1972, The Science Fiction Hall of Fame Vol. III, 1982. With Lindbergh Award Noms. Com. Served to flight lt. RAF, 1941-46; mem. adv. bd. Science Fiction Mus. and Hall of Fame. Recipient Presdl. award U. Ill., 1997. Fellow Royal Astron. Soc., Royal Soc. Arts; mem. Brit. Interplanetary Soc. (chmn. 1947-50, 53), Internat. Council Integrative Studies, AIAA, Inst. Engrs. Sri Lanka (named hon. fellow 1983), Sri Lanka Astron. Soc., Royal Astron. Soc., Assn. Brit. Sci. Writers (life), Internat. Acad. Astronautics, World Acad. Art and Sci., Nat. Space Inst. (dir.), Brit. Sci. Fiction Assn. (pres.), Royal Soc. Arts, Brit. Sub-Aqua Club, Brit. Astron. Assn., H.G. Wells Soc. (hon. v.p.), Sci. Fiction Writers Am., Internat. Sci. Writers Assn., Sci. Fiction Found., Soc. Authors (mem. coun.), Am. Astronautical Assn., Am. Assn. for Advancement of Sci., Nat. Acad. Engring., Third World Acad. of Scis. (assoc. fellow), Sri Lanka Animal Welfare Assn., Sri Lanka Assn. Advancement Sci., Sri Lanka Nat. Inst. Paraplegics, Astron. Soc. Haringey, Soc. Satellite Profls. (hon. chmn., Hall of Fame 1987), Nat. Space Soc. (bd. dirs., R.A. Heinlein Meml. award 1990), Royal Asiatic Soc., Astron. Soc. Pacific, Nat. Acad. Engring. (fgn. assoc.). Office Phone: 9411 2699757.

CLARKE, CHARLES FENTON, lawyer; b. Hillsboro, Ohio, July 25, 1916; s. Charles F. and Margaret (Patton) C.; m. Virginia Schoppenhorst, Apr. 3, 1945 (dec. July 1989); children: Elizabeth, Margaret, Jane, Charles Fenton, IV; m. Lesley Wells, Nov. 13, 1998. AB summa cum laude, Washington and Lee U., 1938; LLB, U. Mich., 1940; LLD (hon.), Cleve. State U., 1971. Bar: Mich. 1940, Ohio 1946. Pvt. practice, Detroit, 1942, Cleve., 1946—; ptnr. firm Squire, Sanders & Dempsey, 1957—, adminstr. litigation dept., 1979-85. Trustee Cleve. Legal Aid Soc., 1959-67; pres. Nat. Assn. R.R. Trial Counsel, 1966-68; life mem. 6th Circuit Jud. Conf.; chmn. legis. com. Cleve. Welfare Fedn., 1961-68; master bencher Manos Inn of Ct., 1991—; bd. dirs. Wheeling and Lake Erie R.R. Co. Pres. alumni bd. dirs. Washington and Lee U., 1970-72; pres. bd. dirs. Free Med. Clinic Greater Cleve., 1970-86; trustee Cleve. Citizens League, 1956-62, Cleve. chpt. ACLU, 1986-93; bd. dirs. citizens adv. bd. Cuyahoga County (Ohio) Juvenile Ct., 1970-73; bd. dirs. George Jr. Republic, Greenville, Pa., 1970-73, Bowman Tech. Sch., Cleve., 1970-91; vice chmn. Cleve. Crime Commn., 1973-75; exec. com. Cuyahoga County Rep. Orgn., 1950—; councilman Bay Village, Ohio, 1948-53; pres., trustee Cleve. Hearing and Speech Ctr., 1957-62, Laurel Sch., 1962-72, Fedn. Cmty. Progress, 1984-90; mem. planning commn. Cleveland Heights, 1994-2003. Fellow Am. Coll. Trial Lawyers; mem. Greater Cleve. Bar Assn. (trustee 1983-86), Cleve. Civil War Round Table (pres. 1968), Cleve. Zool. Soc. (dir. 1970), Phi Beta Kappa. Clubs: Skating, Union (Cleve.); Tavern, Rowfant. Presbyterian. Home: 2262 Tudor Dr Cleveland Heights OH 44106-3210 Office: Squire Sanders & Dempsey 4900 Key Tower 127 Public Sq Cleveland OH 44114-1304 Office Phone: 216-479-8551, 216-479-8500. Business E-Mail: cclarke@ssd.com.

CLARKE, CHARLES J., insurance company executive; Asst. underwriter Travelers Cos. Inc. (formerly Travelers Ins. Group Holdings, Inc.), 1958, sr. v.p. Nat. Accounts Group's property-casualty bus., 1985, chmn. comml. lines, 1990—96, CEO comml. lines, 1996—98, vice chmn., 1998—2001, pres., 2001, chmn., CEO, 2001, vice chmn. Office: Travelers Cos Inc 385 Washington St Saint Paul MN 55102 Office Phone: 651-310-7911.*

CLARKE, CHARLES KENDALL, metallurgical engineer, consultant; b. Ray, Ariz., Apr. 11, 1945; s. Otis Manson Clarke and Flora Beatrice Mayo; m. Carolyn Faye Daniels; 1 child, Valerie Carolyn. BS in Metall. Engring.,

U. Ala., Tuscaloosa, 1968; MS in Metallurgy and Materials Sci., Lehigh U., Bethlehem, Pa., 1971, PhD in Metallurgy and Materials Sci., 1973. Registered profl. engr., Ala. Specialist engr. Boeing Mil. Divsn., Wichita, Kans., 1973—76; assoc. prof. mech. engring. U. South Ala., Mobile, 1976—77; pres. Metall. Consulting, Mobile, 1977—. Past pres. Mobile Chpt. Profl. Engrs., 1987—88. Contbr. articles to profl. jours. Bd. mem. Mobile Symphony, 1987—2000. Fellow: Mobile Kiwanis Club (pres. 1989—90); mem.: Kiwanis (lt. gov. 1991—93). Avocations: woodworking, photography, fishing. Office: Metallurgical Consulting 1146 A LeRoy Stevens Rd Mobile AL 36695

CLARKE, CIANA BERNADINE BENNETT, education educator, researcher; d. John Jose and Hermie Magdalene Bennett; m. Jerry Alexander Clarke, Apr. 4, 1994; children: Ciara children: Jude, James. BA, Houghton Coll., 1988; MS in Tchg., Pace U., 1990; PhD, Fla. State U., 2005. Cert. secondary biology, gen. sci. tchr. NY. Secondary biology, gen. sci. tchr. NYC Bd. Edn., 1990—98; ednl. rschr. Fla. Ctr. Reading Rsch., Tallahassee, 2005—. Summer sci. tchr. trainer LaGuardia C.C., NYC, 1992—92; tchr. mentor NYC Bd. Edn., 1997—98; asst. prof. edn. Warner So. Coll., 2006—. Music dir. local ch., Bklyn., 1991—98. Recipient Ednl. Leadership Award, Phi Delta Kappan, 1990; Empire Challenger fellow, NY State Dept. Edn., 1989—90, Challenger grantee, Pace U., 1989—90, Leslie N. Neilson assistantship in edn., Fla. State U, 1998—99, Delores Auzene fellow, Fla. State U., 2003—04. Mem.: Nat. Assocation Tchr. Edn., Nat. Dropout Prevention Network, Am. Ednl. Rsch. Assn. Avocations: piano, travel, collecting children's books, singing. Home Phone: 850-576-1776.

CLARKE, CORDELIA KAY KNIGHT MAZUY, management consultant, artist; b. Springfield, Mo., Nov. 22, 1938; d. William Horace and Charline (Bentley) Knight; m. Logan Clarke, Jr., July 22, 1978; children by previous marriage: Katharine Michelle Mazuy, Christopher Knight Mazuy. AB in English with honors, U. N.C., 1960; MS in Stats., N.C. State U., 1962; BFA in Painting, Lyme Acad. Coll. Fine Arts, 2005; MFA in Visual Arts, Mass. Coll. Art, 2007. Statistician Research Triangle Inst., Durham, NC, 1960—63; statis. cons. Arthur D. Little, Inc., Cambridge, Mass., 1963—67; dir. mktg. planning and analysis Polaroid Corp., Cambridge, 1967—70; dir. mktg. and bus. planning Transaction Tech. Inc., Cambridge, 1970—72; pres. Mazuy Assos., Boston, 1972—73; v.p. Nat. Shawmut Bank, Boston, 1973—74; sr. v.p., dir. mktg. Shawmut Corp., 1974—78; sr. v.p., dir. retail banking Shawmut Bank, 1976—78; v.p. corp. devel. Arthur D. Little, Inc., 1978—79; v.p. Conn. Gen. Life Ins. Co., 1979—85; pres. CIGNA Securities, 1983—85; exec. v.p. McGraw-Hill Inc., 1988-90; chmn. Templeton, Inc., 1985—92, 1995—; pres. micromarketing divsn. ADVO, 1990—95. Faculty Williams Sch. Banking; adv. com. Bur. of Census, 1978-84; bd. dirs. Guardian Life Ins. Co., Berkshire Life Ins., Providence Jour. Co., Provincetown Fine Arts Work Ctr., 2006—; tchr. Amos Tuck Grad. Sch. Bus., Dartmouth Coll., 1964-65, exec.-in-residence, 1978, 80; bd. overseers, 1979-85; exec.-in-residence Wheaton Coll., 1978; vis. prof. Simmons Grad. Sch. Mgmt., 1978; mem. schs. adv. coun. Bank Mktg. Assn., 1976-78; mem. corp. adv. bd. Hartford Nat. Bank & Trust Co., 1980-87. Columnist Am. Banker, 1976-78. Mem. Mass. Gov.'s Commn. on Status of Women, 1977-79; bd. corporators Babson Coll., 1977-80; adv. bd. Boston Mayor's Office Cultural Affairs, 1977-79; bd. dirs. McGraw-Hill, Inc., 1976-88, Blue Shield of Mass., 1976-79, Greater Hartford Arts Coun., 1979-93, Cybex Internat. Inc., 1996-2000; trustee Children's Mus. Hartford, 1980-82; corporator Inst. of Living, 1981-92; regent U. Hartford, 1982—; bd. dirs. Hartford Art Sch., 1982-94, Hartford Stage Co., 1985-99, Manhattan Theatre Club, 1988-91, Inst. for Future, 1988-92, N.Y. Internat. Festival of Arts, 1988-91, Goodspeed Opera, 1990—, Inst. Design, 1990-98, Aeroflex Found., 1972—. Mem. Artists Assn. Nantucket (elected), Conn. Women Artists (elected), Lyme Art Assn. (assoc.), Essex Art Assn. (assoc.), Provincetown Art Assn., Internat. Womens Forum, Power 10, Phi Beta Kappa, Phi Kappa Phi, Kappa Alpha Theta. Home and Office: 89 River Rd East Haddam CT 06423-1462 Home Phone: 860-526-5300; Office Phone: 860-526-3368.

CLARKE, CYNTHIA THERESE See HARRISS, CYNTHIA

CLARKE, DOUGLAS E., lawyer; b. Houston, 1948; BA, Wash. & Lee U., 1970; JD, U. Houston, 1973. Bar: Tex. 1973; cert. estate planning & probate law Tex. Bd. Legal Specialization. Ptnr., Probate Dept. Andrews & Kurth LLP, Houston. Assoc. editor Houston Law Rev., 1972—73, probate editor Tex. State Bar News (for Real Estate Probate & Trust Sect.), 1986—91. Mem.: Houston Estate Forum, State Bar Tex. (Real Estate, Probate & Trust Law Counsel 1993—97), Houston Bar Assn. (Probate, Trust & Estate Sect.). Office: Andrew Kurth LLP 600 Travis St Ste 4200 Houston TX 77002-3090 Office Phone: 713-220-4474. Office Fax: 713-238-4285. Business E-Mail: dclarke@andrewskurth.com.

CLARKE, EDMUND M., computer scientist, educator; BA, U. Va., 1967; MA in Math., Duke U., 1968; PhD in Computer Sci., Cornell U., 1976. Tchr. Dept. Computer Sci. Duke U.; asst. prof. computer sci. Div. Applied Sci. Harvard U., 1978—82; joined Computer Sci. Dept. Carnegie-Mellon U., Pitts., 1982, prof., 1989—, FORE Sys. prof. computer sci., 1995—. Co-recipient ACM Kanellakis Award, 1999; recipient Technical Excellence Award, Semiconductor Rsch. Corp., 1995, Allen Newell Award for Excellence in Rsch., 1999. Mem.: NAE, IEEE (Harry H. Goode Meml. Award 2004). Office: Carnegie Mellon U Sch Computer Sci 5000 Forbes Ave, Wean Hall 7117 Pittsburgh PA 15213-3891 Office Phone: 412-268-2628. Office Fax: 412-268-5576. E-mail: Edmund.Clarke@cs.cmu.edu.

CLARKE, EDWARD NIELSEN, engineering science educator; b. Providence, Apr. 25, 1925; s. Edward O.A. and Edith (Nielsen) C.; m. Vivian Constance Bergquist, July 23, 1949; children: Sandra J., David E., Allan R., Jeffrey B. BS, Brown U., 1945, PhD, 1951; MS, Harvard U., 1947, M in Engring. Sci., 1948. Mem. tech. staff, sect. head for semiconductors, physics lab. Sylvania Electric Products Co., Bayside, NY, 1950-56; group head for rsch. Sperry Semiconductor divsn. Sperry Rand Corp., Norwalk, Conn., 1956—59; v.p. ops. and dir. Nat. Semiconductor Corp., Danbury, Conn., 1959-65; assoc. dean faculty, assoc. dean grad. studies, dir. rsch. Worcester Poly. Inst., 1965-86, prof. engring. scis., 1968-94, dir. Ctr. Solar Electrification, 1986-94, prof. emeritus, 1995—; tri-coll. coord. rsch. Clark U.-Holy Cross Coll.-Worcester Poly. Inst., 1974-85. Co-founder Nat. Semiconductor Corp.; founder solar electrification ctr. Worcester Poly. Inst.; disting. vis. prof. Nichols Coll., 2002, lectr. history of semiconductors and hybrid-electric cars, 1995—. Trustee Upsala Coll., East Orange, N.J., 1971-74. Served with USNR, 1943-46. Recipient Brown U. Engring. Alumni medal, 1998. Mem. IEEE, Am. Phys. Soc., Torch Club (Worcester), Sigma Xi (past chpt. pres.), Tau Beta Pi. Lutheran. Achievements include patents and inventions in semiconductor technology; pioneering development of solar powered racing car. Home: 85 Richards Ave Paxton MA 01612-1123 Personal E-mail: encvcc@aol.com. *Helping others to achieve has been my own principal achievement. Retain mobility and be willing to use one's skills wherever they are needed. Do not become too comfortable and secure. Move on to find new challenges. Stay young with variety in one's life and a healthy use of the out-of-doors.*

CLARKE, EDWARD OWEN, JR., lawyer; b. Balt., Dec. 19, 1929; s. Edward Owen and Agnes Oakford C.; m. P. Rhea Parker, Dec. 18, 1954; children: Deborah Jeanne, Catherine Ann, Carolyn Agnes, Edward Owen III. AB magna cum laude, Loyola Coll., Balt., 1950; JD with honors, U. Md., 1956. Bar: Md. 1956, U.S. Dist. Ct. Md. 1956. Law clk. U.S. Dist. Ct. Md., 1956-57; assoc. Smith, Somerville & Case, Balt., 1957-62, ptnr., 1962-71, Piper & Marbury, Balt., 1971-94, mem. policy and mgmt. com., 1981-94, mng. ptnr., 1987-90, co-chmn. bus. div., 1991-94. Mem. Gov.'s Com. to Study Blue Sky Law, 1961; mem. Md. Commn. on Revision Corp. Law, 1965-66. Bd. dirs. Bon Secours Hosp., 1964-73, sec., 1968-73; bd. dirs. Hosp. Cost Analysis Svc., 1966-81; bd. pres. exec. coun. Md. Hosp. Assn., 1968-74, chmn. com. on legislation, 1971-73, treas., 1973; trustee St. Mary's Coll. Md., 1983-94, chmn. bd., 1988-94; trustee St. Mary's Sem., U. Balt., 1986-89, Loyola HS, Balt., 1984-90, Hannah More Ctr., 1980-83; bd. dirs. Helix Health Sys., Inc., 1995-98, Med Star Health, 1998-2006; mem. Md. Higher Edn. Commn., 1994-2004, chmn. 1995-2000. Lt. USNR, 1952-55. Recipient Alumni Laureate award Loyola Coll. in Md., 2001. Mem. Order of Coif, Order of the Ark and the Dove, Plantation Golf and Country Club (Venice, Fla.), Phi Beta Kappa, Alpha Sigma Nu, Tau Kappa Alpha. Home: 627 Khyber Ln Venice FL 34293-4456

CLARKE, ERSKINE, religious history professor, writer; AB, Univ. SC; BD, Columbia Theol. Seminary, Decatur, Ga.; ThM, PhD, Union Theol. Seminary, Va. Pastor Belton Presbyn. Ch., SC, 1970—73; now prof. Am. religious history, dir. internat. programs Columbia Theol. Seminary, Decatur, Ga. Vis. fellow Clare Hall, Cambridge. Author: Wrestlin' Jacob: A Portrait of Religion in the Old South, 1979, Our Southern Zion: A History of Calvinism in South Carolina Low Country, 1690-1990, 1996, Exilic Preaching: Testimony of Christian Exiles in an Increasingly Hostile Culture, 1998, Dwelling Place: a Plantation Epic, 2005 (Bancroft prize for history, Columbia Univ., 2006). Presbyn. Office: Columbia Theol Seminary 701 Columbia Dr PO Box 520 Decatur GA 30031 Office Phone: 404-687-4543. Business E-Mail: ClarkeE@CTSnet.edu.

CLARKE, FLORENCE DOROTHY, minister, educator; b. Charleston, SC, Feb. 21, 1941; d. Peter Glover and Janie Etta (Gilliard) Oliver; children: Stephanye R., Jamie J. BS, S.C. State U., 1963. Tchr. bus. Williams Meml. Sch., St. George, SC, 1963—65, Charles A. Brown H.S., Charleston, SC, 1965—68; sr. adminstrv. aide, sr. analyst Electric Boat Corp., Groton, Conn., 1968—96; assoc. min. African Meth. Episcopal Zion Ch., New London, Conn., 1975—98, supply pastor Cambridge, Mass., 1996—97, pastor Waterford, Conn., 1998—. Christian edn. dir. New Haven Dist., 1993—2004; chaplain Conn. Coll., New London, 2002—04; spkr. in field. Contbr. articles to mags. Bd. dirs. Noank (Conn.) Bapt. Group Homes, Inc., 1995—99. Named Outstanding Christian Educator, Walls Temple African Meth. Episcopal Zion Ch., 1997. Mem.: AAUW, NAACP (exec. bd., edn. commn.), Am. Correctional Chaplains Assn., Am. Correctional Chaplains Assn., Christian Edn. (dist. dir. 1990—2005), Nat. Coun. Negro Women (1st v.p. 1996—99, Outstanding Svc. award 1996). Methodist. Avocations: singing, reading, public speaking. Home: 11 Lodus Ct New London CT 06320-4328 Office Phone: 860-443-7561.

CLARKE, FRANK WILLIAM, communications executive; b. Quebec, Que., Can., Apr. 16, 1942; came to U.S., 1946; s. William Frank Clarke and Tolly (English) Wing; m. Barbara Jean Dreher, Mar. 1966 (div. Sept. 1975); children: Kathleen Julienne Clarke Smith, Lori Christine Clarke Genovese; m. Vera Gretel Thol, Nov. 14, 1977; stepchildren: Teo Capriles, Gretel Capriles Saade. Student, U. Va., 1958-61; BS in Commerce, NYU, 1964; MS in Journalism, Northwestern U., 1965. Staff asst., then asst. account exec. Grey Advt. Inc., NYC, 1969-70, account exec., 1970-73, account dir. Caracas, Venezuela, 1973-75, v.p. account svcs., 1975-78, v.p., area dir., 1978-82, NYC, 1982-88, sr. v.p., area dir., 1988-93, exec. v.p., area dir., 1993-99; sr. cons. Strategy XXI Group Ltd., NYC, 1999-2000, ptnr., 2001—. Mem. product mktg. com. U.S. Fund for UNICEF, N.Y.C., 1989-93, nat. adv. coun., 1991-93, bd. dirs., 1994-2000, mem. exec. com., 1996-2000; bd. dirs. Street Law, Inc., Washington, 1999—, chmn. 2001-. Capt. U.S. Army, 1966-69. Mem. Racquet and Tennis Club N.Y. Republican. Avocations: gardening, cross country skiing. Office: Strategy XXI Group Ltd 515 Madison Ave New York NY 10022-5403

CLARKE, GARRY EVANS, composer, educator, academic administrator, musician; b. Moline, Ill., Mar. 19, 1943; s. Clarence Henderson and Gladys Arlene (Hokinson) C.; m. Melissa Jane Naul, May 24, 1975; children: Catharine van Gelder, Margaret Elizabeth Jane. MusB summa cum laude, Cornell Coll., Mount Vernon, Iowa, 1965; MusM, Yale U., 1968; LittD (hon.), Washington Coll., 1988. Asst. prof. music Washington Coll., Chestertown, Md., 1968-73; assoc. prof., 1973-79; prof. Washington Coll., Chestertown, 1979—, dean coll., 1977-83, acting pres., 1981-82. Am. liaison Harrison & Harrison Ltd., Durham, Eng. Composer symphonic, chamber, vocal, piano and organ music and opera; lectr. and recitalist (U.S., Europe): Am. music; condr. piano workshops; opera coach; organist and choir master, St. Paul's Episcopal Parish, Centerville, Md., 1975-88; Chester Parish, Chestertown, Md., 1988—; author: Essays on American Music, 1977; contbr. articles, revs. to profl. jours.; co-editor: Varied Air and Variations (Ives), 1971; editor: Charles Ives. Soc. publs. Trustee Coun. Econ. Edn. Md.; bd. dirs. Talbot Chamber Orch., Ea. Shore Chamber Music Festival. Ford Found. fellow, 1965, Woodrow Wilson fellow, 1965; Carnegie Found. rsch. grantee, 1964, NEH rsch. grantee, 1970; recipient Bronze medal Coun. for Advancement and Support of Edn., 1993. Mem. AAUP, Soc. Music Theory, Assn. Anglican Musicians, Sonneck Soc., Council Higher Edn. in Music, Am. Conf. Acad. Deans, Nat. Assn. Schs. Music, Am. Assn. Higher Edn., Yale Sch. Music Alumni Assn. (exec. com. 1975-80), Assn. Yale Alumni, Yale Club (N.Y.C.), Order of Omega, Pi Kappa Lambda, Omicron Delta Kappa, Phi Delta Theta. Episcopalian. Home: Fairways 7775 Waterview Ln Chestertown MD 21620-4746 Office: Washington Coll 300 Washington Ave Chestertown MD 21620-1197 Office Phone: 410-778-7838. E-mail: gclarke2@washcoll.edu.

CLARKE, GRAY B., psychiatrist; b. Chapel Hill, NC, June 15, 1967; d. Charles Lee and Karen Lee Clarke; 1 child, Benjamin C. Leyba. BS, U. N.Mex., Albuquerque, 1987—92, MD, 1993—98. Cert. Am. Bd. Psychiatry and Neurology, 2004. Asst. prof. U. N.Mex., Albuquerque, 2003—; med. dir., u. hosp. psychiatry consultation/liaison svc. U. N.Mex, Albuquerque, 2003—; attending psychiatrist, dept. psychiatry U. N.Mex., Albuquerque, 2003—. Contbr. chapters to books, papers to profl. jours. and pubs. Mem.: Assn. Academic Psychiatry, Acad. Psychosomatic Medicine, Am. Psychiat. Assn. Office: Univ New Mex Dept Psychiatry 2400 Tucker NE 4th fl FPC Albuquerque NM 87131 Home Phone: 505-899-4566; Office Phone: 505-272-4763. Business E-Mail: gclarke@salud.unm.edu.

CLARKE, HENRY LEE, foreign service officer, ambassador; b. Ft. Benning, Ga., Nov. 15, 1941; s. Edwin Lee and Jane Iredell (Jones) C.; m. Kathleen Ann Smith, May 19, 1973 (div. 1996); children: Ann Marie, Edwin Lee; m. Elena Anatolyevna Fedyai, Jan. 8, 1997; children: Yuliya Chikerenda, Christopher Lee. AB, Dartmouth Coll., 1962; MPA, Harvard U., 1967. U.S. fgn. svc. officer Dept. State, 1967-99; econ. counselor Am. Embassy, Moscow, 1982-85, dep. chief Bucharest, Romania, 1985-89, econ. counselor Tel Aviv, 1989-92, amb. to Uzbekistan, Tashkent, 1992-95; internat. affairs advisor Nat. War Coll., Washington, 1995-98; sr. advisor for property restitution in Europe, Dept. State, Washington, 1998-2000; dep. high rep. for Bosnia and Brcko Supr., 2001—03. Chmn. bd. Am. Sch., Bucharest, 1985-89, Tashkent Internat. Sch., 1994-95.

CLARKE, HUGHETTE NAOMI, elementary school educator; b. Flushing, NY, Jan. 20, 1951; d. Hugh Calvin and Naomi L. Clarke. BA, Queens Coll., Flushing, 1973, MSc, 1977; EdD, Tchrs. Coll. Columbia U., NYC, 2004. Cert. tchr. K-6 N.Y. State Dept. Edn., SPS N.Y. State Dept. Edn. Tchr. pre-K various schs., NYC, 1974—2002; tchr. math. Longwood Mid. Sch., Mid. Island, NY, 2002—. Mem.: L.I. Black Educators, The Links, Inc., Alpha Kappa Alpha (pres. Sigma Psi Omega chpt. 2002—06). Avocations: skiing, reading. Office: Longwood Mid Sch 43 Mid Island-Yaphank Rd Middle Island NY 11953 E-mail: hughette@erols.com.

CLARKE, INGRID GADWAY, retired academic ombudsman, consultant; b. Bad Homburg, Hesse, Germany, Sept. 21, 1942; came to U.S., 1964; d. Johann Kajetan and Irmgard (Schneider) Rebholz BA equivalent, Johann Wolfgang Goethe U., Frankfurt, Germany, 1964; MA, Memphis State U., 1965; postgrad., Tulane U., 1965-69; PhD, So. Ill. U., 1984. Instr. So. Ill. U., Carbondale, 1969-74, univ. ombudsman, 1974—2000, chair, bd. dirs. students' legal assistance program, 1980—86; ret., 2000. Mem. Carbondale Human Rels. Com., 1974-76; chairperson Carbondale Fair Housing Bd., 1978-82. Fulbright scholar, 1964-67. Mem. Fulbright Alumni Assn., Univ. and Coll. Ombudsman Assn. (founder and first pres. 1985-86), Internat. Ombudsman Assn. (disting.), Delta Phi Alpha. Avocations: bicycling, cooking, skiing, hiking. Address: 61348 Bad Homburg Ottilienstr 8 Germany Personal E-mail: taunus@midwest.net.

CLARKE, JAMES WESTON, political science professor, writer; b. Elizabeth, Pa., Feb. 16, 1937; s. Alonzo Peterson and Beatrice (Weston) C.; m. Jeanne Nienaber; children: Julianne, Michael BA, Washington and Jefferson Coll., 1962; MA, Pa. State U., 1964, PhD, 1968. Asst. prof. Fla. State U., 1967-71; assoc. prof. U. Ariz., Tucson, 1971-76, prof. polit. sci., 1976—, chmn. dept., 1973-78, univ. disting. prof., 2000. Author: American Assassins: The Darker Side of Politics, 1982, Last Rampage: The Escape of Gary Tison, 1988, On Being Mad or Merely Angry: John W. Hinckley Jr. and Other Dangerous People, 1990, The Lineaments of Wrath: Race, Violent Crime, and American Culture, 1998, Defining Danger: American Assassins and the New Domestic Terrorists, 2006. Served with USMC, 1955-58 Recipient James Gillespie Blaine prize Washington and Jefferson Coll., 1962, Matthew Brown Ringland prize, 1962, Burlington Northern Found. award for excellence in tchg., 1987, Golden Key Nat. Honor Soc. award for tchg., 1989, Social and Behavioral Scis. award for outstanding tchg., 1991, 96;named to the Elizabeth Forward HS Hall of Fame, 2005; Udall fellow, 1993; Fulbright scholar, Ireland, 1999 Mem. Am. Polit. Sci. Assn. (Outstanding Tchg. in Polit. Sci. 2000). Home: 855 E Placita Leslie Tucson AZ 85718-1960 Office: U Ariz 315 Social Sci Bldg Tucson AZ 85721-0001 Office Phone: 520-621-7600. Business E-Mail: jclarke@email.arizona.edu.

CLARKE, JANET MORRISON, marketing executive; d. Morton and Shirley (Harkinson) Morrison, m. Frederick G.E. Clarke, Oct. 4, 1980. BA in Architecture, Princeton U., 1976. Sales rep. Sci. Press, Ephrata, Pa., 1977-78, R.R. Donnelley & Sons Co., Chgo., 1978, various positions including sr. v.p. Information Technol. and dir. venture capital fund, 1978—97; mng. dir., global database mktg. Citibank, 1997—2000; chmn., CEO KnowledgeBase Marketing, Inc., 2000—01; exec. v.p. Young & Rubicam, Inc, 2000—01; chief mktg. officer DealerTrack, Inc., 2002—03; founder Clarke Littlefield LLC, 2001—, pres., 2001—02, 2003—. Bd. dirs. Cox Communications, 1995—2004, Asbury Automotive Group, Express-Jet Holdings Inc., 2002—, eFunds Corp., 2000—, Forbes.com Inc., Gateway Computers, 2005—, Cox Enterprises, 2006—; mem. sch. bd. Harvard Bus. Sch. Charter trustee, Princeton U.; bd. dirs. YWCA, Westbrook, Conn., 1984—; mem., regional chmn. Nat. Ann. Giving Com. Princeton (N.J.) U., 1985—. Mem.: York Golf & Tennis Club, Landmark (Stamford, Conn.), Princeton (N.Y.C.). Republican.

CLARKE, JOHN, physics professor; b. Cambridge, Eng., Feb. 10, 1942; arrived in U.S., 1968; s. Victor Patrick and Ethel May (Blowers) C.; m. Grethe Fog Pedersen, Sept. 15, 1979; 1 child, Elizabeth Jane. BA, Cambridge U., 1964, MA, PhD, Cambridge U., 1968, ScD (hon.), 2003. Postdoctoral scholar U. Calif.-Berkeley, 1968-69, asst. prof. physics, 1969-71, assoc. prof., 1971-73, prof., 1973—, faculty rsch. lectr., 2005; chair exptl. physics Luis W. Alvarez Meml., 1994—. Contbr. numerous articles to profl. jours. Guggenheim fellow, 1977-78, Sloan Found. fellow, 1970-72, Miller Inst. Basic Rsch. fellow, 1975-76, 94-95; recipient Charles Vernon Boys prize Brit. Inst. Physics, 1977, award Soc. Exploration Geophysics, 1979, Outstanding Tchg. award U. Calif., 1983, Fritz London award for low temperature physics, 1987, Fed. Lab. Consortium award for excellence in technology transfer, 1992, divsn. materials scis. award in solid state physics Dept. Energy, 1986, 92, IEEE U.S. Activities Bd. Electrotechnology Transfer award, 1995, Comstock prize Physics NAS, 1999, Coun. on Superconductivity award IEEE, 2002, Olli V. Lounasmaa prize Finnish Acad. Sci. and Letters, 2004; named Calif. Scientist of Yr., 1987, One of 50, Scientific Am., 2002. Fellow AAAS, Royal Soc. London (Hughes medal 2004), Am. Phys. Soc. (Joseph F. Keithley Advances in Measurement Sci. award 1998), Brit. Inst. Physics, Christ's Coll. (hon.). Office: U Calif Dept Physics 366 LeConte Hall #7300 Berkeley CA 94720-7300

CLARKE, JOHN PATRICK, retired newspaper publisher; b. Mattoon, Ill., Oct. 29, 1930; s. Patrick Joseph Clarke and Lucille (Hennebry) Stoeckinger; m. Roberta June Steiner, July 25, 1959 (div. 1984); children: Shannon, Dana; m. Sheila Cordill, June 24, 1995. BS, Ind. U., 1958; MBA, Harvard U., 1962. With contr.'s staff Ethyl Corp., NYC, 1958-60; bus. mgr. State Jour.-Register, Springfield, Ill., 1962-68, pub., 1968-96; ret., 1996. Sec., bd. dirs. Ill. Ambassadors, 1986—; mem. Atty. Registration and Disciplinary Commn., 1987—; chmn bd. dirs. State Farm Rail Classic (LPGA tour). With USN, 1949-50, 52-54. Mem. Am. Newspaper Pubs. Assn., Inland Daily Press Assn., Sangamo Club (pres. 1978-79). Avocations: sailing, golf. Home: 4301 Gulf Shore Blvd N Apt 504 Naples FL 34103-3477 also: 1240 N Astor St Chicago IL 60610

CLARKE, JUDY, lawyer; b. Asheville, NC, 1953; m. Speedy Rice. B in Psychology, Furman U., 1974; JD, U. S.C., 1977. Trial atty. Fed. Defenders San Diego, Inc., exec. dir., 1983—91; pvt. practice, 1991-92; exec. dir. Fed. Defenders of Ea. Washington & Idaho. Mem. faculty Nat. Criminal Def. Coll., Macon, Ga., bd. regents, 1985—, pres. Nat. Assn. Criminal Def. Lawyers, 1996-97 Author: Federal Sentencing Manual; contbr. articles to profl. jours. Mem. NACDL (pres. 1996-97). Office: Fed Pub Defenders Office 10 N Post St Ste 700 Spokane WA 99201-0705

CLARKE, JULIA L., library director; Student, Millsaps Coll., Jackson, Miss.; MS in Libr. Sci., U. NC, Chapel Hill. Reference libr. U. Memphis, Main Libr., Knoxville, Tenn.; head reference and circulation functions U. of the South Jesse Ball du Pont Libr., Sewanee, Tenn.; head circulation dept. Green Hills br. Nashville Pub. Libr., mgr. Thompson Ln. and Donelson brs.; with Carnegie Libr., Clarksdale, Miss., Albuquerque/Bernalillo County Libr. Sys., 1985—, children's libr. Esperanza Libr., mgr. Lomas-Tramway Libr., mgr. Taylor Ranch Libr., mgr. Wyo. Libr., asst. dir., 2000—06, acting dir., 2006—07, dir., 2007—. Office: Albuquerque Bernalillo County Libr Sys 501 Copper Ave NW Albuquerque NM 87102 Office Phone: 505-768-5122. E-mail: jclarke@cabq.gov.

CLARKE, KENNETH KINGSLEY, retired electronics executive; b. Miami, Fla., June 7, 1924; s. Kenneth Kingsley and Mary (Coffin) Clarke; m. Nona Nelme, Sept. 15, 1945; 1 child, Kenneth Stephen. Student, Cornell U., 1941—42; MSEE, Stanford, 1948; DEE, Bklyn. Poly. Inst., 1959. Rsch. fellow Bklyn. Poly. Inst., 1949-50, faculty, 1955-69, prof. elec. engring., 1965-69, dir. grad. elec. engring. divsn., 1967-69; asst. prof. Madras (India) Inst. Tech., 1950-52; lectr. U. Ceylon, Colombo, 1952-54; asst. prof. Clarkson Coll. Tech., Potsdam, NY, 1954-55; pres. Clarke-Hess Comm. Rsch. Corp., NYC, 1969-99. Cons. in field; vis. prof. Mid. E. Tech. U., Ankara, Turkey, 1961—62; dir. Julie Rsch. Labs., 1966—71. Author (with M. V. Joyce): Transistor Circuit Analysis, 1961; author: (with D. T. Hess) Communication Circuit Analysis, 1971; author: Spoken Speech and the Invention of Writing, 2004. 2d lt. AC US Army, 1943—46. Recipient Svc. award, Parlar Found., 1992. Fellow: IEEE (life), Instrument and Measurement Soc. (mem. adminstrv. com. 1993—96, mem. visitor accreditation bd. 1983—88, bd. dirs. Instrumentation/Measurement Tech. Conf., tech. program chmn. 1995); mem.: AAAS, AAUP, Sigma Xi, Tau Beta Pi. Achievements include co-inventor frequency locked loop. Home: 300 Riverside Dr New York NY 10025-5279 Home Phone: 212-222-0498. Personal E-mail: ken1924@ix.netcom.com.

CLARKE, LEWIS JAMES, landscape architect; b. Eng., Mar. 10, 1927; s. Roland and May (Pringle) C.; children: Lewis Nigel, Jennifer Kay, Rachel May, Lisa Elaine. Dip. Arch., Sch. Architecture, Leicester, Eng., 1950; Dip. L.D., Kings Coll, U. Durham, 1951; M.L.A., Harvard U., 1952. Prof. Sch. Design N.C. State Univ., Raleigh, 1952-68; sr. partner Lewis Clarke Assos., Raleigh, 1952—. Served with Corps Royal Engrs., 1946-49. Smith Mundt fellow, Fulbright fellow, 1951-52. Fellow Inst. Landscape Architects, Am. Soc. Landscape Architects; mem. Royal Inst. Brit. Architects. Home and Office: Lewis Clarke Assocs 1701 Glen Eden Dr Raleigh NC 27612-4335

CLARKE, LOGAN, JR., management consultant; b. Atlanta, May 28, 1927; s. Leonard Warner Moore and Marion (Ray) C.; children: Logan III, Jeffrey Reed, Jonathan, Lisa Beth; m. Cordelia Kay Knight Mazuy. Student, U. Okla., 1944; La., State U., 1945; Stonier Grad., Sch. Banking, 1960; BA, U. Pa., 1949; MS, Hartford Grad. Center, 1981. Salesman Liberty Mut. Ins. Co., Boston, 1949-52; with Nat. Shawmut Bank Boston, 1952-70, asst. v.p., 1955-58, v.p., 1958-70; exec. v.p. County Bank NA, Cambridge, Mass., 1970-71, pres., dir., 1971-75; pres. Shawmut Bank of Boston, N.A.; pres., dir. Shawmut Corp., 1976-78; alt. dir. Atlantic Internat. Bank Ltd., London; alt. rep. Internat. Monetary Conf., 1976-78; lectr. Hartford (Conn.) Grad. Center, 1979-86, dean Sch. Mgmt., 1983-85; exec. v.p. Soc. for Savings, Hartford, 1986-90; acting pres. Hartford Coll. for Women, 1990-91; pres. Templeton Inc., 1991—. Trustee Lyme Acad. Fine Art, 1997-2006; cons. Arthur D. Little, Inc., 1979-85. Mem. Town Meeting Lexington, Mass., 1961-70, appropriations com., 1960-66, sch. com., 1966-70; bd. overseers Children's Hosp. Med. Ctr., Boston, 1967-87; trustee Lesley Coll., Cambridge, 1971-86, Hartford Coll. for Women, 1985-92; chmn. bd. Govs. Higher Edn., Conn., 1992-97, chmn., 1994-97; corporator Northeastern U., Boston, 1976-85. Recipient Outstanding Young Man award Boston Jr. C. of C. Mem. Masons. Episcopalian. Home: 89 River Rd East Haddam CT 06423-1462 E-mail: lclarke4@mindspring.com.

CLARKE, MILTON CHARLES, lawyer; b. Chgo., Jan. 31, 1929; s. Gordon Robert and Senoria Josephine (Carlisa) C.; m. Dorothy Jane Brodie, Feb. 19, 1955; children: Laura, Virginia, Senoria K. BS, Northwestern U., 1950, JD, 1953. Bar: Ill. 1953, Mo. 1956, U.S. Dist. Ct. (we. dist.) Mo. 1961, U.S. Ct. Appeals (8th cir.) 1961. Assoc. Swanson, Midgley, Gangwere, Clarke & Kitchin, Kansas City, Mo., 1955-61, ptnr., 1961-91; of counsel Olsen & Talpers, P.C., Kansas City, 1994—. Served with U.S. Army, 1953-55. Mem. Rotary. Office: Olsen and Talpers PC 1950 Ten Main Ctr 920 Main St Kansas City MO 64105-2011 Office Phone: 816-421-2050. Personal E-mail: miltonclarke@hotmail.com.

CLARKE, NINA HONEMOND, historian, writer, retired principal; b. Dickerson, Md., Nov. 13, 1917; d. Percival James and Sarah Elizabeth (Copeland) Honemond; m. Samuel Ellis Clarke, May 25, 1941 (dec.); 1 child, Camille Clarke Battle. BS, Hampton Inst., Va., 1944; MEd, Boston U., 1952, George Washington U., Am. U., U. Md., Washington and College Park, 1960. Cert. first grade tchr. Bowie State Tchrs. Coll., 1937. Tchr. Montgomery County Pub. Schs., Rockville, Md., 1937—64, reading specialist, 1964—68, vice prin., 1967—68, prin., 1968—73; ret., 1973; cons. Black history Mongomery County Hist. Soc., 1978—. Contbg. author Flower of the Forest, 1982—88. Author: History of Black Public Schools of Montgomery County Maryland 1872-1961, 1978, History of 19th Century Black Churches, 1985. Trustee United Methodist Ch., Rockville, Md. Named Md. Outstanding Vol. award, Sr. Citizens Hall of Fame, 1989; named to Human Rights Hall of Fame, Montgomery County Human Rels. Commn., 2001; recipient Martin Luther King Humanitarian award, 1992, Cmty. Svc. award, Alpha Phi Alpha, 2004, Arthur Wagman award, 2004. Mem.: NAACP (life), Bethune Mus. Archives Inc., Am. Assn. Ret. Persons, Peerless Rockville Hist. Soc. Inc., Montgomery County Hist. Soc., Assn. Study Afro Am. Life and History, Afro Am. Hist. and Geneal. Soc., Md. Hist. Soc., Montgomery County Ret. Tchrs. Assn., Bethune Douglass Mus., Assn. Black Women Historians, Bowie State U. Alumni (county and nat. chpts.), Reginald F. Lewis Mus. Md. African Am. History and Culture, Traveliers Club, Merry Makers Club. Democrat. Methodist. Avocations: gardening, travel, church office. Home: 600 Great Falls Rd Rockville MD 20850

CLARKE, PAULA KATHERINE, anthropologist, researcher, social studies educator; b. Berkeley, Gloucestershire, Eng., July 27, 1946; d. Percy George and Grace Anne C.; m. Warren Ted Hamilton. BA, U. Calif., Berkeley, 1982; PhD, U. Calif., San Francisco, 1991. Prof. anthropology and sociology Columbia Coll., Sonora, Calif., 1997—. Invited participant Oxford Round Table Diversity in Soc., 2006; invited spkr. in field. Contbr.: Men and Masculinities: A Social, Cultural, and Historical Encyclopedia, 2003; contbr. articles to ednl. jours. (Nominated-Kathleen Gregory Klein Award by Women's Caucus/Popular and Am. Culture Assn. for best unpublished article on feminism and popular culture, 1999). Creator Future Promise Award scholarship Columbia Coll., Sonora, 2001. Recipient Excellence in Tchg. award, Tuolumne County Bd. Edn., 2002. Office: Columbia Coll 11600 Columbia College Dr Sonora CA 95370 Office Phone: 209-588-5356. Business E-Mail: clarkep@yosemite.edu.

CLARKE, PETER, communications and health educator; b. Evanston, Ill., Sept. 19, 1936; s. Clarence Leon and Dorothy (Whitcomb) C.; m. Karen Storey, June 4, 1962 (div. 1984); 1 child, Christopher Michael. BA, U. Wash., 1959; MA, U. Minn., 1961, PhD, 1963. Dir., asst. prof. Comm. Rsch. Ctr. U. Wash., Seattle, 1965-68, assoc. prof. Sch. Comm., 1967-72, dir. Sch. Comm., 1971-72; prof. dept. journalism U. Mich., Ann Arbor, 1973-74, chmn., prof. dept. journalism, 1975-78, chmn., prof. dept. comm., 1979-80; dean, prof. Annenberg Sch. Comm., U. So. Calif., LA, 1981-92, prof., 1993—; prof. preventive medicine U. So. Calif. Keck Sch. Medicine, LA, 1985—. Co-dir. From the Wholesaler to the Hungry, 1991—; dir. Ctr. for Health and Med. Comm., 1997—; cons. for various fed. and state govt. commns. on mass media and social problems. Co-author: (with Susan H. Evans) Covering Campaigns: Journalism in Congressional Elections, 1983, Surviving Modern Medicine: How to Get the Best from Doctors, Family and Friends, 1998; editor: New Models for Communication Research, 1973; co-editor: (with Susan H. Evans) The Computer Culture, 1985; contbr. articles to profl. jours. Numerous Fed., corp., pvt. founds. grants. Office: U So Calif Annenberg Sch Comm 3502 Watt Way Los Angeles CA 90089-0054 Home Phone: 310-395-8598; Office Phone: 213-740-0940. E-mail: chmc@usc.edu.

CLARKE, PETER D., lawyer; b. Worcester, Mass. BBA with highest distinction, U. Mich., 1972; JD magna cum laude, Ind. U., 1975. Bar: Ill. 1975, DC. Gen. counsel OGE Energy Corp., 1997—; ptnr. Jones Day, Chgo. Mem.: ABA, Order of the Coif. Office: Jones Day 77 W Wacker Chicago IL 60601-1692 Office Phone: 312-269-1519. Office Fax: 312-782-8585. E-mail: pdclarke@jonesday.com.*

CLARKE, PETER JOHN, computer scientist, educator, educational consultant; s. Joseph Lloyd and Violet Clarke. B, U. WI, Cave Hill, Barbados, 1987; M, Binghamton U., NY, 1996; D, Clemson U., SC, 2003. Lectr. Barbados C.C., Bridgetown, 1987—99; adj. lectr. U. WI, 1996—99; asst. prof. Fla. Internat. U., Miami, 2003—. Contbr. articles to profl. jours. Senator United Faculty Fla., Miami, 2005—06. Recipient Travel award, Ga. Tech., NSF, 2004, Quality Edn. Minorities Network, 2005; grantee, NSF, 2006—; Fulbright scholar, 1994—96, sr. investigator, NSF REU grant, 2006. Mem.: IEEE, ACM, Assn. Software Testing, Phi Kappa Phi. Achievements include research in Classification system for Object-Oriented Languages; development of new Communication Modeling Language (CML). Office: SCIS FLorida International University 11200 SW 8th Street ECS 212A Miami FL 33199 Home: 10945 SW 75th St Miami FL 33173 Home Phone: 305-270-9998; Office Phone: 305-348-2440. Office Fax: 305-348-3549. Business E-Mail: clarkep@cis.fiu.edu.

CLARKE, RICHARD ALAN, former federal official; b. Mass., 1950; BA, U. Pa., 1972; MS, MIT, 1978. Nuclear weapons & European security analyst Office Sec. Def., 1973-77; sr. analyst Pacific Sierra Rsch. Corp., 1978-79, Bur. Politico-Mil. Affairs, U.S. Dept. State, Washington, 1979-85; dep. asst. sec. for intelligence U.S. Dept. State, 1985-89, asst. sec. for politico-mil. affairs, 1989-92; spl. asst. to Pres. for global affairs Nat. Security Coun., Washington, 1992—98, nat. coord. for security, infrastructure protection, & counter-terrorism, 1998—2001, spl. adviser for cyber-space security, 2001—03; chmn. Good Harbor Consulting, LLC, Arlington, Va., 2003—. Chair Critical Infrastructure Protection Bd., 2001—03; adj. faculty Harvard U., Cambridge, Mass., 2003—; security cons. ABC News, Washington, 2003. Author: (non-fiction) Against All Enemies: Inside America's War on Terror, 2004, (novels) The Scorpion's Gate, 2005, Breakpoint, 2007.

CLARKE, RICHARD LEWIS, health science association administrator; b. Indpls., Sept. 9, 1948; s. John Richard and Opal (Emmons) C.; m. Linda DeMattia, Aug. 12, 1972; children: John, Laura, R. Bradley. BS, Bradley U., 1971; MBA, U. Miami, 1972. Bus. mgr. Jackson Meml. Hosp., Miami, 1973-76; controller Palmetto Gen. Hosp., Hialeah, Fla., 1976-80; sr. v.p. fin. Swedish Med. Ctr., Englewood, Colo., 1980-86; pres. Healthcare Fin. Mgmt. Assn., Westchester, Ill., 1986—. Bd. dirs., treas. Colo. Hosp. Assn. Trust, Denver. Fellow Healthcare Fin. Mgmt. Assn.; mem. Am. Soc. Assn. Execs., Econ. Club of Chgo. Avocations: sailboat racing, skiing. Office: Healthcare Fin Mgmt Assn 2 Westbrook Corp Ctr Ste 700 Westchester IL 60154

CLARKE, ROBERT EARLE (BOBBY CLARKE), professional sports team executive; b. Flin Flon, Manitoba, Can., Aug. 13, 1949; m. Sandy Clarke; children: Wade, Lucas, Jody, Jakki. Player Flin Flon Bombers, Phila. Flyers, 1969-84, asst. coach, 1979—82, gen. mgr., 1984-90, pres., gen. mgr., 1994—2006, sr. v.p., 2006—; gen. mgr., v.p. Minn. North Stars, 1990-92; gen. mgr. Fla. Panthers, 1993—94. Winner West Divsn. Rookie of Yr., 1970, Player of Yr. West Divsn. Sporting News, 1972-73, Bill Masterton Meml. trophy, 1972, Hart Meml. trophy, 1973, 75, 76, Player of Yr. Comp. Conf. Sporting News, 1974-75, Player of Yr. Sporting News, 1975-76, Lester B. Pearson trophy, 1973, Frank J. Selke trophy, 1983, NHL Exec. of Yr. Sporting News, 1993-94, 94-95; co-winner Lester Patrick award, 1981; named to Hockey Hall of Fame, 1987. Office: Phila Flyers Wachovia Ctr 3601 S Broad St Philadelphia PA 19148-5250

CLARKE, ROBERT LOGAN, lawyer; b. Tulsa, Okla., June 29, 1942; s. Ralph Logan and Faye Louise (Todd) C.; m. Jean (Puddin) Barrow Talbert, Sept. 23, 1967; 1 child, Robert Logan Jr. BA Econs., Rice U., 1963; LLB, Harvard U., 1966. Bar: N.Mex. 1966, Tex. 1967. Legis. asst. to U.S. Senator Edwin L. Mechem, Washington, 1964; assoc. Hinkle, Bondurant, Cox, Eaton & Hensley, Roswell, N.Mex., 1966, Bracewell & Giuliani, Houston, 1968-73, ptnr., 1973-85, ptnr., head fin. svcs. sect., 1992—; comptr. of currency Washington, 1985-92; dir. FDIC, Washington, 1985-92, Resolution Trust Corp., Washington, 1989-92. Bd. dirs. Cmty. Bancorp. N.Mex., Inc., Cmty. Bank, Eagle Materials, Inc., First Investors Fin. Svcs., Inc., Stewart Info. Svcs. Corp., Encore Trust Co.; sr. advisor to pres. Nat. Bank Poland, 1992-2000; advisor to bank suprs. in Ea. Europe, Mexico, Argentina, Brazil and Kazakhstan. Precinct chmn. Harris County Reps., 1970-74, 76-85, legal counsel, 1984-85; trustee Mus. N.Mex. Found., 1992-06, Southwestern Grad. Sch. Banking Found., 1993—, Internat. Folk Art Found., 1995-02, Rice U., 2006-; dir. Santa Fe Chamber Music Festival, 2003—; founding dir. Houston Rep. Club, 1982-85; bd. dirs. Houston Polit. Action Com., 1983-85; trustee Trout Unltd., 1997-05; mem. adv. com. Harris County Reagan-Bush campaign, 1984; asst. scoutmaster Boy Scouts Am., Houston, 1980-85; deacon 1st Presbyn. Ch. Houston. Capt. U.S. Army, 1966-68. Recipient Disting. Svc. medal U.S. Treasury Dept., 1992, Banking Leadership award Western States Sch. Banking, Albuquerque, 1993. Mem. Houston Bar Assn., Houston Bar Found., State Bar Tex., State Bar N.Mex., Rice U. Alumni Assn. (chmn. area club com. 1984-85, mem. exec. bd. dirs. 1987-89, Disting. Alumnus award 1992), River Oaks Country Club, Chevy Chase Club, Houston Club, Coronado Club, Houston City Club, Rotary (trustee student's ednl. fund). Avocations: tennis, fishing, hiking. Office: Bracewell & Giuliani LLP Pennzoil South Tower 711 Louisiana St Ste 2300 Houston TX 77002-2781 Office Phone: 713-221-1180.

CLARKE, ROY, physicist, researcher; b. Bury, Lancashire, England, 1947; BSc in Physics, U. London, PhD, 1973. Rsch. assoc. Cavendish Lab., Cambridge, U.K., 1973-78; James Franck fellow U. Chgo., 1978-79; prof. U. Mich., Ann Arbor, 1979-86; dir. applied physics program, 1986—2002. Co-founder k-Space Assocs. Inc. Editor: Synchrotron Radiation in Materials Research, 1989. Fellow Am. Phys. Soc. Achievements include development of novel methods for real-time x-ray and electron diffraction studies; patents for quasiperiodic optical coatings and epitaxial spin-valve devices. Office: U Mich Randall Lab Ann Arbor MI 48109-1040

CLARKE, STEPHAN PAUL, retired language educator, writer; b. Watertown, NY, Jan. 18, 1945; s. Albert John and Marjory Ruth (Grieb) Clarke; m. Mary Elizabeth Hawley, May 23, 1970; 1 child, Erin Elizabeth. BS in Edn., SUNY, Geneseo, 1966; MA, Bowling Green State U., 1968. Cert. secondary tchr. N.Y. Dept. Edn. Tchr. English E. J. Wilson HS, Spencerport, NY, 1970-99; ret., 1999. Spkr. in field. Author: (book) The Lord Peter Wimsey Companion, 1985 (Edgar Allan Poe Spl. award, Mystery Writers of Am.), The Lord Peter Wimsey Companion, rev. edit., 2002, Crimes and Clues, 1977. Chmn. supr. com. Spencerport Fed. Credit Union, 1985—2003, bd. dirs., sec. bd., 1999—2004; rec. sec. Ch. and Ministry Com. Genesee Valley Assn. United Ch. of Christ, Rochester, 1983—88. Lt. USNR, 1968—70. Recipient Excellence in Secondary Sch. Tchg. award, U. Rochester Grad. Sch. Edn. and Human Devel., 1991. Mem.: SAR (bd. mgrs. Rochester chpt. 1997—, chpt. historian 1999—2004, chpt. pres. 2001—06, War Svc. medal 1996, Silver Good Citizenship medal 1997, Meritorious Svc. medal 2006, Liberty medal 2007), NY Social Studies Coun., Nat. Coun. Tchrs. English, Kodak Geneal. Soc., Ont. County Geneal. Soc., Rochester Geneal. Soc., USN Meml. Found., Dorothy L. Sayers Soc. U.K., Stratford Shakespearean Festival Found. Can., Sons Union Vets Civil War, U.S. Naval Inst. (life). Democrat. Avocations: reading, travel, photography, model railroads, genealogy. Home: 148 Greenway Blvd Churchville NY 14428-9210 Personal E-mail: sclarke@rochester.rr.com. *Live with the realization that the greatest success is that in which the world partakes, the indestructable good you leave behind.*

CLARKE, STEVEN GERARD, chemistry professor; b. LA, Nov. 19, 1949; BA in Chemistry/Zoology magna cum laude, Pomona Coll., 1970; PhD in Biochemistry & Molecular Biology, Harvard U., 1976. NIH undergrad. fellow Glynn Rsch. Labs., Bodmin, England, summer 1969; NSF predoctoral fellow Harvard U., 1970-73, biochemistry and molecular biology instr., 1973-74; Miller Inst. fellow U. Calif., Berkeley, 1976-78; asst. prof. chemistry and molecular biology UCLA, 1978-83, assoc. prof. chemistry and biochemistry, 1983-87, prof. chemistry and biochemistry, 1987—, dir. Molecular Biology Inst., 2001—. Vis. fellow molecular biology Princeton (N.J.) U., 1986-87, U. Wash., 2004-05; mem. sci. com. 1st Internat. Symposium on Post-Translational Modifications of Proteins and Aging, Lacco Ameno d'Ischia, Naples, Italy, 1987; chair, symposium organizer ann. meeting Am. Soc. for Biochemistry and Molecular Biology, Atlanta, 1991; mem. adv. bd. nutrition and metabolism sect. biol. aging Nat. Inst. Aging, NIH, 1993; co-chair Fedn. Am. Socs. for Exptl. Biology summer rsch. conf., Vt., 1995; dir. Molecular Biology Inst., U. Calif., L.A., Calif., 2001— Assoc. editor Protein Sci., 1995-98, mem. editl. adv. bd., 1994-95; mem. editl. bd. Jour. Biol. Chemistry, 1994-98; contbr. more than 200 articles to profl. jours. Woodrow Wilson fellow, 1970; grantee Am. Heart Assn., 1984-85, 85-86, 87-88, 89, NSF, 1989, 90, 91, NIH, 1995. Mem. Am. Chem. Soc. (Ralph F. Hirschmann award 1996), Am. Soc. Biochemistry and Molecular Biology, The Protein Soc., Assn. Med. and Grad. Depts. Biochemistry, Phi Beta Kappa, Alpha Chi Sigma. Office: UCLA Dept Chemistry & Biochem 607 Charles E Young Dr East Los Angeles CA 90095-1569 Home Phone: 310-820-1106; Office Phone: 310-825-8754. Business E-Mail: clarke@mbi.ucla.edu.

CLARKE, TERENCE MICHAEL, public relations and advertising executive; b. Altoona, Pa., Apr. 9, 1937; s. Robert Ewing and Louise Mercedes (Eckley) C.; m. Judith Ann Lawson, Oct. 15, 1966; children: Lawson Robert, Penn Terence. Student, U. Pitts., 1955-57; cert., Inst. Far Ea. Langs., Yale U., 1958; BS, Boston U., 1963, MS, 1989. Pub. rels. mgr. Pepsi-Cola Co., NYC, 1963, H.P. Hood & Sons, Boston, 1964-66; pres. The Taggart Co., Chgo., 1966-70; dir. pub. rels. Creamer, Trowbridge, Case & Basford, Boston, 1970; v.p., dir. Johnson, Raffin & Clarke Inc., Boston, 1971-76; assoc. prof. Boston U., 1976-77; chmn. Clarke Goward Advt. Inc., Boston, 1977—2004; chmn., CEO Clarke & Co. Inc., Boston, 1997—2004, Red 98 Interactive, 1999—2003; prin., owner Clarke Comm. Group, Inc., 2005—. Bd. dirs. EPROPSHOP, Inc. Chmn. sch. planning, site, constrn. com. Hingham, Mass., 1971-86; exec. com. Coll. Comm., Boston U., 1987—; bd. dirs. Mass. Soc. for Prevention of Cruelty to Children, 1980-94; mem. Hingham Police Sta. Constrn. Com., 1987-90; trustee Belmont (Mass.) Hill Sch., 1988-2003, Boston U., 1995-97; bd. overseers Huntington Theatre Co., Boston, 1992-2004; bd. govs. China Edn. Inst. With USAF, 1957-60. Recipient L.E. Sissman award Greater Boston Advt. Club, 1984. Mem. Greater Boston Advt. Club (bd. dirs. 1980-83), Barbershop Harmony Soc. (Internat. Quartet Champions 1980), Boston U. Alumni (pres. 1995-97, Disting. Alumni award Coll. Comms. 1984), Algonquin Club, Univ. Club. Republican. Presbyterian. Avocation: barbershop quartet singing.

CLARKE, THOMAS E., apparel executive; b. Binghamton, NY, Aug. 8, 1951; married. MS, U. Fla., Gainesville, 1977; D in Biomechanics, Pa. State U., 1980. With Nike, Inc., 1980—, rschr. Sports and Rsch. Lab Exeter, NH, various positions, 1983-94, divisional v.p. mktg., 1987—89, corp. v.p., 1989—90, gen. mgr., 1990, pres., COO Beaverton, Oreg., 1994-2000, bd. dirs., 1994—2004, co-CFO Beaverton, Oreg., 2000, pres. new bus. ventures. Avocation: running (competitive marathon runner). Office: Nike Inc One Bowerman Dr Beaverton OR 97005-6453 Office Phone: 503-671-6453.*

CLARKE, THOMAS HAL, lawyer; b. Atlanta, Aug. 10, 1914; s. James Caleb and Mary Cox (DeSaussure) C.; m. Mary Louise Hastings, July 12, 1951; children: Thomas Hal Jr., Katie Clarke Hamilton, Rebecca DeSaussure Morrison. LLB, Washington and Lee U., 1938. Bar: Ga. 1939, U.S. Dist. Ct. (no. dist.) Ga., U.S. Ct. Appeals (5th cir.), U.S. Supreme Ct., 1973. Ptnr. Clarke & Anderson, Atlanta, 1948-60, Mitchell, Clarke, Pate & Anderson, Atlanta, 1960-69, 73-85; of counsel Gambrell, Clarke, Anderson & Stolz, Atlanta, 1985-92. Copyright trustee Gone With the Wind and sequels, 1983—. Mem. Fed. Home Loan Bank Bd., Washington, 1969-73; past pres., bd. dirs. Atlanta Hist. Soc.; past bd. visitors Emory U.; trustee emeritus Washington and Lee U.; mem. Hibernian United Service Club, Dublin, Ireland. Served with USNR, 1942-46, ETO, PTO. Mem. Internat. Bar Assn. (past chmn. savs. and bldg. socs. com.), ABA (chmn. savs. and loan com. 1970-73, chmn. corp. banking and bus. law sect. 1973-74, mem. ho. of dels. 1974-80, editor The Business Lawyer 1972), Ga. Bar Assn., Atlanta Bar Assn., Am. Law Inst., Atlanta Lawyers Club (past pres.), Selden Soc., English Speaking Union (past pres., chmn. bd.), Metropolitan Club (Washington D.C.), Commerce Club, Piedmont Driving Club (Atlanta). Presbyterian. Home: 186 15th St NE Atlanta GA 30309-3511

CLARKE, TROY A., automotive executive; BEngring., GM Inst., 1978; MBA, U. Mich., 1982. Prodn. mgr. metal fabricating plant GM Corp., Grand Rapids, Mich., 1987—90, dir. México Ramos Arizpe complex Detroit, 1990—92, plant mgr. N.Am. ops. assembly ctr. Kansas City, 1993—97, dir. mfg. México Detroit, 1997, pres., mng. dir. México, corp. v.p., 1997—2001, v.p. labor rels., 2001—02, group v.p., mfg. and labor rels., 2002—04, group v.p., exec. v.p., GM Asia Pacific, 2004, pres., GM Asia Pacific, 2004—06, pres. N.Am. divsn., 2006—. Office: GM Corp 300 Rennaissance Ctr Detroit MI 48265

CLARKE, VICTORIA C. (TORIE CLARKE), former federal agency administrator; b. Pitts., Mar. 1959; m. Brian Graham; children: Colin, Charlie, Devan. BA, George Washington U., 1982. Editl asst., photographer, graphics editor Washington Star newspaper, 1979—82; press asst. to v.p. The White House, 1982; press sec. to Congressman, then Sen. John McCain, 1983—89; asst. U.S. Trade Rep. Exec. Office of the Pres., 1989—92; press sec. for reelection campaign Pres. George Bush, 1992; v.p. for pub. affairs and strategic counsel Nat. Cable TV Assn., 1993—98; pres. Bozell Eskew Advt.; gen. mgr. Hill and Knowlton, Washington; asst. sec. for pub. affairs U.S. Dept. Def., Washington, 2001—03; sr. advisor for comm. & govt. affairs Comcast Corp., Washington, 2003—; analyst CNN. Author: Lipstick on a Pig: Winning in the No-Spin Era by Someone Who Knows the Game, 2006. E-mail: torie@torieclarke.com.

CLARKE, YVETTE DIANE, congresswoman; b. Bklyn., Nov. 21, 1964; d. Una S.T. Clarke. Attended, Oberlin Coll., 1982—86, Medgar Evers Coll. Child care specialist Erasmus Neighborhood Fedn., 1985; legis. aide to Senator Velmanette Montgomery NY State Senate, 1986; exec. asst. to Assemblywoman Barbara Clark NY State Assembly; dir. youth programs Hosp. League / 1199 Training & Upgrading Fund, 1991; dir. bus. develop. Bronx Empowerment Zone; mem. NYC Coun. from 40th dist., 2002—07, co-chair women's caucus; mem. US Congress from 11th NY dist., 2007—; mem. homeland security com., edn. & labor com., small bus. com. Democrat. African Methodist Episcopal. Office: 1029 Longworth House Office Bldg Washington DC 20515 also: 123 Linden Blvd 4th Fl Brooklyn NY 11226 Office Phone: 718-287-1142. Office Fax: 718-287-1223.*

CLARKE-HALL, DEBORAH RENAY, elementary school educator; b. Washington, Aug. 15, 1954; d. Charlie and Claudelia Sweat Barnes; m. McLavern Hall, July 24, 1999. BS in Elem. Edn., Va. Union U., Richmond, 1979. Cert. tchr. Md. Bd. Edn., advanced profl. Md. Bd. Edn., 1982. Science educator Charles County, Md. Pub. Sch. Sys., Waldorf, 1979—95, 1995—. Mem. NAACP, Westmoreland County, Va.; served on numerous Democratic campaigns in Va. Named Outstanding Elem. Sci. Tchr., Md. Assn. Sci. Tchrs., 2002, Charles County Pub. Schs., 2006, So. Md. Elec. Co., 2006; recipient recognition as outstanding sci. educator, Millennium Chems., Frederick, Md., 2002. Mem.: NSTA (elem. sci. com. 2003—05, judge, Explora Vision awards 2004—06, judge, Craftsman Young Inventors 2005), Va. Assn. Sci. Tchrs., Com. on Elem. Sci. Internat., The Girl Friends, Inc. (Richmond chpt.). Democrat. Baptist. Avocations: birdwatching, antiques, tracking hurricanes using online data. Home: 8201 Eva Dr Port Royal VA 22535 E-mail: sweatclarke@hotmail.com.

CLARKIN, JOHN FRANCIS, health care management executive; b. Atlantic City, Dec. 30, 1936; s. John Francis and Agnes (Winterholer) C.; m. Dorothy Louise Piffath, 1 son, John F. BSBA, Rider Coll., 1959; postgrad., Temple U. Cert. mgmt. cons. Inst. Mgmt. Cons., 1968. Mktg. rep. Scott Paper Co., Indpls., 1960-62; systems and mktg. rep. Burroughs Corp., Phila., 1962-67; dir. Mid-Atlantic health care ops. mgmt. practice Coopers & Lybrand, Phila., 1967-92; v.p. corp. fin. svcs. Crozer-Keystone Health Sys., Upland, Pa., 1992-97; pres. The Clarkin Group, West Chester, Pa., 1997-98; v.p. bus. svcs. Thomas Jefferson U. Hosp., Phila., 1998—. Lead instr., spkr. numerous profl. meetings and seminars. Author: Topics in Health Care Financing, 1982; (with others) Handbook of Health Care Accounting and Finance, 1982, 89, Billing Systems, 2 vols., 1982, 89, Managing Accounts Receivable, 1990; contbr. articles to profl. jours. Mem. Grand Oak Run Civic Assn., 1970—. With U.S. Army, 1959. Grantee Rotary Club, 1955—59. Mem. Inst. Mgmt. Cons., Hosp. Mgmt. Systems Soc., Hosp. Fin. Mgmt. Assn., Med. Group Mgmt. Assn., Am. Hosp. Assn., Vesper Club, Pickering Racquet Club. Republican. Roman Catholic. Home: 1421 Grand Oak Ln West Chester PA 19380-5951 Office: Thomas Jefferson U Hosp Bus Svcs 170 S Independence Sq W Philadelphia PA 19106 Office Phone: 215-955-6403.

CLARK-JOHNSON, SUSAN, publishing executive; b. Mount Kisco, NY, Feb. 21, 1947; d. Emile Schurmacher and Elizabeth Woolf; m. Samuel Brooks Johnson. BA in history, SUNY, Binghamton, 1967. With Niagara Gazette, NY, 1970—83; pub. Binghamton Press & Sun-Bulletin, 1983—84; v.p. N.E. region Gannett Co. Inc., 1984—85; pres., pub. Reno Gazette-Jour., 1985—2000; pres. Gannett West Gannett Co. Inc., 1985—94, sr. group pres. Pacific Newspaper Group, 1994—2005; chmn. & CEO Phoenix Newspapers, 2000—05; pub. Ariz. Republic, 2000—05; pres. Gannett Co. newspaper divsn., McLean, Va., 2005—. Bd. dirs. Harrah's Entertainment, Inc.; bd. visitors John S. Knight Fellowships for Profl. Journalists, Stanford U. Office: Gannett Co Newspaper Divsn 7950 Jones Branch Drive Mc Lean VA 22101*

CLARK-JONES, THOMAS REES, musician; b. Wilkes Barre, Pa., Dec. 27, 1948; s. Arthur James Jones and Dorothy May Jenkins; m. Denise Marlene Clark, Feb. 16, 1991; children: Jillian Gail, Jenna Clark, William Clifford. MusB, Wilkes U., Wilkes Barre, 1970; MA in Organ Performance, Coll. NJ, Trenton, 1976. Organist, choirmaster Abington Ch., Pa., 1971—77, 1st Presbyn. Ch., Lynchburg, Va., 1986—96, Knoxville, Tenn., 1996—98, Pine St. Presbyn. Ch., Harrisburg, Pa., 1998—; organist Temple Shalom, Levittown, Pa., 1971—77; organist, dir. music Court St. United Meth. Ch., Flint, Mich., 1977—86; lectr. music Flint Coll., U. Mich., 1977—86. Mem.: Am. Guild Organists (bd. dirs. Phila. chpt. 1974—77, dean Flint chpt. 1979—83, dist. convener 1989—95). Home: 102 Ridgewood Dr Camp Hill PA 17011 Office: Pine St Presbyn Ch 310 N 3d St Harrisburg PA 17101

CLARK-LANGAGER, SARAH ANN, curator, academic administrator; b. Lynchburg, Va., May 14, 1943; m. Craig T. Langager, 1979. BA in Art History, Randolph-Macon Woman's Coll., 1965; postgrad., U. Md., 1968; MA in Art History, U. Wash., 1970; PhD in Art History, CUNY, 1988. Assoc. edn. dept., lectr. Yale U. Art Gallery, New Haven, 1965-67, Albright-Knox Art Gallery, Buffalo, 1967-68; asst. to dir. Richard White Gallery, Seattle, 1969-70; curatorial asst. to curators painting and sculpture San Francisco Mus. Modern Art, 1970; assoc. edn. dept., lectr. Seattle Art Mus., 1971-73, 74-75; asst. curator, and then assoc. curator modern art, lectr. Seatle Art Mus., 1975-79; curator 20th century art, lectr. Munson-Williams-Proctor Inst., Utica, NY, 1981-86; asst. prof. art history, dir. Univ. Art Gallery, U. North Tex., Denton, 1986-88; dir. Western Gallery, curator outdoor sculpture collection Western Wash. U., Bellingham, 1988—, mem. adj. faculty, 1988—. Lectr., cons. in edn. NY Cultural Ctr., NYC, 1973-74; editl. asst. October, MIT Press, NYC, 1980; lectr. art history South Seattle C.C., 1975; lectr. 20th century art Cornish Inst. Fine Arts, Seattle, 1977-78; sole rep. for N.Y. State, Art Mus. Assn. Am., 1984-86; bd. dirs. Wash. Art Consortium; cons. State of Wash. Save Outdoor Sculpture, 1994-2000, others. Contbr. articles to profl. jours.; curator exhbns., 1970—, including Rodney Ripps traveling exhbn., 1983, Sculpture Space: Recent Trends, 1984, Order and Enigma: American Art Between the Two Wars, 1984, Stars over Texas: Top of the Triangle, 1988, Public Art/Private Visions, 1989, Drawing Power, 1990, Focus on Figure, 1992, Chairs: Embodied Objects, 1993, Northwest Native American and First Nations People's Art, 1993, New Acquisitions, 1995, Stars and Stripes: American Prints and Drawings, 1995, Photographs from America, 1996, NW Artists' Books, 1999, Decades of Giving: Virginia Wright and Sculpture at Western, 1999, Surface Tension, 2003, A Sofa and., 2003, Noguchi & Dance, 2005, The Al Vera Lesse Collection, West Wash., 2006, others; author: Master Works of American Art from the Munson-Williams-Proctor Institute, 1989, Audiophone Tour for Sculpture Collection-20 Interviews, 1991, The Outdoor Sculpture Collection: The Development of Public Art at Western, 2000, The Italian Period in Susan Bennerstoom, 2000, Sculpture in Place: A Campus as Site, 2002, Isamu Noguchi: Beyond Red Square, 2004. Recipient Woman of Merit in Arts award Mohawk Valley C.C. and YWCA, Utica, 1985; Kress Found. fellow U. Wash., 1970; Helena Rubenstein Found. scholar CUNY Grad. Ctr., 1980. Office: Western Wash U Western Gallery Fine Arts Complex Bellingham WA 98225-9068 Office Phone: 360-650-3963. Business E-Mail: sarah.clarklangager@wwu.edu.

CLARKSON, ADRIENNE, former Governor General of Canada; b. Hong Kong, 1939; m. John Ralston Saul. BA with honours, U. Toronto, MA in English Lit.; postgrad., Sorbonne, Paris. Host, writer, prodr. CBC TV, 1965-82; first agt.-gen. for Ont. Paris, 1982-87; pres, pub. McClelland & Stewart, 1987-88; exec. prodr., host, writer Adrienne Clarkson's Summer Festival, Adrienne Clarkson Presents, 1988-98; gov. gen. Govt. of Can., 1999—2005. Chair, bd. trustees Can. Museum of Civilization, Hull, Que.; pres. exec. bd. IMZ, Vienna; active numerous arts and charitable orgns. Exec. prodr., host CBC TV program Something Special, others; writer, dir. several films, Can. Named Officer of the Order of Can., 1992, Chancellor and Prin. Companion of the Order of Can., 1999. Office: 12A Admiral Rd Toronto ON Canada M5R 2L5 Office Phone: 416-964-2313. E-mail: ahouse12@rogers.com.

CLARKSON, CHARLES ANDREW, real estate investment executive; b. Grove City, Pa., Sept. 1, 1945; s. Harold William and Jean Henrietta (Jaxtheimer) C.; m. Patricia Holt, June 14, 1969; children: Thomas Byerly, Blair Elizabeth, John Holt. AB, Princeton U., 1967; JD, George Washington U., 1972. With N.Y. Urban League, 1967—68; real estate negotiator Safeway Stores, Washington, 1968-69; mortgage banker J.W. Rouse Co., Washington, 1970-73; pres. Alex Brown Realty, Balt., 1973-76; founder, pres. The Clarkson Group, Jacksonville, Fla., 1976—. Bd. dirs. Ramgow, Inc.; chmn. Intelligenxia, JCCI. Chmn. bd. dirs. Jacksonville Urban League, 1987, The Alliance World Class Edn., Cmtys. in Schs., 1987; hon. trustee UNF Found.; mem. Environ. Land Mgmt. Study Com III, Fla.; chmn. bd. trustees WJCT-TV; mem. Commn. on Future of the South, 1998; chmn. bd. govs. FCCJ Found.; bd. Jacksonville Symphony, The Clarkson Group. Mem.: The Lodge at Ponte Vedra, Sawgrass Club. Office: The Clarkson Group Ste 200 3100 University Blvd S Jacksonville FL 32216-2727

CLARKSON, CHERYL LEE, healthcare executive; b. Chgo., Apr. 14, 1953; d. George Mendenhall and Carol Ann (Fertig) C.; m. Daniel J. Townsend; children: Drew Scott Clarkson-Townsend, Danielle Ann Clarkson-Townsend. BA in Sociology, Ariz. State U., 1975; MS in Mgmt., MIT, 1990. Sales rep. Am. Hosp. Supply, Inc., Phoenix, 1975-78, area sales mgr. Dallas, 1978-79, Edison, N.J., 1979-81, regional mgr. Boston, 1981-83, dir. sales Evanston, Ill., 1983-85; v.p. sales, mktg. Rudolph Beaver, Inc., Waltham, Mass., 1985-88; pres. Beaver Steriseal, Inc., Waltham, 1987-88, Clarkson and Assocs., 1988-90, Abiodent, Inc., Danvers, Mass., 1990-92; CEO, COO, bd. dirs. Peer Review Analysis, Inc., Boston, 1992-95; CEO, pres. SkinHealth, Inc., Wellesley, Mass., 1999—. Bd. overseers Boston U. Med. Ctr. Hosp., 1993-1997; bd. dirs. NMT Med. Inc., Boston. Trustee Kingsley Montessori Sch., Boston, 1996—99; bd. dirs. Northeastern U. Sch. of Bus., 1998—2006; trustee Mass. Eye and Ear Infirmary, Boston, 1998—; mem. global rsch. coun. Children's Hosp. of Boston, 2005—. Mem. Algonquin Club (Boston). Avocations: travel, golf, horseback riding. Office: SkinHealth Inc 251 Washington St Wellesley Hills MA 02481 Office Phone: 781-431-0454. Business E-Mail: cclarkson@skinhealthcenters.com.

CLARKSON, ELISABETH ANN HUDNUT, volunteer; b. Youngstown, Ohio, Apr. 20, 1925; d. Herbert Beecher and Edith (Schaaf) Hadnut; m. William M. E. Clarkson, Sept. 23, 1950; children: Alison H., David B., Andrew E. AB, Wilson Coll., 1947, LHD, 1985; MA, SUNY, 1973, postgrad. With J. L. Hudson Co., Detroit, 1947-50; writer Minute Parade daily Sta. WGR, Detroit, 1948-50. Author: (book) You Can Always Tell a Freshman, 1949, An Adirondack Archive: The Trail to Windover, 1993; contbr. articles to profl. jours. Trustee Wilson Coll., Chambersburg, Pa., 1970—83, chmn. bd. trustees, 1979—82; collector, curator Graphic Controls Corp. art collection, 1976—83; active N.Y. State Mus., 1985—90; past chmn. jr. group Albright Knox Art Gallery; mem. Buffalo Art Commn., 1983—, chmn., 1990—96; sustainer Jr. League, 1983—; mem. exec. bd. arts adv. coun. SUNY, Buffalo, 1985—95; mem. cmty. adv. panel Niagara Frontier Transp. Authority, 1991—94; trustee Clarkson Ctr. Human Svcs., 1995—2000, Irish Classical Theatre Co., 1998—2004; mem. adv. bd. Tannery Pond Cmty. Ctr., North Creek, NY, 2002—; mem. adv. com. Cmty. Fund Gore Mountain Region, 2005; mem. Trinity Episcopal Ch., 1950—, Trinity Vestry, 1996—99, mem. cultural leadership group, 1994—96, 1998—2000; mem. racism commn. Episcopal Diocese of Western N.Y., 1989—92; mem. Companion of the Holy Cross, 1971—, companion-in-charge soc., 1985—90; bd. dirs. Buffalo Mus. Sci., 1972—87, 1990—96, Bischoff Clarkson Hudnut Corp., North Creek, NY, 1973—83, Windover Corp., 1997—2003, pres., 1998—2001; bd. dirs. N.Y. State Mus. Assn., Albany, 1985—90; adv. bd. dirs. North Creek R.R. Mus., 2003—; mem. adv. bd. Adirondack Cmty. Trust Gore Mountain Region, 2007—. Recipient Trustee award for disting. svc., Wilson Coll., 1983, award in the arts, NCCJ, 1998. Mem.: Buffalo Club (art and archives com. 2004—), Sloane Club (London), Buffalo Tennis and Squash Club, Garret Club (bd. dirs. 2000—03, pres. 2001—02). Home: 156 Bryant St Buffalo NY 14222-2003: Log house Windover North Creek NY 12853

CLARKSON, JOHN G., academic administrator, ophthalmologist; m. Diana Teasdale; children: Paige, David. BS, Princeton U.; MD, Miami Sch. Medicine, 1968. Intern U. Hosp., Boston; resident ophthalmology U. Miami/Jackson Meml. Med. Ctr., Fla.; ophthalmic pathology, retinal and vitreous surgery fellow Johns Hopkins U., Balt.; chmn. dept. ophthalmology, dir. Bascom Palmer Eye Inst., 1991—96; sr. v.p. med. affairs, dean Sch. Medicine U. Miami, 1995—2006; exec. dir. Am. Bd. Ophthalmology, 2006—. Mem.: Macula Soc., Retina Soc., Am. Ophthalmol. Soc., Am. Acad. Ophthalmology, Am. Bd. Ophthalmology (bd. dirs.), Club Jules Gonin. Office: U Miami Miller Sch Medicine Profl Arts Ctr 301 1150 NW 14th St Miami FL 33136 Home Phone: 305-666-5796; Office Phone: 305-243-7878. Business E-Mail: jclarkson@miami.edu.

CLARKSON, KELLY BRIANNE, singer; b. Burleson, Tex., Apr. 24, 1982; d. Steve Clarkson, Jeanne and Jimmy Taylor (Stepfather). Winner inaugural Am. Idol contest, 2002; 2d place World Idol contest, 2004. Singer: (albums) Thankful, 2003 (Reached #1 on the Billboard Charts, 2004), Breakaway, 2004, My December, 2007, (songs) Before Your Love/A Moment Like This, 2002 (Billboard best selling single of yr.), Because of You, 2004 (MTV Video Music award for Best Female Video, 2006); actor: (films) Issues 101, 2002, From Justin to Kelly, 2003; singer: (films) Love Actually, 2003, Ella Enchanted, 2004, The Princess Diaries 2: Royal Engagement, 2004. Co-recipient Song Writer award for Miss Independent (with Rhett Lawrence), ASCAP, 2004; recipient Best Female Video and Best Pop Video for Since U Been Gone, MTV Video Music Awards, 2005, Favorite Adult Contemporary Artist, Am. Music Awards, 2005, Favorite Female Performer, People's Choice Awards, 2006, Best Pop Vocal Album, Grammy awards, 2006, Best Female Pop Vocal Performance, 2006, Choice Music: Female Artist, Teen Choice Awards, 2006, Favorite Female Artist, Am. Music Awards, 2006, Favorite Artist Adult Contemporary, 2006. Office: c/o Jeff Kwatinetz The Firm 9465 Wilshire Blvd 6th Fl Beverly Hills CA 90212 Office Phone: 310-860-8000. Office Fax: 310-860-8100.*

CLARKSON, LAWRENCE WILLIAM, air transportation executive; b. Grove City, Apr. 29, 1938; s. Harold William and Jean Henrietta (Jaxtheimer) Clarkson; m. Barbara Louise Stevenson, Aug. 20, 1960; children: Michael, Elizabeth, Jennifer. BA, DePauw U., 1960; JD, U. Fla., 1962. Counsel Pratt & Whitney, West Palm Beach, Fla., 1967-72, program dep. dir., 1972-75, program mgr., 1974-75, v.p., mng. dir. Brussels, 1975-78, v.p. mktg. West Palm Beach, 1978-80, v.p. contracts Hartford, Conn., 1980-82, pres. comml. products div., 1982-87; sr. v.p. Boeing Comml. Airplanes Group, Seattle, 1988-91; corp. v.p. planning and internat. devel. Boeing Co., Seattle, 1992-93, sr. v.p., 1994-99; pres. Boeing Enterprises, Seattle, 1997-99; sr. v.p. Project Internat., Seattle, 2000—. Chmn. Hitco Carbon, 2002—, Interturbine NV, 2000—02; bd. dirs. Partnership for Improved Air Travel, Washington, 1988—91, Atlas Air, Avnet Inc. Trustee DePauw U., Greencastle, Ind., 1987—, vice chmn., 1996—2002; trustee Embry Ridde Aero. U., Daytona Beach, Fla., Seattle Opera, 1990—, chmn., 1991—2002; overseer Tuck Sch. Dartmouth, Hanover, NH, 1993—99; corp. counsel Interlochen (Mich.) Ctr. Arts, 1987, trustee, 1988—, chmn., 1996—2001; pres. Japan-Am. Soc., Wash., 1993, Wash. State China Rels. Com., 1992—93; chmn. Nat. Bur. Asia Rsch., Coun. Fgn. Rels., U.S. Pacific Econ. Corp. Coun., 1993—2000. Mem.: Am. Inst. Contemporary German Studies (bd. dirs. 1997—99), Nat. Assn. Mfrs. (bd. dirs. 1993—99), The Pilgrims of the U.S., Wings Club (bd. govs. 1987—91), Met. Club DC, N.Y. Yacht Club, Order St. John (bd. govs., Knight). Episcopalian. Home: 3795 Lamb Dr NW Marietta GA 30064 Office Phone: 206-979-7001. Personal E-mail: lwc42938@aol.com.

CLARKSON, THOMAS WILLIAM, toxicologist, educator; b. Eng., Aug. 1, 1932; came to U.S., 1957; s. William and Olive (Jackson) C.; m. Winifred Browne, Mar. 4, 1957; children: Ian, Jean, Ann. BSc, U. Manchester, 1953, PhD, 1956; Dr Medicine (hon.), U. Umea, Sweden, 1986. Sci. officer tox research unit Med. Research Council U.K., Carshalton, Surrey, 1962-64; sr. fellow polymer sci. Weizmann Inst. Sci., Rehovot, Israel, 1964-65; mem. faculty U. Rochester (N.Y.) Med. Sch., 1958—, prof. toxicology, 1971—, head div., 1980-86, J. Lowell Orbison Disting. Svc. Alumni prof., 1983—, dir. Environ. Health Scis. Ctr., 1986-98; chmn. Dept. Environ. Medicine, 1992-98. Dir. NASA Ctr. Rsch. and Tng. in Space Environ. Health, 1991-95. Mem. editorial bds. profl. jours.; author articles in field. Recipient Founders' award CIIT, 1997, Arthur Kornberg Rsch. award U. Rochester, 1999. Mem. Inst. Medicine of NAS, Permanent Commn. Internat. Assn. Occupational Health, Soc. Toxicology (Arnold J. Lehman award 1993, Merit award 1999), Brit. Pharm. Soc., Am. Soc. Pharmacology and Exptl. Therapeutics, Internat. Soc. for Trace Element Rsch. in Humans, Ramazzini Collegium, Polish Toxicology Soc. (hon.), La Academia Nacional de Medicina de Buenos Aires (hon. mem.). Office: Dept Environ Medicine U Rochester Med Sch Rochester NY 14642-0001

CLARNO, KEVIN TAYLOR, nuclear engineer; b. Ill. BS, MIT, Cambridge, Mass., 1999; MS, Tex. A&M U., Coll. Sta., 2001, PhD, 2005. Computational nuc. engr. Oak Ridge Nat. Lab., Tenn., 2004—.

CLARREN, STERLING KEITH, pediatrician; b. Mpls., Mar. 12, 1947; s. David Bernard and Lila (Reifel) C.; m. Sandra Gayle Bernstein, June 8, 1970; children: Rebecca Pia, Jonathan Seth. BA, Yale U., 1969; MD, U. Minn., 1973. Pediatric intern U. Wash. Sch. Medicine, Seattle, 1973-74, resident in pediatrics, 1974-77, asst. prof. dept. pediatrics, 1979-83, assoc. prof., 1983-88, prof., 1988, Robert A. Aldrich chair in pediatrics, 1989—2005; clin. prof. pediatrics U. B.C. Faculty of Medicine, Vancouver, 2005—; CEO Can. N.W. FASD Rsch Network, Vancouver, 2005—. Head divsn. congenital defects U. Wash. Sch. Medicine, 1987-95, head divsn. hosp. medicine, 2002-04; dir. dept. congenital defects Children's Hosp. and Med. Ctr., Seattle, 1987-96, dir. fetal alcohol syndrome clinic Child Devel. and Mental Retardation Ctr. U. Wash., 1992-2001, dir. Fetal Alcohol Syndrome Network, 1995-2001; dir. inpatient svcs. Children's Hosp. and Med. Ctr., Seattle, 1996-2004. Contbr. articles to profl. jours.; patentee for orthosis to alter cranial shape. Cons. pediatrician Maxillofacial Rev. Bd., State of Wash., Seattle, 1984-90, chmn. Health-Birth Defects Adv. Com., Olympia, 1980-90; mem. gov.'s task force on FAS State of Wash., 1994-95; mem. fetal alcohol adv. com. Children's Trust Found., Seattle, 1988—; bd. dirs. Seattle Children's Home, 2003—; mem. adv. bd. Nat. Orgn. on Fetal Alcohol Syndrome; mem. fetal alcohol com. Inst. Medicine, NAS, 1994-95. Rsch. grantee Nat. Inst. Alcohol Abuse & Alcoholism, 1982—, Ctrs. for Disease Control, 1992—. Fellow AAAS; mem. Soc. for Pediatric Rsch., Teratology Soc., Rsch. Soc. on Alcoholism (pres. fetal alcohol study group 1993), Am. Cleft Palate Assn., N.Y. Acad. Scis. Avocations: cross country skiing, fishing, hiking, sailing. Office: Sunny Hill Health Ctr for Children 3644 Slocan St Vancouver BC V5M 3E8 Canada Home: 8515 Paisley Dr NE Seattle WA 98115 Office Phone: 604-453-8306, 604-875-2000 x 3390. E-mail: sclarren@cw.bc.ca.

CLARY, BRADLEY G., lawyer, educator; b. Richmond, Va., Sept. 7, 1950; s. Sidney G. and Jean B. Clary; m. Mary-Louise Hunt, July 31, 1982; children: Benjamin, Samuel. BA magna cum laude, Carleton Coll., 1972; JD cum laude, U. Minn., 1975. Bar: Minn. 1975, US Dist. Ct. Minn. 1975, US Ct. Appeals (10th cir.) 1977, US Ct. Appeals (8th cir.) 1979, US Ct. Appeals (6th cir.) 1980, US Ct. Appeals (7th cir.) 1981, US Supreme Ct. 1986, US Ct. Appeals (4th cir.) 1989, US Ct. Appeals (9th cir.) 1991. Assoc. Oppenheimer Wolff & Donnelly, St. Paul, 1975-81, ptnr., 1982-2000; from legal writing dir. Law Sch. to clin. prof. U. Minn., 1999—. Vaughan G. Papke clin. prof. law, 2004—06, dir. applied legal instrn., 2004—. Adj. prof. Law Sch. U. Minn., Mpls., 1985-99; adj. instr. William Mitchell Coll. Law, St. Paul, 1995-96, 98, adj. prof., 1997, 99. Author: Primer on the Analysis and Presentation of Legal Argument, 1992; co-author: Advocacy on Appeal, 2001, 2d edit., 2004, Successful First Depositions, 2001, 2d edit., 2006, Successful Legal Analysis and Writing: The Fundamentals, 2003, 2d edit., 2006. Vestryman St. John Evangelist Ch., St. Paul, 1978-81, 98-00, pledge drive co-chmn., 1989-90, sr. warden, 2000-2002; mem. alumni bd. Breck Sch., Mpls., 1981-85, 89-96, exec. com., 1991-96, dir. emeritus, 1996—; mem. adv. bd. Glass Theatre Co., West St. Paul, Minn., 1982-87; mem. antitrust adv. panel dept. health State of Minn., 1992-93. Mem. ABA (adv. group antitrust sect. 1987-89, corp. counseling com.), Minn. Bar Assn. (program chmn. antitrust sect. 1986-87, treas. 1987-88, vice-chmn. 1989-90, co-chmn. 1990-92, governing coun. appellate practice sect. 2001-03, 2003-06), Phi Beta Kappa Avocations: tennis, sailing. Office: U Minn Law Sch 229 19th Ave S Rm 444 Minneapolis MN 55455-0400

CLARY, RICHARD WAYLAND, lawyer; b. Tarboro, NC, Oct. 10, 1953; s. S. Grayson and Jean (Beazley) C.; m. Suzanne Clerkin, July 21, 1991; children: Grayson Edward, Taryn Fenner. BA magna cum laude, Amherst Coll., Mass., 1975; JD magna cum laude, Harvard U., Cambridge, Mass., 1978. Bar: N.Y. 1981, U.S. Dist. Ct. (so. and ea. dists.) N.Y. 1981, U.S. Dist. Ct. (no. dist.) Calif. 1982, U.S. Ct. Appeals (9th cir.) 1983, U.S. Supreme Ct. 1989, U.S. Ct. Appeals (3d cir.) 1990, U.S. Ct. Appeals (2d cir.) 1994, U.S. Ct. Appeals (fed. cir.) 1995, U.S. Dist. Ct. (no. dist.) N.Y. 1998, U.S. Ct. Appeals (11th cir.) 1999, U.S. Ct. Appeals (6th cir.) 2000, U.S. Dist. Ct. D.C. 2002, U.S. Ct. Appeals (5th cir.) 2003. Law clk. to judge U.S. Ct. Appeals (2d cir.), NYC, 1978-79; law clk. to Justice Thurgood Marshall U.S. Supreme Ct., Washington, 1979-80; assoc. Cravath, Swaine & Moore LLP, NYC, 1980-85, ptnr., 1985—, mng. ptnr. litigation, 1997—2005, head of litigation, 2005—. Bd. dirs. Legal Aid Soc., 1998—.(vice chair, 2003-) John Woodruff Simpson fellow Amherst Coll., 1975-76. Mem. ABA, N.Y. State Bar Assn., Assn. Bar City N.Y., Fed. Bar Coun., London Ct. Internat. Arbitration, Phi Beta Kappa Roman Catholic. Office: Cravath Swaine & Moore LLP Worldwide Plz 825 8th Ave New York NY 10019-7475 Office Fax: 212-474-3700. Business E-Mail: rclary@cravath.com.

CLASSON, ROLF ALLAN, pharmaceutical company executive; b. Nassjo, Sweden, Aug. 20, 1945; s. Allan K.E. and May Britt (Lagerquist) C.; m. Birgitta Larsson, Feb. 3, 1968; children: Peter, Karin, Erik. M in Bus. Econs., Gothenburg U., 1969. Personnel mgr. Pharmacia, Uppsala, Sweden, 1969-74; mgmt. cons. Asbjorn Habberstad, Stockholm, 1974-77; mktg. mgr. Pharmacia, Uppsala, 1977-80; div. gen. mgr. Tarkett, Ronneby, 1980; pres. Pharmacia Infusion, Uppsala, 1981-84, Pharmacia Devel. Co. Inc., Piscataway, NJ, 1984-90; pres., chief oper. officer Pharmacia Biosystems AB, 1990—91; exec. v.p. Bayer Corp., 1995—2002, exec. v.p., worldwide mktg., sales & services, group diagnostics, 1991—92, pres., group diagnostics, 1995—2002, sr. v.p., sales & services, group diagnostics, 1992—95, chmn. exec. comm., health care div., 2002—04; vice-chmn. Hillenbrand Industries, Batesville, Ind., 2004—05, interim pres., CEO, 2005—06, chmn., 2006—. Mem. supv. bd. Bayer HealthCare AG; bd. dir. Enzon Pharmaceuticals, ISTA Pharmaceuticals, Millipore Corp., Auxilium Pharmaceuticals. Office: Hillenbrand Industries Mail Code K71 1069 State Route 46 E Batesville IN 47006-8835*

CLASTER, JILL NADELL, academic administrator, history educator; d. Harry K. and Edith Lillian Nadell; m. Millard L. Midonick, May 24, 1979; 1 child from previous marriage, Elizabeth Claster (dec.). BA, NYU, 1952, MA, 1954; PhD, U. Pa., 1959. Instr. history U. Pa., 1956-58; instr. ancient and medieval history U. Ky., Lexington, 1959-61, asst. prof., 1961-64; adj. asst. prof. classics NYU, NYC, 1964-65, asst. prof. history, 1965-68, assoc. prof., 1968-84, prof., 1984—, acting undergrad. chmn. history, 1972-73, dir. M.A. in liberal studies program, 1976-78; assoc. dean Washington Sq. and Univ. Coll., 1978, acting dean, 1978-79, dean, 1979-86; dir. Hagop Kevorkian Ctr. for Near Eastern Studies, NYU, 1991-96. Appointee N.Y.C. Commn. on Status of Women. Author: Athenian Democracy: Triumph or Travesty, 1967, The Medieval Experience, 1982; Contbr. articles to profl. jours. Danforth grantee, 1966-68; Fulbright grantee, 1958-59 Mem. Am. Hist. Assn., Medieval Acad. Am. Home: 161 W 15th St New York NY 10011-6720 Office: NYU Dept History 53 Washington Sq S Dept History New York NY 10012-1098 Office Phone: 212-243-4445. Business E-Mail: jill.claster@nyu.edu.

CLAUS, CHRISTOPHER W., insurance company executive; BBA, U. Minn.; MBA, U. St. Thomas, St. Paul. Dir. mktg. Norwest Investment Svcs., Mpls., v.p. equity trading and retirement plans; v.p. investment sales and svc. Investment Mgmt. Co. USAA (United Svcs. Automobile Assn.), 1994, sr. v.p. investment sales and svcs. Investment Mgmt. Co., pres. fin. svcs. group and investment mgmt. co., 2001—. Bd. govs. Investment Co. Inst. Office: USAA 9800 Fredericksburg Rd San Antonio TX 78288 Office Phone: 210-498-8222.*

CLAUSELL, DEBORAH DELORIS, artist; b. Mobile, Ala., July 16, 1951; d. Stephen Joseph and Estel Abney Clausell. BA in Sociology, U. Mobile, Ala., 1976; cert., Barbizon Modeling Sch., 1984. Movie extra Century Casting, Santa Monica, Calif., 1984—85; libr. Mobile Pub. Libr., 1996-97. Exhibited in group shows Greater Gulf State Fair, Mobile, 1990, 96 (3d, 2d and 1st prize ribbons), 1997 (3rd prize ribbon), 1999, 2005 (3d prize), Mercy Med. Gallery, Daphne, Ala., 1993, Mus. of City of Mobile, 1993, Fine Art Mus. of the South, Mobile, 1993, Spring Hill Art, Mobile, 1993, Greater Gulf State Fair Exhibit Fine Arts, 1999, Monticello-Thomas Jefferson Meml., 1993; pvt. collection The White House, Heritage Hall, 2000 and Art Auction, Energen Corp. Artpark Exbhn., 2001, Greater Gulf State Fair (Fine Art 3d prize), 2005, Gold Stories of Gold Eagles Letters, 2007. Mem. Smithsonian Inst., 2001, USS Constn. Mus., 2002, U.S. Border Control, 2003. 2d lt. USAF, res. Recipient 3d prize fine art dept., Greater Gulf State Fair, 2005, Gold Eagles and Stars Letters, US Pres. Bush, 2006, 2007. Mem. VFW, Internat. Platform Assn., Nat. D-Day Mus., U.S. Naval Inst., Libr. Congress Assn., Nat. Trust for Hist. Preservation, Civil War Trust, Mt. Vernon Ladies Assn., Navel League, Preservation Alliance. Democrat. Roman Catholic. Avocations: classic guitarist, harmonica, swimming, vocal singing, reading. Home: 5859 Reams Dr N Mobile AL 36608-3652 Office Phone: 251-341-1217.

CLAUSEN, HUGH JOSEPH, retired army officer; b. Mobile, Ala., Dec. 25, 1926; s. Hugh Martin and Elizabeth Hazel (Orrell) C.; m. Betty Sue Richards, June 7, 1949; children: Melinda, Joseph. LL.B., U. Ala., 1950; grad., Advanced Mgmt. Program, Harvard U., 1970. Bar: Ala. 1950, U.S. Supreme Ct. 1959, U.S. Ct. Mil. Appeals 1959. Commd. 1st lt. U.S. Army, 1951, advanced through grades to maj. gen.; various assignments U.S. and Europe, 1951-62; asst. staff judge adv. (8th Army), Korea, 1962-64; judge adv. U.S. Disciplinary Barracks, Fort Leavenworth, Kans., 1964-66; instr. U.S. Army Command and Gen. Staff Coll., 1966-68; staff judge adv. 1st Inf. Div., Vietnam, 1968-69; assigned Office Legis. Liaison, Dept. Army, Washington, 1969-71; chief mil. justice div. Office JAG, 1971-72, exec. officer, 1972-73; staff judge adv. III Corps and Ft. Hood, Tex., 1973-76; chief judge U.S. Army Ct. Mil. Rev., Falls Church, Va., 1976-78; asst. judge adv. gen. for mil. law Dept. Army., 1978-79, asst. judge adv. gen., 1979-81, judge adv. gen., 1981-85. Vice pres. for adminstrn., sec. bd. trustees Clemson U., S.C., 1985-92, v.p. emeritus, 1992—. Decorated Disting. Service Medal, Bronze Star with 3 oak leaf clusters, Meritorious Service medal, Legion of Merit with oak leaf cluster, Air medal with oak leaf cluster, Army Commendation medal with oak leaf cluster; RVN Honor medal; RVN Gallantry Cross with palm; RVN Civic Action Honor medal with palm. Mem. Ala. Bar Assn., Phi Alpha Delta. Address: 333 Kendra Pl Clemson SC 29631 Personal E-mail: hughclausen@nuvok.net.

CLAUSEN, JANE, library director; Pub. svcs. dir. Lubbock Pub. Libr., Tex., dir. Tex. Mem.: Lubbock Area Libr. Assn., Tex. Libr. Assn. Office: Lubbock Pub Libr 1306 9th St Lubbock TX 79401 Office Phone: 806-775-2824. Office Fax: 806-775-2827. E-mail: jclausen@mail.ci.lubbock.tx.us.

CLAUSEN, JEANNE LORRAINE, musician; b. LA, Oct. 16, 1944; BA, Sarah Lawrence Coll., 1967; MA in Music, Cleve. Inst. Music, 1972. Mem. Calif. New Music Ensemble, LA, 1975—78; mem. trio in residence Claremont Grad. Sch., Calif., 1976—79; concert mistress Ensemble Concerto, dir. Roberto Gini, Milan, 1983—86; mem. Amsterdam Baroque Orch., dir. Ton Koopman, Netherlands, 1986—87; founder, 1st violin La Cetra, San Francisco, 1982—2002. Author: Something Has Been Lost In the Passage of Time, (video) The Rhapsodic Art Of The Ancients. Achievements include research on 16th century stringed instrument the lira da braccia. Avocations: hiking, swimming, reading, good conversation, enjoying the mystical beauty of nature. Home: PO Box 2603 Nevada City CA 95959 Personal E-mail: jeannelc@earthlink.net.

CLAUSEN, JERRY LEE, psychiatrist; b. Wausau, Wis., Nov. 5, 1939; s. Douglas William and Florence Jean (Amidon) Clausen; m. Nancy Eileen Longdon, Aug. 3, 1962; children: Keith Rusell, Pamela Dawn. BA, Wesleyan U., Middletown, Conn., 1961; MD, Albany Med. Coll., NYC, 1965. Diplomate in psychiatry and addiction psychiatry Am. Bd. Psychiatry and Neurology, cert. Am. Soc. Addiction Medicine. Psychiatry intern Upstate Med. Ctr., Syracuse, 1965-66, psychiat. resident, 1966-67, 69-71, asst. attending, 1971-72, attending, 1972-80; staff psychiatrist Onondaga Mental Health Clinic, Syracuse, 1971-72; courtesy staff Benjamin Rush Psychiatric Ctr., Syracuse, 1971-84, active staff, 1984—2004; pvt. practice psychiatry Syracuse, 1971—2004; clin. asst. prof. SUNY, 1972—. Staff psychiatrist Onondaga Pastoral Counseling Ctr., Syracuse, 1971—72, Syracuse, 1981—97, psychiat. dir., 1973—81; cons. psychiatrist Loretto Rest Geriatric Ctr., Syracuse, 1972—74. Tchr. 1st Universalist Ch., Syracuse, 1966—. Lt. comdr. USN, 1967—69. Fellow: Am. Psychiat. Assn. (chmn. ins. mktg. com. 1979—88, disting.); mem.: N.Y. State Med. Soc., Onondaga County Med. Soc. Avocations: walking, tennis, cross country skiing. Home Phone: 315-637-9263; Office Phone: 315-727-9263. Personal E-mail: jclausen@twcny.rr.com.

CLAUSEN, MARK A., lawyer; s. Alton B. and Vivian B. Clausen; m. Ann M. Lokey, Jan. 1, 1991; children: David M., William HF, Ellena A. Jones. BS, Oakland U., Rochester, Mich., 1980; JD, Coll. William & Mary, Williamsburg, Va, 1984. Bar: Wash. 1986, Fed. Dist. Ct. (we. dist.), DC 1986, Ct. Claims Fed. Cir. 2005, Vaccine Injury Compensation Bd. 2004, Ct. Appeals (9th cir.) 2004. Law clk. Wash. State Ct. Appeals, Seattle, 1984, Wash. State Supreme Ct., Olympia, 1985—85, Diamond & Sylvester, Seattle, 1985—86; atty. Oles Morrison Rinker Stanislaw & Ashbaugh, Seattle, 1986—89, Bryan Schiffrin & McMonagle, Seattle, 1989—93; pres. Mark A. Clausen, P.S., Seattle, 1993—97; mem. Linville Clausen & Linton, PLLC, Seattle, 1997—2004; prin. Clausen Law Firm, PLLC, Seattle, 2004—. Dir. Vertical World, Inc, Seattle, 1997—98. Coun. mem. U. Luth. Ch., Seattle, 2001—03; dir. NW Chamber Chorus, Seattle, 1985—86. Recipient First Pl., News Reporting award, UPI Ind. Newspapers, 1980, First Pl., Investigative Reporting award, Inland Daily Press Assn., 1981, First Pl. award, John Marshall Law Sch. Moot Ct. Tournament, 1983; fellow, John Marshall Soc., 1984. Mem.: Wash. State Bar Assn. (chmn. consumer Protection Com. 2000—01). Lutheran. Avocations: bicycling, mountain climbing, running, classical music. Office: Clausen Law Firm PLLC 701 Fifth Ave Ste 7230 Seattle WA 98104 Office Phone: 206-223-0335.

CLAUSER, DONALD ROBERDEAU, retired musician; b. Fort Worth, Mar. 2, 1941; s. Donald Milton and Selina Almira (Sizer) C. B.F.A., U. N.M., 1962; Mus.M., Boston U., 1964; diploma, Curtis Inst. Music, 1967. Mem. viola sect., Phila. Orch., 1966—04, ret., 2004. Home: 1609 Chanticleer Cherry Hill NJ 08003-4820 *It is my conviction that music is a universal medium of communication— a factor which is surely of distinct value in these troubled times. Keeping this in mind has constantly been uppermost in the pursuit of my career, wherever this may have led me.*

CLAUSMAN, GILBERT JOSEPH, retired medical librarian; b. Los Angeles, Nov. 8, 1921; s. Pete John and Lila (Mason) C. AB, Willamette U., 1947; BS, Columbia U., 1948, MS, 1952. Med. librarian N.Y. Acad. Medicine, NYC, 1948-55; med. librarian NYU Med. Ctr., NYC, 1955-86, librarian emeritus, 1987—. Cons. Milton Helpern Library Legal Medicine, 1963-88. Served with USN, 1942-45 Mem. Med. Libr. Assn. (pres. 1977-78), Archons of Colophon, N.Y. Acad. Medicine, Acad. Health Info. Profls. Home: 6 Cobble Hill Rd Westport CT 06880-2915

CLAUSON, SHARYN FERNE, consulting company executive, educator; b. Phila., Oct. 4, 1946; d. Eugene and Gertrud Jayn (Besser) C. BA in English, Temple U., 1968; MEd in Psychology, Arcadia U. (formerly Beaver Coll.), 1979; MBA in Marketing, Drexel U., 1982; postgrad. in law, Temple U., 1987. Market analyst Epstein Rsch., Bala, Pa., 1967-69; cons. Ednl. Testing Svc., Princeton, NJ, 1979-80; CEO CCX, Narberth, Pa., 1978-79; mem. faculty Cheltenham Twp. Sch. Dist., Elkins Park, Pa., 1969—2003; dir. Sharyn Clauson Bus. Comm., Narberth, Pa., 1975-85; pres. S. Clauson & Assocs., Inc., King of Prussia, Pa., 1985—; dir. Execuwriter, King of Prussia, 1985—. Adj. faculty Drexel U., Phila., 1979-96, Phila. U., 1985-89, St. Joseph's U., Phila., 1986-92, Phila. Ctr. of Gt. lakes Coll. Assn., 1988; adv. bd. Ergodyne, Inc., 1995-96; talk show host Sta. WDVT-AM, Phila., 1985; bd. dirs. Site Selex, Inc., Doylestown, Pa., dir. comm. and pub. rels., 1988-95. Editor: Curriculum for Optacon Music Reading, 1984; mem. editorial adv. bd. Bus. Communications and Concepts, 2d edit., 1985 Com. mem. Women's Polit. Caucus, Phila.; mem. Phila. Art Alliance; exec. bd., arts and scis. alumni bd. Temple U. Women's Law Caucus; sec., v.p. bd. dirs. VFTW Coun., 2000-02, 04-06, sec. 2000-01, v.p., 2001-02, 04-06; Moore-Irwin taskforce Upper Merion Twp., 2006—, Econ. and Cmty. Devel. Commn., 2007—. Golden Hearts honoree, 1999; recipient U.S. Congl. award, 1999. Mem. ASCD, AAUW, Am. Mktg. Assn., Nat. Spkrs. Assn. (chairperson 1985), Nat. Assn. Profl. Saleswomen (honoree 1982—), Nat. Coun. Tchrs. of English, Delaware Valley Writing Coun., Wallenberg Communicators, Phi Delta Kappa. Office: 21036 Valley Forge Circle King Of Prussia PA 19406 E-mail: Sfc1210@aol.com.

CLAUSS, PETER OTTO, lawyer; b. Knoxville, Tenn., Sept. 23, 1936; s. Alfred and Jane (West) C.; m. Elizabeth Mary Lou Percival, Apr. 28, 1962; children: Andrew Bradford, Victoria Johns. AB, U. Chgo., 1955; LLB, Yale U., 1958. Bar: Pa. 1959, U.S. Dist. Ct. (ea. dist.) Pa. 1959, U.S. Tax Ct. 1959, U.S. Ct. Appeals (3d cir.) 1959, U.S. Supreme Ct. 1963, U.S. Ct. Claims 1960, U.S. Ct. Customs 1962. Assoc. Clark, Ladner, Fortenbaugh & Young, Phila., 1958-65, ptnr., 1966-96, mem. exec. com., 1967-76, mng. ptnr., 1968-72, sr. ptnr., chmn. corp. and bus. dept., 1983-96; sr. ptnr. Pepper, Hamilton LLP, Phila., 1996—2004, of counsel, 2004—. Past dir. Norcross, Inc., Nutrion Corp., Helicrane Constrn. Corp., Mannion Co., Henry Cantor, Inc., Keystone Helicopter Corp., Interactive Graphics, Inc.; asst. sec. Masland Corp., 1974-86; adj. prof. law Villanova U., 2002—; lectr. in field. Contbr. articles to legal jours. Sec., mem. vestry, mem. Outreach Com., stewardship com., search com., Christ Ch., Ithan; past coach Little League Baseball; past treas. Ithan Sch. PTA; past treas. Boy Scouts Am., Ithan, Pa. Ford Found. fellow, 1952-55; chmn. 50th reunion class gift com., U. Chgo., 2004-05. With USNG, 1959-67. Mem. ABA (past chmn. sales, exchanges and basis com. tax sect.), Phila. Bar Assn. (past chmn. unpopular causes com., past vice chmn. pub. svc. com.), Pa. Bar Assn., Juristic Soc. of Phila. (past bd. govs.), Yale Law Sch. Assn. for Ea. Pa. (pres. 1974-82), Assn. Yale Alumni (Phila. del. 1982-84), Phi Gamma Delta (nat. sec., bd. dirs., 1982-88, gen. counsel, 1972-82, gen. counsel ednl. found. 1996-2006), Phi Delta Phi, Yale of Phila. Club (past pres.), Phila. Club, Racquet of Phila. Club, First Troop Phila. City Calvary Club, Univ. Barge Club, Merion Cricket Club, Orpheus Club, First Monday Club (past pres.), Ocean Point and Ocean Creek Golf Club (Fripp Island, S.C.), Dataw Island Golf Club (S.C.), Penn Club (v.p. 2007—). Republican. Episcopalian. Home: 758 Darby Paoli Rd Newtown Square PA 19073-2609 Office: 3000 Two Logan Sq 18th & Arch Sts Philadelphia PA 19103-2799 Home Phone: 610-525-5404; Office Phone: 215-981-4541. Business E-Mail: claussp@pepperlaw.com.

CLAUSS-EHLERS, CAROLINE S., psychologist, educator, journalist; b. Manhasset, NY, July 17, 1967; d. Harold Wilson and Carole (Page) Clauss; m. Julian Charles Edward Clauss-Ehlers; children: Isabel S., Sabrina S. BA with honors, Oberlin Coll., 1989; MA, Columbia U., 1992, EdM, 1993, PhD, 1999. Bilingual clinician Henry St. Settlement, Cmty. Consultation Ctr., NYC, 1992-96; clin. interviewer N.Y. State Psychiat. Inst., NYC, 1995-98; predoctoral intern in clin. psychology NYU Med. Ctr./Bellevue Hosp., NYC, 1996-97; columnist HOY, 2002—; psychologist pvt. practice, 2000—. Adj. asst. prof. psychology and edn. Tchr. Coll., Columbia U., 1998—2001; asst. prof. counseling psychology Rutgers U. Grad. Sch. Edn., 2001—; guest correspondent Univision, 2002—; cons. in field. Author: Diversity Training for Classroom Teaching: A Manual for Students and Educators, 2006; co-editor: Community Planning to Foster Resilience in Children, 2004; contbr. articles to profl. jours. Oberlin Alumni scholar, 1992; Tchrs. Coll. scholar, 1994-96; Leopold Schepp Found. fellow, 1994-97; Rosalynn Carter fellow for mental health journalism, 2004-05. Mem. APA, N.Y. State Psychol. Assn., Assn. Hispanic Mental Health Profls. Office: Rutgers U 10 Seminary Pl New Brunswick NJ 08901 Office Phone: 732-932-7496 ext. 8312. Business E-Mail: csce@rci.rutgers.edu.

CLAUSSEN, ALEX, music educator; b. Tahlequah, Okla., July 23, 1973; s. M. Jerry and Kathleen C. Claussen; m. Amitia A. Peterson, July 13, 1996; children: Abigail Anne, Kathleen Elizabeth. MusB Edn, U. Ctrl. Okla., Edmond, 1996. Dir. mid. sch. band Duncan Pub. Schs., Okla., 1996—2000, head dir. band, 2000—02; coord. instrumental music Sapulpa Pub. Schs., Okla., 2002—; staff mem. Okla. Ambassador of Music European Tour, 2003, 2005, 2007. Guest condr. various honor bands, 1996—; adjudicator, Okla., Ark. Named Outstanding Young Band Dir. Okla., Am. Sch. Band Dirs. Assn., 1999, Outstanding Band Dir. of Yr., SW Okla. Bandmasters Assn., 2002; named to Who's Who Among Am. Tchrs., Outstanding Am. Tchr., Nat. Honor Roll. Mem.: Okla. Music Educators Assn. (chairperson all-state band 2004—05), Okla. Bandmasters Assn. (pres. 2005—06), Phi Beta Mu (Outstanding Young Band Master Okla. 2001). Office: Sapulpa HS Band 3 South Mission Sapulpa OK 74066

CLAUSSEN, EILEEN BARBARA, environmental services administrator, former federal agency administrator; b. NYC, June 9, 1945; d. Louis and Elsie (Young) Lerner; children: Hillary Anne, Geoffrey David. BA, George Washington U., 1966; MA, U. Va., 1967. Systems analyst USN, Washington, 1967-68; cons. Booz, Allen & Hamilton, Inc., Washington, 1968-69; asst. dir. ctr. for comml. devel. Boise Cascade Corp., Washington, 1969-72; various mgmt. positions Office of Solid Waste U.S. EPA, Washington, 1972-83, dir. characterization and assessment div., 1984-87, dir. atmospheric & indoor air programs, 1987-93, acting dep. asst. adminstr. air & radiation, 1988-89, dep. asst. adminstr. Office Air & Radiation, 1990—91; spl. asst. to Pres., sr. dir. global environ. affairs NSC, Washington, 1993—96; asst. sec. oceans, internat. environment & science affairs US Dept. State, Washington, 1996—98; pres. Pew Ctr. on Global Climate Change, Arlington, Va., 1998—. Bd. dirs. Coun. Fgn. Rels., China Coun. for Internat. Cooperation on Environ. & Devel.; commr. Pew Ocean Commn. Recipient Career Achievement award, US Dept. State, Meritorious Exec. award for Sustained Superior Accomplishment, Disting. Exec. award for Sustained Extraordinary Accomplishment, Fitzhugh Green award for Outstanding Contributions to Internat. Environ. Protection. Office: Pew Ctr on Global Climate Change 2101 Wilson Blvd Ste 550 Arlington VA 22201

CLAVER, ROBERT EARL, television producer, director; b. Chgo., May 22, 1928; s. Louis E. and Sara M. (Sosna) C.; 1 child, Nancy Beth. BS in Journalism, U. Ill., 1950. Prodr.-writer: first 1000 Captain Kangaroo shows (Sylvania award, Peabody award); prodr., dir.: (TV shows) Here Comes the Brides, 1968-70, The Interns, 1970-71, Partridge Family, 1970-74, Gloria, CBS-TV, 1982-83, Small Wonder, 1985, New Love American Style, 1985, New Leave It to Beaver, 1986-87, Charles in Charge, 1987, Out of This World, 1987-91, numerous other series; dir.: (TV shows) Welcome Back Kotter, ABC-TV, 1977-78, All's Fair, CBS-TV, Housecalls, CBS-TV, 1979-80, Mork and Mindy, ABC-TV, 1981-82. With U.S. Army, 1951-53. Mem. Dirs. Guild Am.

CLAVERIE, PHILIP DEVILLIERS, lawyer; b. New Orleans, June 29, 1941; s. Louis Barbot and Viola Aimee (Schlegel) C.; m. Laura Lynn McCampbell, Apr. 27, 1974; children: Philip deVilliers Jr., Stephanie McCampbell. AB, Princeton U., 1963; JD, Tulane U., 1966. Bar: La. 1966. Assoc. Phelps Dunbar, New Orleans, 1966-70, ptnr., 1970—. Contbr. articles to profl. jours. Trustee Children's Hosp. New Orleans, 1978-, pres. 1985-87; mem. bd. govs. Isidore Newman Sch., 1982-00, chmn. 1995-98; mem. exec. bd. New Orleans Police Found., 1998—, hon. consul of Finland; bd. dirs. World Affairs Coun. New Orleans, 2004—, World Trade Ctr., 2006-. Served to lt. comdr. JAGC, USNR, 1973-79. Fellow Am. Bar Found., La. Bar Found.; mem. ABA, La. State Bar Assn., New Orleans Bar Assn., Assn. Bar City N.Y., Am. Law Inst., Am. Judicature Soc., La. State Law Inst., World Trade Ctr., Pickwick Club, Stratford Club. Office: Phelps Dunbar LLP Ste 2000 365 Canal St New Orleans LA 70130-6534 Home: 3040 Post Oak Blvd Ste 900 Houston TX 77056-6536 Office Phone: 504-584-9223. E-mail: claverip@phelps.com, claverip@cox.net.

CLAWSON, CURTIS J., manufacturing executive; MBA, Harvard U. Various positions Allied Signal, Arvin Industries; pres. Beverage Cans Am. Bus. Unit Am. Nat. Can Group Inc., 1998—99, pres., COO Chgo., 1999—2000; chmn., pres., CEO Hayes Lemmerz Internat., Northville, Mich., 2001—. Office: Hayes Lemmerz Internat 15300 Centennial Dr Northville MI 48167*

CLAWSON, DAVID KAY, orthopedic surgeon; b. Salt Lake City, Aug. 8, 1927; s. David J. and Elva (Gundry) C.; m. Janet Dorothy Smith, June 1, 1952; children: Kim Debra, David Roger. Student, U. Utah, 1944-45, 47-48; MD, Harvard U., 1952. Diplomate: Am. Bd. Orthopedic Surgery. Intern Stanford U. Hosp., 1952-53, resident gen. surgery, 1953-54; resident orthopedic surgery Stanford U. Hosp., also San Francisco City and County Hosp., 1954-57; fellow in orthopedics Nat. Found. Infantile Paralysis, 1955-58; hon. sr. registrar Royal Nat. Orthopedic Hosp., London, Eng., 1957-58; asst. prof. UCLA Med. Sch., 1958; asst. prof. surgery, head div. orthopedic surgery U. Wash. Med. Sch., 1958-61, assoc. prof. surgery, head div. orthopedic surgery, 1961-65, prof., 1964-83, chmn. dept. orthopedics, 1964-75; dean Coll. Medicine, U. Ky., 1975-83, vice chancellor for clin. profl. services, 1982-83; exec. vice chancellor U. Kans. Med. Ctr., Kansas City, 1983-94, cons. to chancellor, 1994; prof. orthopaedic surgery U. Ky., 1994—, cons. to dean, 1994—. Mem. Accreditation Coun. for Grad. Med. Edn., 1977-88; chmn. residency rev. com. on structure and functions, 1987-88; chmn. coun. of deans Assn. Am. Med. Coll., 1985-86, chmn. of the assembly, 1988-89, immediate past chmn., 1989-90, disting. svc. rep. to exec. coun., 1992-95; active Am. Orthopaedic Soc. for Sports Medicine, 1972-87, founder, 1972; active Assn. Orthopaedic Chmn., 1971-73, founder, 1971. Contbr. med. jours.; mem. editorial bd.: Clin. Orthopedics and Related Research, 1964—. Mem. Heart of Am. coun. Boy Scouts Am., 1989—, mem. adv. bd., 1989-92, Regional Task Force and Edn. Found., 1972—. With USNR, 1945-46. Exchange fellow Am. Orthopedic Assn., 1967 Mem. AMA (coun. for med. affairs 1988—), Am. Acad. Ortho. Surgeons (coun. on health policy 1990-95), Am. Orthopaedic Assn., Assn. Acad. Health Ctrs., Assn. Am. Univs., Assn. Bone and Joint Surgeons (pres. 1977), Harvard Med. Sch. Alumni Assn. (pres. 1984-85). Home: 3785 Jamaica Ct Lexington KY 40509-9506 also: 10 E Roanoke St Seattle WA 98102-3257 Personal E-mail: dkcjd@msn.com. *Look to the past only for the lessons we can learn, live today for the joy of being alive, plan to the future to insure that what should be, will be.*

CLAWSON, JOHN ADDISON, investment company and retired chemicals executive; b. Monaco, Pa., June 4, 1922; s. Ralph S. and Elsie (Winnett) C.; m. Patricia Harmon, July 5, 1947; children: Christine Brandwie, Hunter Winnett. BS, Miami U., 1943, LLD, 1979; postgrad., Harvard U., 1968. Vice pres., nat. mgr. bus. and labor reports div. Prentice-Hall, NYC, 1948-55; with DuBois Chems. div. Chemed Corp., Cin., 1955-78, dist. mgr. NYC, 1955-60, regional mgr. Ea. div., 1960-64, divisional mgrs. v.p., 1964-66, exec. v.p., dir. sales, 1966-70, gen. mgr., 1968-70, pres., chief exec. officer, 1970-79, group exec., 1975-79; v.p. Chemed Corp., 1971-77, exec. v.p., 1978-79, ret., 1979. Chmn. Whitehall Mgmt. Corp., Cin.; bd. dirs. Suburban Fed. Savs. & Loan Assn. Trustee Providence Hosp., 1974-76; dean's assoc. Miami U., 1973—. Lt. (j.g.) USNR, 1943-46. Mem. Cin. C. of C. (city and county planning com. 1971-74), Soap and Detergent Assn. (vice-chmn. bd. 1971-73, chmn. bd., chief exec. officer 1974-75, mem. exec. com., bd. dirs. 1976-79), Delta Sigma Phi, Sigma Alpha Epsilon. Clubs: Queen City (Cin.), Kenwood Country (Cin.); John's Island (Fla.), Cat Cay, Ltd., Commodore (Bahamas). Presbyterian.

CLAWSON, RITA LOUISE, curator; b. Lafayette, Ind., Nov. 10, 1949; d. LaRue Mason Clawson and Geraldine Katherine Mueller. BS, Purdue U., 1971; AS, Vincennes U., 1982. Curatorial asst. Evansville Mus. Arts and Sci., Ind., 1985—88; dir. curator Old Jail Mus., Crawfordsville, Ind., 1988—89; asst. dir., curator Gage County Hist. Soc., Beatrice, Nebr., 1990—. Active Gage County Heritage Preservation, Beatrice, 1990—98, Nebr. History Network, 1992—98. Mem.: Nebr. Mus. Assn., Am. Assn. Mus., Purdue Alumni Assn. Democrat. Roman Catholic. Avocations: history, antiques, reading, walking. Home: 401 N 8 Apt 3 Beatrice NE 68310 Office: Gage County Hist Soc PO Box 793 101 N Second St Beatrice NE 68310

CLAY, CASSIUS MARCELLUS See ALI, MUHAMMAD

CLAY, CLARENCE SAMUEL, acoustical oceanographer; b. Kansas City, Mo., Nov. 2, 1923; s. Clarence Samuel and Mary Else (Hall) C.; m. Andre Jane Edwards, Mar. 27, 1945; children: Arnold, Jo, David, Michael. BS, Kans. State U., 1947, MS, 1948; PhD in Physics, U. Wis., 1951. Asst. prof. U. Wyo., Laramie, 1950-51; physicist Carter Oil Co., Tulsa, 1951-55; rsch. scientist Columbia U., Dobbs Ferry, N.Y., 1955-67; prof. dept. geol. geophysics U. Wis., Madison, 1967-89, emeritus prof., 1989—. Author: Elementary Exploration Seismology, 1990, (with I. Tolstoy) Ocean Acoustics, 1966, (with H. Medwin) Acoustical Oceanography, 1977, Fundamentals of Acoustical Oceanography, 1997; (with I. Tolstoy) Ocean Acoustics, 1987. Fellow Acoustical Soc. Am. (Silver medal in Acoustical Oceanography, 1993); mem. Sigma Xi. Home: 5109 St Cyr Rd Middleton WI 53562 Office: U Wis Weeks Hall 1215 W Dayton St Madison WI 53706-1600

CLAY, CLIFTON FORD, motion picture producer, writer; b. Galveston, Tex., Nov. 2, 1939; s. James Henry and Catherine (Royal) C.; m. Ann Chandler, Oct. 4, 1964; children: Mary Kim, Jason Anthony, Tara Ann. BS, U. Calif., Berkeley, 1962; MA, Am. Film Inst., Beverly Hills, Calif., 1977; postgrad., Citrus Coll., Azusa, Calif., 1978. Actor Screen Actor's Guild, Hollywood, Calif., 1968-75; freelance writer LA, 1972—; film producer Turner-Clay Prodn., LA, 1972-74; v.p. Motion Picture Group, Beverly Hills, 1982-83; chief ops. officer Oak Tree Films, Ltd., London, 1984—. Mem. exec. bd. Park Ave. Entertainment, L.A., 1986, Am. Film Inst. Alumni Writers Workshop, 1984—; v.p. Am. Film Inst. Alumni, 1985-87, pres., 1987-88; lectr. high schs., 1987—; v.p. Courtroom Gunfighters, Inc., 1991—; pres. NKOSI Internat. House, 1992—. Producer: Maxi, 1972; screenwriter: Sunflower, 1973, Sweetwine & Tyree, 1975, This Land Yesterday, 1976, Delaney Street Feud, 1978, Grannie's Rebels, 1978, Destiny's Journey, 1982, Autumn Rain, 1984, Jammer, 1984, Bramber House, 1985, Augusta Rose, 1986, The Concrete Garden, 1990, Courtroom

Gunfighters, 1991, Freeborn-The Roundtable, 1992, The Ebony Rope, 1992, The Dragon's Mouth, 1993, Justice For No One, 1994, Uncle Bubba, 1995, The Cedar Street Boys, 1995, My Lover, My Friend, 1995, Till Tomorrow Comes, 1996, Clear Lake Meadow, 1996, Grandma's Hat, 1997, A Whisper of Truth, 1997, Mama's Song, 1997, Strawberry Kisses, 1998, Bakala, 1998, Moonlight and Soft Waves, 1999, Naked Sisters, 1999, Blood of My Blood, 2000, A Families Garden, 2000, T-Bone Smith, 2001, Right On Time, 2001, Vera Lee, 2002, That Old Oak Tree, 2003; actor: Bullitt, 1968, Take the Money and Run, 1968, Red, White and Black, 1970, Maxi, 1972, Terminal Island, 1972. Den leader Cub Scouts Am., Covina, Calif., 1978; coach Little League Football, Covina, 1979. Mem. Assn. Ind. Video & Filmmakers, Inc., Producers Assn. LA., Britain Film & TV Producers, Vintage Sports Car Club, Ltd. (Eng.). Episcopalian. Avocations: shooting, sky diving, lecturing, racing cars, collecting model trains. Home: 679 Antiquity Dr Suisun City CA 94585-4073 Office: Oak Tree Films Ltd 42a Devonshire Close CM23 5ED London WI England

CLAY, CYNTHIA JOYCE, writer, editor-in-chief; b. Cedar Falls, Iowa, Aug. 4, 1957; d. James Hubert and Delight Clay; m. Guillermo Jose Ramon, Jan. 7, 1987. Attended, Nat. Theater Inst., 1978; BA cum laude, Brandeis U., 1979; MFA, U. Ga., 1979. Editor-in-chief Oestara Pub. LLC, Key Biscayne, Fla., 2004—. Author: Vector Theory and the Plot Structures of Literature and Drama, (novels) Zollocco: A Novel of Another Universe (Eppie Sci. Fiction finalist, 2001), The Romance of the Unicorn, (short stories) New Myths of the Feminine Divine; editor: The Oestara Anthology of Pagan Poetry, 2006 (Eppie winner best poetry, 2006); actor: The First Loebner Prize Competition Touring Test, Lulu, Marriage of Figaro, Has Washington Got Legs?. Mem.: Electronically Pub. Internet Connection. Democrat. Avocations: travel, swimming, reading. Home: 303 Galen Dr #102 Key Biscayne FL 33149 Home Phone: 305-953-3697, 305-365-3917. Personal E-mail: cynthia@oestarapublishing.com.

CLAY, EDWIN S., III, library director; m. Debra Clay; 1 child, Maggie. Grad., Randolph Macon Coll., 1966; MLS, U. NC, 1967. Dir. Va. Wesleyan Coll. Libr., Va. Beach Pub. Libr. and Info. Office, Fairfax County Pub. Libr., Va., 1982—. Asst. to city mgr., Virginia Beach; mem. Nat. Mgmt. and Planning Adv. Com., Libr. of Congress; adj. faculty mem. Cath. U. Sch. of Libr. & Info. Sci. Past. pres. Virginians for the Arts; chmn. Va. Commn. for Arts; bd. dirs. FCPL Found. Recipient Managerial Excellence award, 2000. Mem.: Va. Pub. Libr. Dir.'s Assn. (past pres., Named Outstanding Libr. Dir. 2002), Va. Libr. Assn. (bd. dirs.). Office: Fairfax County Pub Libr Ste 324 12000 Government Center Pky Fairfax VA 22035-0012 Office Phone: 703-324-3100. Office Fax: 703-324-8365.*

CLAY, ERIC L., federal judge; b. Durham, NC, Jan. 18, 1948; BA, U. N.C., 1969; JD, Yale U., 1972. Bar: Mich. 1972, US Dist. Ct. (ea. dist.) Mich. 1972, US Supreme Ct. 1977, US Ct. Appeals (6th cir.) 1978, US Dist. Ct. (we. dist.) Mich. 1987, US Ct. Appeals (DC cir.) 1994. Law clk. to Judge Damon J. Keith US Dist. Ct. (ea. dist.) Mich., 1972—73; atty., shareholder, dir. Lewis, White & Clay, P.C., Detroit, 1973—97; judge US Ct. Appeals (6th cir.), Detroit, 1997—. Hearing panelist Atty. Discipline Bd., State of Mich., 1985—97. Fellow John Hay Whitney, Yale U. Mem.: ABA, Wolverine Bar Assn., Detroit Bar Assn., Nat. Assn. Railroad Trial Counsel, Nat. Bar Assn., US Sixth Jud. Conf. (life), Phi Beta Kappa. Office: Potter Stewart US Cthse 100 E 5th St Cincinnati OH 45202-3988*

CLAY, ORSON C., insurance company executive, director; b. Bountiful, Utah, July 26, 1930; s. George Phillips and Dorothy (Cliff) C.; m. Dianne Jones, June 13, 1961; children: Orson Cliff, Charles Kenneth, Elizabeth Temple. BS, Brigham Young U., 1955; MBA with distinction, Harvard U., 1959. With Continental Oil Co., various locations in, U.S.; mng. dir. Conoco A.G., Zug, Switzerland, 1962-63; dir. econs. divsn. Continental Oil Co. Ltd., London, Eng., 1964-65; gen. mgr. adminstrn. and ops. Continental Oil (U.K.) Ltd., London, 1965-66; asst. mgr. marine transp. Continental Oil, NYC, 1966-68; exec. asst. fin. Pennzoil United, Inc., Houston, 1968-70; exec. v.p. fin., treas. Am. Nat. Ins. Co., Galveston, Tex., 1970-73, sr. exec. v.p., treas., 1973-76, pres., 1977-95, CEO, 1978-91, also bd. dirs., ret., 1995. Past mem. nat. adv. coun. mgmt. Brigham Young U. Past trustee United Way Galveston; past bd. dirs. Tex. Rsch. League; active LDS Ch., missionary in Can., 1951-53. 1st lt. USMCR, 1955-57. Donald Kirk David fellow Harvard U., 1959. Mem. Life Officers Mgmt. Assn. (bd. dirs. 1993-95). Home: 1877 Stone Hollow Dr Bountiful UT 84010-1058

CLAY, PHILLIP L., academic administrator; married; 1 child. AB with honor, U. NC, Chapel Hill, 1968; PhD in City Planning, MIT, 1975. Faculty MIT, Cambridge, Mass., 1975, assoc. dept. head, 1990—92, head, dept. urban svcs., 1992—94, assoc. provost, office of provost, 1994—2001, prof. of city planning, chancellor; asst. dir., Joint Ctr. for Urban Studies MIT and Harvard, 1980—84. Chair Mass. Inst. Tech. Coun.; mem. bd. Media Lab Europe, Cambride-Mass. Inst. Tech. Author: (books) Neighborhood Renewal: Middleclass Resettlement and Incumbent Upgrading in American Neighborhoods; co-author (with Rob Hollister): Neighborhood Politics and Planning. Founding mem. Nat. Housing Trusts; vice pres. bd. Com. Builders; sr. adv. on project in several areas that include pub. housing, cmty. capacity bldg., and urban job initiatives; bd. trustees Roxbury Cmty. Coll.; mem., policy and rsch. adv. coun. Fed. Nat. Mortage Assn. (Fannie Mae); cons. to numerous fed. and state agencies and found. Avocation: gardening. Office: Office of Chancellor Rm 10-200 Mass Inst Tech 77 Mass Ave Cambridge MA 02139-4307 Office Phone: 617-253-9742. Office Fax: 617-258-6261.

CLAY, WILLIAM LACY, JR., congressman; b. St. Louis, July 27, 1956; s. William L. and Carol Ann (Johnson) C.; m. Ivie Lewellen, Jan. 24, 1992; 2 children. BS in Govt. and Politics, U. Md., Coll. Pk., 1983; student, Harvard U. John F. Kennedy Sch. Govt.; LLD (hon.), Lincoln U., Harris-Stowe State U. Cert. paralegal; lic. real estate salesman, Mo. Mem. Mo. State House of Reps., Jefferson City, 1983—91, Mo. State Senate, 1991—2001, US Congress from 1st Mo. dist., 2001—, mem. fin. svcs. com. and govt. reform com., chmn. subcommittee on info. policy, the census and the nat. archives; mem. Congl. Black Caucus. Chmn. Mo. Jesse Jackson 1988 Presdl. Campaign; Jackson del. to 1988 Dem. Nat. Conv.; committeeman to Dem. Nat. Com.; bd. dirs. William L. Clay Scholarship and Rsch. Fund., Congl. Black Caucus Found. Recipient Most Influential Black Americans, Ebony mag., 2006. Mem. Ams. Dem. Action (Outstanding Legis. Mo. chpt. 1985, 86). Democrat. Roman Catholic. Office: US House of Reps 434 Cannon House Office Bldg Washington DC 20515 Office Phone: 202-225-2406.*

CLAYCOMB, CECIL KEITH, biochemist, educator; b. Twin Falls, Idaho, Oct. 19, 1920; s. Cecil R. and Frilla E. (Reams) C.; m. Elizabeth Jane Gregg, Mar. 10, 1943; children: John K., Mary E. BS, U. Oreg., Eugene, 1947, MS, 1948, PhD, 1951. Prof., head dept. biochemistry Dental Sch. U. Oreg., Portland, 1951-82, dir. minority recruitment, 1971-74, asst. to pres./dir. minority student affairs, 1974-84, coordinator basic sci. curriculum, 1951-77, chmn. admissions com., 1959-69, emeritus, 1985—; emeritus prof. biochemistry Oreg. Health and Sci. U., 1986—. Contbr. articles to sci. jours. Served to 1st lt. AUS, 1943-46. Scholar dental bd. New South Wales, Sydney, Australia, 1970 Mem. Am. Chem. Soc., Internat. Assn. Dental Research, AAAS, Res. Officers Assn., Sigma Xi. Home: 3326 SW 13th Ave Portland OR 97239-2922

CLAYMAN, GREG, communications executive; b. 1972; m. Amanda Clayman. Degree in Eng. and Am. Lit., Harvard Coll. V.p., Brand Strategy Sterling Grp., NYC; co-founder, v.p. Mktg., Sales, Bus. Devel. Upoc Networks, 1999; v.p., Wireless Strategy and Ops. MTV Network, NYC. Mem. CTIA Wireless Internet Caucus Leadership Coun.; mem., adv. bd. MECCA, Billboard Mag. Named one of 40 Executives Under 40, Multichannel News, 2006. Office: MTV Network 1515 Broadway New York NY 10036 Office Phone: 212-258-8000. Office Fax: 212-258-8000.

CLAYMAN, PAUL F., lawyer; BA in Polit. Sci., Lewis & Clark Coll., 1978; JD, Am. Univ. Atty. Office of Legal Adv., U.S. State Dept., Washington, 1988—2003; chief counsel Com. Fgn. Rels., U.S. Senate, 2003—. Office: Foreign Relations Committee Room 439 Senate Dirksen Office Building Washington DC 20510-6225

CLAYPOOL, DAVID L., lawyer; b. Springfield, Ill., 1946; BA in History, Ill. Coll., 1968; JD with high distinction, U. Iowa, 1975. Bar: Iowa 1975. Ptnr., pub. fin. practice and ptnr.-in-charge Dorsey & Whitney, LLP, Des Moines. Editor notes and comments Iowa Law Review, 1974-75. Capt. U.S. Army, 1968-72 Mem. Iowa State Bar Assn., Pol County Bar Assn., Nat. Assn. Bond Lawyers, Iowa Mcpl. Attys. Assn., Order of Coif. Office: Dorsey & Whitney LLP 801 Grand Ave Ste 3900 Des Moines IA 50309-2790 Home Phone: 515-440-0773; Office Phone: 515-283-1000. Business E-Mail: claypool.david@dorsey.com.

CLAYTON, CAROL A., lawyer; b. Aug. 11, 1958; BA, Univ. Utah, 1979; JD, Univ. Va., 1982. Bar: DC 1982. Ptnr., environ. law practice Wilmer Cutler Pickering Hale & Dorr, Washington, asst. mng. ptnr., mem. mgmt. com. Editor (articles): Va. Jour. Natural Resources Law; contbr. chapters to books; co-author: Environ. Auditing Handbook. Office: Wilmer Cutler Pickering Hale & Dorr 1875 Pennsylvania Ave NW Washington DC 20006-3642 Office Phone: 202-663-6650. Office Fax: 202-663-6363. Business E-Mail: carol.clayton@wilmerhale.com.

CLAYTON, CLAUDE F., JR., lawyer; b. Tupelo, Miss., June 15, 1948; s. Claude F. and Bronson (Munday) C.; children from a previous marriage: Frances, Claude III Student, Stanton Mil. Acad., 1966; BA, Tulane U., 1971; JD, U. Miss., 1973. Bar: Miss. 1973. Mem. judiciary com. U.S. Senate, Washington, 1968; ptnr. Mitchell, Voge, Clayton and Beasley, Tupelo, 1973-85, Mitchell, McNutt & Sams, Tupelo, 1985—2001; pres. Mitchell, NcNutt & Sams, Tupelo, 1995—97; ptnr. Clayton Law Firm, PLLC, 2001—03, Clayton, O'Donnell, Walsh & Davis, PLLC, 2003—. Mem. complaints tribunal Supreme Ct. Miss., 1990-93; speaker Miss. Jud. Coll., also various trial practice and ethics seminars; special justice Miss. Supreme Ct., 2000. Mem. ABA (young lawyers divsn., chmn. justice dept. liaison com. 1978-79), Miss. State Bar (pres. fellows of young lawyers 1990-91, co-chmn. specialization com. 1990-92, chmn., 1980-82, lawyer econs. com. 1988-89, ethics com. 1982-85, co-chmn. continuing legal edn. com. 1980-81, law jour.-law sch. liaison com. 1974-76, various coms. young lawyers sect. 1985-90, bd. dir. 1975-80), Miss. Def. Lawyers Assn. (bd. dir. 1992-95), Def. Rsch. Inst., Internat. Assn. Def. Counsel. Office: Clayton O'Donnell Walsh & Davis PLLC 115 N Broadway PO Box 755 Tupelo MS 38802-4869 Home Phone: 662-255-0663; Office Phone: 662-620-7938. E-mail: cclayton@northmslaw.com.

CLAYTON, DAVID A(LVIN), biology professor; b. Joliet, Ill., Feb. 5, 1944; m. Lauretta Swanson, 1965; children: Lindsay, Ryan, Megan. BS, No. Ill. U., 1965; PhD in Biophysics and Chemistry, Calif. Inst. Tech., 1970. Asst. prof. pathology Stanford U., 1970—76, assoc. prof., 1976—82, prof., 1982—89, prof. devel. biology, 1989—; sr. sci. officer Howard Hughes Med. Inst., 1996—99, v.p. sci. devel., 2000—02, v.p., chief scientific officer, 2002—. Mem. adv. com. nucleic acids and protein synthesis, Am. Cancer Soc., 1976-80; mem. molecular biology study sect., NIH, 1982-86, chmn., 1984-86; mem. sci. rev. bd. Howard Hughes Med. Inst., 1993-96; mem. nat. adv. bd. Gen. Med. Sci. Coun., 1996-99; Fisher lectr. So. Ill. U., 1989. Recipient Warner-Lambert/Parke Davis award, 1982. Mem. Inst. Medicine Nat. Acad. Sci., Am. Soc. Biochemistry and Molecular Biology.

CLAYTON, JAMES EDWIN, journalist; b. Johnston City, Ill., Nov. 14, 1929; s. John Herman and Vinnie Ethel (Black) C.; m. Elise Brookfield Heinz, June 3, 1961; children— Jonathan Brown, David Lake. BS, U. Ill., 1951; MPA, Princeton, 1956. Reporter So. Illinoisan, Carbondale, Ill., 1953-52; reporter Washington Post, 1956-64, asst. mng. editor, 1964-67, 72-74, editorial writer, 1967-72, assoc. editor, 1974-82; assoc. dir. Reporter's Com. for Freedom of Press, 1984; sr. fellow Airlie Found., 1984-94. Vis. lectr. Northwestern U., 1966-67, Johns Hopkins, 1970. Author: The Making of Justice, 1964; editor: The Rights of Free Men, 1984. Chmn. bd. trustees Sofia Am. Schs., Inc. Served to 1st lt. AUS, 1951-52. Recipient Interpretive Reporting awards Washington Newspaper Guild, 1959, 62, 63, Distinguished Washington Correspondence award Sigma Delta Chi, 1960, Worth Bingham prize, 1970, George Polk Meml. award for editorial writing, 1970 Mem.: Princeton (Washington, N.Y.C.). Baptist. Home: 2728 N Fillmore St Arlington VA 22207-4936

CLAYTON, JOHN DANIEL, mechanical engineer, researcher; b. Annapolis, Md., Jan. 25, 1976; PhD, Ga. Inst. Tech., Atlanta, 2002. Rschr. Worcester Poly. U., Mass., 1997, Sandia Nat. Labs., Livermore, Calif., 2000, U.S. Army Rsch. Lab., Apg, Md., 2003—. Post Doctoral Fellowship, NRC, 2003, Grad. Fellowship, NSF, 1998—2001. Mem.: Soc. Engring. Sci. (assoc.), Am. Phys. Soc. (assoc.), Am. Acad. Mechanics (assoc.). Achievements include research in Physics And Mechanics Of Solids; Mathematical And Computational Modeling. Office: US Army Rsch Lab Impact Physics Br Aberdeen Proving Ground MD 21005-5069 E-mail: jclayton@arl.army.mil.

CLAYTON, JON KERRY, insurance company executive; b. Cin., Dec. 29, 1945; s. Lawrence and Charlotte Marie (Miller) C.; m. Mary-Paige Royer, Aug. 27, 1983; 1 child from previous marriage: Margaret Allyn; children: Thomas Barry, Timothy Jon. B.I.E., Ga. Inst. Tech., 1968; MBA, Harvard U., 1970. Asst. treas. Am. Security Ins. Co., Atlanta, 1970-76, treas., 1976-78; v.p., treas. Am. Security Inc. Co., Atlanta, 1978-80; v.p. fin. Fortis, Inc., NYC, 1980-83, sr. v.p., 1983-85; pres. Fortis Benefits Ins. Co., 1985-93; exec. v.p. Assurant Inc., NYC, 1993—99, pres., 2000—05, CEO, 2000—06, interim CEO, 2007. Served to 1st lt. U.S. Army, 1970. Office: Assurant Inc 1 Chase Manhattan Plz New York NY 10005-1401*

CLAYTON, JOSEPH PAUL, broadcast executive; b. Oct. 11, 1949; married; 4 children. BA in Bus. Admin., Bellarmine U., Louisville, 1971; MBA in Mktg. and Mgmt., Ind. U., Bloomington, 1972. Various mgmt. positions RCA Consumer Electronics, 1973—86; senior v.p. TV div. Thomson Consumer Electronics, 1987—92, exec. v.p. mktg. and sls. Am. & Asia, 1992—97; pres., CEO Frontier Corp. (aquired by Global Crossing Ltd.), Rochester, NY, 1997—99; pres. N. Am. region, vice chmn. Global Crossing Ltd., 1999—2001; pres., CEO SIRIUS Satellite Radio, NYC, 2001—04, chmn., 2004—. Former mem. bd. dirs. Global Crossing, Frontier Corp., E.W. Scripps; mem. bd. dirs. Transcend Services, Atlanta, Sirius Satellite Radio, NYC; former chmn. Consumer Electronics Assn.; mem. bd. dirs., bd. govs. Electronics Industry Assn. Mem. Dean's Advisory Bd. Indiana U. Kelley Sch. of Bus.; mem., former vice chmn. NY State Office of Science, Tech. and Academic Rsch. Advisory Council; trustee Bellarmine U., Louisville, Rochester Inst. of Technology., Rochester, NY. Office: SIRIUS Satellite Radio 1221 Ave of the Americas New York NY 10020 Office Phone: 212-584-5100.*

CLAYTON, JULIA B., academic administrator, musician; b. Salt Lake City, Oct. 27, 1942; d. Ivan Miles and Violet P. Bryson; m. Archer Robert Clayton, Dec. 5, 1963; children: Ned William, April Diane, Christopher Michael; 1 child, Laura Furst. MusM, U. Utah, 1984. Assoc. dir., office of fin. aid and scholarships U. Utah, Salt Lake City, 1988—97, dir. fin. aid and scholarships, 1997—98; dir. student fin. svcs. SUNY Downstate Med. Ctr., Bklyn., 1998—. Cons., website rev. bd. Thompson Pub., Washington, 1995; adv. coun. Utah Higher Edn. Assistance Authority, Salt Lake City, 1990—97. Mem. editl. bd.: Jour. Fin. Aid, 1996—98. Organist, pianist, choir dir., arranger, performer LDS Ch., 1952—2003. Scholar, U. Utah, 1960—64. Mem.: Rocky Mtn. Assn. Fin. Aid Adminstrs., Utah Assn. Fin. Aid Adminstrs. (student newsletter editor, pub. 1992—94), NY Assn. Fin. Aid Adminstrs., Nat. Assn. Fin. Aid Adminstrs. (governance com., profl. devel. com., history com., editl. bd. Transcript mag. 1999), Mu Phi Epsilon, Phi Kappa Phi. Business E-Mail: julia.clayton@downstate.edu.

CLAYTON, M. COURTLAND, management consultant; b. Norwich, Conn., Feb. 19, 1938; s. Marvin C. and Peggy (Farmer) Clayton; children: Cheryll, Michelle, Deborah. BS in Indsl. Engring., Purdue U., 1963; MBA, U. Louisville, 1971; MPA, Penn. State U., 1986; grad., U.S. Army War Coll., 1986. Registered profl. engr., Calif., Ky., Mo., Pa.; cert. purchasing mgr., mfg. engr., mfg. mgr., profl. mgmt. cons., logistician, exec. in logistics. Mgr. shop ops. GE Appliances, Louisville, 1968-69, prog. mgr. mfg. engring., 1969-71, contracting agt. material handling and computer systems, 1973-76, program mgr., material resource systems, 1976-80, mgr., advance and indirect material purchasing, 1980-82, program mgr., purchasing programs, 1982-87, program mgr., sourcing integration, 1987-89, mgr. supplier productivity engring., 1989-93, puchasing mgr. range products bus., 1993; prin. The Clayton Group, Louisville, 1993-94; mgr. range bus. purchasing GE Appliances, Louisville, 1992-94; mgr. Strategic Sourcing, Louisville, 1994; mgr. mfg. engring. Emerson Electric Co., St. Louis, 1971-72; corp. engring. and mfg. cons. AMEDCO, Springfield, Mo., 1972-73; pres. Clayton Cons., Louisville, Ky., 1994—. Prin. The Clayton Group, Global Cons., sr. exec. dir. NuSkin, Pharmanex, Big Planet, 1990—. Patentee in field. Chmn. bd. deacons Bapt. Ch., Louisville, 1975; dir. ch. choir Bapt. Ch., Arkansas City, Kans., 1963. Col. US Army, 1963—93. Named to Honorable Order of Ky. Cols. Mem. Res. Officers Assn. (exec. bd., pres. 1984, nat. councilman 1990-94), Ky. Res. Officers Assn., Inst. Indsl. Engrs., Assn. Internal Mgmt. Cons., Assn. of U.S. Army, Mil. Officers Assn. Am. (pres. Louisville chpt. 2005), Purdue Alumni Assn., U. Louisville Alumni Assn., Pa. State Alumni Assn., Army War Coll. Alumni Assn. Republican. Avocations: piano, gardening, sports. Home and Office: 8215 Camberley Dr Louisville KY 40222-5534 Office Phone: 502-429-6666. Personal E-mail: claytongroup@bigplanet.com.

CLAYTON, MICHAEL F., lawyer; b. Mar. 2, 1954; BA, Wake Forest U., 1977; JD, U. Va. Sch. Law, 1980. Bar: D.C. 1980, Va. 1981, registered: U.S. Supreme Ct. 1988. Ptnr., intellectual property trademark/copyright practice group leader Morgan, Lewis & Bockius LLP. Pro bono gen. counsel Women in Mil. Svc. Am. Meml.; lectr. U. Va. Sch. Law. Recipient Elizabeth D. & Richard A. Merrill Endowment Lectr. Law, U. Va. Office: Morgan Lewis & Bockius LLP 1111 Pennsylvania Ave NW Washington DC 20004 Office Phone: 202-739-5215. Office Fax: 202-739-3001. Business E-Mail: mclayton@morganlewis.com.

CLAYTON, ORVILLE WOOLFORD, surgeon; b. Ft. Payne, Ala., May 30, 1921; s. Olney Walker Clayton and Flora Pauline Wheeler; m. Dorothy Nell Meadows, June 20, 1944; children: Stephen W., Kathy L. Stockham, Shelley E. BA, U. Ala., 1943; B in Medicine, Northwestern U., 1945, MD, 1946. Post surgeon US Army, Huntsville, Ala., 1946—48; chief resident in surgery U. Hosp., Birmingham, Ala., 1948; chief surgery Bapt. Med. Montclair, Birmingham, 1969—74, pres. staff, 1982; clin. assoc. prof. surgery U. Ala., Birmingham, 1973—91; ret., 1991. Capt. US Army, 1946—48. Fellow: ACS, So. Thoracic Soc. Avocations: gardening, genealogy. Home: 3133 Ryecroft Rd Birmingham AL 35223-2715

CLAYTON, RAYMOND EDWARD, municipal official; b. Saskatoon, Sask., Can., Nov. 6, 1942; m. Joan Ann Snodgrass, Sept. 21, 1963; children: Grant, Sheila, Matthew, Daniel. B. of Commerce, U. Sask., 1964; MA in Econs., 1965. Dir. rsch. Dept. Mcpl. Affairs, Govt. Sask., Regina, 1965-67, Dept. Edn., Govt. Sask., Regina, 1967-69, dir. ednl. adminstrn., 1969-77, dep. minister, 1979-84; dir. taxation and fiscal policy Dept. Fin., Govt. Sask., Regina, 1977-78; dep. minister Dept. Urban Affairs, Govt. Sask., Regina, 1978-79; chmn. Govt. Fin. Commn., Regina, 1984-86; asst. dep. minister Dept. Energy & Mines, Govt. Sask., Regina, 1986-94, dep. minister, 1994—2002; pres. Sask. Property Mgmt. Corp., Regina, 2002—04; pres., CEO Sask. Transp. Co., Regina, 2004—. Office Phone: 306-787-2116. E-mail: rclayton@stcbus.ca.

CLAYTON, RICHARD REESE, retired diversified financial services company executive; b. St. Louis, Aug. 26, 1938; s. Lester Cox and Gladys Caroline (Reese) C.; m. Leigh Ila Smith, Feb. 25, 1961; children: Mark, Catherine, Christine. BS in Indsl. Econs., Purdue U., 1960. With Trane Co., 1960-73, mng. dir. Sydney, Australia, 1970-73; pres. Hallowell div. Standard Pressed Steel Co., Hatfield, Pa., 1973-77; exec. v.p. domestic ops., dir. SPS Technologies Inc., Jenkintown, Pa., 1977-84; pres., CEO, dir. Vermont Castings, Inc., Randolph, Vt., 1984-87; exec. v.p., chief adminstrv. officer Ea. Enterprises (formerly Ea. Gas & Fuel Assocs.), Weston, Mass., 1987-89, exec. v.p., COO, 1990-91, pres., COO, 1991-98. Baptist.

CLAYTON, ROBERT NORMAN, chemist, educator; b. Hamilton, Ont., Can., Mar. 20, 1930; came to U.S., 1952, naturalized, 1995; s. Norman and Gwenda (Twist) C.; m. Cathleen Shelburne, Jan. 30, 1971; 1 dau., Elizabeth Jane. B.Sc., Queens U., 1951, M.Sc., 1952; PhD, Calif. Inst. Tech., 1955. Research fellow Calif. Inst. Tech., 1955-56; mem. faculty Pa. State U., 1956-58, U. Chgo., 1958—, prof. chemistry and geochemistry, 1966—. Recipient Medal Sci. in Physical Sciences, 2004. Fellow AAAS, NAS, Royal Soc. (London), Royal Soc. Can., Am. Acad. Arts Scis., Am. Geophys Union, Meteoritical Soc. Achievements include research distbn. stable isotopes of light elements in nature, application to problems in geology.

CLAYTOR, RICHARD ANDERSON, retired federal agency administrator; b. Roanoke, Va., Sept. 4, 1927; s. William Graham and Gertrude (Boatwright) C.; m. Mary Lee Leary, June 18, 1949; children: Gale Catherine, Douglas Gordon, Richard Anderson Jr. BS, U.S. Naval Acad., 1949; BS in Marine Engring., Webb Inst. Naval Architecture, 1956, MS in Naval Architecture, 1956. Registered profl. engr., NJ, Calif. Commd. ensign USN, 1949, advanced through grades to capt., 1969; served in various ships, 1949-53; project mgr. nuclear power div. USN Bur. Ships, Washington, 1956-63; asst. mgr. Pitts. Naval Reactors Office, AEC, 1963-73; ret., 1973; v.p., asst. to pres. Burns and Roe, Inc., Oradell, NJ, 1973-79; pres. Burns and Roe-Humphreys & Glasgow Synthetic Fuels, Inc., Oradell, 1979-81, Burns and Roe Pacific Co., LA, 1981-90; asst. sec. for def. programs U.S. Dept. Energy, Washington, 1990-93; ind. cons. Decorated Legion of Merit. Mem.: Army-Navy Club. Episcopalian. Avocations: golf, bridge, painting.

CLEAGE, PEARL MICHELLE, writer, playwright, journalist; b. Springfield, Mass., Dec. 7, 1948; d. Albert B. Clege Jr. and Doris (Graham) C.; m. Michael Lomax, 1969 (div. 1979); 1 child, Deignan Njeri Lomax; m. Zaron W. Burnett Jr., 1994. Student, Howard Univ., Washington, DC; BA in Drama, Spelman Coll., Atlanta, 1971. Faculty Spelman Coll.; press secy. speechwriter Mayor Maynard Jackson, Atlanta. Contbr. articles to Atlanta Jour. Constitution, Atlanta Tribune; co-founder, editor Catalyst, literary journ.; author (self-published vol.): Mad at Miles: A Blackwoman's Guide to Truth, 1990; author: The Brass Bed, 1991, (collection of essays) Deals with the Devil and Other Reasons to Riot, 1993, (novels) What Looks Like Crazy on an Ordinary Day, 1997 (NY Times Bestseller list, Oprah Book

Club selection, 1998, BCALA Lit. award), I Wish I Had a Red Dress, 2001, Some Things I Thought I'd Never Do, 2003, Babylon Sisters, 2005, Baby Brother's Blues, 2006 (Best Literary Work in Fiction, NAACP Image awards, 2007), (plays) Blues for an Alabama Sky, 1995, Flyin' West, 1992, Bourbon at the Border, 1997; co-author (with husband, Zaron W. Burnett, Jr.): We Speak Your Names: A Celebration, 2006; contbg. editor Essence Mag. Recipient Bronze Jubilee award for lit., 1983, Outstanding Columnist award, Atlanta Assn. Black Journalists, 1991. Office: Spelman College 350 Spelman Ln SW Atlanta GA 30314*

CLEAR, ALBERT F., JR., retired hardware manufacturing company executive; b. NYC, June 9, 1920; s. Albert F. and Edna (Coyle) C.; m. Jeanne Posselt, Aug. 7, 1947; children: Geoffrey Posselt, Gregory Stuart. BS, MIT, 1942; MBA, Harvard U., 1948. V.p., mgr. Mallory div. John B. Stetson Co., Danbury, Conn., 1948-57; mng. assoc. Booz-Allen & Hamilton, NYC, 1957-65; v.p., gen. mgr. hardware div. Stanley Works, New Britain, Conn., 1965-69, v.p. consumer group, chmn. European ops., 1967-69, exec. v.p., 1969-76, pres., 1977-80, vice chmn., 1980-82. Chmn. Ansonia (Conn.) Copper & Brass, 1999-2001; bd. dirs. The Stanley Works, New Britain, Stanley Home Products, Westfield, Mass., Barden Corp., Danbury, Curtis Corp., Sandy Hook, Constructive Workshop, Inc., New Britain, D&L Corp., Danbury; adv. dir. Conn. Nat. Bank. Vice chmn. MIT Ctr. N.Y., 1965; bd. dirs. Danbury chpt. ARC, 1953; trustee Hartford Grad. Ctr., Hartford Coll. for Women, Housatonic Valley Assn., 1976-80. Capt. AUS, 1942-46. Mem. Builders Hardware Mfrs. Assn. (exec. com.), Danbury C. of C. (pres. 1954), New Britain C. of C. (dir. 1967-69, 72-80, pres. 1977).

CLEAR, JOHN MICHAEL, lawyer; b. St. Louis, Dec. 16, 1948; s. Raymond H. and Marian (Clark) Clear; m. Isabel Marie Bone, May 10, 1980; 1 child, Thomas Henry. BA summa cum laude, Washington U., St. Louis, 1971; JD with honors, U. Chgo., 1974. Bar: Mo. 1974, D.C. 1975, U.S. Ct. Appeals (5th and D.C. cirs.) 1975, U.S. Supreme Ct. 1977, U.S. Ct. Appeals (3d cir.) 1978, U.S. Ct. Appeals (8th cir.) 1980, U.S. Ct. Appeals (9th cir.) 1990, U.S. Dist. Ct. (so. dist.) Ill. 1995, U.S. Ct. Appeals (7th cir.) 1997. Law clk. to judge U.S. Ct. Appeals (5th cir.), Atlanta, 1974-75; assoc. Covington & Burling, Washington, 1975-80; jr. ptnr. Bryan, Cave, McPheeters & McRoberts, St. Louis, 1980-81, ptnr., 1982—. Mem. ABA, Mo. Bar Assn., D.C. Bar Assn., St. Louis Met. Bar Assn., Am. Law Inst., Order of Coif., Racquet Club, Noonday Club, Fox Run Golf Club, Phi Beta Kappa. Office: Bryan Cave LLP One Metropolitan Sq Saint Louis MO 63102-2750 Office Phone: 314-259-2283. Business E-Mail: jmclear@bryancave.com.

CLEARFIELD, HARRIS REYNOLD, physician; b. Phila., Aug. 8, 1933; s. Samuel and Rae (Lewis) C.; m. Louise Libby, June 30, 1957; children: Andrea, Jonathan. BS, Franklin and Marshall Coll., 1955; MD, Jefferson Med. Coll., 1959. Intern Grad. Hosp. U. Pa., Phila., 1959-60, resident in internal medicine, 1960-62, resident in gastroenterology, 1962-63, mem. staff, 1963-72, Episcopalian Hosp., Phila., 1967-72, head sect. gastroenterology, until 1972; sr. attending physician Phila. Gen Hosp., 1972-77; mem. faculty U. Pa. Med. Sch., Phila., 1963-72; clin. asst. prof. medicine Temple U. Med. Sch., Phila., 1967-72; dir. div. gastroenterology Hahnemann Hosp., Phila., 1972—, prof. medicine, 1972—. Lectr., cons. Naval Regional Med. Ctr., Phila., 1976-78; sr. cons. Phila. Gen. Hosp., 1972-74; mem. gov.'s adv. com. of ACP, 1980-88; dir. Krancer Ctr. for Inflamatory Bowel Disease Rsch., 1985—. Author: (with Dinoso) Gastrointestinal Emergencies, 1979, (with Borowsky) Case Studies in Gastroenterology, 1989; editorial cons. Am. Jour. Proctology, 1976-86; contbr. articles to profl. jours. Chmn. sci. adv. bd. Nat. Found. Ileitis and Colitis, 1976-80, trustee, 1990—. Recipient Lindback award Phila. chpt. Nat. Found. Ileitis and Colitis, 1979, named Physician of Yr., 1980, Janssen award, 1998. Fellow ACP (mem. bd. regents 1999-2003, chmn. coun. subspecialty socs. 1999-2003), Phila. Coll. Physicians; mem. Am. Gastroenterologic Assn., Bockus Internat. Soc. Gastroenterology (trustee, v.p., pres. 1993-95), Phila. Gastroenterology Group (pres. 1974-75), Am. Coll. Gastroenterology (Master; gov. Ea. Pa. 1990-92, trustee 1992-96), Pa. Soc. Gastroenterology (pres. 1993-95), Delaware Valley Soc. Gastrointestinal Rsch. Forum, Pa. Med. Soc. (commn. on accreditation 1986-92), Phila. Med. Soc. (bd. dirs. 1996—, sec. 1998—, v.p. 1999-, pres. 2001-02), Musical Fund Soc. Phila. (physician, 2003—). Home: 720 Oxford Rd Bala Cynwyd PA 19004-2112 Office: 219 N Broad St Philadelphia PA 19102-1121 Office Phone: 215-762-6070. Personal E-mail: harris.clearfield@drexel.edu.

CLEARO, KELLIE ANNE, internist, pharmacist, psychiatrist; b. Syracuse, NY, Nov. 10, 1969; d. Albert Martin Clearo and Carmen Delia Vazquez. BS in Pharmacy, U. Fla., Gainesville, 1993; MD, U. Wash., Seattle, 2000. Pharmacist Rite-Aid, Seattle, 1994—2000; resident in internal medicine and psychiatry SUNY, Bklyn., 2000—02, Duke U., Durham, NC, 2002—05; physician Emory Hosp., Atlanta, 2005—. Mem.: Am. Coll. Physicians, Am. Psychiat. Assn., Am. Pharmacist Assn. Office: Emory U Hosp Clifton Rd Atlanta GA 30307 Business E-Mail: kellie.clearo@emoryhealthcare.org.

CLEARY, BEVERLY ATLEE (MRS. CLARENCE T. CLEARY), writer; b. McMinnville, Oreg., Apr. 12, 1916; d. Chester Lloyd and Mable (Atlee) Bunn; m. Clarence T. Cleary, Oct. 6, 1940; children: Marianne Elisabeth, Malcolm James. BA, U. Calif., 1938; BA in Librarianship, U. Wash., 1939; LHD (hon.), Cornell Coll., 1993. Children's librarian Pub. Libr., Yakima, Wash., 1939-40; post librarian U.S. Army Regional Hosp., Oakland, Calif., 1942-45. Author: Henry Huggins, 1950, Ellen Tebbits, 1951, Henry and Beezus, 1952, Otis Spofford, 1953, Henry and Ribsy, 1954, Beezus and Ramona, 1955, Fifteen, 1956, Henry and the Paper Route, 1957, The Luckiest Girl, 1958, Jean and Johnny, 1959, The Real Hole, 1960, Hullabaloo ABC, 1960, 98, Two Dog Biscuits, 1961, Emily's Runaway Imagination, 1961, Henry and the Clubhouse, 1962, Sister of the Bride, 1963, Ribsy, 1964, The Mouse and the Motorcycle, 1965, Mitch and Amy, 1967, Ramona the Pest, 1968, Runaway Ralph, 1970, Socks, 1973, (play) The Sausage at the End of the Nose, 1974, Ramona the Brave, 1975, Ramona and Her Father, 1977 (Newbery Honor Book award ALA 1978), Ramona and Her Mother, 1979, Ramona Quimby, Age 8, 1981 (Newbery Honor Book award ALA 1982), Ralph S. Mouse, 1982, Dear Mr. Henshaw, 1983 (ALA Notable Book citation 1984, John Newbery medal 1984), Ramona Forever, 1984, Lucky Chuck, 1984, The Ramona Quimby Diary, 1984, Beezus and Ramona Diary, 1986, Janet's Thingamajigs, 1987, The Growing Up Feet, 1987, A Girl from Yamhill: A Memoir, 1988, Muggie Maggie, 1990, Strider, 1991, Petey's Bedtime Story, 1993, My Own Two Feet: A Memoir, 1995, Ramona's World, 1999. Recipient Disting. Alumna award U. Wash., 1975, Laura Ingalls Wilder award ALA, 1975, Regina medal Cath. Libr. Assn., 1980, De Grummond award U. Miss., 1982, U. So. Miss. medallion, 1982, Hans Christian Andersen medal nominee, 1984, Nat. Medal of the Arts, 2003, Libr. of Congress Living Legent medal, 2003. Mem. Authors Guild of Authors League Am. Office: c/o Harper Collins Children's Books 1350 Sixth Ave New York NY 10019-4702

CLEARY, DAVID MICHAEL, composer, critic, library assistant; b. Chelsea, Mass., Nov. 11, 1954; s. Robert Joseph and Sally Ann (Deuker) C.; m. Janice Tucker Rhoda, Jan. 21, 2001. MusB, New Eng. Conservatory Music, 1976; MusM, U. Hartford, 1978; MusD, U. Cin., 1982. Asst. to composition dept. New Eng. Conservatory Music, Boston, 1974-76; tchg. asst. in music theory U. Hartford, Conn., 1976-78, U. Cin., 1978-80, rotating instr. in music theory, 1980-81; libr. asst. Harvard U., Cambridge, Mass., 1984—. Assoc. prodr. The Composers Show, Sta. WGBH-FM, Boston, 1974-75; co-dir. Composers in Red Sneakers, 1994-2000, pres., 1997-2000. Compositions include Seven Bagatelles for Piano, 1975, Five Character Studies, 1979, A Gathering of Quokkas, 1985 (commd. Dinosaur Annex Ensemble), Lake George Overture, 1988, String Quartet no. 1, 1988, Gryllus, 1988-89, Cruikshank Fantasy, 1989 (commd. Alea III), Woodwind Quintet no. 2, 1990 (commd. Arcadian Winds), String Quartet no. 2, 1991 (commd. Artaria Quartet Boston), Linsner Sextet, 1992 (commd. Northwestern U. Trombone Ensemble), Western Wind Fragments, 1993-94 (commd. Eos Ensemble), Fanfares for Teddy Roosevelt, 1994-95, The Deeper Magic, 1995-96 (commd. Duo Renard), Fourteen Movie Characters, 1996-97 (commd. Am. Composers Forum Boston Area chpt.), Postcards from Annaghmakerrig, 1998, One Chord Wonders, 1999 (commd. Quincy Symphony), composer piano accompaniments ABCs of Strings Method Series, 2001—, Crosscultural Variations, 2002 (commd. Continental Harmony/Am. Composers Forum), SICPP Fantasies, 2002 (commd. SICPP Festival), Woodwind Quintet No. 3, 2003 (commd. Equinox Chamber Players), Opposites Attract (comd. Second Instrumental Unit), 2005; contbg. music writer (website) All-Music Guide, 1997—; (book) All Music Guide to Rock, 3d edit.; contbg. music critic New Music Connoisseur, 1999—, The Enterprise, 1999-2006, 21st Century Music, 2000—, Living Music, 2003—, Boston Herald, 2003—; recs. on Centaur, Vienna Modern Masters, Capstone, Musicians Showcase CD labels; contbr. articles to profl. jours. Mem. fellows coun. Va. Ctr. for the Creative Arts, 1999-02; bd. advisors Kalvos and Damian's New Music Bazaar, 1999-2005. Recipient 1st pl. Rosenberger Meml. Comm. Competition, Cin., 1989, Harvey Gaul Composition Competition, 1990; ASCAP grantee U. Hartford, 1978, grantee Somerville Arts Coun., 1987, 90, Meet the Composer, 1990, ASTRAL grantee Nat. Found. for Advancement in Arts, 1994; rsch. fellow U. Cin., 1980, Douglas W. Bryant fellow, 1988, fellow Va. Ctr. for Creative Arts, 1988-89, Yaddo fellow, 1988, Cummington fellow, 1989, Millay fellow, 1990, fellow Ella Lyman Cabot Trust, 1990, Ragdale fellow, 1992, MacDowell fellow, 1995, Tyrone Guthrie Ctr. fellow, 1998, Djerassi fellow, 2002. Mem. BMI, Am. Music Ctr., Am. Composers Forum, Soc. Composers, Electronic Music Found. Home: 7 Arlington St Apt 34 Cambridge MA 02140-2736 Office: Harvard U JFK Sch Govt Libr 79 JFK St Cambridge MA 02138

CLEARY, EDWARD WILLIAM, retired diversified forest products company executive; b. Sergeant Bluff, Iowa, May 21, 1919; s. Edward D. and Laura Helen (Rich) C.; m. Arita Louise Hefferan, June 12, 1946; children: John William, Kathryn Louise, Patricia Jane. BA, DePauw U., 1941; BSc, Ohio State U., 1947. Sr. acct. Price Waterhouse & Co., Portland, Oreg., 1947-53; treas., contr. Nat. Hosp. Assn., Portland, 1953-55, Valsetz Lumber Co., Portland, 1955-60; asst. compt. Boise Cascade (Idaho) Corp., 1960-63, compt., 1963-68, v.p., compt., 1968, v.p., treas., 1968-80, v.p., 1980-82, ret., 1982. Chmn. bd. dirs. Farmers & Merchants State Bank, 1993-2002. Mem. Pacific N.W. Area coun. YMCA, 1967-70; mem. exec. com. Boise United Fund, 1966-69, chmn. budget com., 1966-69; pres., bd. dirs. YMCA, 1967-69; bd. dirs. Idaho Blue Cross Hosp. Assn., 1969-75, Discovery Ctr. of Idaho, 1990-99; past pres. Bogus Basin Recreation Assn., bd. dirs. 1973-91. With AUS, 1941-42, USNR, 1942-46. Mem. AICPA, Nat. Assn. Accts. (past pres. Boise chpt., past nat. dir.), Idaho Soc. C.P.A.'s, Hillcrest Country Club (past dir., past v.p.). Home: Apt 408 3110 Crescent Rim Dr Boise ID 83706 Personal E-mail: ecclearyl@mindspring.com.

CLEARY, JANE M., not-for-profit developer, consultant; b. Iowa City, May 13, 1960; d. James L. and Mary K. Feeney; m. Brian F. Cleary; children: Kevin A., Joseph J.; m. Kenneth D. Conte, Nov. 0, 1979 (div. Dec. 0, 1987); 1 child, Katharine A. Conte. BS in Decision Scis., George Mason U., Fairfax, Va., 1986. Cne Novell, 1991; cert. project mgmt. profl. Project Mgmt. Inst., 2006, Cabm Assn. Profls. Bus. Mgmt., 2007. Programmer, analyst Burroughs Corp., McLean, Va., 1980; sys. analyst, programmer Anser, Arlington, Va., 1980—87; mgr., info. tech. Nat. Assn. Realtors, Washington, 1987—94; dir. mis Am. Soc. Travel Agts., Alexandria, Va., 1994—96; dir., assn. consulting Light Industries, Panurgy, Millersville, Md., 1996—2001; prin. DataMeleon, LLC, Annandale, Va., 2001—03; product solutions team leader Advanced Solutions Internat., Inc., Alexandria, 2003—. Sec. Columbia Knoll Coun. Co-Owners, Arlington, 1989—91; pres. Columbia Knoll Coun. of Co-Owners, 1991—93, Bristow Village Homeowners Assn., Annandale, 1993—94. Mem.: NAFE, Am. Mgmt. Assn., Am. Soc. Advancement Project Mgmt., Assn. Profls. in Bus. Mgmt. Liberal. Roman Catholic. Home Phone: 703-944-6038.

CLEARY, JOHN JOSEPH (JACK), lawyer; b. Boston, Nov. 24, 1946; s. John Joseph and Mildred Kathleen (Bell) C.; m. Nancy Jean Miller, June 1, 1968; children: Nina Dorothy, Eric John. BS, MIT, 1968; MPhil, Yale U., 1970; JD magna cum laude, Harvard U., 1974. Bar: Mass. 1974. Assoc. Goodwin, Procter & Hoar, Boston, 1974-81; ptnr., employee benefits practice group Goodwin Procter LLP (formerly Goodwin, Procter & Hoar), Boston, 1981—. Dir. N.E. Employee Benefits Coun., Wellesley, Mass., 1988-94. Mem. Needham (Mass.) Youth Commn., 1984-86; dir. Cath. Meml. High Sch., West Roxbury, Mass., 1987-95. Mem. ABA, Mass. Bar Assn., Boston Bar Assn. (past co-chmn. ERISA com. 1987-89), Dedham Country and Polo Club. Roman Catholic. Avocations: golf, theater, travel. Office: Goodwin Procter Exchange Pl Boston MA 02109-2881 Home Phone: 508-668-1353; Office Phone: 617-570-1199. Office Fax: 617-523-1231. Business E-Mail: jcleary@goodwinprocter.com.

CLEARY, MANON CATHERINE, artist, retired educator; d. Frank and Crystal (Maret) C. Attended, U. Valencia, Spain, Cocoran Sch. Art; BFA, Washington U., St. Louis, 1964; MFA, Temple U., 1968. Instr. fine arts SUNY, Oswego, 1968-70; from instr. to assoc. prof. D.C. Tchrs. Coll., Washington, 1970-78; from assoc. prof. to prof. art U. DC, Washington, 1978—2004, 2005, ret., 2005. One woman shows include Mus. Modern Art Gulbenkian Found., Lisbon, Portugal, 1985, Iolas/Jackson Gallery, NYC, 1982, Osuna Gallery, Washington, 1974, 77, 80, 84, 89, Univ. D.C., 1987, Tyler Gallery SUNY at Oswego, 1987, J. Rosenthal Fine Arts, Washington, 1991, Addison/Ripley Gallery, Washington, 1994, 99, Md. Arts Pl., 1997, Kramer Book Afterwords, 1998, Pass Gallery, Washington, 2000, others; group exhibits include Twentieth Century Am. Drawings: The Figure in Context, Traveled Nat. Acad. Design, 1984-85, Butler Inst. Am. Art, Youngstown, Ohio, 1987, Art Inst. Chgo., 1999-00, Huntsville (Ala.) Mus., 1987, Boca Raton (Fla.) Mus. Art, 1987, Corcoran Gallery Art, Washington, 1987, 96, Dimock Gallery, Washington, 1987, Tretyakov Gallery, Moscow, 1990, Nohra Haime Gallery, N.Y.C., 1994, Holter Mus., Helena, Mont., 1996, Gallery Stendahl, NYC, 1996, Alt. Mus., NYC, 1996, Kasteyev Mus., Almaty, Kazakstan, 1996, Alouan Gallery, Almaty, 1997, Art Inst. Chgo., 1999-2000, RAP, Rockville, Md., 2000-01, Nat. Mus. Women in the Arts, Washington, 2000, Wadell Gallery, Sterling, Va., 2005, Corcoran Arthe Warehouse Gallery, Washington, C.C., 2005, Nat. Drawing Invitational Travelling Show, 2005—, others; artist-in-residence Herning Hojskole, Denmark, 1980, Ucross Found., Wyo., 1984, Bridge Assn., Creative Lab. Project, Almaty, 1996, 97. Recipient Mayor's 14th ann. award for excellence in an artistic discipline, 1998; individual artist grantee D.C. Commn. on the Arts, 2000-01. Mem. Coll. Art Assn., Pi Beta Phi. Office Phone: 202-297-5072. Personal E-mail: manonart@aol.com.

CLEARY, MEAGAN BAYLESS, ecologist, educator, researcher; BS in Natural Resources Mgmt., Colo. State U., Fort Collins, 1997; MS in Environ. Studies and Environ. Edn., U. Mont., Missoula, 2000; postgrad., U. Wyo., Laramie, 2003—. Undergraduate rschr. NSF-Rsch. Experience Undergrads., Colo. State U., Fort Collins, 1995—97; technician forest inventory analysis USDA - US Forest Svc., Ogden, Utah, 1997—98; tchg. asst. environ. sci. for educators dept. edn. U. Mont., Missoula, 1999, instr. instrnl. media dept. edn., 1999, k-12 sci. tech. edn. specialist NASA - earth obs. sys. Edn. Project, 1999—2001; instr. Wild Rockies Field Inst., Missoula, 2001—; tchg. asst. earth sys. sci. program U. Wyo., Laramie, 2004—05, fellow Wyo. Space Grant Consortium, 2005—06, rsch. asst. dept. botany, 2006—. Rschr. Progetto Lupo, Parco Valle Pesio, Italy, 2000—01. Represented in permanent collections The Bra Show. Troop pres. Girl Scouts USA, 1986—92; program dir. Fiesta de los suenos en el aire libre Sangre de Cristo Girl Scout Coun., Santa Fe, 1999. Recipient Girl Scout Gold award, Sangre de Cristo Girl Scout Coun., 1992, Best Undergraduate Talk award, Colo. State U. Ecol. Symposium, 1996, Presentation of High Distinction, All-Colo. State U. Undergrad. Rsch. Symposium, 1996, Honor Sr. award, Dept. Forest Scis., Colo. State U., 1997, Robert L. Davis Meml. award, Coll. Natural Resources, Colo. State U., 1997, Cert. of Merit, USDA - US Forest Svc. Rsch. Sta., 1997, 1998, Best Grad. Poster award, Colo. State U. Ecol. Symposium, 2006, Best Grad. Presentation award, U. Wyo. Grad. Symposium, 2006; scholar, Santa Fe County Med. Soc., 1992, Nat. Assn. Secondary Sch. Prins., 1992; Robert C. Byrd scholar, Dept. Edn., State of N.Mex., 1992, Dean's scholar, Colo. State U., 1992—93, President's scholar, 1993—96, Leon H. and Katherine Rust Hurd Endowed scholar, 1994, Philip A. Connolly Meml. scholar, 1995, Thomas C. Evans scholar, 1996, Edwin Payson scholar, Dept. Botany, U. Wyo., 2005. Mem.: Assn. for Women in Sci., Am. Geophys. Union, Am. Inst. Biol. Scis., Ecol. Soc. Am., Golden Key, Xi Sigma Pi (pres. 1995—97, scholar 1997), Mortar Bd., Phi Kappa Phi. Avocations: sports, travel, arts and crafts, pets, cooking. Home Phone: 307-742-2003. Business E-Mail: meagankb@uwyo.edu.

CLEARY, PAUL DAVID, sociomedical educator; b. Toronto, May 14, 1948; s. Frank C. and Janet E. (Sweeney) Cleary; m. Cynthia F. Barnett, May 20, 1982; children: Janet A., Barnett D. BS in Physics, U. Wis., 1970, MS in Sociology, 1973, PhD in Sociology, 1980. Lectr. dept. sociology U. Wis., 1976-77; asst. rsch. prof. grad. sch. of social work Rutgers U., 1979-81, assoc. rsch. prof., 1981-82; asst. prof. dept. social medicine and health policy Harvard Med. Sch., 1982-87, assoc. prof. dept. health care policy and social medicine, 1988-92, prof. dept. health care policy and social medicine, 1993—2006; lectr., prof. dept. behavioral scis. Harvard Sch. of Pub. Health, 1983—2000; vis. assoc. prof. dept. sociomed. scis. Columbia U. Sch. of Pub. Health, 1988—; dean of pub. health Yale U., New Haven, 2006—. Rsch. assoc. dept. medicine Beth Israel Hosp., Boston, 1982—; assoc. epidemiologist dept. medicine, Brigham and Women's Hosp., Boston, 1987—; cons. Marshfield Rsch. Found., 1978-80, Hershey Med. Sch., Nat. Heart, Lung, and Blood Inst., Bundesgesundheitsamt, West Berlin, 1983-85, Harvard Inst. for Internat. Devel. Applied Diarrheal Disease Rsch. Project; mem. study sect. NIMH, 1980, 81, 85-89; study sect. sci. adv. com. Am. Found. AIDS Rsch., 1987-92; mem. program rev. panel Mass. AIDS Office, 1988-91; local adv. com. VIII Internat. Conf. on AIDS, 1989-92, co-chair social sci., policy, and law track, 1990-92; mem. faculty coun. Harvard Med. Sch., 1991-93, com. promotions, reappointments and appointments, 1993-96; vis. prof. Dept. Sociology, U. Stockholm, Sweden, 1982. Author: The Three Mile Island Nuclear Accident, 1988; author: (with others) Heart Disease and Rehabilitation, 1979, Handbook of Health, Health Care and the Health Professions, 1983, Heart Disease and Rehabilitation, 1986, Illness Behavior: A Multidisciplinary Model, 1986, Taking Care: Understanding and Encouraging Self-Protective Behavior, 1987, Gender and Stress, 1987, AIDS: The Safety of Blood and Blood Products, 1987, Evaluating Family Programs, 1988, The Future of Mental Health Services Research, 1989, AIDS and The Health Care System, 1990, Depression in Primary Care: Screening and Detection, 1990, Effectiveness and Outcomes in Health Care, 1990, International Law and AIDS: International Responses, Current Issues and Future Directions, 1992; assoc. editor: Jour. of Health and Social Behavior, 1983—86, 1989—92; editor: The Milbank Quar., 1992—2000. Mem.: AAAS, Inst. of Medicine, Assn. of Health Svcs. Rsch., Am. Sociol. Assn. (med. sociology sect. nominations com. 1985—86, 1989—90). Office: Yale Sch Pub Health 60 College St PO Box 208034 New Haven CT 06520-8034 Office Phone: 203-785-2867. E-mail: oaul.cleary@yale.edu.

CLEARY, SEAN MICHAEL, risk management executive; b. Somerset West, South Africa, Oct. 26, 1948; s. Thomas Stanislaus and Isobel Forsyth Cranston (Bell) C.; m. Sophia Natalie Smit, June 5, 1971; children: Sean Michael, Mary Siobhan. BA, U. South Africa, 1969; MBA, Brunel U., England, 1999. Vice consul, consul SA Consulate Gen., Tehran, Iran, 1971-75; deputy head econ. & fin. rels. divsn. Min. Fgn. Affairs, Pretoria, South Africa, 1976—77, head tng. divsn., 1978; polit. counsellor South African Embassy, Washington, 1978-82; consul gen. SA Consulate Gen., Beverly Hills, Calif., 1982-83; chief dir. Office of Adminstr. Gen., Windhoek, Nambia, 1983-85; mng. dir. Strategic Concepts Ltd., Wellington, South Africa, 1985—. Guest lectr. Grad. Sch. Bus., UNISA, Johannesburg, 1986—, Witwatersrand Bus. Sch., Johannesburg, 2002, Henley Mgmt. Coll., England, 2002—; faculty mem. Grad. Inst. Mgmt. and Tech., Johannesburg, 1996—, Internat. Ctr. for Mgmt. Devel., Johannesburg, Gordon Inst. Bus. Sci., Parmenides Found., Germany, Parmerides Found., Italy; sr. advisor Arab Bus. Coun.; forum fellow, strategic adviser to chmn. World Econ. Forum; vice chmn. Meridian Worldwide LLC, 1998—; mng. dir. Ctr. Advanced Governance; mgmt. bd. Think Tools AG, 1999—2003, supervisory bd., 2003—04, RedIT AG, 2004—; mem. facilitating and prep. com. Nat. Peace Accord; chair Working Group on Code of Conduct for Polit. Parties/Orgn., 1992; mem. bd. Lead Internat.; mem. advisory bd. Abraj Capital Ltd. Author (with Thierry Malleret) Resilience to Risk, 2006, (with Thierry Malleret) Global Risks, 2007; contbr. articles to profl. jours. Bd. mem. Lead Internat. Mem. Africa Task Force, World Econ. Forum, South African Inst. Internat. Affairs, Africa Inst. South Africa, Soc. Advancement Socio-Econs. Avocations: fishing, riding, writing, music. Home: The Lodge Silverhurst Estate Constantia Main Rd Constantia Cape Town 7806 South Africa Office Phone: 27218641560. Personal E-mail: sean.cleary@parmenides-foundation.org. Business E-Mail: scleary@stratconcepts.co.za.

CLEARY, THOMAS CHARLES, technology company executive; b. Chgo., Nov. 15, 1921; s. Thomas Harold and Mary Margaret (Russell) C.; m. Barbara Winnifred Johnson, Dec. 18, 1948; children: Thomas Robert, Margaret Mary Cleary Nurmia, Mary Ann Cleary Robitaille. BS in Mech. Engring., UCLA, 1949. Pres., gen. mgr. Whittaker Corp., Denver, 1950-63; dir. program mgmt. Litton Industries, Woodland Hills, Calif., 1963-65; asst. gen. mgr. Teledyne Sys., Inc., 1965-66; v.p., CEO Viking Industries, Chatsworth, Calif., 1966-67; v.p. Power Conversion, Inc., Long Beach, Calif., 1967-68; chmn. bd. dirs., mng. dir. TRW Electronic Comp. Co., Taiwan, Republic of China, 1968-69; pres., CEO Deutsch Relays, Inc., East Northport, NY, 1969-89, Struthers Dunn-Hi G, Pitman, NJ, 1989-91; chmn., CEO G&H Tech., Inc., Camarillo, Calif., 1992—. Author: Dynamic Management System, 1990, Management By Intent, 1991. Fundraiser Meml. Sloan-Kettering Cancer Ctr., N.Y., 1989—; mem. chancellor's assocs. UCLA, 1992—, mem. exec. com., dean's coun., sch. engring., 1992—; mem. bd. councillors UCLA Found., 1997. Capt. inf. U.S. Army, 1942-50, PTO. Named Entrepreneur of Yr. in mfg. Greater L.A. Area, 1997. Republican. Roman Catholic. Achievements include patents in the gyroscope and relay areas. Office: G&H Tech Inc 750 W Ventura Blvd Camarillo CA 93010-8382

CLEARY, TIMOTHY FINBAR, professional society administrator; b. Cork, Ireland, Sept. 30, 1925; s. John Francis and Nora (Riordan) C.; m. Patricia Agnes Hanley, June 21, 1947; children: Timothy F. X., Maureen P., Therese A., Richard S., Gail P., Eileen P. BS, Fordham U., 1955, JD, 1959. Bar: N.Y. 1959, D.C. 1980. Atty. N.Y.C. Police Dept., 1959-67; asst. counsel Fair Labor Standards div. U.S. Dept. Labor, Washington, 1967-71, chief counsel, 1971-73, mem., 1973-85; cons. in occupational safety and health, 1985—; exec. dir. Nat. Trust for Tng., Edn. and Research in Constrn., 1987-1991; internal campaign contbn. administrator Internat. Brotherhood Elec. Workers. Chmn. U.S. Occupational Safety and Health

Rev. Commn., Washington, 1977-81; mem. Adminstrv. Conf. U.S.; cert. arbitrator Nat. Mediation Bd.; lectr. labor law Practising Law Inst., U. Wis., Washington and Lee U., Cumberland Sch. Law, Ohio No. U., Brookings Instn., AFL-CIO Center for Labor Studies, Gompers-Murray Inst.Trade Assc., numerous others. Contbr. articles to profl. jours. Served with USN, 1943-45. Mem.: Friendly Sons St. Patrick, D.C. Home and Office: 5709 Cheshire Dr Bethesda MD 20814-2207 Office Phone: 301-530-6576. E-mail: tfincleary@yahoo.com.

CLEARY, WILLIAM JOSEPH, JR., lawyer; b. Wilmington, NC, Aug. 14, 1942; s. William Joseph and Eileen Ada (Gannon) C. AB in History, St. Joseph's U., 1964; JD, Villanova U., 1967. Bar: N.J., 1967, Calif. 1982, U.S. Ct. Appeals (3d cir.) 1969, U.S. Ct. Appeals (9th cir.) 1983, U.S. Dist. Ct. (ctrl. dist.) Calif. 1983, U.S. Supreme Ct. 1992. Law sec. to judge N.J. Superior Ct., Jersey City, 1967-68; assoc. Lamb, Blake, H&D, Jersey City, 1968-72; dep. pub. defender State of N.J., Newark, 1972-73; 1st asst. city corp. counsel Jersey City, N.J., 1973-76; assoc. Robert Wasserwald, Inc., Hollywood, Calif., 1984-86, Gould & Burke, Century City, Calif., 1986-87; pvt. practice Hollywood, 1989—. Mem. ABA, FBA, N.J. State Bar Assn., Calif. Bar Assn., L.A. County Bar Assn. (appellate cts. com.), Nat. Jesuit Hon. Soc., Alpha Sigma Nu. Democrat. Roman Catholic. Office: 1853 1/2 Canyon Dr Los Angeles CA 90028-5607 Office Phone: 323-856-0436. E-mail: jmclaw42@aol.com.

CLEAVE, MARY L., environmental engineer, former astronaut; b. Southampton, NY, Feb. 5, 1947; BS in Biol. Scis., Colo. State U., 1969; MS in Microbiol. Ecology, Utah State U., 1975, PhD in Civil and Environ. Engring., 1979. Mem. rsch. staff Utah State U., 1971-80; astronaut NASA, Lyndon B. Johnson Space Ctr., Houston, 1980-90, mission specialist STS 61-B, 1985, mission specialist STS-30, 1989; now dep. project mgr. NASA Ocean Color Satellite Program, Greenbelt, Md. Mem. Tex. Soc. Profl. Engrs., Water Pollution Control Fedn., Sigma Xi, Tau Beta Pi.

CLEAVER, EMANUEL, II, congressman, former mayor, minister; b. Waxahachie, Tex., Oct. 26, 1944; s. Lucky and Marie (McKnight) Cleaver; m. Dianne Donaldson, June 1970; children: Evan Donaldson, Emanuel III and Emiel Davenport (twins), Marissa Dianne. BS in Sociology, Prairie View A&M U., Tex., 1968; MDiv, St. Paul Sch. Theology, Kansas City, Mo., 1974; DD (hon.), Baker U., 1988. Ordained to ministry United Meth. Ch. Sr. pastor St. James United Meth. Ch., Kans. City, Mo., 1969—; coun. mem. Kans. City, Mo., 1979—91, mayor pro-tem, 1987-91, mayor, 1991—99; spl. adv. to Andrew Cuomo US Sec. of Housing and Urban Devel., 1999—2000; host Under the Clock KCUR-FM pub. radio, Kans. City, Mo., 2000—04; mem. US Congress from 5th Mo. dist., 2005—, mem. fin. svcs. com. Lectr. to chs., schs., civic and social orgns. nationwide. Chmn. Kans. City Coun. Plans and Zoning Com., 1984-87, Policy and Rules Com., 1987-91; mid-cen. regional v.p. So. Christian Leadership Conf. (Drum Major for Justice award 1991); founder, co-chair Kans. City Harmony In A World of Difference. Recipient William Yates Disting. Svc. Medallion William Jewel Coll., 1987, Pub. Svc. award Am.-Jewish Com., 1991, Junteenth Man of Yr. award Black Archives of Mid-Am. Inc., 1991, Disting. Citizen award Greater Kans. City Urban Affairs Coun., 1991, Cmty. Svc./Leadership award Webster U., 1991, Disting. Svc. award Park Coll., 1991, Friend of Youth award Boys & Girls Clubs, 1991, Outstanding Contbns. to Black Cmty. award Concerned Citizens Black Clergy of Atlanta, 1991, Rainbow award, 1992, 100 Most Influential Kansas Citizens award Kans. City Globe, 1991, 92, 93, Bridge Builders award Kans. City Globem 1992, Harold L. Holiday Sr. Civil Rights award NAACP, 1992, Disting. Grad. award St. Paul Sch. Theology, 1993, Kans. City Anti-Apartheid award, 1993, James C. Kirkpatrick Excellence for Govt. award, 1993, Disting. Citizen of Midwest award NCCJ, 1993, Gov. award for local elected ofcl. of yr. State of Mo., 1994; named one of Most Influential Black Americans, Ebony mag., 2006. Mem. NAACP, Greater Kans. City C. of C. (Centurions Leadership award 1987), Alpha Phi Alpha. Democrat. Office: US House Reps 1641 Longworth House Office Bldg Washington DC 20515-2505 Office Phone: 202-225-4535.*

CLEAVER, JAMES EDWARD, radiologist, educator; b. Portsmouth, England, May 17, 1938; came to the U.S., 1964; s. Edward Alfred and Kathleen Florence (Cleveley) C.; m. Christine J. Cleaver, Aug. 8, 1964; children: Jonathan, Alison. BA, St. Catharine's Coll., 1961; PhD, U. Cambridge, 1964. Rsch. fellow Mass. Gen. Hosp., Boston, 1964-66; asst. rsch. biophysicist lab. radiobiology environ. health U. Calif., San Francisco, 1966-68, asst. prof. radiology, 1968-70, assoc. prof. radiology, 1970-74, prof. radiology, 1974—; vis. prof. Imperial Cancer Rsch. Fund, London, 1973-74, prof. radiology, 1975-96, prof. dermatology, 1996—. Contbr. over 350 articles to profl. jours. Recipient Lila Gruber award Am. Acad. Dermatology, 1976, Sr. Investigator award Am. Soc. Photobiology, 1995, Luigi Provasoli award Phycol. Soc. Am., 1992, J. Little award for radiation rsch. Harvard U., 2003. Mem. NAS, Nat. Coun. on Radiation Protection, Radiation Rsch. Soc. (councillor 1982-84, Rsch. award 1973).

CLEAVER, WILLIAM LEHN, lawyer; b. Harrisburg, Pa., Dec. 7, 1949; s. Gene Franklin and Goldie Jean (Haldeman) C.; m. Judith Ann McMahon, Aug. 2, 2003; children: Benjamin Neville, Valerie Anne. BA, Augustana Coll., 1971; JD, U. Iowa, 1974. Bar: Iowa 1974, Ill. 1975, U.S. Dist. Ct. (so. dist.) Iowa 1975, U.S. Dist. Ct. (so. dist.) Ill. 1975. Ptnr. Bozeman, Neighbour, Patton & Noe, LLP, Moline, Ill., 1991—. Chmn. bd. govs. BBB Ctrl. Ea. Iowa. Mem. adv. coun. Luth. Social Svcs. of Ill. Adult Day Care Ctr., Rock Island; pres. adv. coun. Ret. Sr. Vol. Program, Moline; commr. and chmn. Rock Island Preservation Commn.; mem. Citizen's Adv. Com., Rock Island; mem., pres. sch. bd. Rock Island/Milan Dist. 41; v.p. bd. dir. United Way of Quad Cities, Rock Island; bd. govs. Rock Island Cmty. Found.; bd. dir. Quad Cities chpt. ARC, Rock Island Pub. Library Found. Col. USAR, ret. Mem. ABA, Ill. State Bar Assn. (mem. assembly), Iowa State Bar Assn., Rock Island County Bar Assn., Scott County Bar Assn. Lodges: Kiwanis (pres. 1983-84, bd. dirs. 1984-85). Lutheran. Avocations: fine arts, racquet sports. Home: 8806 Ridgewood Rd Rock Island IL 61201-7655 Office: Bozeman Neighbour Patton & Noe 1630 5th Ave Moline IL 61265-7910 Home Phone: 309-787-4741; Office Phone: 309-797-0850. E-mail: wcleaver@bnpn.com.

CLEAVES, PETER SHURTLEFF, foundation administrator; b. Washington, Dec. 4, 1943; s. Richard Delaplane and Margaret Grant (Shurtleff) C.; m. Dorothy Barcham, Aug. 31, 1968; children: Geoffrey, Rachel. AB, Dartmouth Coll., 1966; MA, Vanderbilt U., 1968; PhD, U. Calif., Berkeley, 1972. Escort interpreter U.S. Dept. State, Washington, 1966-68; assoc. rep. for Peru, Ecuador and Bolivia, Ford Found., Lima, Peru, 1972-76, rep. for Mex. and C.Am., Mexico City, 1977-82; vis. scholar Yale U., New Haven, 1976-77; v.p. 1st Nat. Bank Chgo., 1982-90; prof. U. Tex., Austin, 1990-99, dir. Inst. Latin Am. Studies, 1990-95, dir. Ctr. for Study Western Hemisphere Trade, 1995-97; exec. dir. Avina Found., Hurden, Switzerland, 1997—2004; pres. DRG Internat., 2005—07; CEO Emirates Found., 2007—. Cons. various corp., multilateral, and non-profit orgns. in Latin Am. and the Middle East, 1990—. Author: Bureaucratic Politics and Administration in Chile, 1974, Agriculture, Bureaucracy and Military Government in Peru, 1980, Profession and the State, The Mexican Case, 1987, Latin America in the 21st Century, 2003; also numerous articles. Chmn., trustee Internat. Sch. Panama, Panama City, 1984-86; mem. Cabot Journalism Com., 1995-2004, LASA Investment Com., 2000-. William Hill Meml. fellow Dartmouth Coll., 1966, NDEA Title VI fellow U. Calif., 1968, rsch. fellow Doherty Found., 1970, Fulbright-Hays fellow, 1971. Mem. L.Am. Studies Assn., Barton Creek Country Club. Avocations: tennis, languages. Home: 3605 Flamevine Cv Austin TX 78735-1544 Office: Emirates Found Chamber of Commerce Bldg Cornish Rd PO Box 45005 Abu Dhabi United Arab Emirates 3 Office Phone: 971-2-616-7788. Home Fax: 512-329-5016 512-329-5016. Personal E-mail: pcleaves@emiratesfoundation.ae.

CLEELAND, CHARLES S., medical educator, researcher; s. Joseph Cawley and Charlotte Swanson Cleeland; m. Xin Shelley Wang, Nov. 27, 2005; children: Sarah Cleeland Knight, Charles Travis. PhD, Washington U., St. Louis, Mo, 1967. Diplomate Amercian Bd. Profl. Psychology, 1976. McCullough prof. cancer rsch. M. D. Anderson Cancer Ctr., Houston; prof. neurology U. Wis., Madison, 1967—95. Dir. Am. Pain Found., Balt., 1997—2007. Mem.: Am. Pain Soc. (pres. 1995—96, Fordyce award). Office: MD Anderson Cancer Ctr 1100 Holcombe Unit 221 Houston TX 77006 Home Phone: 713-745-3470; Office Phone: 713-745-3470.

CLEESE, JOHN MARWOOD, writer, comedian; b. Weston-Super-Mare, Eng., Oct. 27, 1939; s. Reginald and Muriel Cleese; m. Connie Booth, Feb. 20, 1968 (div. 1978); 1 child, Cynthia; m. Barbara Trentham, Feb. 15, 1981 (div. 1990); 1 child, Camilla; m. Alyce Faye Elchelberger, Dec. 28, 1992. Student, Clifton Coll., Bristol, Eng.; MA, Cambridge U., Eng.; LLD (hon.), St. Andrews U. Andrew D. White prof.-at-large Cornell U., 1999—. Writer, performer (TV series) The Frost Report, 1966, At Last the 1948 Show, others; actor: (TV series) Monty Python's Flying Circus, Fawlty Towers, Third Rock from the Sun, 1998 (Emmy nomination), The Human Face, 2001; (TV films) The Taming of the Shrew, 1981, (guest appearance): (TV series) Cheers (Emmy award for Outstanding Guest Performer in a Comedy Series, 1987),: (films) Interlude, 1968, The Magic Christian, 1970, The Rise and Rise of Michael Rimmer, 1970, And Now for Something Completely Different, 1972, Monty Python and the Holy Grail, 1975, Romance with a Double Bass, 1975, Life of Brian, 1979, The Secret Policeman's Ball, 1979, Time Bandits, 1981, Monty Python Live at the Hollywood Bowl, 1982, The Secret Policemen's Other Ball, 1982, Privates on Parade, Yellowbeard, 1983, The Meaning of Life, 1983, Silverado, 1984, Clockwise, 1986, Erik the Viking, 1988, Splitting Heirs, 1992, Mary Shelley's Frankenstein, 1994, Jungle Book, 1994, The Out-of-Towners, Isn't She Great, 1998, The World is Not Enough, 1999, Rat Race, 2000, Harry Potter and the Sourcerer's Stone, 2001, Die Another Day, 2002, Harry Potter and the Chamber of Secrets, 2002, Scorched, 2003, Charlie's Angels: Full Throttle, 2003, (voice) Shrek 2, 2004, Around the World in 80 Days, 2004, (voice) Valiant, 2005, Complete Guide to Guys, 2006, L' Entente cordiale, 2006, (voice) Charlotte's Web, 2006; actor, writer: A Fish Called Wanda, 1988; actor(voice actor): Fierce Creatures, 1997; co-author: (book) The Strange Case of the End of Civilization as We Know It, 1977, Monty Python's Big Red Book, 1975, Families and How to Survive Them, 1983, Life and How to Survive It, 1993, The Human Face, 2001; founder, former dir. Video Arts Ltd., London, 1979—91 (Queen's award for Exports, 1982), creator TV and radio commls. Office: care David Wilkinson 115 Hazlebury Rd London SW6 2LX England*

CLEGG, CHRISTOPHER R., lawyer; BA, U. Calif., Berkeley; MA in Internat. Studies, John Hopkins U.; LLB, Georgetown U. Pvt. practice, Cleve., Seattle; sr. corp. counsel Goodrich Aerospace; v.p. BFGoodrich Performance Materials; sr. v.p., gen. counsel, sec. Noveon Inc., 2001—04, Commonwealth Industries, 2004, Aleris Internat., Inc., Beachwood, Ohio, 2004—. Mem.: Am. Soc. Corp. Secretaries, Am. Corp. Counsel Assn. Office: Aleris Internat, Inc 25825 Science Park Dr Beachwood OH 44122*

CLEGG, JAMES STANDISH, physiologist, biochemist, educator; b. Aspinwall, Pa., July 27, 1933; divorced; 3 children; m. Eileen Clegg; 1 stepchild. AA in Biology, Coffeyville Coll., 1953; BS in Zoology, Pa. State U., 1958; PhD in Biology, Johns Hopkins U., 1961. Rsch. assoc. biologist Johns Hopkins U., 1961-62; asst. prof. zoology U. Miami, 1962-64, from assoc. prof. biology to prof., 1964-70; prof. sect. molecular and cellular biology U. Calif., Davis, 1986—, dir. Bodega Marine Lab., 1986-98. With CNRS Thias France, 1983; pres. Nat. Assn. Marine Labs., 1992-94. With US Army, 1953—55. Recipient Fulbright Sr. Rsch. award U. London, 1978, U. Ghent, 1999; Wilson fellow, 1958-59. Fellow AAAS; mem. Am. Soc. Zoologists, Am. Soc. Cell Biology, Biophys. Soc., Soc. Cryobiology, Sigma Xi. Independent. Achievements include research in comparative biochemistry and biophysics; mechanisms of cryptobiosis; properties and role of water in cellular metabolism; cytoplasmic organization. Office: U Calif Bodega Marine Lab PO Box 247 Bodega Bay CA 94923-0247 Home Phone: 707-875-2215; Office Phone: 707-875-2010. Business E-Mail: jsclegg@ucdavis.edu.

CLEGG, KAREN KOHLER, lawyer; b. Junction City, Kans., Jan. 7, 1949; d. John Emil and Delores Maxine (Letkeman) Kohler; m. Stephen J. Clegg Jr., Mar. 28, 1970. BS, Emporia State U., 1970; JD, U. Kans., 1975; MBA, Rockhurst Coll., 1989. Bar: Kans. 1975, U.S. Dist. Ct. Kans. 1975, Mo. 1977, U.S. Dist. Ct. (we. dist.) Mo. 1977. Asst. atty. gen. State of Kans., Topeka, 1975-77; atty. The Bendix Corp., Kansas City, Mo., 1977-81, sr. atty., 1981-84; counsel Allied Corp. (now Allied Signal, Inc.), Kansas City, 1984-90, v.p. adminstrn., 1990—93, v.p. field svcs. Columbus, Md., 1994—95, v.p. ops. Kansas City, 1995—2001; pres. Honeywell Fed. Mfg. and Technologies Honeywell Internat., 2001—02, v.p. def. and space programs, Honeywell Aerospace; ret. Mem. council human resources mgmt. adv. bd. Commerce Clearing House, Chgo., 1985-88. Sec. Assn. Greater Devel. Coll. Blvd., Shawnee Mission, Kans., 1986-87; bd. dirs. adv. council Avila Coll. Bus., Kansas City, 1984—, Dimension's Unltd., Kansas City, 1985-86. Mem. ABA, Mo. Bar Assn., Am. Soc. Personnel Adminstrn. (v.p., bd. dirs. EEO 1985, profl. services 1986-87), Greater Kansas City C. of C. (centurian leadership program). Avocations: music, theater, art, reading, travel. Office: Honeywell 2000 E 95th St Kansas City MO 64131-3030 Home: 6909 Burnt Sienna Cir Naples FL 34109-7828

CLEGG, MICHAEL TRAN, genetics educator, researcher; b. Pasadena, Calif., Aug. 1, 1941; AA, Sacramento City Coll., 1967; BS, U. Calif., Davis, 1969, PhD, 1972. Asst. prof. Brown U., Providence, 1972—76; assoc. prof. U. Ga., Athens, 1976—82, prof., 1982—84; prof. genetics U. Calif., Riverside, 1984—2004, acting dean Coll. Natural and Agrl. Scis., 1994—97, dean Coll. Natural and Agrl. Scis., 1997—2000, Donald Bren prof. biol. scis., ecology and evolutionary biology Irvine, 2004—. Chmn. biology bd., NRC, mem. commn. on life scis., 1990-96, chmn., 1998-2000. Co-author: Principles of Genetics, 1988; co-editor: Plant Population Genetics, 1989, Molecular Evolution, 1990; contbr. articles to sci. jours. Sgt. US Army, 1960—63. Guggenheim Found. fellow, 1981-82; recipient Darwin prize Edinburgh U., 1995. Fellow Am. Acad. Arts & Scis., Third World Acad. Scis. (assoc.); mem. NAS (fgn. sec. 2002-06), Am. Soc. Naturalists (v.p. 1986), Am. Genetics Assn. (pres. 1987), Soc. for the Study of Evolution (v.p. 1986), Genetics Soc. Am., Soc. Molecular Biology and Evolution (pres.-elect 2001, pres. 2002). Avocations: skiing, flying. Office: Ecology & Evolutionary Biology U Calif 321 Steinhaus Hall Irvine CA 92697-2525 Office Phone: 949-824-4490. Office Fax: 949-824-2181. E-mail: mclegg@uci.edu.*

CLEGG, ROGER BURTON, lawyer; b. Odessa, Tex., Apr. 18, 1955; s. Joe Dunn and Margaret Elisabeth (Blau) C.; m. Joann Ruth Catalfamo, June 15, 1985; 1 child, Paul. BA magna cum laude, Rice U., 1977; JD, Yale U., 1981. Bar: DC 1981. Grad. fellow Office Gen. Counsel, CIA, Langley, Va.; mem. staff editorial and research div. Republican Nat. Com., Washington, 1980; law clk. to presiding judge US Ct. Appeals, Washington, 1981-82; atty.- adviser office of legal policy US Dept. Justice, Washington, 1982, spl. asst. to atty. gen., 1982-83, dep. asst. atty. gen., 1983-84, acting asst. atty. gen., office legal policy, 1984, assoc. dep. atty. gen., 1984-85, spl. litigation counsel, civil div., 1985, asst. to solicitor gen., 1985-87, dep. asst. atty. gen. civil rights div., 1987-91, dep. asst. atty. gen. env. div., 1991-93; v.p., gen. counsel Nat. Legal Ctr. for Pub. Interest, Washington, 1993-97, Ctr. for Equal Opportunity, Washington, 1997—2005, pres. Sterling, Va., 2006—. Editor-in-chief Yale Studies in World Public Order, 1979-80. Mem.: D.C. Bar, Federalist Soc., Phi Beta Kappa. Republican. Methodist. Home: 9703 Flintridge Ct Fairfax VA 22032-1712 Office: Ste 500 14 Pidgeon Hill Dr Sterling VA 20165 Office Phone: 703-421-5443.

CLEGHORN, JOHN EDWARD, bank executive; b. Montreal, July 7, 1941; m. Pattie E. Hart; children: Charles, Ian, Andrea. B in Commerce, McGill U., Montreal, 1962; DCL (hon.), Bishop's U., 1989; LLD (hon.), Wilfrid Laurier U., 1991; DCL (hon.), Acadia U., 1996. Chartered acct. Articled with Clarkson Gordon, chartered Accts., Montreal, 1962-64; sugar and futures trader St. Lawrence Sugar Ltd., Montreal, 1964-66; with Citibank, NY, Montreal, Winnipeg & Vancouver, 1966—74, Royal Bank of Canada, Montreal, Toronto & Vancouver, 1974—86, pres., 1986-90; pres., COO RBC, 1990—94; CEO Royal Bank of Can., Montreal, 1994-95, chmn., CEO, 1995—2001; chmn., bd. dirs. SNC Lavalin Group, Inc., 2001—, Canadian Pacific Railway Ltd., Calgary, Alberta, 2006—. Bd. dirs. Finning Internat. Inc., Nortel Networks, Can. Pacific Ry. Ltd., Molson Inc, McGill U; chmn. internat. adv. bd. McGill Faculty Mgmt.; dir. Can. Spl. Olympics Found.; chancellor emeritus Wilfrid Laurier U. Chmn. Hist. Found. of Can. Fellow Order of Chartered Accts. Quebec, Inst. Chartered Accts. Ont.; mem. Can. Inst. Chartered Accts. Office: Ste 3115 31st Flr S Tower 200 Bay St Royal Bank Plz Toronto ON Canada M5J 2J5 Business E-Mail: john.cleghorn@rbc.com.

CLELAND, CHARLES LESLIE, sociologist, educator; b. Cairo, W.Va., Aug. 26, 1927; s. Ronald Stewart Cleland and Dorothy Catherine Leslie; m. Laurel Elaine Hays, June 6, 1953; children: Rebecca Elizabeth, Linda Hays. BA summa cum laude, U. Charleston, W.Va., 1952; postgrad., Harvard U., Cambridge, Mass., 1952—53; MS, U. Wis., Madison, 1955, PhD, 1958. Asst. prof. rural sociology U. Tenn., Knoxville, 1958—62, assoc. prof. rural sociology, 1962—69, prof. rural sociology, 1969—95, prof. emeritus, 1995—. From participating scientist to chmn. regional rsch. coms. Agrl. Exptl. Sta. so. region, Knoxville, 1963—92. Staff sgt. USAF, 1946—48. Recipient Chancellor's citation, U. Tenn., 1987, Pondergrass award for outstanding svc., Agrl. Exptl. Sta., 1987. Mem.: Rural Sociol. Soc. (Disting. Svc. award 1995), Phi Kappa Phi. Democrat. Presbyterian. Avocations: volunteering, church choir. Home: 5108 Yosemite Tr Knoxville TN 37909

CLELAND, JOSEPH MAXWELL (MAX CLELAND), federal official, former senator; b. Atlanta, Aug. 24, 1942; s. Joseph Hugh and Juanita (Kesler) C. BA, Stetson U., Deland, Fla., 1964; MA, Emory U., 1968; LLD (hon.), Stetson U., Deland, Fla., 1979; degree (hon.), Emory U. Mem. Ga. Senate, Atlanta, 1971-75; cons. Com. on Vets. Affairs, U.S. Senate, Washington, 1975, profl. staff mem., 1975-77; adminstr. VA, Washington, 1977-81; sec. of state State of Ga., Atlanta, 1982-95; U.S. senator from Ga, 1997—2003; mem. armed svcs. com., govtl. affairs com., small bus. com.; disting. adj. prof. Am. Univs. Washington Semester Program, 2003—. Mem. commerce com. U.S. Senate, 1999-2003; strategic cons. The Carmen Group, 2003—, mem. Export-Import Bank of the US, 2003- Author: Strong at the Broken Places, 2000, Going for the Max!: 12 Principles for Living Life to the Fullest, 2002. Candidate U.S. Senate, Ga., 1996. Capt. U.S. Army, 1965-68, Vietnam. Decorated Bronze Star, Silver Star; fellow Ctr. for Congrl. and Presdl. Studies, 2003—; recipient Disting. Alumnus award Stetson U., 1972, Gt. Georgian award WSB Radio, award for gallantry Easter Seal Soc., 1973, Outstanding Handicapped Citizen in Ga. award, 1973, Jefferson award for greatest pub. service by individual under 35 Am. Inst. Pub. Service, 1977, Inspiration award Assn. U.S. Army, Atlanta, 1978, AMP of Yr. award, 1978, Life Inspiration award Religious Heritage Am., 1978, Golden Key award Am. Assn. Sch. Adminstrs., 1978, Gold medallion Chapel of Four Chaplains, 1979, Am. Patriot's medal Valley Forge Freedom's Found., 1979, J.O. Wright award, 1979, Neal Pike award, 1979, Citizen of Yr. award Nat. Conf. Citizenship, 1986; named One of Five Outstanding Young Men in Ga. Ga. Jaycees, Outstanding Disabled Vet. DAV, one of 100 most influential people in Ga. by Ga. Trend mag. Democrat. Office: Export-Import Bank of the US 811 Vermont Ave NW Washington DC 20571

CLELAND, MAX (JOSEPH MAXWELL CLELAND), former senator; b. Atlanta, 1942; BA, Stetson U., doctorate (hon.); MA in Am. History, Emory U., doctorate (hon.). Mem. Ga. State Senate, 1971-75, sec. of state, 1983-96; U.S. senator from Ga., 1996—2003. Head U.S. VA, 1977-81, mgr. GI Bill, VA Home Loan Guaranty program, VA Hosp. program; founder First Stop Bus. Info. Ctr.; mem. Senate Armed Svcs. com., 1997-2003, com. on commerce, sci. and transp., 1999-2003, com. on govtl. affairs, 1997-2003, com. in small bus., 1997-2003. Author: (autobiography) Strong at the Broken Places, 1980, Going for the Max!: 12 Principles for Living Life to the Fullest, 2000. Capt. U.S. Army, 1967, Vietnam. Decorated Bronze Star, Silver Star; named One of Rising Democrats, Time Mag.; recipient Victory award Nat. Rehab. Hosp., Washington, 1996, Nat. award U.S. Small Bus. Adminstrn. Democrat.*

CLELAND, SHERRILL, college president; b. Galion, Ohio, Sept. 21, 1924; s. Fred Burr and Doris Louise (Gregg) C.; m. Betty Irene Chorpenning, July 6, 1946 (dec. June 1986); children: Ann Denise Cleland Feldmeier, Douglas Stewart, Sarah McDermott Cleland Allen, Scott Cameron; m. Diana Ashley Drake, Sept. 3, 1988; stepchildren: Cynthia Rush, Allison Abizaid, Linda Wiener, Carol Abizaid, Amanda Abizaid, Richard Abizaid. AB, Oberlin Coll., Ohio, 1949; MA, Princeton U., NJ, 1951, PhD in Econs., 1957; LLD (hon.), Marietta Coll., Ohio, 1989. Instr. econs. Princeton U., 1951-55; asst. prof. U. Richmond, 1955-56; mem. faculty Kalamazoo Coll., 1956-73, acad. v.p., 1964-67; prof. econs., pres. Marietta Coll., Ohio, 1973—89, now prof. emeritus Ohio, 1989—. Econs. adviser Hashemite Kingdom Jordan, 1963-64; Ford Found. vis. prof. econs. and devel. adminstrn. Am. U. Beirut, Lebanon, 1967-69, hon. prof. Southwestern U. Fin. and Econs., Chengdu Peoples Republic China, 1985; cons. examiner North Ctrl. Assn. Colls., 1960-90; dir. Cleve. Fed. Res. Bank, Cin. br., 1980-85. Co-editor, author: Continuity and Change in the World Oil Industry, 1970; contbg. author: Linear Programming and Theory of Firm, 1962; contbr. to profl. jours. Pres. Kalamazoo chpt. Human Rels. Coun., 1958-60; bd. dirs. Tuition Exch., Inc., 1975—; chmn. Student Loan Funding Corp., 1991-97; bd. dirs. AHEAD Corp., Amideast, Inc.; past pres. Ohio Coll. Assn.; chmn. East Ctrl. Coll. Consortium, Ind. Colls., Univs. Ohio; trustee Oberlin Coll., 1976-82, Mt. Vernon Coll., 1992-97; dir. Knowledge Works Found., Cin., 1997—; mem. Sarasota Coun. of the Blind, 2005-. With AUS, 1944-46. Decorated Bronze Star, Purple Heart.; recipient Kazanjian Found. teaching award econs., 1971; Leadership tng. fellow N. Central Assn. Colls., 1959 Fellow Middle East Studies Assn.; mem. Am. Econ. Assn., UN Assn. (past pres. Kalamazoo chpt.), Ohio Assn. for Freedom to Die. Presbyterian. Home: 4489 Highland Oaks Cir Sarasota FL 34235-5175 Home (Summer): 67 Birch Tree Ln Waitsfield VT 05673 E-mail: dadcleland@yahoo.com.

CLELAND, W(ILLIAM) WALLACE, biochemistry educator; b. Balt., Jan. 6, 1930; s. Ralph E. and Elizabeth P. (Shoyer) C.; m. Joan K. Hookanson, June 18, 1967 (div. Mar. 1999); children: Elsa Eleanor, Erica Elizabeth. AB summa cum laude, Oberlin Coll., 1950; MS, U. Wis., 1953, PhD, 1955. Postdoctoral fellow U. Chgo., 1957-59; asst. prof. U. Wis., Madison, 1959-62, assoc. prof., 1962-66, prof., 1966—, M.J. Johnson prof. biochemistry, 1978—, Steenbock prof. chem. sci., 1982—2002. Contbr. articles to profl. biochem. and chem. jours. Served with U.S. Army, 1957-59. Grantee NIH, 1960—, NSF, 1960-94; recipient Stein and Moore award Protein Soc., 1999. Mem. NAS, Am. Acad. Arts and Scis., Am. Soc. Biochemistry and Molecular Biology (Merck award 1990), Am. Chem.

Soc. (Alfred R. Bader Bioinorganic or Bioorganic Chem. award 1993, Repligen award 1995). Achievements include development of dithiothreitol (Cleland's Reagent) as reducing agent for thiol groups; development of application of kinetic methods for determining enzyme mechanism. Office: Enzyme Inst 1710 University Ave Madison WI 53726-4087 Home Phone: 608-244-3938; Office Phone: 608-262-1373. E-mail: cleland@biochem.wisc.edu.

CLEM, ALAN LELAND, retired political scientist, educator; b. Lincoln, Nebr., Mar. 4, 1929; s. Remey Leland and Bernice (Thompson) Clem; m. Mary Louise Burke, Oct. 24, 1953; children: Andrew, Christopher, Constance, John, Daniel. BA, U. Nebr., 1950; MA, Am. U., Washington, DC, 1957, PhD, 1960. Copywriter, rsch. dir. Ayres Advt. Agy., Lincoln, 1950-52; press sec. to Congressman Carl Curtis of Nebr., 1953-54; press sec. to Congressman R. D. Harrison of Nebr., 1955-58; info. specialist Fgn. Agrl. Svc., Dept. Agr., 1959-60; from asst. prof. to assoc. prof. polit. sci. U. SD, Vermillion, 1960—64, prof., 1965—; assoc. dir. Govtl. Rsch. Bur., 1962-76, chmn. dept. polit. sci., 1976-78; ptnr. Opinion Survey Assocs., 1964-88, ret., 1996. State analyst Comparative State Elections Project, U. N.C., 1968—73; dir. Mt. Rushmore Presdl. Inst., 1970—71; mem. adv. com. state and local govt. stats. US Census Bur., 1970—74. Author: (book) Prairie State Politics: Popular Democracy in South Dakota, 1967, The Making of Congressmen: Seven Campaigns of 1974, 1976, American Electoral Politics: Strategies for Renewal, 1981, Law Enforcement: The South Dakota Experience, 1982, The Government We Deserve, 1985, 5th edit., 1995, Congress: Powers, Processes and Politics, 1989, Government by the People? South Dakota Politics in the Last Third of the 20th Century, 2002; editor: Contemporary Approaches to State Constitutional Revision, 1969; contbr. articles to profl. jours. Active Vermillion City Coun., 1965—69; sr. warden St. Paul's Episcopal Ch., Vermillion, 1971—73, treas., 1996—2006. Recipient Alumni Achievement award, U. Nebr. Coll. Arts and Scis., 1998; Nat. Conv. faculty fellow, 1964. Mem.: Am. Polit. Sci. Assn., Midwest Polit. Sci. Assn. (mem. exec. coun. 1970—72, mem. editl. bd. Am. Jour. Polit. Sci. 1971—72), Mensa, Vermillion Golf Assn. (pres. 1986—87), Alpha Tau Omega, Phi Beta Kappa, Sigma Delta Chi, Pi Sigma Alpha (mem. nat. coun. 1986—89), Phi Alpha Theta. Republican. Home: 608 Colonial Ct Vermillion SD 57069 *Avoid haste, anxiety, contentiousness, and self-centeredness. Care, clarity, persistence, honesty, and grace will prevail in the long run.*

CLEM, ALEXANDER MURPHREE, lawyer; b. Vero Beach, Fla., Nov. 6, 1963; s. Chester Earl and Tilley (Murphree) Clem; m. Carmen Maria Chinchilla, May 18, 1996; children: Cristiana, Isabella, Alexander II. BA in Polit. Sci., Furman U., Greenville, SC, 1986; JD cum laude, Stetson U., St. Petersburg, Fla., 1990. Bar: Fla., Tenn. Assoc. Maguire, Voorhis & Welle, 1991—97; ptnr. Morgan & Morgan PA, Orlando, Fla., 1997—. Bd. overseers Stetson U. Coll. Law, 2007—; lectr. in field. Named Disting. Alumnus, Stetson U. Coll. Law, 2005, Lawyer of Distinction, Orlando Mag., 2006; named one of Fla's. Legal Elite, Fla. Trend mag., 2006, Best of the Bar, Orlando Bus. Jour., 2006, Top 5% Attys., Fla. Super Lawyers mag., 2007; scholar, Rotary. Mem.: ABA, Orange County Bar Assn. (legis. com., fed., state trial practice com., chmn. courtroom tech. subcom.), Acad. Fla. Trial Lawyers (pres. 2004—05, exec. com., bd. dirs.). Republican. Roman Catholic. Office: Morgan & Morgan PA 20 N Orange Ave Ste 160 Orlando FL 32801

CLEM, JOHN RICHARD, physicist, educator; b. Waukegan, Ill., Apr. 24, 1938; s. Gilbert D. and Bernelda May (Moyer) Clem; m. Judith Ann Paulsen, Aug. 27, 1960; children: Paul Gilbert, Jean Ann. BS, U. Ill., 1960, MS, 1962, PhD, 1965. Rsch. assoc. U. Md., College Park, 1965-66; vis. rsch. fellow Tech. U., Munich, 1966-67; from asst. prof. to assoc. prof. physics Iowa State U., Ames, 1967—75, prof., 1975—, disting. prof. in liberal arts and scis., 1989, now disting. prof. emeritus, physics, chmn. dept. physics, 1982-85. Vis. staff mem. Los Alamos Nat. Lab., 1971—83, cons., 1997—2001, Argonne Nat. Lab., Ill., 1971—76, Brookhaven Nat. Lab., Upton, NY, 1980—81, Oak Ridge (Tenn.) Nat. Lab., 1981, Allied-Signal, Torrance, Calif., 1990—92, Am. Superconductor Corp., Westborough, Mass., 1996—97, Pirelli Cable Corp., Lexington, SC, 1996—97; guest prof. U. Tuebingen, Germany, 1978; cons. IBM Watson Rsch. Ctr., Yorktown Heights, NY, 1982—85, vis. scientist, 1985—86, Electric Power Rsch. Inst., Palo Alto, Calif., 1992—93; vis. prof. applied physics Stanford U., 1992—93. Editor: Virtual Jour. Applications Superconductivity; sci. editor: newsletter High-Tc Update, 1987—2003; contbr. articles to profl. jours. Recipient award for sustained outstanding rsch. in solid state physics, U.S. Dept. Energy; Fulbright Sr. Rsch. fellow, 1974—75, NATO grantee, 1979—82. Fellow: London Inst. Physics, Am. Phys. Soc. (chair divsn. condensed matter physics 1994—95); mem.: AAUP, Iowa Acad. Sci., Sigma Xi, Phi Kappa Phi, Tau Beta Pi. Democrat. Presbyterian. Achievements include patents in field. Avocation: singing. Office: Iowa State Univ 17 Physics Ames IA 50011-3160 Home Phone: 515-292-4758. Business E-Mail: clem@ameslab.gov.

CLEM, SARAH LYNN, special education educator; b. Houston, Oct. 5, 1971; d. Russell Clark Sutton and Dina Jemison Smith; m. Chris Turner Clem, Dec. 16, 1995; children: Seth Turner, Amy Elyse. BSc, Sam Houston State U., 1995; MA, Western N.Mex. U., 2005. Cert. Elem., Spl. Edn., English (grades 1-8) State Dept. Tex., 1995, Elem., and Spl. Edn. Pub. Edn. Dept. N.Mex, 1996, Early Childhood Edn. State Dept., Tex., 2001. Presch. tchr. Lordsburg Mcpl. Schs., N.Mex., 1996—99, spl. edn. tchr., 2002—03, lead spl. edn. tchr., 2003—04, spl. edn. coord., 2004—05, iep facilitator, 1998—99, prin. adv. com., 1998—99, Christmas play dir., 2002, positive behavior support team, 2002—04, student asst. team coord., 2002—05, girl power facilitator, 2004—05, adminstrv. team, 2004—, elem. prin., spl. edn. dir., 2005—06; coord. sect. 504 Sierra Blanca Schs., Lordsburg Mcpl. Schs., 2003—; tchr. Sierra Blanca Schs., Tex., 2000—02, one act play dir., 2001, supt. adv. com., 2001—02; prin. R.V. Traylor Elem., 2005—. Leader Girl Scouts Am., Lordsburg, 1997—99; vacation bible sch. tchr. United Meth. Ch., Sierra Blanca, Tex. and Lordsburg, N.Mex, 1998—2004, vacation bible sch. dir., 1998—2004; co-chmn. Adminstrn. Bd., Lordsburg, 2003—05, edn. chmn., 2003—05. Olive Marlowe Smithson scholarship, Western N.Mex U., 2003, Preschool Inclusion grant, Pub. Edn. Dept., 2004, Least Restrictive Environment grant, Pub. Edn. Dept., NM, 2004, Least Restrictive Environment/Positive Behaviro Support grant, 2005—06. Mem.: Delta Kappa Gamma (second v.p. 2003—04, scholarship 2003), Zeta Tau Alpha (treas., rush chmn., jud. chmn., house mgr. 1992—95, White Rose nominee 1995), Beta Sigma Phi (treas., pres. 1997—2000, Woman of Yr. 2000, 2002). R-Consevative. Methodist. Avocations: exercise, reading. Office: Lordsburg Municipal Schs PO Box 430 Lordsburg NM 88045 Home Phone: 505-542-9596; Office Phone: 505-542-3252. Business E-Mail: sclem@lmsed.org.

CLEMENCE, CHERYL LYNN, systems administrator; d. Robert H. and Carolyn Marie Clemence. BS, Mt. Union Coll., Alliance, Ohio, 1987; MPH, U. Miami, Fla., 1990; MBA, U. Miami, 1993. Sr. rsch. assoc. dept. psychiatry and behavioral scis. U. Miami, 1990—94, sr. database tech. specialist, 1994—2000; mgmt. info. sys. and quality improvement dir. U. Miami Behavioral Health, 2000—. Contbr. articles to profl. jours. Mem.: Mensa, Beta Gamma Sigma. Democrat. Methodist. Avocations: travel, music, reading, computers. Office: U Miami Behavioral Health PO Box 016960 (M-861) Miami FL 33101 Office Phone: 305-243-3169. Office Fax: 305-243-3098.

CLEMENCE, ROGER DAVIDSON, landscape architect, educator; b. Worcester, Mass., Jan. 20, 1936; s. Luther Davidson and Dorothy (Kay) C.; m. Margaret Ann Weinandy, Aug. 19, 1961; children: Peter, Benjamin, Ellsabeth. AB, Amherst Coll., 1957; MArch, U. Pa., 1960, M in Landscape Architecture, 1962. Registered landscape architect, Minn. Instr., asst. prof. Coll. Architecture and Design U. Mich., Ann Arbor, 1962-66; assoc. prof. Sch. Architecture and Landscape Architecture U. Minn., Mpls., 1966-73, dir. Urban Edn. Ctr., Sch. Architecture and Landscape Architecture, 1970-77, interim head Sch. Architecture and Landscape Architecture, 1984, mem. urban studies faculty Coll. Liberal Arts, 1973—97, mem. Am. studies faculty Coll. Liberal Arts, 1986—97, dir. grad. studies in architecture Sch. Architecture and Landscape Architecture, 1978-85, prof. dept. architecture, 1973, assoc. dean Coll. of Architecture and Landscape Architecture, 1989-95, acting dean, spring 1993, interim dean, 1995-96. Landscape arch., planner, Mpls., 1963; collegiate program leader Minn. Ext. Svc., 1993-97, prof. emeritus, summer 1997—. Co-creator 10-part TV series The Meanings of Place, 1986. Mem. Minn. Com. on Urban Environment, 1979-88, Designer Selection Bd., 1980-85, chmn., 1983-84; mem. Mpls. Fed. Cts. Master Plan Com., 1991-92. Recipient Morse-Alumni Disting. Tchg. award, 1974, Pub. Svc. award Minn. Soc. Landscape Architects, 1982, Lob Pine award, 1996, CALA Disting. Svc. award, 1995; T.P. Chandler fellow U. Pa. Grad. Sch. Fine Arts, 1960-62; HWS Cleveland Vis. scholar U. Minn., 2000-06. Fellow Am. Soc. Landscape Architects; mem. AIA (prof. affiliate Minn. chapt. 1979), MASLA, Tau Sigma Delta. Democrat. Mem. Unitarian Universalist Assn. Avocations: photography, writing, golf, reading, gardening. Office: U Minn CALA 89 Church St SE Minneapolis MN 55455-0109

CLEMENDOR, ANTHONY ARNOLD, obstetrician, educator, gynecologist, educator; b. Port-of-Spain, Trinidad, Nov. 8, 1933; came to US, 1954, naturalized, 1959; s. Anthony Arnold and Beatrice Helen (Stewart) C.; m. Elaine Browne, May 31, 1958 (dec. May, 1991); children: Anthony Arnold, David Alan; m. Janat Jenkins, Sept. 23, 1993. AB, NYU, 1959; MD, Howard U., 1963. Diplomate Am. Bd. Ob-Gyn. Intern USPHS, SI, NY, 1963-64; resident Met. Hosp. Ctr., NYC, 1964-68, chief outpatient dept. ob-gyn, 1969-73; med. dir. family planning Human Resources Adminstrn., NYC, 1973-74; assoc. dean student affairs, dir. office minority affairs NY Med. Coll., Valhalla, 1974-97, assoc. clin. prof. dept. ob-gyn., 1978-90, prof. clin. ob-gyn., 1990-98, clin. prof. ob-gyn., 1998—. Bd. dirs. Elmcore, Caribbean-Am. Ctr. N.Y.C., Nat. Assn. Minority Med. Educators, Inc., 1978-88, Empire State Med. Sci. and Ednl. Found., Inc., Caribbean Am. Ctr. N.Y., 1988-91; mem. Nat. Urban League, N.Y. Urban League; life mem. NAACP. Fellow ACOG, APHA; mem. AMA (survey team liaison com. on med. edn. 1989—, del. N.Y. State 1998-2005, liaison com. on med. edn. 1989-97), Am. Fertility Soc., Nat. Med. Assn., Med. Soc. State of N.Y. (treas. PAC 1997, councilor 1999-2002, asst. sec. 2002, treas. 2004-05), N.Y. County Med. Soc. (sec. 1989, v.p. 1990, pres. elect 1991, pres. 1992-93, bd. trustees, chmn. bd. trustees 1997-98), N.Y. Acad. Medicine, N.Y. Gynecol. Soc. (v.p. 1986, pres. 1988) Personal E-mail: aclemendor@aol.com.

CLEMENS, BRUCE ARCHER, lawyer; b. San Francisco, Sept. 23, 1946; s. Marion and Alice (Hertzka) C.; m. Brandi Roth, Sept. 4, 1982. BA in Maths., Mich. State U., 1967; MS in Computer Sci., Stanford U., 1971; JD, UCLA, 1974. Bar: Calir. 1974, U.S. Dist. Ct. (ctrl. dist.) Calif. 1974, U.S. Tax Ct. 1977. Systems analyst IBM, Greenbelt, Md., 1967-71; assoc. Loeb and Loeb, LA, 1974-75; ptnr. Clemens, Clemens & Holland, Beverly Hills, Calif., 1975-77, Jaffe, Clemens & Fridkis, Beverly Hills, Calif., 1977-80, Jaffe and Clemens, Beverly Hills, Calif., 1980—. Co-author: Division and Taxation of Retirement Benefits in Dissolution Proceedings, 1979, 2d edit., 1982, 3d edit., 1984, 4th edit., 1986, 5th edit., 1989, Drafting and Litigating Prenuptial, Cohabitation and Marital Settlement Agreements, 1981, Tax Planning for Marital Termination Settlement, 1987. Fellow Am. Acad. Matrimonial Lawyers; mem. L.A. County Bar Assn. (exec. com. 1987-88), Beverly Hills Bar Assn. (exec. com. 1986-87), Beverly Hills Hist. Soc., Moot Ct. Office: Jaffe and Clemens 433 N Camden Dr Ste 1000 Beverly Hills CA 90210-4414*

CLEMENS, DAVID ALLEN, minister; b. Camden, NJ, Aug. 8, 1941; s. Arleigh and Mae C.; m. Janice, Feb. 13, 1965; children: Stephen David, Daniel Lee. BA magna cum laude, Houghton Coll., 1963; MA, Nat. Christian U., 1972; ThD, Clarksville Sch. Theology, 1980; PhD, Christian Bible Coll., 1990. Ordained to ministry Ind. Bapt. Ch., 1963. Missionary Pocket Testament League, Argentina, Paraguay, Chile, Peru, Bolivia, 1963-66; min. Richfield (Pa.) Mennonite Ch., 1966-67; itinerant Bible tchr. Bible Club Movement Inc., Upper Darby, Pa., 1968-2000, nat. rep., 1971-77, dir. Family Adult Ministries dept., 1977-80, min. at large, 1980-99, missionary, Bible tchr., 1999-2000; pres., Bible tchr. David Clemens Bible Tchg. Ministries, Inc., Marlton, , 2000—. Preaching and tchg. tours Eng., Scotland, The Netherlands, Belgium, Sweden, Spain, Ireland, Can., Middle East, The Philippines, Zimbabwe, Poland, Cuba, Italy, Germany, Switzerland, Zambia, Guyana. Author: Steps to Maturity, Vols. I-III, 1973-79, How to Get Along With Impossible People, 1978. Mem. Nat. Home Missions Fellowship. Home and Office: 72 Knox Blvd Marlton NJ 08053-2921 Personal E-mail: drdavidclemens@aol.com. *To know, love, and serve God (as revealed in Jesus Christ) is the highest privilege of life.*

CLEMENS, PETER J., IV, corporate financial executive; BS, Samford Univ., 1987; MBA, Vanderbilt Univ., 1991. V.p., fin. & treas. Caremark Rx, Nashville, 1995—98, sr. v.p., fin., & treas., 1998—2005, exec. v.p., CFO, 2005—07, Caremark Pharm. Services, 2007—. Office: Caremark Rx Ste 800 211 Commerce St Nashville TN 37201*

CLEMENS, RICHARD GLENN, lawyer; b. Chgo., Oct. 8, 1940; s. James Ralston and Jeanette Louise (Moellering) C.; m. Judith B. Clemens, Aug. 19, 1967; 1 child, Kathleen. BA, U. Va., 1962, JD, 1965. Bar: Ill. 1965. Assoc. Sidley Austin LLP, Chgo., 1965—66, Washington, 1968—71, Brussels, 1972—73, ptnr. Chgo., 1973—2005, sr. counsel, 2006—. Capt. US Army, 1966-68. Mem. ABA, Chgo. Bar Assn., Lawyers Club. Office: Sidley Austin LLP 1 S Dearborn St Chicago IL 60603 Office Phone: 312-853-7642. Business E-Mail: rclemens@sidley.com.

CLEMENS, ROGER (WILLIAM ROGER CLEMENS), professional baseball player; b. Dayton, Ohio, Aug. 4, 1962; m. Debbie Lynn Godfrey, May 27, 1963; children: Koby Aaron, Kory Allen, Kacy Austin, Kody Alec. Student, San Jacinto North Jr. Coll., Houston, 1980—81, U. Tex., 1981—83. Baseball player Boston Red Sox, 1984—96, Toronto Blue Jays, 1997—98, NY Yankees, 1998—2003, 2007—, Houston Astros, 2004—06. Pitcher Team USA, World Baseball Classic, 2006. Named Major League Player of Yr., Sporting News, 1986, Pitcher of Yr., 1986, 1991, 1997—98, 2001; named to Am. League All-Star Team, 1986, 1988, 1990—92, 1997—98, 2001, 2003, Nat. League All-Star Team, 2004—05, MLB All-Century Team, 1999; recipient Cy Young award, Am. League, 1986, 1987, 1991, 1997, 1998, 2001, Cy Young Award, Nat. League, 2004, Am. League MVP, 1986, MLB All-Star Game MVP, 1986. Achievements include holds MLB record for strikeouts in a single game (20); recorded 300th career win and 4,000 career strikeouts, June 13, 2003; being a member of World Series Champion New York Yankees, 1999, 2000; holds MLB record for Cy Young Awards (7), 2004; holds MLB record for oldest player to win Cy Young Award (age 42), 2004; became 8th pitcher to reach 350 career wins, July 2, 2007. Office: NY Yankees Stadium E 161 St & River Ave Bronx NY 10451*

CLEMENS, ROSEMARY A., health facility administrator, foundation administrator; m. Mitchel Greenfield Garren, Aug. 30, 1985 (dec. Dec. 2006). BA, St. John's U., 1966; MA, NYU, 1968, PhD, 1973. Assoc. prof. Fordham U. Sch. Social Work and Edn., NYC, 1973—83; dir. strategic planning and mktg. NY Hosp., NYC, 1983—88; clin. instr. Cornell Med. Coll., Dept. Pub. Health, NYC, 1983—88; dir. AIDS and adolscent awareness project Women's City Club, NYC, 1988—92; dep. dir. NY State Inst. Basic Rsch. Devel. Disabilities, SI, 1992—96; devel. and program dir. Skin Cancer Found., NYC, 1996—98; pres., CEO N.Y. divsn. Prevent Blindness Am., NYC, 1998—2001; CEO N.Y.Children's Vision Coalition, NYC, 2001—. Author: (book) Lessons to be Learned - Adolescents and AIDS (Cmty. Achievement Award - NYS Optometric Assn, 2004). Bd. mem. Cmty. Bd. #1, Women's City Club, UN Assn., NYC, 1975—2005; rsch. assoc. Gov. Nelson A. Rockefeller Presdl. Campaign, 1968—69, Mayor John Lindsay's Adminstrn., NYC, 1973—75; dir. decentralization studies State Sen. Roy M. Goodman Commn. on N.Y.C. Governance, 1975—77; rsch. asst. Ford Found., 1968. Mem.: Yale Club of NYC, Nat. Arts Club, Cosmopolitan Club of NY (pub. affairs com. 1997—99). Avocations: travel, reading, gardening, theater, interior decorating. Home: 7 Lexington Ave New York NY 10010 Office: NY Children's Vision Coalition 33 West 42nd St New York NY 10036 Home: 110 Atlantic Ave Palm Beach FL 33480 Office Phone: 212-997-3550. Personal E-mail: rosemaryclemens@aol.com.

CLEMENS, T. PAT, manufacturing executive; b. Hibbing, Minn., July 26, 1944; s. Jack LeRoy and Mildred (Coss) C.; m. 1966 (div. 1992); children: Patrick Michael, Heather Kristen. BS in Econs. and Mgmt., St. Cloud State U., Minn., 1968; student of theology, Coll. St. Thomas, Ft. Worth, Tex., 1985-87. Sales adminstr. Transistor Electronics Co., Eden Prarie, Minn., 1969; head instnl. sales Chiquita Brands, Edina, Minn., 1970; dist. sales mgr. Menley & James Labs., Phila., 1971-75; owner, pres. T.P. Clemens Labs., Eagan, Minn., 1975—. Instr community edn. Rosemount, Minn., 1977-78; bd. dirs. Rosemount Hockey, 1977-78, Relocation Assistance Assn. Am., 1984-85; v.p. Sch. Dist. #196 Booster Club, 1984-85; lectr. econs. to corps., high schs. and colls. in U.S., Scotland, Ireland, and Jamaica, 1979—. Author, editor: How Prejudice and Narcissism Control Economics of the United States and the World, 1979. Mem. Rosemount Cmty. Edn. Bd., 1985, chmn., 1986-87; chmn. speakers bur. Citizens Steering Com., 1984-85; coach Little League, 1970-82, 88-91; coach high sch. weight lifting team, 1975-95; vol. worker with comatose children, 1975-96, 97—. Recipient letter of recognition for stopping armed robbery Dakota County Atty.'s Dept., 1979, 93. Mem. Internat. Platform Assn., Kids-N-Kinship Program 1988-92. Home and Office: 1276 Vildmark Dr Eagan MN 55123-2801 Office Phone: 651-454-6746. Personal E-mail: tpatclemens@cs.com.

CLEMENT, BILL, hockey analyst; b. Buckingham, Que., Can., Dec. 20, 1950; Center Phila. Flyers, 1970-75, Washington Capitals, 1975-76, Atlanta Flames, 1976-80, Calgary Flames, 1980-82; analyst Madison Sq. Garden telecasts NJ Devils; guest commentator NHL telecasts USA Network; NHL game analyst ESPN, 1986-88, NHL studio analyst, 1992—93, game analyst Nat. Hockey Night; analyst Phila. Flyers PRISM, 1988-92; playoff analyst Stanley Cup Finals SportsChannel Am., 1988-92; analyst Flyers Sta. WGBS-TV, 1988-91, Sta. WPHL-TV, 1991-92; ice-level reporter NHL All-Star Game NBC, 1992, 93; analyst Winter Olympics TNT, 1992; studio analyst Can. Cup CTV, Canada, 1991; hockey studio analyst Salt Lake City Olympic Games, CNBC, 2002; host hockey coverage Torino Olympic Games, Italy, 2006; host NHL on NBC, 2005—; studio host Versus (formerly OLN), 2005—07. Participant All-Star Games, 1975-76, 78; motivational spkr., 1990—; model appearing in more than 250 TV ads, including Chevrolet, Deep Woods Off, Hardees, and NAPA; actor appearing in TV shows including All My Children (ABC), 1986. Recipient Cable ACE award, 1992; named Favorite Nat. TV Personality The Hockey News, 1996. Achievements include being a member of Stanley Cup Champion Phila. Flyers, 1974, 1975.

CLEMENT, CLAYTON EMERSON, lawyer; b. Oakland, Calif., Dec. 3, 1943; s. Robert Emerson and Dorothy Winslow (Deacon) C.; m. Barbara Jonas, Sept. 4, 1965 (div. Aug. 1984); children: Robert, Jason; m. Kimberly Anderson, Nov. 30, 1991. BA with honors, U. Pacific, 1965; JD, U. Calif., Berkeley, 1968. Bar: Calif. 1969, U.S. Dist. Ct. (no. dist.) Calif. 1969, U.S. Ct. Appeals (9th cir.) 1969, U.S. Supreme Ct. 1972. Assoc. Cox & Cummins, Martinez, Calif., 1968-71; ptnr. Arata, Misuraca & Clement, Santa Rosa, Calif., 1972-75; pvt. practice Santa Rosa, 1976-78; ptnr. Clement, Fitzpatrick & Kenworthy, Santa Rosa, 1978—. Instr. Santa Rosa Jr. Coll., 1977-85; assoc. prof. law Kennedy U., Martinez, Calif., 1969-72. Dir. Sonoma County Family YMCA, Santa Rosa, 1985-91; treas. BOSCO for Congress Com., Santa Rosa, 1982-90; dir. Blood Bank The Redwoods, 2004—. Fellow Am. Coll. Trial Lawyers; mem. ABA, Assn. Bus. Trial Lawyers, Am. Bd. Trial Advocates. Democrat. Avocations: flying, fishing. Home: 4199 Pine Rock Pl Santa Rosa CA 95409-4014 Office: Clement Fitzpatrick & Kenworthy 3333 Mendocino Ave Ste 200 Santa Rosa CA 95403-2233 Office Phone: 707-523-1181. E-mail: cclement@cfk.com.

CLEMENT, EDITH BROWN, federal judge; b. Birmingham, Ala., Apr. 29, 1948; d. Erskine John and Edith (Burrus) Brown; m. Rutledge Carter Clement Jr., Sept. 3, 1972; children: Rutledge Carter III, Catherine Lanier. BA, U. Ala., 1969; JD, Tulane U., 1972. Bar: La. 1973. Law clk. to Hon. Herbert W. Christenberry US Dist. Ct., New Orleans, 1973-75; ptnr. Jones, Walker, Waechter, Poitevent, Carrere & Denegre, New Orleans, 1975-91; judge US Dist. Ct. (ea. dist.) La., New Orleans, 1991—2001, US Ct. Appeals (5th cir.), New Orleans, 2001—. Fellow La. Bar Found. (life); mem. Am. Law Inst., La. Bar Assn., Federalist Soc. Advisory Bd. Louisiana Chpt., Maritime Law Assn. US, Fed. Bar Assn., Am Inn Ct., Com. Admin. Office of the Judicial Conference of the US, 5th Cir. Judicial Coun, Tulane Law Sch. Inn of Ct. Office: US Ct Appeals 5th Cir 600 Camp Street Rm 200 New Orleans LA 70130-3313*

CLEMENT, EVELYN GEER, librarian, educator; b. Springfield, Mass., Sept. 1, 1926; d. Elihu and Helen (Schenck) Geer; m. J.R. Clement, Sept. 9, 1946 (div. 1972); children: James Randall, Timothy B., Susan Henson, Marc W., Audrey Ethriedge. BA with honors, U. Tulsa, 1965; MLS, U. Okla., 1966; PhD, Ind. U., Bloomington, 1975. Libr. Tulsa City-County Libr., 1960—66; learning resources libr. Oral Roberts U., Tulsa, 1966—68; spl. instr. U. Okla., Norman, 1966—70; prof., chmn. libr. sci. Memphis State U., 1972—85, dir. Ctr. for Instructional Svc. and Rsch., 1985—95, chmn. acad. senate, 1979—80, mem. faculty tenure and promotion appeals com., 1980—82, mem. standing univ. com. on libr., 1975—80, 1986—87, chmn. women's task force, 1984—85; ret., 1995. Dir. media consortium Tenn. Regents, 1993—95; regional trustee Geer Family Assn., 2001—07. Editor: Bibliographic Control of Nonprint Media, 1972; contbr. articles to profl. jours. Treas. bd. adminstrn. Harvard Pk. Village Neighborhood Assn., 2005—. Doctoral fellow, U.S. Office Edn., Title II-B, Ind. U., 1968—71. Mem.: ALA, Afghanistan Perceivers, Pi Gamma Mu, Beta Phi Mu, Phi Alpha Theta. Republican. Avocations: computers, needlepoint, exercise, reading. Home: 5206 S Harvard Ave #336 Tulsa OK 74135-3591 Personal E-mail: erren@aol.com.

CLEMENT, HENRY JOSEPH, JR., diversified building products executive; b. New Orleans, May 14, 1942; s. Henry Joseph Sr. and Margaret (Dowd) C.; m. Kathleen Erin Shean; children: Colleen and Collette (twins). BS, Loyola U., 1973. Sales rep. GE, New Orleans, 1972-77, mgr. product planning Louisville, Ky., 1977-79, mgr. internat. market Tyler, Tex., 1979-83; v.p. internat. sales Phillips Industries, Inc., Dayton, Ohio, 1983-84, pres. internat. div., 1984-88; pres. internat. group Tomkins Industries, Dayton, 1988-94; pres. Crescent Group, Inc., Dublin, Ohio, 1994—. Vice chmn., bd. dirs. Shaanxi-Hytec, Ltd., Xian, Chila, 1988-89. Loan exec. United Way, New Orleans, 1974, Tyler, 1979. Mem. Miami Valley (Ohio) Internat. Trade Assn. (trustee), Blue Key (Cross Key Svc. award 1973). Republican. Roman Catholic. Home: 4666 Chatham Ct Dublin OH 43017-8607 E-mail: cresgroup@cs.com.

CLEMENT, HOPE ELIZABETH ANNA, retired librarian; b. North Sydney, NS, Can., Dec. 29, 1930; d. Harry Wells and Lana (Perkins) Clement. BA, U. King's Coll., 1951, D of Civil Law (hon.), 1992; MA, Dalhousie U., 1953; BLS, U. Toronto, 1955. With Nat. Library of Can., Ottawa, Ont., 1955-92, chief nat. bibliography div., 1966-70, asst. dir. research and planning br., 1970-73, dir. research and planning br., 1973-77, assoc. nat. librarian, 1977-92; ret., 1992. Editor: Canadiana, 1966—69. Recipient Outstanding Svc. Librarianship award, Can. Lib. Assn., 1992, Can. Libr. Assn. (Outstanding Svc. to Librarianship award 1992), Internat. Fedn. Libr. Assns. (medal 1991).

CLEMENT, JOHN EDWARD STRAUSZ, retired minister, retired religious organization administrator; b. Enid, Okla., Jan. 9, 1934; s. Joseph Alvis and Sarah Evelyn (Brown) C.; m. Judith A. Strausz-Clement; children: Stephen W., Paul E., Catherine K., Christopher S. Strausz-Clark, Karen L. Clark. BA, Oberlin Coll., 1956; MDiv, Union Theol. Sem., 1960. Ordained to ministry Presbyn. Ch., 1960. Pastor, Williamsport, Pa., 1960-65, Wilmington, Del., 1965-69; project leader S. Cen. Ministry, Minn., 1969-74; mission enabler Los Ranchos Presbytery, Long Beach, Calif., 1974-78; exec. presbyter Cayuca-Syracuse Presbytery, Syracuse, N.Y., 1978-91, Pitts. Presbytery, 1991-95; interim exec. presbyter Carlisle Presbytery, Camp Hill, Pa., 1995-96; gen. presbyter Blackhawk Presbytery, Oregon, Ill., 1996—2001, ret., 2001. Mem. Ecumenical Execs. of No. Ill., 1996-2001, Campus Ministry Com. of Synod of Lincoln Trails, 1998-2000, Nat. Cooperative Com. on Partnership Funding, Presbyn. Ch. (USA), 1998—2001. Organizing mem. Habitat for Humanity, Syracuse, N.Y.; chmn. ecumenical exec. cabinet and v.p. Syracuse Interreligious Coun., 1985-87; ch.-wide adminstrv. coord. cabinet Presbyn. Ch. (USA), 1986-88, 91-92; chmn. pers. com. N.Y. State Coun. of Chs., 1989-91; chmn. Synod of N.E. Ecumenical Cabinet, 1987-91; mem. AIDS Task Force of Ctrl. N.Y.; mem. nat. com. Bicentennial Fund Campaign, Presbyn. Ch. (USA), 1988-92; organizing mem. Christian Leaders Fellowship, Pitts., 1991-95; exec. com. Coun. of Christian Assocs. of We. Pa., 1991-95; mem. coun. judicatory execs. Ill. Conf. Chs., 1996-2001; mem. Downtown Chs. Ecumenical Com., Sante Fe, 2003-04, N.Mex. Conf. Chs. Faith and Order Task Force, 2003-07; chair Presbytery Santa Fe Task Group on Korean Fellowship, 2003-04; moderator Embudo Presbyn. Ch., Dixon, N.Mex., 2005-07; Presbytery Santa Fe rep. to Luth. Office Govtl. Ministry Lobbying in N.Mex. State Legislature, 2005—; mem. Presbytery of Santa Fe Coun. Com. on Spl. Relations, 2007-. E-mail: johnesclement@comcast.net. *I believe God loves our world and has become one of us to redeem us and guide us toward a new humanity. I see our ministry standing on the side of the poor and oppressed as well as loving the oppressor.*

CLEMENT, PAUL DREW, federal agency administrator, lawyer; b. Milw., June 24, 1966; BSFS summa cum laude, Georgetown U., 1988; MPhil with distinction, Cambridge U., Eng., 1989; JD magna cum laude, Harvard Law Sch., 1992. Intern Office of U.S. Sen. Robert Kasten, Washington, 1985-86; intern White House, Office of Pub. Liaison, Washington, 1987; summer assoc. McGuire, Woods, Battle & Boothe, Washington, 1990, Covington & Burling, Washington, 1991, Gibson, Dunn & Crutcher, Washington, 1992; teaching fellow Harvard U., 1990-92; law clk. to Hon. Laurence H. Silberman U.S. Ct. Appeals (D.C. cir.), Washington, 1992-93; law clk. to Assoc. Justice Hon. Antonin Scalia U.S. Supreme Ct., Washington, 1993-94; assoc. Kirkland & Ellis, Washington, 1994-97; chief counsel U.S. Senate Subcom. on Constitution, Washington, 1997—99; head, appellate div. King & Spalding LLP, Washington, 1999—2001; prin. dep. solicitor gen. US Dept. Justice, Washington, 2001—04, acting solicitor gen., 2004—05, solicitor gen., 2005—, acting atty. gen., 2007—. Adj. prof. Georgetown U. Law Ctr., 1998—; acad. tutor for 1st yr. students Harvard Law Sch., 1991-92. Recipient Olin fellowship in law and econs. Harvard Law Sch., 1991-92, Harvard Law Review, U.K. Fgn. Office scholarship Cambridge U., 1989, Humes Jr. fellowship in diplomacy, Notz medal, Nevils medal Georgetown U., 1988; named one of Litigation's Rising Stars, The Am. Lawyer, 2007. Mem. Phi Beta Kappa. Office: US Dept Justice Robert F Kennedy Bldg 10th St & Constitution Ave NW Rm 5143 Washington DC 20530*

CLEMENT, PAUL PLATTS, JR., performance technologist, educator; b. Geneva, Ill., Aug. 30, 1935; s. Paul P. and Vera Elizabeth (Dahlquist) C.; m. Susan Alice Aikins, June 7, 1958; children: Paul P. IV, Kathleen Elizabeth. BA in Math., Coe Coll., 1957. Sales tech. rep. Burroughs Corp., Chgo., 1960-63; mgr. EDP, Harding-Williams Corp., Chgo., 1963-65; edn. coord. Standard Oil Co., Chgo., 1965-69; mgr. product planning Edutronics Systems Internat., Chgo., 1969-71; interactive video instrn. specialist Advanced Systems Inc., Chgo., 1971-88; ind. cons. in tng., media use, computers Downers Grove, Ill., 1988; prin. instr., developer UNISYS Corp., Lisle, Ill., 1988-89; mgr. employee devel. CNA Ins. Cos., Chgo., 1990-91; cons. media tng. Internet Systems Corp., Chgo., 1990-93; prin. Clement Consulting Group, Downers Grove, 1993—. Part-time data processing faculty Coll. of DuPage and Coll. extension, Harper Coll., Ill., DeVry Inst., Joliet Jr. Coll.; invited spkr. numerous computer and tng. confs., nat. and internat. assns.; developer, presenter workshops in field; mem. adv. bd. Northeastern Ill. U., Chgo. Developer and pub. 12 animated films with supplementary texts, 84 videotapes, 17 interactive videodiscs and over 7000 pages of expository texts; collaborator 100 other videotapes with supplementary texts; prin. developer micro-computer based People Compatability System, 1983; developer Decision Table Algorithms, 1986, 94th Inf. Div. Assn. Info. System, 1977, Basic Computer Programmer Tng. Curriculum for Eng. Govt., 1979, computerized Data Processing Curricula Devel. System, 1973, Early COBOL Lang. precompiler, 1967, AutoMagic Glossary, 1992; contbr. articles to Datamation Mag., Data Tng. Mag. Capt. USAF, 1958-60. Recipient Silver award WPC, 1996, Gold award, 1998. Home and Office: 4942 Linscott Ave Downers Grove IL 60515-3537 Office Phone: 630-969-7957. E-mail: paulclementjr@sbcglobal.net.

CLEMENT, RICHARD JOSEPH, retired obstetrician, gynecologist; b. Crowley, La., Apr. 10, 1937; m. Emily S. Clement. MBA in Bus. Adminstrn. and Statis., McNeese State U., 1959; MD, La. State U., 1963. Diplomate Am. Bd. Ob-Gyn. Intern Charity Hosp., New Orleans, 1963-64, resident in ob-gyn. and anesthesiology, 1964-67; pvt. practice, 1963—97; chief of staff Lake Charles Meml. Hosp., 1993-94; ret. Chmn. bd. Walter O. Moss Regional Hosp., 1994—; clin. asst. prof. La. State U. Sch. Medicine, New Orleans, 1974. Col. US Army. Fellow Am. Coll. Ob-Gyn., Am. Fertility and Sterility Soc., Soc. for Colposcopy and Colpomicroscopy, Internat. Coll. Surgery; mem. AMA, La. State Med. Soc., Calcasieu Parish Med. Soc., New Orleans Parish Med. Soc., La. State U. Postgrad. Ob-Gyn. Soc. (pres.), Royal Soc. Medicine. Home: 517 S Ryan St Lake Charles LA 70601-5724

CLEMENT, ROBERT WILLIAM, retired air force officer; b. Columbus, Ohio, Aug. 8, 1927; s. Coleman Clay and Leola Marie (Barnett) C.; m. Leila Ann Cameron, Dec. 27, 1950 (dec. Nov. 1998); children: Susan Lee, Robert William (dec.), Sandra Gay, Randall Clay; m. Elizabeth deGaris Atherton, June 1999. Student, Yale U., 1945-46; BS, U.S. Mil. Acad., 1950; MS in Aero. Engring., U. Colo., 1957; postgrad., Army War Coll., 1966-67. Commd. 2d lt. USAF, 1950, advanced through grades to maj. gen., 1978; vice comdr. 12th Air Force, Tactical Air Command, Bergstrom AFB, Tex., 1976; dep. chief staff for ops. and intelligence USAF in Europe Ramstein Air Base, Federal Republic of Germany, 1978-80; comdr. 16th Air Force, Torrejon AB, Spain, 1980-84; ret., 1984; asst. prof. math U.S. Air Force Acad., 1956-59. Decorated Air Force DSM, Legion of Merit with 3 oak leaf clusters, DFC with one oak leaf cluster, Bronze Star, Air medal with 9 oak leaf clusters. Home: PO Box 2207 Haines City FL 33845-2207 Home Phone: 863-324-9401.

CLEMENT, STEPHEN LE ROY, agricultural researcher; b. Ventura, Calif., Aug. 25, 1944; s. Edward Le Roy and Eleanor Eileen (Summers) C.; m. Mary Anne Lindeman, Dec. 21, 1981; 1 child, Kevin Matthew. BS in Entomology, U. Calif., Davis, 1967, PhD in Entomology, 1976. Postdoctoral researcher U. Calif., Davis, 1977; asst. prof. entomology Ohio State U., Ohio Agrl. Rsch. Devel. Ctr., Wooster, 1977-81; rsch. entomologist USDA, Agrl. Rsch. Svc., Rome, Italy, 1982-86; mem. agrl. mission U.S. Embassy, Rome, 1982-86; rsch. entomologist USDA, Agrl. Rsch. Svc., Pullman, Wash., 1986—. Seasonal ranger-naturalist U.S. Park Svc., Yellowstone Nat. Park, 1970-72; mem. peer rev. panel agrl. rsch. grants USDA Coop. States Rsch. Svc., Washington, 1987; mem. adv. team FAO, UN, Rome, 1982; mem. review team Internat. Ctr. for Agrl. Rsch. Dry Areas, Aleppo, Syria, 1998. Author (with others): Global Plant Genetic Resources for Insect-Resistant Crops, 1998. Contbr. articles to profl. jours. 1st lt. U.S. Army, 1967-70, Vietnam. Decorated Bronze Star for Valor (Vietnam); grantee Sigma Xi, 1976, U.S. EPA, 1977-81, USDA-CSRS, 1994, USDA-FAS, 1996, US AID, 2005—. Mem.: Entomol. Soc. Am. (governing bd. 2005—). Achievements include research in insect pest management and plant biodiversity. Office: Wash State U USDA Agrl Rsch Svc 59 Johnson Hall Pullman WA 99164-6402 E-mail: slclement@wsu.edu.

CLEMENT, YVONNE MADELINE, librarian; b. Tacoma, June 17, 1924; d. Cecil Edward and Madeline Edith (Wink) DeGuire; m. Ralph Louis Clement, Jr., June 25, 1949 (dec. Dec. 1969); children: Lawrence E., Catherine E. Gilbert, Mary Susan Clement Zimmerman, Michele Y. Clement Cates, David L. BA, Holy Names Coll., 1946; BA in Libr. sci., Rosary Coll., 1947. Asst. br. libr. Tacoma Pub. Libr., 1947—49, Salt Lake County Libr., Salt Lake City, 1967—69, br. libr., 1969—71, assoc. dir., 1971—86; ret., 1986. Author (with B.M. Hepworth): Utah Libraries: Heritage and Horizons, 1976. Bd. dirs. Utah coun. Camp Fire Girls, Salt Lake City, 1983—84.

CLEMENTE, ALICE RODRIGUES, language educator; b. Pawtucket, RI, July 28, 1934; d. Alipio Rodrigues and Maria (Joaquim) C. AB, Brown U., 1956, MA, 1959, PhD, 1967. Instr. Randolph-Macon Woman's Coll., Lynchburg, Va., 1959—61, Wheaton Coll., Norton, Mass., 1964; prof. Spanish and Portuguese, comparative lit. Smith Coll., Northampton, Mass., 1964—96, prof. emeritus, 1996—; mng. editor Gavea Brown Publs., 1996—. Adj. prof. Brown U., Providence, 1996—. Editor: Sweet Marmalade, Sour Oranges-Contemporary Portuguese Women's Fiction; translator: Camilo Castelo Branco, Doomed Love-A Family Memoir; contbr. articles to profl. jours Chmn. Water Supply Citizens Adv. Com.; bd. dirs. Portuguese Am. Scholarship Found., Cumberland Land Trust, Blackstone River Watershed Coun. Home: PO Box 7771 Cumberland RI 02864-0898 Home Phone: 401-723-8828; Office Phone: 401-863-3042. Business E-Mail: alice_clemente@brown.edu.

CLEMENTE, CARMINE DOMENIC, anatomist, educator; b. Penns Grove, NJ, Apr. 29, 1928; s. Ermanno and Caroline (Friozzi) Clemente; m. Juliette Vance, Sept. 19, 1968. AB, U. Pa., 1948, MS, 1950, PhD, 1952; postdoctoral fellow, U. London, 1953—54. Asst. instr. anatomy U. Pa., 1950—52; mem. faculty UCLA, 1952—, prof., 1963—95, chmn. dept. anatomy, 1963—73, dir. brain rsch. inst., 1976—87, prof. pathology, neurobiology and anatomy, 1995—. Disting. prof. neurobiology and anatomy, 2004—; prof. surg. anatomy Charles R. Drew U. Medicine and Sci., LA, 1974—. Hon. rsch. assoc. Univ. Coll., U. London, 1953—54; vis. scientist Nat. Inst. Med. Rsch., Mill Hill, London, 1988—89, London, 1991; cons. VA Hosp., Sepulveda, Calif., 1956—96, NIH; mem. med. adv. panel Bank Am.-Giannini Found., 1963—98; chmn. sci. adv. com., bd. dirs. Nat. Paraplegia Found.; bd. dirs. Charles R. Drew U., 1985—94. Author: Aggression and Defense: Neurol Mechanisms and Social Patterns, 1967, Physiological Correlates of Dreaming, 1967, Sleep and the Maturing Nervous System, 1972, Anatomy: An Atlas of the Human Body, 1975, 5th edit., 2006, Clemente's Anatomy Dissector, 2001, 2d edit., 2006; editor: Gray's Anatomy, 1973, 30th Am. edit., 1985; editor-in-chief: Exptl. Neurology, 1973—86, assoc. editor: Neurol. Rsch., Jour. Clin. Anatomy; contbr. articles to sci. jours. Recipient award for merit in sci., Nat. Paraplegia Found., 1973, 23rd Ann. Rehfuss Lectr. and medal, Jefferson Coll., 1986, award for excellence in med. edn., UCLA, 1996, Award of Extraordinary medit, UCLA Med. Alumni Assn., 1997, Significant Early Contributor award, Sleep rsch. Soc., 2003, Disting. Tchr. award, Alpha Omega Alpha, 2006; fellow John Simon Guggenheim Meml. Found., 1988—89. Fellow: Am. Assn. Anatomists (v.p. 1972, pres. 1976—77, Henry Gray award 1993); mem.: NAS (mem. com. on neuropathology, mem. BEAR coms.), Soc. for Neurosci., Japan Soc. Promotion of Sci. (Rsch. award 1978), NY Acad. Scis., Med. Rsch. Assn. Calif. (bd. dirs. 1976—87), AMA-Assn. Am. Med. Colls. (mem. liason com. on med. edn. 1981—87, AOA Robert Glaser Tchg. award 2006), Internat. Brain Rsch. Orgn., Biol. Stain Commn., Assn. Anatomy Chairmen (pres. 1972), Nat. Bd. Med. Examiners (bd. dirs. 1978—84, mem. anatomy test com. 1980—84), Coun. Acad. Socs. (mem. adminstrv. bd. 1973—81, chmn. 1979—80), Assn. Am. Med. Colls. (mem. exec. com. 1978—81, disting. svc. mem. 1982), Am. Neurol. Assn., Am. Assn. Clin. Anatomists (Honored Mem. of Yr. 1993), Am. Acad. Neurology, Am. Physiol. Soc., Brain Rsch. Inst. (dir. 1976—87), Pavlovian Soc. N.Am. (pres. 1972, Ann. award 1968), Am. Acad. Cerebral Palsy (hon.), Inst. Medicine of NAS (mem. sci. adv. bd.), Alpha Omega Alpha, Sigma Xi. Democrat. Home: 11737 Bellagio Rd Los Angeles CA 90049-2158 Office: UCLA Sch Medicine Dept Neurobiology Los Angeles CA 90095-0001 Office Phone: 310-825-9566. Business E-Mail: cdclem@ucla.edu.

CLEMENTE, CELESTINO, physician, surgeon; b. Penns Grove, NJ, June 11, 1922; s. Ermanno and Caroline (Friozzi) C.; m. Marie Ann Strangio, Nov. 16, 1946; children: Jeffrey, Roderick, Mark, Laurie Ann, Jonathan. BS, Rutgers U., New Brunswick, NJ, 1942; MD, U. Pa., Phila., 1945. Diplomate Am. Bd. Surgery. Intern Jersey City Med. Ctr., 1945-46; resident in gen. surgery Martland Med. Ctr., 1950-53; practice medicine specializing in gen. surgery Newark, 1953—; dir. surgery Children's Hosp., Newark, 1962-70, St. Vincent's Hosp., Montclair, N.J., 1972-83; trustee United Hosps. Med. Ctr., Newark, 1972-88, v.p. med. affairs, 1975-88. Assoc. clinic prof. surgery N.J. Med. Sch., Newark, 1975—; dir. surgery Roseland (N.J) Surg. Ctr., 1983—, also chmn. bd. Rep. candidate for U.S. Ho. of Reps, N.J., 1968; active Nat. Ad Council/HEW, 1970-74. Served to lt. USNR, 1946-48. Fellow ACS, Internat. Coll. Surgeons; mem. AMA, AAAS, Essex Club (Newark). Home and Office: 364 Ridgewood Ave Glen Ridge NJ 07028-1513 Office: 556 Eagle Rock Ave Roseland NJ 07068-1500 Office Phone: 973-743-5188. E-mail: ccmdnj@aol.com.

CLEMENTE, FRANCESCO, artist; b. Naples, Italy, Mar. 23, 1952; arrived in NYC, 1981; m. Alba Primiceri. Studied architecture, U. Rome, 1970. One-man shows include Galleria Valle Giulia, Rome, 1971, James Corcoran Gallery, LA, 1983, Mezzanine Gallery and Met. Mus. Art, NY, 1985, Ringling Mus. Art, Sarasota, Fla., 1985-87, Mus. Modern Art, NY, 1986, Art Inst. Chgo., 1987, Milw. Art Mus., 1988, Phila. Mus. Art, 1990-91, Solomon R. Guggenheim Mus., NY, 1983, San Francisco Mus. Modern Art, 1984, Walker Art Ctr., Mpls., 1984-85, Seattle Art Mus., 1985, Joslyn Art Mus., Omaha, 1985-86, Phila. Mus. Art, 1988, LA County Mus., 1987, Minn. Mus. Art, St. Paul, 1987-88, Milw. Art Mus., 1988, Dolan/Maxwell, Phila., 1990-91, Sidney Mishkin Gallery, Baruch Coll., NY, 1994, Luhring Augustine, NY, 1994, Galerie Graff, Montreal, 1994, Anthony D'Offay Gallery, London, 1994, U. Mo., 1994, others; exhibited works at Mus. Modern Art Paris, 1981, 89, Aldrich Mus. Contemporary Art, Ridgefield, Conn., 1983, Art Inst. Chgo., 1987-2001, Phila. Mus. Art, 1990-2001, Centre Georges Pompidou, Musée national de l'art moderne, Paris, 1994-2002, Solomon R. Guggenheim Mus., NY, 1999-2002, Museo Archeologico Nazionale di Napoli, 2002-03. Office: care Gagosian Gallery 980 Madison Ave New York NY 10021-1848

CLEMENTE, PATROCINIO ABLOLA, secondary school educator; b. Manila, Apr. 23, 1941; arrived in U.S., 1965; s. San Jose Elpidio and Amparo (Ablola) Clemente. BSE, U. Philippines, 1960; MA, Ball State U., 1966, EdD, 1969; postgrad., U. Calif., Riverside, 1970, Calif. State Coll., Fullerton, 1971—72. H.S. tchr. gen. sci. and biology Divsn. City Schs., Quezon City, Philippines, 1960—65; doctoral fellow dept. psychology Ball State U., Muncie, Ind., 1966—67, dept. spl. edn., 1967—68, grad. asst. dept. gen. and exptl. psychology, 1968—69; tchr. educable mentally retarded H.S. level Fontana Unified Sch. Dist., Calif., 1969—70, intermediate level, 1970—73, dist. sch. psychologist, 1973—79, bilingual edn. counselor, 1979—81; resource specialist Morongo Unified Sch. Dist., Calif., 1981—83, spl. day class tchr., 1983—90, tchr. math, sci., Spanish, English, 1990—. Adj. assoc. prof. Chapman Coll., Orange, Calif., 1982—91. Adult leader mem. sch. bd. Blessed Sacrament Sch., Twentynine Palms, Calif. State bd. scholar Ball State U., 1965 Girl Scouts of Philippines, 1963—65; mem. sch. bd. Blessed Sacrament Sch., Twentynine Palms, Calif. State bd. scholar, Ball State U., 1965—66. Mem.: NEA, ASCD, Smithsonian Instn., Morongo Tchrs. Assn., Calif. Tchrs. Assn., Nat. Geog. Soc., Assn. for Children with Learning Disabilities, Found. Exceptional Children, Nat. Assn. of Sch. Psychologists, Am. Assn. on Mental Deficiency, Coun. for Exceptional Children. Roman Catholic. Home: PO Box 637 Twentynine Palms CA 92277-0637 Office Phone: 760-367-9507. Personal E-mail: patclem@msn.com.

CLEMENTS, JERRY K., lawyer; b. Ft. Worth, Feb. 2, 1954; BS magna cum laude, Tex. Christian U., 1975; JD cum laude, Baylor U., 1981. Bar: Tex. 1981, US Ct. Appeals (5th cir.) 1981, US Dist. Ct. (all dists. Tex.) 1981, US Supreme Ct. 1981. Chair litig. dept., mem. mgmt. com. Locke, Liddell & Sapp, LLC, Dallas, 2002—06, mng. ptnr., 2007—. Contbr. articles to profl. publs.; editor-in-chief: Baylor Law Rev., 1981. Bd. mem. Tex. State Bd. Physician Asst. Examiners, 1997—2000. Named one of Top Ten Litigators, Dallas Bus. Jour., Top 50 Female Trial Lawyers in Tex., Tex. Monthly Mag., The 50 Most Influential Women Lawyers in Am., Nat. Law Jour., 2007. Fellow: Dallas Bar Found., Tex. Bar Found., Internat. Soc. Barristers, Am. Coll. Trial Lawyers, Am. Bar Found.; mem.: Tex. Assn. Def. Counsel, Dallas Bar Assn., ABA, Am. Bd. Trial Advs. Office: Locke Liddell & Sapp LLP Ste 2200 2200 Ross Ave Dallas TX 75201 Office Phone: 214-740-8799. Office Fax: 214-740-8800. E-mail: jclements@lockeliddell.com.*

CLEMENTS, JOHN ALLEN, physiologist; b. Auburn, NY, Mar. 16, 1923; s. Harry Vernon and May (Porter) C.; m. Margot Sloan Power, Nov. 19, 1949; children: Christine, Carolyn. MD, Cornell U., 1947; MD (honoris causa), U. Berne, Switzerland, 1990, Philipps U., Marburg, Germany, 1992; ScD (honoris causa), U. Manitoba, 1993. Rsch. asst. dept. physiology Med. Coll. N.Y., Cornell U., Ithaca, 1947-49; commd. 1st lt. U.S. Army, 1949, advanced through grades to capt., 1951; asst. chief clin. investigation br. Army Chem. Ctr., 1951-61; assoc. rsch. physiologist U. Calif., San Francisco, 1961-64, prof. pediat., 1964—2004, Julius H. Comroe Jr. prof. pulmonary biology, 1987—2004; mem. staff Cardiovascular Research Inst. Cardiovasc. Rsch. Inst., San Francisco, 1961—2004, mem. grad. group in biophysics, 1987—2004. Career investigator Am. Heart Assn., 1964-93; mem. group in biophysics and med. physics U. Calif., Berkeley, 1969-87; cons. Surgeon Gen. USPHS, 1964-68, Surgeon Gen. U.S. Army, 1972-79; sci. counselor Nat. Heart and Lung Inst., 1972-75; Bowditch lectr. Am. Physiol. Soc., 1961; 2d ann. lectr. Neonatal Soc., London, 1965; Distinguished lectr. Can. Soc. Clin. Investigation, 1973; mem. Nat. Heart Lung and Blood Adv. Coun., 1990-93; Ulf von Euler Meml. lectr. Karolinska Inst., 1996. Mem. editorial bd.: Jour. Applied Physiology, 1961-65, Am. Jour. Physiology, 1965-72, Physiol. Reviews, 1965-72, Jour. Developmental Physiology, 1979-85; assoc. editor: Am. Rev. Respiratory Diseases, 1973-79; chmn. publs. policy com.: Am. Thoracic Soc., 1982-86; assoc. editor: Ann. Rev. Physiology, 1988-93, Am. Jour. Physiology: Lung Cellular and Molecular Physiology, 1988-94. Recipient Dept. Army R & D Achievement award, 1961, Modern Medicine Disting. Achievement award, 1973, Howard Taylor Ricketts medal and award U. Chgo., 1975, Mellon award U. Pitts., 1976, Calif. medal Am. Lung Assn. Calif., 1981, Trudeau medal Am. Lung Assn., 1982, Internat. award Gairdner Found., 1983, J. Burns Amberson lecture award Am. Thoracic Soc. and Am. Lung Assn., 1991, Christopher Columbus Discovery award NIH, 1992, Albert Lasker Clin. Med. award, 1994, Virginia Apgar award Am. Acad. Pediat., 1994, Warren Alpert Found. award, 1995, Discover award Pharm. Rsch. and Mfrs. of Am.; named Mayo Clinic Disting. Lectr. in Med. Sci., 1993, Am. Physiol. Soc. Julius H. Comroe Disting. Lectr., 2000. Fellow AAAS, Am. Acad. Arts and Scis., Am. Coll. Chest Physicians (hon.), Royal Coll. Physicians (London); mem. NAS, Western Assn. Physicians, Western Soc. Clin. Rsch., Perinatal Rsch. Soc. (councillor 1973-75), Am. Lung Assn. (hon., life) Office: U Calif Sch Medicine Cardiovascular Rsch Inst 3333 California St Ste 150 San Francisco CA 94118-1944 Business E-Mail: john.clements@ucsf.edu.

CLEMENTS, JOHN ROBERT, real estate company executive; b. Richmond, Ind., Nov. 2, 1950; s. George Howard and Mary Amanda (McKown) Clements. Grad. high sch., Phoenix. Sales assoc. Clements Realty, Inc., Phoenix, 1973-75, office mgr. Mesa, Ariz., 1975-78, v.p., co-owner Phoenix, 1978-80; broker, assoc. Ben Brooks & Assocs., Phoenix, 1980-88; pres. John R. Clements, P.C., 1994—; broker Keller Williams Realty, Phoenix and Mesa, Ariz., 1994-96; exec. v.p. real estate/acquisitions CBS Outdoor, Phoenix, 1996—. Real estate dir. Cir. K Corp., Western Region, 1989—92. Bd. dirs., v.p. Big Sisters Ariz., Phoenix, 1974—80; appointee Govtl. Mail Co., Ariz., 1986—2000, commr. chair Ariz., 1991—95; trustee Ariz. Realtors Polit. Action Com., 1975—85, Realtors Polit. Action Com. Ill., 1985—88. Mem.: Coun. Residential Specialists (bd. govs. 1986, v.p. 1990, pres. 1991), Nat. Assn. Realtors (past bd. dirs., mem. exe. com.), Mesa-Chandler-Tempe Bd. Realtors (past bd. dirs., pres. 1978), Ariz. Assn. Realtors (bd. dirs., pres. 1981), Ariz. Country Club. Republican. Presbyterian. Home: 3618 N 60th St Phoenix AZ 85018-6708 Office: CBS Outdoor 3150 N 48th St Ste 200 Phoenix AZ 85040 Office Phone: 602-246-9569.

CLEMENTS, KATHLEEN KILEY, education educator; d. Joseph Frances Jr. and Eileen (Streblow) Kiley; m. Lawrence M. Clements III, Nov. 17, 1984; children from previous marriage: Zachary Lawrence, Deven Lee, Brandice Gergeron. BS, Boston Coll., 1982; MS, U. Houston, Clear Lake, 1987; postgrad., Northcentral U., Prescott, Ariz. Cert. tchr., spl. edn. tchr., adminstr. Tex. Spl. edn. tchr. Houston Ind. Sch. Dist., 1982—85, MADS IS, Gray, Maine, 1987—88; tchr. CIISD, Houston, 1985—87; asst. prin. Poland Sch. Dist., Maine, 1988—91; prin. Phippsburg Sch. Dist., Maine, 1991—93, Windham Sch. Dist., Maine, 2001—02, asst. dir. student svcs., 2001—02; coord. elem. edn. St. Joseph's Coll. Maine, Standish, 2002—06, prof., 2002—. Mem. literacy faculty Maine State Edn. Dept., Augusta, 2005—. Mem. Casey Family Svcs., Portland, 1988—; officer exec. com. MLFSA, Windham, Maine, 2001—. Named Maine Woman of Yr., MWY Orgn., Portland, 1995; recipient Foster Parent Svc. award, Casey Family Svcs., 1991, 1996, 2001. Mem.: ASCD, Coun. Exceptional Children, Nat. Coun. Tchrs. English, Moses Little Farm Assn. Avocations: reading, writing, music. Home: 31 Moses Little Dr Windham ME 04062 Office: St Joseph's Coll Maine 278 Whites Bridge Rd Standish ME 04084

CLEMENTS, LYNNE FLEMING, marriage and family therapist, application developer; b. Bklyn., Aug. 8, 1945; d. Daniel Gillies and Dorothy Frances (Zitzmann) Fleming; m. Louis Myrick Clements, Feb. 19, 1972;

children: Ryan Louis, Glenn Fleming. BA in Sociology, Bradley Univ., 1967; MSW, Fordham Univ., 1973; post grad. studies, Columbia Univ., 1970-71; cert. in family therapy, Inst. for Mental Health Edn., 1990. LCSW NJ, cert. social work mgr. Computer programmer Employer's Comml. Union Group Ins. Co., Boston, 1967-69, Harvard Bus. Sch., Cambridge, Mass., 1969-70, Volkswagon of Am., Englewood Cliffs, NJ, 1971; psychiat. social worker Associated Cath. Charities Family and Children's Svc., Paramus, NJ, 1973-74, Christian Health Ctr., Wyckoff, NJ, 1976; owner, mgr. Wicker Wagon, Bergenfield, NJ, 1977-85; psychotherapist The Psychotherapy Counseling Ctr., Bergenfield, NJ, 1982-89; programmer analyst Atlas Computing Svc., Secaucus, NJ, 1984-86; program coord., family therapist Divsn. Family Guidance, Hackensack, NJ, 1986-91; pres. Corp. Family Resources, Ridgewood, NJ, 1989—; family therapist cons. Family Recovery of Valley View, White Plains, NY, 1992-94, Furman Clinic, Fair Lawn, NJ, 1995-96, Van Ost Inst. for Family Living, Englewood, NJ, 1996; cert. social work mgr., 1997—. Part time family therapist NJ Ctr. Psychotherapy Inc., Ridgefield Pk., NJ, 1990. Chmn. curriculum enhancement com. Bergen County Acad. Advancement Sci. and Tech., NJ, 1992—96; chmn. entertainment Bergen County Children's Festival, 1993; founder, chmn. Bergenfield Coun. of the Arts, 1993; chmn., designer Bergenfield Coun. Arts, 1993—99, chmn. author and poet program, 1996—, Bergenfield Coun. of the Arts, 1996—; mem. fundraising com., arts programming chmn. Bergenfield Cmty. Ctr., 2000—; co-chmn. Bergenfield Film Festival, 2004—; co-chmn., designer Bergenfield A Taste of the Arts Festival, 2003—; sec. Mayor's Beautify Bergenfield Com., NJ, 1991—95; chmn. bd. cmty. play ctr. All Saints Ch., 1977—78, Sunday sch. tchr., 1982—89; mem. Twin Boro Youth Ministry Coun., 1989—. Recipient First and Second Pl. awards, Bergenfield Art Contest, 1980, Best Practice Award for Author/Poet Program, N.J. Dept. Edn., 2003; grantee NIMH, 1973. Mem.: NASW, AAUW, N.J. Coalition Mental Health Profl., N.J. Soc. Clin. Social Workers (bd. dir., chmn. mktg. and vendor 1999—2003, membership chmn. 2003—), N.J. Commerce and Indsl. Assn. (child care com. 1990—, human resources com. 1990—), Fordham U. Alumni Assn., Am. Orthopsychiatric Assn., Acad. Cert. Social Workers, Gifted Child Soc. (parent workshop coord. 1989—, bd dir.), Women of Accomplishments (founder, pres. 1990—, chmn. women's coalition conf. 1993—), Zonta (Amelia Earhart chmn. 1987—88, chmn. status women com. 1993—94, lit. com. 1995—). Episcopalian. Avocations: walking, art, music, crafts, boating, acting. Home: 148 Harcourt Ave Bergenfield NJ 07621-1917 Office: Corp Family Resources 15 Godwin Ave Ste 1 Ridgewood NJ 07450-3739 Office Phone: 201-670-0269. Personal E-mail: lynne.clements@att.net.

CLEMENTS, MICHAEL CRAIG, health services consulting executive, retired renal dialysis technician; b. Cin., Sept. 17, 1945; s. Marvin Hubert and Mildred Helen (Rabe) C.; m. Minnie Faye Pospisil, Dec. 1, 1972; children: Melissa Ayn, Michael Aaron. Student, U. Cin., 1968-70; EMT/paramedic, Good Samaritan Health Ctr., 1980. Cert. renal dialysis technician. Hemodialysis technician Christ Hosp., Cin., 1968-79; tech. svcs. dir. Dialysis Clinic, Inc., Cin., 1980-91; pres. Critical Care Svcs., Inc., Mason, Ohio, 1987—. Firefighter/paramedic Mason Vol. Fire Co., 1978-85, EMS tng. officer, 1984, EMS capt., 1985; coop employers environ. and sci. lab. tech. programs Cin. State Coll. Contbr. articles to profl. jours. Mem. Mason Environ. Adv. Commn., 1990—, vice chmn., 1992-93, bus. and parent curriculum review com. Mason City Schs., 1992; employer advisor coop. program Cin. Tech. Coll. Biomed. Engring. Tech., 1986-91; with U.S. Naval Sea Cadet Corps, 2002—, comdg. officer Cin. divsn., 2006—. With USN, 1964-70. Mem.: Nat. Assn. Nephrol. Tech., Ohio Acad. Sci., Assn. Advancement of Med. Instrumentation. Mem. Ch. of Christ. Office: Critical Care Svcs Inc 7562 Central Parke Blvd Mason OH 45040-6816 Office Phone: 513-573-9901. E-mail: michael.clements@criticalcareservicesinc.com.

CLEMENTS, ROBERT, insurance executive; b. Chgo., Sept. 7, 1932; s. John and Mildred L. (Chapman) C.; m. Marilyn Trexler, Dec. 27, 1955; children: Paula J., John, Jeffrey, Ben T. BA, Dartmouth Coll., 1954. Underwriter Royal Ins. Co., NYC, 1956—59; sr. v.p. Marsh & McLennan, Ltd., Toronto, Ont., Canada, 1959—75; chmn. Marsh & McLennan Inc., NYC, 1975—92; pres. Marsh & McLennan Cos., Inc., NYC, 1992-94; founder, chmn. MMC Capital Corp., 1994-96; chmn. Risk Capital Holdings, Inc., 1996—2000, Arch Capital Group Ltd., 2000—05. Chmn. Island Heritage Holdings, 2002-, Integro Ltd., 2005-; chmn. bd. trustees Risk Found.; chmn. emeritus Coll. Ins. Bd. overseers emeritus Inst. for Civil Justice. With U.S. Army, 1954-56. Democrat. Office: 1 Sound Shore Dr Greenwich CT 06830 Office Phone: 203-862-4343.

CLEMENTS, THOMAS FRANK, writer; b. NYC, Aug. 21, 1936; s. Louis and Frances Clements; m. Laime Parry, Apr. 18, 1992; m. Suzanne Cook (div.); children: Mark, Steven. BA in Polit. Sci., Queen's Coll, NYC, 1963; MA in Am. Studies, Fairfield U., Conn., 1975. Cert. tchr. Hawaii, 1992, NY, 1963. Acad. pub., mktg. mgr., editor Holt, Rhinehart and Winston, NYC, 1966—80; pres. Rsch. Micropubs. Svc., Austin, Tex., 1981—93; social studies, English tchr. Maui Pub. Schs., Hawaii, 1993—98; co-creator, writer Alternative-Hawaii.com, Oahu, Hawaii, 1998—. Mem., recruiter Hawaii Ecotourism Assn., Oahu, 1998—, Hawaii Vis. Conv. Bur., Oahu, 2002—. Author of poems. Mem. over 25 social and environ. orgns. With US Army, 1959—61, Korea. Recipient Kahili award, Hawaii Vis. Conv. Bur., 2002. Mem.: ACLU, Nature Conservancy, Mensa, Sierra Club.

CLEMINS, ARCHIE RAY, career officer; b. Mt. Vernon, Ill., Nov. 18, 1943; s. Archie Cornell and Earline (Pepple) C.; m. Marilyn Paddick, June 30, 1967; children: Becky, Travis. BSEE, U. Ill., 1966, MSEE, 1972. Commd. ensign USN, 1966, advanced through grades to rear adm., 1991; engr. officer USS Tunny, Charleston, S.C., 1972-75; staff engr. Comdr. in Chief, U.S. Pacific Fleet, Pearl Harbor, Hawaii, 1975-78; exec. officer USS Parche, Mare Islands, Calif., 1978-81; comdg. officer USS Pogy, Mare Islands, 1982-85; exec. asst. Dep. Chief of Naval Ops., Washington, 1985-86; comdr. Submarine Group 7, Yokosuka, Japan, 1986-88; chief of staff, comdr. U.S. Seventh Fleet, Yokosuka, 1988-90; comdr. Tng. Command, U.S. Pacific Fleet, San Diego, 1990-2000; pres. Caribou Technologies, Inc., Boise, Idaho, 2000—. Mem.: NAE. Republican. Office: Caribou Technologies, Inc 2041 White Pine Ln Boise ID 83706-4048

CLEMMENSEN, LARRY P., investment company executive; Grad., Calif. State U., Fresno, 1969. V.p., corp. contr. Pertec Computer Corp., 1979; CEO Capital Group Cos., LA. Named Outstanding Alumni, Calif. State U., Fresno, 2001. Office Fax: (213) 486-9217.*

CLEMMER, RICHARD L., electronics executive; b. 1953; BSBA, Tex. Tech U.; MBA, So. Meth. U. Fin. mgmt. positions Tex. Instruments, 1973—88, sr. v.p. & CFO semiconductor group, 1988—96; exec. v.p. fin., CFO, Quantum Corp., Milipitas, Calif., 1996—2001; bd. dir., chmn., pres., CEO, CFO PurchasePro.com Inc., 2001—03; chmn., pres. Venture Capital Tech. LLC, 2003—05; ptnr. Shelter Capital Partners, 2004—05; bd. dir. Agere Systems Inc., Allentown, Pa., 2002—, pres., CEO, 2005—. Bd. dir. i2 Technologies Inc., Excel Switching Corp., u-Nav Microelectronics. Office: Agere Systems Inc 1110 American Pkwy NE Allentown PA 18109

CLEMMONS, JOHN B., bank executive, director, retired mathematics educator; b. Rome, Ga., Apr. 11, 1916; s. Lewis Isaac Clemmons and Bessie Turner; m. Mozelle Dailey; children: John B. Jr., Sheila Mozelle. BS, Morehouse Coll.; MS, Atlanta U.; postgrad., U. So. Calif. Prin. Harlan (Ky.) H.S., 1941—43; asst. prin. Carver H.S., Cumberland, Md., 1943—47; dept. head Savannah (Ga.) State U., 1947—87; chmn. bd. dirs. Carver Bank, Savannah. Bd. dirs. Goodwill, 1975—2001. Recipient Silver Beaver award, Boy Scouts Am., 1963; fellow Mention, Boule Found., 1996—, Russell, 2000; grantee, Ford Found., 1951, NSF, 1960. Mem.: Am. Math. Assn., Masons (32d degree), Beta Kappa Chi, Alpha Kappa Mu. Home: 2201 E Victory Dr Savannah GA 31404 Office: Carver Bank PO Box 2769 Savannah GA 31498-1201

CLEMONS, BARBARA GAIL, history educator; b. Bastrop, Tex., Mar. 27, 1956; d. Robert Simpson and Hattie Aldridge; m. Robert Clemons, Apr. 25, 1986; 1 child, Cheree; 1 child, Monique Duvall. Bachelors, Bishop Coll., 1977; Masters, Tex. State U., San Marcos, 1980. Cert. prin. Prairie View U., 2005. Tchr. Bastrop ISD, 1977—, team leader, 1981—91, dept. head, 1991—. Resdient BEAT Team Bastrop Intermediate Sch., 2004—05. V.p. Mission F Ch. Macedonia Bapt., Bastrop, 2000—04. Named Tchr. of Yr., Bastrop Intermediate, 1998, Walmart Tchr. of Yr., 2001, Cmty. Tchr. of Yr., 2002. Mem.: ATPE. Democrat. Baptist. Avocations: gardening, travel, camping. Home: 2013 Pecan St Bastrop TX 78602 Office: Bastrop ISD Intermediate Sch 509 Old Austin Hwy Bastrop TX 78602 Business E-Mail: bclemons@bastrop.isd.tenet.edu.

CLEMONS, JANE ANDREA, state legislator; b. Poughkeepsie, NY, Apr. 2, 1946; d. Mary (Longendyke) Martin; m. Michael R. Clemons, Oct. 15, 1966; children: Bret, Nick, Benjamin. Student, Moore Gen. Hosp., Grasmere, NH, 1966. Nurse various orgns., Nashua, N.H., 1967-89; mem. N.H. Ho. of Reps., Dist. 31, Nashua, 1990—, dep. Dem. House leader, 2005; dep. Dem. leader N.H. Ho. of Reps.; 2nd vice chair N.H. Dem. State Party, 2005—; ranking dem. election law com. N.H. Ho. of Reps. Sponsor Sr. Citizen Computer Health Care Program, Nashua, 1983-84; ward chair Dem. City Com., Nashua, 1988; del. Dem. State Conv., Nashua, 1988; vol. Merrimack (N.H.) Friars Club, 1990-92; del. State Dem. Pary, 1993, Dem. Nat. Conv., 2004; chair Election Law Com., 2007. Greek Orthodox. Avocations: gardening, reading, camping. Home: 177 Kinsley St Nashua NH 03060-3649 Office: NH House Reps State House Concord NH 03301 E-mail: JCSR119@aol.com.

CLEMONS, JOHN ROBERT, lawyer; b. Oak Park, Ill., June 9, 1948; BA, U. Iowa, 1970; JD, DePaul U., 1975. Asst. village mgr. Village of Riverside, Ill., 1970-72; co-dir. dist. 208 Youth Ctr., Riverside, 1970-73; area dir. S.W. area Cook County OEO, 1972-73; clk., legal rschr. Klein, Thorpe & Jenkins, attys., Chgo., 1974-75; asst. state atty.'s Jackson County, Murphysboro, Ill., 1975-80, state's atty., 1980-88; adj. prof., lectr. So. Ill. U., Carbondale, 1978—; ptnr. So. Ill. Law Ctr.,LLC, Carbondale, 1991—; pres. Mt. Joy Enterprises, Inc. Home: 375 Mount Joy Rd Murphysboro IL 62966-4464 Office: 813 W Main St Carbondale IL 62901-2537 Office Phone: 618-529-4000. Business E-Mail: silc@ll.net.

CLENDENEN, WILLIAM HERBERT, JR., lawyer; b. New London, Conn., Dec. 2, 1942; s. William H. and Ethel L. (Clifford) Clendenen; m. Corinna P. Clendenen; children: William, Patrick, Allison, Derek, Luke. BA, Providence Coll., 1964; JD, Cath. U. Am., 1967. Bar: Conn. 1967, U.S. Dist. Ct. Conn. 1971, U.S. Dist. Ct. (so. dist.) N.Y. 1977, U.S. Dist. Ct. R.I. 1977, U.S. Ct. Claims 1977, U.S. Ct. Appeals (2d cir.) 1971, U.S. Supreme Ct. 1976. Reginald Heber Smith Cmty. Lawyer fellow U. Pa., Phila., 1967—68; staff atty. New Haven Legal Assistance Assn., Inc., 1966—73; prin. William H. Clendenen Jr., PC, New Haven, 1973—2002; mng. mem. Clendenen & Shea LLC, New Haven, 2002—. Supervising atty. Yale Law Sch., 1981; alt. pub. mem. Conn. State Bd. Mediation and Arbitration, 1976—78; co-chmn. U.S. Dist. Ct. Conn. Spl. Masters Com., New Haven, 1985—89. Fellow: Am. Coll. Trial Lawyers, Conn. Bar Found. (life; dir. 1991—2004, treas. 1992—2004); mem.: ATLA, ABA, New Haven County Bar Found. (dir. 1993—2003), Conn. Trial Lawyers Assn., New Haven County Bar Assn. (sec. 1986—87, treas. 1987—88, v.p. 1988—89, pres. 1989—90), Conn. Bar Assn. (chmn. consumer law sect. 1974—78, chmn. lawyer referral com. 1987—89, jud. independence task force 1998—99, chmn. fed. judiciary com.). Home: 102 River Edge Farms Rd Madison CT 06443-2756

CLERGUE, LUCIEN GEORGES, photographer; b. Arles, France, Aug. 14, 1934; s. Etienne and Jeanne (Grangeon) C.; m. Yolande Wartel, Jan. 10, 1963; children: Anne, Olivia. Dr. es Letters in Photography, U. Provence, 1979. Tchr. workshops New Sch., N.Y.C., Art Ctr., Pasadena, Osaka U., Japan, other U.S. univs. and colls. Freelance photographer, 1959—; artistic dir. Arles Festival, 1971-75, 86-88; founder, Rencontres Internat. de la Photographie, Arles, 1969, art dir. XXVth anniversary, 1994; one-man shows include Kunstgewerbe Mus., Zurich, 1958, 63, Mus. Modern Art, NYC, 1961—, Musèe d'Arts Decoratifs, Paris, 1962—, Moderna Museet, Stockholm, 1969—, Art Inst. Chgo., 1970—, Kunsthalle, Düsseldorf, Fed. Republic Germany, 1970—, Gallery Witkin, NYC, 1972-79, Bruxelles Musee d'Ixelles, 1974—, Israel Mus., Jerusalem, 1974—, Ctr. Pompidou, Paris, 1980—, Mus. d'Art Moderne Paris, 1984, George Eastman House, Rochester, 1985, ICP, NY, 1986, Amos Anderson Mus., Helsinki, 1987, Real Maestranza Sevilla, 1991, Houston Photo Fest, 1992, Milw. Art Mus., 1993, Calif. Mus. Photography, Riverside, 1997, Centro de la Imagen, Mexico, 1997, Kunstmuseum Dortmund, 1999, John Stevenson Gallery, NY, 2000, 02, 05, Gallery B. Lebon, Paris, 2000, Vitoria, Spain, 2002, Arles 35th RIP, 2004, Bernheimer Gallery, Munich, 2005, Patrice Trigano, Paris, 2007; works rep. books, movies; represented in permanent collection Fogg Mus., Harvard U., Cambridge, Mass., Mus. Modern Art, NYC, Met. Mus., NYC, Louis Storm Gallery, LA, 2006; films include Picasso War Love and Peace; books include Footprints of the Gods, 1988, Picasso my Friend, 1993, Grands Nus, 1999, Poesie Photographique, 2003; contbr. articles to profl. jours. Decorated chevalier Nat. Order Merit, Legion of Honor; recipient Louis Lumière prize, 1966, Grand Prix of Higashikawa Photo Fest, 1986, 3rd prize World Press Photo Internat., Amsterdam, 1997, Prix Polyedre, Aix, France, 1998, Lucie award Acheivement Fine Art Photography, 2005. Mem. Ste. des Amis Jean Cocteau, Ste des Amis de La Fond, St. J. Perse, Aix en Provence, Rencontres Internat. de la Photographie Arles, Memoire 2000, Union des Photographes Createurs, French Acad. des Beaux Arts (First elected photographer 2006). Roman Catholic. Home: 19 Rue Aristide Briand 13200 Arles France Office Phone: 33 04 90520704. E-mail: lucien.clergue@free.fr, lucienclergue@mac.com.

CLERIHUE, RANDOLPH JAMES, federal agency administrator; b. 1966; BA, Taylor U.; MBA, Northwestern U. Press sec. President's Commn. to Stengthen Soc. Security; comm. dir. Health Assn. Am.; asst. exec. dir. Comm. and Pub. Affairs Office of Policy and External Affairs, Pension Benefit Guaranty Corp.; asst. sec. for pub. affairs US Dept. Labor, Washington, 2006—. Office: US Dept Labor 200 Constitution Ave NW Rm S2514 Washington DC 20210 Office Phone: 202-693-4676. Office Fax: 202-693-5057.

CLERKIN, EUGENE PATRICK, physician, educator; b. NYC, Feb. 22, 1931; s. Eugene and Nance (Fitzsimmons) C.; m. Nancy Lucille Oshirak, Aug. 16, 1958; children: Eugene J., Brian A., Lucille A., Kathryn M. BS, Manhattan Coll., 1952; MD, NYU, 1956. Diplomate Am. Bd. Internal Medicine and Endocrinology. Physician Lahey Clinic Found., Burlington, Mass., 1963—, chmn. dept. internal medicine, 1970-91, also bd. govs., 1981-91; asst. clin. prof. medicine Harvard Med. Sch., Boston, 1976-99; assoc. clin. prof. Tufts Med. Sch., 1999—. Mem. corp. N.E. Deaconess Hosp., 1980-93. Lt. USNR, 1958-60. Fellow ACP; mem. AMA, Endocrine Soc., Am. Diabetes Assn., Mass. Med. Soc. Roman Catholic. Avocations: tennis, hiking. Office: Lahey Clinic Med Ctr 41 Mall Rd Burlington MA 01805-0002 Home Phone: 781-235-0254; Office Phone: 781-744-5100. Business E-Mail: eugene.clerkin@lahey.org.

CLERMONT, KEVIN MICHAEL, law educator; b. NYC, Oct. 25, 1945; s. William Theodore and Rita Ruth (Healy) C.; m. Emily Sherwin; 2 children, Adrienne Shaine, Jian Louise. AB summa cum laude, Princeton U., 1967; postgrad., U. Nancy, France, 1967-68; JD magna cum laude, Harvard U., 1971. Bar: Mass. 1971, NY 1974, US Dist. Ct. (so. and ea. dists.) NY 1974, US Ct. Appeals (2d cir.) 1974. Law clk. to judge U.S. Dist. Ct. (so. dist.) N.Y., 1971-72; assoc. Cleary, Gottlieb, Steen & Hamilton, NYC, 1972-74; asst. prof. Sch. Law Cornell U., Ithaca, NY, 1974-77, assoc. prof., 1977-80, prof., 1980-89, Flanagan prof. law, 1989—. Vis. prof. Sch. Law Harvard U., Cambridge, 1991. Co-author: Law: Its Nature, Functions, and Limits, 3d edit., 1986, Civil Procedure: Territorial Jurisdiction and Venue, 1999, Res Judicata: A Handbook on Its Theory, Doctrine, and Practice, 2001, Civil Procedure, 7th edit., 2004, Civil Procedure Stories, 2004, Principles of Civil Procedure, 2005, Materials for a Basic Course in Civil Procedure, 9th edit., 2007; editor: Harvard Law Rev., 1969—71. Fulbright scholar, 1967-68. Mem. ABA, Assn. Am. Law Schs., Order of Coif, Phi Beta Kappa, Sigma Xi. Home: 100 Iroquois Rd Ithaca NY 14850-2223 Office: Cornell U Sch Law Myron Taylor Hall Ithaca NY 14853 Office Phone: 607-255-5189. Business E-Mail: kmc12@cornell.edu, kevin-clermont@postoffice.law.cornell.edu.

CLERMONT, YVES WILFRID, anatomy educator, researcher; b. Montreal, Que., Can., Aug. 14, 1926; s. Rodolphe and Fernande (Primeau) C.; m. Madeleine Bonneau, June 30, 1950; children— Suzanne, Martin, Stephane B.Sc., U. Montreal, 1949; PhD, McGill U., 1953. Lectr. anatomy McGill U., Montreal, 1953-56, asst. prof., 1956-60, assoc. prof., 1960-63, prof., 1963-97, prof. emeritus, 1997—, chmn. dept., 1975-85. Mem. Nat. Bd. Med. Examiners, Phila., 1979-82; mem. rsch. grant com. Med. Rsch. Coun., Ottawa, 1970-97; cons. WHO, NIH, Ford Found., Fonds pour la formation de chercheurs et l'aide à la recherche, Quebec; sec. Artur Lucian Award Com. for Rsch. in Circulatory Diseases, 1983-97, hon. mem., 1997-2000. Contbr. chpts. to books, numerous articles to profl. jours. Recipient Ortho prize Can. Soc. Study Fertility, 1958, Prix Scientifique Govt. of Que., 1963, S.L. Siegler award Am. Soc. Study Fertility, 1966, Van Campenhout award Can. Fertility and Andrology Soc., 1986, Osler Teaching award McGill U., 1990. Fellow: Royal Soc. Can.; mem.: Can. Assn. Microscopy (v.p. 1982—83), Am. Assn. Andrology (Disting. Andrologist award 1988, Serono award lectureship 1992), Can. Assn. Anatomists (hon. J.C.B. Grant award 1986), Soc. Study of Reprodn., Am. Assn. Anatomists (v.p. 1970—73). Home: 567 Townshend St Saint Lambert PQ Canada J4R 1M4 E-mail: yves.clermont@videotron.ca.

CLEVELAND, DON W., biomedical researcher; BS with highest honors in Physics, N.Mex State U., 1972; PhD in Biochemical Scis., Princeton U., NJ, 1977. Predoctoral fellow NSF, 1972—75; Chaim Weizmann postdoctoral fellow U. Calif., San Francisco, 1978—81; asst. prof. dept. biol. chemistry Johns Hopkins U. Sch. Medicine, Balt., 1981—85, assoc. prof., 1985—88, prof., 1988—94; prof., head lab. cell biology Ludwig Inst. Cancer Rsch. and U. Calif., San Diego, 1995—. Chair molecular cytology study sect. NIH, 1996—98. Contbr. articles to sci. jours.; assoc. editor: Jour. Cell Biology, 1991—98; editor, 1998—. Recipient Rsch. Career Devel. award, NIH, 1982—87, Jacob Javits Neuroscience Investigator, NIH Nat. Inst. Neurol. Disorders and Stroke, 1989—96, Method to Extend Rsch. in Time award, NIH Nat. Inst. Gen. Medicine, 1994—, Sheila Essey prize, Am. Acad. Neurology and Amyotrophic lateral sclerosis (ALS) Assn., 1999. Fellow: Am. Acad. Arts & Sciences; mem.: NAS. Office: Ludwig Inst Cancer Rsch 9500 Gilman Dr La Jolla CA 92093-0670

CLEVELAND, HARLAN, political scientist, public affairs executive; b. NYC, Jan. 19, 1918; s. Stanley Matthews and Marian Phelps (Van Buren) Cleveland; m. Lois W. Burton, July 12, 1941; children: Zoë, Melantha, Alan Thorburn. Grad. cum laude, Phillips Acad., Andover, Mass., 1934; AB in Politics with high honors, Princeton U., 1938; recipient 22 hon. degrees. Intern Office of US Senator Robert M. LaFollette, Jr., 1939-40; writer info. div. Farm Security Adminstrn., Washington, 1940-42; ovcl. Bd. Edn. Warfare and successor Fgn. Econ. Adminstrn., Washington, 1942—44; exec. dir. econ. sect. Allied Control Commn., Rome, 1944-45; mem. US del. 3d session UNRRA Coun., London, 1945; acting v.p. in charge econ. sect. Allied Commn., Rome, 1945-46; dept. chief of mission UNRRA Italian Mission, Rome, 1946-47; dir. China office UNRRA, Shanghai, 1947-48; dir. China program ECA, Washington, 1948-49, dept. asst. adminstr., 1949-51; asst. dir. for Europe Mut. Security Agy., 1952-53; exec. editor The Reporter, NYC, 1953-56, pub., 1955-56; prof. polit. sci., dean Maxwell grad. sch. citizenship and pub. affairs Syracuse U., 1956-61; chmn. Citizens for Kennedy, NY, 1960; asst. sec. for internat. orgn. affairs Dept. State, 1961-65; chmn. Cabinet Com. on Internat. Cooperation Yr., 1965; US amb., rep. to NATO, 1965-69; prof. polit. sci., pres. U. Hawaii, Honolulu, 1969-74, pres. emeritus, 1974—; dir. program in internat. affairs Aspen Inst. Humanistic Studies, Princeton, NJ, 1974-80, disting. fellow, 1988—; chmn. US Weather Modification Adv. Bd., 1977-78; disting. vis. Tom Slick prof. world peace LBJ Sch. Public Affairs, U. Tex., Austin, 1979; prof. pub. affairs and planning Hubert H. Humphrey Inst. Public Affairs, U. Minn., Mpls., 1980-88, prof. emeritus, 1988—, dean, 1980-87. Hon. chmn. The Am. Forum for Global Edn., Vols. in Tech. Assistance; bd. dirs. Mertz-Gilmore Found.; nat. adv. coun. World Learning; del. from NY Dem. Nat. Conv., 1960; electronic faculty Western Behavioral Scis. Inst., 1983—91; faculty Connected Edn., 1987—96; hon. trustee The Atlantic Coun. Author: The Obligations of Power, 1966, NATO: The Transatlantic Bargain, 1970, The Future Executive, 1972 (Louis Brownlow award 1975), China Diary, 1976, The Third Try at World Order, 1977, The Knowledge Executive, 1985, The Age of Choice, 1990, The Global Commons, 1990, Birth of a New World, 1993, Leadership and the Information Revolution, 1997, Nobody in Charge, 2002; co-author: Next Step in Asia, 1948; The Overseas Americans, 1960, Humangrowth, 1978; editor: The Promise of World Tensions, 1961, The Management of Sustainable Growth, 1980, Energy Futures of Developing Countries, 1980; gen. editor: Readings for Leaders (series), 1988; co-editor: The Art of Overseasmanship, 1957, The Ethic of Power, 1962, Ethics and Bigness, 1962, Bioresources for Development, 1980, Prospects for Peacemaking, 1988. Decorated US Medal of Freedom, gold star Order Brilliant Star (China), gran ufficiale Order of Merit (Italy); recipient Woodrow Wilson award, Princeton U., 1968, Prix de Talloires, 1981, Leader for Peace award, US Peace Corps, 1985, Rhodes scholar, Oxford U., 1938—39. Fellow: Internat. Leadership Forum, World Bus. Acad., World Acad. of Art and Sci. (pres. 1991—2000); mem.: ASPA (pres. 1970—71, Dwight Waldo award 1988, Elmer Staats Lifetime Achievement award 2003), Coun. on Fgn. Rels., Am. Polit. Sci. Assn., Century Club (NYC), Phi Beta Kapp. Home: 46891 Grissom St Sterling VA 20165-3593 Personal E-mail: harlancleve@falconresidents.org. *If you try too carefully to plan your life, the danger is that you will succeed—succeed in narrowing your options, closing off avenues of adventure that cannot now be imagined, perhaps because they are not yet technologically possible. When a student asks me for career advice, I can only suggest that he or she opt for the most exciting "next step" without worrying where it will lead, and then work hard on the job in hand, not pine for the one in the bush. When your job no longer demands of you more than you have, go and do something else. Always take by preference the job you don't know how to do. If you build into your life enough variety of experience, you will be training for leadership in the role I have called The Public Executive.*

CLEVELAND, HERBERT BRUCE, minister, consultant; b. Gardner, ND, Feb. 20, 1931; s. Herbert Tedeman Cleveland and Edna Mae Leary; m. Constance Doreen Borlaug, Sept. 9, 1955; children: Laurie, Elizabeth, Robert, Timothy. BA, U. ND, Grand Forks, 1957; BTh, Luther Sem., St. Paul, 1959, MDiv, 1964; diploma in gerontology, U. Mich., Ann Arbor, 1980; cert. in pastoral core, Princeton U., NJ, 1981. Ordained reverend

Evangelical Luth. Ch. Am. Tchr. Sioux County, ND, 1949—51; pastor Evangelical Luth. Ch. Am., Chgo., 1959—. Chaplain VA, Ft. Meade, SD, 1963—83, dep. chief, Washington, 1983—88, chief chaplains, 1988—92, dir. ethics, 1992—93; interim pastor Luth. Ch., SD, 1995—2006. Host (radio talk show) What's Your Opinion, 1972—82; author, editor: History of Ft. Meade, 1978, VA Medical Center, 1978 (commendation); editor: Prof Hospital Ministry, 1990. Pres. United Way, Sturgis-Ft. Meade, Ft. Meade Mus., Sturgis-Ft. Meade; bd. dirs. Luth. Soc. Svc. Found., SD, 1995—2000. Col., chaplain US Army, 1959—91. Decorated Meritorious Svc. medal, Humanitarian Svc. medal; recipient Exceptional Svc. award, Dept. Vet. Affairs, 1991. Mem.: VFW, Mil. Chaplain Assn. (nat. pres. 1992—93), Am. Legion (SD chaplain 1982). Avocations: photography, travel, walking, swimming. Home: 1607 West Blvd Rapid City SD 57701

CLEVELAND, MARY HELOISE, elementary school educator; d. Harry Williams and Josephine Burnett Young; m. Franklin Roosevelt Cleveland, Dec. 4, 1970; 1 child, Kizmet Temeka. BS, Miss. Valley State, Itta Bena, 1970; EdM, Miss. U. for Women, Columbus, 1974. Cert. tchr. Miss. State Bd. Edn. Cert. baby sitter Ladies Aux. North Miss. Med. Ctr., Tupelo, 1963—70; elem. tchr. Coffeeville Elem. Sch., Miss., 1970—72, Tupelo Pub. Sch. Sys., 1972—. Vol. North Miss. Med. Ctr., Tupelo, 1986; ward 3 poll worker Popola Voters League, Tupelo, 1972. Named Tchr. of Distinction, Create Found. N.E. Miss. Cmty. Found., 2003; scholar, Miss. Valley State U. Mem.: NEA, Miss. Assn. Educators (bldg. rep. 2005—06), Alpha Kappa Alpha. Democrat. Baptist. Avocation: antiques. Home: 2403 S Lawndale Tupelo MS 38801 Office: Tupelo Pub Sch Dist PO Box 557 Tupelo MS 38802

CLEVELAND, SUSAN ELIZABETH, library administrator, researcher; b. Plainfield, NJ, Mar. 14, 1946; d. Robert Astbury and Grace Ann (Long) Williamson; m. Stuart Craig Cleveland, Aug. 21, 1971; children: Heather Elizabeth, Catherine Elisa. BA, Rutgers U., 1968, MLS, 1969. Acquisitions libr. Jefferson U., Phila., 1970-71; biomed. libr. VA Hosp., Hines, Ill., 1972; med. cataloger U. Ariz., Tucson, 1973-74; dir. U. Pa. Hosp. Libr., Phila., 1974-87; exec. dir. Cleveland, Lamb, Urban Assocs., 1987-89; libr. dir. Mt. Sinai Hosp., Phila., 1989, West Jersey Health System (now Virtua Health Sys.), Voorhees, NJ, 1990—2002, Our Lady of Lourdes Med. Ctr., Camden, NJ, 2002—. Cons. in field, Phila. USPHS fellow, Detroit, 1969-70; recipient Chapel of 4 Chaplains Legion of Honor. Mem. Med. Libr. Assn. (Phila. chpt.), Spl. Libr. Assn., Basic Health Sci. Libr. Consortium, So. N.J. Consortium for Health Info. Svcs., Health Scis. Libr. Assn. N.J., Acad. Health Info. Profls., Caravan Club. Home: 9 Sylvan Ct Laurel Springs NJ 08021 Office Phone: 856-757-3548. Business E-Mail: clevelands@lourdesnet.org.

CLEVELAND, WILLIE MAE, elementary school educator; d. Robert Morris and Rosa Lee Jones; m. Jimmy Charles Cleveland, Dec. 22, 1973; children: Jimmy Jr., Lynetta. Student, Selma U., Ala., 1970—72; BA, Tuskegee Inst., Ala., 1973; postgrad., U. Ala., Tuskaloosa, 1986—87. Cert. tchr. Ala. Tchr. Perry County Bd. Edn., Marion, Ala., 1987—. Target search coord. Duke U. Youth dir. Lillie Star Dist. Chs.; bd. dirs. Marion/Perry County Libr., 1996—. Named Tchr. of Yr., Marion Elem., 1993. Mem.: NEA, Ala. Edn. Assn., Lit. Fedrated Club (pres. 1996—), Zeta Phi Beta (pres. 2003—, bd. mem. 2006—). Democrat. Baptist. Avocations: reading, travel. Office: Albert Turner Elem 901 Pegues Cir Marion AL 36756

CLEVEN, CAROL CHAPMAN, retired state legislator; b. Hanover, Ill., Nov. 2, 1928; d. Edward William and Vivian (Strasser) Chapman; m. Walter Arnold Cleven; children: Kern W., Jeffrey P. BS, U. Ill., 1950, postgrad., 1950-56. Elem. sch. tchr. Derinda Ctr., Ill., 1946-47; with rsch. staff U. Ill., Urbana, 1950-56; exec. dir. Crittenton Hasting House, Brighton, Mass., 1975-86; mem. Mass. Ho. of Reps., Boston, 1987—2003; ret., 2003. Mem. edn. com., mem. human svcs. com., mem. election laws com. Mass. Ho. of Reps., Boston; mem. Rep. Task Force Pediatric AIDS, Mass. Caucus Women Legislators, Gov.'s Adolescent Health Adv. Coun., Spl. Commn. Pub. Assistance, Spl. Com. Women and Criminal Justice; co-chair Legis. Caucus Older Citizen's Concerns, Dept. Social Svcs. Working Group; mem. steering com. Mass. Legis. Children's Caucuse. Mem. Chelmsford (Mass.) Sch. Com., 1969—87, mem. elem. needs com., 1969—71, mem. sch. bldg. com., 1971—76; bd. dirs. Camp Paul Exceptional Children, 1987—; past pres. Lowell (Mass.) YWCA, Lowell Coll. Club; mem. Merrimack River Watershed Coun., Mass. Coalition Pregnant and Parenting Teens, Alliance Young Families; treas. Boston Ctr. Blind Children; bd. dirs. Chelmsford Ednl. Found., Greater Lowell Alzeimers Assn., Eastern Mass. Alzheimers Assn.; mem. spl. adv. bd. Cmty. Teamwork, Inc. Mem.: Mass. Assn. Sch. Coms. (life), Florence Crittenton League Lowell, Chelmsford LWV, Chelmsford Hist. Soc., Friends of Libr., Sigma Delta Epsilon, Phi Sigma. Congregationalist. Home: 4 Arbutus Ave Chelmsford MA 01824-1113 Personal E-mail: wcleven@comcast.net.

CLEVENGER, RAYMOND CHARLES, III, federal judge; b. Topeka, Aug. 27, 1937; s. Raymond and Mary Margaret (Ramsey) Clevenger; m. Celia Faulkner, Sept. 6, 1961 (div. Mar. 1987); children: Winthrop, Peter. BA, Yale U., 1959, LLB, 1966. Law clk. to Justice Byron S. White US Supreme Ct., Washington, 1966—67; ptnr. Wilmer Cutler & Pickering, Washington, 1967—71, 1972—90; spl. asst. to gen. counsel John W. Barnum US Dept. Transp., Washington, 1971—72; judge US Ct. Appeals (Fed. cir.), Washington, 1990—2006, sr. judge, 2006—. Bd. dir. Markle Found. Mem.: ABA, Bar of Supreme Ct. of US, Bar of US Customs Ct., DC Bar Assn. Office: Howard T Markey Nat Ct Bldg 717 Madison Pl NW Washington DC 20439-0002*

CLEVENGER, SARAH, botanist, consultant; b. Indpls., Dec. 19, 1926; d. Cyrus Raymond and Mary Beth (Stevens) C. AB, Miami U., 1947; PhD, Ind. U., 1957. Tchr sci. Radford Sch., El Paso, Tex., 1949-51, Hillsdale Sch., Cin., 1951-52; asst. prof. Berea (Ky.) Coll., 1957-59, 61-63, Wittenberg U., Springfield, Ohio, 1959-60, Eastern Ill. U., 1960-61, Ind. State U., Terre Haute, 1963-66, assoc. prof., 1966-78, prof., 1978-85, prof. emerita, 1985—. Mem. Am. Inst. Biol. Sci., Am. Soc. Plant Taxonomists, Bot. Soc. Am., Internat. Assn. Plant Taxonomy, Phytochem. Soc. N.Am. (past sec.). Achievements include first to isolate and name the flower pigment aurantinidin. Home: 717 S Henderson St Bloomington IN 47401-4838 Personal E-mail: sclevenger@iquest.net.

CLEVENGER, WILLIAM THOMAS, electrical engineer; b. Chattanooga, Tenn., Nov. 6, 1950; s. Asa Ralph and Effie Clarine (Harris) C.; m. Mary Elizabeth Carman, Sept. 12, 1970; children: Elizabeth Eve, Emily Anne. BS, David Lipscomb Coll., 1972; BSEE, U. Tenn., 1973. Registered profl. engr., Tenn., Ala., Fla., Ind., La., NJ, NC, Va., Wis., Ky., Miss., Ga., SC, Colo., Utah, Ark., Idaho, Ill., Kans., Mich., Minn., Mo., Mont., Neb., NH, Pa., Tex., Wash., W.Va., Ariz., Calif., Del., Md., Ohio, Okla., Alaska, Ariz., Iowa, Oreg., N.Mex. Elec. engr. TVA, Chattanooga, 1973-74; from engr. to v.p. Smith Seckman Reid, Inc., Nashville, 1974-87; dir. bldg. engring. Sverdrup Corp., Nashville, 1987-89; mgr. bldg. facilities Allen and Hoshall, Inc., Nashville, 1990-91; sr. elec. engr. SSOE, Inc., Nashville, 1991-92; prin. Quantum Engring. Group, Inc., Nashville, 1992—2003; engr. TLC Architectural Engring., Brentwood, Tenn., 2004—. Contbr. chpt. to book. Mem. IEEE, NSPE, SAR, Am. Cons. Engrs. Coun. (bd. dirs. 1990-97), Illuminating Engring. Soc., Tenn. Soc. Profl. Engrs. (liaison with state architects/engrs. bd. 1989-93, Young Engr. of Yr. award 1986), Cons. Engrs. Tenn. (various offices 1982—, Presdl. Citation 1985, 88, 91, New Prins. award 1986), Civitans (past pres. Nashville chpt.). Mem. Ch. of Christ. Avocation: bicycling. Home: 4305 Dale Ave Nashville TN 37204-4125 Office: TLC Engring Arch Creekside Crossing 6 Cadillac Dr Ste 200 Brentwood TN 37027-5080 Home Phone: 615-297-0303; Office Phone: 615-297-4554. Business E-Mail: tom.clevenger@tlc-eng.com.

CLEVER, LINDA HAWES, physician; b. Seattle; d. Nathan Harrison and Evelyn Lorraine (Johnson) Hawes; m. James Alexander Clever, Aug. 20, 1960; 1 child, Sarah Lou. AB with distinction, Stanford U., 1962, MD, 1965. Diplomate Am. Bd. Internal Medicine, Am. Bd. Preventive Medicine in Occupl. Medicine. Intern Stanford U. Hosp., Palo Alto, Calif., 1965—66, resident, 1966—67, fellow in infectious disease, 1967—68; fellow in cmty. medicine U. Calif., San Francisco, 1968—69, resident, 1969—70; med. dir. Sister Mary Philippa Diagonostic and Treatment Ctr. St. Mary's Hosp., San Francisco, 1970—77; chmn. dept. occupl. health Calif. Pacific Med. Ctr., San Francisco, 1977—. Clin. prof. medicine U. Calif. Med. Sch., San Francisco; NIIH rsch. fellow Sch. Medicine, Stanford U., 1967—68; mem. nat. adv. panel Inst. Rsch. on Women and Gender, 1990—, chair panel, 1998—2000; mem. San Francisco Comprehensive Health Planning Coun., 1971—76; bd. dirs., mem. Calif.-OSHA Adv. Com. on Hazard Evaluation Sys. and Info. Svc., 1979—85, Calif. Statewide Profl. Stds. Rev. Coun., 1977—81, San Francisco Regional Commn. on White House Fellows, 1979—81, 1983—89, 1992, 95, chmn., 1977—81, 2001—02; bd. sci. counselors Nat. Inst. Occupl. Safety and Health, 1995—2001. Editor We. Jour. Medicine, 1990—98; contbr. articles to profl. jours. Trustee Stanford U., 1972—76, 1981—91, v.p., 1985—91; pres. RENEW, 2000—; bd. dirs. Sta. KQED, 1976—83, chmn., 1979—81; bd. dirs. Ind. Sector, 1980—86, vice chmn., 1985—86; bd. dirs. San Francisco U. H.S., 1983—90, chmn., 1987—88; active Womens Forum West, 1980—, bd. dirs., 1992—93; mem. Lucile Packard Children's Hosp. Bd., 1993—97, Lucile Packard Found. Children, 1997—99; mem. policy adv. com. U. Calif. Berkeley Sch. Pub. Health, 1995—, chair, 1995—2000; bd. dirs. The Redwoods Retirement Cmty., 1996—2001, Buck Inst. for Rsch. in Aging, 2000—; bd. govs. Stanford Med. Alumni Assn., 1997—2002, 2003—, pres., 2003—05; bd. dirs. No. Calif. Presbyn. Homes and Svcs., 2000—. Master: ACP (gov. No. Calif. region 1984—89, chmn. bd. govs. 1989—90, regent 1990—96, vice chair bd. regents 1994—95); fellow: Am. Coll. Occupl. and Environ. Medicine; mem.: APHA, We. Assn. Physicians (pres. 2003), We. Occupl. Medicine Assn., Calif. Acad. Medicine, Calif. Med. Assn., Inst. Medicine NAS, Stanford U. Women's Club (bd. dirs. 1971—80), Chi Omega. Office: 2300 California St Ste 304 San Francisco CA 94115-1931 Office Phone: 415-600-3321. Business E-Mail: linda.clever@ucsf.edu.

CLEVER, MARCIA SUE, psychiatrist; b. Natrona Heights, Pa., Aug. 13, 1956; d. John Stacy and Marjorie Mae (DeBay) Clever; m. James Paul Hickey, June 27, 1987; 1 child, Blair. BS, U. Pitts., 1977; MD, Cornell U., 1981. Diplomate Am. Bd. Psychiatry and Neurology. Intern in surgery U. Calif.-Davis Med. Ctr., Sacramento, 1981-82, resident in surgery, 1982-83, resident in psychiatry, 1983-85; sr. resident in geropsychiatry U. Calif.-San Francisco, Langley Porter Neuropsychiat. Inst., 1985-86; assoc. psychiatrist Timberlawn Psychiat. Hosp., Dallas, 1986-87; pvt. practice Johannesburg, S.Africa, also Rome, 1987—; asst. clin. prof. U. Ill., Chgo., 1989; med. dir. psychiat. emergency screening svc. Kimball Med. Ctr., Lakewood, NJ, 1992-95; asst. clin. prof. psychiatry U. Medicine and Dentistry N.J., Piscataway, 1995—. Psychiat. cons. US Dept. State, Johannesburg, 1987—89. Bd. trustees Monmouth U., West Long Branch, NJ, 2003—. Burroughs-Wellcome fellow, 1984-86. Mem. Am. Psychiat. Assn. Avocations: boating, reading. Office: 25 Bridge Ave Ste 205 Red Bank NJ 07701 Office Phone: 732-345-9100.

CLEWELL, BEATRIZ CHU, director, researcher; arrived in US, 1969; d. Wah Yuck and Ruby Mae Chue; m. Andre Clewell (div.); m. Faustino Romero, Sept. 15, 1984. BA in English Lit., Fla. State U., 1970, MA in Edn. Policy, Planning and Analysis, 1977, PhD, 1980. Rsch. scientist Ednl. Testing Svc., Princeton, NJ, 1983—90, sr. rsch. scientist, 1990—94; prin. rsch. assoc., program dir. Urban Inst., Washington, 1995—. Exec. dir. commn. on the advancement of women and minorities in sci. engring. and tech. NSF, Arlington, Va., 1999—2000. Co-author: Breaking the Barriers, 1992, Good Schools In Poor Neighborhoods, 2007; co-editor: Ednl. Evaluation and Policy Analysis, 1998—2002; contbr. numerous articles to profl. jours. and chpts. to books. Fellow: Assn. Women in Sci.; mem.: Am. Ednl. Rsch. Assn. (Disting. Scholar award 1992), Phi Kappa Phi, Phi Beta Kappa. Avocations: reading, opera. Office: Urban Inst 2100 MST NW Washington DC 20037

CLEWELL, DON B., microbial geneticist, educator; b. Dallas, Sept. 5, 1941; AB, Johns Hopkins U., 1963; PhD, Ind. U., Indpls., 1967. Cert. molecular biologist, microbiologist. From asst. prof. to assoc. prof. schs. dentistry and medicine U. Mich., Ann Arbor, 1970-77, prof., 1977—2004, prof. emeritus, 2004—. Burroughs Wellcome vis. prof. U. Rochester, N.Y., 1982; found. lectr. Am. Soc. for Microbiology, 1985-86; mem. recombinant DNA adv. com. NIH, Bethesda, Md., 1986-90. Mem. editl. bd.: Jour. Bacteriology, 1974—80, Plasmid, 1977—87, Infection and Immunity, 1985—96; contbr. over 200 articles to profl. jours., chapters to books. Recipient Rsch. Career Devel. award USPHS, 1975-80, Disting. Faculty Achievement award U. Mich., 2002, Disting. Faculty Lectureship award Biomed. Rsch. U. Mich. Med. Sch., 2003. Mem.: Am. Acad. Microbiology. Achievements include discovery and characterization of bacterial sex pheromone systems and conjugative transposons. Office: U Mich Sch Dentistry Biol and Materials Scis Ann Arbor MI 48109-1078 Home Phone: 734-769-4870; Office Phone: 734-763-0117. E-mail: dclewell@umich.edu.

CLEWETT, RAYMOND WINFRED, mechanical design engineer; b. Upland, Calif., Nov. 7, 1917; s. Howard Jasper and Pansy Gertrude (Macy) C.; m. Hazel Royer, June 11, 1938; children: Alan Eugene, Patricia Gail, Charles Raymond, Richard Howard, Beverly Lynn. Student, Chaffey Jr. Coll., 1937. Exptl. mechanic Douglas Aircraft Co., Santa Monica, Calif., 1937—45; shop foreman, exptl. designer Lear, Inc., Los Angeles, 1945—51; design engr., shop mgr. The RAND Corp., Santa Monica, Calif., 1951—83; mech. designe cons. Pacific Sierra Rsch. Corp., Santa Monica, Calif., 1981—99; also design cons. The RAND Corp., Santa Monica, Calif.; owner, mgr. HY-TECH Engring. and Devel. Lab., Malibu, Calif., 1983—2001. Works include mech. design of JOHNNIAC early model electronic computer; designer various computer input/output devices, 1953-70; developer low vision reading aids for the blind, 1970-75; design and constrn. spl. equipment for sci. and research, 1983-99; stone sculptor, 1994-2001; exhbns. include Malibu Art Festival, 1998, Art Affair XIII, Pacific Palisades, Calif., 1998 (First Pl. award Ventura County Fair, 2004); patentee in field. Republican. E-mail: ray_clewett@juno.com.

CLIBURN, VAN (HARVEY LAVAN CLIBURN JR.), concert pianist; b. Shreveport, La., July 12, 1934; s. Harvey Lavan and Rildia Bee (O'Bryan) C. Studied music with, mother, 1937-51; studied with, Mme. Rosina Lhevinne; grad. (Frank Damrosch scholar), Juilliard Sch. Music, 1954; MFA, Moscow Conservatory, 1989; HHD (hon.), Baylor U., 1958; D (hon.), The Juilliard Sch. of Music, 1998; D (hon.), Loyola U., Texas Christian U., Michigan State U., U. Cincinnati, Louisiana State U., Southern Methodist U., Boston U., Moscow Conservatory. Helped establish the Van Cliburn Foundation, 1958, first Van Cliburn Internat. Piano Competition, Forth Worth, TX, 1962. Pub. appearances, Shreveport, 1940, debut, Houston Symphony Orch., 1947; appeared with Dallas Symphony Orch., 1952, N.Y. Philharm. Orch., Carnegie Hall, 1954, 58; concert pianist on tour, U.S. & Europe, 1955-78, Soviet Union, 1960-72; retired in 1978; came out of retirement to perform at White House, 1987; on tour U.S., 1994-. recs. RCA Victor; guest TV shows, concert with Symphony of the Air, Carnegie Hall, 1958, concert Brussels Fair, Belgium, 1958, other appearances: Phila., Chgo., Hollywood, Denver, London, Amsterdam, Paris, Athens, Monaco, The Hague, Copenhagen, Stockholm, Bucharest, Oslo, La Scala, Moscow, Leningrad, Kiev, Boston, Washington, Dallas, Rio de Janeiro, Mexico City, Tokyo, Berlin, Munich, Zurich, Geneva, Madrid, Barcelona, Lisbon, Vienna, Tel Aviv; extensive recs. of works by Rachmaninoff, Chopin, Beethoven, others; composer classical music; recordings include My Favorite Encores-Works by Chopin, et. al., A Romantic Collection, World's Favorite Piano Music. Recipient Tex. State prize, 1947; Nat. Music Festival award, 1948; G.B. Dealy award Dallas, 1952; Kosciuszko Found. Chopin award, 1952; grantee Olga Samaroff Found., 1953; 1st place Juilliard Concerto concert, 1953; Edgar M. Leventritt Found. award, 1954; Carl M. Roeder Meml. award Juilliard Sch. Music, 1954; 1st prize Internat. Tchaikovsky Piano Competition Moscow, 1958; citation Am. Assn. Sch. Adminstrs., 1959; U. Mich. Musical Soc. First Disting. Artist award, 1996; Arturo Toscanini award, Classical Music Broadcaster's Assn., 1998, Lifetime Achievement award Texas Cultural Trust, 2001, Kennedy Ctr. Honors Medallion, 2001, President's Merit award Nat. Academy of Recording Arts & Sciences, 2002, Presidential Medal of Freedom, 2003; named number one in classical field Top Artists on Campus Poll (album sales), 1968. Mem. Am. Guild Mus. Artists. Clubs: Thespian (Kilgore, Tex.) (pres.), Rotary (hon.), Lotos (life), Shreveport, Ft. Worth. Baptist. Achievements include performed for numerous US Presidents, royalty and heads of state in Europe, Asia, and South America; inducted into Am. Classical Music Hall of Fame, 2001. Office: Van Cliburn Found 2525 Ridgmar Blvd Ste 307 Fort Worth TX 76116-4583

CLICK, CARRIE, public relations executive; b. 1970; Degree in Humanities, Pepperdine U., degree in Spanish, M in Pub. Policy. Cert. Internat. Bus. Protocol Cons. Protocol Sch. of Washington, DC, profl. certification Susan Peterson Productions, Inc., Comm. Ctr. Intern rsch. Heritage Found., Washington; dep. assoc. dir. for Outreach Office of Faith-Based Cmty. Initiatives, The White House; dir., founder Click on.Etiquette. Mem. Southern Ariz. Ctr. Against Sexual Assault, New Parents Network, South of 45; bd. dirs. El Rio Found. Named one of 40 Under 40, Tucson Bus. Edge, 2006. Office: Click on Etiquette 6719 E Camino Principal Tucson AZ 85715 Office Phone: 800-377-3132. Office Fax: 800-377-3135.

CLICK, DAVID FORREST, lawyer, investment advisor; b. Miami Beach, Fla., Dec. 17, 1947; s. David Gorman and Helen Margaret (McPhail) C.; m. Helaine London, June 2, 1974; children: Kenneth Randall, Adam Elliott. BA, Yale U., 1969, JD, 1973, MA, 1974. Bar: Conn. 1973, Md. 1983, U.S. Supreme Ct. 1983, Fla. 1984, Maine 1984; bd. cert. wills, trusts, estates. Asst. prof. Western New England Sch. Law, Springfield, Mass., 1974-77; assoc. prof. Ind. U., 1977-78, U. Md., Balt., 1978-84; assoc. Nixon, Hargrave, Devans and Doyle, Jupiter, Fla., 1984-86; pvt. practice, Jupiter, 1986—. Pres. Click Capital Mgmt., LLC. Contbr. articles to profl. jours. Mem. Christmas Cove (Maine) Improvement Assn., Palm Beach County Estate Planning Coun., pres. 1988-89; participant Leadership Palm Beach County, 1991-92. Mem. ABA, Fla. Bar Assn., Palm Beach County Bar Assn. (cultural activities award 1992, named a Fla. Super Lawyer), Yale Club of Palm Beaches (pres.), Kiwanis (chmn. scholarship com.). Presbyterian. Home: 19216 Pinetree Dr Jupiter FL 33469-2002 Office: 810 Saturn St Ste 15 Jupiter FL 33477-4456 Office Phone: 561-747-7077.

CLICK, PATRICIA C., historian, educator; BA in History, Mary Baldwin Coll., Staunton, Va., 1972; MA in Am. History, U. Va., Charlottesville, 1974, PhD in Am. History, 1980. Asst. prof. humanities U. Va., Charlottesville, 1983—89, assoc. prof. sci., tech. and society, 1989—. Author: The Spirit of the Times: Amusements in Nineteenth-Century Baltimore, Norfolk, and Richmond, 1989, Time Full of Trial: The Roanoke Island Freedmen's Colony, 1862-1867, 2001, (website) Roanoke Island Freedmen's Colony (Best of History Website, 2002); contbr. chapters to books, articles to profl. jours. History Award for Summer Rsch. grant, NC Humanities Com., 1981, GTE Lectureship Program award, GTE Found., 1985—86, Summer Rsch. grant, NC Divsn. of Cultural Resources, Nat. Pk. Svc., and Ea. Nat. Monument Assn., 1996, U. Seminar Summer Rsch. grant, U. of Va. Provost's Office, 1997, 2002. Mem.: Va. Hist. Soc., So. Hist. Assn., Nat. Coun. History Edn., Va. Coun. History Edn., Humanities and Tech. Assn. (exec. com. 1990—93, mem. editl. bd. Humanities and Tech. Rev.), U. Va. Lychnos Soc., Phi Beta Kappa, Phi Alpha Theta. Office: U Va 351 McCormick Road PO Box 400744 Charlottesville VA 22904-4744 Office Phone: 434-924-6118.

CLIFF, JOHNNIE MARIE, mathematics and chemistry professor; b. Lamkin, Miss., May 10, 1935; d. John and Modest Alma (Lewis) Walton; m. William Henry Cliff, Apr. 1, 1961 (dec. 1983); 1 child, Karen Marie. BA in Chemistry, Math., U. Indpls., 1956; postgrad., NSF Inst., Butler U., 1960; MA in Chemistry, Ind. U., 1964; MS in Math., U. Notre Dame, 1980; postgrad., Martin U., 2000. Cert. tchr. Ind. Rsch. chemist Ind. U. Med. Ctr., Indpls., 1956-59; tchr. sci. and math. Indpls. Pub. Schs., 1960-88; tchr. chemistry, math. Martin U., Indpls., 1989—, chmn. math. dept., 1990—, divsn. chmn. depts. sci. and math., 1993—. Adj. instr. math. U. Indpls., 1991, Ivy Tech State Coll., Indpls., 2002. Contbr. scientific papers. Grantee NSF, 1961-64, 73-76, 78-79, Woodrow Wilson Found., 1987-88; scholarship U. Indpls., 1952-56, NSF Inst. Reed Coll., 1961, C. of C., 1963. Mem. AAUW, NAACP, NEA, Assn. Women in Sci., Urban League, NY Acad. Scis., Am. Chem. Soc., Nat. Coun. Math. Tchrs., Am. Assn. Physics Tchrs., Nat. Sci. Tchrs. Assn., Am. Statis. Assn., Am. Assn. Ret. Persons, Neal-Marshall-Ind. U. Alumni Assn., U. Indpls. Alumni Assn., U. Notre Dame Alumni Assn., Ind. U. Chemist Assn., Notre Dame Club Indpls., Kappa Delta Pi, Delta Sigma Theta. Democrat. Baptist. Avocations: gardening, sewing. Home: 405 Golf Ln Indianapolis IN 46260-4108 Office: Martin U 2171 Avondale Pl Indianapolis IN 46218-3878 Home Phone: 317-253-0129; Office Phone: 317-543-3235.

CLIFF, WALTER CONWAY, lawyer; b. Detroit, Jan. 2, 1932; s. Frank V. and Virginia L. (Conway) C.; m. Ursula McHugh, Nov. 5, 1960; children: Walter C., Mary F., Catherine C. BS, LL.B., U. Detroit, 1955; LL.M., NYU, 1956. Bar: Mich. 1956, N.Y. 1958. Assoc. firm Cahill Gordon & Reindel, NYC, 1958-66, ptnr., 1966-2000; sr. counsel, 2000—. Bd. dirs. Florence Gould Found., N.Y.C., 1983—; bd. dirs. Austen Riggs Center, Stockbridge, Mass., 1983-89, Geoffrey Hughes Found., 1992—; mem. Collections com. Harvard U. Art Mus., 1992—. Served with U.S. Army, 1956-58. J.K. Lasser fellow NYU, 1955-56. Mem. ABA, Assn. of Bar of City of N.Y., N.Y. Bar Assn., Stockbridge Golf Club. Democrat. Roman Catholic. Office: Cahill Gordon & Reindel 80 Pine St Fl 17 New York NY 10005-1790 Business E-Mail: wcliff@cahill.com.

CLIFFORD, DOROTHY RING, journalist; b. Kingsport, Tenn., Jan. 13, 1930; d. Wiley Everett Ring and Mary Lee Barton; m. Gordon Henry, Jr. Clifford, May 11, 1957 (dec.); children: Wiley Howard, Elizabeth Clifford Simmons, Mary Gordon Clifford Cunningham. Diploma, Agnes Scott Coll., Ga., 1950, U. Tenn., 1952. Women's editor, reporter Kingsport Times News, Tex., 1948—57; reporter, editor Savannah News Press, 1957—58, women's editor, 1958—59; assoc. women's editor, women's editor Tallahassee Democrat, 1959—62, acting women's editor, 1970—72, assoc. editor, 1972—73, people's editor and food editor, 1973—84, features reporter, writer, 1985—2001, freelance writer, 2002—. Bd. mem. Fla. Press Club; bd. dirs. Le Mayne Art Found.; pres. Jr. League, 1968—69; bd. dirs. Murat House Mus., Tallahassee, 1970—73; founding pres. Fla. State U., Friends of Dance, Tallahassee, 1987—90. Recipient 1st Pl. in journalism, J.C. Penney and U. Mo., 1961, Dallas Market Ctr., 1982. Mem.: Tallahassee Lit. Club. Republican. Episcopalian. Home: 5353 Tewkesbury Trace Tallahassee FL 32309

CLIFFORD, EUGENE THOMAS, lawyer; b. Utica, NY, July 15, 1941; s. James Anthony and Mary Margaret (Ellard) C.; m. Joyce Victoria Siwinski, Sept. 4, 1965; children: Michael Sean, Elizabeth Joyce, Thomas More. BA, Boston Coll., 1963, LLB, 1966. Bar: N.Y. 1967, U.S. Dist. Ct.

(we. dist.) N.Y. 1967. Assoc. Chamberlain, D'Amanda, Bauman, Chatman & Oppenheimer, Rochester, NY, 1967-72, Lamb, Webster, Walz, Telesca & Donovan, Rochester, 1972-76; ptnr. Webster, Sullivan, Santoro & Clifford, Rochester, 1976-86, Fulreader, Rosenthal, Sullivan, Clifford, Santoro & Kaul, Rochester, 1986-2001, Davidson Fink LLP, Rochester, 2001—. Bd. dirs. N.Y. state divsn. Am. Cancer Soc., Syracuse, 1972-78, 82-88, 90-97, chmn. bd. dirs., 1982-83, nat. bd. dirs., 1991-97; bd. dirs. Urban League of Rochester, 1988-91. Recipient Nat. Bronze award N.Y. state divsn. Am. Cancer Soc., 1984, Hope award Monroe County unit, 1983. Mem.: ABA, Nat. Acad. Elder Law Attys., N.Y. State Bar Assn., Monroe County Bar Assn. (pres. 2002—03). Office: 28 Main St E Ste 1700 Rochester NY 14614 Home Phone: 315-589-4480; Office Phone: 585-546-6448. E-mail: eclifford@dfckg.com.

CLIFFORD, GARI DAVID, engineering educator, biomedical engineer; s. Gareth and Josephine Clifford; m. Rachel Hall, June 21, 2003. BS in Physics, Exeter U., England, 1992; MS in Math. and Theoretical Physics, Southampton U., England, 1995; PhD, Oxford U., England, 2003. Sr. rsch. scientist Ministry Defence, London, Kent, 1995—98; cons. Intel, Hillsboro, Oreg., 2003—; sci. advisor E-Trolz, Lawrence, Mass., 2003—; rsch. engr. mgr. MIT, Cambridge, Mass., 2004—, instr. biomedical engring., 2004—. Cons. Physiostream, Atlanta, 2006—. Author: (textbook) Advanced Methods for ECG Analysis; editor: Jour. Biomed. Engring. Online, 2003—, Jour. Biol. Systems, 2003—. Fellow, Oxford U., 2002—03, MIT, 2003—04. Mem.: IEEE (sr.). Achievements include patents pending for Method to filter, segment, compress and classify biomedical signals. Avocations: paragliding, travel, photography. Office: Massachusetts Institute of Technology 77 Massachusetts Avenue Cambridge MA 02139 Office Phone: 617-253-1000.

CLIFFORD, GERALDINE JONCICH, retired education educator; b. San Pedro, Calif., Apr. 17, 1931; d. Marion and Geraldine Joncich; m. William F. Clifford, July 12, 1969 (dec. 1993). AB, UCLA, 1954, MEd, 1957; EdD, Columbia U., 1961. Tchr., San Lorenzo, Calif., 1954-56, Maracaibo, Venezuela, 1957-58; researcher Inst. Lang. Arts, Tchrs. Coll., Columbia, 1958-61; asst. prof. edn. U. Calif., Berkeley, 1962-67, asso. prof., 1967-74, prof., 1974-94, assoc. dean, 1976-78, chmn. dept. edn., 1978-81, acting dean Sch. Edn., 1980-81, 82-83, dir. edn. abroad program, 1988, 89, prof. grad. sch. Berkeley, 1994—97, prof. emerita, 1994. Author: The Sane Positivist: A Biography of Edward L. Thorndike, 1968, The Shape of American Education, 1975, Ed Sch: A Brief for Professional Education, 1988, Lone Voyagers: Academic Women in Coeducational Universities, 1870-1937, 1989, Equally in View: The University of California, Its Women, and The Schools, 1995. Macmillan fellow, 1958-59, Guggenheim fellow, 1965-66, Rockefeller fellow, 1977-78; recipient Willystine Goodsell award. Mem. History Edn. Soc., Am. Ednl. Rsch. Assn., Phi Beta Kappa, Pi Lambda Theta. Home: Apt 733 1661 Pine St San Francisco CA 94109-0420 Business E-Mail: gcliffor@berkeley.edu.

CLIFFORD, BROTHER PETER, academic administrator, religious studies educator; b. NYC, Feb. 17, 1925; s. Peter and Mary (Lynch) C. AB, Manhattan Coll., 1950; MA, Fordham U., 1957; EdD, Harvard U., 1970; EdD (hon.), St. Mary's Coll., Winona, Minn., 1987. Cert. sch. supt., N.Y. Tchr., prin. Cath. schs., NYC, 1947-57; dean De La Salle Coll., Manila, 1957-61; asst. prin. Bishop Loughlin High Sch., Bklyn., 1962-64; assoc. supt. schs. Diocese Bklyn., 1968-71; exec. sec. Nat. Cath. Edn. Assn., Washington, 1971-74; assoc. dean edn. St. John U., NYC, 1974-76; pres. St. Mary's Coll., Winona, Minn., 1976-84; provincial Bros. Christian Schs., Narragansett, RI, 1984-87; staff asst. higher edn. U.S. Cath. Conf., Washington, 1987-89; pres. St. Mary Coll., Leavenworth, Kans., 1989-94; dir. fin. Narragansett Christian Bros. Ctr., 1994-99; v.p. Metanoia St. Mary's U., Winona, Minn., 2000—02; dir. accreditation studies Ocean Tides Sch., 2002—. Mem. Leavenworth Area Devel., 1989-94; trustee Christian Bros. Investment Svcs., 1994—, Christian Bros. Svcs., 1994-2000; mem. bd. regents La Salle Acad., Providence, 1994-96, 2004-; mem. diocesan sch. bd. Diocese of Providence, 1994-2000; v.p. Metanoia Group, St. Mary's U. of Minn., 2000-02 Recipient Avila award Coll. St. Teresa, Winona. Mem. Am. Fundraising Profls., Kans. Ind. Coll. Assn., Kans. Ind. Coll. Fund, Bros. of the Christian Schs (Christian Bro. 1943—). Office Phone: 401-789-0244 x241. Business E-Mail: clifford@smumn.edu.

CLIFFORD, ROBERT A., lawyer; b. Evergreen Park, Ill., Mar. 24, 1951; s. George Leonard and Shirley Marie (Meyer) C.; m. Joan Elizabeth Makowski, July 29, 1973; children: Erin Elizabeth, Tracy Ann. BS in Commerce, DePaul U., 1973, JD, 1976. Bar: Ill. 1976, US Dist. Ct. (no. dist. Ill.) 1976, US Supreme Ct. 1981, US Dist. Ct. (ea. dist. Wis.) 1993, US Dist. Ct. (ctrl. dist. Ill.) 1993, US Ct. Appeals (7th cir.) 1996. Assoc. Philip A. Corboy & Assocs., Chgo., 1974-82, Corboy & Demetrio, Chgo., 1982-84; ptnr. Clifford & Henely, Chgo., 1984-85; prin. ptnr. Clifford Law Offices, Chgo., 1985—; cons. and lectr. in law; mediation panelist Endispute of Chgo., 1982—; mem. bd. overseers Rand Inst. Civil Justice 1998-. Contbr. articles to profl. jours. Mem. adv. coun., DePaul U. Coll. Law, 1987—; bd. trustees DePaul U. , 1987—; mem. bd. advs. Mercy Hosp. & Med. Ctr. 1988-; mem. adv. bd. Geroulis Ednl. Found. 1990-. Named one of Top Ten Litigators, Nat. Law Jour., 1993, Top Ten Lawyers in Ill., Nat. Law Jour., 1999, Top Ten Most Influential Lawyers in Ill., Am. Rsch. Corp., 2000, 30 Toughest Lawyers, Chgo. Mag., 2002, Top 5 Most Respected and Feared Plaintiff Attys., Corp. Legal Times, 2004. Fellow Chgo. Bar Found; master Chgo. Inn of Ct. (pres. 1994-95); mem. ABA (chair litig. sect. 2001-02, chair Task Force Terrorism & Law 2001-02), Fed. Bar Assn., Ill. State Bar Assn., Chgo. Bar Assn. (bd. mgrs. 1992-94, ABA del. 2003-05), Kane County Bar Assn., Lake County Bar Assn., N.W. Suburban Bar Assn., Am. Law Inst., Inner Cir. Advocates, Nat. Jud. Coll., Am. Inn of Ct., Am. Judicature Soc., Ill. Com. for Jud. Independence, Am. Soc. Law and Medicine, Am. Inst. Aeronautics and Astronautics, Assn. Trial Lawyers of Am. (mem. membership com. 1989-), Ill. Attys. for Criminal Justice, Ill. Inst. Continuing Legal Edn., Soc. Trial Lawyers of Am., Ill. Trial Lawyers Assn. (mem. exec. com. 1986-, pres. 1990), Trial Lawyers Club Chgo., Ill. State and Chgo. Soc. of Phys. Medicine and Rehab., Exec. Club Chgo., DePaul U. Alumni Assn. (past pres.). Roman Catholic. Clubs: Butler Nat. Golf (Oak Brook, Ill.); Inverness Golf (Ill.); Dairymen's Country (Boulder Junction, Wis.). Office: Clifford Law Offices 120 N LaSalle St 31st Fl Chicago IL 60602 Office Phone: 312-899-9090. Office Fax: 312-251-1160. E-mail: rclifford@cliffordlaw.com.*

CLIFFORD, ROBERT WILLIAM, state supreme court justice; b. Lewiston, Maine, May 2, 1937; s. William H. and Alice (Sughrue) C.; m. Clementina Radillo, Jan. 18, 1964; children: Laurence M., Matthew P. BA, Bowdoin Coll., 1959; LLB, Boston Coll., 1962; LLM, U. Va., 1998. Bar: Maine 1962, U.S. Dist. Ct. Maine 1965. Ptnr. Clifford & Clifford, Lewiston, 1964-79; justice Maine Superior Ct., Auburn, 1979-83, chief justice, 1984-86; assoc. justice Maine Supreme Ct., Auburn, 1986—. Mem. Lewiston City Coun., 1968-70, mayor, 1971-72; mem. Maine State Senate, 1973-76; chmn. Lewiston Charter Commn., 1978-79; mem. Maine Probate Law Revision Commn., 1973-79; bd. trustees St. Joseph's Coll. Maine, 2000—. Mem. Maine Bar Assn., Androscoggin County Bar Assn., Am. Judicature Soc. Roman Catholic. Office: Maine Supreme Jud Ct 2 Turner St PO Box 3488 Auburn ME 04212-3488 Home Phone: 207-784-7219; Office Phone: 207-783-5425. Business E-Mail: robert.w.clifford@maine.gov.

CLIFFORD, STEVEN FRANCIS, science administrator, director; b. Boston, Jan. 4, 1943; s. Joseph Nelson and Margaret Dorothy (Savage) C.; children from previous marriage: Cheryl Ann, Michelle Lynn, David Arthur; m. Theresa Kavanagh, Aug. 1996. BSEE, Northeastern U., Boston, 1965; PhD, Dartmouth Coll., 1969. Postdoctoral fellow NRC, Boulder, Colo., 1969-70; physicist Wave Propagation Lab., NOAA, Boulder, 1970-82, program chief, 1982-87, dir. environ. tech. lab., 1987—2001; sr. rsch. scientist emeritus U. Colo., 2001—. Mem. electromagnetic propagation panel, NATO, 1989-93; vis. sci. closed acad. city Tomsk, Siberia, USSR; apptd. mem. NAS Bd. on Atmospheric Sci. and Climate, 1999—. Author: (with others) Remote Sensing of the Troposhpere, 1978; contbr. 130 articles to profl. jours.; patentee in acoustic scintillation liquid flow measurement, single-ended optical spatial filter, acoustic sensor of surface ocean current and waves, high resolution GPS scatterometer. Recipient 5 Outstanding publs. awards Dept. Commerce, 1972, 75, 89, 96, Outstanding Career Performance, U.S. Presidental award, 1998; inducted NAE, 1997. Fellow: Acoustical Soc. Am., Optical Soc. Am. (editor atmospheric optics 1978—84, advisor atmospheric optics 1982—84); mem.: NRC (bd. atmospheric sci. and climate, chair panel on FAA weather forecasting accuracy, study team on homeland security), NAE, IEEE (sr.), Am. Geophys. Union, Internat. Radio Sci. Union. Avocations: running, cross country skiing. Office: CIRES/NOAA Environ Tech Lab 325 Broadway St Boulder CO 80305-3337 Office Phone: 303-497-6291.

CLIFFORD, STEWART BURNETT, banker, director; b. Boston, Feb. 17, 1929; s. Stewart Hilton and Ellinor (Burnett) C.; m. Cornelia Park Woolley, Apr. 26, 1952; children: Cornelia Lee Wareham, Rebecca Lyn Mailer-Howat, Jennifer Leggett Danner, Stewart Burnett Jr. AB, Harvard U., Cambridge, Mass., 1951, MBA, 1956. Asst. cashier Citibank, N.A., NYC, 1958-60, asst. v.p., 1960-63; exec. v.p., gen. mgr. Merc Bank, Montreal, Que., Canada, 1963-67, v.p. planning Overseas div., 1967-68; v.p., adminstr. comml. banking group Citibank, NYC, 1969-72, v.p. head world corp. dept. London, 1973-75, sr. v.p. domestic energy, 1975-80, sr. v.p., head pvt. banking and investment divsn., 1981-87, div. exec., head investment divsn., 1987-93; sr. banker Pvt. Bank US, 1993-94; cons. MB Investment Ptnrs., NYC, 1995—. Trustee Spence Sch., NYC, 1976—98, chair bd. trustees, 1984—86; elder Brick Ch.; trustee Presbyn. Ch. Found., 1996—2001, Auburn Seminary, NYC; bd. dirs. Nat. Inst. Social Scis., NYC; trustee emeritus Princeton Theol. Sem.; com. univ. resources Harvard Coll.; bd. dirs. Monumental Corp., Balt., 1974—89, Harvard Alumni Assn., 1989—91; pres. 120 East End Ave. Corp, Woolley-Clifford Found.; vice chmn. Asphalt Green. 1st lt. US Army, 1951—54. Mem.: Ocean Reef Club (Key Largo, Fla.), Harvard Club (NYC), Union Club (NYC, former pres.), Bath and Tennis Club (Palm Beach), Duxbury Yacht Club (Mass.), Pilgrims (NYC). Republican. Avocations: squash, tennis. Home: 120 E End Ave New York NY 10028-7552 Office: MB Investment Ptnrs 31st Fl 825 3d Ave New York NY 10022 Home Phone: 212-734-7079; Office Phone: 212-370-7300.

CLIFT, ELEANOR, news correspondent, writer; b. Bklyn., July 7, 1940; d. Erk and Inna Roeloffs; m. William Brooks Clift Jr., 1964 (div. 1981); children: Edward, Woodbury, Robert; m. Tom Brazaitis, Sept. 30, 1989 (dec. Mar. 30, 2005). Student, Hofstra U., Hunter Coll. Former sec. to nat. affairs editor Newsweek, NYC, former reporter Atlanta bur., former White House corr., named dep. Washington bur. chief, 1992, contbg. editor, 1994—; with Washington bur. LA Times, 1985—86. Regular panelist The McLaughlin Group, 1983—; polit. analyst Fox News Network; column Capitol Letter appears weekly on Newsweek-MSNBC website; co-chair bd. dirs. Internat. Women's Media Found. Co-author (with Tom Brazaitis): War Without Bloodshed: The Art of Politics, 1996, Madam President: Shattering the Last Glass Ceiling, 2000; author: Founding Sisters and the 19th Amendment, 2003, Election 2004: How Bush Won and What You Can Expect in the Future, 2005. Office: Newsweek Washington Bur 1750 Pennsylvania Ave NW Washington DC 20006-4502 E-mail: eclift@newsweek.com, eclift@aol.com.

CLIFTON, DOUGLAS C., retired newspaper editor; b. Bklyn., July 14, 1943; s. Norman Stanton and Anne Frances (Montesano) C.; m. Margaret E. Clifton, Dec. 18, 1965; children: Amy Elizabeth Clifton Gallup, Clay Norman. BA in Polit. Sci., Dowling Coll., 1965. Positions including reporter, city editor, dep. mng. editor Miami Herald, 1970-87; news editor Washington bur. Knight Ridder, 1987-89; mng. editor Charlotte Observer, NC, 1989-91; sr. v.p., exec. editor Miami Herald, 1991-99; editor Plain Dealer, 1999—2007. Lt. U.S. Army, 1966-69, Vietnam. Named Editor of Yr., Editor & Pub. Mag., 2003; recipient Spl. Recognition award, AP Soc. Ohio, 2007. Mem.: Am. Soc. Newspaper Editors (freedom of info. com. 2003—). E-mail: dclifton@plaind.com.

CLIFTON, GUY L., neurosurgeon, educator; b. Jacksonville, Tex., Apr. 29, 1949; BS, Tex. A&M U., 1971; MD with high honors, U. Tex., 1975. Cert. Am. Bd. Neurological Surgery. Intern in surgery U. Minn. Hosp., Mpls., 1975-76; resident in neurosurgery U. Tex. Med. Br., Galveston, 1976-80; dep. chief neurosurgical svc., dir. neurosurgical ICU Ben Taub Gen. Hosp., Houston, 1980-84; asst. prof. dept. neurosurgery Baylor Coll. Medicine, Houston, 1980-84; assoc. attending surgeon Hunter Holmes McGuire VA Med. Ctr., Richmond, Va., 1984-89, chief neurosurgery svc., 1987-90; assoc. prof. divsn. neurosurgery Med. Coll. Va., Richmond, 1984-89, interim chmn. dept. rehab. medicine, 1988-90, prof. divsn. neurosurgery, 1990; chief neurosurgery Hermann Hosp., Houston, 1990—2004; prof., dir. divsn. neurosurgery Health Sci. Ctr. U. Tex. Houston Med. Sch., 1990-92, prof., chmn. dept. neurosurgery Health Sci. Ctr., 1992—2004, prof. dept. neurosurgery, 2004—, Runnells Disting. chair, neurosurgery. Mem.-at-large med. bd. Harris County Hosp. Dist., 1983-84; dir. Vivian Smith Ctr. Neurologic Rsch., 2000-, Mission Connect, 2002-; mem. exec. com. joint sect. on trauma Am. Assn. Neurol. Surgery/Cong. Neurol. Surgeons, 1986—; cons., reviewer NIH/NINCDS, Nat. Inst. Disability and Rehab. Rsch., Ctrs. for Disease Control; invited lectr. in field. Mem. cons. bd. editors Orthopedics, 1983-90; mem. editl. bd. Jour. Neurotrauma, 1988—; contbr. 110 articles to sci. and profl. jours., 28 chpts. to books. Chmn. Save Our ERs, 2003—. Recipient Roche Neuroscis. award SAMA-UTMB Nat. Student Rsch. Forum, 1975, Nancy, Clive and Pierce Runnells Disting. Prof. in Neurosci., 1999; grantee Yale U., 1980-83, NIH, 1980-84, 94—, 93, 93—, Baylor Coll. Medicine, 1981-82, Mead Johnson, 1982-83, Moody Found., 1982-83, Ross Labs., 1983-84, Med. Coll. Va., 1986, Thomas F. and Kate Miller Jeffress Meml. Trust, 1986, VA, 1987-90, 90, Nat. Inst. on Disability and Rehab. Rsch., 1988-90, NIH/NINDS 1994-99, 2002-; named Robert Wood Johnson Health Policy Fellow, IOM, 2006. Mem. AMA, ACS (Regional reidents Competition award com. on trauma, 1979), Am. Assn. Neurol. Surgeons (liason to Am. Acad. Phys. Medicine Rehab., Nat. Ctr. for Rehab. Rsch.), Am. Assn. Surgery for Trauma, Am. Spinal Injury Assn., Am. Trauma Soc., Soc. of Neurol. Surgeons, Nat. Head Injury Found. (profl. adv. bd. 1992—, Sheldon Berrol Clin. Svc. award 1993), Congress Neurol. Surgeons, Soc. Neurol. Anesthesia and Neurol. Supportive Care, Soc. Neurotrauma (founding officer, v.p. 1988, program chmn. 1991), Tex. Assn. Neurol. Surgeons (bd. dirs. 1991), Tex. med. Assn., Houston Neurol. Soc., Phi Kappa Phi, Alpha Omega Alpha. Office: U Tex Houston Med Sch 6431 Fannin St MSB 7 130 Houston TX 77030 Office Phone: 713-500-6135.

CLIFTON, JAMES ALBERT, physician, educator; b. Fayetteville, NC, Sept. 18, 1923; s. James Albert Jr. and Flora M. (McNair) Clifton; m. Katherine Rathe, June 25, 1949; children: Susan M.(dec.) , Katherine Y., Caroline M. BA, Vanderbilt U., 1944, MD, 1947. Diplomate Am. Bd. Internal Medicine (mem. 1972-81, mem. subsplty. bd. gastroenterology 1968-75, chmn. 1972-75, mem. exec. com. 1978-81, chmn. 1980-81). Intern U. Hosps., Iowa City, 1947—48, resident dept. medicine, 1948—51; staff dept. medicine Thayer VA Hosp., Nashville, 1952—53; asst. clin. medicine Vanderbilt Hosp., Nashville, 1952—53; cons. physician VA Hosp., Iowa City, 1965—93; assoc. medicine dept. internal medicine Coll. Medicine, U. Iowa, 1953—54, chief divsn. gastroenterology, 1953—71, asst. prof. medicine, 1954-58, assoc. prof., 1958—63, prof., 1963—91, prof. emeritus, 1991—, traveling fellow, 1964, vis. prof. dept. physiology, 1964, vice chmn. dept. medicine, 1967—70, chmn. dept. medicine Coll. Medicine, 1970—76, Roy J. Carver prof. medicine, 1974—91, Roy J. Carver prof. emeritus, 1991—, dir. James A. Clifton Ctr. Digestive Diseases, 1985—90, interim dean, 1991—93. Investigator Mt. Desert Isle Biol. Lab., Salisbury Cove, Maine, 1964; vis. faculty mem. Mayo Found. and Mayo Clinic, 1966; vis. prof. dept. medicine U. N.C. Chapel Hill, 1970; cons. gastroenterology and nutrition tng. grants com. Nat. Inst. Arthritis and Metabolic Diseases, NIH, 1964—68, chmn., 1965—68; mem. Nat. Adv. Arthritis and Metabolic Diseases Coun., 1970—73; mem. gastroenterology tng. com. VA, Washington, 1967—71, chmn. tng. grants com., 1971—73; mem. med. adv. bd. Digestive Disease Found., 1969—73; vis. prof. gastroenterology U. London (St. Marks Hosp.), 1984—85; mem. sci. adv. com. Ludwig Inst. Cancer Rsch., Zurich, 1984—95. Internat. editl. bd. Italian Jour. Gastroenterology, 1970—90, Gastroenterology, 1964—68. Recipient Disting. Alumnus of Yr. award, Vanderbilt U. Sch. Medicine, 1984, Disting. Alumnus of Yr. Achievement award, U. Iowa Coll. Medicine, 2000, Disting. Mentoring award, 2002, Disting. Alumni award, U. Iowa Alumni Assn., 2004; fellow, NIH, USPHS, 1955—56, Evans Meml. Hosp., Mass. Meml. Hosps., also Boston U. Sch. Medicine, 1955—56; Phi Connell scholar, Vanderbilt U., 1943—44. Fellow: ACP (bd. regents 1972—79, pres. 1977—78, Alfred Stengel award 1984, Laureate award 1989); mem.: AAUP, AAAS, AMA (liaison com. grad. med. edn. 1976—77), Internat. Soc. Internal Medicine (exec. com. 1978—80), Assn. Profs. Medicine (councillor 1972—73, sec.-treas. 1973—75), Assn. Am. Med. Colls., Am. Physiol. Soc., Soc. Exptl. Biology and Medicine, Assn. Am. Physicians, Am. Clin. and Climatol. Assn. (v.p. 1984), Am. Fedn. Clin. Rsch., Am. Soc. Internal Medicine (Internist of Yr. award Iowa chpt. 1986), Am. Assn. Study Liver Disease, Am. Heart Assn., Am. Gastroent. Assn. (pres. 1970—71), Inst. Medicine NAS, U. Iowa Assn. Emeritus Faculty (pres. 1999—2000), U. Iowa Retirees Assn. (pres. 1999—2000). Home: 39 Audubon Pl Iowa City IA 52245-3437 Office: U Iowa Hosp and Clinics 4 JCP Hawkins Dr Iowa City IA 52242 Home Phone: 319-351-1561; Office Phone: 319-356-1771. Business E-Mail: james-clifton@uiowa.edu. E-mail: zybumjim@mchsi.com.

CLIFTON, JAMES K., market research company executive; m. Susan Clifton; children: Nicole, Jonathan, Jackie. DHL (hon.), Medgar Evers Coll., Jackson State Univ.; DComm (hon.), Bellevue Univ. Chmn., CEO Gallup Org., Washington, 1988—. Chmn. Thurgood Marshall Scholarship Fund. Office: Gallup Organization 901 F St NW Washington DC 20004

CLIFTON, JEAN B., publishing executive; b. Orange, NJ, Feb. 10, 1961; d. Henry T. and Eileen Patricia (Connors) Benedetto; m. Richard Daniel Clifton, Aug. 10, 1985; 1 child, Kevin Thomas. BBA, U. Mich., 1983. Auditor, cons. Ernst & Young, 1983-86; asst. contr. Jour. Register Co., Princeton, NJ, exec. asst. to chmn., exec. v.p., CFO, treas. Trenton, NJ, 1986—2005; pres., COO Platinum Strategic Partners, L.L.C., 2005—06; sr. v.p., CFO The Reader's Digest Assn., Inc, 2007—. Bd. dirs. Jr. Achievement of Ctrl. N.J., Princeton Mem. Newspaper Assn. Am. (postal affairs com.). Office: The Reader's Digest Assn Inc Reader's Digest Rd Pleasantville NY 10570*

CLIFTON, LUCILLE THELMA, author; b. Depew, NY, June 27, 1936; d. Samuel Louis and Thelma (Moore) Sayles; m. Fred James Clifton, May 10, 1958 (dec. Nov. 1984); children: Sidney, Fredrica (dec. 2000), Channing (dec. 2004), Gillian, Graham, Alexia. Student, Howard U., 1953-55, Fredonia State Tchrs. Coll., NY, 1955; DL (hon.), Dartmouth Coll., 2005. Prof. literature and creative writing U. Calif., Santa Cruz, 1985-90; dist. prof. humanities St. Mary's Coll. Md., 1990—, Hilda C. Landers endowed chair in liberal arts, 2000—. Poet-in-residence, Coppin State Coll., Balt., 1972-76, Jenny Moore vis. writer, George Washington U., 1982-83. Author: Good Times, 1969, Good News About The Earth, 1972, An Ordinary Woman, 1974, Generations, 1976, Two-Headed Woman, 1980, Sonora Beautiful, 1981, Next, 1987, Good Woman, 1987, Quilting, 1991, The Book of Light, 1993, Blessing the Boats, 2000 (Nat. Book award); Everett Anderson books and other books for children; co-author: Free to Be You and Me, 1974 (Emmy award), Free To Be A Family. Named Poet Laureate, State of Md., 1979; recipient Discovery award Poetry Center, 1969, winner Nat. Book Award, 2000; YMHA grantee, 1969; Nat. Endowment Arts grantee, 1970, 72 Fellow Am. Acad. Arts and Scis.; mem. Authors League, Author Guild, P.E.N., Acad. Am. Poets (chancellor), Poetry Soc. Am. (bd. dirs., Lila Wallace/Reader's Digest award 1999). Office: St Marys Coll of Maryland Divsn Arts and Letters Montgomery Hall 126 Saint Marys City MD 20686

CLIFTON, MATTHEW P., petroleum refining company executive; b. 1951; V.p. econ. engring. & legal affairs Holly Corp., Dallas, 1988—91, sr. v.p., 1991—95; chmn., CEO Holly Logistic Svcs. LLC; pres. Holly Refining & Mktg. Co., Holly Corp., Dallas, 1995—2005, CEO, 2005—07, chmn., CEO, 2007—. Office: Holly Corp Ste 1600 100 Crescent Ct Dallas TX 75201-6927 Office Fax: 214-871-3566.*

CLIFTON, RICHARD RANDALL, federal judge; b. Framingham, Mass., Nov. 13, 1950; s. Arthur Calvin and Vivian Juanita (Himes) C.; m. Teresa Morano Aleshire, Oct. 15, 1988; children: David Madison, Katherine Kaleilani. AB, Princeton U., 1972; JD, Yale U., 1975. Bar: Ill. 1975, Hawaii 1976, US Dist. Ct. Hawaii 1976, US Ct. Appeals (9th cir.) 1976, US Ct. Appeals (2d cir.) 1979, US Supreme Ct. 1982. Law clk. to judge US Ct. Appeals (9th cir.), Honolulu, 1975-76, judge, 2002—; from assoc. to ptnr. Cades, Schutte, Fleming & Wright, Honolulu, 1977—2002. Adj. prof. law U. Hawaii, Honolulu, 1979-89. Co-author: The Shreveport Plan: An Experiment in the Delivery of Legal Services, 1974. Mem. dist. com. Nancy J. Stivers Meml. Fund, Honolulu, 1984—; bd. dirs. Hawaii Pub. Radio, Honolulu, 1991—, chmn., 1995-2000; mem. Hawaii State Jud. Conf., 1987-90; 1st vice chmn. Hawaii Rep. Party, 1989-93, chmn. rules com., 1987-90, gen. counsel, 1993-2001; bd. dirs. Hawaii Women's Legal Found., 1987—, Ninth Jud. Cir. Hist. Soc., 1996—; mem. Hawaii State Reapportionment Com., 1991-92. Mem. ABA, Hawaii Bar Assn., Am. Law Inst. Office: US Court of Appeals 999 Bishop St #2010 Honolulu HI 96813*

CLIFTON, RUSSELL B., retired mortgage company executive, consultant; b. Maroa, Ill., Jan. 16, 1930; s. Russell Thomas and Clara Leoda (Luckenbill) C.; m. Mary Joyce Hartline, Oct. 10, 1948; 1 son, Steven Shawn. BA, Mich. State U., 1957. Bank auditor Arthur Andersen & Co., Detroit, 1957-59; v.p. Mich. Nat. Bank, Lansing, 1959-65; sr. v.p. Assoc. Mortgages Co., Kansas City, Mo., 1965-69; v.p. Fed. Nat. Mortgage Assn., Washington, 1969-85, ret., 1985; pres., chief exec. officer First Chesapeake Mortgage, Inc., Beltsville, Md., 1985-86, also bd. dirs.; cons. banking and mortgage lending, 1986—. Mem. adv. com. Home Owner's Warranty Corp., Washington, 1978-81; bd. dirs., mem. exec. com., treas. Nat. Acad. Conciliators, Washington, 1979-91; bd. dirs. Lincoln Savs. & Loan (now Seasons Savs. Bank), Richmond, Va., 1987-89; bd. dirs., treas. Nat. Ctr. for Dispute Settlements, Washington, 1987-91. Served with U.S. Army, 1952-54. Named disting. fellow Nat. Assn. Cert. Mortgages Bankers, 1975 Mem. Phi Kappa Phi, Beta Alpha Psi, Beta Gamma Sigma, Tau Sigma. Methodist.

CLIFTON, THOMAS E., academic administrator, minister; m. Audrey Vought; children: Sandra, Jill Clifton Mallard. Student, Duke Divinity Sch.; M in Divinity, Crozer Theol. Sem., Rochester, NY; MS in Personnel Counseling, Wright State U., Dayton; D in Ministry, Princeton Theol. Sem. Pastor First Bapt. Ch., Perry, Ohio, 1967-70, Sidney, Ohio, 1970-73; assoc. pastor Binkley Bapt. Ch., Chapel Hill, N.C., 1973-77; pastor First Bapt. Ch., Lafayette, Ind., 1977-85, Penifield, N.Y., 1985-93; pres. Ctrl. Bapt.

Theol. Seminary, Kansas City, Kans., 1993—2003. Writer: Bapt. Leader, Capitol Report; (curriculum) Judson Press. Office: Ctrl Bapt Theol Sem 741 N 31st St Kansas City KS 66102-3964

CLIJSTERS, KIM, retired professional tennis player; b. Bilzen, Belgium, June 8, 1983; m. Brian Lynch, July 13, 2007. Profl. tennis player WTA, 1999—2007. Winner 32 singles, 11 doubles tennis tournaments including Luxembourg, 1999, Hobart, Leipzig, 2000, Stanford, Leipzig, Luxembourg, 2001, Hamburg, Filderstadt, Luxembourg, 2002, Sydney, Indian Wells, Rome, Rosmalen, Stanford, Los Angeles, Filderstadt, Luxembourg, 2003, Paris, Antwerp, 2004, Indian Wells, Miami, Eastbourne, Stanford, Los Angeles, Toronto, 2005, US Open, 2005, J&S Cup, 2006, Bank of the West Classic, 2006, Gaz de France Stars, 2006,Medibank Internat., 2007; finalist Bratislava, 1999, Filderstadt, 2000, Roland Garros, Indian Well's, Hertogenbosch, 2001; recipient Karen Krantzcke Sportsmanship award, 2005-2006, WTA Player Awards Office: Ste 1500 1 Prospect Plaza Saint Petersburg FL 33701-1500*

CLIMAN, RICHARD ELLIOT, lawyer; b. NYC, July 19, 1953; s. David Arthur and Mary (Vitale) C. AB cum laude, Harvard U., 1974, JD cum laude, 1977. Bar: Calif. 1977. Assoc. Pettit & Martin, San Francisco, 1977-83, ptnr., 1984-94; ptnr., head mergers and acquisitions group Cooley Godward Kronish LLP, Palo Alto, San Francisco, Calif., 1994—. Co-chair Doing Deals Practising Law Inst., 1997-2002, Tech. Mergers and Acquisitions Inst. Glasser LegalWorks, 1999-2001, The New Era in Tech. M&A, 2006; adv. bd. BNA Mergers & Acquisitions Law Report; exec. com. Securities Reg. Inst., Corp. Counsel Ctr., Sch. Law Northwestern U.; lectr. and panelist in field. Contbr. articles to profl. jours. Named one of 500 Leading Lawyers in Am., Lawdragon, 2005, 2006, 100 Most Influential Lawyers in Am., Nat. Law Jour., 2006. Mem. ABA (sect. bus. law, chair com. on negotiated acquisitions 2002-06, co-chair Nat. Inst. on Negotiating Bus. Acquisitions 2003—). Home: 1 Tulip Ln San Carlos CA 94070-1551 Office: Cooley Godward Kronish LLP 5 Palo Alto Sq 3000 El Camino Real Palo Alto CA 94306-2120 Home Phone: 650-594-1641; Office Phone: 650-843-5174. E-mail: rcliman@cooley.com.*

CLIMER, KAREN ELISE, not-for-profit fundraiser; b. Orlando, Fla., July 1, 1977; d. Ronnie Duncan Climer and Frances Mary Demetre. MusB, U. Ala., Tuscaloosa, 1999; MBA, Rollins Coll., Winter Pk., Fla., 2007. Devel. asst. Orlando Opera, 2000—01; dir. ann. giving Art and Culture Ctr., Hollywood, Fla., 2001—02; sales rep. Tempus Resorts Internat., Orlando, 2002—03; ann. giving coord. BETA Ctr., Orlando, Fla., 2006—. Real estate instr., Fla., 2003—. Mem. adv. bd. dist. 3 Orange County Pks. and Recreation, Fla., 2005—07; bd. dirs. Negro-Spiritual Scholarship-Found., Orlando, 2003—04; vol. Leadership Winter Pk., Fla., 2006—07, Heart of Fla. United Way, Orlando, 2006. Mem.: Assn. Fundraising Profl., Toastmasters Internat. (pres. 2000—). Democrat. Roman Catholic.

CLINARD, KEITH A., lawyer; b. High Point, NC, Feb. 25, 1954; BA cum laude, Wake Forest U., 1976, JD cum laude, 1979. Bar: NC 1979, US Dist Ct. Mid. Dist. NC, US Dist. Ct. We. Dist. NC, US Ct. Appeals 4th Cir. Mem. Womble Carlyle Sandridge & Rice PLLC, Winston-Salem, NC, chair product liability litig. practice group. Mem.: ABA, NC Assn. Def. Attorneys (bd. dirs. 1989—92), Forsyth County Bar Assn., NC Bar Assn. Office: Womble Carlyle Sandridge & Rice PLLC PO Box 84 Winston Salem NC 27102 Office Phone: 336-721-3631. Office Fax: 336-733-8376. Business E-Mail: kclinard@wcsr.com.

CLINCH, NICHOLAS BAYARD, III, small business owner; b. Evanston, Ill., Nov. 9, 1930; s. Nicholas Bayard Jr. and Virginia Lee (Campbell) C.; m. Elizabeth Wallace Campbell, July 11, 1964; children: Lee Bridges, Alison Campbell. Student, N.Mex. Mil. Inst., Roswell, 1948-49; AB, Stanford U., 1952, LLB, 1955. Bar: Calif. 1959. Expedition leader First Ascent, Gasherbrum I (26,470 ft.), Pakistan, 1958, First Ascent, Masherbrum (25,660 ft.), Pakistan, 1959-60; assoc. Voegelin, Barton, Harris & Callister, LA, 1961-68; pvt. practice Washington, 1968-70; v.p., counsel Lincoln Savs. & Loan Assn., LA, 1970-74; exec. dir. Sierra Club Found., San Francisco, 1975-81; environ. cons. Fluor Corp., Grass Valley, Calif., 1981-84; v.p., sec. CCA, Inc., Denver, 1984—. Bd. dirs. Growth Stock Outlook Inc., Potomac, Md.; mem. adv. bd. Lowell Obs. Author: A Walk in the Sky, 1982. Leader Am. Antarctic Mountaineering Expdn., Sentinel Range, 1966-67; co-leader Chinese Am. Ulugh Muztagh Expdn., Kun Lun Range, Xinjiang, 1985, Am. Expdns. to Kang Karpo Range, Yunnan-Tibet border, 1988, 89, 92, 93; co-founder, trustee Calif. League Conservation Voters, San Francisco, 1972-97; bd. dirs. Environ. Law Inst., 1981-86, Recreational Equipment Inc., 1985-91, 93-2001. 1st lt. USAF, 1956-57. Recipient John Oliver La Gorce medal Nat. Geog. Soc., Washington, 1967. Fellow Royal Geog. Soc., Explorers Club; mem. ABA, Am. Alpine Club (hon., pres. 1967-70, Gold medal 2006), Appalachian Mountain Club (hon.), State Bar Calif., Roxburghe Club of San Francisco, Alpine Club (hon. London), Chinese Assn. Sci. Expdns. (hon.). Republican. Episcopalian. Avocations: mountain climbing, skiing, book collecting. Home: 2001 Bryant St Palo Alto CA 94301-3714 Office: CCA Inc 220 Josephine St 200 Denver CO 80206

CLINE, ALLEN LEE, endocrinologist, medical educator; b. New Madison, Ohio, Dec. 3, 1934; s. William Ora Cline and Marjoria Ellen Clark; m. Barbara Faye Clendenin, Aug. 25, 1963; children: Jonathan Allen, Elisabeth Leigh, Steven Matthew, Bonny Johanna. BS, Baldwin-Wallace Coll., 1957; MD, Harvard U., 1961. Diplomate Am. Bd. Internal Medicine, Am. Bd. Endocrinology. Intern Buffalo (N.Y.) Gen. Hosp., 1961—62; resident Univ. Hosps., Cleve., 1962—64; fellow metabolism Yale-New Haven (Conn.) Hosp., 1966—67; resident Boston (Mass.) City Hosp., 1967—68; pvt. practice endocrinology Dayton, Ohio, 1968—85; dir. internal medicine residency program Miami Valley Hosp./Wright State U., Dayton, 1985—97; assoc. dir. internal med. residency program Kettering (Ohio) Med. Ctr., 1999—, mem. endocrinology practice, 1999—. With USPHS, 1964—66. Fellow: ACP. Office: Kettering Med Ctr Network 3535 Southern Blvd Kettering OH 45429 Office Phone: 937-395-8693. Personal E-mail: allencline@aol.com.

CLINE, ANDREW HALEY, lawyer; b. Fountain Hill, Pa, Nov. 30, 1951; s. William Matthew and Eleanor Mary (Bosich) m. Sharon (Harlan) C.; children: Haley Andrea, Catherine Anne. BA, Guilford Coll., 1973; JD, U. Ala., 1978. Bar: Pa. 1978, U.S. Dist. Ct. (mid. dist.) Pa. 1982, U.S. Ct. (ea. dist.) 1989, U.S. Ct. Appeals (3rd cir.) 1988, U.S. Supreme Ct. 1990. Law clk. Commonwealth Ct. Pa., Harrisburg, 1978—80; asst. counsel Dept. Transp., Harrisburg, 1980—86; assoc. dep. gen. counsel Gov. Office, Harrisburg, 1986—87, dep. gen. counsel, 1987—89; assoc. Kirkpatrick & Lockhart, LLP, Harrisburg, 1989—91, ptnr., 1992—2001; dep. gen. counsel Gov. Office, Harrisburg, 2001—02; dep. chief counsel Dept. Transp., Harrisburg, Pa., 2003. Editor-in-chief Ala. Law Rev., 1978. Named one of Outstanding Young Men Am. Jaycees, 1978. Mem. Fed. Bar Assn. (pres. Ctrl. Pa. chpt. 1994-95, nat. del. 1995-97), Pa. Bar Assn., Dauphin County Bar Assn. (chmn. continuing legal edn. com. 1992-95, bd. dirs. 1993-95, chmn. govt. law sect. 1994, sec. 1996), Bench and Bar Soc., Am. Inns of Ct. (master emeritus J.S. Bowman chpt.), St. Thomas More Soc. (bd. dirs. 1997-98), Omicron Delta Kappa. Avocation: photography. Office: Office Chief Counsel PO Box 8212 Harrisburg PA 17105-8212 Home Phone: 717-774-4906; Office Phone: 717-787-5473. Business E-Mail: acline@state.pa.us.

CLINE, BOBBY JAMES, insurance company executive; b. Floydada, Tex., Mar. 12, 1932; s. Howard O. and Carrie (Tomlinson) C.; m. Martha Nolen, May 29, 1954; children: Carolyn, Pamela, Millie, Robert, Sean. BBA, U. Tex., 1954. Casualty underwriter Ins. Co. N.Am., Dallas, 1956-59; account exec./ptnr. Munger-Moore & Assocs., Dallas, 1959-68; ptnr. Harris-Moore & Assocs., Dallas, 1968-70; sr. v.p. Alexander & Alexander Inc., Dallas, 1970-72, exec. v.p., 1972-77, pres., 1977-96, vice chmn. bd.; exec. v.p. Aon Risk Svcs. Tex., Dallas, 1997-2000; chmn. bd. Tex. Banc Ptnr., Inc., Tex., 2000—05; ptnr. Tex Cap Ins.-Concord Ins., Dallas, 2005—. Bd. dirs. Vision Bank. Served with USN, 1954-56. Mem. Soc. CPCUs (dir.), U. Tex. Ex-Students Assn. (past pres.), Salesmanship Club, Preston Trail Golf Club, Dallas Club, Dallas Athletic Club, Garland Toastmasters, Riverhill Country Club. Baptist. Avocations: golf, hunting. Home: 1944 Wynn Joyce Rd Garland TX 75043-2542 Office: Tex Cap Ins 4100 McEwen Ste 270 Dallas TX 75244 Office Phone: 972-720-5363. Personal E-mail: bcline@texcap-concord.com.

CLINE, ERIC H., archaeologist, anthropologist, classicist, educator; married; 2 children. BA, Dartmouth Coll.; MA in Near Eastern Archaeology, Yale U.; PhD in Ancient History, U. Pa. Tchr. Stanford U., Xavier U., U. Cin., Calif. State U., Fresno; chair Dept. Classical and Semitic Languages and Lit. George Washington U., assoc. prof. Classics / Semitics dept. and Anthropology dept. Sr. staff archaeologist, dir. George Washington U. Archeol. Field Sch.; co-dir. archeol. excavations in Tel Kabri, Israel. Author: Sailing the Wine-Dark Sea: International Trade and the Late Bronze Age Aegean, 1994, The Battles of Armageddon: Megiddo and the Jezreel Valley from the Bronze Age to the Nuclear Age, 2000, Jerusalem Besieged: From Ancient Canaan to Modern Israel, 2004; co-author: Amenhotep III: Perspectives on his Reign, 1998, The Aegean and the Orient in the Second Millennium BC, 1998, Thutmose III: A New Biography, 2005, The Ancient Egyptian World, 2005; contbr. articles to profl. jours. Recipient Morton Bender Award, 2004, Nat. Excellence in Undergraduate Tchg., Archeol. Inst. Am., 2005. Mem.: Am. Schs. of Oriental Rsch. (bd. trustees), Archeol. Inst. Am. (Excellence in Undergraduate Tchg. Award 2005). Office: George Washington U 345 Phillips Hall, 801 22nd St, NW Washington DC 20052 Office Phone: 202-994-0316. Office Fax: 202-994-2156. E-mail: ehcline@gwu.edu.

CLINE, JANICE CLAIRE, education educator; b. Wausau, Wis., Aug. 22, 1945; m. Brent Buell, Jan. 28, 1979. BS, U. Wis., Madison, 1967; MA, NYU, NYC, 1972. Tchr. Hyde Park HS, Chgo., 1967-69; instr. JOB tng. program Chase Manhattan Bank, NYC, 1969-71; adj. lectr. N.Y.C. CC CUNY, Bklyn., 1971-72; evaluator title I evaluation team York Coll., Jamaica, 1972—, lectr. Lectr. in field; spkr. in field. Contbr. articles to profl. jours. Coord. Conf. Support Liberation South Africa and Namibia York Coll., Jamaica, 1985, coord. Student/Faculty Consortium Ctrl. Am., 1986. Recipient Outstanding Contbn. award, Conf. African People, 1986. Mem.: AAUP, Nat. Action Network, Nat. Coun. Tchrs. English, Am. Fedn. Tchrs. (del. 2000—), Internat. Reading Assn., Profl. Staff Congress (sr. coll. officer, exec. com. 2002—06, chpt. chmn. 2002—), CUNY Women's Coalition. Office: CUNY York Coll Dept English 94-20 Guy R Brewer Blvd Jamaica NY 11451-0001

CLINE, JOHN CARROLL, psychologist; b. Staunton, Va., Sept. 6, 1955; s. Carroll Hubert and Naomi Edith (Hevener) C.; m. Diane Jeannette Goudreau, May 21, 1983; 1 child, Virginia Goudreau Cline. BA, U. Va., 1977; PhD, U. Toledo, 1984. Lic. psychologist, Conn.; cert. biofeedback; clin. assoc. Am. Bd. Med. Psychotherapists; diplomate Am. Acad. Pain Mgmt., Am. Acad. Sleep Medicine. Psychology intern U. Toledo, 1980-81; predoctoral intern VA Med. Ctr., West Haven, Conn., 1981-82, attending psychologist, 1984-85; clinician Alcohol Svcs. Orgn., New Haven, 1982-85; team leader, staff psychologist Elmcrest Hosp., Portland, Conn., 1985-86, asst. unit chief, 1986, dir. behavioral medicine svc., 1986-90; pvt. practice psychologist Hamden, Conn., 1986-94; dir. adult outpatient svcs. Inst. of Living, Hartford, Conn., 1990-93; psychol. svcs. cons. Hamden, Conn., 1994—; clin. dir. dept. counseling and psychiat. svcs. Grove Hill Med. Ctr., New Britain, Conn., 1994-2000, chair quality assurance & outcomes mgmt. dept. psychiat. svcs., 1995-2000; psychologist Gaylord Hosp., Wallingford, Conn., 2000—06, sleep psychologist, 2006—; cons. Conn. Edn. Svcs., Middletown, 2000—; pvt. practice Affiliated Clin. Therapists, Middletown, 1999—2002; sleep psychologist Gaylord Sleep Medicine, North Haven, 2006—. Clin. affiliate Yale Psychol. Svcs. Clinic, Yale U., New Haven, 1985—; cons. psychologist VA Med. Ctr., West Haven, 1985—91; asst. prof. clin. psychiatry U. Conn. Med. Sch., Farmington, Conn., 1991—94; adj. asst. prof. phys. therapy, orthop. phys. therapy program Sch. Grad. and Continuing Edn. Quinnipiac U., Hamden, Conn., 1992—2006; sr. cons. network devel. Inst. of Living, Hartford, 1993—94; affiliate clin. faculty, Grad. Inst. Profl. Psychology U. Hartford, Conn., 1997—99, 2001—06; asst. prof. clin. psychiatry, dept. psychiatry Yale U. Sch. Medicine, New Haven, 2002—. Mem. mission study com. 1st Presbyn. Ch., New Haven, 1990-91; mem. Conn. Coun. Mental Health Providers, 1993-96, chair, 1993-94. Fellow Conn. Psychol. Assn. (chair hosp. practice com. 1990-92, practice directorate coord. 1993, pres.-elect 1994, pres. 1995-96, past pres. 1997); mem. AAAS, APA (coun. rep. 1997-99), N.Y. Acad. Scis., Assn. Psychiat. Clinics of Conn. (mem. polit. com. 1993-94, mem. edn. com. 1993-94), Soc. Behavioral Medicine, Am. Pain Soc. Home: 4 Lamkin St Hamden CT 06517-3309 Office: Gaylor Sleep Medicine Gaylord Hosp PO Box 400 Gaylord Farm Rd Wallingford CT 06492-7048 Office Phone: 203-741-3474. Personal E-mail: jcclineusa@netscape.net.

CLINE, MICHAEL ROBERT, lawyer; b. Parkersburg, W.Va., Oct. 13, 1949; s. Robert Rader and Hazel Mae (Boice) C.; m. Carole R. Davis, Aug. 28, 1972. AB, Morris Harvey Coll., 1972; JD, Wake Forest U., 1975. Project coord. Gov.'s Office Fed.-State Rels., Charleston, W.Va., 1970-72; spl. asst. W.Va. Office Econ. Opportunity, 1973; spl. asst. W.Va.-Dept. Labor, Charleston, 1974; staff asst., hearing officer, 1975-77; sole practice, Charleston, 1977—. Mem. ABA, ATLA, Comml. Law League Am., So. Mems. Assn. (bd. dirs.), Nat. Assn. Criminal Def. Lawyers, W.Va. Trial Lawyers Assn. (bd. dirs. 1982—, treas. 1984, v.p. 1985-86, Outstanding Mem. 1983), W.Va. State Bar (chmn. com. on econs. of law practice 1986, 91-92), W.Va. Bar Found., Elks, Rotary, Pi Kappa Delta, Phi Alpha Delta. Republican. Methodist. Home: 1531 Dixie St Charleston WV 25311-1903 Office: 323 Morrison Bldg Charleston WV 25301 Office Phone: 304-343-5001. Personal E-mail: mcline@mountain.net. Business E-mail: mcline@clinelaw.com.

CLINE, NANCY M., librarian, department chairman; b. Chambersburg, Pa., Sept. 21, 1946; d. Gerald E. and Mary Jane (Koons) C.; m. Laurence Hettich, Dec. 28, 1983; 1 child, Jennifer. AB in English, U. Calif., Berkeley, 1968, MLS in Librarianship, 1970. Pa. documents libr. Pa. State U., University Park, 1970-71, head govt. documents sect., 1971-80, chief bibliographic resources dept., 1980-84, asst. dean, head bibliographic resources and svcs. div., 1984-88, dean univ. librs., 1988—96; Roy E. Larsen libr. Harvard Coll., Cambridge, Mass., 1996—; chmn. Library Digital Initiative Harvard U., Cambridge, Mass., chmn. Widener Renovation Project planning com. Bd. trustees JSTOR; adv. bd. Carnegie Mellon U. Libraries; editl. bd. Encyclopedia Libr. & Info. Sci.; mem. adv. coun. Princeton U. Univ. Libr.; mem. adv. bd. for academic services Carnegie Mellon U. Mem. ALA (Document to the People award 1983, Atkinson Meml. award 2006), Pa. Libr. Assn., Golden Key Hon. Soc. (hon.), Assn. Rsch. Librs. (task force on govt. info. in electronic format 1986-88, chair task force on telecom. 1989-91, info. policy com. 1990-93, rep. nat. steering com. coalition for networked info. 1990-94, bd. dirs. 1992-94, pres.-elect 1994-95), Rsch. Librs. Group (bd. govts. 1988-92, chair fin. and adminstrn. com. 1991-92). Office: Office of the Librarian HCL Widener Libr Rm 110 Harvard Yard Cambridge MA 02138 Office Phone: 617-495-2401. Office Fax: 617-496-4750. E-mail: ncline@fas.harvard.edu.

CLINE, PHILIP J., police superintendent; b. Oct. 10, 1949; m. Kathleen A. Cline. BA, Lewis U., 1993, BA, 1997. With Chgo. Police Dept., 1968—, detective, 1972—77, sgt., 1977—85, lt., 1985—94, comdr. Area 5 Detectives Divsn., 1994—98, comdr. Narcotics & Gang Investigations Sect., 1998—2000, dep. chief organized crime unit, 2000—01, chief of detectives, 2001—03, acting supt., 2003, supt., 2003—. Bd. mem. Ill. Criminal Justice Authority. Achievements include development of the Chicago police department street corner conspiracy initiative. Office: Chicago Police Dept 3510 South Michigan Ave Chicago IL 60653

CLINE, PHILIP LEE, business and economics educator; b. Oklahoma City, Okla., July 10, 1945; s. Maurice Lee and Natha Louise (Craig) C.; m. Julia Ann Semtner, June 8, 1968; children: Benjamin Lee, Susan Elizabeth. BA, Washington and Lee U., 1967; MS, Okla. State U., 1973, PhD, 1975. Assoc. systems engr. IBM, Tulsa, Okla., 1967-69, mktg. rep., 1969-70; rsch. assoc. Okla. State U., Stillwater, 1970-75; from asst. prof. to prof. econs. Washington and Lee U., Lexington, Va., 1975—, head dept. mgmt., 1990-95, The Lewis Whitaker Adams prof. econs. and mgmt., 1995—. Cons. Resources for the Future, Washington, 1975, USDA, Washington, 1975; North River Assocs., Lexington, 1986; bd. dirs Lexington Golf and Country Club. Contbr. articles to profl. jours. Vol. Rockbridge Area Habitat for Humanity. Recipient Outstanding Faculty award Va. Coun. Higher Edn.; grantee Ford Found., 1974, John M. Glenn, 1976, '82, NSF, 1977, '78; Fulbright Sr. Fellow, Trinidad, Tobago, 2000. Mem. Am. Statis. Assn., Am. Mgmt. Assn., Am. Econs. Assn., Beta Gamma Sigma, Omicron Delta Epsilon, Phi Kappa Phi. Office: Washington Lee U Lexington VA 24450

CLINE, RUTH ELEANOR HARWOOD, translator, historian; b. Middletown, Conn., Oct. 31, 1946; d. Burton Henry and Eleanor May (Cash) Harwood; A.B., Smith Coll., 1968; M.A., Rutgers U., 1969; Ph.D., Georgetown U., 2000; cert. translation from French, Georgetown U., 1978; m. William R. Cline, June 10, 1967; children: Alison, Marian. Reviewer, U.S. Dept. State, Washington, 1979-94. Former v.p. Smith Coll. Class of 1968; rsch. assoc. dept. history Georgetown U., 2002-. Mem. Am. Translators Assn. (cert. in French, Spanish and Portuguese), MLA, Internat. Arthurian Soc. Episcopalian. Translator English verse: Yvain; or the Knight with the Lion (Chretien de Troyes), 1975; Perceval; or the Story of the Grail (Chretien de Troyes), 1983, Lancelot or the Knight of the Cart (Chretien de Troyes), 1990 (Lewis Galantiere Prize 1992), Erec and Enide (Chretien de Troyes), 2000, Cliges (Chretien de Troyes), 2000, also articles. Home: 5315 Oakland Rd Chevy Chase MD 20815-6638

CLINE, TERRY L., federal agency administrator; b. Ardmore, Okla., July 31, 1958; B in Psychology, U. Okla., 1980; M in Clin. Psychology, Okla. State U., PhD. Clin. instr. dept. psychiatry Harvard Med. Sch., Boston; staff psychologist McLean Hosp., Belmont, Maine; clin. dir. cmty. health ctr. Cambridge, Mass.; commr. Okla. Dept. Mental Health and Substance Abuse Svcs., Oklahoma City, 2001—04; sec. health State of Okla., Oklahoma City, 2004—06; adminstr. Substance Abuse and Mental Health Svcs. Adminstrn. (SAMSHA), US Dept. Health & Human Services, Rockville, Md., 2006—. Office: Substance Abuse and Mental Health Svcs Adminstrn 1 Choke Cherry Rd Rockville MD 20857*

CLINE, THOMAS WARREN, geneticist, educator; b. Oakland, Calif., May 6, 1946; married, 1986. AB, U. Calif. Berkeley, 1968; PhD in Biochemistry, Harvard U., 1973. Fellow devel. genetics Helen Hay Whitney Found., U. Calif. Irvine, 1973-76; from asst. to prof. biology Princeton U., 1976-90; prof. genetics and devel. U. Calif. Berkeley, 1990—. Recipient Molecular Biology award NAS, 1992. Fellow AAAS, Am. Acad. Arts and Scis.; mem. U.S. Nat. Acad. Scis., Genetics Soc. Am. Achievements include research in development regulation of gene expression in Drosophila melanogaster with emphasis on oogenesis, sex determination, and X-chromosome dosage compensation. Office: U Calif 16 Barker Hall MC 3204 Berkeley CA 94720-3204 Office Phone: 510-643-5632.

CLINE, THOMAS WILLIAM, real estate leasing company executive, management consultant; b. Flint, Mich., Oct. 17, 1932; s. Leo D. and Helen (Wolohan) C.; m. Joanne Greiner, July 18, 1959; children: Robert Arthur, Thomas John, Mary Elizabeth. BS, U. Detroit, 1954, JD, 1956. Bar: Mich. 1957. Gen. atty. Wickes Corp., Saginaw, Mich., 1958-61, sec., gen. counsel, 1961-69, sr. v.p., gen. counsel, 1969-71, sr. v.p., sec., 1971-80, dir., 1964-70, 74-80; sr. v.p., group officer, dir. Wickes Cos. Inc., Saginaw, 1980-83; pres. Cline Mgmt. Co., Saginaw, 1983—; pres., COO Signature Corp., Chgo., 1984-85; exec. v.p., COO Seitner Bros. Inc., Saginaw, 1986—2004. Bd. dirs. Mid-Am. Life Assurance Co., Mich. Nat. Bank, Saginaw, Can. West Fin. Svcs.(U.S.) Inc., Aristar Inc. Chmn. fin. com. Diocese of Saginaw, 1970-72; chmn. Saginaw Cath. Schs. Study Com., 1969, Nat. assn. Boys Clubs Am.; bd. dirs. San Diego Symphony Assn., 1975-78, Econ. devel. Corp. San Diego County, 1975-78, also vice-chmn., Saginaw Japanese Cultural Ctr. and Tea House; vice chmn. Boys Clubs San Diego, 1975-77; trustee Saginaw Gen. Hosp. Assn., 1971-72, 73-75; trustee, fin. chmn. Saginaw Coop. Hosp. Inc., 1972; trustee, v.p. United Way of Saginaw County; bd. fellows Saginaw Valley Coll., 1973-75, chmn. bus. fund dr., 1978; mem. adv. bd. Delta Coll., U. San Diego, 1975-78, San Diego State U. Bus. Sch., 1975-78, Saginaw Art Mus., 1986-94; mem. instnl. rev. bd. Saginaw Valley State U., 2002-07; mem. fin. com. Diocese San Diego, 1975-78; bd. dirs. Mich. State C. of C., 1973-75, Saginaw Symphony Assn. 1984-88, also v.p.; chmn. Saginaw Met. Area Nat. Alliance of Bus., 1979-80; bd. dirs. San Diego C. of C., 1976-77; ann. programs fund stategic advisor Rotary Found., 2001-03; pres. Big Creek Fishing Lodge, 2000-03; bd. dirs. Saginaw Hall of Fame, 2005—, Saginaw Valley State U. Humanities Series. With U.S. Army, 1956-58. Mem. Mich. Bar Assn., Mich. Mfrs. Assn. (bd. dirs. 1980-88), U.S. C. of C. (adv. com.), Saginaw Club (bd. dirs., v.p. 1991), Serra Club Saginaw County (pres., bd. dirs.), Rotary (pres. Saginaw 1990-91, dist. gov. 1994-95, chair dist. found.1996-2000, del. coun. on legis. 1998, nat. advisor to Rotary Found. 2001-03), Blue Key Soc., Delta Sigma Pi, Beta Alpha Psi, Delta Theta Pi. Home and Office: 4640 Ashland Dr Saginaw MI 48603-4605

CLINE, THOMAS WILLIAM, prosecutor; s. James William and Juanita Ernestine Cline; m. Mary Jean Lynch, June 22, 1968; children: Barbara, Terry, Rose. A, Columbia Coll., Mo., 1981; BS in Bus. Adminstrn., Park Coll., Parkville, Mo., 1986; JD, U. Mo., Columbia, 1988. Bar: Mo., Ark. Enforcement officer Audrain County Health Dept., Mexico, Mo., 1973—74; chief dep. sheriff Audrain County, Mexico, 1974—78; county investigator Audrain County P.A., Mexico, 1978—79; pub. works dir. City Mountain Grove, Mo., 1979—81; county investigator Wright County Pros. Office, Mountain Grove, 1981—86; para-legal, law clk. Law Office of Milt Harper, Columbia, 1986—88; pros. atty. Ozark County, Gainesville, Mo., 1989—94, 1998—. Chmn. Citizen's Adv. Com. Family Care and Counseling, Mountain Grove, 1986. V.p. SW Mo. Water and Sewerage Conf., 1986; bd. mem. Child Adv. Coun., Mo., Mountain Grove, 1986, Child Fatality Rev. Team, 1998—. With US Army, 1972—73. Named one of, Outstanding Young Men of Am., 1981, 1984. Mem.: Nat. Dist. Atty. Assn., Mo. Archeol. Soc. Republican. Avocations: fishing, hunting, motorcycling, scuba diving. Office: Ozark County Pros Atty 115 U Hwy Gainesville MO 65655

CLINE, WILLIAM CHAMBERS, automotive executive; b. Elmhurst, Ill., June 15, 1949; s. William Herbert and Polly (Stevens) C.; m. Linda Blair, July 3, 1971; children: Polly Hayes, Sarah McGavock, William Crockett, Blair Chambers. AB, Duke U., 1971; MM, Northwestern U., 1974. CPA, Ill. Audit staff Arthur Young, Chgo., 1974-79, audit mgr., 1979-82; mgr. Borg-Warner Inc., Chgo., 1982-85; asst. controller, 1985-93, v.p., contr., 1993—2004, acting CFO, 2003—04, v.p. acquisition coordination, 2005—. Mem. AICPAs, Ill. Soc. CPAs, Chgo. Athletic Assn. Avocations: horse racing, golf. Office: Borg-Warner Corp 200 S Michigan Ave Ste 1700 Chicago IL 60604-2460

CLINE, WILLIAM RICHARD, economist, educator; b. Denver, Oct. 30, 1941; s. John Russell and Marian Alice (Franklin) C.; m. Ruth Eleanor Harwood, June 10, 1967; children: Alison Margaret, Marian Harwood. AB Pub Affairs summa cum laude, Princeton U., Princeton U., 1963; MA in Econs., Yale U., 1964, PhD, 1969. Lectr. Princeton U., 1967-69, asst. prof., 1969-70; Ford Found. vis. prof. Brazilian Planning Ministry and U. Sao Paulo, 1970-71; dep. dir. trade and devel. research U.S. Treasury Dept., Washington, 1971-73; sr. fellow Brookings Instn., Washington, 1973-81, Inst. for Internat. Econs., Washington, 1982—; pres. Econs. Internat., Inc., Washington, 1981—; dep. mng. dir., chief economist Inst. Internat. Fin., Washington, 1996—2001; sr. fellow Ctr. for Global Devel., Washington, 2002—. Professorial lectr. Johns Hopkins Sch. Internat. Studies, 1981-82, 84; vis. lectr. Princeton U., 1983, 85; vis. prof. Aoyama Gakuin U., Tokyo, 1992-94; adv. bd. U.S. Export-Import Bank, 1986-87. Author: Economic Consequences of a Land Reform in Brazil, 1970, Potential Effects of Income Redistribution, 1972, Trade Negotiations in the Tokyo Round, 1978, World Inflation and the Developing Countries, 1981, International Debt: Systemic Risk and Policy Response, 1984, The U.S.-Japan Economic Problem, 1985, Exports of Manufactures From Developing Countries, 1984, The Future of World Trade in Textiles and Apparel, 1987, Informatics and Development, 1987, United States External Adjustment and the World Economy, 1989, The Economics of Global Warming, 1992, International Economic Policy in the 1990s, 1994, International Debt Reexamined, 1995, Trade and Income Distribution, 1997, Trade Policy and Global Poverty, 2004, The United States as a Debtor Nation, 2005, Global Warming and Agriculture, 2007. Woodrow Wilson fellow, 1964, Ford Found. fellow, 1965; recipient Harold and Margaret Sprout award Internat. Studies Assn., 1993. Mem. Am. Econ. Assn., Council Fgn. Relations. Episcopalian. Office: Inst Internat Econs 1750 Massachusetts Ave NW Washington DC 20036-1903 Office Phone: 202-416-0726. E-mail: wcline@cgdev.org.

CLINES, FRANCIS X., journalist; b. Bklyn. Attended, St. Francis Coll., Fordham Univ., St. John's Univ. News clk. to Long Island corr. NY Times, 1958—70, legis. reporter, Albany bur., 1970—73, bur. chief, Albany, 1973—76, About NY columnist, 1976—79, White House reporter Washington, 1979—86, reporter, London bur., 1986—89, bur. chief, corr., Moscow, 1989—92, now nat. corr., Washington bur., and editl. bd. mem., 2002—. Author: (collection of columns) About New York, 1980. Recipient Meyer Berger award for feature writing, Columbia Univ., 1979, Deadline Writing award, Am. Soc. Newspaper Editors, 1988, George Polk award, 1992. Office: Editorial Board NY Times 229 W 43rd St New York NY 10036 Office Phone: 212-556-3917. Office Fax: 212-556-3815. Business E-Mail: fclines@nytimes.com.

CLINGAN, EDMUND, history professor; b. NYC, Oct. 12, 1962; s. Eldon Ray and Jo Ann Clingan. BA, Queens Coll., NYC, 1985; MA, U. Wis., Madison, 1987, PhD, 1991. Asst. prof. U. ND, 1995—2000, assoc. prof., 2000—04; prof. history CUNY Queensborough CC, Bayside. Author: Finance from Kaiser to Führer, 2001. Filbright scholar, USIA, 1988. Mem.: German Studies Assn., Am. Hist. Assn., Phi Alpha Theta, Phi Beta Kappa. Office: Dept History Queensborough Coll 222 05 56th Ave Bayside NY 11364

CLINGER, WILLIAM DOUGLAS, computer scientist, educator; b. Ft. Worth, June 8, 1954; BS in Math., U. Tex., Austin, 1973; PhD in Math., MIT, Cambridge, 1975—81. Asst. prof. Ind. U., Bloomington, 1981—85; prin. scientist Tektronix, Beaverton, Oreg., 1985—88; asst. prof. U. Oreg., Eugene, 1988—94; assoc. prof. Northeastern U., Boston, 1994—. Achievements include invention of algorithm for correctly rounded conversions from decimal to binary; efficient algorithm for hygienic macro expansion; older-first generational garbage collection. Avocation: music. Office: Northeastern Univ 360 Huntington Ave Boston MA 02115

CLINKENBEARD, JAMES HOWARD, principal; b. Alexandria, Va., Apr. 1, 1950; s. Howard Samuel and Ethel Jane (Schwager) C.; m. Janelle Darlene Turner, May 27, 1972; children: Adam James, Nathan Linton, Evan Joel. BS, Murray State U., 1977; MEd, Xavier U., 1985, postgrad., 1986—87, postgrad., 1989—92. Cert. tchr. and adminstr., Ky. Tchr. art Newport (Ky.) Ind. Schs., 1978-88, chief negotiator, 1985-88, asst. prin., 1988-91, 92-96, dir. Title V, 1991-92, acting prin., 1992, 94-95, prin., 1996—2006, ednl. svcs. coord., 2006—; freelance artist, designer Bellevue, Ky., 1977—. Juror various sch. and profl. art shows; speaker pub. sch. in-service programs. Featured in Kentucky Artist and Craftsman mag., 1977, Inside Kentucky Schools, Ky. Ednl. T.V., 2001; author various documents, ednl. reports. Active Bellevue Civic Assn., 1979—92; state advisor Ky. Imagination Celebration, 1984—85; advisor Ky. Task Force for Comprehensive Arts, 1984, Ky. Task Force on Acad. Competition, 1985; active Ft. Thomas and Newport PTAs, 1992—; chmn. Ky. Foster Care Rev. Bd., 1991—97, Sch. Based Decision Making Coun., 1996—2006; chair com. Ky. Rewards Category Sch., 1996—98, 1998—2000; deacon First Christian Ch., Ft. Thomas, Ky., 1976—, Sunday sch. tchr., 1976—97, chmn. bd., 1982—83, Sunday sch. tchr., 1999—2000; chmn. Citizens Bellevue Schs., 1980—81; bd. dirs. Ky. Citizens for the Arts in Edn., 1983—85; chmn. Arts Subcom, Coun. on Higher Edn., 1985—86; mem. select panel Ky. Disting. Educators Program, 1992—93; chair com. troop 70 Boy Scouts Am., 1997—2001, mem. trailblazer dist. adv. com., 2006—. Recipient commendation Ky. Supt. Pub. Instrn., 1984. Mem.: ASCD, NEA, Washington Evening Star Cartoonists Guild, Newport Adminstrs. Assn. (pres. 1994—97, 2001—), Newport Tchrs. Assn. (sec. 1982—83, vice chmn. polit. action com. 1984, treas. 1985—88, pres. 1988), Ky. Edn. Assn. (svcs. com. 1985—87, del. 1986—88, task force 1987—88), Ky. Art Edn. Assn. (various offices including pres. 1983—84, Project Art Tchr. award 1980), Nat. Art Edn. Assn. (Ky. del. 1976—77, 1981), Ft. Thomas Swim Club (bd. dirs. 1994—2000, pres. 1995—2000), Alpha Tau Omega (chpt. advisor 1987—91, chpt. housing corp. pres. 1993—, chpt. trustee 1995—). Republican. Mem. Christian Ch. (Disciples Of Christ). Avocations: reading, sports, working with children. Home: 30 Kathy Ln Fort Thomas KY 41075-1914 Office: Newport Ind Schs 301 E 8th St Newport KY 41071-1615 Personal E-mail: jclink.nky@fuse.net.

CLINKSCALE, MARTHA NOVAK, music educator, researcher; b. Akron, Ohio, June 16, 1933; d. Joseph John and Ophia May Novak; m. Alfred Thorpe Loeffler, Jr., Apr. 7, 1955 (div. Oct. 1966); children: Alfred Thorpe Loeffler III, Lise Morrison Loeffler-Welton; m. Edward Henry Clinkscale, Mar. 4, 1968 (dec. July 1994). MusB in Piano Performance, U. Louisville, 1953; MusM in Piano Performance, Yale U., 1955; PhD in Musicology, U. Minn., 1970. Music libr., accompanist Chaffey Coll., Alta Loma, Calif., 1965—68; vis. lectr. Calif. State U., San Bernardino, U. Redlands, Calif.; lectr. piano, fortepiano, chamber music U. Calif., Riverside, 1979—96; vis. lectr. Calif. State Poly. U., Pomona, 1989—90; adj. prof. fortepiano emerita So. Meth. U., Dallas, 1998—2004. Presenter in field. Author: Makers of the Piano 1700-1820, 1993, Makers of the Piano 1820-1860, 1999; editor: Jour. of the Am. Musical Instrument Soc., 1993—96; originator, editor: Early Pianos: 1700-1860: A Comprehensive Relational Database, 1983—; contbr. articles to profl. jours. Mem.: Western Early Keyboard Soc., Royal Mus. Assn., Soc. for Seventeenth-Century Music, Galpin Soc., Midwestern Hist. Keyboard Soc., Internat. Musicol. Soc., Internat. Coun. on Museums, Com. Internat. des Musées et Collections d'Instruments de Musique, Am. Musicol. Soc. (treas. Pacific SW chpt. 1985—87, v.p. Pacific SW chpt. 1990—92, mem. nat. chpt. fund com. 1991—94, pres. Pacific SW chpt. 1992—96, chair nat. chpt. fund com. 1993—94), Am. Musical Instrument Soc. (bd. govs. 1991—95), Am. Inst. Verdi Studies, Southeastern Hist. Keyboard Soc. (bd. mem. 1998—2003, chair nominating com. 2003—04, mem. jour. oversight com. 2003—, treas. 2004—), Sigma Alpha Iota, Pi Kappa Lambda.

CLINTON, BILL (WILLIAM JEFFERSON CLINTON), 42nd President of the United States; b. Hope, Ark., Aug. 19, 1946; s. Virginia Dell Cassidy and William Jefferson Blythe IV; m. Hillary Rodham, Oct. 11, 1975; 1 child, Chelsea Victoria. BS in Internat. Affairs, Georgetown U., 1968; postgrad., Oxford U., 1968-70; JD, Yale U., 1973; LHD (hon.), Pace U., 2006, U. NH, 2007. Prof. U. Ark. Sch. Law, Fayetteville, 1973-76; pvt. practice law, 1973-76; atty. gen. State of Ark., Little Rock, 1977-79, gov., 1979-81, 83-92; of counsel Wright, Lindsey & Jennings, Little Rock, 1981-82; pres. US, Washington, 1993-2001; spl. envoy for tsunami recovery UN, 2005—. Chmn. So. Growth Policies Bd., 1985-86. Author: Between Hope and History: Meeting America's Challenges for the 21st Century, 1996, My Life, 2004 (Grammy Award for Spoken Word Album, 2005, Publishers Weekly Bestseller, NY Times Bestseller, Biography of Yr., Brit. Book Awards, 2005, Audiobook of Yr., Audio Publ. Assn., 2005), Giving: How Each of Us Can Change the World, 2007; guest appearance The Fight to be Fit, Nick News, 2005. Chmn. Edn. Commn. of the States, 1986-87, mem. steering com.; mem. Task Force on Adolescent Edn., Carnegie Found.; chmn. Dem. Leadership Coun., 1990-91; hon. co-chair, Club of Madrid; co-chair, Families of Freedom Fund; chmn. Global Fairness Initiative; founder, Am. India Found., 2001-, hon. chair., advisory bd. co-chair, Internat. AIDS Trust Rhodes scholar U. Coll., Oxford U., 1968-70; named Knight Comdr. of the Most Courteous Order of Lesotho, 2005; named One of Most Influential People, TIME mag., 2005-06; recipient Jimmy and Rosalynn Carter award for humanitarian contributions to the health of humankind, Nat. Found. for Infectious Diseases, 2005, Pasteur Found. award, 2005, Citizen of the World award, UN Correspondents Assn., 2006; co-recipient Liberty medal, Nat. Constitution Ctr., 2006. Mem. ABA, Ark. Bar Assn., Nat. Govs. Assn. (vice chmn. 1986, chmn. 1986-87, exec. com., fin. com., com. on human resources, com. on internat. trade and fgn. rels., task force on rural devel., co-chmn. task force for edn. 1990-92); former chmn. Dem. Leadership Coun.; fellow Am. Acad. Arts & Sciences Democrat. Established the William J. Clinton Foundation, which includes the Clinton Presidential Center (library, foundation offices, and Clinton School of Public Service at the University of Arkansas) on November 18, 2004. The foundation's purpose is to focus on four major areas: health security; economic empowerment; leadership development and citizen service; and racial, ethnic and religious reconciliation. Office: William J Clinton Found 55 W 125th St New York NY 10027*

CLINTON, CHELSEA VICTORIA, financial consultant, former first daughter; b. Little Rock, Ark., Feb. 27, 1980; d. William Jefferson and Hillary Rodham Clinton. BA in Hist., Stanford U., 2001; MA in Internat. Rels., Oxford U., 2003. Cons. McKinsey & Co., 2003—06; joined Ave. Capital Grp., NYC, 2006—. Office: Avenue Capital Group 535 Madison Ave 15th Fl New York NY 10022*

CLINTON, EDWARD XAVIER, lawyer; b. Chgo., July 13, 1930; s. Michael Xavier and Mary Agnes (Joyce) Clinton; m. Margaret Mary Clinton, May 1, 1965 (div. Oct. 1978); 1 child, Edward Xavier Jr. Student, DePaul U., 1949-50; JD, John Marshall U., 1953. Bar: Ill. 1953, U.S. Dist. (no. dist.) ill. 1955, U.S. Ct. Appeals (7th cir.) 1955, U.S. Supreme Ct. 1995. Assoc. Schultz & Biro, Chgo., 1955-56; with securities dept. Ill. State Dept., Springfield, 1956-57; assoc. Hough, Young & Coale, Chgo., 1957-65, Keck, Mahin & Cate, Chgo., 1965 92; pvt. practice Chgo., 1992—. Instr. John Marshal Law Sch., Chgo., 1965—74; arbitrator N.Y. Stock Exch.; spkr. in field. Contbr. articles to profl. jours. Mem. adv. bd. Steppenwolf Theatre, Chgo., 1988—89, Chgo. Opera Theatre, 1983—88, Children's Care Found., v.p.; adv. bd. Little Sisters of Poor; pastoral coun. Holy Name Cathedral, 1989—94; bd. dirs. Records Mgmt. Svcs., 1996—97. With US Army, 1953—55. Postgrad. scholar, John Marshall Law Sch., 1953, John Jewell scholar, 1953. Mem.: ABA, Nat. Lawyers Assn., Bar Assn. 7th Cir., Chgo. Bar Assn., Ill. Bar Assn., Evanston Golf Club, Execs. Club Chgo. (bd. dirs. 1985—95), Union League Club, Mid Day Club, Lawyers Club Chgo., KC, Am. Legion, Rotary. Roman Catholic. Avocations: golf, prisoner appeals (pro bono). Home: 990 N Lake Shore Dr Chicago IL 60611-1366 Office: 19 S La Salle St Ste 1300 Chicago IL 60603-1406 Office Phone: 312-357-1515. Personal E-mail: eclinton@mac.com.

CLINTON, HILLARY (HILLARY DIANE RODHAM CLINTON), senator, lawyer, former First Lady of United States; b. Chgo., Oct. 26, 1947; d. Hugh Ellsworth and Dorothy (Howell) Rodham; m. William J. Clinton, Oct. 11, 1975; 1 child, Chelsea Victoria. BA in Polit. Sci., with high honors, Wellesley Coll., 1969; JD, Yale U., 1973; LLD (hon.), U. Ark., Little Rock, 1985, Ark. Coll., 1988, Hendrix Coll., 1992, U. Sunderland, 1993, U. Pa., 1993, U. Mich., 1993, U. Ill., 1994, U. Minn., 1995, San Francisco State U., 1995, U. Ulster, 2004; LLD, Marymount Manhattan Coll., 2005, Rensselaer Poly. Inst., 2005; D Pub. Svc. (hon.), George Washington U., 1994, U. Md., College Park, 1996; DHL (hon.), Drew U., 1996, Ohio U., 1997, Pace Univ., 2003, Manhattanville College, 2004. Bar: Ark. 1973, admitted to practice: US Dist. Ct. (Ea. Dist.) Ark. 1973, US Dist. Ct. (We. Dist.) Ark. 1973, US Ct. Appeals (8th Cir.) 1973, US Supreme Ct. 1975. Atty. Children's Def. Fund, Cambridge, Mass. and Washington, 1973-74; legal cons. Carnegie Coun. on Children, New Haven, 1973-74; counsel, impeachment inquiry staff Judiciary Com. US Ho. of Reps., Washington, 1974; asst. prof. law, dir. Legal Aid Clinic U. Ark. Sch. Law, Fayetteville, 1974-77, asst. prof. law Little Rock, 1979-80; ptnr. Rose Law Firm, Little Rock, 1977-92; First Lady of the US, 1993—2001; chair Presdl. Task Force on Nat. Health Care Reform, 1993; US Senator from NY, 2001— Com. security and cooperation in Europe US Senate, com. armed forces, com. environ. and public works, com. health, edn., labor and pensions, spl. com. on aging; candidate for Dem. party nomination 2008 Presidential Election, 2007—. Author: Handbook on Legal Rights for Arkansas Women, 1977, 87, It Takes a Village: And Other Lessons Children Teach Us, 1996, Dear Socks, Dear Buddy: Kids' Letters to the First Pets, 1998, An Invitation to the White House, 2000, Living History, 2003; syndicated columnist Talking It Over, 1995-2000; contbr. articles to profl. journals. Bd. dirs. Childrens Def. Fund, Washington, 1976-92, chair, 1986-91, Legal Svcs. Corp., Washington, 1977-81, chair, 1978-80; founder, pres., bd. dirs. Ark. Advs. for Children and Families, 1977-84; bd. dirs. Wal-Mart Stores, Inc., 1986-92, TCBY, 1986-92, Child Care Action Campaign, 1986-92, Nat. Ctr. on Edn. and the Economy, 1987-92, Ark. Children's Hosp., 1988-92, Franklin and Eleanor Roosevelt Inst., 1988-92, Children's TV Workshop, 1989-92, Public/Private Ventures, 1990-92; chmn. Ark. Edn. Stds. Com., 1983-84; mem. commn. on quality edn. So. Regional Edn. Bd., 1984-92; chair ABA Commn. on Women in the Profession, 1987-91; former hon. pres. Girl Scouts of Am.; mem. adv. bd. HIPPY, 1988-92, bd. dirs.; former hon. chair Pres.' Com. on the Arts and Humanities, US Del., UN Fourth World Conf. on Women, 1995; hon. mem. The Pen and Brush, 1996—; hon. chair, NY Acad. Sciences Gala, 2005. Named Outstanding Layman of Yr. Phi Delta Kappa, 1984, Health Educator of Yr., Ryan White Found., 1995; recipient Lewis Hine award Nat. Child Labor Law Com., 1993, Albert Schweitzer Leadership award Hugh O'Brian Youth Found., 1993, Iris Cantor Humanitarian award UCLA Med. Ctr., 1993, Friend of Family award Am. Home Econs. Assn., 1993, Charles Wilson Lee Citizen Svc. award Com. for Edn. Funding, 1993, Claude D. Pepper award Nat. Assn. for Home Care, 1993, Commitment to Life award AIDS Project LA, 1994, Disting. Svc., Health Edn. and Prevention award Nat. Ctr. for Health Edn., 1994, First Ann. Eleanor Roosevelt Freedom Fighter award, 1994, Brandeis award U. Louisville Sch. of Law, 1994, Social Justice award United Auto Workers, 1994, Ernie Banks Positivism trophy Emil Verban Meml. Soc., 1994, Humanitarian award Alzheimer's Assn., 1994, Elie Wiesel Found., 1994, Internat. Broadcasting award Hollywood Radio and TV Soc., 1994, Ellen Browning Scripps medal Scripps Coll., 1994, Disting. Pro Bono Svc. award San Diego Vol. Lawyer Program, 1994, HIPPY USA award, 1994, C. Everett Koop medal Am. Diabetes Assn., 1994, Women's Legal Def. Fund award, 1994, Martin Luther King, Jr. award Progressive Nat. Bapt. Conv., 1994, 30th Anniversary Women at Work award in Pub. Policy, Nat. Commn. on Working Women, 1994, Greater Washington Urban League award, 1995, Servant of Justice award NY Legal Aid Soc., 1995, Presdl. award Bklyn. Coll., 1995, Outstanding Mother award Nat. Mother's Day Com., 1995, Dedication, Annual Survey Am. Law, NYU, 1995, Nat. Breast Cancer Coalition Leadership award, 1995, Faith in Humanity award Nat. Coun. Jewish Women, 1996, NICHE Humanitarian award, 1996, Nat. Assn. Elem. Sch. Prins. Dist. Svc. award, 1996, Grammy award, 1997, Bully Pulpit award Nat. Coun. for Adoption, 1997, Nat. Family Advocate award Parents' Plus Newspaper, 1997, Disting. Svc. to Edn. award Coll. Bd., 1997, Disting. Svc. award Columbia U. Ctr. of Addiction and Substance Abuse, 1997, Commitment to Children award The Elizabeth Glaser Pediat. AIDS Found., 1997, Eleanor Roosevelt Living World award Peace Links, 1997, Humanitarian award Am. Found. Suicide Prevention, 1999, Lifetime Humanitarian Achievement award Children of Chernobyl Relief Fund and Ukrainian Inst. Am., 1999, Mother Teresa award, Govt. Albania, 1999, Shalom Chaver award internat. leadership, Yitzhak Rabin Ctr. Israel Studies, 1999, Disting. Am. award John F. Kennedy Libr. Found., 2004, Woman of Yr. award Met. Coun. on Jewish Poverty, NY, 2004, German Media prize, 2004, Health Quality award Nat. Com. Quality Assurance, 2005, Intrepid Freedom award Intrepid Sea, Air and Space Mus., 2005, President's Vision and Voice award Am. Med. Women's Assn., 2005, President's award Reserve Officers Assn., 2005, Remembrance award Alzheimer's Assn., 2006, Energy Leadership award U.S. Energy Assn., 2006; Paul Harris fellow Rotary Found., 1996; named one of Most Powerful Women, Forbes mag., 2005, 100 Most Influential People, Time Mag., 2006; named to Nat. Women's Hall of Fame, NY, 2005; honored with life-sized figure, Madame Tussauds' wax museum, Times Square, NYC, 2006. Fellow: Am. Bar Found.; mem.: ABA (chair, commn. on women in the profession), Assn. Trial Lawyers Am., Pulaski County Bar Assn., Ark. Women Lawyers Assn., Ark. Trial Lawyers Assn., Ark. Bar Assn. Democrat. Meth. First First Lady elected to the US Senate and the first woman elected statewide in NY. Office: US Senate 476 Russell Senate Office Bldg Washington DC 20510 also: District Office Ste 2601 780 Third Ave New York NY 10017-2154 Office Phone: 202-224-4451, 212-688-6262. Office Fax: 202-228-0282, 212-688-7444.*

CLINTON, JACK W., dean; DMD, Oreg. Health and Sci. U. Sch. Dentistry, 1964. Assoc. dean clin. affairs Oreg. Health and Sci. U. Sch. Dentistry, interim dean, 2003—04, dean, 2004—. Pres. Sch. of Dentistry Alumni Assn., 1979—80. Mem.: ADA, Internat. Coll. Dentists (vice regent), Am. Assn. Dental Schools, Am. Assn. Dental Examiners. Office: Oreg Health and Sci U Sch Dentistry 611 SW Campus Dr Portland OR 97239

CLINTON, LAWRENCE PAUL, psychiatrist; b. Lubbock, Tex., Apr. 27, 1945; s. Lewis Paul Clinton and Dorothy E. (Higgins) Clinton-Billingslea; m. Bonnie Gail Orenstein, June 22, 1969; children: Kerry Elizabeth, Andrew James, Alexander Geoffrey, Kaylin Lee. BA with honors, So. Conn. State Coll., 1966; postgrad., Ohio State U., 1966-68; MD, Hahnemann U., 1972. Diplomate Am. Bd. Psychiatry and Neurology, Am. Bd. Forensic Examiners, Am. Acad. Experts in Traumatic Stress, Am. Bd. Psychotherapy, 2000, Am. Psychiat. Assn. Teaching asst. Ohio State U., Columbus, 1966-68, research fellow, 1966-68; clin. instr. psychiatry Hahnemann U., Phila., 1975-82, asst. clin. prof., 1982—. Chief exec. officer Bldg. Mgmt. Group, Vineland, NJ, 1986—; psychiat. dir. James Guiffre Med. Ctr., Phila., 1976-79; med. dir. PSI Group, 1990-2003; cons. Superior Ct. NJ, 1975—, Ranch Hope, Alloway, NJ, 1989-92. Contbr. articles to profl. jours. Mem. Am. Security Coun., 1975—, Rep. Senatorial Com., 1978—, Rep. Nat. Com., 1978, The Pres. Club, 1990—. Recipient awards Am. Security Coun., 1982, Buena Regional Sch. Dist., NJ, 1983, Vineland Parent Support and Adv. Group, 1990, Rep. Presdl. Legion of Merit medal, 1992; decorated Chevalier Comdr. Ordre Souverain et Militaire de la Milice du Saint Sepulcre, 1990—, The DaVinci Diamond award, Cambridge Eng., 2004 Fellow Am. Bd. Forensic Examiners, Phila. Coll. Physicians and Surgeons, Am. Psychiat. Assn. (disting.); mem. AMA, Internat. Assn. Group Psychotherapy, NJ Psychiat. Soc., Med. Club Phila., World Fedn. Mental Health, InterAm. Coll. Physicians and Surgeons, Hahnemann Undergrad. Rsch. Soc. (treas. 1971-72), Confedn. of Chivalry, Am. Chem. Soc., Soc. d'Chemie (pres. 1965-66), South Jersey Psychiat. Soc. (sec.-treas. 1994-2001, pres. 2001-03, exec. program chmn. 2003—, Disting. Svc. award 2006), Internat. Churchill Soc., The Heritage Found., SPQR Club (pres. 1961-62) (Milford, Conn.), Union League Phila., Union League Phila. Yacht Club, Phi Lambda Kappa (v.p. 1972). Avocations: gardening, art collecting, book collecting, historical biography, golf, sailing. Office: 1138 E Chestnut Ave Bldg 6 Ste A Vineland NJ 08360-5053 Office Phone: 856-696-2660. Personal E-mail: lpclinton@mindspring.com.

CLINTON, STEPHEN MICHAEL, academic administrator; b. Wichita, Kans., Aug. 21, 1944; s. Thomas Francis and Bettie Lee (Harrison) C.; m. Virginia Ann Schoonover, Aug. 30, 1964; children: Matthew, Michael, Shanna. MA in Philosophy, Trinity Evang. Div. Sch., Deerfield, Ill., 1969, MDiv, 1970; PhD in Theology, Calif. Grad. Sch. Theology, 1979; postgdoc. in philosophy, U. Calif., Riverside, 1985-87, PhD in Edn., 1997; MA in Counseling, Internat. Sch. Theology, San Bernardino, Calif., 1987; MA in Edn., Calif. State U., San Bernardino, 1988. Ordained to ministry Evang. Free Ch. Am., 1973; cert. gifted edn. tchr., Calif. Pastor Lake Zurich (Ill.) EFC, 1967-69, Faith Presbyn. Ch., Wichita, Kans., 1972-74, Highlander Evang. Free Ch., 1974—78, East Cmty. Ch., Orlando, Fla., 1993-94, First Bapt. Ch., St. Cloud, Fla., 1999-2000; dir. extension degree programs Internat. Sch. Theology, 1974-86, assoc. prof., 1978-86; dir. Internat. Leadership Coun., 1986—; pres. Orlando (Fla.) Inst., 1991—, prof. edn. and religion, 1992—; dir. EdD program Iberia-Am. U. Leadership, 1998—2004; exec. dir. Vision Orlando, 2005—, bd. dirs., 1992—. Pres Ministry Devel., Inc., San Bernardino, 1978-86; chmn. bd. dirs. Masterlife Internat., 1999-2000; bd. reference Am. All Stars, 2000—; prof. Belhaven Coll., 2000-01; adj. prof. Moody Bible Inst., Phoenix U., 2001—, Valenia C.C., 2000—, Asbury Theol. Sem., 2000. Author: The Doctrine of the Christian Life, 1981, Cultural Apologetics, 1983, Calvinism and Arminianism, 1985, The Everlasting God, 1989, Movements Which Changed History, 1993, Theistic Realism, 1998, The Role of the Holy Spirit in Spiritual Development, 2001; also 40 articles. Pres. Advs. for Gifted and Talented Edn., San Bernardino, 1979-85; chmn. state parent coun. Calif. Assn. for Gifted, 1978-83; pres. advocates for gifted and talented edn. San Bernardino Unified Sch. Dist., 1984-87; chmn. bd. dirs. Ctr. for Individuals with Disabilities, San Bernardino, 1984-88; Maitland C. of C., bd. dirs., 2002—, pres., 2006. Mem. Evang. Philos. Soc. (editor 1979-81, 84-98, pres. 1983), Evang. Free Ch. Ministerial Assn., Evang. Theol. Soc. (chmn. 1982, 03), Philosophy of Edn. Soc. Office: Orlando Inst 100 Lake Hart Dr Ste 3000 Orlando FL 32832 Office Phone: 407-721-0111. Business E-Mail: sclinton@toi.edu.

CLIPPARD, RICHARD F., prosecutor; Graduate, U. Miss., 1976; JD, U. Miss. Law Sch., 1980. Private practice Butler, Lackey, Holt and Snedeker, 1980—83; special asst. US atty. US Small Bus. Adminstrn., 1983—88; asst. US atty. US Atty. Office, Nashville, 1988—2000, chief of Civil Division, 2000—01; interim U.S. atty. Middle Dist., Tenn., 2001—02; U.S. trustee for Tenn. & Ky. Exec. Off. for U.S. Trustees, 2003—. Office: 200 Jefferson Ave Ste 400 Memphis TN 38103

CLIPPERT, CHARLES FREDERICK, lawyer; b. Detroit, May 21, 1931; s. Harrison Frank and Ethelyn (Reuss) C.; m. Lynne Davison, June 6, 1959; children: Martha G. Shannon, Charles Frederick III, Thomas Harrison. BA, U. Mich., 1953, LLB, 1959. Bar: Mich. 1959. Assoc. Dickinson, Wright, Moon, Van Dusen & Freeman, Bloomfield Hills, Mich., 1959-67, ptnr., 1967-97, mem. exec. com., 1986-89; mem. Dickinson Wright PLLC, Bloomfield Hills, Mich., 1998-2000, cons. mem., 2001—. Commr. City of Birmingham, Mich., 1964-70, mayor, 1969-70; gov. Cranbrook Schs., Bloomfield Hills, 1978-99; trustee Cranbrook Ednl. Community, Bloomfield Hills, 1980-98, sec., 1989-93. Lt. (j.g.) USNR, 1953-56; mem. endowment com. The Consortium of Endowed Episcopal Parishes, 1998-2003. Fellow Am. Bar Found., Mich. Bar Found.; mem. ABA, State Bar Mich. (real property law coun. 1980-85, mem. select com. on professionalism 1992-99, mem. alternate dispute resolution coun. 1999-2006), Oakland County Bar Assn. (bd. dirs. 1985-91, pres. 1990-91), Orchard Lake Country Club (gov. 1986-92, pres. 1991-92), Am. Arbitration Assn. (panel of neutral arbitrators 1997—), Pi Sigma Alpha. Office: Dickinson Wright PLLC Ste 2000 38525 Woodward Ave Bloomfield Hills MI 48304-2971 Mailing: PO Box 509 Bloomfield Hills MI 48303-0509 Office Phone: 248-433-7212. Business E-Mail: cclippert@dickinsonwright.com.

CLIZBE, JOHN ANTHONY, psychologist, social services administrator; b. Council Bluffs, Iowa, June 28, 1942; s. Harold George and Margaret Jane (Fariday) C.; m. Rebecca Rose Maddox, Jan. 30, 1965; children: Mark Andrew, Diane Christine. BA, William Jewell Coll., Liberty, Mo., 1964; PhD, Washington U., St. Louis, 1967. Clin. psychology resident Norfolk (Nebr.) State Hosp. and Northeast Mental Health Clinic, 1967-68; cons. psychologist Nordli, Wilson Assocs., Worcester, Mass., 1968-97, gen. ptnr., 1975-97, resident mgr., 1978-83, mng. ptnr., 1983-93, sr. ptnr., 1993-97; v.p. disaster svcs. ARC, Falls Church, Va., 1997—2002, interim exec. dir. Triangle Area chpt., 2003, interim CEO Price George's County chpt., 2003; emergency planner City of Alexandria Health Dept., Va., 2004—. Pres. PCMS, Inc., 1984-97; dir., treas. PSI, Inc., 1983-97, Human Interface Group, Inc., 1986-97; dir., v.p., treas. Student Achievement Inst., Worcester, 1973-97. Columnist Bus. Times. Dir., treas., pres. Nat. Psychol. Cons. to Mgmt.; mem. bd. edn. Town of Madison, Conn., 1980-86; trustee Calvin K. Kazanjian Econ. Found., Inc., 1986—; dist. chmn. 101st Assembly Dist., 1992-97, Conn. Party, 1992—; chmn. Conn. Red Cross Disaster Mental Health Com., 1992-97, Nat. Bd. Emergency Ford and Shelter Program, 1997—; facilitator Vision Project City of New Haven, 1994; coord. Mental Health Svcs., 1995, Spl. Olympics World Games; mem. exec. com. Nat. Hurrican Conf., 1997—; chmn. waterfront com. City of New Haven Vision Project; others; nat. chmn. disaster svcs. ARC, 1995-97; mem. exec. com. Internat. Conf. on Disaster Mgmt., 2000; mem. adv. com. Natural Hazards Rsch. and Applications Ctr., 1998—; chmn. bioterrorism emergency planners subcom. Washington Area Coun. Govts. NDEA fellow Washington U., 1967. Mem. APA (membership com. div. 14), Mass. Psychol. Assn., Am. Mgmt. Assn. (faculty President's Assn. 1987-97), New Haven C. of C. (bd. dirs. 1989-95), Sigma Xi, Pi Gamma Mu, Pi Kappa Delta. Office: ARC 8111 Gatehouse Rd Falls Church VA 22042-1203 Home: 25533 Bushey Heath Rd Royal Oak MD 21662 Office Phone: 703-838-4400. Business E-Mail: john.clizbe@udh.virginia.gov.

CLODFELTER, DANIEL GRAY, state legislator, lawyer; b. Thomasville, NC, June 2, 1950; s. Billy G. and Marie Lorene (Wells) C.; m. Elizabeth Kay Bevan, Aug. 20, 1974; children: Julia Elizabeth, Catherine Gray. BA, Davidson Coll., 1972; AB, Oxford U., 1974; JD, Yale U., 1977. Bar: N.C. 1977, U.S. Dist. Ct. (we. dist.) N.C. 1977, U.S. Dist. Ct. (ea. dist.) N.C. 1979, U.S. Ct. Appeals (4th cir.) 1984, U.S. Dist. Ct. (mid. dist.) N.C. 1985. Law clk. to presiding judge U.S. Dist. Ct., Charlotte, NC, 1977—78; assoc. Moore & Van Allen, Charlotte, 1978—82, ptnr., 1983—. Mem. N.C. Senate, 1999—. Mem. Charlotte City Coun., 1987-93, Charlotte-Mecklenburg Planning Commn., 1984-87, chmn., 1986-87; state sec. Rhodes Scholarship Trust, N.C., 1986-97; trustee Z. Smith Reynolds Found., Inc., Winston-Salem, N.C., 1983—; bd. dirs. N.C. Ctr. for Pub. Policy Rsch., 1994-96. Rhodes scholar, 1972. Mem. N.C. Bar Assn. (antitrust law com., bankruptcy sect. coun.). Office: Moore & Van Allen 100 N Tryon St 4700 Charlotte NC 28202-4003 E-mail: clodfelterd@mvalaw.com.

CLODIUS, ROBERT LEROY, retired economist; b. Walla Walla, Wash., Mar. 10, 1921; s. Hans Friedrich and Emma (Wellman) C.; m. Joan Elizabeth Coyle, Aug. 27, 1949; children: Catherine, Mark. Student, Whitman Coll., 1938-40, LLD, 1970; BS, U. Calif., Berkeley, 1942, PhD, 1950. Lectr. econs. U. Calif., 1949-50; mem. faculty U. Wis., 1950-90, prof. agrl. econs., 1958-90, chmn. dept., 1960-62, v.p. univ., 1962-71, acting pres., 1970, prof. agrl. econs. emeritus, 1990—, prof. econs., 1971-90, prof. econs. emeritus, 1990—, prof. ednl. adminstrn., 1971-90, prof. ednl. administr. emeritus, 1990—, prof. univ., 1971-90, prof. univ. emeritus, 1990—, v.p. univ. emeritus, 1990—; pres. Nat. Assn. State Univs. and Land Grant Colls., 1979-91, pres. emeritus, 1992—. Vis. assoc. Harvard Bus. Sch., 1954; lectr. Am. Coun. Edn., Inst. Coll. and Univ. Adminstrs.; State Dept. specialist in South Am., 1961; cons. Dept. Agr., 1961; mem. com. agr. scis. to Sec. Agr., 1961-69; cons. Rockefeller Found., 1963-67; adviser U. East Africa, 1963-67; chmn. Com. Instnl. Coop., 1968; cons. Ford Found., Philippines, 1970; chmn. exec. bd. commn. instns. higher edn. North Ctrl. Assn., 1972-74; v.p. Midwest Univs. Consortium Internat. Activities, Inc., 1964-70, chmn. bd., 1970-71; mem. Commn. on Higher Edn., Govt. Sierra Leone, 1969; adminstr. Indonesian Higher Agr. Edn. Project, 1971-77; adv. commr. Edn. Commn. of the States, 1980-91; mem. Nat. Commn. on Higher Edn. Issues, 1981-82, chmn. adv. com. Nat. Ctr. Food and Agrl. Policy, Resources for the Future, 1984-89; nat. adv. com. Adult Learning Svc. PBS, 1987-91, Debt for Devel. Coalition, Inc., 1988-92, chmn., 1988-91, chmn. adv. com., 1992-97; cons. U.S. Info. Agy., 1991-94; v.p. WM Acad. Search Cons. Internat. Inc., 1991-94. Author articles, monographs, chpts. in books; editor: Jour. Farm Econs, 1958-60. Bd. dirs. U. Corp. Atmospheric Rsch., 1962-67, Ctr. for Rsch. Librs., 1969-71, Argonne U. Assocs., 1978-84, USN Meml. Found., 1995-2000, sec., 1998-2000, trustee, 2001-05; adv. bd. Rockford Coll. Music Acad., 2002—; docent Navy Mus., Washington Navy Yard, 1997-2000, Andersen Japanese Gardens, 2002—; bd. dirs. Music Acad. Found., 2007—. Lt. USNR, 1942-55. Decorated Commendation medal; recipient Kiekhofer Teaching award U. Wis., 1953. Mem.: AAUP (pres. U. Wis. 1957), Nat. Assn. Scholars, Am./Schleswig Holstein Heritage Soc. (adv. com. 1999—), U.S.-Indonesian Soc. Washington, Am. Agrl. Econs. Assn. (v.p. 1960), Navy Club of USA-Ship 1 (chaplain 2002—), Rotary Internat., Phi Beta Kappa, Phi Kappa Phi, Alpha Zeta. Home: 1909 Shaw Woods Dr Rockford IL 61107-1729

CLOGAN, PAUL MAURICE, English language and literature educator; b. Boston, July 9, 1934; s. Michael J. and Agnes J. (Murphy) C.; m. Julie Sydney Davis, July 27, 1972 (dec. 1982); children: Michael Rodger, Patrick Terence, Margaret Murphy. BA, Boston Coll., 1956, MA, 1957; PhD, U. Ill., 1961; F.A.A.R., Am. Acad. in Rome, 1966; MDiv, Blessed John XXIII Sem., 1999. Asst. prof. Duke U., 1961-65; assoc. prof. Case Western Res. U., Cleve., 1965-72; prof. English U. North Tex., Denton, 1972—. Vis. prof. U. Keele, Eng., 1965, U. Pisa, Italy, 1966, U. Tours, France, 1978; vis. mem. Inst. Advanced Study, Princeton, N.J., 1970, 77; cons. Library of Congress, Ednl. Testing Service, NEH, Nat. Acad. Scis., NRC Commn. Human Resources, Nation Rsch. Council Com. for the Study of Rsch.-Doctorate-Programs in the U.S., Am. Council Learned Socs., Nat. Enquiry into Scholarly Comm., Chilton Rsch. Services; mem. Am. Arts Assn., Inst. Internat. Edn., nat. screening com. 1984-88. Author: The Medieval Achilleid of Statius, 1968, Social Dimensions in Medieval and Renaissance Studies, 1972, In Honor of S. Harrison Thomson, 1970, Medieval and Renaissance Studies in Review, 1971, Medieval and Renaissance Spirituality, 1973, Medieval Historiography, 1974, Medieval Hagiography and Romance, 1975, Medieval Poetics, 1976, Transformation and Continuity, 1977, Byzantine and Western Studies, 1984, Fourteenth and Fifteenth Centuries, 1986, The Early Renaissance, 1987, Literary Theory, 1988, Spectrum, 1992, Columbian Quincentenary, 1992, Renaissance and Discovery, 1993, Breaching the Boundaries, 1994, Convergences, 1994, Diversity, 1995, Historical Inquiries, 1997, Transitions, 1998, Civil Strife and National Identity in the Middle Ages, 1999, Literacy and the Lay Reader, 2000, Ethnicity and Self-Identity, 2002, Papal Letters, Manual for Confessors and Romance, 2003, Humanist Educational Theory, Gregory the Great, and Culinary Comedy, 2004, Reengagement with History, 2005, Dialogue, Discussion and Development, 2006; editor: Medievalia et Humanistica, Studies in Medieval and Renaissance Culture, 1970—; contbr. articles to profl. jours. Grantee Duke Endowment 1961-62, Am. Coun. Learned Socs., 1963-64, 70-71, 88, Am. Philos. Soc., 1964-69, U. North Tex., 1972-75, 80-81, 89; sr. Fulbright-Hays postdoctoral rsch. fellow, Italy, 1965-66, France, 1978, fellow Prix de Rome, 1966-67, Bollingen Found., 1966, NEH, 1969-70, 86, 90-91. Mem. Internat. Assn. Univ. Profs. English, MLA (exec. com. 1980-86, del. assembly 1981-86), Internat. Comparative Lit. Assn., Internat. Arthurian Soc., Modern Humanities Research Assn., Medieval Acad. Am. (nominating com. 1975-76, John Nicholas Brown Prize com. 1981-83), Internat. Assn. for Neo-Latin Studies, The New Chaucer Soc., Fulbright Assn. Democrat. Roman Catholic.

CLOHESY, WILLIAM WARREN, philosopher, educator; b. Chgo., July 31, 1946; s. John Cecil and Mary Evelyn (Ahern) Clohesy; m. Stephanie June Jagucki, June 19, 1971. BS, Loyola U., Chgo., 1964-68; MA, So. Ill. U., 1968-71; PhD, New Sch. Social Rsch., NYC, 1981. Instr. Loyola U., Chgo., 1967, asst. prof., 1982-83; tchg. asst. So. Ill. U., Carbondale, 1969; adj. prof. Montclair State Coll., Upper Montclair, NJ, 1981-82; asst. prof. Rochester (N.Y.) Inst. Tech., 1983-86, rsch. assoc., 1986-87; lectr. U. Belgrano, Buenos Aires, 1987; asst. prof. U. No. Iowa, Cedar Falls, 1987-93, assoc. prof., 1993—2006, prof., 2006—. BSN adv. com. Allen Coll., Waterloo, Iowa, 1991—2002; instnl. rev. bd. U. No. Iowa, 2002—. Editor: (book) Ethics at Work, 1992; contbr. articles to profl. jours. Recipient Kurt Riezler Meml. award, New Sch. for Social Rsch., 1982, Faculty Excellence award, Iowa Bd. Regents, 2001; fellow Fulbright fellowship to Argentina, 1987; grantee W.K. Kellogg Found., 1995—2001, Iowa Humanities Bd., 1991—92, NEH, 1991—92. Mem.: Soc. Advancement Am. Philosophy, N.Am. Kant Soc., N.Am. Soc. Social Philosophy, Hume Soc., Am. Philos. Assn., Internat. Soc. 3d Sector Rsch. Democrat. Roman Catholic. Avocation: Irish language, literature, and music. Office: U No Iowa Dept Philosophy & Religion Cedar Falls IA 50614-0501 Office Phone: 319-273-6123. Business E-Mail: william.clohesy@uni.edu.

CLONEY, TERENCE J., lawyer; b. Chgo., Oct. 29, 1953; s. John Edward and Helen (Junginger) C.; m. Katherine Giam, 1985; children: Sean Christopher, Michael Brendan. AB, Columbia U., 1975; JD, NYU, 1979. Bar: N.Y. 1980, Ill. 1989. Assoc. Milbank, Tweed, Hadley & McCloy, NYC, 1979-83, Hong Kong, 1983-86, Singapore, 1986-89; ptnr. Gardner, Carton & Douglas, Chgo., 1989-97, Altheim & Gray, Chgo., 1997—2003; assoc. gen. counsel Freddie Mac, 2004—06, HSBC Fin. Corp., Prospect Hts., Ill., 2006—. Bd. dirs. Juvenile Diabetes Found., Chgo., 1993-2001, mem. exec. com., 1994-96. Mem. ABA. Home: 421 Concord Ln North Barrington IL 60010-2207 Office: HSBC Fin Corp 2700 Sanders Rd Prospect Heights IL 60070 Office Phone: 847-291-7890. Business E-Mail: terence.j.cloney@us.hsbc.com.

CLONINGER, CLAUDE ROBERT, psychiatrist, epidemiologist, educator, researcher; b. Beaumont, Tex., Apr. 4, 1944; s. Morris Sheppard and Marie Concetta (Mazzagatti) Cloninger; m. Sharon Lee Rogan, July 11, 1969; children: Bryan Joseph, Kevin Michael. BA, U. Tex., 1966; MD, Washington U., St. Louis, 1970; degree (hon.), U. Umea, Sweeden, 1983. Diplomate Am. Bd. Psychology and Neurology. Instr. psychiatry Washington U., St. Louis, 1973—74, asst. prof., 1974—78, assoc. prof., 1978—81, prof., 1981—, prof. genetics, 1978—, prof. psychology, 1989—, Wallace Renard prof. psychiatry, 1991—, head dept. psychiatry, 1989—94, dir. ctr. psychobiology personality, 1994—. Psychiatrist-in-chief Barnes and Renard Hosps., St. Louis, 1989—94; vis. prof. U. Hawaii, Honolulu, 1978—79, U. Umea, Sweden, 1980; chmn. NIMH Psychopathology Rev. Com., Washington, 1980—84; cons. WHO, Geneva, 1981—, Am. Psychiat. Assn., Washington, 1978—, Nat. Inst. on Alcohol Abuse and Alcoholism, 1984—99, Inst. Medicine, 1986; chmn. genetics initiative schizophrenia NIMH, 1989—97; mental health commr. State of Mo., 1990—95. Author: Feeling Good: The Science of Well-Being, 2004, others; editor: Jour. Behavior Genetics, 1980—86, Am. Jour. Human Genetics, 1980—83; assoc. editor Genetic Epidemiology, 1983—92, Human Heredity, 1989—, mem. editl. bd. Arch. Gen. Psychiatry, Comprehensive Psychiatry, Neuropsychopharmacology, Jour. Comprehensive Psychiatry, Jour. Psychiat. Rsch., Jour. Med. Genetics; contbr. articles to profl. jours. Recipient Rsch. Scientist award, NIMH, 1975, 1980, 1985, Strecker award, Inst. Pa. Hosp., 1988, James B. Isaacson award, ISBRA, 1992, Lifetime Achievement award, Am. Soc. Addiction Medicine, 2000, Finnish Psychiatry Assn. Annual medal, Lifetime Achievement award, Internat. Soc. Psychiat. Genetics, 2003. Fellow: AAAS, Am. Psychopathol. Assn. (treas. 1984—89, v.p. 1990, pres. 1991—93, sec. 1994—96, Samuel Hamilton award 1993), Am. Psychiat. Assn. (Adolph Meyer award 1993); mem.: Rsch. Soc. Alcoholism (bd. dirs. 1987—90), Inst. Medicine of NAS, Behavior Genetics Assn. (editl. bd. 1980—), Am. Soc. Human Genetics (editl. bd. 1980—83). Avocations: gardening, reading, travel. Office: Washington U Dept Psychiatry 4940 Childrens Pl Saint Louis MO 63110-1002 Home: 12950 Huntbridge Forest Dr Saint Louis MO 63131 Home Phone: 314-863-1338; Office Phone: 314-362-7005. Business E-Mail: clon@tci.wustl.edu.

CLONINGER, KRISS, III, insurance company executive; b. Houston, Oct. 21, 1947; s. Kriss and Jewel JoAnn (Jones) C.; m. Lisa L. Welch; children: Laura Kay, Kriss Alan; stepchildren: J. Tanner Prewit, Presley N. Lanier. BBA, U. Tex., 1969, MBA, 1971. Actuary KPMG Peat Marwick, Dallas, 1973-74, Atlanta, 1977-92, Rudd & Wisdom, Austin, Tex., 1974-77; CFO AFLAC Inc., 1992—, sr. v.p. Columbus, Ga., 1992—93, exec. v.p., 1993—2001, pres., 2001—, bd. dirs. Columbus, Ga., 2001—. Bd. dirs. Tupperware Corp., Total Sys. Svcs., Inc., Little Blessings Nurturing Ctr., 2002—. Served to 1st lt. USAF, 1971-73. Fellow Soc. Actuaries; mem. Am. Acad. Actuaries. Office: AFLAC 1932 Wynnton Rd Columbus GA 31999 Office Phone: 706-323-3431. E-mail: kcloninger@aflac.com.*

CLONTZ, DONNA, lawyer, writer, consultant; b. Pensacola, Fla., Oct. 21, 1946; d. Clarence E. and Anita I. Clontz; m. Norm Howard, Mar. 15, 1995; children: Chris Howard, Debbie Prestininzi. BA, UCLA, 1969; JD cum laude, San Francisco Law Sch., 1976. Cert. tchr. Calif. Dep. dist. atty. Ventura County Dist. Attorney's Office, Ventura, Calif., 1977—86; freelance cons. Washington, 1983—. Cons. State of Calif., Sacramento, 1986—96; police auditor City of Reno, 2003—05. Co-author: The Need to Know, Juvenile Record Sharing, 1989, School Safety: A Planning Guide for Action, 1989; editor: Law in the School, 1989; author: (Calif. juvenile justice legislation) Serious Habitual Offender Program. Tchr., facilitator Office Juvenile Justice and Delinquency Prevention, Washington, 1983—99. Named Outstanding Woman in Law and Law Enforcement, Ventura County, 1985; recipient Outstanding Svc. award, Ventura County Peace Officers Assn., 1986. Mem.: AAUW (v.p. 2005—), Phi Beta Kappa. Avocations: travel, photography, golf. Home: PO Box 33244 Reno NV 89533 Personal E-mail: donnanorm1@yahoo.com.

CLOONAN, JAMES BRIAN, investment company executive; b. Chgo., Jan. 28, 1931; s. Bernard V. and Lauretta D. (Maloney) C.; m. Edythe Adrianne Ratner, Mar. 26, 1970; children: Michele, Christine, Mia; stepchildren: Carrie Madorin, Harry Madorin. Prof. Sch. Bus. Loyola U., Chgo., 1966-71; pres. Quantitative Decision Sys., Inc., Chgo., 1972-73; chmn. bd. Heinold Securities, Inc., Chgo., 1974-77; prof. grad. sch. bus. DePaul U., Chgo., 1978-82; chmn. Investment Info. Svcs., 1981-86; pres. Mktg. Sys. Internat. Inc., 1985-87, Analytics Sys. Inc., 1987—. Bd. dirs., chmn. Mktg. Svcs. Internat., Inc. Author: Estimates of the Impact of Sign and Billboard Removal Under the Highway Beautification Act of 1965, 1966, Stock Options-The Application of Decision Theory to Basic and Advanced Strategies, 1973, An Introduction to Decision Making for the Individual Investor, 1980, Expanding Your Investment Horizons, 1983, A Lifetime Strategy for Investing in Common Stocks, 1988, Maximum Return Minimum Risk, 2003. Mem.: Am. Assn. Individual Investors (pres. 1979—92, chmn. 1992—), Am. Mktg. Assn. Home: 1242 N Lake Shore Dr Chicago IL 60610-2361 Office: Am Assn Individual Investors 625 N Michigan Ave Chicago IL 60611-3110 Office Phone: 312-280-0170. E-mail: jbcaaii@aol.com.

CLOONAN, MICHELE V., library director; BA in Lit. and Language, Bennington Coll., 1975; MA in Gen. Studies Humanities, U. Chgo., 1979; MSLIS, U. Ill., 1984, PhD in Libr. Sci., 1998. Preservation officer Brown U. Libr., Providence, 1987—90; head rare books dept. Smith Coll. Libr., Northampton, Mass., 1995—96; asst. prof., Dept. of Libr. and Info. Sci. UCLA, 1991—95, 1995—2002, chair, Dept. Info. Sci., 2001—02; dean, prof. Simmons Coll. Grad. Sch. Libr. Info. Sci., Boston, 2002—. Recipient Donald G Wing award, GSLIS, U Ill., 1984, Berner-Nash award, 1988, Career Devel. award, UCLA, 1991—92, Comm. Rsch. awards, 1992—2001, Faculty Staff Ptnr. award, 2000; fellow Va. Ctr. Creative arts, 1989. Mem.: Assn. Libr. Info. Sci. Edn. (v.p., pres. elect). Office: Simmons Coll Grad Sch Libr Info Sci 300 The Fenway Boston MA 02115-5898

CLOONEY, GEORGE, actor; b. Lexington, Kentucky, May 6, 1961; s. Nick and Nina Clooney; m. Talia Balsam, Dec. 15, 1989 (div. Sept. 1993). Student, No. Ky U. Actor: (TV series) E/R, 1984—85, The Facts of Life, 1985—86, Roseanne, 1988—89, Sunset Beat, 1990, Baby Talk, 1991, Sisters, 1992—94, ER, 1994—99; (films) Grizzly II: The Predator, 1987, Return to Horror High, 1987, Return of the Killer Tomatoes, 1988, Red Surf, 1990, Unbecoming Age, 1992, One Fine Day, 1996, From Dusk Till Dawn, 1996, Batman & Robin, 1997, The Peacemaker, 1997, The Thin Red Line, 1998, Out of Sight, 1998, Three Kings, 1999, (voice) South Park: Bigger, Longer and Uncut, 1999, O Brother, Where Art Thou, 2000 (Golden Globe award for Best Peformance by an Actor in a Motion Picture, 2001), The Perfect Storm, 2000, Ocean's Eleven, 2001, Spy Kids, 2001, Solaris, 2002, Spy Kids 3-D: Game Over, 2003, Intolerable Cruelty, 2003, Ocean's Thirteen, 2007; actor, dir. (films) Confessions of a Dangerous Mind, 2002, actor, dir., writer Good Night and Good Luck, 2005 (named best film Nat. Bd. Rev., 2005, George Selvin award, Writer Guild Am, 2006), actor, exec. prodr. Ocean's Twelve, 2004, Syriana, 2005 (Best Performance by an Actor in a Supporting Role in a Motion Picture, Hollywood Fgn. Press Assn., (Golden Globe award), 2006, Performance by an Actor in a Supporting Role., Acad. Motion Picture Arts & Sciences, 2006), (TV films) Fail Safe, 2000, prodr., writer (films) Kilroy, 1999; exec. prodr.: (films) Rock Star, 2001, Insomnia, 2002, Welcome to Colinwood, 2002, Far From Heaven, 2002, The Jacket, 2005; prodr.: Criminal, 2004; exec. prodr.: (TV series) K Street, 2003; dir.: Unscripted, 2005. Recipient SAE awards, 1998, 99, Freedom award Broadcasting Film Critics Assn., 2006, Am. Cinematheque award, 2006; named one of 50 Most Powerful People in Hollywood, 2003-06; named one of The World's Most Influential People, TIME mag., 2006-07, 100 Most Powerful Celebrities, Forbes.com, 2007; named Sexiest Man Alive, People mag. 1997, 2006; named a WIRED Renegade, WIRED Rave Awards, 2006. Office: Creative Artist Agy 9830 Wilshire Blvd Beverly Hills CA 90212-1804

CLOPINE, GORDON ALAN, consulting geologist, educator; b. LA, Nov. 28, 1936; s. Walter Gordon and Sara Elizabeth (Donahue) C.; m. Margaret Anne Umbach, 1959; m. Sara Rose Lapinski, 1979; children: William: Susan, Russell, Cynthia. BS, U. Redlands, Calif., 1958; MS, U. Houston, 1960. Registered geologist, Calif., 1970, Ariz., 1985, Alaska, 1991, Utah, 2004; cert. profl. geologist, Calif., 1982; registered environ. assessor, Calif., 1992. CEO, Clopine Geol. Svcs., Inc., Cons. Geologists, Redlands, 1961—. Prof. San Bernardino Valley Coll., San Bernardino, Calif., 1961-84, dean instrn., 1978-81, prof. Crafton Hills Coll., Yucalpa, Calif., 1982-92, dean administrv. svcs., 1992-93, v.p. 1993-97, 2002-03; v.p. instruction, 2000, adminstrv. svs., 2002-03; bd. dirs. Crafton Hills Coll. Found., 2003, v.p. 2006-; rsch. assoc. San Bernardino County Mus., 1986—; adj. faculty U. Redlands, 1961—; mem. extension faculty U. Calif.-Riverside, 1965—. field leader geol. field studies and natural environ. series; lectr., rschr. on geol. and land use conditions. Author reports and studies on geol. hazards and land use and environ. geology land use. Pres., San Bernardino County Mus. Assn., 1972. Fellow Geol. Soc. Am.; mem. Am. Inst. Profl. Geologists. Republican. Achievements include research on geologic field studies, Calif., Mich., Alaska, Hawaii, Washington, Idaho, Arizona, Utah and Wyoming; land use and volcanic hazards in Hawaii and Ground Water in California; beach erosion and volcanic hazards in Pacific Northwest. Home and Office: 13093 Burns Ln Redlands CA 92373-7415 E-mail: gclopine@aol.com.

CLORE, LAWRENCE HUBERT, lawyer; b. Tulsa, July 31, 1944; s. Hubert Charles and Jessie Louada (Fowler) Clore; m. Carol Jean Roegelein, July 3, 1967 (div. 1981); children: Robert William, James Lawrence; m. Martha Jo Lawyer; children: Kathryn Denise, Michael Hubert. BBA, Tex. Christian U., 1966; JD, U. Tex., 1969. Bar: Tex. 1969, cert.: Tex. Bd. Legal Specialization (specialist in labor and employment law). Assoc. Fulbright & Jaworski, Houston, 1971-77, ptnr., 1977—. Capt. US Army, 1969—71, Vietnam. Mem.: ABA, Houston Mgmt. Lawyers Forum (chmn. 1976—77), Indsl. Rels. Rsch. Assn., Tex. Bar Assn. (labor and employment sect., coun. 1990—93, vice chair 1993—94, chair 1994—95). Republican. Methodist. Avocations: hunting, fishing, golf. Office: Fulbright & Jaworski 1301 Mckinney St Ste 5100 Houston TX 77010-3031 Home Phone: 713-465-1660; Office Phone: 713-651-5403. Business E-Mail: lclore@fulbright.com.

CLOSE, CAROLE LYNNE, education educator, consultant; b. Coshocton, Ohio, Dec. 27, 1943; d. Robert Linn and Ruth Ann Close; m. Douglas Fabish, Aug. 27, 1977 (div. Dec. 30, 1982); 1 child, Coriana Lynne. BS in Edn., Bowling Green State U., 1966; MEd in Post-Secondary Edn. Adminstrn., Cleve. State U., 1979. Mediator Cmty. Youth Mediation Program, 1983. Advisor, coord. Winning Against Violent Environments (W.A.V.E.) Conflict Resolution Program, Cleve., 1983—; cons. and trainer Ohio Commn. on Dispute Resolution and Conflict Mgmt., Columbus, 1994—. Co-chair, mediation com. of the labor mgmt. coun. Cleve. Teachers Union, 1997—2004; ind. edn. and conflict resolution cons., 1983—; social studies tchr. Cleve. Pub. Schools, 1966—93. Edn. com. Assn. Conflict Resolution, 2002—02; civil rights and peace and justice activist Ohio, 1964—; mem. Hate Crime Com., Cleve., 1997—2004; steering com. mem. People Empowered Against Child Endangerment (PEACE), 1992—96; advisor Gov.'s Commn. Peace and Conflict Mgmt., Columbus, 1988—88. Named to Cleve. Mcpl. Sch. Dist. Educators and Alumni Hall of Fame, Grads Net, 2001; recipient The Global Peace award, Twenty-first Congl. Dist. Caucus, 1986, Leadership award, Cleve. Teachers Union, 1988, 1990, Governor's Spl. Recognition award for Outstanding Achievements in Mediation Edn., Gov. of Ohio, 1989, The Ghandi-King Peace award, Cath. Ch., 1989, Margaret Herrman Founder's award, Nat. Conf. on Peacemaking and Conflict Resolution, 1997, Liberty Bell Law

Week award, Cleve. and Cuyahoga Bar Assn., 2001, Peace Works award, Strategies Against Violence Everywhere, 2003, Outstanding Tchr. award, Jr. Ahievement and the P.T.A. Mem.: Mediation Assn. No. Ohio, Women's Speakout for Peace and Justice. Achievements include development of school district-wide comprehensive peer mediation program. Avocations: reading, movies, travel. Home: 2184 Briarwood Rd Cleveland Heights OH 44118 Home Phone: 216-321-4284. Personal E-mail: cclose@aol.com.

CLOSE, CHUCK (CHARLES THOMAS CLOSE), artist; b. Monroe, Wash., July 5, 1940; s. Leslie Durwood and Mildred Emma (Wagner) C.; m. Leslie Rose, Dec. 24, 1967; children: Georgia Molly, Maggie Sarah. BA, U. Wash., 1962; BFA, Yale U., 1963, MFA, 1964; postgrad. (Fulbright grantee), Akadamie der Bildenen Kunste, Vienna, Austria, 1964-65; ArtsD (hon.), Art Inst. of Boston, 1992, U. Mass., 1995; LHD (hon.), Skidmore Coll., 1992; DFA (hon.), Colby Coll., 1994. Faculty U. Mass., 1965-67, Sch. Visual Arts, NYC, 1967-71, N.Y.U., 1970-73. Mem. Bykert Gallery, NYC, 1969-74, Pace Gallery, NYC, 1977— One-man shows include Los Angeles County Museum, 1971, Mus. Contemporary Art, Chgo., 1972, 81, Mus. Modern Art, NYC, 1973, San Francisco Mus. Art, 1975, Balt. Mus. Art, 1976, Georges Pompidou Centre/Musée Nationale d'Art Moderne, Paris, 1979, Univ. Art Mus., Berkeley, Calif., 1982, Richard Gray Gallery, Chgo., 1982-83, Milw. Art Mus., 1984, Contemporary Arts Mus., Houston, 1985, Fuji Gallery, Tokyo, 1985, Aldrich Mus., Yokohama Museum of Art, Japan 1989, Pace Gallery, NYC, 1991, No Boundries, Denver Art Mus., 2004, Printed Light, Nat. Gallery of Australia, 2004, Neue Editionen, Munich, 2004, others; retrospective Walker Art Center, Mpls., 1980, St. Louis Art Mus., 1981, Whitney Mus., NYC, 1981, Aldrich Mus., Art Inst. Chgo., 1989, Butler Inst., Youngstown, Ohio, 1989, Mus. Modern Art, NYC, 1991, Kunsthalle Baden Baden, Germany, 1994, Lenbachhaus House, Munich, 1994, Cartier Found., Paris, 1994, Photographs by Chuck Close, Worcester Mus. of Art, 1999, 2000, traveling exhibition originating in Mus. Modern Art, NYC, 1998-99, Chuck Close Prints: Process and Collaboration, Met. Mus. of Art, 2004; group shows include, Whitney Mus., NYC., 1969, 70, 72, 77, 79, 91, Whitney Biennial Exhbn., Documenta 5 & 6, Kassel, Fed. Republic Germany, 1972, 77, Tokyo Biennale, 1974, Contemporary Voices: Works from the UBS Art Collection, Mus. Modern Art, NYC, 2005. Trustee Whitney Mus. Am. Art, NYC. Recipient Showhegan medal Nat. Acad. Arts and Letters, 1991, Infinity award Internat. Ctr. of Photography, 1990, Skowhegan medal, 1991, Acad. and Inst. of Arts and Letters prize, 1991; Nat. Endowment for Arts grantee, 1973 Office: Pace Wildenstein 32 E 57th St Fl 3 New York NY 10022-2513

CLOSE, DONALD PEMBROKE, management consultant; b. Orange, NJ, July 11, 1920; s. Charles Mollison and Simah Close; m. L. Carolyn Reck, Apr. 22, 1950 (dec. Mar. 1983); children: Geoffrey Stuart, Cynthia Leigh, Sara Carolyn; m. Diane M. Wisdo Kendzor, Dec. 31, 1996. BS in Econs., U. Pa., 1942. Sales rep. IBM, Newark, 1946-47; asst. budget dir. L. Bamberger & Co., Newark, 1947-53; staff exec. Am. Express, NYC, 1953; contr., sec. Ciba Co., Inc., NYC, 1953-59; dir. fin. and control Avon Products Inc., NYC, 1960-72; pres. Corp. Fin. Assocs., Inc., NYC, 1973-76; v.p. Nelson Walker Assocs., NYC, 1973-76, Internat. Mgmt. Advisors, Inc., NYC, 1976-86; prin. Deven Assocs. Internat. Inc., NYC, 1986-91, The Pembroke Close Mgmt. Group, NYC, 1991—. Mem. Pvt. Sector Study on Cost Control in Fed. Govt., 1982. Trustee Morristown Beard Sch., NJ, 1974-77; pres. Jr. Essex Troop Calvary, 1964-68 With 102nd div. US Army, 1942—45. Decorated Bronze Star with oak leaf cluster, Letter of Commendation, NJ Disting. Svc. medal with oak leaf cluster. Mem. Fin. Execs. Inst., Am. Soc. Corp. Secs., Systems and Procedures Assn., Internat. Assn. Accts., Human Resources Planning Soc., Group for Strategic Organizational Effectiveness, St. Andrews Soc. NY, St. George's Soc. NY, Navy League US, 102d Inf. Divsn. Assn., U.S. Naval Inst., Campbell Soc., Internat. Assn. Corp. and Profl. Recruiters, Human Resources Exch. Assn., Univ. Club (NYC), Morristown Club, Wharton Club, Essex Hunt Club, Burnt Mills Polo Club, Phi Sigma Kappa (past sec.). Republican. Episcopalian. Office: The Pembroke Close Mgmt Group PO Box 226 Gladstone NJ 07934-0226 Office Phone: 908-781-2135.

CLOSE, GLENN, actress; b. Greenwich, Conn., Mar. 19, 1947; d. William and Bettine Close; m. Cabot Wade 1969 (div. 1971); m. James Marlas, 1984 (div. 1987); 1 child, Annie Maude Starke; m. David Shaw, Feb. 3, 2006. BA in drama and anthropology, Coll. William and Mary, 1974. Joined New Phoenix Repertory Co., 1974. Co-owner The Leaf and Bean Coffee House, Bozeman, Montana, 1993-94. Actor: (Broadway debut) Love for Love, 1974; (Broadway plays) The Rules of the Game, 1974, The Member of the Wedding, 1975, Rex, 1976, Barnum, 1980—81 (Tony award nomination for best featured actress in a musical, 1980), The Real Thing, 1984—85 (Tony award for best actress in a play, 1984), Benefactors, 1985—86, Death and the Maiden, 1992 (Tony award for best actress in a play, 1992), Sunset Boulevard, 1994—95 (Tony award for best actress in a musical, 1995), (other theatre appearances include) Uncommon Women and Others, The Singular Life of Albert Nobbs, 1982, Childhood, 1985, Joan of Arc at the Stake, 1985, Sunset Boulevard (LA), 1993—94, The Vagina Monologues, 1998; (films) The World According to Garp, 1982, The Big Chill, 1983, Greystoke: The Legend of Tarzan, Lord of the Apes (voice), The Natural, 1984, The Stone Boy, 1984, Jagged Edge, 1985, Maxie, 1985, Fatal Attraction, 1987, (voice) Gandahar, 1988, Dangerous Liaisons, 1988, Immediate Family, 1989, Reversal of Fortune, 1990, Hamlet, 1990, Meeting Venus, 1991, Hook, 1991, The House of the Spirits, 1993, The Paper, 1994, Mary Reilly, 1996, 101 Dalmations, 1996, Mars Attacks!, 1996, Paradise Road, 1997, Air Force One, 1997, Cookie's Fortune, 1999, (voice) Tarzan, 1999, Things You Can't Tell Just by Looking at Her, 2000, 102 Dalmations, 2000, The Safety of Objects, 2001, (voice) Pinocchio, 2002, Le Divorce, 2003, The Stepford Wives, 2004, Nine Lives, 2005, Heights, 2005, The Chumscrubber, 2005, (voice) Hoodwinked, 2005, Tarzan II, 2005, Evening, 2007; (TV films) The Rules of the Game, 1975, Too Far to Go, 1979, Orphan Train, 1979, The Elephant Man, 1982, Something About Amelia, 1984, Stones for Ibarra, 1988, She'll Take Romance, 1990, In the Gloaming, 1997, The Lion in Winter, 2003 (Golden Globe Award for best actress in a mini-series or TV movie, 2005, Screen Actors Guild Award for best actress in a TV movie or miniseries, 2005), Strip Search, 2004; (TV series) The Shield, 2005, Damages, 2007—; actor, exec. prodr. (TV films) Sarah, Plain and Tall, 1991, Skylark, 1993, Serving in Silence: The Margarethe Cammermeyer Story, 1995 (Emmy award for best actress in a miniseries or special, 1995), Sarah, Plain and Tall: Winter's End, 1999, Baby, 2000, The Ballad of Lucy Whipple, 2001, South Pacific, 2001; exec. prodr.: (TV films) Journey, 1995. Recipient Woman of Yr. Award Hasty Pudding Theatricals, Harvard U., 1990, Dartmouth Film Award, 1990. Mem. Phi Beta Kappa. Office: Creative Artists Agy 9830 Wilshire Blvd Beverly Hills CA 90212-1804*

CLOSE, LANNY GARTH, otolaryngologist, educator; b. San Antonio, Aug. 13, 1946; s. James Garth and Nona Lee (Galbraith) C.; m. Sharron Maredith Smith, Nov. 22, 1980; children: Hunter, Maredith. BA summa cum laude, Tex. Tech. U., 1968; MD cum laude, Baylor Coll. Medicine, 1972. Diplomate Am. Bd. Otolaryngology. Resident in surgery Johns Hopkins Hosp., Balt., 1972-74; resident in otolaryngology Baylor Affiliated Hosps., Houston, 1974-77; asst/assoc. prof. otolaryngology U. Tex., Houston, 1977-82; asst. surgeon dept. head & neck surgery M.D. Anderson Hosp., Houston, 1978-79; from assoc. prof. to prof. otolaryngology U. Tex. Southwestern Med. Sch., Dallas, 1982-94; prof., chmn. dept. otolaryngology/head and neck surgery Columbia U., NYC, 1994—. Guest examiner Am. Bd. Otolaryngology, 1993, 94, 96, 97; pres.-elect Columbia-Presbyn. Med. Bd. Contbr. numerous articles to profl. jours. Fellow ACS, Am. Laryngological Assn., The Triological Soc., Am. Rhinological Assn., Am. Broncho Esophageal Assn., Am. Soc. for Head and Neck Surgery, Soc. of Head and Neck Surgery; mem. Royal Soc. Medicine, Johns Hopkins Soc. Scholars, Alpha Omega Alpha. Office: Coll Physicians & Surgeons Columbia U 630 W 168th St New York NY 10032-3702 Business E-Mail: lgc6@columbia.edu.

CLOSE, MICHAEL JOHN, property manager, lawyer; b. Sandusky, Ohio, Jan. 24, 1943; s. Robert J. and Mary Lee (Graefe) C.; m. Nancy L. Schelp, June 18, 1995; children: Christina C., Karen L. AB in History, Lafayette Coll., Easton, Pa., 1965; JD cum laude, U. Mich., 1968. Assoc. Dewey, Ballantine, Bushby, Palmer & Wood, NYC, 1968-76; ptnr. Dewey Ballantine, NYC, 1976-96; pres., CEO Balmer Parc LLC, NYC, 2003—. Chmn. Tax Rev., N.Y.C. Author: Tax Aspects of Oil and Gas Drilling Funds, 1972, Drilling Funds: The 1977 Perspective, 1977, Special Allocations in Oil and Gas Ventures, 1982, The Final Section 704 (b) Regulations: Special Allocations Reach New Heights of Complexity, 1986, Fringe Benefit Regulation and the New York Law Firm Culture: A New Era, 1989, Off Balance Sheet Financings, 1994; contbr. articles to profl. jours. Bd. dirs., adminstrv. vice-chmn. Conn. Swimming, Inc., 1992-99; chmn. ad-hoc com. on by-laws USA Swimming, Inc., 1995-96; bd. dirs. Sharks Swim Team, Inc., 1991-94, pres., 1992-94; trustee Asolo Theatre Repertory Endowment Fund, 2005—; bd. dirs. Asolo Repertory Theatre, Inc., 2006—, mem. exec. com., 2006—. Mem. ABA (mem. tax sect. com. on partnerships), Assn. of Bar of City of N.Y., N.Y. Law Inst. (life mem.), N.Y. State Bar Assn. (mem. tax sect. com. partnerships), Ohio State Bar Assn., Real Estate Bd. N.Y.(assoc.), India House (N.Y.C.), Burning Tree Country Club (Greenwich, Conn.), Meadows Country Club (Sarasota, Fla.), Phi Delta Phi, Theta Chi. Republican. Home: 4951 Windsor Park Sarasota FL 34235-2610 Office: Balmer Parc LLC 18th Fl 445 Park Ave New York NY 10022 Office Phone: 212-486-8500. Personal E-mail: thecloses@comcast.net. Business E-Mail: mclose@dakotarealtyny.com.

CLOSEN, MICHAEL LEE, retired law educator; b. Peoria, Ill., Jan. 25, 1949; s. Stanley and Dorothy Closen. BS, MS, Bradley U., 1971; JD, U. Ill., 1974. Bar: Ill. 1974. Instr. U. Ill., Champaign, 1974; jud. clk. Ill. Appellate Ct., Springfield, 1974-76, 77-78; asst. states atty. Cook County, Chgo., 1978; prof. law John Marshall Law Sch., Chgo., 1976—2003; notary pub. State of Fla., 2004—, State of Ill., 1990—2003. Reporter Ill. Jud. Conf., Chgo., 1981—2002; arbitrator Am. Arbitration Assn., Chgo., 1981—2003; lectr. Ill. Inst. Continuing Legal Edn., Chgo., 1981—2002, BRI, 1985—; vis. prof. No. Ill. U., 1985—86, adj. prof., 1990, St. Thomas U., 1991, Loyola U., Chgo., 1999—2002; vis. prof. U. Ark., 1993, 96; arbitrator Cook County Cir. Ct. Mandatory Arbitration Program, 1990—2002, Will County Cir. Ct. Mandatory Arbitration Program, 1996—2002; dir. Ctr. for Legal Edn., Ltd., 1995—96. Author: (casebook) Agency and Partnership Law, 1984, Agency and Partnership Law, 3d edit., 2000; author: (with others) Contracts, 1984, Contracts, 3d edit., 1992, AIDS Cases and Materials, 1989, AIDS Cases and Materials, 3d edit., 2002, Notary Law and Practice, 1997, Contract Law and Practice, 1998; co-author: (book) The Shopping Bag: Portable Art, 1986, AIDS Law in a Nutshell, 2d edit., 1996, Legal Aspects of AIDS, 1991; contbr. articles to profl. jours. Named One of Outstanding Young Men in Am., 1981; recipient Svc. award, Am. Arbitration Assn., 1984—85, 5-Yr. Cmty. Achievement award, Ill. Politics Mag., 1998. Mem.: Nat. Notary Assn. (cons. 2004—, Achievement award 1998).

CLOSIUS, PHILLIP J., dean, law educator; BA, U. Notre Dame; JD, Columbia U. Atty. Kelley Drye & Warren, New York, NY; faculty mem. U. Toledo Sch. Law, 1979—, dean, prof. law, 1999—. Contbr. articles to law jours.; pub. in fields of Sports Law, Constl. Law and Law and Lit. Mem.: ABA, Toledo Bar Assn., Ohio State Bar Assn., Assn. Am. Law Sch. Office: U Toledo Sch Law 2801 W Bancroft Toledo OH 43606 Office Phone: 419-530-2379. Office Fax: 419-530-4526. E-mail: Phillip.Closius@utoledo.edu.

CLOSSON, WALTER FRANKLIN, child support prosecutor; b. Phila., Dec. 24, 1944; s. David Mayard Jr. and Florence Louise (Anderson) C.; m. Irene Veronica Jones, Aug. 10, 1968; children: Forrest Troy, Carey-Walter Franklin. BS in Music Edn., West Chester U., 1967; JD, Potomac Sch. Law, Washington, 1981. Bar: Ga. 1983, Md. 1985. Tchr. music D.C. Pub. Schs., Washington, 1967-77; tchr. woodwinds D.C. Youth Orch. Program, Washington, 1969-71; dist. ct. commr. Dist. Ct. of Md., Ellicott City, 1978-89; supervising dist. ct. commr. Dist. Ct. of Howard County, Ellicott City, 1984-89; asst. state's atty. State's Atty.'s Office, Ellicott City, 1989-99, chief child support divsn., 1999-2000; supervising atty. Bur. of Supoort Enforcement, Howard County Dept. Social Svcs., Columbia, Md., 2000—. Mem. Howard County Bar Assn., Waring-Mitchell Law Soc. (pres. 1992-94, Man of Yr. 1990), Masons (sr. deacon 1996-97, sr. warden 1997-98, worshipful master, 1998-99, Lodge treas. 2002-05), Delta Theta Phi (v.p. 1979-80). Office: Howard County Dept Social Svcs 7121 Columbia Gateway Dr Columbia MD 21046 Home Phone: 410-997-5319; Office Phone: 410-872-8769. Business E-Mail: WClosson@dhr.state.md.us.

CLOTHIAUX, PIERRE LAURENT, orthopedic surgeon; b. Aug. 28, 1956; married; 3 children. Student, Auburn U., Ala.; MD, U. Ala., Birmingham, 1982. Cert. Am. Bd. Orthop. Surgery, 1990. Intern orthop. surgery Mayo Clinic, Rochester, Minn., 1982—83, resident, 1983—87; fellow Beth Israel Hosp./Harvard Med. Sch., Boston, 1987—88; with Ferrell-Duncan Clinic CoxHealth, Springfield, Mo. Mem. adv. bd. and joint ops. com. CoxHealth, 1996—2007, mem. surg. exec. com., mem. bldg. and grounds com. of bd. dirs., 2003—, bd. dirs., 2007—, advisor to settlement com. Contbr. articles to med. jours. Named one of Top Docs, 417 Mag., 2006. Avocations: gardening, bicycling. Office: CoxHealth Ferrell-Duncan Clinic 1423 N Jefferson Ave Springfield MO 65802 Office Phone: 417-875-3800. Office Fax: 417-875-3176.

CLOTHIER, ROBERT CLARKSON, lawyer; b. Bryn Mawr, Pa., Apr. 26, 1961; s. Robert Clarkson Jr. and Maree (Horgan) Clothier; m. Anne Chandler Freeman, Feb. 7, 1964; children: Sarah Freeman, Caleb Hume. AB, Princeton U., NJ, 1983; JD with honors, U. Chgo., 1989. Bar: Pa. 1990. Law clk. to Hon. Robert Chapman US Ct. Appeals (4th cir.), Columbia, SC, 1989—90; ptnr. Dechert LLP, Phila., 1990—2003, High Swartz Roberts & Seidel LLP, Norristown, Pa., 2003—05, Fox Rothschild LLP, Phila., 2005—. Co-author: (pamphlet) The Media Survival Kit, 2001, Defamation Issues in Higher Education, 2004. Trustee Haverford Sch., Pa., 1995—. Mem.: Nat. Assn. Coll. and Univ. Attys., Media Law Resource Ctr., Order of Coif. Office: Fox Rothschild LLP 2000 Market St Philadelphia PA 19103

CLOTWORTHY, JOHN HARRIS, oceanographic consultant; b. Balt., Mar. 23, 1924; s. Harris A. and Violet (Klein) C.; m. Martha D. Wilson, Mar. 22, 1947; 1 child, John S. B.E.E., U. Va., 1946; certificate, Harvard Bus. Sch., 1956. Registered profl. engr., Md. With Westinghouse Electric Corp., 1948-67, v.p. def. and space center, gen. mgr. underseas div., 1963-67; chmn. div. ocean engring. U. Miami, Fla., 1967-68; cons. to oceanographic industry, 1967-68; founder, pres. Oceans Gen., Inc., Miami, 1968-71; dir. office congl. and legislative affairs NOAA, Washington, 1971-78; v.p., gen. mgr. Joint Oceanographic Instns. Inc., Washington, 1978-88, cons., 1988—. Sec., v.p. Oak Bldg. & Savs. Assn., 1946-56; Bd. govs. Va. Engring. Found., 1965-68, 72-78; bd. dirs. Historic Organ Restoration Com., Inc., 2006—. Trustee, co-chmn., bd. advisors Mare Nostrum Found., 1986-88. Fellow Marine Tech. Soc. (founding mem., bd. dirs. 1966-69, chmn. silver anniversary com. 1986-88, Lockheed award for ocean sci. and engring. 1992); mem. AAAS, Am. Geophys. Union, Am. Guild Organists, Nat. Oceanography Assn. (pres. 1966-69), Internat. Club Annapolis (pres. 1995-96), Annapolis Yacht Club, Atlantic City Convention Hall Organ Soc. (sec.-treas. 1998—), Alpha Tau Omega. Home: 2014 Gov Thomas Bladen Way Apt #201 Annapolis MD 21401 E-mail: jclotwor@comcast.net.

CLOUD, BRUCE BENJAMIN, SR., retired construction executive; b. Thomas, Okla., Feb. 15, 1920; s. Dudley R. and Lillian (Sanders) Cloud; m. Virginia Dugan, June 5, 1944 (dec.); children: Sheila Marie Cloud Kiselis, Karen Susan, Bruce Benjamin, Deborah Ann Cloud McKenzie, Virginia Ann Cloud Treadwell. BCE, Tex. A&M U., 1940. Registered profl. engr., Tex. With H.B. Zachry Co., San Antonio, 1940-42, 55-99, exec. v.p., 1963-87, pres., 1987-93, vice chmn., 1993-94, sr. corp. advisor, 1995-99, adv. dir., 1999—2004; ptnr., bd. dirs. Dudley R. Cloud & Son, Constrn., San Antonio, 1946-55; owner Cloud Enterprises, San Antonio; ret. Mem. adv. bd. dirs. Capitol Cement Co./Aggregate Co., 1999—2004. Mem. adv. coun. Boysville Inc., 1978—79; bd. dirs. Tex. State Tech. Coll. Found., 1983—97, 1998—, hon. life bd. dirs. Lt. col. C.E. US Army, 1942—46, ETO. Recipient Pro Deo Et Juventute award, Nat. Coun. Cath. Youth, Soyr Svc. award, 2003. Mem.: NSPE, Cons. Contractors Coun. Am. (chmn. 1989), Tex. Engring. Ext. Svc. (adv. bd. 1995—97), Tex. Transp. Inst. (adv. bd. 1993—97), Am. Mgmt. Assn., Tex. Good Rds.-Transp. Assn. (bd. dirs. 1974—79, mem. exec. com. 1975—81, 1985—89), Tex. Soc. Profl. Engrs., Nat. Assn. Gen. Contractors (mem. bur. reclamation com. 1968—97, mem. environ. com. 1971—76, mem. enrgy and materials 1976—86, bd. dirs. 1976—88, life dir., mem. exec. com. 1978—79, mem. equipment mgmt. com. 1978—97, chmn. heavy divsn. 1979, mem. ethics rules legis. com. 1979, mem. fin. com. 1979, mem. water and power resource com. 1980—81, mem. transp. policy com. 1980—95, mem. engring. documentation rev. com. 1985, mem. corps engrs. com. 1988—97, mem. quality constrn. com. 1993—96, Nat. AGC Oustanding Com. chmn. 1997), Tex. Hotmix Paving Assn. (bd. dirs. 1972), Nat. Asphalt Paving Assn., Am. Concrete Paving Assn. (v.p. 1970—74, bd. dirs., 1st v.p. 1975, pres. 1976), Am. Inst. Mgmt., San Antonio Livestock Assn. (life), Tex. Assn. Gen. Contractors (life; dir. hwy. and heavy br. 1947—48, 1972—76, pres. 1974, chmn. corps engrs. joint com. 1989—90), San Antonio C. of C. (chmn. better rds. task force 1978—79, 1985—93, bd. dirs. 1993—94), Nocturnal Adoration Soc., Holy Name Soc. (v.p. 1962—63), KC (3d degree).

CLOUD, JOHN ALBERT, JR., ambassador; married; 2 children. BA, U. Conn., 1975; MA in Internat. Affairs, George Washington U., 1977. Mem. US Dept. State, Washington, 1988—91, economic counselor, Am. Embassy in Bonn Germany, 1991—95, dep. chief mission Warsaw, 1996—99, dep. chief mission to EU, 1999—2001; spl. asst. to pres., sr. dir. internat. affairs NSC, Washington, 2001—03; dep. chief mission US Dept. State, Berlin, 2003—05, interim chargé d'affaires, 2005, US amb. to Lithuania Vilnius, 2006—. Recipient Superior Honor award (3), US Dept. State. Office: US Embassy 4510 Vilnius Pl Washington DC 20521

CLOUD, ROBERT ROYCE, surgeon; b. Houston, Feb. 12, 1954; s. Albert Hadden and Emily Ann (Royce); m. Connie Jo, Aug. 4, 2001; children: Ashley, Tyler. BS, Northeast La. U., 1976; MD, Tulane U., New Orleans, 1980. Intern gen. surgery Baylor Med. Ctr., Dallas, 1980-81, resident gen. surgery, 1981-85, fellow colon rectal surgery, 1985-86; private practice Dallas, 1986—. Mem. staff Med. City Hosp., Dallas, 1986—, Baylor Hosp., 1986—, Presbyn. Hosp., Dallas, 1988—. Bd. dirs. Wednesday's Child, Am. Cancer Soc. Fellow ACS, Am. Soc. Colon Rectal Surgeons; mem. Tex. Surgical Soc., Tex. Med. Assn., Tex. Soc. Colon Rectal Surgeons, Dallas County Med. Soc. Avocations: golf, tennis. Office: 12200 Park Central Dr Ste 100 Dallas TX 75251-2102 Personal E-mail: dcloudmd@ultradsl.net.

CLOUDSLEY, DONALD HUGH, retired library administrator; b. Buffalo, Jan. 11, 1925; s. James Rowland and Helen Margaret (Macgregor) C. BA, Bethany Coll., W.Va., 1948; MLS, Carnegie Inst. Tech., 1949. Jr. librarian Buffalo Pub. Library, 1949-52; sr. librarian I Erie County Pub. Library, Buffalo, 1952-58; sr. librarian II Buffalo and Erie County Pub. Library, 1958-59, dep. dir., 1974-83, dir., 1983-95; reference librarian Grosvenor Library, Buffalo, 1959-61; head Brighton br. Tonawanda Library, NY, 1961-65; dir. Tonawanda Library, 1965-73; trustee West N.Y. Libr. Resources Coun., Buffalo, 1983-93, treas., 1976-89. Mem. N.Y. State Regent's Adv. Coun. on Librs., 1988-93, chmn., 1990-91; mem. adv. com. on pub. librs. Online Computer Libr. Ctr., 1991-94. Mem. citizens adv. coun. SUNY-Buffalo, 1983-95. Named Boss of Yr., Am. Bus. Women's Assn., Buffalo, 1984; recipient Alumni Achievement award Bethany Coll., 1991, Buffalo (N.Y.) News Citizen of Yr. award, 1992. Mem. ALA, N.Y. Libr. Assn., N.Y. State Pub. Librs. Assn. (cert. com. 1971-75), Rotary (treas. Kenmore, N.Y. club 1975-76), Beta Theta Pi. Methodist. Home: 152 Hidden Ridge Cmn Williamsville NY 14221-5765

CLOUES, EDWARD BLANCHARD, II, lawyer; b. Concord, NH, Dec. 28, 1947; s. Alfred Samuel and H. Jeannette (Callas) C.; m. Mary Anne Matthews, Aug. 21, 1971; children: E. Matthew, M. Elizabeth. BA, Harvard U., 1969; JD, NYU, 1972. Bar: Pa. 1972, U.S. Dist. Ct. (ea. dist.) Pa. 1973. Law clk. to hon. judge James Hunter III U.S. Ct. Appeals (3d cir.), Phila. and Camden, NJ, 1972-73; assoc. Morgan, Lewis & Bockius LLP, Phila., 1973-79, ptnr., 1979-98; chmn., CEO K-Tron Internat., Inc., Pitman, NJ, 1998—. Bd. chmnn, CEO K-Tron Internat., Pitman, NJ, 1996-, vice chmn. bd., 1987-94; bd. dirs. AMREP Corp., chmn., 1995—; bd. dirs. Penn Va. Corp., Penn Va. Resource Ptnrs., L.P. Republican. Lutheran. Avocations: travel, reading. Office: K-Tron Internat Inc PO Box 888 Rtes 55 & 553 Pitman NJ 08071 Home Phone: 215-643-6516; Office Phone: 856-256-3310. Business E-Mail: ecloues@ktron.com.

CLOUGH, RAY WILLIAM, JR., civil engineering educator; b. Seattle, July 23, 1920; s. Ray William and Mildred (Nelson) Clough; m. Shirley Claire Potter, Oct. 30, 1942; children: Douglas Potter, Allison Justine, Meredith Anne. BSCE, U. Wash., 1942; MS, Calif. Inst. Tech., 1943; SM, MIT, 1947, ScD in Civil Engring., 1949; DTech (hon.), Chalmers U., Goteborg, Sweden, 1979, Norges Tekniske Høgskole, Trondheim, Norway, 1982. Registered engr., Wash. Faculty U. Calif.-Berkeley, 1949—, prof. civil engring., 1959—, chmn. div. structural engring. and structural mechanics, 1967—70, dir. Earthquake Engring. Rsch. Ctr., 1973—76, Nishkian prof. structural engring., 1983—87, prof. emeritus, dept. civil engring., 1987—. Cons. in field; adv. com. NAS-NAE Environ. Sci. Svcs. Adminstrn., 1967—70; mem. U.S. C.E. Structural Design Adv. Bd., 1967—79. Capt. USAF, 1942—46. Named Hon. Rschr., Lab. Nat. De Engenharia Civil Lisbon, 1972; recipient Benjamin Franklin medal in Civil Engring., Franklin Inst., 2006, Sr. Rsch. award, Am. Soc. for Engring. Edn., 1986, Congress medal, Internat. Assn. Computer Mechanics, 1986, citation, U. Calif., 1987, A.C. Eringen medal, Soc. of Engring. Sci., 1992, U.S. Nat. Medal of Sci., presented by Pres. William J. Clinton, 1994, Prince Philip medal, Royal Acad. Engring., 1997, George W. Housner medal, Earthquake Engring. Rsch. Inst., 1996, Top Seismic Engr. of 20th Century award, Applied Tech. Coun. San Francisco, 2006; Fulbright fellowship, NTH Norway, 1956—57, Overseas fellow, Cambridge (Eng.) U., 1963—64. Fellow: ASCE (hon.; chmn. engring. mechanics divsn. 1964—65, Rsch. award 1960, Howard award 1970, Newmark medal 1979, Moissieff medal 1980, T. VonKarman medal 1980), Inst. Water Conservation and Hydroelectric Power Rsch. (hon.); mem.: NAE, NAS (dynamics panel adv. bd. on hardened electric power sys. 1964—70), Chinese Acad. Engring., Seismol. Soc. Am. (bd. dirs. 1970—73), Structural Engrs. Assn. No. Calif. (bd. dirs. 1967—70).

CLOUGH, (GERALD) WAYNE, academic administrator; b. Douglas, Ga., Sept. 24, 1941; married; 2 children. BSCE, Ga. Inst. Tech., 1964, MSCE, 1965; PhD, U. Calif., Berkeley, 1969. Registered prof. engr., Calif., Va. Assoc. prof. Duke Univ.; assoc. prof. to prof. civil engring. Stanford U.,

Calif., 1974—82; prof. civil engring., coord. geotech. program Va. Polytechnic Inst. and State U., 1982—83, prof. civil engring., head dept. civil engring., 1983—90, dean Coll. Engring., 1990—93; provost, prof. civil engring. U. Wash., Seattle, 1993—94; pres. Ga. Inst. Tech., Atlanta, 1994—. Bd. dirs. Noro-Moseley Ptnrs., TSYS, Columbus, Ga., Nat. Sci. Bd.; spl. cons. San Francisco Bay Area Rapid Transit Sys.; apptd. Pres. Coun. Adv. on Sci. & Tech., 2001—; chmn. nanotechnology task force. Contbr. articles to profl. jours., chapters to books. Trustee Ga. Rsch. Alliance; chmn. Gov. Perdue's Telecomm. Task Force; mem. exec. com., co-chair Nat. Innovation Initiative U.S. Coun. Competitiveness; mem. exec. com. Metro Atlanta C. of C. Named one of 100 Most Influential People in Ga., Ga. Trend Mag.; recipient George Westinghouse award, Am. Soc. Engring. Edn., 1986, Nat. Engring. award, Am. Assn. Engring. Societies, 2001, Norman Medal, 1982, 1996. Mem.: NAE (chmn., Engr. of 2020 project), ASCE (hon. OPAL award Lifetime Achievement in Edn. 2004), Metro Atlanta C. of C. (exec. com.). Home: Ga Inst Tech Office of the Pres 225 N Ave NW Carnegie Bldg Atlanta GA 30332-0325*

CLOUGH, WILLIAM ROBERT, minister, educator; b. Tarpon Springs, Fla., Aug. 4, 1949; s. William James and Mildred Wyngarden Clough; m. Elizabeth McCracken Clough, June 20, 1971; children: William Patrick, David Ian. BS, Fla. Presbyn. Coll., St. Petersburg, FL, 1971; DMin, Louisville Presbyn. Theol. Sem., 1974; MDiv, Louisville Presbyn. Theol. Sem., 1978; MA, Salve Regina U., Newport, RI, 1989. Ordained minister Presbyn. Ch., USA, 1975, Senior Fellow Inst. for Interdisciplinary Rsch. Commd. ensign USN, 1974, advanced through grades to comdr., ret., 2000; assoc. prof., program chair, pastoral cmty. counseling program Argosy U., Sarasota, Fla., 2000—. Chaplain US Navy, 1974—2000. Contbr. articles to profl. jours. Mem.: Am. Assn. Pastoral Counselors, Fla. Ctr. Sci. and Religion, Presbyn. Assn. Sci., Tech. and the Christian Faith (founding mem.). Democrat-Npl. Presbyterian. Avocations: writing, scuba diving. Office: Argosy Univ Sarasota 5250 17th St Sarasota FL 34235 Office Phone: 941-379-0404.

CLOUS, JAMES M., electrical equipment company executive, engineer; b. Traverse City, Mich., July 22, 1959; s. August J. and Beverly J. (Kroetsch) C.; m. Mimi M. O'Connell, June 28, 1979 (div. July 1983). AS, Northwetern Mich. Coll., 1979; BSME, Mich. Tech. U., 1981. Sales engr. Louis Allis-Litton, Houston, 1981-83; dist. mgr. Louis Allis-Magnetek, Baton Rouge, 1984-85, GEC Automation Projects, Houston, 1986-88; regional mgr. Ross Hill Controls, Houston, 1989-91; nat. sales mgr. ABB Indsl. Systems, New Berlin, Wis., 1991-94; v.p. sales and mktg. Ideal Electric, Mansfield, Ohio, 1994-96; pres. Clous Cons., Traverse City, Mich., 1996—; fin. advisor Waddell & Reed, Traverse City, 2001—03, First Asset Fin., 2004—. Pvt. practice mktg. cons., Houston, 1987-91. Mem. Nat. Rep. Com., Washington, 1988. Mem.: IEEE, Traverse Bay Twilight Rotary Club (charter mem., chmn. charter night com., club svc., chmn. bd. dirs.). Republican. Roman Catholic. Home: 887 Carver St Traverse City MI 49686 Office: First Asset Fin 945 E 8th St Traverse City MI 49686 Office Phone: 231-631-1571. Personal E-mail: jimclous@aol.com.

CLOUSE, JOHN DANIEL, lawyer; b. Evansville, Ind., Sept. 4, 1925; s. Frank Paul and Anna Lucille (Frank) C.; m. Georgia L. Ross, Dec. 7, 1978; 1 child, George Chauncey. AB, U. Evansville, 1950; JD, Ind. U., 1952. Bar: Ind. 1952, US Supreme Ct. 1962, US Ct. Appeals (7th cir.) 1965. Assoc. Firm of James D. Lopp, Evansville, 1952-56; pvt. practice Evansville, 1956—. Guest editorialist Viewpoint, Evansville Courier, 1978—86, Evansville Press, 1986—98, Focus, Radio Sta. WGBF, 1978—84; 2d asst. city atty. Evansville, 1954—55; mem. Com. for Implementation of Criminal Justice Act of 1964, 1965; mem. appellate rules sub-com. Ind. Supreme Ct. Com. on Rules of Practice and Procedure, 1980. Pres. Civil Svc. Commn. Evansville Police Dept., 1961-62, v.p., 1988; pres. Ind. War Memls. Com., 1963-69; mem. jud. nominating com. Vanderburgh County, Ind., 1976-80; dir. Ind. Fed. Cmty. Defender Project, Inc., 1993-98. With inf. US Army, 1943-46. Decorated Bronze Star; named one of World's Most travelled Man Guinness Book of Records, 1993, Most Travelled Man, 1995-2001; named to Bar Register of Preeminent Lawyers. Mem. Evansville Bar Assn. (v.p. 1972, James Bethel Gresham Freedom award 1997), Ind. Bar Assn. (chmn. com. on civil rights 1991-92), 87th Inf. Divsn. Assn., Internat. Wood Collectors Soc., Register Preminent Lawyers, Club Internat. Des Grand Voyageurs, Travelers Century Club (LA), Pi Gamma Mu. Republican. Methodist. Office: 123 NW 4th St Ste 317 Evansville IN 47708-1712 Home Phone: 812-473-3748; Office Phone: 812-424-6671. Personal E-mail: jdcmjs@aol.com.

CLOUSTON, ROSS NEAL, retired food and related products company executive; b. Montreal, Que., Can., Sept. 13, 1922; came to U.S., 1965, naturalized, 1973; s. Alan Roy and Maude (Neal) C.; m. Brenda Kerson, Feb. 12, 1944; children: Robert, Brendan. B.Sc., McGill U., 1949; MBA, Harvard U., 1951. With fisheries plant, N.S., Canada, from 1940; founder LaSalle Foods Ltd., 1953, Blue Water Sea Food Ltd., Montreal, 1959, Blue Water Sea Food Ltd. (merged into Gorton Corp., 1963, merged into Gen. Mills, Inc. 1968); pres. Gorton Group div. Gen. Mills, Inc., 1969-86, chmn., 1986-87, corp. v.p. parent co., 1970-87; v.p. Gen. Mills Can. Ltd. Pres. Nat. Fisheries Inst., 1975, Fisheries Council Can., 1962. Served with RCAF, 1941-45. Decorated Royal Norwegian Order of Merit; recipient Man of Yr. award Nat. Fisheries Inst., 1985. Mem. The Oaks.

CLOUTMAN, EDWARD BRADBURY, III, lawyer; b. Lake Charles, La., Dec. 8, 1945; s. Edward Bradbury Jr. and Evelyn (Daniel) C.; m. Kathryn Sue Robinson, Aug., 1967 (div. 1974); children: Michael Edward, Chad Edward; m. Elizabeth Katherine Julian, June 11, 1976; 1 child, Edward Bradbury IV. JD, La. State U., 1969. Bar: La. 1969, U.S. Dist. Ct. (we. dist.) La., U.S. Ct. Appeals (5th cir.) 1970, Tex. 1971, U.S. Dist. Ct. (no., we., and ea. dists.) Tex., U.S. Supreme Ct. 1973, U.S. Ct. Appeals (10th cir.) 1974, U.S. Ct. Appeals (6th cir.) 1980, U.S. Ct. Appeals (11th cir.) 1982. Reginald Heber Smith fellow CENLA Legal Aid Soc., Alexandria, La., 1969-70, Dallas Legal Svcs. Found., 1970-71; ptnr. Johnston, Polk, Larson, Cloutman & Dixon, Dallas, 1971-73; assoc. Mullinax, Wells, Mauzy and Baab, Inc., Dallas, 1973-74; ptnr. Mullinax, Wells, Baab and Cloutman, P.C., Dallas, 1975-90; pvt. practice Dallas, 1990—. Adj. prof. So. Meth. U. Sch. Law, 1990-98. Mem. ABA, Inns of Ct. (master 1990—). Democrat. Office: 3301 Elm St Dallas TX 75226-2562 Home Phone: 214-826-3674; Office Phone: 214-939-9222. E-mail: crawfish11@prodigy.net.

CLOVER, HAWORTH ALFRED, elementary school educator, historian; b. Woodland, Calif., Feb. 18, 1933; s. Herman Alfred and Anna Margaret (Powell) C.; m. Carol Ann Anderson, June 17, 1961 (dec. Jan. 26, 2005); children: Haworth Alfred, John Allan, Catherine Alette. Student, U. Calif., Davis, 1950-51; MusB, U. Pacific, Stockton, Calif., 1954, BA, 1957, MA, 1960, EdD, 1977; postgrad., Stanford U., Calif., 1962, U. Vt., Burlington, 1963. Cert. spl. secondary music tchr., gen. elem. tchr., elem. adminstr. Elem. tchr. San Joaquin (Calif.) County Schs., 1957-60, Hillsborough (Calif.) City Sch. Dist., 1960—96. Landmark cons. Yolo County Hist. Soc., Woodland, 1984-86; mem. adj. faculty history dept. U. Pacific, 1995—. Author: Hesperian College 1861-1896, 1973; compiler: (book) Haytime, 1974, reprinted, 2006, Hesperian College Landmarks, 1995, We're Only Here For A Visit the Story of the Feather River Inn Golf Course, 2004, The Matthews Family-Community Builders From Coast to Coast, 2007. Mem. San Francisco Mus. Soc., 1976-2003, San Francisco Zool. Soc., 1976-1996. With U.S. Army, 1954-56. Recipient Kirkbride Calif. History award U. of the Pacific, Stockton, 1957, Outstanding Svc. to U., U of the Pacific, 2005. Mem. NEA, Calif. Sch. Adminstrn. Assn., Calif. and Pa. Geneal. Soc., Hillsborough Tchrs. Assn. (treas. 1961-63), Jedediah Smith Rsch. Assn. (bd. dir. 1994-96, exec. dir. 1996—, career change telecommuter), Commonwealth Club Calif., Westerner's Internat. (sheriff San Francisco corral 1983), San Mateo County Men's Garden Club (pres. 1972-73), U. Pacific Alumni (bd. dir., sec. 1985-1998), Masons (past master 1986, past patron 1993-94), Phi Mu Alpha, Phi Delta Kappa, Phi Kappa Phi, Sigma Alpha Epsilon. Republican. Presbyterian. Avocations: wood working, gardening, photography, travel. Office: Hesperia Press 8366 Mediterranean Way Sacramento CA 95826 Office Phone: 916-388-9422.

CLOVIS, SAMUEL HARVEY, JR., academic administrator; b. Salina, Kans., Sept. 18, 1949; s. Samuel Harvey and Mildred Marie (Baize) C.; m. LaVeta Roos, Nov. 27, 1971 (div. Mar. 2000); children: Travis Justin, Matthew Allen; m. Charlotte Anne Chase, July 21, 2000; 1 stepson, Robert Khan Rosenberger. BS in Polit. Sci., USAF Acad., 1971; MBA, Golden Gate U., 1984; D of Pub. Adminstrn., U. Ala., Tuscaloosa, 2006. Commd. 2d lt. USAF, 1971, advanced through grades to col., 1992, ret., 1996; mgr. tech. support Betac Corp., Colorado Springs, Colo., 1996-97; mgr. strategic solutions divsn. Logicon Inc., Herndon, Va., 1997-2000; assoc. dean, dir. of faculty Coll. Working Adults William Penn U., Oskaloosa, Iowa, 2000—02, founding dean Coll. of Bus. and Mgmt. Sci., 2002—03; mgr. bus. devel. Northrop Grumman Corp., 2003—04; assoc. Booz Allen Hamilton, 2004; chair, prof. dept. bus. adminstrn. and econ. Morningside Coll., Sioux City, Iowa, 2004—. Mem. affiliate faculty Regis U., Denver, 1995—; cons. Rand Corp., Santa Monica, Calif., 1996-2000; prin. analyst Homeland Security Inst., Arlington, Va., 2004-. Mem. ASPA, Am. Polit. Sci. Assn., Assn. of Grads. USAF Acad., Assn. for Pub. Policy Analysis and Mgmt. Avocations: fishing, golf, weightlifting. Office: Morningside Coll 1501 Morningside Ave Sioux City IA 51106 Office Phone: 712-274-5437. E-mail: clovis@morningside.edu.

CLOW, LEE, advertising agency executive; With Chiat/Day, LA, 1972—, exec. v.p., creative dir., pres., chief creative officer; chmn., worldwide chief creative officer TBWA/Chiat/Day, LA, 1995—. Bd. dir. Oakley Inc., 2002—. Named Creative Exec. of Yr., USA Today, 1997; named to One Club Hall of Fame, Art Dir. Hall of Fame, Advt. Hall of Fame, Mus. Modern Art; recipient Lifetime Achievement Award, Clio Awards Fest., 2004. Office: TBWA Chiat/Day 5353 Grosvenor Blvd Los Angeles CA 90066*

CLOWER, DONNA, music company executive; b. 1970; Grad., U. NC. Ind. cons. Capitol Records; assoc. dir. spl. markets Arista Records, 1999—2000; sr. dir. strategic mktg. J Records, 2000—03; v.p. strategic mktg. & artist devel. RCA Music Group, 2003—07; sr. v.p. strategic mktg. & artist devel. BMG Label Group, 2007—. Office: BMG Label Group Sony BMG Music Entertainment 550 Madison Ave New York NY 10022*

CLOWES, EDITH W., language educator, consultant, literature educator, consultant; b. Cleve., Dec. 23, 1951; BA, Oberlin U., 1973; MPhil, Yale U., 1977, PhD, 1981. Asst. prof. Russian lang. and lit. Knox Coll., Galesburg, Ill., 1981—82; asst. prof. U. Va., Charlottesville, 1983—84; from asst. prof. to assoc. prof. Purdue U., West Lafayette, Ind., 1984—94, prof., 1994—98, dir. program in comparative lit., 1992—94; prof. Slavic langs. and lit. U. Kans., Lawrence, 1999—. Author: (book) Maksim Gorky, 1987, The Revolution of Moral Consciousness, 1988, Russian Experimental Fiction: Resisting Ideology after Utopia, 1993, Fiction's Overcoat: Russian Literacy Culture and the Question of Philosophy, 2004; editor: Between Tsar and People, 1991, Doctor Zhivago: A Critical Companion, 1995, Collaborator: Merchant Moscow, 1998; translator: Private Wealth-National Vision: The Memoirs of a New Russian Entrepreneur (Aleksandr Panikin), 2000. Fellow, NEH, 2001; grantee, ITT, Munich, 1973—74, IREX, Moscow, 1978—79, 1993, 1994, 1997, NEH, 1986—88, 2005, German Acad. Exch. Svc., 1998, German Acad. Exch. Svc, 2004, ACLS, 2006—. Mem.: MLA, Am. Comparative Lit. Assn., N.Am. Nietzsche Soc., Am. Assn. Tchrs. Slavic and E. European Lang., Am. Assn. Advancement Slavic Studies, Phi Beta Kappa. Office: U Kans Dept Slavic Langs and Lits Lawrence KS 66045

CLOWES, GARTH ANTHONY, electronics executive, consultant; b. Didsbury, Eng., Aug. 30, 1936; came to U.S., 1957; s. Eric and Doris Gladys (Worthington) C.; m. Katharine Allman Crewdson, July 29, 1950 (dec. Jan. 1998); children: John Howard Brett, Peter Miles, Vicki Anne. BSc, Stockport Coll., Cheshire, Eng., 1953; postgrad., UCLA, 1965-66; higher nat. cert., Birmingham U., Eng., 1955-56. Gen. mgr., v.p., dir. Eldon Industries, Inc., El Segundo, Calif., 1962-69; CEO, founder Entex Industries, Inc., Compton, Calif., 1969-83; pres., founder Entex Electronics, Inc., Camano Island, Calif., 1983—. Pres., founder TTC, Inc., Carson, Calif., 1984-86; pres. Universal Telesis Electronics, Inc., Carson, 1986-87; gen. mgr. Matchbox Toys (U.S.A.) Ltd., Moonachie, N.J., 1987-88; dir. gen. Matchbox Spain, S.A., Valencia, 1988-89; cons. Matchbox Internat. Ltd., worldwide, 1986-89; spkr. in bus. field. Inventor electronic voice recognition devices, numerous others. Mem. pres.'s com. UNICEF, N.Y., 1972-74, Senate Adv. Bd., Washington, 1982-83; cons. Interracial Coun., L.A., 1967-69; mem. adv. bd. Santa Rosa Coll., 1993-99. Decorated Knight of Malta. Avocations: antiques, gardening, art, breeding scotch highland cattle. Home: 68 W Cross Island Rd Camano Island WA 98282-6667 Home Phone: 306-387-5497. E-mail: sonoma@webtv.net.

CLOWES, JOHN HOWARD, lawyer; BA, U. Calif., Santa Barbara, 1976; JD, U. Calif., Berkeley, 1982. Bar: Calif. 1982. Ptnr., co-chmn. Emerging Growth & Venture Capital practice group DLA Piper Rudnick Gray Cary, San Francisco. Named a No. Calif. Super Lawyer, San Francisco mag., 2004. Mem.: ABA. Office: DLA Piper Rudnick Gray Cary Suite 800 153 Townsend St San Francisco CA 94107 Office Phone: 415-836-2510. Office Fax: 415-836-2501. Business E-Mail: howard.clowes@dlapiper.com.

CLOYD, G. GIL, information technology executive; Joined Proctor & Gamble Co., 1970—; v.p. Proctor and Gamble Distributing Co., Cin.; global v.p. for consumer products, v.p. corporate R&D in Asia; chief technology officer Proctor and Gamble Co., 2000—. Named Technology Leader of Yr., Industry Week, 2004. Office: Proctor and Gamble 1 Proctor & Gamble Plz Cincinnati OH 45202 Office Phone: 513-983-1100. Office Fax: 513-562-4500.

CLOYD, J. TIMOTHY, academic administrator; m. Rebecca Davis Cloyd; 2 children. BA in Philosophy and Polit. Sci. magna cum laude, Emory and Henry Coll., 1985; MA in Polit. Sci., U. Mass., 1990, PhD in Polit. Sci., 1991. Rsch. fellow Inst. for the Study of World Politics, Washington, 1990—91; mem. polit. sci. faculty, coord. program in social and polit. thought Vanderbilt U., 1991—94; mgr. U.S. Senate Race, Tenn., 1994; exec. dir. devel. and alumni rels. U. Ark., Little Rock, 1994—97; from asst. prof. to prof. politics Hendrix Coll., Conway, Ark., 1997—, v.p. for devel. and coll. rels., 1997—2001, pres., 2001—. Chair exec. com. So. Collegiate Athletics Conf., 2004—. Author: The Gulf War and Just War: A Study Guide on the Persian Gulf War; co-editor: (collection of essays) Politics and the Human Body, 1995. Office: Hendrix Coll 1600 Washington Ave Conway AR 72032 Office Phone: 501-450-1351. E-mail: cloyd@hendrix.edu.*

CLUBB, BRUCE EDWIN, retired lawyer; b. Blackduck, Minn., Feb. 6, 1931; s. Ernest and Abigail (Gordy) Clubb; m. Martha Lucia Trapp, Dec. 19, 1954 (dec. Nov. 2001); children: Bruce Allen, Christopher Wade. BBA, U. Minn., 1955, LL.B. cum laude, 1958. Bar: DC 1959. Atty. Covington & Burling, 1958-61, Devel. Loan Fund, 1961-62, Chapman, DiSalle and Friedman, 1962-67; commr. U.S. Tariff Commn., 1967-71; ptnr. firm Baker & McKenzie, Washington, 1971-96; disting. lawyer in residence U. Minn. Law Sch., 1981-82. Chmn. bd. dirs. Sunrise Properties, Inc., 1989—99. Author: (treatise) United States Foreign Trade Law (2 vols.), 1991; contbr. law revs. With US Army, 1952—54. Mem. D.C. Bar Assn., Am. Arbitration Assn. (arbitrator 1994-2000), Order of Coif, Cosmos Club (pres. 1986), Met. Club, Army Navy Club. Republican. Personal E-mail: bclubb2@aol.com.

CLUFF, LLOYD STERLING, earthquake geologist; b. Provo, Utah, Sept. 29, 1933; s. Colvin Sterling and Melba Cluff; m. Janet L. Peterson, Dec. 21, 1976; children: Tanya, Sasha, Branden. BS in Geology, U. Utah, 1960. Registered profl. geologist, Calif.; cert. engring. geologist, Calif. Jr. geologist El Paso Natural Gas Co., Salt Lake City, 1957-59; tchg. asst. dept. geology U. Utah, Salt Lake City, 1958-60; geologist Lottridge Thomas & Assocs., Salt Lake City, 1960; v.p., prin. geologist Woodward-Clyde Cons., San Francisco, 1960—85; assoc. prof. geology and geophysics U. Nev., Reno, 1967-73; dir. dept. geoscis. Pacific Gas and Electric Co., San Francisco, 1985—. Cons. Trans-Alaska Pipeline Siting Study, 1972-74; Aswan High Dam seismic safety evaluation, Govt. of Egypt, 1982-86; mem. com. Nat. Earthquake Hazards Reduction Program, Washington, 1987, Decade for Natural Disaster Reduction, Washington, 1989; advisor Venezuela Pres.'s Earthquake Safety Com., 1967-72; advisor Joint Legis. Com. on Seismic Safety, State of Calif., 1970-74; chmn. seismic rev. panel Calif. Pub. Utilities Commn., San Francisco, 1980-81; mem. Calif. Seismic Safety Commn., 1985-99, chmn., 1988-90, 95-97; adv. bd. So. Calif. Earthquake Ctr., 1996-2001, 04—; chmn. Tech. Adv. Bd. on Earthquake Risk, Israel, 1996-2004; adv. panel on earth scis. NSF, 1992-95; chmn. com. on practical lessons from the Loma Prieta Earthquake, 1994; organizing com. for Pub. Policy Partnership 2000-White House Confs. on Natural Disaster Loss Reduction, 1997-98; com. on assessing costs of natural disasters NAS, 1998-99, bd. natural disasters NAS, 1997-2000, Natural Disaster Roundtable, 2000—; nat. pre-disaster mitigation program adv. panel FEMA, 1998-99; external adv. panel for Pacific Earthquake Engring. Rsch. Ctr., 1998-99, implementation adv. bd., 1999—; natural disaster panel Heinz Ctr. Inst. for Natural Disasters, 2000-02; chmn. sci. earthquake studies adv. com. USGS Nat. Earthquake Hazards Reduction Program, 2002—. Recipient Hogentagler award ASTM, 1968, Alfred E. Alquist medal, Calif. Earthquake Safety Found., 1998, John Wesley Powell award, USGS, 2000, William Joyner Meml. Lecture award Seismol. Soc. Am. and Earthquake Engring. Rsch. Inst., 2003, Lifetime Achievement award Western States Seismic Policy Coun., 2006; named Woodward lectr., San Francisco, 1979, Sinotech Dist. lectr., Taiwan, 2002. Fellow Calif. Acad. Scis.; mem. NAE, Seismol. Soc. Am. (pres. 1982-83), Assn. Engring. Geologists (pres. 1968-69), Earthquake Engring. Rsch. Inst. (hon., pres. 1993-95, chmn. Internat. Conf. on Seismic Zonation, Nice, France 1995), Geol. Soc. Am., Structural Engrs. Assn. No. Calif. (H.J. Degenkolb award 1992), Nat. Acad. Delegation Islamic Rep. of Iran, 2000. Republican. Avocations: photography, skiing, mountain climbing, hiking, bicycling. Office: Pacific Gas & Elec Co 245 Market St San Francisco CA 94105-1797 Office Phone: 415-973-2791. E-mail: lsc2@pge.com.

CLUMP, MICHAEL ADEN, psychologist, educator; s. Aden H. and Dee Clump; m. Keli Braitman, Aug. 2, 2001. BA, Wabash Coll., 1997; PhD, So. Ill. U., 2001. Asst. prof. psychology Boise (Idaho) State U., 2001—03, Marymount U., Arlington, Va., 2003—, chair undergrad. psychology program, 2004—. Vis. asst. prof. psychology St. Mary's Coll., Notre Dame, Ind., 2001. Contbr. articles to profl. jours. Mem.: APA, Am. Psychol. Soc., Ea. Psychol. Assn., Coun. Tchrs. Undergrad. Psychology, Phi Beta Kappa, Psi-Chi (pres. Wabash Coll. chpt.). Avocations: travel, collecting Native American artifacts. Office: Marymount U Dept Psychology 2807 N Glebe Rd Arlington VA 22207 Business E-Mail: michael.clump@marymount.edu.

CLUTE, ROBERT EUGENE, political science professor; b. Earlville, Iowa, July 12, 1924; s. Henry and Leta (Allen) C.; m. Doris Reams, 1947; children: Robert Eugene, Andrea Reams. BA, U. Ala., 1947; MA, George Washington U., 1948; PhD, Duke U., 1957. Selector U.S. Displaced Persons Commn., Frankfurt, Fed. Republic Germany, 1948-50; analyst USAF, Austria, 1950-54; rsch. assoc. Duke U., Durham, N.C., 1957-58; vis. asst. prof. Tulane U. La., New Orleans, 1958-59; asst. prof. U. Nev., 1959-62; assoc. prof. U. Ga., Athens, 1962-68, prof. polit. sci., 1968—, head dept. polit. sci., 1972-75, grad. coord., 1975-88, chmn. social scis. div., 1982-93, prof. emeritus, 1993—. Am. specialist to Anglophone Africa, Cultural Affairs div. U.S. Dept. State, 1977. Author: The International Legal Status of Austria, 1962; (with others) The International Law Standard and Commonwealth Developments, 1966, De lege pactorum, 1970, Law and Justice, 1970; contbr. articles to profl. jours. With U.S. Army, 1943-46. Fulbright scholar 1967-68; Danforth assoc. 1972. Mem. Am. Soc. Internat. Law, Am. Polit. Sci. Assn., Ga. Polit. Sci. Assn., So. Polit. Sci. Assn., Internat. Studies Assn., African Studies Assn., Phi Kappa Phi, Phi Alpha Theta, Pi Sigma Alpha, Phi Beta Delta. Democrat. Episcopalian. Home: Ste 214 Arbor Terr 3736 Atlanta Hwy Athens GA 30606-3159 Office: U Ga Dept Polit Sci Athens GA 30602 *It is important for me to have career opportunities which help people. The preservation, analysis and dissemination of the knowledge of the past is as essential as the creation of new knowledge. Practical application of knowledge is extremely important. One must be loyal to one's colleagues and the institutions in which one participates.*

CLYBURN, JAMES ENOS (JIM CLYBURN), congressman; b. Sumter, SC, July 21, 1940; m. Emily England; children: Mignon, Jennifer, Angela. BS, SC State U., 1962; LHD (hon.), Winthrop Coll., 1987; DSc (hon.), Coll. Charleston, 1992, Med. U. SC, 1993; LHD (hon.), St. Augustine Coll., 1994; LLD (hon.), Claflin Coll., 1995; LHD (hon.), SC State U., 1995; LLD (hon.), Voorhees Coll., 1996. Tchr. Charleston County Pub. Sch. Sys.; employment counselor SC Employment Security Commn., 1965—66; dir. Charleston County Neighborhood Youth Corps/New Careers Projects, 1966—68; exec. dir. SC Commn. Farmworkers Inc., 1968—71; mem. staff Staff of Gov. John C. West, Charleston, SC, 1971-74; commr. SC Human Affairs Commn., Columbia, 1974-92; mem. US Congress from 6th SC dist., 1993—, majority whip, 2007—. Pres. Nat. Assn. Human Rights Workers, 1980-81, Internat. Assn. Ofcl. Human Rights Agencies., 1985-87. Active So. Regional Coun., Atlanta; bd. dirs. Wofford Coll., Spartanburg, Allen U., Columbia, Brookgreen Gardens Murrell's inlet, James R. Clark Sickle Cell Anemia Found., Ctr. for Cancer Treatment and Rsch., SC Literacy Assn. Recipient ann. award for disting. svc. to state gov. Nat. Govs. Assn.; named Pub. Adminstr. of Yr. Am. Soc. Pub. Adminstrn. SC chpt.; named one of Most Influential Black Americans, Ebony mag., 2006. Mem. NAACP (life), Masons, Shriners, Omega Psi Phi. Democrat. Office: US House Reps 2135 Rayburn House Office Bldg Washington DC 20515 Office Phone: 202-225-3315. Office Fax: 202-225-2313. E-mail: jclyburn@mail.house.gov.*

CLYBURN, LUTHER LINN, real estate broker, appraiser; b. Evansville, Ind., May 17, 1942; s. Luther and Robbie (Cobb) C.; children: Lisa Michelle, Luther Brent. Grad., Am. Savs. and Loan Inst., 1970; ABA, Pontiac Bus. Inst., Mich., 1972; BS, Detroit Coll. Bus., 1972; M of Bus. Mgmt., Ctrl. Mich. U., 1983. Lic. merchant marine; cert. scuba instr.; cert. Profl. Assn. Dive Instrs. Chief loan officer First Fed. Savs. and Loan Assn. Oakland, Pontiac, 1964-74; assoc. broker Bateman Real Estate Corp., Pontiac, 1975-77; regional rep. United Guaranty Residential Ins., Troy, Mich., 1977-83; sr. account mgr. Investors Mortgage Ins. Co., Boston, 1983-87; real estate broker, appraiser White Lake, Mich., 1977—, Clyburn Appraisal Svcs., White Lake, 1987—; project dir. Norwood Project, 2004, Great Lakes Ancient Shores Sink Holes, 2006. Dir. sea ops. Mirek Standowicz shipwreck recovery expedition, Lake Mich., 2001, Drowned

River project, Straits of Mackinac, 2001; project dir. sea ops. Norwood Project, 2004; founder, pres. Noble Odyssey Found. Inc., 2002—; project dir. Underwater Ancient Shores, Lake Huron, 2006, Underwater Ancient Shores Ancient Land Bridges, 2007; ship capt. Pride of Michigan expedition of Jean-Michel Cousteau's Ocean Futures Soc. Thunder Bay Film. Project dir., capt.: (documentary film) Angels of the Sea, 1982 (N.Y. Film Festival award 1983); photographer for Tundra Tours 25th anniversary of Alaska's Iditarod dog sled race, 1997, 2000; contbr. articles to profl. jours. Capt., comdr. Noble Odyssey Tng. Ship, Mt. Clemens, Mich., 1977-89; dir., comdr. U.S. Naval Sea Cadet Corps Great Lakes div., Mt. Clemens, Mich., 1973—; nat. bd. dirs. U.S. Naval Sea Cadet Corps, 1988; project dir. Interseas Inc., Pontiac, 1982; ship capt. Great Lakes Botanical Island research project for Cranbrook Inst. Sci. (Thunder Bay Islands, Lake Huron, 1987, Islands of Green Bay, 1989, 90); dir. of Underwater Cinitofu; capt. Pride of Mich., 1989—; capt. Great Lakes Island Rsch. Project for Oakland U., Fox Islands, 1996; project dir. In Search of the Griffin, Great Lakes Rsch. Bd., Pride of Mich., 1998—; founder, pres. Inter-Seas Exploration Ltd., 1999—. Recipient Cert. Appreciation award Southfield Bicentennial Commn., 1976, Letter of Commendation award Sec. of Navy, 1983, Quality People award Meritorious Cmty. Svc., 1993, Oakland County Q2 award, 1993, Unsung Hero award Mich. Ho. of Reps., 1994, Cert. Congl. Recognition, U.S. Senate, 2006 Mem. Internat. Ship Masters Assn. (pres. Detroit Lodge 7 2006), Navy League of U.S., Am. Soc. Appraisers, Mich. Assn. Real Estate Appraisers, Detroit Lodge Internat. Ship Masters Assn., Am. Acad. Underwriter Scis. Home and Office: 9000 Gale Rd White Lake MI 48386-1411 Office Phone: 248-666-9359. Personal E-mail: lclyburn@comcast.net.

CLYDE, LARRY FORBES, banker; b. Heber City, Utah, Nov. 19, 1941; s. Don and Kathryn (Forbes) C.; m. Barbara Eliason, Dec. 23, 1963 (div. Jan. 1985); children: Lynne, Karen Lee; m. Katharyn L. Decker, July 3, 1986. BA, Utah State U., 1963, MS, 1965. With Pitts. Nat. Bank, 1965-68, Crocker Nat. Bank, San Francisco, 1968-86, mgr. investment banking, 1973-75, mgr. capital markets divsn., 1975-86, sr. v.p., 1976-78, exec. v.p., mem. policy com., 1978-86; mng. dir., chief exec. US capital markets activities Midland Bank Group, NYC, 1986-87; CEO Midland Montagu Govt. Securities, Midland Montagu Mcpl. Securities, Midland Montagu Trust Co., 1986-87; exec. v.p., mgr. fin. institutions American Express Bank, 1987—88, Mellon Bank N.A., Pitts., 1988—2000, exec. v.p., mem. sr. mgmt. com., mgr. capital markets and portfolio and fund mgmt. divsns., 1988—96, mgr. global securities lending divsn., 1996—2000. Bd. dirs. Pub. Securities Assn. 1976-83, vice chmn., 1981, chmn., 1982; mem PSA Govt. Borrowing com., 1980-87; Am Bankers Assn. bank investment and Funds mgmt. exec. comm. 1979-83, vice chmn. 1981, chm. 1982,; treas., dir. No. Calif. chpt. Invest-In-Am., 1975-86; bd. dir. Dealer Bank Assn. 1986-87; bd. dirs. Fed. Farm Credit Funding Corp, 2000-; chmn. audit com 2004-; mem. Fed. Farm Credit Sys. Audit Com., 2000-, vice chmn. 2004—; mem. adv. bd. Las Campanas, 2006—. San Francisco Bond Club, Club at Las Campanas. Office: 12 Mustang Mesa Santa Fe NM 87506-7702

CLYDE, ROBERT ALLAN, computer software engineer; b. Salt Lake City, June 9, 1959; s. Allan Roy and Janet (Wright) C.; m. Lisa Marie DeFranco, July 14, 1981; children: Elizabeth, Julie. BS in Computer Sci., Brigham Young U., 1984. V.p. engring./mktg. Clyde Digital Systems, Orem, Utah, 1981-91; v.p., gen. mgr. Security Products divsn. Raxco, Orem, 1991-94; v.p. security svcs. Axent Techs., Orem, 1994-96; v.p., gen. mgr. Security Mgmt. Bus. unit Axent, Orem, 1996—2000; v.p., chief tech. officer Symantec Corp., Cupertino, Calif., 2001—. Author: (software product) Contrl, Audit, KBlock; inventor systems for parallel monitoring. Mem. IEEE, Info. Security Assn., EDP Auditors Assn., Assn. for Computing Machinery. Avocations: fishing, camping. Office: Symantec Corp 20330 Stevens Creek Blvd Cupertino CA 95014

CLYMER, ADAM, journalist, writer; b. NYC, Apr. 27, 1937; s. Kinsey and Eleanor (Lowenton) Clymer; m. Ann Wood Fessenden, June 3, 1961; 1 child, Jane Emily (dec.). AB, Harvard U., 1958; postgrad., U. Cape Town, South Africa, 1959; LHD (hon.), U. Vt., 2005. Reporter Virginian-Pilot, Norfolk, Va., 1960—62, Balt. Sun, 1963—76, N.Y. Daily News, Washington, 1977; reporter, editor N.Y. Times, NYC and Washington, 1977—90, asst. Washington editor, 1991—97, Washington editor, 1997—99, Washington corr., 1999—2003. Vis. scholar Annenberg Pub. Policy Ctr., 2003—05; adj. prof. George Washington U., 2006. Author: (book) Edward M. Kennedy: A Biography, 1999; co-author: Reagan: The Man, The President, 1981; editor: N.Y. Times Yr. in Rev., 1986—87. Mem. Harvard Crimson Grad. Bd., Cambridge, Mass., 1958—, chair, 2005—; bd. dirs. Washington Press Club Found., 1995—, pres., 2000—03. With US Army, 1960—62. Recipient Everett Dirksen award, Dirksen Congl. Rsch. Ctr., 1994, Carey McWilliams award, Am. Polit. Sci. Assn., 2003. Mem.: Nat. Press Club, Delhi Golf Club (India), Phi Beta Kappa. Avocation: fly fishing. Office Phone: 202-549-7161. E-mail: adam.clymer@earthlink.net.

CLYMER, BRIAN WILLIAM, diversified financial services company executive, retired state official; b. Camden, NJ, May 16, 1947; s. Howard Young and Jean (Hatch) C.; children: Kathleen Norris, Richard Hatch; m. Valerie Clymer; children: Caitlin, Emily, Daniel Scott. AA in Bus., Mitchell Coll., 1968; BS in Bus. and Econs., Lehigh U., 1969; DSc in Commerce (hon.), Drexel U., 1999. CPA, Pa. Ptnr. Clymer, Merves & Amon, CPAs, 1982-89; adminstr. Fed. Transit Adminstrn., Dept. Transp., Washington, 1989-93; pres., CEO Railway Systems Designs Inc., 1993-94; treas. State of N.J., 1994-97; sr. v.p. external affairs Prudential Fin., 1997—. Vice chmn. Southeastern Pa. Transp. Authority, 1981—89; exec. com. Am. Pub. Transit Assn., 1993—95; bd. dirs. Longport, Inc., N.J. Alliance Action, N.J. Ind. Coll. Fund, Commerce and Industry Assn. NJ, Hill Internat. With Pa. N.G., 1970-76. Mem. AICPA, Pa. Inst. CPA, N.J. Soc. CPA. Republican. Presbyterian. Avocations: fishing, golf. Home: 62 Brookville Hollow Rd Stockton NJ 08559-2006 Office: Prudential Fin 751 Broad St Newark NJ 07102-3777 Office Phone: 973-367-2510.

COADY, MICHAEL ANTHONY, surgeon, department chairman; b. Balt., Jan. 17, 1967; s. James Michael and Jacqueline Annette Coady. BA, Bennington Coll., Vt., 1989; MD, George Washington U., Washington, 1993; MPH, Yale U., New Haven, Conn., 1997. Asst. prof., dir. cardiac transplantation Yale U., New Haven, 2003—05; chmn. surgery Landmark Med. Ctr., Woonsocket, RI, 2005—. Mem. med. exec. com. Landmark Med. Ctr., 2006—. Contbr. articles to profl. jours., chapters to books; reviewer Jour. Thoracic and Cardiovasc. Surgery, Circulation, Annals of Thoracic Surgery. Dir. surg. rotation for students Woonsocket HS, RI, 2006—. Named one of 40 Under 40, Providence Bus. News, 2006; grantee Yale U., 2004. Mem.: Am. Heart Assn. (grantee 1997—99), Soc. Thoracic Surgeons. Avocations: skiing, sailing, classical music. Home: 54 Pratt St Providence RI 02906 Office: Landmark Med Ctr Cardiac Surgery 115 Cass Ave Woonsocket RI 02895 Office Phone: 401-767-1503. Office Fax: 401-767-1508. Personal E-mail: macoady@gmail.com.

COAKLEY, DEIRDRE, columnist, writer; b. Detroit, Aug. 10, 1927; d. Cecil Francis and Elizabeth Kearney Coakley. Grad., Hollywood (Calif.) H.S., 1944. Mem. editl. staff L.A. Examiner, 1943-46; mem. editl. staff various other newspapers LA, to 1954; advt. exec., mag. editor Las Vegas (Nev.) Sun, 1954-66, Sunday mag. editor, 1977-85; freelance advt. and pub. rels. exec. Las Vegas, 1966-68; pub. rels. exec. Jimmy Snyder Info. Unltd. Tropicana Hotel, Las Vegas, 1968-74; pub. rels. dir. Desert Springs Hosp., Las Vegas, 1974-77; writer, columnist Gadsden (Ala.) Times, 1985—. Editor: The Way it Was: Diary of a Pioneer Woman, 1979-80; author: The MGM Grand Hotel Fire, 1982, Portrait of a City: An Informal History of Gadsden, Alabama 1846-1996, 1996; writer, curator Voices and Images of World War II. Publicist United Way of Etowah County, Gadsden, 1994—; bd. dirs. Metro. Arts Coun., 1988-95, Gadsden Symphony Orch., 1990-96; mem. Gadsden Ctr. Cultural Arts. Mem. Gadsden Art Assn., Etowah Hist. Soc. Democrat. Roman Catholic. Avocation: genealogy. Office: 6148 Stewart Ridge Walk Buford GA 30518 Home Phone: 770-271-3482. E-mail: deirdrecoakley@bellsouth.net.

COAKLEY, JAMES A., atmospheric science educator; b. Long Beach, Calif., Dec. 14, 1946; s. James A. and Beverly A. Coakley; m. Stella M. Coakley; children: Sarah C. Lewis, Miriam A. Riherd, Martha V. BS in Physics, UCLA, 1968; MA in Physics, PhD in Physics, U. Calif., Berkeley, 1972. Scientist Nat. Ctr. for Atmospheric Rsch., Boulder, Colo., 1972—88; prof. COAS, Oreg. State U., Corvallis, 1988—. Editor: Jour. Climate. Recipient Exceptional Sci. Achievement award, NASA, 1995. Fellow: AAAS (sect. chair 2004—04), Am. Meteorol. Soc.; mem.: Am. Geophys. Union, Phi Beta Kappa. Avocations: amateur radio, swimming. Office: COAS Oregon State University 104 COAS Admin Bldg Corvallis OR 97331-5503 Office Phone: 541-737-5686. Office Fax: 541-737-2540. Business E-Mail: coakley@coas.oregonstate.edu.

COAKLEY, MARTHA, state attorney general, former prosecutor; b. North Adams, Mass., July 14, 1953; m. Thomas F. O'Connor, Jr. BA cum laude, Williams Coll., Williamstown, Mass., 1975; JD, Boston U. Sch. Law, 1979. Assoc. civil litig. Parker, Coulter, Daley & White, Boston, 1979—80, Goodwin, Proctor & Hoar, Boston, 1981—86; asst. dist. atty. Middlesex Dist. Atty.'s Office, Lowell, Mass., 1986—87, asst. dist. atty. criminal and pub. protection bur. Cambridge, Mass., 1989—90, asst. dist. atty., team capt. Somerville/Malden region, 1991, chief Child Abuse Prosecution Unit Somerville, Mass., 1991—96, sr. trial counsel Cambridge, Mass., 1997; spl. atty. Boston Organized Crime Strike Force US Dept. Justice, Boston, 1987—89; dist. atty. Middlesex County, Mass., 1999—2006; atty. gen. Commonwealth of Mass., Boston, 2007—. Recipient Shining Star Leadership award, Victim Rights Law Ctr., 2005, Eleanor Roosevelt Humanitarian award, Shrewsbury Dem. Town Com., 2005, Voices Against Violence award, 2005. Democrat. Avocations: baroque music, classical music, bicycling, skiing. Office: Office of Atty Gen McCormack Bldg One Ashburton Pl Boston MA 02108-1698 Office Phone: 617-727-2200.*

COAKLEY, RICHARD WALKER, retired chemical engineer; b. Havre de Grace, Md., Feb. 28, 1926; s. William C. and Margaret Walker Coakley; m. Martha Hildreth Coakley, Sept. 19, 1959; children: Virginia C. Price, Janice F. Student, Franklin & Marshall Coll., Lancaster, Pa., 1944, Northwestern U., Chgo., 1945; BSChemE, U. Md., College Park, 1946—50. Rsch. engr. E.I. duPont de Nemours, Wilmington, Del., 1950—51, chem. shift supr. Aiken, SC, 1951—56, chem. engr. Niagara Falls, NY, 1956—58; sr. chem. engr. Olin-Mathieson Corp., Youngstown, NY, 1958—60; rsch. chem. engr. Dow-Badische Co., Williamsburg, Va., 1960—69; supervisory chem. engr. Naval Explosives Devel. Engring. Dept., Yorktown, Va., 1974—93. Mem. Naval Res. Divsn., Youngstown, 1957—60; developer naval weapons, 1980—93. Pres. Birchwood Civic Assn., James City County, Va., 1962—70, James City Civic Assn., James City County, 1972—2000; chmn., vice chmn. James City County Bd. Suprs., 1968—72; chmn. James City County Rep. Com.; nominee Va. Gen. Assembly. Lt. j.g. USN, 1943—80. Mem.: VFW (comdr. 1995—97), AIChE (chmn. AIChE Synthetic Fiber Symposium 1966, chmn. Tidewater chpt.), Nat. Assn. Ret. Fed. Employees (chmn. 1995—97), Williamsburg Stamp Soc. (chmn. 1964—98). Methodist. Avocations: stamp collecting/philately, photography. Home: 110 Redbud Ln Williamsburg VA 23185 Personal E-mail: coakleyrwmh@aol.com.

COALTER, MILTON J., JR., library director, educator; b. Memphis, July 5, 1949; s. Milton J. and Jewel (Mitchel) C.; children: Martha Claire, Siram Jacob. BA, Davidson Coll., 1971; MDiv, Princeton Theol. Sem., 1975, ThM, 1977; PhD in Religion, Princeton U., 1982. Asst. prof. Am. religion N.C. State U., Raleigh, 1981-82; pub. svcs. libr. The Iliff Sch. Theology, Denver, 1982-84, acting libr. dir., 1984-85; libr. dir., prof. bibliography and rsch. Louisville Presbyn. Theol. Sem., 1985—2004, acting pres., 2002—03; libr. dir., prof. bibliography and rsch. Union Theol. Sem.-PSCE, Richmond, Va., 2004—. Bd. dirs. Louisville Inst., Scholars Press; gen. assembly coun. task force on ch. membership growth Presbyn. Ch., Louisville, 1989-91. Author: (with John M. Mulder) The Letters of David Avery, 1979, Gilbert Tennent, Son of Thunder, 1986; (with John M. Mulder and Louis B. Weeks) The Presbyterian Presence in the Twentieth Century, 7 vols., 1989-92, Vital Signs, 1996, Resources for American Christianity, 2002, website for religion divsn. Lilly Endowment, 2000--; editor: (with Virgil Cruz) How Shall We Witness?, 1995; contbr. articles to profl. jours. Mem. Gen. Assembly Theol. Task Force on Peace, Unity and Purity of the Ch., 2001—06. Recipient Jonathan Edwards award Princeton U., 1977-80, Tchg. award Assn. Princeton Grad. Alumni, 1979-80, Francis Makemie award Presbyn. Ch. Dept. History; Lilly Endowment grantee, 1987-90, 99—, N.J. Hist. Commn. grantee, 1979-80, Pew Charitable Trust grantee, 1990-93; Princeton U. Whiting fellow, 1980-81. Mem. Am. Theol. Libr. Assn. (bd. dirs. 1997-03, pres. 1998-00). Presbyterian. Office: William Smith Morton Libr Union Theol Sem-PSCE 3401 Brook Rd Richmond VA 23227 Home Phone: 804-358-4168; Office Phone: 804-278-4311.

COAN, CARL A.S., JR., lawyer; b. Phila., Sept. 1, 1934; s. Carl A.S. and Flora M. Coan; m. Patricia Ann Lacey, June 25, 1955; children: Carl A.S. III, Christopher, Timothy, Sheila, Kenneth. AB, Georgetown U., Washington, 1954; LLB, Georgetown U., 1958. Atty. FHA, Washington, 1958—61, Urban Renewal Adminstrn., Washington, 1961—67; atty., asst. gen. counsel HUD, Washington, 1967—69; dep. legis. counsel Nat. Assn. Home Builders, Washington, 1969—71, staff v.p., legis. counsel, 1971—77; ptnr. Coan & Lyons, Washington, 1977—. Dir. Nat. Housing Conf., Washington; trustee CHF Internat., Silver Spring, Md. Chmn., mem. Consumer Protection and Pub. Utilities Commn., Fairfax County, Va., 1967—74, Redevel. and Housing Authority, Fairfax County, 1975—86; mem. Planning Commn., Fairfax County, 1995—99. 1st lt. US Army, 1954—56. Mem.: ABA. Office: Coan and Lyons 1100 Connecticut Ave NW Washington DC 20036-4112

COAN, PATRICIA A., judge; b. NYC, July 21, 1945; 2 children. BSN, Georgetown U., 1967; JD, U. Denver, 1981. Bar: Colo. 1982; RN N.Y., Conn., Mont. Pvt. practice, Denver, Colo., 1982-96; magistrate judge U.S. Dist. Ct. for Dist. Colo., Denver, 1996—. Bd. dirs. Colo. Lawyers Health Program. Mem. Women's Bar Assn., Colo. Bar Assn., Denver Bar Assn., Sigma Theta Tau, Alpha Sigma Nu. Office: 901 19th St Denver CO 80294-1929 Office Phone: 303-844-4892.

COAN, RICHARD WELTON, psychologist, educator; b. Martinez, Calif., Jan. 24, 1928; s. Otis Welton and Esta Dorothy (Wilson) C.; m. Edith Margaret Vedova, Oct 17, 2003; children: Lisa Cooper, Cynthia, Angela Lambert, Abbie. BA in Psychology, U. Calif., Berkeley, 1948, MA in Psychology, 1950; PhD in Psychology, U. So. Calif., 1955. Psychology instr. L.A. City Coll., 1950-55; rsch. assoc. psychology U. Ill., Urbana, 1955-57; from asst. prof. to prof. psychology U. Ariz., Tucson, 1957-89, prof. emeritus, 1989—. Author: The Optimal Personality, 1974, Hero, Artist, Sage, or Saint?, 1977, Psychologists: Personal and Theoretical Pathways, 1979, Psychology of Adjustment, 1983, Human Consciousness and Its Evolution, 1987, A Princess for Larkin, 2001, Shaul of Tarsos, 2004, Horatio, 2006. Democrat. Avocations: musical composition, writing novels and poetry. Home: 2992 W Royal Copeland Dr Tucson AZ 85745 E-mail: rwcoan@cox.net.

COAR, RICHARD JOHN, mechanical engineer, aerospace transportation executive, consultant; b. Hanover, NH, May 2, 1921; s. Herbert Greenleaf and Anne (Langille) C.; m. Cecilie Berle, 1942 (dec. 1971); children— Gregory, Candace, Andrea, Kenneth; m. Lucille Hicks, 1972. BS in Mech. Engring., Tufts U., 1942. Engr. Pratt & Whitney Aircraft, East Hartford, Conn., 1942-56; chief engr. Fla. Research and Devel. Ctr., 1956-70, asst. gen. mgr., 1970—72; v.p. engring. Pratt & Whitney Aircraft, East Hartford, 1972—76, exec. v.p., 1976-83, pres., 1983-84; sr. v.p. United Techs., Hartford, 1983-84, exec. v.p., 1984-86. Patentee aircraft engines and controls Corporator Hartford Hosp., 1983; bd. dirs. Hartford Symphony, 1985-87. Recipient Franklin W. Kolk Air Transp. Progress award Soc. Automotive Engrs., 1985, Daniel Guggenheim medal for contbns. to aeronautic and space propulsion sys., 1998. Mem. ASME (George Westinghouse Gold medal 1986), NAE, Am. Soc. Metals (disting. life mem.), Tau Beta Pi, Water's Edge Country Club. Avocations: sailing, golf.

COASE, RONALD HARRY, economist, educator; b. Willesden, Eng., Dec. 29, 1910; arrived in U.S., 1951; s. Henry Joseph and Rosalie (Giles) Coase; m. Marian Ruth Hartung, Aug. 7, 1937. B of Commerce, London Sch. Econs., 1932; DSc in Econs., U. London, 1951; D Rer. Pol. (hon.), Cologne U., Germany, 1988; D of Social Sci. (hon.), Yale U., 1989; LLD (hon.), Washington U., St. Louis, 1991, U. Dundee, Scotland, 1992; DSc (hon.), U. Buckingham, Eng., 1995; DHL (hon.), Beloit Coll., 1996; PhD (hon.), U. Paris, 1996; DHum (hon.), Clemson U., 2003. Sir Ernest Cassel Travelling scholar, 1931—32; asst. lectr. Dundee Sch. Econs., 1932—34, U. Liverpool, England, 1934—35; from asst. lectr. to lectr. to reader London Sch. Econs., 1935—51; prof. U. Buffalo, 1951—58, U. Va., Charlottesville, 1958—64, U. Chgo., 1964—, now Clifton R. Musser prof. emeritus, sr. fellow in law and econs. Law Sch. Statistician, then chief statistician Ctrl. Statis. Office, Offices War Cabinet, England, 1941—46. Author: British Broadcasting, A Study in Monopoly, 1950, The Firm, the Market and the Law, 1988, Essays on Economics and Economists, 1994; editor: Jour. Law and Econs., 1964—82. Mem. hon. com. Eurosci. Named Rockefeller fellow, 1948; recipient Nobel prize in econs., 1991, Innovations award, The Economist, 2003; fellow Ctr. for Advanced Study Behavioral Scis., 1958—59; Sr. Rsch. fellow, Hoover Instn., Stanford U., 1977, hon. fellow, London Sch. Econs. Fellow: European Acad., Am. Econ. Assn. (disting.), Brit. Acad. (corr.), Am. Acad. Arts and Scis.; mem.: Internat. Soc. for New Instnl. Econs. (founding pres. 1997), Mont Pelerin Soc., Royal Econ. Soc. Office: U Chgo Laird Bell Law Quadrangle 1111 E 60th St Chicago IL 60637-2776 Home: The Hallmark 2960 N Lake Shore Dr Chicago IL 60657 Home Phone: 773-755-0409; Office Phone: 773-702-7342.

COATES, ANNE V., film editor; b. Reigate, Surrey, Eng., Dec. 12, 1925; m. Douglas Hickox (dec.). Grad., Bartrum Gables Coll. Editor: (films) The Pickwick Papers, 1952, Forbidden Cargo, 1954, To Paris with Love, 1955, Wicked Wife, 1955, Tears for Simon, 1957, The Horse's Mouth, 1958, The Truth about Women, 1958, Tunes of Glory, 1960, Lawrence of Arabia, 1962 (Academy award best film editing 1962), Becket, 1964 (Academy award nomination best film editing 1964), Why Bother to Knock, 1964, Those Magnificent Men in Their Flying Machines, 1965, Young Cassidy, 1965, Hotel Paradiso, 1966, The Bofors Gun, 1968, Great Catherine, 1968, The Adventurers, 1970, Friends, 1971, The Public Eye, 1972, The Nelson Affair, 1973, Murder on the Orient Express, 1974, 11 Harrowhouse, 1974, Man Friday, 1975, Aces High, 1976, The Eagle Has Landed, 1977, The Medusa Touch, 1978, The Legacy, 1979, The Elephant Man, 1980 (Academy award nomination best film editing 1980), Ragtime, 1981, The Bushido Blade, 1982, The Pirates of Penzance, 1983, Greystoke: The Legend of Tarzan, Lord of the Apes, 1984, Raw Deal, 1986, Lady Jane, 1986, Masters of the Universe, 1987, Farewell to the King, 1989, Listen to Me, 1989, I Love You to Death, 1990, What About Bob?, 1991, Chaplin, 1992, In the Line of Fire, 1993 (Academy award nomination best film editing 1993), Pontiac Moon, 1994, Congo, 1995, Striptease, 1996, Out to Sea, 1997, Out of Sight, 1998 (Academy award nomination best film editing 1999), Passion of Mind, 2000, Erin Brockovich, 2000, Sweet November, 2001, Unfaithful, 2002, Taking Lives, 2004, Catch and Release, 2006. Recipient Officer of the Brit. Empire, 2003; grantee Acad. fellowship, Brit. Acad. Film and TV Arts, 2007. Mailing: United Talent Agy 9560 Wilshire Blvd Beverly Hills CA 90212*

COATES, ARDITH WILLIAMS, language educator; b. Anniston, Ala., Dec. 9, 1950; d. Theron Hollis and Edna Evelyn Williams; m. Joseph M. Coates, Sept. 11, 1993. BS in Secondary Edn., Jacksonville State U., Ala., 1973; MS in Secondary Edn., Jacksonville State U., 1979; MRE, New Orleans Bapt. Seminary, 1982. English & math. tchr. Northside Jr. HS, Anniston, 1973—74, White Plains HS, Oxford, Ala., 1974—75, Cobb Jr. HS, Anniston, 1975—76, Weaver HS, Ala., 1976—77, Sycamore Jr. HS, Ala., 1977—78; tchr. Constantine Day Care Ctr., Anniston, 1979—80; camp dir. Guest Svcs. Va. Bapts., Richmond, Va., 1982—96; English tchr. Liberty U., Lynchburg, Va., 1997—. Author: (tchg. guide for film on missions in China) Winter is Past Teaching Guide, 1986. Mem.: Nat. Coun. Tchrs. English. Republican. So. Bapt. Avocations: reading, piano, cooking, sewing. Office: Liberty Univ 1971 University Blvd Lynchburg VA 24502

COATES, DONALD ROBERT, geologist, educator; b. Grand Island, Neb., July 23, 1922; s. Frank Jefferson and Harriet (Ferris) C.; m. Jeanne Louise Grandison, Mar. 18, 1944 (dec. Jan. 1993); children: Cheryl D., Donald Eric, Lark J.; m. Marilyn Hilton Williams, Jan. 12, 1998 (dec. Jan. 2004). BA, Coll. Wooster, Ohio, 1944; MA, Columbia U., NYC, 1948, PhD, 1956. Faculty Earlham Coll., Richmond, Ind., 1948—51; geologist, project chief US Geol. Survey, Tucson, 1951—54; faculty Harpur Coll. (now Binghamton U./SUNY), 1954—90, chmn. dept. geology, 1954—63, prof., 1963—90; prof. emeritus SUNY Binghamton, 1990—; rsch. geologist US Geol. Survey, Vestal, NY, 1958—61; vis. geoscientist Am. Geol. Inst., 1963—85; cons. Engring. Corps US Army, 1965—86. Cons. Empire State Electric Energy Rsch. Corp., Consol. Edison NY, Niagara Mohawk Power Corp., Mohonk Preserve Corp., Protector Pine Oak Woods Inc., US Army C.E., Town of Islip, NY State Dept. Environ. Conservation, NY State Electric & Gas Corp., NY State Dept. Transp., NY State Atty. Gen., NY State Power Authority, NY Low Level Nuc. Waste Siting Commn., Town of Vernon, NY, Broome County, Chemung County, Town of Vestal, NY, Town of Trenton, NY, Town of Deerfield, NY, Town of Norwich, Adastra West Pubs., 1999, Facts on File, Inc., 1987, 99, also pvt. cos.; assoc. program dir. NSF Found., 1963-64; vis. prof. Ind. U., 1955, U. Ill., 1963, Guangdong Seismol. Bur., China, 1987; vis. scholar Chinese Acad. Sci., 1995. Editor: Geology of South-Central New York, 1963, Environmental Geomorphology and Landscape Conservation, 3 vols., Coastal Geomorphology, Glacial Geomorphology, Geomorphology and Engineering, Landslides, (with John Vitek) Threshholds in Geomorphology, Urban Geomorphology, Environmental Geomorphology, 1971, Environmental Science Workbook, 1972, (with Charles Higgins) Ground Water Geomorphology, 1990; editor, author: Environmental Geology; author: Geology and Society; contbr. to Science - A Process Approach, 1965; also articles, reports. Lt. USN, 1943—46, lt. USNR, 1946—54. Recipient award for Sustained Superior Performance NSF, 1964; Rsch. grantee NSF, US Dept. Commerce, US Geol. Survey, NY State Atomic and Space Devel. Authority, Rsch. Found. SUNY, 1958-61. Fellow AAAS, Geol. Soc. Am. (Merit cert. engring. geology divsn. 1980, E.B. Burwell Jr. award 1995); mem. Assn. Engring. Geologists, Nat. Assn. Geology Tchrs. (pres. Ea. sect. 1962, Ralph Digman award 1972, Coll. Tchr. of Yr. award 1971), Am. Inst. Profl. Geologists, NY State Geol. Assn. (pres. 1963, 81), Phi Beta Kappa. Home: 6608 17th Ave Court West Bradenton FL 34209 Office: Binghamton U SUNY Dept Geol Scis Binghamton NY 13902 Personal E-mail: profcoates@earthlink.net.

COATES, GLENN RICHARD, lawyer; b. Thorp, Wis., June 8, 1923; s. Richard and Alma (Borck) C.; m. Dolores Milburn, June 24, 1944; children— Richard Ward, Cristie Joan Student, Milw. State Tchrs. Coll., 1940-42, NMA and MA, 1943-44; LLB, U. Wis., 1949, SJD, 1953. Bar: Wis. 1949. Atty. Mil. Sea Transp. Service, Dept. Navy, 1951-52; pvt. practice Racine, Wis., 1952—. Sec., gen. counsel Racine Federated Inc.; lectr. U. Wis. Law Sch., 1955—56. Author: Chattel Secured Farm Credit, 1953; contbr. articles to profl. publs. Chmn. bd. St. Luke's Meml. Hosp., 1973-76, bd. dirs., 1990-91; pres. Racine Area United Way, 1979-81; bd. curators State Hist. Soc. Wis., 1986-2001, pres., 1995-97; bd. dirs. Racine County Area Found., 1983-89; bd. dirs. Wis. History Found., Inc., 1983-99, Hist. Sites Found., Inc., 1987-89, St. Luke's Hosp./St. Mary's Med. Ctr. Healthcare Found., 1992-96. With U.S. Army, 1943-46. Fellow Am. Bar Found. (life); mem. ABA, State Bar Wis. (bd. govs. 1969-74, chmn. bd. 1973-74), Wis. Jud. Coun. (chmn. 1969-72), Am. Law Inst. (life), Racine Country Club, Masons, Order of Coif. Methodist (chmn. fin. com. 1961-67). Home: 2830 Michigan Blvd Racine WI 53402-4254

COATES, ROBERT JAY, retired electronics executive; b. Lansing, Mich., May 8, 1922; s. Archie Louis and Ruth Agnes (Hutchings) C.; m. Gladys Buchhorn, Aug. 17, 1946; (dec.); 1 child, Bonnie; m. H. Regina Thorsen, Oct. 17, 1999. BSEE, Mich. State U., 1943; MSEE, U. Md., 1948; PhD in physics, Johns Hopkins U., 1957. Radio engr. U.S. Naval Research Lab., Washington, 1943—46, electronic scientist, 1946—49, 1952—59; instr. physics Johns Hopkins U., Balt., 1949—52; assoc. chief tracking sys. divsn., chief space data acquisition, advt. devel. divsn., advt. data sys. divsns., mgr. Pacific plate motion experiment Goddard Space Flight Ctr., NASA, Greenbelt, Md., also mgr. Crustal Dynamics Project, 1959—88, ret., 1988. Cons. in field Vol. Habitat for Humanity, 1996-99. Served with USN, 1944-45. Recipient Outstanding Performance award NRL, 1959, Group Achievement award NASA, 1973, 1968, 1986, Apollo Achievement award, 1969, Exceptional Performance award Goddard Space Flight Center, 1971, Exceptional Service medal, 1986; Outstanding Leadership medal NASA, 1989. Fellow IEEE; mem. Am. Phys. Soc., Am. Geophys. Union, AAAS, Sigma Xi, Phi Kappa Phi, Tau Beta Pi. Home: 3112 Gracefield Rd Apt 313 Silver Spring MD 20904

COATES, THOMAS J., medical association administrator; BA in Philosophy, San Luis Rey Coll., 1968; MA in Psychology, San Jose State U., 1971; PhD in Counseling Psychology, Stanford U., 1977. Mem. faculty Stanford Heart Disease Prevention Program; with Johns Hopkins U.; dir. behavioral medicine unit div. gen. internal medicine U. Calif., San Francisco, 1984—, mem. med. attending staff, 1984—, prof. div. gen. internal medicine dept. medicine, 1990—, dir. Ctr. AIDS Prevention Studies, 1991—. Spl. advisor family health internat.'s AIDS prevention project USAIDS; chair global programme on AIDS steering com. social and behavioral studies unit WHO. Contbr. articles to profl. jours. Mem.: NAS (mem. Inst. Medicine). Office: UCLA Dept Med Divsn Infectious Dis Prevention & Policy Rsch 10940 Wilshire Blvd Ste 1220 Los Angeles CA 90024-7320

COATES, WAYNE EVAN, agricultural engineer; b. Edmonton, Alta, Canada, Nov. 28, 1947; arrived in U.S., 1981; s. Orval Bruce Wright and Leora (Raesler) C.; m. Patricia Louise Williams, Aug. 28, 1970 (dec. May, 6, 2004); m. Patricia Wiercinski, Apr. 15, 2006. BS in Agr., U. Alta., 1969, MS in Agrl. Engring., 1970; PhD in Agrl. Engring., Okla. State U., 1973. Registered profl. engr., Ariz., Sask. Forage systems engr. Agr. Can., Melfort, Saskatoon, Canada, 1973-75; project engr., tech. advisor, asst. sta. mgr. Prairie Agrl. Machinery Inst., Humboldt, Saskatoon, Canada, 1975-81; pvt. practice cattle, grain farmer Humboldt, 1975-81; assoc. prof. U. Ariz., Tucson, 1981-91, prof., 1991—; prof. titular ad honorem U. Nat. de Catamarca, Argentina, 1993—. Cons. Vols. in Coop. Assts. and Ptnr. of Am., 1991-98, Paraguayan Govt. UN Devel. Program, 1987-90, Argentine Govt., univ. and pvt. industry, 1991—, govt., univ. and agrl. orgn., Mid East agrl. projects, 1986-89, 98-99; pres. Ariz. Chia, Inc., 2006—; spkr. at internat. conf., Australia, Paraguay, Argentina, Peru, Chile, US expert witness in field. Designer farm equipment primarily for alternative crops and tillage; patentee in field; contbr. articles to profl. jour. Pres. Sunrise Ter. Village Townhomes Homeowners Assn., Tucson, 1990-92, 98-00. Grantee USDA, Washington, 1981-07, Ariz. Dept. Environ. Quality, Phoenix, 1989-98, US Dept. Energy, Washington, 1991-98, agrl. industries western US, 1982-06. Fellow: Can. Soc. Agrl. Engring. (webmaster 2002—); mem.: Coun. Agrl. Sci. and Tech. (bd. mem. 2002—04, exec. com. 2004—), Am. Kenaf Soc. (newsletter editor 2000—02, webmaster 2001—05, treas. 2002), Soc. Automotive Engr. (chmn. farm machinery com. 2000—05), Assn. Advancement Indsl. Crops (pres. 1994—95, rep. to CAST 2003—04, Outstanding Rschr. award 1997), Am. Soc. Agrl. Engr. (chmn. Ariz. sect. 1984—85, vice-chmn. Pacific region 1988—89, dir. dist. 4 1991—93, internat. dir. 1994—96, rep. CAST 2002—04), Sigma Xi. Avocations: running, hiking. Office: U Ariz Office Arid Lands Studies PO Box 506 Sonoita AZ 85637 Home Phone: 520-455-0707; Office Phone: 520-455-5050. Business E-Mail: wcoates@ag.arizona.edu.

COATES, WINSLOW SHELBY, JR., lawyer; b. Bayville, NY, Mar. 4, 1929; s. Winslow Shelby and Jane (Brush) C.; m. Frances Ward White, Feb. 16, 1959; children: Susan F. White, Trevor D. BA, Yale U., New Haven, Conn., 1952; LLB, U. Va., Charlottesville, 1959. Bar: N.Y. 1961, U.S. Dist. Ct. (so. dist.) N.Y. 1962. Assoc. Dow & Stonebridge, NYC, 1961-67; pvt. practice NYC, 1967-77; ptnr. Miller, Montgomery, Sogi, Brady & Taft, NYC, 1977-80; shipping exec. Oceanic Fleet Carriers S.A., NYC, 1980-86; pvt. practice Oyster Bay, NY, 1986—; counsel Dickerson, Tomaselli & Mullen, LLP, NYC, 2007—. Founder Trident Maritime Svcs., Ltd., Oyster Bay, 1994—. Author: Maritime Product Liability, 1979; contbr. articles to local newspapers. Co-founder Friends of the Bay, 1988; active Bd. Zoning Appeals, Matinecock, N.Y. Lt. USN, 1953-56. Mem. Maritime Law Assn. of the U.S., Piping Rock Club, Army and Navy Club, Navy League U.S. Republican. Avocations: chess, tennis, reading, travel, yachting. Home: 200 Piping Rock Rd Locust Valley NY 11560-2509 Office: 115 South St PO Box 186 Oyster Bay NY 11771-0186 Office Phone: 516-674-1556.

COATNEY, LOUIS ROBERT, librarian, historian; s. Robert Marlin and Grace Jack Coatney; life ptnr. Reidun Boeasaeter. BA in Philosophy, Augustana Coll., Rock Island, Ill., 1972; MS in Libr. Sci., U. Ill., Urbana, 1973; MA in History, Western Ill. U., Macomb, 1994. Docs. and reference libr. Alaska State Libr., Juneau, 1973—89; libr. Western Ill. U. Libr., 1989—94; LRC asst. Carl Sandburg Coll., Galesburg, 1999—. Author: (internet discussion forum) Guardian Unlimited Talk: The Kelly Inquiry: A Sham or the Start of an Ethical Cleansing of the West?. With US Army, 1964—69. Mem.: Heart of Ill. Libr. Consortium (coord. 2005—), West Point Soc. of Prairies. Achievements include design of Sturm Nach Osten military history boardgame; 1st Alamein and Battles for Alamein military history boardgame; Webpage with free boardgames and cardstock model ship plans, http://LCoat.tripod.com, 1997-present; Leyte Gulf Naval Chess Game; Moscow Attacked! boardgame on webpage; Naval Action, naval miniature rules; research in H-Diplo, May 14, 1999, re: Appendix B of Rambouillet Treaty, which helped end the Kosovo War. Home: 626 Western Ave Macomb IL 61455 Office: Carl Sandburg Coll 2400 Tom L Wilson Blvd Galesburg IL 61401 Home Phone: 309-836-1447; Office Phone: 309-341-5206. Personal E-mail: elcoat@hotmail.com. Business E-Mail: lcoatney@sandburg.edu.

COATS, ANDREW MONTGOMERY, dean, lawyer, former mayor; b. Oklahoma City, Okla., Jan. 19, 1935; s. Sanford Clarence and Mary Ola (Young) C.; m. Linda M. Zimmerman; children: Andrew, Michael, Jennifer, Sanford BA, U. Okla., 1957, JD, 1963. Assoc. Crowe and Dunlevy, Oklahoma City, 1963-67, ptnr., 1967-76, sr. trial ptnr., 1980—96; dist. atty. Oklahoma County, Oklahoma City, 1976-80; mayor City of Oklahoma City, 1983-87; dean U. Okla. Coll. Law, 1996—; dir. IBC Bank Okla., 2004—. Pres. Okla. Young Lawyers Conf., 1968-69; dir. Local Okla. Bank, Oklahoma City. Democratic nominee US Senate, 1980; pres. Oklahoma County Legal Aid Soc., 1972-73. Served to lt. USN, 1960-63 Named Outstanding Lawyer in Okla., Oklahoma City U., 1977, Phi Beta Kappa of Yr., 2003, U. Okla. Coll. Law bldg. named in honor of Andrew M. Coats; named to Okla. Hall of Fame, 2006. Fellow Am. Coll. Trial Lawyers (pres. 1996-97, 10th Cir. regent 1992-96), Am. Bar Found., Internat. Acad. Trial Lawyers; mem. ABA, US Supreme Ct. Hist. Soc. (trustee), Okla. Bar Assn. (pres. 1992-93), Okla. County Bar Assn. (pres. 1976-77), Am. Bd. Trial Advs. (charter pres. Okla. Chap.) Order of Coif, Oklahoma City Golf and Country Club (bd. dirs. 1977-80, 93-96), Petroleum Club (pres. 1995), Phi Beta Kappa (pres. 1975), Pi Kappa Alpha (pres. 1956), Phi Delta Phi (pres. 1962). Clubs: Oklahoma City Golf and Country, Petroleum. Democrat. Episcopalian. Avocations: music, golf. Office: Crowe and Dunlevy 20 N Broadway Ave Ste 1800 Oklahoma City OK 73102-8273 also: U Okla Coll Law 300 Timber Dell Rd Norman OK 73019-5081 Office Phone: 405-325-4720. Business E-Mail: acoats@ou.edu.

COATS, DANIEL RAY, lawyer, former ambassador, senator; b. Jackson, Mich., May 16, 1943; s. Edward R. and Vera E. C.; m. Marcia Crawford, Sept. 4, 1965; children: Laura, Lisa, Andrew. BA, Wheaton Coll., Ill., 1965; JD cum laude, Ind. U., 1971. Bar: Ind. 1972. Asst. v.p., counsel Mutual Security Life Ins. Co., Ft. Wayne, Ind., 1969—75; Dist. rep. U.S. Congressman Dan Quayle, 1976-80; mem. 97th-100th Congresses from 4th Dist. Ind., Washington, 1981-89; U.S. senator from Ind., 1989-99; lobbyist Pharm. Rsch. and Mfrs. of Am.; spl. counsel Verner, Liipfert, Bernhard, McPherson and Hand, 1999—2001; U.S. amb. to Germany U.S. Dept. State, Berlin, 2001—05; sr. counsel King & Spaulding LLP, Washington, 2005—, co-chmn. govt. rels. group, 2005—. Mem. Armed Svcs. Com., Labor and Human Resources Com., Intelligence Com.; bd. dirs. IPALCO. Lear Siegler Svcs., Inc., Internat. Repub. Inst., The Empowerment Network. Pres., Big Bros./Big Sisters of Am., Ind. Served with U.S. Army, 1966-68. Office: King & Spaulding LLP 1700 Pennsylvania Ave NW Washington DC 20006 Office Phone: 202-731-6262. Business E-Mail: dcoats@kslaw.com.

COATS, JANET S. (JANET WEAVER), executive editor; m. Mark Weaver, 1993 (div. Jan. 2007); children: Sam, Rachel; m. Rusty Coats, Apr. 2007. B in journalism, U. Mo., 1984. Reporter, asst. city editor Stuart (Fla.) News, 1986—89; from reporter to dep. mng. editor/features and sports Virginian-Pilot, Norfolk, Va., 1989—94; mng. editor The Wichita (Kans.) Eagle, 1994—97, Sarasota (Fla.) Herald-Tribune, 1997—99, exec. editor, 1999—2003; dean faculty Poynter Inst., St. Petersburg, Fla., 2003—04; mng. editor Tampa (Fla.) Tribune, 2004—05, exec. editor, v.p., 2005—. Mem.: Am. Soc. Newspaper Editors (bd. dirs.). Office: Tampa Tribune 200 S Parker St Tampa FL 33606 also: Tampa Tribune PO Box 191 Tampa FL 33601*

COATS, NATHAN B., state supreme court justice; m. Mary Ricketson; 1 child, Johanna. BA in Econs., U. Colo., 1971, JD, 1977. Assoc. Hough, Grant, McCarren and Bernard, 1977-78; asst. atty. gen. Appellate Sect., Colo., 1978-83, dep. atty. gen. Colo., 1983-86; adj. prof. U. Colo., Colo., 1990; chief appellate dep. dist. atty. 2d Jud. Dist., Denver, 1986-2000; justice Colo. Supreme Ct., 2000—. Chief reporter Erickson Commn. on Officer-Involved Shootings, 1996-97; lectr. Denver Police Acad., 1986-97; reporter Govs. Columbine Commn., 1999-2000; mem. Colo. Supreme Ct. Criminal Rules Com., 1983-2000, chmn., 1997-2000, Colo. Bd. Law Examiners, 1984-94, Colo. Supreme Ct. Appellate Rules Com., 1985-2000, Colo. Supreme Ct. Civil Rules Com., Colo. Supreme Ct. Criminal Pattern Jury Instructions Com., 1987-2000, Colo. Supreme Ct. Jury Reform Pilot Project Com., 1998-2000, Colo. Dist. Attys. Coun. Legis. Com., 1990-2000. Office: Colo State Supreme Ct Judicial Bldg 2 E 14th Ave Denver CO 80203-2115*

COATS, ROBERT NOYCE, hydrologist; b. Berkeley, Calif., July 28, 1943; s. Robert Roy and Mary Elizabeth (Robinson) C.; m. Kathleen Garrett Silber, May 18, 1980; children: Zachary Thomas, Noah Robert. BS, U. Calif., Berkeley, 1965; PhD, U. Calif., 1975; MS, U. Minn., 1967. Tchg. assoc. Dept. Conservation and Resources Studies U. Calif., Berkeley, 1974-78; scientist John Muir Inst., Napa, Calif., 1978-83; assoc. Philip Williams & Assocs., San Francisco, 1983-86, prin., 1986—97; sr. scientist Stillwater Scis., Berkeley, Calif., 1997—99; owner Hydroikos Ltd., Berkeley, Calif., 1999—. Contbr. articles to profl. jours. Fellow Rockefeller Found., 1978-79. Mem. AAAS, Am. Geophys. Union, Soc. for Ecol. Restoration, Internat. Limnology Soc. Avocations: poetry, music, photography. Office: Hydroikos Ltd 2560 Ninth St Ste 216 Berkeley CA 94710 Home Phone: 510-524-6717; Office Phone: 510-845-0435. Business E-Mail: coats@hydroikos.com.

COATSWORTH, JOHN HENRY, history professor, writer, dean; b. NYC, Sept. 27, 1940; s. Joseph Samuel Coatsworth and Janet Whedon (Bell) Barr; m. Patricia Ann Sopiak, June 13, 1964; 1 child, Anna Catherine. BA, Wesleyan U., 1963; MA, U. Wis., 1967, PhD, 1972; MA, Harvard U., 1993. Asst. prof. history U. Chgo., 1969—77, assoc. prof., 1977—80, prof., 1980—92, chair Dept. History; prof. history, Monroe Gutman prof. L.Am. affairs Harvard U., Cambridge, Mass., 1992—2007, founding dir. David Rockefeller Ctr. for L.Am. Studies, 1994—2006, chair Com. on Human Rights Studies; prof. internat. and pub. affairs and history Sch. Internat. and Pub. Affairs, Columbia U., NYC, 2007—, interim dean, 2007—. Mem. Coun. on Fgn. Rels., 2000—; bd. dirs. Tinker Found. Author: Growth Against Development, 1981, The United States and Central America, 1994; co-editor: Images of Mexico in the United States, 1989, Latin America and the World Economy Since 1800, 1998, The Cambridge Economic History of Latin America, 2006 John Simon Guggenheim fellow Guggenheim Found., 1986-87. Mem. Am. Hist. Assn. (pres. 1995), L.Am. Studies Assn., Econ. History Assn., Conf. on L.Am. History, Am. Acad. Arts and Scis. Office: Sch Internat and Pub Affairs Fayerweather Hall, Rm 612 420 West 118th Street New York NY 10027 Office Fax: 212-854-4646. E-mail: jhc2125@columbia.edu.*

COBABE, ALVIN FRED, retired surgeon, small business owner; b. Ogden, Utah, Nov. 7, 1917; s. Frederick James and Hazel (Hudman) Cobabe; m. June Heslop, Nov. 10, 1937; children: Carolyn, Gayla, Shawna, Aleta. AS, Weber State Coll., Ogden, 1959; BS, U. Utah, Salt Lake City, 1960, MD, 1963. Cert. Am. Soc. Clin. Hypnosis, 1966, lic. Calif., 1968, Utah, 1969. Elec. engr. KLO Radio Sta., Ogden, 1936—37; owner, operater, ranching and equipment co. Weber and Cache County, Utah, 1937—; owner, operater, earth moving constrn. co. Utah, 1950—, Ariz., 1950—, Nev., 1950—, Calif., 1950—; owner, operater Powder Mountain Ski Resort, Weber and Cache County, 1958—; pvt. practice Weber County, 1963—; intern Thomas D. Dee Meml. Hosp., 1963—64; pvt. practice Ogden, Utah, 1963—88. Mem.: Ogden Exec. Assn. (pres.), Utah Ski Assn. (founding mem. 1965—), Weber County Med. And Surg. Soc. Achievements include first person to ever have angioplastic surgery performed on July 6, 1967 at Cleveland Clinic as experimental surgery. Avocation: flying.

COBB, BRIAN ERIC, broadcast executive; b. Berlin, NH, Jan. 3, 1945; s. Everett Bryan and Eleanore (Bouchard) C.; m. Denise Leclair, Sept. 20, 1986; children: Jennifer, Heather. BS, U. Nev., 1967. Gen. sales mgr. Sta. WNGE-TV, Nashville, 1972, mktg. mgr., 1973-76, v.p., gen. mgr., 1977, Sta. WSIX AM/FM, Nashville, 1977, Gen. Electric Broadcasting of Colo., stas. KOA-AM, KOAQ, KOA-TV, Denver, 1978-81; v.p. TV Chapman Assocs., Washington, 1982-87; ptnr. Media Venture Ptnrs., Naples, Fla., 1987-2001; pres. Cobb Corp., NYC, 2001—. Cons. Denver Broncos, 1982—2000; pres. Media Ventur Mgmt., Biltmore Broadcasting. Comml. chmn. Mile-Hi United Way, 1980; bd. dirs. Vanderbilt Children's Hosp., 1973-76; founder, chmn. Naples Children and Edn. Found.; trustee Fla. Gulf Coast U., 2001—. Named an Outstanding Young Man of Yr., Nashville Jaycees, 1978. Mem. Nat. Assn. Broadcasters, Nat. Assn. TV Program Execs., Tenn. Assn. Broadcasters (bd. dirs. 1975-77), Nat. Assn. Media Brokers (pres. 1993-95), Rotary. Republican. Roman Catholic. Avocations: golf, reading. Office: Cobb Corp LLC Ste 210 800 Laurel Oak Dr Naples FL 34108-7512 Office Phone: 202-478-3737, 212-812-5020. Business E-Mail: briancobb@cobbcorp.tv.

COBB, CALVIN HAYES, JR., lawyer; b. San Diego, Aug. 2, 1924; s. Calvin Hayes and Frances King (Halm) Cobb; m. Olive Latimer Watson, Mar. 19, 1955; children: Alice Cobb Parte, Joan Cobb Pettit, Calvin Hayes III, Robert Watson, Olive Latimer Waxter. BS with distinction, U.S. Naval Acad., 1944; LLB, Georgetown U., 1950. Bar: DC 1950, Md. 1950, U.S. Supreme Ct. 1953. Assoc. Law Offices Elisha Hanson, Washington, 1950-55; ptnr. Hanson, Cobb & O'Brien, Washington, 1955-69, Steptoe & Johnson, Washington, 1969—2005, of counsel, 2006—. Leading article editor: Georgetown Law Jour., 1949; contbr. articles to law revs. and profl. jours. Trustee Found. Mid. East Peace, 1969—, Naval Hist. Found., 1983—2003; chmn. Found. Mid. East Peace, 2004—. Lt. (j.g.) USN, 1944—47. Recipient Disting. Pub. Svc. award, U.S. Sec. of Navy, 1979, 1991, USCG, 1991. Mem.: Soc. Cin., U.S. Naval Acad. Alumni Assn. (trustee 1955—58), Navy League U.S. (nat. judge adv. 1975—89, bd. dirs. 1975—, sr. v.p. 1988—89, pres. 1989—91, Nat. Pres.'s award 1976, 1983, 1986), Naples Athletic Club, Forum Club (bd. dirs. 2000—03), Barristers Club (pres. 1974), Naples Bath and Tennis Club, Royal Poinciana Golf Club (pres. 2003—05), Gibson Island Club, Chevy Chase Club (pres. 1974—75). Republican. Roman Catholic. Avocations: tennis, golf, bridge. Office: 1330 Connecticut Ave NW Washington DC 20036-1704 Home Phone: 239-649-4352. Personal E-mail: chcobbjr@aol.com. Business E-Mail: ccobb@steptoe.com.

COBB, CHARLES KENCHE, JR., lawyer, real estate broker; b. Canton, Ga., Aug. 23, 1934; s. Charlie Kench and Alice (Enloe) Cobb; m. Carolyn Webb, Aug. 31, 1963; children: Charlie Kenche III, Catherine Elizabeth Fryman. BS, Ga. Tech., 1956; MBA, Harvard U., 1962; postgrad., Emory U., 1963, Georgetown U., 1959; LLD, Woodrow Wilson, 1968. Bar: Ga. 1969. Pres. C. Cobb Properties, Atlanta, 1969—, Sterling Land Co., Atlanta, 1973—; dir. Canton Textile Mills, Inc., 1991—. Mem. exec. com. Ga. Tech. Wesley Found., Atlanta, 1983—2003; treas. Reinhardt Coll., Waleska, Ga., 1984—87, sec., 1987—90, trustee, 1974—; bd. dirs. Ga. Tech. YMCA, Atlanta, 1976—89; lay leader Northside United Meth. Ch., 1978, trustee, 2007—. Served to 1st lt. USAF, 1956—59, ETO. Mem.: Ga. Assn. Exchangors (former pres., Ga. Exchangor of Yr. 1971, 1990), Atlanta Bd. Realtors (bd. dirs. 1983—90, Outstanding Transaction of Yr. award 1986), Ga. Bar Assn., Ga. Tech. Alumni Assn. (trustee 1976—79), Ga. Hist. Trust, Buckhead 50 Club (pres. 1997), Canton Golf Club, Shriners, Masons. Home: 2851 Howell Mill Rd NW Atlanta GA 30327-1333 Office: 1 Northside 75 NW Ste 102 Atlanta GA 30318-7715 Office Phone: 404-355-0889.

COBB, DAVID KEITH, accountant; b. Calhoun City, Miss., Mar. 2, 1941; s. Bayne and Frances (Clements) C.; m. Dorothy Hill, June 15, 1963; children: Paul J., John D., Mark F. BS, U. So. Miss., 1963. Nat. mng. ptnr. fin. svcs. KPMG Peat Marwick, NYC, 1963-95; CEO, vice chmn. Alamo Rent A Car, Inc., 1995-97. Bd. dirs. RHR Internat., Inc., BankAtlantic Bancorp, Alliance Data Sys., Inc., BFC Fin. Corp. Bd. dirs. Nova Southeastern U. Grad. Sch. Bus. Republican. Presbyterian. Home and Office: 2521 Del Lago Dr Fort Lauderdale FL 33316-2303 Business E-Mail: kcobb@cobbcorner.com.

COBB, HENRY NICHOLS, architect; b. Boston, Apr. 8, 1926; s. Charles Kane and Elsie Quincy (Nichols) C.; m. Joan Stewart Spaulding, June 5, 1953; children: Sara Quincy, Emma Trow, Pamela Codman. AB, Harvard U., 1947, MArch, 1949; DFA (hon.), Bowdoin Coll., 1985; D Tech. Scis (hon.), Swiss Fed. Inst. Tech., 1990. Designer in office Hugh Stubbins, 1949-50; mem. archtl. divsn. Webb & Knapp, Inc., 1950-60; ptnr. Pei Cobb Freed & Ptnrs. (formerly I.M. Pei & Ptnrs.), NYC, 1960—. Vis. critic Yale U., 1963-66, Bishop vis. prof. architecture, 1973, 78, Davenport vis. prof., 1975; studio prof., chmn. dept. architecture Harvard U. Grad. Sch. Design, Cambridge, Mass., 1980-85. Prin. works include Pl. Ville Marie, Montreal, Can., 1962, Ctr. for Govt. and Internat. Studies, Harvard U., 2005; acad. ctr. and residence halls State U. Coll., Fredonia, N.Y., 1967, John Hancock Tower, Boston, 1972, Collins Place, Melbourne, Australia, 1976, Wilson Commons, U. Rochester, 1976, World Trade Ctr., Balt., 1977, Dallas Ctr., 1979, Johnson & Johnson World Hdqrs., New Brunswick, N.J., 1981, 16th St. Mall, Denver, 1982, Mobil Rsch. Lab., Farmers Branch, Tex., 1983, Portland (Maine) Mus. Art, 1983, Arco Tower, Dallas, 1984, hdqrs. Pitney Bowes Corp., Stamford, Conn., 1985, Fountain Place, Dallas, 1986, Columbia Sq., Washington, 1986, Commerce Sq., Phila., 1987, First Interstate World Ctr., L.A., 1989, Anderson Grad. Sch. Mgmt. UCLA, 1994, AAAS Hdqrs., Washington, 1997, U.S. Courthouse, Boston, 1998, World Trade Ctr., Barcelona, 1999, Head Office ABN-AMRO Bank, Amsterdam, 1999, Coll.-Conservatory of Music, U. Cin., 1999, Tour EDF, Paris, 2001, 2099 Pennsylvania Ave., Washington, 2001, Friend Ctr. for Engring. Edn., Princeton U., 2001, U.S. Courthouse, Hammond, Ind., 2002, World Trade Ctr. and Grand Marina Hotel, Barcelona, 2002, Nat. Constn. Ctr., Phila., 2003, Hyatt Ctr., Chgo., 2005, Ctr. Govt. and Internat. Studies Harvard U., 2005. Trustee Am. Acad. in Rome, 1972-90, Brearley Sch., 1975-80. Served with USNR, 1944-46. Recipient Topaz medallion for excellence in archtl. edn. Assn. Collegiate Schs. of Architecture/AIA, 1995. Fellow AIA (medal of honor N.Y. chpt. 1982), Am. Acad. Arts and Scis.; mem. AAAL (Arnold W. Brunner Meml. prize in architecture 1977), NAD. Office: Pei Cobb Freed & Ptnrs 88 Pine St New York NY 10005

COBB, JAMES E., lawyer; b. Quitman, Ga., Jan. 20, 1930; s. W. Fred and Rose S. Cobb; m. Virginia Wenz Cobb, Sept. 10, 1955; children: Laurence, Jeffrey, Linda. BA, U. Fla., Gainesville, 1952, JD cum laude, 1958. Assoc. Bedell & Bedell, Jacksonville, Fla., 1958—62, Mathews Osborne & Ehrich, Jacksonville, Fla., 1962—64, ptnr., 1964—91, Peek & Cobb, Jacksonville, 1991—98, Peek Cobb Edward & Peshten, Jacksonville, 1998—2003, Peek Cobb & Edwards, Jacksonville, 2003—. Pres. Jacksonville Bar Assn., 1969. Pres. North Fla. Heart Assn., Jacksonville, 1970, Meninak Club, Jacksonville, 1972; gen. counsel Jacksonville C. of C., 1994. Capt. USAF, 1952—65, Korea. Named one of, Best Lawyers in Am., 1989—2006; recipient Fla. Blue Key, 1958, Justice Raymond Ehrlich Trial Advocacy award, Jacksonville Bar Assn., 2003—04. Fellow: Am. Coll. Trial Lawyers; mem.: Fla. Bar Found. (pres. 1978—), Fla. Supreme Ct. Hist. Soc. (pres. 1991—), U. North Fla. Found. (pres. 1993—). Avocations: golf, travel. Home: 4242 Ortega Blvd #15 Jacksonville FL 32210 Office: Peek Cobb & Edwards 1301 Riverplace Bk 32207 Jacksonville FL 32210

COBB, JAMES G., editor; BA, Butler CC, El Dorado, KS, 1974. Automobiles editor NY Times, 1994—. Office: NY Times 229 W 43rd St New York NY 10036 Office Phone: 212-556-4045. E-mail: autos@nytimes.com.

COBB, JILL, pathologist; b. Wichita, Kans., Nov. 3, 1942; d. Neville Norwood Cobb and Mary Margaret Abercrombie; m. George Edward Thomas, Jan. 25, 1993. B Gen. Studies, Wichita State U., 1977; MD, U. Kans. Med. Ctr., Kansas City, 1981; MPH, Johns Hopkins U., Balt., 1998. Diplomate Am. Bd. Pathology, Anatomic, Clin. Pathology, 1985, Am. Bd. Forensic Pathology, 1986. Dep. coroner Denver Coroner's Office,

1986—89, Wedgwick County, Wichita, Kans., 1999—2000; coroner Arapahoe County, Littleton, Colo., 1987—93, Harvey, McPherson County, Kans., 1995—97, Douglas County, Kans., 1996—97; coroner's pathologist Capital Coast Dist. Health Bd., Wellington, New Zealand, 2004—06; pathologist Sedick County Regional Forensic Sci. Ctr., Wichita. Cons. in field. Forensic pathologist Physicians for Human Rights, Bahrain, 1998—99. Mem.: Oreg. Med. Assn., Am. Acad. Forensic Scis. Avocations: lapidary, ceramics, mosaics, knitting. Office: Sedick County Regional Forensic Sci Ctr 1109 N Minneapolis Wichita KS 67214

COBB, JOHN BOSWELL, JR., clergyman, educator; b. Kobe, Japan, Feb. 9, 1925; s. John Boswell and Theodora Cook (Atkinson) C.; m. Jean Olmstead Loftin, June 18, 1947; children: Theodore, Clifford, Andrew, Richard. MA, U. Chgo. Div. Sch., 1949, PhD, 1952. Ordained to ministry United Meth. Ch., 1950. Pastor Towns County Circuit, N.Ga. Conf., 1950-51; faculty Young Harris Coll., Ga., 1950-53, Candler Sch. Theology and Emory U., 1953-58, Sch. Theology, Claremont, Calif., 1958-90; Avery prof. Claremont Grad. Sch., 1973-90; ret., 1990; mem. commn. on doctrine and doctrinal standard United Meth. Ch., 1968-72; mem. commn. on mission, 1984-88. Author: A Christian Natural Theology, 1965, The Structure of Christian Existence, 1967, Christ in a Pluralistic Age, 1975, (with Herman Daly) For the Common Good, 1989. Dir. Ctr. for Process Studies. Fulbright prof. U. Mainz, 1965-66; fellow Woodrow Wilson Internat. Ctr. for Scholars, 1976 Mem. Am. Acad. Religion, Am. Metaphys. Soc. Business E-Mail: cobbj@cgu.edu.

COBB, JOHN CANDLER, medical educator; b. Boston, July 8, 1919; s. Stanley and Elizabeth Mason (Almy) C.; m. Helen Imlay-Franchot, July 27, 1946; children: Loren, Nathaniel, Bethany, Julianne. BS in Astronomy cum laude, Harvard U., 1941, MD, 1948; MPH, Johns Hopkins U., 1954. Diplomate Nat. Bd. Med. Examiners, Am. Bd. Preventive Medicine and Pub. Health; lic. physician, Conn., Md., N.Mex. Intern Yale New Haven Hosp., 1948-49, fellow in pediatrics, 1949-50; jr. asst. resident Yale Psychiatric Clinic, 1950-51; instr. pediatrics Johns Hopkins U., 1951-56, asst. prof. hygiene, 1954-56; cons. Indian Health divsn. USPHS, Albuquerque, 1956-60; prof. preventive medicine U. Colo., Denver, 1965-85, emeritus prof., 1985—, chmn. dept., 1966-73. Dir. med. social rsch. project on population Govt. of Pakistan, 1960-64; cons. Am. Friends Svc. Com., Algeria, 1964; short term cons. WHO, Indonesia and Western Pacific Region, 1969, 70-73, USAID, Togo and Niger, 1979; exch. prof. Guangxi Med. Coll., Nanning, China, 1985-86; coord. ethics seminars U. Health Scis. Ctr., 1980-85; pres. World Hand Assocs., 1985--; cons. in field. Contbr. numerous articles to profl. jours. Bd. dirs., pres. Am. Assn. Planned Parenthood Physicians, 1966-67; chmn. Task Force for Preparing 314(b) Agy. Grant Application, 1969; mem., chmn. health com. of Gov. Lamm and U.S. Congressman Wirth's Task Force on Rocky Flats Nuc. Weapons Plant, Denver, 1974-75; mem. Gov.'s Task Force on Health Effects of Air Pollution, 1978-79; commr. Air Pollution Control Commn. of Colo., 1976-79; mem. air quality policy com. Denver Regional Coun. of Govts., 1978-80, environ. council, U. Colo., 1970-75, Gov.'s Sci. adv. Counc., Colo., 1973-80, Gov.'s Blue Ribbon Task Force on Transp., Colo., 1977; bd. dirs. ROMCOE Ctr. for Environ. Problem Solving, 1978-81, Colo. Coalition for Full Employment, 1978-80; mem. Am. Friends Svc. Com. Adv. Group on Rocky Flats/Nuclear Weapons Project, 1979-85; owning mem. Chaordic Commons. Recipient Florence Sabin award Colo. Pub. Health Assn., 1979, Jack Gore Meml. Peace award Am. Friends Svc. Com., 1980; U.S. EPA grantee, 1975-82. Mem. AAAS, WHO, Internat. Solar Energy Soc., Am. Solar Energy Soc., Internat. Physicians for Prevention of Nuclear War (del. to Congresses in Moscow and Montreal), Appropriate Rural Tech. Assn. (bd. dirs. 1987-2002, v.p. 1991-92), Nat. Resources Def. Coun. (bd. advisors 1991-92), N.Mex. Solar Energy Assn. (bd. dirs. 1995-98), Physicians for Human Rights, Physicians for Social Reponsibility. Home and Office: # 4320 10501 Lagrima De Oro NE Albuquerque NM 87111

COBB, JUDY LYNN, elementary school educator; b. Fresno, Calif., July 31, 1940; d. V.W. and Ruth (Benight) Keim; m. Jeffrey, Jay. BA, Calif. State U., Fresno, 1962. Tchr. Fresno (Calif.) Unified Sch. Dist., 1963-68, Lodi (Calif.) Unified Sch. Dist., 1976—2002, Chpt. I ESL resource tchr., 1981-87. Designer, implementor curriculum for elem. students, using literature, oral and written language, and art to teach reading, social studies, science and multi-cultural activities; nat. grant participant Program Academic Excellence, 1984-87; mem. Lodi Dist. Yr. Round Sch. Com., Art Task Force; artist dist. and cmty. activities; spkr., presenter in field. Contbg. author: Language Literature Approach to English as a Second Language; Represented in permanent collections Lodi Unified Sch. Dist. Named Mentor Tchr., 1986-88 Mem. San Joaquin Reading Assn., Calif. Reading Assn., Internat. Reading Assn. Home: 9531 Springfield Way Stockton CA 95212-2016 Personal E-mail: judylcobb@aol.com.

COBB, KAY BEEVERS, state supreme court justice, retired state senator; b. Quitman County, Miss., Feb. 28, 1942; m. Larry Cobb. BS, Miss. U. for Women; JD, U. Miss. Atty. priv. practice, Oxford, Miss., 1978—84; dir. prosecutors prog. U. Miss. Law Sch.; atty. Miss. Bur. of Narcotics, 1984—88; various positions including coord. SWEEPS anti-drug prog. Office of Miss. Atty. Gen., 1988—92; senator State of Miss., 1992—96; atty. priv. practice, Oxford, 1996—99; assoc. justice Miss. Supreme Ct., 1999—, presiding justice, 2004—. Former mem. President's Commn. on US Model State Drug Laws, Nat. Alliance for Model State Drug Laws. Mem. Miss. Bar Assn. (Chief Justice award 2003), Vets. Aux., C. of C. Baptist. Office: Miss Supreme Ct PO Box 117 450 High St Jackson MS 39205 Home Phone: 601-957-3291; Office Phone: 601-359-2099.

COBB, MELANIE H., biomedical researcher; PhD in Biol. Chemistry, Wash. U., St. Louis, 1976. Fellow Mt. Sinai Sch. Medicine, 1976—80, Albert Einstein Coll. Medicine, 1980—83; prof. dept. pharmacology U. Tex. Southwestern Med. Ctr., Dallas. Jane and Bill Browning, Jr. chair med. sci. U. Tex. Southwestern Med. Ctr.; Haberecht Dean Southwestern Grad. Sch. of Biomedical Scis. Contbr. articles to sci. jours. Recipient Max Planck award, 1994. Mem.: Am. Soc. Microbiol., Am. Soc. Pharmacology and Exptl. Therapeutics (Goodman and Gilman award in drug receptor pharmacology 2000), Am. Soc. Cell Biology, Am. Soc. Biochemistry and Molecular Biology, NAS. Office: U Tex Southwestern Med Ctr 5323 Harry Hines Blvd Dallas TX 75390-9041

COBB, MILES ALAN, retired lawyer; b. Salt Lake City, May 8, 1930; s. Miles Cobb and June (Ray) Cobb Wilson; children: Jennifer, Melissa, Mary. BS, U. Calif.-Berkeley, 1953, LL.B., 1958. Bar: Calif. 1958. Assoc. Bronson, Bronson & McKinnon, San Francisco, 1958-65, ptnr., 1965-76, 78-84; gen. counsel FDIC, Washington, 1976-78; pres. Bell Savs & Loan Assn., San Mateo, Calif., 1984-85. Author: Federal Regulation of Depository Institutions, 1984. Served to 1st lt. U.S. Army, 1953-55; Korea Democrat. Avocations: photography, golf, gardening. E-mail: macobb@sbcglobal.net.

COBB, SHIRLEY ANN DODSON, public relations consultant, journalist; b. Oklahoma City, Jan. 1, 1936; d. William Ray and Irene Dodson; m. Roy Lampkin Cobb, Jr., June 21, 1958; children: Kendra Leigh, Cary William, Paul Alan. BA in Journalism with distinction, U. Okla., 1958, postgrad., 1972, Jacksonville U., 1962. Info. specialist Pacific Missile Test Ctr., Point Mugu, Calif., 1975-76; reporter, splty. editor Religion and Fashion News Chronicle, 1977-81; cons. pub. rels., cable TV, telecom. Camarillo, Calif., 1977—; media mgr. pub. info. cable TV and telecom. City of Thousand Oaks, Calif., 1983-99. Contbr. articles to profl. jours. Pres. Point Mugu Officers' Wives Club, 1975-76; trustee Ocean View Sch. Bd., 1976-79; bd. dir. Camarillo Hospice, 1983-85, Long Term Care of Ventura County, Inc., 2001-03; sec. Ednl. TV for Conejo, 1997-98, pres., 1998-2000, bd. dir., 1997-2002; vice chair Greater Thousand Oaks Telecmty., 1999-2000; treas. Thousand Oaks Rep. Women Federated, 2001-03, pres., 2004; with Ventura County Leadership Acad., 1999-2002; bd. dir. LWV Ventura County, 1999-2003, v.p., comm. dir., 2002-03, Calif. Luth. Univ. Cmty. Leaders Assn., 1987-. Recipient Spot News award San Fernando Valley Press Club, 1979, First Pl. spl. program Calif. Assn. Pub. Info. Ofcls., 1985, Helen Putnam award League of Calif. Cities, 1989, Telecom. Proj. award, League of Calif. Cities Telecom., 1998, 1st pl. award Best Practice award Govt., Bus., Edn. Tech. Expo '98. Mem. Pub. Rels. Soc. Am. (LA chpt. liaison 1991), Calif. Assn. Pub. Info. Ofcls. (pres. 1989-90, Paul Clark Lifetime Achievement award 1993), Conejo Valley Hist. Soc. (sec. 1993-96, co-chair oral history com. 2001-, chair 2003-, bd. dirs. 2003—, dir.-at-large 2006), Las Posas Country Club, Spanish Hills Country Club, Town Hall of Calif. Club, Westlake Womens Club (publicity chair 2006), Phi Beta Kappa, Chi Omega (v.p. 1957-58, mem. mortar bd.). Republican. Home: 2481 Brookhill Dr Camarillo CA 93010-2112 Personal E-mail: cobbweb@aol.com.

COBB, STEPHEN A., lawyer; b. Moline, Ill., Jan. 27, 1944; s. Archibald William and Lucile Bates C.; m. Nancy L. Hendrix, Dec. 18, 1971. AB cum laude, Harvard U., 1966; MA in Sociology, Vanderbilt U., 1968, PhD in Sociology, 1971, JD, 1977. Bar: Tenn. 1978, U.S. Dist. Ct. (mid. dist.) Tenn. 1978. Asst. prof. Tenn. State U., Nashville, 1970-74, dept. head, 1972-74; mem. edn. oversight com. Tenn. Ho. Reps., Nashville, 1974—86, chair edn. oversight com., 1985—86; pvt. practice law Nashville, 1978-86; with Waller Lansden Dortch & Davis, Nashville, 1986-90, ptnr., 1990—2005. Fulbright Jr. lectr. U. Caen, France, 1977—78; lectr. dept. sociology Fisk U., 1981—86. Former pres. Sister Cities of Nashville, Inc.; mem. So. Regional Edn. Bd., former vice chmn commn. ednl. quality. Decorated officer Ordre des Palmes Academiques (France); recipient Paul Simon Internat. award, 1990, Edwin Cudeki Internat. Bus. award, 1992; NDEA fellow, NIMH fellow, 1966-70. Mem. ABA, Tenn. Bar Assn., Tenn Fgn. Lang. Inst., Nashville Bar Assn. (former pres.), Fedn. Alliances Francaises (former pres.), Order of Coif. Home: 1929 Castleman Dr Nashville TN 37215-3901

COBB, SUE BELL, state supreme court justice; b. Evergreen, Ala. d. Otis and Thera Bell; m. William J. Cobb; children: Bill, Andy, Caitlin. BA, U. Ala.; JD, U. Ala. Sch. Law. Dist. judge Conecuh County, Ala., 1981—94; judge Ct. Criminal Appeals, Ala., 1995—2006; alt. chief justice Ct. of the Judiciary, Ala., 1997—2000; chief justice Ala. Supreme Ct., 2007—. Recipient Disting. Svc. award, Nat. Juvenile Detention Assn., Outstanding Svc. award, Juvenile Probation Officer Inst., Children's Voice award, Jud. Conservationist award, Ala. Wildlife Fedn., 1992, Polit. Achievement award, NAACP, Conecuh County br., 1996, Pub. Citizen of Yr. award, Nat. Social Workers Assn., Ala. ch., 1999. Office: Ala Supreme Ct 300 Dexter Ave Montgomery AL 36104 Office Phone: 334-229-0600. Business E-Mail: cjcobb@appellate.state.al.us.

COBB, TY, lawyer; b. Great Bend, Kans., Aug. 25, 1950; s. Grover Cowling and Elizabeth Anne (McCleary) C.; m. Leigh Elliott Stevenson, Aug. 21, 1976; children: Chance Wyatt, Chelsea Leigh, Brady Elliott, Chloe Elizabeth. AB, Harvard U., 1972; JD, Georgetown U., 1978. Bar: D.C. 1979, U.S. Dist. Ct. D.C. 1979, U.S. Dist. Ct. Md. 1979, U.S. Ct. Appeals (4th and D.C. cirs.) 1979, U.S. Ct. Internat. Trade 1980, U.S. Ct. Appeals (3d cir.) 1987, U.S. Supreme Ct. 1986, Md. 1987, Colo. 1998, U.S. Ct. Appeals (10th cir.) 1999. Legis. adminstrv. asst. U.S. Ho. of Reps., Washington, 1974-75; law clk. to fed. judge U.S. Dist. Ct., Balt., 1978-79; assoc. Collier, Shannon, Rill & Scott, Washington, 1979-81; asst. U.S. atty. Office of U.S. Atty., Balt., 1981-86; chief criminal cases Office U.S. Attorney, Balt., 1984-86; mid-Atlantic regional coord. Organized Crime Drug Enforcement Task Force U.S. Dept. Justice, Balt., 1985—86; ptnr. Hogan & Hartson LLP, Washington and Balt., 1988-98, mng. ptnr. Denver, 1998—, dir. litig. practice group. Spl. trial counsel Office of Ind. Counsel HUD, 1994-95; instr. U.S. Atty. Gen.'s Adv. Inst., U.S. Dept. Justice, 1983-86; mem. Jud. Conf. of U.S. Ct. Appeals (4th cir.); trustee Grand Canyon Trust, 2004—. Contbr. articles to profl. jours. Chmn. Md. lawyers Dole for Pres., 1986-87; counsel Forest Glen Park Civic Assn., Montgomery County, Md., 1981-84, Colo. Fed. Jud. Selection Com., 2001—; bd. trustees Grand Canyon Trust, 2004—. Fellow Am. Coll. Trial Lawyers (com. on fed. criminal procedure); mem. ABA, Internat. Bar Assn., Harvard Alumni Assn. (bd. dirs. 1990-92), Congress of Fellows Ctr. for Internat. Legal Studies. Republican. Office: Hogan & Hartson LLP 555 13th St NW Ste 800 E Washington DC 20004-1161 also: Hogan & Hartson LLP One Tabor Ctr 1200 17th St Ste 1500 Denver CO 80202-5835 Office Phone: 202-637-6437, 303-899-7300. Office Fax: 202-637-5910. Business E-Mail: tcobb@hhlaw.com.

COBB, VANESSA WYVETTE, elementary school educator; b. Sanford, NC, May 27, 1953; d. Ernest and Frances Olivia Cobb. BS, Hampton U., Va., 1976; MA, Mich. State U., East Lansing, 1977. Tchr. basic skills improvement East Orange Sch. Dist., NJ, 1977—94, tchr. math, soc. studies, 1994—95, tchr. 2nd grade, 1995—96, tchr. 5th grade sci., 1996—97, tchr. 1st, 2nd grade, 1997—98, tchr. 1st grade, 1998—2000, tchr. pre-K, 2000—02, 2003—05, tchr. 5th grade, 2002—03, tchr., kindergarten, 1st grade, 2005—. Mem. Newark Mus.; contbg. mem. UNICEF. Mem.: NEA, Am. Counseling Assn., NJ Sch. Counselor Assn., Am. Sch. Counselor Assn., Essex County Edn. Assn., NJ Edn. Assn., East Orange Edn. Assn., Gordon Parks Acad. Sunshine Club. Avocations: photography, ballet, reading, music, theater. Home: 9 Mill Rd Burlington NJ 08016

COBB, VIRGINIA HORTON, artist, educator; b. Oklahoma City, Nov. 23, 1933; d. Wayne and Ruth (Goodale) Horton; m. Bruce L. Cobb, Dec. 30, 1951 (div. 1985); children: Bruce Wayne, Juliann, William Stuart, M. Jerrold Friedman, 1988. Student, U. Colo., 1966-67, Community Coll., Denver, 1967; student of, William Schimmel, Ariz., 1965-66, Edgar Whitney, NYC, 1966, Chen Chi, 1974. Comml. artist and designer Ruth Horton Studios, Oklahoma City, 1954-63; instr. seminars, 1974—, N.Mex. Watercolor Soc., Albuquerque, 1976, Okla. Mus. Art, Oklahoma City, 1976, Upstairs Gallery Workshops, Arlington, Tex., 1977, 78, 79, 80, St. Louis Art Guild, 1980, Alaska Water Color Soc., Anchorage, 1981, Needham (Mass.) Art Center, 1981, N.C. Watercolor Soc., Charlotte, 1981, San Diego Watercolor Soc., 1981, S.C. Water Color Soc., Florence, 1981, Hawaii Water Color Soc., 1989, Trillium Workshops, Toronto, 1989, 90, Baffin Island, 1992, Maui, Hawaii, 1993, Vancouver Island, 1990, 91. Guest instr. Crafton Hills Coll. Master Seminars, Yucaipa, Calif., 1979, 80, 81, U. Alaska, Anchorage, 1981, Master Class/Santa Fe Painting Workshops/Friedman Cobb Studios, 1989—; guest lectr. Watermedia 2000, Houston; lectr. Sta. KRDO-TV, 1977, Francis Marion Coll., Florence, 1981, Sta. KAKM, Anchorage, 1981; guest spkr. Watermedia, Houston, 2003. Author: Discovering The Inner Eye, 1988; author (with Jerrold Friedman) Alice.on bristol, 1996, (with Polly Hammett) Designsense, 2003; contbr. articles to art publs.; one-woman shows include Jack Meier Galleries, Houston, 1979-81, 83-85, San Juan Coll., 1995, Art Resources, St. Paul, 1988, Sturh Mus., Grand Island, Nebr., 1982; exhibited in group shows at Nat. Acad., 1982, 1985, NAD, NYC, 1978-81, San Bernardino (Calif.) County Mus., 1978, Nat. Watercolor Invitational, Rochester, NY, 1981, Rocky Mountain Nat. Watermedia Exhbt., Golden, Colo., 1978-79, 81, Albuquerque Mus. Art, 1985, Am. Watercolor Soc., 1985, Internat. Waters: A Touring Exhibit, Canada, 1991, USA, 1992, Great Britain, 1992, Scotland, 1993; represented in permanent collections, NAD, Jefferson County (Colo.) Public Libr., Foothills Art Ctr., Golden, Colo., St. Lawrence U., Canton, NY, N.Mex. Watercolor Soc., Albuquerque, Santa Fe Mus. Fine Arts. Recipient Foothills Art Ctr. award, 1976, Edgar Fox award Watercolor U.S.A., 1973, Denver award Rocky Mountain Nat. Exhbn., 1981, Am. Artist Achievement award, 1994. Mem. NAD (Walter Biggs Meml. award 1978, 81), Nat. Watercolor Soc. (Strathmore Paper Co. award 1975), Am. Watercolor Soc. (Paul B. Remmey Meml. award 1974,. Arches Paper Co. award 1977, Edgar Whitney award 1978, Mary Pleishner Meml. award 1980, High Winds medal 1981, Silver medal of Honor 1983, guest demonstrator 1980, nat. juror 1981, Dolphin fellow 1982, juror Watercolor West 1990, Juror award 1999), N.Mex. Watercolor Soc. (hon.), Rocky Mountain Watermedia Soc. Personal E-mail: veacobb@yahoo.com.

COBB, WILLIAM C., Internet company executive; BSc, U. Pa.; MBA, Northwestern U. From v.p. new bus. to sr. v.p., chief mktg. officer Tricon Restaurants Internat. PepsiCo, sr. v.p., chief mktg. officer Tricon Restaurants Internat.; sr. v.p. global mktg. eBay Inc., San Jose, Calif.; pres. eBay N. Am., San Jose, Calif., 2005—. Office: eBay Inc 2145 Hamilton Ave San Jose CA 95125-5905

COBBAN, WILLIAM AUBREY, paleontologist; b. Anaconda, Mont., Dec. 31, 1916; s. Ray Aubrey and Anastacia (McNulty) C.; m. Ruth Georgina Loucks, Apr. 15, 1942; children: Georgina, William, Robert. BA, U. Mont., 1940; PhD, Johns Hopkins U., 1949. Geologist Carter Oil Co., Tulsa, 1940—46; paleontologist U.S. Geol. Survey, Washington, 1948—92, emeritus scientist, 1992—. Contbr. numerous articles to profl. jours. Recipient Meritorious Svc. award Dept. Interior, 1974, Disting. Svc. award US Dept. Interior, 1986; honoree 6th Internat. Symposium, Cephalopods--Recent and Past, 2004, Dallas Peck Outstanding Sci. Emeritus award, US Geol. Survey, Dallas, 2006. Fellow AAAS, Geol. Soc. Am.; mem. Soc. Econ. Paleontologists and Mineralogists (hon.; Disting. Pioneer Geologist award 1985, Raymond C. Moore Paleontology medal 1990), Rocky Mountain Assn. Geologists (hon.), Mont. Geol. Soc. (hon.), Wyo. Geol Assn. (hon.), Paleontol. Soc. Am. (Paleontol. medal 1985), Assn. Petroleum Geologists, Paleontol. Rsch. Inst. (Gilbert Harris award 1996), Rocky Mountain Assn. Geologists (Outstanding award 2001), Phi Beta Kappa, Sigma Xi. Republican. Mem. United Ch. of Christ. Office: US Geol Survey Federal Ctr PO Box 25046 # 980 Denver CO 80225 Office Phone: 303-236-5670.

COBBLEDICK, SUSIE DIANE, librarian; b. Decatur, Ill., Oct. 27, 1963; d. David Stanley Cobbledick and Willetta Louise Finley. BA, BFA, Kent State U., 1987; MFA, Temple U., 1992; MLS, Kent State U., 1994. Librarian Bklyn. Pub. Libr., 1995—98; reference librarian Worthington (Ohio) Pub. Libr., 1998—2001; librarian Lorain Pub. Libr. Sys., North Ridgeville, Ohio, 2002—. Mem.: Ohio Libr. Coun., Progressive Librarians Guild, Svc. Employees Internat. Union (v.p. Lorain Pub. Libr. Sys. chpt. 2003—). Democrat. Avocations: bookbinding, drawing, weaving. Office: Lorain Pub Libr Sys North Ridgeville Br 35700 Bainbridge Rd North Ridgeville OH 44039 Office Phone: 440-327-8326. Personal E-mail: 110162.1737@compuserve.com.

COBB-MYERS, JANET LEA, music educator; b. Beardstown, Ill., Jan. 4, 1946; d. Lawrence Elmer and Virginia Lee (Sinnock) Cobb; m. John Merrill Myers, July 2, 1994; stepchildren: Barbara, Jonathan. AA, Springfield Coll., 1966; MusB in Music Edn., Am. Conservatory Music, 1969, Degree in Bach Applied Piano Performance, 1972. Music tchr. Villa Mid. Sch., Villa Pk., Ill., 1970—71; exec. admin. asst. State of Ill. Dept. Pub. Aid, 1977—2002; pvt. piano tchr. Pvt. Practice, 1985—. Pres., sec., treas. Evening Etude Music Club, Springfield, 1990—2002; judge piano competitions, performances, and recitals throught Europe and US. Dir., creator Springfield Handel Choir, 1996. Found. for Arts scholarship, Three Arts Club, Chgo., 1967—72, scholarship, Mozarteum-Salzburg, Austria, 1971, Dutch Min., Belgium, 1980. Mem.: Evening Etude Music Club, Ill. Fedn. Music Club. Independent. Roman Cath. Avocations: reading, gardening, swimming. Home and Office: 530 Overton Rd Springfield IL 62711 Home Phone: 217-726-8030; Office Phone: 217-725-1676. Business E-Mail: jcobb@springfieldlaw.com.

COBBS, CHARLES GLENN, retired medical educator; b. Birmingham, Ala., Mar. 30, 1934; s. John Hariner Cobbs and Marie Augustine Glenn; m. Naneita McEachfrow Leach, July 30, 1960; children: John Glenn, Charles Stringfellow, Archibald Leach. AB, Princeton U., NJ, 1955; MD, Harvard Coll., Cambridge, Mass., 1963. Dir. U. Ala., Birmingham, 1969—90, prof. medicine, 1990—2000, prof. emeritus, 2000—. 1st lt. USMC Res., 1955—59.

COBBS, NICHOLAS HAMNER, lawyer, judge; b. NYC, June 28, 1946; s. John Lewis and Phyllis Cobbs; children: Robert White, Rebecca Ann. AB cum laude, Amherst Coll., Mass., 1968; JD, U. Pa., 1974. Bar: N.Y. 1975, D.C. 1982, Md. 1984, Va. 1990, U.S. Dist. Ct. (so. dist.) N.Y. 1975, U.S. Dist. Ct. D.C. 1982, U.S. Dist. Ct. (ea. dist.) Va. 1990, U.S. Dist. Ct. (we. dist.) Va. 1990, U.S. Dist. Ct. Md. 1989, U.S. Supreme Ct. 1984. Assoc. Burlingham Underwood & Lord, NYC, 1974-77, Haight, Gardner, Poor & Havens, NYC, 1977-83; ptnr., of counsel Tigert & Roberts, Washington, 1984-89; ptnr. Law Offices of Nicholas H. Cobbs, Washington, 1989—2005; adminstrv. law judge D.C. Office of Administrv. Hearings, 2005—. Steering com. DC Bar Law Practice Mgmt., 2000-05, litigation steering com., 2001-07, co-chmn., 2002-04. Contbr. articles to profl. jours. Arbitrator, mediator DC Superior Ct., Washington, 1990-05; instr. DC Bar Continuing Legal Edn., 1993—. Lt. USNR, 1969-73. Recipient Spl. Merit award, D.C. Bar, 2003. Mem. ABA, Fed. Bar Assn. Episcopalian. Office: 941 N Capitol St Ste 9100 Washington DC 20002

COBBS, PRICE MASHAW, social psychiatrist; b. LA, Nov. 2, 1928; s. Peter Price and Rosa (Mashaw) C.; m. Evadne Priester, May 30, 1957 (dec. Oct. 1973); children: Price Priester, Marion Renata; m. Frederica Maxwell, May 26, 1985 AB, U. Calif.-Berkeley, 1953; MD, Meharry Med. Coll., 1958. Intern San Francisco Gen. Hosp., 1958-59; psychiat. resident Mendocino State Hosp., Talmage, Calif., 1959-61, Langley Porter Neuro-Psychiat. Inst., San Francisco, 1961-62; pres., CEO Pacific Mgmt. Systems, San Francisco, 1967—; CEO Cobbs, Inc. Mgmt. cons. in workforce diversity numerous cos., govt. agys. and community projects; conducted seminars UN, Dept. State; guest lectr. leading colls. and univs.; chair 1st Ann. Nat. Diversity Conf., San Francisco, 1991; speaker 1st Internat. Diversity Conf., Johannesburg, South Africa, 1991; vis. cons., lectr. workforce diversity, South Africa, 1993; co-founder, pres. Renaissance Books, Inc.; adv. bd. Black Scholar. Author: My American Life: From Rage to Entitlement, 2005, (with William H. Grier) Black Rage, 1968, The Jesus Bag, 1971, (with Judith L. Turnock) Cracking the Corporate Code: From Survival to Mastery, 2000; contbr. State of Black America 1988, 89. Bd. dirs. Shared Interest; founding mem. Diversity Collegium. Served to cpl. U.S. Army, 1951-53 Recipient Pathfinder award Assn. Humanistic Psychology, 1993, Al Martins Heritage award, The Exec. Leadership Coun., Harvey Russell award, PepsiCo, 2003. Fellow Am. Psychiat. Assn.; mem. Nat. Med. Assn., NAACP (life), Nat. Acad. Scis.; charter mem. Nat. Urban League. Achievements include pioneering in discipline of ethnotherapy to understand differences in race, culture and ethnicity. Office: Pacific Mgmt System 3528 Sacramento St San Francisco CA 94118-1850 Personal E-mail: cozycobbs@aol.com.

COBEN, HARLAN, writer; b. Newark; m. Anne Armstrong-Coben; 4 children. BS in Polit. Sci., Amherst Coll., 1984. Author: (novels) Drop Shot, 1996, Back Spin, 1997, One False Move, 1999 (Fresh Talent award, W.H. Smith booksellers, UK), The Final Detail, 1999, Darkest Fear, 2000, Deal Breaker, 2000, Tell No One, 2001 (NY Times, London Times, Le Monde, Publishers Weekly, LA Times, San Francisco Chronicle bestseller lists, nominee Edgar award, nominee Macavity award, nominee Anthony award, nominee Barry award, recipient Le Grand Prix des Lectrics de Elle for fiction, France), Gone For Good, 2002 (NY Times, London Times, Le Monde, Publishers Weekly, LA Times, San Francisco Chronicle bestseller lists, Thumping Good Read award, W.H. Smith, UK), No Second Chance, 2003 (NY Times, London Times, Le Monde, Publishers Weekly, LA Times, San Francisco Chronicle bestseller lists, Internat. Book of the Month Club pick), Fade Away, 2004, Just One Look, 2004 (NY Times, London Times, Le Monde, Publishers Weekly, LA Times, San Francisco Chronicle bestseller lists), The Innocent, 2004 (Publishers Weekly bestseller list, 2005), (short stories) A Simple Philosophy (nominee Anthony award, nominee Macavity award, nominee Agatha award), The Key to My Father. Recipient Edgar Allan Poe award, Mystery Writers of Am., Anthony award, World Mystery Conf., Shamus award, Private Eye Writers of Am. Office: c/o Dutton Books Penguin Group USA 375 Hudson St New York NY 10014 Personal E-mail: me@harlancoben.com.

COBERLY, LEANN, internist; b. July 1, 1963; MD, Univ. Cin., 1989. Resident Duke Univ. Med. Ctr., asst. chief resident; with Univ. Cin., 1992—, dir. student edn. for internal medicine, co-chairperson, R-1 Selection Com.; practices Hoxworth Faculty Practice, Ohio, Jewish Hosp. Cholesterol Ctr., Ohio. Office: Hoxworth Faculty Practice Hoxworth Ctr 2nd Fl 3130 Highland Ave Cincinnati OH 45219 Office Phone: 513-584-4503. Office Fax: 513-584-0462.*

COBEY, JOHN GEOFFREY, lawyer, consultant; b. Cleve., Aug. 16, 1943; s. Herbert Todd and Phyllis Jean (Weston) C.; m. Jan M. Frankel, 1983; children: Max Todd, David William. BS, Cornell U., 1966; postgrad., U. de Deusto, Balbao, Spain, 1968, Exeter U., Eng., 1969; JD, U. Cin., 1969. Bar: Ohio 1969, U.S. Dist. Ct. (so. dist.) Ohio 1969, U.S. Ct. Appeals (6th cir.) 1970, Ky. 1978, U.S. Dist. Ct. (no. dist.) Ky. 1978. Mem. Cohen, Todd, Kite and Stanford LLC, 1969—. Bd. dirs. Armstel Corp., Armstrong Coffee Co.; sec. bd. dirs. Elegant Fare; former counsel coop. housing City of Cin. Founder, pres. Young Men's Wing, Mercantile Libr., 1971, regional amb. Cornell U., 1998-2007; trustee Ohio chpt. Nature Conservancy, 1974-82, Hillel of Cin., 1980-86, Women's Def. Fund, 1977, Holmes House, 1978-80; sec. Arts Consortium, Cin., 1975-77, trustee, 1975-78; mem. exec. com. Cin. chpt. Am. Jewish Com., 1981—; trustee Hillel House, Better Housing League; chmn. bd. Friends Cin. Parks, 1982-84, pres. 1977-79; chmn. bd. dirs. Washington Park Housing Co., 1997—; bd. dirs. Cin. Law Libr., Greater Cin./No. Ky. Apt. Assn., 1975-94, Chinese Music Festival, 1996-00, Greater Cin. Oral Health Commn., 2000—, United Jewish Cemetary, 1999-2002, Friends of Spl. Treatment Ctr. for Juvenile Arthritis, Children's Hosp. Cin., 2000—, Opn. Smile, 1998; mem. Cathedral Com. on Reconciliation, Nat. Coun. Civil Justice. Mem. Ohio State Bar Assn., Ky. Bar Assn., Cin. Bar Assn., No. Ky. Bar Assn., Fed. Bar Assn., U. Coll. Life Scis. and Agr. Alumni Assn. (dist. dir. 1977-79), Ohio Apt. Assn. (bd. dirs. 1986-87), Cin. Apt. Assn. (bd. dirs. 1983-90, pres. 1986-87), U. Cin. Law Sch. Alumni Assn. (bd. dirs. 1973-76), 32d Degree Masons Scottish Rite, Cornell Club Southern Ohio (bd. mem. 1998-2006). Home: 231 Oliver Rd Cincinnati OH 45215-2638 Office: Cohen Todd Kite and Stanford 250 E 5th St Ste 1200 Cincinnati OH 45202-3121 Office Phone: 513-333-5234. Business E-Mail: jcobey@ctks.com.

COBEY, RALPH, industrialist; b. Sycamore, Ohio, Aug. 15, 1909; m. Hortense Kohn, Feb. 28, 1944; children: Minnie, Susanne. ME, Carnegie Inst. Tech., 1932; DSc (hon.), Findlay Coll., 1958. Pres. Perfection Steel Body Co., Galion, Ohio, 1945-70, Perfection-Cobey, Co., Galion, Ohio, 1949-70, Eagle Crusher Co., 1954-90, chmn. bd., 1990—; pres. Philips-Davies Co., 1965-70, Cobey Co., 1946-70, Diamond Iron Works, 1972-90, Austin-Western Crusher Co., 1974-90, Scoopmobile Co., 1978-90, Madsen Co., 1979-90, World Wide Investment Co., 1950—. Aide in preparation of prodn. and design of Army tanks OPM, 1939-42. Mem. contbg. com. NCCJ, 1951-55, now area chmn. spl. gifts com.; founder, pres. Harry Cobey Found.; area chmn. U.S. Savs. Bonds; mem. pres.'s adv. coun. for devel. Ashland Coll., Ohio, mem. Ohio Gov.'s Citizens' Task Force on Environ. Protection, 1971-72, Pres.'s Tax Com., 1962-66; pioneer chaplain svcs. in indsl. plants; mem. Ohio Expns. Commn., 1964, Radio Free Europe Com.; chmn. Cmty. Heart Fund Campaign, 1971-72; pres., spl. gifts chmn. Crawford County Heart Fund, 1972-78; mem. Ohio fin. bd. Heart Fund, 1973—; mem. Ohio Rep. Fin. Com.; mounted dep. sheriff, Morrow County (Ohio), 1974-84; bd. dirs., chmn. long range planning com. Johnny Appleseed Area coun. Boy Scouts of Am.; hon. life mem. Galion Cmty. Ctr.; trustee Galion City Hosp. Found. Bd.; mem. pres.'s coun. Ohio State U.; chmn., founder Minnie Cobey Meml. Libr.; founder, chmn. bd. trustees Louis Bromfield Malabar Farm Found.; bd. dirs. Morrow County United Appeals; State of Ohio amb. of natural resources; numerous other civic activities. Capt. USAAF, 1942-46, 51, Korea. Baden-Powel World fellow King Carl Gustaf of Sweden, 1992; recipient Disting. Citizen of Yr. award Heart of Ohio Coun., Boy Scouts Am., 1995, Lifetime Commitment to Humanitarianism award from Rep. Joan Lawrence, Ohio Ho. Reps., 1996, award Louis Bromfield Soc., 2001, resolution from Ohio Dist. 5 Agy. on Aging, Cert. of Appreciation USDA, 2003; inductee Ohio State Fair Hall of Fame, 1992, Ohio Agrl. Hall of Fame, 1999, Ohio Natural Resources Hall of Fame, 2001, Ohio Sr. Citizens Hall of Fame, 2002, N. Ctrl. Ohio Entreprenureal Hall of Fame, 2003; Ralph Cobey Day in City of Galion, 1995, City of Bucyrus, 1999. Mem. NAM, Nat. Assn. 4-H Clubs, Future Farmers Am., U.S. C. of C. (mem. taxation, fgn. affairs, labor rels. coms.), Masons (32 degree, awarded 75 yr. pin 2007), Shriners (sec.-treas.). Home: 4270 State Route 309 Galion OH 44833-9618 Office: Eagle Crusher Co Inc PO Box 537 Galion OH 44833-0537

COBEY, VIRGINIA BRANUM, artist, collector, civic leader; b. Chgo.; d. Albert Marshall and Hope (Engelhard) B.; m. James Alexander Cobey, Aug. 1, 1942; children: Hope Cobey Batey (dec.), Christopher Earle Cobey, Lisa Cobey Kelland. AFA, Stephens Coll., 1939; BFA in Drama, U. Iowa, 1941. Hostess, Stage Door Canteen, NYC, 1942-43; mem. Am. Theatre Wing, NYC, 1942-43; actress Little Theater of the Rockies, 1939-40; model I. Magnin, LA, 1943-44; stylist Macy's, NYC, 1945; curator, Pacific Asia Mus., 1970; importer Va. Cobey Art/Antiques, Pasadena, Calif., 1978—. Bd. dirs. Women's Council KCET-PBS, LA, 1968; v.p. Pasadena Art Alliance, 1971-73; chmn., bd. dirs. Friends of Occidental Coll., LA, 1975-76; bd. dirs. Costume Council LA County Mus. Art, 1981-82, Friends of Vielles Maisons Françaises, LA, 1986; bd. dirs. Internat. Student Ctr., UCLA, 1985—; founder, chmn. Southwestern Affiliates Southwestern Sch. Law, 1983-85, named Outstanding Friend, 1985. Ford Found. grantee Tamarind lithography, 1971. Mem. League Women Voters (founder 1956), Hosp. Assistance League (founder 1958), Legis. Wives (pres. 1964), Mother's Club (bd. mem.), Pacific Asia Mus. (mem.), Beta Sigma Phi, Pi Beta Phi. Episcopalian. Clubs: Valley Hunt (Pasadena), Smoke Tree Ranch.

COBLE, ALICIA SHARON, retired elementary and secondary school educator; b. De Land, Fla., July 4, 1948; d. Paul W. and Helen (Brown) C. BA, U. South Fla., 1969; MAT, Stetson U., 1971. Cert. tchr. elem.; elem. through jr. coll. level English and music; secondary level humanities. Tchr. secondary level English, music Volusia County Sch. Bd., DeLand; elem. tchr. Lighthouse Christian Acad., Deland; tchr. Deland H.S., Seabreeze H.S.; ret. Home: 920 Westridge Dr Debary FL 32713-2109 Personal E-mail: aliciascoble@yahoo.com.

COBLE, (JOHN) HOWARD, congressman, lawyer; b. Greensboro, NC, Mar. 18, 1931; s. Joseph Howard and Johnnie (Holt) Coble Student, Appalachian State U., Boone, NC, 1949-50; BA in Hist., Guilford Coll., Greensboro, NC, 1958; JD, U. NC Sch. Law, Chapel Hill, 1962. Bar: NC 1966. Field claim rep., supt. State Farm Mut. Automobile Ins. Co., 1961-67; asst. county atty. Guilford County, NC, 1967-69; asst. US atty. Mid. Dist. NC, 1969—73; mem. NC Ho. Reps., 1969, 1979—84; sec. NC Dept. Revenue, 1973—77; atty. Turner, Enochs & Sparrow, Greensboro, NC, 1979—83; mem. US Congress from 6th NC dist., 1985—, mem. transp. and infrastructure com., mem. judiciary com., ranking mem. cts. and intellectual property subcommittee. Served to capt. USCG, 1952-56, commdg. officer USCGR. Mem. NC Bar Assn., Greensboro Bar Assn., Masons (33 degree; master Mason), Am. Legion, VFW, Lions, SAR. Republican. Presbyterian. Office: US House Reps 2468 Rayburn House Office Bldg Washington DC 20515-3306 Home Phone: 336-852-4956; Office Phone: 202-225-3065. Office Fax: 202-225-8611.*

COBURN, D(ONALD) L(EE), playwright; b. Balt., Aug. 4, 1938; s. Guy Dabney and Ruth Margaret (Somers) C.; m. Nazlee Joyce French, Oct. 24, 1964 (div. Sept. 1971); children: Donn Christopher, Kimberly; m. Marsha Woodruff Maher, Feb. 22, 1975. Student pub. schs., Balt. Propr. Don Coburn & Assocs., Balt., 1966-70; with Stanford Agy., Dallas, 1970-73; propr. Donald L. Coburn Corp. Cons., Dallas, 1973-75; ind. playwright, 1975—. Playwright: The Gin Game, 1977 (Pulitzer prize in drama 1978, Tony award nomination 1978, Golden Apple 1978), Bluewater Cottage, 1979, The Corporation Man, 1981, Currents Turned Awry, 1982, Guy, 1983, Noble Adjustment, 1986, Anna-Weston, 1988, Return to Blue Fin, 1991; (screenplays) Flights of Angels, 1987, A Virgin Year, 1992; (teleplay) Hollywood Presents: The Gin Game, 2002. Served with USNR, 1958-60. Mem. Authors League Am., Writers Guild Am., Tex. Inst. Letters, Soc. des Auteurs et Compositeurs Dramatiques. Office Phone: 646-486-4600. E-mail: dlcoburn@thegingame.com.

COBURN, LEWIS ALAN, mathematics professor; b. Austin, Tex., Aug. 16, 1940; s. Nathaniel and Ann (Block) C.; m. Charlaine Elizabeth Ackerman, June 19, 1966; 1 child, Elinor Nadia. BS, U. Mich., 1961, MS, 1962, PhD, 1964. Asst. prof. NYU, NYC, 1964-65, Purdue U., West Lafayette, Ind., 1965-66, Yeshiva U., NYC, 1966-68, assoc. prof., 1968-72, prof. math., 1972-79; prof. SUNY, Buffalo, 1979—, chmn. dept. math., 1979-97. Mem. editorial bd. Jour. Integral Equations and Operator Theory, 1978—; contbr. over 40 articles to math. rsch. jours. NSF grantee, 1966—. Mem. Am. Math. Soc. Office: SUNY Dept Of Math Buffalo NY 14260-0001 Home Phone: 716-836-8518. Business E-Mail: lcoburn@buffalo.edu.

COBURN, MARJORIE FOSTER, psychologist, educator; b. Salt Lake City, Feb. 28, 1939; d. Harlan A. and Alma (Ballinger) Polk; m. Robert Byron Coburn, July 2, 1977; children: Robert Scott, Kelly Anne; children: Polly Klea Foster, Matthew Ryan Foster. BA in Sociology, UCLA, 1960; Montessori Internat. Diploma with honors, Washington Montessori Inst., 1968; MA in Psychology, U. No. Colo., 1979; PhD in Counseling Psychology, U. Denver, 1983. Lic. clin. psychologist. Probation officer Alameda County, Oakland, Calif., 1960—62; dir. Friendship Club, Orlando, Fla., 1963—65; probation officer Contra Costa County, El Cerrito, Calif., 1966, Fairfax County, Va., 1967; tchr. Va. Montessori Sch., Fairfax, 1968—70; spl. edn. tchr. Leary Sch., Falls Church, Va., 1970—72, sch. administr., 1973—76; tchr. Aseltine Sch., San Diego, 1976—77, Coburn Montessori Sch., Colorado Springs, 1977—79; pvt. practice psychotherapy Colorado Springs, 1979—82, San Diego, 1982—. Cons. in field. Author (with R.C. Orem): Montessori: Prescription for Children with Learning Disabilities, 1977; contbr. articles to profl. jours. Mem.: APA, Mensa, The Charter 100, San Diego Psychol. Assn., Calif. Psychol. Assn., Coun. Exceptional Children, Phobia Soc., Am. Orthopsychiat. Assn., Rotary. Episcopalian. Office: 836 Prospect St Ste 101 La Jolla CA 92037-4206 Home Phone: 858-454-0817; Office Phone: 858-456-5065.

COBURN, RICHARD JOSEPH, electronics executive, electrical engineer; b. NYC, Nov. 4, 1931; s. Elmer Roswell and Marie Veronica (Greenan) C.; m. Catherine Elizabeth Wilkinson (div. 1992); children: Jenifer, Catherine, Steven; m. Elizabeth A. Semmler, Jan. 1993. BSEE, Yale U., 1954. Devel. engr. Hamilton Standard, Windsor Locks, Conn., 1954-59; chief engr. Dynamic Controls Corp., South Windsor, Conn., 1959-66; mgr. digital logic Fairchild Industries, Germantown, Md., 1966-68; co-founder, pres. Scan Optics, East Hartford, Conn., 1968-72; pres. Coburn Tech., East Hartford, 1972-77, KCR Tech., East Hartford, Conn., 1977-91; co-founder, chmn. Accent Color Sciences, Inc., East Hartford, Conn., 1993—2001; mgr. SentryTec, LLC, Bloomfield, Conn., 2001—. Mgr. Iconical Sys. LLC, 2004—; advisor bd. dirs. Ecoair, Inc., North Haven, Conn. Mem. Yale Club, Franklin & Eleanor Roosevelt Inst. Republican. Roman Catholic. Achievements include invention of electronic back pressure control, radio noise free switch, apparatus for image reproduction. Home: 15 Stratford Park Bloomfield CT 06002-2143 Office Phone: 860-205-7757. Personal E-mail: dickacs@aol.com.

COBURN, ROBERT CRAIG, philosopher, educator; b. Mpls., Jan. 25, 1930; s. William Carl and Esther Therice C.; m. Martha Louise Means, July 12, 1974. BA, Yale U., 1951; BD, U. Chgo., 1954; MA, PhD, Harvard U., 1958. Asst. prof. philosophy U. Chgo., 1960-65, assoc. prof., 1965-68, prof., 1968-71; prof. philosophy U. Wash., Seattle, 1971—2005, emeritus prof. philosophy, 2005—. Vis. assoc. prof. philosophy Cornell U., 1966, U. Bergen, Norway, spring 1986; condr. NEH summer seminar, 1983; cons. ERDA. Author: The Strangeness of the Ordinary: Issues and Problems in Contemporary Metaphysics, 1989; contbr. articles to philos. jours., chpts. to books. Ordained elder Rocky Mountain Conf. United Methodist Ch. Andrew Mellon postdoctoral fellow in philosophy U. Pitts., 1961-62; NSF grantee, 1968-69 Mem. Am. Philos. Assn. (exec. com. Pacific div. 1973-74), AAUP, Soc. Values in Higher Edn., Phi Beta Kappa. Home: 6852 28th Ave NE Seattle WA 98115-7145

COBURN, RONALD MURRAY, ophthalmologist, surgeon; b. Detroit, Aug. 25, 1943; s. Sidney and Jean (Goldberg) C.; m. Barbara Joan Levy, Feb. 21, 1969; children: Nicholas Scott, Lauren Joy. BS, Wayne State U., 1965, MD, 1969; postgrad., Kresge Eye Inst., 1971—74. Diplomate Am. Bd. Ophthalmology, Am. Bd. Eye Surgery (surg. examiner). Dir. The Coburn Clinic, Dearborn, Mich., 1976—; chief ophthalmology Straith Hosp. for Spl. Surgery, Southfield, Mich., 1985—2000; dir. Cataract Specialty Surgery Ctr., Berkley, Mich., 2003—. Cons. CooperVision, Inc., Bellevue, Wash., 1985-88, Alcon Surg., Inc., Ft. Worth, 1988—. Co-author: Lens-Stat Intraocular Lens Modeling System; editorial advisor Phaco and Foldables, 1990. Trustee Straith Hosp. for Spl. Surgery, 1986—. Capt. Mich. N.G., 1969-76. Fellow ACS, Internat. Coll. Surgeons, Soc. Eye Surgeons, Royal Soc. Medicine (London), Leadership Soc. ACS, Soc. for Excellence in Eye Care; mem. AAAS, Am. Soc. Cataract and Refractive Surgery, Am. Diabetes Assn., Mich. Ophthal. Soc., Wayne County Med. Soc., Rsch. To Prevent Blindness, N.Y. Acad. Scis., Internat. Assn. Ocular Surgeons, Internat. Eye Found., Soc. Geriatric Ophthalmology, Internat. Glaucoma Congress, Phi Beta Kappa. Achievements include design of Am. Med. Optics PC19LB intraocular lens, CILCO CPLU CP20 intraocular lenses, CooperVision CP10BG posterior chamber intraocular lens, Alcon CZ20BD intraocular lens. Home: 1490 W Long Lake Rd Bloomfield Hills MI 48302-1340 E-mail: ronaldcoburn@mac.com.

COBURN, STEVEN D., composer, musicologist, educator, pianist; b. Albany, NY, Aug. 7, 1955; s. Richard and Nancy Coburn; m. Lynn K. Osro, May 14, 1989; 1 child, Maxwell R. MusB, SUNY, Potsdam, 1978; MA, NYU, 1992, PhD, 2002. Adj. instr. Pace U., NYC, 2003—. Accompanist, asst. dir. Pk. Slope Singers, Bklyn., 2000—; accompanist Cmty. Chorus Bklyn., 2002—, Bklyn. Philharmonia Chorus, 2006—; piano instr. BrooklynPianoLessons.com; music dir. Stageworks Summer Repertory Theatre. Author: (book) Mahler's Tenth Symphony: Form and Genesis, Essential Exercises for the Development of Piano Technique; composer: (choral) Aspects of Prospect Park, Dreams, Jubilation, Motet, (chamber) String Quartet, Scherzo for Septet, Brass Quartet, Trumpet Sonata, Prelude and Allegro for Clarinet and Piano, (orchestral) Fantasy, (piano) Four Bird Songs, Alleluia-Étude, (vocal) Progress. Mem.: Soc. for Music Theory, Am. Musicol. Soc. Avocation: painting. Personal E-mail: stevendcoburn@aol.com.

COBURN, TOM (THOMAS ALLEN COBURN), senator; b. Casper, Wyo., Mar. 14, 1948; m. Carolyn Denton; 3 children. BS in Acctg., Okla. State U., 1970; MD, U. Okla., 1983. Mfg. mgr. ophthalmic divsn. Coburn Optical Industries, 1970-78; resident surgery St. Anthony's Hosp., 1983-84; resident in family practice U. Ark. Area Health and Edn. Ctr., 1984-86; family practice physician, obstetrician, 1986—94; mem. U.S. Congress from 2d Okla. dist., 1995-2001; US Senator from Okla., 2005—. Bd. dirs Optical Mfrs. Assn., 1973—74, Better Vision Inst., 1976—77, Family Rsch. Coun., Optical Manufacturers' Assn., 1973—74, Saxon Publishing Co., Norman, Okla.; mem. com. homeland security and govtl. affairs US Senate, com. Indian affairs, com. judiciary; co-chmn. President's Advisory Coun. on HIV/AIDS, 2001—. Author (with John Hart): Breach of Trust: How Washington Turns Outsiders Into Insiders, 2003. Recipient Spl. Legis. award, Okla. Psychol. Assn., 1999. Mem.: Pan Am. Allergy Soc., Southern Med. Assn. (vice counselor), East Ctrl. County Med. Soc. (former pres.), Ark. Med. Soc., Okla. Med. Assn., AMA, Am. Acad. Otolaryngic Allergy, Am. Acad. Family Practice. Republican. Baptist. Office: US Senate 172 Russell Senate Office Bldg Washington DC 20510 also: District Office Ste 800 1800 South Baltimore Tulsa OK 74119 Office Phone: 202-224-5754, 918-581-7651. Office Fax: 202-224-6008, 918-581-7195.*

COCANOUGHER, ARTHUR BENTON, academic administrator; b. Lubbock, Tex., July 6, 1938; s. Arthur Clifton and Bonnie Odell (Ford) C.; m. Dianne Esther Reisenauer, May 27, 1967; children: Carolyn, David. Mgr. Gen. Electric Co., NYC, 1962-67; asst. prof. U. So. Calif., Los Angeles, 1970-72; assoc. prof. So. Meth. U., Dallas, 1972-73; prof. mktg. U. Houston, 1973-75, chmn. dept., 1975-76, dean Coll. Bus., 1976-85, sr. v.p., provost, 1985-87; dean Tex. A&M U. Coll. Bus., College Station, 1987-2001, emeritus, disting. prof., 2001—; interim chancellor Texas A&M U. System, 2003—04. Trustee fixed income mutual funds Legg Mason Ptnrs.; cons. in field. Contbr. articles to profl. jours. Bd. dirs. Better Bus. Bur., Houston, 1979-87, West Houston Assn., 1984-87. Served to 1st lt. U.S. Army, 1960-62. Recipient Nicholas Salgo award So. Meth. U., 1973, Outstanding Service award U. Houston Alumni Assn., 1982, Disting. Alumnus award Coll. Bus. U. Tex.-Austin, 1981. Mem. Am. Mktg. Assn., Acad. Mktg. Sci. Home: 4409 Nottingham Ln Bryan TX 77802-5904 Office: Tex A&M U Coll Bus Coll Bus 4112 Tamu College Station TX 77843-4112

COCCARO, STEPHEN F., plastic surgeon; b. Bklyn., Mar. 13, 1959; BA in Biology cum laude, NYU, 1981; MD, SUNY, Syracuse, 1985. Lic. NJ, 1987, NY, 1991, diplomate Am. Bd. Plastic Surgery, 1999. Resident plastic surgery U. N.Mex., Albuquerque, 1990—93; resident gen. surgery St. Barabus Med. Ctr., Livingston, NJ, 1985—90; attending physician John T. Mather Meml. Hosp., Port Jefferson, NY, St. Charles Hosp., Port Jefferson, Brookhaven Mem. Hosp. Med. Ctr., Patchogue, NY, North Shore Surgi Ctr., Smithtown, NY, Stony Brook U. Hosp., NY, Stony Book U. Hosp. Ambulatory Surgery Ctr. Clin. asst. prof. surgery SUNY, Stony Brook; lectr. in field; gen. practice physician Urgent Cre Med. Ctr., Dover, NJ, 1989—90, Budd Lake, NJ, 1989—90; ACLS instr. SBMC, Livingston, 1989—90. Contbr. articles to profl. jours. Fellow: Internat. Coll. Surgeons; mem.: AMA, Suffolk County Med. Soc., Med. Soc. NY, NY Regional Soc. Plastic and Reconstructive Surgery, N.E. Soc. Plastic Surgeons, Am. Soc. Aesthetic Plastic Surgery, Am. Soc. Plastic Surgeons, Nassau Surg. Soc., Am. Soc. Laser Medicine and Surgery, Suffok Acad. Medicine, Little Bay Beach Assn. (trustee), Beta Lambda Sigma. Office: Suffolk Plastic Surgeons PC Suffolk Ambultory Surgery PLLC 179 Belle Meade Rd East Setauket NY 11733

COCCHI, WAYNE PAUL, special education educator; b. Mineola, NY, Sept. 25, 1954; s. Paul and Helen Gloria C. AA, Nassau C.C., Garden City, NY, 1974; BS in Edn., SUNY, Geneseo, 1976; MA in Edn., Ohio State U., 1980. Tutor, resource ctr. aid Columbus (Ohio) State C.C. Dept. Disability Svcs., 1979-82, adaptive edn. specialist, 1982-94, dir., 1994—. Treas. steering com. Transition Comm. Consortium Learning Disabilities, 1988—; adv. bd. HEATH Resource Ctr., 1993-98; mktg. dir. Disability Network Ohio-Solidarity, Inc., 1993-97; apptd. commr. Ohio legal rights svcs. commn., Pres. Ohio Senate, 2004—. Mem. editl. bd. Postsecondary LD Report, 1997-2003. Instr. braille Westerville Pub. Libr. Cmty. Svc., 1995-2000; mem. ops. efficiency task force Columbus Pub. Schs., 1997; apptd. mem. Ohio Gov.'s Coun. People with Disabilities, 1998-2004, chmn., 2001-03. Recipient Leadership award Ohio Ednl. Svc. Ctr. Assn., 1998. Mem. Assn. Higher Edn. Disability (pres. 1992-93, Past Pres. award, 1993, Ronald E. Blosser Dedicated Svc. award 1994). Roman Catholic. Office: Columbus State Cmty Coll Dept Disability Svcs 550 E Spring St Columbus OH 43215-1722 Office Fax: 614-287-6054. Business E-Mail: wcocchi@cscc.edu.

COCCHIARELLA, ANTONIO, physician, educator; arrived in U.S., 1956, naturalized; s. Francesco Saverio Cocchiarella and Yolanda Padoan; m. Teresa Marie Arzonetti, Nov. 8, 1957; 1 child, Francesca Yolanda Militeau. MD, U. Padova & Bari, Italy, 1953. Diplomate Am. Bd. Phys. Medicine & Rehab. Resident rehab. medicine NYU & Columbia U., 1960—63; attending physiatrist Yonkers Gen. Hosp., NY, 1964—80; med. dir. rehab. svcs. Phelps Meml. Hosp., Sleepy Hollow, NY, 1976—92, Cabrini Med. Ctr., NYC, 1992—97; attending physician Presbyn. Hosp., NYC, 1999—. Pvt. practice, NYC, 1965—75; med. dir. Arthritis Ctr. Riverside Gen. Hosp., Secaucus, 1977—81; attending physiatrist Jacoby Med. Ctr., Bronx, NY, 2002—05; prof. clin. rehab. medicine Columbia U., NYC, 1999—. Flight lt. med. corp. Italian Airforce, 1953—56. Mem.: N.Am. Spine Assn. (hon.), N.Y. Acad. Sci. (hon.), Ea. Pain Soc. (assoc.), Acad. Phys. Medicine Rehab. (sr.), Am. Rheumatism Assn. (sr.), Westchester Med. Soc. (sr.), N.Y. State Med. Soc. (sr.). Avocations: stamp collecting/philately, cooking. Office: 200 S Broadway Tarrytown NY 10591 Office Phone: 914-674-1497. Personal E-mail: ninoter@aol.com.

COCCIA, MICHEL ANDRE, retired lawyer; b. Sept. 17, 1922; BS in Indsl. Engring., Ill. Inst. Tech., 1944; JD, John Marshall Law Sch., 1951; docteur, l'Universite de Paris, 1965. Bar: Ill. 1951, U.S. Supreme Ct. 1951. Ptnr. litigation Baker & McKenzie, Chgo., 1951-88; justice Ill. Appellate Ct., Chgo., 1988-91. Lectr. in fields. Contbr. articles to profl. jours. With USNR. Fellow: Internat. Soc. Barristers, Internat. Acad. Trial Lawyers, Am. Coll. Trial Lawyers; mem.: ABA (various coms., past ho. of dels.), Justinian Soc. (Man of Yr. 1981), Def. Rsch. Inst. (chmn. products liabiltiy com. 1971—77, bd. dirs. 1977—80), Internat. Assn. Ins. Counsel (sec., treas. 1975—78, products liability com., fed. ruls com.), Soc. Trial Lawyers (past pres.), Am. Judicature Soc., Chgo. Bar Assn. (various coms.), Ill. Bar Assn. (pres. 1981—82, past bd. govs., various coms.), John Marshall Law Sch. Alumni Assn. (past pres., Citation of Merit 1971), Ill. Inst. Tech. Alumni Assn. (past. pres., past trustee, various awards), Mid Am. Club, Union League Club. Avocations: french, barbershop chorus, amateur radio, boating.

COCHÉ, JUDITH, psychologist, educator; b. Phila., Sept. 2, 1942; d. Louis and Miriam (Nerenberg) Milner; m. Erich Coché, Oct. 16, 1966 (dec. 1991); 1 child, Juliette Laura; m. John Anderson, Jan. 1, 1994. BA, Colby Coll., 1964; MA, Temple U., 1966; PhD, Bryn Mawr Coll., 1975. Diplomate Am. Bd. Profl. Psychology, lic. psychologist Pa., Md., N.J., Fla., cert. in group psychotherapy Nat. Registry Group Psychotherapists. Rsch. asst. Jefferson Med. Coll., 1965-66; diagnostician Law Ct., Aachen, Germany, 1967-68; staff psychologist N.E. Community Mental Health Ctr.,

Phila., 1969-74; family clinician Inst. Pa. Hosp., 1974-76; instr. psychology Drexel U., 1976-77; lectr. Med. Coll. Pa., 1977-78; asst. clin. prof. Hahnemann Med. Coll., Phila., 1979—; pvt. practice Phila., 1974—, N.J., 1985—; assoc. prof. psychiatry U. Pa., 1985—, clin. coord. psychology, 1999—; clin. prof. psychology in psychiatry U. Pa. Med. Coll., 1986—; mem. faculty Family Inst. of Phila., 1990—; sr. cons. Phila. Child Guidance Clinic, 1992-96; assoc. clin. prof. psychology in psychiatry U. Pa. Med. Coll., 1986—. Clin. cons. Hilltop Prep Sch., 1977—86; clin. supr. Am. Assn. Marriage and Family Therapy. Co-author: Couples Group Psychotherapy, A Clinical Practice Model, 1990, Powerful Wisdom: Voices of Distinguished Women Psychotherapists, 1993; contbr. chapters to books, articles to profl. jours. Bd. dirs. Whitemarsh Art Ctr., 1977-78, Please Touch Museum, 1982-89; profl. adv. bd. Parents Without Ptnrs., 1977-86; adv. com. Pa. Ballet/Shirley Rock. Named Women of Distinction, Phila. Bus. Jour., 2004; grantee, Del. Children's Bur. Bryn Mawr Coll., 1974—75, Pa. Hosp., 1975—77. Fellow Am. Group Psychotherapy Assn.; mem. APA, Am. Assn. Marriage and Family Therapy (approved supr.), Am. Family Therapy Assn., Phila. Soc. Clin. Psychologists (pres. 1980-81), Family Inst. Phila., Pa. Psychol. Assn. (chmn. legis. com. 1982), Soc. Rsch. in Psychotherapy, Women's Exec. Forum (Phila.). Address: Acad House 1420 Locust St Ste 410 Philadelphia PA 19102-4202 also: Price Waterworks Bldg Ste 3023 359 96th St Stone Harbor NJ 08247 Home Phone: 215-859-1050; Office Phone: 215-735-1908. E-mail: jmcoche@gmail.com.

COCHELL, GARY G., mathematician, educator; BS in Math., Colo. Sch. of Mines, 1971; MS in Math., Okla. State U., 1973, EdD in Higher Edn./Math., 1976; postgrad., Cornell U., 1986—87. Grad. asst. Okla. State U., 1971—76; asst. prof. math. Quincy Coll., 1976—77, St. Norbert Coll., 1977—78; vis. asst. prof. math. Colo. Sch. of Mines, 1978—79; prof., head dept. math. Culver-Stockton Coll., Canton, Mo., 1979—, calculus reader, 2001—07. Vis. prof. math. Cornell U., Ithaca, NY, 1986—87, summer vis. prof., 1987—95, 1997—2004; adj. prof. U. Md. Univ. Coll., 2004—; evaluator Eisenhower grant proposals Coordinating Bd. of Higher Edn. in Mo., 1996—99; participant Supporting Secondary Stds. in Mo. Math. Project, Mo. Dept. Elem. and Secondary Edn., 1997—98; presenter in field. Mem. sch. bd. Canton R-V Schs., Mo., 1988—2003; track coach Canton R-V HS, 1998—2002; past elder Canton Christian Ch. Recipient Gov.'s award for tchg., Mo. Dept. Higher Edn., 1994. Mem.: Can. Soc. History of Math., Mo. Coun. Tchrs. Math. (bd. dirs. 2002—04), Nat. Coun. Tchrs. Math (manuscript reviewer 2000, 2002, Com. for Comprehensive Math. Edn. of Every Child 1998). Avocations: running, motorcycling. Office: Culver-Stockton Coll 1 College Hill Canton MO 63435 Business E-Mail: gcochell@culver.edu.

COCHETTI, ROGER JAMES, international communications and internet company executive; b. Albany, NY, Apr. 11, 1950; s. Roger Peter and Mary Ann Cochetti. BS in Fgn. Svc., Georgetown U., 1972; postgrad., Johns Hopkins U., 1975; cert., Cambridge U., 1976, U. Va., 1986. Dir. Washington office UN Assn. of U.S.A., 1972-77; asst. dir. for legis. and pub. affairs U.S. Internat. Devel. Coop. Agy., Washington, 1978-81; dir. pub. and investor rels. Communications Satellite Corp., Washington, 1981-85, dir. investor and internat. rels., 1985-87, v.p. maritime bus. planning and devel., 1987-88, v.p. mobile bus. planning and devel., 1989-93; author, cons., lectr., 1993—; program dir. Internet policy and bus. planning IBM Corp., 1994-2000; sr. v.p. policy Network Solutions, Inc., 2000; sr. v.p. Veri Sign, 2001—03; cons. to Internet and technology industries, 2003; group dir. pub policy CompTIA Computing Tech. Industry Assn., 2004—. Cons. to John D. Rockefeller III, N.Y.C., 1975; bd. dirs. Truste, Inc., Internet Law and Policy Forum, Internet Edn. Found., Internet Content Rating Assn., Electronic Authentication Partnership, The Pub. Affairs Coun., Inc., Family Online Safety Inst. Author: Mobile Satellite Handbook, 1994. N.Y. State Regents scholar, 1968. Mem. Pacific Telecommn. Coun., Nat. Press Club (Washngton), Princeton Club (N.Y.C.). Democrat. Roman Catholic. Home Phone: 301-369-7247. E-mail: roger@cochetti.us.

COCHRAN, DEBORAH DONICK, lawyer; b. Cleve., 1963; married; 4 children. BA with honors, Franklin and Marshall Coll., 1985; JD with honors, George Washington U., 1988. CPA Md., 1985; bar: Md. 1988, Va. 1989, DC. Ptnr. Squire, Sanders & Dempsey, Miles & Stockbridge, Cochran & Owen, LLC. Named one of Top 100 Attys., Worth mag., 2005—06. Mem.: Order of the Coif. Office: Cochran & Owen 8000 Towers Cresent Dr Ste 160 Vienna VA 22182 Office Phone: 703-847-4480. Office Fax: 703-847-4499.*

COCHRAN, FIELDING B., III, lawyer; b. Corpus Christi, Tex., Nov. 14, 1949; BA, So. Meth. U., 1971; JD, U. Tex., 1975. Bar: Tex. 1975. Ptnr. Vinson & Elkins LLP, Houston. Mem.: ABA, Houston Bar Assn., Tex. Bar Assn. Office: Vinson & Elkins LLP First City Tower 1001 Fannin St, Ste 2300 Houston TX 77002 Office Phone: 713-758-2817. E-mail: fcochran@velaw.com.

COCHRAN, GEORGE MOFFETT, retired judge; b. Staunton, Va., Apr. 20, 1912; s. Peyton and Susie (Robertson) C.; m. Marion Lee Stuart, May 1, 1948; children— George Moffett, Harry Carter Stuart. BA, U. Va., 1934, LLB, 1936; LLD (hon.), James Madison U., 1991. Bar: Va. 1935, Md. 1936. Asso. law firm, Balt., 1936-38; partner firm Peyton Cochran and George M. Cochran, Staunton, 1938-64, Cochran, Lotz & Black, Staunton, 1964-69; justice Supreme Ct., Richmond, Va., 1969-87. Pres. Planters Bank & Trust Co., Staunton, 1963-69 Chmn. Woodrow Wilson Centennial Commn. Va., 1952-58, Va. Cultural Devel. Study Commn., 1966-68, Frontier Culture Mus. Va., 1986-98; mem. Va. Commn. Constl. Revisi on, 1968-69, Jud. Coun. Va., 1963-69, Va. Ho. Dels., 1948-66, Va. Senate, 1966-68; chmn. bd. dirs. Stuart Hall, 1971-86; mem. bd. visitors Va. Poly. Inst., 1960-68; trustee Mary Baldwin Coll., 1967-81, U. Va. Law Sch. Found., 1975-89, Woodrow Wilson Birthplace Found., 1955-93. Lt. comdr. USNR, 1942-46. Recipient Algernon Sydney Sullivan award Mary Baldwin Coll., 1981. Mem. ABA, Va. Bar Assn. (pres. 1965-66), Raven Soc., Soc. of Cin., Phi Beta Kappa, Phi Delta Phi, Beta Theta Pi. Episcopalian. Home and Office: 24 Ridgewood Dr Staunton VA 24401-2424

COCHRAN, J. GUYTON, JR., corporate financial executive; BBA, U. Ga., 1988; MBA, Ga. State U., 1995. Wire and cable controller bus. process design team Southwire, 1995—99, dir. fin., 1999—2000, v.p. fin., 2000—03, chief fin. officer, 2003—. Mem.: AICPA, Alumni Club Ga. State U., Alumni Club U. Ga. Office: Southwire 1 Southwire Dr Carrollton GA 30119

COCHRAN, JAMES ALAN, mathematics professor, department chairman, dean; b. San Francisco, May 12, 1936; s. Commodore Shelton and Gwendolyn Audrey (Rosenau) C.; m. Katherine Koehler Kern, Sept. 6, 1958; children: Cynthia Royal, Sarah Lynn. BS in Physics, Stanford U., 1956, MS in Physics, 1957, PhD in Math., 1962. Mem. tech. staff, supr. applied math. Bell Telephone Labs. Inc, Whippany, NJ, 1962-72; prof. math. Va. Poly. Inst. and State U., Blacksburg, 1972-78; prof., chmn. dept. math. Wash. State U., Pullman, 1978-84, prof., 1978-89, prof. math. Richland, Wash., 1999—2003, prof. emeritus, 2003—, campus exec. officer and founding dean tri-cities, 1989-98; staff assoc. First Presbyn. Ch., Kennewick, Wash., 2001—. Vis. prof. math. Stanford U., 1968-69, Wash. State U., 1977, U. NSW, Sydney, Australia, 1985, Southeast U., Nanjing, China, 1994; fgn. scholar math. and mechanics Nanjing Inst. Tech., 1984; vis. fellow Deakin U., Victoria, Australia, 1985, 87. Author: Analysis of Linear Integral Equations, 1972, Applied Mathematics: Principles, Techniques, and Applications, 1982, Advanced Engineering Mathematics, 1987; also articles. Mem. nat. coun. Boy Scout Am., 1973-76, 99-2001, mem. local coun., 1974-77, 82-84, 93—, coun. pres., 1999-2001, mem. western region, 1996-02; chmn. bd. commrs. Morris County (N.J.) Area Libr. Sys., 1971-72; mem. bd. dirs. Tri-Cities Sci. and Tech. Park Assn., 1990-2003, chmn., 1990-93; bd. dirs. Wash. Environ. Industry Assn., 1990-95, TRIDEC, 1996-2001; dir. state bd. Math. Engring. Sci. Achievement, 1992-2001; mem. Am. Pub. TV Stas. Bd., 1992-96; exec. com. Tri-Cities Commercialization Partnership, 1993-97; mem. Hanford Adv. Bd., 1994-2003; sr. advisor Tri-Cities Corp. Coun. for the Arts, 1991-2000; bd. trustees Tri-Cities Prep Found., 2003—. Recipient Silver Beaver award Boy Scouts Am., 1997, Disting. Eagle Scout award, 1997, Founders award Wash. State U., Tri Cities, 2003, God and Svc. award Presbyn. Ch. U.S.A., 2004; Gordon vis. fellow, Deakin U., Victoria, Australia, 1985. Mem. Am. Math. Soc., Math. Assn. Am., Soc. Indsl. Applied Math., Nat. Eagle Scout Assn. (young man pres. 1957-58, adviser 1958-71, Disting. Service award 1976), Phi Beta Kappa, Sigma Xi, Golden Key, Alpha Phi Omega. Republican. Presbyterian. Home: 1927 Cypress Pl Richland WA 99354-2414 Office: First Presbyn Ch 2001 W Kennewick Ave Kennewick WA 99336 Personal E-mail: cochran.ja@gmail.com.

COCHRAN, JAMES J., mathematics professor, researcher; BS in Econs., Wright State U., Dayton, Ohio, 1982, MS in Econs., 1984, MBA in Quantitative Analysis, 1985; PhD in Stats. & Ops. Rsch., U. Cin., 1997. Assoc. prof. stats. & ops. rsch. La. Tech U., Ruston, 2000—. Vis. scholar Stanford U., Palo Alto, Calif., 2002—02; vis. prof. decision scis. Miami U., Oxford, Ohio, 1998—99; vis. asst. prof. stats. U. Cin., 1997—98, 1999—2000. Editor (author): (nonfiction) Anthology of Statistics in Sports; author: Active Learning for Quantitative Courses, chapter 9 of TutORials. Mem.: Inst. Math. Stats., Am. Statis. Assn., Inst. Ops. Rsch. & Mgmt. Scis. (pres. edn. forum 2000—05, founding chair 2005—07), Internat. Stats. Inst. (life). Office: La Tech U College & Railroad Ave Ruston LA 71272 Office Phone: 318-257-3445. Office Fax: 318-257-4253. E-mail: jcochran@cab.latech.edu.

COCHRAN, JAMES KIRK, dean, oceanographer, educator, geochemist; BS summa cum laude, Fla. State U., 1973; M in Philosophy, Yale U., 1975, PhD in Geochemistry, 1979. Rsch. staff geochemist Yale U. dept. geology and geophysics, New Haven, 1979-81; asst. scientist dept. chemistry Woods Hole (Mass.) Oceanographic Instn., 1981-83; asst. prof. marine scis. SUNY, Stony Brook, 1985-90, assoc. prof., 1985-90, prof., 1990—, assoc dir. for rsch., 1990-92; assoc. dean for rsch. Marine Scis. Rsch. Ctr., SUNY, Stony Brook, 1992-94, dean, dir., 1994-98; rsch. assoc. dept. invertebrate paleontology Am. Mus. Natural History, NYC, 1986—. Invited lectr., UCLA, 1979, vis. scholar, Dept. Oceanography, U. Wash., Seattle, 1982, vis. scientist Ctr. des Faibles Radioactivités CNRS, Gif sur Yvette, France, 1989; vis. fellow Program in Oceanic and Atmospheric Scis., Princeton (N.J.) U., 1990, vis. prof. Inst. di Geol. Marina, Bologna, Italy, 1992, 98; assoc. rschr. European Ctr. for Environ. Geoscis., Aix-en-Provence, France, 1998, 2000, 04, vis. scientist Internat. Atomic Engr. Agency, Monaco, 1999; mem. Group of Experts on Sci. Aspects of Marine Pollution and Internat. Atomic Energy Agy. working group to formulate an oceanographic model for dispersion of wastes disposed in the deep sea, 1980-82; sci. rep. to Phys. Oceanography Task Group of the Internat. Seabed Working Group, 1983-87; mem. Alvin Rev. Com., 1984-87, Joint Global Ocean Flux Steering Com., 1990-93; dir. summer course Processes in the Coastal Ocean, Bologna, Italy, 2000. Contbr. more than 100 articles to profl. jours. Mem. Am. Geophys. Union, Geochem. Soc., Oceanography Soc., Sigma Xi. Office: SUNY at Stony Brook Marine Sciences Rsch Ctr Stony Brook NY 11794-5000

COCHRAN, JOHN EUELL, JR., aerospace engineer, educator, lawyer; b. Dawson, Ala., May 22, 1944; s. John Euell and Beatrice Ann (Raley) Cochran; m. Gladys Carol Holdbrooks, Dec. 26, 1965; children: Christopher, Jonathan. BAE., Auburn U., 1966, MS, 1967; PhD, U. Tex.-Austin, 1970; JD, Jones Law Inst., 1976. Registered profl. engr., Ala.; bar: Ala. 1977. Asst. prof. aerospace engring. Auburn (Ala.) U., 1970-75, assoc. prof., 1975-78, alumni assoc. prof., 1978-80, alumni prof., 1980-81, prof., 1981—, assoc. athletic dir., 1981-84, interim head aerospace engring., 1992-93, head aerospace engring., 1993—. Cons. Northrup Svcs., Huntsville, Ala., 1970—71, U.S. Army Missile Command, Redstone Arsenal, Ala., 1975—82, SRS Tech., Huntsville, 1984—89, Dept. Justice, 1996—97, Boeing Co., 1998, others; pres. Eaglemark, Inc.; legal cons. Sigmatech, Inc. Assoc. editor: Jour. Guidance Control and Dynamics, 1989—91; contbr. articles to profl. jours. Tau Beta Pi fellow, 1965, Nat. Coll. Athletic Assn. fellow, 1965, NSF fellow, 1968. Fellow: AIAA, Am. Astronautical Soc.; mem.: NSPE, ABA, Ala. Soc. Profl. Engrs. (v.p. Auburn chpt. 1985, pres. 1986, Young Engr. of the Yr. 1980), Am. Helicopter Soc. Methodist. Achievements include analysis, simulation and reconstruction of aircraft accidents; research in areas of dynamics and control, spacecraft attitude dynamics and control; stability and control of aircraft including towed vehicles; missile launcher dynamics; simulation using hardware-in-the-loop (HWIL); simulation of aerospace and transportation systems; short courses/seminars on engineering topics and engineering law and ethics. Home: 1887 Prim Dr Auburn AL 36830-7545 Office: Auburn U 211 Aerospace Engring Buil Auburn AL 36849 Business E-Mail: jcochran@eng.auburn.edu.

COCHRAN, JOHN P., economics professor; b. Ft. Collins, Colo., Dec. 22, 1949; s. Ira Williams and Elizabeth Ann C.; m. I. Ann Cochran, Aug. 23, 1977. BA in Econs., Met. State Coll., Denver, 1978; MA in Econs., U. Colo., 1981, PhD in Econs., 1985. Intern as sr. economist Colo. Pub. Utility Commn., summer 1986; asst. prof. econs. Met. State Coll. of Denver, 1986-90, chair of econs., 1990-94, assoc. prof. econs., 1990-96, prof. econs., 1996-97, chair and prof. econs., 1997—2003, interim dean sch. bus., 2004—06; dean Met. State Coll. Sch. Bus., 2006—. Vis. lectr. econs. Met. State Coll. of Denver, 1981-82, vis. asst. prof., 1982-86, dir. Ctr. for Econ. Edn., 1997-2003; adj. asst. prof. econs. Regis U., Denver, 1986-90; adj. scholar Ludwig von Mises Inst., 1997—; vis. prof. U. Colo., Boulder, 2001-2003; Mises Meml. lectr. at Austrian Scholars' Conf. 9, Ludwig Von Mises Inst., 2003; mem. faculty Young Am.'s Rd. to Freedom: The Friedrich Hayek Seminar at the Reagan Ranch Ctr., 2003; participant Liberty Fund Conf. and the Austman Bus. Cycle Theory, 2007; presenter in field. Co-author: The Hayek-Keynes Debate: Lessons for Current Business Cycle Research, 1999; mem. editl. bd. Quar. Jour. Austrian Econ., 2004—, Indian Jour. Econs. and Bus., 2002—; contbr. articles to profl. jours. Mem.: Golden Key Honor Soc. (Outstanding Scholar/Rsch. award 2002). Office Phone: 303-556-3218. Business E-Mail: cochranj@mscd.edu.

COCHRAN, JOHN R., III, bank executive; b. 1951; married. Graduate, Loyola College. Sr. v.p. MBNA Am. Bank Nat. Assn., Newark, Del., 1985-87; bd. dirs. MBNA Am. Bank N.A., Del., 1986—, exec. v.p. Del., 1987-91, CEO Del., 1990-91; exec. v.p. MBNA Corp., Del., 1991; vice-chmn. bd. MBNA Am. Bank N.A., Del., 1991, chmn., CEO Del., 2003—06; card services marketing bus. develop. exec. Bank of Am., Charlotte, NC, 2006—. Office: Bank of America 100 N Tryon St Charlotte NC 28255

COCHRAN, JUDY ANNE, psychiatric nurse practitioner; b. Springfield, Mass., Aug. 18, 1954; d. John and Marie Theresa (Roy) Cochran. RN Clin. Psychiatry, Bay State Med. Ctr. Sch. Nursing, Springfield, 1980. RN N.Y. State Edn. Dept. Profl. Licensing Svcs. divsn. Nurse psychiatry Inst. Living, Hartford, Conn., 1980—81, NYU Hosp., 1982—83; nurse psychiatry, coord. Longmont United Hosp., Colo., 1983—85; nurse psychiat. clinic Columbine Psychiat. Hosp., Highlands Ranch, Colo., 1987—93; nurse psychiatry West Pines Psychiat. Hosp., Wheat Ridge, Colo., 1993—97, Porter Hosp., Denver, 1997—2001. Nurse psychiatry Gilliam Juvenile Detention Ctr., Denver, 1995—97. Author (screenplay): Graven Images, 2000, The Garden, 2002; author: (teleplay) Twin Forks, 2003, For Heaven's Sake, 2000. Mem.: Women in Film, TV, Video (v.p. 1996, charter), Mensa. Avocations: fencing, art, horseback riding, dogs. Office: PO Box 625 Orient NY 11957

COCHRAN, KATHY HOLCOMBE, music educator, conductor; d. Bobby Neal and Louise Bryant Holcombe; m. Alan Randolph Cochran, June 14, 1975. AA, North Greenville Coll., 1973; MusB, Furman U., 1975; M in Music Edn., U. SC, 1978; postgrad., Clemson U., 1997—. Cert. tchr. pub. sch. choral music K-12 SC, elem. sch. educator SC. Gen. and choral music specialist grades 6-8 Lexington Intermediate Sch., SC, 1975—76; elem. music specialist K-2 Pierce Ter. Elem. Sch., Ft. Jackson, SC, 1976—78; elem. music specialist grades 1-5 Greenville County Schs., 1978—90, lead tchr. for choral dirs., 1996—97; choral dir. Berea HS, Greenville, 1991—97, fine arts dept. chair, 1995—97; tchg. intern, asst. Clemson U., SC, 1999—2000; tchr. choral music edn. Furman U., Greenville, 2001—. Dir. Young Artists Piano Competition Greenville Symphony Orch., 1990—91; sec. choral divsn. SC Music Educators Assn., 1996—97, pres.-elect, 1997—98. Author, composer Music for All Ages, 1985. Mem. Greenville County Legal Aux., 1978—; trustee North Greenville Coll., Tigerville, SC, 1996—2001, bd. advisors, 1994—96. Named Outstanding Young Educator, Greenville Jaycees, 1987, Wade Hampton Jaycees, Taylors, SC, 1980. Mem.: Soc. Rsch. in Music Edn., Internat. Soc. for Music Edn., Choristers Guild, SC Music Educators Assn., NY Acad. Scis., Am. Choral Dirs. Assn., Assn. for Supr. and Curriculum Devel., Nat. Reading Conf., Internat. Reading Assn., Music Educators Nat. Conf. (SC Music in Our Schs. coord. 1980), Pi Kappa Lambda, Kappa Delta Pi, Phi Delta Kappa. Avocations: reading, cooking, boating.

COCHRAN, KENNETH WILLIAM, toxicologist; b. Chgo., Nov. 2, 1923; m. Martha Louise Wells, May 10, 1945; children: Kenneth W. III, Kimberley W. Cochran Nelson (dec.). SB, U. Chgo., 1947, PhD, 1950. Rsch. asst. to instr., toxicity lab. and dept. pharmacology U. Chgo., 1946-52; from rsch. assoc., instr. to prof. emeritus U. Mich., Ann Arbor, 1952—. Contbr. articles to profl. jours. Pvt. 1st lt. US Army, 1943—46. Fellow AAAS; mem. Am. Soc. for Microbiology, Am. Soc. for Pharmacology and Exptl. Therapeutics, Mycol. Soc. of Am., N.Am. Mycol. Assn. (exec. sec. 1988-97, award for contributions to amateur mycology, 2004). Home: 3556 Oakwood St Ann Arbor MI 48104-5213 Office Phone: 734-971-2552. Personal E-mail: kwcee@umich.edu.

COCHRAN, MONA SHEINFELD, retired economics professor; b. Phila., Dec. 3, 1934; d. Samuel and Sara (Baram) Sheinfeld; m. Kendall Pinney Cochran, Dec. 19, 1975; children: Paula, Susan, Kenneth, Hersh BA, Rutgers U., New Brunswick, NJ, 1956; MA, Temple U., Phila., 1968; PhD, So. Meth. U., Dallas, 1966. Systems analyst RemingtonRand UNIVAC, Phila., 1956-58; rsch. analyst Coopers & Lybrand, NYC, 1958-60; tchg. asst. So. Meth. U., Dallas, 1961-65; vis. rsch. scholar London Sch. Econs., 1981-82; acad. visitor U. York, Eng., 1981-82; prof. econs. Tex. Woman's U., Denton, Tex., 1965-91, prof. emerita, 1991—. Avocations: travel, sewing, entertaining. Home: 3765 Weeburn Dr Dallas TX 75229-2716

COCHRAN, ROBERT LEE, music educator; b. King City, Mo., Nov. 24, 1956; s. Buford Ralph and Edna Edith Cochran; children: Laura Danell McDavitt, Zachary Lee, Anthony Richard Rodriguez. BS in Edn., Mo. Western State U., 1980; MEd, NW Mo. State U., 1987. Tchr., dir. bands Savannah Sch. Dist., Mo., 1981—96, Raytown Sch. Dist., 1996—2006; ret., 2006. Mem.: Mo. Music Educator Assn., Mo. Band Masters (pres. NW dist. 1987—88), Phi Beta Mu. Avocation: outdoor activity. E-mail: Bandman_2@netzero.com.

COCHRAN, STEVE, lawyer; b. LA, Mar. 18, 1957; BA, U. Calif., Santa Cruz, 1979; JD, U. Calif., Berkeley, 1982. Bar: Calif. 1982, US Dist Ct. 1983, Ctrl. Dist. Calif., US Ct. Appeals, Ninth Cir. 1986, US Dist. Ct., Ea. Dist. Calif. 1991. Law clk. Hon. William P. Gray Ctrl. Dist. of Calif.; extern clk. Hon. Cecil F. Poole U.S. Ct. Appeals, 9th Cir.; ptnr. Katten Muchin Rosenman, LA, 1991—. Mem. adv. bd. Nat. Circuit Judicial Conf. Mem. adv. bd. 9th Cir. Jud. Conf., 2004—. Mem.: LA Criminal Cts. Bar Assn., Calif. Attys. Criminal Justice, State Bar of Calif. Office: Katten Muchin Rosenman Ste 2600 2029 Century Park E Los Angeles CA 90067-3012 Office Phone: 310-788-4455. Office Fax: 310-712-8455. Business E-Mail: steve.cochran@kattenlaw.com.

COCHRAN, SUSAN MILLS, research librarian; b. Grinnell, Iowa, Nov. 21, 1949; d. Lawrence Omen and Louise Jane (Morgan) Mills; m. Stephen E. Cochran, July 1, 1972; children: Bryan, Jeremy. Libr. Iowa Geneal. Soc., Des Moines, 1987-96; rsch. libr. Royal Gorge Regional Mus. & History Ctr. (formerly Local History Ctr., Canon City Pub. Libr.), Colo., 1997—. Editor: Mingo, Iowa 1884-1984, 1984; contbr. articles to profl. jours. Past mem. Jasper County Cemetery Commn., Newton; mem. Jasper County His. Soc.; past bd. dirs. Jasper County Libr., Newton, Iowa. Mem. Iowa Geneal. Soc., Jasper County Geneal. Soc., State Assn. for the Preservation of Iowa Cemeteries (charter), Fremont County Geneal. Group (coord.), Colo. Coun. Geneal. Socs. Avocations: genealogy, history, birding. Office: Royal Gorge Regional Mus & History Ctr 612 Royal Gorge Blvd Canon City CO 81212 Address: PO Box 1460 Canon City CO 81215 Office Phone: 719-269-9036. E-mail: historycenter@canoncity.org.

COCHRAN, THAD (WILLIAM THAD COCHRAN), senator; b. Pontotoc, Miss., Dec. 7, 1937; s. William Holmes and Emma Grace (Berry) C.; m. Rose Clayton, June 6, 1964; children: Thaddeus Clayton, Katherine Holmes. BA in Psychology, U. Miss., 1959, JD cum laude, 1965; postgrad. (Rotary Found. fellow), U. Dublin, Ireland, 1963-64. Bar: Miss. 1965. Practiced in Jackson, 1965-72; assoc. firm Watkins & Eager, 1965-72; mem. 93d-95th congresses from Miss., 1973—78; US Senator from Miss., 1978—; chmn. Rep. conf. 104th Congress, 1995. Mem. agr. nutrition and forestry com., appropriations com., govtl. affairs com., rules and adminstrn. com., senate Rep. conf. com. Mem. exec. bd. Andrew Jackson council Boy Scouts Am., 1973-. Served to lt. USNR, 1959—61. Named Outstanding Young Man of Jackson, 1971, One of Three Outstanding Young Men of Miss., 1971, Conservation Achievement award, Nat. Wildlife Fedn., Conservationist of the Year, Dicks Unlimited, 1994, Congl. Leadership award, Airports Coun. Internat. N. Am., 2004; Named Honored Cooperator Nat. Cooperative Bus. Assn., 2003, Congressional Leadership award Airports Coun. Internat.-N.Am., 2004. Mem. ABA, Miss. Bar Assn. (pres. young lawyers sect. 1972-73), Omicron Delta Kappa, Phi Kappa Phi, Pi Kappa Alpha. Clubs: Rotarian. Republican. Baptist. Office: US Senate 113 Dirksen Senate Office Building Washington DC 20510-0001 also: District Office Ste 614 188 East Capitol St Jackson MS 39201-2137 Office Phone: 202-224-5054, 601-965-4459. Office Fax: 202-224-9450, 601-965-4919.

COCHRAN, WENDELL ALBERT, science editor; b. Carthage, Mo., Nov. 29, 1929; s. Wendell Albert and Lillian Gladys (Largent) C.; m. Agnes Elizabeth Groves, Nov. 9, 1963; remarried Corinne Frances Des Jardins, Aug. 25, 1980. AB, U. Mo., Columbia, 1953, A.M. in Geology, 1956, B.J., 1960. Geologist ground-water br. U.S. Geol. Survey, 1956-58; reporter, copyeditor Kansas City Star, Mo., 1960-63; editor Geotimes and Earth Sci. mags., Geospectrum newsletter, Alexandria, Va., 1963-84; v.p. Geol. Survey Inc., Bethesda, Md., 1984-86; tech. editor Okla. Geol. Survey, 1998—2006; freelance editor, cons., 2006—. Co-author: Into Print: A Practical Guide to Writing, Illustrating, and Publishing, 1977; sr. editor: Geowriting: A Guide to Writing, Editing and Printing in Earth Science, 1973; contbr. articles to profl. jours. and encys. Mem. Earth Sci. Editors

(Outstanding Contbns. award 1982), Dog in the Night-time. Home: 4351 SW Willow St Seattle WA 98136-1769 Office Phone: 206-932-8227. Personal E-mail: atrypa@eskimo.com.

COCHRAN, WILLIAM MICHAEL, librarian; b. Nevada, Iowa, May 6, 1952; s. Joseph Charles and Inez (Larson) Cochran; m. Diane Marie Ohm, July 24, 1971. BLS, U. Iowa, Iowa City, 1979, MA with distinction in Libr. Sci., 1983; MA in Pub. Adminstrn., Drake U., Des Moines, Iowa, 1989. Dir. Red Oak Pub. Libr., Iowa, 1984; patron svcs. libr. Pub. Libr. of Des Moines, 1984-87; LSCA program coord. State Libr. of Iowa, Des Moines, 1987-88, dir. libr. devel., 1988-89, asst. state libr., 1989-90; dir. Parmly Billings Libr., 1990—. Mem. White House Conf. on Libr. and Info. Svcs. Mem. mayor's com. on homelessness, 2006—. Mem.: Mont. Ctr. for Book Adv. Com., Libr. Adminstrn. and Mgmt. Assn., Pub. Libr. Assn., Mont. Gov.'s Blue Ribbon Telecommunications Task Force, Mont. Libr. Assn. (chair, pub. libr. divsn. 1991—92, legis. com. chair 1992—93, pres. 1998—99, named Libr. of Yr. 1998), ALA, Beta Phi Mu. Office: Parmly Billings Libr 510 N Broadway Billings MT 59101-1156

COCHRANE, BETSY LANE, former state senator; b. Asheboro, NC; d. William Jennings and Bobbie (Campbell) Lane; m. Joe Kenneth Cochrane, 1958; children: Lisa, Craig. BA cum laude, Meredith Coll., Raleigh, 1958. Tchr. Winston-Salem Sch. Sys., NC, Highland Presbyn. Ch. Sch.; mem. NC Ho. of Reps., Raleigh, 1980-88, house minority leader, 1985-88; mem. NC Senate, 1988-2001, chmn. Commn. on Aging, 1989-99, vice chmn. higher edn. com., 1991-92, senate minority whip, 1993-94, senate minority leader, 1995-96, vice chmn. senate appropriations, 1995—2000, vice chmn. senate commerce commn., 1995—2000, ranking minority mem. senate agr., 1995—2000. Mem. comm. on Future of South, 1985—86, Nat. Rep. Platform Com., Joint Legis. Ethics Com., 1989—2000, chmn., 1989—90; mem. NC Parks Commn., 1989—96, Retail Mchts. Adv. Bd., 1989—2000, Govtl. Ops., 1989—97, Gov.'s Advocacy Coun. on Children and Youth, 1990—2000, Select Com. on Redistricting, 1991, 92, 94, Revenue Law, 1992—2000, Order of LongLeaf Pine, 1992, Environ. Rev. Com., 1997—2001, Utility Rev. Com., 1997—2000, Gov.'s Blue Ribbon Task Force Environ. Indicators, 1989—91; spkr. in field. Trustee Davie County Hosp.; bd. advisors Z. Smith Reynolds Found., 1996—99, Meredith Coll., chmn. pres.'s adv. coun., 1999—2001, govs. adv. budget com., 1989—93, pub. sch. forum, 1985—99, mem. Meredith Challenge Bd., 2005—, year book editor, 1958—, mem. student govt., 1955—58; mem. Davie County Schs. Task Force on Facilities, 2001—02, So. Regional Edn. Bd., 1987—2001, Meredith May Ct., 1957, 1958; del. GOP Nat. Conv., 1976, 1988, 1992, 1996; trustee CUMC, 2006—, trustee sec., 2007—; mem. Bible Study Fellowship, discussion leader, 2003—; mem. Faith Works Task Force, 2005—; bd. dir. Davie County Sch. Mebane Challenge, 2004—07, Forks of the Yadkin Mus., 2002—, vice chmn., 2004—. Named Disting. Citizen of Yr., NC Libr. Dirs., 1991, Legislator of Yr., NC Divsn. Aging, 1991, NC Assn. for Home Care, 1992, NC Health Facilities Assn., 1993, NC Wildlife Fedn., 1995, Autism Found., 1995, Disting. Alumnae of the Yr., Meredith Coll., 1996; named one of 10 Outstanding Legislators in Nation, 1987, 100 Outstanding Graduates, Meredith Coll.; named to NC GOP Hall of Fame, 2001, GOP Hall of Fame, Davie County, 2003; recipient Woman in Govt. award, NC Jaycees, 1985, Myers-Honeycutt award for excellence in pub. svc., 1996, Dr. Ewald W. Busse award, Aging Advocates of N.C., 1997, Women Achievement award, FWC NC, 2002. Mem.: Kappa Nu Sigma, Seekers Book Club, Bermuda Run Garden Club. Baptist. Home and Office: 331 Orchard Pk Dr Advance NC 27006-9582 Personal E-mail: betsycochrane@triad.rr.com. Business E-Mail: betsyc@ncleg.net.

COCHRANE, EUGENE W., JR., foundation administrator; BA in History, Erskine Coll., 1970; MA in Econ. and Bus. Admin., Appalachian State U., 1972. Residency Charlotte Memorial Hospital; former hospital administrator; admin., hospital div. Duke Endowment, 1980—91, dir. health care div., 1991—96, v.p., dir. health care div., 1996—2003, exec. v.p., dir. health care div., 2003—05, pres., 2005—. Bd. dirs. Southeastern Council of Found., Grantmakers in Health; mem. N.C. Inst. of Medicine, N.C. Med. Care Commn.; adv. bd. mem. Kate B. Reynolds Health Trust. Bd. of visitors Davidson Coll. Fellow: Am. Coll. of Healthcare Executives. Office: Duke Endowment 100 N Tryon St Ste 3500 Charlotte NC 28202

COCHRANE, PAUL HOLLIS, general practice physician; b. Boston, Oct. 23, 1953; s. Joseph Xavier and Bernadette Anne (Abbott) C.; children: Gregory, Jennifer, Amanda, Casey; m. Dorian Cochrane, Oct. 22, 1999; 1 child, Katie. BA, U. Mass., 1974; OD, N.Eng. Coll. Optometry, 1979; D Naturopathy, Clayton Sch. Natural Healing, Birmingham, Ala., 1986; D Chiropractic, Palmer Coll. Chiropractic, 1988; A in Paralegal Sci., Southland U., 1983; DO, New England Coll. Osteopathic Medicine, 1992; JD, Monticello U., 1997. Resident in osteopathy Community Hosp. R.I., Cranston, 1992-93; med. examiner Nicholas County, W.Va., 1995-96; physician pvt. practice, 1997—. Real estate developer, Mass., 1981—; instr. diagnosis Palmer Coll. Chiropractic, Davenport, Iowa, 1986-88; instr. U. N.Eng. Coll. Osteopathic Medicine, Biddeford, Maine, 1990—. Coord. glaucoma, pediatric eye screenings, Lions Club, Arlington, 1980— (disting. svc. award 1984); player, coach pro baseball Bangor Blue Ox Northeast League, 1996. Fellow Internat. Acad. Clin. Acupuncture; mem. Am. Osteopathic Assn., Am. Acad. Osteopathy, Am. Coll. Osteopathic Family Physicians, Mass. Osteopathic Soc., N.Eng. Coll. Osteopathic Medicine. Democrat. Roman Catholic. Avocations: sports, reading. Home: 34 Snow Creek Dr Hyannis MA 02601

COCHRANE, ROBERT LOWE, biologist; b. Morgantown, W.Va., Feb. 10, 1931; s. Thomas Joseph and Isabelle Durston (Lowe) C. BA, W.Va. U., 1953; MS, U. Wis., 1954, PhD, 1961. Rsch. asst. genetics U. Wis., Madison, 1953—55, rsch. asst. zoology, 1957—60; with Fur Animal Exptl. Sta., Petersburg, Alaska, 1955; agt. in animal husbandry USDA, Madison, Wis., 1955—61; biologist FDA, Washington, 1961—62; sr. research fellow dept. anatomy U. Birmingham (Eng.), 1962—65; project assoc. dept. physiology U. Pitts., 1965—66; sr. endocrinologist Eli Lilly & Co., Indpls., 1966—80; rsch. assoc. G.D. Searle & Co., Skokie, Ill., 1980—81; with Short's Fur Farm, Granton, Wis., 1981—83; rsch. assoc. Marshfield (Wis.) Med. Found., 1983—84; biologist Northwood Fur Farms, Inc., Cary, Ill., 1984. Participant Internat. Mink Show, Wis., 1976—2006, W.Va. Fox Show, Morgantown, 1989; FAO cons. Wildlife Inst. India, Dehra Dun, 1985; adj prof. divsn. animal and vet. sci. W.Va. U., Morgantown, 1987—; ad hoc reviewer competitive rsch. grants U.S. Dept. Agr. Ad hoc reviewer (various sci. jours.). Recipient Knight of Golden Horse Shoe award W.Va. Pub. Sch. System, 1945, W.Va. Boy's State, 1948; U. Birmingham (Eng.) sr. rsch. fellow, 1962-65. Mem. AAAS, Am. Inst. Biol. Scis., Soc. Exptl. Biology and Medicine, Soc. Reprodn. and Fertility, Soc. Study Reprodn., Am. Soc. Animal Sci., Endocrine Soc., N.Y. Acad. Sci., Soc. Endocrinology, Coun. Agrl. Sci. and Tech., Internat. Platform Assn., NRA (life), Sigma Xi, Pi Kappa Alpha, Gamma Sigma Delta. Presbyterian. Achievements include discovery of the ovarian hormonal requirements for ova-implantation and embryonic diapause in the rat, the elucidation of the role played by prostaglandins in corpus luteum function, parturition and ductus arteriosus closure in the rat; discovery of timing, duration and pattern of reproductive cycles in martens; development of steroid synthesis inhibitors for controlling reproduction in mammals; rsch. in the successful raising of ruffed grouse in captivity, dissemination of scientific information on fur farming and raising ruffed grouse to the commercial trade and public. Home: 404 Junior Ave Morgantown WV 26505-2208 Office Phone: 304-293-2406 ext 4408. Business E-Mail: rcochra2@wvu.edu.

COCHRANE, WALTER E., academic administrator, conductor, music supervisor, clarinet soloist; b. Phila. s. Earl and Martha (Binder) C. BS, MS, U. Pa., Phila.; grad. study, Harvard U., 1956, NYU, 1957, Columbia U., 1960; studied with, Pierre Monteux and Leopold Stokowski. Cert. sch. dist. adminstr., NY, Pa., NJ, Mass., Maine, Va.; cert. music supr., NY, Pa., Conn., Va.; supt. schs., NY, Mass., Maine; sch. prin., NY, Pa., Mass. Clarinet soloist Phila. Brahms Cycle, 1950; dir. bands Upper Darby Pa. Schs., 1950-51; prof. clarinet and chamber music Phila. Musical Acad., 1950-52; solo clarinetist Phila. Symphonic Band, 1950-58; dir. music Alexandria Va. City Schs., 1951—58; clarinet soloist Alexandria String Quartet, 1952; dist. music dir. Sch. Dist. II, LI, NY, 1958-60; supr. music NY State Edn. Dept., Albany, 1960-67; conductor NY State Bands, 1960—63; v.p. Found. Am. Art Song, Albany, 1965-70; supr. music Hartford City Schs., Conn., 1967-69; faculty music edn. U. Hartford, 1967—69; asst. supt. Sch. Dist. 5, LI, 1970-78; supt. schs. Maine Sch. Adm. Dist. 19, Lubec, Maine, 1978-80; v.p. and dean Inst. Security and Tech., Phila., 1980-87; corp. dir. edn. PTC Career Insts., Phila., 1987; pres. Career Guidance Corp., 1988-91, dir. GED home study program N.Y. State, 1992—. Founder, dir. Stony Brook Conservatory Music, LI, 1958—61. Author: GED Home Study Program, 2000, Meet The Great Composers, 2000, The Gulf War, 1994, World Wars I and II, Mathematics Mastery Manual, 1998, Science Mastery Manual, 1997, Understand Music, 1990, Women Composers, 1991, Literature Mastery Manual, 1997, Who Was the Killer Composer?, 1992, Clarinet Curriculum, 1951, Flute Curriculum, 1951, Graded Music for Wind and String Chamber Music, 1952, Graded Music for Brass Instruments, 1960, Public Schools Can Help You, 1960, The AAA Method in American Education-Analysis, Action and Alleviation of Attrition, 1960, CATP: Cooperative Analysis of Teacher Performance, 1966, Non-Traditional Employment for Women, 1982, A Philosophy and Basic Procedures for Supervision, 1982, Understanding Students for the Improvement of Learning, 1983, Encyclopedia of Conductors, 2001. Recipient Humanitarian award Chgo. PTC, Music Edn. Svc. award, NY State Sch. Music Assn, 1999. Mem. ASCD, NEA, SAR, NY State Sch. Music Assn. (adjudicator, all-state conductor, Svc. to Music Edn. award), Nat. Assn. of Secondary Sch. Prins., Am. Assn. Sch. Adminstrs., Music Educators Nat. Conf., Nat. Assn. Trade and Tech. Schs. (adminstrv. advancement com. 1981), NY ASCD, Phila. Musical Soc.

COCHRUM, ELLEN JOAN, language educator; b. Tianjin, China, Jan. 19, 1929; arrived in U.S., 1947; d. Ivan Trofimovich Lukashik and Eleonore Elizabeth Mirksch; m. John Cochrum, Aug. 13, 1947 (dec.); children: Julie A. Bauer-Cook, J. Paul, Jeane M. Cabral, James R. BA in Fgn. Langs., Calif. State U., Fullerton, 1966; MA in Russian Lang. and Lit., Middlebury Coll., 1968; PhD in Russian Lang. and Lit., Mich. State U., 1977; AA in Exercise Sci., Santa Ana Coll., 2003. Instr. Russian Berlitz Sch. Langs., Santa Ana, Calif., 1959—60, Oceanside-Carlsbad Coll., Calif., 1960—61, Chapman U., Orange, Calif., 1961—62; instr. German and Russian Calif. State U., Fullerton, 1962—69, assoc. prof. German and Russian, 1985—91; instr. Russian Mich. State U., East Lansing, 1969—77, asst. prof. Russian, 1977—79; assoc. prof. Russian Calif. State U., Long Beach, 1979; lectr. Russian U. Calif., Irvine, 1980, UCLA, 1980—81. Chmn. Russian sect. Modern and Classical Langs. So. Calif., 1965—69; rsch., lang. specialist computer translation of sci. Russian texts, 1965—69; asst. prof. Russian Middlebury Coll., Vt., 1973, 74, 75, 76, 79, 80, 81, 82; sec.-treas. Mich. chpt. Am. Assn. Tchrs. Slavic and East European Langs., 1974—77. Translator: Ministry to the Hospitalized, 1980; author: (monograph) The Modern Teaching of Russian, 1963, (bibliography) A Bibliography of Works by and about Jurij Nagibin 1940-1978, 1979. Recipient Disting. Tchg. award, Calif. State U., Fullerton, 1967—68, Alumni Achievement award, Santa Ana Coll., 1997. Mem.: Tau Sigma, Phi Kappa Phi (life). Avocations: aqua aerobics, hiking, gardening, church secretarial work. Address: Apt 3 13641 Fairview St Garden Grove CA 92843-4225 Personal E-mail: ejcochrum@aol.com.

COCKE, WILLIAM MARVIN, JR., plastic surgeon, educator; b. Balt., Aug. 2, 1934; s. William M. and Clara E. (Bosley) C.; m. Sue Ann Harris, Apr. 25, 1981; children: Gregory William, Laura Marie, Julie Ann; children by previous marriage: William Marvin III, Catherine Lynn, Deborah Kay, Brian Thomas. BS with honors in Biology, Tex. A&M U., 1956; MD, Baylor U., 1960. Diplomate: Am. Bd. Plastic Surgery (guest examiner 1978). Intern surgery Vanderbilt U. Hosp., Nashville, 1960-61; fellow gen. surgery Ochsner Clinic and Found. Hosp., New Orleans, 1961-64; chief resident surgery Monroe (La.) Charity Hosp., 1963-64; resident reconstructive surgery Roswell Park Meml. Inst., Buffalo, 1965-66; chief resident plastic surgery VA Hosp., Bronx, NY, 1966; practice medicine specializing in plastic surgery Nashville, 1968-75, Sacramento, 1976-79; pvt. practice medicine specializing in plastic surgery Bryan, Tex., 1980-92; prof. surgery, head div. plastic/reconstructive surgery Marshall U. Sch. of Medicine, Huntington, W.Va., 1992—. Mem. staff Cabell-Huntington Hosp., Huntington Vets. Med. Ctr.; asst. prof. plastic surgery Vanderbilt U. Sch. Medicine, Nashville, 1968-69, asst. clin. prof. plastic surgery, 1969-75; assoc. prof. plastic surgery Ind. U. Sch. Medicine, Indpls., 1975-76; chief plastic surgery service Wishard Meml. Hosp., Ind. U., 1975-76; assoc. prof. surgery U. Calif. Sch. Medicine, Davis, 1976-79, chmn. dept. plastic surgery, 1976-79; prof. surgery, chief div. plastic surgery Tex. Tech. U. Sch. Medicine, Lubbock, 1979-80, dir. Microsurg. Research Lab., 1979-80; clin. prof. surgery Tex. A&M U. Sch. Medicine, 1983-92; prof. plastic surgery, 1986-89; chief plastic surgery svc., dept. surgery, Olin Teague VA Med. Ctr., Temple, Tex., 1986-92; prof. head surgery divsn. plastic and reconstruction Marshall U. Sch. Medicine, 1992—. Author textbooks on plastic surgery; contbr. articles to profl. jours. Served with M.C. USAF, 1966-68. Recipient Dean Echols award Ochsner Hosp. Found., 1963 Mem. ACS, Am. Assn. Plastic Surgeons, Soc. Head and Neck Surgeons, Assn. Acad. Surgery, Alton Ochsner Surg. Soc., Alpha Omega Alpha. Episcopalian. Home: 45 Olde Farm Rd Ona WV 25545-9747 Office: Marshall U Sch Medicine Dept Surgery 1600 Medical Center Dr Huntington WV 25701-3656

COCKERHAM, SIDNEY JOE, professional society administrator; b. Waxahachie, Tex., Aug. 17, 1951; s. Sidney Julius and Joan (Barlow) C. BS in Biology, U. Tex., Arlington, 1973. Cert. tchr., Tex. Tchr. Tex. Pub. Schs., Waxahachie, 1973-77; dir., founder U.S. Nat. Tennis Acad., Dallas, 1982—. Lt. USN, 1977-82. Avocation: tennis. Home and Office: 3523 McKinney Ave # 208 Dallas TX 75204 Office Phone: 214-887-5999. E-mail: sjcntx_sohw@yahoo.com.

COCKERHAM, WILLIAM CARL, sociologist, educator; b. Oklahoma City, Mar. 31, 1939; s. Carl Reese and Eva Louise C.; m. Frances Louise Coats, Jan. 20, 1960 (div. April 1964); children: Laura, Bruce; m. Cynthia (Ross) Cockerham, April 2, 1969; children: Geoffrey, Sean, Scott. BA, U. Okla., 1962; MJ, U. Calif., Berkley, 1969, PhD, 1971. Commd. 2d lt. U.S. Army, 1962, advanced through grades to capt., 1966, ret., 1995; prof. sociology and medicine U. Ill., Urbana, 1975-91; prof. sociology U. Wyo., Laramie, 1971-75; prof. sociology, chair U. Ala., Birmingham, 1991—, disting. prof. sociology, 2005—. Author: Medical Sociology, 10th ed., 2007 (included in Internat. Sociol. Assn.'s List of Books of the Century), Social Causes of Health and Disease, 2007, Sociology of Mental Disorder, 7th edit., 2005. Maj. Gen. U.S. Army Res., 1962-95. Decorated DSM, Legion of Merit; recipient Connor prize, History of Ideas, 1996, Ireland award Scholarly Distinction, 2004; Fulbright scholar, Germany, 1985. Office: U Alabama Dept Sociology 1530 3d Ave S Birmingham AL 35294-0001

COCKING, JILL HAGER, protective services official; b. Tucson, Ariz., Dec. 1, 1978; d. Lee and Ann Hager; m. Jeffery David Cocking, May 20, 2005. BS (hon.), No. Ariz. U., Flagstaff, 2001. Rsch. tech., lab. mgr. U. Ariz., Tucson, 2001—03; criminalist I Ariz. Dept. Pub. Safety, Phoenix, 2004—. Mentor Ariz. Quest Kids, Phoenix, 2006. Mem.: Am. Acad. Forensic Scis. (assoc.). Office: Arizona Department of Public Safety 2102 W Encanto Blvd Phoenix AZ 85009 Office Phone: 602-223-2934. E-mail: jcocking@azdps.gov.

COCKRAM, SUZANNE M., elementary school educator; d. Joseph and Kathleen Rabedeaw; m. Donald R. Cockram, June 13, 1981; children: Joshua, Jason. BS, Ea. Mich. U., 1977, M in Reading, 1982. Cert. in reading recovery Mich. Tchr. Hillsdale (Mich.) Cmty. Schs., 1977—, reading recovery tchr., 1996—2001; tchr. literacy tng. Hillsdale Ind. Sch. Dist., 2002—. Den leader Boy Scouts Am., Hillsdale, coun. mem.

COCKRELL, KENNETH DALE, astronaut; b. Austin, Tex., Apr. 9, 1950; s. Dale and Jewell Cockrell; 2 children. BSc in Mech. Engring., U. Tex., 1972; MSc in Aeronautical Sys., U. W. Fla., 1974. Commd. lt. USN, 1972, naval aviator Pensacola, Fla., 1974—75; served on USS Midway, 1975—78; various assignments naval air test ctr. USN, 1979—82; comdr. USS Ranger Naval Sta., San Diego, 1982—85; aerospace engr., rsch. pilot Ellington Field, Houston, 1987—90; astronaut NASA, Houston, 1991—. Astronaut Discovery, 1993, Endeavour, 1995, Columbia, 1996, Atlantis, 2001, Endeavour, 2002. Decorated Humanitarian Svc. medal USNR, Def. Meritorious Svc. medal, Disting. Flying Cross; scholar, Alcoa Found., 1968. Mem.: Assn. Space Explorers, Soc. Exptl. Test Pilots. Avocations: sport flying, skiing, tennis, water-skiing. Office: Astronaut Office CB NASA Johnson Space Center Houston TX 77058

COCKRELL, SANFORD ALONZA, III, accountant; b. Raleigh, NC, Feb. 2, 1959; s. Sanford Alonza Jr. and Vivian Mercer Cockrell; m. Louise Heath, Dec. 5, 1960; children: L. Heath, Morgan. M. BSBA, U. N.C., 1982. CPA, N.Y. Staff acct. Rackley & Parker CPAs, Raleigh, N.C., 1982-84; mgr. Deloitte Haskins & Sells, Raleigh, 1984-89; sr. mgr. Deloitte & Touche, NYC, 1989-93, ptnr., 1993—, bd. dirs., 2001—. Vice chmn. bd. dirs. Deloitte Touche Tohmatsu, 2003—; Grad. Leadership Raleigh I, Greater Raleigh C. of C., 1985-86; pres., treas. NC Soc. NY, 1996—, chmn. fin. com.; chmn. Younger Mem.'s Activities Com.; mem. Coun. Nominating Com., Univ. Club, exec. com. coun., v.p.; adv. bd. U. NC, Inst. for Arts and Humanities, Chapel Hill, NC, 1999—; co-chair cons. adv. bd., Youth, Inc.; coun. mem. U. NC Chapel Hill Nat. Devel. Coun., 1995—; coach girls' basketball and T-ball Yorkville Youth Athletic Assn., NYC, 2000—; elder, deacon Brick Presbyn. Ch., N.Y.C., 1994-2000; 2d v.p., NY area dir. U. NC, Chapel Hill Gen. Alumni Assn. Bd. Dirs., 1996-2000; reunion gift com. U. NC, Chapel Hill, 1991-92. Recipient Mac Disting. Alumni award, Kenan-Flager Bus. Sch., 2004. Mem. N.C. Soc. CPAs (chmn. com. on taxation 1986-88), Coral Beach Club (Bermuda), Rockaway Hunting Club, Lawrence Beach Club, Madison Beach Club. Presbyterian. Avocations: golf, running, sailing, travel, reading. Office: Deloitte Tax LLP 1633 Broadway New York NY 10019 Home: 359 Mansfield Ave Darien CT 06820-2113 Office Phone: 212-492-3804. Office Fax: 212-492-3881. Business E-Mail: scockrell@deloitte.com.

COCKRILLE, STEPHEN, art director, business owner; b. Washington, Jan. 19, 1945; s. Donald Herbert and Dorothy Charlotte (Hoover) Cockrille; m. Éva Vágréti, May 17, 1987; children: Christopher Lewis, Micki Lee. BA, W.Va. State Coll., 1968; MA, U. N.D., 1972. Grad. tchg. asst. U. N.D., Grand Forks, 1971; design asst. Thomas Clayton Printing, NYC, 1974-75; art dir. West Side Printing & Graphics, NYC, 1975-76; studio mgr. Graphic Concern, Inc., NYC, 1976-78; ind. art dir. NYC, 1978-84; pres. Textart, Inc., NYC, 1984-97; ind. art dir. Woodland Park, Colo., 1997—2004; pres., mng. dir. Miro Design, Inc., Colorado Springs, 2004—. Prodr.: numerous basal ednl programs for nat. distbn., 1984—97. Selected for presentation to the Jordanian Min. Edn. and staff on US textbook industry, NYC, 1995; judge New Eng. Book Show, Boston, 1987. With Ctrl. Intelligence Ctr. US Army, 1968—70, Vietnam. Recipient Hon. mention, New Eng. Book Show, Boston, 1992, Pupil's Edit. and Theme Posters, Boston, 1992, bronze award, Dimensional Illustrators Awards Show, NYC, 1992, 1st pl. award, Ednl. Sch. Divsn. NY Book Show, 1994. Independent. Avocations: painting, reading, skiing. Home: 1150 Kings Crown Rd Woodland Park CO 80863-7731 Office Phone: 719-634-5222. Personal E-mail: scockrille@mirodesign.net.

COCKRUM, WILLIAM MONROE, III, investment banker, educator; b. Indpls., July 18, 1937; s. William Monroe C. II and Katherine J. (Jaqua) Moore; children: Catherine Anne Cockrum Dean, William Monroe IV AB with distinction, DePauw U., 1959; MBA with distinction, Harvard U., 1961. With A.G. Becker Paribas Inc., LA, 1961-84, mgr. nat. corp. fin. div., 1968-71, mgr. pvt. investments, 1971-74, fin. and adminstrv. officer, 1974-80, sr. v.p., 1975-78, vice chmn., 1978-84; prin. William M. Cockrum & Assocs., LA, 1984—; faculty Northwestern U., 1961—63. Vis. lectr. Anderson Grad. Sch. Mgmt. UCLA, 1984—88, adj. prof., 1988—; vis. prof. Warwick U., England, 2004—, Cranfield U., England, 2006—. Mem. Deke Club (NYC), UCLA Faculty Club, Alisal Golf Club (Solvang, Calif.), Bel-Air Country Club (LA), Delta Kappa Epsilon. E-mail: bcockrum@anderson.ucla.edu.

COCKS, GEOFFREY CAMPBELL, history professor; b. New Bedford, Mass., Nov. 13, 1948; s. James Fraser and Lillias (Campbell) C.; m. Sarah Rogers, Aug. 28, 1971; 1 child, Emily Anne. AB, Occidental Coll., 1970; MA, UCLA, 1971, PhD, 1975. Instr. Occidental Coll., LA, 1974-75; asst. prof. history Albion (Mich.) Coll., 1975-83, assoc. prof., 1983-87, prof., 1987-94, Royal G. Hall prof., 1994—2002, Juilian S. Rammelkamp prof., 2002—. Vis. asst. prof. UCLA, 1980. Author: Psychotherapy in the Third Reich, 1985, 2d edit., 1997, Treating Mind and Body, 1998, The Wolf at the Door, 2004; co-editor: German Professions, 1990, Medicine and Modernity, 1996, Depth of Field, 2004; editor: The Curve of Life, 1994. Fellow German Acad. Exch. Svc., 1973-74, 85, NEH, 1980, 87, 88-89, Fulbright fellow, 1989; Nat. Libr. Medicine grantee NIH, 1991-92. Mem. Am. Hist. Assn., German Studies Assn. Office: Albion Coll Dept History Albion MI 49224

COCKS, GEORGE GOSSON, retired chemical microscopy professor; b. Sioux City, Iowa, Mar. 22, 1919; s. George Green and Nellie Patricia (Gosson) C.; m. Marian L. Singer, May 11, 1942; children: Gary, Kathleen (Mrs. Thomas Sadlowski), Francis, Kenneth. BS in Chemistry, Iowa State U., 1941; PhD in Chem. Microscopy, Cornell, 1949. Researcher Battelle Meml. Inst., Columbus, Ohio, 1949-64; prof. chem. microscopy Cornell U., 1964-81, prof. emeritus, 1981—; cons. Los Alamos (N.Mex.) Nat. Lab., 1980-81, staff mem., 1981-90; ret., 1990. Scoutmaster Central Ohio council Boy Scouts Am., 1956-64. Served to lt. comdr. USNR, 1942-45. NSF grantee to study crystallization inorganic materials in polymers, 1966-68, to study biomed. uses collagen, 1972—, DOE grantee in hot dry rock geothermal energy project, 1981-90. Fellow AAAS (coun. 1970-75); mem. Am. Optical Soc., Am. Chem. Soc., Microscopy Soc. Am. (exec. sec. 1964-76), Sigma Xi, Phi Kappa Phi. Achievements include patents in field. Home: 1719 Hyland St Bayside CA 95524-9302

COCKWELL, JACK LYNN, finance company executive; b. East London, South Africa, Jan. 12, 1941; s. William Henry and Daphne (Cound) C.; children: Linda, Lorie, Leslie, Tessa, Malcolm, Gareth. M.Com., U. Cape Town, 1964, postgrad. with distinction, 1966. Chartered Acct. Mgr. Touche Ross & Co., Cape Town and Montreal, 1959-67; exec. v.p., chief oper. officer Edper Enterprises Ltd., Toronto, Ont., Canada, 1968-90, Brascan Corp. (now Brookfield Asset Mgmt. Inc.), Toronto, 1979-91, pres. and CEO, 1991—2002, group chmn., 2002—. Bd. dirs. Norbord, Inc., Fraser Papers, Inc., Great Lakes Power, Inc., Brookfield Properties, Inc.,

Astral Media Inc. Chmn. bd. trustees Royal Ont. Mus.; bd. dirs. C.D. Howe Inst. Office: Brookfield Asset Mgmt Inc 181 Bay St Ste 300 PO Box 762 Toronto ON Canada M5J 2T3 Office Phone: 416-556-5130. E-mail: dhorton@brookfield.com.

COCOVES, ANITA PETZOLD, psychotherapist; b. Princeton, NJ, June 2, 1957; d. Charles Bernard and Kathleen Marie (McDonald) Petzold; m. Nicholas John Cocoves, Oct. 11, 1997; 1 child, Nicholas Euthymius. AS in Bus., Indian River C.C., Fla., 1986; BS in Liberal Studies, Barry U., 1988; MS in Human Svcs. Adminstrn., Nova U., 1989, postgrad., 1989—91; PhD in Human Svcs. Adminstrn., LaSalle U., 1994. Lic. mental health counselor, Fla.; cert. addictions prevention profl.; internat. cert. alcohol and drug abuse counselor; nat. cert. counselor; cert. employee assistance counselor; nat. cert. clin. mental health counselor; nat. cert. addictions counselor; cert. DUI instr.; cert. family and county ct. mediator. Admissions coord. Palm Beach Inst., West Palm Beach, Fla., 1985—86; dir. admissions Heritage Health Corp., Jensen Beach, Fla., 1986—89; coord. rug abuse strategy Martin County Bd. of County Commrs., Stuart, Fla., 1989—2001; adminstr. health and human svcs. Martin County Bd. of County Commr., Stuart, 2001—. Mem. Drug Resource Team for the 12th Congl. Dist., Fla., 1990—, Juvenile Justice Assn. of the 19th Jud. Ct., Fla., 1993—, vice chmn. 1999—; grant writer in field. Vol. Hist. Soc. Martin County, Stuart, 1986—; mem. United Way Martin County, Stuart, 1993; mem. bd. dirs. Cmty. AIDS Adv. Project, Stuart, 1993; chmn. treatment com. Martin County Task Force on Substance Abused Children, Stuart, 1993; chmn. Legis. Subcom. Martin County Juvenile Justice Com., 1998—. Recipient Outstanding Cmty. Svc. award United Way Martin County, Stuart, 1993. Mem. NASW, Am. Mental Health Counselors Assn., Nat. Criminal Justice Assn., Nat. Assn. Alcoholism and Drug Abuse Counselors, Nat. Consortium Treatment Alternatives to St. Crime Programs, Am. Coll. Addiction Treatment Adminstrs., Am. Labor-Mgmt. Adminstrs., Fla. Alcohol and Drug Abuse Assn. Republican. Roman Catholic. Avocations: walking, reading. Home: 38 SE Ocean Blvd Stuart FL 34994-2215 Office Phone: 772-288-5785, 772-463-2868. Business E-Mail: acocoves@martin.fl.us.

CODDING, FREDERICK HAYDEN, lawyer; b. Hopewell, Va., Dec. 13, 1938; s. Francis Chadwick and Ruthcille Sharon (Craven) C.; m. Judith Willis Hawkins, Apr. 30, 1966; children: Forrest Hayden, Judith Chadwick, Cally Willis, Clare Catharine. AB, Coll. William and Mary, 1962; JD, Georgetown U., 1966. Bar: Va. 1966, D.C. 1968, U.S. Supreme Ct. 1979. Legal asst. Vet. Adminstrn., Washington, 1963-65; Capitol Hill reporter, editor Congressional Monitor, Washington, 1966; law clk. to chief judge D.C. Ct. Appeals, 1966-68; individual practice law Va. and Washington; v.p., counsel Nat. Assn. Miscellaneous, Ornamental and Archtl. Products Contractors, Fairfax, Va., 1970—; counsel, dir. Nat. Assn. Reinforcing Steel Contractors, Fairfax, 1970—. Editor pub. legis., adminstrv., bldg. and constrn. industry newsletters, reports. Mem. federally established rev. bds. for constrn., OSHA and industry; counsel, pres. Fairfax Police Youth Club; appointee Fairfax City Sch. Bd., 1983-88. Mem. ABA, D.C. Bar Assn., Va. Bar Assn., Fairfax Bar Assn., Nat. Coun. Erectors, Fabricators and Riggers, Sigma Nu. Office: Law Office 10382 Main St Fairfax VA 22030-2412

CODDINGTON, ARTHUR MICHAEL, JR., pediatrician, dermatologist; b. Johnson City, NY, Apr. 19, 1920; s. Arthur Michael and Marie Corwin Coddington; m. Margaret Mary Nealon, Sept. 6, 1954; children: Jane, Arthur III, Mary. BA, Princeton U., NJ, 1943; MD, U. Pa., Phila., 1946. Cert. pediatrician U. Pitts., 1952, diplomate Am. Bd. Pediats., 1952. Pvt. practice pediats., Johnson City, 1952—, Ithaca, NY, 1982—88; pvt. practice, pediat. dermatology Cortland, NY, 1984—89, Norwich, NY, 1991—. Pres. pediat. staff Wilson Meml. Hosp., Johnson City, 1963—74. Mem. sch. bd. Johnson City Sch. Sys., 1958—63. Capt. US Army, 1944—49, US, Korea, Japan. Mem.: Rotary. Independent. Roman Catholic. Office: Arthur M Coddington MD 394 Main St Johnson City NY 13790 Office Phone: 607-797-0603.

CODDINGTON, CLINTON HAYS, lawyer; b. Honolulu, July 8, 1939; s. L. Clinton and Patricia Carolyn (Richer) C.; m. Martha Anne Stevens, June 20, 1970; children: Clinton Stevens, Catherine Hadley. BSCE, US Mil. Acad., 1961; JD, U. Calif., Berkeley, 1968. Bar: Calif. 1969, US Ct. Appeals (2nd, 5th, 7th, 8th and 9th cirs.), US Supreme Ct. 1974. Assoc. Bronson, Bronson & McKinnon, San Francisco, 1969-70, Ropers Majeski Kohn Bentley & Wagner, Redwood City, Calif., 1970-77; ptnr. Tucker & Coddington, Palo Alto, Calif., 1977-78; ptnr., chmn. Coddington, Hicks & Danforth, Redwood City, 1978—. Contbr. articles to profl. jours. Chmn. Easter Seals; vestryman, sr. warden, chancellor various Episcopal chs.; pres. Chinquapin Homeowners Assn., Lake Tahoe, Calif., 1991-92, Stanford Hills Homeowners Assn., Palo Alto, Calif. Capt. US Army, 1961-64. Mem. ABA, Assn. Def. Counsel, Lawyer/Pilot Bar Assn., Internat. Assn. Def. Counsel, San Mateo County Bar Assn., Calif. Bar Assn., Def. Rsch. Inst., Am. Bd. Trial Advocates. Republican. Avocations: guitar, classical music, aviation, boating, reading. Office: Coddington Hicks & Danforth 555 Twin Dolphin Dr Ste 300 Redwood City CA 94065-2133 Personal E-mail: chc@coddington.org. Business E-Mail: ccoddington@chdlawyers.com.

CODEN, DANIEL JAY, ophthalmologist; b. Detroit, Feb. 20, 1958; s. Theodore Paul and Barbara Joan Coden; m. Elizabeth Ann Nederlander-Coden, June 1, 1984; children: Lauren, Jacqueline, Benjamin. BS, U. Mich., Ann Arbor, 1980; MD, Wayne State U., Detroit, 1984. Diplomate Am. Acad. Ophthalmology. Resident ophthalmology U. Calif., San Diego, 1988; fellow oculoplastic surgery Manhattan Eye, Ear and Throat Hosp., NYC, 1989; sr. staff surgeon Henry Ford Hosp., Detroit, 1989—90; med. dir. La Jolla Laser Vision, Calif., 1990—. Named Young Leader in Ophthalmology, Ophthalmology Mgmt., 1989. Fellow: ACS; mem.: Am. Soc. Cataract and Refractive Surgery, Am. Acad. Ophthalmology (Honor award 2002), Am. Soc. Ophthalmic Plastic and Reconstructive Surgery, Alpha Omega Alpha (pres. 1983). Office: LaJolla Laser Vision 9850 Genesee Ste 310 La Jolla CA 92037

CODEY, RICHARD JAMES (DICK CODEY), state senator, former acting governor; b. Orange, NJ, Nov. 27, 1946; m. Mary Jo Rolli, Nov.28, 1981; children: Kevin, Christopher. Student Trenton Jr. Coll.; BA in Edn., Fairleigh Dickinson U., 1981; LHD (hon.), Drew U., 2007. Mem. N.J. Gen. Assembly, Trenton, 1974—81, chmn. Assembly State Govt Com.; mem. NJ State Senate (dist. 27), Trenton, 1982—; chmn. Senate Institutions, Health and Welfare Com NJ State Senate, 1982—92, asst. minority leader, 1992—98, minority leader, 1998—2001, Dem. Senate pres. Trenton, 2002—03, pres., 2004—; acting gov. State of NJ, Trenton, 2002, 2004—06, 2007. Pres. Olympic Insurance Agy., 1983—. Recipient Svc. award N.J. Mental Health Assn., Svc. award N.J. Prosecutor's Assn.; named Citizen of Yr., N.J. Psychiat. Assn. Mem. Nat. Assn. Funeral Dirs., State Assn. Funeral Dirs. Democrat. Office: NJ Senate PO Box 099 State Capitol Trenton NJ 08625 also: 449 Mount Pleasant Ave West Orange NJ 07052-2734*

CODINA, ARMANDO M., real estate developer; b. Cuba; US, 1960; m. Margarita Codina; children: Ana, Ali, Andri, Amanda. Student, Jacksonville U. Clerk Am. Nat. Bank; bank officer Republic Bank, Miami, Fla.; founder, pres. Professional Automated Services, Inc., 1970—78; founder, chmn., CEO Codina Group, Coral Gables, Fla., 1979—. Bd. dirs. BellSouth Corp., 1992—, GM Corp., 2002—, AMR Corp., Merrill Lynch, 2005—. Office: Codina Group 355 Alhambra Circle Ste 900 Miami FL 33134

CODINA, FRANCISCO, automotive executive; b. Cuba; arrived in U.S., 1965; BBA, Univ. Ala. Mgmt. positions Ford Motor Co., Dearborn, Mich., 1977—95; mktg. & customer svc. dir. Ford of Mexico, 1995—98; mng. dir. Ford of Argentina, 1998—99, pres., 1999—2001; gen. mktg. mgr. Ford div. Ford Motor Co., Dearborn, Mich., 2001—03, v.p. customer svc. div., 2003—06, group v.p. N.Am. mktg., sales & svc., 2006—. Mem. bd. vis. Univ. Ala. Sch. Commerce; chmn. Detroit Regional Council, Boy Scouts Am. Office: Ford Motor Co 1 American Rd Dearborn MI 48126*

CODINHA, J. WILLIAM, lawyer; b. NYC, 1947; BA, Ohio Wesleyan U., 1969; JD, Boston U., 1972. Bar: Mass. 1972, DC 1994, Fed. Dist. Ct. Mass., First Cir. Ct. Appeals. First asst. dist. atty., chief trial div. Middlesex County Dist. Atty.'s Office; spl. asst. atty. gen. Ward Commn., 1980—81; mem. Nixon Peabody LLP, Boston, 1981—, ptnr., practice group co-leader. Chief counsel US Senate Select Com. on POW/MIA Affairs, 1991—93, US Senate Com. on Banking, Housing and Urban Affairs (Whitewater Investigation), 1994. Mem.: DC Bar Assn. Office: Nixon Peabody LLP 100 Summer St Boston MA 02110 Office Phone: 617-345-1325. Office Fax: 866-947-1684. E-mail: jcodinha@nixonpeabody.com.

CODISPOTI, ANDRE JOHN, allergist, immunologist; b. Bklyn., Apr. 27, 1938; s. Bruno Mario and Antoinette (Savarese) C.; m. Miranda Babini, June 14, 1967; children: Rita, Elisa, Andrew. BA, Coll. of Holy Cross, 1959; MD, U. Bologna, Italy, 1965. Diplomate Am. Bd. Pediatrics, Am. Bd. Allergy and Immunology. Rotating intern Long Island Coll. Hosp., Bklyn., 1966, resident in pediatrics, 1967-69, fellow in allergy and immunology, 1971-73; pvt. practice Suffern, NY, 1972—. Maj. M.C., U.S. Army, 1969-71. Fellow Am. Coll. Allergy, Asthma and Immunology, Am. Acad. Allergy, Asthma and Immunology. Republican. Roman Catholic. Avocations: reading, music, travel, tennis, skiing. Office: 7 Hemion Rd Suffern NY 10901-4903 also: 70 Gilbert St Monroe NY 10950-1538 E-mail: acodispotimd@aol.com.

CODO, CHRISTINA, securities executive; b. Evanston, Ill., Jan. 13, 1960; d. Norman Fredric and Charlotte Jean (Bailey) Codo; m. Patrick Joseph Maloney; children: Beatrice Grace Codo Maloney, Daniel Patrick Codo Maloney. BA in Econs., Northwestern U., 1980; MBA, Yale U., 1987. Exec. officer in lending Lloyds Bank Internat. Inc., Miami, Fla., 1982-85; exec. officer high yield capital markets Salomon Inc., NYC, 1987-89; with instnl. sales Whitehill Capital Inc., NYC, 1989, v.p. instnl. sales, 1989-91; mem. instnl. adv. staff Euromobiliare, SpA, Milan, 1991-92; assoc. fgn. securities group JP Morgan, NYC, 1992-93, v.p. Emerging Markets, 1993-94, Chgo., 1994-98; assoc., controller's divsn. Continental Ill. Bank and Trust Co. Inc., 1999—. Fin. dir. Jr. League of Evanston-North Shore, Winnetka, 1999—2001, co-chmn. fundraising com., 1997—98; mem. exec. bd. Ronald Knox Montessori Sch., chair fundraising com., 2001—02, pres. bd. dirs., 2003—04; vice chair New Trier Township Youth Com., 2000—. Mem.: Chgo. Coun. Fgn. Rels. Avocations: opera, golf, tennis, internat. travel.

CODRON, MICHAEL VICTOR, theater producer; b. June 8, 1930; s. I. A. and Lily (Morganstern) Codron. Student, St. Paul's Sch.; MA, Worcester Coll., Oxford U. Mem. adv. coun. Hampstead Theatre; adminstr. Aldwych Theatre; Cameron Mackintosh prof. contemporary theatre Oxford (Eng.) U., 1993, emeritus fellow St. Catherine's Coll., 2003—. Prodr.: (plays) Breath of Spring, 1957, The Birthday Party, 1958, Pieces of Eight, 1959, The Caretaker, 1960, The Tenth Man, 1961, Rattle of a Simple Man, 1962, Next Time I'll Sing to You, Private Lives, The Lovers and the Dwarfs, Cockade, 1963, Poor Bitos, The Formation Dancers, Entertaining Mr. Sloane, 1964, Loot, The Killing of Sister George, Ride a Cock Horse, 1965, Little Malcolm and His Struggle Against the Eunuchs, The Anniversary, There's a Girl in My Soup, Big Bad Mouse, 1966, The Judge, The Flip Side, Wise Child, The Boy Friend, 1967, Not Now Darling, The Real Inspector Hound, 1968, The Contractor, Slag, The Two of Us, The Philanthropist, 1970, The Foursome, Butley, A Voyage Round My Father, The Changing Room, 1971, Veterans, Time and Time Again, Crown Matrimonial, My Fat Friend, 1972, Collaborators, Savages, Habeas Corpus, Absurd Person Singular, 1973, Knuckle, Flowers, Golden Pathway Annual, The Nomran Conquests, John Paul George Ringo.and Bert, 1974, A Family and a Fortune, Alphabetical Order, A Far Better Husband, Ashes, Absent Friends, Otherwise Engaged, Stripwell, 1975, Funny Peculiar, Treats, Donkey's Years, Confusions, Teeth 'n' Smiles, Yahoo, 1976, Dusa Stas, Fish & Vi, Just Between Ourselves, Oh, Mr. Porter, Breezeblock Park, The Bells of Hell, The Old Country, 1977, The Rear Column, Ten Times Table, The Unvarnished Truth, The Homecoming, Alice's Boys, Night and Day, 1978, Joking Apart, Tishoo, Stage Struck, 1979, Dr. Faustus, Make and Break, The Dresser, Taking Steps, Enjoy, 1980, Hinge & Bracket, Rowan Atkinson in Revue, House Guest, Quartermaine's Terms, 1981, Season's Greetings, Noises Off, Funny Turns, 1982, The Real Thing, 1982, The Hard Shoulder, 1983, Look, No Hans!, Benefectors, 1984, Jumpers, Who Plays Wins, Made in Bangkok, 1986, Woman in Mind, 1986, Hapgood, Uncle Vanya, Re Joyce!, The Sneeze, Henceforward, 1986, The Cherry Orchard, 1989, Man of the Moment, Look, Look, Hidden Laughter, Private Lives, 1990, What the Butler Saw, 70 Girls 70, The Revengers Comedies, 1991, The Rise and Fall of Little Voice, 1992, Time of My Life, 1993, Jamais Vu, 1993, Dead Funny, 1994, Arcadia, 1994, The Sisters Rosensweig, 1994, Indian Ink, 1995, The Killing of Sister George, 1995, Dealer's Choice, 1995, The Shakespeare Revue, 1995, A Talent to Amuse, 1996, Tom and Clem, 1997, Silhoutte Heritage, 1997, Things We Do for Love, 1998, Elton John's Glasses, 1998, Alarms and Excursions, 1998, The Invention of Love, 1998, Copenhagen, 1999 (Tony award, 2000), Quartet, 1999, Comic Potential, 1999, Peggy for You, 2000, Blue/Orange, 2001, Life After George, 2002, Bedroom Farce, 2002, Damsels in Distress, 2002, My Brilliant Divorce, 2003, Dinner, 2003, Democracy, 2004, Ying Tong, 2005, Losing Louis, 2005, Glorious!, 2005, Entertaining Angels, 2006; (films) Clockwise, 1965. Decorated comdr. Brit. Empire. Mem.: Garrick Club. Office: Aldwych Theatre London WC2B 4DF England

CODY, ALDUS MORRILL, retired editor, journalist, typographer; b. Somerville, Mass., Jan. 11, 1915; s. Luther Morrill and Josephine Belle (Morrill) C.; m. Dorothy Gifford, Dec. 25, 1936; 1 child, Raymond Gifford; m. Bertha Hood Carnahan, June 1, 2002 (dec Sept. 2005). BA in Journalism, U. Fla., 1936. Editor Suwannee Dem., Live Oak, Fla., 1936-37, Williamson County News, Franklin, Tenn., 1937, Marion County News, Ocala, Fla., 1938-39, Kissimmee (Fla.) Gazette, 1939-41, Share Your Knowledge Rev. (later Rev. Graphic Arts), Cin., 1970-80, The High Twelvian, St. Louis, 1989-95; mng. editor Ocala Morning Banner, 1937-38; editor, pub. The Fla. Cattleman, Kissimmee, 1940-45; founder, CEO, Cody Publs., Kissimmee, 1946-77; editor News of Masonic Cmty., Kissimmee, 1989-96; ret., 1996; editor The Quadrangle, Good Samaritan Retirement Village, Kissimmee, 1996—2000. Author: (with Robert Cody) Osceola County—First 100 Years, 1996; editor The Connector, 1st United Meth. Ch., 2001—. Former commr. and mayor City of Kissimmee. Mem. Internat. Assn. Printing House Craftsmen (dist. gov. 1968-70, nat. editor 1970-80), Fla. Assn. Square Dancers (founder, pres.), Masons (past master), Shriners, Rotary (past pres. Kissimmee). Democrat. Methodist. Avocation: genealogy. E-mail: aldus@kua.net.

CODY, DANIEL SCHAFFNER, lawyer; b. Columbus, Ohio, Nov. 21, 1948; s. Ralph Eugene and Grace (Schaffner) C.; 1 child, Sean. Student, Kent State U., 1977; BA, Ohio State U., 1970, BSEd, 1973; JD, U. Akron, 1990. Bar: Ohio 1990, U.S. Dist. Ct. (no. dist.) Ohio 1990, U.S. Ct. Appeals (6th cir.) 1990, U.S. Ct. Appeals (4th cir.) 1992. Tchg. Archbishop Hoban H.S., Akron, Ohio, 1973-88, athletic dir., 1980-84; rsch. asst. Hon. Arthur Goldberg (ret.) U.S. Supreme Ct., U. Akron, 1989, staff intern Appellate Rev. Office, 1990-91; jud. clk. Ohio Ct. Appeals (9th dist.), Akron, 1990-91; assoc. Jacobson, Maynard, Tuschman & Kalur, Cleve., 1991-93; pvt. practice Akron, 1993—. Trustee U. Akron Law Alumni Assn., 1992—, pres., 2000-01; trustee Archbishop Hoban H.S., 1995-2001. Mem.: Akron Bar Assn., Ohio State Bar Assn. Democrat. Roman Catholic. Office: 17 S Main St Ste 201 Akron OH 44308-1803 Home: 230 Mineola Ave Akron OH 44313-7861

CODY, FRANK JOSEPH, education educator, consultant; b. Detroit, Sept. 13, 1940; s. Burns J. and Margaret (Dowley) C.; m. Shirley Black, May 16, 1992. AB, Loyola U., 1962, PhL, 1965, MA, 1966, MDiv, 1975; PhD, Ohio State U., 1980. Cert. tchr., prin., supr., Ohio, Mich. Headmaster St. Ignatius HS, Cleve., 1977-81; dir. Chapel Sch., Sao Paulo, Brazil, 1981-83, U. Detroit Ctr. Econ. Edn., 1988-91; assoc. prof., tchr. adminstrv. edn. U. Detroit, 1983-91; adminstr. Grand Rapids Cath. Secondary Schs., 1991-95; headmaster Woodside Priory Sch., Portola Valley, Calif., 1995—97; tchr. Kalamazoo Ctrl. HS, 1997—2005, asst. prin., 1998-99; dir. Small Learning Cmtys. Project, 2002—03; instr., acad. coord. Spring Arbor U., 2005—. Trustee Wheeling Coll., 1980-82, mem. Coun. Entrance Svcs. Coll. Bd., 1978-81; mem. Mich. Supt.'s Com. on Accreditation, 1984-88; commr. Nat. Assn. Secondary Sch. Prins./Carnegie Found. Commn. on Future of Am. H.S., 1994-96; dir. rsch. English lang. studies Unified Coll. Guarulhos, Sao Paulo, Brazil, 1998-2002; instr. U. Phoenix, 2005—. Co-author: Manual of Educational Risk Management, 1991, Escola e Communidade: Uma Parceria Necessaria, 1997, O Professor Do Terceiro Milenio, 2000, Um Novo Ensino Para Uma Nova Era, 2006; contbr. articles to profl. jours. Trustee Trinity Sch., Menlo Park, Calif., 1996-97; vice chair planning commn. City of Kalamazoo, 2003—; exec. com. Kalamazoo Assn. Ret. Sch. Personnel, 2007—. Roman Catholic. E-mail: buffcody@ameritech.net.

CODY, THOMAS GERALD, management consultant, writer; b. Holyoke, Mass., Feb. 18, 1929; s. John Francis and Mary Gertrude (Scanlon) C.; m. Kathleen Mary Maguire, Nov. 17, 1956 (dec. June 2004); children—Kathleen, Joseph. AB, Coll. of Holy Cross, 1950; postgrad., Boston Coll., 1950—52; MBA, Harvard U., 1957. Various corp. mgmt. positions, 1955—62; cons., prin., v.p. Fry Cons., Inc., Chgo., L.A., Washington, 1962—72; exec. dir. U.S. EEOC, Washington, 1972—74; asst. sec. for admin. HUD, Washington, 1974—76; Washington v.p. L.B. Knight & Assoc., Inc., 1976—79; pres. Lester B. Knight Mgmt. Cons. Group, 1979—81, Thomas Cody & Assoc., Annapolis, Md., 1981—84; v.p. human resources Baxter Travenol Labs. Inc., Deerfield, Ill., 1984—86, corp. v.p., 1985—87; exec. v.p., Chgo. office Jannotta Bray & Assoc. Inc., 1987—, ptnr. Washington office, 1989—96; prin. The Washington Group, 1996—. Author: Management Consulting: A Game Without Chips, 1986, Strategy of a Megamerger, 1990, Innovating For Health, 1994. Mem. U.S. Arch. and Transp. Barriers Compliance Bd., 1974-76, Anne Arundel Commn. on Women, 1977-79, U.S. Comptr. Gen. Adv. Panel, 1983-88; bd. dirs. Found. for Jr. Blind, L.A., 1968-70, Baxter Am. Found., 1986-88, Suburban Cook County Area Agy. on Aging, 1988-89; trustee St. Mary of the Woods Coll., Terre Haute, Ind., 1987-90; mem. panel on employers and working families NAS. 1st lt. USMC, 1953-55. Mem. Harvard Club of NYC. Home: 5450 Whitley Park Ter Apt 303 Bethesda MD 20814-2054 Personal E-mail: thomas-cody@hotmail.com.

CODY, THOMAS GERALD, retail executive, lawyer; b. NYC, Nov. 4, 1941; s. Thomas J. Cody and Esther Mary Courtney; m. Mary Ellen Palmer, Nov. 26, 1966; children: Thomas Jr., Mark, Amy, Anne. BA in Philosophy, Maryknoll Coll., 1963; JD, St. John's U., 1967; LLD (hon.), Cen. State U., Wilberforce, Ohio, 1985. Bar: N.Y. 1967. Assoc. Simpson Thacher & Bartlett, N.Y., 1967-72; asst. prof. law sch. St. John's U., N.Y., 1972-76; sr. v.p., gen. counsel, sec. Pan Am. Airways, N.Y., 1976-82; sr. v.p. law and pub. affairs Macy's Inc. (formerly Federated Dept. Stores Inc.), Cin., 1982-88; exec. v.p. legal & human resources Macy's Inc., Cin., 1988—2003, vice chmn. legal, human resources and external affairs, 2003—. Trustee Xavier U., Cin., Children's Hosp. Med. Ctr., Cin; bd. dirs. Cin. USA Regional Chamber Mem. ABA, Bankers Club, Queen City Club, Hyde Park Country Club, Commonwealth Club of Cin. Roman Catholic. Office: Macy's Inc 7 W 7th St Cincinnati OH 45202-2424 Office Phone: 513-579-7768.*

CODY, WILLIAM BERMOND, political science professor; b. Brunswick, Ga., Jan. 15, 1949; s. Bermond Hamp and Dorothy Jane (Satterfield) C.; m. Mildred Ann McInnis, Sept. 5, 1970; children: Margaret Jae, Elizabeth Joelle. AB, U. Ga., 1971, MA, 1973, JD, 1986; PhD, New Sch. Social Rsch., 1980. Bar: Ga. 1986. Student advisor New Sch. Social Rsch., NYC, 1978-79; asst. to pres. Robeal Mgmt. Co., Charleston, SC, 1983-85; assoc. Carr, Tabb & Pope, Atlanta, 1987; legal asst. Ga. Ct. Appeals, Atlanta, 1987-89; asst. prof. polit. sci. U. Ga., Athens, 1989-90; asst. prof. Oxford (Ga.) Coll. Emory U., 1990-93; assoc. prof. Oxford (Ga.) Coll. Emory U., 1993—. Adj. instr. Coll. New Rochelle, N.Y., 1978-79; vis. asst. prof. Clemson (S.C.) U., 1980-83; mem. Emory U. Senate, 1995-97, pres.-elect, 1996-97, pres., 1997-98. Vestryman St. Bede's Episcopal Ch., Atlanta, 1988-92, jr. warden, 1990, sr. warden, 1991; bd. dirs. Interfaith, Inc., Atlanta, 1989-90. Mem. ABA, Am. Polit. Sci. Assn., Ga. Polit. Sci. Assn., So. Polit. Sci. Assn., Am. Hist. Assn., Acad. Polit. Sci., Ga. Bar Assn. Democrat. Office: Polit Sci Dept Oxford Coll Emory U Oxford GA 30054 E-mail: bcody@emory.edu.

CODY, WILMER ST. CLAIR, educational policy researcher; b. Mobile, Ala., Jan. 1, 1937; s. Wilmer St. Clair and Madeline (Maygarden) C.; m. Caroline Marie Burns, Aug. 16, 1958; children: David Marshall, Alison Marie. AB, Harvard U., 1959, EdM, 1960, EdD, 1968. Tchr. Newton (Mass.) Schs., 1960, Mobile County Schs., 1960-62, prin., 1962-64; dir. tchr. edn. Atlanta Schs., 1966-67; supt. Chapel Hill (N.C.) Schs., 1967-71; sr. rsch. assoc. Nat. Inst. Edn., 1971-73; supt. Birmingham (Ala.) City Schs., 1973-83, Montgomery County Schs., Rockville, Md., 1983-87; dir. nat. assessment project Council Chief State Sch. Officers, 1987-88; supt. edn. State of La., 1988-92; exec. dir. Nat. Edn. Goals Panel, Washington, 1992-93; dir. Nat. Faculty/So. Region, New Orleans, 1993-95; commr. edn. State of Ky., Frankfort, 1995-99; pres. Cody Assocs., Inc., 1999—. Cons. in field; mem. Nat. Assessment Governing Bd., 1998—2002, Smithsonian Nat. Bd., 2005—. Mem. Nat. Adv. Com. on Juvenile Justice and Delinquency Prevention, 1976-78; bd. dirs. Comty. Chest, Campfire Girls; trustee Nat. Coun. Econ. Edn., So. Assn. Colls. and Schs., 1990-92; chmn. Nat. Assessment Edn. Policy Com., 1983-87; dir. S.W. Edn. Devel. Lab., 1988-92; steering com. Edn. Commn. of the States, 1990-92, So. Region Edn. Bd., 1990-92, 96-99; exec. bd. Nat. Coun. for Accreditation of Tchr. Edn., 1990-92, 96-98, chair 1998; pres. Coun. Chief State Officers, 1997-98; mem. Frazier Mus. Adv. Com., 2006—; pres. Harvard Club La., 2006. Named Educator of Yr. ALA, 1977. Mem.: Am. Assn. Sch. Adminstrs., Phi Delta Kappa. Methodist. Home: 1535 Eleonore St New Orleans LA 70115-4242

COE, BENJAMIN PLAISTED, retired state official; b. Long Beach, Calif., Aug. 24, 1930; s. Benjamin and Mary Plaisted (Ricker) C.; m. Margaret Jane Butler, Sept. 5, 1953; children: Benjamin B., Elizabeth C., Mary Susan, Margaret Jane. AB, Bowdoin Coll., 1953; BS, Ch.E., MIT, 1953. Lic. profl. engr., N.Y. With silicone products dept. Gen. Electric Co., Waterford, NY, 1953-65, process econs. engr., 1963-65; exec. dir. Vols. for Internat. Tech. Assistance, Schenectady, 1965-68, exec. dir. U.S.A. div., 1969-73, v.p., 1971-73; exec. dir. Tug Hill Commn., N.Y. State, 1973-93; ret. Tug Hill Commn., 1993. Vestry Trinity Episcopal Ch., 1978-81, warden, 1981-86, 93-96; bd. dirs. Schenectady Symphony, 1969; chmn. pub. svc. divsn. Jefferson County United Way, 1982-84, bd. dirs., 1985-88, 2d v.p., 1988-89, 1st v.p., 1990-91, pres., 1992-94; pres. Vol. Ctr. Jefferson County, 1994-96, 98—. Named Exec. of Yr. Watertown Profl. Secs.

Internat., 1978-79; recipient Ageless Achievers award, N.Y. State, 2002. Mem. AIChE (chmn. N.E. N.Y. sect. 1965), Rotary (pres. Watertown 1989-90, dist. gov. 1996-97, Paul Harris fellow, Citation for Meritorious Svc. 2002), Phi Beta Kappa, Sigma Xi, Tau Beta Pi. Home: 627 Stone Cir Watertown NY 13601 *I have come to think that success should be measured internally, between man and his maker, rather than by external signs. My goals are to involve myself with mankind in a worthwile way and at the same time keep my family fed, healthy, and in a position to work toward their own goals.*

COE, DONALD KIRK, retired academic administrator; b. Tuscaloosa, Ala., Nov. 21, 1934; s. Glen Dale and Hazel Mae (Coley) C.; m. Frances Ellen Truman, May 31, 1958; children: Mark William, Sandra Elizabeth, Bonnie Lee. BA, U. Ala., 1957. Wire editor Xenia (Ohio) Daily Gazette, 1958-59; reporter, county editor Sharon (Pa.) Herald, 1959-61; asst. wire editor Pitts. Press, 1961-66; in public relations and fund raising Carnegie-Mellon U., Pitts., 1966-70; editorial writer St. Petersburg (Fla.) Times, 1970-75; chief editorial writer Chgo. Sun-Times, 1975-84; univ. dir. pub. affairs U. Ill., 1984-98, spl. asst. to pres., 1998-2000; ret., 2000. Pres. Nat. Conf. Editorial Writers Found., 1989-91. Capt. USAR, 1958-68. Recipient Ill. UPI award, 1977 Mem. Sigma Delta Chi (pres. coll. chpt. 1957) Presbyterian. Home: 723 Bonnie Brae Pl River Forest IL 60305-1930

COE, DOUG, religious organization administrator; b. 1930; 1 child, David. Head Fellowship Found., Inc. (also callled Internat. Found.), Arlington, Va. Founder Nat. Prayer Breakfast. Named one of 25 Most Influential Evangelicals in America, Time Magazine, 2005. Christian. Office: Fellowship Found 2145 N 24th St Arlington VA 22207 Office Phone: 703-536-6591.*

COE, EMMA A., finance educator; d. Maximo L. Almo and Gliceria de Veyra Tarrius; m. Armando Sy; 1 child, Armando Co Jr. BS in Commerce, Banking & Fin./Bus. Mgmt., Divine Word U., Tacloban City, 1962; BA in English, Divine Word U., 1962, MA in English, 1981, MBA, 1981. Cert. bus. mgmt. LA Cmty. Coll., 1989, English LA Cmty. Coll., 1989, vocational edu. tchg. Calif. Commn. Tchr. Credentialing, 1999, ESL LA Cmty. Coll., 1990, authorization svc. Bur. Pvt. Postsecondary & Vocat. Edn., 2005, small-scale industries Ateneo de Manila U., TESOL Victoria U., Wellington, New Zealand. Instr. Divine Word U., Tacloban, Leyte, Philippines, 1962—79, chmn. banking & fin., 1979—81, registrar, 1981—82, chmn. bus. mgmt./banking & fin. depts., 1982—85; sec. pub. adminstrn. office Calif. State U., Dominguez Hills, Carson, 1985—87; mktg. sec. Arthur B. Laffer & Assocs., Lomita, Calif., 1987—89; instr., evening coord. Am. Bus. Inst., LA, 1989—91; sr. word processor Seeley Co., Diamond Bar, Calif., 1991—95; instr. United Edn. Inst., Huntington Park, Calif., 1996—98; bus. instr. Monterey Pk. Coll., Calif., 1997—2004; gen. edn. on campus instr. ITT Technical Inst., San Dimas, Calif., 2003—; online adj. prof. Mt. Sierra Coll., Monrovia, 2005—07. Organizer, resource spkr. Bur. Domestic Trade, Tacloban, 1972—74; barangay elected sec. Barangay Nula-Tula, Tacloban, 1973—75; tng. conf. spkr. Local Police Commn., Tacloban, 1980—82; workshop resource spkr. Philippine Constabulary Seminars, Tacloban City, 1980—83; chmn. Roy Montejo deserving students' scholarship com. Divine Word U., 1983—83; chmn. scholarship com. Leyte-Samar Civic Orgn., LA, 1987—88. Chmn. scholarship com. Leyte-Samar Assn., LA, 1989—90; donor Gliceria Tarrius Scholarship, Tacloban, 1985, Tarrius Sisters' Academic Scholarship, Tacloban, 1990. Named one of Top 10 Tchrs. award, Divine Word U., 1980; recipient Instr. of Month award, ITT, 2007.

COE, FREDRIC L., internist, educator, researcher; b. Chgo, Dec. 25, 1936; s. Lester J. and Lillian (Chaitlen) C.; m. Eleanor Joyce Brodny, May 5, 1965; children: Brian, Laura. AB, U. Chgo., 1955, MS, 1957, MD, 1961. Diplomate Am. Bd. Internal Medicine. Intern Michael Reese Hosp., Chgo., 1961-62, resident, 1962-65, U. Tex. S.W. Med. Sch., 1967-69; chmn. nephrology Michael Reese Hosp., 1972-82; prof. medicine U. Chgo., 1977—, prof. physiology, 1979—; chmn. nephrology A.M. Billings Hosp., Chgo., 1982—; founder, pres. Litholink Corp., 1995—. Author: Nephrolithiasis, 1978, 2d edit. (with J. Parks), 1987, (with B. Brenner and F.C. Rector) Renal Physiology, 1986, Clinical Nephrology; editor: Renal Therapeutics, 1978, Nephrolithiasis, 1980, Hypercalciuric States, 1983, (with M. Favus) Disorders of Bone and Mineral Metabolism, 1993, 2d edit., 2001; editor-in-chief Yearbook of Nephrology, 1991-96; editor: (with others) Kidney Stones: Medical and Surgical Management, 1996. Served to capt. USAF, 1961-67. Recipient Belding Scribner medal for lifetime achievement in clin. rsch. Am. Soc. Nephrology, 2000; Univ. of Chgo. Distingguished Svc. Award, 2001; grantee NIH, 1977-. Fellow ACP; mem. Am. Soc. Clin. Investigation, Am. Physiol. Soc., Assn. Am. Physicians Jewish. Achievements include first evidence for hyperuricosuria as cause of calcium renal stones; discovery of nephro calcin a protein inhibitor of crystal growth; first demonstration that human idiopathic hypercalciuria is hereditary. First evidence that apatite plaque begins inthe basement membranes of the renal thin limbs of Henle's loop. Home: 5490 S Shore Dr Chicago IL 60615-5984 Office: U Chgo Med Ctr 5841 S Maryland Ave Chicago IL 60637-1463 Office Phone: 773-702-1475. Business E-Mail: f-coe@uchicago.edu.

COE, JACK MARTIN, lawyer, consultant; b. Orange, NJ, 1945; AB, U. Va., Charlottesville, 1967; AM, Brown U., Providence, RI, 1969; cert., Oxford U., Eng., 1972; JD, U. Fla., Gainesville, 1975; cert., U. Nev., Reno, 1989. Bar: Fla. 1975, DC 1978, US Dist. Ct. (so. dist.) Fla. 1976, US Dist. Ct. (mid. dist.) Fla. 1993, US Ct. Appeals (5th cir.) 1976, US Ct. Appeals (11th cir.) 1981, US Supreme Ct. 1978; cert. family and cir. ct. mediator, Fla., 2002-, arbitrator, Fla., 2002-. Assoc. Adams, George, Wood, Lee & Schulte, 1975-77, Thomas E. Lee, Jr., P.A., 1977-78; shareholder Lee, Murphy & Coe, P.A., 1979-88; acting circuit judge, county court judge Dade County, Fla., 1988-93; shareholder Fowler, White, Burnett, Hurley, Banick & Strickroot, P.A., 1993-94; of counsel Silver & Garvett, P.A., 1994-2000; pvt. practice Coral Gables, Fla., 2000—. Mem. civil rules com. County Court Judges Conf., 1988-92, criminal rules com., 1988-92; lectr. Bridge the Gap seminar, 1988; lectr. on various circuit and county court practices and procedures; chair Dade County Bar Civil Litigation Com., 1993-1996; judicial mentor, apptd. by Fla. Supreme Ct., 1990-91. Mem. Coral Gables Planning and Zoning Bd., Fla., 1993-2001, 06—, Hist. Preservation Bd., 1993, Code Enforcement Bd., 2001-06. Mem. Bar Assn. (appellate rules com. 1986-90, appellate practice and advocacy sect. 1993—), Fla. Acad. Profl. Mediators, Peter T. Fay Am. Inns of Ct. (bencher), Kiwanis (bd. dirs. 1989-92, Key Club chmn. 1989-92), Federalist Soc., Nat. Lawyer Honor Soc. Avocations: golf, hunting, fishing. Office: The Law Ctr 3081 Salzedo St SE 301 Coral Gables FL 33134 Office Phone: 305-445-3200. Personal E-mail: coejack@bellsouth.net.

COE, MICHAEL DOUGLAS, retired anthropologist; b. NYC, May 14, 1929; s. William Rogers and Clover (Simonton) Coe; m. Sophie Dobzhansky, June 5, 1955; children: Nicholas, Andrew, Sarah, Peter, Natalie. AB, Harvard, 1950, PhD, 1959. Asst. prof. U. Tenn., 1958-60; mem. faculty Yale U., 1960—, prof. anthropology, 1968-90, Charles J. MacCurdy prof. anthropology, 1990-94, prof. emeritus, 1994—. Adviser Robert Woods Bliss Collection Pre-Columbian Art, Dumbarton Oaks, Harvard, 1963—80. Author: La Victoria, An Early Site on the Pacific Coast of Guatemala, 1961, Mexico, 1962, The Jaguar's Children: Pre-Classic Art of Central Mexico, 1965, The Maya, 1966, America's First Civilization, 1968, The Maya Scribe and His World, 1973, Classic Maya Pottery at Dumbarton Oaks, 1975, Lords of the Underworld, 1978, Young Lords and Old Gods, 1982, Breaking the Maya Code, 1992, Angkor and the Khmer Civilization, 2003, Final Report, An Archaeologist Excavates His Past, 2006, The Line of Forts, Historical Archaeology on the Colonial Frontier of Massachusetts, 2006; author: (with Kent V. Flannery) Early Cultures and Human Ecology in South Coastal Guatemala, 1967; author: (with Richard A. Diehl) In the Land of the Olmec, 1980; author: (with Dean R. Snow and Elizabeth P. Benson) Atlas of Ancient America, 1986; author: (with Sophie D. Coe) The True History of Chocolate, 1996; author: (with Justin Kerr) The Art of the Maya Scribe, 1998; author: (with Mark Van Stone) Reading the Maya Glyphs, 2001; contbr. articles to profl. jours. Chmn. bd. dirs. Planting Fields Found., 1985—; pres. Heath Hist. Soc., Mass., 1984—90. Recipient Tatiana Proskouriakoff award, Harvard U., 1989, James D. Burke prize in fine arts, St. Louis Art Mus., 2001, Order of Quetzal award, Rep. Guatemala, 2005, Orden del Pop, Popol Vuh Mus., Guatemala, 2006. Fellow: Royal Anrthop. Soc.; mem.: NAS, Conn. Acad. Scis. and Engring., Conn. Acad. Arts and Scis., Anglers Club N.Y., Limestone Trout Club, Sigma Xi. Home: 376 St Ronan St New Haven CT 06511-2251 Home Phone: 203-562-7956. Personal E-mail: olmecC@aol.com.

COE, RODNEY MICHAEL, medical educator; b. Marquette, Mich., Nov. 10, 1933; s. Roy Arthur and Renee Adelaide (Reeder) C.; m. Elaine Elwell, Sept. 6, 1954; children: Kevin Elwell, Curtis Daniel, Andrea, Douglas Arthur. BS, Iowa State Coll., 1955; MA, So. Ill. U., 1959; PhD, Wash. U., 1962. From asst. to assoc. prof. Wash. U., St. Louis, 1962-70; from assoc. prof. to prof. St. Louis U., 1970—, chmn. cmty. and family medicine, 1989—, prof. emeritus, 1999. Exec. dir. Med. Care Rsch. Ctr., St. Louis, 1963-73; vis. prof. L.Am. Faculty Social Scis., Santiago, Chile, 1969-70; cons. Chilton Rsch. Svcs., Radnor, Pa., 1970-79, NIH, Bethesda, Md., 1976—. Author: Sociology of Medicine, 1970, and eighteen others; contbr. articles to profl. jours. Mem. Health Care for the Homeless, St. Louis, 1985—; mem., past pres. SSM Rehab. Inst., St. Louis, 1968—. Capt. U.S. Army, 1956-58. Recipient Geriatric Leadership Acad. award NIH, 1986-92; grantee NIH, Dept. Vets. Affairs, pvt. funds. Avocations: swimming, golf.

COE, SUE, artist, journalist; b. Tamworth, England, 1951; Grad., Royal Coll. Art, London, 1973. Illustrator Time Magazine, N.Y. Times. Exhibitions include Thumb Gallery, 1979, Moira Kelly Fine Art, London, 1982, P.P.O.W. Gallery, 1982, 1985, Contemporary Art Ctr., 1986, Phyllis Kind Gallery, 1986, Anderson Gallery, Commonwealth U., Knight Gallery, Portland Art Mus., Wesleyan U., Contemporary Arts Mus., Ohio State U., San Francisco Art Inst., 1987, City Gallery of Contemporary Art, 1988, Mus. Modern Art, 1989, Oxford, Eng., 1989, Cornerhouse, Manchester, Eng., 1989, Orchard Gallery, Derry, Ireland, 1989, Herbert Art Gallery, Coventry, Eng., 1989, Galerie St. Etienne, 1989, Joan Whitney Payson Gallery of Art, Portland, Maine, 1990—91, Ind. U. Fine Arts, 1990—91, U. Mo., 1990—91, Wash. State U., 1990—91, Inter Am. Art Gallery, 1990—91, Miami Dade CC, 1990—91, Ga. State U. Art Gallery, 1990—91, Santa Monica Mus. Art, 1990—91, Brody's Gallery, 1990, 1994, Md. Art Place, 1993, Hirschhorn Mus., 1994, Galerie St. Etienne, 1992, 1994, 1996, 1999, 2000—01, NYC, 2005, Mead Art Mus., Amherst Coll., Mass., 1993, Mesa Coll. Gallery, 1995, Salt Lake City Art Ctr., 1996, Nelson Fine Arts Ctr., Ariz. State U. Art Mus., 1996—99, U. Ill., 1996—99, Guilfort Coll. Art Gallery, 1996—99, Tacoma Art Mus., 1996—99, Lewis and Clark U., William Benton Mus. Art, 2000—01, Tyler Art Gallery, 2002, David Winton Bell Gallery, 2002, Ctr. Contemporary Art, 2003, Fairbanks Gallery, Oreg., 2004, Overtones Gallery, Calif., 2004, Galerie St. Etienne, NY, 2005, Emmannuel Gallery, Denver, 2006, Pacific Northwest Coll. of Art, Portland, 2007, exhibited in group shows at Am. Inst. Graphic Arts, 1977, Georges Pompidou Ctr., 1978, U.N. HQ, 1980, P.S.1, LI, 1984, Avery Arts Ctr., 1984, San Francisco Mus. Art, 1984, Holly Solomon Gallery, 1985, Mus. Modern Art, Italy, 1985, Art Inst. Chgo., 1986, LA County Mus. Art, 1987, Mus. Modern Art, NYC, 1988, Duke U., 1991, Drawing Ctr., NYC, 1992, Katonah Mus., 1992, Hood Mus., 1992, Montgomery Mus. Fine Art, 1992, Walker Art Ctr., 1993, Inst. Contemporary Art, 1993, Valentine Mus., 1993, Anacostia Mus., 1993, Nexus Contemporary Art Ctr., 1993, Ctr. Arts Yerba Buena, 1993, Md. Art Pl., 1993, Meud Art Mus., Amheart Coll., Mass., 1993, Mus. Modern Art, NYC, 1996, 1997, 2001, Galerie St. Etienne, NY, 2000, 2004, Colgate U., Hamilton, NY, 2001, St. Lawrence U., Canton, NY, 2002, Neue Galerie am landes Museum Jeanneum, Graz, Austria, 2003, Lois & Richard Rosenthal Ctr. for Contemporary Art, Cin., 2004, Parker's Box, Bklyn., 2004, The Katherine K. Herberger Coll. of Fine Arts, Tempe, Ariz., 2004, Grey Art Gallery, NY, 2005, at Andy Warhol Mus., Pitts., 2006, at Austin Mus. Art, 2007. Represented in permanent collections Galerie St. Etienne; author: (books) How to Commit Suicide in South Africa, 1983, Paintings and Drawings, 1985, X (The Life and Times of Malcom X), 1986, Dead Meat, 1996, Pits Letter, 2000, Bully: Master of the Global Merry-Go-Round, 2004, Sheep of Fools.A Song Cycle for 5 Voices, 2005, (exhbn. catalogue) Police State, 1987. Named National Academician, 1994. Office: Galerie St Etienne 24 West 57th Street New York NY 10019

COE, TUCKER See WESTLAKE, DONALD

COELHO, SANDRA SIGNORELLI, secondary school educator, consultant, elementary school educator; b. Torrington, Conn., Nov. 19, 1940; d. Ernest J. and Linda M. (Zanolli) Signorelli; m. Walter S. Coelho, July 11, 1964. BS, Cen. Conn. State U., 1962, MS, 1969; cert. intermediate adminstrn., Cen. Conn. State, 1980; PhD, Richmonds U., 2006. Tchr. Torrington Bd. Edn., 1962-65; K-12 tech./math. coord. East Windsor (Conn.) Bd. Edn., 1965—2002; cons. Enfield Town Hall, 2002, Conn. Acad., 2003—04, PIMMS, 2003—; assoc. dir. math PIMMS Wesley U., 2004—. Assistive tech. task force State of Conn.; presenter C.A.B.E.; cons. Town of Enfield, Conn. Acad.; co-pres. CCLM, 2005; ednl. reviewer Corwin Press. Chmn. townwide curriculum com. East Windsor; chmn. East Windsor Tech. Com. Recipient Golden Apple award; BEST Mentor-Assessor; Apple Computer scholar; PIMMS fellow. Mem. NEA, Conn. Edn. Assn., Conn. Educators Computing Assn. (adviser), Conn. Coun. Leaders Math. (pres.), East Windsor Edn. Assn. (past pres.), Atomic (sec. exec. bd., past chmn. ann. meeting), Coun. for Leaders of Math, Pi Lambda Theta, Phi Delta Kappa (exec. bd.), Delta Kappa Gamma (past v.p. Rho chpt., cons. edn. & tech.) Home and Office: 50 Smalley Rd Windsor Locks CT 06096-1134 Office Phone: 860-685-6466. Personal E-mail: sandrac101@aol.com, scoelho4@cox.net. Business E-Mail: scoelho@wesleyan.edu. *Think about what you do before you decide to do it. People are most important. Try to do what you believe in and proceed in a respectful manner on your own merits and not at the expense of others.*

COEN, JESSICA, blog writer, editor; Grad., U. Mich., 2002. Tchr. South LA HS, Teach for America; exec. asst. major TV studio; editor Gawker-.com, Gawker Media, NY, 2004—06; dep. online editor Vanity Fair mag., NYC, 2006—. Blog writer (personal blog site) jessicacoen.com, freelance writer NY Times, NY Observer, NY Post, ELLE, guest appearances Today Show, Topic A with Tina Brown. Named one of 100 Media People You Need to Know for 2005, Media Mag. Office: Vanity Fair Online Conde Nat Publications 4 Times Sq 7th Floor New York NY 10036 Office Phone: 212-286-2860.*

COERPER, MILO GEORGE, lawyer, priest; b. Milw., May 8, 1925; s. Milo Wilson and Rose (Schubert) Coerper; m. Lois Hicks, Apr. 11, 1953; children: Milo Wilson, Allison Lee, Lois Paddock. BS, U.S. Naval Acad., 1946; LLB, U. Mich., 1954; MA, Georgetown U., 1957, PhD, 1960. Bar: DC 1954, Md. 1960. Pvt. practice, Washington; assoc. Wilmer & Broun, 1954-60; with Coudert Bros. Assoc., 1961—63, ptnr., 1964—96, ret., 1996—; ordained deacon Episcopal Ch., 1978, priest, 1979. Cathedral chaplain Washington Nat. Cathedral, 1986—. Contbr. articles to profl. jours. Trustee, vice chmn. U.S. Canterbury Cathedral Trust Am., 1982—97, acting chmn., 1991, 1997; mem. coun. Friends Canterbury Cathedral US, 1999—2005, trustee, 2005—. Ensign USN, 1946—49, served to lt. USN, 1951—53. Recipient Cross of the Order of Merit of Fed. Rep. of Germany, Pres. Dr. Richard von Weizsacker, 1993. Mem.: ABA, Internat. Assn. Protection Indsl. Property, Am. Soc. Internat. Law, Am. Law Inst., Md. State Bar Assn., Bar Assn. DC, Chevy Chase Club, Met. Club (pres. 1986), Army and Navy Club. Home: 7315 Brookville Rd Chevy Chase MD 20815-4057 Office Phone: 202-857-6208. Personal E-mail: wmcoerp@verizon.net.

COEY, JOHN MICHAEL DAVID, physicist, educator; b. Belfast, Northern Ireland, Feb. 24, 1945; s. David Stuart Coey and Joan Elizabeth Newsam; m. Wong May, Sept. 1, 1973; children: James, Dominic. BA, Cambridge U., Eng., 1966; PhD, U. Man., Can., 1971; diplôme d'habilitation, INPG, Grenoble, France, 1986; ScD, U. Dublin, Ireland, 1987; D (hon.), Institut Nat. Poly., Grenoble, 1994. With CNRS, Grenoble, 1971—78, attaché de recherché, 1972—75, chargé de recherché, 1975; with IBM, Yorktown Heights, 1976—77; lectr. Trinity Coll., Dublin, 1978—81, assoc. prof., 1981—87, prof., 1987—, head dept., 1991—94, dep. dir. Centre Rsch. Adaptive Nanostructure and Nanodevices, 2004—. Vis. prof. IBM, Yorktown Heights, 1979, Inst. Physics, Peking, 1980, McGill U., 1982, U. Bordeaux, 1984, CEN, Grenoble, 1985, Johs Hopkins, 1986, U. Paris VI, 1992, U. Calif., San Diego, 1997, Fla. State U., 1998, U. Paris XI, 1998, Le Mans U., 1999, 2001, 03; chmn. IUPAP Commn. Magnetism, 2002—05, Joint European Magnetics Symposium, 2001—06; mem. acad. com. Magnetism Lab. CAS, Peking; mem. various rev. panels. Contbr. articles to profl. jours. Fellow, Trinity Coll. Dublin, 1982; grantee, EU, 1966—2000, 1985—95, 1995—98, SFI, 2001—; Fulbright fellow, 1997. Fellow: Royal Soc., Am. Phys. Soc., Am. Mineral. Soc., Inst. Physics (Charles Cree medal and prize 1997); mem.: NAS (fgn. assoc. 2005), Royal Irish Acad. (Gold medal 2005). Achievements include research in magnetic, electronic and structural properties of solids; spin electronics; magnetoelectrochemistry; amorphous materials; physical properties of minerals; permanent magnet applications. Avocation: gardening. Office: Trinity Coll Sch Physics Dublin 2 Ireland Business E-Mail: jcoey@tcd.ie.

COEYTAUX, REMY RENE, physician, researcher; s. Paul Alfred and Sylvia Nelly Coeytaux; m. Kristen DiMambro Coeytaux, June 30, 1990; children: Alex Arthur, Ethan Arthur. AB, Brown U., Providence, RI, 1986; MD, Stanford U., Calif., 1992—96; PhD, U. N.C., Chapel Hill, 2004. Lic. physician NC Med. Bd., 1999. Asst. prof. family medicine U. N.C. Sch. of Medicine, Chapel Hill, 2001—; founder Integrated Health Ctr., Chapel Hill. Dir. clin. trials program U. N.C. Dept. of Family Medicine, 2003—. Office: Univ NC Manning Dr Chapel Hill NC 27599 Business E-Mail: remy_coeytaux@med.unc.edu.

COFER, JONATHAN H., career officer; b. Pa., July 13, 1950; Commd. 2d lt. U.S. Army, 1972, advanced through grades to brig. gen., 1998; dir. joint rear area coord. U.S. Ctrl. Command, MacDill AFB, Fla., 1998—2000; dep. dir. ops., combating terrorism U.S. Army, Washington, 2000—02; sr. exec. v.p. MZM Inc., Washington, 2002—. Office: MZM Inc 1523 New Hampshire Ave NW Washington DC 20036

COFFARO, STEVEN C., lawyer; b. Cin., July 31, 1970; BA, Miami U., 1992; JD, U. Cin. Law, 1995. Bar: Ohio 1995, US Dist. Ct. Southern Dist. Ohio 1995, Ky. 1996, Ind. 1997, US Dist. Ct. Northern Dist. Ind. 1997, US Dist. Ct. Southern Dist. Ind. 1997, US Dist. Ct. Western Dist. Ky. 1998, US Dist. Eastern Dist. Ky. 1998, US Ct. of Appeals Sixth Cir. 2002, US Dist. Ct. Northern Dist. Ohio 2005, US Ct. of Appeals Second Cir. 2005. Ptnr. Keating Muething & Klekamp PLL, Cin. Involved with St. Xavier High Sch. Named Leading Lawyer, Cincy Bus. Mag., 2005, 2006; named one of Ohio's Rising Stars, Super Lawyers, 2006. Mem.: St. Francis Xavier Soc., Ohio State Bar Assn., Ky. Bar Assn., Ind. State Bar Assn., Cin. Bar Assn., ABA, Order of Coif. Office: Keating Muething & Klekamp PLL One E Fourth St Ste 1400 Cincinnati OH 45202 Office Phone: 513-579-6400. Office Fax: 513-579-6457.

COFFEE, JOHN COLLINS, JR., legal educator; b. Albany, NY, Nov. 15, 1944; s. John Collins and Mary E. (Morse) C.; 1 dau., Megan Purcell. BA, Amherst Coll., 1966; LLB, Yale U., 1969; LLM in Taxation, NYU, 1976. Bar: N.Y. 1970, U.S. Dist. Cts. (so. and ea. dists.) N.Y. 1974, U.S. Ct. Appeals (2d cir.) 1974, D.C. 1980. Assoc. Cravath, Swaine & Moore, NYC, 1970-76; assoc. prof. law Georgetown U. Law Ctr., Washington, 1976-79; vis. prof. U. Va. Law Sch., Charlottesville, 1978, U. Mich. Law Sch., 1979; Adolph A. Berle prof. law Columbia U. Law Sch., NYC, 1980—; vis. prof. Harvard Law Sch., 2001. Vis. prof. Stanford U. Law Sch., Palo Alto, Calif., 1987. Author: (with others) Knights, Raiders, and Targets: The Impact of the Hostile Takeover, 1988, Business Organization and Finance, 5th edit., 1995, Cases and Materials on Securities Regulation, 8th edit., 1998, Cases and Materials on Corporations, 4th edit., 1995. Contbr. articles to legal jours. Mem. panel on sentencing research Nat. Acad. Scis., 1980-83; mem. SEC Adv. Com. on Capital Formation, 1995-96, Subcoun. on Capital Markets, U.S. Competitiveness Policy Coun., 1994, Standong Com. On Law and Justice Nat. Rsch. Coun., 1992-95; legal adv. com. N.Y. Stock Exch., NADS, 1996—; gen. coun. Am. Econ. Assn.; mem. legal advb. bd. NASD; mem. market regulation com. NASD Regulation, Inc.; mem. adv. bd. LENS, Inc.; mem. standong com. on law and justice NAS. Reginald Heber Smith fellow, 1969-70; named one of 100 Most Influential Lawyers, Nat. Law Jour., 2006. Fellow AAAS, Am. Bar Found.; mem. Am. Law Inst. (reporter project on corp. governance), ABA (reporter minimum standards for criminal justice), Am. Assn. law Sch. (chmn. sect. on bus. assns. 1981-82, chmn. com. on sects. 1984-85, chmn. audit com.), Assn. Bar City of N.Y. (com. on securities laws 1981-92). Office: Columbia U Sch Law 435 W 116th St New York NY 10027-7201 E-mail: jcoffee@law.columbia.edu.*

COFFEE, JOSEPH DENIS, JR., retired college chancellor; b. Glens Falls, NY, Dec. 8, 1918; s. Joseph Denis and Kathryne Grace (Dwyer) C.; m. Margaret Mary Jennings, Oct. 7, 1941 (dec. Aug. 1998); children: John Allan (dec.), James Jennings, Mary Joyce Coffee, Barbara Grace Coffee Wolf, Matthew Brian, Margaret Erin Coffee Giovannini, Ann Ellen Coffee Beach. AB, Columbia U., 1941. Asst. to gen. sec. Columbia U., NYC, 1946-50, dir. devel., 1950-60, founder corp. matching gift program of alumni support, 1953, assoc. dean, 1959-60, asst. to pres. for alumni affairs, 1960-66; v.p. Eisenhower Coll., Seneca Falls, N.Y., 1966-69, exec. v.p., 1969-76, acting pres., 1975-76, pres., 1976-80, chancellor, 1980-81, chancellor emeritus, 1981—. Dir. scholarship program Joint Industry Bd., Elec. Industry of N.Y., 1947-81; exec. sec. Com. for Corporate Support Am. Univs., 1962-64 Chmn. March Dimes campaign, Closter, N.J., 1953; active Boy Scouts Am.; former treas., dir. Anglo-Am. Hellenic Bur. Edn.; pres. Seneca County United Way, 1973-75; Chmn. Teaneck Polit. Assembly, 1967-68; Trustee Teaneck Bd. Edn., 1961-64, 65-68, Columbia U., 1978-84; bd. dirs. Nat. Women's Hall of Fame. Served from ensign to lt. comdr. USNR, 1941-46. Mem.: Seneca Falls Hist. Soc. (past trustee), Rotary (past pres. Seneca Falls, Paul Harris fellow 1988, 2002). Roman Catholic.

COFFEE, VIRGINIA CLAIRE, civic worker, former mayor; b. Alliance, Nebr., Dec. 8, 1920; d. James Maddigan and Adelaide Mary (Forde) Kennedy; m. Bill Brown Coffee, June 21, 1942; children: Claire, Sara, Virginia Anne, Sue. BS, Chadron State Coll., Nebr., 1942. Prin. Whitman (Nebr.) H.S., 1942; bookkeeper Coffee & Son, Inc., Harrison, Nebr., 1965—, officer, 1967, pres., 1987-97, v.p., 1998—2005, pres., 2005—; dir. Friends of Agate Fossil Beds, Inc., Harrison, 1988, v.p., 1988-2001. Chmn. compilation com. book Sioux County Memoirs of Its Pioneers, 1967; coord. Harrison sect. book Nebraska Our Towns, 1988. Mayor City of Harrison, 1978-80; leader Girl Scouts U.S.A., 1953-63; sch. bd. Harrison Elem., 1958-64; liason com. Chadron State Coll., 1975, pub. rels. chmn.

Nebr. Cowbelles, 1968; hon gov. Nebr. Centennial, 1967; sec. NW Stock Growers, 1971-73; corp. officer Ft. Robinson Centennial, 1973-88; officer Gov's Ft. Robinson Centennial Commn., 1973-75; chmn. Sioux County Bicentennial, 1973-77; trustee Nebr. State Hist. Soc. Found., 1975—, Village of Harrison, 1973-80; bd. dirs. Chadron State Coll. Found., 1996—, sec., 2003; bd. dirs. Harrison Cmty. Club, Inc., 1983-86, officer, 1984-86; bd. dirs. Running Water Ranching Coalition, 2005—; apptd. Sioux County Vis. Com. 1989-2003, adm. Nebr. Navy, 1992; com. for marker to honor Harrison Centennial 1985-86; mem. Sioux County History Book Com. 1985-86 Recipient Disting. Svc. award, Chadron State Coll., 1994. Mem. Nebr. State Hist. Soc. (life, dir. 1979-85, 2d v.p. 1982-84, 1st v.p. 1984-85), Wyo. State Hist. Soc., Sioux County Hist. Soc. (life, bd. dirs. 1975-81, 83-84, 87-90, 97-2003, pres. 1988-90, co-pres., 2d v.p.), Nebr. Cattle Women, Harrison Cmty. Inc., Cardinal Key. Roman Catholic. Address: PO Box 336 Harrison NE 69346-0336

COFFEY, CHARLES MOORE, communication research professional, writer; b. Chgo., July 8, 1941; s. Charles Adams and Helen Marie (Moore) C. BA in Econs., Beloit Coll., 1963; postgrad., Purdue U., 1980. WDBJ radio and TV reporter Times-World Corp., Roanoke, Va., 1964-65; reporter, anchor, prodr. WHAS AM FM TV, Louisville, 1967-72; asst. to chancellor Ind. U. S.E., New Albany, 1972-77; dir. spl. events Ind. U., Bloomington, 1977-82; dir. alumni affairs Ind. U.-Purdue U., Indpls., 1982-88; comm. advisor Bayh-O'Bannon Campaign, Indpls., 1988; comm. asst. Lt. Gov. of Ind., Indpls., 1989-97; dir. comm. rsch. Ind. Dept. Adminstrn., Indpls., 1997—2005. Lt. gov.'s rep. Intelenet Commn., Indpls., 1990-97, gov.'s rep., 1997-2004; gov.'s rep. Enhanced Data Access Rev. Com., Indpls., 1997-2005 Contbr. articles to profl. jours. Pres. Coun. for Retarded Children, Clark County, Ind., 1975—76, Bloomington Restorations; chmn. Clark-Floyd Conv. Bur., Jeffersonville, Ind., 1977; bd. dirs. YMCA Greater Indpls., 1989—95, 1997—98, 2000—03, 2004—05, sec. bd., 1998—2000, trustee, 1999—2004. With USAF, 1963. Recipient AP award for comprehensive reporting Va. AP Broadcasters, 1964-65. Mem. Internat. Assn. Protocol Cons., Soc. Profl. Journalists. Democrat. Home: 3922 Alsace Pl Indianapolis IN 46226-5413 Home Phone: 317-848-3728; Office Phone: 317-752-0234. Personal E-mail: ccoffey2@indy.rr.com.

COFFEY, JAMES FRANCIS, lawyer; b. Lewiston, Maine, Aug. 8, 1962; s. Thomas Francis and Mary Ann (Amnott) C.; m. Christina Beau Coursen, June 17, 1995; children: Bridget Catherine, Caroline Claire, Meredith Coursen. BA, Providence Coll., 1984; JD, New Eng. Sch. Law, Boston, 1988; LLM, NYU, 1989. Bar: Mass. 1988, U.S. Dist. Ct. Mass. 1990, U.S. Ct. Appeals (1st cir.) 1990, D.C. 1991. Assoc. Boroff & Assocs., Boston, 1989-93; ptnr. Coffey & Shea, Boston, 1993-97, Curran, Coffey & Tavenner, LLP, Boston, 1997-99, Curran, Coffey & Moran, LLP, Boston, 1999—, Verrill Dana, LLP, Boston, 2006—. Lectr., panel chair Mass. Continuing Legal Edn., Inc., Boston, 1992—; adj. prof. corp. fin. New Eng. Sch. Law, 2001-05. Mem. Mass. Pub. Edn. Nominating Coun.; gen. counsel Mass. Rep. Party, 2006—. Recipient Gerald L. Wallace Scholarship NYU, N.Y.C., 1988. Mem. ABA (bus. law divsn.), D.C. Bar, Mass. Bar Assn. (bus. law sect. 1989—), Boston Bar Assn., Boston Racquet Club. Roman Catholic. Avocations: history, golf, squash, skiing. Office: Verrill Dana LLP One Boston Pl Boston MA 02108 Office Phone: 617-309-2600.

COFFEY, JOHN LOUIS, federal judge; b. Milw., Apr. 15, 1922; s. William Leo and Elizabeth Ann (Walsh) Coffey; m. Marion Kunzelmann, Feb. 3, 1951; children: Peter, Elizabeth Mary Coffey-Robbins. BA, Marquette U., 1943, JD, 1948; MBA (hon.), Spencerian Coll., 1964, D (hon.) in Bus., 1973. Bar: Wis. 1948, US Dist. Ct. 1948, US Supreme Ct. 1980. Asst. city atty. City of Milw., 1949—54; judge Civil Ct., Milw. County, 1954—60, Milw. County Mcpl. Ct., 1960—62; judge criminal divsn. Cir. Ct., Milw. County, 1962—72, sr. judge criminal divsn., 1972—75, chief presiding judge criminal divsn., 1976, judge civil divsn., 1976—78; justice Wis. Supreme Ct., Madison, 1978—82; judge US Ct. Appeals (7th cir.), Chgo., 1982—2004, sr. judge, 2004—. Mem. Wis. Bd. Criminal Ct. Judges, 1960—78, Wis. Bd. Circuit Ct. Judges, 1962—78. Mem. adv. bd. St. Mary's Hosp., 1964—70; mem. Milw. County com. Boy Scouts Am., 1970—78; chmn. vol. svcs. adv. com. Milw. County Dept. Pub. Welfare, 1970—72; chmn. St. Eugene's Sch. Bd., 1967—70; pres. St. Eugene's Ch. Coun., 1974; bd. dirs., mem. exec. bd. Milw.-Waukesha chpt. ARC; chmn. adv. bd. St. Joseph's Home for Children, 1958—65. With USNR, 1943—46. Named Outstanding Young Man of Yr., Milw. Jr. C. of C., 1951, 1 of 5 Outstanding Young Men of Yr., Jr. C. of C., Wis. State, 1957; recipient Outstanding Law Alumnus of Yr. award, Marquette U., 1980, Merit award, Marquette U. Alumni Assn., 1985, Alumni Merit award, Marquette U. HS, 2001. Fellow: Am. Bar Found.; mem.: State Bar Assn. Wis., Ill. State Bar Assn., 7th Cir. Bar Assn., Marquette U. Law Alumni Assn. (Disting. Profl. Achievement Merit award 1985), Marquette U. M Club (former dir.), Nat. Lawyers Club, Am. Legion (Disting. Svc. award 1973), Alpha Sigma Nu (Marquette U. chpt.), Phi Alpha Delta (hon.). Roman Catholic. *I have tried to the best of my ability to render justice to all and remember that "We are a country of laws, not of men" and while protecting the individual's rights I have not lost sight of the common good of all mankind and cautioned each and every one who appeared before me that with every right there is a corresponding obligation.**

COFFEY, JOHN P. (SEAN COFFEY), lawyer; b. Bronx, NY, July 15, 1956; BS with merit in Ocean Engring., US Naval Acad., Annapolis, Md., 1978; JD magna cum laude, Georgetown U., 1987. Bar: NY 1988, US Dist. Ct. (so. dist. NY) 1989, US Ct. Appeals (2nd cir.) 1992, US Dist. Ct. (we. dist. NY) 1995, US Dist. Ct. (ea. dist. NY) 1998, NJ 1999, US Dist. Ct. (dist. NJ) 1999. Asst. US atty. (so. dist. NY) US Dept. Justice, 1991—95; ptnr. litig. Latham & Watkins; ptnr. class action litig., securities litig. Bernstein, Litowitz, Berger & Grossmann, LLP, NYC, 1998—. Adj. prof. Fordham U. Law Sch., 1993—94. Articles editor: Georgetown Law Jour. Served USN, 1978—86, served to Capt. USNR, 1986—2004. Named an Top 10 Trial Lawyers in Am., Nat. Law Jour., 2005. Mem.: ABA, Assn. Bar City of NY, Order of the Coif. Office: Bernstein Litowitz Berger & Grossmann LLP 1285 Ave of the Americas New York NY 10019 Office Phone: 212-554-1409. Office Fax: 212-554-1444. E-mail: sean@blbglaw.com.*

COFFEY, JOSEPH IRVING, political scientist, educator; b. St. Louis, Feb. 13, 1916; s. Joseph Aloysius and Catherine Elizabeth (Burns) C.; m. Marjorie Ann Strode, Nov. 15, 1939 (div. 1963); m. Rosemary Klineberg, June 28, 1963 (div. 1976); m. Maryann Bishop, May 13, 1978; children: John Patrick, Catherine Elizabeth, Judith Ann, Megan Forbes, Susan Fox, James Odell; 1 stepchild, Janet Lynn Bishop. BS, U.S. Mil. Acad., 1939; postgrad., Columbia U., 1943-45; PhD in Internat. Relations, Georgetown U., 1954. Asst. dir. programs, spl. studies project Rockefeller Bros. Fund, 1956-57; exec. asst. to spl. asst. to Pres. for security ops. coordination, Washington, 1958-60; mem. staff Pres.'s Com. on Info. Activities Abroad, White House, 1960; rsch. analyst Inst. for Def. Analyses, Washington, 1960-63; chief office of nat. security studies Bendix Systems div., Ann Arbor, Mich., 1963-67; prof. pub. and internat. affairs U. Pitts., 1967-80, Disting. Svc. prof., 1980-82, prof. emeritus, 1982—, dir. Ctr. for Internat. Security Studies, 1975-81; sr. rsch. fellow Univ. Ctr. Internat. Studies, 1981-90; vis. prof. internat. peace and security studies Carnegie-Mellon U., 1986-91. Adj. prof. Carnegie Mellon U., 1991—92; sr. vis. fellow Ctr. for Internat. Studies Princeton U., 1990—91, sr. rsch. assoc., 1993—95, vis. lectr. Woodrow Wilson Sch., 1992; cons. AID, ACDA, Dept. Def. Dept. State, Internat. Comm. Agy.; dir. program on religion and conflict resolution Tanenbaum Ctr. Interreligious Understanding, 1999—2001. Author/editor books in field including Strategic Power and National Security, 1971, Arms Control and European Security, 1977, Allied Perceptions of Threat, 1983, Deterrence and Arms Control: American and West German Perspectives on INF, 1985, The Atlantic Alliance and the Middle East, 1989, Defense and Détente: U.S. and West German Perspectives on Defense Policy, 1989, Germany, the EU and the Future of Europe, 1995, The Future Role of NATO, 1997, Religion, Law and the Role of Force, 2002. Served to col. U.S. Army, 1939-60. Internat. Inst. Strategic Studies rsch. assoc., 1972-73; Stockholm Internat. Peace Rsch. Inst. fellow, 1977, NATO rsch. fellow, 1981, 89 Mem.: Istituto Affari Internat. Home: 102 Marten Rd Princeton NJ 08540 Office Phone: 609-497-2882. E-mail: mbricec@aol.com.

COFFEY, LELA, advertising executive; b. 1972; m. Maurice Coffey, 2001; children: Mikaela, Mikenzi. Assoc. mktg. dir. Tampax Proctor & Gamble, 2004—. Named one of 40 Under 40, Advt. Age, 2007; recipient Silver Effie Award, Healthcare OTC Category, 2007. Office: Proctor & Gamble One Proctor & Gamble Plz Cincinnati OH 45202*

COFFEY, MATTHEW B., senior advisor to industry; b. Cumberland, Md., Jan. 20, 1941; s. Francis Wade and Mary Agnes (Stegmaier) C.; m. Sharon Harriet West, May 20, 1971; children: Julia Katherine West, Francis Matthew West. AA, Potomac State Coll., 1960; BS, W.Va. U., 1962, MBA, 1969. Investigator U.S. CSC, Washington, 1964-65; staff asst. to Pres. Johnson The White House, Washington, 1965-69; dir. planning Corp. for Pub. Broadcasting, Washington, 1969-73; dir. recruiting Carter-Mondale Transition, Washington, 1976-77; pres. Assn. of Pub. Radio Stas., Washington, 1973-77; sr. v.p. Nat. Pub. Radio, Washington, 1977; exec. v.p. Nat. Alliance of Bus., Washington, 1977-78; dir. Washington Office Textron, Inc., Washington, 1978-79; v.p., CFO Bridgeport-Textron, Bridgeport, Conn., 1979-83; exec. dir. Nat. Assn. Counties, Washington, 1983-85; pres. Nat. Tooling and Machining Assn., 1985—2005, Coffey & Co., 2005—. Bd. dirs. Coun. for Adult and Experiential Learning, 1996-97; co-chmn. Commn. on Workforce Skills in Indsl. Found. Firms, 1992-94; mem. Nat. Alliance Bus. Coun. on Work Force Excellence, 1992-97; mem. industry adv. bd. D.O.E. Labs., 1993-96. Author: Toward a Clinical Method of Executive Selection, 1969; pub. Precision Mag., 1992-96; contbr. articles to profl. jours. Chmn., bd. dirs. Pub. Interest Groups, Washington, 1985; bd. dirs. Bridgeport Econ. Devel. Corp., 1981-83, Naugatuck Valley Indsl. Devel. Com., 1980-83; chmn. Pvt. Industry Coun., Bridgeport, 1981-83; bd. govs. Nat. Cathedral Sch., 1988; mem. bldg. com. Washington Nat. Cathedral, 1989—, co-chair long range planning task group, 1994-98, chmn. bldg. com., 1998—; trustee Protestant Episcopal Cathedral Found., 1998-; prin. Ctr. for Excellence in Govt., 1988-98; bd. dirs. Small Bus. Legis. Coun., 1990—2005, chmn., 1998-99. Fellow Nat. Acad. Pub. Adminstrn., Congl. Country Club, Univ. Club. Home: PO Box 367 Marshall VA 20116 Office: 3602 Massachusetts Ave NW Washington DC 20007-1449 Office Phone: 202-329-2340. Personal E-mail: mattcoffey@earthlink.net. Business E-Mail: coffey&compnay@msn.com.

COFFEY, NANCY, real estate broker; b. Palm Springs, Calif. d. Arthur Johnson and Joan (Hunter) Coffey. BA, Stanford U., 1967, MS in Engring., 1977. Comml. broker Coldwell Banker, San Francisco, 1980-87, Cushman & Wakefield, NYC, 1987—90; model Gilla Roos, NYC, 1991—96; real estate broker, 1990-96; comml. real estate broker Rolfe Group, NYC, 1997—98, Cushman & Wakefield, Inc., NYC, 1998—2000, Halstead Property, NYC, 2001—. Active Jr. League, San Francisco, 1981—87, NYC, 1987—2000, sustainer, 1999—2000, Palo Alto Jr. League, 2000—01; mem. exec. com. NYC, 2003—05, mem. children's com., 2006—07; vice chair membership com. Soc. Meml. Sloan Kettering, 1999—2000, mem. adminstrv. bd., 2002—; v.p. Class of 1967 Stanford U.; parish life com. mem. St. James Ch., 1997—2000. Mem.: River Club NY, Rockaway Hunting Club. Achievements include first female industrial real estate broker in Houston. Home: Smoke Tree Ranch Palm Springs CA 92264 Office Phone: 212-381-3355.

COFFEY, PAUL, retired professional hockey player; b. Weston, Ont., Can., June 1, 1961; married; 3 children. Defenseman Edmonton Oilers, 1980-87, Pitts. Penguins, 1987-92, LA Kings, 1992, Detroit Red Wings, 1993-97, Phila. Flyers, 1997—98, Chgo. Blackhawks, 1998, Carolina Hurricanes, 1998—2000, Boston Bruins, 2000. Mem. Team Canada, Canada Cup, 1984, 87, 91, Team Canada, World Cup of Hockey, 1996; player NHL All-Star Game, 1982—86, 1988—94, 1996—97. Named to Second All-Star Team, NHL, 1982—84, 1990, First All-Star Team, 1985, 1986, 1989, 1995; recipient James Norris Meml. Trophy, 1985, 1986, 1995. Achievements include being a member of Stanley Cup Champion Edmonton Oilers, 1984, 1985, 1987, Pittsburgh Penguins, 1991; having his number 7 retired by the Edmonton Oilers, 2005; being inducted into the Hockey Hall of Fame, 2004. Office: Paul Coffey's Bolton Toyota 12050 Albion-Vaughan Rd Bolton ON Canada

COFFEY, SHARON MARIE, music educator; d. Billy Bolan and Audra LaVerne Hale; m. Loy Clark Coffey, Aug. 14, 1992; children: Richard Clark, Michael Bolan, Rachael Marie. B.Mus.Edn., Baylor U., Waco, Tex., 1987. Cert. txhr. Tex., 1987. Choir tchr. Garland Independent Sch. Dist., Tex., 1987—88, Irving Independent Sch. Dist., Tex., 1988—94, Navasota Independent Sch. Dist., Tex., 2004—. Pvt. voice instr., Navasota, 1994—2004; music minister New Hope Cmty. Ch., Navasota, 2005—. Social chairperson Jaycees, Navasota, Tex., 1994—99; music dir. New Hope Cmty. Ch., Navasota, 2005—06. Grantee Sound Sys. of Music grantee, Navasot Edn. Found., 2005. Mem.: Tex. Choral Dirs. Assn., Tex. Music Educator's Assn. (assoc.). D-Conservative. Baptist. Avocations: pianist, singer, travel, movies, cooking. Office: Navasota ISD PO Box 511 Navasota TX 77868 Home Phone: 936-825-8341; Office Phone: 936-825-4225.

COFFEY, SUSANNA JEAN, artist, educator; b. New London, Conn. d. Edwin Raymond and Magel C. (Willingham) C. BFA magna cum laude, U. Conn., 1977; MFA, Yale U., 1982. Tchg. asst. Yale U., 1982—; F.H. Sellers prof. painting Art Inst. Chgo., Oxbow, Mich., 1985—. Vis. artist various schs., 1983—; adj. assoc. prof. U. Ill., 1983; vis. critic Royal Coll. Art, London, 1995, Vt. Studio Ctr., 1994; panel mem. Harvard Ctr. Religious Studies, 2001. Illustrator: The H Hymn to Demeter, 1989, Monovassia (Eleni Fourtouni), 1979; one-woman shows include The Cultural Ctr. of the Chgo. Pub. Libr., 1986, Weatherspoon Gallery, Greensboro, N.C., 1993, Alpha Gallery, 1995, 2001, 04, Galeria Alejandro Sales, Barcelona, 1995, Tibor De Nagy Gallery, 1996-97, 2001, 2003, others; represented in permanent collections Northwestern U., Evanston, Ill., Art Inst. Chgo., Mpls. Mus. Art, Bryn Mawr (Pa.) Coll., Boston Mus. Fine Arts, Weatherspoon Gallery, and pvt. collections. Individual Artists grant Conn. Commn. on the Arts, 1980, Chgo. Artists Abroad grant, 1990, Ill./Arts Coun. grant, 1985, 92, Studio Program grant Marie Walsh Sharpe Found., 1992, Nat. Endowment for the Arts grant, 1993; Guggenheim fellow, 1996; recipient Louis Comfort Tiffany Found. award, 1993, Acad. award in art Am. Acad. of Arts and Letters, 1995; named to Nat. Acad. Design, 2001. Office: Sch of the Art Inst of Chgo 37 S Wabash Ave Chicago IL 60603-3002

COFFEY, THOMAS FRANCIS, JR., retired writer; b. Walthourville, Ga., Feb. 14, 1923; s. Thomas Francis and Julian (Bacon) Coffey; m. Mary Corley, Apr. 6, 1946 (dec. July 1988); 1 child, Mary Cynthia Smith; m. Marjorie Kinsner Guice, Nov. 11, 1989. Student Am. Press Inst., Columbia U., 1964; student program for urban execs., MIT, 1970. Reporter Savannah Eve. Press, Ga., 1940-42, asst. city editor, sports editor, 1945-55, city editor, 1960-64, mng. editor, 1964-67; dir. civilian pub. rels. US Army, Camp Stewart, Ga., 1942; news dir. Sta. WSAV-TV, Savannah, 1955-57; sports editor Savannah Morning News, 1957-60, mng. editor, 1967-69, assoc. editor, 1974-87, editor, 1987-89, columnist, 1989-98; ret., 1998. Commnetator Sta. WJCL-TV, Savannah, 1990—99. Author: Working for God, 1992, Only in Savannah, 1995, Savannah Lore and More, 1997. Bd. dirs. United Way Savannah; asst. city mgr. City of Savannah, 1969—74; lay leader Episc. Ch. With US Army, 1943—45. Decorated Bronze Star, Purple Heart. Mem.: Midway Soc. Ga. (pres. 1985), Nat. Soc. Newspaper Columnists, Nat. Conf. Edit. Writers, Internat. City Mgmt. Assn., Ga. A.P. News Coun., Greater Savannah Hall of Fame Assn. (pres. 1969), Am. Bus. Club (past pres. Savannah chpt.), Am. Legion, SR (pres. Ga.), Sigma Delta Chi. Home: 6401 Habersham St Unit 1B Savannah GA 31405-5632 Office: Savannah News Bldg 1375 Chatham Pkwy Savannah GA 31405 *Dedication to the task at hand/Compassion and concern for others/Gratitude to those who have built this nation/Faith in God.*

COFFEY, THOMAS WILLIAM, lawyer; b. Cin., Jan. 19, 1959; s. Joseph Paul and Doris June (Adams) C. MusB, U. Cin., 1981, JD, 1987. Bar: Pa. 1987, U.S. Dist. Ct. (we. dist.) Pa. 1987, U.S. Ct. Appeals (3d cir.) 1988, Ohio 1990, U.S. Dist. Ct. (so. dist.) Ohio 1990, (no. dist.) Ohio 2004, (ea. dist.) Mich., 2005, U.S. Ct. Appeals (6th cir.) 1990. Dir. band Ea. Local Sch., Brown County, Ohio, 1981-83, Goshen (Ohio) High Sch., 1983-84; assoc. Buchanan Ingersoll, P.C., Pitts., 1987-90; chmn. bankruptcy group Cors & Bassett, Cin., 1990—2004; sr. counsel bankruptcy practice group head Tucker Ellis & West LLP, Cleve., 2004—. Mem. ABA, Ohio Bar Assn., Cin. Bar Assn., Am. Fedn. Musicians, Masons, Shriners. Avocation: symphonic and dixieland jazz. Office: Tucker Ellis West LLP 925 Euclid Ave 1150 Huntington Bldg Cleveland OH 44115 Home: 1011 Literary Rd Cleveland OH 44113 Office Phone: 216-696-4244. Business E-Mail: thomas.coffey@tuckerellis.com.

COFFEY, TIMOTHY, physicist; b. Washington, June 27, 1941; s. Timothy and Helen (Stevens) C.; m. Paula Marie Smith, Aug. 24, 1963; children: Timothy, Donna, Marie. BS in Elec. Engring. (Cambridge scholar 1958), MIT, 1962; MS in Physics, U. Mich., 1963, Evening News Assn. fellow, 1964, PhD, 1967. Rsch. physicist Air Force Cambridge Rsch. Lab., 1964; theoretical physicist EGG, Inc., Boston, 1966-71; head plasma dynamics br., then supt. plasma physics div. Naval Rsch. Lab., Washington, 1971-80, assoc. dir. rsch. for gen. sci. and tech., 1980-83, dir. rsch., 1983—2001; sr. rsch. scientist U. Md., Coll. Pk., 2001—. Recipient award Naval Rsch. Lab., 1974, 75, Disting. Civilian award Dept. Defense, 1991, Robert Dexter Conrad medal Dept. of Navy, 2000. Fellow Am. Phys. Soc., Washington Acad. Scis.; mem. AAAS, Franklin Inst. (com. for sci. and arts, Delmar S. Fahrney medal 1991), Am. Phys. Soc. Office: Univ Md 2133 Lee Bldg College Park MD 20742

COFFIELD, SHIRLEY ANN, lawyer, educator; b. Portland, Oreg., Mar. 31, 1945; BA, Willamette U., 1967; MA, U. Wisc.-Madison, 1969; JD, George Washington U., 1974. Bar: D.C. 1975. Clk. Stitt, Hemmendinger and Kennedy, Washington, 1973-74; asst. gen. counsel Office U.S. Trade Rep., Washington, 1975-79; ptnr. Reaves & Coffield, Washington, 1979-82; sr. counsel to dep. asst. sect. textiles and apparel U.S. Dept. Commerce, Washington, 1982-85; spl. counsel Skadden, Arps, Slate, Meagher and Flom, Washington, 1985-87; ptnr. Piper & Marbury, Washington and Balt., 1987-90, Baker & Hostetler, Washington, 1990-94, Keller and Heckman, L.L.P., Washington, 1994-98, Duane, Morris & Heckscher, 1998-2000, Coffield Law, Washington, 2000—. Adj. prof. internat. econ. law Georgetown U. Law Sch., 1982—. Mem. Fed. Bar Assn., Am. Soc. Internat. Law, D.C. Bar, Pi Gamma Mu, Phi Delta Phi. Office: Coffield Law Ste 315 666 11th St NW Washington DC 20001-4530 Office Phone: 202-331-3097. Personal E-mail: coffieldlaw@yahoo.com.

COFFIN, ANNE GAGNEBIN, arts administrator, editor; d. Albert Paul and Genevieve (Hope) G.; m. John Devereux Coffin; children: Samuel Devereux, Thomas Huguenin. BA, Smith Coll. Asst. editor, feature writer Look mag., NYC, 1961-71; N.Y. rep. Villa I Tatti, Harvard U. Ctr. for Italian Renaissance Studies, Florence, 1984-92; dir. Internat. Print Ctr., NYC, 2000—. Curator, exhbn. organizer Am. Art: The Last 4 Decades, London, 1977. Bd. dirs N.Y. Landmarks Conservancy, N.Y.C., 1981—; bd. dirs. Chamber Music Soc. Lincoln Ctr., N.Y.C., 1984—, Leopold Schepp Found., 1991—, Brit.-Am. Arts Assn., 1985—; co-chmn. Contemporary Arts Coun., Mus. of Modern Art, N.Y.C.; mem. Art Table, Villa I Tatti Coun., 1992—. Mem.: The Century Assn., Cosmopolitan Club. Mailing: 20 E 9th St 3AB New York NY 10003

COFFIN, BEATRIZ DE WINTHUYSEN, landscape architect; b. Madrid, July 20, 1930; came to U.S., 1952; d. Javier de Winthuysen and Maria Hector; m. Laurence E. Coffin Jr., Jan. 4, 1958; children: Thomas A., Alisa W. BS, Furman U., Greenville, SC, 1954; M in Landscape Arch., Harvard U., 1957. Cert. landscape architect, Md., Va. Landscape architect A. Carl Stelling, NYC, 1957-58, Vorhees-Walker-Smith-Haines Architects, NYC, 1958-60; ptnr. Coffin & Coffin, Washington, 1963—. Landscape architect USN, Washington, 1968; instr. George Washington U., 1974, U. Md., 1985; pres. Internat. Inst. Site Planning, Washington, 1976—; lectr. U. Guanajuato, Mex., 1989, 92; lectr., cons. City of Quito, Ecuador (sponsored by USIA), 1990, 1994, 99, La Paz, Bolivia (sponsored by USIA), 1995. Co-author: A Maryland New Town Turns 50, Arquitectura Paisajista, Quito, Conceptos y diseños, 1991, Lexicon 2001 Multi-Lingual Dictionary of Landscapes and Urban Planning, 2001; contbr. numerous articles to profl. publs. Mem. design adv. steering com. D.C. Commn. on the Arts and the Humanities, 1986-94; bd. dirs. The World Charter Pub. Sch., Washington, 1998-2001. Fellow Am. Soc. Landscape Archs.; mem. Latin Am. Mgmt. Assn. (treas. 1990-95), Grupo Cultural San Gil. Office: Internat Inst Site Planning 715 G St SE Washington DC 20003-2853 Office Phone: 202-546-2322. Personal E-mail: iisitep@aol.com.

COFFIN, BERTHA LOUISE, retired telecommunications industry executive; b. Atlanta, Aug. 19, 1919; d. William Wesley and Bertha Louise (Marsh) Mendenhall; m. J. Donald Coffin, Feb. 14, 1943 (dec. Sept. 1978). BA, U. Kans., 1940. Med. technologist Midwest Rsch. Lab., Emporia, Kans., 1940—43; ins. agt. Coffin Ins. Agy., Council Grove, Kans., 1943—99, sole owner, mgr., 1978—82; treas. Council Grove Tel. Co., 1947—50, sec.-treas., 1950—78, pres., chmn. bd., 1978—98, gen. mgr., 1978—99. Del. legis. confs. Nat. Tel. Coop. Assn., 1986, 88, 91-92, 94, 97, comem. comml. co. com., 1987-91, mem. govt. affairs com., 1991-98, exec. com., 1996-98; founder, pres., chmn. bd. Kans. Personal Comm. Svcs. Ltd., 1995-2005; officer Cities Unltd., Inc., 1999—. Copy preparation for book The Story of the Santa Fe Trail, 1982; author: History of Council Grove Telephone Company, 1991; ann. civic sects. tel. directory. Pres. various lit. clubs, Council Grove, 1945-72; speaker various civic, polit. and religious groups, 1962—; mem. adv. coun. Manhattan Christian Coll., 1983-86, trustee, 1986-92, 93-99, 2000-2006, chmn., 1991-92; active Dramatic Impact Ministries. Mem. Kans. Telecomm. Assn. (bd. dirs. 1992-95), Ind. Tel. Pioneers (dir. 1984-92). Avocations: travel, church related activities.

COFFIN, DWIGHT CLAY, retired grain company executive; b. Evansville, Ind., Aug. 21, 1938; s. Dwight DeWitt and Ruth Robertson (Clay) Coffin; m. Carol Ann Elsaesser, Dec. 27, 1986; 1 child from previous marriage, John Charles. Student, DePauw U., 1959—61; BA, U. Pitts., 1963; MBA, NYU, 1970; postgrad., Harvard U., 1976; cert. in counseling, Postgrad. Ctr. Mental Health, NYC, 2001. With Chase Manhattan Bank, NYC, 1964-72, employee rels. officer, 1968-70, mgmt. svcs. officer, 1970-72; dir. employment and tng. Continental Grain Co., NYC, 1972-73, dir. internat. pers. Paris, 1973-75, v.p. pers. NYC, 1975-85, v.p., sec., 1985-86, v.p. human resources, 1986-99; ret., 1999. Mem global adv coun Am Grad Sch Int Mgt, 1986—. Pres Bishop's Fund for Children; dir Greenwich Found; pres Greenwich chpt English Speaking Union; warden St Barnabas Episcopal Ch, 1992—; bd dirs St Luke's Life Works,

Stamford, 1989—. Mem.: SAR (treas Capt Mead chpt), Human Resource Planning Soc, Nat Foreign Trade Coun (chmn mgt resources comt 1984), Innis Arden Golf Club. Republican. Home: 115 Oak Tree Pl Santa Barbara CA 93108 Personal E-mail: dwightcc@sover.net.

COFFIN, FRANK MOREY, retired federal judge; b. Lewiston, Maine, July 11, 1919; s. Herbert Rice and Ruth (Morey) Coffin; m. Ruth Ulrich, Dec. 19, 1942; children: Nancy, Douglas, Meredith, Susan. AB, Bates Coll., 1940, LLD, 1959; postgrad. indsl. adminstrn., Harvard U., 1943, LLB, 1947; LLD, Bates Coll., 1959, U. Maine, 1967, Bowdoin Coll., 1969; degree (hon.), Colby Coll., 1975. Bar: Maine 1947. Law clk. to fed. judge Dist. of Maine, 1947—49; engaged in practice Lewiston, 1947—52; with Verrill, Dana, Walker, Philbrick & Whitehouse, Portland, Maine, 1952—56; mem. 85th-86th Congresses from 2d Dist. Maine, House Com. Fgn. Affairs; mng. dir. Devel. Loan Fund, Dept. State, Washington, 1961; dep. adminstr. AID, 1961—64; U.S. rep. devel. assistance com. Orgn. Econ. Coop. and Devel., 1964—65; judge 1st circuit US Ct. Appeals, 1965—2006, chief judge, 1972—83, sr. judge, 1989—2006; chmn. com. jud. br. US Jud. Conf., 1984—90. Adj. prof. U. Maine Sch. Law, 1986—89. Author: Witness for Aid, 1964, The Ways of a Judge-Reflections from the Federal Appellate Bench, 1980, A Lexicon of Oral Advocacy, 1984, On Appeal, 1994. Emeritus Bates Coll.; dir. The Governance Inst., 1987—; mem. emeritus The Examiner; chair Maine Justice Action Group, 1996—2001. Lt. USNR, 1943—46. Recipient Edward J. Devitt Disting. Svc. to Justice award, 2001. Mem.: ABA, ABA (co-chmn. com. on loan forgiveness and repayment 2001—02), Am. Acad. Arts and Sci., Am. Acad. Arts and Sci.*

COFFIN, GRANGE SIMONS, pediatrician; b. Kinston, NC, Jan. 18, 1923; s. Francis Joseph Howells and Annie Roulhac Coffin; m. Heidi von Unger Coffin, July 19, 1971; children: Peter, Susanna, Carl Phillip; m. Ann Casselberry Coffin, Dec. 23, 1949 (dec.); children: William, Priscilla, Hope, John. BS, Yale U., 1943, MD, Columbia U., 1947. Intern in medicine Roosevelt Hosp., NYC, 1947—48; fellow in microbiology U. Chgo., 1948—50; asst. resident pediatrics Johns Hopkins U., Balt., 1950—51, intern pediatrics, 1953—54; resident pediatrics U. Md., Balt., 1954—55, instr., asst. prof. pediatrics, 1955—62; pediatrician pvt. practice, 1955—92; ret., 1992. Physician Sonoma State Hosp., Sonoma Devel. Ctr., 1962—97; asst. prof., assoc. prof. pediatrics U. Calif., San Francisco, 1962—. Contbr. articles various profl. jours. Cpt. USAF, 1951—53, La. Republican. Episcopalian. Achievements include discovery of Coffin-Lowry Syndrome; Coffin-Siris Syndrome. Home: 679 Colusa Ave Berkeley CA 94707

COFFIN, JOHN MILLER, medical researcher, biology professor; b. Boston, Apr. 20, 1944; s. Louis Fussell and Mary Elizabeth (McCarthy) C.; m. Marion Clair Szurek, June 22, 1968; children: Erica Mary, Heather Rachel. BA, Wesleyan U., 1967; PhD, U. Wis., 1972. Fellow U. Zurich, Switzerland, 1972—75; asst. prof. molecular biology to assoc. prof. Tufts U. Sch. Medicine, Boston, 1975—82, prof., 1982—, Am. Cancer Soc. Rsch. Prof. Molecular Biology and Microbiol., 1994—; dir. HIV Drug Resistance Prog. Ctr. Cancer Rsch., Nat. Cancer Inst., NIH, Bethesda, Md., 1997—. Mem. virology study sect. NIH, Bethesda, Md., 1980-84; mem. sci. adv. bd. Viagene, Inc., San Diego, 1988. Editor: RNA Tumor Viruses, 2 vols., 1985, Retroviruses, 1997; mem. editl. bd. Jour. Virol, Virology, Oncogene, Oncogene Res., Leukemia; editor Jour. Virol, 1991-97; contbr. articles to profl. jours. Trustee Leukemia Soc. Am., NY, 1987. Recipient Outstanding Investigator award Nat. Cancer Inst., 1987, Method to Extend Rsch. in Time (MERIT) award NIH, 2006. Mem. AAAS, NAS, Am. Soc. Microbiol. Office: Tufts U Sch Medicine Dept Molecular Biology and Microbiol 136 Harrison Ave Boston MA 02111 also: HIV Drug Resistance Prog Nat Cancer Inst Bldg 535 Rm 109 PO Box B Frederick MD 21702-1201 Office Phone: 617-636-6526, 301-846-5943. Office Fax: 617-636-4086, 301-846-6013. E-mail: jcoffin@ncifcrf.gov, john.coffin@tufts.edu.

COFFINA, SCOTT A., lawyer; b. NYC, June 27, 1967; m. Kim Coffina; 1 child. BA with distinction in Govt., Cornell U., Ithaca, NY, 1989; JD, U. Pa., 1992. Bar: Pa. 1993, DC 1994, NJ 2006. Staff asst. to assoc. dir. polit. affairs The White House, Washington, 1988—89, assoc. counsel to Pres., 2007—; assoc. Wiley, Rein & Fielding LLP, 1992—95; asst. US atty. (ea. dist.) Pa. US Dept. Justice, 1997—2001; atty. Montgomery, McCracken, Walker & Rhoads, LLP, Phila., 2001—03, ptnr., 2003—07. Mem. hearing com. Supreme Ct. Pa. Disciplinary Bd. Office: The White House 1600 Pennsylvania Ave NW Washington DC 20502

COFFMAN, EDWARD MCKENZIE, retired history professor; b. Hopkinsville, Ky., Jan. 27, 1929; s. Howard Beverly and Mada (Wright) C.; m. Anne Nelson Rouse, June 30, 1955; children: Anne Wright, Lucia Page, Edward McKenzie. AB, U. Ky., 1951, MA, 1955, PhD (So. Faculty fellow), 1959. Instr., asst. prof. Memphis State U., 1957-61; research asso. George C. Marshall Research Found., 1960-61; asst. prof., assoc. prof., prof. history U. Wis., Madison, 1961-92, prof. emeritus, 1992—. Dwight D. Eisenhower vis. prof. Kans. State U., 1969-70; vis. prof. mil. history U.S. Mil. Acad., 1977-78; disting. vis. prof. USAF Acad., 1982-83; Harold K. Johnson vis. prof. U.S. Army Mil. History Inst., 1986-87; mem. adv. com. Dept. Army Mil. History Program, 1971-76, 87-89, chair, 1989-93; mem. Nat. Hist. Publs. and Records Commn., 1972-76; John F. Morrison vis. prof. U.S. Army Command and Gen. Staff Coll., 1990-91. Author: The Hilt of the Sword: The Career of Peyton C. March, 1966, The War to End All Wars: The American Military Experience in World War I, 1968, The Old Army: A Portrait of the American Army in Peacetime, 1784-1898, 1986, The Regulars: The American Army, 1898-1941, 2004; mem. editl. bd. Mil. Affairs, 1974-77, Arno Press series The American Military Experience and The George C. Marshall Papers; chmn. editl. bd. Jour. Mil. History, 1995-99. Served with U.S. Army, 1951-53. Recipient Outstanding Civilian Svc. medal Dept. Army, 1978, Comdr.'s Pub. Svc. award, 1987, Disting. Civilian Svc. medal, 1991; Guggenheim fellow, 1973-74; Harmon Lectr. USAF Acad., 1976; Am. Philos. Soc. grantee, 1960; named U. Ky. Disting. Alumnus, 1995. Mem. Soc. for Mil. History (pres. 1983-85, Samuel Eliot Morison prize 1990, Moncado prize 1995, Disting. Book award, 2005), U.S. Commn. Mil. History, So. Hist. Soc., Orgn. Am. History, Phi Beta Kappa. Democrat. Home: 1089 Lakewood Dr Lexington KY 40502-2523

COFFMAN, JAMES RICHARD, academic administrator, veterinarian, educator; b. Lyndon, Kans., July 19, 1938; s. Harry Thomas and Eleanor Louise (Lowe) C.; m. Sharon Sue Neill, June 10, 1960; children: David Neill, Michael James, Scott Thomas. BS, Kans. State U., 1960, DVM, 1962, MS, 1969. Pvt. practice equine vet., Wichita, Kans., 1962-65, Oklahoma City, 1969-71; inst. vet. medicine Kans. State U., Manhattan, 1965-69, prof., head dept. surgery and medicine, vet. medicine, 1981-84, prof. vet. medicine, dean, 1984-87, provost, 1987—2004; assoc. prof. vet. medicine and surgery U. Mo., Columbia, 1971-75, prof., 1975-81, dir. Equine Ctr., 1973-78; prof., head dept. surgery and medicine Sch. Vet. Medicine Kans. State U., Manhattan, 1981-84, prof., dean, 1984-87, provost, 1987—2004, provost emeritus vet. clin. sci., 2004—. Chair Nat. rsch. Coun., Bd. on Agr. subcom., 1999. Author: Equine Chemistry and Pathophysiology, 1991; editor Compendium on Continuing Edn. 1980-83, mem. editorial bd., 1980-85; editor in chief Equine Sportsmedicine, 1981-85; mem. editorial bd. Jour. Equine Medicine and Surgery, 1979-80; adv. bd. Equine Vet. Jour., 1980—; contbr. numerous articles to profl. jours. Bd. dirs. St. Mary Hosp., Manhattan, 1989—. Recipient Disting. Tchr. award Norden Labs., 1969. Mem. Am. Coll. Vet. Internal Medicine (diplomate, pres. 1978-79, chmn. bd. regents 1979-80), Am. Assn. Equine Practitioners (dir. at large 1982-83, v.p. 1984, pres. 1986-87), Am. Vet. Med. Assn. (trustee profl. liability ins. trust 1978-85, chmn. 1980-82), Nat. Acads. Practice Vet. Medicine (exec. bd. 1985-87, founding com. mem. 1985-97), Kans. Vet. Med. Assn., Nat. Assn. State Univs. and Land Grant Colls. (coun. chief acad. officers 1987-2004, exec. coun. on acad. affairs), Rotary (bd. dirs. 1989-90), Phi Kappa Phi, Gamma Sigma Delta, Phi Zeta. Avocation: painting. Home: 200 Waterbridge Rd Manhattan KS 66503-2512

COFFMAN, JENNIFER BURCHAM, judge; b. 1948; BA, U. Ky., 1969, MA, 1971, JD, 1978. Ref. libr. Newport News (Va.) Pub. Libr., 1972-74, U. Ky. Libr., 1974-76; atty. Law Offices Arthur L. Brooks., Lexington, Ky., 1978-82; ptnr. Brooks, Coffman and Fitzpatrick, Lexington, 1982-92, Newberry, Hargrove & Rambicure, Lexington, 1992-93; judge U.S. Dist. Ct. (ea. dist. and we. dist.) Ky., 1993—. Adj. prof. Coll. Law, U. Ky., 1979-81. Bd. dirs. YWCA Lexington, 1986—92, Shepherd Ctr., 2000—05. Mem. Ky. Bar Assn., Fayette County Bar Assn., U. Ky. Law Sch. Alumni Assn. Office: 136 US Courthouse 101 Barr St Lexington KY 40507-1313 Office Phone: 859-233-2453.

COFFMAN, MICHAEL S., international organization official, ecologist; b. 1943; m. Susan Coffman; children: Jonathan, Tamera. BS in forestry, No. Ariz. U., 1966, MS in biology, 1967; PhD in forest sci., U. Idaho, Moscow, 1970. Faculty Mich. Tech. U.; former mgr. Champion Internat. (now Internat. Paper), Stamford, Conn.; pres. Environmental Perspectives, Inc.; exec. dir. Sovereignty Internat. Pub. Discerning the Times Digest, 1999—. Author: Saviors of the Earth. Bd. mem. Nazarene Ch. Nazarene. Office: Environmental Perspectives Inc 6 Heather Rd Bangor ME 04401 also: Sovereignty International PO Box 191 Hollow Rock TN 38342 Office Phone: 731-986-0099.*

COFFMAN, MIKE (MICHAEL H. COFFMAN), state official, former state legislator; b. Ft. Leonard Wood, Mo., Mar. 19, 1955; s. Harold and Dorothy Coffman; m. Cynthia Coffman. B, U. Colo., 1979. Small bus. entrepreneur; mem. Colo. State Ho. Reps., 1988—94, Colo. State Senate, 1994—98; treas. State of Colo., Denver, 1998—2006, sec. state, 2007—. Chmn. fin. com. Colo. State Senate. Served in US Army, 1972—74 USAR, 1975—78, major USMC, 1979—82, major USMC, 1994, civil officer USMC, 2005—06, served in USMCR, 1983—94. Republican. Office: Office Sec State Dept State 1700 Broadway Denver CO 80290*

COFFMAN, RICHARD C., retired protective services official; s. Marvin Curtis and Winifred Ruth (Smith) Coffman; m. Jean Trzcinski; children: Richard Bruce, Lizbeth Lee. BS, U. Mo., Columbia, 1949, MS, 1950. Spl. agent US Army Counter Intelligence Corps, Japan, 1945—47, FBI, Washington, 1950—80; investigator Dept. Def., Salt Lake City, 1980—, NSA, 1980—, US Treasury, 1980—. Dir. security Commorative Air Force, Salt Lake City, 1986—96. Mem.: NRA, FBI Agents Assn. Republican. Presbyterian. Avocations: photography, flying, auto racing, history. Office: Invescon Inc 2508 Dickinson St Miles City MT 59301

COFFMAN, ROBERT LEE, pharmaceutical executive; AB, Ind. U.; PhD, U. Calif., San Diego. Postdoctoral fellow Stanford U. Med. Sch., Calif.; various positions up to Disting. Rsch. fellow DNAX Rsch. Inst., Palo Alto, Calif., 1981—2000; v.p., chief sci. officer Dynavax Technologies Corp., Berkeley, Calif., 2000—. Contbr. articles to sci. jours.; adv. editor: Jour. Exptl. Medicine. Co-recipient William S. Coley award for rsch. in basic and clin. immunology, Cancer Rsch. Inst., NYC, 1997. Mem.: NAS. Achievements include fundamental discoveries about regulation of immune responses in allergic and infectious diseases. Office: Dynavax Technologies 2929 Seventh St Ste 100 Berkeley CA 94710

COFFMAN, TERRENCE J., retired academic administrator; b. 1945; m. Wallis Coffman. Student, Corcoran Coll. Art and Design, Lacoste Sch. Arts. Dean then pres. Md. Coll. Art and Design, Silver Spring, 1973—83; pres. Milw. Inst. Art & Design, 1983—2003; ret., 2003. Instr. Smithsonian Instn., Washington; artist-in-residence Milw. Inst. Art & Design. Author: A Walk Through the Wheatfields: The Missing Journals of Vincent van Gogh. Recipient Milw.'s Frank Kirkpatrick award, 2001. Avocation: playing acoustic guitar. Office: Milw Inst Art & Design 273 E Erie St Milwaukee WI 53202-6003

COFIELD, ROBERT HAHN, orthopedic surgeon, educator; b. Cin., Oct. 24, 1943; s. Robert Hedrick and Virginia (Hahn) C.; m. Pamela Joyce Haarbauer, Aug. 12, 1967; children: Robert, Stacey, Virginia. BA, Washington and Lee U., 1965; MD, U. Ky., 1969; MS, Mayo Grad. Sch. Medicine, 1976. Diplomate Am. Bd. Orthopedic Surgery. Intern Charity Hosp./Tulane U., New Orleans, 1970; cons. Mayo Clinic, Rochester, Minn., 1975—; from instr. to assoc. prof. Mayo Med. Sch., Rochester, 1975-88, prof., 1988—; vice chmn. dept. orthopedics Mayo Clinic, Rochester, 1992-97, Frank R. and Shari Caywood prof. orthopedic surgery, 1993, chmn. dept. orthopedics, 1997—2005; assoc. dean Mayo Grad. Sch., Rochester, 1992-94, dean, 1994-98; pres. Am. Bd. Orthopaedic Surgery, Chapel Hill, 1999-2000. Editor-in-chief Jour. Shoulder and Elbow Surgery, 1990-96; contbr. chpts. to books, more than 200 articles to profl. jours.; co-inventor humeral resect. guide; co-designer Cofield total shoulder sys. Lt. comdr. USNR. Mem. AMA, Am. Acad. Orthopedic Surgery, Am. Bd. Orthopedic Surgery (dir. 114—), Am. Orthopedic Assn., Am. Shoulder and Elbow Surgeons (founding sec.-treas. 1982-87, pres. 1988-89). Republican. Presbyterian. Office: Mayo Clinic 200 1st Ave NW Rochester MN 55901-3004 Office Phone: 507-284-2995.

COFONI, PAUL MICHAEL, information technology executive; b. Westerly, RI, Oct. 14, 1948; s. Sylvester James and Sarah Eleanor (Castagna) Cofoni; m. Karen Sue Tapley, May 31, 1970; 2 children. BS in Math., U. R.I., 1970; student in Sr. Exec. Program, MIT, 1989. With Gen. Dynamics, 1974—91; from v.p. Tech. Mgmt. Group Ea. Region to pres. Tech. Mgmt. Group Computer Scis. Corp., El Segundo, Calif., 1991—2001, with, 2001—05, pres. Fed. Sector, 2001—05; pres. U.S. ops. CACI Internat. Inc., Arlington, Va., 2005—07, pres., CEO, 2007—. With US Army, 1970—74. Mem.: AIAA, Info. Tech. Assn. Am. (bd. dirs.), Armed Forces Comms. and Electronics Assn. (bd. dirs.), Nat. Def. Indsl. Assn. (bd. dirs.), The Bus. Roundtable. Office: CACI Internat Inc Three BallStrom Plz 1100 N Glebe Road Arlington VA 22201*

COGAN, BRIAN M., federal judge; BA, U. Ill. Chapaign-Urbana, 1975; JD, Cornell Law Sch., 1979. Law clk. to judge Sidney M. Aronovitz US Dist. Ct. (So. dist.) Fla., 1979—80; assoc. Stroock & Stroock & Lavan LLP, 1980—2006, ptnr., 1988—2006, gen. counsel, 2004—06; judge US Dist. Ct. (Ea. dist.) NY, 2006—. Office: US Dist Ct Ea Dist NY 225 Cadman Plaza E Brooklyn NY 11201 Office Phone: 718-613-2230. Office Fax: 718-613-2236.*

COGAN, JOHN FRANCIS, JR., lawyer; b. Boston, June 13, 1926; s. John Francis and Mary (Galligan) C.; m. Mary T. Hart, May 1, 1951 (div.); m. Mary L. Cornille, June 24, 1989; children: Peter G., Pamela E., Jonathan C., Gregory M. AB cum laude, Harvard U., 1949, JD, 1952. Bar: Mass. 1953. Ptnr. Hale and Dorr, Boston, 1957—2000, mng. ptnr., 1976—84, chmn., 1984—96, of counsel, 2000—04, Wilmer, Cutler, Pickering, Hale, and Dorr, Boston, 2004—; dep. chmn. Pioneer Global Asset Mgmt., SpA, Milan, 2000—; non-exec. chmn. Pioneer Investment Mgmt., USA, Inc., Boston, 2000—. Trustee various Pioneer Funds, Inc., Boston, 1963—; pres. Pioneer Group, Inc., Boston, 1963—2000; chmn. bd. dirs. Teberebie Goldfields, Inc., 1986—2000; chmn. exec. com. bd. dirs. Pioneer Western Corp., 1968—79; sr. v.p., bd. dirs. Western Res. Life Assurance Co., Ohio, 1968—79; chmn. bd. dirs. ICI Mutual Ins. Co., 1987—94, 2004—. Trustee Boston Symphony Orch., 1989—, overseer, 1984—92, chmn., 1989—92, vice chmn., 2003—; overseer Mus. Fine Arts, 1989—90, trustee, 1990—, chmn., 1994—98; trustee Boston Ballet, 1986—89; mem. Mass. Dem. State Com., 1968—80; trustee Univ. Hosp., Boston, 1965—95, chmn. bd., 1972—89; trustee Boston Med. Ctr., 1995—; bd. dirs. Wendell P. Clark Meml. Assn., Walker Home for Children, 1972—, Brigham Surg. Group, Inc., 1981—95, The Med. Found., 1986—90; trustee Boston U. Med. Ctr., 1973—90; bd. govs. Investment Co. Inst., 1971—74, 1975, 1981, 1982, chmn. bd. govs., 1978—80, 1982—85, 1986—89, 1991—. With USNR, 1944—46. Fellow Am. Acad. Arts and Scis.; mem. ABA, Internat. Bar Assn., Mass. Bar Assn. (chmn. corp. banking and bus. law com. 1973-76), Boston Bar Assn. (past chmn. profl. svcs. sect., mem. bench-bar com.), Boston Estate and Bus. Planning Coun. (past pres.), Boston Probate and Estate Planning Forum (sec. 1958-73), Nat. Assn. Security Dealers (bd. dirs. 1983-86, legal adv. bd. 1988-94). Home: 975 Memorial Dr Apt 802 Cambridge MA 02138-5755 Home Phone: 617-876-1845; Office Phone: 617-422-4802.

COGAN, TOM (THOMAS J. COGAN), aerospace engineer; BS in Aerospace Engring., Tex. A&M U., College Station. Positions in aerodynamics on 737, 757 and 7J7 programs Boeing Co., 1977—89, mktg. mgr. 757 and 737 programs, 1989, various positions including interiors integrated product team leader 757-300, crown systems leader 737-600/-700/-800 and sr. mgr. payloads, dep. chief project engr. 757 programs, 1996—98, mfg. bus. unit mgr. Devel. Mfg., chief project engr. Boeing 757, chief project engr. Sonic Cruiser program, chief project engr. Boeing 7E7, 2003, chief project engr. 787 Dreamliner. Named one of The 50 Who Matter Now, Bus. 2.0, 2007. Office: Boeing Comml Airplanes PO Box 3707 Seattle WA 98124 Office Phone: 206-655-2121.

COGBILL, JOHN VALENTINE, III, lawyer; b. Munich, Jan. 30, 1948; m. Janet Mary Cogbill; children: John, Jamie, Chrissy. BS in Engring., USMA, 1970; JD, U. Richmond, 1979. Bar: Va. 1979, admitted to practice: US Fed. Ct. 1979. Joined McGuireWoods LLP, Richmond, Va., 1987, ptnr., real estate & environ. dept., mng. ptnr. Richmond office. Mem. Commonwealth Transp. Bd., 1995—99, Richmond Met. Authority Bd., 1995—99; chmn. Nat. Capital Planning Commn., 2001—; bd. trustees The Henricus Found., 2001—. Served US Army, 1970—76. Fellow: Va. Law Found.; mem.: Urban Land Inst., Chesterfield-Colonial Heights Bar Assn., Am. Coll. Real Estate Lawyers, Richmond Bar Assn., Va. Bar Assn., Greater Richmond C. of C. (bd. dirs. 1998—2002, Bernard L. Savage Cmty. Svc. Award 2003). Office: McGuireWoods LLP One James Ctr 901 E Cary St Richmond VA 23219-4030 Office Phone: 804-775-4383. Office Fax: 804-698-2031. Business E-Mail: jcogbill@mcguirewoods.com.

COGDILL, RICHARD A., food products executive; Exec. v.p., CFO, sec., treas. Pilgrim's Pride Corp., Pittsburg, Tex., 1996—. Office: Pilgrim's Pride Corp 110 S Texas St Pittsburg TX 75686*

COGEN, RICHARD M., lawyer; b. NYC, 1955; BA cum laude, U. Rochester, 1976; JD, Cornell U., 1979. Bar: NY 1980. Ptnr. Nixon Peabody LLP, Albany, NY. Mem.: ABA, Albany County Bar Assn., Environ. Auditing Roundtable, Inst. Environ. Auditing (mem. bd. dirs. 1985—94), Air and Waste Mgmt. Assn. (chmn. Legal Com. 1990—92, vice chair Environ. Auditing Com. 1995—98), NY State Bar Assn. Office: Nixon Peabody LLP Omni Plaza 30 S Pearl St Albany NY 12207-3425 Office Phone: 518-427-2665. Office Fax: 866-947-1278. E-mail: rcogen@nixonpeabody.com.

COGGIN, CHARLOTTE JOAN, cardiologist, educator; b. Takoma Park, Md., Aug. 6, 1928; d. Benjamin and Nanette (McDonald) C. BA, Columbia Union Coll., 1948; MD, Loma Linda U., 1952, MPH, 1987; DSc (hon.), Andrews U., 1994. Diplomate Am. Bd. Pediatrics. Intern L.A. County Gen. Hosp., 1952-53, resident in medicine, 1953-55; fellow in cardiology Children's Hosp., LA, 1955-56, White Meml. Hosp., LA, 1955-56; rsch. assoc. in cardiology, house physician Hammersmith Hosp., London, 1956-57; resident in pediatrics and pediatric cardiology Hosp. for Sick Children, Toronto, Ont., Canada, 1965-67; cardiologist, asst. prof. medicine, co-dir. heart surgery team Loma Linda (Calif.) U., 1961-73, assoc. prof., 1973-91, prof. medicine, 1991—. Asst. dean. Sch. Medicine Internat. Program, 1973—75; v.p. for global outreach Loma Linda U. Health Scis. Ctr., 1998—; assoc. dean. Sch. Medicine Internat. Program, 1975—, spl. asst. to univ. pres. for interat. affairs, 1991; co-dir., cardiologist heart surgery team missions to, Pakistan and Asia, 63, Greece, 67, Greece, 69, Saigon, Vietnam, 1974—75, Saudi Arabia, 1976—87, China, 1984, China, 1989—91, Hong Kong, 1985, Zimbabwe, 88, Zimbabwe, 93, Kenya, 88, Nepal, 92, China, 92, Myanmar, 95, North Korea, 96. Author: Atrial Septal Defects, motion picture (Golden Eagle Cine award and 1st prize Venice Film Festival 1964); contbr. articles to med. jours. Recipient award for service to people of Pakistan City of Karachi, 1963, Medallion award Evangelismos Hosp., Athens, Greece, 1967, Gold medal of health South Vietnam Ministry of Health, 1974, Charles Elliott Weinger award for excellence, 1976, Wall Street Jour. Achievement award, 1987, Disting. Univ. Svc. award Loma Linda U., 1990; named Honored Alumnus Loma Linda U. Sch. Medicine, 1973, Outstanding Women in Gen. Conf. Seventh-day Adventists, 1975, Alumnus of Yr., Columbia Union Coll., 1984, Outstanding Achievement in Edn., Adventist Alumni Achievement award, 1999. Mem. AAUP, AAUW, Am. Coll. Cardiology, AMA (physicians adv. com. 1969—), Calif. Med. Assn. (com. on med. schs., com. on member svcs.), San Bernardino County Med. Soc. (chmn. comm. com. 1975-77, mem. comm. com, 1987-88, editor bull., 1975-76, William L. Cover, M.D. Outstanding Contbn. to Medicine award 1995), Am. Heart Assn., Med. Rsch. Assn. Calif., Calif. Heart Assn., Am. Acad. Pediatrics, World Affairs Coun., Internat. Platform Assn., Calif. Museum Sci. and Industry MUSES (Outstanding Woman of Yr. in Sci. 1969), Am. Med. Women's Assn., Loma Linda Sch. Medicine Alumni Assn. (pres. 1978), Alpha Omega Alpha, Delta Omega. Democrat. Home: 25052 Crestview Dr Loma Linda CA 92354-3415 Personal E-mail: jcoggin@verizon.net.

COGGINS, PAUL EDWARD, JR., lawyer; b. Hugo, Okla., May 21, 1951; s. Paul E. and Rebecca (Cates) C.; m. Regina T. Montoya, June 12, 1976; 1 child, Jessica Chandler. BA summa cum laude in Polit. Sci., Yale U., New Haven, Conn., 1973; BA with 1st class honors, Oxford U., 1975; JD cum laude, Harvard U., Cambridge, Mass., 1978. Bar: Tex. 1978. Tchr. Project New Gate N.Mex. State Penitentiary, 1973; law clk. Mass. Ct. Appeals, 1978-79; fed. prosecutor US Atty.'s Office, Dallas, 1980-83; assoc. Johnson & Swanson, Dallas, 1979-80, ptnr., 1983-86, Meadows, Owens, Collier, Reed & Coggins, Dallas, 1986-93; US atty. US Dept. Justice, Dallas, 1993-2001; prin. Fish & Richardson, P.C., Dallas, 2001—. Mem. adv. com. Magnet Sch. in Dallas, 1984—. Author: The Lady is the Tiger, 1987; co-author: Out of Bounds, 1992. Pres. bd. dirs. Dem. Forum, Dallas, 1985—; mem. North Tex. Crime Commn., chair, 2004. Named a Rhodes scholar, 1973—76; named one of Best Lawyers in Dallas, D Mag., 2005. Mem. ABA, CASA (pres. 2005), Dallas Bar Assn. (mem. pro bono panel), Dallas County Hist. Found., Town and Gown (pres., 2003-04). Office: Fish & Richardson PC 5000 Bank One Ctr 1717 Main St Dallas TX 75201-4612 Office Phone: 214-292-4003. Fax: 214-747-2091. Business E-Mail: coggins@fr.com.

COGHILL, WILLIAM THOMAS, JR., retired lawyer; b. St. Louis, July 20, 1927; s. William Thomas and Mildred Mary (Crenshaw) C.; m. Patricia Lee Hughes, Aug. 7, 1948; children: James Prentiss, Victoria Lynn, Cathryn Anne. Undergrad., U. Mo., Columbia, 1944-45, 46-47, JD, 1950. Bar: Mo. 1950, Ill. 1958. Pvt. practice, Farmington, Mo., 1950-51; spl. agt. FBI, 1951-52; ptnr. Smith, Smith & Coghill, Farmington, 1952-57; assoc. Coburn & Croft, St. Louis, 1957-58; ptnr. Thompson Coburn (formerly

Thompson & Mitchell and predecessor firm), Belleville, Ill., 1958—2001, ret., 2001. Co-author: Illinois Products Liability, 1991, Cavaliers, 1999. With USN, 1945-46. Fellow Am. Coll. Trial Lawyers; mem. ABA, Ill. State Bar Assn., Mo. State Bar Assn. Home: 715 W Moon Valley Dr Phoenix AZ 85023-6234 Personal E-mail: tcoghill@cox.net.

COGHLAN, JOHN PHILIP, corporate financial executive; b. San Francisco; life ptnr. Tina Vindum; children: Kearney, Callan. BA in Psychology, with honors in social thought, Stanford U.; MA in Economics and Public Policy, Princeton U.; MBA, Harvard U. Founder, COO San Francisco Grocery Express. Ltd.; joined Charles Schwab & Co., 1986, gen. mgr. Schwab Instl., 1992—97, exec. v.p., 1992—2005, enterprise pres. retirement plan services, 1997—2001, enterprise pres. services for investment managers, 1998—2001, enterprise pres. Schwab Instl., 2001—02, vice chmn., 1999—2005, enterprise pres. individual investor's bus., 2002—05; pres. CEO Visa USA, 2005—. Bd. dirs. Success Metrics, San Francisco, CollectAmerica, Denver. Pres. bd. dirs. San Francisco Lighthouse for the Blind; bd. dirs. Glide Meml. Ch. Mem.: Internat. Bd. of Practices and Standards for Certified Financial Planners (Nat. Advisory Coun.). Office: Visa USA 900 Metro Center Blvd Foster City CA 94404*

COGHLAN, KELLY JACK, lawyer; b. Longview, Tex., Sept. 3, 1952; s. Howard and Peggy Coghlan. BBA with honors, So. Meth. U., 1975, JD cum laude, 1978. Bar: Tex. 1978, U.S. Dist. Ct. (so. dist.) Tex. 1979, U.S. Tax Ct. 1981, U.S. Ct. Appeals (5th cir.) 1981, U.S. Supreme Ct. 1984. Law clk. to presiding judge Finis E. Cowan U.S. Dist. Ct. (so. dist.) Tex., 1978-79; assoc. Vinson & Elkins, Houston, 1979-84; equity ptnr. Dotson, Babcock & Scofield, Houston, 1984-88, chmn. risk mgmt. com., head gen. litigation group, 1987-88; pvt. practice, Houston, 1988—. Bd. dirs. Sta. KSBJ, Houston, sec., 1990-93, chmn. long range planning com., 1989-93, mem. exec. com., 1990-97, v.p., 1994-97. Mem. So. Meth. U. Law Sch. Southwestern Law Jour. Mem. steering com. Palmer Drug Abuse Program, Houston, 1980-82; vol. jr. high and H.S. youth programs, 1990—, 2d Bapt. Ch., Houston, 1990—; mem. 1st Meth. Ch., Longview, Tex., 1962—; youth min., Wesley United Meth. Ch., Longview, 1972-77. Recipient So. Meth. U. M award, 1975, Russell Baker Moot Ct. 1st pl. award So. Meth. U. Law Sch., 1976; named Players of 1999, Tex. Lawyer. Fellow: Pro Bono Coll. State Bar Tex., Coll. State Bar Tex., Houston Bar Found. (life), Tex. Bar Found. (life); mem.: ABA, Houston Young Lawyers Assn. (chmn. com. on consumer rights 1981—82), Houston Bar Assn., Tex. Bar Assn., Gulf Coast Mensa, Nat. Eagle Scout Assn. (life), Am. Mensa, So. Meth. U. Student Found. (hon.), Lambda Chi Alpha, Phi Delta Phi (hon.), Beta Gamma Sigma (hon.), Blue Key Soc. (hon.; pres. 1974—75), Order of Coif (hon.). Avocations: drumming, singing, youth work. Office: 505 Lanecrest Ln Ste 1 Houston TX 77024-6716 Office Phone: 713-973-7475.

COGMAN, DON V., public relations executive; Grad. with honors, U. Okla. Chief of staff to US Senator Dewey Bartlett, 1972-76; v.p. govt. affairs MAPCO Inc., 1980-89; founder RCF Group, Washington, 1988—92; pres., CEO Washington region Burson-Marsteller, 1991-94; pres., CEO The Americas, 1995; vice-chmn., COO Burson-Marsteller Worldwide; pres., COO Burson-Marsteller, 1998—2000; exec. v.p. corp. affairs Young & Rubicam Inc., NYC, 2000; chmn. CC Investments LLC, Scottsdale, Ariz.; sr. counselor Feldman & Ptnrs., LA, 2007—. Bd. dir. Am. Coun. Young Polit. Leaders, White House Adv. Bd. on Pvt. Sector Iniatives; former pres. Vote Am. Found.; chmn. Nat. Fed. of Ind. Bus. Edn. Found.; mem., Nat. Coun. on the Arts Nat. Endowment for the Arts; bd. dir. Fund for am. Studies, Washington, Acting Co., NYC. Fellow: Hudson Inst.; mem.: Juilliard Ovation Soc. Office: Nat Endowment for the Arts 1100 Pennsylvania Ave NW Washington DC 20506-0001 also: Feldman & Ptnrs Ste 2000 8491 Sunset Blvd Los Angeles CA 90069 Office Phone: 310-360-0211. E-mail: don@feldmanandpartners.com.*

COGSWELL, JAMES A., library director; BA, Bowdoin Coll.; MLS, Rutgers U. Libr. Johns Hopkins U., Balt.; mgr. integrated libr. sys. Princeton U., NJ; dir. collection devel., mgmt. and preservation U. Minn.; dir. libr**s**. U. Mo., Columbia, 2002—. Bd. mem. Mo. Libr. Network Corp., St. Louis, 2006—. Contbr. articles to profl. jours. Mem.: ALA, Assn. Coll. and Rsch. Librs., Assn. Libr. and Collections and Tech. Svcs., Beta Phi Mu. Office: MU Librs U Mo-Columbia 104 Ellis Library Columbia MO 65203 Office Phone: 573-882-4701. E-mail: CogswellJA@missouri.edu.*

COGSWELL, JIM, library director; BA, Bowdoin Coll., Brunswick, Maine; MLS, Rutgers U., New Brunswick, NJ. Libr. mgr. Johns Hopkins U., Princeton U., U. Minn.; dir. librs. U. Mo., Columbia, 2002—. Contbr. articles to profl. jours. Mem.: ALA, Assn. Coll. and Rsch. Librs., Assn. Libr. and Collections and Tech. Svcs., Beta Phi Mu. Office: MU Librs Adminstrv Offices U Mo-Columbia 104 Ellis Library Columbia MO 65201-5149 Office Phone: 573-882-4701. Office Fax: 573-882-8044. Business E-Mail: cogswellja@missouri.edu.*

COGSWELL, JOHN HEYLAND, retired telecommunications industry executive, financial consultant; b. Southampton, NY, Oct. 18, 1933; s. John W. and Lucy A. (McCurdy) C.; m. Patricia A. Morrissey, June 18, 1955; children: Julie A., Catherine J. AB, Dartmouth Coll., 1955, MS, 1956. Registered profl. engr., Mass. Engr. New Eng. Telephone Co., Boston, 1956-61, planning engr., Pittsfield, Mass., 1961-63, staff acct., Boston, 1963-65, constrn. program engr., 1969-71, div. mgr. fin., 1971-83, sec.-treas., 1983-90; engr. Am. Telephone Co., NYC, 1965-68, mgr. econs., 1968-69. Treas., bd. dirs. Neighborhood Health Plan, Boston, 1986-88, 90-98, pres. 1988-90. Active Needham Bd. Selectmen, 1996—, Needham Town Meeting, 1975—; pres. bd. dirs. Health Action Forum, Greater Boston, 1992—97, treas., 1983—92, 1997—98; treas., bd. dirs. Muscular Dystrophy Assn., Greater Boston, 1978—91, Needham Hist. Soc., Inc., Mass., 1975—95, trustee Mass., 1995—; treas., bd. dirs. Cmty. Health Ctr. Capital Fund, 1992—99; chmn. Needham Planning Bd., 1977—87; active Needham Bd. Appeals, 1987—91; chmn. Needham Bd. Selectmen, 1998, 2001, 2006; bd. dirs. Pathway Health Networks, 1995—96, Care Group, 1996—. Health Agys. of Mass., 1996—99, Cmty. Health Charities, 1999—2005, pres., 2001; bd. dirs. Mass. Hosp. Assn., 2000—03, Bridgewater Goddard Park Med. Assocs., 2000—02, chmn., 2000—02; bd. dirs. Combined Health Appeal of Mass., 1991—96, pres., 1993—95; chmn. bd. dirs. Provider Svc. Network, 2003—05; bd. dirs. Ctr. Cmty. Responsive Care, 1994—98, treas., 1994—95; trustee Deaconess-Glover Hosp., 1991—99, vice-chmn., 1992—94, chmn., 1994—99; bd. dirs. Mass. Health Data Consortium, 1991—96, treas., 1994—96; bd. dirs. HealthPoint, 2001—04, Deaconess-Waltham Hosp., 2002, Living Care Villages of Mass., 2005—, New Eng. Health Care Found., 1992—96, North Hill Retirement Cmty., 2005—, treas., 2007—; bd. dirs., treas. Cogswell Family Assn., 1989—. Recipient Class of 1955 award Dartmouth Coll., 2003; named Vol. of Yr., Combined Health Appeal Am., 1992. Mem. Fin. Mgmt. Assn. (bd. dirs. 1977-79), Fin. Exec. Inst. (bd. dirs. 1988-90), Treas.'s Club Greater Boston (pres. 1987-88), Republican Club (New Providence, N.J.; pres. 1966-68). Episcopalian. Avocations: gardening, golf. Home and Office: 1479 Great Plain Ave Needham MA 02492-1217 Home Phone: 781-444-0852. Personal E-mail: j.cogswell@verizon.net.

COHAN, CHRISTOPHER J., professional sports team owner; b. Salinas, Calif., 1951; s. Helen; m. Angela Cohan; 3 children. BA, Ariz. State U., 1973. With Feather River Cable TV Corp., Orinda, Calif., 1973-77; founder, owner Sonic Comm., 1977—98; owner, CEO NBA Golden State Warriors, Calif., 1995—. Mem. adv./fin. com. NBA Bd. Govs. Founder Warriors Found., 1997—; established Ann. Angela and Christopher Cohan Cmty. Svc. Award, 2000. Office: Golden State Warriors 1011 Broadway Oakland CA 94607*

COHAN, GEORGE SHELDON, advertising and public relations executive; b. Oak Park, Ill., May 30, 1924; s. Charles and Ann (Holt) C.; m. Natalie Holmes, Dec. 14, 1974; children: Barry, Gail, Charles, Victoria. Student, Colo. Sch. Mines, 1941-42, Ind. U., 1942-43; BS in Mech. Engring, U. Cin., 1948; postgrad., John Marshall Law Sch., 1954-56. Certified bus. communicator. Field engr. Indsl. Erectors, Inc., Chgo., 1948-50; sales engr. Fairbanks-Morse & Co., Chgo., 1950-56; v.p., account supr. Hoffman & York Advt. Agy., Milw., 1956-62, Tobias & Olendorf, Chgo., 1962-65; sr. v.p., gen. mgr. Bozell & Jacobs, Inc., Chgo., 1965-74; chmn. bd., pres. Cohan & Paul, Inc., Chgo., 1975-84; pres. Fletcher, Mayo & Assocs., Chgo., 1984-87, Doremus & Co., Chgo., 1987-89, George Cohan Co., Chgo., 1989—; chmn. Cohan Seafood Co., San Francisco, 1988—. Bd. dir. Forest Labs., N.Y.C., Universal Gift Cert., Inc. Author: (play) Black Mutiny, 1948; contbr. articles to profl. jours. Mem. Cen. Ind. coun. Boy Scouts Am., 1965-69; mem. exec. com. March of Dimes, 1965-69, ANTA, 1948-51. 1st lt. C.E. AUS, 1943-45, CBI. Recipient Outstanding Merit award 8th Pan Am. Ry. Congress, 1954, 1st pl. Nat. Lithographic Soc., 1955, 15th ann. G.D. Crain award, 1981, gold award Chgo. Assn. Direct Mktg., 1979, 80, Pres.'s Cup award, 1986; named to Advt. Hall of Fame, 1981. Mem. ASME, Bus. and Profl. Advertisers Assn. (internat. pres. 1976-77, Best Seller award 1954, Best of Show 1962, Best of Show Indpls. 1966-67, ABP award 1971, Addy Gold award 1979, Profl. Excellence award 1978, Gold medal 1979, 80, Pro-Com. Gold award, 1981, 83, 84, Career of Excellence Spl. award 1989, Lifetime Career of Excellence award 1989), Pub. Rels. Soc. Am., Screen Actors Guild. Unitarian Universalist. Avocations: flying, cooking, fishing, opera, acting. Home: 2048 Foxfire Ct Henderson NV 89012-2190 Office Phone: 702-260-4244. E-mail: geocoh@aol.com.

COHAN, LEON SUMNER, lawyer, retired electric company executive; b. Detroit, June 24, 1929; s. Maurice and Lillian (Rosenfeld) C.; m. Heidi Ruth Seelmann, Jan. 22, 1956; children: Nicole, Timothy David, Jonathan Daniel. BA, Wayne State U., 1949, JD, 1952. Bar: Mich. 1953. Pvt. practice, Detroit, 1954-58; asst. atty. gen. State of Mich., Lansing, 1958-61, dep. atty. gen., 1961-72; v.p. legal affairs Detroit Edison Co., 1973-75, v.p., 1975-79, sr. v.p., gen. counsel, 1979-93; counsel Barris, Sott, Denn & Driker, Detroit, 1993—. Bd. dirs. Oakland Commerce Bank. Trustee Mich. Cancer Found.; bd. dirs. Concerned Citizens for Arts in Mich., U. Mich. Musical Soc.; mem. arts commn. Detroit Inst. Arts; mem. Race Rels. Coun. Met. Detroit. With U.S. Army, 1952-54. Recipient Disting. Alumni award Wayne State U. Law Sch., 1972, Disting. Svc. award Bd. Govs., Wayne State U., 1973, Judge Ira W. Jayne award NAACP, 1987, Israel Histadrut Menorah award, 1987, Knights of Charity award Pontifical Inst. for Fgn. Missions, 1989, Fellowship award Am. Arabic and Jewish Friends of Met. Detroit, Judge Learned Hand Human Rels. award, 1991, Gov.'s Arts award for Civic Leadership in the Arts, Michiganian of Yr. award Detroit News, 1993. Mem. ABA, Detroit Bar Assn., State Bar Mich. (Champion of Justice award 1993), Mich. Gen. Counsel Assn., Detroit Club. Democrat. Jewish. Home: 17 Eastbury Ct Ann Arbor MI 48105-1402 Office: Barris Sott Denn & Driker 15th Fl 211 W Fort St Lbby 15 Detroit MI 48226-3244 Business E-Mail: lscohan@comcast.com.

COHANE, HEATHER CHRISTINA, publishing executive, editor; b. Camberley, Surrey, Eng. came to US, 1982; d. William Willoughby and Naomi Mary (Winder) Fausset; m. John Philip Cohane, May 13, 1961 (dec. Dec. 1981); children: Alexander, Candida, Ondine; m. Ossian Kare Berga, Nov. 2, 1985. (dec. Oct. 2000). Student pvt. schs., Isle of Wight, Eng. and Neuchatel, Switzerland. Founding editor, pub. Quest mag., NYC, 1987—; exec. v.p. Gotham Mag., NYC, 1999—2001; editor-at-large Avenue Mag., 2002—04; contbg. editor NY Dog, 2004—. Office Phone: 212-249-7872. Personal E-mail: hcohane@aol.com.

COHEE, KEVIN, bank executive; b. Kans. City, Mo., 1958; m. Teri A. Cohee. BA, U. Wis., MBA, 1985; JD, Harvard Law Sch., 1985. Founder cons. firm, 1979; investment banker Salomon Bros., Inc., 1985—88; acquired Military Profl. Svcs., Inc., 1985—93, Boston Bank of Commerce, 1995—96; chmn., CEO OneUnited Bank, 1996—. Office: OneUnited Bank 3683 Crenshaw Blvd Los Angeles CA 90016 Office Phone: 323-290-4848. Office Fax: 323-293-7746.

COHELEACH, GUY JOSEPH, artist; b. NYC; s. Gaetan Guy and Flavia Marie (Aymong) Coheleach; m. Patricia Arlene McGauley; children: George G., Coleen P., Hugh G., Guy G.(dec.) , Elizabeth P.(dec.). Grad., Cooper Union, NYC; ArtsD (hon.), Coll. William and Mary, Williamsburg, Va., 1975. Bd. dirs. Soc. Animal Artists. One-man shows include over 100 exhbns. from NY to LA including LA County Mus., 1991, Carnegie Mus., Pitts., 1995-96, Newark, NJ, Mus., 1996, West Valley Art Mus., Phoenix, 2000, Vero Beach Mus. Art, Fla., 2004-05; group shows include Bird Artists of World, Tryon Gallery, London, Mammal Artists of World, Nairobi, Kenya, Bird Artists of Am., Graham Gallery, NYC, Am. Mus. Natural History, Denver Mus., Nat. Collection of Fine Art, Washington, Corcoran Gallery, Washington; represented in permanent collections, White House, Nat. Wildlife Fedn. Gallery, Am. Mus. Natural History, Nat. Audubon Soc. Gallery; master artist from Leigh Yawkee Woodson Art Mus., 1983, Nat. History Mus. of LA, 1991, R.W. Norton Art Gallery Glassmere Wildlife Park, 1992, Cin. Mus. of Natural History, 1992, Cultural Ctr. Gallery, Stuart, Fla., 1993, Ctrl. Park Gallery, NYC, 1993, Internat. Wildlife Mus., Tucson, 1993, Dayton Mus., 1994, Houston Mus., 1994, Cleve. Mus., 1994, Blauvelt Art Mus., 1995, Carnegie Mus., 1995, Newark Mus., 1996, John James Audubon Mus., 1997, Roger Tory Petersen Inst., 1997, Haley Mus., 1997, Ft. Worth Zoo Mus., 1998, Neville Pub. Mus., Green Bay, Wis., 1998, Michelson Mus., Marshall, Tex., 1999, Burpee Mus., Rockford, Ill., 1999, West Valley Art Mus., Surprise, Ariz., 2000, Cultural Ctr., Stuart, Fla., 2001, RT Peterson Inst., Jamestown, NY, 2002, Wildlife Experiences Mus., Parker, Colo., 2003, RW Norton Gallery, Shreveport, La., 2003, Vero Beach, Fla., Art Mus., 2004, Oskosh Pub. Mus., 2005-06, Ward Mus. Wildfowl Art, 2005, Oshkosh Pub. Mus., 2006, Schiele Mus., Gastonia, NC, 2007. Served with AUS. Recipient Mzuri Safari Internat. Wildlife Artist's Magnum Opus award, 1974; Conservation award African Safari Club, 1976; Blue ribbon Printing Industries Am., 1969-81; named Artist of Yr., Gt. Lakes Art Festival, Milw., 1985 Fellow Explorers Club; mem. Soc. Animal Artists (v.p., 8 awards of excellence, 1980—), Nat. Audubon Soc. (life), Nat. Wildlife Fedn. (life, Artist of Yr. 1985), East African Profl. Hunters Assn. (hon.), Adventurers Club, Boone and Crocket Club, Campfire (NY), Pres.'s Club (U. Tenn.), Phila. Gun Club. Prints of work American Eagle chosen by Dept. State as gifts for vis. fgn. heads of state. Personal E-mail: guymbogd@aol.com. Business E-Mail: guysart@patmedia.net. *I believe anyone can attain a very high degree of success in any field as long as they love their chosen field and are not afraid of work.*

COHEN, ABBY JOSEPH, investment company executive; b. NYC, Feb. 29, 1952; d. Raymond and Shirley (Silverstein) Joseph; m. David M. Cohen. AB in Econs., Cornell U., 1973; MA in Econs., George Washington U., Washington, 1976. CFA. Economist Fed. Res. Bd., Washington, 1973-76; economist/analyst T. Rowe Price Assocs., Balt., 1976-83; investment strategist Drexel Burnham Lambert, NYC, 1983-90, Goldman, Sachs & Co., NYC, 1990—, mng. ptnr., 1998—. Trustee/fellow Cornell U.; bd. overseers Cornell Med. Sch. Named one of Most Powerful Women, Fortune Mag., 1998, Most Powervul, Smart Money Mag., 1998—2002, Most Powerful People, Forbes mag., 2005; named to top 50 in Global Fin., 1996; recipient Woman Achiever (Woman of Yr.), YWCA, NYC, 1989, Wall St. Week Hall of Fame, 1998. Mem. Nat. Assn. Bus. Economists, Inst. Chartered Fin. Analysts (chair), N.Y. Soc. Security Analysts (mem. bd. govs.), Nat. Economists Club (bd. govs.), Assn. for Investment Mgmt. and Rsch. (chair bd. govs. 1997-98), Coun. on Fgn. Rels., Coun. on Excellence in Govts. (bd. dirs.). Office: Goldman Sachs & Co 85 Broad St New York NY 10004-2456

COHEN, ADAM, reporter, lawyer; b. Manhattan; AB, Harvard Univ., 1984, JD, 1987. Edn. reform lawyer; lawyer So. Poverty Law Ctr., Montgomery, Ala.; sr. writer Time Mag., NYC; asst. editl. page editor The NY Times, 2002—. Co-author (with Elizabeth Taylor): American Pharaoh: Mayor Richard J. Daley, His Battle for Chicago and the Nation, 2000; author: The Perfect Store: Inside eBay, 2002. Office: Editl Bd The NY Times 229 W 43rd St New York NY 10036 Office Phone: 212-556-3626. Office Fax: 212-556-3815.

COHEN, ALAN, investment banker; b. NYC, Jan. 1, 1945; s. Harold and Edith (Schneider) Cohen; m. Carolyn Zacks, Jan. 3, 1970; children: Davi Melissa, Michael Jarrett. BA in Econs., Bklyn. Coll., 1967; postgrad, NYU. Commodity broker Reynolds Securities Inc., NYC, 1977—78; v.p., regional commodity mgr. Loeb Rhoades Hornblower, NYC, 1978—79; v.p., regional commodity dir. E.F. Hutton Co., NYC, 1979—80; v.p., nat. commodities sales mgr., ltd. ptnr. and assoc. dir. Bear, Stearns & Co., NYC, 1980—91; sr. mktg. dir. Stamford Co., NYC, 1991—. Home: 7 Hemlock Ln Marlboro NJ 07746-1212 Office: Independence Cmty Bank Corp 182 Atlantic Ave Brooklyn NY 11201-5604

COHEN, ALAN BARRY, researcher, educator; b. Bklyn., Nov. 3, 1952; s. Max B. and Blanche (Katz) C.; m. Helaine Francine Hartman, Dec. 22, 1973; children: Jeremy Todd, Bradley Daniel, Melanie Ann, Brandon Adam. BA, U. Rochester, 1973; MS, Harvard U., 1975, ScD, 1983. Rsch. asst. Beth Israel Hosp. and Harvard Med. Sch., Boston, 1974-75; sr. analyst Urban Systems Rsch. & Engring. Inc., Cambridge, Mass., 1975-79; rsch. assoc. Harvard Sch. Pub. Health, Boston, 1979-81, Johns Hopkins Sch. Hygiene and Pub. Health, Balt., 1981-82, asst. prof., 1982-84; assoc. dir. John Hopkins Ctr. for Hosp. Fin. and Mgmt., Balt., 1983-84; program officer Robert Wood Johnson Found., Princeton, NJ, 1984-87, sr. program officer, 1987-88, v.p., 1988-92; rsch. prof. Heller Grad. Sch. Brandeis U., 1992-94; prof. health policy and mgmt. Boston U. Sch. Mgmt., 1994—, dir. health care mgmt. program, 1994—2003; exec. dir. Health Policy Inst. Boston U., 2003—; prof. health svcs. Boston U. Sch. Pub. Health, 2004—. Nat. program dir. Robert Wood Johnson Found. Scholars in Health Policy Rsch. Program, 1992—; mem. nat. adv. com. Robert Wood Johnson Found. Info. for State Health Policy Program, 1994-98; cons. NJ Dept. Health, 1993; chmn. commr.'s cardiac svc. com. State of NJ, Trenton, 1990-92; mem. Inst. Medicine, Tech. Monitoring Panel on Access to Care, 1989-91; cons. DC State Health Planning and Devel. Agy., 1984, Nat. Ctr. Health Svc. Rsch., 1984. Mem. editl. bd. Inquiry, Health Affairs; contbr. articles to profl. jours. Recipient Charles F. Wilinsky award Harvard Sch. Pub. Health, 1979; Kaiser fellow in health policy and mgmt., 1973-74; Dissertation grantee Nat. Ctr. Health Svc. Rsch., 1979-80. Fellow Acad. Health; mem. APHA, ASHE, APPAm, Am. Econ. Assn., Am. Polit. Sci. Assn., Nat. Acad. Social Ins., Health Tech. Assessment Internat., Zeta Beta Tau (pres. Gamma Pi chpt. 1972-73, treas. 1970-72), Beta Gamma Sigma. Jewish. Avocations: reading, travel, cinema, basketball, gardening. Office: Boston U Health Policy Inst 53 Bay State Rd Boston MA 02215

COHEN, ALAN H., retail executive; b. Indpls., Mar. 5, 1947; m. Linda Cohen; children: Nathan, Lauren. BS, Ind. U., 1969, JD, 1973. Atty., 1976—80; chmn., CEO The Finish Line, Inc., Indpls., 1976—, pres., 1976—2003. Mem. bd. vis. Ind. U. Law Sch.; mem. dean's adv. coun. Kelley Sch. Bus.; bd. dirs. Ctrl. Ind. Corp. Partnership. Nat. trustee Boy's and Girl's Clubs Am.; bd. dirs. Ind. C. of C. Named Entrepreneur of Yr., Inc. mag., 1991, Ernst & Young, 1991; recipient Spirit of Philanthropy award, Ind. U., 2002, Purdue U., 2002. Office: The Finish Line Inc 3308 N Mitthoeffer Rd Indianapolis IN 46235 Office Phone: 317-899-1022.

COHEN, ALAN SEYMOUR, internist; b. Boston, Apr. 9, 1926; s. George I. and Jennie (Laskin) C.; m. Joan Elizabeth Prince, Sept. 12, 1954; children: Evan Bruce, Andrew Hollis, Robert Adam AB magna cum laude, Harvard Coll., Cambridge, Mass., 1947; MD magna cum laude, Boston U., 1952. Intern Harvard Med. Svc., Boston City Hosp., 1952-53, resident, 1953-55; exch. registrar in medicine Dundee Royal Infirmary and U. St. Andrews, Scotland, 1955-56. Rsch. and clin. fellow in rheumatology Mass. Gen. Hosp., Boston, 1956-58; instr. Med. Sch. Harvard Coll. and Mass. Gen. Hosp., 1958-60; head arthritis and connective tissue disease sect. Evans dept. clin. rsch. Mass. U. Hosp., Boston, 1960-72; Conrad Wesselhoeft prof. medicine Sch. Medicine Boston U., 1972-93, prof. pharmacology, 1974-92, disting. prof. medicine in rheumatology, 1993—; dir. Arthritis Ctr., 1977-94; dir. divsn. medicine Boston City Hosp., 1973-93; dir. Thorndike Meml. lab., 1973-93; bd. dirs. Hemagen Diagnostics Inc.; scientific bd. Neurochem. Inc., Can., 1997-2001. Editor: Laboratory Diagnostic Procedures in the Rheumatic Diseases, 1967, rev. edit., 1975, 3d edit., 1985, (with others) Symposium on Amyloidosis, 1968, (With R. Friedin and M. Samuels) Medical Emergencies: Diagnostic and Management Procedures from Boston City Hospital, 1977, (with J. Combes and H. Koh) 2d edit., 1983, Rheumatology and Immunology, 1979, (with J.C. Bennett) 2d edit., 1986, Progress in Clinical Rheumatology, 1984, (with D. Goldenberg) Drugs in the Rheumatic Diseases, 1986, Amyloidosis, 1986, Clinical Problems in Acute Care Medicine (J.J. Heffernan, R.A. Witzburg, A.S. Cohen), 1989; founder, editor-in-chief Amyloid Jour. Protein Folding Disorders, 1994—; contbr. more than 700 articles to profl. jours. Trustee Arthritis Found., Atlanta, 1976-82, trustee Mass. chpt., 1966-85, vice chmn., 1971-84, pres., 1981-94; vice sec. for N.Am., mem. exec. com. Pan Am. League Against Rheumatism, 1982-85; chmn. Boston City Hosp. Physician Alumni Reunion Com., 1992; pres. Boston City Hosp. Fund for Excellence, 1992. Served to surg. USPHS, 1953-55. Recipient Outstanding Alumnus award Boston U. Sch. Medicine, 1975, Purdue Frederic Arthritis award, 1979, James H. Fairclough Jr. award for disting. svc. to Mass. chpt. Arthritis Found., 1981, Alumni award for spl. distinction Boston U., 1981, Jan Van Bremeen Gold medal Dutch Rheumatism Soc., 1990, Commrs. Disting. Physician award Boston City Hosp., 1991, Gold medal Am. Coll. Rheumatology, 1994, Dr. Marian Ropes award Arthritis Found., 1995, Socius Honoris Causa, Hungarian Amyloid Soc., 2001, Hero award Arthritis Found., 2001, Millenium Medal of Hungarian Rsch. Group Amuloidosun, HSFR, 2001, Outstanding Achievement award Internat. Soc. Amyloidosis 2006. Master Am. Coll. Rheumatology (pres. 1978-79); fellow ACP; mem. Internat. Soc. Amyloidosis (bd. dirs. 2004—), Am. Soc. Clin. Investigation, Assn. Am. Physicians, Am. Fedn. Clin. Rsch., Am. Soc. Exptl. Pathology, Soc. Exptl. Biology and Medicine, Electron Microscopy Soc. Am., New Eng. Soc. for Electron Microscopy, Am. Soc. Cell Biology, N.Y. Acad. Sci., AMA, Mass. Med. Soc., New Eng. Rheumatism Assn. (past pres.), Italian Rheumatism Soc. (hon.), Spanish Rheumatism Soc. (hon.), Finnish Rheumatism Soc. (hon.), Brazilian Rheumatism Soc. (hon.), Irish Soc. Rheumatism and Rehab. (hon.), Italian Soc. Amyloidosis (hon.), Boston U. Sch. Medicine Alumni Assn. (past pres.), Harvard Club (Boston), Wightman Tennis Ctr. (Weston, Mass.), Interurban Clin. Club, Boulders Club (Carefree, Ariz.), Phi Beta Kappa, Alpha Omega Alpha. Jewish. Office: Boston U Sch Medicine Amyloid Program 715 Albany St Bradston 204 Boston MA 02118-2307 Office Phone: 617-638-8900. Business E-Mail: jlienert@bu.edu.

COHEN, ALBERT, musician, educator; b. NYC, Nov. 16, 1929; s. Sol A. and Dora Cohen; m. Betty Joan (Berg) Aug. 28, 1952; children: Eva Denise, Stefan Berg. BS, Juilliard Sch. Music, 1951; MA, NYU, 1953, PhD, 1959; postgrad., U. Paris, 1956-57. Mem. faculty U. Mich., Ann Arbor, 1960-70, assoc. prof. music, 1964-67, prof., 1967-70; prof. music, chmn. dept. SUNY, Buffalo, 1970-73, Stanford U., 1973-87, William H.

Bonsall prof. music, 1974—, prof. emeritus, 2000—. Editor: Broude Bros. Ltd., N.Y.C., Info. Coordinators, Detroit. Author: Treatise on the Composition of Music, 1962, Elements or Principles of Music, 1965; (with J.D. White) Anthology of Music for Analysis, 1965; (with L.E. Miller) Music in the Paris Academy of Sciences, 1666-1793, An Index, 1979, Music in the French Royal Academy of Sciences, 1981, Music in the Royal Society of London 1660-1806, 1987; editor: J.B. Lully, Ballet de Flore, 2001; contbr. articles to profl. jours. Guggenheim fellow, 1968-69; NEH fellow, 1975-76, 82-83, 85-89, Fulbright fellow, 1956-1957. Mem. Internat. Musicol Soc., Am. Musicol Soc., French Musicol Soc., Music Libr. Assn. Office: Stanford U Dept Music Stanford CA 94305

COHEN, ALBERT DIAMOND, retail executive; b. Winnipeg, Man., Can., Jan. 20, 1914; s. Alexander and Rose (Diamond) C.; m. Irena Kankova, Nov. 6, 1953; children: Anthony Jan, James Eduard, Anna-Lisa. LLD (hon.), U. Man., 1987. Pres. Gendis Inc., Winnipeg, Canada, 1953-87, chmn., CEO, 1987-99, chmn., pres., CEO, 1999—. Author: The Entrepreneurs (Cert. of Merit Nat. Bus. Book award 1986), The Story of SAAN, 2002, The International Distinguished Entrepreneur Award--What Business Award has the Whole World Talking?, 2006. Past pres. Winnipeg Clin. Rsch. Inst., 1975-80, Paul H.T. Thorlakson Rsch. Found., 1978-80, Man. Theatre Ctr., 1968-71, 76-81; past hon. chmn. St. John's Ravenscourt Sch., 1984-94; commr. Metric Bd. Ottawa, 1978. Named mem. Order of Can., 1983, promoted to officer, 1995; recipient Internat. Disting. Entrepreneur award U. Man., 1983, Man. of Yr. award Sales and Advt. Club, Winnipeg, 1974, Commemorative medal 125th Ann. Can. Fedn., 1992, Sony Lifetime Achievement award, 2000; inducted into Can. Bus. Hall of Fame, 1994. Office: Gendis Inc PO 9400 1370 Sony Pl Winnipeg MB Canada R3T 1N5 E-mail: finance@gendis.ca.

COHEN, ALLAN RICHARD, broadcast executive; b. Bklyn., Dec. 27, 1947; s. Ike and Fae C.; m. Roberta Segal, July 12, 1970; children: Evan, Stacie. BS, Hofstra U., 1970; MM, Poly. Inst. Bklyn., 1976. Electronics engr. Sperry Systems Mgmt. Div., Great Neck, NY, 1970-74; with CBS/Viacom, 1974—; dir. planning and adminstrn. WCBS-TV, 1977-79; v.p. personnel CBS Broadcast Group, 1979-80; v.p., gen. mgr. Sta. KMOX-TV, St. Louis, 1980-86, Sta. KMOV-TV, St. Louis, 1986—. Lectr. in comm. and journalism Washington U., St. Louis; mem. affiliates adv. bd. CBS. Restaurant critic, travel editor St. Louis Bus. Jour. Vice chmn. bd. dirs. St. Louis Symphony; bd. dirs. Paraquad, Jewish Hosp., United Way, Variety Club; mem. adv. bd. Nat. Coun. Jewish Women, St. Louis. Recipient Flair awards, Emmy awards. Mem. NATAS (v.p. St. Louis chpt. 1987-88, pres. 1989-91), Mo. Broadcasters Assn. (bd. dirs.), Ill. Broadcasters Assn., Nat. Assn. Broadcasters, St. Louis Jr. League (adv. bd.), Westwood Club, St. Louis Variety Club (bd. dirs.).

COHEN, ANDREW, news analyst, lawyer; b. Montreal; BA, Boston U., 1988, JD, 1991. Assoc. Gorsuch Kirgis, Boston, 1991; legal analyst, commentator CBS News Radio, 1997—, CBS News, CBS 4, Denver. Author: (law column) Gavel to Gavel, Bench Conference. Recipient S.P.J. Award for Best Spot News coverage. Office: CBS 4 1044 Lincoln St Denver CO 80203

COHEN, ANN ELLEN, librarian; b. Binghamton, NY, June 11, 1949; d. Leonard Francis and Shirley Frances (Greenhouse) C. Student, Elmira Coll., 1967-69; BA, George Washington U., 1971; MSLS, Syracuse U., 1972. N.Y. State Librarian's Cert. Br. libr. Binghamton Pub. Libr., 1973-77, info. services libr., 1977-84, Broome County Pub. Libr., Binghamton, 1985-88; asst. div. head Rochester (N.Y.) Pub. Libr., 1988—. Dir. Temple Israel Libr., Binghamton, 1982-85, cons., 1982—, cons. children's libr., 1985-86. Author book revs., Libr. Jour., 1983-97, Booklist's Reference Books Bulletin, 1989—. Mem. 123d Dist. of N.Y. State Assembly's Edn. Aid Task Force, 1986-88, Broome County (N.Y.) Com. of U.S. Commn. for Bicentennial Celebration of U.S. Constn., 1987; bd. dirs. Jewish Cmty. Ctr., Binghamton, 1982-85, Temple Beth Am, Henrietta, N.Y., 1996—. Mem. AAUW, ALA (affiliates coun. rep. jr. mems. round table 1984-86, editl. bd. reference books bulletin 1989-92), N.Y. Libr. Assn. (pres. jr. mems. round table 1985-86), Hadassah, Jewish Genealogy Soc. of Greater Rochester. Office: Rochester Pub Libr 115 South Ave Rochester NY 14604-1896

COHEN, ARNOLD NORMAN, gastroenterologist; b. NYC, Nov. 5, 1949; s. Norman and Edna Clara (Arnold) C.; m. Colleen Ruth Carey, children: Eric Arnold, Leslie Carey. BA summa cum laude, Hobart Coll., 1971; MD, Harvard U., 1975. Diplomate Am. Bd. Internal Medicine, Am. Bd. Gastroenterology. Resident internal medicine U. Pa., Phila., 1975-78, asst. instr. medicine, 1977-78; fellow gastroenterology, instr. medicine Northwestern U., Chgo., 1978-80; asst. clin. prof. medicine U. Wash. Med. Sch., Seattle, 1980—; mem. faculty Spokane (Wash.) Family Medicine Residency, 1980—; pvt. practice gastroenterology Spokane, 1980—. Mem. various coms. St. Lukes-Deaconess Hosp., Spokane, 1980—; pres. med. staff St. Lukes Hosp., 1985-86. Contbr. articles to profl. jours. and textbooks. Fellow ACP, Am. Coll. Gastroenterology; mem. Am. Soc. Gastrointestinal Endoscopy, Am. Gastroent. Soc., Wash. Med. Soc., Spokane Internal Med. Soc., Phi Beta Kappa, Alpha Omega Alpha. Avocations: shooting sports, martial arts, swimming. Home: 3514 S Jefferson St Spokane WA 99203-1441 Office: Spokane Digestive Disease Ctr 801 W 5th Ave Spokane WA 99204-2823 Office Phone: 509-747-5145.

COHEN, ARYELL, music educator; b. Bronx, NY, Aug. 20, 1952; s. Aaron Moses Cohen and Phyllis Novik; m. Maxine Judith Hersh (div.); children: Michelle, Erica. BA in Music, Calif. State U., 1978. Tchg. credential Calif., 2000. Tchr. Sinai Temple, LA, 1970, organist, choir dir., 1975—; tchr. L.A. Unified Sch. Dist., 1995—. Mem. Music Educators Nat. Conf. Mem.: Guild Temple Musicians, Am. Choral Directors Assn., Am. Guild Organists. Democrat. Jewish. Office Phone: 310-474-1518. Business E-Mail: acohen@sinaitemple.org.

COHEN, BENEDICT S., lawyer; BA, Yale U., 1980; JD, U. Chgo., 1983. Dep. gen. counsel environ. and installations US Dept. Def.; chief of staff com. homeland security US Ho. of Reps.; sr. adv. to chmn. SEC; gen. counsel Dept. Army US Dept. Def., 2006—. Office: US Dept Def 104 Army Pentagon Rm 2E520 Washington DC 20310-0104 Office Fax: 703-697-9235.

COHEN, BERNARD IRVIN, plastic surgeon; b. Pottsville, Pa., Jan. 6, 1936; DDS, U. Pitts., 1960, MD, 1964. Cert. Am. Bd. Gen. Surgery, Am. Bd. Plastic Surgery. Intern, gen. surgery South Side Hosp., Pitts., 1964—65; resident Colo. Med. Ctr., Denver, 1965—69, Norfolk Gen. Hosp., Va., 1969—71; hosp. appointment Butler Meml. Hosp., Pitts.; asst. clin. prof. U. Pitts.; private practice Pitts., 1971—. Fellow: ACS; mem.: Am. Soc. Aesthetic Plastic Surgery, Am. Soc. Plastic Surgeons. Office: Roesch-Taylor Bldg 2100 Jane St Pittsburgh PA 15203*

COHEN, BERNARD LEONARD, physicist, researcher; b. Pitts., June 14, 1924; s. Samuel and Mollie (Friedman) C.; m. Anna Foner, Mar. 30, 1950 (dec. 1998); children: Donald, Judith, Frederick, Ernest. BS, Case Inst. Tech., 1944; MS, U. Pitts., 1948; PhD, Carnegie Inst. Tech., 1950. With Oak Ridge (Tenn.) Nat. Lab., 1950-58; prof. physics U. Pitts., 1958-94, prof. emeritus, 1994—, adj. prof. chemistry, chem. engring., radiation health, environ. and occupl. health; dir. Sarah Mellon Scaife Nuc. Physics Lab., 1965-78. On leave with Gen. Atomic Lab., San Diego, 1959-60, Inst. for Def. Analysis, Washington, 1962, Brookhaven Nat. Lab., 1965, Los Alamos Sci. Lab., 1969, Inst. Energy Analysis, Oak Ridge, 1974-75, Electric Power Rsch. Inst., 1975, Argonne Nat. Lab., 1978-79; cons. numerous govtl. agys. and pvt. corps. Author: Heart of the Atom, 1967, Concepts of Nuclear Physics, 1971, Nuclear Science and Society, 1974, Before It's Too Late: A Scientist's Case for Nuclear Power, 1983, A Homeowner's Guide to Radon, 1987, The Nuclear Energy Option: Alternative For The Nineties, 1990; contbr. numerous articles to profl. jours. Fellow AAAS, Am. Phys. Soc. (chmn. divsn. nuc. physics 1974-75, Bonner prize for nuc. physics 1981); mem. NAE, Am. Assn. Physics Tchrs. (nat. coun. 1973-78), Am. Nuc. Soc. (chmn. divsn. environ. scis. 1980-81, Pub. Info. award 1984, Walter Zinn award 1996, Spl. award 1996), Soc. Risk Analysis, Health Physics Soc. (Disting. Sci. Achievement award 1992). Home: 307 S Dithridge St Apt 204 Pittsburgh PA 15213-3514 Office Phone: 412-624-9245. Fax: 412-624-9163. Business E-Mail: blc@pitt.edu.

COHEN, BETSY Z., bank executive; m. Edward C. Cohen; children: Daniel, Jonathan, Abigail. BA cum laude, Bryn Mawr Coll.; JD cum laude, U. Pa. Law clk. hon. John Biggs chief judge U.S. Ct. Appeals 3rd Cir.; law prof. Rutgers U. Law Sch.; co-founder Spector, Cohen, Gadon & Rosen, Phila.; dir. First Union Corp. of Va., Dominion Bancshares, Inc., 1985—93; founder, chmn., CEO Jefferson Bank, Downingtown, Pa., 1974—; founder Jefferson Bank NJ, 1987; chmn., CEO JeffBanks, Inc., 1993—; founder, chmn., CEO, trustee RAIT Investment Trust, 1997—; dir. Hudson United Bancorp, 1999—2000; CEO Bancorp Bank, 2000—, chmn., 2003—; CEO Bancorp Inc., 2000—, dir., 2000—. Bd. dirs. Aetna US Healthcare, The Opera Co. Phila., WHYY-TV; trustee Phila. Mus. Art, Jewish Theol. Sem.; vice chair Bryn Mawr Coll., chair fin. com.; chair Phila. Mus. Art Corp. Ptnrs. Article editor The Law Rev. Recipient Paradigm award Greater Phila. C. of C., 1997, Elizabeth Dole Glass Ceiling award Southeastern Pa. ARC, 1998; named Delaware Valley Master Entrepreneur of the Yr., 1994, one to Top 50 Bus. Women in Commonwealth of Pa., 1996, one of 50 Leading Female Entrepreneurs of the World, Nat. Found. for Women Bus. Owners, 1997, A Woman of Distinction, Cmty. Women's Edn. Project, 1998; ranked 103 Working Woman Mags. Top 500 Bus. Women, 1998. Mem. Order of the Coif. Office: The Bancorp Bank 405 Silverside Rd Wilmington DE 19809 E-mail: bcohen@jeffbanks.com.

COHEN, BETTY L., former broadcast executive; b. Racine, Wis. BA in Comm., Stanford U., 1977. Broadcast prodr. Pub. Media Ctr., San Francisco, 1977; mgr. sr. prodr. on-air promotion Lifetime Television Services; writer-prodr. on-air promotion Cable Health Network; dir. on-air promotion and interstitial programming Nickelodeon/Nick at Nite, 1984—88; sr. v.p. & gen. mgr. Turner Network Television, 1988—92; founder, exec. v.p. Cartoon Network Worldwide, 1992—2001, pres., 1994—2001; with AOL Time Warner Inc., 2001—02; pres. Betty Cohen Media Consulting, LLC, 2002—05; pres., CEO Lifetime Entertainment Services, 2005—07. Bd. trustees AOL Time Warner Found.; exec. com. Cable in the Classroom Nat. Cable Television Assn. Bd. dir. Anti-Defamation League; mentor Teach for Am.; bd. adv. Atlanta Girls' Sch., Roadtrip Nation. Named PROMAX Internat. Marketer of Yr., 1997; named one of Top 100 Marketers, Advertising Age, 1999, 50 Most Powerful Women in Bus., Fortune mag., 2000, 100 Most Powerful Women in Entertainment, Hollywood Reporter, 2006; recipient Vanguard award, NCTA, 2000, Pinnacle award, PROMAX/BDA, 2001, Global Programming award, Multichannel News, 2001. Mem.: Phi Beta Kappa.*

COHEN, BRAM, web programmer; b. 1975; Summer studies in math., Hampshire Coll., 1992; attended, SUNY, Buffalo, 1993. Database programming and maintenance Travel Tours Internat., 1994; rsch. asst. in artificial intelligence AT&T Bell Lab., Murray Hill, NJ, 1993, 1995; software engr. Earthweb Inc., 1996; chief java programmer db-Centric Corp., 1997; chief software developer Signet Assurance Co., 1997—99; software engr. Evil Geniuses for a Better Tomorrow, 2000—01, MojoNation, 2000—01, Valve Software, 2003—04; CEO, co-founder, software developer BitTorrent Inc., Bellevue, Wash., 2001—. Co-founder CodeCon. Creator BitTorrent peer-to-peer (P2P) file distribution protocol; co-author: Codeville. Named one of World's 100 Most Influential People, Time Mag., 2005. Fellow: World Tech. Network (World Tech. Network award (Entertainment) 2005). Achievements include development of BitTorrent, software for downloading & sharing large files. Avocations: juggling, oragami. Office: BitTorrent Inc 201 Mission St Ste 900 San Francisco CA 94105

COHEN, BRETT I., health products executive; b. Bronx, NY, Aug. 13, 1962; s. Gilbert Victor and Phyllis C. C.; m. Elissa Bloom, Aug. 23, 1986; children: Harley Lennon, Jake Aaron. BS, SUNY, Albany, 1984, PhD in Chemistry, 1987. Postdoctoral fellow Rutgers U., New Brunswick, NJ, 1988; CEO, v.p. dental rsch. Essential Dental Systems, South Hackensack, NJ, 1989—2003. Mem. dental magnets subcom. Am. Dental Assn./ISO Specification No. 81 Magnets and Keepers, 1993—. Contbr. articles to profl. jours.; patentee in field. Mem. Am. Chem. Soc., Soc. for Dental Materials, Soc. for Lasers, Am. Soc. Quality Control. Avocations: reading, running, movies. Office: Essential Dental Systems 89 Leuning St South Hackensack NJ 07606-1326 Business E-Mail: eds@pipeline.com.

COHEN, BRUCE MICHAEL, psychiatrist, educator, scientist, health facility administrator; b. Univ. Heights, Ohio, Sept. 1, 1947; s. Herschel and Natalie (Marshall) C.; m. Marian A. Oliner, July 11, 1970; children: Matthew, Laura. BS, MIT, Cambridge, Mass., 1969; MD, Case Western Res. U., Cleveland, Ohio, 1975; PhD, Case Western Res. U., Dept. Biology, Cleveland, Ohio, 1975. Diplomate Am. Bd. Psychiatry and Neurology, 1979, Nat. Bd. Med. Examiners, 1976, Mass. Lic., 1976. Clin. fellow in psychiatry Harvard Med. Sch., Boston, 1975—78, instr. in psychiatry, 1978-81, asst. prof. psychiatry, 1981-85, assoc. prof. psychiatry, 1985-95, prof. psychiatry, 1995—; resident in psychiatry McLean Hosp., Belmont, Mass., 1975-78, chief resident in psychiatry, 1977-78, asst. psychiatrist, 1978—83, assoc. psychiatrist, 1984—88, spec. asst. to the gen. dir./psychiatrist-in-chief, 1987—88, assoc. gen. dir., 1988-94, psychiatrist, 1988—, sr. v.p. rsch. & tng., 1994-97, pres., psychiatrist in chief, 1997—2005, head dept. psychiatry Med. Sch. Harvard U., 1997—2005, dir. Shervert Frazier Rsch. Inst., 2006—; dir. combined Mass. Gen. Hosp./McLean Hosp., Belmont, Mass., 1995—97. Vis. physician MIT Clin. Rsch. Ctr., Cambridge, Mass., 1979—85, vis. sci., 1993—; asst. chief clin. rsch. sect. Mailman Rsch. Ctr., Belmont, 1979—81, assoc. chief clin. rsch. sect., 1981—85, chief clin. rsch. sect. Clin. Biochemistry Lab., 1981—85, dir. Molecular Pharmacology Lab., 1985—; cons. psychiatrist Westwood Lodge, Westwood, Mass., 1986—88; assoc. dir. Mental Health Clin. Rsch. Ctr. McLean Hosp., Belmont, 1981—88, program dir. Biomedial Rsch. Support Grant, 1988—92, dir. residency training program, 1993—97, dir. brain imaging program, 1993—97; pres. McLean Health Svcs., Belmont, 1998—99, dir. & CEO, 1999—2006. Contbr. numerous sci. articles and abstracts to peer-reviewed jours.; author 20 book chpts.; adv. editor, Psychopharmacology, 1980-2002; assoc. editor Am. Jour. of Psychiatry, 2000- Laureate investigator Nat. Alliance for Rsch. on Schizophrenia and Depression, 1989. Predoctoral fellow NSF, Case Western Res. U., 1971-73, Ethel duPont Warren fellow in psychiatry Harvard Med. Sch., McLean Hosp. 1977-78, fellowship, Scottish Rite Schizophrenia Rsch. Program, NMJ, USA, 1978-80, recipient 6 grants NIMH, 3 grants Scottish Rite Schizophrenia Program, 7 projects program grants NIMH. Fellow Mass. Psychiatric Soc., Soc. Magnetic Resonance, Am. Psychiat. Assn., Am. Coll. Neuropsychpharmacology; mem. AAAS, AMA, Soc. Biological Psychiatry Office: McLean Hosp Adminstrn bldg Rm 118 115 Mill St Belmont MA 02478-1048 Office Phone: 617-855-3227. Office Fax: 617-855-3670. Business E-Mail: cohenb@mclean.harvard.edu.

COHEN, BURTON DAVID, food service executive, lawyer; b. Chgo., Feb. 12, 1940; s. Allan and Gussy (Katz) C.; m. LInda Rochelle Kaine, Jan. 19, 1969; children: David, Jordana. BS in Bus. and Econs., Ill. Inst. Tech., 1960; JD, Northwestern U., 1963. Staff atty. McDonald's Corp., Oak Brook, Ill., 1964-69, asst. sec., 1969-70, asst. gen. counsel, 1970-76, asst. v.p., 1976-78, dep. dir. legal dept., 1978-80, v.p. franchising, asst. gen. counsel, asst. sec., 1980-89, sr. v.p., chief franchising officer, 1989-98; mng. ptnr. Burton D. Cohen & Assoc. LLC. Adv. dir., 1992-93, McDonald's Corp., 1992—; adv. bd. La. State U. Franchise U.; dir. Goodwill Enterprises Devel. Corp.; franchise mediator CPR Inst. for Dispute Resolution; adj. prof. Kellogg Grad Sch. Mgmt., Northwestern U.; bd. dirs. Dwyer Group, Cotlete; cons. Exec. Svc. Corps. Chgo.; sr. cons. Ifranchise Group; lectr., cons. in field. Author: Franchising: Second Generation Problems, 1969. With AUS, 1963-64. Mem. ABA, Ill. Bar Assn., Chgo. Bar Assn., Internat. Franchise Assn. (lectr.), Assn. Nat. Advertisers, Chgo. Coun. Fgn. Rels., Execs. Club (Chgo.), Tau Epsilon Phi, Phi Delta Phi. Office: 300 Cedar Ave Highland Park IL 60035

COHEN, BURTON JACK, otolaryngologist, educator; b. Louisville, 1936; MD, U. Louisville, 1962. Diplomate Am. Bd. Otolaryngology. Intern Detroit Receiving Hosp., 1962-63; resident in ear nose and throat U. Louisville Hosp., 1965-69; staff Jewish Hosp., Louisville, 1969—. Clin. prof. U. Louisville. Fellow: ACS, Am. Neurotologic Soc., Am. Acad. Otolaryngology-Head and Neck Surgery, Assn. Acad. Physicians, Am. Acad. Pediat. Office: 225 Abraham Flexner Way Louisville KY 40202-1846 Home Phone: 502-426-2371; Office Phone: 502-583-9425. Personal E-mail: burton.cohen@insightbb.com.

COHEN, CAROLYN A., healthcare educator; BS, Boston U., 1965; postgrad., Boston State Coll., U. Mass., 1978, Boston Leadership Acad., 1989, Boston Leadership Inst., 1997. Tchr., coach health and phys. edn. coord. girls athletics Roslindale H.S., Boston, 1965—76; tchr., coach health and phys. edn. coord. athletics West Roxbury H.S., Boston, 1976—87; asst. dir. health phys. edn. athletics Madison Park Campus, Boston, 1979—87; health educator dept. phys. edn./athletics West Roxbury H.S., Boston, 1989—90, 1990—, lead tchr., 1995—2000; commr. girls' basketball Boston Pub. Schs., 1979—. Cheerleading judge various orgns., 1963, 64, 65, 70, 74, 80, 69-74; coach recreational programs N.E. Deaconess Hosp. Sch. Nursing, 1962-64, Beth Israel Hosp. Sch. Nursing, 1961-64; basketball ofcl. Bay State League, Pvt. Sch. League, Cath. H.S., 1961-80; coach phys. edn. dept. Boston U., 1962-65, 65-68, programming guild chmn., 2005-; ofcl. Boston Park and Recreation Dept., 1962-75, summer playgrounds instr., 1961-65; instr. garening, athletic specialist agr. dept. Boston Schs., 1965-76. Trustee Adaptic Environ. Ctr., Boston, 1986—, treas., mem. exec. bd., 1990—; trustee Friends of Boston Harbor Islands, Inc.; instr. ARC, 1965—; rep. Office Children-Area IV, Roslindale, Boston, 1974—76; liaison West Roxbury H.S. and Cmty. Sch. New Move Unlimited Theatre, Boston, 1981—84; liaison spl. arts project West Roxbury H.S., 1993—94. Named to Boston U. Scarlet Key Soc., 1998, N.E. New Agenda Hall of Fame, 2003; recipient Spl. Citation, Boston U. Sargent Coll. Alumni Assn., 1980, Cert. of Appreciation, ARC Mass. Bay, 1986, New Agenda award, Boston Salute to Women in Sport, 1993, Disting. Svc. to Alma Mater award, Boston U., 1994, Citation, Mass. Celebration Women in Sports Day, 2002, citation, Mil. Order of World Wars, 2002, Youth Patriotic & Leadership, 2002, Patrick Henry award, YPAL Program of Officer's of World Wars, 2004. Mem.: Sargent Coll. Alumni Assn. (class sec., editor class newsletter 1965—, Spl. Citation 1980, Black Gold award 1995), Boston U. Nat. Alumni Coun., Boston U. Alumni Assn. (v.p. 1980—82, 1987—89, v.p. cmty. 1995—97, sec. 1997—, named to North East New Agenda Hall Fame 2003), Mass. Assn. Health, Phys. Edn., Recreation and Dance (state and exec. com. 1969—74, coord. registration ann. state conv. 1975—94, treas. 1981—94, Honor award recognition 1978, Presdl. Citation 1988, Joseph McKenney award 2002), AAHPERD (bud. mgr. nat. conv. 1988—89), Boston U. Women's Grad. Club (v.p. for scholarship 1981—83, 2005—).

COHEN, CHARLES EMIL, art historian, educator; b. NYC, July 11, 1942; s. Philip and Hannah (Abramson) Cohen; m. Sondra Eileen Cohen, Sept. 27, 1964; children: Joshua K., Jonathan E. BA, Columbia U., 1963; MFA, Princeton U., 1965; PhD, Harvard U., 1971. Tutor Harvard U., Cambridge, Mass., 1967-68, head teaching fellow, 1969-70; asst. prof. art U. Chgo., 1970-75, assoc. prof., 1975-80, chmn. art dept., 1985—89, Resident Master Pierce Hall, Mary L. Block prof. art, 1980—, chmn. com. visual arts. Curator of drawings Pordenone 500th Anniversary, 1984; resident master Pierce Hall U. Chgo. Author: I Disegni di Pomponio Amalteo, 1975, Drawings of Giovanni Antonio da Pordenone, 1980, Art of Giovanni Antiorio da Pordenone: Between Dialect & Lang.; contbr. articles to profl. jours. Fellow Guggenheim Found., 1983, Am. Coun. Learned Socs., 1980, Gladys Krieble Delmas Found., 1989, NEH, summer 1983; Univ. fellow NEH, 1989-90. Mem.: Renaissance Soc. Am., U. Chgo. Renaissance Seminar, Midwest Art History Soc., Coll. Art Assn. Am. Jewish. Office: U Chgo Dept Art 5540 S Greenwood Ave Chicago IL 60637-1506 Office Phone: 773-702-5880. E-mail: cac5@uchicago.edu.

COHEN, CHERYL DIANE DURDA, communications executive; b. Mpls., Jan. 26, 1947; d. Joseph and Dolores Catherine (Monahan) Durda; m. Miles Jon Cohen, June 24, 1967; children: Christopher, Michael, Brian, Katherine Kelly. BA, U. Minn., 1978; grad. Owner/Pres. Mgmt. program, Harvard Bus. Sch., 1992. Writer Aeration Industries Internat. Inc., Chaska, Minn., 1982—85, communications asst., 1985—86, communications mgr., 1986—88, v.p. pub. rels., 1988—93, v.p. mkgt., 1993—97, cons. environ. mktg., 1997—2003, v.p. mktg., 2003—, corp. sec., 2003—, also bd. dirs. Bd. dirs. Aeration Industries Internat., Inc. Editor AIRE-02 News, 1985—, AQUA-02 News, 1988—; contbr. articles on water restoration and aquaculture to profl. jours.; film editor, producer, 1986—. Bd. dirs. Minn. Assn. Retarded Citizens, Mpls., 1984-85, Joseph Durda Found., 1990—; St. David's Sch. for Exceptional Children, Minnetonka, 1980-85; adv. bd. Minnetonka Schs. CARE, Minn., 1982-92; dir. communications Minnetonka Football Assn., 1986-92, founding mem., 1986; adv. coun. U. Minn. Women's Intercollegiate Athletics; founding mem. Minnetonka Basketball Club, 1984; active legis. testimony, lobbying, pub. speaking Adv. for Severely Disabled, 1981-93; active U. Minn. Gopher Football Team's Parent Club, 1988-92, USAF Acad. Parents Club, 1992-93, Harvard-Radcliffe Club Minn., 1992-96; co-facilitator Devel. Capable Young People series for Minnetonka community, 1983-84. Mem. World Aquaculture Soc., Asian Fisheries Soc., Women of Water, U. Minn. Alumni Assn., U. Minn. Presidents Club (chartered), Booster Club (producer cable TV sports show 1988-92, co-chair publicity 1988-92), Harvard Bus. Sch. Club Minn. (alumni mem.). Roman Catholic. Avocations: reading, sports, music. Office: Aeration Industries Internat Inc 4100 Peavey Rd Chaska MN 55318-2353 Home Phone: 952-935-2987. Business E-Mail: cheric@aireo2.com.

COHEN, CHRISTOPHER B., lawyer; b. Washington, July 10, 1942; m. Judith Calder; 2 children. B.A., U. Mich., 1964, JD, 1967. Bar: Ill. 1968, Wis. 1986, D.C. 1972, U.S. Dist. Ct. D.C. 1969, U.S. Dist Ct. (no. dist.) Ill. 1968, U.S. Ct. Mil. Appeals 1977, U.S. Supreme Ct. 1974; lic. real estate broker, 1986. Clerk; lawyer Legal Aid Bur.-United Charities of Chgo., 1967-68; adminstrv. asst. to pres. Cook County Bd. Commrs., 1969-71; hearing officer Liquor Commn. Cook County, Chgo., 1970-71; alderman 46th ward Chgo. City Coun., 1971-77; atty. Schwartzberg, Barnett & Cohen, Chgo., 1973-77; midwest regional dir. U.S. Dept. HHS, Chgo., 1977-81; atty. Hinshaw, Culbertson, Moelmann, Hoban & Fuller, Chgo., 1981-82, Cassiday, Shade & Gloor, Chgo., 1982-85; ptnr. Holleb & Coff, Chgo., 1985-98; of counsel Buyer & Rubin, Chgo., 1998—2005; prin. Cohen Law Firm, Chgo., 1998—. Lectr. Northwestern U., 1973, 04, DePaul U., Chgo., 1981, U. Ill., Chgo., 1981, 82; adult edn. tchr. Francis Parker Sch., Chgo., 1979, 80, 81; bd. dirs. State of Ill. Hosp. Licensing Bd., 1987-97; bd. dirs. State of Ill. Med. Ctr. Commn., 1985-90; mem. fed. regional coun. 1977-81; nursing home adv. coun. Office of Ill. Atty. Gen., 1988-94; Dem. candidate U.S. Ho. Reps., 10th Congressional Dist. Ill.,

1999; Wis. State Pub. Defender, 2005—; rep. administrv. appeals divsn. Ill. Sec. State, 2002—; adminstrv. law judge Ill. Dept. Employment Security, 2003-05, bd. rev., 2005-07. Contbr. articles to profl. jours. and nat. newspapers. Field organizer Humphrey for Pres., Chgo., 1968; asst. to Ill. field dir. Jimmy Carter for Pres., Chgo., 1976; active spl. projects, polit. unit Clinton/Gore Campaign, Little Rock, 1992; mem. govt. affairs com. Jewish Fedn. Met. Chgo., 1988—; mem. U. Mich. Law Sch. Alumni Fund, 1967—, Glenview Concert Band, 2001-02; fin. exec. bd. New Trier Township Dem. Orgn., 1993-98; bd. dirs. UNICEF Chgo., 1996-97. Mem. ABA (adminstrv. law and regulatory practice sect. 1990-95), Ill. State Bar Assn. (founding mem., chair health care sect. coun. 1986-87, mem. legis. com. 1988-90, assembly 1991-97, local govt. sect.), Chgo. Bar Assn. (vice chair urban affairs com. 1991, chair health law com. 1983, mem. real estate tax com.), D.C. Bar Assn., State Bar Wis. Home Phone: 847-835-4002; Office Phone: 847-867-8500. Business E-Mail: chris@chriscohen.com.

COHEN, CLAIRE GORHAM, investment company executive; b. St. Johnsbury, Vt., May 9, 1934; d. John David and Muriel (Somers) Gorham; m. Richard D. Cohen, Nov. 26, 1959; 1 son, James H. Student, U. Vt., 1953—54; BA, Radcliffe Coll., 1956. Proofreader Dun & Bradstreet, Inc., 1956, mcpl. bond analyst, 1957-64, sr. state analyst, 1965-66, sr. analyst, 1970-71, Moody's Investors Svc. Inc., NYC, 1971-75; v.p., assoc. dir. rsch. Mcpl. Bond Rsch. Divsn., NYC, 1975-86, v.p. mng. dir. state ratings, 1986-89; exec. mng. dir. govtl. fin. Fitch Investors Svc., Inc., NYC, 1989-91, exec. v.p., 1991-94, vice chmn., 1994-97, Fitch IBCA, NYC, 1997—2004; cons., 2005—07. Mem. Govt. Acctg. Stds. Adv. Bd., 1999-2002; mem. Fed. Acctg. Stds. Adv. Bd., 2002-07; mem. Task Force on N.Y. State Pub. Authorities, 1974-75. Mem. N.Y. Harvard-Radcliffe Schs. Com.; 1952 class agt. St. Johnsbury Acad., 1981-86; 1956 class agt. Radcliffe Coll., 1981-86. Recipient Disting. Svc. award State Debt Mgmt. Network, 1999, Lifetime Achievement award Women in Pub. Fin., 2007. Mem. Mcpl. Forum N.Y. (Career Svc. award 2002), Mcpl. Analysts Group N.Y. (treas. 1983-84, chmn. 1984-85, Career Achievement award 2004), Nat. Fedn. Mcpl. Analysts (bd. govs. 1984-86, chmn. awards com. 1984-85, Career Achievement award 1991), Soc. Mcpl. Analysts, India House Club (bd. govs. 2003—).

COHEN, CORA, artist; b. NYC, Oct. 19, 1943; d. George and Anne (Lenarsky) C. BA, Bennington Coll., 1964, MA, 1972. Vis. artist U. Pa., 1969-70, U. Chgo., 1983-95, Art Inst. Sch. Chgo., 1983-85, 97, Boston Mus. Sch. Fine Arts, 1994-95, U. Minn., 1996, Kunsthögskolan, Stockholm, 1996, Corcoran Mus. Sch. Art, 2000, Washington U., St. Louis, 2003; vis. prof. Art Inst. Sch. Chgo., 1992-93; adj. faculty NYU, 1990-2000, Rutgers U., Newark, 2004, Md. Inst. Coll. Art, 2005-06; assoc. prof. art U. N.C., Greensboro, 1998-2003, Vt. Studio Ctr., 1999-2002, 06; nat. focus artist Emory and Henry Coll., Emory, Va., 2003-04; guest lectr. New Sch., 2004; 4th yr. adviser Md. Inst. Coll. Art, 2005, 06. One-person shows include Everson Mus. Art, Syracuse, N.Y., 1974, Max Hutchinson Gallery, N.Y.C., 1979-80, 84, Wolff Gallery, 1988, Holly Solomon Gallery, 1990, New Arts Program, Kutztown, Pa., 1993, Jason McCoy Gallery, N.Y.C., 1993-94, David Beitzel Gallery, N.Y.C., 1994, Sarah Moody Gallery Art, Tuscaloosa, Ala., 1996, Joslyn Art Mus., Omaha, 1996, Hering Raum, Bonn, Germany, 1997-98, Rena Bransten Gallery, San Francisco, 1997, Jason McCoy Gallery, N.Y.C., 1997, Belvedere Strasse, 1999, Bentley Gallery, Scottsdale, Ariz., 1999, 2002, 05, Stefanie Hering, Berlin, 2000, McCoy Chelsea, 2001, Emory (Va.) and Henry Coll., 2003-04, Jason McCoy Inc., N.Y.C., 2004, Abaton Garage, Jersey City, 2005, Galerie Martius Winter, Berlin, 2007; exhibited in group shows at Baxter Art Gallery, Pasadena, Calif., 1985, Am. Acad. and Inst. Arts and Letters, N.Y.C., 1987, Barbara Krakow Gallery, Boston, 1987, Pamela Auchincloss Gallery, Contemporary Surfaces, N.Y.C., 1992, A/C Project Room, An Esemplastic Shift, N.Y.C., 1992, Sandra Gering Gallery, 1992, Piccolo Spoleto Festival, Charleston, S.C., 1992, The Fetish of Knowledge, A/C Project Room, N.Y.C., 1992, Daniel Weinberg Gallery, L.A., 1989, Wolff Gallery, N.Y.C., 1991, Feigen Gallery, 1991, Sytsema Galleries, Baarn, Holland, 1992, Jason McCoy Gallery, N.Y.C., 1993, The Painting Ctr., N.Y.C., 1993, White Columns, N.Y.C., 1993, Bill Maynes Contemporary Art, N.Y.C., 1994, Penine Hart Gallery, N.Y., 1994, Trans Hudson Gallery, Jersey City, Out of the Blue Gallery, Edinburgh, Scotland, 1994, Cepa Gallery, Buffalo, 1995, 2000, the Smart Fair, Stockholm, 1995, NYU, N.Y.C., 1995, Newhouse Ctr. Contemporary Art, S.I., N.Y., 1997, Galleri Mariann Ahnlund Umea, Sweden, 1996, Accrochage, Hering Raum, Bonn, 1996, Galerie Brigitte Schenk, Köln, Germany, Köln Art Fair, 1997, Cepa Gallery, Buffalo, Galleri Mariann Ahnlund, Stockholm, Stalke Out of Space, Copenhagen, Barbara Davis Gallery, Houston, 1998, Oppenhoff & Rädler, Leipzig, Stockholm Art Fair, Hunter Coll., Times Square Gallery, N.Y., The Art Fair, The 69th Regiment Armory, N.Y., 1999, 2002, 04, 06, McCoy, Kansas City, 2000, Open Studio to Benefit the Coalition for the Homeless, N.Y., 2000, U. Ariz. Mus. Art, Tucson, 2001, The Five and Dime Series, Jan Van de Donk, NY, 2001, Cynthia Broan Gallery, N.Y., 2002, Painting Painting N3 Project Space, Williamsburg, Brooklyn, N.Y., 2003, Sheldon Art Galleries, St. Louis, 2003, Stalke Collection Gallery, Gallery Kirke, Sonnerup, Denmark, 2006; photgrapher: Cohen, Cora: The Record, The Death, The Surprise, 1999. Recipient N.Y. Found. Arts Gottlieb Found. award, 1990, 2006, Pollock Krasner award, 1998, Kohler Fund award U. NC, 1999, Adolph and Esther Gottlieb Found. award, 2006; Painting fellow Nat. Endowment for the Arts, 1987; Yaddo Residence grantee, 1982, 95, New Faculty grantee U. N.C., 1999. Mem. Simon Wiesenthal Ctr., Coll. Art Assn. Jewish. Home: 287 Broadway New York NY 10007-2004 Office Phone: 212-267-9430. Personal E-mail: ccohen287@earthlink.net.

COHEN, CYNTHIA MARYLYN, lawyer; b. Bklyn., Sept. 5, 1945; AB, Cornell U., 1967; JD cum laude, NYU, 1970. Bar: N.Y. 1971, U.S. Ct. Appeals (2nd cir.) 1972, U.S. Dist. Ct. (so. and ea. dists.) N.Y. 1972, U.S. Supreme Ct. 1975, U.S. Dist. Ct. (ctrl. and no. dists.) Calif. 1980, U.S. Ct. Appeals (9th cir.) 1980, U.S. Dist. Ct. (so. dist.) Calif. 1981, U.S. Dist. Ct. (ea. dist.) Calif. 1986. With Paul, Hastings, Janofsky & Walker LLP, L.A., NYC. Bd. dirs. N.Y. chpt. Am. Cancer Soc., 1977-80; active Pres.'s Coun. Cornell Women; lawyer rep. Ninth Cir. Jud. Conf. Recipient Am. Jurisprudence award for evidence, torts and legal instns., 1968-69; John Norton Pomeroy scholar NYU, 1968-70, Founders Day Cert., 1969. Mem. ABA, Assn. Bar City N.Y. (trade regulation com. 1976-79), Assn. Bus. Trial Lawyers, Fin. Lawyers Conf., N.Y. State Bar Assn. (chmn. class-action com. 1979), State Bar Calif., Los Angeles County Bar Assn., Order of Coif, Delta Gamma. Avocations: tennis, bridge, rare books, wines. Home: 4531 Dundee Dr Los Angeles CA 90027-1213 Office: Paul Hastings Janofsky & Walker LLP 515 S Flower St 25th Fl Los Angeles CA 90071 Home Phone: 323-663-1869; Office Phone: 213-683-6000. Business E-Mail: cynthiacohen@paulhastings.com.

COHEN, DANIEL EDWARD, writer; b. Chgo., Mar. 12, 1936; s. Milton M. and Sue Greenberg C.; m. Susan Lois Handler, Feb. 2, 1958; 1 child, Theodora (dec.). BA in Journalism, U. Ill., 1958. Mng. editor Sci. Digest mag., NYC, 1959-68; writer, 1968—. Author: Myths of the Space Age, 1967, Secrets from Ancient Graves, 1968, Vaccination and You, 1968, The Age of Giant Mammals, 1969, Animals of the City, 1969, Mysterious Places, 1969, A Modern Look at Monsters, 1970, Night Animals, 1970, Conquerors on Horseback, 1970, Talking with Animals, 1971, Superstition, 1971, A Natural History of Unnatural Things, 1971, Ancient Monuments and How They Were Built, 1971, Masters of the Occult, 1971, Voodoo, Devils, and the New Invisible World, 1972, Watchers in the Wild, 1972, In Search of Ghosts, 1972, The Magic Art of Foreseeing the Future, 1973, How Did Life Get There?, 1973, Magicians, Wizards and Sorcerers, 1973, How the World Will End, 1973, reissued as Waiting for the Apocalypse, 1983, Shaka: King of the Zulus, 1973, ESP: The Search Beyond the Senses, 1973, The Black Death, 1974, The Magic of the Little People, 1974, Curses, Hexes, and Spells, 1974, Intelligence: What Is It?, 1974, Not of the World, 1974, Human Nature, Animal Nature, 1974, The Far Side of Consciousness, 1974, The Mysteries of Reincarnation, 1975, The Greatest Monsters in the World, 1975, The Body Snatchers, 1975, The Human Side of Computers, 1975, Monsters, Giants, and Little Men from Mars, 1975, The New Believers, 1975, The Spirit of Lord, 1975, Animal Territories, 1975, Mysterious Disappearances, 1976, The Ancient Visitors, 1976, Dreams, Visions, and Drugs, 1976, Gold, 1976, Biorhythms in Your Life, 1976, Supermonsters, 1977, Ghostly Animals, 1977, The Science of Spying, 1977, Real Ghosts, 1977, Meditation, 1977, What Really Happened to the Dinosaurs?, 1977, Creativity: What Is It?, 1977, Ceremonial Magic, 1978, The World of UFO's, 1978, The World's Most Famous Ghosts, 1978, Young Ghosts, 1978, rev. edit., 1994, Frauds, Hoaxes, and Swindles, 1979, Missing, 1979, Mysteries of the World, 1979, What's Happening to Our Weather, 1979, Dealing with the Devil, 1979, Famous Curses, 1979, Great Mistakes, 1979, Close Encounters with God, 1979, The Monsters of "Star Trek", 1980, Monsters You Never Heard Of, 1980, The Tomb Robbers, 1980, Bigfoot: America's Number One Monster, 1980, Everything You Need to Know about Monsters and Still Be Able to Sleep, 1981, Ghostly Terrors, 1981, The Headless Roommate and Other Tales of Terror, 1981, The Last Hundred Years' Medicine, 1981, The Great Airship Mystery, 1981, Re-Thinking, 1982, America's Very Own Monsters, 1982, How to Buy a Car, 1982, Horror in the Movies, 1982, How to Test Your ESP, 1982, Real Magic, 1982, The Last Hundred Years' Household Technology, 1982, Monster Hunting Today, 1983, The Encyclopedia of Monsters, 1983, The Simon and Schuster Question and Answer Book on Computers, 1983, Southern Fried Rat and Other Gruesome Tales, 1983, Monster Dinosaur, 1983, The Restless Dead, 1983, The Encyclopedia of Ghosts, 1984, Musicals, 1984, Horror Movies, 1984, Hiram Bingham and the Dream of Gold, 1984, Masters of Horror, 1984, America's Very Own Ghosts, 1985, Henry Stanley and the Quest for the Source of the Nile, 1985, The Encyclopedia of the Strange, 1985; (with Susan Cohen) The Kids' Guide to Home Computers, 1983, Teenage Stress, 1984, The Kids' Guide to Home Video, 1984, Screen Goddesses, 1984, Hollywood Hunks and Heroes, 1985, Rock Video Superstars, 1985, Wrestling Superstars, Vol. 1, 1985, Vol. 2, 1986, Heroes of the Challenger, 1986, A Six-Pack and a Fake ID, 1986, The Encyclopedia of Movie Stars, 1986, A History of the Oscars, 1986, ESP: The New Technology, 1986, Strange and Amazing Facts About Star Trek, 1986, (with Susan Cohen) Wrestling Superstars II, 1986, Teenage Competition, 1986, Hollywood's Newest Superstars, 1987, The Encyclopedia of Unsolved Crimes, 1988, UFO's: The Third Wave, 1988, (with Susan Cohen) What Kind of Dog is That, 1989, Zoo Superstars, 1989, When Someone You Know is Gay, 1989, Ancient Egypt, 1990, The Ghosts of War, 1990, Ancient Greece, 1990, The Magical World of Monsters, 1991, Beverly Hills 90210: Meet the Stars, 1991, (with Susan Cohen) Going for the Gold: Medal Hopefuls for Winter '92, 1991, Zoos, 1992, Where to Find Dinosaurs Today, 1992, Ancient Rome, 1992, Ghostly Tales of Love and Revenge, 1992, Prophets of Doom, 1992, Ghosts of the Deep, 1993, Ghost in the House, 1993, Animal Rights, 1993, Dinosaur Discovery, 1993, The Beheaded Freshman and Other Nasty Rumors, 1993, The Ghost of Elvis and other Celebrity Spirits, 1994, Cults, 1994, 101 of the World's Strangest Mysteries, 1994, Into The Darkness, 1994, Real Vampires, 1995, The Phantom Hitchhiker, 1995, Riddle of the Stones, 1995, Prohibition, 1995, The Modern Ark, 1995, Gus the Bear, The Flying Cat and the Lovesick Moose, 1995, Allosaurus and Other Jurassic Meat Eaters, 1995, Stegosaurus and Other Jurassic Plant Eaters, 1995, Tyrannosaurus Rex and Other Cretaceous Meat Eaters, 1995, Triceratops and Other Cretaceous Plant Eaters, 1995, Werewolves, 1996, The Alaska Purchase, 1996, Joseph McCarthy: The Misuse of Political Power, 1996, Ghostly Warnings, 1996, Dangerous Ghosts, 1996, Screaming Skulls: 101 of the World's Great Ghost Stories, 1996, (with Susan Cohen) Gold Medal Glory: The Story of America's 1996 Women's Gymnastics Team, 1996, Hollywood Dinosaur, 1997, Great Conspiracies and Elaborate Cover-ups., 1997, Raising the Dead, 1997, The Millennium, 1997, Watergate: Deception in the White House, 1998, Cloning, 1998, The Alien Files 1, 1998, Contact, 1998, The Alien Files 2, Conspiracy, 1998, Are You Ready, The Best and Worst Predictions for the Millennium, 1998, The Manhattan Project, 1999, Prophets of Doom, The Millennium Edition, 1999, Wrestling Renegades, Civil War Ghosts, 1999, The Impeachment of William Jefferson Clinton, 1999, Yellow Journalism, 2000, George W. Bush, 2000, Apatosaurus, 2000, Pteranodon, 2000, Velociraptor, 2000, Stegosaurus, 2000, Triceratops, 2000, Tyrannosaurus, 2000, (with Susan Cohen) PanAm 103, 2000, rev. edit., 2001, Jesse Ventura, 2001, Hauntings and Horrors, 2002, Ankylosaurus, 2002, Brachiosaurus, 2002, Diplodocus, 2002, Ichythosaurus, 2002, Iguanoden, 2002, Allosaurus, 2002, Spinosaurus, 2003, Miasaurus, 2003, Pachcephalosaurus, 2003, Parasauiolophus, 2003, Trodon, 2003, Sarcosuchus imperator, 2003. Mem. Authors Guild, Watson's Erroneous Deductions Club, The Wodehouse Soc. (editor Plum Lines), Chapter One, The Capers of Sherlock Holmes Club, Clumber Spaniel Club Am. Avocation: dogs. Home and Office: 877 W Hand Ave Cape May Court House NJ 08210-1865 E-mail: bladgscast@aol.com.

COHEN, DANNY, computer engineer; PhD, Harvard U. Faculty mem. computer sci. Harvard U., 1969—73, Info. Scis. Inst., U. So. Calif., 1973—93; co-founder Myricom, 2001; disting. engr. Sun Microsystems Inc., 2001—. Mem.: NAE. Office: Sun Microsystems Inc M/S UMPK16-160 16 Network Cir Menlo Park CA 94025 Office Phone: 650-786-0006. E-mail: danny.cohen@sun.com, dannycohen@ieee.org.

COHEN, DAVID, lawyer; b. Miami; m. Erika Cohen; 2 children. Bachelor's degree, Fla. Internat. U.; JD, U. Fla., 1989; LLM, Columbia U. Atty. Alston & Bird, Atlanta, 1989—93; assoc. judge Fulton County Ga. Juvenile Ct., 1993—95; legal counsel NY Mets, 1995—98, gen. counsel, 1998—, v.p., 2005—. Office: NY Mets 123-01 Roosevelt Ave Flushing NY 11368-1699*

COHEN, DAVID BLAIR, lawyer; b. Glen Ridge, NJ, Mar. 27, 1958; BA, U. Tex., 1980, JD, 1983. Bar: Tex. 1983, DC 1989. Ptnr., co-head Bus. & Internat. Sect. Vinson & Elkins LLP, Washington, DC. Office: Vinson & Elkins LLP Willard Office Bldg 1455 Pennsylvania Ave NW, Ste 600 Washington DC 20004 Office Phone: 202-639-6566. E-mail: DCohen@velaw.com.

COHEN, DAVID HARRIS, neuroscientist, educator, academic administrator; b. Springfield, Mass., Aug. 26, 1938; s. Nathan Edward and Sylvia (Golden) C.; m. Arline Wyler, June 17, 1960 (div. Aug. 1980); children: Bonnie, Daniel, Ian; m. Anne Helena Remmes, Jan. 17, 1981; 1 child, Kaitlin. BA, Harvard U., 1960; PhD, U. Calif., Berkeley, 1963. Postdoctoral fellow UCLA, 1963—64; asst. prof. physiology Western Res. U., Cleve., 1964—68; assoc. prof. to prof. physiology U. Va. Med. Sch., Charlottesville, 1968—79; prof., chmn. neurobiology SUNY, Stony Brook, 1979—86; v.p. rsch., dean grad. sch. Northwestern U., Evanston, Ill., 1986—91, provost, 1992—95, prof. neurobiology and physiology, 1986—95; v.p. arts and scis., dean of faculty emeritus Columbia U., NYC, 1995—2003, prof. biol. scis. and psychiatry, 1995—. Mem. adv. com. directorate biol., behavioral and social scis. NSF, 1982-89; mem. life scis. rsch. adv. bd. Air Force Office Sci. Rsch., 1985-91; mem. bd. govs. Argonne Nat. Lab., 1986-92; bd. dirs. Zenith Electronics, Inc., 1990-95, Rsch. Librs. Group, 1993-97, 2001—06, Columbia U. Press, 1996-2005, Thuris Corp., 2000—, Trevor Day Sch., 2000—, Socratic Arts, 2003—, KLi, 2004-06, The Grass Found., 2006—, Eduventures, 2006—; mem. adv. bd. Knowledge Investment Ptnrs., 2003—, Identity Theft 911, 2004—. Mem. various editl. bds. profl. jours.; contbr. articles to profl. jours. Bd. overseers Fermi Nat. Accelerator Lab., Batavia, Ill., 1987-94; exec. com. Ill. Gov.'s Sci. Adv. Com., 1989-95; mem. Liaison Com. Med. Edn., 1987-89; bd. dirs. N.Y. Structural Biology Ctr., 1999-2003. Fellow AAAS; mem. Soc. Neurosci. (pres. 1981-82), Pavlovian Soc. (pres. 1978-79), Assn. Neurosci. Depts. and Programs (pres. 1981-82), Nat. Soc. Med. Rsch. (v.p. 1984-85), Nat. Assn. Biomed. Rsch. (bd. dirs. 1985-87), Coun. Acad. Socs. (adminstrv. bd. 1982-87, chmn. 1985-86), Assn. Am. Med. Colls. (exec. coun. 1984-91, chmn. 1989-90), Internat. Brain Rsch. Orgn. (ctrl. coun. 1978-82), Inst. Medicine Forum of Neurosci. Nervous Sys. Disorders. Jewish. Home: 445 Riverside Dr Apt 72 New York NY 10027-6801 Home Phone: 212-316-6242. Business E-Mail: dhc14@columbia.edu.

COHEN, DAVID JOEL, medical educator; b. New Haven, Nov. 2, 1960; AB summa cum laude, Harvard U., 1982, MD, 1986, MSc, 1994. Diplomate Am. Bd. Internal Medicine; lic. physician, Mass. Intern then resident Brigham and Women's Hosp., Boston, 1986-89; clin. rsch. fellow Beth Israel Hosp., Boston, 1989-94, now asst. dir. interventional cardiology; fellow Harvard Sch. Pub. Health, Boston, 1992-94, instr. health policy and mgmt., 1995—; instr. medicine Harvard Med. Sch., Boston, 1993-96, asst. prof., 1996—. Asst. dir. invasive cardiology sect. Beth Israel Hosp., 1994—. Contbr. chpts. to books and numerous articles to profl. jours. Grantee Johnson and Johnson, 1993-94, Am. Heart Assn., 1995—. Mem. Phi Beta Kappa. Home: 29 Reservoir Ave Chestnut Hill MA 02467-1329

COHEN, DAVID JOHN, cardiothoracic surgeon; b. San Antonio, Jan. 13, 1947; s. Melvin David and Betty (Brown) C.; m. Deborah Milton, May 29, 1976; children: John, Christopher, Scott, Joshua, Benjamin. BA in Biochemistry, Rice U., Houston, 1968; MD, Washington U., 1972; BS in Mech. Engring. summa cum laude, U. Tex., San Antonio, 1999; grad., US Army Command and Gen. Staff Coll., 2001; MPA, Harvard U., Cambridge, Mass., 2003. Intern Johns Hopkins Hosp., Balt., 1972-73, resident in gen. surgery, 1973-74, U. Wash. Affiliated Hosps., Seattle, 1976-79; resident in cardiothoracic surgery Hosp. of U. Pa., Phila., 1979-81; chief dept. cardiovasc. physiology Walter Reed Army Inst. of Rsch., Washington, 1981-83; staff Brooke Army Med. Ctr., Ft. Sam Houston, Tex., 1983-84, asst. chief cardiothoracic surgery San Antonio, 1992-93, dir. heart transplant program, 1994—2001, chief cardiothroacic surgery, 1993—2002, cardiothoracic surgeon, 2005—06, ret., 2006; staff U. Wis. Hosp., Madison, 1984-87, William S. Middleton VA Hosp., Madison, 1984-87, chief thoracic surgery svc., 1986-87; staff Med. Ctr. Hosp., San Antonio, 1987-92, Audie L. Murphy VA Hosp., San Antonio, 1987-92, chief cardiothroacic surgery, 1991-92, dir. surg. ICU, 1988-92; sr. clin. cons. for combat doctrine and devel. US Army Med. Ctr. and Sch., Ft. Sam Houston, 2003—05; dep. comdr. for clin. svcs. 86th Combat Support Hosp., Iraq, 2004—05; pvt. practice cardiothoracic surgery San Antonio, 2006—. Bd. dirs. Tex. Organ Sharing Alliance, San Antonio, 1994—2002; cardiac transplant fellow Tex. Heart Inst., Houston, 1993; cons. thoracic and cardiovasc. surgery US Army Surgeon Gen., 1999—2002; pres. Alamo Cardiothoracic Surg. Assocs., P.A., San Antonio, 2006—. Mem. nat. health and safety com. Boy Scouts Am., 2006—, asst. scoutmaster San Antonio, 1990—2002. Decorated Legion of Merit, Bronze Star, Meritorious Svc. medal (4), Army Commendation medal (6), Order of Mil. Med. Merit; recipient Nat. Collegiate Engring. award, US Achievement Acad., 1998. Fellow ACS, Am. Coll. Cardiology, Am. Coll. Chest Physicians; mem. Am. Assn. Thoracic Surgeons, Soc. Thoracic Surgeons, Soc. Univ. Surgeons, San Antonio Cardiology Soc. (sec.-treas. 1997-98, pres. 1998-99), Golden Key, Tau Beta Pi. Jewish. Avocations: horseback riding, camping, skiing. Office: Alamo Cardiothoracic Surgery Assocs PA 525 Oak Ctr Ste 270 78258-3917 Office Phone: 210-495-4200. Personal E-mail: david_j_cohen@hotmail.com.

COHEN, DAVID LEON, physician; b. St. Louis, Feb. 2, 1947; s. Benjamin David and Hannah (Finfer) C.; m. Sheila Zeisel, July 2, 1974; children: Robin, Lori, Jonathan, Jennifer. BS, Roosevelt U., 1967; MS, Chgo. Med. Sch., 1972; MD, Mt. Sinai Sch. Medicine, 1976. Diplomate Am. Bd. Dermatology. Intern in internal medicine Michael Reese Hosp., Chgo., 1976—77; resident Mt. Sinai Hosp., NYC, 1977—80; pvt. practice Hewlett and Jamaica, NY, 1980—. Clin. instr. dept. dermatology Mount Sinai Sch. Medicine, NYC, 1980—. Office: 1800 Rockaway Ave Ste 208 Hewlett NY 11557-1645 also: 86-78 Midland Pky Jamaica NY 11432 Office Phone: 516-887-4343. Business E-Mail: david.l.cohen@mssm.edu.

COHEN, DAVID LOUIS, communications executive; b. NYC, Apr. 11, 1955; s. Arthur Stanley and Barbara (Cohen) C.; m. Rhonda Resnick, Aug. 14, 1977; children: Benjamin Jeffrey, Joshua Scott. BA, Swarthmore Coll., Pa., 1977; JD summa cum laude, U. Pa., Phila., 1981; LLD (hon.), Drexel U., Phila., 1997. Bar: Pa. 1981, US Dist. Ct. (ea. dist. Pa.) 1982, US Ct. Appeals (3rd cir.) 1982, US Supreme Ct. 1983. Press sec. US Rep. James H. Scheuer, Washington, 1976, adminstrv. asst., chief of staff, 1977-78; law clk. to Hon. Joseph S. Lord III US Dist. Ct., Phila., 1981-82; assoc. to ptnr. Ballard Spahr Andrews & Ingersoll, LLP, Phila., 1982-92, ptnr., 1997—2002, chmn., 1998—2002; exec. v.p. Comcast Corp., 2002—. Co-author: Continuing Care Retirement Communities: An Empirical, Financial and Legal Analysis, 1984; contbr. articles to profl. jours. Dir. comm. Rendell for Mayor, Phila., 1987, campaign mgr., 1991; chief of staff Hon. Edward G. Rendell, Mayor, Phila., 1992-97; bd. dirs. Wistar Inst., Phila., 1994, Stratford Friends Sch., Phila., 1993, Regional Performing Arts Ctr., 1997, United Way of Southeastern Pa., Phila., 1993, first vice chair, 1997-98, chair 1998; bd. dirs. Greater Phila. C. of C., 1998-; bd. dirs., exec. com. Port Wardens of the Ind. Seaport Mus., 1998; trustee Phila. Bar Found., 1999, Hosp. U. Pa., 1999, Overseers Sch. Medicine U. Pa., 1999; mem. health sys. trustee bd. U. Pa., 1999; co-chair Phila. 2000, 1998. Recipient Hatikvah award Jewish Nat. Fund, 1993, Americanism award Anti-Defamation League, 1993, Cmty. Leader of Yr. award Arthritis Found., 1994, Citizen of Yr. award March of Dimes, 1994, ARC, 1999, Outstanding Young Leader award Jaycees, 1995, Jerusalem Covenant award State of Israel Bonds, 1996, Clarence Farmer Svc. award Phila. Commn. Human Rels., 1997, Phila. Bar medal, 1997, Champions award Cmty. Legal Svcs., 1997, Cora Svcs. award, 1997, Cmty. Svc. award Episcopal Hosp., 1997, Golden Heart Humanitarian award Variety Club, 1998, Cmty. Svcs. Recognition award Phila. Tribune Charities, 1998, Success award March of Dimes Found., 1999, Cmty. Svc. award Operation Understanding, 1999, Vision for Phila. award Phila. Hospitality, 1999, Dr. John Kearsley award, 1999. Mem. ABA, Pa. Bar Assn., Phila. Bar Assn. Dem. Office: Comcast Corp 1500 Market St Philadelphia PA 19102-2148*

COHEN, DAVID WALTER, academic administrator, educator, periodontist; b. Phila., Dec. 15, 1926; s. Abram and Goldie (Schlein) C.; m. Betty Axelrod, Dec. 19, 1948 (dec. Mar. 1992); children: Jane Ellen, Amy Sue, Joanne Louise. DDS, U. Pa., 1950; DSc (hon.), Boston U., 1975; PhD (hon.), Hebrew U., Jerusalem, 1977, U. Athens, 1979; Dr Honoris Causa, U. Louis Pasteur, Strasbourg, France, 1986; DHL (hon.), U. Detroit, 1989. Diplomate: Am. Bd. Periodontology (chmn. 1972). Research fellow pathology and periodontia Beth Israel Hosp., Boston, 1950-51; mem. faculty U. Pa. Sch. Dentistry, Phila., 1951—, prof. periodontics, 1962-86, chmn. dept., 1962-73; dean Sch. Dental Medicine U. Pa., Phila., 1972-83; dean emeritus U. Pa. Sch. Dentistry, Phila., 1983—; pres. Med. Coll. Pa., 1986-93; chancellor Allegheny U. of Health Scis., 1993-98; chancellor emeritus Coll. Medicine Drexel U., 1998—; mem. staff Albert Einstein Med. Center, Phila., Children's Hosp., Phila.; pres. Jewish Publ. Soc., 1993-96. Vis. prof. Boston U. Sch. Grad Dentistry, 1972—; nat. cons. periodontics USAF, 1965-70; bd. govs. Hebrew U., Jerusalem, Betty and Walter Cohen chair in periodontal rsch., 1986; D. Walter Cohen endowed chair in periodontics U. Pa., 1995. Author: (with H.M. Goldman) Periodontia, 1957, (with others) An Introduction to Periodontia, 1959, Periodontal Therapy, 1960, (with R. Genco and Goldman) Contemporary Periodontics, 1990, (with Genco, L. Rose and B. Mealey) Periodontal

Medicine, 1999, Periodontics, Medicine Surgery and Implants, 2001; also numerous articles and chpts. V.p. Jewish Publ. Soc., 1985-89, pres., 1993-96; pres. Nat. Mus. Am. Jewish History, Phila., 1996—. Served with USN, 1944-45. Named to Ctrl. H.S. Hall of Fame, 1976; 1st Presdl. scholar U. Calif., San Francisco, 1985-86; named for him Hebrew U. Betty and D. Walter Cohen Chair in Periodontal Rsch., 1986, U. Pa. D. Walter Cohen Endowed Chair in Periodontics, 1995; D. Walter Cohen Mid. East Ctr. for Dental Edn. dedicated by Hebrew U. of Jerusalem, 1997. Fellow AAAS, Am. Acad. Oral Pathology, Am. Acad. Periodontology, Inst. of Medicine of Nat. Acad. Scis.; mem. Am. Soc. Periodontists (pres. 1967), Friends of Nat. Inst. Dental Rsch. (pres. 1998—). Office: Drexel Univ Coll Medicine 1601 Cheery St Ste1050 Philadelphia PA 19102

COHEN, EDMUND STEPHEN, lawyer; b. Newark, June 25, 1946; s. Louis William and Edna (Medresch) C.; m. Lisa Beth Sonenthal, June 30, 1968; children: Ellen Paige, Paul Lawrence. BA cum laude, Dartmouth Coll., 1968; JD cum laude, Harvard U., 1971; LLM in Taxation, NYU, 1975. Bar: N.Y. 1972, U.S. Ct. Appeals (2d cir.) 1972, U.S. Ct. Claims, 1973, U.S. Tax Ct. 1973, U.S. Dist. Ct. (so. dist.) N.Y. 1975. Assoc. Davis Polk & Wardwell, NYC, 1971-78; ptnr. Cole & Deitz, NYC, 1978-81, Coudert Bros. LLP, NYC, 1981—2005; chmn. Global Tax practice, ptnr. Winston & Strawn, NYC, 2005—. Adj. prof. law grad. tax program NYU Law Sch., 1977-86; chmn. seminars World Trade Inst., N.Y.C., 1977—, Practicing Law Inst., N.Y.C., 1977—, NYU Fed. Tax Inst. Contbr. articles to profl. jours. Mem. ABA, N.Y. State Bar Assn., Assn. Bar City N.Y., Internat. Fiscal Assn. Office: Winston & Strawn LLP 200 Park Ave Fl 41 New York NY 10166 Office Phone: 212-294-2634. Office Fax: 212-294-4700. Business E-Mail: ecohen@winston.com.

COHEN, ELAINE HELENA, pediatrician, cardiologist, educator; b. Boston, Oct. 14, 1941; d. Samuel Clive and Lillian (Stocklan) C.; m. Marvin Leon Gale, May 7, 1972; 1 child, Pamela Beth Gale. AB, Conn. Coll., 1963; postgrad., Tufts U., 1963—64; MD, Woman's Med. Coll. Pa., 1969. Diplomate Am. Bd. Pediat. Pediat. intern Children's Hosp. of L.A., 1969-70, resident in pediat., 1970-71; fellow in pediat. cardiology UCLA Ctr. Health Scis., 1971-72, L.A. County/U. So. Calif. Med. Ctr., LA, 1972-74; pediatrician Children's Med. Group of South Bay, Chula Vista, Calif., 1974—. Clin. instr. dept. pediat. UCLA Sch. Medicine, 1971-72, U. So. Calif., L.A., 1972-74; asst. clin. prof. dept. pediat. U. Calif., Calif. Sch. Medicine, San Diego, 1974-98, preceptor dept. pediat., 1992—, assoc. clin. prof. dept. pediat., 1998—. Fellow Am. Acad. Pediat.; mem. Calif. Med. Assn., San Diego County Med. Soc. Avocations: sketching, design. Office: Children's Med Group South Bay 280 E St Chula Vista CA 91910-2945 Office Phone: 619-425-3951. Personal E-mail: leongalemarvin@msn.com.

COHEN, ERIC L., lawyer; b. NYC, Oct. 19, 1958; BA cum laude, Brandeis U., 1980; JD magna cum laude, Yeshiva U., 1983. Bar: NY 1984, DC 1990. Assoc. Robinson, Silverman, Pearce, Aronsohn & Berman, LLP (now Bryan Cave, LLP), NYC, 1983—92, ptnr., 1992—98; sr. v.p., gen. counsel, sec. Terex Corp., Westport, Conn., 1998—. Mem.: Bar of the DC Ct. Appeals, NY State Bar Assn. Office: Terex Corp 200 Nyala Farm Rd Westport CT 06880*

COHEN, EZECHIEL GODERT DAVID, physicist, researcher; b. Amsterdam, Holland, Jan. 16, 1923; came to U.S., 1963; s. David Ezechiel and Sophia Louisa (de Sterke) C.; m. Marina Arnoldina Linnekamp, Apr. 19, 1950; children: Michael Benjamin, Andrea Margaret. BS in Math., Physics and Astronomy, U. Amsterdam, 1947, PhD, 1957. First asst. U. Amsterdam, 1950-61, assoc. prof., 1961-63; research assoc. U. Mich., 1957-58, Johns Hopkins, 1958-59; prof. Rockefeller U., 1963-93, prof. emeritus, 1993—. Vander Waals prof. U. Amsterdam, 1969; Lorentz prof. U. Leiden, 1979; vis. prof. Coll. de France, 1969, 72, 79, 83, 90, Inst. for Advanced Studies, Australian Nat. U., Canberra, 1982, 88, 92, 96, 99, U. Florence, Italy, 1999, 2000; Donders prof. U. Utrecht, 1988; Francqui prof. interuniversitaire U. Brussels and U. Leuven, 1997. Editor: Fundamental Problems in Statistical Mechanics, Vol. I, 1961, Vol. II, 1968, Vol. III, 1975, Vol. IV, 1978, Vol. V, 1980, Vol. VI, 1985, Statistical Mechanics at the Turn of the Decade, 1971, The Boltzmann Equation, Theory and Applications, 1973. Recipient Royal Decoration as Knight, Order of Dutch Lion, 2004. Fellow Am. Phys. Soc.; mem. Royal Dutch Acad. Scis., Johns Hopkins Soc. of Scholars, Mexican Acad. Molecular Engrng. (corr.), Internat. Union of Pure and Applied Physics (Triann. Boltzmann Medal of the Commn. on Statis. Physics 2004). Office: Rockefeller U 1230 York Ave New York NY 10065-6399 Business E-Mail: egdc@rockefeller.edu.

COHEN, EZRA HARRY, lawyer; b. Macon, Ga., Mar. 13, 1942; s. Harry M. and Rena C. Cohen; m. Bonnie E. Cohen, Feb. 1, 1969 (div. Mar. 1988); children: Aaron M., Eileen R.; m. Katherine C. Meyers, June 18, 1989. BA, Columbia U., 1964; JD, Emory U., 1969. Bar: Ga. 1969. Ptnr. Troutman, Sanders, Lockerman & Ashmore, Atlanta, 1969-76, 79—; judge U.S. Bankruptcy Ct., U.S. Dist. Ct. (no. dist.) Ga., Atlanta, 1976-79. Dir. S.E. Bankruptcy Law Inst., Atlanta. Contbg. author: Cowan's Bankruptcy Laws & Practices, 1979. Mem. Emory U. Law Sch. Coun., Atlanta, 1988—. With U.S. Army, 1964-66, ETO. Fellow Am. Coll. Bankruptcy; mem. Ga. Bar Assn. (chmn. bankruptcy law sect.), Assn. Former Bankruptcy Judges (bd. dirs.), Nat. Assn. Bank Judges (assoc.), Atlanta Bar Assn. (bd. dirs. 1988-90), Lawyers Club of Atlanta. Home: 546 W Wesley Rd Atlanta GA 30305-3534 Office: Troutman Sanders 600 Peachtree St NE Ste 5200 Atlanta GA 30308-2216 E-mail: ezra.cohen@troutmansanders.com.

COHEN, FELIX ASHER, lawyer; b. Pitts., Aug. 11, 1943; s. Alex Harry and Audrey Gwen (Williams) C.; m. Nancy Ann Wills, July 24, 1971; children: Timothy Asher, Blair Wills Lavey. AB, Princeton U., 1965; JD, U. Pitts., 1971. Bar: Pa. 1972, U.S. Dist. Ct. (we. dist.) Pa. 1972, U.S. Tax Ct. 1972. Systems engr. IBM Corp., Pitts., 1965-68; law clk. U.S. Dist. Ct., Pitts., 1971-72; assoc. Buchanan Ingersoll, Pitts., 1972-75; sr. v.p., sec., counsel, bd. dirs. Signal Fin. Corp., Pitts., 1975-92; counsel CoreStates Fin. Corp., Phila., 1994-98; ptnr. Wolf Block Schorr & Solis-Cohen, Phila., 1999—. Mem. ABA, Pa. Bar Assn., Allegheny County Bar Assn., Phila. Bar Assn., Del. State Bar Assn. Home: 3 Black Rock Rd Chadds Ford PA 19317-9271

COHEN, FERN K., music educator; b. Hartford, Conn., Jan. 24, 1944; d. Anne L. Kent-Wald and Felix Wald (Stepfather); m. Joel S. Cohen, June 19, 1966; children: Michael H., Rachel S. Cohen-Rodney, Naomi R. BA in Music Edn., Johns Hopkins U., 1966; MS in Music Edn., Ctrl. Conn. State U., 1991, postgrad., 2001. Cert. K-12 music tech. State Dept. Edn., Conn., 1966. Music tchr. k-8 Hartford (Conn.) Pub. Schools, 1966—69; music tchr. Plainville (Conn.) Pub. Schs., 1983—84, Newington (Conn.) Pub. Schs., 1984—, program leader music dept., 1996—. Dir. summer music program Newington (Conn.) Pub. Schs., 1999. Nominee Tchr. of Yr., Newington, 2004, Excellence in Music Tchg. award, New Haven Symphony Orch., 2005; recipient Tchr. of Yr., Martin Kellogg Mid. Sch., 1985; grantee, Music Academy, 2001. Mem.: Conn. Music Edn. Assn. (assoc.; region dir., chairperson No. region orch., No. region dir., adjudicator all-state and region festivals), MENC (assoc.), Am. String Tchrs. Assn. (assoc.; mem. at large, past pres.), Ctrl. Conn. U. Alummni (assoc.), Johns Hopkins Alumni (assoc.), Mu Phiu Epsilon (assoc.), Alpha Delta Kappa (assoc.). Independent. Jewish. Avocations: swimming, knitting, music. Home: 22 Jeffrey Ln Newington CT 06111 Office: Newington Pub Sch 131 Cedar St Newington CT 06111 Home Phone: 860-667-3143; Office Phone: 860-667-5888. Personal E-mail: stringteacher@cox.net. Business E-Mail: fcohen@newington-schools.org.

COHEN, FLORENCE EMERY, retired financial services executive; b. Paterson, NJ, Mar. 6, 1944; d. Claude John and Esther (Belber) Emery; m. Harvey H. Cohen, Sept. 5, 1965; children: John Aaron, Jason Matthew. AB in History, Temple U., 1965; MA in Social Scis., U. Chgo., 1970. Product planning mgr. Penn. Mut. Ins. Co., Phila., 1970-77; dir. mktg. sys. Prudential Co., Newark, 1978-80, v.p. mktg. analysis, 1980-82, v.p. tax adminstrn., 1983-84, v.p. market devel., 1984-88, v.p. enterprise planning, 1988-90; sr. v.p. individual pensions Pruco Life Co., 1990-93, v.p., Prudential annuity svcs. exec., 1993—94; ret. Lectr. numerous industry assns.; mem. exec. coun. Jersey City (N.J.) State Coll., 1985; mem. bd. visitors St. Andrew's Presbyn. Coll., N.C. grad. study fellow U. Del., 1965, Temple U., 1965, U. Chgo. 1970. Rep. committeewoman West Windsor; elder First Presbyn. Ch. Dutch Neck, mission com., deacon; bd. dir. Project Freedom; chmn. Affordable Housing Com., West Windsor; pres. Welcoming Svcs., L.L.C., 1999—. Recipient Prudential Cmty. Champions award, 2001, 02, 03, 04, 05, Project Freedom Spirit award, 2000, 03. Fellow Life Office Mgmt. Assn., Limra Life Inst.; mem. Am. Soc. CLUs, Soc. Advancement Mgmt. (N.J. chpt., exec. of yr. 1986), Rotary (Princeton Corridor), Friends of West Windsor Open Space, West Windsor Hist. Soc. Republican. Avocations: cooking, gardening, swimming. Home: 3 Stonelea Dr Princeton Junction NJ 08550 also: 1621 A Spoonbill Ln Naples FL 34105

COHEN, FRED EHRENKRANZ, biophysics professor; b. Miami Beach, Fla., Sept. 10, 1956; s. James Cohen and Ruth Belle (Ehrenkranz) Levkoff; m. Carolyn Beth Klebanoff, July 19, 1981; 1 child, Alison. BS, Yale U., 1978; MD, Stanford U., 1984; PhD, Oxford U., Eng., 1980. Asst. prof. U. Calif., San Francisco, 1985-91, assoc. prof., 1991—94, prof. Medicine, Cellular & Molecular Pharmacology, Pharm. Chemistry, and Biochemistry & Biophysics, 1994—, chief, Div. of Endocrinology and Metabolism, 1995—96. Mem. sci. and med. adv. bd. Chiron Corp., Emeryville, Calif., 1988—, sci. adv. bd. Procept, Inc., Cambridge, Mass., 1988—. Assoc. editor Jour. Molecular Biology, London, 1990—; mem. editorial bd. Protein Engring., 1992—, Perspectives in Drug Discovery & Design, 1993—. Recipient Silver Knight in Math. award The Miami Herald, 1974, Robert C. Bates fellowship Yale U., 1977, Merriman prize Yale U., 1978; Rhodes scholar, 1978, Searle scholar, 1988. Fellow ACP; mem. Am. Soc. Clin. Investigation, Endocrine Soc. (Weitzman Young Investigator award 1992), Western Assn. of Physicians, Biophys. Soc., Inst. Medicine (2004). Office: U Calif San Francisco 600 16th St N472J Box 2240 San Francisco CA 94143-2240 E-mail: cohen@cmpharm.ucsf.edu.

COHEN, FREDERICK H., lawyer; b. Chgo., Feb. 28, 1965; BA in Fin., U. Ill., 1987; JD with honors, U. Chgo., 1990. Bar: Ill. 1990, US Dist. Ct. (no. dist. Ill.) 1991, US Ct. Appeals (7th cir.) 1991, US Supreme Ct. 2001. Prin. Goldberg, Kohn, Bell, Black, Rosenbloom & Moritz, Chgo. Adj. prof. Kent Coll. Law. Named one of The Nation's Top Litigators, Nat. Law Jour., 2007; recipient Equal Justice award, Sargent Shriver Nat. Ctr. Poverty Law, 2004, Child Health Adv. of Yr. award, Acad. Pediat., 2005, Excellence in Pro Bono award, US Dist. Ct. (no. dist. Ill.), 2006. Office: Goldberg Kohn Ste 3700 55 E Monroe St Chicago IL 60603-5802 Office Phone: 312-201-3929. Office Fax: 312-863-7429. E-mail: frederick.cohen@goldbergkohn.com.*

COHEN, GARY J., lawyer; b. Tucson, 1968; Grad., Northwestern U. Atty. Mesch, Clark & Rothschild, P.C., Tucson, 1993—, ptnr., litig. section. Bd. mem. Tucson Jewish Cmty. Ctr.; mem. Tucson Fiesta Bowl com., Tucson City Magistrate Merit Selection Com., City of Tucson Anti-Hate Crime Task Force, Pima County Teen Ct., Lawyers for Literacy. Mem.: Southwest Section of US Tennis Assn. Office: Mesch, Clark & Rothschild PC 259 N Meyer Ave Tucson AZ 85701-1090 Office Phone: 520-624-8886. Office Fax: 520-798-1037.

COHEN, GEORGE LEON, lawyer; b. Covington, Ga., June 20, 1930; s. Leon and Callie (Harrison) C.; m. Jacqueline Lanier Edwards, Nov. 17, 1951 (dec. May 2001); children— George Leon, Gardner Edwards; m Martha Starr Daniels, Nov 20, 2004. AB, Va. Mil. Inst., 1951; LLB, U. Va., 1956. Bar: Ga. 1957, U.S. Ct. Appeals (11th cir.). Assoc. Sutherland, Asbill & Brennan, Atlanta, 1956-62, ptnr., 1962—. Editorial bd. Va. Law Rev., 1954-56 Mem.: ABA (various coms.), Am. Law Inst. (advisor to corp. governance project), Lawyers Club Atlanta, Atlanta Bar Assn., Ga. State Bar (chmn. corp. and banking law sect. 1968—69, chmn. Ga. bus. corp. code revision com. 1986—89, various coms.), Omicron Delta Kappa, Order of Coif. Office: Sutherland Asbill & Brennan 999 Peachtree St NE Ste 2300 Atlanta GA 30309-3996 Home Phone: 404-351-3677; Office Phone: 404-853-8035. Business E-Mail: george.cohen@sablaw.com.

COHEN, GLORIA ERNESTINE, elementary school educator; b. Bklyn., July 6, 1942; d. Victor George and Marion Theodosia (Roberts) C. BS in Edn., Wilberforce U., 1965; MA in Elem. Edn., Adelphi U., 1975; Profl. Diploma in Ednl. Adminstrn., L.I. U., 1984; MS in Edn., Bklyn. Coll., 1986. Tchr. Bd. Edn., Bklyn., 1965—; case worker Dept. Welfare, Bklyn., 1965—. Mem. comprehensive sch. improvement program Pub. Sch. 149, 1990—91, mem. open corridor planning com., 1990—91, mem. consultation com., 1990—; tchr. in charge of after sch. reading and math. tutorial program, 1995—96; dean grades 4-6, 1996—98; supr. Sat. Acad.; tchr. in charge of Read Extended Day program, 1997—98; cons. tchr. for 4th grade class, 1999; tchr. in charge of food and nutrition distbn. Maxwell H.S., Bklyn., 1999, P.S. 64 Dist. 27, Queens, 2000; tutorial tchr. Pub. Sch. 149, 2001—02; tutorial reading tchr. P.S. 149, Bklyn., 2004; tchr. in charge of food and nutrition distbn. P.S. 174 Dist. 19, Bklyn., 2001—04, Dist. 27, Pub. Sch. 60, Queens, 2005—06. Mem.: US Tennis Assn., Rockville Racquet Club, Kappa Delta Pi, Zeta Phi Beta. Democrat. Roman Catholic. Avocation: tennis.

COHEN, GORDON S., health products executive; b. NYC, May 18, 1937; s. Leon Lewis and Irene (Lipton) C.; m. Marjorie Rennick, June 12, 1960; children: Terri Susan, Lisa Michelle, Bonnie Lynne. AB, Brown U., 1959; MD, Yale U., 1963. Diplomate Am. Bd. Pathology, Anatomic Pathology and Clin. Pathology. Instr. dept. pathology Yale U., New Haven, 1967-70, asst. prof. pathology, 1970-71, asst. clin. prof. pathology, 1971-76; pres. Jeneric Industries, Wallingford, Conn., 1975-86; chmn. Pentron Corp., Wallingford, 1977—; pres. Jeneric/Pentron, Inc., Wallingford, 1987—. Attending pathologist Yale-New Haven Hosp., 1970-71, Hosp. St. Raphael, New Haven, 1971-76; pathologist The Charlotte Hungerford Hosp., Torrington, Conn., 1967-70. Author numerous articles in field. Sr. edn. officer Milford (Conn.) U.S. Power Squadron, 1987; mem. Congressman DeNardis's Small Bus. Adv. Com., 1982; bd. dirs. Mary Wade Home, 2002—. Capt. (M.C.) USAR, 1964-70. Mem. Internat. Acad. Pathology, NY Acad. Scis., Phi Beta Kappa, Sigma Xi, Alpha Omega Alpha. Avocations: sailing, shooting, book collecting. Office: Pentron Corp 53 N Plains Industrial Rd Wallingford CT 06492-5841 Business E-Mail: gordon@pentron.com.

COHEN, HARLAN P., lawyer; b. Boston, Mass., Mar. 26, 1948; BA magna cum laude, Harvard U., 1970, JD cum laude, 1974. Bar: Tex. 1974. Ptnr. Locke Purnell Rain Harrell P.C., Dallas, 1974—98, Gibson Dunn Crutcher. Mem. ABA, Phi Beta Kappa. Office: Gibson Dunn Crutcher 2100 McKinney Ave Ste 1100 Dallas TX 75201 Office Phone: 214-698-3109. Office Fax: 214-571-2983. Business E-Mail: hcohen@gibsondunn.com.

COHEN, HARRIET NEWMAN, lawyer; b. Providence, Dec. 8, 1932; d. Morris and Marion Newman. BA in Latin and Greek, cum laude, Barnard Coll., 1952; MA in Latin and Greek, cum laude, Bryn Mawr Coll., 1953; JD cum laude, Bklyn. Law Sch, 1974. Bar: NY 1975, US Dist. Ct. (So. Dist. NY) 1975, US Dist. Ct. (Ea. Dist. NY) 1975, US Ct. Appeals (2nd Cir.), US Supreme Ct. Assoc. Squadron, Gartenberg, Ellenoff & Plesent, NYC, 1974—76, Phillips, Nizer, Benjamin, Krim & Ballon, NYC, 1976—80, Golenbock & Barell, NYC, 1980—83; ptnr. Golenbock and Barell, 1984—86, Solin & Breindel, 1986, Cohen, Hennessey, Bienstock & Rabin PC, 1994—. Tchr. domestic relations law Continuing Edn. Divsn. CUNY, 1980, mem. adv. bd., 82; lectr. Assn. Bar City NY, 1982, NY Women's Bar Assn, 1981—82, NY State Trial Lawyers Assn., 1981—82; mem. Child Support Commn. State NY, 1984—90, Commn. Foster Care in City NY, 1991—94. Author: The Equitable Distribution Law in Divorce: The New York Experience, The Divorce Book for Men and Women: How to Gain Your Freedom Without Losing Everything Else, 1994; feature article writer NY Law Jour., spl. sect. on matrimonial law, 1999—2006. Bd. mem. In Motion, Inc., 2002—05, Legal Momentum; chair lawyers' com. Bernard Coll. Alumnae Assn., 2000—02. Mem.: NY County Lawyers' Assn., ABA, Coalition on Women's Legis. Issues (co-chair 1986), NY State Bar Assn., Assn. Bar City NY, NY Women's Bar Assn. (v.p. 1983—84, pres. 1985—86). Office: Cohen Henessey Bienstock & Rabin PC Floor 19 11 West 42nd St New York NY 10036-8002 Office Phone: 212-575-0007. Office Fax: 212-764-3925.*

COHEN, HARRIS L., diagnostic radiologist, consultant; b. Bklyn., Sept. 18, 1951; s. Samuel G. and Lola Estera (Altman) C.; m. Sandra Wilensky, Oct. 18, 1979; children: David Matthew, Lauren Elizabeth, Benjamin Adam. BA cum laude in Chemistry, CUNY, Bklyn., 1969—73; MD in Medicine, SUNY, Bklyn., 1972—76. Diplomate Am. Bd. Radiology, Nat. Bd. Med. Examiners; cert. added qualifications in pediatric radiology Am. Bd. Radiology. Asst. prof. radiology SUNY Health Sci. Ctr., Bklyn., 1981-88; asst. chief of imaging Brookdale Hosp. Med. Ctr., Bklyn., 1983-85; med. dir. diagnostic med. imaging program Coll. Health Related Professions, SUNY Health Sci. Ctr., Bklyn., 1985—88, 1994—; assoc. prof. radiology Cornell U. Med. Coll., NYC, 1988-93; chief pediatric CT and ultrasound North Shore U. Hosp.-Cornell, Manhasset, NY, 1988-93, assoc. dir. divsn. CT/ultrasound/magnetic resonance imaging, 1988-93; assoc. dir. radiology Kings County Hosp., Bklyn., 1993-2000; prof. radiology SUNY Health Sci. Ctr., Bklyn., 1993-2000, assoc. chmn. acad. affair and clin. rsch., 1998-2000; vis. prof. radiology, dir. divsn. pediat. imaging Johns Hopkins U., Balt., 2000—02; prof. radiology, vice chmn. dept. radiology, dir. divsn., body imaging, chief pediatric body imaging SUNY, Stony Brook, 2002—, dir. abdominal imaging fellow program, 2003—. Dir. divsn. ultrasound U. and Kings County Hosps., Bklyn., 1985-88, 93-2000, dir. divsn. pediat. radiology, 1999-2000; cons. ultrasound and pediatric imaging Brookdale Hosp. Med. Ctr., Bklyn., 1988—; RSNA internat. vis. prof., India, 2005; RSNA Eyler editl. fellow, 2004-05. Author, editor, co-editor: Ultrasonography of the Prenatal and Neonatal Brain, 1996, 2d edit., 2002, Spanish transl., 2002, Obstetrics & Gynecology (Ultrasound), 1997, Fetal and Pediatric Ultrasound, 2001, Chinese Transl., 2003, Spanish Transl., Ecografia Fetal y Pediatrica, 2004, Gastrointestinal Disease VI, 2004, Ultrasound III, 2005, Neurology III, 2006, mem. editl. bd.: Jour. Diagnostic Med. Sonography, 1985—, Jour. Ultrasound in Medicine, 2002—, Ultrasound Quarterly, 2002—, reviewer: Radiographics, 1991 (Editors cert. recognition, 1990-2003); contbr. chapters to books, articles to profl. jours., ednl. CDs and videos. Named one of Best Drs. in NY, Castle Connoly, 2003—, listed in Radiology Editors Forum, 2006, Best Drs. in NY, NY Mag., 2003, Best Drs. in Am., 2007; recipient Master Tchr. award in radiology, SUNY Health Sci. Ctr. at Bklyn. Alumni Assn., 1996, Tchr. of Yr. award, SUNY Stony Brook Radiology, 2006. Fellow: Am. Inst. Ultrasound in Medicine (chmn. pediat. sect. 1994—95, chmn. ctrl. program com. 1995—97, bd. dirs. 1999—2002, bd. govs. 1999—2002, co-chair emergency ultrasound 2001—04), Am. Acad. Pediat. (chmn. radiology sect. 1992—94), Soc. Radiologists in Ultrasound (chmn. constn. com. 1996—98, program com. 2004—), Am. Coll. Radiology (stds. and accreditation com. 1992—98, commn. ultrasound edn. com. 1998—, task force on disaster planning 2001—05, disting. cmty. svc. award 1998, 2004); mem.: Radiologic Soc. N.Am. (audiovisual com. 1992—96, exhibits com. 2002—04, coord. ultrasound cases of day 2004—06, exhibits com. 2007—, Eyler editl. fellow 2004—05, internat. vis. prof. 2006), Soc. Radiology in Ultrasound (program com. 2004—), Soc. Pediat. Radiology (liaison to Am. Acad. Pediat. 1993—94, liaison to Am. Inst. Ultrasound in Medicine 1995, program com. 2004), SUNY-Downstate Alumni Assn. (councillor, bd. mgrs. 1998—2001), Alpha Omega Alpha. Avocations: computers and computer education, basketball, baseball, american and jewish history. Home: 78 Grove Ave Cedarhurst NY 11516-2311 Personal E-mail: hcohenmb@optonline.net. Business E-Mail: harris.cohen@stonybrook.edu.

COHEN, HARVEY JAY, geriatrician, hematologist, oncologist, educator; b. Bklyn., Oct. 21, 1940; s. Joseph and Anne (Margolin) C.; m. Sandra Helen Levine, June 1964; children: Ian Mitchell, Pamela Robin. BS, Bklyn. Coll., 1961; MD, Downstate Med. Coll., Bklyn., 1965. Diplomate Am. Bd. Internal Medicine, Am. Bd. Hematology. Intern, then resident internal medicine Duke U. Med. Ctr., Durham, NC, 1965-67, fellow hematology and oncology, 1969-71; chief hematology-oncology VA Med. Ctr., Durham, NC, 1975-76, chief med. svc., 1976-82, assoc. chief staff-edn., 1982—2007, geriatric rsch., edn. and clin. ctr.; assoc. prof. medicine Duke U. Med. Ctr., Durham, 1976-80, now prof. medicine, also dir. Ctr. for Study of Aging, chair dept. medicine, 2007—. Chair bd. sci. counselors Nat. Inst. Aging, 1999—2003; chair Women's Health Initiative, Observational Study Monitoring Bd., 2005. Author: Medical Immunology, 1977; co-author: (with H.G. Koenig) The Link Between Religion and Health: Psychoneuroimmunology and the Faith Factor, 2002, Taking Care After 50, 2000; editor: Cancer I and II, 1987, Jour. Gerontology: Med. Scis., 1988-92, Geriatric Medicine, 1997; contbr. articles to profl. jours. Served as surgeon USPHS, 1967-69. Fellow ACP, Am. Geriat. Soc. (bd. dirs. 1987-96, chair bd. dirs. 1995-96, sec. 1991-93, ethics com. 1992-96, pres. 1994-95, Dennis W. Jahnigen Meml. award 2005), Gerontology Soc. Am. (clin. sec., rsch. com. 1987-92, chair publs. com. 1996-98, program chair 1994, pres. 2000, Donald P. Kent award, 2005); mem. Am. Soc. Clin. Oncology, Am. Soc. Hematology, Am. Assn. Cancer Rsch. (cancer and acute leukemia group B, chair cancer in the elderly com.), Assn. Am. Physicians, Internat. Soc. Geriat. Oncology (bd. dirs. 2000-, pres. 2004-). Home: 2811 Friendship Cir Durham NC 27705-5521 Office: Duke U Med Ctr for Study Aging & Human Devel Box 3703 Durham NC 27710-0001 Business E-Mail: cohen015@mc.duke.edu.

COHEN, HARVEY JOEL, pediatric hematology and oncology educator; b. NYC, July 4, 1943; s. Phillip and Ida (Teitel) C.; m. Ilene Verne Bookseger, Aug. 15, 1965; children: Philip Jason, Jonathan Todd. BS, Bklyn. Coll., 1964; MD, PhD, Duke U., 1970. Intern Children's Hosp., Boston, 1970-71, resident, 1973-74; instr. pediatrics Harvard U. Med. Sch., Boston, 1974-76, asst. prof., 1976-79, assoc. prof., 1979-81; assoc. prof. pediatrics U. Rochester (N.Y.) Med. Ctr., 1981-84, prof., 1984-93, assoc. chmn. dept., 1987-93, chief pediatric hematology and oncology, 1981-93; chmn. dept. pediatrics Stanford (Calif.) U. Sch. Medicine, 1993—2006, prof., 1993—; chief staff Lucile Salter Packard Children's Hosp. at Stanford, 1993—2006. Med. advisor Montgomery Med. Ventures, San Francisco, 1984—97; sci. advisor St. Jude Children's Rsch. Hosp., Memphis, 1985—90, 2001—; chmn. hematology study sect. NIH, Washington, 1986—88. Editor: Hematology: Basic Principles and Practice, 1991, 94, 99, 2005. Med. dir. Camp Good Days and Spl. Times, Rochester, 1981—93, Monroe County chpt. Am.Cancer Soc., Rochester, 1983—93; med. dir. Rochester br. Cooley's Anemia Found., 1984—93; bd. dirs. Lucile Pakcard Children's Hosp., 1993—97, Lucile Packard Found. for Children's Health, 1997—2000, Lucile Pakcard Children's Hosp., 2000—06, Ronald McDonald House of Palo Alto, Calif., 1995—2005, Children's Health Coun., 1996—2005. Tng. grantee Nat. Inst. Gen. Med.

Scis., 1983-90, Nat. Inst. Child Health and Human Devel., 1990-94. Mem. Soc. for Pediatric Rsch. (pres. 1988-89), Am. Soc. for Clin. Investigation, Am. Pediatric Soc. Democrat. Jewish. Achievements include research in on continuous assay for superoxide production, effect of selenium on synthesis of glutatnione peroxidase; relationship of in vitro and in vivo killing of leukemic cells by asparagase clinical trials in childhood leukemia; comparative proteomics in pediatric diseases. Office: Stanford U Sch Medicine Dept Pediatrics Rm H-310 Stanford CA 94305 Office Phone: 650-723-5104 can't process batch details. Business E-Mail: punko@stanford.edu.

COHEN, HENRY RODGIN (H. RODGIN COHEN), lawyer; b. Charleston, W.Va, May 7, 1944; s. Louis W. and Bertie (Rodgin) C.; m. Barbara Latz, Aug. 31, 1969; children: Sarah Abigail, Jonathan David. BA, Harvard U., 1965, LLB, 1968; LLB (hon.), U. Charleston, 1998. Bar: W.Va. 1968, NY 1970. Assoc. Sullivan & Cromwell, NYC, 1970-77, ptnr., 1977—, vice chmn., 1999-2000, chmn., 2000—. Contbg. editor Fin. Svcs. Regulation Newsletter, 1985; bd. advisors Banking Law Rev.; mem. nat. bd. contbrs. Am. Lawyers Newspaper Group. Trustee NY Presbyn. Hosp., Hampton Coll., Econ. Club, Deerfield Acad., Hackley Sch.; mem. adv. bd. Wall St. Rising, United Way of Westchester-Putnam, U. Charleston. With US Army, 1968—70. Named a leader of BTI Consulting Group's Law Firm Client Svc. All-Star Team, 2006, Dealmaker of Yr., Am. Lawyer mag., 2007; named one of Global 100, CFO Mag., 100 Most Influential Lawyers, Nat. Law Jour., 2000, 2006, Top 100 NY Super Lawyers, NY Super Lawyers, 2006; named to The Lawdragon 500: The Leading Lawyers in Am. Office: Sullivan & Cromwell 125 Broad St Fl 28 New York NY 10004-2489 Office Phone: 212-558-3534, 202-956-7500. Business E-Mail: cohenhr@sullcrom.com.

COHEN, HERBERT JESSE, pediatrician, educator; b. NYC, Apr. 27, 1935; s. Barnet and Edith (Lepolstat) C.; m. Marion E. Finger, Aug. 29, 1960; children— Linda Elizabeth, Gerald Daniel, Seth Michael. BA (Ford Found. scholar), Columbia, 1955; MD, State U. N.Y., 1959. Intern Bellevue Hosp., NYC, 1959-60; resident NY Hosp., 1960-62; asst. instr. Cornell Med. Sch., 1961-62; instr. Tulane Med. Sch., 1962-64; NIH fellow Albert Einstein Coll. Medicine, 1964-66, asst. prof. pediatrics and rehab. medicine, 1966-71, assoc. prof., 1971-76, prof., 1976—; dir. Children's Evaluation and Rehab. Ctr., Rose F. Kennedy Center for Mental Retardation and Human Devel., Bronx, NY, 1968, 1978—2006, Bronx Developmental Services, N.Y. State Dept. Mental Hygiene, 1971-80, Rose F. Kennedy U. Ctr. for Excellence in Devel. Disabilities Tng. Svcs. and Rsch., 1974—2006, dir. div. child devel. and devel. disabilities dept. pediatrics, 1981—2006. Vice chmn. Pres.'s Com. on Mental Retardation, 1978-81; mem. study sect. human devel. NIH, 1978-82; mem. profl. adv. bd. various founds. and profl. orgns. Author 4 books; contbr. over 85 articles to profl. pubs. With USPHS, 1962—64. Recipient Disting. Humanitarian R&D awards Mental Retardation Svc. Orgns., Disting. Svc. award Assn. of Univ. Ctrs. on Disability, 2005; United Cerebral Palsy Rsch. and Edn. Found. fellow, 1966-68 Fellow Am. Acad. Pediatrics (chmn. child devel. sect., chmn. com. on children with disabilities, Arnold J. Capute award sect. on children with disabilities 2004) Assn. U. Ctrs. Disabilities (Disting. Svc. award); mem. AAAS, Am. Acad. Cerebral Palsy, Am. Assn. Univ. Affiliated Facilities (pres. 1980-81, dir. 1977-84), Am. Assn. Mental Retardation (Leadership award 1996), Am. Assn. Ctrs. on Disability (Disting. Leadership award). Office: R F Kennedy Ctr 1410 Pelham Pky S Bronx NY 10461-1101 Office Phone: 718-430-8522. Business E-Mail: hcohen@aecom.yu.edu.

COHEN, HERMAN NATHAN, private investigator; b. Bklyn., June 3, 1949; s. Stanley and Hannah (Persky) C.; m. Carolyn P. Grillo, Jan. 8, 1989. BA, Bklyn. Coll., 1970; MS in Ednl. Adminstrn., Hofstra U., 1975. Investigator IRS, NYC, 1970-72, adminstrv. intern Washington, 1972-73, employee devel. specialist Uniondale, NY, 1973-75, br. chief Bklyn., 1975-79; pers. officer Home Ins. Co., NYC, 1979-81; asst. v.p. City Investing Co., NYC, 1981-85; prin. H.N. Cohen Enterprises, Inc., NYC, 1985-86; human resources dir. Empire Blue Cross Blue Shield, NYC, 1986-89; v.p. adminstrn. ASPCA, NYC, 1989-90, sr. v.p., 1990, exec. v.p., 1990-91, chief adminstrv. officer, 1991-92, chief law enforcement, 1992-94; CEO, pvt. investigator Due Diligence Plus, Amherst, NY, 1994—, pvt. investigator West Hartford, Conn., 1994—; chief oversight U.S. Dept. Vets. Affairs, Washington, 2000—. Arbitrator Am. Arbitration Assn., 1986—; bd. dirs. Ashfield Corp.; adj. faculty Conn. Criminal Law Found. Bd. dirs. Owen Sch.; adjutant, dir. at large Centennial Legion of Hist. Mil. Commands; mem. amb.'s coun. Wadsworth Atheneum, Conn., 1st co. Gov. Foot Guard, Conn.; vol. Montgomery County (Md.) Police Dept. Mem. Internat. Assn. Chiefs of Police (chmn. pvt. security com.), Conn. Police Chiefs Assn., Vet. Corps. Arty., Nat. Assn. Investigative Specialists, World Affairs Coun., Mensa, Ancient Free and Accepted Masons, Am. Soc. Indsl. Security, Md. Police Chiefs Assn. Democrat. Jewish. Office: US Dept Vets Affairs 810 Vermont Ave NW 264C Washington DC 20420 E-mail: cyberpi@msn.com.

COHEN, HOWARD A., cardiologist; B cum laude, Yale U.; MD, NYU, 1970. Intern internal medicine Bellevue Hosp., resident internal medicine, chief resident; fellow cardiology Johns Hopkins Hosp.; cardiologist Nat. Naval Med. Ctr., Bethesda, Md.; dir. interventional cardiology St. John's Hosp., Calif., dir. Cardiac Catheterization Lab. Calif., chief of staff Calif.; prof. medicine U. Pitts., dir. clin. cardiology, dir. The Cardiac Catheterization Lab., assoc. dir. Cardiovascular Inst.; dir. cardiac catheterization lab. Lenox Hill Hosp., NYC, dir. divsn. cardiovascular intervention. Med. adv. bd. Biopure Corp.; lectr. area percentaneony left venticular assist, radial artery access; prin. investigator Nat. Heart, Lung and Blood Inst. Dynamic Registry. Named Best Doctor, NY Mag., 2003—06. Fellow: So. Cardiac Angiography and Interventions, Am. Coll. Cardiology; mem.: So. Calif. Soc. Interventional Cardiology (founder and pres.). Office: Lenox Hill Hosp 100 East 77th St New York NY 10021 Office Phone: 212-434-2400.

COHEN, IRA MYRON, retired aeronautical and mechanical engineering educator; b. Chgo., July 18, 1937; s. Harry Nathan and Esther (Lenchner) C.; m. Linda Barbara Einstein, June 12, 1960; children: Susan Ellen Bolstad, Nancy Beth Cavanaugh. B in Aero. Engring., Poly. Univ., Bklyn., 1958; MA, Princeton U., NJ, 1961, PhD in Aero. Engring., 1963; MA (hon.), U. Pa., 1971. Mem. tech. staff Sandia Labs., Albuquerque, summers 1971, 74, 77; asst. prof. engring. Brown U., Providence, 1963-66; asst. prof. mech. engring. U. Pa., Phila., 1966-67, assoc. prof., 1967-76, prof., 1976—2006, chmn. dept., 1992-97; ret., 2006. Guest prof. Technische Hochschule Aachen, Germany, 1966; cons. fluid mechanics related problems to industry, 1966—, attys., 1966—; mem. bd. The Sch. in Rose Valley, Moylan, Pa., 1969-74. Author: (with P.K. Kundu) Fluid Mechanics, 2d edit., 2002, 3d edit., 2004; contbr. articles to various publs. Recipient Sustained Svc. award, AIAA, 2006; Travel grant, Fulbright, 1966. Fellow AIAA (sect. sec. 1977-80, 85—), ASME; mem. AAUP, Am. Phys. Soc., Sigma Xi. Office: U Pa Dept Mech Engring & Applied Mechanics 233 Towne Bldg Philadelphia PA 19104-6315 Business E-Mail: imcohen@seas.upenn.edu. *Persistent hard work and uncompromising high standards will eventually overcome greed, corruption, and evil. Never forget to treat every human being with dignity, respect, kindness, and compassion. A loving mate is a lifelong inspiration.*

COHEN, IRWIN, economist; b. Bronx, NY, Feb. 29, 1936; s. Samuel and Gertrude (Levy) C. BS in Acctg., NYU, 1956, MBA in Fin., 1964, MA in Econs., 1969; BS in Math., CCNY, 1970. Fin. analyst US SEC, NYC, 1965-67, Fed. Res. Bank NY, NYC, 1967-72, Prudential Ins. Co. Am., 1973-74, SEC, 1974—98; ret. Mem. Internat. Platform Assn. (life), Math. Assn. Am., Am. Fin. Assn., Econ. History Assn. Home: 372 Central Park Ave Apt #2K Scarsdale NY 10583-1308

COHEN, JAY M., federal agency administrator, retired military officer; Grad., U.S. Naval Acad., 1968; MS in Marine Engring. and Naval Arch., MIT. Commd. ensign USN, 1968, advanced through grades to rear adm., 1997, ret., 2005; diver SEALAB Group, San Diego; supply and weapons officer USS Diodon, San Diego; with engring. dept. USS Nathanal Greene, New London; engr. officer USS Nathan Hale, Bremerton, Wash.; staff Comdr. Submarine Force, U.S. Atlantic Fleet; exec. officer USS George Washington Carver, New London; comdr. USS Hyman G. Rickover, New London; sr. mem. nuclear propulsion examining bd. Comdr. in Chief, U.S. Atlantic Fleet; dir. operational support Dir. Naval Intelligence, Pentagon, Washington; comdr. USS L.Y. Spear, 1991—93; dep. chief Navy Legis. Affairs SECNAV; dep. dir. ops. Joint Staff SECNAV, 1997—99, dir. Navy Y2K Project Office, 1999—2000; chief, Naval Rsch. Naval Rsch. Lab., Washington, 2000—06; dep. comdt. for sci. and tech. USMC, 2000—06; under sec. for sci. & tech. US Dept. Homeland Security, 2006—. Decorated Legion of Merit, Def. Superior Svc. medal, Meritorious Svc. medal.

COHEN, JEFF, editor, publishing executive; b. Cheyenne, Wyo. m. Kathryn M. Kase. BA in journalism, U. Tex., 1976. Sports and feature writer San Antonio Light, 1976—89, mng. editor, 1989—93; spl. projects editor new media Hearst Newspaper Divsn., NYC, 1993—94; editor Times Union, Albany, NY, 1994—2002; exec. v.p., editor Houston Chronicle, 2002—. Juror Pulitzer Prize, 1999, 2000. Fellow Multicultural Mgmt. Program, U. Mo. Sch. Journalism, 1987, Newspaper Mgmt. Ctr., Kellogg Grad. Sch. Mgmt., Northwestern U., 1990. Office: Houston Chronicle 801 Texas Ave Houston TX 77002*

COHEN, JEFFREY E., lawyer; b. NYC, Feb. 14, 1951; AB, Princeton Univ., 1972; JD, Harvard Univ., 1982. Bar: NY 1983. Ptnr., head of Global Securities practice Coudert Bros., NYC. Mem.: ABA. Office: Coudert Bros LLP 1114 Ave of the Americas New York NY 10036 Office Phone: 212-626-4936. Office Fax: 212-626-4120. Business E-Mail: cohenj@coudert.com.

COHEN, JEFFREY MICHAEL, lawyer; b. Dayton, Ohio, Nov. 13, 1940; s. H. Mort and Evelyn (Friedlob) C.; m. Betsy Z. Zimmerman, July 3, 1966; children: Meredith Sue, Seth Alan. AB, Colgate U., 1962; JD, Columbia U., 1965. Bar: Fla. 1965, U.S. Supreme Ct. 1969; cert. civil trial lawyer Fla. Bar Bd. Cert.; diplomate Nat. bd. Trial Advocacy. Asst. pub. defender Dade County (Fla.), 1968-70, asst. state's atty., 1970-72, spl. asst. state's atty., 1973; ptnr. Fromberg Fromberg Gross Cohen Shore & Berke, P.A., 1972-84, Cohen, Berke, Bernstein, Brodie & Kondell, P.A., Miami, Fla., 1984-2000, Carlton Fields, 2000—. Adj. prof. litigation skills U. Miami Sch. Law, 1989—, adj. prof. trial skills Nova Southeastern U. Law Sch.; chair bd. of legal specialization and edn. Fla. Bar. Trustee Miami-Dade County Alliance for Ethical Govt. Mem. ABA, Dade County Bar Assn. (bd. dirs.), Acad. Fla. Trial Lawyers, Assn. Trial Lawyers Am., Am. Judicature Soc., Nat. Inst. Trial Advocacy (chair and faculty mem.), Fla. Criminal Def. Attys. Assn. Home: 3628 Saint Gaudens Rd Miami FL 33133-6533 Office: 4000 Internat Pl 100 SE 2d St Miami FL 33131 Office Phone: 305-530-0050. E-mail: jmcohen@carltonfields.com.

COHEN, JOEL EPHRAIM, biologist, educator, demographer; b. Washington, Feb. 10, 1944; s. Hymen Ezra and Alice. C.; children: Zoe, Adam. BA, Harvard U., 1965, MA, 1967, MPH, PhD, Harvard U., 1970, DrPH, 1973; MA (hon.), Cambridge U., 1974. Jr. fellow in math. biology and sociology Soc. of Fellows Harvard U., 1967-71, asst. prof. biology, 1971-72, assoc. prof., 1972-75; prof. populations Rockefeller U., NYC, 1975—, Abby Rockefeller Mauzé prof., 1996—; prof. populations Columbia U., NYC, 1995—; dir.'s visitor Inst. for Advanced Study, Princeton, 1989-90. Chmn. bd. Societal Inst. Math. Scis., 1973—88; mem. ednl. adv. bd. John Simon Guggenheim Meml. Found., 1985—2001, mem. com. selection of fellows, 1990—99; mem. Mayor's Commn. for Sci. and Tech. City of N.Y., 1984—90; mem. sci. adv. bd. Inst. Sci. Interchange, Torino, Italy, 1991—; mem. bd. math. scis. NRC, 1991—92, mem. exec. com, panel on sci., tech. and law, 2000—, mem. governing bd., 2001—05; mem. bd. The Nature Conservancy, Arlington, Va., 2000—; trustee N.Y. Nature Conservancy, 2001—; mem. exec. com. Tyler Prize for Environ. Achievement, 2001—04, 2005—06; mem. adv. bd. Sci. for Judges Project Bklyn. Law Sch., 2002—07. Author: A Model of Simple Competition, 1967, Casual Groups of Monkeys and Men, 1971, Food Webs and Niche Space, 1978, Community Food Webs, 1990, Absolute Zero Gravity, 1992, How Many People Can the Earth Support?, 1995, Comparisons of Stochastic Matrices, 1998, Plants and Population: Is There Time?, 1999, Forecasting Product Liability Claims in the Manville Asbestos Case, 2004, Educating All Children: A Global Agenda, 2007; mem. editl. bd.: Am. Scholar, 1994—99. Trustee Russell Sage Found., 1989-99, vice chmn. bd., 1996-99; trustee Black Rock Forest Preserve, 1989—, Population Reference Bur., Washington, 2004—. Recipient Mercer award Ecol. Soc. Am., 1972, disting. statis. ecologist award 6th Internat. Congress of Ecology, 1994, Olivia Nordberg award for excellence in writing on population scis. Population Coun., N.Y.C., 1997, Fred L. Soper award Pan Am. Health & Edn. Found., Washington, 1998, Tyler prize Environ. Achievement, 1999, N.Y.C. Mayor's award for excellence in sci. and tech., 2002; fellow Ctr. for Advanced Study in Behavioral Scis., Stanford, 1981-82, John Simon Guggenheim Meml. fellow, 1981-82, MacArthur Found. fellow, 1981-86. Fellow AAAS, Am. Acad. Arts and Scis. (mem. coun. 2000—04), Am. Statis. Assn.; mem. Population Assn. Am. (Mindel Sheps award 1992), Cambridge Philos. Soc., Am. Philos. Soc., U.S. Nat. Acad. Scis. (mem. coun. 2001—04). Office: Rockefeller U 1230 York Ave Ste 20 New York NY 10021-6399

COHEN, JOEL J., lawyer, investment banker; b. NYC, Feb. 8, 1938; s. David M. and Eva (Weinstein) C.; m. Lillian Zeisel, June 30, 1963; children: Peter, Andrew Daniel, Nancy Elizabeth. BBA, CCNY, 1959; JD, Harvard U., 1962. Bar: N.Y. 1963. Assoc. Davis, Polk & Wardwell, NYC, 1963-69, ptnr., 1969-87; mng. dir. investment banking, co-head global mergers and acquisitions Donaldson, Lufkin & Jenrette Securities Corp., NYC, 1989-2000; chmn. bd. dirs. Chubb Corp., Warren, NJ, 2002—03; chmn., co-CEO Sagent Advisors Inc., NYC, 2003—. Bd. dirs. Maersk Inc., Madison, N.J., Chubb Corp., Warren, N.J., Borders Group Inc., Ann Arbor, Mich.; gen. counsel Presdl. Task Force on Market Mechanisms, 1987-88. Served with USAR, 1962-68. Mem. Assn. of Bar of City of N.Y. Home Phone: 212-737-7847; Office Phone: 212-904-9450. Business E-Mail: jcohen@sagentadvisors.com.

COHEN, JON STEPHAN, lawyer; b. Omaha, Nov. 9, 1943; s. Louis H. and Bertha N. (Goldstein) C.; children: Carolyn, Sherri, Barbara, Shayna, Jordan; m. Cheryl A. Jiroux, Oct. 7, 1994. Student, London Sch. Econs., 1963-64; BA, Claremont Men's Coll. (now Claremont McKenna Coll.), 1965; JD, Harvard U., 1968. Bar: Ariz. 1968. Assoc. Snell & Wilmer, Phoenix, 1968-73, ptnr., 1973—. Bd. dirs. Vika Corp., Phoenix, Ariz. Tech. Coun., Phoenix, Ariz. Sci. Ctr., Phoenix, Ariz. Bus. Leadership, Phoenix. Bd. dirs. Kronos Rsch. Inst., Phoenix. Fellow Ariz. Bar Found.; mem. ABA, Ariz. Bar Assn., Maricopa County Bar Assn., Village Athletic Club. Avocations: record collecting, skiing, racquetball. Home: 6901 E Northern Ave Paradise Valley AZ 85253 Office: Snell & Wilmer One Arizona Ctr Phoenix AZ 85004-0001 Office Phone: 602-382-6247. Business E-Mail: jcohen@swlaw.com.

COHEN, JONATHAN LITTLE, investment banker; b. NYC, Feb. 18, 1939; s. Reuben and Marjorie (Little) C.; children: Gregory David, Suzanne Elizabeth; m. Allison B. Morrow, 1998. AB, Dartmouth Coll., 1960, MBA, 1961. Asst. v.p. Irving Trust Co., NYC, 1963-68; assoc. Goldman, Sachs & Co., NYC, 1969-73, v.p., 1973-84, gen. ptnr., 1984-96; ltd. ptnr. The Goldman Sachs Group, L.P., NYC, 1996-99, adv. dir., 1999—. Trustee 1st Presbyn. Ch., NYC, 1996—99, Wildlife Conservation Soc., NYC, 2000—, Oberlin Coll., 1995—97, Pa. Acad. Fine Arts, 1998—; bd. overseers Amos Tuck Sch. Bus. Adminstrn., Dartmouth Coll., 1991—2004, chmn., 1995—2001; bd. overseers Hopkins Ctr. and Hood Mus. Art, Dartmouth Coll., 2001—05, Hood Mus. Art, Dartmouth Coll., 2006—; mem. pres.'s leadership coun. Dartmouth Coll., 1998—, mem. coun. alumni, 1983—86; mem. sch. com. Friends Sem., NYC, 1985—91. Lt. USN, 1961—63. Mem.: Coral Beach and Tennis Club (Bermuda), Bond Club, Bellport Bay Yacht Club, India House. Office: Goldman Sachs & Co 22nd Fl 85 Broad St New York NY 10004-2456 Business E-Mail: jonathan.cohen@gs.com.

COHEN, JOSEPH I., forensic pathologist; s. Melvin L. and Malkah Cohen; m. Julia I. Silva, May 24, 1987. MEd, Med. Coll. Wis., Milw. Lic. anatomic, clinical & forensic pathology Am. Bd. Pathology, 1996. City med. examiner Office Chief Med. Examiner, NYC, 1994—99; chief forensic pathologist Riverside County Sheriff-Coroner, Perris, Calif., 1999—. Forensic cons., Riverside, Calif., 1996—. Mem.: Calif. State Coroners' Assn., Am. Acad. Forensic Scis., Nat. Assn. Med. Examiners. Office: Riverside County Sheriff-Coroner 800 S Redlands Ave Perris CA 92570 Home Phone: 951-369-0540. Office Fax: 951-443-2303; Home Fax: 951-346-3245. Personal E-mail: nyc4jc@aol.com. Business E-Mail: jicohen@riversidesheriff.org.

COHEN, JOSHUA ROBERT, lawyer; b. East Patchogue, NY, Aug. 20, 1963; s. Abraham Cohen and Elizabeth Joan Caufield; m. Robin Renee Conlon, Feb. 28, 1967; children: Rhylan Ethan, Khyla Mia. BA, Hartwick Coll., 1985; JD, Fordham U., 1991. Bar: Conn. 1991, N.Y. 1992, U.S. Dist. Ct. (so. and ea. dists.) N.Y., 1992. Sr. assoc. Belair & Evans LLP, NYC, 1991-99; ptnr. Garson, Gerspach, DeCorato & Cohen, LLP, NYC, 1999—. Office: Garson Gerspach De Corato & Cohen LLP 110 Wall St New York NY 10005 Office Phone: 212-742-8700. Business E-Mail: cohen@ggdc.com.

COHEN, JUDITH R., realtor; d. Erwin Nat and Edith Helen Rosenblum; m. Richard Loeb Cohen, June 15, 1958; children: David Rosenblum, Rachel Susan Ennis, Jonathan Lee, Jennifer Leah Estlin. BS in Elem. Edn., U. Vt., Burlington, 1955—58. Lic. realtor Nat. Assn. Realtors, 1985, cert. accredited buyer rep. Nat. Assn. Realtors, 1992, residential specialist Nat. Assn. Realtors, 1992, new home sales profl. Cleve. Area Bd. Realtors. Tchr. Shaker Hts. Bd. Edn., Ohio, 1977—81; realtor, broker HGM Hilltop (now Realty One), Shaker Hts., 1981—88, Howard Hanna Smythe Cramer, Pepper Pike, Ohio, 1989—. Dir. Cleve. Area Bd. Realtors, 1992—94; gov. NE Ohio Multiple Listing Svc., Cleve., 1993—94. Dir. City of Shaker Heights Recreation Bd., Shaker Heighs, Ohio, 1972—77; mem. Nat. Coun. Jewish Women, Cleve., 1966; trustee Suburban Temple, Beachwood, Ohio, 1973—79; v.p. Mt. Sinai Hosp. Jr Aux., Cleve., 1966; pres. Greater Cleve. Dental Soc. Aux., Cleve., 1970—71; mem. Met. Health Planning Corp Dental Health Com., Cleve., 1971—77; trustee, bd. trustees Jewish Vocat. Svc., Cleve., 1975—80; dir. Cleve. Health & Edn. Mus. Women's Bd., 1986—88; cert. narrator taping for blind program Libr. Congress, Cleve., 1979—92; vol. rec. artist Cleve. Soc. Blind, 1967; leader Girl Scouts Am., Shaker Hts., 1969—77; chmn. Shaker Hts. All City Girl Scout Camporee, 1976—77. Mem.: Real Estate Buyers Agt. Coun. (licentiate), Coun. Residential Specialists (licentiate), Cleve. Area Bd. Realtors (licentiate; bd. dirs. 1992—94, Rookie of Yr. award 1982), Ohio Assn. Realtors (licentiate), Nat. Assn. Realtors (assoc.). Jewish. Avocations: travel, tai chi, crossword puzzles, dance. Office: Howard Hanna Smythe Cramer 30300 Chagrin Blvd Pepper Pike OH 44124 Business E-Mail: judyjudyjudy@realtor.com.

COHEN, JULES, former dean, internist, educator; b. Bklyn., Aug. 26, 1931; s. Samuel S. and Dora (Goldstein) C.; m. Doris Eidlin, Mar. 25, 1956; children: Stephen E., David E., Sharon C. Anisfeld. AB, U. Rochester, 1953, MD, 1957. Intern Beth Israel Hosp., Boston, 1957-58; resident, fellow in medicine U. Rochester (N.Y.) Strong Meml. Hosp., 1958-60, mem. faculty, 1963—, prof. medicine, 1973—; NIH research asso. Bethesda, Md., 1960-62; research fellow Postgrad. Med. Sch., London, 1962-63; physician in chief Rochester Gen. Hosp., 1976-82; sr. asso. dean med. edn. U. Rochester Sch. Medicine, 1982-97. USPHS research grantee, 1963-69; USPHS research grantee, 74-77; recipient USPHS Research Career Devel. award, 1970-75; Am. Heart Assn. grantee-in-aid, 1969-71 Fellow ACP, Am. Coll. Cardiology; mem. Am. Physiol. Soc., Am. Heart Assn. (fellow coun. on clin. cardiology), Monroe County Med. Soc., N.Y. State Med. Soc., Rochester Acad. Medicine. Home: 152 Burkedale Cres Rochester NY 14625-1704 Office: U Rochester Sch Medicine and Dentistry 601 Elmwood Ave Rochester NY 14642-0001 Home Phone: 585-381-5413; Office Phone: 585-273-4536. Business E-Mail: Jules_Cohen@urmc.rochester.edu.

COHEN, KARL PALEY, nuclear energy consultant; b. NYC, Feb. 5, 1913; s. Joseph M. and Ray (Paley) C.; m. Marthe H. Malartre, Sept. 20, 1938; children: Martine-Claude Lebouc, Elisabeth M. Brown, Beatrix Josephine Cashmore. AB, Columbia U., 1933, MA, 1934, PhD in Phys. Chemistry, 1937; postgrad., U. Paris, 1936—37. Rsch. asst. to Prof. H. C. Urey Columbia U., 1937-40; dir. theoretical divsn. SAM Manhattan Project, 1940—44; physicist Std. Oil Devel. Co., 1944-48; tech. dir. H.K. Ferguson Co., 1948-52; v.p. Walter Kidde Nuc. Lab., 1952-55; cons. AEC, sr. sci. Columbia U., 1955; mgr. advance engring. atomic power equipment dept. GE, 1955-65, gen. mgr. breeder reactor devel. dept., 1965-71, mgr. strategic planning, nuc. energy divsn., 1971-73, chief scientist, nuc. energy group, 1973-78; cons. prof. Stanford U., 1978-81. Author: The Theory of Isotope Separation as Applied to Large Scale Production of U-235, 1951; contbr. articles to profl. jours. Recipient Energy Rsch. prize, Alfried Krupp Found., 1977. Fellow AAAS, Am. Nuc. Soc. (pres. 1968-69, bd. dirs.), Am. Inst. Chemists (Chem. Pioneer award 1979); mem. NAE, IEEE, Am. Phys. Soc., Phi Beta Kappa, Sigma Xi, Phi Lambda Upsilon. Home and Office: 928 N California Ave Palo Alto CA 94303-3405 Personal E-mail: karlpc@comcast.net.

COHEN, KENNETH A., lawyer; b. Washington, Jan. 27, 1945; BA cum laude, Harvard U., 1967, JD magna cum laude, 1970. Bar: Mass. 1971, US Dist. Ct. Mass., US Ct. of Appeals (1st, 11th and fed. cirs.), US Tax Ct., US Supreme Ct. Law clk. to Hon. Bailey Aldrich U.S. Ct. Appeals (1st. cir.), 1970-71; assoc. prof. of Law Boston U., 1976-79; mem. Goodwin, Procter & Hoar, Boston; counsel Goodwin Procter LLP, Boston. Lectr. Boston U Sch. of Law, 1981-88. Mem. ABA, Mass. Bar Assn. Mem. Harvard Law Review 1969-70. Mailing: Goodwin Procter LLP 53 State St Exchange Pl Boston MA 02109 Office Phone: 617-570-1000, 617-570-1270. Office Fax: 617-523-1231. Business E-Mail: kcohen@goodwinprocter.com.

COHEN, LARRY, film director, producer, screenwriter; b. Chgo., Apr. 20, 1947; TV writer: (series) Kraft Mystery Theatre, The Defenders, Arrest and Trial, NYPD Blue, 87th Precinct Ice, Heatwave; (movies) Cool Million, 1972, Shootout in a One-Dog Town, 1974, Man on the Outside, 1975, Desperado: Avalanche at Devil's Ridge, 1988; creator: Branded, 1965-66, The Invaders, 1967-68; film writer: The Return of the Seven, 1966, Daddy's Gone A-Hunting, 1969, El Condor, 1970, I, The Jury, 1982, Best Seller, 1987, Deadly Illusion, 1987, Guilty as Sin, 1993, Phone Booth, 2003; dir., prodr., writer: Bone, 1972, Black Caesar, 1973, Hell in Harlem,

1973, It's Alive, 1974, Demon, 1976, The Private Files of J. Edgar Hoover, 1978, It Lives Again, 1978, Full Moon High, 1982, Q, 1982, Perfect Strangers, 1984; story: Success, 1979, The Man Who Wasn't There, 1983, Scandalous, 1984, Body Snatchers, 1984; dir., writer: Special Effects, 1984, The Ambulance, 1990; exec. prodr., dir., writer: The Stuff, 1985, It's Alive III: Island of the Alive, 1987, Return to Salem's Lot, 1987, Wicked Stepmother, 1989; prodr., writer: Maniac Cop II, 1990; writer, dir.: As Good As Dead, 1996; dir.: Original Gangstas. 1997, Pick Me Up, 2005.

COHEN, LARRY, labor union administrator; b. Phila. State worker, NJ; staff rep. Communications Workers of Am., 1980—82, dir. NJ area, 1982—85, asst. to v.p. for Dist. 1, 1985—86, asst. to pres. & dir. organizing, 1986—98, nat. mobilization coord., 1988, exec. v.p. organizing, edn. & tng., mobilization, internat. affairs, health & safety, 1998, pres. Washington, 2005—. Pres. Union Network Internat. Telecom Sector, 2001—; founder Jobs with Justice, 1987. Office: Communications Workers of America 501 3rd St NW Washington DC 20001-2797*

COHEN, LAURA, lawyer; b. Pitts., Feb. 26, 1958; d. Alfred and Rita K. Cohen; (div.); children: Sarah Hackney, Beth Hackney. BA in Polit. Sci. with honors, Chatham Coll., 1993; JD, U. Pitts., 1996. Bar: Pa. 1996, US Dist. Ct. (we. dist.) Pa. 1996, US Supreme Ct., 2000. Lawyer, owner Family Legal Ctr., Monroeville, Pa., 1996—. Mem.: Neighborhood Legal Svcs. Assn. (bd. dirs. 2004—), Greater Pitts. Bus. Connection (v.p. 1997—99, pres. 2000—), Allegheny County Bar Assn., Pa. Bar Assn. (hearing com., mem. Pa. disciplinary bd.). Office: Family Legal Ctr 2526 Monroeville Blvd Monroeville PA 15146-2133 Office Phone: 412-824-0100. Business E-Mail: laura@familylegalcenter.com.

COHEN, LAWRENCE ALAN, health facility administrator; b. NYC, Nov. 29, 1953; s. Irwin Wolf Cohen and Ernestine Jacqueline (Rosenbloom) Chaut; m. Ilene Beth Rosen, May 27, 1979; children: Bari, Kerri, Andrew. BBA in Acctg., George Washington U., 1975; JD, St. Johns U., 1979; LLM in Taxation, NYU, 1982. Bar: N.Y.; CPA. Assoc. Rogers & Wells, NYC, 1979-82, Battle Fowler, NYC, 1982-84; 1st v.p. VMS Realty Ptnrs., NYC, 1984-88; exec. v.p. PaineWebber Properties Inc., NYC, 1989-90, pres., CEO, 1991-96; vice chmn., CFO Capital Sr. Living Corp., NYC, 1996-98, CEO, 1999—. Mem. Nat. Realty Com. (exec. com. 1990—), Nat. Multi Housing Coun. (exec. com. 1992—), Am. Srs. Housing Assn. (exec. bd. dirs. 1992—). Jewish. Home Phone: 516-374-1549; Office Phone: 212-551-1770. E-mail: lcohen@capitalsenior.com.

COHEN, LAWRENCE EDWARD, sociologist, educator, criminologist; b. LA, July 20, 1945; s. Louis and Florence (White) C. BA, U. Calif., Berkeley, 1969; MA, Calif. State U., 1971; PhD, U. Wash., 1974; postdoctorate study, SUNY, Albany, 1973-75. Rsch. assoc. Sch. of Criminal Justice, SUNY, Albany, 1973-76; asst. prof. U. Ill., Urbana, 1976-80; assoc. prof. U. Tex., Austin, 1980-85; prof. Ind. U., Bloomington, 1985-88, U. Calif., Davis, 1988—. Cons. editor Social Forces, 1981-84, Jour. Criminal Law and Criminology, 1982-2000, Am. Sociol. Rev., 1982-84, Am. Jour. Sociology, 1990-98, Criminology, 1996-98; contbr. numerous articles to profl. jours. Sgt. USMC, 1963-66, Vietnam. Grantee NIMH, 1978-80, NSF, 1983-89. Mem. Am. Sociol. Assn., Am. Soc. Criminology, Acad. Criminal Justice Scis., Soc. for Study Social Problems. Office: U Calif Dept Sociology Davis CA 95616 Business E-Mail: lecohen@ucdavis.edu.

COHEN, LAWRENCE SOREL, internist, educator; b. NYC, Mar. 27, 1933; s. Max and Fannie (Cooper) C.; m. Jane Abramson, Aug. 5, 1961; children: Melanie, Wendy. AB, Harvard U., 1954; MD, N.Y. U., 1958; MA (hon.), Yale U., 1970. Diplomate: Am. Bd. Internal Medicine, Sub Bd. Cardiovascular Diseases. Intern, then resident in medicine Yale-New Haven Hosp., 1958-60, 64-65; asst. in medicine Harvard U. Med. Sch., 1962-64; sr. investigator Nat. Heart, Lung and Blood Inst., 1965-68, mem. task force on arteriosclerosis, 1978-80, chmn. clin. trials rev. com., 1984-85, 87-89; assoc. prof. medicine U. Tex. Med. Sch., Dallas, 1968-70; prof. medicine Yale U. Med. Sch., 1970-81, Ebenezer K. Hunt prof. medicine, 1981—, dep. dean, 1991-95, spl. advisor to dean, 1995—. Mem. editorial bd. Circulation, Am. Jour. Cardiology, Am. Heart Jour.; contbr. over 160 articles to med. jours. Active Am. Heart Assn., chpt. pres., 1980-81, affiliate pres. Conn. chpt., 1984-86. With USPHS, 1960-62. Recipient Francis Gilman Blake award for Teaching of Med. Scis., 1973 Fellow ACP, Am. Coll. Cardiology (trustee 1978-83, mem. editorial bd. jour.); mem. Assn. Univ. Cardiologists (pres.-elect 1990, pres. 1991), Brit. Cardiac Soc., Ombudsman Assn., Interurban Clin. Club (pres. 1988), Alpha Omega Alpha. Home: 633 Whitney Ave New Haven CT 06511-2218 Office: Yale U Sch Medicine 333 Cedar St I-207 New Haven CT 06510-3289 Office Phone: 203-785-4128. Business E-Mail: lawrence.s.cohen@yale.edu.

COHEN, LEONARD (NORMAN COHEN), poet, writer, musician; b. Montreal, Que., Can., Sept. 21, 1934; s. Nathan B. and Masha (Kline) C. BA, McGill U., 1955; postgrad., Columbia.; LLB (hon.), Dalhousie U., 1971; LLD (hon.), McGill U., 1992. Author: (poetry) Let Us Compare Mythologies, 1956, The Spice Box of Earth, 1961, Flowers for Hitler, 1964, Parasites of Heaven, 1966, Selected Poems, 1956-68, 1968, The Energy of Slaves, 1972, Death of a Lady's Man, 1979, Book of Mercy, 1984, Stranger Music: Selected Music and Songs, 1993, Dance Me to the End of Love, 1995, Book of Longing, 2006, (novels) The Favorite Game, 1963, Beautiful Losers, 1966, also articles, songs including music for McCabe and Mrs. Miller, 1971, Natural Born Killers, 1994; rec. artist for Sony Music; albums include I'm Your Man, 1988, The Future, 1992, Cohen Live, 1993, More Best Of, 1997, Field Commander Cohen: Tour of 1979, 2001, Ten New Songs, 2001, Dear Heather, 2004. Decorated Order of Can.; recipient McGill Lit. award, 1956, Que. Lit. award, 1964, Gov. Gen.'s Performing Arts award, Can., 1993, Hall of Fame award, Can. Songwriters, 2006. Office: c/o Macklam Feldman Mgmt 200-1505 W 2nd Ave Vancouver BC Canada V6H 3Y4 E-mail: leonardinfo@mfmgt.com.

COHEN, LEWIS CARROLL, sculptor, educator; b. Mpls., Apr. 19, 1936; s. Irving and Celia (Tolchiner) C.; m. Adrianne Luther; children: Julia, Aaron. Student, U. Minn., 1952-53; postgrad., Ecole des Arts Decoratif, Paris, 1962-63; diploma with honors, Mus. Sch., Boston, 1962; MFA, Claremont Coll., Calif., 1976. Instr. Boston U., 1964-67; lectr. Calif. State U., Long Beach, 1970-87; instr. Laguna Beach (Calif.) Coll. Art, 1973-85; asst. prof. Scripps Coll., Claremont, 1974-75; assoc. prof., then prof. Coll. of William and Mary, Williamsburg, Va., 1987—. Interim dir. Laguna Beach Sch. Art, 1980. Exhibited sculpture in solo exhbns. Four Oaks Gallery, Pasadena, Calif., 1985, Twentieth Century Gallery, Williamsburg, 1988, Martin Sumers Gallery, N.Y.C., 1990, Muscarelle Museum of Art, Williamsburg, 1993; commd. works include Portrait of Henry Mudd, Harvey Mudd Coll., sculpture of Reverand James Blair, Tercentenary of Coll. of William and Mary, 1993. Recipient Prix de Rome Am. Acad. in Rome, 1967-70; named National Academician, 1992. Mem. Nat. Acad. Design. Office: Coll of William and Mary Dept Fine Arts Williamsburg VA 23185

COHEN, LORI G., lawyer; b. Boston, May 18, 1965; BA cum laude, Duke U., 1987; JD with distinction, Emory U., 1990. Bar: Georgia, Am. Bar Assoc. Ptnr., products liability, medical malpractice def. litig. Alston & Bird LLP, Atlanta, 1990—2005; ptnr., litig. products liability, life sciences Greenberg Traurig LLP, Atlanta, 2005—. Editor Medical Malpractice & Strategy, Product Liability Law & Strategy, Pharmaceutical and Medical Device Law Bulletin. Named one of The 50 Most Influential Women Lawyers in Am., Nat. Law Jour., 2007; recipient Top Defense Wins Award, Top 10 Under 40, 1999—2000. Mem.: Product Liability Advisory Council, Defense Research Institute. Office: Greenberg Traurig LLP Ste 400 The Forum 3290 Northside Pkwy Atlanta GA 30327 Home Phone: 404-355-3781; Office Phone: 678-553-2385. Office Fax: 678-553-2386. Business E-Mail: cohenl@gtlaw.com.*

COHEN, LOUIS RICHARD, lawyer; b. Washington, Nov. 28, 1940; s. Milton Howard and Rowna (Chaffetz) C.; m. Bonnie Rubenstein, Aug. 29, 1965; children: Amanda Carroll Leiter, Eli Augustus. AB, Harvard U., 1962, LLB, 1966; student, Wadham Coll., Oxford, Eng., 1962-63. Bar: DC. Law clk. to Hon. John M. Harlan US Supreme Ct., Washington, 1967-68; assoc. Wilmer Cutler Pickering LLP, Washington, 1968—74, ptnr., 1974—86, 1988—2004; dep. solicitor gen. US Dept. Justice, Washington, 1986—88; ptnr. Wilmer Cutler Pickering Hale and Dorr LLP, Washington, 2004—05, sr. counsel, 2006—. Vis. prof. Stanford Law Sch., Calif., 1981; lectr. Harvard Law Sch., Cambridge, Mass., 1986; bd. dirs. Pinhead Inst., 2006—. Editor: Regulating Campaign Finance, Annals of the American Academy, 1986; author: Book Review Michigan Law Review, 1993, (with C. Boyden Gray) The Need for Secular Choice in The Future of School Choice, Hoover Institution, 2003. Chair Harvard Law Sch. Fund, 1993-96; overseers com. to visit Harvard Law Sch., 1986-92; bd. dirs. Woolly Mammoth Theatre Co., Washington, 1988-91, 96—. Ptnrs. for Sacred Places, 2002-, Pinehead Inst., 2006-; bd. govs. Folger Shakespeare Libr., 2007—. Mem.: Telluride Soc. for Jazz (bd. dir. 2001—), Am. Law Inst., Am. Acad. Appellate Lawyers, Supreme Ct. Hist. Soc. Jewish. Avocation: hiking. Office: Wilmer Cutler Pickering Hale and Dorr LLP 1875 Pennsylvania Ave NW Washington DC 20006 Office Phone: 202-663-6700. Business E-Mail: louis.cohen@wilmerhale.com.

COHEN, MALCOLM MARTIN, psychologist, researcher; s. Nathan and Esther Cohen; m. Marilyn Jerrow, Jan. 2, 1959 (dec. 1967); m. Eleanor Johnson, June 30, 1969 (div. 1988); m. Suzana Gal, Feb. 14, 1961. BA, Brandeis U., Waltham, Mass., 1959; MA, U. Pa., Phila., 1961, PhD, 1965. Lic. psychologist, Pa. Asst. instr. U. Pa., Phila., 1961-63; rsch. psychologist Naval Air Engring. Ctr., Phila., 1963-67; supervisory rsch. psychologist Naval Air Devel. Ctr., Warminster, Pa., 1967-82; asst. chief biomed. rsch. divsn. NASA-Ames Rsch Ctr., Moffett Field, Calif., 1982-85, chief neurosci. br., 1985-88, rsch. scientist, 1988—2005, chief human info. processing rsch., 2000—05, Ames assoc., 2005—; pvt. practice, 2006—. Lectr. dept. aeros. and astronautics Stanford U., 1983—92, lectr., cons. prof. human biology program, 1994—2005; cons. in field. Assoc. editor Habitation Jour., 2004-; contbr. articles to profl. jours. Founding mem. Common Cause of Phila., 1973. Recipient Exceptional Sci. Achievement medal NASA 1994. Fellow AIAA (assoc.), Aerospace Med. Assn. (editl. bd. Aviation Space and Environ. Medicine 1985-93, assoc. editor 2001-03, Environ. Sci. award 1985, William F. Longacre award 1989), Aerospace Human Factors Assn. (pres. 1992); mem. AAAS, NY Acad. Scis., Psychonomics Soc., Sigma Xi. Jewish. Achievements include patents for light bar to monitor human acceleration tolerance. Avocations: scuba diving, photography, chess. Office: NASA Ames Rsch Ctr Mail Stop 262-2 Moffett Field CA 94035 Personal E-mail: malcohen@aol.com.

COHEN, MALCOLM STUART, economist; b. Mpls., Jan. 17, 1942; s. Jack Alvin and Lorraine Ethel (Hill) Cohen; m. Judith Ann Arenson, Sept. 25, 1965; children: Laura, Randall, Ilona. BA in Econs. summa cum laude, U. Minn., 1963; PhD in Econs., MIT, 1967. Labor economist U.S. Bur. Labor Stats., Washington, 1967-68; lectr. U. Md., College Park, 1968; asst. to v.p. state rels. and planning U. Mich., Ann Arbor, 1968-70, various tchr. positions, 1968-85, co-rsch. dir. Inst. Labor and Indsl. Rels., 1973-80, dir. Inst. Labor and Indsl. Rels., 1980-93; cons. Corp. Pub. Broadcasting, 1994-97; lectr. indsl. rels. ctr. U. Minn., 1994-96; pres. Employment Rsch. Corp., Ann Arbor, 1997—. Project dir. various projects, Washington, 1968—92; expert witness discrimination and econ. loss various clients, 1982—; cons. Mich. Senate Fiscal Agy., Lansing, 1988, U.S. Dept. Labor, 1995—2001, EEOC, 1996—. Co-author: A Micro Model of Labor Supply, 1970, Global Skill Shortages, 2002; author: Labor Shortages: As Am. Approaches the 21st Century, 1995; contbr. articles to profl. jour. Mem.: Internat. Indsl. Rels. Assn., Labor and Employment Rels. Assn., Nat. Assn. Forensic Economists. Avocations: jogging, genealogy. Office: Employment Rsch Corp Ste 250 3820 Packard Rd Ann Arbor MI 48108-3348 Office Phone: 734-477-9040. Business E-Mail: malco@umich.edu. E-mail: mc@employmentresearch.com.

COHEN, MARC R., lawyer; b. 1959; BA, Yale U., New Haven, 1981; JD, Yale U. Law Sch., New Haven, 1984. Bar: Conn. 1985, DC 1991. Law clk. to Hon. José A. Cabranes US Dist. Ct. (dist. Conn.), 1984—85; atty. Brenner, Saltzman, Wallman & Goldman, New Haven, 1985—90, Wilmer, Cutler & Pickering, 1990—99, Pillsbury, Winthrop, Shaw & Pittman, LLP, Washington, 1999—2006; ptnr. Mayer, Brown, Rowe & Maw, LLP, Washington, 2006—. Office: Mayer Brown Rowe & Maw LLP 1909 K St NW Washington DC 20006-1101 Office Phone: 202-263-3206. Office Fax: 202-263-3300. E-mail: mcohen@mayerbrownrowe.com.*

COHEN, MARCUS, allergist, immunologist; b. Appleton, Wis., June 8, 1937; s. Frank and Hannah (Weinstein) C.; m. Sheila Terman, July 14, 1963; children: Kimberly Ellyn, Louis Jeffrey. BA, U. Wis., Madison, 1959, MD, 1962. Rotating intern San Francisco Gen. Hosp. and U. Calif., 1962—63; resident in pediat. U. Calif., San Francisco, 1963—65; fellow in allergy and immunology U. Wis., Madison, 1965—66; pvt. practice allergy and immunology, 1966—; clin. prof. pediat. U. Wis. Med. Sch., 2006—. Pres. Madison Gen. Hosp. Med.-Surg. Found., 1986-91; pres. Quisling Clinic S.C., 1973-86; vice chair Physicans Plus Med. Group, 1987; vice chair, mem. exec. com. Physicians Plus Ins. Co., 1993-98, bd. chair, 1996-98; chair dept. pediat. Madison Gen. Hosp., 1969-70; sr. med. flight examiner FAA, 1981-2003; mng. ptnr. Quisling Clinic Real Estate Partnership. Bd. dir. Meriter Found., 1994-95; mem. U. Wis. Med. Found., 1989-. Named one of Am.'s Top Physicians, Consumers Rsch. Coun., 2003. Fellow Am. Acad. Pediat., Am. Acad. Allergy, Asthma and Immunology, Am. Coll. Allergy, Asthma and Immunology, Wis. Allergy Soc. (pres. 1993-95), Bascom Hill Soc., Univ. Wis. Found. Jewish. Avocations: skiing, bicycling, sailing, fishing, photography. Office: 20 S Park St 4th Fl South Bldg Madison WI 53715-1375 Office Phone: 608-287-2600. Business E-Mail: mcohen1@facstaff.wisc.edu.

COHEN, MARK HERBERT, broadcast executive; b. Boston, Mar. 27, 1932; s. Henry I. and Francis C.; m. Mary Jane Pitman, July 30, 1961; children: Patricia Beth, H. Jonathan, Cathy Ann. BA in Bus. Adminstrn., U. Maine, 1954; MS in TV Prodn., Syracuse U., NY, 1958. Announcer Sta. WGUY-AM-FM, Bangor, Maine, 1954, Sta. WGAN-AM-TV, Portland, Maine, 1954-55; various positions in sales, planning and station clearance ABC-TV network, NYC, 1958-68, v.p. sales planning, 1967-70, v.p., assoc. dir. planning, bus. and fin. analysis, 1970-76, sr. v.p. fin. and planning, 1976-77, sr. v.p., 1977-85; v.p. Am. Broadcasting Cos. Inc., 1981-83, sr. v.p., 1983-85, exec. v.p. broadcast group, 1985-86; bd. dirs. ESPN, 1983—85; exec. v.p. ABC Network Div., 1986-88; v.p. Capital Cities/ABC, 1986-88; pres. distbn. and prodn. co. D.L. Taffner Ltd., NYC, 1990-91; broadcasting cons., 1991—. Mem. exec. com. of alumni coun. U. Maine, 1980-86. Mem. adv. bd. Newhouse Sch., Syracuse U., 1985-88; mem. exec. com. of pres.'s coun. U. Maine, 1988, vice chmn. of pres.'s coun., 1992-93, chmn., 1993-95, vice chmn. Campaign for Maine, 1991-96. 1st lt. inf. US Army, 1954—57. Fellow Nat. Acad. Arts and Scis. (pres. internat. coun. 1984-85, exec. com. 1986-92); mem. Internat. Radio and TV Soc. (gov. 1980-81, v.p. 1983-85), Whipporwill Club. Personal E-mail: mhc001@aol.com.

COHEN, MARK STEVEN, dentist; b. NYC, Dec. 10, 1948; s. Lawrence and Yetta (Grossman) C.; m. Arlene Debbie Deutsch, Aug. 23, 1970 (div. May 1984); 1 child, Aaron Philip; m. Donna Lynn Poissonnier, Nov. 27, 1985. BS, CCNY, 1971; DDS, Columbia U., 1975, cert. in Pedodontics, 1976. Practice dentistry, Yonkers, NY, 1975-76, Bristol, Conn., 1976-79, Brookfield, Conn., 1977—. Dir. dental service N.Y. Inst. for the Edn. Blind, Bronx, 1976-78; assoc. attending dentist Danbury (Conn.) Hosp., 1976-82, Blythdale Children's Hosp., Valhalla, N.Y., 1986-87; assoc. clin. prof. dentistry Columbia U., N.Y.C., 1976—, mem. quality assurance com., 1982-85. Patentee in field. Active Dental Guidance Council for Cerebral Palsy, N.Y.C., 1976-81. Chemistry fellow NSF, Washington, 1969-71, research fellow NIH, 1971, United Cerebral Palsy, 1975-76. Mem. ADA, Conn. State Dental Assn., Greater Danbury Dental Soc., Am. Dental Vols. for Israel, OKU Dental Honor Soc. Democrat. Jewish. Avocations: travel, photography, biking, collecting antiques. Office: Mark S Cohen 940 Federal Rd Brookfield CT 06804-1144 Office Phone: 203-775-5533. Personal E-mail: mscddspc@aol.com, mscddspc@mindspring.com.

COHEN, MARLENE LOIS, pharmacologist; b. New Haven, May 5, 1945; d. Abraham David and Jeanette (Bader) C.; m. Jerome H. Fleisch, Aug. 8, 1976; children: Abby Fleisch, Sheryl Fleisch. BS, U. Conn., 1968; PhD, U. Calif., San Francisco, 1973. Registered pharmacist, Calif., Conn. Postdoctoral fellow Roche Inst. of Molecular Biology, Nutley, NJ, 1973-75; sr. pharmacologist Eli Lilly & Co., Indpls., 1975-80, rsch. scientist, 1980-85, sr. rsch. scientist, 1985-89, rsch. advisor, 1989-94, disting. rsch. fellow, 1994—2002; co-founder Creative Pharmacol. Solutions LLC, Carmel, Ind., 2002—. Adj. asst. prof. dept. pharmacology and toxicology Ind. U. Sch. Medicine, Indpls., 1976-82, adj. assoc. prof., 1982-86, adj. prof., 1987—; rsch. asst. Pfizer Labs., Groton, Conn., 1967; cons. Drug Dependence Inst., Yale U., New Haven, 1974. Mem. editl. bd. Jour. Clin. and Exptl. Hypertension, 1978—99, Procs. of the Soc. for Exptl. Biology and Medicine, 1979-84, Life Sci., 1984—, Jour. Pharmacology and Exptl. Therapeutics, 1987-2006, Current Drugs: Serotonin 1992-2000, Current Topics in Pharmacology, 1994-2000; mem. Molecular Interventions Adv. Bd., 1999-2005; ad hoc reviewer for profl. jours.; author: (with others) Principles of Medicinal Chemistry, 1974, 3d edit., 1989, New Antihypertensive Drugs, 1976, The Serotonin Receptors, 1988, The Peripheral Actions of 5-Hydroxytryptamine, 1989, Central and Peripheral 5-HT3 Receptors, 1992; contbr. articles to profl. jours. Recipient Disting. Alumni award, U. Conn. Sch. Pharmacy, 2002. Mem. Soc. for Exptl. Biology and Medicine, Am. Soc. for Pharmacology and Exptl. Therapeutics (chair subcom. on women in pharmacology 1984-89, chairperson nominating com. 1984, com. on profl. affairs 1984-89, membership com. 1989-92, bd. publs. trustees 1989—95, pres. 2001), Serotonin Club (councilor 1987-90, nomenclature com. 1988—2000), Alpha Lambda Delta, Phi Kappa Phi, Rho Chi. Office: Creative Pharmacol Solutions LLC 10532 Coppergate Ste 101 Carmel IN 46032 Office Phone: 317-571-9878. Personal E-mail: marlenelcohen@aol.com.

COHEN, MARTIN BRUCE, physician; b. Bayshore, NY, Nov. 2, 1954; BA, Brandeis Univ., 1976; MD, SUNY, 1980. Diplomate Am. Bd. Internal Medicine, Am. Bd. Cardiovasc. Disease, Am. Bd. Interventional Cardiology, Am. Bd. Clinical Cardial Electrophysiology. Attending physician Westchester County Medical Ctr., Valhalla, N.Y., 1985—. Fellow Am. Coll. Cardiology. Office: Cardiology Cons Westchester Westchester County Med Ctr Valhalla NY 10595 Office Phone: 914-593-7800.

COHEN, MARY ANN, federal judge; b. Albuquerque, July 16, 1943; d. Gus R. and Mary Carolyn (Avriette) C. BS, UCLA, 1964; JD, U. So. Calif., 1967. Bar: Calif. 1967. Ptnr. Abbott & Cohen, P.C. and predecessors, LA, 1967-82; judge US Tax Ct., Washington, 1982—, chief judge, 1996-2000. Mem. ABA (sect. taxation), Legion Lex. Republican. Office: US Tax Ct 400 2nd St NW Washington DC 20217-0002 Office Phone: 202-521-0655.

COHEN, MELANIE ROVNER, lawyer; b. Chgo., Aug. 9, 1944; d. Millard Jack and Sheila (Fox) Rovner; m. Arthur Wieber Cohen, Feb. 17, 1968; children: Mitchell Jay, Stephanie Tomasky, Jennifer Sue, Jason Canel. AB, Brandeis U., 1965; JD, DePaul U., 1977. Bar: Ill. 1977, U.S. Dist. Ct. (no. dist.) Ill., US Ct. Appeals (7th cir.), US Supreme Ct. 1998. Law clk. to Justice F.J. Hertz U.S. Bankruptcy Ct., 1976-77; ptnr. Antonow & Fink, Chgo., 1977-89, Altheimer & Gray, Chgo., 1989—2003, Quarles & Brady, Chgo., 2003—. Mem. Supreme Ct. Ill. Atty. Registration and Disciplinary Commn. Inquiry Bd., 1982-86, Hearing Bd., 1986-94; instr. secured and consumer transactions creditor-debtor law DePaul U., Chgo., 1980-90, 1994-96; instr. real estate and bankruptcy law John Marshall Law Sch. LLM program, Chgo., 1996-98, 2004-06; bd. dir. Bankruptcy Arbitration and Mediation Svcs. Contbr. articles to profl. jours. Panelist, spkr., bd. dir., v.p. Brandeis U. Nat. Alumni Assn., 1981-90; life mem. Brandeis Nat. Women's Com., 1975—, pres. Chgo. chpt., 1975-82; mem. Glencoe (Ill.) Caucus, 1977-80; chair lawyers com. Ravinia Festival, 1990-91, chmn. sustaining com., 1991, mem. annual fund, 1991—. Fellow, Brandeis U. Fellow: Am. Coll. Bankruptcy; mem.: ABA (co-chair com. on enforcement of creditors' rights and bankruptcy), Leading Lawyer's Network, Internat. Women's Insolvency and Restructuring Confederation, Internat. Fedn. Insolvency Profls., Internat. Insolvency Inst., Turnaround Mgmt. Assn. (pres. Chgo./midwest chpt. 1990—92, internat. bd. dirs. 1990—2004, mem. mgmt. com. 1995—2003, pres. internat. bd. dirs. 1999—2000, chmn. internat. bd. dirs. 2000—01, Leading Lawyer 2004—), Comml. Fin. Assn. Edn. Found. (bd. govs.), Ill. Trial Lawyers Assn., Comml. Law League, Chgo. Bar Assn. (chmn. bankruptcy reorgn. com. 1983—85, Super Lawyer 2005—), Ill. State Bar Assn. Home: 167 Park Ave Glencoe IL 60022-1351 Office: Quarles & Brady 500 W Madison Ave Ste 3700 Chicago IL 60661 Office Phone: 312-715-5050. Business E-Mail: mcohen@quarles.com.

COHEN, MELVIN IRWIN, retired communications systems and technology executive; b. NYC, June 25, 1936; s. Alexander and Fannie (Becker) C.; m. Elaine Chesin; children: Daniel Marc, Martha Rachel. SB, MIT, Cambridge, Mass., 1957; SM, MIT, 1958; PhD, Rensselaer Poly. Inst., 1965. Engr. Pratt & Whitney Aircraft, East Hartford, Conn., 1958-61; mem. tech. staff, supr. Bell Telephone Labs., Murray Hill, NJ, 1964-72; asst. dir. Western Elec. Co., Princeton, NJ, 1972-79; dept. head AT&T Bell Labs., Murray Hill, 1979-82, dir. Whippany, NJ, 1982-87, Murray Hill, 1987, v.p. mfg. R&D Princeton, 1987-88, exec. dir., 1988-90, exec. dir. electronics and photonics div. Breinigsville, Pa., 1990-93, v.p. rsch. effectiveness Murray Hill, NJ, 1993-96, Bell Labs/Lucent Techs., Murray Hill, 1996-2000; ret., 2000. Mem. panel on assessment of Nat. Inst. Standards and Tech. Programs, NRC, 1990-96; trustee AT&T Found., 1993-96; mem. sci. policy bd. Rutgers U., Newark, 1993-96. Patentee in laser tech. Trustee Temple Sinai Summit, N.J., 1977-79, N.J. Prison Complex, Trenton, 1975-83; bd. advisors Rahway Lifers Program, 1979-83; mem. deptl. adv. bd. Rensselaer Poly. Inst., 1988-92, mem. exec. bd. Anderson Ctr. for Innovation in Undergrad. Edn., 1992-98. Named Key Exec., Rensselaer Poly. Inst., 1986-99, chmn. Key Exec. Program, 1994-95; recipient Clarence E. Davies medal for engring. achievement, 1993, Fellow award Rensselaer Poly. Inst. Alumni Assn., 1993. Fellow IEEE (3d Millennium medal), Optical Soc. Am.; mem. AAAS, IEEE Lasers and Electrooptics Soc. (pres. 1989, Disting. Svc. award 2000). Home: 188 High Tor Dr Watchung NJ 07069-5412 Personal E-mail: micohenmj@aol.com.

COHEN, MELVIN R., physician, educator; b. Chgo., May 24, 1911; s. Louis M. and Anna S. (Friedman) C.; m. Miriam, May 19, 1946; children: Nancy, Alan BS, U. Ill., 1931, MS in Pathology, 1933, MD, 1934. Diplomate: Am. Bd. Ob-Gyn. Practice medicine specializing in infertility, Chgo.; sr. attending physician Michael Reese Med. Ctr., Chgo., Northwestern Meml. Hosp., Chgo.; founder, dir. Fertility Inst. Ltd., Chgo.; prof.

Northwestern U. Med. Sch., Chgo., prof. emeritus; guest vis. prof. first Martin Clyman postgrad. course in infertility Mount Sinai Hosp., NYC, 1982. Author: Laparoscopy, Culdoscopy and Gynecography: Technique and Atlas, 1970; contbr. numerous chpts. in med. books and articles to med. jours. on infertility, endometriosis and Spinnbarkeit. Dir., producer: 8 teaching films on infertility; video films during surgery; ektochrome slides established world-wide technique. Pioneer use of Pergonal for stimulating ovulation. Served with MC, AUS, 1942-45. Co-recipient Gold Medal for Infertility exhibit AMA, 1951; recipient award for film on endometriosis 10th World Congress of Fertility and Sterility, Madrid, Spain, 1980, Lifetime Achievement award for contbns. to gynecologic endoscopy and women's health care Internat. Congress of Gynecologic Endoscopy, 1994; named honoree Internat. Soc. Gynecologic Endoscopy for pioneering work in laparoscopy, 1996, named Father of Modern American Laparoscopy, 1974. Fellow Chgo. Gynecol. Soc. (life); mem. AMA, Am. Fertility Soc., Am. Coll. Ob-Gyn., Am. Assn. Gynecol. Laparoscopists (Lifetime Achievement award Internat. Congress 1994), Internat. Fertility Assn., Internat. Family Planning Research Assn., Ill. State Med. Soc., Chgo. Gynecol. Soc., Kansas City Gynecol. Soc. (hon.), Los Angeles Gynecol. Soc., Inst. Medicine Chgo., Midwest Bio-Laser Inst., Indian Assn. Gynecol. Endoscopists (hon.), Soc. Reproductive Surgeons, Chgo. Assn. Reproductive Endocrinologists (pres. 1984-85), Sigma Xi, Alpha Omega Alpha. Address: 990 N Lake Shore Dr # 26C Chicago IL 60611-1366

COHEN, MICHAEL, educational association administrator; married; 2 children. BA in Sociology, SUNY, Binghamton; student, Ont. Inst. Studies in Edn., Johns Hopkins U., Balt. With Nat. Inst. Edn.; dir. policy devel. and planning Nat. Assn. State Bds. of Edn.; dir. edn. policy Nat. Govs. Assn., 1986—90; dir. Nat. Alliance for Restructuring Edn., 1990—93; various sr. edn. policy positions The White House, Washington, 1993—2001, spl. asst. to the Pres. edn. policy, 1996—99; sr. adv. to Sec. of Edn. US Dept. Edn., asst. sec. edn. for elem. and secondary edn., 1999—2001; sr. fellow Aspen Inst., 2001—03; pres. Achieve, Inc., Washington, 2003—. Office: Achieve Inc 1775 Eye St NW Ste 410 Washington DC 20006 Office Phone: 202-419-1540. Office Fax: 202-828-0911. E-mail: mcohen@achieve.org.*

COHEN, MICHAEL, urologist; b. Freehold, NJ, Aug. 24, 1976; s. Saul Abraham and Carol Marcia Cohen; m. Judith Steenbergen, July 8, 2001; children: Gabriella Helen, David Morris. MD, Cornell U., NYC, 1998—2002. Urology resident Lahey Clinic Med. Ctr., Burlington, Mass., 2002—.

COHEN, MICHAEL PAUL, statistician; b. San Mateo, Calif., July 8, 1947; s. Herman Charles and Evadna Fern (Tull) C. BA, U. Calif. San Diego, La Jolla, 1969; MA, UCLA, 1971, PhD, 1978. Math. statistician Bur. Labor Stats., Washington, 1978-87; math. statistician, cons. Nat. Ctr. Edn. Stats., Washington, 1987-2000, Bur. Transp. Stats., Washington, 2000—06, asst. dir. for survey programs, 2002—06; ret., 2006; ind. statis. cons., 2006—; adj. prof. George Mason U., 2007—. Reviewer Inst. Statis. Math., Tokyo, 1988-92, Jour. Bus. and Econ. Stats., Washington, 1988, Annals of Stats., Hayward, Calif., 1991, Survey Methodology, 1998-2003, Jour. Ofcl. Stats., 1998-2003; tech. adv. bd. Nat. Ctr. Edn. Stats., Washington, 1987-2000; invited spkr. Internat. Stats. Inst., Seoul, Republic of Korea, 2001, Joint Statis. Meetings, Toronto, 2005; adj. prof. George Mason U., 2007-. Assoc. editor: Jour. Ofcl. Stats., 2003—, Jour. Am. Stats. Assn., 2004—06; contbr. articles to profl. jours. Recipient cash awards U.S. Dept. Edn., 1987, 89, 90, 92, 93, 97, 98, 99, Quality Step Increases, U.S. Dept. Edn., 1988, 91, 94, 96, U.S. Dept. Transp., 2003. Fellow Washington Acad. Scis. (bd. mgrs. 1996—, sec. 1997-2000, pres.-elect 2002-03, pres. 2003-04), Am. Statis. Assn. (program chair govt. stats. sect., 2006); mem. Internat. Statis. Inst., Inst. Math. Stats., Am. Statis. Assn., Am. Math. Soc., Soc. Indsl. and Applied Math., Washington Statis. Soc. (bd. dirs. 1990—, pres.-elect 2006-07, pres. 2007—, Pres. award 1999), Calif. State Soc., Capital PC Users Group, Philos. Soc. of Washington (bd. dirs. 1999-2003), Washington Acad. Scis. (bd. mgrs. 1996—), Am. Assn. Pub. Opinion Rsch. (assoc. treas. D.C. chpt. 2003, treas. 2004). Achievements include significant statistical contributions to index aggregation and expenditure weights; significant statistical contributions to consumer price index revision; proof of admissibility of empirical distribution function. E-mail: mcohen@cpcug.org.

COHEN, MICHAEL R., health facility administrator, pharmacist; BS, Temple. U., 1968, MS, 1984; degree in Sci. (hon.), U. Scis. Phila., 2001, Long Island U., 2005; degree in Pub. Svc. (hon.), U. Md., 2005. Various leadership positions in pharmacy Temple U. Hosp., 1970—83, Quakertown Cmty. Hosp., 1983—92; faculty mem. Temple U. Sch. Pharmacy, 1976—; pres., founder Inst. for Safe Medication, Huntingdon Valley, Pa., 1993—. Mem. Sentinel Event Adv. Group, Joint Commn. on Accreditation of Healthcare Orgns.; mem. Drug Safety and Risk Mgmt. Adv. Panel FDA; mem. Nat. Quality Forum's Evidence-Based Practices Steering Com. Editor: Medication Error, 1999; co-editor: ISMP Medication Safety Alert!; assoc. editor Hosp. Pharmacy jour., mem. editl. bd. Jour. Intravenous Nurse Soc., Healthcare Risk Control, Joint Commn. Jour. on Quality Improvement. Named Am. Druggist Top 50, 1997, 1998, MacArthur fellow, John D. and Catherine T. MacArthur Found., 2005; recipient Prof. Anthony J. Amadio Disting. Lecture Award, Duquesne U., 1994, Nicholas Tucci Memorial Lecture Award, U. Pittsburgh, 1996, 1999, Sr. M. Gonzales Duffy Award, Penn. Society of Health-System Pharmacists, 1997, Am. Druggist Top 50, 1999, Award for Achievement, Sustained Contbn.- Lit. Pharmacy Practice in Health Systems, Am. Society of Health-System Pharmacists, 1998, Pharmacist of the Year, Am. Druggist, 1999. Office: Inst Safe Medication Practices 1800 Byberry Rd Ste 810 Huntingdon Valley PA 19006 E-mail: mcohen@ismp.org.

COHEN, MILDRED THALER, art gallery director; b. NYC, Oct. 30, 1921; d. William and Dora (Snow) Intner; m. Seymour R. Thaler, June 17, 1945 (dec. 1976); children: Frederic I., Joan Thaler Zimmer; m. Sidney Cohen, Mar. 20, 1982. BA, Hunter Coll., 1942; BLS, Pratt Inst., 1943. Libr. Queens Borough Pub. Libr., NYC, 1943-44, Mus. of French Art, French Inst., NYC, 1944-46; dir. Marbella Gallery, Inc., NYC, 1971—. Author: (catalogues) Women Students of William Merritt Chase, 1973, Robert Hallowell, 1983, Eliot Clark, 1990, Tonalism, America's Gift to Landscape Painting, 1993, (brochures) Ethel Paxson, 1976, Three Generations of Wiggins, 1981, Samuel Rothbart, 1989, Rachel V. Hartley, 1991, Frank Kleinholz, 1992, Anthony Springer, 1996, Joseph Margulies, 1997, Allen Blagden, 1998, Hildegarde Hamilton, 1999, Samuel Brecher, 1999, 2003, James Bowman Consor, 2001, 2004, Tsar (Valery Tsarikovsky), 2007. Bd. dirs. Lenox Hill Settlement House, NYC, 1955—77. Mem. Appraisers Assn. Am., Hunter Coll. Alumni (pres. Queens chpt. 1951-54, past bd. dir., pres. scholarship and welfare fund 1958-60, mem. coll. art adv. com., named to Hall of Fame 1973). Democrat. Jewish. Home and Office: 28 E 72nd St New York NY 10021-4234 Office Phone: 212-288-7809. Personal E-mail: marbella_gallery@aol.com.

COHEN, MITCHELL S., political science professor; b. NYC; PhD, Columbia Univ. Prof Weissman Sch, Baruch Col, NYC. Co-editor: Dissent Mag; author: The Wager of Lucien Goldmann, 1994, Zion and State, 1987; editor: Princeton Readings in Political Thought, 1995, Rebels and Reactionaries: An ANthology of Great Political Stories, 1992; contbr. articles in prof jours, columns in newspapers. Office: Dissent 310 Riverside Dr Apt 2008 New York NY 10025-4129 E-mail: mitchellcohen@aol.com.

COHEN, MORREL HERMAN, physicist, biologist, educator; b. Boston, Sept. 10, 1927; s. David and Rose (Kemler) C.; m. Sylvia Zwein, June 18, 1950; children: Julie, Robert, Daniel, Lisa. BS in Physics, Worcester Poly. Inst., 1947, DSc (hon.), 1973; MA in Physics, Dartmouth Coll., 1948; PhD in Physics, U. Calif., Berkeley, 1952. Faculty U. Chgo., 1952-57, assoc. prof. physics, 1957-60, prof., 1960-72, prof. theoretical biology, 1968-72, Louis Block prof. physics and theoretical biology, 1972-81, com. developmental biology, 1973-74, publs. bd., 1969-70; acting dir. James Franck Inst., 1965-66, dir., 1968-71; dir. materials rsch. lab. NSF, 1977-81; sr. sci. advisor Corp. Rsch. Lab. Exxon Rsch. and Engring. Co., 1981-96. Vis. scientist NRC, Can., 1960, Xerox Corp., 1975, 78; disting. vis. scientist Rutgers U., 1998-99, disting. scientist 1999—, grad. faculty, 2004—; disting. scientist Princeton U., 2003-05, sr. chemist, 2006-; vis. fellow Clare Hall U., Cambridge, 1972-73; Shrum lectr. Simon Fraser U., 1973; assoc. Clare Hall U. Cambridge, Eng., 1973-; vis. prof. U. Va., 1976, Kyoto U., 1979; disting. visitor Scottish Univs. Physics Alliance, 2007; adv. panel electrophysics NASA, 1962-66; adv. com. Nat. Magnet Lab., 1963-66; rev. com. solid state sci. and metallurgy divsn. Argonne Nat. Lab., 1964-67, chmn., 1966, bd. govs., 1982-89, sci. and tech. adv. com., 1983-91; chmn. Gordon Conf., 1968, 4th Internat. Conf. Armorphous and Liquid Semiconductors., 1971; adv. com. Inst. Amorphous Studies, 1982—; mem. Army Basic Rsch. Com., 1979-85, steering com., 1980-85; adv. com. dept. physics U. Tex., Austin, 1982-91; chmn. vis. com. dept. Physics Colo. Sch. of Mines, 1987-94; vice chmn. IUPAP commn. on stats. mechanics, 1987-93; van der Waals prof. U. Amsterdam, 1991-92; panelist workshop on effective utilization of solar energy DOE, 2005; cons. in field. Contbr. articles on physics of solids, liquids, gases, theoretical and developmental biology, geophysics, materials sci., chem. physics, chem. engring. and econophysics; assoc. editor Jour. Chem. Physics, 1960-63; mem. editl. bd. McGraw-Hill Co., 1963-70, Physics of Condensed Matter, 1962-74, Advances in Chem. Physics, 1960-93, U. Chgo., 1969-70, Jour. Statis. Physics, 1970-75. AEC fellow, 1951-52, Guggenheim fellow, 1957-58, NSF sr. postdoctoral fellow Rome, 1964-65, Spl. fellow NIH, 1972-73. Fellow AAAS, Am. Phys. Soc. (divsn. coun. 1978-82, exec. com. solid state physics divsn. 1968-71, chmn. 1970, mem. panel on pub. affairs, 2002-05); mem. AAUP, Am. Inst. Physics, Nat. Acad. Scis. (class mem. com. 2003), N.Y. Acad. Scis., Sigma Xi (nat. lectr. 1966). Home: 1100 Crim Rd Bridgewater NJ 08807-1872 Office: Dept Physics and Astronomy Rutgers The State Univ NJ 136 Frelinghuysen Rd Piscataway NJ 08854-8019 E-mail: mhcohen@prodigy.net.

COHEN, MURRAY, aerospace engineer, consultant; s. Benjamin and Mollie Cohen; m. Thelma Florence Fishback (div.); children: Eleanor, Gary, Robert; m. Josephine Marie Morici, Aug. 31, 1968; children: Joseph, Susan, Sandy. B Aero. Engring., Poly. U., Bklyn., 1953. Registered profl. engr., NY, 1983. Asst. to chief engr. Colonial Airlines, LaGuardia Airport, NY, 1946—48; design engr. TAAG Design, Mineola, NY, 1948—51; unit leader armament engring. Rep. Aviation Corp., Farmingdale, NY, 1951—57; group leader flight control engring. Grumman Aerospace Corp., Bethpage, NY, 1958—90; pvt. practice cons. engr. Middle Island, NY, 1990—. Condr. seminar in field. Contbr. articles to profl. jours. Organizer fundraisers Commn. Social Justice Order Sons of Italy in Am., Farmingdale, 1972—. With USAF, 1942—45. Recipient Project Sterling award, Grumman Aerospace Corp., 1978. Mem.: AIAA, NSPE (2d v.p. Suffolk County chpt.), Birchwood Computer Club (v.p.). Achievements include patents for aircraft rod end double locking device; aircraft rod end integrated locking device. Avocations: chess, photography, computers.

COHEN, N. JEROLD, lawyer; b. Pine Bluff, Ark., June 13, 1935; s. Maurice and Gertrude L. Cohen; children: Pamela, Lindsey L., Giles T. BBA, Tulane U., 1957; LLB magna cum laude, Harvard U., 1961. Bar: N.Y. 1962, Ga. 1966, D.C. 1966. Assoc. Cleary, Gottlieb, Steen and Hamilton, NYC, 1961-65, Sutherland, Asbill, and Brennan, Atlanta, Washington, 1965, ptnr., 1968-79, 81—; chief counsel IRS, 1979-81, adv. coun., 1999-2000, chmn. Former pres., former mem. nat. bd. dirs. ACLU Ga.; chmn. Atlanta Cmty. Rels. Commn., 1976-79. 1st lt. US Army, 1958. Recipient Gen. Counsel's award U.S. Dept. Treasury, Commrs. award IRS. Fellow Am. Bar Found.; mem. ABA (past chair tax sect.), FBA, Am. Law Inst., Am. Tax Policy Inst. (mem. bd.), Am. Coll. Tax Counsel (regent, former chair). Office: Sutherland Asbill & Brennan 999 Peachtree St NE Ste 2300 Atlanta GA 30309-3996 Office Phone: 404-853-8038. Business E-Mail: jerry.cohen@sablaw.com.

COHEN, NEAL S., air transportation executive; BA, MBA, U. Chgo. Various positions in internat. fin., banking, planning GM, NYC, 1984-91; dir. corp. planning Northwest Airlines Corp., St. Paul, 1991, from dir. mkt. planning to v.p. fin. and contr., 1992-99, sr. v.p., treas., 1999—2000, Eagan, Minn., 2004—05, exec. v.p., CFO, 2005—07, exec. v.p. strategy, internat., CEO Regional Airlines, 2007—; exec. v.p., CFO Budget Group Inc., 2000, Sylvan Learning Systems, 2000—01, Conseco Fin., 2001—02; exec. v.p., fin., CFO US Airways, Inc., Arlington, Va., 2002—04. Office: Northwest Airlines Corp 2700 Lone Oak Pkwy Eagan MN 55121 Office Phone: 612-726-2111.*

COHEN, NELSON CRAIG, lawyer; b. Harrisburg, Pa., Nov. 8, 1947; s. Raymond and Rhea (Jaschik) C. BS in Acctg., Pa. State U., 1969; JD, George Washington U., 1973. Bar: Md. 1973, D.C. 1974. Assoc., ptnr. Levitan Ezrin West & Kerxton, Bethesda, Md., 1973-84; ptnr. Kerxton & Cohen Chartered, Bethesda, 1984-87, Zuckerman Spaeder LLP, Washington, 1987—. Speaker on bankruptcy matters. Mem. ABA (bus. banking sec.), Bankruptcy Bar Assn. Md., Montgomery County Bar Assn., Md. State Bar Assn. Republican. Jewish. Avocation: golf. Office Phone: 202-778-1823. E-mail: ncohen@zuckerman.com.

COHEN, NELSON P., prosecutor; b. 1949; B in Polit. Sci, U. Pitts.; law degree, Duquesne U. Prosecutor Allegheny County dist. atty.'s office; dep. criminal chief we. dist. Pa.; fed. prosecutor Pitts.; US atty. dist. Alaska US Dept. Justice, 2006—. Office: US Attys Office Federal Bldg & US Courthouse 222 W 7th Ave #9 Rm 253 Anchorage AK 99513-7567*

COHEN, NICHOLAS, immunologist, educator; b. NYC, Nov. 20, 1938; s. Saris and Frances (Pakett) C.; m. Jayne Sevin Rogal, July 1, 1962 (div. 1972); children: Jaime Anne, Jessica Sevin; m. Catharina Johanna van der Harst, Oct. 23, 1974; children: Misha Thomas, Mark Sebastian. AB, Princeton U., 1959; PhD, U. Rochester, 1965. Asst. prof. microbiology and immunology Sch. Medicine and Dentistry U. Rochester, NY, 1967-73, assoc. prof. NY, 1973-80, prof. microbiology, immunology and psychiatry NY, 1980—2004, dir. divsn. immunology NY, 1980—2004, prof. oncology NY, 1997—2004, prof. emeritus NY, 2004—; assoc. dir. Ctr. for Psychoneuroimmunology Rsch., Rochester. Vis. prof. Agrl. U., Wageningen, The Netherlands, 1982-83; mem. Basel Inst. for Immunology, Switzerland, 1975-76; mem. peer rev. bds. NIH, 1976-80; cons. NIH study sects., NIMH study sects., NSF. Assoc. editor Brain, Behavior and Immunity Jour., Devel. Comparative Immunology; editor 5 books; contbr. articles to profl. jours. Postdoctoral scholar in immunology UCLA, 1965-67, Fulbright scholar, 1982-83; grantee NIH, NIMH, NSF, 1967—; recipient Rsch. Career Devel. award NIH, 1974-78, NIH Merit award, 1987-97. Mem. Am. Soc. Zoologists (chmn. divsn. comparative immunology 1977-79), Transplantation Soc., Am. Soc. Immunologists, Brit. Soc. Immunology, Internat. Soc. Devel. and Comparative Immunology (v.p. the Americas 1994-2000), Psychoneuroimmunology Rsch. Soc. (councilor 1993-97). Democrat. Avocations: music, travel. Home: 211 Highland Pkwy Rochester NY 14620-2544 Office Phone: 585-275-3412.

COHEN, NOEL LEE, otolaryngologist, educator; b. NYC, Sept. 20, 1930; s. Victor Max and Esther Lily (Schonfeld) C.; m. Baukje Philippina Boersma, June 1, 1957; 1 child, Mark Bennett. AB, NYU, 1951; MD, U. Utrecht, The Netherlands, 1957; MD (hon.), U. Freiburg, Germany, 2002. Cert. Am. Bd. Otolaryngology, 1963. Intern Stads-en Academi Ziekenhuis, Utrecht, 1955-57; resident in otolaryngology Bellevue Med. Ctr. NYU, NYC, 1959-62, instr. Sch. Medicine, 1962-64, asst. prof., 1964-69, assoc. prof., 1969-73, clin. prof., 1973-80, prof. otolaryngology, 1980—, chmn. dept. otolaryngology, 1981—2003, interim dean, provost Sch. Medicine, 1997-98, vice dean for clin. affairs, 1998-99, sr. advisor to dean, 2000—, Mendik Found. prof., 1999—2003, prof. otolaryngology, 2003—; pres. NYU Hosp. Ctr., 1998. Bd. dir. League Hard of Hearing, Am. Auditory Soc.; mem. adv. bd. Self Help for Hard of Hearing People, 1995, Alexander Graham Bell Assn., Acoustic Neuroma Assn.; sci. adv. bd. Sci. Deafness Rsch. Found., 2000-; mem. med. adv. bd. Cochlear Corp., 1986-2007; lectr. in field, spkr. at profl. confs. Mem. editl. bd. Jour. of Otology & Neurotology, 1986-2004, Otolaryngology-Head and Neck Surgery, Internat. Cochlear Implant Jour., 1999—; reviewer articles and books for profl. jours.; contr. chpts. to books, articles to profl. jours. Lt. USNR, 1957—59. Fellow: ACS; mem.: N.Y. Acad. Scis., N.Y. Otol. Soc. (pres. 1998—99), Soc. Acad. Depts. Otolaryngology, Soc. Univ. Otolaryngologists, Am. Neuro-Otol. Soc., N.Am. Skull Base Soc., N.Y. Head and Neck Soc. (charter mem., pres. 1984), N.Y. State Soc. Otolaryngology-Head and Neck Surgery (pres. 1988—89), N.Y. Acad. Medicine, Am. Otol. Soc., Am. Bronchoesophagol. Assn., Am. Soc. Head and Neck Surgery, Rhinol. and Otol. Soc., Am. Laryngol., Am. Acad. Otolaryngology-Head-Neck Surgery (Honor award 1985, Disting. Svc. award 2001). Democrat. Jewish. Avocations: tennis, skiing, gardening, carpentry. Office: NYU Med Ctr NYU Cochlear Implant Ctr 660 1st Ave New York NY 10016-6402 Office Phone: 212-263-3301. Business E-Mail: noel.cohen@nyumc.org.

COHEN, NORM, chemist; b. NYC, Dec. 13, 1936; s. Moshe and Yetta (Pickman) C.; m. Anne Elizabeth Billings, July 11, 1959 (div. 1987); children: Alexandra Elizabeth Rachel, Carson Benjamin; m. Verni Greenfield, Feb. 6, 1987; 1 child, Matthew Jonathan Greenfield. BA in Chemistry, Reed Coll., 1958; MA in Math., U. Calif., Berkeley, 1960, PhD in Chemistry, 1963. Mem. tech. staff Aerospace Corp., El Segundo, Calif., 1963—72, head dept. chem. kinetics, 1972—84, sr. scientist, 1984—94; adj. asst. prof. chemistry U. Portland, 1995—99, Portland C.C., 1995—. Exec. sec. John Edwards Mem. Forum, LA, 1969—94. Author: Long Steel Rail, 1981, 2d edit., 2000 (Chgo. Folklore prize 1982, Deems Taylor award ASCAP 1982, Botkin prize Am. Folklore Soc. 1983), Traditional Anglo-American Folk Music: An Annotated Discography of Published Recordings, 1994, A Finding List of American Secular Songsters Published 1860-99, 2002, Folk Music: A Regional Exploration, 2005; editor: Ozark Folk Songs, 1982, John Edwards Meml. Forum Quar., 1966-83, 85-86; asst. editor Internat. Jour. Chem. Kinetics, 1977-83, editor, prodr. album Minstrels and Tunesmiths, 1982 (Grammy nomination 1982); contbr. articles and revs. to chemistry and folk, music jours. Grantee NEA, NEH, DOE, EPA, NIST. Mem.: Am. Chem. Soc., Assn. for Recorded Sound Collections, Soc. Am. Music. Democrat. Jewish. Achievements include research and publications in combustion chemistry, atmospheric chemistry, thermochemistry, chemistry of high energy chemical lasers. Home: 6507 SE 31st Ave Portland OR 97202-2687 E-mail: ncohen@teleport.com.

COHEN, NORTON JACOB, lawyer; b. Detroit, Nov. 5, 1935; s. Norman and Molly Rose (Natinsky) Cohen; m. Lorelei Freda Schuman, June 16, 1957 (dec. Jan. 1996); children: Debrah Anne, Sander Ivan. Student, U. Mich., 1953-55, U. Detroit, 1955-56; JD, Wayne State U., 1959. Bar: Mich. 1959, Tex. 1962, U.S. Dist. Ct. (ea. dist.) Mich. 1963, U.S. Ct. Appeals (6th cir.) 1966, U.S. Supreme Ct. 1970. Law clk. to presiding justice Mich. Supreme Ct., Lansing, 1959; assoc. Zwerdling, Miller, Klimist & Maurer, Detroit, 1963—68; legal dir. ACLU of Mich., Detroit, 1968—69; sr. dir. Miller, Cohen, Martens, Ice & Geary, P.C., Southfield, Mich., 1971—97, Miller Cohen, P.L.C., Detroit, 1997—. Mem. exec. bd. Met. Detroit ACLU, 1969—93, chmn., 1972—74; vice chair Equal Justice Coun., Detroit, 1970—74; spl. counsel workers compensation Mich. AFL-CIO, 1983—86; mem. dir.'s adv. coun. Workers Compensation Bur. Mich. Dept. Labor, 1986—99; chmn. Southfield Dem. Party, Mich., 1965—67; co-chair Robert F. Kennedy for Pres., Oakland County, Mich., 1968; mem. B'nai B'rith, Am. Jewish Com. Served to capt. JAGC US Army, 1960—63. Decorated Army Commendation medal; named to Mich. Worker's Compensation Hall of Fame, 2000; recipient Spirit of Detroit award, Detroit Common Coun., 1982. Fellow: Coll. Workers' Compensation Lawyers; mem.: ABA (labor co-chair workers compensation sect. labor & employment law 1989—96, 2005—), Fed. Bar Assn. Jewish. Office: Miller Cohen PLC 600 W Lafayette Blvd Fl 4 Detroit MI 48226-3125 Home Phone: 248-626-9133; Office Phone: 313-964-4454. Business E-Mail: yourlawyers@millercohen.com.

COHEN, PATRICIA, editor, critic; Ideas editor NY Times, theater editor Culture Desk and Arts and Leisure. Office: NY Times 229 W 43rd St New York NY 10036 Office Phone: 212-556-4427. Office Fax: 212-556-1516.

COHEN, PHILIP HERMAN, accountant; b. Bklyn., Dec. 4, 1936; s. David J. and Toby (Jaeger) C.; m. Susan Rudd; children: Davina Ellen, Tobias Samuel Dory. BS, NYU, 1957. From acct. to ptnr. Touche Ross & Co., NYC, 1957-81; exec. v.p. fin., CFO Integrated Resources, Inc., NYC, 1981-86, sr. exec. v.p. fin., CFO, 1986-90; fin. and real estate cons. Philip H. Cohen & Co., 1990—. Chmn. bd. dirs., pres., CEO FRMT Ltd. (A Bermuda Mut. Ins. Co.), 1996—99; bd. dirs. FMRT Ltd. (A Bermuda Mut. Ins. Co.); chmn. exec. com. FRMT Ltd. (A Bermuda Mut. Ins. Co.), 1999—2001; bd. dirs. Diwal Corp., Mitcor Corp., Odin Mgmt. Corp., Sy Sims Sch. Bus. Yeshiva U.; chmn. bd. dirs. Fraternity Risk Mgmt. Trust, 1994—99, chmn. exec. com., 1999—2000. Bd. dirs. Alpha Epsilon Pi Found., Inc., 1976—2005, Nat. Interfrat. Conf., 1975-86, Nat. Interfrat. Found., 1996—, State of Israel Bonds, N.Y.; bd. dirs. Sutton Pl. Synagogue, 1984-99, v.p., 1993-99; bd. dirs. joint purchasing com. Fedn. Jewish Philanthropies, 1977-78; mem. Cmty. Bd. Manhattan, N.Y., 1992-2006; internat. bd. dirs. Hillel Found. for Jewish Student Campus Life, 1999—, mem. exec. com. of bd. dirs., 2005—. Recipient State of Israel Bond Peace award 1983, Accts. Bankers and Fin. award Am. Jewish Congress, 1984, Gold medal Nat. Interfraternity Conf., 1994, Disting. Svc. award Fraternity Exec. Assn., 1999. Mem. Found. Acctg. Edn., Am. Inst. CPA's (real estate com. 1987-90), N.Y. State Soc. CPA's (admissions com. 1968-69, chmn. fin. and leasing com. 1972-74, com. on rels. with the bar 1974-76, com. on real estate acctg. 1976-79, com. ins. 1980-81, fin. acctg. standards com. 1983-86, chmn. mem.-in-industry com. 1981-83, chief fin. officers com. 1984-86, furtherance com. 1986, annual conf. com. 1985-87, com. on ops. 1987-88, bd. dirs. 1983-86, v.p. 1985-86, Outstanding CPA in Industry award 1986), Fin. Execs. Inst., Am. Acctg. Assn., Nat. Assn. Accts., Soc. Ins. Accts., Alpha Epsilon Pi (supreme gov. 1966-73, nat. pres. 1974-76, mem. fiscal control bd. 1977-81, vice chmn. 1981-92, chmn. 1992-2005), Beta Alpha Psi, Areopagus Clubs: South Fla. Alumni Alpha Epsilon Pi. Lodges: Masons. Jewish. Home: 1500 Ocean Dr Ste 903 Miami Beach FL 33139 Office Phone: 305-532-5872.

COHEN, PHILIP N., sociologist, educator; s. Marshall M. and Avis H. Cohen; m. Judy F. Ruttenberg, Aug. 23, 1992; 1 child, Charlotte. BA, U. Mich., Ann Arbor, 1992; MA, U. Mass., Amherst, 1995; PhD, U. Md., Coll. Pk., 1999. Asst. prof. sociology U. Calif., Irvine, Calif., 1999—2005; assoc. prof. sociology U. NC, Chapel Hill, 2005—. Fellow: Carolina Population Ctr.; mem.: Coun. Contemporary Families, Popluattion Assn. Am., Am. Sociol. Soc. Office Phone: 919-843-4791.

COHEN, POLLY, film company executive; Degree in Chinese Studies, U. Calif. San Diego; MFA, U. Southern Calif. With Jersey Films; creative exec. Warner Bros. Pictures, 1997—98, prodn. exec., 1998—99, v.p. prodn., 1999—2003, sr. v.p. prodn., 2003—06, exec. v.p. prodn., 2006; pres. Warner Ind. Pictures, 2006—. Named one of 100 Most Powerful

Women in Entertainment, Hollywood Reporter, 2006. Achievements include fluency in Chinese language. Office: Warner Independent Pictures 4000 Warner Blvd Burbank CA 91522 Office Phone: 818-954-6000. Office Fax: 212-954-7667.*

COHEN, RACHEL RUTSTEIN, financial planner; b. Phila., June 10, 1968; d. Charles Lawrence and Ronna (Newman) Rutstein (Stepmother), Susan Ellen (Yokel) Sansweet; m. Kipp B. Cohen, Nov. 22, 1995; children: Brandon Erik, Ryan Cameron. BS in Bus. Adminstrn., Pa. State U., 1990; student, U. Tel Aviv, 1989; MBA in Fin., Temple U., 1997. CFP; cert. wealth mgmt. advisor. V.p. Merrill Lynch, Bala Cynwyd, Pa., 1990—. Author: Creating Workplace Community, 2004. V.p. bd. dirs. Phila. chpt. Shaare Zedek Hosp.Charity, 1992-96, co-chair Phone-A-Thon, 1993; active Childrens Hosp. Found., 2004, Merrill Lynch Make a Wish Fundraiser; co-chmn. playground campaign Or Ami Mem.: The Forum of Exec. Women, Phila. Fin. Assn. (co-chair dinner com.), Phila. C. of C. (diplomate 1991—95, nursery sch. com. 2003—, co-chmn. playground campaign 2004—), Green Valley Country Club. Republican. Avocations: golf, tennis, travel, language (spanish), reading. Office: Merrill Lynch 2 Bala Plz Bala Cynwyd PA 19004 Home Phone: 610-834-1890. Personal E-mail: kicohen@comcast.net. Business E-Mail: rachel_cohen@ml.com.

COHEN, RACHELLE SHARON, journalist; b. Phila., Oct. 21, 1946; d. Hyman and Diane Doris (Schultz) Goldberg; m. Stanley Martin Cohen, June 22, 1968; 1 child, Avril Heather. BS, Temple U., 1968. Editor Somerville (Mass.) Jour., 1968—70; reporter Lowell (Mass.) Sun, 1970—72, AP, Boston, 1972—79; state house bur. chief Boston Herald Am., 1979—80, editl. page editor, 1980—82; editl. page editor, columnist Boston Herald, 1982—. Mem.: Mass. Assn. Mental Health (bd. dirs. 1993—), Mass. Bar Assn. (bench, bar, press com.), Women's Lunch Place (bd. dirs. 2006—). Office: Boston Herald 1 Herald St Boston MA 02118-2200 Home Phone: 617-236-1315; Office Phone: 617-619-6492.

COHEN, RAYMOND, retired mechanical engineer, educator; b. St. Louis, Nov. 30, 1923; s. Benjamin and Leah (Lewis) C.; m. Katherine Elise Silverman, Feb. 1, 1948 (dec. May 1985); children: Richard Samuel, Deborah Elise, Barbara Beth; m. Lila Lakin Cagen, Nov. 30, 1986. BS, Purdue U., 1947, MS, 1950, PhD, 1955. Profl. engr., Ind., 1955. Instr. mech. engrng. Purdue U., 1948-55, asst. prof., 1955-58, assoc. prof., 1958-60, prof., 1960-98, asst. dir. Ray W. Herrick Labs., 1970-71, dir., 1971-93, acting head Sch. Mech. Engring., 1988-89, Herrick prof. engring., 1994-99, Herrick prof. emeritus engring., 1999—. Cons. to industry. Departmental editor: Ency. Brit., 1957-62; editorial bd. Jour. Sound and Vibration, 1971-87; editor Internat. Jour. of Heating, Ventilating, Air Conditioning and Refrigerating Rsch., 1994-98. Served as sgt. inf. AUS, 1943-46. Recipient Kamerlingh Onnes gold medal, 1995; NATO sr. fellow in sci., 1971 Fellow ASME, ASHRAE; mem. NSPE, Am. Soc. Engring. Edn., Soc. Exptl. Mechanics, Internat. Inst. Refrigeration (chmn. U.S. nat. com. 1992-95, U.S. del. 1992-99, Merit medal 2003), Acoustical Soc. Am., Inst. Noise Control Engring. (pres. 1990), Sigma Xi, Pi Tau Sigma, Tau Beta Pi. Home: 2501 Spyglass Dr Valparaiso IN 46383 Office: Purdue U Ray W Herrick Labs 140 S Intramural Dr West Lafayette IN 47907-2031 Personal E-mail: rcohen81@comcast.net.

COHEN, RICHARD B., grocery company executive; b. Worcester, Mass., July 25, 1952; s. Lester and Norma (Russem) Cohen. BA in Acctg., U. Pa., 1974. V.p. fin. C&S Wholesale, Worcester, Mass., 1977-81, gen. mgr., 1981-83, pres., CEO, 1983—, now chmn. bd., dir. Bd. dirs. The Food Distbn. Inst.; bd. trustees Deerfield Acad. Bd. overseers U. Pa. Wharton Sch. Bus., 2005. Named Entrepreneur of the Yr., Ernst & Young, 2002. Jewish. Avocations: fishing, tennis, travel. Office: C & S Wholesale Grocers Inc 7 Corporate Dr Keene NH 03431 Office Phone: 603-354-7000. Office Fax: 603-354-4690.*

COHEN, RICHARD MARTIN, journalist; b. NYC, Feb. 6, 1941; s. Harry Louis and Pearl (Rosenberg) C.; m. Barbara Stubbs, May 3, 1969 (div.); 1 son, Alexander Prescott. BS, N.Y. U., 1967; MS in Journalism, Columbia U., 1968. With UPI, 1967-68; gen. assignment reporter Washington Post, 1968-76, syndicated columnist, 1976—. Author: A Heartbeat Away, 1973. Office: Washington Post Co 251 W 57th St New York NY 10019-1802 Office Phone: 212-445-4901. E-mail: cohenr@washpost.com.

COHEN, RICHARD NORMAN, insurance executive; b. NYC, Oct. 28, 1923; s. Norman M. and Janet (Goldsmith) C.; m. Ann Robertson, Oct. 25, 1975; children: Daniel Hays, James Matthew; 1 stepchild, Mark Thompson. Grad., Phillips Exeter Acad., 1941; BA, Yale U., 1945. Salesman Cohen, Goldman & Co., NYC, 1947-50; mens fashion editor Fawcett Publs., NYC, 1951-52; life ins. broker Mass. Mut. Life Ins. Co., NYC, 1954—; account exec. John M. Riehle, Inc., NYC, 1961-63, v.p., 1963-83, Leonard Newman Agy. Inc., White Plains, NY, 1984-94, Arthur Gallagher & Co., White Plains, 1994-2000; dir. Silver Hill Hosp., New Canaan, Conn., 1997—2004. Dir. NY Times, 1960—72. Served to 2d lt. USAAF, 1943-45. Mem. Country Club of New Canaan, Yale Club (N.Y.C.), Century Country Club (White Plains, N.Y.), Beta Theta Pi. Republican. Jewish. Home: 1062 Ponus Rdg New Canaan CT 06840-3420 Personal E-mail: RNCI@optonline.net.

COHEN, ROBERT, medical device and pharmaceutical manufacturing and marketing executive; b. Glen Cove, NY, Sept. 23, 1957; s. Alan and Selma (Grossman) C.; m. Nancy A. Arey, Jan. 17, 1981. BA, Bates Coll., 1979; JD, U. Maine, 1982. Bar: N.Y. 1983, U.S. Dist. Ct. (so. and ea.) N.Y. 1983. Atty. Pfizer Inc., NYC, 1982-86; asst. corp. counsel, asst. sec. Pfizer Hosp. Products Group, Inc., NYC, 1986-88; v.p. bus. devel., dir. for med. device mfr. and marketer Deknatel Inc., Fall River, Mass., 1988-92; pres., CEO GCI Med., Braintree, Mass., 1992-93; v.p. bus. devel. Sulzermedica USA, Inc., Angleton, Tex., 1993-94, group v.p., 1994-98; v.p. bus. & tech. devel. St. Jude Med., Inc., St. Paul, 1998—2002; CEO, dir. Advanced Circulatory Sys., Inc., Eden Prairie, Minn., 2003—04; dir. Horizon Med. Products, Inc., Atlanta, 1998-2001, CardioFocus, Inc., Boston, 1999-2000; pres., CEO, bd. dirs. Travanti Pharma Inc., Mendota Heights, 2004—. Author: 19th Century Maine Authors, 1978. Mem.: ABA. Republican. Home: 18683 Bearpath Trl Eden Prairie MN 55347-3476 Office: Travanti Pharma Inc 2520 Pilot Knob Rd Ste 100 Mendota Heights MN 55120 Personal E-mail: rcohenmeddev@aol.com.

COHEN, ROBERT, plastic surgeon; BA, Emory U., 1995; MD, Tulane U., 1999. Diplomate Am. Bd. Plastic Surgery, lic. Ariz. Med. Bd., Med. Bd. Calif. Intern & resident in gen. surgery Dartmouth-Hitchcock Med. Ctr., Lebanon, NH, 1999—2002, resident in plastic & reconstructive surgery, 2002—03, chief resident, 2003—04; fellow in aesthetic surgery/laser surgery Marina Plastic Surgery Assocs., Marina Del Rey, Calif., 2004—05; pvt. practice Scottsdale Ctr. Plastic Surgery, Paradise Valley, Ariz., 2005—. Affiliated Dartmouth-Hitchcock Med. Ctr., Lebanon, NH, 1999—2003, U. Southern Calif. U. Hosp., LA, 2004—05, Daniel Freeman Hosp., Marina Del Rey, Calif., 2004—05, Marina Outpatient Surgery Ctr., Marina Del Rey, Calif., 2004—05, Paradise Valley Cosmetic Surgery Ctr., Paradise Valley, Ariz., 2005—, Scottsdale Healthcare Osborn/Greenbaum Specialty Hosp., Scottsdale, Ariz., 2005—, Scottsdale Healthcare Shea/Piper Surgery Ctr., Scottsdale, Ariz., 2005—. Contbr. chapters to books, articles to profl. journals. Founding mem. Tulane ch. Doctors Ought to Care, 1995; vol. Brantley Ctr. Homeless Shelter, 1995—97, Ozanam Inn Homeless Shelter, 1995—99, Project Vietnam Med. Mission, Ha Nam Province, 2004. Mem.: Maricopa County Plastic Surgeons' Soc., Ariz. Soc. Plastic & Reconstructive Surgeons, Alpha Epsilon Delta, Plastic Surgery Ednl. Found., Am. Soc. Plastic Surgeons, Order of Omega, Phi Sigma, Phi Sigma Tau. Office: Scottsdale Ctr for Plastic Surgery Ste A-500 5410 N Scottsdale Rd Paradise Valley AZ 85253 Office Phone: 480-423-1973.*

COHEN, ROBERT ABRAHAM, retired physician; b. Chgo., Nov. 13, 1909; s. Ezra Harry and Catherine (Kurzon) C.; m. Mabel Jean Blake, Mar. 21, 1933 (dec. Oct. 1972); children— Donald Edward, Margery Jean; m. Alice L. Muth, Mar. 31, 1974. BS, U. Chgo., 1930, PhD, MD, 1935. Intern Michael Reese Hosp., Chgo., 1936-37; resident Henry Phipps Psychiat. Clinic Johns Hopkins U., 1937-38; resident Sheppard-Pratt Hosp., Towson, Md., 1938-39, 40-41; sr. fellow Inst. Juvenile Research, Chgo, 1939-40; pvt. practice psychiatry Washington, 1946-48; clin. dir. Chestnut Lodge, Rockville, Md., 1948-53, dir. psychotherapy, 1981-91; dir. clin. investigations NIMH, Bethesda, Md., 1953-69, dir. div. clin. and behavioral research, 1969-81, dep. dir. intramural research program, 1969-81; ret., 1991. Pres. Washington Sch. Psychiatry, 1973-82; bd. dirs. Founds. Fund for Rsch. in Psychiatry, 1960-63, chmn. bd., 1962-63; trustee William Alanson White Psychiat. Found. Served from lt. (j.g.) to comdr. M.C. USNR, 1941-46. Recipient HEW Disting. Svc. award, 1970, Salmon medal N.Y. Acad. Scis., 1978, Fromm-Reichmann award Am. Acad. Psychoanalysis, 1979, Woodley House award, 1982. Fellow Am. Psychiat. Assn. (disting. life); mem. Am. Psychoanalytical Assn., Am. Psychopathol. Assn., Assn. Rsch. in Nervous and Mental Disease, Washington Psychoanalytic Soc. (pres. 1951-53), Washington Psychiat. Soc. (pres. 1958-59), Washington Psychoanalytic Inst. (chmn. edn. com. 1955-59), Washington Acad. Medicine, Cosmos Club. Home: 5216 Elsmere Ave Bethesda MD 20814-5734 Personal E-mail: alibob@rcn.com.

COHEN, ROBERT EDWARD, chemical engineering professor, consultant; b. Oil City, Pa., Jan. 21, 1947; s. David M. and Minnie E. Cohen; m. D. Jane Woodman, Nov. 18, 1978; children: Genevieve Elizabeth, Eliot Lee. BS with distinction, Cornell U., 1968; MS, Calif. Inst. Tech., 1970, PhD, 1972. Postdoctoral rsch. fellow Calif. Inst. Tech., Pasadena, 1972; ICI rsch. fellow Oxford (Eng.) U., 1972-73; asst. prof. chem. engring. MIT, Cambridge, 1973-75, Harold and Esther Edgerton asst. prof., 1975-77, assoc. prof., 1977-82, prof., 1982—, founding dir. program in polymer sci. and tech., 1985-88, Bayer prof. chem. engring., 1988-95, St. Laurent prof. chem. engring., 1995—, assoc. chmn. of faculty, 1989-91, chem. engring. grad. officer, 1992-01, founding dir. PhD in Chem. Engring. Practice degree program; co-dir. DuPont-MIT Alliance, 2000—. Vis. appt. Sandia Nat. Labs., Albuquerque, summer 1979, Istituto Guido Donegani, Novara, Italy, 1981-82; vis. prof. dept. chemistry Harvard U., 1989; vis. prof. Balliol Coll., Oxford U., 2006; co-founder, bd. dirs., cons. MatTek Corp., Ashland, Mass., 1985—; bd. dirs. Kiser Rsch., Inc., Washington, 1992-94; chmn. sci. adv. bd. William and Mary Greve Found., NYC, 1988—, bd. dirs., 1997—. Co-editor: Jour. Polymer Engring.; mem. editorial adv. bd. Jour. Applied Polymer Sci., 1989—, Chemistry of Materials, 1989-93; cons. editor AIP Series on Polymers and Complex Fluids, 1992-97; contbr. articles to profl. jours.; patentee in field. Trustee The Advent Sch., Boston, 1996-99 Recipient Camille and Henry Dreyfus Tchr. Scholar award Dreyfus Found., 1977; Robert W. Vaughan Meml. lectr. Calif. Inst. Tech., 1984, Shell Disting. lectr. dept. materials sci. Northwestern U., 1996, Capers and Marion McDonald award MIT, 2006. Fellow AIChE (program chair materials divsn. polymer sect. 1993-97, dir. materials divsn. 1998-2001, Charles M.A. Stine award 2000), Am. Phys. Soc.; mem. Am. Chem. Soc., Materials Rsch. Soc., Soc. Rheology, N.Y. Acad. Scis. Jewish. Avocation: golf. Office: MIT Dept Chem Engring Bldg 66 Rm 554 Cambridge MA 02139

COHEN, ROBERT L., film producer; b. NYC, July 7, 1936; s. Edward I. and Shirley (Schiff) C. BA, Pratt Coll., 1959. Baseball player Pitts. Pirates, 1961-63; advt. photographer Ladies Home Journal, NYC, 1963-67; unit prodn. mgr. ABC Network, NYC, 1967-74; producer, pres. Duo Prodns., Inc., NYC, 1974-77; prodn. mgr. various major motion picture orgns., NYC, 1977-80; dir., producer Robert L. Cohen, Inc., NYC, 1980-98; pres., CEO Prodn. Link Internat., 1998—. Producer TV commls., 1967— (4 Clio awards); prodn. mgr. feature film, 1978 (Cannes Best Acting award). Dir. Clean Water Coun. N.J.; East Pa. rep. Monmouth County N.J. to Aberdeen N.J., 1998—. Sgt. U.S. Army, 1959-62. Mem. Dirs. Guild Am., Theodore Gordon Flyfishers (dir.), Atlantic Salmon Fedn. Clubs: Friars. Avocations: fly fishing, sailing, golf. Home and Office: 120 Warren Dr Matawan NJ 07747-1844

COHEN, ROBERT SONNÉ, physicist, philosopher, educator; b. NYC, Feb. 18, 1923; m. Robin Gertrude Hirshhorn, June 18, 1944; children: Michael, Daniel, Deborah. BA, Wesleyan U., Middletown, Conn., 1943, LHD, 1986; MS, Yale U., 1943, PhD (NRC fellow), 1948. Instr. physics Yale U., 1943-44, instr. philosophy, 1949-51; sci. staff, war research div. Columbia U. and Communications Bd., U.S. Joint Chiefs Staff, 1944-46; asst. prof. physics and philosophy Wesleyan U., 1949-57; assoc. prof. physics Boston U., 1957-59, prof. physics and philosophy, 1959-93, chmn. dept. physics, 1959-73, chmn. dept. philosophy, 1986-88, prof. emeritus, 1993—; acting dean Coll. Liberal Arts, 1971-72. Chmn. Boston U. Center for Philosophy and History Sci., 1970-93, chmn. emeritus, 1993—; vis. lectr. humanities and philosophy of sci. Mass. Inst. Tech., 1958-59, 61-62; vis. prof. history of ideas Brandeis U., 1959-60; lectr. history and philosophy of sci. Am. U., Washington, summers 1958-68; vis. fellow Polish and Yugoslav Acad. Sci., 1963, Hungarian Acad. Sci., 1964; vis. prof. philosophy U. Calif., San Diego, 1969, Yale U., 1973; rsch. fellow history of sci. Harvard U., 1974; mem., chmn. U.S. Nat. Com. for Internat. Union History and Philosophy of Sci., 1969-75; trustee Wesleyan U., 1968-84, emeritus, 1984—; trustee Tufts U., 1984-93, emeritus, 1993—. Author, editor articles, books and jours. in field.; Editor: Boston Studies in Philosophy of Sci., Vienna Circle Collection, Sci. in Context. Trustee Bill of Rights Found. Am. Coun. Learned Soc. fellow philosophy and sci., 1948-49, First faculty fellow Cambridge, Eng., 1955-56, fellow Wissenschaftskolleg zu Berlin, 1983-84, Inst. fur Wissenschaften dem Menschen, Vienna, 1994; papers collected in Robert S. Cohen Collection at Howard Gotlieb Archival Rsch. Ctr., Boston U., selection archived Inst. Vienna Cir., U. Vienna. Fellow AAAS (chmn. sect. L history and philosophy of sci. 1978-79), Am. Phys. Soc.; mem. AAUP, Am. Assn. Physics Tchrs., Am. Philos. Assn. (exec. com. 1988-91), History Sci. Soc., Philosophy Sci. Assn. (v.p. 1972-75, pres. 1982-84), Nat. Emergency Civil Liberties Com. (mem. nat. coun.), Am. Inst. Marxist Studies (chmn. 1964-82), Fedn. Am. Scientists (nat. coun. 1967-70), Inst. for Unity of Sci. (exec. com. 1960-74). Home: 44 Adams Ave Watertown MA 02472-1391 Office: Boston U Dept Philosophy 745 Commonwealth Ave Boston MA 02215-1401 Personal E-mail: robertscohen@hotmail.com.

COHEN, ROBERT STEPHAN, lawyer; b. NYC, Jan. 14, 1939; s. Abraham and Florence C.; children: Christopher, Ian, Nicholas; m. Stephanie J. Stiefel, Jan. 29, 1998. BA, Alfred U., 1959; LLB, Fordham U., 1962. Bar: N.Y. 1963, U.S. Dist. Ct. (so. and ea. dists.) N.Y. 1964, U.S. Ct. Appeals (2d cir.) 1965. Sr. ptnr. Cohen Lans LLP and predecessor firms, NYC, 1968—. Mem. faculty Am. Acad. Psychiatry and the Law, 1984-03; lectr.-at-law U. Pa. Law Sch., 2003-. Author: Reconcilable Differences, 2002; contbr. articles to legal jours. 1st lt. JAG USAR, 1965—67. Fellow Am. Coll. Family Trial Lawyers; mem. ABA, N.Y. State Bar Assn., N.Y.C. Bar Assn., N.Y. Acad. Matrimonial Lawyers, Univ. Club (N.Y.C.). Office: Cohen Lans LLP 885 3d Ave New York NY 10022 Office Phone: 212-326-1701. Business E-Mail: rscohen@cohenlans.com.

COHEN, ROBERTA JANE, think-tank associate; b. NYC, Feb. 5, 1940; d. George H. and Ethel (Israel) Cohen; m. David A. Korn, Apr. 8, 1981; stepchildren: Marie Korn, David Korn, Philip Korn, Stephen Korn. BA, Barnard Coll., 1960; MA, Johns Hopkins U., 1963; Doctorate (hon.), U. Bern, Switzerland, 2005. Exec. dir. Internat. League for Human Rights, NYC, 1971-78; sr. adviser to U.S. del. to UN and human rights officer Dept. of State, Washington, 1978-80, dep. asst. sec. state for human rights, 1980-81; head pub. affairs office U.S. Embassy, Addis Ababa, 1982-85; hon. sec. Parliamentary Human Rights Group, London, 1985-86; sr. advisor to refugee policy group Washington, 1989-96; sr. advisor NAS Com. on Human Rights, Washington, 1991-95; sr. advisor on internally displaced to rep. UN Sec.-Gen., 1994—; co-dir. project on internal displacement Brookings Instn., Washington, 1994—2007, sr. advisor to project on internal displacement, 2007—, sr. fellow, 2001—07, nonresident sr. fellow, 2007—. Cons. World Bank, various govt. and non-govt. orgns., 1991—94; chmn. task force on human rights UN Assn., Washington, 1993—94; chair task force on China Internat. Human Rights Law Group, Washington, 1997—99, vice chair, 1992—96; bd. dirs. Jacob Blaustein Inst. for Advancement Human Rights; mem. adv. com. Human Rights Watch/Africa, RFK Meml. on Human Rights, Internat. League Human Rights, Acad. on Human Rights and Humanitarian Law, Am. Univ. Washington Coll. Law, Trinity Coll. Human Rights Program; mem. Coun. Fgn. Rels., Women's Fgn. Policy Group, Brookings Coun.; commr. Women's Commn. on Refugee Women & Children; sr. fellow Inst. for Study of Internat. Migration, Georgetown U., 2007—. Author: People's Republic of China: The Human Rights Exception, 1987; co-author (with Francis Deng): Masses in Flight: The Global Crisis of Internal Displacement, 1998; co-editor: The Forsaken People, 1998; co-editor: The Guiding Principles on Internal Displacement and the Law of the South Caucasus: Georgia, Armenia and Azerbaijan, 2003; mem. adv. com. Jour. Refugee Studies, adv. com. Forced Migration Rev. Pub. mem. U.S. del. UN Commn. on Human Rights, 1998, Orgn. for Security and Cooperation in Europe, 2003. Co-recipient The Grawemeyer award for Ideas Improving World Order, U. Louisville, 2005; recipient Superior Honor award, USIA, Addis Abada, 1985, Human Rights award, UN Assn., 1994, Fiftieth Ann. award for Exemplary Writing on Fgn. Affairs and Diplomacy, Diplomats and Consular Officers Ret., 2002, Disting. Alumna award, Barnard Coll., 2005, Social Scis. award, Washington Acad. Scis., 2005. Mem.: Cosmos Club. Personal E-mail: rcohen@brookings.edu.

COHEN, ROBIN L., lawyer; b. Phila., Oct. 27, 1961; BA magna cum laude, U. Pa., 1983, JD, 1986. Bar: Pa. 1986, NJ 1989, NY 1989. Ptnr. Anderson, Kill, Olick & Oshinsky, P.C., NYC, Dickstein Saphiro Morin Oshinsky LLP, NYC, 1996, mem. exec. com., mng. ptnr. NY office. Named one of The 50 Most Influential Women Lawyers in Am., Nat. Law Jour., 2007. Office: Dickstein Shapiro Morin & Oshinsky LLP 1177 Avenue of the Americas New York NY 10036-2714 Office Phone: 212-835-1440. Office Fax: 212-997-9880. Business E-Mail: cohenr@dsmo.com.*

COHEN, RONALD J., lawyer; b. Englewood, NJ, Dec. 16, 1950; s. Irwin and Shirley (Kushel) C.; m. Jeanne K. Houser, June 22, 1981; children: Shay, Emily. BA, U. Fla., 1973; JD, U. Miami, 1976. Asst. city atty. City of Miami, 1979-83; assoc. Paul, Landy, Beiley & Harper, Miami, 1983-87; ptnr. Klausner & Cohen, PA, Hollywood, Fla., 1987-97; pvt. practice Ronald J. Cohen, PA, Miami, 1997—. Office: 8100 Oak Ln Ste 403 Miami Lakes FL 33016-7051 Office Phone: 305-823-1212. Business E-Mail: rcohen@roncohenlaw.com.

COHEN, RONALD S., accountant; b. Lafayette, Ind., July 13, 1937; s. William and Stella (Fleischman) C.; m. Nancy Ann Plotkin, May 29, 1960; children: Philip, Douglas. BS in Acctg., Ind. U., 1958. CPA Ind. Staff acct. Crowe, Chizek & Co., South Bend, Ind., 1958—65, ptnr., 1965—2003, mng. ptnr., 1982—94, chmn. bd. dirs., 1994—2000. Chmn. Horwath Internat., 1999—; mem. dean's adv. coun. Ind. U. Sch. Bus., 1996—. Commr. Housing Authority of South Bend, 1976-85, also vice-chmn.; pres. Jewish Fedn., 1979-82; bd. dirs. United Way of South Bend, 1987-90. Served to lt. USAR, 1958-66. Mem. AICPA (bd. dirs. 1990-97, vice-chmn. 1994, chmn. 1995), Ind. Soc. CPAs, Ind. U. Sch. Bus. Alumni Assn. (bd. dirs. 1992-95). Democrat. Jewish. Office: Crowe Chizek & Co PO Box 7 330 E Jefferson Blvd South Bend IN 46601-2366 Office Phone: 574-236-8677. E-mail: rcohen@crowechizek.com.

COHEN, ROSALIE, civic worker; b. New Orleans, May 27, 1910; d. Leon and Fannie (Brener) Palter; m. Joseph Cohen, July 7, 1929 (dec. Oct. 1979); children: Carmel Jonathan, Sharon Cohen Leviton. BA, Tulane U., 1940. Cert. Hebrew language Hebrew Univ., Jeruselem. Chmn. women's divsn. campaign New Orleans Jewish Welfare Fund, 1945; chmn. family svc. New Orleans Jewish Fedn., 1950-56, pres., 1959-61; vice chmn. women's divsn. Heart Campaign, 1950; pres. New Orleans B'nai B'rith Hillel Corp., 1954—, pres. New Orleans B'nai B'rith Hillel Found., 1954-59, Isidore Newman Sch. PTA, 1950-51; nat. vice chmn. women's divsn. United Jewish Appeal, 1954-60, mem. adv. bd., 1960—; mem. regional bd. Anti-Defamation League, 1956—; mem. B'nai B'rith Adult Jewish Edn. Commn., 1960-66; bd. dirs. Nat. Found. Jewish Culture, 1960—; founder Willow Wood Home for Jewish Aged, New Orleans, 1962-97; mem. Orleans Parish Bd. Welfare, 1958-66, New Orleans Bd. Wefare, 1958, Citizens Com. for Juvenile Ct., 1963-66; organizer year-round women's divsn. Jewish Welfare Fedn., New Orleans, 1965, hon. pres., 1966—; organizer citizens steering com. Orleans Parish Welfare Dept., 1966; v.p. Coun. Jewish Fedns. and Welfare Funds, 1963-66, sec., 1966—; bd. overseers Philip Lown Ctr. Judaic Studies, Brandeis U., Waltham, Mass., 1966—; sec. Fgn. Rels. Assn., 1966-67, bd. dirs., 1967—; chpt. pres. Hadassah, 1932-36, 40-42, 47, hon. v.p., 1950; founder Am.-Christian Palestine Com., New Orleans, 1945-48, Hillel chpt., Tulane U., New Orleans, Lemann-Stern Young Leadership, New Orleans; founding mem. Nat. Found. for Jewish Culture, N.Y.C. Recipient svc. award United Jewish Appeal, award of honor Govt. of Israel Bonds, 1954, citation Orleans Parish Bd. Welfare, 1966, cert. of merit U.S. Office Censorship, 1944, hon. award Tulane U. Sch. Social Work, Hebrew U. Mem. Am. Assn. for Jewish Edn. (v.p. 1965—), Jewish Publs. Soc. Am. (bd. dirs.). Democrat.

COHEN, SANFORD IRWIN, physician, educator; b. NYC, Sept. 5, 1928; s. George A. and Gertrude (Slater) C.; m. Jean Steinbruecker, Nov. 30, 1952; children— Jeffrey, Debra, John, Robert. AB magna cum laude, N.Y. U., 1948; M.B., MD, Chgo. Med. Sch., 1952. Intern Jackson Meml. Hosp., Miami, Fla., 1952-53; resident psychiatry U. Colo. Med. Center, 1953-54; resident Duke Med. Center, 1954-55, 57-58, mem. faculty, 1956-68, prof. psychiatry, 1964-68, head div. psychosomatic medicine and psychophysiol. research, 1964-68, lectr. psychology, 1960-68; instr. Washington Psychoanalytic Inst., 1964-68; cons. VA Hosp., Durham, NC, 1957-65, NIMH, 1963-66; prof. psychiatry Boston U. Med. Sch., 1970-86, chmn. dept., 1970-86; vis. research scientist health and behavior br., div. basic scis. NIMH, 1986-88; prof. psychiatry U. Miami (Fla.) Sch. Medicine, 1988-2000, vice chmn. dept., 1990-2000, prof. emeritus, 2000—. Markle scholar med. sci., 1957-62; Commonwealth fellow, Czech Republic and USSR, 1966. Contbr. articles to profl. jours., chpts. to books. Recipient Robert Morse award excellence in sci. writing, 1965 Fellow Am. Psychiat. Assn. (disting. life), Am. Coll. Clin. Pharmacology (life); mem. AAAS, Am. Psychosomatic Soc., Acad. Behavioral Medicine Rsch. Home: 15110 Rollinmead Dr Darnestown MD 20878-3906 Home Phone: 301-527-0821; Office Phone: 305-355-9106. Business E-Mail: scohen@med.miami.edu.

COHEN, SANFORD NED, pediatrician, educator, academic administrator; b. NYC, June 12, 1935; s. George M. and Fannie Leah (Epstein) Cohen; m. Judith Luskind, June 22, 1958 (div. 1984); m. Sandra Hoffman, June 13, 1992. AB, Johns Hopkins U., Balt., 1956, MD, 1960. Diplomate Am. Bd. Pediatrics. Intern in pediat. Johns Hopkins Hosp., 1960-61, resident, 1961-63; from instr. to assoc. prof. NYU Sch. Medicine, NYC, 1965-74; chmn., prof. pediat. Wayne State U. Sch. Medicine, Detroit,

1974-81, prof. pediat., 1991-98, prof. emeritus, 1998—, dir. Child Rsch. Ctr., 1975—81, assoc. dean, 1981-86, dir. Devel. Disability Inst., 1983—86, sr. v.p. acad. affairs, provost, 1986-91. Pediatrician-in-chief Children's Hosp. Mich., Detroit, 1974—81; adj. faculty U. Mich. Sch. Pub. Health, Ann Arbor, 1980—90; chair steering com. NIH Network Pediat. Pharmacology Rsch. Units, 1994—98, mem. adv. com., 1999—2002; reviewer Inst. Medicine Nat. Acad. Sci.; mem. profl. adv. coun. Children's Med. Rsch. Inst., Oklahoma City, 1999—; vol. cons. Lee Meml. Health Sys., Ft. Myers, Fla., 2000—; mem. adv. bd. Children's Hosp. S.W. Fla., 2003—; chmn. adv. com. to dean Fla. Gulf Coast U., 2006—. Editor: Progress in Drug Therapy in Children, 1981; contbr. articles to profl. jours. Mem. bd. health, Leonia, NJ, 1972—74; mem. Bd. Police Commrs., Detroit, 1995—99, chmn., 1997—98; co-pres. Temple Judea, 2004—. John and Mary R. Markle scholar acad. medicine, 1968—74. Mem.: Soc. Pediat. Rsch. (v.p. 1980—81), Sr. and Ret. Physicians Assn. (pres. 2001—06), Midwest Soc. Pediat. Rsch. (pres. 1979—80), Am. Pediat. Soc. Avocations: reading, golf. Office: Children's Hosp Mich 3901 Beaubien St Detroit MI 48201-2119 Office Phone: 313-745-5214. Business E-Mail: scohen@med.wayne.edu.

COHEN, SASHA (ALEXANDRA PAULINE COHEN), ice skater; b. Westwood, Calif., Oct. 26, 1984; d. Roger and Galina Cohen. Appeared in films: Blades of Glory, 2007; author: (book) Sasha Cohen: Autobiography of a Champion Figure Skater, 2005. Achievements include Recipient Gardena Winter Trophy, 1999; winner, Junior Grand Prix, Stockholm, Sweden, 1999; 2nd place, U.S. Championships, 2000; winner, Pacific Coast Sectional, 2000; Finlandia Trophy, 2001; 3rd place, Trophee Lalique, 2001; Silver medalist, U.S. Nats. Championship, 2001-2002; 2nd place, U.S. Championships, 2002; 4th place, World Championships, 2002; 4th place, Olympic Winter Games, 2002; 2nd place, Hersheys Kisses Challenge, 2002; 4th place, Campbells Classic, 2002; 1st place, Skate Can., 2002; 1st place, Trophee Lalique, 2002; 2nd place, Cup of Russia, 2002; 1st place, Crest White Strips Challenge, 2002; bronze medalist, U.S. Nats., 2003; 4th place, Worlds, 2003; champion, Grand Prix Finals, 2003; 1st place, Trophee Lalique, 2004; 1st place, Skate Can., 2004; 1st place, Skate Am., 2004; 1st place, Campbells Soup, 2004; silver medallist, World Championships, 2004-2005; 1st Place, U.S. Nats., 2006; silver medallist, Torino Olympics, Italy, 2006. Avocations: art, jewelry making, reading, designing costumes. Office: 9 Journey c/o Ice Palace Aliso Viejo CA 92656*

COHEN, SAUL BERNARD, retired academic administrator, geographer; b. Malden, Mass., July 28, 1925; s. Barnett and Anna (Kaplinsky) C.; m. Miriam Friederman, June 11, 1950; children: Deborah Fae, Louise Esther. AB, Harvard U., 1947, AM, 1949, PhD, 1955; DSc (hon.), Queens Coll., 1986; LLD (hon.), CUNY, 1986; DSc (hon.), Clark U., 1991, DHL (hon.), 2004; DPhil (hon.), Haifa U., Israel, 2004. From instr. to prof. geography Boston U., 1952-65; vis. prof. U.S. Naval War Coll., 1957; prof. geography, dir. Grad. Sch. Geography, Clark U., Worcester, Mass., 1965-78; dean Grad. Sch. Geography, Clark U. (Grad. Sch.), 1967-70, chmn. faculty, 1973-76, 77-78; pres. Queens Coll., Flushing, NY, 1978-85; univ. prof. geography Hunter Coll., NYC, 1986-96, univ. prof. emeritus, 1996—. Vis. prof. Hebrew U., Jerusalem, 1971, 74, 75; adj. prof. Haifa U., 1977; cons. social sci. div. NSF, 1966-74, U.S. Office Edn., 1966-77; prof. Haifa U., 2006—; mem. U.S. nat. delegation Internat. Geog. Union, 1966-69; chmn. com. geography Nat. Acad. of Scis.-NRC, 1966-69. Author: Geography and Politics in a World Divided, 1963, rev. edit., 1973, Problems and Trends in American Geography, 1967, Experiencing the Environment, 1976, Resources and Human Networks, 1977, Jerusalem-Bridging the Four Walls, 1977, Jerusalem Undivided, 1980, Israel's Defensible Borders: A Geopolitical Map, 1983, The Geopolitics of Israel's Border Question, 1987, Geopolitics of the World System, 2003, also articles; geog. editor The Oxford World Atlas, 1973; geog. advisor New Columbia Ency., 1991, 93; editor-in-chief Columbia Gazetteer of the World, 1998. Chmn. N.Y.C. Early Childhood Commn., 1985-86; co-chmn. N.Y. State Sch. and Bus. Alliance, 1986-94; mem. Temp. State Commn. on N.Y.C. Sch. Governance, 1989-91; at-large mem. N.Y. State Bd. Regents, 1993—, chmn. Regents Telecom. Policy Commn., 1994-97, Regents Elem., Secondary and Continuing Edn. Com., 1995-98, Regents Higher Edn. and Profession com., 1999-2003, co-chmn. critical issues workgroup, 2004-05, chmn. quality com., 2005-06, policy integration and innovation com., 2006—; mem. N.Y. State Archives Partnership Trust, 1994—; chmn. vis. com. N.Y. State Mus., 1997—. Mem. Consortium Profl. Assns. (chmn. 1965-71), Assn. Am. Geographers (exec. officer 1964-65, del. Am. Coun. Learned Socs. 1964-66, mem. coun. 1966-70, chmn. com. coll. geography 1965-67, v.p. 1988-89, pres. 1989-90, past pres. 1990-91, chmn. com. on geog. curriculum internat. exch. 1990-96), Am. Geog. Soc. (coun. 1970-79). Home: 82 Taymil Rd New Rochelle NY 10804-2802 Personal E-mail: sbcohen1@optonline.net.

COHEN, SAUL G., chemist, educator; b. Boston, May 10, 1916; s. Barnet M. and Ida (Levine) C.; m. Doris E. Brewer, Nov. 27, 1941 (dec. July 1971); children— Jonathan Brewer, Elisabeth Jane; m. Anneliese F. Kissinger, June 1, 1973. AB summa cum laude, Harvard U., 1937, MA, 1938, PhD, 1940; ScD, Brandeis U., 1986. Research fellow Harvard, 1939-40, 41-43, instr., 1940-41; NRC fellow, lectr. U. Calif. at Los Angeles, 1943-44; research chemist Pitts. Plate Glass Co., 1944-45, Polaroid Corp., 1945-50, cons., 1950—98; with Brandeis U., 1950—, prof. chemistry, 1952—, Univ. prof., 1974-86, prof. emeritus, 1986—, chmn. Sch. Sci., 1950-55, dean faculty, 1955-59, chmn. dept. chemistry, 1959-66, 68-72; vis. prof. Havard Med. Sch., 1965, Hebrew U., Jerusalem, 1972. Contbr. articles on reaction mechanisms, free radicals, photochemistry, enzymology to profl. jours. Bd. overseers Harvard U., 1983-89; mem. Joint Com. on Appointments, 1984-89. Fulbright sr. scholar, 1958-59; Guggenheim fellow, 1958-59; Centennial medalist Harvard Grad. Sch. Arts and Scis., 1992. Fellow Am. Acad. Arts and Scis. (council), AAAS; mem. Am. Soc. Biol. Chemists, Am. Chem. Soc. (James F. Norris award 1972, trustee Northeastern sect. 1976-84), Chem. Soc. London, AAUP, Fedn. Am. Scientists, Phi Beta Kappa, Sigma Xi. Achievements include patents in polymers, hyroxylamines as photographic developers, heterocyclic silver solvents, dye-developers, diagnostic assays. Home: 90 Commonwealth Ave Apt 7 Boston MA 02116

COHEN, SELMA, retired librarian; b. NYC, Mar. 14, 1930; d. George and Rose (Cohen) Unger; m. Irwin H. Cohen, Nov. 19, 1950; children: Barbara Katzeff, Joel. Asst. bookkeeper acctg. dept. Severud, Perrone et al, NYC, 1970—75, Russell Reynolds Assoc., Inc., 1976—77, rsch. asst., 1977—2006, reference libr., 1985—2006; ret., 2006. Home: 3400 Paul Ave 10H Bronx NY 10468-1042

COHEN, SEYMOUR MARTIN, oncologist, hematologist, educator; b. NYC, Dec. 19, 1936; s. Harry and Rose (Ehrlich) C.; m. Carole J. Pomerantz, Aug. 16, 1976; children: Roger, Michael. BA, Bklyn. Coll., 1957; MD, U. Pitts., 1962. Diplomate Am. Bd. Internal Medicine and Subspecialty in Med. Oncology. Intern Montefiore Hosp., NYC, 1962-63, asst. resident in medicine, 1963-64; resident in medicine Mt. Sinai Hosp., NYC, 1964-65, Am. Cancer Soc. fellow in hematology, 1965-66, mem. staff, 1969—. Fellow in hematology L.I. Jewish Hosp., 1968-69; pvt. practice medicine specializing in med. oncology and hematology, N.Y.C., 1969—; clin. assoc. in medicine Mt. Sinai Med. Sch., 1969-73, sr. clin. asst. physician in medicine, 1969-73, asst. clin. prof. medicine, 1973-78, assoc. clin. prof. medicine, 1979—; bd. dirs. Cmty. Oncology Alliance, 2004-, Lung Cancer Alliance, 2001-04. Assoc. editor Cancer Investigation, 1993-2002; contbr. articles to profl. publs., research on malignant melanoma. Mem. exec. com. Jewish Am. Polit. Action Com., 1975-79, v.p., 1979-81, pres., 1981-83; bd. govs. State of Israel Bonds, 1979-92. Capt. M.C., USAF, 1966-68. Fellow A.C.P.; mem. AMA, Am. Soc. Clin. Oncology, Internat., Am. Socs., Hematology, NY Cancer Soc. (sec. 1983-86, v.p. 1987, pres. 1989), NY State Soc. Med. Oncologists and Hematologists (pres. 1989-92, bd. dirs. 1992—), NY Alliance of Physicians and Surgeons (bd. dirs. 1988-89, co-chmn. 1990—), NY County Med. Soc. Office: 1045 5th Ave New York NY 10028-0138 Office Phone: 212-249-9141. Business E-Mail: smonc@aol.com.

COHEN, SEYMOUR STANLEY, biochemist, educator; b. NYC, Apr. 30, 1917; s. Herman and Lena (Tanz) Cohen; m. Elaine Pear, July 12, 1940; children: Michael, Sara. BS, CCNY, 1936; PhD in Biol. Chemistry, Columbia U., 1941; Dr.h.c., U. Louvain, 1972, U. Kuopio, 1982. NRC fellow Rockefeller Inst., 1941—42; mem. faculty U. Pa., 1943—71, prof. biochemistry in pediat., 1954—71, Charles Hayden-Am. Cancer Soc. prof. biochemistry, 1957—71, Hartzell prof., chmn. dept. therapeutic research Sch. Medicine, 1963—71; Am. Cancer Soc. prof. microbiology U. Colo. Sch. Medicine, Denver, 1971—76; disting. prof., Am. Cancer Soc., prof. pharm. scis. SUNY, Stony Brook, 1976—85, prof. emeritus, 1985—. Chmn. coun. analysis and projection Am. Cancer Soc., 1972—74, adviser rsch., 1974—76; Guggenheim fellow Pasteur Inst., Paris, 1947—48; Jesup lectr. Columbia U., 1967; guest investigator Institut du Radium, Paris, 1967—68; vis. prof. Collège de France, Paris, 1970; vis. fellow Smithsonian Instn., 1973—74, 1986; vis. prof. U. Tokyo, 1974, Hadassah Med. Sch., 1974, Zuckerman lectr. tropical disease, 79; Guggenheim and Lady Davis fellow Faculty Agr., Israel, 1983; fellow Nat. Humanities Ctr., NC, 1982—83, NC, 1985; rsch. assoc. history of sci. Smithsonian Instn., 1986; presdl. scholar U. Calif., San Francisco, 1988; lectr. Academia Sinica, Taiwan, 1989; trustee Marine Biol. Lab., Woods Hole, Mass.; bd. sci. cons. Sloan-Kettering Inst. Author: Virus-Induced Enzymes, 1968, Introduction to the Polyamines, 1971, Guide to the Polyamines, 1998, Biography of Thomas Cooper, 1999; editl. bd.: Virology, 1954—59, Jour. Biol. Chemistry, 1959—65, Jour. Cell Physiology, 1966—71, Bacteriol. Revs, 1969—73, Hist., Philos. Life Scis., 1985. Named Fogarty scholar, NIH, 1973—74; recipient cert. for war research, OSRD, 1945, War Manpower Commn., 1945, War Research medal, Columbia U., 1943, Eli Lilly award and medal, Am. Soc. Bacteriology, Immunology and Pathology, 1951, 1st Mead Johnson award, Am. Acad. Pediatrics, 1952, medal, Soc. de Chimie Biologique France, 1964, Borden award, Am. Assn. Med. Colls., 1967, Passano award, 1974, Townsend Harris medal, CCNY Alumni Assn., 1978, Forster award, German Acad. Sci. and Letters, Mainz, 1978. Master: Am. Acad. Arts and Scis.; fellow: AAAS (Newcomb Cleveland award 1955), Am. Acad. of Microbiology; mem.: NAS, Am. Assn. Cancer Rsch. (bd. dirs. 1974—77), French Soc. Microbiology (hon.), Inst. Medicine, Soc. Gen. Physiologists (councilor, pres. 1967—88), Phi Beta Kappa. Home: 10 Carrot Hill Rd Woods Hole MA 02543-1206

COHEN, SHARON CLAIRE, history educator, consultant; b. West Palm Beach, Fla., Nov. 4, 1959; d. Sidney Alexander Cohen and Helene Held Cohen-Saffar; m. Elliot D. Rosen, Oct. 14, 1984; children: Lillian, Joseph. B in History, Washington U., St. Louis, 1981; M in East Asian Studies, George Washington U., DC, 1985. Cert. secondary history tchr. Md. Program specialist NEH, Washington, 1985—91; classroom tchr. Walter Johnson H.S., Bethesda, Md., 1993—2003, Springbrook H.S., Silver Springs, Md., 2003—. Sr. dir. East Asia Nat. Com. for Tchg. About Asia, College Park, Md., 2000—; tchg. cons. Coll. Bd., NYC, 2001—, AP world history test devel. com., 2002—06; curriculum writer World History for Us All, San Diego, 2002—06; exec. bd. World History Connected, 2002—. Author: AP World History Teaching Units, 2005, AP World History Teacher's Guide, 2007; editor: Latin America and Africa in World History, 2007. Named Montgomery County Tchr. of Yr., Montgomery County Hist. Soc., 1999. Mem.: Nat. Coun. for the Social Studies, Am. Hist. Assn. (chair tchg. prize com. 2004—07), World History Assn. (program com. 2004, 2005). Avocations: gardening, cooking. Home: 7013 Poplar Ave Takoma Park MD 20912 Office: Springbrook HS 201 Valley Brook Dr Silver Spring MD 20904

COHEN, SHELDON, psychologist, psychology professor; b. Detroit, Oct. 11, 1947; PhB, Monteith Coll., Wayne State U., 1969; PhD, NYU, 1973. Asst. prof., dept. psychology U. Oreg., 1973—82; prof., dept. psychology Carnegie Mellon U., Pitts., 1982—, Robert E. Doherty prof. psychology, 2003—; co-dir. U. Pitts.-Carnegie Mellon U. Brain, Behavior & Immunity Ctr., 1989—; adj. prof. pathology & psychiatry U. Pitts. Sch. Medicine, 1990, mem. Pitts. Cancer Inst., 1992—; interim dir. Pitts. (Pa.) Cancer Inst., 1992—93. Contbr. articles, chapters to books, scientific papers; mem. editorial bd. scientific journals. Named one of 20 psychologists with greatest impact on the field, Inst. Scientific Info., 1996, world's most cited authors, 2003; recipient Patricia R. Barchas award, Am. Psychosomatic Soc., 2006, Sr. Scientist award, NIMH, 1997—2002, Rsch. Scientist Devel. awards, 1987—97. Fellow: Soc. Behavioral Medicine, Acad. Behavioral Medicine Rsch. (exec. coun. 1989—2002), Am. Psychological Soc., APA (James McKeen Cattell fellow award 2002—03, Disting. Scientific Contbn. award 2004, Disting. Scientist Lectr. 1997); mem.: Soc. Exptl. Social Psychology, Inst. Medicine. Office: Dept Psychology Carnegie Mellon U 5000 Forbes Ave Baker Hall Rm 335-D Pittsburgh PA 15213 Office Phone: 412-268-2336, 412-268-2781. E-mail: scohen@cmu.edu.

COHEN, SHELDON GILBERT, physician, historian, immunologist; b. Pittston, Pa., Sept. 21, 1918; s. Samuel H. and Dorthy (Goldberg) C. Grad., Wyo. Sem., 1936; student, Syracuse U., 1936-37; BA, Ohio State U., 1940; MD, NYU, 1943; DSc (hon.), Wilkes U., 1976. Diplomate Am. Bd. Allergy and Immunology. Intern Bellevue Hosp., NYC, 1944; resident internal medicine Ft. Howard VA Hosp., Balt., 1947-48; resident in allergy VA Hosp., Aspinwall, Pa., 1948-49, U. Pitts. Med. Ctr., 1948-49; rsch. fellow U. Pitts. Sch. Medicine, 1949-50; rsch. assoc. U. Pitts., 1950-51; attending physician Allergy Clinic, Falk Clinics, 1950-51; chief of allergy Mercy Hosp., Wilkes-Barre, 1951-72; attending physician in allergy VA Hosp., Wilkes-Barre, 1951-60, cons. in internal medicine and rsch., 1960-72; assoc. prof. biol. rsch. Wilkes U., Wilkes-Barre, 1952-62, prof. biol. rsch., 1962-68, prof. exptl. biology, 1968-72, adj. prof. immunology, 1991—; cons. extramural programs Nat. Inst. Allergy and Infectious Diseases, 1972-73, chief allergy and immunology br., 1973-76, dir. immunology, allergic and immunologic diseases program, 1977-88, sci. advisor div. of intramural rsch. office of dir., 1988—; bd. sci. advisors Allergy and Immunology Inst. of Internat. Life Scis. Inst., 1989-97; sr. staff physician NIAID-NIH Clin. Ctr., 1974—; 21. Adj. prof. medicine Northwestern U., 1988-98; scholar Nat. Libr. Medicine, 1988-99, vis. scholar history of medicine, 1999--; regional med. cons. Children's Asthma Research Inst. and Hosp., Denver, 1969-72; mem. medico adv. bd. CARE, 1977-89; cons. to Ministry Public Health, State of Kuwait, 1981-83; mem. expert adv. panel on immunology WHO, Geneva, Switzerland, 1979-2004, dir. WHO Collaborating Ctr. for Allergy, 1985-89; bd. dirs. Asthma and Allergy Found. Am., 1969-81, mem. com. public edn., 1976-81; bd. dirs. Lupus Found. Am., 1978-85, exec. v.p., 1981-85, mem. med. council, 1978-93; mem. aeroallergens com. NRC, 1976-80. Author: Excerpts from Classics in Allergy, 2d edit., 1992, Asthma Among the Famous, 1995—2002, A Journey Through the World of Allergy, 2007; mem. editl. bd. Jour. Devel. and Comparative Immunology, 1976—81, Allergy Proc., 1983—93; editor: Hist. Notes, Allergy and Asthma Proc., 1988—93, Allergy Archives, Jour. Allergy and Clin. Immunology, 2001—; cons. editor Am. Jour. Rhinology, 1986—93; contbr. articles to profl. jours., chapters to books. Trustee Marywood Coll., Scranton, Pa., 1983-89; bd. govs. adv. coun. Wilkes U., Wilkes-Barre, 1991-92. Capt. M.C., USAF, 1944-46. Recipient Disting. Svc. award Wyo. Sem., 1978, Asthma and Allergy Found. Am., 1981, Clemens von Pirquet award Georgetown U., 1981, NIH Centennial award, Terri Gottheif Lupus Rsch. Inst., 1987, NYU Med. Alumni Achievement award in health sci., 1988, Achievement award Internat. Assn. Allergology and Clin. Immunology, 1988, Spl. Recognition award Am. Acad Allergy and Immunology, 1989, 2002, recognition citation ILSI Allergy and Immunology Inst., 1992. Fellow: Am. Acad. Allergy (chmn. rsch. coun. 1963—66, historian 1963—69, v.p. 1979—80, Disting. Svc. award 1971), ACP, Coll. Physicians Phila., Am. Coll. Allergists (hon.); mem.: Washington Soc. History of Medicine (v.p. 1993—94, pres. 1994—96), Am. Assn. History of Medicine, Am. Fedn. Clin. Rsch., Collegium Internat. Allergolicum, Soc. Exptl. Biology and Medicine, Am. Coll. Rheumatology, Clin. Immunology Soc., Assn. Am. Physicians, Am. Assn. Immunologists, Cosmos Club, Alpha Omega Alpha (NYU alumni), Sigma Xi. Home: 5500 Friendship Blvd Apt 1927N Chevy Chase MD 20815-7272 Office: Nat Libr Medicine Bldg 38 HMD Room 1 E21 Bethesda MD 20892 also: NIH NIAID 6700 B Rockledge Dr Rm 1105 Bethesda MD 20892-7600 Office Phone: 301-496-0705. Business E-Mail: scohen@niaid.nih.gov.

COHEN, SHELDON IRWIN, lawyer; b. Newark, July 25, 1937; BS in Ceramic Engring., Rutgers U., 1959, AB in Humanities, 1959; LLB, Georgetown U., 1964. Bar: Va. 1964, D.C. 1964, U.S. Ct. Appeals (D.C. and 4th cirs.) 1964, U.S. Supreme Ct. 1967. Assoc. Chapman, Disalle & Friedman, Washington, 1964-70; pvt. practice law Washington, Arlington, Va., 1970—. Author: Security Clearances and the Protection of National Security Information, Law and Procedure, 2000. Vice chmn. Arlington Dem. Com., 1968-70; mem. Va. Dem. Cen. Com., 1969-70. Capt. USAR, 1959-67. Mem. ABA (chmn. govt. pers. com. 1986-89, chmn. nat. security interests com. 1990-95), D.C. Bar Assn. (chmn. civil svc. law com. 1984-86), Cosmos Club. Democrat. Office: 2009 14th St N Ste 708 Arlington VA 22201-2514 Home Phone: 703-716-1277; Office Phone: 703-522-1200. E-mail: sicohen@sheldoncohen.com.

COHEN, SHELDON STANLEY, lawyer; b. Washington, June 28, 1927; s. Herman and Pearl (Jaffe) C.; m. Faye Fram, Feb. 21, 1951; children: Melinda Ann Cohen Goetzl, Laura Eve Cohen Apelbaum, Jonathan Adam, Sharon Ruevena Cohen Liebman. AB with spl. honors, George Washington U., 1950, JD with highest honors (Charles W. Dorsey scholar), 1952; DLit (hon.), Lincoln Coll.; LLD (hon.), George Washington U., 2003. Bar: D.C. 1952, U.S. Dist. Ct. D.C. 1952, U.S. Ct. Appeals (D.C. cir.) 1952, U.S. Claims Ct. 1956, U.S. Tax Ct., 1956, U.S. Supreme Ct. 1956, U.S. Ct. Appeals (fed. cir.) 1986; CPA, Md. Acct., 1950-52; legis. atty. Office Chief Counsel, IRS, Dept. Treasury, 1952-56, chief counsel, 1963-65, commr. internal revenue, 1965-69; assoc. Paul, Weiss, Rifkind, Wharton & Garrison, 1956-60; ptnr. Arnold, Fortas & Porter, Washington, 1960-63, Cohen & Uretz, Washington, 1969-85, Morgan, Lewis & Bockius, Washington, 1985—2005; prof. George Washington U. Sch. Pub. Policy and Pub. Adminstrn., 2005—; counsel Farr, Miller & Washington; prof. George Wash. Law Sch., 2006—. Lectr. Howard U. Law sch., 1957-58; professorial lectr. George Washington U. Law Sch., 1958-81, 2005—; adj. prof. U. Miami Law Sch., Fla., 1974-85; adv. com. Inst. Estate Planning, U. Miami Law Ctr., 1969-86; chmn. exec. compensation com. U.S. Pay Bd., 1971-72; cons. Commn. for Revision of Tax Laws, 1969-71; cons. Filer Commn. on Pvt. Philanthropy and Pub. Needs, 1975-76; mem. Commn. on Founds. and Pvt. Philanthropy, 1969-70; adv. group to commr. IRS, 1969-70; chmn. steering com. Adminstrv. Conf. U.S., 1974-84; mem. exec. com. Washington Lawyer's Com. for Civil Rights Under Law, 1975—, co-chmn., 1988-90; mem. Jimmy Carter Tax Task Force, 1976; advisor on tax and econs. Walter F. Mondale Campaign, 1984, Albert Gore campaign, 2000, John Kerry campaign, 2004; cons. UN Devel. Program on Tax Adminstrn., 1990-96; cons. panel to controller gen. U.S. Gen. Acctg. Office, 1982-2000, chmn. Audit Adv. Com, 1995—; pres. Am.-Israel Tax Found., 1969-80; mem. coun. Sch. Govt. and Bus. Adminstrn. George Washington U., 1969-79, commn. on governance, 1970, trustee, 1980-2002, chmn. bd. of trustees, 2000-02, chmn. emeritus, 2003; pres. Law Assn., 1978-79; rapporteur CIAT Conf. in Can., 1987; adv. bd. The Lincoln Legals, 1988—; v.p. presdl. Inaugural Found., 1992-93; bd. dirs. Supreme Ct. Hist. Soc., treas. 1995—; adv. bd. Sch. Public Affairs & Public Policy, Geo. Washington U., 2004—. Editorial and bus. sec.: George Washington U. Law Rev, 1952; case notes editor, 1951-52; mem. editl. bd. Nat. Law Jour., 1978—85, Corporate Taxation. Sec., tax counsel Ctr. for Nat. Policy, 1981—2000; mem. adv. com. D.C. Ct. Appeals Admission Com.; adviser Lincoln Bicentennial Commn., 2003—; counsel Project Judaica Found., Inc., 1980—; bd. regents Omar N. Bradley Found., U.S. Army Hist. Collection, 1970—73; v.p. Am. Jewish Hist. Soc., 1980—92, chmn., 1993—2000, hon. chair, 2001—; v.p. trustees Walter Mondale;s Blind Trust, 1976—81; treas. Nat. Jewish Dem. Coun., 1991—; spl. tax counsel Dem. Nat. Com., 1969—72, gen. counsel, 1972—77; v.p. Presdl. Inaugural Found., 1992—93; past pres. Jewish Social Service Agy., Washington; chmn. endowment steering com. Coun. Jewish Fedns., 1991—2000, Am. Jewish Hist. Soc., 1993—; past v.p. Jewish Cmty. Ctr. Greater Washington; bd. overseers Jewish Theol. Sem. Am., 1972—; trustee United Jewish Endowment Fund, 1980—2002, trustee emeritus, 2003—; bd. dirs., past v.p. Jewish Cmty. Found.; trustee B'nai B'rith Found. of U.S.; bd. dirs. Adas Israel Congregation, Jewish Welfare Bd., United Synagogues Am., Common Cause, Nat. Council for a Responsible Firearms Policy, Inc., Nat. Found. for Jewish Culture, 1968-72, Am. Jewish Joint Distbn. Com., United Jewish Appeal Found. of D.C., 1969—2002, Supreme Ct. Hist. Soc., 1993—, treas., 1997—; bd. dirs., chmn. devel. com. Cmty. Found. Greater Washington, 1982—90; bd. dirs. Am. Assocs. Ben-Gurion U. of the Negev, Israel, v.p., 1988—90; bd. dirs. Gomez Found. for Mill House, 1982—95, Ulysses S. Grant Assn., 1976—, v.p., 1994—; bd. dirs. B'nai B'rith, 1979—85. With USNR, 1945—46. Recipient Young Person Under 40 in Govt. award, Downtown DC Jr. C. of C., 1964, Alumni Achievement award George Washington U., 1965, Arthur Flemming award, 1966, Alexander Hamilton award U.S. Treasury Dept., 1969, Joseph Ottenstein Cmty. Svc. award Jewish Social Agy., 1976. Ourisman award for comm. svc. 1999. Mem. Nat. Acad. Pub. Adminstrn. (chmn. com. on energy 1978-79, trustee, sec. 1983-90, com. on ethics, chair study Holocaust Mus. 1999), ABA (chmn. spl. com. on retirement benefits legis. tax csect. 1972-73), Fed. Bar Assn. (coun. tax sect.), DC Bar Assn. (bd. dirs. 1969-72), DC Bar (Unified) (bd. govs. 1972-75, tax counsel 1972-, chair Iolta Study), Am. Coll. Tax Counsel, Am. Law Inst., J. Edgar Murdock Am. Inn of Ct. (counselor 1988—), DC Inst. CPAs (hon.), Inter-Am. Ctr. for Tax Adminstrs. (pres. 1967-68), Am.-Israel C. of C. (chmn. tax com.), Cosmos Club (chmn. admissions com. 2005-07), Tournament Players Assn., Golf Avenel Club, Masons. Home: 5518 Trent St Bethesda MD 20815-5512 Office: Farr Miller & Washington 1020 19th St NW Washington DC 20035 Home Phone: 301-654-7473; Office Phone: 202-530-5609. Business E-Mail: sscohen@gwu.edu, sscohen@farrmiller.com.

COHEN, SIDNEY MAXIMILIAN, neurologist; b. Morristown, NJ, May 26, 1919; s. Abraham Isaac and Shaina Rachel C.; m. Lea Ostrojinsky, Feb. 26, 1955; children: Ron, Navah, Oren. BS, Columbia U., NYC, 1939, DMS, 1952; MD, L.I. Med. Coll., Bklyn., 1943. Diplomate Am. Bd. Psychiatry and Neurology. Rotating intern Cumberland Hosp., Bklyn., 1943, asst. resident medicine, 1944; resident in neurology Mt. Sinai Hosp., NYC, 1947; asst. resident Neurol. Inst., NYC, 1948; fellow dept. neurology Columbia U., NYC, 1949-54; attending neurologist Roosevelt/St. Luke's Hosp., NYC, 1952-91; sr. attending neurologist Roosevelt St. Luke's Hosp., 1991—; assoc. neurologist Neurol. Inst., 1952—. Contbr. articles to profl. jours. Capt. M.C., U.S. Army, 1944-46. Recipient Scroll of Honor United Jewish Appeal, 1971. Fellow Am. Acad. Neurology; mem. Am. Psychiat. Assn., Assn. for Rsch. Nervous & Mental Diseases. Avocations: art, coin and antique collecting, ballet, opera, theater. Office: 1213 Park Ave New York NY 10128-1703 Home Phone: 212-876-2522; Office Phone: 212-876-2522.

COHEN, STANLEY, pathologist, educator; b. NYC, June 4, 1937; s. Herman Joseph and Eva (Lapidus) C.; m. Marion Doris Cantor, Aug. 30, 1959; children: Laurie Ellen, Ronald Nelson, Kenneth Stuart. AB, Columbia U., 1957, MD, 1961. Diplomate Am. Bd. Pathology (mem. immunopathology com.). Intern Albert Einstein Med. Ctr., Bronx, NY, 1961-62; resident Mass. Gen. Hosp., 1962-64; fellow NYU Med. Ctr., 1964-66; prof. pathology SUNY, Buffalo, 1968-74; acting dir. Ctr. for Immunology, Buffalo, 1973-74; prof. pathology U. Conn. Health Ctr., Farmington, 1974-87, assoc. chmn., 1976-80; prof., chmn. bd. Hahnemann U., Phila., 1987-94; prof., chmn. U. Medicine Dentistry-N.J. Med. Ctr., 1994—. Mem. study sect. allergy and immunology, 1981-85; chair study sect. tumor immunology ahd therapy TRDRP, 1992-94; co-chmn. 3d, 4th and 5th Internat. Lymphokine Workshops, 1982, 84, Congress on Cytokines, 1987, UCLA colloquium: molecular pathways of cytokines, 1990—, Keystone Symposium, 1992. Author: Mechanisms of Cell-Mediated Immunity, 1974, Mechanisms of Tumor Immunity, 1976, Mechanisms of Immunopathology, 1978, Biology of the Lymphokines, 1979, Interleukins, Lymphokines and Cytokines, 1983, Molecular Basis of Lymphokine Action, 1987, Role of Lymphokines in the Immune Response, 1989; assoc. editor-in-chief Clin. Immunology and Immunopathology; mem. editorial bds. 8 profl. jours.; contbr. more than 195 articles to profl. jours. Served to capt. U.S. Army, 1966-68. Recipient Kinne award, 1954, Borden award, 1961, Parke-Davis award in Exptl. Pathology, 1977, Outstanding Investigator award Nat. Cancer, Inst., 1986; Witobsky Meml. lectr., 1995. Mem.: Pluto Soc., Am. Soc. Exptl. Biology (fin. com. 2001—), Am. Soc. Investigative Pathology (sec.-treas. 2001—07, v.p. 2007—), Clin. Immunol. Soc. (councilor), Am. Assn. Immunologists, Am. Assn. Pathologists. Home: 79 Ettl Cir Princeton NJ 08540-2334 Office: UMDNJ Med Sch Newark NJ 07103 Business E-Mail: cohenst@umdmj.edu.

COHEN, STANLEY, retired biochemistry educator; b. Bklyn., Nov. 17, 1922; s. Louis and Fannie (Feitel) C.; m. Olivia Larson, 1951 (div.); children: Burt Bishop, Kenneth Larson, Cary; m. Jan Elizabeth Jordan, 1981. BA, Bklyn. Coll., 1943; MA, Oberlin Coll., 1945, PhD, 1989; PhD in Biochemistry, U. Mich., 1948; PhD, U. Chgo., 1985, Washington U., 1993. Instr. dept. biochemistry and pediatrics U. Colo., Denver, 1948-52; Am. Cancer Soc. fellow in radiology Washington U., St. Louis, 1952-53, assoc. prof. dept. zoology, 1953-59; asst. prof. biochemistry, sch. medicine Vanderbilt U., Nashville, 1959-62, assoc. prof., 1962-67, prof. biochemistry, 1967-86, disting. prof., 1986-2000, disting. prof. emeritus, 2000—. Charles B. Smith vis. rsch. prof. Sloan Kettering, 1984; Feodor Lynen lectr. U. Miami, 1986, Steenbock lectr. U. Wis., 1986. Mem. editorial bd. Abstracts of Human Developmental Biology, Jour. of Cellular Physiology. Cons. Minority Rsch. Ctr. for Excellence. Recipient Rsch. Career Devel. award NIH, 1959-69, William Thomson Wakeman award Nat. Paraplegia Found., Earl Sutherland Research Prize Vanderbilt U., 1977, Albion O. Bernstein MD award Med. Soc. State N.Y., 1978, H.P. Robertson Meml. award Nat. Acad. Sci., 1981, Lewis S. Rosentiel award Brandeis U., 1982, Alfred P. Sloan award Gen. Motors Cancer Research Found., 1982, Louisa Gross Horwitz prize Columbia U., 1983, Disting. Achievement award UCLA Lab. Biomed. and Environ. Scis., 1983, Lila Gruber Meml. Cancer Research award Am. Acad. Dermatology, 1983, Bertner award MD Anderson Hosp. U. Tex., 1983, Gairdner Found. Internat. award, 1985, Fred Conrad Koch award Endocrine Soc., 1986, Nat. Medal Sci., 1986, 89, Albert and Mary Lasker Found. Basic Med. Research award, 1986, Nobel prize in physiology or medicine, 1986, Tennessean of Yr. award Tenn. Sports Hall of Fame, 1987, Franklin Medal, 1987, Albert A. Michaelson award Mus. Sci. and Industry, 1987. Fellow Jewish Acad. Arts and Sci.; mem. Nat. Acad. Sci., Am. Soc. Biol. Chemists, Am. Chem. Soc., AAAS, Internat. Inst. Embryology, Internat. Acad. Sci. (hon. internat. coun. for sci. devel.).

COHEN, STANLEY, commercial real estate developer; b. Cin., Jan. 4, 1929; s. Robert Lieb and Celia (Gordon) C.; m. Rae A. Cohen, Aug. 28, 1960; children: Gordon Alan, Gary Louis, Sharon Diann. BA, U. Cin., 1950. Promotion assoc. Ziv TV Programs, Inc., Cin., 1953-57; program dir. WDSU-TV, New Orleans, 1957-64; pres. Royal Street Devel. Co., Inc., Newport Beach, Calif., 1965-73, Mission Hills Ranch, Inc., Newport Beach, 1969-73; vice chair Greater Park City Co., Inc., Park City, Utah, 1971-74; sr. v.p. E.M. Warburg, Pincus & Co., Inc., Newport Beach, 1973-75; mng. ptnr. Stanley Cohen/Crocker/Pacific Assocs., Newport Beach, 1978-85, Shoreline Sq. Assocs., Newport Beach, 1985-94; owner Stanley Cohen & Assocs., Costa Mesa, Calif., 1975—. Bd. dirs. Flowline, Inc., Los Alamitos, Calif.; mem. exec. com. The Olson Co., Seal Beach, Calif., 1995—; guest lectr. UCLA Grad. Sch. Bus., U. So. Calif. Grad. Sch. Bus., U. Calif. San Diego Grad Sch. Bus. Contbr. articles to L.A. Times, Orange County Register. Bd. dirs. Calif. State U. Found., Long Beach, 1987-95; trustee St. Mary Med. Ctr., Long Beach, 1984-90; chmn. ednl. resources adv. com. Newport-Mesa Unified Sch. Dist., Newport Beach, 1982-83. Recipient Disting. Achievement award U. Cin., 1993, Disting. Bus. and the Arts award Pub. Corp. for the Arts, Long Beach, 1989, Outstanding Achievement award Long Beach Area C. of C., 1983, Outstanding Leadership award Newport Harbor Coun. PTA Pres., 1983, Outstanding Leadership award Newport-Mesa Unified Sch. Dist. Bd. Edn., 1983. Mem. Nat. Assn. TV Program Execs. (hon. life; founding pres. 1963-65). Lincoln Club of Orange County. Home: 1501 Antigua Way Newport Beach CA 92660-4917 Office: Stanley Cohen and Assocs 2183 Fairview Rd Ste 219 Costa Mesa CA 92627-5674

COHEN, STANLEY NORMAN, geneticist, educator; b. Perth Amboy, NJ, Feb 17, 1935; s. Bernard and Ida (Stolz) Cohen; m. Joanna Lucy Wolter, June 27, 1961; children: Anne, Geoffrey. BA, Rutgers U., 1956, ScD (hon.), 1994; MD, U. Pa., 1960, ScD (hon.), 1995. Intern Mt. Sinai Hosp., NYC, 1960-61; resident Univ. Hosp., Ann Arbor, Mich., 1961-62; clin. assoc. arthritis and rheumatism br. Nat. Inst. Arthritis and Metabolic Diseases, Bethesda, Md., 1962-64; sr resident in medicine Duke U. Hosp., Durham, NC, 1964-65; Am. Cancer Soc. postdoctoral rsch. fellow Albert Einstein Coll. Medicine, Bronx, 1965-67, asst. prof. devel. biology and cancer, 1967-68; mem. faculty Stanford (Calif.) U., 1968—, prof. medicine, 1975—, prof. genetics, 1977—, chmn. dept. genetics, 1978-86, K.-T Li Prof., 1993—. Mem. com. recombinant DNA molecules NAS-NRC, 1974; mem. com. on genetic experimentation Internat. Coun. Sci. Unions, 1977—96. Mem. editl. bd. Jour. Bacteriology, 1973—79, Molecular Microbiology, 1986—2005, Procs. Nat. Acad. Sci., 1996—, Current Opinion in Microbiology, 1997—. Trustee U. Pa., 1997—2002. With USPHS, 1962—64. Named to Nat. Inventors Hall of Fame, 2001; recipient Burroughs Wellcome Scholar award, 1970, Mattia award, Roche Inst. Molecular Biology, 1977, Albert Lasker basic med. rsch. award, 1980, Wolf prize, 1981, Marvin J. Johnson award, 1981, Disting. Grad. award, U. Pa. Sch. Medicine, 1986, Disting. Svc. award, Miami Winter Symposium, 1986, Nat. Biotech award, 1989, de la Vie prize, LVMH Inst., 1988, Nat. Medal Sci., 1988, City of Medicine award, 1988, Nat. Medal of Tech., 1989, Spl. award, Am. Chem. Soc., 1999, Lemelson MIT Prize, MIT, 1996, Albany Med. Ctr. prize in medicine and biomedical rsch., 2004, The Shaw prize in Life Sci. and Medicine, 2004, Innovation Biosci. award, The Economist, 2005, John Stearns Medicine Lifetime Achievement award, NY Acad. Medicine, 2007; Guggenheim fellow, 1975, faculty scholar, Josiah Macy, Jr., 1975—76. Fellow: AAAS, Am. Acad. Microbiology; mem.: NAS (chmn. genetics sect. 1988—91), Am. Philos. Soc., Inst. Medicine, Assn. Am. Physicians, Am. Soc. Clin. Investigation, Am. Soc. Pharmacology and Exptl. Therapeutics, Am. Soc. Microbiology (Cetus award 1988), Genetics Soc. Am., Am. Soc. Biol. Chemists, Am. Philos. Soc., Alpha Omega Alpha, Phi Beta Kappa, Sigma Xi. Achievements include obtaining, with Herbert Boyer, first patent in the field of recombinant deoxyribonucleic acid (DNA), 1980. Office: Stanford U Sch Med Dept Genetics Rm M-322 Stanford CA 94305

COHEN, STEPHEN FRAND, political scientist, writer, historian, educator, commentator; b. Indpls., Nov. 25, 1938; s. Marvin Stafford and Ruth (Frand) C.; m. Katrina vanden Heuvel; children: Andrew, Alexandra, Nicola. BS, Ind. U., 1960, MA, 1962; PhD, Columbia U., 1969; cert., Russian Inst., 1969. Instr. Columbia U., NYC, 1965-68; asst. prof. politics Princeton U., NJ, 1968-73, assoc. prof., 1973-80, prof., 1980-98, prof. emeritus, 1998—; dir. Russian studies Princeton (N.J.) U., 1973-80, 88-94; prof. Russian studies and History NYU, 1998—. Cons. on Russia, CBS news TV commentator, 1989-2006; corr., chief cons. PBS WNET films on Russia, 1994-2001; adv. coun. U.S. Acad. Scis., Washington, 1979-82. Author: Bukharin and the Bolshevik Revolution, 1973 (Nat. Book Award nominee 1974, Bukharin prize 1989), Rethinking the Soviet Experience, 1985, Sovieticus: American Perceptions and Soviet Realities, 1985 (Page One award 1985), Failed Crusade: America and the Tragedy of Post-Communist Russia, 2000, 2d edit., 2001, The Question of Questions: Why did the Soviet Union End? (in Russian), 2007; editor: (with Robert C. Tucker) The Great Purge Trial, 1965, (with Rabinowitch and Sharlet) The Soviet Union Since Stalin, 1980, An End to Silence, 1982, (with Katrina vanden Heuvel) Voices of Glasnost: Interviews with Gorbachev's Reformers, 1989; mem. editl. bd. Slavic Rev., 1977-82, Post-Soviet Affairs, 1992-2002; assoc. editor World Politics, 1972-88; columnist The Nation Mag., 1982-87; contbg. editor, 1994-; mem. editl. coun. Svobodnaya Mysl (Moscow), 2004-. Adv. bd. Guggenheim Meml. Found., 2003-. Recipient Page One award Column Writing, 1985, Ind. U. Disting. Alumn award, 1998, Columbia U. Harriman Inst. Alumnus of Yr. award, 2002; fellow Am. Coun. Learned Socs., 1971, 72-73; fellow John Simon Guggenheim Found., 1976-77, 88-89, Rockefeller Found., 1980-81; NEH fellow, 1985-86; Fulbright-Hays fellow, 1988-89. Mem. Coun. Fgn. Relations, Am. Polit. Sci. Assn., Am. Hist. Assn., Am. Assn. for Advancement Slavic Studies. Home: 340 Riverside Dr Apt 8B New York NY 10025-3436 Office Phone: 212-998-8289. Personal E-mail: sfc1@nyu.edu.

COHEN, S(TEPHEN) MARSHALL, philosophy educator; b. NYC, Sept. 27, 1929; s. Harry and Fanny (Marshall) C.; m. Margaret Dennes, Feb. 15, 1964; children: Matthew, Megan. BA, Dartmouth Coll., Hanover, NH, 1951; MA, Harvard U., 1953, Oxford U., 1977. Jr. fellow, Soc. of Fellows Harvard U., Cambridge, Mass., 1955-58, asst. prof. philosophy and gen. edn., 1958-62; asst. prof. U. Chgo., 1962-64, assoc. prof., 1964-67, acting chair Coll. Philosophy, 1965-66; assoc. prof. Rockefeller U., NYC, 1967-70; prof. philosophy Richmond Coll. (now Coll. of S.I.), 1970-83; exec. officer program in philosophy Grad. Ctr. CUNY, 1975-83; prof. philosophy and law U. So. Calif., LA, 1983—97, dean divsn. humanities, 1983-94, interim dean Coll. Letters, Arts and Sci., 1993-94, Univ. prof. philosophy and law emeritus, 1998—, dean emeritus Coll. Letters, Arts and Sci., 1998—. Lectr. Lowell Inst., Boston, 1957-58; vis. fellow All Souls Coll., Oxford, Eng., 1976-77; mem. Inst. for Advanced Study, Princeton, N.J., 1981-82. Editor: The Philosophy of John Stuart Mill, 1961, Philosophy and Public Affairs, 1970-99, Philosophy and Society series, 1977-83, Ethical, Legal and Political Philosophy series, 1983-99; co-editor: Film Theory and Criticism, 1974, 79, 85, 92, 98, 2004, War and Moral Responsibility, 1974, The Rights and Wrongs of Abortion, 1974, Equality and Preferential Treatment, 1977, Marx, Justice and History, 1980, Medicine and Moral Philosophy, 1982, What Is Dance?, 1983, International Ethics, 1985, Punishment, 1995. Rockefeller Found. humanities fellow, 1977, Guggenheim fellow, 1976-77. Mem. Am. Philos. Assn., Am. Coun. Learned Socs. (bd. dirs. 1987-91, 93-2004), Coun. on Internat. Ednl. Exch. (bd. dirs. 1991-94). Democrat. Jewish. Office: U So Calif Law Sch Los Angeles CA 90089-0071 Home Phone: 310-276-4399; Office Phone: 213-740-4794. Business E-Mail: mcohen@law.usc.edu.

COHEN, STEVE (STEPHEN IRA COHEN), congressman, former state legislator; b. Memphis, May 24, 1949; s. Morris David and Genevieve (Goldsand) C. BA, Vanderbilt U., 1971; JD, U. Memphis, 1973. Bar: Tenn. 1974. Sole practice, 1974-75; legal adv. Memphis Police Dept., 1975-78; mem. Shelby County Commn., 1978-80; sole practice Memphis, 1978—; mem. Tenn. State Senate from Dist. 30, 1983—2007, dep. spkr., 2000—07, chair, Senate State & Local Govt. Comm., 1991, mem., Senate Judiciary, Transp. & Fiscal Review Comm.; mem. US Congress from 9th Tenn. dist., 2007—, mem. judiciary com., transp. & infrastructure com. Interim judge Gen. Sessions Ct., 1980; v.p. Tenn. Constnl. Conv., 1977; del. Democratic Nat. Conv., 1980, 92; chair lottery info. and recommendation com.; mem. coun. state govts. exec. com., 2002, exec. com. Nat. Conf. State Legislators. Trustee Memphis Coll. Art, 2000, bd. trustees, 1988-2002; mem. Redbirds Found., Memphis Shelby County Center City Commn, Memphis Zoological Soc., 1998-, (bd. dirs. 1988-). Recipient Public Leadership award, Tenn. Human Rights Campaign, 2002, Legislator of the Year, Boys & Girls Clubs of Tenn., 2003, Leadership Award, Gov.'s Awards in the Arts. Mem. Memphis Bar Assn., Shelby County Charter Commn. Democrat. Jewish. Office: 1004 Longworth House Office Bldg Washington DC 20515 also: Clifford Davis Fed Bldg Ste 369 167 N Main St Memphis TN 38103*

COHEN, STEVEN A., investment company executive; b. 1956; m. Alexandra Cohen; 7 children. BS in Econ., U. Penn. Trader Gruntal & Co., 1978—92; founder, chmn. SAC Capital Advisors, 1992—. Bd. mem. Michael J. Fox Found.; co-founder Steven and Alexandra Cohen Found.; mem. painting & sculpture com. Mus. Modern Art. Named one of top 200 collectors, ARTnews Mag., 2004, Richest Americans, Forbes, 2003—, World's Richest People, 2004—, The World's Most Influential People, TIME mag., 2007. Avocation: collector of impressionism, modern & contemporary art. Office: SAC Capital Advisors 72 Cummings Pt Rd Stamford CT 06902 Office Phone: 203-614-2000.*

COHEN, STEVEN PAUL, anesthesiologist, researcher; b. Phila., Dec. 9, 1963; s. Allen Theodore Cohen and Harriet Ruth Hershfeld; m. Eun-Kyung Im, July 7, 2001; children: Berklee Kordell, Zared Orion. BA, SUNY, Stony Brook, 1985; MD, Mt. Sinai U., 1989. Diplomate Am. Bd. Anesthesiology. Intern Beth Israel Med. Ctr., NYC, 1990—93; resident in anesthesia Presbyn. Hosp. Columbia U., NYC, 1993; commd. 2d. lt. U. S. Army, 1993; asst. chief anesthesia & operavice svc. 121st Gen. Hosp., Seoul, Republic of Korea, 1993—95; chief anesthesia & operative svc. Wverzburg (Germany) MEDDAC, 1995—96, 121st Gen. Hosp., Seoul, Republic of Korea, 1996—99; fellow in pain mgmt. Mass. Gen. Hosp./Harvard Med. Sch., Boston, 1999—2000; dir. acute pain svc. Walter Reed Army Med. Ctr., Washington, 2000—; dir. inpatient pain svcs. NYU Med. Ctr., NYC, 2002—04; assoc. prof. Divsn. Pain Medicine Sch. Medicine Johns Hopkins U., Balt., 2004—. Assoc. prof. Walter Reed Army Med. Ctr., Washington, 2004—. Contbr. articles to profl. jours and newspapers. Col. USAR. Recipient 1st pl., U.S. Army Photography Contest, 1998, 2d. pl., U.S. Army Forces Photography Contest, 1998, 2d ranked in black belt form N.Y./N.J. region, Karate Illustrated Mag., 1984. Mem.: N.Y. Acad. Scis., Am. Soc. Anesthesiologist, Am. Pain Soc. Avocations: martial arts, photography, writing, travel. Office: Johns Hopkins Divsn Pain Management 550 N Broadway Ste 301 Baltimore MD 21205 Office Phone: 410-955-1818. Business E-Mail: scohen40@jhmi.edu.

COHEN, STUART F., investment company executive; BS in Quantitative Bus. Analysis, Ariz. State U. Sr. positions in US sales and mktg. divsn., IBM Personal Computer Co. and Networking Divsn. IBM; v.p. worldwide mktg., corp. officer InFocus Corp.; v.p. mktg. and bus. devel. RadiSys Corp.; CEO Open Source Devel. Labs, Beaverton, Oreg., 2003—06; with OVP Venture Partners, 2006—. Office: OVP Venture Partners 5550 SW Macadam Ave Ste 300 Portland OR 97239 Office Phone: 503-626-2455. Office Fax: 503-626-2436. Business E-Mail: stuartcohen@osdl.org.*

COHEN, SUSAN LOIS, writer; b. Chgo., Mar. 27, 1938; d. Martin and Ida Handler; m. Daniel E. Cohen, Feb. 2, 1958; 1 child, Theodora (dec.). BA, New Sch. for Social Rsch., 1960; MA in Social Work, Adelphi U., 1962. Social worker, NYC, 1962-67; various social work positions in N.Y.C., 1962-68. Author: The Liberated Couple, 1969, reassued under title Liberated Marriage, 1973; author: (under name Elizabeth St. Clair) Stonehaven, 1974; author: The Singing Harp, 1975, Secret of the Locket, 1975, Provenance House, 1976, Mansion in Miniature, 1977, Dewitt Manor, 1977, The Jeweled Secret, 1978, Murder in the Act, 1978, Sandcastle Murder, 1979, Trek or Treat, 1980, Sealed with a Kiss, 1981; author: (with Daniel Cohen) The Kids' Guide to Home Computers, 1983; author: The Kids' Guide to Home Video, 1984, Teenage Stress, 1984, Screen Goddesses, 1984, Rock Video Superstars, 1985, Wrestling Superstars, Vol. 1, 1985, Vol. 2, 1986, Hollywood Hunks and Heroes, 1985, Heroes of the Challenger, 1986, A Six-Pack and a Fake ID, 1986, The Encyclopedia of Movie Stars, 1986, A History of the Oscars, 1986, Teenage Competition: A Survival Guide, 1987, Young and Famous: Hollywood's Newest Superstars, 1987, Going for the Gold, 1987, What You Can Believe about Drugs, 1988, What Kind of Dog is That, 1989, When Someone You Know is Gay, 1989, Zoo Superstars, 1989, Zoos, 1992, Where to Find Dinosaurs Today, 1992, Going for the Gold: Medal Hopefuls for Winter '92, 1992, Gold Medal Glow: The Story of America's Women's Gymnastic Team, 1996, Pan Am 103, 2000, rev. edit., 2001, Hauntings and Horrors, 2002. Mem.: Wodehouse Soc. (pres.), Watson's Erroneous Deductions, Chapter One, The Capers of Sherlock Holmes, Clumber Spaniel Club of Am. Avocation: cats. Address: 877 W Hand Ave Cape May Court House NJ 08210-1865 Personal E-mail: BldgsCast@aol.com.

COHEN, TED, philosopher, educator; b. Danville, Ill., Dec. 13, 1939; s. Sam and Shirley E. Cohen; m. Julie Simon, Apr. 18, 1940 (div. 1992); children: Shoshannah, Amos; m. Ann Rutherfurd Collier Austin, 1994. AB, U. Chgo., 1962; MA, Harvard U., 1965, PhD, 1972. Prof. philosophy U. Chgo., 1967—, chmn. dept. philosophy, 1974-79. Author: Jokes, 1999, Korean transl., 2002, Dutch transl., 2005; editor: Essays in Kant's Aesthetics, 1982, Pursuits of Reason, 1993; contbr. articles to profl. jours. Bd. dirs. Ctr. Rehab. and Tng. Disabled, B'nai Brith Hillel Found. of U. Chgo., KAM Isaiah Israel Congregation, Chgo., 1980—, mem. faculty religious sch.; chmn. com. gen. studies humanities U. Chgo., 1991—. Named William R. Kenan Jr. Disting. Prof. Humanities, Coll. William and Mary, 1986—87; grantee, Am. Coun. Learned Socs., 1980, 1985. Mem.: Am. Philos. Assn. (v.p. 2005, pres.-elect 2005), Am. Soc. Aesthetics (pres. 1997—), Phi Beta Kappa (vis. scholar 2000—01). Avocation: baseball theory and practice. Office: U Chgo Dept Philosophy 1050 E 59th St Chicago IL 60637-1559 Home: 5816 S Blackstone Ave Chicago IL 60637 Home Phone: 773-288-4694; Office Phone: 773-702-8506. Business E-Mail: tedcohen@midway.uchicago.edu.

COHEN, WALTER STANLEY, financial consultant; b. Bklyn., Oct. 24, 1936; s. Harry and Ruth (Spitz) Cohen; m. Barbara Lee Cooper, June 18, 1960; children: Howard H, Andrea Sue. BS, U. Buffalo, 1958; postgrad., NYU, 1960-64. Jr. acct. Morris, Sherwood & May (CPAs), NYC, 1958-59; semi-sr. acct. H. Merdinger & Co. (CPAs), 1960-61; sr. acct. Skillman & Michaels (CPAs), NYC, 1961-62; with Blessings Corp., NYC, 1962-84, sr. acct., 1962-66, asst. contr., 1966-69, asst. sec., 1969-70, sec., 1970-79, sec.-treas., 1979-84; v.p. fin. Sketchley Am., Inc., 1984-86; fin. cons. Thomson-McKinnon Securities, 1987-89; assoc. v.p. investments Prudential Securities, Bridgewater, NJ, 1989-94; assoc. v.p. Morgan Stanley Dean Witter, Somerville, NJ, 1994—2003; retired, 2003. With AUS, 1959—60. Mem.: B'nai B'rith, Kappa Nu (v.p. 1956—57, treas. 1955—56). Republican. Jewish. Home: 9 Hazeltine Ln Jackson NJ 08527 Office Phone: 732-928-7398. Personal E-mail: waltbarb@optonline.net.

COHEN, WARREN I., history professor; b. Bklyn., June 20, 1934; s. Murray and Fay (Phillips) C.; m. Janice Prichard, June 22, 1957 (div. Mar. 1986); children: Geoffrey Scott, Anne Leslie; m. Nancy Bernkopf Tucker, June 12, 1988. AB, Columbia U., 1955; A.M., Fletcher Sch. Law and Diplomacy, Tufts U., 1956; PhD, U. Wash., 1962. Lectr. U. Calif.-Riverside, 1962-63, asst. prof., 1963-67, assoc. prof., 1967-71; prof. history Mich. State U., East Lansing, 1971-93, univ. disting. prof., 1990-93, dir. Asian Studies Ctr., 1979-89; disting. univ. prof. U. Md., Baltimore County, 1992—. Vis. prof. Nat. Taiwan U., Taipei, 1964-66, Columbia U., N.Y.C., 1971, Fgn. Affairs Coll., Beijing, 1986; mem. Com. on Am.-East Asian Rels., Balt., 1973—; mem. adv. com. on hist. diplomatic documentation Dept. State, 1986-90, chmn., 1988-90; scholar-in-residence Assn. for Diplomatic Studies and Tng., 1994-95; acting dir. Asia program Wilson Ctr., 1995-99. Author: The American Revisionists, 1967, America's Response to China, 1971, The Chinese Connection, 1978, Dean Rusk, 1980, Empire without Tears, 1987, East Asian Art and American Culture, 1992, America in the Age of Soviet Power, 1945-1991, 1993, East Asia the the Center, 2000, Asian American Century, 2002, America's Failing Empire, 2005; editor Diplomatic History, 1979-82, New Frontiers in American-East Asian Relations, 1983, (with Akira Iriye) Japan and the United States in the Postwar World, 1988, Great Powers in East Asia, 1953-60, 1990, (with Nancy Bernkopf Tucker) Lyndon Johnson Confronts the World, 1994, Pacific Passage, 1996, (with Li Zhao) Hong Kong Under Chinese Rule, 1997. Bd. dirs. Mich. China Council, East Lansing, 1978-92; exec. sec. Gov's Mich. and China Com., Lansing, 1982-84; mem. Gov's Commn. on China, 1984-88; bd. dirs. Japan Council, 1979-92. Served to lt. (j.g.) USNR, 1956-59, PTO. Fulbright lectr. Tokyo, 1969-70; rsch. grantee Am. Coun. Learned Socs., 1968, Ford Found., 1976-77, Henry Luce Found., 1983-84; recipient Disting. Faculty award Mich. State U., 1988; Wilson Ctr. fellow, 1990-91, sr. scholar, 1999—; Presdl. rsch. scholar UMBC, 2001-. Mem. ACLU, Coun. on Fgn. Rels., Orgn. Am. Historians, Soc. for Historians of Am. Fgn. Rels. (v.p. 1983, pres. 1984, Graebner prize 2004). Democrat. Jewish. Office: U Md Balt County Dept History Baltimore MD 21250-0001 also: 11500 S Glen Rd Potomac MD 20854-1852 Office Phone: 410-455-2312. Business E-Mail: wcohen@umbc.edu.

COHEN, WAYNE R., lawyer; b. 1966; m. Jill F. Cohen. BBA with distinction, U. Mich., 1988; JD cum laude, U. Miami, 1991. Admitted: 1991. Founder, mng. ptnr. Cohen & Cohen, PC, Washington. Assoc. professorial lectr. law George Washington U. Sch. Law, 1993—; appointed to peer review comm. Atty. Grievance Commn. Md., 2002—04. Named Washington's Top Lawyers, Washingtonian Mag., 2004; named one of Top 50 Lawyers in Washington, 2002, Top 75 Best Lawyers in Washington, 2002, Washington's Top Trial Lawyers. Mem.: DC Bar Assn. (former chmn., litig. sect., former chair, injury to persons and property), Assn. Trial Lawyers Am., Trial Lawyers Assn. Metropolitan Washington, DC (immediate past pres., former bd. gov.). Office: Cohen & Cohen PC 1717 K St NW Ste 502 Washington DC 20006 Office Phone: 202-955-4529. Business E-Mail: wrc@cohenandcohen.net.

COHEN, WILLIAM, law educator; b. Scranton, Pa., June 1, 1933; s. Maurice M. and Nellie (Rubin) C.; m. Betty C. Stein, Sept. 13, 1952 (div. 1976, dec. 2000); children: Barbara Jean, David Alan (dec. 1995), Rebecca Anne; m. Nancy M. Mahoney, Aug. 8, 1976; 1 dau., Margaret Emily. BA, UCLA, 1953, LLB, 1956. Bar: Calif. 1961. Law clk. to U.S. Supreme Ct. Justice William O. Douglas, 1956-57; from asst. prof. to assoc. prof. U. Minn. Law Sch., 1957-60; vis. assoc. prof. UCLA Law Sch., 1959-60, mem. faculty, 1960-70, prof., 1962-70, Stanford (Calif.) Law Sch., 1970—, C. Wendell and Edith M. Carlsmith prof. law, 1983-99, Carlsmith prof. emeritus, 1999—. Vis. prof. law European U. Inst., Florence, Italy, fall 1977; Merriam vis. prof. Ariz. State U. Law Sch., Spring 1981 Author: Constitutional Protection of Expression and Conscience: The First Amendment, 2003; co-author: The Bill of Rights, a Source Book, 1968, Comparative Constitutional Law, 1978, Constitutional Law Cases and Materials, 1981, 7th edit., 2005, Constitutional Law: The Structure of Government, 1981, Constitutional Law: Civil Liberty and Individual Rights, 1982, 5th edit., 2007. Home: 698 Maybell Ave Palo Alto CA 94306-3819 Office: Stanford Law Sch Nathan Abbott Way Stanford CA 94305 Business E-Mail: wcohen@stanford.edu.

COHEN, WILLIAM MARK, lawyer; b. NYC, May 22, 1951; s. Martin and Annabelle (Turner) C.; m. Melinda Pauline Salomon, Aug. 3, 1975; children: Jessica, Adam. AB, Rutgers U., 1973; JD, Georgetown U., 1976. Bar: Tenn. 1976, U.S. Dist. Ct. (mid. dist.) Tenn. 1976, U.S. Ct. Appeals (6th cir.) 1977, U.S. Supreme Ct. 1980. Law clk. to chief judge U.S. Dist. Ct. (mid. dist.) Tenn., Nashville, 1976-78; asst. U.S. atty. U.S. Atty.'s Office, 1978—83, 1st asst. U.S. atty., 1983—92, chief criminal divsn., 1992—98, asst. U.S. atty., 1998—2002, 2003—05, sr. litigation counsel, 2002—03, 2005—; adj. prof. law Vanderbilt U. Law Sch., 2003—. Home: 6021 Foxland Dr Brentwood TN 37027-5733 Office: US Attys Office 110 9th Ave S Ste A961 Nashville TN 37203-3870

COHEN, WILLIAM NATHAN, radiologist; b. Balt., Dec. 10, 1935; s. Herbert and Lillian (Goldberg) C.; m. Sylvia Weinstein, Feb. 9, 1964; children: Elaine, Shirah, Jonathan. Student, Johns Hopkins U., 1952—55; MD, U. Md., 1959. Intern U. Mich. Hosp., Ann Arbor, 1959-60; resident in radiology Mallinckrodt Inst., Washington U., St. Louis, 1960-63; chief radiology sect. Gallup Indian Hosp., USPHS, 1963-65; asst. prof. radiology U. Iowa, Iowa City, 1965-69, asso. prof., 1969-73, prof., 1973-76; prof. radiology SUNY Upstate Med. U., Syracuse, 1976-83, clin. prof. radiology, 1983—. Attending radiologist Crouse Hosp., Syracuse; vis. prof. radiology Hebrew U., Jerusalem, 1971-72; examiner Am. Bd. Radiology, 1981-87. Contbr. articles in field to med. jours. Fellow Am. Coll. Radiology; mem. Radiol. Soc. N. Am., Am. Roentgen Ray Soc., Am. Inst. Ultrasound in Medicine (sr.), Alpha Omega Alpha. Business E-Mail: wcohen1@twcny.rr.com.

COHEN, WILLIAM SEBASTIAN, consultant, former Secretary of Defense; b. Bangor, Maine, Aug. 28, 1940; s. Reuben and Clara (Hartley) C.; m. Diana Dunn, 1962 (div. 1987); children: Kevin, Christopher; m. Janet Langhart, Feb. 14, 1996 AB cum laude, Bowdoin Coll., 1962; LLB cum laude, Boston U., 1965; LLD, St. Joseph's Coll., Windham, Maine, 1974, U. Maine, 1975, Western New Eng. Coll., 1975, Bowdoin Coll., 1975, Nasson Coll., 1975, Thomas Coll., 1988, Colby Coll., 1988. Bar: Maine, Mass., D.C. Ptnr. Paine, Cohen, Lynch, Weatherbee & Kobritz, Bangor, 1966-72; instr. U. Maine, 1968-72; asst. county atty. Penobscot County, Maine, 1968-70; US Senator from Maine, 1979-96; sec. US Dept. Def., Washington, 1997-2001; chmn., CEO The Cohen Group, Washington, 2001—. Mem. Bangor Sch. Com., 1970-71, Bangor City Council, 1969-72, mayor, 1971-72; Trustee Unity Coll.; bd. overseers Bowdoin Coll., 1973-85; trustee and counselor Ctr. Strategic and Internat. Studies, Washington, 2001—; chmn. bd. advisors MIC Industries Author: Of Sons and Seasons, 1978, Roll Call, 1981, A Baker's Nickel, 1986, One-Eyed Kings, 1991, Easy Prey: the Fleecing of America's Senior Citizens and How to Stop It, 1997, Dragon Fire, 2006; co-author: (with Kenneth Lassoon) Getting the Most Out of Washington: Using Congress to Move the Federal Bureaucracy, 1982 (with Gary Hart) The Double Man, 1985, (with George Mitchell) Men of Zeal: The Inside Story of the Iran-Contra Hearings, 1988, (with Thomas B. Allen) Murder in the Senate, 1993, (with Janet Langhart Cohen) Love in Black and White: A Memoir of Race, Religion, and Romance, 2007 Recipient Alumni award for disting. pub. service Boston U., 1976; named to N.E. Hall of Fame Basketball Team, 1962, Silver Anniversary award Nat. Collegiate Athletic Assn., 1987; Outstanding Young Man of Yr. Nat. Jaycees, 1975; James Bowdoin scholar, 1961-62; Alumni Fund scholar, 1962, selected for Balfour Silver Anniversary All-Am. Team, Nat. Assn. Basketball Coaches U.S., 1987. Republican. Office: The Cohen Group 1200 19th St NW Ste 400 Washington DC 20030*

COHEN-DEMARCO, GALE MAUREEN, pharmaceutical executive; b. Rochester, NY, June 4, 1947; d. Maurice Cohen and Florence Michaels; m. David Earl McCarty, June 16, 1975 (div. Nov. 1979); 1 child, Brock Adam; m. Peter Francis DeMarco, Aug. 3, 1984. BA, U. Rochester, 1969; MA, SUNY, Buffalo, 1971. Various pharm. cos.; hosp. rep., dist. mgr., med. liaison Glaxo Pharms., 1987—97; regional bus. mgr. Axcan Pharma, 1997—2003, sr. regional account mgr., 2003—07, sr. nat. account mgr., 2007—. Democratic com. person Congressional Dist. #352, Ill.; democratic twp. chair Wauconda, Ill. Named Employee of Quarter, Axcan, 2006; named to Pres.'s Club, 2001, Glaxo, 1987, 1988; grantee, NIH, 1969; scholar, NY State Regents, 1964. Democrat. Jewish. Avocations: environmental activities, charity organizations. Home: 27621 W Lakeview Dr N Wauconda IL 60084-2362 Office: Axcan Pharma 22 Inverness Ctr Pkwy Ste 310 Birmingham AL 35242 Office Phone: 847-987-6603. Personal E-mail: jap19472002@yahoo.com.

COHEN-GADOL, AARON, neurosurgeon; b. Tehran, Iran, Nov. 23, 1970; arrived in US, 1989; s. Soleiman Cohen-Gadol and Hemda Shofet. BA with honors in Biomed. Engring., U. Calif., San Diego, 1993; MD, U. So. Calif., LA, 1997; M, Mayo Grad. Sch., Rochester, Minn., 2005. Lic. Ind., Calif., Minn., Ark. Resident Mayo Clinic, Rochester, 2004—05, chief resident assoc., 2004—05; attending UCLA, 2005—06, Meth. Hosp., Indpls., 2006—, St. Vincent Hosp., Indpls., 2006—. Instr. U. Ark. Med. Sci. Ctr., Little Rock, 2005—06; presenter in field. Co-author: The Legacy of Harvey Cushing: Profiles of Patient Care, 2007; contbr. scientific papers to numerous profl. jours., chapters to books. Grantee, Baxter Found., 1995, Am. Diabetes Assn., 1995; Crowley scholar, Widney scholar. Mem.: Am. Epilepsy Soc. (mem. com. 2002—05), Coun. State Neurosurg. Soc. (rep. 2004—, midwestern del. 2002—03), Congress Neurol. Surgeons, Ind. State Med. Assn., Am. Assn. Neurol. Surgeons (exec. com. mem. 2007—, pub. com. 2005—, history sect. exec. com. 2004—07, asst. editor newsletter 2004—), Phi Beta Delta, Alpha Omega Alpha, Sigma Xi. Avocations: basketball, running, weightlifting. Office: Indpls Neurosug Group 1801 N Senate Blvd #535 Indianapolis IN 46202

COHEN-SCHWARTZ, DAWN SHERI, radiologist; MD, Albert Einstein Coll. Medicine, Bronx, NY, 1994. Diplomate Am. Bd. Radiology. Intern New Rochelle Med. Ctr., NY, 1994—95; radiology resident Montefiore Med. Ctr., Bronx, 1995—99; breast imaging fellow NYU Med. Ctr., NYC, 1999—2000. Attending physician Summit Radiol. Assocs., Westfield, NJ, 2005—. Avocation: aerobics. Home Phone: 973-994-2705; Office Phone: 908-232-0290.

COHEN-VADER, CHERYL DENISE, municipal official; b. Ft. Bragg, NC, Mar. 23, 1955; BA, Princeton U., 1977; MBA, Columbia U., 1983. Treas. internat. divsn. commodity import-export financing Bank of N.Y., NYC, 1977-81; v.p. Citicorp Securities Markets, Inc. Citicorp, NYC, 1983-90; v.p. Weldon, Sullivan, Carmichael & Co., 1990-92; asst. v.p. Kirkpatrick Pattis, 1993-95; mgr. revenue dept. City of Denver, 1996—, dep. mayor, 2003—04. Mem. Mcpl. Securities Rulemaking Bd., 1998-2001. Bd. dirs. Mile High chpt. ARC, Colo. Episcopal Found., 1998-2001; bd. dirs. Black Ch. Intitiatives, 1998—. Recipient Consortium of Grad. Mgmt. Edn. fellowship, 1981-83, Recognition of Achievement award Five Points Bus. Assn., Inc., 1995, Leadership Denver award Denver C. of C., 1994; honored in Living Portraits of African-Am. Women Nat. Coun. Negro Women, 1997. Mem. Govt. Finance Officers Assn. Office: City Denver Revenue Dept McNichols Bldg Rm 300 144 W Colfax Ave Denver CO 80202-5391

COHILL, MAURICE BLANCHARD, JR., federal judge; b. Pitts., Nov. 26, 1929; s. Maurice Blanchard and Florence (Clarke) C.; m. Suzanne Miller, June 27, 1952 (dec. May 1986); m. Anne D. Mullaney, May 26, 2005; children: Cynthia Cohill Plattner, Jonathan, Jennifer Cohill O'Connor, Victoria. AB, Princeton U., 1951; LLB, U. Pitts., 1956. Bar: Pa. 1957. Judge family div. Common Pleas Ct., Allegheny County, Pitts., 1965-76; judge U.S. Dist. Ct. Pa. (we. dist.), 1976-94, chief judge, 1985-92, sr. judge, 1994—. Bd. dirs. Pa. George Jr. Republic, Grove City; chmn. bd. fellows Nat. Ctr. for Juvenile Justice. Served to capt. USMCR, 1951-53. Mem. ABA, Pa. Bar Assn. Allegheny County Bar Assns., Nat. Coun. Juvenile Ct. Judges (past v.p.), Pa. Coun. Juvenile Ct. Judges (past pres.), Phi Delta Phi. Republican. Presbyterian. Office: US Dist Ct US Courthouse 700 Grant St 8th Fl Rm 803 Pittsburgh PA 15219 Office Phone: 412-208-7380.

COHLER, BERTRAM JOSEPH, psychologist, educator; b. Chgo., Dec. 3, 1938; s. Jonas Robert and Betty (Cahn) C.; m. Anne Meyers, June 11, 1962 (dec. Dec. 1989); children: Jonathan Richard, James Joseph. BA, U. Chgo., 1961; PhD, Harvard U., 1967; cert. in adult analysis, Inst. Psychoanalysis, 1989. Diplomate Am. Bd. Psychoanalysis, Am. Bd. Examiners in Profl. Psychology. Lectr. social relations Harvard U., Cambridge, Mass., 1967-69; assoc. dir. Sonia Shankman Orthogenic Sch., 1969-72, 94-96; dir. Orthogenic Sch. U. Chgo., 1969-72, 94—; asst. prof. U. Chgo., 1969—75, assoc. prof., 1975—81, William Rainey Harper dept. chair, 1977—, prof. depts. psychology, edn. and psychiatry, 1981—. Co-dir. Univ. Ctr. Health anf Aging Soc., 1987—; sci. and profl. staff dept. psychiatry Michael Reese Hosp., Chgo., 1980-90; cons. The Tresholds, Chgo., 1972-81, Inst. Psychoanalysis, Chgo., 1972—, Ill. State Psychiat. Inst., Chgo., 1977-82; pres. bd. Ctr. Religion and Psychotherapy, Chgo. Author (with H. Grunebaum et al.): Mentally Ill Mothers and Their Children, 1975, 1982, Mothers, Grandmothers and Daughters, 1981; author: (with others) Parenthood as an Adult Experience, 1983, The Invulnerable Child, 1987, Handbook of Clinical Research on Adolescence, 1993; author: (with R. Galatzer-Levy) The Essential Other, 1993; author: The Course of Gay and Lesbian Lives, 2000; author: (with R. Galatzer-Levy) The Psychoanalytic Study of Lives Over Time, 1999; author: (with others) Rethinking Psychoanalysis and the Homosexualities, 2002; author: Writing Desire, 2007. Bd. dirs. Horizons Cmty. Svcs., Chgo.; mem. initial rev. group in aging NIMH, Washington, 1982—86, Mental Health Spl. Projects, 1988—2003. Recipient Quantrell prize for disting. tchg. U. Chgo., 1975, 99, Lily Gondor award Postgrad. Ctr. for Mental Health, 2000, Henry A. Murray award APA and Soc. for Personology, 2006; fellow Inst. Medicine, 1975. Fellow Gerontol. Soc., Soc. Projective Techniques Am. Orthopsychiat. Assn. (bd. dirs. 1981-84, pres. elect 1991, pres. 1992), Am. Psychol. Assn. (chmn. profl. affairs com. divsn. 39 1981-83, editor Psychoanalytic Psychology 1987-97, pres. sect. II 1992); mem. Am. Sociol. Assn., Am. Anthrop. Assn., Am. Assn. Psychiat. Svcs. to Children (Alexander Gralnick award), Soc. Rsch. in Child Devel., Chgo. Assn. Psychoanalytic Psychology (pres. 1983-84), Am. Psychoanalytic Assn. Home: 5408 S Blackstone Ave Chicago IL 60615-5407 Office: U Chgo 5730 S Woodlawn Ave Chicago IL 60637-1603 Office Phone: 773-702-3574. Business E-Mail: bert@midway.uchicago.edu. *Emphasis on community services has been an important tradition in my family for several generations. This concern includes making knowledge and skills available to others, providing leadership and giving of time where needed. Teaching, writing, and research and clin. svc. are all involved in making the world better for my having been a part of it. My own goal has been to improve the human condition and to inspire my students to carry on this concern for the welfare of others.*

COHN, ALBERT LINN, lawyer; b. Paterson, NJ, June 18, 1928; s. David and Rose (Yolken) C.; m. Sylvia J. Jacoby, June 14, 1959; children: Melissa Lynn, Joshua Peter, Priscilla Betsy, Liza-Faith Michaelis, Thaddeus Augustus David. BS, Georgetown U., 1948; JD, Harvard U., 1951. Bar: D.C. 1951, N.J. 1954, cert.: (civil trial atty.). Assoc. David Cohn, Paterson, 1954—59; ptnr. David & Albert L. Cohn, 1959—66; sr. ptnr. Cohn & Lifland, Saddle Brook, NJ, 1967—. Adj. prof. law Rutgers U., Newark, 1979—2005, Inst. Cont. Legal Edn., 1980, 1982—, chmn. curriculum adv. com., 1984—85; vis. instr. Mass. Cont. Legal Edn., Nat. Inst. Trial Advocacy, Harvard U. Law Sch., 1981; trustee NJ Inst. Cont. Legal Edn., chair, 1993—2006; master Arthur T. Vanderbilt Inn. Ct., 1988—90, Morris Pashman Inn of Ct., 1990—98, mem. coord. com., 1992—98. Mem. editl. bd. Divorce Litigation, 1996—; contbr. articles. Trustee emeritus NY Gilbert and Sullivan Players, 2006—; pres. Temple Shomrei Emunah, 1968—70; overseer Jewish Theol. Seminary, 1969—79. 1st lt. USAF, 1951—53. Named Superlawyer, NJ Monthly, 2005, 2006—07; named to Best Lawyers in Am., NY Magazine, 2006, 2007; recipient Alfred C. Clapp award, NJ Inst. Continuing Legal Edn., 1994. Fellow: Am. Bar Found.; mem.: ABA, Bergen County Bar Found., Harvard Law Sch. Assn. N.J. (pres. 1998), Saddle Brook C. of C. (past pres., trustee), Million Dollar Advs. Forum, Trial Attys. N.J., Soc. Med. Jurisprudence, N.J. State Bar Assn., Bergen County Bar Assn. (trustee 2007—), Passaic County Bar Assn. (trustee 1978—86), Hamilton Club (Paterson), Harvard Club (N.Y.C.). Home: Llewellyn Park 74 Mountain Ave West Orange NJ 07052 Office: Cohn & Lifland Park 80 Plz W One Saddle Brook NJ 07663-5830 Home Phone: 973-325-9255; Office Phone: 201-845-9600. Business E-Mail: alc@njlawfirm.com.

COHN, ANDREW HOWARD, lawyer; b. NYC, Jan. 17, 1945; s. Maurice John and Margaret Ethel (Gordon) C.; m. Marcia Bliss Leavitt, July 10, 1977; children: Marisa Leavitt, David Herman. BA, U. Pa., 1966; AM, Harvard U., 1970, PhD, 1972; JD, Yale U., 1975. Bar: Mass. 1975, U.S. Dist. Ct. Mass. 1976, U.S. Ct. Appeals (1st cir.) 1976. Law clk. to presiding justice U.S. Ct. Appeals (1st cir.), Providence and Boston, 1975-76; assoc. Hill & Barlow, Boston, 1976-80; sr. ptnr. Hale and Dorr, Boston, 1980—. Chmn. exec. com. Hale and Dorr, 1990-91, real estate dept., 1991-97, energy group, 1992—; cons. for juvenile justice standards project ABA and Inst. for Judicial Adminstrn., NYC, 1973-74; rsch. fellow MIT-Harvard U. Joint Ctr. for Urban Studies, Cambridge, Mass., 1969-71, Univ. Coll., Nairobi, Kenya, 1968. Contbr. articles to profl. jours.; note and project editor Yale Law Jour., New Haven, 1974-75. Advisor Newton Cmty. Schs. Found., Mass., 1987—88. Named Law and Social Sci. fellow, Russell Sage Found., 1972—74. Mem. ABA (environ. controls com., bus. law sect.), Am. Coll. Real Estate Lawyers, Boston Bar Assn. (chmn. real estate sect. 95-97), Yale Law Sch. Assn. Mass. (treas. 1985-87). Democrat. Jewish. Office: Wilmer Hale 60 State St Boston MA 02109-1816 Office Phone: 617-526-6218. Business E-Mail: andrew.cohn@wilmerhale.com.

COHN, AVERN LEVIN, district judge; b. Detroit, July 23, 1924; s. Irwin I. and Sadie (Levin) C.; m. Joyce Hochman, Dec. 30, 1954 (dec. Dec. 1989); m. Lois Pincus Cohn, June 1992; children: Sheldon, Leslie Cohn Magy, Thomas. Student, John Tarleton Agrl. Coll., 1943, Stanford U., 1944; JD, U. Mich., 1949. Bar: Mich. 1949. Practiced in, Detroit, 1949-79; mem. firm Honigman Miller Schwartz & Cohn, Detroit, 1961-79; sr. judge U.S. Dist. Ct., 1979—. Mem. Mich. Civil Rights Commn., 1972-75, chmn., 1974-75; Mem. Detroit Bd. Police Commrs., 1975-79, chmn., 1979; bd. govs. Jewish Welfare Fedn., Detroit, 1972—. Served with AUS, 1943-46. Mem. ABA, Mich. Bar Assn., Am. Law Inst. Office Phone: 313-234-5160. E-mail: avern_cohn@mied.uscourts.gov.

COHN, BERTRAM JOSIAH, portfolio manager; b. Newark, Sept. 12, 1925; s. Julius Henry and Bessie Ruth (Einson) C.; m. Barbara Biard, June 20, 1956; children: Daniel, Susan, Diana. AB cum laude, Harvard, 1949; MBA, NYU, 1957. Vice pres. Decatur Iron & Steel Co., Ala., 1951-67; chmn. bd. Schuylkill Lead Corp., Baton Rouge, 1968-70, DPF, Inc., Hartsdale, NY, 1970—, Interstate Bakeries Corp., 1970-82. Mem. internat. adv. com. Cohn Inst. for History and Philosophy Sci., Tel Aviv U. Trustee Washington Inst. for Near East Policy. With AUS, 1943-46. Mem. Wilderness Soc. (governing coun.). Home: 125 Woodbine Ave Larchmont NY 10538-3523 Office: First Manhattan Co 437 Madison Ave New York NY 10022-7001 Office Phone: 212-756-3380.

COHN, BRUCE, film and television company executive; b. San Francisco, Apr. 8, 1931; s. Theodore and Rosebud Enid (Schmulian) C.; 1 child, Mitchell Barry. M of Journalism, U. Calif., Berkeley, 1954. Writer, producer Clete Roberts News Sta. KTLA-TV, Hollywood, Calif., 1957-62; west coast producer Huntley-Brinkley and Today Show NBC, Burbank, Calif., 1962-63; news dir. Sta. KNBC-TV, Burbank, 1963-66; Washington producer ABC Evening News, 1966-68; west coast producer Los Angeles, 1968-71; exec. producer Nat. Pub. Affairs Ctr. for TV Pub. Broadcasting System, Washington, 1971-73; ind. producer, writer various film studios, Burbank, 1973-75, 1973—; pres. Bruce Cohn Prodns., Inc., Mill Valley, Calif., 1975—. Instr. US history, critical thinking Fashion Inst. for Design and Merchandising, San Francisco, 2004. Screenwriter: Good Guys Wear Black, 1979; writer, producer (TV documentary) 1968-A Crack in Time, 1978, Secret Files of J. Edgar Hoover, 1990; producer (documentary series) Time Was, 1980; producer, dir. (documentary series) Rember When, 1981; writer, producer, dir. (documentary) Kisses with Lauren Bacall, 1991; writer, producer (documentary) Tom Clancy Presents John Ehrlichman In the Eye of the Storm, 1998, Couples, 2000. Recipient Cable Ace award, 1979, 81, 2 Gold medals N.Y. Internat. Film Festival, 1981, Gold plaque Chgo. Internat. Film Festival, 1982, Emmy award NATAS, 1984, 97. Mem. Writers Guild Am., Am. Film Inst. Home and Office: 125 Via Lerida Greenbrae CA 94904-1211 Personal E-mail: bcp333@aol.com.

COHN, CHARLES ERWIN, retired physicist; b. Chgo., Apr. 25, 1931; s. Sam and Rose (Schwartz) Cohn; m. Margaret Klaer Hunt, June 1, 1976. AB, U. Chgo., 1950, SM, 1953; PhD, U. Chgo., 57. Physicist Argonne Nat. Lab., Ill., 1956—85; ret., 1985. Contbr. numerous articles to profl. jours. Achievements include patents in field. Avocation: race walking marathons. Home: 6311 Mark Tr Austell GA 30168 Home Phone: 770-944-7510.

COHN, CINDY A., lawyer; b. Detroit, Nov. 30, 1963; d. Robert M. and Norma Rose (Arkin) C. Student, London Sch. Econs., 1984; BA in English, U. Iowa, 1986; JD, U. Mich., 1989. Bar: Calif. 1989. Internat. instruments intern UN Ctr. for Human Rights, Geneva, 1989-90; assoc. Farella, Braun & Martel, San Francisco, 1990-91; devel. dir. Unrepresented Nations & Peoples Orgn., San Francisco, 1991; assoc. McGlashan & Sarrail, San Mateo, Calif., 1991—99; legal dir., gen. counsel Electronic Frontier Found., San Francisco, 2000—. Vol. counsel Seva Svc. Orgn., Plymouth, Mich., 1988-89, Unrepresented Nations and Peoples Orgn., 1989-1991. Editor Mich. Jour. Internat. Law, 1989; contbr. articles to profl. jours. Bates fellow U. Mich., 1989. Named one of the Lawyers of the Year, California Lawyer Mag., 1997, Top 100 Influential Lawyers, Nat. Law Jour., 2006, The 50 Most Influential Women Lawyers in Am., Nat. Law Jour., 2007. Mem. Human Rights Advs. (bd. dirs., pres.), Verified Voting Found. (bd. dirs.). Office: Electronic Frontier Foundation 454 Shotwell St San Francisco CA 94110-1914*

COHN, DANIEL ROSS, physicist; b. Berkeley, Calif., Nov. 28, 1943; s. Roy Wolfsohn and Betty (Black) C.; m. Helen Desfosses, Aug. 25, 1967 (div. 1974); 1 child, Adam Robsohn; m. Joanne Brecker, June 10, 1978. BA, U. Calif., Berkeley, 1966; PhD, MIT, 1971. Rsch. scientist, gp. leader Francis Bitter Nat. Magnet Lab., MIT, Cambridge, Mass., 1971-80; divsn. head Plasma Fusion Ctr., MIT, Cambridge, 1980—; sr. rsch. scientist Nuc. Sci. and Engring. Dept., MIT, Cambridge, 1980—; acting asst. dir. plasma fusion ctr. MIT, Cambridge, 1992-96; pres., CEO Integrated Environ. Techs., 1996—2000. Cons. in field. Editor Jour. of Fusion Energy, 1984-92; contbr. more than 150 articles to profl. jours. Recipient Discover award for Technol. Innovation, Discover Mag., 1999. Fellow Am. Phys. Soc.; mem. Am. Nuc. Soc., Phi Beta Kappa. Achievements include more than 25 US patents on environmental, energy and monitoring technology; development of new energy and environmental technology. Office: MIT Plasma Fusion Ctr 167 Albany St Cambridge MA 02139-4213 Home: 100 Memorial Dr Apt 11-22b Cambridge MA 02142-1334 Business E-Mail: cohn@psfc.mit.edu.

COHN, DAVID STEPHEN, lawyer; b. Richmond, Va., June 19, 1945; s. Alfred Jerome and Jane Shaffer Cohn; m. Jane Boyle, Nov. 22, 1970; children: Elizabeth, Sarah. AB, U. Pa., 1967; JD, Harvard U., 1971. Bar: Pa. 1971, Va. 1973, NY 2005, U.S. Dist. Ct. (ea. dist.) Pa. 1971, U.S. Ct. Appeals (3d cir.) 1971. Assoc. Schnader, Harrison, Segal & Lewis, Phila., 1971-73; asst. prof. law T.C. Williams Sch. Law, U. Richmond, 1973-75; counsel Hunton & Williams, Richmond, 1975-84; mem., chmn., real estate dept. Browder, Russell, Morris & Butcher, P.C., Richmond, 1984-89; ptnr. Troutman Sanders LLP, Richmond, 1989—, NYC, 2005—, chmn. real estate investments practice group, 2007—. Arbitrator Am. Arbitration Assn., 1972—; lectr. Marshall Wythe Sch. Law, Coll. William and Mary, Williamsburg, Va., 1977—81; mem. Va. Gov.'s Regulatory Reform Adv. Bd., 1983—85, Va. Gov.'s Com. on Efficiency in Govt., Richmond, 1985—87; chmn. Va. com. Harvard Law Sch. Fund, Cambridge, Mass., 1986—88, 2002—03. Editor: (book) The Residential Real Estate Transaction, 1975. Bd. dirs., pres. Sci. Mus. Va. Found., 1987—2002; mem. Va. Hist. Landmarks Bd., 1988—89; chmn., pres. Richmond Goodwill Industries, Inc., 1988—2002, 2004—; mem. Va. Vol. Formulary Bd., 1989—2003; mem. adv. coun. Va. Gov.'s Sch. Govt. and Internat. Studies for Gifted, 1991—93; mem. regulatory climate subcom. Va. Gov.'s Econ. Recovery Coun., 1991—92; mem. orgnl. structure team Gov.'s Commn. on Efficiency and Effectiveness, 2002; bd. dirs. Va. Nonprofit Housing Coalition, 1990—, sec., 1990—; mem. state ctrl. com. Va. Dem. Party, Richmond, 1985—93; assoc. trustee U. Pa., Phila., 1984—94; bd. dirs. Better Housing Coalition, 1988—99; chmn. trustees Sci. Mus. Va., 2002—. Mem.: ABA (chmn. govtl. assistance for real estate programs com. 1989—93), NY State Bar, Pa. State Bar, Va. State Bar (mem. bd. govs. real estate sect. 1984—87), Va. Bar Assn. (chmn. real estate com. 1985—87), Am. Coll. Real Estate Lawyers (chmn. affordable housing com. 1991—97). Jewish. Office: Troutman Sanders LLP Chrysler Bldg 405 Lexington Ave New York NY 10174 Office Phone: 212-704-6492. Business E-Mail: david.cohn@troutmansanders.com.

COHN, GARY D., diversified financial services company executive; b. Cleve., Aug. 27, 1960; m. Lisa Pevaroff Cohn. BSBA in Finance, American U., 1982. Former silver trader; sr. trader J. Aron Futures unit Goldman, Sachs & Co., London, 1990, ptnr., 1994—96, mng. dir., 1996, co-head of global sales and trading, mem. mgmt. com., 2002—, head, FICC commodities and emerging markets, 2002—06; pres., co-COO The Goldman Sachs Group, Inc, NYC, 2006—. Treas. Commodity Exch. Inc., 1990; bd. dirs. London Medal Exch., 1994, NY Mercantile Exch., 1998—2000. Trustee NYU Sch. Medicine Found., American U., Harlem's Children Zone, NYU Hosp., NYU Child Study Ctr., Gilmour Academy, Cleveland. Recipient Effecting Change award, 100 Women in Hedge Funds, 2005. Office: The Goldman Sachs Group Inc 85 Broad St New York NY 10004

COHN, GARY DENNIS, journalist, educator; b. Bklyn., Mar. 9, 1952; s. Morton J. and Claire Cohn; m. Sally Denton, 1980 (div. 1983); 1 child, Jacob Max Cohn. BA in Psychology and Polit. Sci., SUNY, Buffalo, 1974; postgrad., U. Calif., Berkeley, 1974-75. Reporter Jack Anderson Column, Washington, 1975-80, Lexington (Ky.) Herald-Leader, 1980-84, Miami bur. Wall St. Jour., NYC, 1984-86, Phila. Inquirer, 1986-93, Balt. Sun, 1993—2001, LA Times, 2003—07. Atwood chair dept. journalism and pub. comm. U. Alaska, Anchorage, 2001—03; adj. prof. Sch. Journalism U. So. Calif., 2004—. Recipient Edward W. Scripps 1st Amendment award,

1980, Inter-Am. Press Assn. award, 1996, Overseas Press Club of Am. award, 1995, 97, Selden Ring award, 1996, 98, 1st Amendment award Soc. Profl. Journalists, 1997, 1st prize for investigative reporting Sigma Delta Chi, 1997, Investigative Reporters and Editors award, 1997, George Polk award, 1997, Pulitzer Prize for Investigative Reporting, 1998, finalist, Pulitzer Prize for Public Svc., 1996, finalist, Pulitzer Prize for Nat. Reporting, 2002. Mem.: Investigative Reporters & Editors. Personal E-mail: garycohn@gci.net. Business E-Mail: garycohn@usc.edu.

COHN, HOWARD, retired magazine editor; b. NYC, Nov. 1, 1922; s. Morris and Vivian (Siegel) C.; m. Regina Levy, Apr. 2, 1949; children—Steven B., Robert D. BA, Am. U., 1947. Assoc. editor Sportfolio mag., 1947-48; assoc. editor, then mng. editor Am. Lawn Tennis mag., 1948-50; assoc. editor Quick mag., 1950-51, Collier's mag., 1951-56; freelance writer, 1957-59; articles editor Pageant mag., 1959, exec. editor, 1959-63; mng. editor True mag., 1964-68, Med. World News mag., 1968, exec. editor, 1968-75, editor, 1975-77; exec. editor McGraw-Hill Newsletter Center, 1977-79; sr. staff editor McGraw-Hill Pub. Co., NYC, 1979-81; editor-in-chief Graduating Engr. mag., 1981-88. Served with AUS, 1943-46. Home: 750A Heritage Hls Somers NY 10589-4009

COHN, IAN J., architect; b. Phila., Jan. 9, 1950; s. Isidore Jr. and Jacqueline (Heymann) C.; m. Vicki Hertzberg, June 23, 1973; children: Kevin Aton, Adrian Kirrin. Grad., The Gunnery, Washington, Conn.; BA, Washington U., St. Louis, 1971, MArch, 1974. Registered arch., N.Y. Staff arch. Howell, Killick, Partridge & Amis, London, 1974-76, George Nelson & Co., NYC, 1977; assoc. Perkins & Will, NYC, 1977-80; founding ptnr. Ian-Aaron Archs., NYC, 1980-89, Ian-Aaron Architects Internat. (in assn. with Sheehan & Barry, Dublin, Ireland), Dublin, Ireland, 1985-89; prin. Diversity: Architecture & Design, NYC, 1989—. 1st vis. young artist-in-residence The Gunnery Sch., 1989, vis. prof., 1992. Author: Structures: A Rule of Thumb Handbook, 1973; designs exhibited in mus. and mags. Bd. dirs. Kids of NYU Found., Inc.; chair comm. com. Ctrl. Synagogue, N.Y., 1997-2000. Mem. The Gunnery Alumni Assn. Democrat. Jewish. Avocations: photography, tennis, travel, wine, gourmet foods. Office: Diversity: Architecture & Design 250 E 87th St Apt 22A New York NY 10128-3101 E-mail: ddiversity@aol.com.

COHN, ISIDORE, JR., surgeon, educator; b. New Orleans, Sept. 25, 1921; s. Isidore and Elsie (Waldhorn) C.; m. Jacqueline Heymann, July 4, 1944 (div. Aug. 1971); children: Ian Jeffrey, Lauren Kerry; m. Marianne Winter Miller, Jan. 3, 1976. MD, U. Pa., Phila., 1945; M.Med. Sci. in Surgery, 1952, DMS in Surgery, 1955; LHD (hon.), U. SC, 1995. Diplomate Am. Bd. Surgery (bd. dirs. 1969-75). Intern Grad. Hosp. U. Pa., 1945-46, resident in surgery, 1949-52; fellow dept. surg. rsch. U. Pa., 1947-48; vis. surgeon Charity Hosp., New Orleans, 1952-62, sr. vis. surgeon, 1962-2000, hon. sr. vis. surgeon, 2000—; surgeon in chief La. State U. Svc., Charity Hosp., New Orleans, 1962-89; prof. surgery La. State U. Sch. Medicine, New Orleans, 1959-2000, emeritus chmn., emeritus prof. surgery, 2000—. Cons. surgeon VA Hosp., New Orleans, Touro Infirmary, New Orleans; instr. surgery La. State U. Sch. Medicine, New Orleans, 1952-53, asst. prof., 1953-56, assoc. prof., 1956-59, prof., 1959-2000, chmn. dept. surgery, 1962-89; mem. surg. rsch. rev. com. VA, Washington, 1967-68; dir. Nat. Pancreatic Cancer Project, 1975-84; mem. Soc. Surg. Chairmen, 1962-89. Mem. editl. bd. Am. Surgeon, 1963-87, Current Surgery, 1964-90, Am. Jour. Surgery, 1968-96, emeritus, 1997—, Digestive Diseases and Scis., 1978-82, Surg. Gastroenterology, 1982—, Cancer, 1992—2002, Digestive Surgery, 1995—. Bd. dirs. New Orleans Met. Conv. and Visitors Bur., 1998-2000, New Orleans Mus. Art, 2004—, Jewish Endowment Found., 2006—. Served to capt. M.C., AUS, 1946-47. Isidore Cohn, Jr. Professorship named in his honor at La. State U., 1987, Isidore Cohn, Jr., M.D. Student Learning Ctr. at La. State U. Health Sci. Ctr. Sch. Medicine dedicated in his honor, 2002, Spirit of Charity award Med. Ctr. La., 2003; named Outstanding Alumnus, Isidore Newman Sch., New Orleans, La., 2003, Role Model, Young Leadership Coun. New Orleans, 2006. Fellow ACS (exec. com., bd. govs. 1987-91, vice-chmn. 1989-90, chmn. 1990-91, 1st v.p. 1993-94); mem. AMA, Am. Surg. Assn., So. Surg. Assn. (1st v.p. 1979-80, treas.-recorder 1981-82, pres. 1982-83), La. Surg. Assn. (pres. 1968), So. Med. Assn., La., Orleans Parish med. socs., Soc. Univ. Surgeons, Southeastern Surg. Congress (chmn. forum on progress in surgery 1967-69, councillor for La. 1967-73, pres. 1972), Surg. Biology Club II, Assn. Acad. Surgery, Isidore Cohn, Jr.-James D. Rives Surg. Soc., Internat. Surg. Soc., Am. Gastroenterol. Assn., Bockus Soc. Gastroenterology, Soc. Surgery Alimentary Tract (trustee 1969-80, recorder 1973-76, pres. 1976-77, chmn. bd. 1977-78, Founders medal 2004), Am. Soc. Microbiologists, Soc. Surg. Oncology, NY Acad. Scis., Am. Assn. Cancer Research, Southeastern Cancer Research Assn. (pres. 1975), Collegium Internationale Chirurgiae Digestivae, Am. Cancer Soc. (vice chmn. clin. investigation adv. com. 1969, chmn. clin. investigation adv. com. 1969-73), Tex. Surg. Soc. (hon.), Sigma Xi, Phi Beta Kappa, Alpha Omega Alpha, Omicron Delta Kappa. Home: 510 Iona St Metairie LA 70005-4430 Office: La State U Med Sch New Orleans LA 70112 Home Phone: 504-835-6135. Personal E-mail: drdrdrjr@aol.com.

COHN, JOSEPH DAVID, surgeon; b. NYC, Jan. 26, 1937; s. Samuel Theodor and Gertrude (Emsheimer) C.; m. Barbara Ester Forst, July 27, 1966; children: Michael, Russell. SB, MIT, 1957; MD, NYU, 1961; MBA, Rutgers U., 1993. Diplomate Am. Bd. Surgery, Am. Bd. Thoracic Surgery, Am. Bd. Critical Care Surgery. Intern Duke Hosp., Durham, NC, 1961-62; surg. resident Bronx Mcpl. Hosp. Ctr., NY, 1962-67; thoracic surgery resident U. Calif., San Diego, 1969-71; from asst. dir. surgery to dir. St. Barnabas Med. Ctr., Livingston, NJ, 1971-83; thoracic surgeon Northfield Surg. Assn., Livingston, 1978-99; mem. staff Santa Rosa Meml. Hosp. Sutter Med. Ctr., Santa Rosa, Calif., 2001—. Clin. asst. prof. surgery UMDNJ, Newark, 1972—79, assoc. prof., 1979—90, prof., 1990—99. Editor sci. jours.; author software programs, 1988; contbr. articles to profl. jours. Capt. USAF, 1967-69. Fellow Am. Heart Assn. 1966-67, NIH 1964-66. Fellow ACS, Am. Coll. Critical Care Medicine; mem. Sigma Xi, Phi Lambda Upsilon, Alpha Omega Alpha. Avocations: skiing, scuba, flying. Office: 5773 Shiloh Ridge Road Santa Rosa CA 95403-7802 Office Phone: 707-578-6714. Business E-Mail: jcohn@alum.mit.edu.

COHN, KATHLEEN MANDRY, writer; b. Utica, NY, Feb. 22, 1944; d. Alphonse and Helen Cudilo Mandry; m. Martin Cohn, Dec. 29, 1972; 1 child, Aaron. BA English Lit., Harpur Coll., 1965. Copywriter Benton & Bowles Advt., NYC, 1965—71; copywriter, v.p. creative McCaffrey & McCall Advt., NYC, 1972—78; freelance writer NYC, 1978—80; assoc. creative dir. Foote Cone Belding, San Francisco, 1980—82; v.p. creative Dancer Fitzgerald Sample, San Francisco, 1982—84. Creative cons., San Francisco, 1983—86. Author: How to Make Elephant Bread, 1971, The Cat & The Mouse & The Mouse & The Cat, 1972, How Does it Feel to Live Next Door to a Giraffe?, 1973, (play) I Don't Want to be Like My Father, 1973, How to Grow a Jelly Glass Farm, 1974, The World on My Windowsill, 1975, (adult non-fiction) First American Peanut Growing Book, 1976, (children's TV) ABC's Schoolhouse Rock, 1976; lyricist Rufus Xavier Sarsaparilla. Vol., parent bd., chair sch. events French Am. Internat. Sch.; vol. The Urban Sch., 826 Valencia. Avocations: growing lavender, hiking, swimming, yoga, reading. Home: 1524 Willard St San Francisco CA 94117

COHN, LAWRENCE H., cardiothoracic surgeon; b. San Francisco, Mar. 11, 1937; s. Harold Edward and Dorothy Harriet (Cohen) C.; m. Roberta Lee Cohn, June 26, 1960; children— Leslie Anne, Jennifer Lynne BA, U. Calif., Berkeley, 1958; MD, Stanford U., 1962. Diplomate Am. Bd. Surgery, Am. Bd. Thoracic Surgery. Sr. cardiothoracic surgeon Brigham & Woman's Hosp., Boston, 1980-87, chief div. cardiac surgery, 1987—; prof. surgery Harvard Med. Sch., Boston, 1980—. Chmn. bd. regents Nat. Libr. Medicine, 1991-92; chmn. Physicians Orgn., Brigham & Women's Hosp., 2000-04. Served to lt. comdr. USPHS, 1964-66. Fellow Am. Coll. Cardiologists, Am. Coll. Chest Physicians (pres. 1987), Soc. Thoracic Surgeons, Am. Assn. Thoracic Surgery (pres. 1999), Am. Surg. Soc. Office: Brigham Womens Hosp 75 Francis St Boston MA 02115-6106 Office Phone: 617-732-7678. Business E-Mail: lcohn@partners.com.

COHN, M. JAMES, radiologist; s. Arthur and Dora Cohn; m. Beverly Cohn. BA in Biophysics, U. Calif., Berkeley, 1984; MD, Harvard U., Boston, 1989. Bd. cert. diplomate diagnostic radiology Am. Bd. Radiology, 1994, bd. cert. diplomate Nat. Bd. Med. Examiners, 1989, fellow magnetic resonance imaging U. Calif., Irvine, 1995, fellow computed radiology Harvard Med. Sch., Mass. Gen. Hosp., 1989. Dir. MRI West Boca Med. Ctr., Boca Raton, Fla., 1995—99; pres. Palm Desert Radiology Med. Group, Rancho Mirage, Calif., 2000—05. Mem.: Am. Coll. Radiology, Radiology Soc. N.Am. Avocations: jazz musician, travel. Office: Eisenhower Medical Center 39000 Bob Hope Dr Rancho Mirage CA 92270 Home Phone: 760-250-5886; Office Phone: 760-250-5886.

COHN, MARIANNE WINTER MILLER, civic activist; b. Denver, Jan. 15, 1928; d. Henry Abraham II and Esther (Sheflan) Winter; m. Benjamin K. Miller, Dec. 29, 1948 (dec. Dec. 1972); children: Judy Ellen, Philip Henry (dec. 1996); m. Isidore Cohn Jr., Jan. 3, 1976; stepchildren: Ian Jeffrey Cohn, Lauren Kerry Cohn Fouros. Student, Colo. U., 1946-47. Chmn. spouse program arrangements ACS, La., 1985; mem. exec. bd. NCCJ, New Orleans, 1987—96, sec., 1991—92, treas., 1993—94, nat. bd. dir., 1993; chmn. Odyssey Ball of New Orleans Mus. Art, 1992—; mem. exec. bd. Greater New Orleans Tourist and Conv. Commn., 1985; mem. Sisterhood of Temple Emanuel Denver, pres., 1957—60; women's bd. dir. Nat. Jewish Hosp. at Denver, 1951—60, pres. women's divsn., 1960—61, mem., sec. gov. bd., 1972—76; mem. nat. bd. Nat. Jewish Ctr., 1976—, regional vice chmn., 1999—; bd. dir. New Orleans Symphony Aux., 1980; chmn. Exhibit Sun King, Louis XIV La. State Mus., 1984, mem. governing bd., 1992—2005, bd. dir., 1994—2001, Jewish Endowment Found., New Orleans, 1987—88; mem. Arts Coun. of New Orleans, 1988—, v.p. devel., 1991—92, v.p. grants, exec. bd., 1995—96; pres. La. Mus. Found., 1989—90; bd. dir. La. Coun. Music and Performing Arts, 1991—92; pres. Arts Coun. of New Orleans, 1997—98, chmn. bd., 1999, v.p. grants, 2001, vice chair, 2007; bd. dir. La. ArtWorks of Arts Coun. of New Orleans, 2000—06. Recipient Edgar L. Feinberg Meml. award James D. Rives Surg. Soc., 1988, Woman of Fashion award Men of Fashion, 1989, Humanitarian award Nat. Jewish Ctr. Immunology and Respiratory Medicine, 1995, role model award Young Leadership Coun. New Orleans, 1998—, Nat. Jewish Ctr. Chmn.'s award, 1999, Robert S. Daniels M.D. Alumni Svc. award, La. State U. Sch. Medicine, 2006. Republican. Avocations: travel, cooking. Personal E-mail: sunkingmc@aol.com.

COHN, MARJORIE F., law educator, legal association administrator; b. Pomona, Calif., Nov. 1, 1948; d. Leonard L. and Florence Cohn; m. Pedro López children: Victor, Nicolas; m. Jerome P. Wallingford. BA, Stanford U., 1970; JD, Santa Clara U., 1975. Bar: Calif. 1975, U.S. Dist. Ct. (so. dist.) Calif. 1982, U.S. Dist. Ct. (no. dist.) Calif. 1983. Staff atty. Nat. Lawyers Guild, San Francisco, 1975-76, Agrl. Labor Rels. Bd., Sacramento, 1976-78, Appellate Defenders, Inc., San Diego, 1987-91; dep. pub. defender Fresno County Pub. Defender's Office, Fresno, Calif., 1978-80; pvt. practice Monterey and San Diego Counties, San Diego, 1981-87; prof. law Thomas Jefferson Sch. Law, San Diego, 1991—. Legal analyst on TV, radio and in print media. Co-author: Cameras in the Courtroom: Television and the Pursuit of Justice, 1998; editor-in-chief Guild Practitioner, 1994-2003. Recipient Golden Apple award, Student Bar Assn., Thomas Jefferson Sch. Law, 1995—98, Svc. to Legal Edn. award, San Diego County Bar Assn., 2005, Top Attys. award, San Diego, 2006. Mem. Nat. Lawyers Guild (nat. exec. com. 1996-2006, exec. v.p., pres. 2006-), Calif. Attys. for Criminal Justice. Office: Thomas Jefferson Sch Law 2121 San Diego Ave San Diego CA 92110-2986 Office Phone: 619-374-6923. Business E-Mail: marjorie@tjsl.edu.

COHN, MILDRED, retired biochemist, educator; b. NYC, July 12, 1913; d. Isidore M. and Bertha (Klein) Cohn; m. Henry Primakoff, May 30, 1938; children: Nina, Paul, Laura. BA, Hunter Coll., 1931, DSc (hon.), 1984; MA, Columbia U., 1932, PhD, 1937; DSc (hon.), Women's Med. Coll., 1975, Radcliffe Coll., 1978, Washington U., St. Louis, 1981, Brandeis U., 1984, U. Pa., Phila., 1984, U. N.C., 1985; PhD (hon.), Weizmann Inst. Sci., 1988; DSc (hon.), U. Miami, 1990. Rsch. asst. biochemistry George Washington U. Sch. Medicine, 1937—38; rsch. assoc. Cornell Med. Coll., 1938—46, Washington U. Sch. Medicine, 1946—58, assoc. prof. biol. chemistry, 1958—60; assoc. prof. biophysics and phys. biochemistry U. Pa. Med. Sch., 1960—61, prof., 1961—71, prof. biochemistry and biophysics, 1971—82, Benjamin Rush prof. physiol. chemistry, 1978—82, prof. emerita, 1982—; sr. mem. Inst. Cancer Rsch., Phila., 1982—85; chancellor's vis. prof. biophysics U. Calif., Berkeley, 1982; vis. prof. biol. chemistry Johns Hopkins U. Med. Sch., 1985—91. Rsch. assoc. Harvard U. Med. Sch., 1950—51; established investigator Am. Heart Assn., 1953—59; career investigator, 1964—78; vis. prof. chemistry Yale U., 1973. Mem. editl. bd. Jour. Biol. Chemistry, 1958—63, 1967—72. Recipient Hall of Fame award, Hunter Coll., 1973, Disting. Alumni award, 1975, Cresson medal, Franklin Inst., award, Internat. Assn. Women Biochemists, 1979, Humboldt award, Germany, 1980, 1982, Nat. Medal Sci., 1983, award, Am. Acad. Achievement, 1984, Mack award, Ohio State U., 1985, Chandler medal, Columbia U., 1986, Women in Sci. award, N.Y. Acad. Sci., 1992, Gov.'s award for excellence in sci., Pa., 1993, Founders medal, Magnetic Resonance in Biology, 1994, Stein-Moore award, Protein Soc., 1997. Mem.: NAS, Inst. de Biologie Physico-Chimique, Coll. Physicians of Phila. (Disting. Svc. award 1987), Am. Biophys. Soc., Am. Soc. Biochemistry and Molecular Biology (pres. 1978—79), Harvey Soc., Am. Chem. Soc. (chmn. divsn. biol. chemistry 1975—76, Garvan medal 1963, Remsen award Md. sect. 1988, Cinn. sect. Oesper award 2000), Am. Philos. Soc. (v.p. 1994—2000, sec. 2005—), Am. Acad. Arts and Scis., Iota Sigma Pi (hon. nat. mem. 1988), Sigma Xi, Phi Beta Kappa. Office: U Pa Med Sch 242 Anat Chem Bldg Dept Biochemistry & Biophys Philadelphia PA 19104-6059 Business E-Mail: cohn@mail.med.upenn.edu.

COHN, MORTON RAY, lawyer; b. Toledo, July 19, 1923; s. Jay and Martha Cohn; m. Jeane Marie Dushane, Sept. 29, 1960; children: Morton R., Laura Ann. BA, U. Mich., Ann Arbor, 1948; JD, U. Toledo, 1980. Bar: Mich. Exec. dir. Port of Monroe, Mich., 1970—71; pres. retail jeweler Best Jewelers, 1956—70; v.p. sales Buckeye Furniture, Monroe, 1948—56; pvt. practice law Monroe, 1981—. Del. Dem. Nat. Conv., Chgo., 1968; mayor City of Monroe, 1966—67. 1st lt. USAAF, 1943—46. Mem.: Monroe County Bar Assn., State Bar of Mich., Lettermen's M Club/U. Mich. Avocations: golf, tennis, bowling. Home: 1704 Strasburg Rd Monroe MI 46161-9720 Office: 19 E Front St Monroe MI 48161-6206

COHN, SHERMAN LOUIS, lawyer, educator; b. Erie, Pa., July 21, 1932; s. Jacob and Bella (Kaufman) C.; m. Lucy Diaz, July 5, 1998 (dec. Sept. 2003); children by previous marriage: Ronald Bruce, Jerald Seth, Joshua Biber, Steven David, Leah Sura Guihen. BS in Fgn. Svc. summa cum laude, Georgetown U., 1954, JD, 1957, LLM, 1960, M of Acupuncture (hon.), 1993. Bar: Va. 1957 (ret.), D.C. 1957, Md. 1978. Law clk. to Judge Burton R. Laub Erie County Ct., Pa., 1955, Walton H. Hamilton, 1957, Judge Charles Fahy, U.S. Ct. of Appeals for D.C. Circuit, 1957-58; staff atty. Appellate sect. Civil divsn. Dept. Justice, Washington, 1958-62, asst. chief, 1962-65; prof. law Georgetown U. Law Ctr., Washington, 1965—, dir. continuing legal edn., 1977-84. Lectr. Cath. U. Law Sch., 1963-65; vis. prof. Am. U. Law Sch., 1969-78, 92-95; adminstr. Preview of U.S. Supreme Ct. Cases, 1975-79; cons., litigation counsel Select Com. on Presdl. Campaign Activities U.S. Senate, 1973-74; mem. Jud. Conf. D.C. Circuit, 1965-73, 75, 77-78, 86, Jud. Conf. D.C. Ct. Appeals, 1979-81; reporter Nat. Conf. on Appellate Justice, San Diego, 1976. Contbr. articles to profl. jours. Chair Tai Sophia Inst., 2006—; bd. dirs. Jewish Coun. Aging, 2003—, Nat. Acupuncture Found., 2000—, pres., 2004—; chmn. Nat. Accredited Commn. Schs. and Colls. Acupuncture and Oriental Medicine, 1983—94; pres. Traditional Acupuncture Found., 1984—88, Charles Fahy Am. Inn of Ct., 1985—86, Am. Inns Ct. Found., 1985—98, trustee, 1985—96; chmn. bd. dirs. Tai Hsuan Found., 1998—2001; bd. dirs. Acupuncture and Oriental Medicine Alliance, 1999—2003; trustee Rule of Law Found., 2002—; pres. H.M. and A.E. Himmelfarb Found., 2002—06; mem. bd. overseers Tai Sophia Inst., 2003—06, chmn. bd. trustees, 1996—. Recipient A. Sherman Christensen award Am. Inns of Ct., 1990, Younger Fed. Lawyer award for outstanding service to U.S., 1964, Civil Justice award Am. Bd. Trial Advocates, 1993. Mem. ABA, D.C. Bar Assn., Am. Law Inst., Internat. Assn. Jewish Lawyers and Jurists (pres. Am. sect. 1983-87, dep. pres. internat. 1985-91), Jewish Law Assn. (pres. 1998-2002), Soc. Am. Law Tchrs., Georgetown U. Alumni Assn. (chmn. alumni fund 1985-87, Presdl. citation 1978, 87, John Carroll award 1980), B'nai B'rith. Office: Georgetown U Law Ctr 600 New Jersey Ave NW Washington DC 20001-2075 Office Phone: 202-662-9069. Business E-Mail: cohn@law.georgetown.edu.

COHN, STEPHEN ANDREW, publishing executive; b. New Haven, Conn., Aug. 30, 1949; s. Robert Greer and Dorrit Claire Cohn; m. Edith Joan Steudel, Aug. 14, 1971; children: Travis, Rachel, Marlon. BA, Yale U., 1970; MA, Stanford U., 1974; EdS, George Peabody Coll. for Tchrs., 1978. Mng. editor Jour. Health Politics, Policy and Law, Durham, NC, 1981—84; journals mgr. Duke U. Press, Durham, 1984—93, dir., 1993—. Home: 1406 Pennsylvania Ave Durham NC 27705 Office: Duke U Press 905 W Main St Ste 18-B Durham NC 27701 Office Phone: 919-687-3606.

COHN, STEVEN FREDERICK, sociology educator, consultant; b. Chgo., Sept. 5, 1939; s. William Wolf and Sylvia Ann (Wechsler) C.; m. Kathleen Marie Cusick, May 8, 1968 (div. Jan. 1974); 1 child, Iain. BA, Dartmouth Coll., 1961; PhD, Columbia U., 1975. Lectr. U. Strathclyde, Glasgow, Scotland, 1968-69, U. Glasgow, 1969-71; asst. prof. U. Maine, Orono, 1971-77; policy analyst NSF, Washington, 1978-79; assoc. prof. U. Maine, Orono, 1980-85, prof., 1986—. Cons. ACTION, Washington, 1970-72, The Royal Soc., London, 1984. Contbr. articles to profl. jours. Fulbright fellow Coun. for Internat. Exch. Scholars, 1984. Mem. Am. Sociol. Assn. (sect. program com. 1995-96), Ea. Soc. Assn. (publs. com. mem. 1990), Phi Beta Kappa. Jewish. Home: 99 N Main Ave Orono ME 04473-4430 Office: U Maine 201 Fernald Orono ME 04469-0001 Business E-Mail: steve.cohn@umit.maine.edu.

COHN, WILLIAM ETTLINGER, cardiologist, thoracic surgeon, product designer; b. New York, Ny, Sept. 2, 1960; s. Hugh Karl and Judith Ettlinger Cohn; m. Mishaun Victoria Drever, May 30, 1961; children: Benjamen Mycroft, Elizabeth Emily, William Ettlinger, Robert Huntington, Christopher Michael. Grad., Oberlin Coll.; MD, Baylor Coll. of Medicine, Houston, Tex., 1982—86. Diplomate Board of Thoracic Suregry Soc. of Thoracic Surgery, 1994. Assoc. prof. Harvard Med. Sch., Boston, 1991—2002; chief of minimally invasive cardiac surgery Beth Israel Deaconess Med. Ctr., Boston, 2001—04; dir. Minimally Invasive Surgical Tech.; co-dir. Cullen Cardiovascular Rsch. Lab, Tex. Heart Inst., St. Luke's Episcopal Hosp., Houston, 2004—. Author (investigator): (scientific publications) 1)use of ultrasonic welding in cardiac surgery, 2) myocardial revascularization with a pedicaled gastric submucosal flap 3)The Hgraft as a varient of minimally invasive coronary artery bypass; mem. med. team Miracle Workers (ABC), 2006, guest appearance The View, 2006. Achievements include invention of Coronary artery stabilizer to allow bypass surgery without stopping the heart; Nextstitch suture chain for cardiac valve implantation; Catheters For Percutaniously Attaching One Blood Vessel To Another Without Requiring An Operation; Distinguished Inventor of the year, 2000, Intellectual Property Owner's Association; Multiple Patents For Cardiac Valve Procedures Without Stopping The Heart. Office: St Luke's Episcopal Health Sys 6770 Bertner Ave Houston TX 77030 Office Phone: 832-355-3005. Office Fax: 832-355-9004. Business E-Mail: wcohn@heart.thi.tmc.edu. E-mail: wcohn@caregroup.harvard.edu.*

COHON, JARED L., academic administrator; m. Maureen Cohon; 1 child, Hallie. BA in Civil Engring., U. Pa., 1969; MA in Civil Engring., MIT, 1972, PhD in Civil Engring., 1973. Legis. asst. for energy and environment U.S. Senator Daniel P. Moynihan, 1997—98; from faculty to assoc. dean engring. to vice provost rsch. Johns Hopkins; prof. environ. systems analysis, dean Sch. Forestry and Environ. Studies Yale U., 1992—97; pres. Carnegie Mellon U., Pitts., 1997—; apptd. chmn. by Pres. Clinton Nuclear Waste Tech. Review Bd., 1997—2002. Bd. dir. Mellon Fin. Corp. Recipient Joan Queneay Hodges award, Nat. Audubon Soc. and Am. Assn. Engring. Scis., Pareto-Edgeworth award, Multiple Criteria Decision Making Soc. Mem.: Am. Soc. of Civil Engr., Am. Water Resources Assn., Inst. for Ops. Research and Mgmt. Sci., Am. Geophysical Union, Sigma Xi, Tau Beta Pi. Office: Carnegie Mellon Univ 5000 Forbes Ave Pittsburgh PA 15213-3890 Office Phone: 412-268-2600.*

COIFMAN, RONALD R., mathematician, educator; b. Tel Aviv; PhD, U. Geneva, 1965. Former prof. U. Chgo., Washington U.; prof. math. and computer sci. Yale U., New Haven, 1980—, chair math dept., 1986—89, Phillips prof. math., 1998—. Vis. prof. Tel Aviv U., Israel, U. Chgo. Co-author 3 books; contbr. articles and papers to profl. jours. Recipient State of Conn. medal of Sci., Gov. John G. Rowland, 1996, Nat. medal of Sci., 1999. Fellow: NAS; mem.: Conn. Acad. Sci. and Engring., Am. Acad. Arts and Scis. Office: Yale U Dept Math PO Box 208285 New Haven CT 06520-8283 Office Phone: 203-432-1213.

COILE, RUSSELL CLEVEN, electrical engineer, consultant; b. Washington, Mar. 11, 1917; s. Cecil Roy and Gunda Cristoffersen Coile; m. Ruth Ledig, 1942 (div. 1951); children: Russell Cleven Jr., Christopher Christoffersen, Benjamin Paul; m. Ellen Miller Coile, Dec. 27, 1951; children: Jennifer Norah Miller, Jonathan Roy Miller, Andrew Cleven Miller. SB, MIT, 1938, SM, 1939, EE, 1950; PhD, City U., London, 1978; Grad., Naval War Coll., 1959, Air War Coll., 1964. Registered profl. engr., Pa., 1947, DC, 1951, lifetime instr. credential in engring., Calif. Cmty. Colls., 1989; cert. emergency mgr. Internat. Assn. Emergency Mgrs., 1993, lic. pvt. pilot FAA. Rsch. asst. Elec. Engring. Rsch. Lab., MIT, Cambridge, 1938—39; magnetician Cargnegie Instn. Wash./Huancayo (Peru) Magnetic Obs., 1939—42; engr. Colton & Foss, Inc., Washington, 1946—47; ops. rsch. scientist Ops. Evaluation Group, MIT, Washington, 1947—62; dir. rsch. Ops. Rsch. Group, Office Naval Rsch., Washington, 1953—57; dir. marine corps ops. analysis group Ctr. For Naval Analyses, Franklin Inst., Washington, 1962—67; ops. rsch. analyst Ctr. for Naval Analyses, U. Rochester, Arlington, Va., 1967—78; sr. rsch. analyst Ketron, Arlington, 1978—81; dep. exec. dir./chief scientist Planning Rsch. Corp., Fort Ord, Calif., 1982—87; sr. analyst Evaluation Tech. Inc., Monterey, Calif., 1988—90; disaster coord./emergency program mgr. Pacific Grove Fire Dept., Pacific Grove, Calif., 1990—2000; adj. prof. Inst. for Joint Warfare Analysis, Naval Postgraduate Sch., Monterey, 1998—2000; dir. disaster svcs. Carmel Chpt., ARC, Carmel-by-the-Sea, Calif., 2000—01; disaster cons., 2002—. Lectr. US Naval War Coll., 1949, 56, 59, Anthropol. Soc. Hawaii, Honolulu, 1951, US Naval Postgrad. Sch., 1951, 54, 1984—86, Japanese Maritime Def. Force Staff Coll., 1956, NATO Sci. Affairs Conf., London, 1964, US Naval Acad., 1965, UK Royal Mil. Coll. Sci., 1989, 92, 93, UK Inst. Civl Def., 1994, 95, UK Emergency Planning Soc., 1995, UN Dept. Humanitarian Affairs, 1996, Monterey Inst. Internat. Studies, 2000,

05; expert witness FCC Broadcast Station Hearing, 1946; Am. del. Internat. Fedn. Operational Rsch. Socs., Oslo, 1963, World Agy. Planetary Monitoring and Earthquake Risk Reduction, Geneva, 2001; mem. small arms adv. com. Advanced Rsch. Projects Agy., Dept. Def., Washington, 1968—70; cons. Pres. Sci. Adv. Counsel, 1965, IEEE, 1966—67, Purdue U., Lafayette, Ind., 1978, NSF, Washington, 1997, Monterey Inst. Internat. Studies, 2005, Nat. Organ. Disability, 2005, Fed. Emergency Mgmt. Agy., Washington, 2000—02, Assn. Monterey Bay Area Govts., Marina, Calif., 2002—, others; instr. Neighborhood Emergency Response Teams, Pacific Grove, 1994—97; mem. Nat. Civil Def., Emergency Mgmt. Monument Commn., 2001—02. Asst. editor: Quality Control and Applied Statistics Abstracts, 1956—57, mem. editl. adv. bd.: Hungarian Acad. Scis. Internat. Jour. Scientometrics, 1978—97; contbr. articles to profl. jours. Chmn. cmty. working group Global Disaster Info. Network Conf., Mexico City, 1999, Ankara, Turkey, 2001; acredited vol. examiner FCC Amateur Radio Lic. Exams, 1993—; Am. del. founding conf. World Agy. Planetary Monitoring and Earthquake Risk Reduction, Geneva, 2001. Commd. 2nd lt. US Army, 1938, active duty, 1942—46, WWII, with US Army, 1945, advanced through grades to col. USAF, 1962, ret., 1977. Recipient Exemplary Practices in Emergency Mgmt. award, Fed. Emergency Mgmt. Agy., 1998, 1999, 2000; fellow, NSF, 1997. Fellow: Fellowship Operational Rsch., Inst. Civil Def. and Disaster Studies, Am. Geog. Soc.; mem.: IEEE (life; cons. 1955), Nat. Orgn. Disability, Nat. Orgn. on Disability, Am. Soc. Profl. Emergency Planners, Internat. Test and Evaluation Assn. (bd. dirs. 1985—88), U.K. Emergency Planning Soc., Inst. for Ops. Rsch. and the Mgmt. Scis., Am. Soc. for Info. Sci., Internat. Emergency Mgmt. Soc., Internat. Assn. Emergency Mgrs. (cert. emergency mgrs. comm. 1998—2003, assessor Emergency Mgmt. Accreditation Program 2003—), Island Sailing Club (Cowes, Eng.), Marine Meml. Club (San Francisco). Achievements include world speed record holder for flight from Washington to Rome, NY. Avocations: sailing, amateur radio. Home: 970 Egan Ave Pacific Grove CA 93950-2406 Office: Sand City Police Dept 1 Sylvan Park Sand City CA 93955 Office Phone: 831-394-1467. Personal E-mail: russell@coile.com.

COINER, MARYROSE C., psychologist; b. Newark, Dec. 14, 1949; d. William J. and Margaret (Queenan) Carew; m. H. Michael Coiner, Mar. 8, 1975; children: John P., Thomas M. BS, St. Peter's Coll., Jersey City, NJ, 1971; PhD, Yale U., 1978. Lic. psychologist, Mass. Asst. prof. psychology Millersville State U., Pa., 1978-80; staff psychologist Framingham Union Hosp., Mass., 1980-90; pvt. practice Marlboro and Framingham, Mass., 1981—. Bd. dirs. Together Inc., Marlboro, 1983-91, Advocates Inc., Framingham, 1991—. NSF fellow, 1971-74. Mem. APA, Mass. Psychol. Assn. Office: 14 Vernon St Ste 206 Framingham MA 01701-4733 Home Phone: 508-485-7732; Office Phone: 508-620-9948. E-mail: m.coiner@verizon.net.

COIROLO, CHRISTINA, writer, author representative; arrived in US, 1964, naturalized, 1972; d. Jose M. Coirolo and Ilia Barrios; m. Mikel Goodwin (div.); children: Lucy Abdo, Paulette Maloney, Mikel Goodwin, Christine Goodwin, Richard Goodwin. BA, Utah State U., Logan, 1971, MEd, 1972. Cert. interpreter Lang. Line Svc., Monterey, Calif. Mng. dir. Britannia Rds., Lansing, Mich., 1982—2000, The Writing Clinic, Charlotte, Mich., 2004—; author rep. Outskirts Press, Parker, Colo., 2006—. Cons. CNC Consulting, Lansing, 2001—. Author: Old Sins Cast Long Shadows, 2005, A Nice and Quiet Place, 2006, Double Dealing, 2006, (manuals) Tour Management, 2000, Guide to Hispanics in the US, 2004, The Writing Clinic, 2004. Mem.: ACLU, Am. Assn. Univ. Women. Democrat. Avocations: writing, reading, interior decorating. Home: 1420 Jack Henry Dr Charlotte MI 48813 Fax: 517-541-3868. E-mail: criscoi@juno.com.

COKELET, GILES ROY, biomedical engineering educator; b. NYC, Jan. 7, 1932; s. Roy S. and Anna M. (Trippel) C.; m. Sarah Drew, June 15, 1963; children: Becky, Bradford BS, Calif. Inst. Tech., 1957, MS, 1958; ScD, MIT, 1963. Rsch. engr. Dow Chem. Co., Williamsburg, Va., 1958-60; asst. prof. Calif. Inst. Tech., Pasadena, 1964-68; assoc. prof. Mont. State U., Bozeman, 1969-76, prof., 1976-78, U. Rochester, NY, 1978-98; rsch. prof. Mont. State U., Bozeman, 1998—. Contbr. articles to profl. jours. With U.S. Army, 1954-55, Japan. Recipient Sr. U.S. Scientist award Humboldt-Stiftung, Bonn, Fed. Republic Germany, 1981-82, 88. Fellow AAAS; mem. Biomed. Engrng. Soc., Microcirculatory Soc., No. Am. Soc. Biorheology, Internat. Soc. Biorheology (past pres., Poiseuille medal 1999). Avocations: stamp collecting/philately, hiking. Office: Mont State U Dept Chem and Biol Engrng Bozeman MT 59717-0001 Office Phone: 406-994-5928. Business E-Mail: giles_c@coe.montana.edu.

COKER, HOWARD COLEMAN, lawyer; b. Jacksonville, Fla., Apr. 30, 1947; BS in Journalism, U. Fla., 1969, JD, 1971. Bar: Fla. 1972, cert.: Fla. (in civil trial practice) 1985, Nat. Bd. Trial Advocacy (civil trial specialist) 1987. Asst. state atty. Fourth Jud. Cir., 1972; assoc. Howell, Kirby, Montgomery, D'Aiuto & Dean, P.A., 1973-76; pres., dir. Coker, Schickel, Sorenson & Daniel, P.A., Jacksonville, Fla., 1976—. Guest lectr. more than 40 CLE seminars on litig. and trial matters throughout Fla., for Fla. Bar Assn., Fla Justice Assn. (formerly Acad. Fla. Trial Lawyers); advisor mock trial team U. Fla. Law Sch., 1991-98; adj. prof. U. North Fla.; mem. Nat. Conf. Bar Pres., 1997-2003. Chair ednl. adv. coun. U. North Fla., 1992-94, chair adv. bd. for paralegals, 1990-92; bd. dir. Jacksonville Zool. Gardens, 2000-, chair, 2006-07; mem. adv. bd. Parks, Recreation, Entertainment & Conservation, Jacksonville, 2006-; bd. dir. Spina Bifida Assn. Jacksonville, 2000-. Named Lawyer of Yr., The Daily Record, 2007; named one of Best Lawyers in Am., Million Dollar Advocates Forum, 1999—2000, Top Lawyers in Fla., Fla. Monthly, 2003, Fla. Legal Elite, 2005—07, Jacksonville Best Lawyers, 2007. Fellow Am. Bar Found., Internat. Soc. Barristers; mem. ABA (ho. of dels., jud. qualifications commn.), ATLA, Am. Arbitration Assn. (panel arbitrators 1983—), Fla. Bar Assn. (pres. 1998-99, bd. govs. 1994-99, exec. com. 1995-97, all bar fconf. del. 1990-92, 94, 96, 97, budget com. 1995-97, bd. rev. coml. on profl. ethics chair 1995-96, disciplinary rev. com. 1994-95, jud. qualification screen com. 1994-95, legis. com. 1994-95, profl. retreat chair 1996, program evaluation com. chair 1996-97, 4th jud. cir. grievance com. reviewer 1994-97, coun. sects. 1991-94, chair 1993-94, sect. leadership conf. chair 1995, trial lawyers sect. exec. coun. 1987-94, bd. govs. liaison 1996, chair 1992-93, exec. co. 1989-93, legis. com. 1988-93), Am. Bd. Trial Advocates (pres. Jacksonville chpt. 1988—, media rep. 1988, exec. com. 1988—, diplomate; Jacksonville chpt. Trial Lawyer of Yr. 2003), Am. Judicature Soc., Chester Bedell Meml. Found. (trustee 1996-2001), First Coast Trial Lawyers Assn. (Pres. award 1996), Fla. Justice Assn. (formerly Acad. Fla. Trial Lawyers; bd. dirs. 1995—, pres. 2002-2003, Eagle sponsor 1990—; Silver Eagle award 1996, 1997, 2004, Legislative Shoe Leather award 1998, 2000, Golden Eagle award 1998, Eagle Workhorse award 1999, Wings of Justice award 2000, Staff Appreciation award 1999, B. J. Masterson award 2005, Perry Nichols award 2006, M. McKinley Smiley award 2006, Tiger in the Bush award 2007), Fla. Lawyers Assn. for Maintenance of Excellence (bd. dirs. 1995-97), So. Trial Lawyers, Fla. Supreme Ct. Hist. Soc., Jacksonville Bar Assn., Roscoe Pound Found., U.S. Supreme Ct. Hist. Soc., Internat. Acad. Trial Lawyers, Fla. Conservation Assn. (pres. 1993-94), Fla. Ducks Unltd. — (chmn. 1991-93; Sportsman of Yr. 1994), Fla. Wildlife Fedn., Seminole Club (bd. dirs. 1988, pres., 1989), U. Fla. Nat. Alumni Assn. (pres.'s coun. 1992-2001), Sigma Alpha Epsilon, Phi Delta Phi. Office: PO Box 1860 136 E Bay St Jacksonville FL 32201 Home: 4931 River Point Rd Jacksonville FL 32207 Office Phone: 904-356-6071. Office Fax: 904-353-2425. Business E-Mail: hcoker@cokerlaw.com.

COKER, LARRY E., former college football coach; b. June 23, 1948; m. Dianna Bryant; 1 child, Lara. BS in History, Northeastern St. Univ., Tahlequah, Okla., 1970; MS in Guidance Counseling and Phys. Edn., Northeastern St. Univ., 1973. Offensive backfield coach Tulsa U., 1979—82; offensive coord. Okla. St. U., 1983—88, U. Okla., 1990—92; defensive backfield coach Ohio State U., 1993—94; quarterbacks coach, offensive coord. U. Miami, 1995—2000, head coach, 2001—06. Recipient Paul "Bear" Bryant award, Nat. Sportscasters & Sportswriters Assn., 2001. Achievements include coaching U. Miami to the 2001 BCS Nat. Championship.

COKER, MICH, lawyer; b. Gulfport, Miss., 1975; BS in Spanish, Millsaps Coll., 1997; postgraduate diploma in Sci., U. Queensland, Brisbane, Australia, 1998; studied Internat. Law & Comparative Constl. Law, U. Nairobi, Kenya, 2000; JD, James E. Rogers Coll. of Law, U. Ariz., 2002; LLM in Taxation, U. Washington Sch. of Law, 2003. Legal cons. Wash. Environ. Coun., Seattle; atty. Snell & Wilmer LLP, Tucson. Author: (publications) Saving the Sierra: Alternative Mechanisms for Conserving Northern Mexico's Last Wild Places, 2003, Avoiding Employee Lawsuits 101: Top Ten Employee Mistakes, 2006. Bd. dir. Tucson Audubon Soc., Tucson Hispanic Chamber of Commerce, chair, Pub. Policy Com. Named one of 40 Under 40, Tucson Bus. Edge, 2006. Mem.: Pima County Bar Assn., FBA, ABA, State Bar of Ariz. Avocation: hiking. Office: Snell & Wilmer LLP One S Church Ave Ste 1500 Tucson AZ 85701 Office Phone: 520-882-1209.

COKUSLU, LYNDA ELIZABETH MCCORD, medical assistant; b. Atlanta, June 11, 1956; d. Joseph Adair and Yvonne (Champagne) McCord; m. Fethi Cokuslu, Aug. 24, 1985; children: Sasha, Sedef, Samantha. Cert. med. asst., Bryman Sch., 1975; MBA/MHA, U. Phoenix. Lic. GAINS for Health and Life Ins. 2007; cert. med. asst. 2004, AAS, 2006, BAS, 2007. Casuality/liability claims processor Continental Ins./UAC, Atlanta, 1978—82; nutrition asst. Fayette County Edn., Peachtree City, Ga., 2001—03. Mem. adv. bd. Clayton State U. Host benefit Hapeville (Ga.) Hist. Soc., 1988; officer PTA, Hapeville, 1997; catechist Youth/Adult Sch. Religion, Hapeville, 1996—2002, Fayetteville, 2003—04. Mem.: Am. Health Info. Mgmt. Assn., Am. Med. Asst. Assn., Travelers Protective Assn., Midtown Bus. Assn., Internat. Poet Soc. Roman Catholic. Home: 105 Buckeye Ln Fayetteville GA 30214 Office: Audvi Elecs 140 A Robinson Dr Fayetteville GA 30214 Office Phone: 404-780-6424. Personal E-mail: lcokuslu@bellsouth.net.

COLABUFO, STEVEN JAMES, mathematics educator; b. Syracuse, NY, June 24, 1977; s. Michael and Sharon Anne (Militello) Colabufo; m. Krista Leslie Pearse, July 27, 2002; 1 child, Joseph Robert. BA in Math., St. John Fisher Coll., Rochester, NY, 1999, MS in Math., Sci., Tech. in Edn., 2003; postgrad., SUNY, Brockport, 2007. Cert. math. tchr. NY. Math. tchr. Rochester City Sch. Dist., 1999—. Graphing calculator cons. Tex. Instruments, Rochester, 2003—. Mem. Hilton Fire Dept. Marching Band. Mem.: Nat. Coun. Math. Tchrs., Rochester Curling Club, KC. Republican. Roman Catholic. Home: 11 Saddleback Dr Rochester NY 14624

COLACELLO, BOB (ROBERT JOHN COLACELLO), magazine editor, writer; b. Bklyn., May 8, 1947; s. John and Liberina (Alberino) C. BS in Fgn. Service, Georgetown U., 1969; MFA, Columbia U., 1971. Mng. editor Interview Mag., NYC, 1971-72, spl. contbg. editor, 1972-74, exec. editor, 1974-83; contbg. editor Parade Mag., NYC, 1983—, Vanity Fair Mag., NYC, 1984-86, 88—, sr. editor, 1986-87. Cons. Random House, N.Y.C., 1985-86. Author: Holy Terror: Andy Warhol Closeup, 1990, Ronnie & Nancy: Their Path to the White House, 2004; co-author: From A to B and Back Again: The Philosophy of Andy Warhol, 1975; co-author, exec. editor Andy Warhol's Exposures, 1979. Republican. Roman Catholic.

COLACINO, MICHAEL, real estate company executive; BA cum laude, Harvard Coll., 1979; MS in Real Estate, NYU. Pres. Studley, NYC, 2002—. Faculty mem. NYU, mem. Real Estate Roundtable; comml. alliance adv. bd. Realtors; mem. Real Estate Bd. NY. Contbr. articles to profl. publications. Bd. dirs. Internat. Ctr. Photography; mem. Horace Mann Sch., Children's Aid Soc., Film Soc. Lincoln Ctr., Nat. Acad. Design, Tuberous Sclerosis Alliance, Jazz at Lincoln Ctr.; adv. bd. Zell-Lurie Real Estate Ctr. Wharton U. Office: Studley 300 Park Ave 3rd Floor New York NY 10022 Office Phone: 212-326-1008. E-mail: mcolacino@studley.com.*

COLACURCIO, MICHAEL J., English professor; BA, Xavier Univ., 1958, MA, 1959; PhD, Univ. Ill., 1963. Disting. prof. English UCLA. Fellow: Am. Acad. Arts & Scis. Office: 299 Humanities Building UCLA PO Box 951530 Los Angeles CA 90095-1530 Office Phone: 310-825-9612. Business E-Mail: COLACURC@humnet.ucla.edu.*

COLAIANNI, JOSEPH VINCENT, judge; b. Detroit, Mar. 19, 1935; s. Pasquale and Marie D. (Mastrantonio) C.; m. Rita Milena Roll, Oct. 13, 1962; children: Marie Elena, Joseph Vincent, Michael Philip, Vincent Gerard. BEE, U. Detroit, 1956; postgrad., Wayne State U., 1956—58; JD with honors, George Washington U., 1961. Bar: Mich. 1962, Ohio 1963, Washington 1964. Assoc. firm Fay and Fay, Cleve., until 1965; trial atty. civil divsn. Dept. Justice, Washington, 1965-70; commr. US Ct. Claims, Washington, 1970-73, trial judge, 1973-77; judge US Ct. Claims DC, 1977-84; mng. ptnr. Pennie & Edmonds, Washington, 1984-98; chair intellectual property Patton Boggs LLP, Washington, 1998—. Sci. liaison com. Sci. Ct., 1976-84; prof. grad. sch. Patent Resources Inst.; adj. prof. Am. U., 1984-87, Cath. U. Sch. Law, 1997—; adv. com. patents and trademarks US Dept. Commerce, 1987-89; sr. adviser US Claims Ct. Adv. Coun., 1984—; adv. com. US Patent and Trademark Office. Adv. bd. Patent, Trademark and Copyright Jour., 1984-91. District Heights Recreation Coun., Md., 1969-70; bd. dirs. Henson Valley Montessori Sch.; pres. Tilden PTA, 1979-81; pres. Lido Civic Club, 1981, bd. dirs., 1982-90, 2000—; trustee Western Coll. Medicine, 1982-85; adv. bd. Holy Rosary, Washington, 1984-; co-pres. U. Md. at College Park Parents Assn., 1991-97; mem. pres. cabinet U. Detroit Mercy, 1982—, commn. on future Coll. Engrng., 1995-96. Mem. Am., Fed. Bar Assns., Patent Office Soc., Mich., Ohio, Washington Bars, Phi Delta Phi, Eta Kappa Nu, Omicron Delta Kappa, Phi Delta Kappa, George Washington U. Law Rev. (1960-61). Office Phone: 202-457-6174. Business E-Mail: jcolaianni@pattonboggs.com.

COLAIANNIA, LOUIS MARIO, dentist, composer, pianist; b. Denver, Colorado, Jan. 28, 1955; s. Louis Andrew and Rose Marie C.; 1 child, Louis Adam. DDS, U. Colo., 1980. Dentist, Denver, 1980-98; dental dir., exec. dir. Safeguard Health Plans, Anaheim, Calif., 1996; pres. Colaiannia Enterprises Inc., Wheatridge, Colo., 1999—; CEO Mountain Home Health Care, Inc., 1999—. Advisor Songs Across the Sea, Littleton, Colo., 1998. Composer, pianist (music CD) Corners of the Soul, 1996; Sailing on a Dream, 1998; Colaiannia's First Symphony, 2000; internat. concert pianist. Bd. dir. Evergreen, Colo. Music Festival, 2000; presenter numerous benefit concerts nationwide, 1996—; founder, bd. dir. Angel Care Found. Mem. Sons of Italy Lodge. Avocations: mountain climbing, sports. Home: 5753 W 61st Dr Arvada CO 80003-5158 Office: Colaiannia Enterprises Inc 1300 Carr St Lakewood CO 80214

COLAIZZI, JOHN LOUIS, medical educator; b. Pitts., May 10, 1938; s. Peter Richard and Lena M. (Sebastian) C.; m. Maria Rose Santoro, Aug. 12, 1967; children: James J., Patricia R., John Louis. BS, U. Pitts., 1960; MS, Purdue U., 1962, PhD, 1965. Asst. prof. Sch. Pharmacy, W.Va. U., Morgantown, 1964—65; asst. prof., assoc. prof. Sch. Pharmacy, U. Pitts., 1965—76, prof., chmn., assoc. dean, 1976—78; prof., dean Sch. Pharmacy Rutgers U., Piscataway, NJ, 1978—2007, acting v.p. acad. affairs, 2003, prof., 2007—. Bd. dirs. Rahway Hosp., N.J., 2003—; bd. dirs. Robert Wood Johnson Univ. Hosp., New Brunswick, N.J., 1984—, chmn., 1997-2000; mem. Medicaid Drug Utilization Rev. Bd. N.J., 1996-97; bioavailability cons. Drug Utilization Rev. Coun. N.J., 1997-2000. Mem. Am. Pharm. Assn., Am. Assn. Pharm. Scis., Am. Soc. Health-Sys. Pharmacists, Am. Assn. Coll. Pharmacy, Pharm. Care Mgmt. Assn. (dean's adv. coun. 1998-2003), Somerset County Tech. Inst. (pharm. techn. adv. bd. 2007—), Am. Inst. History of Pharmacy, Rho Chi, Alpha Zeta Omega, Sigma Xi. Democrat. Roman Catholic. Home: 21 Jason Dr East Brunswick NJ 08816-3342 Office: Rutgers U Sch Pharmacy 160 Frelinghuysen Rd Piscataway NJ 08854-8020 Office Phone: 732-445-5215. Personal E-mail: j.colaizzi@comcast.net. Business E-Mail: jlcolaiz@rci.rutgers.edu.

COLAIZZI, ROGER A., lawyer; b. Rochester, Pa., June 16, 1958; BA, Dickinson Coll., 1980; JD, Widener U., 1983. Bar: Pa. 1983, Md. 1984, DC 1988, NY 1991, Va. 1991, US Dist. Ct. (ea. dist.) Va. 1991, US Dist. Ct., DC 1992. Prosecutor honors prog. Civil Rights Div. Employment Litig. Sect., US Dept. Justice, 1983—87; spcl. asst. US Atty. for DC, 1986—87; ptnr. Intellectual Property Litig. Dept. Venable LLP, Washingotn, DC, 1992—. Mem. No. Va. Tech. Coun. Recipient Del. Law Forum Award. Mem.: ABA (mem. Litig. Sect.), Alexandria Bar Assn., NY Bar Assn., Pa. Bar Assn., Va. Bar Assn., Md. Bar Assn., DC Bar Assn. Office: Venable LLP 575 7th St NW Washington DC 20004 Office Phone: 202-344-8051. Office Fax: 202-344-8300. E-mail: racolaizzi@venable.com.

COLALUCA, BETH, pediatric neurpsychologist; b. Dayton, Ohio, June 1, 1969; d. Mario Anthony and Janet Mae Colaluca; m. Michael R. Hooper, Oct. 19, 2002. BS, Tex. A&M U., 1991; MS, U.North Tex., Denton, 1996; PhD, U. North Tex., Denton, 1998. Lic. psychologist Tex. State Bd. of Examiners of Psychologists, registered nat. register health svc. provider Coun. for Nat. Register of Health Svc. Providers in Psychology. Pediat. psychologist Tex. Scottish Rite Hosp. for Children, Dallas, 2000—02; pediat. neuropsychologist Cook Children's Med. Ctr., Ft. Worth, 2002—. Mgr, hematology/oncology Cook Children's Med. Ctr., Ft. Worth, 2002—. Recipient rsch. grant, North Tex. Cancer Rsch. Found., 2003. Mem.: APA, Dallas Psychol. Assn., Tex. Psychol. Assn., Internat. Neuropsychology Soc., Nat. Acad. of Neuropsychology. Office: Cook Children's Med Ctr 1516 Cooper St Fort Worth TX 76104 Home Phone: 817-745-0012; Office Phone: 682-885-1480. Office Fax: 682-885-3600. Business E-Mail: bethc@cookchildrens.org.

COLAN, JOANNE, video blogger, television personality; b. Lancashire, UK, Mar. 20; Rschr., host, writer, prodn. coord. BBC TV, BBC Radio; Europe VJ MTV, 2000—04; music/DJ curator Table 50 club, Manhattan; travel adventure series host, Any Given Latitude Fine Living Network; and host, co-prodr. Rocketboom.com, 2006—. Named one of Top 10 Savvy Women in Podcasting, Podonomics, 2006; recipient Best European Satellite Music Programme award, What Satellite UK & Europe TV Poll, 2001. Office: Rocketboom Planetarium Sta PO Box 804 New York NY 10024-0545 Business E-Mail: hi@rocketboom.com.*

COLANDER, DAVID CHARLES, economist, educator; b. Jamestown, NY, Nov. 16, 1947; s. Fred J. and Elsie J. (Clauson) C. Student, U. Birmingham, Eng., 1968-69; BA, Columbia U., 1970, MPhil, PhD, 1976. Policy fellow Brookings Instn., Washington, 1977-78; cons. U.S. Govt., Washington, 1977-82; assoc. prof. U. Miami, Coral Gables, Fla., 1979-82; Christian A. Johnson Disting. prof. Middlebury (Vt.) Coll., 1982—; Kelley profl. disting. tchr. Princeton U., 2001—02. Author: (with Harry Landreth) The Coming of Keynesianism to America, 1989, (with Abba Lerner) MAP: A Market Anti-Inflation Plan, 1980, Macroeconomic Theory and Policy, 1986, (with Elgin Hunt) Social Science, 1984, 87, 90, 93, 96, 99, (with Harry Landreth) History of Economic Thought, 1988, 93, 2000, 2004, (with Arjo Klamer, The Making of an Economist, 1990, Why Aren't Economists as Important as Garbagemen?, 1991, Economics, 1993, 96, 98, 2001, 2004, (with Dewey Dane) The Art of Monetary Policy, 1994, (with Ed Ganber) Macroeconomics, 2002, The Lost Art of Economics, 2000; contbr. articles to profl. jours. With U.S. Army, 1970. Mem. Am. Econ. Assn., Ea. Econ. Assn. Avocation: biking. Office: Middlebury Coll Dept Econ Munroe 215 College St Middlebury VT 05753 Home Phone: 802-388-0015; Office Phone: 802-443-5302. E-mail: colander@middlebury.edu.

COLANGELO, BRYAN, professional sports team executive; b. June 1, 1965; s. Jerry John and Joan E. (Helmich) Colangelo; m. Barbara Colangelo; children: Mattia, Sofia. BS in Bus. Mgmt. and Applied Econ., Cornell U., 1987. Scout Phoenix Suns, 1990—92, asst. dir. player pers., 1992—95, v.p. adminstrn., gen. mgr., 1995—97, exec. v.p., 1997—99, gen. mgr., 1997—2006, pres., 1999—2006; pres., gen. mgr. Toronto Raptors, 2006—. Alt. gov. bd. govs. NBA; tournament dir. NIKE Desert Classic; pres. Phoenix Arena Sports; bd. dirs. Ariz. Sports Coun., Phoenix Suns Charities, Home Base Youth Svcs. Bd. dirs. Phoenix C. of C., vice chmn. econ. devel., mem. exec com. Named one of Top 25 Valley Bus. Leaders, Ariz. Bus. Jour., 1995, NBA Exec. of Yr., The Sporting News, 2005, 2007. Office: Toronto Raptors Air Canada Ctr 40 Bay St Ste 400 Toronto ON M5J 2X2 Canada*

COLANGELO, CARMON, artist, printmaker, educator; b. Toronto, Oct. 29, 1957; came to U.S., 1981; s. Patrick and Coreen (Ciciretto) C.; m. Susan Jane Berry, Oct. 6, 1984; children: Jessica Lynn, Ashley Coreen, Chelsea Michelle. BFA in printmaking & painting, U. Windsor, Ontario, Can., 1981; MFA in printmaking, La. State U., 1983. Instr. La. State U., Baton Rouge, 1984; asst. prof. art W.Va. U., Morgantown, 1984—88, grad. coord., 1986—99, assoc. prof., 1988—94, dir. grad. studies in art, 1989—2006, assoc. chair div. art, 1993, chair, prof. art, 1993—97; dir., prof. art Lamar Dodd Sch. Art, U. Ga., Athens, 1997—2006; disting. rsch. prof. U. Ga., Athens, 2003—06; dean, Sam Fox Sch. Design and Visual Arts Washington U., St. Louis, 2006—, Desmond Lee prof. collaboration in arts, 2006—. Founding dir. Ideas for Creative Exploration, U. Ga. Exhibited prints in shows U.S.-Korea Internat., 1989, Boston Printmakers 42d, 1990, Silvermine Internat., 1992, New World Contemporary Prints, Balt., 1993; solo exhbns.: Re-tracings, John and Jane Allcott Gallery, U. Chapel Hill, NC, 2001, Street Gallery, Liverpool Contemporary Biennial, Eng., Fountain of Age, Sandler-Hudson Gallery, Atlanta, 2002, Phantasmasoria, Scuola Internat. di Grafica, Venice, Italy, 2003, Laura Mesaros Gallery, W.Va., 2004, Phantasmasoria, Maseo de Pueblos, Guanajuato, Mex., 2004, Bruno David Gallery, St. Louis, 2006; represented in collections Nat. Mus. Am. Art, Wash. DC, Whitney Mus. of Am. Art, Fla. State Art Mus., Musco Nat. del Grabado, Buenos Aires, Kennedy Mus. Art, Butler Mus. Am. Art, Fogg Art Mus., Bibliotechue Internat. Recipient Clemson Nat. award, 1993, 65th Nat. SAGA Purchase award, NY, 1993; featured in Printmaking: A Primary Form of Expression, 1992, Sr. Rsch. Fine Arts grant, U. Ga., 1998; named Disting. Rsch. prof., U. Ga., 2003, Deem Disting. lectr. W.Va. U., 2004. Mem. Boston Printmakers, L.A. Printmaking Soc., Phila. Print Club, Mo. Print Consortium, Coll. Art Assn, Coll. Art Assn. (bd. mem.), Nat. Coll. Art Adminstrs., Ga. Mus. Art (bd. mem.), So. Graphics Coun. (bd. mem., 1995-1997), Art Papers (bd. mem, 1998). Avocation: sports. Office: Wash Univ St Louis Campus Box 1213 One Brookings Dr Saint Louis MO 63160-4899 Office Phone: 314-935-9300. Business E-Mail: colangelo@wustl.edu.

COLANGELO, JERRY JOHN, professional sports team executive; b. Chgo. Heights, Ill., Nov. 20, 1939; s. Larry and Sue (Drancek) C.; m. Joan E. Helmich, Jan. 20, 1961; children: Kathy, Kristen, Bryan, Mandie. BA, U. Ill., 1962. Ptnr. House of Charles, Inc., 1962—63; assoc. D.O. Klein & Assocs., 1964—65; dir. merchandising Chgo. Bulls, 1966—68; gen. mgr.

Phoenix Suns, 1968—87, exec. v.p., 1987, pres., 1987—99, CEO, 1987—2007, chmn., 1999—; CEO Arizona Diamondbacks, Phoenix, 1998—2004, exec. emeritus, 2004—. Mng. dir. USA Basketball Men's Sr. Nat. Team prog., 2005—. Named Most Influential Sports Figure in Ariz. for Twentieth Cent., Ariz. Republic, Top Businessperson, Phoenix Bus. Jour., NBA Exec. of Yr., 1976, 1981, 1989, 1993; named to Naismith Meml. Hall of Fame, 2004. Mem. Basketball Congress Am. (former exec. v.p., dir.), Phi Kappa Psi. Clubs: Univ., Phoenix Execs. Republican. Baptist. Office: USA Basketball 5465 Mark Dabling Blvd Colorado Springs CO 80918-3842*

COLANGELO-BRYAN, JEREMY PAUL, urban planner, transportation executive; b. NY, Mar. 1, 1973; s. Nicholas Bryan and Juliette Colangelo; m. Bridget Anderson, Dec. 15, 2006. BA, Macalester Coll., St. Paul, Minn., 1995; MA, Rutgers U., New Brunswick, NJ, 2000. Fellow East Bay Conservation Corps., Oakland, Calif., 1995—97; mgr. workforce transp. NJ Transit, Newark, 1999—2001, analyst policy and planning, 2003—05, mgr. access to region's core, 2005—; staff transp. group Gov.'s Transition Team, Trenton, NJ, 2001—02; policy specialist commissioner's office NJ Dept. Transp., Trenton, 2002—03. Cons. Green Lake 2020, Seattle, 1998. Vol. Election Protection, Columbus, Ohio, 2004, NY, 2006. Fellow, Rutgers U., 1998—2000; DeWitt Wallace Disting. scholarship, Macalester Coll., 1991—95. Mem.: Phi Beta Kappa. Office: NJ Transit One Penn Plz East Newark NJ 07105 Home Phone: 973-229-2225; Office Phone: 973-491-7743.

COLANTUONO, THOMAS PAUL, prosecutor, former state legislator; b. Newton, Mass., Oct. 4, 1951; m. Pamela E. Chaloge. BA, Duke U., 1973; JD, Boston Coll., 1976. Bar: NH 1976. Assoc. Hamblett & Kerrigan, Nashua, NH, 1976-78; asst. atty gen. NH Atty. Gen.'s Office, 1978-81; pvt. practice Derry, 1981—2001; state senator State of NH, 1990-96; vice chmn. exec. dept., adminstrn. coms.; exec. councilor State of NH, 1999—2001; US atty. dist. NH US Dept. Justice, NH, 2002—. Former chmn ways and means com., NH Senate, mem. capitol budget, fin., judiciary, ins. coms., vice chmn. exec. dept., adminstrn. coms. Mem. ABA, NH Bar Assn., Derry Rotary, Londonderry and Hudson C. of C. Office: US Attys Office 55 Pleasant St Rm 352 Concord NH 03301*

COLASURD, RICHARD MICHAEL, lawyer; b. Navarre, Ohio, Apr. 1, 1928; s. Michael and Adeline (Manack) C.; m. Jane Cooley, Dec. 20, 1986; children: Steven Michael, David Gerard, Cathie Marie. AB, U. Notre Dame, 1950; JD, Harvard U., 1953. Bar: Ohio 1953. Practice in, Toledo, 1960-99; spl. agt. FBI, 1953-56; asst. U.S. atty. charge Northwestern Ohio, 1956-60; mem. firm Shumaker, Loop & Kendrick, 1960-64; asst. city law dir. Toledo, 1964; mem. firm Mulholland, Hickey & Lyman, 1964-73; U.S. commr., 1963-67. Mem. Ohio Bar Assn., Toledo Bar Assn., Soc. Former Spl. Agts. FBI, Lexington C.C., Rotary. Roman Catholic. Home: 16133 Edgemont Dr Fort Myers FL 33908-3651

COLASURDO, IRMA LOUISE, secondary school educator, department chairman; b. Houma, La., Feb. 9, 1946; d. Irma Menard Dover; m. Charles Lewis Colasurdo, June 30, 1984. BA, Nicholls State U., Thibodaux, La., 1967, MEd, 1978. Tchr. Terrebonne HS, Houma, 1967—70, Vandebilt Cath. HS, Houma, 1970—, dept. chmn., 1970—. Named Tchr. of Yr., Vandebilt Cath. HS, 2006, Tchr. of Excellence, Diocese of Houma-Thibodaux; named to Hall of Fame, Vandebilt Cath. HS; recipient You Make a Difference award, Nicholls State U., 2006. Mem.: Am. Coun. Tchg. Fgn. Langs. Roman Catholic. Avocations: rock hunting, writing, cooking, antiques. Home: 510 Sunset Ave Houma LA 70360 Office: Vandebilt Cath HS 209 S Hollywood Rd Houma LA 70360 E-mail: chasco@peoplepc.com.

COLBERG, LINDA, physical education educator; d. Harold Colberg and Jeanne Woudenberg. BS in Edn., Ea. Ill. U., Charleston, 1974; MEd, U. Ill., Champaign, 1992. Cert. personal trainer Am. Coun. Exercise. Instr. phys. edn. and health Wauconda Schs. # 118, 1974—77; sales rep. Maybelline Co., Chgo., 1979—80; instr. phys. edn. and life skills Glenview Schs. # 34, 1980—94; instr. phys. edn. Schaumburg Schs. # 54, 1994—2006, field leader elem. phys. edn., 2006—. Fitness supr., personal trainer Rolling Meadows Fitness Ctr., 2002; tchr. English Family Camp, Czech Republic, 2006. Editor articles for health and fitness publs. Named Sales Rep. of Yr. for Midwestern U.S., Maybelline Corp., 1979; recipient Florence McAfee scholarship, Ea. Ill. U., 1972. Mem.: AAHPERD, Am. Assn. for Health Edn., Am. Assn. for Active Lifestyles and Fitness, Ill. Assn. Health, Phys. Edn. and Recreation. Home: 1339 S Parkside Dr Palatine IL 60067 Office: Schaumburg Sch Dist 54 524 Schaumburg Rd Schaumburg IL 60194 E-mail: LColberg710@comcast.net.

COLBERG, TALIS J., state attorney general; b. AK, 1958; m. Krystyna Colberg; 2 children. BA in Oriental Hist., Pacific Lutheran U., 1979; JD, Pepperdine U., 1983; PhD student in No. Studies, U. Alaska. Bar: Alaska 1984. Assoc. atty. Kopperud and Hefferan, Wasilla, Alaska, 1984—85; staff counsel Travelers Ins. Cos., 1985—92; pvt. practice atty., 1992—2006; atty. gen. State of Alaska, 2006—. Adj. hist. instr. ea. and western civilization Matanuska-Susitna Coll., 1992—. Mem. Greater Palmer C. of C., 1992—, Matanuska-Susitna Valley State Pk. Adv. Bd., 1998—2001; dir. bd., sec., pres. Alaska State Fair, Inc., 1995—2001; bd. dirs. Alaska Humanities Forum, 2002—06, chmn., 2004—05. Mem.: Rotary (past pres.). Republican. Office: Office of Atty Gen Diamond Courthouse PO Box 110300 Juneau AK 99811-0300 Office Phone: 907-465-3600. Office Fax: 907-465-2075. E-mail: Attorney_General@law.state.ak.us.*

COLBERN, STEVEN GARRETT, chemist, researcher; s. Robert John and Mildred Elaine (Garrett) Colbern; m. Heather Noel Ebersole, Dec. 20, 1997; 1 child, Garrett James. BS in Chemistry, UCLA, 1989. Hazardous materials cert. Calif. Specialized Tng. Inst. Electronics technician USN, Point Mugu, Calif., 1978—79; owner exotic animal bus., Glendale, Calif., 1984—89; biotech. rschr. LA Neuropsychiat. Inst., 1989—92, Cedars-Sinai Inst., Beverly Hills, Calif., 1992—94; owner vitamin bus., Oxnard, Calif., 1994—97; chemist, rschr. Applied Silicones, Ventura, Calif., 1997—98, YTC Am., Camarillo, Calif., 1998—. Patentee in field. Mem.: Internat. Soc. Optical Engrs., Am. Chem. Soc., Exptl. Aircraft Assn. Libertarian. Roman Catholic. Achievements include development of sol-gel process for the manufacture of ultra-pure, fluorinated silica glass; high and low pressure drying processes for sol-gel materials and monoliths; applied silicones; process for encapsulation of any desired metal inside single-walled carbon nanotubes; novel carbon nanotube purification process. Avocations: model building, scuba diving, weightlifting. Business E-Mail: scolbern@ytca.com.

COLBERT, ALICE TAYLOR, history professor; b. Atlanta, May 11, 1955; d. Codie Artez and Fay (Waits) Taylor; m. James Early Colbert Jr., May 18, 1991. BA, Shorter Coll., 1977; MA, Emory U., 1983, PhD, 1988. Adminstrv. asst. Atlanta Hist. Soc., 1980-81, mus. asst., 1981-83; contract curator Gulf Islands Nat. Seashore, Nat. Pk. Svc., Fla. and Miss., 1983-84; prof. history, dir. mus. Shorter Coll., Rome, Ga., 1984—2005, dean Sch. Edn. and Social Scis., 2002—05; chair dept. history, geography, polit. sci. U. Ark., Ft. Smith, 2005—. Mus. cons. Chieftains Mus., Rome, 1986-2005; project dir. Ga. Women Meeting Challenges symposium; mem. Southeastern Mus. Conf. Editor Jour. Cherokee Studies, 1988-2005, Jour. Ga. Assn. Historians, 1995-2002; regional coord. New Ga. Guide, 1993-96; contbr. articles to profl. jours. Mem. Ga. Rev. Bd. Nat. Register of Historic Places, 1995—98, Ga. Hist. Records Adv. Bd., 2001—05. Exhibit and program grantee Ga. Humanities Coun., 1987, 88, 93. Mem.: Nat. Coun. on Pub. History, Am. Hist. Assn., Orgn. Am. Historians, So. Hist. Assn., Pi Gamma Mu (sec. 1985—2005). Avocations: public speaking, historical research. Office: Univ Ark Ft Smith 5210 Grand Ave PO Box 3649 Fort Smith AR 72913-3649 Business E-Mail: acolbert@uafortsmith.edu.

COLBERT, DEBORA A., director; d. Neil R. Montgomery; m. Jonathan L. Colbert; children: Robert N., Kathryn L., Curtis L. M in Mgmt., Regis U., 1999; PhD in Ednl. Leadership, Colo. State U., 2003. Cert. program planner LERN, 2002, program planner cert. programs LERN, 2004. Cmty. edn. coord. Nat. Technol. U., Fort Collins, Colo., 1996—2000; dir. distance degrees Colo. State U. Continuing Edn., Fort Collins, 2000—. Mem. Leadership Ft. Collins, 2004—05. Mem.: U. Continuing Edn. Assn., Nat. U. Degree Consortium (v.p. 2004—05). Office: Colorado State Univ Continuing Edn Spruce Hall Campus Delivery 1040 Fort Collins CO 80523-1040 Home Phone: 970-491-2645; Office Phone: 970-491-2645. Business E-Mail: dcolbert@learn.colostate.edu.

COLBERT, JAMES, JR., academic administrator; b. Berkeley, Calif., Dec. 12, 1953; s. Darline V. and Lloyd B. Mahoney (Stepfather); m. Nancy L. Inman, July 11, 1993; children: Kayla M., Matthew J. BA in Biol. Scis., U. Calif., Berkeley, 1977; PharmD in Clin. Pharmacy, U. Calif., San Francisco, 1981. Registered pharmacist Calif. State Bd. Pharmacy, 1981. Asst. clin. prof. nursing San Diego State U. Sch. Nursing, 1995—99; asst. clin. prof. pediat. UCSD Sch. Medicine, San Diego, 1998—; edn. coord. UCSD Med. Ctr., San Diego, 2001—03, clin. coord., 2003—06; assoc. clin. prof. pharmacy UCSF Sch. Pharmacy, San Francisco, 2004—, asst. dean experiential edn., 2006—. Vol. Stand Down Vietnam Veterans, San Diego, 2002. Maj. US Army, 1990—99, San Diego. Decorated Armed Forces Svc. medal US Dept. Def., Nat. Def. Svc. medal, Hon. Discharge US Army Dept., SW Asian Svc. medal US Dept. Def., Kuwait Liberation medal Kingdom Saudi Arabia, Kingdom Kuwait, Army Commendation medal U.S. Army Dept., Army Achievement medal US Dept. Def., Army Commendation medal U.S. Army Dept.; recipient Outstanding Tchr. award, Divsn. Family Medicine Residency Program, UCSD Sch. Medicine, 1992—93, Preceptor of Yr. award, UCSD Dept. Pharmacy Gen. Practice Residency Program, 1997—98, Mem. Hall of Fame award, Calif. Soc. Health-Sys. Pharmacists, 1998, Pharmacist of Yr. award, San Diego Soc. Health-Sys. Pharmacists, 1999—2000, Outstanding Tchg. award, Dept. Pediat. Residency Program, UCSD Sch. Medicine, 2001, Health Hero, Sickle Cell Disease Assn. United Way, 2002; grantee Novartis-Pediatric Pharmacy Advocacy Grp. scholar, Novartis Pharms., Pediatric Pharmacy Advocacy Grp., 1998. Fellow: Calif. Soc. Health-Sys. Pharmacists, Am. Soc. Health-Sys. Pharmacists; mem.: Sickle Cell Disease Assn. Am. (med. advisor San Diego chpt. 1995), UC Berkeley Alumni Assn., UCSF Sch. Pharmacy Alumni Assn., San Diego Soc. Health-Sys. Pharmacists (pres. 2000—02), VFW (life), Am. Inst. History Pharmacy, Am. Assn. Colls. Pharmacy, Pediatric Pharmacy Advocacy Grp., Assn. Mil. Surgeons US, Am. Legion, Kappa Psi. D-Liberal. Methodist. Achievements include research in pain management in sickle cell anemia; development of advanced pharmacy practice education; introductory pharmacy practice education. Avocations: sports, coin collecting/numismatics, genealogy. Office: UCSD Sch Pharmacy 9500 Gilman Dr La Jolla CA 92093-0657 Home Phone: 858-486-3912. Office Fax: 858-822-5591. Business E-Mail: jcolbert@ucsd.edu.

COLBERT, KEVIN LEROY, lawyer; b. Decatur, Ill., June 6, 1960; s. Jerry Lee Colbert and Kathleen Branham; m. Cynthia Rebecca Loop, May 26, 1985 (div. Apr. 23, 2001); m. Maria Lynnette Richard, Jan. 1, 2002; children: Kevin, Jr. LeRoy, Lauren Rebecca, Georgia Lynnette. BS, U. SC, 1983; JD with hon., U. Tulsa, 1990; LLM, U. Houston, 2007. Bar: Tex. 1990, US Dist Ct. (so. dist.) Tex. 1994. Staff atty. Shell Oil Co., Houston; assoc. Akin, Gump, Stauss, Hauer & Feld, LLP, Houston, 1994—96, Gardere Wynne Sewell, LLP, Houston, 1996—99, ptnr., environ. practice group leader, 1999—. Spkr. in field. Contbr. articles to profl. jours. Vol. Big Bros. Big Sisters Greater Houston, 2006—; bd. dirs. Fund Devel. Task Force; chair Lawyers Initiative Task Force; mem. World Affairs Coun., Houston. Capt. US Army, 1979—87, Fed. Rep. Germany. Mem.: ABA (vice chair toxic torts and environ. law com.), Phi Alpha Delta, Sigma Alpha Epsilon. Home: 4 Sleepy Oaks Houston TX 77024 Office: Gardere Wynne Sewell LLP 1000 Louisiana Ste 3400 Houston TX 77002 Office Phone: 713-276-5680. Office Fax: 713-276-6680. Business E-Mail: kcolbert@gardere.com.

COLBERT, MARVIN JAY, retired internist, educator; b. Spokane, Wash., Nov. 6, 1923; s. John B. and Elizabeth (Peters) C.; m. Eleanor Ruth Rott, June 2, 1951 (dec. July 2000); children: Janet Lynn, James Lee, Lawrence Jay. Student, U. Utah, 1940-43; BS, Yale U., 1946; MD, Boston U., 1949. Diplomate: Am. Bd. Internal Medicine. Intern, resident in internal medicine Presbyn. Hosp., Chgo., 1949-50, VA Hosp., Boston, 1953-54, U. Ill. Rsch. and Ednl. Hosp., 1954-55; pvt. practice internal medicine Belmond, Iowa, 1955-56; mem. faculty U. Ill., Chgo., 1956-58; dir. health svc. Med. Ctr., 1959-78, prof. medicine, 1969-78; dir. employee health svcs. Evang. Hosp. Assn., Oak Brook, Ill., 1978-86. Cons. internal medicine radiol. and environ. rsch. div. Argonne (Ill.) Nat. Lab., 1978-79. Pres. Hillcrest PTA, Downers Grove, Ill., 1960-62; Parent-Tchrs. Group Chiengmai Co-Ednl. Ctr., Thailand, 1965-66. Capt. M.C. AUS, 1943-46, 50-52. Fellow ACP; mem. Assn. for Advancement of Automotive Medicine (dir. 1969-76). Home: 1700 Robin Ln #544 Lisle IL 60532 Office Phone: 630-969-1139. Personal E-mail: ERColbert@aol.com. *While on leave from The University of Illinois, Marvin Jay Colbert was a Visiting Professor of Internal Medicine. Between the years of 1965-66 he taught at The Chiengmai Medical School and Hospital in Chiengmai, Thailand.*

COLBERT, STEPHEN, comedian, actor; b. Charleston, SC, May 13, 1964; m. Evelyn McGee; 3 children. Grad., Northeastern U., 1986. Performer Second City, Chgo., Annoyance Theatre, Chgo. Actor: (films) Snow Days, 1999, Nobody Knows Anything, 2003, Bewitched, 2005, (voice): (TV series) Harvey Birdman, Attorney at Law, 2001—, Crank Yankers, 2002, Tough Crowd with Colin Quinn, 2002—; actor, writer: Exit 57, 1995—96; The Dana Carvey Show, 1996; (co-creator and voice of Ace, The Ambiguously Gay Duo) Saturday Night Live, 1996—; actor: (TV series) The Daily Show with Jon Stewart, 1997—; writer: TV series The Daily Show with Jon Stewart, 2003—; actor, writer: (TV films) Strangers with Candy: Retardation, a Celebration, 1998; actor, writer, co-prodr.: (TV series) Strangers with Candy, 1999—2000; actor, writer The Colbert Report, 2005—; co-author (with Amy Sedaris and Paul Dinello): Wigfield, 2003. Named Person of Yr., US Comedy Arts Festival, 2007; named one of 100 Most Influential People, Time mag., 2006.*

COLBERT, THOMAS, state supreme court justice; b. Oklahoma City, Okla., Dec. 30, 1949; m. Doretha Guion; 3 children. Grad., Eastern Okla. State Coll., 1970; BS, Ky. State U., 1972, MA in Ed., 1976; JD, U. Okla. Coll. of Law, 1982. Asst. dean Marquette U. Law Sch., 1982—84; asst. dist. atty. Okla. County, 1984—86; atty. Miles-LaGrange & Colbert, 1986—89, Colbert and Associates, 1989—2000, Okla. Dept. Human Services, 1988—89, 1999—2000; judge Okla. Ct. of Civil Appeals, 1999—2004, chief judge, 2004; justice Okla. Supreme Ct., 2004—. Served in criminal investigation div. US Army, 1973—75. Mem.: ABA, Nat. Bar Assn., Tulsa County Bar Assn., Okla. Bar Assn. Office: Okla Supreme Ct Rm 204 State Capitol Bldg Oklahoma City OK 73105*

COLBERT, VIRGIS W., food products executive; b. Jackson, Miss., Oct. 13, 1939; m. Angela Colbert; three children. BS in Indsl. Mgmt., Ctrl. Mich. U. Mfg. gen. supt. Chrysler Corp.; asst. to plant mgr. Miller Brewing Co., Reidsville, NC, 1979-80, prodn. mgr. Ft. Worth, 1980-81, profn. mgr. Milw., 1981, plant mgr., 1981-87, asst. dir. can mfg., 1987-88, dir. can. mfg., 1988, dir. container and support mfg., 1988-89, v.p. materials mfg., 1989-90, v.p. plant ops., 1990-93, sr. v.p. ops., 1993-95, sr. v.p. worldwide ops., 1995-97, exec. v.p., 1997—, also bd. dirs. and exec. com. Bd. dirs. Manitowoc Co., The Stanley Works, Sara Lee Corp., Merrill Lynch Co. Past chmn. bd. Thurgood Marshall Scholarship Fund; past chmn. bd. trustees Fisk U., Nashville; bd. dirs. Bradley Sports and Entertainment Corp. Ctr., Greater Milw. Open; exec. adv. com. Nat. Urban League's Black Exec. Exch. Program. Recipient various awards Jarvis Christian Coll., Tyler, Tex., So. U., New Orleans, N.C. AT&T, Greensboro, Clark Coll., Atlanta, Grambling (La.) State Coll., Fla. Meml. Coll., Miami, U. N.C., Greensboro, Young Program of Nat. Alliance Bus., Svc. award Nat. Urban Leage, Trumpet award Turner Broadcasting Sys., 1996, Exec. Leadership Coun. Achievement award, 1998; named Harlem YMCA Black Achiever, Milw. YMCA Black Achiever, Phi Beta Sigma Fraternity Black Achiever, one of 50 Top Black Execs. in Corp. Am., Ebony Mag., 1992, one of 24 To Watch in '94, Ebony Mag., 1994, one of 12 Most Powerful Blacks in Corp. Am., Ebony Mag., 1998, one of Am.'s 40 Most Powerful Black Execs., Black Enterprise Mag., 1993, One of 50 Top Black Execs. in Corp. Am., Black Enterprise Mag., 2000, Beverage Exec. of Yr., Beverage Industry Mag., 2001, One of 50 Most Powerful Balck Execs. in Am., Fortune Mag., 2002, One of 75 Most Powerful African Ams. in Corp. Am., Black Enterprise Mag., 2005; inductee Scott H.S. Hall of Fame, Toledo, 1987. Mem. NAACP (life, Svc. award), 100 Black Men of Am. (hon.), Omega Psi Phi. Office: Miller Brewing Co 3939 W Highland Blvd Milwaukee WI 53201 Office Phone: 414-931-3823.

COLBERT-CORMIER, PATRICIA A., secondary school educator; b. Lake Charles, La., Nov. 12, 1943; 4 children. BS in Biology, U. La., 1965, MS in Microbiology, 1975. Edn. specialist cert. in reading 1978. Tchr. biology dept. Lafayette (La.) H.S., 1975—, mem. health acad. com., 2003—; lead sci. tchr. H.S. 802 Lafayette Parish. Mem. editl. adv. panel Cold Spring Harbor Labs. DNA Learning Ctr. Mem. Nat. Academics Tchrs. Adv. Group; past bd. dirs. Nat. Bd. Profl. Tchg. Stds. Finalist, Nat. Tchr. Hall Fame; DuPont fellow, 1994, Albert Einstein fellow, NASA, Washington, 2000—01, Disney Ch. Am. Tchr. and Tandy Tech. scholar, 1996. Office: Lafayette HS Biology Dept 3000 W Congress St Lafayette LA 70506 Office Phone: 337-984-5284. Personal E-mail: p53colbert@aol.com.

COLBORN, GENE LOUIS, anatomy educator, researcher; b. Springfield, Ill., Nov. 23, 1935; s. Adin Levi and Grace Downey (Tucker) C.; divorced; children: Robert Mark, Adrian Thomas, Lara Lee Colborn Russell; m. Sarah Ellen Crockett, Aug. 14, 1976; children: Jason Matthew, Nathan Tucker. BA with honors, Ky. Christian Coll., Grayson, 1957; BS with honors, Milligan Coll., Tenn., 1962; MS in Anatomy, Wake Forest U., Winston-Salem, NC, 1964, PhD in Anatomy, 1967. Postdoctoral fellow U. N.Mex. Sch. Medicine, Albuquerque, 1967—68; asst. prof. U. Tex. Health Sci. Ctr., San Antonio, 1968—72, assoc. prof., 1972—75; assoc. prof. anatomy Med. Coll. Ga., Augusta, 1975—88, prof. anatomy, 1988—2000, prof. surgery, 1993—2000, emeritus prof. anatomy and surgery, 2000—, dir. Ctr. for Clin. Anatomy, 1987—2000, dir. med. gross anatomy, 1975—2000, cons. dept. surgery, 1977—2000; clin. prof. surgery Emory U. Sch. Medicine, Atlanta, 1996—; chmn. divsn. anat. scis. Ross U. Sch. Medicine, Dominica, 2000—01; prof. Am. U. Caribbean Sch. Medicine, St. Maarten, Netherlands Antilles, 2002—04, chmn. anatomy, 2002—04. Pres. Ga. State Anat. Bd., 1983-93; cons. Eisenhower Army Med. Ctr., 1990-96; founder, pres. Gelco Med. Pub. Co., 2004-. Author: Practical Gross Anatomy, 1982, Surgical Anatomy, 1987, Hernias, 1988, Musculoskeletal Anatomy, 1989, Workbook of Surgical Anatomy, 1990, Clinical Gross Anatomy, 1993, Modern Hernia Repair, 1996, The Embryological and Anatomical Basis of Surgery, 2002; mem. editl. bd.: Clin. Anatomy Jour.; contbr. numerous articles on cardiac conduction, nervous sys., primate anatomy, cell culture and clin. and surg. anatomy to profl. jours. Active San Antonio Symphony Mastersingers, 1970-75, Augusta Opera, 1975—, Augusta Choral Soc., 1975-95; judge Regional Sci. Fairs, Augusta, 1978-90. Recipient Golden Apple award, U. Tex. Health Sci. Ctr., 1975, Outstanding Med. Educator award, Med. Coll. Ga., 1976, 1977, 1978, 1982, 1987, 1988, 1990, 1991, 1997, Disting. Faculty award, 1978, 2000, Excellence in Tchg. award, 1997, 1999, Regents' award in tchg., 1998, others. Mem. AAUP, Am. Assn. Clin. Anatomists (membership chmn. 1982-86, mem. editl. bd. Jour. Clin. Anatomy 1994—), Am. Assn. Anatomists, Columbia County Choral Soc. (founding mem.), KC (4th degree). Republican. Avocations: opera, chorales, chess, tennis, camping. Address: 178 Creekview Ct Martinez GA 30907 Personal E-mail: glcolb@yahoo.com.

COLBURN, DAVID DUNTON, investment advisor; b. San Mateo, Calif., Aug. 18, 1958; s. Richard Dunton and Joan Francis (Garber) C.; m. Carolyn Louise Hadley, Sept. 30, 1989; children: Margaret Hadley, Ethan Dunton. BA, Harvard U., 1980; MBA, U. Pa., 1989. V.p. Bank of Am., LA, 1981-87; investment mgr. CED Mgmt. Svcs. Inc., Northbrook, Ill., 1989-91; mng. ptnr. Lincolnshire Assocs., Ltd., 1991—, Miranda Investors, LLC, Northbrook, 2000—. Trustee R.L. Stevenson Sch., 2003—. Mem. Young Pres. Orgn. Office: 555 Skokie Blvd Ste 555 Northbrook IL 60062-2854 Home Phone: 847-691-9094. E-mail: davidcolburn@mac.com.

COLBURN, DAVID R., academic administrator; BA, MA, Providence Coll.; PhD, U. N.C., 1971. Joined U. Fla., Gainesville, 1972, chairperson dept. history, 1981—89, assoc. dean Coll. Liberal Arts and Scis., 1989—95, provost, 2000—05. Author: Government in the Sunshine State: Florida Since Statehood, 1999, African American Mayors: Race, Politics and the American City, 2000, Florida's Megatrends: Critical Issue Facing Florida in the Twenty-First Century with Lance deHaven-Smith, 2001; contbr. chapters to books, articles to profl. jours., to newspapers. With US Army, 1966, Vietnam.

COLBURN, KEITH W., electronics executive; Chmn. bd., CEO Consolidated Electrical Distributors, Thousand Oaks, Calif., 1999—. Office: Consolidated Electrical Distributors Inc 31356 Via Colinas Ste 107 Westlake Village CA 91362

COLBURN, KENNETH HERSEY, retired financial executive; b. Melrose, Mass., Jan. 8, 1952; s. Warren Edward and Maybelle (Hersey) C.; married. AB, Brown U., 1975; MPPM, Yale U., 1978. Assoc. Credit Suisse 1st Boston Corp./(formerly First Boston Corp.), NYC, 1978-83, v.p., 1983-88, mng. dir., 1988—94; v.p. project and internat. fin. Raytheon Co., Lexington, Mass., 1995-98; COO Highfields Capital Mgmt. L.P., Boston, 1996—2005; ret., 2005. Trustee Huntington Theatre Co., Boston, Bentley Coll., Waltham, Mass. Mem. Yale Club, Boothbay Harbor Yacht Club, Dedham Polo and Country Club, Southport Yacht Club. E-mail: kcolburn@105600.com.

COLBURN, MARTHA, animator, filmmaker, artist; b. 1979; BA in Art, Md. Inst. Coll. Art, Balt., 1994; MA equivalent, Rijksakademie Van Beeldende Kunst (Royal Acad. Art), Holland, 2002. Several presentations and lectures in many fine art schools and art groups in the U.S.A., 2001; vis. prof. animation San Francisco Art Inst., 2001; Filmwerkplaats, Basics of Subversive and Traditional Animation, Rotterdam, Netherlands, 02; vis. artists, lecture Kunstakademie of Bergen, Norway, 2003, Statenskunst Akademie, Norway, 2003; vis. tutor Dutch Art Inst., Enschede, Netherlands, 2003; lectr., animation workshop Nanjing Art Inst., China, 2004; vis. artist, prof. Calif. Inst. Arts, 2004; vis. artist MIT, Mass., 2005, Sch. Mus. Fine Arts, Boston, 2005. Mus./archive/gallery film screenings Anthology Fim Archive, NY, Film Series, 1997, MoMA, NY Five Films Screened in Big As Life: An American History of 8 mm Films, 1998, Whitney Mus., NY, 2001, Pacific Film Archive, Calif., 2002, Mus. Contemporary Art,

Lyon, France, 2002, Art Space, Auckland, New Zealand, 2004, and several others; solo visual exhibitions, De Kabinetten of De Vleeshal, Middelburg, Netherlands, INSE(X)CTS Major Art Fair, Amsterdam, Netherlands, 2002, Frankfurter Kunstverein, Young and Upcoming, Frankfurt, Germany., 2003, W.I.N.D.O.W. gallery, Walter Van Beirendonk Fashion shop, Antwerp, Belgium, 2003, group visual art exhbns., Courthouse Gallery, Anthology Film Archive, NYC, 2000, Las Palmas, Transmission: Emerging Artists living around the North Sea, Rotterdam, Netherlands, 2001, Outline Gallery, Haunted House Of Art, Amsterdam, Netherlands, 2002, Group Show, Diana Stigter Gallery, Amsterdam, 2003, Site Specific, Deiska, Amsterdam, Netherlands, 2003, Luggage Nanjing Art Institute Gallery, Nanjing, China, 2004, Vixens, Diana Stigter Gallery, Amsterdam, Netherlands, 2004, Liste Art Fair, Diana Stigter Gallery, Basel, Switzerland, 2004, Sideshow Gallery, Williamsburg, NY. US. group show with Jonas Mekas, 2004, and several others; film screenings Women in Film Series, Washington, DC, 1996, Oberlin Coll., Independent Film Series, Ohio, 1996, Halcyon Gallery, Balt., 1997, Layers in Time, Cin(E) Poetry Film Festival, San Francisco, 1997, NY Women's Film Festival, 1998, Contemporary Issues Film Festival, Portugal, 1999, NY and Chgo. Underground Film Festivals, 1999, Sundance Film Festival, Utah, 2000, MIX Film Festival (NY and Brazil), 2001, Traditional and Subversive Animation, Worm Cinema, Rotterdam, Netherlands, 2002, MIX Gay and Lesbian Film Festival, NY, 2002, Rhodes Coll., Memphis, Tenn., 2003, Phila. Film Festival, 2003, Netherlands Film Festival, 2004, LA Film Festival, Egyptian Theater, Calif., 2004, Utah Arts Festival, 2004, Super 8 Special 2004, Basel, Switzerland, 2004, Rotterdam Internat. Film Festival, Netherlands, 2005, DUTCH OPEN, Amsterdam, 2005, Brampton Indie Arts Festival, Calif., 2005, and several others; watercolors, films and large photgraphic works toured Norway with Nat. Touring Exhbns., 2001—05, commissions, Channel Four, GB, Titles for Animation Babylon, 1998, Park TV, Amsterdam, Berlin, NY, Two one hour programs, 2001, collections, BBC TV, One Film Purchased, 1999, Dibendetto Collection, private, video, 2000, private collection, Jonas Mekas, US, 2001; filmaker, animator Acrophobic Babies, 1994, First Film In X-tro, 1994, Feature Presentation, 1994, Alcohol, 1995, Asthma, 1995, Live Frazz, 1995, Zig Zag, 1995, Caroline Kraabel Solo, 1995, Caffine Jam, 1995, Improvisation, 1995, Killer Tunes, 1996, Kiwi and Wally, 1996, Who Knows?, 1996, My Secret Shame, 1996, I'm Gonna, 1996, Uberfail: Pee Poo and Flies, 1996, Hey Tiger, 1996, Dog Chow, 1996, Cholesterol, 1996, Persecution in Paradise, 1997, I Can't Keep Up, 1997, Ode to a Busdriver, 1997, Evil of Dracula, 1997, What's On?, There's a Pervert in our Pool!, 1998, A Toetally Soleful Feeture Pedsintation, 1998, Lift Off, 1999, Spiders In Love: An Arachnogasmic Musical, 2000, Skelehellavision, 2001, Cats Amore, 2002, Groscher Lansangriff: Big Bug Attack, 2002, Secrets of Mexuality, 2003 (Dutch Film Fund completion grant, 2004), XXX Amsterdam, 2004, A Little Dutch Thrill, 2004, Cosmetic Emergency, 2005 (Dutch Film Fund production grant, 2004), several compact disc recordings; Whitney Biennial: Day for Night, Whitney Mus. Am. Art, NYC, 2006. Recipient Kenneth Patchen award, Nat. Poetry Film Festival, 1997, Juries Choice award, Super Super 8 Film Festival, 1997, Juries Choice award for no budget film making, Hamburg Short Festival, Del., 1998, Best Animated Film, NY Underground Film Festival, 1999, 2003, Chgo. Underground Film Festival, 1999, Sarah Lawrence Coll. Film award, 2002; Md. State Arts Grant, 1997, Filmcore Grant, NY Underground Film Festival, 1998, Chgo. Underground Film Festival Grant, 2000, Thaw Film Festival Grant, 2000, Rockefeller Grant Nominee, 2001, Dutch Ministry Edn., Culture and Sci., 2000—02, Stadsdeel de Baarsjes Grant Project: xxx Amsterdam, 2004. Address: c/o Diana Stigter Gallery Elandsstraat 90 1016 SH Amsterdam Netherlands Mailing: c/o Stux Gallery 530 W 25th St New York NY 10001 E-mail: info@marthacolburn.com, spidersinlove@hotmail.com.

COLBY, KAREN LYNN **See WEINER, KAREN**

COLBY, WILLIAM MICHAEL, lawyer; b. Pontiac, Mich., Jan. 24, 1942; s. Orville Edgar and Jeannette (Nadon) C.; m. Brenda Schneckenburger, Nov. 28, 1964; children: Kathleen C. Scott, Thomas Brownell. AB, U. Mich., 1963, JD, 1966. Bar: N.Y. 1966, U.S. Tax Ct. 1969, U.S. Supreme Ct. 1972, Fla. 1982. Assoc. Harter, Secrest & Emery, Rochester, NY, 1966—74, ptnr., 1975—99, counsel, 2000—. Cons. various tax pubs. Contbr. articles to profl. jours.; editor various tax publs. Bd. dirs., hon. mem. Rochester Mus. and Sci. Ctr.; chmn. bd. dirs. Genesee Cmty. Charter Sch. Fellow Am. Bar Found.; mem. Monroe County Bar Found. (pres. 1980-81), Oak Hill Country Club. Avocations: golf, wine tasting, travel. Home: 39 Granite Dr Penfield NY 14526-2851 Office: Harter Secrest & Emery LLP 1600 Bausch & Lomb Pl Rochester NY 14604-2711 Office Phone: 585-232-6500. Business E-Mail: wcolby@hselaw.com.

COLBY-HALL, ALICE MARY, language educator; b. Portland, Maine, Feb. 25, 1932; d. Frederick Eugene and Angie Fraser (Drown) C.; m. Robert A. Hall, Jr., May 8, 1976 (dec. 1997); stepchildren: Philip, Diana Hall Goodall, Carol Hall Erickson. BA, Colby Coll., 1953; MA, Middlebury Coll., 1954; PhD, Columbia U., 1962. Tchr. French, Latin Orono (Maine) HS, 1954-55; tchr. French Gould Acad., Bethel, Maine, 1955-57; lectr. French Columbia U., 1959-60; instr. Romance lit. Cornell U., Ithaca, NY, 1962-63, asst. prof., 1963-66, assoc. prof., 1966-75, prof. Romance studies, 1975-97, prof. emerita, 1997—, chmn. Romance studies, 1990-96. Author: The Portrait in Twelfth Century French Literature: An Example of the Stylistic Originality of Chrétien de Troyes, 1965; mem. editl. bd. Speculum, 1976-79, Olifant, 1974—. Fulbright grantee, 1953-54; NEH fellow, 1984-85; recipient Médaille des Amis d'Orange, 1985; decorated chevalier de l'Ordre des Arts et Lettres, 1997. Mem. Modern Lang. Assn., Medieval Acad. Am. (councillor 1983-86), Internat. Arthurian Soc., Société Rencesvals, Académie de Vaucluse, Phi Beta Kappa. Republican. Congregationalist. Home: 308 Cayuga Heights Rd Ithaca NY 14850-2107 Office: Cornell U Dept Romance Studies Ithaca NY 14853 Business E-Mail: amc12@cornell.edu.

COLCORD, HERBERT NATHANIEL, III, (SKIP), corporate communications executive; b. Quincy, Mass., Mar. 21, 1951; s. Herbert Nathaniel Jr. and Audrey Louise (Gunn) C.; m. Deborah Sue O'Brien, Nov. 8, 1975; children: Heather Michele, Jared Scott, Devon Elizabeth. BA in Journalism cum laude, Northeastern U., Boston, 1973; MA in Journalism, U. Mo., Columbia, 1975. Accredited bus. communicator. Staff reporter The Patriot Ledger, Quincy, Mass., 1970-73, Columbia (Mo.) Daily Tribune, 1974-75; pub. affairs asst. Nat. Fire Protection Assn., Boston, 1975-77, mgr. editorial programs, 1977-79; mgr. pub. affairs Ocean Spray Cranberries, Inc., Plymouth, Mass., 1979-82, mgr. consumer affairs, 1982-89, mgr. mktg. comms. Lakeville, Mass., 1990-97, mgr. corp. comm. and pub. affairs, 1998-99; sr. mgr. corp. comm. Polaroid Corp., Cambridge, Mass., 1999—2001, dir. corp. comm., 2002—05; dir. global media rels. Am. Std. Cos., Piscataway, NJ, 2005—. Bd. dirs. Plymouth County Devel. Coun., Pembroke, Mass., 1989-92; bd. dirs. Nat. Guest Rels. Assn., 1984-86, pres., 1984-85. Contbr. articles to profl. jours. Recipient Gold Quill award for Excellence Internat. Assn. Bus. Communicators, 1983, Writing Excellence award Coop. Communicators Assn., 1980-81, Writing Excellence award Nat. Coun. Farmer Coop., 1981-82, 1st pl. Spl. Project Awards, Coop. Communicators Assn., 1992; named Pub. Rels. Allstar, Food and Beverage Mag., 1995, one of Top 10 Food Industry Pub. Rels. Profls., Food Bus. Mag., 1992, Pub. Rels. Week's Corporate Comm. Team of Yr., 2007. Mem. Internat. Assn. Bus. Communicators, Kappa Tau Alpha. Avocations: basketball, golf, genealogy. Home: 322 Nichols Dr Taunton MA 02780-4373 Office: Am Std Cos 1 Centennial Ave Piscataway NJ 08855-6820 Office Phone: 732-980-3065. Business E-Mail: hcolcord@americanstandard.com.

COLDEWEY, JOHN CHRISTOPHER, English literature educator; b. Beloit, Wis., June 13, 1944; s. George Henry and Frances Mary (McLoughlin) C.; m. Carolyn Culver (div.); children: Christopher, Devin; m. Christine May Rose, Sept. 9, 1989. BA, Lewis U., 1966; student, U. London, Eng., 1966; MA, No. Ill. U., 1967; PhD, U. Colo., 1972. Acting asst. prof. English U. Wash., Seattle, 1972-73, asst. prof. English, 1973-79, assoc. prof. English, 1979-91, prof. English, 1991—, dir. grad. studies, 1995-99; postdoctoral rsch. fellow Nottingham (Eng.) U., 1979-80; Fulbright exchange prof. U. East Anglia, Norwich, Eng., 1986-87. Lectr., speaker and reader in field. Author: Pseudomagia: A 17th Century Neo-Latin Tragicomedy by William Mewe, 1979, Renaissance Latin Drama in England, Vol. IV, 1987, Vol. 14, 1991, Contexts for Early English Drama, 1989, Early English Drama: An Anthology, 1993, Drama: Classical Through Contemporary, 1998, rev., 2001, Medieval Drama: Critical and Cultural Studies (4 Vols.), 2007; editor: Modern Lang. Quar., 1983-93; contbr. chpts. to books, articles to profl. jours. Bd. dirs. Friends U. Wash. Libr., 1991-99 (pres. 1995-97); hon. advisor Brit. Univs. Summers Schs. Program, 1977-94. Fellow Medieval Acad. Am., 1974-75; grantee Am. Coun. Learned Socs., 1974-75, 1976-77, 86-87, 89-90, grantee NEH, 1979-80, 82-83, 92-93, fellow, 1999-2000. Mem. Coun. Editors Learned Jours. (pres. 1992-94, v.p. 1990-92, sec.-treas. 1989-90), Medieval and Renaissance Drama Soc. (exec. coun. 1997-98, v.p. 1998-00), Medieval European Drama Coun. (Am. rep. 1997-99). Avocations: skiing, bicycling, mountain travel, running. Home: 333 35th Ave E Seattle WA 98112-4923 Office: U Wash Dept English Box 354330 Seattle WA 98195-0001 Office Phone: 206-543-2183. Business E-Mail: jcjc@u.washington.edu.

COLDREN, IRA BURDETTE, JR., lawyer; b. Uniontown, Pa., June 15, 1924; s. Ira Burdette and Eleanor Clarke (Lincoln) C.; m. Phyllis Miles, Sept. 7 (div. Oct. 1970); children: Kathy, Lee Ellen, Janice, David; m. Frances Thomas, Aug. 27, 1971. BS, U.S. Mil. Acad., 1945; LLB, U. Pa., 1952; LLM in Estate Planning, U. Miami, 1982. Bar: Pa. 1952, U.S. Dist. Ct. (we. dist.) Pa. 1953, U.S. Ct. Appeals (3d cir.) 1983. Commd. 2d lt. U.S. Army, 1945, advanced through grades to lt. col., 1952, ret., 1956; assoc. Ray, Coldren & Buck, Uniontown, Pa., 1956-59; ptnr. Coldren & Coldren, Uniontown, 1959-62, Coldren & Adams, Uniontown, 1962—83, Coldren, Adams, DeHaas & Radcliffe, Uniontown, 1983-92, Coldren Adams, Uniontown, 1992—2003, Coldren Adams & Vernon, 2003—. Pres. Greater Uniontown United Fund, 1962, Fayette County Devel. Council, 1971-75. Fellow Am. Bar Found., Am. Coll. Trust and Estate Counsel; mem. Pa. Bar Assn. (ho. of dels. 1976-79, bd. govs. 1979-82, v.p. 1985-86, pres. 1986-87), Pa. Bar Inst. (pres. 1982-83), Fayette County Bar Assn. (pres. 1983), Am. Law Inst., Am. Judicature Soc., Internat. Assn. Ins. Counsel, Pa. Jaycees (pres. 1959), Club: Uniontown Country (pres. 1969-71). Lodges: Rotary (pres. Uniontown club 1964), Masons (master 1964, 69, mem. Scottish Rite Supreme Coun. 1991—). Democrat. Presbyterian. Home: 117 Belmont Cir Uniontown PA 15401-4759 Office: Coldren Adams 55 E Church St Uniontown PA 15401-3530 Home Phone: 724-438-9337; Office Phone: 724-437-2711. E-mail: CALawFirm@aol.com.

COLDREN, LARRY ALLEN, electrical engineering educator, consultant; b. Lewistown, Pa., Jan. 1, 1946; s. Roscoe Calvin and Mary (Hutchinson) C.; m. Donna Kauffman, Sept. 4, 1966; children: Christopher William, Bret Allen. BS, AB, Bucknell U., 1968; MS, Stanford U., 1969, PhD, 1972. Registered profl. engr., N.J. Mem. tech. staff Bell Labs., NJ, 1968-84, supr. NJ, 1984; prof. U. Calif., Santa Barbara, 1984—, Fred Kavli prof. optoelectronics and sensors Dept. Engring.; chmn., chief tech. officer Agility Commns., 1998—. Contbr. over 500 papers to tech. jours.; patentee in field. Recipient John Tyndall award, 2004. Fellow IEEE (mem. ad com. 1988-94), Optical Soc. Am., IEE; mem. NAE, Phi Beta Kappa, Tau Beta Pi, Pi Mu Epsilon, Sigma Pi Sigma. Presbyterian. Avocation: flying. Home: 4665 Via Vistosa Santa Barbara CA 93110-2333 Business E-Mail: coldren@ece.ucsb.edu.

COLE, ANN HARRIET, psychologist, consultant; b. Phila., Feb. 27, 1949; d. Albert and Deborah (Mann) Brawerman; m. Stephen Cole, June 4, 1969 (div. June 18, 1987); children: Richard David, Robert Walter; m. Allan J. Besbris, Aug. 4, 1998. BA, SUNY, Stony Brook, 1971, MA, 1975. Dir. field rsch. Opinion Rsch. Assocs., 1974-76; v.p. Social Data Analysts, Inc., 1976-86; rsch. assoc. Jay Schulman, Inc., NYC, 1986-87; cons. Litigation Scis., Inc., NYC, 1988-90, Stanley S. Arkin, P.C., NYC, 1990, Chadbourne & Parke, NYC, 1990-91; pres. Ann Cole Opinion Rsch. and Analysis, 1991—. CBS news cons., 1994-95. Mem. Am. Soc. Trial Cons. (bd. dirs. 1994-99, v.p. 1996-97, pres. 1997-99), Qualitative Rsch. Cons. Am. Office: 8913 Pennystone Ave Las Vegas NV 89134 also: Ann Cole Opinion Rsch and Analysis 860 Crow Hill Rd Arlington VT 05250-9043 Office Phone: 212-302-1650, 702-363-0390. E-mail: ahcole@acoraweb.com.

COLE, BERNARD F., community and family medicine professor; BA, Boston U., 1985, MA, 1986, PhD, 1992. Assoc. prof. cmty. and family medicine Dartmouth Med. Sch., Lebanon, NC. Contbr. articles to profl. jours. Office: Dartmouth Med Sch Sect Biostatistics & Epidemiolog 1 Medical Center Drive 7927 Rubin Bldg Lebanon NH 03756 Office Phone: 603-650-7247. Office Fax: 603-653-9093. Business E-Mail: Bernard.F.Cole@Dartmouth.edu.

COLE, BRAD, mayor; b. Decatur, Ill., Nov. 27, 1971; s. Neal and M. Sue Cole. BA, So. Ill. U., Carbondale, 1994, M in Legal Studies, 2006. Commr. Ill. Student Assistance Commn., Springfield, 1993-95; asst. dir. So. Ill. U. Alumni Assn., Carbondale, 1995-99; city councilman City of Carbondale, 1999—2003; asst. dep. chief of staff Office of Gov., State of Ill., Springfield, 1999—2001; dep. chief of staff Office of the Gov., State of Ill., Springfield, 2002—03; mayor City of Carbondale, 2003—. Dir. Lower Miss. Delta Devel. Ctr., Memphis, 2000—. Trustee Carbondale Pub. Libr., 1997-99; commr. Carbondale Park Dist., 1997-99; v.p. Ill. Mcpl. League, 2005—; bd. dirs. Sister Cities Internat., 2005—. Named one of Outstanding Young Men of Am., 1996, 98. Mem. So. Ill. U. Alumni Assn., Rotary (Club Rotarian of Yr. 1998), Masons (sec. lodge 2000-04, grand orator 2003—, Delta Chi (ritual com. 1997-), So. Ill. Mayor's Assn. (pres. 2005—). Home: PO Box 1071 Carbondale IL 62903 Office: City of Carbondale 200 S Illinois Ave Carbondale IL 62901

COLE, BRIAN JARED, orthopedist; b. Chgo., Ill., Dec. 7, 1962; m. Emily Cole; children: Ethan, Adam. BS in Bio., Psychol., U. Ill., 1985; MBA in Health Admin., U. Chgo., 1989; MD, U. Chgo. Pritzker Sch. Medicine, 1990. Cert. Advanced Cardiac Life Support, 1992, Am. Bd. Orthop. Surgery, 1999, National Bds. Parts 1-3, 1991, lic. Ill., 1990, NY, 1992, Penn., 1996, Ind., 2000. Intern, orthop. Loyola U. Med. Ctr, Maywood, Ill., 1990—91; resident, sports medicine Hosp. Spl. Surgery, Cornell U., NYC, 1992—96; sports med. fellow U. Pitts., 1996—97; staff mem. Rush U. Med. Ctr., Chgo., 1997—, asst. prof., dept. orthopedic surgery, 1997—2004, assoc. prof., dept. anatomy and cell bio., prof., dept. anatomy and cell biology, assoc. prof., dept. orthopedic surgery, 2002, prof., dept. orthop., dir., sports med. divsn., Cartilage Restoration Ctr., 1997—2004, sect. head, cartilage rsch. program, Cartilage Restoration Ctr., 2004—. Com. mem., cost containment Hosp. Spl. Surg., 1991—96, med. records, 1993—96; med. care evaluation Rush Presbyterian-St. Luke's Med. Ctr., 1997; dir., exec. com. Midwest Orthopaedics, Rush U. Med. Ctr., 1998—2000, dir., coding practices com., 1997, dir. mktg. com., 98; subcommittee sports evaluation AAOS, 2000, com. elec. media, 00; exec. mem. Univ. Chgo. Grad. Program Health Admin., 1997; consul. The Pitts. Ballet Co., 1997—98, Elmhurst Coll., 2001; team doctor Univ. Pitts. Football, 1997—98, NE Ill. Univ. Basketball, 1997—98; team orthopedic surgeon Chgo. Rush Profl. Arena Football, 2001—; team physician Chgo. Bulls, 2004—; co-team physician Chgo. White Sox, 2001—. Contbr. articles to numerous profl. jours.; editor: (profl. jours.) Sports Med. Reports, 2001, Atlas Surg. Techniques in Sports Med., 2001, Sports Med., Arthroscopy, 2001, Orthopedic Quarterly; reviewer: profl. jours. Am. Jour. Sports Med., 2002, Jour. Knee Surgery, 2003. Named Chicago's Top Doctor (placed on cover), Chgo. Mag., 2006; named one of Best Doctors in Am., 2004, 2005, Top Doctor in the Chgo. Metro Area, 2003, 2004, 2005; recipient Golden Key, Univ. Ill., 1985, Lewis Clark Wagner award, 1996, Best Rsch. Project award, Rush Univ., 2001, 2003, 2004, 2005, OREF Career Devel. award, 2001, Clin. Rsch. Poster award, AMSA, 2002. Mem.: Mid Am. Orthop. Assn., Chgo. Sports Med. Soc., Ill. Orthop. Soc., NY State Orthop. Soc., Chgo. Med. Soc., Ill. State Med. Soc., NBA Team Physicians Society, Am. Orthop. Soc. Sports Med., Internat. Soc. Arthroscopy, Knee Surgery and Orthop. Sports Med., Am. Shoulder and Elbow Soc., Orthop. Rsch. Soc., Am. Orthop. Soc. Sports Med., Arthroscopy Assn. No. Am., Internat. Cartilage Repair Soc., Am. Acad. Orthop. Rsch., Am. Soc. Bone Mineral Rsch., AMA. Office: Rush Univ Hosp Ste 1063 1725 W Harrison Chicago IL 60612 Office Fax: 312-432-2381, 312-942-1517.*

COLE, BRUCE MILAN, federal agency administrator, art historian; b. Cleve., Aug. 2, 1938; s. Jerome I. and Selma (Kaufman) C.; m. Doreen Luff, July 15, 1962; children: Stephaine Wren, Ryan Lawrence. BA, Western Res. U., 1962; MA, Oberlin Coll., 1964; PhD, Bryn Mawr Coll., 1969. Asst. prof. U. Rochester, 1969-73; assoc. prof. Ind. U., Bloomington, 1973-77, prof., 1973-88, disting. prof. fine arts, 1988—2001; chmn. Nat. Endowment for the Humanities, Nat. Found. on the Arts & the Humanities, Washington, 2001—. Author: Giott and Florentine Painting 1280-1575, 1976, paperback edit., 1977, Agnolo Gaddi, 1977, Italian Majolica from Midwestern Collections, 1977, Masaccio and the Art of Early Renaissance Florence, 1980, Sienese Painting from Its Origins to the Fifteenth Century, 1969, The Renaissance Artist at Work, 1983, London, John Murray, 1983, Sienese Painting in the Age of Renaissance, 1985, Italian Art 1250-1550: The Relation of Renaissance Art to Life and Soc., 1987, Art of the Western World, Piero della Francesca, 1991, Giotto: The Scrovegni Chapel, Padua, 1993, Studies in Italian Art 1250-1550, 1996, Titian and Venetian Painting, 1450-1590, 1998, The Informed Eye, 1999. Recipient Pres.' award Am. Assn. Italian Studies, 1987; NEH fellow, 1972, Guggenheim Found. fellow, 1975, Am. Coun. Learned Socs. fellow, 1981. Fellow Accademia Senese degli Intronati; mem. Nat. Coun. on the Humanities, 1992-99. Avocation: walking. Office: Nat Endowment for the Humanities Ste 503 1100 Pennsylvania Ave NW Washington DC 20506 Office Phone: 202-606-8310. Office Fax: 202-682-5603. E-mail: bcole@neh.gov.

COLE, CAROLYN, photojournalist; b. Boulder, Colo., Apr. 24, 1961; BA in Photojournalism, U. Tex., 1983. Staff photographer El Paso Herald Post, 1986—88, San Francisco Examiner, 1988—90; freelance photographer Mexico City, 1990—92; staff photographer Sacramento Bee, 1992—94, L.A. Times, 1994—. Contbr. (photographs) Holy Lands, Life Books, Time Inc., The American Spirit, Life--The Year in Pictures, 2002. Recipient Pictures of the Year, newspaper portrait/personality award of excellence, U. Mo., 1986, first place, feature pictures story for "Cadet McKeag: Wentworth Academy's Only Female", Calif. Press Photographers Assn., 1993, Mark Twain Award, first place picture story for "Haiti: Crisis in the Caribbean", AP News Execs. Coun., 1994, best spot news photo or photographic series for "Haiti: Crisis in the Caribbean", LA Times Editl. Award, 1994, best feature photo or photographic series for "Health Crisis in Russia", LA Time Editl. Award, 1995, first place, newspaper feature picture & newspaper feature story award of excellence, Pictures of the Year, U. Mo., 1994, issue reporting picture story award of excellence for "California's Fragile Future", 1996, third place issue reporting, 1998, Journalist of the Year Award, Times Mirror Corp., 1998, Pulitzer Prize, breaking news for LA Times team coverage of the North Hollywood shootout, 1998, newspaper feature story, second place for "In the Shadow of War", Pictures of the Year, U. Mo., 1999, global news picture story, award of excellence for "No Winners in War, 1999, general news picture award of excellence for "Face of Conviction", 2000, newspaper photographer of the year, Nat. Press Photographers Assn., 2002, Mark Twain Award for best of show, AP News Execs. Coun., 2002, first place, people in the news for "Church of the Nativity", World Press Photo, 2003, first place, mag. news story editing & second place, feature picture story for "Church of the Nativity", Pictures of the Year, U. Mo., 2003, Robert Capa Award for courage in photography for covering the siege at the Church of the Nativity, Bethlehem, Overseas Press Club, 2003, Newspaper Photographer of Yr., U. Mo., 2003, Nat. Press Photographers Assn., 2003, award for news photography for church of the nativity, Sigma Delta Chi, 2003, Pulitzer Prize for feature photography, 2004, George Polk award for photojournalism, 2004, Robert Capa award for courage in photography for Iraq war and civil conflict in Liberia, 2004, award for news photography Iraq war, Sigma Delta Chi, 2004, 2d pl. people in the news Iraq War, 3d pl. for civil conflict in Liberia, World Press Photo, 2004, 2d pl. natural disaster story, Hurricane Katrina, Pictures of the Yr., U. Mo., 2005, award of excellence for "Exhausted, But Alive", 2005, Photojournalist of Yr. award, Nat. Press Photographers Assn., 2007. Office: LA Times 202 W First St Los Angeles CA 90012*

COLE, CAROLYN JO, brokerage house executive; b. Carmel, Calif. d. Joseph Michael Jr. and Dorothea Wagner (James) C. AB, Vassar Coll., 1965. Sr. v.p. UBS Painewebber, Inc., NYC, 1975—95; exec. v.p. Tucker Anthony, Inc., Boston, 1995—97; chmn. Inst. Econ. & Fin., Inc., NYC, 1997—98; mng. dir. Citigroup, NYC, 1998—. Guest lectr. Harvard U. Bus. Sch.; lectr. Securities Industry Inst., Wharton Sch. U. Pa.; past chmn. bd. dirs. NY Women's Bldg.; past bd. dirs. Women's Venture Fund. Named to YWCA Acad. Women Achievers. Mem. NOW, DAR, N.Y. Soc. Security Analysts (past bd. dirs.), The CFA Inst., Aspen Inst. Humanistic Studies, Fin. Women's Assn., Women's Econ. Roundtable, Econ. Club N.Y., Women in Need (past bd. dirs.), Vassar Club, Univ. Club. Democrat. Office: Citigroup Private Equity 388 Greenwich St New York NY 10013-2339 Office Phone: 212-816-4766. Business E-Mail: cali.cole@citi.com.

COLE, CHARLES CHESTER, JR., academic administrator; b. Altoona, Pa., Sept. 12, 1922; s. Charles Chester and Kathryn Platt (Snyder) C.; m. Mary Elizabeth Ewald, Apr. 20, 1944 (div. 1979); children: Phyllis, Dorothy, Barbara, Elizabeth.; m. Gael Monie O'Brien, Jan. 14, 1983 (dissolved 1988). AB, Columbia U., 1943, MA, 1947, PhD, 1951; LLD, Lafayette Coll., 1970. Lectr. history Columbia U., 1946-49; asst. dean Columbia Coll., 1949-57, assoc. dean, 1957-58; instr. history Briarcliff Jr. Coll., 1949; dean Lafayette Coll., 1958-70, provost, 1967-70; pres. Wilson Coll., Chambersburg, Pa., 1970-75; exec. dir. Ohio Humanities Council, Columbus, 1976-89, exec. dir. emeritus, 1990—. Trustee Ednl. Testing Svc., 1968-72, Coll. Entrance Exam. Bd., 1965-68, Cedar Crest Coll., 1972-79, Nat. Cultural Alliance, 1989-91; cons. coll. entrance exam. bd. State U. N.Y., Fedn. of State Humanities Couns. Author: The Social Ideas of the Northern Evangelists, 1826-60, 1954, Encouraging Scientific Talent, 1956, Flexibility in the Undergraduate Curriculum, 1962, To Improve Instruction, 1978, Effective Learning, 1980, Improving Instruction, 1982, Active Group Learning, 1985, Lion of the Forest: James B. Finley, Frontier Reformer, 1994, A Fragile Capital: Identity and the Early Years of Columbus, Ohio, 2001. Active Ohio Northwest Ordinance Commn., 1986-88. 1st lt. 8th Air Force USAAF, 1944-45. Adminstrv. Travel grantee Carnegie Corp., 1957, NSF grantee, 1954. Mem. Am. Hist. Assn., Assn. Higher Edn. (exec. com. 1955-58), Ohio Acad. History, Phi Beta Kappa. Home and Office: 111 Owens Ln Wayne PA 19087 Office Phone: 614-281-2512. *Who can really say how successful one's life has been? If there is a secret to success, I believe it is found in the right combination of patience, persistence, humility, high ideals, a sense of humor, a capacity to learn from mistakes, and a willingness to work hard.*

COLE, CHARLES DEWEY, JR., lawyer; b. Lower Merion Twp., Pa., Aug. 12, 1952; s. Charles Dewey and Margaret Ann (Leach) C. AB, Columbia U., 1974; JD, St. John's U., Jamaica, NY, 1979; ML Info. Sci., U. Tex., 1982; LLM, NYU, 1988; LLM in Environ. Law, Pace U., 1993; LLM in Trial Advocacy, Temple U., 1999; LLM in Advanced Litigation, Nottingham Trent U., 2003. Bar: N.Y. 1980, Tex. 1980, N.J. 1986, D.C. 1988, U.S. Dist. Ct. (we. and ea. dists.) Tex. 1980, U.S. Dist. Ct. (so. and ea. dists.) N.Y. 1980, U.S. Dist. Ct. (no. dist.) Tex. 1982, U.S. Dist. Ct. (no. dist.) N.Y. 1983, U.S. Dist. Ct. (we. dist.) N.Y. 1984, U.S. Dist. Ct. N.J. 1986, U.S. Dist. Ct. D.C. 1994, U.S. Ct. Internat. Trade 1980, U.S. Tax Ct. 1984, U.S. Ct. Appeals (5th and 11th cirs.) 1981, U.S. Ct. Appeals (Fed. cir.) 1982, U.S. Ct. Appeals (2d cir.) 1984, U.S. Ct. Appeals (D.C. cir.) 1987, U.S. Ct. Appeals (3d cir.) 1993, U.S. Supreme Ct. 1984; solicitor, Eng. and Wales, 1995; Higher Rights of Audience (civil procs.) Qualification, 2002. Law clk. to chief judge U.S. Dist. Ct. (ea. dist.), Beaumont, Tex., 1979-80, U.S. Ct. Appeals (5th cir.), Austin, Tex., 1981-82; assoc. Moore, Berson, Lifflander & Mewhinney, Garden City and NYC, NY, 1982-85; assoc. and ptnr. Newman Schlau Fitch & Burns P.C., NYC and Mineola, NY, 1985-88; assoc. Meyer, Suozzi, English & Klein, P.C., Mineola and NYC, 1988-95; of counsel, ptnr. Newman Fitch Altheim Myers, P.C., NYC and Newark, 1995—. Instr. trial techniques program Hofstra Law Sch., 1994—2000; instr. intensive trial advocacy program Widener Law Sch., 1999—. Author: Law Books as a Charitable Contribution, 1975, The EPA Lender Liability Regulations: EPA's Questionable Authority to Promulgate the Regulations as Part of the National Contingency Plan, 1993, Charging the Jury on Damages in Personal-Injury Cases: How New York Can Benefit from English Practice, 2004; contbr. book revs. to profl. publs. Mem.: Legal Writing Inst., Solicitors Assn. of Higher Ct. Advs., Coll. of State Bar Tex., State Bar Tex., Selden Soc., Supreme Ct. Hist. Soc., Soc. Advanced Legal Studies, Osgoode Soc. for Can. Legal History, Brit. and Irish Assn. Law Librs., Law Libr. Assn. Greater N.Y., Am. Assn. Law Librs., Fed. Bar Coun., Bar Assn. 5th Fed. Cir., Maritime Law Assn. U.S. (proctor), DC Bar, N.Y. State Bar Assn., Law Soc. (reference group on multi-party actions), Clarity, Scribes (dir., brief-writing competition com.). Republican. Home: 16 94th St Apt 3B Brooklyn NY 11209-6643 Office: Newman Fitch Altheim Myers PC 14 Wall St New York NY 10005-2101 Office Phone: 212-619-4350. Business E-Mail: dcole@nfam.com.

COLE, CHARLES DUBOSE, II, law educator; b. Monroeville, Ala., May 14, 1938; BSBA, Auburn U., 1960; JD cum laude, Samford U., 1966; LLM, NYU, 1971; D (hon.), Faculdade Marcelo Tupinamba, Sao Paulo, Brazil, 1991. Bar: Ala. 1966, U.S. Supreme Ct., 1971, U.S. Ct. Appeals (fed. cir.) 1997, U.S. Ct. Internat. Trade, 1997. Law clk., assoc. atty. Porterfield & Sch., Birmingham, Ala., 1965-66; prof. law Cumberland Sch. Law Samford U., Birmingham, 1966-75, 81—; Lucille S. Beeson prof. law and dir. internat. programs, master comparative law degree program Cumberland Sch. Law, Birmingham, Ala., 1993—; dir. permanent study commn. Ala. Jud. System, 1972-74; dir. Ala. Jud. Conf. Criminal Justice Survey, 1973; dir. adv. com. Ala. jud. article implementation Ala. Dept. Ct. Mgmt., 1974-75; dir. so. regional office Nat. Ctr. for State Cts., Atlanta, 1975-79; adminstrv. dir. cts. Commonwealth of Ky., Frankfort, 1979-81. Lectr. Cumberland Inst. for Continuing Legal Edn., Ala. Continuing Legal Edn., Josephson/Kluwer Bar Rev. Ctr. Am., Inc., 1967-87; law and social sci. adv. coun. Coll. Liberal Arts/Auburn U., 1991-96, dean's coun., 1996—07; chmn. profl. adv. com. Office Advancement Auburn U., 1992-93; reporter civil justice adv. group Middle Dist. Ala., 1991-93; del. Moscow Conf. on Law and Econ. Coop., The Kremlin Palace, 1990; legal specialist (pro bono) Parliament of Ukraine, 1993; v.p. faculty Samford U., 1989-90; policy com. mem. Cumberland Sch. Law, 1989-92, 2000-02, 2003-2004; mem. faculty exec. com. Samford U., 1988-89; del. U.S./Japan Bilateral Session, 1988; presenter USIA, Internat. Meeting Brazil/U.S., 1988; participant seminar Claremont McKenna Coll./NEH, 1986; presenter in field. Author (with Brewer): Alabama Constitutional Law, 1992, 2d edit., 1997; author: Comparative Constitutional Law: The United States and Brasil, 2006; contbr. articles to profl. jours.; mem. editl. bd. Ala. Lawyer, 2000—04. Bd. dirs. Auburn U. Bar Assn., 1991—2004. Named Outstanding Prof. Student Bar Assn. and Cumberland Sch. Law, 1972-73, 83-84, 2005-06, Outstanding Alumnus, Phi Alpha Delta, 1973, Samford U. Cumberland Sch. Law, 1998; recipient Jackson Outstanding Law Sch. Tchg. award Samford U., 2006. Mem. ABA (lectr. appellate judges seminar 1977-78), Am. Judicature Soc. (bd. dirs. 2000-05, exec. com. 2000-05, editorial com. 2003-2004, v.p. 2004-05), Supreme Ct. Hist. Soc., Am. Trial Lawyers Assn. (faculty mem.), Ala. Bar Assn. (action group mem. 1984-85, chmn. 1985-88, reporter task force on jud. selection 1988-89, com. on the future of the profession 1990-91, task force on legal edn. 1992-93, com. on judicial and legal reform 1994-95, chmn. 1995-96), Ukrainian Legal Found. (bd. fgn. advisors 1993-98), Birmingham Bar Assn. (mem. civil ct. rules com. 1998-99), Auburn U. Bar Assn. (adv. bd. 1992-2004), Phi Alpha Delta. Home: 1824 Mountain Laurel Ln Birmingham AL 35244 Office Phone: 205-726-2420. Personal E-mail: colecdII@aol.com. Business E-Mail: cdcole@samford.edu.

COLE, CHARLES EDWARD, lawyer, state attorney general; b. Yakima, Wash., Oct. 10, 1927; married; 3 children. BA, Stanford U., 1950, LLB, 1953. Law clk. Vets. Affairs Commn. Territory of Alaska, Juneau, 1954, Territorial Atty. Gen.'s Office, Fairbanks, Alaska, 1955-56, U.S. Dist. Ct. Alaska, Fairbanks, 1955-56; city magistrate City of Fairbanks, 1957-58; pvt. practice law, 1957-90; atty. gen. State of Alaska, 1990-94; pvt. law comml. litigation, 1995—. Profl. baseball player, Stockton, Calif. and Twin Falls, Idaho, summers of 1950, 51, 53. With U.S. Army, 1946-47. Mem. Calif. State Bar, Washington State Bar Assn., Alaska Bar Assn. Office: Law Dept State of AK Office of Atty Gen PO Box 110300 Juneau AK 99811-0300 also: Law Offices of Charles E Cole 406 Cushman St Fairbanks AK 99701-4632

COLE, CLARENCE RUSSELL, college dean; b. Crestline, Ohio, Nov. 20, 1918; s. Arthur Leroy and Anita Emma (Stephan) C.; m. Mary Piper, Mar. 15, 1945; children: Carole Ann, Larry Lee, Pamela Sue. Student pre-med., Otterbein Coll., Westerville, Ohio, 1937-39; DVM, Ohio State U., 1943, MS, 1944, PhD, 1947. Instr. dept. vet. pathology Coll. Vet. Medicine Ohio State U., Columbus, asst. prof., 1947-49, chmn. dept., 1947-67, assoc. prof., 1949-54, prof., 1954-67, asst. dean Coll. Vet. Medicine, 1960-67, dean Coll. Vet. Medicine, 1967—, prof. pathology Coll. Medicine, 1952—, prof. comparative pathology Grad. Sch., 1954—, now prof. emeritus. Regents prof. Ohio Bd. Regents, 1966—; chmn. Mershon Ctr. Nat. Security, Ohio State U., 1965-67; mem. U. Coun. Rsch., 1960-67; adminstr. cons. Vet. Rsch., Archtl. Engring. Planning, Animal Med. Ctr., N.Y.C.; cons. nat. adv. rsch. resources coun. NIH, 1972—, NIH Health Manpower Grants Br; mem. nat. adv. com. Nat. Ctr. for Primate Biology, 1967-70; mem. com. on comparative pathology NRC, NAS, 1971—; mem. fellowship com. NATO. Recipient Herzfeld lectr. award Auburn U.; 1st award sci. exhibit Ohio State Med. Assn., 1956; 2nd award AMA. Mem. Men and Women of Sci., Internat. Acad. Pathology (mem. exec. coun.), Internat. Toxoplasmosis Com. (vice-chmn. 1959—), AVMA (Gold award, chmn. adv. bd. vet. med. spltys. 1960-75), Am. Coll. Vet. Pathologists (Disting. citation 1967, pres. 1957, Disting. Mem. 1989), Assn. Am. Vet. Med. Colls. (sec.-treas. 1969—), Sigma Xi, Phi Zeta, Omega Tau Sigma. Clubs: Torch Internat. Home: 2869 Welsford Rd Columbus OH 43221

COLE, DAVID EDWARD, automotive executive, educator; b. Detroit, July 20, 1937; s. Edward Nicholas and Esther Helen (Engman) C.; m. Carol Hutchins, July 9, 1965; children: Scott David, Christopher Carl. BS in Mech. Engring. and Math., U. Mich., 1960, MS in Mech. Engring., 1961, PhD, 1966. Engr. GM, Detroit, 1960—65; prof. U. Mich., Ann Arbor, 1967—, dir. Office for Study of Automotive Transp., 1978—2000; entrepreneur 6 cos., 1975—95; pres. Ctr. Auto Rsch. and Mgmt., ptnr. The Altarum Inst. Mich, 2000—03; chmn. Ctr. for Automotve Rsch. (ind. not for profit), 2003—. Bd. dirs. MSX Internat., Detroit, Saturn Electronics, Aurburn Hills, Mich., Plastech, Dearborn, R.L. Polk, Southfield, Mich., Campfire Interactive, Ann Arbor, Mich., Mich. Econ. Devel. Corp., Lansing, Mich. Ctr. Automotive Rsch., Ann Arbor, Strategic Econ. Investment & Commercialization Orgn., Denso Corp., Charitable Found., Mich. Renewable Fuels Commn., U. Mich. Energy Rsch. Coun.; mem. energy engring. bd. NRC, 1989-94; select panel U.S.-Can. Free trade Pact, 1988-91; co-chair Detroit Rennaisance Mobility Com. Author: Elementary Vehicle Dynamics, 1972; contbr. articles to profl. jours. Bd. trustees Hope Coll., 1994—2006; mem. Mich. Renewable Fuels Commn.; former bd. dirs. Automotive Hall of Fame, Dearborn. Fellow Soc. Automotive Engrs. (dir. 1980-83, 85-88, Teetor award 1969), Engring. Soc. Detroit (Horace H. Rackham medal 2000); mem. Chevalier of the Nat. Order of Merit from France, 1999, Soc. Mktg. Execs. (Mktg. Educator of Yr. 1998, Rene Dubos Environ. award 1998), Nat. Auto Dealers Assn. Found. (Freedom of Mobility award 1993), Swedens Royal Order of the Polar Star. Republican. Presbyterian. Avocations: hunting, fishing, boating, running, golf. Office: Ctr Auto Rsch 1000 Victors Way Ste 200 Ann Arbor MI 48108 Home Phone: 734-665-7990. E-mail: dcole@cargrop.org.

COLE, DAVID MACAULAY, journalist, consultant; b. Richmond, Calif., Feb. 17, 1954; s. Frederick George and Norma Ann C. Student, San Francisco State U., 1972-77. Mng. editor Feed/Back Mag., San Francisco, 1974-78, exec. editor, 1978-83; asst. music editor Rolling Stone Mag., San Francisco, 1976-77; from copy editor to asst. mng. editor The San Francisco Examiner, 1979-87, asst. mng. editor, 1987-89; prin., owner The Cole Group, Pacifica, Calif., 1989—. Editor, publisher The Cole Papers, 1989—, NewsInc., 1997—; author: Cole's Notes--Profiles in Pagination, 1996, Cole's Guide to Publishing Systems, 1994, 95, 96, 97; contbg. editor Presstime Magazine, 1994-2005, TechNews Mag., 1994-2003; columnist, Publish Mag., 1997. Trustee Jr. Statesman Found, San Mateo, Calif., 1997—, exec. com., 2001-05. Mem. Nat. Press Photographers Assn., Soc. News Design, Soc. Profl. Journalists (v.p. local chpt. 1979). Avocation: steam train preservation. Office: The Cole Group PO Box 719 Pacifica CA 94044-0719 Fax: 650-475-8479. E-mail: dmc@colegroup.com.

COLE, EMRIED DARGAN, JR., lawyer; b. Hattiesburg, Miss., Nov. 6, 1945; m. Wandaleen Poynter. BA in History with high honors, Emory U., 1967; JD, Harvard U., 1970. Bar: Md. 1990, US Ct. Appeals (5th, 6th, 7th, 11th and DC cir.) 1974, US Supreme Ct. 1974. Assoc. Powell, Goldstein, Frazer and Murphy, Atlanta, 1970—73; asst. gen. atty., asst. gen. solicitor Louisville and Nashville R.R. Co., Louisville, 1973—77; gen. atty. Seaboard System R.R., Jacksonville, 1977—83, gen. solicitor, 1983—86; v.p. law and risk mgmt. CSX Transp.-Equipment Group, Balt., 1986—90; of counsel, ptnr. Venable LLP, Balt., 1990—. Adj. faculty Johns Hopkins Univ. Sch. of Profl. Studies in Bus. and Edn., 2002; adj. faculty, dir. Luth. Theol. Sem., Gettysburg, 2004. Contbr. articles to profl. jours. Trustee, bd. pensions Evangelical Luth. Ch. in Am., 2003—; chair bd. dirs. Biakon Luth. Soc. Ministries; cabinet mem. Cmty. Investment Vision, United Way, Ctrl. Md. Mem.: ABA, Assn. Transp. Practitioners (chmn. com. profl. ethics 1982—84), State Bar Ga., Nat. Assn. R.R. Trial Counsel, Fla. Bar Assn. Office: Venable LLP 1800 Mercantile Bank & Trust Bldg 2 Hopkins Plz Baltimore MD 21201-3805 also: 575 7th St NW Washington DC 20004 Office Phone: 410-224-7787, 202-344-4887. Office Fax: 410-244-7742, 202-334-8300. Business E-Mail: edcole@venable.com.

COLE, ERIK, professional hockey player; b. Oswego, NY, Nov. 6, 1978; m. Emily Cole; 1 child, Bella. Attended, Clarkson U. Left wing Carolina Hurricanes, 2001—. Mem. USA Olympic Hockey Team, Torino, Italy, 2006. Achievements include being a member of Stanley Cup Champion Carolina Hurricanes, 2006. Office: Carolina Hurricanes RBC Ctr 1400 Edwards Mill Rd Raleigh NC 27607

COLE, GEORGE THOMAS, lawyer; b. Orlando, Fla., Mar. 14, 1946; s. Robert Bates and Frances (Arnold) C.; m. Peggy Ellen Stimson, May 23, 1981; children: Leslie Elizabeth, Ashley Ellen, Robert Warren. AB, Yale U., 1968; JD, U. Mich., 1975. Bar: Ariz. 1975. With Fennemore, Craig, von Ammon, Udall & Powers, Phoenix, 1975-81; ptnr. Fennemore Craig, P.C., Phoenix, 1981—. Mem. Ariz. State U. Coun. for Design Excellence. Served to lt. (j.g.) USN, 1968-71. Named one of, Best Lawyers in Am. Real Estate, 2007, S.W. Super Lawyers Real Estate, 2007. Fellow: Ariz. Bar Found. (founding); mem.: Maricopa Bar Assn., Ariz. Bar Assn. (coun. real property sect. 1985—88, chmn. 1987—88), Cmty. Assns. Inst., Nat. Golf Found. (assoc.), ULI (cmty. devel. coun. 1995—2001, 2003—), Ariz. Assn. Home Bldrs., Nat. Assn. Home Bldrs., Phoenix Cmty. Alliance (bd. mem.), White Mountain Country Club (Pinetop, Ariz.), Paradise Valley Country Club (Phoenix), Yale Club (pres. 1984). Republican. Methodist. Home: 5102 E Desert Park Ln Paradise Valley AZ 85253-3054 Office: Fennemore Craig 3003 N Central Ave Ste 2600 Phoenix AZ 85012-2913 Office Phone: 602-916-5308. E-mail: gcole@fclaw.com.

COLE, GLEN DAVID, minister; b. Tacoma, Dec. 21, 1933; s. Ray Milton and Ruth Evelyn (Ranton) C.; m. Mary Ann Von Moos, June 6, 1953; children: Randall Ray, Ricky Jay. BA in Theology, Cen. Bible Coll., 1956; DD, Pacific Coast Bible Coll., 1983. Assoc. pastor Bethel Temple, Dayton, Ohio, 1956—57; pastor Assembly of God, Marion, Ohio, 1957-60, Maple Valley, Wash., 1960-65; assoc. pastor Calvary Temple, Seattle, 1965-67; sr. pastor Evergreen Christian Ctr., Olympia, Wash., 1967-78, Capital Christian Ctr., Sacramento, 1978-95, pastor emeritus, 1995—; dist. supr. Assemblies of God, Sacramento, 1997—. Exec. presbyter Assemblies of God, Springfield, 1985-95; bd. mem., ch. extension plan, Salem, Oreg., 1997-; bd. mem. fin. svcs. group, Assemblies of God, Springfield, Mo., 1998-; trustee Bethany Bible Coll., Santa Cruz, Calif., 1979—; bd. dirs. Cen. Bible Coll., Springfield, Mo., 1988-99; bd. dirs. Calif. Theol. Sem., Fresno, 1985-90. Mem. Rotary (pres. Olympia chpt. 1977-78). Republican. Mem. Assemblies Of God Ch. Office: Assemblies of God 6051 S Watt Ave Sacramento CA 95829-1304 *It seems that the people God uses most are not those with greater ability, or more education, or superior talent but those who become totally dependent on him.*

COLE, HEATHER ELLEN, librarian; b. Rochester, NY, Nov. 7, 1942; d. Donald M. and Muriel Agnes (Kimball) Cole; m. Stratis Haviaras; 1 child, Elektra Maria Muriel. BA, Cornell U., 1964; MS, Simmons Coll., 1973. Mgr. Brentano's, Boston, 1968-70; intern Harvard Coll. Libr., Cambridge, Mass., 1970-73, reference libr., 1973-77; libr. Hilles Libr., 1977—2005. Mem.: AAUW, ALA, Assn. Coll. Rsch. Librs. Democrat. Episcopalian. Avocation: gardening. Home: 19 Clinton St Cambridge MA 02139-2303 Office: Harvard Coll Lamont Library Cambridge MA 02138 Office Phone: 617-495-2455. Business E-Mail: hcole@eas.harvard.edu.

COLE, HENRY PHILIP, educational psychology educator; b. Buffalo, Jan. 5, 1937; s. Raymond James and Hannah Christina (Shapleigh) C.; m. Marion Margaret Montgomery, Aug. 19, 1961; children: Mark Douglas, David Arthur, Debra Lynn. BS in Chemistry, Nasson Coll., 1958; MEd, SUNY, Buffalo, 1966, EdD, 1968. Chemistry technician WASCO Chem. Co., Sanford, Maine, 1957-58; tchr. physics and sci. Holland (N.Y.) Ctrl. Sch., 1958-59; med. rsch. technician Buffalo Gen. Hosp., 1959-61; tchr. sci. Griffith Inst. and Ctrl. Sch., Springville, NY, 1961-65; instr. ednl. psychology SUNY, Buffalo, 1966-68; ednl. psychologist Ea. Regional Inst. for Edn., Syracuse, NY, 1968-71; prof. ednl. psychology U. Ky., Lexington, 1971—, prof. preventive medicine, 1990—, head behavioral rsch. aspects safety-health group (BRASH), 1984-97. Vis. prof. Syracuse U., 1968-70; rsch. psychologist U.S. Bur. Mines, Pitts., 1988-89; U.S. del. MINESAFE Internat. Conf., Western Australia, 1993; behavioral safety expert ILO, China, 1993. Author: Measuring Learning in Continuing Education for Engineers and Scientists, 1984; contbr. more than 200 tech. reports, articles to profl. jours., chpts. to books. Cubmaster Boy Scouts Am., Lexington, 1975-77, round table commr., 1976-78; v.p., team. rep. Little League Baseball, Lexington, 1975-78. With U.S. Army, 1959-61. Recipient Disting. Author award Jour. Allied Health, 1981, Best Paper award Am. Soc. Engring. Edn., 1985, Pub. of Yr. award Bur. of Mines-Pitts. Rsch. Ctr., 1987, Tech. Transfer award, 1989, Unsung Hero's award for outstanding rsch. contbns. U. Ky., Exceptional Achievement award for Rsch., Tchg., and Svc. Coll. of Edn., U. Ky., 2000, 03. Mem. APA, APHA, Am. Ednl. Rsch. Assn., Am. Soc. Agrl. Engrs. Republican. Presbyterian. Avocations: hiking, reading, farming. Office: University Kentucky Dept Preventive Medicine 1141 Red Mile Rd Ste 102 Lexington KY 40504-9842 Office Phone: 859-323-5202. Business E-Mail: hcole@uky.edu.

COLE, JACK ELI, physician; b. Matamoras, Pa., Jan. 7, 1915; s. Eli Martin and Louise (Henneberg) Cole; m. Evelyn Gaston Darragh, Apr. 26, 1941; children: Jack Eli, Thomas, Beverly, Martin, Robert, Leslie, Christopher, Candace, Champa. BS, Pa. State U., 1937; MD, U. Pa., 1941. Diplomate Am. Bd. Family Practice. Intern Wilkes-Barre (Pa.) Gen. Hosp., 1941-42; pvt. practice Matamoras, Pa., 1946—48, Bethlehem, Pa., 1952-68, 1973-89; staff St. Luke's Hosp., Bethlehem, 1948—, sec. dept. family practice, 1973-88; incorporator, mem. med. staff Muhlenberg Hosp., Bethlehem, 1960—, pres. med. staff, 1961-62; student health physician Lehigh U., Bethlehem, 1948-52; physician Peace Corps, Afghanistan, Swaziland, India, 1968-73; leader mission med. team United Ch. Christ, Honduras, 1987, 1993; preceptor Temple U. Med. Sch., Phila., 1978-86. Author: Wandering Voices, 1999, Richard and Sabina, 2001; contbr. poetry to anthologies, children's stories and articles to profl. publs. Charter mem. mission partnership com. N.E. Pa. Conf. United Ch. of Christ, 1984. With US Army, 1942—45. Decorated Purple Heart, Combat Medic badge; recipient Recognition award, Temple U. Med. Sch., 1979, Boss of Yr. award, Allentown Bus. Women's Assn., 1975. Fellow: Am. Acad. Family Physicians; mem.: AMA, Am. Acad. Family Physicians, Pa. Acad. Family Physicians, Lehigh Valley Acad. Family Physicians (v.p. 1979—81, pres. 1981—83), Pa. Med. Soc., Northampton County Med. Soc. Democrat. Avocation: opera. Home: 782 Barrymore Ln Bethlehem PA 18017-2522 Personal E-mail: jackcolesr@aol.com.

COLE, JAMES S., dean, dental educator; b. Mpls., Minn. m. Barbara Cole. BS, Stephen F. Austin State U., 1967; DDS, Baylor Coll. Dentistry, 1975. Instr., restorative sciences Baylor Coll. Dentistry, Texas A&M U., Dallas, 1977—81, v.p., dir. computer services, 1981—92, prof., restorative sciences, 1992—, interim pres. and dean, 1990, exec. v.p., assoc. dean, CFO, COO, vice dean, interim dean, 1999—2000, dean, 2000—; pres., treas. Baylor Oral Health Found., 1997—99; interim pres. Tex. A&M U. Sys. Health Sci. Ctr., 2000—01. Bd. mem. Friends of the Nat. Inst. of Dental and Craniofacial Rsch., 2005—. Lt. USN, 1967—71. Recipient Dentist of Yr., Dallas County Dental Soc., 2000. Fellow: Internat. Coll. Dentists, Am. Coll. Dentists. Office: 3302 Gaston Ave Dallas TX 75246 Office Phone: 214-828-8300. Office Fax: 214-828-8496. Business E-Mail: JCole@bcd.tamhsc.edu.

COLE, JAMES YEAGER, foundation administrator; b. Cleve., Sept. 20, 1957; s. Charles and Nancy Cole. JD, Blackstone Sch. Law, Dallas, 1980, U. N.C., 1989; MA, M.C.I., London, 1981; PhD, N.W. London U., 1981. CEO Cole Corp., Tallahassee, 1979-81; judge Inst. Advanced Law Study, Las Vegas, 1981-84; cons., sentencing adv. Cullowhee, NC, 1984-2001; firm pres. ForLegalHelp.com, 2001—. Decorated knight comdr. Royal Knights Justice, London, knight chevalier Venerable Order of Knights of Michael the Archangel; recipient Presdl. medal of Merit, U.S. Pres. Ronald Reagan, Washington, 1980, Disting. Leadership award, ABA jud. divsn., 1997. Mem.: N.C. Fraternal Order Police, N.C. Sheriff's Assn., Nat. Sherriff's Assn., Am. Fedn. Police, Internat. Bar Assn., Nat. Judges Assn., World Judges Assn., Am. Judges Assn., Maggic Valley C. of C., Island Found., Human Rights Inst., Haywood County C. of C., Heirs, Inc. Avocations: swimming, skiing, volleyball, tennis, movies. Home: 389 Chestnut Walk Dr Waynesville NC 28786 Home Phone: 828-551-5699; Office Phone: 828-470-5299. Business E-Mail: judge.cole@abanet.org.

COLE, JESSIE MAE, nursing assistant, freelance/self-employed writer; b. McGehee, Ark., Nov. 19, 1925; d. Alonso Smith and Estelle Hursey; m. Amos Burns, May 15, 1942; children: Bobbie D., Joyce R.; m. Mose Eddie Cole (div. Nov. 1972). AA, Fresno City Coll, 1985; BA, Charter Oak State Coll., 1999. Cert. tchr. Calif., 1979. Beautician Beauty Culture, Chgo., 1956—76; nursing asst. Hope Manor Facility, Fresno, Calif., 1983—. Pvt. piano tchr., Fresno, 1981—. Author: (website) How to Read Sheet Music, 1997; contbr. articles. Mem. Wall of Tolerance Nat. Campaign for Tolerance, 2002—03; bible study instr. Coll. Ch. of Christ, Fresno, 1975—. Recipient Employee of Year, Calif. Assn. Health Facilities. Mem.: Nat. Assn. Black Journalists. Home: 284 N Logsdon Pky Radcliff KY 40160

COLE, JOHN ADAM, insurance executive; b. Odessa, Tex., May 6, 1951; s. Alling and Millicent (McWilliam) C.; m. Karen Elisabeth Jones, June 28, 1974 (dec. May 2002); children: J. Adam Jr., Robert H., Kathryn E. A in Occupational Studies in Acctg., Bus.i, Utica (N.Y.) Sch. Commerce, 1973; postgrad., New Sch. Social Rsch., 1984, Am. Coll., Bryn Mawr, Pa. ChFC, CLU. Sales mgr. Mohawk Frozen Foods, Marcy, NY, 1973-77; sole propr. From the C's, Inc., Rome, NY, 1975-77; agt., dist. asst. Equitable Fin. Svcs., Rome, 1978-83; advanced mktg. specialist Farm Family Ins. Cos., Albany, NY, 1984, dir. agt. and mgr. devel., 1985-87, dir. devel. and advanced life sales, 1987-96, dir. advanced markets, 1996-97, dir. life sales, 1997—2003, dir. life and fin. svcs., 2003—; v.p. life ops. Farm Family Ins. Co., 2004—; mem. mktg. com. Farm Bur. Bank, 1998—. Adj. instr. various profl. tng. orgns., Rome, Utica and Albany, 1981—. Pres. Rome Cmty. Concerts Assn., 1978-80, Voorheesville (N.Y.) Ctrl. Sch. Bd., 1990—2005; cubmaster Boy Scouts Am.; mem. Holland Patent (N.Y.) Ctrl. Sch. Bd., 1982-85; mem. parents adv. bd. Pine Bush Little League, New Scotland Pop Warner, Guilderland Babe Ruth League; coach Ea. N.Y. State Champions team Babe Ruth Allstars, 1995; found. dir. Voorheesville Cmty. Schs. Found., 1999—. Mem. Ea. N.Y. Soc. CLUs & ChFCs (bd. dirs. 1986-91), Ea. N.Y. Soc. Fin. Svcs. Profls. (bd. mem. 2003—), Albany Assn. Life Underwriters (bd. dirs. 1987-92), Mohawk Valley Life Underwriters (pres., chmn. 1980-84), Kiwanis, N.Y. State Newsletter award 1992), Masons. Republican. Methodist. Office: Farm Family Ins Co PO Box 656 Albany NY 12201-0656 Office Phone: 518-431-5185. E-mail: john_cole@farmfamily.com.

COLE, JOHN FRANKLAND, electrical engineer, educator; s. Roger Powell Cole and Josephine Coleman Rogers; m. Teresa Ellen Parker, Nov. 30, 1956; children: John David, Charles Christopher, Amy Catherine Belew, Kathleen Grace. BSEE, U. Tenn., Knoxville, 1970. Proiect engr. Owens Corning Fiberglas, Jackson, Tenn., 1970—73, advanced glass technologist Granville, 1973—76, supr. instrument shop Jackson, 1976—78, supr. maintenance ops., 1978—87; mgr. engring., maintenance mgr. Bekaert Steel Wire Corp., Dyersburg, 1987—89; sr. elec. engr. Kaiser Aluminum & Chem. Corp., Jackson, 1989; mgr. engring. Kaiser Aluminum & and Chem. Corp., 1989—. Adj. prof. engring. Union U., Jackson, 2004—; coop. engr. Jackson Utility Divsn., 1966—68. Contbr. articles to profl. jours. Bd. mem. Trinity Chritian Acad., Jackson, 1992—2005; bd. pres. Trinity Christian Acad., 1998—98. Mem.: IEEE, Tenn. Soc. Profl. Engrs., Eta Kappa Nu, Tau Beta Pi. Baptist. Achievements include development of trade secret on winder speed control. Office: Kaiser Aluminum Fabricated Products 309 Industrial Drive Jackson TN 38301 Home Phone: 731-668-8077; Office Phone: 731-423-2811. Business E-Mail: john.cole@tennalum.com.

COLE, JOHN POPE, JR., lawyer; b. Washington, Jan. 12, 1930; s. John Pope and Helen (Gorman) C.; m. Patsy Nan Moss, Mar. 20, 1960; children— John Moss, Nina Gorman. BS, Auburn U., 1953; LL.B., George Washington U., 1956. Bar: D.C. 1956, Md. 1956, Ga. 1961. Atty. FCC, Washington, 1956-57; ptnr. Smith & Pepper, Washington, 1957-66; staff U.S. Ho. Reps., Washington, 1961-62; founding ptnr. Cole, Raywid & Braverman, Washington, 1966—2006, ret., 2006; ptnr. Davis Wright Tremaine, Washington, 2007—. Served with USAF, 1948-49. Home: 5309 Portsmouth Rd Bethesda MD 20816-2930 Office: Davis Wright Tremaine 1919 Pennsylvania Ave NW Washington DC 20006-3458 Office Phone: 202-973-4200. Business E-Mail: jackcole@dwt.com.

COLE, JOHN PRINCE, lawyer, academic administrator; b. Carrollton, Ga., Mar. 18, 1963; m. Mary Stewart Donovan. AB, Harvard U., 1985; JD magna cum laude, Mercer Law Sch., 1991. Bar: Ga. 1991, US Dist. Ct. (no., mid. dist.) Ga. 1991, US Ct. Appeals (11th cir.) 1991. Law clerk Mitchell, Coppedge, Wester, Bisson & Miller, Dalton, Ga., 1989, Ga. Atty. Gen., Atlanta, 1990; assoc. Anderson, Walker & Reichert, Macon, Ga., 1991-94; gen. asst. to pres. Mercer U., Macon, Ga., 1994—2000, v.p. univ. admissions, 2001—03, 2004—, v.p. charitable and estate planning, 2003—04. Trustee First Bapt. Ch., Macon, 1993-97, deacon, 2006—; trustee Ga. Children's Home, 1996-2000, bd. chair, 1999-2000; funds allocation com. United Way Ctrl. Ga., 1992-94. Maj. US Army, Bosnia, 2001. Mem. ABA, Nat. Assn. Coll. and Univ. Attys., Macon Bar Assn. (treas. 1997-98, sec. 1998-99, pres. elect 1999-2001, pres. 2001-02), Lawyers Found. Ga., Leadership GA, Phi Kappa Phi. Democrat. Avocations: hiking, music, golf. Office: Mercer U 1400 Coleman Ave Macon GA 31207-0003 Home Phone: 478-738-0858; Office Phone: 478-301-2570.

COLE, JOHNNETTA BETSCH, former academic administrator, educator; b. Jacksonville, Fla., Oct. 19, 1936; d. John Thomas and Mary Frances (Lewis) Betsch; m. Robert Eugene Cole (div. 1982); children: David, Aaron, Ethan; m. Arthur J. Robinson, Jr. (div. 2002). Student, Fisk U., 1953; BA in Sociology, Oberlin Coll., 1957; MA in Anthropology, Northwestern U., Evanston, Ill., 1959, PhD, 1967. Instr. UCLA, 1964; dir. black studies Wash. State U., Pullman, 1969-70; prof. anthropology U. Mass., Amherst, 1970-83, assoc. provost undergrad. edn., 1981-83; vis. prof. Hunter Coll., NYC, 1983-84, prof. anthropology, 1983-87, dir. Inter-Am. Affairs Program, 1984-87; pres. Spelman Coll., Atlanta, 1987-97, pres. emeritus, 1997—; pres. Bennett Coll. Women, Greensboro, NC, 2002—07, chair bd. dirs. Johnnetta B. Cole Global Diversity and Inclusion Inst. Corp. bd. dirs. Merck & Co., Inc.; presdl. disting. prof. anthropology, women's studies and Afro-Am. studies Emory U., 1998-2001. Author, editor: Anthropology for the Eighties, 1982, All American Women, 1986, Anthropology for the Nineties, 1988, Conversations: Straight Talk with America's Sister President, 1993, Dream the Boldest Dreams, 1998; author: (with Beverly Guy-Sheftall) Gender Talk: The Struggle for Women's Equality in African American Communities, 2003; mem. editl. bd. The Black Scholar. Immediate past chair bd. trustees United Way. Am. Recipient numerous hon. degrees. Fellow Am. Anthrop. Assn.; mem. Am. Acad. Arts and Scis., Assn. Black Anthropologists (past pres.). United Methodist. Office: Johnnetta B Cole Global Diversity & Inclusion Inst 900 E Washington St Greensboro NC 27401 Office Phone: 336-517-2272. Office Fax: 336-517-2221. Business E-Mail: jcole@bennett.edu.

COLE, JONATHAN EDWARD, lawyer; b. Atlantic, Iowa, July 21, 1945; s. Edward Perine and Edna Lorraine (Gilman) C.; m. Patricia Ann Meredith, June 9, 1967; children: Matthew Edward, Meredith Asher. Student, Universite de Strabourg, France, 1965-66; BA with distinction, Brown U., 1968; JD cum laude, Harvard U., 1971. Bar: RI 1971, Fla. 1981, NY 1985, Mass. 1986. Assoc. Edwards & Angell, Providence, 1971-75, ptnr., 1975-81, ptnr. in charge Palm Beach, Fla., 1981—2002; ptnr. Edwards Angell Palmer & Dodge, Fort Lauderdale, Fla., 2002—. Bd. dirs., chmn. U. Miami Venture Coun. Forum, Miami, 1984—. Contbr. articles to profl. journs., spkr. in fields. Trustee Young Audiences of Palm Beach County, West Palm Beach, Fla., 1987-89, Land Preservation Trust of Palm Beach County, West Palm Beach, 1989—; trustee, v.p. South Fla. Sci. Mus., West Palm Beach, 1986—; trustee, chmn. Trinity Sq. Repertory Co., Providence, 1972-82, Actors Workshop and Repertory Co., West Palm Beach, 1982-86; bd. dirs., sec. Citizens for Environ. Land Preservation, West Palm Beach, 1991—, Town of Palm Beach United Way. Mem. Nat. Assn. SBICs (assoc.), Assn. for Corp. Growth (bd. dirs., pres. elect Boca Raton, Fla. chpt. 1982—), Palm Beach County Bar Assn. (Svc. to Arts award 1987), Brown U. Alumni Assn. (bd. dirs., exec. com. Providence chpt. 1982-86), Brown U. Club (bd. dirs. Palm Beach chpt. 1984-90), ABA, Vision Broward (steering com.), Bus. Devel. Bd. Palm Beach County, Inc., Enterprise Devel. Corp. South Fla., Fla. Bar Assn., Fla. Venture Forum, Inc. Avocations: fly fishing, bird hunting, tennis, Asian. Office: Edwards Angell Palmer & Dodge 350 E Las Olas Blvd Ste 1150 Fort Lauderdale FL 33301 Office Phone: 954-667-6124. Office Fax: 954-727-2601. Business E-Mail: jcole@eapdlaw.com.

COLE, KATHLEEN ANN, advertising executive, social worker; b. Nov. 22, 1946; d. James Scott and Kathryn Gertrude (Borisch) Cole; m. Brian Brandt, Mar. 21, 1970. BA, Miami U., 1968; MSW, U. Mich., 1972; MM, Northwestern U., 1978. Social worker Hamilton County Welfare Dept., Cin., 1969—70, Lucas County Children Svcs. Bd., Toledo, 1970—74, East Maine Sch. Dist., Niles, Ill., 1974—77; account supr. Leo Burnett Advt. Agy., Chgo., 1978—93; primary therapist Lifeline, Chgo., 1994—95; acct. dir. GreenHouse Comm., 1995—2001; program coord. North Shore Sr. Ctr., 2004—. Field instr. Loyola U., Chgo., 1976—77. Mem. North Shore United Meth. Congregation. Mem.: NASW (chair pub. rels. task force), Kellogg Alumni Assn., Northwestern U. Prof. Women's Assn., Miami U. Alumni Assn. (dir. 1976—78), Acad. Cert. Social Workers. Home: 414 Kelling Ln Glencoe IL 60022-1113 Office: 1779 Winnetka Rd Winnetka IL 60093 Personal E-mail: colemarketing@comcast.net.

COLE, K.C., journalist, writer; BA, Barnard Coll. Writer, editor Saturday Rev., San Francisco; editor Newsday; sci. commentator Pasadena Pub. Radio (KPCC); sci. writer L.A. Times, 1994—. Adj. prof. UCLA; tchr. sci. writing Yale U., Wesleyan U.; mem. Jour. Women Symposium; dir. PEN West; vis. prof. U. So. Calif. Annenberg, 2006—. Author: (book) The Hole in the Universe: How Scientists Peered Over the Edge of Emptiness and Found Everything, The Universe and the Teacup: The Mathematics of Truth and Beauty, First You Build a Cloud: Reflections on Phyics as a Way of Life, Mind Over Matter: Conversations with the Cosmos, 2003; contbg. writer: The New Yorker, The New York Times, Washington Post, Newsday, Esquire, Newsweek, others. Recipient Writing prize, Am. Inst. Physics, Edward R. Murrow award, Skeptics Soc., Elizabeth A. Wood Sci. Writing award, Am. Crystallographic Assn., 2001; fellow Math. Sci. Rsch. Inst., Exploratorium. Office: LA Times 202 W First St Los Angeles CA 90012 Office Phone: 213-237-7354. Office Fax: 213-237-4712. Business E-Mail: kc.cole@latimes.com.

COLE, KENNETH D., apparel designer; b. 1954; s. Charles Cole; m. Maria Cuomo; 3 children. BA, Emory Univ., Atlanta, 1976. Sr. exec. El Greco, Inc., 1976-82; CEO, pres., chmn. bd. dirs. Kenneth Cole Prodns., Inc., NYC, 1982—. Bd. dir. Coun. Fashion Designers Am., Sundance Inst. Bd. dirs. Am. Found. for AIDS Rsch., 1985- (vice chmn., 2002-2005, chmn., 2005-), H.E.L.P. for homeless, 1987-. Recipient Spotlight award for dedication to increasing public awareness, Creative Coalition , Media Spotlight award, Amnesty Internat., 1992, Award for Humanitarian Excellence, Coun. Fashion Designers Am., 1996, Extraordinary Voice award, Mother's Voices for his continued efforts in AIDS awareness, Humanitarian Leadership award, Coun. on Foundations, 1996, Fashion Medal of Honor award, Fashion Footwear Assn. NY (FFANY), 1997, Emory Medal for disting.svc., 1999., amfAR's Award of Courage, 2000; named Humanitarian of Yr., Divine Design, footwear industry's highest honor as Footwear News' Person of Yr. Office: Kenneth Cole Prodns Inc 603 West 50th St New York NY 10019 Office Phone: 212-265-1500. Fax: (212) 713-6666; Office Fax: 212-830-7422.*

COLE, KENNETH W., automotive executive; Grad., U. Tex., Austin; JD, U. Houston. Reg. dir. pub. govt. affairs Amoco Corp.; joined as v.p. pub. affairs Allied Corp., 1981; joined Washington office Allied Signal Inc., 1983, staff v.p. Washington office, 1985, v.p. govt. relations, 1988; v.p. govt. rels. GM Corp., 2001—, v.p. global public policy and govt. rels., 2007—, mem. automotive strategy bd., 2007—. Mem.: Nat. Assn. Bus. Polit. Action (past pres.), Business-Govt. Rels. Coun. (past pres.), Congl. Inst. (bd. dirs.), European Inst. (bd. dirs.), Coun. Pub. Affairs Execs. (bd. dirs.), Pub. Affairs Coun. (bd. dirs.), Nat. Fgn. Trade Coun. (bd. dirs.), U.S. Capital Hist. Soc. (bd. dirs.), Wolf Trap Found. (bd. dirs.). Office: GM Corp 1660 L St NW Washington DC 20036 also: 300 Renaissance Ctr PO Box 300 Detroit MI 48265-3000*

COLE, LEWIS GEORGE, lawyer; b. NYC, Mar. 9, 1931; s. Ralph David and Emma (Balterman) C.; m. Sara Livingston, June 22, 1952; children: Elizabeth, Peter. BS in Econ., U. Pa., 1951; LLB, Yale U., 1954. Bar: N.Y. 1954. Ptnr. Stroock & Stroock & Lavan, LLP, NYC, 1958—. Bd. dirs. Ametek, Inc. Served as 1st lt. U.S. Army, 1954-57. Mem. ABA, Assn. Bar City NY, NY State Bar Assn. Office: Stroock & Stroock & Lavan LLP 180 Maiden Ln New York NY 10038-4925 Office Phone: 212-806-6050.

COLE, LORRAINE, women's association executive; b. Chgo. m. Vincent Stovall; 1 child. Bachelor's degree, No. Ill. U.; PhD, Northwestern U. Cert. Assn. Exec. Exec. dir. Nat. Med. Assn., 1994—2000; pres., CEO Black Women's Health Imperative, 2000—06; CEO YWCA USA, Washington, 2006—. Mem. key philanthropic organizations com. ASAE & The Ctr. for Assn. Leadership. Office: YWCA USA 1015 18th St NW #1100 Washington DC 20036 Office Phone: 202-467-0801.*

COLE, LUTHER FRANCIS, former state supreme court associate justice; b. Alexandria, La., Oct. 25, 1925; s. Clem and Catherine (Wiley) C.; m. Juanita Barton, Mar. 9, 1945; children: Frances Jeannette, Jeffrey Martin, Christopher Warren. Student, La. Tech. U., 1943—44; JD, La. State U., 1950. Ptnr. Cole, Mengis & Durant, Baton Rouge, 1950-66; judge 19th Jud. Dist., Baton Rouge, 1966-75, chief judge, 1975-79; judge Ct. Appeals, Baton Rouge, 1979-86; assoc. justice Supreme Ct. La., New Orleans, 1986-92. Chmn. Jud. Budgetary Control Bd., 1990-92; mem. La. Bd. Ethics for Elected Ofcls., 1994-95, La. Commn. on Law Enforcement and Adminstrn. of Criminal Justice, 1996—2004. Rep. La. Legis., Baton Rouge, 1964-66; v.p. Merchants Assn., Baton Rouge, 1954; chmn. awards Boy Scouts Am., Baton Rouge, 1956; mem. Civic Ctr. com., Baton Rouge, 1971-74; bd. dirs. Blundon Home, Baton Rouge, 1984-86. Served to lt. (j.g.) USN, 1943-46. Mem. ABA (ann. meeting 1991, Jury Standards award 1991), La. Bar Assn., Baton Rouge Bar Assn. (pres. 1966), La. Dist. Judges Assn. (pres. 1972-73). Clubs: Exchange (Baton Rouge) (pres. 1954). Democrat. Baptist. Avocations: hunting, cooking. Home and Office: 9213 Hilltrace Ave Baton Rouge LA 70809-2614

COLE, MAX, artist; b. Hodgeman County, Kans., Feb. 14, 1937; BA, Fort Hays State U., 1961; MFA, U. Ariz., 1964. One-man shows include Louver Gallery, LA, 1978, 80, Sidney Janis Gallery, NYC, 1977, 80, Zabriskie Gallery, NY, 1987, Haines Gallery, San Francisco, 1988, 93, 96, 98, 2007, Galerie Schlegl, Zurich, 1990, 96, 99-2000, Mus. Folkwang, Essen, Germany, 1993, Kunstraum Kassel (Germany), 1992, Roswell (N.Mex.) Mus. and Art Ctr., 1996, Stark Gallery, NY, Galerie Michael Strum, Stuttgart, 1997, 99, Mus. Modern Art, Otterndorf, Germany, 1998, Haus Konstructive und Konkrete Kunst, Zurich, 2001, Walter Storms Gallery, Munich, 2002, Kunstverein, Aschaffenberg, Germany, 2002, Diozesan Museum, Cologne, 2004, Mus. Chasa Juara Val Chava, Switzerland, Studio La Citta, Verona, Italy, 2006, Haines Gallery, San Francisco, 2007, Galerie Lindner, Vienna, 2007; exhibited in group shows including LA County Mus. Art, 1976, Corcoran Gallery Art, Washington, 1977, La Jolla Mus., 1980, Santa Barbara Mus., 1980, Mus. Fine Arts of N.Mex., 1984, Neuberger Mus., Purchase, NY, 1984, Marilyn Pearl Gallery, NYC, 1985, Pratt Manhattan Ctr. Gallery, 1985, UCLA, 1988, Nat. Gallery Modern Art, New Delhi, 1988, Panza Found., Verese, Italy, 1995, Aagauer Kunsthaus, Aarau, Switzerland, 1995, Trento (Italy) Mus., 1996, Galerie Schlegl, Zurich, 1996, Manif, 1997, Internat. Art Forum, Seoul, 1997, Mus. Modern Art, Otterndorf, Germany, 1998, Haines Gallery, San Francisco, 1998; represented in permanent collections LA County Mus. Art, Newport Harbor Mus. Art, La Jolla Mus. Contemporary Art, Mus. N.Mex., Dallas Mus. Art, Santa Barbara Mus., Everson Mus., Tel Aviv Mus., La. Mus., Van Der Heyt Mus., Wuppertal, Germany, Denmark, Panza Collection, Italy, Diozesan Mus., Cologne, Chiat Found., NY, Panza Collection, Italy, Lembach Haus, Munich, Ingolstaadt Mus., Germany. Address: PO Box 56 Ruby NY 12475

COLE, MICHAEL H., food products executive; Law degree, U. Va., Charlottesville, 1985. Bar: Va. 1985. With McGuireWoods LLP, Smithfield Foods, Inc., Va., 1996—, sec., 1999—, v.p., dep. gen. counsel, v.p., chief legal officer. Bd. dirs. Pennexx Foods, Inc., 2001. Office: Smithfield Foods Inc 200 Commerce St Smithfield VA 23430 Office Phone: 757-365-3000. Office Fax: 757-365-3017.*

COLE, NANCY STOOKSBERRY, educational research executive; b. Brenham, Tex., Nov. 29, 1942; d. Joe Brady and Grace Darling (Pyburn) S.; m. James W.L. Cole, June 4, 1966; 1 child, David Leverett. BA, Rice U., 1964; MA, U. N.C., 1967, PhD, 1968. Rsch. psychologist Am. Coll. Testing Program, Iowa City, 1968-71, dir. test devel., 1971-73, asst. v.p., 1973-74; from assoc. prof. to prof. U. Pitts., 1975-85; prof., dean edn. U. Ill., Champaign, 1985-89; exec. v.p. Ednl. Testing Svc., Princeton, N.J., 1989-93; pres., 1994-2000; sr. advisor, 2000—04; ret., 2004. Contbr. articles on ednl. testing to profl. jours. Fellow Am. Psychol. Assn.; mem. Nat. Acad. Edn., Nat. Coun. on Measurement in Edn. (pres. 1983-84), Am. Ednl. Rsch. Assn. (pres. 1988-89).

COLE, NATALIE MARIA, singer; b. LA, Feb. 6, 1950; d. Nathaniel Adam and Maria (Harkins) Cole; m. Marvin J. Yancy, July 31, 1976 (div. 1980); 1 child, Robert Adam; m. Andre Fischer, Sept. 16, 1989 (div. 1995); m. Rev. Kenneth Dupress, Oct. 12, 2001 (div. 2004). BA in Child Psychology, U. Mass., 1972. Rec. singles and albums, 1975—; albums include Dangerous, 1985, Everlasting, 1987, The Natalie Cole Collection, 1987, Inseparable, Thankful, Good To Be Back, 1989, Unforgettable, 1991 (4 grammys, 3 grammys 1992), Too Much Weekend, 1992, I'm Ready, 1992, I've Got Love On My Mind, 1992, Take A Look, 1993 (Grammy award nominee best jazz vocal 1994), Holly and Ivy, 1994, Stardust (2 Grammy awards), Magic of Christmas, 1999, Snowfall on the Sahara, 1999, Greatest Hits, 2000, Ask a Woman Who Knows, 2002; television appearances include Big Break (host), 1990, Lily in Winter, 1994; appeared in TV movies The Wizard of Oz in Concert (as Glinda), 1995, Always Outnumbered, 1998, Freak City, 1999; co-author: Angel on My Shoulder, 2000; composer Easter Egg Escapade, 2005. Recipient Grammy award for best new artist, 1975, best Rhythm and Blues female vocalist 1976; recipient 1 gold single, 3 gold albums; recipient 2 Image awards NAACP 1976, 77; Am. Music award 1978, other awards. Mem.: Nat. Assn. Rec. Arts & Scis., AFTRA, Delta Sigma Delta. Baptist. Home: 700 N San Vicente Blvd Ste G910 West Hollywood CA 90069-5061

COLE, NIKKI JO, music educator; b. Mansfield, Pa., July 29, 1971; d. Clifton Thomas and Phyllis Eleanor Griffin; m. John Arthur Cole, July 23, 1994. MusB in Music Edn., U. Pa., Mansfield, 1993; MusM in Music Edn., Ithaca Coll., NYC, 1999. Lic. music educator N.Y. State, 1993. Instrumental music educator Elmira (N.Y.) City Sch. Dist., 1993—2000, Bath (N.Y.) Ctrl. Sch. Dist., 2000—. Workshop presenter on assessment in music edn. various sch. dists., NY, Pa., 1996—; mentor, cooperating tchr. U. Pa., Mansfield, Pa., 1997—. Contbr. Music- A Resource Guide for Standards-Based Instrn. Recipient Commissioner's Acad. for Tchg. and Learning award, N.Y. State Edn. Dept., 2000. Mem.: N.Y. State Band Dir.'s Assn., N.Y. State Sch. Music Assn. (curriculum com. 2006), Music Educator's Nat. Conf. Avocation: flute. Home Phone: 607-962-5292. Business E-Mail: jcole32@stny.rr.com.

COLE, RANSEY GUY, JR., federal judge; b. Birmingham, Ala., May 23, 1951; s. Ransey Guy and Sarah Nell (Coker) Cole; m. Kathleine Kelley, Nov. 26, 1983; children: Justin Robert Jefferson, Jordan Paul, Alexandra Sarah. BA, Tufts U., 1972; JD, Yale U., 1975. Bar: Ohio 1975, D.C. 1982. Assoc. Vorys, Sater, Seymour and Pease, Columbus, Ohio, 1975—78, ptnr., 1980—86, 1993—95; trial atty. US Dept. Justice, Washington, 1978—80; judge US Bankruptcy Ct., Columbus, 1987—93, US Ct. Appeals (6th cir.), Cinn., 1995—. Bd. trustee March of Dimes, Ohio, 1985—88, YMCA, 1984—88, Neighborhood House, 1985—88, Columbus Area Internat. Prog., 1986—94, Children's Hospital, 1990—. Mem.: ABA, Columbus Bar Assn., Nat. Bar Assn. Office: US Courthouse 85 Marconi Blvd Rm 127 Columbus OH 43215-2823*

COLE, RICHARD A., retired lawyer; b. Syracuse, NY, Feb. 21, 1951; s. Victor and Marie (Pogacar) C.; m. Lois Hallonquist, Sept. 27, 1975. AB, Brown U., 1973; JD, Cornell U., 1976. Bar: Ill. 1976, U.S. Dist. Ct. (no. dist.) Ill. 1976. Assoc. Mayer, Brown, Rowe & Maw, Chgo., 1976—82, ptnr., 1983—2002. Trustee U. Notre Dame, London, 1981-2002. Avocation: travel. Home: 131A Farmholme Rd Stonington CT 06378 Home Phone: 860-535-2089. Personal E-mail: rlcole51@sbcglobal.net.

COLE, RICHARD CARGILL, language educator; b. Kansas City, Kans., Apr. 16, 1926; s. Horace Richard and Iris Verner (Cargill) C.; m. Florence Adaline Mason, June 27, 1956; children: Celia Elizabeth Cole Shaw, Paul Richard. BA, Hamilton Coll., 1950; MA, Yale U., 1951, PhD in English, 1955. English tchr. Manlius (N.Y.) Sch., 1951-52; asst. to dean of freshmen Yale U., New Haven, 1953-54; instr. English U. Tex., Austin, 1954-57; assoc. prof. Radford Va. Coll. (now Univ.), 1957-59, prof. English, 1959-61, Davidson (N.C.) Coll., 1961-93, prof. emeritus, 1993—. Author: Irish Booksellers and English Writers, 1740-1800, 1986; author, editor: Robert Colvill's Atalanta and Savannah, 1987, John Singleton's Grand Tour, 1815-1817, 1988, The General Correspondence of James Boswell, 1766-1767, 1993, Thomas Mante, Writer, Soldier, Adventurer, 1993, The General Correspondence of James Boswell, 1768-1769, 1997; contbr. articles to profl. jours. Sgt. USAAF, 1944-46, ETO. Robert Warnock Rsch. fellow Yale U., 1975-76, Rsch. fellow Yale U. Div. Sch., 1978; rsch. grantee Bd. Higher Edn., Presbyn. Ch., 1968, Piedmont U. Ctr. NC, 1968; grantee Am. Coun. Learned Socs., 1976, Nat. Endowment for the Humanities, 1985, 89. Mem. Phi Beta Kappa. Republican. Presbyterian. Home: 400 Avinger Ln Apt 101 Davidson NC 28036-9700

COLE, RICHARD CHARLES, lawyer; b. Albany, NY, Apr. 23, 1950; s. Charles Stanley and Doris Jean (Hatch) Cole; children: Jack Patrick, Charles Michael, Will. BA magna cum laude, Cornell U., 1972; JD, Harvard U., 1975. Bar: N.Y. 1976, Calif. 1989, U.S. Dist. Ct. (so. and ea. dits.) N.Y. 1977, U.S. Ct. Apeals (D.C. cir.) 1980, U.S. Ct. Appeals (2d and 5th cirs.) 1981, U.S. Dist. Ct. (no, ea., so. and ctrl. dists.) 1989, U.S. Supreme Ct. 1995. Assoc. LeBoeuf, Lamb, Leiby & MacRae, NYC, 1975-83, ptnr., 1984-89, LeBoeuf, Lamb, Greene & MacRae, San Francisco, 1989-95; pvt. practice Mill Valley, 1996—. Mem.: ABA. Avocations: woodwind instruments, school volunteering, jazz. Office: 111 Stanford Ave Mill Valley CA 94941-3562 Office Phone: 415-383-2558. Personal E-mail: dickcc@pacbell.net.

COLE, RICHARD JOHN, marketing executive; b. NYC, Oct. 18, 1926; s. Arthur and Anna C.; m. Birgitta Ofling, Aug. 26, 1961; children— Catherine Ann, Richard Arthur, John Eric, Christopher Arne. BA, Yale U., 1946. Pres. Richard J. Cole, Inc., NYC, 1954-61; gen. mgr. Dynasty of Hong Kong, NYC, 1961-67; CEO, M.I. Group div. Manhattan Industries, Inc., 1967—89; mng. dir. B. Barclay Internat., Inc., 1989—92; prin. Sources Unltd., 1991—, R.&R. Internat., Inc., NYC, 1992—. Served with USNR, 1943-46, 52-53. Congregationalist. Home and Office: 72 Main St Newtown CT 06470 Office Phone: 917-756-0972. E-mail: rcole054@earthlink.net.

COLE, RICHARD LOUIS, political scientist, educator; b. Dallas, Jan. 25, 1946; s. Louis Ray and Mary (Steely) C.; children: Jonathan, Ashley. BA, North Tex. State U., Denton, 1967, MA, 1968; PhD, Purdue U., 1973. Asst. prof. George Washington U., 1973-78, assoc. prof., 1978-79; research scholar Yale U., New Haven, Conn., 1979-80; prof. polit. sci., dean Sch. Urban and Pub. Affairs U. Tex., Arlington, 1980—; acting dean Coll. Liberal Arts, 2001—. Cons. Office Revenue Sharing Rand Corp. Author: Citizen Participation, 1974, Revenue Sharing, 1976, Introduction to Political Inquiry, 1980, Urban Life in Texas, 1986, Texas Politics and Public Policy, 1987, The Politics of American Government, 1994, Introduction to Political and Policy Research, 1996; mem. editl. bd. Am. Politics Quar., 1977-88, Jour. Cmty. Action, 1981—, Pub. Adminstrn. Rev., 1986-89, Jour. Urban Affairs, 1988—; contbr. articles to profl. jours. Mem. Leadership Arlington. Mem. Am. Soc. Pub. Adminstrn. (pres. N. Tex. chpt. 1989-90), S.W. Polit. Sci. Assn. (v.p. 1983-84, pres.-elect 1990, pres. 1991-92), Am. Polit. Sci. Assn. Democrat. Methodist. Home: 614 Portofino Dr Arlington TX 76012-2759 Office: Inst Urban Studies U Tex PO Box 19588 Arlington TX 76019-0001 E-mail: cole@uta.edu.

COLE, RICHARD RAY, communications educator, former dean; b. Forney, Tex., Apr. 20, 1942; s. Richard W. and G. Gladys C.; m. Lynda F. Painter, May 31, 1968. BJ, U. Tex., 1964, MA, 1966; PhD, U. Minn., 1971. Asst. city editor The News, Mexico City, 1966-67; freelance writer, 1966-67; reporter Harrow Observer, Harrow-on-the-Hill, England, 1968; asst. prof. W.Va. U., 1967-68; instr. U. Minn., 1968-71; mem. faculty U. NC, Chapel Hill, 1971—, prof. journalism, 1979—, John T. Kerr Jr. disting. prof., 2002—, dean Sch. Journalism and Mass Comm., 1979—2005. Nat. scholarship com. Freedom Forum, 1980-86, chmn., 1987-93; chief judge H.L. Mencken Nat. Writing Award Competition, 1983-90; mem. journalism awards program steering com. William Randolph Hearst Found., 1981-2005, chmn., 1991-2005; chmn. accrediting teams US journalism schs.; mem. faculty adv. com. World Press Inst.; mem. Nat. Accrediting Coun. on Edn. in Journalism and Mass Comm., 1987-96, v.p., 1989-95; cons. in field; creator cooperative programs with univs. in Mexico City, Santiago, Chile, Brazil, State of Parana, Havana, Cuba, United Arab Emirates; apptd. adh., coun. facultad comunicaciones Pontificial Cath. U. Chile, 1999—. Co-author: Gathering and Writing The News: Selected Readings, 1975; editor: Communication in Latin America: Journalism , Mass Communication, and Society, 1996; asst. editor Journalism Quar., 1973-85; contbr. articles to profl. jours. Chmn. U. NC Bicentennial Observance Planning Com., 1986-87; mem. Bicentennial Policy Com., 1988-94. Recipient Excellence award in undergrad. tchg.

Amoco Found., 1978, Freedom Forum medal for lifetime accomplishments in journalism-mass comm. adminstrn., 1992, Earl Gluck award for disting. svc. to broadcasting, 2004, Dist. Svc. medal UNC-Chapel Hill General Alumni Assn., 2005, Order of Long Leaf Pine, Govt. of NC, 2005; named to NC Journalism Hall of Fame, 2005, Order of Long Leaf Pine award NC Gov., 2005; grantee U. Minn., U. NC Dept. State, Internat. Comm. Agy., Internat. Media Fund, US AID, others; Fulbright fellow, Brazil, 2001 Mem. Assn. Edn. Journalism and Mass Comm. (exec. com. 1977-79, 81-84, chmn. coms. 1974-75, 77-79, pres. 1982-83, nat. task force on future mass comm. of edn. 1983-84), Internat. Assn. Mass Comm. Rsch. (coun. 1980-88, v.p. 1984-88), Assn. Schs. Journalism and Mass Comm. (exec. com. 1983-88, 1992-93, pres. 1986-87, mem. nat. steering com. to select 1st journalist in space NASA 1985-86), Inter Am. Press Assn., Order of Golden Fleece, Sigma Delta Chi, Kappa Tau Alpha. Office: U NC Sch Journalism & Mass Communication PO Box 3365 Chapel Hill NC 27599-0001 Home Phone: 919-929-2436; Office Phone: 919-843-8289. Business E-Mail: richard_cole@unc.edu.

COLE, RICHIE THOMAS, musician, composer, educator; b. Trenton, NJ, Feb. 29, 1948; s. Thomas and Emily Cole; m. Rise Cole, July 4, 1999; children: Amy Marrazzo, Shawn Shaw. Degree in Saxaphone, Berklee Coll. Music, 1969. Musician Alto Madness Music, Pensacola, Fla., 1969—2005. Cons., arranger, composer, educator Alto Madness Music, Pensacola, Fla., 1969—. Composer over 5000 musical compositions. Mem.: United Fedn. Musicians, Chamber Music Assn., Rec. Acad., Internat. Assn. Jazz Educators (Lifetime Jazz Educator award 2003), Nat. Jazz Svc. Orgn. (assoc.). Achievements include spreading a colorblind musical vision throughout the world of americas only artform, jazz. Home: 209 Nancy Ln Trenton NJ 08638 Home Phone: 609-882-3462; Office Phone: 305-495-1809. Office Fax: 609-882-2078; Home Fax: 609-882-2078. Personal E-mail: richiecolealtomadness@yahoo.com.

COLE, ROBERT K., diversified financial services company executive; MBA, Wayne State U. Pres. NBD Bancorp and Pub. Storage, Triple Five Inc., real estate devel., 1990—94; pres., COO-fin. Plaza Home Mortgage Corp., 1994—95; co-founder New Century Fin. Corp., Irvine, Calif., 1995, chmn., CEO, 1995—2006, chmn., 2006—. Bd. dirs. Option One Mortgage Corp. (subs. Plaza Home Mortgage), 1994—95, New Century Mortgage, 1995—. Office: New Century Fin Corp Ste 1000 18400 Von Karman Ave Irvine CA 92612 Office Phone: 949-440-7032.

COLE, ROBERT THEODORE, lawyer; b. Bklyn., Mar. 16, 1932; s. Harold I. and Bella (Weissman) C.; m. C. Margaret Hall, Oct. 25, 1959; children: Elizabeth, Tanya, Judith Amy. BS in Econs., U. Pa., 1953; LLB magna cum laude, Harvard U. Law Sch., 1956; diploma in law, London Sch. Econs., 1958. Bar: NY 1956, DC 1972. Assoc. Law Office Frank Boas, Brussels, 1960-62, Nixon Mudge Rose et al, NYC, 1962-67; atty. U.S. Treasury Dept., Washington, 1967-73, internat. tax counsel, 1971-73; ptnr. Cole Corette & Abrutyn, Washington, 1973-96; ptnr., sr. counsel, internat. tax group Alston & Bird LLP, Washington, 1997—, chmn. internat. tax group, 1997—2000; co-owner The Little Gyms, No. Va. Lectr. on internat. tax. Editor, prin. author Practical Guide U.S. Transfer Pricing; contbr. articles on internat. taxes to legal jours. Capt. USAF, 1957-59. Recipient exceptional svc. award US Treasury Dept., 1973. Fellow Am. Coll. Tax Counsel; mem. Assn. Bar City NY, Nat. Fgn. Trade Coun. (vice-chair tax com. 1989-95), Harvard Club (NYC). Avocations: hiking, theater. Office: Alston & Bird LLP 950 F St Washington DC 20004 Office Phone: 202-756-3306. Business E-Mail: bob.cole@alston.com.

COLE, ROLAND JAY, lawyer; b. Seattle, Dec. 15, 1948; s. Robert J. and Josephine F. C.; m. Elsa Kircher, Aug. 16, 1975; children: Isabel Ashley, Madeline Aldis. AB in Econs. magna cum laude, Harvard U., 1970, M in Pub. Policy, 1972, PhD in Pub. Policy, JD, 1975. Bar: Wash. 1975, U.S. Supreme Ct. 1980, U.S. Dist. Ct. (we. dist.) Wash. 1984, Mich. 1989. Rsch. scientist Battelle Human Affairs Rsch. Ctrs., Seattle, 1975-83; assoc. Appel and Glueck, P.C., Seattle, 1984-89; gen. counsel Indsl. Tech. Inst., Ann Arbor, Mich., 1990-94; founder, exec. dir. Software Patent Inst., Indpls., 1994—, exec. dir., 2005—; of counsel Shughart Thomson & Kilroy PC, Overland Park, Kans., 1997-2000, Barnes & Thornburg, Indpls., 2000—05; dir. tech. policy Sagamore Inst. Policy Rsch., 2006—. Co-author: Government Requirements of Small Business, 1980, The Containment of Organized Crime, 1984; co-programmer Quadrant I software program, 1983. HUD fellow, 1970-71. Mem. Assn. Personal Computer User Groups (dir., founding pres. 1986), Wash. Athletic Club. Congregationalist. Avocations: squash, racquetball, volleyball, music. Office: Software Patent Inst 5315 N Washington Blvd Indianapolis IN 46220-4462 Home Phone: 317-259-4462; Office Phone: 317-727-8940. Business E-Mail: cole@spi.org.

COLE, SCOTT L., lawyer; b. Ft. Lee, Va., Dec. 19, 1967; BA, U. Tex., Austin, 1990, JD, 1994. Bar: Tex. 1994, US Ct. Appeals (5th cir.), US Dist. Ct. (ea., no. and we. dists. Tex.). Atty. McKool Smith, P.C., Austin, Tex. Staff mem.: Tex. Law Rev., 1992—94. Named a Rising Star, Tex. Super Lawyers mag., 2006. Mem.: Tex. Bar Assn., ABA, Travis County Bar Assn. Office: McKool Smith PC 300 W 6th St Ste 1700 Austin TX 78701 Office Phone: 512-692-8705. E-mail: scole@mckoolsmith.com.*

COLE, SOLON ROBERT, pathologist, educator; b. McComb, Miss., Sept. 18, 1937; s. Robert Walter and Thelma Rebecca (Price) C. BS, Tulane U., 1959, MD, 1962. Diplomate Am. Bd. Pathology. Intern St. Vincent's Hosp., NYC, 1962-64; resident in pathology Boston City Hosp., 1964-67; rsch. fellow Harvard Med. Sch., Boston, 1967-69; pathologist pulmonary sect. Armed Forces Inst. Pathology, Washington, 1970-72; sr. pathologist Hartford Hosp., 1972—2002, dir. electron microscopy, 1972—. Assoc. prof. pathology U. Conn. Health Ctr., Farmington, 1974-2003, prof., 2004—; with Hartford Pathology Assocs., 1992—; com. on nomenclature of lung disease WHO, Geneva, Switzerland, 1978—; lung pathology cons. Regional Hosps., Hartford, 1972—. Contbr. chapters to books. Bd. dirs. Hartford Symphony Orch., 1985. Royal Hort. Soc. fellow, London, 1985; grantee HEW, 1976, Nat. Heart and Lung Assn., 1978, Combined Hosp. Fund, 1983; named one of the Top Doc. in Am., 2001, 02, Internat. Scientist of Yr., 2003. Fellow: Coll. Am. Pathologists; mem.: Soc. Pulmonary Pathologists, New Eng. Cancer Soc., Electron Microscopy Soc. Am., Internat. Acad. Pathology, Sigma Xi. Democrat. Avocation: landscaping. Home: 1 Gold St Apt 23E Hartford CT 06103-2932 Office: Dept Pathology Hartford Hosp 80 Seymour St Hartford CT 06115-2701 Personal E-mail: solonc@snet.net.

COLE, STEVEN, psychiatrist, educator; b. NYC, July 02; s. John and Clara Cole; m. Mary DeGenaro, May 7, 1984; children: Jamie Nace Cohen-Cole, Ethan Benson Cohen-Cole, Anna Sioni Cohen-Cole, Kristen Andrea Raju, MaryBeth Raju. MD, MA, Duke U., Durham, NC, 1974. Lic. psychiatrist Am. Bd. Psychiatry and Neurology, 1978, in geriatric psychiatry Am. Bd. Psychiatry and Neurology, 1980, in psychosomatic medicine Am. Bd. Psychiatry and Neurology. Prof. psychiatry med. ctr. Stony Brook U., NY, 2003—. Author: (book) The Medical Interview: The Three Function Approach. Fellow: Am. Psychiat. Assn. Office: Dept Psychiatry Health Scis Ctr Level 10-042 Stony Brook NY 11794-8101 Office Phone: 631-444-2861.

COLE, SUSAN A., academic administrator, language educator; m. David Cole, two children. BA in English and Am. Lit., Columbia U., 1962; MA in English and Am. Lit., Brandeis U., 1964, PhD in English and Am. Lit., 1972. Tchg. asst. Clark U., 1964-65; assoc. prof. CCUNY-N.Y.C. Tech. Coll., 1968-77; assoc. dean for acad. affairs Antioch U., 1977-80; v.p. for univ. adminstrn. and pers. Rutgers U., New Brunswick, N.J., 1980-92; pres., prof. English Met. State U., Mpls. and St. Paul, 1993-98; pres. Montclair State U., Upper Montclair, NJ, 1998—. Guest adj. assoc. prof. Pace U., fall 1977; vis. sr. fellow in acad. adminstrn. Office Acad. Affairs, CUNY, 1991-93; bd. dirs. Western State Bank; presenter in field. Contbr. articles to profl. jours. Chmn. edn. resolutions sessions, coord. edn. panels N.Y. State meeting Internat. Women's Year, Albany, 1977; agy. mem. N.J. Gov.'s Mgmt. Improvement Program, 1982; v.p., bd. dirs. Bklyn. Ecumenical Coops., 1988-90; mem. cmty. health care policy task force Robert Wood Johnson Univ. Hosp., New Brunswick, 1991; mem. blue ribon task force Mpls. Pub. Libr., 1994-95; mem. steering com. Greater St. Paul Tomorrow, 1994—; trustee Twin Cities Pub. TV, 1994—, Sci. Mus. Minn., 1994; bd. dirs., mem. exec. com. St. Paul Riverfront Corp., 1994—; v.p., founding bd. dirs. St. Paul Pub. Schs. Found., 1995—; bd. dirs. St. Paul Found., 1995—. Mem. Am. Assn. State Colls. and Univs. (urban and met. steering com. 1993—), Am. Coun. on Edn. (Commn. on Women in Higher Edn. 1993—), Greater Mpls. C. of C. (enterprise devel. task force 1994—). Office: Montclair State U 235 College Hall 1 Normal Ave Montclair NJ 07043-1624 Office Phone: 973-655-4212. Office Fax: 973-655-7195. E-mail: coles@mail.montclair.edu.*

COLE, SUSAN STOCKBRIDGE, retired theater educator; b. San Francisco, Jan. 26, 1939; d. Elmer Leroy Stockbridge and Martha Louise Rosenauer; m. John Michael Day, June 28, 1965 (div. May 1968); m. Willie Robert Cole, June 12, 1976. AB, Stanford U., Calif., 1960, MA, 1961; PhD, U. Oreg., 1972. Asst. prof. theatre Bakersfield (Calif.) Coll., 1962-69; grad. tchg. fellow U. Oreg., Eugene, 1969-72; asst. prof. theatre Keuka Coll., Keuka Park, NY, 1972-75; prof. Appalachian State U., Boone, NC, 1975—2005, dept. chair theatre and dance, 1989—2005; ret., 2005. Cons. Dept. Pub. Instrn., Raleigh, N.C., 1980—2005, N.C. Arts Coun., Raleigh, 1989-93. Author: American National Biography, 1999, Notable Women in American Theatre, 1990; designer more than 100 play prodns., 1962—; dir. more than 60 play prodns. Recipient Outstanding Svc. award, Coll. Fine and Applied Arts, Appalachian State U., 2005. Mem.: Am. Soc. for Theatre Rsch., Assn. for Theatre in Higher Edn., N.C. Theatre Conf. (pres. 1991—92, Svc. award 1997, Disting. Career award 2005), Southeastern Theatre Conf. (pres. 1998—99, Suzanne Davis award 2002), Lions Club Internat. (dist. officer 1997—, treas. 1999—2004, past pres.), Alpha Psi Omega (pres. 1997—2002). Democrat. Episcopalian. Avocation: reading. Home: PO Box 220 Todd NC 28684-0220 Personal E-mail: coless@appstate.edu.

COLE, THOMAS AMOR, lawyer; b. Phila., Nov. 2, 1948; s. George Lough and Elizabeth (Bush) C.; m. Carol L. Owen, Dec. 27, 1969 (div. 1979); children: Kirsten E., Lauren E.; m. Constance J. Ward, Nov. 17, 1979; children: Lindsay W., Emily C. BA with honors, Johns Hopkins U., 1970; JD with honors, U. Chgo., 1975. Bar: Ill. 1975, U.S. Dist. Ct. (no. dist.) Ill. 1975. Assoc. Sidley & Austin, Chgo., 1975-81; v.p. law Northwest Industries, Chgo., 1982-85; ptnr. Sidley & Austin, Chgo., 1981—, mgmt. com., 1988—, chair exec. com., 1998—2001, Sidley Austin Brown & Wood LLP, Chgo., 2001—06, Sidley Austin LLP, Chgo., 2006—. Adj. prof., U. Chgo. Law Sch.; chmn. exec. com. Northwestern U. Sch. Law, Garrett Corp., Securities Law Inst.; co-chair Tulane Corp. Law Inst.; bd. dirs. U. Chgo., Northwestern Meml. Hosp., Chgo. Coun. Global Affairs U. Chgo. Mem. ABA, Chgo. Bar Assn., Am. Law Inst., Chgo. Club, Econ. Club, Comml. Club, Law Club of Chgo., Order of Coif, Phi Beta Kappa. Democrat. Mem. Soc. Friends. Office: Sidley Austin LLP 1 S Dearborn St Chicago IL 60603-2000 Office Phone: 312-853-7473. Office Fax: 312-853-7036. Business E-Mail: tcole@sidley.com.

COLE, THOMAS L., retail executive; Grad., Kent State U., Ohio. With Macy's, Inc. (formerly Federated Dept. Stores, Inc.), 1972—, v.p., contr. I. Magnin San Francisco, 1980, sr. v.p. fin. and adminstrn. Merchandising Group, sr. v.p. fin. svcs. Lazarus divsn. Cin., pres. Merchandising Group NYC, chmn. Logistics and Ops., 1995, chmn. Systems and Tech., 2001, chmn. Credit and Customer Svcs., 2002, vice chmn. support ops., 2003—. Office: Macys Inc 7 W Seventh St Cincinnati OH 45202 Office Phone: 513-579-7000. Office Fax: 513-579-7897.*

COLE, TODD GODWIN, management consultant transportation; b. Coushatta, La., Mar. 5, 1921; s. Ira and Lucie (Triche) C.; m. Inez Hamilton, Feb. 9, 1953 (div. 1974); children: Michael H., Diane Cole Janusz (dec. 1994); m. Josephine Giovanetti, Oct. 1974 (dec. 1985); m. Pamela Wilds, Mar., 1987. Student, La. State U., 1935—37; LLB, Woodrow Wilson Coll., 1947. CPA, Ga. With Delta Airlines, 1940-63, dir., exec. v.p. adminstrn., 1955-63; sr. v.p. fin. and adminstrn., dir. Ea. Airlines, 1963-67, vice chmn., chmn. fin. com., dir., 1967-69; v.p., asst. to pres., dir. C.I.T. Fin. Corp., NYC, 1969, v.p. fin., 1969-71, mem. exec. com., 1970-86, exec. v.p., 1971-73, pres., chief adminstrv. officer, 1973-80, pres., COO, 1980-83, pres., CEO, 1984-86; CEO, bd. dirs. Frontier Air Lines D.I.P., 1987-89; vice chmn., dir. Ea. Air Lines D.I.P., 1989-91; mng. dir. Simat, Hellesen & Eichrer, Inc., 1992-96; pres. Cole & Wilds Assocs., Miami, 1996—; vice chmn. Hawaiian Airlines, Inc., 2002—03; founding dir. Coral Gables Trust Co., 2004. Chmn. Arrow Air, Inc., 1997-98; bd. dirs. Kaiser Ventures, LLC. Mem. Ga. Bar Assn. Office: Todd G Cole 60 Edgewater Dr #14E Coral Gables FL 33133-6975 Office Phone: 305-666-8136. Personal E-mail: coletg@bellsouth.net.

COLE, TOM, congressman; b. Shreveport, La., Apr. 28, 1949; s. John D. and Helen Gale Cole; m. Ellen Decker; 1 child, Mason. BA, Grinnell Coll., Iowa, 1971; MA, Yale U., New Haven, 1974; PhD, U. Okla., Norman, 1984. Founding ptnr., pres. CHS & Assocs., Okla. City; fellow Yale U., 1974; instr. U. Okla., 1975-78, Okla. Bapt. U., 1981; exec. dir. Okla. Rep. Com., 1980-81; dist. dir. Staff of US Rep. Mickey Edwards of Okla., 1982—84; exec. dir. Reagan-Bush Campaign, Okla., 1984; chmn. Okla. State Rep. Party, 1985-89; mem. Okla. State Senate, 1988—91; pres. Cole, Hargrave, Snodgrass & Assocs., 1989—; sec. state Okla., 1995-99; chief of staff Rep. Nat. Com., Washington, 1999; mem. US Congress from 4th Okla. dist., 2003—, mem. armed svcs. com., 2003—, mem. natural resources com., dep. whip, chmn. Nat. Rep. Congl. Com. Lectr. Grinnell Coll., 1977, 79; campaign mgr. Helen Cole for State Rep., 1978, 80, 82, Ken Wilson for County Commr., 1981, Evelyn Orth for County Commr., 1981, Helen Cole for State Senate, 1984; mem. Cleve. County Rep. Exec. Com., 1979-85, Okla. County Rep. Exec. Com., 1983-85; dep. campaign mgr. Daxon for Gov., 1981-82. Mem. nat. bd. Fulbright Assn. Fulbright fellow U. London; Watson fellow Inst. Hist. Rsch., London; recipient Robert A. Taft award Okla. Rep. Party, Guardian Small Bus. award Nat. Fedn. Ind. Bus. Mem. Am. Hist. Assn., Inst. Hist. Rsch., Soc. Study Labor Hist., Ea. London Hist. Soc., Okla. C. of C., Phi Alpha Theta, Chickasaw Nation. Republican. Methodist. Office: US House Reps 236 Cannon House Office Bldg Washington DC 20515 Office Phone: 202-225-6165. Office Fax: 202-225-3512.*

COLE, VINCENT J., lawyer; b. Binghamton, NY, Nov. 25, 1956; s. Joseph F. and Allene J. (Van Gordon) C.; m. Lenore Ymer, May 14, 1994; children: Joseph, Chrisopher, Lisa. BA in polit. sci. & philosophy, Syracuse U., 1978, JD, 1981. Bar: N.Y. 1982, U.S. Dist. Ct. (so. dist.) N.Y. 1982. Assoc. Cahill Gordon & Reindel, NYC, 1981-91; corp. counsel Lexmark Internat., Inc., Greenwich, Conn., 1991-96, asst. gen. counsel, sec., 1996, v.p., gen. counsel, sec. Lexington, Ky., 1996—. Office: Lexmark Internat Inc 740 W New Circle Rd Lexington KY 40550-0001 Office Phone: 606-232-2700.*

COLE, WAYNE STANLEY, historian, educator; b. Manning, Iowa, Nov. 11, 1922; s. Roy Eldon and Gladys Evelyn (Granseth) Cole; m. Virginia Rae Miller, Dec. 24, 1950; 1 child, Thomas Roy. BA with high honors, Iowa State Tchrs. Coll., 1946; MS, U. Wis., 1948, PhD, 1951. From instr. to asst. prof. history U. Ark., 1950-54; from asst. prof. to prof. Iowa State U., 1954-65; prof. U. Md., College Park, 1965-92, Disting. scholar tchr., 1989-90, prof. history emeritus, 1992—; Fulbright lectr. U. Keele, England, 1962-63. Author: (book) America First, 1953, Senator Gerald P. Nye and American Foreign Relations, 1962, An Interpretive History of American Foreign Relations, 1968, An Interpretive History of American Foreign Relations, 2d edit., 1974, Charles A. Lindbergh and the Battle Against American Intervention in World War II, 1974, Roosevelt and the Isolationists 1932-1945, 1983, Norway and the United States, 1905-55, 1989, Determinism and American Foreign Relations During the Franklin D. Roosevelt Era, 1995, A Life in Twentieth Century America, 2002. Served to 1st lt. USAAF, 1943—45. Fellow Woodrow Wilson Internat. Ctr. for Scholars, 1973, NEH, 1978—79. Mem.: Soc. Historians Am. Fgn. Rels. (pres. 1973, Graebner award 1994). Lutheran. Home: 10203 Mcgovern Dr Silver Spring MD 20903-1612 Business E-Mail: wcole@umd.edu. *Work hard. Give your best. Never give up. Empathize with those who are different. Remember you stand on shoulders of those who came before. Leave the world a better place than it was. Never forget that you could be wrong.*

COLE, WILLIAM LOUIS, lawyer; b. LA, May 13, 1952; AB magna cum laude, U. Calif., Irvine, 1974; JD, Stanford U., 1977. Bar: Calif. 1977. Atty. Mitchell, Silberberg & Knupp, LA, mng. ptnr., 1991—97, mem. exec. com., 1997—. Mem. ABA (co-chair sports and entertainment com. 2003-05), State Bar Calif., Los Angeles County Bar Assn. (mem. exec. com. labor law sect. 1989-90), Order of Coif, Phi Beta Kappa. Office: Mitchell Silberberg & Knupp 11377 W Olympic Blvd Los Angeles CA 90064-1625 Office Phone: 310-312-2000. Business E-Mail: wlc@msk.com.

COLE, WILLIE, artist; b. Somerville, NJ, 1955; Student, Boston U., 1974—75; BFA, Sch. Visual Arts, NYC, 1976; student, Art Students League, NYC, 1976—79. Artist-in-residence Studio Mus., Harlem, NY, 1989, The Contemporary, Balt., 1994, Pilchuck Glass Sch., Seattle, 1994, Capp St. Project, San Francisco, 1995. One-man shows include Ednl. Testing Svc. Corp., Princeton, N.J., 1986, Inst. Contemporary Arts, L.I., 1990, Peter Miller Gallery, Chgo., 1991, 1993, Newark Mus., 1992, St. Louis Art Mus., 1992, Brooke Alexander, N.Y., 1992, 1994, Balt. Mus. Industry, 1994, Capp St. Project, San Francisco, 1995, U. Arts, Phila., 1995, Fabric Workshop Mus., 1995, Alerie Almine Rech, Paris, 1997, Alexander and Bonin, N.Y., 1997, John Berggruen Gallery, San Francisco, 1998, Mus. Modern Art, N.Y.C., 1998, Birmingham (Ala.) Mus. Art, 1998, Morris Mus., Morristown, N.J., 1999, Alexander and Bonin, 2002, exhibited in group shows at Littlejohn-Smith Gallery, N.Y., 1986, Robeson Ctr. Gallery, Rutgers U., 1987, Palais Exposition, Nice, France, 1988, Artworks, Princeton, 1989, Art in General, N.Y., 1990, Brooke Alexander, 1991; author: Brooke Alexander, 1993; Exhibited in group shows at Weatherspoon Art Gallery, Greensboro, N.C., 1992, Tokushima Modern Art Mus., Japan, 1992—94, Newark Mus., 1993, 1997, N.J. Ctr. Visual Arts, Summit, 1994, 1996, Josh Baer Gallery, N.Y., 1994, Neuberger Mus. Art, Purchase, N.Y., 1994, 1997, Mus. Modern Art, N.Y.C., 1995, 1996, K&E Gallery, N.Y., 1995, Whitney Mus. Am. Art, Champion, 1995, City Gallery Chastain, Atlanta, 1996, Rhona Hoffman Gallery, Chgo., exhibited in group shows, N.Y., 1998, exhibited in group shows, Paine Webber Art Gallery, N.Y., 1998, Alexander and Bonin, 1998—99, Represented in permanent collections Bronx Mus. Art, Mus. Contemporary Art, Chgo., Dallas Mus. Art, Milw. Art Mus., Newark Mus. Art, N.J. Mus. Modern Art, N.Y.C., Whitney Mus. Am. Art, N.Y., St. Louis Art Mus., State Mus., Trenton, N.J., Nat. Gallery Art, Washington, FRAC Lorraine, Metz. Recipient Joan Mitchell Found. award, 1996; fellow Rutgers Ctr. Innovative Printmaking fellow, Rutgers U., 1991; Penny McCall Found. grantee, 1991, Wheeler Found. grantee, 1994, Louis Comfort Tiffany Found. grantee, 1995. Office: c/o Alexander & Bonin 132 10th Ave New York NY 10011-4727

COLELLA, PHILIP, mathematician; BS, MS, PhD, U. Calif. Head applied numerical algorithms group Lawrence Berkeley Nat. Lab. Recipient Sidney Fernbach award, IEEE, 1998, SIAM/ACM prize for computational sci. and engring., 2003. Mem.: NAS (mem. bd. math. scis. and their applications). Office: Lawrence Berkeley Nat Lab 1 Cyclotron Rd MS 50A-1148 Berkeley CA 94720 Office Phone: 510-486-5412. Office Fax: 510-495-2505. E-mail: PColella@lbl.gov.

COLEMAN, ANITA S., professor of library science; BA in English Lit., U. Madras, India, 1980, MS in Libr. and Info. Sci, 1982; MS in Edn., Southern Ill. U., 1988; PhD in Libr. and Info. Sci., U. Ill., Urbana-Champaign, 1996. Intern Am. Consulate Libr., Madras, India, 1982; academic libr. and dir. tech. services, 1983—2000; vis. rschr. Alexandria Digital Libr. Dept Computer Sci. U. Calif., Santa Barbara, 2000—01; asst. prof. Sch. Info. Resources and Libr. Sci. U. Ariz., Tucson, 2001—. Co-editor: Jour. Edn. for Libr. and Info. Sci., 2005—; founding editor: Digital Libr. Info. Sci. and Tech., 2002—, theme editor: Digital Libraries Jour. Digital Info., 2002—. Named one of the Movers & Shakers, Libr. Jour., 2007. Office: School of Info Resources and Library Sci Univ Ariz 1515 E First St Tucson AZ 85719 Office Phone: 520-621-3565. Office Fax: 520-621-3279. E-mail: asc@u.arizona.edu.

COLEMAN, ARLENE FLORENCE, retired pediatrics nurse; b. Braham, Minn., Apr. 8, 1926; d. William and Christine (Judin) C.; m. John Dunkerken, May 30, 1987. Diploma in nursing, U. Minn., 1947, BS, 1953; MPH, Loma Linda U., 1974. RN, Calif. Operating room scrub nurse Calif. Luth. Hosp., LA, 1947-48; indsl. staff nurse Good Samaritan Hosp., LA, 1948-49; staff nurse Passavant Hosp., Chgo., 1950-51; student health nurse Moody Bible Inst., Chgo., 1950-51; staff nurse St. Andrews Hosp., Mpls., 1951-53; pub. health nurse Bapt. Gen. Conf. Bd. of World Missions, Ethiopia, Africa, 1954-66; staff pub. health nurse County of San Bernadino, Calif., 1966-68, sr. pub. health nurse Calif., 1968-73, pediatric nurse practitioner Calif., 1973—. Contbr. articles to profl. jours. Mem. bd. dist. missions Bapt. Gen. Conf., Calif., 1978-84; mem. adv. coun. Kaiser Hosp., Fontana, Calif., 1969-85, Bethel Sem. West, San Diego, 1987—; bd. dirs. Casa Verdugo Retirement Home, Hemet, Calif., 1985—; active Calvary Bapt. Ch., Redlands, Calif., 1974—; mem. S.W. Bapt. Conf. Social Ministries, 1993—. With Cadet Nurse Corps USPHS, 1944-47. Calif. State Dept. Health grantee, 1973. Fellow Nat. Assn. Pediatric Nurse Assocs. and Practitioners; mem. Calif. Nurses Assn. (state nursing coun. 1974-76). Democrat. Avocations: gardening, travel, reading. Home: 622 Esther Way Redlands CA 92373-5822

COLEMAN, BARBARA MCREYNOLDS, artist; b. Omaha, May 5, 1956; d. Zachariah Aycock and Mary Barbara (McCulloh) McR.; m. Stephen Dale Dent, Mar. 12, 1983 (div. Dec. 20, 1992); children: Madeleine Victoria, Matthew Stephen; m. Ross Coleman, Oct. 16, 1993; 1 child, Mia Jeanne Coleman. Student, U. N.Mex., 1979, MA in Cmty. and Regional Planning, 1984. Lectr. U. N.Mex. Sch. Arch., Albuquerque, 1979—82, 1991—2000; assoc. planner, urban designer planning divsn. City of Albuquerque, 1982-84, city planner, urban designer N.Mex. redevel. divsn., 1984-88; v.p. Hydra Aquatic, Inc., Albuquerque, 1997—. Cons. City of Albuquerque Redevel. Dept., 1987-88; urban design cons. Southwest Land Rsch., Albuquerque, 1991, instr. at Ctr. for Action and Contemplation, Albuquerque, NM, 1999—. Columnist: Kids and Art, 1990-92; author: Coors Corridor Plan (Albuquerque Conservation Assn. Urban Design award 1984), Electric Facilities Plan, Downtown Core Revitalization Strategy and Sector Development Plan; contbr. articles to profl. jours. and mags.; chpts. to books; exhibited at Dartmouth St. Gallery Fine Art, Albuquerque, 1992—, Chimayo Trade and Mercantile, N.Mex.,

JoAnne Chappel Gallery, San Francisco, Southwest Arts Festival, Albuquerque, Act I Gallery, Taos, N.Mex., Nat. Arts Club, NYC, Hermitage Mus., Norfolk, Va., Schimmel Ctr. for the Arts, Pace U., NYC, Musée Granet, Aix-en-Provence, France, Fine Arts Gallery, Albuquerque, 1999 (1st pl.), Florence Biennial, 2005. Vol. art tchr. A. Montoya Elem. Sch., Roosevelt Mid. Sch., Albuquerque, 1989—. Recipient First Pl. for pastels N.Mex. Art League, 1991, Merit award Pastel Soc. of S.W., 1989, 1st pl. award N.Mex. State Fair Fine Arts Gallery, Albuquerque, 1999; finalist Nat. Cath. Reporter Jesus 2000 contest. Mem. Pastel Soc. of Am. (signature mem.), Pastel Soc. N.Mex. (pres. 1991-92, Best of Show 1990 award, 4th pl. Am. Artist Mag. award 1999). Democrat. Episcopalian. Avocations: hiking, skiing, running. Office: U NMex Sch Architecture Albuquerque NM 87131-0001

COLEMAN, BENJAMIN JOSEPH, music educator; b. Miami, Dec. 23, 1966; s. Joseph Hampton and Evelyn Coleman; m. Pilar Quintina Kelley, Aug. 9, 2001; children: Isabella Angelita, Eliana Teodora. MusB, Queens Coll. Aaron Copland Sch. Music, 1992; MS in Edn., Queens Coll., 1997. Woodwinds instr. The Amadeus Sch. Music, Flushing, 1993—97; band dir. Prospect Elem. Sch., Hempstead, NY, 1997—2003, Hempstead H.S., 2003—. Woodwind adjudicator Sewanhaka Ctrl. HS Dist., Floral Park, 1996—; tchr. mentor Hempstead Pub. Schs., 2005—; clarinet tutor Barbados Nat. Cultural Found., Saint James, 1995, 96. Clarinetist The Rockaway Five Towns Symphony Orch., Flushing. Named Nat. Honor Roll Outstanding Am. Tchr., 2005—06; recipient Discimus ut Serviamus Music award, Queens Coll., 1990, 1992, Gold With Distinction, NY State Schs. Music Assn., 2002, Gold medal, 1999, 2000, Silver medal, NY State Schs. Music Assn., 2001, 2005. Mem.: NY State Schs. Music Assn. (Bronze medal 2007), Nassau Music Educators Assn., Internat. Clarinet Assn., Phi Delta Kappa. Achievements include performing at Carnegie Hall, Weill Recital Hall, Alice Tully Hall, and Steinway Hall; conducting Hemstead High School Concert Band at Avery Fisher Hall. Avocations: reading, exercise, travel. Home: 712 Thrush Ave West Hempstead NY 11552 Office: Hempstead High School 201 President St Hempstead NY 11550 Home Phone: 516-485-4432; Office Phone: 516-292-7111 ext. 2244. Office Fax: 516-292-4368. Personal E-mail: krommer@optonline.net.

COLEMAN, BERNELL, physiologist, educator; b. Jefferson County, Miss., Apr. 26, 1929; s. Percy and Julia (Nailor) C.; m. Annie C. Richardson, Jan. 30, 1962; children— Rochelle, Ronald. BS, Alcorn A&M Coll., 1952; PhD, Loyola U., 1964. Rsch. asst. in biochemistry U. Chgo., 1956-57; rsch. in cancer Hines (Ill.) VA Hosp., 1957-59; instr. St. Louis U. Sch. Medicine, 1963-65, asst. prof. physiology, 1965-67; asst. prof. Chgo. Med. Sch., 1967-69, assoc. prof., 1969-76, prof., 1976, Howard U. Coll. Medicine, Washington, 1976—, chmn. dept. physiology and biophysics, 1979—. Lectr. Cook County Grad. Sch. Medicine, U. Ill. Med. Sch.; vis. prof. Rush Med. Coll.; external examiner Godfrey Huggins Sch. Medicine, U. Zimbabwe, Salisbury, 1981; mem. cardiovasc. and pulmonary study sect. Nat. Heart, Lung and Blood Inst./NIH, 1982-83, rsch. tng. rev. com., 1990-94. Peer rev. com. Am. Heart Assn., 1988-93, 95—, rsch. com., 1993—. With U.S. Army, 1953-56, Korea. Recipient rsch. award Chgo. Med. Sch. Bd. Trustees, 1975; NIH rsch. fellow, 1960-61; NIH grantee, 1966-68, 69-74, 74-76, 79—; USPHS fellow, 1961-63; Univ. fellow Loyola U., 1964; Dept. Def. grantee, 1965-67 Mem.: AAAS, AAUP, Heart Failure Soc. Am., Am. Soc. Hypertension (charter), N.Y. Acad. Scis., Internat. Soc. of Hypertension in Blacks, Assn. Black Cardiologists, Fedn. Am. Socs. Exptl. Biology (vis. scientist for minority instns. programs 1982—83, 1989—90), Am. Heart Assn. (basic sci. coun.), Am. Physiol. Soc. (cardiovascular fellow 1985), Phi Rho Sigma, Sigma Xi. Democrat. Achievements include research numerous publs. in cardiovascular physiology. Home: 14200 Myer Ter Rockville MD 20853-2350 Office: 520 W St NW Washington DC 20001-2337 Office Phone: 202-806-6330. Business E-Mail: bcoleman@howard.edu.

COLEMAN, BRITTIN TURNER, lawyer; b. Tuscaloosa, Ala., Dec. 12, 1942; s. Jefferson Jackson and Rose Wallace (Turner) C.; m. Johanna M. Nicol, June 1963 (div. 1967); 1 child, Anna M. Shields; m. Jane M. Kirkman, June 27, 1970; children: Mary Elizabeth, Emily Jane. BA in Am. Studies, U. Ala., 1964, LLB, 1967. Bar: Ala. 1967, U.S. Dist. Ct. (no. dist.) Ala. 1972, U.S. Ct. Appeals (5th cir.) 1975, U.S. Ct. Appeals (11th cir.) 1981, U.S. Dist. Ct. (mid. and so. dists.) Ala. 1986. With Bradley, Arant, Rose & White, Birmingham, Ala., 1971—, ptnr., 1976—. Adj. prof. law, coach Nat. Mock Trial teams Cumberland Sch. Law, 1979-84 (2 Nat. Championships); former mem. faculty Ala. Def. Lawyers Assn. Trial Acad., 1992; former mem. Ala. Pattern Jury Instructions Com.; mem. ct.'s adv. group No. Dist. Ala., 1997; mem. Product Liability Adv. Coun. Bd. dirs. Downtown YMCA, 1993-99; active Canterbury United Meth. Ch. Capt. JAGC, U.S. Army, 1967-71. Decorated Bronze Star with first oak leaf cluster, Army Commendation medal with first oak leaf cluster, Vietnam Svc. medal, Vietnam Campaign medal, Vietnam Civil Action Honor medal. Master: Birmingham Inn of Am. Inns of Ct.; fellow: Ala. Law Found., Am. Bar Found.; mem.: ABA, Farrah Law Soc., Def. Rsch. Inst., Ala. Def. Lawyers Assn., Am. Bd. Trial Advocates, Ala. Law Inst., Birmingham Bar Found. (bd. dirs. 2000—02), Birmingham Bar Assn. (chmn. grievance com. 1989, exec. com. 1992—94, pres.-elect 1998, pres. 1999, past chmn. civil cts. com., past chmn. CLE com., past chmn. ins. com., past Liberty Bell award com., past chmn. election com., past exec. com. young lawyers sect., past chmn. long range planning com.), Am. Judicature Soc., Ala. Law Sch. Found. (pres. 1994—96, exec. com. 1997—), The Summit Club, The Club, Ala. Alumni of Order of Coif (pres. 1992—94). Office: Bradley Arant Rose & White One Federal Pl 1819 5th Ave N Birmingham AL 35203 Business E-Mail: bcoleman@bradleyarant.com.

COLEMAN, CATHERINE G., astronaut; b. Charleston, SC, Dec. 14, 1960; d. James J. Coleman and Ann L. Doty; m. Josh Simpson. BS in Chemistry, MIT, 1983; D in Polymer Sci. and Engring., U. Mass., 1991. Commd. 2nd lt. USAF, 1983, advanced through grades to lt. col.; rsch. chemist materials directorate Wright Lab., Wright Patterson AFB; astronaut NASA Johnson Space Ctr., Houston, 1992—, with astronaut office mission support br., spl. asst. to ctr. dir., with astronaut office payloads and habitability br., mission specialist on STS-73, 1995, mission specialist on STS-83, lead mission specialist on STS-93, 1999. Surface analysis cons. for Long Duration Exposure Facility; vol. test subject centrifuge program Crew Sys. Directorate Armstrong Aeromedical Lab. Mem. ACS, AAUW, Soc. Photo-Optical Instrumentation Engrs., Internat. Womens' Air and space Mus. Avocations: flying, scuba diving, sports, music. Office: NASA Lyndon B Johnson Space Ctr Houston TX 77058

COLEMAN, CHARLES PAYSON, JR., (PAYSON COLEMAN), lawyer; b. NYC, May 9, 1950; C. Payson and Mimi (Wainwright) C.; m. Catherine C. Coleman, June 23, 1972; children: Charles P. III, Avery W., Phillips Reed. BA, Williams Coll., 1972; JD, Hofstra U., 1976. Bar: N.Y. 1976. Assoc. Winthrop, Stimson, Putnam & Roberts, NYC, 1976-84, ptnr., 1985—2001, Pillsbury Winthrop LLP, NYC, 2001—05; fin. execs. ptnr. Pillsbury Winthrop Shaw Pittman LLP, NYC, 2005—, mem. mng. bd. Mem. aviation working group Cape Town Convention. Articles editor Hofstra Law Rev., 1975-76. Chmn. Greenwood Cemetery, Bklyn., 1982—, North Shore Univ. Hosp., Manhasset, N.Y., 1993. Named Best of the Best among Aviation lawyers, Expert Guide to the World's Aviation Lawyers, 2004. Mem.: ABA (mem. sub-com. on aircraft financing). Office: Pillsbury Winthrop Shaw Pittman LLP 1540 Broadway New York NY 10036 Office Phone: 212-858-1426. Office Fax: 212-858-1500. Business E-Mail: payson.coleman@pillsburylaw.com.

COLEMAN, CLAIRE KOHN, public relations executive; b. New Castle, Pa., Nov. 19, 1924; d. Louis and Florence (Frank) Kohn; m. Frederick H. Coleman, Mar. 10, 1957; children: Franklin, Elliot. BA, Pa. State U., 1945. Market editor Fairchild Publs., NYC, 1945—48; asst. home editor NY Times, 1949—50; pub. rels. dir. United Wallpaper, Chgo., 1950—53, Assoc. Am. Artists, NYC, 1953—54; dir. Wallpaper Info. Bur., NYC, 1954; dept. head Roy Bernard, Inc., NYC, 1955—58; pub. rels. dir. Siesel Co., NYC, 1972—, sr. v.p., 1988; pres. Tisch Trask Comm. Resources Pub. Rels. Group, 1988—89; sr. v.p. Anthony M. Franco, NYC, 1989—90; pres. Coleman Comm., NYC, 1990—. Ctrl. steering com. Sch. Dist. Critical Assessments, New Rochelle, NY, 1969—71; active Mayor's Adv. Coun. on Aging, 1966, Mayor's Adv. Coun. on Bd. Edn. Appts., 1969; v.p. Coun. of PTAs, 1969—70; chmn. women's divsn. United Jewish Appeal, New Rochelle, 1971; v.p. Found. Women Execs. Pub. Rels., 1992—93, pres., 1993—94, bd. dirs., 1998—2006; bd. dirs., v.p. Beechmont Assn., 1969—74, adv. bd., 1990—. Fellow: Internat. Furnishings and Design Assn. (formerly Home Fashions League) (founder 1947, exec. chmn. 1947, pres. 1947, v.p. 1948—50, v.p. Chgo. chpt. 1950—53, nat. treas. 1977—78, nat. pres. 1980—81, v.p. NY chpt. 1994, nat. v.p. mktg. 1998—2000, v.p. NY chpt. 2006—07, dir. at large NY chpt. 2007—, Cir. of Excellence award 1994, Internat. Hon. Recognition award 1998); mem.: Women Execs. Pub. Rels. (bd. dirs 1983—84, sec. 1986—87, pres.-elect 1994—95, pres. 1996—97). Home Phone: 914-576-6885. Home Fax: 914-633-6914. E-mail: ckcpr@aol.com.

COLEMAN, CLAUDIA L., marketing executive; b. Dec. 1947; m. William T. Coleman. With Hewlett-Packard, 1971—91, dist. mgr., mktg. mgr. Named to President's Com. for People with Intellectual Disabilities. Co-founder Coleman Inst. for Cognitive Disabilities, U. Colo.

COLEMAN, COURTNEY STAFFORD, mathematician, educator; b. Ventura, Calif., July 19, 1930; s. Courtney Clemon and Una (Stafford) C.; m. Julia Wellnitz, June 26, 1954; children: David, Margaret, Diane. BA, U. Calif., Berkeley, 1951; PhD, Princeton U., 1955. Asst. prof. Wesleyan U., Middletown, Conn., 1955-58; from asst. prof. to full prof. Harvey Mudd Coll., Claremont, Calif., 1959-98. Lectr. Princeton (N.J.) U., 1954-55; rsch. in field. Author, editor: Differential Equations Models, 1983; editor, translator: Local Methods in Nonlinear Differential Equations, 1988; author: (with others) Differential Equations, 1987, Differential Equations Laboratory Workbook, 1992 (EDUCOM award for best math./computer course materials), Ordinary Differential Equations: A Modeling Perspective, 1998, 2d edit., 2004, ODE Architect, 1999 (award of excellence and Gold medal for best CD-ROM in edn.); mem. editl. bd. Jour. of Differential Equations, 1964—, UMAP Jour., 1980—. Mem. Am. Math. Soc., Math. Assn. Am., Soc. Indsl. Applied Math. Office: Harvey Mudd Coll Math Dept 1250 N Dartmouth Ave Claremont CA 91711 E-mail: coleman@hmc.edu.

COLEMAN, DABNEY W., actor; b. Austin, Tex., Jan. 3, 1932; s. Melvin Randolph and Mary (Johns) C.; m. Ann Courney Harrell, Dec. 21, 1957 (div. June 1959); children: Kelly Johns, Randolph, Mary; m. Carol Jean Hale, Dec. 11, 1961 (div. 1983); 3 children. Student, Va. Mil. Inst., 1949-51, U. Tex., 1951-57, Neighborhood Playhouse Sch. Theatre, 1958-60. Actor N.Y., Los Angeles, 1960—. Films include: The Slender Thread, 1965, The Scalp Hunters, 1968, Rolling Thunder, 1977, North Dallas Forty, 1979, Nothing Personal, 1980, How to Beat the High Cost of Living, 1980, Melvin and Howard, 1980, Nine to Five, 1980, Tootsie, 1982, War Games, 1983, Cloak and Dagger, 1984, On Golden Pond, 1981, The Man with One Red Shoe, 1985, Dragnet, 1987, Hot to Trot, 1988, Where the Heart Is, 1990, Short Time, 1990, Meet the Applegates, 1991, There Goes the Neighborhood, 1992, Amos and Andrew, 1993, The Beverly Hillbillies, 1993, Clifford, 1994, Devil's Food, 1996, Casanova Falling, 1998, You've Got Mail, 1998, Casanova Falling, 1999, Inspector Gadget, 1999, Stuart Little, 1999, The Climb, 2002, Moonlight Mile, 2002, Where the Red Fern Grows, 2003, Hard Four, 2005, Domino, 2005; TV includes: (TV series) Mary Hartman, Mary Hartman, 1976-78, Forever Fernwood, 1977-78, Apple Pie, 1978, Buffalo Bill, 1983-84, The Slap Maxwell Story, 1987, Drexell's Class, 1991-92, Madman of the People, 1994, Madman of the People, 1996, Recess (voice), 1997-01, Exiled, 1998, The Guardian, 2001-04, Courting Act, 2006-, (TV films) Maybe Baby, 1988, Never Forget, 1991, Columbo and the Murder of a Rock Star, 1991, In the Line of Duty: Kidnapped, 1995, Target Earth, 1998, My Date with the President's Daughter, 1998, Exiled, 1998, Must Be Santa, 1999, How to Marry a Billionaire: A Christmas Tale, 2000, Kiss My Act, 2001; author: two scripts Bright Promise, NBC, 1972; TV guest appearances include The Fugitive, 1963, I Dream of Jeannie, 1965, The Invaders, 1967, McMillan and Wife, 1971, The Streets of San Francisco, 1972, Love Boat, 1977, others. Served with U.S. Army, 1953-55. Recipient Emmy nomination Buffalo Bill, 1983, 84, Sworn to Silence; Golden Globe award, Slap Maxwell; Three Golden Globe Nominations. Mem. Phi Delta Theta Episcopalian.

COLEMAN, DEBI (DEBORAH ANN), investment and former computer company executive; b. Central Falls, RI, Jan. 22, 1953; d. John Austin and Joan Mary Coleman. BA, Brown U., 1974; MBA, Stanford U., 1978; PhD in Engring. (hon.), Worcester Poly., Mass., 1987. With fin. mgmt. tng. program Gen. Electric, Providence, 1975-76; with fin. mgmt. Hewlett-Packard Co., Cupertino, Calif., 1978-81; contr. Macintosh/Apple 32 group Apple Computer Inc., Cupertino, Calif., 1981-84, dir. ops., 1984-85, v.p. worldwide mfg., 1985-87, CFO, 1987-89, chief info. officer, 1990-92, CIO, 1990-92; v.p. materials ops. Tektronix Inc., Wilsonville, OR, 1992-94; pres., CEO Merix Corp., Forest Grove, Ill., 1994—2001, chmn., 1999—2001; mng. ptnr. SmartForest Ventures, Portland, Oreg., 2001—. Mem. U.S. Dept. Def. Mfg. Sci. Tech. Bd., 1988-91; bd. dirs. VMX, Inc., Software Pub Corp., Octel, Reply! Inc., 2006- Mem. adv. coun. Stanford Inst. Mfg. Automation, 1985-87; mem. Harvard U. Bus. Sch. Vis. Com., 1987—, Com. of 200, 1987—; trustee San Jose/Cleve. Ballet, 1989-92, Brown U., 1994—. Named a Henry Crown Fellow, Aspen Inst., 1997. Mem. Internat. Women's Forum. Democrat. Roman Catholic. Office: SmartForest Ventures 319 SW Washington St Ste 720 Portland OR 97204*

COLEMAN, DEBORAH ANN, lawyer; b. Chgo., July 19, 1951; d. Louis J. and Gloria (Bryskier) C.; m. Dan A. Polster, May 29, 1977; 3 children. AB magna cum laude, Radcliffe Coll., 1973; JD, Harvard U., 1976. Bar: Ohio 1976, US Dist. Ct. (no. dist.) Ohio, 1976, US Ct. Appeals (6th cir.) 1982, US Ct. Appeals (5th cir.) 2001, US Ct. Appeals (fed. cir.) 2005. Assoc. Hahn Loeser & Parks LLP, Cleve., 1976—83, ptnr., 1984—. Mem. task force on rules of profl. conduct Ohio Supreme Ct., 2003—06. Contbr. articles to legal jours. Mem. ABA (chair standing com. on ethics and profl. responsibility 1997-98), Ohio Bar Assn., Cleve. Bar Assn. (past chair profl. ethics com., Hon. William K. Thomas Profl. award 2007). Office: Hahn Loeser & Parks LLP 3300 BP Tower 200 Public Sq Ste 3300 Cleveland OH 44114-2303 Office Phone: 216-274-2220. Business E-Mail: dacoleman@hahnlaw.com.

COLEMAN, DENIS PATRICK, JR., investment banker; b. NYC, Jan. 6, 1946; s. Denis Patrick and Muriel (Clark) C.; m. Annabelle Giellerup, Sept. 15, 1972; children: Denis P. III, Nicholas A., Timothy W., Matthew T. BSBA, Georgetown U., 1967; MTS in Marriage and Family, John Paul II Inst. for Studies, Washington, DC. Former exec. v.p. Bear Stearns Cos. Inc., NYC, 1967-89; vice-chmn. Discount Corp. N.Y., NYC, 1991-93; exec. v.p. sr. mng. dir. Bear Stearns Cos. Inc., NYC, 1989; pvt. investor, 1993—; US consul gen. Bermuda, 2002—04. Coun. mem. Palm Beach, Fla., 2005—, coun. pres., 2006—. Bd. dirs., chmn. Covenant House, N.Y.C., Canterbury Sch., New Milford, Conn., Norton Gallery & Sch. of Art, Palm Beach. Mem. Mcpl. Bond Club N.Y., Bond Club N.Y. Roman Catholic. Office: 360 S County Rd Palm Beach FL 33480

COLEMAN, DENNIS M., lawyer; b. Mar. 5, 1953; AB, Brown Univ., 1975; JD, Georgetown Univ., 1978. Bar: R.I. 1979, US Dist. Ct. (Fed. dist.). Assoc. Ropes & Gray, Boston, 1988—93, ptnr. corp. dept., 1993—, head sports law practice group. Pres. Brown Univ. Hall of Fame; incorporator Kent Meml. Hosp. Mem.: ABA (sports & entertainment forum), R.I. Black Lawyers Assn., Boston Bar Assn., Sports Lawyers Assn. Office: Ropes & Gray 1 International Pl Boston MA 02110-2624 Office Phone: 617-951-7361. Office Fax: 617-951-7050. Business E-Mail: dennis.coleman@ropesgray.com.

COLEMAN, DONALD JACKSON, ophthalmologist, educator; b. Waverly, NY, Dec. 1, 1934; s. Max Elliot and Frances Agnes (Henton) C.; m. Jane Marie Holmes, July 6, 1963; children: Jeffrey, Jonathan, Jeremy. BS, Union Coll., 1956; MD, U. Buffalo, 1960. Bd. cert. opthalmology. Intern Columbia Med. Div., Bellevue Hosp., NYC, 1960-61; lt. comdr. USPHS Bur. State Services Heart Disease Control Program, Washington, 1961-64; resident in ophthalmology Edward S. Harkness Eye Inst., Columbia Presbyn. Med. Center, NYC, 1964-67, mem. faculty, staff, 1967-79; John Milton McLean prof. Cornell U. Med. Coll., NYC, 1979—; chmn. dept. ophthalmology N.Y. Hosp.-Cornell Med. Ctr., 1979—2006, ophthalmologist-in-chief, 1979—2006; chmn. emeritus, 2006—. Sr. author: Ultrasonography of Eye and Orbit, 1977, 2d edit., 2006; contbr. articles to med. jours. Recipient Wacker award of Club Jules Gonin Internat. Retina Soc., 1976, Lucien Howe medal, 1988, Weisenfeld award, Assn. Vision and Rsch. in Opthalmology; named hon. doctor of med. sci., U. Ferrara; NIH grantee. Fellow ACS, Am. Acad. Ophthalmology; mem. Am. Inst. Ultrasound Medicine (bd. govs. 1970-73), Am. Ophthamolgy Soc., Am. Retina Soc. (v.p. 1989-91, pres. 1991-93), Assn. Rsch. Ophthamology (Weisenfeld award 1996), Societas Interationalis de Diagnostic Ultrasonica in Ophthalmology (exec. bd. 1971-81), World Fedn. Ultrasound Medicine and Biology (exec. bd. 1973-82, sec.treas. 1973-77, treas. 1977-82), Am. Intraocular Lens Soc. (sci. advisor 1976-79), Am. Soc. Ophthalmic Ultrasound (bd. govs. 1976—), AMA, N.Y. County Med. Soc., Am. Eye Study Club, Jules Gonin Club (exec. com. 1992—, v.p. 1993-98, pres. 1998-2004). Republican. Methodist. Office: NY-Presbyterian Hosp-Weill-Cornell Med Ctr 520 E 70th St New York NY 10021-4870 Office Phone: 212-746-5588. Business E-Mail: djceye@aol.com.

COLEMAN, DOROTHY CHARMAYNE, nurse; b. July 13, 1958; BS in Nursing, Mich. State U., 1981; MS in Nursing, Wayne State U., Detroit, 1988. RN. Obstet. high risk staff nurse Hutzel Hosp., Detroit, 1983—; ob-gyn. nurse practitioner The Wellness Plan, Detroit, 1991-98; clin. nursing instr. Wayne State U., Detroit, 1994, 95, 99. Named Nurse of Yr., Hutzel Hosp., 2001. Home: 20801 Kipling St Oak Park MI 48237-2747

COLEMAN, DOUGLAS, research scientist, educator; b. Stratford, Ontario, Can. BSc, McMaster U., 1954; PhD, U. Wis., 1958. Sr. staff scientist emeritus Jackson Labs., Bar Harbor, Maine. Recipient Claude Bernard Medal, 1977, Gairdner award, Gairdner Found., 2005. Mem.: NAS. Achievements include research in the existence of a hormone system that contributed to controlling fat cell homeostasis.

COLEMAN, EARL MAXWELL, publishing company executive; b. NYC, Jan. 9, 1916; s. Samuel Sidney and Rose (Ensleman) C.; m. Frances Louise Allan, Mar. 23, 1942 (div. Mar. 15, 1965); children: Allan Douglass, Dennis Scott; m. Ellen Schneid, Aug. 19, 1973. Student, NYU, 1933-34, CCNY, 1934-35, Columbia U., 1946. Founder, pres. Plenum Pub. Corp. (and predecessors), NYC, 1946-77, chmn. bd. dirs., 1960-77, cons., 1977—. Founder Earl M. Coleman Enterprises, Inc. (Pubs.), 1977—; pres. Nat. Pubs. The Black Hills Inc., 1984-89; cons. Prentice Hall Coll. div., 1989-90. Contbr. poems, short stories to mags. Served with USAAF, 1941-45. Mem. Info. Industry Assn. (dir. 1971—), Assn. Am. Publishers (exec. com. tech.-sci.-med. div. 1970—), Sci. Tech. Med. Publishers (Holland). *Do whatever you do passionately. Never be astonished at the fact that literally all the worldly affairs with which humans busy themselves and into which they pour so much energy, are games, sometimes bloody games, but games. Not only does the passionate player have a greater chance to get ahead in the game, he also enjoys it more than the passive player. Only the person who is willing to be stark naked before his own eyes, which can be the cruelest of mirrors, gets to savor his life to the fullest. Here too, passion serves, for ruthless honesty with self is key to an honest appraisal of anything else.*

COLEMAN, ELIZABETH, college president; b. NYC, Nov. 23, 1937; d. Lewis and Sophie (Brantman) Ginsburg; m. Aaron Coleman, June 14, 1959; children: Daniel, David. BA, U. Chgo., 1958; MA, Cornell U., 1959; PhD, Columbia U., 1965; Doctorate (hon.), Hofstra U.; LLD (hon.), U. Vt. Instr. humanities SUNY, NYC, 1960-65; assoc. dean faculty New Sch. Social Research, NYC, 1966-76, dean Coll. Arts and Scis., 1977-84, prof. literature and humanities, 1984-87; pres. Bennington (Vt.) Coll., 1987—. Vis. lectr. Hebrew U., 1972, SUNY-Stony Brook, 1975; curriculum cons. Howard U., 1973; chmn. outside evaluating com. CUNY, 1976 Contbr. articles to profl. pubs. Mem. nat. adv. coun. Woodrow Wilson Found., 1990; bd. dirs. Ctrl. Vt. Pub. Svc. Corp., 1990-96; bd. trustees Inst. Ecosystem Studies, 1994. Fellow Ford Found., 1954-58; Woodrow Wilson fellow, 1958-59; F.J.E. Woodbridge fellow Columbia U., 1963-64; Pres.'s fellow Columbia U., 1964-65 Mem. MLA, Am. Assn. Colls. Home and Office: Bennington Coll Office of Pres Rte 67A Bennington VT 05201

COLEMAN, ERNEST ALBERT, plastics and materials consultant; b. NYC, Nov. 21, 1929; s. Del Rey and Rozelle (Weed) C.; m. Sonia Dimon, Aug. 22, 1953 (div. 1967); children: Donna Leslie, David Winslow; m. Ann G. Royer, Jan. 20, 1968. BS in Chemistry, Rensselaer Poly. Inst., 1951; MS in Phys. Organic Chemistry, U. Pa., Phila., 1955, PhD in Phys. Organic Chemistry, 1959. Sr. rsch. chemist DuPont, Wilmington, Del., 1957-71; phys. scientist Libr. of Congress, Washington, 1971-73; mgr. tech. svc. GAF, Wayne, NJ, 1973-79; mgr. thermoplastics R & D Dart & Kraft Corp., Paramus, NJ, 1979-82; rsch. mgr. Union Carbide, Tarrytown, NJ, 1982-86, Norton Performance Plastics, Wayne, NJ, 1986-88; key technologist Norton Co., Worcester, Mass., 1986-88. Cons., 1986—; adj. prof. U. Conn., Stamford, 1982-86, Naugatuck State Tech. Coll., 1992-2002; CEO CP Tech., Inc. Inventor over 50 patents (U.S. and fgn.) engring. thermoplastics composites, fast crystallizing PET, improvement of mech., chem. and thermal properties of thermoplastic resins and abrasives; assoc. editor Jour. Vinyl & Additive Tech., 1994-96. V.P. consistory Reformed Ch., Kinnelon, NJ, 1982; elected elder, Turn of River Presbyn. Ch., Stamford, 2000. Fellow Soc. Plastics Engrs. (edn. chmn. 1985-86, 91-92, chmn. tech. program 1987-89, 93-95, seminar chmn. 1990-92, nat. publs. com. 1991-96, nat. edn. com. 1991-96, polymer modifiers and additives divsn. coun. 2001—, nat. intellectual property com. 2002-03, chair tech. vols. com., 2003-04, sec. mktg. and mgmt. divsn. 2000—, adv. com. Stamford, Conn., 2003—, chair nat. publ. com., 2004—, Honored Svc. mem. 2005); mem. AAAS, Am. Chem. Soc. (chair southwestern Conn. sect. 2002), Assn. Cons. Chemists and Chem. Engrs. (pres. 1996-98), Inventors Assn. Conn., Sigma Xi, Phi Lambda Upsilon. Avocations: rehabilitation of injured/orphaned animals, coin collecting/numismatics, woodworking. Home and Office: 950 Willow Valley Lakes Dr H-211 Willow Street PA 17584

COLEMAN, FAY, literature and language educator, director; b. Detroit, May 8, 1949; d. Hiter Carrington and Etta Jewel (Roberts) Coleman. BS in English and History, Ea. Mich. U., 1971, MA in English Lit. and Langs., 1972. Tchr. adult edn. Melvindale High Sch., Mich., 1973—84; substitute tchr. Taylor Pub. Schs., Mich., 1974—77; tchr. English, history Taylor Ctr. HS, 1977—80, tchr. English, yearbook advisor, 1993—97; tchr. English, history West Jr. HS, Taylor, 1984—85, Brake Jr. HS, Taylor, 1985—93;

tchr. English, dept. chair John F. Kennedy HS, Taylor, 1997—. Social chair Brake Jr. HS, 1985—92, union rep., 1991—92; class advisor John F. Kennedy HS, 2003; presenter in field. Recipient Golden Apple award, Wayne County Regional Svc. Agy., 2000; grant, Taylor Ctr. High, Mich., 1994—97. Baptist. Avocations: travel, gardening, sewing. Home: 21609 Bayside Saint Clair Shores MI 48081 Office: John F Kennedy High Sch 13505 Kennedy Dr Taylor MI 48180

COLEMAN, FRANCES MCLEAN, secondary school educator; b. Jackson, Miss., Feb. 17, 1940; d. Robert Beatty and Dorothy Trotter (Witty) McLean.; m. Thomas Allen Coleman, Aug. 29, 1964; children: James Plemon, Robert McLean, Dorothy Witty McLean, Josiah Dennis, Leonidas McLean. BA, U. Miss., Oxford, 1962; MS, U. Miss., Jackson, 1964, PhD, 1970. Cert. tchr., Miss.; cert. in young adult/adolescent sci., Nat. Bd. Prof. Tchg. Stds. Adolescent/Young Adult Scis. Coord. Title I ESEA Choctaw County, Ackerman, Miss., 1970-73; instr. anatomy and physiology Wood Jr. Coll., Mathiston, Miss., 1977-78; instr. math. Miss. State U., Starkville, 1978-81; tchr. Choctaw City Sch. Dist., Ackerman, 1982—2003, dist. tech. coord., 1995—2003; facilitator PBS Teacherline, 2002—. Adj. faculty Lesley U., Cambridge, Mass., 2002—; cons. JBHM Edn. Group, LLC, 2003—, liaison, 2005—. Contbr. articles to profl. jours. including Surgery, T.H.E. Jour., Learning and Leading with Tech. Active Miss. State Bd. of Health, Jackson, 1980-94. Recipient Presdl. award for excellence in sci. teaching NSF, 1990, Sci. Tchr. awards Disney, 1993; named to Women Hall of Master Tchrs. Miss. U., 1994; named Educator of Yr. Milken Family Founds., 1991; Tandy scholar, 1991; Tapestry grantee, 1995; Coun. for Basic Edn. Sci.-Math. fellow, 1994, Access Excellence fellow Genentech, 1995, Am. Physiol. Soc. fellow, 1995, Einstein Disting. Educator fellow Dept. of Energy, 2000. Mem. Nat. Sci. Tchrs. Assn., Am. Assn. German Tchrs., Am. Assn. French Tchrs., Am. Assn. Physics Tchrs., Nat. Assn. Biology Tchrs., Miss. Edn. Computer Assn. (Miss. Computer Educator of Yr. 1990, pres.-elect 1995, pres. 1996), Miss. Fgn. Lang. Assn. (pres. secondary sect. 1992-94). Episcopalian. Avocations: reading, travel. Home: PO Box 268 Ackerman MS 39735-0268 Office: Choctaw County Sch Dist PO Box 398 Ackerman MS 39735-0398 Personal E-mail: fcoleman@telepak.net. *We advise students to do what they like in life. Perhaps we should advise them that with imagination and hard work they can transform almost any job so that they like what they do.*

COLEMAN, GARY WILLIAM, retired elementary school educator; b. Davenport, Iowa, Dec. 16, 1945; s. Robert Earl and Mildred Margaret (Mast) C.; m. Janice Marie Jamtgaard, Dec. 29, 1973; children: Heidi Marie Howard, Sean Robert. BS in Elem. Edn., U. SD, Vermillion, 1987; BSBA, Ariz. State U., Tempe, 1969. Cert. elem. tchr., S.D. Tchr. Marty Indian Sch., SD, 1987-91, Parkston Elem. Sch., SD, 1991-2000; acct./bookkeeper Ulland Bros Constrn., Austin, Minn.; realtor assoc. Myre-Sorenson Real Estate, Albert Lea, Minn.; bldg. constrn. contractor, landscaper, Alcester, SD; site mgr. Heritage Ct. Apts., Oak Leaf Real Estate Mgmt. Ltd., 2001—03; preschool tutor South Ctrl. Edn. Coop., 2002—03; tutor Avon Elem. Sch., SD, 2003—04; human resources coord. Boys and Girls Club, Wagner, SD, 2003—04; tchr. Marty Elem. Sch., SD, 2005—07; ret., 2007. E.M.T., 1982—2003. Sgt. USAF, 1969-73. Mem. NEA, Parkston Edn. Assn. (v.p. 1995-96, pres. 1996-97, founder scholarship fund 1997), Am. Legion (vice-comdr. SD 7th Dist. 2003-05, comdr. 2005-07). Achievements include establishing Coleman/Jamtgaard scholarship, 2006. Personal E-mail: gcolemanmis@hotmail.com.

COLEMAN, GEORGE A., school system administrator; m. Carrie Coleman; 1 child, Olga Coleman Williams. BS in History, Tuskegee Inst.; MA in Early Childhood Edn. and Curriculum and Instruction, Columbia U. Edn. cons. kindergarten and primary grades Conn. Dept. Edn., Hartford, 1987, chief Bur. of Curriculum and Instrn. and Bur. of Early Childhood Edn. and Social Svcs., assoc. commr. Div. Teaching and Learning Programs and Svcs., 1998—, interim commr. edn., 2006—07. Tchr. early childhood edn. and history Tufts U., Western Conn. State U., U. New Haven. Contbr. articles to profl. jours. Coun. mem. United Way, Conn. State Birth-to-Three Coun., Conn. Commn. on Children and Jr. Achievement; chair bd. dirs. Hord Found., Danbury. Office: Office of Commr Dept Edn 165 Capitol Ave Hartford CT 06106 Office Phone: 860-713-6500.*

COLEMAN, GEORGE EDWARD, musician; b. Memphis, Mar. 8, 1935; s. George Edward and Indiana (Lyle) C.; m. Gloria Bell, Aug. 3, 1959; children: George, Gloria; m. Carol Ann Hollister, Sept. 7, 1985. Grad. high sch., Memphis. Ind. saxophonist with numerous jazz combos, 1952-74; leader George Coleman Quartet/Quintet/Octet, 1974—. Cons. Lenox (Mass.) Jazz Sch. Music, 1958, L.I. U., 1984—, NYU, 1987—, New Sch. Social Rsch., 1987—, Thelonious Monk Inst., 1996, New Eng. Conservatory, 1998; judge Thelonious Monk Inst. Internat. Jazz Competition, Washington, 2002; pvt. instr. Saxophonist B.B. King Band, 1952-53, 55, Max Roach Quintet, 1958-59, Miles Davis quintet, 1963-64, Lionel Hampton Orch., 1965-66, Lee Morgan quintet, 1969, Elvin Jones Quartet, 1970; composer, arranger mus. shows, films: Sweet Love Bitter, 1970, Comedie (French), 1985, Freejack, 1991, The Preacher's Wife, 1996. Grantee NEA, 1975, 81, 85; recipient award for contbns. to music Beale St. Assn., 1977, Tip of the Derby awards, 1978, 79, NY Jazz Audience award, 1979, Gold Note Jazz award, 1985, Key to the City of Memphis, 1991, Lifetime Achievement award Jazz Found. Am., 1997, Concertgebow Jazz award, 2002, Excellence in Jazz award Manhattan Assn. Cabarets and Clubs, 2005; selected by Internat. Jazz Critics Poll, 1958; named Artist of Yr., Record World mag., 1969. Personal E-mail: nysax@aol.com.

COLEMAN, GERALD CHARLES, judge, educator; b. Phila., Apr. 23, 1935; s. Francis Eugene and Mary Veronica Coleman; m. Mary Lou Coleman, Sept. 3, 1960; children: Margaret Mary, Miriam, Christine. BS in econ., Villanova U., 1957; JD, Georgetown U. Law Ctr., 1963, LLM, 1976; MA in internat. rels., Boston U., 1971; MS in sys. mgmt., U. So. Calif., 1983. Bar: Va. 1963, Pa. 1991, Supreme Ct. US 1970. Apptd. mil. law judge, 1970; law educator Rutgers U., Camden, NJ, 1992—95; adminstrv. law judge Commonwealth Pa., Phila., 1995—. Contbr. articles to profl. jours. Legacy mem. Nat. Constn. Ctr., Phila., 2003; founding supporter Kimmel Ctr. Performing Arts, Phila., 2003. Officer US Army, 1964—92, lt. colonel US Army, 1963—92, Vietnam, Japan, Germany. Decorated Bronze Star US Army, Phan Rang, Vietnam, Master Parachute Wings US Army, Ft. Bragg, NC, Legion Merit US Army, Tokyo. Mem.: Federalist Soc., Am. Soc. Internat. Law. Avocations: mountain climbing, boating. Home: 233A Bainbridge St Philadelphia PA 19147 Office: Bureau Hearings and Appeals Commonwealth of Pa State Office Bldg 1400 Spring Garden St Philadelphia PA 19130

COLEMAN, GREGORY G., former magazine publisher, Internet company executive; BS in Bus. Adminstrn., Georgetown U.; MBA, NYU. V.p., nat. sales mgr., Women's Day advert CBS, Inc.; founding pub., Memories mag. Diamandis Comm.; v.p., worldwide pub. Reader's Digest, Pleasantville, NY, pres., US mag. publishing, 1991—97; sr. v.p. Reader's Digest Assn., Pleasantville, NY, 1997—2001; exec. v.p., global sales Yahoo! Inc., 2001—. Co-chair, internal ad coun. Yahoo!; bd. advisor missoandfriends.com. Office: Yahoo! Inc 701 1st Ave Sunnyvale CA 94089*

COLEMAN, GREGORY S., lawyer; b. 1963; BS in Applied Math. Sci., Tex. A&M U., 1987, MBA, 1989; JD, U. Tex. Sch. Law, 1992. Cert.: civil appellate law. Law clk. to Hon. Edith Hollan Jones US Ct. Appeals (5th Cir.), 1992—93; law clk. to Justice Clarence Thomas US Supreme Ct., 1995—96; solicitor gen. State of Tex., 1999—2001; ptnr. Weil, Gotshal & Manges L.L.P., Austin, 2001—07, Yetter & Warden L.L.P., Austin, 2007—; adj. prof. South Tex. Coll. Law, U. Tex. Sch. Law. Named one of Litigation's Rising Stars, The Am. Lawyer, 2007. Office: Yetter & Warden LLP Two Houston Ctr 909 Fannin Ste 3600 Houston TX 77010 E-mail: gcoleman@yetterwarden.com.*

COLEMAN, HENRY EDWIN, artist, educator; b. Charlottesville, Va., Oct. 26, 1938; s. Albin Clayton and Mary Louise (Nay) C.; m. Charlotte Heyne, Dec. 29, 1962 (dec. 1984); children: Edwin Randolph, Mary Clayton; m. Leslie W. Rose, Jan. 4, 1993; 1 stepson, John A. Rose. AB in Fine Arts, Coll. William and Mary, 1961; MA, U. Iowa, 1963. Instr. art Lawrence Coll., Appleton, Wis., 1963-64; mem. faculty Coll. William and Mary, Williamsburg, Va., 1964-99, prof. fine arts, 1989—91, chair dept. fine arts, 1987—91. Cons. for purchasing CSX Corp. Art Collection, Richmond, Va., 1985. Illustrator: Oscar Wilde's Remarkable Rocket, 1974; one-man shows include Radford Coll., Va., 1975, Gallery II West, St. George, Utah, 1984, U. Maine, Presque Isle, 1989, Andrew & Laura McLain Mus., Florenceville, N.B., Can., 1989, Muscarelle Mus. Art William & Mary Coll., Williamsburg, Va., 1999, exhibited in group shows at Patio Show, Iowa City, 1962—63, Des Moines Art Ctr., 1963, Lawrence Coll., Appleton, 1964, 20th Century Gallery, Williamsburg, 1964—66, Chrysler Mus., Norfolk, Va., 1972, So. Ill. U., Carbondale, 1975, Peninsula Art Ctr., Newport News, Va., 1980, Nat. Small Image Exhbn., Spokane, Wash., 1984, Am. Drawing Biennial Muscarelle Mus. of Art, Coll. William and Mary, Williamsburg, 1988, 1990 (Honorable Mention award), 1992, Internat. Cultural Exch. Art Exhibit, Neyagawa, Japan, 1988, Bowery Gallery, N.Y.C., 1988, Invitational D'Art Ctr., Norfolk, 1991, Peninsula Fine Arts Mus., Newport News, 1995—96, 2001, The Charles H. Taylor Art Ctr., Hampton, Va., 2006. Commr. Williamsburg Arts Commn., 1985-91; bd. dirs. Yorktown (Va.) Arts Found., 1989-93; juror Occasion for the Arts, Williamsburg, 1988, 27th Regional Art Exhbn., W.C. Rawls Libr. & Mus., Courtland, Va., 1990; commr. archtl. rev. bd., City Williamsburg, 1994-2000. Summer Rsch. grantee Coll. William & Mary, 1976, Semester Faculty grantee, 1985, Faculty Rsch. grantee, 1991-92. Office: Coll William and Mary Andrews Hall Williamsburg VA 23185 E-mail: coleman1@whro.net.

COLEMAN, J. EDWARD, computer company executive; B in Economics, Coll. William and Mary, 1973; MBA, Ind. U. With IBM Corp., 1976—93; v.p., gen. mgr., Channel Financing IBM Credit Corp.; systems integrator McCollister's Tech. Services, Inc., 1993—95; various leadership roles Computer Sciences Corp., bus. develop. exec., dir. mktg., 1995—99; CEO CompuCom Systems, Inc., Dallas, 1999—2004, pres., 2000—04, chmn., 2001—04; sr. v.p. Arrow Electronics, Inc., Melville, NY, 2005—06; pres. Arrow Enterprise Computing Solutions, Arrow Electronics, Inc., Englewood, Colo., 2005—06; CEO Gateway, Inc., Irvine, Calif., 2006—, also bd. dir., 2006—. Bd. dir. Red Oak Software. Bd. advisors Coll. William and Mary Sch. Bus. Named one of Top 25 Executives, Computer Reseller News, 2003; recipient Lifetime Achievement award, VARBusiness 500, 2004. Office: Gateway Inc 7565 Irvine Center Dr Irvine CA 92618*

COLEMAN, JACK ANDREW, JR., otolaryngologist; b. Mpls., Oct. 17, 1951; s. Jack Andrew and Patricia Marie Coleman; m. Margaret Overton, June 14, 1987; children: Kelley Anne, Jennifer Allison, Jack Andrew Christian. BA, U. Va., 1973; postgrad., U. Autonoma Guadalajara, Mex., 1973-77; MD, U. Cin., 1979. Diplomate Am. Bd. Gen. Otolaryngology, Nat. Bd. Med. Examiners, cert. Am. Acad. Facial Plastic and Reconstructive Surgery. Intern, surgery U. Cin. Gen. Hosp., 1979—80, resident in surgery, 1980—81; resident in otolaryngology U. Pitts. Eye and Ear Hosp., 1981-84; staff physician Southside Cmty. Hosp., Farmville, Va., 1984-85, Univ. Med. Ctr., Lebanon, 1985-88; instr. Vanderbilt U. Med. Ctr., Nashville, 1988-93, asst. prof., 1993-96; chief otolaryngology Nashville Gen. Hosp., 1988-93; staff physician Centennial Med. Ctr., St. Thomas Hosp., Nashville, 1996-2000, Chesapeake Gen. Hosp., 2000-01, Sentera Bayside Hosp., 2000—; asst. clin. prof. otolaryngology Eastern Va. Med. Sch., 2000-01. Mem. edn. com. Laser Inst. Am., Cin., 1991—96; cons. InFLUENT, San Francisco, 1998—99, 2000—03, Ethicon Endo-Surgery, 2001—03; mem. med. adv. bd. Pj Med., 2000—03; physician Police S.W.A.T. Team, Chesapeake, Va. Editor: Management of Lower Airway Stenosis, 1995, Sleep Apnea Vols. 1 and 2, 1998—99. Cubscout leader Boy Scouts Am., 1998—99; hon. chmn. physician adv. bd. Nat. Rep. Congl. Com., 2001. Comdr. USNR. Grantee, Laserscope Co., 1988, Karl Storz Instruments, 1989, Vanderbilt U. Rsch. Coun., 1994. Fellow: ACS (mem. history and archives com. 1988—93), Am. Acad. Facial Plastic and Reconstructive Surgery, Am. Acad. Otolaryngology and Head and Neck Surgery (mem. relative value scale com. 1988—90, chmn., mem. com. sleep disorders 1990—98, mem. com. on infectious diseases 1990—98, mem. polit. contact network 1991—96, mem. self-instructional packages subcommittee 1991—96, mem. allergy and immunology com. 1991—96, mem. subcommittee on core edn. 1992—93, chmn. sleep disorders com. 1995—96); mem.: AMA, Wilson County Med. Soc., Tenn. Soc. Otolaryngology, Tenn. Med. Soc., Soc. Univ. Otolaryngologists-Head and Neck Surgeons (membership com. 1990—96), Pan-Am. Soc. Otolaryngology, Laser Inst. Am. (sr.; mem. edn. com. 1991), Assn. Military Surgeons US (life), Nashville Acad. Otolaryngology, Am. Rhinologic Soc., Am. Broncho-Esophagologic Soc., Am. Acad. Sleep Medicine (mem. clin. practice review com. 1999—2001), Am. Acad. Otolaryngic Allergy, H. William Scott, Jr. Soc., Amateur Athletic Union (coach, ofcl. Tae Kwon Do program 1998—2001), Rotary. Avocations: military history, military awards, military miniatures, skydiving. Home: 2832 Sulphur Springs Rd Murfreesboro TN 37129

COLEMAN, JAMES EDWIN, JR., lawyer; b. Atlanta, May 23, 1923; s. James Edwin and Demis Cecelia (Thrower) C.; m. Margaret Copeland Sutherland, June 24, 1947; children: J. Hamilton, Margaret S., Sarah C., James Edwin III. BS, Ga. Inst. Tech., 1948; LL.B., U. Va., 1951. Bar: Ga. 1952, Tex. 1954. Mem. Carrington, Gowan, Johnson, Bromberg & Leeds, Dallas, 1953—58; ptnr. Carrington, Johnson & Stephens, Dallas, 1958—70, Carrington, Coleman, Sloman & Blumenthal LLP, Dallas, 1970—. Decorated Silver Star; named Outstanding 50 Yr. Lawyer Award, Tex. Bar Found., 2005; named one of Tex. Super Lawyers, Tex. Monthly, 2003, 2004, The Best Lawyers in Am., 2005—06; recipient Pres. Award, State Bar Tex., 1997, Trail Lawyer of the Yr., Dallas Bar Assoc., 1997, Professionalism Award, Fifth Cir. Am. Inns Ct. Found., 1997, Lola Wright Found. Award, 1999, Samuel E. Gates Litigation Award, Am. Coll. Trial Lawyers, 2002, Fellows Award, Dallas Bar Found., 2002. Fellow: Tex. Bar Found., Am. Bar Found.; mem.: Univ. VA Law School Found. (bd. trustees), S.W. Legal Found. (research fellow 1976—, bd. dir. 1979—98, chmn. bd. trustees 1995—98), Am. Coll. Trial Lawyers, Internat. Acad. Trial Lawyers, Am. Law Inst., Nat. Inst. for Trial Advocacy (bd. dir. 1981—, chmn. bd. trustees 1991—93), Dallas Bar Assoc. (v.p. 1965, sec., treas. 1972), State Bar of Tex. (chmn. Antitrust 1977—78, bd. dir. 1980—81), Am. Bar. Assoc. (council of litigation 1973—75, dir. litigation 1975—81). Methodist (ofcl. bd. 1965-66, 68-71, chmn. trustees 1967).

COLEMAN, JAMES H., JR., lawyer, former state supreme court justice; b. Lawrenceville, VA, May 4, 1933; s. James H. Sr. and Neda Coleman; m. Sophia Coleman, May 12, 1962; 2 children. BA cum laude, Va. State U., 1956, LLD (hon.), 1995; JD, Howard U., 1959. Bar: N.J. 1960, U.S. Dist. Ct. N.J. 1960, U.S. Supreme Ct. 1963. Asst. and/or cons. various N.J. commns. and divs., 1960-64; pvt. practice law Elizabeth and Roselle, NJ, 1960-70; judge N.J. Workers' Compensation Ct., 1964-73, Union County Ct., 1973-78, Law div. N.J. Superior Ct., 1978-81; mem. spl. three-judge resentencing panel N.J. Superior Ct., 1979-81; judge Appellate div. N.J. Superior Ct., 1981-87, presiding judge, 1987-94; assoc. justice Supreme Ct. of N.J., Springfield, 1994—2003; atty. Porzio, Bromberg & Newman, Morristown, 2004—. Mem. various Supreme Ct. coms.; lectr. in field. Chmn. Elizabeth Good Neighbor Coun.; mem. Elizabeth Adv. Bd. on Urban Renewal; incorporator, bd. dirs. Union County Legal Svcs., Elizabeth Anti-Poverty Program; v.p., bd. dirs., counsel to Urban League of Union County; counsel to Elizabeth NAACP; v.p. Scotch Plains-Fanwood Human Rights Coun.; Mem. N.J. Com. on Hiring the Handicapped; mem. Union County Coordinating and Adv. Com. on Higher Edn.;mem. Essex County Coll. Equal Edn. Opportunity Fund Bd., others; chair bd. trustees N.J. Legal Svcs. Fellow ABA; mem. Nat. Bar Assn. (judicial coun.), N.J. Bar Assn., Union County Bar Assn., Am. Law Inst., Am. Judicature Soc., Garden State Bar Assn., Omega Psi Phi. Baptist. Avocations: tennis, gardening. Office: Porzio Bromberg & Newman 100 Southgate Pkwy PO Box 1997 Morristown NJ 07962-1997 Office Phone: 973-889-4088. Business E-Mail: jhcoleman@pbnlaw.com.

COLEMAN, JAMES JULIAN, lawyer; b. New Orleans, May 5, 1915; s. William Ballin and Millie (Davis) C.; m. Dorothy Louise Jurisich, July 30, 1940; children: James Julian, Thomas Blaise, Peter Dee, Dian Judith. BA, Tulane U., 1934, JD, 1937; LLD (hon.), Hampden-Sydney Coll., 1982. Bar: La. 1937. Sr. ptnr. Coleman, Johnson, Artigues & Jurisich, New Orleans. Past pres. Internat. Trade Mart, New Orleans Philharmonic Symphony; hon. consul gen. Republic of Korea; chmn. La. Jud. Compensation Commn. Past pres. New Orleans C. of C., Jr. Achievement New Orleans, Adult Edn. Ctr.; past bd. dirs. U.S. C. of C., Internat. House, Fed. Rels. Assn.; past chmn. New Orleans coordinating com. NASA; founder Peoples League; trustee emeritus Principia Coll.; past chmn. Tulane U. Bus. Sch. Coun.; chmn. bd. trustees Crimestoppers. Decorated Order of Oranje-Nassau Diplomatic Service Merit Republic Korea; recipient Nat. Achievement award Jr. Achievement, Loving Cup award New Orleans Times-Picayune, 1980, Joseph W. Simon, Jr. award, 1981, Disting. Alumnus award Tulane U., 1982, New Orleans Activist award, 1984, C. Alvin Bertel award, 1985; named to Bus. Hall of Fame, 1984; named Pres. Emeritus, World Trade Ctr., N.Y.C., Chmn. Emeritus, The City Energy Club, Humanitarian of Yr. ARC, 2000; recipient Benemerenti Papal Honor, 1989. Mem. ABA, Internat. Bar Assn., La. Bar Assn., New Orleans Bar Assn., Am. Judicature Soc. (past dir.), Beta Gamma Sigma (hon.) Christian Scientist (1st reader 1953-56). Home: 10 Audubon Pl New Orleans LA 70118-5526 Office: 321 Saint Charles Ave New Orleans LA 70130-3145 *Success in Family Enterprises depends on an inbred family loyalty supported by love, compassion and understanding for and between family members and their spouses from generation to generation.*

COLEMAN, JAMES JULIAN, JR., lawyer, industrialist, real estate company executive; b. New Orleans, May 7, 1941; s. James Julian Sr. and Dorothy Louise (Jurisich) C.; m. Carol Campbell Owen, Dec. 19, 1970 (dec. Sept. 1979); 1 child, James Owen; m. Mary Olivia Cochrane Cushing, Oct. 12, 1985. BA, Princeton U., 1963; postgrad. in law, Oxford U., Eng., 1963-65; JD, Tulane U., 1968. Bar: La. 1969, U.S. Supreme Ct. 1969. Chmn. Internat.-Matex Tank Terminals, New Orleans, 1969—; pres. Coleman Devel. Co., New Orleans, 1969—, IMTT, Quebec, 1993—, Nfld. Transhipment Terminal Inc.; sr. ptnr. Coleman, Johnson & Artigues, New Orleans, 1972—2006, mng. ptnr., 2006—; pres. City Ctr. Properties, New Orleans, 1980—. Mng. ptnr. Windsor Ct. Hotel, New Orleans Hilton Hotel, Exxon Bldg., Chevron Bldg., Freeport Cooper Gold Bldg., Internat. River Ctr.; chmn. East Jersey R.R. and Terminal Co., 1993; trustee Coleman Family Found., New Orleans, Owen-Coleman Found., New Orleans; dir., v.p. USCG Found.; pres. Nat. Coast Guard Mus. Assn., 2001—. Author: Gilbert Antoine de St. Maxent: The Spanish Frenchman of New Orleans, 1975. Mem. history coun. Princeton U., 1982—2007; mem. N.J. Commn. on Sci. and Tech., 1992—, chmn. 2003—; bd. dirs. Hampden Sydney Coll., 1982-92, Liberty Sci. Ctr., Liberty State Park, N.J., 1999—; bd. overseers N.J. Inst. Tech., 1999—. Named H.M. Hon. Brit. Consul for La., Brit. Consulate, New Orleans, 1975—, to Order of Brit. Empire, Queen Elizabeth II, London, 1986. Mem. ABA, La. Bar Assn., Interant. Yacht Restoration Assn. (bd. dirs.), N.Y. Yacht Club, N.Y. Racquet Club, Newport Reading Room, So. Yacht Club, New Orleans Lawn Tennis Club, USN League (bd. dirs. New Orleans), Union League Club, N.Y. Racquet Club. Office: Coleman Johnson & Artigues 321 St Charles Ave 10th Fl New Orleans LA 70130-3145 Office Phone: 504-586-1979. E-mail: jjcjr@imtt.com.

COLEMAN, JEFFREY PETERS, lawyer; b. Providence, Nov. 21, 1959; s. Gerard Giles and Molly Claire (Armbrecht) C.; children: Chelsea Adelle, Rebecca Rose, Martin Daniel, Angelyn Marie. BA in Psychology, Davidson Coll., 1981; postgrad., Exeter U., Eng., 1984; JD, Coll. of William and Mary, 1985. Bar: Fla. 1985, US Dist. Ct. (mid. dist.) Fla. 1986, US Supreme Ct. 2005, US Tax Ct. 2007. Assoc. Harris, Barrett, Mann & Dew, St. Petersburg, Fla., 1985-86; ptnr. Bonner, Hogan & Coleman, P.A., Clearwater, Fla., 1986-97; pres. Coleman Law Firm, 1997—. Prin. Investment Fraud Recovery Network. Author: Spotting Those Bad Apples: Investment Fraud in the New Millenium, 1999. Counsel Pinellas County Habitat for Humanity, Fla., 1989, Boy Scouts Am. Pinellas County; advisor Philmout Expdn., 2002, troop com. chmn., 2005; mem. adv. coun. Pinellas County Schs., 2005; worship leader Heritage United Meth. Ch. Recipient Eagle Scout, Jessup Internat. Moot Ct. Competion, Order of the Arrow Brotherhood Level Disting. Svc. award, Pinellas County Schs., 2007. Mem. Fla. Bar Assn., Clearwater Bar Assn. (pres. young lawyers divn., coord. pub. rels. com. 1989-90), Publ. Investors Arbitration Bar Assn. (chmn. 1999 Fla. mid-year conf., presenter ann. meeting 2000-2005), Nat. Assn. Securities Dealers (arbitrator 2000), ATLA (nat. chmn. securities litigation sect.). Democrat. Methodist. Avocations: scuba diving, camping, boating, swimming. Office: Coleman Law Firm 581 S Duncan Ave Clearwater FL 33756 Office Fax: 727-461-7474. Business E-Mail: jeff@colemanlaw.com.

COLEMAN, JO-ANN S.E., social worker; d. Joseph B. Edwards and Annie M. Pimble-Edwards. A in Theology, Ch. of Christ Bible Inst., 1951; B in Religious En., Cmty. Bible Inst., 1957, M in Christian Counseling; DD, Wayne Theol. Sem., 2005. Ordained minister, cert. chaplain. Clerical Health and Hosp. Corp., NYC, 1981—89; caseworker Dept. Homeless Svcs., NYC, 1989—2002, supr., 2002—. Assoc. pastor White Rock Bible Ch., Inc., NYC, 1972. Singer: Timoth Wright's Concert Choir. Mem. concert choir N.Y. Fellowship Mass Choir; mem. James Cleveland Gospel Mus. Workshop Am., Women of Substance, Bereavement Consortium Ctrl. Harlem, Inc. Baptist. Avocations: reading, singing, bowling, travel. Office: NYC DHS/Yale Holel 316 W 97th St New York NY 10025

COLEMAN, JOEL CLIFFORD, lawyer; b. Reading, Pa., Nov. 6, 1930; s. Thomas and Lee (Jason) Iscovitz; m. Lois M. Schulman, Feb. 4, 1960; children: Teri, Thomas. BS in Econs., U. Pa., 1952, LLB cum laude, 1955. Bar: N.Y. 1956. Assoc. Kaye, Scholer, Fierman, Hays & Handler, NYC, 1955-67; atty. Twentieth-Century Fox Film Corp., NYC, 1967-69; gen. counsel Internat. Playtex, Inc., NYC and Stamford, Conn., 1969-86, sec., 1975-86, v.p., 1980-86, also dir.; v.p., gen. counsel, sec. Playtex Inc., 1986-88, Playtex Family Products Corp., 1989-94, Playtex Products, Inc., 1994, assoc. gen. counsel, asst. sec., 1994-95. Editor U. Pa. Law Rev., 1953-55, case editor, 1954-55. Trustee Larchmont (N.Y.) Temple, 1973-75; bd. dirs. Jewish Home for the Elderly of Fairfield County, 1996—, Bruce Mus., Greenwich, Conn., 1997—. Mem. Order of Coif. Home: 61 Ridgeview Ave Greenwich CT 06830-4755

COLEMAN, JOHN DANIEL, political strategist; s. Thomas Mabra and Ruth Strohm Coleman; m. Marie Lokey, Mar. 23, 1985. BS, Mid. Tenn. State U., Murfreesboro, 1969—73. V.p., bd. dir. Am. Laser Tech., Inc, Alexandria, Va., 1993—98; COO, sr. ptnr. J.D. Coleman & Assoc., LLC, DC, 1998—; with Polit. Campaign Creative Mgmt. Resources, 2006—.

Cons. on judgmental shooting Law Enforcement Industry, Clearwater, Fla., 1995—2002. Mem. Nashville Area Jr. C. of C., Nashville, 1973—82, Dem. Exec. Com., St. Petersburg, Fla., 2001—03, Castle Heights Found., Lebanon, Tenn., 1974—76. Col. USAR. Mem.: ABA (assoc.), Tenn. Farm Bur. (assoc.), Minn. Bar Assn. (assoc.), Shriner (assoc.), Alpha Tau Omega (life). D-Conservative. Methodist. Achievements include development of a simulator to train law enforcement personnel. Avocations: golf, skiing. Office: Polit Campaign Creative Mgmt Resources PO Box 308 Whites Creek TN 37189 Business E-Mail: dan@jdcolemanassociates.com.

COLEMAN, JOHN JAMES, III, lawyer, educator; b. Birmingham, Ala., Apr. 10, 1956; s. John James Jr. and Yonceil Oden (Foster) C.; m. Lizabeth Gaines, Aug. 24, 1985; 1 child, John J. IV. AB in History and Econs. magna cum laude, Duke U., 1978, JD, 1981. Bar: Ala. 1981, U.S. Dist. Ct. (no. and mid. dists.) Ala., U.S. Ct. Appeals (4th and 11th cirs.) 1982, U.S. Supreme Ct. 1987, Ga. 2000, Tex. 2001. Law clerk Judge Donald Russell, U.S. Ct. Appeals 4th cir., Richmond, Va., 1981-82; assoc. Balch & Bingham, Birmingham, 1982-88, ptnr., 1989-2000, Burr & Forman LLP, Birmingham, 2000—. Adj. instr. Cumberland Sch. Law, Birmingham, 1990—, Birmingham Sch. Law, 1994—; v.p. Indsl. Rels. Rsch. Assn., Birmingham, 1990-91; bd. dirs. Indsl. Health Coun. of Ala., Inc., Birmingham, 1991—. Author: Employment Discrimination in Alabama, Supplement to Employment Discrimination in Alabama, 1991, Disability Discrimination in Employment, 2001; co-author: (guide publ.) Workers Compensation Practice, 1994; contbr. articles to profl. jours. Ballot security atty. Rep. Party, Ala., 1988, 92, 94; co-chmn. Kidschance Scholarship, Birmingham, 1992. Mem. ABA (labor and employment law sect. OSHA com.), Am. Arbitration Assn. (mem. panel arbitrators), Ala. State Bar (exec. com. labor and employment sect. treas. 1995-96, vice chmn. 1996-97, chmn. 1997-98), Shades Mountain Sunrise Rotary Club (treas. 1994-96), Redstone Club. Republican. Roman Catholic. Avocations: tennis, bicycling, riding, writing. Office: Burr & Forman LLP 3100 SouthTrust Tower 420 N 20th St Birmingham AL 35203 Home: 2917 Carlisle Rd Birmingham AL 35213-3419 Fax: (205) 458-5100. E-mail: jcoleman@burr.com.

COLEMAN, JOHN JOSEPH, III, surgery educator; b. Boston, Nov. 15, 1947; Grad., Harvard U., 1969, MD, 1973. Intern Emory U. Affiliated Hosp., Atlanta, 1973-74, resident in gen. surgery, 1974-78, resident in plastic surgery, 1978-80; fellow in surg. oncology U. Md., Balt., 1980; prof. surgery Ind. U., Indpls., 1980—86; chief plastic surgery Ind. U. Med. Ctr., Indpls., 1980—86, James E. Bennett prof. of plastic surgery & Wadley R. Glenn chair in surgery, 1986—91, prof. of surgery & chmn. plastic surgery, 1991—. Mem.: Am. Head and Neck Soc., Am. Bd. of Plastic Surgery (chmn. 2002—03). Office: U Plastic Surg Assocs 235 Emerson Hall 565 Barnhill Dr Indianapolis IN 46202-5112

COLEMAN, JOHN MICHAEL, lawyer, consumer products company executive; b. Boston, Dec. 28, 1949; s. John Royston Coleman and Mary Norrington Irwin; m. Susan Lee Lavine, Oct. 29, 1978; children: William L., Anne H. L. BA, Haverford Coll., Pa., 1975; JD, U. Chgo., 1978. Bar: N.Y. 1978, Pa. 1979, U.S. Ct. Appeals (3rd and 4th cirs.) 1979, U.S. Dist. Ct. (ea. dist.) Pa. 1979, U.S. Dist. Ct. (so. dist.) N.Y. 1981, U.S. Supreme Ct., 1982, N.J. 1988. Law clk. to judge U.S. Ct. Appeals, Richmond, Va., 1978-79; law clk. to chief justice Warren Burger U.S. Supreme Ct., Washington, 1980-81; assoc. Dechert Price & Rhoads, Phila., 1981-86, ptnr., 1986-89; v.p., gen. counsel Campbell Soup Co., Camden, NJ, 1989-90, sr. v.p. law and pub. affairs, 1990-97; sr. v.p., gen. counsel The Gillette Co., Boston, 1997-99; mng. dir., CEO, Cambridge (Mass.) Capital Ptnrs. LLP, 1999-2000, chmn., CEO, 2000—05, Matlack Capital Partners, LLC, Moorestown, NJ, 2005—. Adj. prof. law U. Pa., Phila., 1985-88; bd. dirs. CDI Corp., NCI Consulting, Inc. Contbr. articles to profl. jours. Chmn. bd. trustees Campbell Soup Found., 1990-97; trustee N.J. State Aquarium, 1991-94, Food and Drug Law Inst., 1991-98, Inst. for Law and Econs., 1993-97, Am. Judicature Soc., 1995—; mem. vis. com. U. Chgo. Law Sch., 1993-95; mem. corp. Haverford Coll., 1994—; bd. dirs. The Guidance Ctr., treas., 2000-04. Mem. Am. Law Inst., Order of the Coif, Phi Beta Kappa. Mem. Religious Soc. of Friends. Office Phone: 856-778-9398. Business E-Mail: ceo@matlackcaptial.com.

COLEMAN, JOHN ROYSTON, writer; b. Copper Cliff, Ont., Can., June 24, 1921; came to U.S., 1946, naturalized, 1954; s. Richard Mowbray and Mary Irene (Lawson) C.; m. Mary N. Irwin, Oct. 1, 1943 (div. 1966); children: John M., Nancy J., Patty A., Stephen W. BA, U. Toronto, 1943; MA, U. Chgo., 1949, PhD, 1950; LLD (hon.), Beaver Coll., 1963, U. Pa., 1968, Gannon Coll., 1975; LHD (hon.), Manhattanville Coll., 1975, Emory and Henry Coll., 1977, Green Mountain Coll., 1984; DLitt (hon.), Haverford Coll., 1980, Elizabethtown Coll., 1987, Marlboro Coll., 1991; DSL (hon.), U. Toronto Victoria Coll., 1994. Rsch. assoc. U. Chgo., 1947-49; instr. econs. Mass. Inst. Tech., 1949-51, asst. prof., 1951-55; asso. prof., asst. head dept. econs. Carnegie Inst. Tech., 1955-60, prof., head dept. econs., 1960-63, dean div. humanities and social sci., 1963-65; assoc. dir. econ. devel. and adminstrn. Ford Found., 1965-66, program officer in charge social devel., 1966-67; pres. Haverford Coll., Pa., 1967-77, Edna McConnell Clark Found., NYC, 1977-86; chmn. Coleman Assocs. Inc., 1985-97; pres. Home Town Press, Inc., 1995-2001. Chmn. bd. dirs. Fed. Res. Bank Phila., 1973-76; labor arbitrator, cons., 1953-85; cons. indsl. rels. rsch. Ford Found. in India, 1960-61; tchr. Am. Economy CBS-TV, 1962-63 Author: Goals and Strategy in Collective Bargaining, 1951, Readings in Economics, 1952, 55, 58, 64, 67, Labor Problems, 1953, 59, Working Harmony, 1955, The Changing American Economy, 1967, Comparative Economic Systems, 1968, Blue Collar Journal, 1974, The Ballad of Clarence Adams, 1992, Pieces from the Quilt, 1993, The Play of the Three Kings, 1995, Takeoff at the North Pole, 2002; contbr. numerous articles to mags. Justice of peace, chmn. bd. civil authority Town of Chester, Vt., 1991—; prodr., dir. Chester Players Guild, 1991—; dir. Green Mountain Union H.S. Bd., 1998—; v.p. So. Windsor United Way, 1997-2003; chmn. Reparative Parole Bd., Springfield, Vt., 1997-2006. Lt. Royal Can. Navy, Vol. Res., 1943-46 Mem. Religious Soc. of Friends. Home: PO Box 995 Chester VT 05143-0995

COLEMAN, LEWIS WALDO, film company executive, former bank executive; b. San Francisco, Jan. 2, 1942; s. Lewis V. and Virginia Coleman; children: Gregory, Peter. BA, Stanford U., 1965. With Bank Calif., San Francisco, 1965-73, Wells Fargo Bank, San Francisco, 1973-86, exec. v.p., chmn. credit policy com., until 1986; vice chmn., CFO, treas. Bank Am., San Francisco, 1986-95; sr. mng. dir. Montgomery Securities, San Francisco, 1995-98; CEO Nations Bank Montgomery Securities, San Francisco, 1998; chmn. Banc Am. Securities LLC, 1995—2000; pres. Gordon and Betty Moore Found., 2000—04, trustee, 2004—; pres. Dreamworks Animation SKG, 2005—. Bd. dirs. Northrop Grumman. Bd. mem. Conservation Internat.; nat. dir. Trout Unlimited. Office: Dreamworks Animation SKG 1000 Flower St Glendale CA 91201

COLEMAN, LORING W., artist; b. Boston, 1918; Grad., Middlesex School, Scott Carbee School of Art, Boston. Prof., painting, sculpture Middlesex School; represented Francesca Anderson Find Art, Lexington, Mass. Exhibitions include Retrospective, Concord Art Assoc., Francesca Anderson Fine Art, St. Botolph Club, Central Place Galleries, Shore Galleries, exhibited in group shows, Am. Watercolor Soc., Knickerbocker Artists, High Art Museum, Munson Gallery, Milton College, Museum of Fine Arts, Addison Gallery of Am. Art, Represented in permanent collections, Salmagundi Club, Museum of Fine Arts, Butler Institute of Am. Art, Parrish Art Museum, Canton Art Institute, Fitchburg Art Museum, Concord Public Library. Named National Academician, 1994; recipient Strathmore Paper Co Award, Elizabeth K. Ellis Artists Fellowship Award, Salmagundi Club, Lifetime Achievement Award, New England Watercolor Soc. Office: c/o Francesca Anderson Fine Art 56 Adams Street Lexington MA 02420

COLEMAN, MARSHALL DONALD, psychiatrist, psychoanalyst; b. Utica, NY, Dec. 27, 1925; s. Jacob and Lucille (Smith) C.; m. Beverly Sitrin, June 28, 1949; children: Charles Theodore, Jacqueline Sue. BA, Harvard Coll., 1947; MD, Harvard Med. Sch., 1952. Diplomate Am. Bd. Psychiatry and Neurology. Intern Mass. Meml. Hosps., Boston, 1952-53; resident Boston Psychopathic Hosp., Boston, 1953-56; tchg. fellow Med. Sch. Harvard U., Boston, 1953-56; instr. Albert Einstein Sch. Medicine, Bronx, N.Y., 1956-57, asst. prof., 1957-63, asst. clin. prof., 1963—; sr. vis. staff Jacobi Hosp., Bronx, N.Y., 1962—; pvt. practice Mamaroneck, N.Y., 1968—. Dir. walk-in psychiat. clinic Albert Einstein Sch. Medicine, 1956; pres. N.Y. State Psychoanalytic Coordinating Com., 1988-2005. Author: Winston S. Churchill: Overcoming Childhood Adversities Help Form the Heroic Character of the Statesman, 1994; contbg. editor: Generations of Holocaust, 1982; editor articles on psychiat. walk-in clinics, brief psychotherapy and agoraphobia. Co-chairperson mental health profls. N.Y. area United Jewish Appeal, 1990-2003, chmn. emeritus, 2003—. With U.S. Army, 1944-46, ETO. Recipient M. Jucovy Lifetime Achievement award, 2000. Fellow Am. Psychiat. Assn. (life); mem. N.Y. Psychoanalytic Soc., Internat. Psychoanalytic Soc., Westchester Psychoanalytic Soc. (pres. 1978-79), Internat. Psychoanalytic Soc. Office: 1030 Greacen Point Rd Mamaroneck NY 10543-4609 Home Phone: 914-698-8818.

COLEMAN, MARSHIA ADAMS, social sciences educator; b. Conway, Ark., Oct. 22, 1956; d. Marshall and Lucille Wolford Adams; m. George Coleman Jr., July 22, 1996; 1 child, Adam Joseph McClung. BS in Edn., U. Ctrl. Ark., 1988, MS in Edn., 1991. Cert. tchr. Ark. Tchr. Sacred Heart Sch., Morrilton, Ark., 1988—90, Little Rock (Ark.) Sch. Dist., 1990—. Tchr. Park U. Little Rock (Ark.) AFB, Jacksonville, 2000—; writer curriculum Little Rock (Ark.) Sch. Dist., 1990—; creater, writer Holocaust curriculum Park U.; Holocaust rschr. Charles U., Prague, Czech Republic, Jagiellonian U., Krakow, Poland; field rschr. U. Western Cape, Cape Town, South Africa; spkr. in field. Co-author: Celebrating Arkansas, 1997, 2002. Mem. PTA, Forest Heights Mid. Sch., mem. Ark. coun. social studies; mem. food team Bethlehem House St. Peter's Episc. Ch., Conway, Ark.; pres. bd. Knowing Our Past Found. Recipient Stephens Outstanding Tchr. award, City Edn. Trust, 2004. Fellow: Delta Tchr. Acad.; mem.: APA, NEA, Little Rock Classroom Tchrs. Assn., Ark. Edn. Assn., U.S. Holocaust Meml. Mus. Republican. Episcopalian. Avocations: horseback riding, reading, writing, music, walking. Home: 109 Cedar Valley Dr El Paso AR 72045 Office: McClellan High Sch 9417 Geyer Springs Rd Little Rock AR 72209 Office Phone: 501-447-2755. Business E-Mail: marshia.coleman@lrsd.org.

COLEMAN, MARY ELLEN, quality assurance professional; b. Rochester, Minn., May 1, 1955; d. Louis James and Rosalyce Mae (Molacek) Hoppa; m. Michael A. Coleman, Nov. 15, 1975; children: Brenna Anne, Timothy Michael. Degree in liberal arts, Coll. St. Benedict, St. Joseph, Minn., 1973—74. Ecg outreach/quality control coord. Mayo Found., Rochester, 1975—. Contbr. articles to profl. jours. Office: Mayo Clinic 200 1st St SW Rochester MN 55905 Home Phone: 507-282-2267.

COLEMAN, MARY H., state legislator; b. Noxapater, Miss., July 25, 1946; m. Cayle Coleman, children Marcus, Crystal, Arqullas. Student, L.A. Trade-Tech. Coll., Tougaloo Coll. Mem. Miss. Ho. of Reps., 1987—; mem. edn., ins., pub. bldgs., pub. health coms.; mem. ways and means com. Exec. asst. to State Auditor, 1987-92; pres. Nat. Black Caucus of State Legislators. Recipient 100 Most Influential Black Americans, Ebony mag., 2006. Mem. NAACP, NOW, SCLC, Women in Govt., Alpha Kappa Alpha (Beta Delta Omega chpt.). Democrat. Baptist. Home: 308 Lynwood Ln Jackson MS 39206-3931 Office: State Capitol Bldg PO Box 1018 Jackson MS 39215-1018 Office Phone: 601-359-3360. E-mail: mcoleman@mail.house.state.ms.us.

COLEMAN, MARY SUE, academic administrator; b. Richmond, Ky, Oct. 2, 1943; m. Kenneth Coleman; 1 child, Jonathan. BA, Grinnell Coll., 1965; PhD, U. N.C., 1969; DSc (hon.), Dartmouth Coll., 2005. NIH postdoctoral fellow U. N.C., Chapel Hill, 1969—70, U. Ky., 1971—72, instr., rsch. assoc. depts. biochemistry and medicine, 1972—75, asst. prof. dept. biochemistry, 1975—80, assoc. prof. dept. biochemistry, 1980—85, prof. dept. biochemistry, 1985—90; prof. dept. biochemistry and biophysics U. N.C., Chapel Hill, 1990—93; provost, v.p. for academic affairs, prof. biochemistry U. N.Mex., 1993—95; pres., prof. biochemistry, prof. biol. scis. U. Iowa, Iowa City, 1995—2002; pres. U. Mich., Ann Arbor, 2002—. NSF summer trainee Grinnell Coll., 1962; acting dir. basir rsch. U. Ky. Cancer Ctr., 1980—83; scientific cons. Abbott Labs., 1981—85, Collaborative Rsch., 1983—88; assoc. dir. rsch. L.P. Markey Cancer Ctr. U. Ky., 1983—90, dir. grad. studies biochem., 1984—87, trustee, 1987—90; assoc. provost, dean rsch. U. N.C., 1990—92; scientific cons. Life Techs., Inc., 1992; vice chancellor grad students and rsch. U. N.C., 1992—93; pres. Iowa Health Sys., 1995—2002; mem. Big Ten Coun. Pres.'s, 1995—2002; chair undergrad. edn. com. Am. Assn. Univs., 1997—; bd. trustees Univs. Rsch. Assn., 1998—; mem. task force on tchrs. edn. Am. Coun. Edn., 1998—; mem. Gov.'s Strategic Planning Coun., 1998—2000, Imagining Am. Pres.'s Coun., 1999—, Bus.-Higher Edn. Froum, 1999—; mem. rsch. accountability task force Am. Assn. Univs., 2000—; mem. stds. success adv. bd. Am. Assn. Univs. and he Pew Charitable Trusts, 2000—; co-chair Inst. Medicine Com. on Consequences of Uninsurance, 2000—; mem. Knight Commn., 2000—01; mem. exec. com. Am. Assn. Univs., 2001—; mem. bd. dirs. Johnson & Johnson, 2003—; bd. dirs. Meredith Corp., Am. Coun. Edn.; presenter in field. Mem. editl. bd.: Jour. Biol. Chemistry, 1989—93; contbr. articles to profl. jours. Trustee Crinnell Coll., 1996—; mem. bd. govs. Warren G. Magnuson Clin. Ctr., NIH, 1996—2000, State of Iowa Gov.'s ACCESS Edn. Commn., 1997; bd. dirs. United Way, Albuquerque, 1995; trustee John S. and James L. Knight Found., 2005—. Fellow postdoctiral fellow, Clayton Found. Biochem. Inst., U. Tex., 1970—71. Fellow: AAAS, Am. Acad. Arts and Scis.; mem.: Nat. Coll. Athletic Assn. (bd. dirs. 2002—), Nat. Assn. State Univs. ans Land Grant Colls. Coun. Cchief Acad. Officers (exec. com. 1993—95), Am. Soc. Biochem. and Molecular Biology, Am. Assn. Cancer Rsch.*

COLEMAN, MAURICE L., bank executive; b. Trenton, NJ; BA cum laude, Columbia U., MS. Dean of students Noble & Greenough Prep Sch., Dedham, Mass.; founder & exec. dir. U. Mass. Math & Sci. Upward Bound Program; sr. v.p. & dir. Cmty. Econ. Devel. Unit FleetBoston Fin., NYC; sr. v.p. & cmty. devel. market mgr. Bank of Am., NYC. Vice-chmn. Abyssinian Devel. Corp.; mem. Harlem Edn. Activities Fund; mem. exec. bd. Initiative for a Competitive Bklyn. Named one of 40 Under 40 Rising Stars, Crain's NY Bus., 2007; recipient YMCA Black Achievers award, FleetBoston, 2001, Forward Thinking award. Office: Bklyn Econ Devel Corp Ste 350 175 Remsen St Brooklyn NY 11201

COLEMAN, MICHAEL BENNETT, mayor; b. Indpls., Nov. 18, 1954; s. John and Joan Coleman; m. Frankie L. Coleman; children: Kimberly, Justin, John-David. BA in polit. sci., U. Cin., 1977; JD, U. Dayton, 1980. Pvt. practice; mayor City of Columbus, Ohio, 2000—, Mem. city coun. City of Columbus, 1992—99, pres., 1997—99. Mem. Columbus Convention Ctr. Citizens Adv. Group, 1986; bd. mem. Columbus Youth Corps, Inc., Rosemont Ctr., Veterans Meml. Convention Ctr., Black Family Adoption, Ctrl. Ohio Transit Authority. Recipient Cmty. Svc. Award, Columbus Bar Assn., Citizen's Leadership Award. Mem.: ABA (mem. Minority Coun. Demonstration Program 1990—), Nat. Conf. Black Lawyers, Ohio State Bar Assn. (mem. coun. of delegates 1990—), Robert B. Elliot Law Club (v.p. 1989). Office: Mayors Office 90 W Broad St Rm 247 2nd Fl Columbus OH 43215-9014 Office Phone: 614-645-7671. Office Fax: 614-645-5818. Business E-Mail: mac@columbus.gov.*

COLEMAN, MICHAEL MURRAY, polymer science educator; b. Herne Bay, Eng., Jan. 24, 1938; s. Ronald and Winifred L. (Legg) C.; m. Mary Jane Ogorek, June 25, 1977; 1 child, David Spencer. BSc in Polymer Sci., Borough Poly., London, 1968; MS in Macromolecular Sci., Case Western Res. U., 1971, PhD in Macromolecular Sci., 1973. Analytical chemist Rhokana Corp. Ltd., Nkana, Zambia, 1955-61, Johnson-Mathey Ltd., Wembley, Eng., 1963-64; rsch. chemist Revertex Ltd., Harlow, Eng., 1968-69, E.I. du Pont de Nemours & Co., Wilmington, Del., 1973-75; asst. prof. polymer sci. Pa. State U., 1975-78, program chmn. polymer sci., 1976-84, assoc. prof., 1978-82, prof., 1982—2002, head, dept. materials sci. and engring., 1983-91, prof. emeritus, 2002—. Author: (with others) The Theory of Vibrational Spectroscopy and its Application to Polymeric Materials, 1982, Specific Interactions and the Miscibility of Polymer Blends, 1991, Fundamentals of Polymer Science, 1994, 2d edit., 1997; contbr. over 200 tech. articles to profl. jours. Fellow Am. Phys. Soc. (high polymer physics divsn.); mem. Am. Chem. Soc. (polymer and polymeric materials sci. and engring. divsns.), Soc. Plastics Engrs. Office: Pa State Univ 330 Steidle Bldg University Park PA 16802-5007 Home Phone: 814-466-7773; Office Phone: 814-865-3117. Fax: (814) 865-2917. E-mail: MMC4@psu.edu.

COLEMAN, MILTON, editor; b. Milw. BFA, U. Wis.-Milw. Reporter Milw. Courier; reporter, editor African World newspaper, Greensboro, NC, All-African News Svc., WHUR-FM, Washington, Cmty. News Svc., NY, Mpls. Star; Metro staff reporter Washington Post, 1976—80, city editor, 1980—83, nat. news staff, 1983—86, asst. mng. editor met. news, 1986—96, dep. mng. editor, 1996—. Active in Boy Scouts Am., 1982—, scoutmaster Troop 1650 S.E. Washington, DC, scoutmaster Troop 544 N.W. Washington, DC. Named a Disting. Alumnus, U. Wis.-Milw., 1998; recipient Dist. award of Merit, Boy Scouts Am., Silver Beaver award, Spirit of Scouting award, 1994; fellow, So. Edn. Found., 1971, Michele Clark Summer Program for Minority Journalists, Columbia U. Grad. Sch. Journalism, 1974. Mem.: Am. Soc. Newspaper Editors (bd. dirs. 2003—, treas. designate 2006—07, treas. 2007—08, chmn. Diversity Com. 2004—), Inter-Am. Press Assn., Nat. Assn. Minority Media Execs., Nat. Assn. Black Journalists. Office: Washington Post 1150 15th St NW Washington DC 20071*

COLEMAN, M.L. (MICHAEL LEE), artist; b. Livingston, Mont., May 11, 1941; s. Lee Lambert and Alma Phylis (Samson) Coleman; m. Sheri Donita Short, Dec. 31, 1981; m. Linda Kay Savage (div.); children: Diane Marie Ehlert, Kimberly Ann. BS, U. Wyo., Laramie, 1963. CPA Colo. Staff acct. Arthur Andersen, Denver, 1965—69, mgr., 1969—73; self-employed artist Big Fork, Mont., 1973—81, Sedona, Ariz., 1982—. Exhibitions include Cattleman's Found. Art Show and Auction, Calgary, Can., 1981 (Best of Show). Bd. dir. Sedona Arts Festival, Ariz., 1998—2001, Marilyn Sunderman Found., Sedona, Ariz., 2002—04. Capt. US Army, 1963—65. Avocation: travel. Home and Studio: Sunset Pass Studios 200 Sunset Pass Rd Sedona AZ 86351-9519 Office Phone: 928-284-5803. E-mail: mlcolemanstudios@gmail.com.

COLEMAN, MORTON, oncologist, hematologist, educator; b. Norfolk, Va., Sept. 15, 1939; s. Isadore and Bessie (Levin) C.; m. Joyce Goodman, May 26, 1968; children: Ingrid Alexandra, Benjamin Lee, Abigail Rachael. AA, Coll. William and Mary, 1958; BA, Johns Hopkins U., 1959; MD, Med. Coll. Va., 1963. Diplomate Nat. Bd. Med. Examiners, Am. Bd. Internal Medicine, Am. Bd. Hematology, Am. Bd. Clin. Oncology. Intern Grady Meml. Hosp.-Emory U. Med. Ctr., Atlanta, 1963-64, resident, 1964-65, N.Y. Hosp.-Cornell U. Med. Ctr., NYC, 1967-68; NIH fellow in hematology Cornell U. Med. Coll., 1968-70, asst. prof. medicine, 1970-74, assoc. prof., 1974-86, clin. prof., 1986—; asst. attending N.Y. Hosp., NYC, 1970-74, assoc. attending, 1974-86, attending, 1986—99, assoc. dir. oncology svc., 1974-86; assoc. program dir. Nat. Cancer Inst. Clin. Chemotherapy Program Cancer Control, 1974-80; attending N.Y. Presbyterian Hosp., 1999—. Dir. Ctr. for Lymphoma and Myeloma, divsn. hematology-oncology, 1997—; attending staff Manhattan Eye and Ear Hosp., 1972—82, Doctors Hosp., 1973—90, Beth Israel NorthMed. Ctr., 1990—94. Assoc. editor: Cancer Investigation, 1987—2006; mem. editl. adv. bd. Hem/Onc Today, 1999—, internat. adv. bd. Indian Jour. Med. and Pediatric Oncology, 1994—, mem. editl. bd. Acta Haematologica, 2005—; contbr. articles to rsch. publications on blood and cancer. Chmn. new agts. com. Cancer and Leukemia Group B, 1975—82; chmn. bd. dir. Fund for Blood and Cancer Rsch., 1975—; sci. advisor United Leukemia Fund, 1976—82; co-chmn. clin. rsch. rev. com. Israel Cancer Rsch. Fund, 1988—93; mem. exec. com. NY State Soc. Med. Oncology and Hematology, 1991—99; program chmn. NY Cancer Soc., 1993—94, sec., 1994—95, treas., 1995—96, v.p., 1996—97, pres.-elect, 1997—98, pres., 1998—99, coun. of advisors, 2002—; chmn. Lymphoma/Hodgkins' Diseases symposium com. Internat. Union Against Cancer Congress, 1993—94; internat. adv. bd. Cancer Care Trust and Rsch. Found., India, 1995—; chmn. bd. dir. Affiliated Physicians Network, 1996—2001; mem. clin. practice com. Am. Soc. Clin. Oncology, 1997—2001, mem. pub. com., 2001—04, mem. program com., 2001—03, chmn. policy and procedures subcom., 2002—04, chmn. hematol. malignancy subcom., 2002—03; bd. dir., chmn. med. affiliates bd. Cure for Lymphoma Found., 1997—2001; mem. sci. adv. com. Lymphoma Rsch. Found., 1998—, exec. com. bd. dirs., chmn. med. affiliates bd., 2001—; bd. dirs. Immunomedics Inc., 2000—, BML Pharmaceuticals Inc., 2003—05; mem. adv. bd. The Lymphoma Found., 2006—. Lt. comdr. USN, 1965—67. Recipient Disting. Alumni award, Old Dominion U., 1994, Together award, Cure for Lymphoma Found., 2000, 2001, Rosetta Cir. award, Lymphoma Rsch. Found., 2002. Fellow: ACP; mem.: AMA, AAAS, N.Y. County Med. Soc., NY State Med. Soc., Soc. Study of Blood, NY Acad. Sci., Internat. Soc. Hematology, Harvey Soc., Cornell U. Med. Ctr. Alumni Assn., Am. Soc. Hematology, Am. Radium Soc., Am. Fedn. Clin. Rsch., Am. Assn. Cancer Rsch., Explorers Club, Sigma Zeta, Alpha Omega Alpha. Office: 407 E 70th St 3rd fl New York NY 10021-5302 also: NY Presbyn Hosp-Weill Cornell U Med Ctr Div Hematology-Oncology 525 E 68th St New York NY 10021-4870 Personal E-mail: mortoncolemanmd@aol.com.*

COLEMAN, NORMAN, JR., senator, former mayor; b. Bklyn., Aug. 17, 1949; m. Laurie Casserly; children: Jacob, Sarah. BA in Political Sci., Hofstra U., 1971; JD, U. Iowa, 1976. Bar: Minn. Criminal prosecutor, civil litig. supr., chief lobbyist Minn. Atty. Gen.'s Office, 1976—86, asst. atty. gen., chief prosecutor & solicitor. gen., 1986—92; mayor City of St. Paul, 1994—2002; US Senator from Minn., 2003—. Active in creation of Minn. Drug Abuse Resistance Edn. program, also The Partnership for a Drug Free Minn.; adj. prof., William Mitchell Coll. Law, 1983-92; mem. com. agr., nutrition and forestry, US Senate, com. fgn. affairs, com. homeland security and govtl. affairs, com. small bus. and entrepreneurship. Humphrey fellow U. Minn.; Award Pub. Svc Woodrow Wilson Internat. Ctr. for Scholars, Award Excellence in Pub.-Pvt. Partnerships US Conf. Mayors, 2001, Mondale award Japan-Am. Soc. of Minn., 2001, Urban Innovator award Ctr. for Civic Innovation, The Manhattan Inst., 2001, Award Leadership in Inter-American Understanding Hudson Inst. Ctr. Latin Am. Studies, 2005. Republican. Jewish. Office: US Senate 320 Hart Senate Office Building Washington DC 20510 also: District Office Ste 100N 2550 University Ave West Saint Paul MN 55114-1098 Office Phone: 202-224-5641, 651-645-0323. Office Fax: 202-224-1152, 651-645-3110.*

COLEMAN, ORNETTE, jazz musician; b. Ft. Worth, Mar. 9, 1930; s. Randolph and Rosa C.; 1954; m. Jayne Cortez (div. 1964); 1 child, Denardo. Doctorate (hon.), U. Pa., Bard Coll., New Sch. Social Rsch., Berklee Sch. Music. Founder Sound Grammar music label, NYC. Player alto and tenor saxophone, trumpet, violin, bassoon; toured with Clarence Samuels, 1949, with Pee Wee Crayton, 1950; led quartet with Don Cherry, Eddie Blackwell and Charlie Haden; appeared in numerous major festivals throughout the world including JVC Jazz Festival, NYC, 1991; toured Japan, Europe, and Africa; recs. for small jazz ensemble include Something Else, 1958, The Shape of Jazz to Come, 1959, Art of the Improvisors, 1959-61, Free Jazz, 1960, Chappaque Suite, 1965, Live at the Tivoli, 1965, Paris Concert-Nov. 4, 1965, Empty Foxhole, 1966, Live in Milano, 1968, Love Call, 1968, New York is Now, 1968, Dancing in Your Head, 1976, Fashion Faces, 1979, Of Human Feelings, 1979, (with Pat Metheny) Song X, 1985, At the Golden Circle, Stockholm, Vol. I, 1987, Vol. II, 1987, Naked Lunch, 1992, (with Jerry Garcia) Virgin Beauty, 1988, Beauty is a Rare Thing, 1993, Languages, 1993, Tone Dialing, 1995, Sound Museum: Hidden Man, 1996, Sound Museum: Three Women, 1996, Rock the Clock, 2006, Sound Grammar, 2006; others include Broken Shadows, Change of the Century, Dedication to Poets and Writers, Ornette on Tenor, Tomorrow is the Question, Town Hall Concert; played with own group, Prime Time; over 100 compositions for small jazz group and larger ensembles including Music of Ornette Coleman containing his works for string quartet and woodwind quintet recorded by London Symphony Orch.; composer symphony Skies of America; appeared in film Ornette: Made in America, 1986. Guggenheim Found. fellow, 1967, 1974; recipient Poses Creative arts award Brandeis U., 1985, Letter of Distinction, Am. Music Ctr., 1987, Genius award, MacArthur Found., 1994, Dorothy & Lillian Gish prize, 2004, NY State Gov. Arts award, Grammy Lifetime Achievement award, 2007, Pulitzer Prize for Music, 2007; named Jazz Man of Yr. by Jazz and Pop 3d Ann. Readers Poll, 1968; inducted to Downbeat Hall of Fame, Big Band & Jazz Hall of Fame, 1989, Am. Acad. Arts & Sciences, 1997. Mem.: ASCAP. Achievements include developing musical theory concept called Harmoldic theory for composers and players. Office: c/o Phrase Text Inc PO Box 20071 London Terrace Sta New York NY 10011 also: c/o Ken Weinstein Big Hassle Media 44 Wall St 22nd Fl New York NY 10005 Office Phone: 646-238-9942. Office Fax: 212-431-1753. E-mail: phrasetext@gmail.com.*

COLEMAN, PAUL DARE, physics and electrical engineering educator; b. Stoystown, Pa., June 4, 1918; s. Clyde R. and Catharine (Livengood) C.; m. Betty L. Carter, June 20, 1942; children— Susan Dare, Peter Carter. AB, Susquehanna U., 1940; MS, Pa. State U., 1942; PhD, MIT, 1951, DSc (hon.), 1978. Asst. physics Susquehanna U., 1938-40, Pa. State U., 1940-42; physicist USAF-WADC, Wright Field, Ohio, 1942-46, Cambridge Air Research Center, also; grad. research assoc. Mass. Inst. Tech., 1946-51; prof. elec. engring., dir. electro-physics lab. U. Ill. at Urbana, 1951—. Recipient meritorious civilian award, USAAF, 1946, Disting. Alumni award, Susquehanna U., 1980. Fellow AAAS, IEEE, MTT (Disting. Educator award 1994, Centennial medal 1984), Optical Soc. Am., Am. Phys. Soc.; mem. Sigma Xi, Pi Mu Delta, Pi Mu Epsilon, Eta Kappa Nu. Achievements include research on millimeter waves, submillimeter waves, relativistic electronics, far infrared molecular lasers, beam wave guides and detectors, chem. lasers, nonlinear optics, solid state electronics; inventor of the magnetic wiggler, the key component of the free electron laser. Home: 710 Park Lane Dr Champaign IL 61820-7633 Office: Univ Ill 133 Everitt Lab 1406 W Green St Urbana IL 61801-2918

COLEMAN, PAUL DAVID, neurobiology educator, researcher; b. NYC, Dec. 2, 1927; s. A. Barnett and Martha L. (Michaels) C.; m. Zinia J. Cereska, Mar. 13, 1955 (div. Sept. 1978); children: Laura A., Paul David; m. 2d Dorothy G. Flood, Feb. 26, 1983. AB, Tufts U., 1948; PhD, U. Rochester, 1953. Asst. prof., research assoc. Tufts U., Medford, Mass., 1956-59; assoc. Computer Ctr. MIT, Cambridge, 1957-59; spl. fellow Johns Hopkins Sch. Medicine, Balt., 1959-62; assoc. prof. Sch. Medicine U. Md., Balt., 1962-67; prof. neurobiology and anatomy Sch. Medicine, U. Rochester, NY, 1967—. Editor in chief Neurobiology of Aging, 1988—; contbr. articles to profl. jours. 1st lt. US Army, 1953—56. Recipient award for leadership and excellence in Alzheimer's disease Nat. Inst. Aging, NIH, 1990, Pioneer award Alzheimers Assn., 2000; Rsch. grantee NSF, 1958-67, NIH, 1963—; NIH spl. fellow Johns Hopkins U. Sch. Medicine, 1959-62. Mem. Soc. for Neurosci., Am. Assn. Anatomists, AAAS, Gerontol. Soc., Am. Psychol. Assn., Sigma Xi. Clubs: Yacht (Rochester, N.Y.) (bd. dirs. 1971-72). Home: 7 Durham Way Pittsford NY 14534

COLEMAN, PAUL JEROME, JR., physicist, researcher; b. Evanston, Ill., Mar. 7, 1932; s. Paul Jerome and Eunice Cecile (Weissenberg) C.; m. Doris Ann Fields, Oct. 3, 1964; children: Derrick, Craig. BS in Engring. Math., U. Mich., 1954, BS in Engring. Physics, 1954, MS in Physics, 1958; PhD in Space Physics, UCLA, 1966. Rsch. scientist Ramo-Wooldridge Corp. (name now Northrop Grumman), El Segundo, Calif., 1958-61; instr. math. U. So. Calif., LA, 1958-61; mgr. interplanetary scis. program NASA, Washington, 1961-62; rsch. scientist UCLA, 1962-66, prof. geophysics, space physics, 1966—; asst. lab. dir., mgr. Earth and Space Scis. divsn., chmn. Inst. Geophysics and Planetary Physics Nat. Lab., Los Alamos, N.Mex., 1981-86; dir. Inst. Geophysics and Planetary Physics UCLA, 1989-92; dir. Nat. Inst. for Global Environ. Change, 1994-96; pres. Univs. Space Rsch. Assn., Columbia, Md., 1981-2000, Girvan Inst. Tech., 2002—. Bd. dirs. Axcess Inc., Dallas, Knowledge Vector, Inc., Durham, N.C., others; mem. adv. bd. San Diego Supercomputer Ctr., 1986-90, chmn., 1987-88, others; trustee Univs. Space Rsch. Assn., Columbia, Md., 1981-2000, Am. Tech. Alliances, 1990-2002, Internat. Small Satellite Orgn., 1992-96; vis. scholar U. Paris, 1975-76; vis. scientist Lab. for Aeronomy Ctr. Nat. Rsch. Sci., Verrieres le Buisson, France, 1975-76; com. mem. numerous sci. and ednl. orgns., cons. numerous fin. and indsl. cos. Co-editor: Solar Wind, 1972; co-author: Pioneering the Space Frontier, 1986; mem. editorial bd. Geophysics and Astrophysics Monographs, 1970—; assoc. editor Cosmic Electrodynamics, 1968-72; contbr. revs. to numerous profl. jours. Apptd. to Nat. Commn. on Space, Pres. of U.S., 1985, apptd. to Space Policy Adv. Bd., Nat. Space Coun., v.p. of U.S., 1991; bd. dirs. St. Matthew's Sch., Pacific Palisades, Calif., 1979-82, v.p., 1981-82. 1st lt. USAF, 1954-56, Korea. Recipient Exceptional Sci. Achievement Medal NASA, 1970, 1972, spl. recognition for contributions to the Apollo Program, 1979; Guggenheim fellow 1975-76, Fulbright scholar, 1975-76, Rsch. grantee NASA, NSF, Office Naval Research, Calif. Space Inst., Air Force Office Sci. Research, U.S. Geol. Survey. Mem. Internat. Acad. Astronautics, Bel Air Bay Club (L.A.), Birnam Wood Golf Club (Monteceito, Calif.), Cosmos Club (Washington), Valley Club (Montecito, Calif.), Eldorado Country Club (Indian Wells, Calif.), Tau Beta Pi, Phi Eta Sigma. Avocations: flying, skiing, racquetball, tennis, golf. Home: 1323 Monaco Dr Pacific Palisades CA 90272-4007 Office: UCLA Inst Geophysics & Planetary Physics 405 Hilgard Ave Los Angeles CA 90095-9000 Home Phone: 310-474-8702; Office Phone: 310-825-1776. Business E-Mail: pcoleman@igpp.ucla.edu.

COLEMAN, PHYLLIS, law educator; b. Bronx; d. Harvey and Amy Davis Gallub. BS in Journalism, U. Fla., 1970, MEd, 1975, JD, 1978. Bar: Fla. 1978, Fla. Supreme Ct. 1978. Reporter, news editor Gwinnett Daily News, Lawrenceville, Ga., 1972—73; assoc. Broad & Cassel, Bay Harbor, Fla., 1978—79; from asst. to full prof. law Nova Southeastern U., Fort Lauderdale, Fla., 1979—. Editor: Family Law: Text and Commentary (annual), 1997—; co-author: (casebook) Sports Law: Cases and Materials, 1999, Bush v. Gore: The Fight for Florida's Vote, 2001; contbr. articles to profl. jours., chapters to books. Mem. Broward County Managed Care Ombudsman Com., Fort Lauderdale, 2002; selection com. Hall of Fame Ind. Fla. Alligator, Gainesville, Fla., 2003—05; founding mem. animal law com. Fla. Bar, 2003—05. Named Outstanding Faculty Mem., Black Law Students, Nova Southeastern U., 1994, Prof. of Yr., Student Bar Assn., Nova Southeastern U., 2004—05; named to Hall of Fame, U. Fla., 1971, Alligator Hall of Fame, Ind. Fla. Alligator, 1999. Liberal. Jewish. Avocation: scuba diving. Office: Nova Southeastern U 3305 College Ave Fort Lauderdale FL 33314-7721 Office Phone: 954-262-6166. Office Fax: 954-262-3835. E-mail: colemanp@nsu.law.nova.edu.

COLEMAN, RICHARD WILLIAM, retired lawyer; b. Brookline, Mass., Dec. 9, 1935; s. Michael John and Mary Ellen (Motherway) C.; m. Mary M. Kilcommins, June 3, 1961; children: Lauren, Christopher. BS, Boston Coll., Newton, Mass., 1957; JD, Boston Coll., Brighton, Mass., 1960. Bar: Mass. 1960, U.S. Dist. Ct. Mass. 1961, U.S. Ct. Appeals (1st cir.) 1981. Field atty. NLRB, Newark, 1960-61; assoc. Segal & Flamm, Boston, 1961-69; labor rels. advisor Scott Paper Co., Phila., 1969-70; labor rels. mgr. Harvard U., Cambridge, Mass., 1970-72; ptnr. Segal, Roitman & Coleman, Boston, 1972-93; pres. Richard W. Coleman, P.C., Needham, 1994—2002; ret. Contbg. editor Development of Law Under National Labor Relations Act, 1988. Bd. dirs. Little Bros. of St. Francis, 1998-2001. Recipient Cushing award Cath. Labor Guild Boston, 1976. Mem. ABA, Am. Prepaid Legal Svcs. Inst. (bd. dirs. 1997—), Indsl. Rels. Rsch. Assn., Mass. Bar Assn., Boston Bar Assn., AFL-CIO Lawyers Coord. Com. Democrat. Roman Catholic. Avocations: golf, reading, choir singing. E-mail: rcolegolf@aol.com.

COLEMAN, ROBERT GRIFFIN, geology educator; b. Twin Falls, Idaho, Jan. 5, 1923; s. Lloyd Wilbur and Frances (Brown) C.; m. Cathryn J. Hirschberger, Aug. 7, 1948; children: Robert Griffin Jr., Derrick Job, Mark Dana. BS, Oreg. State U., 1948, MS, 1950; PhD, Stanford U., 1957. Mineralogist AEC, NYC, 1952-54; geologist U.S. Geol. Survey, Washington, 1954-57, Menlo Park, Calif., 1958-80; prof. geology Stanford U., Calif., 1981-93, prof. emeritus Calif., 1993—. Vis. petrographer New Zealand Geol. Survey, 1962-63; br. chief isotope geology U.S. Geol. Survey, Menlo Park, 1964-68, regional geologist, Saudi Arabia, 1970-71, br. chief field geochemistry and petrology, Menlo Park, 1977-79; vis. scholar Woods Hole Oceanographic Inst., Mass., 1975; vis. prof. geology Sultan Qaboos U., Oman, 1987, 89; cons. geologist, 1993—; instr. geobotany field sch. Siskiyou Inst., Oreg., 1998-99. Author: Ophiolites, 1977, Geologic Evolution of the Red Sea, 1993, Ultrahigh Pressure Metamorphism, 1995; contbr. articles to profl. jours. Named Outstanding Scientist, Oreg. Acad. Sci., 1977; Fairchild scholar Calif. Inst. Tech., Pasadena, 1980; recipient Meritorious award U.S. Dept. Interior, 1981 Fellow AAAS, Geol. Soc. Am. (coun.), Am. Mineral Soc. (coun., editor), Am. Geophys. Union; mem. Nat. Acad. Scis., Russian Acad. Sci. (fgn. assoc.). Republican. Avocations: wood carving, art. Home: 2025 Camino Al Lago Atherton CA 94027-5938 Business E-Mail: coleman@pangea.stanford.edu.

COLEMAN, ROBERT HEMPHILL, III, theater educator; b. Augusta, Ga., Sept. 7, 1952; s. Martin Teague and Virginia Baldwin Coleman. MFA in Drama, Yale U., New Haven, Conn., 1998; BA in English Lit., Augusta Coll., 1994. Tech. dir., asst. prof. Dept. Drama U. Tenn., Knoxville, Tenn., 1998—2000; dir. tech. prodn. program Sch. Theatre Fla. State U., Tallahassee, 2000—. With tech. and global resources Cirque du Soleil, Montreal, Canada, 2003—06; tech. dir. Opera Festival N.J., Princeton, 1995—99, dir. prodn., 1999—2000. Mem.: ASCE (assoc.), Southeastern Theatre Conf., U.S. Inst. Theatre Tech., Am. Inst. Steel Constrn. (corr.), Am. Mensa, Ltd. Episcopalian. Office: FSU School of Theatre 239 Fine Arts Bldg Tallahassee FL 32306 Home: 106 5th St NE Havana FL 32333 Home Phone: 850-212-3202; Office Phone: 850-644-4305. Business E-Mail: rcoleman@fsu.edu.

COLEMAN, ROBERT J., lawyer; b. Phila., Dec. 24, 1936; s. Francis Eugene and Mary Veronica (McCullough) C.; m. Mary Patricia Coleman, June 26, 1955; children: Debra, Robert P., Linda, Martin S. AB, Villanova U., 1959; JD, Temple U., 1964. Bar: Pa., U.S. Dist. Ct. (ea. dist.) Pa., 1964, U.S. Ct. Appeals (3d cir.), U.S. Supreme Ct., 1973. With First Pa. Bank, Phila., 1955-57; underwriter Employer's Mut. Co., Phila., 1957-59; claim adjuster Safeco Ins. Co., Phila., 1959-62; claim supr. Gen. Accident Ins., Phila., 1962-64; assoc. Rappaport & Lagakos, Phila., 1964; trial atty. Allstate Ins. Co., Phila., 1964-67; chmn., CEO Marshall, Dennehey, Warner, Coleman & Goggin, Phila., 1967—2004, chmn. emeritus, 2005—. Chmn. hearing com. Pa. Disciplinary Bd., Phila., 1986-94; mem. Pa. Bd. Law Examiners, 1997-2003; bd. dirs. Republic First Bancorp, 2003-. Assoc. editor Phila. County Reporter, 1984-96; contbr. articles to legal publs. Bd. vis. Temple U. Law Sch. With USAR, 1954-62. Mem. ABA, Pa. Bar Assn., Phila. Bar Assn., Phila. Bar Found. (past trustee), Pa. Def. Inst., Internat. Assn. Def. Lawyers, Def. Rsch. Inst. Republican. Roman Catholic. Avocations: tennis, boating, travel. Home: 908 Penn Valley Rd Media PA 19063-1652 Office: Marshall Dennehey Warner Coleman & Goggin 1845 Walnut St Philadelphia PA 19103-4797 Business E-Mail: rjcoleman@mdwcg.com.

COLEMAN, ROBERT LEE, retired lawyer; b. Kansas City, Mo., June 14, 1929; s. William Houston and Edna Fay (Smith) C. B of Music Edn., Drake U., 1951; LLB, U. Mo., 1959. Bar: Mo. 1959, Fla. 1973. Law clk. to judge U.S. Dist. Ct. (we. dist.) Mo., Kansas City, 1959-60; assoc. Watson, Ess, Marshall & Enggas, Kansas City, 1960-66; asst. gen. counsel Gas Svc. Co., Kansas City, 1966-74; v.p., corp. counsel H & R Block, Inc., Kansas City, 1974-94; ret., 1994. With U.S. Army, 1955-57. Mem.: ABA.

COLEMAN, ROBERT WINSTON, lawyer; b. Oklahoma City, Mar. 1, 1942; s. Clint Sheridan and Genevieve (Ross) C.; m. Judith Moore, Sept. 7, 1963; children: Robert Winston, Jr., Claire Elizabeth. BA, Abilene Christian Coll., 1964; JD with hons., U. Tex., 1968. Bar: Tex. 1968, Ga. 1970. Law clk. to presiding justice U.S. Ct. Appeals (5th cir.), Montgomery, Ala., 1968-69; assoc. Kilpatrick, Cody, Rogers, McClatchey & Regenstein, Atlanta, 1969-75; ptnr. Meyers, Miller, Middleton, Weiner & Warren and predecessor, Dallas, 1975-80, Jones, Day, Reavis & Pogue, Dallas, 1981-85; dir. Baker, Glast and Middleton, P.C., Dallas, 1985-92; ptnr. Vial, Hamilton, Koch & Knox, LLP, Dallas, 1992-2000, Brown McCarroll LLP, Dallas, 2000—. Mem. exec. com. Dallas County Dem. Com., 1980-87. Mem. ABA, Dallas Bar Found., Dallas Bar Assn., Tex. Bar Assn., Ga. Bar Assn., Am. Judicature Soc. Office: Brown McCarroll LLP 2000 Trammell Crow Ctr 2001 Ross Ave Dallas TX 75201 Office Phone: 214-999-6100. Business E-Mail: rcoleman@mailbmc.com.

COLEMAN, RODNEY ALBERT, political scientist, consultant; b. Newburgh, NY, Oct. 12, 1938; s. Samuel and Rebecca (Belden) Coleman; children: Terri Lynn, Stephen Anthony. BArch, Howard U., 1963; grad. exec. devel. program, U. Mich., 1988. Commd. 2nd lt. USAF, 1963, advanced through grades to capt., separated, 1973; White House fellow Washington, 1970-71; exec. asst. to chmn. D.C. City Coun., Washington, 1973-78; archtl. design cons. Pennsylvania Ave. Devel. Corp., Washington, 1978-80; dir. govt. rels. Gen. Motors, Detroit, 1980-85, dir. mcpl. govt. affairs, 1985-90, exec. dir. urban and mcpl. affairs, 1990-94; asst. sec. of Air Force for manpower, Res. affairs, installations, and environ. Dept. of Air Force, Washington, 1994-98; exec. v.p. ICF Kaiser Internat., Fairfax, Va., 1998-99; ptnr. Alcalde & Fay, Arlington, Va., 1999—. Chmn. bd. adv. Mus. Aviation of Ga., 1998—; trustee Air Force Aid Soc., 1998—2005; bd. dirs. Washington Hosp. Ctr., 2002—05. Decorated Bronze Star medal, Air Force Commendation medal Republic of Vietnam, Honor medal First Class, Air Force Meritorious Svc. medal; recipient Disting. Alumni award for postgrad. achievement in corp. and govt. svc. Howard U., 1996, Disting. Alumnus award Newburgh Free Acad., 1994, Black Engr. of Yr. dean's award, 1996, Lt. Gen. Benjamin O. Davis Jr. Disting. Achievement award of The Tuskegee Airmen, 1996, decoration for exceptional civilian svc. Dept. of Air Force, 1997, Eagle award Nat. Guard Bur., 1998. Mem. White House Fellows Assn., Exec. Leadership Coun. Air Force Assn., Tuskegee Airmen. Methodist. Avocation: golf. Home: 17519 Edinburgh Dr Tampa FL 33647 Home Phone: 813-929-7370; Office Phone: 813-929-7370. Personal E-mail: honrc@aol.com. Business E-Mail: coleman@alcalde-fay.com.

COLEMAN, RONALD LEE, insurance claims executive; b. Danville, Va., June 10, 1941; s. Raymond Lee and Mildred Sue (Floyd) C.; m. Stephanie Walther Barton Ewalt; children: Ronald Lee, Christopher Brent. BSBA summa cum laude, Va. Poly. Inst. and State U., 1964; BS in Pub. Adminstrn. summa cum laude, U. Richmond, 1964, postgrad., 1971; postgrad. law sch., U. Va., 1980. Pres. Johnson & Coleman, Ltd., Richmond, 1974—79; v.p. Schnell, Johnson & Coleman, Ltd., Richmond, 1979—81; pres. Ron Coleman & Assocs., Ltd., Richmond, Va., 1981—. Adj. prof. U. Tex., Austin, Pa. State U., State College; adv. coun. Pamplin Bus. Sch., Va. Tech. Author: Investigation and Handling of Aviation Claims, 1981, Presentation of Evidence in Accident Reconstruction Cases, 1989, others; editor-in-chief Claimsman mag., 1971-76; contbr. articles to profl. jours. Mem. U.S. Senatorial Bus. Adv. Bd., 1988; mem. adv. coun. Paplin Coll. Bus., Va. Tech.; mem. Rep. Presdl. Task Force, 1988; mem. Va. Rep. Com., Chesterfield County, 1984; mem. The Pres.'s Coun., 1990, Pres. Club Rep. Party; bd. dirs. Va. Tech. Found., Va. Tech. Athletic Fund., Va. Tech. Athletic Bd.(exec. com.). Mem. ABA (exec. bd.; exec. com., torts and ins. practice sect.), Richmond Claims Assn. (pres. 1971-72, Man of Yr. award 1971), Va. Claims Assn. (Bob Anderson Humanitarian award), Def. Law Inst., Atlanta Claims Assn., Profl. Claims Assn. Richmond, Truck Ins. Def. Assn., 1872 Soc. at Va. Poly. Inst. and State U., Assn. Lloyds Mems. London, Pilon Soc. at Va. Poly. Tech. Inst. and State U., Ut Prosim Soc. at Va. Poly. Tech. Inst. and State U., Bowman Soc. Va. Poly. Tech. Inst. and State U., Candwell Soc. at Va. Poly. Tech. Inst. and State U., Va. Tech. Found., 1789 Soc. at Hampden-Sydney Coll., Soc. of Founders Hampden-Sydney Coll., Va. Hist. Soc., Rotunda Soc. U. Va., Reform Club London, St. James Club London, Salisbury Country Club, Hurlingham Club London, Sloane Club London, Quinnipiack Club New Haven, Yale Club NYC, Bowman Soc. at Va. Tech., Oxford-Cambridge Club London. Methodist. Avocations: jazz, golf.

COLEMAN, SHANNON DESHAE, lawyer, educator; b. Middlesboro, Ky., Apr. 21, 1975; d. James Emory and Judy Carol Coleman. BA in English, Lincoln Meml.U., 1996; JD, U. Tenn., 1999. Bar: Tenn. 1999, US Dist. Ct. (ea. dist. Tenn.) 2000, US Tax Ct. 1999. Assoc. Gentry, Tipton & McLemore, PC, Knoxville, 1999—2005, Holifield & Assocs., P.C., Knoxville, 2005—06; spl. counsel Kramer Rayson LLP, Knoxville, Tenn., 2006—. Adj. prof. law U. Tenn., Knoxville, 2003—06; lectr. in field. Mem.: ABA, Knoxville Bar Assn., Tenn. Bar Assn., Am. Health Lawyers Assn. Avocations: skiing, running, reading, travel. Home: 6656 Bay Circle Dr Knoxville TN 37918 Office: Kramer Rayson LLP 800 South Gray St Ste 2500 Knoxville TN 37929 Business E-Mail: scoleman@kramer-rayson.com.

COLEMAN, STEPHEN BEASLEY, JR., real estate broker, writer; b. Birmingham, Ala., Aug. 7, 1941; s. Stephen Beasley and Marietta Randolph Coleman; m. Alexandra Sammons Vandiver, Aug. 10, 1971 (div. Apr. 15, 1998); children: Stephen Beasley III, Sammons Randolph, William Wilkes Young. BA, Duke U., 1963; MA, U. Ala., 1968. Cert. Cert. Comml. Investment Mem. Inst., 1998. English instr. U. Tenn., Knoxville, 1968—69; tchr. of english Christ Ch. Episcopal Sch., Greenville, SC, 1969—75; sales rep. Overhead Door Co. of Greenville, SC, 1975—76; owner, gen. mgr. Overhead Door Co. of Anniston-Gadsden, Ala., 1977—82; v.p., gen. mgr. Overhead Door Co. of Birmingham, Ala., 1982—91; assoc. broker Sloss Real Estate Group, Inc., Birmingham, Ala., 1991—99, LAH Comml. Real Estate, Birmingham, Ala., 1999—. Bd. dirs. Ala. chpt. Cert. Comml. Investment Mem., Birmingham, Ala., 2004—. Author: (short stories) Winter on the Mountain, 1968, The Colemans of Greene County, 1984, Clarence W. Allgood: My Brother's Keeper, 1988, Saint Luke's Episcopal Church: The First Fifty Years, 1999, The Best Poems and Poets of 2004, 2005. Vestryman, jr. warden Grace Episcopal Ch., Anniston, Ala., 1979—82; bd. mem., chmn. of music edn. Ala. Symphony Orch., Birmingham, 1987—90; bd. mem. Shades Valley Edn. Found., Birmingham, Ala., 1993—2006; pres. Oak Hill Meml. Assn., Birmingham, Ala., 2004—06. Lt. USNR, 1963—65. Mem.: Rotary Club of Shades Valley (pres. 1995—96). Office: LAH Comml Real Estate 2850 Cahaba Rd Ste 200 Birmingham AL 35223 Home Phone: 205-533-0523; Office Phone: 205-423-3107. Personal E-mail: sbcoleman@ccim.net.

COLEMAN, STEVEN ANDREW, surveyor; b. Columbus, Ga., Aug. 29, 1958; s. Jim, Jr. and Jackie Coleman; m. Deborah Louise Jones, June 10, 1979; children: Stefanie Lynn, Jessica Ann, James Andrew. Cert., Mid. Ga. Coll., 1990. Registered land surveyor Ga. State Bd. Registration for Profl. Engrs., 1996, broker Ga. Real Estate Bd., 1994. V.p. Mercer Land Surveying, Inc., Forsyth, Ga., 1985—95; dir. of constrn. Ocmulgee Fields, Inc., Macon, Ga., 1996—97; pres., owner Steve Coleman & Assoc., Inc., Forsyth, 1997—. Mem. Mary Persons H.S. Coun., Forsyth, 2001—03; bd. dir. Monroe County Recreation Bd., Forsyth, 1995—97. Recipient Torch award for Marketplace Ethics, BBB of Mid. Ga., 2002. Mem.: Nat. Soc. Profl. Surveyors, Am. Congress on Surveying and Mapping, Surveying and Mapping Soc. Ga., Forsyth-Monroe County C. of C. (bd. dirs. 1996—2001, Golden Nail award 2000), Jaycees (bd. dirs. 1982—83), Mary Persons Touchdown Club (v.p. 2000—01, pres. 2002—03, v.p. 2006), Forsyth Golf Club (bd. dirs. 1999—2002), Rotary (bd. dirs. Forsyth-Monroe county chpt. 1996—97, charter mem.). Avocation: outdoor sports. Office: Steve Coleman & Assoc Inc 38 EJohnston St PO Box 892 Forsyth GA 31029-0892 Office Phone: 478-992-9900. Business E-Mail: steve@steve-coleman.com.

COLEMAN, STUART H., lawyer; b. NYC, Nov. 24, 1954; BA magna cum laude, Wesleyan Univ., 1976; JD cum laude, NYU, 1979. Bar: NY 1980. Assoc. Stroock & Stroock & Lavan LLP, NYC, 1979—87, mem. operating exec. com., 1986—, ptnr., 1988—, co-mng. ptnr., 2003—. Mem.: ABA (Task Force on Fund Director's Guidebook, Task Force on Independent Dir. Counsel), Assn. Bar City NY (chmn., investment mgmt. com.), Order of Coif. Office: Stroock & Stroock & Lavan LLP 180 Maiden Ln New York NY 10038-4982 Office Phone: 212-806-6049. Office Fax: 212-806-9049. Business E-Mail: scoleman@stroock.com.

COLEMAN, TERRY LEWIS, state legislator; b. Dodge County, Ga., Dec. 5, 1943; m. Carol Cofield Coleman; 2 children. AA, Reinhardt Coll., 1979; BS, Brenau Coll., 1981; JD, Woodrow Wilson Coll. Law, 1981. Rep. 144th dist. Ga. Ho. of Reps., 1973—, spkr., 2003—04. Chmn. pub. safety com. Ga. Ho. Reps., 1978—86, chmn. natural resources com., 1987—88, chmn. ways and means com., 1989—90, chmn. appropriations com., mem. budget conf. com., chmn. joint com. budget responsibility oversight com., 1991—2002; pres. Coleman & Co. Benefits; bd. dirs. Bank Dodge County, Colony Bank Corp. Mem. Eastman Vol. Fire Dept.; pres. C. of C., 1985—87; bd. govs. Mercer Med. Sch., 1990—2002. With Ga. N.G. Mem.: Million Dollar round Table, Pacific Mutual Nat. Leaders Club. Democrat. Home: PO Box 157 Eastman GA 31023-0157 Office: Rm 436 18 Capitol Sq Atlanta GA 30334 Office Phone: 478-374-5594. Business E-Mail: terry.coleman@house.ga.gov.

COLEMAN, THOMAS YOUNG, lawyer; b. Richmond, Va., Jan. 6, 1949; s. Emmet Macadium and Mary Katherine (Gay) C.; m. Janet Clare Norris, Aug. 30, 1980; children: Dana Alicia (dec.), Amanda Gay, Blair Norris. BA, U. Va., 1971, JD, 1975. Bar: Va. 1975, U.S. Dist. Ct. (we. dist.)

Va. 1975, U.S. Ct. Appeals (4th cir.) 1976, Calif. 1977, U.S. Dist Ct. (no. dist.) Calif. 1977. Law clk. to Hon. James C. Turk, chief judge U.S. Dist. Ct. (we. dist.) Va., Charlottesville, 1975-76; assoc. Morrison & Foerster LLP, San Francisco, 1976-79; v.p., counsel Calif. 1st Bank (now Union Bank of Calif.), San Francisco, 1979-85; of counsel Orrick, Herrington & Sutcliffe LLP, San Francisco, 1985-86, chmn. profl. devel. com., ptnr., 1987—, gen. counsel, ptnr. in charge profl. devel. Speaker in field; vis. atty. Clifford-Turner Solicitors (now Clifford Chance), London, 1984. Mem. bus. gifts com. San Francisco Symphony. Mem. Internat. Bankers Assn. in Calif. (co-counsel). Office: Orrick Herrington & Sutcliffe LLP 405 Howard St San Francisco CA 94105-2669 Office Phone: 415-773-5870. Office Fax: 415-773-5759. Business E-Mail: tycoleman@orrick.com.

COLEMAN, VIRGINIA FLOOD, lawyer; b. Mt. Kisco, NY, Jan. 1, 1945; d. John Randolph and Enid (Anderson) C. AB magna cum laude, Radcliffe Coll., 1966; JD cum laude, Harvard U., 1970. Bar: Mass. 1970. Law clk. Supreme Jud. Ct. Mass., Boston, 1970-71; assoc. Ropes & Gray, Boston, 1971-84, ptnr., 1984—. Mem. estate planning curriculum adv. com. Mass. Continuing Legal Edn., Boston, 1985—. Treas. Neighborhood Assn. Back Bay, Boston, 1986-88, sec., 1988-90; mem. human subject com. Brigham & Women's Hosp., Boston, 1978—. Recipient Best Lawyers in Am., 1997—2007, Estate Planner of the Year, Boston Estate Planning Coun., 2002, Mass. Super Lawyers, 2004—06, Mass. Super Lawyers Top 50 Women, 2006. Fellow Am. Coll. Trust and Estate Counsel, Internat. Acad. Trust and Estate Counsel (academician); mem. ABA (chmn. com. on fiduciary income taxation of real property, probate and trust law sect. 1989-93), Boston Bar Assn. (tax sect.), mem. Am. Law Inst., Editl. Bd Estate Planning mag., mem. Estate Planning Curriculum Adv. Com. for MCLE, Editl. Bd. Practical Tax Lawyer, Phi Beta Kappa. Avocations: tennis, singing, piano. Office: Ropes & Gray 1 Internat Place Boston MA 02110-2624 Office Phone: 617-951-7213. Office Fax: 617-235-0045. Business E-Mail: virginia.coleman@ropesgray.com.

COLEMAN, WADE HAMPTON, III, management consultant, mechanical engineer, retired banker; b. Tuscaloosa, Ala., June 24, 1932; s. Wade Hampton, Jr. and Margaret Pauline (James) C.; m. Kate Shannon Stabler, June 2, 1958 (div. 1966); children— Shannon Hunter, Wade Hampton IV; m. Eileen Marie Lincoln, Dec. 23, 1967; 1 child, Lydie Elizabeth BA, U. N.C., 1954; BS and BSM.E., U. Ala., 1960; MSI.E., Lehigh U., 1965. Registered profl. engr., Pa. Rsch. engr. Western Electric Co., Princeton, NJ, 1960-65; tech. staff mem. MITRE Corp., Arlington, Va., 1965-66; mgmt. cons. Booz, Allen & Hamilton, Washington, 1967-70; prin. Auerback Corp., Phila., 1970-72; spl. asst. to sec. HEW, Washington, 1972-73; sr. v.p. Citibank, NA, NYC, 1973-85; chmn., chief exec. officer Asbestos Claims Facility Inc, Princeton, NJ, 1985-87; pres. ELW Devel. Group, Lawrenceville, NJ, 1987-89, Coleman & Evans Inc., Princeton, 1989—. Mem. Civic Assn., Lawrenceville, N.J., 1973— , bd. dirs. Lower Eastside Services Ctr., N.Y.C., 1978— , pres. 1986-90; bd. dirs. Capstone Found., Tuscaloosa, 1980—. Served with USN, 1954-57, lt. comdr. res. ret. Mem. Nat. Soc. Profl. Engrs., Am. Bankers Assn., Sigma Pi Sigma, Tau Beta Pi, Delta Kappa Epsilon Republican. Episcopalian. Home: 4 Monroe Ave Lawrenceville NJ 08648-1606

COLEMAN, WILLIAM T., information technology executive; b. Oct. 1947; m. Claudia L. Coleman. BS, US Air Force Acad.; MS, Stanford U. With Sun Microsystems, Inc., 1985—95, v.p., gen. mgr. Sun Profl. Svcs.; co-founder BEA Sys., Inc., 1995, CEO, 1995—2001, chmn. bd. dirs., 1995—2002, chief strategy officer, 2001—02; co-founder, chmn. bd., CEO Cassatt Corp., 2003—. Bd. dirs. Symantec Corp., 2003—. Co-founder Coleman Inst. Cognitive Disabilities, U. Colo. Office: Cassatt Corp 1740 Technology Dr, 6th Fl San Jose CA 95110

COLEMAN, WILLIAM THADDEUS, JR., lawyer, former secretary of transportation; b. Germantown, Pa., July 7, 1920; s. William Thaddeus and Laura Beatrice (Mason) Coleman; m. Lovida Hardin, Feb. 10, 1945; children: William Thaddeus III, Lovida Hardin Jr., Hardin L. AB summa cum laude, U. Pa., 1941; LLB magna cum laude, Harvard U., 1943. Bar: Pa. 1947, DC 1977. Law sec. Judge Herbert F. Goodrich, U.S. Ct. of Appeals, 3d Cir., 1947—48, Justice Felix Frankfurter (assoc. justice Supreme Ct. U.S.), 1948—49; assoc. Paul, Weiss, Rifkind, Wharton & Garrison, NYC, 1949—52, Dilworth, Paxson, Kalish, Levy & Green, Phila., 1952—56; ptnr. Dilworth, Paxson, Kalish, Levy & Coleman, 1956—75; sec. US Dept. Transp., Washington, 1975—77; sr. counselor, sr. ptnr. O'Melveny & Myers, various locations, 1977—. Spl. counsel for transit matters City of Phila., 1952—63; rep. atty. gen. Pa. and Commonwealth of Pa. in litig. to remove racial restrictions at Girard Coll., 1965; mem. Pres.'s Com. on Govt. Employment Policy, 1959—61; cons. ACDA, 1963—74; sr. cons., asst. counsel Pres.'s Commn. on Assassination of Pres. Kennedy, 1964; co-chmn. planning sessions White House Conf. to Fulfill These Rights, 1965—66; mem. U.S. del. 24th Session UN Gen. Assembly, 1969; mem. legal adv. com. Coun. on Environ. Quality, 1970; pub. mem. Pres.'s Nat. Commn. on Productivity, 1970; commr. Price Commn., 1971—72, Phila. Fairmount Pk. Commn., 1967—75, White House Commn. Aviations Safety and Security, 1996—97; mem. Gov.'s Commn. on Constl. Revision, 1963—65; mem. mil. tribunal, appellate, maj. Guantanamo Bay, Cuba, 2004—. Contbr. articles to profl. jours. Former chmn. bd. NAACP Legal Def. and Ednl. Fund; v.p., trustee, mem. exec. com. Phila. Art Mus.; trustee Brookings Instn., Nat. Gallery Art, 1999; mem. Trilateral Commn.; mem. exec. com. Lawyers Com. for Civil Rights Under Law; bd. overseers Harvard U., 1975—81; bd. dirs., adv. dir. NY City Ballet. Decorated officer French Legion of Honor; recipient Joseph E. Beale prize, 1946, Presdl. Freedom medal, Pres. Clinton, 1995, NAACP Legal Def. Fund Thurgood Marshall Lifetime Achievement award, 1997, Marshall Wythe medallion, 2003, Chief Justice John Marshall award, ABA, Lifetime Achievement award, The Am. Lawyer, 2004, Golden Plate award, Acad. Achievement, 2006; Langdell fellow, 1946—47. Fellow: Am. Coll. Trial Lawyers; mem.: Coun. Fgn. Rels., Am. Arbitration Assn. (gov.), Am. Acad. Arts and Scis., Am. Philos. Soc., Phila. Bar Assn. (past chmn. jud. com.), Am. Law Inst. (coun., Henry J. Friendly medal 2000), Am. Acad. Appellate Lawyers, Met. Club (Washington), Jr. Legal Club (Phila.), Alfalfa Club, Cosmos Club, Order of Coif, Harvard Law Sch. Club, Pi Gamma Nu (Wickersham award 1997, The Fordham-Stein prize 2000), Phi Beta Kappa. Office: O'Melveny & Myers 1625 Eye St NW Washington DC 20006 Office Phone: 202-383-5325. E-mail: wcoleman@omm.com.

COLEMAN SMITH, SALAAM, communications executive; b. 1970; m. Christopher Smith; 1 child, Asa. BS in Indsl. Engring., Stanford U. Mgmt. cons.; v.p., Programming Nickelodeaon/Nick at Nite; programming and creative exec. MTV Networks; sr. v.p., Programming E! Networks, 2003—06; sr. v.p. Style Network, E! Entertainment, Inc., 2006, exec. v.p., 2006—. Prin. mem. strategic planning team, Nickelodeon Networks. Named one of Top 35 Executives Under 35, Hollywood Reporter, 2003, 40 Executives Under 40, Multichannel News, 2006; Walter Kaitz Found. Cable TV Industry fellowship. Office: E! Entertainment Television Inc 5750 Wilshire Blvd Los Angeles CA 90036

COLEN, DAN, artist; b. Leonia, NJ, 1979; BFA in Painting, RI Sch. Design, 2001. Prin. works include Secrets and Cymbals, Smoke and Scissors (My Friend Dash's Wall in the Future), 2004—06, Untitled (going, going, go.), 2005, Holy War, 2006, The Awesome Power of Nature, 2006, Rama Lama Ding Dong, 2006, Untitled (Vete al Diablo), 2006, Self Portrait as the Wanderer, Madonna and the Fairy, The Cloud and the Ghost, Me, Jesus and the Children, The Firecracker and the Old Man, solo exhibitions, Seven Days Always Seemed Like Bit of An Exaggeration, Rivington Arms, NY, 2003, Potty Mouth, Potty War, Pot Roast, Pot is a Reality Kick, Gagosian Gallery, NYC, 2006, Secrets and Cymbals, Smoke and Scissors (My Friend Dash's Wall in the Future), Deitch Projects, NY, 2006, Secrets and Cymbals, Smoke and Scissors (My Friend Dash's Wall in the Future), Peres Projects, LA, 2006, group exhibitions, First Show, Rivington Arms, NY, 2002, Art Works for Hard Money, Gavin Brown's Enterprise, 2003, Galerie du Jour, Paris, Whitney Biennial: Day for Night, Whitney Mus. Am. Art, NYC, 2006, The Armory Show with Peres Projects, NY, 2005, Bridge Freezes Before Road, Barbara Gladstone Gallery, 2005, Interstate, Nicole Klagsbrun Gallery, NY, 2005, Infinate Painting with Villa Manin-Centre for Contemporary Art, Passariano, Codroipo, Italy, 2006, Axis of Praxis, Midway Contemporary Art, Mpls., Minn., 2006, USA Today, Royal Acad. Arts, London, 2006, Fantastic Politics, Nat. Mus. Art, Architecture and Design, Oslo, Norway, 2006. Mailing: c/o Rivington Arms 102 Rivington St New York NY 10002

COLEN, FREDERICK HAAS, lawyer; b. Pitts., May 16, 1947; married, 1972. BSChemE, Tufts U., 1969; JD, Emory U., 1975. Bar: Pa. 1975, Ga. 1975, U.S. Patent Office 1976, U.S. Dist. Ct. (we. dist.) Pa. 1975, U.S. Dist. Ct. (no. dist.) Ga. 1975, U.S. Ct. Appeals (fed. and 3d cirs.) 1975, U.S. Supreme Ct. 1980. Chem. engr. Shell Oil Co., New Orleans, 1969-71; san. engr. USPHS, Morgantown, W.Va., 1971-73; patent atty. Mobay Chem. Corp., Pitts., 1975-79; assoc. Reed Smith, LLP, Pitts., 1979-86, ptnr., 1986—. Contbr. articles to profl. jours. Mem. ABA, Allegheny County Bar Assn., Pa. Bar Assn., Ga. Bar Assn., Am. Intellectual Property Law Assn. Home: 4940 Ellsworth Ave Pittsburgh PA 15213-2807 Office: Reed Smith LLP 435 6th Ave Pittsburgh PA 15219-1886 Office Phone: 412-288-4164. Business E-Mail: fcolen@reedsmith.com.

COLEN, HELEN SASS, plastic surgeon; b. Bytom, Poland, Jan. 9, 1947; came to the U.S., 1963; d. Karl Julius and Sabina (Orgel) Sass; m. Stephen Robert Colen, Mar. 25, 1972; children: Kari, Michael. BA, NYU, 1968, MD, 1972. Diplomate Am. Bd. Plastic Surgery. Intern Jefferson U. Hosp., 1972-74; gen. surgeon U. Colo., Denver, 1974-79; plastic surgeon U. Columbia-St. Lukes, NYC, 1979-81; microsurgeon Bellevue Hosp., NYC, 1981-82; practice medicine specializing in plastic surgery NYC, 1982—. Fellow ACS; mem. Am. Soc. Plastic Surgeons, Am. Soc. Aesthetic Plastic Surgery, Phi Beta Kappa. Office: 742 Park Ave New York NY 10021-3553 Home Phone: 212-249-8376; Office Phone: 212-772-1300.

COLEN, STEPHEN R., plastic and reconstructive surgeon; b. NYC, Feb. 11, 1947; s. Leslie Colen and Ruth Mintz; m. Helen Sass, Mar. 25, 1972; children: Kari, Michael. Bachelor's degree, St. Lawrence U., 1967; DDS, NYU, 1971; MD, Hahnemann U., 1974. Surgeon NYU Hosp., NYC, 1982—; clin. asst. plastic surgery Bellvue Hosp., NYC, 1982—; attending physician plastic surgery N.Y. Vets. Hosp., NYC, 1983—; attending surgeon Manhattan Eye, Ear & Throat, NYC, 1983—, Beth Israel North Hosp., NYC, 1994—; assoc. prof. plastic surgery NYU Med. Ctr., 2003—; chief dept. plastic surgery Hackensack U. Hosp., 2003—. Attending N.Y. Eye and Ear Infirmarmy, N.Y.C., 1983—; mem. surg. case rev. com. NYU Med. Ctr., N.Y.C., 1987—, mem. ednl. com., 1988—; mem. utilization rev. com. Bellvue Hosp., N.Y.C., 1984—. Mem. Am. Assn. Plastic Surgeons, Am. Soc. Plastic Surgeons, N.Y. Regional Med. Soc., Westchester Country Club, Olde Fla. Golf Club, Univ. Club. Office: 742 Park Ave New York NY 10021 Home Phone: 212-249-8376; Office Phone: 212-988-8900. E-mail: scolen47@aol.com.

COLES, ANNA LOUISE BAILEY, retired dean, nurse; b. Kansas City, Kans., Jan. 16, 1925; d. Gordon Alonzo and Lillie Mai (Buchanan) Bailey; children: Margot, Michelle, Gina. Diploma, Freedmen's Hosp. Sch. Nursing, 1948; BSN, Avila Coll., Kansas City, Mo., 1958; MSN, Cath. U. Am., 1960, PhD in Higher Edn., 1967. Instr. VA Hosp., Topeka, 1950—52, supr. Kansas City, Mo., 1952—58; asst. dir. in-service edn. Freedmen's Hosp., Washington, 1960—61, adminstrv. asst. to DON, 1961—66, assoc. dir. nursing services, 1966—67, DON, 1967—69; dean Howard U. Coll. Nursing, Washington, 1968—86, dean emeritus, 1986—; pvt. practice Kansas City, Kans.; dir. minority devel. U. Kans., 1991—95. Pres. Nurses Examining Bd., 1967—68; cons. Gen. Rsch. Support Program, NIH, 1972—76; mem. Inst. Medicine, NAS, 1974—; cons. VA Ctrl. Office continuing edn. com., 1976—; mem. D.C. Health Planning Adv. Com., 1967—68, Tri-State Regional Planning Com. for Nursing Edn., 1969, Health Adv. Coun., Nat. Urban Coalition, 1971—73; bd. dirs. Hilton Grand Vacation CLub Seaworld Internat. Ctr. Contbr. articles to profl. jours. Trustee Cmty. Group Health Found., 1976—77, cons., 1977—; bd. regents State Univ. Sys. Fla., 1977; adv. bd. Am. Assn. Med. Vols., 1970—72; bd. dirs. Iona Whipper Home for Unwed Mothers, 1970—72, Nursing Edn. Opportunities, 1970—72. Recipient Sustained Superior Performance award, HEW, 1962, Meritorious Pub. Svc. award, Govt. of D.C., 1968, medal of honor, Avila Coll., 1969, Disting. Alumni award, Howard U. Nat. Assn. for Equal Opportunity in Higher Edn., 1990, Cmty. Svc. award, Black Profl. Nurses Kansas City, 1991, Lifetime Achievement award, Assn. Black Nursing Faculty in Higher Edn., 1993, Svc. award, Midwest Regional Conf. on Black Families and Children, 1994, Alumni award in Nursing, Avila U., 2006. Mem.: ANA, Am. Assn. Colls. Nursing (sec. 1975—76), Am. Congress Rehab. Medicine, Nat. League Nursing, Societas Docta (charter, pres. 1996—99), Freedmen's Hosp. Nursing Alumni Assn., Alpha Kappa Alpha, Sigma Theta Tau. Home: 15107 Interlachen Dr Apt 315 Silver Spring MD 20906-5627

COLES, DONALD EARL, retired engineering educator; b. St. Paul, Feb. 8, 1924; s. Courtney J. and Lorna (Addison) C.; m. Ellen Searight, Sept. 11, 1947; children: Christopher Lee, Elizabeth Anne, Kenneth Spencer, Janet Jacqueline. B.Aero. Engring., U. Minn., 1947; MS, Calif. Inst. Tech., 1948, PhD, 1953. Research engr. Jet Propulsion Lab., Pasadena, Calif., 1950-53; research fellow Calif. Inst. Tech., Pasadena, 1953-56, mem. faculty, 1953-96, prof. aeros., 1964-96; ret., 1996. Cons. to industry, 1954—; mem. Nat. Com. Fluid Mechs. Films, 1960 Producer ednl. film Channel Flow of a Compressible Fluid, 1966. With US Army, 1943—46. Fellow AIAA (Lawrence Sperry award 1953, Dryden medal 1985), Am. Phys. Soc. (Otto Laporte award 1996); mem. Nat. Acad. Engring., Sigma Xi. Home: 1033 Alta Pine Dr Altadena CA 91001-1409

COLES, GRAHAM, conductor, composer; b. London, May 7, 1948; arrived in Canada, 1951; s. Walter Harold and Phyllis Irene Gwendoline (Conn) C. MusB, U. Toronto, 1972, MusM, 1974, EdB, 1991. Music dir. Kitchener-Waterloo (Ont.) Chamber Orch., 1985—; rental agt. Berandol Music Ltd. Examiner emeritus coll. of examiners Royal Conservatory of Music, Toronto. Composer numerous instrumental and vocal compositions. Mem. Can. League Composers, Can. Music Ctr. (assoc. composer), Assn. Can. Orchs. Home: 86 Weber St E Kitchener ON Canada N2H 1C7 Office Phone: 519-744-3828. E-mail: kwchamberorchestra@on.aibn.com.

COLES, JOANNA, magazine editor-in-chief; BA in British & Am. Lit., U. East Anglia. With The Daily Telegraph, BBC2 TV, BBC Radio, The Guardian; NY bur. chief The Times of London, 1998—2001; articles and features editor New York mag., 2001—04; exec. editor More, 2004—06; editor-in-chief Marie Claire, NYC, 2006—. Co-host on XM Radio's Take Five channel. Mem.: Am. Friends of Royal Ct. Theater (founding mem.). Office: Marie Claire 1790 Broadway, 3rd Fl New York NY 10019 Office Phone: 212-649-5000. Office Fax: 212-649-5050.

COLES, LAVERANUES, professional football player; b. Jacksonville, Fla., Dec. 29, 1977; s. Sirretta Willaims. Degree, Fla. State U. Wide receiver NY Jets, 2000—02, 2005—, Washington Redskins, 2003—04. Named to Pro Bowl, 2003. Office: NY Jets 1000 Fulton Ave Hempstead NY 11550

COLES, MARTIN, beverage company executive; b. Cardiff, Wales, July 24, 1955; BS biochemistry, U. of Wales, 1977. Mgr. prodn. Proctor & Gamble; v.p. manufacturing, logistics, customer service, and franchised bottling ops. PepsiCo, 1987—92; dir, Logistics for Europe NIKE Inc., 1992—94; v.p., gen. mgr. Nike Europe, 1994—97; exec. v.p., global sales Nike Inc., 1997—2000; pres., CEO Letsbuyit.com, 2000—01; sr. v.p. Internat Ops. Gateway, Inc., 2001; exec. v.p. of Global Operating Units Reebok Internat., Ltd., 2001—02, exec. v.p., 2001—04, pres., CEO, 2002—04; pres. Starbucks Coffee Internat., 2004—07; COO Starbucks Corp., 2007—. Office: Starbucks Corp 2401 Utah Ave S Seattle WA 98134 Office Phone: 206-447-1575. Office Fax: 206-682-7570.*

COLES, ROBERT, child psychiatrist, educator, writer; b. Boston, Oct. 12, 1929; s. Philip and Sandra (Young) C.; m. Jane Hallowell; children— Robert, Daniel, Michael. AB, Harvard U., 1950; MD, Columbia U., 1954; MD (hon.), Temple U., 1972, Bates Coll., Notre Dame U., Holy Cross Coll.; MD, Wayne State U., 1973, Western Mich. U., 1974, Hofstra U., 1975, Coll. William and Mary, 1976, Rutgers U., 1977, Knox Coll., 1978, Colby Coll., 1981, Sienna Heights Coll., 1983, Beloit Coll., 1984, Emory U., 1986, Dartmouth Coll., 1987. Intern U. Chgo. Clinics, 1954-55; resident in psychiatry Mass. Gen. Hosp., Boston, 1955-56, McLean Hosp., Belmont, Mass., 1956-57, Judge Baker Guidance Center-Children's Hosp., 1957-58; mem. staff children's Unit Met. State Hosp., Waltham, Mass., 1957-58; mem. staff alcoholic clinic Mass. Gen. Hosp.; teaching fellow in psychiatry, mem. psychiat. staff and clin. asst. in psychiatry Harvard Med. Sch., 1955-58; research psychiatrist Harvard U. Health Services, 1963—; lectr. gen. edn. Harvard U., 1966—, prof. psychiatry and med. humanities, 1977—; founder and editor DoubleTake Magazine, 1995—. Child psychiat. fellow Judge Baker Guidance Center, Children's Hosp., Boston, 1960-61; mem. Nat. Adv. Com. on Farm Labor, 1965—; cons. Appalachian Vols., 1965— , Rockefeller Found., 1969— , Ford Found., 1969—; mem. Inst. of Medicine, Nat. Acad. Scis., 1973-78; vis. prof. public policy Duke U., 1973—; cons. supr. dept. psychiatry Cambridge (Mass.) Hosp., 1976—; cons. Center for Study of So. Culture, U. Miss., 1979—; bd. dirs. Ctr. for Documentary Studies, Duke U.; vis. prof. psychiatry, Dartmouth Coll., 1989. Author: Children of Crisis: A Study of Courage and Fear, 1967, Dead End School, 1968, Still Hungry in America, 1969, The Grass Pipe, 1969, The Image is Yours, 1969; Wages of Neglect, 1969, Uprooted Children: The Early Lives of Migrant Farmers, 1970, Teachers and the Children of Poverty, 1970, Erik H. Erikson: The Growth of His Work, 1970, The Middle Americans, 1970, Migrants, Sharecroppers and Mountaineers, 1972, The South Goes North, 1972, Saving Face, 1972, Farewell to the South, 1972, A Spectacle Unto the World, 1973, Riding Free, 1973, The Darkness and the Light, 1974, The Buses Roll, 1974, Irony in the Mind's Life: Essays on Novels by James Agee, Elizabeth Bowen and George Eliot, 1974, Headsparks, 1975, The Mind's Fate, 1975, Eskimos, Chicanos and Indians, 1978, Privileged Ones, Vol. V of Children in Crisis book series, 1978, (with Jane Hallowell Coles) Women of Crisis Lives of Struggle and Hope, 1978, Walker Percy: An American Search, 1978, Flannery O'Connor's South, 1980, Women of Crisis; Lives of Work and Dreams, 1980, Dorothea Lange: Photographs of a Lifetime, 1982, (with Ross Spears) Agee, 1985, The Political Life of Children, 1986, Dorothy Day: A Radical Devotion, 1987, Simone Weil: A Modern Pilgrimage, 1987, Times of Surrender: Selected Essays, 1988, Harvard Diary, 1988, That Red Wheelbarrow, 1988, The Call of Stories: Teaching and the Moral Imagination, 1989, Rumors of Separate Worlds, 1989, The Spiritual Life of Children, 1990; contbg. editor: The New Republic, 1966— , Am. Poetry Rev, 1972— , Aperture, 1974— , Lit. and Medicine, 1981— , New Oxford Rev, 1981—; mem. editorial bd.: Integrated Edn., 1967— , Child Psychiatry and Human Devel., 1969— , Rev. of Books and Religion, 1976— , Internat. Jour. Family Therapy, 1977— , Grants mag., 1977— , Learning mag., 1978— , Jour. Am. Culture, 1977— , Jour. Edn., 1979—; bd. editors: Parents' Choice, 1978—; editor: Children and Youth Services Rev., 1978—. Bd. dirs. Field Found., 1968—; trustee Robert F. Kennedy Meml., 1968— , Robert F. Kennedy Action Corps, State of Mass., 1968— , Miss. Inst. Early Childhood Edn., 1968— , Twentieth Century Fund, 1971—; bd. dirs. Reading is Fundamental, Smithsonian Inst., 1968— , Am. Freedom from Hunger Found., 1968— , Am. Parents Com., 1971—; mem. corp. Boston Children's Service, 1970; mem. adv. council Inst. for Nonviolent Social Change of Martin Luther King, Jr. Meml. Center, 1971— , Ams. for Children's Relief, 1972—; mem. nat. com. for Edn. of Young Children, 1972—; mem. nat. adv. council Rural Am., 1976—; trustee Austen Riggs Found., Stockbridge, Mass., 1976—; mem. nat. adv. com. Ala. Citizens for Responsive Public Television, 1976—; mem. adv. com. Nat. Indian Edn. Assn., 1976—; visitor's com. mem. Boston Mus. Fine Arts, 1977; bd. dirs. Boys Club Boston, 1977; vis. com. Boston Coll. Law Sch., 1977; adv. Center for So. Folklore, 1978—; mem. children's com. Edna McConnell Clark Found., 1978—; bd. dirs. Lyndhurst Found., 1978—; mem. nat. adv. bd. Foxfire Fund, Inc., 1979—. Recipient Ralph Waldo Emerson prize Phi Beta Kappa, 1967; Anisfield-Wolf award in race relations Saturday Rev., 1968; Hofheimer award Am. Psychiat. Assn., 1968; Sidney Hillman prize, 1971; Weatherford prize Berea Coll. and Council So. Mountains, 1973; Lilliam Smith Award So. Regional Council, 1973; McAlpin medal Nat. Assn. Mental Health, 1972; Pulitzer prize, 1973 (all received for Children of Crisis, Vols. II, III); disting. scholar medal Hofstra U., 1974; William A. Shonfeld award Am. Soc. Adolescent Psychiatry, 1977; MacArthur Found. award, 1981; Josepha Hale award, 1986; fellow Davenport Coll., Yale U., 1976— Fellow Am. Acad. Arts and Scis., Inst. Soc., Ethics and the Life Scis.; mem. Am. Psychiat. Assn., Am. Orthopsychiat. Assn. (past dir.), Acad. Psychoanalysis, Nat. Orgn. Migrant Children. Home: PO Box 674 Concord MA 01742-0674

COLES, ROBERT NELSON, SR., religious organization administrator; b. Aug. 1, 1929; married; 6 children. Grad., Salvation Army Officers Coll., 1956; postgrad., DePaul U., 1968. Ordained minister 1956. Field officer Salvation Army, 1960-68; with Vols. Am., 1946-55, 60-80; editor-in-chief Rescue Herald Orgn. Am. Rescue Workers, Phila., 1981-92, ordination com. chmn., dir. spl. svcs., 1988-96; nat. comm. sec. Am. Rescue Workers, 1980—, nat. info. officer, 2003—, also nat. bd. mgrs., 1956-2001. Chmn. ordination com., 2002, aid-de-camp to gen. Am. Rescue Workers, 1985-96. Editor-in-chief Rescue Herald 1988-2003. Nat. info. officer Comty. Svc. Coun.; organizer numerous youth baseball and basketball teams, and semi-profl. football team Vols. Am., Elmira, N.Y.; established 3 group homes for children from broken homes, Hagerstown, Md., 1969-81; dir. food program Am. Rescue Workers, Phila., 1981-92. Named to Elmira Sports Hall of Fame, 1990. Mem. Am. Correctional Chaplains Assn., Am. Correction Assn., Md. State Sheriff's Assn., Washington County Ministerial (treas. 1993-94), Scottish Rite Bodies, Masons (32 degree), Hagerstown Exch. Club. Office: Am Rescue Workers Nat Field Office 11116 Gehr Rd Waynesboro PA 17268 Office Phone: 717-762-2965. Personal E-mail: bigchief@comcast.net.

COLES, ROBERT TRAYNHAM, architect; b. Buffalo, Aug. 24, 1929; s. George Edward and Helena Vesta (Traynham) C.; m. Sylvia Rose Meyn, Mar. 28, 1953; children: Marion Brigette, Darcy Eliot. Student, Hampton Inst., Va., 1949; BA, U. Minn., Mpls., 1951, BArch, 1953; MArch, MIT, Cambridge, 1955; DLitt (hon.), Medaille Coll., Buffalo, 1977. Designer, Perry, Shaw, Hepburn and Dean (Architects), Boston, 1956-57, Shepley, Bulfinch, Richardson and Abbott (Architects), Boston, 1957-58, Carl Koch and Asso., Cambridge, Mass., 1958-59; architect, custom design mgr. Techbuilt, Inc. (housing prefabricators), Cambridge, 1959-60; coordinating architect Deleuw, Cather and Brill, Engrs., Buffalo, 1960-63; prin. Robert Traynham Coles, Architect, P.C., Buffalo, 1963—; Langston Hughes Disting. prof. architecture and urban design U. Kans., 1989. V.p. Buffalo Archtl. Guidebook Corp., 1979-82; cons. housing rsch. Union Carbide Corp., 1963; vis. prof. SUNY, Buffalo, summer 1967, U. Kans., 1969; v.p.

Eastside Cmty. Orgn. Inc., 1965-68, pres., 1968-77; chmn. Com. for an Urban U., 1966-67, Goals for Met. Buffalo, 1967-68; pres. Cmty. Planning Assistance Ctr. Western N.Y., Inc., 1972-74, Archtl. Mus. and Resource Ctr., 1980-84; mem. N.Y. State Bd. for Architecture, 1984-94, vice chmn., 1990, chmn., 1991; assoc. prof. architecture Carnegie Mellon U., Pitts., 1990-95; mem. jury U.S. Post Office Nat. Design Competition, Wash., D.C., 1994, City Plaza Nat. Design Competition, Lexington, Ky., 2001; chair jury, N.Y. State Assn. Architects Design Awards, N.Y.C., 1995. Treas., v.p., editor (newsletter) Nat. Orgn. Minority Architects, 1972—80, contbr. The Urban Ecosystem: A Holistic Approach, 1974, exhibitor Design Diaspora, Black Architects and International Architecture, 1970-1990, Chgo. Athenaeum, 1993, Robert Traynham Coles: Architect, Buffalo, N.Y., 1996, Between Tradition and Memory: Constructed Shleters, Black Architects, Inst. Rsch. African Diaspora in Americas and Caribbean, N.Y.C., 1999, Robert Traynham Coles: Inner City Architect, Buffalo and Erie County Hist. Soc., Buffalo, N.Y., 2002. Mem. coun. Burchfield Art Ctr., Buffalo, 1989-92, nat. adv. com. Arts in Am., 1989, Erie County Horizons Waterfront Commn., 1988-91; bd. dirs. Build a New City, Inc., 1973-75; trustee Preservation League N.Y. State, sec., 1978; trustee Western N.Y. PBS, 1981-87, hon. trustee, 1987—. Named Citizen of Distinction, Mayor of Buffalo, NY, 1997, An Uncrowned King, The Uncrowned Queens Inst. for Rsch. and Edn. on Women, Inc., 2007; recipient Centennial award, Medaille Coll., 1975, Alumni Achievement award, U. Minn. Coll. Architecture and Landscape Architecture, 1997, William Wells Brown award, Afro-Am. Hist. Assn. of the Niagara Frontier, Inc., 2007; Edward H. Moeller scholar, 1949—53, Rotch Traveling scholar, Boston Soc. Archs., 1955. Fellow AIA (mem. nat. housing com. 1969-71, nat. urban design and planning com. 1971-73, chmn. social responsibility com. Buffalo-Western N.Y. chpt. 1970-71, dir. 1978-81, nat. dep. v.p. minority affairs 1974-75, sec. Coll. of Fellows 1991-93, vice-chancellor 1993-94, chancellor 1995, Whitney E. Young award 1981, James William Kideney award N.Y. State chpt. 2004); mem. Nat. Orgn. Minority Architects (treas. 1976-78, dir. 1978, v.p. 1978), Alpha Kappa Mu. Home: 321 Humboldt Pkwy Buffalo NY 14208-1023 Office: 730 Ellicott St Buffalo NY 14203-1102 Office Phone: 716-842-2280. Personal E-mail: rtcoles.arch@dservmail.com. *Because they have the ability to see things as they can be, today's architects have a special task which goes beyond simply designing the physical environment. They must be activists involved in the social and political life of the community. They must address their efforts to change in these areas as well, so that people can make the needed adjustments to an increasingly challenging and rich urban world. They must, in their works, build the demonstrative alternative to the way we live today. They must be initiators as well as implementors—leaders more than followers. They must truly be revolutionaries who see their architecture as a broad movement to enchance the quality of life of urban people.*

COLES, WILLIAM HENRY, ophthalmologist, educator; b. Rochester, NY; BA, Ohio Wesleyan U., 1958; MD, Emory U., 1962; MS, La. State U., 1970. Diplomate Am. Bd. Ophthalmology. Intern Grady Hosp., Atlanta, 1962-63; resident Charity-La. State U., New Orleans, 1966-70; prof. ophthalmology Emory U., Atlanta, 1980-86, dir. postgrad. edn., 1981-86; prof. ophthalmology SUNY, Buffalo, 1986—, chmn. dept., 1986—. Clin. assoc. prof. Med. Univ. S.C., Charleston, 1980-86; chief of svc. Grady Meml. Hosp., Atlanta, 1981-84; chief ophthalmology svc. VA Hosp., Atlanta, 1984-86; chmn. adv. coun. Ophthalmic Surgery, 1998. Author: Ophthalmology: A Diagnostic Text, 1989; sect. editor: Medicine for the Practicing Physician, 1984 (Med. Textbook of Yr. award). Dir. Inst. Health Assessment, 1997—2000. Nat. Eye Inst. grantee, 1975-78. Mem. AMA, ACS (chair adv. coun. 1997—99, regent 1998-2004), AAUP, Am. Acad. Ophthalmology (Disting. Svc. award 1989, sr. honor award 1998), Med. Soc. State of N.Y., Assn. Rsch. and Vision in Ophthalmology, Assn. Univ. Profs. in Ophthalmology (trustee, pres. 1996-97). Home: 303 Old Franklin Grove Chapel Hill NC 27514

COLESCOTT, WARRINGTON WICKHAM, artist, printmaker, educator; b. Oakland, Calif., Mar. 7, 1921; s. Warrington W. and Lydia (Hutton) C.; m. Frances Myers, Mar. 15, 1971; children by previous marriage: Louis Moore, Julian Hutton, Lydia Alice. AB, U. Calif., Berkeley, 1942, MA, 1947; postgrad., Acad. de la Grand Chaumiere, Paris, France, 1950-53, Slade Sch. Art, U. London (Eng.), 1957. Mem. faculty U. Wis., Madison, 1949-86, prof. art, 1957-86, Leo Steppat chair, prof., 1979-85, Leo Steppat chair (emeritus prof.), 1986—. Printmaker emeritus So. Graphics Coun., 1991; academician Nat. Acad. One-man shows include Perimeter Gallery, Chgo., 1985, 87-88, 91, 93, 95, 99, 2002, 05, Elvehjem Mus., Madison, Wis., 1989, Peltz Gallery, Milw., 2001, 04, 06, Quedlinburg, Germany, 2006; exhibited in group shows at Nelson-Atkins Mus., Kansas City, 1990, New Orleans Mus. Art, 2003, Milw. Art Mus. Retrospective, 2005, Ark. State U., Jonesboro, 2005 (Purchase award); represented in permanent collections Mus. Modern Art, Victoria and Albert Mus., London, Bibliotechque Nat., Paris, Met. Mus., Chgo. Art Inst., Bklyn. Mus., Phila. Mus. Art, Milw. Art Mus., Elvehjem Art Mus., Whitney Mus. Am. Art, Corcoran Gallery Art, Fogg Art Mus. Harvard U., Nat. Acad., NY; co-author (with Arthur Hove) Progressive Printmakers, 1999; etchings commd. Milw. Art Mus., NY Print Club, 2002, Corcoran Gallery Art, Washington, 2005 Fulbright fellow, 1957, Guggenheim fellow, 1965, Nat. Endowment Arts Printmaking fellow, 1975, Artist fellow, 1979, 83-84, 93-94; recipient Print award NAD, 1991-92, 95, 97, NSAL Award of Excellence, 1993, 99, award Internat. Triennial of Print, Cracow, Poland, 1997, award Boston Printmakers, 2003, Lifetime Achievement in Printmaking award So. Graphics Coun., 2006, Andrew Carnegie prize Printing, 2006. Fellow Wis. Acad. Sci. Arts and Letters. Office: 8788 County Hwy A Hollandale WI 53544-9801

COLESSIDES, NICK JOHN, lawyer; b. Kavala, Greece, Jan. 14, 1938; came to U.S., 1958; s. John T. and Maroula C.; m. Sophia Simons Symeonidis, Oct. 5, 1970. BS in Polit. Sci., U. Utah, 1963, MS Polit. Sci., 1967, JD, 1970. Bar: Utah 1970, U.S. Dist. Ct. Utah 1970, U.S. Ct. Appeals (10th cir.) 1970, U.S. Dist. Ct. (so. dist.) Ohio 1975, U.S. Ct. Appeals (9th cir.) 1976. Chief deputy county atty. Salt Lake County (Utah) Atty.'s Office, 1970-74; city atty. West Jordan (Utah) City Atty.'s Office, 1971-78, Park City (Utah) Atty.'s Office, 1976-80; atty. pvt. practice, Salt Lake City, 1970—. Bd. dirs. Merrill Lynch Bank, U.S.A., Salt Lake City City. Trustee Greek Orthodox Ch., SaltLake City, 1976, 77, 87, 88, 98, 99, Utah Cmty. Reinvestment Corp. Mem. Assn. Trial Lawyers Am., Utah Trial Lawyers Assn., U. Utah Coll. of Law Alumni Assn. (trustee 1995-98), Utah State Bar Assn., Salt Lake County Bar Assn., Am. Inn of Ct. VII (master of the bench, pres. 1997, 98). Greek Orthodox. Avocations: gardening, cooking, reading. Office: 466 S 400 E Ste 100 Salt Lake City UT 84111-3301 Home: Apt 410 150 S 300 E Salt Lake City UT 84111-2087

COLETTA, GERARD CHARLES, management consultant; b. Cambridge, Mass., Dec. 9, 1944; s. Gerard Charles and Eileen Gertrude (Barrett) C.; m. Pamela S. Wight, June 30, 1984; children: Nadine, Sean. BSChemE, Tufts U., 1966; MSChemE, MIT, 1968; postgrad., U. Calif., Berkeley, 1969-71. Design engr. Standard Oil of Calif., San Francisco, 1968-71; staff cons. Arthur D. Little, Inc., Cambridge, 1971-78; corp. dir. of safety and health Nat. Semiconductor Corp., Santa Clara, Calif., 1978-81; sr. cons. Risk Planning Group, Darien, Conn., 1981-83; pres. Risk Control Services, Tiburon, Calif., 1983-86; prin. and practice mgr. Tillinghast div. Towers Perrin Co., San Francisco, 1986-91; sr. v.p., nat. practice mgr., bus. continuity cons. Marsh USA (formerly Sedgwick of Calif.), San Francisco, 1991-2000; v.p., nat. practice leader, bus. continuity cons. Palmer & Cay, Boston, 2000—04; nat. practice leader bus. continuing cons. Milliman Inc., Wakefield, Mass., 2004—. Spkr. in field. Contbr. articles to profl. jours. Mem. ASTM (chmn. com. 1980-85, bd. dirs. sub-com. 1987-91, Spl. Service award 1985, Achievement award 1986), Am. Soc. Safety Engrs., Nat. Safety Mgmt. Soc., Tufts U. Chem. Engring. Alumni Council, Tau Beta Pi. Republican. Avocations: tennis, skiing, jogging. Office: Milliman Inc 289 Edgewater Dr Wakefield MA 01880 Home Phone: 978-369-6789; Office Phone: 781-213-6277. Business E-Mail: jerry.coletta@milliman.com.

COLETTA, RALPH JOHN, retired lawyer; b. Chillicothe, Ill., Dec. 13, 1921; s. Joseph and Assunta Maria (Aromatario) C.; m. Ethel Mary Meyers, Nov. 19, 1949; children: Jean, Marianne, Suzanne, Joseph, Robert, Michele, Renee. BS, Bradley U., 1943; JD, U. Chgo., 1949. Bar: Ill. 1949. Practice law, Peoria, Ill., 1949-99; gen. ptnr. Ralet Ltd. Partnership, Peoria; ret., 1999. Pres. White Star Corp., Mark Tidd, Inc.; asst. state's atty. Peoria County. Chmn. United Fund. Served to 1st lt. AUS, 1943-46. Mem. ABA, Ill. State Bar Assn., Peoria County Bar Assn., Chgo. Bar Assn., Creve Coeur Club, Mt. Hawley Country Club, KC, Union League Club. Republican. Roman Catholic. Home: 301 W Crestwood Dr Peoria IL 61614-7328 E-mail: roletltdptship@aol.com.

COLETTE, S., artist; b. Tunisia, Aug. 10, 1954; One-woman shows include Sefonatty Gallery, NYC, 1973, Frauen Mus., Germany, 1988, Found. Starke, Berlin, 2001, Maison Lumiere, NYC, 2001, exhibited in group shows at Carol Johnssen Gallery, Munich, 2002, 2003, 2005, 2006, PPOW Gallery, NYC, 2002, UNESCO, Paris, 2003, 2005, Lowen Palais, Berlin, 2003, 2005, Rosenthal Showroom, NYC, 2004, Colette Inst. Art, 2004, Grey Art Gallery, 2006, Haus der Kultur, Germany, 2006, Frauen Mus., Bonn, Germany, 2006, Pablo's Birthday Gallery, NYC, 2006, Vivian Horan Gallery, 2007, HPGRP Gallery, 2007, Represented in permanent collections Gugenheim, Ludwig Mus., Cologne, Germany, Berlin Mus. Art, Larry Aldrich Mus, prin. works include Collette Lounge, Starke Found., Berlin, Colette Salon, Ginza, Tokyo, exhibitions include Paris Biennale Mus. Modern Art, 1977, NYC Mus. Modern Art, 1977, Whitney Mus. Art, NYC, 1978, New Mus., NY, 1981, Ludwig Mus., Cologne, 1986, Mus. Contemporary Art, Lausanne, Switzerland, 1995, Kim Foster Gallery, 1999, Merck and Finck Bank, Berlin, 2000, Montreal Biennale, Can., 2005, Sante Fe Art Inst., 2005.

COLETTI, JOHN ANTHONY, lawyer, retail and real estate company executive; b. Cherry Point, NC, Sept. 22, 1952; s. Joseph Nicholas and Gloria Lucy (Fusco) Coletti; m. Barbara Nancy Carlotti, July 20, 1975; children: Lisa M., Kristen B. Student, Biscayne Coll., 1970-72; BA summa cum laude, Boston Coll., 1974, JD, 1977. Bar: R.I. 1977, U.S. Dist. Ct. R.I. 1977. Assoc. Resmini, Fornaro, Colagiovanni & Angell, Providence, 1979-81; ptnr. Coletti & Tente, Cranston, RI, 1981—. Pres. Coletti's Furniture, Inc., Johnston, RI, 1983—96, Coletti's Realty, Inc., Johnston, 1983—96. Legal counsel Cranston Housing Authority, 1988—; with alumni admissions coun. Boston Coll., 1980—; bd. dirs. Smithfield Girls Basketball League, 2001—, pres., 2004. Mem.: ABA, Nat. Assn. Retail Collection Attys., R.I. Conveyancers Assn., R.I. Bar Assn., Phi Beta Kappa. Roman Catholic. Avocations: horseback riding, golf, figure skating. Home Phone: 401-231-5949; Office Phone: 401-941-4050. E-mail: jjacolaw@cox.net.

COLEY, BETTY See FREDEMAN, BETTY

COLEY, JAN BRUMBACK, biology educator; d. Clifton and Violet Brumback; m. Bob Coley, June 23, 1979; children: Kimberly, Chad. MS, Auburn U., Ala., 1973. Tchr. biology, chmn. sci. dept. Jefferson County H.S., Dandridge, Tenn., 1986—. Recipient Disting. Sci. Tchg. award, Tenn. Acad. Sci., 2004. Office: Jefferson County High School 115 West Dumplin Valley Road Dandridge TN 37725 Home Phone: 865-933-6526; Office Phone: 865-397-3182. Office Fax: 865-397-4121. Personal E-mail: coleyj@k12tn.net.

COLEY, PHYLLIS DEWING, biology professor; m. Tom Kursar. BA in Biology, Hampshire Coll., Amherst, Mass., 1974; MA in Evolutionary Ecology, U. Chgo., 1980, PhD in Evolutionary Ecology, 1981. NSF postdoctoral fellow Smithsonian Tropical Rsch. Inst., Panama, 1982—83, rsch. assoc., 1995—; asst. prof. dept. biology U. Utah, Salt Lake City, 1982—87, assoc. prof., 1987—93, prof., 1993—. Vis. scholar Scripps Instn. Oceanography, La Jolla, Calif., 1994. Contbr. articles to sci. jours. Recipient George R. Mercer award, Ecol. Soc. Am., 1984, Career Advancement award, NSF, 1994—95, Biology in Excellence Tchg. award, 1995; grantee Guggenheim fellowship, 1989—90. Fellow: Am. Acad. Arts & Scis. Office: Biology Dept U Utah 257 S 1400 East Salt Lake City UT 84112-0840 E-mail: coley@biology.utah.edu.

COLEY, RANDOLPH C., lawyer; b. Atlanta, Feb. 20, 1947; BA, Vanderbilt U., 1969, JD, 1978. Bar: Ga. 1978, Tenn. 1997, Tex. 1999. Ptnr. King & Spalding LLP, Atlanta, 1978—96; exec. dir. Morgan Keegan & Co., Memphis, 1996—99; ptnr. King & Spalding LLP, Houston, 1999—, mng. ptnr. Houston office & mem. Oper. Com., 1999—2005, mem. policy com., 2001—04. Exec. student writing editor: Vanderbilt Law Review 1977-78. Bd. dir. Jung Ctr., The Alley Theatre. Mem. ABA, Order of the Coif., State Bar Tex. Office: King & Spalding LLP 1100 Louisiana Houston TX 77002 Office Phone: 713-751-3256. Office Fax: 713-751-3290. Business E-Mail: rcoley@kslaw.com.

COLFIN, BRUCE ELLIOTT, lawyer, video producer; b. Bklyn., June 9, 1951; s. Abraham and Sylvia (Laykin) C.; m. Virginia Mary Faszczewski, Sept. 27, 1981. BA, CUNY, 1977; JD, N.Y. Law Sch., 1980. Bar: N.Y. 1982, U.S. Dist. Ct. (so., ea. dists.) N.Y., 1987, U.S. Ct. Internat. Trade, 1990. Audio engr. Snowball Sound Systems, N. Bergen, NJ, 1974-77; producer, dir. cable TV program What's On, NYC, 1976-84; stage mgr. Peter Tosh U.S. tour Rolling Stones Records, 1978; v.p., producer Upswing Artists Mgmt., NYC, 1979-86; pres., producer, dir. LegalVision, Inc., NYC, 1982-87; ptnr. Jacobson & Colfin, NYC and Washington, 1985-90; mem. Jacobson & Colfin, P.C., NYC and Washington, 1990—; pres. Fifth Ave. Media, Ltd., NYC, 1996—. Assoc. prof. music bus. and tech. Five Towns Coll., 1999—; spkr. Discovery Ctr., N.Y., 1st Ann. Musicians Seminar, L.I., N.Y. Law Sch. Media Law Soc., 1986; vis. lectr. SUNY, Oneonta, 1988—; panelist New Eng. Music Orgn. Conf., 1998, Emerging Artists and Talent in Music, 1999, 2002; judge semi-final round Benjamin Cardozo Law Sch./Broadcast Music Inc., Entertainment and Comm. Law Moot Ct. Competition, 2003; judge various competitions; guest lectr. JamPro, Kingston, Jamaica, 2005, 06; coach Lynbrook Roller Hockey, 2002—, asst. coach Lynbrook H.S. Ice Hockey, 2006—. Assoc. prodr. music video Blues Alive, 1982; exec. prodr., dir. video series Entertainment Law Video Primer, 1984; exec. prodr. (CD) Zen Tricksters, 1999; co-author Music and the Internat: Some Thoughts from a Copyright Perspective, 2007; contbr. (chpt.) Real Law@Virtual Space Regulation in Cyberspace, 2d edit., 2005; monthly columnist Ind. Music Producers Soc. Jour., NARAS N.Y. chpt. newsletter; columnist: Replication News, 1998, Medialine, 2000; contbr. articles to profl. jours. Mem. ABA (com. entertainment sports law, subcom. chmn. patent, trademark and copyright com. 1989, subcom. chmn. internat. law and practice, internat. intellectual property rights com., spl. subcom. on multimedia 1994—, editl. advisor pubs. com. internat. law sect. 1990-92, exec. com. entertainment law cir. 1989-91, com. on authors of intellectual property law sect. 2001—), Nat. TV Acad. (NY chpt., mem. new media com., internet sub-com.), NY State Bar Assn. (entertainment, arts and sports law sect., com. on talent agys. and talent mgmt., com. on rights of publicity 1994—), Nassau County Bar Assn. (vice chmn. sports, entertainment and media law com. 2002-04, chmn. 2004-06, organizer CLE program on entertainment law 2006), Spkrs. Bur. Entertainment and Sports Law Comm., Copyright Soc. USA (editl. bd. 1986-88), Nat. Acad. of Recording Arts and Scis. (NY chpt.). Jewish. Avocations: travel, writing, stamp collecting/philately, hockey. Office: Jacobson & Colfin PC 1208 West Broadway Hewlett NY 11557 also: 60 Madison Ave Ste 1026 New York NY 10010-1666 Office Phone: 212-691-5630. Business E-Mail: bruce@thefirm.com.

COLGATE, CATHARINE PAMELLA, secondary school educator; b. Cedar Rapids, Iowa, Dec. 17, 1939; d. Fred Joseph and Emma H. Petrick; children: Shannon Colgate, Stephen Colgate, Stewart Colgate, Stanley Colgate. BA, Ariz. State U., 1973, MA, 1977, postgrad., 1977—94. Cert. tchr., jr. coll. educator, Ariz. Tchr. English Mesa Pub. Schs., Ariz., 1975—99; instr. English Mesa C.C., 1982—2004; prof. English Chandler/Gilbert C.C., Mesa, 2005—; English instr. Shelterwood H.S., Westminster, Colo., 2006—07, English chair, 2006—07. Writing specialist Associacao Escola Graduada, São Paulo, Brazil, 1990; vis. prof. edn. U. São Paulo, 1988; mem. med. mission, Chiappas, Mexico, 2004; mem. ea. Iowa Presbytery mission, Forteleza, Brazil, 05; vis. English tchr. Secondary Fed. Sch., Chiappas, Mexico, 2004; instr. writers workshop Chandler/Gilbert Cmty. Coll., 2005—. Patentee sch. lecterns. V.p. Temple Union H.S. Dist. 213, 1974—79. Mem.: AAUP, NEA, Ariz. Sch. Bd. Assn., Mesa Edn. Assn., Nat. Coun. Tchrs. English, Nat. Sch. Bds. Assn., Adj. Faculty Assn. (life), USAF Acad. Alumni Parents' Orgn. and Assn., Phi Lambda Theta, Phi Delta Kappa, Beta Sigma Phi. Home: PO Box 27626 Tempe AZ 85285-7626 Personal E-mail: Cpcolgate@aol.com.

COLGATE, DORIS ELEANOR, sailing school owner, administrator; b. Washington, May 12, 1941; d. Bernard Leonard and Frances Lillian (Goldstein) Horecker; m. Richard G. Buchanan, Sept. 6, 1959 (div. Aug. 1967); m. Stephen Colgate, Dec. 17, 1969. Student, Antioch Coll., 1958-60, NYU, 1960-62. Rsch. supr. Geyer Moyer Ballard, NYC, 1962-64; administrv. asst. Yachting Mag., NYC, 1964-68; v.p. Offshore Sailing Sch. Ltd., Inc., NYC, 1968-78, pres. Ft. Myers, Fla., 1978—2001; pres., CEO On and Offshore, Inc., Ft. Myers, 1984-2001; v.p. Offshore Travel, Inc., City Island, 1978-88; pres., CEO Offshore Sailing Sch. Ltd., Inc., Ft. Myers, 2001—. Pres. bd. dirs. Women's Sailing Found., 1998-2000, chair 2000-02, adv. coun., 2002—; chair US Saling Comml. Sailing Schs., 2005-07. Author: The Bareboat Gourmet, 1983, Sailing: A Woman's Guide, 1999; co-author: Fast Track to Cruising, 2004; contbr. articles to profl. jours. Bd. dirs. Fla. Repertory Theatre. Recipient Betty Cook Meml. Lifetime Achievement award, 1994, Sail Industry Leadership award, 1996, Timothea Larr award, U.S. Sailing, 2003. Mem. Royal Ocean Racing Club (London chpt.), Nat. Women's Sailing Assn. (founder, chair nat. women's adv. bd. 1990-94, pres. 1994-00, chair 2000-02, Leadership in Women's Sailing award 2004), Am. Women's Econ. Devel. Corp. (adv. bd. 1980-86), Boat US (nat. adv. coun. 1995—), Sail Am. (bd. dirs. 2000-06, chair mktg. com. 2005-06), Internat. Sailing Summit (exec. com. 2000—, chair comml. sailing com. US Sailing 2005-07). Avocations: piano, sailing, photography, writing, cooking. Office: Offshore Inc 16731 McGregor Blvd Fort Myers FL 33908-3843 Office Phone: 239-985-7511. Business E-Mail: doris@offshoresailing.com.

COLGATE, J. EDWARD, mechanical engineering educator; b. Sept. 30, 1962; SB, MIT, 1983, SM, 1986, PhD in mech. engring., 1988. Asst. prof. Northwestern U., Evanston, Ill., 1988—94, assoc. prof., 1994—2002, prof. dept. mech. engring., 2002—; co-founder, dir., tech. adv. Stanley Cobotics Inc., pres., 1999—2000. Co-editor: Advances in Robotics, Mechatronics & Haptic Interfaces, 1993; editor (assoc.): IEEE Transactions on Robotics & Automation, 1998—, Jour. of Dynamic Systems, Measurement & Control, 1995—98; editor: (U.S.) Robotics & Computer Integrated Mfg., 1995—99; contbr. chapters to books, articles to profl. jours. Recipient Henry Hess award ASME, 1995. Mem.: ASEE, IEEE, ASME. Office: Northwestern U Dept Mech Engring 2145 Sheridan Rd Dept Mech Evanston IL 60208-0834

COLGATE, STEPHEN, small business owner; b. NYC, June 25, 1935; s. Gilbert Colgate and Nina (King) Heiner; m. Doris Eleanor Horecker, Dec. 17, 1969. BA, Yale U., 1957. CEO, owner Offshore Sailing Sch., Ltd., Ft. Myers, Fla., 1964—, Offshore Travel, Inc., NYC, 1978-88, On and Offshore, Inc., Captiva Island, Fla., 1975—, Cafe Offshore Inc., City Island, Fla., 1981-84. Author: (book) Colgate's Basic Sailing Theory, 1973, Fundamentals of Sailing, Cruising and Racing, 1978, The Yachtsman's Guide to Racing Tactics, 1981, Steve Colgate on Sailing, 1991, Steve Colgate on Cruising, 1991, Steve Colgate on Racing Rules, 1991, Fast Track to Cruising, 2005. Served to capt. USAF, 1958—60. Mem.: Nat. Marine Mfrs. Assn., U.S. Olympians (Fla. chpt.), Internat. Sailing Schs. Assn. (pres.), Internat. Sailing Fedn., U.S. Sailing Assn., St. Charles Yacht Club, Cruising Club Am., Royal Ocean Racing Club (London), N.Y. Yacht Club (N.Y.C.). Republican. Episcopalian. Avocations: bicycling, sailing. Office Phone: 239-454-1700. Business E-Mail: steve@offshoresailing.com.

COLGRASS, MICHAEL CHARLES, composer; b. Chgo., Apr. 22, 1932; s. Michael Clement and Ann (H) C.; m. Ulla Damgaard, Nov. 25, 1966; 1 child, Neal. MusB, U. Ill., 1956; studied with Paul Price, studied with Eugene Weigle, studied with Darius Milhand, studied with Lukas Foss, studied with Wallingford Riegger, studied with Ben Weber. Author: Tuning the Human Instrument, 1993-94, My Lessons with Kumi-How I Learned to Perform with Confidence in Life and Work, 2000; freelance solo percussionist maj. N.Y. mus. orgns., 1956—, Narrator, Boston Symphony, 1969, Phila. Orch, 1970; dir.: Virgil's Dream, Brighton Festival; Soloist, Danish Radio Orch., 1965; dir. opera Nightingale Inc, U. Ill. Contemporary Music Festival, 1975; author, poet own theatre works, 1966—; composer: Divertimento, 1961, Fantasy Variations, 1961, Wind Quintet, 1962, Light Spirit, 1963, Rhapsody, 1963, Rhapsodic Fantasy, 1965, Sea Shadow, 1966, As Quiet As, 1966, Virgil's Dream, 1967, Three Brothers, 1951, Percussion Music, 1953, Chamber Music for Four Drums and String Quintet, 1954, Chamber Music for Percussion Quintet, 1955, Variations for Four Drums and Viola, 1957, The Earth's a Baked Apple, 1968-69, New People for mezzosoprano, viola, piano, 1969, Nightingale, Inc, Auras for Harp and Orch, 1973, Image of Man, 1974, Concertmasters for 3 violins and orch, 1975, Best Wishes U.S.A. for black and white choruses, folk instruments, jazz band and orch, 1976, Theatre of the Universe for soloists, chorus and orch, 1976, Wolf for solo cello, 1976, Letter from Mozart for orch, 1976, Déjà Vu, 1977 (Pulitzer prize 1978), Mystery Flowers of Spring for soprano and piano, 1978, Something's Gonna Happen, children's musical theatre, 1978; Flashbacks, musical play for 5 brass, 1979; Night of the Raccoon, 5 songs for soprano and 4 players, 1979, Ghosts of Pangea-A Fantasy of Cultures Meeting for full orchestra, 2000; Delta, for violin, clarinet, percussion and orch, 1979; Tales of Power, a mus. drama for solo piano on the writings of Carlos Castaneda 1980; Metamusic for solo piano, 1981; Memento for 2 pianos and orch., 1982; Demon for amplified piano, tape, radios and orch., 1983; Chaconne for viola and orch., 1984, Winds of Nagual, for wind ensemble, 1985; Strangers: Irreconcilable Variations for clarinet, viola and piano, 1986, (Jules Legèr Chamber Music Prize 1988), Déjà Vu for percusssion quartet and wind ensemble, 1987; Folklines: A Counterpoint of Musics for string quartet and wind ensemble, 1988, The Schubert Birds, 1989, Snow Walker for organ and orch., 1990, arctic Dreams for symphonic band, 1991, Wild Riot of the Shaman's Dreams for solo flute, 1991, Arias for clarinet and orchestra, 1992, Te Tuma Te Papa for solo percussionist, 1994, a Flute in the Kingdom of Drums and Bells, 1994, Urban Requiem for four saxophones and wind ensemble, 1995, "Hammer & Bow" for violin and marimba, 1997, 98, Dream State for solo piano, 1998, Baroque Blues for solo piano, 1998, Drummers for solo piano, 1998, "Chameleon" for solo saxophone, 1999, Memento Trio for flute, cello and piano, 1999, "Old Churches" for young band, 1999, Crosswords for flute, piano and orch., 2002 "The Beethoven Machine" for young band, 2003, "Apache Lullaby" for young band, 2003, "Bach-Goldberg Variations" for chamber orchestra, 2003, "Gotta Make Noise" for percussion ensemble and young band; works commd. N.Y. Philharm., CBC, U. Ill. Symphonic and Concert Bands, Boston Symphony, Toronto Symphony Orch., Lincoln Center Chamber Mus. Soc., New Eng. Conservatory Wind Ensemble, Fromm Found., Corp. for Pub. Broadcasting, Ford Found., Spokane, Detroit, Springfield, Minn. symphony orchs., Musica Aeterna Orch. N.Y., Young Concert Artists N.Y., Nat. Arts Centsre Orch. of Can., Calgary Internat. Organ Festival, New World Festival Arts, Delos, Manhattan and Muir string quartets, U. Miami, Nexus percussion ensemble: works recorded various cos.: contbr. articles to publs.; columnist Music Mag.; author: My Lessons with Kumi- How I Learned to Perform with Confidence in Life and Work, 2000, Ghosts of Pangea (for orchestra), 2000, Dream Dancer (for saxophone and wind ensemble), 2001, Bali (for wind ensemble), 2005, RAAG MALA: Music of India through Western Ears (for wind ensemble), 2006, Side by Side (for harpsichord, altered piano and orch.), 2007. With AUS, 1954-56. Scholar Tanglewood, Mass., 1952, 54, Aspen, Colo., 1953; Guggenheim fellow, 1964-65, 68-69; recipient Fromm award, 1966, Chem. Bank award, 1971, Emmy award for Sta. WGBH-TV film Soundings: The Music of Michael Colgrass for best documentary Nat. Acad. TV Arts and Scis., 1982; Rockefeller grantee, 1967-69; Ford Found. grantee, 1972; recipient Pulitzer prize, 1978; Winds of Nagual winner Louis B. Sudler Internat. Wind Band Composition Competition, 1985, De Moulin prize Nat. Band Assn., 1985, Barlow Internat. prize, 1986. Office: 55 Harbor Sq #2011 Toronto ON Canada MSJ 2L1 E-mail: colgrass@interlog.com. *I see the composer as a person not separate from life and community but indigenous to it. How to bridge the gap that has developed between the artist and people is the biggest challenge I know, but I find the more I reach out to people the less indifferent they are to the artistic experience.*

COLI, GUIDO JOHN, chemical company executive; b. Richmond, Va., Sept. 12, 1921; s. Guido and Rena (Pacini) C.; m. Vonda L. Coli; children: Pamela, Patricia, Deborah, Rebecca Smith. BS, Va. Poly. Inst., 1941, MS, 1942, PhD, 1949. Registered profl. engr., N.Y., Va. Asst. engr. Va. Health Dept. bur. indsl. hygiene, 1941; assoc. chemist Naval Research Lab., 1942-43; instr. chem. engrng. Va. Poly. Inst., 1947-48; chem. engr. Mobil Oil Co., Paulsboro, NJ, 1949-50; with Allied Chem. Corp., NYC, 1950-72, group v.p. corp., 1968-72, dir., 1970-72; pres. Am. Enka Co., Enka, NC, 1979-82; dir. Akzo Am. Inc., 1979-86, pres., chief exec. officer, 1982-86; chmn., chief exec. officer Armira, Inc., Asheville, NC, 1986—; pres., CEO Sisters of Mercy Svcs. Corp., Asheville, 1999—. Mem. Gov. Va. Commn. to Establish Urban Univ. in Richmond Area, 1966-67; mem. adv. council Coll. of Engring., Va. Poly. Inst. Lt. USN, 1943-46. Fellow Am. Inst. Chemists; mem. Am. Chem. Soc. (chmn. Va. 1957), Am. Inst. Chem. Engrs., Sigma Xi, Phi Lambda Upsilon, Tau Beta Pi, Phi Kappa Phi, Alpha Kappa Psi. Clubs: University (N.Y.C.); Country of Asheville. Home: 314 Town Mountain Rd Asheville NC 28804-3821 Office: Sisters of Mercy Svcs Corp 445 Biltmore Ave Asheville NC 28801-4119 Personal E-mail: v.coli@home.com.

COLIBAZZI, TIZIANO, psychiatrist; arrived in US, 1999; s. Sandro Colibazzi and Daniela Petrocchi. D Medicine and Surgery, Cath. U., Rome, 1999; postgrad., Northwestern U., Chgo., 2005. Diplomate Am. Bd. Psychiatry and Neurology, 2006. Postdoctoral fellow NIMH, Bethesda, Md., 2000—01; intern Northwestern U., Chgo., 2001, resident in psychiatry, 2001—05, chief resident, 2005; asst. clin. psychiatry NY Presbyn. Hosp., NYC, 2005—; rsch. fellow in neuroimaging Columbia U., NYC, 2005—. Named Resident of Yr., Evanston Hosp., 2003. Fellow: Am. Psychoanalytic Assn.; mem.: AMA, Med. Soc. NY, Soc. Practitioners Columbia U. Med. Ctr., Orgn. AIDS Psychiatry, Am. Psychiat. Assn. Avocation: Latin American literature. Office: 333 W 57th St Ste 1H New York NY 10019 Office Phone: 212-265-5009.

COLICCHIO, TOM, chef, food service executive; b. Elizabeth, NJ; Sous-chef Quilted Giraffe; chef Gotham Bar and Grill, Rakel; exec. chef. Mondrian; co-owner, founder, exec. chef. Gramercy Tavern, NYC, 1994—2006; chef, owner Craft Restaurant, NYC, 2001—, Craftbar, 2002—, CraftSteak, Las Vegas, 2002—, NYC, 2006—, Craft, 2006—, LA, 2007—, WichCraft, NYC, Las Vegas, San Francisco, 2003—. Head judge Bravo's Top Chef, 2006—07. Author: Think Like a Chef (James Beard Best Gen. Cookbook, 2001), Craft of Cooking, 2003; host, judge: (TV series) Top Chef, 2006—. Named one of Top Ten Chefs in Am., Food & Wine mag.; recipient James Beard award Best Chef NYC, 2000, James Beard Outstanding Service award, 2001, James Beard award for Best New Restaurant in Am., 2002. Office: Craft Restaurant 43 E 19th St New York NY 10003 Office Phone: 212-780-0666.*

COLIHAN, JAMES CHARLES, lawyer; b. Bridgeport, Conn., Sept. 7, 1953; s. John Charles and Eileen (Walsh) C.; m. Jane Richards, Sept. 28, 1985; children: Katherine, Leigh, John. BA magna cum laude, Holy Cross Coll., 1975; M. Internat. Affairs, Columbia U., 1977; JD, U. Va., 1979. Bar: N.Y. 1980, Conn. 1980. Assoc. Coudert Bros., NYC, 1979-82, 85-87, London, 1983-85, ptnr. NYC, 1988—, head Global Mergers & Acquisitions practice. Counsel Coun. for the U.S. and Italy, N.Y.C., 1986—; hiring ptnr. Coudert Bros., 1990—. Fundraiser New Eng. chpt. Cystic Fibrosis Found., Maine, 1987—. Internat. fellow Columbia U., 1975-76. Mem. ABA, NY State Bar Assn., Conn. State Bar Assn., Phi Beta Kappa. Avocations: golf, music, travel. Office: Coudert Bros 1114 Avenue Of The Americas Fl 4 New York NY 10036-7710 Office Phone: 212-880-4680. Office Fax: 212-626-4120. Business E-Mail: colihanj@coudert.com.

COLISH, MARCIA LILLIAN, history professor; b. Bklyn., July 27, 1937; d. Samuel and Daisy (Karch) Colish. BA magna cum laude, Smith Coll., 1958; MA, Yale U., 1959, PhD, 1965; DHL (hon.), Grinnell Coll., 1999. Instr. history Skidmore Coll., Saratoga Springs, NY, 1962-63; instr. Oberlin Coll., Ohio, 1963-65, asst. prof., 1965-69, assoc. prof., 1969-75, prof. history, 1975-2001, Frederick B. Artz prof. history, 1985-2001, chmn. dept. history, 1973-74, 78-81, 85-86; vis. fellow Yale U., 2001—, lectr. in history, 2004—05. Vis. prof. history and religious studies Yale U., 2002—03; lectr. history Case Western Res. U., Cleve., 1966—67; vis. scholar Am. Acad. Rome, 1968—69, 2006; Phi Beta Kappa vis. scholar, 2006—07; editl. cons. W.W. Norton & Co., 1973, John Wiley & Sons, Inc., 1981, SUNY Press, 1983, 85, U. Chgo. Press, 1988, U. Calif. Press, 1988, Princeton U. Press, 1988, 96, 98, U. Notre Dame Press, 1991, 92, 94, 2005, U. Ill. Press, 1995, U. Pa. Press, 1995, 97, 99, Yale U. Press, 1997, 98, Oxford U. Press, 1998, 2001, 05, Blackwell's, 1998, Liturgical Press, 1999, Cambridge U. Press, 2002, 05, E. J. Brill, 2003, 04, Palgrave Macmillan, 2003, 05; cons. dept. history Grinnell Coll., 1974, Knox Coll., 1981, St. John's U., 1981, Whitman Coll., 1982, Hope Coll., 1995, Kenyon Coll., 1996; mem. exec. bd. Ohio Program Humanities, 1976—81, 1978—81, vice chmn., 1979—81; writing residency Villa Serbelloni, Bellagio, 1995; mem. Sch. Hist. Studies, Inst. Advanced Study, Princeton, 1986—87. Author: The Mirror of Language: A Study in the Medieval Theory of Knowledge, 2d rev. edit., 1983, paperback edit., 2004, The Stoic Tradition from Antiquity to the Early Middle Ages, 1985, enlarged paperback edit., 1990, Peter Lombard, 1994, Medieval Foundations of the Western Intellectual Traidtion, 400-1400, 1997, 2d printing, 1998, paperback edit., 1999, La Cultura del Medioevo, 2001, Ambrose's Patriarchs: Ethics for the Common Man, 2005, Studies in Scholasticism, 2006. Mem. exec. bd. Oberlin ACLU, 1970—74, chmn., 1972—74, rec. sec., 1976—77, vice chmn., 1979—80; mem. exec. bd. Oberlin YWCA, 1966—70. Named Etienne Gilson lectr., Pontifical Inst. Mediaeval Studies, Toronto, 2000; recipient Wilbur Cross medal, Yale Grad. Sch. Alumni Assn., 1993, Marianist award, U. Dayton, 2000; Samuel S. Fels fellow, Yale U., 1961—62, Younger Scholar fellow, Inst. Rsch. Humanities, U. Wis., 1974—75, Nat. Humanities Ctr. fellow, 1981—82, Guggenheim fellow, 1989—90, Woodrow Wilson Ctr. fellow, 1994—95, NEH fellow, 1968—69, 1981—82, NEH Summer grantee, U. Calif., 1993. Fellow: Medieval Acad. Am. (coun. 1987—89, 2d v.p. 1989—90, 1st v.p. 1990—91, pres. 1991—92, Haskins medal 1998); mem.: Internat. Soc. Intellectual History, Internat. Soc. Classical Tradition, Soc. Internat. pour Etude Philosophie Medievale, Ctrl. Renaissance Conf., Renaissance Soc. Am., Midwest Medieval Conf. (pres. 1978—79), Medieval Assn. Midwest (coun. 1978—81), Am. Hist. Assn. Home: 80 Seaview Terr #29 Guilford CT 06437 E-mail: marcia.colish@yale.edu.

COLIZZA, WAYNE ANTHONY, orthopaedic surgeon; b. Hamilton, Ont., Can., Sept. 12, 1958; came to the U.S., 1992; s. Vincent Patrick and Velma Louise C.; m. Marlene Catherine Morin, Aug. 13, 1983; children: Wayne Jr., Christina, Michael. BSc in Biochemistry with honors, McGill U., Montreal, 1982, MD, 1987. Diplomate Am. Bd. Orthopaedic Surgery. Fellow Insall Scott Kelly Inst. for Orthopedics and Sports Medicine, NYC, 1992-93; attending surgeon St. Clares Med. Ctr., Denville, NJ, 1993—, Beth Israel Med. Ctr., NYC, 1995-99, Morristown (N.J.) Meml. Hosp., 1996—; pvt. practice Newton, Cedar Knolls, NJ, 1996—. Contbr. articles to profl. jours. Pres. Canadian Orthopaedic Residents Assn., 1992. Recipient Zimmer Travelling Fellows award Am. Orthopaedic Assn., 1994. Fellow ACS, Internat. Coll. Surgeons, Royal Coll. Surgeons Can. (cert.), Am. Acad. Orthopaedic Surgeons; mem. Can. Orthopaedic Assn., Can. Med. Assn., N.J. Med. Soc., N.J. Orthopedic Soc. (bd. dirs.). Office: 63 Newton Sparta Rd Newton NJ 07860-2745 also: Ste 101 218 Ridgedale Ave Cedar Knolls NJ 07927-2109 Office Phone: 973-300-5960.

COLKER, DAVID A., former stock exchange executive; Grad., U. Va., 1979; JD, U.Va., 1982. Gen. counsel Nat. Stock Exch. (formerly Cin. Stock Exch.), 1984—90, exec. v.p., 1991—95, COO, 1995—98, pres., COO, 1998—2001, pres., CEO, 2001—06.

COLKER, EDWARD, artist, educator; b. Phila., Jan. 5, 1927; Grad., Phila. Coll. Art, 1949; BS, NYU, 1965, MA, 1985. Instr., critic Phila. Coll. Art, Cooper Union, NYC, 1949-66; assoc. prof. Grad. Sch. Fine Arts, U. Pa., 1968-70; dir. Sch. Art and Design, U. Ill., Chgo., 1972-78, research prof. art, 1977-80; dean of visual arts SUNY, Purchase, 1980-85; chmn. dept. art Cornell U., 1985-86; provost Univ. of the Arts, 1986-91, Cooper Union for the Advancement of Sci. and Art, NYC, 1991—95, Pratt Inst., Bklyn., 1995—98, 2003. Cons. Nat. Endowment Arts, USIA; cons. in field One-person shows, Print Club, Phila., 1961, 89, Amel Gallery, N.Y.C., 1965, East Hampton Gallery, N.Y.C., 1969, Douglas Kenyon Gallery, Chgo., 1975, Ctr. Book Arts, N.Y.C., Neuberger Mus., Purchase, U. Ill., Chgo., 1985, 86, SUNY, Albany, 1990, Cooper Union, 1993, U. of Ariz. Mus. of Art, Bates Coll. Mus. of Art, 1998, Neuberger Mus. of Art, 1999, Poets House, 2002-03, others; represented in permanent collections, Mus. Art, Phila., Library of Congress, Washington, Mus. Modern Art, N.Y.C., Nat. Mus., Stockholm, Rosenwald Collection, NYU, U. Ariz., others. Guggenheim Found. fellow, 1961-62; Ill. Arts Council grantee, 1973, 80; Graham Found. grantee, 1977, R. Florsheim Art Fund grantee, 1997. Mem. Coll. Art Assn. Am., Caxton Club, Grolier Club.

COLL, EDWARD GIRARD, JR., university president; b. Pitts., Aug. 9, 1934; s. Edward G. and Alive V. (Ebeling) C.; m. Carole Hulse, Feb. 3, 1958; children— Thomas, Jean Coll Mendenhall, Peter, Karen, Kelly. BA, Duquesne U., 1960, LHD (hon.), 1983, Alfred U., 2000. Div. dir. United Fund Allegheny County, Pitts., 1959-61; asst. to exec. v.p. United Fund Dade County, 1961-63; asst. to v.p. for devel. affairs U. Miami, 1963-66, dir. corp. and found. relations, 1966-67, dir. devel., 1967-72, sec. univ. corp., 1972-73, v.p. for devel. affairs, 1973-82; pres. Alfred U., NY, 1982-2000; ret., 2000. Bd. dirs. Steuben Trust Co.; lectr. in field. Contbr. articles to profl. jours. Chmn. zoning bd. appeals Dade County, 1973-82; bd. dirs. Nat. Ctr. Child Abuse and Neglect, 1985-90; pres. com. NCAA, 1988-92, coun. mem. 1993-97, vice-chair divsn. III, 1990, v.p., 1994-96; trustee Coun. for Support and Advancement Edn., Washington, 1981-82, 87-89, chair, 1991-92. With U.S. Army, 1953-56. Univ. Adminstr. Fulbright fellow U. Warwick, Coventry, Eng., 1985. Mem. Ind. Colls. and Univs. N.Y. (bd. dirs. 1982-86), Duquesne Univ. Alumni Assn., Am. Mktg. Assn. (hon.), Miami Club, University Club, Genesee Valley Club, Wellsville Country Club, Delta Mu Delta, Phi Kappa Phi, Beta Gamma Sigma. Roman Catholic. Home: 4202 Dunham Pk Flowery Branch GA 30542 Office: 4202 Dunham Park Flowery Branch GA 30542 Personal E-mail: edcarolecoll@bellsouth.net.

COLL, JOHN PETER, JR., lawyer; b. Pitts., Oct. 5, 1943; s. John Peter and Lelia (Nicolussi) C.; m. Nancy Kaye Swan; children: John Peter III, Alexis S. AB in Polit. Sci., Duke U., 1965; JD, Georgetown U., 1968. Bar: N.Y. 1969, U.S. Dist. Ct. (so. dist.) N.Y. 1970, U.S. Dist. Ct. (ea. dist.) N.Y. 1974, U.S. Ct. Appeals (2d cir.) 1972, U.S. Supreme Ct. 1974, U.S. Ct. Appeals (5th cir.) 1981, U.S. Ct. Appeals (11th cir.) 1981, U.S. Ct. Appeals (8th cir.) 1980, U.S. Ct. Appeals (6th cir.) 1991, U.S. Ct. Appeals (1st cir.) 1993, U.S. Ct. Appeals (3d cir.) 1994, U.S. Ct. Appeals (9th cir.) 1994, U.S. Dist. Ct. (no. dist.) Calif. 1983, U.S. Dist. Ct. (no. dist.) N.Y. 1984, U.S. Dist. Ct. (we. dist.) N.Y. 1988, U.S. Tax Ct. 1990, U.S. Ct. Appeals (fed. cir.) 1999. Assoc. Donovan Leisure Newton & Irvine LLP, NYC, 1968-76, ptnr., 1976-98, chmn. exec. com., 1989-98; ptnr. Orrick, Herrington & Sutcliffe, LLP, NYC, 1998—; mem. exec. com. Orrick, Herrington & Sutcliffe LLP, NYC, 2000—; office leader-N.Y.C. Orrick, Herrington & Sutcliffe, LLP, NYC, 2002—05. Bd. advisors product safety and liability rep. BNA, 1991—; mem. litigation steering com. Def. Rsch. Inst., 1991—97. Contbg. author: Products Liability in New York, Strategy and Practice, 1997, 2d. edit., 2004, Commercial Litigation in New York State Courts, 2d edit., 2004. Named one of Top Ten Litigators in NYC, Nat. Law Jour., 1999, Top 500 Leading Litigators in Am., Law Dragon, 2006. Mem. ABA (litigation sect. 1983—), Fed. Bar Coun., N.Y. State Bar Assn., Assn. of Bar of City of N.Y., N.Y. Coun. Law Assn., Legal Aid Soc. N.Y. (bd. dirs. 2003—), Lawrence Beach Club (bd. govs. 1991-2000), Cherry Valley Club, Univ. Club. Democrat. Roman Catholic. Office: Orrick Herrington and Sutcliffe LLP 666 5th Ave New York NY 10103-1798 Office Phone: 212-506-3790. Office Fax: 212-506-5151. Business E-Mail: pcoll@orrick.com.

COLL, STEPHEN WILSON, journalist; b. Wash., Oct. 8, 1958; s. Robert Wilson and Shirley Lee (Baldwin) Coll; m. Susan Keselenko, May 17, 1984; children: Alexandra, Emma, Maxwell. BA cum laude, Occidental Coll., 1980. Contbg. editor Calif. mag., LA, 1983—85; staff writer The Washington Post, 1985—87, Wall St. corr., 1987—89, New Delhi bur. chief, 1989—93, investigative journalist, London bur., 1993—95, mng. editor, 1998—2004, assoc. editor, 2005; editor & pub. The Washington Post Mag., 1995—98; staff writer The New Yorker Mag., Washington, 2005—. Author: (books) The Deal of the Century: The Breakup of AT&T, 1986, The Taking of Getty Oil: From the Oil Patch to Wall Street - The Full Story of the Most Spectacular and Catastrophic Takeover of All Time, 1987, On the Grand Trunk Road: A Journey into South Asia, 1993, Ghost Wars: The Secret History of the CIA, Afghanistan, and Bin Laden, from the Soviet Invasion to September 10, 2001, 2004 (Pulitzer Prize for gen. non-fiction, 2005); co-author (with David A. Vise): Eagle on the Street: Based on the Pulitzer Prize-Winning Account of the SEC's Battle with Wall Street, 1991. Recipient Pulitzer Prize for explanatory journalism, 1990, Gerald Loeb Award, UCLA, 1990, Livingston Award, Molly Parnell Livingston Found., 1992, Ed Cunningham Award, Overseas Press, 2000, Robert F. Kennedy Internat. Print Award, 2001, Journalism Leader Award, South Asian Journalists Assn., 2002. Mem.: Phi Beta Kappa. Office: The Washington Post 1150 15th St NW Washington DC 20071-0002

COLLAMORE, THOMAS JONES, corporate financial executive; b. Hartford, Conn., Jan. 29, 1959; s. H. Bacon Jr. and Elizabeth Caldwell (Jones) C.; m. Jacqueline Ann Kelly, Nov. 21, 1992; children: Thomas Jones Jr., Pauline Elizabeth, Sallie Ann, Katherine Muse. BA magna cum laude, Drew U., 1981. Personal aide Rome for Gov., Bloomfield, Conn., 1978, dep. dir., 1982; staff asst. George Bush for Pres., Hartford, 1979-80; confidential asst. to sec. commerce Malcolm Baldrige Washington, 1981-82; spl. asst. to sec. commerce, 1982-85; dep. asst. to V.p. of U.S. The White House, Washington, 1985-87, asst. to V.p. of U.S., 1987-89; dir. secretariat Office of Pres.-elect of U.S., Washington, 1988-89; asst. sec. for adminstrn. U.S. Dept. Commerce, Washington, 1989-91, chief of staff, asst. sec. commerce, 1991-92; v.p. corp. affairs policy and adminstrn. Philip Morris Cos. Inc., NYC, 1992-95, v.p. corp. pub. affairs, 1995—. Chmn. govt. ops. com. Pres.'s Coun. on Mgmt. Improvement, Washington, 1989-91; mem. bd. advisors George Bush Presdl. Libr., 1996—. Bd. dirs. Malcolm Baldrige Scholarship Fund, Hartford, 1988—, City Meals-on-Wheels of N.Y.; trustee Kingswood-Oxford Sch., West Hartford, 1991—, Drew U., Madison, N.J., 1992—; alt. del. Rep. Nat. Conv., Detroit, 1980, del., Houston, 1992. Mem. Pi Sigma Alpha. Episcopalian. Home: 5206 Norway Dr Chevy Chase MD 20815-6672 Office: Atria Group Inc 101 Constitution Ave NW 4th Fl Washington DC 20001

COLLAR, EMILIO, JR., information systems consultant; b. Astoria, Queens, NY, Jan. 7, 1969; s. Emilio and Luisa Collar. BBA in Mgmt. Info. Sys., Pace U., 1993, MS in Info. Sys., 1998; PhD in Info. Sys., U. Colo., Boulder, 2005. Claims analyst Gen. Reins., Stamford, Conn., 1993—95; cons. worldwide olympic games tech. IBM, Somers, NY, 1996—98; asst. prof. mgmt. info. sys. Ancell Sch. Bus., Western Conn. State U., 2005—; founder, CEO ADD Advisors, LLC, Danbury, Conn., 2006—. Recipient Outstanding Student of Yr. award, Pace U., 1998; fellow, U. Colo. at Boulder, 1998—2000; scholar, KPMG, 1998—2003. Mem.: IEEE, Internat. Group e-Business Rsch. Applications, Assn. Info. Sys., Assn. Computing and Machinery, Attention Deficit Disorder Assn., Attention Deficit Disorder Orgn., Children and Adults with Attention Deficit Hyperactivity Disorder. Home: 11 Aunt Hack Rd Danbury CT 06811 Office: Western Connecticut State Univ Ancell Sch Business 181 White St Danbury CT 06810 Office Phone: 203-947-0344, 203-837-8903. Business E-Mail: collare@wcsu.edu.

COLLEN, JOHN, lawyer, educator; b. Chgo., Dec. 26, 1954; children: Joshua, Benjamin, Sarah, Joel. AB summa cum laude, Dartmouth Coll., 1977; JD, Georgetown U., 1980. Bar: Ill. 1980, U.S. Dist. Ct. (no. dist.) Ill. 1980, Trial 1982, U.S. Ct. Appeals (7th cir.) 1984, U.S. Supreme Ct. 1990. Ptnr. Duane Morris, LLP, Chgo. Mem. editl. adv. bd. Jour. Bankruptcy Law and Practice; adj. prof. law St. John's U. Author: Buying and Selling Real Estate in Bankruptcy, 1997; contbr. articles to profl. jours.; lectr. in field. Fellow Am. Coll. Bankruptcy; mem. ABA, Chgo. Bar Assn., Am. Bankruptcy Inst. (chmn. emeritus com. real estate bankruptcy), Phi Beta Kappa. Avocations: water sports, magic. Office: Duane Morris LLP 227 W Monroe St Chicago IL 60606-5016 Office Phone: 312-499-6700. Fax: 312-499-6701. Business E-Mail: jcollen@duanemorris.com.

COLLEN, MORRIS FRANK, retired medical association administrator, physician, consultant, researcher; b. St. Paul, Nov. 12, 1913; s. Frank Morris and Rose Collen; m. Frances B. Diner, Sept. 24, 1937; children: Arnold Roy, Barry Joel, Roberta Joy, Randal Harry. BEE, U. Minn., 1934, MB with distinction, 1938, MD, 1939; DSc (hon.), U. Victoria, BC, Can., 2004. Diplomate Am. Bd. Internal Medicine. Intern Michael Reese Hosp., Chgo., 1939—40; resident LA County Hosp., 1940—42; chief med. service Kaiser Found. Hosp., Oakland, Calif., 1942—52, chief of staff, 1952—53; med. dir. West Bay divsn. Permanente Med. Group, Oakland, 1953—79, dir. med. methods rsch., 1962—79, dir. tech. assessment, 1979—83, cons. divsn. rsch., 1983—. Chmn. exec. com. Permanente Med. Group, Oakland, 1953—73; dir. Permanente Svcs., Inc., Oakland, 1958—73; adj. asst. prof. biomed. informatics Uniformed Svcs. U. Health Scis., 2000—; chmn. health care sys. study sect. USPHS, 1968—72, mem. adv. com. demonstration grants, 1967, advisor VA, 68; mem. adv. com. Automated Multiphasic Health Testing, 1971; discussant Nat. Conf. Preventive Medicine, Bethesda, Md., 1975; mem. com. on tech. in health care NAS, 1976; mem. adv. group Nat. Commn. on Digestive Diseases, U.S. Congress, 1978; mem. adv. panel to U.S. Congress Office of Tech. Assessment, 1980—85; mem. peer rev. adv. group TRIMIS program Dept. Def., 1978—90; program chmn. 3rd Internat. Conf. Med. Informatics, Tokyo, 1980; chmn. bd. sci. counselors Nat. Libr. Medicine, 1985—87, mem. lit. selection tech. rev. com., 1997—2002, chmn., 2000—02; chmn. tech. evaluation group Application of Advanced Network Infrastructure in Health and Disaster Mgmt., 2002, chmn. tech. group, 02; program chmn. Internat. Conf. Health Promotion, Atlanta, 2003; lectr. in field; cons. in field. Author: Treatment of Pneumococcic Pneumonia, 1948, Hospital Computer Systems, 1974, Multiphasic Health Testing Services, 1978, History of Medical Informatics, 1995; editor: Permanente Med. Bull., 1943—53; mem. editl. bd.: Preventive Medicine, 1970—80, Jour. Med. Sys., Methods Info. Medicine, 1980—97, Diagnostic Medicine, 1980—84, Computers in Biomed. Rsch., 1987—94; contbr. articles to profl. jours., chpts. to books. Fellow Ctr. Advanced Studies in Behavioral Scis., Stanford U., 1985—86; scholar Johns Hopkins Centennial scholar, 1976, scholar-in-residence, Nat. Libr. Medicine, 1987—2002. Fellow: ACP, Am. Coll. Med. Informatics (pres. 1987—88, Morris F. Collen medal named in his honor 1993), Am. Inst. Med. and Biol. Engring., Am. Coll. Chest Physicians, Am. Coll. Cardiology; mem.: NAS, AMA, Salutis Unitas (v.p. 1972), Internat. Health Evaluation Assn. (pres. 1995—96, Morris F. Collen Permanente Rsch. award named in his honor 2003, Lifetime Achievement award 1992, Computers in Health Care Pioneer award 1992, David E. Morgan award for achievement in health care info. 1998, Japan Shigeaki Hinohara award for preventive medicine 2001, Cummings Psyche award for behavioral medical rsch. 2001), Am. Med. Informatics Assn. (bd. dirs. 1985—96), Nat. Acad. Practice in Medicine (chmn. 1982—88, co-chmn. 1989—91), Soc. Adv. Med. Sys. (pres. 1973), Am. Fedn. Clin. Rsch., Inst. Medicine (chmn. tech. subcom. for improving patient records 1990, chmn. workshop on informatics in clin. preventive medicine 1991), Internat. Med. Informatics Assn. Sr. Officers Club, Tau Beta Pi, Alpha Omega Alpha. Home: 4155 Walnut Blvd Walnut Creek CA 94596-5834 Office: 2175 Ygnacio Valley Rd #228 Walnut Creek CA 94598 Personal E-mail: mfcollen@aol.com.

COLLEN, TOM, women's college basketball coach; b. Dec. 21, 1953; m. Nicki Taggert; children: Connor David, Reese Elizabeth. B in Phys. Edn., Bowling Green State U., 1977; M in Recreation Edn., Miami U., Ohio, 1983. Asst. coach Miami U., Ohio, 1982-84, U. Utah, 1984-86, Purdue U., 1986—93, U. Ark., 1993—95, assoc. head coach, 1995—97, head coach, 2007—, Colo. State U., Ft. Collins, 1997—2002, U. Louisville, 2003—07. Named Coach of Yr., Western Athletic Conf., 1999, Dist. VII Coach of Yr., Women's Basketball Coaches Assn., 1999, Nat. Coach of Yr., Women's Basketball Jour., 1999, Women's Basketball News Svc., 1999. Office: U Ark Womens Basketball Athletics Dept 131 Barnhill Arena Fayetteville AR 72701*

COLLENS, LEWIS MORTON, retired academic administrator, law educator; b. Chgo., Feb. 10, 1938; m. Marge Collens; 1 child, Steven. BS, U. Ill., Urbana, 1960, MA, 1963; JD, U. Chgo., 1966. Bar: Ill. 1966. Assoc. Ross, Hardies, Chgo., 1966-67; spl. asst. to gen. counsel EEOC, Washington, 1967-68; asst. prof. Ill. Inst. Tech., Chgo. Kent Coll. Law, 1970-72, assoc. prof., 1972-74, prof., 1975—90; dean Coll. Law, Ill. Inst. Tech., 1974-90, pres., 1990—2007. Bd. dirs. Amsted Industries, Inc., Dean Foods Co., Inc.; trustee Latin Sch. Chgo. Dir. Ill. Coalition; bd. dirs. Alion Sci.

and Tech. Mem. ABA, Ill. Bar Assn., Chgo. Bar Assn., Am. Law Inst., Mayors Coun. Tech. Advs., Econ. Club of Chgo. Office Phone: 312-567-5198. Office Fax: 312-567-3004. E-mail: collens@iit.edu.*

COLLER, BARRY SPENCER, internist, pathologist, hematologist, educator, department chairman; b. NYC, Nov. 21, 1945; s. Arthur L. and Ruth (Degenshein) Coller; m. Barbara Nan Gelfand; children: Hilary Ann, Alyssa Brook. BA magna cum laude, Columbia U., 1966; MD, NYU, 1970; DSc (hon.), Mount Sanai Sch. Medicine, 2002, SUNY Stony Brook, 2003. Diplomate in internal medicine and hematology Am. Bd. Internal Medicine, 1973, in hematology Am. Bd. Pathology, 1974, Am. Bd. Pathology, 1975. Intern, resident Bellevue Hosp., NYC, 1970—71, resident in medicine, 1971—72; clin. assoc., hematology svc., clin. pathology dept. NIH, Bethesda, Md., 1972—74, staff physician, hematology svc., clin. pathology dept., 1974—76; asst. prof. medicine SUNY Health Scis. Ctr., Stony Brook, 1976-78, clin. chief hematology lab., 1976-93, assoc. prof., 1978-82, clin. dir. hematology div. dept. medicine, 1978-83, prof. medicine and pathology, 1982-93, head hematology div., 1984-93, Disting. Svc. prof., 1993, adj. prof.; assoc. dir. biomed. rsch. Advanced Ctr. Biotech. SUNY, 1992-93; Murray M. Rosenberg prof. medicine Mt. Sinai Sch. Medicine, NYC, 1993—2001, chmn. dept. medicine, 1993—2001, clin. prof. medicine, 2001—; dir., chief medicine Mt. Sinai Hosp., NYC, 1993—2001; David Rockefeller prof. medicine, head lab. blood and vascular biology, v.p. med. affairs Rockefeller U., NYC, 2001—; physician-in-chief Rockefeller U. Hosp., NYC, 2001—. Surgeon USPHS, NIH, Bethesda, Md., 1972—76; clin. instr. Georgetown U. Sch. Medicine, Washington, 1972—76; Anna and Leo Roon lectr. Scripps Clinic and Rsch. Found., La Jolla, Calif., 1986; Martin Rosenthal lectr. Mt. Sinai Hosp., NYC, 1991; vis. prof. Cornell U., Ithaca, NY, 1992, Ithaca, 96, U. Nebr., Omaha, 1994, SUNY, Bklyn., 1994, U. Wash., 1999, U. Utah, 2002, U. Calif., San Francisco, 2002; Hymie Nossel Meml. lectr. Columbia U., NYC, 1994; Herion-Walker lectr. U. N.C., Chapel Hill, 1997; Oscar D. Ratnoff lectr. Case Western Reserve U., 1997; vis. lectr. U. Okla., 1997; Teichman lectr. Tel Aviv U., 2002; dir. Stony Brook Found., 1991—93, 2001—, L.I. High Tech. Incubator Facility, Stony Brook, 1991—93; scientific advisor Ariad Pharm., Cambridge, Mass., 1991—; cons. Centocor Inc., Malvern, Pa., 1986—95, Northport VA Med. Ctr., NY, 1986—94, Genentech, South San Francisco, 1994—95; scientific adv. bd. mem. Otsuka Pharm. Co., Rockville, Md., 1985—93, N.Y. Blood Ctr., NYC, 1994—, N.Y. Biotech. Assn., 1995—99, Oxford Found., 1996—98, Accumetrics, San Diego, 1996—2001; bd. govs. NIH Clin. Ctr., 2002—05; bd. extamural advisors Nat. Heart, Lung and Blood Inst., 2000—; mem. adv. bd. clin. rsch. NIH, 2005—. Editor: Progress in Hemostatis and Thrombosis, Vol. 8, 1986, Vol. 9, 1988, Vol. 10, 1990, Williams' Hematology, 5th edit., 1995, 6th edit., 2000; mem. editorial bd. Blood, 1981-85, Current Opinion in Hematology, 1991-2005, Blood Cells, Molecules & Diseases, 1999-, Circulation, 1993-2004, Mt. Sinai Jour. Medicine, 1994-, Haemostasis, 1996-2002, Thrombosis and Haemostasis, 1999-2003, Pathophysiology of Haemostasis and Thrombosis, 2003-; reviewing editor Jour. Lab. and Clin. Medicine, 1991-; cons. editor Jour. Clin. Investigation, 1992-97; contbr. over 100 articles, revs. and abstracts to sci. jours., chpts. to books. Councilor east sect. Am. Fedn. Clin. Rsch., 1981—86; bd. gov. Clin. Ctr. NIH, 2002—; adv. in field; sec. bd. dir. SUNY Stony Brook, 1978—83, sec. treas. bd. dir., 1983—87. Recipient citation Fight for Sight, 1977, Jane Nugent Cochems prize, 1977, Internat. Investigator recognition award, 1987, Solomon A. Berson Med. Alumni Achievement award NYU Med. Ctr., 1991, Inventor of Yr., N.Y. Intellectual Property Law Assn., 1997, Jacobi medallion Mt. Sinai Sch. Medicine, 1997, Disting. Career award Internat. Soc. on Thrombosis and Haemostasis, Nat. Rsch. Achievement award Am. Heart Assn., 1998, Therapeutic Frontiers award, Am. Coll. Clin. Pharmacy, Alexander Richman award Humanism, Mount Sanai Sch. Medicine, Spl. Achievement award, 2001, Warren Alpert Found. award, 2001, Coltove award, Acad. Clin. Lab, Physicians and Scientists, Gold Humanism Hon. Soc., Arnold P. Gold Found.; named Man of Year Village Times Pub., 1998; grantee NIH, 1976—, Am. Heart Assn., 1983-86, SUNY, 1987-89; Guggenheim fellow Weizmann Inst. Sci., Rehovot, Israel, 1982. Master: Am. Coll. Physicians; fellow: AAAS, Coll. Am. Pathologists, NY Acad. Medicine; mem.: NAS, Am. Heart Assn., Am. Acad. Arts & Scis., NY Acad. Sci., Inst. Medicine, Assn. Profs. Medicine (bd. dirs. 2000—01), Internat. Soc. on Thrombosis and Haemostasis (councilor 1986—92, publs. com. 1986—92, chmn., fin. com. 1990—92), Harvey Soc., Am. Soc. Hematology (treas. 1983—87, fin. com. 1983—90, exec. com. 1984—87, corp. adv. com. 1986—87, adv. com. 1987—92, com. on pub. info. and govtl. affairs 1988—98, chmn., com. on pub. info. and govtl. affairs 1992—94, fin. com. 1993—, v.p. 1995—96, pres.-elect 1996—97, exec. com. 1996—98, edn. com. 1996—98, com. on practice 1996—98, pres. 1997—98, adv. com. 1998, chair, adv. com. 1999—2000, Stratton medal 2005), Am. Fedn. Med. Rsch. (councilor, ea. sect. 1981—86), Assn. Am. Physicians, Am. Soc. Clin. Investigation, Alpha Omega Alpha (sec.-treas., MU chpt. 1985—86, councilor, MU chpt. 1985—90), Phi Beta Kappa (v.p., Alpha Beta N.Y. 1990—91, pres., Alpha Beta N.Y. 1991—92). Achievements include discovery of a monoclonal antibody that was modified to produce the drug abciximab which was approved by the FDA in 1994 and the verify now rapid platelet function assays approved by the FDA in 1999-2005; patents in field. Office: Rockefeller U Lab Blood/Vasc Bio 1230 York Ave New York NY 10021

COLLETT, WALTER LEE, electrical engineer, educator; b. Morristown, Tenn., Oct. 11, 1968; s. William and Bonnie June (Lefevers) C.; m. Candi Renea Henry, July 11, 1992; children: Aaron Shaw, Ian Christopher. BSEE, Tenn. Tech. U., Cookeville, 1990, MSEE, 1992, PhD in Engring., 1999. Instrumentation engr. Quaker Oats Co., Newport, Tenn., 1992-94; grad. rsch. asst. Ctr. for Electric Power, Cookeville, 1994-99; sr. elec. engr. Square D Co., Nashville, 1999-2000, supr. engring., 2000—03, mgr. engring., 2003—04; asst. prof. elec. engring. Western Ky. U., Bowling Green, 2004—. Adj. faculty Nashville State Tech. Inst., 1995—99, Vol. State CC, 2002—04; tchg. assoc. dept. elec. and computer engring. Tenn. Tech. U., 1997; presenter in field; cons. in field. Contbr. articles to profl. jours. Mem. IEEE (sr. mem. student chpt. treas. 1989-91), Am. Phys. Soc., Internat. Soc. for Environ. Info. Scis., Sigma Xi, Eta Kappa Nu (student chpt. treas. 1990-91). Baptist. Home: 105 Seminole Lane White House TN 37188 Office: 1906 Coll Heights Blvd Bowling Green KY 42101 E-mail: walter.collett@wku.edu.

COLLETTE, TONI, actress, singer; b. Sydney, Nov. 1, 1972; m. Dave Galafassi, Jan. 11, 2003. Actor: (films) Efficiency Expert, 1991, Spotswood, 1992, This Marching Girl Thing, 1994, Muriel's Wedding, 1994, Lilian's Story, 1995, (voice only) Arabian Knight, 1995, Cosi, 1996, The Pallbearer, 1996, Emma, 1996, The Boys, 1997, Clockwatchers, 1997, The James Gang, 1997, Diana & Me, 1997, Velvet Goldmine, 1998, Hotel Sordide, 1999, Dead by Monday, 1999, 8 1/2 Women, 1999, The Sixth Sense, 1999, Shaft Returns, 2000, Changing Lanes, 2002, About a Boy, 2002, Hotel Splendide, 2000, Dirty Deeds, 2002, The Hours, 2002, Japanese Story, 2003, The Last Shot, 2004, In Her Shoes, 2005, The Night Listener, 2006, Little Miss Sunshine, 2006 (Outstanding Performance by a Cast in a Motion Picture, SAG, 2007), Like Minds, 2006, Evening, 2007; (TV appearances) The Panel, 1998, Frontline, 1994, Dinner With Friends, 2001; singer: (albums) Beautiful Awkward Pictures, 2006 Office: United Talent Agy care Adam Isaacs 9560 Wilshire Blvd Ste 500 Beverly Hills CA 90212-2427*

COLLETTI, NED, professional sports team executive; m. Gayle Colletti; children: Lou, Jenna. BA, No. Ill. Univ. With media rels., baseball ops. dept. Chgo. Cubs, 1982—94; v.p., asst. gen. mgr. San Francisco Giants, 1995—2005; gen. mgr. LA Dodgers, 2005—. Spkr. in field. Author: Golden Glory: Notre Dame vs. Purdue, 1983, You Gotta Have Heart: Dallas Green's Rebuilding of the Cubs, 1985. Vol. Salesian Boys and Girls Club, San Francisco; Charlie Wedemeyer Family Outreach Program. Named to Triton Coll. Sports Hall of Fame, 1993. Office: LA Dodgers 1000 Elysian Park Ave Los Angeles CA 90012

COLLETTI, RONALD F., chemist, researcher; b. Phila., May 28, 1959; M in Analytical Chemistry, U. Del., Newark, 1986; PhD in Polymer Sci, U. So. Miss., Hattiesburg, 1990. Rsch. chemist Monsanto, Pensacola, Fla., 1990—94, rsch. engr. Greenwood, SC, 1994—96, sr rsch. chemist St. Louis, 1996—. Scholar, German Acad. Exch. Svc., 1984. Mem.: Am. Chem. Soc. Office: Monsanto 800 N Lindbergh Blvd Saint Louis MO 63167 Office Phone: 314-694-8237. Office Fax: 314-694-7178. E-mail: rfcoll@monsanto.com.

COLLEY, KAREN J., medical educator, researcher; b. Nov. 3, 1958; BS in Chemistry, Duke U., 1981; PhD in Molecular Biology, Washington U., St. Louis, 1987. Postdoctoral fellow dept. biol. chemistry UCLA, 1987—91; postdoctoral fellow NIH, 1990; asst. prof. dept. biochemistry U. Ill., Chgo., 1991—97, assoc. prof., 1997—. Mem. med. adv. bd. Leukemia Rsch. Found., 1994—, reviewer study sect., 1994—; outside reviewer NSF Grants, 1995—, VA Rsch. Grants, 1995—; mem. pathiobiochemistry study sect. NIH, 1998—. Reviewer: Jour. Biol. Chemistry, Jour. Cell Biology, Molecular and Chem. Neuropathology, Jour. Cell Sci., Devel. Biology; contbr. articles to profl. jours.; patentee in field. Recipient Established Investigator award, Am. Heart Assn., 1996; fellow (sr.), Am. Cancer Soc., 1991; grantee, 1992, U. Ill., 1992, 1996, Leukemia Rsch. Found., Inc., 1993. Mem.: AAAS, Soc. Glycobiology, Am. Soc. Biochemistry and Molecular Biology, Am. Soc. Cell Biology, Sigma Xi. Office: U Ill Dept Biochemistry and Molecular Biology 1819 W Polk St Chicago IL 60612-7331

COLLEY, MARK DOUGLAS, lawyer; b. Alexandria, Va., Aug. 6, 1955; s. Wilfred Raymond and Alice Mildred (Hook) C.; m. Deborah A. Harsch, Aug. 13, 1977; 1 child, Arden Meredith Harsch Colley. BA, William & Mary Coll., 1977; JD, U. Va., 1980. Bar: Va. 1980, DC 1981, US Ct. Appeals (4th cir.) 1981, US Ct. Appeals (DC cir.) 1981, US Ct. Appeals (11th cir.) 1989, US Dist. Ct. (DC dist.) 1981, US Dist. Ct. (ea. dist.) Va. 1989. Law clk. Hon. John W. Kern DC Ct. Appeals, Washington, 1980-81; assoc. Peabody, Lambert & Meyers, Washington, 1981-84, Davis, Graham & Stubbs, Washington, 1984-88, ptnr., 1989, Holland & Knight, Washington, Arnold & Porter LLP, Washington, 2007—, mem. govt. contracts & bus. litigation practice groups, 2007—. Counsel Humane Soc. US, Washington, 1984-91. Recipient Humane Soc. US award, 2006. Mem. ABA (vice-chmn. Pub. Contract Law Sect. Bid Protest com., mem. Litig. Sect.), Fed. Cir. Bar Assn., Boards Contract Appeals Bar Assn. Office: Arnold & Porter LLP 555 12th St NW Washington DC 20004-1206 Office Phone: 202-942-5720. Office Fax: 202-942-5999. E-mail: Mark.Colley@aporter.com.*

COLLI, BART JOSEPH, lawyer; b. Englewood, NJ, Feb. 13, 1948; s. Bart Joseph and Marie (Burns) C.; m. Mary Ellen Diemer, May 20, 1972; 1 son, Michael John. BA summa cum laude, Fordham Coll., 1968; JD cum laude, Harvard U., 1971. Bar: N.Y. 1972, Tex. 1975, N.J., 1988, Pa. 2002. Assoc. White & Case, NYC, 1971-75; ptnr. Hughes & Luce, Dallas, 1976-85, McCarter & English, L.L.P., Newark, 1985—2000; exec. v.p., gen. counsel, sec. ARAMARK Corp., Phila., 2000—. Judge Entrepreneur of the Yr. awards program, 1993, 95, 96, North Jersey Venture Fairs, 1993, 94, N.J. Family Bus. of Yr. awards program, 1997, 99; lectr. in field; mem. resources com. Edison Partnership Tech.; chmn. 1st annual Mergers and Acquisitions Conf., 1999, spkr. 2d annual Conf.; lectr. in field. Contbr. numerous articles to legal publs. Trustee Tri-County Scholarship Fund, No. N.J. chpt. Leukemia Soc. Am., Inc.; coun. Lincoln Ctr. Bus. Coun. of the Consol. Fund. Capt. M.I., USAR, 1968-76. Mem. ABA (fed. regulation of securities com., sect. on corp.), N.J. State Bar Assn. (securities law com., bus. orgn. com. of the corp. and bus. law sect.), Phi Beta Kappa. Office: ARAMARK Corp ARAMARK Tower 1101 Market St Philadelphia PA 19107-2934 Business E-Mail: colli-bart@aramark.com.

COLLIER, ALBERT M., pediatrician, educator, director; b. Elba, Ala., May 3, 1937; s. Milford William and Ida Ruth C.; m. Mary Gaynell Wehler, July 17, 1960; children: Albert Mark, Dennis Murray, Jonathan Lee. BS, U. Miami, 1959, MD, 1963. Pediatric resident U. Miami, Coral Gables, Fla., 1963-66; fellow infectious diseases U. NC, Chapel Hill, 1968-70, from asst. prof. to assoc. prof., 1971-80, prof., 1980—, chief divsn. infectious disease, 1980—2004, assoc. dir. Ctr. Environ. Med. Lung Bio, 1980—2004, acting dir. Frank Porter Graham Child Devel. Ctr., 1990-92, assoc. chmn. pediat. rsch., 1997—2003, med. sch. sci. integrity officer, 2000—. Contbr. over 100 articles to profl. jours. Recipient Louis Dienes award Internat. Orgn. Mycoplasmology, Vienna, Austria, 1988. Mem. Gideons (zone leader 1990-93). Baptist. Office: U NC Chapel Hill Dept Pediatrics 5135 Bioinformatics Cb 7220 Chapel Hill NC 27599-0001 E-mail: uncacl@med.unc.edu.

COLLIER, ALICE ELIZABETH BECKER, retired social services administrator; b. Akron, Ohio, June 09; d. Christian and Virginia (Schulmeister) Becker; m. John Robert Fenwick, Aug. 28, 1954 (dec. 1980); 1 child, Beth Alice; m. Thomas Collier, Mar. 8, 1980. BA in Edn., Heidelberg Coll., Tiffin, Ohio, 1949; MA in Edn. Adminstrn., U. Akron, 1968. Cert. tchr., ednl. adminstr., Ohio. Tchr. Air Force Dependent Schs., Fed. Republic Germany and Eng., 1960-64, Akron Pub. Schs., 1964-68, adminstr., 1968-80; dep. mayor City of Akron, 1980-84; pres. Collier Pub. Rels./Mktg., Akron, 1984-86; gen. mgr., broker Coldwell Banker Real Estate, Akron, 1986-90; dir. comms. Area Agy. on Aging, Akron, 1990-94; v.p. Mktg. and Creative Solutions, 1994-97; ret., 1997. Author, editor: (Manual) Visual-Motor Training for the Developmentally Disabled Child, 1972, Different Strokes for Little Folks, 1974. Chmn. adv. coun. U. Akron, 1977-88; mem. Akron Health Commn., 1978-80, Akron Sr. Citizens Commn., 1980—94, Nat. Adv. Coun. on Aging, Bethesda, Md., 1982-84; pres. Tri-County Employee Assistance Program, Summit, Medina and Portage, 1985-97; charter rev. commn. Summit County, 1991; mem. women's adv. coun. Summa Health Sys., 1994—2003; v.p. Women's Network, Akron, 1987-88; trustee Comty. Health Rsch. Group, Inc., 1980—2002, Cuyahoga Falls Gen. Hosp. Found., 1992-2005; pub. rels. chmn. State of Ohio Atty. Gen. Health Info. Com.; trustee No. Ohio Golf Charities Found., Firestone Country Club, 1999—2004, World Series of Golf, Firestone Country Club, 1983—2000; vol. World Golf Championships, 2001—04. Recipient Svc. to Elderly award Am. Gerontol. Soc., 1982, Excellence in Comm. award Nat. Assn. Area Agys. on Aging, 1991. Mem.: AAUW, Akron Bd. Realtors (Salesperson of Yr. award 1988, Hall of Fame award 1988), Ohio Assn. Realtors (trustee 1988—90), Am. Mktg. Assn. (pres. Akron-Canton chpt. 1988—89, Spl. Merit award 1990), Ohio State Alumni Assn., Medina Country Club, Heidelberg Coll. Alumni Assn., Akron Women's City Club, Mission Valley Country Club, Woman's Golf Assn. (9 hole divsn. Mission Valley Country Club treas. 2002—05, v.p. 2006—), Pi Lambda Theta (founding, charter). Republican. Avocations: church organist, golf, tennis, collecting hummel figurines. Home (Summer): 333 N Portage Path Beechwood #11 Akron OH 44303-1218 Home (Winter): 25 The Esplanade N Apt 204 Venice FL 34285-1518 Personal E-mail: atcollier4@comcast.net.

COLLIER, ANNA, photographer; b. LA, Calif., 1970; BFA, Calif. Inst. Arts, Valencia, Calif., 1993; MFA, U. Calif., LA, 2001. Vis, faculty Art Ctr., Pasadena, Calif., 2002—03, Calif. Coll. Arts, San Francisco, 2002—; vis, faculty, New Genres dept. San Francisco Art Inst., Calif., 2003. Solo exhibitions, One on One, Three Day Weekend, LA, Calif., 1995, Inst. Visual Arts, U. Wis., Milw., 1998, MARC FOXX, West Gallery, LA, Calif., 2001, MARC FOXX, 2002, Jack Hanley Gallery, San Francisco, Calif., 2004, group exhibitions, L.A.C.E., video screening of LA video artists, 1993, Summer Group Show, Three Weekend, LA, Calif., 1994, Thank!; Three Day Weekend, 1994, Dave's Not Here; Three Day Weekend, 1995, Eros Travel Com., Studio Neuwirth, Vienna, Austria, 1996, Art Dogs, George's, LA, Calif., 2000, Summer Group Show, Goldman Tevis, 2000, I Want More, Temple Bar Gallery, Dublin, Ireland, 2001, New Wight Art Gallery, UCLA, 2001, MARC FOXX, LA, Calif., 2001, 2003, Group Show, MARC FOXX, 2002, A Show That Will Show That a Show Is Not Only a Show, The Project, 2002, Bay Area Now III, Yerba Buena Ctr. for the Arts, San Francisco, Calif., 2002, Portraiture, Karyn Lovegrove Gallery, LA, Calif., 2003, Makeshift World, Stephen Wirtz Gallery, San Francisco, Calif., 2003, 17 Reasons, Jack Henley Gallery, 2003, Nicole Klagsbrun Gallery, NY, 2004, Whitney Biennial: Day for Night, Whitney Mus. Am. Art, NYC, 2006, mus. collections, San Francisco Mus. Modern Art, Mus. Contemporary Art San Diego, La Jolla, Calif., LA County Mus. Art; curatorial projects Black Rainbow, Lucky Tackle Gallery, Oakland, Calif., 2003, Version, New Langton Arts, San Francisco, Calif., 2004. Address: c/o MARC FOXX Gallery 6150 Wihshire Blvd Los Angeles CA 90048 also: c/o Jack Hanley Gallery 395 Valencia St San Francisco CA 94103

COLLIER, BRIAN, history professor; b. Sept. 15, 1972; BA, Loyola U., Chgo., 1995; MA, Colo. State U., Ft. Collins, 1999; PhD, Ariz. State U., Tempe, 2006. Faculty assoc. Ariz. State U., 2003—06; asst. prof. Grand Valley State U., Allendale, Mich., 2006—. Book rev. editor: Jour. of West, 2004—. Recipient Svc. award, Grad. and Profl. Student Assn., Tempe, 2002—03, Cert. Appreciation, Gov. of Ariz., Phoenix, 2003. Mem.: Western History Assn. Home: 430 Rosewood Ave SE Grand Rapids MI 49506

COLLIER, CHARLES ARTHUR, JR., lawyer; b. Columbus, Ohio, Apr. 18, 1930; s. Charles Arthur and Gertrude Clara (Roe) C.; m. Linda Louise Biggs, Aug. 5, 1961; children: Sheila Collier Rogers, Laura Collier Prescott. AB magna cum laude, Harvard U., 1952, LLB, 1955. Law clk. U.S. Dist. Ct. (cen. dist.) Calif., LA, 1959-60; assoc. Freston & Files, LA, 1960-66; assoc., ptnr. Mitchell, Silberberg & Knupp, LA, 1967-82; ptnr. Irell & Manella, LA, 1982-95, of counsel, 1995—2003; ret., 2003. Lectr. Calif. Continuing Edn. of Bar, 1976-89; advisor Restatement of Property, Donative Transfers, 1990—; speaker numerous local bar assns. Contbr. articles to profl. jours Recipient Arthur K. Marshall award Probate and Trust sect. L.A. County Bar Assn. Fellow Am. Coll. Trust and Estate Counsel (chmn. state laws com. 1986-89, regent 1989-98, joint editl. bd. uniform trust and estate acts 1988-2006, chmn. expanded practice com. 1989-92, chmn. nominating com. 1998-99, spkr. 1988, exec. com. 1989-98, treas. 1992-93, sec. 1993-94, v.p. 1994-95, pres.-elect 1995-96, pres. 1996-97, immediate past pres. 1997-98), ABA Found.; mem. ABA (mem. real property, trust and probate law sect. spkr. 1985, 89, moderator teleconf. 1998, coun. 1989-93, chmn. com. trust adminstrn. 1982-85, chmn. task force on fiduciary litigation 1986-89, sr. lawyers divsn., vice chair wills, probate and trusts com. 1999-2000, chair 2000-01, vice chair book pub. com. 2000-06, chair editl. bd. 2001—06, sec. 2005-07, vice chmn. 2007—, others), Estate Planning, Trust and Probate Law Sect. of State Bar Calif. (chmn. 1980-81, vice chmn. 1979-80, mem. exec. com. 1977-82, advisor 1982-85, chmn. probate com. 1977-78, mem. legislation com. 1977-80, sect. liaison to Calif. Law Revision Commn. 1982-88), Harvard Alumni Assn. (dir. 1975-77, v.p. 1979-82), Harvard Club So. Calif. (pres. 1970-72). Office: Irell & Manella LLP 1800 Ave Of Stars Ste 900 Los Angeles CA 90067-4276 Home Phone: 626-792-5914. Business E-Mail: ccollier@irell.com.

COLLIER, CHARLIE, communications executive; b. 1970; BA, Bucknell U.; MBA, Columbia U. Nat. sales account exec. TeleRep Inc.; v.p., Advt. Sales A&E TV Networks, NYC; sr. v.p. Oxygen Media; exec. v.p., gen. mgr., Advt. Sales Court TV, NYC, 2001—. Named one of 40 Executives Under 40, Multichannel News, 2006. Office: Courtroom TV Network LLC 600 Third Ave New York NY 10016

COLLIER, DAVID, political science professor; b. Chgo., Feb. 17, 1942; s. Donald and Malcolm (Carr) C.; m. Ruth Berins, Mar. 10, 1968; children: Stephen, Jennifer. BA, Harvard U., 1965; MA, U. Chgo., 1967, PhD, 1971. From instr. to assoc. prof. Ind. U., Bloomington, 1970—78; from assoc. prof. to Robson prof. polit. sci. U. Calif., Berkeley, 1978—, chmn. dept. polit. sci., 1990—93, 2003. Faculty fellow U. Notre Dame, 1986, 87; vis. prof. U. Chgo., 1989; chmn. Ctr. for Latin Am. Studies U. Calif., Berkeley, 1980-83; co-dir., co-founder Stanford-Berkeley Joint Ctr. for Latin Am. Studies, 1981-83, founding transitional pres. qualitative methods sect., 2002-03 Author: Squatters and Oligarchs: Authoritarian Rule and Policy Change in Peru, 1976; co-author: Shaping the Political Arena, 1991 (Prize, Best Book on Comparative Politics, Am. Polit. Scis. Assn. 1993—), Rethinking Social Inquiry, 2004 (Best Book award Am. Polit. Sci. Assn.); co-author, editor: The New Authoritariansim in Latin America, 1979; contbr. articles to profl. jours. Fellow Social Sci. Rsch. Coun. and Am. Coun. Learned Socs., 1974-75, 79-80, 88-89, Guggenheim Found., 1988-89, Ctr. for Advanced Studies in Behavioral Scis., Stanford, 1994-95; grantee NSF 1975-77, 80-83 Fellow: Am. Acad. Arts and Sci.; mem.: Latin Am. Studies Assn., Am. Polit. Sci. Assn. (pres. comparative politics sect. 1997, founding transitional pres. qualitative methods sect. 2002—03). Office: Univ Calif Dept Polit Sci 210 Barrows Hall Berkeley CA 94720-1950

COLLIER, DAVID ALAN, management educator; b. Lexington, Ky., Aug. 3, 1947; s. J. Hamlet Jr. and Dorothy (Gifford) C.; children: Christopher David, Thomas Andrew. BSME, U. Ky., 1970, MBA, 1972; PhD, Ohio State U., 1978. Materials mgr. Babcock & Wilcox Co., Barberton, Ohio, 1972-74; asst. prof. mgmt. Duke U., Durham, NC, 1978-81; assoc. prof. U. Va., Charlottesville, 1981-86; prof. Ohio State U., Columbus, 1986—2007; chair ops. mgmt., Alico eminent scholar Fla. Gulf Coast U., 2007—. Cons. numerous corp. exec. programs, 1980—; mem. bd. examiners Malcolm Baldrige Nat. Quality Award, 1991, 92. Author: Service Management: Automation of Services, 1985 (Freedom Found. for Econ. Excellence award, 1985), Service Management: Operating Decisions, 1987, The Service/Quality Solution, 1994, Operations Management: Goods, Services and Value Chains, 2005; contbr. over 70 articles to profl. jours. (numerous awards). Ameritech Faculty fellow, 1989, U. Warwick Vis. Faculty fellow, 1995. Mem. Am. Soc. Quality Control, Decision Scis. Inst., Sigma Alpha Epsilon. Home: 1354 Hickory Ridge Ln Columbus OH 43235-1131 Office: Ohio State U 2100 Neil Ave Columbus OH 43210-1144 Office Phone: 614-292-8305. Business E-Mail: collier.4@osu.edu.

COLLIER, DAVID BEEBE, lawyer, consultant; b. Concord, Mass., Aug. 21, 1967; s. Dana Monroe Collier II and Jean Littlefield Fairbanks; m. Shonya A. Kowal, May 29, 1993; children: Isabella A., Gager A. BS in Info. Tech., Ea. Conn. State U., Windham, 1999, BS in Bus. Adminstrn., 1999; JD, U. Conn., Hartford, 2005. Cert. sys. engring. Microsoft, 2000, sys. engring. trainer Microsoft, 2001, A+ CompTIA Computing Tech. Industry Assn., 1999. PC game developer and adminstr. Gate M.U.D., British Columbia, Canada, 1994—97; systems integrator cons. Pfizer Inc.'s Legal Divsn., various locations, Conn., 1999—2005; atty. Garcia & Milas, PC, New Haven, 2005—. Fin. cons. Mayflower Montessori Sch., Norwich, Conn., 2000—04; instr. Ridley Lowell Tech. Inst., New London, Conn., 2000—01. Pro bono atty. Statewide Legal Aid, New Haven, 2006—07. With US Army, 1990—93. Decorated Army Achievement medal US Army, Good Conduct medal. Mem.: IEEE (assoc.), ABA (assoc.), Assn. for Computing Machinery, NY County Lawyers Assn. (assoc.), NY State Bar Assn. (assoc.), NY Acad. Scis. (assoc.), Am. Chem. Soc. (assoc.), New

Haven County Bar Assn. (assoc.), Am. Intellectual Property Assn. (assoc.), Conn. Bar Assn. (assoc.), Fairbanks Family in Am. (assoc.), Armstrong Clan Assn. (assoc.), Internat. Sled Dog Racing Assn. (assoc.), Manchester Regional Police and Fire Bagpipe Band (assoc.; piper 2000—07), Malt Adv. Soc. (assoc.), Soc. of Mayflower Descendants Conn., Am. Mensa (assoc.; comm. com. 2006—07), Phi Delta Phi (assoc.). Achievements include research in theft of wireless services in conjunction with crimes. Avocations: genealogy, bagpipes, animal welfare/rescue. Office: Garcia & Milas PC 44 Trumbull St New Haven CT 06510 Home Phone: 860-887-4640; Office Phone: 203-773-3824.

COLLIER, EARL MILLER, JR., biotechnology company executive; b. Richmond, Va., Aug. 31, 1947; s. Earl Miller and Emily Wallace (Webb) Collier; m. Frances C. Utterback, June 11, 1978 (div. Apr. 1991); children: Emily F., Braxton L.; m. Maren D. Anderson, Aug. 23, 1992; children: Maxwell A. Brooks, William E. BA, Yale U., 1969; JD, U. Va., 1973. Dep. adminstr. Dept. HEW, Health Care Financing Adminstrn., Washington, 1979-81; ptnr. Hogan & Hartson, Washington, 1981-91; pres. Vitas Healthcare, Miami, Fla., 1991-95, Clark Point Co., Washington, 1995-97; exec. v.p. Genzyme Corp., Cambridge, Mass., 1997—. Bd. dirs. deCode Genetics, Pervasis, Inc., Newton Willeslzy Hosp. Mem. Yale Club NY, Causeway Club, DC Bar Assn. Home: 240 Otis St West Newton MA 02465-2525 Office: Genzyme Corp 500 Kendall St Cambridge MA 02142 Office Phone: 617-252-7500. Office Fax: 617-252-7600. Business E-Mail: duke.collier@genzyme.com.

COLLIER, HERMAN EDWARD, JR., retired college president; b. St. Louis, Aug. 8, 1927; s. Herman E. and Evelyn (Saville) C.; m. Jerline L. Weston, Mar. 25, 1948; children: Herman Edward III, Michael F., Thomas W. BS, Randolph-Macon Coll., Ashland, Va., 1950, ScD, 1977; MS, Lehigh U., Behtlehem, Pa., 1952, PhD, 1955, LLD, 1971; LittD, Coll. Charleston, SC, 1976; LHD, Muhlenberg Coll., Allentown, Pa., 1986, Moravian Coll., Behtlehem, Pa., 1987. Chmn. dept. chemistry Moravian Coll., 1955-57; research chemist E. I. duPont de Nemours Co., Wilmington, Del., 1957-63; prof. chemistry, chmn. div. natural scis. Moravian Coll., 1963-69, pres., 1969-86; pres., dir. I&I Planning Assocs., 1987—89; interim pres. Salem Acad. and Coll., 1991, N.C., Wesleyan Coll., 1994-95, Chowan Coll., 1995-96, Lees-McRae Coll., 1997-98. Sr. cons. Acad. Search Consultation Svc., 1998—; bd. dirs. Horizon Health Sys. Inc., First Health Found., chair bd. dirs., 2007-; cons. sci. adv. bd. EPA, 1979-85; chmn. Commn. Ind. Colls. and Univs. Pa.; bd. dirs. First Health Moore Regional Hosp. Bd. Patentee mfg. tech. and product quality organo-lead compounds; sodium tetraphenyl boron for potassium detection; periodic table for lecture room, 1953; flame spectra Metallic ions from the H-F Flame, 1957. Mem. Com. to Employ the Handicapped, 1970-75; mem. Northampton County Citizens for Regional Progress; bd. dirs. United Fund Bethlehem, Hist. Bethlhem, Inc., Moravian Music Found., 1992-94, Roanoke Island Hist. Assn., Inc., 1996—98; trustee St. Luke's Hosp., R.K. Laros Found., Moravian Acad., Salem Acad. & Coll., 1995-2007. With USN, 1945-46. Mem. Lehigh Valley Assn. Ind. Colls. (dir.), Am. Chem. Soc., AAUP, Lehigh Valley Automobile Assn. (dir. 1981-86), Bethlehem C. of C. (dir.), Phi Beta Kappa, Sigma Xi, Omicron Delta Kappa, Kappa Alpha. Home Phone: 910-695-9953. Personal E-mail: hcollier2@earthlink.net.

COLLIER, NATHAN MORRIS, musician, educator; b. Clinton, Okla., July 23, 1924; s. Lotan Morris and Annie Carlletta (Willsey) C.; m. Frances Aleta Snell, June 24, 1955; children: Susan Aleta Kowalski, Ray Morris. MusB, U. Okla., 1949; MusM, U. Rochester, 1951. String music cons. Lincoln (Nebr.) Pub. Schs., 1951-68; asst. concertmaster Lincoln Symphony Orch., 1953-2001, emeritus asst. concertmaster, 2002—; 1st violinist Lincoln String Quartet, Nebr., 1955—; first violin Omaha (Nebr.) Symphony, The Nebr. Sinfonia, 1956-79; asst. prof. violin, theory Nebr. Wesleyan U., Lincoln, 1968-84; asst. concertmaster Nebr. Chamber Orch., 1973-91; assoc. concertmaster Omaha (Nebr.) Symphony, The Nebr. Sinfonia, 1977-78; concertmaster Lincoln Symphony, Lincoln Little Symphony, 1977-78; acting concertmaster Omaha (Nebr.) Symphony, The Nebr. Sinfonia, 1978; prin. second violinist Des Moines Symphony, 1979—; asst prof. music, condr. symphony orch. Kans. State U., Manhattan, 1980-81, pvt. tchr., 1st violinist Resident String Quartet, 1980-81; string tchr. St. John Luth. Sch., Seward, Nebr., 1983-89; acting concertmaster on occasion Nebr. Chamber Orch.; concertmaster Omaha Pops Orch., 1988-90; 1st violinist Avanti String Quartet, 1990; sect. I violinist Nebr. Symphony Chamber Orch., 1995—. Vis. instr. music Concordia U., Seward, 1985, 90; 1st violinist Lincoln String Quartet, 1951—; guest prin. violinist Des Moines Symphony, 1979, 87; guest violinist, violist Myron Cohen Met. and the Midlands String Quartets, Omaha, 1988—, Hastings (Nebr.) Symphony, 1990—; concertmaster and solo violinist with Collegium Musicum Concordia, 1999—; viola instr. chamber music coach summer course U. Nebr., Lincoln, 1991; concertmaster, soloist Nebr. Camerata-Orch. Berlin tour, 1992; mem. adv. bd. Rocky Ridge Music Ctr., 1972; cons., lectr. in field. Composer various mus. pieces; arranger numerous compositions for string quartet, 1980. Tchr., co-organizer Brownville (Nebr.) Summer Music Festival, 1972-77. With USN, 1943-46. Grantee U.S. Govt., 1966; inducted into Nebr. Music Educators Hall of Fame, 2002. Mem. NEA, Am. String Tchrs. assn. (Nebr. Pvt. Studio Tchr. of Yr. 1994), Music Tchrs. Nat. Assn. (nationally cert. 1994—), Music Educators Nat. Conf., Violin Soc. Am., Chamber Music Am., Lincoln Music Tchrs. Assn., Nat. Sch. Orch. Assn., Nebr. Music Tchrs. Assn. (Music Tchr. of Yr. 2003), Nebr. State Edn. Assn., Lincoln Musicians Assn., Omaha Musicians Assn., Lincoln Arts Coun. (co-recipient Lincoln Mayor's Arts award 1995), Pi Kappa Lambda. Democrat. Methodist. Home: 4544 Mohawk St Lincoln NE 68510-4838 Office Phone: 402-488-4721. E-mail: acorelli@aol.com.

COLLIER, SAMUEL MELVIN, aerospace engineer; b. Atlanta, Aug. 19, 1941; s. Samuel Roland Collier and Dixie Pauline (Sorrells) Terry; m. Gail Lee Grenfel Simmons, Sept. 22, 1962 (div. 1982); children: Phyliss, Sheri, Suzan, Samuel, Donica, Michele; m. Betty Lou Morris, Feb. 22, 1985. Grad., Officer's Candidate Sch., 1964; BS, U. Tex., 1973; MS in Bus. Adminstrn., U. No. Colo., 1977. Enlisted U.S. Army, 1959, advanced through grades to maj., ret., 1979; sr. staff engr. LTV Missiles & Electronics, Grand Prairie, Tex., 1979-85; engrng. project mgr. LTV Aircraft, Dallas, 1985-93; tech. transfer mgr. La. State U., Shreveport, 1996-97; sr. staff engr. Lockheed-Martin, Dallas, 1999-2000; cons. sys. engr. joint strike fighter devel. Lockheed Martin Aeronautics Corp., Ft. Worth, 2002—04. Grants cons. Town of Vivian, 1993-95. Author, pub. Terrapin Neck, Frog Level, Horseshoe, 2000, North Caddo Parish, 2007. Pres. Hist. Soc. North Caddo, Vivian, 1995—99, 2005—06, bd. dirs., 2005—; cons. Caddo Lake Heritage Awareness Program, 2007; grants rev. panelist Shreveport Regional Arts Coun., 1996, 1997; mem. Vivian Preservation Commn., 1995—96. Mem. Ret. Officers Assn., Inst. Ops. Rsch. and Mgmt. Sci. Republican. Baptist. Achievements include leading the operations research engineering team in a highly competitive tactical missile system production program won by the company; managing research and development programs that defined future military aircraft designs based upon the application of stealth technologies; authoring winning grant applications for small, local non-profit corporations. Avocations: bass fishing, archery, genealogy. Home: 1701 N Pine St Vivian LA 71082-9515 Personal E-mail: scollier@cmaaccess.com.

COLLIER, TOM WARD, musician, educator; b. Puyallup, Wash., June 30, 1948; s. Ward L. and Ethel M. (Turner) Collier; m. Cheryl Anne Zilbert, May 31, 1970; children: Cara, Nina. BA, MusB, U. Wash., 1971. Freelance musician Seattle Symphony/N.W. Chamber Orch., 1967-74; drummer, vibraphonist Northwest Jazz Quintet, Seattle, 1972-80; studio musician various artists and shows including Barbra Streisand, Ry Cooder, American Music Awards, Harry O., LA, 1975-78; timpanist LA Repertoire Orch., 1976-77; jazz drummer Howard Roberts Quartet/Bill Smith Trio, LA, Seattle, 1975-82; freelance percussionist various artists including Johnny Mathis, Paul Williams, Jermaine Jackson, Sammy Davis Jr., Bob Hope, Barbra Streisand, Ry Cooder, Olivia Newton-John, The Beach Boys, Bud Shank, Earl "Fatha" Hines, Diane Schurr, LA, Seattle, 1976-91; jazz vibraphonist Collier/Dean Duo, Seattle, 1977—; faculty, dir. percussion studies U. Wash., 1980—, dir. Jazz Inst., 1989—92, sound prodn. evening degree adv. bd. dirs., 1994-2000, dir. jazz studies, 2001—04, adv. bd. dirs. Songwriting Cert. program, 2004—; rec. artist, leader band Tom Collier, 1987—. Leader Tom Collier Duo/Trio Wash. State Arts Commn. Cultural Enrichment Program, 1980—95, Arts Edn. Program, 1996—2001; owner Mallet Head Music, 1979—, T.C. Records, 1987—91; dir. N.W. Percussion Inst., Seattle; acad. cons. Experience Music Project Mus., Seattle, 1990—2000; music amb. Tour Western Japan, 2005. Musician: (albums) Whistling Midgets, 1981, Illusion, 1987, Pacific Aire, 1991, Mallet Jazz, 2004, Duets, 2005; author: Jazz Improvisation and Ear Training, 1983, rev. edit., 2003, Studio Call Simulated Recording Sessions, 1984, History of Jazz, Lecture Notes, Overheads and Listening Examples, 1997; composer: Quintet for Percussion Ensemble, 1972, Xenolith for Jazz Quartet and String Quartet, 1973, Piece for Electric Bass, Vibraphone and Orch., 1979, Nina's Joy, Busy Body, Tightwad, Subito Sox, 1991; musician: with Larry Coryell, Buddy DeFranco, Eddie Daniels, Emil Richards, 1975—2000, (film soundtrack) with John Williams, Oliver Nelson, Kim Richmond, Henry Mancini; world premier performance of own composition: Three Movements for Solo Marimba, 2000, pub.: Bar Code, Springtide, Day In, Day Out, Studio 4 Music Pub. Bd. dirs. S. Ctrl. Sch. Dist., Seattle, 1987—91; mem. arts adv. bd. Fed. Way Sch. Dist., 1992—94. Rockefeller Rsch. grantee, U. Wash., 1967—71, Royalty Rsch. Fund grantee, 2003. Mem.: ASCAP (Spl. award 1981—97), Music Educators Nat. Conf. (faculty advisor 1986—88), Nat. Assn. Jazz Educators (Outstanding Svc. award 1980), Percussive Arts Soc., Musicians Union. Office: U Wash Sch Music 353450 Seattle WA 98195-0001 Office Phone: 206-543-8259. Business E-Mail: tomcollier@tomcolliervibes.com.

COLLIER, WILLIAM GAYLE, psychology professor, researcher; b. Albuquerque, July 31, 1970; s. William Robert and Judith Church Collier. BS in Psychology, Okla. Christian U., 1992; MA in Exptl. Psychology, U. Ctrl. Okla., 1994; MS in Exptl. Psychology, Tex. Christian U., 1997, PhD in Gen. Exptl. Psychology, 1998. Grad. asst. Multimedia Ctr., Coll. Edn., U. Ctrl. Okla., Edmond, 1994; dep. asst. dept. psychology Tex. Christian U., Ft. Worth, 1995-96, acad. tutor athletic dept., 1997-98, dep. asst. dept. psychology, 1998; lectr. psychology U. Tex., Tyler, 1998-99, vis. asst. prof., 1999—2002; asst. prof cognitive psychology U. NC, Pembroke, 2002—, undergrad. student advisor dept. psychology and counseling, 2003—. Undergrad. student advisor dept. psychology U. Tex., Tyler, 1999-2002. Author poetry; contbr. articles to profl. jours. Mem.: Soc. Edn., Music and Psychology Rsch., Southwestern Psychol. Assn., Assn. Psychol. Sci., European Soc. Cognitive Scis. Music (assoc.; affiliate mem.), Psi Chi, Alpha Chi. Avocations: science fiction, history, poetry, music, theater. Office Phone: 910-521-6458. Business E-Mail: william.collier@uncp.edu.

COLLIGAN, EDWARD T., computer company and communications executive; Bachelor Degree, U. Oreg. V.p., strategic and product marketing Radius Corp.; v.p. marketing Palm Inc.; former pres., COO Handspring, Inc. (acquired by palmOne, Inc. in 2003), 1998—2003; sr. v.p., gen. mgr., Wireless Bus. Unit Palm Inc., Sunnyvale, Calif., 2003—04, pres., 2004—, interim CEO, 2005, CEO, 2005—. Office: Palm Inc 950 W Maude Ave Sunnyvale CA 94085 Office Phone: 408-503-7000.*

COLLIN, THOMAS JAMES, lawyer; b. Windom, Minn., Jan. 6, 1949; s. Everett Earl and Genevieve May (Wilson) C.; m. Victoria Gatov, Oct. 11, 1985; children: Arielle, Elise, Sarah. BA, U. Minn., 1970; AM, Harvard U., 1972; JD, Georgetown U., 1974. Bar: Ohio 1975, U.S. Dist. Ct. (no. and so. dists.) Ohio 1975, U.S. Ct. Appeals (10th cir.) 1977, U.S. Supreme Ct. 1980, U.S. Ct. Appeals (6th cir.) 1981, U.S. Ct. Appeals (8th cir.) 1982, U.S. Ct. Appeals (7th cir.) 1997, U.S. Ct. Appeals (11th cir.) 1999. Law clk. to Judge Myron Bright U.S. Ct. Appeals, 8th Cir., St. Louis, 1974-75; assoc. Thompson, Hine LLP, Cleve., 1975-82, ptnr., 1982—. Author: Ohio Business Competition Law, 1994, (with others) Criminal Antitrust Litigation Manual, 1983; editor: Punitive Damages and Business Torts: A Practitioner's Handbook, 1998, Antitrust Law and Economics of Product Distribution, 2006; contbr. articles to profl. jours. Active Citizens League, Cleve., bd. trustees, 1994-99, v.p., 1995-97, pres. 1997-99; bd. trustees Citizens League Rsch. Inst., Cleve., 1999-2002. Mem. ABA (chair bus. torts and unfair competition com. antitrust sect. 1995-98, chair annual mtg. com. 2001-02, chmn. distbn. and franchising com. 2002-05), Ohio State Bar Assn. (bd. govs. antitrust sect. 1988-98). Republican. Avocations: book collecting, music. Home: 7879 Oakhurst Dr Cleveland OH 44141-1123 Office: Thompson Hine LLP 127 Public Sq Cleveland OH 44114-1216

COLLINGS, CHRIS D., lawyer; b. McAllen, Tex., July 2, 1970; B of Social Work with honors, U. Tex., Austin, 1997; JD, South Tex. Coll. Law, 2001. Bar: Tex. 2002, US Dist. Ct. (so. dist. Tex.) 2002, US Dist. Ct. (we. dist. Tex.) 2003, US Dist. Ct. (ea. dist. Tex.) 2004. Jud. intern Fifth Dist. Ct. Appeals, 1999; with Kirk Law Firm, 2002—03; assoc. Brown Sims P.C., 2003—. Cpl. USMC, 1989—94. Named a Rising Star, Tex. Super Lawyers mag., 2006. Mem.: Am. Inns of Ct., VFW, Pearl and Area Rep. Pachyderm Club. Office: Brown Sims 1177 West Loop South 10th Fl Houston TX 77027 Office Phone: 713-629-1580. Office Fax: 713-629-5027. E-mail: ccollings@brownsims.com.*

COLLINGS, ROBERT BIDDLECOMBE, judge; b. Aug. 31, 1942; s. Harry Biddlecombe and Juanita Beatrice (Huber) C.; m. Mary Clare Flintoft, Sept. 14, 1968; children: John Richard Biddlecombe, Christopher James More, Clare Yung Hee. AB, Hamilton Coll., 1964; JD, Harvard U., Cambridge, Mass., 1967. Bar: Mass. 1968, NH 1970, US Ct. Mil. Appeals 1970, US Dist. Ct. Mass. 1971, US Ct. Appeals (1st cir.) 1971, US Ct. Appeals (5th cir.) 1979, Temporary Emergency Ct. Appeals 1980. Asst. U.S. atty. Dept. Justice, Boston, 1971-82, chief criminal divsn., 1976-82, 1st asst. U.S. atty., 1978-81; U.S. magistrate judge US Dist. Ct., Boston, 1982—, chief magistrate judge, 1999—2001. Lectr. law Harvard Law Sch., 1988—92, Northeastern U. Sch. Law, 1989—90; guest lectr. Stanford Law Sch., 2000—; mem. Magistrate Judge Ednl. Com. of Fed. Jud. Ctr., 1990—96, Def. Svcs. Com. Jud. Conf. U.S., 1991—97; mem. joint adv. group Adminstrv. Office of U.S. Cts., 1998—2000; mem. Fed. Jud. Ctr. Bd., 2001—05. Co-editor: Federal Court Civil Litigation in the First Circuit, 1994. Lt. USNR, 1967-71. Mem. ABA (chair magistrate judges' com. nat. conf. fed. trial judges 1999-2000, exec. com. 2000-02, sec. 2002-03, vice-chmn. 2003-04, chair elect 2004-05, chair 2005-06), Nat. Coun. US Magistrates (treas. 1990-91), Fed. Magistrate Judges Assn. (2d v.p. 1991-92, 1st v.p. 1992-93, pres.-elect 1993-94, pres. 1994-95, past pres. 1995-96, legis. chmn. 1995—, Founders award 1998), Mass. Bar Assn., Boston Bar Assn. Office: US Courthouse 1 Courthouse Way Ste 7420 Boston MA 02210-3002 Office Phone: 617-748-9228. Business E-Mail: honorable_robert_collings@mad.uscourts.gov.

COLLINGS, ROBERT L., lawyer; b. May 22, 1950; AB, Harvard U., 1972; JD, Boston Coll., 1977. Bar: Pa. 1977, U.S. Ct. Appeals (D.C. cir.) 1981, U.S. Dist. Ct. (ea. dist.) Pa. 1985, U.S. Ct. Appeals (3d cir.) 1984, U.S. Dist. Ct. (mid. dist.) 1992. Atty. U.S. EPA, 1977-84, sect. chief, 1979—81, br. chief, 1981-84; ptnr. Morgan, Lewis & Bockius LLP, 1984—98, Schnader, Harrison, Segal & Lewis LLP, Phila., 1998—, mem. exec. com., 2003—. Editor: Environmental Spill Reporting Handbook; contbr. Municipal Solicitors Handbook, 1994, 1999, 2003, Brownfields: A Comprehensive Guide, 1997, 2d edit., 2002. Bd. dirs. Pa. Environ. Coun., 2003. Mem. ABA (vice chair enforcement com. sect. environment, energy and resources 2003), Phila. Bar Assn. (chair environ. law com. 1986), Water Resources Assn. (sec. exec. com. 1990—). Office: Schnader Harrison Segal & Lewis LLP 1600 Market St Ste 3600 Philadelphia PA 19103-7287 Office Phone: 215-751-2074. E-mail: rcollings@schnader.com.

COLLINGSWORTH, CONNIE RENEE, lawyer; b. Lincoln, Nebr., 1958; m. Allen D. Wilcox; children: Alexa, Elise. B, Andrews U., Berrien Springs, Mich., 1979; JD, U. Nebr. Coll. Law, 1982; ML in Internat. Bus. Legal Studies, U. Exeter, Eng. Corp. lawyer Chamberlain, Hrdlicka, White, Williams & Martin, Houston, 1982—85, Hall Estill, Tulsa, Okla., 1985—87, Preston Gates & Ellis, Seattle, 1987—2002; gen. counsel The Bill & Melinda Gates Found., Washington, 2002—. Mem. bd. dirs. Attenex Corp.; co-chairwoman Social Ventures Partners. Co-founder French Am. Sch. Puget Sound, Mercer Island. Office: The Bill and Melinda Gates Foundation Ben Franklin Station PO Box 6176 Washington DC 20044*

COLLINS, ALISON, opera singer, music educator; d. Joseph Stephen and Linda Louise Collins; m. Aaron Hradec Alpar, Jan. 1, 2005. MusB, San Francisco Conservatory, 1993; MA, San Jose State U., 2004. Prin. artist Townsend Opera Players, Modesto, 1991—; apprentice artist Sarasota (Fla.) Opera, 1995—97; guest artist Am. Opera Projects, NYC, 1995—99, Opera San Jose, Calif., 2002—03, asst. stage dir., 2005—06; instr. San Jose State U., 2005—. Recipient Brian F. Soctt award, Am. Opera Projects, 1997, Richard F. Gold award, Shoshana Found., NYC, 1995. Mem.: Music Tchrs. Assn. Calif., Nat. Assn. Tchrs. Singing. Office: San Jose State U Sch Music and Dance 1 Washington Sq San Jose CA 95112

COLLINS, ALLAN MEAKIN, education educator; b. Orange, NJ, Aug. 7, 1937; s. Clinton and Sarah Amy (Meakin) C.; m. Anne Marjorie Linstead, Aug. 24, 1963; children: Antony, Elizabeth. MA in Comm. Scis., U. Mich., Ann Arbor, 1962, PhD in Psychology, 1970. Sr. scientist Bolt, Beranek & Newman Inc., Cambridge, 1967-82, prin. scientist, 1982-2000; prof edn. and social policy Northwestern U., Evanston, Ill., 1989—2005, emeritus, 2005—. Co-dir. Ctr. for Tech. in Edn., Bank St. Coll. Edn., NYC, 1991—94; rsch. prof. edn. Boston Coll., 1998—2002; vis. sr. lectr. Harvard Grad. Sch. Edn., 2005—06; lectr. various colls. and univs. Editor: Representation and Understanding, 1975, Cognitive Science, 1976-80, Readings in Cognitive Science, 1988; author: The Cognitive Structure of Emotions, 1988. Guggenheim fellow, 1974, Sloan fellow, 1980. Fellow AAAS; mem. Nat. Acad. Edn., Cognitive Sci. Soc. (chmn. 1979-80, goving. bd. 1979-87), Am. Assn. for Artificial Intelligence (fellow 1990), Am. Ednl. Rsch. Assn. Achievements include launched research on human semantic memory (with R. Quillian); development of first intelligent tutoring system (with J.R. Carbonell); development of cognitive apprenticeship (with J.S. Brown). Home: 135 Cedar St Lexington MA 02421-6516 Business E-Mail: collins@bbn.com.

COLLINS, ALLEN HOWARD, psychiatrist; b. Washington, Sept. 6, 1942; s. Murray and Bertha (Baccalman) C.; m. Stephanie Evelyn Awn, May 22, 1976; children: Sasha Marie, Matthew Allen, Alyssa Beth. AB, Columbia Coll., 1964; MD, Tufts U., 1968; MPH, Columbia U., 1974. Diplomate Am. Bd. Psychiatry and Neurology, Nat. Bd. Med. Examiners; cert. in psychoanalysis. Mental health career develop. fellow NIMH, Rockville, Md., 1968—74, staff psychiatrist Region II NYC, 1972—74, psychiat. cons., 1974—90; chief psychiat. consultation liaison svcs. Lenox Hill Hosp., NYC, 1974—76, chief psychiat. inpatient svc., 1976—78, chief psychiatry svc., 1978—86, chmn. dept. psychiatry, 1986—2005, pres. med. bd., 1994—96, 2000—02. Examiner in psychiatry Am. Bd. Psychiatry and Neurology, Evanston, Ill., 1979-2005, chief proctor, 1991-2005; clin. prof. psychiatry N.Y. Med. Coll., Valhalla, 1988-90; tng. and supervisory psychoanalyst divsn. psychoanalytic tng., 1986-90; assoc. clin. prof. psychiatry Cornell U. Med. Coll., 1990-93; clin. prof. psychiatry NYU Med. Ctr., 1993—; vis. prof. psychiatry SUNY/Downstate Health Sci. Ctr., 1998—. Author: (with others) Provider's Guide To Hospital-Based Services, 1986; contbr. articles to profl. jours. Trustee Lenox Hill Hosp., 1994-2004. With USPHS, 1968-74. Fellow Am. Psychiatr. Assn., Am. Acad. of Psychoanalysis, N.Y. Acad. Medicine. Avocations: tennis, golf, reading biographies, history. Office Phone: 212-588-1205. Personal E-mail: ahcolmd@aol.com.

COLLINS, ALMA JONES, language educator, writer; d. Walter Melville Jones and Anne Teresa Harrington; m. Daniel Francis Collins, Apr. 9, 1994. BA, Conn. Coll., 1943; MA, Trinity Coll., 1952, U. Conn., 1962. Tchr., counselor West Hartford (Conn.) Bd. Edn., 1947-72; pres. Arts Universal Rsch. Assocs., 1978—. Interviewed Salvador Dali (CD located in archives Wadsworth Atheneum Mus. Art), 1978, 79; cons. for corp. product devel.; rep. for artists. Author: Danielle at the Wadsworth, 2004; contbr. articles to profl. jours. Mem. Phi Beta Kappa, Delta Kappa Gamma Internat. Avocation: writing poetry and fiction. Home and Office: 275 Steele Rd A318 West Hartford CT 06117-2763

COLLINS, ANNAZETTE R., state representative; b. Chgo., Apr. 28, 1962; m. Keith Langston; children: Angelique, Taylor. BS in Sociology, Chgo. State U., MS in Criminal Justice, 1983. Social worker Ada S. McKinley Interventions, 1982—83; correctional officer Fed. Bur. Prisons, 1983—86; social worker Cook County Social Svcs., 1986—90; adminstr. Dept. Children Family Svcs., 1990—2000, Chgo. Pub. Schs., 2000; mem. Ill. Ho. of Reps., 2000—. Mem. St. Joseph Sch. Bd., 1992—95; v.p. pres.'s club Cosmopolitan Cmty. Ch., 2001. Democrat. Baptist. Office: 252-W Stratton Office Bldg Springfield IL 62706 Home: 3235 W Warren Blvd Apt 2 Chicago IL 60624-2494 Home Phone: 773-342-1912; Office Phone: 773-533-0010. Personal E-mail: annazette@sbcglobal.net.

COLLINS, ANTHONY G. (TONY COLLINS), academic administrator; b. Australia; m. Karen Collins; 4 children. B in Civil Engring., Monash U., Melbourne, Australia, 1971; Master's Degree, Lehigh U., 1973, PhD, 1982. With environ. engrng. consulting firm, Australia, Utah Devel. Co.; from asst. prof. to prof. civil and environ. engrng. Clarkson U., Potsdam, NY, provost, 2001—03, pres., 2003—. Bd. mem. Ctrl. NY Metro. Devel. Authority, CITEC Mfg. & Tech. Solutions, NY Indoor Environ. Quality Ctr.; chair Associated Colleges St. Lawrence Valley. Recipient John W. Graham Faculty Rsch. award, Clarkson U., Disting. Teaching award, Outstanding Advising award. Office: Clarkson Univ Office of the Pres PO Box 5500 Potsdam NY 13699-5500*

COLLINS, ARLENE, secondary school educator; b. Mandan, ND, Sept. 7, 1940; d. John Marcellus and Cecelia Magdalena (Schaaf) Weber; m. Abdul Rahman Rana (dec.); children: Fazale Rahman, Habeeb Rahman; m. Freddie L. Collins. BS in math., N.D. State U., 1962; postgrad., W.Va. Inst. Tech., 1974; M in Edn. Adminstrn., WVCOGS, 1988. Cert. mid. sch. tchr., W.Va. Tchr. physics, math. Montgomery (W.Va.) H.S., 1970; tchr. math., sci. Spencer (W.Va.) Jr. H.S., 1974-80; sci. tchr. Poca (W.Va.) Mid. Sch., 1980—, team leader, 1983-96. W.Va. textbook adoption com., W.Va. Bd. Edn., 1984-90. Leader Girl Scouts U.S.A., Montgomery, 1966-70, 99—, Boy Scouts Am., Montgomery, 1966; bd. dirs. Violet Twp. Womens League, 2002—; vol. Am. Cancer Soc. Fellow: African Am. Law Enforcement Agts. Assn., Inc.; mem.: NOW (bd. dirs. 1986), Am. Fedn. Tchrs., Laurel Soc., VFW Aux., Am. Legion Aux. (sec. 2002—), Buckeye Sertoma, Soroptimists Internat. Home: 355 Drexel Pl Pickerington OH 43147 Home Phone: 614-920-4066; Office Phone: 614-920-4066. Personal E-mail: ac090@aol.com.

COLLINS, ARTHUR D., JR., medical products executive; b. Lakewood, Ohio, Dec. 10, 1947; BS, Miami U., Oxford, Ohio, 1969; MBA, U. Pa., 1973. With Abbott Laboratories, 1978—84, div. v.p., 1984—89, corp. v.p. diagnostic products, 1989—92; pres. Medtronic Internat., 1992—94; exec. v.p. Medtronic Inc., Mpls., 1992—94, COO, 1994—96, pres., COO, 1996—2001, pres., CEO, 2001—02, chmn., CEO, 2002—07, chmn., 2007—. Bd. dir. U.S. Bancorp, Cargill Inc.; chmn. Advanced Med. Tech. Ind. Assn. Mem. bd. overseers Wharton Sch., Univ. Pa. Office: Medtronic Inc 710 Medtronic Pkwy Minneapolis MN 55432-5604*

COLLINS, AUDREY B., judge; b. 1945; BA, Howard U., 1967; MA, Am. U., 1969; JD, UCLA, 1977. Asst. atty. Legal Aid Found. LA, 1977-78; with Office LA County Dist. Atty., 1978-94, dept. dist. atty., 1978-94, asst. dir. burs. ctrl. ops. and spl. ops., 1988-92, asst. dir. atty., 1992-94; judge. US Dist. Ct. (Ctrl. Dist.) Calif., 1994—. Dep. gen. counsel Office Spl. Acad. scholar Howard U.; named Lawyer of Yr., Langston Bar Assn., 1988; honoree Howard U. Alumni Club So. Calif., 1989; recipient Profl. Achievement award UCLA Alumni Assn., 1997, Ernestine Stahlhut award Women Lawyers Assn., 1999, Bernard S. Jefferson Justice of Yr. award John M. and Langston Bar Assn., 2006. Mem. FBA, Nat. Assn. Women Judges, Nat. Bar Assn. (life), Assn. Bus. Trial Lawyers (bd. dirs. 2004—), State Bar Calif. (com. bar examiners, chmn. subcom. on moral character 1992-93, co-chmn. 1993-94), LA County Bar Assn. (exec. com. litig. sect. 1999-2002, task force on criminal justice sys. 2002-03), Assn. LA County Dist. Attys. (pres. 1983), Black Women Lawyers LA County, Women Lawyers LA (life, bd. dirs. 2005-, bd. govs. 2005-06), Calif. Women Lawyers (life), Order of Coif, Phi Beta Kappa. Office: US Dist Ct Edward R Roybal Fed Bldg 255 E Temple St Ste 670 Los Angeles CA 90012-3334

COLLINS, BOBBY MCMANUS, II, dental educator; s. Bobby McManus Collins, Sr. and Gail Patrick Collins; m. Lisa Joye Dixon, Oct. 14, 1978. BA, U. NC, 1978, DDS, 1983; MS, U. Pitts., 2004. Diplomate Am. Bd. of Oral and Maxillofacial Pathology, 1998, cert. Oral and Maxillofacial Pathology U. Fla. Coll. Dentistry, 1995. With US Army Dental Corps, 1984, advanced through grades to maj., 1989, dental officer, 1984—92; resident in oral pathology U. Fla., Gainesville, 1992—95; fellow in head and neck pathology U. Pitts. Med. Ctr., 1995—96; asst. prof. U. Pitts. Sch. Dental Medicine, 1996—2005, assoc. prof., 2005—. Guest lectr. US.-Saudi Aramco, Dhahran, Saudi Arabia, 1997, Pa. Dental Assn., 2004—; cons. US Army Dental Corps, 1999—, USN Dental Corps, Bethesda, Md., 2000—; oral pathology cons. VA Med. Ctr., 2005—, Allegheny Gen. Hosp., 2007—. Contbr. articles to profl. jours., chapters to books. Decorated 2 Army Commendation medals, Expert Field Med. badge US Army 18th Airborne Corps, 5 Army Achievement medals, Nat. Def. Svc. medal, Meritorious Svc. medal; named to Best Dentists in Am., Woodward/White, 2004—05, Best of US Dentists/Oral and Maxillofacial Pathology, Pittsburgh's Best Dentists, 2007; recipient Faculty Award of Excellence/Appreciation, U. Pitts. Sch. Dental Medicine, 2000, 2003, 2004, 2005. Fellow: Acad. of Gen. Dentistry (Master 2004); mem.: Student Clinicians of the ADA, Am. Acad. of Oral and Maxillofacial Pathology (chmn., profl. and pub. rels. 2004—05), Omicron Kappa Upsilon (chmn. membership com. 2004—). Avocations: guitar, travel, volksmarching. Office: Univ Pitts Sch of Dental Med G-135 Salk 3501 Ter Pittsburgh PA 15261 Business E-Mail: bcollins@pitt.edu.

COLLINS, BRUCE W., lawyer; b. Dallas, Nov. 8, 1953; BA, Stanford U., 1975; JD with high honors, U. Tex., 1978. Bar: Tex. 1978. Law clk. to Hon. Robert M. Hill U.S. Dist. Ct. (no. dist.) Tex., 1978-79; ptnr. Carrington, Coleman, Sloman & Blumenthal LLP, Dallas. Mem. Tex. Law Review, 1976—78; approved arbitrator Nat. Assn. Securities Dealers Regulation, NY Stock Exch., Am. Stock Exch. Named one of Tex. Super Lawyer, 2003. Fellow: ABA, Tex. Bar Found., Dallas Bar Found.; mem.: Order of Coif. Office: Carrington Coleman Sloman Blumanthal 901 Main St 5500 Dallas TX 75202-3707 Office Phone: 214-855-3018. Office Fax: 214-758-3718. E-mail: bcollins@ccsb.com.

COLLINS, CARDISS, retired congresswoman; b. St. Louis, Sept. 24, 1931; m. George W. Collins (dec.); 1 child, Kevin. Student, Northwestern U.; LLD (hon.), John Marshall Law Sch., 1969, Winston-Salem State U., 1980, Spelman Coll., 1981, BarberScotia Coll., 1986; DHL (hon.), Rosary Coll., 1996; DrPsychology (hon.), Forest Inst. Profl. Psychology, 1993. Barber Scotia Coll.; mem. 93d-104th Congresses from 7th Ill. Dist., 1973-97; ret., 1997. Ranking minority mem. govt. reform & oversight com.; former chair. govt. activity and transp. subcom.; former chair commerce, consumer protection and competition subcom.; former majority whip-at-large; former asst. regional whip; former chair Congl. Black Caucus, sec.; dir. emeritus, former chair Congl. Black Caucus Found.; former chair Mems. Congress for Peace through Law; chairwoman Nielsen Media Rsch. Taskforce TV Measurement. Recipient award Roosevelt U., Loyola U., Scroll of Merit Nat. Med. Assn.; named to Hall of Fame Women's Sports Found. Mem. NAACP, Nat. Coun. Negro Women (past v.p.), Chgo. Urban League, Black Women's Agenda, The Chgo. Network, The Links, Dem. Nat. Com., Alpha Kappa Alpha. Democrat. Baptist. Home: 1110 Roundhouse Ln Alexandria VA 22314-5934

COLLINS, CARL RUSSELL, JR., industrial engineer; b. Williamsport, Pa., Dec. 29, 1926; s. Carl Russell, Sr. and Annis (Kilmer) C.; m. Rita Thomas, Oct. 3, 1959; children— James, Michael, Nancy BS in Indsl. Engring., Pa. State U., 1953. Div. sales mgr. Fla. Power Corp., St. Petersburg, 1961-64, asst. div. mgr., 1964-65, dist. mgr., 1965-67, div. mgr., 1967-79, v.p., 1979-85, George F. Young Inc., Architects and Engrs., St. Petersburg, 1986-91. Bd. dirs. Abilities, Inc. Bd. dirs. United Way, St. Petersburg, 1978, Com. of 100, 1981; v.p. Suncoasters, Inc., St. Petersburg, 1982; mem. adv. bd. Salvation Army, 1964—; active Meth. Ch., pres. Meth. Men, chmn. adminstrv. bd., lay leader, chmn. fin. com. With USN, 1944-46, as lt., 1953-56. Mem. Pa. State U. Alumni Club (life), Tau Beta Pi. Lodges: Kiwanis (pres. 1984). Republican. Avocations: photography, fishing, boating. Home: 5937 Tangerine Ave S Saint Petersburg FL 33707-4059

COLLINS, CARON LEE, music educator; d. James and Evelyn Fitch; m. Philip Collins, Oct. 15, 1978; children: Richard, Daniel. BA in Music Edn., Ind. U. Sch. of Music, 1978; MA, Marygrove Coll., 2002; PhD in Music, Ohio State U., 2007. Cert. profl. tchg. Dept. of Edn./Ohio, 2002. Dir. bands Diocese of Columbus, Ohio, 1980—2005; grad. tchg. assoc. Ohio State U. Sch. Music, 2005—07. Coord. instrumental music Diocese of Columbus, Ohio, 1983—2005. Dir.: (music) Columbus Diocese Summer Music Program, Hartley Area Jr. High Jazz-Rock Group, Columbus Diocese Music Marathon, Columbus Diocese Honor Band Program, Columbus Diocese Solo and Ensemble Contest. Vol. Meals on Wheels, Columbus, 2002—04; leader, merit badge counselor, vol. Boy Scouts Am., Columbus, 1995—2000; vol. Dem. Party, Columbus, 1992—2004; musician Redeemer Luth. Ch., Columbus, 1990—. Mem.: Coll. Music Soc., Ctrl. Ohio Assn. Cath. Educators (assoc.; negotiation com. mem. 2002—03), Music Educators Nat. Conf. (assoc.), Phi Kappa Phi. Avocations: hiking, camping, environment advocate. Personal E-mail: bandtchr1@hotmail.com.

COLLINS, CHRISTOPHER CARL, manufacturing executive; b. Schenectady, NY, May 20, 1950; s. Gerald Edward and Constance (Messier) Collins; m. Margaret Elizabeth Busby Cox, May 20, 1972 (div. Apr. 1978); 1 child, Carly Elizabeth; m. Mary Sue Kuhn, Jan. 9, 1988; children: Caitlin Christine, Cameron Christopher. BSME, N.C. State U., 1972; MBA, U. Ala., 1975. Sales engr. Westinghouse Elec. Corp., Birmingham, Ala., 1972-76, market rsch. analyst Buffalo, 1976-77, mgr. market planning, 1978-79, mgr. gearing divsn., 1980-82; pres., chmn., CEO Nuttall Gear Corp., Niagara Falls, NY, 1983-97; pres. Nuttall Gear, LLC, Niagara Falls, 1997-98; v.p. corp. devel. Wilson Greatbatch Ltd., Clarence, NY, 1999; chmn. bd., CEO, Bloch Industries LLC, Rochester, NY, 1999—; chmn. bd. Zepto Metrix Corp., Buffalo, 1999—; treas. Volland Electric Equipment Corp., Buffalo, 2001—; v.p. Easom Automation Sys., Detroit, 2003—. Mem. small bus. adv. coun. Fed. Res. Bank, NY, 1992—95; treas. Frontier Indsl. Supply, Buffalo, 2001—, Mead Supply, Buffalo, 2002—; chmn. Niagara Machinery Corp., Wilson, NY, 2003—04; chmn. and CEO Audubon Machinery Corp., Buffalo, 2004—; treas. Niagara Ceramics Corp., Buffalo, 2004—; chmn. Bio Clin. Partners, Boston, 2004—; chmn., CEO Oxygen Generating Sys. Internat., Buffalo, 2004—; treas. Lang & Washburn Electric, Buffalo, 2004—; pres., CEO Buckler Biodefense Corp., Buffalo, 2006—; v.p., bd. dirs. Virionyx Ltd., Auckland, New Zealand, 2006—; chmn. Starboard Sun Corp., Buffalo, 2007—. Bd. dirs. Kenmore Mercy Hosp., 1986-93; mem. ho. of dels. United Way, Buffalo, 1986-2003; mem. Buffalo Fin. Planning Com., 1994; v.p. adminstrn., exec. bd. dirs. Greater Niagara Frontier coun. Boy Scouts Am., 1998—; Rep. and Conservative candidate for U.S. Congress, 1998; mentor Ctr. for Entrepreneurial Leadership, SUNY, 1999— Mem. Chief Execs. Orgn., World Pres.'s Orgn., Young Pres. Orgn. (chmn. edn. com. 1988-89, chpt. chmn. 1989-90, chmn. membership 1990-91, chmn. exec. com. 1991-96), Brookfield Country Club, Holimont Ski Club. Republican. Roman Catholic. Avocations: golf, skiing, aviation. Home: 9660 Cobblestone Dr Clarence NY 14031-1576 Office: Bloch Industries LLC 140 Commerce Dr Rochester NY 14623-3592 Home Phone: 716-759-2591; Office Phone: 716-656-9900. Personal E-mail: ccc9660@prodigy.net.

COLLINS, DANIEL FRANCIS, lawyer; b. NYC, Mar. 5, 1942; s. Daniel Joseph and Madeline Elizabeth (Berger) C.; m. Margaret Mary Heyden, Jan. 15, 1966; children: Matthew C., Elizabeth C. BA in History and Polit. Sci., Hofstra U., 1964; JD, Am. U., 1967. Bar: D.C. 1968. Law clk. to E. Barrett Prettyman U.S. Ct. Appeals, Washington, 1967-68; assoc. Ross, Marsh & Foster, Washington, 1970-74, mem., 1974-78; ptnr. Brackett & Collins, P.C., Washington, 1978-87; v.p. regulatory law The Coastal Corp., Washington, 1987-2001; sr. v.p., dep. gen. counsel El Paso Corp., Washington, 2001—03; of counsel Fulbright & Jaworski, L.L.P., Washington, 2004—. Office: Fulbright & Jaworski LLP 801 Pennsylvania Ave NW Washington DC 20004 Home Phone: 301-229-2172; Office Phone: 202-662-4586. Personal E-mail: dfcollins@fulbright.com.

COLLINS, DANIEL W., accountant, educator; b. Marshalltown, Iowa, Sept. 1, 1946; s. Donald E. and Lorine R. (Metge) C.; children: Melissa, Theresa BBA with honors, U. Iowa, Iowa City, 1968, PhD, 1973. Asst. prof. acctg. Mich. State U., East Lansing, 1973-76, assoc. prof., 1976-77; vis. assoc. prof. U. Iowa, Iowa City, 1977-78, assoc. prof., 1978-81, prof., 1981-83, Murray chaired prof. acctg., 1983-88, Henry B. Tippie prof. of acctg., 1989—; vis. IBM prof. bus. Fuqua Sch. Bus., Duke U., 1988-89, chmn. dept. acctg., 1995—2003; vis. full prof. Kellogg Sch. Mgmt., Northwestern U., 2005. Mem. Fin. Acctg. Stds. Adv. Coun., acad. adv. bd. Deloitte & Touche; mem. Arthur Andersen doctoral dissertation awards com., 1996-99; bd. dirs. Ira B. McGladrey Inst., U.S. Bank, Iowa City, Christian Ret. Svcs., Iowa City. Assoc. editor Acctg. Rev., 1980-86; mem. editl. bd. Jour. Acctg. and Econs., 1978-2006, Jour. Acctg. Rsch., 2001-06; contbr. articles to profl. jours. 2d lt. US Army, 1972. Recipient All Univ. Tchr. scholar award Mich. State U., 1976, Gilbert Maynard Excellence in Tchg. award U. Iowa, 1985, Collegiate Tchg. award, 1998; Univ. Faculty scholar U. Iowa, 1980-82, Faculty Excellence award Iowa Bd. Regents, 2000, Outstanding Acctg. Alumnus award, U. Iowa, 2003. Mem. Am. Acctg. Assn. (disting. vis. faculty mem. Doctoral Consortium 1980, 89, dir. Doctoral Consortium 1987, program dir. ann. conv. 1988, dir. publs. 1989-91, exec. com. 1989-91, Outstanding Acctg. Educator award 2001), Acctg. Rschrs. Internat. Avocations: jogging, gardening. Office: U Iowa Coll Bus W262 PBAB Iowa City IA 52242-1000 Home: 2301 Muddy Creek Ln Coralville IA 52241

COLLINS, DAVID BROWNING, religious institution administrator; b. Hot Springs, Ark., Dec. 18, 1922; s. Charles Frederick and Agnes Elizabeth (George) C.; m. Maryon Virginia Moise, Oct. 14, 1945; children: Melissa, Christopher, Matthew, Geoffrey. BA, U. of the South, 1943, BD, 1948, STM, 1962, DD, 1974. Ordained to ministry Episcopal Ch. as deacon, 1948, as priest, 1949. Rector St. Andrew's Episc. Ch., Marianna, Ark., 1948-53; priest-in-charge Holy Cross Episc. Ch., West Memphis, Ark., 1949-53; chaplain and assoc. prof. of religion U. of the South, Sewanee, Tenn., 1953-66; dean Cathedral of St. Philip, Atlanta, 1966-84; exec. dir. Windsong Ministries, Inc., 1984—; pres. House of Deps. Episcopal Ch., 1985-91. Trustee Ch. Pension Fund, N.Y.C., 1976-88; mem. Bd. of Clergy Deployment, N.Y.C., 1971-76. Contbr. articles to profl. jours. Pres. Christian Council of Met. Atlanta, 1977-78; chaplain Atlanta Braves Booster Club, 1966-84. Served to lt. (j.g.) USNR, 1943-46. Episcopalian. Avocation: baseball. Home and Office: 132 Hearthstone Dr Woodstock GA 30189-5298 E-mail: davidbrev@bellsouth.net.

COLLINS, DENNIS ARTHUR, retired foundation administrator; b. Yakima, Wash., June 9, 1940; s. Martin Douglas and Louise Constance (Caccia) C.; m. Mary Veronica Paul, June 11, 1966; children: Jenifer Ann, Lindsey Kathleen. BA, Stanford U., 1962, MA, 1963; LHD, Mills Coll., 1994, U. San Diego, 2002. Assoc. dean admissions Occidental Coll., Los Angeles, 1964-66, dean admissions, 1966-68, dean of students, 1968-70; headmaster Emma Willard Sch., Troy, N.Y., 1970-74; founding headmaster San Francisco U. High Sch., 1974-86; pres. James Irvine Found., San Francisco, 1986—2002; ret. Trustee Coll. Bd., N.Y.C., 1981-85, Ind. Ednl. Svcs., Princeton, N.J., 1981-85, Calif. Assn. Ind. Schs., L.A., 1982-86, Branson Sch., 1987-89, Aspen Inst. Nonprofit Sector rsch. Fund, 1992—; chmn. bd. So. Calif. Assn. Philanthropy, L.A., 1989-91, No. Calif. Grantmakers, 1987-90; dir. Rebuild L.A., 1992-93. Trustee Cathedral Sch. for Boys, San Francisco, 1976-82, Marin Country Day Sch., Corte Madera, Calif., 1978-84, San Francisco Exploratorium, 1984-86, Ind. Sector, Washington, 1987-95, Am. Farmland Trust, Washington, 1992—, Occidental Coll, Nat. Ctr. for Pub. Policy and Higher Edn., Ctr. for Philanthropy and Pub. Policy; bd. dirs., vice chmn. Children's Hosp. Found., San Francisco, 1984-86; chmn. bd. dirs. Coun. for Cmty. Based Devel., Washington, 1989-92. Mem. Council on Founds., World Trade Club, Univ. Club, Calif. Club (LA). Democrat. Episcopalian. Home: PO Box 1248 Belvedere Tiburon CA 94920-4248

COLLINS, DENNIS GLENN, mathematics professor; b. Gary, Ind., June 26, 1944; s. Glenn and Irene Martha (Richman) C.; m. Barbara Jean Hamilton, July 14, 1979; 1 child, Glenn H. BA, Valparaiso U., 1966; MS, Ill. Inst. Tech., 1970, PhD, 1975. Temp. instr. Mich. State U., East Lansing, 1975-76; instr. U. New Orleans, 1976-79; asst. prof. Valparaiso U., Ind., 1979-82; from asst. prof. to prof. math. U. PR, Mayaguez, 1982—, chmn. math. dept. pers. com., 1994-95. Vis. scholar U. PR, Mayaguez, 2003-2004; vis. assoc. prof. dept. math. Mich. State U., 1988-89; judge computer sci. Internat. Sci. and Engring. Fair, San Juan, PR, 1987; presenter, lectr. in field. Created postcards of 120 mathematicians and physicists, 1983-2001, New Orleans Serenade, 2006; composed short Columbus Cantata and short Spaceship Cantata, Short Cosmic Cantata, One Size Fits All, 2001. NSF fellow, 1966—67, vis. scholar, Mich. State U., 1988—89, 1996—97. Mem.: NY Acad. Scis., Soc. Indsl. and Applied Mathematicians, Am. Math. Soc. (informatics and cybernetics 1990, dialog com. to rector 1997—2003, 4th Energy Conf. 2006), Internat. Soc. for Optical Engring., Soc. Photo-optical Instrumentation Engrs., Internat. Soc. for Sys. Sci., Sigma Xi (treas. local chpt. 2000—, pres. 2003—04). Lutheran. Achievements include patents in field. Home: 7108 Grand Blvd Hobart IN 46342-6628 Office: U PR Dept Math Mayaguez PR 00681 Personal E-mail: d-collins-pr@hotmail.com.

COLLINS, DUANE E., manufacturing executive; BSME, U. Wis.; postgrad., Harvard U. Sales engr. Parker Hannifin Corp., Cleve., 1961, gen. sales mgr., ops. mgr. hose products divsn., gen. mgr., 1973-76, v.p. ops. fluid connectors group, 1976-80, pres. fluid connectors group, 1980-83, corp. v.p., 1983-87, pres. internat., 1987-88, corp. exec. v.p., pres. internat., 1988-92, vice chmn., 1992-93, CEO, 1993—2001, chmn., 2001—04. Bd. dirs. Parker Hannifin Corp., Sherwin-Williams Co., MeadWestvaco, MTD Holdings. Office: Parker Hannifin Corp 6035 Parkland Blvd Cleveland OH 44124-4141

COLLINS, E. DALE, surgeon, educator; d. Curtis David and Vera Virginia Collins; m. George L. Kachikis, Oct. 3, 1981; children: Isabella Maria Kachikis, Moskoula Virginia Kachikiks. MD, Emory U., Atlanta, 1989. Cert. Am. Bd. Plastic Surgery, 1997. Asst. prof. surgery Dartmouth-Hitchcock Med. Ctr., Lebanon, NH, 1995—2001, assoc. prof. surgery, 2001—; and dir. comprehensive breast oncology program Norris Cotton Cancer Ctr., Lebanon, NH, 1999—. Dir. comprehensive breast program Dartmouth-Hitchcock Med. Ctr., 1999—. Author: (monograph) Collaborative Surgical Management of Breast Cancer; editor (author): (book) Manual of Acute Hand Injuries; author: (chpt.) New Trends in Clinical Research, (article) The health burden of breast hypertrophy (James Barrett Brown award for Best Paper, 2001). Named one of Outstanding Young Women of Am., Emory U. Sch. Medicine, 1989, Best Doctors for Women in Am., Ladies Home Jour. mag., 2002; recipient Am. Med. Women's Assn. award for Academic Achievement, Emory U., 1989, Harmes Surg. Scholar award, Dartmouth-Hitchcock Med. Ctr. Dept. Surgery, 1997-2000, Mosenthal Tchg. award, Dartmouth Med. Sch., 2003, William H. Kadel Alumni Medal, Eckerd Coll., 2004. Mem.: Soc. for Med. Decision Making, New Eng. Soc. Plastic and Reconstructive Surgeons (counselor 2004—), Am. Soc. Plastic Surgeons, Am. Assn. Plastic Surgeons, Alpha Omega Alpha Nat. Med. Honor Soc. Achievements include development of an Internet-based utility assessment to determine patient preference for breast hypertrophy. Office: Dartmouth Hitchcock Medl Ctr One Med Ctr Dr Lebanon NH 03755 Office Phone: 603-653-3500. Office Fax: 603-653-3502. Business E-Mail: e.dale.collins@hitchcock.org.*

COLLINS, EILEEN MARIE, astronaut; b. Elmira, NY, Nov. 19, 1956; d. James Edward and Rose Marie (O'Hara) C.; m. James Patrick Youngs, Aug. 1, 1987; 2 children. AS in Math., Sci., Corning C.C., 1976; BA in Math., Econs., Syracuse U., 1978; grad., USAF Undergrad. Pilot Tng., Vance AFB, Okla., 1979, USAF Test Pilot Sch., Edwards AFB, Calif., 1990; MS in Ops. Rsch., Stanford U., 1986; MA in Space Systems Mgmt., Webster U., 1989; student, Air Force Inst. Techology, 1986; grad., Air Force Test Pilot Sch., Edwards AFB, Calif., 1990. Commd. 2d lt. USAF, 1978, advanced through grades to col., 1993, T-38 instr. pilot 71st flight tng. wing Vance AFB, 1979-82, C-141 aircraft comdr. and instructor pilot, 86th mil. airlift squadron Travis AFB, Calif., 1983-85, ret., 2005; asst. prof. math., T-41 instr. pilot USAF Acad., Colorado Springs, Colo., 1986-89; astronaut Johnson Space Ctr. NASA, Houston, 1991—2006. Served on astronaut support team responsible for Orbiter prelaunch check-out, final launch configuration, crew ingress/egress, landing/recovery; spacecraft communicator, CAPCOM, also served as the astronaut office spacecraft systems branch chief, chief information officer, shuttle branch chief, astronaut safety branch chief; pilot, space shuttle Discovery (STS-63), 1995 (first women pilot of space shuttle), space shuttle Atlantis (STS-84), 1997; comdr. space shuttle, Columbia (STS-93), 1999 (first women shuttle comdr.); crew comdr. space shuttle, (STS-114) Discovery; during this Return To Flight mission, the crew tested and evaluated new procedures for flight safety, shuttle inspections and repair techniques, 2005. Col. USAF. Decorated Air Force Commendation medal with one oak leaf cluster, Air Force Meritorious svc. medal with one oak leaf cluster, Armed Forces Expeditionary medal for svc. in Grenada (Operation Urgent Fury, 1983), Def. Superior Svc. medal, Def. Meritorious Svc. medal, Disting. Flying Cross, French Legion Honor, Disting. Flying Cross, NASA Outstanding Leadership medal, NASA Space Flight medals; recipient Harmon Trophy, 1995, Free Spirit award, 2006. Mem.: Am. Inst. Aeronautics and Astronautics, US Space Found., Order of Daedalians, Air Force Assn., The Ninety-Nines, Women Military Aviators. Avocations: running, golf, hiking, camping, reading, photography, astronomy.

COLLINS, ELSIE MARTHA, apparel designer, costume designer; d. Thomas Baird Mehaffey and Irene Clorinda Orsini; Student, RI Sch. Design, Providence, 1980—81. Costume seamstress Trinity Repertory Co., Providence, 1977—78; costume designer Barker Playhouse, Providence, 1985, Opera RI, Providence, 1986, Looking Glass Theater, Providence, 1986, Montanaro Mime Ensemble, South Paris, Maine, 1986; costume cutter, draper The Walnut St. Theater, Phila., 1987; costume designer, cutter Shakespearean Theater Maine, Monmouth, 1998; costumer designer Opera Providence, 2007; costume designer Michelangelo Performing Arts Ctr., 2007, Cornerstone Theatre, RI, 2007. Owner, designer Samsara Designs, Providence, 1987—95. Artistic dir. (exhibitions) One Hundred Yrs. Fashion: 1850-1950, 2002. Grantee, RI State Coun. on the Arts. Avocations: guitar, reading, writing, poetry, antiques. Office Phone: 401-330-0674.

COLLINS, ELWOOD F., lawyer; BA, Fordham Univ., 1968; JD, NYU, 1971. Bar: N.Y. 1972, Fla. 1979. Adminstrv. ptnr. & mem. mgmt. com. Kirkpatrick & Lockhart Nicholson Graham LLP, NYC. Office: Kirkpatrick & Lockhart Nicholson Graham LLP 599 Lexington Ave New York NY 10022-6030 Office Phone: 212-536-4005. Office Fax: 212-536-3901. Business E-Mail: ecollins@klng.com.

COLLINS, FRANCIS S., federal agency administrator, geneticist, physician; b. Apr. 14, 1950; BS in Chemistry, U. Va., 1970; PhD in Physical Chemistry, Yale U., 1974; MD, U. N.C., Chapel Hill, 1977. Residency and chief residency in internal medicine N.C. Memorial Hospital, Chapel Hill, 1978—81; fellow in human genetics Yale U., 1981—84; prof. internal med. and human genetics, chief med. genetics U. Michigan, Howard Hughes Med. Inst, 1984—93; dir. Human Genome Project, 1992—2003; chief, genetic and molecular biology NIH, 1993; dir. Nat. Ctr. for Human Genome Rsch. (became Nat. Human Genome Rsch. Inst. in 1997), NIH, Bethesda, Md., 1993—; sr. investigator, Genome Technology Br. Nat. Human Genome Rsch. Inst., NIH, Bethesda, Md. Overseer Internat. Human Genome Sequencing Consortium; lectr. in field. Contbr. articles to profl. jours.; contbd. foreward Coming to Peace with Science: Bridging the Worlds Between Faith and Science, 2004. Vol. physician rural missionary hosp., Nigeria. Co-recipient Gairdner Found. Internat. award for work on cystic fibrosis, 1990; recipient Mendel medal, Biotechnology Heritage award, Chemical Heritage Found. and Biotechnology Industry Orgn., 2001, Gairdner Found. Internat. award for merit, 2002, Allan award, Am. Soc. Human Genetics, 2005; named Va. Outstanding Scientist of Yr., Sci. Mus. of Va., 2001 Mem.: IOM, NAS, AMA (Scientific Achievement award 2001). Achievements include working on methods of crossing large stretches of DNA to identify disease genes, which was named "positional cloning"; identifying the gene for cystic fibrosis with Lap-Chee Tsui and Jack Riordan in 1989; identifying the neurofibromatosis gene with colleagues in 1990; identifying the defective gene that causes Huntington's Disease with colleagues in 1993; identifying the gene for multiple endocrine neoplasia type 1 and the M4 type of adult acute leukemia with colleagues; overseeing a complex multidisciplinary project, Human Genome Project, aimed at mapping and sequencing the entire human DNA, and determining aspects of its function. A working draft of the human genome sequence was announced in June, 2000, an initial analysis was published in February, 2001, and the completed sequence was announced in April, 2003; founding of the National Human Genome Research Institute Division of Intramural Research (DIR) in 1994, which has developed into one of the nation's premier research centers in human genetics; serving as strong advocate for protecting privacy of genetic information and as a national leader in efforts to prohibit gene-based insurance discrimination. Office: Nat Human Genome Rsch Inst NIH Bldg 31/4B09 31 Center Dr 9000 Rockville Pike Bethesda MD 20892 Office Phone: 301-496-0844. Fax: 301-402-2218. Business E-Mail: francisc@mail.nih.gov.

COLLINS, FRANK, JR., dentist, educator; b. Jackson, Miss., Mar. 1, 1965; s. Frank Collins, Sr. and Emma H. Collins. BS in Biology, U. So. Miss., 1988; DDS, Howard U., 1996; cert. in gen. dentistry, Luth. Med. Ctr., Bklyn., 2002. Instr. Hinds C.C., Raymond, Miss., 1997—2000; gen. practice resident St. Mary's Hosp., Waterbury, Conn., 2001. Mem.: ADA (Am. Dental Assn.), Acad. Gen. Dentistry. Avocations: music, jogging.

COLLINS, FRANK EDWIN, lawyer; b. Jackson, Mo., Apr. 10, 1954; s. Arthur Black and Margaret Collins; m. Barbara Jo Justice, Oct. 26, 1974; children: Justin, Eric, Keith, Garrett. BA, U. Mo., Kansas City, 1976, JD, 1979. Bar: Mo. 1979. Counsel Mo. Divsn. Ins., Jefferson City, 1979-81; assoc. gen. counsel Blue Cross/Blue Shield, Kansas City, Mo., 1981—86; gen. counsel, sec. Prime Health, Inc., 1986—97; exec. v.p., gen. counsel, sec. Sierra Health Svcs., Las Vegas, Nev., 1997—. Pres. Sierra Health Holdings, Inc.; sec. S.W. Realty, Inc., Sierra Acquisition Corp., Prime Holdings, Inc., others; bd. dirs. numerous subsidiaries of Sierra Health Svc. Bd. dirs. United Way, Las Vegas. Mem. Mo. Bar Assn. Office: Sierra Health Svcs 2724 N Tenaya St PO Box 15645 Las Vegas NV 89128 Office Phone: 702-242-7189. Office Fax: 702-242-1532. E-mail: leg104@sierrahealth.com.

COLLINS, FREDERICK GEORGE, music educator, secondary school educator; b. Pitts., Pa., Feb. 8, 1960; s. Frederick George and Barbara Eleanor Collins; m. Mary Nicollet Yackovich, Aug. 6, 1983; children: Catherine Nicole, Lauren Elyse, Megan Elizabeth, Kristen Marie. BS in Music Edn., Duquesne U., Pitts., Pa., 1983; MA in Music Edn., Ind. U. Pa., Ind., Pa., 1997. Cert. tchr. Pa., 1983. Dir. bands North Cath. H.S., Pitts., 1983—84, Wapahani H.S., Selma, Ind., 1984—85, Jasper (Ind.) H.S., 1985—87, Walkersville (Md.) H.S., 1987—92, Mt. Pleasant (Pa.) Area H.S., 1992. Mem.: NEA, KC, Music Educators Nat. Conf. Home: 775 Hecla Rd Mount Pleasant PA 15666 Home Phone: 724-423-1263; Office Phone: 724-547-4100 1660. Office Fax: 724-547-0526. Business E-Mail: fcollins@mpasd.net.

COLLINS, GAIL, former newspaper editor; b. Cin., Nov. 25, 1945; m. Daniel J. Collins. BA in Journalism, Marquette U., 1967; MA in Govt., U. Mass., 1971. Founder Conn. State News Bur., 1972—77; freelance writer, 1977—79; sr. editor Conn. Mag.; columnist Conn. Bus. Jour., 1977—79; host pub. affairs program Conn. Pub. TV, 1977—79; instr. journalism So. Conn. State Coll., 1977—79; fin. reporter UPI, NYC, 1982—85; columnist NY Daily News, NYC, 1985—91, NY Newsday, NYC, 1991—95; mem. editl. bd. The NY Times, NYC, 1995—2007, host This Week Close-Up cable news program, 1997—, columnist op-ed page, 2000—01, editl. page editor, 2001—07. Author: Scorpion Tongues: Gossip, Celebrity, and American Politics, 1998, America's Women: Four Hundred Years of Dolls, Drudges, Helpmates and Heroines, 2003; co-author (with Dan Collins): The Millennium Book, 1991. Recipient Meyer Berger award, Columbia U., 1987, Matrix award, Women in Comm, 1989, award for commentary, AP, 1994; Bagehot fellow, Columbia U., 1981—82.*

COLLINS, GORDON DENT, recording industry executive; b. Berkeley, Calif., Mar. 27, 1924; s. Edward Everett and Dorothy Janet C.; m. Louise Norma Krivicich, July 23, 1960; children: Daniel Edward, Patrick Doyle, Christine Anne, Gordon Jr. Student, U. Maine, 1943-44; BSEE magna cum laude, U. Wash., 1948; postgrad., Stanford U., 1960-63. Registered profl. engr., N.Y. Founder, chief executive officer Collins Rec. Co., Los Altos, Calif., 1962—. Assigned to Comissariat à l'energie Atomique, Ctr. Nuclear Studies, France. Served to lt. U.S. Army Signal Corps, 1943-52. Named Sr. of Yr. Elfun Soc., San Jose, Calif., 1980. Mem Soc. Engrs. and Scientists of France, Phi Beta Kappa, Tau Beta Pi, Phi Kappa Psi, Sigma Xi. Clubs: No. Calif. Golf Assn. (Pebble Beach). Achievements include patents in field of nuclear power, sodium technology, fast breeder reactors; development of atomic power. Avocations: golf, travel, photography, genealogy. Office: PO Box 934 Los Altos CA 94023-0934

COLLINS, HARKER, retired economist, manufacturing and publishing executive; b. Denver, Nov. 24, 1924; s. Clem Wetzel and Marie (Harker) C.; m. Emily Harvey, Aug. 23, 1957; children: Catherine Emily, Cynthia Lee, Constance Marie. BS, U.S. Naval Acad., 1945. Asst. buyer Montgomery Ward & Co., NYC, 1947-51; prodn. mgr. Diamond Hosiery Mills, High Point, NC, 1953-55; v.p. Vanette Hosiery Mills, Dallas, 1955-59; v.p., dir. Grote Mfg. Co., Madison, Ind., 1959-71; group v.p., gen. mgr. Bendix Corp., South Bend, Ind., 1971-73; pres., dir. Bandag, Inc., Muscatine, Iowa, 1973-78, chief exec. officer, 1974-78; pres., chief exec. officer, bd. dirs. Harker Collins & Co., Lubbock, Tex., 1978-98; pub. newsletters The Economy and You, Update, 1978-96; econ. counsel Automotive Svc. Industry Assn., 1978-91; exec. v.p., bd. dirs. Indsl. Molding Corp., Lubbock, 1993-97; pres., bd. dirs. Indl. Molding Corp., Lubbock, 1997; ret., 1997. Instr. U. Denver, 1948; chmn. automotive industry liaison com. with Dept. Transp., 1968-86, automotive industry excise tax com., 1964-70, automotive industry tariff com., 1964-70, joint operating com. for automotive trade shows, 1969-77 Mem. Pres.'s Com. Hwy. Safety, 1966-68; Bd. dirs. Iowa Ind. Coll. Found., 1976-86; bd. fellows Northwood Inst., 1974—; alderman City of Rancho Viejo, Tex., 1980-87. Served to ensign USN, 1945-47; to lt. USNR, 1951-53. Recipient Automotive Industry Leadership award, 1965, 74; Fin. World award as chief exec. of yr., 1975, 77 Mem. Automotive Svc. Industry Assn. (vice chmn. 1966-67, chmn. 1968-69, chmn. heavy duty exec. com. 1969-71, chmn. safety and environ. protection com. 1962-67, 70-78), Automotive Sales Coun. (bd. dirs. 1966-67, sec. 1971-72, v.p. 1972-73, pres. 1973-74), Am. Nat. Standards Inst. (chmn. task force on used vehicle standards 1966-74), Home Products Safety Coun. (pres. 1960-63), Medicine Cabinet Mfg. Coun. (pres. 1960-63, bd. dirs. 1960-68), Truck Safety Equipment Inst. (pres. 1960-63, dir. 1960-68).

COLLINS, HAROLD R., director; b. Hartland, Ala., Mar. 14, 1919; s. Francis A. Collins and Vestie Gertrude Kinsaul; m. Ruth Collins (dec.); children: Harold Ray Jr., Gene Bassett. BS, Troy U., Ala.; MA, EdS, U. Ala., Tuscaloosa; postgrad., Columbia U., NYC. Tchr. sci. Freeport Jr. H.S., Fla.; tchr. biology Jay H.S., Fla.; prin. Zion Chapel Jr. H.S., Jack, Ala., Goshen H.S., Ala.; asst. supt. Pike County Schs., Troy, Ala., supt.; prof. adminstrn. and curriculum grad sch. Troy State U.; supt. Mobile City and County Schs., Ala.; exec. dir. Spring Hill Edn. Lab., Mobile. Adj. prof. U. Ala., Coll. Edn., U. South Ala., Troy State U., Spring Hill Coll., Ala. State U. Mem. State Indsl. Adv. Coun.; mem. exec. bd. Boy Scouts Am.; mem. Mobile United, Inc., Mobile Area Cmty. Action Com., Mobile Mental Health Adv. Bd., State Adv. Coun. Spl. Edn., State Adult Edn. Adv. Coun.; bd. dirs. Jr. Achievement. Mem.: NEA, Mobile Area C. of C., Internat. Platform Assn., Nat. Fedn. Urban-Suburban Sch. Dists., Ala. Assn. Elem. Sch. Prins., Ala. Assn. Sch. Adminstrs., Nat. Assn. Secondary Sch. Prins., Nat. Assn. Sch. Bds., Am. Assn. Secondary Sch. Adminstrs., Mobile County Edn. Assn., Ala. Edn. Assn., Rotary, Mensa, Phi Delta Kappa, Kappa Phi Kappa. Office: Springhill Edn Lab 4307 Old Shell Rd Mobile AL 36608

COLLINS, HARRY DAVID, forensic, mechanical and nuclear engineer, claims consultant; b. Brownsville, Pa., Nov. 18, 1931; s. Harry Alonzo and Cecilia Victoria (Morris) Collins; m. Suzanne DyLong, May 11, 1956; children: Cynthia L., Gerard P. BSME, Carnegie Mellon U., 1954; MS in Physics, U.S. Naval Postgrad. Sch., 1961; postgrad., U.S. Army Command and Gen. Staff Coll., 1970, George Washington U., 1971—72. Registered profl. engr., Miss., La. Commd. 2nd lt. C.E. US Army, 1954, advanced through grades to lt. col., 1969; sr. advisor Vietnam Engr. Sch., 1968—69; comdr. 802d Heavy Engr. Constrn. Bn., Republic of Korea, 1972—73; dep. dist. engr. and acting dist. engr. Army Engr. Dist., New Orleans, 1973—75; v.p. deLaureal Engrs., Inc., New Orleans, 1975-78; v.p. Near East mktg. and project mgmt. Kidde Cons., Inc., 1978—82; dir. new bus. devel. and project mgmt. North Africa, Mid. East Am. Mid. East Co., Inc., 1982—84; sr. cons. Wagner, Hohns, Inglis, Inc., 1984—91; chief engr. bd. commrs. Orleans Levee Dist. State of La., 1981—82; pres. Harry D. Collins and Assoc., New Orleans, 1992—. Pres. La. Security Products & QuTech, 1994—97. Contbr. articles to profl. jours. Decorated Legion of Merit, Bronze Star, Meritorious Svc. medal with oak leaf cluster, Vietnam Nat. Commendation medal. Mem.: NSPE, ASME, N.Y. Acad. Sci., Assn. Profl. Genealogists, Nat. Acad. Forensic Engrs. (diplomate, cert.), Am. Arbitration Assn. (mem. panel arbitrators), Am. Nuc. Soc., La. Engring. Soc., Am. Soc. Mil. Engrs., Sigma Xi. Home: 3814 Camp St New Orleans LA 70115-2629 Home Phone: 504-621-8605. Personal E-mail: hdc1@cox.net.

COLLINS, IZOLA E., retired music educator; b. Galveston, Tex., Oct. 26, 1929; d. Brister Marshall and Viola Cornelia Fedford; m. Roy L. Collins Jr., Dec. 26, 1952 (dec.); children: June Viola Collins Pulliam, Roy Lester III, Cheryl Lynette Marguerite Collins Crayton. BA in Music, Prairie View A&M U., 1948; MusM, Northwestern U., 1953. Band dir. Hilliard HS, Bay City, Tex., 1948—53, Lorraine Crosby HS, Hitchcock, Tex., 1958—65; music instr. Golaid Elem. Sch., Galveston, 1966—68; music tchr., choir dir. Stephen F. Austin Jr. HS, Galveston, 1968—84; band dir., music tchr. Galveston Cath. Sch., 1986—87, 1987—88; ret., 1988. Trustee, v.p., pres., sec. Galveston Ind. Sch. Dist., 1985—95. Author: Divine Light Never Goes Away, 2001, Island of Color: Where Juneteenth Started, 2004. Mem. governing bd. St. Mary's Hosp., Galveston, 1993—96; v.p. Galveston Partnership, 2000—02; bd. dirs. Old Ctrl. Cultural Ctr., Marcus Netherly Scholarship, Galveston Cultural Arts Coun., St. Vincent's House, Galveston Historical Found. Named Citizen of Yr., Nat. Pan-Hellenic Coun., Galveston, 2000; recipient Steel Oleander award, Galveston Hist. Found., 2006, Dr. Martin Luther King Humanitarian award, Kingfest Com., Galveston, 2006. Mem.: Galveston County Assn. Black Sch. Educators (founder), Nat. Assn. Black Sch. Educators, Galveston Musical Club (pres. 1996—98, 2003—05), Tex. Fedn. Music Clubs (life; legislative chmn. 2000—06, 4th v.p. 2005—, dist. V pres. 2005—07, state parliamentarian 2007), Delta Sigma Theta (Golden Life mem.). Democrat. Mem. African Methodist Episcopal Ch. Avocations: jazz, dance, cruising, theater.

COLLINS, J. BARCLAY, II, lawyer, oil industry executive; b. Gettysburg, Pa., Oct. 21, 1944; s. Jennings Barclay and Golda Olevia (Hook) C.; m. Janna Claire Fall, June 25, 1966; children: J. Barclay III, L. Christian. AB magna cum laude, Harvard U., 1966; JD magna cum laude, Columbia U., 1969. Bar: NY 1969. Law clk. to presiding judge US Ct. Appeals (2nd cir.), NYC, 1969-70; assoc. Cravath, Swaine & Moore, NYC, 1970-78; v.p., asst. gen. counsel City Investing Co., NYC, 1978-84; exec. v.p., gen. counsel Amerada Hess Corp., NYC, 1984—, bd. dir. Bd. dirs. Premier Oil plc, Nuvera Fuel Cells Inc. Trustee Bklyn. Hosp., Bklyn.; bd. dirs. United Hosp. Fund NY, past gov. Bklyn. Heights Assn. Mem. ABA, NY Bar Assn., NYC Yacht Club. Clubs: Heights Casino (Bklyn.); Harvard NYC. Office: Amerada Hess Corp Ste 810 1185 Avenue Of The Americas New York NY 10036-2601*

COLLINS, J. MICHAEL, retired public broadcasting executive; b. Buffalo, Feb. 17, 1935; s. John Lloyd and Celestine (Buhrle) C.; m. Marilyn Anne Mercer, Aug. 5, 1961; children: Kevin Michael, Timothy David, Sheila Anne, Jeanne Mary, Julie Lynn. BS in Social Scis., Canisius Coll., 1957, LHD (hon.), 1978; postgrad., Mich. State U., 1957-58. Promotion mgr. Western N.Y. Pub. Broadcasting Assn. (Stas. WNED-TV-AM-FM, WNEQ-TV, WNJA-FM), Buffalo, 1959-60, dir. devel., 1961-62, asst. sta. mgr., 1963-65, gen. mgr., 1966-69, pres., 1970-98; sr. cons., 1998-99; ret., 1999. Co-author: ETV: The Farther Vision, 1967. Mem. ho. of dels. United Way of Buffalo and Erie County, 1967-98; trustee Ea. Ednl. Network, 1965-95, treas., 1967-70, exec. com., 1967-74, 78-81, 84-85, 88-90, 92-94, chmn. budget and fin. com., 1967-70, pres., 1971-72, chmn., 1973-74, v.p., 1980-81, 88-90, 92-93, adv. bd. interregional progam svc., 1984-90; trustee Am. Program Svc., 1993-96, exec. com., 1993-96, fin. com., 1994-96; mem. CATV com., devel. adv. com. NAEB; exec. bd. Niagara Frontier coun. Boy Scouts Am., 1971-76; exec. com. Cantalician Ctr., 1978-85; trustee St. Joseph's Collegiate Inst., 1978-85 (mem. steering com. capital campaign, 1998-2000); chmn. PBS Border Sta.Consortium, 1986-88; bd. dirs. PBS, 1972-78, 80-86, vice-chmn., 1975, nat. program policy com., 1990-95; mem. Governance Task Force, 1996; bd. dirs. PBS Enterprises, 1985-90, Nat. Data Cast, Inc., 1989-90; trustee Assn. Am. Pub. TV Stas., 1987-93, exec. com., 1989-93, chmn. nominating com., 1989; mem. Kenmore-Tonawanda Pub. Schs. Bd. Edn., 1974-81, v.p., 1977, pres., 1978; trustee Chautauqua Instn., 1988-96, devel. com., 1989, program com., 1986-95, exec. com., 1989-95, personnel com., 1990-95, mktg. com., 1994-95, fin. com., 1995-96, bldg. and grounds com., 1995-96, edn./youth/recreation com., 1989-93, 96-97, chmn., 1989-93, mission policy com., 1997-98; bd. dirs. Buffalo Coun. World Affairs, 1994-95, Blue Shield West N.Y., 1990-92, Buffalo Broadcasters, 2006—, Legal Svcs. for the Elderly, 2006—; mem. fin. com. St. Amelia Ch., 1990-, mem. stewardship com., 1993—, chmn., 1993-2001, trustee, 2001—, mem. bishop's com. laity, Roman Cath. Diocese Buffalo, 1995—; bd. dirs. John Lodge McHugh Endowment, 2000—, chmn., 2000-06; trustee Kenmore-Tonawanda Pub. Libr., 2006—. Recipient Focus award Buffalo Courier Express, 1978, Signum Fidei award St. Joseph's Collegiate Inst., 1984, Man of Yr. award Nat. Columbus Day Com., 1985, 92, Matrix award Women in Comm., 1985; named one of 100 Most Influential People in Western N.Y., Bus. First, 1996; inducted into Buffalo Broadcast Pioneers Hall of Fame, 1999. Mem. N.Y. State Ednl. Radio and TV Assn. (trustee, pres. 1964-65, treas. 1963, editor newsletter 1962), Pub. Rels. Assn. Western N.Y. (pres. 1966), Nat. Assn. Ednl. Broadcasters, Buffalo Broadcasters Assn. (bd. dirs. 2005-), Canisius Coll. Alumni Assn. (bd. govs. 1960-62, 70-73). Avocations: reading, collecting and tasting wine, photography.

COLLINS, JACK ADAM, mechanical engineer; b. Columbus, Ohio, Nov. 23, 1929; married, 1958; 4 children. BSME, Ohio State U., 1952, MSc, 1954, PhD in Mech. Engring., 1963. From rsch. asst. to rsch. assoc. mech. engring. Ohio State U., 1952-63, assoc. prof. mech. engring., 1972-74; assoc. prof. Ariz. State U., 1963-72, chmn. mech. design sect. dept. mech. engring., 1975-92, prof., 1974-92; ret. Cons. Babcock & Wilcox Rsch. Ctr., GE Co., AiRsch. Mfg. Co., Worthington Industries, Owens/Corning Fiberglass. Author: Failure of Material in Mechanical Design: Analysis Prediction Prevention, 1981, rev., 1993, Mechanical Design of Machine Elements and Machines: A Failure Prevention Perspective, 2003. Mem. ASME (Machine Design award 1997), Am. Soc. Engring. Edn., Am. Soc. Testing and Materials. Achievements include experimental and analytical stress and deflection analysis; experimental and analytical failure analysis, including fatigue, creep, wear and fretting. Home: 4447 E Via Dona Rd Cave Creek AZ 85331 Business E-Mail: collins.13@osu.edu.

COLLINS, JAMES DUFFIELD, marine engineer, editor; b. Logansport, Ind., Dec. 20, 1919; s. Louis Duffield and Gaynelle May (Mobley) C.; m. Barbara Cook, Mar. 12, 1949; children: Barbara Cook Jr., James Duffield II. BS in Marine Engring., U.S. Mcht. Marine Acad., 1946. Process engr. Gen. Motors Corp., Indpls., 1940-44; marine engr. Moore McCormack Lines, NYC, 1946; sr. project engr. rsch. and devel. Gen. Motors Corp., Indpls., 1946-82; editor-at-large Marcel Dekker, Inc., NYC, 1986—. Contbg. author: Materials and Processes, 1985; author: Bowline Knot, 1972, The Double Bowline Knot, 2006; contbr. articles to profl. jours; patentee in field. Mem. pres.' coun. Purdue U. Lt. j.g. USNR, 1946—57. Mem. Soc. Naval Architects and Marine Engrs., U.S. Naval Inst., Masons. Avocations: music, concert master, orchestra and symphony member. Personal E-mail: jcollin9@ix.netcom.com.

COLLINS, JAMES FRANKLIN, retired ambassador; b. Aurora, Ill., June 4, 1939; AB cum laude, Harvard Coll., 1961; MA, Ind. U., 1964, postgrad., 1964-67, Moscow State U., 1965-66. Asst. prof. history US Naval Acad., Annapolis, Md., 1967—69; vice consul Am. consulate gen. US Dept. State, Izmir, Turkey, 1969—71, polit. officer European Affairs Bur. Washington, 1971—73, polit. officer Moscow, 1973—75, polit. analyst Bur Intelligence and Rsch. Washington, 1975—78, staff asst., polit. officer Near East Affairs Bur., 1978—82, polit. counselor Am. embassy Amman, Jordan, 1982—84, dir. ops. ctr. Washington, 1984—87; dir. for intelligence policy Nat. Security Coun., Washington, 1987—88; dep. exec. sec. for Europe and L.Am. US Dept. State, Washington, 1988—90, dep. chief of mission Am. embassy Moscow, 1990—93, coord. for regional affairs for new ind. states Washington, 1993—94, sr. coord. office amb.-at-large new ind. state, 1994—95, amb.-at-large, spl. advisor to sec. state new ind. states, 1995—97, U.S. amb. to Russian Fedn. Moscow, 1997—2001, ret., 2001; sr. internat. advisor Akin, Gump, Strauss, Hauer & Feld LLP, Washington, 2001—07; sr. assoc. dir. Russian Eurasia program Carnegie Endowment Internat. Peace, Washington, 2007—. Writer cons., 2001— Address: 1779 Massachusetts Ave Washington DC 20036 Office Phone: 202-939-2284, 202-483-7600. Personal E-mail: jfcollins@aol.com. Business E-Mail: jcollins@ceip.org.

COLLINS, JAMES H., JR., architectural firm executive; BArch, Rensselaer Poly. Inst., MBA with distinction. Joined Payette Assocs. Inc., Boston, 1979, pres., 1998—. Lectr. in field. Author: Design Process for the Human Workplace, in The Architecture of Science. Recipient Fellows award, Rensselaer Alumni Assn., 2003. Office: Payette Assocs Inc 285 Summer St Boston MA 02210-1522

COLLINS, JAMES WILLIAM, health science association administrator, director, epidemiologist, mechanical engineer; b. Atlanta, Oct. 19, 1962; s. Thomas Allen and Mary Frank Collins; m. Maria Joao Ponte, Oct. 25, 1992; children: Karina Maria, James Seth. B of Mech. Engring., Ga. Inst. Tech., 1984; MSME, W.Va. U., 1989; PhD in Health Policy and Mgmt., Johns Hopkins U., 1998. Rsch. mech. engr. Ctrs. Disease Control and Prevention, Nat. Inst. Occupl. Safety and Health, Morgantown, W.Va., 1984—90, rsch. epidemiologist, 1992—2004; assoc. dir. sci. Ctrs. Disease Control and Prevention, Nat. Inst. Occupl. Safety and Health, Divsn. Safety Rsch., 2004—. Bd. editors Jour. Injury Control and Safety Promotion, Amsterdam, 2004—; guest lectr. occupational epidemiology Johns Hopkins U; guest lectr. occupational safety and health W.Va. U. Pres. Exch. Club, Fairchance, Pa., 2000—06; fin. com. Mt. Moriah Bapt. Ch., Smithfield, 2004—06. Capt. USPHS, 1984—2005. Recipient Spl. Assignment award, USPHS, 1991, Surgeon Gen Exemplary Svc. medal, 1992, Achievement medal, 1996, Pub. Health Svc. citation, 1996, Crisis Response Ribbon, 2002, Outstanding Unit citation, 2002, U. S. Pub. Health Svc. Engring. Lit. award, Chief Engr. USPHS, 2000, Partnering award Worker Safety and Health, Nat. Inst. Occupl. Safety and Health, 2003, 2006, Alice Hamilton Excellence in Occupl. Safety and Health Human Studies Rsch. award, 2005. Mem.: Commd. Officers Assn. USPHS (pres., v.p., treas. 1984—2005, Mem. of Yr. 1988). Conservative. Baptist. Achievements include research in intervention trials demonstrating highly effective programs to prevent back and other musculoskeletal injuries among health care workers due to patient lifting and slips and falls. Avocations: travel, hunting, fishing, softball, coaching. Home: 70 South Morgantown St Fairchance PA 15436 Office: Ctrs Disease Control & Prevention 1095 Willowdale Rd Mail stop 1900 Morgantown WV 26505 Home Phone: 724-564-1234; Office Phone: 304-285-5998. Business E-Mail: jcollins1@cdc.gov.

COLLINS, JASON L., psychologist; b. Rochester, NY, Apr. 12, 1978; s. M. and S. Collins. BS in Psychology, St. John Fisher Coll., Rochester, NY, 2001; MS in Sch. Psychology, Rochester Inst. Tech., NY, 2005. Cert. sch. psychologist Nat. Assn. Sch. Psychologists, 2006, N.J. Dept. Edn., 2006. Sch. psychologist Bruce St. Sch. for the Deaf, Newark, 2004—. Mem.: Nat. Assn. Sch. Psychologists. Avocation: bowling. Office: Bruce Street Sch for the Deaf 333 Clinton Pl Newark NJ 07112 Home Phone: 585-233-0329; Office Phone: 973-705-3805. Office Fax: 973-705-3818. Business E-Mail: jcollins@nps.k12.nj.us.

COLLINS, JEAN KATHERINE, language educator; b. Norfolk, Va., June 14, 1928; d. Elwood Brantley and Katherine Belle (Lambertson) C. BA in Liberal Arts, James Madison U., Harrisonburg, Va., 1945-49; MA in English, U. Richmond, 1950-51; edn. credits, U. Va., Eastern Shore of Va., 1950-60; art edn. credits, Millersville State Tchrs. Coll, summer 1970. Continuity writer Radio Station WLEE, Richmond, Va., 1949; English, critic tchr. Farmville H.S., Longwood Coll., Va., 1951-53; English tchr., art tchr. Hermitage H.S., Richmond, Va., 1953-55; prin., art tchr. Cape Charles (Va.) H.S., 1957-59; head English dept., tchr. Northampton H.S., Eastville, Va., 1960-63; art tchr. Pvt. Studio, Cape Charles, Va., 1964-90. Pres. Lambda chpt. Delta Kappa Gamma Soc., Eastern Shore of Va., 1966-68; recording sec. Iota State Delta Kappa Gamma Soc., Headqtrs., Richmond, Va., 1967-69; adv. bd. Eastern Shore Pub. Libr., Accomac, Va., 1981-89; bd. dirs. Eastern Shore of Va. Hist. Soc., Onancock, Va., 1957-60. Author: (poetry) Madison Quarterly, 1948, 49; author, illustrator: An Eastern Shore Sampler, 1975; author: History of Trinity United Methodist Church, 1993. Named Woman of Yr. Young WOmen's Club of Cape Charles, Va., 1958. Mem. Eastern Shore of Va. Hist. Soc., Cape Charles Hist. Soc., Trinity United Meth. Ch., Delta Kappa Gamma Soc. Republican. Methodist. Avocations: painting, needlecrafts, history, theater, dance, writing.

COLLINS, JEFFREY G., lawyer, former prosecutor; b. Detroit, Mar. 16, 1959; m. Lois Collins; 2 children. BA in Psychology, Northwestern U., 1981; JD, Howard U. Sch. Law, 1984. Pvt. practice, 1984—94; appointed judge Detroit Recorder's Ct., 1994—96; cir. judge Wayne County Cir. Ct., 1997—98; judge Mich. Supreme Ct., 1998—2000, Mich. Ct. Appeals, 2000—01; U.S. atty. (ea. dist.) Mich. US Dept. Justice, 2001—04; atty., ptnr. litigation dept. Foley & Lardner LLP, 2004—. Mentor Man to Man program Paul Robeson Acad.; mem. Plymouth United Ch. of Christ, Detroit. Mem.: Mich. Assn. for Leadership Devel. (founder, dir. Wayne County chpt.).

COLLINS, JESSICA ANN, military officer; b. Tulsa, Okla., May 31, 1981; d. Kenneth Matthew Collins, Jr. and Mai Hoa Collins. BS in Sociology, U. Tulsa, 2005, cert. in womens studies, 2005. Vol. Veterans Assistance Hosp., Tampa, Fla., 2005, VFW, Tulsa, 2001—03. Cpl. USMC, 1999—. Decorated Selected Marine Corps Res. medal USMC, Nat. Def. medal, Global War on Terrorism Svc. medal, Marine Corps Good Conduct medal, Armed Forces Res. medal with M Device, Global War on Terrorism Expeditionary medal, Sea Svc. Deployment ribbon, Navy and Marine Corps Commendation medal U.S. Sec. of Navy; Simon Estes Merit scholar, Simon Estes Ednl. Found., Inc., 1999—2003. Mem.: NOW, Women Marine Assn. Okla. Chpt., Women in Mil. Svc., Nat. Coalition Against Domestic Violence. Office: US Marine Forces Central Command 7115 S Boundary Blvd Tampa FL 33621 Home Phone: 918-406-5377. Office Fax: 813-827-7011. Business E-Mail: collinsja@marcent.usmc.mil.

COLLINS, JOAN HENRIETTA, actress; b. London, May 23, 1933; came to U.S., 1938; d. Joseph William and Elsa (Bessant) C.; m. Maxwell Reed (div.); m. Anthony Newley (div.); children: Tara, Sacha; m. Ronald S. Kass, Mar., 1972 (div.); 1 child, Katy; m. Peter Holm (div.); m. Percy Gibson, 2002. Student, Francis Holland Sch., London, Royal Acad. of Dramatic Art. Actor: (films) Cosh Boy, 1952, Our Girl Friday, 1953, I Believe in You, 1952, The Good Die Young, 1954, Land of the Pharoahs, 1955, The Virgin Queen, 1955, Girl in the Red Velvet Swing, 1955, The Opposite Sex, 1956, Sea Wife, 1957, Island in the Sun, 1957, Rally Round the Flag Boys!, 1958, The Bravados, 1958, Seven Thieves, 1960, Esther and the King, 1960, Road to Hong Kong, 1962, Warning Shot, 1967, Subterfuge, 1969, The Executioner, 1970, Up in the Cellar, 1970, Revenge, 1971, Quest for Love, 1971, Tales From the Crypt, 1972, Tales That Witness Madness, 1973, Drive Hard, Drive Fast, 1973, Dark Places, 1973, I Don't Want to be Born, 1975, The Bawdy Adventures of Tom Jones, 1976, Empire of the Ants, 1977, The Stud, 1978, The Big Sleep, 1978, The Bitch, 1979, Sunburn, 1979, Game for Vultures, 1979, Homework, 1982, Nutcracker, 1982, Decadence, 1994, In the Bleak Mid-Winter, 1995, The Clandestine Marriage, 1998, The Flintstones-Viva Rock Vegas, 1999, Joseph and His Technicolor Dreamcoat, 1999, Ozzie, 2001, Ellis in Glamourland, 2004, and several others; (TV films) Drive Hard, Drive Fast, 1973, The Man Who Came to Dinner, Paper Dolls, 1982, The Wild Women of Chastity Gulch, 1982, The Cartier Affair, 1983, Making of a Male Model, 1983, Her Life as a Man, 1984, Hart to Hart: Two Harts in Three Quarters Time, 1995, and several others; (TV miniseries) The Moneychangers, 1976, Sins, 1986, Monte Carlo, 1986, Tonight at 8:30, 1991, Dynasty: The Reunion, 1992, Dynasty Reunion:Catfights & Caviar, 2006; (TV series) Dynasty, 1981—89, Faerie Tale Theater, 1982, Pacific Palisades, 1997, Footballers Wives, 2005, Hotel Babylon, 2005; (TV films) Mama's Back, 1993, Annie: A Royal Adventure, 1995, Hart to Hart, 1995; actor, actor: (TV films) Sweet Deception, 1998, These Old Broads, 2000, (video) Secrets of Fitness and Beauty, 1994, (theater) Jassey, Claudia, The Skin of Our Teeth, The Praying Mantis, The Last of Mrs. Cheyney, The 7th Veil, A Doll's House, Private Lives, 1990, Love Letters, 2000, Over the Moon, 2001, Full Circle, 2004, An Evening With Joan Collins, 2006, Legends, 2006; guest appearances Mission Impossible, 1969, Baretta, 1976, Police Women, 1976, Starsky & Hutch, 1977, Fantasy Island, 1980, The Love Boat, 1983, The Nanny, 1996, Roseanne, 1993, Will & Grace, 2000, Guiding Light, 2002, Who Wants to Be a Millionaire, 2005, Loose Women, 2005, Footballers Wives, 2006, and several others, others; author: Past Imperfect, 1978, Second Act, 1996, Katy, A Fight for Life, Joan Collins Beauty Book, 1980, Prime Time, 1988, Love and Desire and Hate, 1991, My Secrets, 1994, Too Damn Famous, 1995, My Friends Secrets, 1999, Star Quality, 2002, Joan's Way, 2002, Misfortune's Daughters, 2005, Ellis in Glamourland, 2005, others. Decorated Order of Brit. Empire; recipient Emmy nomination, Golden Globe award, Ace award, People's Choice award; named to Order Brit. Empire. Avocations: travel, 18th century art. Address: 16 Bulbecks Walk South Woodham Ferrers Essex CM3 52N England Office Phone: 011 44 1245 328367. E-mail: pkeylock@aol.com.

COLLINS, JODA LEE, minister; b. Modesto, Calif., May 3, 1949; s. Joda William and Retha Mae Collins; m. Laura Carmela Collins. DD, Universal Bible Inst., 1976; BA, Golden State U., 1980, PhD, 1982; BA in Psychology, Calif. State U., 1988. So. Baptist pastor various chs., Calif., Fla., Tenn., 1974—. Author: (book) Dynamic Discipleship, 1996, The Biblical Role of Woman in the Church, 1998, How to Successfully Pastor a Difficult Church, 1998, The Chronology of Revelation, 1999, Every Word Spoken by Jesus on How to do Church, 2000, A Kingdom Based Church, 2002, Introduction to New Testament Greek, 2003. With USAF, 1968—72, Vietnam. Republican. Baptist. Avocations: Karate, water-skiing, bowling, fishing. Home: 4033 Buttonbush Dr Milton FL 32583-5020 Office Phone: 850-623-3954. E-mail: DrJLCollins@aol.com.

COLLINS, JOE LENA, retired secondary school educator; b. Mt. Pleasant, Tenn., Nov. 18, 1922; d. Morton Daniel and Rosetta Francis C. BS in English, Tenn. Tech., Cookeville, 1949; MA in English, George Peabody, Nashville, 1968, EdS in English, 1975. Cert. tchr. Sec. to Dr. G.C. English and Dr. C.D. Walton, Mt. Pleasant, Tenn., 1942-46; tchr. Maury Co. Schs., Mt. Pleasant, Tenn., 1949-51, Tenn. Tech., Cookeville, Tenn., 1951; acct. Cookeville Prodn. Credit, Tenn., 1951-52; tchr. Metro Nashville Schs., 1952-88; ret., 1988. Lectr. Ret. Learning Vanderbilt U., 2000—. Com. worker Dem. Party, 1980—2003. Mem. AAUW (pres. 2000), Tenn. Writers Alliance, Tenn. Hist. Soc., Women in the Arts, United Meth. Women (Woman of Purpose award), Belle Meade Book Club (leader), Metro Ret. Tchrs. Assn. Avocations: reading, writing, painting, sports. Home: 6212 Henry Ford Dr Nashville TN 37209-1738

COLLINS, JOHN ALFRED, retired obstetrician, gynecologist, educator; s. John Bandel and Vera Collins; m. Carole Joanne Sedwick West; children: John, Blayne, Anne. MD, U. West Ont., 1960. Resident ob-gyn. U. West Ont., 1961—65; McLaughlin Found. fellow U. Coll. Hosp., London, U. Edinburgh, Scotland, Middlesex Hosp., London, 1965—67; clin. rsch. fellow Ont. Cancer Found. London Clinic, 1967—76; with dept. ob-gyn. U. West Ont., 1967—77, asst. dean undergrad. edn. faculty medicine, 1975—77; prof., head dept. ob-gyn. Dalhousie U., 1977—83; prof., chmn. dept. ob-gyn. McMaster U., Hamilton, Ont., 1983—93; vis. chair internat. Francqui Found. Brussels Free U., 2000—01. Mem. editl. bd. New Eng. Jour. Medicine, 1991-96, Fertility and Sterility, 1991-96, Obstetrics and Gynecology, 2004—07; editor-in-chief Human Reproduction Update, 2007—; contbr. articles to profl. jours. Mem. Royal Coll. Physicians and Surgeons Can., Royal Belgium Acad. Medicine, Royal Coll. Ob-Gyn. U.K., Am. Coll. Ob-Gyn., Am. Soc. Reproductive Medicine, Can. Fertility and Andrology Soc., Soc. Ob-Gyn. Can. Home: 400 Maders Cove Rd RR 1 Mahone Bay NS Canada B0J 2EO

COLLINS, JOHN F., lawyer; b. NYC, Dec. 15, 1948; AB, Fordham U., 1970; JD, U. Chgo., 1973. Bar: N.Y. 1974, US Dist. Ct. (no. dist. Calif., ea., so., no. dist. NY), US Ct. Appeals (2d, 3d, 9th, Fed. cir.), US Ct. Fed. Claims, US Supreme Ct. Ptnr., antitrust & trade regulation practices Dewey Ballantine LLP, NYC. Editor (asst.): Antitrust Law Jour., Annual Rev. of Antitrust Law Developments. Mem. ABA, N.Y. State Bar Assn., Assn. Bar of City of N.Y., Phi Beta Kappa. Office: Dewey Ballantine 1301 Avenue Of The Americas New York NY 10019-6022 Office Phone: 212-259-7080. Office Fax: 212-259-8201. Business E-Mail: jcollins@dbllp.com.

COLLINS, JOHN R., energy executive; BBA, Univ. Del.; MBA, Univ. Pitts. Fin. mgmt. positions with Bell Atlantic Corp., Perdue Farms Inc.; fin. mgmt. positions Balt. Gas & Elec. Co., 1988—95, asst. treas., dir. fin. mgmt., 1995—97; CFO Constellation Commodities Group, 1997—2002; v.p., chief risk officer Constellation Energy, Balt., 2002—04, sr. v.p., chief risk officer, 2005—07, sr. v.p., CFO, chief risk officer, 2007—. Bd. dir. Constellation Energy Partners. Bd. mem. Roland Park Pl., Spl. Olympics Md.; bd. vis. Lerner Coll. Bus. Univ. Del. Office: Constellation Energy 750 E Pratt St Baltimore MD 21202*

COLLINS, JOHN W., JR., retired military officer, technologist, educator; b. Lackawanna, NY, Jan. 27, 1958; m. Simona E Aschenbrenner, Apr. 12, 1980; children: Mary, John III. AS, N.Y. Regents (now Excelsior) Coll., Albany, 1979; BA, Columbia Coll., Mo., 1982; MPA, U. Okla., Norman, 1984; EdD, Seton Hall U., South Orange, NJ, 1999. Cert. prin., supt., chief sch. adminstr., sch. bus. adminstr., JROTC Mil. Tchr. standard cert. 1998. Enlisted U.S. Army, 1975, commd. 2d lt., 1978, advanced through grades to lt. col., retired, 1998; assoc. acad. dir. SetonWorldWide, Seton Hall U., South Orange, NJ, 1998—2001; faculty assoc. Seton Hall U., South Orange, NJ, 1998—2004, asst. prof., 2005—06, acting dept. chair, 2005—06; assoc. prof. NJ City U., 2006—. Edn. tech. cons. Seton Hall U., South Orange, NJ, 1998—. Author: (essay) Proud to Serve, 1991; contbr. articles to edn. and mil. logistics jours., chapters to books. Patron USAF CAP; Vol. Am. Overseas Schs., Germany, 1992—94. Named to Officer Candidate Sch. Hall Fame, US Army, 2006; recipient Legion of Merit, 1988-1998, Cert. of Appreciation, President U.S., 1998, N. Y. State Conspicuous Svc. Cross (12 awards), Gov. N.Y., 1999, N. Y. State Conspicuous Svc. Star (3 awards), 2000, N.J. Meritorious Svc. medal, Adj. Gen. of N.J., 2003, Meritorious Svc. medal (4 awards), Pres. of U.S., 1987-1996. Mem.: VFW, FOP (assoc.), Am. Legion, Assn. US Army (life), Am. Legion, Disabled Am. Vets. (life). Avocations: fishing, travel. Home: 12 Hunterdon Road West Orange NJ 07052-1604 Office: NJ City U 2039 Kennedy Blvd Jersey City NJ 07305-1597 Office Phone: 201-200-3179. Personal E-mail: john.collins6@us.army.mil. Business E-Mail: jcollins2@njcu.edu.

COLLINS, JOYCE A.P., minister, librarian, educator, realtor; b. Memphis, June 12, 1948; d. Joe Harry (Stepfather) and Lelia Mae (Strickand Powell) Armstrong; m. Warren Eugene Collins, Sept. 4, 1971 (div. 1994); adopted children: Evangeline, Warren Gabriel. BA cum laude, LeMoyne-Owen U., Memphis, 1970; MLS, Western Mich. U., Kalamazoo, 1971. Cert. tchr. Tenn., 1970, lifetime tchr. cert. La., cert. realtor La. Circulation libr. Tenn. State U., Nashville, 1971—72; catalog libr. La. State U., Baton Rouge, 1972; dir. info. and rsch. ARIC, Nashville, 1973—74; asst. prof., head libr. media svcs. Fisk U., Nashville, 1974—75; libr., lectr. Pub. Schs. Davidson Co., Nashville, 1975—77; libr., head circulation dept. Southern U., Baton Rouge, 1977—78, social sci. libr., 1978—80; realtor Baton Rouge, 1980—; dir. JACPO Ministries, Nashville, 1997—. Faculty sen. La. State U., Baton Rouge, 1970—80; reader svcs. coord. Fisk U., Nashville, 1975. Mem.: AAUW, Nat. Assn. U. Women, La. Libr. Assn. Baptist. Home: PO Box 1601 Madison TN 37116-1601

COLLINS, KATHLEEN, academic administrator, art educator; b. Chgo., BA in psychology, minor in fine arts, Stanford U.; MFA in photography. Chmn. applied photography dept. Sch. Photographic Arts & Sci., Rochester Inst. Tech., coord. summer workshops; dean Sch. Art & Design, NY State Coll. Ceramics, Alfred U., prof.; pres. Kans. City Art Inst., 1996—. Represented in permanent collections, Art Inst. Chgo., Cleve. Art Mus., Centro Cultural/Arte Contemporaneo, Mex. City, Mex., Chrysler Mus., Norfolk Va. Office: Office of President Kansas City Art Inst 4415 Warwick Blvd Kansas City MO 64111*

COLLINS, KATHLEEN ANNE, artistic director; b. Elmira, NY, Dec. 20, 1951; d. James G. and Joyce (Balmer) C.; m. Andrew Stephen Elston, May 28, 1977; children: Megan, Kate. BA, SUNY, Albany, 1974; MA in Theatre, U. Wash., 1976, MFA in Theatre, 1979. Dir. edn. Seattle Children's Theatre, 1975-78; instr. drama Lakeside Sch., Seattle, 1978-79; artistic dir. Honolulu Theatre for Youth, 1979-83, Fulton Opera House, Lancaster, Pa., 1983-98; prof. Cornish Coll. of Arts, Seattle, 1999—. Guest lectr. U. Hawaii, Honolulu, 1981, U. Wash., Seattle, 2002—04; guest dir. Seattle Children's Theatre, 2002—06; adj. faculty Lesley U., 2000—06; guest dir. Six Minutes, Seattle Rep. Woman's Playwriting Festival, Seattle, 2004. Contbg. author: Drama With Children, 1979. Bd. dirs. PTO, Lancaster, 1990-98; pres. Winifred Ward Found. Mem. Am. Assn. Theatre Educators, Assn. and Soc. for Theatre and Children. Democrat. Personal E-mail: kalcollins@comcast.net.

COLLINS, KERRY, professional football player; b. Lebanon, Pa., Dec. 30, 1972; Student, Pa. State U. Quarterback Carolina Panthers, 1995-98, New Orleans Saints, 1998-99, N.Y. Giants, 1999—2004, Oakland Raiders, 2004—06, Tenn. Titans, 2006—. Named to NFL Pro-Bowl, 1996. Office: Tenn Titans One Titans Way Nashville TN 37213

COLLINS, KEVIN HEATH, lawyer; b. Cedar Rapids, Iowa, May 7, 1958; s. Thomas Martin and Joanne (Heath) C.; m. Sally A. Stephenson, June 11, 1985. BA, Creighton U., 1978; JD, U. Iowa, 1980. Bar: Iowa 1981, Hawaii 1982, U.S. Dist. Ct. (no. and so. dist.) Iowa 1981, U.S. Dist. Ct. Hawaii, 1982, U.S. Ct. Appeals (8th cir.) 1981, U.S. Ct. Appeals (9th cir.) 1982, U.S. Supreme Ct. 1984. Sr. v.p. Shuttleworth & Ingersoll, P.C., Cedar Rapids, 1980-82, 84—; assoc. Dinman & Yokoyama, P.C., Honolulu, 1982-84. Exec. com. United Way of East Cen. Iowa, Cedar Rapids, 1986-87, Retired Sr. Vol. Program, Cedar Rapids, 1986-89. Fellow Iowa Acad. Trial Lawyers, Assn. Am. Bd. Trial Advocates, Fedn. of Insurance & Corp. Counsel; mem. ABA, Am. Arbitration Assn. (panel mem.), Iowa State Bar Assn. (co-chair com. on delivery of legal svcs. to the elderly 1989-90, mem. law practice mgmt. sect. 1991-98, bd. govs. 1998-2001, v.p. 2001-02, pres.-elect 2002-03, pres. 2003-04), Hawaii State Bar Assn. Office: Shuttleworth Ingersoll PLC PO Box 2107 Cedar Rapids IA 52406-2107

COLLINS, KEVIN LLOYD, lawyer; s. Eldon Lloyd and Delores Ann Collins; m. Heather Maloy; children: Liam, Colman. JD, U. Mo., Kansas City, 1986. Bar: Tex. 1993, bd. cert. in criminal law and juvenile law: Bd. Legal Specialization. Jud. law clk. U.S. Dist. Ct., Springfield, Mo., 1987; asst. dist. atty. Bexar County Dist. Atty.'s Office, San Antonio, 1992—96; pvt. practice San Antonio, 1996—. Contbr. articles to profl. jours. Mem.: Inns of Ct., Mensa (pres. San Antonio chpt. 2004—05). Avocations: travel, sports. Office: Kevin L Collins PC 600 Navarro Ste 250 San Antonio TX 78205 Office Phone: 210-223-9480. Personal E-mail: kevc11@yahoo.com.

COLLINS, KEVIN T., lawyer; b. 1954; BA in Comm., Fordham U., 1976; JD, Seton Hall U., 1980. Bar: NY 1981. Ptnr., corp. group Dorsey & Whitney LLP, NYC, chmn., life sci. and health care group, mem., policy com.; shareholder Heller Ehrman LLP, NYC, 2005—. Office: Heller Ehrman LLP Times Sq Tower 7 Times Sq New York NY 10036 E-mail: kevin.collins@hellerehrman.com.*

COLLINS, LARRY RICHARD, artist, educator, art gallery director; b. Spokane, Wash., July 15, 1945; s. Richard Thurman and Glorious Blossom (Kingbay) C. BFA, U. Okla., 1967; postgrad., Ind. U., 1970; MFA, Mass. Coll. Art, 1980. Instr. anatomy, design, figure drawing, drawing Vesper George Sch. Art, Boston, 1980-81; instr. anatomy, figure drawing Brockton (Mass.) Art Mus. Sch., 1980-81; prof. anatomy, drawing, figure drawing Mass. Coll. Art, Boston, 1980-82, 86-95; instr. anatomy, drawing, figure drawing U. N.H., Durham, 1987-88; prof. figure drawing Montserrat Coll. Art, Beverly, Mass., 1994—95, Provincetown Art Assn. and Mus., Mass.; dir. Driskel Gallery, Schoolhouse Ctr., Provincetown, Mass., 1998—2004, Larry Collins Fine Art, Provincetown, 2004—. Combat artist First Air Cavalry Divsn., U.S. Army, Vietnam, 1968-69; guest lectr. in anatomy, Boston U., 1986; figure drawing Mus. Sch. Provincetown Art Assn. and Mus., 2006-07. One-man shows include Bazza Gallery, Oklahoma City, 1962, Northeastern State Coll., Talequah, Okla., 1962, U. Okla., Norman, 1963, 1967, Mass. Coll. Art, Boston, 1979, Mabee-Gerrer Mus. Art, Shawnee, Okla., 1984, First St. Gallery, N.Y.C., 1986, N.Y. Pub. Libr., 1987, Michael Allen Gallery, Brookline, Mass., 1995, East End Gallery, Provincetown, 1996, Tiffany & Co., N.Y.C., 1996, Wohlfarth Galleries, Washington, 1997, Schoolhouse Ctr., Provincetown, 1999, 2001, Carrie Haddad Gallery, Hudson, N.Y., 1998, Hampshire Coll., Amherst, Mass., 2004, exhibited in group shows at Mus. Art, U. Okla., Norman, 1961—63 (Purchase awards in painting, 1962, 1963), Springfield (Mo.) Art Mus., 1962, Okla. Art Ctr., Oklahoma City, 1962—63, 1965—66, Philbrook Art Ctr., Tulsa, 1963, 1966, Joslyn Art Mus., Omaha, 1966, Brockton Art Mus., Mass., 1980, Wistariahurst Mus., Holyoke, Mass., 1980, Mass. Coll. Art, Boston, 1981, El Paso (Tex.) Mus. Art, 1982, Fairleigh Dickinson U., Teaneck, N.J., 1982, Pa. State U., University Park, 1983, Sheldon Meml. Art Gallery, Lincoln, Nebr., 1983, Gump's Gallery, San Francisco, 1983—85, Camera di Commercio, Lucca, Italy, 1984, Boston Visual Artists' Union, 1984, Provincetown Art Assn. and Mus., 1984, 1986, Provincetown Art Assn. & Mus., 1996—2007, Butler Inst. Am. Art, Youngstown, Ohio, 1984, Nat. Acad. Design, N.Y.C., 1984, 1986, First St. Gallery, NYC, 1984—88, Indiana U. Pa., 1985, NYU, 1985, Amos Eno Gallery, NYC, 1986—87 (1st prize, 1986), John Pence Gallery, San Francisco, 1987, St. Louis Artists Guild, 1987, Grand Ctrl. Galleries, N.Y.C., 1987, Mass. Coll. Art, Boston, 1993, Schoolhouse Ctr., 1998—2001, Worcester Art Mus., 2006, U. RI, Providence, 2007, Represented in permanent collections Mus. Art U. Okla., Norman, Sheldon Meml. Art Gallery, Lincoln, Nebr., Mabee-Gerrer Mus. Art, Shawnee, Print Collection, Boston Pub. Libr., Photographs Collection, Berg Collection, N.Y. Pub. Libr., Worcester (Mass.) Art Mus., Spl. Collection Libr., U. N.C., Chapel Hill, reprodns. of paintings appear in, Human Anatomy and Figure Drawing (Jack N.Kramer), 1984, Old Love Story (Allen Ginsberg), 1986, The Am. Painting Collection Sheldon Meml. Art Gallery (Norman A. Geske), The Hopper House at Truro (Lawrence Ferlinghetti), Tow (Eileen Myles), 2005. Served with U.S. Army, 1967-69, Vietnam. Decorated Bronze Star, Combat Infantryman Badge, Army Commendation medal with Valor-device; grantee Individual Artists' Painting N.H. State Coun., 1987-88, Artists' Opportunity, 1989-90; travel fellow Creative Art Studies, Rome, Florence, Pisa, Arezzo, Italy, 1984. Mem. Provincetown Art Assn. Home: PO Box 2 Provincetown MA 02657-0002 Home Phone: 508-487-9849. Business E-Mail: larry@larrycollinsfineart.com.

COLLINS, LAURA JANE, music educator, singer; d. Horace R. and Mary J. Collins; m. Thomas H. Buchholz, Dec. 1977 (div. 1982); 1 child, Erik. Student, Viterbo Coll., LaCrosse, Wis., 1977; BA, Cameron U., Lawton, Okla., 1979. Cert. music educator K-12 Okla., 1979, Yamaha Music Sch. Tchr. Yamaha Internat. Corp., 1980. Yamaha music sch. tchr. Keynote Music Co., Tulsa, Okla., 1980—82; vocal, gen. music educator Tulsa Pub. Schs., Okla., 1981—; tchr. Tulsa Opera Children's Workshop, 1986—87; pvt. piano and voice instr. Jazz ensemble vocalist: R.F. Singers, 2003—04, Tulsa Opera Chorus, 2003. Vol. Tulsa Boy Singers; co-mgr. office Anderson for Pres., Tulsa, 1980; pres., co-mgr. Tulsa oOffice Jones for US Senate, 1980; vol. Orza for Gov., 2002; liason Dem.Tulsa Pub. Sch. Tchrs.; church organist Altus, Okla., 1977—82, Tulsa, 1989—94; founding mem. Children's Advocacy Team All Souls Unitarian Ch., Tulsa, 1993, chapel accompanist, 1993—95, choir accompanist, 1995—96; chapel organist Hillcrest Hosp., 1998—. Mem.: NEA (del. 2002—05), Okla. Music Educators Assn., Okla. Edn. Assn. (del. 2003—07), Tulsa Classroom Tchrs. Assn. (bd. dir.). Democrat. Universalist. Avocations: gardening, reading, creative writing, politics. Home: 3903 S Rockford Ave Tulsa OK 74105 Office: Hoover Elementary Sch 2327 S Darlington Tulsa OK 74114 Office Phone: 918-746-9120. Business E-Mail: collila@tulsaschools.org.

COLLINS, MARQUIS TYRONE, investment company executive; b. Balt., Apr. 22, 1977; s. Ashley Collins and Linda Oliver. Grad., Marine Mil. Acad., Harlingen, Tex., 1995. CEO Collins Investments, Balt., 2000—. CEO K-Money Music, Balt., 1996—. Recipient Songwriter award, ASCAP, NY, 2001, 2002, 2003. Avocations: basketball, football, drag racing, golf. Home: 3823 Elmley Ave Baltimore MD 21213 Office: K-Money Music 1723 E 35th St Baltimore MD 21218

COLLINS, MARTHA, English language educator, writer; b. Omaha, Nov. 25, 1940; d. William E. and Katheryn (Essick) C.; m. Theodore M. Space, Apr. 1991. AB, Stanford U., 1962; MA, U. Iowa, 1965, PhD, 1971. Asst. prof. NE Mo. U., Kirksville, 1965-66; from instr. to prof. English U. Mass., Boston, 1966—2002, co-dir. creative writing, 1979—2000; Pauline Delaney prof., co-dir. creative writing Oberlin Coll., Ohio, 1997—2007. Author (poetry): The Catastrophe of Rainbows, 1985, The Arrangement of Space, 1991, A History of Small Life on a Windy Planet, 1993, Some Things Words Can Do, 1998, Blue Front, 2006; translator: The Women Carry River Water, 1997 (winner, American Literary Translators Assn. award, 1998), Green Rice, 2005. Fellow Bunting Inst., 1982-83, Ingram Merrill Found., 1988, NEA, 1990; grantee Witter Bynner/Santa Fe Art Inst., 2001, Lannan Found. Residency, 2003; recipient Pushcart prize, 1985, 96, 98, Di Castagnola award, 1990, Anisfield-Wolf award, 2007. Mem. Poetry Soc. Am., Assoc. Writing Programs. Democrat.

COLLINS, MARY ANN, lawyer; b. Aurora, Colo., May 12, 1953; d. Harold Ernest and Gertrude Elizabeth (Shannon) C.; m. Ronald Jay Sklar, Jan. 20, 1984; 1 child, Jacob Michael. BA, Western Ill. U., 1974; MA in Polit. Sci., U. Ill., 1976; JD, Loyola U., 1980. Bar: Ill. 1980, Calif. 1984. Assoc. Chapman and Cutler, Chgo., 1980-83, Orrick, Herrington & Sutcliffe, San Francisco, 1983-88, ptnr., 1988—. Chair transp. fin. group. Orrick, Herrington & Sutcliffe, San Francisco, co-chair health care, higher edn., and 501(c) revenue transactions group. Contbr. articles to profl. jours. Mem. ABA, Calif. Bar Assn., San Francisco Mcpl. Forum. Office: Orrick Herrington & Sutcliffe 405 Howard St San Francisco CA 94105 Office Phone: 415-773-5998. E-mail: marycollins@orrick.com.

COLLINS, MARY LYNN, education educator; d. William and Catherine Lynn; m. James Francis Lynn, June 16, 1962; children: Daniel Patrick, Catherine Anne Bona, James Francis Jr., Mary Lynn Callanan, Robert William, Maureen Jane Novaco. BA in Elem. Edn., SUNY, Cortland, 1957, MS in Secondary Edn., 1960; MS in Guidance Counseling, Syracuse U., NY, 1962, PhD, 1976. Prof. edn. LeMoyneCollege, Syracuse, 1979—97, chmn. dept. edn., 1979—97; prof. Nova Southeastern U., Ft. Lauderdale, Fla., 1997—. Home: 13061 NW 1st St Plantation FL 33325 Office: Nova Southeastern Univ Davie FL 33314 Home Phone: 954-472-9406; Office Phone: 954-262-8635. Business E-Mail: mcollins@nova.edu.

COLLINS, MICHAEL, aerospace consultant, astronaut; b. Rome, Oct. 31, 1930; s. James L. and Virginia (Stewart) C. (parents Am. citizens); m. Patricia M. Finnegan, Apr. 28, 1957; children: Kathleen, Ann Stewart, Michael L. BS, U.S. Mil. Acad., 1952; grad., Advanced Mgmt. Program, Harvard U., 1974; DSc, Northeastern U., 1970, Stonehill Coll., 1970; LLD, St. Michael's Coll., 1970, Southeastern U., 1975. Commd. officer U.S. Air Force, advanced through grades to maj. gen., 1969; fighter pilot, flight comdr. U.S., Europe; exptl. flight test officer Edwards AFB, Calif.; astronaut NASA, 1963-69, Gemini 10, 1966; astronaut, space walker, comdr., Command Module pilot Apollo 11, 1969; apptd. asst. sec. state for pub. affairs Washington, 1970-71; dir. Nat. Air and Space Mus., Smithsonian Instn., Washington, 1971-78; undersec. Smithsonian Instn., 1978-80; v.p. LTV Aerospace & Def. Co., 1980-85; pres. Michael Collins Assocs., Washington, 1985—. Author: Carrying the Fire, 1974, Flying to the Moon and Other Strange Places, 1976, Liftoff, 1988, Mission to Mars, 1990. Decorated D.S.M., D.F.C.; recipient Presdl. Medal of Freedom, NASA Distinguished Service and Exceptional Service medals, Hubbard medal, Collier trophy, Goddard Meml. trophy, Harmon trophy, Gen. Thomas D. White USAF Space trophy, gold space medal Fedn. Aeronautique Internat. Mem. Soc. Exptl. Test Pilots. Clubs: Alfalfa, Alibi.

COLLINS, N. DANA, art gallery owner, consultant, retired art educator; d. Harold Emile and Nathalie Margaret Collins; m. C. Stephen Rhoades, May 20, 2000 (dec. 2004); children: Jenny Rose, Caitlin Dane(dec.). Student, Yale U., 1964, Sch. Art Inst. Chgo.; BFA, Washington U., 1965; MFA, Pratt Inst., 1967; postgrad., U. Tenn., Columbia Coll., U. Ill., North Adams Coll., Gov.'s State U., Ea. Ill. U., Ill. State U. Prof. fine arts Ill. Valley C.C., Oglesby, 1981—2004, ret., 2004; prin., owner Collins & Co. Studio, Princeton, Ill., 2003—. Tchr. L.I. U., Bklyn., 1967—68, Bay Path Coll., Longmeadow, Mass., 1973—74; prof. humanities Ill. Consortium Internat. Edn., London, 1987, Coll. St. Francis, Joliet, Ill., 1991, 94; prof. art Berkshire C.C., Pittsfield, Mass., 1970—80; presenter, tchr., cons. in field. Author: Teaching Studio Art to Diverse Students, 1998; co-editor: The Second Berkshire Anthology, 1975; one-woman shows include The Bklyn. Ctr., 1967, Becket Art Ctr., Mass., 1971, Berkshire Athenaeum, 1979, The Art Gallery, Boston, 1980, McAuley Gallery, Iowa, 1988, The Row Ho. Gallery, Ill., 1993, Prairie Arts Ctr., Princeton, 2006, exhibited in group shows at Pratt Inst., 1968, 1969, 1970, SUNY, New Paltz, 1970, Pratt Manhattan Ctr., 1970, The Bklyn. Mus., 1970, Berkshire Mus., 1975, 1976, 1980, Berkshire C.C., Pittsfield, 1975, Paddlewicker Gallery, Lenox, Mass., 1976, Williams Coll., Williamstown, Mass., 1979, Art Gallery Boston, 1981, Rockford Coll., 1989, Thomas Gallery, Ill., 1991, 1992, Tri-State Gallery, Platteville, Wis., 2003, Art Space, Muscatine, Iowa, 2005—07, Prairie Art Ctr., Ill., 2006. Dir. mural projects St. Margaret's Hosp., Spring Valley, Ill.; hot line crisis counselor Battered Woman's Task Force, Pittsfield, 1978—80; bd. dirs. Against Domestic Violence, Streator, Ill., 1983—87, Prairie Arts Ctr., Princeton, Ill.; adv. bd. Ill. Valley Fine Arts Trust, LaSalle, 1992—97. Scholar, Norfolk Sch. Painting, 1964. Mem.: NOW (v.p. 1993—89), Bur. County Big Sister Program, Ill. Fedn. Tchrs. Democrat. Avocations: music, poetry. Home: 19186 Norwood Dr Princeton IL 61356 Office: Collins & Co Studio Gallery 537 S Main St Princeton IL 61356 Office Phone: 815-878-5995.

COLLINS, NANCY WHISNANT, foundation administrator; b. Dec. 20, 1933; d. Ward William and Marjorie Adele (Blackburn) Whisnant; m. James Quincy Collins, Jr., Apr. 25, 1959 (div. 1974); children: James Quincy III, Charles Lowell, William Robey;. Student, Queens Coll., Charlotte, 1951—53; AB in Journalism, U. N.C., Greensboro, 1955, MS in Pers. Adminstrn., 1967; postgrad., Cornell U., Ithaca, NY, 1955—56. Pers. asst. R.H. Macy & Co., Inc., NYC, 1955; jr. exec. placement dir. Scofield Placement Agy., San Francisco, 1956—57; freelance journalist London, Paris, and Frankfurt, Germany, 1957—59; program dir. Girl Scouts U.S.A., Hampton, Va., 1959—61; dir. tour Tokyo, Hong Kong, Singapore, 1965—66; asst. dir. Sloan Exec. Program Stanford (Calif.) U., 1968—78; asst. dir. Hoover Instn., 1979—81; asst. to pres. Palo Alto (Calif.) Med. Found., 1981—2000; asst. to chmn. Novo Ventures, Menlo Park, Calif., 2000—; exec. dir. Marconi Soc., 2006—. Bd. dir. Am. Healthway Sys.; fund raising cons. Stanford U. Equestrian Ctr., 1994—2004; mgr. Marconi Soc. Ann. Mtg., 2006. Author: Professional Women and Their Mentors, 1988, Women Leading: Making Tough Choices on the Fast Track, 1988, Love at Second Sight, 2003, Playing the MidLife Dating Game, 2003; editor: Have a Great Day: Today and Every Day of Your Life; contbr. articles short stories, and poems to mags. and newspapers. Fundraiser Cornell U., NYC, 1975—81; fundraising consultant Stanford Univ., Equestrian Cender, 1994—2004; mem. coun. Trinity Episcopal Ch., Menlo Park, Calif., 1975—80; mem. leadership team Menlo Park Presbyn. Ch.; bd. dirs. Santa Clara County coun. Girl Scouts U.S.; mem. exec. coun. Stanford area coun. Boy Scouts Am., 1980—81; mem. San Mateo County Charter Rev. Com.; mem. pers. bd. City of Menlo Park, 1979—; mem. women's program bd. Coro Found.; trustee Pacific Grad. Sch. Psychology; sec.-treas. Chapman Rsch. Fund. Fellow, Cornell U.; grantee, Richardson Found., 1967. Mem.: AAUW, Catalyst, Peninsula Profl. Women's Network, Am. Mgmt. Assn., Menlo Circus Club, Overseas Press Club, Commonwealth Club, Mayflower Soc. Club, Kappa Delta. Home: 1850 Oak Ave Menlo Park CA 94025-5842 E-mail: collinsnw@aol.com.

COLLINS, PAMELA MARIE, forensic specialist, educator; b. Detroit, Aug. 12, 1962; d. James Edward and Angiline Sarah (Virgilio) Callaway; m. Shaun Michael Collins, Nov. 23, 2005; 1 child, Sara Rene' Russell stepchildren: Adam Michael, Kayla Michele. BS in Criminal Justice, Jacksonville State U., Ala., 1991, MS in Criminology, 1993; M in Forensic Sci., George Wash. U., Washington, 1999; MS in Orgnl. Psychology and Tng. Devel., St. Joseph's U., Phila., 2004. Spl. agt. Wuerzburg Resident Agy., US Army Criminal Investigation Command, Germany, 1987—88; spl. agt. charge Ft. McClellan Resident Agy., US Army Criminal Investigation Commd., Ala., 1990—93; team chief, gen. crimes Schofield Barracks Field Office, US Army Criminal Investigation Commd., Hawaii, 1993—96; spl. agt. in charge Ft. McClellan Resident Agy., U.S. Army Criminal Investigation Command, Fort McClellan, Ala., 1996—98; bn. ops. officer, forensic sci. officer Bavaria Bn., US Army Criminal Investigations Commd., Germany, 1999—2002; master instr. forensic sci. US Army Mil. Police Sch., Fort Leonard Wood, Mo., 2002—07; mil. analyst, 2007—. With US Army, 1982—2007. Decorated Meritorious Svc. medal Achievement Tng. and Doctrine Comdr., Meritorious Svc. medal Commdg. Gen., US Army Criminal Investigation Command, Army Commendation medal, Army Achievement medal, Legion of Merit Tng. and Doctrine Command. Fellow: Armed Forces Inst. Pathology, Am. Acad. Forensic Sci.; mem.: Criminal Investigation Command Agt. Assn. (assoc.), Internat. Assn. Blood Pattern Analysis (assoc.). Achievements include Provided VIP protection for Secretaries of Defense Weinberger, Cheney, and Carlucci. Avocations: hiking, running, reading, golf. Office: US Army Mil Police Sch 401 MANSCEN Loop Fort Leonard Wood MO 65473-9085 Personal E-mail: pcollins@cablemo.net. Business E-Mail: pamela.m.collins1@us.army.mil.

COLLINS, PATRICIA ANN, pastor, pastoral counselor; d. Verner and Mittie Bell Patton; m. Raymond Collins, Sept. 13, 1971; children: Raymond Jr., Annetra Deonette, Sonja Raynette Anthony, Kimberly Dianne, Teon Lavance. A. in Nursing, Lawson State Coll., 1975; BA in Christian Edn., Birmingham-Eastonian Bible Coll., 1988; MDiv, Samford U-Beeson Div., 1994. Registered nurse, Ala., 1975; pastoral counselor Carraway/United Meth. Counseling Ctr., Ala., 1997, bereavement coord. Am. Acad. Bereavement, N.Y., 2003. Registered nurse Cooper Green Hosp., Birmingham, 1975—77; nursing supr. Lloyd Nolan Hosp., Fairfield, Ala., 1977—83; trauma registered surg. nurse Carraway Meth. Hosp., Birmingham, 1983—92; nurse chaplain Carraway Med. Ctr., Bessemer, Ala., 1992—93, chaplain hospice, 1994—; asst. dir. pastoral svcs. UAB Med. West, Bessemer, 2004—; sr. pastor Faith Missionary Bapt. Ch., Birmingham, 2004—. Bereavement coord. UAB Med. West Hosp., 1995—; pastoral counselor U. Ala. Bessemer Hosp., 1997—, dir. cancer support group touch, 1998—. Mem. Nat. Bapt. Conv., Nashville, 1980—2005, Peace Bapt. Assn., Birmingham, 2005. Mem.: Ala. Nurses Assn. (assoc.), Mary Mahoney Nurses Assn. (assoc.; chaplain 1993—2004, Leadership), Racial - Ethnic Multicultural Assn. of Chaplains (assoc.), Assn. Clin. Pastoral Edn. (assoc.). Baptist. Achievements include first African American woman to become senior pastor of a Black Baptist Church in the state of Alabama. Avocations: singing, reading, music, painting, travel. Home: 1301 Ave H Birmingham AL 35218 Office: UAB Medical West 995 9th Ave Hwy 11 South Bessemer AL 35021 Home Phone: 205-781-1232; Office Phone: 205-481-7531. Office Fax: 205-481-7498; Home Fax: 205-780-9128. Personal E-mail: pac4567@aol.com. Business E-Mail: pcollins@uabmw.org.

COLLINS, PAUL JOHN, banker; b. West Bend, Wis., Oct. 26, 1936; s. Curtis Alvin and Adele (Stopenbach) C.; m. Carol Lee Hoffmann, May 8, 1965; children: Ronald Alvin, Julia Downing. BBA, U. Wis., 1958; MBA, Harvard U., 1961. With Citibank, NYC, 1961-2000, investment analyst, portfolio mgmt., 1961-70, sr. v.p., chmn. investment policy com., 1970-75, sr. v.p., head corp. planning, 1976-77, sr. v.p., head fin. div., 1977-79, exec. v.p. acctg. and control, 1980-81, group exec. investment bank, 1982-85, sr. corp. officer N.Am., 1985-88, vice chmn., 1988-98, also bd. dirs., Citigroup vice chmn., 1998-2000. Vice chmn. Nokia Corp.; bd. dirs. BG Group, Enstar Group, Actis Capital LLP. Bd. dirs. Glyndebourne Arts Trust, U. Wis. Found.; mem. adv. bd. Welch Carson Anderson & Stowe. Republican. Congregationalist. Home: 29 Wilton Crescent London SW1 X8SA England E-mail: pcollins@pjcpartners.com.

COLLINS, PAUL STEVEN, vascular surgeon; b. Portsmouth, Ohio, July 24, 1954; s. Paul Whitney and Geralda Pearl (Hoskins) Collins; m. Cathy Ann McWicker, Jan. 17, 1981; children: Lauren Elizabeth, Paul McWicker, Andrew Steven. BS, Davidson Coll., NC, 1976; MD, U. South Fla., Tampa, 1979. Diplomate Am. Bd. Surgery, spl. qualifications in gen. vascular surgery and surg. critical care; diplomate Nat. Bd. Med. Examiners; lic. surgeon, Fla., Va. Commd. 2d lt. US Army, 1979, advanced through grades to lt. col., 1990, resident in gen. surgery Walter Reed Army Med. Ctr. Washington, 1979-84, chief gen. surg. Würzburg, Germany, 1984-86, fellow peripheral vasc. surgery Walter Reed Army Med. Ctr. Washington, 1986-87, chief vascular surgery Letterman Army Med. Ctr. San Francisco, resigned, 1992; pvt. practice St. Petersburg, Fla., 1990—; asst. clin. prof. surgery U. South Fla., 1995—. Asst. clin. prof. surgery Uniformed Svcs. U. Health Scis., Bethesda, Md., 1984—; chief of surgery St. Anthony's Hosp., St. Petersburg, 1998—2000, dir. vascular lab., 1994—97, chmn. dept. surgery, 1998—2000, chief of staff, 2005—; profl. mem. Keystone, Tampa, Fla., 1993—97; pres. Bay Plaza Outpatient Surgery, 1994—2001; bd. dirs., trustee St. Anthony's Found.; team surgeon Tampa Bay Devil Rays Baseball Team, 1996—. Contbr. chpts. to books, articles to med. jours. Bd. dirs. St. Anthony's Found. Recipient Physicians Recognition award AMA, 1992, Sigvaris award Camp Internat., 1987. Fellow: ACS (Regional Trauma award 1984), Internat. Soc. Cardiovasc. Surgeons; mem.: Pinellas County Med. Soc. (bd. govs.), Fla. Med. Assn., Fla. Vascular Soc. (sec., treas. 2002—04, pres.-elect 2004, pres. 2005), So. Assn. Vascular Surgery (Pres.'s award 1992). Avocations: golf, tennis, snow and water skiing, gardening. Office: 960 7th Ave N Saint Petersburg FL 33705 Personal E-mail: sclpac@aol.com, stevec@tampadsl.net.

COLLINS, PHIL (PHILIP DAVID CHARLES COLLINS), singer, songwriter, drummer, record producer; b. London, Jan. 30, 1951; s. Greville and June Collins; m. Andrea Collins, 1975 (div. 1982); 1 child, Simon; step child, Joely; m. Jill Collins, 1984 (div. 1996); 1 child, Lily Jane; m. Orianne Cevey, July 24, 1999 (separated March 15, 2006); 1 child: Nicholas. Drummer rock band Genesis, 1971-75, lead singer, songwriter, 1975—. Albums with Genesis include: Nursery Cryme, 1971, Foxtrot, 1972, Selling England by the Pound, 1973, Genesis Live, 1973, The Lamb Lies Down on Broadway, 1974, Trick of the Tail, 1976, Wind and Wuthering, 1977, Seconds Out, 1977, Spot the Pigeon, 1977, And Then There Were Three, 1978, Duke, 1980, Abacab, 1981, Three Sides Live, 1982, Genesis, 1983, Invisible Touch, 1986, We Can't Dance, 1991, The Way That We Walk Volume One: The Shorts, 1992, The Way That We Walk Volume Two: The Longs, 1993; solo albums include: Face Value, 1981, Hello, I Must be Going, 1982, No Jacket Required (Grammy award 1986), 1985, 12"Ers, 1987,.But Seriously, 1989, Serious Hits-Live, 1990, Both Sides, 1993, Dance into the Light, 1996, Hits, 1998, Big Band-A Hot Night in Paris, 1999, Testify, 2002, The Platinum Collection, 2004, Love Songs: A Compilation.Old and New, 2004; composer film: Against All Odds (Acad. award nomination), 1984, White Nights, 1985, Buster, 1988, (voice) Balto, 1995, Tarzan, 1999, Moulin Rouge!, 2001, Brother Bear, 2003; TV movie Hook, 1991, Frauds, 1993, Calliope, 1993, And the Band Played On, 1993; composer, lyricist (broadway) Tarzan, 2006. Winner Grammy award for Best Song (Against All Odds), 1985, Grammy award for Two Hearts, 1989, 5 others, 2 Silver Clef awards, 2 awards Variety Club of Gt. Britain, 1 Elvis award, Golden Globe for the song Two Hearts from the movie Buster, 1989, Oscar and Golden Globe for the song You'll be in my Heart from the movie Tarzan, 2000, numerous others, Star on the Hollywood Walk of Fame, 1999, Diamond award RIAA, 1999, City of Life award, 2002. Office: Atlantic Records 1290 Avenue Of The Americas New York NY 10104-0184

COLLINS, PHILIP A., management consultant; Regional dir. third-party eligibility Medstandard, Inc., 1992—2000, exec. dir. billing svcs., 1998—2000; sr. bus. cons. Medcath, Inc., 2001—02, ctrl. bus. office dir., 2002—03; sr. healthcare cons. Unicare Corp., 2003—04; dir. quality assurance Medstandard, Inc., 2004—05. Mem. Gerson Lehrman Group Healthcare Coun. Mem.: Soc. Industry Leaders. Address: 9117 Windy Crest Dr Dallas TX 75243 E-mail: philipacollins@aol.com.

COLLINS, RICHARD LAWRENCE, editor; b. Little Rock, Nov. 28, 1933; s. Leighton Holden Collins and Sarah Aloysia (Banks) Polk; m. Ann Terry Slocomb, Feb. 14, 1958; children— Charlotte, Sarah, Richard Jr. Chief pilot Ben M. Hogan Co., Little Rock, 1957-58; mng. editor Air Facts mag., Princeton, NJ, 1958-68; sr. editor Flying mag., NYC, 1968-77, editor in chief, 1977-88; editor in chief, pub. Pilot, sr. v.p. Aircraft Owners and Pilots Assn., Frederick, Md., 1988-89; aviation cons., 1989—. Editor-at-large Flying Mag.; editor, cons. Sportsman's Market, Inc. Author numerous aviation books including: Flying Safely, 1977, Tips to Fly By, 1980, Thunderstorms and Airplanes, 1982, Flight Level Flying, 1985, Air Crashes, 1986, The Perfect Flight, 1988, Pilot Upgrade, 1989, Mastering the Systems, 1991; contbr. articles to mags. Chmn. Ark. Aero. Commn., Little Rock, 1976. Served with U.S. Army, 1955-57 Recipient Earl D. Osborn award Aviation Writers, 1978, Sherman Fairchild award Flight Safety Found., 1965, platinum wing award NBAA, 2000; named to Ark. Aviation Hall of Fame, 1988 Mem. Flying Physicians Assn. (hon.), Lawyer Pilots Bar Assn. (hon.), Civil Aeromed. Assn. (hon.) Clubs: Quiet Birdmen. Avocation: sailing. Office: 1633 Broadway 45th Fl New York NY 10019

COLLINS, RICHARD STRATTON (DICK COLLINS), retired public relations executive; b. Smith Center, Kans., Dec. 11, 1929; s. Edgar Wesley and Rosina Ann (Allbert) C.; children: Ann Michelle, Jennifer Lee, Logan Reed. BA, U. Tex., 1952. Editor of Lookout Look Mag., NYC, 1952-53, asst. circulation promotion mgr., 1953-57, circulation promotion mgr., 1957-64, pub. rels. mgr., 1964-67; v.p., dir. corp. pub. rels. Cowles Comm., NYC, 1967-74; assoc. The Jonathan Rinehart Group, NYC, 1974-76; dir. pub. rels. ABA, Chgo., 1976-80, dir. comms., 1980-89, dir. comms./pub. affairs, 1989-94, ret., 1994. Writer mag. advts. (award of Excellence Communication Arts Mag. 1971); contbr. articles to profl. jours.; newspaper columnist. Bd. dirs., pres. Family Counseling Svcs., Bergen County, N.J., 1968-76. Recipient Silver Screen award U.S. Indsl. Film Festival, 1979, The Chris Plaque, Columbus Film Festival, 1979. Mem. Pub. Rels. Soc. of Am. (Silver Anvil award 1964). Avocations: golf, gardening, reading, civil liberties organizations, recording for the blind.

COLLINS, ROBERT ELLWOOD, surgeon; b. Cottage City, Md., Aug. 4, 1932; s. Edward Clarence and Edith (Blough) C.; m. Barbara Kauffmann Murray, June 28, 1964; children: Garret, Randy, Robin, Bill, Bruce, Brad, Beth. BS, Ea. Mennonite Coll., 1954; MD, Med. Coll. Va., 1958. Diplomate Am. Bd. Orthop. Surgeons. Intern Washington Hosp. Ctr., 1958-59, orthopaedic resident, 1961-64; pvt. practice medicine Broadway, Va., 1959-60; resident in gen. surgery Med. Coll. Va., Richmond, 1960-61; pvt. practice medicine specializing in orthop. surgery Washington, 1964—. Acting orthopaedic chief Children's Hosp., 1970—72; chief orthopaedics Washington Hosp. Ctr., 1973—75, vice-chmn. dept. orthopaedics, 1975—80, bd. dirs., pres. med. and dental staff, 1981, 1983—85; assoc. prof. Georgetown U. Hosp., 1975—; courtesy staff Sibley Meml. Hosp.; pres. med. staff Nat. Rehab. Hosp., Washington, 1988—2001; bd. dirs. Medlantic Health Corp., Washington. Bd. dirs. Easter Seal Soc. of Washington and Md., 1986—, chmn. bd. dirs., 1990—92; bd. dirs. Nat. Orthopedic Hosp., Washington, 1990, Nat. Easter Seals Soc., 1995—2001. Recipient Tchg. award Georgetown U., Washington, 1985; Children's Orthop.'s fellow Children's Hosp., 1963, Cerebral Palsy fellow Children's Rehab. Inst. Johns Hopkins U., 1965. Fellow ACS (chmn. DC trauma com.), Am. Acad. Cerebral Palsy, Am. Acad. Orthop. Surgeons, Am. Acad. Orthop. Foot Surgeons; mem. Med. Soc. DC (pres. 1985-86), Washington Clin. Club (past pres.), Georgetown Club, Congl. Country Club (Bethesda, Md.). Presbyterian. Office: Nat Orthopaedics Inc Drs Collins Johnson & Tozzi PC 106 Irving St NW Ste 215 Washington DC 20010-2993 Home Phone: 703-237-5329; Office Phone: 202-291-9260. E-mail: granbobc@aol.com.

COLLINS, RONALD LESLIE LEOPOLD, neurosurgeon; b. Nov. 19, 1944; Came to U.S., 1979; MB BS, U. W.I., Kingston, Jamaica, 1968. Diplomate Am. Bd. Neurological Surgery, Am. Bd. Minimally Invasive Spinal Surgery. Intern Harlem Hosp. Ctr., 1979-80, resident, 1980-81, King/Drew Med. Ctr., 1985-88; fellow Cook County Hosp., 1984-85, Robert Wood Johnson U. Hosp., 1988-89; neurosurgeon NYC, 1989—. Contbr. articles to profl. jours.; inventor in field. Fellow Royal Coll. Surgery (Edinburgh), Internat. Coll Surgeons, Oxford Med. Alumni, Masons. Home: 681 E 78th St Brooklyn NY 11236-3307 Home Phone: 718-251-7141; Office Phone: 917-538-2680. E-mail: rllcolins@aol.com.

COLLINS, RUTH ANN, principal; d. Carl Alvin Pettis, Jr. and Lois Marie Pettis; m. Timothy Paul Collins; children: Thomas Paul, Megan M., Deanna M., Brandon J. BSc, Minn. State U., 1985, MSc cum laude, 1994; postgrad., U. St. Thomas, 1997, postgrad., 1998, postgrad., 2000, U. Loyola, 2000, U. Minn., 2001—04, postgrad., 2005—. Lic. adminstrv. leadership Minn., tchr. Minn., spl. edn. Minn. Tchr. grade 5, 1985—87; tchr. spl. edn., 1987—2005; specialist autism resource Waterville Elysian Morristown Pub. Schs., 1996—2000; intern spl. edn. Roosevelt Sch., Faribault, 2003—04, coord., 2005—; dir. Faribault Spl. Edn. Office, 2005—. Mem. resource and referral com. Gov.'s Coun.; presenter in field. Co-editor: FOCUS - Parent Newsletter, 1996—2000, Faribault Edn. Assn. Newsletter, 2000—02; contbr. A Taste of McKinley, A Quilter's Christmas Cookbook. Mem.: Tchrs. Retirement Assn., Twin Cities Autism Soc., Minn. Assn. Sch. Adminstrs., Nat. Elem. Sch. Prins. Assn., Edn. Minn. (state com., chmn. membership com., co-editor, editor newspaper, bldg. rep., v.p. local chpt., co-chmn. com.), Cath. Dau. of Am., Minn. Deer Hunters Assn., Rotary. Avocation: quilting. Office: Fairbault Pub Schs 925 Parshall St Faribault MN 55021

COLLINS, SAMUEL W., JR., judge; b. Caribou, Maine, Sept. 17, 1923; s. Samuel Wilson Collins & Elizabeth Black C; m. Dorothy Small, 1952; children: Edward, Elizabeth, Diane. BA, U. Maine; JD, Harvard U. Lawyer, Rockland, Maine, 1947—; justice Supreme Jud. Ct., Portland, Maine. Trustee Rockland Sch. Dist, 1949-61; Maine State Senate Dist. 21, 1975-84, majority leader, 1981-82, minority leader, 1983-84. Recipient Disting. Svc. award Jaycees, 1978. Mem. Maine Bar Assn., Rotary, Phi Beta Kappa, Phi Kappa Phi, Delta Tau Delta. Unitarian Universalist. Republican. Office: Knox County Courthouse 62 Union St Rockland ME 04841-2836 Office Phone: 207-594-2254.

COLLINS, STEPHEN, actor; b. Des Moines, Oct. 1, 1947; s. Cyrus Stickney and Madeleine (Robertson) C.; m. Faye Elizabeth Yoe Grant, Apr. 21, 1985; 1 child, Katherine Donovan. BA, Amherst Coll., 1969. Appeared in films including All The President's Men, 1976, Between the Lines, 1977, Fedora, 1978, The Promise, 1979, Star Trek-The Motion Picture, 1979, Loving Couples, 1980, Brewster's Millions, 1985, Choke Canyon, 1986, Jumpin' Jack Flash, 1986, The Big Picture, 1989, Stella, 1990, My New Gun, 1992, The First Wives Club, 1996, Drive Me Crazy, 1999, Blood Diamond, 2006, Because I Said So, 2007, (TV series) Tattinger's, 1989, Tales of the Gold Monkey, 1982, Working It Out, 1990, Sisters, 1995-96, 7th Heaven, 1996-2006, (TV films) including The Henderson Monster, 1980, Summer Solstice, 1981, Inside The Third Reich, 1982, The Two Mrs. Grenvilles, 1987, Weekend War, 1988, A Woman Scorned: The Betty Broderick Story, 1992, Her Final Fury: Betty Broderick, the Last Chapter, 1992, The Disappearance of Nora, 1993, Remember, 1993, A Family Divided, 1995, For Love Alone: The Ivana Trump Story, 1996, The Babysitter's Seduction, 1996, On Seventh Avenue, 1996, An Unexpected Family, 1996, An Unexpected Life, 1998, As Time Runs Out, 1999; stage prodns. including (Broadway) Moonchildren, The Ritz, (off Broadway) Beyond Therapy, Love Letters, and various other prodns. Bd. dirs. The Creative Coalition, N.Y.C., 1989—, Am. Clean Water Found., Washington, 1990—. Mem. Acad. Motion Picture Arts and Scis.*

COLLINS, STEVE ANTHONY, oil industry executive; b. Houma, La., May 18, 1973; s. Frankie P. and Hilda E. Collins. Grad., South Lafourche HS, Galliano, La., 1991. Gen. laborer Tidewater Dock, Golden Meadow, La., 1992—94; owner, operator Better Bodies Health Club, Larose, La., 1994—99; v.p. Global Contractors, Lockport, La., 1998—2000; owner, pres. So. Oilfield Svcs., Cut Off, La., 2000—03, Universal Svcs. LLC, Cut Off, 2003—; co-owner Better Bod Smoothies, Houma, La., 2006—. Cons., owner Internat. Labor Cons., Chennai, India, 2002—. Bd. dirs. Larose Civic Ctr., 2000—02. Mem.: Larose C. of C. Republican. Roman Catholic. Achievements include patents pending for solar powered devices. Avocations: fishing, exercise, investing. Home Phone: 985-258-0490. Personal E-mail: stevecollinsceo@yahoo.com.

COLLINS, STEVEN M., lawyer; b. Atlanta, Oct. 22, 1952; s. E.B. and Judith (Morse) C.; divorced; 1 child, Erin M.; m. Anne Frances Garland, Oct. 31, 1987; 1 child, Timothy G. AB, Harvard U., 1974, JD, 1977. Bar: Ga. 1977, U.S. Dist. Ct. (no. dist.) Ga. 1977, U.S. Ct. Appeals (11th cir.) 1981, U.S. Dist. Ct. (mid. dist.) Ga. 1982, U.S. Tax Ct. 1984, U.S. Ct. Appeals (4th cir.) 1986, U.S. Ct. Appeals (6th cir.) 2001, U.S. Supreme Ct. 1994. Assoc. Alston & Bird, Atlanta, 1977-83, ptnr., litig., trial practice group, 1983—. Editor-in-chief Ga. State Bar Journal, Atlanta, 1982-84. Mem. ABA, State Bar Ga., Atlanta Bar Assn. Office: Alston & Bird One Atlantic Ctr 1201 W Peachtree St NW Atlanta GA 30309-3424 Office Phone: 404-881-7149. Business E-Mail: steve.collins@alston.com.

COLLINS, SUSAN MARGARET, senator; b. Caribou, Maine, Dec. 7, 1952; BA in Govt. magna cum laude, St. Lawrence U., 1975. Prin. advisor bus. affairs to Senator William S. Cohen US Senate, 1975—78; commr. Maine Dept. Profl. and Fin. Regulation, 1987—92; dir. New England ops. U.S. Small Bus. Adminstrn., 1992—93; exec. dir. Ctr. Family Bus., Husson Coll., Bangor, Maine, 1993—96; US Senator from Maine, 1997—. Staff dir. Senate Subcom. on Oversight Govt. Mgmt., 1981-87; chair Cabinet Coun. on Health Care Policy, State of Maine; mem. U.S. Senate com. health, edn., labor and pensions, 1997—, subcom. on children and families, 1997—, subcom. on pub. health and safety, 1997—, com. on govtl. affairs, 1997—; chmn. permanent subcom. on investigations, 1997—; mem. spl. com. on aging; spl. inspector gen. to handle Hurricane Katrina Relief, 2005- Author (with Catherine Whitney): (Books) Nine and Counting: The Women of the Senate, 2000. Rep. candidate for Gov., State of Maine, 1994. Recipient Outstanding Alumni award St. Lawrence U., 1992, Nat. Public Policy Leadership award Am. Diabetes Assn., Tchr. Leader award Reading Recovery Coun. N. Am., 2004, Public Svc. award Emergency Nurses Assn., 2004, Outstanding Legis. award Triangle Coalition Sci. and Technology Edn., 2005, Port Person of Yr. Am. Assn. Port Authorities, 2006, Congressional Leadership award Nat. Urban League, 2006. Mem. Bangor Rotary Club, Phi Beta Kappa. Republican. Roman Catholic. Office: US Senate 461 Dirksen Sen Office Bldg Washington DC 20510 also: Margaret Chase Smith Fed Bldg 202 Harlow St Rm 204 PO Box 655 Bangor ME 04402-4919 Office Phone: 202-224-2523, 207-945-0417. Office Fax: 202-224-2693, 207-990-4604.*

COLLINS, THEODORE JOHN, lawyer; b. Walla Walla, Wash., Oct. 2, 1936; s. Robert Bonfield and Catherine Roselle (Snyder) C.; m. Patricia Spengler Pasieka, May 11, 1968; children: Jonathan, Caitlin, Matthew, Patrick, Flannary. BA, U. Notre Dame, 1958; postgrad., U. Bonn, Fed. Republic Germany, 1959; LLB, Harvard U., 1962. Bar: Wash. 1962, U.S.

Supreme Ct. 1982, U.S. Ct. Appeals (fed. cir.) 1982, U.S. Dist. Ct. (ea. dist.) Wash. 1965, U.S. Dist. Ct. (we. dist.) Wash. 1962. Ptnr. Perkins Coie Law Firm, Seattle, 1962-86; v.p., gen. counsel The Boeing Co., Seattle, 1986-98, sr. v.p., gen. counsel, 1998-2000; of counsel Perkins Coie Law Firm, 2001—. Adj. prof. Seattle U. Law Sch. Mem. ABA, Wash. State Bar Assn., King County Bar Assn., Wash. Athletic Club. Office Phone: 206-359-3578. E-mail: tcoll10236@aol.com, collt@perkinscoie.com.

COLLINS, THOMAS WILLIAM, caterer, consultant; b. Lewiston, Idaho, Nov. 4, 1926; s. William James and Mary (Egan) C.; m. Mary Charlene Tracy, Aug. 1, 1947 (dec. Apr. 1984); children: Kathleen, William, Charles. Grad. high sch., Staples, Minn., 1944. Owner Collins Cafe, Park Rapids, Minn., 1947-63, Tom Collins Restaurant, Walker, Minn., 1963-83, Tom Collins Catering, Walker, 1983—. Author: Collins Cooking Secrets, 1981. Fundraiser DFL, 1976-83; adv. bd. Lake Country Food Bank, Mpls., 1981-86, bd. dirs., 1987-98. Served with USN, 1945-46, 51-52. Recipient Recognition award Mont. Gov., 1978, cert. of Spl. Congl. Recognition, 1995; Tom Collins Day proclaimed by Minn. Gov., 1977. Mem. Assn. Great Lakes Outdoor Writers, Am. Legion. Lodges: Masons (sr. warden 1958), Shriners. Avocations: hunting, fishing, photography. Home and Office: PO Box 33 Walker MN 56484-0033

COLLINS, TUCKER, pathologist, molecular biologist; b. Lorain, Ohio, Nov. 3, 1952; s. Robert James and Catherine (Meisner) C.; m. Mary Judith Whitley, June 15, 1985. BA, Amherst Coll., 1975, DSc (hon.), 1998; MD, PhD, U. Rochester, 1981. Diplomate Am. Bd. Pathology. Clin., rsch. fellow Brigham and Women's Hosp., Boston, 1981-85; from instr. to prof. pathology Harvard Med. Sch., Boston, 1985-98, prof. pathology, 1998—; Wolbach prof., chmn. dept. pathology Children's Hosp., Boston, 1992-99. Staff pathologist Brigham and Women's Hosp., 1992-2001; charter mem., chmn. pathology study sect. NIH. Author: Pathologic Basis of Disease, 1999; mem. editl. bd. Am. Jour. Pathology; contbr. articles to profl. jours. Scholar Pew Scholars Program, 1987-91; grantee NIH, 1985, 1990, 1993, 1996, 1997, 2002, 2005, 2006, Am. Heart Assn. Established Investigator, 1991-96; recipient Warner-Lambert/Parke-Davis award Am. Soc. for Investigative Pathology, 1994; assoc. master Francis Weld Peabody Soc. Mem. Am. Soc. Investigative Pathology (pres.), Am. Assn. Univ. Pathologists, N.Am. Vascular Biology Orgn., New England Soc. Pathologists (pres.), Acad. Harvard Med. Sch. Achievements include research in the structure and function of SCAN family of transcription factors. Home: 120 Jerusalem Rd Cohasset MA 02025 Office: Children's Hosp Boston MA 02115 Home Phone: 781-383-4708; Office Phone: 617-919-2662. Personal E-mail: tcoll02115@aol.com. Business E-Mail: tcollins@rics.bwh.harvard.edu.

COLLINS, WALTER LLOYD GEORGE, editor; b. Broken Arrow, Okla., Dec. 6, 1917; s. Dow Otho and Myrtle Hester (Campbell) C.; m. Ruth Leona Hamilton, Sept. 3, 1935; children: Mary, Walter, Alvin, Shirley. BA, Pan Am. U., 1966; MA, U. Tulsa, 1975. Aviation cadet USAAF, 1942; advanced through grades to maj. USAF, 1962; exec. in charge C-E Installation Project NATO, Europe, North Africa, Mid. East, 1956-57; sr. editor radar and missiles project USAFE, 1957-58; ops. officer C-E divsn. Def. Atomic Support Agy., Alburquerque, 1959-63; dir. comm.-elec., spacetrack NORAD, Colorado Springs, 1963-64; ret., 1964; gen. mgr. Desert Lodge, Moab, Utah, 1967-68; design engr. planner Beech Aircraft Corp., Wichita, Kans., 1968-72; dir. internat. student affairs Spartan Sch. Aeronautics, Tulsa, 1979-83; pres. R&W Internat., Tulsa, 1984-88, Alpha-Omega Press, Tulsa, Ponca City, Okla., 1990—. Adv. bd. edn. com. Okla. Acad. State Goals, 1977—95. Author: On the Razor's Edge, 1990, Manner of Man, 2001, Into Fields of Fire, 2004. Active Kay County Rep. Com., 1993—, Okla., Ponca City Traffic Commn., 1997-2000. Mem. Acad. Am. Poets, Nat. Order Battlefield Commns., Am. Air Mus. in Great Britain, Air Force Assn., Mil. Officers Assn. Am. Avocations: writing, editing, photography. Personal E-mail: wgcollins@cableone.net.

COLLINS, WAYNE DALE, lawyer; b. Portsmouth, Va., Dec. 23, 1951; s. Wayne D. Sr. and Mary L. (Higdon) C.; m. Mary Ann Bradshaw, Aug. 9, 1981; children: Laura, Melissa, Christopher. BS with honors, Calif. Inst. Tech., 1973, MS, 1974; JD, U. Chgo., 1978; postgrad., U. Minn., 1979. Bar: N.Y. 1979, U.S. Supreme Ct. 1983, D.C., 1991. Assoc. Shearman & Sterling, NYC, 1978-81, 83-86, ptnr., 1987—; spl. asst. to V.P. George Bush, Washington, 1981-82; dep. asst. atty. gen. antitrust div. U.S. Dept. Justice, Washington, 1983. Vis. lectr. Yale Law Sch., 1991-95; vis. com. U. Chgo. Law Sch., 2003—. Co-author: Horizontal Mergers: Law and Policy, 1986, Non-Horizontal Mergers: Law and Policy, 1988, State Antitrust Practice and Statutes, 1991. White House fellow, 1981-82. Fellow Am. Bar Found.; mem. ABA (chmn. antitrust sect. subcom. on fin. markets and instns. 1983-87, chmn. pub. com. 1987-91, coun. mem. antitrust sect. 1991-94, officer antitrust sect. 1994-1999), Am. Law Inst., Assn. of Bar of City of N.Y., Am. Econ. Assn., Econometric Soc., Coun. Fgn. Rels., Am. Coun. Nationalities Svc. (bd. dirs. 1988-1999). Republican. Roman Catholic. also: 801 Pennsylvania Ave NW Washington DC 20004-2615 Office Phone: 212-848-4127.

COLLINS, WILLIAM EDWARD, JR., aeromedical administrator, researcher, psychologist; b. Bklyn., May 16, 1932; s. William Edward and Loretta Agnes (Brasier) C.; m. Corliss Jean Barnes, June 20, 1970; 1 child, Corliss Adora. BS, St. Peter's Coll., Jersey City, 1954; MA, Fordham U., Bronx, NY, 1956, PhD, 1959. Lic. psychologist, Okla. Psychol. rsch. asst. Fordham U., 1954-56, tchg. fellow, 1958, grad. instr., 1958-59, rsch. asst., 1958-59; rsch. psychologist US Army Med. Rsch. Lab., Ft. Knox, Ky., 1959-61; rsch. psychologist Aviation Psychology Lab. FAA Civil Aeromed. Inst., Oklahoma City, 1961-63, chief sensory integration sect., 1963-65, lab. supr., 1965-86, human resources rsch. br. mgr., 1986-88, dep. dir., 1988-89, dir., 1989-2001; adj. assoc. prof. psychology U. Okla., Norman, 1963-70, adj. prof., 1970-89; adj. assoc. prof. rsch. psychology dept. psychiatry and behavioral scis. U. Okla. Health Scis. Ctr., Oklahoma City, 1965-71, adj. prof., 1971—. Mem. Nat. Acad. Sci.-NRC Com. on Vision, 1963-82, mem. exec. coun., 1973-81; mem. Nat. Acad. Sci.-NRC Com. on Hearing, Bioacoustics and Biomechanics, 1963-87; appearances before House Sub-Com. on Pub. Health and Environ., 1971, House Sub-Com. on Investigations and Oversight, 1983, House Sub-Com. on Transp., Aviation and Materials, 1987, 88; judge Okla. State Sci. and Engring. Fair, Ada, 1980, 81, 82; mem. Okla. Bd. Examiners Psychologists, 1981-84, chmn., 1982-84; evaluator proposals NSF, 1968-82, HEW, 1971-80; presenter, lectr. in field. Contbr. articles to profl. jours., chapters to books. Served to res. capt. Med. Services Corps, US Army, 1959-61. Recipient citation for svc. to aviation medicine Okla. State Legislature, 1999, Disting. Career Svc. award FAA, 2001; named to Okla. Aviation and Space Hall of Fame, 2004; named in his honor Ann. award Most Outstanding Sscientific, Tech. Pub. Aerospace Medicine, 2003. Fellow AAAS, APA (abstractor Psychol. Abstracts 1962-2002, citation 1973), NY Acad. Scis., Aerospace Med. Assn. (Raymond F. Longacre award 1971, presdl. exec. com. 1982-84, exec. coun. 1982-85, editl. bd. Aviation, Space and Environ. Medicine 1974-2000, assoc. editor 1980-2000, Pres.'s Citation 1993, Harry G. Moseley award 1998, Life Scis. and Biomed. Engring. Profl. Excellence award 1989, Pres.'s award 1999, Louis H. Bauer Fonders award 2007), Am. Psychol. Soc. (charter), Aerospace Human Factors Assn. (charter, Paul T. Hansen award 1998, William E. Collins award for excellence in human factors named in his honor 2002); mem. Assn. Aviation Psychologists (pres. 1974-75), Okla. Psychol. Assn. (Disting. Psychologist award 1984), South African Soc. Aerospace and Environ. Medicine (Silver Medal award 1998), Nat. Mus. Am. Indian (charter, cert. of appreciation 1995), So. Poverty Law Ctr., Nat. Campaign Tolerance (founding mem.). Home: 8900 Sheringham Dr Oklahoma City OK 73132-4764 Office: Dept Psychiat Behavior Sci Okla U Health Sci Ctr Room ORI-332 PO Box 26901 Research Building Oklahoma City OK 73190-3048

COLLINS, WILLIAM F., JR., neurosurgery educator; b. New Haven, Jan. 20, 1924; MD, Yale U., 1947. Diplomate Am. Bd. Neurol. Surgery. Intern Barnes Hosp., St. Louis, 1947-49, asst. resident in neurosurgery, 1951-52, resident, 1952-53; fellow neurophysiology Washington U., 1953-54; instr. neurosurgery Western Res. U., Cleve., 1954-55, sr. instr., 1955-57, asst. prof., 1957-60, assoc. prof., 1960-63; prof., chmn. divsn. neurosurgery Med. Coll. Va., 1963-67; prof. Yale U., New Haven, chief sect. neurosurgery, 1963—86, chmn. dept. surgery, 1986-93, prof. neurosurgery emeritus, 1994—; clin. prof. neurosurgery U. Calif. Sch. Medicine, San Diego, 1997—. With M.C., U.S. Army, 1949-51. Office: Yale Sch Medicine Dept Neurosurgery PO Box 208082 New Haven CT 06520-8082 Home Phone: 203-473-9025; Office Phone: 203-785-2806. Personal E-mail: wfcollin@aol.com.

COLLINS, WILLIAM J. (BILLY COLLINS), poet, educator; b. NYC, Mar. 1941; Prof. English Lehman Coll., CUNY. Author: (books of poetry) Pokerface, 1977, Video Poems, 1980, The Apple That Astonished Paris, 1988, Questions About Angels, 1991 (Selected by Edward Hirsch for Nat. Poetry Series), The Art of Drowning, 1995 (finalist for Lenore Marshall Poetry Prize), Picnic, Lightning, 1998, Taking Off Emily Dickinson's Clothes, 2000, Sailing Alone Around the Room: New and Selected Poems, 2001, Nine Horses, 2002; contbr. poetry to profl. jours. and publs.; editor: Poetry 180: A Turning Back to Poetry, 2003; reader (recording) The Best Cigarette, 1997. Named a Literary Lion, N.Y. Pub. Libr., 1992; named U.S. Poet Laureate, 2001; recipient Oscar Blumenthal Prize, Bess Hokin Prize, Frederick Bock Prize, Levinson Prize; fellow, N.Y. Found. for the Arts, NEA, Guggenheim Found. Home Phone: 914-248-6613; Office Phone: 718-960-8550.

COLLINS, WILLIAM LEROY, retired telecommunications engineer; b. Laurel, Miss., June 17, 1942; s. Henry L. and Christene E. (Finnegan) C. Student, La Salle U., 1969; BS in Computer Sci., U. Beverly Hills, 1984. Sr. computer operator Dept. Pub. Safety, Phoenix, 1975-78, data communications specialist, 1978-79, supr. computer ops., 1981-82; mgr. network control Valley Nat. Bank, Phoenix, 1979-81; mgr. data comm. Ariz. Lottery, Phoenix, 1982-85; mgr. telecomm. Calif. Lottery, Sacramento, 1985—2004; ret., 2004. Mem. Telecomm. Study Mission to Russia, Oct. 1991. Contbr. to profl. publs. Served as sgt. USAF, 1964-68. Mem. IEEE, Nat. Sys. Programmers Assn., Centrex Users Group, DMS Centrex User Group, Accunet Digital Svcs. User Group, Telecomms. Assn. (v.p. edn. Sacramento Valley chpt. 1990-94, pres. 1995, chpt. assn. dir. 1996-97, chpt. past pres. 1996, Prestigious Svc. award 1997), Telecom. Assn. (chmn. corp. edn. com. 1994-95, conf. com. 1994-95, co-chair conf. program com. 1996, program dir. edn. 1996, corp. dir. edn. 1996-97, pres.-elect 1998, pres. and ceo, 1999), SynOptics User Group, Timeplex User Group, Assn. Data Comm. Users, Soc. Mfg. Engrs., Data Processing Mgmt. Assn., Am. Mgmt. Assn., Assn. Computing Machinery, Am. Soc. for Quality Control, Bldg. Industry Cons. Svc. Internat., Assn. for Quality and Participation, KC, Calif. Integrated Svcs. Digital Network User Group, Computer Security Inst., Assn. Pub. Comms. Officials, Armed Forces Comms. and Electronics Assn., Assn. Info. Tech. Profls., H.P. Open View Forum. Roman Catholic. Home: 503 Mointain Shadow Dr Bayfield CO 81122 E-mail: wlc0617@wmconnect.com.

COLLINSON, DALE STANLEY, lawyer; b. Tulsa, Okla., Sept. 1, 1938; s. Harold Everett and Charlotte Elizabeth (Bonds) C.; m. Susan Waring Smith, June 7, 1969; children: Stuart, Eleanor. AB in Politics and Econs. summa cum laude, Yale U., 1960; LLB, Columbia U., 1963. Bar: NY 1963, DC 2004, US Tax Ct. 1977. Law clk. US Ct. Appeals (2d cir.), NYC, 1963-64; law clk. to Justice Byron R. White US Supreme Ct., Washington, 1964-66; asst. prof. Stanford Law Sch., Calif., 1966-68, assoc. prof., 1968-72; atty.-advisor Office of Tax Policy, US Dept. Treasury, Washington, 1972-73, assoc. tax legis. counsel, 1973-74, dep. tax legis. counsel, 1974-75, tax legis. counsel, 1975-76; tax ptnr. Willkie Farr & Gallagher, NYC, 1976-2000; spl. counsel fin. instns. and products IRS, Washington, 2000—06; dir. fin. instns. and products KPMG LLP, Washington, 2006—. Panel mem. Practising Law Inst. programs, 1981, 82, 84, 86, 88, Am. Law Inst.-ABA program, 1984, Investment Co. Inst. programs, 1992, 94, 97, 2003, others. Contbr. articles to legal jours Fellow Am. Coll. Tax Counsel; mem. ABA, NY State Bar (chmn. tax sect. 1985), Assn. of Bar of City of NY (tax coun. 1990-93, vice chmn. taxation of corps. com. 1990-93), Nat. Assn. Bond Lawyers. Republican. Home: 5480 Wisconsin Ave Apt 922 Chevy Chase MD 20815 Office: KPMG LLP 2001 M St NW Washington DC 20036 Home Phone: 301-652-3087; Office Phone: 202-533-3000. Business E-Mail: dale.collinson.td.60@aya.yale.edu, dcollinson@kpmg.com.

COLLINSWORTH, CRIS, sportscaster, retired professional football player; b. Dayton, Ohio, Jan. 27, 1959; m. Holly Collinsworth; 4 children. BS, U. Fla., Gainesville, 1981; law degree, U. Cin. Wide receiver Cin. Bengals, 1981—88; feature reporter HBO Inside the NFL, 1989, co-host; analyst NBC Sports, 1990—98, studio analyst Sunday Night NFL, 2006—; studio analyst Fox NFL Sunday, 1998—2002, game analyst, 2002. Named to NFL Am. Football Conf. Pro Bowl Team, 1981—83; recipient Sports Emmy award, Outstanding Studio Analyst, 1998, 1999, Sports Emmy award, Outstanding Sports Personality/ Studio Analyst, 2003—07, Sports Emmy award, Outstanding Sports Personality/ Sports Event Analyst, 2007. Office: NBC Sports 30 Rockefeller Plz New York NY 10112*

COLLIS, DENNIS K., orthopedic surgeon; b. Wall Lake, Iowa, Mar. 2, 1937; s. Kennth O. and Blanche Marie Collis; m. Jeanne Camille Tyack, Aug. 28, 1994; children: Randall, Amy. BA in Chemistry and Biology, Grinnell Coll., Iowa, 1959; MD, Washington U., St. Louis, 1963. Diplomate Am. Bd. Orthop. Surgery. Intern, resident Hennepin County Gen. Hosp., Mpls., 1963—65; resident in orthop. surgery U. Iowa, Iowa City, 1967—70; pvt. practice orthopedic surgery Eugene, 1970—; clin. instr. to sr. clin. instr. dept orthops. U. Oreg. Med. Sch., Portland, 1971—78; adj. assoc. prof. dept phys. edn. U. Oreg., Eugene, 1972—78; asst. clin. prof. to assoc. clin. prof. dept. orthops. Oreg. Health Scis. U., Portland, 1978—. Cons. Letterman Gen. Hosp., 1977—79; cons. Hip Clinic, Portland VA Hosp., 1984—. Contbr. chapters to books, articles to profl. jours. Capt. USAF, 1965—67. Decorated Air Force Commendation medal. Mem.: AMA, Orthop. Rsch. and Edn. Found. (treas. 1994—95, chmn. bd. 1995—98), Am. Orthop. Assn. (v.p. 1999), Assn. of Bone and Joint Surgeons (pres. 1994), North Pacific Orthop. Assn. (pres. 2004), Russell Hibbs Soc. (pres. 1990), The Hip Soc. (pres. 1996), Oreg. Med. Assn., Lane County Med. Soc., Western Orthop. Assn. (pres. Oreg. chpt. 1983), Am. Acad. Orthop Surgeons (membership com. 1987, chmn. com. on the hip 1988—94), Eugene Arts Found. (trustee 1984—86), Support Hult Ctr. Orgn. (pres. 1984—85), Eugene Rotary Club, Eugene Country Club (bd. dirs. 1989—92). Presbyterian. Avocations: golf, racquetball, travel, spectator sports. Home: 3265 Riverplace Dr Eugene OR 97401 Office: Orthopedic Healthcare Northwest 1200 Hilyard St Ste 600 Eugene OR 97401 Home Phone: 541-686-0401; Office Phone: 541-485-8111. Business E-Mail: dkcollis@ohn.com.

COLLIS, SIDNEY ROBERT, retired telephone company executive; b. Oak Park, Ill., Mar. 24, 1924; s. Sidney John and Celia (Steele) C.; m. Lois E. Harding, Feb. 23, 1946 (dec.); children— Robert H., Elizabeth A., Gail M., April L. Student, Ill. Inst. Tech., 1941-43, U. Santa Clara, 1943-44; BS in Elec. Engring, Northwestern U., 1947. Registered profl. engr., Ill. With Ill. Bell Telephone Co., 1947-54, 60-61; with Am. Tel. & Tel. Co., 1954-60, 61-62, asst. v.p., 1968-83; v.p. Am. Tel. & Tel. Communications, 1984. Asst. v.p. N.Y. Telephone Co., 1962-63, v.p., 1963-68. Home: 70 Fieldstone Dr Basking Ridge NJ 07920-1607

COLLISCHAN, JUDY KAY, art gallery and museum director, critic, artist; b. Red Wing, Minn., Oct. 19, 1940; d. Michael J. and Olive Amanda (Sundberg) Collischan; 1 son, Brien Grey Collischan Van Wagner. BA, Hamline U., 1962; postgrad. Nat. U. Mex., summer 1963; MFA, Ohio U., 1964; PhD, U. Iowa, 1972. Asst. prof. art history U. No. Iowa, Cedar Falls, 1970-71, U. Nebr.-Omaha, 1971-75; assoc. prof. SUNY-Plattsburgh, 1975-82; dir. Hillwood Art Gallery, LI U., C.W. Post Campus Greenvale, N.Y., 1982—94; assoc. dir. Neuberger Mus. Art, SUNY, Purchase, N.Y., 1995-2000; pvt. practice cons., 2001—; art critic Arts, Art Express, NYC, 1982-; field rep. N.Y. State Council on Arts, NYC, 1983, mem. visual arts panel, 1986—; cons. Gen. Motors art collections, NYC 1983. Author: Women Shaping Art, 1984, Lines of Vision: Drawings by Contemporary Women, 1989, Welded Sculpture of The 20th Century, 2000; contbr. articles to profl. jours. Fellow Kress Found., 1970; recipient award SUNY, 1981. Mem. Am. Assn. Mus. Office Phone: 212-505-9657. Personal E-mail: jcollischan@gmail.com.

COLLISON, JIM, publishing executive; b. Blue Earth, Minn., May 24, 1933; s. Elliott Eugene and Rosa Theresa (Whitcomb) C.; m. Valerie Ann Thul, Oct. 28, 1954; children: Judith, Michelle, Daniel, Michael, Rebecca, David. BA, St. John's Univ., 1955. Sports editor Blue Earth Post and Faribault County Register, 1953; staff writer St. Cloud Daily Times, Minn., 1953-55, Waterloo Courier, Iowa, 1955-57, Mason City Globe Gazette, Iowa, 1958-63; bus. and edn. cons. Jim Collison Assoc., Mason City, Iowa, 1963-77; exec. dir. Employers of Am., Mason City, Iowa, 1978-81, pres., 1981—; pres., pub. Sunburst Publ., Mason City, Iowa, 1990—. Co-founder Employers of Am., 1978; chmn. bd. ISBE Ins. Alliance, Mason City, 1986—, Select Advantage, Inc., ISBE Bus. Ins. Assn., ISBE Employer Benefits Assn.; pres. Am. Corp. Advisors, Inc.; workshop presenter. Author: Skill Building in Advanced Reading, 1968, Mental Power in Reading, 1970, Complete Employee Handbook Made Easy, 1994, 97, 2001, The Employer Protection Workshop, 1996, No-How Coaching, 2001, Complete Suggestion Program Make Easy, 2001; pub., sr. editor (e-newletter) HRmadeEasy; creator IdeaTracker software, 2003, Suggestion ProSoftware, 2006. Asst. min. Orchard (Iowa) Congreg. Ch., 1985—; designer Adult Literacy and Employment Reading Training Program. Democrat. Avocations: flower gardening, hiking. Home: 310 Meadow Ln Mason City IA 50401-1717 Office: Employers of Am PO Box 1874 Mason City IA 50402-1874

COLLMAN, JAMES PADDOCK, chemistry professor; b. Beatrice, Nebr., Oct. 31, 1932; married. B.Sc., U. Nebr., 1954, MS, 1956; PhD (NSF fellow), U. Ill., 1958; Docteur Honoris Causa, U. Dijon, France, 1988, U. Borgogne, 1988; D (hon.), U. Nebr., 1988. Instr. chemistry U. N.C., Chapel Hill, 1958-59, asst. prof., 1959-62, asso. prof., 1962-67; prof. chemistry Stanford U., 1967—; George A. and Hilda M. Daubert prof. chemistry Stanford U., 1980—. Frontiers in Chemistry lectr., 1964, Nebr. lectureship, 1968; Venable lectr. U. N.C., 1971; Edward Clark Lee lectr. U. Chgo., 1972; vis. Erskine fellow U. Canterbury, 1972; Plenary lectr. French Chem. Soc., 1974; Dreyfus lectr. U. Kans., 1974; Disting. inorganic lectr. U. Rochester, 1974; Reilley lectr. U. Notre Dame, 1975; William Pyle Philips lectr. Haverford Coll., 1975; Merck lectr. Rutgers U., 1976; FMC lectr. Princeton, 1977; Julius Steiglitz lectr. Chgo. sect. Am. Chem. Soc., 1977; Pres.'s Seminar Series lectr. U. Ariz., 1980; Frank C. Whitmore lectr. Pa. State U., 1980; Plenary lectr. 3d IUPAC Symposium on Organic Synthesis, 1980, 2d Internat. Kyoto Conf. on New Aspects Inorganic Chemistry, 1982, Internat. Symposium on Models of Enzyme Action, Brighton, Eng., 1983, Internat. Symposium, Italy, 1984; Brockman lectr. U. Ga., 1981; Samuel C. Lind lectr. U. Tenn., 1981, Syntex Disting. lectr. Colo. State U., 1983; Disting. vis. lectr. U. Fla., 1983; vis. prof. U. Auckland, New Zealand, 1985; Nelson J. Leonard lectr. U. Ill., 1987; plenary lectr. Internat. Symposium on Activation of Dioxygen and Homogeneous Catalytic Oxygenations, Tsukuba, Japan, 1987; plenary lectr. 12th Internat. Symposium on Macrocyclic Chem., Hiroshima, Japan, 1987; lectr. Texas A&M, 1988; J. Clarence Karcher lectr. U. Okla., 1989; Musselman lectr. Gettysburg Coll., 1990; Davis lectr. U. New Orleans, 1991; PLU lectr. Okla. State U., 1991; lectr. 5th Internat. Fischer Symposium, Karlsruhe, Ger., 1991; lectr. Euchem Conf., 1991; Pratt lectr. U. Va., 1992, others; lectr. series Harvard/MIT, 1992, Yale U., 1993; invited speaker symposia, univs., confs. Recipient Disting. Teaching award Stanford U., 1981, Calif. Scientist of Year award, 1983, Allan V. Cox medal for excellence in fostering undergrad. rsch., 1988, LAS Alumni Achievement award Coll. Liberal Arts and Scis. U. Ill., 1994, John C. Bailar Jr. medal, 1995, Joseph Chatt medal Royal Soc., 1998 Hans Fischer award in polyphrin chemistry Internat. Conf. Porphyrins and Phthalocyanines, 2002, Oesper award, 2007; named George A. and Hilda M. Daubert Prof. Chemistry (endowed chair, Stanford U.), 1980; Guggenheim fellow, 1977-78, 85-86, Churchill fellow, Cambridge, 1977—, Bing fellow, 1996. Fellow AAAS, Calif. Acad. Sci. (hon.); mem. Am. Chem. Soc. (Calif. sect. award 1972, Soc. award in inorganic chemistry 1975, Arthur C. Cope scholar 1986, Pauling award Puget Sound and Oreg. sect. 1990, Disting. Svc. award in inorganic chemistry 1991, Alfred Bader award 1997, Joseph Chatt lectr. 1998, Marker lectr. medal 1999), NY Acad. Sci. (Basolo medal 2000, Hans Fischer Porphyrin Chemistry award 2002), Chem. Soc. (London), Nat. Acad. Sci., Am. Acad. Arts and Scis., Phi Beta Kappa, Sigma Xi, Phi Lambda Upsilon, Alpha Chi Epsilon (Hans Fischer award 2002). Office: Stanford U Dept Chemistry Stanford CA 94305 Office Phone: 650-725-0283. Business E-Mail: jpc@stanford.edu.

COLLMER, ROBERT GEORGE, retired language educator; b. Guatemala, Nov. 28, 1926; (parents Am. citizens); s. G. Russell and Constance Ethel (Cravener) Collmer; m. Linnie Maffett Burney, Jan. 5, 1948 (dec. 1979); children: Carol Linda Collmer McLaren, Mark Wesley; m. Alys Edney, July 4, 1981. BA, Baylor U., Waco, Tex., 1948, MA, 1949; PhD, U. Pa., Phila., 1953. Asst. instr. U. Pa., Phila., 1949—52; instr. Phila. Bibl. U., 1952—54; from assoc. prof. to prof., chmn. dept. English Hardin-Simmons U., Abilene, Tex., 1954-58, 61; Smith-Mundt vis. prof. Inst. Tecnologico, Monterrey, Mexico, 1958—60; ind. rschr. U. Leiden, Netherlands, 1960; acad. dean, prof. Wayland Bapt. U., Plainview, Tex., 1961—66; Fulbright vis. prof. Universidad Nacional, Asuncion, Paraguay, 1966—67; prof. English Tex. Tech U., Lubbock, 1967—73; prof., chmn. dept. English Baylor U., Waco, Tex., 1973—80, disting. English prof., 1992—97, emeritus disting. English prof., 1997—, dean grad. studies and rsch., 1979—92. Vis. English prof. U. Jordan, 1997. Editor (with others): Am. Bypaths, 1980, The English Journals of Lodewijck Huygens, 1982, Bunyan in Our Time, 1989; contbr. articles to profl. jours. With US Army, 1945—46. Fellow, Rockefeller Found., 1958, Smith-Mundt, 1958—60, Fulbright-Hays, 1966—76; grantee, Am. Philos. Soc., 1976, Dutch Ministry Edn. Scis., 1981; Hon. Rsch. fellow, U. Glasgow, 1994, Sr. Rsch. grantee, Fulbright-Hays, 1982. Mem.: Conf. Coll. Tchrs. English (pres. 1983—84), Conf. Christianity and Lit. (pres. 1982—85), Assn. Tex. Grad. Schs. (pres. 1982—83), S. Ctrl. Renaissance Conf. (pres. 1970—71), Deans Conf. So. Assn. Bapt. Schs. (pres. 1963—64). Democrat. Avocations: traveling to Latin America and Europe, book collecting. Home Phone: 512-869-6949; Office Phone: 512-869-6949. Personal E-mail: rcoll1017@aol.com.

COLLOMS, VERGENE JENKINS, music educator, composer, musician, music producer, arranger; b. Hamilton County, Ill., Apr. 12, 1917; d. Herbert and Laura (Jenkins) Meadows; m. Lester H. Colloms (dec. 1971); 1 child, Beverly Jo Patterson. AA, McKendree Coll., Lebanon, Ill., 1940, BA, 1945; M in Music Edn., Northwestern U., Evanston, Ill. and Chgo.,

1969. Developer music and music courses, U. Singers U. SC, Spartanburg, 1970; instr. Matthew Whaley Sch. -conjunct William and Mary Coll., Williamsburg, Va.; head music dept. Tenn. Wesleyan Coll., Athens; music instr. Lima campus Ohio State U.; music prof. Spartanburg Meth. Coll. and U. SC, chartered music fraternity. Pres. SC chpt. Nat. Assn. Tchr. Singing, 1948, Cmty. Concerts, Bus. and Profl. Women, 1983, Breakfast Bus. and Profl. Women, 1984; dir. music Charles Lea Ctr., 1970—78; advisor Spartanburg Jr. Philharm., 1972—; state advisor SC youth divsn. SC Fedn. Music Clubs, 1975; organizer music club Cedar Springs Sch. Blind; asst. dir. The Shepherd Ctr. Chorus. Author: This Is The Army, Mrs. Jones, 1945, The Builder, 1956; leading soprano (Operas) Converse Coll., 1949—52; performer: (mother-daughter team) The Accordionettes, 1952—95; composer: Bicentennial, 1976; prodr., arranger (musical setting) Dixieland Music, 1965, Dixieland Firsthand, 1967, 1968, 1978, 1982; singer: (Operas) The Marriage of Figaro, Menotti's Medium, Falstaff, Madame Butterfly. Pres. Tuesday Reading and Spartanburg Garden Club Coun.; brownie leader Girl Scouts US, 1955—58, badge instr., 1958—90, Boy Scouts Am., 1958—90; chartered Jr. Garden Club Z.L. Madden Sch., 1988—95; chartered Bus. Profl. Women's Breakfast Club; developer Woman's History Month, Spartanburg, 1976. Named Career Women in Bicentennial Yr., Spartanburg, 1976, Spartanburg Sr. Citizen of Yr., 1990, Spartanburg Career Women of Bicentennial Yr., Woman of Yr., March of Dimes, Outstanding Achiever Woman's History Month; recipient Order of the Palmetto, Gov. SC, Order of the Crescent cmty. svc., Clio award. Mem.: Delta Kappa Gamma. Home: 666 Palmetto St Spartanburg SC 29302-2636

COLLOTON, STEVEN M., federal judge; b. Iowa City, Iowa, Jan. 9, 1963; AB, Princeton U., 1985; JD, Yale Law Sch., 1988. Law clk to Hon. Laurence H. Silberman US Ct. Appeals, DC cir., Washington, 1988—89; law clk. to Hon. William H. Rehnquist US Supreme Ct., Washington, 1989—90; special asst. to Asst. Atty. Gen. Dept. Justice Office Legal Counsel, 1990—91; asst. U.S. Atty. No. Dist. Iowa, 1991—99; assoc. counsel Office Ind. Counsel Kenneth W. Starr, 1995—96; ptnr. Belin Lamson McCormick Zumbach Flynn, Des Moines, 1999—2001; U.S. Atty. So. Dist. Iowa, 2001—03; judge US Ct. Appeals (8th cir.), Des Moines, 2003—. Office: US Courthouse Annex 110 E Court Ave Ste 461 Des Moines IA 50309-2053*

COLLUM, RICK DANIEL, lawyer; b. Atlanta, Sept. 25, 1969; s. Wesley Daniel and Mary Elizabeth Collum; m. Donna Lee Rogers, Sept. 12, 1992; children: Danielle Elizabeth, Jared Lee. BS in Criminal Justice, Valdosta State U., 1992, BA in Sociology, 1992; JD, Cleve. State U., 1999. Bar: Ga. 2000, U.S. Dist. Ct. (no., mid. and so. dists.) Ga. 2001, U.S. Tax Ct. 2001, U.S. Ct. Appeals (11th cir.) 2001, U.S. Surpeme Ct. 2004. Dep. U.S. marshal U.S. Marshals Svc., Cleve., 1992—99; legal instr. Fed. Law Enforcement Tng. Ctr., Brunswick, Ga., 1999—2000; jud. law clk. Hon. W. Louis Sands, Mid. Dist. Ga., Albany, 2000—02; lawyer Hall, Booth, Smith & Slover, Albany, 2002—04, The Collum Law Firm, Moultrie, 2004—. Magistrate judge Colquitt County, Ga., 2006—. Tchr. Sunday Sch. Autryville (Ga.) Bapt. Ch., 2001—. Baptist. Avocations: golf, fishing, hunting, weightlifting. Office: The Collum Lawfirm PO Box 1867 Moultrie GA 31776 Office Phone: 229-891-3000.

COLLYER, ROBERT B., retired trade association administrator; b. Decatur, Ill., Oct. 16, 1932; s. Murray Gordon and Frances Mary (Evans) C.; m. Margaret Mary Hebel, Feb. 27, 1960; 1 son, Bryan. BA, Humboldt Coll., 1956. Cons. DeLeuw Cather & Co., 1957-59; claims and mgr. govt. relations Indsl. Indemnity Co. Calif., San Francisco, San Jose, Sacramento, 1960-73; exec. asst. UBA Inc., Washington, 1974-81; dep. under sec. Employment Standards Adminstrn. U.S. Dept. Labor, Washington, 1981-84; pres. The Collyer Co., 1984—2007; exec. dir. Internat. Assn. Indsl. Accident Bds. and Commns., 1990-96; exec. dir., sec.-treas. Internat. Workers' Compensation Found., 1990—2007; dean Internat. Workers' Compensation Coll., 1990-96; ret., 2007. Co-founder, dir. Nat. Symposium Workers Compensation U. Maine, 1976-80; dir. Western States Self-Ins. Colloquim, Inc., Nat. Employers' Adv. Council on Workers Compensation; cons. Nat. Indsl. Council; mem. Nat. Adv. Commn. on State Workers Compensation Law Compliance U.S. Dept. Labor; mem. Nat. Adv. Commn. on Indsl. Rehab. Research and Tng. Program U. N.C.; mem. steering com. Nat. Workers Compensation Info. Exchange Group; mem. steering com. Permanent Disability Study Adv. Commn. NSF; mem. steering com. U.S. Longshoremen and Harbor Workers' Reform Group Pres. Marin county Republican Council, (Calif.), 1973; mem. Calif. Rep. Central Com., 1970-73; asst. county chmn. Com. to Re-elect Pres., 1972. Named Republican of Yr. Marin County, 1972 Home and Office: Spruce Creek Fly In 25 Lazy Eight Dr Port Orange FL 32128

COLMAN, CHARLES KINGSBURY, academic administrator, criminologist; b. Nashua, NH, May 14, 1929; s. Charles David Colman and Lela (Bessey) Sproul; m. Marjorie Gertrude Bahe, Aug. 19, 1950 (dec. May 2003); children: Charles David, Cathleen Ann. Diploma, Yale U., 1961; BA, U. Md., 1963; MEd, Stetson U., 1972; EdD, Fla. Atlantic U., 1978. Spl. agt. USAF, U.S. Army, 1947-67; asst. prin. Satellite High Sch., Satellite Beach, Fla., 1969-81, dean acad. edn., 1981-85; ctr. dir. Brevard C.C., Patrick AFB, Fla., 1985-92, provost Palm Bay, Fla., 1992-94; pres. emeritus, 1994—. Mem. Fla. State Adv. Com. on Mil. Edn., Patrick AFB, 1985—; edn. rep. Semiconductor Mfg. Tech., Dallas, 1985—. Author: Formative Years, 1970; author computer software. Co-founder Boys Club Am., Melbourne, Fla, 1968. Grantee Fla. Dept. Edn., 1987, 89, 90, 91, U.S. Dept. Edn., 1991-92; recipient Ace award Fla. Dept. Edn., 1991. Mem. ASCD, Ret. Officers' Assn., Assn. Former Intelligence Officers (v.p. 1998-2000, pres. 2001-02, Fla. chpt.), Assn. Former OSI Spl. Agts. (sec. 1998—, Space Coast chpt.), Phi Delta Kappa (chpt. pres. 1983-84). Avocations: golf, computer programming. Home: 1717 Timberline Ln SE Salem OR 97306-9564 Office: Brevard Community Coll Palm Bay Campus 250 Community College Pky Palm Bay FL 32909-2206

COLMAN, JENNY MEYER, psychiatrist; b. Livingston, NJ, Apr. 23, 1968; d. Robert Osborne and Margaret Saur Meyer; m. William Woodruff Colman, June 20, 1998; children: Thomas Emory, Sean Robert, Jackson Schuyler. BA, Harvard Coll., Cambridge, 1990; MD, Columbia Coll., NYC, 1997. Diplomate Am. Bd. Psychiatry and Neurology. Resident in psychiatry Columbia Presbyn./NY Hosp., NYC, 1997—2000, U. Calif., San Francisco, 2000—01; attending psychiatrist St. Mary's Med. Ctr., San Francisco, 2001—03, med. dir. adolescent inpatient unit, 2002—03; pvt. practice San Francisco, 2001—03, Poughkeepsie, NY, 2003—04, Fishkill, NY, 2004—. Mem.: Am. Acad. Child and Adolescent Psychiatry, Am. Psychiatric Assn. Avocations: hiking, skiing, running. Office Phone: 845-896-5400.

COLMAN, ROBERT WOLF, hematologist, educator; b. NYC, June 7, 1935; s. Jack K. and Miriam (Greenblatt) C.; m. Roberta Fishman, June 16, 1957; children: Sharon, David. AB summa cum laude, Harvard U., Cambridge, Mass., 1956; MD cum laude, Harvard U., 1960. Cert. Internal Medicine, Hematology. Intern Boston City Hosp., 1960-61; resident Beth Israel, Brookline, Mass., 1961-62; clin. assoc. USPHS, NIH, 1962-64; resident Barnes Hosp., St. Louis, 1964-65, fellow in hematology, 1965-67; assoc. in medicine Harvard Med. Sch., Cambridge, Mass., 1967-69, asst. prof., 1969-73, assoc. prof., 1973, U. Pa., Phila., 1973-77, prof. medicine, 1977-78, Temple U. Sch. Medicine, Phila., 1978—, dir. Sol Sherry Thrombosis Rsch. Ctr., 1979—2005, prof. thrombosis rsch., 1981—, Sol Sherry prof. of medicine, 1989—, prof. physiology, 1992—. Hematology study sect. NIH, Bethesda, Md., 1977-81; parent com. to review SCORs in Ischemic Heart Disease; chemistry spl. emphasis panel to review SBIR, STTR grants, NIH, study sect. rev. therapeutic modulation angiogensis disease, study sect. to rev. tng. grants and careeer devel. awards; invited lectr. Gordon confs., Internat. Congress Hemostasis and Thrombosis, Fedn. Am. Socs. Exptl. Biology; plenary lectr. and chair Gordon Conf. Internat. Soc. Kallikreins and Kinins, others. Editor: Hemostasis and Thrombosis, 5th edit., 2005; editor Platelet Jour.; mem. editorial bd. Jour. Clin. Investigation, Blood, Procs. Soc. Exptl. Biology, Thrombosis Rsch. Platelets, Thrombosis Hemostasis; contbr. numerous articles to profl. jours. Surgeon USPHS, 1962—64. Recipient Leon Resnick prize Harvard U., Career Devel. award NIH, Sr. Investigator award S.E. Pa. chpt. Am. Heart Assn., Disting. Career award Internat. Soc. Thrombosis and Hemostasis. Fellow ACP; mem. Assn. Am. Physicians. Am. Soc. Clin. Investigation, Am. Soc. Biochemistry and Molecular Biology, Internat. Soc. Hemostasis and Thrombosis (councillor 1989-95), Peripatetic Club, Interurban Clin. Club, Phi Beta Kappa, Sigma Xi, Alpha Omega Alpha. Achievements include 8 patents in field. Avocation: travel. Office: Temple U Sch Medicine Sol Sherry Thrombosis Rsch Ctr 3400 N Broad St Philadelphia PA 19140-5104 Home Phone: 610-566-1318; Office Phone: 215-707-4665. Business E-Mail: colmanr@temple.edu.

COLMANT, ANDREW ROBERT, lawyer; b. Bklyn., Oct. 10, 1931; s. Edward J. and Mary Elizabeth (Byrne) C.; children: Elizabeth, Carolyn, David (dec.), Stephen, Robert. BBA, St. Johns U., Jamaica, NY, 1957, LLB, 1959. Bar: N.Y. 1959, U.S. Dist Ct. (so. and ea. dists.) N.Y. 1961, U.S. Ct. Appeals (2nd cir.) 1969, U.S. Ct. Appeals (4th cir.) 1977, U.S. Supreme Ct. 1991. Assoc. Hill, Rivkins, Carey, Loesberg O'Brien & Mulroy and predecessor firms, 1959-73, ptnr., 1973-87; of counsel Jerrold E. Hyams, 1988—91, Peter F. Broderick, 1992. Proctor in admiralty; active USMC amphibious reconnaissance; Amtrac Driver, Army Gen. Intelligence Sch. Interpretive vol. Sandy Hook Lighthouse and History House, Fort Hancock, NJ, Navesink Light Sta., Highland, NJ; active Conservation Coun. for Hawaii, Honolulu, St. Stephans Indian Sch., Am. Indian Mus. Natural History, Deep Cut Gardens, Middleton, NJ; vol. Twin Lighthouse, NJ, Highlands Hist. Soc., Highlands, NJ; VIP Nat. Park Svc.; vol. Sandy Hook Lighthouse, History House, Hancock, NJ, 2002—, Cmty. St. Benedict, Holmdel, NJ; rep., leader Bayshore Comty. Hosp., Holmdel, NJ, 1978—; min. of eucharist St. Benedict Parish, Holmdel, NJ; extraordinary min. Holy Eucharist Asssigned; Sunday contingent; mem., track chmn. Parish Coun., Fin. Funding, Constl. Lance cpl. USMC, 1952—54. Recipient Social Min. award, Diocese Trenton Bishop Riess, VIP award, Dept. Interior. Mem.: ACLU, ABA (torts and ins. and admiralty com. , sr. com.), St. John's Sch. Law Admiralty Soc., Social Security Com., Assn. Internationale de Droit des Assurances, Pacific Rim Maritime Law Assn., Asia Pacific Lawyers Assn., NY State Bar Assn. (admiralty), Maritime Law Assn. U.S. (life; proctor in admiralty 1960, carriage goods com.), NY County Lawyers Assn. (life; admiralty com. 1963,), Nat. Trust for Hist. Preservation, Nat. Maritime Hist. Soc., Navy League U.S., Amnesty Internat., Anti-defamation League, Nat. Park Conservation Assn., Twin Light Hist. Soc., Nat. Wildlife Fedn., ATLA (admiralty com. 1995), Sierra Club. Home: Bayshore Health Ctr 715 N Beers St Holmdel NJ 07733-1503

COLMES, ALAN, political commentator, radio personality; Overnight host Sta. WABC, NYC, 1982—84, morning host, 1984—85; with Sta. WNBC, NYC, Sta. WMCA, NYC; morning host Sta. WZLX, Boston; ptnr, on-air host Daynet radio network, 1990—94; worked in develop. of radio divsn. United Stations, 1996; co-host Hannity & Colmes FOX News Channel, NYC, 1996—; host The Alan Colmes Show FOX New Radio, NYC, 2003—; host Sta. WEVD, NYC, 1998—2001. Author: Red, White & Liberal: How Left Is Right & Right Is Wrong, 2003. Office: FOX News Channel 1211 Avenue of the Americas New York NY 10036

COLODNY, EDWIN IRVING, lawyer, retired air transportation executive; b. Burlington, Vt., June 7, 1926; s. Myer and Lena (Yett) Colodny; m. Nancy Dessoff, Dec. 11, 1965; children: Elizabeth, Mark, David. AB with distinction, U. Rochester, 1948; LLB, Harvard U., 1951; D in Comml. Sci. (hon.), Robert Morris Coll., 1985; LLD (hon.), Middlebury Coll., 1986; HHD (hon.), Kings Coll., 1988; LLD (hon.), U. Vt., 2004. Bar: N.Y. 1951, DC 1958. With CAB, 1954-57, USAirways Inc. (formerly Allegheny Airlines Inc.), 1957-91; exec. v.p. mktg. and legal affairs USAirways, Inc. (formerly Allegheny Airlines Inc.), 1969-75, pres., 1975-90, CEO, 1975-91, chmn. bd. dirs., 1978-92; also chmn. USAirways Group, Inc., 1978-92; ret., 1992; of counsel Paul, Hastings, Janofsky and Walker, Washington, 1991—2002; chmn. Comsat Corp., 1997-2000; of counsel Dinse, Knapp & McAndrew, Burlington, Vt., 2004—. Interim pres. U. Vt., 2001—02; interim pres., CEO Fletcher Allen Health Care, Burlington, 2002—03. Trustee Vt. Law Sch. Lt. US Army, 1952—54. Recipient James D. McGill Meml. award, U. Rochester, Wright Bros. Meml. award, 1990, Tony Jannus award, 1990. Mem.: ABA, U. Rochester (bd. trustees). Personal E-mail: eic8225@aol.com.

COLOMBÍ-MONGUIÓ, ALICIA DE, language and humanities educator; b. Buenos Aires; came to the U.S., 1967; d. Carlos and Rosa de Colombí; m. Luis Monguió, Aug. 8, 1979. BA in History, U. Santa Clara, 1969; MA in Spanish and Portuguese, Stanford U., 1971, PhD in Spanish and Humanities, 1973. Asst. prof. Spanish Mills Coll., Oakland, Calif., 1973-79; faculty Bennington (Vt.) Coll., 1979-82; prof. Spanish SUNY, Albany, 1982-84, 86-98, chair dept. Hispanic and Italian studies, 1986-90, rsch. prof. Hispanic and humanistic studies, 1998—; prof. Spanish U. Ariz., 1984-86. Chair divsn. letters Mills Coll., Oakland, 1975-79; chair fgn. langs. and lits. Bennington Coll., 1979-82; head dept. Spanish and Portuguese U. Ariz., Tucson, 1984-86; chair dept. Hispanic and Italian studies SUNY, Albany, 1986-90, rsch. prof. Hispanic and humanistic studies, 1998—. Author: De amor y poesia en la Espana Medieval, 1976, Petrarquismo Peruano, 1985, Del exe antiguo a nuestro nuevo polo, 2003, 3 books poetry; contbr. more than 90 articles to profl. jours. Recipient Diploma de Honor, U. P.R., Mayagüez, 1981; Guggenheim fellow, 1978-79. Mem. MLA, Assn. Internat. Hispanistas, Renaissance Soc. Am. Avocations: gardening, travel. Office: Office VP Acad Affairs Ad Bldg 203 State U Albany Albany NY 12222 Personal E-mail: amonguio@aol.com.

COLOMBO, MICHAEL ALLEN, lawyer; b. Lumberton, NC, Sept. 2, 1948; BS, NC State Univ., 1970; JD, Univ. SC, 1979. Bar: NC, SC, US Ct. of Appeals, US Dist. Ct., US Tax Ct. Ptnr. Colombo Kitchin Attys., Greenville, NC. Capt. fighter pilot USAF, 1970—75. Mem.: ABA, Am. Coll. of Trust and Estate Counsel, Pitt County Bar Assn. (pres. 1988—89), NC Bar Assn. (pres. 2005—06). Office: Colombo Kitchin Attys 1698 E Arlington Blvd Greenville NC 27858 Office Phone: 252-321-2020.

COLOMBO, ROSE MARIE, freelance/self-employed newswriter, television personality; d. James Santo Colombo and Maria Vigil; children: Robert, Rochelle, Theresa Lee, Holly Strickland. Grad., Elegance Acad. Profl. Makeup, 1984; postgrad., Dermatol. Inst. Advanced Skin Care, Torrance, Calif., 1986. Cert. and lic. esthetician, manicurist, aromatherapist, reflexologist, accupressurist. Founder, pres., CEO Women Fight Back for Legal Justice, Inc., Calif., 1989—. Freelance writer, 1980—; pres., CEO Jovone Skin Care, 1984—; TV host, prodr., writer Issues of the Day, Calif., 1989—; columnist Sunset Pub., Costa Mesa, Calif., 1995—2003. Author: How to Protect Yourself From Your Own Attorney, 2005; author: (poems). Mem. LEADS Businesswomen's Club, 1984—85, LA Press Club, 1980—, Southern Calif. Motion Picture Coun., 2004—, Anaheim Businesswomen's Club, 1984—85; v.p., editor No. Long Beach Fedn. Rep. Women's Club, Calif., 1970—74; mem. Com. to Oppose Recall of Judge Nancy Stock, Orange County, Calif., 1997; past mem. Pres. Reagan's Task Force. Named Silver Poet, 1990, Golden Poet, 1988; recipient Journalism of Arts award, City News Svc., 1996, Jeanne Angel award, So. Calif. Motion Picture Coun., 2005, Media Breakfast Club Appreciation award, 1997, Bronze Poet award, Internat. Soc. Poets, 2006, Fellow Poet Noble House award, London, Eng., 2006, Editor's Choice award, Internat. Soc. Poets, 2006. Mem.: Internat. Soc. Poets, Cmdrs. Club Disabled Am. Veterans, L.A. Press Club. Avocations: poetry, music. Office Phone: 714-223-9895. Personal E-mail: jovoneskincare@aol.com, rosies411@sbcglobal.net.

COLÓN, ERNIE, comic book artist; b. Puerto Rico, July 13, 1931; Attended, Sch. Indsl. Arts. With Harvey Comics; freelancer Marvel Comics, DC Comics, editor. Artist (comic series) Monster in My Pocket, Richie Rich, Casper the Friendly Ghost, Amethyst: Princess of Gemworld, Arak, Magnus: Robot Fighter, Grim Ghost, Damage Control, (books) The 9/11 Report: A Graphic Adaptation, 2006 (Libr. Jour. Fall Editors' Pick, 2006), contbr. (documentaries) Adventures Into Digital Comics, 2006. Office: Komikwerks 205 Beech St Belmont MA 02478

COLON, JOSE ERNESTO, pathologist; b. Arecibo, PR, May 3, 1957; s. Ernesto Colon and Raquel De Jesus. BS, U. PR, Mayaguez, 1975—79. Lic. dental medicine U. PR Sch. Dental Medicine, 1991, oral & maxillofacial pathology & medical scis. Harvard Sch. Dental Medicine, Boston, 2002. Asst. prof. U. PR Sch. Dental Medicine, 1991—98, general practice residency, 1992; oral & maxillofacial pathologist/forensic odontologist Armed Forces Inst. Pathology, DC, 2004—; forensic odontologist Office Armed Forces Med. Examiner, Rockville, Md. Mem. Instl. Rev. Bd. Armed Forces Inst. Pathology, DC, mem. rsch. com. Maj. Dental Corps, 1997, Devens, Mass. Grantee Ocular Pemphigoid Mechanism Pathogenesis grant, NEI, 2000—02. Mem.: Am. Acad. Forensic Scis., Am. Soc. Forensic Odontology, Am. Acad. Oral & Maxillofacial Pathology. Achievements include research in characterization of pathogenic autoantibodies in mucous membrane pemphigoid using in-vitro organ culture model. Office: Armed Forces Inst Pathology 6825 16th St NW Bldg 54 Rm 3055 Washington DC 20306-6000 Home Phone: 301-920-0015. Office Fax: 202-782-3140. Business E-Mail: colonj@afip.osd.mil.

COLONEY, WAYNE HERNDON, civil engineer; b. Bradenton, Fla., Mar. 15, 1925; s. Herndon Percival and Mary Adore (Cramer) C.; m. Anne Elizabeth Benedict, June 21, 1950; 1 child, Mary Adore. B.C.E. summa cum laude, Ga. Inst. Tech., 1950. Registered profl. engr. and surveyor, Fla., Ga., Ala., N.C. Project engr. Constructora Gen. S.A., Venezuela, 1948-49, Fla. Rd. Dept., 1950-55; hwy. engr. Gibbs & Hill, Inc., Guatemala, 1955-57, project mgr. Tampa, Fla., 1957-59; project engr., then assoc. J.E. Greiner Co., Tampa, 1959-63; ptnr. Barrett, Daffin & Coloney, Tallahassee, 1963-70; pres. Wayne H. Coloney Co., Inc., Tallahassee, 1970-78, chmn., bd. chief exec. officer, 1978-85; pres., sec. Tesseract Corp., 1975-85; dep. chmn. Howden Airdynamics Am., Tallahassee, 1985-90; pres. Coloney Co. Cons. Engrs., Inc., 1978—; v.p., dir. Howden Coloney Inc., Tallahassee, 1985-90; prin. Coloney-Von Soosten & Assocs. Inc., Tallahassee, 1990—2002, Aurora Mgmt. Ptnrs., Tallahassee, 2002—03; prin. engr. Coloney Bell Engring., 1996—. Chmn. adv. com. Area Vocat. Tech. Sch., 1965-78; pres. Retro Tech. Corp., 1983-93, Profl. Mgmt. Con. Group, 1983-87; pres., bd. dirs. Internat. Enterprises Inc., 1967-73; bd. dirs., exec. com. GTO, Inc., 1990-2006. Patentee roof framing system, dense packing external aircraft fuel tank, tile mounting structure, curler rotating device, bracket system for roof framing; contbr. articles to profl. jours. Pres. United Fund Leon County, 1971-72; bd. dirs. Springtime Tallahassee, 1970-72, pres., 1981-82; bd. dirs. Heritage Found., 1965-71, pres., 1967; mem. Pres.'s Adv. Council on Indsl. Innovation, 1978-79; bd. dirs. LeMoyne Art Found., 1973, v.p., 1974-75; bd. dirs. Goodwill Industries, 1972-73, Tallahassee-Popoyan Friendship Commn., 1968-73; mem. Adv. Com. for Hist. and Cultural Preservation, 1969-71; vice chmn. Govs. Commn. for Purchase from the Blind, 1980-2002. Served with AUS, 1943-46. Fellow ASCE, Nat. Acad. Forensic Engrs. (pres.); mem. NSPE, Am. Def. Industries Assn., Fla. Engring. Soc. (sr.), Fla. Inst. Cons. Engrs., Fla. Surveying and Mapping Soc., ANAK, Koseme Soc., Fla. Small Bus. Assn. (pres. 1981), Gov.'s Club, Phi Kappa Phi, Omicron Delta Kappa, Sigma Alpha Epsilon, Tau Beta Pi. Anglican. Home: 1304 Hollow Oak Cir Tallahassee FL 32308 Office: Coloney Bell Engineering 1624 Vlg Sq Blvd Ste 101 Tallahassee FL 32309-2767 Home Phone: 850-222-5798; Office Phone: 850-222-8193. E-mail: whc@coloneybell.com.

COLONNIER, MARC LEOPOLD, retired anatomist; b. Quebec, Can., May 12, 1930; m. Lise De Gagne, Oct. 24, 1959; 1 son, Jean. BA, B.Ph., U. Ottawa, 1951, MD, 1959, MS, 1960; PhD, U. Coll. London, 1963. Asst. prof. anatomy U. Ottawa, 1963-65; asst. prof. dept. physiology U. Montreal, Que., Canada, 1965-67; assoc. prof., assoc. fellow neurol. scis. group Med. Research Council Can., 1967-69; prof., head dept. anatomy U. Ottawa, 1969-76; prof. dept. anatomy Laval U., Quebec City, Que., 1976-91; ret., 1991. Recipient Lederle Med. Faculty award, 1966, Charles Judson Herrick award Am. Assn. Anatomists, 1967 Fellow Royal Soc. Can.; mem. Am. Assn. Anatomists; Mem. Soc. Neurosci.; mem. Can. Assn. Anatomists (pres. 1973-75) Clubs: Cajal.

COLP, NORMAN BARRY, artist, curator; b. Bronx, NY, Sept. 3, 1944; s. Joseph Johnny Colp and Martha (Berman) Colp Levine; m. Marsha Stern, July 18, 1981. BA in Art, CUNY, 1967; postgrad., Pratt Inst., 1967, Parsons Sch. Design, 1971. Archtl. modelmaker Milton Glaser Inc., NYC, 1978—80; assoc. curator Alternative Mus., NYC, 1979—80; curator exhibits Ctr. Book Arts, NYC, 1980—83, exhbn. coord., 1983; instr. Pratt Graphics Ctr., NYC, 1983—84, Sch. Visual Arts, NYC, 1982—86, acad. advisor, 1984—87; photog. artist, curator NYC, 1978—. Cons. curator Anchorage Mus. History and Art, 1990, Golden & Dresnin Design, Phila., 1990, Islip Art Mus., East Islip, N.Y., 1990, Boca Raton (Fla.) Mus. Art, 1991; cons. on book Exploring Color Photography, 1991, 97, The Girls' Guide to Hunting and Fishing, 1999-2000; artist-in-residence Pub. Sch. 1, Long Island City, N.Y., 1977-78, Cabin Creek Ctr. for Work and Environ. Studies, N.Y.C., 1979; workshop presenter-in-residence Mus. Holography, N.Y.C., 1985; cons. Artists Found., Inc., Boston, 1986, juror, 1989; lectr. in field. Author: Freud's Recipe, Crazy Hair, A Primer on Art Criticism, 1983; one-man shows include Victoria and Albert Mus., London, 1991, Islip Art Mus., 1993, UCLA, 1994, Coll. of Charleston, 1997, Hugo de Pagano Gallery, NYC, 1998, The Tiny Cinema, Red Mills, Claverack, NY, 2001, exhibited in group shows at Mus. Modern Art Libr., Mus. Fine Arts, St. Petersburg, Fla., Boca Raton Mus., Corcoran Gallery of Art, Washington, U. Art Mus., U. Calif., Berkeley, Wadsworth Atheneum, Hartford, Conn., The Ralls Collection, Washington, FotoFest 2002, Houston, 2002, Art in Embassies Program, U.S. Dept. State, Havana, Cuba, 2003, Lima, Peru, 2003, Fine Print Auction FotoFest Internat., Houston, 2004, U. Calif. Berkeley Art Mus., Martha Stewart Incarcerated Living Eyewear Promotional Mailing, 2005, The Flipbook Show, Kunsthalle, Düsseldorf, Germany, 2005, Foto Mus., Antwerp, Belgium, 2006, Fine Print Auction, Foto Fest Internat., Houston, 2006, Represented in permanent collections Nat. Libr., Paris, Victoria and Albert Mus., Corcoran Gallery, Libr. Congress, Mus. Modern Art Libr., NYC, NY Pub. Libr., Queens Mus. of Art, Flushing, NY, Islip Art Mus., East Islip, NY, Bklyn. Mus. Art, Smithsonian Archives Am. Art, Washington, Whitney Mus. Am. Art, Internat. Ctr. Photography, NYC. Grantee, Com. for Visual Arts, 1980, Met. Transit Authority, 1991, Fieldcrest Cannon Inc., 1991, The Merchant and Ivory Found., 2002, FotoFest, 2002. Avocations: art, pottery. Home: 180 W End Ave Apt 3R New York NY 10023-4913

COLSON, CHARLES WENDELL, lay minister, writer; b. Boston, Oct. 16, 1931; s. Wendell Ball and Inez (Ducrow) C.; m. Nancy Billings, June 3, 1953; children: Wendell Ball II, Christian B., Emily Ann; m. Patricia Ann Hughes, Apr. 4, 1964. AB, Brown U., 1953; JD with honors, George Washington U., 1959; DD, Gordon Conwell Theol. Sem., 1997; LLD (hon.), Wheaton Coll., 1982, Houghton Coll., 1983, Ea. Coll. 1983, Anderson Coll., 1984, Taylor U., 1985, Geneva Coll., 1987, John Brown U., 1988, Palm Beach Atlantic Coll., 1989, LeTourneau U., 1990; LLD (hon.), King Coll., 1995, Dallas Bapt., 1998, Union U., Tenn., 2001. Pvt. practice, Washington, 1961-69; asst. to asst. sec. Navy, 1955-56; adminstrv. asst. Senator Leverett Saltonstall U.S. Senate, 1956-61; sr. ptnr. Gadsby & Hannah, 1961-69; spl. counsel to pres. of U.S., 1969-72; ptnr. Colson & Shapiro, Washington, 1973-74; assoc. Fellowship House, Washington, 1975-76, Prison Fellowship, 1976—. Author: Born Again, 1975, Life Sentence, 1979, Crime and the Responsible Community, 1980, Loving God, 1983, Who Speaks for God?, 1985, Kingdoms in Conflict, 1987, Against the Night, 1989, (with Dan Van Ness) Convicted, 1989, The God of Stones and Spiders, 1990, (with Jack Eckerd) Why America Doesn't Work, 1991, (with Ellen Santilli Vaughn) The Body, 1992, Dance With Deception, 1993, (with Nancy Pearcey) A Dangerous Grace, 1994, (with Richard John Neuhaus) Evangelicals & Catholics Toward a Common Mission Together, 1995, (with Ellen Santilli Vaughn) Gideon's Torch, 1995, (with Anne Morse) Burden of Truth, 1997, The Line Between Right and Wrong, 1997, (with Nancy Pearcey) How Now Shall We Live?, 1999, (with Harold Fickett) Answers to Your Kid's Questions, 2000, Chuck Colson Speaks, 2000, Justice That Restores, 2001, Being the Body, 2003, The Good Life, 2005. Campaign mgr. Saltonstall campaign, 1960. Capt. USMCR, Korea. Recipient Religious Heritage award Freedom Found., 1977, Abe Lincoln award So. Bapt. Conv., 1984, Poverello award U. Steubenville, 1986, Disting. Svc. award Salvation Army, 1990, Humanitarian award So. Bapt. Conv., 1991, Domino's Pizza award, the Templeton Prize for Progress in Religion, 1993; named Layman of Yr., Nat. Assn. Evangs., 1983, Disting. Sr. Fellow Coalition for Christian Colls. and Univs., 1997; named one of 25 Most Influential Evangelicals in Am. Time mag., 2005. Mem. Order of Coif, Beta Theta Pi. Baptist. Office: Prison Fellowship 44180 Riverside Pkwy Lansdowne VA 20176*

COLSON, EARL MORTON, lawyer, educator; b. Bklyn., Mar. 8, 1930; s. Abraham and Rebecca (Hecker) C.; m. Helen Theresa Austern, Apr. 24, 1960; children: Adam Thomas, Amy Esther, Deborah Austern. BS magna cum laude, Syracuse U., 1950; LLB magna cum laude, Harvard U., 1957. Bar: N.Y. 1958, D.C. 1960. Assoc. Chadbourne, Parke, Whiteside & Wolff, NYC, 1957-60, Arent, Fox, Kintner, Plotkin & Kahn, Washington, 1960-68, ptnr., 1968—91, of counsel, 1992—. Adj. prof. law Georgetown U., 1970—2003; lectr on tax subjects. Author: Capital Gains and Losses, 1975; co-author: Federal Taxation of Estates, Gifts and Trusts, 1975. Bd. dirs. Washington Hebrew Congregation, 1979—, v.p., 1984-90, pres., 1990-92; trustee Kingsbury Ctr., 1978-81; mem. N.Y. bd. overseers Hebrew Union Coll., 1995-97; bd. dirs. D.C. chpt. Am. Jewish Com., 1995-98. Mem. ABA (chmn. estate and gift tax com. sect. taxation 1972-73), D.C. Bar Assn. (chmn. tax com. 1971-72, treas., bd. govs. 1974-76), Am. Law Inst., Assn. of Bar of City of N.Y., Cosmos Club Washington. Office: 1050 Connecticut Ave NW Washington DC 20036-5303

COLSON, JOHN R., electric power industry executive; With PAR Elec. Contractors Inc. (subs. of Quanta Svcs.), 1971—97, pres., 1997—97; CEO Quanta Svcs., Houston, 1997—, chmn., 2002—. Bd. dir. Quanta Svcs., 1998—, US Concrete Inc., 1999—. Mem.: Mo. Valley Chpt. Nat. Elec. Contractors Assn. (bd. dir.). Office: Quanta Svcs 1360 Post Oak Blvd Houston TX 77056 Office Phone: 713-629-7600.*

COLSON, RANDALL ELWIN, lawyer; s. Elwin and Joanne Colson; m. Valerie Colsen, Aug. 13; children: Catherine, Christopher. BA in Liberal Arts, Wheaton Coll., Ill., 1986; BSEE, U. Ill., 1986; JD, Northwestern U., 1991. Lic.: U.S. Patent and Trademark Office 1995, bar: Ill. 1991, Tex. 1995. Engr. Data Gen. Corp., Westboro, Mass., 1986—88; atty. D'Ancona & Pflaum, Chgo., 1991—94, Haynes and Boone LLP, Dallas, 1994—. Bd. dirs. Turtle Creek Manor, Dallas, 2004—, pres., 2007. Named Tex. Super Lawyer, Tex. Monthly Mag. Mem.: Dallas (Tex.) Bar Assn. Office: Haynes and Boone LLC 901 Maine St Ste 3100 Dallas TX 75202

COLSON, ROSEMARY, music educator; b. Madison, Ind., July 15, 1937; d. Howard Paul and Mary Wilder Colson. Student, Georgetown Coll., 1955—56; MusB, George Peabody Coll., 1960; MusM, Yale U., 1965. Tchr. piano Wilmington Music Sch., Del., 1965—66, Settlement Music Sch., Phila., 1966—77, Chestnut Hill Acad., Phila., 1969—78; piano tchr. Acad. Cmty. Music, Ft. Washington, Pa., 1993—; tchr. pvt. piano Phila., 1967—; organist, choir master Grace Epiphany Episcopal Ch., Phila., 1987—2000. Contbr. articles to profl. jours. Treas. West Ctrl. Germantown Neighbors, Phila., 1981—83; bd. dirs. YWCA Germantown, Phila., 1990—94, Women's Sacred Music Project, 2003—05. Mem.: Am. Guild Organists, Delta Omicron (advisor to U. Pa. chpt. 1963—64). Democrat. Presbyterian. Avocations: gardening, reading, travel. Home: 6021 McCallum St Philadelphia PA 19144 Personal E-mail: rsmrclsn@aol.com.

COLSTON, FREDDIE CHARLES, political science professor; b. Gretna, Fla., Mar. 28, 1936; s. Henry Bill and Willie Mae (Taylor) C.; m. Doris Marie Suggs, Mar. 13, 1976; 1 child, Deirdre Colston Graddick BA, Morehouse Coll., 1959; MA, Atlanta U., 1966; PhD, Ohio State U., 1972. Chmn. dept. social studies Attucks H.S., Hollywood, Fla., 1960—64; instr. social sci. Ft. Valley (Ga.) State Coll., 1966-68; assoc. prof. polit. sci. So. U., Baton Rouge, 1972-73, U. Detroit, 1973-76; assoc. prof., chmn. div. social sci. Dillard U., New Orleans, 1976-78; asst. prof. polit. sci. Delta Coll., University Center, Mich., 1978-79; assoc. dir. Exec. Seminar Ctr. U.S. Office Pers. Mgmt., Oak Ridge, 1980-87; prof. Inst. of Govt. Tenn. State U., Nashville, 1987-88; prof., dir. pub. adminstrn. program N.C. Ctrl. U., Durham, 1988-91; prof. dept. history and polit. sci. Ga. Southwestern State U., Americus, 1992-97. Pres. Broward County (Fla.) Social Studies Coun., 1961-62; mem. constn. com. Fla. State Tchrs. Assn., 1963-64; chmn. human rels. coun. Ga. Southwestern State U., 1997. Author: Dr. Benjamin E. Mays Speaks: Representative Speeches of a Great American Orator, 2002; contbr. articles to profl. jours. Mem. bd. mgmt. Northwestern Br. YMCA, Detroit, 1976; mem. govt. subcom. Task Force 2000, City of Midland, Mich., 1979. Scholar Morehouse Coll., 1955, Atlanta U., 1965, Nat. Def. Edn. Act, 1964; fellow Ford Found., 1967, So. Fellowships Fund, 1968-71; grantee C-Span, 1994, 95, 96; recipient Mr. Psi award Psi chpt., Omegi Psi Phi, 1959, Outstanding Faculty award Kappa Delta Sorority, Ga. Southwestern State U., 1995, Outstanding Faculty award Sabu orgn. Ga. Southwestern State U., 1997 Mem. Am. Polit. Sci. Assn. (com. on the status of blacks in the profession 1977-80), Nat. Conf. Black Polit. Scientists, Ctr. for Study of Presidency, Assn. for Study of Afro-Am. Life, Am. Soc. Pub. Adminstrn., Pi Sigma Alpha, Alpha Phi Gamma. Avocations: reading, photography, sports. Home and Office: 126 Hazleton Ln Oak Ridge TN 37830-7929 Personal E-mail: freddie12@comcast.net.

COLTHUP, NORMAN BERTRAM, retired spectroscopist; b. Paris, July 6, 1924; BS, Antioch Coll., 1949; DS (hon.), Fisk U., 1974. Co-author: Introduction to Infrared and Raman Spectroscopy, 3d edit., 1990, The Handbook of Infrared and Raman Characteric Frequencies of Organic Molecules, 1991. Recipient Williams-Wright award, Coblentz Soc., 1979, Maurice Hasler award, 1999. Address: 71 Strawberry Hill Ave Apt 704 Stamford CT 06902-2723

COLTMAN, EDWARD JEREMIAH, communication executive; b. Boston, Aug. 20, 1948; s. Edward Philip and Eleanor (Dwyer) C. BA, Harvard U., 1969, M of City and Regional Planning, 1979. Reporter The Hartford (Conn.) Courant, 1970; asst. to Alfred G. Aronowitz, NYC, 1970-72; reporter The Evening Capital, Annapolis, Md., 1973-74, The Sun, Balt., 1974-77; sr. assoc. Richard Grefé Assocs., Washington, 1979-83; dep. dir. policy Corp. for Pub. Broadcasting, Washington, 1983-89; dir., 1989-95; exec. dir. new media Corp. for Pub. Broadcasting, Washington, 1995-97, exec. dir. strategic planning, 1997-99, exec. dir. spl. projects, 1999—2005, sr. dir. comms., 2005—. Avocation: hand bookbinding. Home: 122 6th St SE Washington DC 20003-1132 Office: Corp for Pub Broadcasting 401 9th St NW Washington DC 20004-2129 Office Phone: 202-879-9670. Business E-Mail: tcoltman@cpb.org.

COLTMAN, JOHN WESLEY, physicist; b. Cleve., July 19, 1915; s. Robert White and Louise (Tyroler) C.; m. Charlotte Waters Beard, June 10, 1941; children: Sally Louise Condit, Nancy Jean Horner. BS in Physics, Case Inst. Tech., 1937; MS, U. Ill., 1939, PhD in Physics, 1941. Rsch. scientist Rsch. Labs. Westinghouse Electric Corp., Pitts., 1941—49, mgr. electronics and nuc. physics dept., 1949—60, assoc. dir. rsch. labs., 1960—64, dir. rsch. math. and radiation, 1964—69, dir. rsch. industry, def. and pub. sys., 1969—74, dir. rsch. and devel. planning, 1974—80. Mem. adv. group on electron devices Dept. Def., 1958-62; mem. Naval Intelligence Sci. Adv. Com., 1971-73, NRC Commn. on Human Resources, 1977-80; privately sponsored rschs. on acoustics of the flute. Contbr. articles to profl. jours. Recipient Longstreth medal Franklin Inst., 1960; Roentgen medal Remscheid, W. Ger., 1970; Gold medal Radiol. Soc. N.Am., 1982 Fellow Am. Phys. Soc., IEEE; mem. Nat. Acad. Engring., Am. Musical Instrument Soc. Presbyterian. Achievements include inventing x-ray image amplifier, universally used world-wide for fluoroscopy, and the scintillation counter. Home: 3319 Scathelocke Rd Pittsburgh PA 15235-5122 Personal E-mail: coltmanjw@verizon.net.

COLTON, CLARK KENNETH, chemical engineering professor; b. NYC, July 20, 1941; s. Sidney and Goldie (Chases) C.; m. Ellen Ruth Brandner, June 20, 1965; children: Jill Erin, Jason Adam, Michael Ross, Brian Scott. B of Chem. Engring., Cornell U., 1964; PhD, MIT, 1969. Asst. prof. chem. engring. MIT, Cambridge, 1969-73, assoc. prof., 1973-76, prof., 1976—, Bayer prof. chem. engring., 1980-85, dep. head dept. chem. engring., 1977-78, chmn. centennial chem. engring. edn., 1988. Cons. to NIH, FDA, various indsl. orgns.; mem. adv. bd. mil. personnel supplies NRC, 1971-75 Mem. editl. bd. Jour. Membrane Sci., 1975-81, 97, Jour. Bioengring., 1976-79, Preparative Chromatography, 1988-94, Isolation and Purification, 1994—, ASAIO Jour., 1985-94; mem. editl. bd. Cell Transplantation, 1991-94, 97, assoc. editor, 1997—; contbr. articles to sci. jours. Ford found. fellow, 1969-70; recipient Tchr./Scholar award Camille and Henry Dreyfus Found., 1972, Lifetime Contbn. award in bioartificial organs Engring. Found., 1998. Fellow AAAS; mem. AIChE (dir. food, pharm. and bioengring. div. 1978-81 (food, Pharm. and Bioengring. div. award, 1999, Allan P. Colburn award 1977), N.Y. Acad. Scis., Am. Soc. Artificial Internal Organs (editorial bd. 1978-84), Am. Diabetes Assn., Am. Soc. for Apheresis, Am. Soc. for Engring. Edn. (Curtis W. McGraw rsch. award 1980), North Am. Membrane Soc., Am. Heart Assn., Cell Transplantation Soc. (sec. 1994-2001, treas. 2001—), Transplantation Soc., Internat. Pancreas and Islet Transplant Assn., Internat. Soc. on Oxygen Transport to Tissue, Am. Chem. Soc., Am. Inst. Med. and Biol. Engring. (founding mem.), Internat. Soc. Articificial Organs, Internat. Soc. Blood Purification (Gambro award 1986), Biomed. Engring. Soc., Cornell Club, Sigma Xi, Tau Beta Pi, Phi Lambda Upsilon. Home: 279 Commonwealth Ave Chestnut Hill MA 02467-1012 Office: MIT Dept Chem Engring Cambridge MA 02139 Office Phone: 617-253-4585. Business E-Mail: ckcolton@mit.edu.

COLTON, DAVID LEM, mathematician, educator; b. San Francisco, Mar. 14, 1943; s. Ellis and Myrl (Crowder) C.; m. Renate, Dec. 20, 1968; children— Claire, Natasha. BS, Calif. Inst. Tech., 1964; MS, U. Wis., 1965; PhD, U. Edinburgh, Scotland, 1967, DSc, 1977. Asst. prof. math. Ind. U., 1967-71, assoc. prof., 1972-74; prof. U. Strathclyde, Glasgow, Scotland, 1975-78, U. Del., Newark, 1978—, Unidel prof., 1996—. Vis. prof. McGill U., 1968-69, U. Glasgow, 1971-72, U. Konstanz, 1974-75 Author various rsch. monographs; rschr. numerous publs. in field; mem. adv. bd. Springer Verlag series: Interaction of Mechanics and Math.; mem. editl. bd. Inverse Problems and Imaging. Office: U Del Dept Math Newark DE 19716 Business E-Mail: colton@math.udel.edu.

COLTON, ELIZABETH WISHART, government agency administrator; b. Rockville Centre, NY, June 25, 1929; d. Ronald Sinclair Wishart and Elizabeth Lathrop Phillips. BA cum laude, We. Coll. for Women, 1951; postgrad., Am. U., 1951—52, Bowie State Coll., 1989—90. Jr. mgmt. asst. U.S. C.S.C., Washington, 1954, test developer, 1954—55, civil svc. insp., 1955—58, stds. developer and writer of qualification and classification stds., 1958—59, developer and implementer nationwide evauation plans of maj. fed. depts., 1958—62; developed and implemented bureauwide pers. mgmt. improvement programs Bur. of Reclamation Dept. of Interior, Washington, 1962—65, asst. dir. of pers. for nat. pk. svc., 1965—70, staff specialist dir. equal opportunity Office of Equal Employment Opportunity Programs, 1970; dep. dir. of pers. for pers. mgmt. evaluation and asst. to dep. dir. for classification and pay Dept. of Treasury, Washington, 1970—78; dir. divsn. pers. sys. imrprovement Office Asst. Sec. Health and Human Svcs., Washington, 1978—85. Real estate broker, Annapolis, Md., 1985—2003; antique dealer, Annapolis, 1985—2003. Job counselor displaced homemakers YWCA, Annapolis, 1985—92, active, 1985—92; ct. -apptd. spl. advocate for a foster child; developer and leader inner-city boys cooking class N.Y. Ave. Presbyn. Ch., Washington, 1960—69. Mem.: We. Coll. Alumnae Assn. Miami U. (trustee 2004—06), Victoria Walk Unit Owners Assn. (sec. treas. 2003—). Presbyterian. Avocations: ancient history, gardening, travel, genealogy. Home: Greens of Cross Court 1200 S Washington St Apt 304 Easton MD 21601 E-mail: bcolton@goeaston.net.

COLTON, JOEL, historian, educator; b. NYC, Aug. 23, 1918; s. Philip and Theresa (Cotler); m. Shirley Baron, May 8, 1942 (dec. Dec. 2003); children— Valerie Beth, Kenneth Richard. BA magna cum laude, CCNY, 1937, MS, 1938; MA, Columbia U., 1940; PhD, 1950. Lectr. history Columbia U., 1946-47; successively instr., asst. prof., assoc. prof., prof. history Duke U., 1947-89, prof. emeritus, 1989—, chmn. dept. history, 1967-74, chmn. acad. council, 1971-73; dir. for humanities Rockefeller Found., 1974-81. U.S. mem. Internat. Commn. on History of Social Movements and Social Structures, 1975—, v.p., 1980-85, co-pres., 1985-90, hon. pres., 1990—; vis. prof. U. Wis., Makerere U., Uganda; lectr. Cadi-Ayyad U., Morocco. Author: Compulsory Labor Arbitration in France, 1936-39, 1951, (Japanese transl. 1999), Léon Blum: Humanist in Politics, 1966 (French transl. 1968), rev. edit., 1987, Twentieth Century: Time-Life Great Ages of Man Series, 1968, rev. edit., 1980; co-author: (with R.R. Palmer) A History of the Modern World, 2d - 8th edits., 1956-95 (transl. into Arabic, Persian, Swedish, Finnish, Spanish, Italian and Chinese), (with R.R. Palmer and L. Kramer), 10th edit., 2007, Study Guide for A History of the Modern World, 10th edit., 2007; editor: The Humanities in an International Context, 1976, The Search for a Value Consensus, 1978, Toward the Restoration of the Liberal Arts Curriculum, 1979; co-editor: Technology, The Economy and Society, 1987; bd. editors: Jour. Modern History, 1967-70, Third Republic/Troisième République, 1975-85, French Hist. Studies, 1985-88; mem. adv. bd. Hist. Abstracts, 1981--; contbr. articles to profl. jours., encys., internat. conf. procs. and yearbooks. Mem. adv. bd. Duke U. Press, 1982-88; trustee Triangle Univs. Ctr. for Advanced Studies, N.C., 1982-85. U.S. Army, 1942-46, 1st lt. M.I., 1944-46, ETO. Recipient book award Mayflower Soc., 1967, Townsend Harris medal CCNY Alumni Assn., 1980, Disting. Tchg. award Duke U., 1986, award for contbns. to study and tchg. French history Western Soc. for French History, 1994; Guggenheim fellow, 1957-58, fellow Rockefeller Found., 1961-62, sr. fellow NEH, 1970-71. Fellow Am. Acad. Arts and Scis. elected 1979, Phi Beta Kappa (vis. scholar 1983-84), Phi Beta Kappa Soc.; mem. Am. Hist. Assn. (com. on internat. hist. activities 1980-85), So. Hist. Assn. (chmn. European sect. 1975-76, Disting. Svc. award European History sect., 2005), Soc. French Hist. Studies (v.p. 1972-73), PEN Am. Ctr. Home: 2701 Pickett Rd # 3044 Durham NC 27705 Office: Duke U Dept History Box 90719 Durham NC 27708-0719 Personal E-mail: jcolton2@earthlink.net.

COLTON, JOHN P., nuclear scientist, engineering executive; b. Vernal, Utah, Jan. 3, 1937; s. Hugh W. and Marguarite Maughan Colton; m. Barbara Snyder Colton, Dec. 24, 1962; children: Nancy, Marcelle, Jeannie(dec.) , John S. BS in Metallurgical Engring., U. Utah, Salt Lake City, 1962; postgrad., U. Idaho, Idaho, 1962—66, U. Mo., St. Louis, 1966—74. Engr. Phillips Nuc. Divsn., Idaho Falls, 1962—66; engring. mgr. United Nuc. Corp., St. Louis, 1966—72, mgr. corp. quality assurance New Haven, 1972—74; sr. scientist US AEC, Washingtin, 1974—76; field officer Internat. Atomic Energy Agy., Vienna, 1976—81; sr. scientist US State Dept., Washington, 1981—91; divsn. mgr. Internat. Atomic Energy Agy., 1991—99; sr. scientist US State Dept., 1999—2000. Advisor to gov. Energy Adv. Bd., Salt Lake City, 2004—; cons. Internat. Atomic Energy Agy., 2003—. Col. US Army, 1954—91. Mem.: Res. Officer Assn. Mem. Lds Ch. Avocations: scuba diving, gardening.

COLTON, MINDY ZIMMERMAN, artist, art director, consultant; b. NYC, Aug. 6, 1951; s. Louis and Helen Helfstein Zimmerman; m. Paul Franklin Colton, July 21, 1985. Student, Art Students' League, NYC, Parsons Sch. Design, 1968—70; BFA, Wash. U., St. Louis, 1974; MA in Instrnl. Systems, U. Ctrl. Fla., Orlando, 1996. Permanent tchg. cert. art Mo. Art dir. L.G. Wells Art and Advt., Lexington, Ky., 1978—80, Coun. State Govts., Lexington, 1980—81; graphics and photography comm. specialist Tobacco and Health Rsch. Inst. U. Ky., Lexington, 1982—84; dir. publs. Kennesaw Coll., Ga., 1984—85; dir. creative svcs., asst. dir. mktg. U. Ctrl. Fla., Orlando, 1987—2002, profl. cons., art dir. Office Coop. and Experiential Learning, 2004—; graphic artist Lockheed-Martin, Orlando, 2002—03. Exhibit organizer Fla. chpt. Women's Caucus for the Arts, Orlando, 2000, pub. rels./newsletter editor Ctrl. Fla. chpt.; exhibit organizer Fla. chpt. Nat. Mus. Women in the Arts, Deland, 2005—06; area coord. Region 3 US Dressage Found.; instr. Wellston Sch. Sys., St. Louis, 1975, Fayette County Adult Edn. Program, Lexington, 1980—81, Orlando Coll., 1993, U. Ctrl. Fla., 1998, 2002; spkr. and presenter in field. Artist, designer (sculpture) The Long Walk, 2002 (1st pl. sculpture Titusville Artists' League, Best in Show, Fla. Forest Mus., 2003), Lyric, 2003 (Best of Fla. Artists, 1st pl. in sculpture, 2006), Leap of Faith, 2004 (award of excellence Deland Mus. Art, 2006), Renewal, 2005 (Best of Show, Kissimmee (Fla.) Outdoor Sculpture Experience, 2006), American Art Collector, 2007; one-woman shows include U. Ctrl. Fla., 1998, Main St. Gallery, Titusville, Fla., 2005, 2-person show, U. Ctrl. Fla. Libr., 2002, Atlantic Ctr. for the Arts at Harris Ho., New Smyrna Beach, Fla., 2004, Mt. Dora Ctr. for the Arts, 2004, 3-person show, Art League of Daytona Beach, 2006 (76th Ann. Exhibit award of Achievement, 2007), one-woman shows include Bank of Am., Casselberry, 2004, Winter Springs, Fla., 2004, also numerous others, Represented in permanent collections Crealdé Sch. Art Outdoor Sculpture Garden, Darden Co., Orlando, Coca-Cola Corp., Atlanta, Mt. Dora Ctr. for the Arts, U. Ctrl. Fla. Honors Coll., U. Ctrl. Fla. Credit Union, City of Casselberry City Hall, U. Ctrl. Fla. Coll. Arts and Scis. Organizer fundraising exhibit Freedom Ride, Casselberry, Fla., 2003; exhibit cons., advisor Deland Mus. Art, 2004—06; donor, participant Golden Rule Found., Orlando, 2004—06; advisor Jewish Fedn. Outreach Com., Orlando, 2006. Recipient Addy 1st pl. award, 1978, Addy 1st pl. and Merit award, 1979, Golden Image award of distinction, Fla. Pub. Rels. Assn. of Ctrl. Fla., 1986, Bronze Quill awards of excellence and awards of merit, IABC, 1989, 1990, 1993, Case History award, Dynamic Graphics Found. Inc., 1991, 1992, award of excellence, CASE, 1994, 1998, 2000, 2002, Grand award of excellence, 1996, 1997, award of merit, 2001, Regional Merit award, Potlach Paper Co., 1997, 1st pl. sculpture, Best of Fla. Artists, 2006, Osceola Ctr. for Arts, 2007; Profl. Devel. grantee for sculpture, United Arts of Ctrl. Fla., Orlando, 2003, 2005, Profl. Devel. Enhancement grantee, State of Fla. Divsn. Cultural Affairs, 2005, Profl. Devel. grant retreat, 2007. Mem.: Art League of Daytona Beach, Indiana Arts League, United Arts of Ctrl. Fla., Deland Mus. Art, Equine Artist Guild, Crealde Sch. of Art and Contemporary Sculpture Garden (Cheryl Bogdanowitsch Sculpture scholar 2000, permanent installation in sculpture garden 2003), Nat. Mus. Women in the Arts (show chmn. 2004—06), Fla. Artists' Group, Artists' League of Titusville, Orlando Mus. Art, Phi Kappa Phi, Kappa Delta Pi. Avocations: horseback riding, travel, theater, art, water sports. Home Fax: 407-568-7335. Personal E-mail: equusartist@aol.com.

COLTON, ROY CHARLES, management consultant; b. Phila., Feb. 26, 1941; s. Nathan Hale and Ruth Janis (Baylinson) C. BA, Knox Coll., 1962; MEd, Temple U., 1963. With Sch. Dist. of Phila., 1963-64; sys. analyst Wilmington Trust Co., 1967-69; exec. recruiter Atwood Consultants Inc., Phila., 1969-71; pres. Colton Bernard Inc., San Francisco, 1971—. Occasional lectr. Fashion Inst. Tech., Phila. Coll. Textiles and Scis. Served with AUS, 1964-66. Mem. San Francisco Fashion Industries, San Francisco C. of C., Calif. Exec. Recruiter Assn., Nat. Assn. Exec. Recruiters, Am. Apparel Mfrs. Assn., Am. Arbitration Assn. (panel arbitrators). Office: Colton Bernard Inc 870 Market St Ste 822 San Francisco CA 94102-2921 Office Fax: 415-399-0750. Business E-Mail: rcolton@coltonbernard.com.

COLTON, STERLING DAVID (DAVID COLTON), lawyer; b. 1955; s. Sterling Don and Ellie Colton. BA in economics, Brigham Young U., 1979, JD, 1982. Bar: Utah 1982. Ptnr. VanCott, Bagley, Cornwall & McCarthy, Salt Lake City; sr. counsel for exploration and devel. group Phelps Dodge Mining Co., 1988-95; v.p., counsel Phelps Dodge Exploration Corp., 1995-98; v.p., gen. counsel Phelps Dodge Corp., Phoenix, 1998-99, sr. v.p., gen. counsel, 1999—. Mem. ABA, Utah Bar Assn. Office: Phelps Dodge Corp 1 N Ctrl Ave Phoenix AZ 85004-2306

COLTON, STERLING DON, retired lawyer, hotel executive; b. Vernal, Utah, Apr. 28, 1929; s. Hugh Wilkins and Marguerite (Maughan) Colton; m. Eleanor Ricks, Aug. 6, 1954; children: Sterling David, Carolyn, Bradley Hugh, Steven Ricks. BS in Banking and Fin., U. Utah, 1951; JD, Stanford U., 1953. Bar: Calif. 1954, Utah 1954, DC 1967. Ptnr. Van Cott, Bagley, Cornwall & McCarthy, Salt Lake City, 1957—66; vice chair, sr. v.p., gen. counsel, bd. dirs. Marriott Corp. and Marriott Internat., 1966—95; ret., 1995. Nat. adv. counsel Ballet W.; mem. adv. coun. Nat. Conservancy; v.p. Colton Ranch Corp., 1987—; pres. Can. Vancouver Mission Ch. of Jesus Christ of Latter Day Saints, 1995—99, Washington D.C. Temple, 1999—2002; former chmn. nat. adv. coun. U. Utah; trustee So. Va. U., 2003—. Maj. JAG US Army, 1954—57. Mem.: ABA, Washington Met. Corp. Counsel Assn. (former pres., dir.), DC Bar Assn., Utah Bar Assn., Calif. Bar Assn., Sigma Chi. Republican. Mem. Lds Ch. Personal E-mail: sdercolton@yahoo.com.

COLTON SKOLNICK, JUDITH A., artist; b. Washington, Jan. 31, 1947; d. Bernard and Helen (Glick) Colton; 2 children. Student, Corcoran Sch. Art, 1964, student, 1993—94; BA in Art and Art History with honors, U. Md., 1972; postgrad., Montgomery Coll., 1990—91. Tchr. faux painting workshop The Artful Framer, 1991, Craft Country, Olney, Md., 1991; artist guest lectr. Radford U., spring 1996; supr. painting Paint Out Aids Ea. Market, Washington, 1992; asst. to art cons. Capitol Arts, Washington, 1992-96; tech. illustrator Vitro Corp., 1981-86; artist assoc. Mary Anne Reilly, 1995; founder Unity in Diversity Women's Exhibn. Group; interviewer, active Va. Juvenile Detention Ctr., 1993; spkr., presenter in field. One-woman shows include Beltone Hearing Aid, Washington, 1963, New Trends, Springfield, Va., 1971, Artful Framer, Olney, Md., 1991, Kurz, Koch, Doland and Dembling, Washington, 1992, Heartland Cafe, 1992, "R" St. Gallery Jackson Sch., 1993, Franklin Ct. Gallery, 1994, Parish

Gallery, 1995, Flossie Martin Gallery Radford U., Blacksburg, Va., 1996, Sunrise Gallery, Kilmarnock, Va., 1997, Nat. Press Club Bldg., Washington, 1997—98, Art Mine Agora Gallery, N.Y.C., 1998—2005, Very Spl. Arts Online Gallery, Washington, 1998—2001, Articulate Gallery, 1999, exhibited in group shows at Castel S. Pietro Terme, Italy, 1999—2006, Feminist Expo, Balt., 2000, Art Expo N.Y., 2000, King St. Stephen Mus., Hungary, 2000, Jemison-Carnegie Heritage Hall Mus., Ala., 2001, Attleboro Mus., Mass., 2001, Maison Francois de Bologne, Italy, Sung Kyun Kwan U., Seoul, Korea, Amsterdam Whitney Gallery, NYC, 2002—03, Nat. Assn. Women Artists, 2002—03, Poughkeepsie Art Mus., N.Y., 2004, Kostia, Palkane, Finland, 2005, Centro Culturale, Campamation, Italy, 2005, Forean Mus., Maramores, Romania, 2006, U. De Algarve, Portugal, 2006, Park Gallery, Lahtpur, Nepal, 2006, Mediteranean Ctr. Art, Alimera, Italy, 2006, Cluube Milleniuume, Vila Nova de Gaia, Portugal, 2007, others; (command murals, faux painting); contbr. to profl. mags. and pubs. Mem. Nat. Assn. Women Artists Inc., Nat. Mus. Women in Arts, Corcoran Sch. Art Alumni Assn. (presenter). Republican. Jewish. Avocations: poetry, reading, walking, boating. Home: 2301 E St NW A1115 Washington DC 20037

COLUMBRO, MADELINE M., education educator; d. Nicola and Nancy DeNicola Columbro. BA, Notre Dame Coll., Cleve., 1956; MA, Cath. U. Am., Washington, 1967; PhD, Case Western Res. U., Cleve., 1974; postgrad., Brown U., Providence, 1976, Yale U., New Haven, 1980. Cert. tchr. Ohio, lifelong learning Harvard U. Sch. Edn. Prof., adminstr. Notre Dame Coll., 1963—91; from academic dean to grant writer St. Mary Coll., Orchard Lake, Mich., 1991—2007, grant writer, 2007—. Music dir. Pontifical North Am. Coll., Rome, 1990—91. Chmn. Eleanor B. Rainey Meml. Inst., Cleve., 1999—2007; bd. dirs. Alta Ho., 1999, Geauga United Way Svcs., Chardon, Ohio, 2000. Neighborhood Leadership Cleve. scholar, Cleve. State U., 1999—2000. Avocations: medieval manuscripts, keyboard performances. Office: Sisters of Notre Dame 13000 Auburn Rd Chardon OH 44024 Office Phone: 440-279-1172. Office Fax: 440-279-1179. Business E-Mail: mcolumbro@ndec.org.

COLUMBUS, CHRIS J., film director, screenwriter; b. Spangler, Pa., Sept. 10, 1958; s. Alex Michael and Mary Irene (Puskar) C., m. Monica Devereux, 1983; 4 children. BFA, NYU, 1980. Writer: (films) Reckless, 1983, Gremlins, 1984, Goonies, 1985, Young Sherlock Holmes, 1985, Little Nemo, 1992; dir.: (films) Adventures in Babysitting, 1987, Home Alone, 1990, Home Alone 2: Lost in New York, 1992, Mrs. Doubtfire, 1993; dir., writer: Heartbreak Hotel, 1988, Only the Lonely, 1991; prodr., writer: Christmas with the Kranks, 2004; dir., writer, prodr.: Nine Months, 1995; dir., prodr.: Stepmom, 1998, Bicentennial Man, 1999, Rent, 2005; dir. exec. prodr: Harry Potter and the Sorcerer's Stone, 2001 (Las Vegas Film Critics award, 2001, Broadcast Film Critics Award, 2001), Harry Potter and the Chamber of Secrets, 2002; exec. prodr.: Fantastic Four, 2005; prodr.: Jingle All the Way, 1996, Harry Potter and the Prisoner of Azkaban, 2004, 3-D Rocks, 2005. Recipient Golden Plate award, Acad. Achievement, 2006. Democrat. Office: Creative Artists Agy c/o Beth Swofford 9830 Wilshire Blvd Beverly Hills CA 90212-1804*

COLUSSI, VALDIR CARLOS, physicist; b. São Paulo, Brazil, Mar. 28, 1966; arrived in US, 1997; s. Valdir and Mercedes Elizabeth (Perini) Colussi; m. Larissa Sapia, Feb. 1, 1991; children: Lara Sapia, Nubia Sapia. B, U. São Paulo, 1990, M with distinction, 1992; PhD, U. Campinas, 1997. Cert. therapeutic radiol. med. physicist Am. Bd. Radiology. Postdoctoral fellow Case Western Res. U., Cleve., 1997—98, rsch. assoc., 1998—2000; med. physicist, rsch. assoc. U. Hosps. Cleve., 2000—01, med. physicist, 2002—, clin. dir. physics dept. radiation oncology, 2006—. Mem.: Am. Soc. for Therapeutic Radiology and Oncology, Am. Assn. Physicists in Medicine, Am. Soc. for Laser Medicine and Surgery, Am. Soc. for Photobiology, Brazilian Soc. Physics. Office: Univ Hosps Cleve 11100 Euclid Ave Cleveland OH 44106 Office Phone: 216-844-2531. Personal E-mail: valdir.colussi@uhhospitals.org. Business E-Mail: valdir.colussi@case.edu.

COLUSSY, DAN ALFRED, aviation executive; b. Pitts., June 3, 1931; s. Dan and Viola E. (Andreis) C.; m. Helene Graham, June 6, 1953; children: Deborah, Jennifer. BS U.S. Coast Guard Acad., 1953; MBA, Harvard U., 1965. Applications engr. Jet Propulsion div. Gen. Electric Co., 1956-63; dir. ops. Am. Airlines, NYC, 1965-66; v.p. mktg. N.E. Airlines, Boston, 1966-69; v.p. Wells, Rich, Green Advt. Agy., NYC, 1969-70; v.p. mktg. devel. Pan Am. World Airways, NYC, 1970-72, v.p. passenger mktg., 1972-74, sr. v.p. passenger mktg., 1974, sr. v.p. field ops., 1974-75, sr. v.p. mktg. and services, 1975-76, exec. v.p. mktg. and services, dir., 1976-78, pres., chief operating officer, mem. exec. com., 1978-80; chmn., chief exec. officer Columbia Air, Balt., 1981-82; pres., CEO Can. Airlines Internat., Vancouver, B.C., 1982-84, chmn., 1985-86; bd. dirs., mem. exec. com. Can. Pacific Hotels, 1983-84; pres., chief exec. officer UNC Inc., Annapolis, Md., 1985-97, chmn. bd., chmn. exec. com., 1989-97; chmn. Gemini Capital, Palm Beach Gardens, Fla., 1997, Iridium Holdings, LLC, Arlington, Va., 2000—03; ret., 2003. Mem. bd. visitors Coll. Bus. and Mgmt. U. Md.; pres. adv. bd. St. John's Coll.; mem. Johns Hopkins Medicine Bd. Visitors.; bd. dirs. Balt. Gas and Electric Co., Hist. Annapolis Found.; chmn. Care First Inc. Mem. Campaign Cabinet, U.S. Naval Ist., Chesapeake Bay Found. (pres.' coun.), Larchmont Yacht, Annapolis Yacht, Harvard (N.Y.C.) Club, Old South Country Club, Wings Club (N.Y.C.), Econ. Club Washington, Met. Club Washington, Order of St. John (Can.), Chartwell Country Club, Ballen Isles Country Club. Office: CareFirst Inc 10455 Mill Run Cir Owings Mills MD 21117-5559

COLVIN, DONALD BERNARD, surgeon; b. Irvin, NC, Sept. 27, 1949; s. John Harley and Marie Josephine Colvin; m. Rosalind Mary Rodgers, Apr. 8, 1978; children: Renee, Kira. BS, U. Fla., Gainesville, 1971, MD, 1975. Surgeon, pres. Fairfax Colon & Rectal Surgery, Va., 1983—. Sect. chief Inova Fairfax Hosp., Falls Church, Va., 2005—. Lt. comdr. USN, 1975—80. Fellow: Am. Coll. Surgeons (pres. 2006—07), Am. Soc. Colon & Rectal Surgeons. Avocations: fly fishing, photography, boat building. Office: Fairfax Colon & Rectal Surgery 8316 Arlington Blvd #401 Fairfax VA 22031

COLVIN, HARRY WALTER, JR., physiology educator; b. Schellsburg, Pa., Dec. 5, 1921; s. Harry Walter and Maude Elizabeth (Girven) C.; m. Marie Catherine McNinch, Apr. 8, 1950; children: Sarah Lee, William McNinch. BS, Pa. State U., 0950; PhD, U. Calif., Davis, 1957. Instr. Okla. State U., Stillwater, 1955-57; assoc. prof. physiology U. Ark., Fayetteville, 1957-65; prof. U. Calif., Davis, 1965—. Cons. Pel-Freez Biologicals, Inc., Rogers, Ark., 1960-65. Assoc. editor Hilgardia, 1981-92; contbr. articles to profl. jours. Served with U.S. Army, 1942-45, ETO. Decorated Bronze Star, Purple Heart; recipient Outstanding Advisor award, 1982—83, 1984—85, 1987—88, Magnar Ronning award for Outstanding Tchg.; grantee Fulbright award, Yugoslavia, 1972, Argentina, 1986. Mem. Am. Dairy Sci. Assn., Am. Soc. Animal Sci., Sigma Xi, Phi Kappa Phi, Alpha Zeta, Gamma Sigma Delta, Phi Sigma , Phi Eta Sigma. Avocations: golf, flying. Home: 1515 Shasta Dr Apt 3326 Davis CA 95616 Office: U Calif Davis Dept Neurobiology Physiol & Behavior Davis CA 95616 E-mail: hwcolvin@ucdavis.edu.

COLVIN, JOHN O., federal judge; b. 1946; AB, U. Mo., 1968; JD, Georgetown U., 1971, LLM in Taxation, 1978. Tax counsel Office. of Senator Bob Packwood, 1975-84; senate fin. com. chief counsel, 1985-87; chief minority counsel US Senate, 1987-88; judge US Tax Ct., Washington, 1988—, chief judge, 2006—. Adj. prof. law Georgetown U. Law Ctr., 1987—. Served with USCG, 1971-75. Mem. Fed. Bar Assn. Office: US Tax Ct 400 2nd St NW Washington DC 20217-0002*

COLVIN, O. MICHAEL, medical association administrator, medical educator; b. Princeton, Ind., June 15, 1936; s. Jack Gene and and Evelyn Mae (Satkamp) C.; m. Arline Mae Lockerbie, Aug. 23, 1959; children: Michael Eric, Jennifer Susan, Kimberly Anne, Christopher Andrew. BA in Chemistry, Ind. U., 1957; MD, Washington U., St. Louis, 1961. Intern, resident Johns Hopkins Hosp., Balt., 1961-64; clin. assoc. Nat. Cancer Inst., Bethesda, Md., 1964-66; fellow in pharmacology Johns Hopkins U., Balt., 1966-68, physician, 1968-95, from asst. prof. to prof. medicine, 1968-95; dir. Duke Comprehensive Cancer Ctr. Duke U. Med. Ctr., Durham, NC, 1995—2002; Wm. Shingleton prof. cancer rsch. Duke U. Sch. Medicine, Durham, 2002—. Grant rev. study sect. Nat. Cancer Inst., Bethesda, 1968—. Recipient Career Devel. award Nat. Cancer Inst., 1975-80. Mem. AAAS, Am. Soc. Clin. Oncology, Am. Soc. Bone Marrow Transplantation, Am. Assn. Cancer Rsch. Home: 208 Arcadia Ln Chapel Hill NC 27514-1472 Office: Duke U Med Ctr 419 Jones Bldg PO Box 3843 Durham NC 27702-3843 Office Phone: 919-684-4167. Business E-Mail: colvi003@mc.duke.edu.

COLVIN, RUTH JOHNSON, literacy organization founder; b. 1916; Attended, Thornton Jr. Coll., Harvey, Ill., Mosier Bus. Coll., Chgo., Ill., Northwestern U., Evaston, Ill.; BS, Syracuse U., NY. Founder non-profit orgn. Literacy Volunteers, Inc. (then Literacy Volunteers, Am., Inc., now ProLiiteracy Worldwide), Syracuse, NY, 1962; bd. dir. (life) ProLiteracy Worldwide, Syracuse, NY. Vol. literacy instr. Internat. Exec. Corps, mission groups, websites. Named to Nat. Women's Hall of Fame, 1993; recipient President's Svc. award, Points of Light Found., 1987, Presdl. Medal of Freedom, 2006. Achievements include development of new methods of teaching, including tutoring manuals, which are used in adult education programs, libraries, schools and correctional facilities throughout the country; volunteer work in 26 countries giving training in both native language and English literacy to speakers of other languages. Address: Proliteracy Worldwide 1320 Jamesville Ave Syracuse NY 13210

COLVIN, SHERRILL WILLIAM, lawyer; b. Jeffersonville, Ind., Sept. 13, 1938; s. Hewitt L. and Mary (Sutton) C.; m. Sarah Albin, Aug. 12, 1962; children: John, Betsy. AB, Wabash Coll., 1960; JD, Ind. U., 1965. Bar: Ind. 1965, U.S. Supreme Ct. 1968. Ptnr. Haller & Colvin PC, Fort Wayne, Ind., 1965—. Mem. disciplinary commn. Ind. Supreme Ct., 1986-96; mem. faculty Nat. Inst. Trial Advocacy Fellow Am. Coll. Trial Lawyers; mem. Ind. State Bar Assn. (pres. 2003-2004), disciplinary commn. Supreme Ct. (chair 1995-96), Ind. Trial Lawyers Assn. (pres. 1991-92). Methodist. Office: Haller & Colvin 444 E Main St Fort Wayne IN 46802-1910 Home Phone: 260-456-6234; Office Phone: 219-426-0444. E-mail: scolvin@hallercolvin.com.

COLVIN, THOMAS STUART, agricultural engineer, farmer; b. Columbia, Mo., July 17, 1947; s. Charles Darwin and Miriam Elizabeth (Kimball) C.; m. Sonya Marie Peterson, Sept. 11, 1982; children: Christopher, Kristel. BS, Iowa State U., 1970, MS, 1974, PhD, 1977. Registered profl. engr., Iowa. Farmer, Hawkeye and Cambridge, Iowa, 1970—; rsch. assoc. Iowa State U., Ames, 1972-77; agrl. engr. USDA/Agrl. Rsch. Svc., Ames, 1977—2005. Cons. WillowCreek Cons., Manning, Iowa, 1978-85. Sgt. USAF, 1970-72, Vietnam. Recipient Air Force Commendation medal USAF, 1971. Mem. Am. Soc. Agrl. Biol. Engrs. (power machinery stds. com. St. Joseph, Mich. 1989—, Iowa sec., Young Engr. of Yr. 1986, Engr. of Yr. 2004), Soil and Water Conservation Soc., Iowa Acad. Sci. (chair agrl. scis. sect. 1991-92), Sigma Xi, Alpha Epsilon (pres. 1978), Gamma Sigma Delta, Phi Mu Alpha. Achievements include design and development of first computer program to help farmers manage tillage and residue cover for erosion control. Office: Oxford Farms 55670 290th St Cambridge IA 50046-8617

COLVIN, VICKI LEIGH, chemistry professor, educator; BS in Chemistry and Physics, Stanford U., Calif., 1988; PhD in Phys. Chemistry, U. Calif., Berkeley, 1994. Mem. tech. staff Bell Labs., Murray Hill, NJ, 1994-96; asst. prof. dept. chemistry to prof. chemistry and chem. engring. Rice U., Houston, 1996—. Dir. Rice U. Ctr. Biol. and Environ. Nanotechnology, Houston. Contbr. articles to profl. jours., chpts. to books. Named one of Top 20 Young Scientists to Watch, Discover mag., 2000; Rsch. fellow, Alfred P. Sloan Found., 2000. Mem. Am. Chem. Soc. (Victor K. LaMer award 1995). Achievements include patents in field. Office: Dept Chemistry Rice U MS-60 PO Box 1892 Houston TX 77251-1892 Office Phone: 713-737-5741. Office Fax: 713-348-2578. E-mail: colvin@rice.edu.*

COLVIS, JOHN PARIS, aerospace engineer, mathematician, research scientist; b. St. Louis, June 30, 1946; s. Louis Jack and Jacqueline Betty (Beers) C.; m. Nancy Ellen Fritz, Mar. 15, 1969 (div. Sept. 16, 1974); 1 child, Michael Scott; m. Barbara Carol Davis, Sept. 3, 1976; 1 child, Rebecca Jo; stepchildren: Bruce William John Zimmerly, Belinda Jo Zimmerly Little. Student, Meramec Community Coll., St. Louis, 1964-65, U. Mo., 1966, 72-75, Palomar Coll., San Marcos, Calif., 1968, U. Mo., Rolla, 1968-69; BS in Math., Washington U., St. Louis, 1977. Assoc. system safety engr. McDonnell Douglas Astronautics Co., St. Louis, 1978-81; sr. system safety engr. Martin Marietta Astronautics Group-Strategic Systems Co., Denver, 1981-87; sr. engr. Martin Marietta Astronautics Group-Space Launch Systems Co., Denver, 1987-95, Lockheed Martin Astronautics Co.-Space Launch Sys., Denver, 1995—2006; staff engr. United Launch Alliance, Denver, 2007—. Rschr. in field. Lance cpl. USMC, 1966-68, Vietnam. Mem. VFW (post 4171), Colo. Home Educators' Assn. (pres. 1989), Khe Sanh Vet Incorp. Evangelical. Achievements include research in the quantum postulate; the quantum philosophy of science and mathematics. Avocations: camping, hiking, swimming. Home: 4978 S Hoyt St Littleton CO 80123-1988 Personal E-mail: john.colvis888@yahoo.com.

COLWELL, BRYAN YORK, private investor, philanthropist; BA magna cum laude, Harvard U., Cambridge, Mass., 1983; postgrad., U. Pa. Wharton Sch., 1985; MBA with distinction, Columbia U., NYC, 1986. Strategic planner SmithKline Beckman Corp., Phila., 1983-85; v.p. Goldman, Sachs and Co., NYC, 1986—2000; mng. dir., head of global power and utilities ABN Amro Inc., NYC, 2000—02; pres. Colwell Found., 2002—. Mem. bd. Archtl. Rev. and Planning for Tuxedo Pk., NYC; chmn. utilities com. Village Tuxedo Park, NY. Author: The Public-Private Partnership, 1983. Mem. dirs. coun. Mus. of City of NY; bd. dir., chmn. assocs. com. Lenox Hill Neighborhood House, 1994—; bd. dir. Tuxedo Park Archtl. Rev. Bd., Nat. Hypertension Assn. Named Outstanding Young Am., WSB-Radio-TV Network, Atlanta, 1979; recipient Young Scholar award Harvard Club of Atlanta, 1979, Outstanding Student cup Atlanta Jour., 1979. Mem. Am. Fin. Assn. (v.p. 1985-86), Columbia Bus. Sch. Alumni Assn., Harvard U. Inst. Politics, World Affairs Coun., Harvard Architecture Soc. (pres. 1980), Brook Club, Links Club (membership com.), Owl Club, Hasty Pudding Club (v.p. 1981-83), Harvard Club NY, Racquet and Tennis Club, Tuxedo Club (membership com.), Sea Island Club, Southampton Club, Corviglia Club St. Moritz, (life) St. Moritz Tobogganing Club/Cresta (life).

COLWELL, GENE THOMAS, engineering educator; b. Chattanooga, Aug. 3, 1937; s. William Clarence and Mary Virginia (Smith) Colwell; m. Peggy Ann Fletcher, June 1, 1973. BSME, U. Tenn., 1959, MSME, 1962, PhD, 1966. Rsch. engr. Oak Ridge Nat. Lab., Tenn., 1959—62, 1965—68; instr. U. Tenn., Knoxville, 1962—65; asst. prof. Ga. Inst. Tech., Atlanta, 1966—71, assoc. prof., 1971—77, prof., 1977—95, prof. emeritus, 1995—, assoc. dir. Atlanta, 1984—87. Vis. prof. U. Carabobo, Venezuela, 1971; cons. in field. Contbr. articles to profl. jours. Numerous rsch. grants. Fellow: ASME (life); mem.: Sigma Xi, Pi Tau Sigma. Achievements include patents in field. Avocations: tennis, golf, hiking. Home: 9145 Prestwick Club Dr Duluth GA 30097-2442

COLWELL, HOWARD OTIS, advertising executive; b. New Rochelle, NY, Sept. 16, 1929; s. Robert Talcott and Louise (Otis) C.; m. Barbara Elaine Hrosenchik, Aug. 14, 1954 (dec. Feb. 27, 2001; children: John Robert, Christian, Mary Louise; m. Lydia Macdonald, April 6, 2002. AB, Colgate U., Hamilton, NY, 1953. Copy group head Batten, Barton, Durstine & Osborn, NYC, 1953-59; v.p., creative dir. Tatham-Laird & Kudner, NYC, 1959-68; sr. v.p., creative dir. William Esty Advt., NYC, 1968-87; v.p., corp. creative dir. Combe, Inc., White Plains, NY, 1987-98, sr. creative cons., 1998—. Guest lectr. NYU, 1979-81, Pace U., 1980-84, adj. prof., 1982-83 Chmn. YMCA Indian Guides Norwalk-Wilton, 1966; chmn. Wilton Voice on Edn., 1972-75, Wilton Arts Council, 1980-83; v.p. bd. dirs. Wilton Orch., 1985—, pres., 1986-87. Mem. Phi Beta Kappa. Congregationalist. Office: 1101 Westchester Ave White Plains NY 10604-3503 Personal E-mail: hcolwell@optonline.net.

COLWELL, RITA ROSSI, microbiologist, former federal agency administrator, medical educator; b. Nov. 23, 1934; BS in Bacteriology with distinction, Purdue U., 1956, MS in Genetics, 1958; PhD in Oceanography, U. Wash., 1961; DSc (hon.), Heriot-Watt U., Edinburgh, Scotland, 1987, Hood Coll., 1991; DSc, Purdue U., 1993; DSc (hon.), U. Surrey, Eng., 1995, U. Bergen, Norway, 1999, Coastal Carolina U., 1999, U. Md. Balt. County, 1999, St. Mary's Coll., 1999, Mich. State U., 2000, Washington Coll., 2000, U. Conn., 2000, Williams Coll., 2000, SUNY, Albany, 2000, U. Ancona, Italy, 2001, George Washington U., 2001, Mount Holyoke, 2001, Washington U., St. Louis, 2001, Calif. Poly. Inst., San Luis Obispo, 2001, Renssalaer Poly. Inst., 2001, U. Newcastle, UK, 2001, Mercy Coll., 2002, U. Queensland, Australia, 2002; DSc, U. Glasgow, 2002, Weizmann Inst. Sci., Israel, 2002, Tuskegee Inst., 2003, U. Ill., 2003, Dartmouth Coll., 2003; DSc (hon.), U. Del., Newark, 2003, Ariz. State U., Tempe, 2004, Georgetown U., Washinton, 2004, St. Joseph's U., Phila., 2004, Smith Coll., Northapmton, Mass., 2004, U. Mass., Dartmouth, North Dartmouth, 2004, Bates Coll., Lewiston, Maine, 2004, Cedar Crest Coll., Allentown, Pa., 2004, Pa. State U., Univ. Pk., 2004, Rutgers U., New Brunswick, 2005, Chatham Coll., Pitts., 2007, Skidmore Coll., Saratoga Springs, NY, 2007; LLD (hon.), Notre Dame Coll., 1994, U. Nebr., 2003; LHD (hon.), U. Ala., 2001; LittD (hon.), Ariz. State U., 2004; DHC (hon.), U. Naples, Italy, 2006. Rsch. asst. genetics lab. Purdue U., West Lafayette, Ind., 1956—57; rsch. asst. U. Wash., Seattle, 1957—58, predoctoral assoc., 1959—60, asst. rsch. prof., 1961—64; asst. prof. biology Georgetown U., Washington, 1964—66, assoc. prof. biology, 1966—72; prof. microbiology U. Md., 1972—98, v.p. for acad. affairs, 1983—87; dir. Ctr. Marine Biotech., 1987—91; founder, pres. Biotech. Inst. U. Md., 1991—98; dir. NSF, Arlington, Va., 1998—2004; chmn. Canon US Life Scis., Inc., 2004—; Disting. Univ. prof. U. Md., College Park, 2004—, Johns Hopkins Bloomberg Sch. Pub. Health, 2004—. Hon. prof. U. Queensland, Brisbane, Australia, 1988; mem. ocean scis. bd. NAS, 1977—80; hon. prof. Quindao U., China, 1995; cons. Washington area comms. media, congressman, legislators, 1978—; external examiner various univs. abroad, 1964—; vice chmn. polar rsch. bd. NAS, 1990—94; mem. Nat. Sci. Bd., 1984—90; mem. sci. adv. bd. Oak Ridge Nat. Labs., 1988—90, 1993—96; adv. com. FDA, 1991—92, food adv. com., 1993—96, sci. bd., 1996—; Koch lectr., Berlin, 2000. Author (manual numerical taxonomy): Collecting the Data, 1970; author: (with M. Zambruski) Rodina-Methods in Aquatic Microbiology, 1972; author: (with L.H. Stevenson) Estuarine Microbial Ecology, 1973; author: (with R.Y. Morita) Effect of the Ocean Environment on Microbial Ecology, 1973; author: (with A. Sinsky and N. Pariser) Marine Biotechnology, 1983; author: Vibrios in the Environment, 1985, Nucleic Acid Sequence Data, 1988; author: (with others) Marine Biotechnology, 1995; Microbial Diversity, 1996; author: Viable But Nonculturable Microorganisms in the Environment, 2000, others; mem. editl. bd.: Microbial Ecology, 1972—91, Applied and Environ. Microbiology, 1969—81, Oil and Petrochemical Pollution, 1980—91, Jour. Washington Acad. Scis., 1981—87, Johns Hopkins U. Oceanographic Series, 1981—84, Revue de la Fondation Oceanographique Ricard, 1981—, Estuaries, 1983—89, Zentralblatt fur Bacteriologie, 1985—, Jour. Aquatic Living Resources, 1987—, Sys. Applied Microbiology, 1985—2000, World Jour. Microbiology and Biotech., 1988—95, Environ. Microbiology, 2001—; contbr. articles to profl. jours.; (Koch lecture) Anatomy Lesson, Amsterdam, 2002. Named Prof. Extraordinairo, U. Catolica Valparaiso, Chile, 1976, Scholar of Yr., Phi Kappa Phi, 1992, 2006 Nat. Medal Sci. Laureate, NSF, 2007; recipient Gold medal, Internat. Biotech. Inst., 1990, Purkinje Gold medal for achievment in sci., Czechoslavakian Acad. Sci., 1991, Civic award, Gov. Md., 1990, Woman of the Yr. award, Women Legis. of Md., 1996, Cert. of Recognition, NASA, 1984, Alice Evans award, Am. Soc. Microbiol., 1988, Andrew White medal, Loyola Coll., 1994, medal of distinction, Barnard Coll./Columbia U., 1996, Gold medal, Charles U., Prague, 2000, Gold medals, UCLA, 2000, Alumna Summa Laude Dignata award, U. Wash., 2000, Achievement award, AAUW, 2001, Carey award, Am. Assn. Adv. Sci., 2001, Thomas award, Explorer's Club Lowell, 2000, Stone award, Boston, 2007, Nat. Medal Sci., Pres. USA, 2007. Fellow: AAAS (chmn. sect. biol. scis. 1993—94, pres. 1995, chmn. bd. 1996, Carey award 2001), Marine Tech. Soc. (exec. com. 1982—88), Washington Acad. Scis. (bd. mgrs. 1976—79, pres. 1996—98), Am. Acad. Microbiology (chmn. bd. govs. 1989—99), Grad. Women. Sci., Can. Coll. Microbiologists; mem.: Nat. Acad. Scis., Am. Philos. Soc., Royal Swedish Acad. Sci., Soc. Gen. Microbiology, Internat. Coun. Sci. Unions, Am. Soc. Limnology and Oceanography, World Fedn. Culture Collections, Classification Rsch. Group Eng. (charter), Am. Soc. Microbiology (hon.; various sci. coms. 1961—, pres. 1985, chmn. program com. REGEM-1 1988, Fisher award 1985), U.K. Soc. Applied Microbiology (hon.), Bangladesh Soc. Microbiology (hon.; fgn.), French Soc. Microbiology (hon.), Israeli Soc. Microbiology (hon.), Australian Soc. Microbiology (hon.), Soc. Indsl Microbiology (bd. govs. 1976—79, Charles Thom award 1998), U.S. Fedn. Culture Collections (governing bd. 1978—88), Internat. Coun. Sci. Unions (exec. bd. 1993—96, gen. com.), Am. Inst. Biol. Scis. (bd. govs. 1976—82), Internat. Union Microbiol. Soc. (v.p. 1986—90, pres. 1990—94), World Fedn. Culture Collections, Royal Soc. Can., Explorers Club (Lowell Thomas award 2000), Omicron Delta Kappa, Phi Beta Kappa, Sigma Delta Epsilon, Sigma Xi (nat. pres. 1991, Ann. Achievement award 1981, Rsch. award 1984), Delta Gamma (Delta Gamma Rose award 1989). Achievements include research in marine biotechnology; marine and estuarine microbial ecology; survival of pathogens in aquatic environments; ecology of Vibrio cholerae and related organisms; microbial systematics; marine microbiology; antibiotic resistance; environmental aspects of Vibrio cholerae in transmission of cholera; global climate and cholera transmission. Address: John Hopkins Bloomberg Sch Pub Health 615 N Wolfe St Ste W1102 Baltimore MD 21205 Office Phone: 301-405-9550. Business E-Mail: colwell@umbi.umb.edu.

COLWELL, ROBERT L., computer architect, consultant; BSEE, U. Pitts.; MSEE, PhD, Carnegie Mellon U. CPU architect Multiflow Computer; chief IA32 microprocessor architect Intel Corp., Hillsboro, Oreg., 1992—2000; ind. cons. R&E Colwell & Assoc., Inc., Portland, Oreg. Contbr. articles to profl. jours. Mem.: IEEE (perspectives editor IEEE Computer Mag.), NAE. Office: R&E Colwell & Assoc Inc 3594 NW Bronson Crest Loop Portland OR 97229-7062

COLWILL, JACK MARSHALL, physician, educator; b. Cleve., June 15, 1932; s. Clifford V. and Olive A. (Marshall) Colwill; m. Winifred Stedman, 1954; children: James F., Elizabeth Ann, Carolyn. BA, Oberlin Coll., 1953; MD (George Whipple scholar), U. Rochester, 1957. Diplomate Am. Bd. Med. Examiners, Am. Bd. Internal Medicine, Am. Bd. Family Practice. Intern Barnes Hosp., Washington U. Sch. Medicine, St. Louis,

1957—58; resident in medicine U. Washington Affiliated Hosps., Seattle, 1958—60; chief resident U. Hosp., 1960—61; instr. medicine, dir. med. outpatient dept. U. Rochester Sch. Medicine and Dentistry, 1961—62, sr. instr. medicine, dir. med. outpatient dept., 1962—64; asst. dean, asst. prof. medicine, asst. prof. cmty. health and med. practice U. Mo. Sch. Medicine, Columbia, 1964—67, assoc. dean, asst. prof., 1967—69, assoc. dean for acad. affairs, asst. prof., 1969—70, assoc. dean, assoc. prof., 1970—76, interim chmn. dept. family and cmty. medicine, 1976—77, prof., 1976—97, prof. emeritus, 1999—, chmn. dept., 1977—97, interim dean, 2000. Cons. Bur. Health Manpower, NIH, 1969—75, Office Divsn. Dir. USPHS, 1977—; mem. Coun. on Grad. Med. Edn. Health Resources and Svcs. Adminstrn., 1990—96. Contbr. articles to profl. jours. Chair commn. on Gulf War and Health Inst. of Medicine, NAS, 1999—2003; dir. Robert Wood Johnson Found. Generalist Physician Initiative, 1991—2000; bd. dirs. Am. Bd. Family Medicine, 1998—2003. Mem.: AMA, Inst. Medicine NAS, Am. Acad. Family Physicians (commn. on govtl. legis. affairs 1984—87), Soc. Tchrs. Family Medicine (bd. dirs. 1978—82, 1983—87, pres.-elect 1987—88, pres. 1988—89), Assn. Med. Am. Colls. (chmn. Midwest-Gt. Plains Group on Student Affairs 1971—73, nat. vice chmn. group 1973—74, chmn. working group on non-cognitive assessment 1974—77, adv. to com. on admissions assessment 1974—77), Alpha Omega Alpha. Office: U Mo-Columbia Sch Medicine Dept Family And Medicine Columbia MO 65212-0001 Office Phone: 573-882-2165.

COLYER, KIRK KLEIN, insurance and real estate investment executive; b. Fayetteville, NC, Jan. 30, 1956; s. Joe Bill and Charlotte (Klein) C. Assoc. in Bus., SUNY, Albany, 1977; BBA in Polit. Sci., U. Incarnate Word, 1980; student, Leonard's Tng. Sch., 1985, Tex. Crime Prevention Inst., 1985. Lic. recording agt.; lic. mortgage loan officer Tex. Councilman City of Balcones Heights, San Antonio, 1977-82, mayor, 1982-86, mayor emeritus, 1986; pres. Colyer Real Estate Investments, San Antonio, 1980—; pres., founder Colyer Ins. Agy., San Antonio, 1982—; pres. Colyer Oil Co., San Antonio, 1982—; loan officer Spinner Mortgage, 2002; founder, pres. Healthysa.com, 2003—; assoc in training Weichert Realtors; Rep. del. State Senatorial District 25; del. Texas, 2006, Rep. Conv., 2006; Rep. PCT chmn. PCT 3070 Huntercreek, 2006; campaign mgr. Wayne Christian for Judge, County Ct., 2006, Jason Wentworth for Gov., PCT 3049, 2006; campaign vol. Carleton Spears for Judge, Dist. Ct. 150, 2006; assoc. in tng. Weighert Realtors, Lisa Kay Assocs., 2006. Pres. Dominion Village, San Antonio, Tex., 1991—, ABC Colyer Nursery, 1999; adv. coun. US Postal Svc., 1994, Nat. Consumers, 1998-99; campaign dir. Congl. Rep. nominee Carl Bill Colyer, San Antonio; campaign treas. Gerry Richkoff County Clk., Bexar County, 1994, Leon M. Hernandez Dem. precinct chmn., campaign treas./mgr., 2000; chmn. elect Rep. precinct, 2006; mem. dinner com. US Congress Dist. 20 Charlie Gonzalez, 1998—; founder, pres. Healthysa.com, 2005. Featured extra (films) Miss Congeniality, 2000, speaking role Reason to Believe, 2001, appeared in TV comml., 2004. V.p. Balcones C. of C., San Antonio, 1978, San Antonio Young Reps., 1991; bd. dirs. Beautify San Antonio, 1982, South Tex. Charities, 1998; exec. bd. Alamo Area Coun. Govts., 1979-84; pres. Tex. Mcpl. League Region 7, San Antonio, 1985; founder Bexar County Young Reps., 1995; bd. dirs. San Antonio March of Dimes, 1985; grad. Leadership San Antonio, 1985; pres. Lulac Coun. 602, 1998-2000; host. Com. for Nat. Rep. Conv. 2000 Bid for San Antonio, Tex.; campaign treas. Leon Hernandez Dem. Precinct, 2000—; campaign worker Mayor Clint Eastwood, Carmel, Calif., 1986, Campaign for George Gervin for Mud King, San Antonio, 1997; treas. Hunters Creek North Homeowners Assn., 1995, bd. dirs., 2005-06; bd. dirs. US Postal Adv. Com., San Antonio, 1994; raffle com. corp. donations San Antonio Stock Show Rodeo, 2001, life mem. raffle com., 2004—; judge Miss San Antonio US Galaxy, 2004; chmn. Tex. largest halloween party benefit kids South Tex. Charities, 2004; bd. dirs. San Antonio Martini Found., 1992—; hon. deputy constable Bexar County, Tex., 2003; campaign exec. mgr. Miss Tex. Kristin Howsley, 2004; campaign exec. mgr. Kristin Howsley Miss Galaxy, 2004, Miss San Antonio Galaxy, 2005; fin. com., silent auction chmn. Bexar County Rep. Party, 2005; mem. nat. panel Home Testing Inst. Am., 2005; founder San Antonio Bar Owners Assn., 2006, San Antonio Bar Owners Assn. Found., 2006; precinct chmn. Bexar County Reps., 2006; del. Bexar County Senatorial Com. 26, 2006, Tex. Rep. State Conv., 2006; founder God's Found. for Cancer Rsch., 2006. Named one of Outstanding Mems. of Am., U.S. Jaycees, 1977-91; USANA Health Scis. Dist. Achiever, 2003; Rey Feo XLIX, 1996-97. Mem. IHIO Corridor (founder, pres. 1984-86), San Antonio Ind. Car Dealers Assn. (founder, pres. 1993—), Tex. Auto Dealers Assn. (bd. dirs. 1994—), San Antonio City Club, San Antonio Plaza Club (life), Rey Feo '97, Distributive Edn. Clubs of Am. (life), Lions (bd. dirs. Balcones chpt. 1976-78), Tex. Jaycees (dist. bd. dirs. 1978, pres. Balcones Hts. chpt. 1977, Top Recruiter 1980), San Antonio Crime Stoppers (bd. dirs. 1984—), San Antonio Martini Found. (bd. dirs. 1988—), San Antonio Parrot Head Club, San Antonio P.A.R.T.I. Found. (bd. dirs. 1998—), South Tex. Charities., Shoppers Voice Consumer Product Survey Am., God's Found. Cancer Rsch.com (founding mem., 2006). Republican. Avocations: fishing, hunting, hiking, jogging, roller blading. Home: 13290 Hunters View St San Antonio TX 78230-2032 Office: Colyer Ins Agy 4311 Ih 10 W San Antonio TX 78201 Office Phone: 210-789-2258. Personal E-mail: kirk.k.colyer@aol.com.

COMANOR, WILLIAM S., economist, educator; b. Phila., May 11, 1937; s. Leroy and Sylvia (Bershad) C.; children: Christine, Katherine, Lauren, Gregory. Student, Williams Coll., 1955—57; BA, Haverford Coll., 1959; MA, PhD, Harvard U., 1964; postgrad., London Sch. Econs., 1963—64. Spl. econ. asst. to asst. atty. gen. Antitrust divsn. U.S. Dept. Justice, Washington, 1965-66; asst. prof. econs. Harvard U., Cambridge, Mass., 1966-68; assoc. prof. Stanford (Calif.) U., 1968-73; dir. bur. econs. FTC, Washington, 1978-80; prof. econs. U. Calif., Santa Barbara, 1975—, dept. chmn., 1984-87; prof. Sch. Pub. Health UCLA, 1990—. Author: National Health Insurance in Ontario, 1980, Advertising and Market Power, 1974, Competition Policy in Europe and North America, 1990, Competition Policy in the Global Economy, 1997, Law and Economics of Child Support Payments, 2004; contbr. articles to profl. jours. Recipient Dist. fellow award, Indsl. Orgn. Soc., 2003. Mem.: Indsl. Orgn. Soc. (pres. 1991, Disting. Fellow award 2003), Am. Econ. Assn. Office: U Calif Dept Econs Santa Barbara CA 93106 Home: 14701 Valley Vista Blvd Sherman Oaks CA 91403 Office Phone: 310-206-1694. Business E-Mail: comanor@ucla.edu.

COMAS, DANIEL L., manufacturing executive; m. Leigh Carnahan. BA, Georgetown Univ., 1986; MBA, Stanford Univ., 1991. Fin. analyst Paine Webber; mgmt. positions Danaher Corp., Washington, 1991—96, v.p. corp. develop., 1996—2004, sr. v.p. fin. & corp. develop., 2004—05, exec. v.p., CFO, 2005—. Office: Danaher Corp 2099 Pennsylvania Ave NW Washington DC 20006*

COMBE, JOHN CLIFFORD, JR., lawyer; b. New Orleans, Jan. 5, 1939; s. John Clifford and Gladys Ann (Reine) C.; m. Lynne Wendel Watson, July 11, 1964; children: John, Wendy, Holly. BBA, Tulane U., 1960, LLB, 1965. Bar: La. 1965, U.S. Dist. Ct. (ea. and mid. dists.) La. 1965, U.S. Ct. Appeals (5th cir.) 1965, U.S. Supreme Ct. 1971, U.S. Ct. Appeals (11th cir.) 1981, U.S. Dist. Ct. (we. dist.) La. 1986. Assoc. Jones, Walker, Waechter, Poitevent, Carrere & Denegre, New Orleans, 1965—, ptnr., 1970—, sr. ptnr., 1989—. Editor: La. Bar Jour., 1975-77; contbr. articles to legal jours. Organizer, mem. Crestmont Pk. Improvement Assn.; organizer Greater New Orleans Law Explorer program Boy Scouts Am., 1974; mem. St. Catherine of Siena Parish Sch. Bd., 1976-89; trustee Acad. of Sacred Heart, 1993-96. Lt. (j.g.) USN, 1960-62. Recipient Monte M. Lemann award, La. Civil Svc. League, 1990. Fellow: ABA (mem. ho. of dels. 1982—88), La. State Bar Found., Am. Bar Found., Am. Coll. Trial Lawyers (state chair 1999—2000); mem.: La. Bar Assn. (mem. bd. govs. 1973—74, sec.-treas. 1975, mem. bd. govs. 1975—76, 1977—78, 1978—80, pres. 1979—80, Outstanding Young Lawyer award 1978, pres. award 1989), So. Regional Conf. Bar Pres., Nat. Conf. Bar Pres., Def. Rsch. Inst., Am. Judicature Soc. (mem. bd. govs. 1982—86), La. Assn. Def. Counsel (bd. dirs. 1969—75, faculty trial acad. 2000—02), Internat. Assn. Def. Counsel (speaker 1989, mem. faculty trial acad. 1991), Stratford Club (pres. 1993—95), Boston Club. Republican. Roman Catholic. Office: Jones Walker Waechter Poitevent Carrere 8555 United Plaza Blvd Ste 500 Baton Rouge LA 70809-7028 Office Phone: 504-582-8144. Business E-Mail: jcombe@joneswalker.com.

COMBEE, SUSAN, assistant principal; m. Todd Wayne Combee, May 22, 1982; children: Matthew Todd, Jacob Scott. MS, James Madison U., Harrisonburg, Va., 1982. Cert. elem. supervision and adminstrn. Va., 1996. Speech pathologist Henry County Pub. Sch., Collinsville, Va., 1988—96, Hanover County Pub. Schs., Ashland, Va., 1998—2001, asst. prin., 2001—. Supr. ASHA certification James Madison U., Harrisonburg, Va., 1997—98. Dir. children's activities New Bethesda Bapt. Ch., Mechanicsville, 2005—07, pianist, 2001—07; bd. dirs. Battlefield Green Swim Team, Mechanicsville, Va., 1997—2001. Recipient Ednl. Leadership award, Hanover County Pub. Sch., 2006. Office: Cool Spring Elementary School 9964 Honey Meadows Rd Mechanicsville VA 23116 Home Phone: 804-730-4610; Office Phone: 804-723-3560.

COMBS, ANN LAINE, investment company executive, former federal agency administrator; b. 1956; BA, U. Notre Dame, 1978; JD, George Washington U., 1981. With Price Waterhouse, Inc., Nat. Assn. Mfrs.; prin. William M. Mercer, Inc.; v.p., chief counsel retirement & pension issues Am. Coun. Life Insurers; dep. asst. sec. Employee Benefits Security Adminstrn., US Dept. Labor, Washington, 1987—93; asst. sec. Employee Benefits Security Adminstrn., U.S. Dept. Labor, Washington, 2001—06; mng. dir., Instl. Strategic Consulting Group The Vanguard Group, Inc., Valley Forge, Pa., 2007—. Mem. adv. coun. on social security, 1994—96; bd. dirs. Nat. Acad. Social Insurance, Am. Benefits Coun., Am. Coun. Life Insurer's Internat. Pension Found. Mem.: ABA, DC Bar. Office: The Vanguard Group Inc PO Box 1110 Valley Forge PA 19482

COMBS, CHARLES DONALD, academic administrator; b. Levelland, Tex., Mar. 28, 1952; s. Harold Bloyd and Emma Laura (Cole) C.; m. Pamela Quattlebaum, Mar. 31, 1983. BA with high honors, Tex. Tech U., 1972, MA, 1974; PhD, U. N.C., 1980; PhD (hon.), State Univ. Medicine and Dentistry, Moldova, 2003. Instr. polit. sci. Tex. Tech U., Lubbock, 1973-76, Elon Coll., NC, 1975-76; instr. pub. adminstrn. NC Ctrl. U., Durham, 1976-77; sr. program assoc. Robert Wood Johnson Found., Chapel Hill, NC, 1977-79; adminstr. Surry Family Health Group, Va., 1978-81; program dir. Ea. Va. Med. Sch., Old Dominion U., Norfolk, 1980-85; asst. v.p. adminstrn. and svcs. Ea. Va. Med. Sch., Norfolk, 1985-87; assoc. v.p. instl. advancement Med. Coll. Hampton Rds., Norfolk, 1987-88, v.p. instl. advancement, 1988-92, v.p. planning and program devel., 1992—2006, co-dir. Nat. Ctr. Collaboration Med. Modelling and Simulation, 2000—06, assoc. dean planning and health professions, 2006—. Cons. numerous health and human svc. orgns., Va., N.C., Tex., Kans., Eastern and Ctrl. Europe, Africa, Asia and C.Am.; chmn. exec. com. Va. Statewide Health Edn. Adv. Com., 1992-2000; chmn. Regional Perinatal Coordinating Coun., 1989—; treas. Women's Health Va., 1998-2000. Contbr. articles to profl. jours. Grantee City of Durham, 1976, Kresge Found., 1979, Dept. Health and Human Svcs., 1981-85, 90—, Champus Mental Health Demonstration Program, 1986-89; sr. fellow Naval Postgrad. Sch., 1996-2003; recipient Disting. Alumni award South Plains Coll., 1998. Mem. APHA, Am. Assn. Univ. Adminstrs., Am. Hosp. Assn., Am. Soc. Pub. Adminstrs., Hampton Rds. C. of C. (mem. regional legis. affairs com. and health care task force 1985-96), Assn. of Acad. Health Ctrs. (nat. program chair 1996). Methodist. Home: 7800 N Shore Rd Norfolk VA 23505-1735 Office: Ea Va Med Sch PO Box 1980 Norfolk VA 23501-1980 E-mail: combscd@evms.edu.

COMBS, ERIC A., social studies educator; m. Elizabeth Ann Haver; 1 child, Olivia. Grad., Air Force Senior NCO Acad.; MEd, Univ. Dayton; Masters student in Ednl. Leadership, Antioch-McGregor Univ. Social studies tchr. Fairborn (Ohio) H.S. Served to sr. master sgt. (ret.) USAF. Decorated Meritorious Svc. Medal (three devices), Air Force Commendation Medal (three devices), Air Force Achievement Medal (one device), Air Force and Navy Marksman awards, Outstanding Airman of Yr. Ribbon; named Ohio Tchr. of Yr., 2007. Office: Fairborn High Sch 900 East Dayton-Yellow Springs Rd Fairborn OH 45324 Business E-Mail: ecombs@fairborn.k12.oh.us.*

COMBS, ERIC K., lawyer; b. West Union, Ohio, Aug. 10, 1971; BA, Miami U., 1993; JD, U. Madison-Wis., 1996. Bar: Ohio 1996. Ptnr., Litig. Dept. Taft, Stettinius & Hollister LLP, Cin. Trustee West End Health Ctr., 1998—2003, mem., Adv. Bd.; assoc. mem., Allocation Com. Fine Arts Fund; tutor Taft Elem. Sch.; deacon Knox Presbyn. Ch. Named one of Ohio's Rising Stars, Super Lawyers, 2006. Mem.: Cin. Acad. of Leadership for Lawyers, Cin. Bar Assn. (bd. trustee), Order of Coif, Phi Beta Kappa. Office: Taft, Stettinius & Hollister LLP 425 Walnut St Ste 1800 Cincinnati OH 45202-3957 Office Phone: 513-381-2838. Office Fax: 513-381-0205.

COMBS, HOLLY MARIE, actress; b. San Diego, Dec. 3, 1973; m. Bryan Travis Smith, Feb. 28, 1993 (div. 1997); m. David W. Donoho, Feb. 14, 2004; children: Finley Arthur, Riley. Actor: (films) Walls of Glass, 1985, Sweet Hearts Dance, 1988, New York Stories, 1989, Born on the Fourth of July, 1989, Simple Men, 1992, Dr. Giggles, 1992, Chain of Desire, 1993, A Reason to Believe, 1995; (TV films) A Perfect Stranger, 1994, Sins of Silence, 1996, Love's Deadly Triangle: The Texas Cadet Murder, 1997, Daughters, 1997, See Jane Date, 2003; (TV series) Picket Fences, 1992—96 (best young actress in a new TV series Young Artist award, 1993), Charmed, 1998—2006; prodr.:, 2000—06.

COMBS, LINDA MORRISON, federal official; b. Lenoir, NC, June 29, 1946; d. Robert Hugh and Vera Ludema (Bryant) Morrison; m. David Michael Combs, June 20, 1970. AA, Gardner Webb Coll., 1966, PhD (hon.), 1985; BS, Appalachian State U., 1968, MA, 1978; EdD, Va. Poly. Inst. and State U., 1985. Tchr., adminstr. Winston-Salem (N.C.)/Forsyth County Schs., 1968-79, sch. bd mem., 1980-82; exec. sec., dep. U.S. Dept. Edn., Washington, 1982-84, dep. under-sec. mgmt., 1984-86; pub. edn. advisor State of N.C., Raleigh, 1986-87; owner Combs Group Cons., Winston-Salem, 1987; acting asst. dir. for mgmt. U.S. Dept. Vet. Affairs, Washington, 1987-89; asst. sec. mgmt. U.S. Dept. Treasury, Washington, 1989—91; CFO EPA, Washington, 2002—04; asst. sec., budget & fin. mgmt., CFO U.S. Dept. Transport., Washington, 2004—05; contr., Office Fed. Fin. Mgmt. Office Mgmt. & Budget, Washington, 2005—. Pres., founder Combs Music Internat., Winston-Salem, NC, 1991—2001. Gov.'s advocate Com. for Children and Youth, Winston-Salem, 1974-75; treas. Michael Britt for N.C. Senate, Forsyth County, 1976; v.p. Forsyth County Young Reps. Club, 1980-81. Recipient Honor and Outstanding Svc. award Combined Fed. Campaign, Washington, 1983, Alumnus of Yr. award Gardner Webb Coll., Boiling Springs, N.C., 1987, Disting. Alumnus of Yr. Appalachian State U., Boone, N.C., 1986. Mem. Forsyth County Rep. Womens Club, Pres.'s Coun. on Mgmt. Improvement (vice chair, Outstanding Leadership award 1989), Phi Delta Kappa, Delta Kappa Gamma. Republican. Baptist. Avocations: running, cooking, tennis. Office: Office Mgmt & Budget 1650 Pennsylvania Ave NW Rm 263 Washington DC 20503

COMBS, PHILIP JUDSON, lawyer; b. Atlanta, June 22, 1966; m. Dawn Michelle Baker, July 22, 2001; children: Walker, Isaac. BA with honors, Emory U., Atlanta, 1988; JD with high honors, Duke U., Durham, NC, 1993. Bar: W.Va. 1992, US Dist. Ct. (so. dist.) W.Va., US Dist. Ct. (no. dist.) W.Va. 1999, US Ct. Appeals (4th cir.) 1992. Law clk. US Ct. Appeals 4th Cir., Charleston, W.Va., 1992—93; asst. atty. Dept. Justice, Charleston, W.Va., 1994—98; assoc. Farmer, Clive and Arnold, 1999; ptnr. Allen Guthrie McHugh & Thomas, Charleston, W.Va., 2000—. Pres. Walker Isaac Investments, LLC, Charleston. Bd. dirs. W.Va. Internat. Film Festival, Charleston, 2000—05. Nat. Merit scholar, Emory U., 1984—88, Parkinson scholar, Duke U. Sch. Law, 1989—92. Mem.: Products Liability Adv. Coun., Def. Rsch. Inst., Order of the Coif, Phi Alpha Theta. Office: Allen Guthrie McHugh & Thomas 500 Lee St Ste 800 Charleston WV 25301 Office Phone: 304-345-7250. Office Fax: 304-345-9941. Business E-Mail: pjcombs@agmtlaw.com.

COMBS, ROBERTA, religious organization administrator; b. Charleston, SC, 1946; m. Andy Combs (dec.); children: Karen, Michele. Bus. home-builder, developer, 1976—90; polit. cons., 1990—99; exec. v.p. Christian Coalition of Am., 1999—2001, chmn., pres., 2001—. Office: Christian Coalition of America PO Box 37030 Washington DC 20013 Home Phone: 843-797-3085; Office Phone: 202-479-6900. Business E-Mail: roberta.combs@cc.org.

COMBS, SEAN (DIDDY), record company executive, producer; b. Harlem, NY, Nov. 4, 1969; s. Melvin and Janice Combs; 1 child (with Misa Hylton-Brim), Justin; children (with Kim Porter), Christian, D'Lila Star, Jessie James. Attended, Howard U., Washington, DC. Various pos. including intern, head A&R dept. Uptown Records, 1988—93; CEO, founder Bad Boy Entertainment, 1993—; launched clothing line Sean John, 1998—; launched fragrance, Unforgivable, 2006. Prodr.: Forever My Lady (Jodeci), 1991, Diary of a Mad Band (Jodeci), 1993, What's the 411? (Mary J. Blige), 1993, My Life (Mary J. Blige), 1994, Project: Funk Da World (Craig Mack), 1994, Ready to Die (The Notorious B.I.G.), 1994, Think of You (Raymond Usher), 1994, Faith (Faith Evans), 1995; also prodr. records by Supercat, 1996, Keith Sweat, Caron Wheeler, Mix Tape Volume 2, 1997, Money Talks, 1997, Diana, Princess of Wales: Tribute, 1997, Chef Aid: The South Park Album, 1998; performer: (albums) In Tha Beginning.There Was Rap, 1997, No Way Out, 1997 (Grammy Award, Best Rap Album); performer, prodr. (albums) Forever, 1999, The Saga Continues, 2001, Press Play, 2006; exec. prodr.: (TV series) Making the Band II, 2002, Making the Band III, 2005—06, Run's House, 2005; actor: (films) Made, 2000, Monster's Ball, 2001, Death of a Dynasty, 2003; exec. soundtrack prodr.: Bad Boys II, 2003; actor: (Broadway plays) A Raisin in the Sun, 2004. Named Menwear Designer of Yr., Coun. of Fashion Designers of Am., 2004; named one of 50 Most Influential African-Americans, Ebony Mag., 2004, Most Influential Black Americans, 2006, 100 Most Influential People, Time Mag., 2006, 100 Most Powerful Celebrities, Forbes.com, 2007; recipient ASCAP, Songwriter of the Year, 1996.*

COMBS, STEPHEN PAUL, pediatrician, health facility administrator; b. Bristol, Tenn., Feb. 11, 1966; s. Paul Willis and Janis Rose C. BS, East Tenn. State U., 1988, MD, 1992. Cert. physician exec. Am. Coll. Physician Execs.; diplomate Nat. Bd. Med. Examiners. Resident pediat. Duke U., Durham, NC, 1992—95, asst. chief pediat. residents Duke Children's Hosp., 1994—95; ptnr. Mountain Region Pediats., Kingsport, Tenn., 1995—98, sec., 1998—; pediatrician Gray Sta. Pediat., Tenn., 1999—; v.p. med. affairs Holston Valley Med. Ctr., 2006—. Dir. pediat. intensive care Wellmont Health Sys., 1998—2006, chmn. pediat. critical care, 1996—2006; chmn. dept. pediat. Indian Path Med. Ctr., 1999—2003; mem. med. adv. bd. Am. Homepatient, Nashville, 1995—98; mem. child fatality rev. bd. jud. Dist. II State of Tenn., 1995—; bd. dirs. Wellmont Holston Valley Med. Ctr., chief staff, 2006; med. dir. clin. trials program Highlands Physicans Inc., 2001—04, bd. dirs., mem. various coms.; assoc. clin. prof. pediat. East Tenn. State U., 2002—05, clin. prof. pediat., 2005—; bd. dirs. Highlands Wellmont Health Network; vice chair, physicians exec. com. Wellmont Physician Svcs., 2005—, pres., CEO, 2007—. Contbr. articles to profl. jours. Recipient Forty Under 40 award, Bus. Jour., Health Care Hero award, 2003. Fellow Am. Acad. Pediat. (resident rep. 1993-95, program chmn. Tenn. chpt. 2000, nominating chair Tenn. chpt. 2001, fellow at large 2005—), Am. Soc. Clin. Pediat., Am. Bd. Pediat., Am. Bd. Forensic Examiners, Am. Soc. Clin. Pediat.; mem. AMA, Tenn. Med. Assn., N.C. Med. Assn., Duke Med. Alumni Assn., East Tenn. State U. Med. Alumni Assn. (rep. 1992—), History of Appalachia Soc., Alpha Omega Alpha. Republican. Baptist. Avocations: civil war, revolutionary war, gardening, skiing, golf. Home: 405 Westfield Pl Kingsport TN 37664-6410 Office: Gray Sta Pediat 2103 Forest Dr Ste 5 Gray TN 37615-8423 Business E-Mail: stephen_p_combs@wellmont.org.

COMBS, SUSAN, state agency administrator; married; 3 children. Grad., Vassar Coll.; JD, U. Tex. Formerly asst. dist. atty., Dallas; mem. Tex. Legislature, 1993-96; owner, operator ranch in West Tex.; commr. of agr. State of Tex., 1999—2006, comptr. pub. acct., 2007—. Named Outstanding Legis. Crimefighter, Greater Dallas Crime Commn., 1993. Mem. Tex. Wildlife Assn. (bd. dirs., Tex. and Southwestern Cattle Raisers Assn. (bd. dirs.). Office: Tex Comptroller Pub Acct P O Box 13528 Capitol Station Austin TX 78711-3528 Business E-Mail: commissioner@agr.state.tx.us.*

COMBS, W(ILLIAM) HENRY, III, lawyer; b. Casper, Wyo., Mar. 18, 1949; s. William Henry and Ruth M. (Wooster) Combs; 1 child from previous marriage, J Bradley. Student, Northwestern U., 1967—70; BS, U. Wyo., 1972, JD, 1975. Bar: Wyo. 1975, U.S. Dist. Ct. Wyo. 1975, U.S. Ct. Appeals (10th cir.) 1990, U.S. Supreme Ct. 1990. Assoc. Murane & Bostwick, Casper, 1975—77, ptnr., 1978—. Mem. com. resolution fee disputes, 1990—92. Mem.: ABA (tort and ins. practice sect., law office mgmt. sect.), US Handball Assn., Nat. Bd. Trail Advocacy (cert.), Am. Judicature Soc., Def. Rsch. Inst., Natrona County Bar Assn., Waterski USA. Republican. Episcopalian. Avocations: handball, water-skiing, skiing, climbing, driving. Office: Murane & Bostwick 201 N Wolcott St Casper WY 82601-1922

COMEAU, CAROL SMITH, school system administrator; b. Berkeley, Calif., Sept. 4, 1941; d. Floyd Franklin and Bessie Caroline (Campbell) Smith; m. Dennis Rene Comeau, Dec. 27, 1962; children: Christopher, Michael, Karen. BS in Edn., U. Oreg., 1963; M in Pub. Sch. Adminstrn., U. Alaska, 1985. Third grade tchr., Springfield, Oreg., 1963-64; elem. sch. tchr. Ocean View Elem. Sch., Anchorage, 1975-84, 2d-6th grade tchr.; 6th grade tchr. Spring Hill Elem. Sch., Anchorage, 1985-86; adminstrv. intern Tudor Elem. Sch., Anchorage, 1986-87; prin. Orion Elem. Sch., Anchorage, 1987-89; prin. Spring Hill Elem. Sch., 1989-90; exec. dir. elem. edn. Anchorage Sch. Dist., 1990-93; asst. supt. instrn., 1993-2000; supt., 2000—; mem. exec. com. Coun. Great City Schools, 2003—; community activist ednl. issues. Chair Anchorage United Way, 2004—; bd. dirs. KAKM pub. TV, 1990-92, Alaska Ctr. Performing Arts. Named Tchr. of Yr., Anchorage Sch. Dist. PTA Coun., 1976, Top 25 Most Powerful Alaskans, 2002, Alaska Supt. of Yr., 2003; recipient ATHENA award, Anchorage C. of C., 2004; Mem. NEA (Alaska Renowned Educator, 2003, Nat. Assn. Elem. Sch. Prins., Alaska Assn. Elem. Sch. Prins., Anchorage Edn. Assn. (Tchr. of Yr. 1986), Phi Delta Kappa, Kappa Delta Pi. Democrat. Home: 13632 Jarvi Dr Anchorage AK 99515-3934 Office: Anchorage Sch Dist Adminstrn Bldg 4600 Debarr Rd Anchorage AK 99519-6614 Home Phone: 907-345-4916; Office Phone: 907-742-4312. Business E-Mail: comeau_carol@asdk12.org.

COMEAU, MICHAEL GERARD, lawyer; b. Balt., July 13, 1956; s. Joseph Gerard and Irma (Cullison) C.; m. Penny Lee Derrickson, Apr. 14, 1984; children: Joseph Gerard, Nicole Lee. BA, Randolph-Macon Coll., 1978; JD, U. Balt., 1981; postgrad., George Washington U., 1982-83, U.S. Army Judge Advocate Gen.'s Basic Course, 1992; Advanced Course, 1994, command and gen. staff course, 2002. Bar: Md. 1981, U.S. Dist Ct. Md. 1982, U.S. Ct. Mil. Appeals 1982, U.S. Ct. Appeals (4th and D.C. cirs.) 1982, D.C. 1984, U.S. Dist Ct. D.C. 1984, U.S. Supreme Ct. 1985. Law clk. Balt. County Solicitor's Office, Towson, Md., 1980-81; assoc. county atty. Prince George's County, Upper Marlboro, Md., 1981-84, 86-89; assoc. Knight, Manzi, Brennan & Ostrom, Upper Marlboro, 1984-86; chief dep. clk. Ct. Spl. Appeals, Annapolis, Md., 1986; asst. atty. gen. State of Md., Towson, 1989-94; chief of litigation, asst. county atty. Balt. County Atty.'s Office, Towson, Md., 1994—2000, 2003—; mng. atty. Law Offices of Michael G. Comeau, Balt., 2000—02. Mem. gen. assembly's task force on gaming laws in Prince George's County, 1987. Mem. ch. coun. All Saints Luth. Ch., Bowie, Md., 1986-88, pres., 1987-88, St. John's Sweet Air, 2003-06; mem. Dem. State Ctrl. Com. for Harford County, 1995-98, 2002-, chmn. 2003-; procurement adv. coun. State of Md., 1995-98, Gubernatorial Transition Team, 1994-95; judiciary com. Md. Ho. of Dels., Harford County, 1997-99. Lt. col. Md. Army N.G., 1991—. Recipient Exceptional Svc. award, Md. Atty. Gens.'s Office, 1991. Mem. Md. Bar Assn., Harford County Bar Assn., Prince George's County Bar Assn. (bd. dirs. 1988-90), Kappa Alpha. Democrat. Avocations: baseball card collecting, softball. Home: 3509 Glen Oak Dr Jarrettsville MD 21084-1837 Office: Old Court House Fl 2 Towson MD 21014 Home Phone: 410-692-2432; Office Phone: 410-887-4420. E-mail: mcomeau@co.ba.md.us, mikeco@clearviewcatv.net.

COMER, BETH MEGAN-SIMKINS, forensic scientist; b. KI Sawyer Air Force Base, Mich., Apr. 30, 1975; d. Louis Harry and Virginia McGregor Simkins; m. Michael Jon Comer, July 7, 2001 (div. Oct. 31, 2005). BS in Biology, Ind. U., Bloomington, 1993—97; MEd, U. Minn., Mpls., 1998—2006. Cert. life sci. tchr. Minn. Dept. Edn. Lab. technician Dept. Surgery, U. Minn. Med. Sch., Mpls., 1998—99; sci. tchr. Thomas Jefferson Sr. HS, Bloomington Pub. Schs., Minn., 1999—2001, Coon Rapids HS, ISD Anoka-Hennepin #11, Minn., 2001—04; forensic scientist Minn. Bur. Criminal Apprehension, St. Paul, 2004—. Mitochondrial DNA testing and analysis for regional lab. program FBI, Quantico, Va. Mem.: Midwestern Assn. Forensic Scientists, Am. Acad. Forensic Scis. R-Consevative. Luth. Avocations: travel, reading, walking, cooking. Home: 15593 Early Bird Cir Apple Valley MN 55124 Office: Minn Bureau Criminal Apprehension 1430 Maryland Ave E Saint Paul MN 55106 Home Phone: 612-501-8667. Business E-Mail: beth.comer@state.mn.us.

COMER, CLARENCE C., gas industry executive; b. 1948; married. BBA, Lamar U, 1971. Auditor Arthur Andersen & Co., 1971-75; contr. Stratford Tex., Inc., 1975-77; v.p. fin. Southdown Sugars Inc., 1977-79; treas. Southdown Inc., Houston, 1979-80, controller, then v.p., 1980-85, exec. v.p., 1985-86, pres., 1986—, COO, 1986—87, CEO, 1987—, pres., CEO, 1989—.

COMER, DONALD, III, investment company executive; b. NYC, June 23, 1938; s. Donald and Isabel (Anderson) C.; m. Jane Stephens, May 4, 1962; children: Jason Legare, Luke McDonald, Carrie St. George. BS, U. Ala., 1962. With Cowikee Mills, Eufaula, Ala., 1962-82, plant mgr., 1965-66, v.p., 1966-68, pres., treas., dir., 1968-82; pres., dir. Aurizon Inc., 1982—; past pres., treas., dir. Avondale Mills., Sylacauga, Ala. Past chmn. Ala. Ethics Commn. With USAF, 1961-64. Mem.: Mountain Brook Country (Birmingham). Home: 3905 Hillock Dr Birmingham AL 35213-3223

COMER, EVAN PHILIP, manufacturing executive; b. Cumberland Gap, Tenn., May 29, 1927; s. Evan Mitchell and Margaret Nola (Estep) C.; m. Mary Blanc, Aug. 28, 1948; children: Vivian, Jane. BA, Carson-Newman Coll., Jefferson City, Tenn., 1948; MA, Columbia U., NYC, 1949. Asst. prof. psychology, dir. student personnel and placement Furman U., Greensville, SC, 1949-52; self-employed writer, 1952-53; supervisory conf. leader Union Carbide Nuclear Co., Oak Ridge, 1953-55; instr. in-plant tng. U. Tenn., Knoxville, 1955-56; with Foote Mineral Co., 1956-67, 69-84, v.p., gen. mgr. chems. and minerals div., 1970-80, pres., chief exec. officer Exton, Pa., 1980-84, also bd. dirs.; pres., chief exec. officer, chmn. bd. Ashram Farm, Inc., Rutledge, Tenn., 1984-98. Mem. Pa. adv. bd. Liberty Mut. Ins. Co.; chmn. exec. com. , dir. Phila. Mfrs. Mut. Ins. Co. Pres. Southeastern C.C., Whiteville, NC, 1967-69; mem. adv. bd. Carson-Newman Coll.; bd. dirs. Pa. Sci. and Engring. Found.; mem. Pa. Gov's Sci. Adv. Com.; mem. adv. coun. Pa. Tech. Assistance Program, Pa. State U.; chmn. bd. Chester County Pvt. Industry Coun., 1983-84; mem. Jefferson County Planning Commn., Tenn., 1998—, Jefferson County Zoning Appeals Bd., 1998—; mem. regional resource stewardship coun. TVA, 2000—; pres. Jefferson County Hist. Soc., 2003-, bd. dir., treas. Dandridge Mcpl. Pub. Libr., 2006—; With USNR, 1945-46. Mem.: AIME, Am. Mining Congress, Ferroalloys Assn. (chmn. bd. dirs. 1983—84), Mining Club (NYC). Republican. Baptist. Personal E-mail: comanevan@bellsouth.net.

COMER, JAMES PIERPONT, psychiatrist, educator; b. East Chicago, Ind., Sept. 25, 1934; s. Hugh and Maggie (Nichols) C.; m. Shirley Ann Arnold, June 20, 1959 (dec. Apr. 1994), Bettye Fletcher Comer, July 11, 2004; children: Brian Jay, Dawn Renee. AB, Ind. U., 1956; MD, Howard U., 1960; MPH, U. Mich., 1964; DSc (hon.), U. New Haven, 1977; LittD (hon.), Calumet Coll., 1978; LHD (hon.), Bank St. Coll., NYC, 1987, Albertus Magnus Coll., 1989, Quinnipiac Coll., 1990, DePauw U., 1990; DSc (hon.), Ind U., 1991, Wabash Coll., 1991; EdD (hon.), Wheelock Coll., 1991; LLD (hon.), U. Conn., 1991; LHD (hon.), SUNY Buffalo, 1991, New Sch. for Social Rsch., 1991; DPed (hon.), R.I. Coll., 1991; DSc (hon.), Amherst Coll., 1991; LHD (hon.), John Jay Coll. Criminal Justice, 1991, Wesleyan U., 1991; DH (hon.), Princeton U., 1991; DSc (hon.), Northwestern U., 1991, Worcester Poly. Inst., 1991; LHD (hon.), U. Pa., 1992; DPed (hon.) (hon.), Niagara U., 1992; LHD (hon.), Hamilton Coll., 1992; DSc (hon.), Brown U., 1992; LHD (hon.), U. Mass. Lowell, 1992; DSc (hon.), Med. Coll. Ohio, 1992, Howard U., 1993, W.Va. U., 1993; LLD (hon.), Lawrence U., 1993; DSc (hon.), Morehouse Sch. Medicine, 1993; LLD (hon.), Columbia U., 1994, Boston Coll., 1994; LHD (hon.), Briarwood Coll., 1994, Cleve. State U., 1996; DSc (hon.), St. Mary's Coll., Md., 1996, Albion Coll., 1997, Conn. Coll., 1997, So. Conn. State Coll., 1998; DPed (hon.), Long Island U., 1999; LHD (hon.), Ea. Mich. U., 2000; LHD (hon.), N.C.State Univ., Rosemont Coll., 2002. Served with USPHS, Washington and Chevy Chase, Md., 1961-68; intern St. Catherine's Hosp., East Chicago, 1960-61; resident Yale Sch. Medicine, 1964-67; asst. prof. psychiatry Yale Child Study Center and dept. psychiatry, 1968-70, assoc. prof., 1970-75, prof., 1975-76, Maurice Falk prof. child psychiatry, 1976—; assoc. dean Yale Med. Sch., New Haven, 1969—. Dir. pupil svcs. Baldwin-King Sch. Project, New Haven, 1968-73; dir. sch. devel. program Yale Child Study Ctr., 1973-97, founder sch. devel. program adv. bd., 1997—; dir. Conn. Energy Corp., 1976-2000, Nat. Acad. Found. N.Y., N.Y.C., 1993-98; co-dir. Black Family Roundtable Greater New Haven, 1986-90; cons. Joint Commn. on Mental Health of Children, 1967-68, Nat. Commn. on Causes and Prevention of Violence, NIMH; 1976-77. Author: Beyond Black and White, 1972, Black Child Care, 1975, 2d edit., 1992, School Power, 1980, 2d. edit., 1993, Maggie's American Dream, 1988, Rallying the Whole Village: The Comer Process for Reforming Education, 1996, Waiting For a Miracle: Why Schools Can't Solve Our Problems-And How We Can, 1997, Child by Child: The Comer Process for Change in Education, 1999, The field guide to Corner Schools in Action, 2004, Leave No Child Behind: Preparing Today's Youth for Tomorrow's World, 2004; mem. editl. bd. Am. Jour. Orthopsychiatry, 1969-76, Youth and Adolescence, 1971-87, Jour. Negro Edn., 1973-83, rev. Africal Am. Edn., 2003-; guest editor Jour. Am. Acad. Child Psychiatry, 1985; columnist Parents mag.; contbr. articles to profl. jours. Bd. dirs. Yale Afro-Am. House, 1970-72, trustee Hazen Found., 1974-78 Field Found., 1981-88, Nellie Mae, Mass., 2002-, Wesleyan U., 1978-84, Nat. Coun. for Effective Schs., 1985-90, Albertus Magnus Coll., 1989-2000, Carnegie Corp., 1990-98, Milton S. Eisenhower Found., Washington, 1991—, Conn. State U., 1991-94, Tchrs. Coll, Columbia U., 1999-; profl. adv. bd. Children's TV Workshop, 1970-86; mem. adv. coun. Nat. Assn. Mental Health, Nat. Com. for Citizens in Edn., Hogg Found. for Mental Health, 1983-86, , Nat. Com. for Citizens in Edn., 1983—; mem. Nat. Bd. for Profl. Teaching Standards, Carnegie Forum on Edn. and the Economy, 1987-1991; mem. Nat. Commn. on Teaching and America's Future, Teachers College, Columbia U., 1994; mem. edn. adv. bd., bd. dirs. (hon.) Kids Voting USA, 1997—; mem. nat. evaluation adv. coun. Kellogg Youth Initiative Partnerships W.K. Kellogg Found., 1997—; adv. bd., Energy East, Bridgeport, Conn., 2000-04; mem. Com. Nat. Rsch. Coun., Institute of Med. of the Nat. Academies, 2001-2003; mem. Chair's Exec. Com., Yale U. Child Study Center, 2002-; mem. Blue Ribbon Panel Carroll and Milton Petrie New York City Teacher Fellowship Program, Teachers Coll., Columbia U., 2004-. Recipient Child Study Assn.-Wel-Met Family Life book award, 1975, Howard U. Disting. Alumni award, 1976, Rockefeller Public Svc. award, 1980, Media award NCCJ, 1981, Cmty. Leadership award Greater New Haven C. of C., 1983, Disting. Fellow award Conn. chpt. Phi Delta Kappa, 1984, Elm and Ivy award New Haven Found., 1985, Disting. Svc. award Conn. Assn. Psychologists, 1985, Outstanding Leadership award Children's Def. Fund, 1987, Whitney M. Young Jr. Svc. award Boy Scouts Am., 1989, Prudential Leadership award Prudential Found., 1990, Harold W. McGraw Jr. prize in Edn., 1990, James Bryant Conant award Edn. Commn. States, 1991, Disting. Svc. award Coun. Chief State Sch. Officers, 1991, Family Focus Nat. award, 1991, Charles A. Dana award for pioneering achievement in edn., 1991, Ind. U. Disting. Alumni Svc. award, 1992, Burger King Disting. Svc. to Edn. award, 1992, Conn. Assn. for Human Svcs. Pres. award, 1992, Golden Acorn award Bronx C.C., 1994, Presdl. citation Am. Ednl. Rsch. Assn., 1995, Health Trac Found. prize, 1996, Heinz Family award, 1996, Lehigh U. Outstanding Svc. to Coll. Edn. award, 1996, Ann Vanderbilt Achievement award for ednl. leadership, 1997, Great Friend to Kids award Assn. Youth Mus., 1997, Disting. Svc. medal Tchrs. Coll., 1997, Friends of the Family citation, Working Mother Mag., 1997, World of Children award Judge Baker Children's Ctr., 1997, Michael Bolton Lifetime Achievement award, 1997, Edn. award Inst. Student Achievement, 1999, Disting. Pub. Svc. award Conn. Bar Assn., 1999, Martin Luther Freedom award New Haven Chpt. NAACP, 2000; John and Mary Markle Found. scholar, 1969-74; James Comer NIMH Minority Fellowship established in his honor, 1991.; Disting. Svc. Award, Covenant Care, Inc., 2001, Disting. Life award, Am. Psychiatric Assn., 2003, Assn. Yale Alumni Med., Appreciation award, 2003, John P. McGovern Behavioral Science award, Smithsonian, 2004, Disting. Citizen award, West Haven Black Coalition, 2004, First Annual Tapestry award, New Haven Family Alliance, 2004, Conn. Black Nurses Assn. award, 2004, Friend of Public Edn. award, Conn. Assn. of Bds. of Edn., 2004. Mem. APA (Disting. Svc. award 1993), Am. Acad. Child Adolescent Psychiatry, Nat. Med. Assn., Nat. Mental Health Assn. (Lela Rowland Prevention award 1989), Am. Psychiat. Assn. (Agnes Purcell McGavin award 1990, Solomon Carter Fuller award 1990, Spl. Presdl. Commendation 1990, Disting. Svc. award 1993), Am. Orthopsychiat. Assn. (Vera S. Paster award 1990), Am. Acad. Child Psychiatry, Black Psychiatrists of Am., NAACP, Black Coalition of New Haven, Greater New Haven Black Family Roundtable (co-dir. 1986—), Alpha Omega Alpha, Alpha Phi Alpha. Avocations: photography, travel, sports. Office: Yale U Child Study Ctr 230 S Frontage Rd PO Box 207900 New Haven CT 06520-7900 E-mail: james.comer@yale.edu. *As a black child, I sometimes had doubts about my future opportunities for success in our predominantly white country. My parents counselled me never to let the issue of race stand in my way; that the time of greater opportunity for blacks would come. They advised me to work hard, prepare myself, to strive to be the best or among the best in every undertaking, and at the same time be respectful of all people, regardless of their abilities, race, beliefs, or station in life. I have lived by this advice and it has served me well. I have learned not to strive for top position but to let my work take me where it will in line with my interests.*

COMER, JAMES V., academic administrator; s. Forrest Eugene and Ruby Marie Comer; m. Susan J. Beeman, June 14, 1969; children: Jason E., Jami S. Long. MA, Assemblies of God Theol. Sem., Springfield, Mo., 1992. Prof. Am. Indian Coll. Assemblies of God, Phoenix, 1996—, pres., 2005—. Avocations: antique cars, woodworking. Home: 10020 N 15th Ave Phoenix AZ 85021 Home Phone: 602-284-0531; Office Phone: 602-944-3335.

COMERFORD, CRISTETA, chef; b. Philippines; naturalized, US; m. John Comerford; 1 child. B in Food Tech., U. Philippines; studied classic French cooking, Vienna. Chef La Ciel Restaurant, Vienna, Westin Restaurant, Washington, ANA Restaurant, Washington; asst. to exec. chef The White House, Washington, 1995—2005, exec. chef, 2005—. Achievements include being first woman appointed head chef of The White House. Office: The White House 1600 Pennsylvania Ave Washington DC 20500

COMEROTA, ANTHONY JAMES, vascular surgeon, biomedical researcher; b. Newark, Aug. 4, 1948; s. Louis Anthony and Eleanor Dorothy (Dombroski) C.; m. Elsa Benavides, Aug. 18, 1973; children: Anthony James, Maya Christine, Mark Anthony. BA, Millikin U., 1970; MD, Temple U., 1974. Diplomate Am. Bd. Surgery. Surg. resident Temple U. Hosp., Phila., 1974-78; vascular surgery fellow Good Samaritan Hosp., Cin., 1979-81; from asst. prof. to prof. surgery Temple U. Hosp, Temple U. Sch. Medicine, Phila., 1981-88, prof. surgery, chief vascular surgery, 1988—2002; dir. Ctr. for Vascular Diseases Temple U. Hosp., Temple U. Sch. Medicine, Phila., 1995—2002; dir., chief vascular surgery Jobst Vascular Ctr., Toledo; clin. prof. U. Mich., Ann Arbor, 2002—. Editor: Thrombolytic Therapy for Peripheral Vascular Disease, 1995; co-editor: Prevention of Venous Thromboembolism, 1994. Fellow ACS, Royal Australian Coll. Surgeons; mem. Am. Surg. Assn., Soc. Vascular Surgery, Peripheral Vascular Soc. (pres. 1988-89), Am. Venous Forum (pres. 2000-01), Phila. Acad. Surgery (pres. 1996-97), Temple U. Sch. Medicine Alumni Assn. (pres. 1993-95), Alpha Omega Alpha. Office: Jobst Vascular Ctr 2109 Hughes Dr # 400 Toledo OH 43606 Office Phone: 419-291-2088. Business E-Mail: acomerota@jvc.org.

COMEY, JAMES B., JR., lawyer, aerospace company executive, former federal agency administrator; b. Yonkers, NY, Dec. 14, 1960; m. Patrice Comey; 5 children. BS in Chemistry & Religion, Coll. William and Mary, 1982; JD, U. Chgo., 1985. Law clk. to Hon. John M. Walker US Dist. Ct., Manhattan, 1985—85; assoc. Gibson, Dunn & Crutcher, 1986—87; asst. U.S. atty. (So. dist.) N.Y. US Dept. Justice, Manhattan, 1987—93; ptnr. McGuire Woods, LLP, Richmond, Va., 1993—96; mng. asst. U.S. Atty. Office (Ea. dist) Va. US Dept. Justice, 1996—2002, U.S. atty. (So. dist.) N.Y., 2002—03, dep. atty. gen. Washington, 2003—05; sr. v.p., gen. counsel Lockheed Martin Corp., Bethesda, Md., 2005—. Former adj. prof. law U. Richmond; former chmn Corp. Fraud Task Force US Dept. Justice. Recipient Henry L. Stimson Medal, NYC Bar Assn., 1993. Avocations: squash, bicycling, New York Giants and Knicks, teaching Sunday school. Office: Lockheed Martin Corp 6801 Rockledge Dr Bethesda MD 20817-1877*

COMFORT, IRIS TRACY, writer; b. Racine, Wis. d. Arnold Thomas and Iva Dorothea Tracy; widowed; 1 child, Alain James. Student, U. Wis., Madison, U. Minn. Reporter St. Paul Dispatch, 1937-38; mem. pub. rels. staff Allis-Chalmers, Milw., 1942-45; editor-in-chief Where Mag., Chgo., 1946-47; owner, operator pub. rels. agy. Milw., 1948-49; freelance writer Milw. and Orlando, Fla., 1948—. Lectr. Dept. Def. Schs., Germany, 1991-92; lectr., presenter workshops in field. Author: Earth Treasures, 1970, Joey Tigertail, 1973, Lets Grow Things, 1974, Let's Read About Rocks, 1975, Echoes of Evil, 1981 (Book Club choice), repub. 2001, Shadow Masque, 1982 (Book Club choice), repub. 2001, Florida's Geological Treasures, 1998, also others. Mem. Mystery Writers Am., Authors' Guild, Nat. Speleological Soc., Ctrl. Fla. Mineral and Gem Soc., Fla. Mineral Friends, Romance Writers Am. Avocations: caving, photography, exotic and tropical gardening, rock and mineral collecting, psychic investigation. Home and Office: 2902 Oxford St Orlando FL 32803-6821 Office Phone: 407-894-3545. Personal E-mail: iriscomfort@earthlink.net.

COMFORT, WILLIAM TWYMAN, JR., banker; b. Ellsworth, Kans., Aug. 3, 1937; s. William Twyman and Leoti Dora (Shackleford) C.; m. Nathalie Pierrepont, June 6, 1964; children: Nathalie Pierrepont, William Twyman III, James Theodore, Stuyvesant Pierrepont. BA, Okla. U., 1959, LLB, 1961; DHL (hon.), Okla. U., 2001; LLM, NYU, 1964. With W.E. Hutton & Co., NYC, 1962-73, ptnr., 1969-73, sr. v.p., 1973-74, Citibank, NYC, 1974—; exec. dir. Citicorp Internat. Bank Ltd., London, 1976-78; chmn. bd. dirs. 399 Venture Ptnrs. Inc., Citigroup Venture Capital, Ltd. Chmn. investment com. CourtSquare Capital Ltd., Worldspan Corp.; adj. prof. Columbia Bus. Sch., NYC; bd. dirs. I-Flex, India; trustee John A. Hartford Found., Inc. Trustee NYU Law Ctr. Found.; former trustee Pine Mano Coll., Chestnut Hill, Mass.; advisor to bd. dirs. Old Westbury (L.I.) Gardens. With US Army, 1961. Mem. N.Y. Bar Assn., Okla. Bar Assn., Piping Rock Club (Locust Valley, N.Y.), Jupiter Island Club (Hobe Sound, Fla.). Home: 340 Duck Pond Rd Box 507 Locust Valley NY 11560-2404

COMFORT, WILLIAM WISTAR, mathematics professor; b. Bryn Mawr, Pa., Apr. 19, 1933; s. Howard and Elizabeth (Webb) Comfort; m. Mary Constance Lyon, Mar. 30, 1957; children: Martha Wistar, Howard III. BA, Haverford Coll., 1954; MS, U. Wash., 1957, PhD, 1958; MA ad eundem gradum, Wesleyan U., Middletown, Conn., 1969. Tchg. asst., rsch. asst. U. Wash., Seattle, 1954-58; B. Peirce instr. Harvard U., Cambridge, Mass., 1958-61; asst. prof. U. Rochester, NY, 1961-65; assoc. prof. U. Mass., Amherst, 1965-67; prof. math. Wesleyan U., 1967—2007, Edward Burr Van Vleck prof. math., 1982—2007, chmn. dept., 1969-70, 80-82, 96-97; ret., 2007. Vis prof Univ Ark, 1965, McGill Univ, Montreal, Canada, 1970—71, Univ Heidelberg, 1974, Istituto Matematico Leonida Tonelli, Pisa, Italy, 1974, Athens Univ, Greece, 1978, Univ Nacional Autonoma de Mex, 1983, Univ São Paolo, 1983, 99, Vrije Univ, Amsterdam, 1984, 95, Technische Hochschule Darmstadt, Germany, 1991, Univ Jaume I Castellon, Spain, 1995. Author (with S Negrepontis): The Theory of Ultrafilters, 1974, Continuous Pseudometrics, 1975, Chain Conditions in Topology, 1982; mem. editl. bd.: Procs Am Math Soc, 1972—75; editor (managing ed), 1974—75; mem. editl. bd.: Topology Procs, 1976—, Am Math Monthly, 1983—86, Karachi Jour Math, 1984—, Scientiae Mathematicae, 1992—, Topology and Its Applications, 1993—, Jour. Kerala Math. Assoc., 2004—; contbr. articles to profl. jours. Bd mgrs Haverford Col, 1971—74; trustee Ind Day Sch, Middlefield, Conn., 1972—75. Recipient Excellence-in-Teaching Award, Univ Rochester, 1966. Mem.: AAUP, Asn Concerned Scientists, Conn Acad Sci and Eng, Am Math Soc (coun 1972—75, 1982—93, assoc secy eastern region 1982—93), Math Asn Am, Phi Beta Kappa. Mem. Soc. Of Friends. Home: 3 Ball Ln Old Lyme CT 06371 Office Phone: 860-685-2632. Business E-Mail: wcomfort@wesleyan.edu.

COMINI, ALESSANDRA, art historian, educator; b. Winona, Minn., Nov. 24, 1934; d. Raiberto and Megan (Laird) C. BA, Barnard Coll., NYC, 1956; MA, U. Calif., Berkeley, 1964; PhD with distinction, Columbia U., NYC, 1969. Tchg. asst. U. Calif., Berkeley, 1964, vis. instr., 1967; preceptor Columbia U., 1965-66, 67-68, instr., 1968-69, asst. prof., 1969-74; vis. asst. prof. So. Methodist U., summers 1970, 72, assoc. prof. art history, 1974-75, prof., 1975—, univ. disting. prof., 1983—. Alfred Hodder resident humanist Princeton U., 1972-73; disting. vis. lectr. Oxford U., 1996; vis. asst. prof. Yale U., 1973; vis. humanist various univs.; lectr. in English, German and Italian; keynote spkr. Gewandhaus Symposia, Leipzig, Germany, 1983, 85, 87, 89, Mahler Internat Congress, Amsterdam, 1988, 95, Hamburg, 1989, Oxford, 1996, Montpellier, 1996, Internat. Mahler Fest, Boulder, Colo., 1998; featured spkr. Purchase, NY, 1989, Leningrad, 1990, Stockholm, 1991, Berlin, 1993, Bethoven Extravaganza, Milw., 1994, Schiele Symposium, Indpls., 1994, Helsinki, 1996, Schubertiads at Curtis Inst., Phila., Reed Coll., Oreg. and So. Meth. U., 1997, Santa Fe Opera, 1997-02, 06, Dallas Symphony Orch., 1998-2006, Indpls. Symphony Orch., 2007, Brahmsfest of So. Meth. U., 2005, Mozart Internat. Symposium U. Dublin, Ireland, 1999, San Diego Mus., 1999-2005, Giacometti Symposium, Nasher Sculpture Ctr., Dallas, 2005, 06, Neu Galerie, 2005, 06, 07, Mozartfest of So. Meth. U., 2006, Klimt Atelier, Vienna, 2006; panelist NEH Mus. and Pub. Programs, 1978—; vis. scholar Kalamazoo Coll., 1999. Author: Schiele in Prison, 1973, Egon Schiele's Portraits, 1974 (Nat. Book award nominee 1975, reissued 1990, Charles Rufus Morey Book award 1974), Gustav Klimt, 1975, reissued 1986, 90, 93, 01, also German, French and Dutch edit., Egon Schiele, 1976, reissued 1986, 94, 01, also German, French and Dutch edits., The Fantastic Art of Vienna, 1978, The Changing Image of Beethoven, 1987, Egon Schiele: Nudes, 1995, In Passionate Pursuit: A Memoir, 2004; contbg. author: World Impressionism, 1990, Käthe Kollwitz, 1992, Egon Schiele, 1994, Violetta and her Sisters, 1994, Salome, 1996, By a Finnish Fireside: An Evening with Akseli Gallen-Kallela and Gustav Mahler, 1997, The Visual Wagner, 1997, Irony and Gustav Mahler, 2000, Toys in Friend's Attic, 2001, Beethoven and His World, 2000, Pilgrimage to Schiele, 2005, The Two Gustavs: Klimt, Mahler, and Vienna's Golden Decade, 1897-1907; contbr. numerous articles to Stagebill, Arts Mag., English Nat. Opera, Chgo. Lyric Opera; also author various catalogue and book introductions, also book revs. for NY Times, Women's Art Jour. Awarded Grand Decoration of Honor for svcs. to Republic of Austria, 1990; recipient Charles Rufus Morey Book award Coll. Art Assn. Am., 1974, Laural award AAUW, 1979; named Outstanding Prof., 1977, 79, 83, 85, 86, 87, 88, 90, 98, 99, 2000, 01, 02, 03, 04, Laurence Perrine prize Phi Beta Kappa Gamma of Tex., 2003; AAUW travel fellow, 1966-87; NEH grantee, 1975; named Meadows Disting. Tchg. Prof., 1986-87, Tchr./Scholar of Yr., United Meth. Ch., 1996; Comini Lectr. Series in Art History named in her honor So. Meth. U., 2005. Mem. ASCAP, Nat. Mus. for Women in the Arts (nat. bd. 1997—), Coll. Art Assn. Am. (bd. dirs. 1980-84), Women's Caucus for Art (bd. dirs. 1974-78, Life Achievement award 1995, Tex. Women's Hall of Fame 2002), Tex. Inst. Letters. Democrat. Home: 2900 McFarlin Blvd Dallas TX 75205-1920 Office: So Meth U Divsn Art History Dallas TX 75275 Office Phone: 214-369-8523. Business E-Mail: acomini@smu.edu.

COMINOS, DION NICHOLAS, lawyer; b. LA, Dec. 4, 1962; AB, U. Calif. Berkeley, 1985; JD, U. Calif. Hastings Coll. Law, 1988. Bar: Calif. 1988. Ptnr. Gordon & Rees, LLP, San Francisco, 1987—, mng. ptnr., 2006—. Mem. steering com. profl. liability sect. Def. Rsch. Inst.; mem. steering com. Profl. Liability Underwriting Soc. No. Calif. Chpt., Assoc. of Def. Counsel No. Calif. Constrn. Practice Chpt. Mem.: ABA (mem. tort and practice sect.), Calif. Bar Assn. (bus. law practice sect.). Office: Gordon & Rees LLP Embarcadero Ctr West 275 Battery St 20th Fl San Francisco CA 94111 Office Phone: 415-986-5900 ext. 3133. Office Fax: 415-262-3714. E-mail: dcominos@gordonrees.com.

COMISKEY, MICHAEL PETER, lawyer; b. Oak Park, Ill., Oct. 13, 1948; s. John B. and Jeanne M. (Platt) C.; m. Barbara A. Twardowski, Apr. 24, 1981; children: Julianne, Bridget, Eleanor, Michael Patrick. BA, U. Notre Dame, 1970; JD magna cum laude (hon.), Harvard U., 1975. Bar: Ill. 1975, US Dist. Ct. (no. dist.) Ill. 1975, US Dist. Ct. (ctrl. dist.) Ill., US Court of Appeals (6th, 7th & 8th cirs), Supreme Ct. of Ill. Ptnr. Lord, Bissell & Brook, Chgo., 1983—. Spkr. in field. Contbr. articles to profl. jour. Mem. Notre Dame Alumni Assn., Notre Dame Club of Chgo.; bd of trustees Fenwick H.S. Mem.: Phi Beta Kappa, ABA (antitrust law, bus. law and ins. practice sect.), Chgo Bar Assn. Office: Lord Bissell & Brook 111 S Wacker Dr Chicago IL 60606 Office Phone: 312-443-0427. Office Fax: 312-896-6427. Business E-Mail: mcomiskey@lordbissell.com.

COMISKY, HOPE A., lawyer; b. Phila., Apr. 23, 1953; married; three children. BA with distinction, Cornell U., 1974; JD, U. Pa., 1977. Bar: Pa. 1977, U.S. Dist. Ct. (ea. dist.) Pa. 1978, D.C. 1979, U.S. Ct. Appeals (3d cir.) 1979, (6th cir.) 1996, (7th cir.) 2005, U.S. Supreme Ct. 1987, U.S. Dist. Ct. (mid. dist.) Pa. 1991, N.Y. 1993. Law clerk ea dist. U.S. Dist. Ct., Pa., 1977-78; assoc. Dilworth, Paxson, Kalish & Kauffman, Phila., 1978-84, ptnr., 1985-91, Anderson Kill & Olick, P.C., Phila., 1992-98, mng. ptnr. Phila. office, 1995-98; ptnr. labor and employment law group Pepper Hamilton LLP, Phila., 1998—. Co-chair ERISA and employment litigation practice group Pepper Hamilton LLP, 2005—06, mem. profl. responsibility coun., 2007—; spkr. in field. Contbr. articles to profl. jours. Bd. dirs. Phila. Sch., 1989-2003, pres. 2001-03, hon. bd. dirs., 2004—; bd. dirs. Fedn. Day Care Svcs., 1991-97, mem. exec. com., chmn. pers. practices com., 1985-91; bd. dirs. Ctr. for Literacy, 1996-, v.p., 2004-06, pres. 2006-, chmn. pers. com. 2000-; bd. dirs. Women's Law Project, 1998-2004, Fedn. Early Learning Svcs., 2003-. Mem. Am. Arbitration Assn. (comml. and employment arbitrator), the Coll. of Labor and Employment Attys. (elected mem.), Mortar Board, Phi Beta Kappa. Office: Pepper Hamilton LLP 3000 Two Logan Sq 18th & Arch Sts Philadelphia PA 19103-2799

COMISKY, IAN MICHAEL, lawyer; b. Phila., Feb. 5, 1950; s. Marvin and Goldye (Elving) C. BS magna cum laude, U. Pa., 1971, JD, 1974; LLM in Taxation, U. Miami, 1984. Bar: Pa. 1974, Fla. 1976, D.C. 1976, U.S. Ct. Appeals (3rd and 11th cirs.), U.S. Ct. Claims, U.S. Tax Ct., U.S. Supreme Ct., U.S. Dist. Ct. (ea. and mid. dist.) Pa., U.S. Dist. Ct. (so. dist.) Fla., U.S. Dist. Ct. (mid. dist.) Fla. Law clk. to Hon. Alfred Luongo Jr. U.S. Dist. Ct. Pa., Phila., 1974-75; asst. dist. atty. Office of Dist. Atty., Philadelphia County, Phila., 1975-78; asst. U.S. atty. So. Dist. Fla., 1978-80; spl. asst. Office of Dist. Atty., So. Dist. Fla., 1980; ptnr., white collar internal and govt. investigations group Blank Rome LLP, Phila., 1980—. Presenter various profl. seminars; guest TV and radio programs Co-author: Tax Fraud and Evasion (2 vols.); contbr. articles to profl. publs. Sec. Mann Ctr. Performing Arts. Mem. ABA (chmn. spl. projects com., past chmn. civil and criminal tax penalties com. tax sect., mem. CLE com. tax sect., mem. various coms. criminal justice and litig. sect.), ATLA, Am. Law Inst., Am. Coll. Tax Counsel, Fed. Bar Assn., Pa. Bar Assn., Fla. Bar Assn. (bd. govs. 1998-, chair investment com.), D.C. Bar Assn., Phila. Bar Assn., Assn. Fellows and Legal Scholars, Ctr. for Internat. Legal Studies (hon.). Avocations: gardening, jogging. Office Phone: 215-569-5646. Business E-Mail: icomisky@blankrome.com.

COMISO, JOSEFINO CACAS, research scientist; b. Narvacan, Philippines, Sept. 21, 1940; arrived in U.S., 1964; s. Severino Cacho and Silvestra (Cacas) C.; m. Diana Parreñas Jimenez, June 27, 1970; children: Glen Arnold, David Arnel, Melissa Jane. BS in Physics, U. Philippines, Quezon City, 1962; MS in Physics, Fla. State U., 1966; PhD in Physics, UCLA, 1972. Scientist Philippine Atomic Rsch. Ctr., Quezon City, 1962-63; instr. U. The Philippines, Quezon City, 1963-64; asst. rsch. physicist UCLA, 1972-73; rsch. assoc. U. Va., Charlottesville, 1973-77; sr. mem. tech. staff Computer Scis. Corp., Greenbelt, Md., 1977-79; phys. scientist Goddard Space Flight Ctr. NASA, Greenbelt, 1979—. Co-author: Arctic & Antarctic Sea Ice, 1992; contbr. articles to profl. jours. Pres. Philippine-Am. Acad. Sci. and Engrs., Washington, 1987. Fellow Japan Soc. Promotion Sci.; mem. Am. Geophys. Union, Am. Phys. Soc., Internat. Glaciol. Soc., Com. Polar Meteorology and Oceanography, Electromagnetics Acad. Achievements include space based assessments and studies of surface temperatures, sea ice distributions, heat and salinity fluxes in polynyas, and phytoplankton blooms in the polar regions and the development of satellite sensor algorithms. Home: 11013 Elon Dr Bowie MD 20720-3509 Office: NASA/GSFC Lab for Hydrospheric and Biospheric Scis Code 614.1 Greenbelt MD 20771-0001 Home Phone: 301-262-1148; Office Phone: 301-614-5708. Business E-Mail: josefino.c.comiso@nasa.gov.

COMITAS, LAMBROS, anthropologist, educator; b. NYC, Sept. 29, 1927; s. Dennis and Magdaline (Livanis) C.; m. Irene Mousouris. AB, Columbia U., 1948, PhD in Anthropology, 1962. Instr. anthropology Columbia U., NYC, 1958-61, asst. prof., 1962-64, assoc. prof. anthropology and edn. Tchrs. Coll., 1965-67, prof., 1967-87, Gardner Cowles prof. anthropology and edn., 1988—, dir. div. philosophy, social scis. and edn., 1979-96, dir. Inst. Latin Am. and Iberian studies, 1977-84; dir. Rsch. Inst. study of man, 1985-2001; adminstr. Ruth Landes Meml. Rsch. Fund, 1991—2006; pres. Comitas Inst. Anthrop. Study, 2003—. Mem. drug abuse, clin., behavioral and psychosocial rsch. rev. com. Nat. Inst. Drug Abuse, 1977-81. Author books and articles in field. With U.S. Army, 1946-47. Office Edn. fellow, 1968-69, Guggenheim fellow, 1971-72; Fulbright grantee, 1957-58, Nat. Inst. Drug Abuse grantee, 1975-79. Mem. Soc. Applied Anthropology (pres. 1970-71), Am. Anthrop. Assn., Am. Ethnol. Soc., Nat. Acad. Edn. (chmn. com. anthropology and edn.), N.Y. Acad. Scis. Home: 1107 5th Ave New York NY 10128-0145 Office: Teachers Coll Columbia U New York NY 10027 Office Phone: 212-678-4040. Business E-Mail: lc137@columbia.edu.

COMMANDER, CHARLES EDWARD, lawyer, real estate consultant; b. Jacksonville, Fla., Aug. 17, 1940; s. Charles Edward Jr. and Eleanor (Wood) C.; m. Victoria Coxe, Aug. 10, 1963; children: Eleanor, Charles IV, Christopher. BS in Commerce, Washington & Lee U., 1962; JD, U. Fla., 1965. Bar: Fla. 1966. Atty., assoc. ptnr. Mahoney, Hadlow, Chambers and Adams, Jacksonville, 1966-73; pres. Barnett Winston Properties, Jacksonville, 1973-74; founding ptnr. Commander, Legler, Werber, Dawes, Sadler & Howell, Jacksonville, 1974-91; ptnr., mgmt. com. Foley & Lardner, 1991—2003. Cons. First Union Nat. Bank Fla., Jacksonville, 1990-95; chmn. bd. dirs. First Nat. Bank, Jacksonville, 1979-84; chmn. Property Investment Svcs., Inc., Jacksonville, 1974—; bd. Everbank Fin. Corp., 1994- , Everbank FSB, 2002-; trustee Builders Investment Group, King of Prussia, Pa. and Fullerton, Calif., 1977-80; dir. Koger Equity Inc., 1993-95, Computer Power, 1974-79, 86-92; bd. dirs. U. Fla. Law Ctr. Assn., 2002- , Patriot Transp. Holding Co., 2004-; mem. bd. advisors Lanier Upshaw, Inc. Editor Law Review U. Fla., 1964-65; reporter Fla. Law Revision Comm., 1975-76. Trustee The Bolles Sch., Jacksonville, 1980-90, U. Fla. Law Ctr. Assn., 2004-, Delta Waterfowl Found., 2005—; pres. U. No. Fla. Found., 1994-97, Cummer Gallery of Art, 1993—2002; bd. dirs. Jacksonville Housing Authority, 1995—2003; vice chmn. Mus. Sci. and History, Jacksonville, 1968-73, Jacksonville Zool. Soc., 1972-76, Jacksonville Housing Comm., 2006—; pres. bd. dirs. The River Club, Jacksonville, 1977-84. Episcopalian. Avocations: fishing, hunting, boating, farming. Office: Foley & Lardner Ste 1300 One Independent Dr Jacksonville FL 32202-5017 E-mail: ccommander@foley.com.

COMMANDER, CLAYTON W., computer scientist; b. Fort Walton Beach, Fla., Aug. 23, 1982; s. Warren F. and Deborah I. Commander; m. Leah A. Susi, June 18, 2005. BS in Math., U. Fla., Gainesville, 2003, PhD in Ops. Rsch., 2007. Computer scientist U.S. Air Force Civil Svc., Eglin AFB, Fla., 2003—. Mem.: U. Fla. Alumni Assn., Phi Beta Kappa. Jewish.

COMMENT, ANNA MAE, retired principal; b. St. Thomas, VI, Jan. 26, 1947; d. Warren Elson and Eugenia Eudora Brown; m. Denis X. Comment, May 16, 1970; children: Angela Jeanne McRae, Xavier Warren. BA in English, St. Mary-of-the-Woods Coll., Terre Haute, Ind., 1969. Cert. French/English transls. Nestle Co., Vevey, Switzerland, 1972. Coord. Farley Manning Pub. Rels. Firm, NYC, 1969—70; typist, transl. Nestle Co. S.A., Vevey, Switzerland, 1971—72; adminstrv. asst. Petro Cons. S.A., Geneva, 1973—74; tchr. English grade 12 Eudora Kean HS, St. Thomas, VI, 1982—84; exec. asst. Dept. Econ. Devel., St. Thomas, VI, 1984—89; prin. Sts. Peter and Paul Cath. Sch., St. Thomas, VI, 1989—94; ret. Commr. 1st Bd. Civil Rights Commn., VI, 1985; coord. for VI 1st VI Smithsonian Exhibit on Washington Mall, 1989; cons. World of Difference/Anti-Defamation League, Palm Beach, Fla., 1995—. Columnist: newspaper column; contbr. poetry to anthologies. Active Journey to Justice St. Jude Cath. Ch. Named Woman of Yr., Bus. and Profl. Women of US VI, 1994. Mem.: LWV (Vol. award 2003). Avocations: reading, writing, travel, music appreciation. Home: 4551 NW 26 Pl Boca Raton FL 33434

COMMIRE, ANNE, playwright, writer, editor; b. Wyandotte, Mich., Aug. 11, 1939; BS, Eastern Mich. U., 1961; postgrad., Wayne State U., NYU. Author: (plays) Shay, 1973, Transatlantic Bridge, 1977, Put Them All Together, 1978, Sunday's Red, 1982, Melody Sisters, 1983, Starting Monday, 1988; author: (with Mariette Hartley) (book) Breaking the Silence, 1990; editor: Something About the Author, 1970—90, Yesterday's Authors of Books for Children, 1977—78, Historic World Leaders, 1994, Women in World History: A Biographical Encyclopedia, 1999—2002 (Dartmouth medal, 2002), Dictionary of Women Worldwide, 2006. Recipient Eugene O'Neill Theatre award, 1973, 1978, 1983, 1988; grantee, Creative Artists Program, 1975; playwriting grant, Rockefeller Found., 1979. Mem.: PEN, Writers Guild Am., Dramatists Guild, Authors Guild. Home: 11 Stanton St Waterford CT 06385-1400

COMMON, (LONNIE RASHID LYNN, COMMON SENSE), rap artist; b. Chgo., Mar. 13, 1972; Singer: (albums) Can I Borrow a Dollar?, 1992, Resurrection, 1994, One Day It'll All Make Sense, 1997, Like Water for Chocolate, 2000, Electric Circus, 2002, Be, 2005, Finding Forever, 2007, (songs) Love of My Life (An Ode to Hip Hop), 2002 (Grammy award for Best R&B Song, 2003); actor: (films) Smokin' Aces, 2006.*

COMMONER, BARRY, biologist, educator; b. Bklyn., May 28, 1917; s. Isidore and Goldie (Yarmolinsky) C.; m. Lisa Feiner, 1980; children by previous marriage: Lucy Alison, Frederic Gordon. AB with honors, Columbia U., 1937; MA, Harvard U., 1938, PhD, 1941; DSc (hon.), Hahnemann Med. Coll., 1963, Clark U., 1967, Grinnell Coll., 1968, Lehigh U., 1969, Williams Coll., 1970, Ripon Coll., 1971, Colgate U., 1972, Cleve. State U., 1980; LLD (hon.), U. Calif., 1974, Grinnell Coll., 1981; DSc (hon.), St. Lawrence U., 1988; DHL (hon.), Lowell U., 1990; DSc (hon.), Conn. Coll., 1992, Queens Coll., 2001. Asst. biology Harvard, 1938-40; instr. biology Queens Coll., 1940-42; asso. editor Sci. Illus., 1946-47; asso. prof. plant physiology Washington U., St. Louis, 1947-53, prof., 1953-76, chmn. dept. botany, 1965-69; dir. Washington U. (Center for the Biology of Natural Systems), 1965-81, Univ. prof. environ. sci., 1976-81; prof. dept. geology Queens Coll., Flushing, NY, 1981-87, prof. emeritus, 1987—, dir. Center for the Biology of Natural Systems, 1981-2000, sr. scientist, 2000—. Vis. prof. cmty. health Albert Einstein Coll. of Medicine, N.Y.C., 1981-87; disting. univ. prof. indsl. policy U. Mass., Lowell, 1992-95; pres. St. Louis Com. for Nuclear Info., 1965-66, bd. dirs., 1966; mem. Nat. Tb Commn. on Air Conservation, 1966-68; bd. dirs. Scientists Inst. Pub. Info., 1963—, co-chmn., 1967-69, chmn., 1969-78, chmn. exec. com., 1978—; chmn. spl. cons. group sonic boom Dept. Interior, 1967-68; mem. adv. coun. on environ. edn. Office Edn., HEW, 1971; mem. internat. sponsoring com. Chaim Weizmann Centenary Celebration, 1974-75; mem. adv. com. Coalition Health Communities, 1975; mem. sec.'s adv. coun. Dept. Commerce, 1976; mem. sci. adv. coun. on dioxin Vietnam Vets. Am. Found., 1985—; mem. sci. adv. N.Y. State Com. on Sci. and Tech., 1981—; mem. adv. bd. Com. for Responsible Genetics, 1983—. Author: Science and Survival, 1966, The Closing Circle, 1971 (Phi Beta Kappa award), (Internat. prize City of Cervia, Italy), La Technologia del Profitto, 1973, The Poverty of Power, 1976 (Premio Iglesias award, Sardinia, Italy 1978), Ecologia e Lotte Sociali, 1976, l'energia alternativa, 1978, The Politics of Energy, 1979 (Premio Iglesias award 1982), Se Scoppia La Bomba, 1984, Il Cerchio Da Chiudere, 1986, Making Peace With the Planet, 1990; editorial bd. World Book Ency., 1968-73, Environment mag., 1977; mem. adv. bd. Science Year, 1967-72; editorial adv. bd. Hon. Chemosphere, from 1972; bd. sponsors In These Times, 1976—. Bd. cons. experts Rachel Carson Trust for Living Environment, 1967—; adv. com. Center for Devel. Policy, 1978; mem. bd. Univs. Nat. Anti-War Fund; adv. bd. Fund for Peace, 1978, Citizens Party candidate for pres. of U.S., 1980. Served to lt. USNR, 1942-46. Recipient Newcomb Cleveland prize AAAS, 1953; 1st Humanist award Internat. Humanist and Ethical Union, 1970; medal AIA, 1979; decorated comdr. Order of Merit Italy, 1977 Fellow AAAS (chmn. com. sci. in promotion of human welfare 1958-65, dir. 1967-74, chmn. com. on environ. alterations 1969-72), Am. Sch. Health Assn. (hon.); mem. Soc. Biol. Chemists, Soc. Gen. Physiologists, Am. Soc. Plant Physiologists, Sierra Club, Nat. Parks Assn. (trustee 1968-70), Soil Assn. Eng. (hon. life v.p.), Am. Chem. Soc., Am. Soc. Biol. Chemists, Fedn. Am. Scientists, Ecol. Soc. Am., Inst. Environmental Edn. (trustee), Phi Beta Kappa, Sigma Xi. Office: Queens Coll Ctr for Biol Natural Systems Flushing NY 11367 E-mail: commoner@qc.cuny.edu.

COMMONS, RICHARD B., headmaster; m. Lindsay Commons. BA, U. Va.; MA, Stanford U., Breadloaf Sch. of English, Middlebury Coll. Former staff mem. Camp Dudley, YMCA, Woodberry Forest Sch., Va., McDonough Sch., Md.; headmaster Groton Sch., Groton, Mass., 2002—. Bd. trustees Groton Sch., 2004—05. Office: Groton School PO Box 991 Groton MA 01450-0991 Office Phone: 978-448-3363. Office Fax: 978-448-6355.*

COMP, PHILIP CINNAMON, medical researcher; b. Kewanee, Ill., Feb. 28, 1945; s. Franklin Howard and Alberta (Cinnamon) C.; m. Carol Lee Winter, May 11, 1974; children: Vanessa Cinnamon, Justin Philip, Aubrie Elizabeth. BA, Reed Coll., 1967; MD, U. Wash., 1971; PhD, U. Okla., 1978. Intern, then resident U. Pa. Hosp., Phila., 1971-74; fellow allergy sect. U. Okla. Health Sci. Ctr., Oklahoma City, 1974-76, asst. prof. medicine, 1976-82, assoc. prof. medicine, 1982-88, prof. medicine, 1988—, dir. thrombosis/coagulant lab., 1979—99, dir. gen. clin. rsch. ctr., 2000—04; attending physician med. svc. VA Med. Ctr., Oklahoma City, 1976—, assoc. chief of staff rsch., 1992—; dir. adult sect. Okla. Comprehensive Hemophilia Treatment Ctr., Oklahoma City, 1980—. Affiliated mem. cardiovasc. biology rsch. program Okla. Med. Resident Found., Oklahoma City, 1988—; program dir. Gen. Clin. Rsch. Ctr., 2000—04. Avocations: amateur mycology, breadmaking. Office: VA Med Ctr 921 NE 13th St (151) Oklahoma City OK 73104 Home Phone: 405-720-9326; Office Phone: 405-271-6466.

COMPAGNON, ANTOINE MARCEL, French language educator; b. Brussels, July 20, 1950; came to U.S., 1985; s. Jean and Jacqueline (Terlinden) C. Ecole, Nat. des Ponts et Chaussees, Paris, 1975; D es Lettres, U. Paris VII, 1985. Rsch. attache Centre Nat. de la Recherche Scientifique, Paris, 1975-78; lectr. Ecole Poly., Paris, 1978-85, French Inst., London, 1980-81, U. Rouen, France, 1981-85; prof. Columbia U., NYC, 1985—, Blanche W. Knopf prof., 1991—; prof. U. Le Mans, France, 1989-90, U. Paris, Sorbonne, 1994—2006, Coll. France, 2006—. Vis. prof. U. Pa., Phila., 1986, Phila., 90. Author: La Seconde Main, 1979, Ferragosto, 1985, Proust entre deux Siecles, 1989; editor: Marcel Proust, Sodome et Gomorrhe, 1988. Fellowship Found. Thiers, 1975-78, Guggenheim Found., 1988, All Souls Coll., Oxford U., 1994. Mem. Am. Acad. Arts and Scis. Office: Columbia U 517 Philosophy Hall New York NY 10027 E-mail: amc6@columbia.edu.

COMPAIN, RITA, librarian; b. NYC, Dec. 4, 1926; d. Benjamin and Sara (Modell) Romer; m. Ernest A. Compain, Apr. 17, 1948 (div. 1987); children: Michael, Daniel, Andrew. BS, CUNY, 1947; MLS, L.I. U., 1963; Profl. Dipl., St. John's U., NYC, 1975; postgrad., Columbia U., 1969-70, Lang. & Lit. Inst. Genosee, 1985. Children's librarian Bklyn. Pub. Library, 1947-49; library coordinator Oceanside (N.Y.) pub. schs., 1959-61; librarian Franklin Sq. (N.Y.) pub. schs., 1961-71; staff developer BOCES Nassau, Jericho, N.Y., 1974-76, BOCES Ulster County, N.Y., 1992-93; serials librarian Am. Mus. Natural History, NYC, 1977-79; library cons. Rita Compain Agy., NYC, 1980-85; project dir. "Open Sesame" Am. Reading Council, NYC, 1985-88; staff developer library media Kingston (N.Y.) pub. schs., 1988-93. Asst. prof. L.I. U., Greenvale, 1969-75; libr. cons. Great Neck Pub. Schs., 1975-76; adj. prof. SUNY, New Paltz, 1988-94, U. South Fla., Sarasota, 1996-99; cons., lectr. in field; mem. com. nassau County Jail Libr. Pilot Program, East Meadow, 1979. Contbg. author: Open Sesame Guide to Implementation, 1987; contbg. author, dir. video: Teacher Training Film, 1986; author: New Connections: An Integrated Approach to Literacy, 1994, Giants a Thematic Guide, 1992. Recipient Educator award, Young Playwrights Festival, 2001, 2002. Mem. Nassau-Suffolk Sch. Libr. Assn. (pres. 1969-70), Amnesty Internat., Ringling Mus. Art, Delta Kappa Gamma. Avocations: tennis, golf, travel. Home: 7742 Whitebridge Gln University Park FL 34201-2244 Personal E-mail: becbev@comcast.net.

COMPANS, RICHARD W., microbiology educator; b. Syracuse, NY, Sept. 15, 1940; m. Marian Merly Compans. BA magna cum laude, Kalamazoo Coll., 1963; PhD, Rockefeller U., 1968. Asst. prof. The Rockefeller U., 1969-73, assoc. prof., 1973-75; prof. dept. microbiology The U. Ala., Birmingham, 1975-92, prof. dept. biochemistry, 1985-92; prof., chmn. dept. microbiology and immunology Emory U., 1992—. Guest investigator Inst. Cancer Rsch., Villejuif, France, 1968; hon. fellow John Curtin Sch. Med. Rsch., Canberra, Australia, 1968-69; vis. scientist Nat. Inst. Med. Rsch., Mill Hill, U.K., 1998-99; vis. investigator Scripps Clinic and Rsch. Found., 1982; vis. prof. U. Geneva, 1988-89, U. Marburg, Germany, 1999; numerous univ. appointments including sr. scientist Cancer Ctr., U. Ala., 1975-92; dir. Electron Microscope Core Facility, 1975-92dir. Molecular Cell Biology Grad. Program, 1982-92, others; mem. various virology task forces. Editor: Virus Research, 1983—2002; mem. editl. bd. Jour. Gen. Virology, 1972—77, Jour. Virology, 1974—82, 1991—94, Intervirology, 1974—90, Virology, 1974—76, 1992—, CRC Handbook Series in Clin. Lab. Sci., Archives of Virology, 1980—83, Jour. Biol. Chemistry, 1983—88, Current Topics Microbiology and Immunology, 1985—; contbr. numerous articles to profl. jours. Recipient Wright A. Gardner award Ala. Acad. Scis., 1988, Alexander von Humboldt Rsch. award, 1999; grantee NIH, 1972—, others. Mem. Am. Acad. Microbiology, Am. Soc. Virology, Am. Soc. Biol. Chemists, Am. Soc. Cell Biology, Am. Assn. Immunologists, Soc. Gen. Microbiology, Am. Soc. Microbiology, Soc. Mucosal Immunology, Phi Beta Kappa. Office: Emory U Sch Med Dept Micro & Immunology Rm 3001 1510 Clifton Rd NE Atlanta GA 30322-4218 Office Phone: 404-727-8230. E-mail: rcompan@emory.edu.

COMPTE, MARIA EMILIA, physician, educator, administrator; b. Buenos Aires, Jan. 17, 1958; arrived in U.S., 1989, naturalized, 2002; d. Alberto J. Compte and Hilda M. Hostansky. MD, U. Buenos Aires, 1984; MPH, TM, Tulane U., 1992. Cert. Ednl. Commn. for Fgn. Med. Grads., 1995, in tropical medicine and travel health Am. Soc. Tropical Medicine and Hygiene, 2000, lic. Ministry of Health, Argentina, 1984, physician U.S. Med. Licensing Exam. Bd., 1997. Pvt. med. practice, Buenos Aires, 1985—87; med. dir. & program adminstr. Dooley Found. -Intermed, Departamento de Gracias a Dios, Honduras, 1988—91; dep. med. dir. Item Home-Hosp. Corp., Buenos Aires, 1993—94; vol. program dir. Dooley Found.-Intermed Internat., NYC, 1994—2003, v.p. for programs, 2004—; dir. cmty. medicine Mercy Coll., Dobbs Ferry, NY, 1998—2004, asst. prof., 1998—2004; v.p. programs Intermed Internat., 2004—. Bd. dirs. Intermed Internat., NYC; adj. assoc. prof. St. John's U., NYC, 1998—2000, CUNY, NYC, 1998—2001, Adelphi U., Garden City, NY, 1999. Recipient Excellence in Vol. Med. Work award, Friends of the Americas, 1991; fellow, NY Acad. Medicine, 2002. Mem.: AAUP, APHA, Argentine-Am. Med. Soc., The Global Health Coun., Am. Com. on Clin. Tropical Medicine & Traveler's Health, Am. Soc. Tropical Medicine & Hygiene, Soc. Tchrs. of Family Medicine (assoc.), Infectious Disease Soc. Am. (assoc.), Tulane Med. Alumni Assn., The Cornell Club, Tulane Club NY. Independent. Roman Catholic. Achievements include design, development, implementation, and evaluation of comprehensive rural health and emergency programs for refugees in Central America. Avocations: anthropology, tennis, trekking. Office: Dooley Found Intermed Internat 420 Lexington Ave Rm 2331 New York NY 10170

COMPTON, ALLEN T., retired state supreme court justice; b. Kansas City, Mo., Feb. 25, 1938; 3 children. BA, U. Kans., 1960; LL.B., U. Colo., 1963. Pvt. practice, Colorado Springs, 1963-68; staff atty. Legal Svcs. Office, Colorado Springs, 1968-69, dir., 1969-71; supervising atty. Alaska Legal Svcs., Juneau, Alaska, 1971-73; pvt. practice Juneau, 1973-76; judge Superior Ct., Alaska, 1976-80; justice Alaska Supreme Ct., Anchorage, 1980-98, state supreme ct. chief justice, 1995-97, ret., 1998. Office Phone: 907-783-3189. E-mail: atcgwd@aol.com.

COMPTON, ANN WOODRUFF, news correspondent; b. Chgo., Jan. 19, 1947; d. Charles Edward and Barbara (Ortlund) C.; m. William Stevenson Hughes, Nov. 25, 1978; children: William Compton, Edward Opie, Ann Woodruff, Michael Stevenson. BA, Hollins Coll., Va., 1969. Reporter, anchorwoman WDBJ-TV (CBS), Roanoke, Va., 1969-70, polit. reporter, state capitol bur. chief Richmond, Va., 1971-73; corr. ABC News, 1973—, NYC, 1973-74, White House corr. Washington, 1974—79, 1981—84, 1989—, Congl. corr., 1979—81, 1984—86, chief Ho. of Reps. corr., 1987-88. Trustee Washington Journalism Ctr., 1978-93, Hollins Coll., 1987-93; bd. dirs. Freedom Forum Ctr. for Media Studies, NY, 1984-2000. Co-recipient Alred I. duPont-Columbia U. award, 2002, Emmy award, 2002, George F. Peabody award, 2002; named Mother of Yr., Mother's Day Com., 1988; named to Journalism Hall of Fame, Soc. Profl. Journalists, 2000, Radio Hall of Fame, 2005; fellow, Washington Journalism Ctr., 1970. Mem. White House Corrs. Assn. (dir. 1977-79, v.p. 2006-07, pres. 2007-), Radio-TV Corrs. Bd. (chmn. 1987). Office: ABC News Washington Bur 1717 DeSales St NW Washington DC 20036-4407 also: White House Corrs Assn Ste 300 1920 N St NW Washington DC 20036*

COMPTON, CHARLES (KIP), communications executive; b. 1972; BS in Computer Sci., Mass. Inst. Tech., MEE in EE and Computer Sci. Dir., Tech. Strategy Cisco Systems, Inc., 1998—2001, dir., Entertainment Solutions, 1998—2001, sr. dir., Video & IPTV Devel., 2006—; v.p., Vide and Media Engring. Comcast Cable Comm., 2003—06. Named one of 40 Executives Under 40, Multichannel News, 2006. Office: Cisco Systems Inc 170 W Tasman Dr Bldg 10 San Jose CA 95134-1706 Office Phone: 408-526-4000. Office Fax: 408-526-4100.

COMPTON, CLYDE D., lawyer; BA in Polit. Sci., DePauw Univ.; JD, Ind. Univ. Sch. of Law, Bloomington. Bar: US Supreme Ct. Atty. Portage

City Coun. and Portage Twp. Trustee, Hodges & Davis PC, Merrillville, Ind. Bd. dir. (past pres.) Vis. Nurse Assn.; bd. dir. Salvation Army, Goodwill Industries; mem. (past pres.), Ind. Univ. Law Sch. Alumni Assn.; master Calumet Am. Inn of Ct. Mem.: Am. Trial Lawyers Assn., Ind. Bar Found. (dir., treas., sec., pres.), Lake County Bar Assn., Am. Bar Assn., Indiana State Bar Assn. (pres.-elect 2004, bd. mgrs., mem., Ho. of Del., treas.). Presbyn. Office: Hodges & Davis PC 8700 Broadway Merrillville IN 46410 Office Phone: 219-641-8700. Office Fax: 219-641-8710. Business E-Mail: ccompton@hodgesdavis.com.*

COMPTON, DIANE GROAT, professional counselor, researcher; b. Long Branch, NJ, July 25, 1958; d. Richard Boyd and Alicia Elizabeth (Winsch) Groat; m. Robert Dale Compton, Aug. 21, 1977; 1 child, Robert Dale Jr. AA with spl. honors, Gulf Coast CC, Miss., 1992; BS summa cum laude, U. So. Miss., Hattiesburg, 1994, MS in Counseling Psychology, 1997. Cert. Nat. Bd. Cert. Counselors, 1998, lic. profl. counselor Miss. State Bd. Lic. Profl. Counselors, 1999. Lic. profl. counselor Meml. Behavioral Health, Gulfport, 1998—2003, Renaissance Counseling Ctr., Gulfport, 2003—04; lic. profl. counselor in pvt./solo practice Changes, Biloxi, Miss., 2004—06, Synergy Behavioral Health Gulf Coast, Biloxi, 2006—. Intrusive thought and social-cognitive devel. following hurricane Katrina rsch. asst. USM Prof., Dr. Manuel Sprung, Long Beach, Miss., 2006—. Author: (poster presentation) Measuring Religiosity: Differences in Liberals and Conservatives, (paper presentation) Physical Child Abuse and Religion: A Look at the Effect of Religious Values on the Perception of Corporal Punishment and Abuse. Vol. Harrison County Family Ct. Youth Shelter, Gulfport, 1991—96; various local ch. positions Christ United Meth. Ch., Long Beach, Miss., 1989—; bd. mem. Harrison County Habitat for Humanity, Gulfport, 1991—94. Named to Hall of Fame, Gulf Coast C.C., 1991—92, Nat. Deans List, 1992, Pres.'s List, U. So. Miss., 1992—94; recipient Honors Program scholarship, Gulf Coast C.C., 1992, Morton scholarship, Bd. Higher Edn. and Ministry of the United Meth. Ch., 1992—93, Jr. Coll. Achievement award, U. So. Miss., 1992—94, Nat. Deans List, 1993, Fielding Grad. U. Psychology Faculty Honors award, Fielding Grad. U., 2006. Mem.: APA (assoc.), U. SO. Miss. Alumni Assn. United Methodist. Avocations: hiking, backpacking, travel. Home Phone: 601-914-4895; Office Phone: 601-914-4895.

COMPTON, DORIS MARTHA, lay worker; b. Eudora, Kans., July 9, 1927; d. Roscoe John and Mabel Ann Robinson; 1 child, Christine Lee Compton-Smith. BA, Ft. Hays State U., Hays, Kans., 1949; MA, U. Ark., Fayetteville, 1951; Cert. Lay Pastor, Sterling Coll., Kans., 2000. Commissioned Lay Pastor Presbytery of No. Kans./Kans., 2000; life credential tchr. Dept. of Edn./Kans., 1951. Tchr. of English, speech, journalism, drama, and Latin Kans. Pub. Schs., Winfield, Ashland, Marysville, Washington, 1951—71; English instr. Am. U. Cairo, 1972—74; founder and dir. Colegio Internacional Miguel Otero Silva, Ciudad Guayana, Venezuela, 1975—80; speech and linguistics U. P.R./Interamerican U., Rio Piedras, PR, 1982—84; temp. English instr. Kans. State U., Manhattan, 1987—89; chmn. English dept. Ramses Coll. for Girls, Cairo, 1989—93; stated supply pastor Little Blue River Parish, Narka, Kans., 1993—97; commd. lay pastor Faith United Ch. Presbyn., Clifton, Kans., 2000—. English instr. for an immersion sch. for ESL Fordham U., San Juan, 1982; completed evaluation for Commonwealth HS, Rio Pedro, P.R. Mid. States Assn., Phila., 1981—82, mem. evaluation team for St. Dunstan's Sch., St. Croix, U.S. Virgin Islands, 1982. Author: (book of poetry) Whisper In The Pines (awards for individual poems); contbr. poems to lit. jours. ($1000 by Am. Poetry Assn., San Francisco, 1985, $200 by Internat. Soc. Poets, Washington, D.C., 1996, First Pl. by Kans. Author's Club, 2000); singer: (solo vocal concerts) Egypt, Venezuela, Am.; performer: (47 dramatic prodns.) Egypt, Venezuela, P.R., Am. Spkr. Presbyn. Ch., 81 cities in Kans., Nebr., Iowa, Mo., Ill.; author of VBS curriculum Presbyn. Ch., Clifton, Kans., 2001—03; display of art and antiquities for schools pub. schs., 5 cities in Kans., 1996—2003. Recipient numerous scholarships for internat. peace-making, Presbyn. Ch., 1994—. Mem.: Synod of Mid Am. (assoc.; commr. of higher edn. 2001—03), Presbytery of No. Kans. (assoc.), Clifton (Kans.) C. of C. (assoc.). Presbyterian. Avocations: music, collecting art and antiquities, poetry, travel, caring for two grandchildren. Home: 207 East Bartlett Clifton KS 66937 Office: Faith United Ch Presbyterian PO Box 156 Clifton KS 66937 Office Phone: 785-455-3482.

COMPTON, J. DOUGLAS, lawyer; b. Norfolk, Va., July 5, 1951; s. Emmett Mobley and Alice Elizabeth Compton; m. Nina Nickerson, June 19, 1982. BS, U. Va., Charlottesville, 1973; JD, Mercer U., Macon, Ga., 1978. Bar: N.Mex. 1979, Ga. 1980, U.S. Ct. Appeals (10th cir.) 1979, U.S. Ct. Appeals (11th. cir.) 1983, U.S. Dist. Ct. N.Mex. 1979, U.S. Dist. Ct. (mid dist.) 1980. Assoc. Bivins, Weinbrenner & Regan, Las Cruces, N.Mex., 1979—81, Bovis, Kyle & Burch, Atlanta, 1982—83, Kemp Smith Duncan & Hammond, Albuquerque, 1983—85; shareholder, dir. Butt, Thornton & Baehr, Albuquerque, 1985—2003; ptnr. Cuddy, Kennedy, Albetta & Ives, LLP, Santa Fe and Albuquerque, N.Mex., 2003—04; of counsel Lewis and Roca Jontz Dawe LLP, Albuquerque, 2005—06, Compton & Assocs., Albuquerque, 2007. Named to Nat. Moot Ct., Macon, 1976—78; mem. Mercer Law Rev., 1977—78; adj. prof. N.Mex State U., Las Cruces, 1981—82; guest lectr. Ga. State U., Atlanta, 1983. Author: Medical Malpractice, Annual Survey Edition, 1988, Vaccine Manufacturer Liability: Chipping Away at Strict Liability to Save the Product, 1990; contr.: articles to profl. jours. including N.Mex. Law Rev. Mem.: ABA (litigation, tort and ins. sects., trial practice com.), N.Mex Bar Assn., Albuquerque Bar Assn., Order of Barristers, Atlanta Bar Assn., Ga. Bar Assn., Fedn. of Def. and Corp. Counsel, Def. Lawyers Assn. N.Mex., UVA Club of N.Mex. Republican. Office: Compton & Assocs 400 Gold Ave SW Ste 1300W Albuquerque NM 87102 Office Phone: 505-243-5755. Office Fax: 505-243-5855. Personal E-mail: jdouglascompton@msn.com.

COMPTON, JAMES E., air transportation executive; married; 2 children. B in Econs., M in Econs., U. Ill., Chgo. Mgr. forecasting and revenue analysis United Airlines, 1984—93; with United Parcel Svc. of Am., 1993—95; sr. dir. pricing Continental Airlines, Inc., Houston, 1995, sr. v.p. mktg., 2003—04, exec. v.p. mktg., 2004—. Bd. dirs. Airline Tariff Pub. Co. Office: Continental Airlines Inc PO Box 4607 Houston TX 77210*

COMPTON, JOHN JOSEPH, philosophy educator; b. Chgo., May 17, 1928; s. Arthur Holly and Betty Charity (McCloskey) C.; m. Marjorie Ann Yaple, July 8, 1950; children: Elizabeth Holly, Catherine Marchus, John Arthur. BA, Coll. of Wooster, 1949; MA, Yale U., 1951, PhD, 1953. Asst. prof. philosophy Vanderbilt U., Nashville, 1952-55, assoc. prof., 1955-68, prof., 1968-98, prof. emeritus, 1998—, chmn. or acting chmn. dept., 1966-73, 84-85, 88-89, 93-95. Vis. prof. Colo. Coll., Colorado Springs, 1977, Wesleyan U., Middletown, Conn., 1984. Contbr. articles to profl. jours. and chpts. in books. Mem. bd. advisers Matchette Found., 1968—; trustee Coll. of Wooster, Ohio, 1975—. Recipient Harbison award for disting. teaching Danforth Found., 1966; fellow Belgian-Am. Edn. Found., 1956-57, sr. fellow NEH, 1974-75, fellow Ctr. for Humanities, Wesleyan U., 1974-75. Mem. AAAS, AAUP, Am. Philos. Assn. (sec. ea. div. 1970-73, v.p. 1974), Metaphys. Soc. Am. (pres. 1979), Soc. for Phenomenology and Existential Philosophy, So. Soc. for Philosophy and Psychology, Philosophy of Sci. Assn., Soc. for Values in Higher Edn. (Kent fellow 1951), Phi Beta Kappa. Democrat. Avocations: hiking, camping, gardening, choral singing, cooking. Home: 3708 Whitland Ave Nashville TN 37205-2430 Personal E-mail: jjcompton@aol.com.

COMPTON, NORMA HAYNES, retired dean, artist; b. Washington, Nov. 16, 1924; d. Thomas N. and Lillian (Laffin) Haynes; m. William Randall Compton, Mar. 27, 1946; children: William Randall, Anne Elizabeth. AB, George Washington U., 1950; MS, U. Md., 1957, PhD, 1962; D of Letters, Purdue U., 1996. Rschr. Julius Garfinckel & Co., Washington, 1955; tchr. Montgomery Blair High Sch., Silver Spring, Md., 1955-57; instr. U. Md., 1957-60, teaching and rsch. fellow Inst. Child Study, 1960-61, assoc. prof., 1962-63; psychology extern St. Elizabeths Hosp., Washington, 1962-63; assoc. prof. Utah State U., 1963-64, prof., 1964-68, head dept. clothing and textiles, 1963-68, dir. Inst. for Rsch. on Man and His Personal Environment, 1967-68; dean Sch. Home Econs. Auburn (Ala.) U., 1968-73; dean Sch. Consumer and Family Scis. Purdue U., 1973-87, prof. family studies, 1987-90; faculty The Edn. Ctr., Longboat Key, Fla., 1991-2000, mem. ednl. adv. bd., 1995-98. Cons. Burgess Pub. Co., Mpls., 1975-81, Nat. Advt. Rev. Bd., N.Y.C., 1978-82; bd. dirs. Armour & Co., Phoenix, 1976-82, Home Hosp., Lafayette, Ind., 1983-89; adv. com. Women's Resource Ctr. of Sarasota, Fla., 1992-96; chair Adv. Commn. Status Women, Sarasota, 1993-96; mem. advocates coun. Family Law Network Sarasota, 1994-2000; exec. bd. Sarasota-Manatee Phi Beta Kappa Assn., 1996-99. Author: (with Olive Hall) Foundations of Home Economics Research, 1972, (with John Touliatos) Approaches to Child Study, 1983, Research Methods in Human Ecology/Home Economics, 1988; contbr. articles to profl. jours. Trustee Plymouth Harbor Inc., Sarasota, 2003—; pres. Plymouth Harbor Residents Assn., Sarasota, 2005—07. Recipient Woman of Impact Lifetime Achievement award, 1997. Mem.: PEO, APA, Nat. League Am. Pen Women (v.p. Sarasota br. 2000—04), Am. Assn. Family and Consumer Sci., Sigma Xi, Phi Beta Kappa, Psi Chi, Omicron Nu, Phi Kappa Phi. Congregational United Ch. Christ. E-mail: normahc@aol.com.

COMPTON, OLIN RANDALL, consulting electrical engineer, researcher; b. Parsons, W.Va., Apr. 12, 1925; s. Troy William and Strauda Belle (Robinson) C.; m. Patricia Ruth Osborne, June 3, 1947; children: Patricia Randall, Olin Bryan, Lisa Adrienne, Barry Christopher. BSEE, W.Va. U., Morgantown, 1949; Cert., Advanced Sch. Electric Utility Engring., Pitts., 1961. Registered profl. engr., Va. Jr. engr. Va. Electric & Power Co., Richmond, 1949-56, asst. supt elec. equipment, 1956-59, supt. elect. equipment, 1959-64, asst. substa. engr., 1965-79, elec. systems coord., 1979-83, corp. engring. advisor, 1983-85, prin. engr., 1985-91; pvt. practice cons., elec. rsch. Richmond, 1991—. Chmn. C76 Am. Nat. Standards Inst., Washington, 1968-72, C29, 1983-86; U.S. expert on transformers Internat. Electrochem. Commn., Geneva, Switzerland, 1982-86, on insulators, 1986-89. Contbr. 60 articles to profl. jours. Dir. Ctrl. Va. Ednl. TV Group, Richmond, 1972-79; commr. Tuckahoe Little League, Richmond, 1972-80; dir. United Meth. Lay Tng. Sch., Richmond, 1973-79; Native Am. Ministries coord. Va. Conf. United Meth. Ch., 1995—; chmn. State Spl. Edn. Adv. Com., Richmond, 1976-79; constrn. chmn., 1995-97, bd. dirs. Richmond Metro Habitat for Humanity, Inc., 1995—. 2d lt. USAAF, 1943-47. Fellow IEEE (chmn. substa. com. 1976-78, chmn. transformer com. 1985-88, Disting Svc. awards, best paper prizes 1948, 89). Republican. Avocation: bible study. Home and Office: 8423 Kalb Rd Richmond VA 23229-4133 Office Phone: 804-270-3732. Personal E-mail: olincompton@comcast.net.

COMPTON, R. BRIAN, finance company executive; s. Ralph Lewis and Marilynn Ruth Compton; m. Theresa Ann Bardwil, Feb. 11, 1984; children: Andrew Brian, Jack Henry. BA in Econs., UCLA, 1982. CPA Calif., 1986. CPA KPMG, LA, 1982—88; mgr. planning analysis PepsiCola Co. East, Phila., 1988—92; contr. Villeroy & Boch, Princeton, NJ, 1992—94; dir. ops. fin. Coach, NYC, 1994—99; sr. v.p. fin., CFO, CIO Universal Studies Hollywood, Universal City, 1999—2004; pres. Tax Resolution Svcs. Co., Encino, Calif., 2004—. Bd. mem. Discover A Star Found., LA, 2002—04; scout leader Boy Scouts Am., LA, 2002—. Mem.: AICPA, Calif. Soc. CPAs.

COMPTON, RALPH THEODORE, JR., electrical engineering educator; b. St. Louis, July 26, 1935; s. Ralph Theodore and Ethel (Evans) C.; m. Lorraine Fielding, Nov. 9, 1957; children: Diane Marie, Ralph Theodore III, Richard Thomas. S.B., MIT, 1958; M.Sc., Ohio State U., 1961, PhD, 1964. Jr. engr. DECO Electronics, Leesburg, Va., 1958-59; sr. engr. Battelle Meml. Inst., Columbus, Ohio, 1959-62; asst. supr. Antenna Lab., Columbus, 1962-65; asst. prof. Case Inst. Tech., Cleve., 1965-67; guest prof. Tech. Hochschule, Munich, 1967-68; assoc. prof. Ohio State U., Columbus, 1968-78, prof. elec. engring., 1978-91; pres. Compton Rsch., Inc., Columbus, 1992—. Cons. to various orgns., U.S., Europe, Israel, 1969—. Author: Adaptive Antennas-Concepts and Performance, 1988; contbr. chpts. to books, articles to profl. jours. Fellow Battelle Meml. Inst., 1961; NSF fellow, 1967; recipient Outstanding Paper awards Ohio State Electro-Sci. Lab., 1978, 80, 82, M. Barry Carlton award IEEE Aerospace and Electric Systems Soc., 1983, Sr. Research award Ohio State U. Engring. Coll., 1983 Fellow IEEE (assoc. editor Jour. Trans. on Antennas Propagation 1970); mem. Antenna and Propagation Soc. (chmn. Columbus chpt. 1971-72), Sigma Xi (sec.-treas. Case Inst. Tech. chpt. 1965-67), Pi Mu Epsilon Home and Office: 477 Poe Ave Worthington OH 43085-3036 Office Phone: 614-885-0907. Business E-Mail: compton@ieee.org.

COMPTON, ROBERT H., lawyer; Adminstrv. v.p., gen. counsel Ashland (Ky.) Petroleum Co., until 1988; adminstrv. v.p. Ashland Oil, Inc., Russell, Ky., 1988-92; bus. cons., atty pvt. practice, Ashland, 1992—. Chmn. West Penn/W.Va. AAA, 1999—; magistrate Juvenile Ct., Lawrence County, Ohio.

COMPTON, W. DALE, physicist, researcher, engineer; b. Chrisman, Ill., Jan. 7, 1929; s. Roy L. and Marcia (Wood) D.; m. Jeanne C. Parker, Oct. 14, 1951; children: Gayle Corinne, Donald Leonard, Duane Arthur. BA, Wabash Coll., 1949; MS, U. Okla., 1951; PhD, U. Ill., 1955; DEng (hon.), Mich. Technol. U., 1976. Physicist U.S. Naval Ordnance Test Sta., China Lake, Calif., 1951-52, U.S. Naval Research Lab., Washington, 1955-61; prof. physics U. Ill. at Urbana, 1961-70, dir. coordinated sci. lab., 1965-70; dir. chem. and phys. scis., exec. dir. sci. research staff, v.p. research Ford Motor Co., Dearborn, Mich., 1970-86; sr. fellow Nat. Acad. Engring., 1986-88; disting. prof. indsl. engring. Purdue U., West Lafayette, Ind., 1988—2004, disting. prof. indsl. engring. emeritus, 2004—, interim head Sch. Indsl. Engring., 1998-2001. Mem. Presdl. Commn. for Award of Medal of Sci., 1978—80; vis. com. Nat. Bur. Stds., 1975—79, chmn. vis. com., 1979; mem. coun. Nat. Acad. Engrs., 1990—96, coun. mem., home sec., 2000—; bd. govs. NRC, 1991—95, 2000—06, com. engring. and tech. sys., 1996—97, chmn., 1997—99. Author: (with J.H. Schulman) Color Centers in Solids, 1962; editor: Interaction of Science and Technology, 1969, Design and Analysis of Integrated Manufacturing Systems, 1988; co-editor (with J. Heim): Manufacturing Systems, Foundations of World Class Practice, 1992, Engineering Management: Creating and Managing World Class Operations, 1997. Mem. energy rsch. adv. bd. Dept. Energy, 1979—80; bd. dirs. Mich. Cancer Found., 1975—86; Coordinating Rsch. Coun., 1983—85; adv. com. Combustion Rsch. Facility Sandia Nat. Lab., 1983—86; bd. govs. Argonne Nat. Lab., 1983—86; mem. Coun. Energy Engring. Rsch., 1983—2001. Recipient M. Eugene Merchant Mfg. medal, ASME/SME, 1999, Disting. Svc. award, U. Ill. Coll. Engring. Alumni, 2002. Fellow AAAS, Am. Phys. Soc., Soc. Automotive Engrs., Engring. Soc. Detroit, IC2 Inst. U. Tex.; mem. NAE, Rsch. Soc. Am.

COMPTON, WILLIAM F., retired air transportation executive; b. Apr. 1947; m. Dreana Compton. A in Aerospace, Miami-Dade Coll. Flight instr., 1966; pilot TWA, 1968; exec. v.p. ops. Trans World Airlines, Inc., St. Louis, 1996—97, pres., COO, 1997—99, pres., CEO, 1999—2001, TWA LLC (subsidiary Am. Airlines), 2001; ret. Chmn. TWA br. Air Lines Pilots Assn., 1991-95, mem. exec. bd.; dir., gen. mgr., exec. v.p. Opa Locka Flight Ctr.; pilot Iran Air and Nigeria Airways; chief pilot Make Believe Farm/Arabian Horse World mag.; guest lectr. Stanford U. Grad. Sch. Bus./Law Sch., Midwest Acad. Mgmt.

COMPTON, WILLIAM HENRY, JR., mental health services professional; b. Rockford, Ill., Oct. 6, 1945; s. William Henry and Rosella Louise Compton; 1 child, Edward Errol Ellis-Compton. BA, U. Akron, 1969, MA, 1986. Dir. Project Return: the Next Step, LA, 1994—. Chmn. bd. Pacific Clinics, Arcadia, Calif., 2003—; bd. mem. Nat. Mental Health Assn., Alexandria, Va., 2002—, Protection and Advocacy Inc., Sacramento, 2002—. Exec. com. mem. Southland Theatre Artists Goodwell Event, LA, 2000—03. Recipient Clifford Beers award, Nat. Mental Health Assn., 2001, Consumer Adv. award, Internationa Assn. Psychosocial Rehab. Svcs., 2002, The Howie Harp award, Calif. Network Mental Health Clients, 2002, Helping Move Lives Forward Reintegration award (2nd Pl.), Eli Lilly, 2003. Office: Project Return: The Next Step 1138 Wilshire Suite 100 Los Angeles CA 90017 Personal E-mail: bilbelvoir@aol.com.

COMPTON, WILLIAM THOMAS, real estate investor; b. Bedford, Ind., Dec. 1, 1945; s. Thomas Franklin and Dorothy Jane (Smith) C.; m. Nancy Marie Radocchia, Sept. 13, 1969 (div. Aug. 1994); children: Kimberly Dawn, Lindsay Ann; m. Mary Elizabeth Thody, Aug. 17, 2006. BS in Mgmt., MIT, 1968, Postgrad., 1968-70. Cert. data processor. Sr. systems analyst First Nat. Bank Boston, 1970-73; systems analyst Gen. Computer Systems, Wellesley, Mass., 1973-76; bus. systems analyst Fram Corp., East Providence, R.I., 1976-78; v.p. Span Mgmt. Systems, East Providence, 1978; project leader Prime Computer Inc., Natick, Mass., 1979-81; owner Compton Software Solutions, Tiverton, R.I., 1981-88; prodn. foreman Tillotson Rubber Co., Inc., Fall River, Mass., 1988-89. Author several computer software programs, 1982-85. Loaned officer United Fund Boston, 1970. Mem. Data Processing Mgmt. Assn. (cert. data processing instr. 1985-86). Lodges: Kiwanis (local v.p. 1985, pres. 1985-86). Democrat. Methodist. Avocation: model railroading.

COMRAS, REMA, retired library director; b. NYC, Oct. 26, 1936; d. Manuel and Zita (Kessel) C.; m. Jose Simonet, June 22, 1981. BA, U. Fla., 1958; MLS, Syracuse U., 1960. Libr. Queensborough (N.Y.) Pub. Libr., 1960-61, Spl. Svcs., U.S. Army, Germany and France, 1962-64; asst. head libr. City of Hialeah, Fla., 1964-73, libr. dir. Fla., 1973-89; ret., 1989. Mem. Beta Phi Mu. Home: 1735 Lenox Ave Miami FL 33139-2414 Personal E-mail: remacom@aol.com.

COMSTOCK, AMY L., social services administrator; BA, Bard Coll.; JD, U. Mich. Atty., U.S. Dept. Edn., 1988—93; asst. gen. counsel for ethics Dept. of Education, 1993—98; assoc. counsel to the Pres. White House, 1998—2000; dir. U.S. Office of Govt. Ethics, 2000—03; CEO, Parkinson's Action Network, Washington, 2003—. Office: Parkinsons Action Network Ste 1120 1025 Vermont Ave NW Washington DC 20005 Home Phone: 301-871-9652; Office Phone: 202-638-4101. Business E-Mail: acomstock@parkinsonsaction.org.

COMSTOCK, BETH (ELIZABETH J.), marketing executive; b. Aug. 30, 1960; married; 2 children. BS in Biology, Coll. of William and Mary, 1982. Program dir. Nat. Cable TV Assn., Washington, Arlington Cmty. TV, Va.; publicist, media mgr. NBC, Washington, 1986, corp. comm. mgr. NYC; publicity dir. media rels. Turner Broadcasting, NYC, 1990-92; dir. entertainment publicity CBS/Broadcast Group, NYC, 1992-93; v.p. news media rels. NBC, NYC, 1993-96, sr. v.p. corp. comm. and media rels., 1996—98; v.p., corp. communications GE Co., NYC, 1998—2003, corp v.p. mktg., chief mktg. officer, 2003—05, pres., NBC Universal digital media, mkt. devel., 2005—. Bd. dir. Genworth Financial, 2004—, Healthline Networks, 2007—; invited spkr. in field. Trustee Smithsonian Cooper-Hewitt Nat. Design Mus. Named a Rising Star, 50 Most Powerful Women in Bus., Fortune, 2006; named Mktg. Executive of the Year, BtoB mag., 2003, PR Professional of the Year, PR Week mag., 2004; named one of Magnificent Seven Gurus of Innovation, BusinessWeek, 2005, 100 Most Powerful Women in Entertainment, Hollywood Reporter, 2006, America 's Top Women in Bus.-Game Changers, Pink mag. & Forté Found., 2007; recipient Clarion award Women in Comm., 1995, Aiming High award, Legal Momentum, 2005, Matrix award for Corp. Comm., NY Women in Comm. Inc., 2006. Mem.: Assn. of Nat. Advertisers, Inc. (bd. dir.). Office: NBC Universal 30 Rockefeller Plz Ste 4225 New York NY 10112-4225*

COMSTOCK, DALE ROBERT, mathematics professor; b. Frederic, Wis., Jan. 18, 1934; s. Walter and Frances (Lindroth) C.; m. Mary Jo Lien, Aug. 18, 1956; children— Mitchell Scott, Bryan Paul. BA, Ctrl. Wash. State Coll., 1955; MS, Oreg. State U., 1962, PhD, 1966. Tchr. math. Kennewick (Wash.) High Sch., 1955-57, 59-60; instr. Columbia Basin Coll., Pasco, Wash., 1956-57, 59-60; programmer analyst Gen. Electric Co., Hanford Atomic Works, Richland, Wash., 1963; prof. math. Cen. Wash. U., Ellensburg, 1964—, dean Grad. Sch. and Research, 1970-90; on leave as sr. program mgr. U.S. ERDA, also Presdl. interchange exec., 1976-77; mem. Pres.'s Commn. on Exec. Devel., 1976-77; bd. mem. Grad. Record Exam/Ednl. Testing Svc., 1980—83; bd. dirs. Council Grad. Schs. in U.S., 1981-84, dean in residence, 1984-85. Cons. Indian program NSF, 1968, 69, USIA, India, 1985, NSF, Saudi Arabia, 1986; mem. grant proposal rev. panels NSF, 1970, 71, 76, 77, 89, 90; pres. Western Assn. Grad. Schs., 1979-80, sec.-treas. 1984-90; pres. N.W. Assn. Colls. and Univs. for Sci., 1988-89; Russian exch. prof., St. Petersburg, 1993; vis. prof. U. Wash., 1990-91. With U.S. Army, 1957-59. NSF fellow, 1960-61; grantee, summer 1964 Mem. Am. Math Soc., Math. Assn. Am., Assn. Computing Machinery (exec. com.), Soc. Indsl. and Applied Math., Northwest Coll. and Univ. Assn. for Sci. (pres. 1980-83) Methodist.

COMSTOCK, ROBERT DONALD, JR., real estate executive; b. Miami, Fla., Sept. 28, 1921; s. Robert Donald Sr. and Gertrude C.; m. Mary Evans, Oct. 12, 1949; children: Carol Frances, Robert Donald III (dec.). BS in Commerce, U. Miss., 1943. Lic. real estate broker. Acct. New Orleans Pub. Service Co., 1946-47; salesman, br. mgr. Capitol Records, Inc., New Orleans and Charlotte, N.C., 1948-51; regional v.p. Atlanta, 1952-57; owner, pres. Comstock Distbg. Co., Atlanta, 1957-74, Comstock and Assocs., Atlanta, 1968-74, Cartridge Control Corp., Atlanta, 1968-80, Comstock Properties, Atlanta, 1980—. Pres. Ctr. for Rehab. Tech., Ga. Tech. U., Atlanta, 1987-91, chmn. bd., 1991—. Mem. Atlanta Arts Alliance, 1970—, Atlanta Symphony, 1970—; bd. dirs. Christian Council Met. Atlanta, 1975-77; trustee So. Ctr. for Internat. Studies; mem. Atlanta Hist. Soc. Served to exec. officer U.SS. Pollux, 1943-46, PTO. Named #1 Distbr. CBS Records, Columbia Broadcasting, N.Y.C., 1965, 69, Outstanding Distbr. Columbia Phonographs, Columbia Broadcasting, 1968, 70-72. Mem. Atlanta Bd. Realtors, Capital City Club, Commerce Club, Breakfast Club (pres. 1970-71), Trinity Presbyn. Ch. Men's Club (pres. 1977, Rotary (pres. Atlanta Midtown 1978-79), Omicron Delta Kappa. Avocations: golf, swimming, foreign affairs. Home and Office: 3400 Ridgewood Rd NW Atlanta GA 30327-2418

COMSTOCK, ROBERT FRANCIS, lawyer; b. Lincoln, Ill., June 4, 1936; s. William Bryan and Mary Euceba (Durham) C.; m. Jean Joyce Herring, May 9, 1970; children: James, Michael, Kelly, Jennifer, Margaret. AB, Cath. U., 1958, LLB, 1964. Bar: U.S. Dist. Ct. 1965, U.S. Ct. Appeals (DC cir.) 1965, U.S. Tax Ct. 1971. Ptnr. Comstock & Reilly LLP, Washington, 1965—. Chmn. bd. dirs. Balt. Bancorp, 1991, Met. Fed. Savs. & Loan, Bethesda, Md., 1986-87, Met Holding Co., Bethesda, 1985-87, First Continental Bank, Silver Spring, Md., 1983-86; dir. Nat. Capital Bank Washington, 1999—. Trustee, vice chmn. bd. trustees Cath. U. Am., Washington, 1987—; bd. dirs. Cath. Cemeteries Washington, 1986—, Cath. Youth Orgn. Capt. USAF, 1958-61. Named Knight of St. Gregory, Knight of Holy Sepulchre, Papal Award of Holy See, named to Athletic Hall of Fame, Cath. U., 1985. Mem. ABA, DC Bar Assn., Cath. U. Alumni Assn. (bd. govs.), Columbia Country Club (Chevy Chase, Md.), Univ. Md. M. Club. Roman Catholic. Avocation: sports. Home: 7707 Brookville Rd

Chevy Chase MD 20815-3933 Office: Comstock & Reilly LLP Ste 300 5225 Wisconsin Ave NW Washington DC 20015-2014 Office Phone: 202-966-5788. E-mail: rfcomstock@aol.com.

COMTE DE BOISDAUPHIN, LORD OF QUENDON, See SERVIEN, LOUIS-MARC

COMUS, LOUIS FRANCIS, JR., lawyer; b. St. Marys, Ohio, Feb. 26, 1942; BA, Antioch Coll., 1965; JD, Vanderbilt U., 1968. Bar: N.Y. 1969, Ariz. 1973. Dir. Fennemore Craig P.C., Phoenix, 1975—. Notes editor Vanderbilt Law Rev., 1967-68. Fellow Am. Coll. Trust and Estate Counsel; mem. ABA, State Bar Ariz., Maricopa County Bar Assn. Office: Fennemore Craig PC 3003 N Central Ave Ste 2600 Phoenix AZ 85012-2913 Home Phone: 602-996-9391; Office Phone: 602-916-5314. E-mail: lcomus@fclaw.com.

CON, ADAM JONATHAN, choral conductor, music educator; b. Vancouver, British Columbia, Canada, Sept. 14, 1962; s. William and Loretta Con; life ptnr. Christopher Kent Bowen, May 1, 2003; 1 child, Andrew Bowen. B in Music Edn., U. BC, Vancouver, 1986, M Music Edn., 1988; Ph.D, Choral Music Edn., Fla. State U., Tallahassee, Florida, 1999—2002. Cert. tchr. levels I-III Am. Orff Schulwerk Assn. Dir. of choirs and bands York Ho. Sch., Vancouver, 1994—99; condr. Statesboro (Ga.) So. Cmty. Chorus, Statesboro, Ga., 2002—; educator, chmn. music edn. Ga. So. U., Statesboro, 2005—. Chmn. music edn. Ga. So. U., Statesboro, 2005—. Mem.: Am. Choral Directors Assn. (Ga. state chmn. multicultural music 2003—06), Omicron Delta Kappa. Home Phone: 912-681-1162. Personal E-mail: ajcphd@hotmail.com. Business E-Mail: adamcon@georgiasouthern.edu.

CONA, LOUIS, publishing executive; married; 3 children. BS, NYU. Advt. sales positions USA Today, Scholastic Inc.; sales rep. to advt. divsn. mgr. People mag., 1989—94; assoc. pub. InStyle, pub., 1996—2001, Vanity Fair, 2001—02, v.p., pub., 2002—05, The New Yorker mag., 2005—. Office: The New Yorker Conde Nast Publs 4 Times Sq New York NY 10036*

CONABOY, RICHARD PAUL, federal judge; b. Scranton, Pa., June 12, 1925; m. Marion Hartnett; children: Mary Ann, Richard, Judith, Conan, Michele, Kathryn, Patrick, William, Margaret, Janet, John, Nancy. BA, U. Scranton, 1945; LLB, Cath. U. Am., 1950. Bar: Pa. 1951. Ptnr. firm Powell & Conaboy, Scranton, 1951—54; dep. atty. gen., 1953—62; assoc. firm Kennedy O'Brien & O'Brien, 1954—62; judge Pa. Ct. Common Pleas, 1962—79, pres. judge, 1978—79; judge U.S. Dist. Ct. (mid. dist.) Pa., Scranton, 1980—, chief judge, 1989—93, sr. judge, 1993—. Pres. Pa. Joint Council on Criminal Justice System, 1971-79; mem. Nat. Conf. Juvenile Justice, Nat. Conf. Corrections. Contbr. articles to legal jours. Bd. dirs. Marywood Coll., U. Scranton; apptd. chmn. U.S. States Sentencing Commn., 1994. Mem. Pa. Conf. State Trial Judges (pres. 1976-77, v.p. 1973-76, sec. 1968-73), ABA, Pa. Bar Assn., Am. Judicature Soc. Office: US Dist Courthouse & Post Office Bldg PO Box 189 Scranton PA 18501-0189

CONANT, ALLAH B., JR., lawyer; b. Waco, Tex., July 24, 1939; s. Allah B. and Frances Louise (James) C.; m. Sheila Conant; children: Heather Lee Arsham, Lisa Lynn, Leslie Marie Thorne; stepchild, Thomas R. Bone II. BA, N. Tex. State Coll., Denton, 1961; JD cum laude, Baylor U., 1963. Bar: Tex. 1963, US Tax Ct. 1963, US Dist. Ct. (no. dist.) Tex. 1964, US Dist. Ct. (so. dist.) Tex. 1969, US Ct. Appeals (5th cir.) 1970, US Supreme Ct. 1971, US Ct. Appeals (8th cir.) 1975, US Ct. Appeals (4th and 7th cirs.) 1978, US Ct. Appeals (3d and 11th cirs.) 1981, US Dist. Ct. (ea. dist.) Tex. 1986, US Dist. Ct. (we. dist.) Tex. 1986, US Ct. Appeals (10th cir.) 1987, US Ct. Appeals (2d cir.), 2004; bd. cert. Tex. Trial Law, Tex. Bd. Legal Specialization. Since practiced in, Dallas; ptnr. Shank, Irwin, Conant, Lipshy & Casterline, 1964-90; owner ABC Ranch, 1981-89; of counsel Whittenburg Whittenburg and Schachter, 1990; mem. Conant Whittenburg French & Schachter, Dallas, 1991-99; ptnr. Conant French & Chaney, LLP, Dallas, 1999—2005; ret., 2006—. Contbr. to legal jours. Trustee St. John's Episcopal Sch., 1987-90; bd. dirs. The Libr. at Cedar Creek, 2007—. With USMC Res., 1957—63. Fellow Am. Bar Found. (life), Tex. Bar Found. (life), Dallas Bar Found. (life); mem. ABA (coun. gen. practice sect. 1977-80, chmn. 1982-83, del. 1983-86), Dallas Bar Assn., State Bar Tex., Trial Attys. Am., Baylor Law Sch. Counsellors, Baylor Law Alumni Assn. (dir. 1979-82), Baylor Law Rev. Ex-Editors Assn., N.Tex. State U. Alumni Assn. (dir., v.p.), Henderson County Bar Assn., Sigma Phi Epsilon, Omicron Delta Kappa, Phi Delta Phi (historian 1962). Clubs: Petroleum (Dallas). Avocations: reading, travel, boating. Home: 98 Tanda Trail Trinidad TX 75163 Office Phone: 903-778-2289. Personal E-mail: abconant@msn.com.

CONANT, BRIAN, secondary school educator; b. Denver, Sept. 4, 1977; MS in English Edn., Ill. State U., Normal, 2000. Faculty assoc. U. H.S., Normal, 2000—. Office: University High School 500 W Gregory Normal IL 61790 Office Phone: 309-438-2828. Business E-Mail: conantbrian@hotmail.com.

CONANT, DOUGLAS R., food products executive; b. Chgo., 1952; married; 3 children. BA, Northwestern U., 1973, MBA, 1976. With mktg. dept. Gen. Mills, 1976—86; mgmt. Kraft General Foods, 1986—92; sr. v.p. mktg. Nabisco Biscuit Co., 1992—95; pres. Nabisco Foods Co., 1995—2000; pres., CEO Campbell Soup Co., 2001—. Bd. dirs. Campbell Soup Co., 2001—, Applebee's Internat. Inc., NJ Network. Bd. dirs. Safe Am. Found., Students in Free Enterprise; vice chmn. Conference Bd.; trustee Seeing Eye NJ, Intern. Tennis Hall Fame, Newport, RI. Mem.: NJ C. of C. (bd. dirs.). Office: Campbell Soup Co Campbell Place Camden NJ 08103-3878*

CONANT, HOWARD SOMERS, artist, educator; b. Beloit, Wis., May 5, 1921; s. Rufus P. and Edith B. (Somers) C.; m. Florence C. Craft, June 18, 1943; children: Judith Lynne Steinbach, Jeffrey Scott; m. Virginia E. Lusk, June 7, 1999. Student, Art Students League of N.Y., 1944-45; BS, U. Wis.-Milw., 1946; MS, U. Wis.-Madison, 1947; EdD, U. Buffalo, 1950. Instr. art, asst. head housefellow U. Wis., 1946-47; asst. prof. art SUNY, Buffalo, 1947-50, prof. art, 1950-55; chmn. dept. art and art edn. also chmn. art collection NYU, 1955-76; head dept. art U. Ariz., Tucson, 1976-86, prof. art, 1986-87; profl. artist, 1987—. Art edn. cons. NBC-TV, also Girl Scouts Am. TV series, 1958-60; field reader, also Title III program cons. U.S. Office of Edn.; adviser N.Y. State Council on Arts, 1962-63, Conn. Commn. on Arts, 1967-68; cons. Ford Found., 1973, Children's Theatre Assn., 1973, Getty Trust, 1985; examiner Internat. Baccalaureate Orgn., 1998. Moderator: weekly TV program Fun to Learn About Art, WBEN-TV, Buffalo, 1951-55; numerous one man shows; represented maj. group exhbns. pub. art mus. and coll. art collections; represented by Sol Del Rio Gallery, San Antonio, Art Source Inc., Tulsa, Ideas and Products, Tucson, Shana Steinbach, Lexington, Ky; executed mural Sperry High Sch., Henrietta, NY, 1971, Good Samaritan Med. Ctr., Phoenix, 1982, Valley Nat. Bank, Tucson, 1983; one-man retrospectives, Amarillo (Tex.) Art Mus., 1989, Tucson Jewish Cmty. Ctr., 1995, Sun City (Ariz.) Art Mus., Prescott (Ariz.) Fine Arts Assoc., 1996; author: (with Arne Randall) Art in Education, 1959, 63; author, editor: Art Workshop Leaders Planning Guide, 1958, Masterpieces of the Arts, New Wonder World Cultural Library, Vol. 4, 1963, Art Education, 1964, Seminar on Elementary and Secondary School Education in the Visual Arts, 1965, Lincoln Library of the Arts (2 vols.), 1973, Evaluation Reports, Metropolitan Museum of Art and Guggenheim Art Museum Children's Art Programs, 1971-73; art editor: USA Today, Intellect, 1978-85; assoc. editor Arts mag., 1973-75; contbr. articles profl. publs. Dept. State lectr., India, 1964; Dir. Waukesha County (Wis.) YMCA Art Program, 1946-48; pres., dir. Children's Creative Art Found., 1959-60; mem. adv. com. Coll. of Potomac, 1966; mem. cultural exchange mission to Mex., Ptnrs. of the Ams., 1988, 90; Lt. USAAF, 1943-46. Recipient 25th Ann. medal Nat. Gallery Art, 1966, Disting. Alumnus award U. Wis.-Milw., 1968, Purchase award Richard Florsheim Art Fund, 1992; Disting. fellow Nat. Art Edn. Assn., 1985, Nat. Endowment Arts sr. fellow in painting, 1985. Mem. Coll. Art Assn., Nat. Art Edn. Assn., Internat. Art Critics Assn., Alliance for Arts in Edn., Nat. Assn. Schs. Art and Design, AAUP, Nat. Com. Art Edn. (council, chmn. 1962-63), Inst. Study of Art in Edn. (bd. govs. 1965-72, pres. 1965-68) Clubs: Torch (N.Y.C.) (pres. 1965-66). Studio: 6954 E Cicada Ct Tucson AZ 85750-1395 *I have learned to freely follow my interests from one area of concern or involvement to another without feeling guilty about "putting off until tomorrow what one can do today." I have learned to be an innovator and an explorer, rather than a solemn plodder. I have learned how to do two or three things more or less at once, much like an organist handling contrapuntal melodies. As a result, I am a happy artist, author, lecturer and private human being whose multiple interests seem highly compatible and, indeed, essential to one another.*

CONANT, JAN ROYCE, artist; b. Boston, Sept. 14, 1930; d. Frank A. and Margaret (Newlin) Royce; m. Richard W. Conant, Mar. 22, 1952 (div. 1977); children: Peter Ames, Stephen Wright. Student, Milton Acad., 1948, Boston Mus. Sch., 1951; MFA, Cin. Art Acad., 1954. Owner, mgr. Tinker Hill Farm, Glastonbury, Conn., 1956-73, Stonefield Farm, East Haddam, Conn., 1973—; mng. dir. Chukka Cove Farm, Jamaica, W.I., 1982-84; owner Stonefield Farm and Studio LLC, East Haddam, 1985—. Author, illustrator: Half Pint & Others, 1962, Children of Light, 1998, 2d edit., 2005; illustrator The Winning Streak, 1962, Judge & Jr. Exhibitor, 1964; exhibited in solo shows at Chester Art Gallery, 1987, Lyman Allyn Mus., 1989, W. Graham Arader Gallery, NYC, 1994, Mut. Life Gallery, Kingston, Jamaica, 1997; group show at Lyme Art Assocs. Friend Lyme Acad. Coll. Fine Arts; bd. dirs. Lyme Art Assn. Mem. Am. Acad. Equine Art (patron), U.S. Equestrian Fed. (lic. eventing), US Eventing Assn., US Pony Clubs Inc. (life, v.p. 1974-78, gov. 1966-78, nat. examiner 1968-78). Independent. Avocations: animal behaviorist, dowser. Home and Office: Stonefield Farm 23 Three Bridges Rd East Haddam CT 06423-1732 Personal E-mail: janroyce@aol.com.

CONANT, KIM UNTIEDT, retired elementary school educator; b. Del Norte, Colo., July 26, 1944; d. Warren Malvern and Annine (Gredig) Untiedt; m. Spicer Van Allen Conant, July 9, 1966 (div. Mar. 1983); children: Spicer V., Reid F., Lee G. BA in Am. Studies, Scripps Coll., 1966; MA in Secondary Reading, San Diego State U., 1996. Cert. elem. tchr., Calif. Tchr. asst. Greenwich (Conn.) Country Day Sch., 1966-67; tchr. Katherine Delmar Burke Sch., San Francisco, 1969-70, Cupertino (Calif.) Schs., 1968-69, Kachina Country Day Sch., Phoenix, 1980-83, Paterson (N.J.) Schs., 1985, Black Mountain Mid. Sch., San Diego, 1985-89, Bernardo Heights Mid. Sch., San Diego, 1989—2004, ELD coord., 2000—04; ret., 2004. Tchr. trainer Poway (Calif.) Unified Schs., 1996—2004. Fulbright Exch. tchr. Exeter, Eng., 1998-99. Avocations: swimming, reading, gardening. Home: 14735 Poway Mesa Dr Poway CA 92064-2961

CONARD, ALFRED FLETCHER, legal educator; b. Grinnell, Iowa, Nov. 30, 1911; s. Henry S. and Laetitia (Moon) C.; m. Georgia Murray, Aug. 7, 1939; children— Joy L., Deborah J. AB, Grinnell Coll., 1932, LL.D., 1971; postgrad., U. Iowa, 1932-34; LL.B., U. Pa., 1936; LL.M., Columbia, 1939, J.S.D., 1942. Bar: Pa. 1937, Mich. 1967. Practice in Phila., 1937-38; asst. prof. U. Kansas City (Mo.) Law Sch., 1939-42, acting dean, 1941-42; atty. OPA, 1942-43, Office Alien Property Custodian, 1945-46; asso. prof., then prof. law U. Ill. Law Sch., 1946-54; prof. law U. Mich. Law Sch., 1954-81, prof. emeritus, 1981—. Vis. prof. U. Tex., 1952, U. Colo., 1957, 84, U. Ariz., 1982, U. Calif., Berkeley, 1983, Pepperdine U., 1985-86, U. San Diego, 1989; vis. prof. Stetson U., 1990, vis. scholar, 1991-93; lectr. U. Istanbul, 1958-59, Luxembourg, 1959, Mex., 1963, Brussels, 1965, Salzburg, 1971, Saarbrucken U., 1988, 90; chmn. editorial adv. bd. Bobbs-Merrill Co., 1962-78; exec. com. Am. Assn. Law Schs., 1964-65, chmn. rsch. com., 1968-70, pres. 1971, chmn. bus. assns. sect., 1979. Author: Studies in Easements and Licenses, 1942, Cases on Business Organization, 3d edit., 1965, Automobile Accident Costs and Payments: Studies in the Economics of Injury Reparation, 1964, Corporations in Perspective, 1976, Enterprise Organization, 4th edit., 1987; editor-in-chief Am. Jour. Comparative Law, 1968-71; chief editor bus. and pvt. orgns.: Internat. Ency. Comparative Law, 1965-82; editorial adv. bd. Am. Bar Found. Rsch. Jour., 1976-86. Served OSS AUS, 1943-45. Decorated Purple Heart; Ordre des Chevaliers de la Couronne Belgium; recipient Kulp Meml. award Am. Risk & Ins. Assn., 1965; Guggenheim fellow, 1975 Mem. AAUP (chpt. pres. 1963-64), NRC, Am. Bar Assn. (exec. com. corp. law sect. 1967-71, com. on corp. laws 1974-80, com. on clin. legal edn. 1981-84), Internat. Acad. Comparative Law, State Bar Mich., Am. Law Inst., Law and Soc. Assn. (trustee 1968-75), Council on Law-Related Studies (trustee 1969-74), Phi Beta Kappa, Order of the Coif. Clubs: Rotarian (club pres. 1976-77). Mem. Soc. Of Friends. Address: 80 Kendal Dr Kennett Square PA 19348-2326

CONARD, JANE REISTER, lawyer; b. Eldora, Iowa, Apr. 10, 1947; d. Eugene Lowell and Lois Sylvia (Reed) Reister; m. William Jarrett Conard, June 12, 1971 (div. 1980); 1 child, Tacy Jane; m. Richard A. Maneval, Apr. 8, 1985. BA, Macalester Coll., 1969; MA, U. Iowa, 1971; JD, U. Calif., Davis, 1976. Bar: Calif. 1976, Utah 1983. Legal counsel Calif. State Dept. Health, 1976—78; staff counsel Calif. Dept. Mental Health, Sacramento, 1978—82; counsel Intermountain H ealth Care, Inc., Salt Lake City, 1982—. Chair Utah Dept. Workforce Svcs. Ctrl. Region Coun., 2002—03; mem. State of Utah Health Adv. Coun., 2002—. Trustee Wasatch Canyons Hosp., Utah Disability Law Ctr., 2001—. Mem.: Utah Women Lawyers (exec. bd. 1984—86, Woman Lawyer of Yr. 2006), Am. Health Lawyers Assn. (exec. bd. 2002—), Salt Lake County Bar Assn. (pres. 1992—93). Democrat. Unitarian. Home: 829 Grandridge Dr Salt Lake City UT 84103-3306 Office: Intermountain Health Care Inc 36 S State St 22d Fl Salt Lake City UT 84111

CONARD, JOHN JOSEPH, finance company executive; b. Coolidge, Kans., June 30, 1921; s. Joseph Harvey and Jessie May (Shanstrom) C.; m. Virginia Louise Powell, Sept. 13, 1947; children— Joseph Harvey II (dec.), James Powell, Spencer Dean, John Joseph. BA, U. Kans., 1943, MA, 1947; D Internat. Law, U. Paris, 1951. Instr. polit. sci. U. Kans., 1946-49, asst. to chancellor, 1970-75; spl. asst. U.S. Mut. Security Agy., Paris, France, 1951-54; editor, pub. Kiowa County Signal, Greensburg, Kans., 1955-70; exec. officer bd. regents State of Kans., Topeka, 1976-82; pres. Higher Edn. Loan Program of Kans., Inc., Overland Park, Kans., 1982-86; v.p. Higher Edn. Assistance Found., 1982-86; legis. liaison Gov. of Kansas, 1987-88. Dir. Haviland (Kans.) State Bank. Mem. Kans. Ho. of Reps., 1959-69; mem. State Fin. Council, 1961-69; speaker of House, 1967-69; exec. asst. to Gov. Kans., 1975-76; trustee William Allen White Found., 1959—. Served to ensign USNR, 1943-45. Summerfield scholar, 1939-42; Rotary Found. fellow, 1949-50 Mem. VFW, Rotary, Am. Legion, Phi Beta Kappa, Sigma Delta Chi, Pi Sigma Alpha, Tau Kappa Epsilon. Republican. Methodist. Home: 904 Joseph Dr Lawrence KS 66049-3255 Home Phone: 785-830-8191. Personal E-mail: jcvc@sunflower.com.

CONARD, NORMAN DALE, secondary school educator; BS, Azusa Pacific U.; MA in Edn., Pepperdine U., 1976; MS in History, Pittsburg State U., 1990. Tchr. social studies Mara HS, LA, 1976—81, LAB HS, LA, 1981—85; tchr. social studies, creative art Uniontown HS, Kans., 1987—. Named to Nat. Tchrs. Hall of Fame, 2007; recipient Kans. State Tchr. of Yr., 1992, 100 Most Influential Educators in Am., Northern Life, 2000, Social Studies Outstanding Educator, Kans. Coun. for the Social Studies, 2001, Kans. City Save a Child Award, 2001, Civil Rights Award, NEA, Gov.'s Award for Excellence in Edn., 2004, Kansas History Date Tchr. of Yr., 2007. Office: Uniontown High Sch 601 E 5th St Uniontown KS 66779-0070*

CONARROE, JOEL OSBORNE, foundation administrator, editor, educator; b. West Orange, NJ., Oct. 23, 1934; s. Elvin Hamn and Elizabeth (Lofland) C. BS, Davidson Coll., 1956, LHD (hon.), 1987; MA, Cornell U., 1957; PhD, NYU, 1966; LHD (hon.), Rhodes Coll., 1983; PhD (hon.), U. Md., 1989, Tulane U., 1996. Asst. prof. English U. Pa., 1966-71, assoc. prof., 1971-77, prof., 1977—, ombudsman, 1971-73, chmn. dept. English, 1973-77, master Van Pelt Coll. House, 1974-77, dean faculty arts and scis., 1983-85; pres. John Simon Guggenheim Meml. Found., 1985—2003, pres. emeritus, 2003—. Exec. dir. MLA, NYC, 1978-83; selection com. Commonwealth Award in Lit., 1980-83; v.p. Nat. Book Critics Circle, 1981-85; chmn. Nat. Book Award Fiction Jury, 1988, Pulitzer Prize Fiction Jury, 1989, 94, 97, 2000, 02, Nat. Book Found., 1991-94; bd. dirs. PEN, pres. PEN Am. Ctr., 2002-04, Am. Acad. Poets, Yaddo. Author: William Carlos Williams' Paterson: Language and Landscape, 1970, John Berryman: An Introduction to the Poetry, 1977, Six American Poets, 1992, Eight American Poets, 1994, essays and revs.; editor PMLA, 1978-83. With U.S. Army, 1957-58. Recipient Founders Day award NYU, 1966, Lindback Tchg. award U. Pa., 1970, Disting. Alumni award NYU, 1995; Yaddo fellow, 1973, 76, Guggenheim fellow, 1977-78. Mem. MLA, Am. Acad. Arts Sci., Century Assn., Phi Beta Kappa. Home: 126 W 11th St New York NY 10011-8330

CONARY, DAVID ARLAN, investment company executive; b. South Paris, Maine, Mar. 3, 1937; s. Wilfred Grindle and Arline (Whitney) C.; m. Frances Jane Harrison, June 8, 1957; children: Lee Harrison, Neil Whitney. AB, Bowdoin Coll., 1959; postgrad., Northeastern U., 1965-66, MIT, 1966-67, Boston U., 1967. Registered investment advisor, 1999-04. Securities trader H.C. Wainwright & Co., Boston, 1959-60, May & Gannon, Boston, 1960-65, v.p., dir. rsch., 1968-71; securities analyst, adminstr. investment tech. group Boston Co., Boston, 1965-68; mgr. instl. trading Fahnestock & Co., Boston, 1971-72; resident mgr. G.A. Saxton & Co., Boston, 1972-75; instl. trader Baker, Weeks & Co., NYC, 1975; equities trader State St. Rsch. & Mgmt. Co., Boston, 1976-87; v.p. Howard, Weil, Inc., 1987-88; sr. v.p. Boettcher & Co., Inc., Denver, 1989-90; founder, pres., chmn. Conifer Holding Corp. Inc., 1990—; dir. Astra Corp., Security 1 Specialists, Inc.; pres., chmn. Granite Solid State; mng. ptnr. Hawthorne Investment Mgmt., 1999—2004. Founder Lo-Jack Corp.; lectr. in field. Dist. dir. Mass. Bay United Fund, 1966; founder Bethel Fireworks Com., 2000, Lovell Area Watch, 2002. Named to Internat. Poetry Hall of Fame, 1996. Mem. Nat. Security Traders Assn., Boston Securities Traders Assn. (gov. 1972-73, 81-82), Boston Investment Club (pres. 1985-94), Bethel Area C. of C. (pres. 2001), Bowdoin Club of Boston (dir. 1965-66, dir. 175th anniversary campaign 1973-74), Weymouth Sportsment's Club (sec. 1965-66, 71-72), Mensa, Theta Delta Chi. Avocations: flying, skiing, scuba diving, piano, woodworking. Home: 86 Rumford Ave PO Box 69 Bryant Pond ME 04219-0069 Personal E-mail: david127@megalink.net.

CONATON, MICHAEL JOSEPH, diversified financial services company executive; b. Detroit, Aug. 3, 1933; s. John Martin and Margaret Alice (Cleary) C.; m. Nancy D. Kelley, June 13; children: Catherine, Macaira (dec.), Michael, Margaret, Elizabeth. BS, Xavier U., 1955. Public accountant Stanley A. Hitter, C.P.A., Cin., 1956-58; controller The Moloney Co., Albia, Iowa, 1958-61; v.p. fin. The Midland Co., Cin., 1961-80, sr. v.p., chief fin. officer, 1980-83, exec. v.p., chief fin. officer, 1983-88, pres., chief operating officer, 1988—, also dir., vice-chmn., 1998—. Interim pres. Xavier U., 1990-91. City councilman, Albia, 1959-61; trustee, chmn. bd. Xavier U., 1972. Served to lt. USMC, 1955-56. Mem. Fin. Execs. Inst., New Ohio Inst. (chmn.), Cin. Soc. Fin. Analysts, Athenaeum of Ohio (trustee), Met. Club (chmn. bd.). Home: 736 Elsinboro Dr Cincinnati OH 45226-1706 Office: The Midland Company PO Box 1256 Cincinnati OH 45201-1256 Home Phone: 513-871-3276; Office Phone: 513-947-5211.

CONAWAY, MARGARET GRIMES (PEGGY CONAWAY), library administrator; b. Minot, ND, June 6, 1944; d. John Francis and Veronica Ann (McCarthy) Grimes; m. Steven L. Conaway, July 15, 1967 (div. July 1991); 1 child, Anne Marie. BS in Edn., Minot State Coll., 1966; MA in English, San Jose State U., 1978, MLS, 1988. Cert. secondary tchr., Calif.; cert. c.c. tchr., Calif. Instr. Boise (Idaho) Ind. H.S., 1966-67, Santa Maria (Calif.) Joint Union H.S. Dist., 1967-72; libr. asst. San Jose (Calif.) Pub. Libr., 1984-86, libr., 1986-89, sr. libr., 1989-97, divsn. mgr., 1997—2000; libr. dir. Los Gatos (Calif.) Pub. Libr., 2000—. Oper. design project mgr. San Jose Pub. Libr./San Jose State U. Joint Libr., 1998—2000; vice chmn. adminstrv. coun. Silicon Valley Libr. Sys., 2001—02, chmn. adminstrv. coun., 2002—03. Contbr. articles to encys., to profl. jours.; author: Images of America: Los Gatos, 2004, Images of America: Los Gatos Generations, 2007; co-author: Images of Rail: Railroads of Los Gatos, 2006. Recipient Helen Putnam award for excellence League of Calif. Cities, 1997. Mem. ALA, Calif. Libr. Assn., Pub. Libr. Assn., Libr. Adminstrn. and Mgmt. Assn. Avocations: writing, antiques, history, travel. Home Phone: 831-420-1748; Office Phone: 408-354-6895. Business E-Mail: pconaway@losgatosca.gov.

CONAWAY, MIKE, congressman; b. Borger, Tex., June 11, 1948; m. Suzanne Conaway; 4 children. BBA, Tex. A&M U., 1970. CPA. Acct. Price Waterhouse, Midland, Tex.; CFO Bush Exploration, Midland, Tex.; mem. US Congress from 11th Tex. dist., 2005—, mem. agr. com., mem. armed svcs. com., mem. budget com., mem. def. rev. threat panel. Mem. Tex. State Bd. Pub. Accountancy, 1995—2002. Served in US Army, 1970—72. Named Vol. of Decade, Midland, Tex., YMCA, 1990. Republican. Baptist. Office: US Ho Reps 511 Cannon Ho Office Bldg Washington DC 20515-4311 Office Phone: 202-225-3605.*

CONBOY, KENNETH, lawyer, retired federal judge; b. 1938; BA, Fordham Coll., 1961; JD, U. Va., 1964; MA in History, Columbia U., 1980. Asst. dist. atty., exec. asst. dist. atty. Manhattan Dist. Atty.'s Office, 1966-77; dep. commr., gen. counsel N.Y. Police, 1978-83; criminal justice dir. NYC, 1984-86; N.Y.C. commr. of investigation, 1986-87; judge U.S. Dist. Ct. (so. dist.) N.Y, 1987-93; ptnr. Mudge, Rose, Guthrie, Alexander & Ferdon, NYC, 1994-95, Latham & Watkins, NYC, 1995—. Author: Grand Jury Examination of the Recalcitrant Witness, 1977; contbr. articles to profl. jours. Mem. N.Y. State Crime Control Planning Bd., N.Y. Sovern Commn. Capt. U.S. Army, 1964-66. Fellow: W.B. Yeats Soc., Royal Soc. Arts (Eng.); mem.: Fed. Bar Coun., Assn. of Bar City of NY, NY State Bar Assn., Am. Soc. Legal History, Univ. Club (NY). Office: Latham & Watkins 885 3rd Ave Ste 1000 New York NY 10022-4834 Office Phone: 212-906-1850.

CONBOY, KEVIN PATRICK, lawyer; b. Amityville, NY, Feb. 23, 1952; BA cum laude, Le Moyne Coll., 1974; JD cum laude, U. Ga., 1979. Bar: Ga. 1979. Law clk. to Hon. Marvin H. Shoob U.S. Dist. Ct. (no. dist.) Ga., 1979-82; mem. Powell, Goldstein, Frazer & Murphy, Atlanta; ptnr. Paul, Hastings, Janofsky& Walker LLP, Atlanta. Contbr. articles to profl. jours. Trustee Southern Cath. Coll. Mem. State Bar Ga., Atlanta Bar Assn., Internat. Bar Assn., Ireland C. of C. U.S. (pres. Atlanta chpt.). Office: Paul Hastings Janofsky & Walker LLP 600 Peachtree St NE Ste 2400 Atlanta GA 30308-2222 Office Phone: 404-815-2211. Office Fax: 404-685-5211. Business E-Mail: kevinconboy@paulhastings.com.

CONCANNON, CHRISTOPHER R., stock exchange executive; BA, Catholic U. Am., 1989; MBA, St. John's U., 1991; JD, Catholic U. Am. Columbus Sch. Law, 1994. Bar: NY, NJ, DC. Legis. analyst Am. Stock Exchange, 1992—95; atty. US SEC, Market Regulation divsn., 1994—97; assoc. Morgan, Lewis & Bockius LLP, 1997—99; spl. coun. & sr. v.p. bus. devel. Island ECN, 1999—2002; spl. coun. & sr. v.p. bus. devel., pres. Instinet Clearing Svcs., Inc., 2002—03; exec. v.p. transaction svcs. NASDAQ Stock Market, Inc., NYC, 2003—. Mem. adv. bd. Jour. Trading. Named one of 40 Under 40 Rising Stars, Crain's NY Bus., 2007. Office: NASDAQ Stock Market Inc 50th Fl 1 Liberty Plaza New York NY 10006 Office Phone: 212-401-8742.*

CONCANNON, JAMES M., lawyer, educator, dean; b. Columbus, Ga., Oct. 2, 1947; s. James M. Jr. and Mary Jane Concannon; m. Melissa P. Masoner, June 9, 1988. BS, U. Kans., 1968, JD, 1971. Law clk. Kans. Ins. Commn., Topeka, 1971; rsch. atty. Kans. Supreme Ct., Topeka, 1971-73; asst. prof. law Washburn U., Topeka, 1973-75, assoc. prof. law, 1976-81, prof., 1981—2006, disting. prof., 2006—, dean, 1988-2001. Vis. prof. law Washington U., St. Louis, 1979; active Kans. Commn. on Pub. Understanding of Law, 1983-89, Task Force on Law Enforcement Consolidation, Topeka, 1991-92; mem. Nat. Conf. Commrs. on Uniform State Laws, 1998—, Pattern Instrns. for Kans.-Civil and Criminal Com., Kans. Jud. Coun., 2001—; mem. Kans. Commn. on Jud. Performance, 2006—. Co-author: Kans. Appellate Practice Manual, 1978, Kansas Statutes of Limitations, 1988; sr. contbn. editor: Evidence in America-Federal Rules in the States, 1987. Coord. Citizens to Keep Politics Out of Our Courts, Topeka, 1984; mem. bd. dirs. Kans. Legal Svcs. for Prisoners, 2003—; co-reporter Citizens Justice Initiative, 1997-99; chmn. legal com. Concerned Citizens Topeka, 1995-99; bd. dirs. Mut. Funds Waddell and Reed, Inc., 1997—. Master: Topeka Am. Inn. of Ct. (pres. 2001—02); fellow: Kans. Bar Found., Am. Bar Found. (state chair 2002—05); mem.: Assn. Am. Law Schs. (com. on bar admission, lawyer performance 1994—97), Kans. Bar Assn. (CLE com. 1976—2001, Outstanding Svc. award 1982, 2003), Washburn Law Sch. Alumni Assn. (life), Order of Coif. Office: Washburn U Law Sch 1700 SW College Ave Topeka KS 66621-0001

CONCEMI, ALFRED P., marketing professional; s. Paul T. Concemi and Etta M. Nadeau; children: Emily Ann, Nicholas Andrew. BS in Biomedical Engring., Rensselaer Poly. Inst., Troy, NY, 1990; MA, U. Redlands, Calif., 1992. Sr. engr. Global Therapeutics, Broomfield, Colo., 1995—97; product devel. mgr. InterVascular, Inc, Clearwater, Fla., 1997—99; product specialist W.L. Gore & Assocs., Flagstaff, Ariz., 1999—2004; mktg. dir. AngioDynamics, Inc, Queensbury, NY, 2004—. Achievements include patents for relating to endovascular grafts. Home: 31 Apple Tree Ln Wilton NY 12831 Home Phone: 518-587-4476; Office Phone: 518-798-1215.

CONCIBIDO, VERGEL C., research and development company scientist, plant geneticist, writer, inventor; b. San Pablo City, Laguna, Philippines, Mar. 28, 1965; arrived in US, 1988, naturalized, 2007; s. Bibiano Concibido, Sr. and Esmelisinda Cierte; m. Kerstin Breitmoser, Mar. 25, 1991. BS in Agr., U. Philippines, Los Banos, 1987; MS in Horticulture, ND State U., Fargo, 1990; PhD in Plant Pathology, U. Minn., St. Paul, 1995. Rsch. asst. Inst. Plant Breeding, U. Philippines, 1987—88; rsch. asst. dept. horticulture ND State U., 1988—90; rsch. asst. dept. plant pathology, U. Minn., 1991—95, rsch. assoc., 1995—97; project lead, soybean molecular breeding Monsanto Co., St. Louis, 1997—2005, soybean agronomic traits mgr., 2005—. Contbr. articles to profl. jours.; reviewer profl. jour. articles. Recipient Gerry Roxas Leadership award, Philippines, 1982, M.F. Kernkamp Scholarship award, U. Minn., 1995, Pres. Hasselmo's Student Leadership award, 1995, Above & Beyond award, Monsanto Co., 2005, Tech. People Initiative award, 2004; Monsanto fellow, 2007. Mem.: Am. Seed Assn., Commercial Soybean Breeders, Am. Soc. Agronomy, Crop Sci. Soc. Am., Am. Phytopathological Soc., Sigma Xi (assoc.), Phi Sigma Biol. Honor Soc. (assoc.). Achievements include patent for the identification of seeds or plants using phenotypic markers for breeding and proprietary trait quantitation; genetically mapped the most important resistance genes to soybean cyst nematode (SCN), a damaging pest of soybean and other agronomically important traits of soybean including yield and soybean rust. Avocations: gardening, running, reading, martial arts. Office: Monsanto Co 800 N Lindbergh Blvd Saint Louis MO 63167 Office Fax: 314-694-4888.

CONCOFF, GARY O., lawyer; b. LA, June 28, 1936; m. Jean F. Concoff, June 23, 1963; children: Cory N., Andrew L. BS, UCLA, 1958; JD, Harvard Law Sch., 1962. Bar: Calif. 1963, cert.: LA Assn. 1963. Assoc. O'Melveny & Myers, LA, 1962—65; assoc., ptnr. Kaplan, Livingston et al, Beverly Hills, 1965—81; ptnr. Sidley & Austin, 1981—88, Mitchell Silberberg, 1988—95; atty. Troy & Gould, 1996—. Founder, co-chair UCLA Entertainment Symposium, 1976—78; law lectr. UCLA Law Sch., 1980—82. Contbr. articles and papers to various law pubs. 2d lt., 1958. Mem.: ABA (chmn. forum com.motion picture and TV divsn. 1987—92), Calif. Bar, British Acad. Film and TV Arts (bd. dir. 2001—02). Office: Troy & Gould 1801 Century Park East Los Angeles CA 90067 Business E-Mail: goconcoff@troygould.com.

CONDAYAN, JOHN, foreign service officer; b. Addis Ababa, Ethiopia, Sept. 1, 1933; s. Vahram Hagop and Sirvart (Parthog) C.; m. Eileen Mary Ferguson, Nov. 6, 1965; children: Christopher Charles, Alicia Elizabeth BS, Bucknell U., 1955; MPA, Syracuse U., 1974; postgrad., Nat. Def. U., 1978. Mng. dir. V.H. Condayan & Co., NYC, 1955-63; joined fgn. svc. Dept. State, Washington, 1965, spl. asst. to dep. asst. sec., 1969-71; adminstrv. officer Am. Embassy, Niamey, Niger, 1965-67, gen. svcs. officer Manila, 1967-69, adminstrv. officer Copenhagen, 1971-73, exec. dir. Office Fgn. Bldgs., 1974-75, spl. exec. dir. to asst. sec. of state for adminstrn., 1975-77, counselor of embassy Moscow, 1978-80, Bangkok, 1980-82, minister-counsellor London, 1989-91; exec. dir. Bur. E. Asian and Pacific Affairs, 1982-83; dep. asst. sec. for ops. bur. adminstrn. US Dept. State, Washington, 1983-87, dir. office fgn. missions, 1987-89; assoc. dir. for mgmt. USIA, Washington, 1991-94, acting dir., 1994; pvt. cons., 1994—. Bd. dirs. Internat. Sch., Copenhagen, 1970-71, Anglo-Am. Sch., Moscow, 1978-80, Am. Employee Assn., Moscow, 1978-80, Am. Employee Support Orgn., Bangkok, 1980-82; mem. assets and liability com. State Dept. Fed. Credit Union, 1985, 92-93, bd. dirs., 1993-98, treas., 1994-95. Recipient Presdl. Humanitarian award (The Philippines), 1968, Meritorious Honor award Dept. State, 1975, Superior Honor award, 1985, 92, Presdl. Meritorious award, 1987, Dir.'s award for Superior Achievement, 1993.

CONDE, CRISTOBAL I., computer company executive; b. Santiago, Chile; BS in Astronomy and Physics, Yale U. Co-founder Devon Sys. Internat., Inc., 1987—90; head trading sys. divsn. SunGard Data Sys., Inc., Wayne, Pa., 1991—98, exec. v.p., 1998—99, COO, 1999—2000, bd. dir., 1999—, pres., COO, 2000—02, pres., CEO, 2002—. Office: Sungard Data Sys Inc 680 E Swedesford Rd Wayne PA 19087*

CONDE, YVONNE M., freelance journalist, writer; b. Havana, Cuba, Oct. 28, 1950; came to the U.S., 1961; d. Pedro M. and Maria L. Conde; m. B. Loret de Mola, Apr. 10, 1989. BA in Communication, SUNY, NYC, 1989; MA in Journalism, NYU, 1991. Freelance journalist, NYC, 1991—. Author: Operation Pedro Pan, 1999, The Wisdom of Our People, 2006. Recipient award for best news and pub. affairs work Nat. Assn. Coll. Broadcasters, 1991. Mem.: Nat. Assn. Hispanic Journalists. Roman Catholic. Avocation: sporting clays. Home: 340 E 64 St Apt 23B New York NY 10065 E-mail: yvonneconde@aol.com.

CONDIE, CAROL JOY, anthropologist, science administrator; b. Provo, Utah, Dec. 28, 1931; d. LeRoy and Thelma (Graff) Condie; children: Carla Ann, Erik Roy, Paula Jane. BA in Anthropology, U. Utah, 1953; MEd in Elem. Edn., Cornell U., 1954; PhD in Anthropology, U. N.Mex., 1973. Edn. coord. Maxwell Mus. Anthropology, U. N.Mex., Albuquerque, 1973, interpretation dir., 1974-77; asst. prof. anthropology U. N.Mex., 1975-77; cons. anthropologist, 1977-78; pres. Quivira Rsch. Ctr., Albuquerque, 1978—. Cons. anthropologist U.S. Congl. Office Tech. Assessment, chair Archeol. Resources Planning Adv. Com., Albuquerque, 1985-86; leader field seminars Crow Canyon Archeol. Ctr., 1986-97; appointee Albuquerque dist. adv. coun., bur. land mgmt. U.S. Dept. Interior, 1989; study leader Smithsonian Instn. Tours, 1991; mem. Albuquerque Heritage Conservation Adv. Com., 1992. Author: The Nighthawk Site: A Pithouse Site on Sandia Pueblo Land, Bernalillo County, New Mexico, 1982, Five Sites on the Pecos River Road, 1985, Data Recovery at Eight Archeological Sites on the Rio Nutritas, 1992, Data Recovery at Eight Archeological Sites on Cabresto Road Near Questa, 1992, Archeological Survey in the Rough and Ready Hills/Picacho Mountain Area, Dona Ana County, New Mexico, 1993, Archeological Survey on the Canadian River, Quay County, New Mexico, 1994, Archeological Testing at LA 103387, Nizhoni Extension, Gallup, McKinley County, New Mexico, 1995, Two Archeological Sites on San Felipe Pueblo Land, New Mexico, 1996, Four Archeological Sites at La Cienega, Santa Fe County, New Mexico, 1996, A Brief History of Berino, Berino Siding, and Early Mesilla Valley Agriculture, Dona Ana County, New Mexico, 1997, Main Street Project, Aztec, New Mexico, 2004, Testing and Data Recovery at Seven Sites Cabezon Subdivision Sandoval Co., 2005, Archeological Survey of 355 Acres.on the San Clemente Grant, Valencia County, N.Mex., 2006; author: (with M. Kent Stout) Historical and Architectural Study of the Old Peralta Elementary School, Valencia County, New Mexico, 1997, Archeological Survey of 720 Acres on Ball Ranch, Sandoval County, New Mexico, 1998; author: (with H.H. Franklin and P.J. McKenna) Results of Testing at Three Sites on Tesuque Pueblo Land, Santa Fe County, New Mexico, 1999, Cultural Resources Investigations at the Old Roswell Airport for the Proposed Cielo Grande Recreation Area, Chaves County, New Mexico, 2000, Archeological Survey in Las Lomas de la Bolsa, Santa Fe County, New Mexico, 2001, A Plethora of Walls.the Vigil Properties, Old Town Albuquerque, 2002; author: (with P.W. Bauer, R.P. Lozinsky and L.G. Price) Albuquerque: A Guide to Its Geology and Culture, 2003; author: (with Carol Raish) Indigenous and Traditional Use of Fire in Southwestern Grassland, Woodland, and Forest Ecosystems, 2003; author: (with Susan Dewitt) Doves Along the Ditchbank: La Orilla de la Acequia Historic District, 2003; co-editor: Anthropology in the Desert West, 1986. Mem. Downtown Core Area Schs. Com., Albuquerque, 1982. Ford Found. fellow, 1953-54; recipient Am. Planning Assn. award, 1985-86, Gov.'s award, 1986. Fellow: Am. Anthrop. Assn.; mem.: Albuquerque Archaeol. Soc. (pres. 1992), N.Mex. Archaeol. Coun. (pres. 1982—83, Hist. Preservation award 1988), Archaeol. Soc. N.Mex. (trustee 2001—), Soc. Am. Archaeology (chmn. Native Am. rels. com. 1983—85), Hist. Albuquerque Inc., The Archaeol. Conservancy (bd. dirs. 2003—), N.Mex. Heritage Preservation Alliance, Maxwell Mus. Assn. (bd. dirs. 1980—83), Las Arañas Spinners and Weavers Guild (pres. 1972). Democrat. Avocations: spinning, weaving, gardening. Home and Office: Quivira Research Ctr 1809 Notre Dame Dr NE Albuquerque NM 87106-1011 Office Phone: 505-255-9264. E-mail: cjc1540@qwest.net.

CONDIT, LINDA FAULKNER, retired economist; b. Denver, May 30, 1947; d. Claude Winston and Nancy Isabel (McCallum) Faulkner; m. John Michael Condit, Dec. 20, 1970; 1 child, David Devin. BA, U. Ark., 1969; MA, U. Wis., 1970; postgrad., U. Minn., 1974-77. Rsch. asst. U. Wis., Madison, 1969—70; economist St. Louis Fed. Res. Bank, 1971—73; ops. analyst No. States Power co., Mpls., 1973-76; energy economist, 1976—78; from ecomist to v.p. Pennzoil Co., Houston, 1978—95, v.p., 1995—98; v.p., corp. sec. Pennzoil-Quaker State Co., Houston, 1998—2002. Econ. cons. Jr. Achievement, 1983. Recipient Alumni award, U. Ark., 1969. Mem. Internat. Assn. Energy Economists (pres., v.p., treas.), Nat. Assn. Bus. Economists, Internat. Bus. Coun. (v.p.), Am. Econ. Assn., N.Am. Soc. Corp. Planners, Am. Soc. Corp. Secs. (membership chmn.), Hits Theatre (bd. dirs.), Corp. Alliance To Eliminate Ptnr. Violence (bd. dirs.), Leadership Am., Harvard Discussion Group Indsl. Economists, Forst Club, River Oaks Women's Breakfast Club (v.p., pres.), Mortar Bd., Phi Beta Kappa, Kappa Alpha Theta. Home: 11822 Village Park Cir Houston TX 77024-4418

CONDO, JAMES ROBERT, lawyer; b. Somerville, NJ, Mar. 2, 1952; s. Ralph Vincent and Betty Louise (MacQuaide) C. BS in Bus. and Econs., Lehigh U., 1974; JD, Boston Coll., 1979. Bar: Ariz. 1979, Colo. 2001, U.S. Dist. Ct. Ariz. 1979, U.S. Ct. Appeals (9th cir.) 1982, U.S. Supreme Ct. 1983, U.S. Ct. Appeals (D.C. cir.) 1989, U.S. Ct. Appeals (10th cir.) 1989, U.S. Ct. Appeals (6th cir.) 1991, U.S. Ct. Appeals (4th cir.) 1994. Assoc. Snell & Wilmer, Phoenix, 1979-84, ptnr., 1985—. Judge pro tem Maricopa County Superior Ct. Active Ariz. Town Hall, 1985—. Mem.: ABA, Defense Rsch. Inst., Maricopa County Bar Assn., State Bar Ariz. Office: Snell & Wilmer One Arizona Ctr Phoenix AZ 85004-2202 Office Phone: 602-382-6353. Business E-Mail: jcondo@swlaw.com.

CONDON, ANN BLUNT, psychotherapist; b. Brockton, Mass., Sept. 25, 1938; d. Hugh Francis and Ann Collins Blunt; m. John Weston Condon, Jan. 2, 1965 (div. Feb. 1966); 1 child, Pamela Condon Porter. BA, Newton Coll. Sacred Heart, 1960; MSW, Boston U., 1981. LCSW Mass. Pvt. practice psychotherapy, Centerville, Mass., 1982—; pvt. career coach, 1998—; profl. coach, owner The Joy of Success. Seminar leader Landmark Edn., Quincy, Mass., 1986—92; workshop leader Greening Prodns., Centerville, 1988—. V.p. Svc. Employees Internat. Union, Boston, 1965—69; town meeting mem. Town of Barnstable, 1973—75; trustee Cape Cod C.C., 1975—82, BNI Osterville Village Ptnrs., Hashpee, Mass., 2006—. Mem.: NASW (ACSW, diplomate), Am. Bus. Women Assn., Cape Cod C. of C., Altrusa Club Cape Cod (founding mem., 1st pres.). Democrat. Roman Catholic. Avocations: gardening, writing, cooking, baseball. Office: PO Box 58 7 Woodvale Ln Centerville MA 02632 Office Phone: 508-775-2059. E-mail: thejoyofsuccess@comcast.net.

CONDON, FRANCIS EDWARD, retired chemistry professor; b. Abington, Mass., Oct. 12, 1919; s. Maurice Francis and Eva Isabel (Cole) C.; m. Mary Anna Medvetz, Jan. 9, 1943; children: Francis E., Mary Ellen Condon Laessig, John M., Arthur T., Dorothy A. Condon Waldt, James M., Rita C. Condon McCarthy. AB, Harvard U., 1941, PhD, 1944. Rsch. chemist Phillips Petroleum Co., Bartlesville, Okla., 1944—52; asst. prof. chemistry CCNY, 1952—61, assoc. prof., 1962—66, prof., 1967—82; ret., 1982. Vis. prof. Purdue U., 1960; Louis J. Curtman prof. CCNY, 1976-78; founder, chmn. Seven Siblings Found., Ltd., 1977-94 Author: (with H. Meislich) Introduction to Organic Chemistry, 1960, Study Projects in Physical Chemistry, 1963, Chess monographs, 1992—; contbr. articles to profl. jours., chpts. to books. Planning bd. Borough of Bogota, NJ, 1963; trustee, pres. Bogota Swim Club, Inc., 1967-71 Petroleum Rsch. Fund grantee, 1967-70; NSF Sci. Faculty fellow U. So. Calif., 1964-65 Mem. Am. Chem. Soc. (dir. N.Y. sect. 1967-68), U.S. Chess Fedn. (life), Glen Rock (N.J.) Chess Club (pres. 1975-79, Washington Twp. (N.J.) Chess Club (pres. 1990-92), Dumont (N.J.) Chess Mates (sec. 1992-99), St. Joseph's Holy Name Soc. (pres. 1974-75, sec. 1992—), Alpha Chi Sigma, Sigma Xi. Home: 471 Larch Ave Bogota NJ 07603-1058

CONDON, GEORGE EDWARD, journalist; b. Fall River, Mass., Nov. 6, 1916; s. John Joseph and Mary Agnes (O'Malley) C.; m. Marjorie Philona Smith, May 9, 1942; children— Theresa, John, George, Katherine, Mary, Susan. BSc in Journalism, Ohio State U., 1940. Publicity dir. Mt. Union Coll., Alliance, Ohio, 1941; info. dir. Agrl. Adjustment Adminstrn. for Ohio, 1941-42; mem. staff Cleve. Plain Dealer, 1943-84; TV critic, 1948—62; gen. columnist Cleve. Plain Dealer, 1962-84; pres. George Condon & Assocs., Inc., 1985—. Author: Cleveland-The Best-Kept Secret, 1967, Laughter from the Rafters, 1968, Stars in the Water, 1972, Yesterday's Cleveland, 1976, Yesterday's Columbus, 1977, Cleveland: Prodigy of the Western Reserve, 1979, History of Ohio Farmers Insurance Company, 1985, Gaels of Laughter and Tears, 1995, The Man in the Arena, 1995, West of the Cuyahoga, 2006. Recipient Ohioana Library Assn. Lit. award, 1975, Cleve. Women's City Club Lit. award, 1975, Emily Gray Burke Meml. award lit., 1979; award Cleve. Newspaper Guild; awards for public service, copy editing and column writing Press Club Cleve.; Disting. Service award Nat. Soc. Profl. Journalists, 1980; named to Cleve. Journalism Hall of Fame, Press Club Cleve., 1990. Mem. Sigma Delta Chi, Pi Sigma Alpha. Home: The Waterford 12500 Edgewater Dr Lakewood OH 44107 E-mail: georgec@apk.com.

CONDON, JOSEPH DENNIS, broadcasting executive; b. Albany, NY, Apr. 12, 1946; s. Joseph O. and Loretta (Halleran) C.; m. Kathleen M. Sullivan, Jan. 25, 1969; 1 child, Daniel J. Assoc. Degree in Bus. Adminstrn., Hudson Valley C.C., Troy, NY, 1966; BA in Mktg. and Acctg., Siena Coll., 1969; Degree in Pub. Rels., Albany Bus. Coll., 1975. Cert. TV prodn. specialist, USARNG, 1970. Announcer, disc jockey WTRY Kopps/Monahan Corp., Troy, 1963-67; announcer, news and weathercaster WAST-TV RKO Gen., Albany, 1967-68; announcer, disc jockey WABY Radio, Albany, 1967-69; announcer WTEN/WROW Capital Cities Comm., Albany, 1969-83; with WROW/WYJB Radio Albany Broadcasting, 1969—, pub. affairs dir., 1982—; owner Radio Albany.com, Albany, 2000—. N.E. corr. Voice of Am., Washington, 1983-87; owner radioalbany.com, 2000—; cons. in field, 1991—; owner, operator racioalbany.com comml. internet sta. Pub. rels. chmn. bicentennial com. St. Mary's Ch. Sgt. N.Y. Nat. Guard, 1969-75. Recipient first place for best pub. affairs show N.Y. State Broadcasters, Albany, 1995, second place Nori award Ad Club, Albany, 1995, Best Sta. Event award N.Y. State Broadcasters, Albany, 1996, Best Pub. Affairs Series, 1997, 1998, Best Pub. Affairs Show, 1998, awd. Albany Broadcasting Co., 1998, cmty. svc. award for pub. affairs Nat. Broadcast Assn., 1998, 99, Proclamation, N.Y. State Senate, 1999, Proclamation, N.Y. Senator Neil Breslin, 1999; nominee Marconi award 1997, 98; recipient awards N.Y. State Broadcasters, 1999, silver microphone nat. finalist award, 1999, Best Pub. Affairs show award, 2000, Best Pub. Affairs Series award, 2000. Mem. AFTRA, NAACP, Am. Broadcast Pioneers Broadcast Found., N.Y. State Broadcasters (advisor job fair com.), Holocaust Survivors and Friends, R.R. Hist. Soc., Ad Club, Nat. Music Found. Avocations: broadcast historian, wwii historian, photographer, railroad historian. Home: 48 Glenwood Rd Menands NY 12204-2407 Office: Albany Broadcasting 6 Johnson Rd Latham NY 12110-5638

CONDON, ROBERT EDWARD, surgeon, educator, consultant; b. Albany, NY, Aug. 13, 1929; s. Edward A. and Catherine (Kilmartin) C.; m. Marcia Jane Pagano, June 16, 1951; children: Sean Edward, Brian Robert. AB, U. Rochester, 1951, MD, 1957; MS, U. Wash., 1965. Diplomate Am. Bd. Surgery, Nat. Bd. Med. Examiners. N.Y. Bd. Regents scholar U. Rochester, 1957; intern King County Hosp., Seattle, 1957-58; resident dept. surgery U. Wash. Sch. Medicine (and affiliated hosps.), 1958-65; postdoctoral rsch. fellow Nat. Heart Inst., 1961-63; asst. prof. surgery Baylor Coll. Medicine, Houston, 1965-67; assoc. prof. surgery U. Ill. Coll. Medicine, Chgo., 1967-69, prof., 1969-70; prof., head dept. surgery U. Iowa Coll. Medicine, Iowa City, 1971-72; prof. surgery Med. Coll. Wis., Milw., 1972—98, prof. emeritus, 1998, chmn. dept. surgery, 1979-95; chief surg. svcs. Wood VA Hosp., Milw., 1972-81. Attending surgeon Froedtert Meml. Luth. Hosp., 1982-98; cons. Columbia Hosp., Milw., St. Joseph Hosp., Milw.; clin. prof. surgery U. Wash., 2000—. Author: (with others) Abdominal Pain: A Guide to Rapid Diagnosis, 2d edit., 1995, Manual of Surgical Therapeutics, 9th edit., 1996, Hernia, 4th edit., 1995, Surgical Care, 1980. Recipient sr. class award as Outstanding Faculty Mem. Baylor U. Coll. Medicine, 1966, Excellence in Tchg. award Phi Chi, 1967, Cert. Appreciation U. Iowa Coll. Medicine, 1971, Tchr. of Yr. award U. Iowa Coll. Medicine, 1972, Tchr. of Yr. award Med. Coll. Wis., 1983, 95, Disting. Svc. award Med. Coll. Wis., 1993, Disting. Alumnus award U. Wash., 1998; rsch. fellow Guggenheim Found., 1963-64. Mem. ACS (bd. govs.), Am. Surg. Assn. (v.p.) , Surg. Infection Soc. (pres.), Am. Assn. Surgery of Trauma, Internat. Soc. Surgery, Collegium Internationale Chirurgiae Digestivae (pres.), Assn. for Acad. Surgery, Ctrl. Surg. Assn. (pres.), So. Surg. Assn., We. Surg. Assn., Wis. Surg. Soc. (pres.), Milw. Surg. Soc. (pres.), Chgo. Surg. Soc., Soc. Univ. Surgeons, Soc. Clin. Surgery, Milw. Acad. Medicine, Soc. Surgery Alimentary Tract (v.p.), Milw. Acad. Surgery (pres.). Home and Office: 2722 86th Ave NE Clyde Hill WA 98004-1653 Office Phone: 425-453-7860. E-mail: recrecmd@comcast.net.

CONDON, STANLEY CHARLES, gastroenterologist; b. Glendale, Calif., Feb. 1, 1931; s. Charles Max and Alma Mae (Chinn) C.; m. Vaneta Marilyn Mabley, May 19, 1963; children: Lori, Brian, David. BA, La Sierra Coll., 1952; MD, Loma Linda U., Calif., 1956. Diplomate Nat. Bd. Med. Examiners, Am. Bd. Internal Medicine, Am. Bd. Gastroenterology; recertified Nutritional Support Physician 2002. Intern LA County Gen. Hosp., 1956-57, resident gen. pathology, 1959-61, active jr. attending staff, 1964-65; resident in internal medicine White Meml. Med. Ctr., LA, 1961-63, attending staff out-patient clinic, 1963-64; dir. intern-resident tng. program Manila Sanitarium and Hosp., 1966-71, med. dir., 1971-72; chief resident internal medicine out-patient clinic Loma Linda U. Med. Ctr., 1972-74, attending staff, asst. prof. medicine, 1976-91, med. dir. nutritional support team, 1984—2007, assoc. prof. medicine, 1991—; fellow in gastroenterology Barnes Hosp./Wash. U., 1974-76. Contbr. articles to profl. jours. Capt. U.S. Army, 1957-59. Fellow: ACP; mem.: AMA, San Bernardino County Med. Soc., So. Calif. Soc. Gastroenterology, Calif. Med. Assn., Am. Gastroent. Assn., Am. Soc. for Parenteral and Enteral Nutrition. Republican. Seventh-day Adventist. Avocations: trombone, choral singing, camping, hiking, gardening. Home: 11524 Ray Ct Loma Linda CA 92354-3630 Office: Loma Linda U Med Ctr 11370 Anderson St Loma Linda CA 92354-3450 Office Phone: 909-558-4000 ext. 4905. Business E-Mail: vcondon@llu.edu.

CONDON, THOMAS JOSEPH, university historian; b. New Haven, July 27, 1930; m. Ann Kathleen Gorman, 1962 (dec. June 2001); children: Katherine, Caroline, Gregory. BA, Yale U., 1952; MA, Boston Coll., 1953; PhD, Harvard U., 1962. Teaching fellow history Harvard U., 1959-62; asst. prof. history U. N.B. (Can.), Fredericton, 1962-66; exec. asso. Am. Council Learned Socs., NYC, 1966-70; vis. asso. prof. history Ind. U., 1967-68, City U. N.Y., 1968-69; prof. history, dean of Arts U. N.B., 1970-77; prof. history, dean and v.p. U. N.B. (St. John Campus), 1977-79, acting pres., 1979-80, v.p., 1980-87, prof. history, 1977-96, v.p. emeritus, gov. emeritus, 1996—, acting v.p., 2001—03. Hon. rsch. fellow Inst. U.S. Studies, U. London, 1975-76; mem. Humanities Rsch. Coun. Can., 1972-73, Commn. on Fgn. Students Policy, Can. Bur. Internat. Edn., Ottawa, 1980-83, Maritime Provinces Higher Edn. Commn., 1982-85; chmn. adv. com. on arts in N.B. Min. of Youth, 1973-75; bd. govs. Rothesay Collegiate Sch., 1977-88, U. N.B., 1977-87, 90-96; chmn. engring. task force Maritime Provinces Higher Edn. Commn., 1977-78; chmn., pres. Bi-Capitol Project, Inc., 1982-91; chmn. Festival by the Sea, Sur Mer, 1985, Bi-Capitol Found., 1984—; bd. govs., exec. com. Can. Conf. Arts, 1988-94; bd. dirs. Writers Devel. Trust; bd. govs. Internat. Scholarship Found., 1996—. Author: New York Beginnings: The Commercial Origins of New Netherland, 1968; Mem. editorial bd.: Computers and the Humanities, 1969-70, Acadiensis, 1970—; contbr. articles to profl. jours. V.p. St. John Can. Games, 1977—87; pres. Symphony New Brunswick, 2003—; chair New

Brunswick Jud. Remuneration Commn.; bd. dirs. N.B. Found. for the Arts, New Brunswick Mus., 2004—. With USNR, 1953—57. Decorated Order of Can.; recipient Lescarbot award Can. govt., 1991, Commemorative medal for 125th anniversary of Confedn. of Can., 1992, Queen's Golden Jubilee medal, 2002; Can. Coun. grantee, 1964, 65. Mem. Hist. Assn. Home: 268 Princess St Saint John NB Canada E2L 1L3 Office: Box 5050 Saint John NB Canada E2L 4L5 Home Phone: 506-693-0133; Office Phone: 506-648-5694. Business E-Mail: tjc@unbsj.ca.

CONDON, TOM, sports agent; b. 1953; married; 1 child, Tom. Grad., Boston Coll., 1974; JD, U. Kans. Profl. football player Kans. City Chiefs, 1974—84, New England Patriots, 1985; sports agent IMG Talent Agy., Cleve., 1991—2006, Creative Artists Agy., Beverly Hills, 2006—. Pres. NFL Players Union, 1984—86. Achievements include acting as an agent for over 24 first-round NFL Draft picks. Office: Creative Artists Agy 9830 Wilshire Blvd Beverly Hills CA 90212-1825

CONDON, WILLIAM (BILL), director, writer, producer; b. NYC, Oct. 22, 1955; Degree in philosophy, Columbia Coll. T.V. and motion picture dir., writer, prodr. Writer, dir. Gods and Monsters, 1998 (Best Writing Oscar award 1999, Flanders Internat. Film Festival award 1998, Golden Satellite award 1999, Ind. Spirit award 1999, others), Kinsey, 2004, Dreamgirls, 2006 (Best Dir., African-American Film Critics Assn., 2006); dir. films Candyman: Farewell to the Flesh, 1995; T.V. films include Murder 101, 1991, White Lie, 1991, Dead in the Water, 1991, Deadly Relations, 1993, The Man Who Wouldn't Die, 1995; dir. TV series The Others, 2000; actor: Now You See Him: The Invisible Man Revealed, 2000; actor, writer, prodr. Strange Behavior, 1981; actor, writer, Strange Invaders, 1983; actor, writer, dir. Sister, Sister, 1987; writer F/X2, 1991, The Devil & Daniel Webster, 2002, Chicago: The Musical, 2002, Chicago, 2002. Office: c/o Adam Shulman The Firm 9465 Wilshire Blvd Ste 600 Beverly Hills CA 90212*

CONDON, WILLIAM FRANCIS, JR., literacy educator; s. William Francis Condon, Sr. and Betty Brewer Kidder; children: Jennifer, Margaret, Nicholas, Michael. BA in English, U. Ga., 1972; MA in English, Miami U., Ohio, 1977; PhD in English, Brown U., 1982. Tchr. The Pine Sch., Stuart, Fla., 1974—75; instr. English Okla. U., Norman, Okla., 1979—81; assoc. prof. English Ark. Tech. U., Russellville, Ark., 1981—87; assoc. dir. Eng. Composition Bd. U. Mich., Ann Arbor, Mich., 1987—94, dir. Eng. Composition Bd., 1994—96; dir. writing programs Wash. State U., Pullman, Wash., 1996—2007. Bd. dirs. Coun. Writing Program Admistrs., Oxford, Ohio, 1999—2002. Co-author: Writing The Information Superhighway, 1997, Assessng the Portfolio, 2001; co-editor: Assessing Writing, 2003—05; editor (cons.), 2006—. Recipient Excellence in Edn. award, U. Mich., 1993, 1995. Mem.: Conf. Coll. Composition Comms. (chmn. selection com. 2005, chmn. com. computers composition 1995—98), Nat. Coun. Tchrs. English, Phi Kappa Phi. Avocations: swimming, skiing, music. Office: Washington State Univ 305E CUE Pullman WA 99164

CONDOS, BARBARA SEALE, real estate broker, developer, investor; b. Kenedy, Tex., Feb. 24, 1925; d. John Edgar and Bess Rochelle (Ainsworth) Seale; m. George James Condos, Dec. 24, 1955 (dec.); 1 child, James Alexander. MusB magna cum laude, U. Incarnate Word, San Antonio, 1946. Lic. real estate broker, Tex. Ptnr., CEO Mountain Top-V.I. Devel. Properties, V.I., 1977-85; pres. Investment Realty Co., L.C., San Antonio, 1978—. Choreographer, dancer San Antonio Symphony's Youth Concerts and Opera Festival; actress San Antonio Little Theatre-Patio-Players 1948—. Trustee San Antonio Little Theatre, 1953-76; mem. coun. McNay Mus., 1986—, chmn. coun., 1987—, chair coun., 1988—, trustee, 1989-97, trustee emerita, 1997—; bd. dirs. San Antonio Performing Arts Assn., 1978—; mng. trustee Russell Hill Rogers Fund for Arts. Mem. Internat. Real Estate Fedn., Internat. Real Estate Inst., Nat. Assn. Realtors, Tex. Assn. Realtors, San Antonio Bd. Realtors, Tex. Watercolor Soc. (signature mem.), The Argyle Club. Avocation: painting. Home: 217 Geneseo Rd San Antonio TX 78209-5913 Office: Investment Realty Co 1635 NE Loop 410 San Antonio TX 78209-1625 Business E-Mail: bsc@investmentrealty.com.

CONDOS, J. ALEXANDER, mortgage company executive; b. San Antonio, Nov. 19, 1959; s. George James and Barbara Seale Condos; m. Linda Sue Warner, Aug. 18, 1990 (div. Dec. 12, 2001); children: Elliot Warner, Alexa Nicole. BA with honors, U. Tex., 1981; MBA, U. Chgo., 1984. Lic. real estate broker Tex. and Ill. Sr. investment officer Lomas Fin. Corp., Chgo., 1984—88; owner Alexander Condos Real Estate, San Antonio, 1989—92; prin. Investment Realty Co., L.C., San Antonio, 1993—. Bd. dirs. N.E. YMCA/San Antonio & the Hill Country, 2002; confidence index panelist Tex. Bus. Leaders; corp. campaign com. McNay Art Mus. Mem.: San Antonio Bd. Realtors (comml. investment div.), Internat. Coun. Shopping Ctrs., Chgo. Real Estate Coun., Tex. Assn. Realtors (comml. investment divsn. 1993—), Nat. Assn. Realtors, Real Estate Coun. of Austin, Real Estate Coun. of San Antonio (govt. affairs com. 1996—), Mortgage Bankers Assn. of Am. (capital markets com. 2000—), Rotary. Methodist. Avocation: running. Office: Investment Realty Co LC 1635 NE Loop 410 Ste 910 San Antonio TX 78209-1622 Office Phone: 210-828-9261 20.

CONDRA, ALLEN LEE, retired lawyer, state official; b. Middlesboro, Ky., Apr. 11, 1950; s. Allen and Dorothy Dell (Douglas) C. BA, We. Ky. U., 1972; JD, No. Ky. U., 1978. Bar: Ky. 1979, U.S. Dist. Ct. (we. dist.) Ky. 1980. Staff atty. West Ky. Legal Svcs., Madisonville, 1979—81; dist. atty. dept. transp. Commonwealth of Ky., Madisonville, 1981—2003; ret., 2003. Mem. Ky. Bar Assn., Elks, Masons, K.T., Phi Alpha Delta. Democrat. Methodist.

CONDRATE, ROBERT ADAM, SR., spectroscopy educator; b. Jan. 19, 1938; s. Adam Vincent and Angela Marian (Talacka) C.; m. Judith Campbell, Aug. 13, 1960; children: Barbara Louise, Robert Adam, Laura Angela. BS, Worcester Poly. Inst., 1960; PhD, Ill. Inst. Tech., 1965. Rsch. assoc. U. Ariz., Tucson, 1966—67; from asst. prof. spectroscopy to assoc. prof. N.Y. State Coll. Ceramics, Alfred U., 1967—78, prof., 1978—. Vis. prof. Los Alamos Sci. Lab., 1972, GTE, Towanda, N.Y., 1980; summer lectr. Korea Inst. Sci. & Tech., Seoul, 1989; cons. ceramic cos.; spectroscopy cons. Statue of Liberty/Ellis Island Found., 1984-86. Co-editor: Advances in Materials Characterization, 1983, Vol. II, 1985; mem. editl. bd. Nat. Forum, Asian Jour. Spectroscopy; assoc. editor Am. Ceramic Soc., 1989—; contbr. articles to profl. jours. Mem. parents adv. bd. secondary edn. Alfred-Almond Ctrl. Sch., 1975—80; mem. Danforth Found. Assn. for Higher Edn., 1976—85. Recipient Scholes award Alfred U., 1972, commendation Statue of Liberty/Ellis Island Found., 1984-86; grantee Inland Steel-Ryerson Found., 1963-64, NSF, 1966-67, 84-86, 86-87, Coll. Ctr. Finger Lakes, 1969, Alfred U. Rsch. Found, 1975; NIH fellow, 1964-65; SUNY faculty exch. scholar, 1988—. Fellow: Can. Ceramic Soc., Am. Ceramic Soc., Royal Soc. Chemistry, Am. Inst. Chemists; mem.: AAAS, Materials Rsch. Soc., Clay Minerals Soc., N.Y. Acad. Scis., Coblentz Soc., Am. Phys. Soc., Soc. Applied Spectroscopy (Spectroscopy award Chgo. sect. 1964), Am. Chem. Soc., Internat. Lions Club, Masons, Sigma Xi, Keramos, Tau Beta Pi, Sigma Alpha Epsilon, Psi Lambda Upsilon, Phi Kappa Phi. Home: 5761 Random Rd Alfred Station NY 14803-9793 Office Phone: 607-871-2446. Business E-Mail: fcondrate@alfred.edu.

CONDRELL, WILLIAM KENNETH, lawyer; b. Buffalo, Sept. 19, 1926; s. Paul Kenneth and Celia Olga (Schinas) C.; m. Stacie J. Oliver, June 9, 1991; children: Paul, William, Alexander. BS, Yale U., 1946; S.M., MIT, 1947; JD, Harvard U., 1950. Bar: N.Y. 1951, D.C. 1964, U.S. Ct. Appeals (4th cir.) 1974, U.S. Ct. Appeals (Fed. cir.) 1982, U.S. Ct. Appeals (D.C. cir.) 1984, U.S. Supreme Ct. 1965. Assoc. econ. adv. Exec. Office Pres., Washington, 1951—54; mgmt. cons. McKinsey and Co., Chgo., 1954-55; mgr. budgets Hotpoint div. GE, Chgo., 1955—59; sole practice, 1959-68; ptnr. Steptoe & Johnson, Washington, 1968—90, of counsel, 1990—. Adj. prof. Duke U., Durham, NC, 1975—95, chmn. Ctr. for Forestry Investment, 1980—93; chmn. Ctr. for Continuing Edn., Washington, 1980—. Bd. trustees Hope Housing, 1992—96, Kingsbury Ctr., 1994—98; dir. mediation D.C. Pub. Schs., 1998—99. Lt (j.g.) USNR, 1944—46. Mem.: ABA, Congl. Country Club (Bethesda, Md.). Home: 2510 Virginia Ave NW # 502 Washington DC 20037-1904

CONDRILL, JO ELLARESA, freelance/self-employed small business owner, writer, consultant; b. Hull, Tex., Oct. 25, 1935; d. Freddie (dec.) and Ida (Donatto) Founteno; m. Edwin Leon Ellis, Jan. 9, 1955 (div. 1979); children: Michael Edwin, James Alcia, Resa Ann, Thomas Matthew; m. Donald Richard Condrill, Sept. 21, 1980 (div. 1985). BSBA, Our Lady of the Lake U., 1982; MS in Pub. Adminstrn., Ctrl. Mich. U., 1987; grad., U.S. Army War Coll., 1993. Editorial asst. Airman Mag., San Antonio, 1978; mgmt. analyst San Antonio Air Logistics Ctr., San Antonio, 1979-82; inventory mgr. ground fuels Detachment 29, Alexandria, Va., 1982-83; logistics plans officer Mil. Dist. Washington, 1983-85, chief logistics plans ops. and mgmt., 1985-88; chief integration br. Office of the Dep. Chief of Staff for Logistics, 1990-95; deputy chief logistics plans and ops. div. Hdqs. U.S. Army, The Pentagon, 1995-97; owner Seminars by Jo, Alexandria, Va., 1984-86, GoalMinds, Beverly Hills, Calif., 1997—. Author: Leadership: From Vision to Victory in Six Powerful Steps, 1996, 101 Ways to Improve Your Communication Skills Instantly, 1998, A Millennium Primer: Take Charge of Your Life, 1999, From Book Signing to Best Seller: An Insider's Guide to a Successful Low-Cost Booksigning Tour, 2001 (Best Writer's Ref. Guide, Bay Area Ind. Pubs. Assn. 2001-2002), Take Charge of Your Life: Dare to Pursue Your Dreams, 2003. Civilian v.p. student coun. Army War Coll., Carlisle, Pa. Recipient decoration for Exceptional Civilian Svc., US Army, 1997, Best Speaker award Def. Logistics Agy., Wow award Ford Motor Co. and Greater San Antonio C. of C., 2007. Mem. NAFE, Nat. Spkrs. Assn., Rotary Internat., Toastmasters Internat. (dist. 27 gov. 1991-92, internat. dir. 1994-96, top ranking dist. gov. in internat. orgn. 1991-92, Internat. Pres. Disting. Dist. award 1991-92). Roman Catholic. Avocations: travel, dance, reading. Office: Goal Minds Inc 6300 Rue Marielyne #308 San Antonio TX 78238 Office Phone: 310-993-7553. Business E-Mail: condrill@goalminds.com.

CONDRIN, J. PAUL, insurance company executive; Exec. v.p., personal market mgr. Liberty Mut. Ins. Group, Boston. Office: Liberty Mutual Group 175 Berkeley St Boston MA 02116-5066

CONDRON, BARBARA O'GUINN, philosopher, educator, academic administrator, writer; b. New Orleans, May 1, 1953; d. Bill Gene O'Guinn and Marie Gladys (Newbill) Jackson; m. Daniel Ralph Condron, Feb. 29, 1992; 1 child, Hezekiah Daniel. BJ, U. Mo., 1973; MA, Coll. Metaphysics, Springfield, Mo., 1977, DD, D in Metaphysics, 1979. Cert. counselor; ordained min. Interfaith Ch. Metaphysics. Field rep. Sch. Metaphysics, New Orleans, 1978-80; dir. Interfaith Ch. Metaphysics, 1884-89; pres. Nat. Hdqs., Sch. Metaphysics, Windyville, Mo., 1980-84, prof., 1989—, chmn. bd. dirs., 1991-98, mem. coun. elders, bd. govs. internat. edn., 1998—; CEO SOM Pub., Windyville, 1989-98. Creator Sch. Metaphysics Assocs., 1992; initiator Universal Hour Peace, 1995; initiator, internat. coord. Nat. Dream Hotline, 1988—; radio and TV guest, 1977—; creator Maker's Dozen-Visionary Schs. Recognition, 1999, Taraka Yoga Psi Counseling Program, Powers of Ten Day Experience, 2006; initiator Spiritual Focus Sessions, 1997—; internat. coord. Peace Dome dedication and One Voice Initiative, 2003, Soc. for Intuitive Rsch., 2003—; presenter in field; lectr. in field. Author: What Will I Do Tomorrow?, Probing Depression, 1977, Search for a Satisfying Relationship, 1980, Strangers in My Dreams, 1987, Total Recall: An Introduction to Past Life & Health Readings, 1991, Kundalini Rising, 1992, Dreamers Dictionary, 1994, The Work of the Soul: Past Life Recall & Spiritual Enlightenment, 1996, Uncommon Knowledge, 1996, Firsst Opinion: 21st Century Wholistic Health Care, 1997, Spiritual Renaissance Elevating Your Conciousness for the Common Good, 1999, The Bible Interpreted in Dream Symbols, 2000, Remembering Atlantis: The History of the World Vol. 1, 2002, How to Raise an Indigo Child, 2002, Peacemaking: 9 Lessons for Changing Yourself, Your Relationships and Your World, 2003, The Wisdom of Solomon, 2004, The Invitation: A Play and Film in Four Acts, Satyagraha: A Play Based on the Life of Mohandas K. Gandhi, Every Dream is About the Dreamer, 2004, Master Living: 10 Essential Life Skills for Health, Prosperity, Success and Peace of Mind, 2005; author series When All Else Fails, editor-in-chief Thresholds Jour., 1990—2001, editor Wholistic Health and Healing Guide, 1992—2000, dir. film Making Peace, 2003, prodr., dir. films The Silver Cord, 2004, The Invitation-8 Nobel Peace Laureates Meet in the Peace Dome, 2006, dir. documentary Vision Quest, 2005, numerous poems. Mem. Internat. Platform Assn., Am. Bus. Women's Assn., Interfaith Ministries, Kundalini Rsch. Network, Planetary Soc., Heritage Found., Mo. Writers Guild, Sigma Delta Chi. Office: Sch Metaphysics World Hdqs Windyville MO 65783 Office Phone: 417-345-8411. Business E-Mail: bcondron@som.org, bgc@dreamschool.org.

CONDRON, CHRISTOPHER M. (KIP), investment company executive; b. Scranton, Pa. m. Margaret Condron; 3 children. B in bus., U. Scranton, 1970. Sr. v.p. C.S. McKee & Co., Pitts., 1972—78; founder Condron Assoc., 1978—85; co-pres. AYCO Corp., 1985—89; head priv. client group Boston Co., 1989; pres. Boston Safe Deposit and Trust Co., 1989—99; exec. v.p. Mellon Bank Corp. (Mellon acquires Boston Co.), 1993—94; vice chmn. Boston Co., 1994—95, chmn., CEO, 1995—99; vice chmn. Mellon Bank Corp., 1994—98; chmn., CEO The Dreyfus Corp., 1995—99; pres., COO Mellon Fin. Corp. (formerly Mellon Bank Corp.), 1999—2001; pres., CEO, mem. Group Mgmt. Bd. AXA Fin. Inc., 2001—; chmn., CEO AXA Equitable Life Ins. Co. Bd. govs. Investment Co. Inst., 1997—, exec. com., 1998—2000; bd. dirs. Fin. Svcs. Roundtable. Former trustee U. Scranton, head Pres.'s Coun.; trustee St. Sebastian's Country Day Sch., Needham, Mass, University Pitts.; dir., treas. Am. Ireland Fund, 1999-. Office: AXA Financial 1290 Avenue of the Americas New York NY 10104

CONDRON, DANIEL RALPH, academic administrator, metaphysics educator; b. Chillicothe, Mo., Jan. 30, 1953; s. Ralph Wesley and Rosa Irene (Garber) C.; m. Barbara Gail O'Guinn, Feb. 29, 1992; 1 child, Hezekiah Daniel. BS, U. Mo., 1975, MS, 1978; DDiv, Coll. Metaphysics, Springfield, Mo., 1982, D in Metaphysics, 1985. Cert. counselor; ordained to ministry Interfaith Ch. of Metaphysics. Dir. Sch. Metaphysics, Des Moines, 1980, Kansas City, Mo., 1981, regional dir. Colo., 1982-85, Chgo. and Detroit, 1985-90, pres. bd. nat. hdqs. Windyville, Mo., 1988—; chancellor, prof. Coll. Metaphysics, Windyville, Mo., 1990—97, chmn bd., 1997—. Tchg. asst. U. Mo., Columbia, 1977; sales and mgmt. cons. Am. Media, Des Moines, 1980-83; spkr. in field. Author: Dreams of the Soul, 1991, Permanent Healing, 1992, Universal Language of Mind, 1994, Understanding Your Dreams, 1994, Seven Secret Keys to Prosperity and Abundance, 1996, Superconscious Meditation, 1997, The Four Stages of Growth, 2001, Atlantis: The History of the World, Vol. 1, 2002, Tao Te Ching, Interpreted and Explained, 2003, The Purpose of Life, 2004, The Secret Code of Revelation, 2006, The Emptiness Sutra, 2007; pub. jour. Thresholds Quar., 1988-; internat. radio and TV guest including BBC, Radio Hong Kong, Voice of Am., 1979—. Mem. Sch. Metaphysics Assocs. (pres.), Nat. Space Soc., Planetary Soc., Alpha Gamma Rho, Alpha Zeta. Achievements include implementer and designer of organic and biodynamic farming and agriculture at the 1500 acre College of Metaphysics campus, landscape designer and creator of energetic campus using sacred geometry, including octahedrons, cosehedrons and dodecahedrons placed along ley lines for 1500 acre college of metaphysics campus, discoverer and developer of the Universal language of mind as it applies to dreams, to the Bible and other holy works; discoverer of specific attitudes that cause specific disease and disorders in the body. Home: 163 Moon Valley Rd Windyville MO 65783 Office: Sch Metaphysics Nat Headquarters Windyville MO 65783

CONDRY, ROBERT STEWART, retired hospital administrator; b. Charleston, W.Va., Aug. 16, 1941; s. John Charles and Mary Louise (Jester) C.; m. Mary Purcell Heinzer, May 21, 1966; children: Mary-Lynch, John Stewart. BA, U. Charleston, 1963; MBA, George Washington U., 1970. Asst. hosp. dir. Med. Coll. of Va., Richmond, 1970-73, assoc. adminstr., 1973-75; assoc. hosp. dir. McGaw Hosp., Loyola U., Maywood, Ill., 1975-84, hosp. dir., 1984-93, ret., 1993. Pres. Inter-Hosp. Planning Assn. of Western Suburbs, Maywood, 1983-93; bd. dirs. PentaMed, Inc., San Antonio. Bd. dirs. Met. Chgo. Healthcare Coun., 1985-93, mem. exec. com., 1989-93; bd. dirs. Cath. Hosp. Alliance, 1992, chmn. bd. dirs., 1992, mem. exec. com. 1988-94; mem. Ill. Gov.'s Adv. Bd. on Infant Mortality Reduction, 1988-93, Rev. Bd. on Emergency Medicine Svcs., 1989-93. With U.S. Army, 1964-66. Recipient preceptorship George Washington U., 1985, U. Chgo., 1984, St. Louis U., 1984, Tulane U., 1984, Yale U., 1991. Fellow Am. Coll. Healthcare Execs., Am. Acad. Med. Adminstrs.; mem. Am. Hosp. Assn., Cath. Hosp. Assn., Am. Mgmt. Assn. Republican. Roman Catholic. Avocations: golf, tennis, camping, travel. E-mail: carmelcondry@comcast.net.

CONE, GEORGE WALLIS, lawyer; b. Augusta, Ga., Aug. 20, 1945; s. William Harry and Agnes M. (Hill) Cone; children: Jennifer Lee, Laura Katherine, David Willis. Student, Clemson Coll., 1963—64; BS in PHarmacy, U. Ga., 1967, JD, 1973. Bar: Ga. 73, SC 74. Pharmacist-in-charge Walterboro Drug, Inc., 1967—76; atty. firm McLeod, Fraser & Unger, Walterboro, 1976—84, McLeod, Fraser & Cone, Walterboro, 1985—; city atty. City of Walterboro, 1995—. Bd. dirs. Found. for Human Svcs., 1986—90, Bank of Walterboro, sec. corp., vice chmn.; sec. corp., vice chmn., bd. dirs. Communitycorp, 1995—. Notes editor: Ga. Jour. Internat. and Comparative Law, 1971—72, revs. and comments editor:, 1972—73. Mem. SC Bd. Pharmacy, 1981—87; chmn. SC Bd. PHarmacy, 1986—87; bd. dirs. SC Humane Assn., 1978—85, treas., 1979—84, PRES., 1984—85; bd. dirs. Colleton County SPCA, 1975—85, pres., 1975—77; mem. Colleton County Alcohol and Drug Abuse Com., 1979—81, chmn., 1980—81; bd. dirs. Pub. Defender Corp. Colleton County, 1978—, sec., 1979—; mem. Colleton County Bd. Voter Registration, 1982—84; bd. dirs. Nat. Assn. Bds. Pharm. Found./Bur. Voluntary Compliance, 1983—85, Low Country Cmty. Action Agy., Inc., 1980—85, sec., 1983—85; chmn. Colleton County Old Jail Restoration and Preservation Com., 1984—95; mem. City of Walterboro Downtown Rev. Bd. With SC Army NG, 1970—76. Mem.: ABA, Omar Temple A.A.O.N.M.S., 14th Dist. Pharm. Assn. (pres. 1980—82), SC Pharm. Assn., SC Bar Assn. (ho. of dels. 1975—76, 1977—78, 1979—85), State Bar Ga. (ho. of dels. 1985—89), Am. Soc. Pharm. Law, Colleton County Hist. Soc. (past pres.), Sertoma, Lowcountry Sertoma Club, Dogwood Hills Country Club (pres. 1979—81), Unity Lodge, A & A Scottish Rite Freemasonry, Coastal Shrine Club, Grand Lodge Masons, Phi Alpha Delta, Delta Chi. Democrat. Baptist. Office: PO Box 230 Walterboro SC 29488 Mailing: PO Box 233 Walterboro SC 29488 Personal E-mail: george@coneonline.com. Business E-Mail: gcone@lowcountry.com.

CONE, LAWRENCE ARTHUR, medical educator; b. NYC, Mar. 23, 1928; s. Max N. and Ruth (Weber) C.; m. Julia Haldy, June 6, 1947 (dec. 1956); m. Mary Elisabeth Osborne, Aug. 20, 1960; children: Lionel Alfred. AB, NYU, 1948; MD, U. Berne, Switzerland, 1954; DSc (hon.), Rocky Mountain Coll., 1993. Diplomate Am. Bd. Internal Medicine, Am. Bd. Infectious Diseases, Am. Bd. Allergy and Immunology, Am. Bd. Med. Oncology. Intern Dallas Meth. Hosp., 1954-55, resident internal medicine, 1955; resident Flower 5th Hosp., NYC, 1957-59, Met. Hosp., NYC, 1959-60; rsch. fellow infectious diseases and immunology NYU Med. Sch., NYC, 1960-62; from asst. prof. to assoc. prof. NY Med. Coll., NYC, 1962-72, chief sect immunology and infectious diseases, 1962-72; assoc. clin. prof. medicine Harbor UCLA Med. Sch., 1984—2004; clin. prof. internal medicine U. Calif., Riverside, 1998—; clin. prof. medicine UCLA, 2004—. Career scientist Health Rsch. Coun. N.Y.C., 1962-68; chief sect. immunology and infectious diseases Eisenhower Med. Ctr., Rancho Mirage, Calif., 1973-2002, chmn. dept. medicine, 1976-78, pres. elect, pres., past pres. med. staff, 1984-90; cons. infectious disease Desert Hosp., Palm Springs, Calif., 1980-85; lectr. basic sci. U. Calif., Riverside Biomed. Scis.; mem. mycosis study group NIAID, 1993—, co-investigator Coccidioidomycosis study group, 1993—, eastern coop. oncology group affil. Stanford U., 1994, 2003-. Contbr. articles to profl. jours. Bd. dirs., trustee Desert Bighorn Rsch. Inst., Palm Desert, Calif., pres., bd. dirs., 1995-99; nat. adv. coun., trustee Rocky Mountain Coll., Billings, Mont., 2001—; mem. med. adv. staff Coll. of Desert, Palm Desert; Pres. Cir. Desert Mus., Palm Springs, Calif., Idaho Conservation League, Gilcrease Mus., Tulsa, Sun Valley Ctr. for Arts and Humanities. L.A. County Mus., Smithsonian Inst., Buffalo Bill Historic Mus., Cody, Wyo.; mem. Nat. Mus. Wildlife Art, Yellowstone Art Mus., Billings, Mont.; life mem. The Living Desert, Palm Desert, L.A. County Mus.; mem. cmty. adv. coun. Jr. League; CEO Genetic Rsch. Inst. of Desert; sustaining mem. Rep. Nat. Com. Recipient Outstanding Contbn. to Medicine award Riverside County Med. Assn., 1998, Disting. Achievement award AMC Cancer Rsch. Ctr., 1998, Steven Chase award, 2000, Eisenhower Med. Ctr. award. Fellow ACP, Royal Soc. Medicine, Interam. Soc. Chemotherapy, Am. Coll. Allergy, Am. Acad. Allergy and Immunology, Infectious Diseases Soc. Am., Am. Geriatric Soc. (founding fellow we. divsn.); mem. AAAS, Internat. AIDS Soc., Am. Fedn. Clin. Rsch., Am. Soc. Microbiology, Reticulocudothelial Soc., Am. Fedn. for Clin. Rsch., Faculty Soc. UCLA, Surg. Soc. N.Y. Med. Coll. (hon.), Woodstock Artists Assn., Harvey Soc., N.Y. Acad. Scis., European Soc. Clinical Microbiology and Infectious Disease, Internat. Soc. Infectious Disease, NYU Alumni Assn., Berne Alumni Assn., Hoover Found., Yellowstone Art Mus., Autry Mus. Western Heritage, Nat. Mus. Am. Indian, Palm Springs Art Mus., Lotos Club, Tamarisk Country Club, Coachella Valley Gun and Wildlife Club, Faculty Soc. UCLA Harbor Med. Ctr., O'Donnell Golf Club, Sigma Xi. Republican. Avocations: golf, fishing, hunting, skiing. Home: 765 Via Vadera Palm Springs CA 92262-4170 Office: Probst Profl Bldg #308 39000 Bob Hope Dr Rancho Mirage CA 92270-3221 also: Larkspur Condominiums PO Box 1503 Sun Valley ID 83353-1503 also: 5004 Rt 213 Olivebridge NY 12461 Personal E-mail: lacmedicine@aol.com.

CONELLI, MARIA ANN, art educator, dean, architect; b. Bklyn., Nov. 1, 1957; d. Carmine S. and Mary Conelli; m. Kim J. Hartswick, May 11, 1990. BA in Art History, Bklyn. Coll., 1980; MA, NYU, 1983; MPhil, Columbia U., PhD in Archtl. History, 1992. Educator Met. Mus. Art, NYC, 1981—84; instr. Parsons Sch. Design, NYC, 1983—2001; chair Parsons/Smithsonian Inst., NYC, Washington, 1992—2001; dean Fashion Inst. Tech., NYC, 2001—05; dir. Am. Folk Art Mus., NYC, 2005—. Co-editor: Newsletter Decorative Art Soc., 1995—2005; contbr. articles to profl. jours., books. Trustee Skyscraper Mus., NYC, 1999—2005; mem. mus. com. Coll. Art Assocs., NYC, 2003—. Pub. Works Challenge grantee, Nat. Endowment for the Arts, Washington, 2002—03, J. Paul Getty Postdoctoral fellow, 1997. Fellow: Am. Acad. in Rome (fellow 1987—88); mem.: Coll. Art Assn. Roman Catholic. Office: Am Folk Art Mus 45 W 53d St New York NY 10019-5401 Office Phone: 212-265-1040 ext. 114. Office Fax: 212-265-2350. Business E-Mail: mconelli@folkartmuseum.org.

CONERLY, RICHARD PUGH, retired manufacturing executive; b. Jackson, Ala., May 6, 1924; s. William L. and Eunice (Pugh) C.; m. Iva Jean Brightwell, Aug. 12, 1956; children: William Edward, Robert Andrew, Christopher Brightwell, Elizabeth Anne. Student, Howard Coll., Birmingham, Ala., 1942; B.J., U. Mo., 1948; LL.B., Harvard U., 1952. Bar: Mo. 1952. Practice in, St. Louis, 1952-65; assoc., partner Thompson & Mitchell, 1952-65; v.p., gen. counsel, exec. v.p. Peabody Coal Co., St. Louis, 1965-69; pres. Pott Industries Inc., St. Louis, 1969-87; vice-chmn. Houston Natural Gas Corp., 1979-85; chmn. Orion Capital Inc., St. Louis, 1988-94. With USAAF, 1943—46. Home: 22 Webster Oaks Dr Webster Groves MO 63119 Personal E-mail: rconerly@earthlink.net.

CONETTA, TAMI FOLEY, lawyer; b. Akron, Ohio, Aug. 29, 1965; d. Charles David and Roxanne (Onyett) Foley; m. Anthony Joseph Conetta, July 29, 1989 (div.); 1 child, Emory Elizabeth Conetta; m. Barry Frank Spivey, June 8, 2002. BA in Polit. Sci., Furman U., 1987; JD with honors, U. Fla., 1990. Bar: Fla. 1991; bd. cert. estates, trusts and wills Fla. Bar Bd. Legal Specialization. Ptnr. Gassman & Conetta, PA, Clearwater, Fla., 1990-98, Ruden, McClosky, Smith, Schuster & Russell, PA, Sarasota, Fla., 1998—. Contbr. articles to profl. jours. Mem. planned giving com. All Children's Hosp. Found.; Early Learning Coalition of Sarasota County, vice chmn., 2004-06; chair United Way Women's Initiative Leadership Coun. Recipient Am. Jurisprudence awards in Estate Planning and Taxation of Gratuitous Transfers, 1990. Fellow Am. Coll. Trust and Estate Counsel; mem. Am. Bus. Womens Assn. (pres. Sunrise chpt. 2002-03, Woman of Yr. 2003), Sarasota County Bar Assn. (chair probate and estate planning sect. 2000-01), Clearwater Bar Probate Com. (chair 1996-98), Southwest Fla. Estate Planning Coun., Fla. Bar Assn. (chair probate rules com. 2003-05, Real Property, Probate and Trust Law sect. exec. coun., power of atty. com., chair). Avocation: reading. Office: Ruden McClosky Smith Schuster & Russell PA Ste 700 1515 Ringling Blvd Sarasota FL 34236-6772 Address: PO Box 49017 Sarasota FL 34230-6017 Office Phone: 941-316-7600. E-mail: tami.conetta@ruden.com.

CONEWAY, PETER RICHARD, ambassador, retired diversified financial services company executive; b. Cleve., Apr. 13, 1944; s. Albert Earl and Clara Laroux (Durham) C.; m. Marsella Lynn Martin, July 29, 1967; children: Natalie, Cecile. BBA, U. Tex., 1966; postgrad., U. Hong Kong, 1967; MBA, Stanford U., 1969. Advisory dir. Goldman, Sachs & Co., Dallas, 1969—75, in instl. sales, 1969-75, v.p., resident mgr. Houston, 1975-78, ptnr., 1978—92, mng. dir. equity divsn. Tokyo, 1987—88; amb. to Switzerland & Liechtenstein US Dept. State, Bern, 2006—. Trustee Stanford Bus. Sch., 1983—; trustee Houston Ballet Found., 1983— , Houston Lyric Theatre, 1983— , Mus. Fine Arts, 1983—; bd. dirs. Houston Symphony Soc., 1983—; vice chmn. Houston Bapt. U. President's Council, 1979; bd. visitors U. Tex Anderson Cancer Ctr. Outstanding Young Tex. Ex award, 1983 Allied mem. N.Y. Stock Exchange; mem. Houston C. of C. (bd. dirs.); Clubs: River Oaks (Houston), Tejas (Houston), Coronado (Houston). Baptist. Office: US Dept State 5110 Bern Pl Washington DC 20521-5110*

CONEY, AIMS C., JR., lawyer, labor-management negotiator; b. Cleve., Sept. 22, 1929; s. Aims Chamberlain and Elizabeth (Lee) C.; m. Rita Newbold Platt, Feb. 20, 1954; children: Aims C. III, Sylvia L., Anne F. BA, Yale U., 1951; JD, U. Pa., 1954. Bar: Pa. Assoc. Kirkpatrick, Lockhart, Johnson & Hutchison, Pitts., 1956-69; ptnr. Kirkpatrick & Lockhart, Pitts., 1969-89, of counsel, 1990—. Contbr. articles in field of union-management relations and legal ethics to profl. jours. Bd. dirs. Arthritis Found., Pitts., 1967—, pres., 1972-75; bd. dirs. Ellis Sch., Pitts., 1974-91, Freedom House Amb. Svc., 1968-75, Indian Lake (N.Y.) Zoning Commn., 1993-95, Transitional Svcs. Inc., 1992-98; bd. dirs. Pace Sch., Pitts., 1980-94, pres., 1990-91. With U.S. Army, 1954-56. Mem. Pa. Bar Assn. (co-chmn. ethics com. 1999-2001), Allegheny County Bar Assn. Republican. Home: 516 Glen Arden Dr Pittsburgh PA 15208-2809 Office: Kirkpatrick & Lockhart Preston Gates Ellis LLP 535 Smithfield St Pittsburgh PA 15222-2312 Office Phone: 412-355-6406. Business E-Mail: aims.coney@klgates.com.

CONFER, ANTHONY WAYNE, veterinary pathologist, educator; b. Hot Springs, Ark., July 29, 1947; s. Edwin M. and Gloria V. (Parker) C.; m. Carolyn Gay Pope, Aug. 15, 1970; children: Andrew W., Aaron J., Michael E., Christina A. DVM, Okla. State U., 1972; MS, Ohio State U., 1974; PhD, U. Mo., 1978. Diplomate Am. Coll. Vet. Pathologists. Assoc. prof. La. State U., Baton Rouge, 1978-81, Okla. State U., Stillwater, 1981-85, prof., 1985—, dept. head, 1986-99, 2004—, assoc. dean for rsch. Coll. Vet. Medicine, 1999-2001, Sitlington endowed chair food animal rsch., 1995—, regents prof., 2003—. Vis. prof. U. BC, Vancouver, 1990-91; cons. Ft. Dodge Lab., Iowa, 1987-92, 2003—, Baxter Healthcare Corp., Round Lake, Ill., 1988-89, Vet. Reference Lab., Dallas, 1988-89, Smith Kline Beechan Ltd., Lincoln, Nebr., 1990; mem. Conf. Rsch. Workers-Animal Diseases, 1981—; cons. Diamond Animal Health, Des Moines, 1994-98, Pfizer Animal Health, Lincoln, Nebr., 1997—. Mem. editl. bd. Am. Jour. Vet. Rsch., 1993-2004, 2006—, Vet. Pathology, 1995-97, 2005—; contbr. over 170 sci. publs. in field. V.p. Stillwater Soccer Assn., 1987-91, pres., 1992-93; pub. rels. specialist Stillwater H.S. Soccer Club, 1990-96; cub master Cub Scout pack 22, Stillwater, 1987-89; panel mgr. USDA-NRI, 2006-. Capt. USAF, 69-77. Recipient Beecham award for rsch., SmithKline Beecham Lab., 1985, Norden Disting. Tchr. award, Pfizer, Inc., 1987, 2002, Eminent Faculty award, Okla. State U., 2003. Mem. AVMA (Vet. Rsch award 1992), Am. Coll. Vet. Pathologists (chair standing edn. com. 1994-96, program chair 1995), Morris Animal Found. (sci. advisor 1991-95), Am. Soc. Microbiology, Sigma Xi (chpt. lectr. 1993). Mem. Lds Ch. Avocations: physical fitness, guitar, cooking. Home: 2817 W 28th Ave Stillwater OK 74074-2212 Office: Okla State U Dept Vet Pathobiology Stillwater OK 74078-2007 Office Phone: 405-744-4542. Business E-Mail: aconfer@cvm.okstate.edu.

CONFESSORE, NICHOLAS, journalist; BA magna cum laude, Princeton Univ. Editor Washington Monthly; sr. corr. Am. Prospect; polit. reporter New York Times. Editor USC Annenberg Inst. for Justice and Journalism. Contbr. articles to numerous profl. jours. including Atlantic Monthly, Rolling Stone, The New Republic, The Los Angeles Times, The Boston Globe, and Salon magazine. Recipient Livingston Award, 2003. Office: The New York Times 229 W 43rd St New York NY 10036

CONFORTI, MICHAEL PETER, museum director, art historian; b. Bradford, Mass., Apr. 3, 1945; s. Sven and Cecile Conforti; m. Licia Peterson; children: Peter, Julia. BA, Trinity Coll., Hartford, Conn., 1968; MA, Harvard U., 1973, PhD, 1977. Cataloguer Sotheby & Co., London, 1968-69, dir. tng. program NYC, 1969-71; curator sculpture and decorative arts Fine Arts Mus., San Francisco, 1977-80; chief curator, Bell curator decorative arts and sculpture Mpls. Inst. Arts, 1980-94; dir. Sterling and Francine Clark Art Inst., Wiliamstown, Mass., 1994—. Curated (exhibitions) Sweden: A Royal Treasury, 1988, The American Craftsman and the European Tradition, 1620-1820, 1989, Art and Life on the Upper Mississippi, 1890-1915, 1994, A Grand Design--The History of London's Victoria and Albert Museum, 1997, organizer Uncanny Spectacle: The Public Career of John Singer Sargent, 1997, Impression: Painting Quickly in France 1820-1890, 2001, Gustav Klimt: Landscapes, 2002, Turner: The Late Seascapes, 2003, Jacques-Louis David: Empire to Exile, 2005, The Clark Brothers Collect: Impressionist and Modern Paintings, 2006; contbr. articles on sculpture, decorative arts, collecting and mus. history. Trustee Am. Acad. Rome, 2000—; mem. exec. com. Am. Acad. Rome, Carter Mus., 2003—; vice chmn. Nat. Com. for the History of Art, 2000—; trustee Com. Internat. d'Histoire de L'Art, 2004—, Internat. Coun. Mus., Am. Assn. Mus., 2005—; chair Art Mus. Image Consortium, 2003—05. Decorated Order of Polar Star (Sweden); recipient Robert Smith award, 1987, Charles Montgomery award, 1990; Nat. Endowment Arts Mus. fellow, 1974, Am. Acad. in Rome fellow, 1975-77; Bush fellow, 1985; Getty guest scholar, 1988; Andrew Mellon fellow Ctr. for Advanced Study in the Visual Arts, Nat. Gallery of Art, 1993. Mem.: Assn. Art Mus. Dirs. (trustee 2001—04). Office: Sterling & Francine Clark Art Inst 225 South St Williamstown MA 01267-2878 Office Phone: 413-458-9545.

CONG, JASON JINGSHENG, computer scientist, educator, consultant, researcher; b. Beijing, Feb. 20, 1963; came to U.S., 1986; m. Jing Chang, Jan. 28, 1995. BS, Peking U., China, 1985; MS, U. Ill., 1987, PhD, 1990. Rsch. asst. U. Ill., 1986-90; asst. prof. UCLA, 1990-94, assoc. prof., 1994-98, prof., 1998—, chair, dept. computer sci., 2005—. Cons. Intel Corp., Santa Clara, 1994—; tech. adv. bd. Mentor Graphics, San Jose, Calif., 1994-96, Magma Design Automation, Palo Alto, 1997-2001; founder, pres. Aplus Design Techs., Inc., 1998-2003; chief tech. advisor Magan Design Automation, 2004-. Author: Yield Enhancement of Reconfigurable VlSI Systems, 1992; contbr. over 130 articles to profl. jour. Recipient Young Investigator award NSF, 1993. Fellow IEEE (assoc. editor 1999—, Best Paper award 1995); mem. Assn. Computing Machinery (adv. bd. 1993-99, assoc. editor 1995—, Meritorius Svc. award 1998, Best Paper award 2005). Office: UCLA 4731J Boelter Hl Los Angeles CA 90095-0001

CONGALTON, CHRISTOPHER WILLIAM, lawyer; b. NYC, Apr. 8, 1946; s. William Alexander and Jacqueline Rose (Ryan) C.; m. Susan Tichenor, May 29, 1971. AB, Fairfield U., Conn., 1968; JD, Georgetown U., 1971. Bar: N.Y. 1972, U.S. Dist. Ct. (so. dist.) N.Y. 1974, U.S. Ct. Appeals (2d cir.) 1974, U.S. Supreme Ct. 1976, Ill. 1988, Colo. 1990. Assoc. Dunnington, Bartholow & Miller, NYC, 1971-78; asst. gen. counsel Diamond Internat. Corp., NYC, 1978-82; gen. counsel, v.p. Children's TV Workshop, NYC, 1987-88; chmn. and ceo Moffitt Co., Schiller Park, Ill., 1988—. Mem. ABA, (corp. banking & bus. sect.), Am. Corp. Counsel Assn., N.Y. State Bar Assn., Assn. of Bar of City of N.Y., Chgo. Bar Assn., Eagle Springs Golf Club. Home: 1500 N Lake Shore Dr Chicago IL 60610-6657

CONGALTON, SUSAN TICHENOR, lawyer; b. Mt. Vernon, NY, July 12, 1946; d. Arthur George and M. Marjorie Tichenor; m. Christopher William Congalton, May 29, 1971. BA summa cum laude, Loretto Heights Coll., 1968; JD, Georgetown U., 1971. Bar: NY 1972, Ill. 1986, Colo. 1990. Assoc. Reavis & McGrath (now Fulbright & Jaworski), NYC, 1971-78, ptnr., 1978-85; v.p., gen. counsel, sec. Carson Pirie Scott & Co., Chgo., 1985-87, sr. v.p. fin. and law, 1987-89; mng. dir. Lupine LLC (formerly known as Lupine Ptnrs.), Chgo., 1989—; chmn., CEO Calif. Amforge Corp., 2002—. Bd. dirs. Harris Fin. Corp., Harris Bankcorp, Inc.; chmn. Cmty. Reinvestment Act Com., 1990-97, chmn. audit com., 1997—; chmn. bd., CEO, Calif. Amforge Corp., 2002—. Mem. editorial staff Georgetown U. Law Jour., 1969-70, editor, 1970-71. Bd. overseers Ill. Inst. Tech., Chgo., Chgo. Kent Coll. Law, 1985-89; bus. adv. coun. Bus. Sch., U. Ill., Chgo., 1987-90; planning com. Ann. Corp. Counsel Inst., 1986-89; bd. dirs. Ill. Inst. Continuing Legal Edn., 1992-95; mem. Chgo. Workforce Bd., 1995-98; chmn. Strategic Planning Task force, 1995-96, chmn. Performance Rev. Com., 1996-98. Mem. ABA, Nat. Assn. Corp. Dirs. (bd. dirs. Chgo. chpt. 2001—), Econ. Club Chgo., Chgo. Club (bd. dirs. 1996—2004, treas. 1999-02, sec. 2002—04). Office: Lupine LLC 1520 Kensington Rd Ste 112 Oak Brook IL 60523-2140

CONGDON, AMANDA, actress, web video blogger, writer; b. NYC, 1981; Grad. magna cum laude, Northwestern U., Evanston, Ill., 2004; additional edn., King's Coll., London, Eng., U. New South Wales, Sydney, Australia. With Saatchi & Saatchi Advertising Agy.; co-scripter, co-prodr. Jet Set Show, 2006; co-prodr., anchor, daily online news show Rocketboom.com, 2004—06, part owner, 2004—; co-pres. Oxmour Entertainment. Comp. mem. Playground Improv Troupe, NY Comedy Club. Weblog Amanda UnBoomed, 2006, amandacongdon.com, starringamandacongdon.com, weekly news vlog ABCNews.com/Amanda, co-star CSI, Las Vegas, spl. guest Attack of the Show!, season regular The Restaurant, Season 2, guest appearance The Chris Rock Show, Hey Ya, My Coolest Years, co-host Jean Carlo Cooking Show, Northstar Music video, host (videoblog) Amanda Across America, lead performer (theatre) Independence, Manhattan Theatre Source, Waafrica, Red Room Theatre, Manhattan. Named one of Top 25 Web Celebs, Forbes mag., 2007. Avocations: writing, videoblogging, sketching, improv, bungee-jumping, hula hooping, horseback riding, swimming, volleyball, skiing, rollerskating, kayaking, soccer, hiking. Address: c/o Endeavor Agy 9601 Wilshire Blvd Beverly Hills CA 90210 Personal E-mail: oxmour@gmail.com.*

CONGDON, CHARLES B., lawyer; b. Phila., 1957; BA, Univ. Pa., 1979; JD, Villanova Univ., 1984. Bar: Pa. 1984. Joined Drinker Biddle & Reath LLP, Phila., 1984, now ptnr., bus., fin. dept. Mem.: Pa. Assn. Bond Lawyers, Nat. Assn. Bond Lawyers. Office: Drinker Biddle & Reath LLP One Logan Sq 18th & Cherry Sts Philadelphia PA 19103-6996 Office Phone: 215-988-2659. Office Fax: 215-988-2757. Business E-Mail: charles.congdon@dbr.com.

CONGDON, JOHN RHODES, transportation executive; b. Balt., Feb. 17, 1933; s. Earl Everett and Lillian Francis (Herbert) C.; m. Barbara Natalie Neblett, June 17, 1952; children: Susan Lee, John Rhodes, Jeffrey Whitefield. Student, U. Richmond, 1952-53. Driver Old Dominion Freight Line, 1951; founder, chmn. Old Dominion Truck Leasing, 1963—; vice chmn. Old Dominion Freight Line. Deacon River Rd. Ch., 1981; pres. Dorset Woods Civic Assn., 1973-74. With U.S. Army, 1953-55. Mem. Va. Hwy. Users Assn. (pres. 1976-78), River Rd. Citizens, Country Club of Va., Masons, Shriners. Home: Randolph Sq 112 W Square Dr Richmond VA 23238 Office: 7511 White Pine Rd Chesterfield VA 23832 Home Phone: 804-784-4034; Office Phone: 804-275-7832.

CONGER, HARRY MILTON, mining company executive; b. Seattle, July 22, 1930; s. Harry Milton Jr. and Caroline (Gunnell) C.; m. Phyllis Nadine Shepherd, Aug. 14, 1949 (dec.); children: Harry Milton IV, Preston George; m. Rosemary L. Scholz, Feb. 22, 1991. Degree in Bus. Adminstrn. (hon.), SD Sch. Mines Tech., 1983; degree in Engring. (hon.), Colo. Sch. Mines, 1988, degree (hon.). Registered profl. engr., Ariz., Colo. Shift foreman Asarco, Inc., Silver Bell, Ariz., 1955-64; mgr. Kaiser Steel Corp. Eagle Mountain Mine, 1964-70; v.p., gen. mgr. Kaiser Resources, Ltd., Fernie, B.C., Canada, 1970-73, Consolidation Coal Co. (Midwestern div.), Carbondale, Ill., 1973-75; v.p. Homestake Mining Co., San Francisco, 1975-77, pres., 1977-78, pres., chief exec. officer, 1978-82, chmn., pres., chief exec. officer, 1982-86, chmn., chief exec. officer, 1986-96, chmn., 1996-98, chmn., CEO emeritus, also bd. dirs., 1998, ret., 1998, PG& E Corp., 1982—2001, Baker Hughes Inc., 1987—97, Calmat Inc., 1986—97. Bd. dir., ASA Ltd., Apex Silver Mines; chmn. Am. Mining Congress, 1986—89, World Gold Coun., 1995—97. Trustee Calif. Inst. Tech. With C.E. US Army, 1956. Recipient Disting. Achievement medal Colo. Sch. Mines, 1978, Am. Mining Hall of Fame, 1990, Disting. Svc. award Am. Mining Congress, 1995. Mem. NAE, Nat. Mining Assn. (hon. bd. dirs.), Am. Inst. Mining Engrs. (disting., Charles F. Rand gold medal 1990), Mining and Metallurgy Soc. Am., Mining Club, Bohemian Club, Pacific Union Club. Republican. Episcopalian. Personal E-mail: hmcongerIII@sbcglobal.net.

CONGER, J. WILLIAM, lawyer; b. Shreveport, La., Mar. 6, 1945; BA, Univ. Okla., 1967, JD, 1970. Bar: Okla. 1971, US Dist Ct. (we., no. ea. dist Okla.), US Ct. Appeals (10th cir.). Of counsel, co-founder, past sr. ptnr. & pres. Hartzog Conger Cason & Neville, Okla. City, Okla., 1979—; adj. prof. Okla. City Univ., 2000—, gen. counsel, 2003—. Trustee, past pres. Heritage Hall Sch., Okla. City. Recipient commendation award, Internat. Acad. Trial Lawyers, 1970—71. Fellow: Am. Bar Found., Am. Coll. Trial Lawyers, Okla. Bar Found.; mem.: William J. Holloway Jr. Am. Inn of Ct. (master emeritus, & past pres.), ABA, Okla. Bar Assn. (bd. gov., pres.-elect 2006—07), Okla. County Bar Assn. (past pres. & dir.), Phi Alpha Delta. Office: Hartzog Conger Cason & Neville Ste 1600 201 Robert S Kerr Ave Oklahoma City OK 73102 also: Oklahoma City Univ 2501 N Blackwelder Oklahoma City OK 73106 Office Phone: 405-235-7000, 405-521-5845. Office Fax: 405-996-3403. Business E-Mail: bconger@hartzoglaw.com. E-mail: bconger@okcu.edu.

CONGER, LUCINDA, retired librarian; b. Ft. Bragg, NC, June 11, 1941; d. Meredith Moore and Ann Oliver (Mumford) Dickinson; m. Bruce C. Conger, June 25, 1966. BA, Radcliffe Coll., 1963; MLS, Rutgers U., 1964; student, Wesley Sem., Washington, 1990. Reference libr. U. Calif., Davis, 1964-65; cataloger Libr. of Congress, Washington, 1965, reference libr., 1966; compact storage libr. Princeton (N.J.) U., 1966-70; dir. reclassification Albion (Mich.) Coll., 1970-71, serials libr., 1971-73; reference libr. Yale U., New Haven, 1973-75, U.S. Dept. State, Washington, 1976—2000; chief Reader Svcs. Br., 1994—2000; ret., 2000. Author: Online Command Chart, 1977, 81; columnist Database Mag., 1980-90; contbr. articles to profl. jours. Vol., Washington Cathedral, 1976—, Smithsonian, 2001—. Recipient Govt. Computer News award, 1992, Sec. Career Achievement award, 2000. Mem.: DAR, Archaeological Inst. Am., Harvard Club Washington, Nat. Soc. Colonial Dames. Democrat. Episcopalian. Avocations: classical greek, archaeology, genealogy, travel. Home: 4906 Jamestown Rd Bethesda MD 20816-2709 Personal E-mail: congerld@msn.com.

CONGER, SUE ANN, computer information systems educator; b. Akron, Ohio, Nov. 6, 1947; d. Scott Stanley and Norma Marie (Bauknecht) Summerville; m. David Boyd Conger, July 3, 1971 (dec. June 1997); 1 child, Kathryn Summerville. BS, Ohio State U., 1970; MBA, Rutgers U., 1977; PhD, NYU, 1988. Programmer, analyst USDA, Washington, 1970-72; project leader Ednl. Testing Svc., Princeton, NJ, 1972-73; 2d v.p. Chase Manhattan Bank, NYC, 1973-77; tech. dir. Lambda Technology, Inc., NYC, 1977-80; sr. cons. Mobil Corp., NYC, 1980-83; asst. prof. computer info. systems Ga. State U., Atlanta, 1988-90; asst. prof. Baruch Coll. CUNY, 1990-94; assoc. prof. So. Meth. U., Dallas, 1994-99; dir. electronic commerce Sewell Automotive Cos., Dallas, 1999—2001; assoc. prof., dir. and project mgr. IT programs U. Dallas, Irving, 2001—. Cons. in field. Author: The New Software Engineering, 1994, Planning and Designing Effective Web Sites, 1998, Process Mapping and Management, 2007; contbr. articles to profl. jours. Grantee US Army Info. Systems Engrng. Command, 1989, CMI Group, 2002, Soc. for Info. Mgmt. Advanced Practices Coun., 2006-. Mem. IEEE, AIS, ITSMF, ISACA, PMI, Assn. for Computing Machinery, Acad. of Mgmt. Avocations: reading, sports, cooking. Office: Univ of Dallas 1845 W Northgate Dr Irving TX 75062

CONGER, WILLIAM FRAME, artist, educator; b. Dixon, Ill., May 29, 1937; s. Robert Allen and Catherine Florence (Kelly) C.; m. Kathleen Marie Onderak, May 23, 1964; children: Sarah Elizabeth, Clarisa Lynn. Student, Art Inst. Chgo., 1954, 56-57, 60, 62; BFA, U. N.Mex., 1960; MFA, U. Chgo., 1966. Asst. prof. Rock Valley Coll., Rockford, 1966-71; vis. lectr. Beloit Coll., 1969; prof., chmn. dept. art DePaul U., Chgo., 1971-85; vis. artist U. Chgo., 1976, 83, Cornell U., 1980; Sch. Art Inst. Chgo., 1985, Univ. Iowa; adj. prof. So. Ill. U., 1984; chmn. dept. art theory and practice Northwestern U., Evanston, Ill., 1985-99, prof., 1985—2006, prof. emeritus, 2006-; numerous lectures. One man shows Burpee Mus., Rockford, Ill., 1971, Douglas Kenyon Gallery, Chgo., 1974, 75, Krannert Ctr. for Arts, Urbana, Ill., 1976, Zaks Gallery, Chgo., 1978, 80, 83, Roy Boyd Gallery, Chgo., 1985, 87, 90, 92, 94, 96, 97, 98, 99, 2000, 01, 02, 04, 07, Janus Gallery, Santa Fe, 1992, Tarbel Mus., Ill., 1993, Univ. Club Chgo., 1998, Jonson Mus., Albuquerque, 1998, Walters Art Ctr., Tulsa, 2000, 01, Tadu Contemporary Santa Fe, 2003, 04, 05, Metropolitan Capitol Bank, Chgo., 2006; group shows include Art Inst. Chgo., 1963, 71, 73, 78, 80, 84-85, Mus. Contemporary Art, Chgo., 1976, 96-97, Krannert Mus., Urbana, 1976, Ill. State Mus., 1978, 88-89, E.B. Crocker Gallery, Sacramento, 1977, Phoenix Mus., 1977, Mitchell Mus., 1980, Notre Dame U., 1981, Sonoma State U., 1983, Cowles Mus., 1983, Arts Club Chgo., 1983-97, Sheldon Meml. Gallery, U. Nebr., 1984, Anchorage Fine Arts Mus., 1985, Ark Art Ctr., 1985, Block Mus., Northwestern U., 1986, 90, 96-97, 2005, 06, Smart Mus., 1996, Friatworks Gallery, Chgo., 2001, 03, 05; represented in permanent collections Art Inst. Chgo., Mus. Contemporary Art, Chgo., Smart Mus., U. Chgo., Ill. State Mus., Chgo., No. Ill. U., DePaul U., Jonson Mus., U. N.Mex., Block Mus., City of Chgo. Public Art Collection, Bucknell U., Wellesley Coll., others; also pvt. collections U.S. and worldwide; numerous catalogs, revs. and commentary in Arts mag., Art Forum, Art in Am., Ciamese, Art News, Art Criticism, Art & Antiques; others; author essays in Whitewalls, Chicago/Art/Write, Psychoanalytic Perspectives on Art, Psychoanalytic Studies of Biography, Critical Inquiry, other jours. Bd. dirs. Ox Bow Art Sch., 1982-86; adv. bd. Renaissance Soc., 1988-99; bd. trustees St. Benedict H.S., Chgo., 1994—2000; vis. com., DePaul U. Art Mus., 2004-; referee NEH, 1989; interviewee TV and radio programs including Am. Art Forum. Recipient Bartels award Art Inst. Chgo., 1971; Clusmann award, 1973; Friedman awards U. Chgo., 1965, 66. Mem. Coll. Art Assn. Am., Sons of Am. Revolution, Soc. Mayflower Descendants, Aldren Kindred of Am., Arts Club Chgo., Phi Sigma Tau. Office: Northwestern U Dept Art Theory & Practice Rm 244 Kresge Hall Evanston IL 60201 Home: 3500 N Lake Shore Dr 15A Chicago IL 60657-1815 Studio: 3711 N Ravenswood Chicago IL 60613 Office Phone: 773-296-4595. Personal E-mail: w-conger@sbcglobal.net. Business E-Mail: w-conger@northwestern.edu.

CONGISTRE, JOHN HUBER, electronics engineer, retired military officer; b. San Francisco, Calif., Mar. 7, 1942; s. Jerry Nmn and Wilma Nmn Congistre; m. Kathleen Ann Copley, Apr. 2, 1966; children: Jacqueline Ann Soto, Peter Joseph. BSEE, U. Calif., Berkeley, 1963; MEE, Santa Clara U., Calif., 1972. Commd. lt. USAF, 1964, advanced through grades to lt. col., ret., 1995; electronics engr. Link Sys., Sunnyvale, Calif., 1965—72, Peripheral Tech. Inc, Sunnyvale, 1972—75; sr. electronics engr. Argos Sys., Sunnyvale, 1975—93, EDO-RSS, Morgan Hill, Calif., 1993—. Treas. Am. Judo and Jujitsu Fedn., Santa Clara, 1966. Mem.: Assn. Old Crows (assoc.). Achievements include patents for solid state four quadrant multiplier. Office: Edo-Rss 18705 Madrone Pkwy Santa Clara CA 95037 Home Phone: 408-988-3017; Office Phone: 408-201-8000.

CONIGLIARO, LAURA CLAIRE, securities analyst; b. N.Y.C., Oct. 24, 1945; d. Julius and Edna (Schechner) Gerber; m. Michael Gardham, June 9, 1968; children— Alison Leigh, Andrew Warren. B.A. summa cum laude, Boston U., 1966; M.B.A., Fairleigh Dickinson U., 1979. Intelligence analyst Nat. Security Agy., Fort Meade, Md., 1966-70; securities analyst, assoc. dir. rsch., Prudential-Bache Securities, Inc., NYC, 1979—1996, venture capital and coverage of design and mfg. automation industries; securities analyst Goldman Sachs, NYC, 1996-, enterprise server & storage industry. Named One of Best Stock Pickers & #1 earnings estimator, Forbes mag., 2007. Contbr. articles to profl. jours.; mem. adv. bd. Jour. Computer-Integrated Mfg., 1984. Mem. Robot Inst./Soc. Mfg. Engrs., Computer and Automated Systems Assn., Environ. Info. Ctr. Robotics (mem. adv. bd 1984), Phi Beta Kappa. Office: Goldman Sachs 85 Broad St New York NY 10004*

CONINE, ERNEST, columnist; b. Dallas, Dec. 31, 1925; s. Ernest and Myrtle Conine; m. Phyllis Joan Hoyland, Nov. 28, 1953 (dec.); m. Ulla Fisher, Jan. 10, 1981. BS, So. Methodist U., 1948. Staff writer UPI, Dallas, 1948-51; Washington corr. Dallas Times Herald, 1952-55; successively

Washington corr., Moscow corr., New Eng. mgr. Bus. Week mag., 1955-63; fgn. corr. L.A. Times, Vienna, 1963-64, public affairs columnist, mem. editorial bd., 1964-87, contbr., 1988-92. Mem. Ctr. Internat. and Strategic Affairs, UCLA, 1975-90, Internat. Inst. for Strategic Studies, 1984-98; mem. Calif. Seminar Internat. Security and Fgn. Affairs, 1970-93, L.A. Com. Fgn. Affairs, 1973-93. Contbr. articles to popular mags. Served with Army Air Corps, 1944-46, AUS, 1951-52. Mem. Soc. Profl. Journalists. Home and Office: 205 Dasher Dr Austin TX 78734-5040

CONINO, JOSEPH ALOYSIUS, lawyer; b. Hammond, La., Aug. 17, 1920; s. Dominic and Catherine (Tamborella) C.; m. Mae Evelyn Moragas, Feb. 27, 1943; children: Joseph Aloysius Jr., Robert Carl. BBA, Tulane U., 1950; MBA, U. Pa., 1951; JD, Loyola U., 1961. Bar: La. 1961, U.S. Dist. Ct. (ea. dist.) La. 1961, U.S. Ct. Appeals (5th cir.) 1972, U.S. Supreme Ct. 1989. Pvt. practice, Jefferson, La., 1961—. County judge State of La. Parish, Jefferson, 1970; del. State of La. Constl. Conv., Baton Rouge, 1973-74; asst. atty. Parish of Jefferson, 1977-2006. With USN, 1942—45. Mem. La. Bar Assn. (ho. of dels. 1963-92, bd. dirs. 1981-83, 96-99, 2005—), Jefferson Bar Assn. (pres.), New Orleans C. of C. (bd. dirs. 1974-77), Kiwanis (pres. Metairie, La. chpt.). Avocations: golf, swimming, tennis. Office: 1920 Jefferson Hwy Jefferson LA 70121-3816 Office Phone: 504-834-9010.

CONKEL, ROBERT DALE, lawyer, consultant; b. Oct. 13, 1936; s. Chester William and Marian Matilda (Ashton) Conkel; m. Elizabeth A. Cargill, June 15, 1958; children: Debra Lynn, Dale William, Douglas Alan; m. Brenda Jo Myers, Aug. 2, 1980; 1 child, Chelsea Ashton. BA, Mt. Union Coll., 1958; JD cum laude, Cleve. Marshall Law Sch., 1965; LLM, Case Western Res. U., 1972. Bar: Ohio 1965, U.S. Ct. Appeals (5th cir.) 1979, U.S. Tax Ct. 1974, U.S. Supreme Ct. 1974, Tex. 1978. Supr. Social Security Adminstrn., Cleve., 1958—65; trust officer Harter Bank & Trust Co., Canton, Ohio, 1965—70; exec. v.p. Am. Actuaries, Inc., Grand Rapids, Mich., 1970—73; mgr. plans and rsch. A.S. Hansen, Inc., Dallas, 1973—74; pvt. practice Dallas, 1973—; pension cons., southwest regional dir. Am. Actuaries, Inc., Dallas, 1974—88. Sr. cons. Coopers & Lybrand, Dallas, 1989; pres. Robert D. Conkel, Inc., 1989—; mem. devel. bd. Met. Nat. Bank, Richardson, Tex.; instr. Am. Mgmt. Assn., 1975, Am. Coll. Advanced Pension Planning, 1975—76; enrolled actuary Joint Bd. Enrollment U.S. Depts. Labor and Treasury. Contbr. articles to legal publs.; mem. editl. adv. bd.: jour. Jour. Pension Planning and Compliance, 1974—83. Chmn. Zoning Bd. Adjustments, Richardson, Tex.; sustaining mem. Rep. Nat. Com., 1980—2004. Mem.: ABA (employee benefit com. sect. taxation), Am. Acad. Actuaries, Am. Soc. Pension Actuaries (dir. 1973—81), Dallas Bar Assn., Tex. Bar Assn., Ohio State Bar Assn. Office: 100 N Central Expy # 519 Richardson TX 75080-5332 Home Phone: 972-644-0410; Office Phone: 972-997-8211.

CONKIN, PAUL KEITH, history professor; b. Chuckey, Tenn., Oct. 25, 1929; s. Harry Thomas and Dorothy (Staten) C.; m. Dorothy L. Tharp, 1954; 3 children. BA, Milligan Coll., 1951; MA, Vanderbilt U., 1953, PhD, 1957. Asst. prof. history U. Southwestern La., 1957-59; asst. prof., assoc. prof., prof. U. Md., 1959-67; prof. U. Wis., Madison, 1967-76, Merle Curti prof., 1976-79; disting. prof. history Vanderbilt U., Nashville, 1979—2000, emeritus, 2000—, chmn. dept. history, 1984-87. Author: The New Deal, 1967, F.D.R. and the Origins of the Welfare State, 1967, Puritans and Pragmatists, 1968, Self-Evident Truths, 1974, Prophets of Prosperity, 1980, Gone with the Ivy: A Biography of Vanderbilt U., 1985, Big Daddy from the Pedernales: Lyndon Baines Johnson, 1986, The Southern Agrarians, 1988, Cane Ridge: America's Pentecost, 1991, Four Foundations of American Government, 1994, The Uneasy Center: Reformed Christianity in Antebellum America, 1995, American Originals: Homemade Varieties of Christianity, 1997, When All the Gods Trembled: Darwinism, Scopes, and American Intellectuals, 1998, Requiem for the American Village, 2000, Peabody College: From a Frontier Academy to the Frontiers of Teaching and Learning, 2002, The State of the Earth: Environmental Challenges on the Road to 2100, 2007; co-author: The Heritage and Challenge of History, 1971; author: (with others) A History of Recent America, 1974; co-editor: New Directions in American Intellectual History, 1979. Guggenheim fellow, 1965-66; sr. fellow Nat. Endowment for Humanities, 1972-73, 90. Mem. Am. Hist. Assn. (Beveridge award 1958), Orgn. Am. Historians, So. Hist. Assn. (pres. 1996-97). Home: 1003 Tyne Blvd Nashville TN 37220-1026 Office Phone: 615-322-1088. Business E-Mail: paul.k.conkin@vanderbilt.edu.

CONKLIN, DONALD DAVID, academic administrator; b. Waynesburg, Pa., Oct. 29, 1944; s. Donald David and Esther Louise (McCracken) C.; children: Donald David III, Elizabeth Ann. BA, Pa. State U., 1966, MEd, 1967; EdD, NYU, 1975. Asst. dean. instrn. SUNY, Farmingdale, 1970-72, exec. asst. to pres., 1972-78; spl. asst. N.J. Dept. Higher Edn., Trenton, 1978-80; dean for planning and devel. Mercer County Community Coll., Trenton, 1980-83, dean for adminstrn., 1983-86, dean for acad. affairs, 1986-92; pres. Dutchess Community Coll., Poughkeepsie, NY, 1992—. Cons. AAA of No. N.J., Morristown, 1984, Harrisburg Area C.C., 1983, Ednl. Testing Svc., Princeton, N.J., 1990, Educom Cons. Svcs., Princeton, 1985-90, Md. Higher Edn. Commn., 1992-95. Contbr. articles to profl. jours., chpts. to books. Chair Dutchess County Empire Zone Bd.; chmn. bd. dirs. United Way of Dutchess County; vice chmn., bd. dirs. St. Francis Hosp., Cmty. Fund of Dutchess County, Hudson Valley Philharm., Hudson Valley coun. Boy Scouts Am., Dutchess County Econ. Devel. Corp.; mem. SUNY Coun. of Pres.; chmn. Coll. Bd. CC Adv. Com.; trustee Poughkeepsie Day Sch. trustee Vassar Bros. Med. Ctr. Recipient Adminstrs. award for excellence in aviation edn. FAA, 1989, award Dutchess County Hist. Soc., 2006. Mem. Poughkeepsie C. of C., Rotary, Phi Theta Kappa, Alpha Mu Gamma, Phi Delta Kappa, The Club. Presbyterian. Avocations: tennis, golf, reading. Home: 57 Pendell Rd Poughkeepsie NY 12601-1512 Office: Dutchess CC Pendell Rd Poughkeepsie NY 12601 Office Phone: 845-431-8980. Business E-Mail: conklin@sunydutchess.edu.

CONKLIN, DONALD RANSFORD, retired pharmaceutical executive; b. Bound Brook, NJ, Sept. 10, 1936; s. Walter Ransford and Dorothy Ann (Haase) C.; m. Louise Sealey, July 13, 1960; children: Elizabeth, Edward. BA, Williams Coll., 1958; MBA, Rutgers U., 1961; grad. program for mgmt. devel., Harvard U., 1970. Dir. mktg. Schering Corp. U.S.A. (name changed to Schering-Plough 1971), Kenilworth, NJ, 1970-74; dir. mktg. Europe div. Schering-Plough, Lucerne, Switzerland, 1975-76, v.p. internat. mktg. Kenilworth, 1977-79, regional dir., sr. v.p. Latin Am. div. Miami, Fla., 1980-83, sr. v.p. internat. hdqrs. Kenilworth, 1984—, pres., 1985, group v.p. pharm. ops., 1986, exec. v.p. pharm. ops., 1987-89, pres. pharm. ops., 1989-94, pres. healthcare products, 1994-96; ret., 1996. Bd. dirs. Ventiv Inc., Alfacell Inc. Home: 66 Youngs Rd Basking Ridge NJ 07920

CONKLIN, GEORGE HENRY, sociologist, educator; b. Dumont, NJ, Apr. 9, 1941; s. Richard Brown and Heloise Sealey Conklin; m. Verna Gibble, Aug. 21, 1966; children: Heather, Wendy, Dawn. AB, Colgate U., 1963; PhD, U. Pa., 1971. Asst. prof. Syracuse (N.Y.) U., 1969—74; assoc. prof. Sweet Briar (Va.) Coll., 1974—78; prof. sociology N.C. Ctrl. U., Durham, 1978—, chair faculty senate, 1999—2000. Vice chmn. faculty assembly U. N.C., 2002—03. Contbr. articles to profl. jours., chapters to books and ednl. software; editor: Sociation Today, 2003—. Airport commr. Raleigh-Durham Airport Authority, 1990—99; chair bd. of adjustment Durham County Planning Dept., 1984—90; planning commr. Durham City/ County Planning Dept., 2000—05. Grantee Fulbright grantee, U.S. Ednl. Found. in India, 1963—64, rsch. grantee, Am. Inst. Indian Studies, 1968, Coll. Tchg. Improvement grantee, Fund for Improvment of Postsecondary Edn. (FIPSE), 1982—86, Computer-Based Instrnl. Materials grantee, NSF, Lilly Endowment, 1982—93. Mem.: Internat. Sociol. Assn., So. Sociol. Assn., N.C. Sociol. Assn. (pres. 1998—99, webmaster, editor Sociation Today, Contbns. to Sociology award 1998). Liberal. Presbyterian. Avocation: collecting antique phonographs. Home: 2905 Scuppernong Ln Durham NC 27703-9264 Office: NC Ctrl U Fayetteville St Durham NC Office Phone: 919-530-7327. Business E-Mail: gconkin@nccu.edu.

CONKLIN, GEORGE MELVILLE, retired food products executive; b. Roselle Park, NJ, Dec. 29, 1921; s. Melville Guy and Anna Elizabeth (McMahon) Conklin; m. Jean Austin Wiley, Feb. 19, 1944; children: Andrea(dec.) , Blair. BS, Clarkson Coll. Tech., 1947; MS, Newark Coll. Engring., 1951; DSc (hon.), Clarkson U., 1987. Draftsman Babcock & Wilcox, NYC, 1939-42; indsl. engr. Johns-Manville Co., Manville, NJ, 1947-48, Western Electric Co., Kearny, NJ, 1948-50, Gen. Ceramics, Keasby, NJ, 1950-51; indsl. engring. supr. Gen Electric Co., Bloomfield, NJ, 1951-52; with M & M/Mars, Hackettstown, NJ, 1952—, pres., 1968-78, chmn., 1980-82; group pres. Mars, Inc., 1979-80; ret., 1982. Trustee Clarkson U., 1976—86. With inf. AUS, 1943—45. Decorated Combat Inf. badge; named Hon. Commodore, Lake Waco, Tex.; recipient Key to City of Cleveland, Tenn. Mem.: Tex. Rangers (hon.), Evergreen Club (Palm City, Fla.), Tau Beta Pi. Home: Apt 2227 1221 SW Shoreline Dr Palm City FL 34990-4555 *Be a leader that most people do not notice so that when a job is done well, the people believe that they did it themselves.*

CONKLIN, HAROLD COLYER, anthropologist, educator; b. Easton, Pa., Apr. 27, 1926; s. Howard S. and May W. (Colyer) C.; m. Jean M. Morisuye, June 11, 1954; children: Bruce Robert, Mark William. AB, U. Calif.-Berkeley, 1950; PhD, Yale U., 1955. From instr. to assoc. prof. anthropology Columbia U., 1954-62; lectr. anthropology Rockefeller Inst., 1961-62; prof. anthropology Yale U., 1962-96, chmn. dept., 1964-68, Crosby prof. anthropology, 1990-96; curator of anthropology Yale Peabody Mus. Natural History, 1974-96, dir. divsn. anthropology, 1994-96, Crosby prof. emeritus, curator emeritus, 1996—. Mem. Inst. for Advanced Study, Princeton, N.J., 1972; fellow Ctr. for Advanced Study in Behavioral Scis., Stanford, Calif., 1978-79; field rsch. in Philippines, 1945-48, 52-54, 55, 57-58, 61, 62-63, 64, 65, 68-69, 70, 73, 80-81, 82-85, 90-91, 95, 2000-01, 04, 06, Malaya, Malaysia and Indonesia, 1948, 57, 83, Melanesia, 1987, N.Y., 1942, 48, 52, Calif., 1943, 48, 51, Guatemala, 1959, Peru, 1987; dir., com. problems and policy Social Sci. Rsch. Coun., 1963-70; bd. dirs. Survival Internat. USA, 1985-90; spl. cons. Internat. Rice Rsch. Inst., Los Baños, Philippines, 1962—; book rev. editor Am. Anthropologist, 1960-62; mem. Pacific sci. bd. Nat. Acad. Scis.-NRC, 1962-66. Author: Hanunóo Agriculture, 1957, Folk Classification, 1972, Ethnographic Atlas of Ifugao, 1980; other publs. on ethnol., linguistic and ecol. topics. Served with AUS, 1944-46. Guggenheim fellow, 1973; recipient Internat. Sci. prize Fyssen Found., 1983. Mem. NAS; Fellow Am. Acad. Arts and Scis., Am. Anthrop. Assn. (exec. bd. 1965-68), Royal Anthrop. Inst., N.Y. Acad. Scis. (sec. sect. anthropology 1956); mem. Am. Ethnol. Soc. (councilor 1960-62, pres. 1978-79), Koninklijk Inst. voor Taal- Land- en Volkenkunde, Conn. Acad. Arts and Scis., Linguistic Soc. Am., Kroeber Anthrop. Soc., Phila. Anthrop. Soc., Am. Geog. Soc., Am. Oriental Soc., Assn. Asian Studies, Classification Soc., Linguistic Soc. Philippines, Indo-Pacific Prehistory Assn., Soc. Econ. Botany (Disting. Econ. Botanist award 2005), Internat. Assn. Plant Taxonomy, AAAS, Phi Beta Kappa, Sigma Xi. Home: 106 York Sq New Haven CT 06511-3625 Address: Yale U Dept of Anthropology PO Box 208277 New Haven CT 06520-8277 Office Phone: 203-432-3667. Business E-Mail: harold.conklin@yale.edu.

CONKLIN, HOWARD LAWRENCE, lawyer; b. NYC, Apr. 16, 1943; s. Weldon F. and Gladys (Meyer) C. BS, Fairleigh Dickinson U., 1961; MBA, Syracuse U., 1969; JD, Fordham U., 1974. Bar: Fla. 1974, U.S. Dist. Ct. (so. dist.) 1976, U.S. Supreme Ct. 1978, U.S. Dist. Ct. (mid. dist.) Fla. 1980; lic. pilot FAA; lic. capt. USCG. Mktg. planning specialist Trans World Airlines, NYC, 1969-71; sr. transp. analyst Paine Webber, NYC, 1971-74; ptnr. Tripp, Scott, Conklin & Smith, Ft. Lauderdale, Fla., 1974-97; v.p. govt. and airport rels. Alamo Rent-a-Car, Inc., Ft. Lauderdale, 1997; v.p. govt. rels. AutoNation, Inc., Ft. Lauderdale, 1997—. Chmn. Ft. Pierce Area Coun. C. of C.; chmn. investment advisory com. St. Lucie County; vice chair Ft. Pierce Port Advisory Com.; bd. dirs. ARC; elected del. Dem. Party Nat. Conv., 2004. Col. USAF, 1964—68, Vietnam. Decorated Bronze Star, Legion of Merit. Mem. ABA, Air Force Assn., Res. Officers Assn., St. Lucie County Bar Assn., Indian River County Bar Assn., Mil. Officers Assn. (life), Army Navy Club (Washington), Pelican Yacht Club, Sons of Norway. Avocations: flying, sailing. Office: Howard L Conklin Atty 2030 Harbortown Dr Ste A Fort Pierce FL 34946-1438

CONKLIN, JACK L., education educator; b. Pt. Jefferson, NY, Dec. 9, 1942; s. John A. and Jeanne C.; m. Susan J. Kuceluk, July 25, 1981; children: Susanne, Danielle, Genevieve, Michelle. BA, Dowling Coll., 1967; MA, Adelphi U., 1970; PhD, U. So. Calif., LA, 1972. Tchr. Comsewogue Sch. Dist., Pt. Jefferson Sta., N.Y., 1967-70; asst. prin. intern Toll Jr. H.S., Glendale, Calif., 1971-72; prof. edn. Mass. Coll. Liberal Arts, 1972—2002; chmn. edn. dept. North Adams (Mass.) State Coll., 1982-92, cert. officer, 1988-93; prin. Chester Brook Acad., NJ, 2002—04; prof. edn. Georgian Ct. U., Lakewood, NJ, 2004—. Chmn. Commonwealth Tchr. Edn. Consortium, 1981-83; cons. U.S. Dept. Edn. Drug Free Schs. and Communities, 1989-94; field reader safe and drug-free schs. program U.S. Dept. Edn., 1990—; bd. regents Joint Commn. on Tchg. Preparation in Mass., 1999-2002. Bd. dirs. Berkshire Ctr. for Families and Children, Pittsfield, Mass., 1977, South Forty Alternatives, North Adams, 1978, Old Castle Theatre Co., Bennington, Vt., 1994-98; vestry mem. St. John's Episcopal Ch., Williamstown, Mass., 1983-84, St. John's Episcopal Ch., N. Adams, Mass., 1996-98, Pumpkin Hollow Farm Conf. Ctr. Retreat, 1998-2002; cons. N.E. Regional Ctr. for Drug Free Schs., 1988-94; mem. sch. coun. Mt. Greylock Regional Sch. Dist., Williamstown, 1996-99. Mem. Am. Assn. Colls. for Tchr. Edn. (adv. coun. state reps.), Mass. Assn. Colls. for Tchr. Edn. (pres. 1988-89), North Adams State Faculty Assn. (pres. 1980-83), Cmty. Edn. Legis. Task Force, Mass. State Senate, 1998—Joint Task force on Tchr. Preparation, Phi Delta Kappa, Pi Lambda Theta (nat. officers nominating com., Outstanding Faculty Advisor award 1998-99). Democrat. Avocations: jazz-cocktail piano, sailing. Office: Georgian Ct Univ Raymond W Rm 207 900 Lakewood Rd Lakewood NJ 08701 Home: 85 Hawthorne Rd Williamstown MA 01267 Office Phone: 732-987-2710.

CONKLIN, JOHN EVAN, sociology educator; b. Oswego, NY, Oct. 2, 1943; s. Evan Nelson and Susan Estelle (Brenner) C.; m. Ruth Tiffany Edmonds, July 10, 1965 (div. Oct. 1974); children: Christopher Perry, Anne Tiffany; m. Sarah Hubbard Belcher, Jan.2, 1982; children: Lydia Catherine, Gillian Jane. AB, Cornell U., 1965; PhD, Harvard U., 1969. Research assoc. Harvard U. Law Sch., Cambridge, Mass., 1969-70; asst. prof. sociology Tufts U., Medford, Mass., 1970-76, assoc. prof. sociology, 1976-81, prof. sociology, 1981—, chmn. dept. sociology, 1981-86, 90-91. Author: Robbery and the Criminal Justice System, 1972, The Impact of Crime, 1975, Illegal But Not Criminal, 1977, Criminology, 1981, 9th edit., 2007, Sociology: An Introduction, 1984, 2d edit., 1987, Art Crime, 1994, Why Crime Rates Fell, 2003; editor: The Crime Establishment, 1973, New Perspectives in Criminology, 1996. Mem. Am. Soc. Criminology, Acad. Criminal Justice Scis. Avocations: collecting books, movie memorabilia. Office: Tufts U Dept of Sociology 115 Eaton Hall Medford MA 02155 Office Phone: 617-627-3561. Business E-Mail: john.conklin@tufts.edu.

CONKLIN, JOHN ROGER, retired electronics company executive; b. Poughkeepsie, NY, Dec. 20, 1933; s. Leland Thomas and Eleanor (Warren) C.; m. Catharine Becker, Dec. 28, 1956 (div. Apr. 1976); children: Thomas Stephen, Todd Roger; m. Nancy Plank, July 16, 1983. BS in Mil. Sci., U.S. Mil. Acad., 1956; postgrad., Xavier U., Cin., 1961-62, Northeastern U., 1974. Engr. Procter & Gamble Co., Cin., 1960-64; sales engr. Orville Simpson Co., Cin., 1964-67; pres. DeLaval Separator Co., Poughkeepsie, 1967—78, Standard Gage Co., Poughkeepsie, 1979-86; pres., owner Discount Data Products, Inc., Poughkeepsie, 1988-97; ret., 1997. Adv. bd. Dutchess divsn. Bank of N.Y., Poughkeepsie, 1974-98. Contbr. articles to profl. jours.; patentee basket centrifuge. Bd. dirs. Area Fund-Dutchess County, Poughkeepsie, 1975, Poughkeepsie C. of C., 1981-86, YMCA, Poughkeepsie, 1982; campaign chair United Way, Dutchess County, N.Y., 1986; dir., pres. West Point Soc. of Mid-Hudson Region, 2003. 1st lt. U.S. Army, 1956-60. Mem. D.C. Hist. Soc. Avocations: skiing, trout fishing, gardening, mycology. Home: 5 Dutchess Ter Rhinecliff NY 12574

CONKLIN, THOMAS WILLIAM, lawyer; b. Chgo., Mar. 1, 1938; s. Clarence Robert and Ellen Pauline (Gleason) C.; children: Thomas William, Sarah Adrienne. BA, Yale U., 1960; JD, U. Chgo., 1963. Bar: Ill. 1964, Mich. 1997. Ptnr. Upton, Conklin & Leahy, Chgo., 1969-72, Conklin, Leahy & Eisenberg, Chgo., 1972-79, Conklin & Adler, Ltd., Chgo., 1979-87, Conklin & Roadhouse, Chgo., 1988-95; Rivkin, Radler & Kremer, Chgo., 1995-97; ptnr. Conklin, Murphy, Conklin & Snyder, Chgo., 1997—2004, Conklin & Snyder LLC, Chgo., 2004—05, Conklin & Conklin LLC, Chgo., 2005—. Contbr. numerous articles to legal jours. With USAF, 1963-64. Mem. ABA, Fed. Bar Assn., Am. Arbitration Assn., Internat. Assn. Ins. Counsel, Chgo. Bar Assn., Maritime Law Assn., Mich. Bar Assn., Chgo. Bar Assn., Union League Club Chgo. Home: PO Box 189 Bangor MI 49013-0189 Office: Conklin & Conklin LLC 53 W Jackson Blvd Ste 1150 Chicago IL 60604-3790 Office Phone: 312-341-9500. E-mail: tconk@msn.com.

CONKLIN, WILLIAM FRANK, writer; b. Cambridge, Mass., Apr. 8, 1926; s. Frank Alvin and Helen Pearl (Harvison) Conklin; m. Celia Bass, Aug. 13, 1948. Student, Bucknell U., U. Colo., U. Va. Lic. comml. pilot FAA; master U.S. Mcht. Marine. Enlisted USN, 1944, naval aviator, combat missions in Korea and Vietnam, 1947—68, exch. officer Fleet Air Arm, Royal Navy, 1956—58, ret. comdr., 1968; sys. analyst Ctr. Naval Analyses, Rosslyn, Va., 1968-71; freelance writer various publs., 1971-80; capt. Am. Cruise Lines, Haddam, Conn., 1981; founder Conklin Marine Ctr. and Chesapeake Area Profl. Capts. Assn., Annapolis, Md., 1982-91; owner, writer BBC Comm., Naples, Fla., 1991—. Decorated 2 Disting. Flying Cross, Bronze Star, 17 Air medals. Personal E-mail: bbccomm@earthlink.net.

CONKLING, ROGER LINTON, management consultant, business administration educator, retired utilities executive; b. Bloomington, Ill., July 12, 1917; s. Robert Edwin and Helen (Ricketts) C.; m. Meta Baskerville, Apr. 4, 1941; children: Mary Beth, Jane Linton, Roger Marc. BBA, Northwestern U., Evanston, Ill., 1941; MA, U. Oreg., Eugene, 1948; LLD, U. Portland, 1972. With Pub. Svc. Co. No. Ill., Chgo. and Joliet, 1936-42; economist Bonneville Power Adminstrn., Portland, Oreg., 1945-47, asst. to power mgr., 1948-51, chief system devel., 1952-53, chief customer svc., 1954, dir. budget and mgmt., 1955-56, asst. to adminstr., 1957; v.p., assoc. H. Zinder & Assocs., Inc., Washington, 1958-61; pres., cons. Conkling, Inc., Portland, 1962-67; v.p. N.W. Natural Gas Co., Portland, 1967-76, sr. v.p., CFO, 1976-82; ret., 1982. Adj. prof. bus. adminstrn. U. Portland, 1988—; former pres., dir. Pacific Western Pipeline Corp., Portland; mem. grad. faculty Oreg. System Higher Edn., Portland, 1946-56; cons. in field. Author: Marginal Cost in the New Economy, 2004. Past pres., chmn. Oreg. United Appeal; pres. Delauney Inst. Mental Health, 1964; mem. Gov.'s Com. Child Care, 1964; bd. dirs. Cath. Charities, Inc., Portland, 1957-58, 61-64; pres. Oreg. State Soc., Washington, 1960; chmn. exec. com. Nat. Found., 1958-60; chmn. March of Dimes campaign, Portland, 1957; bd. dirs. Mental Health Assn., 1957-58, Cath. Services for Children, 1954-57, Oreg. Symphony Assn., NCCJ, 1980-82, Found. Oreg. Research and Edn., 1967-80; chmn. bd. regents U. Portland; trustee Providence Children's Center; chmn. ann. fund dr. Oreg. Symphony, 1981; mem. fin. council Archdiocese of Portland, 1988-98. With USNR, 1942-45. Recipient Distinguished Service award Dept. Interior, Arthur S. Fleming award Jr. C. of C., Papal honor, Benemerenti medal. Mem. Am. Econ. Assn., Western Econ. Assn., Fed. Govt. Accts. Assn., Am. Gas Assn., Pacific Coast Gas Assn., Assn. Wash. Gas Utilities (trustee, past pres.), Beta Gamma Sigma, Delta Mu Delta. Home and Office: 2539 SW Hill Crest Dr Portland OR 97201-1749 Home Phone: 503-223-4304; Office Phone: 503-223-4304. Business E-Mail: conklingr@comcast.net.

CONKLYN, ELIZABETH D., insurance company executive; PhD. Sr. v.p. human resources and orgn. Mobile Telecom. Techs. Corp., Jackson, Miss.; sr. v.p. human resources USAA (United Svcs. Automobile Assn.), exec. v.p. people svcs. Mem. Conf. Bd. Adv. Coun. Human Resource Mgmt., 2000. Bd. trustees United Way San Antonio. Office: USAA 9800 Fredericksburg Rd San Antonio TX 78288 Office Phone: 210-498-8222.*

CONLEY, JAMES W., English language educator, language arts educator; b. Chgo., Feb. 23, 1945; s. E. Dean and Mildred Casey Conley; m. Kathleen Marie Gallo, Dec. 29, 1971; children: James Roland, Danielle Jeanne. BA in English, Georgetown U., Washington, 1966; MA in Italian, Middlebury Coll., Vt., 1968; PhD in Comparative Lit., U. of Wis., Madison, 1974. Instr. Gonzaga-in-Florence, Italy, 1971—74; adj. instr. Villanova U., 1974—76, Montgomery County C.C., Blue Bell, 1974—76; prof. English and comm. arts St. Thomas U., Miami Gardens, Fla., 1976—. NEH fellow Princeton U., NJ, 1980, Huntington Libr., San Marino, Calif., 1983, UCLA, LA, 1989, Northwestern U., Evanston, Ill., 1990; dir. honors program St. Thomas U., Miami Gardens, Fla., 1985—, dir. study abroad for Earth program, Assisi, Italy, 1999—2002; editor Biscayne Coll. Instnl. Self Study for Re-affirmation of Accreditation by the So. Assn. of Colls., 1982—83. Contbr. articles to profl. jours. and confs.; prodr.: (weekly radio show) The Round Table from St. Thomas University, 1999—2002. Vol. soccer coach Miami Lakes Optimist Club, 1982—87; bd. of advisers Father Solanus Casey Guild, Detroit, 1995—96; lector, eucharistic min. Our Lady of the Lakes Cath. Ch., Miami Lakes, 1980—2006. Named Tchr. of the Yr., Office of Student Affairs, St. Thomas U., 2005; recipient John Cardinal Newman Award for Excellence in Tchg., Office of Campus Ministry, St. Thomas U., 1997, Frank R. Esposito Award for Commitment to Student Athletics, Intercollegiate Athletics Office, St. Thomas U., 1997, Robert M. Sullivan Award for Excellence in Tchg., Office of Acad. Affairs, Biscayne Coll., 1979, Thomas Sessa Award for Dedication to U. Students, Student Govt. Assn., Biscayne Coll., 1979. Mem.: MLA, KC, Milw. Rd. Soc. of Am., Georgetown U. Alumni Assn., U. of Wis. Alumni Assn., Delta Epsilon Sigma (nat. pres. 2005—, mem. bd. advisers 1998—2001). Roman Catholic. Avocations: poetry, travel, theater, canoeing. Home: 7378 Big Cypress Dr Miami Lakes FL 33014 Office: St Thomas Univ 16401 NW 37th Ave Miami Gardens FL 33054 Home Phone: 305-823-5985; Office Phone: 305-628-6640. Office Fax: 305-628-6757; Home Fax: 305-628-6757. Business E-Mail: jconley@stu.edu.

CONLEY, JOHN WALLACE, academic administrator; b. Portsmouth, Ohio, Feb. 15, 1932; s. Hollie Conley and Dora Lee COnley; m. Dolores Holton Conley, July 13, 1954; 1 child, Konni Lee Gargour. AB, Asbury Coll., 1956; MTH, St. Thomas U., 1974; DD (hon.), Asbury Coll., 1974. Pastor First Ch. God, Morehead, Ky., 1960—66, 1991—94, 5th Ave. Ch. God, South Charleston, W.Va., 1966—73; pres. Gulf Coast Bible Coll., Houston, 1973—84, Mid-Am. Bible Coll., Oklahoma City, 1984—90, Circlesville Bible Coll., Ohio, 1994—2004. With US Army, 1951—52. Home: 592 Sycamore Dr Circleville OH 43113

CONLEY, MARK A., lawyer; b. Phila., Nov. 22, 1951; BA magna cum laude, U. Pa., 1973; JD, Columbia U., 1977. Bar: NY 1978, Calif. 1989.

With Debevoise & Plimpton, Will and Emery; ptnr. corp. law Katten Muchin Zavis Rosenman, LA. Mem.: U. So. Calif. Inst. for Corp. Counsel, LA Venture Assn., LA County Bar Assn., Calif. State Bar Assn. Office: Ste 2600 2029 Century Park E Los Angeles CA 90067 Office Phone: 310-788-4690. Office Fax: 310-712-8225. E-mail: mark.conley@kmzr.com.

CONLEY, PATRICK T., lawyer, writer, historian, educator, real estate developer; b. Branford, Conn., June 22, 1938; s. William Lincoln Conley and Edith Mae De Stasio; m. Gail C. Cahalan-Conley, Dec. 30, 1994; m. Virginia M. Anderson (div.); children: Patrick Jr., Kathleen, Carolyn, Sharon; m. Donna L. Arruda (div.); m. Ruth E. Trainor (div.); children: Thomas, Colleen. AB, Providence Coll., 1959; JD, Suffolk U., 1973; MA, U. Notre Dame, 1963, PhD, 1970. Bar: RI; lic. real estate broker. Prof. history and constitutional law Providence Coll., 1963—88, dir. grad. rsch. Am. history, 1964—94, spl. lectr. history, 1988—94; spl. lectr. constitutional law Salve Regina Coll., 1972—81; tchr. LaSalle Acad., Providence, 1961—62; teaching asst. U. Notre Dame, 1962—63; mem. corp., law sch. adv. com., chmn. libr. adv. com. Roger Williams Coll.; proproetor P.T. Conley Books, 1963—97; ptnr. Foreseeable Devel., Providence. Pres. Phoenix Realty, Four Seas Realty, Hardscrabble Land Co., Sedona Assocs., Options Realty, Phoenix Gambino, Zeus Realty Co.; spkr. in field; developer Conley's Wharf at State Pier No 1, Providence. Author: Democracy in Decline: Rhode Island's Constitutional Development, 1776-1841, 1977, Rhode Island Profile, 1982, An Album of Rhode Island History, 1986, First in War: Last in Peace: Rhode Island and the Constitution, 1786-1970, 1987, Liberty and Justice: A History of Law and Lawyers in Rhode Island, 1636-1998, 1998, Neither Separate Nor Equal: Legislature and Executive in Rhode Island Constitutional History, 1999, Rhode Island in Rhetoric and Reflection, 2002; co-author (with Matthew Smith): Catholicism in Rhode Island: The Formative Era, 1976; co-author: (with Paul Campbell) Providence: A Pictorial History, 1982, Firefighters and Fires in Providence, 1954-1984 and South Providence, 1985; co-author: (with William MacKenzie Woodward and Robert Jones) The Statehouses of Rhode Island: An Architectural and Historical Survey, 1988; editor: Proceedings of Rhode Island Constitutional Convention of 1973, 1973, R.I. Ethnic Heritage Pamphlet series (13 vols.); co-editor: The Constitution and the States, 1988, The Bill of Rights and rhe States, 1992, South Providence, 2006, The Rhode Island State Constitution: A Reference Guide, 2007; mem. editl. bd.: Rhode Island Bar Jour., 1980—81, 1985—88, 1990—93, 1998—. Bd. trustees Bicentennial Coun. Thirteen Original States, 1970—92, vice chmn., 1986—87; chmn. US Constitution Coun., 1988—90; pres. Cath. Assn. Coll. Alumni, 1976; chmn. Cranston Historic Dist. Commn., 1970—72; mem. Gov.'s Justice Commn., 1967—69; chmn. Cranston Charter Rev. Commn., 1972—73; policy advisor Gov. Frank Licht, Gov. Philip Noel, Lt. Gov. J. Joseph Garrahy, Atty. Gen. Herbert F. DeSimone, 1966—76; chmn. RI Bicentennial Commn. and Found., 1974—77; dir. Provicence Crime Commn., 1977—84; v.p. Human Rels. Commn. Diocese Providence, 1968—69; bd. trustees RI Hist. Soc.; chmn. libr. adv. com. Roger Williams Coll., 1990—93, mem. law sch. adv. bd., 1991—97; pres. RI Heritage Hall Fame, 2003—; chmn. RI Sr. Olympics, 2004—; spl. asst., chmn. adv. coun. US Congressman Robert O. Tiernan, 1967—74; sec., del. RI Constitutional Convention, 1973, gen. counsel to pres., 1986; bd. dirs. Heritage Harbor Mus., 1999—. Named Historian Laureate of RI, 2005. Mem.: Bristol Train Artillery Found. (bd. dirs. 2001—), Providence Maritime Heritage Found. (v.p., dir. 1998—), Bristol Statehouse Found. (founder, pres. 1995—99), RI Pubs. Soc. (chmn. 1981—), Bristol Hist. and Preservation Soc. (life), RI Hist. Soc. (life), Am. Hist. Assn. (life), Orgn. Am. Historians (life), RI Heritage Hall of Fame (pres. 2003—, inducted 1995), RI Sr. Olympics (chmn. 2004—), Fabre Line Club (founding pres. 2007—), Elks, Delta Epsilon Sigma. Roman Catholic. Avocations: track and field, travel, interior decorating, book collecting. Home: 1 Bristol Point Rd Bristol RI 02809 Office: 1445 Wampanoag Trail Providence RI 02918 also: Conley's Wharf at State Pier No 1 200 Allens Ave Providence RI 02905 Office Phone: 401-273-1787. Personal E-mail: ptconley@aol.com.

CONLEY, PHILIP JAMES, JR., retired air force officer; b. Providence, May 22, 1927; s. Philip James and Lillian Loretta (Burns) C.; m. Shirley Jean Andrews, Jan. 26, 1956; children: Sharon, Kathleen, Anne, James. BS, U.S. Naval Acad., 1950; MS, U. Mich., 1956, Rensselaer Poly. Inst., 1963. Commd. 2d lt. USAF, 1950, advanced through grades to maj. gen., 1979; dep. chief staff, ops. Air Force Systems Command, Andrews AFB, Washington, 1974-75, chief staff, 1975-78; comdr. Air Force Flight Test Center, Edwards AFB, Calif., 1978-82; vice-comdr. Electronic Systems Divn. Hanscom AFB, Mass., 1983; ret., 1983. Decorated Disting. Svc. medal (2), Legion of Merit (2), Disting. Flying Cross, Bronze Star, Air medal (3). Mem. Air Force Assn., Order of Daedalians, U.S. Naval Acad. Alumni Assn., Am. Legion, Vikings Club (L.A.), Santa Barbara Yacht Club, Monticeto Country Club. Roman Catholic. Home: 930 Camino Viejo Santa Barbara CA 93108-1920

CONLEY, RUTH IRENE, poet; b. Seattle, Jan. 26, 1920; d. Irving Birch Anderson and Gertrude Evelyn Unsworth Edwins; m. Samuel Glenn Conley, June 12, 1946 (div. Nov. 1963); children: Joan Evelyn, Mary Jacquelyn, James Harper. BA in Gen. Studies, U. Wash., 1964, BA in English, 1965, MA in English, 1966, MA in Comparative Lit., 1970; studied with Theodore Roethke. Editor publs. office U. Wash., Seattle, 1965—66, acctg. asst., 1973—86. Author numerous poems; author: (poet) (chapbooks) Time of Apple Harvest, Icicle River, and Short Poems from the Japanese. With US Army, 1944—46. Democrat. Avocation: gardening.

CONLEY, SHAWN, agriculturist; BS, MS, PhD, U. Wis., Madison. Cropping sys. specialist U. Mo., Columbia, 2001—04; state soybean ext. specialist Purdue U., W. Lafayette, Ind., 2004—. Office: Purdue U 915 W State St Lafayette IN 47907 Office Phone: 765-494-0895. Business E-Mail: conleysp@purdue.edu.

CONLEY, TERENCE P., human resources specialist; BA, NYU, 1985. Various postions in human resources RH Macy & Co.; with PepsiCo, Inc., 1990—99; human resources mgr. to dir. Kentucky Fried Chicken, 1990—92; v.p. human resources PepsiCo, Inc., 1994—96; regional dir. Frito-Lay, 1996—98; exec. v.p. human resources and corporate svcs. Cendant Corp., NYC, 1999—. Dir. Cendant Charitable Found. Office: Cendant Corp 9 W 57th St New York NY 10019

CONLEY, TOM CLARK, literature educator; b. New Haven, Dec. 7, 1943; s. Walter Frederick and Hazel Mason (Hatch) C.; m. Verena Andermatt; children: David, Francine. BA, Lawrence U., 1965; MA, Columbia U., 1966; PhD, U. Wis., 1971. Prof. U. Minn., Mpls., 1971-95; prof. renaissance lit., cinema Harvard U., Cambridge, Mass., 1995—, dir. grad. studies in French. Vis. prof. U. Calif., Berkeley, 1978-79, CUNY Grad. Ctr., 1985-87, Miami U., Ohio, 1989, UCLA, 1995; instr. Folger Inst., 1998; summer seminar leader NEH, 1998; seminar leader Sch. Critical Theory, 2003. Author: Lectura de Bunuel, 1988, Film Hieroglyphs, 1991, Graphic Unconscious, 1992, Self-Made Map, 1995, Cartographic Cinema, 2006; translator 5 books, editor 2 books; editor jour. Lendemains, 1985—, Diacritics, 2000—; corr. jour. Litterature, 1988—; contbr. articles to profl. jours. Woodrow Wilson fellow, 1965-66, Fulbright fellow, 1968-69, study fellow Am. Coun. Learned Socs., 1975-76, summer fellow NEH, 1974, 89, Inst. for Rsch. in Humanities fellow, 1990, Newberry Libr. fellow, 1992, Soc. Humanities fellow, 1998, Harvard Cabot fellow, 2002, Guggenheim fellow, 2003—. Mem. MLA, Renaissance Soc. Am., Assn. Study Dada/Surrealism, Midwest MLA (mem. exec. com. 1977-80), Sixteenth Century Studies Soc. (exec. com. 1994—), Alpha Omega Alpha. Avocations: handball, fishing, mycology. Office: Harvard U Romance Langs 201 Boylston Hall Cambridge MA 02138 Office Phone: 617-495-2274. Business E-Mail: tconley@fas.harvard.edu.

CONLEY, WILLIAM CLELAND, statistician, educator; b. Lansing, Mich., June 19, 1948; s. William Cleland Conley Sr. and Joan Joyce Conley. BA in Math. cum laude, Albion Coll., Mich., 1970; MA in Math., Western Mich. U., Kalamazoo, 1971; MSc in Math., U. Windsor, Can., 1973, PhD, 1976. From lectr. to asst. prof. U. Windsor, 1973—77; from asst. prof. to assoc. prof. U. Wis., Green Bay, 1977—99, prof., 1999—. Cons., presenter in field. Author: Computer Optimization Techniques, 1980, 1984, Optimization: A Simplified Approach, 1981, Basic for Beginners, 1982, Basic II Advanced, 1983, Computer Optimization Techniques Revised Edition, 1984; contbr. articles to profl. jours., 195 publs. worldwide. Named to Albion Coll. Athletic Hall of Fame for soccer, 1995, Albion Coll. Athletic Hall of Fame for golf, 2005; recipient Faculty award, Founders Assn., 2001. Fellow: Instn. Electronic and Telecomm. Engrs.; mem.: Am. Chem. Soc., Soc. for Computer Simulation Internat. (sr.), Phi Beta Kappa, Phi Kappa Phi. Achievements include discovery of multi stage monte carlo optimization, TSP statis. for multivariate work. Avocations: jogging, golf, tennis, music. Office: Univ Wis 2420 Nicolet Dr Green Bay WI 54311 Office Phone: 920-465-2051, 920-465-2499. Office Fax: 920-465-2660. Business E-Mail: conleyw@uwgb.edu.

CONLIN, LINDA MYSLIWY, bank executive, former federal agency administrator; b. Springfield, Mass. m. Joseph F. Conlin Jr. Pres. Park-Main Travel Agy.; protocol visits officer US Dept. State; from corp. liaison officer for US/USSR intiatives to assoc. dir. Office of Pvt. Sector Coms. U.S. Info. Agy.; asst. sec. commerce for mktg. U.S. Travel and Tourism Adminstrn., 1989—93; dir. Office Travel and Tourism NJ Dept. Commerce, 1994—98; exec. dir. Office Travel and Tourism NJ Commerce & Econ. Growth Commn., 1998—99; dep. to program chmn. 2000 Rep. Nat. Conv.; sr. campaign coord. Bush/Cheney 2000-Southeastern Pa. Region; asst. sec. trade devel. US Dept. Commerce, Washington, 2001—04; v.p. Export-Import Bank of the US, 2006—. Bd. dirs. Export-Import Bank of the US, 2004—. Republican. Office: Export Import Bank of the US 811 Vermont Ave NW Washington DC 20571

CONLIN, MICHAEL JOSEPH, physician; s. Armetta and Henry Joseph Conlin; m. Terri Conlin; children: Sean, Kathleen, Kyle, Ryan. MD, U. Tex., San Antonio, 1989. Physician Oreg. Health & Scis. U., Portland, 1989—. Office: Oregon Health & Scis Univ 3303 SW Baond Ave Portland OR 97201 Office Phone: 503-494-4779. Office Fax: 503-494-8671.

CONLIN, ROXANNE BARTON, lawyer; b. Huron, SD, June 30, 1944; d. Marion William and Alyce Muraine (Madden) Barton; m. James Clyde Conlin, Mar. 21, 1964; children: Jacalyn Rae, James Barton, Deborah Ann, Douglas Benton BA, Drake U., 1964, JD, 1966, MPA, 1979; LLD (hon.), U. Dubuque, 1975. Bar: Iowa 1966. Assoc. Davis, Huebner, Johnson & Burt, Des Moines, 1966-67; dep. indsl. commr. State of Iowa, 1967-68, asst. atty. gen., 1969-76; U.S. atty. So. Dist. Iowa, 1977-81; ptnr. Conlin, P.C., Des Moines, 1983—. Adj. prof. law U. Iowa, 1977-79; chmn. Iowa Women's Polit. Caucus, 1973-75, del. nat. steering com., 1973-77; cons. U.S. Commn. on Internat. Women's Year, 1976-77; gen. counsel NOW Legal Def. and Edn. Fund, 1985-88, pres., 1986-88; lectr. in field. Co-editor: ATLAs Litigating Tort Cases, 6 vols., 2003; contbr. articles to profl. jours. Nat. committeewoman Iowa Young Dems.; pres. Polk County Young Dems., 1965-66; del. Iowa Presdl. Conv., 1972; Dem. candidate for gov. of Iowa, 1982; bd. dirs. Riverhills Day Care Ctr., YWCA; chmn. Drake U. Law Sch. Endowment Trust, 1985-86; bd. counselors Drake U., 1982-86; pres. founder Civil Justice Found., 1986-88; pres. Roscoe Pound Found., 1994-97; chair Iowa Dem. Party, 1998-99; chair Edwards For Pres. Iowa, 2004. Named scholarship in her honor, Kansas City Women Lawyers; named one of Top Ten Litigators, Nat. Law Jour, 1989, 100 Most Influential Attys., 1991, 50 Most Powerful Women Attys., Nat. Law Jour., 1998, 10 Most Influential Women Attys., 2002; recipient award, Iowa ACLU, 1974, Alumnus of Yr. award, Drake U. Law Sch., 1989, Ann. award, Young Women's Resource Ctr., 1989, Verne Lawyer Outstanding Mem. award, Iowa Trial Lawyers Assn., 1994, Rosalie Wahl award, Minn. Women Lawyers, 1998, Marie Lambert award, 2000, Mary Louise Smith award, YWCA, 2001, Lifetime Achievement award, Des Moines Human Rights Commn., 2003, Ruth Bader Ginsberg award, 2004, Iowa Juneteenth award, State of Iowa, 2005, Feminist Activist award, Bus. Record and Drake U., 2006; scholar Reader's Digest scholar, 1963—64, Fishcher Found., 1965—66. Mem.: ATLA (chmn. consumer and victims coalition com. 1985—87, chmn. edn. dept 1987—88, parliamentarian 1988—89, sec. 1989—90, v.p. 1990—91, pres.-elect 1991—92, pres. 1992—93, Lifetime Achievement award 2003, Champion of Justice award 2006, Leonard Ring Champion of Justice award 2006), ABA, NOW, Nat. Ctr. State Ct. Lawyers Com. (com. mem. 2003—), Nat. Inst. Trial Advocacy (bd. trustees 2003—06), Trial Lawyers Care (bd. dirs.), Inner Circle of Advocates, Higher Edn. Commn. Iowa (co-chmn. 1988—90), Iowa Acad. Trial Lawyers, Internat. Acad. Trial Lawyers, Assn. Trial Lawyers Iowa (bd. dirs.), Iowa Bar Assn., Chi Omega, Alpha Lambda Delta, Phi Beta Kappa. Office: Griffin Bldg 319 7th St Ste 600 Des Moines IA 50309-3826 Office Phone: 515-283-1111. Business E-Mail: rconlin@roxanneconlinlaw.com.

CONLIN, THOMAS, conductor; b. Arlington, Va., Jan. 29, 1944; BMus, Peabody Conservatory Music, 1966, MMus, 1967; studied with Leonard Bernstein, Erich Leinsdorf, Sir Adrian Boult. Artistic dir. Chamber Opera Soc., Balt., 1966-72; assoc. condr. N.C. Symphony Orch., 1972-74; music dir. Queens (N.Y.) Orchestral Soc., 1974-76; condr. Amarillo (Tex.) Symphony Orch., 1976-84, W.Va. Symphony Orch., 1983-2001, condr. laureate, 2001—; prin. condr. Toledo Opera, 2002—. Asst. prof. mus. CUNY, 1974-76. Recording: Naxos and Bridge. Recipient Grammy award for Contemporary Classical Composition, 2001, Indie award nomination for Best Orch. Rec., 2002. Mem. Am. Symphony Orch. League, Nat. Opera Assn., Condrs. Guild, Opera America. Studio: 8440 Augusta Ln Holland OH 43528 Office Phone: 419-867-6977. E-mail: thomas@thomasconlin.com.

CONLON, BRIAN THOMAS, promotion executive; b. Oceanside, NY, Mar. 19, 1958; s. Thomas James and Joan Anna (Erickson) Conlon; m. Mary Jane Lewis, Nov. 12, 1988; children: Brendan Lewis, Ryan Bradshaw Erickson, Emily Rose Mary. BA in English, Hofstra U., 1979. Asst. account exec. DR Group, NYC, 1981-82, account supr., 1982—83; account exec. D.L. Blair, Inc., Garden City, NY, 1983—85, v.p./account supr., 1985—90, sr. v.p., 1990—91, exec. v.p., 1991—2002, pres., 2002—05, vice chmn., CEO, 2005—. Roman Catholic. Office: DL Blair Inc 1051 Franklin Ave Garden City NY 11530-2931 Office Phone: 516-746-3700. Business E-Mail: bconlon@dlblair.com.

CONLON, JAMES EDWARD, retired art educator, sculptor; b. Cin., Dec. 9, 1935; s. Ralph Leroy and Elvera Ann Conlon; m. Joanne Lois Kuhns, June 12, 1959; children: Kevin, Kathleen, Kristopher. BS in Art Edn., Ohio State U., 1959, MA in Fine Arts, 1962. Art tchr. Cin. Pub. Schs., 1960—61; grad. asst. Ohio State U., Columbus, 1961—62; lectr. Ind. U., Bloomington, 1962—65; asst. prof. art U. South Ala., Mobile, 1965—72, assoc. prof., 1972—80, prof., 1980—97, prof. emeritus, 1998—. Designer Mobile Terrace Playground, 1971—72; 14 ft. mirrored site-piece, Gateway, Mobile 1st Night Celebration, cold cast bronze sculpture, Seventh Day Adventist Ch., St. Elmo, Ala., 1982—83, fiberglass wall relief, Mobile Airport Terminal, 1987—88, life-size sculpture, Children and Women's Hosp., Mobile, 1995—97. Bd. dirs. Habitat for Humanity, Mobile, 1995—97. Grantee, Samuel H. Kress Found., 1969—78. Mem.: Water Color and Graphic Arts Soc. Mobile. Avocations: photography, numismatics. Home: 1613 Sugar Creek Dr W Mobile AL 36695 Personal E-mail: jjconlon@bellsouth.net.

CONLON, MICHAEL WILLIAM, lawyer; b. Wilkes Barre, Pa., Nov. 9, 1946; s. William Peter and Dorothy Conlon; m. Alice Cario, June 14, 1969; children: Michele, Stacia. AB magna cum laude, Cath. U., 1968; JD, Duke U., 1971. Bar: Tex. 1971. Ptnr. Fulbright & Jaworski, Houston, 1978-93, 98—, ptnr. in charge Washington, 1993-98, co-head corp., banking and bus. practice dept., 1999—, co-ptnr. in charge Houston Office, 2001—06, ptnr. in charge Houston Office, 2007—. Named to Order of the Coif. Office: Fulbright & Jaworski LLP 1301 McKinney St Houston TX 77010-3031 Home Phone: 713-520-7610; Office Phone: 713-651-5427. Office Fax: 713-651-5246. Business E-Mail: mconlon@fulbright.com.

CONLON, PEGGY EILEEN, publisher; b. Santa Monica, Calif., Mar. 2, 1951; d. Daniel Francis and Mary Eileen (Garrity) C.; m. Robert J. Reale, May 21, 1993. AA, Victor Valley Jr. Coll., Apple Valley, Calif.; BA, Calif. State U., Fullerton; MA, U. So. Calif.-Annenberg, LA. Account exec. Dozier Eastman, Santa Ana, Calif., 1973-75; advt. and pub. rels. mgr. ITT Marine Divsn., Costa Mesa, Calif., 1975-80, EECO, Santa Ana, 1980-82; group pub. CMP Publs., Manhasset, N.Y., 1982-92; pub. Broadcasting & Cable, NYC, 1992—; pres. The Advt. Coun., 1999—. Lt. USNR, 1974-81. Mem. Internat. Radio and TV Soc. (bd. dirs. 1993-96), exec. coun. The Quills. Office: Advertising Council Fl 11 261 Madison Ave New York NY 10016 also: Broadcasting And Cable 360 Park Ave S New York NY 10010-1710

CONLON, SUZANNE B., federal judge; b. 1939; AB, Mundelein Coll., 1963; JD, Loyola U., Chgo., 1968; postgrad., U. London, 1971. Law clk. to judge U.S. Dist. Ct. (no. dist.) Ill., 1968-71; assoc. Pattishall, McAuliffe & Hostetter, 1972-73, Schiff Hardin & Waite, 1973-75; asst. U.S. atty. U.S. Dist. Ct. (no. dist.) Ill., 1976-77, 82-86, U.S. Dist. Ct. (cen. dist.) Calif., 1978-82; exec. dir. U.S. Sentencing Commn., 1986-88; spl. counsel to assoc. atty. gen., 1988; judge U.S. Dist. Ct. (no. dist.) Ill., 1988—. Asst. prof. law De Paul U., Chgo., 1972-73, lectr., 1973-75; adj. prof. Northwestern U. Sch. Law, 1991-95; vice chmn. Chgo. Bar Assn. Internat. Inst., 1993—; vis. com. U. Chgo. Harris Grad. Sch. Pub. Policy, 1997—; bd. mem. DePaul U. Coll. Law, Internat. Human Rights Law Inst. Bd. mem. Ill. St. Andrew Soc. Mem. ABA, FBA, Am. Judicature Soc., Internat. Bar Assn. Judges Forum, Lawyers Club Chgo. (pres. 1996-97). Office: US Dist Ct No Dist Everett McKinley Dirksen Bldg 219 S Dearborn St Ste 2356 Chicago IL 60604-1878

CONLON, THOMAS JAMES, marketing executive; b. NYC, July 30, 1935; s. Kenneth Charles and Catherine (Gavaghan) C.; m. Joan Anna Erickson, Jan. 19, 1957; children: Brian T., Michael K., Keith J.K. Ed., Art Students' League, NYC, 1951-53, St. Peter's Coll., Jersey City, 1953-56. Staff artist N.Y. News, NYC, 1953-57, spl. features writer-reporter, 1957-59; mktg. mgr. Tricolator Inc., Wantagh, NY, 1959-64; assoc. dir. promotion Benton & Bowles, NYC, 1964-68; chmn. D.L. Blair Inc., Garden City, NY, 1968—, PMI, Inc., Atlanta, 1986—, DLB/W, Beverly Hills, Calif., 1987—; mng. dir./gerant Blair Europe, Paris, 1991-98; mng. ptnr. Conlon Holdings Inc., 1999—; pres. Conlon Assocs., LP, 1999—. Illustrator for various mags., 1952-53. Mem. Brookville Country Club; mem. Squadron A, Vets. Corps. 69th Regiment. Home: Wolver Hollow Rd Oyster Bay NY 11771-4301 Office: DL Blair Inc 1051 Franklin Ave Garden City NY 11530-2931 Business E-Mail: tconlon@dlblair.com.

CONLON, WILLIAM F., lawyer; b. Chgo., Jan. 14, 1945; AB, Ind. U., 1967; JD, U. Ill., 1970. Bar Ill. 1970, Iowa 1970, U.S. Supreme Ct. 1975. Asst. U.S. Atty. U.S. Attys. Office (no. dist.) Ill., 1974-79, chief civil divsn., 1977-79; ptnr. corp. criminal def. and internal investigations Sidley Austin Brown & Wood, Chgo., gen. counsel and mem. exec. com. Chmn. Ill. State Bd. Ethics, 1986-88, active, 1982-88, Jud. Inquiry Bd., 1992—97; adj. prof. law Northwestern U., 1991—. Pres. Glencoe (Ill.) Sch. Bd., 1987-88, active, 1981-89. 1st lt. US Army, 1970-72. Fellow Am. Coll. Trial Lawyers. Office: Sidley Austin Brown & Wood LLP Bank One Plz 10 S Dearborn St Chicago IL 60603 Office Phone: 312-853-7384. Office Fax: 312-853-7036. Business E-Mail: wconlon@sidley.com.

CONLY, JOHN FRANKLIN, retired engineering educator; b. Ridley Park, Pa., Sept. 11, 1933; s. Harlan and Mary Jane (Roberts) Conly; m. Jeannine Therese McDonough, Apr. 14, 1967; children: J. Paul, Mary Ann. BS, U. Pa., 1956, MS, 1958; PhD, Columbia U., 1962. Instr. U. Pa., Phila., 1956-58; rsch. asst. Columbia U., NYC, 1959-62; asst. prof. engring. San Diego State U., 1962-65, assoc. prof., 1965-69, prof., 1969—2003, prof. emeritus, 2003—, chmn. dept., 1971-74, 77-85, wind tunnel dir., 1978—2001. D. and F. Guggenheim fellow, 1958. Fellow: AIAA (assoc.; sect. chmn. 1970, best U.S. sect.). Republican. Episcopalian. Office: San Diego State U Dept Aerospace Engring San Diego CA 92182

CONN, ERIC EDWARD, plant biochemist; b. Berthoud, Colo., Jan. 6, 1923; s. William Elmer and Mary Anna (Smith) C.; m. Louise Carolyn Kachel, Oct. 17, 1959; children: Michael E., Kevin E. BA in Chemistry cum laude, U. Colo., Boulder, 1944; PhD in Biochemistry, U. Chgo., 1950. Instr. biochemistry U. Chgo., 1950-52; instr. U. Calif., Berkeley, 1952-53, asst. prof., 1953-58, assoc. prof. Davis, 1958-63, prof., 1964—. Author: (with P.K. Stumpf) Outlines of Biochemistry, 1963, 5th edit., 1987; editor: (with P.K. Stumpf) (book series) Biochemistry of Plants, 1980-90. With U.S. Army, 1945-46. Recipient Pergamon Phytochemistry prize and cert., 1994;, USPHS fellow, 1960, Fulbright Rsch. grantee, 1965, Australian acacia "Acacia conniana" named in his honor, 1984. Mem. NAS, Phytochem. Soc. N.Am. (hon. life mem., pres. 1971-72, editor in chief 1984-89), Am. Soc. Plant Biology (pres. 1986-87, Charles Reid Barnes life mem.), Am. Soc. Biol. Chemistry, Am. Chem. Soc. Democrat. Avocations: gardening, stamp collecting/philately. Office: Univ Calif Sect Molecular & Cellular Biol Davis CA 95616 Home Phone: 530-753-4174; Office Phone: 530-752-3611. Business E-Mail: eeconn@ucdavis.edu.

CONN, MARGARET ELBOW, human resources specialist; b. Albany, NY, Jan. 5, 1951; d. Matthew H. and Margaret A.B. Elbow; m. Richard E. Conn, Apr. 3, 1982. BA, Tufts U., Medford, Mass., 1972; MBA, Columbia U. Grad. Sch. Bus., NYC, 1977. Cert. arbitrator BBB. Asst. to provost Simmons Coll., Boston, 1972—75; human resources mgmt. Ford Motor Co., Dearborn, Mich., 1977—90. Charter mem. Women in Philanthropy, Hilton Head Island, SC, 2005—; vol. First Presbyn. Ch., Hilton Head Island, 1993—; mem. Prayer Shawl Ministry, Hilton Head Island, 2005—. Presbyterian. Avocation: travel. Home: 2 Village N Dr #7 Hilton Head Island SC 29926

CONN, REX BOLAND, JR., pathologist, educator; b. Marengo, Iowa, Aug. 3, 1927; s. Rex Boland and Helena Dorothea (Schoenfelder) C.; m. Victoria Grace Sellens, Dec. 28, 1950; children: Elizabeth Marian, Victoria Anne, Mary Catherine. BS, Iowa State U., 1949; MD, Yale U., 1953; BSc, U. Oxford, Eng., 1955; MS, U. Minn., 1960. Prof. pathology, dir. clin. labs. W.Va. Med. Center, Morgantown, 1960-68; prof. lab. medicine, dir. dept. Johns Hopkins Med. Instns., Balt., 1968-77; prof. pathology and lab. medicine, dir. clin labs. Emory U., Atlanta, 1977-87; prof. and vice chmn. dept. pathology and cell biology, dir. clin. labs. Thomas Jefferson U., Phila., 1987-97; prof. emeritus Jefferson Med. Coll., Phila., 1997—. Mem. pathology tng. com. NIH, 1972-73, mem. pathology A study sect., 1968-72; cons. Walter Reed Army Med. Center, 1972-77; cons. Armed Forces Inst. of Pathology, 1984-88. Editor: Current Diagnosis, 1997, Yearbook of Pathology and Clinical Pathology, 1980, Applied Laboratory Medicine,

1992. Served with USNR, 1945-46. Mem. Coll. Am. Pathologists, Am. Soc. Clin. Pathologists (dir. 1975-81, pres. 1993-94), Acad. Clin. Lab. Physicians and Scientists (pres. 1972). Office: Thomas Jefferson Univ Jefferson Alumni Hall 212 Philadelphia PA 19107 Office Phone: 215-238-1977. Business E-Mail: rex.conn@mail.tju.edu.

CONN, RICHARD LEE, computer scientist, educator; b. Logansport, Ind., Apr. 11, 1954; s. Harry Richard and Forest Geneva Conn. BS in Computer Sci., Rose-Hulman Inst. Tech., 1976; MS in Computer Sci., U. Ill., 1978. Cert. instr., GE Aircraft Engines. Tech. cons. U.S. Army Satellite Comm. Agy., Ft. Monmouth, N.J., 1978-80; instr. Air Force Inst. Tech., Wright-Patterson AFB, Ohio, 1980-82; computer scientist U.S. Army Software Devel. and Support Ctr., Ft. Monmouth, 1982-84; software design engr. Tex. Instruments, Dallas, 1984-85; mgr. Ada Software Repository Project, White Sands, N.Mex., 1984-93; pvt. practice Plano, Tex., 1986; software engr. advanced engring. tech. dept. software engring. section GE Aircraft Engines, Cin., 1986-92; mgr. Mgmt. Assistance Corp. Am., White Sands Missile Range, 1987-91; with Defense Advanced Rsch. Projects Agy./Ada Joint Program Office, Washington, 1991-92; mem. fed. adv. bd. Ada Joint Program Office The Pentagon, Washington, 1992-93; mgr. Pub. Ada Libr. Monmouth Coll., West Long Branch, N.J., 1993-97; prof. software engring. dept. Monmouth U., 1995-97; sr. software process engr. Lockheed Martin Aeronautics, Marietta, Ga., 1997—2003; rsch. prof. info. sci. and tech. Monmouth Coll., West Long Branch, N.J., 1993-95; mem. tech. staff MITRE Corp., Eatontown, N.J., 1992-95; acad. liaison Microscoft, Atlanta, 2003—. Adj. prof. dept. elec. and computer engring. U. Cin., 1990-92; adj. prof. computer sci. and info. sys. Kennesaw (Ga.) State U., 1998—; adj. prof. computing and software engring. So. Polytech. State U., 2002—; instr. dept. elec. engring. Air Force Inst. Tech., Wright-Patterson AFB, 1980-82, human resources dept. GE Aircraft Engines, Cin., 1987-92; co-chair Assn. Computing Machinery/Spl. Interest Group Ada Edn. Working Group; mem. DoD Ada Awareness Group; working group on Ada as design lang. IEEE; mem. Ada quality and style guide team Software Productivity Consortium. Author: ZCPR3: The Manual, 1985, The Ada Software Repository and the Defense Data Network: A Resouce Handbook, 1987; editor Walnut Creek Ada CDRom; editor, lead Ada and Software Engring. Libr. and CDRom. Lead Software Devel. and Engring. SIG, Atlanta PC User's Group, Atlanta, Ga., 2001—03. Capt. US Army Signal Corps, 1976—82, Wright-Patterson AFB, OH. Recipient 2 Army Commendation medals. Master: Software Devel. and Engring. SIG, Atlanta PC User's Group (lead 2001—02); mem.: IEEE, Am. Legion, Assn. Computing Machinery (edn. co-chair Spl. Interest Group in Ada 1984—95), Masons, Tau Beta Pi. Achievements include development of Created the ZCPR series of Operating and Software Development Systems; research in Performed funded research in software reuse; developed the ZCPR3, CSPARTS, SCATC, and DCS3 Domain Specific Software Development Kits; first to Played a role in the development of the Ada programming language; served on Federal Advisory Board for Ada; Reviewer for DoD Software Reuse Initiative; Awarded Outstanding Contributions to the Ada C; development of Wrote numerous courses distributed world-wide in the Public Ada Library, the Ada and Software Engineering Library, and the ACM Journal for Educational Resources in Computing. Avocations: chess, swimming.

CONN, SALLEE J., minister, educator; d. Walter Abbott and Diane Wilson Gose Schroeder; m. James D. Conn, June 5, 1971; 1 child, Ryan. BA, NW U., Kirkland, Wash., 1972; BA in Edn., We. Wash. U., Bellingham, Wash., 1976; MA, Fuller Theol. Sem., Pasadena, Calif., 1997; PhD, Gonzaga U., Spokane, Wash., 2004. Lic. minister Assemblies of God, 1984, ordained minister Assemblies of God, 1993; cert. tchr. Wash., 1976, in acute traumatic stress mgmt. Am. Acad. Experts Traumatic Stress, 2006. Tchr. seconday English Calvary H.S., Majuro, Marshall Islands, 1978—79; office mgr. King Moving Svc., Mount Vernon, Wash., 1979—83; min., missionary Assemblies God World Missions, Nuku'alofa, Tonga, 1983—93; assoc. pastor Shoreline Cmty. Ch., Seattle, 1993—98; assoc. dir. Missionary Renewal Asia Pacific, Kirkland, Wash., 1998—. Bd. dirs. NW U., constn. and bylaws task force, 2004—05, academic planning commn., 2004—, chmn. bd. standing com., 2006—; sec. Tongan Concordance Working Com., Nuku'alofa, Tonga, 1989—92; co-founder, chmn. leadership com. NW Women Ministers' Network, Wash., 1995—; assoc. Ctr. Orgnl. Reform, Spokane, Wash., 2002—; adv. bd. Ministry Resources Internat., Kirkland, 2004—, Inst. Congl. Leadership, Spokane, 2006—, Ctr. Pentecostal Rsch., Kirkland, 2006—. Nat. dir. dept. women's ministries Assemblies of God of Tonga, Nuku'alofa, 1985—86; pastoral advisor Royal Family Kids' Camp, Seattle, 1996—98. Mem.: Assn. Psychol. Type, Am. Acad. Experts in Traumatic Stress, Am. Assn. Pastoral Counselors, Acad. Mgmt., Soc. Pentecostal Studies, Delta Epsilon Chi.

CONNALLY, MARK, statistician, psychometrician; b. Athens, Ga., Mar. 31, 1964; s. Bobby Ray Connally and Barbara Towers; m. Gail Lynn, Dec. 3, 1955; children: Jonathan, Emylee. BS, U. Ga., Athens, 1986, M in Applied Math. Sci., 1989, PhD, 2004. Adj. instr. Truett-McConnell Coll., Watkinsville, Ga., 1992—97; instr. U. Ga., Athens, 1997—2000; sr. statistician Chauncey Group Internat., Princeton, NJ, 2000—03; psychometrician Measurement Inc., Durham, NC, 2003—. Mem.: Am. Ednl. Rsch. Assn. (assoc.). Republican. Home: 253 Northlands Dr Cary NC 27519 Home Phone: 919-460-6261; Office Phone: 919-683-2413.

CONNALLY, SANDRA JANE OPPY, freelance/self-employed artist, educator; b. Crawfordsville, Ind., Feb. 10, 1941; d. Thomas Jay and Helen Louise (Lane) Oppy; m. Thomas Maurice Connally, Nov. 9, 1962 (dec. May 2004); children: Leslie Erin Connally Hosier Dakins, Tyler Maurice. BS, Ball State U., 1963, MA, 1981. Freelance writer, Muncie, Ind., 1971-76; art/freelance, 1964-81; substitute tchr. Muncie (Ind.) Cmty. Schs., 1980—81, art tchr., 1981—2003; ret., 2003. Lectr. Ind. U. Art Mus., Ind., docent; substitute tchr. Monroe County Cmty. Sch. Corp. Two women shows include Emens Auditorium, Ball State U., 1983; exhibited in group shows at Ball State U., 1964, Alford House/Anderson (Ind.) Fine Arts Ctr., 1979-81, Historic 8th St. Exhbn., 1981, Patrons Watercolor Gala, Oklahoma City, 1983, Whitewater Valley Annual Drawing, Painting and Printmaking Competition, Richmond, Ind., 1983; represented in pvt. collections; contbr. short stories to profl. publs. Bd. dirs. Bay Pointe Home Owners Assn. Grantee Container Corp. Am., 1981, Ball State U. Mus. Art/Margaret Ball Meml. Fund, 1992, Robert B. Bell, 1993-95; recipient Achievement award Ind. Dept. Edn., 1992-94, Nat. Gallery Videodisc Competition, 1993; named dising. UniverCitizen Ball State U., 1992, Tchr. Intergalactic Art First Place Ind. State winner, 1998. Mem. Nat. Art Edn. Assn. (del. nat. conv. 1998, 2000-03), Bay Pointe Home Owners Assn. (dir. bd.). Republican. Methodist. Avocations: computers, painting, handmade paper and glass fusing, travel. Home: 1932 Bay Pointe Dr E Bloomington IN 47401-8136

CONNAUGHTON, JAMES L., federal official; m. Susanna Connaughton; children: Spencer, Grace. Grad., Yale U.; JD magna cum laude, Northwestern U. Law clk. U.S. Dist. Judge Marvin Aspen No. Dist. Ill.; U.S. negotiator ISO 14000, 1993—2001; ptnr. environ. practice group Sidley Austin Brown & Wood; chmn. Coun. on Environ. Quality Exec. Office of the Pres., Washington, 2001—. Lectr. in field. Coordinating articles editor: Northwestern U. Law Rev. Scholar Austin scholar, Northwestern U. Mem.: Order of the Coif. Avocations: sailing, singing, beach combing. Office: Exec Office of the Pres Coun on Environ Quality 730 Jackson Pl NW Washington DC 20503

CONNAUGHTON, JAMES PATRICK, psychiatrist; b. Dublin, Mar. 13, 1931; arrived in U.S., 1958; s. Patrick and Julia (Barrett) Connaughton; m. Monica T. Keaveny, 1957; children: Bernadette, Eileen, James, Paul, John. MB, ChB, MD, Univ. Coll., Dublin., 1956; MS in Bus. of Medicine, Johns Hopkins U., 2002. Diplomate Am. Bd. Psychiatry & Neurology, Am. Bd. Child & Adolescent Psychiatry. Intern Mater Univ. Hosp., Dublin, 1956—57; resident in psychiatry Seton Psychiat. Inst., Balt., 1958—61; sr. staff psychiatrist Milw. Psychiat. Hosp., 1961—65; fellow dept. child psychiatry, dept. pediatrics Johns Hopkins Hosp., Balt., 1965—67, sr. staff div. child psychiatry, 1967—. Family practice medicine, Manchester, England, 1957—58; psychiat. cons. VA Hosp., Wood, Wis., 1961—65, Peace Corps Tng. Projects, 1963—64; dir. adolescent program Milw. Psychiat. Hosp., 1961—65; cons. dept. medicine West Allis Meml. Hosp., Milw., 1962—65; ass.t prof. psychiatry Marquette U., 1962—65; treas. Milw. Psychiat. Clinic Chartered, 1963—64, v.p., 1964—65; dir. Dundalk Mental Health Clinic, Baltimore County, Md., 1966—67; cons. Assoc. Cath. Charities, 1966—81, Oldfields Sch., 1968—78, Children's Guild, 1969—78, John F. Kennedy Inst., 1971—, Villa Maria-Residential Treatment Ctr., 1981—, Francis Scott Key Cmty. Psychiatry Program, 1994—; dir. child in-patient neuropsychiatric unit and psychiatric unit Johns Hopkins U. Med. Sch., 1969—72, assoc. prof. psychiatry and pediat., 1972—, liaison-cons. svcs., children-adolescents, 1972—74, dir. psychiat. and mental health scis., 1972—82; dir. child & adolescent neuropsychiat. unit Johns Hopkins Hosp., 1969—73, assoc. dir. divsn. child psychiatry, 1971—, mem. child care com., 1971—73, bed utilization com., 1971—74, pediatric intern selection com., 1971—74; psychiat. svcs. and mental health svcs. Comprehensive Pediatric Child Care Clinic, 1973—81, mental health com., 1974—81, chmn. child abuse and neglect com. dept. pediats., 1975—80, directorate com. cmty. mental health programs, 1981—, dir. child and adolescent cmty. mental health program, 1981—93; psychiat. svcs. and mental health svcs. Children and Adolescent Mental Health Ctr., 1981—93, psychosomatic clinic divsn. child adolescent psychiatry, 1993—. Mem. divsn. spl. edn. City of Balt. Dept. Edn.; directorate com. cmty. mental health programs City of Balt. Health Dept., 1981—, mem. children's mental health planning com.; mem. steering com. East Balt. Mental Health Ctr.; goals and objectives com. Villa Maria Children's Inst., med. adv. com. Fellow: Royal Coll. Psychiatrists, Am. Acad. Child Psychiatry (Disting. fellow), Am. Psychiat. Assn. (life Disting. Life fellow); mem.: AAAS, Md. Psychiat. Soc., Balt. County Med. Soc. Roman Catholic. Home: 45 Thornhill Rd Lutherville MD 21093-5806 Office: Johns Hopkins Hosp 600 N Wolfe St Baltimore MD 21287-0005 Personal E-mail: jimmoncon@comcast.net.

CONNAUGHTON, SEAN THOMAS, federal agency administrator; b. Mar. 23, 1966; s. Eugene and Patricia Connaughton; m. Teresa Voda, 1984; children: Courtney, Sean Jr. BS, U.S. Merchant Marine Acad., 1983; master's degree, George Washington U., 1988; JD, George Mason U., 1992; grad., U.S. Naval War Coll., 1998. Bar: Va. 1992. Def. contractor, Arlington, Va.; civil servant Office Maritime Safety, Security, and Environ. Protection U.S. Coast Guard, Washington; atty. Troutman Sanders LLP, 2000; maritime adminstr. U.S. Dept. Transp., 2006—. Chmn. at large Prince William Bd. County Supervisors, 1999—; bd. dirs. Met. Washington Council of Govts.; chief elected official No. Va. Workforce Investment Bd., bd. dirs. Skillsource Group; mem. No. Va. Transp. Authority; mem. steering com. large urban county caucus Nat. Assn. of Counties; mem. U.S. Merchant Marine Adv. Bd. Mem. Prince William County adv. bd. George Mason U., mem. com. for performing arts ctr.; mem. Woodbridge Campus adv. bd. No. Va. CC; chmn. 9/11 Meml. Fund, Potomac Hosp. Capital Campaign; bd. dirs. Homeland Protection Inst., Ltd., No. Va. Sci. Ctr. Belmont Bay, Conservation Leaders Network; mem. Prince William C. of C., Prince William-Greater Manassas C. of C., Prince William County Rep. Com., Nat. Conf. Rep. County Officials. With U.S. Coast Guard, 1983—86, comdr. USNR. Mem.: Propeller Club of U.S., Reserve Officers Assn., Naval Reserve Assn., Veterans Pro Bono Consortium, Maritime Law Assn., DC Bar Assn., Va. Bar Assn. Office: US Maritime Adminstrn US Dept Trasp 400 7th St SW Washington DC 20590

CONNELL, ALASTAIR MCCRAE, physician; b. Glasgow, Scotland, Dec. 21, 1929; came to U.S., 1970; s. Alex McCrae and Maud (Crawford) C.; m. Joyce Dethlefs, 1983; children: Stewart, Fiona, Alison, Iain, Andrew. BS, U. Glasgow, 1951, MB, ChB, 1954, MD, 1969. Intern Western Infirmary, Glasgow, 1954-55; resident in gastroenterology Cen. Middlesex and St. Mark's Hosp., London, 1957-60; practice medicine specializing in gastroenterology, 1960—91; mem. med. staff Med. Rsch. Coun., 1960-64; sr. lectr. clin. sci. Queen's U., Belfast, No. Ireland, 1964-70; Mark Brown prof. medicine Med. Ctr., U. Cin., 1970-79, dir. div. digestive diseases, 1970-79, prof. physiology, 1972-79, assoc. dean, 1975-77; dir. Office Clin. Affairs, 1975-77; dean Coll. Medicine, U. Nebr. Med. Ctr., 1979-84, prof. internal medicine, 1979-84; v.p. health scis. Va. Commonwealth U., Richmond, 1984-88; scholar-in-residence Inst. Medicine, 1988-89; vice chancellor health scis. Ea. Carolina U., 1989-90; dir. Office Healthcare Inspections, Dept. Vets. Affairs, Washington, 1991-96; adj. prof. med. George Washington U., 1992-97; prof. kinesiology Coll. William and Mary, 2005—. Vis. prof. dept. moral philosophy U. St. Andrews, Scotland, 1984-86; mem. sci. adv. bd. Nat. Found. for Ileitis and Colitis, 1974-80, chmn. rsch. devel. com., 1974-78; mem. Personal Health Com. Ohio, 1974-76; trustee Medco Peer Rev., 1974-79; adj. prof. health adminstrn. Va. Commonwealth U., 1996-2000; med. dir. Williamsburg Landing, 1999-02; chair Sr. Svcs. Coalition, Williamsburg, Va., 2005-06. Author: Clinical Tests of Gastric Function, 1973; author: (with T. Wan) Monitoring the Quality of Health Care, 2002; assoc. editor Am. Jour. Digestive Diseases; contbr. articles to profl. jours. Served with M.C. Royal Army, 1955-57. Fellow Royal Coll. Physicians (Edinburgh), ACP; mem. Am. Assn. Home Care Physicians, Brit. Soc. Gastroenterology, Internat. Group for Study Intestinal Motility (past pres.). Address: 6728 Tarpleys Tavern Rd Williamsburg VA 23188 E-mail: amconn@wm.edu.

CONNELL, CAROL MATHESON, corporate communications specialist, consultant; d. David Matheson and Marion Elizabeth Frances Connell. MBA in Mktg., Columbia U., 1992; PhD, U. Glasgow, Scotland, 2001. Dir. corp. comms. and rsch. Seagram Co. Ltd., NYC, 1980-96; dir. mktg. and rsch. Juvenile Diabetes Found., NYC, 1996-98; sr. strategy cons. IBM, Armonk, NY, 1998—2004; asst. prof. Dept. Econs. Bklyn. (N.Y.) Coll. CUNY, 2004—. Peer coach profl. tchg. act, 2001—. NDEA and Columbia U. fellow Columbia U. Grad. Faculties, 1971, 72. Mem. IEEE, AAAS, Airplane Owner and Pilot Assn. (assoc.). Roman Catholic. Avocation: aviation (private pilot). Office Fax: 973-484-8598. Personal E-mail: templetuttle@aol.com.

CONNELL, GEORGE EDWARD, retired academic administrator, research scientist; b. Saskatoon, Sask., Can., June 20, 1930; s. James Lorne and Mabel Gertrude (Killins) C.; m. Sheila Harriet Horan, Dec. 27, 1955; children: James, Caroline, Thomas, Margaret. BA, U. Toronto, Ont., Can., 1951, PhD in Biochemistry, 1955; DSc, U. Toronto, 1993; LLD (hon.), McGill U., 1987. NSF postdoctoral fellow, 1956-57; asst. prof. biochemistry U. Toronto, 1957-62, assoc. prof., 1962-65, prof., chmn. dept. biochemistry, 1965-70, assoc. dean faculty of medicine, 1972-74, v.p. rsch. and planning, 1974-77, pres., 1984-90, U. Western Ont., London, 1977-84; chair Nat. Round Table on Economy and Environ., 1990-95; vice chair Environ. Assessment Bd., Ont., 1990-93. Bd. dirs. Southam, Inc., 1985-95; chmn. TC207, Internat. Stds. Orgn., 1993-96; prin. adviser Commn. Inquiry on Blood Sys. Can., 1993-95; chmn. bd. protein engring. Nat. Ctr. Excellence, 1995-97; chmn. Task Force on Funding and Delivery Med. Care in Ont., 1995-96; sr. policy advisor Can. Found. for Innovation, 1997; bd. dirs. Allelix Biopharms., Inc., 1994-99; mem. Ont. Press Coun., 1996-2002; trustee McLaughlin Found., 1996-2002; vice-chair Premier's Rsch. Excellence Awards, Ont., 1999-02; chair mgmt. com. Can. Prostate Cancer Rsch. Initiative, 2000-02; mem. rsch. adv. panel Walkerton Inquiry; bd. dirs. Lake Simcoe Region Conservation Found., 2001-05, Energy Probe Found., 2002-. Recipient Order of Can., 1987. Fellow Chem. Inst. Can., Royal Soc. Can.; mem. Am. Soc. Biol. Chemists, Can. Biochem. Soc. (pres. 1973-74). E-mail: george.connell@sympatico.ca.

CONNELL, MARY ELLEN, diplomat; b. Laconia, NH, Jan. 20, 1943; d. Howard Benjamin and Jessie Louise Smith Naylor; m. O. J. Connell III, Nov. 4, 1969 (div. Aug. 1988); 1 child, Piers Andrew. BA, Smith Coll., Northampton, Mass., 1964; MPhil, U. Kans., 1969; MS, Nat. War Coll., 1992. Info. ctr. dir. U.S. Fgn. Svc., Nairobi, Kenya, 1978-80, pub. affairs officer Bujumbura, Burundi, 1980-82; officer African affairs USIA, Washington, 1982-85, exec. asst. to assoc. dir. for policy, 1985-86; counselor pub. affairs U.S. Fgn. Svc., Copenhagen, 1986-90; vis. scholar St. Deiniol's Wales, 1991; exec. sec. USIA, Washington, 1992-95; pub. affairs advisor U.S. Mission to NATO, Brussels, 1995-97; spl. asst. to asst. sec. defense for pub. affairs Washington, 1997-99; mem. policy planning staff Dept. of State, Washington, 1999—; sr. policy analyst Ctr. for Naval Analyses, 2001—. Mem. Internat. Inst. Strategic Studies, Am. Fgn. Svc. Assn., Atlantic Coun., Army and Navy Club. Episcopalian. Office: CNA 4825 Mark Ctr Dr Alexandria VA 22311-1850 Home Phone: 202-337-2639; Office Phone: 703-824-2281. E-mail: connellme@aol.com.

CONNELL, PHILIP FRANCIS, food industry executive; b. Hamilton, Ont., Can., Jan. 20, 1924; s. Maurice W. and Kathleen (Richardson) C. BA, McMaster U., Can., 1946. Chartered acct. With Clarkson Gordon & Co. (Ernst & Young), Hamilton and Toronto, 1946-57; comptroller Canadian Westinghouse Co. Ltd., Hamilton, 1957-67; controller Domtar Ltd., Montreal, 1967-68; v.p. fin. George Weston Ltd., Toronto, Ont., 1968-75, Loblaw Cos., Ltd., Toronto, Ont., 1972-75; exec. v.p. Oshawa Group Ltd., Toronto, Ont., 1976-92, dir., 1976-97. Fellow Inst. Chartered Accts.; mem. Fin. Execs. Inst. (pres. Hamilton chpt. 1966-67), Ont. Inst. Chartered Accts., Hamilton Club, Nat. Club. Home: 400 Walmer Rd Apt 2510 Toronto ON Canada M5P 2X7 also: 606 Locust St Burlington ON Canada L7S 1V8 Fax: 416-920-3638.

CONNELL, SHIRLEY HUDGINS, public relations professional; b. Washington, Oct. 5, 1946; d. Orville Thomas and Mary (Beran) H.; m. David Day Connell, Dec. 13, 1980 (div. 1985). BA, U. R.I., 1968, MA, 1970. Lic. property, casualty broker, N.Y. Clk., editor MGM Studios, Culver City, Calif., 1970-72; scriptor, talent Monarch Records, Studio City, 1972-73; communications specialist U. So. Calif., LA, 1973-81; dir. pub. rels. Six Flags Movieland, Buena Park, Calif., 1981-82, Donald J. Fager & Assocs., NYC, 1982-93, dir. policy holder/pub. rels., 1993-99, asst. v.p., 1999—. Cons. Children's TV Workshop, N.Y.C., 1978; ind. beauty cons. Mary Kay Cosmetics, 1991—; instr. Princeton Rev., 1990-91. Editor: Coastal Ocean Space Utilization III, 1995; contbr. articles to profl. jours.; contbg. editor Greater N.Y. Doctor's Shopper mag., 1987—. Pres. bd. trustees Oaks at North Brunswick Condominium Assn., 1987-2000; founding mem. Mcpl. Svcs. Com., North Brunswick; mgr. Animal Rescue Force, 1988—; chair environ. com. Twp. of North Brunswick, 1990-2001, vice chair, 2001—06; snuggler pediat. and neonatal units St. Peter's Hosp.; Blue Belt Tiger Schulmann's Karate, 1997; founding mem., trustee, bd. dirs. Lawrence Brook Watershed Partnership, 1998—. Mem. NAFE, Marine Tech. Soc. (vice chmn. 1980-81), Mensa (pub. rels. adv. com. 1989—, pub. rels. coord. Ctrl. N.J. chpt. 1992—, bd. dirs. 1992—), Oceanic Soc. (bd. dirs. 1979-81), Stony Brook Millstone Watershed Assn. (water qualification monitor 1994—), Ctrl. N.J. Mensa (trustee, chair pub. rels. 1990—). Avocations: photography, reading, swimming, wood finishing, writing. Office Phone: 212-576-9843. E-mail: sconnell@mlmic.com.

CONNELL, WILLIAM D., lawyer; b. Palo Alto, Calif., Apr. 1, 1955; s. Robert Charles and Audrey Elizabeth (Steele) C.; m. Kathy Lynn Mleko, Aug. 13, 1977; children: Hilary Anne, Andrew James. BA in Polit Sci. with honors, Stanford U., 1976; JD cum laude, Harvard U., 1979. Bar: Calif. 1979, U.S. Dist. Ct. (cen., no. and ea. dists.) Calif. 1979, U.S. Ct. Appeals (9th cir.) 1979. Assoc. Gibson, Dunn & Crutcher, LA, 1979-80, San Jose, Calif., 1980-87, ptnr., 1988-97, GCA Law Ptnrs. LLP, 1997—. Mem. Christian Legal Soc. Mem. Stanford Alumni Assn. (life), Commonwealth Club Calif., U.S. Golf Assn., The Federalist Soc., Phi Beta Kappa. Republican. Avocations: photography, golf. Business E-Mail: bconnell@gcalaw.com.

CONNELL, WILLIAM TERRENCE, lawyer, judge; b. Montclair, NJ, July 29, 1949; s. Raymond Charles and Kathryn (Hanley) C.; m. Honor Marilyn McMahon, July 19, 1975; children: Sean William, Heather Erin, Lauren Blythe. AB, Providence Coll., 1971; JD, Seton Hall U., 1976. Bar: NJ 1977, DC 1979, US Dist. Ct. NJ 1977, US Ct. Appeals (3d cir.) 1984, cert.: (civil trial atty.). Investigator Comml. Union Ins. Co., West Orange, N.J., 1971, Essex County Prosecutors Office, Newark, 1971-77; ptnr. Dwyer, Connell & Lisbona, Montclair, NJ, 1977—, Fairfield, NJ, 1997—. Arbitrator Middlesex County Superior Ct., New Brunswick, NJ, 1984—; judge Mcpl. Ct. Borough of Roseland, NJ, 1988—. Mem.: Def. Rsch. Inst., Trucking Ind. Def. Assn., Middlesex County Trial Lawyers Assn., Middlesex County Bar Assn., Essex County Bar Assn., N.J. Bar Assn., Am. Bd. Trial Attys. (adv.), Assn. Trial Lawyers Am., ABA, Bear Lakes Country Club (Fla.), Essex Fells Country Club (N.J.). Roman Catholic. Home: 18 Ford Ln Roseland NJ 07068-1456 also: 3360 S Ocean Blvd Palm Beach FL 33480 Office: Dwyer Connell & Lisbona Greenbrook Corp Ctr 100 Passaic Ave Fairfield NJ 07004-3508 Home Phone: 973-228-3025; Office Phone: 973-276-1800. Business E-Mail: wconnell@dcllaw.com.

CONNELLY, COLIN CHARLES, lawyer; b. Hopewell, Va., Nov. 1, 1956; s. Charles Bernell and Doris Louise (Beasley) C.; m. Stephanie Paige Lowder, May 9, 1981. AA, Richard Bland Coll., Petersburg, Va., 1977; BA, Va. Commonwealth U., Richmond, 1979; JD, U. Richmond, 1983. Bar: Va. 1983, US Ct. Appeals (4th cir.) 1983. Assoc. Tuck, Freasier, & Herbig, Richmond, Va., 1984-87; ptnr. Tuck & Connelly Profl. Assocs., Inc., Richmond, Va., 1988-95, Connelly & Assocs., PC, Chester, Va., 1996—. Bd. dirs., v.p. Cen. Title Ins. Agy., Richmond, 1988—; agt. Chgo. Title Ins. Corp., Richmond, 1988—. Mem., assoc./counsel Home Builders Assn. South Side Va. Mem. ABA, Va. Bar Assn., Richmond Bar Assn., Southside Bd. Realtors (affiliate), Chester Jaycees, Omicron Delta Kappa, Phi Kappa Phi, Phi Alpha Delta (justice 1983-86). Baptist. Avocations: bicycling, racquetball, basketball. Home: 14206 Masada Ct Chesterfield VA 23838-8725 Office: Connelly & Assocs 4830 W Hundred Rd Chester VA 23831-1746 Office Phone: 877-748-3544. Business E-Mail: cconnelly@connelly-assoc.com.

CONNELLY, DAVID O'BRIEN, museum administrator, journalist; b. Canton, Ohio, Apr. 25, 1952; s. Harold O'Brien and Mary Louise (Wells) C. BA summa cum laude with honors in English, Mt. Union Coll., 1974; MA in Coll. Student Pers., Bowling Green State U., 1975; MA in Latin Am. Studies, U. Tex., Austin, 1995, postgrad., 1977-78. Dir. men's housing Southwestern U., Georgetown, Tex., 1975-76; cmty. educator, publicist Planned Parenthood Assn. Summit County, Akron, Ohio, 1976-77; arts/entertainment editor Shreveport (La.) Jour., 1978-90; asst. grants dir. Mus. Fine Arts, Houston, 1991-93; pub. rels. dir. Mus. of Fine Arts, St. Petersburg, Fla., 1996—. Staff writer The Archer M. Huntington Art Gallery, U. Tex., Austin, 1993-95; staff rep. long-range plan and devel./mktg. coms. bd. trustees Mus. Fine Arts, St. Petersburg. Editor, chief writer Mosaic; arts critic The Daily Texan, 1977-78; contbr. articles to profl. jours. Organizing com. Inner City Soup Kitchen, Shreveport, 1986-87; organizing com., first sec. exec. com., grants writer N.W. La. AIDS Task Force, Shreveport, 1988-91. Harmon O. DeGraff Meml. scholar Akron YMCA, 1977; Emmett Walter fellow U. Tex., 1977-78, Music Critics Inst. fellow, 1980, Aspen Summer Music Festival; named one of Outstanding Young Men of Am., 1989; grantee Tinker Found., 1994. Mem.

Am. Assn. Mus., St. Petersburg Mus. Consortium, Fla. Assn. of Mus., Blue Key, Phi Kappa Phi, Psi Kappa Omega. Democrat. Jewish. Avocations: reading, travel, swimming, films, the arts. Home: 801 65th Ave S Saint Petersburg FL 33705 Office: Mus Fine Arts 255 Beach Dr NE Saint Petersburg FL 33701-3498 Office Phone: 727-896-2667 ext 224. Business E-Mail: david@fine-arts.org.

CONNELLY, DEIRDRE P., pharmaceutical executive; b. San Juan; BA in Econs. and Mktg., Lycoming Coll., Williamsport, Pa., 1983; grad. Advanced Mgmt. Program, Harvard U., 2000. Sales rep. Eli Lilly & Co., 1983—84, mktg. assoc. San Juan, 1984—89, sales supr. Phila., 1989—90, product mgr. diabetes San Juan, 1990—91, nat. sales mgr., 1991—92, mktg. & sales dir., 1992—93, mktg. & sales dir. Caribbean, 1993—95, gen mgr. Eli Lilly PR SA, 1995—97, regional sales dir., exec. dir. global mktg. Evista Indpls., 1997—2001, leader women's health bus. Lilly USA, 2001—03, exec. dir. human resources Lilly USA, 2003, v.p. human resources, 2004, sr. v.p. human resources, 2004—05, pres. Lilly USA, 2005—. Named one of 50 Most Powerful Women in Bus., Fortune mag., 2006. Office: Eli Lilly & Co Lilly Corp Ctr Indianapolis IN 46285 Office Phone: 317-276-2000.*

CONNELLY, GAIL, educational association administrator; COO NAESP, Alexandria, Va., interim exec. dir., 2007—. Office: NAESP 1615 Duke St Alexandria VA 22314 Office Phone: 703-684-3345. Office Fax: 800-396-2377. E-mail: naesp@naesp.org.*

CONNELLY, JENNIFER, actress; b. Catskill Mountains, NY, Dec. 12, 1970; d. Gerard and Eileen Connelly; m. Paul Bettany, Jan. 1, 2003; children: Stellan Bettany, Kai Dugan. Actress: appeared in Italian, Canadian, British, Argentinian, and U.S.; (films) Once Upon a Time in America, 1984, Phenomena, 1985, The Valley, 1985, Labyrinth, 1986, Seven Minutes in Heaven, 1986, Some Girls, 1988, Etoile, 1988, The Hot Spot, 1990, Career Opportunities, 1991, The Rocketeer, 1991, Higher Learning, 1994, Far Harbor, 1996, Mulholland Falls, 1996, Of Love and Shadows, 1996, Dark City, 1997, Inventing the Abbots, 1997, Waking the Dead, 2000, Requiem for a Dream, 2000, Pollock, 2000, A Beautiful Mind, 2001 (Best Supporting Actress Acad. award 2001, Golden Globe, 2001, Am. Film Inst. award, Brit. Acad. award, Golden Satellite award, KCFCC award, OFCS award, SEFCA award and BFCA award 2001-2002, nominee Best Actress SAG award 2001, Featured Actor of Yr. Female Movies AFI Film award 2002), The Hulk, 2003, House of Sand and Fog, 2003, Dark Water, 2005, Little Children, 2006, Blood Diamond, 2006; (TV films) The Heart of Justice, 1993; (TV series) The $treet, 2000. Office: Internat Creative Mgmt 8942 Wilshire Blvd Beverly Hills CA 90211-1934*

CONNELLY, JOHN J., metal products executive; B in History, Duquesne U., Pitts., M in African Affairs. Mgmt. trainee comml. dept. US Steel Internat., NY, 1971—72, svc. rep., 1972—73, v.p., 1988—89, pres., 1989—99; with comml. dept. US Steel, NY, 1973—74, sales position Milw., 1974—78, product rep. std. pipe Ea. Steel Divsn. Houston, 1978—79, asst. mktg. mgr. tin mill products Ctrl. Steel Divsn., 1979, mgr. mktg. std. pipe Tubular Products staff Pitts., 1979—81, asst. gen. mgr. mktg. std. and line pipe, 1981, gen. mgr. tubular products, 1981—86, gen. mgr. Ea. sales, 1986—88, v.p. internat. bus., 1994—99, v.p. long range planning and internat. bus., 1999—2001, v.p. bus. devel. and long range planning, 2001—02, v.p. strategic planning and bus. devel., 2002—04, sr. v.p. strategic planning & bus. devel., 2004—; pres. USX Engrs. and Consultants, Inc., 1994—96. Bd. dirs. World Affairs Coun., Pitts. Mem.: Am. Iron and Steel Inst. Office: US Steel 600 Grant St Pittsburgh PA 15219-2800 Office Phone: 412-433-1121.*

CONNELLY, MARK, writer, educator; b. Phila., July 8, 1951; s. Edward James and Hilda Virginia (Pfleger) C. BA in English and History, Carroll Coll., 1973; MA in Creative Writing, U. Wis., Milw., 1974, PhD in English, 1984. Instr. English Milw. Area Tech. Coll., 1986—. Cons. Great Lakes Precision Products. Author: The Diminished Self: Orwell and the Loss of Freedom, 1987, The Sundance Reader, 1997, Orwell and Gissing, 1997, The Sundance Writer, 1999, Deadly Closets, 2000, Get Writing, 2005, Sundance Choice, 2005, Fifteen Minutes, 2005. V.p. Irish Cultural and Heritage Ctr. of Wis., 2000—. Recipient Ann. Fiction award Milw. Mag., 1982, 1st Place Fiction award Ind. Mag., 1982. Presbyterian. Avocations: reading, travel, Irish studies. Office: Milw Area Tech Coll 700 W State St Milwaukee WI 53233-1419 E-mail: markconn@earthlink.net.

CONNELLY, MARY, television producer; Cons. prodr. Caroline Rhea Show; exec. prodr. The Ellen Degeneres Show, 2003—. Recipient Best Television Series or Specialty (Variety), The Producers Guild of America, 2006. Office: The Ellen Degeneres Show Warner Bros Studios 4000 Warner Blvd Burbank CA 91522

CONNELLY, MARY JO, lawyer, nurse; b. Chgo., May 19, 1949; d. Joseph Anthony and Veronica Colette (Casey) C. BSN, Coll. St. Teresa, 1971; JD, DePaul U., 1980. Bar: Ill. 1980, U.S. Dist. Ct. (no. dist.) Ill. 1980, U.S. Dist. Ct. (ctrl. dist., no. dist.) Ill. 1990; RN, Ill.; RN, Ill. Head nurse neurosurgery St. Mary's Hosp., Rochester, Minn., 1971—73; head nurse ambulatory care U. Calif., San Francisco, 1973—77; ptnr. Sweeney & Riman Ltd., Chgo., 1980—98; pvt. practice law Chgo., 1998—. Mem. ABA, Women's Bar Assn. Ill., Ill. Bar Assn., Chgo. Bar Assn. (investigator hearing, bd. dirs. jud. evaluation com. 1984-89). E-mail: mconnelly@rcn.com.

CONNELLY, MICHAEL, writer; b. Phila., July 21, 1956; BA in Journalism, minor in Creative Writing, U. Fla., 1980. Newspaper reporter, Daytona Beach, Fla., Ft. Lauderdale, Fla.; crime reporter LA Times. Author: (novels) The Black Echo, 1992 (Edgar award, 1992), The Black Ice, 1993, The Concrete Blonde, 1994, The Last Coyote, 1995, The Poet, 1996, Trunk Music, 1997, Blood Work, 1998, Angels Flight, 1999, Void Moon, 2000, A Darkness More Than Night, 2001, City of Bones, 2002 (Notable Book of Yr., NY Times, 2002), Chasing The Dime, 2002, Lost Light, 2003, The Narrows, 2003, The Closers, 2005 (Publishers Weekly Bestseller list, 2005, NY Times Bestseller list, 2005), Echo Park, 2006, The Lincoln Lawyer, 2005, The Overlook, 2007, (articles collection) Crime Beat: A Decade of Covering Cops and Killers, 2006; writer, creator (TV series) Level 9, 2000. Mem.: Mystery Writers Am. (pres. 2003—04). Office: c/o Author Mail Little Brown & Co 1271 Ave of the Americas New York NY 10020*

CONNELLY, MICHAEL C., lawyer, energy executive; married; 2 children. BA in Econs., Carleton Coll., Northfield, Minn.; JD, U. Chgo. Assoc. Oppenheimer, Wolff and Donnelly, St. Paul, 1986—90; atty. No. States Power Co., 1990—93, sr. atty., 1993—2000; v.p., dep. gen. counsel Xcel Energy (merger of No. States Power Co. and New Century Energies), Mpls., 2000—05, v.p. human resources, 2005—07, v.p., gen. counsel, 2007—. Bd. dirs. Twin Cities Housing Devel. Corp. Office: Xcel Energy 414 Nicollet Mall Minneapolis MN 55401-1993*

CONNELLY, SHARON RUDOLPH, lawyer; b. Kingwood, W.Va. d. John E. and Lorene E. Rudolph; 1 child, John. BS, W.Va. State U., 1966; MBA, Ind. U., 1968; JD, Cath. Univ., 1976; LLM in Taxation, Georgetown U., 1995. Bar: Va. 1977. Mgr. IRS, Washington, 1969-76; asst. contr. Mfrs. Hanover, NYC, 1976-77; compliance chief D.C. Dept. Labor, Washington, 1977-79; dir. compliance U.S. Dept. Commerce, Washington, 1979-82; asst. insp. gen. NASA, Washington, 1982-84; dir. insp. office Nuc. Regulatory Commn., Washington, 1984-89, spl. asst. internal controls, 1989-98. Financier, 1998—. Contbr. articles to profl. jours.

CONNELLY, TERRENCE JOHN, SR., broadcast executive; b. Chgo., Aug. 23, 1947; s. Charles Bernard, Jr. and Margaret Agnes (Gilmore) C.; m. Andrea Susan Hahn, Feb. 12, 1972; children: Terrence John, Jr., Bridget Colleen. BS in Comms., U. Ill., 1970. Reporter WITI-TV, Milw., 1970-73, WRGB-TV, Schenectady, N.Y., 1973-74; news dir. WNYT-TV, Albany, N.Y., 1974-76, WDAF-TV, Kansas City, Mo., 1976-78; exec. news producer WMAQ-TV, Chgo., 1978-80; v.p. TV news Taft Broadcasting, Cin., 1980-86; v.p., gen. mgr. WCPO-TV, Cin., 1986-88, WKRC-TV, Cin., 1988-92, WSYX-TV, Columbus, Ohio, 1992-95; pres., gen. mgr. WJLA-TV, Washington, 1995-98; sr. v.p., gen. mgr. The Weather Channel, Atlanta, 1999—. Dir. teletext, Taft Broadcasting, Cin., 1981-86; mem. broadcast adv. bd. UPI, N.Y.C., 1983-85. Editor/gen. mgr.: WCPO TV news, 1987 (Peabody award for investigative report 1987). Bd. dirs. United Way, Washington, 1995-99, Easter Seals Bd., Washington, 1995-97, Muscular Distrophy Assn., Columbus, 1992-95; chmn. Neediest Kids, Inc., Washington, 1995-99. With U.S. Army, 1970-76. Mem. Soc. Profl. Journalists, Radio-TV News Dirs. Assn., Nat. Assn. TV Program Execs., Rotary. Roman Catholic. Office: The Weather Channel 300 Interstate North Pkwy SE Atlanta GA 30339-2403

CONNELLY, THOMAS JOSEPH, lawyer; b. Kansas City, Kans., Jan. 31, 1940; s. Edward J. and Mary (McCallum) C.; m. Barbara Helen Marciniak, Aug. 1, 1964; children: Catherine, Jennifer. AB, U. Detroit, 1963, JD, 1968. Bar: Mich. 1969, US Dist. Ct. (so. and ea. dists.) Mich. 1969, US Ct. Appeals (6th cir.) 1969. Sr. ptnr. Connelly, Crowley, Groth & Seglund, Walled Lake, Mich., 1975—. Exec. bd. dirs. Oakland County (Mich.) Reps., 1979-82. Mem. Mich. Bar Assn. (rep. assembly 1978—), Oakland County Bar Assn., Internat. Arabian Horse Assn. (pres.), Mich. Arabian Horse Assn. (pres. 1986—), Am. Horse Shows Assn. (bd. dirs., exec. com. 1996—). Roman Catholic. Home: 1635 S Garner Rd Milford MI 48380-4127 Office: Connelly Groth & Seglund 2410 S Commerce Rd Walled Lake MI 48390-2129 Office Phone: 248-624-4505. Business E-Mail: tjconnelly@ccgs-law.com.

CONNELLY, THOMAS M., JR., chemicals executive; b. Toledo, Ohio, 1952; m. Patricia Connelly; 2 children. Grad. with highest honors, Princeton U.; PhD in Chem. Engring., U. Cambridge, 1977. Rsch. engr. DuPont, 1977—85; global product mgr. Permasep, Del., 1985—87; mgr. polymer products, dir. Euro Tech. Ctr. DuPont, Geneva, 1987—94, bus. dir. Delrin Geneva & Hong Kong, 1992—97, bus. dir. Kevlar Richmond, Va., 1997—99, v.p., gen. mgr. fluroproducts, 1999—2000, sr. v.p. & chief sci. and technology officer, 2001—06, exec. v.p., chief innovation officer, 2006—. Office: DuPont 1007 Market St Wilmington DE 19898*

CONNELLY, WARREN E., lawyer; b. Mt. Vernon, NY, Nov. 18, 1946; BA cum laude, Dartmouth Coll., 1968; JD, Georgetown U., 1973. Bar: DC 1973. Atty. Cost of Living Coun., 1973-74; mem. Akin, Gump, Strauss, Hauer & Feld LLP, Washington, 1975—, now ptnr. internat. trade. Active NAFTA Binat. Panel. 1st lt. U.S. Army, 1968-70. Mem. DC Bar. Office: Akin Gump Strauss Hauer & Feld LLP 1333 New Hampshire Ave NW Washington DC 20036-1564 Office Phone: 202-887-4046. Office Fax: 202-887-4288. Business E-Mail: wconnelly@akingump.com.

CONNER, CHARLES F., federal agency administrator; b. Lafayette, Ind., Dec. 30, 1957; m. Druscilla Conner; 4 children. BS in Agriculture, Purdue U., 1980. Agrl. aide to Sen. Richard Lugar US Senate, 1980—87; minority staff dir. Com. on Agrl., Nutrition & Forestry, US Senate, 1987—95, majority staff dir., 1995—97; pres. Corn Refiners Assn., 1997—2001; spl. asst. to the Pres. for Agrl., Trade, & Food Assistance Nat. Econ. Coun., 2001—05; dep. sec. USDA, Washington, 2005—. Office: USDA 12th & Jefferson Dr SW Rm 202-B Washington DC 20250

CONNER, DAVID MICHAEL, lawyer; b. Savannah, Ga., Feb. 18, 1970; BBA magna cum laude in acctg., Univ. Ga., JD cum laude, 1995. Bar: Ga. 1995, So. Dist. Ga., U.S. Dist. Ct. 1995. Ptnr., comml. litig. Bouhan, Williams & Levy, LLP, Savannah, Ga. Spkr. in field. Contbr. articles to numerous profl. jours. Named Ga. Rising Star, SuperLawyer Mag., 2006. Mem.: ABA, Ga. State Bar Assn. Office: Bouhan Williams Levy Armstrong House 447 Bull St Savannah GA 31402-2139 Office Phone: 912-236-2491. Business E-Mail: dmconner@bouhan.com.

CONNER, FRANK M. (RUSTY), III, lawyer; b. Richmond, Va., Sept. 30, 1956; BA, Univ. Va., 1978, JD, 1981. Bar: Va. 1981, Ga. 1981, DC 1990. Ptnr., chmn. exec. com. Alston & Bird LLP, Washington. Mem.: ABA, DC Bar Assn., Raven Soc., Omicron Delta Kappa, Phi Beta Kappa. Office: Alston & Bird LLP Atlantic Bldg 950 F St NW Washington DC 20004-2601 Office Phone: 202-756-3303. Office Fax: 202-756-3333. Business E-Mail: fconner@alston.com.

CONNER, LEWIS HOMER, JR., lawyer; b. Chattanooga, Mar. 21, 1938; s. Lewis H. Sr. and Cleo (Johnson) C.; m. Ashley Whitsitt, June 1, 1960; children: Holland Ashley, Lewis Forrest. BA, Vanderbilt U., 1960, JD, 1963. Bar: Tenn. 1963, U.S. Dist. Ct. (all dists.) Tenn. 1963, U.S. Ct. Appeals (6th cir.) 1963, U.S. Ct. Mil. Appeals 1964, U.S. Supreme Ct. 1990; cert. mediator, Tenn. Founding ptnr., atty. Dearborn & Ewing, Nashville, 1972-80; judge Ct. Appeals Middle Dist., Nashville, 1980-84; sr. ptnr., atty. Waller Lansden Dortch & Davis, Nashville, 1985-89, 2005—, Boult, Cummings, Conners & Berry, Nashville, 1989-96; of counsel Stokes & Bartholomew, Nashville, 1997—2005. Chmn. Willis Coroon, Tenn., 1996—99; spl. chief justice Supreme Ct. Tenn., 1980—81; lectr. law Vanderbilt U. Sch. Law, Nashville, 1984—93; life del. Sixth Cir. Ct. Appeals Jud. Conf. Mng. editor Vanderbilt Law Rev. Elder Westminster Presbyn. Ch.; bd. dirs. Tenn. Golf Assn., Nashville, 1965—, pres., 1985; chmn. Tenn. Golf Found., 1992-93, 96-97, 2000-01; fin. co-chmn. Alexander for Gov., 1974-78; chmn. Tenn. Rep. Fin. Com., 1975, Tenn. Corrections Overcrowding Commn., 1985-86; bd. dirs. Boys & Girls Club Middle Tenn., 1980—, pres., 1991-92; bd. govs., chmn. Tenn. State Mus., 1987-91; bd. govs. Gaylord Music City Bowl, 1998- , chmn., 2002—. Recipient Tennesseean of Yr. award, Tenn. Golf Found., 2001, Nat. Lifetime Achievement award, Boys & Girls Club Mid. Tenn., 2003, Hope award, Multiple Sclerosis Soc., 2006. Fellow Am. Acad. Matrimonial Lawyers, Am. Bar Found., Tenn. Bar Found., Nashville Bar Found.; mem. ABA, Am. Arbitration Assn. (bd. dirs. 1990-96, chmn. Tenn. large complex case panel 1992—, panel of arbitrators 1975—, panel of mediators 1995—), Tenn. Bar Assn., Tenn. Jud. Conf., Nashville Bar Assn. (pres. 1986-87, bd. dirs., 1984-87), Comm. on the Future of the Cts. in Tenn., Order of the Coif, PGA of Am. (hon. Tenn. sect.), The Golf Club Tenn. (founder, exec. com. 1991-2003), Richland Country Club (bd. dirs. 1976-79, pres. 1978-79), Belle Meade Country Club, The Honors Course, Naples Grande Golf Club, Nashville City Club, Nashville Cumberland Club, Nashville Stadium Club, Tenn. Golf Assn. (amateur player of yr., 1973). Republican. Avocations: golf, basketball, softball, politics. Home: 163 Charleston Park Nashville TN 37205-4703 Office: Waller Lansden Dortch and Davis PO Box 150039 Nashville TN 37215-0039 Office Phone: 615-850-8495. Business E-Mail: lew.conner@wallerlaw.com.

CONNER, LINDSAY ANDREW, lawyer; b. NYC, Feb. 19, 1956; s. Michael and Miriam Conner. BA summa cum laude, UCLA, 1976; MA, Occidental Coll., 1978; JD magna cum laude, Harvard U., 1980. Bar: Calif. 1980, U.S. Dist. Ct. (cen. dist.) Calif. 1983. Assoc. Kaplan, Livingston, Goodwin, Berkowitz & Selvin, Beverly Hills, Calif., 1980—81, Fulop & Hardee, Beverly Hills, 1982—83, Wyman, Bautzer, Kuchel & Silbert, LA, 1983—86; ptnr., entertainment dept. head Hill Wynne Troop & Meisinger, LA, 1986—93; screenwriter and prodr. 54 St. Prodns., LA, 1994—99; COO, I-Drop, Inc., LA, 1999—2005; ptnr. Dickstein Shapiro, LA, 2006—, head Dept. Entertainment, 2006—. Author: (with others) The Courts and Education, 1977; editor: Harvard Law Rev., 1978-80. Trustee L.A. Community Coll., 1981-97, bd. pres., 1989-90; pres. Calif. Community Coll. Trustees, 1992-93. Mem. ABA, UCLA Alumni Assn. (life), Harvard-Radcliffe Club, Phi Beta Kappa.

CONNER, STEWART EDMUND, lawyer; b. Louisville, Oct. 7, 1941; s. James Pleasant and Lucille (Winter) C.; m. Joan E. Fish, May 20, 1989; children: Shannon Lynn, Erin Eileen, Margaret Eisele; stepchildren: Hunt Rounsavall, Gibbs Rounsavall, Christine Rounsavall. BS, U. Louisville, 1963, JD cum laude, 1966. Bar: Ky. 1966, U.S. Dist. Ct. (ea. and we. dists.) Ky. 1966, U.S. Tax Ct. 1967. Assoc. Wyatt, Tarrant & Combs, Louisville, 1966-72, ptnr., 1972—, chmn. gen. corp. sect., 1980-90, mng. ptnr., 1988-2001, chmn. exec. com., 1988—2004. Bd. dirs. DNP Select Income Fund, 2004—, Louisville Water Co., 1990—, chmn., 2004—. Author, editor: Kentucky Business Practice Handbook, 1988; editor Kentucky Legal Forms, 1988; contbr. to U. Ky. Law Rev. Bd. dirs. Coun. on Higher Edn., 1992-95, Lincoln Heritage coun. Boy Scouts Am., 1989—, chair, 2005-, dePaul Sch., 1996-2004. With U.S. Army, 1968-69, Vietnam. Fellow Am. Bar Found., Ky. Bar Found.; mem. ABA (banking com. 1983), Ky. Bar Assn., Louisville Bar Assn. (chmn. ethics com. 1980), Ky. C. of C. (bd. dirs. 1992-96), Greater Louisville Inc. (bd. dirs. 1996-2001), Law Club, Lawyers Club, Harmony Landing Country Club. Republican. Office: Wyatt Tarrant & Combs 2800 PNC Plz Louisville KY 40202 Home Phone: 502-228-4795; Office Phone: 502-562-7223. Business E-Mail: sconner@wyattfirm.com.

CONNER, TERRY W., lawyer; b. Houston, Feb. 27, 1951; BA, U. Tex., 1972, JD with honors, 1975. Bar: Tex. 1975. Ptnr., Fin. Haynes and Boone LLP, Dallas. Adj. prof. So. Meth. U. Sch. Law, 1987-92, also co-dir. ann. comml. lending inst. Note and comment editor Tex. Law Rev., 1974-75; spl. contbg. editor: Comml. Loan Documentation Guide, 1988. Mem. ABA (mem. corporation, banking and bus. law sect.), State Bar Tex. (mem. fin. instns. com. 1981—), Tex. Assn. Bank Counsel (bd. dirs. 1987-91), Dallas Bar Assn. Office: Haynes & Boone LLP 3100 Nationsbank Plz 901 Main St Ste 3100 Dallas TX 75202-3789 Office Phone: 214-651-5604. Office Fax: 214-200-0408. Business E-Mail: terry.conner@haynesboone.com.

CONNER, WILLIAM BRUCE, facilty engineer; b. Des Moines, Feb. 26, 1955; s. Edward Everett Conner and Harriet Joy Fisher. Student, Coll. of the Desert, Palmdale, Calif., 1974—75, East Carolina U., NC, 1975—76, Iowa State U., 1978—79, Drake U., Des Moines, 1985—86, Des Moines Area CC, 1999—2003; degree, Excelsior Coll., Albany, NY, 2003. Lic. 1st class power engr. Des Moines, 1982, cert. CPO, CFC, HAZWOPER, West Des Moines Police Dept. Citizen's Acad., 2003. Utility engring. dept. City of West Des Moines, 1969—73; civil engring. aid Veenstra & Kimm Cons. Engrs., West Des Moines, 1973—74; shift engr. Young Women's Christian Assn., Des Moines, 1982—83; specialist food security act US Dept. Agrl., Des Moines, 1985—88; mfg. engr. DASE Designs, Des Moines, 1990—95; supr. census data collections US Dept. Commerce, Kansas City, Kans., 1995—96; facility engr. West Des Moines Sch. Dist., 1996—. Sgt. USMC, 1974—81, P02 USNR, 1986—93. Mem.: Am. Legion, Am. Radio Relay League, Am. MENSA Ltd, Vietnam Vets. of Am. (life), Vets. of Fgn. Wars (life), Marine Corp. League (life). Republican. Roman Catholic. Avocations: amateur radio, martial arts. Home: 321 8th St West Des Moines IA 50265 Office: West Des Moines Sch Dist Ops Ctr 2102 Delavan Dr West Des Moines IA 50265 Office Phone: 515-633-4294. Personal E-mail: wbconner@juno.com.

CONNER, WILLIAM CURTIS, federal judge; b. Wichita Falls, Tex., Mar. 27, 1920; s. D.H. and Mae (Weeks) C.; m. Janice Files, Mar. 22, 1944; children: William Curtis, Stephen, Christopher, Molly. BBA, U. Tex., 1941, LLB, 1942; student, Harvard, 1942-43, MIT, 1943. Bar: Tex. bar 1942, N.Y. State bar 1949. Asso., mem. firm Curtis, Morris & Safford (and predecessor firm), NYC, 1946-73; judge U.S. Dist. Ct. (so. dist.) N.Y., White Plains, 1973—, now sr. judge. Editor Tex. Law Rev. Served to lt. USNR, 1942-45, PTO. Recipient Jefferson medal N.J. Patent Law Assn., Outstanding Pub. Svc. award N.Y Intellectual Property Law Assn. Mem. NY Patent Law Assn. (pres. 1972-73), St. Andrews Golf Club. Presbyterian (elder). Office: US Dist Ct US Courthouse 300 Quarropas St White Plains NY 10601-4140

CONNER, WILLIAM HERBERT, lawyer; b. Columbus, Ohio, Jan. 29, 1940; s. Herbert Lee and Beulah Doris C.; m. Julie Ann Katzan, Aug. 13, 1966; children: W. David, Kristen Ann. Student, Purdue U., 1960-61; AB magna cum laude, Miami U., Oxford, Ohio, 1964; JD cum laude, U. Mich. Law Sch., 1967. Bar: Ohio 1967, U.S. Dist. Ct. (no. dist.) Ohio 1967. Assoc. Squire, Sanders & Dempsey L.L.P., Cleve., 1967-77, ptnr., 1977—. Contbr. articles to profl. jours. Mem. ABA (tax exempt financing com. 1981--), Ohio Bar Assn. (chmn. taxation com. 1981-84), Cleve. Bar Assn. (chmn. gen. tax com. 1983-84), Nat. Assn. Bond Lawyers (bd. dirs. 1991, 94-99, treas. 1995-96, pres. elect 1996-97, pres. 1997-98, immediate past pres. 1998-99). Republican. Methodist. Home: 3139 Falmouth Rd Shaker Heights OH 44122-2844 Office: Squire Sanders & Dempsey LLP 4900 Key Tower 127 Public Sq Ste 4900 Cleveland OH 44114-1304

CONNER, WILLIAM J., III, diversified financial services company executive; s. William J. and Margaret M. Conner. AB, Dartmouth Coll., Hanover, NH, 1985; MBA, Amos Tuck Sch. of Bus. Adminstrn., 1987. Intern bd. govs. FRS, Washington, 1983—84; asst. v.p. True BASIC, Inc., Hanover, NH, 1984—87; internal cons. Prog. Corp., Tampa, Fla., 1986, product support specialist Mayfield Heights, Ohio, 1987—89, product mgr., 1990—91, Prog. Casualty Ins. Co. of Can., Toronto, Ont., 1991—97, pres., ceo & gen. mgr., 1997—99; sr. v.p. Associates First Capital Corp., Irving, 1999—2000, Citigroup, Inc., Irving, 2000—01; mng. dir. Trilogy, Inc., Austin, 2001; pres. Aspen Extreme Holdings LLC, 2002—04; COO, v.p. Plymouth Rock Assurance Corp., Boston, 2004—06; pres. Mt. Washington Assurance Corp., Concord, NH, 2004—06; pvt. practice, 2006—. Mem. Ont. com. Ins. Bur. of Can., Toronto, 1995—99. Contbr. preface to exhibition catalogue Waste Management. Sponsor Art Gallery of Ont., Toronto, 1998—99. Grantee, Rockefeller Endowment at Dartmouth, 1983—84. Mem.: IEEE (assoc.), Boston Coll. Club, Cum Laude Soc. (life), Dartmouth Ednl. Assn. (life). Achievements include invention of channel-independent all-risk auto insurance. Avocations: aviation, music, sailing, scuba diving, technology.

CONNERY, MICHAEL M., lawyer; b. Providence, 1943; Student, U. Fribourg, Switzerland; BSFS, Georgetown U., 1968; JD with high honors, U. Conn., 1975. Bar: Conn. 1975, NY 1976. Ptnr., practice leader labor and employment law Skadden, Arps, Slate, Meagher & Flom LLP, NYC. Office: Skadden Arps Slate Meagher & Flom LLP 4 Times Sq New York NY 10036 Office Phone: 212-735-2920. Office Fax: 917-777-2920. Business E-Mail: mconnery@skadden.com.

CONNERY, SIR SEAN (THOMAS SEAN CONNERY), actor; b. Edinburgh, Aug. 25, 1930; s. Joseph and Euphamia C.; m. Diane Cilento, Dec. 6, 1962 (div. Sept. 6, 1973); 1 son, Jason; m. Micheline Roquebrune, 1975; 1 stepdaughter. DLitt (hon.), Heriot-Watt U., 1981, St. Andrews U., 1988. Founder Fountainbridge Films, Los Angeles, 1992—2002. First theater appearance in road show co. of South Pacific, Eng., 1953, also in Macbeth, Judith; Actor (films)Let's Make Up, 1955, No Road Back, 1956, Action of the Tiger, 1957, Hell Drivers, 1957, Time Lock, 1957, Another Time, Another Place, 1958, Tarzan's Greatest Adventure, 1959, Darby O'Gill and the Little People, 1959, The Frightened City, 1961, Operation Snafu, 1961, The Longest Day, 1962, Dr. No., 1962, From Russis With

Love, 1963, Marnie, 1964, Woman of Straw, 1964, Goldfinger, 1964, The Hill, 1965, Thunderball, 1965, A Fine Madness, 1966, You Only Live Twice, 1967, Shalako, 1968, The Molly Maguires, 1970, The Red Tent, 1971, The Anderson Tapes, 1971, Diamonds are Forever, 1971, The Offence, 1973, Zardoz, 1974, The Terrorists, 1974, Murder on the Orient Express, 1974, The Wind and the Lion, 1975, The Man Who Would be King, 1975, Robin and Marian, 1976, The Next Man, 1976, A Bridge Too Far, 1977, The Great Train Robbery, 1979, Cuba, 1979, Meteor, 1979, Outland, 1981, Time Bandits, 1981, Sword of the Valiant, 1982, Wrong is Right, 1982, Five Days One Summer, 1982, Never Say Never Again, 1983, Highlander, 1986, The Name of the Rose, 1986, The Untouchables, 1987 (Acad. award for Best Supporting Actor), The Presidio, 1988, Indiana Jones and the Last Crusade, 1989, Family Business, 1989, The Hunt for Red October, 1990, The Russia House, 1990, Highlander 2: The Quickening, 1991, Robin Hood: Prince of Thieves, 1991, Rising Sun, 1993, A Good Man in Africa, 1994, Just Cause, 1995, First Knight, 1995, The Rock, 1996, (voice only) Dragon Heart, 1996, Playing By Heart, 1998; actor, prodr., Entrapment, 1999, Finding Forrester, 2000; actor, exec. prodr. The Avengers, 1998, The League of Extraordinary Gentlemen, 2003; actor, co-exec. prodr.: Medicine Man, 1992; (TV movies) Requiem For a Heavyweight, 1957, Women in Love, 1957, The Square Ring, 1959, The Crucible, 1959, Colombe, 1960, Without the Grail, 1961, MacBeth, 1961, Anna Karenina, 1961, Male of the Species, 1969, Blitz, 2006; prodr., dir.: The Bowler and the Bonnet (film documentary), I've Seen You Cut Lemons (London stage); prodr.: Something Like the Truth, Playing by Heart, 1998, (narrator) Macbeth, 1999; actor (video games) James Bond 007: From Russia with Love (voice only), 2005 With Brit. Royal Navy. Named Star of the Yr., Nat. Assn. Theater Owners, 1987, Commander of Arts, France; recipient Tribute award Brit. Acad. Film and Television Arts, 1990, Career Achievement award Nat. Bd. Rev., 1993, Cecil B. DeMille Golden Globe award Hollywood Fgn. Press Assn., 1996, Lifetime Achievement award ShoWest Conv., 1999, Order Brit. Empire (OBE), 2000, Life Achievement award Am. Film Inst., 2005, Campidoglia prize, 2006 Office: Creative Artists Agy 9830 Wilshire Blvd Beverly Hills CA 90212-1804

CONNEY, ALLAN HOWARD, pharmacologist, researcher; b. Chgo., Mar. 23, 1930; s. Leo Younkers and Celia (Gasway) Conney; m. Diana Conney, Sept. 5, 1954; children: Michael Raymond, Steven Herbert. BS, U. Wis., 1952, MS, 1954, PhD, 1956. Research asst. McArdle Lab., Madison, Wis., 1952—56; guest investigator Nat. Heart Inst., Bethesda, Md., 1957—58, pharmacologist, 1958—60; head dept. biochem. pharmacology Burroughs Wellcome & Co., Tuckahoe, NY, 1960—70; dir. dept. biochemistry Hoffmann-La Roche Inc., Nutley, NJ, 1970—71, dir. dept. biochemistry and drug metabolism, 1971—83, assoc. dir. exptl. therapeutics, 1979—83, dir. lab. exptl. carcinogenesis and metabolism, 1983—85; head Lab. of Exptl. Carcinogenesis and Metabolism Roche Inst. Molecular Biology, Nutley, NJ, 1985—87; chmn. dept. chem. biology Rutgers U. Coll. Pharmacy, Piscataway, NJ, 1987—2002; NJ Prof. Chem. Biology and Garbe Prof. of Leukemia and Cancer Rsch., Dept. Chem. Biology, Ernest Mario Sch. Pharmacy Rutgers U. , The State U. NJ, dir., Susan Lehman Cullman Lab. for Cancer Rsch. Claude Bernard Medal and Claude Bernard Vis. Professorship U. Montreal, 1970. Assoc. editor Cancer Rsch.; contbr. articles to profl. publications. Recipient Achievement award in Pharmacodynamics, Acad. of Pharmaceutical Scis., 1968, Outstanding Investigator award, NCI, 1990, Thomas Alva Edison Sci. award, NJ Acad. Sci. and Gov. NJ, 1992, Ernest H. Volwiler award, Am. Assn. Colleges Pharmacy, 1993. Mem.: AAAS, NAS, Internat. Soc. for the Study of Xenobiotics, Soc. Toxicology, Inc. (Rsch. Achievement award 1968, Arnold J. Lehman award 1980), Am. Assn. Cancer Rsch. (G.H.A. Clowes award 1981, DeWitt S. Goodman Lectr. award 2002), Am. Soc. Pharmacology and Exptl. Therapeutics (award for Rsch. in Exptl. Therapeutics 1977), Am. Soc. Biol. Chemists. Office: Rutgers U Coll Pharmacy/Lab Cancer Rsch 170 Frelinghuysen Rd Rm 129 Piscataway NJ 08854-8020 Office Phone: 908-445-4940. Office Fax: 732-445-0687. Business E-Mail: aconney@rci.rutgers.edu.*

CONNICK, HARRY, JR., musician, actor, vocalist, composer, lyricist; b. New Orleans, Sept. 11, 1967; s. Harry Connick, Sr. and Anita Connick; m. Jill Goodacre, Apr. 16, 1994. Studied with Ellis Marsalis, studied with James Booker; student, New Orleans Ctr. Creative Arts, Hunter Coll., Manhattan Sch. Music. Musician: (albums) Harry Connick, Jr., 1987, 20, 1988, We Are in Love, 1990 (Grammy award for Best Jazz Vocal Performace, 1991), Lofty's Roach Souffle, 1990, Blue Light, Red Light, 1991, Eleven, 1992, 25, 1992, When My Heart Finds Christmas, 1993, She, 1994, Star Turtle, 1996, To See You, 1997, Come By Me, 1999, 30, 2001, Songs I Heard, 2001 (Grammy Award for Best Traditional Pop Vocal Album, 2002), Harry for the Holidays, 2003, Other Hours, 2003, Only You, 2004; musician: (with Branford Marsalis) Occasion, 2005; contributed music to soundtrack When Harry Met Sally, 1989 (Grammy award for Best Jazz Vocal Male, 1990), The Godfather Part III, 1991 (nom. for Golden Globe award, 1991), Sleepless in Seattle, 1993, The Mask, 1994; contributed music to album/video: Simply Mad About the Mouse, 1991; actor: (films) Memphis Belle, 1990, Little Man Tate, 1991, Copycat, 1995, Independence Day, 1996, Excess Baggage, 1997, Hope Floats, 1998 (nom. Favorite Actor-Drama/Romance Blockbuster Awards, 199), The Iron Giant, 1999, My Dog Skip, 2000; (TV series) Cheers, 1991, Will & Grace, 2002—; (TV films) South Pacific, 2001; (plays) Pajama Game, 2006 (Theatre World award, 2006); appeared on (TV spl.) PBS' Great Performances (nom. for Emmy award Best Performance Variety Special, 1991), PBS presents Harry Connick, Jr.: Romance In Paris, 1998, The Worlds of Harry Connick, Jr., 1999; performer: (TV spl.) The Harry Connick, Jr. Christmas Special, 1993; guest performer (TV spl.) PBS Evening Pops, 2001, band leader Harry Connick's Big Band; musician: (videos) Singin' & Swingin', 1990, Swingin' Out Live, 1991, The New York Big Band Concert, 1993, The Harry Connick, Jr. Christmas Special, 1994; writer/arranged music: (Broadway plays) Thou Shalt Not, 2000; co-prodr.(with Tracey Freeman): (soundtrack), 2002 (Tony nom. Best Original Score (Music & Lyrics) Written for the Theatre, 2002). Office: Wilkins Mgmt Inc 323 Broadway Cambridge MA 02139

CONNICK, ROBERT ELWELL, retired chemistry professor; b. Eureka, Calif., July 29, 1917; s. Arthur Elwell and Florence (Robertson) C.; m. Frances Spieth, Dec. 19, 1952; children: Mary Catherine, Elizabeth, Arthur, Megan, Sarah, William Beach. BS, U. Calif., Berkeley, 1939, PhD, 1942. Mem. faculty U. Calif., Berkeley, 1942-88, researcher Manhattan project, 1942—46, asst. prof. then assoc. prof. chemistry, 1945-52, prof., 1952-88, chmn. dept. chemistry, 1958-60, dean Coll. Chemistry, 1960-65, vice chancellor acad. affairs, 1965-67, vice chancellor, 1969-71, acting dean Coll. Chemistry, 1987-88. Contbr. articles profl. jours. Guggenheim fellow, 1949, 59 Mem. Am. Chem. Soc., Nat. Acad. Scis., Phi Beta Kappa, Sigma Xi, Pi Mu Epsilon. Home: 45 Marguerita Rd Kensington CA 94707-1020 Business E-Mail: connick@berkeley.edu.

CONNIFF, ALEXANDRA ACOSTA, secondary school educator; b. Eufaula, Ala., June 2, 1970; d. Yamandu Pereyia and Syliva Viroga Acosta; children: Robert Nicholas-Acosta, Stephen Daniel-Acosta. BS, Auburn U., 1993, ME, 1997, postgrad., 2003—. Tchr. Eufalua City Bd. Edn., Morris, Ala., 1997—2003, Eufaula City Bd. Edn., 2003—. Roads scholar, Divsn. Learning Disabilities, 2004. Mem.: NEA, Coun. Exceptional Children, Delta Kappa Gamma. Democrat. Methodist. Avocations: travel, reading, cooking. Home: 403 N Randolph Ave Eufaula AL 36027 Office: Eufaula High Sch 530 Lake Dr Eufaula AL 36027 Office Phone: 334-687-1110 x132. Personal E-mail: conniffaa@yahoo.com.

CONNIFF, GREGORY, photographer; b. May 3, 1944; BA, Columbia U., NYC, 1966; LLB, U. Va., Charlottesville, 1969. Bar: Colo. 1969, Wis. 1971. Author: Common Ground, 1985, Wild Edges, 2006. Fellow, NEA, 1981, 1992, John Simon Guggenheim Meml. Found., 1989. Home: 1426 Rutledge St Madison WI 53703

CONNOLA, DONALD PASCAL, JR., management consultant; b. New Brunswick, NJ, Sept. 25, 1948; s. Donald Pascal and Josephine (Montalbano) C. AB, Rutgers U., 1970, MBA, 1973; JD, Bklyn. Law Sch., 1977. Mktg. control analyst Gen. Foods Corp., White Plains, NY, 1973—74, product analyst, 1974, sr. fin. analyst, 1974—75, fin. assoc., 1975—79, fin. specialist, 1979, internal mgmt. cons., 1979—82, mgmt. cons., 1983—. Prof. mgmt. Fairleigh Dickinson U., Rutherford, N.J., 1983-86, dir. MBA program, dir. undergrad. student svcs., 1986-94; prof. bus. adminstrn. Concordia Coll., Bronxville, N.Y., 1995-97; team leader Verizon Comm., 2000—. Mem. ASTD, NJ State Bar Assn., Assn. MBA Execs., Soc. for Human Resource Mgmt. Home: 1220 Cellar Ave Apt 12 Clark NJ 07066-2044 Office: 1500 Teaneck Rd Teaneck NJ 07666

CONNOLLY, COLM F., prosecutor; BA, U. of Notre Dame; MSc, London Sch. Econs.; JD, Duke U. Asst. US atty. dist. Del. US Dept. Justice, 1992—99, US atty. dist. Del., 2001—; ptnr. Morris, Nichols, Arsht and Tunnel, Wilmington, Del., 1999—2001. Recipient Director's award for Superior Performance as Asst. US Atty., US Atty. Gen., 1996. Office: US Attys Office Nemours Bldg PO Box 2046 Wilmington DE 19899-2046*

CONNOLLY, GERALD EDWARD, lawyer; b. Boston, Oct. 13, 1943; s. Thomas E. and Grace J. (Fitzgerald) C.; m. Elizabeth Heidi Eckert, Jan. 6, 1968; children: Matthew F., Dennis F., David D., Edward F. BS, Coll. of Holy Cross, 1965; JD, U. Va., 1972. Bar: Wis. 1972, U.S. Tax Ct. 1973. From assoc. to ptnr. Whyte & Hirschboeck S.C., Milw., 1972-78; ptnr. Minahan & Peterson S.C., Milw., 1978-91, Quarles & Brady, 1991—. Bd. dirs., sec. Reinhart Real Estate Group, Inc., Reinhart Retail Group; sec. Hometown Inc.; bd. dirs. Hatco Corp., Milw., Adaptive Engring. Lab., Inc., Diversatek, Inc., Medovations Inc., Sunlite Plastics, Inc., Milw.; sec. Radisson LaCrosse Hotel, Water Blasting Inc. Trustee Emory T. Clark Family Charitable Found., D.B. Reinhart Family Found.; mem. Circle of Care Children's Hosp. Wis.; vice chmn., bd. dirs. Children's Hosp. Wis. Found. Lt. USN, 1966-69. Mem.: ABA, Kiawah Island Club, North Shore Country Club, Order of Coif. Home: 10134 N Range Line Rd # 27W Mequon WI 53092-5435 Office: Quarles & Brady LLP 411 E Wisconsin Ave Ste 2040 Milwaukee WI 53202-4497 Office Phone: 414-277-5373. Business E-Mail: gec@quarles.com.

CONNOLLY, JANET ELIZABETH, retired sociologist, retired criminal justice educator; b. New Rochelle, NY, June 28, 1929; d. Michael A. and Vincentia (Bonitatibus) Dandry; m. Edward C. Connolly, June 7, 1952; children: Michael, Matthew, Christopher, Benedict, Andrew. BA, Chestnut Hill Coll., Phila., 1951; MA, Temple U., Phila., 1970, PhD, 1975; degree (hon.), Rilski Neofit U., Blagoevgrad, Bulgaria, 1992. Intelligence clk. CIA, Washington, 1951-52; tchr. Prince George's County Bd. Edn., Hyattsville, Md., 1952-53; rsch. assoc. Pa. Prison Soc., Phila., 1974-76; field dir. rsch. Georgetown U. Law Sch., Washington, 1976-77; rsch. dir. Phila. Commn. for Effective Criminal Justice, 1977-78; mem. faculty dept. criminal justice Temple U., Phila., 1980-91; mem. faculty dept. sociology Am. U. in Bulgaria, Blagoevgrad, 1991-96; guest lectr. Sch. Law Kiril E Metodi Univerzitet, Skopje, Macedonia, 1993. Cons. Bucks County Correctional Facility, Doylestown, Pa., 1987-91; evaluator Phila. Prison System, 1973. Campaign chairperson, Doylestown, Pa., 1980, 82, 84, 86, 90; pres. Bucks County Assn. for Corrections and Rehab., Doylestown, 1988-91; trustee Bucks County Community Coll., Newtown, Pa., 1989-91; bd. dirs. ARC, Bucks County chpt., Doylestown, 1980-82; mem. New Hope (Pa.) Civil Svc. Commn., 1986-91; bd. dirs. Planned Parenthood, 1986-88. U.S. Justice Dept. dissertation grantee, Washington, 1972. Mem. ACLU, LWV, Law and Soc. Assn., Am. Correctional Assn., Balkan Ednl. and Sci. Assn. (mem. sci. senate). Democrat. Avocations: gardening, embroidery, painting. Home: 762 Fairview Ave Apt C Annapolis MD 21403-2962 E-mail: janet.r.connolly@comcast.net.

CONNOLLY, JOHN EARLE, surgeon, educator; b. Omaha, May 21, 1923; s. Earl A. and Gertrude (Eckerman) C.; m. Virginia Hartman, Aug. 12, 1967; children: Peter Hart. John Earle, Sarah. AB, Harvard U., 1945, MD, 1948. Diplomate: Am. Bd. Surgery (bd. dirs. 1976-82), Am. Bd. Thoracic and Cardiovascular Surgery, Am. Bd. Vascular Surgery. Intern. in surgery Stanford U. Hosps., San Francisco, 1948-49, surg. research fellow, 1949-50, asst. resident surgeon, 1950-52, chief resident surgeon, 1953-54, surg. pathology fellow, 1954-55, 1957-60, John and Mary Markle Scholar in med. scis., 1957-62; surg. registrar professional unit St. Bartholomew's Hosp., London, 1952-53; resident in thoracic surgery Bellevue Hosp., NYC, 1955; resident in thoracic and cardiovascular surgery Columbia-Presbyn. Med. Ctr., NYC, 1956; from instr. to assoc. prof. surgery Stanford U., 1957-65; prof. U. Calif., Irvine, 1965—, chmn. dept. surgery, 1965-78; attending surgeon Stanford Med. Ctr., Palo Alto, Calif., 1959-65; chmn. cardiovascular and thoracic surgery Irvine Med. Ctr. U. Calif., 1968—; attending surgeon Children's Hosp., Orange, Calif., 1968—, Anaheim (Calif.) Meml. Hosp., 1970—. Vis. prof. Beijing Heart, Lung, Blood Vessel Inst., 1990, A.H. Duncan vis. prof. U. Edinburgh, 1984; Hunterian prof. Royal Coll. Surgeons Eng., 1985-86, Kinmonth lectr., 1987, Hume Lectr. Soc. for Clin. Vascular Surgery, 1998; King James IV lectr. Royal Coll. Surgeons Edinburgh, 2003; Dist. Prof. Lectr. Uniformed Svcs. U. Health Scis., Bethesda, 1998; adv. coun. Nat. Heart, Lung, and Blood Inst.-NIH, 1981-85; Emile F. Holman lectr. Stanford U. Sch. Medicine, 2005; cons. Long Beach VA Hosp., Calif., 1965—. Contbr. articles to profl. jours.; mem. editl. bd.: Jour. Cardiovascular Surgery, 1974-03, chief editor, 1985-96; mem. editl. bd. Western Jour. Medicine, 1975—, Jour. Stroke, 1979—, Jour. Vascular Surgery, 1983-95. Bd. dirs. Audio-Digest Found., 1974—, Franklin Martin Found., 1975-80; regent Uniformed Svcs. U. Health Scis., Bethesda, 1992-03. Served with AUS, 1943-44. Recipient Cert. of Merit, Japanese Surg. Soc., 1979, 90. Fellow ACS (gov. 1964-70, regent 1973-82, vice chmn. bd. regents 1980-82, v.p. 1984-85), Royal Coll. Surgeons Eng., 1982 (hon.), Royal Coll. Surgeons Ireland, 1988 (hon.), Royal Coll. Surgeons Edinburgh, 1983 (hon.); mem. Japanese Surg. Soc. (hon.), Vascular Soc. of Great Britian & Ireland (hon.), Am. Surg. Assn., Soc. U. Surgeons, Am. Assn. Thoracic Surgery (coun. 1974-78), Pacific Coast Surg. Assn. (pres. 1985-86), San Francisco Surg. Soc., L.A. Surg. Soc., Soc. Vascular Surgery, Western Surg. Assn., Internat. Cardiovascular Soc. (pres. 1977), Soc. Internat. Chirurgie, Soc. Thoracic Surgeons, Western Thoracic Surg. Soc. (pres. 1978), Orange County Surg. Soc. (pres. 1984-85), James IV Assn. Surgeons (councillor 1983—), San Francisco Golf Club, Pacific Union Club, Bohemian Club (San Francisco), Harvard Club (N.Y.C.), Big Canyon Club (Newport Beach, Calif.), Cypress Point Club (Pebble Beach). Home: 7 Deerwood Ln Newport Beach CA 92660-5108 Office Phone: 714-456-5756. E-mail: jeconnol@uci.edu.

CONNOLLY, JOHN JOSEPH, publishing executive; b. Worcester, Mass., Feb. 4, 1940; s. Nicholas John and Margaret Anne (Flynn) Connolly; m. Ingrid Schlemminger, Apr. 11, 1964; children: Sean Timothy, Cheryl Lea. BS, Worcester State Coll., 1962; MA, U. Conn., 1963; EdD, Columbia U., 1972; LLD, Mercy Coll., 1980. Pres. Dutchess CC, Poughkeepsie, NY, 1972—81; pres., CEO NY Med. Coll., Valhalla, 1981—92, Castle Connolly Med. Ltd., NYC, 1992—. Bd. dirs. Morton Restaurant Group, Inc.; chmn. Alpha Gene Inc. Chmn. Dutchess County Indsl. Devel. Agy., 1978—81; hon. chmn. Dutchess/Columbia br. Am. Lung Assn., 1993—; pres. Westchester Hist. Soc., 1985—88; pres.'s adv. coun. United Hosp. Fund; bd. advisors Whitehead Inst. for Biomed. Rsch.; adv. com. Funding First, Inc.; bd. dirs., chmn. Profl. Exam. Svc., 1998—; bd. dirs. United Way of Dutchess County, pres., 1978; chmn. bd. trustees St. Francis Hosp., Poughkeepsie, 1976—80; trustee Culinary Inst. Am., 1976—2002, chair, 1996—98; trustee Poughkeepsie Area Fund, 1973—78, St. Agnes Hosp, White Plains, 1988—99; bd. dirs., chmn. Econ. Devel. Corp. Dutchess County; bd. dirs. Westchester County Mental Health Assn., Lupus Found., Am. Lyme Disease Found., 1993—2001, founder, chair, 1994—99. Named Man of the Yr., Dutchess County Legislature, 1980; named one of 100 Outstanding Young Leaders in Higher Edn., Change Mag., 1979; recipient Disting. Svc. award, Poughkeepsie Jaycees, 1974, Marie Y. Martin award, Assn. CC Trustees, 1978. Fellow: Westchester County Assn., Assn. Colls. Mid-Hudson Area (pres. 1976—79), NY Acad. Sci., NY Acad. Medicine, Friends Hudson Valley (chmn. 1990), Friends Nat. Libr. Medicine (dir. 1994—96); mem.: Phi Delta Kappa. Roman Catholic. Office: Castle Connolly Med Ltd 42 W 24th 2nd Floor New York NY 10010 Office Phone: 212-367-8400.

CONNOLLY, JOSEPH FRANCIS, II, academic administrator, government consultant; b. Quincy, Mass., Feb. 15, 1944; s. Joseph Francis and Flora Frances C.; m. Donna M. Cameron, May 4, 1968; children: Jennifer S., Joseph F. III. BA magna cum laude, Park Coll., Parkville, Mo., 1971; LLB, Blackstone Sch. Law, Chgo., 1972, JD, 1977; postgrad., U. South Fla., 1977-79, Fla. Inst. Tech., Melbourne, Liberty U., Lynchburg, Va., Am. Mil. U., Manassas, Va.; MEd, Nat. Coll. Edn., 2000; MMA, Coll. of Higher Edn. for, Martial Arts, UK, 2001; MS, Knightsbridge U., 2002; PhD in Mil. Studies, Internat. Inst. Specialized Edn. and Rsch., Manchester, Eng., 2005. Cert. EMT, firefighter and law enforcement officer, Fla.; cert. in homeland security Level V, Am. Bd. for Cert. in Homeland Security; diplomate Homeland Security, Am. Bd. Cert., 2005. Former coord. emergency med. svcs. City of Quincy, 1971-73; former EMT Boston Ambulance Squad, 1973-74; former coord. 14-community emergency med. svcs. program, 1974; formerly safety tng. coord., lead instr. Fire Tng. Acad. Orange County Pub. Schs., Fla., 1979-82; former dir. pub. safety Poinciana, Fla., 1985-86; sr. cons. Resource, Studies, and Devel. Internat., Inc., 1988-91; CEO Connolly, Hudson, Taylor & Assocs., Orlando, Fla., 1988-91; pres. Joseph F. Connolly II, P.A., Fla., 1982-95; internat. radio show host Internet Radio Network, 2004—. Adj. faculty mem. Pikes Peak C.C., Valencia C.C., Fla. Inst. Tech., Nat. Fire Acad., So. Coll.; tng. counselor emeritus NRA; med. cons. State of Bahrain Def. Force; former mem. Health Planning Coun. Greater Boston; dir. Royal Nat. Lifeboat Instn., Ireland, U.K.; dir. U.S. Jujitsu Fedn. Mem. Orange County subcom. Health Systems Agy. of East Ctrl. Fla.; fire commr. Conway Fire control Dist. of Orange County, 1980-84; former combat lt., staff capt. res. program Orange County Fire Dept.; com. chmn. Orange County Rep. Exec. Com., 1985-93; former Safety Tng. Coord. Orange County Pub. Schs., Fla., pres. Coun. of Vol. Coords., Orange County, 1987; mem. Rep. Presdl. Task Force, Nat. Rep. Senatorial Commn.; active Boy Scouts Am., 1954—; life mem. Nat. Eagle Scout Assn.; chmn. bd. trustees Inst. of Mil. Arts, 1999—. Master sgt. Spl. Forces US Army, 1961—96, col. Fla. Guard, 2003—, lt. col. CAP, 1989, ret., ret. USCG Aux., 1999. Decorated Purple Heart with two oak leaf clusters, 24 other U.S. and fgn. mil. decorations or citations, Knight Sovereign Mil. Order St. John of Jerusalem (Austria); recipient Gill Robb Wilson award CAP, Aerospace Edn. Achievement award, 1987, Resolution of Tribute award Orange County Sch. Bd., 1989, Presdl. Sports award for martial arts, 1999, Pres.'s Leadership award and gold medal U.S. Ju-Jitsu Fedn., 2003, cert. of commendation Nat. Mus. of U.S. Army; named Vietnam Vet. of the Yr., Vietnam Vets. Ctrl. Fla., Inc., 1988; named to Order Knights Templar, 1985; inducted into state, nat. and internat. martial art halls of fame. Fellow Soc. Martial Arts U.K., Royal Soc. Arts; mem. Aircraft Owners and Pilots Assn., Boat/US, Sons of the Union Vets. of the Civil War, Ducks Unltd., VFW (life), DAV (life), Nat. Fire Acad. Alumni Assn. (pres. 1984-92), Internat. Assn. Counselors and Therapists, Nat. Eagle Scout Assn. (life), Am. Coll. of Forensic Examiners Inst., Legion of Frontiersmen of the British Commonwealth, Third Order St. Francis, Mil. Order of Purple Heart, Mensa, Masons, U.S. Judo Assn. (life, 8th degree black belt in jujitsu, 9th degree black belt in judo, inducted into World Martial Arts Hall of Fame, 1996), Asahi Internat. Dojo (pres.), Midori Yama Budokai, U.S. Yudo Assn. (founder 1998, chmn. bd. trustees 1998—), Internat. Yudo Fedn. (founder 2000, chmn. bd. trustees 2000—). Mem. Celtic Ch. Office: 4409 Hoffner Ave Ste 327 Orlando FL 32812-2331

CONNOLLY, JOSEPH THOMAS, retired lawyer, judge; b. Montclair, NJ, Mar. 22, 1938; s. Patrick Joseph and Ethelyn Marie (Dilkes) Connolly; m. Phyllis Jane Marturano, June 25, 1966; children: James V., Michael J., Victoria L. BS, St. Peter's Coll., Jersey City, 1959; JD, Fordham U., 1966. Bar: N.J. 1967, U.S. Dist. Ct. N.J. 1967, U.S. Supreme Ct. 1972. Claim adjuster Md. Am. Gen. Group, East Orange, NJ, 1962—66; jud. clk. Superior Ct. N.J., Newark, 1966—67; assoc. Feuerstein & Sachs, Newark, 1967—68; trial lawyer Office Pub. Defender N.J., Newark, 1968—69; assoc. Donohue & Donohue, Nutley, NJ, 1969—71; ptnr. Brown, Connolly & Karosen, Bloomfield, NJ, 1971—88; judge Mcpl. Ct., Glen Ridge, NJ, 1980—; sole practitioner Glen Ridge, 1989—2006; acting judge Irvington Mcpl. Ct., Newark Mcpl. Ct.; judge Bloomfield Mcpl. Ct., NJ, 2005—; acting judge Orange Mcpl. Ct., NJ, 2005—. Instr. William Paterson Coll., Wayne, NJ, 1980; lectr. Inst. for Continuing Legal Edn., Trenton and Newark, 1975—82; moot ct. judge Seton Hall U. Sch. Law, Newark, 1980—94. Pres. Glen Ridge Cmty. Fund, 1978—79; former trustee League for Family Svc., Bloomfield and Glen Ridge; mem. Mcpl. Alliance Com., Glen Ridge; pres. Bloomfield Jaycees, 1971—72. Served US Army, 1959—65. Mem.: N.J. Bar Assn. (consultor 1979—84), Bloomfield Lawyers (pres. 1976—77, Outstanding Service award 1977), Kiwanis (pres. 1979—80, treas. 2005, Disting. Pres. award). Home: 13 Windsor Pl Glen Ridge NJ 07028-2124

CONNOLLY, KENNETH THOMAS, lawyer; b. Spokane, Wash., Jan. 23, 1940; s. Lawrence Francis and Kathleen Dorothea (Hallahan) C.; m. Laurie Samuel, June 24, 1967; children: Kevin, Megan, Amy, Matthew. BBA, Gonzaga U., Spokane, Wash., 1962; JD, Gonzaga U., 1966; LLM in Taxation, NYU, 1972. Bar: Wash. 1966, U.S. Ct. Mil. Appeals 1967, U.S. Tax Ct. 1983. Assoc. Witherspoon, Kelley, Davenport & Toole, Spokane, 1967-77, ptnr./prin., 1977—. Assoc. prof. law Gonzaga Sch. Law, 1973-77. Bd. overseers Gonzaga Prep. Sch., Spokane, 1988-89; trustee Spokane Guild Sch. Neuromuscular Ctr., 1975-78, Wash. State U. Found. Bd., 1992-97, Whitman Coll. Planned Giving Coun., 1994-2001, Holy Family Adult Day Care Bd., 2001—. Capt. U.S. Army, 1966-70. Recipient Wall St. Jur. award, 1962; decorated Bronze Star medal. Mem. Wash. State Bar Assn. (founder, chmn. health law sect. 1989-92, health law coun. 1989-94, pres. Washington State tax sect. 1987-88, mem. tax coun. 1984—), ABA (chmn. health care subcom. 1990-94). Independent. Avocations: tennis, astronomy. Office: Witherspoon Kelley Davenport & Toole 1100 US Bank Bldg Spokane WA 99201 Business E-Mail: ktc@wkdtlaw.com.

CONNOLLY, KEVIN JUDE, lawyer; b. NYC, May 25, 1954; s. John William and Beatrice Joan (Fallon) C.; m. Audrey Mason, May 25, 1995; children: Shea Alexander, Ciaran Jude. BA cum laude, Fordham Coll., 1976; JD, Fordham U., 1985. Bar: NY 1990, N.Mex., 2007. Assoc. Stroock & Stroock & Lavan, NYC, 1985-89, Robinson, Silverman, Pearce, Aronsohn & Berman LLP, NYC, 1998—2001; pres. Imagetronics, Inc., Mineola, NY, 1989-92; counsel Schreiber, Simmons, MacKnight & Tweedy, NYC, 1992-94, Eaton & Van Winkle, NYC, 1994-97; ptnr. Duval & Stachenfeld LLP, NYC, 2001—05; counsel Zetlin & DeClearia, 2006, Anderson Kill Rolich PC, 2007—. Vis. lectr. Sch. Visual Arts, NYC, 1996—2000; dir. Internet Soc., NYC chpt., 1997—2000; outside counsel Internet Policy Adv. Body, Geneva, 1997—99, Internet Coun. Registrars, Geneva, Hatewatch, Inc., 1998—2002; faculty mem. Practising Law Inst.,

2003—. Author: Law of Internet Security and Privacy, 2003; contbr. Handling Constrn. Risks, 2003, articles to profl. jours. Avocations: antiques, paintball. Home: 20 Apache Creek Santa Fe NM 87505 Personal E-mail: kjconnolly@yahoo.com.

CONNOLLY, MELISSA KANE, public relations executive; b. Wilmington, Del., Aug. 8, 1967; BA, Hofstra U., 1989. Bus. mgr. Fairchild Pub., NYC, 1990—93; VISTA vol. Project Challenge, Long Beach, NY, 1993—94; dir. circulation and mktg. Richner Pub., Lawrence, NY, 1994—97; dir. mktg. Farrell Fritz P.C., Uniondale, NY, 1997—2001; dir. comm. Senator Kemp Hannon, Albany, NY, 2001—03; v.p. u. rels. Hofstra U., Hempstead, NY, 2003—. Mem. govt. affairs team. Commn. Indep. Coll. and U., Albany, NY, 2003—; adv. bd. Inst. Devel. and Advancement of Edn. in Sci., Hempstead, 2004—. Adv. bd. PULSE, NY, 2003—; pres. legis. affairs Long Island Women's Agenda, Plainview, NY, 2004—07. Named one of Top 50 Women on L.I., L.I. Bus. News, 2006, 40 Under 40, 2000—01. Mem.: Internat. Assn. Bus. Comm. (pres. L.I. chpt. 2000—01, com. chmn., Achievement in Comm. award 1998, 1999, Pres. Achievement award 2001, Achievement in Comm. award 2006), Pub. Rels. Soc. Am. Office: Hofstra Univ 202 A Hofstra Hall Hempstead NY 11549

CONNOLLY, PAUL K., JR., lawyer, energy executive; b. San Francisco, June 7, 1944; s. Paul K. C.; m. Nancy Connolly; children: Paul, Daniel. AB, Holy Cross Coll., 1966; JD, Boston Coll., 1969. Bar: Mass. 1969, U.S. Ct. Appeals (1st cir.) 1970. Assoc. Crane, Inker & Oteri, Boston, 1969-75; asst. atty. gen. State of Mass., 1971-75; assoc. Connolly & Johnson, Boston, 1975-80, LeBoeuf, Lamb, Greene & MacRae LLP, Boston, 1981, chmn. energy/utilities dept., mng. ptnr. Boston office; v.p., gen. counsel Energy East Corp., New Gloucester, Maine, 2005—. Instr. Boston U., Boston, 1973-74, Suffolk Law Sch., Boston, 1974-78. Mem. ABA, Fed. Energy Bd., Mass. Trial Law Assn., Mass. Mental Health Legal Advisors (bd. dirs.). Office: Energy East Corp 52 Farm View Dr New Gloucester ME 04260 Office Phone: 617-748-6868. Office Fax: 617-439-0341. Business E-Mail: connolly@llgm.com.*

CONNOLLY, THOMAS EDWARD, judge; b. Boston, Nov. 7, 1942; s. Thomas Francis and Catherine Elizabeth (Skehill) Connolly. AB, St. John's Coll., Brighton, Mass., 1964; JD, Boston Coll., 1969. Bar: Mass. 1969. Assoc. Schneider & Reilly, Boston, 1969-73; ptnr. Schneider, Reilly, Zabin, Connolly & Costello, P.C., Boston, 1973-85, Connolly Leavis & Rest, Boston, 1986-90; judge Mass. Superior Ct., Boston, 1990—. Instr. law Northeastern Law Sch., Boston, 1975—76. Mem. governing coun. Boston Coll. Law Sch. Alumni Coun., 1980—82, 2001—03. Fellow Am. Coll. Trial Lawyers; mem. ABA (vice chmn. products liability sect. 1978-80), Trial Lawyers Assn. Am. (nat. gov. 1977-80), Mass. Acad. Trial Lawyers (gov. 1976-90), Univ. Club (Boston). Roman Catholic. Home: 253 Marlborough St # 4 Boston MA 02116-1731 Office: The Superior Ct Boston MA 02109 Office Phone: 617-788-8130. Personal E-mail: tommyc57@aol.com.

CONNOLLY, VIOLETTE M., small business owner; b. NYC, Nov. 25, 1918; d. Gysbert Martens and Marie Therese dePont; m. Joseph Vincent Connolly Jr., Feb. 27, 1957 (dec.). BA, Hunter Coll., 1940; MS, Columbia U., 1941. Accredited Pub. Rels. Soc. Am. Analyst The Payne Fund, NYC, 1941-53; ptnr. Elser & Assocs., NYC, 1954-56, The J.V. Connolly Co., NYC, 1957-64; cons. on pub. rels., radio and TV Assn. of the Jr. Leagues of Am., NYC, 1964-72; asst. dir. N.Y. Assn. for Brain Injured Children, NYC, 1973-74; circulation mgr. Plants and Gardens Bklyn. Botanic Garden, NYC, 1974-82; adminstr. Nat. Broadcasting Co., NYC, 1983-86; owner, mgr. The White House, Block Island, R.I., 1986—; clk. Town of New Shoreham, Block Island, 1986—. Bd. mem., publicist The Village Art Ctr., N.Y.C., 1944-54; pres. Washington Sq. Bus. and Profl. Women's Club, N.Y.C., 1953-55; founder, chair House and Garden Tours Com., Block Island Hist. Soc., 1971-96; pres. Block Island Gardeners, 1986-97. Capt. First Assembly Dist., Rep. Club, N.Y.C., 1945-57; mem. Bishop's com. St. Ann's Ch., 1995—. Republican. Avocations: antiques, travel.

CONNOLLY, WILLIAM M., state supreme court justice; b. 1938; Undergrad., Creighton U., 1956—59, JD, 1963. Dep. atty. Adams County, 1964—66, atty., 1967—72; pvt. law practice Hastings, 1972—91; former judge Nebr. Ct. of Appeals, Lincoln, 1992—94; assoc. justice Nebr. Supreme Ct. , Lincoln, justice, 1994—. Mem.: Nebr. State Bar Assn. Office: Nebr Supreme Ct Room 2210 State Capital Bldg Lincoln NE 68509*

CONNOR, CAROL J., library director; BA in Hist., Molloy Coll., 1964; MA in Hist., Georgetown U., 1970; MLS, Drexel U., 1972. Various adminstrv. positions in ednl. fields, various US Cities, 1964—72; spl. asst. tech. processes divsn. Lincoln City Librs., Nebr., 1972—73, coord. tech. processes divsn., 1973—76, asst. dir., 1976—78, dir., 1978—. Mem. Mayor's Com. for Internat. Friendship, Lincoln, 1973—; adv. com. U. Nebr., search for dean of librs., 1984-85; del. to cmty. retreat, Star Venture, 1986, edn. task force, 1987-88, vocat. edn. task force, 1988-89, downtown child care task force, 1988-89; mem. cmty. adv. com. Lincoln Pub. Schs. Search for English Cons., 1991, Search for Media Dir., 1992; mem. Nebr. Ctr. for Book Bd., 1990-95, Nebr. Libr. Commn. state adv. coun. 1985-86, Nebr. Lit. Festival Com., 1990-92; bd. dirs. Postsecondary Ednl. Librs. and Resource Ctrs. of Nebr. 1981-84, chair 1982; mem. edn. com. Am. Cancer Soc., Lancaster County, Nebr., 1989-91, Family Svcs. Bd., 1991—, vice chair chair elect 1992, chair, 1994; leadership Lincoln VI 1990-91; mem. Lincoln Cancer Ctr. adv. bd., 1988-94, vice chair 1991-94. Mem. ALA, (bylaws com., membership com., LITA/LAMA conf. com. 1996-97), Mountain Plains Libr. Assn. (chair continuing edn. com. 1984-85; membership devel. com. 1986-87, vice chair and chair of pub. libr. sect. 1975-77, v.p./ pres. elect 1996-97, pres. 1997-98), Nebr. Libr. Assn. (chair intellectual freedom com. 1975-76, state rep. to Mountain Plains Libr. Assn., 1984-86, vice chair and chair of pub. libr. sect. 1987-89), Urban Librs. Coun. (leadership progs. 1994-95), Capitol Bus. and Profl. Women (v.p. 1983), Downtown Lincoln Assn. (mktg. com. 1988-89). Office: Lincoln City Librs 136 S 14th St Lincoln NE 68508-1899 Office Phone: 402-441-8500. E-mail: library@lincolnlibraries.org.

CONNOR, CHRISTOPHER M., manufacturing executive; b. Pensacola, Fla., Mar. 24, 1956; m. Sara Connor; 3 children. BS, Ohio State U., 1978. Dir. advt. Sherwin-Williams' Paint Stores Group, 1983—85, pres., gen. mgr. western divsn., 1985—92, sr. v.p. mktg. group, 1992—94, pres., gen. mgr. diversified brands divsn., 1994—97, pres., 1997—99; vice chmn., CEO Sherwin-Williams Co., 1999—2000, chmn., CEO, 2000—. Bd. dir. Diebold Inc., Nat. City Corp. Chmn. bd. trustees Keep Am. Beautiful, Univ. Hosp. Health Sys., Cleve.; mem. Dean's adv. council Fisher Coll. Bus, Ohio State Univ.; bd. mem. Rock & Roll Hall of Fame & Mus, Cleve. Growth Assn., Catholic Diocese Cleve. Found., Music Arts Assn., Cleve. Orch., Walsh Jesuit H.S. Office: Sherwin-Williams Co 101 Prospect Ave NW Cleveland OH 44115-1075

CONNOR, GEOFFREY MICHAEL, lawyer; b. Washington, Oct. 2, 1946; s. John Thomas and Mary (O'Boyle) C.; m. Maud Holly Pyne, July 24, 1976; children: Taylor Pyne, Michael Buck, Grafton Wright. BA, Williams Coll., 1968; JD, Harvard U., 1973. Bar: N.Y. 1974, N.J. 1975. Clk. to presiding judge U.S. Ct. Appeals (2d cir.), NYC, 1973; assoc. Cleary, Gottlieb, Steen & Hamilton, NYC and London, 1974-79, Shanley & Fisher, NJ, 1979-83; v.p. Carteret Savs. Bank, FA, NJ, 1984-86, sr. v.p. Morristown, NJ, 1987-90; commr. N.J. Dept. Banking, Trenton, 1990-94; ptnr. Reed Smith LLP, Princeton, NJ, 1994—2007, of counsel, 2007—. Lt. (j.g.) USN, 1968-70. Mem. N.J. State Bar Assn. Home: 52 Potterstown Rd PO Box 355 Oldwick NJ 08858-0355 Office: 136 Main St Princeton Forrestal Village Princeton NJ 08543-7839 Office Phone: 609-520-6002. E-mail: gconnor@reedsmith.com.

CONNOR, GEOFFREY SCOTT, former state official, lawyer; b. Ballinger, Tex., July 24, 1963; s. Michael Lynn Connor and Pamela Sue Underwood Hodges. BA, Tex. State U., San Marcos, 1985; student, U. London, 1985; JD, U. Tex., 1988. Bar: Tex. 1988. Asst. gen. counsel Office of the Gov., Austin, Tex., 1988-90, dep. gen. counsel, 1990-91; asst. commr. legal affairs Dept. Agr., Austin, Tex., 1991-95; gen. counsel Tex. Natural Resource Conservation Commn., 1995-99; atty. Akin, Gump, Strauss, Hauer and Feld, 1999—2000; dep. sec. of state State of Tex., 2000—03, sec. of state, 2003—05; counsel bus. transaction sect. Jackson Walker LLP, Austin, Tex., 2005—. Del., Rep. Conv., Austin, 1982-96, alt. del., Houston, 1992; del. Nat. Rep. Conv., San Diego, 1996; bd. dirs. Helping Our Brothers Out, Inc., 1995; trustee Sigma Tau Gamma; mem. bd. advisors. Internat. Ctr. Tex. State U.; mem. Austin Coun. Fgn. Affairs, Austin World Affairs Coun., Dallas World Affairs Coun., Am. Coun. Young Polit. Leaders, Brit.-Am. Bus. Coun. World Congress on Info. and Tech., 2006. Mem. ABA, State Bar Tex. (bd. cert. in adminstrv. law by Tex. Bd. Legal Specialization), Tex. Young Lawyers Assn, Nat. Assn. Secs. of State (internat. affairs com.). Episcopalian. Avocations: travel, reading, hunting, gardening. Office: Jackson Walker LLP Ste 1100 100 Congress St Austin TX 78701-4099 Office Phone: 512-236-2022. Office Fax: 512-236-2002. E-mail: gconnor@jw.com.

CONNOR, HOLLY PYNE, curator, art historian; b. Augusta, Ga., Feb. 5, 1952; d. John Wright and Nancy Buck Pyne; m. Geoffrey Michael Connor, July 24, 1976; children: Taylor Pyne, Michael Buck, Grafton Wright. BA cum laude, Boston U., 1974; MA, Courtauld Inst., London, 1978; PhD, Rutgers U., New Brunswick, NJ, 1996. Asst. curator Bklyn. Mus., 1978—85; cons. curator Newark Mus., 1996—2002, assoc. curator, 2002—05, curator 19th century Am. art, 2005—. Lectr. on Am. art, 1998—. Editor, author: Off the Pedestal: New Women in the Art of Homer, Chase and Sargent, 2006; exhibitions include Picturing America, Newark Mus., 2001—, American Art in the Dutch Tradition, 2001—02. Trustee NJ Hist. Soc., Newark, 1983—88, Far Hills Country Day Sch., NJ, 1988—92; active Tewksbury Hist. Preservation Commn., Oldwick, NJ, 1995—2005. Mem.: Assn. Art Mus. Curators, Coll. Art Assn. Avocations: reading, tennis, skiing. Office: Newark Mus 49 Washington St Newark NJ 07102 Office Phone: 973-596-6664. Business E-Mail: hconnor@newarkmuseum.org.

CONNOR, JAMES RICHARD, retired academic administrator; b. Indpls., Oct. 31, 1928; s. Frank Elliott and Edna (Felt) C.; m. Zoe Ezopov, July 7, 1954; children: Janet K., Paul A. BA with highest distinction, U. Iowa, 1951; MS, U. Wis., 1954, PhD, 1961. Asst. prof. history Washington and Lee U., 1956-57, Va. Mil. Inst., 1958-61; asst. dir. Salzburg Seminar in Am. Studies, 1961-62; joint staff mem. Wis. Coordinating Com. Higher Edn., 1962-63; dir. Inst. Analysis; asst. prof. history U. Va., 1963-66; assoc. prof. history, assoc. provost No. Ill. U., 1966-69; provost, acad. v.p., prof. history Western Ill. U., 1969-74; chancellor, prof. history U. Wis., Whitewater, 1974-91, chancellor, prof. emeritus, 1991. Exec. dir. James S. Kemper Found., Long Grove, Ill., 1991-99; assoc. dir. Va. Higher Edn. Study Com., 1964-65; intern acad. adminstrn. Am. Coun. Edn., Stanford U., 1965-66; staff dir. Study of Governance of Acad. Med. Ctr., Josiah Macy Jr. Found., 1968-70; mem. commn. on higher edn. North Ctrl. Assn. 1970-75, 79-84, cons.-examiner, 1972-91; chair adv. com. on alcohol and drug use U. Wis. System, 1984-85; mem. nat. adv. com. Woodrow Wilson Nat. Fellowship Found., 1990-96, trustee, 1996-2005, trustee emeritus, 2005-; dir. Fairhaven Retirement Corp., 1994—. Author: Studies in Higher Education, 1965; contbr., Ency. Brit. Served with AUS, 1946-47, 51-53. Woodrow Wilson fellow, 1953-54; So. fellow, 1957-58 Mem. AAUP, Orgn. Am. Historians, Blue Key, Golden Key, Order of Omega, Phi Beta Kappa, Phi Eta Sigma, Phi Kappa Phi, Phi Delta Kappa, Beta Gamma Sigma, Phi Alpha Theta, Delta Sigma Pi. Home: N7447 Linden Dr Whitewater WI 53190-4357 Personal E-mail: j31z29connor@webtv.net.

CONNOR, JAMES WILLIAM, lawyer; b. Seminole, Okla., Aug. 21, 1932; s. William Michael Connor and Gertrude Margaret Smith; m. Louise Allen Rucker, Feb. 27, 1960; children: James William Jr., Laura Louise, Patrick Michael, Andrew Allen. BS in Bus. Adminstrn., St. Benedicts Coll., Atchisin, Kans., 1954; LLB, Okla. U., Norman, Okla., 1959. Atty. Wash. County, Bartlesville, Okla., 1959—63; city atty. Bartlesville, 1973—75; ptnr. Selby, Connor Muddux and Janer, Bartlesville, 1963—. Bd. dirs. The Lyon Found., 1977—, pres., 1989—. State rep. Okla. Ho. Reps., Okla. City, 1963—71, fl. leader, 1965—71. With US Army, 1954—56. Named one of Top 10 Legis. 1963-71, Cap. Press Corp. Mem.: ABA, Okla. Bar Assn. Avocations: golf, gardening, reading. Home: 522 E 16th St Bartlesville OK 74003 Office: Selby Connor Maddux and Janer 416 E 5th St Bartlesville OK 74003 Office Phone: 918-336-8114.

CONNOR, JOHN MURRAY, economics professor; b. Attleboro, Mass., July 7, 1943; s. John Murray Sr. and Victoria Rose (Moro) C.; m. Ulla Maija Niemelä, Apr. 3, 1972; 1 child, Timo. BA cum laude, Boston Coll., 1965; MA, U. Fla., 1974; MS, U. Wis., 1974, PhD, 1976. Vol. U.S. Peace Corps, Nigeria, Uganda, 1966—68; agrl. economist Econ. Rsch. Svc.1979 USDA, Madison, 1976, head food mfg. rsch. Econ. Rsch. Svc. Washington, 1979—83; assoc. prof. agrl. econs. Purdue U., West Lafayette, Ind., 1983—89, prof., 1989—, asst. dept. head, 1985—88. Adj. prof. Cath. U. Sacred Heart, Piacenza, Italy, 1991—; vis. prof. Åbo (Finland) Akademi U., 1994; cons. subcom. on multinats. U.S. Senate, Washington, 1974-76, select com. on nutrition, 1977-78, UN Ctr. on Transnats., 1981-82, U.S. Dept. Justice, 1999, Nat. Assn. Attys. Gen., 2000-03; chair Orgn. and Performance World Food Systems, 1988-93. Author: Market Power of Multinationals, 1977, Food Processing: An Industrial Powerhouse in Transition, 1988, 2d edit., 1997, Global Price Fixing, 2001, 2d edit., 2006; (with others) Food Manufacturing Industries, 1985; contbr. articles to profl. jours., chpts. to books. Grantee US Office Tech. Assessment, 1984-85, Inst. Food Technologists, 1986-88, 94-95, Ind. Dept. Commerce, 1987-91, Econ. Rsch. Svc., USDA, 1988-89, Coop. State Rsch. Svc., USDA, 1989—; recipient Antitrust Writing award Jerry S. Cohen Meml. Trust, 2003, Hon. Mention award, 2007. Mem. AAUP (pres. Purdue U. chpt. 1988-90, exec. bd. incl conf. 1990-94, nat. coun. 1991-92), ACLU, Am. Agrl. Econs. Assn. (Policy award 1980, Quality Comm. award 1985, 02, Disting. Extension Program award 1993), Indsl. Orgn. Soc., Am. Econs. Assn. Home: 4355 Creekside Pass Zionsville IN 46077-9292 Office: Purdue U 403 W State St West Lafayette IN 47907-2056 Office Phone: 765-494-4260.

CONNOR, JOHN THOMAS, JR., portfolio manager; b. NYC, June 16, 1941; s. John Thomas and Mary (O'Boyle) Connor; m. Susan Scholle, Dec. 18, 1965; children: Seanna, Marin, John. BA cum laude, Williams Coll., 1963; JD, Harvard U., 1967. Bar: N.Y. 1968, D.C. 1980. Assoc. Cravath, Swaine & Moore, NYC, 1967-71; dep. dir. Office Econ. Policy and Case Analysis, Pay Bd., Washington, 1971-72, Bur. East-West Trade, U.S. Dept. Commerce, Washington, 1972-73; sr. v.p. U.S.-USSR Trade and Econ. Coun., Moscow, 1973-76; assoc. Milbank, Tweed, Hadley & McCloy, NYC, 1976-79; ptnr. Curtis, Mallet-Prevost, Colt and Mosle, Washington, 1980-82; v.p., gen. counsel, sec. PHH Corp., 1982-88; v.p., asst. gen. counsel Prudential Ins. Co. Am., Newark, 1988-90; ptnr. Sills Cummis, Newark, 1990-94; counsel Chadbourne & Parke, NYC, 1994-96, Patterson, Belknap, Webb & Tyler, LLP, 1996-98; portfolio mgr. Third Millennium Russia Fund, 1998—. Bd. dirs., chmn. audit com. Teton Energy, 2003—. Pres., trustee Newark Boys Chorus Sch.; Fulbright tutor Ferguson Coll., Poona, India, 1963—64; chmn. Coun. Econ. Priorities; mem. Am. Law Inst., 1984—2004; exec. dir. N.J. Dems., 1969—70. Mem.: Coun. Fgn. Rels., DC Bar Assn., N.Y. State Bar Assn., Mountain Lake Club (Fla.), Union Club (N.Y.C.), Baltusrol Golf Club N.J., Chevy Chase Club (Md.), Wianno Club (Cape Cod), Phi Beta Kappa. Home: PO Box 832 Lake Wales FL 33859-0832 Office Phone: 863-679-7800. Personal E-mail: jtconnor@tampabay.rr.com, jtconnor@tmrussia.com.

CONNOR, JOSEPH ROBERT, editor; b. NYC, Jan. 31, 1927; s. Joseph M. and Ethel May (Ball) Connor; m. Marie Louise Zolezzi, Sept. 6, 1952; children: Jeanne Marie, Robert Brian, Ellen Louise. BA, Hunter Coll., 1951. Copy editor sports desk N.Y. Mirror, NYC, 1950-52; mng. editor Mechanix Illustrated Mag. div. Fawcett Publs., NYC, 1953-70; editor in chief CBS Publs., NYC, spl. interest publs., 1970-72; editor in chief Motor Mag. div. Hearst Corp., NYC, 1972-77; editor Construction Contracting, 1978-79; editor in chief Graduating Engr. McGraw-Hill, Inc., 1979-81, 88-90; editor Bus. Week New Product Devel., 1981—, Bus. Week Almanac, 1981—; editor in chief Bus. Week Careers, 1982-87; editor-in-chief Graduating Engr., 1988-90; exec. editor Graduating Engr. Peterson's-Cog Publs., 1990-91; freelance writer, editorial cons., 1991—; editor MOTORScoop Mag., GRG Publs. Inc., 1995-96. Author: A Job With a Future in Automative Mechanics, 1969; author: (with Heinz Ulrich) The National Job-Finding Guide, 1981; author: Cracking the Over-50 Job Market, 1992, Living with Your Bulldog, 2001; contbr. articles to popular mags. With AUS, 1945—46. Mem.: Am. Soc. Mag. Editors, Internat. Motor Press Assn. (pres. 1966—67). Home: 8 Woodvale Ln Huntington NY 11743-2324 Personal E-mail: scoop09@aol.com.

CONNOR, KEVIN M., lawyer; b. 1962; BA, Vanderbilt U.; JD, U. Kans. Bar: 1988. Shareholder Seigfreid, Bingham, Levy, Selzer, and Gee, 1994, ptnr., 1995—2002; sr. v.p. legal AMC Entertainment, Kans. City, Mo., 2002—03, sr. v.p., gen. counsel, sec., 2003—. Office: AMC Entertainment Inc 920 Main St Kansas City MO 64105-2017 Office Phone: 816-221-4000. Office Fax: 816-480-4700.

CONNOR, LAURENCE DAVIS, retired lawyer; b. Columbus, Ohio, May 14, 1938; s. Laurence R. and Gladys C. (Davis) Connor; m. Clare Elizabeth Hartwick, Aug. 8, 1964; children: Jeffrey H., Lynne D. Scoville. BA, Miami U., Oxford, Ohio, 1960; JD, U. Mich., 1965. Bar: Mich. 1966, U.S. Dist. Ct. (ea. dist.) Mich. 1966, U.S. Ct. Appeals (6th cir.) 1973, U.S. Supreme Ct. 1979. Assoc. Dykema Gossett, Detroit, 1965-73, ptnr., 1973—2002, mem. exec. com., 1984-90, dir. litigation sect., 1987-91, ret., 1991. Pres. Vis. Nurse Assn. Met. Detroit, 1980—81, Vis. Nurse Corp., Detroit, 1986—88; mem. coun. sect. alternative dispute resolution State Bar Mich., 1992—, chairperson, 1996—97; asst. clin. prof. law U. Mich., 2002—05. Mem.: ABA, Oaks Club, Yondotega Club, Detroit Athletic Club, Country Club Detroit. Office Phone: 313-568-6573. Business E-Mail: lconnor@dykema.com.

CONNOR, MICHAEL S., lawyer; b. Gastonia, NC, Sept. 13, 1962; Student, US Naval Acad.; BSME cum laude, Clemson Univ., 1984; JD, Univ. NC, 1987. Bar: NC 1988. Ptnr., co-leader, intellectual property litig. group Alston & Bird LLP, Charlotte, NC. Frequent speaker and author in field. Bd. dir. Metrolina Entrepreneurial Coun. Named a NC Super Lawyer, 2006; named one of Legal Elite, Bus. NC Mag., 2003. Mem.: Fed. Circuit Bar Assn., Am. Intellectual Property Law Assn., NC Bar Assn. Office: Alston & Bird LLP Ste 4000 Bank of Am Plz 101 S Tryon St Charlotte NC 28280-4000 Office Phone: 704-444-1022. Office Fax: 704-444-8588. Business E-Mail: mconnor@alston.com.

CONNOR, ROGER ARTHUR, retired dermatologist; s. Arthur Joseph and Angelina Marie Connor; m. Mary Madgalene Monahan; children: Michael, Kathleen, Mary Elizabeth, Timothy, Christopher, Matthew. BA, St. Anselm Coll., Manchester, NJ, 1942; MD, Laval U., Que., Can., 1946. Med. intern Mercy Hosp., Springfield, Mass., 1946—47; resident in obstetrics St. Ann Hosp., Fall River, Mass., 1947—48; gen. practice medicine Claremont, NH, 1948—50; resident in dermatology Boston City Hosp., 1954—56; pvt. practice dermatology Pittsfield, Mass., 1956—85; ret., 1985. Vol. dermatologist Sr. Friendship Clinic, Naples, Fla., 1986—; town auditor Allenstown, NH, 1940. Comdr. USN, 1942—50, comdr. USNR, 1950—53. Mem.: Mass. Med. Soc., New Eng. Dermatol. Assn., Am. Dermatol. Assn. Roman Catholic. Avocations: tennis, golf, travel. Personal E-mail: skinconnor@naples.net.

CONNOR, TERENCE GREGORY, lawyer; b. Chelsea, Mass., Dec. 28, 1942; s. Joseph Gerard Sr. and Rosalie Cecilia (Ryan) C.; m. Julie Kaye Berry, Dec. 18, 1971; children: Cormac, Kristin, Etain, Brendan. AB, Georgetown U., 1964; LLB, Seton Hall U., 1967; LLM, Georgetown U., 1975. Bar: D.C. 1968, U.S. Supreme Ct. 1976, Fla. 1980. Trial atty. U.S. Dept. Justice, Washington, 1973-76; labor counsel Nat. Airlines Inc., Miami, Fla., 1976-79; practicing atty. Morgan, Lewis & Bockius, Miami, 1979-96, mng. ptnr., 1996—2002. Mem. firm wide governing bd., 1996-2000. Chmn. Miami: Dade citizen com. for Observance Bicentennial of U.S. Constitution, 1986. Served to capt. JAG, USAF, 1968-73. Mem. Fla. Bar Assn. (chair labor and employment law sect. 1994-95, mem. exec. coun. 1986-93), Miami C. of C. (co-chair pers. and Labor mgmt. com. 1993-94) Home: 1517 San Rafael Ave Miami FL 33134-6241 Office: Junton & Williams LLP 1111 Brickell Ave Ste 2500 Miami FL 33131 Office Phone: 305-415-3316. Business E-Mail: tconnor@morganlewis.com.

CONNOR, ULLA M., linguistics educator; m. John M. Connor; 1 child, Timo. BA in English Philology, U. Helsinki, 1970, MA in English Philology magna cum laude, 1974; MA in English Lit., U. Fla., 1971; MA in Comparative Lit., U. Wis., 1973, PhD in Edn., English Linguistics, 1978. Asst. prof. Georgetown U., Washington, 1980—83, Ind. U.-Purdue U. Indpls., 1984—87, assoc. prof., 1987—93, prof., 1993—, founder, dir. ESL program, 1985—94, 1997—98, dir. Ind. Ctr. Intercultural Comm., 1997—, Barbara E. and Karl R. Zimmer chair in intercultural communication, 2003—. Asst. dean grad. sch. Purdue U., West Lafayette, Ind., 1988—90; donner guest prof. Abo Akademi U., Finland, 1994, 2000; vis. prof. Temple U. Japan, 1995; vis. rschr. U. Jyvaskyla, Finland, 1995; guest prof. Lund U., Sweden, 1998; academic advisor dept. of fgn. langs. Poly. U. Hong Kong, China, 1999—2001. Author: Contrastive Rhetoric: Cross-cultural Aspects of Second Language Writing, 1996; co-author (with others): Successful Grant Proposals. A Guide for Researchers in the European Union; co-editor (with R.B. Kaplan): Writing Across Languages: Analysis of L2 Text, 1987; co-editor: (with A.M. Johns) Coherence in Writing: Research and Pedagogical Perspectives, 1990; co-editor: (with D. Belcher) Reflections on Multiliterate Lives, 2001; co-editor: (with T.A. Upton) Applied Corpus Linguistics: A Multidimensional Perspective, 2004, Discourse in the Professions: Perspectives from Corpus Linguistics; guest editor: Multilingua: Jour. Cross-Cultural and Interlanguage Communication, 2004, Jour. English Academic Purposes Spl. Issue, guest editor with T. Seiler: jour. New Directions for Philanthropic Fundraising. Understanding and Improving Lang. Fundraising. Recipient Glenn Irwin Experience Excellence Recognition award, Ind. U. -Purdue U. Indpls., 1992; Internat. Peace scholarship, U. Fla., 1970-1971, grant, Exxon Edn. Found., 1985-1987, Finland's Acad. Scis. and Tech. (TEKES), 1995, Philanthropy grant, Ind. U., 1999. Mem.: Finnish Soc. Scis. and Letters (elected fgn. mem. 2000), Tchrs. English to Spkrs. of Other Langs., Nat. Coun. Tchrs. English, Am. Assn. Applied Linguistics. Office: Indiana Ctr Intercultural Comm 620 Union Dr Rm 411 Indianapolis IN 46202 Home Phone: 317-733-1938; Office Phone: 317-278-2441. Office Fax: 317-274-5616. Business E-Mail: uconnor@iupui.edu.

CONNOR, W(ALTER) ROBERT, foundation administrator, classicist, educator; b. Worcester, Mass., Aug. 30, 1934; m. Carolyn Loessel; children: Christopher, Stephan. BA, Hamilton Coll., 1956, LHD, 1991; PhD in Classics, Princeton U., 1961; LHD, Knox Coll., 1993. Instr. U. Michigan, Ann Arbor, 1960-63; jr. fellow Ctr. Hellenic Studies, 1963-64; asst. prof. Princeton U., Princeton, NJ, 1964-70, assoc. prof., 1970-72, prof., 1972-89, Andrew Fleming West prof. classics, 1978-89, chmn. dept. classics, 1972-77, chmn. com. Hellenic studies, 1979-85, chmn. coun. humanities, 1982-89; pres., dir. Nat. Humanities Ctr., Rsch. Triangle Pk., NC, 1989—2002; prof. classics Duke U., Durham, NC, 1989-99; pres., CEO The Teagle Found. Inc., NYC, 2003—. Vis. prof. U. Mich., U. Colo., Breadloaf Sch. of English, Inst. Advanced Study, 1985-86; ad hoc com. Radcliffe Inst. Advanced Study, Harvard U., 2000; mem. univ. coun. com. on lit. Yale U., 1979-83; mng. com. Am. Sch. Classical Studies in Athens, 1973-89, exec. com., 1976-80, 85-89; trustee William Alexander Procter Found., 1980-89, Princeton U. Press, 1989, NC Glaxo SmithKline Found., 1995—, Athens Coll., 1995-98, Inst. for Advanced Study, 2002-06, pres. com. on the Arts and Humanities, 2000-02; adv. bd. U. NC, Asheville, 1990-94. Author: Greek Orations, 1966, Theopompus and Fifth Century Athens, 1968, The New Politicians of Fifth Century Athens, 1971, Thucydides, 1984; (with C.L. Connor) Life of St. Luke of Steiris, 1994. Alumni trustee Princeton U., 1993-97. Fulbright fellow U. Coll., Oxford, 1956-57, U. Melbourne; Woodrow Wilson fellow, Danforth Fellow, Am. Coun. Learned Socs. fellow, NEH fellow; recipient Howard Behrman award, 1986. Fellow Am. Acad. Arts and Scis.; mem. Am. Philos. Soc., Am. Philol. Assn. (pres. 1987-88), The Century Assn., Phi Beta Kappa. Office: The Teagle Found Ten Rockefeller Plz Rm 920 New York NY 10020 Business E-Mail: wrconnor@teaglefoundation.org.

CONNOR, WILLIAM EDWIN, II, finance company executive; b. Tokyo, Dec. 19, 1949; s. William Edwin and Jacqueline Ann (Treis) C. BA, Stanford U., 1971; MBA, U. So. Calif., 1973; JD, U. Santa Clara, 1976. Bar: Calif. Sole practice, Los Angeles, 1976-78; rep. dir. W.E. Connor (Japan), Ltd., Tokyo, 1978-81, Connor Group, Tokyo, 1981—. Named one of Forbes' Richest Americans, 2006. Mem. ABA, Calif. Bar Assn. Clubs: Tokyo, Tokyo-Am.

CONNOR-DOMINGUEZ, BILLIE MARIE, science information professional; b. Brighton, Mo., Oct. 4, 1934; d. Clifford Delmar and Naomi Marie (Calhoun) Batten; m. John Michael Connor, Dec. 18, 1968 (dec. 1978); m. Ramon Rosa Dominguez, Sept. 10, 1999. BS, S.W. Mo. State U., Springfield, 1955; MLS, Rutgers U., NJ, 1959. Tchr. Auburn (Ill.) H.S., 1955-58; ext. libr. S.W. Regional Libr., Bolivar, Mo., 1959—62; info. specialist, bus. and tech. svc. Wichita (Kans.) Pub. Libr., 1962-68; subject specialist, SCAN L.A. Pub. Libr., 1969-70, sr. librarian, bus./econ., 1970-77, subject dep. mgr. bus./econs., 1977-79, subject dept mgr. sci./tech./patents, 1979-96, mgr. bus./econs., sci./tech./patents, water and power libr., 1996—. Editor: Communicator, 1971-74, 95—; Co-compiler Ottemiller's Index to Plays in Collections, 5th edit., 1971, 7th edit., 1988; contbr. articles to profl. jours. Bd. dirs. Cmty. Career Devel., Inc., L.A., 1995-02. Recipient Supporter of Support Staff award, Libr. Mosaics and Coun. Libr./Media Technicians, 2002. Mem. AAAS, Spl. Librs. Assn. (bd. dirs. 1992-95, Billie Connor award for Outstanding Contbns. So. Calif. chpt. 1994, Rose Vormelker award 2002), Patent and Trademark Depository Libr. Assn. (pres. 1988), Culinary Historians So. Calif. (libr. liaison 1995—). Achievements include redevelopment of major science and technology collection following devastating fire. Home: 1707 Micheltorena St Apt 312 Los Angeles CA 90026-1142 Office: Sci/Tech/Patents LA Pub Libr 630 W 5th St Los Angeles CA 90071-2002 Home Phone: 323-660-6399; Office Phone: 213-228-7201. Business E-Mail: bconnor@lapl.org.

CONNORS, ALFRED FRANCIS, internist, researcher; b. Bklyn., May 14, 1950; s. Alfred Francis and Mary Elizabeth Connors; m. Mimi Lam, June 10, 1978; children: Lisa Marie, Christopher Hin-Laam. BA, St. Louis U., 1971; MD, Med. Coll. of Ohio, 1974. Diplomate Am. Bd. Internal Medicine, Am. Bd. Pulmonary Diseases, Am. Bd. Critical Care Medicine. Prof. health evaluation scis. and internal medicine U. Va. Sch. Medicine, Charlottesville, 1996—2002; Charles H. Rammelkamp Jr. prof. medicine Case Western Res. U., Cleve., 2002—, chmn. dept. medicine Metrohealth campus, 2002—. Dir. pulmonary and critical care medicine Metrohealth Med. Ctr. /Case Western Res. U., Cleve., 1995—96. Contbr. articles to profl. jours. Office: MetroHealth Med Ctr / CWRU 2500 MetroHealth Dr Cleveland OH 44109

CONNORS, EUGENE KENNETH, lawyer, educator; b. Dobbs Ferry, NY, Oct. 3, 1946; s. Edward Micheal and Eileen (Burke) C.; children: Kevin Patrick, Kathryn Margaret. BA in English, Holy Cross Coll., Worcester, Mass., 1968; JD, Columbia U., 1971. Bar: Pa. 1971. Assoc. Reed Smith Shaw & McClay, Pitts., 1971-76; ptnr. Reed Smith LLP (formerly Reed Smith Shaw & McClay), Pitts., 1977—. Adj. prof. St. Francis U. Grad. Sch., Loretto, Pa., 1975—; ski instr. Holiday Valley Ski Area, Ellicottville, N.Y., 1987—; bd. dirs. Green Garden Inc., 1985—, arbitrator, Am. Arbitration Assn.; spkr. in field. Contbr. articles to profl. jours. Bd. dirs. Sch. Vol. Assn. Pitts., 1973-78, Pitts. Human Resources Assn., 1988-95, TEC/Pa. Smallers Mfrs. Coun., 1993-94, Pitts. Pub. Theater, 1999—, exec. com., 2000—. With USMC. Named one of the Best Lawyers in Am.; named to Chambers' Am. Leading Lawyers in Bus.; named a Pa. Super Lawyer Phila. Mag. Mem. ABA, Pa. Bar Assn., Allegheny County Bar Assn., Pitts. Human Resources Assn. (bd. dirs. 1988-95, treas. 1987-95), Tri-State Employers Assn. (bd. dirs. 1992-93), Profl. Ski Instrs. Am. Avocations: alpine (downhill) skiing, scuba diving, golf. Office: Reed Smith LLP PO Box 2009 435 6th Ave Pittsburgh PA 15219-1886 Home Phone: 412-963-6125; Office Phone: 412-288-3375. Business E-Mail: econnors@reedsmith.com.

CONNORS, FRANK JOSEPH, lawyer; b. NYC, Oct. 8, 1944; s. Frank Joseph and Nina Florence (Kirk) C.; m. Evelyn Noreen Mills, Oct. 14, 1983. BA summa cum laude, UCLA, 1965; MA, Columbia U., 1966; JD cum laude, Harvard U., 1969. Bar: N.Y. 1970, Fla. 1982, Mass. 1986, U.S. Supreme Ct. 1973. Assoc. Dewey, Ballantine, Bushby, Palmer & Wood, NYC, 1969-75; asst. atty. gen. N.Y. State Spl. Prosecutor, NYC, 1975-77; gen. atty. Am. Broadcasting Cos., Inc., NYC, 1977-85; atty. Harvard U., Cambridge, Mass., 1985—; acting gen. counsel, 1992. Arbitrator NYC Civil Ct., 1980-85; comml. arbitrator Am. Arbitration Assn., NYC, 1984-85; trust adv. com. Harvard Mgmt. Co., 1993-. Bd. dirs. World Teach, Inc., 1992-2002. Mem. Am. Judicature Soc., N.Y. State Bar Assn. (copyright com. 1981-85), Assn. of Bar of City of N.Y. (profl. discipline com. 1983-85). Republican. Methodist. Office: Harvard U 1350 Massachusetts Ave Cambridge MA 02138-3846 Office Phone: 617-495-8210. Business E-Mail: frank_connors@harvard.edu.

CONNORS, JACK, JR., advertising executive; m. Eileen Connors; 4 children. Grad., Boston Coll. Founding ptnr., chmn. Hill, Holliday, Connors, Cosmopulos, Inc., Boston, 1968, CEO. Bd. dirs. Navic Networks, 2000—. Chmn. bd. dir. Partners HealthCare Sys.; chmn. bd. trustees Boston Coll.; bd. dir. Nativity Preparatory Sch., Greater Boston C of C, Newton Country Day Sch., Belmont Hill Sch.; trustee, past chmn. Wang Ctr. for Performing Arts. Recipient Heritage Soc. award, Brigham & Women's Hosp., 2003, John Joseph Moakley Pub. Svc. award, 2004, Eternal Light honoree, Jewish Theol. Sem., 2004. Fellow: Am. Acad. Arts & Sciences. Office: Hill Holliday 200 Clarendon St Boston MA 02116

CONNORS, JAMES PATRICK, lawyer; b. NYC, May 28, 1952; s. Joseph Patrick Connors and Edna Theresa Fitzgerald; m. Gloria Ann Ciccarelli, Jan. 12, 1974; children: Nicholas, Patrick, Jamie Cathleen. BA, Herbert H. Lehman Coll., 1974; JD, N.Y. Law Sch., 1977; LLM, NYU, 1985. Bar: N.Y. 1978, U.S. Dist. Ct. (so. and ea. dists.) N.Y. 1978. Assoc. Bower & Gardner, NYC, 1978-80, Joseph W. Conklin, NYC, 1980-82; ptnr. Jones, Hirsch, Connors & Bull, NYC, 1982—. Lectr. NYU Sch. Medicine, 1983, N.Y. Law Jour., 1984, Bellevue Hosp., 1984, Hillcrest Gen. Hosp., 1984, Mt. Sinai Hosp., 1985, Am. Coll. Ophthalmologists, 1986—88. Contbr. Founder Wings of Angels. Recipient Am. Jurisprudence award, Lawyers Pub. Coop., 1977. Mem.: ABA, Internat. Assn. Def. Counsel, Lawyer Pilot Bar Assn., Def. Assn. of N.Y., N.Y. County Bar Assn., N.Y. State Bar Assn. Home: 85 Mayflower Dr Yonkers NY 10710-3801 Office Phone: 212-527-1000. E-mail: jconnors@jhcb.com.

CONNORS, JOHN G., former computer software company executive; m. Kathy Connors. BA in Acctg., U. Mont., 1984. CPA. Corp. contr. PIP Printing, Inc.; with fin. dept. Safeco Corp., Deloitte, Haskins and Sells; mgmt. Microsoft Corp., 1989, gen. mgr. worldwide fin. ops., corp. controller, 1994-96, v.p. worldwide enterprise group, sr. v.p. fin., CFO, 1999—2005; ptnr. Ignition Partners LLC, Bellevue, Wash., 2005—. Recipient Disting. Alumni award, U. Mont., 1997. Office: Ignition Partners LLC 11400 SE 6th St Ste 100 Bellevue WA 98004

CONNORS, JOSEPH ALOYSIUS, III, lawyer; b. Washington, June 24, 1946; s. Joseph Aloysius Jr. and Charlotte Rita (Fox) C.; m. Mary Louise Bucklin, June 14, 1969. BBA, U. Southwestern La., 1970; JD, U. Tex., 1973. Bar: Tex. 1973, U.S. Dist. Ct. (so. dist.) Tex. 1975, U.S. Supreme Ct. 1976, U.S. Ct. Appeals (5th cir.) 1976, U.S. Dist. Ct. (ea., we. and no. dists.) Tex. 1981, U.S. Ct. Appeals (11th cir.) 1981, U.S. Ct. Appeals (3d, 4th, 6th, 7th, 8th, 9th, 10th and D.C. cirs.) 1986. Law clk. to assoc. justice Tex. Ct. Civil Appeals, Amarillo, 1973-74; assoc. Rankin & Kern, McAllen, Tex., 1974-76; asst. criminal dist. atty. Hidalgo County, Tex., 1976-78; pvt. practice, McAllen, 1978—. Faculty Criminal Trial Advocacy Inst., Huntsville, Tex., 1981-84; spkr. seminars State Bar Tex., 1980-81, 84; adj. prof. Reynaldo G. Garza Sch. Law, Edinburg, Tex., 1988-89. Contbg. editor Criminal Trial Manual, Tex., 1984-95; contbr. articles to profl. jours. Bd. dirs. Tex. RioGrande Legal Aid, 1991—, pres. bd. dirs., 1994-96. With USMCR, 1965-71 Mem. NACDL, State Bar Tex. (grievance com. 12B 1984-91, chmn. com. 1989-90, profl. enhancement program 1997-2000), Tex. Assn. Criminal Def. Lawyers (bd. dir. 1982-89, Excellence award 1983, medal of honor 1987), Hidalgo County Bar Assn. (bd. dir. 1981-83), Am. Soc. Writers on Legal Subjects, Hidalgo County Criminal Def. Lawyers Assn. (bd. dir. 1991-98). Democrat. Roman Catholic. Home: 605 E Violet Ave Ste 3 Mcallen TX 78504-2469 Office: Law Offices Joseph A Connors III 605 E Violet Ave Ste 3 Mcallen TX 78504 Office Phone: 956-687-8217. Business E-Mail: connors@innocent.com.

CONNORS, KENNETH ANTONIO, retired pharmacy educator; b. Torrington, Conn., Feb. 19, 1932; s. Peter Francis and Adeline (Gioia) C.; m. Patricia R. Smart, Dec. 30, 1972. BS, U. Conn., 1954; MS, U. Wis., 1957, PhD, 1959. Rsch. assoc. dept. chemistry Ill. Inst. Tech., Chgo., 1959-60, Northwestern U., Evanston, Ill., 1960-61; asst. prof. U. Wis. Sch. Pharmacy, Madison, 1962-65, assoc. prof., 1965-72, prof., 1972-97, prof. emeritus, 1997—, acting dean, 1991-93. Author: A Textbook of Pharmaceutical Analysis, 3d edit., 1982, Reaction Mechanisms in Organic Analytical Chemistry, 1973, Chemical Stability of Pharmaceuticals, 2d edit., 1986, Binding Constants, 1987, Chemical Kinetics, 1990, Thermodynamics of Pharmaceutical Systems, 2002. Served with U.S. Army, 1961. Fellow AAAS, Acad. Pharm. Scis., Am. Assn. Pharm. Scis.; mem. Am. Chem. Soc. Office: U Wis Sch Pharmacy 777 Highland Ave Madison WI 53705-2222

CONNORS, MARY JEAN, communications executive; V.p. human resources Phila. Newspapers, Inc., 1989—95; asst. to sr. v.p. news and ops. Knight Ridder, Inc., San Jose, Calif., 1988—89, sr. v.p. human resources, 1996—2003, sr. v.p., 2003—. Chmn. bd. Bd. Calif. Strategic Human Resources Partnership. Office: Knight Ridder Inc 50 W San Fernando St Ste 1500 San Jose CA 95113-2429 Office Phone: 408-938-7700. Office Fax: 408-938-7766.

CONNORS, MICHELE PERROTT, wholesale beverage company executive; b. Ft. Lauderdale, Fla., June 28, 1952; d. Samuel R. and Mariette (Larouche) Perrott; m. Robert Gary Connors, Apr. 14, 1973; children: Eva Marie, Colleen Elizabeth. AA, Daytona Beach Community Coll., Fla., 1972. Legal sec. Richard Krause, Ormond Beach, Fla., 1972-74; sec. S.R. Perrott, Inc., Ormond Beach, 1974-79, v.p., ops. mgr., 1979-83, pres., chief exec. officer, 1983—. Prin., pres. Michele & Group Modeling Talent Agy., 1989—. Bd. dirs. Daytona Beach Easter Seals Soc., 1985—, chmn. fundraising, 1983-86; bd. dirs. Am. Cancer Soc., 1989—; tennis dir., coach Father Lopez H.S., 1995—. Mem. Beer Industry Fla. Assn. (bd. dirs. 2003—), Nat. Beer Wholesalers, Ormond Beach C. of C. (pres. 1984), Oceanside Country Club, Trails Racquet Club. Republican. Roman Catholic. Office: S R Perrott Inc PO Box 836 Ormond Beach FL 32175-0836 Office Phone: 386-672-2275. Business E-Mail: K.Ceglarski@srperrott.com.

CONNORS, PETER J., lawyer; b. Huntington, NY, June 25, 1951; s. John Anthony and Jeanne (Labate) Connors; m. Claudine Minieri, Nov. 13, 1979; children: Priscilla, Grayson. BA, Cath. U., 1973; JD, U. Richmond, 1976; LLM, NYU, 1979. CPA N.Y., 1979, Va., 1979; bar: N.Y. 1977. Mgr. JC Penney & Co., NYC, 1983—87; sr. mgr. KPMG, NYC, 1987—90; prin., dir. Ernst & Young LLP, NYC, 1990—95; ptnr. Baker & McKenzie, NYC, 1995—2001, Orrick, Herrington & Sutcliffe LLP, NYC, 2001—. Fellow: Am. Coll. Tax Counsel; mem.: ABA (coun. mem. tax sect. 2005), Internat. Fiscal Assn. (coun. mem. 2006), N.Y. State Bar Assn. (exec. com. tax sect.). Avocation: squash. Office: Orrick Herrington & Sutcliffe LLP 666 5th Ave New York NY 10103 Home Phone: 609-799-7423; Office Phone: 212-506-5120. Business E-Mail: pconnors@orrick.com.

CONNORS, ROBERT LEO, city official; b. Kings County, NY, June 11, 1940; s. John Leo and Emma Mae (Bayers) C.; children from former marriage: Anne, Laura, Kathleen; m. Sharon M. Skeels, Jan. 20, 1996; 1 child, Sarah. B Profl. Studies, Pace U., NYC, 1974, MS in Indsl. Labor Rels., 1976. Police officer, trustee, fin. sec. exec., 1st v.p. Patrolmen's Benevolent Assn., N.Y.C. Police Dept., 1965-77; dep. commr., dir. labor rels. Dept. Gen. Services City N.Y.C., 1977-83; dir. personnel adminstrn. City of Fall River, Mass., 1984-85, city adminstr. Mass., 1985-2000; chief of staff Bristol County Sheriff's Office, Dartmouth, Mass., 2005—; orgnl. cons., 2000—05. Lectr. field. Co-author: Comprehensive Reorganization of Municipal Government, 1986. Mem. Fall River Regional Task Force, 1984—; treas. Seekonk (Mass.) Water Dist., 2005. Served with USAF, 1957-61. Recipient Cmty. Rels. Svc. award, US Justice Dept., Boston, 1985. Mem. Am. Mgmt. Assn., Nat. League Cities, Internat. City Mgmt. Assn., Greater Fall River Personnel Council, Internat. Personnel Mgmt. Assn., Soc. Profls. Dispute Resolution. Lodges: Masons. Independent. Avocations: golf, carpentry. Home: 26 Primrose Dr Seekonk MA 02771-5916 Office: Bristol County Sheriff's Office Dartmouth MA 02747 Office Phone: 508-995-1311. Business E-Mail: RobertConnors@BCSO-MA.org.

CONNORS, TERRENCE M., lawyer; b. NYC, Oct. 18, 1946; BA, Canisius Coll., 1968; JD, State U. NY, 1971. Bar: NY 1973. Ptnr. Connors & Vilardo LLP, Buffalo. Instr. trial technique State U. NY, Buffalo, 1992—, mem. dean's adv. coun., 1996—; mem. bd. regents Canisius Coll., 1995—; mem. com. on character and fitness for bar admission applicants Eighth Jud. Dist., 1986—; mem. merit selection com. We. Dist. NY, 1994; mem. screening panel jud. candidates for Hon. Patrick J. Moynihan U.S. Senate. Fellow: NY Bar Found., Am. Coll. Trial Lawyers (state chair upstate NY 1996—98); mem.: ABA, NY State Bar Assn. (mem. com. jud. selection 1992—, chmn. criminal justice sect., mem. ho. of delegates), NY State Assn. Criminal Def. Lawyers (charter life mem.), Nat. Assn. Criminal Def. Lawyers (life), Assn. Trial Lawyers Am., We. NY Trial Lawyers Assn., Erie County Bar Assn. (bd. dirs. 1984). Office: Connors & Vilardo LLP 1020 Liberty Bldg 420 Main St Buffalo NY 14202 Office Phone: 716-852-5533. Office Fax: 716-852-5649. E-mail: tmc@connors-vilardo.com.

CONNORS, WILLIAM FRANCIS, JR., academic administrator; b. Mar. 31, 1945; s. William Francis and Ethel Lucille (Sester) C.; m. Susan Edwards, Nov. 20, 1971; children: Terence, Corinne, Kristin, Jessica. AB, St. Anselm Coll., 1966; MEd, Springfield Coll, 1967; MPA, L.I. U., 1980. From counselor to exec. dean Suffolk C.C., Selden, NY, 1967—, exec. dean, 2005—. Trustee, v.p. Emma S. Clark Meml. Libr., 1984-92; pres. sch. bd. Sts. Philip and James Sch., St. James, NY, 1984-93; mem. pres. Three Village Bd. Edn., 1994—2006. Roman Catholic. Home: 39 Cinderella Ln East Setauket NY 11733-1708 Office: Suffolk County CC Selden NY 11784 Office Phone: 631-451-4330. Business E-Mail: connorw@sunysuffolk.edu.

CONNOR-WARD, DANNETTE VAUDRILYN, research biologist; b. Heathsville, Va., Sept. 25, 1952; d. Daniel Vaudrielle and Ilva (Thompson) Connor; m. Harry Ward, Nov. 28, 1984; children: LeNette, Daniel. BS, Mary Washington Coll., 1974; MS, U. Mo., St. Louis, 1981. Rsch. biologist Monsanto Agrl. Co., St. Louis, 1974-79; rsch. biologist II, Monsanto Corp. Rsch., St. Louis, 1980-84; sr. rsch. biologist Monsanto Co., St. Louis, 1985-94; sr. rsch. biologist, team leader Monsanto Life Sci. Co., Chesterfield, Mo., 1995-96; sr. rsch. biologist, supr. Office of Sci. and Tech., Monsanto Life Scis., Chesterfield, Mo., 1997—2000, sr. scientist, 2000—. Tech. advisor St. Louis CC, Florissant, Mo., 1995—, St. Louis CC. Mentor S. Louis Pub. Schs., 1988—; sci. advisor St. Louis Regional Sci. and Tech. Career Access Ctr., 1990-93; vol. Insvc. Sci. Tchr. Enhancement Project, St. Louis, 1995—; vol. tutor various schs. St. Charles (Mo.), 1995—. Recipient Leadership award YWCA, St. Louis, 1989, Excellence in Sci. award St. Louis Am. Newspaper, 1988; named One of Leading Scientists in St. Louis met. area, 1992, A Futurist of Tech. and Sci., Black Enterprise Mag., 1990. Mem. Soc. InVitro Biology (co-chair edn. com. 1998—, mem. program planning com. 1988-98), Sigma Xi. Achievements include patents in field; first to transgenic soybean plant using Agrobacterium mediated DNA delivery. Office: A2NE 800 N Lindberg Saint Louis MO 63167 Office Phone: 314-694-6024. Office Fax: 314-694-4028. Business E-Mail: dannette.c.ward@monsanto.com.

CONOBY, JOSEPH FRANCIS, chemist; b. Albany, June 12, 1930; s. Joseph Francis and Helen Emma (Brucker) C.; m. Mary Joan A. Ryan, June 21, 1958; children: James Francis, Mark Joseph. BS, Union Coll., 1952. Sr. tech. svc. engr. Allied Chem. Corp., Syracuse, NY, 1956-66; rsch. chemist Conversion Chem. Corp., Rockville, Conn., 1966-69; environ. engr., indsl. hygienist Honeywell Bull, Billerica, Mass., 1969-87, mgr. environ. and health engring., 1969-87; mgr. environ. engring. Bull HN Worldwide Info. Sys., 1987-95; sr. scientist Concorp, Inc., Acton, Mass., 1996—. Adv. bd. Mass. Water Resources Authority Sewer Use (rules and regulations, policy and procedures, and facilities planning task forces); cons. exptl. project course Mass. Inst. Tech., 1977-78. Contbr. articles to profl. jours.; patentee in field. Lt. USN, 1952-56. Mem. Am. Indsl. Hygiene Assn. Home: 5 Samuel Parlin Dr Acton MA 01720-3206 Office: Concorp Inc PO Box 2766 Acton MA 01720-6766 Office Phone: 978-263-8530. E-mail: jfconoby@concorp.com.

CONOMY, JOHN PAUL, neurologist, educator, lawyer; b. Cleve., July 31, 1938; s. John and Marie Conomy; m. Sharon Sopata; children: John, Lisa, Christopher, Francesca Maria. BS cum laude, John Carroll U., 1960; MD, St. Louis U., 1964; JD, Case Western Res. U., 1992. Diplomate Am. Bd. Psychiatry and Neurology (examiner 1975—). Student rsch. fellow in neurology St. Louis U., 1963-64; intern in straight medicine St. Louis U. Hosps., 1964; resident in neurology U. Hosps. of Cleve., 1965-68; fellow in neuropathology Cleve. Met. Gen. Hosp. and Case Western Res. U., Cleve., 1968; career teaching fellow U. Pa., 1970; asst. prof. neurology Case Western Res. U. Med. Sch., Cleve., 1972-77, assoc. clin. prof., 1979, prof. clin. neurology, 1992—; chmn. dept. neurology Cleve. Clinic Found., 1975-92, chmn. clin. rsch. projects and instl. rev. com., 1978-82, founder, dir. Mellen Ctr. Multiple Sclerosis Treatment and Research, 1984-92, exec. dir., 1987—, also exec. dir. consortium of multiple sclerosis ctrs.; assoc. prof. neurology Pa. State U., 1989—; prof. clin. neurology, adj. prof. law Case Western Res. U., 1992—; dir. clin. neurosci., dir. Office of Profl. Affairs Innova Med. Svcs., Cleve., 1994—. Attending physician Highland View Hosp., Cleve., 1968, U. Hosps. Cleve., 1968, attending neurologist, 1972-78, bd. govs. dept. medicine, 1974-75; assoc. neurologist Hosp. U. Pa., 1970; sr. staff neurologist Scott and White Clinic and Hosp., Temple, Tex., 1971; cons. in neurology VA Ctr., Temple, 1971; clins. attending neurologist Parkland Hosp., Dallas, 1971-72; clin. instr. neurology U. Tex. Southwestern Med. Sch., Dallas, 1971-72; vis. lectr. neurosci. U. Tex. Med. Sch., San Antonio, 1971-72; cons. physician evaluation bd. Whittaker Internat. Services for Saudi Arabia and United Arab Emirates, 1980; physician evaluation bd. Whittaker Corp., 1980-85, sci. adv. bd. Communicative Disorders Found., 1980—; med. advisor Huntington's Disease Found., Cleve., 1984-87; biotech. adv. bd. State of Ohio, 1983-85; cons. HHS, SSA, 1990—; participant Manpower in Neurology Conf., San Diego, 1985; vis. prof. London Hosp. Med. Sch., 1982-83, U. Louvain, Belgium, 1983, Oxford (Eng.) U., 1983, Nat. Ctr. Nervous, Mental and Muscular Disorders, Tokyo, 1984, Kyoto (Japan) U., 1984, Kyushu U., Fukuoka, Japan, 1984, U. Bursa, Turkey, 1985, U. Istanbul, 1985, 86, 88, vis. neurologist Christian Med. Coll., Vellore, India, 1986, vis. export Ministry of Health, Singapore, 1988; hon. cons. London Hosp. and Tower Hamlets Health Dist., 1982-83; co-investigator neurogenic factors in the pathogenesis of arterial hypertension NIH, 1978; sr. investigator Quantitation of Cutaneous Sensation VA Hosp., Cleve., 1974, neuroscis. rsch. program Cleve. Clinic Found., 1975—; adj. prof. law Case Western Res. U., 1992—; pres. Health Systems Design Inc., 1992—, CompEval Corp., True North Med. Svcs.; cons. Atty. Gen. State of Ohio, 1992—, FTC, 1994—, U.S. Dept. Justice, U.S. Dept. Social Security. Contbr. articles to profl. jours.; mem. editorial bd. Postgrad. Medicine, 1985—, Jour. Neurologic Rehab., 1987—, Surg. Neurology, 1986—, Health Matrix, 1990; reviewer Neurology, 1977—, Cleve. Clin. Quar., 1977—, Neurosurgery, 1979—Am. Jour. Physiology, 1980-81, Archives of Neurology, 1982—, Residency Rev. Com. in Psychiatry and Neurology, 1983—. Served as capt. USAF, 1968-70. Recipient Francis M. Grogan prize St. Louis U. Med. Sch., 1964, Clin. Tchr. of Yr. award U. Hosps. Cleve., 1973; grantee Mary B. Lee Fund, 1973, Reinberger Found., 1976-82, Mellen Fund, 1976, 84, Hostetler Found., 1989, NIH, 1978—. Fellow ACP (invited speaker 1979, 85, reviewer health care delivery programs 1984), Royal Soc. Medicine (London), Am. Acad. Neurology, Am. Heart Assn. (stroke coun.); mem. AAAS, AMA (sect. coun. on neurology 1977-81, vice chmn.-sec. 1979-81; del. Health Policy agenda for the Am. People, 1983), Soc. Neurosci. (pres. Cleve. chpt. 1975-79), ABA, Am. Assn. History Medicine, Ohio State Med. Assn., Cleve. Acad. Medicine, No. Ohio Neurologic Soc., Assn. Rsch. in Nervous and Mental Disease, Internat. Soc. Tech. Assessment in Health Care , Am. Neurol. Assn. (chmn. pub. rels. com. 1981-85), Soc. Clin. Neurologists (councillor 1976-79, program chmn. 1982), Assn. U. Profs. Neurology, Am. Electroencephalographic Soc., Internat. Assn. Study Pain, Am. Acad. Neurology, Cleve. Med. Libr. Assn. (trustee 1980—, chmn. pubs. com. 1984), Clin. Neurosci. Soc. (pres. elect 1992), Cleve. Health Scis. Libr. (exec. com. 1984-86), Behavioral Neurology Soc., Nat. Multiple Sclerosis Soc., Worshipful Soc. Apothecaries London, Coun. Med. Specialty Socs., 1985—), Nat. Multiple Sclerosis Soc. (med. adv. bd. 1987-92), Internat. Fedn. Multiple Sclerosis Socs. (med. adv. bd. 1989—), Health Svcs. Rsch. Com. (chmn. 1986), Am. Assn. Neurol. Surgeons (assoc. membership bd. 1982—), Inst. Clin. Neuroscis. London, Internat. Med.

Scholar's Program, European Neurol. Soc. (pres. 1991), Can. Neurol. Assn. (hon.), Am. Soc. Law and Medicine, Am. Coll. Legal Medicine, ABA, Ohio State Bar Assn., World Assn. for Med. Law (co-chair sect. history health law), Alpha Omega Alpha. Avocations: travel, bicycling, racquetball, photography, music. Office Phone: 216-765-8393. Personal E-mail: 2br02b@msn.com.

CONOUR, WILLIAM FREDERICK, lawyer; b. Indpls., June 21, 1947; s. William E. and Marian L. (Smith) C.; m. Jennifer Conour; children: Tonja, Andrea, Erin, Rachel, Tyler, Elise. BA in History, Ind. U., 1970, JD cum laude, 1974; MTh, U. Edinburgh, Scotland, 2006. Bar: Ind. 1974, U.S. Dist. Ct. (so. dist.) Ind. 1974, U.S. Dist. Ct. (no. dist.) Ind. 1996, U.S. Ct. Appeals (7th cir.) 1975, U.S. Supreme Ct., 1982; cert. mediator Ind. Supreme Ct., 1992—. Dir. tng. Ind. Pros. Attys. Coun., Indpls., 1974-82; ptnr. Conour & Davis, Indpls., 1974-86; assoc. prof., adj. faculty Ind. U., 1975—89; pvt. practice Indpls., 1986-88; spl. dep. prosecutor State of Ind. v. Ford Motor Co. (Ford Pinto Prosecution); ptnr. Conour Doehrman, Indpls., 1988—2003; ptnr., owner Conour-Daly, Indpls., 2003—. Assoc. prof., adj. faculty Ind. U. Purdue U. Indpls., 1976-86; lectr. Ind. Law Enforcement Acad., otehr lectrs. in field; rsch. analyst Ind. Criminal Law Study Commn., 1973-74. Contbg. author Indiana Criminal Procedure Sourcebook, 1974, Indiana Penal Code, 1974, Indiana Prosecuting Attorney's Deskbook, New Indiana Penal Code, 1976, Lawyers Cooperative Publishing, 1996, The Indiana Lawyer, 2000; editor profl. bulletins; editor, contbg. author: Indiana Prosecuting Attorney's Deskbook, 1978; contbr. articles to profl. jours.; author: Indiana Penal Code, 1977, Res Gestae Mag., 1977-90, The Prosecutor, 1980, Verdict mag., 1992, The Indiana Lawyer, 1996, 99. Guarantor Butler U. Clowes Hall; patron Ind. Repertory Theatre, Indpls. Symphony Orch.; mem. Gov.'s club Ind. Dems., Conner Prairie Pioneer Settlement, Nat. Safety Coun., Hoosier Safety Coun.; mem., co-chmn. task force cmty. based missions second Presbyn. ch.; mem. bd. dirs. U. HS; chess coach U. HS Chess Team; life mem.U.S. Chess Fedn.; life mem. Ind. U. Alumi Assn.; life mem. Woodburn Guild Ind. U.; life mem., mem. bd dirs. Hoosier Salon, U.S. Centenial Olympic Com., Ind., 1996; mem. Five Seasons Country Club; life mem. Ind. Dressage Soc., U.S. Dressage Fedn., NA/WPN, Am. Horse Show Assn.; mem. gold club U.S. Equestrian Team. Recipient commendation Drug Enforcement Adminstrn. U.S. Dept. Justice, 1977, Commendation award Hoosier Safety Coun., 1989, Commendation award Ind. State Bar Assn. Criminal Justice Sect., 1990. Fellow Roscoe Pound Found. (life), Found. Am. Bd. Trial Advocates (sr. life), Indpls. Bar Found. (life); mem. ABA (litigation sect.), Am. Bd. Trial Advocates (pres. Ind. chpt., honoree, charter sr. life fellow 1996), Am. Soc. Safety, Ind. Bar Assn. (sec. litigation 1981-82, ad hoc com. on legal cert., mem. litigation sect., criminal justice sect., sec. 1977-78, treas. 1981-82), Am. Coll. Legal Medicine (assoc.), Indpls. Bar Assn. (grievance com. 1983-91, litigation sect.), Assn. Trial Lawyers Am. (cert. Nat. Coll. Advocacy 1979, Advanced Coll. Advocacy 1981, cons. site litigation group, M Club, lectr., cert. civil trial advocate), Ind. Bar Assn. (grievance com. 1984-91), Coll. of Legal Medicine, Am. Coll. of Legal Medicine, Ind. Trial Lawyers Assn. (sustaining mem., bd. dirs., lectr., amicus curie com., rule of evidence com.), Ind. Lawyers Commn. (ad hoc com. on criminal justice standards and goals 1976-80), Am. Bd. Trial Advs., Ind. U. Alumni Assn. (life), Ind. State Bar Assn. (litig. sect. 1983-, appellate law sect. 1996-, ad hoc com. legal cert., chmn. lawyers adv. com. 1996-98, commendation criminal justice sect. 1990), Trial Lawyers Pub. Justice (sustaining founder), Indpls. Law Club, Indpls. Athletic Club, US Equestrian Team (contbg. mem.), Nat. and Hoosier Safety Coun. (commendation 1989), US Dressage Fedn. Ind. Dressage Soc. (dir.), Indpls. Mus. Art, Sagamore Am. Inn of Ct. (pres. 1999-2001, pres.-elect 1997-99, counselor 2001-), Nat. Am. Inns Ct. Found. (trustee 2001-), Am. Coll. Barristers (sr.counsel), Phi Delta Phi (hon.). Clubs: Inpls. Athletic; Ind. Soc. Chgo., Atla "M". Democrat. Office: Conour-Daly Ste 150 500 E 96th St Indianapolis IN 46240-3765 Home: 2701 Oglethorpe Ct Indianapolis IN 46268-1247 Office Phone: 317-846-5550. Business E-Mail: wfc@tortsurfer.com.

CONOVER, LLOYD HILLYARD, retired research scientist; b. Orange, NJ, June 13, 1923; s. John Howard and Marguerite Anna (Cameron) C.; m. Virginia Rogers Kirk, Aug. 24, 1944 (dec. Dec. 1988); children: Kirk Howard, Roger Lloyd, Heather Cameron, Craig Scott; m. Marie Strauss Solomons, Oct. 18, 1990 (dec. May 2003); m. Katharine Miller Meacham, Dec. 29, 2005. BA, Amherst Coll., 1947, PhD, U. Rochester, 1950. Rsch. chemist, mgr. Chas. Pfizer & Co., Bklyn. and Groton, Conn., 1950—68; dir. chem. rsch. and chemotherapy Pfizer Cen. Rsch., Groton, 1968-71, rsch. dir. Europe, Sandwich, Eng., 1971-74, v.p. agrl. R & D Groton and Sandwich, 1975-84. Contbr. articles on antibiotics, anthelmintics and animal health drugs to sci. jours.; patentee tetracycline and pyrantel. Chmn. Waterford Planning, 1961-63. Lt. (j.g.) USNR, 1943-46, PTO. Recipient Eli Whitney award Conn. Patent Law Assn., 1983, Third Century award Found. Creative Am., 1990; inductee Nat. Inventors Hall of Fame, 1992. Fellow Royal Soc. Chemistry, Royal Soc. Arts; mem. Am. Chem. Soc., Phi Beta Kappa, Sigma Xi. Independent. Achievements include directing research resulting in new drugs for infectious diseases. Avocations: travel, gardening.

CONOVER, RICHARD CORRILL, lawyer; b. Jan. 12, 1942; s. John Cedric and Mildred (Dunn) C.; m. Cathy Harlan, Dec. 19, 1970; children: William Cedric, Theodore Cyril. BS, U. Nebr., Lincoln, 1965, MS, 1966, JD, Cornell U., 1969. Bar: N.Y. 1970, Mont. 1982, U.S. Dist. Ct. (so. and ea. dists.) N.Y. 1971, U.S. Supreme Ct. 1977, U.S. Ct. Customs and Patent Appeals 1979, U.S. Dist. Ct. Mont. 1984, U.S. Tax Ct. 1986. Assoc. Brumbaugh, Graves, Donohue & Raymond, NYC, 1969—73, Townley, Updike, Carter & Rodgers, NYC, 1974—75; assoc. gen. counsel legal office Automatic Data Processing, Inc., Clifton, NJ, 1975—77; assoc. Nims, Howes, Collison & Isner, NYC, 1977—81; pvt. practice Mont., 1981—. Lectr. indsl. and mech. engring. dept. Mont. State U., 1981—97. Mem.: ABA, Am. Patent Law Assn., Mont. Bar Assn. Home: PO Box 1329 Bozeman MT 59771-1329 Office: Ste 404 104 E Main St Bozeman MT 59715-4787 Home Phone: 406-586-1249; Office Phone: 406-587-4240.

CONOVER, WILLIAM JAY, statistics educator; b. Hays, Kans., Dec. 6, 1936; s. William Joseph Conover and Viola Marie (Herman) Beishline; m. Patricia Louise Solomon, June 11, 1960 (div. Apr. 1994); children: Christopher Michael, Robert Andrew, Judith Ann, Therese Marie, William Joseph; m. Susan Theresa Mole, Dec. 27, 1996; 1 child, Chloe Theresa. BS, Iowa State U., 1958; MA, Cath. U., 1962, PhD, 1964. Asst. prof. stats. Kans. State U., Manhattan, 1964-67, assoc. prof. stats., 1967-73; vis. prof. stats. U. Zürich, Switzerland, 1970-71; prof. stats. Tex. Tech U., Lubbock, 1973-81, Horn prof., 1981—, area coord. of info. systems/quantitative scis., assoc. dean, 1978-88. Vis. prof. U. Calif., Davis, 1976-77; vis. staff mem. Los Alamos (N.Mex.) Sci. Lab., 1976—; cons. Sandia Lab., Albuquerque, 1979—. Author: Practical Nonparametric Statistics, 1971, 3rd edit., 1999, Modern Bus. Stat., 1983, 2d edit., 1989; co-author 9 textbooks on statistics; contbr. articles to profl. jours. Lt. (j.g.) USN, 1958-61. Recipient Rushing Faculty Rsch. award Tex. Tech Dad's Assn., 1983, Samuel Wilks award US Army, 1997. Fellow Am. Statis. Assn. (Don Owen award San Antonio chpt. 1986); mem. Inst. Math. Stats., Biometric Soc., Inst. Decision Scis. Roman Catholic. Avocations: chess, basketball. Office: Tex Tech U Coll Bus Adminstrn Lubbock TX 79409 Office Phone: 806-742-1546. Business E-Mail: jay.conover@ttu.edu.

CONOVER-CARSON, ANNE, writer; d. George Richards and A. Louise (Pinkerton) Conover; m. Thomas N. Ambrose, June 22, 1959 (div. Oct. 1967); 1 child, Natalie Anne Ambrose; m. Thomas B. Carson, Nov. 14, 1970 (dec. June 2002). BA, Stanford U., 1959, MA, 1966. Editor Curtis Pub. Co., Phila., 1959—61, Johns Hopkins Press, Balt., 1966—68; editor, writer Libr. Congress, Washington, 1968—76, U.S. Info. Agy., 1976—90; editor-in-chief Anne Carson Assocs., 1990—. Author: Caresse Crosby: From Black Sun to Roccasinibalda, 1990, Ezra Pound and the Crosby Continental Editions, 1993; author: (with Julia Montgomery Walsh) Risks and Rewards: A Memoir, 1998; author: Olga Rudge and Ezra Pound: What Thou Lovest Well, 2001, Olga Rudge: Pound's Muse and the Circe of the Cantos in Ezra Pound: Nature and Myth, 2003. Nominee Best Scholarly Biography of Yr., Yale Press, 2001. Mem.: MLA, Author's Guild, Am. Acad. Poets, Nat. Coalition Ind. Scholars, Chevy Chase Club, Knickerbocker Club (NYC), Met. Club (Washington). Democrat. Episcopalian. Avocations: chamber and early music, Chinese brush painting, travel.

CONQUEST, CLAIRE M., secondary school counselor; d. Archie Jones and Cabelle Harris-Smith; m. John E. Conquest, Apr. 8, 1972; 1 child, Alicia 1 stepchild, Troy. BA, So. U., 1966; MA, Queens Coll., NY, 1974; degree in Adminstrn., Coll. New Rochelle, 1990. Cert. in counseling edn. N.Y. Tchr. home econs. Dawnwood Jr. H.S., Centereach, NY, 1967—69; counselor Bellport (N.Y.) H.S., 1969—71, Ea. H.S., Balt., 1971—73, Longwood H.S., Middle Island, NY, 1974—2001, ret., 2001. Spkr. in field. Co-editor: The African American Church, 1996. Commr. Brookhaven Black History Commn., Medford, 1997—; chmn. scholarship com. Faith Bapt. Ch., Coram, NY, 2000—; adv. bd. Brookhaven Town Office Women's Svcs., Medford, NY, 1999—. Recipient Outstanding Educator award, Bus. and Profl. Women, 1998, Educator of Yr. award, Brookhaven Town NAACP, 1999, Outstanding Educator award, Brookhaven Town Office Women's Svcs., 2000. Mem.: We. Suffolk Counselors Assn., Ea. L.I. Black Educators Assn. (treas. 1990—, chmn. scholarship com. 1990—), L.I. Urban League High Achievers (mem. com. 1999—), Delta Sigma Theta (pres. 2000—02, chmn. scholarship com. 2002—). Democrat. Baptist. Avocations: travel, theater, Scrabble, mahjong.

CONQUEST, ROBERT (GEORGE ROBERT ACWORTH CONQUEST), writer, historian, poet; b. Malvern, Worcestershire, Eng., July 15, 1917; s. Robert Folger Westcott and Rosamund Alys (Acworth) C.; m. Joan Watkins, 1942 (dis. 1948); children: John, Richard; m. Tatiana Mihailova, 1948 (dis. 1963); m. Caroleen Macfarlane, 1964 (dis. 1978); m. Elizabeth Neece, Dec. 1, 1979. Student, Winchester Coll., Eng., 1931-35, U. Grenoble, France, 1935-36, U. Oxford, 1936-39; MA, U. Oxford, Eng., 1972; DLitt, U. Oxford, 1975. First sec. H.M. Fgn. Svc., Sofia, Bulgaria, U.N., London, 1946-56; rsch. fellow London Sch. Econs., 1956-58; vis. poet U. Buffalo, NY, 1959-60; lit. editor The Spectator, London, 1962-63; sr. fellow Russian Inst. Columbia U., NYC, 1964-65; fellow Woodrow Wilson Internat. Ctr., Washington, 1976-77; sr. rsch. fellow Hoover Inst., Stanford (Calif.) U., 1977-79, 81—. Disting. vis. scholar Heritage Found., Washington, 1980-81; adv. bd. Freedom House, N.Y.C., 1980—; rsch. assoc. Ukrainian Rsch. Inst. Harvard U., Cambridge, Mass., 1983—; adj. fellow Washington Ctr. Strategic Studies, 1984—. Author: Poems, 1955, A World of Difference, 1955, Common Sense About Russia, 1960, Power and Policy in the USSR, 1961, The Pasternak Affair, 1962, Between Mars and Venus, 1962, (with Kingsley Amis) The Egyptologists, 1965, Russia after Khrushchev, 1965, The Great Terror, 1968, Arias from a Love Opera, 1969, The Nation Killers, 1970, Where Marx Went Wrong, 1970, V I Lenin, 1972, Kolyma: The Arctic Death Camps, 1978, Coming Across, 1978, The Abomination of Moab, 1979, Forays, 1979, Present Danger: Towards a Foreign Policy, 1979, We and They: Civic and Despotic Cultures, 1980, (with Jon M. White) What to do When the Russians Come, 1984, Inside Stalin's Secret Police: NKVD Politics 1936-39, 1985, The Harvest of Sorrow: Soviet Collectivization and the Terror-Famine, 1986, New and Collected Poems, 1988, Stalin and the Kirov Murder, 1988, Tyrants and Typewriters, 1989, The Great Terror: A Reassessment, 1990, Stalin: Breaker of Nations, 1991, Demons Don't, 1999, Reflections on a Ravaged Century, 1999, The Dragons of Expectation, 2005. Capt. inf. Brit. Army, 1939-46, ETO. Decorated officer Order Brit. Empire, companion Order St. Michael and St. George; recipient Alexis de Tocqueville award, 1992, Light Verse award Acad. Arts and Letters, 1997, Presdl. Medal of Freedom, The White House, 2005; Jefferson Lecture Humanities, Washington, 1993, Richard M. Weaver prize for scholarly letters, 1999; Royal Soc. Lit. fellow, 1972. Fellow Brit. Acad., Brit. Interplanetary Soc., AAAL-Michael Braude Award Light Verse, Royal Soc. Lit., Am. Acad. Arts & Sci., Soc. Promotion Roman Studies; Mem. Literary Soc.; Clubs: Travellers (London). Home: 52 Peter Coutts Cir Stanford CA 94305-2506 Office: Stanford U Hoover Inst Stanford CA 94305-6010

CONRAD, DAVID PAUL, business broker, real estate developer, retired food service executive; b. Greensboro, NC, Jan. 11, 1946; s. Lucas Lee and Elizabeth Gertrude (Kincaid) Conrad; 1 child, Lucas Wilfong. BSBA, East Carolina U., 1970; cert. in Real Estate, Forsyth Tech. Coll., 1979. From cashier to cook Libby Hill Seafood, Greensboro, 1962—64; plant mgr. Libby Hill Seafood Restaurants, Inc., Greensboro, 1970—76, mgr. Winston-Salem, NC, 1976—85, v.p., dir. ops. Greensboro, 1985—93, also bd. dirs., 1985—93; comml. real estate broker Allied Comml. Real Estate, Kernersville, NC, 1993; franchise owner Swisher Maids of West Greensboro, NC, 1994—99, regional dir. NC, 1996—98; broker-in-charge VR Bus. Brokers, 1998—2000; founder, former owner Triad Bus. Brokerage, Greensboro, 2002—04, Star Video Games, Greensboro, High Point and Wilkesboro, NC, 2002—05; founder, owner CedarMountain Log Homes, Beech Mountain, NC, 2005—, Blue Ridge Bus. Brokerage Co., Boone, NC, 2005—. Pvt. pilot. Mem. Greensboro Jaycees, 1973—81; vol. Wesley Long Hosp. Staff sgt. NC N.G., 1968—74. Mem.: Inst. Cert. Bus. Counselors, Masons. Republican. Methodist. Avocation: music. Office: 161-K Howard St Boone NC 28607 Business E-Mail: david@blueridgebrokerage.com. E-mail: blueridgebrokerage@charterinternet.com.

CONRAD, DAVID WILLIAMS, retired lawyer; b. St. Louis, Jan. 10, 1930; s. Lawrence Henry and Roberta (Williams) C.; m. Marilyn Russo, Sept. 26, 1959; children: Roberta Lucy, Philip Lloyd, Angela Beth. AB, Colgate U., 1951; JD, Harvard U., 1954. Bar: NJ 1954, US Supreme Ct. 1973. Assoc. McCarter & English, Newark, 1956-59; ptnr. Conrad & Jones, Montclair, NJ, 1964-71; pvt. practice Montclair, 1959-64, 71-93; ptnr. Conrad & Boutillier, Montclair, 1993—2005, ret., 2005. Counsel Montclair State U. Found., 1959-2005, Homes of Montclair Ecumenical Corp., 1988-2005. Legis. candidate NJ State Assembly, 1971; pres. NJ Chamber Music Soc., 1984-86, Union Congl. Ch., Montclair, 1988-91. With US Army, 1954-56. Mem.: N.J. State Bar Assn. Democrat. Congregationalist. Avocations: piano, music, travel.

CONRAD, DONALD GLOVER, insurance executive; b. St. Louis, Apr. 23, 1930; s. Harold Armin and Velma Glover (Morris) C.; m. Stephania Shimkus, Feb. 8, 1980; 1 child, Christina; 1 stepchild, Alexa Sanzone Paolella; children by previous marriage: Marcy Conrad, Suzanne Conrad, Mark. Student, Wesleyan U., Middletown, Conn., 1948-49; BS, Northwestern U., Evanston, Ill., 1952; MBA, U. Mich., 1957. With Exxon Co., 1957-70; fin. adv. Exxon Co. (Esso Natural Gas), The Hague, Netherlands, 1965-66; treas. Exxon Co. (Esso Europe), London; 1966-70; sr. v.p. Aetna Life & Casualty Co., Hartford, Conn., 1970-72, exec. v.p., dir., 1972-88, ret., 1988; prin. owner, chmn. Hartford Whalers Hockey Club, 1988-92; sr. advisor to the pres. World Bank, Washington, 1995—2003. Bd. dirs. Chevy Chase F.S.B., Md., Sovereign Exploration Assocs. Internat., Inc.; ptnr. Kanturk Ptnrs., Washington. Chmn. emeritus Am. Coun. for Arts NY; founder Greater Hartford Arts Coun. Lt. USNR, 1952-55. Mem. Watch Hill Yacht Club, The Club at Windermere, Bath and Tennis Club (Palm Beach), Teton Pines Country Club (Jackson Hole), Chevy Chase Club (Washington). Home: PO Box 242 3855 Curtis Dr Teton Village WY 83025 Personal E-mail: donaldcon@mac.com.

CONRAD, GEOFFREY WENTWORTH, archaeologist, educator; b. Boston, Dec. 24, 1947; s. Albert Austin and Ruth Wentworth (Cadieux) C.; m. Karen Ann Hildebrant, June 12, 1971; children: Matthew, Peter, Marc. AB, Harvard U., 1969, PhD, 1974. Curatorial asst. Smithsonian Inst., Washington, 1974-75; asst. prof. and asst. curator Harvard U., Cambridge, Mass., 1976-81, assoc. prof. and assoc. curator, 1981-83; dir. William Hammond Mathers Mus. Ind. U., Bloomington, 1983—, assoc. prof. anthropology, 1983-91, prof., 1991—, chair, 1991-95, assoc. dean faculties, 2003—05, spl. advisor for arts and humanities, office v.p. for rsch., 2004—06, assoc. vice provost for rsch., 2007—. Cons. Nat. Geog. Soc., Washington, 1982-83. Co-author: Religion and Empire, 1984, The Andean Heritage, 1982; co-editor: Ideology and Precolumbian Civilizations, 1992; contbr. articles to profl. jours.; mem. editl. bd. Jour. of Field Archaeology, 1986-96. Bd. dirs. Monroe County Hist. Soc., Bloomington, 1989-92. Grantee NSF, 1978, 85, Ind. Humanities Coun., 1983, 86, 88, 95, 2006, Wenner-Gren Found., 1987, Inst. Mus. and Libr. Svcs., 2000, 04, Howard Heinz Endowment, 2004. Fellow AAAS; mem. Archaeol. Inst. Am. (pres. Ctrl. Ind. chpt. 1989-91, acad. trustee 1994-97), Soc. Am. Archaeology, Assn. for Field Archaeology, Am. Assn. Mus., Internat. Assn. for Caribbean Archaeology, Assn. Midwest Mus., Assn. Coll. and Univ. Mus. and Galleries (Midwest rep. 1990-91) Home: 3130 Saint James Ct Bloomington IN 47401-7105 Office: Mathers Mus Ind U 601 E 8th St Bloomington IN 47408-3812 also: Ind U Dept Anthropology Student Bldg Bloomington IN 47405 Address: Ind U Office VP Rsch Franklin Hall 116-Y Bloomington IN 47405 Home Phone: 812-334-7681; Office Phone: 812-865-5340, 812-855-6066. Business E-Mail: conrad@indiana.edu.

CONRAD, HANS, materials science and engineering educator; b. Konradstahl, Germany, Apr. 19, 1922; came to U.S., 1926, naturalized, 1944; s. K. Henry and Martha Ann (Bader) C.; m. Emma Ann Bort, June 10, 1944; children: Sandra Joy, Roberta Lee, Gary Richard. Student, Washington and Jefferson Coll., 1940-42; BS in Metall. Engring, Carnegie Inst. Tech., 1943; MEng, Yale, 1951, DEng, 1956. Research metallurgist Chase Copper & Brass Co., Waterbury, Conn., 1953-55; supervisory engr. Westinghouse Research Labs., Churchill Boro, Pa., 1955-59; sr. research specialist Atomics Internat., Canoga Park, Calif., 1959-61; head dept. physics Aerospace Corp., El Segundo, Calif., 1961-64; tech. dir. Franklin Inst. Research Labs., Phila., 1964-67; prof., chmn. dept. metall. engring. and materials sci., assoc. dir. Inst. Mining and Minerals Research, U. Ky., Lexington, 1967-80; prof., head dept. materials engring., dir. minerals and materials research programs N.C. State U., 1981-85, prof., 1985—. Japan Soc. Promotion Sci. vis. prof. 1976; Disting. vis. prof. Am. U., Cairo, 1983, Soviet Acad. Scis, 1984; Ministry Metall. Industry, PRC, 1986. Contbr. articles to profl. jours. and books. Recipient Rsch. award U. Ky., 1971, U.S. Sr. Scientist award Alexander von Humboldt-Stiftung, 1974; Alcoa Rsch. award N.C. State U., 1985, Alumni Rsch. award, 1991. Fellow: Am. Soc. Materials, The Minerals, Metals and Materials Soc. (Structural Materials Disting. Sci. award 2000); mem.: Tau Beta Pi, Sigma Xi. Home: 205 Glasgow Rd Cary NC 27511-6517 Office Phone: 919-515-7443. E-mail: hans_conrad@ncsu.edu.

CONRAD, HAROLD AUGUST, retired religious pension board executive; b. Cleve., Dec. 18, 1928; s. August and Olga (Heise) C.; m. Anne Chernosky, July 10, 1948 (dec. Mar. 1956); children: Deborah Anne Hamer, Loren Harold, Rebecca Faith Towle; m. Naomi Ruth Sweeny, Dec. 31, 1960; 1 child, Paul Alan. BA, Anderson U., Ind., 1952; MDiv, Christian Theol. Sem., Indpls., 1970; DD, Mid-Am. Christian U., Oklahoma City, 1975. Pastor Akron Ch. of God, Akron, Ind., 1952-63, First Ch. of God, Winchester, Ky., 1963-66, Glendale Ch. of God, Indpls., 1966-74; exec. sec. treas. Bd. of Pensions of Ch. of God, Anderson, Ind., 1974-93; ret., 1993. State chmn. Ind. Ministerial Assembly, Indpls., 1961-62; vice chmn. Ky. Ministerial Assembly, Winchester, 1965-66; mem. Bd. of Pensions of Ch. of God, Anderson, Ind., 1964-74; bd. dirs. Exec. Coun. of Ch. of God, Anderson, Ind., 1976-84, 87-90. Mem. Nat. Ch. Pensions Conv. (pres. 1985). Republican. Mem. Ch. Of God. Avocations: stamp collecting/philately, gardening, walking, reading, travel. Home: 810 Northwood Dr Anderson IN 46011-1072 E-mail: conradhn@cs.com.

CONRAD, HAROLD THEODORE, psychiatrist; b. Milw., Jan. 25, 1934; s. Theodore Herman and Alyce Barbara Conrad; m. Elaine Marie Blaine, Sept. 1, 1962 (dec.); children: Blaine, Carl, David, Erich, Rachel. *Wife Elaine, deceased, was an accomplished musician. She studied piano in Rome and at Newcomb College. Son Blaine is a graduate in Economics and is currently studying computer applications for health data management. Son Carl is an attorney in private practice. Son David is an expert in environmental preservation and safety. He has a graduate degree in the field and works for a Native American group. Daughter Rachel is a physician. Son Erich is a physician.* AB, U. Chgo., 1954, BS, 1955, MD, 1958. Diplomate Am. Bd. Psychiatry. Intern USPHS Hosp., San Francisco, 1958-59, commd. sr. asst. surgeon, 1958, advanced through grades to med. dir., 1967, resident psychiatry Lexington, Ky., 1959-61, Charity Hosp., New Orleans, 1961-62; chief of psychiatry USPHS Hosp., New Orleans, 1962-67, clin. dir., 1967; dep. dir. divsn. field investigation NIMH, Chevy Chase, Md., 1968; chief NIMH Clin. Rsch. Ctr., Lexington, 1969-73; cons. psychiatry region IX USPHS, HEW, San Francisco, 1973-79; dir. adolescent unit Alaska Psychiat. Inst., Anchorage, 1979-81, supt., 1981-85; clin. assoc. prof. psychiatry U. Wash. Med. Sch., 1981-85; psychiatrist pvt. practice, Houma, La., 1985—2004, ret., 2005. Contbr. articles to profl. jours. Recipient cmty. awards for contbns. in field of drug abuse and equal employment opportunity for minorities. Fellow: Am. Psychiat. Assn. (Disting. life), Royal Soc. Medicine; mem.: AMA, Alpha Delta Phi, Alpha Omega Alpha.

CONRAD, JACOB B., curator, historian; b. Milw., Sept. 14, 1957; s. Arthur Baier Conrad and Dorothy Dolores Jankowski. BA in History, U. Wis., Madison, 1985; MA in History, Columbia U., NYC, 1987. Assoc. curator Wis. Hist. Soc., Eagle, 1995—2006; curator of collections Genesee Country Village and Mus., Mumford, NY, 2006—. Mem.: Am. Assn. for State and Local History, Am. Assn. Museums, Phi Beta Kappa. Office: Genesee Country Village and Museum 1410 Flint Hill Rd Mumford NY 14511

CONRAD, JIMMY, professional soccer player; b. Arcadia, Calif., Feb. 12, 1977; m. Lyndsey Conrad. Attended, San Diego State Univ., UCLA. Defender San Jose Earthquakes, 1999—2003, Kansas City Wizards, 2003—. 15 caps U.S. Nat. Soccer team, 2005—; mem. U.S. World Cup team, 2006. Contbr. column for espn.com. Named Defender of the Yr., Major League Soccer, 2005; named to All-Star team, 2004—05. Mailing: US Soccer Fedn 1801 S Prairie Ave Chicago IL 60616

CONRAD, KENT (GAYLORD KENT CONRAD), senator; b. Bismarck, ND, Mar. 12, 1948; m. Lucy Calautti, Feb. 1987; 1 child, Jessamyn Abigail. Student, U. Mo., 1967; BA in Govt. and Polit. Sci., Stanford U., 1972; MBA, George Washington U., 1975. Asst. to tax commr. State of N.D. Tax Dept., Bismarck, 1974-80, dir. mgmt. planning and personnel, 1980, tax commr., 1981-87; US Senator from ND Washington, 1987—. Com. Indian affairs US Senate, com. fin., com. budget, com. agr., nutrition and forestry. Recipient Award of Appreciation, ND Dry Pea and Lentil Assn., Nat. Health Leadership award, Am. Assn. Nurse Anesthetists, 1994, Hero Rural Edn. award, Nat. Rural Edn. Assn., 2002, Outstanding Support for Rural Edn. award, ND Coun. Edn. Leaders, 2002, Congressional Spl. Recognition award, Nat. Sch. Boards Assn., 2003, Cmty Health Defender award, Nat. Assn. Cmty. Health Centers, 2005, John M. Agrey award, Upper Great Plains Transp. Inst., ND State U., 2005. Democrat. Unitarian.

Office: US Senate 530 Hart Senate Office Bldg Washington DC 20510-0001 also: US Federal Bldg Rm 104 102 North 4th St Grand Forks ND 58203 Office Phone: 202-224-2043, 701-775-9601. Office Fax: 202-224-7776, 701-746-1990.*

CONRAD, MARCEL EDWARD, hematologist, oncologist, educator; b. NYC, Aug. 15, 1928; s. Marcel Edward and Lulu Marie (Geraghty) C.; m. Marcia Louise Grove; children: Marcel Edward, III, Mark E., Carol J., Erin E., Julia P. BS, Georgetown U., 1949, MD cum laude, 1953. Diplomate Am. Bd. Internal Medicine, Am. Bd. Hematology. Commd. 1st lt. M.C. U.S. Army, 1953, advanced through grades to col., 1968; intern Walter Reed Gen. Hosp., Washington, 1953-54, resident, then chief resident in internal medicine, 1955-60; mem. staff Walter Reed Army Inst. Rsch., 1961-74, chief dept. hematology, 1965-74; chief clin. investigation svc. Walter Reed Army Med. Ctr., 1971-74; clin. asst. prof., then clin. assoc. prof. medicine Georgetown U. Med. Sch., 1964-74; prof. medicine U. Ala. Med. Sch., Birmingham, 1974-83, also dir. div. hematology and oncology, 1974-83; prof. medicine, pathology, dir. divsn. hematology, oncology U. South Ala., Mobile, 1983-2001, dir. USA Cancer Ctr., 1985-2001, disting. prof. medicine, 2001; cons. Mobile, 2001—. Prin. investigator Minority Based Cmty. Cancer Oncology Program, 1990—2004. Contbr. numerous articles to med. publs. Advanced from 1st lt. to col. US Army, 1953—75. Decorated Legion of Merit with oak leaf cluster; recipient Skinner medal U.S. Army, 1955, Hoff medal, 1962, John Shaw Billings award, 1967, William Beaumont award, 1972, Walter Reed award, 1974, Harry Hines award Nat. Cancer Inst., 2003, Eagle Scout. Fellow Internat. Soc. Hematology, ACP (Laureate award 1989, named Disting. Prof. Medicine, 2001); mem. AAAS, Assn. Am. Physicians, Internat. Soc. Hematology, Am. Soc. Clin. Investigation, Am. Physiol. Soc., Internat. Soc. Blood Transfusion, Am. Soc. Hematology, Am. Soc. Clin. Oncology, Am. Chem. Soc., Soc. Exptl. Biology and Medicine, So. Soc. Clin. Investigation, Am. Fedn. Clin. Rsch., Alpha Omega Alpha. Roman Catholic. Achievements include basic and clinical contributions in hematology hepatology and oncology. Avocation: sailing. Home and Office: 28451 Perdido Pass Dr Orange Beach AL 36561-3602 Office Phone: 251-209-5902. Personal E-mail: mconrad2@comcast.net.

CONRAD, MARY TRENCH, elementary school educator; b. St. Louis, Sept. 25, 1940; d. Joseph Michael and Rosemary O'Reilly Flynn; m. Robert Daniel Conrad, June 13, 1964; children: Elizabeth Colleen Mortimer, Sean Robert. BA in Elem. Edn., Webster U., Webster Groves, Mo., 1962. Tchr. Bayless Sch. Dist., St. Louis, 1962—63, Diocese San Francisco, 1963—67, Ritenaur Sch. Dist., St. Louis, 1968—71, Archdiocese St. Louis, 1971—86, 1990—, Diocese Trenton, Mo., 1986—88. Vice prin. Ascension Sch., Chesterfield, Mo., 1983; dir. religion St. Blaise, Maryland Heights, Mo., 1986—88; chmn. sch. self study St. Angela Merici, Florissant, Mo., 1997—98. Nominee Tchr. of Yr. award, Disney, 2000. Mem.: Assn. Cath. Elem. Tchrs., Nat. Cath. Tchr. Assn., U.S. Golf Assn., Ladies Ancient Order Hibernians (pres. St. Louis chpt. 1995—96, v.p. St. Louis chpt. 1992—95, chmn. freedom for Ireland St. Louis chpt. 1991—99, chmn. state missions Mo. chpt. 1999—2001). Avocations: golf, travel, reading. Office: St Angela Merici 3860 North Hwy 67 Florissant MO 63034

CONRAD, PAUL ERNEST, transportation consultant; b. Hartford, Conn., June 11, 1927; s. Ernest and Agnes Anita (Eis) C.; m. Audrey Grace Lindner, June 17, 1947; children: Cynthia Dale, Robin Sue, Kristen Diane. BS, U. Conn., 1949. Hwy. engr. Fed. Hwy. Adminstrn., Southeast U.S., Conn. and N.Y., 1949-55; prin. assoc. Wilbur Smith & Assocs., Columbia, S.C., 1955-69, sr. v.p., 1969-72, exec. v.p., 1972-91, also bd. dirs. Bd. dirs. Spring Valley Homeowners Assn., 1976-77, 97-98, Enclave Comty. Assn., 1999-2004. With USN, 1945-46. Mem. NSPE, ASCE, Inst. Transp. Engrs., Am. Cons. Engrs. Coun., Spring Valley Country Club (bd. govs. 1993-96, v.p. house), Country Club at Wildewood and Woodcreek Farms. Lutheran. Home: 103 Enclave Loop Columbia SC 29223-3260

CONRAD, PAUL FRANCIS, cartoonist; b. Cedar Rapids, Iowa, June 27, 1924; s. Robert H. and Florence G. (Lawler) C.; m. Barbara Kay King, Feb. 27, 1954; children: James, David, Carol, Elizabeth. BA, U. Iowa, 1950. Editorial cartoonist Denver Post, 1950-64, L.A. Times, 1964-93; cartoonist L.A. Times Syndicate, 1973-2000, Tribune Media Svcs., 2000—. Richard M. Nixon chair Whittier Coll., 1977-78 Exhibited sculpture and cartoons LA County Mus. Art, 1979, Libr. of Congress, 1999; permanent collection Am. Treasures Libr. of Congress; author: The King and Us, 1974, Pro and Conrad, 1979, Drawn and Quartered, 1985, CONArtist: Thirty Years With The Los Angeles Times, 1993, Drawing The Line, 1999. Served with C.E. AUS, 1942-46, PTO. Recipient Editl. Cartoon award, Sigma Delta Chi, 1963, 1969, 1971, 1981—82, 1988, 1997, Pulitzer prize editl. cartooning, 1964, 1971, 1984, Overseas Press Club award, 1970, 1981, Journalism award, U. So. Calif., 1972, Robert F. Kennedy Journalism award 1st prize, 1985, 1990, 1992, 1993, Hugh M. Hefner 1st Amendment award, 1990, Lifetime Achievement award, Am. Assn. Editl. Cartoonists, 1998, Lifetime Pub. Svc. award, Edmund G. Brown Inst. Pub. Affairs, 2000; fellow sr. fellow, Sch. Pub. Policy and Social Rsch., UCLA, 2001—03. Fellow Soc. Profl. Journalists; mem. Phi Delta Theta. Democrat. Roman Catholic. Office: 904 Silver Spur Rd 358 Rolling Hills Estates CA 90274 Home Phone: 310-377-1806; Office Phone: 310-544-0497.

CONRAD, PHILIP JEFFERSON, social worker; b. New Iberia, La., Nov. 30, 1957; s. Karl Donovan and Dolores Beatrice (Bienvenu) C.; children: Siobhan, Turner; m. Chun Hae Pyon; stepchildren: Gina, Audrey. BSME, U. Southwestern La., 1979; postgrad., U. Okla., 1992-93, U. Tex.-Pan Am. Commd. 2nd lt. USAF, 1979, advanced through grades to capt., 1983, structural engr. Dayton, Ohio, 1979-81, safety officer, investigator, specialist, 1983-89, A-10 pilot Suwon AFB, Korea, 1983-84, RAF Bentwaters, England, 1984-87, E-3 pilot Oklahoma City, 1987-89, supv. Command Ctr., 1989-92; software engr. Texas Instruments, Dallas, 1993-96, DSC Comms. Co., Plano, Tex., 1996-98, Alcatel, Plano, 1998-99, Santera Systems Inc., Plano, 1999—2002, Rapport Techs. Inc., Carrollton, 2003—04. Vol. ct. apptd. spl. advocate Collin County, Tex. Decorated Air medal, Meritorious Svc. medal. Mem.: Coun. Social Work Edn., Nat. Assn. Social Workers, Phi Kappa Phi. Avocations: bicycling, personal computers. Home: 2308 S 45th St Mcallen TX 78503-8104 Home Phone: 956-222-7925. Personal E-mail: philipconrad@gmail.com.

CONRAD, ROBERT DAVID, broadcast executive, educator; b. Kankakee, Ill., July 17, 1933; s. Clarence P. and Geneva (Beatty) C.; m. Jean Smith, July 11, 1959; children: Caroline, Allison, Christopher (dec.), Susan, Andrea. BS, Northwestern U., 1955; DFA (hon.), Baldwin Wallce Coll., 1983; MusD (hon.), Cleve. Inst. Music, 1998; DHum (hon.), Oberlin Coll., 2002. Announcer KULA, KAIM, Honolulu, 1956-57, WKAN, Kankakee, 1947-51; announcer, program dir. WEAW AM/FM, Evanston, Ill., 1951-54; announcer WFMT, Chgo., 1954-55, announcer, ops. mgr., 1957-60; program dir. WDTM, Detroit, 1960-62; v.p., program mgr. WCLV, Cleve., 1962-92, pres., broadcast mgr., 1992—. Prodr., commentator Cleve. Orch., 1965—; broadcasting instr. Cuyahoga C.C., Cleve., 1984-91; adj. prof. broadcasting Case We. Res. U./Cleve. Inst. Music, 1991—. Bd. dirs., trustee Cleve. Music Sch. Settlement, 1995—; bd. dirs. Rainey Inst., Cleve. Sch. Arts, 1998-2006, Cleve. Playhouse, 2006-, Music Theatre Ednl. Programming, 2007, Cliffside Found., 2007—; bd. trustees Cleve. Orch., 2002—. Named Program Dir. of Yr., Billboard Mag., N.Y., 1982, Excellence in Broadcasting award Cleve. Assn. Broadcasters, 2001; named to No. Ohio Radio Hall of Fame, 1993, City Club Hall of Fame, 2000; recipient award of achievement Cleve. Radio Broadcasters Assn., 2000, Lifetime Achievement award Cleve. Achievement in Radio Awards, 2002. Mem. Concert Music Broadcasters Assn. (bd. dirs., pres. 1980-83), City Club Cleve. (past bd. dirs., v.p. 1975-78). Office: WCLV 26501 Renaissance Pkwy Cleveland OH 44128-5798 Office Phone: 216-464-0900. E-mail: rconrad@wclv.com.

CONRAD, ROBERT J., JR., federal judge; b. Chgo., May 17, 1958; BA Clemson U., 1980, JD U. Va., 1983. Law clk. Michie, Hamlett, Donato and Lowry, 1981—83, assoc., 1983—86; ptnr. Horn and Conrad, 1986—87; sole practice Robert J. Conrad Jr., PA, 1987—88; ptnr. Bush, Thurman and Conrad, 1988—89; asst. U.S. atty. (we. dist.) N.C. U.S. Dept. Justice, 1989—2001, U.S. atty. (we. dist. N.C.), 2001—04; ptnr. Mayer, Brown, Rowe & Maw LLP, Charlotte, NC, 2004—05; judge US Dist. Ct. (we. dist.) NC, 2005—, chief judge, 2006—. Office: US Dist Ct 235 Charles R Jonas Fed Bldg 401 W Trade St Charlotte NC 28202 Business E-Mail: robert_conrad@ncwd.uscourts.gov.

CONRAD, STEVEN ALLEN, critical care and emergency physician, biomedical engineer, educator; b. St. Martinville, La., Aug. 23, 1953; s. Karl Donovan and Dolores Beatrice (Bienvenu) C.; m. Mona Theresa Hollier, Aug. 9, 1974; children: David, Lesley, Taylor. BS, U. S.W. La., 1974; MD, La. State U., Shreveport, 1978; MS, Case Western Reserve U., Cleve., 1980, PhD, 1985; MS in Engring., La. Tech. U., 1981; MBA, La. State U., 2001, MS in Info. Sys. Tech., 2003; MSc in Bioinformatics, U. Manchester, 2006. Diplomate Am. Bd. Internal Medicine, Critical Care Medicine, Am. Bd. Emergency Medicine; cert. nutritional support physician; cert. clin. rsch. investigator Assn. Clin. Rsch. Investigators, 2004. Postdoctoral trainee in biomed. computing Case Western Res. U., 1979—80; resident internal medicine La. State U., Shreveport, 1981-84; fellow in critical care medicine Mayo Grad. Sch. Medicine, Rochester, Minn., 1984-86; from asst. prof. medicine to prof. bioinformatics and computational biology La. State U. Med. Ctr., Shreveport, La., 1986—2003, prof. medicine, emergency medicine, pediatrics, anesthesiology, bioinformatics and computational biology, 2003—, dir. critical care medicine tng. program, 1987—; instr. computer sci. Winona State U., 1985—86. Cons. physician critical care VA Med. Ctr., 1986—2003, dir. extracorporeal life support program, 1993—, co-dir. nutritional support svc., 1994—, transplant intensivist Willis Knighton Regional Heart Transplant Program, 1994—2004, attending physician in pediat. ICU, 1994—; mem. emergency med. svcs. task force Shreveport Fire Dept., 1992—; prin. investigator in multiple device and drug trials. Editor: Pulmonary Function Testing: Principles and Practice, 1984; mem. editl. bd. Internat. Jour. Electronic Healthcare, 2003—, ASAIO Jour., 2004—; manuscript reviewer ASAIO Jour., 2004-, Artificial Organs, Intensive Care Medicine, Critical Care Chest Medicine, Chest; abstract reviewer Critical Care Medicine; contbr. chpts. to books and articles to profl. jours. Grantee, Am. Heart Assn., NHLBI. Fellow ACP, Am. Coll. Critical Care Med., Am. Coll. Chest Physicians, Am. Coll. Emergency Physicians, Am. Acad. Emergency Physicians; mem. IEEE (sr.), Biomed. Engring. Soc., Shock Soc., Am. Soc. Artificial Internal Organs, Internat. Soc. for Artificial Organs, Soc. for Acad. Emergency Medicine, Am. Soc. for Parenteral and Enteral Nutrition, Internat. Soc. for Computational Biology, Assn. Clin. Rsch. Profls., Alpha Omega Alpha, Sigma Xi, Phi Kappa Phi, Beta Gamma Sigma, Sigma Iota Epsilon. Office: La State U Health Scis Ctr 1501 Kings Hwy Shreveport LA 71103-4228 Office Phone: 318-675-6885. Business E-Mail: sconrad@lsuhsc.edu.

CONRAD, WINTHROP BROWN, JR., lawyer; b. Detroit, May 26, 1945; s. Winthrop Brown and Dolores Conrad; m. Ellen Rouse, May 12, 1973; children: Parker Rouse, Louisa Katherine, Frances Winthrop. AB, Yale U., 1967; JD, Harvard U., 1971. Bar: N.Y. 1972, U.S. Dist. Ct. (so. dist.) N.Y. 1975, U.S. Ct. Appeals (2d cir.) 1975. Ptnr. Davis, Polk & Wardwell, NYC, 1979—, Paris Office, 1985-88. Bd. dirs. Found. for Joffrey Ballet, N.Y.C., 1985-86, British-Am. Ednl. Found.; former trustee Estate and Property of the Conv. of the Diocese of N.Y., Episcopal Diocese of N.Y., Ch. Pension Fund; trustee, chair Vt. Studio Ctr.; dir., BAR Vermont Inc. Mem. ABA, Assn. of Bar of City of N.Y. Home: 1120 5th Ave New York NY 10128-0144 Office: Davis Polk & Wardwell 450 Lexington Ave Fl 31 New York NY 10017-3982 also: 856 Old Post Rd Bedford NY 10506-1215

CONRAD-ENGLAND, ROBERTA LEE, pathologist; b. Meriden, Conn., Aug. 25, 1950; d. Hans and Emma Ann (Bort) Conrad; m. Gary Thomas England, June 6, 1976; children: Eric Bryan, Christopher Ryan. BS in Microbiology, U. Ky., 1972, MD, 1976. Diplomate Nat. Bd. Med. Examiners, Bd. Am. Pathologists. Resident anatomic and clin. pathology Emory U. Affiliated Hosps., Atlanta, 1976-80; pathologist Western Bapt. Hosp., Paducah, Ky., 1980—2005. Cons. Marshall County Hosp., Benton, Ky., 1985-2005, chair infection control com., 1985-2005 Mem., com. chairperson PTA, Poducah, Ky., 1993-94; mother's asst. Boy Scouts Am., Poducah, 1991-94. Fellow Coll. Am. Pathologists, Am. Soc. Clin. Pathologists; mem. Ky. Med. Assn., Ky. Soc. Pathologists, Ky. Women Mentors in Sci., Alpha Omega Alpha, Phi Beta Kappa. Avocations: swimming, snorkeling, interior decorating.

CONRADER, CONSTANCE RUTH, artist, writer; b. Vandalia, Mo., Apr. 13, 1919; d. Gilbert Fordyce and Elizabeth Florence (Cleghorn) Stone; m. Jay Merten Conrader, Nov. 29, 1941 (dec. 1996). Student, Carroll Coll., 1938-40, North Park Coll., 1940-41. Cert. pub. libr. Artist, author, Oconomowoc, Wis., 1940—. Libr. Oconomowoc Pub. Libr., 1947-82, vol. 1982—; illustrator Turtox classroom charts Gen. Biol. Supply House, Chgo., 1940-60; manuscript critique Baha'i Pub. Trust, Wilmette, Ill., 1970-89, editor, 1988. Author, illustrator: Blue Wampum, 1958; co-editor: Tokens From the Writings of Baha'u'llah, 1973; illustrator: Northwoods Wildlife Region, 1983; co-author, illustrator articles to profl. jours.; co-editor regional Baha'i Newsletter, 1997-2006 Chair UN Day, Oconomowoc, 1976-86. Avocations: gardening, music, reading, cooking. Home: 738 E Washington St Oconomowoc WI 53066-3110

CONRADT, JODY, retired women's college basketball coach; b. Goldthwaite, Tex., May 13, 1941; BS in Phys. Edn., Baylor U., 1963, MS in Phys. Edn., 1969. Women's basketball, volleyball and track head coach Sam Houston State U., Huntsville, Tex., 1969—73; women's basketball, volleyball and softball head coach U. Tex., Arlington, 1973—76, head women's basketball coach Austin, 1976—2007, women's athletic dir., 1992—2001. Mem. Coaches vs. Cancer/Am. Cancer Soc.; hon. chair Susan B. Komen Race for the Cure fundraising walk/run, Austin, 2003; vol. ann. walk Austin's SafePlace. Named one of Top 50 Women's Sports Execs. in the nation, Street & Smith's Sports Bus. Jour., 1998; named to Tex. Women's Hall of Fame, 1986, Internat. Women's Sports Hall of Fame, NYC, 1995, Naismith Meml. Basketball Hall of Fame, 1998, Women's Basketball Hall of Fame, 1999, Tex. Sports Hall of Fame, 1998, U. Tex. Women's Athletics Hall of Honor, 2000, Internat. Scholar-Athlete Hall of Fame, 2003; recipient Carol Eckman award, Women's Basketball Coaches Assn., 1987, Nat. Award for outstanding commitment to women's athletics, Nat. Assn. for Girls and Women in Sports, 1991, award for contbn. to sports, NCAA, 1992, John and Nellie Wooden Nat. Coach of Yr. award, 1996—97, Nat. Coach of Yr. award, ESPN.com, 2002—03, Harvey Penick award for Excellence in the Game of Life, Caritas, Austin, 2003. Home: 9614 Leaning Rock Cir Austin TX 78730-2725*

CONRAN, JOSEPH PALMER, lawyer; b. St. Louis, Oct. 4, 1945; s. Palmer and Theresa (Bussmann) C.; m. Daria D. Conran, June 8, 1968; children: Andrew, Lizabeth, Theresa. BA, St. Louis U., 1967, JD with honors, 1970. Bar: Mo. 1970, U.S. Ct. Mil. Appeals 1971, U.S. Ct. Appeals (8th cir.) 1974. Assoc. Husch and Eppenberger, St. Louis, 1974-78, ptnr., 1978—, chmn. litigation dept., 1980-95, chmn. mgmt. com., 1995—. Mem. faculty Trial Practice Inst. Capt., JAGC, USAF, 1970-74. Mem. Bar Assn. Met. St. Louis (Merit award 1976, 77), Mo. Bar Assn. (bd. govs. 1987-92), Mo. Athletic Club (pres. 1986-87), Norwood Hills Country Club, St. Louis Club. Roman Catholic. Home: 53 Hawthorne Est Saint Louis MO 63131-3035 Office: Husch Eppenberger 190 Carondelet Plz Ste 600 Saint Louis MO 63105-3433 Office Phone: 314-480-1900. Business E-Mail: joe.conran@husch.com.

CONRATH, BARNEY JAY, astrophysicist; b. Quincy, Ill., June 23, 1935; s. Frederick Barney and Jayme Wilson (Cason) C.; m. Marjorie Ann Hilder, Sept. 3, 1962; children: Ann, Frederick, Susan. BA, Culver-Stockton Coll., Canton, Mo., 1957; MA, U. Iowa, 1959; PhD, U. N.H., 1966. Astrophysicist Goddard Space Flight Ctr., NASA, Greenbelt, Md., 1960-90, sr. fellow, 1990-95; vis. sr. scientist Ctr. Radiophysics Space Rsch., Cornell U., Ithaca, NY, 1995—. Co-author: Exploration of the Solar System by Infrared Remote Sensing, 1991, Exploration of the Solar System by Infrared Remote Sensing, 2d edit., 2003. Recipient Exceptional Sci. Achievement medal NASA, 1982, 90. Mem. Am. Astron. Soc. (Gerard P. Kuiper prize 1996), Am. Geophys. Union, Sigma Xi. Achievements include serving as principal investigator of Voyager infrared spectroscopy experiment which determined helium abundance, thermal structure, energy balance, and atmospheric composition of Jupiter, Saturn, Uranus and Neptune. Home Phone: 434-591-1355; Office Phone: 434-591-1055. Business E-Mail: Conrath@astro.cornell.edu.

CONRON, MICHAEL WILLIAM, lawyer; b. Teaneck, NJ, Apr. 22, 1964; s. Michael John and Madelyn Mary (Higgins) C. BS in Econs., U. Pa., 1986; JD cum laude, U. Md., 1993. Bar: Md. 1993, DC 1999, admitted to practice: US Dist. Ct. (Dist. Md.) 1994. Assoc. Venable, Baetjer and Howard, LLP, Balt., 1993—; ptnr., Bus. Trans. Dept. & Mergers and Acquisitions Dept. Venable LLP, Balt. Adj. prof., Securities Regulation U. Md. Sch. Law. Articles editor & exec. bd. mem. The Business Lawyer. Mem. festival com. Fed. Hill-Fells Point Preservation Soc., Balt., 1994—; bd. dir. USS Constellation Mus.; chmn., Basic Securities Law Program Md. Inst. for Continuing Prof. Edn. of Lawyers. Lt. USN, 1986—90, comdr. USN. Recipient Navy Commendation medal, Navy Achievement medal, Navy Expeditionary medal. Mem.: DC Bar, Am. Law Inst., Balt. Jr. Assn. Commerce, Bar Assn. Balt. City (fee arbitration com.), Md. Bar Assn., ABA, Order of Coif. Roman Catholic. Office: Venable LLP 575 7th St NW Washington DC 20004 Office Phone: 202-344-4752. Office Fax: 202-344-8300. Business E-Mail: mwconron@venable.com.

CONROY, DAVID JEROME, lawyer; b. New Orleans, Dec. 27, 1929; s. George E. and Lilyon (Bowling) C.; m. Ann Kathryn Gunderson, May 15, 1954; children: Kathryn Ann, David Michael, Elizabeth Helen, Mary Daire, Peter George Edward, Patrick Frank. BA, Tulane U., 1950, JD, 1952. Bar: La. 1952. Ptnr. Milling, Benson, Woodward, Hillyer, Pierson & Miller, New Orleans, 1956—, mng. ptnr., 1974-84; sec. Jahncke Svc. Inc., New Orleans, 1961-69, Public Grain Elevator New Orleans, 1964-83; sec., dir. C.B. Fox Co., New Orleans, 1965—. Mem. planning com. Tulane Tax Inst., 1975-79; del. La. Constl. Conv., 1973; bd. dirs. New Orleans Speech and Hearing Ctr., 1968-74, pres., 1970-72; bd. dirs. Louise S. McGehee Sch., 1970-77, pres., 1975-77; trustee Pub. Affairs Rsch. Coun. La., 1974-80; bd. dirs. Family Svc. Soc., 1972-77, United Way Greater New Orleans, 1974-80; bd. dirs. Human Svcs. on Cable, Inc., 1982-87, v.p., 1985-87; bd. dirs. Coun. for A Better La., 1974-, pres., 1987-88; bd. dirs. Greater New Orleans Ednl. TV Found., 1986-92; bd. dirs., exec. com. Greater New Orleans Found., 1985-96, chmn., 1993-95; bd. dirs Comm. for a Better New Orleans, 1999-; bd. suprs., exec. com. La. State U., 1988-94, chmn. bd. suprs., 1990-91; mem. gov's. spl. task force on pub. higher edn., 1989-90; mem. mayor's adv. com. on charter revision, City of New Orleans; role model (law) Young Leadership Coun., 1996; chmn. bd. commrs. La. Stadium and Exposition Dist., 1998-2004; bd. dirs. Jefferson Libr. Inst., J. Bennett Johnson Sci. Found. Served with AUS, 1952-54. Fellow Am. Bar Found., La. Bar Found; mem. ABA, New Orleans Bar Assn. (chmn. jr. bar comm. 1956, chmn. com. on profl. ethics and grievances 1985-87, Pres. award 1998), Am. Law Inst., La. Bar Assn. (chmn. sect. corp. law 1968-69 , mem. com. law reform 1974-84, chmn. com. law reform 1977-78, Bd. Gov. award 1980), La. Law Inst. (adv. com. on conflicts of law 1984,), St. Thomas More Cath. Lawyers Assn. (bd. govs. 1969-72, 78-80, 1st v.p. 1971-72). Roman Catholic. Clubs: Pickwick (bd. dirs. 1985-91, pres. 1989-90), New Orleans Country. Office: 909 Poydras St Ste 2300 New Orleans LA 70112-1010 Home: 437 Dorrington Dr Metairie LA 70005 Office Phone: 504-569-7000. Business E-Mail: dconroy@millinglaw.com.

CONROY, J. MICHAEL, lawyer, judge; b. 1945; m. Claudia Marie Remington, 1979; children: John, Aindrea. BA, Univ. of Notre Dame, 1967; JD, Georgetown Univ. Law Ctr., 1971, LLM in Taxation, 1986. Ptnr. Conroy & Williams, 1972—80; public defender State of Md., Montgomery County, 1976—79; ptnr. Conroy, FitzGerald, Ballman & Ridgway, 1980—82, Conroy, Fitzgerald & Ballman, 1982—87, Conroy, Fitzgerald, Ballman & Dameron, 1987—90, Conroy, Ballman & Dameron, 1990—2004, prin., 2004—06; Judge Dist. Ct. Md., 2006—. Mem. Assn. of Trial Lawyers of Am., 1973—2000. Vol. Ronald McDonald House, Cath. Youth Orgn. With US Army, 1968—69 USAR, 1969—74. Recipient Leadership in Law award, Daily Record, 2005. Mem.: ABA (delegate 2003—07), Montgomery County Bar Found. (dir. 1985—98, treas. 1989—90, pres. 1995—96), Montgomery County Bar Assn. (pres. 1994—95), Md. State Bar Assn. (pres.-elect 2004, pres. 2005—06). Avocations: running, tennis, rugby. Office: 27 Courthouse Sq Rockville MD 20850 Office Phone: 301-279-1468. Personal E-mail: mikeconroy4@yahoo.com.

CONROY, MARGARET M., library director; B., Quincy U., Ill.; MPA, U. Mo., Columbia; MLS, Dominican U., Ill. Dir. Little Dixie Regional Libraries, Moberly, Mo., Mo. River Regional Libr., Jefferson City; state libr. Mo. State Libr., Jefferson City, 2006—. Bd. dirs. Mo. Libr. Network Corp., MOREnet. Active River City Habitat for Humanity. Mem.: Mo. Libr. Assn. (former pres.), Ashland Optimist, Jefferson City Rotary. Office: Mo State Libr 600 W Main St PO Box 387 Jefferson City MO 65101 Office Phone: 573-751-2751. E-mail: margaret.conroy@sos.mo.gov.

CONROY, MARY ELIZABETH, history professor; b. Hammond, Ind., Sept. 2, 1937; d. Edward Michael and Branche Gisela (Schellenbauer) Schaeffer; m. Thomas Francis Conroy, June 19, 1965; children: Alexandra Blanche, Margaret Eleanor. BA, St. Mary's Coll., South Bend, Ind., 1959; MA, Ind. U., Bloomington, 1962, PhD, 1964. Asst. prof. Kans. State U., Manhattan, 1964—65, U. Ill., Chgo., 1965—68, U. Colo., Denver, 1975—78, assoc. prof., 1978—85, prof. Russian and Soviet hist., 1985—2005, prof. emerita, 2005. Author: P.A. Stolypin: Practical Politics in late Tsarist Russia, 1977, In Health and In Sickness: Pharmacy, Pharmacists and the Pharmaceutical Industry in late Imperial Russia, 1994 (George Urdang award, 1997), The Soviet Pharmaceutical Business During Its First Two Decades 1917-1937, 2006; editor: Emerging Democracy in Late Imperial Russia, 1998. Grantee, Ford Found., 1960—64, Internat. Rsch. and Exchange, 1990. Mem.: Slovak Soc. Colo. (pres. 2006), Assn. Study of Health Democracy in Former Soviet Union, Am. Inst. Hist. Pharmacy, Am. Hist. Assn., Am. Assn. Advancement Slavic Studies. Republican. Roman Catholic. Avocations: art, music, architecture, travel. Home: 3825 Colorado Blvd Cherry Hills Village CO 80113-4202 Home Fax: 303-761-6273. Personal E-mail: maryesconroy@earthlink.net. Business E-Mail: mary.conroy@cudenver.edu.

CONROY, PAT (DONALD PATRICK CONROY), writer; b. Atlanta, Oct. 26, 1945; s. Donald and Frances Dorothy (Peek) C.; m. Barbara

Bolling, 1969 (div. 1977); children: Jessica, Melissa, Megan; m. Lenore Gurewitz, 1981 (div. 1995); children: Gregory, Emily, Susannah. BA in English, The Citadel, 1967. Author: The Boo, 1970, The Water Is Wide, 1972 (Anisfield-Wolf award Cleve. Found. 1972), The Great Santini, 1976, The Lords of Discipline, 1980 (Lillian Smith award for fiction So. Regional Council 1981), The Prince of Tides, 1986, Beach Music, 1995, The Losing Season, 2002, The Pat Conroy Cookbook: Recipes of My Life, 2004; screenwriter: (TV movie) Invictus, 1988, (with Becky Johnson) The Prince of Tides, 1991 (Academy Award nomination best adapted screenplay 1991). Ford Found. Leadership Devel. grantee, 1971; recipient NEA award for achievement in education, 1974, Ga. Gov.'s award for Arts, 1978, Golden Plate award Am. Acad. Achievement, 1992, Thomas Cooper Libr. Soc. Literary award U. S.C., 1995, S.C. Gov.'s award in the Humanities for disting. achievement, 1996, Humanitarian award Ga. Commn. on the Holocaust, 1996, Lotos medal of Merit for outstanding literary achievement, 1996. Mem. Authors Guild Am., Writers Guild, PEN. Democrat. Office: care Doubleday 1540 Broadway New York NY 10036-4039

CONROY, TAMARA BOKS, artist, retired special education educator; b. Most, Czechoslovakia; came to U.S., 1947; d. Alois and Tatiana (Shapilova) Boks; m. John P. Conroy, Aug. 19, 1950 (dec. Oct. 1973); 1 child, Michael Thomas (dec.). Student, U. Graz, Austria, 1945-47; RN, New Rochelle (N.Y.) Med. Ctr., 1950; student, Coll. of William & Mary, 1958-59, Cath. U. Am., 1960; BS in Nursing Edn., Columbia U., 1963, MA in Spl. Edn., 1965. RN, N.Y.; cert. spl. edn. tchr., N.Y. Nurse accident rm. New Rochelle Hosp./Med. Ctr., 1950-51; pub. health nurse Va. Dept. of Health, Richmond, 1958-59; tchr. spl. edn. Southern Westchester Bd. Coop. Edn. Svcs., Portchester, NY, 1965-83; freelance artist and painter NYC and Pelham, NY, 1969—. Asst. to chmn. math. dept. Columbia U., N.Y.C., 1975-76. Author math. program Learning Numbers-Step by Step, 1977. Pres., founder Classical Music Lovers' Exch., Pelham, N.Y., 1980-98. Mem. Am. Fedn. Tchrs., N.Y. State United Tchrs., BOCES Tchrs. Assn. (profl.), Women's Mus. Group, Mamaroneck Artists Guild, Silvermine Artists Guild, Westchester Musicians Guild (assoc.), Kappa Delta Pi. Avocations: flying, reading, music, fashion designing, painting and drawing.

CONROY, THOMAS FRANCIS, insurance company consultant; b. Chgo., Sept. 26, 1938; s. Thomas Francis and Eleanor Althea (Heatherly) C.; m. Mary Elizabeth Schaeffer, June 19, 1965; children: Alexandra B., Margaret E. BSc, De Paul U., 1959; MBA, U. Chgo., 1969. CPA, CDP. Mgr. Ernst & Whinney, Chgo., 1959-74; exec. v.p. fin., treas., contr. Security Life of Denver, 1974-93; prin. Ea. Hemisphere Trading Corp., Denver, 1990—2003; pres. Security Life Reins., 1993-99, ING Re Internat., 2000-01; mng. prin. Strategic Reins. Cons. Internat., Englewood, Colo., 2001—; mng. ptnr. Mann Conroy Eisenberg & Assoc., LLC, Greensboro, 2002—. Bd. dirs. Teton Petroleum Co., Auspice Corp. Trustee Denver Chamber Orch., 1988-93; bd. dirs. Buffalo Mountain Met. Dist., 1984-95, Denver affiliate Susan G. Komen Found., 2002-06. Capt. U.S. Army, 1960-62. Fellow Life Mgmt. Inst. Roman Catholic. Home Phone: 303-761-6238; Office Phone: 303-762-8812. Business E-Mail: tomconroy@strategicre.com.

CONRY, THOMAS FRANCIS, mechanical engineering educator; b. West Hempstead, NY, Mar. 7, 1942; s. Thomas and Bridget Anne (Walsh) C.; m. Sharon Ann Silverwood, June 10, 1967; children: Christine Elizabeth, Carolyn Danielle, Anne Marie. BS, Pa. State U., 1963; MS, U. Wis., Madison, 1967, PhD, 1970. Registered profl. engr., Wis., Ill. Engr. Gen. Motors Corp., Milw., 1963-66, sr. research engr. Indpls., 1969-71; asst. prof. gen. engring. U. Ill., Coll. Engring., Urbana, 1971-75, assoc. prof. gen. and mech. engring., 1975-81, prof. gen. and mech. engring., 1981—2006, co-dir. mng. engring. program, 1986-89, head dept. gen. engring., 1987-98, founding coord. program in tech. and mgmt., 1995—98, prof. emeritus indsl. and enterprise sys. engring., 2006—. Sr. visitor U. Cambridge, Eng., 1978; cons. Zurn Industries, 1974-83, Ruhl Forensic, 2006-; staff cons. Sargent & Lundy, Engrs., 1977, 79; cons.-evaluator commn. on instns. of higher edn. North Ctl. Assn., 1983—; cons. indsl. firm on machine dynamics, optimization and tribology. NSF trainee, 1968-69; NASA/ASEE summer faculty fellow, 1974-75. Contbr. articles to profl. jours. Mem. Bd. Edn. St. Matthews Parish Roman Catholic Ch., Champaign, 1981-84. Recipient Edmond E. Bisson award, Soc. Tribologists and Lubrication Engrs., 2007. Fellow ASME (chmn. design engring. divsn. 1979-80, tech. editor Jour. Vibration, Acoustics, Stress and Reliability in Design, 1984-89, mem. bd. on comm. 1989-93, 96-00, mem. com. on fin. and investment 1999-04); mem. Am. Soc. Engring. Edn., Rotary, Sigma Xi, Lambda Chi Alpha, Phi Kappa Phi. Home: 3301 Lakeshore Dr Champaign IL 61822-5205 Office: 104 S Mathews Ave Urbana IL 61801-2925 Business E-Mail: tconry@uiuc.edu.

CONSAGRA, SOPHIE CHANDLER, academic administrator; b. Radnor, Pa., Apr. 28, 1927; d. Alfred D. and Carol (Ramsay) Chandler; children: Maria, Pierluigi, Francesca, George. BA, Smith Coll., 1949; MA, Cambridge U., Eng., 1952. Exec. dir. Del. Arts Coun., 1972-78; dir. visual arts and architecture NY State Coun. Arts, 1978-80; dir. Am. Acad. in Rome, 1980-84, pres., 1984-88, pres. emerita, vice chmn./spl. projects, 1988-90. Cons. Nat. Endowment Arts. Recipient Smith Coll. award, 1986, Centennial medal Am. Acad. in Rome, 1995. Address: 955 Lexington Ave New York NY 10021-5128

CONSER, WALTER HURLEY, JR., religion and philosophy educator; b. Riverside, Calif., Apr. 4, 1949; s. Walter Hurley and Barbara Healy C.; m. Janet Gunter, June 7, 1986; 1 child, Emily. BA, U. Calif., Irvine, 1971; MA, Brown U., Providence, 1974, PhD, 1981. From vis. asst. prof. to prof. U. N.C., Wilmington, 1985—. Author: Church and Confession, 1984, God and the Natural World, 1993, Sacred Spaces, 1999, A Coat of Many Colors, 2005; editor: Experiences of the Sacred, 1992, Religious Diversity and American Religious History, 1997; mem. adv. bd. Jour. So. Religion, 1997—. Mem. Am. Hist. Assn. Mem. Am. Acad. Religion. Office: Dept Philosophy and Religion U NC 601 S College Rd Wilmington NC 28403-5601

CONSEY, KEVIN EDWARD, museum administrator; b. NYC, Jan. 15, 1952; s. Edward and Dorothy (Kemmann) C.; m. Susan Mary Kirsch, Aug. 26, 1972. BA, Hofstra U., 1974; M in Mus. Practice, MA, U. Mich., 1977; MBA, Northwestern U., 1999. Dir. Emily Lowe Gallery, Hofstra U., Hempstead, N.Y., 1977-80, San Antonio Mus. Art., 1980-83; dir., chief exec. officer Newport Harbor Art Mus., Newport Beach, Calif., 1983-89, Mus. Contemporary Art, Chgo., 1989-2000; dir. art mus. and pacific film archive U. Calif., Berkeley, 2000—. Panelist profl. devel. Nat. Endowment for Arts, Washington, 1987-88, John D. and Catherine T. MacArthur Found., Nat. Arts Journalism Fellowship program, 45th Venice Biennale Sch. of Curators, Mus. Studies Program at the Art Inst. of Chgo., Ill. Arts Alliance, Calif. Arts Coun., Tex. Commn. on the Arts, NY State Coun. on the Arts, panelist challenge grant, 1988, panelist mus. program, 1989-90, panelist F.A.C.I.E., 1991-94; bd. dir. Com. Internat. Mus. Modern Art. Bd. dir. Nat. Audubon Soc., Chgo. Latin Sch., Golden Gate Chpt., Berkeley Cmty. Found.; advisory com. Girls Inc., Oakland, Calif. Hofstra U. scholar, 1970-74, Guggenheim Mus. intern, 1976; grantee Nat. Mus. Act, 1976-77; teaching fellowships U. Va., Toledo Mus. Art, Ohio, U. Mich. Mus. Art, Nat. Gallery Art, Wash., DC, Solomon R. Guggenheim Mus., NYC. Mem. Assn. Art Mus. Dirs., Coll. Art Assn., Internat. Assn. Art Critics Office: BAM/FFA U Calif Berkeley 2625 Durant Ave Berkeley CA 94720-2250 Office Phone: 510-642-1295. Business E-Mail: kconsey@berkeley.edu.

CONSIDINE, JILL M., securities trader; b. Aug. 14, 1944; m. Martin Rettinger; 1 child, Danielle. BS in Biology, St. John's U., 1965, LLD (hon.), 1986; postgrad. in biochemistry, Bryn Mawr Coll., 1965-67; MS, Grad. Sch. Bus., Columbia U., 1980. V.p. Chase Manhattan Bank, NYC, 1971-81, Bankers Trust, NYC, 1981-83; pres., CEO The First Women's Bank, NYC, 1984-85; supt. banks N.Y. State Banking Dept., NYC, 1985-91; mng. dir., chief admin. officer American Express Bank Ltd., 1991—93; pres. New York Clearing House Assn., NYC, 1993-99; chmn., CEO The Depository Trust Co., NYC, 1999—. Bd. dirs. Fed. Res. Bank N.Y., 2002—, Atlantic Mut. Ins. Comps., Ambac Fin. Corp., The Interpublic Group of Cos. Mem. Coun. Fgn. Rels., Japan Soc., Group of 30 Steering Com., N.Y.C. Partnership, Securities Industry Found. Econ. Devel.; dir., cons. Sept. 11 Fund, Alliance Downtown N.Y. Named equities achiever of the yr., Equities Mag., 2000; named one of 100 Most Influential Women in Bus., Crain's NY mag., 1999; recipient Star award, NY Women's Agenda, 1995, Six Sigma CEO of the Yr. award, 2006. Mem.: Coun. Fgn. Rels. Office: The Depository Trust Co 55 Water St New York NY 10041-0001*

CONSIDINE, JOHN R., pharmaceutical company executive; Attended, Villanova Univ., Pace Univ. With Arthur Andersen, 1973—83; mgmt. positions through sr. v.p., CFO Am. Home Products Corp., Madison, NJ, 1983—2000; exec. v.p., CFO Becton Dickinson & Co., Franklin Lakes, NJ, 2000—06, sr. exec. v.p., CFO, 2006—. Bd. mem. St. Vincent's Svc., Animal Cancer Found. Office: Becton Dickinson & Co 1 Becton Dr Franklin Lakes NJ 07417-1880*

CONSIDINE, RUSSEL A., executive recruiter, photographer; BA, Hofstra U. Investment officer TIAA-CREF, NYC, 1977-88; pres., founder BMR Corp., Hastings-on-Hudson, NY, 1988-2000; exec. recruiter, 2001—. Founder, CEO Considine Real Estate Adv. Group Inc., Hastings-on-Hudson, N.Y., 2001—; co-founder www.globalcalm.com., 2000—. Co-author, co-illustrator: (photography) The Moonlight Lullaby. Coach Colts Youth Club, Yonkers, NY, 1996—99; dir. golf, football, track and field Metro NY Scholar Athlete Awards, NYC. Recipient Investor of Yr. award First Interstate Mortgage Co., 1987. Avocations: golf, skiing, writing, hiking, reading, photography. Home: 83 Rosedale Ave Hastings On Hudson NY 10706 Personal E-mail: russ@rockefeller.tv, russ@considinephotos.com.

CONSIDINE, TERRY, real estate company executive; m. Betsy Considine. BA, Harvard College, 1968; JD, Harvard Law Sch., 1971. Founder, CEO Considine Co., Denver, 1975—87; state senator Colo., 1987—92; CEO Property Asset Mgmt., Denver, 1987—94; chmn., pres., CEO AIMCO, Denver, 1994—. Rep. candidate for U.S. Senate, 1992. Office: AIMCO Ste 1100 4582 S Ulster St Pkwy Denver CO 80237 Office Phone: 303-757-9101.*

CONSOLI, MARC-ANTONIO, composer; b. Catania, Italy, May 19, 1941; came to U.S., 1956, naturalized, 1967; s. Francesco Gabriele Settimio and Rosa (Puglisi) C. BMus, N.Y. Coll. Music, 1966; MMus, Peabody Conservatory, 1967; MMus Arts, Yale U., 1971, DMus Arts, 1977. Lectr. Bridgeport U.; vis. prof. U. Western Ont., 1975 Composer, works performed by Balt. Symphony Orch., N.Y. Philharm., Los Angeles Philharm., Louisville Orch., Ensemble Kontrapunkte, Vienna, Austria, Monday Evening Concerts, Los Angeles, Berkshire Music Center, Yale Players for New Music, Gaudeamus Festival, Netherlands, Royan Festival, France; commns. for Graz (Austria) radio sta., Royan Festival, others; performer, dir.-mem., Yale Players for New Music, 1969-71, The Experiment, 1974, Equinox I, 1967, Equinox II, 1968, Isonic, 1970, Interactions I-V, 1970-71, Profiles, 1972-73, Music for Chambers, 1974, Canti Trinacriani, 1975, Sciuri Novi I, 1974, Sciuri Novi II, 1975, Tre Canzoni, 1976, Odefonia, 1976, Vuci Siculani, 1979, Tre Fiori Musicali, 1979, Naked Masks, 1980, The Last Unicorn, 1981, Orpheus' Meditation, 1981, Saxlodie, 1981, Afterimages, 1982; String Quartet, 1983, Fantasia Celeste, 1983, Ancient Greek Lyrics, 1984, Musiculi II (summer), 1985, Reflections, 1986, Eyes of the Peacock, 1987, Sans Parole I and II, 1988, Cello Concerto, 1988, String Quartet II, 1989, Arie Mutate, 1990, Musiculi IV (winter), 1990/92, Musiculi III (autumn), 1992/94, Games for 2 and 3, 1994/95, Cinque Canti, 1995, Varie Azioni, Di-ver-ti-mento (Games for 4), 1995, Sciuri Novi III, 1997, Pensieri Sospesi, 1997, Rounds & Relays, 1997, Varie Azioni II, 1998, Varie Azioni III, 1999, Four Shades of Tango, 1999, Rounds' Separation, 1999, Passaggi Obbligati, 2000, Estratti Obbligati I, II and III, 2001, Night Whispers, 2002, Sciuri Novi IV, 2004, Varie Azioni IV, 2004, Collected Moments II, 2005. Recipient award Nat. Inst.-Am. Acad. Arts and Letters, 1975; Guggenheim Found. fellow, 1971-72, 79-80; Fulbright fellow Poland, 1972-74; Creative Artists Pub. Service grantee, 1975; Nat. Endowment for Arts grantee, 1979, 81, 85. Mem. Broadcast Music Inc., Am. Composers Alliance, Am. Music Center. Business E-Mail: mc29@nyu.edu.

CONSOLO, FAITH HOPE, real estate company executive; b. Ohio; BFA, NYU; MFA, Parsons Sch. Design; AA in Real Estate Studies, NYU. Owner internat. promotional modeling agy.; owner interior design studio; small stores real estate broker; joined Garrick-Aug Assocs. Store Leasing Inc., NYC, 1985, sr. mng. dir., vice chmn., 1999—2005; founder, vice chmn. Garrick-Aug Worldwide; chmn. retail leasing and sales divsn. Prudential Douglas Elliman, NYC, 2005—. Apptd. cons. The 42nd St. Redevelopment Corp., NYC, Penn Sta. Redevelopment, NYC, The Downtown Alliance, NYC; lectr. Assn. Women on Econ. Devel., Nat. Assn. Women Bus. Owners, The Women's Econ. Roundtable, Inst. Internat. Rsch., Nat. Assn. Appraisers & Planners, Women Inc.; bd. dirs. The Real Estate Bd. NY, Internat. Coun. Shopping Ctrs., Nat. Broker's Network; advisor Mayor's Coun. on the Aging Related Issues; instr. NYU Parsons Sch. Design, Wharton Bus. Sch.; contr. Luxury Inst.; lectr. in field. Author: (internet newsletter) The Faith Report; contbr. articles to NY Post, to NY Times, to Crain's NY Bus., to Real Estate Weekly, NY Real Estate Jour., to Real Estate NY. Named Woman of Yr., Associated Builders and Owners of Greater NY, 1999, Woman of Outstanding Achievement, Assn. Real Estate Women, 2003, Woman of Valor, Capuchin Food Pantries of St. John the Bapt. Friary, 2003; named one of NY Most Influential Women in Bus., Crain's NY Bus., 1996, 1999. Mem.: Young Men's/Women's Real Estate Assn., Assn. Real Estate Women (past pres., creator The Founder's award). Office: Prudential Douglas Elliman 575 Madison Ave 3rd Fl New York NY 10022 Address: Care of Alyssa Beaver Rubenstein Assoc Inc 1345 Ave Americas New York NY 10105-0109 Office Phone: 212-418-2000. Business E-Mail: fconsolo@elliman.com.

CONSTANTELOS, DEMETRIOS JOHN, priest, educator; b. Spilia, Messinia, Greece, July 27, 1927; came to U.S., 1955; naturalized, 1958; s. John and Christine (Psilopoulos) C.; m. Stella Croussouloudis, Aug. 15, 1954; children: Christine, John, Eleni, Maria. BTh, Holy Cross Sch. Theology, Brookline, Mass., 1958; ThM, Princeton Theol. Sem., NJ, 1959; MA, Rutgers U., New Brunswick, NJ, 1963, PhD, 1965; DD, Hellenic Coll./Holy Cross, Brookline, Mass., 1991. Ordained priest Greek Orthodox Ch., 1955. Pastor St. Demetrios, Perth Amboy, NJ, 1955—64, St. Nicholas Ch., Lexington, Mass., 1965—67; interim pastor St. Barbara Ch., Toms River, NJ, 1972—74, St. Anthony Ch., Vineland, NJ, 1975—82, Holy Trinity Ch., Egg Harbor Twp., NJ, 1982—89; prof. Hellenic Coll., Brookline, Mass., 1965—71; prof. history Richard Stockton Coll. N.J., Pomona, 1971—86, Charles Cooper Townsend Disting. prof., 1986—97, prof. emeritus, 1997—, disting. rsch. scholar in residence, 2001—. Mem. Orthodox-Cath. Theol. Consultation, 1965-84, New Rev. Standard Version Bible Com., 1974—, Anglican-Orthodox Theol. Consultation; vis. lectr. Boston Coll., Chestnut, Mass., 1967-68; vis. prof. religion, Onassis vis. prof. Hellenic studies NYU, NYC, 1991. Author: Byzantine Philanthropy, 1968, 2d edit., 1991, Understanding the Greek Orthodox Church, 1982, 4th edit., 2005, Poverty, Society and Philanthropy in the Late Mediaeval Greek World, 1992, Christian Hellenism, 1998, Christian Faith and Cultural Heritage, 2005, Interrelationship Between Christianity and Hellenism in Greek, 2007, Renewing the Church: The Historical Significance of the Council in Trullo, 2006, The Greeks: Their Heritage and its value today, 2d edit., 2006; editor: Encyclicals, 1976, Orthodox Theology, 1981, Archbishop Iakovos, Visions and Expectations for a Living Church, 1998, Archbishop Iakovos: The Torch Bearer, vol. 1, 1999, vol. II, 2001, Archbishop Iakovos, Paideia, 2002, Archbishop Iakovos, He Merimnamou, 2006, Archbishop Iakovos, That They May Be One, 2007; editor Greek Theol. Rev., 1965-71, assoc. editor Jour. Ecumenical Studies, 1976—. Lane Cooper fellow Rutgers U., 1962, Jr. fellow Dumbarton Oaks, 1964. Mem. Orthodox Theol. Soc. (pres. 1968-71), Modern Greek Studies Assn., Parnasos Philol. Soc. (corr.), Medieval Acad. Am., U.S. Nat. Com. Byzantine Studies. Home: 304 Forest Dr Linwood NJ 08221-1511 Office: Richard Stockton Coll NJ Dept History Pomona NJ 08240 Office Phone: 609-652-4433. Business E-Mail: constand@stockton.edu. E-mail: djconstantelos@aol.com.

CONSTANTIN, EMILIA, physicist, researcher; b. Turia Covasma, Romania, Dec. 5, 1933; arrived in France, 1977; d. Dumitru and Ilona (Jakabos) Strungaru; m. Gilles Constantin, 1957; 1 child, Marie. Diploma in phys. scis., Jassy, Roumanie, 1957; DSc, Cluj, Roumanie, 1973. Rschr. Chem. Inst., Jassy, 1959-61; asst. U. Cluj, 1961-63, 1st degree prof., 1963-77; assoc. asst. ULP, Strasbourg, France, 1979, assoc. prof., 1979-87, prof., 1987—2002. Dir. MS lab. ULP, 1982—2002; sci. edn. films prodr., 1998—. Author: Mass Spectrometry, 1986, 90, 96, Atomistique, 1965, Molecular Structure, 1976; editor: Mass Spectrometry in Cancer Rsch., 1994; 2 patents in field. Roman Catholic. Home and Office: 12 Sq Jean Thébaud 75015 Paris France E-mail: moldaconstantin@noos.fr.

CONSTANTINE, ANDREW, conductor; b. England, 1964; Studied, with John Carewe; studied with Norman Del Mar, Royal Coll. Music Conducting Class; studied with Ilya Musin, Leningrad State Conservatory. Condr. London Philharm., Royal Philharm. Orch.; asst. condr. Stats Oper, Munich, 1993; asst. condr. to assoc. condr. Balt. Symphony Orch. Vis. condr. Prague Spring Festival, Tivoli Festival-Copenhagen, Norway Musik Festival, St. Petersburg Symphony, Arthus Symfonleorkester, Sonderjyllands Symfonierorkester, Albog Symfonierorkester, Trondheim Symphony Orch., Talich Chamber Orch., Nat. Symphony Orch., Ireland. Recordings with Talich Chamber Orch., London Symphony Orch. Recipient Donatella Flick/Academia Italiana Conducting Competition, 1991; fellow NESTA, Brit. Govt. Office: Baltimore Symphony Orchestra 1212 Cathedral St Baltimore MD 21201-5545*

CONSTANTINE, JAN FRIEDMAN, lawyer; b. NYC, Jan. 22, 1948; d. Howard J. and Elayne (Sercus) Friedman; m. Lawrence Levien, Oct. 11, 1970 (div. Sept. 1974); m. Lloyd E. Constantine, June 22, 1975; children: Isaac, Sarah, Elizabeth. BA, Smith Coll., Northampton, Mass., 1970; JD, George Washington U., 1973. Bar: N.Y. 1974, U.S. Dist. Ct. (so. and ea. dists.) N.Y. 1975, U.S. Ct. Appeals (2d cir.) 1975. Staff atty. div. spl. projects FTC, Washington, 1973-75, staff atty. N.Y. office NYC, 1975-77; asst. atty. U.S. Dist. Ct. (ea. dist.) N.Y., Bklyn., 1977-82; litigation counsel Macmillan, Inc., NYC, 1982-84, assoc. gen. counsel, 1985-90, dep. gen. counsel, 1990-91; exec. v.p. and dep. gen. counsel News Am. Inc., NYC, 1992—; sr. gen. counsel News Am. Mktg. and Pub. Groups, NYC; sr. v.p. The News Corp. Ltd., NYC, 1996—. Vis. asst. prof. George Washington U. Law Sch., Washington, 1974; bd. mem. The Feminist Press. Mem. Assn. of Bar of City of N.Y. (mem. consumer protection com. 1981-84, corp. law com. 1987-90, media law com. 1991-94, women in the law com. 1994-96, comm. and media law com. 1996—, chair 1999-2001). Avocations: tennis, singing. Home: 10 W 66th St New York NY 10023-6206 Office: The News Corp Ltd Ste 300 1211 Avenue Of The Americas New York NY 10036-8795

CONSTANTINE, KATHERINE A., lawyer; b. 1955; BS in Fgn. Svc. magna cum laude, Georgetown U., 1977, JD, 1980. Bar: Minn. 1980. Assoc., gen. litig. Nichols, Kruger, Starks and Carruthers, 1980—83; assoc. Fabyanske Svoboda & Westra PA, 1983—85, Dorsey & Whitney LLP, Mpls., 1986—88, ptnr., banking comml. dept., 1989—, and co-chair, bus. restructuring and bankruptcy. Assoc. editor Georgetown's The Tax Lawyer, 1979—80. Named a Leading Atty. in bankruptcy law, Minn. Bus. Guidebook to Law and Leading Attorneys, 1994—96, Guide to Leading Am. Attorneys, 1998, Minn. Super Lawyer, 2000—03. Mem.: ABA, Am. Bankruptcy Inst., Minn. Women Lawyers, Hennepin Co. Bar Assn., Minn. State Bar Assn., Phi Beta Kappa. Office: Dorsey & Whitney LLP Ste 1500 50 S Sixth St Minneapolis MN 55402-1498 Office Phone: 612-340-8792. Office Fax: 612-340-2868. Business E-Mail: constantine.katherine@dorsey.com.

CONSTANTINE, KEVIN, professional hockey coach; b. International Falls, Minn., Dec. 27, 1958; children: Mathew, Jeffrey, Nicholas. Head coach Rochester USHL, Minn., 1987-88, Kansas City IHL, 1991-92, San Jose Sharks, 1993-94, 95-96; asst. coach Calgary Flames, 1996-97; head coach Pitts. Penguins, 1997—2000; founder, gen. mgr, co-coach Pitts. Forge, 2001—03; head coach NJ Devils, 2002, Everett Silvertips, 2003—07, Houston Aeros, 2007—. Runner-up for Jack Adams award as NHL Coach of Yr., 1993-94, IHL Coach of Yr., 1991-92; career NHL coaching record (all with the Sharks) is 55-78-24; coached USHL championship team in 1987-88, and IHL championship team in 1991-92. Office: Houston Aeros Hockey Club Ste 1100 1221 Lamar St Houston TX 77010*

CONSTANTINE, LARRY L., software designer, design and consultanting company executive; Grad., MIT Sloan Sch. Mgmt. Dir. lab. Usage-Centered Software Engring.; prof. U. Madeira, Funchal, Portugal; faculty mem., prof. info. tech. U. Tech., Sydney; co-founder, prin., dir. R&D, chief scientist Constantine & Lockwood, Ltd., Rowley, Mass., 1993—. Presenter in field. Co-author (with Ed Yourdon): Structured Design, 1979; co-author: (with Lucy Lockwood) Software for Use, 1999 (Jolt award as best book, 1999); author: The Peopleware Papers, 2001, others; contbr. articles to profl. jours. Achievements include patents for human-machine interaction; first to help construct the foundation of modern software engineering theory and practice; research in structured design and analysis. Business E-Mail: lconstantine@alum.mit.edu.

CONSTANTINI, LOUIS O., financial consultant, stockbroker; b. Columbus, Ga., Jan. 12, 1948; s. Louis T. and Edna G. (Spears) C.; m. Mary Ann Jennings, Feb. 9, 1974; children: Rachel J., Emily J. BA, U. Fla., 1972. Cert. fin. mgr. Intelligence officer CIA, Washington and overseas, 1972-76; v.p., fin. cons. Merrill Lynch & Co., El Paso, Tex., 1976-84, fin. cons. Las Cruces, N.Mex., 1984—, v.p., 1988—. Chmn. El Paso Estate Planning Coun., 1982. Decorated Bronze Star, Combat Infantryman Badge, Cross of Gallantry with Gold Star (Republic of Vietnam). Mem. Sigma Phi Epsilon (Disting. Alumnus award 1999, dist. gov. s.w. dist.), Frederick A. Cook Soc. (bd. dirs.). Avocation: Arctic exploration. Home: 5155 Hunters Chase Rd Las Cruces NM 88011-2553 Office: Merrill Lynch & Co 425 S Telshor Blvd Ste 101C Las Cruces NM 88011-8211 Office Phone: 505-521-5110. Personal E-mail: newmex@comcast.net.

CONSTANTINIDES, MINAS SPIROS, otolaryngologist, plastic surgeon; b. Thessaloniki, Greece, Jan. 17, 1961; BA in biochemistry magna cum laude, Brown U.; MD, Coll. Physicians and Surgeons, Columbia U., 1987. Bd. cert. facial plastic surgery and otolaryngology. Intern and resident in gen. surgery Harvard U. Surgical Svc., New England Deaconess Hosp., Boston, 1987—89; resident in otolaryngology- head and neck surgery NYU Sch. Medicine, 1989—93; fellow U. Toronto, 1993—94; dir.

facial plastic and reconstructive surgery Dept. Otolaryngology, NYU Med. Ctr., 1994—; asst. prof. otolaryngology NYU Sch. Medicine, 1994—. Named one of Top Cosmetic Surgeons in US, Town and Country Mag., 1999, Top Drs. NY, Converse and Connolly, 2000, NY Mag., 2001, 2004, Best Beauty Drs., 2003. Fellow: ACS, Am. Acad. Otolaryngology - Head and Neck Surgery, Am. Acad. Facial Plastic and Reconstructive Surgery (mem. nat. task force domestic violence 1999); mem.: AMA, Hellenic Med. Soc. NY, Facial Plastic Surgery Soc. NY. Office: NYU Med Ctr 530 First Ave Ste 7U New York NY 10016 Office Phone: 212-263-5882, 212-263-8490. E-mail: minas.constantinides@med.nyu.edu.

CONSTANTINO, JOHN NICHOLAS, medical educator, researcher; b. St. Louis, Aug. 30, 1962; s. Henry Franklin and Julia Shamia Constantino; m. Michele Ann McDermott. BA, Cornell U., 1984; MD, Wash. U., 1988. Diplomate bd cert. pediat. Am. Bd. Pediat., 1993, gen. psychiatry Am. Bd. Psychiatry and Neurology, 1999, subsplty. child and adolescent psychiatry Am. Bd. Psychiatry and Neurology, 2000. Assoc. prof. psychiatry and pediat. Wash. U. Sch. Medicine, St. Louis, 1996—. Author: A Poor Man's Proof for the Existence of God; contbr. articles to profl. jours. Grantee, Nat. Inst. Child Health and Human Devel. Pub. Health Svc. Rsch., 2003; Cornell U. scholar, 1980. Office: Washington U Sch Medicine 660 South Euclid Ave Campus Box 8134 Saint Louis MO 63110 Office Phone: 314-747-6768. Business E-Mail: constantino@wustl.edu.

CONSTANTINO, KAREN MARIE, elementary school educator; b. Seattle, Oct. 23, 1959; d. Frank Joseph Constantino and Margaret Eileen Ingo. BA in Edn., Ctrl. Wash. U., Ellensburg, 1989. Cert. tchr. Wash., 1989. Various positions Bank of Am., Seattle, 1981—96; 3rd grade tchr. St. Brendan Parish Sch., Bothell, Wash., 1993—. Leadership team St. Brendan Parish Sch., Bothell, Wash., 2001—04. Tchr. Leadership grant, Gates Found., 2000. Mem.: Assn. of Curriculum and Instrn. Home: 11423 23rd Ave SW Seattle WA 98146 Office: St Brendan Parish Sch 10049 NE 195th Bothell WA 98011 Home Phone: 206-439-8348; Office Phone: 425-483-8300. Personal E-mail: kcon@msn.com. Business E-Mail: kmc@saintbrendan.org.

CONSTANTS, DOROTHY MARIE, manufacturing executive; b. Newark, Feb. 3, 1928; d. Henry J. and Marie (McNamee) Trautfetter; m. Alfred C. Constants, Jr., July 14, 1951; children: Alfred C. III, David, Michael, Stephen. Student, Drake Secretarial Sch., 1948, Traphagen Sch. Design, 1949. Exec. sec. Westinghouse Lamp Divsn., Bloomfield, NJ, 1945-51. Pres. Oakland Woman's Club, N.J., 1967-69, Don Bosco HS Mothers Guild, Ramsey, N.J., 1971, Valley PTO, Oakland, N.J., 1972, Friends of Pub. Libr., Oakland, 1982-84, N.J. State Fedn. Women's Clubs, New Brunswick, 1984-86; trustee Oakland Libr. Bd., 1987-89, pres. Regency Oaks Civic Assn., Spring Hill, Fla., 1994-97, 2003-04, dir., sec. United Cmtys. Hernando County, Inc., Spring Hill, Fla., 1999-04; pres. Brooksville Women's Club, Fla., 1992-94. Named Oakland's Woman of Yr., 1975. Mem. Douglas Coll. Alumni Assn. (hon.), Nat. and State Assn Parliamentarians, Gen. Fedn. Women's Clubs (chmn. resolutions com.1986-88). Roman Catholic. Avocations: cruising, reading, creative handiwork. Home: 437 Shore Acres Rd Apt 1B Arnold MD 21012-1908 Personal E-mail: dmconstants@peoplepc.com.

CONSTON, HENRY SIEGISMUND, lawyer; b. Dresden, Germany, Dec. 18, 1928; arrived in U.S., 1947, naturalized, 1952; BSBA, NYU, 1955, JD, 1958, LLM, 1961. Bar: N.Y. 1959. With Calif. Tex. Oil Corp., NYC, 1947—61; sr. ptnr. Walter, Conston, Alexander & Green PC, NYC, 1961—95; sr. counsel, corp. tax, estate law Alston & Bird, NYC, 2001—. Contbr. articles to profl. jours. Bd. dirs. Margaret Tietz Ctr. for Nursing Rehab. With US Army, 1953—54. Office: 90 Park Ave New York NY 10016-1301 Home Phone: 516-883-5922; Office Phone: 212-210-9420.

CONSUL, VINCENT A., lawyer; b. Alameda, Calif., June 7, 1953; BA, Univ. Calif., Berkeley, 1975; JD, Univ. Pacific, 1980. Bar: Calif. 1980, Nev. 1981, US Dist. Ct. (Dist. Nev.) 1981, US Ct. Appeals (9th Cir.) 1984, US Supreme Ct. 2003. Dep. dist. atty. Clark County, Nev., 1980—83; asst. US atty. Dist. of Nev., 1983—85; ptnr. Dickerson, Dickerson, Consul & Pocker, Boies Schiller & Flexner, Las Vegas. Bd. dirs. 8th Judicial Dist. Pro Bono Found., 1997—2005. Recipient Am. Jurisprudence award for family law. Mem.: ABA, Eighth Judicial Dist. Pro Bono Found. (mem, bd. dir. 1997—), State Bar of Calif., State Bar of Nev. (bd. gov. 1997—, pres. 2005—06). Office: Boies Schiller & Flexner Ste 800 300 S 4th St Las Vegas NV 89101 Office Phone: 702-382-7300. Office Fax: 702-382-2755. E-mail: vconsul@bsfllp.com.*

CONTA, RICHARD VINCENT, actuary; b. NYC, Sept. 4, 1946; s. Antonio and Eugenia Theresa (Cavally) C.; m. Joanne Shultis, July 14, 1979 (div. 1990); children: Kerry, Gregory; m. Maureen Fitzgerald, June 8, 1991; 1 child, Tracy. BA, Fordham U., Bronx, NY, 1968. Pension clk. Tchrs. Retirement Sys., City of N.Y., 1968-69; actuarial student U.S. Life Ins. Co., NYC, 1969-74; pension actuary Laiken, Siegel & Co., NYC, 1974-75; enrolled actuary Guardian Life Ins. Co., NYC, 1975-99; ptnr. Fitzgerald & Conta Pension Svcs., Bloomfield, N.J., 1990—. Mem.: Am. Acad. Actuaries, Am. Soc. Pension Actuaries. Roman Catholic. Office: Fitzgerald & Conta Pension Svcs 104 Davis Ave Bloomfield NJ 07003-4140 Office Phone: 973-338-7757. Office Fax: 973-338-7834. Personal E-mail: Fitzconta@aol.com.

CONTADOR VELASCO, ALBERTO, professional cyclist; b. Spain, Dec. 6, 1982; Profl., 2003—; mem. Liberty Seguros-Wurth Team, Team Astana, 2006, Discovery Channel Pro Cycling Team, 2007—. Recipient Best Young Rider award, Tour de France, 2007. Achievements include winning the 2007 Tour de France; winner, Setmana Catalana, 2005; winner, various stages including Stage 8, Tour de Pologne, 2003, Stage 4, Tour de Romandie, 2005, Stage 6, Vuelta a Pais-Vasco, 2005, Stage 5, Tour Down Under, 2005, Stage 8, Tour de Suisse, 2006, Stage 3, Tour de Romandie, 2006. Mailing: Discovery Channel Pro Cycling Team 98 San Jacinto Blvd Ste 430 Austin TX 78701 Office Phone: 512-478-7211. Office Fax: 512-476-0611.

CONTE, JULIE VILLA, nurse, administrator; b. Manila, July 4, 1951; came to U.S., 1970; d. Gregorio Cortes and Lourdes (Villa) Dirige. BSN, Calif. State U., LA, 1974; MBA, U. Phoenix, San Diego, 1993. RN, Calif. Staff nurse Santa Monica (Calif.) Hosp., 1976-78; pub. health nurse Kaiser Found. Hosp., Panorama City, Calif., 1978-85; nursing supr. Nat. Med. Homecare, LA, 1985-86; dir. home health Holy Cross Hosp., Mission Hills, 1986-88; dir. profl. svcs. Care Home Health, San Diego, 1988; dir. nursing Health Prime Home Health Svcs. of San Diego, Inc., 1988-92; dir. home health svcs. Alvarado Home Health Agy., San Diego, 1993-94; expert consulting Home Health and Bus. Cons., San Diego, 1994—; dir. patient care svcs. Unlimited Care, Inc., 1995-96; CEO, pres., adminstr. We Care Home Health Svc., Inc., 1996—. Cons. in field. Mem. Bapt. Nursing Fellowship (pres. Calif. chpt. 1997-2004, nat. pres., pres.-elect 1999-2003), Alpha Delta Chi Republican. Avocations: travel, foreign language, collecting, piano, organ. Office Phone: 619-229-3800. Personal E-mail: julieconte7@aol.com.

CONTE, TONY, chef; b. New Haven; Assoc. Occupl. Sci. Culinary degree, Culinary Inst. Am., Hyde Park, NY. Cook Sole E Luna Ristorante, Westport, Conn.; exec. sous chef Greenwich Country Club, Belmont Country Club, Jean Georges; chef de partie JoJo; exec. chef, co-owner Pesce, Branford, Conn.; exec. chef The Oval Room, Washington. Named one of Washington DC's Rising Stars, StarChefs.com, 2006. Office: The Oval Room 800 Connecticut Ave NW Washington DC 20006 Office Phone: 202-463-8700. Office Fax: 202-785-9863.*

CONTEH, NABIE Y., information systems and computer technology educator; s. Abdul Rahman and Haja Ramatu Conteh; children: Abdul Rahman, Ramatu. BS, Inst. Info. and Comm. Tech., Enschede, Netherlands, 1998; MBA, Ferris State U., Mich., 2000; MS, U. Md., Balt., 2003, PhD, 2004. IT specialist ABN AMRO Bank, Amsterdam, Netherlands, 1998—99; coord. Getronics Trans. Svcs., Netherlands, 1999—2000; rsch. asst. U. Md., Balt., 2001—04, adj. asst. prof., 2005—; asst. prof. Shenandoah U., Winchester, Va., 2005—. Recipient Unix Specialist Tng. award, European Social Funds, 1998; Fellowship, The Netherlands Govt., 1994—95, Rsch. Grants, NSF, 2002—04, Dissertation Fellowship, U. Md., 2004. Home: 9737 Mount Pisgah Rd Apt T13 Silver Spring MD 20903 Office: Shenandoah U 1460 University Dr Winchester VA 22601 Home Phone: 240-417-9258; Office Phone: 540-665-4503. Home Fax: 301-408-7565. Personal E-mail: nconteh1@umbc.edu. Business E-Mail: nconteh@su.edu.

CONTI, CHARLES RICHARD, medicine and cardiology educator; b. Bethlehem, Pa., Oct. 26, 1934; s. Charles Richard and Olga Louise Conti; m. Ruth Ellen Wursta, Aug. 24, 1957; children: Jill, Jamie, Jennifer, Richard III. AB magna cum laude, Lehigh U., 1956; MD, Johns Hopkins U., 1960. Diplomate Am. Bd. Internal Medicine, Am. Bd. Cardiovasc. Disease. Intern, resident Johns Hopkins, chief resident, cardiology fellow, dir. cardiac catheterization lab., 1968-74; prof. medicine and cardiology, eminent scholar U. Fla. at Shands, Gainesville, 1974—. Author: Coronary Artery Spasm, 1981, Introduction to Clinical Cardiology, 1991; editor-in-chief Clin. Cardiology, 1988—; contbr. numerous articles to med. jours. Capt. M.C., U.S. Army, 1962-64. Master Am. Coll. Cardiology (trustee, v.p., editor chmn. pres. 1989-90, Gifted Tchr. award Fla. chpt. 1999); fellow Coll. Physicians South Africa (hon.); mem. Johns Hopkins Soc. Scholars, numerous others. Republican. Roman Catholic. Avocations: golf, skiing, running. Home: 7900 SW 43d Dr Gainesville FL 32608 Office: U Fla Health Sci Ctr 1600 SW Archer Rd PO BOX 100277 Gainesville FL 32610-0277 Fax: 352-374-6831. E-mail: conticr@medicine.ufl.edu.*

CONTI, INDALICIO PALOMAR, finance educator; b. Dinas, Philippines, Dec. 22, 1953; s. Ismael Hernandez Conti and Irenea Demit Palomar. BS in Mgmt., Philippine Coll. of Commerce, Manila, 1976, BSc in Acctg., 1977; LLB, U. of the East, Manila, 1985; MBA, Polytechnic U. of Philippines. CPA; cert. cons. BCS Sys. & Technologies Inc., 2006. Jr. acct. Gen. Textile Mills, Inc., Libis, Quezon City, Philippines, 1978; dir., acct. Supreme Traders, Inc., Manila, 1978-79; auditor PUP Credit Union, Manila, 1978-83; legal rschr. Polytechnic U. Philippines, Manila, 1992; prof. Coll. Accountancy, Polytechnic U. Philippines, Manila, 1993—; mng. ptnr. Conti & Assoc. CPA's, Quezon City, Philippines. Fin. cons., bd. trustees Fieldridge Learning Ctr., Brgy. San Felipe, Batangas, 1999; tax cons., legal rschr. V.C. Ramirez Law Office, Quezon City, 1997—; external auditor N.F.K. Constrn., Merto Manila, Vincent Mark Security Agy., Quezon City, 1998—, Psychol. Ext. Evaluation Rsch. Svcs., Quezon City, 1999—; fraud auditor Kendeigh Fgn. Exch. Internat. Corp., 2002; assoc. prof. CBIBE Philippine Women's U., Manila, 1999; mem. faculty Colegio San Lorenzo Project 6, Quezon City, 2000—; CPA, tax practitioner, chief legal rschr., Fabella & Assocs. Law Office, Quezon City, 2002; profl. lectr., Trinity Grad. Sch. (Cmty. Outreach), 2000; prof. Polytechnic U. Philippines Coll. Accountancy, Manila, 2003—. Author: (textbooks) Income Taxation Law, 1984, Transfer and Business Taxes, 1986, Fundamentals of Transfer and Business Taxes, 1987, Fundamentals of Income Tax, 1988, Fundamentals of Philippine Income Taxation, 2007. Mem. Philippine Inst. CPA's. Roman Catholic. Avocations: martial arts, dance, playing chess, bowling, reading. Personal E-mail: ipc-cpa@yahoo.com.

CONTI, JAMES JOSEPH, retired chemical engineer, educator; b. Coraopolis, Pa., Nov. 2, 1930; s. James Joseph and Mary (Smrekar) Conti; m. Concetta Razziano, May 13, 1961; children: Lori Ann, James Robert. BChem Engring. summa cum laude, Poly. Inst. Bklyn., 1954, MChem Engring., 1956, D Chem. Engring., 1959. Sr. engr. Bettis atomic power divsn. Westinghouse Electric Corp., 1958—59; mem. faculty Polytech. U. N.Y., 1959—90, prof. chem. engring., 1965—90, chmn. dept., 1964—70, provost, 1970—78, v.p. ednl. devel., 1978—90; pres. Webb Inst. Naval Architecture, Glen Cove, NY, 1990—99, ret., 1999. Cons. in field. Contbr. articles to profl. jours.; patentee in field. Trustee Webb Inst. Naval Architecture, 1974—99. Fellow: AAAS, Am. Inst. Chemists; mem.: AIChE, Am. Soc. Engring. Edn., Omega Chi Epsilon, Phi Lambda Upsilon, Tau Beta Pi, Sigma Xi. Home: 26 Miami Rd Bethpage NY 11714-2229

CONTI, JOY FLOWERS, judge; b. Kane, Pa., Dec. 7, 1948; d. Bernard A. Flowers and Elizabeth (Tingley) Rodgers; m. Anthony T. Conti, Jan. 16, 1971; children: Andrew, Michael, Gregory. BA, Duquesne U., 1970, JD summa cum laude, 1973. Bar: Pa. 1973, U.S. Dist. Ct. (we. dist.) Pa. 1973, U.S. Ct. Appeals (3d cir.) 1976, U.S. Supreme Ct. 1993. Law clk. Supreme Ct. Pa., Monessen, 1973-74; assoc. Kirkpatrick & Lockhart, Pitts., 1974-76, 82-83, ptnr., 1983-96; shareholder Buchanan, Ingersoll, P.C., Pitts., 1996—2002; dist. judge U.S. Dist. Ct.(we. dist.) Pa., Pitts., 2002—. Prof. law Duquesne U., Pitts., 1976-82; hearing examiner Pa. Dept. State, Bur. Profl. Occupation and Affairs, 1978-82; chairperson search com. for judge U.S. Bankruptcy Ct. (we. dist.) Pa., 1987, 95; active Pa. Futures Commn. on Justice in 21st Century, 1995-97. Contbr. articles to profl. jours. Mem. disciplinary hearing com. Supreme Ct. Pa., 1982-88; v.p. Com. for Justice Edn., Pitts., 1983-84; mem. Leadership Pitts., 1987-88. Named one of Ten Outstanding Young Women in Am., 1981. Fellow Am. Bar Found. (Pa. state chair 1991-97); mem. ABA (ho. of dels. 1980-86, 91-97), Am. Law Inst., Am. Coll. Bankruptcy, Pa. Bar Assn. (gov. 1993-95, ho. of dels. 1978—, corp. banking and bus. law sect. coun. 1983-89, treas. 1991-93, v.p. 1993-95, chair-elect 1995-97, chmn. 1997-99, chmn. commn. comml. law 1990-93, co-chair 1995-2002, chair civil rights and responsibilities com. 1986-89, Achievement award 1982, 87, 99, Anne X. Alpern award 1995), Nat. Conf. Bar Pres. (exec. coun. 1993-96), Am. Inns Ct. (Pitts. chpt., counselor 2004—), Nat. Assn. Women Judges, Fed. Judges Assn., Allegheny County Bar Assn. (adminstrv. v.p. 1984-86, 90, chairperson corp. banking and bus. law sect. 1987-89, treas. 1988-90, gov. 1991, pres.-elect 1992, pres. 1993), Internat. Women's Insolvency and Restructuring Confedn. (chair Tri-State Network 1996), Pa. Bar Inst. (dir. 1991-97), Duquesne Club. Roman Catholic. Office: US Dist Judge 5250 US Courthouse and Post Office 700 Grant St Pittsburgh PA 15219 Office Phone: 412-208-7330.

CONTI, LOUIS THOMAS MOORE, lawyer; b. Phila., Aug. 31, 1949; s. Alexander and Yolanda (DiLorenzo) Conti; m. Christina M.S. Moore, May 1, 1982; children: Charles Alexander, Whitney Caroline. BS, LaSalle Coll., 1971; MBA, Drexel U., Phila., 1972; JD, Creighton U., Omaha, 1975; LLM, Temple U., Phila., 1981. Bar: Pa. 1975, US Claims Ct. 1975, US Tax Ct. 1975, US Dist. Ct. (ea. dist.) Pa. 1978, US Ct. Appeals (3d cir.) 1979, US Supreme Ct. 1981, Fla. 1982, US Dist. Ct. (mid. dist.) Fla. 1988. Tax atty. Office Chief Counsel IRS, Washington and Phila., 1975-81; tax mgr. Touche Ross & Co., Phila., 1981-84; assoc. Saul, Ewing, Remick & Saul, Phila., 1984-87; shareholder Swann & Haddock, P.A., Orlando, Fla., 1987-89; ptnr., chmn. corp. tax and securities dept. Holland & Knight, Orlando, 1989—. Mem. fin. com. S.E. Pa. chpt. ARC, Phila., 1984—87; advisor Vol. Lawyers for Arts, Phila., 1984—87; bd. dirs. Fla. Hosp. Found., Ctrl. Fla. Planned Giving Coun., 1989—97, Cmty. Found. Ctrl. Fla. Inc., World Trade Ctr., Orlando, 1992—95; mem. internat. bus. adv. bd. Metro Orlando; grad. Leadership Orlando, 1994, Leadership Fla., 1996; chair recruiting com. East Ctrl. Region of Leadership Fla., 1997; bd. dirs. Orlando Performing Arts and Edn. Ctr., Inc., 1998—2001. Mem.: ABA (chmn. task force on drafting prototype ltd. liability co. operating ag 1998—, chmn. Fla. Bar drafting com. 1999, tax and bus. law sect.), Orange County Bar Assn. (chmn. tax sect. 1990—91), Fla. Bar Assn. (chmn. drafting com. ltd. liability co. statutes 1998—, bus. law sect. 1999—2001, chair tax sect. 2001—02, tax and bus. law sect., chair corps. and securities com.), Seminole County C. of C. (bd. dirs. 1994—97). Republican. Avocation: travel, skiing, golf, tennis, theatre. Home: 603 Genius Drive Winter Park FL 32779 Office: Holland & Knight PO Box 1526 Orlando FL 32802-1526 Office Phone: 407-244-5118. Business E-Mail: louis.conti@hklaw.com.

CONTI, PAUL LOUIS, management consulting company executive; b. Utica, NY, Sept. 3, 1945; s. Louis Joseph and Dorothy Mae (Kellogg) C.; m. Lee Ann Scheuerman, Apr. 18, 1970; children: Meghan Elizabeth, Dawn Michelle. BA, So. Ill. U., 1972, MBA, 1974. Sr. cons. Lester B. Knight & Assocs., Chgo., 1974-76; dir. pers. Applied Info. Devel., Oak Brook, Ill., 1976-80; v.p. Comsi, Inc., Oak Brook, 1980-82; CEO Prestige Mgmt. Sys., Inc., Glen Ellyn, Ill., 1982-86; v.p. human resources Rand McNally & Co., Skokie, Ill., 1986-87; assoc. dir. Ernst & Young (formerly Ernst & Whinney), Chgo., 1987-93; regional v.p. Alexandria Alexander, Inc., Chgo., 1993-97; COO, sr. v.p. AON Corp., 1997-99; sr. v.p. Apropos Tech., Inc., Oak Brook, Ill., 1999—; pres., chief assets officer Vericlaim, Inc., Chgo., 1999—. Bd. dirs. So. Ill. U. Coll. Bus. Adminstrn. Lobbyist Invest in the Future, Invest in Edn., State of Ill., 1988; bd. dirs., exec. com. So. Ill. U.-Carbondale Found., 1991—, pres., 1994-97. Named to So. Ill. U. COBA Hall of Fame, 1988; named Cmty. Ambassador So. Ill. U., 1980. Mem. Soc. Human Resource Profls., Soc. Human Resources Mgmt., Human Resources Mgmt. Assn. of Chgo., Employment Mgmt. Assn., Pontikes Ctr. for Mgmt. Info. (bd. dirs. 1989—), So. Ill. U. Alumni Assn. (pres. 1986-88, bd. dirs. 1986—, exec. com. 1991—), Ideal Club (pres. 1986-88), McCullom Lake Club. Republican. Roman Catholic. Avocations: hunting waterfowl and upland game, golf, various participative sports, coaching women's fast pitch softball. Home: 635 S Park Blvd Glen Ellyn IL 60137-6977 Office Phone: 630-245-7005. Business E-Mail: pconti@vericlaiminc.com. E-mail: contip@msn.com.

CONTIGUGLIA, JOSEPH JUSTIN, preventive medicine physician, internist; b. NYC, Jan. 8, 1948; s. Joseph and Doris (Justin) C.; m. Sylvie Blaise, Nov. 23, 1982; children: Dorothy Justine, Joseph Henry, Catherine Emily. AB in Sociology, Columbia Coll., NYC, 1969; MD, Sienna U., Italy, 1975; MPH and Tropical Medicine, Tulane U., 1981; MBA, St. Mary's U., San Antonio, 1990. Diplomate Am. Bd. Preventive Medicine, Am. Bd. Med. Mgmt. Resident internal medicine Cabrini Med. Ctr., NYC, 1975-78; commd. USAF, advanced through grades to col.; chief hyperbaric medicine USAF Clinic, Kadena AFB, Okinawa, Japan, 1978-80; resident aerospace medicine USAF Sch. Aerospace Medicine, Brooks AFB, San Antonio, 1980-82; chief aeromed. svcs. USAF Hosp., Seymour Johnson AFB, Goldsboro, N.C., 1982-85; chief occupational medicine and environ. health Royal Australian Air Force, Canberra, Australia, 1985-87; chief aerospace medicine div. Air Tng. Command, Randolph AFB, San Antonio, 1987-90; hosp. comdr. USAF Hosp., Reese AFB, Lubbock, Tex., 1990-92; dep. comdr. 5th med. group comdr. 5th aerospace medicine squadron, Minot AFB, N.D., 1992-96; comdr. 5th Air Transportable Hosp.; clin. assoc. prof. preventive medicine and rural health U. N.D. Sch. Medicine, 1992—; dir. med. ops. USAF-Europe, 1996—. Editor: Flight Surgeons Check List, 1982. Fellow Royal Soc. Medicine, Am. Coll. Preventive Medicine, Aerospace Med. Assn. (chmn. mil. aviation safety subcom., chmn. AIDS subcom.); mem. ACP, Am. Col. Physician Execs., Am. Soc. Tropical Medicine and Hygiene, Royal Aero. Soc., Aviation Med. Soc. Australia and New Zealand. Republican. Roman Catholic. Avocations: flying, shooting, riding, wine and beer making, amateur radio.

CONTINETTI, ROBERT E., chemistry professor; Prof. dept. chemistry and biochemistry U. Calif. San Diego, La Jolla, 1992—. Kurt Schuler scholar, chmn. dept. Recipient Packard Found. fellow, 1994. Fellow: Am. Phys. Soc. Office: U Calif San Diego Dept Chem & Biochem MC-0340 9500 Gilman Dr La Jolla CA 92093-0340 Office Phone: 858-534-5559. E-mail: rcontinetti@ucsd.edu.

CONTRACTOR, FAROK, business and management educator; b. Bombay, Dec. 24, 1946; arrived in US, 1967; s. Jamshed Phirozshaw and Hilla C. Contractor; children: Cyrus, Sahm, Eric. BSME, U. Bombay, 1967; MS in Indsl. Engring., U. Mich., 1968; MBA, U. Pa., 1977, PhD in Managerial Sci. and Applied Econs., 1980. Staff indsl. engr. Max Factor, Inc., LA, 1969; rsch. fellow U. Mich., Ann Arbor, 1969-70; exec. officer, asst. to mng. dir. TATA Group subs. TATA Adminstrv. Svcs., India, 1970-74; asst. instr. bus. and mgmt. Wharton Sch. Bus., U. Pa., Phila., 1975-77, instr., 1977-80; chmn. internat. bus. dept. Grad. Sch. Mgmt., Rutgers U., Newark and Piscataway, NJ, 1986-88, 90-93, assoc. prof., 1980-90, prof. internat. bus., 1991—. Lectr. Wharton Sch. Bus., U. Pa., 1985-86; vis. scholar UN Ctr. on Transnat. Corps., N.Y., fall 1988; mem. Internat. Bus. Inst., Rutgers U., 1986—, rsch. dir. CIBER, 1997-99, com. mem., 1980-90; NSF reviewer, 1980, 84, 94; organizer, co-chmn. joint conf. on coop. ventures in internat. bus. Rutgers U. and Wharton Sch. Bus., U. Pa., 1986, co-chmn. conf. on coop. strategies and alliances, Lausanne, Switzerland, 2001; licensing and tech. transfer agreements cons.; Unilever Group vis. fellow, vis. prof. Indian Inst. Fgn. Trade, New Delhi, spring 1994; vis. prof. Copenhagen Bus. Sch., 1995, Lubin Sch. Pace U., 1997, Fletcher Sch. Law and Diplomacy, Tufts U., 2000; presenter in field. Author: International Technology Licensing: Compensation, Costs and Negotiation, 1981, Licensing In International Strategy: A Guide for Planning and Negotiation, 1985, Government Policies And Foreign Direct Investment, 1991, Cooperative Strategies in International Business, 1988, Economic Transformation in Emerging Countries: The Role of Investment, Trade and Finance, 1998, the Valuation of Intangible Assets in Global Operations, 2001, Cooperative Strategies and Alliances, 2003, others; co-author: Introduction to International Business, 1986. Grantee, The German Marshall Fund of U.S., 1986, Carnegie Bosch Found., 1996—98; Esmee Fairbairn fellow, U. Reading, Eng., 1982, Fulbright fellow, 1991—92. Fellow Acad. Internat. Bus. (bd. dirs., sec.-treas. 1992-94); mem. Licensing Execs. Soc., Acad. Mgmt. (exec. bd. 1997—2002, pre-conf. workshop chair San Diego meeting 1998, program chmn. Chgo. meeting 1999, pres. internat. mgmt. divsn. 2000—), European Internat. Bus. Assn., Zoroastrian Assn. Greater N.Y., Internat. Trade and Fin. Assn. (bd. dirs. 1995-97). Avocations: antique restoration, skiing, trekking, canoeing, interior design. Office: Rutgers Univ Sch Mgmt 81 New St Newark NJ 07102 Office Phone: 973-353-8348.

CONTRENI, JOHN JOSEPH, JR., humanities educator; b. Savannah, Ga., Aug. 31, 1944; s. John Joseph Sr. and Elfriede Johanna (Hille) C.; m. Margarita Lee Partridge, July 3, 1986; children: Judith, Rachel, Daniel, Maureen, Jennifer Rogers, Paul Rogers. BA, St. Vincent Coll., 1966, HHD (hon.), 1996; PhD, Mich. State U., 1971. From asst. prof. to prof. history Purdue U., West Lafayette, Ind., 1971—, head dept. history, 1985-97, asst. dean Sch. Humanities, Social Sci. and Edn., 1981-85, interim head dept. fgn. langs. and lits., 1983—85, interim dean, Grad. Sch., 2002—04, dean, Grad. Sch., 2004—06, dean, Coll. Liberal Arts, 2006—. Pres. Midwest Medieval Conf., 1980-81. Author: The Cathedral School of Laon from 850 to 930: Its Manuscripts and Masters, 1978, (John Nicholas Brown prize 1982), Codex Laudunensis 468: A Ninth-Century Guide to Virgil, Sedulius, and the Liberal Arts, 1984; co-author: Glossae Divinae Historiae: The Biblical Glosses of John Scottus Eriugena, 1997; translator: Education and Culture in the Barbarian West, Sixth Through Eighth Centuries (Pierre Riché), 1976, Carolingian Learning, Masters, and Manuscripts, 1992; co-editor: Religion, Culture, and Society in the Early Middle Ages: Studies in Honor of Richard E. Sullivan, 1987, French Historical Studies, 1991-2000, Word, Image, Number: Communication in the Middle Ages, 2002; mem. editl. bd. Internat. History Rev., 2001-03; contbr. articles to profl. jours. and chpts. to books. Pres., bd. trustees Brookston-Prairie Twp. Pub. Libr., 1995-01. Grantee Am. Philos. Soc., 1973, 76, 82, 86, NEH, 1973, 86, Am. Coun. Learned Socs., 1975, 77-79, 83, 89, Purdue U., 1973, 75-76, 81, 83, 89, 99. Mem. Soc. for Promotion Eriugenian Studies, Medieval Acad. of Am. (councillor 1987-90, grantee 1973, fellow, 2003), Grad. Record Exam. Bd., Test English as a Fgn. Lang. Bd., Phi Beta Kappa. Home: 504 W 5th St Brookston IN 47923-8100 Office: Coll Liberal Arts Beering Hall 100 N Univ St West Lafayette IN 47907-2098 E-mail: contreni@purdue.edu.

CONTRERAS, FRANK R., musician; s. Francisco Javier Contreras and Arquelina Rodríquez Elorriaga. MusB, Millikin U., 1965; MusM, E. Carolina U., 1966; D in Musical Arts (fellow 1970-73), W.Va. U., 1977. Instr. piano Millikin U., Decatur, Ill., 1966—67, Alderson Broaddus Coll., Phillippi, W.Va., 1973—76, U. Ala., Huntsville, 1977—94, Oakwood Coll., Huntsville, 2000—. Tchr. Colors Fine Arts Ctr. Musician (pianist): Huntsville Symphony, Pitts. Symphony, E. Carolina U. Symphony, W.Va. Symphony, W. N.Mex U. Symphony. Organist 1st Presbyn. Ch., Huntsville, 1988—. Temple B'Nai Shalom, Huntsville, 1994—. With US Army, 1968—69, Vietnam. Recipient Anne M. Gannett award, Nat. Fed. Music Clubs, 1970. Mem.: Am. Guild Organists, Am. Fedn. Musicians, Nat. Guild Piano Tchrs. (adjudicator). Democrat. Episcopalian. Avocations: history, literature, travel. Home: 4312 Chalet Cir Huntsville AL 35810 Office: 1st Presbyn Ch 307 Gates Ave Huntsville AL 35801

CONTRERAS-SWEET, MARIA, bank executive; b. Guadaljara, Mex., Dec. 24, 1955; came to U.S., 1960; d. Rafael Quintero and Maria Guadalupe (Torres) Contreras; m. Raphael Raymond Sweet, Feb. 7, 1981; children— Rafael, Francesca, Antonio. A.S. in Sec. Legal, Mt. San Antonio Coll., 1975; B.S. in Polit. Sci., Calif. State U.-Los Angeles, 1977. Field rep. Calif. State Speaker State Legis., Los Angeles, 1974-75; adminstrv. asst. to Senator Joseph Montoya, Calif. State Senate, Los Angeles, 1975-79; dist. mgr. U.S. Census Bur., US Dept. Commerce, Los Angeles, 1979-80; former dir. pub. affairs 7-Up Bottling Co., Westinghouse Beverage Group, Los Angeles, former sec., Dept. Bus., Transport. & Housing Agy, State of Calif., mng. ptnr, co-founder, FORTIUS Holdings, LLC, chmn., Promerica Bank, 2006-; Bd. Mex.-Am. Opportunity Found., Los Angeles, 1982— , Rossi Youth Found., Los Angeles, 1978—; fund com. mem. E. Los Angeles Little Sisters, 1983; adv. council Hispanic Women's Council, Los Angeles, 1982—; active Industry Environ. Council, Sacramento, Recipient Mother of Yr. award La Clinica Famillar del Barrio, Los Angeles, 1983; Humanitarian award Rossi Youth Found., 1983; Woman of Yr. award Mex.-Am. Opportunity Found., 1983. Mem. Internat. Assn. Bus. Communicators, Calif./Nev. Soft Drink Assn., RecyCal (fin. chair.). Democrat. Roman Catholic. Office: FORTIUS Holdings LLC 13191 Crossroads Pkwy N Ste 565 City Of Industry CA 91746

CONVERSE, PHILIP ERNEST, retired social sciences educator; b. Concord, NH, Nov. 17, 1928; s. Ernest Luther and Evelyn (Eaton) C.; m. Jean Gilmore McDonnell, Aug. 25, 1951; children: Peter Everett, Timothy McDonnell. BA, Denison U., 1949, DHL (hon.), 1974; MA, State U. Iowa, 1950; cert., U. Paris, 1954; MA, U. Mich., 1956, PhD, 1958; DHL (hon.), U. Chgo., 1979; LLD (hon.), Harvard U., 2006; DSc (hon.), U. Mich., 2007. Asst. prof. sociology U. Mich., 1960-65, prof. sociology and polit. sci., 1965-89, Robert C. Angell Disting. prof., 1975-89; ret., 1989. Asst. study dir. Inst. Social Rsch. U. Mich., 1956-58, study dir., 1958-65, program dir., 1965-82, dir. Ctr. for Polit. Studies, 1982-86, dir. Inst. Social Rsch., 1986-89; dir. Ctr. Advanced Study in Behavioral Scis., 1989-94; trustee Ctr. Advanced Study in Behavioral Scis., 1980-86, 94-2000, Russell Sage Found., 1982-92. Co-author: The American Voter, 1960, Elections and the Political Order, 1966, The Human Meaning of Social Change, 1972, The Quality of American Life, 1976, Political Representation in France, 1986; contbr. articles to profl. jours. Served with U.S. Army, 1950-52. Recipient Disting. Faculty Achievement award U. Mich., 1973; Fulbright fellow, 1959-60; NSF fellow, 1967-68; Guggenheim fellow, 1975-76; Ctr. Advanced Study in Behavioral Scis. fellow, 1979-80 Mem. AAAS, Am. Sociol. Assn., Am. Polit. Sci. Assn. (pres. 1983-84), Internat. Soc. Polit. Psychology (pres. 1980-81), Nat. Acad. Scis., Am. Acad. Arts and Scis., Am. Philos. Soc. Home: 9 Haverhill Ct Ann Arbor MI 48105-1406 Personal E-mail: pconvers@umich.edu.

CONVERSE, SANDRA, city finance director, financial planner; b. Galion, Ohio, July 23, 1949; d. Mervin E. Harper and Phyllis R. Bowden (dec.); m. Robert W. Marsh, June 19, 2001; children: Kimberly Spencer, Kelly Converse. Payroll clk. Neighborhood Youth Corps., Mansfield, Ohio, 1977-78; asst. fin. dir. Mansfield City, 1978-93, fin. dir., 1993—. Charter commn. mem. City of Mansfield, 1988. Mem. NAFE, La. Edn. Assn., Govt. Fin. Officers Assn. U.S. and Can., Mcpl. Treas. Assn. U.S. and Can., Nat. Assn. Tax Preparers, Ohio Govt. Fin. Officers Assn., Mcpl. Fin. Officers Assn. Ohio (at-large bd. mem.). Democrat. Pentecostal. Avocations: reading, learning, sewing, painting. Office: City of Mansfield 30 N Diamond St Mansfield OH 44902-1738 Home: 155 W Prospect St Mansfield OH 44907-1305 Office Phone: 419-755-9775. E-mail: sconverse@CI.mansfield.oh.us.

CONVEY, BOBBY (ROBERT FRANCIS CONVEY), professional soccer player; b. Phila., May 27, 1983; Midfielder DC United, 2000—04, Reading FC, England, 2004—. 39 caps, 1 goal U.S. Nat. Soccer team, 2000—; mem. U.S. World Cup team, 2006. Mailing: US Soccer Fedn 1801 S Prairie Ave Chicago IL 60616

CONVEY, JOHN J., academic administrator; Provost Cath. U. Am., Washington. Author: Catholic Schools Make a Difference: Twenty-Five Years of Research, 1992, Catholic Schools Still Make a Difference: Ten Years of Research, 1991-2000, 2002; co-author: Catholic Schools and Society, 1991, Strategic Planning for Catholic Schools: A Diocesan Model of Consultation, 1996, Benchmarks of Excellence: Effective Boards of Catholic Education, 1997, Assessment of Catholic Religious Education Weaving Christ's Seamless Garment, 1999, Catholic Schools at the Crossroads: Survival and Transformation, 2000; co-editor: Catholic Character of Catholic Schools, 2000. Office: Provost 103 McMahon Hall The Cath Univ Am Washington DC 20064*

CONWAY, CONNIE ANNE See HELLYER, CONSTANCE

CONWAY, CRAIG A., retired computer company executive; b. Ft. Wayne, Ind., Oct. 17, 1954; m. Tina Conway; 2 children. BS in Math. & Computer Sci., SUNY, Brockport, 1976. Applications cons. Tymeshare, 1976—79; with Atari, 1979—83; dir. worldwide distbn. Digital Research, 1983—85; exec. v.p. mktg., sales & ops. Oracle Corp., 1985—93; pres., CEO TGV Software, Inc., 1993—96, OneTouch Systems., 1996—99, PeopleSoft Inc., Pleasanton, Calif., 1999, 1999—2004. Bd. dirs. Aspect Telecomm. Corp., SalesLogix Corp., Salesforce.com Inc., 2005-. Recipient Cap Gemini Ernst & Young Leadership award for Global Integration, 2002. Address: Salesforce.com Inc One Market Ste 300 San Francisco CA 94105

CONWAY, DAVID ANTONY, marketing professional; b. NYC, Dec. 31, 1941; s. David A. and Elizabeth (Reidy) C.; m. Rosanne Kearney, July 30, 1966; children: Jennifer Stanton, Caroline Sloane. BS in Econs., Fordham Coll., 1963, MS in Econs., 1965. With Allied Chem. Corp., NYC, 1967-68, CBS, Inc., NYC, 1968-75, Goldman Sachs & Co., NYC, 1975-76; v.p. adminstrn. Keene Corp., NYC, 1976-86; v.p. adminstrn., bd. dirs. KDI Corp., Cin., 1986-93; pres. Modern Edn. Svcs., NYC, 1994-97; pres., CEO WaterChef, Inc., Glen Head, NY, 1998—, also chmn. bd. dirs. 1st lt. U.S. Army, 1965-67. Mem. Manhasset Bay Yacht Club (Port Washington, N.Y.). Republican. Roman Catholic. Office: WaterChef Inc 1007 Glen Cove Ave Glen Head NY 11545-1589 Personal E-mail: conway@waterchef.net.

CONWAY, DWIGHT COLBUR, retired chemistry professor; b. Long Beach, Calif., Nov. 14, 1930; s. Dee A. and Ruth (Mills) Conway; m. Diane Faye Coulter, Aug. 25, 1962; children: Kathleen Conway Jurell, Karyn Conway Hasselbrinck, Michael Dwight, Patrick Hugh. BS, U. Calif., Berkeley, 1952; MS, U. Chgo., 1953, PhD, 1956. Postdoctoral student Purdue U., West Lafayette, Ind., 1956-57, asst. prof., 1957-63; assoc. prof. chemistry Tex. A.&M. U., College Station, 1963-67, prof., 1967—2006; ret., 2006. Recipient Excellence in Tchg. award, Std. Oil Co. of Ind., 1969, Disting. Achievement award, Assn. of Former Students, 2003; fellow, U.S. Rubber Co., 1953—54; DuPont tchg. fellow, 1954—55. Mem. Am. Chem. Soc. (chmn. local chpt.), Am. Phys. Soc., Am. Soc. Mass Spectrometry, Phi Beta Kappa, Sigma Xi (pres. local chpt.), Alpha Chi Sigma. Home: 1138 Brunes Blvd Brownsburg IN 46112 E-mail: conway@mail.chem.tamu.edu.

CONWAY, E. VIRGIL, financial consultant, lawyer; b. Southhampton, NY, Aug. 2, 1929; m. Elaine Wingate, June 28, 1969; children: Allison, Sarah, William, John BA Philosophy and Religion magna cum laude, Colgate U., 1951; LLB cum laude, Yale U., 1956; LLD (hon.), Pace U., 1990; LHD (hon.), SUNY, Stony Brook, 1998; LLD (hon.), Colgate U., 2002. Bar: N.Y. 1956. Assoc. Debevoise & Plimpton, NYC, 1956—64; supt. 1st dept. Banks of State N.Y., 1964—67; exec. v.p. Manhattan Savs. Bank, NYC, 1967—68; pres., chmn. The Seamen's Bank for Savs., 1969—88; chmn. Rittenhouse Advisors LLC, 2001—. Bd. dirs. Union Pacific Corp., chmn. exec. compensation com., mem. exec. com. 1978-2002; bd. dirs. J.P. Stevens & Co., Inc., 1974-88; trustee, mem. exec. com., chmn. audit com. mut. funds managed by Phoenix Funds, 1990-; dir., mem. audit com. of mut. funds managed by Phoenix Duff & Phelps Funds, 1990-; trustee, mem. exec. com., chmn. exec. devel. & comp. Atlantic Mut. Ins. Co., 1974-2002; trustee, mem. exec., chmn. exec. pers. and pension coms. Consol. Edison Co. N.Y., 1970-2002; trustee, chmn. compensation com., mem. exec. com. Urstadt Biddle Property Co., 1989—; adv. dir. Blackrock BFM, Freddie Mac Securities Mortgage Fund, 1968-2001; N.Y. rep. Conf. of State Bank Suprs., 1970-77, mem. adv. coun., 1973-74, mem. adv. com. to N.Y. State Supt. Banks, 1967-70; chmn. Fin. Acct. Stds. Adv. Coun., 1992-1995; adv. dir. Fund Directions; dir. chmn. comp. com. Trism, Inc., 1995-2001; dir., mem. exec. com., audit com., chmn. stock option com. Accuhealth, Inc., 1995-2002; sec. N.Y. State Banking Bd., 1964-67; vice chmn., bd. dirs. Seaman's Corp., 1986-89 Editor: Yale Law Jour Mem. Met. Transp. Authority, chmn. audit and real estate coms., mem. Metro North L.I. R.R. and N.Y.C. Transit coms., 1992-95; chmn. Met. Transp. Authority, L.I. R.R., Metro North, Transit Authority of City of N.Y., Triborough Bridge and Tunnel Authority, 1995-2001; mem. N.Y. State Thruway Authority, chmn. audit and fin. com.; chmn. Temporary State Commn. on Water Supply Needs of Southeastern N.Y., 1970-75; mem. Audit Com. N.Y.C., 1981-1996, chmn., 1990-1996, Mayor's Mgmt. Adv. Bd., N.Y.C., 1975-77; mem., chmn. meml. design com. N.Y.C. Korean Vets. Meml. Commn.; del. Rep. State Conv. N.Y., 1962, 66; pres. N.Y. Young Rep. Club, 1962-63; mem. adv. bd. NYU Real Estate Inst.; bd. dirs. Realty Found. N.Y.; bd. dirs., chmn. audit, fin., exec. coms. Josiah Macy, Jr. Found.; trustee, former vice chmn., mem. exec. com. Citizens Budget Commn.; life trustee N.Y.C. Police Found., Pace U., N.Y.C., Colgate U.; trustee N.Y. coun. Boy Scouts Am.; hon. life trustee South St. Seaport Mus.; bd. govs., pres. Fed. Hall Meml. Assocs., Inc., 1981-84; bd. dirs., vice chmn, treas., mem. audit and fin., compensation, project planning and pub. policy com., N.Y.C. Partnership, Inc., 1980-91, hon. ptnr., 1991—; elder Reformed Ch. of Bronxville Recipient Humanitarian award Jewish Hosp. and Rsch. Ctr., Denver, 1977, Montauk Playhouse Cmty. Ctr., 2005, Good Scout award Greater N.Y. couns. Boy Scouts Am., 1980, Eagle Scout award, 1988, Silver Beaver award, 1989, Spl. Recognition award NAACP, 1980, Disting. Svc. to Higher Edn. medal Brandeis U., 1976, Urban Leadership award NYU, 1981, Hundred Yr. Assn. Gold Medal award, 1986, Alexander Hamilton award Bowling Green Assn., Disting. Svc. award Bklyn. Bur. Cmty. Svc., 1995, Family of Yr. award Family Svc. Westchester, Inc., 1996, Norman Vincent Peale award, Insts. Religion and Health, 1998, Ellis Island medal of honor, Nat. Ethnic Coalition, 1998; Gov.'s Parks and Preservation award, 1999, March of Dimes Svc. to Humanity award, 2000, Urban Visionaries award, Cooper Union, 2002, Hudson Valley Hero's award, Historic Hudson Valley, 1998; named Man of Yr. Realty Found. N.Y., 1978 Mem. ABA, N.Y. State Bar Assn., Assn. of Bar of City of N.Y., Nat. Assn. Mut. Savs. Banks (past dir.), Savs. Banks Assn. N.Y. State (pres. 1978-79, past dir. and chmn. legis.), N.Y. C. of C. and Industry (bd. dirs., exec. com., sec.-treas. 1974-91, chmn. mission rev. com. 1985), Real Estate Bd. N.Y. (bd. govs. 1976-79), Econ. Club N.Y., Knights of St. Patrick (bd. dirs., co-chmn.), Union League Club, Links Club, Siwanoy Country Club, Hillsboro Club, Phi Beta Kappa. Office: 101 Park Ave Rm 2500 New York NY 10178-3099 Office Phone: 212-808-7155.

CONWAY, EARL CRANSTON, business educator, retired manufacturing company executive, educator; b. Asbury Park, NJ, Nov. 14, 1931; s. Earl Cranston and Alda Evelyn (Hendrickson) C.; m. Nancy Lou Schucker, Oct. 23, 1954; children: Karen Marie, Anne Margaret, Earl Edward, Nancy Maureen. BA in Polit. Sci. and Internat. Rels., U. Pa., Phila., 1954. Sales-mktg. rep. Procter & Gamble, Phila., 1957-59, unit mgr. Balt. and Chgo., 1960-64, dist. mgr. Minn., Pa., 1964-69, divsn. mgr., nat. sales mgr. Cin., 1970-81, gen. sales mgr. Europe Brussels, 1981-85, corp. dir. world-wide quality Cin., 1985-92. Co-chmn. U.S. Quality Coun. of Conf. Bd., N.Y.C., 1989-92; adj. prof. U. Cin., 1990-2005; adj. faculty Indian River C.C., Indian River County, Fla., 1996-99; lectr. quality and strategic planning Ministry of Light Industry, Hong Kong, Shanghai, Guangzhou and Wuxi, Peoples Republic of China, 1992—, Moscow and Kirov, Russia, 1994—; vis. lectr. bus. and engring. schs.; advisor quality mgmt. V.P. Gore, U.S. and Gov. Jim Hunt, N.C., 1992-93, 93-94. Vice chmn. nat. bd. dirs. Vols. of Am., New Orleans, 1991-96; mem., bd. trustees Ursuline Acad., Cin., 1992-93; mem. planning and zoning bd. City of Vero Beach, Fla., 1995-99; bd. dirs., v.p. Civic Assn., Indian River County, Fla., Vero Beach, Fla., 1995—; vice chmn., bd. dirs. Indian River Meml. Hosp., Indian River County, 1999-2004. 1st lt., inf. U.S. Army, 1955-56. Recipient Taguchi Quality Engring. award Am. Supplier Inst., 1989, Recognition by Ministry of Light Industry, People's Republic of China, Guangzhou and Wuxi, 1992-93. Mem. Am. Soc. Quality. Republican. Roman Catholic. Home: 1020 Olde Doubloon Dr Vero Beach FL 32963-2449

CONWAY, HOBART MCKINLEY, JR., futurist; b. Hackleburg, Ala., Nov. 1, 1920; s. Hobart McKinley and Eva (Kelly) C.; m. Rebecca Warner Kellam, Sept. 17, 1942; children: Linda, Laura. BS, Ga. Inst. Tech., 1940, BA in Engring., 1941. Rsch. engr. NASA, 1941-44, 46-47; dir. So. Assn. Sci. and Industry, Atlanta, 1948-53; pres. Conway Rsch., Inc., Atlanta, 1954—; dir. Sitenet, 1983—. Mem. U.S. Devel. Mission to S.E. Asia, 1962; cons. AID, 1963-68; chmn. Ga. Sci. and Tech. Commn., 1965-66, Caracas Interam. Devel. Seminar; indsl. devel. cons., 15 countries. Editor: Indsl. Devel. mag, 1954-64, Site Selection Handbook, 1954-64, Weather Handbook, 1974, Industrial Facility Planning, 1976, Industrial Park Growth, 1979, Site Net World Guide, 1988—; editor Site World, 1990, 92; author: The Airport City, 1977, 93, Pitfalls in Development, 1978, Marketing Industrial Buildings and Sites, 1980, Disaster Survival, 1981, The Good Life Index, 1981, Facility Planning Technology, 1987, A Glimpse of the Future, 1992, Geo-Economics, The New Science, 1994, The Telcom Coup, 1994, Development Highlights of the Twentieth Century, 1997, Three Tomorrows, 2002; also rsch. reports on facilities planning. Mem. Ga. Senate from 41st Dist., 1963-64, 67-68; sponsor The Safe Skies award, 1989—. With USNR, 1944-46. Recipient medal Time mag., 1953 Fellow AAAS; mem. World Devel. Fedn. (chmn.), Internat. Devel. Rsch. Coun. (founder, dir., recipient award 1979), Aircraft Owners and Pilots Assn. Methodist. Office: Conway Data Inc 6625 The Corners Pky Ste 200 Norcross GA 30092 Home: 10952 Country Road 320 #3 Micanopy FL 32667

CONWAY, JAMES JOSEPH, radiologist, educator; b. Chgo., July 1, 1933; s. Frank and Mary (Tuohy) Conway; m. Dolores Mazer, June 30, 1956; children: Laurie, John, Cheryl. BS, DePaul U., 1959; MD, Northwestern U., 1963. Asst. instr. U. Pa., 1964—68; assoc. in radiology McGaw Med. Ctr. Northwestern U., Chgo., 1968—71, asst. prof. to assoc. prof. radiology, 1974—80; attendant radiology Children's Meml. Hosp., Chgo., 1968—98, prof. radiology, 1980—. Contbr. articles over 110 to profl. jours. With US Army, 1953—55. Recipient Gold medal, Chgo. Radiol. Soc., 1993, Scroll of Appreciation award, Radiol. Soc. N.Am., 1983. Fellow: Am. Coll. Radiology, Am. Coll. Nuc. Physicians, P.R. Soc. Nuc. Medicine (hon.); mem.: Soc. Nuclear Medicine (pres. 1994—95). Avocation: collector of Chicago memorabilia. Office: Childrens Meml Hosp 2300 N Childrens Plz Chicago IL 60614-3394 Personal E-mail: nukedr@comcast.net.

CONWAY, JAMES TERRY, career military officer; b. Walnut Ridge, Ark., Dec. 1947; m. Annette Drury; children: Brandon, Scott, Samantha. BS in Psychology, Southeast Mo. State U., 1969; grad. with honors, Basic Sch., U.S. Army Inf. Officers' Advan, Marine Corps Command and Staff, Air War Coll. Commd. 2nd lt. USMC, 1970, advanced through grades to gen., 2006; rifle platoon comdr., 106mm recoilless-rifle platoon comdr. 3rd Bn. 1st Marines, Camp Pendleton; weapons platoon comdr. Basic Inf. Tng. Sch., Camp Pendleton; co. comdr. Inf. Tng. Regiment, Camp Pendleton; exec. officer of marine detachment USS Kitty Hawk; series and co. comdr. in Recruit Tng. Regiment Marine Corps Recruit Depot, San Diego; aide to comdg. gen., dir. Sea Sch.; regiment's asst. 3rd Bn. 2nd Marines 2nd Marine Divsn., Camp Lejeune; sect. head tactics group Basic Sch.; ops. officer 31st MAU; with ops. divsn. Hdqs. Marine Corps.; sr. aide to Chmn. Joint Chiefs of Staff The Pentagon; divsn. G-3 ops. officer 2nd Marine Divsn.; comdr. 3rd Bn. 2nd Marines, 1990; pres. Marine Corps U., Quantico, Va., 1998—2000; commdr 1st Marine Divsn., 2000—02; commdr. I Marine Expeditionary Force, 2002—04; dir. ops. (J-3), The Joint Staff The Pentagon, Washington, 2004—06; comdt. USMC, Washington, 2006—. Decorated Def. Disting. Svc. medal, Disting. Svc. medal, Legion of Merit, Def. Meritorious Svc. medal, Meritorious Svc. Medal, Navy Commendation medal, Navy Achievement medal, Combat Action Ribbon Office: USMC Comdt 9999 JCS Pentagon Washington DC 20318*

CONWAY, JILL KATHRYN KER, historian, writer, former academic administrator; b. Hillston, New South Wales, Australia, Oct. 9, 1934; d. William Innis and Evelyn Mary (Adames) Ker; m. John James Conway, Dec. 22, 1962 (dec. 1995). BA, U. Sydney, Australia, 1958; PhD, Harvard U., 1969; degree (hon.), St. Thomas U., 1974, Mt. Holyoke Coll., 1975, Amherst Coll., 1976, York U., Toronto, 1977, U. NH, 1977, Westfield State Coll., 1979, Mt. St. Vincent U., Halifax, NS, 1980, Wesleyan U., 1980, U. Mass., 1981, Williams Coll., 1982, Queen's U., 1983, U. Toronto, 1984, McGill U., 1984, SUNY, 1986, Providence Coll., 1987, Smith Coll., 1988, Miami U., 1989, U. Rochester, 1990, Dartmouth Coll., 1990, Notre Dame U., 1990, Manhattanville Coll., 1991, Elms Coll., 1991, Keene State U., 1991, Lake Forest Coll., 1992, Tufts U., 1992, Brock U., 1992, Bentley Coll., 1993. Lectr. history U. Toronto, Ont., Canada, 1964-68, asst. prof. Ont., 1968-70, assoc. prof. Ont., 1970-75, v.p. Ont., 1973-75; pres. Smith Coll., Northampton, Mass., 1975-85, Sophia Smith prof., 1975-85; vis. prof. sci., tech., and soc. MIT, Boston, 1985—. Bd. dirs. Merrill Lynch Co., Arthur D. Little, Inc., Colgate-Palmolive Co., Nike, Inc., Allen Group Inc. Author: Merchants and Merinos, 1960, Women Reformers and American Culture: 1870-1930, 1972, The Female Experience in Eighteenth-and Nineteenth-Century America: A Guide to the History of American Women, 1982, Women Reformers and American Culture, 1987, Utopian Dream or Dystopian Nightmare? Nineteenth Century Feminist Ideas About Equality, 1987, The Road from Coorain, 1989, Autobiographies of American Women: An Anthology, 1992, True North: A Memoir, 1995, Modern Feminism: An Intellectual History, 1997, When Memory Speaks, 1998, In Her Own Words: Women's Memoirs from Australia, New Zealand, Canada, and the United States, 1999, Earth, Air, Fire, Water: Humanistic Studies of the Environment, 2000, Women on Power: Leadership Redefined, 2001, A Woman's Education, 2001, Felipe the Flamingo, 2006; co-author (with Susan Bourque and Joan Scott): Learning About Women, 1989; co-author: (with Susan Bourque) The Politics of Women's Education, 1993; co-author: (with Russell Baker and William Zinsser) Inventing the Truth: The Art and Craft of Memoir, 1995; co-author: (with Elizabeth Topham Kennan as Clare Munnings) Overnight Float, 2000; editor: Written by Herself, 1995, Written By Herself, vol. 2, Autobiographies of Women from Britain, Africa, Asia and the US, 1996. Trustee Mt. Holyoke Coll., The Kresge Found., The Knight Found., New Eng. Med. Ctr.; former trustee Clarke Sch. for Deaf, Coll. Retirement Equities Fund, Acad. of Music, Northampton, Hampshire Coll., Northfield Mt. Hermon Sch.; bd. dirs. Ctr. Communications. Mem. Am. Hist. Assn., Can. Hist. Assn., Am. Antiquarian Soc. Home Phone: 617-253-4062. Personal E-mail: kerconway@aol.com.

CONWAY, JOHN E., federal judge; b. 1934; BS, U.S. Naval Acad., 1956; LLB magna cum laude, Washburn U., 1963. Assoc. Matias A Zamora, Santa Fe, 1963-64; ptnr. Wilkinson, Durrett & Conway, Alamogordo, N.Mex., 1964-67, Durrett, Conway & Jordon, Alamogordo, 1967-80, Montgomery & Andrews, P.A., Albuquerque, 1980-86; city atty. Alamogordo, 1966-72; mem. N.Mex. State Senate, 1970-80, minority leader, 1972-80; chief fed. judge U.S. Dist. Ct. N.Mex., Albuquerque, 1994—2000, sr. fed. judge, 2000—. Mem. Jud. Resources Com., 1995—98. 1st lt. USAF, 1956-60. Mem. 10th Cir. Dist. Judges Assn. (pres. 1995-98), Fed. Judges Assn. (bd. dirs. 1996-2001), Nat. Commrs. on Uniform State Laws, N.Mex. Bar Assn., N.Mex. Jud. Coun. (vice chmn. 1973, chmn. 1973-75, disciplinary bd. of Supreme Ct. of N.Mex. vice chmn. 1980, chmn. 1981-84.). Office: US Dist Ct Chambers #740 333 Lomas Blvd NW Albuquerque NM 87102-2272 Office Phone: 505-348-2200. Business E-Mail: jconway@nmcourt.fed.us.

CONWAY, JOHN K., lawyer; Gen. counsel Kemper Ins. Co., Long Grove, Ill. Office: Lumbermens Mutual Casualty Co 1 Kemper Dr Long Grove IL 60049-0001

CONWAY, JOHN S., history professor; b. London, Dec. 31, 1929; s. Geoffrey S. and Elsie (Philips) C.; m. Ann P. Jefferies, Aug. 10, 1957; children— David, Jane, Alison BA, Cambridge U., Eng., 1952; MA, Cambridge U., 1955, PhD, 1956. Asst. prof. U. Man., Can., 1955-57; asst. prof., assoc. prof., then prof. history U. B.C., Vancouver, 1957-94, prof. emeritus, 1995—. Mem. editl. bd. dirs. Holocaust and Genocide Studies, Kirchliche Zeitgeschichte; Smallman Disting. vis. prof. history U. Western On., 1998. Author: The Nazi Persecution of the Churches, 1968, 2d edit., 1997. Contbr. numerous articles on churches and the holocaust to topical publs. Pres. Tibetan Refugee Aid Soc., Can., 1971-81; chmn. Vancouver Coalition with World Refugees, 1982-84. Recipient Queen's Silver Jubilee medal, 1977. Mem. Can. Inst. Internat. Affairs, German Studies Assn., Can. Hist. Assn. Anglican. Home: 4345 Locarno Crescent Vancouver BC Canada V6R 1G2 Office: U BC Dept History East Mall Vancouver BC Canada V6T 1Z1 E-mail: jconway@interchange.ubc.ca.

CONWAY, JOHN THOMAS, federal agency administrator, lawyer, engineer; b. NYC, May 10, 1924; s. John Joseph and Johannah (Stanley) C.; m. Priscilla Harris, Sept. 13, 1947 (div. 1978); children: John, Daniel, Sean, Thomas, Christopher, Johannah; m. Virginia McLaughlin, Mar. 17, 1989. BNS, Tufts U., 1945, BS in Engring., 1947; JD, Columbia U., 1949. Bar: N.Y. 1949, U.S. Supreme Ct. 1952. Spl. agt. FBI, Washington, 1950-56; asst. dir. US Congress Joint Com. on Atomic Energy, Washington, 1956-62, exec. dir., 1962-68; exec. asst. to chmn. Consol. Edison, NYC, 1968-78, exec. v.p., 1982-89; chmn. Def. Nuc. Facilities Safety Bd., Washington, 1989—2005, chmn. emeritus, 2005—. Pres. Am. Nuc. Energy Coun., Washington, 1978-82, chmn. bd., 1983-89; bd. dirs. Empire State Energy Rsch. Com., N.Y., 1970-76, Atomic Indsl. Forum, 1976-78; mem. oversight com. U.S. Com. Energy Awareness, Washington, 1982-89. Bd. dirs. Americans for Energy Independence, Washington, 1982-89, Youth for Energy Independence, Washington, 1982-89, Assn. For A Better N.Y., 1982-89, N.Y. Fire Safety Found., 1984-89; mem. N.Y.C. Mayor's Com. for Sci., 1969-76. Lt. (j.g.) USNR, 1943—52. Mem. Am. Legion (life), U.S. Army Ft. Meyer Officer Club, Dem. Club (Washington). Democrat. Roman Catholic. Office: Def Nuc Facilities Safety Bd 625 Indiana Ave NW Ste 700 Washington DC 20004-2909

CONWAY, JOHN W., manufacturing executive; BA in Econ., U. Va., 1967; JD, Columbia Law Sch., 1970. Pres. Continental Can Internat. Corp., 1988; sr. v.p. Crown Cork & Seal (acquired Continental Can Internat. Corp.), Phila., 1991-93; exec. v.p., pres. internat. divsn. Crown Cork & Seal, Phila., 1993-96, pres., exec. v.p. Am. divsn., 1997-2001; chmn. bd., pres., CEO Crown Holdings Inc., Phila., 2001—. Bd. dirs. Crown Cork & Seal, Nat. Food Processors Assn., The West Co.; chmn. Can Mfrs. Inst. Office: Crown Cork & Seal 1 Crown Way Philadelphia PA 19154-4599*

CONWAY, KEVIN, actor, performing company executive; b. NYC, May 29, 1942; s. James John C. and Margaret O'Brien; m. Mila Quiros, Apr. 5, 1966. Broadway and Off-Broadway appearances include: Dinner at Eight, Elephant Man, Of Mice and Men, Moonchildren, Red Ryder, One Flew Over the Cuckoo's Nest, Life Class, Other Places, King John, Other People's Money, 1988 (Outer Critics Circle award for best actor, 1989), On the Waterfront, Lawyers; films include: Slaughterhouse Five, Portnoy's Complaint, FIST, Paradise Alley, The Funhouse, Flashpoint, Homeboy, Jesse, One Good Cop, Ramblin Rose, Jennifer 8, Gettysburg, Lawnmower Man II, Whipping Boy, The Quick and the Dead, Rage of Angels, The Scarlet Letter, The Deadliest Season, The Lathe of Heaven, Elephant Man, Something About Amelia, When Will I Be Loved, Breaking the Silence, Train Wreck; (miniseries) Mark Twain, Gettysburg, Streets of Laredo, Flamingo Rising, Calm at Sunset, Sally Hemmings, Oz, Brotherhood; (films) Black Knight, Gods and Generals, 13 Days, Looking for Richard, Mercury Rising, The Confession, Mystic River, Invincible; (TV miniseries) The Bronx Is Burning, (TV) Miami Vice, Law and Order, Jag, Equalizer, Law and Order/Criminal Intent, The Black Donnellys; voice of Mark Twain in Ken Burns Documentary; dir.: (plays) Off-Broadway and Lincoln Ctr. Mecca, Old Flames, Milk Train Doesn't Stop Here, Chgo. and L.A. prodn. Other Peoples Money, 1990; star, dir.: (feature film) The Sun and the Moon, 1985. Bd. dirs. Second Stage Co. Served with USN, 1960-62. Recipient Village Voice Obie award, 1973; recipient Drama Desk award, 1973-74. Mem. Screen Actors Guild (bd. dirs. 1979-81), Nat. Acad. TV Arts and Scis. Home and Office: 25 Central Park W New York NY 10023-7253 Office Phone: 212-582-9235. E-mail: gemicon@aol.com.

CONWAY, LYNN, computer scientist, electrical engineer, educator; b. Mt. Vernon, NY, Jan. 2, 1938; BS, Columbia U., 1962, MSEE, 1963; D (hon.), Trinity Coll., 1997. Rsch. staff IBM Corp., Yorktown Heights, NY, 1964-68; sr. staff engr. Memorex Corp., Santa Clara, Calif., 1969-73; rsch. staff Xerox Corp., Palo Alto, Calif., 1973-78, rsch. fellow, mgr. VLSI systems area, 1978-82, rsch. fellow, mgr. knowledge systems area, 1982-83; asst. dir. for strategic computing Def. Advanced Research Projects Agy., Arlington, Va., 1983-85; prof. elec. engring. and computer sci., assoc. dean U. Mich. Coll. Engring., Ann Arbor, Mich., 1985—98, prof. emerita elec. engring. and computer sci., 1999—. Vis. assoc. prof. elec. engring. and computer sci. MIT, Cambridge, Mass., 1978-79; sci. adv. bd. USAF, 1987-90. Co-author: textbook Introduction to VLSI Systems, 1980; contbr. articles to profl. jours.; patentee in field. Mem. coun. Govt.-Univ.-Industry Rsch. Roundtable, 1993-98; mem. corp. Charles Stark Draper Lab., 1993—; mem. bd. visitors USAF Acad., 1996-2000, presdl. appt.; mem. Air Force Sci. and Tech. Bd., Nat. Acads., 2000—. Recipient Ann. Achievement award Electronics mag., 1981, Harold Pender award U. Pa., 1984, Wetherill Medal Franklin Inst., 1985, Sec. of Def. Meritorious Civilian Svc. award, 1985; named to Electronic Design Hall of Fame, 2002. Fellow IEEE; mem. NAE, AAAS (named Engr. of Yr. 2005), Soc. Women Engrs. (Ann. Achievement award 1990), Assn. Computing Machinery. Avocations: canoeing, natural landscaping, travel. Office: U Mich 3640 CSE Bldg Ann Arbor MI 48109 Business E-Mail: conway@umich.edu.

CONWAY, MARK ALLYN, lawyer; b. Dayton, Ohio, Dec. 13, 1957; s. Allyn Walter and Doris Jean (Wright) C.; m. Dawn Elizabeth Manning, July 31, 1982; children: Ashley Wright, Alexandra Mills. BA, Denison U., 1980; JD, Calif. Western Sch. of Law, 1983; LLM in Taxation, Georgetown U., 1984. Bar: D.C. 1983, U.S. Tax Ct. 1983, Calif. 1988, Ohio 1991. Ptnr. Thompson Hine LLP, Dayton, 1990—. Fellow Am. Coll. of Trust and Estate Counsel; mem. ABA (real property, probate and trust law sect.), D.C. Bar Assn., Calif. Bar Assn. (real property, probate and trust law sect. 1988—), Dayton Racquet Club. Republican. Presbyterian. Avocations: tennis, skiing, sailing. Office: Thompson Hine LLP 2000 Courthouse Plz NE Dayton OH 45402 Home: 1545 Ridgeway Rd Dayton OH 45419 Office Phone: 513-443-6840. E-mail: Mark.Conway@Thompsonhine.com.

CONWAY, MICHAEL MAURICE, lawyer; b. St. Joseph, Mo., Mar. 11, 1946; s. Michael Maurice and Genevieve (Hepburn) C.; m. Kathleen Stevens; children: Michael, Cara, Mary. BS in Journalism, Northwestern U., 1968; JD, Yale U., 1973. Bar: Ill. 1973, U.S. Dist. Ct. (no. dist.) Ill. 1973, U.S. Tax Ct. 1975, U.S. Ct. Claims 1976, U.S. Ct. Appeals (7th cir.) 1976, U.S. Ct. Appeals (1st cir.) 1979, U.S. Supreme Ct. 1980, U.S. Ct. Appeals (5th and 11th cirs.) 1981, U.S. Ct. Appeals (fed. cir. 1982). Ptnr. Hopkins & Sutter now Foley & Lardner, Chgo., 1979—, chmn. Chgo. litigation dept. Counsel U.S. Ho. Reps. com. on judiciary impeachement inquiry Richard M. Nixon, 1974. Chmn. Ill. Lawyers Com. Clinton/Gore, Chgo., 1992; alt. del. Dem. Nat. Conv., 1992, del., 1996. Mem. Am. Coll. Trial Lawyers. Roman Catholic. Avocation: baseball. Office: Foley & Lardner LLP 321 N Clark St Chicago IL 60610 Office Phone: 312-832-4351. Business E-Mail: mconway@foley.com.

CONWAY, NANCY ANN, newspaper editor; b. Foxboro, Mass., Oct. 15, 1941; d. Leo T. and Alma (Goodwin) C.; children: Ana Lucia DaSilva, Kara Ann Martin. Cert. in med. tech., Carnegie Inst., 1962; BA in English, U. Mass., 1976, cert. in secondary edn., 1978. Tchr. Brazil-Am. Inst., Rio de Janeiro, 1963-68; freelance writer, editor Amherst, Mass., 1972-76; staff writer Daily Hampshire Gazette, North Hampton, Mass., 1976-77; editor Amherst Bull., 1977-80, Amherst Record, 1980-83; features editor Holyoke (Mass.) Transcript/Telegram, 1983-84; gen. mgr. Monday-Thursday Newspapers, Boca Raton, Fla., 1984-87; dir. editorial South Fla. Newspaper Network, Deerfield Beach, 1987-90; pub., editor York (Pa.) Newspapers, Inc., 1990-95; metro editor Denver Post, 1995-96; exec. editor, v.p. Alameda Newspaper Group Oakland (Calif.) Tribune, 1996—2003; editor The Salt Lake (Utah) Tribune, 2003—. Bd. dirs. Math.: Opportunities in Engring., Sci. and Tech.-Pa. State, York, 1991-95. Recipient writing awards, state newspaper assns. Mem. Am. Soc. Newspaper Editors, Soc. Profl. Journalists. Avocations: literature, photography, gardening. Office: The Salt Lake Tribune 90 S 400 W Ste 700 Salt Lake City UT 84101-1431 Business E-Mail: nconway@angnewspapers.com.

CONWAY, RICHARD FRANCIS, investment company executive; b. Greenwich, Conn., Jan. 4, 1954; s. Francis Xavier and Marie (Bohan) C.; m. Greta Weil, Oct. 29, 1988; children: Signe Charlotte Weil, Anna Augusta Weil. BA, Harvard Coll., 1976; MBA, Yale U., 1981. Mgmt. trainee Citibank, NYC, 1976-79; assoc. L.F. Rothschild, Unterberg, Towbin Inc., NYC, 1981-83, v.p., 1983-86, prin., 1986-88; v.p. Salomon Bros. Inc., NYC, 1988-90, Security Pacific Mcht. Bank, NYC, 1990-91; sr. v.p. Needham and Co. Inc., NYC, 1992-94; v.p. Smith Mgmt. Co., NYC, 1994-97, Lone Star Securities Mgmt., Inc., NYC, 1998-99; ptnr. Lampe, Conway & Co., LLC, NYC, 1999—. Trustee Choate Rosemary Hall Sch., Wallingford, Conn., 1974-78; class com. Harvard Coll. Fund, Cambridge, Mass., 1991, 01, 06. Mem. Harvard Club (N.Y.C.), Knickerbocker Club (N.Y.C.), Georgica Assn. (Wainscott, N.Y.). Roman Catholic. Home: 1361 Madison Ave New York NY 10128-0713 Office: 680 5th Ave Ste 12th Fl New York NY 10019 Home Phone: 212-534-3319; Office Phone: 212-581-8989. Personal E-mail: richardconway@nyc.rr.com. Business E-Mail: conway@lampeconway.com.

CONWAY, THOMAS WILLIAM, biochemist, educator; b. Aberdeen, SD, June 6, 1931; s. James L. and Agnes (Mullen) C.; m. Mary Patricia Leadon, July 6, 1957; children: Catherine A., James M. BS, Coll. St. Thomas, St. Paul, 1953; MA, U. Tex., 1955, PhD, 1962. Postdoctoral fellow Rockefeller U., NYC, 1962-64; asst. prof. U. Iowa, Iowa City, 1964-68, assoc. prof., 1968-73, prof. biochemistry, 1973-96, prof. emeritus, 1996—. Mem. NIH Physiol. Chem. Study Sect., 1975-79, chmn., 1976-78; Am. Cancer Soc. vis. scholar ICRF Labs., London, 1980-81, vis. prof. U. Chile, 1968. Co-author: Biochemistry: A Case-Oriented Approach, 1974, 6th rev. edit., 1996. 1st Lt. USAF, 1953-58. Named Rosalie B. Hite fellow, U. Tex. Austin, 1958-62, NSF fellow Rockefeller U., N.Y.C., 1962-64, vis. scholar Am. Cancer Soc., London, 1980-81. Mem. Am. Soc. Biol. Chemists, Am. Chem. Soc., Soc. de Biologia de Chile (hon.), Sigma Xi (pres. U. Iowa chpt. 1978-79). Roman Catholic. Home: 1 Wellesley Way Iowa City IA 52245-3830 Business E-Mail: thomas-conway@uiowa.edu.

CONWAY, WILLIAM E., JR., telecommunications industry executive, venture capitalist; b. Lowell, Mass., 1949; m. Joanne Conway; 1 child. BA in Econ., Dartmouth U., 1971; MBA, U. Chgo., 1974. Various positions The Nat. Bank of Chgo., 1974—84; pres., treas. MCI Comm. Corp., 1981—84, sr. v.p. CFO, 1984—87; founding ptnr., mng. dir. The Carlyle Group, Washington, 1987—; chmn. Nextel Comm., Inc., Reston, Va., 2001—. Chmn. bd. United Defense Inst.; bd. dirs. several pvt. co. Co-founder Bedford Falls Found. Office: Nextel Commn Inc 2001 Edmund Halley Dr Reston VA 20191*

CONWAY, WILLIAM GAYLORD, zoologist, zoo director, conservationist; b. St. Louis, Nov. 20, 1929; s. Frederick Eldridge and Alice Harriet (Gaylord) C. AB, Washington U., 1951; ScD (hon.), St. Lawrence U., 1979, Fordham U., 1981, Trinity Coll., 1984. Curator birds St. Louis Zoo, 1951-56, NY Zool. Soc. (now The Wildlife Conservation Soc.), NYC, 1956-72, assoc. dir., 1960-61, zoo dir., 1962-99, gen. dir., 1966-99, pres., 1992-99; sr. conservationist, 1999—. Mem. expdns. to Trinidad, Argentina, Chile, Bolivia, China; advisor Fundación Patagonia Natural, Argentina; mem. advisory bd. Internat. Zoo Yearbook, 2004; bd. dirs. Caribbean Conservation Corp. Contbr. articles to profl. jours. Decorated comdr. Order of the Golden Ark (The Netherlands); recipient Mayor's award of honor for arts and culture, 1979, Marlin Perkins award AAZPA, 1986, Disting. Achievement award Soc. for Conservation Biology, Disting. Svc. medal Am. Assn. Mus., 1998, Heini Hediger award World Zoo Orgn., 1999, IUCN-Survival Svc. Commn., 2001, Henry Shaw medal Mo. Botanical Gardedn, 2002; hon. fellow Zool. Soc. London, 2002. Mem.: Conservation Breeding Specialist Grp., Wildlife Conservation Soc. (bd. dirs., bd. advisors 2004—, Gold medal 2000), Nat. Audubon Soc. (Audubon medal 1999), Am. Zoo and Aquarium Assn., Am. Assn. Zool. Pks. and Aquariums (past pres.), Am. Assn. Museums (medal 1998), Am. Conservation Assn. (bd. dirs., St. Louis Zoo 1st Conservation medal 2005), Cultural Instns. Group (past pres.), Internat. Survival Svc. Commn. (Peter Scott medal 2000), Wilson Ornithol. Club, Brit. Avicultural Soc., Cooper Ornithol. Soc., Am. Ornithologists Union. Personal E-mail: wgcwcs@optonline.net.

CONWAY DE MACARIO, EVERLY, immunologist, molecular biologist; b. Buenos Aires, Apr. 20, 1939; d. Delfin E. and Maria Gloria (Benatuil) Conway; m. Alberto J. L. Macario, Mar. 16, 1963; children: Alex, Everly. PhD in Pharmacy, Nat. U. Buenos Aires, 1960, PhD in Biochemistry, 1962. Rsch. fellow Nat. Acad. Medicine Argentina, Buenos Aires, 1962-63; head lab. oncology and immunology Argentinian Assn. against Cancer, Buenos Aires, 1966-67; chief of immunology Sch. Medicine, Buenos Aires, 1967-68; rsch. fellow dept. tumor-biology Karolinska Inst., Stockholm, 1969-71; sr. rsch. scientist Lab. Cell Biology, NRC Italy, Rome, 1971-73; vis. scientist Internat. Agy. Rsch. on Cancer, WHO, Lyon, France, 1973-74, Brown U., Providence, 1974-76; rsch. scientist Wadsworth Ctr. NY State Dept. Health, Albany, 1976—2006; prof. dept. biomed. scis. Sch. Pub. Health, Albany, 1986—2002, mem. admission com., 1986-89. Grant referee in field. Co-editor: Monoclonal Antibodies against Bacteria, 1985-86, vols. I-III, Gene Probes for Bacteria, 1990; assoc. editor profl. jour. 1986—; mng. editor Frontiers on Biosci.; contbr. articles to profl. jours.; contbr. chpts. to books and encyclopedias. Recipient Prof. J.M. Mezzadra award Nat. U. Buenos Aires, 1969, Travel award to Eng., 2nd Internat. Immunology Congress, 1974, Gold medal Argentinian Soc. Biochemistry, 1980, Hans Osterman Found. grantee, Sweden, 1969, Sir Samuel Scott of Yews Trust grantee, Sweden, 1970, Winifred Cullis grantee Internat. Fedn. Univ. Women, 1972, NATO rsch. grantee, 1975, 81, U.S. Dept. Energy grantee, 1981, 84; Travel award to China, 1985, Spain, 1993, South Africa, 1994. Mem. Scandinavian Soc. Immunology, Italian Assn. Immunologists, French Soc. Immunology (travel award 1974), Am. Assn. Immunologists (chmn. com. on status of women 1980-86, edn. com. 1982-87, awards com. 1991-92, travel award to Australia 1977), Am. Soc. Microbiology (sr. editor Manual Clin. Lab. Immunology 4th-5th edits.), Internat. Soc. Microbial Ecology, Cell Stress Soc. Internat., Nat. Acad. Microbiology (chmn. Morrison Rogosa awards com. 2002-06, chmn. internat. subcom. on taxonomy of methanogens). Achievements include patents for microcircle system, microsample holder and carrier; invention of ultrasensitive micro-immunoenzyamtic assay and multipurpose modular system for use in lab and field settings, of the antigenic fingerprinting method; creation of immuntechnology for rapid identification of microbes directly in samples of complex microbial mixtures; first to establish the antigenic cohesiveness of methanogenic and halophilic archaea and demonstrate clusters overlapping phylogenetic branches; sequenced for the first time archaeal transportes and chaperone genes; found new morphotype of methanosarcina; created an integration vector for transformation of methanogens; participated in the sequencing of the genomes of two methanogens; discovered an archaeon with the four main chaperoning systems in the cystol.; found two new chaperonins' in archaea; discovered that ashaeal hsp70 (dnak) genes belong to various evolutionary lineages. Home: 9 Travilah Terr Potomac MD 20854 Office: Ctr of Marine Biotech Columbus Ctr 701 E Pratt St Baltimore MD 21202 Business E-Mail: macarioe@umbi.umd.edu.

CONWELL, ESTHER MARLY, physicist, researcher; b. NYC, May 23, 1922; d. Charles and Ida (Korn) C.; m. Abraham A. Rothberg, Sept. 30, 1945; 1 son, Lewis J. BA, Bklyn. Coll., 1942, DSc, 1992; MS, U. Rochester, NYC, 1945; PhD, U. Chgo., 1948. Lectr. Bklyn. Coll., 1946-51; mem. tech. staff Bell Tel. Labs., 1951-52; physicist GTE Labs., Bayside, NY, 1952-61, mgr. physics dept., 1961-72; vis. prof. U. Paris, 1962-63; Abby Rockefeller Mauze prof. MIT, Cambridge, 1972; prin. scientist Xerox Corp., Webster, NY, 1972-80, rsch. fellow, 1981-98. Adj. prof. U. Rochester, 1990—2001, prof., 2001—; cons., mem. adv. com. engring. NSF, 1978—81. Author: High Field Transport in Semiconductors, 1967, also rsch. papers; mem. editl. bd. Jour. Applied Physics, Proc. of IEEE, patentee in field. Fellow IEEE (Edison medal 1997), Am. Phys. Soc. (sec.-treas. divsn. condensed matter physics 1977-82); mem. AAAS, NAS, NAE, Soc. Women Engrs. (Achievement award 1960, Susan B. Anthony Lifetime Achievement award 2006). Office: U Rochester Dept Chemistry and Physics Rochester NY 14627 Business E-Mail: conwell@chem.rochester.edu.

CONWELL, HALFORD ROGER, physician; b. Cin., Jan. 28, 1924; s. Halford Fredrick and Erma Pearl (Cornelius) C.; m. Margaret Ann King, Dec. 15, 1965; children: Mark A., Sherri L., John H. BA, U. Wooster, 1948; MA, U. Louisville, 1950; MD, U. Cin., 1955. ATP; diplomate crew coordination tng. Continental Airlines. Practice in aviation medicine, Huntsville, Tex., 1959—; mem. staff Huntsville Meml. Hosp., chief of staff, 1974-75, chief medicine, 1976-80, bd. trustees, 1991—2005. Sr. U.S. med. officer Brit. Caledonian Airways, 1977-89; cons. Aeromexico; chief flight surgeon Continental Airlines, 1996—; mem. Walker County Hosp. Dist., 1975-79, chmn., 1976-79; asst. dean of men, instr. psychology Heidelberg U., Tiffin, Ohio, 1950-51; instr. psychology Cin. Coll.; sr. med. examiner FAA; sr. examiner C.A.A. (U.K.), C.A.A. (Australia); newspaper columnist, 1992—. Trustee Biol. Analysis and Rsch. Found.; capt. (hon.) Tex. Internat. Airline, Continental Airlines Golden Eagles, 2007; founder Bomber Command Mus. (R.A.F.) Lt. USNR, 1942-46. Recipient safe pilot award Nat. Pilots Assn., Pilot Proficiency award FAA (Continental Airlines Golden Eagles Hon. award 2007), Profl. Svc. Citation. Fellow Aerospace Med. Assn. (John A. Tamisiea award 2000, Bernice Audie Davis award 2005), Civil Aviation Medicine Assn. (v.p. 1968-80, dir. 1968—, pres. 1980-81, award of merit 1994, 97); mem. Brit. Assn. Aerospace Medicine, Latin Am. Aviation Med. Assn., Scottish Assn. Aviation Med. Examiners, Airline Med. Dirs. Assn., Mitchell Pediatric Soc., Academie Internationale de Medicine Aeronatque et Spatiale, Aircraft Owners and Pilots Assn. (med. adv. panel), Confederate Air Force (founding mem.), Air Transp. Assn. (med. com.), Order Ky. Cols., Quiet Birdmen, Masons, Psi Chi, Alpha Psi Omega. Office: 2800 Lake Rd Huntsville TX 77340-5632 Office Phone: 936-295-5222.

CONWILL, KINSHASHA HOLMAN, museum director; d. Moses Carl and Mariella (Ama) Holman; m. Houston Conwill. Nat. Achievement Scholar Mount Holyoke Coll.; BFA magna cum laude, Howard Y.; MBA, UCLA. Coord. activities Frank Lloyd Wright Hollyhock Ho., LA, 1976—78; asst. exhibit coord. Mus. of the Am. Indian, NYC, 1979; dep. dir. Studio Mus., Harlem, 1980—88, dir., 1988—99; project dir. NY Found. for the Arts' Cultural Blueprint for NYC, 2000—02; sr. policy advisor Museums & Cmty. Initiative, Am. Assn. Museums, 2002—03; dep. dir. Nat. Mus. African Am. History & Culture, Smithsonian Inst., Washington, 2005—. Bd. dirs. Provisions Libr.; bd. overseers Calif. Inst. Arts. Named to Centennial Honor Roll, Am. Assn. Mus., 2006. Office: Smithsonian Inst PO Box 37012 Washington DC 20013-7012 E-mail: kinshashac@aol.com.*

CONYERS, CLAUDE BRUNSON, publishing consultant, editor, dance historian; b. Cartersville, Ga., June 19, 1934; s. Claude Brunson and Rachel Keith (Stephens) C. BA, Vanderbilt U., 1956; MA, Columbia U., 1962; dance tng., New Dance Group, NYC, 1959, Sch. of Am. Ballet, 1960, Ballet Russe Sch., 1961-64. Sr. editor Prentice-Hall, Inc., Englewood Cliffs, NJ, 1960-64; dancer PACT Ballet, Johannesburg, 1965-66, Les Grands Ballets Canadiens, Montreal, 1967; editl. dir. Greystone Press, NYC, 1968-70; editl. cons. NYC, 1970-74; spl. projects editor Praeger Pubs., NYC, 1975; sr. projects editor Macmillan Pub. Co., NYC, 1975-87; editl. dir., scholarly and profl. reference Oxford U. Press, NYC, 1988-98, v.p., 1995-99. Mem. publs. com. N.Y. Acad. Scis., 1990-95. Bd. dirs. George Balachine Found., 1999—, Hillbrow Pub. Svcs., 2001—; project dir. Popular Balanchine, 2000-04. Lt. (j.g.) USNR, 1956-58. Recipient R.R. Hawkins award Profl. and Scholarly Pub./Assn. Am. Pubs., 1991, 93, 96, 98, Dartmouth medal ALA, 1987, 99. Mem. ASPCA, People for the Ethical Treatment of Animals, Internat. Assn. History Religions, Am. Soc. for Theatre Rsch., Congress on Rsch. in Dance, Soc. Dance History Scholars (editl. bd. 1989-94, 2000-06), Clan Keith Soc., World Dance Alliance, Soc. for Scholarly Pub., Alley Cat Allies, Humane Soc. U.S., Humane Farming Assn., Pawling Garden Club, Kappa Alpha Order. Democrat. Unitarian. Home and Office: 116 S White Rock Rd Holmes NY 12531-5409 Office Phone: 845-878-9451. E-mail: cconyers1@comcast.net.

CONYERS, JOHN, JR., congressman; b. Detroit, May 16, 1929; s. John and Lucille (Simpson) C.; m. Monia Estes; children: John Jr., Carl Edward. BA, Wayne State U., 1957, JD, 1958; LLD, Wilberforce U., 1969. Bar: Mich. 1959. Legis. asst. to Congressman John Dingell, 1959-61; sr. ptnr. firm Conyers, Bell & Townsend, 1959-61; referee Mich. Workmen's Compensation Dept., 1961-64; mem. U.S. Congress from 14th Mich. dist., 1964—; former chmn. Govt. Ops. Com., former chmn. subcom. on legis. and nat. security; ranking mem. Judiciary Com. Past dir. edn. Local 900, United Auto Workers; mem. adv. council Mich. Liberties Union; gen. counsel Detroit Trade Union Leadership Council; vice chmn. nat. bd. Ams. for Democratic Action; vice chmn. adv. council ACLU; an organizer Mems. Congress for Peace through Law; bd. dirs. numerous other orgns. including African-Am. Inst., Commn. Racial Justice, Detroit Inst. Arts, Nat. Alliance Against Racist and Polit. Repression, Nat. League Cities. Sponsor, contbg. author: Am. Militarism, 1970, War Crimes and the American Conscience, 1970, Anatomy of an Undeclared War, 1972; contbr. articles to profl. jours. Trustee Martin Luther King Jr. Ctr. for Non-Violent Social Change. Served to 2d lt. U.S. Army, 1950-54, Korea. Recipient Rosa Parks award SCLC; named one of Most Influential Black Americans, Ebony mag., 2006 Mem. NAACP (exec. bd. Detroit), Kappa Alpha Psi. Democrat. Baptist. Office: 2426 Rayburn Bldg Washington DC 20515-2214 also: District Office 669 Federal Building 231 W Lafayette Detroit MI 48226 Office Phone: 202-225-5126. E-mail: johnconyersjr@gmail.com.*

COOGAN, PHILIP SHIELDS, pathologist; b. Peoria, Ill., Feb. 13, 1938; s. Paul Mathew and Elizabeth Ann (Shields) C.; m. Carol Jean Gerlach, June 18, 1960 (div. 1985); children: Mary Brighid, Philip Gerlach, Joseph Baker, Clare Ann; m. Joan C. Storozynski, Dec. 24, 1987. Student, U. Notre Dame, 1955—58; MD, St. Louis U., 1962. Diplomate: Am. Bd. Pathology. USPHS summer rsch. trainee pathology St. Louis U. Med. Sch., 1958—61; intern Presbyn.-St. Luke's Hosp., Chgo., 1962—63, resident, 1963—67; rsch. pathologist, chief histopathology U.S. Air Force Sch. Aerospace Medicine, 1967—69; asst. prof. pathology Rush Med. Coll., Chgo., 1971—73, assoc. prof., 1972—75; assoc. prof. pathology Northwestern U., Chgo., 1974—78; dir. anatomic pathology Northwestern Meml. Hosp., Chgo., 1974—78; prof. pathology James H. Quillen Coll. Medicine, East Tenn. State U., Johnson City, 1978—2004. Cons. FDA, 1972-81, USPHS, 1962-67 Assoc. editor: Year Book Pathology and Clinical Pathology, 1978-80. Served with USAF, 1967-69. Recipient Hektoen award Chgo. Path. Soc., 1969; named Outstanding Tchr. East Tenn. State U. Coll. Medicine, 1980, 81, 83, 84, 85 Mem. AMA, AAAS, U.S. and Can. Acad. Pathology, Am. Soc. Exptl. Pathology, Am. Soc. Clin. Pathology, Coll. Am. Pathology, Am. Soc. Investigative Pathology, Alpha Omega Alpha. Roman Catholic. Office: East Tenn State U Dept Pathology Johnson City TN 37614 Home Phone: 423-282-6770; Office Phone:

423-439-6789. E-mail: coogan@etsu.edu. *"Don't shoot the wounded." As a teacher of medical students and residents, it is advisable to treat those struggling under adversity with special care. They often become the most empathetic physicians.*

COOK, ADDISON GILBERT, chemistry professor; b. Caracas, Venezuela, Apr. 1, 1933; s. Harold Reed and Florence (Sloan) C.; m. Nancy Lois Spriggs, Aug. 18, 1956; children: Virginia Lynn, Shirley June, Diane Joyce. BS, Wheaton Coll., 1955; PhD, U. Ill., 1959. Rsch. assoc. Cornell U., 1959-60; from asst. prof. to prof. chemistry Valparaiso U., 1960—2004, sr. rsch. prof., 2004—, chmn. dept., 1970-93. Cons. chemistry divsn. Argonne Nat. Lab., Ill., 1961-69; rsch. assoc. Amoco, Whting, Ind., 1960. Editor, contbr.: Enamines: Synthesis, Structure, and Reactions, 1969, 2d edit., 1988; Contbr. articles profl. jours. Recipient Research Corp. grant, 1960-61; Petroleum Research Fund grant, 1963-69. Mem. Am. Chem. Sco., Chem. Soc. (London), Ind. Acad. Sci., Sigma Xi, Phi Lambda Upsilon, Pi Mu Epsilon. Mem. Evangel. Free Ch. Am. Home: 2308 Shannon Dr Valparaiso IN 46383-2427 Office: Valparaiso U Dept Chemistry 210 Neils Sci Ctr Valparaiso IN 46383 Home Phone: 219-462-3339; Office Phone: 219-464-5389. Business E-Mail: Gil.Cook@valpo.edu.

COOK, ALBERT THOMAS THORNTON, JR., financial advisor; b. Cleve., Apr. 24, 1940; s. Albert Thomas Thornton and Tyra Esther (Morehouse) C.; m. Mary Jane Blackburn, June 1, 1963; children: Lara Keller, Thomas, Timothy. BA, Dartmouth Coll., 1962; MA, U. Chgo., 1966. Asst. sec. Dartmouth Coll., Hanover, NH, 1972-77; exec. dir. Big Bros., Inc., NYC, 1977-78; underwriter Boettcher & Co., Denver, 1978-81; asst. v.p. Dain Bosworth Inc., Denver, 1981-82, Colo. Nat. Bank, Denver, 1982-84; pres. The Albert T.T. Cook Co., Denver, 1984—. Arbitrator Nat. Assn. Securities Dealers, NYC, 1985—, Mcpl. Securities Rulemaking Bd., Washington, 1987-98. Pres. Etna-Hanover Ctr. Cmty. Assn., Hanover, NH, 1974-76; active Mayor's Task Force, Denver, 1984; bd. dir. Rude Park Cmty. Nursery, Denver, 1985-87, Willows Water Dist., Colo., 1990-2004, pres., 1998-99, 2003-04; trustee The Iliff Sch. Theol., Denver, 1986-92; mem. com. on trustees Dartmouth Coll., 1990-93; bd. dirs. U. Denver Humanities Inst., 2006—. Mem.: Dartmouth Assn. of Alumni (trustee 2005—), Dartmouth Alumni Coun. (chmn. nominating and trustee search coms. 1987—89, exec. com.), Yale Club, Dartmouth Club of NYC, Cactus Club, Univ. Club (chmn. admissions com. 1997—98), Lions (bd. dir. Denver chpt. 1983—85, treas. 1986—87, pres. Denver Found. 1987—88, 2d v.p. 2001—02, 1st v.p. 2002—03, pres. 2003—04), Delta Upsilon. Congregationalist. Avocations: fly fishing, furniture making, skiing, backpacking, bicycling. Home: 7099 E Hinsdale Pl Centennial CO 80112-1610 Office: One Tabor Ctr 1200 17th St Ste 960 Denver CO 80202-5835

COOK, ALEXANDER BURNS, curator, artist, educator; b. Grand Rapids, Mich., Apr. 16, 1924; s. Gorell Alexander and Harriette Florence (Hinze) C.; m. Marilyn Bierschwal Coffey, Aug. 11, 1992. BA, Ohio Wesleyan U., 1949; MS, Case Western Res. U., 1967. Editl. cartoonist, artist Cleve. Plain Dealer, 1949-55; account exec. Edward Howard & Co., Cleve., 1955-61; spl. art tchr. Cleve. Pub. Schs., 1964-88; curator exhibits Inland Seas Maritime Mus. (formerly Gt. Lakes Mus.), Vermilion, Ohio, 1970-78, curator, 1978—, chmn. mus. oper. com., 1977—. Contbr. editl. cartoons to Reid Cartoon Collection, U. Kans. Jour. Hist. Ctr., The Critique, 1975-88; editl. advisor, columnist Inland Seas Quar. Jour., 1957—, The Chadburn, 1976—; cover illustrations for Ohioana Quar., 1979—; book cover illustrations Dodd, Mead & Co., 1984; paintings represented in pvt. collections, 1960—; executed murals depicting Gt. Lakes shipping Gt. Lakes Mus., 1969, Great Lakes shipwreck Inland Seas Maritime Mus., 2001. Trustee Berkshire Condominium Owners Assn., 1981-83, pres., 1982-83; trustee Shaker Hist. Soc., 1999—. With AUS, 1943-45. Recipient award of honor Ohio Wesleyan U., 1955, Disting. Achievement award Gt. Lakes Hist. Soc., 1973, 1st pl. award for editl. cartoons Union Tchr. Comm. Assn., 1980, 81, 82, 87, Vermilion C. of C. Svc. Award, 2000, Disting. Mus. Profl. award Ohio Museums Assn., 2001. Mem. Gt. Lakes Hist. Soc. (exec. v.p. 1959-64, v.p. 1964-95, trustee, mem. exec. com. 1959—), Ohioana Libr. Assn., Cleve. Mus. Art, Am. Soc. Marine Artists (artist mem.), Assn. for Great Lakes Maritime History, Chgo. Maritime Soc., English Speaking Union, Ohio Acad. History, Northeastern Ohio Inter-Mus. Coun., Vermilion Boat Club, The Union Club, Detroit Marine Hist. Soc., Delta Tau Delta, Pi Delta Epsilon, Pi Sigma Alpha. Republican. Episcopalian. Avocations: gardening, sailing, model railroading. Home: 2449 Saybrook Rd University Heights OH 44118

COOK, ANN JENNALIE, literature educator, cultural organization administrator; b. Wewoka, Okla., Oct. 19, 1934; d. Arthur Holly and Bertha Mable (Stafford) C.; children: Lee Ann Merrick, Amy Ceil Leonard; m. Gerald George Calhoun, Apr. 1994. BA, U. Okla., 1956, MA, 1959; PhD, Vanderbilt U., 1972. Instr. English U. Okla., 1956-57; tchr. English NC, 1958—61, Conn., 1958—61; instr. So. Conn. State Coll., 1962-64; asst. prof. U. SC, 1972—74; adj. asst. prof. Vanderbilt U., Nashville, 1977-82, assoc. prof., 1982-89, prof., 1990-98, prof. emerita, 1999—. Exec. sec. Shakespeare Assn. Am., 1975-87; chmn. Internat. Shakespeare Assn., 1988-96, v.p. 1996—. Author: Privileged Playgoers of Shakespeare's London, 1981, Making a Match: Courtship in Shakespeare and His Society, 1991; assoc. editor Shakespeare Studies, 1973-80; contbr. articles to profl. jours. Trustee Folger Shakespeare Libr., 1985—90, Shakespeare Birthplace Trust (life), Friends of the Shakespeare Birthplace Trust, Nashville Symphony, 2000—06, Univ. Sch. Nashvillle, 2000—04, Nashville Opera Guild, 2000—03, Nashville Shakespeare Festival, 2002—, Shakespeare League of Nashville; pres. English-Speaking Union, 2003—07, nat. bd. dirs., 2004—. Recipient Letseizer award, 1956, Nat. Leadership award Delta Delta Delta, 1956; Danforth fellow, 1968-72, Folger summer fellow, 1973, Donelson fellow, 1974-75, fellow Rockefeller Found., 1984, Guggenheim Found., 1984-85; grantee Folger seminar NEH, 1992-93. Mem. MLA, AAUP, Shakespeare Assn. Am., Shakespeare Inst., Vanderbilt Libr. Heard Soc. (pres. 2004-06), Phi Beta Kappa. Episcopalian. Office: Vanderbilt U Dept English Nashville TN 37235 Home: 6666 Brookmont Terr Apt 207 Nashville TN 37205 Office Phone: 615-322-2541. Personal E-mail: gercalhoun@aol.com.

COOK, AUGUST JOSEPH, lawyer, accountant; b. Devine, Tex., Sept. 25, 1926; s. August E. and Mary H. (Schmidt) C.; m. Matie M. Brangan, July 12, 1952; children: Lisa Ann, Mary Beth, John J. BS, Trinity U., 1949; BBA, U. Tex., 1954; JD, St. Mary's U., 1960. Bar: Tex. 1960, Tenn. 1975. Bus. mgr., corp. sec. Life Enterprises, Inc. and affil. cos., San Antonio, 1950-58, also bd. dirs.; mgr. Ernst & Young, San Antonio, 1960-69, ptnr., Memphis, 1970-84; ptnr. McDonnel Boyd, Memphis, 1984-91; of counsel Harris, Shelton, Dunlap and Cobb, Memphis, 1991-97, Pietrangelo Cook, Memphis, 1997—. Author: A.J. $ Tax Court, 1987; author newspaper column A.J.'s Tax Fables, 1983—; contbr. articles to profl. jours. Alderman City of Castle Hills, Tex., 1961-63, mayor, 1963-69; chmn. Bexar County Coun. Mayors, 1967-69; v.p. Tex. Mcpl. League, 1968-69; bd. dirs. San Antonio Met. YMCA. With U.S. Army, 1945-46, PTO. Mem. AICPA, Tex. Soc. CPAs, Tex. Bar Assn., Estate Planning Coun. San Antonio (pres. 1967), Tenn. Soc. CPAs, Tenn. Bar Assn. (chmn. tax, probate and trust sect., 1993-95), Estate Planning Coun. Memphis (pres. 1983-84), Toastmasters (pres. 1963), Delta Theta Phi, Kappa Pi Sigma, University Club (Memphis), Canyon Creek Country Club (San Antonio, bd. dirs.), Chickasaw Country Club, Optimists (bd. dirs.), Rotary (treas. 1978, 99, bd. dirs. 1986-87, 96-97). Home: 6785 Slash Pine Cv Memphis TN 38119-5617 Office: Pietrangelo Cook PLC 6410 Poplar Ave Ste 190 Memphis TN 38119-4841

COOK, BARBARA K., music educator; b. Manitowoc, Wis., Oct. 8, 1953; d. Robert L. and Donna J. Franz; m. John E. Cook, May 15, 1976; children: Brennan, Brady. Grad., Silver Lake Coll., Manitowoc, 1976, Masters, 2004. K-12 music tchr. Elcho Sch., Wis., 1977—83, 1986—88; music tchr. White Lake Sch., Wis., 1996—. Musician various chs., 1968—2003, 2006—. Composer: (hist. musical) Musical Millenium: A History of White Lake, 2000, Railroad Runnings, 2002, The History of the Wolf River, 2003. Choral dir. Pickerel Christmas Concerts, 2002, 2003. Mem.: NEA, Daughters the King, Eastern Star. Episcopalian. Avocations: reading, cooking, music. Home: 8537 City Rd DD Pickerel WI 54465

COOK, BLANCHE WIESEN, historian, educator, journalist; b. NYC, Apr. 20, 1941; d. David Theodore and Sadonia (Ecker) Wiesen. BA, Hunter Coll., 1962; MA, Johns Hopkins U., 1964, PhD, 1970; DHL (hon.), Russell Sage Coll., 1998. Instr. Hampton Inst., Va., 1963; instr. Stern Coll. for Women, Yeshiva U., NYC, 1964-67; prof. history John Jay Coll., Grad. Faculty CUNY, 1968—, disting. prof., 1995—. Prodr., broadcaster program stas. WBAI and WKPFK Radio Pacifica, N.Y.C. and L.A., 1978—; prodr.-host Jewish Women in Am., CUNY-TV, 2004-05; vis. prof. UCLA, 1982-83; syndicated journalist; bd. dirs. Women's Fgn. Policy Adv. Coun., v.p., co-chair Fund for Open Info. and Accountability; mem. freedom to write com. PEN; elected univ.-wide union officer PSC-CUNY, 2000. Author: Crystal Eastman on Women and Revolution, 1978, Declassified Eisenhower, 1981 (N.Y. Times Notable Book), Biography of Eleanor Roosevelt, vol. 1, 1992 (L.A. Times Book award, N.Y. Times Notable Book, Lambda Lit. prize for biography), vol. 2, 1999, ER I, ER II (Best Books), Christian Sci. Monitor, 1999 (Notable Book award 1999), Intro to Owen Lattimore, Ordeal by Slander, 2004; sr. editor: The Garland Library of War and Peace, 360 vols., 1970-80, Bella Abzug in Jewish Women's Encyclopedia, 1997; contbr. articles to various publs. Appointed to com. on documents for fgn. rels. U.S. Dept. State, 1986-90. Named Scholar of the Yr. NY Coun. Humanities, 1996, Alumna of Yr. Hunter Coll. Hall of Fame, 1999; recipient Breakthrough award Women, Men and Media, 1992, Feminist of Yr. award Feminist Majority Found., 1992, Lambda Lit. Pioneer award, 2005; faculty fellow CUNY, 1978, 84, 91. Mem. Orgn. Am. Historians (co-chair freedom of info. com.), Am. Hist. Assn. (v.p. for rsch. 1991-94), Coordinating Com., Women in Hist. Profession (pres. N.Y.C. chpt. 1969-71), Berkshire Women Historians, Soc. Historians Am. Fgn. Rels., Conf. on Peace Rsch. in History (bd. dirs., v.p.), Peace History Soc. Women's Internat. League for Peace and Freedom, Pi Sigma Alpha, Phi Alpha Theta. Office: CUNY John Jay Coll Dept History 445 W 59th St New York NY 10019-1104 Office Phone: 212-237-8827.

COOK, BRUCE LAWRENCE, editor; b. Chgo., Dec. 12, 1942; s. David Charles, III and Anna Mae (Lawrence) Cook; m. Carolyn Winslow Smith Hammock (div. Dec. 1972); 1 child, Steven Winslow; m. Eileen Clare McPeak, Jan. 3, 1973; children: Christopher David, Helen Clare, Bruce Michael. BA in Radio-TV, Ohio Wesleyan U., Delaware, 1965; MA in Speech Arts, San Diego State U., 1967; PhD in Comm., Temple U., Phila., 1979. Trustee comm. rsch. David C. Cook Found., Elgin, Ill., 1972-83; dir. Ill. Mcpl. Inst., Dundee, 1983-88; mng. editor Sr. Am. Newspapers, Dundee, 1988-90; dir. Cook Comm., Dundee, 1990—; rsch. analyst Copley Chgo. Newspapers, Plainfield, 1995-2000; sr. rsch. analyst Reach Chgo. , Hollinger Inc. Chgo. (Ill.) Sun-Times, 2000—04, sr. rsch. analyst, 2004—. Instr. Columbia Coll., Chgo., 1989—, DeVry U./Keller Grad. Sch. Mgmt., Oak Brook, Ill., 1991—. Author: (monograph) Understanding Pictures in Papua, 1981, (booklet) Serving Mentally Impaired People, 1983; founder, editor (website) author-me.com. Trustee Village of Sleepy Hollow, Ill., 1983—87; alt. bd. rev. Kane County, Batavia, Ill., 1993—95; pres. World Writers Resources, Inc., 2007—; v.p. gen. edn. adv. bd. DeVry Inst. Tech., 1997—. Capt. USAF, 1967—72. Mem.: IEEE, Am. Legion. Republican. Home: 1211 Carol Crest Dr Sleepy Hollow IL 60118-2643 Office: Chgo Sun Times 350 N Orleans St Chicago IL 60654 Personal E-mail: cookcomm@gte.net.

COOK, BRYSON LEITCH, lawyer; b. Balt., Apr. 17, 1948; s. A. Samuel Cook. BA magna cum laude, Princeton U., 1970; JD cum laude, U. Pa., 1973, MBA, 1973. Bar: Md. 1974, U.S. Dist. Ct. Md. 1976, U.S. Tax Ct. 1977. Assoc. Alex Brown & Sons, Balt., 1973-75, Venable, Baetjer & Howard, Balt., 1975-81, ptnr., 1981—; ptnr., Bus. Trans. Dept. and Taxation Dept. Venable LLP, Balt. Adj. prof. U. Md. Law Sch., Balt., 1981, Loyola U. Bus. Sch., Balt., 1980-82. Contbr. articles to legal jours.; author tax mgmt. portfolios. Trustee Balt. Ballet, 1980-83, Keswick Home for the Incurables, Balt., 1983—; bd. dirs. Balt. City Jail, 1980-82; counsel Md. Hist. Soc., Balt., 1981—. Recipient Gordon A. Block award U. Pa. Law Sch., 1973. Mem. ABA, Bar Assn. Balt. City, Md. State Bar Assn., Internat. Fiscal Assn., Order of Coif, Elkridge Club (Balt.). Republican. Methodist. Office: Venable LLP Mercantile Bank & Trust Bldg 2 Hopkins Plz Ste 1800 Baltimore MD 21201-2971 also: Venable LLP 575 7th St NW Washington DC 20004 Office Phone: 410-244-7522. E-mail: blcook@venable.com.

COOK, C. COLLEEN, librarian, dean; BA, MLS, U. Tex.; MA, Tex. A&M U., PhD Higher Edn. Adminstrn. Serials cataloger Tex. A&M Univ. Librs., assoc. dean adminstrn. tech. svcs., 1993, exec. assoc. dean, 1996—2003, interim dean, 2003—04, dean, 2004—. Co-prin. investagator LibQUAL+ project; lectr. in field. Mem. editl. adv. bd. Performance measurement and metrics; contbr. articles to profl. jours. Recipient Disting. Librarianship Award, Tex. A&M U. Assn. of Former Students, 1992. Mem.: ALA, Am. Edn. Rsch. Assn., Tex. Libr. Assn. Office: Tex A&M U Librs College Station TX 77843-5000 Office Phone: 979-845-5741. E-mail: ccook@tamu.edu.*

COOK, CAMILLE WRIGHT, retired law educator; b. Tuscaloosa, Ala. d. Reuben Hall and Camille Tunstall (Searcy) Wright; children: Sydney, Reuben, Cade, Camille. AB, U. Ala., 1945, JD, 1948. Bar: Ala. 1948. Asst. prof. law, Law Sch. Auburn (Ala.) U., 1968; mem. faculty Sch. Law U. Ala., 1968-93, assoc. dean, dir. continuing legal edn., prof. law, Law Sch., 1975-93, asst. acad. v.p., 1984-85; prof. emeritus, 1993—. Bd. dirs. U. Ala. Law Sch. Found., Am/South. Mem. Smithsonian Coun., Washington, 1972-78, Ala. Air Pollution Commn., 1971-81; vestry Christ Episcopal Ch. Recipient outstanding commitment to tchg. award U. Ala., 1990, disting. alumni award, 1996, Algernon Sydney Sullivan award, 1999. Fellow Am. Bar Found., Ala. Bar Assn. (award merit 1973); mem. ABA (Rawles Spl. Merit award 1983), Farrah Law Soc. (trustee 1972—, disting. alumnae award 1992), Am. law Inst. (coun., Rawles Spl. Merit award 1983). Episcopalian. Home: 32 Ridgeland Tuscaloosa AL 35406-1607 Personal E-mail: camillewcook1@comcast.net.

COOK, CHARLES EDWARD, JR., editor, political analyst; b. Shreveport, La., Nov. 20, 1953; s. Charles Edward and Mary Elizabeth (Hudgens) C.; m. Lucy Gerald, Apr. 17, 1982. Student, Georgetown U., 1972-77. Rsch. dir. Dem. Senatorial Campaign Com., Washington, 1977-79; so. regional desk person Kennedy for Pres. Campaign, Washington, 1979-80; pub. opinion analyst, polit. cons. William R. Hamilton & Staff, Washington, 1980; asst. dir. for polit. affairs Nat. Assn. of Home Builders, Washington, 1981-82; mem. profl. staff Senate Dem. Policy Com., Washington, 1982-84; editor The Cook Polit. Report, Washington, 1984—, publisher; polit. analyst Nat. Jour. Group. Election night analyst C-Span, 1986, 88, NBC News, 1988, CBS News, 1990, 92, NBC, 1994, 96, 98, 2000, 2002 and 2004; polit. analyst CNN, 1996-2002, NBC, 2002—. Columnist Roll Call, 1986-98, Nat. Jour., 1998—. Methodist. Office: Cook Political Report The Watergate 600 New Hampshire Ave NW Washington DC 20037*

COOK, CHARLES WILKERSON, JR., bank executive, retired municipal official; b. Nashville, Sept. 10, 1934; s. Charles Wilkerson and Virginia (Jones) C.; m. Sally Randolph Frierson, June 24, 1961 (dec. May 2001); children: Charles Wilkerson III, John Stephenson Frierson; m. Mary Hawkins, Jan. 18, 2003. BS, Yale U., 1956; postgrad., Rutgers U., 1964-66. With Third Nat. Bank, Nashville, 1959-85, pres., 1979-83, chmn., 1983-85, also dir.; with Third Nat. Corp., Nashville, 1985-89, pres., chief exec. officer, 1985-87, chmn. bd. dirs., chief exec. officer, 1987-89, dir., 1983-90; exec. v.p. Sun Trust Banks, Inc., 1989-90; dir. fin. Met. Govt. of Nashville-Davidson County (Tenn.), Nashville, 1991-93; pres., CEO, dir. Union Planters Bank of Mid. Tenn., N.A., Nashville, 1993-99, chmn., bd. dirs., 2000—01; ret., 2001; vice chmn. Nashville Bank and Trust Co., 2004—, dir., 2004—; mem. Met. Govt. Bd. Equalization, 2004—. Bd. dirs. Nashville Electric Power, chmn. bd. dirs., 1997-2003; bd. dirs. Quality Industries, Inc., Richland Place, Inc. Author: History of a Bank Merger, 1969. Active Nashville-Davidson County Govt. Social Svcs. Commn., 1970-85; sr. warden Christ Episcopal Ch., Nashville, 1970-71; pres. Episc. Churchmen of Tenn., 1974; mem. bishop and coun. Episc. Diocese of Tenn., 1979-81; chmn., bd. dirs. United Way Nashville, 1984-85, 1993-97; chmn. Project PENCIL, 1988-89, Jr. Achievement of Nashville, Bill Wilkerson Hearing and Speech Ctr., Nashville, 1970-80, Ensworth Sch., 1978-81, Better Bus. Bur. Nashville, 1980-83, Nashville Meml. Hosp., 1974-89, Tenn. Performing Arts Mgmt. Corp., 1985-89, vice-chmn., 1987-89, Tenn. State Mus. Found., 1986-89; adv. bd. Salvation Army, Nashville, 1976-79; bd. dirs. Episcopal Ch. Found., 1991-92, St. Luke's Cmty. House, 1999-2004, chmn., 2002-03; bd. dirs. Nashville Pub. TV Corp., 1998—, chmn., 2006—, Nashville Cmty. Found., 2000—, Tenn. Hist. Soc., 2000—; campaign chmn. United Way Mid. Tenn., 1994. With USN, 1956-59; capt. Res., 1977-84. Mem. Nashville C. of C. (bd. govs. 1982-84, 95-2000), Belle Meade Country Club (bd. dirs. 1996-2000, pres. 1999-2000), Army-Navy Club (Washington), Yale Club NYC, Univ. Club (Nashville). Home Phone: 615-292-0011.

COOK, CHARLES WILLIAM, aerospace engineer, consultant, educator; b. Yankton, SD, Sept. 27, 1927; s. William O. and Kathryn S. (Eymer) C.; m. Virginia M. Fosness, May 30, 1950 (dec. Jan. 2005); children: Jennifer Cook Clark, William O. II, Amy Cook Lewandowski. AB summa cum laude, U. S.D., Dean Akeley fellow, 1951; MS, Calif. Inst. Tech., 1954, PhD, 1957. Head nuclear physics Convair Corp., San Diego, 1957-60; chief Ballistic Missile Def. br. Advanced Rsch. Project Agy., Washington, 1961; corp. dir. elec. rsch. and devel. No. Am. Aviation Inc., El Segundo, Calif., 1961-67; dep. div. chief. CIA, Washington, 1961-71; asst. dir. def. rsch. and engring. Dept. Def., Washington, 1971-74; dep. under sec. for space systems, acting dir. NRO Air Force, 1974-79, dep. asst. sec. for space plans and policy, 1979-88. Adj. prof. George Mason U., Fairfax, Va., 1988-90; cons. aerospace engring., plans and policy Inst. Def. Analyses, Alexandria, Va., Sys. Planning Corp., Arlington, Def. Sci. Bd., Pentagon, Global Outpost Inc., Alexandria, ANSER, Arlington, George Washington U., VEDA, Alexandria, Kistler Aerospace, Kirkland, Wash., McGraw-Hill Inc., 1988—. Contbr. articles to profl. jours., chpts. to books. With A.C. AUS, 1944-47. Decorated Air Force Exceptional Civilian Svc. award with three oak leaf clusters; named to Coyote Hall of Fame, U. SD, 1976; recipient Meritorious Civil Svc. award, Sec. Def., 1974, DSM, 1976, Disting. Alumni award, U. S.D., 1982, cert. of appreciation, Intelligence R&D Coun., 1987, Disting. Svc. medal, NASA, 1988, Nat. Intelligence medal of achievement, 1988, Disting. Svc. award, Nat. Reconnaissance Office, 1998; fellow Dean Akeley, U. SD, 1951, Dobbins, Calif. Inst. Tech., 1953, 1954—56. Fellow AIAA; mem. IEEE (sr.), Am. Phys. Soc., Am. Inst. Physics, Sigma Xi, Phi Beta Kappa, Sigma Pi Sigma. Achievements include determination of astrophysical significance of B12 with respect to element synthesis in stellar interiors. Home: 1180 Daleview Dr Mc Lean VA 22102-1540 Office: Inst for Def Analyses 4850 Mark Center Dr Alexandria VA 22311-1882 Office Phone: 703-845-2312. Personal E-mail: cwcook22102@aol.com. Business E-Mail: ccook@ida.org.

COOK, COLIN BURFORD, psychiatrist; b. London, Jan. 20, 1927; arrived in U.S., 1952, naturalized, 1975; s. Bertram William and Anna Marie (Forster-Jones) C. MD, London U., 1951. Diplomate Am. Bd. Psychiatry and Neurology. Rotating intern Bridgeport (Conn.) Hosp., 1952-53; resident Goodmayes Hosp., Warlingham Park Hosp., London, 1955-57; gen. med. practitioner London, 1960-66; resident in psychiatry Marquette (Wis.) Sch. Medicine, 1968-69, Cornell U., White Plains, NY, 1969-71; fellow Nat. Hosp. Neurol. Disease, U. London, 1973; practice medicine specializing in psychiatry, Stamford, Conn., 1975—. Prof. psychiatry Columbia U., NYC, 1992-95; attending physician, psychiatrist Regional Network Programs, Inc., Conn., 1995-96. Author: (as Alan Phillips) Jazz Improvisation and Harmony, 1965, 4th edit., 1998. Served with Brit. Navy, 1953-55, 57-59. Fellow: Am. Soc. Psychoanalytical Physicians; mem.: AMA, Authors League, Masons (32d degree). Address: 373 Strawberry Hill Ave Stamford CT 06902-2512 Office Phone: 203-348-9091. Personal E-mail: ccookie3210@aol.com.

COOK, DANE (DANE JEFFREY COOK), comedian, actor; b. Boston, Mar. 18, 1972; Comedian, dir., exec. prodr. nationwide tour Tourgasm, 2005. Actor: (films) Flypaper, 1997, Buddy, 1997, Mystery Men, 1999, Simon Sez, 1999, L.A.X., 2002, The Touch, 2002, Stuck On You, 2003, Torque, 2004, Mr. 3000 (voice), 2004, London, 2005, Waiting., 2005, Employee of the Month, 2006, Mr. Brooks, 2007; (TV films) Windy City Heat, 2003, Humor Me, 2004; actor, writer, prodr. (films) Spiral, 1999, comedian, writer (TV specials) Comedy Central Presents: Dane Cook, 2000, comedian (CD/DVDs) Harmful If Swallowed, 2003, Retaliation, 2005, host Saturday Night Live, 2005, headlined Comedy Central Insomniac Tour Movie, voice Crank Yankers, Shorties Watchin' Shorties, Duck Dodgers, 2005, guest appearances Maybe This Time, 1996, Suddenly Susan, 1998, The Man Show, 2002, co-host Teen Choice Awards, 2006. Named Hot Comic, Rolling Stone mag., Coolest Comic of Yr., Stuff mag.; named one of 100 Most Influential People, Time mag., 2006; recipient Comedy Central Stand-Up Showdown. Office: c/o Creative Artists Agy Tracy Brennan/Steve Smooke 9830 Wilshire Blvd Beverly Hills CA 90212 E-mail: DC@DANECOOK.com.*

COOK, DAVID, editor; b. Boston, Dec. 28, 1946; s. Theodore N. and Charlotte M. (Stachelhaus) Cook; m. Linda Markarian, Dec. 19, 1981; children: Matthew D., Christopher E., Timothy T. BA, Principia Coll., 1969; postgrad., Columbia U., 1977; Mich. State U., 1979-81. Staff writer Christian Sci. Monitor, Boston and Washington, 1971-77, bus. corr. Boston, 1981-82, Washington corr., 1982-88; chief bur. McGraw Hill World News, Detroit, 1977-79, dep. chief Chgo., 1980-81; corr. Bus. Week Mag., Detroit, 1979-80; mng. editor Monitor TV, Boston, 1988-92; editor Monitor Radio, Boston, 1992-94, The Christian Sci. Monitor, Boston, 1994—2001, Washington bur. chief, sr. editor, 2001—. With US Army, 1969—71. Christian Scientist. Avocation: reading. Office: Christian Sci Monitor Washington Bur 910 16th St Washington DC 20006 Office Phone: 202-481-6680. Business E-Mail: cookd@csmonitor.com.

COOK, DEBORAH L., federal judge, former state supreme court justice; b. Pitts., Feb. 8, 1952; BA in English, U. Akron, 1974, JD, 1978, LLD (hon.), 1996. Ptnr. Roderick & Linton, Akron, 1976-91; judge 9th dist. Ohio Ct. Appeals, 1991-94; justice Ohio Supreme Ct., 1995—2003; judge US Ct. Appeals, (6th cir.), Cincinnati, Ohio, 2003—. Bd. trustees Summit County United Way, Vol. Ctr., Stan Hywet Hall and Gardens, Akron Sch. Law, Coll. Scholars, Inc.; bd. dirs. Women's Network; vol. Mobile Meals, Safe Landing Shelter. Named Woman of Yr., Women's Network, 1991. Fellow Am. Bar Found.; mem. Omicron Delta Kappa, Delta Gamma (pres., Nat. Shield award). Office: 532 Potter Stewart US Courthouse 100 E Fifth St Cincinnati OH 45202-3988*

COOK, DEBRA JO, counseling administrator, elementary school educator; b. May 21, 1965; BS in Bus. Edn., W.Va. Inst. Tech., Montgomery, 1987; MA in Counseling, Marshall U., Charleston, 1993. Educator, cons. pvt. industry, Chas, W.Va., 1988—99; counselor, educator Kanawha Co. Schs., Chas, W.Va., 2000—. Mem.: Am. Fedn. Tchrs., Am. Sch. Counseling Assn., W.Va. Sch. Counseling Assn. (pres. 2006—). Home: 708 Oxford Cir Charleston WV 25314 Personal E-mail: debcook@suddenlink.net.

COOK, DON W., human resources specialist, retired military officer, risk management consultant; b. Lancaster, Calif., Mar. 28, 1967; s. Donald W. Abrams and Dianne C. Willerford-Norton; life ptnr. Robert P. Cook, July 12, 2006; children: Brendon Wilsey, Joshua Wilsey, Nickolas Wilsey-Timko. BA in Secondary Edn., Ariz. State U., Tempe, 1997; PhD in Polit. Sci., Concordia U., NY, 2000; MSW, Concordia U., Wis., 2003. Registered counselor Wash., 2000. Commd. lt. USCG, Long Beach, Calif., 1986, advanced through grades to lt. comdr., ret., 2006; risk mgr., recruiter Manpower, Bellingham, Wash., 2005—; mgr. human resources Trident Seafoods, Anacortes, Wash., 2005—. Mem.: DeMolay Internat. (juris. master councilor So. Calif. chpt. 1985—86). Democrat. Roman Catholic. Avocations: travel, boating. Home: 1151 Lisa St Oak Harbor WA 98277 Office: Trident Seafoods 1400 4th St Anacortes WA 98221 Home Phone: 360-678-3213; Office Phone: 360-299-7036. Home Fax: 360-293-0185. Personal E-mail: whidbeydon@msn.com.

COOK, DONALD EVAN, pediatrician, educator; b. Pitts., Mar. 24, 1928; s. Merriam E. and Bertha (Gwin) C.; m. Elsie Walden, Sept. 2, 1951; children: Catherine, Christopher, Brian, Jeffrey. BS, Colo. Coll., 1952; MD, U. Colo., 1955. Diplomate Am. Bd. Pediat., 1961. Intern Fresno County Gen. Hosp., Calif., 1955-56; resident in gen. practice Tulare (Calif.) County Gen. Hosp., 1956-57; resident in pediatrics U. Colo., 1957-59; practice medicine specializing in pediatrics Aurora, Colo., 1959—64, Greeley (Colo). Med. Clinic, 1964—86, Greeley Sports Medicine Clinic, 1988—93; med. adv. Centennial Develop. Svcs., Inc., 1993-95; clin. faculty U. Colo., clin. prof., 1977—; pres. Am. Acad. Pediatrics, Elk Grove Village, Ill., 1999-2000; ret. from practice, 2004. Organizer, dir. Sports Medicine Px Exam. Clinic for Indigent Weld Co. athletes, 1990—96; mem. adv. bd. Nat. Ctr. Health Edn., San Francisco, 1978—80; mem. adv. com. innaternal and child health programs Colo. State Health Dept., 1981—84, chmn., 1981—84; preceptor Sch. Nurse Practitioner program U. Colo., 1978—88; affiliate prof. nursing U. No. Colo., 1996; vol. physician Monfort Children's Clinic, 2002—05. Mem. Weld County Dist. 6 Sch. Bd., 1973—83, pres., 1973—74, 1976—77, chmn. dist. 6 accountability com., 1972—73, mem. adv. com. dist. 6 teen pregnancy program, 1983—85; mem. Weld County Task Force on Teen-aged Pregnancy, 1986—89, Dream Team Weld County Task Force on Sch. Dropouts, 1986—92; mem.Weld County Interagy. Screening Bd., Weld County Cmty. Ctr. Found., 1984—89; mem. Weld County Task Force Spkrs. Bur. on AIDS, 1987—94, Weld County Task Force Adolescent Health Clinic, Task Force Child Abuse, C. of C.; bd. dirs. No. Colo. Med. Ctr., 1993—98, No. Colo. Med. Ctr. Found., 1994—; med. advisor Weld County Sch. Dist. VI-Nurses, 1987—2004; mem. Sch. Dist. 6 Health Coalition, Task Force on Access to Health Care; group leader neonatal group Colo. Action for Healthy People Colo. Dept. Pub. Health, 1985—86; co-founder Colorodians for Seatbelts on Sch. Buses, 1985—90; co-founder, v.p. Coalition of Primary Care Physicians Colo., 1986; mem. adv. com. Greeley Ctrl. Drug and Alcohol Abuse, 1984—86; bd. dirs. Rocky Mtn. Ctr. for Health Promotion and Edn., 1984—2006, v.p., 1992—93, pres., 1994—95; med. cons. Sch. Dist. 6, 1989—2004; mem. bd. dirs. United Way Weld County, 1993—98; founder, med. dir. Monfort Children's Clinic, 1994—98, vol. physician, 1998—2004. With USN, 1946—48. Recipient Disting. Svc. award, Jr. C. of C., 1962, Svc. to Mankind award, Sertoma Club, 1972, Disting. Citizenship award, Elks, 1975—76, 2000—01, Spark Plug award, U. No. Colo., 1981, Mildred Doster award, Colo. Sch. Health Coun. for Sch. Health Contbns., 1992, Svc. award, Eta Sigma Gamma, 1996, Citizen of Yr. award, No. Colo. Med. Ctr. Found., 1996, Humanitarian of Yr. award, Weld County United Way, 1996, Alfred Winchester Humanitarian award, Greeley/Weld Sr. Found., Inc., 1996, Silver and Gold award, U. Colo. Med. Alumni Assn., 1997, Franklin Geggenbach award, 1997, Denver Children's Hosp. Pediatric Alumni award, 1997, Benezet award, Colo. Coll., 2000, Edn. Ptnr. of the Yr. award, Greeler-Weld C. of C., 2004, 2006, Leeann Anderson Cmty. Care award, Greeley C. of C., 2006. Mem.: AMA (chmn. sch. and coll. health com. 1980—82, James E. Strain Cmty. Svc. award 1987, 1994), Centennial Pediatric Soc. (pres. 1982—86), Colo. Med. Soc. (com. in sports medicine 1980—90, com. chmn. 1986—90, chmn. com. sch. health 1988—91, A.H. Robbins Cmty. Svc. award 1974), Weld County Med. Soc. (pres. 1968—69), Adams Aurora Med. Soc. (pres. 1964—65), Am. Acad. Pediat. (chmn. sch. health com. 1975—80, mem. task force on new age of pediatrics 1982—85, chmn. Colo. chpt. 1982—87, media spokesperson Speak Up for Children 1983—, Ross edn. and award com. 1985—86, alt. dist. VIII chmn. 1987—93, mem. coun. sects. mgmt. 1991—92, chmn. alt. dist. chmn. com. 1991—93, dist. chmn. dist. VIII 1993—98, mem. search com., exec. dir. candidate for pres. 1998, pres. elect 1998—99, v.p. AAP 1998—99, pres. 1999—2000, 1999—2000, immediate past pres. 2000—01, dist. VIII catch facilitator 2000—06, tomorrows children's task force 2001—04, reimbursement task force 2002—04), Colo. Med. Soc. Sch. Health Com. (chmn. 1967—78), Colo. Coll. Alumni Assn. (bd. dirs. 2003—, co-chmn. class 52 50th reunion com.), Rotary (bd. dirs. Greely chpt. 1988—91, chmn. immunization campaign Weld County 1994, mem. immunization com. 1994—, mem. adv. bd. Greeley Promises for Children 2001—, bd. dirs. Greely chpt. 2003—05, mem. task force on indigent care 2004—, mem. sch. readiness task force 2004—, William D. Farr award 2007, Cmty. Svc. award 2007). Republican. Methodist. Office: Monfort Children's Clinic 100 N 11th Ave Greeley CO 80631 Office Phone: 970-352-0072. Personal E-mail: ecook4130@msn.com. Business E-Mail: dcook@aap.org.

COOK, DORIS MARIE, retired accountant, educator; b. Fayetteville, Ark., June 11, 1924; d. Ira and Mettie Jewel (Dorman) Cook. BSBA, U. Ark., Fayetteville, 1946, MS, 1949; PhD, U. Tex., Austin, 1968. CPA Okla., Ark. Jr. acct. Haskins & Sells, Tulsa, 1946-47; instr. acctg. U. Ark., Fayetteville, 1947-52, asst. prof., 1952-62, assoc. prof., 1962-69, prof., 1969-88, Univ. prof. and Nolan E. Williams lectr. in acctg., 1988-97, emeritus disting. prof., 1997—. Mem. Ark. State Bd. Pub. Accountancy, 1987-92, treas., 1989-91, vice chmn. 1991-92; mem. Nat. Assn. State Bds. of Accountancy, 1987-92; appointed Nolan E. Williams lectureship in acctg., 1988-97; Doris M. Cook chair in acctg. U. Ark., Fayetteville, 2000. Mem. editl. bd. Ark. Bus. Rev., Jour. Managerial Issues; contbr. articles to profl. jours. Recipient Bus. Faculty of Month award Alpha Kappa Psi, 1997, Outstanding Faculty award Ark. Tchg. Acad., 1997, Charles and Nadine Baum Outstanding Tchr. award, 1997, Outstanding Leadership and Svc. award for Women's History Month, 1999, AAUW, others. Mem. AICPA, Ark. Bus. Assn. (editor newsletter 1982-85), Am. Acctg. Assn. (chmn. nat. membership 1982-83, Arthur Carter scholarship com. 1984-85, membership Ark. 1985-87), Am. Women's Soc. CPAs., Ark. Soc. CPAs (life, v.p. 1975-76, pres. N.W. Ark. chpt. 1980-81, sec. Student Loan Found. 1981-84, treas. 1984-92, pres. 1992-97, chmn. pub. rels. 1984-88, 93-95, Outstanding Acctg. Educator award 1991, Outstanding Com. Svc. award 1995, Student Loan Found. Bd. award 2001, 21 Yrs. Outstanding Svc. award 2001), Acad. Acctg. Historians (life, trustee 1985-87, rev. bd. of Working Papers Series 1984-92, sec. 1992-95, pres.-elect 1995, pres. 1996), Ark. Fedn. Bus. and Profl. Women's Clubs (treas. 1979-80), Fayetteville Bus. and Profl. Women's Clubs (pres. 1973-74, 75-76, Woman of Yr. award 1977) Mortar Bd., Beta Gamma Sigma, Beta Alpha Psi (editor nat. newsletter 1973-77, nat. pres. 1977-78, Outstanding Alumni in Edn. Iota chpt. 1999, Outstanding Svc. award Iota chpt. 1997), Phi Gamma Nu, Alpha Lambda Delta, Delta Kappa Gamma (sec. 1976-78, pres. 1978-80, treas. 1989-2000), Phi Kappa Phi. Home: 1655 Amy Ave Glendale Heights IL 60139

COOK, E. GARY, manufacturing executive; BS, Univ. Va., 1966; PhD in Chemistry, Va. Polytechnic Inst., 1970. Sr. mgmt. positions, including v.p., printing, pub., v.p., med. products, v.p., corp. plans E.I. DuPont de Nemours & Co., 1969—92; sr. v.p., pres.-chem., bd. dir. Ethyl Corp., 1992—94; pres., COO Albemarle Corp., 1994—96; chmn., pres., CEO Witco Corp. (merged with Crompton Knowles to become CK Witco), 1996—99; chmn. Integrated Environ. Tech. LLC, 2002—, Louisiana Pacific Corp., 2000—. Bd. dir. Trimeris Corp. Office: Louisiana Pacific Corp 414 Union St Nashville TN 37219 Office Phone: 515-986-5600.*

COOK, EDDIE WALTON, army chaplain, military officer; b. Fayetteville, NC, Sept. 18, 1970; s. Eddie Ray and Eugenia Marie Cook; m. Jennifer L. Cook, Dec. 18, 1999; 1 child, Edward J. B of Mgmt., NC State U., Raleigh, 1992, B of Econs., 1992; MDiv, S.E. Bapt. Theol. Seminary, Wake Forest, NC, 2002; DD, Erskine Theol. Seminary, Due West, SC, 2007. Army inf. officer, 82nd airborne divsn. US Army, Ft. Bragg, NC, 1992—95, army ordnance officer 82nd airborne divsn., 1995—97, army chaplain, 82nd airborne divsn., 2002—05; asst. pastor Evangelism First Assembly God, Raleigh, 1998—2002; army chaplain Walter Reed Army Med. Ctr., Washington, 2005—06, Gen. Leonard Wood Army Hosp., Md., 2007—. Hosp. chaplain Clin. Pastoral Edn., Washington, 2005—06. Chaplain Boy Scouts Am. Troop 747, Fayetteville, NC, 1993—2005. Decorated Bronze Star medal US Army. Mem.: Am. Assn. Pastoral Counselors. Republican. Assembly Of God. Avocations: camping, outdoor activities.

COOK, EDWARD JOSEPH, college president; b. NYC, July 8, 1925; s. Clinton J. and Catherine A. (Cullen) C.; m. Dorothy A. Collins, July 21, 1951; children: Barbara A., Thomas E., Patricia M. BS summa cum laude, Fordham U., 1949, PhD, 1958; MA, Columbia U., 1950. Assoc. prof., chmn. dept. econs. Sch. Bus., Fordham U., NYC, 1950-62; asst. dean Sch. Bus., chmn. econs. dept. St. John's U., NYC, 1962-64; prof. econs., dir. div. bus. C.W. Post Coll., Greenvale, N.Y., 1964-69, exec. dean Sch. Bus. Adminstrn., 1969-73; pres. C. W. Post Center, L.I. U., Greenvale, 1973-86. Mgmt. cons. to U.S. Navy and pvt. industry, 1969-73 Author: Causes of Commercial Bank Failures in New York State, 1958, (with R. Vizza) The Marketing Concept, 1968, (with A.F. Chapman) Peter Drucker, Contributions to Business Enterprises, 1970, (with J.N. Macri) Maternal Serum Alpha-Fetoprotein Patient-Specific Risk Reporting: Its Use and Misuse, 1990, (with J.N. Macri) Maternal Serum Down Syndrome Screening: Free Beta Protein, 1990. Chmn., L.I. Regional Planning Bd. Served with U.S. Army, 1942-45. Decorated Purple Heart. Mem. Am. Econ. Assn. Roman Catholic.

COOK, FRANCES D., management consultant; b. Charleston, W.Va., Sept. 7, 1945; d. Nash and Vivian Cook. BA, Mary Washington Coll. of U. Va., 1967; MPA, Harvard U., 1978; LLD, Shenandoah U., 1998. Certificats d'Etudes, Université d'Aix-Marseille (France), 1966. Commd. fgn. svc. officer Dept. State, 1967; spl. asst. to R.S. Shriver amb. to France, Paris, 1968-69; mem. U.S. Del. Paris Peace Talks on Viet-Nam, 1970-71; cultural affairs officer, consul Am. Consul Gen., Sydney, Australia, 1971-73; cultural affairs officer, first sec. Am. Embassy, Dakar, Senegal, 1973-75; personnel officer for Africa USIA, Washington, 1975-77; dir. office public affairs African Bur. Dept. State, Washington, 1978-80, amb. to Republic of Burundi at Bujumbura, 1980—83, consul gen. Alexandria, Egypt, 1983-86, dep. asst. sec. of state for refugees Washington, 1986-87, dir. Office of West African Affairs, 1987-89, amb. to Cameroon Yaoundé, 1989-93, U.S. coord. for Sudan, 1993; dep. asst. sec. of state for political-military affairs Dept. of State, Washington, 1993-95, amb. to Oman Muscat, 1996-99; founder The Ballard Group, LLC, 2002. Bd. dirs. ATK, Corp. Coun. in Africa. Recipient various honor awards Dept. State and Def. Mem. Am. Fgn. Svc. Assn., Coun. of Fgn. Rels., Harvard Club of N.Y.C., Washington Inst. Fgn. Affairs, Phi Beta Kappa (alumni). Home: PO Box 40882 Washington DC 20016-0882 Home Phone: 202-237-7446; Office Phone: 202-237-7446. Business E-Mail: francesdcook@ballardgroupllc.com.

COOK, GARETH, reporter; b. Ann Arbor, Mich. m. Amanda Cook; 1 child. BA in Internat. Rels., Brown Univ., 1991, BA in Math. Physics, 1991. Asst. editor Fgn. Policy Mag., 1991—93; reporter US News & World Report, 1993—94; editor position Washington Monthly, 1995; news editor Boston Phoenix; New England editor, city desk Boston Globe, 1999, Sunday metro editor, 1999—2000, sci. writer, 2000—. Recipient Pulitzer Prize for explanatory reporting, 2005. Mem.: Sigma Xi, Phi Beta Kappa. Office: Boston Globe 135 Morissey Blvd PO Box 55819 Boston MA 02205-5819 Office Phone: 617-929-2000.

COOK, GARY RAYMOND, academic administrator, minister; b. Little Rock, Ark., Sept. 27, 1950; s. Raymond C. and Vada (James) C.; m. Sheila Gayle Raymer, Dec. 28, 1974; children: David Daniel, Mark Andrew. BA, Baylor U., 1972; MDiv, So. Sem., Louisville, 1975; MA, U. North Tex., 1977; D in Ministry, Southwestern Sem., 1977. Pastor 1st Bapt. Ch., McGregor, Tex., 1976-78; dir. denomination and community rels. Baylor U., Waco, Tex., 1978-88; pres. Dallas Bapt. U., 1988—. Author: Retirees in Mission, 1977; co-editor: Abner McCall: One Man's Journey, 1981. Mayor pro tem City of Waco, 1983-84, mem. city coun., 1981-84; past bd. dirs. Tex. Dept. on Aging; past internat. bd. dirs. Habitat for Humanity. Recipient Humanitarian award Waco Conf. Christians and Jews, 1986, Disting. Alumnus award Southwestern Sem., 2000, Baylor U., 2003. Mem. Rotary (sustaining). Home and Office: 3000 Mountain Creek Pkwy Dallas TX 75211-6700

COOK, GEORGE VALENTINE, lawyer, consultant; b. Glendale, NY, Feb. 14, 1927; s. Walter Preston and Ida Ruth (Smith) C.; m. Edith Wengler, Sept. 4, 1948 (dec. Dec. 2002); children: George V., James, Robert, Laura, Barbara, Mary, Walter, Elizabeth. BA, Columbia U., NYC, 1949, LL.B., 1952. Bar: N.Y. 1953, U.S. Dist. Ct. (so. dist.) N.Y. 1955, U.S. Dist. Ct. (ea. dist.) N.Y. 1955, U.S. Ct. Appeals (2d cir.) 1955, U.S. Ct. Appeals (3d cir.) 1982, US. Dist. Ct. (no. dist.) N.Y. 1987. Assoc. Dewey, Ballantine, Bushby, Palmer & Wood, NYC, 1952-56; mem. legal staff N.Y. Telephone Co., NYC, 1956-59, 60-61; atty. AT&T, NYC, 1959-60, 61-65, v.p., 1972—76; v.p. regulatory matters Western Electric Co., Inc., NYC, 1966-72, v.p. gen. counsel, 1976-83, also dir.; exec. v.p., gen. counsel AT&T Technologies, Inc., NYC, 1984-85; counsel Hunton & Williams, 1985-90; cons., 1990—. Contbr. articles to profl. jours. Active alumni activities Columbia U. Served to 2d lt. U.S. Army, 1945-47. Fellow Am. Bar Found.; mem. ABA, N.Y. State Bar Assn., Assn. Gen. Counsel, Assn. Bar City of N.Y. Home: 127 Somerset Ave Garden City NY 11530-1348

COOK, GERALD, electrical engineering educator; b. Hazard, Ky., Oct. 31, 1937; s. Rudolph H. and Rose I. (Boyer) C.; m. Nancy Anne Gillespie, June 9, 1962; children: Gerald Boyer, Allan Binford. BS, Va. Poly. Inst., 1961; MS, MIT, 1962, ScD, 1965. Registered profl. engr., Va. Lectr. U. Colo., Colorado Springs, 1966—68; asst. prof. U.S. Air Force Acad., Colorado Springs, 1966—68; assoc. prof. U. Va., Charlottesville, 1968—73, prof., 1973—81; prof., chmn. dept. Vanderbilt U., Nashville, 1981—85; Earle C. Williams prof. elec. engring. George Mason U., Fairfax, Va., 1985—, chmn. dept. elec. and computer engring., 1990—98. Vis. prof. Tech. U. Denmark, 1979-80; vis. rschr. Night Vision Lab., Ft. Belvoir, 1998-99. Editor-in-chief IEEE Trans. on Indsl. Electronics, 1984-91. Recipient Outstanding Rsch. award USAF Office Aerospace Rsch., 1968, Cert. of Achievement, U.S. Army, 1981; NSF fellow, 1961-64. Fellow IEEE (life, pres. Indsl. Electronics Soc. 1981-83, Centennial medal 1984, Eugene Mittelmann Achievement award 1989), Am. Soc. Engring. Edn. (Outstanding Rsch. awrd S.E. sect. 1971), Sigma Xi, Eta Kappa Nu, Phi Kappa Phi, Tau Beta Pi. Home: 4821 Fox Chapel Rd Fairfax VA 22030-4508 Office: George Mason U Dept Elec Engring Fairfax VA 22030 Office Phone: 703-993-1699. Business E-Mail: gcook@gmu.edu.

COOK, GLORIA HOUSTON, civic leader; b. Portland, Maine, Aug. 22, 1933; d. Ellwyn Kenelm and May Elvera (Delay) Houston; m. James Thomas Cook Jr., Jan. 28, 1952; children: Victoria Cook Leonhardt, Sheryl Ann. Student, U. Fla., 1950-52. Invitee, White House Conf. on Food, Nutrition and Health, 1969, cons. to Fla. conf., 1970; Gen. Synod del. from Fla., United Ch. of Christ, 1975-77; dir. pub. rels., trustee, chmn. nominating com., mem. pulpit com., tchr. Sunday sch., mem. stewardship bd., Seabreeze United Ch.; legis. appointee, sec. exec. bd., Volusia County Charter Rev. Commn., 1975-77; mem. Volusia County Pers. and Merit Bd., 1974-85, chmn., 1980-83; bd. counselors, Bethune-Cookman Coll., 1977-84; bd. dirs., Atlantic Ctr. for Arts, New Smyrna Beach, Fla.; pres., bd. dirs., exec. com. Meml. Health Care Systems, Ormond Beach, Fla., 1980-2000, mem. hosp. estate planning com., chmn., treas. pers. com., chmn. fin. com., v.p., CEO search, evaluation and compensation com.; hon. life dir. Volusia/Flagler Easter Seals, 1955—, fundraising capital campaign chmn., 1999-2004; past pres., v.p., sec. Fla. Easter Seals; past pres., v.p., chair, vice chmn. Ho. of Dels. Nat. Easter Seals; mem. nat. adv. child health and human devel. Coun. Nat. Insts. Health, 1990-94; past pres., sustaining mem. Jr. League Daytona Beach, Civic League Halifax Area, Women's Network. Recipient Meritorious Service and Outstanding Vol. Service awards Nat. Easter Seals, Humanitarian of Yr. Meml. Health Sys., 1991, Easter Seal Lily award, 2004; named Layman of Yr., Fla. Med. Soc., 1985, one of 100 Outstanding Jr. League Mems. Internat. Jr. Leagues, named Vol. of Distinciton, Centennial Yr., 1995. Mem. Nat. League Am. Pen Women (patron), Highlands Country Club (N.C.), Hammock Dunes Country Club (Fla.). Republican. Avocations: collecting perfume bottles, photography, gardening. Home: 15 Madeira Ct Palm Coast FL 32137-2103 also: 78 S Sassafras Ct Highlands NC 28741-6635

COOK, HARDY MERRILL, III, literature and language professor; b. Balt., July 21, 1947; s. Hardy Merrill Cook, Jr. and Elizabeth (Frierson) Cook; m. Kathleen Mary Kelley, Apr. 25, 1975 (dec. Oct. 30, 2004); children: Melissa Lauren Cook Ralph, Rebecca Mary Elizabeth. BA, U. Md., College Pk., 1969, MA, 1972, PhD, 1988. English prof. Bowie State U., Md., 1977—. Co-editor (with Ian Lancashire): (electronic edit.) Shake-speares Sonnets and Lovers Complaint 1609; contbg. editor: Shakespeare Newsletter, 1990—98; mem. editl. bd.: Internet Shakespeare Edits., 1996—, Multicultural Shakespeare: Translation, Appropriation and Performance, 2003—, mem. adv. bd.: Digital Renaissance Edits., 2006—; contbr. articles to profl. jours. Recipient Regents' Faculty Excellence award, U. Sys. Md., 1999. Mem.: Malone Soc., Internat. Shakespeare Assn., Shakespeare Assn. Am. Office: Bowie State U MLK Bldg Bowie MD 20715 Personal E-mail: editor@shakspear.net. Business E-Mail: hcook@bowiestate.edu.

COOK, HARRY CLAYTON, JR., lawyer; b. Washington, Mar. 25, 1935; s. Harry Clayton and Lillian June (A'harrah) Cook; m. Jane Clare Mellius, 1963 (div. 1974); children: Christianne Pier, Nicole, Harry Clayton III; m. Judith Ann Taber, 1994; children: Rebecca Lyeth Kelsey, Parker Burr Kelsey. BSChemE, Princeton U., 1956; LLB, U. Va., 1960. Bar: Colo. 1960, N.Y. 1961, Pa. 1966, D.C. 1973. Assoc. Sullivan & Cromwell, NYC, 1960—63, Holme Roberts & Owen, Denver, 1964, Pepper Hamilton & Scheetz, Phila., 1965—69, ptnr., 1969—70, 1973; on assignment as sr. tax counsel Sun Oil Co., Phila., 1970; ptnr. Cadwalader Wickersham & Taft, Washington, 1974—87, Bishop, Cook, Purcell & Reynolds, Washington, 1988—90; pvt. practice H.C. Cook Law Offices, Langley, Va., 1991; of counsel Bastianelli, Brown & Touhey, Washington, 1992—2002; sr. counsel Fulbright & Jaworski LLP, Washington, 2002—04; counsel Seward & Kissel LLP, Washington, 2004—. Page to U.S. Sen. E. D. Millikin, Colo., 1950—52; gen. counsel Maritime Adminstrn.; mem. Maritime Subs. Bd., U.S. Dept. Commerce, Washington, 1970—73; U.S. del. to Soviet Union Maritime Agreement between U.S. and USSR, 1971—73; mem. Adminstrv. Conf. U.S., 1980—90, chmn. com. jud. rev., 1982—88, sr. fellow, 1988—90; mem. U.S. Office Tech. Assessment, Nat. Def. Exec. Res., U.S. Mil. Sealift Command, 1983—91; mem. citizens adv. panel U.S. Maritime Ind., 1982—85, cargo policy workshop particpant, 1984—85; short sea shipping workshop participant Nat. Shipbuilding Rsch. Program, 2007. Mem. editl. bd.: Va. Law Rev., 1958—60, exec. editor:, 1959—60; contbr. articles to profl. jours. Bd. dirs. Com. on the Present Danger, 1978—87; bd. govs. United Svc. Orgns., 1998—2002; bd. dirs. SeaBridge Inc., 2002—; bd. adv. QuadTech Marine, Inc., 2004—; bd. dirs. New World Inst., 2003—, Inst. Fgn. Policy Analysis, 1975—87. Mem.: ABA, Maritime Law Assn. U.S. (marine fin. com., proctor in admiralty), D.C. Bar Assn., Am. Law Inst. (life), Raven Soc., Univ. Club (N.Y.C.), Fishers Island Club (N.Y.), Chevy Chase (Md.) Club, Cosmos Club (Washington), Hay Harbor Club (N.Y.), Met. Club (Washington), Order of Coif, Phi Delta Phi. Office: Seward & Kissel LLP Ste 350 1200 G Ste NW Washington DC 20005 Office Phone: 202-661-7185. Personal E-mail: PlimsollDC@aol.com.

COOK, HARVEY CARLISLE, law enforcement official; b. Cambridge, Md., June 19, 1936; s. John Morrison and Lula Arbelia (Warfield) C.; m. Shirley Marie Cox, Aug. 4, 1973; children: Brenda, Claudine, John, Anne. AA in Police Sci., Charles Ct. C.C., La Plata, Md., 1973; BBA, U. Md., College Park, 1979, cert. in paralegal, 1980; cert. in criminal justice, FBI Nat. Acad., Quantico, Va., 1983. lic. USCG Masters, 1988. Insp. Tidewater Fisheries Dept., Hughesville, Md., 1958—61, dist. insp., 1962—64; lt. Md. State Marine Police, Hughesville, 1965—69, capt. LaPlata, 1970—72, Md. Natural Resources Police, LaPlata, 1973—75, maj. Annapolis, 1976—86, dep. supt., 1986—88; dir. Hovercraft tng. and ops. Hover Sys., Inc., 1988—93; dir. health & indsl. safety Mech. Constrn. Inc., 1994—; dir. marine & indsl. safety & security Cook & Assocs., 1995—. Liaison officer Emergency Mgmt. Agy., Pikesville, Md., 1974-86. Bd. dirs. Charles County Fair, LaPlata, 1985. Recipient Instr. Svc. award, 2001, Pa. Fish and Boat Commn. Instr. award, 2003, 2004; Disting. Svc. award Gov. of Md., 1987, Sustained Aux. Svc. award USCG Aux., 2000; named Best Engring. Soldier Md. Nat. Guard 121st Engr. Bn., 1967, Disting. Citizen, Mass. Gov.'s Office, 1983; Ky. Col., 1983. Mem. Fraternal Order Police, NRA (life), Nat. Police Officers Assn. Am. (charter), Hoverclub Am., U.S. Hovercraft Soc. Inc. (bd. dirs. 1987, v.p. 1990-92, pres. 1993), USCG Aux. (Ann. Safe Boating award 1975, Pub. Educator award 1999, 04, 05, 06, Pa. Inst. Svc. award 2004, 05, 06, state liaison officer 1982-86, vice Flotilla comdr. 1996, comdr. 1997-98, Flotilla staff officer 1998-07, staff officer marine safety divsn. 4 2007—), Chesapeake Bay Profl. Capts. Assn., Potomac River Pilots Assn., FBI Nat. Acad. Assocs., Dr. Samuel A. Mudd Soc. Inc. (treas. 1987), So. Md. Bd. Realtors, Md. Chiefs Police Assn., Charles County C.C. Alumni Assn. (pres. 1984). Republican. Methodist. Avocations: hunting, fishing, power boating, antiques. Office: Cook & Assocs 408 Briarwood Rd Wallingford PA 19086-6503 Office Phone: 610-999-4286. Personal E-mail: hscook1@comcast.net.

COOK, IAN AINSWORTH, psychiatrist, researcher, educator; b. NYC, May 1, 1960; s. Charles David and Bobette Cook; m. Hallie Houck; children: Natalie, Abigail. BS in Engring. magna cum laude, Princeton U., 1982; MD, Yale U., 1987. Diplomate Nat. Bd. Med. Examiners, Am. Bd. Psychiatry and Neurology. Resident in surgery U. Colo., Denver, 1987-88; resident in psychiatry Neuropsychiat. Inst. UCLA, 1991-94, chief resident in liaison psychiatry, 1993-94, instr. dept. psychiatry, 1995-96, assoc. dir.

residency edn. dept. psychiatry, 1995-96, asst. prof psychiatry, 1996—2003, assoc. prof. psychiatry, 2003—; registrar Neuropsychiat. Inst., 1999—2001; dir. NPI Acad. Info. Tech. Core, 1999—; assoc. dir. Office of Profl. and Cmty. Edn., 1998—. Examiner Am. Bd. Psychiatry and Neurology, 1998—.; chmn. departmental Curriculum Com., 2005-07; assoc. dir. Lab. of Brain, Behavior, and Pharmacology, 2006—; dir. UCLA Depression Rsch. Program, 2007—; mem. task force on professionalism David Geffen Sch. Medicine, UCLA, 2007—. Mem. editl. bd. Jefferson Jour. Psychiatry, 1992-94; editor: Mood Disorders, Cogent Medicine, 2005-; contbr. articles to profl. jours. Rsch. fellow Nat. Inst. Mental Health, 1993-96; recipient Young Investigator award Nat. Alliance Rsch. Schizophrenia and Depression, 1995, 97. Fellow: West Coast Coll. Biol. Psychiatry (mem. exec. bd 2005-, pres. 2007—, Jr. Faculty Rsch. award 2003); mem.: Am. Psychiat. Assn. (Burroughs-Wellcome fellow 1992, mem. com. of resident and fellows 1992-94, mem. steering com./practice guidelines 1994—, mem. exec. com. 2002—), So. Calif. Psychiat. Soc. (councilor 2004—), Nat. Eagle Scout Assn., Sigma Xi, Tau Beta Pi. Achievements include four patents in biomed. devices and methods. Office: UCLA Neuropsychiat Inst & Hosp 760 Westwood Plz Los Angeles CA 90095-8353

COOK, IAN M., consumer products company executive; b. 1952; With Colgate, United Kingdom, 1976, mktg. dir. Philippines, gen. mgr. Dominican Republic, Colgate's Nordic Group, Copenhagen; exec. v.p. mktg., Colgate N. Am. Colgate-Palmolive Co., NYC, 1994—97, pres. Colgate-N. Am., 1997—2002, exec. v.p., 2000—04, COO, 2004—05, pres., COO, 2005—07, pres., CEO, 2007—. Bd. dirs. Colgate-Palmolive Co., 2007—. Office: Colgate-Palmolive Co 300 Park Ave New York NY 10022*

COOK, J. VINCENT, lawyer; JD, U. Ga. Sr. mng. ptnr. Cook Noell Tolley Bates & Michael, Athens, Ga. Adj. prof. med. malpractice U. Ga. Mem.: Athens-Western Cir. Bar Assn. (past pres.), Ga. Civil Justice Found. (past pres.), Am. Bd. Trial Advocates (past pres. Ga. chpt.), Ga. Trial Lawyers Assn. (past pres.), State Bar Ga. (pres. 2007, treas.). Office: Cook Noell Tolley Bates & Michael LLP PO Box 1927 Athens GA 30603 Office Phone: 706-549-6111.

COOK, JAMES IVAN, clergyman, educator; b. Grand Rapids, Mich., Mar. 8, 1925; s. Cornelius Peter and Cornelia (Dornbos) C.; m. Jean Rivenburgh, July 8, 1950; children: Mark James, Carol Jean, Timothy Scott, Paul Brian (dec.). BA, Hope Coll., 1948; MA, Mich. State U., 1949; BD, Western Theol. Sem., 1952; ThD, Princeton Theol. Sem., 1964. Ordained to ministry Reformed Ch. America, 1953. Pastor Blawenburg Reformed Ch., NJ, 1953-63; from instr. to asst. prof. bibl. langs. Western Theol. Sem., Holland, Mich., 1963-67, prof. bibl. langs. and lit., 1967-77, Anton Biemont prof. New Testament, 1977-95, prof. emeritus, 1995—; chmn. Theol. Commn., Reformed Ch. Am. N.Y.C., 1980-85; pres. Gen. Synod-Reformed Ch. Am., NYC, 1982-83. Author: Edgar Johnson Goodspeed, 1981, Shared Pain and Sorrow: Reflections of a Secondary Sufferer, 1991, One Lord/One Body, 1991; editor Reformed Rev., 1987-2002; contbg. editor: Grace Upon Grace, 1975, Saved by Hope, 1978, The Church Speaks, 1985; founding editor Perspectives: A Jour. of Reformed Thought, 1986-90, The Church Speaks, vol. 2, 2002. Served with U.S. Army, 1943-45, ETO. Recipient Disting. Alumni award, Hope Coll., 1985, Western Theol. Sem., 2004. Home: 1004 S Shore Dr Holland MI 49423-4539 Office: Western Theol Sem 101 E 13th St Holland MI 49423-3622

COOK, JENIK ESTERM (JENIK ESTERM COOK SIMONIAN), artist, educator; b. Rezaieh, Iran, July 7, 1940; came to U.S., 1964; d. Sameual Amijon and Nanajan (Amreh Sarkissian) Simonian; m. Carrol Ross Cook, Sept. 28, 1961; children: Fiona Gitana Cook Anderson, Herold H. Studied with Hossein Delrish, Iran, 1968-70; studied with Barbara Lae, Scotland, 1970-78; studied with Chalita Robinson, 1981-87, studied with Jake Lee, 1987-90, studied with Dr. Alex Vilumsons, 1988-94. Tchr. art. Resident artist Orlando Gallery, L.A.; art tchr. U. Judaism, Bel Air. One-woman shows include Pacific Design Ctr., L.A., 1996, Orlando Gallery, 1997, 98, Bakery Digital Post Prodn. Ctr., L.A., West Wood Fed. Bldg., L.A., 1999, Hilton Hotel, L.A., 1999; exhibited in groups shows at Orlando Gallery, 1998, L.A. Conv. Ctr., 1998. Rheinfelden (Germany) Town Hall, 1998, Gallery Merkel, Grenzack, Germany, 1998, L.A. Art Expo, 1998, MGM Conf. Ctr., 1999, Long Beach Conv. Ctr., 1999, Art 21, Las Vegas MGM Conv. Ctr., 1999, Art Expo, N.Y., 2000; set designer, scenic artist North Hollywood Ch. of Religious Sci., 1999. Office: Everywomans Village 5650 Sepulveda Blvd Van Nuys CA 91411-2981 Home: 5643 Norwich Ave Van Nuys CA 91411-3233

COOK, JOANN CATHERINE, computer professor; children: Jeffrey, James, Joseph, Jodie Gray, Janet. AS in Data Processing, Jefferson Jr. Coll., Hillsboro, Ill., AA in Bus. Adminstrn.; BS in Info. Mgmt., Maryville U., St. Louis; MBA, North Ctrl. Coll., Naperville, Ill. Regional computer analyst Prime Computer, St. Louis, 1983—87; regional tech. support mgr. Prime Computer/Computervision, Oakbrook, Ill., 1987—94; assoc. prof. Coll. DuPage, Glen Ellyn, Ill., 1995—. Computer cons., Naperville, 1994—99. Office: Coll DuPage 425 Falwell Blvd Glen Ellyn IL 60137 Home Phone: 630-499-8831; Office Phone: 630-942-2674. Business E-Mail: cookjo@cod.edu.

COOK, JOEL, radiologist; (parents Am. citizens); m. Cheryl Cook. MD, U. Ark., Little Rock, 1974—78. Diplomate Am. Bd. Radiology, 1999. Family physician self-employed, Newport, Ark., 1979—81, Osceola, Ark., 1971—84; emergency medicine physician, 1984—90; mc officer US Navy, 1990—2001; radiologist Norma J. Vinger Ctr. Breast Care, LaCrosse, Wis., 2004—06; med. dir. Athens Regional Breast Health Ctr., Ga., 2006—. Vol. Habitat Humanity, Athens, 2006, Ducks Unlimited, Athens, 2006. Comdr. USN, 1990—2001. Mem.: Soc. Breast Imaging, Am. Roentgen Ray Soc., Am. Coll. Radiology. Office: Athens Regional Breast Health Ctr 1199 Prince Ave Athens GA 30606 Business E-Mail: jcook@armc.org.

COOK, JOHN, mayor; b. Bklyn., Feb. 27, 1946; m. Tram Cook, 1970; 6 children. ABA Bus. Arts, El Paso Community Coll., 1973; BA Bus. Conferred Mgmt., Univ. Texas El Paso, 1973—77; Alternative Cert Spl Edn, Univ. Tex. El Paso, 1992—93. Ctrl. office installer Western Electric Co., 1965—72; ctrl. office foreman Mountain States Telegraph Co., 1972—83; mgr. network options Southwestern Bell Telephone Co., 1983—91; teacher El Paso Independent Sch. Dist., 1992—93; v.p. and marketing plant mgr. Hoang Food Products Inc., 1993—95; pres. mktg. mng. and fundraising consultants Cook and Assoc., 1994—99; quality assurance coord. and v.p. mktg. Bienvivir Senior Hlth. Svc, 1996—97; pres. El Paso Housing Fin. Corp., 1999—2001, El Paso Hlth. Care Facilities Fin. Corp., 1999—; mayor City of El Paso, Tex., 2005—. Vol. exec. dir. El Paso Charities Comm. Chest, 1994—. M.d. counterintelligence US Army, 1971, Vietnam. Named Newsmaker of Yr., El Paso Times, 2005; recipient Gen. Mgr. award for comm. svc., SW Bell Tel. Co., 1989, Golden Hammer award, Habitat for Humanity, 2002, Annual Bravo award, Women Voters of El Paso, 2007. Mem.: United Way El Paso, El Paso Transp. Collaborative (pro-bono cons. 1996—), Am. Legion, LULAC Project Amistad (chmn. 2000—). Office: Office of the Mayor 10th Fl 2 Civic Ctr Plz El Paso TX 79901 Fax: 915-541-4501. E-mail: mayor@elpasotexas.gov.*

COOK, J(OHN) ROWLAND, lawyer; b. Dallas, July 20, 1942; s. John Hubbard and Nancy Eva Cook; m. April Beall, Dec. 24, 1966 (div. 1984); children: Matthew Rowland, Samantha, Joshua Malcolm, Abigail; m. Diane E. Ireson, Aug. 10, 1990; stepchildren: Eric Perlmutter, Lindsay Perlmutter. Student, Tex. A&M U., 1960, So. Meth. U., 1961; BBA, U. Tex., 1964, LLB, 1965. Tax law specialist IRS, Washington, 1965-66; adminstrv./legis. asst. U.S. congressman J. J. Pickle, 1966-69; spl. counsel, staff atty. div. corp. fin. SEC, 1969-76, chief, asst. dir. Office of Disclosure Policy and Proceedings div. corp. fin., 1976-79; asst. atty. gen. ins., banking and securities dept. State of Tex., Austin, 1979-80; from assoc. to ptnr. Salmanson, Smith & Mouer, 1980-81; ptnr., mem. Johnson & Wortley, P.C., 1981-95; shareholder Jenkens & Gilchrist, P.C., 1995—2007, mng. shareholder, 2003—07, Winstead PC, 2007—. Bd. dirs., pres. Travis County Dispute Resolution Ctr., 1990-95. Contbr. articles to profl. jours. Bd. dirs. Peoples' Cmty. Clinic. Office: Jenkens & Gilchrist PC Ste 2500 401 Congress Ave Austin TX 78701-3238 Office Phone: 512-370-2808.

COOK, KAREN S., sociologist, professor; Prof. Ray Lyman Wilbur Prof. of Sociology, dept. of sociology. Fellow Ctr. for Advanced Study in the Behavioral Sci. Co-author: (novels) Equity theory: psychological and sociol. perspectives; editor Social exchange theory, 1987; co-editor The Future of sociology, 1988; co-author Social Capital, 2001, The Russell Sage Found. Series on Trust; editor Trust in Soc., 2001; contbr. articles to profl. jour. Mem.: NAS, American Acad. of Arts and Sci. Office: Stanford U Prof of Sociology Bldg 120 Rm 238/240 Stanford CA 94305 Office Phone: 650-723-1194. E-mail: kcook@stanford.edu.*

COOK, KARLA JOAN, elementary school educator; b. LA, June 24, 1939; d. Charles Paul and Helen Barbara (Hamel) Belanger; m. John Rencoret, Aug. 1962 (div. 1964); 1 child, Renee; m. John Cook, Mar. 15, 1973 (div., 1983); children: Michael Donovan, Melody Marie. AB, Compton Jr. Coll., 1963; BA, Calif. State U., LA, 1970. Cert. life tchr., Calif. Bookkeeper, asst. 1st Nat. Bank, NYC, 1957-58; bookkeeper, vault teller 1st Western Bank, LA, 1958-61; Blue-line operator County Sanitation, LA, 1963-66; tchr. Long Beach Unified Sch. Dist., Calif., 1971-72, L.A. Unified Sch. Dist., Calif., 1974—94, 1996—98, Anaheim Sch. Dist., Calif., 1994-96; ret., 2006; film background artist many casting cos., 1994—. Founder, dir. Crisis Intervention Resource and Referral Agy., South Gate, Calif., 1991—95; dir. Sunday sch. program Lynnwood Ch. of God, 1995; coord. Adult Sunday Sch., Tabernacle of Praise, Long Beach, 2004—05. Mem. Christian Blue Collar Workers (pres. 1990-91), United Tchrs. L.A. (chpt. chair 1990-91), Creative Actors Alliance, Film Actors Co. Democrat. Avocations: painting, dance, acting, creative writing, sculpting. Home: 1602 E Harding St Long Beach CA 90805 Personal E-mail: karlacook1@verizon.net.

COOK, KATHRYN ANNE, secondary school educator; b. Coral Gables, Fla., Dec. 5, 1951; d. Raymond Clarence Cook and Dorothea Pauline Glühr-Cook; 1 child, Kimberley Spinney. BA, Marquette U., 1973; diploma in German lang., Goethe Inst., Germany, 1973; EdM, Cambridge Coll., 1998. English tchr. Goethe Inst., Germany, 1973; liason office Royal Embassy Saudi Arabia, London, 1973—76; adminstrv. asst. Dr. Kenneth G. Robbins, DDS, Springfield, Mass., 1988—96; computer tchr. Mount Carmel Sch., Springfield, 1989—95; telemarketer Media One, Springfield, 1991—98; tchr. City of Springfield Dept. Edn., 1996—. Tutor Mass. Comprehensive Assessment Sys. Dept. Edn., Springfield, 2000—; tchrs. tutor City of Springfield, 2000—; athletes tutor Play It Smart, Springfield, 2001—, sr. class advisor, 2003—04. Author: Journey Through the Abyss, 2000. Co-chairperson Resources Team Accreditation Coord., 2000—03; Mass. state advisor Rep. Nat. Com., Springfield, 2001. Mem.: Alumni Assn. Marquette, Phi Mu, Alpha Delta Kappa (historian elect 2000—). Republican. Lutheran. Avocations: writing, horseback riding, rowing, travel, cooking. Home: 151 White St Springfield MA 01108

COOK, KENNETH RAY, radiologist; b. Sublette, Kans., Sept. 16, 1953; s. Curtis Carl and Carmen Madonna (Countryman) Cook; m. Paula Rose Petryszyn, July 22, 1978; children: Erin Michelle, Leah Nicole, Tara Rachelle. AA, Hutchinson CC, Kans., 1976; BA, U. Kans., 1979, MD, 1983. Diplomate Am. Coll. Radiology; lic. pvt. pilot. Resident in diagnostic radiology U. Kans. Med. Ctr., 1983-87; pvt. practice, Corpus Christi, Tex., 1987—; chmn. mgmt. com. Radiology Assocs., Corpus Christi, 1997—2002. Staff radiologist Spohn Meml. Med. Ctr., Columbia N.W., Corpus Christi, 1987-99; chief radiology Bay Area Med. Ctr., 1993-99, vice chmn., trustee, 1993-94, chmn., 1994-96; chief radiology Rehab. Hosp. South Tex., 1989-91; asst. clin. prof. family practice U. Tex., San Antonio; med. dir. Del Mar Coll. Ultrasound Technol. Sch.; chief Corpus Christi Med. Ctr., 1998-99 Recipient Resident Tchg. award U. Kans. Dept. Radiology, Kansas City, 1985-86, Resident Tchg. award, Med. Ctr. Kans. U., 1986-87 Mem. AMA, Am. Coll. Radiology, Radiologic Soc. N. Am., Tex. Med. Soc., Tex. Radiologic Soc., Am. Inst. Ultrasound in Medicine, Nueces County Med. Soc. Republican. Roman Catholic. Avocations: fishing, hunting, camping, flying. Office: Radiology Assocs PO Box 5608 Corpus Christi TX 78465-5608 Home Phone: 361-850-9151; Office Phone: 361-561-3100. Personal E-mail: kcook963@msn.com. Business E-Mail: kcook@xraydocs.com.

COOK, LESLIE PAM, music educator; b. Milw., Jan. 11, 1966; d. Marvin Ben and Janice Ina Blitstein; m. David J. Cook, Nov. 12, 2005. BA in English, U. Wis., Madison, 1988; MS in Ednl. Psychology, U. Wis., Milw., 1994, BFA in Music Edn., 1997. Cert. tchr. Wis. Paralegal Foley & Lardner, Milw., 1989—90; pub. Hal Leonard Music Publ., Milw., 1991—93; sales mgr. Roadway Express, Milw., 1997—98; tchr. Kenosha Unified Sch. Dist., Wis., 1998—. Flute player Knigthwind Ensemble, Milw., 1999—. Scholar, U. Wis., Madison, 1988. Mem.: Nat. Assn. Music Edn. Avocations: bicycling, horseback riding, hiking, kayaking. Office: Lincoln Mid Sch 6729 18th Ave Kenosha WI 53143-4918

COOK, LEWIS ANDERSON, physician, anthropologist; b. Beckley, W.Va., June 22, 1942; s. Wilson and Anne (Legato) C.; m. Vicki Miles, May 23, 1966; children: Wilson, Tiffany Anne. BA, W.Va. U., 1968, MD, 1973; MS, U. Coll. London, 1999. Diplomate Am. Bd. Family Practice, Nat. Bd. Med. Examiners. Intern, resident in family practice Med. Coll. Va./Va. Commonwealth U., Richmond, 1973-76; family practice physician Fayetteville, W.Va., 1976-97, 2000—; clin. asst. prof. W.Va. Sch. Medicine, 1990-2000. Cons., reviewer W.Va. Med. Inst., 1980-86, bd. dirs., pres. bd. dirs., 2005—; chmn. dept. family practice Raleigh Gen. Hosp., 1984-97, pres. bd. trustees, 1988, chief of staff, 1985, 91. Author: History of Fayetteville, 1983; contbr. articles to profl. jours. Chmn. pk. bd. City of Fayetteville, W.Va., 1981-84; pres. Keep Am. Beautiful, Fayette County, 1900-98; chmn. Fayetteville Hist. Bd.; chmn. Fayette County Litter Control, 1992-97; physician Fayetteville Sports, 1976-97; mem. W.Va. Gov.'s Adv. Bd. for State Health Policy, 1996; mem. Regional Health Adv. Com. for State of W.Va., 1990-95; mem. Fayette Fine Arts Coun., 1990-97. With U.S. Army, 1962-65. Fellow Am. Acad. Family Practice; mem. W.Va. State Med. Assn., Raleigh County Med. Soc., Fayette County Med. Soc. (pres. 1980), Am. Anthrop. Assn., W.Va. Archaeol. Soc., Soc. Primitive Tech., Early Am. Industries Assn. (bd. dirs. 1995-98), Sci. Instrument Soc. (Eng.), Surveyors Hist. Soc., Med. Collectors Assn., Mid-West Tool Collectors Assn. (v.p. 1994-97), Oughtred Soc., Ohio Tool Collectors Assn., Astron. Soc. of Pacific, Kanawha Valley Astron. Soc., Astron. League, Rotary (pres. W.Va. chpt. 1984, Fayetteville chpt. 1984-2002). Avocations: woodworking, astronomy, architecture, tennis, golf. Home: RR 3 Box 4-a Fayetteville WV 25840-9502 Office Phone: 304-574-1888. E-mail: miles2@earthlink.net.

COOK, LINDA Z., utilities executive; b. Kansas City, June 1958; m. Steve Cook; 3 children. Grad. degree in Petroleum Engring., U. Kans. Various tech. and managerial positions Shell Oil Co. (Houston and Calif.), 1980—98; dir., strategy & bus. develop. Shell Exploration & Prodn. Global Exec. Com., The Hague, Netherlands; CEO Shell Gas & Power, 2000—03, 2004—; pres., CEO, bd. dir. Shell Can. Ltd., 2003—04; mng. dir. Royal Dutch Petroleum Co., 2004—; group exec. dir., gas and power Royal Dutch/Shell Group, 2004—. Bd. dir. Boeing Co., 2003—. Named one of 100 Most Powerful Women in World, Forbes Mag., 2005—06, 50 Women to Watch, Wall Street Journal, 2005, 50 Most Powerful Women in Global Bus., Fortune Mag., 2005. Mem.: Soc. Petroleum Engrs. Office: Shell International BV FSK Division PO Box 162 2501 AN The Hague Netherlands

COOK, LISA MARIE, mathematics professor, mathematics learning center coordinator; b. Manhasset, NY, Apr. 7, 1980; BS in Applied Math. with Computer Sci., L.I. U.-C.W. Post Campus, 2002, MS in Applied Math., 2004. Academic asst. L.I U.-C.W. Post Campus, Brookville, NY, 2001—02, grad. asst., 2002—04, student coord. tutoring program, 2002—04; instr. Suffolk County CC, Selden, NY, 2004—, coord. math. learning ctr., 2004—. Mem. mediated math. com. Suffolk County CC, 2004—, mem. precalculus com., 2004—. Mem.: Am. Math. Soc., N.Y. State Math. Assn. Two-Year Colls., Kappu Mu Epsilon (sec. 2002, N.Y. Lambda chpt., Nat. Honor Soc., treas. 2004). Roman Catholic. Achievements include guest presenter of honors thesis, Hot Hands in Basketball: Myth or Math?, at the Annual Kappa Mu Epsilon Banquet, 2002. Avocations: cooking, sports. Home: 2678 Martin Ave Bellmore NY 11710 Office: Suffolk County Community Coll 533 College Rd Selden NY 11784 Home Phone: 516-785-4988; Office Phone: 631-451-4717. Office Fax: 631-451-4887. Business E-Mail: cookl@sunysuffolk.edu.

COOK, MARY MARGARET, steamfitter, educator; b. Royal Oak, Mich., Apr. 28, 1944; d. John Patrick and Agnes Hannah (Anderson) McMahon; m. Barney Albert Cahill, Aug. 19, 1967 (div. Apr. 1971); m. Frank Melvin Cook, Jan. 26, 1974. BA in Elem. Edn., Ariz. State U., 1971; cert. United Assn. instr., Mich. State U., 1990; Cert., Ariz. C.C. Cert. elem. tchr., Ohio, Ariz.; mech. lic. journeyman and steamfitter. Tchr. St. Agnes Elem. Sch., Phoenix, 1967-71, Bevis Elem. Sch., Cin., 1971-73; GED instr. Scottsdale, Ariz., 1975-78; steamfitter United Assn. Local 469, Phoenix, 1978—. Instr. apprentices Rio Salado C.C., Phoenix, 1984-90; math. cons. Ariz. Dept. Edn., 1988-90; state dir. AFL-CIO Apprenticeship Awareness Program, 1990-92. Chair State Con. Emerging Careers for Women, 1992—98; mem. Apprenticeship Adv. Coun., 1990—97, chair, 1995—97; staff dept. commerce Workforce Devel. Coun., 1997—; mem. Gov.'s Commn. on Nontraditional Employment for Women; state dir. Project Nontraditional Assistance and Info. Link, 1992—99; extended staff Gov.'s Workforce Devel. Policy, 1997—2004; cons. Pro Max, 1999—; apprenticeship and tng. rep. Ariz. Dept. Commerce, 2000—04; program mgr. Ariz. Dept Transp., 2004—, contract compliance officer, 2007—. Mem.: Ariz. State U. Alumni Assn. (life), Toastmasters Internat. (Advanced Toastmaster silver). Avocations: computers, reading, weightlifting. Home: 22452 N 80th Ln Peoria AZ 85383-2149

COOK, SISTER MARY MERCEDES, school system administrator, director; b. Hagerstown, Md., Dec. 18, 1939; d. Garland and Anita Rideoutt (Willis) C. Student, Fordham U.; BA, Ea. Conn. State U., 1974, MS, 1983; grad., Norwich Dicocesan Prins. Acad., Conn., 1991; postgrad., U. Dayton, 1999. Joined Sistes of Charity of Our Lady of Mother of the Ch., Roman Cath. Ch.; cert. tchr., Conn. Tchr., prin. St. Joseph Sch., Baltic, Conn., 1959-61; tchr. Sacred Heart Sch., Byram, Conn., 1961-63, Bloomfield, Conn., 1963-66, Taftville, Conn., 1966-67, Acad. of Holy Family, Baltic, 1967-84; vice-prin., tchr., chair dept. English, guide counselor Acad. of the Holy Family, Baltic, Conn., 1990—2000; tchr., vice prin. Assumption Sch., Manchester, 1984—; dir. Sacred Heart Ednl. Ctr., Baltic, 2003—. Mem.: Nat. Cath. Ednl. Assn., Math. Assn. Am., Nat. Coun. Tchrs. English. Republican. Avocations: reading, writing, painting, cooking, interior decorating.

COOK, MAURICE GAYLE, soil science educator, consultant; b. Frankfort, Ky., Dec. 26, 1931; s. Price Cash and Evelyn (Moore) C.; m. Eva Nancy Blalock, Aug. 27, 1966; 1 child, Stephen Price. BS, U. Ky., 1957, MS, 1959; PhD, Va. Poly. Inst., 1961. From asst. prof. to prof. N.C. State U., Raleigh, 1961-92, Alumni Disting. prof., 1975; ret., 1992. Spl. advisor Gov. N.C., 1999-2000. Author: Concepts in Soil Science, 1973; contbr. numerous articles to profl. jours. With U.S. Army, 1957; col. USAR, 1962-90. Named to Hall of Disting. Alumni, U. Ky., 2000, Hall of Fame, NC Assn. Soil and Water Conservation Dists., 2006 Fellow Soil Sci. Soc. Am., Am. Soc. Agronomy, Soil and Water Conservation Soc. (bd. dirs. 1979-88, pres. 1986-87, Hugh Hammond Bennett award 2006), Nat. Assn. Colls. and Tchrs. Agr.; mem. Soil Sci. Soc. N.C. (Achievement award 1991), N.C. Divsn. Soil and Water Conservation (exec. dir. 1982-84), Am. Water Resources Assn., Internat. Erosion Control Assn., Gamma Sigma Delta (Merit award 1986), Epsilon Sigma Phi, Alpha Zeta (pres. 1976-85). Democrat. Baptist. Home: 3458 Leonard St Raleigh NC 27607-6827 Personal E-mail: mgcook@mindspring.com.

COOK, MELANIE K., lawyer; b. Salt Lake City, June 3, 1953; BS, UCLA, 1974, JD, 1978. Bar: Calif. Ptnr. Bloom Hergott Cook Diemer & Klein, Beverly Hills, Calif., 1987—2002, Bloom Hergott Diemer & Cook, Beverly Hills, Calif., 1992—2002, Ziffren, Brittenham, Branca, Fischer, Gilbert-Lurie, Stiffelman & Cook, LLP, LA, 2004—. Named one of 100 Most Powerful Women in Entertainment, Hollywood Reporter, 2006. Office: 1801 Century Park W Los Angeles CA 90067-6406 Office Phone: 310-552-6535.*

COOK, MICHAEL ALLAN, social sciences educator; b. Newark, Eng., Dec. 24, 1940; s. John Manuel and Enid May (Robertson) Cook. BA, Cambridge U., Eng., 1963. Lectr. Sch. Oriental and African Studies U. London, 1966—84, reader, 1984—86; Cleveland E. Dodge prof. Near Ea. studies Princeton (N.J.) U., 1986—. Author: Early Muslim Dogma, 1981, Muhammad, 1983, The Koran, 2000, others. Fellow: Am. Acad. Arts and Scis., Royal Asiatic Soc.; mem.: Am. Philos. Soc., Am. Oriental Soc. Office: Princeton Univ Dept Near Eastern Studies Princeton NJ 08544 Home Phone: 609-683-0130; Office Phone: 609-258-5360. Business E-Mail: mcook@princeton.edu.

COOK, MICHAEL BLANCHARD, government executive; b. Buffalo, May 8, 1942; s. Gerhard Albert and Lura (Lincoln) C.; m. Le Thi Kim Oanh, Feb. 10, 1942; children: Arthur, Benjamin. BA, Swarthmore Coll., 1963; postgrad., Princeton U.; B in Philosophy, Oxford U., 1966. Field advisor Agy. for Internat. Devel., Saigon, Vietnam, 1966-68; model cities rep. HUD, Phila., 1968-70; consular officer Dept. of State, Udorn, Thailand, 1971-73; exec., Water Programs EPA, Washington, 1973-80, superfund dir., 1980-81, dep. dir. hazardous waste, 1981-85, dir. drinking water, 1985-91, dir. wastewater enforcement and compliance, 1991-94, dir. wastewater mgmt., 1994—2002, dir. superfund remediation and technology innovation, 2002—. Author numerous articles on sewage treatment, hazardous waste and drinking water. Rhodes scholar Rhodes Trust, Oxford U., Eng., 1964; recipient Meritorious Honor awards U.S. Dept. of State, 1967, 72, Gold, Silver, Bronze medals EPA, 1975-87, Disting. Exec. award, Pres. Ronald Reagan, 1987. Avocations: running marathons, triathlete. Home: 3406 Rose Ln Falls Church VA 22042-4015 Office: EPA Superfund Remediation 5201G 1200 Pennsylvania Ave NW Washington DC 20460-4201 Home Phone: 703-237-9699; Office Phone: 703-603-8960. Business E-Mail: cook.mike@epa.gov.

COOK, MICHAEL HARRY, lawyer; b. June 9, 1947; s. Leonard James and Ethel (Shapiro) C.; m. Michele Anne Reday, Apr. 21, 1979; children: Noah Reday, Megan Rose. Student, U. Wis., 1965—66; BA with honors cum laude, Temple U., 1969; JD, Villanova U., 1973. Bar: Pa. 1973, DC

1979, US Dist. Ct. (no. dist.) Ill. 1977, US Dist. Ct. DC 1981, US Ct. Claims 1982, US Ct. Appeals (3d cir.) 1982, US Ct. Appeals (5th cir.) 1981, US Ct. Appeals (9th cir.) 1979, US Ct. Appeals (11th cir.) 1981, US Ct. Appeals (7th cir.) 1984, US Ct. Appeals (10th cir.) 1984, US Ct. Appeals (fed. cir.) 1984, US Ct. Appeals (DC cir.) 1981, US Supreme Ct. 1976. Atty. Gen. Counsel's Office US Dept. Health and Human Svcs., Washington, 1973—80; assoc. Wood, Lucksinger & Epstein, Washington, 1981—85, ptnr., 1985—90, Katten, Muchin & Zavis, Washington, 1991—97, Baker & McKenzie, Washington, 2003—06, Epstein Becker & Green, P.C., Washington, 2006—; mem. Mintz, Levin, Cohn, Ferris, Glovsky and Popeo, P.C., Washington, 1997—98; shareholder Jenkens & Gilchrist, P.C., Washington, 1998—2003. Lectr. Am. Health Lawyers Assn., Aspen Sys., Inc., various state and nat. hosps. and long-term care assns. Contbg. author (book) Integrated Health Care Law, 1993, Handbook of Subacute Health Care, 1995; contbg. author: book Subacute Care: A Guide to Devel., Implementation and Mgmt., 1995; contbg. author (book) St. Anthony's Compliance Reference Manual, 1995, Managed Care Contracting: A Looseleaf Guide, 1995, Health Law and Compliance Update, 2004; contbg. author: book The Long Term Care Handbook: Regulatory, Operational, and Fin. Guideposts, 2nd edit., 2000, 3rd edit., 2005; mem. editl. bd. McKnight's Long Term Care News; contbr. articles to profl. health care jours. V.p. Taylor Run Citizens Assn., Alexandria, Va., 1982-84, pres., 1984-85, bd. dirs., 1985—; home care work group for candidate for Gov. of Va. Timothy Kaine, 2005, health care transition team, 2005-06; long term care work group Gov. Kaine's Health Reform Commn., 2006—; active No. Va. Dem. Bus. Coun. Named one of 100 Most Influential People in Long Term Care, McKnight's Long Term Care News, 1996; Pres.'s scholar, Temple U., Phila., 1969. Mem.: ABA, Assisted Living Fedn. Am. (former managed care task force, former pub. policy task force, former leadership coun., pres. coun., legal com.), Nat. Assn. for Support of Long Term Care, Sword Soc., Tau Epsilon Phi, Phi Eta Sigma. Democrat. Jewish. Home: 2724 King St Alexandria VA 22302-4009 Office: Epstein Becker & Green PC 1227 25th St NW Ste 700 Washington DC 20037 Office Phone: 202-861-1865. Business E-Mail: mcook@ebglaw.com.

COOK, MICHAEL L., lawyer; b. De Leon, Tex., May 13, 1940; BBA, Tex. Tech U., 1962; JD, U. Tex., 1968. CPA Tex., 1965; bar: Tex. 1968. Shareholder Jenkens & Gilchrist, P.C., Austin, firm leader tax practice group. Co-author: Federal Tax Aspects of Cancellation of Indebtedness and Foreclosures, 1993. Fellow: Tex. Bar Found.; mem.: ABA, Am. Coll. Tax Counsel (bd. regents), State Bar Tex. Office: Jenkens & Gilchrist PC Ste 2500 401 Congress Ave Austin TX 78701 Office Phone: 512-499-3849. Office Fax: 512-499-3810. Business E-Mail: mcook@jenkens.com.

COOK, MICHAEL LEWIS, lawyer; b. Rochester, NH, Mar. 5, 1944; s. Israel J. and Molly L. Cook; m. Roberta Tross, Feb. 25, 1995; children: Jonathan, Alexander. AB, Columbia U., 1965; JD, NYU, 1968. Bar: NY 1969, registered: US Dist. Ct. (So. Dist.) NY 1970, US Dist. Ct. (Ea. Dist.) NY 1970, US Ct. Appeals (2nd Cir.) 1972, US Supreme Ct. 1973, US Ct. Appeals (7th Cir.) 1984, US Ct. Appeals (4th Cir.) 1986, US Dist. Ct. (No. Dist.) NY 1996, US Ct. Appeals (3rd Cir.) 2001. Assoc. Weil, Gotshal & Manges, NYC, 1970-75, ptnr., 1975-80; ptnr., chair restructuring group Skadden, Arps, Slate, Meagher & Flom, LLP, NYC, 1980-2000; ptnr., chair bus. reorganization group Schulte Roth & Zabel LLP, NYC, 2000—. Lectr. bus. law Herbert H. Lehman Coll., CUNY, 1968—70; adj. prof. law NYU Law Sch., 1975—2001. Co-author: A Practical Guide to the Bankruptcy Reform Act, 1979, Creditors' Rights, Debtors' Protection and Bankruptcy, 1985, rev. edit., 1997; contbr.: Collier on Bankruptcy, 1979, rev. edit., 2003, Collier Bankruptcy Practice Guide, 2003; lead editor and contbg. author: Bankruptcy Litigation Manual, rev. edit., 2006-07. Former bd. dirs. Goddard Riverside Cmty. Ctr.; former bd. dirs., former chair Lawyers Alliance for NY. Fellow: Am. Bar Found., Am. Coll. Bankruptcy; mem.: NYC Bankruptcy Assistance Project (chair steering com.), Lawyers Alliance NY (former chair), Practicing Law Inst. (bankruptcy law adv. com.), Assn. Bar City NY, ABA (chmn., creditors' rights litig. com.), Bankruptcy Litig. Inst. (chmn. 1980—96), Columbia Coll. Alumni Assn. (bd. dirs.). Office: Schulte Roth & Zabel LLP 919 Third Ave New York NY 10022 Home Phone: 212-722-1195; Office Phone: 212-756-2150. Office Fax: 212-593-5955. Business E-Mail: michael.cook@srz.com.

COOK, MYRTLE, special education and elementary school educator; b. New Orleans, June 15, 1936; d. John Henry and Angeline (Gray) C.; m. Marshall Butler, Dec. 22, 1979 (dec. July 1981). Student, So. U., 1954-55; BA, Southeastern La. U., 1960, MEd, 1971, postgrad., 1975. Cert. elem. tchr., tchr. mentally retarded, student tchr. supr., prin., La., reading specialist. Tchr. Tangipahoa Parish Sch. Sys., La., 1961—2006; elem. tchr. Tangipahoa Parish Sch. System, Hammond, La., Ponchatoula, La., Kentwood, La., tchr. Headstart Ponchatoula, prin. Headstart, tchr. spl. edn., Hammond, mem. spl. edn. adv. coun. Amite, La.; 1st and 3d grade tchr. Greenville Park Elem. Sch.; elem. tchr. 1st, 4th and 6th grades O.W. Dillon Elem. Sch., Crystal St. Sch., D.C. Reeves Elem. Sch., Ponchatoula, La., spl. edn. tchr.; 6th grade tchr. Perion Jr. HS, Ponchatoula; 7th and 8th grade tchr. spl. edn. Hammond Jr. HS. Participant and presenter workshops in field. Vol., coach La. Spl. Olympics; active Girl Scouts U.S.A., United Way Tangipahoa Parish, La. Heart Fund; music dir., pianist, piano tchr. children's choir cmty. Greenfield Bapt. Ch., Hammond, La., 1961—, sec. sr. women's aux., 1961—; music dir., organist choirs Little Bethel Bapt. Ch., Amite, 1961—; organist, chmn. music La. Home and Fgn. Mission Bapt. Sr. Women's Aux., 1961—; tchr. Parish Tangipahon; also others. Named Tangipahoa Parish Tchr. of Yr., La. Edn. Assn., 1974, Educator of Yr. award, Amite, 1975; Spl. Edn. Tchr. of Yr, Tangipahoa Parish Sch. System, 1987; T.H. Harris scholar So. U., 1954-55. Mem. Tangipahoa Parish Edn. Assn., Tangipahoa Fedn. Tchrs. Democrat. Achievements include being one of the frist African American students at Southeastern Louisiana University. Avocations: reading, piano, singing, aerobics, music.

COOK, NENA, lawyer; b. Salt Lake City, Jan. 25, 1966; BA, Gonzaga U., 1988; JD, Willamette U., 1991. Bar: Oreg. 1991, Wash., US Supreme Ct., US Ct. Appeals (9th Cir.), US Dist. Ct. (Dist. Oreg.) 1992, US Dist. Ct. (Ea. Dist. Wash.) 2000, US Dist. Ct. (We. Dist. Wash.) 2000. Ptnr. Sussman Shank LLP, Portland, Oreg. Chair employment law group Sussman Shank LLP; spkr. in field. Prodn. editor: Willamette Law Rev., 1990—91; contbr. articles to profl. jours. Chair Leadership Coll. Adv. Bd., 2006. Named one of Forty under 40 Outstanding Leadership in Bus. and Civic Affairs, Portland Bus. Jour., 2002. Mem.: ABA, Soc. Human Resource Mgmt., Portland Human Resource Mgmt. Assn., Fed. Bar Assn., Oreg. Women Lawyers, Oreg. State Bar Assn. (mem. fed. practice procedure com. 1997—99, chmn. 1998—99, ninth cir. jud. conf. rep. 2000—03, mem. bd. govs. 2002—05, pres.-elect 2004, pres. 2005, mem. jud. screening com.), Wash. State Bar Assn. Office: Sussman Shank LLP 1000 SW Broadway Ste 1400 Portland OR 97205 Office Phone: 503-227-1111, 503-243-1626. Office Fax: 503-248-0130. E-mail: nena@sussmanshank.com.*

COOK, NOEL ROBERT, manufacturing executive; b. Houston, Mar. 19, 1937; s. Horace Berwick and Leda Estelle (Houghton) C.; children: Laurel Jane, David Robert. Student, Iowa State U., 1955-57; BS in Indsl. Engring., U. Mich., 1960. Registered profl. engr., Mich.; cert. Fluid Power Engr. Engr. in tng. Eaton Mfg., Saginaw, Mich., 1960-61; mgr. mfg. and contracting J.N. Fauver Co., Madison Heights, Mich., 1961-65; pres. Newton Mfg., Royal Oak, Mich., 1965—; sec. Indsl. Piping Contractors, Birmingham, Mich., 1969-75; pres. RNR Metal Fabricators, Inc., Royal Oak, 1974-78; chmn. bd. dirs. Kim Internat. Sales Co., 1978-88; pres. Newton Sales Co., Royal Oak, 1978-90, Power Package Windsor Ltd., Windsor, Ont., Can., 1981—. Patentee in field. With U.S. Army, arty. officer, 1960-61. Mem. ASME, Fluid Power Soc., Nat. Fluid Power Assn., Birmingham Jr. C. of C. (past bd. dirs.), Delta Tau Delta. Home: 4481 Cherry Hill Dr Orchard Lake MI 48323-1615 Office: Newton Mfg Co 4249 Delemere Blvd Royal Oak MI 48073-1897 Office Phone: 248-549-9600. Personal E-mail: ncook@newtonmfgco.com.

COOK, PAMELA MARGARET, French educator; b. Gateshead, Eng., Apr. 11, 1955; came to U.S., 1983; d. John Andrew and Doreen Cook; m. Philip Edward Mirowski, June 14, 1986; 1 child, Alexander John Daniel Mirowski. BA with honors, U. Nottingham, Eng., 1977; MA, MPhil, PhD, Yale U., 1991. Tchr. Sawston Coll., Cambridge, Eng., 1978-83; asst. head dept. Hitchin Sch., Herts, Eng., 1983-85; part-time asst. prof. French St. Mary's Coll., Notre Dame, ind., 1990—. Mem. Hoosier Environ. Coun., Indpls., 1997—; mem. Ind. Opera North. Christine Jankowski fellow, 1984. Mem. MLA. Avocations: singing, flute, piano, theater. Home: 3015 Hilltop Dr South Bend IN 46614-2213

COOK, PATRICIA L., finance company executive; Grad., St. Mary's Coll.; MBA, NYU. Various mgmt. positions Salomon Bros., Inc., Fisher Francis Trees & Watts; mng. dir., chief investment officer fixed income Prudential Investment Mgmt.; mng. dir., chief investment officer global fixed income JPMorgan Fleming Asset Mgmt., 2003—04; exec. v.p. investments Fed. Home Loan Mortgage Corp., 2004—, chief. bus. officer, 2007—. Mem. Treasury Borrowing Adv. Com. Office: Fed Home Loan Mortgage Corp 8200 Jones Branch Dr Mc Lean VA 22102-3110 Office Phone: 703-903-2000.*

COOK, PAUL CHRISTOPHER, intelligence officer; b. Corpus Christi, Tex., Mar. 24, 1953; s. William Eckford and Nelle (Gladney)C. AA, Ocean City Coll., Md., 1973; BA, U. Ariz., Tucson, 1978; MA, U. Ariz., 1981, PhD, 1987. Oceanographer Dept. Natural Resources State of Md., Annapolis, 1973—75; rschr. Child Psychology Lab., Tucson, 1977—78; behavioral and video cons. Intermt. Ctrs. for Human Devel., Tucson, 1978—79; rsch. assoc. Family & Community Medicine Ariz. Health Sci. Ctr., Tucson, 1982—84, rsch. cons., 1989—98; rsch. and analysis assoc. U. Ariz., Tucson, 1980—87, rsch. cons. Coll. Medicine, 1989—98; sr. human factors engr. U.S. Army Electronic Proving Ground, Ft. Huachuca, Ariz., 1986—87; engring. psychologist U.S. Army Yuma Proving Ground, Ariz., 1988; cons. engr. Cook Enterprises, Tucson, 1989—91; pres. World Trade Assocs. Ltd. Sterling, Inc., Tucson, Lake Havasu, Ariz., 1991—97; pres., ptnr. Unicus Imports, Inc., 1997—2000; candidate, sr. exec. svcs., sr. rsch. scientist U.S. Navy Space and Naval Warfare Sys. Ctr., San Diego, 1999; ops. specialist, intelligence warfare test directorate commd. Ft. Huachuca (Az.), Ft Hood (Tex.), 2000—01; ops. rsch. analyst intelligence electronic warfare Theatre Missle Def., Fort Huachuca, 2000—00; ops. analyst U.S.A. Intelligence Electronic Warfare Reconnaissance, Spl. Projects, Ft. Huachuca, 2001—02; intelligence officer U.S. Army Intelligence Ctr., Ft. Huachuca, 2002—. Rsch. cons. Coll. Medicine Ariz. Health Scis. Ctr., U. Ariz., Tucson, 1989—; pres. World Trade Assocs. Ltd. of Sterling, Inc., Tucson, Sterling, Va. and Lake Havasu, Ariz., 1990-98. Scuba diver Pima County Sheriff's Dept., 1985-90; plank owner USN Meml., Washington. Mem. Navy League (life), U.S. Naval Inst., Human Factors Soc., Internat. Platform Assn., Profl. Assn. Diving Instrs., U.S. C. of C. Republican. Methodist. Home: 6537 E Santa Elena Tucson AZ 85715-3132 Office: Trail Dust Town #10 PO Box 10 6541 E Tanque Verde Rd Tucson AZ 85715-3813 Office Phone: 520-533-6304. Personal E-mail: paul.c.cook@us.army.mil. Business E-Mail: cookp@hua.army.mil. E-mail: tombstone_arizona@msn.com.

COOK, PAUL MAXWELL, technology company executive; b. Ridgewood, NJ; BSChemE, MIT, 1947. With Stanford Rsch. Inst., Menlo Park, Calif., 1948-53, Sequoia Process Corp., 1953-56, Raychem Corp., Menlo Park, Calif., 1957-95, founder, former pres., CEO, until 1990, chmn., bd. dirs., until 1995; chmn., CEO CellNet Data Sys., San Carlos, Calif., 1990-94; chmn., bd. dirs. SRI Internat., 1993-98; chmn. DIVA Sys. Corp., Menlo Park, Calif., 1995—, CEO, 1995-99; founder, CEO, Agile TV Corp., 2000—. Mem. exec. com. San Francisco Bay Area Coun., 1988-94, chmn., 1990-91. Recipient Nat. Medal Tech., 1988; named to San Francisco Bay Area Bus. Hall of Fame, 1999. Mem. NAE, Am. Acad. Sci., Environ. Careers Orgn. (past chmn., bd. trustees), MIT Corp. (life, emeritus). Office: Diva Sys Corp 15233 Ventura Blvd 9th Fl Sherman Oaks CA 91403-2201 E-mail: pcook@agile.tv.

COOK, PETER HALSEY, architect; Grad., Rensselaer Poly. Inst., Troy, NY, 1982. Lic. NY, 1987. Designer William G. Thompson, Bridgehampton, NY; apprentice Eugene L. Futterman Arch., 1982—87; owner, prin. Peter Cook Arch., 1987—. Mem.: AIA, NY State Assn. Archs. Office: Peter Cook Arch PO Box 1431 Bridgehampton NY 11932 Office Phone: 631-283-0077 ext. 108. Office Fax: 631-283-5960.*

COOK, PHILIP CARTER, lawyer; b. Atlanta, Nov. 4, 1946; BS, Ga. Inst. Tech., 1968; JD cum laude, Harvard U., 1971. Bar: Ga. 1972. Law clk. to Hon. Lewis R. Morgan U.S. Ct. Appeals (5th cir.), 1971-72; mem. Alston & Bird, Atlanta, dep. mng. ptnr. Atlanta & Washington. Pres. Harvard Journal of Legislation 1970-71. Fellow Am. Coll. Tax Counsel; mem. ABA (chmn. sect. taxation, com. on banking and savs. instns. 1995), D.C. Bar, State Bar Ga. (chmn. taxation sect.), Am. Law Inst., Atlanta Tax Forum (trustee 1986-91, pres. 1991), Phi Kappa Phi, Omicron Delta Kappa. Office: Alston & Bird 1 Atlantic Ctr 1201 W Peachtree St NW Atlanta GA 30309-3424 Office Phone: 404-881-7491. Office Fax: 404-881-7777. Business E-Mail: pcook@alston.com.

COOK, PHILIP JACKSON, economist, educator; b. Buffalo, Oct. 15, 1946; s. Gerhard Albert and Lura (Lincoln) C.; m. Judith Walmsley, June 27, 1966; children: Elizabeth Camden, Brian Lincoln. BA, U. Mich., 1968; PhD, U. Calif., Berkeley, 1973. Prof. Duke U., Durham, NC, 1973—, dir. Inst. Policy Scis., 1985-89, dir. Sanford Inst. Pub. Policy, 1997-99. Vis. scholar Inst. Rsch. in Social Sci. U. NC, Chapel Hill, 1980; expert Office Poly. and Mgmt. Analysis, criminal divsn. U.S. Dept. Justice, 1982; mem. rsch. adv. com. U.S. Sentencing Commn., 1986—91, chair rsch. adv. com., 1986; mem. adv. bd. Injury Prevention Rsch. Ctr. U. NC, 1990—; mem. adv. bd. H. John Heinz III Sch. Pub. Policy and Mgmt. Carnegie Mellon U., 1992—; mem. Ctr. Gun Policy Rsch. Johns Hopkins U., 1995—2003; cons. enforcement divsn. U.S. Dept. Treasury, 1999—2000; rsch. assoc. Nat. Bur. Econ. Rsch., 1996—; mem. adv. com. Harvard Injury Control Ctr. Author: Selling Hope, 1989, The Winner-Take All Society, 1995, Gun Violence, 2000, Evaluating Gun Policy, 2003, Paying the Tab: The Economics of Alcohol Policy, 2007. Recipient Kenneth J. Arrow award for best paper published in health econ., 1993, Vernon Prize in Pub. Policy, 1997; grantee, US Dept. Justice, Robert Wood Johnson Found.; Spl. Career fellow, Ford Found., 1968—72. Fellow: Am. Soc. Criminology; mem.: Inst. Medicine of NAS, Am. Econ. Assn., Assn. Pub. Policy and Mgmt. (treas. 1985—93). Office: Duke Univ Inst Pub Policy PO Box 90245 Durham NC 27708-0245 Business E-Mail: pcook@duke.edu.

COOK, PHILLIP H., chemicals executive; Grad. in Mech. Engring., U. Tex., Austin. Rsch. engr. urethanes devel. lab. Dow Chem. Co., Freeport, Tex., 1970, rsch. engr., grp. leader epoxy resins tech. svc. & devel., 1979, market devel. mgr. epoxy resins Midland, Mich., 1983, grp. mktg. mgr. structural and design resins, 1985, bus. ops. mgr. epoxy resins and intermediates Corp. Product dept., 1987, comml. v.p. Dow-United Technologies Composite Products, 1989, global bus. mgr. epoxy products, 1993, v.p. bus. devel. for Greater China, 1995, v.p., global bus. dir. ethylene dichloride, vinyl chloride monomer, chlorine, caustic soda and HCL, 1998, global bus. v.p. epoxy products & intermediates, 2000, sr. v.p. performance chems. and thermosets, 2003, mem. Office of the Chief Exec. Midland, Mich., 2004—, corp. v.p. strategic devel. and new ventures, 2005, sr. adv., 2006—. Bd. dirs. Methanex Corpn.; bd. mgrs. Univation Technologies; mem. members com. Dow Agrosciences; Office of Chief Exec.'s rep. diversity & inclusion steering team Dow Chem. Co., corp. sponsor Gays, Lesbians and Allies at Dow Employee Network. Mem. vis. com. dept. chem. engring. U. Tex., Austin, mem. Coll. Engring. Found. Adv. Coun. Mem.: Nat. Paint and Coatings Assn. (bd. dirs., mem. exec. com.), Midland Country Club (bd. dirs.). Office: Dow Chem Co 2030 Dow Ctr Midland MI 48674

COOK, QUENTIN LAMAR, lawyer, church administrator, healthcare executive; b. Sept. 8, 1940; s. J. Vernon and Bernice (Kimball) Cook; m. Mary Gaddie, Nov. 30, 1962; children: Kathryn Cook Knight, Quentin Laurence, Joseph Vernon III. BS, Utah State U., 1963; JD, Stanford U., 1966. Bar: Calif. 1966. Assoc. Carr, McClellan, Ingersoll, Thompson & Horn, Burlingame, Calif., 1966-69, ptnr., 1969-93; interim pres., CEO Calif. Healthcare Sys., San Francisco, 1993-94, pres., CEO, 1994-95; vice chmn. Sutter Health/Calif. Healthcare Sys., San Francisco, 1996; gen. authority LDS Ch., 1996—. City atty. Town of Hillsborough, Calif., 1982—93; mem. adv. bd. Utah State U., Logan, 1985—95; mem. bd. visitors Brigham Young U. Law Sch., Provo, 1994—96.

COOK, RICHARD JAMES, academic administrator; b. Alpena, Mich., Oct. 20, 1947; s. George Robert and Edith Mabel C.; m. Teresa Marie Lahti, Jan. 4, 1997. BS in Chemistry, U. Mich., 1969; MS, Princeton U., 1971, PhD in Chemistry, 1973. Prof. of chemistry Kalamazoo Coll., 1973-89, provost, 1989-96; pres. Allegheny Coll., Meadville, Pa., 1996—. Vice-chmn. Mich. Toxic Substance Control Commn., Lansing, Mich., 1984-90; mem. Gov.'s Environ. adv. bd., Lansing, 1992-96; bd. dirs. Assn. of Ind. Colleges and Univs. of Pa., 2000—. Contbg. author: Municipal Solid Waste Incineration-Risk Management, 1991. Bd. dirs. Am. Lung Assn. of Mich., Lansing, 1990-96, Kalamazoo Nature Ctr., 1984-88. Recipient Gov.'s cert. of merit Gov. John Engler, Lansing, 1994, Lucasse Rsch. award Kalamazoo Coll., 1987. Mem. Hist. Soc. of W. Pa. (bd. dirs. 1997—), Allegheny Coll. (bd. dirs. 1996—), Coun. of Ind. Colls. (bd. dirs. 1999—). Office: Allegheny Coll 520 N Main St Meadville PA 16335-3903 Home Phone: 814-332-8642; Office Phone: 814-332-5380. E-mail: rcook@alleeny.edu.*

COOK, RICHARD KELSEY, aerospace transportation executive; b. White Plains, NY, Nov. 14, 1931; s. Albert James and Frances Elizabeth (Butler) C.; m. Marjorie S. Schellabarger, Sept. 10, 1959 (div.); children: Geoffrey, Patrick, Sarah, Catherine; m. Fleur Wales-Baillie, Oct. 14, 1987. BA, George Washington U., 1958; postgrad., Stanford U., 1979. Legis staff Am. Trucking Assn., 1959-61; adminstrv. asst. Rep. Edwin B. Dooley, 1961; legis. asst. Rep. Oliver P. Bolton, 1963-65; profl. minority staff mem. Banking and Currency Com., U.S. Ho. of Reps., Washington, 1965-69; spl. asst. to Pres. of U.S., Washington, 1969-71, dep. asst., 1971-73; v.p. Lockheed Corp., Washington, 1973-94, sr. v.p., 1994-95; pres. RKC Ltd., 1995—. Spl. adv. O'Connor & Hannan, Washington, 1995-98; cons. Thorlock Corp. Ltd., Perth, Australia, 1999-01; Pacific Digital, LA; registered lobbyist; pioneered internet lobbying with PanAmSat Corp., 1998-00; def. cons. Citadel Hedge Fund, Chgo., 2004-; internet cons. European Aerospace Def. Space Co.-N.Am., 2004-05; v.p., dir. Grove Tactical Tng. Ctr., 2005-. Served with USAF, 1949-53. Mem. Aero. Club (pres. 1979), Met. Club, 116 Club (D.C.), Burning Tree Club (Bethesda, Md.), Captiva Island Yacht Club (Fla.), Inanda Club (Johannesburg, South Africa), Tau Kappa Epsilon. Personal E-mail: rkcook1@aol.com.

COOK, RICHARD W. (DICK COOK), film company executive; b. Bakersfield, Calif., Aug. 20, 1950; BA in Polit. Sci., U. So. Calif., 1972. Ride operator Disneyland, Anaheim, Calif., sales rep., 1971-74, sales mgr., 1974-77; mgr. pay TV and non-theatrical releases Disney Studios, 1977-80; asst. domestic sales mgr. Buena Vista, 1980-81, v.p., asst. gen. sales mgr., 1981-84, v.p., gen. sales mgr., 1985-88, sr. v.p. domestic distbn., 1988-94; pres. Buena Vista Pictures Distbn., 1994; pres. worldwide mktg. Buena Vista Pictures Mktg., 1994-97; chmn. Walt Disney Motion Pictures Group, Burbank, Calif., 1997—2002, Walt Disney Studios, 2002—. Bd. dirs. Found. Motion Picture Pioneers, Verdugo Hills Hosp., Will Rogers Found.; pres. The Chandler Sch.; pres. bd. trustees Flintridge Prep. Sch.; trustee U. So. Calif., 1998—. Named one of 50 Most Powerful People in Hollywood, Premiere mag., 2004—06; recipient George Washington Medal of Freedom, Freedoms Found. Valley Forge. Mem.: Acad. Motion Picture Arts and Scis. Office: Walt Disney Studios 500 S Buena Vista St Burbank CA 91521-0006

COOK, ROBERT CROSSLAND, chemist, researcher; b. New Haven, June 5, 1947; s. Russell C. and Tensia (Veazey) C. BS in Chemistry, Lafayette Coll., 1969; MPh in Phys. Chemistry, Yale U., 1971, PhD in Theoretical Chemistry, 1973. Mem. faculty Lafayette Coll., Easton, Pa., 1973-81; staff scientist Lawrence Livermore (Calif.) Nat. Lab., 1981—. Instr. Calif. State U., Hayward, 1985-86, 94, Chabot Coll., 1986-90, Las Positas Coll., 1990-92; mem. vis. faculty Dartmouth Coll., Hanover, N.H., 1977, 78, 79, Colo. State U., Ft. Collins, 1980. Contbr. articles to profl. jours. Grantee in field. Mem. Am. Chem. Soc., Am. Phys. Soc., Sigma Xi. Office: Lawrence Livermore Nat Lab L-479 PO Box 808 Livermore CA 94551-0808 Business E-Mail: bobcook@llnl.gov.

COOK, ROBERT S., JR., lawyer; b. Syracuse, NY, 1940; m. Sally Williams. BA, Amherst Coll., 1962; LLB, Yale U., 1965. Bar: N.Y. 1966. Assoc. Hancock, Ryan, Shove & Hust, Syracuse, NY, 1965-68; urban renewal rep. HUD, NYC, 1968-71; exec. dir. The Parks Coun., Inc., NYC, 1972-73; v.p., co-founder Project for Pub. Spaces, Inc., NYC, 1974-77; cons. NYC, 1978-80; assoc. Tufo & Zuccotti, NYC, 1981-86; assoc., then ptnr. Brown and Wood, NYC, 1986-94; ptnr. DeForest & Duer, NYC, 1995—2001, Anderson, Kill & Olick, P.C., NYC, 2002—. Author: Zoning for Downtown urban Design, 1980. V.p., bd. dirs. Citizens Housing and Planning Coun., 1985; cons. The Denver Partnership, 1981; mem. N.Y. State Freshwater Wetlands Appeals Bd., 1991-94. Design project fellow Nat. Endowment for Arts, Washington, 1978-79; Graham Found. for Advanced Studies in the Fine Arts fellow, Chgo., 1979. Mem. N.Y. State Bar Assn., Assn. Bar City N.Y. (com. environ. law 1979-82, com. land use planning and zoning, 1994-2000, chmn. 1997-2000, com. N.Y.C. affairs 2000-01). Office: Anderson Kill & Olick PC 1251 Ave of the Americas New York NY 10020-1182 E-mail: rcook@andersonkill.com.

COOK, ROBIN, writer; b. NYC, May 4, 1940; s. Edgar Lee and Audrey (Koons) C.; m. Barbara Ellen Mougin, July 18, 1979. BA, Weslyan U., 1962; MD, Columbia U., 1966. Resident in gen. surgery Queen's Hosp., Honolulu, 1966-68; resident in ophthalmology Mass. Eye and Ear Infirmary, Boston, 1971-75, mem. staff, from 1975; clin. instr. Harvard U. Med. Sch., 1972. Author: The Year of the Intern, 1972, Coma, 1977, Sphinx, 1979, Brain, 1981, Fever, 1982, Godplayer, 1983, Mindbend, 1986, Outbreak, 1987, Mortal Fear, 1988, Mutation, 1989, Harmful Intent, 1990, Vital Signs, 1990, Blindsight, 1991, Terminal, 1992, Fatal Cure, 1994, Acceptable Risk, 1995, Invasion, 1997, Chromosome 6, 1997, Toxin, 1998, Vector, 1999, Shock, 2001, Abduction, 2002, Seizure, 2003, Marker, 2005 (Publishers Weekly Bestseller list, 2005). Lt. comdr. USN, 1969-71. Avocations: skiing, surfing, painting, cooking.

COOK, SCOTT DAVID, computer software company executive; b. Glendale, Calif., July 26, 1952; m. Signe Ostby; children: David, Karl, Annie. BA in Economics and Math., U. So. Calif.; MBA, Harvard U. Various mktg. positions to brand mgr. Procter & Gamble; cons. Bain Co.; co-founder Intuit Inc., Menlo Park, Calif., 1983, pres., CEO, 1984-94, chmn. bd., 1993—98, chmn. exec. com., 1998—. Bd. dirs. Intuit Inc.,

1984—, eBay, 1998—, The Procter & Gamble Co., 2000—. Bd. trustees Asia Found.; bd. visitors Harvard Bus. Sch., Ctr. Brand and Product Mgmt., Intuit Scholarship Found. Named one of Forbes' Richest Americans, 2006; recipient Lifetime Achievement award, Software Publishers Assn., 1994, PC mag., 2003. Mem.: Phi Beta Kappa. Office: Intuit Inc 2632 Marine Way Mountain View CA 94043 Office Phone: 650-944-6000.*

COOK, SHARLA J., career officer; BS in Edn. with honors, Brigham Young U., 1971; disting. grad., Officer Tng. Sch., 1972; aircraft maintenance officer course, Chanute AFB, Ill., 1973; M in Logistics Mgmt., Air Force Inst. of Tech., 1977; grad., Air Command and Staff Coll., 1985; disting. grad., Indsl. Coll. of Armed Forces, 1993. Commd. 2d lt. USAF, 1972, advanced through grades to brigadier gen., 1998; wing job control officer U-Tapao Air Base, Thailand, 1975-76; aide-de-camp air logistics ctr. comdr. Sacramento Air Logistics Ctr., McClellan AFB, Calif., 1981-82, dep. br. chief inventory and scheduling br., 1982-84; comdr. 374th Orgnl. Maintenance Squadron, Clark Air Base, The Philippines, 1985-87; maintenance ops. officer 58th Tactical Tng. Wing, Luke AFB, Ariz., 1988-90, asst. dep. comdr. for maintenance, 1990-91; dep. comdr. 58th Support Group, Luke AFB, 1991-92; comdr. 8th Logistics Group, Kunsan Air Base, South Korea, 1993-94; chief maintenance engring. Hdqs. Pacific Air Forces, Hickam AFB, Hawaii, 1994-95, asst. dir. logistics, 1995-96; dir. aircraft directorate Ogden Air Logistics Ctr., Hill AFB, Utah, 1996-97; dir. logistics Hdqs. Air Edn. and Tng. Command, Randolph AFB, Tex., 1997—; comdr. 82d tng. wing Air Edn. and Tng. Command, Sheppards AFB, Tex., 1999—. Decorated Legion of Merit, Meritorious Svc. medal with 4 oak leaf clusters. Address: 82 TRW/CC Sheppard Afb TX 76311

COOK, SHARON LEE DELANCEY, retired elementary school educator, musician; b. Manchester, Iowa, May 15, 1939; d. Donald Wesley Delancey and Alta Grace Haynes; children: Eric LeRoy, Melanie Mae Mead, Keith Delancey. At, Iowa State Tchr's Coll., Cedar Falls, 1956—58; BA, Upper Iowa U., Fayette, 1971. Cert. tchr. Iowa. Tchr. pre-kindergarten Valleybrook Sch., Falls Church, Va., 1958—59; typist-receptionist Libr. of Congress, Washington, 1959—60, 1966—68; tchr. grade 1 Maquoketa Valley Schs, Hopkinton, Iowa, 1968—69; tchr. grades 2.3 and 5 West Del. Schs., Manchester, 1969—97. Accompanist West Del. Pub. Schs., Manchester, Iowa, 1969—2000; repertoire asst. Pvt. Music Tchr's Assn., Cedar Rapids, 1999—; ch. organist and pianist, Manchester, Iowa, 1969—. Chairperson McGee Brick Sch. Found., Manchester, Iowa, 1999—; prayer chairperson Christian Women's Club, 2005—. Mem.: Fed. Women's Club (v.p. 2005—). Achievements include restoration of historic one-room brick school. Avocations: poetry, writing. Office: McGee Brick Sch Found 608 E Union St Manchester IA 52057

COOK, SHARON WARREN, social worker, educator; d. Shirley Whitaker and Johnnie Warren; 1 child, Talia Senai. M in Social Work, U. N.C., Chapel Hill, 1992—95. Asst. prof. social work Winston-Salem State U., NC, 1995—, asst. chair, dept. social sciences, 2003—. Bd. mem. Mental Health Assn. Forsyth County, Winston-Salem, 2000—, Youth Opportunities Homes, Inc., Winston-Salem, 2001—; cons./trainer Novant Healthcare Sys., Winston-Salem, 2005—. Author: (book chapter) Mary Church Terrell. Bd. mem. Mental Health Assn. Forsyth County, Winston-Salem, 2001—06. Recipient Faculty Tchg. awards, Wisnton-Salem State U., 2004, 2003, 2001, 1999, Nat. Recipient, Founding Mem. of Rosa PArks Wall of Tolerance, So. Poverty Law Ctr., 2004. Avocations: boating, pool, golf. Office: Winston-Salem State Univ 601 Martin Luther King Dr Winston Salem NC 27110 Home Phone: 336-778-1044; Office Phone: 336-750-2625. Office Fax: 336-750-2647; Home Fax: 336-778-1044. Personal E-mail: swarrencook@yahoo.com. Business E-Mail: cooksw@wssu.edu.

COOK, STANTON R., media company executive; b. Chgo., July 3, 1925; s. Rufus Merrill and Thelma Marie (Borgerson) C.; m. Barbara Wilson, Sept. 23, 1950 (dec. Nov. 1994). BS in Mech. Engring., Northwestern U., 1949. With Shell Oil Co., 1949-51, Chgo. Tribune Co., 1951-81, v.p., 1967-70, exec. v.p. and gen. mgr., 1970-72, pres., 1972-74, pub., 1973-90, CEO, 1974-76, chmn., 1974-81; dir. Tribune Co., 1972-96, v.p., 1972-74, pres., 1974-88, chmn., 1989-92, CEO, 1974-90; chmn. Chgo. Nat. League Ball Club, Inc., 1990-94. Bd. dirs. AP, 1975-84, 2d vice chmn., 1979-84; bd. dirs. Newspaper Adv. Bur., 1973-92, Am. Newspaper Pubs. Assn., 1974-82; dep. chmn., bd. dirs. Fed. Res. Bank Chgo., 1980-83, chmn., 1984-85; bd. dirs. Robert R. McCormick Tribune Found., 1990-2001. Trustee Robert R. McCormick Trust, 1972-90, Savs. and Profit Sharing Fund of Sears Employees, 1991-94, U. Chgo., 1973-87, Mus. Sci. and Industry, Chgo., 1973—, Field Mus. Natural History, Chgo., 1973—, Gen. Douglas MacArthur Found., 1979—, Northwestern U., 1987—, Shedd Aquarium Soc., 1987—, Am. Newspaper Pubs. Assn. Found., 1973-82. Mem. Newspaper Assn. Am. (bd. govs. 1992), Chgo. Coun. Fgn. Rels. (bd. dirs. 1973-93), Comml. Club (past pres.), Econ. Club (life, past pres.), Glen Lake Assn. (pres. 2001-04). Home: 224 Raleigh Rd Kenilworth IL 60043-1209

COOK, STEPHEN ARTHUR, mathematics and computer science educator; s. Gerhard Albert and Lura C.; m. Linda Marie Craddock, May 4, 1968; children— Gordon, James. BS in math., U. Mich., 1961; S.M. in math., Harvard U., 1962, PhD in math., 1966. Asst. prof. U. Calif.-Berkeley, 1966-70; assoc. prof. U. Toronto, 1970-75, prof., 1975—, univ. prof., 1985—. Contbr. articles to profl. jours. E.W.R. Staecie Meml. fellow, 1977-78; Killam research fellow Can. Council, 1982-83; recipient ACM Turing award Assn. Computing Machinery, 1982, Killam prize Can. Coun., 1997. Fellow Royal Soc. Can., Royal Soc. London; mem. Nat. Acad. Scis., Am. Acad. Arts and Scis. Office: Dept Computer Sci U Toronto Toronto ON Canada M5S 3G4 Office Phone: 416-978-5183. Business E-Mail: sacook@cs.toronto.edu.

COOK, STEPHEN CHAMPLIN, retired shipping company executive; b. Portland, Oreg., Sept. 20, 1915; s. Frederick Stephen and Mary Louise (Boardman) C.; m. Dorothy White, Oct. 27, 1945 (dec. Sept. 1998); children: Mary H. Cook Goodson, John B., Samuel D., Robert B. (dec.). Student, U. Oreg., Eugene, 1935-36. Surveyor U.S. Engrs. Corp., Portland, Oreg., 1934-35; dispatcher Pacific Motor Trucking Co., Oakland, Calif., 1937-38; manifest clk. Pacific Truck Express, Portland, 1939; exec. asst. Coastwise Line, San Francisco, 1940-41, mgr. K-Line svc., 1945-56; chartering mgr. Ocean Svc. Inc. subs. Marcona Corp., San Francisco, 1956-75, 1975—. Author 1 Charter Party, 1957. Steering com. Dogwood Festival, Lewiston, Idaho, 1985-92; sec. Asotin County Reps., Clarkston, Wash., 1986-88; adv. bd. Clarkston Pt. Commrs., 1989-92. Lt. USN, 1941-45, PTO; grand marshall Asotin Christmas Parade, 2006. Recipient Pres.'s award Marin (Calif.) coun. Boy Scouts Am., 1977, Order of Merit, 1971, 84, Skillern award Lewis Clark coun., 1982, Silver Beaver award 1987; Lewis-Clark Valley Vol. award, 1987, Youth Corps award Nat. Assn. Svc. and Conservation Corps, 1990, Pres.'s Spl. award Clarkston C. of C., 1983, Asotin Citizen of Yr. award, 1999. Mem. VFW, Asotin County Hist. Soc. (hon. life pres. 1982-83, bd. dirs.), Asotin C. of C. (v.p. 1994-95). Republican. Mem. Stand for United Ch. of Christ. Avocations: hiking, camping, stamp collecting/philately.

COOK, STEVEN M., lawyer, construction executive; With Sears, Roebuck and Co., 1996—2006; v.p., dep. gen. counsel, corp. sec. Sears Holdings Corp.; v.p., gen. counsel, sec. Pulte Homes, Inc., Bloomfield Hills, Mich., 2006—. Office: Pulte Homes Inc 100 Bloomfield Hills Pky Bloomfield Hills MI 48304*

COOK, STUART DONALD, neurologist, educator; b. Boston, Oct. 23, 1936; s. Martius and Nina (Schwartzman) C.; m. Josepha Emdin, June 26, 1960; children— Andrew, Peter, Jonathan. AB, Brandeis U., 1957; MS, U. Vt., 1959, MD, 1962. Diplomate: Am. Bd. Psychiatry and Neurology. Intern Upstate Med. Center, Syracuse, NY, 1962-63; resident in neurology Albert Einstein Coll. Medicine, Bronx, NY, 1965-67, chief resident, 1967-68, instr. dept. neurology, 1968-69; asst. prof. neurology Coll. Physician and Surgeons, Columbia U., NYC, 1969-71; prof. medicine NJ Med. Sch., Newark, 1971, chmn. dept. neuroscis., 1972-98, prof. neurology, neurosciences, 1972—; chief neurology svc. VA Med. Ctr., East Orange, NJ, 1971-86; acting dean NJ Med. Sch., 1987-89; pres. U. Medicine and Dentistry N.J., 1998—2004. Vis. scientist div. virology Nat. Inst. Med. Research, London, 1977-78; vis. scientist Swiss Inst. for Cancer Research, 1985. Contbr. articles to profl. jours. Served with USN, 1963-65. Mem. Am. Acad. Neurology (S. Weir Mitchell award 1968), AAUP, Harvey Soc., Am. Neurol. Assn., Sigma Xi, Alpha Omega Alpha. Home: 26 Dogwood Dr Morristown NJ 07960-3310 Office: U Medicine and Dentistry Rm 1435 65 Bergen St Newark NJ 07101-1709 Office Phone: 973-972-9181. Business E-Mail: cooksd@umdnj.edu.

COOK, SUSAN DEBORAH, language educator, writer; b. London, Sept. 8, 1969; d. Michael John and Barbara Ann Cook; m. Edward Tauscher Dobson, July 16, 1994; children: Magdalen Ruth Cook Dobson, Beatrice Rose Cook Dobson. BA in English, Cambridge U., Eng., 1992, MPhil in English, 1993; PhD in English, U. London, 1997. Sr. libr. asst. Queens Coll., Cambridge, 1993—94; libr. assoc. Hill Meml. Libr. La. State U., Baton Rouge, 1995—97; cataloguing asst. Stillwater Pub. Libr., Okla., 1998; tchr. Grace Christian Sch., Louisville, Miss., 1999—2005; lectr. in English Miss. State U., Starkville, 2005—. Author: The Book of Galahad, 2005, Sir Gawain and the Green Knight and Ivanhoe, 2007. Recipient Star Tchr. award, 2003; Le Bas Rsch. grantee, Cambridge U., 1991, Found. scholar, Queens Coll., 1990. Mem.: Hist. Novel Soc. (book reviewer 2006—), Order of Daus. of King. Anglican. Office: Miss State U Mississippi State MS 39762

COOK, SUSAN FARWELL, director; b. Boston, Apr. 28, 1953; d. Benjamin and Beverly (Brooks) Conant; m. James Samuel Cook Jr., Aug. 17, 1985; children: Emily Farwell, David McKendree. AB, Colby Coll., Waterville, Maine, 1975; MBA, Thomas Coll., Waterville, Maine, 2002. Bank teller Boston 5 Cent Savs. Bank, 1975-76; asst. technician plan cost John Hancock Mut. Life Ins. Co., Boston, 1976-77, technician plan cost, 1977-78, sr. technician plan cost, 1978-79, asst. mgr. group pension plan cost, 1979-81; assoc. dir. alumni rels. Colby Coll., Waterville, Maine, 1981-86, dir. alumni rels., 1986-97, assoc. dir. planned giving, 1997—2005, asst. dir. campaign, 2005, dir. planned giving, 2005—. Co-dir. adv. bd. women's studies Colby Coll., 1987-89, adv. women's group, 1987-89; bd. dirs. Maine Planned Giving Coun., 2001-04, treas., 2002-04. Bd. dirs., newsletter sec. Literacy Vols. Am., Waterville, 1986—89, 1991—92, v.p., 1995—97, pres., 1997—99; treas. Pitcher Pond Improvement Assn., 1988—95, Gagnon/100 Campaign, 1996, 1998; coach Waterville Area Youth Hockey Assn., 1997—2001; bd. dirs. Youth Hockey Assn., 2001—05; treas. Gagnon for Senate, 2000, 2002; trustee Universalist-Unitarian Ch., Waterville, 2001—, v.p., 2003—05, pres., 2005—07; bd. dirs. Congress Lake Assns., Yarmouth, Maine, 1988—92, Waterville Youth Soccer Assn., 2001—07, pres., 2002—05; bd. dirs. Kennebec Montessori Sch., 1999—2001, Soccer Maine, 2004—07, sec., 2005—07. Mem. AAUW (sec. Waterville br. 1989-91, pres. 1991-93, co-pres. 1993-95, treas. 2003-06), Coun. Advancement and Support of Edn., CASE Dist. I (awards com. chair 1994-96, exec. bd. dirs. 1994-97, chair awards com. 1994-96, sec. 1996-97, nominating com. 1997-99). Avocations: skiing, sewing, golf. Home: 6 Pray Ave Waterville ME 04901-5339 Office: Colby Coll 4372 Mayflower Hl Waterville ME 04901-8843

COOK, TERRANCE, business executive; BSBA, U. Louisville. Client devel. and rels. mgr. Greenebaum Doll & McDonald PLLC, Louisville, 1999—. Team capt. Mar. of Dimes, Louisville. Mem.: Legal Mktg. Assn. (assoc.). Office: Greenebaum Doll & McDonald PLLC 3500 National City Tower 101 S 5th St Louisville KY 40202 Office Phone: 502-587-3528.

COOK, TIMOTHY D., computer company executive; b. 1960; BS in Indsl. Engring., Auburn U.; MBA, Duke U. With IBM, 1982—94; sr. v.p. fulfillment Intelligent Electronics Inc., 1994—96, COO, Reseller divsn., 1996—97; v.p. corp. materials Compaq Computer Corp., 1997—98; sr. v.p. worldwide ops. Apple Computer Inc., Cupertino, Calif., 1998—2002, exec. v.p. worldwide sales & ops., 2002—05; COO Apple Inc. (formerly Apple Computer Inc., Cupertino, Calif., 2005—. Fuqua scholar Duke U. Office: Apple Inc 1 Infinite Loop Cupertino CA 95014-2083*

COOK, VICTOR JOSEPH, JR., business educator, consultant; b. Durant, Okla., June 25, 1938; s. Victor Joseph and Athelene Ann (Arduser) C.; m. Linda Lee Potter, June 6, 1960 (div. 1971); children: Victor Joseph III, William Randall, Christopher Phelps; m. barbara Brainard, Dec. 29, 1989 (div. 1997). BA, Fla. State U., 1960; MS, La. State U., 1962; PhD, U. Mich., 1965. Rsch. assoc. Mktg. Sci. Inst., Phila., 1965-68; assoc. rsch. dir. Boston, 1968-69; asst. prof. U. Chgo., 1969-75; pres., dir. Mgmt. & Design, New Orleans, 1975-78; prof. Freeman Sch. Bus. Tulane U., 1978—. Pres. Styjl Furniture, 1998—; cons. Ford Motor Co., Dearborn, Mich., 1964-67, IBM, NYC, 1968-72, Sears, Roebuck & Co., Chgo., 1975-77, Internat. Computers Ltd., ICL, London, 1982-91, DuPont Co., Wilmington, 1986-95, Bases Group, Cin., 1986-89. Author: Brand Policy Determination, 1967, Readings in Marketing Strategy, 1989, Competing for Customers and Capital, 2006. Mem. Am. Mktg. Assn., Am. Econ. Assn., Inst. for Ops. Rsch. and The Mgmt. Scis., Beta Gamma Sigma, Phi Beta Kappa. Republican. Achievements include patents for furniture The Style. Office: Tulane U AB Freeman Sch Bus New Orleans LA 70118 Office Phone: 504-865-5476. Personal E-mail: v2@thestyle.com. Business E-Mail: victor.cook@tulane.edu.

COOK, VIOLETTA BURKE, university administrator; b. Monroe, Mich., Dec. 13, 1941; d. Vangel and Jordonna (Tomova) Dimeff; m. Dock D. Burke Jr., Nov. 30, 1963 (div. Apr. 1976); children: Jennifer, Jonathan; m. Earl Ferguson Cook, Aug. 9, 1981 (dec. Oct. 1983). Student, U. Mich., 1959-62; BA, Tex. A&M U., 1970, MA in Polit. Sci., 1974. Legis. asst. U.S. Senate, Washington, 1962-64; instr., reseach assoc. geoscience Tex. A&M U., Coll. Sta., 1970-82; instr. Blinn Coll., Coll. Sta., 1982—98; dir. sponsored student programs Tex. A&M U., Coll. Sta., 1982—. Precinct chair Dem. Party, Brazos County, Tex., 1978—; vice-chmn. Planning and Zoning Commn., Coll. Sta., 1976-79; chmn. Zoning Bd. Adjustments, Coll. Sta., 1980-84. Groundwater Shell fellow, 1978. Mem. Southwest Social Sci. Assn., Assn. Univ. Dirs. Internat. Agrl. Programs (bd. dirs. 1985-87). Democrat. Avocation: internat. travel. Office: Sponsored Student Programs Tex A&m U College Station TX 77843-1226 Office Phone: 979-845-2550.

COOK, VIRGINIA, real estate company executive; b. Corpus Christi, Tex. m. Firman Cook. Pres. Henry S. Miller Realtors, Dallas, 1971—99; cofounder (with Sheila Rice) Virginia Cook Realty, Tex., 2000, CEO Tex. Named one of Real Estate's 25 Most Influential Thought Leaders, Realtor Mag., 2006. Mem.: Greater Dallas Assn. Realtors (sec.-treas. 1980, v.p. 1981, pres. 1982, Realtor of Yr. 1984), Women's Coun. of Realtors (pres. Dallas Chpt. 1970, Realtor of Yr. 1989, Woman of Yr. 1982), Tex. Assn. Realtors (dir. 1978—, sec.-treas. 1987, v.p. 1988, pres. 1989, Realtor of Yr. 1991), Nat. Assn. Realtors (chair Multiple Listing Policy 1986, chair Big City SubForum 1990, v.p. and liaison to committees 1992—93, v.p. and liaison to affiliates 1994, exec. com. 1997, chair strategic thinkers planning com. 2002, bd. dirs., Disting. Svc. Award 2003). Office: Virginia Cook Realtors 5950 Sherry Lane Ste 110 Dallas TX 75225 Office Phone: 214-696-8877. Office Fax: 214-691-7779. E-mail: info@virginiacook.com.*

COOK, WILLIAM ALFRED, medical products executive; b. Matoon, Ill., 1931; m. Gayle Cook; 1 child, Carl. BS, Northwestern U., 1953; post-grad., Trinity U., Tex. Hypodermic needle salesman, Chgo.; co-founder Cook Inc. (now Cook Group, Inc.), Bloomington, 1963. Co-recipient Nat. Preservation award, W. Baden Springs Hotel, 1998; named one of 400 Richest Americans, Forbes mag., 1998—, World's Richest People, 2001—. Achievements include producing and marketing catheters, wire guides, and needles, thus becoming the first medical supplier for early American angiographers. Office: Cook Group Inc PO Box 489 Bloomington IN 47402-0489*

COOK, WILLIAM E., JR., lawyer; AB, Duke Univ., 1984; JD, Harvard Univ., 1987. Bar: D.C. Law clk. Chief Judge Richard C. Erwin, US Dist. Ct., Middle Dist. N.C.; ptnr., Diversity Affairs Arnold & Porter, Washington. Office: Arnold & Porter 555 Twelfth St NW Washington DC 20004-1206 Office Phone: 202-942-5996. Office Fax: 202-942-5999. Business E-Mail: william.cook@aporter.com.

COOK, WILLIAM HOWARD, architect; b. Evanston, Ill., Dec. 19, 1924; s. Clare Cyril and Matilda Hermine (Schuldt) C.; m. Nancy Ann Dean, Feb. 1, 1949; children: Robert, Cynthia, James. BA, UCLA, 1947; BArch, U. Mich., 1952. Chief designer Fabrica de Muebles Camacho-Roldan, Bogota, Colombia, S.Am., 1949-52; assoc. architect Orus Eash, Traverse City, Mich., Ft. Wayne, Ind., 1952-60; ptnr. Cook & Swaim (architects), Tucson, 1961-68; project specialist in urban devel. Banco Interamericano de Desarrollo, Buenos Aires, Argentina, 1968-69; pres. Cain, Nelson, Wares, Cook and Assocs., architects, Tucson, 1969-82. Vis. lectr. architecture U. Ariz., 1980-89; coord. archtl. exch. with U. LaSalle, Mexico City, 1983, 85, 87, 89, 93. Served to lt. (j.g.) USNR, 1943-46. Fellow AIA (pres. So. Ariz. 1967); mem. Ariz. Soc. Architects (pres. 1970), Ariz. Soc. of AIA (Architect's medal 1981) Home and Office: PO Box 347 Sonoita AZ 85637-0347 Home Phone: 520-455-5867.

COOK, WILLIAM M., manufacturing executive; b. Aug. 1954; BSBA, MBA, Va. Tech. Univ. Sr. v.p., comml. & indsl. Donaldson Co., Mpls., 1996—2000, sr. v.p. internat., CFO, 2001—04, pres., CEO, 2004—05, chmn., pres., CEO, 2005—. Office: Donaldson Co 1400 W 94th St Minneapolis MN 55431*

COOK-BENNETT, GAIL, pension fund administrator; BA in Econ., Carleton U., 1962; MA in Econ., U. Mich.; PhD in Econ., U. Mich.; LLD honoris causa, Carleton U., 2004. Former acad. positions U. Toronto; former sr. exec. position C.D. Howe Inst.; vice-chair Bennecon Ltd., 1982—98; chair, investment mgr. Can. Pension Plan Investment Bd., Toronto, Ont., 1998—. Bd. dirs. Manulife Fin. Corp., Petro-Can, Emera Inc. Recipient Honour for Contbn. to Working Women, Montreal YWCA, 1977; fellow, Can. Inst. Corp. Dirs., 2000. Office: Can Pension Plan Investment Bd Ste 2700 PO Box 101 1 Queen St E Toronto ON M5C 2W5 Canada Office Phone: 416-868-4075. E-mail: gcook-bennett@cppib.ca.

COOK-DEEGAN, ROBERT MULLAN, physician, educator; s. William Raymond Cook and Merry (Mullan) Low. BA in Chemistry, Harvard Coll., 1975; MD, U. Colo., 1979. Intern U. Colo., Denver, 1979-80, postdoctoral fellow, rsch. pathologist, 1980-82; sr. assoc. Office Tech. Assessment, U.S. Congress, Washington, 1982-88; acting exec. dir. biomed. ethics adv. com. U.S. Congress, Washington, 1988-89; expert Nat. Ctr. Human Genome Rsch., Bethesda, Md., 1989-90; dir. div. bio-behavioral scis. and mental disorders Inst. Medicine, NAS, Washington, 1991-94; sr. program officer NAS, 1994-96; Cecil and Ida Green fellow U. Tex., Dallas, 1996; dir. Nat. Cancer Policy Bd., 1996-2000, Robert Wood Johnson Health Policy Fellowship Program, 2001—02, Ctr. Genome Ethics Law and Policy, Duke U., 2002—. Author: The Gene Wars: Science, Politics, and the Human Genome, 1994; contbr. articles and chpts. in field. Bd. dirs. Physicians for Human Rights, Boston, 1987-96; dir. ctr. excellence Ethical, Legal & Social Implications Rsch., NIH, 2004—. Recipient Robert Johnson Health Policy Rsch. Investigator award, 1999—2002; grantee Alfred P. Sloan Found., Georgetown U., 1988—91, NSF, 1990—91, Nat. Cancer Inst. and Robert Wood Johnson, 1992—2000, Burroughs Wellcome Fund, 2000—01. Fellow AAAS. Achievements include research in history of human genome project, public policy in cancer, health policy, tobacco control, neurology, psychiatry, behavioral medicine, neuroscience and addiction; U.S. federal policy on Alzheimer's disease and other dementing disorders, public policy on human gene therapy and bioethics. Office: Duke Univ Box 90141 Durham NC 27708-0141 Office Phone: 919-668-0793.

COOKE, CARLTON LEE, JR., mayor; b. Marion, Ala., July 12, 1944; s. Carlton Lee and Willie (Rinehart) Cooke; married; 1 child, Kimberly Ann. Student, U. Hawaii, 1962-65; BA, La. Tech. U., 1966; postgrad., U. Tex., 1970-72. Mfg. engr. Tex. Instruments, Austin, 1972-75, site personnel mgr., 1975-81, mktg. mgr., 1981-83; pres., CEO Greater Austin C. of C., 1983-87; mayor City of Austin, Austin, 1988—91. CEO, pres. good2CU.com, Inc., 1999—2000; chmn., CEO Habitek Internat., Inc., 1991—, Tanisys Tech. Corp., 2002—03; pres., CEO U.S. Med. Sys., Inc., 1992—, The Life Store Med. Group, LLC, 2004—06; bd. dirs. New Century Equity Holdings Corp., Bill Concepts Corp., U.S. Long Distance Corp., Sharps Compliance Corp., Med. Polymers Tech., Inc., ProActive Med. Techs., Inc., CUville.com, Inc., FIData.com, Inc., Staubach Co., Tanisys Tech. Corp., Stewart Title, Reliability, Inc.; participant U.S. Conf. Mayors, Washington, 1991; mem. Anthony Commn., U.S. Congress. Contbg. editor: to mags. Co-chmn. Jerry Lewis Telethon, Austin, 1986—87; chmn. United Negro Telethon, 1991, Tex. Housing Fin. Corp., 1992—94, Austin Charter Com., 1993—94, Tex. Walk of Stars, 1991—2003; mem. Austin City Coun., 1977—91, mayor pro tem, 1979; mem. adv. bd. U. Miami Rosenstiel Sch. Ctr. Sustainable Fisheries, 2001—02. Capt. USAF, 1966—72, Vietnam. Decorated Bronze Star; named Jaycee of the Yr., Austin Jaycees, 1976; named one of Five Outstanding Young Texans, Tex. Jaycees, 1979; recipient Carl Burnett Cmty. award, 1981, Disting. Austin Citizen's award, 1992, Excellence award, Real Estate Coun. Austin, 1992. Mem.: VFW (life), Austin-San Antonio Corridor Coun. (pres. 1988, 1991), Tex. Mcpl. League (pres. 1991), Nat. League Cities (chair fin. steering com.). Baptist. Avocations: travel, reading, civic work, movies, art. Home: PO Box 50442 Austin TX 78763-0442 Office: Office of Mayor 3160 Bee Cave Rd Ste 300C Austin TX 78746 Office Phone: 512-347-8800 ext 3. Business E-Mail: usmedsys@sbcglobal.net.

COOKE, CATHERINE E., pharmacist, consultant; PharmD, Med. U. SC., 1994. Lic. pharmacist Bd. Pharmacy, 1992. Ind. cons. RxSvs., Ellicott City, Md., 2007—. Office: RxSvcs 5106 Bonnie Branch Rd Ellicott City MD 21043 Home Phone: 410-480-5012; Office Phone: 410-480-5012.

COOKE, EDMUND, lawyer; BA, Kent State U., 1965; JD, U. Mich. Law Sch., 1973. Bar: Mich. 1973, DC 1979. Atty., Appellate Ct. Divsn. Nat. Labor Relations Bd.; spl. asst. to vice-chair EEOC, dep. dir., Field Svc. Office; staff counsel US Ho. of Reps.; ptnr., Labor & Employment Dept. Venable LLP, Washington. Contbr.; co-editor: Disability Law Reporter Svc. Capt. USAF, 1966—70. Office: Venable LLP 575 7th St NW Washington DC 20004 Office Phone: 202-344-4983. Office Fax: 202-344-8300. Business E-Mail: edcooke@venable.com.

COOKE, JACKIE (JACQUELINE MARIE COOKE), elementary school educator; BS, Portland State U., Oreg., 1981, MA, 1992. Tchr. Portland Metro area, 1981—; first grade tchr. West Gresham Elem. Sch., Gresham. Co-editor (and webmaster): Oreg. Coun. Tchrs. of Math. profl. jour. Named Oreg. Tchr. of Yr., 2007. Office: West Gresham Elem Sch 330 W Powell Blvd Gresham OR 97080 Business E-Mail: jackie_cooke@gbsd.gresham.k12.or.us.*

COOKE, MICHAEL, editor-in-chief, publishing executive; b. England; m. Barbara Cooke; 3 children. BA, Auckland U., 1969. Joined Toronto Star, 1974, copy editor, city editor; co-mng. editor Montreal Gazette; mng. editor Edmonton Jour., 1992—95; editor-in-chief The Vancouver Province, 1995—2000, The Fin. Post, Canada, 1998; founding editor The Nat. Post, 1998; editor-in-chief Chgo. Sun-Times, 2000—05, 2006—, NY Daily News, NYC, 2005; v.p. editl. Sun-Times News Group, Chgo., 2006—. Office: Chicago Sun Times 350 N Orleans St Ste 1270 Chicago IL 60654-2148 Office Phone: 312-321-3000. Office Fax: 312-321-3084. E-mail: mcooke@suntimes.com.*

COOKE, NICOLE, school librarian; BA in Comm., Rutgers U., 1997, MLS, 1999; MA in Adult Edn., Pa. Sate U., 2006. Asst. supr. Laurie Music Libr. Rutgers U., 1995—98, ind. study Ctr. for Alcohol Studies Libr., 1999; info. specialist Montclair Pub. Libr., NJ, 1999—2001, acting mgr. youth services dept. NJ, 2000—01, info. specialist NJ, 2001—03; info. and edn. libr. U. Medicine and Dentistry of NJ, Newark, 2001—03; evening reference libr., asst. prof. Montclair State U., NJ, 2003—. Logistics coord. NJ Train-the-Trainer Program, 2005, program coord., 2005—; mem. libr. standards task force NJ Commn. Higher Edn., 2006—; libr. adv. bd. Oxford U. Press, 2005—. Reviewer (books) Internet Reference Svcs. Quarterly, 2004—, Libr. Jour., 2002—, (audio book), 2004—, (materials) Jour. Libr. & Info. Services in Distance Learning, 2004—, (audiovisual material) Ednl. Media Reviews Online, 2004—. Named one of the Movers & Shakers, Libr. Jour., 2007. Mem.: Assn. Coll. and Rsch. Libraries, ALA, Black Caucus of Am. Libr. Assn. - NJ Chpt. (founding mem. 2005, v.p. and programming chair 2006), Infolink Libr. Coop. (diversity com. 2004—05), NJ Libr. Assn. Office: Sprague Library Montclair State Univ Normal Ave Montclair NJ 07043 Office Phone: 973-655-4058. Office Fax: 973-414-0909. E-mail: cooken@mail.montclair.edu.

COOKE, ROBERT WILLIAM, retired science journalist; b. Alhambra, Calif., Mar. 26, 1935; s. Loren Elvin and Edith (Mason) C.; m. Sue B. Cato, Sept. 10, 1960; children: Gregory, Karen, Emily. BS in English, Calif. State Poly. Coll., 1961; MS in Journalism, UCLA, 1962; postgrad. in advanced sci. writing (Univ. fellow), Columbia U., 1969-70. Reporter-photographer Pomona (Calif.) Progress-Bull., 1962-63; newsman AP, Los Angeles, 1963-67; sci. writer Calif. Inst. Tech., 1967-69, Pasadena (Calif.) Star-News, 1970-73; sci. editor Boston Globe, 1973-84; sci./medicine writer Atlanta Jour. and Constn., 1984-86; sci. writer Newsday, LI, NY, 1986—2003; ret., 2003. Author: Improving on Nature, The Brave New World of Genetic Engineering, 1977, Earthfire; the Eruption of Mt. St. Helens, 1982, Dr. Folkman's War, 2001. With USCG, 1954—58. Recipient James T. Grady award Am. Chem. Soc., 1981, Lewis Thomas award for communicating life scis. Woods Hole Marine Biology Lab., 1991, Sci. Writing award AAAS/Westinghouse, 1991. Mem.: Nat. Assn. Sci. Writers, Kappa Tau Alpha. Democrat. Methodist.

COOKE, SARA MULLIN GRAFF, daycare provider, kindergarten educator, medical assistant; b. Phila., Dec. 29, 1935; d. Charles Henry and Elizabeth (Mullin) Brandt Graff; m. Peter Fischer Cooke, June 29, 1963 (div. July 1994); children: Anna Cooke Smith, Peter Fischer Jr., Elizabeth Cooke Haskins, Sara Cooke Lowe; m. Laina Cooke Driscoll, Dec. 18, 1999. AA, Bennett Coll., 1955; BE in Child Edn., Westchester State Tchrs. Coll., 1956. Asst. to tchr. 1st grade The Woodlyn Sch., 1956-58; tchr. Sara Bircher's Kindergarten, Germantown, Pa., 1958-62, Chestnut Hill Acad., Pa., 1962-63, Tarleton Sch., Devon, Pa., 1963-64; with F.C.I. Mktg. Co-ordinators Inc., NYC, New Canaan, Conn., 1980-86; fundraiser Children's Hosp., Phila., 1989-92, pres. women's com., 1987-88; coord., master of ednl. ceremonies Phila. Soc. for Preservation Landmarks, 1991-93; coord. Elderhostel Program Landmarks Soc., 1992-93. Pvt. day caretaker Spl. Care, Inc., 1988—; pvt. daycare and doctor's asst., 1994—. Kindergarten tchr. Sunday Sch., 2004-06; bd. aux. Children's Hosp. Phila., 1970-76, women's bd., 1977—, pres., 1987-88; commonwealth bd. Med. Coll. Pa., 1984-99, Gimbel award com., 1994; alt. del. Rep. Nat. Conv., 1992; co-chmn. benefit St. Martin in the Fields, London, 1997, usher, 2003-06, tchr. Chestnut Hill Sunday Sch., 2005-; vol. with parents of very sick children Connelly Family Resource Ctr./Children's Hosp. of Phila., 1999—, chmn., 2003; vol. pediat. oncology sect. Children's Hosp. Phila., 2007; vol. Rep. Nat. Conv., 2000; press vol. Polit. Fest in Laura Bush Libr., 2000. Nominee Pa. Soc., 2004; recipient Silver Cup award, Children's Hosp. Phila., 2002. Mem. Pa. Assn. Hosp. Auxs. (health rep.) Nat. Soc. Colonial Dames (garden com. 1988—), Alumnae Assn. Madeira Sch. (class sec., 1997-2003, class agt., Vol. Svc. award 1997), Pa. Soc. (life), Phila. Cricket Club, Jr. League Garden Club (co-chmn. Daisy Day Children's Hosp. 2001), Colonial Dames Pa., Pa. Soc. Reps. Republican. Episcopalian. Home and Office: Penns Wood G-26 20 Haws Ln Flourtown PA 19031

COOKE, STEVEN JOHN, chemical engineer, consultant, scientist; b. Grand Rapids, Mich., Oct. 1, 1954; s. Edward G. and Annette M. (Minnema) C.; m. Marguerite K. Oldenburger, June 18, 1977; children: Allison, Jonathan. BS in Chemistry, Calvin Coll., 1977; M in Chem. Engring., Ill. Inst. Tech., 1987; postgrad. in Engring., Calif. Coast U. Registered profl. engr., Ill.; cert. profl. chemist, quality engr., quality auditor. Chemist, lab. supr. Matheson Gas Products, Joliet, Ill., 1977-80; chief chemist Cardox, Countryside, Ill., 1980-85; scientist Am. Air Liquide, Countryside, 1985-92; asst. quality mgr. Alphagaz Divsn. of Liquid Air, Countryside, 1992-93; quality assurance/quality control mgr. Am. Air Liquide, Countryside, 1993-95; quality mgr. Carbonic Industries Corp., 1995-98, Airgas Carbonic, Duluth, Ga., 1998—2000; pres. Process Systems Consulting, 2000—. Online faculty U. Phoenix, 2003—; chemistry mentor Thomas Edison State Coll., 2005—. Contbr. chpt. to book, articles on quality systems to profl. jours. Group leader Hazardous Materials Emergency Response Team; treas. Christian Reformed Ch. Mission, Western Springs, Ill., 1982-93, Chicagoland Diaconal Task Force Bd., Palos Heights, Ill., 1989-92. Fellow Am. Inst. Chemists; mem. Am. Soc. Quality Control, Am. Chem. Soc. (publicity chair I&EC divsn. 1989-95, chair I&EC divsn. 1999-2001, chair small chem. bus. divsn. 2004-05), Compressed Gas Assn. (CO2 task force, gas specifications com.) Achievements include patent for portable gas analyzer. Address: 1117 Mineral Springs Rd Charlotte NC 28262 Office Phone: 704-598-4819. Business E-Mail: scooke@sprynet.com.

COOKE, WARREN F., lawyer; b. Phila., 1946; BA, Dartmouth U., 1968; JD, Yale U., 1972. Bar: N.Y. 1973. Mem. Milbank, Tweed, Hadley & McCloy, NYC, Hongkong, 1978—87, Milbank, Tweed, Hadley & McCloy (long range planning Com.), 1988—91, Milbank, Tweed, Hadley & McCloy LLP (compensation com.), 1991—95; ptnr. Milbank, Tweed, Hadley & McCloy, 1980—. Mem. IBA, ABA, Assn. Bar NYC, NY State Bar Assn., Am. Soc. Internat. Law. Office: Milbank Tweed Hadley & McCloy 1 Chase Manhattan Plz New York NY 10005-1413 Office Phone: 212-530-5220. Office Fax: 212-530-5219. Business E-Mail: wcooke@milbank.com.

COOKS, R(OBERT) GRAHAM, chemist, educator; b. Benoni, South Africa, July 2, 1941; came to U.S., 1968; s. Audrey Owen Eva Mitchie; m. Maria-Luisa Raduan Ripoll, Aug. 19, 1967; children: Owen, Barry, Jude. BSc, U. Natal, 1961, PhD, 1965, Cambridge U., 1967. Asst. prof. Kansas State U., Manhattan, 1968-71; from assoc. dir. to disting. prof. Purdue U., Lafayette, Ind., 1971—. Author: Metastable Ions, 1973; contbr. articles to profl. jours.; patentee in field. Recipient ACS award in analytical chemistry Am. Chem. Soc., 1997. Mem. Am. Soc. Mass Spectrometry (pres. 1984-86), Internat. Mass Spectrometry Soc. (pres. 1997-2000). Home: 177 Prophet Dr West Lafayette IN 47906-1235 Office: Purdue U Dept Chemistry West Lafayette IN 47907 Business E-Mail: cooks@purdue.edu.

COOKSEY, JOHN CHARLES, ophthalmologist, retired congressman; b. Aug. 20, 1941; s. Henry Oscar and Ruth (Lee) C.; m. Dorothy Ann Grabill, Dec. 30, 1969; children: Karen, Carol Ann, Catherine. MD, La. State U., New Orleans, 1966; MBA, U. Tex., Austin, 1994. Mem. Congress from 5th La. Dist., 1996—2002, mem. agr. and internat. rels. coms.; practice medicine specializing in ophthalmology Monroe, La., 1972—; assoc. clin. prof. La. State U. Sch. Medicine, New Orleans, 1982—90, clin. prof., 1990—. Mem. teaching staff E.A. Conway Hosp., Monroe , 1972—; vis. lectr. Alton Ochsner Med. Found., New Orleans, 1978—; asst. clin. prof. La. State U. Med. Sch., New Orleans, 1979-82. Republican. Address: 1310 N 19th St Monroe LA 71201 Business E-Mail: jcooksey@cookseymd.com.

COOKSON, ALAN HOWARD, electrical engineer, researcher; b. London, July 3, 1939; arrived in U.S., 1968; s. Joseph and Rachel Cookson; m. Elizabeth Rosamond Ritblat, Oct. 24, 1965; children: Richard Jonathan, Simon Charles. BSc in Engring. with 1st class honors, Queen Mary Coll., London U., 1961, PhD of Elec. Engring., 1965. Chartered engr., Gt. Brit. Rsch. fellow Queen Mary Coll., London, 1964—65; rsch. officer Ctrl. Elec. Rsch. Labs., Leatherhead, England, 1965—69; sr. engr. Westinghouse R & D Ctr., Pitts., 1968—75; mgr. gas cable rsch. Westinghouse Power Circuit Breaker, Westborough, Mass., 1975—80; mgr. polymers, dielectrics and advanced batteries Westinghouse Sci. & Tech. Ctr., Pitts., 1980—92; dep. dir. Electronics and Elec. Engring. Lab. divsn. Nat. Inst. Stds. and Tech., Gaithersburg, Md., 1992—. U.S. rep. advanced materials for electro tech. com. Internat. Conf. Large Elec. Systems, 1996—; mem. US nat. com. Internat. Electrotech. Commn.; convener Working Group on Gas Insulated Cables, Internat. Conf. Large Elec. Systems, 1980-90. Editor: Digest of Literature on Dielectrics, 1970; contbr. articles to profl. jours.; patentee in field. Mem. adv. com. Miss. State U., 1983. Fellow IEEE (pres. Dielectrics and Elec. Insulation Soc. 1993-94), Inst. Elec. Engrs. London; mem. Phys. Soc., Inst. Physics London. Home: 15717 Bondy Ln Darnestown MD 20878-2114 Office: Nat Inst Standards/Tech Rm B358 Bldg 220 Gaithersburg MD 20899-8100 Office Phone: 301-975-2220. Business E-Mail: cookson@nist.gov.

COOLEDGE, RICHARD CALVIN, lawyer; b. Charleston, SC, Apr. 20, 1943; s. Russell Clarence and Lorena Ann (Weymuth) C.; m. Nancy Jean Western, June 15, 1965 (div. Dec. 1986); children: Dean Richard, Mark Alan, Jocelyn Joy; m. Jeanine Diana Smith, Apr. 12, 1989 (div. Nov. 1993). BA in Econs. with honors, U. Mo., Columbia, 1965; JD, U. Mich., 1968. Bar: Ariz. 1969, U.S. Dist. Ct. Ariz. 1969, U.S. Ct. Appeals (9th cir.) 1973, U.S. Supreme Ct. 1973. Mem. Brown & Bain P.A., Phoenix, 1968—2004, Perkins Coie Brown & Bain, Phoenix, 2004—. Contbg. editor: Banking and Lending Institutions Forms, Business Workouts Manual; contbr. articles to profl. jours. Fellow Ariz. Bar Found.; mem. Motorcycle Safety Found. (instr. 1994-2003), BMW Owners Assn. Avocations: motorcycling, golf, music, aviculture. Office: Perkins Coie Brown & Bain PA 2901 N Central Ave Fl 20 Phoenix AZ 85012-2700 Home Phone: 602-791-9996; Office Phone: 602-351-8425. Business E-Mail: rcooledge@perkinscoie.com.

COOLEY, ANDREW LYMAN, computer company executive; b. St. Louis, Oct. 14, 1934; s. Andrew L. and Algretta R. (Carr) C.; m. Joan Lynn Wheatley, Jan. 9, 1958; children: Cathleen Wheatley, Caroline Carr. BA, George Washington U., 1964, MA, 1967; MS, U.S. Army Command and Gen. Staff Coll., 1966; postgrad., U.S. Army War Coll., 1972-73. Commd. 2d lt. U.S. Army, 1955, advanced through grades to maj. gen. Continental U.S. and Hawaii, 1955-64; bn. adv. Vietnam, 1964-65; aide to chief of staff SHAPE, Belgium, 1967-69; tank bn. comdr. Germany, 1969-70; mem. staff Dept. of Army Pentagon, 1970-72; brigade comdr. and div. chief of staff Korea, 1975-77; exec. to comdr. in chief Pacific Hawaii, 1978-79; asst. div. comdr. 101st Airborne Div., 1979-81; asst. dep. dir. for politico-mil. affairs, plans and policy directorate Joint Chiefs of Staff, Washington, 1981-83; mil. adviser Habib-Draper Mission, Lebanon, 1982-83; dir. strategy, plans and policy Dept. Army, Washington, 1983-85; comdg. gen. 24th Inf. Div. (Mech.) and Fort Stewart, Hunter Army Air Field, Fort Stewart, Ga., 1985-87; chief Office Military Cooperation, Cairo, 1987-89; ret., 1989; program mgr. Vinnell Brown Root, Turkey Base Maintenance Agreement, 1989-91; project mgr. ops. and maintenance Brown and Root Svcs. Corp., Houston, 1991-94; program mgr. Project Restore Hope Somalia, 1993. Ind. cons. with expertise in Africa, Croatia, Bosnia and Haiti, 1994-97; dir. ops. Dyncorp Internat. Tech. Svcs. LLC, 1998—. Author: Diplomatic Significances of the Great White Fleet, 1966, Realistic Deterrence in NATO, 1973. Decorated Def. D.S.M. with oak leaf cluster, Legion of Merit with oak leaf cluster, Bronze Star, Air medal, others; Fed. Exec. fellow Brookings Instn., 1977-78; named to Officer Candidate Sch. Hall of Fame, 1979. Mem. Assn. U.S. Army, Armor Assn. Episcopalian. Home: 13235 W Pine Creek Sedalia CO 80135-9450 Home Phone: 303-647-2195; Office Phone: 972-871-6754. Business E-Mail: andy.cooley@dyn-intl.com.

COOLEY, CHARLES P., chemicals executive; married; 3 children. BA in Philosophy, Yale Coll.; MBA, Dartmouth Coll. With nat. banking div. Mfrs. Hanover Trust Co., NYC; various positions Atlantic Richfield; controller and v.p. fin. and adminstrn. ARCO Products Co.; asst. treas. corp. fin. Atlantic Richfield Co., LA; v.p., treas., CFO The Lubrizol Corp., Wickliffe, Ohio, 1998—. Office: The Lubrizol Corp 29400 Lakeland Blvd Wickliffe OH 44092

COOLEY, DENTON ARTHUR, surgeon, educator; b. Houston, Aug. 22, 1920; s. Ralph C. and Mary (Fraley) C.; m. Louise Goldsborough Thomas, Jan. 15, 1949; children: Mary, Susan, Louise, Florence, Helen. BA, U. Tex., 1941; MD, Johns Hopkins U., 1944; Doctorem Medicinae (hon.), U. Turin, Italy, 1969; HHD (hon.), Hellenic Coll., 1984, Holy Cross Greek Orthodox Sch. of Theology, 1984; DSc honoris causa, Coll. of William and Mary, 1987. Diplomate: Am. Bd. Surgery, Am. Bd. Thoracic Surgery. Intern Johns Hopkins Sch. Medicine, Balt., 1944-45, resident surgery, 1945-50; sr. surg. registrar thoracic surgery Brompton Hosp. for Chest Diseases, London, Eng., 1950-51; assoc. prof. surgery Baylor U. Coll. Medicine, Houston, 1954-62, prof. surgery, 1962-69; clin. prof. surgery U. Tex. Med. Sch., Houston, 1975—; founder, surgeon-in-chief Tex. Heart Inst., 1962—. Served as capt., M.C., 1946-48. Named one of ten Outstanding Young Men in U.S., U.S. C. of C., 1955, Man of the Yr. award Kappa Sigma, 1964; recipient Rene Leriche prize Internat. Surg. Soc., 1967, Billings Gold medal Am. Surg. Soc., 1967, Vishnevsky medal Vishnevsky Inst., USSR, 1971, Theodore Roosevelt Award, 1980, Presdl. Medal of Freedom, presented by Pres. Reagan, 1984, Gifted Tchr. award Am. Coll. Cardiology, 1987, Disting. Svc. award AMA, 1997, Nat. Medal of Tech., U.S. Dept Commerce, 1998 Hon. fellow Royal Coll. Physicians and Surgeons of Glasgow, Royal Coll. Surgeons of Ireland, Royal Australasian Coll. Surgeons, Royal Coll. Surgeons of Eng.; mem. ACS, Am. Surg. Assn., Internat. Cardiovascular Soc., Am. Assn. Thoracic Surgery, Soc. Thoracic Surgery, Soc. Univ. Surgeons, Am. Coll. Cardiology, Am. Coll. Chest Physicians, Soc. Clin. Surgery, Soc. Vascular Surgery, Western Surg. Assn., Tex. Surg. Soc., Halsted Soc. Achievements include performance of numerous heart transplants; implanted 1st artificial heart, 1969. Office: Tex Heart Inst PO Box 20345 Houston TX 77225-0345 Business E-Mail: dcooley@heart.thi.tmc.edu. *As a person progresses along the path of life, he may achieve certain goals he set for himself as a youth. But to be more completely fulfilled, he must forever extend hid goals to utilize his talents ans accomplishments more fully. Too often, a man receives recognition for his deeds early in life and contents himself prematurely with living in peace and self-satisfaction.*

COOLEY, JACK CRAIN, cadriovascular surgeon; b. Redfield, SD, Sept. 4, 1924; s. Frank Henry and Crystal Cooley; m. Gloria Gamage Cooley, Dec. 23, 1947; children: Crystal, Carolyn Stamm, Craig. BA, Northwestern U., 1942, MD, 1947; BS, U. Minn., 1954. Diplomate Am. Bd. Surgery, 1954, 1955. Surgery fellow Mayo Clinic, Rochester, Minn., 1949—57; staff surgeon Carle Clinic, Urbana, Ill., 1957—90; assoc. prof. surgery U. Ill., 1965—80. Adv. bd. Mayo Clinic Alumni Bd., Rochester, Minn. Contbr. articles to profl. jours. Bd. governors YMCA, Urbana. Capt. USAF, 1951—53. Mem.: ACS, Ill. Coll. Surgeons, Ill. Surg. Soc., Soc. Thoracic Surgeons, Ctrl. Surg. Assn., Western Surg. Assn. Republican. Presbyterian. Avocations: golf, tennis. Home: 4055North Recker #12 Mesa AZ 85215 Business E-Mail: jackfrommesa1@cox.net.

COOLEY, JAMES WILLIAM, retired executive researcher; b. NYC, Sept. 18, 1926; s. William F. and Anna (Fanning) C.; m. Ingrid Uddholm, May 1, 1957; children: William, Anna-Carin, Lars. BA, Manhattan Coll., Riverdale, NY, 1949; MA, Columbia U., 1951, PhD, 1961. Programmer Inst. Advanced Study, Princeton, NJ, 1953-56; research staff Courant Inst., NYU, 1956-62; research staff mem. IBM Watson Research Ctr., Yorktown Heights, NY, 1962-91; with dept. elec. engring. U. R.I., Kingston, 1991-93; ret., 1993. Inventor fast fourier transform. Served with USAAF, 1945-46. Fellow IEEE (life, Third Millennium medal, Jack Kilby medal 2002); mem. NAE.

COOLEY, RICHARD EUGENE, lawyer; b. Flint, Mich., Apr. 28, 1935; s. Eugene J. and Helen Frances (Lumbert) C.; m. Wanda Lee Ford, Feb. 20, 1965; children: Scott Richard, Courtney Cooley Breaugh. AB, Albion Coll., 1957; JD, Duke U., 1960. Bar: Mich. 1960, U.S. Supreme Ct. 1970. Asst. pros. atty. Genesee County, Mich., 1962-64; city atty. Linden, Mich., 1964—89; ptnr. Bellairs, Dean & Cooley, 1964—2004; township atty. Fenton Township, 1970—; spl. asst. atty. gen. State of Mich., 1975-81; ptnr. Cooley, Mouton & Smith, Flint, Mich., 2005—. Village atty. Village of Gaines, Mich., 1989-96 Past pres. Child and Family Svcs. Mich., Flint. Mem. State Bar Mich., Genesee County Bar Assn. (pres. 1977-78), Genesee County Bar Found. (life), Flint Estate Planning Coun. (pres. 1999-2000), Rotary, Masons. Republican. Presbyterian. Avocations: skiing, sailing, travel. Office: Cooley Moulton & Smith 412 S Saginaw St Ste 300 Flint MI 48502-1810 Home: 906 E Kearsley St Flint MI 48503-6119 Office Phone: 810-767-1520.

COOLEY, STEVE, prosecutor; b. LA, May 1, 1947; m. Jana Cooley; 2 children. BA, Calif. State U., LA, 1970; JD, U. So. Calif., 1973. Joined Dist. Attys. Office, 1973; dist. atty. L.A. County, 2000—. Named Alumnus of Yr., Calif. State U., L.A., 1998, Pros. of the Yr., Century City Bar Assn., 2001, L.A. County Bar Assn., 2005, Champion of the People, Nat. Black Pros. Assn., Crime Victims Star of the Yr., Justice for Homicide Victims; recipient Leaders in Pub. Svc. award, Encino C. of C., Cmty. Justice award, Calif. NAACP. Mem.: Phi Kappa Phi. Office: County of Los Angeles Foltz Justice Ctr 210 W Temple St Ste 18000 Los Angeles CA 90012-3210 Business E-Mail: scooley@lacountyda.org.

COOLEY, THOMAS F., dean, economist, educator; b. Rutland, Vt., Jan. 3, 1943; s. Thomas J. and Marjorie (Batcheldor) C.; m. Patricia Bower; children: Noah, Joshua, Aaron, Frederika Prott. BS, Rensselaer Polytech., 1965; MA, U. Pa., 1969, PhD, 1971; doctorate (hon.), Stockholm Sch. Econs., 1987. Systems engr. IBM Corp., 1965—66; asst. prof. econs. Tufts U., Medford, Mass., 1970—76; rsch. assoc. Nat. Bur. Econ. Rsch., 1973—77; vis. asst. prof. Carnegie-Mellon U., 1973—74; vis. prof. U. Western Australia, 1974; faculty assoc. Joint Ctr. for Urban Studies, MIT and Harvard, 1976—80; assoc. prof. econs. U. Calif., Santa Barbara, 1976—79, prof. econs., 1980-87; vis. prof. Birbeck Coll., U. London, 1979—80, Stockholm Sch. Econs., 1984, 1985; prof. econs and applied stats. Simon Sch. Bus. and prof. econs. Dept. Econs. U. Rochester, 1987—92; prof. econs. U. Pa., 1995—97; Fred H. Gowan Prof. Econs. Simon Sch. Bus. and prof. econs. Dept. Econs. U. Rochester, 1992—2000, dir. Bradley Policy Rsch. Ctr., 1995—2000; Paganelli-Bull Prof. Econs. Stern Sch. Bus. and prof. econs. Faculty Arts and Scis. NYU, 1999—, Richard R. West Dean Stern Sch. Bus., 2002—. Mem. editl. bd. Jour. Monetary Econs., 1988—; coordinating editor Review of Econ. Dynamics. Author: Frontiers of Business Cycle Research, 1995. Recipient Superior Teaching Award, Rochester-Erasmuc Exec. MBA program, 1990, 1992, MBA Class of 1993, Simon Sch. Bus., 1992, MBA class of 1996, Simon Sch. Bus., 1995; fellow NSF, 1967—70, Econometric Soc., 1998; grantee, US Dept. Labor, 1970—72, 1974—76, 1978—79, Nat. C. of C. Found., 1976—77, NSF, 1976—78, 1990—93, 1993—95, 1997—2000, 2001—03, US Dept. Housing and Urban Devel., 1978—79, 1981—82, Nat. Inst. Justice, 1984—86; Irving Scholar, 1963—65. Mem. Am. Econ. Assn., Econometric Soc., Soc. for Econ. Dynamics (pres. 2000-03). Office: Dept Econs Leonard N Stern Sch Bus NYU 44 W 4th St New York NY 10012-1126

COOLEY, WILLIAM EDWARD, research scientist, consultant; b. St. Louis, Mar. 7, 1930; s. Charles Frederic and Lillian Marie (Williams) C.; m. Marion Grace Sherman, June 5, 1952; children: Charles, Marilyn, Harold, Noele. AB, Cen. Coll., 1951; PhD, U. Ill., 1954. Rsch. chemist Procter & Gamble Co., Cin., 1954-61, product devel. chemist, 1961-65, product devel. group leader, 1965-75, product devel. regulatory sect. mgr., 1975-90, regulatory affairs sect. mgr., 1990-91; worldwide regulatory coordination sect. mgr., 1991-94; pres. Cooley Cons., Inc., 1994—. Contbr. articles to profl. jours. Mem. Am. Assn. Dental Rsch., Internat. Assn. Dental Rsch., Drug Info. Assn., Assn. Food Drug Ofcls., Regulatory Affairs Profl. Soc. (bd. editors 1990), Consumer Healthcare Products Assn. (bd. dirs. 1987-91), Food and Drug Law Inst. Republican. Achievements include patents in field. Avocations: music, motorcycling, railroading, flying, astronomy. Home and Office: Cooley Cons Inc 531 Chisholm Trail Wyoming OH 45215-2517 Home Phone: 513-522-2491; Office Phone: 513-522-3797.

COOLEY, WILLIAM EMORY, JR., radiologist; b. Charlottesville, Va., Jan. 28, 1941; s. William Emory Sr. and Madelle Elizabeth (Fullen) C.; m. Janella Mahoney Haney, Dec. 26, 1966; children: Angela Janette, William Emory, James Haney. BA, Emory U., 1963; MD, U. Va., 1967. Diplomate Am. Bd. Radiology. Rotating intern. U.S. Naval Hosp., Phila., 1967-68; resident radiology U.S. Naval Regional Med. Ctr., Phila., 1972-75, radiologist Portsmouth, Va., 1975-76, asst. chief radiology, 1976-77; radiologist Bloomington Radiology S.C., Ill., 1977-79, pres., 1979—2005. Chief radiologist Brokaw Hosp., Normal, Ill., 1979-85, St. Joseph Hosp., Bloomington, Ill., pres. med. staff, 1981, med. dir. radiology, 2000—; med. dir. radiology Bromenn Health Care System, Bloomington, 1985—, pres. med. staff, 1990; founding mem. bd. Ft. Jesse Imaging Ctr., Normal, 2002—, chmn., 2006; bd. dir. Bloomington-Normal Healthcare. Mem. citizens adv. coun. Sch. Dist. 87, Bloomington, 1981-84; v.p. McLean County unit Am. Cancer Soc., 1989-90, pres., 1990-94. Comdr. USN, 1966-77. Fellow Am. Coll. Radiology (alt. councillor 1987-92, councillor 1993-99, mem. commn. on small and rural practices 2000, fellowship com. 2004-); mem. AMA, Radiol. Soc. N.Am., Am. Roentgen Ray Soc., Am. Inst. Ultrasound Medicine, Ill. Radiol. Soc. (exec. com. 1986-99, pres. 1994-95), Ctrl. Ill. Radiol. Soc. (pres. 1990-91), Clin. Magnetic Resonance Soc., Soc. Nuc. Medicine, Soc. Breast Imaging, Bloomington Country Club, Masons. Republican. Presbyterian. Avocations: book collecting, tennis, personal computers. Office: Bloomington Radiology SC 2200 Fort Jesse Rd Ste 280 Normal IL 61761-2155

COOLIDGE, DANIEL SCOTT, lawyer; b. Portland, Maine, Sept. 20, 1948; s. John Walter and Mary Louise (Arnold) C.; m. Carolyn Stiles, Nov. 23, 1984; children: Lillian Mae, Lydia Stiles. BS summa cum laude, U. Bridgeport, 1976; JD, Harvard U., 1980. Bar: Conn. 1980, N.H. 1982, Mass. 2001, U.S. Patent Office 1999, U.S. Ct. Appeals (1st cir.) 1983, U.S. Supreme Ct. 1985. Assoc. Cummings & Lockwood, Stamford, Conn., 1980-82, Sheehan, Phinney, Bass & Green PA, Manchester, NH, 1982-87, ptnr., 1987—. Chmn. juvenile diversion com. Pittsfield (N.H.) Dist. Ct., 1982-85. Author: Survival Guide for Road Warriors, 1996; mem. editl. bd. Law Tech. News; columnist Law Office Computing, 1997—; patentee tel. test equipment. Chmn. Bradford Constitution Bicentennial Com.; mem. Pittsfield Planning Bd., 1984-85; treas., trustee First Congl. Ch., Pittsfield, 1984-85, First Bapt. Ch. Bradford; pres. Pittsfield Arts Coun., 1985; del. N.H. Constl. Conv., Concord, 1984-94; moderator Town of Bradford, N.H., 1999-, Kearsarge Reg. Sch. Dist, 2002-; founding bd. dirs., officer U.S. Found. for Inspiration and Recognition of Sci. and Tech. Mem. ABA (environ. law sect., intellectual property law sect., acting chmn., chmn. computer and tech. divsn., vice-chmn. sys. and tools law practice mgmt. sect. 1994—, governing coun. 1996—, advisor UCC article 2B drafting com. 1995-99), N.H. Bar Assn. (vice-chmn. tech. sect. 1993-96, chmn. lex mundi intellectual property sect. 1992-93), Manchester Bar Assn. Avocations: computers, physics, fly fishing, hiking, machining. Home: 106 Bible Hill Ln Warner NH 03278-3701 Office: Coolidge and Graves 108 Bible Hill Warner NH 03278 Office Phone: 603-456-2532. Personal E-mail: dancoolidge@yahoo.com. Business E-Mail: dancoolidge@ipbizlaw.com.

COOLIDGE, ROBERT TYTUS, deacon, historian, educator; b. Boston, Mar. 30, 1933; s. Lawrence and Victoria Stuart (Tytus) C.; m. Ellen Osborne, Sept. 10, 1960 (div.); children: Christopher, Miles, Matthew. Grad., Groton Sch., Mass., 1951; AB, Harvard U., 1955; MA, U. Calif., Berkeley, 1957; BLitt, U. Oxford, Eng., 1966. Ordained deacon Episcopal Ch., 1967. Non-stipendiary min. Christ Ch. Cathedral, Montreal, Que., Can., 1967-69, 71—, dir. Montreal Fund for the Diaconate, 1984—; non-stipendiary min. St. Marylebone Ch., London Clin., 1969-71; mem. faculty Loyola Coll. (now Concordia U.), Montreal, 1963—, assoc. prof. history, 1968-88, adj. assoc. prof., 1988—2000, assoc. prof. emeritus, 2000—; non-stipendiary min. St. George's Ch., Montreal, 2004—. Non-stipendiary min. Diocese Montreal, 1971—; historian Monticello Assn., 1975-2002, historian emeritus, 2003—. Contbr. to hist. vols. Fellow Royal Hist. Soc.; mem. Am. Soc. Ch. History, Ecclesiastical History Soc., Medieval Acad. Am., Am. Hist. Assn., Soc. d'Histoire de l'Eglise de France, Oxford and Cambridge Club (London), Univ. Club (Montreal), Royal St. Lawrence Yacht Club, N.Am. Assn. Deacons, N.Am. Assn. for the Diaconate, St. Andrew's Soc., Assn. Angelican Deacons Can. Home: POB 4070 Westmount PQ Canada H3Z 2X3 *If you really want to help your fellow humans, don't think it is their fault if they refuse or reject your help. Look instead at how you react to help offered to you.*

COOLS, ANNE C., Canadian senator; b. Barbados, Aug. 12, 1943; BA, McGill U., 1981; LLD (hon.), Can. Christian Coll., 2004. Social worker; senator Senate of Canada, Ottawa, 1984—. Named Spiritual Mother of Year, Internat. Jewish Women's Orgn., 1997, Person of Year, REAL Women of Can., 1999, Greatest Canadian, CBC-TV, 2004, Top Twenty Canadian Women, 2004, 10 Top Women, Toronto Sun Newspaper, 2004; named to These 50 Made a Difference, 2006; recipient Outstanding Achievement award politics, Pride Mag., 1997, Toronto Bob Marley Day award, 2001, Women of Excellence Leadership award, Nat. Ctr. Strategic Nonprofit Planning and Cmty. Leadership, 2004. Conservative. Avocations: reading, classical music, piano, gardening, dogs. Office: 178-F Centre Block The Senate of Canada Ottawa ON Canada K1A 0A4 Office Phone: 613-992-2808. Business E-Mail: coolsa@sen.parl.ca.

COOMBE, BOB (ROBERT D.), academic administrator; BA in Chemistry, Williams Coll., 1970; PhD in Phys. Chemistry, U. Calif., Berkeley, 1973. Postdoctoral rsch. assoc. U. Toronto, Canada, 1973—74; tech. staff Rockwell Internat. Sci. Ctr., 1974—81; asst. prof. U. Denver, 1981—85, assoc. prof., 1985—89, prof., 1989—, dean grad. studies, 1985—87, chair dept. chemistry and biochemistry, 1988—95, dean natural scis., math. and engring., 1995—2001, provost, 2001—06, chancellor, 2006—. Office: U Denver Office of Chancellor 2199 S University Blvd Denver CO 80208 Office Phone: 303-871-2111. E-mail: tcoe@du.edu, chancelr@du.edu.*

COOMBE, GEORGE WILLIAM, JR., lawyer, retired bank executive; b. Kearny, NJ, Oct. 1, 1925; s. George William and Laura (Montgomery) Coombe; m. Marilyn V. Ross, June 4, 1949; children: Susan, Donald William, Nancy. BA, Rutgers U., 1946; LLB, Harvard U., 1949; MLA, Stanford U., 2005. Bar: NY 1950, Mich. 1953, Calif. 1976. Practice US Supreme Ct., NYC, 1949—53, Detroit, 1953—69; atty., mem. legal staff Gen. Motors Corp., Detroit, 1953—69, asst. gen. counsel, sec., 1969—75; exec. v.p., gen. counsel Bank of Am., San Francisco, 1975—90; ptnr. Graham and James, San Francisco, 1991—95; sr. fellow Stanford Law Sch., 1995—. Lt. USNR, 1942—46. Mem.: NYC Bar Assn., Los Angeles Bar Assn., San Francisco Bar Assn., Calif. Bar Assn., Mich. Bar Assn., Am. Bar Assn., Phi Gamma Delta, Phi Beta Kappa. Presbyterian. Home: 2190 Broadway St Apt 2E San Francisco CA 94115-1312 Personal E-mail: gwcoombe@sbcglobal.net.

COOMBS, ALICE A. TOLBERT, anesthesiologist, internist; b. LA, Dec. 6, 1955; d. Roosevelt and Elba Louise (Simmons) Tolbert; m. Albert A. Coombs III, Aug. 20, 1983; children: Albert, Andrew, Angela. BS, U. So. Calif., 1977; MD, UCLA Sch. Medicine, 1981. Cert. anesthesiologist. Intern Mass. Gen. Hosp., resident, internal medicine, anesthesia and critical care; internist, anesthesiologist, intensivist, critical care specialist NEMC Tufts U.-South Shore Hosp., Boston & South Weymouth, Mass., 1990—. Nursery worker New Covenant Christian Ctr.; head of youth anti-smoking program, Smoking-Don't Go There, 1999- Mem. AMA (Found. award for Health Edn. 2006), Mass. Med. Soc. (del., asst. sec.-treas., 2006-07, Cmty. Clinician Yr. award, 2002, Henry Bowditch Pub. Health award, 2005); Norfolk South Dist. Med. Soc. (pres. 1998, bd. trustees, 2003-) Office: South Shore Hospital 55 Fogg Rd South Weymouth MA 02190-2432*

COOMER, MERLE JOAN, retired language educator; b. Greenville, SC, July 17, 1941; d. Boyce Lee and Pearl Wofford Calvert; m. James Claudus Coomer, Feb. 20, 1960; children: Sharon Elaine Coomer Mattingly, James Calvin, Jeffrey Claudus. BA, Berea Coll., Ky., 1963; MA in Spanish for Coll. Tchg., Western Ky. U., Bowling Green, 1970. Secondary Edn., Adminstrn. Ky. Dept. Edn., 1984. HS tchr. Rockcastle County Bd. Edn., Mt. Vernon, Ky., 1963—64, Barren County Bd. Edn., Glasgow, 1964—2000; adj. fgn. lang. instr. Western Ky. U., Glasgow, Ky., 1988—2005; ret. Sec. Glasgow/Barren County Ret. Tchrs. Assn., Glasgow, 2001—03, pres., 2003—05. Sunday sch. tchr. Temple Hill Bapt. Ch., Glasgow, 1964—2006. Mem.: Am. Coun. Tchrs. Fgn. Langs. (assoc.), Ky. Ret. Tchrs. Assn. (assoc.), NEA (life). Avocations: travel, knitting, reading. Home: 8265 Tompkinsville Rd Glasgow KY 42141 Home Phone: 270-427-2363.

COONERTY, MARY ELIZABETH, special education educator; b. Mineola, NY, Oct. 24, 1954; d. Thomas Bartholomew and Vivian Irene Coonerty; m. John Charles Coppola, Aug. 7, 2004; children: Patrick David Hait, Meaghan Elizabeth Hait. BS in Spl. Edn. summa cum laude, Dowling Coll., 1995; MA in Liberal Studies, SUNY, Stony Brook, 1999. Cert. sch. dist. adminstr. Queens Coll., N.Y., 2004. Spl. educator Ea. Suffolk Bd. Cooperative Ednl. Svcs., West Hampton Beach, NY, 1998—99, curriculum tchr. Bellport, NY, 1999—2006, LI regional transition coord., 2006—. Co-chair Mid East Suffolk Tchr. Ctr., Riverhead, NY, 2003—06; tchr. Our Lady of Snow, 2004—06. Tchr. Our Lady of Snow RC, Blue Point, NY, 2004—04. Mem.: ASCD, Nat. Staff Devel. Coun. Roman Catholic. Avocations: travel, reading, embroidery, knitting, gardening. Home: 90 Corey Ave Blue Point NY 11715 Office: Eastern Suffolk BOCES 350 Martha Ave Bellport NY 11713 Home Phone: 631-363-8343; Office Phone: 631-286-6535. Personal E-mail: marysail5@att.net. Business E-Mail: mcoonert@esboces.org.

COONEY, CHARLES HAYES, lawyer; b. Nashville, Apr. 25, 1937; s. Robert G. and Annie Lee (Hayes) C.; m. Patsy M. Cooney, Dec. 25, 1986; children: Susan, Hayes Jr. BA, Vanderbilt U., 1959, JD, 1963. Bar: Tenn. 1963. Pvt. practice Cornelius & Collins, Nashville, 1963-67; chief def. atty. gen. State of Tenn., Nashville, 1967-80; ptnr. Watkins & McNeilly, 1980—. Staff mem. Vanderbilt U. Law Review, 1961-62. Capt. U.S. Army, 1959. Mem. ABA, Rotary, Tenn. Bar Assn. (pres. young lawyers sect., 1961), Nashville Bar Assn. (bd. dirs. 1985-87), Tenn. Bar Found., Nashville Bar Found. Presbyterian. Avocations: golf, travel. Office: Watkins McNeilly 214 2nd Ave N Ste 300 Nashville TN 37201-1638 Office Phone: 615-255-2191. Business E-Mail: jeanne@watkinsmcneilly.com.

COONEY, JOAN GANZ, broadcast executive, director; b. Phoenix, Nov. 30, 1929; d. Sylvan C. and Pauline (Reardan) Ganz; m. Timothy J. Cooney, 1964 (div. 1975); m. Peter G. Peterson, 1980. BA, U. Ariz., 1951; degrees (hon.), Boston Coll., 1970, Hofstra U., Oberlin Coll., Ohio Wesleyan U., 1971, Princeton U., 1973, Russell Sage Coll., 1974, Harvard U., 1975, Allegheny Coll., 1976, Georgetown U., 1978, U. Notre Dame, 1982, Smith Coll., 1986, Brown U., 1987, Columbia U., 1991, NYU, 1991, Dartmouth U., 2006. Reporter Ariz. Republic, Phoenix, 1953—54; publicist NBC, 1954—55, U.S. Steel Hour, 1955—62; prodr. Sta. WNET, Channel 13, pub. affairs documentaries NYC, 1962—67; TV cons. Carnegie Corp. N.Y., NYC, 1967—68; exec. dir. Children's TV Workshop (producers Sesame Street, Electric Company, others) (name changed to Sesame Workshop 2000), NYC, 1968—70, pres., trustee, CEO, 1970—88, chmn., CEO, 1988—90, chmn. exec. com., 1990—. Bd. dirs. Johnson & Johnson; bd. dirs. Met. Life Ins. Co. Mem. Pres.'s Commn. on Marijuana and Drug Abuse, 1971—73, Nat. News Coun., 1973—81, Pres.'s Commn. for Agenda for 80's, 1980—81, Adv. Com. for Trade Negotiations, 1978—80, Carnegie Found. Nat. Panel on High Sch., 1980—82, Gov.'s Commn. on Internat. Yr. of the Child, 1979; Mus. TV and Radio; trustee N.Y. Presbyn. Med. Ctr. Named to Hall of Fame, Acad. TV Arts and Scis., 1990, Nat. Women's Hall Fame, 1998; recipient numerous awards for Sesame Street and other TV programs including Nat. Sch. Pub. Rels. Assn. Gold Key, 1971, DSM, Columbia Tchrs. Coll., 1971, Soc. Family Man award, 1971, Nat. Inst. Social Scis. Gold medal, 1971, Frederick Douglass award, N.Y. Urban League, 1972, Silver Satellite award, Am. Women in Radio and TV, Woman of Yr. in Edn. award, Ladies Home Jour., 1975, NAEB Disting. Svc. award, NEA Friends of Edn. award, Kiwanis Decency award, 5th Women's Achiever award, Girl Scouts U.S.A., Stephen S. Wise award, 1981, Harris Found. award, 1982, Ednl. Achievement award, AAUW, 1984, Disting. Svc. to Children award, Nat. Assn. Elem. Sch. Prins., 1985, DeWitt Carter Reddick award, Coll. Comm., U. Tex.-Austin, 1986, Emmy Lifetime Achievement award, Acad. TV Arts and Scis., 1989, Presdl. medal of Freedom, 1995, Nat. Humanities Medal, 2003. Mem.: NATAS, Am. Women in Radio and TV, Internat. Radio and TV Soc., Nat. Inst. Social Scis. Office: Sesame Workshop 1 Lincoln Plz New York NY 10023-7129

COONEY, JOHN FONTANA, lawyer; b. Worcester, Mass., Jan. 1, 1949; s. John Joseph and Ida (Fontana) Cooney. AB magna cum laude, Brown U., 1970; JD, U. Chgo., 1973. Bar: Mass. 1973, DC 1977, admitted to practice: US Supreme Ct. 1978, US Dist. Ct. (DC) 1978, US Dist. Ct. (Dist. Mass.) 1977, US Ct. Appeals (DC Cir.) 1977, US Ct. Appeals (1st Cir.), US Ct. Appeals (3rd Cir.), US Ct. Appeals (4th Cir.), US Ct. Appeals (9th Cir.), US Ct. Appeals (Fed. Cir.). Atty. Gaston Snow & Ely Bartlett, Boston, 1973-75; asst. to solicitor gen. Dept. Justice, Washington, 1975-76; atty. Wilmer, Cutler & Pickering, Washington, 1977-82; dep. gen. counsel Office Mgmt. & Budget, Washington, 1982-87; atty. Dickstein, Shapiro & Morin, Washington, 1987-88, Venable, Baetjer, Howard & Civiletti, Washington, 1988—; ptnr., Econ. Regulatory Litig. Dept. and Adminstrv. Regulation Dept. Venable LLP, Washington. Co-author: Environmental Crimes Deskbook, 1995; assoc. editor U. Chgo. Law Rev., bd. editors Adminstrv. Law Rev. Mem.: ABA (Counsel Sect., Adminstrv. Law & Regulatory Policy 2000—03), DC Bar, Order of Coif, Phi Beta Kappa. Fluent in French. Office: Venable LLP 575 7th St NW Washington DC 20004 Office Phone: 202-344-4812. Office Fax: 202-344-8300. Business E-Mail: jfcooney@venable.com.

COONEY, J(OHN) GORDON, JR., lawyer; b. Alexandria, Va., Mar. 22, 1959; s. John Gordon Sr. and Patricia Ruth (McEwen) C.; m. Gretchen Smith Millspaugh, July 17, 1999. BA, Wesleyan U., 1981; JD magna cum laude, Villanova U., 1984. Bar: Pa. 1984, US Dist. Ct. (ea. dist.) Pa. 1986, US Ct. Appeals (5th cir.) 1997, US Ct. Appeals (3d cir.) 1988, US Supreme Ct. 2002, US Ct. Appeals (10th cir) 2004. Law clk. to hon. judge J. William Ditter Jr. U.S. Dist. Ct. (ea. dist.) Pa., Phila., 1984-86; assoc. Morgan, Lewis & Bockius, LLP, Phila., 1986-92, ptnr., 1992—2006, mng. ptnr. Phila. office, 2006—. Adj. lectr. Villanova U. Sch. Law, 1993-04, The Acad. Advocacy, 2004-05, lawyers adv. com. Third Cir., 2006—; master Villanova U. Inn of Ct., 1999—; barrister U. Pa. Law Sch. Inn of Ct., 1994-96. Editor-in-chief Villanova U. Law Rev., 1983-84; mem. editl. bd. The Legal Intelligencer, 1997-2001. Trustee Rosemont Sch. of the Holy Child, 1997-, chmn., 2001—; alumni bd. mgrs. Episcopal Acad., 1996-2002; trustee Gesu Sch., 2002—, World Affairs Coun. Phila., 2005—. Mem. ABA (com. on class actions and derivative suits), Pa. Bar Assn., Phila. Bar Assn. (profl. guidance com., fed. cts. com.), Union League Phila., Merion Cricket Club, Pyramid Club, Wesleyan U. Alumni Assn. (pres. Phila. area 1993-96), Arthritis Found. (bd. dirs Ea. Pa. chpt. 1993-96), Order of Coif. Republican. Roman Catholic. Office: Morgan Lewis & Bockius LLP 1701 Market St Philadelphia PA 19103-2903 Office Phone: 215-963-4806. Business E-Mail: jgcooney@morganlewis.com.

COONEY, JOHN THOMAS, retired banker; b. Warren, Pa., Jan. 20, 1927; s. Willis Edward and Elaine Cooney; m. Clara Jean Ellberg, Dec. 22, 1950; children: John B., Michael T., Lisa J. BSBA, Gannon U., 1951. Asst. personnel mgr. Nat. Biscuit Co., Houston, 1951-52; v.p. Bank of Southwest, Houston, 1956-80, exec. v.p., and sr. trust officer, 1980-85; vice chmn. M Trust Corp., 1985-90, Ameritrust Tex. N.A., Houston, 1990-92. Adv. dir. Legacy Trust Co., 1993—; bd. dirs. Marine Safety Systems, Inc., 1996-2005; mem. SEI II Bd. of Trustees, 1994-06. Pres. Mental Health Assn., Houston; bd. dirs. Am. Heart Assn., state treas., Tex.; established TBA Tex. Sch. of Trust Banking (chmn. 1978). Served as cpl. U.S. Army, 1945-46. Recipient Medal of Honor Gannon U., 1951. Mem. Tex. Bankers Assn. (trust divsn. chmn. 1982-83), Lakeside Country Club, The Houstonian Club. Republican. Roman Catholic.

COONEY, KEVIN L., lawyer; b. 1969; BS in Chem. Engring., Purdue U., 1992; JD, Washington U., 1997. Bar: Ind. 1997, US Dist. Ct. Southern Dist. Ind. 1997, US Dist. Ct. Northern Dist. Ind. 1997, Ohio 1998. Mem. Shared Harvest Foodbank; trustee Liberty Twp. Parks Com., Purdue Club of Cin.; pres., trustee Friends of Liberty Twp. Parks & Recreation. Named one of Ohio's Rising Stars, Super Lawyers, 2006. Mem.: Greater Mutual Funds Assn., ABA, Ohio State Bar Assn., Ind. State Bar Assn., Cin. Bar Assn. Office: Frost Brown Todd LLC 2200 PNC Ctr 201 E Fifth St Cincinnati OH 45202-4182 Office Phone: 513-651-6800. Office Fax: 513-651-6981.

COONEY, MIKE, former secretary of state; b. Wash., Sept. 3, 1954; s. Gage Rodman and Ruth (Brodie) C.; m. Dee Ann Marie Gribble; children: Ryan Patrick, Adan Cecelia, Colin Thomas. BA in Polit. Sci., U. Mont., 1979. State rep. Mont. Legislature, Helena, 1976-80; exec. asst. U.S. Sen. Max Baucus, Butte, Mont., 1979-82, Washington, 1982-85, Helena, Mont., 1985-89; sec. of state State of Mont., Helena, 1988—2001; coord. Lewis & Clark Bicentennial Public Safety Project, 2001; ex. dir. Healthy Mothers/ Healthy Babies: The Montana Coalition, 2001—. Bd. dirs. YMCA; mem. adv. panel Fed. Clearinghouse. Mem. Nat. Secs. of State (pres.), Nat. Assns. Secs. of State (pres. 1997) Democrat. Office: 1235 Birch St, Ste 1 Helena MT 59601

COONEY, PATRICIA RUTH, civic worker; b. Englewood, NJ; d. Charles Aloysius and Ruth Jeannette (Foster) McEwen; m. J. Gordon Cooney, June 8, 1957; 1 child, J. Gordon, Jr. Student, Fordham U., 1950-51; DHL honoris causa, Phila. Theol. Sem. St. Charles Boromeo, 1991. Blood bank chmn. Strafford Village Civic Assn., 1968-69, sec., 1970-71; chmn. spl. gifts com. cath. charities appeal Archdiocese of Phila., 1985, vice chmn. spl. gifts com. cath. charities appeal, 1980—. Mem. Coun. Mgrs. Archdiocese, Phila., 1982-88, sec., exec. com., 1983-88; bd. dirs. Cath. Charities Archdiocese of Phila., sec., exec. com., 1988-90, v.p., exec. com., 1991-2006; bd. dirs. Village Divine Providence, Phila., sec., 1983-85, v.p. exec. com., 1990-2006; bd. dirs. St. Edmond's Home Crippled Children, Phila., v.p. exec. com., 1990-2006; bd. dirs. Don Guanella Village of Archdiocese of Phila., v.p. exec. com., 1990-2006; v.p. exec. com. St. Francis Homes for Boys, 2000-06, St. Joseph House Boys, 2000-06, St. Vincent Svcs. Women and Children, 2000-06, St. Joseph Cath. Home Children, 2000-06, St. Gabriel's Sys., 2000-06, St. Vincent's Home, Tacony, 2003-2006; mem. Archdiocesan Adv. Com. on Renewal, 1991-2000; Women's Com. Wills Eye Hosp., 1973-, mem.-at-large, 1st v.p.; mem. Women's Aux. St. Francis Country House, Darby, Pa., 1976—, treas., 1978-82; exec. com. United Way Southeastern Pa., 1984-90, sec., 1986-88; bd. dirs. Chapel of Four Chaplains, 1984-89, Phila. Criminal Justice Task Force, 1989-90. Decorated Cross Pro Ecclesia et Pontifice, 1982, Lady Order St. Gregory the Gt., 1998. Republican. Avocations: reading, tennis, sailing. Home: 1400 Waverly Rd Villa 26 Gladwyne PA 19035

COONEY, PATRICK RONALD, bishop; b. Detroit, Mar. 10, 1934; s. Michael and Elizabeth (Dowdall) C. BA, Sacred Heart Sem., 1956; STB, Gregorian U., Rome, 1958, STL, 1960; MA, Notre Dame U., 1973. Ordained priest Roman Cath. Ch., 1959, ordained bishop Roman Cath. Ch., 1983. Assoc. pastor St. Catherine Ch., Detroit, 1960—62; asst. chancellor Archdiocese of Detroit, 1962—69, dir. dept. worship, 1969—83; rector Blessed Sacrament Cathedral, 1977—83; regional bishop Roman Cath. Ch., Detroit, 1983—89; apptd. bishop Diocese of Gaylord, Mich., 1989—. Office: Diocese of Gaylord Pastoral Ctr 611 W North St Gaylord MI 49735-8349

COONEY, SONDRA MILEY, literature and language educator; b. Mt. Vernon, Ohio, May 31, 1936; d. Wilbert H. and Orpha K. Miley; m. James F. Cooney, June 16, 1968; children: Margaret Cecilia, Charles Michael. BA, Manchester Coll., Ind., 1958; MA, U. Mich., Ann Arbor, 1959; PhD, Ohio State U., Columbus, 1970. Instr. U. Wis., Madison, 1967—68; asst. prof. English Kent State U., Ohio, 1970—79, assoc. prof. English, 1979—2005. Author: Oxford Dictionary of National Biography, 2005, Dictionary of Literary Biography, 1991, 3d edit., 1995. John Hill Burton fellow, Scottish Centre of Book, 1998. Mem.: Nat. Conf. Tchrs. English, AAUW (fellow 1966—67), Rsch. Soc. for Victorian Periodicals, AAUP, Soc. History of Authorship, Reading, and Pub. Episcopalian. Avocations: gardening, sewing. Home: 384 Burr Oak Dr Kent OH 44240 Office: Kent State Univ/Stark Campus 6000 Frank Ave NW North Canton OH 44720 Home Phone: 330-678-0510. Personal E-mail: scooney@kent.edu.

COONEY, WILLIAM J., lawyer; b. Augusta, Ga., July 31, 1929; s. John F. and Ellen (Joy) C.; m. Martha L. Whaley, May 1, 1971; children: William J. IV, Sarah C. BS, U. Notre Dame, 1951; JD, Georgetown U., 1954, LLM, 1955. Bar: D.C. 1954, Calif. 1961, Ga. 1963. Law clk. U.S. Ct. Appeals, Washington, 1954, U.S. Claims Ct., Washington, 1955; asst. U.S. atty. Washington, 1958-60, San Francisco, 1960-63; sole practice Augusta, 1963—. Capt. JAGC US Army, 1955—58. Mem. State Bar Ga., Spl. Master State Bar Ga., Augusta Bar Assn. (mem. exec. com.), Am. Arbitration Assn. (arbitrator). Roman Catholic. Office: 1 Habersham Sq 3602 Wheeler Rd Augusta GA 30909-1826 Office Phone: 706-860-6600. Business E-Mail: 3210martha@bellsouth.net.

COONING, CRAIG R., career officer; BSc in Engring., Auburn U., 1973; grad. student, U. Ala., 1976—77, MBA, 1977; student, Squadron Officer Sch., 1979, Air Command and Staff Coll., 1982, Armed Forces Staff Coll., 1986; course, Nat. Security Mgmt. course, 1986; student, Indsl. Coll. Armed Forces, 1993—94; sr. acquisition course, Nat. Def. U., 1994. Vice comdr. Space and Missile Sys. Ctr., L.A. Air Force Base, 1973; sys. program officer dir., warranted contract officer, plant rep. office comdr., comd. ROTC program Auburn U., 1973—; procurement contracting officer San Antonio Air Logistics Ctr., Kelly AFB, Tex., 1973—76; contracting and mfg. career mgmt. assignment officer Air Force Mil. Personnel Ctr., Randolph AFB, Tex., 1982—86; dep. comdr. Detachment 48 Air Force Contract Mgmt. divsn. Air Force Plant Rep. Office Hughes Missile Sys. Group, Tucson, 1986—88; comdr. Detachment 43 Air Force Contratc Mgmt. divsn. Air Force Plant Rep. Office Morton Thiokol Inc., Brigham City, Utah, 1988—90; chief Commodities Contracting divsn. Contracting Directorate, Hill AFB, Utah, 1990—91; dir. Directorate Specialized Mgmt., Hill AFB, Utah, 1991—93, Space Acquisition, Office Undersec. Air Force, Wash., 1993—. Decorated Legion of Merit, Meritorious Svc. medal with five oak leaf clusters.

COONROD, DELBERTA HOLLAWAY (DEBBIE), retired elementary school educator, consultant; b. Eldon, Mo., Oct. 21, 1937; d. Delbert Leland and Zealoth (Stevens) Hollaway; m. Charles Ralph Coonrod, Aug. 26, 1961; children: Charles Leland, Marcia Renee. BS in Edn., U. Kans., 1961; MS in Edn., Ind. U., 1972, EdD in Edn., 1977; postgrad., U. Tex., Tex. Women's U. Cert. elem. tchr., Kans. Classroom tchr. Hood Sch. & Heizer Elem., Barton County, Kans., 1957-60, Emporia (Kans.) Pub. Schs., 1961-62, Lincoln (Nebr.) Pub. Schs., 1964-66, South Bend (Ind.) Sch. Corp., 1967-72; assoc. instr., vis. asst. prof. Ind. U., Bloomington, 1972-79; asst. prof. Ind. State U., Terre Haute, 1975-76; pres. Debcon, Inc., Bloomington, 1979-81; pvt. practice cons. Bloomington, 1981-85; classroom tchr. Ft. Worth Ind. Sch. Dist., 1985—2001; assoc. prof., dir. tchr. edn. Culver-Stockton Coll., Canton, Mo., 2001—02; ret., 2002. Cons. Ft. Hays State U., Kans., 1990, Edison C.C., Piqua, Ohio, 1994; instr. Tarrant County (Tex.) Jr. Coll., 1992-94; adj. asst. prof. Tex. Woman's U., Denton, 1987-2000; adj. prof. Tex. Christian U., Ft. Worth, 1991-92; adminstrv. project dir. Monroe County Sch. Corp., Bloomington, 1983-85; instr. Weatherford (Tex.) Coll., 1996-97; kindergarten cons. Penn-Harris-Madison Sch. Corp., Mishawaka, Ind., 1970-71; head adminstr. Hoosier Cts. Nursery Sch., Ind. U., 1978-79; nat. approved trainer Head Start, 1982-85; chair emeritus Who's Who in Am. Edn. adv. bd.; mem. FWISD Dist. adv. com., 1996-98. Reporter Shelby County Herald, Shelbyville, Mo., 2003—; contbr. articles to profl. jours. Bd. dirs. 4C's of Monroe County, 1979—85; mem. Greater Ft. Worth Lit. Coun., 1990—99; mem. Hist. Commn. City of Bedford, Tex., 1993—97; chmn. early literacy com. Tex. State Reading Assn., 1993—96; com. co-chair Campaign for Children, 1st Tex. coun. Camp Fire, 1992—94; educator Ft. Worth Sister Cities, 1991—2001; Harashin Educator scholar Nagaoka, Japan, 1992; bd. dirs. Ft. Worth Assn. Edn. Young Children, 1986—87; chmn. spkrs. bur. Ind. Gov.'s Com. for Internat. Yr. of the Child, 1979—80; mem. Shelby County

Outreach and Ext. Coun. U. Mo., 2003—; host parent Am. Field Svc., 2003—; media chair Relay For Life, Shelby County, Mo., 2004—; mem. policy bd. Douglass Cmty. Svcs., Hannibal, Mo., 2006—; others. Recipient Excellence in English Edn. award Tex. Joint Coun. Tchrs. English, 1990, Ethel M. Leach award Tex. Woman's U., 1990, Outstanding Tchr. award Fort Worth Bus. Cmty./Adopt-A-Sch. Adv. Com., 1991; named Woman of Yr., Monroe County (Ind.) Girls Club, 1985, Yellow Rose of Tex., 1989, Dillard Tchr. of Week, 1992-93; named to Hon. Order Ky. Cols., 1987; Joe E. Mitchell Disting. Educator honoree Tex. Wesleyan U., 1991; honored Tex. Edn. Agy. Early Childhood Promising Practices (inclusion model), 1993-94, NYL Care Health Plans Chair for Tchg. Excellence in Early Childhood Edn., 1997-98, Extension Leaders Honor Roll, U. Mo.-Columbia, 2004. Mem. Ind. Assn. Edn. Young Children (bd. dirs. 1974-80, pres. 1979-80), Pi Lambda Theta (nat. v.p. 1985-89, pres. 1982-84, pres. Great Lakes Region II 1993-97, internat. 1st v.p. 2003, Greater Ft. Worth area chpt. Internat. Recognition award region VII Outstanding Pi Lambda Thetan 1992, pub. adv. bd. 1995-97, Edn. Endowment bd. 1996-2002), PEO (M chpt.), Delta Theta Tau, Delta Kappa Gamma; Am. Field Svc. Host parent, 2003-04. Republican. Baptist. Avocations: poetry, piano, photography, public speaking, journalism. Home: 1362 J Spur Bethel MO 63434-2312 Office Phone: 573-633-2166. Personal E-mail: coonrod@marktwain.net.

COONS, BARBARA LYNN, public relations executive, librarian; b. Peoria, Ill., June 1, 1948; d. Harold Leroy and Norma (Brauer) C. BA, Stephens Coll., Columbia, Mo., 1970; MA, U. N.C., 1972; MLS, Cath. U., 1982. Rsch. asst. Am. Revolution Bicentennical Office Libr. of Congress, Washington, 1974-76, editl. asst., office of the Asst. Librarian, 1976-78; ednl. liaison specialist Libr. of Congress, Washington, 1978-82; dir. rsch. svc. Gray and Co., Washington, 1982-85, v.p., 1985-86; from v.p., dir. rsch. svcs. to sr. mng. dir. Hill and Knowlton Pub. Affairs Worldwide, Washington, 1986—96; U.S. dir. rsch. svcs. Hill and Knowlton USA, 1996—2004; sr. v.p., dir. media analysis and competitive intelligence Strategy One, Washington, 2004—. Pres. Library of Congress Profl. Assn., 1982. Mem. Spl. Libraries Assn., Stephens Coll. Alumnae Club of Greater Washington (pres. 1987). Lutheran. Home: 709 Arch Hall Ln Alexandria VA 22314-6208 Office Phone: 202-326-1733. E-mail: barbara.coons@strategyone.net.

COONS, RONALD EDWARD, historian, educator; b. Elmhurst, Ill., July 24, 1936; s. William A. and Madeline Louise (Theisen) C. BA, DePauw U., Greencastle, Ind., 1958; A.M., Harvard U., 1959, PhD, 1966. Teaching fellow history Harvard U., 1961-62, 63-66; research fellow Inst. Europäische Geschichte, Mainz, Germany, 1962-63; mem. faculty U. Conn., Storrs, 1966—2002, prof. history, 1979—2002, prof. emeritus, 2002—, dir. grad. studies, dept. history, 1983-87, 90-98, assoc. chmn., 1993—94, 2000—02, interim chmn., summer 1994. Author: Steamships, Statesmen and Bureaucrats: Austrian Policy Towards the Steam Navigation Company of the Austrian Lloyd, 1836-1848, 1975, I primi anni del Lloyd Austriaco, 1983; editor: Over Land and Sea. Memoir of an Austrian Rear Admiral's Life in Europe and Africa, 1857-1909 (Ludwig Ritter von Höhnel), 2000; mem. editl. bd. Austrian History Yearbook, 1992-94, 96-97, mem. adv. bd., 1994-96, also articles and revs. Mem. exec. com. St. Mark's Episcopal Ch., Storrs, 1976-82, 83-85, asst. organist, 1980-87; mem. exec. com. U. Conn. Friends of Soccer, 1989-98, v.p., 1993-95, pres. 1995-97; mem. exec. com. New Eng. Hosta Soc., 1989-92; co-chair interim com. St. Paul's Episcopal Ch., Willimantic, 1998-2001, mem. vestry, 2001-04, 07—, sr. warden, 2005—07. NEH summer fellow, 1969; Am. Coun. Learned Socs. grantee, 1974,85, Am. Philos. Soc. grantee, 1974; NIH grantee, 1979; Gladys K. Delmas Found. grantee, 1983-84. Mem. AAUP, Am. Hist. Assn., Conf. Group Cen. European History, German Studies Assn., Soc. for Austrian and Habsburg History (exec. com. 1992-97, exec. sec. 1994-96), New Eng. Hist. Assn., Vienna Hist. Soc., Conn. Acad. Arts and Scis., Conn. Hort. Soc., Phi Beta Kappa (chpt. sec. 1976-86, v.p. 1987-88, 99-2000, pres. 1988-89, 2000-2001, historian, 2007—), Phi Alpha Theta, Phi Mu Alpha. Democrat. Office: U Conn Dept History 241 Glenbrook Rd Storrs Mansfield CT 06269-2103 Home: 1 Gin Still Ln West Hartford CT 06107-2647 Office Phone: 860-486-3722. Personal E-mail: recoons@hotmail.com.

COONTZ, STEPHANIE JEAN, history professor, writer; b. Seattle, Aug. 31, 1944; d. Sidney Coontz and Patricia (McIntosh) Waddington; 1 child, Kristopher. BA with honors, U. Calif., Berkeley, 1966; MA, U. Wash., Seattle, 1970. Mem. faculty Evergreen State Coll., Olympia, Wash., 1975—. Dir. rsch. and pub. edn. Coun. Contemporary Families, 1993—. Author: The Way We Never Were: American Families and the Nostalgia Trap, 1992, The Social Origins of Private Life: A History of American Families, 1988, The Way We Really Are: Coming to Terms With America's Changing Families, 1997, Marriage, A History: From Obedience to Intimacy, or How Love Conquered Marriage, 2005; (with others) Women's Work, Men's Property: On the Origins of Gender and Class, 1986, History and Family Theory, vol. II, 1989; contbr. numerous articles to profl. jours. Woodrow Wilson Found. fellow, 1968-69; recipient Washington Gov's. Writer's award, 1989, Dale Richmond award Am. Acad. Pediatrics, 1995, Visionary Leadership award Coun. Contemporary Families, 2004. Mem. Am. Studies Assn., Am. Hist. Assn., Orgn. Am. Historians. Office: Evergreen State Coll 2700 Evergreen Pwy NW Olympia WA 98505-0001 Address: c/o Viking Publicity 375 Hudson St New York NY 10014 Office Phone: 360-867-6703. Business E-Mail: coontz@evergreen.edu.

COOP, FREDERICK ROBERT, retired city manager; b. San Diego, Mar. 1, 1914; s. Ernest Frederick and Hazel (Angier) C.; m. Jean Haven, Feb. 11, 1939; children: Susan, Robert, Thomas, Elizabeth. AB, U. Calif., Berkeley, 1935; MS in Pub. Adminstrn, U. So. Calif., 1937. Pers. technician Calif. State Pers. Bd., 1937-41; pers. dir. Pasadena, Calif., 1941-49; pers. cons. UN, 1947; city mgr. Inglewood, Calif., 1949-56, Fremont, Calif., 1956-58; chief pub. svcs. divsn. U.S. Ops. Mission to Yugoslavia, 1958-61; city mgr. Newport Beach, Calif., 1961-64, Phoenix, 1964-69; regional dir. HEW, San Francisco, 1969-71; dir. pub. adminstrn. svcs. Arthur D. Little, Inc., San Francisco, 1972-78; pres. Coop Mgmt. Svcs. Inc., 1978—91. Pres., bd. dirs. Pub. Svc. Skills Inc. Served to lt. comdr. USNR, WW II. Named Young Man of Yr. Pasadena Jr. C. of C., 1947. Mem. Internat. City Mgmt. Assn. (regional v.p. 1965-67, Disting. Svc. award 2000), Am. Soc. Pub. Adminstrn. (bd. dirs.), Nat. Acad. Pub. Adminstrn., League Calif. Cities (hon. life, city mgrs. dept.).

COOPER, ALAN SAMUEL, lawyer, educator; b. June 13, 1942; s. Rudey and Rosalie (Schwartz) C.; m. Maxine Jacobs, Aug. 13, 1966 (dec.); children: Lauren K., Jennifer D.; m. Linda Morguelan Klein, April 18, 1999. BA, Vanderbilt U., 1964, JD, 1968. Bar: Tenn. 1968, D.C. 1969, U.S. Dist. Ct. D.C. 1969, U.S. Supreme Ct. Appeals (Fed. cir.) 1975, U.S. Supremem Ct. 1980. Law clk. U.S. Dist. Ct. (mid. dist.), Tenn., 1967-68; assoc. Browne, Schuyler & Beveridge and Browne, Beveridge & DeGrandi, Washington, 1968—72, Schyler, Birch, Swindler, McKie & Beckett, Washington, 1972-74; ptnr. Schyler, Banner, Birch, McKie & Beckett, Washington, 1974-94; mem. bd. dirs., shareholder Banner & Witcoff, Ltd., Washington, Chgo., Boston, 1995-97; ptnr. Shaw Pittman Potts & Trowbridge, Washington, NYC, L.A., London, 1997—2005, Howrey LLP, 2005—. Adj. prof. Georgetown U. Law Ctr., 1985-2003; adviser on trademark law to U.S. del. to Diplomatic Conf. on Revision of Paris Conv. for Protection of Indsl. Property, Nairobi, Kenya, 1981. Mem. ABA (faculty Nat. Insts. on Trademark Litigation 1978-79), Internat. Trademark Assn., D.C. Bar, Bar Assn. D.C., Tenn. Bar Assn., Bethesda Country Club. Jewish. Office: 1299 Pennsylvania Ave NW Washington DC 20004 Personal E-mail: cooper.alan@comcast.net. Business E-Mail: coopera@howrey.com.

COOPER, ALICE (VINCENT DAMON FURNIER), popular musician; b. Detroit, Feb. 4, 1948; m. Sheryl Cooper, Mar. 3, 1976; children: Calico, Dashiell, Sonora Rose. PhD (hon.), Grand Canyon Univ, Phoenix, 2004. Radio show presenter Planet Rock, London, 2006—, FM-MGK 102.9, Bala Cynwyd, Pa., 2006—. Albums include Pretties for You, 1969, Love It to Death, 1971, Killer, 1971, School's Out, 1972, Billion Dollar Babies, 1973, Muscle of Love, 1973, Welcome to My Nightmare, 1975, Alice Cooper Goes to Hell, 1976, Lace and Whiskey, 1977, From the Inside, 1978, Special Forces, 1981, DaDa, 1982, Zipper Catches Skin, 1983, Constrictor, 1986, Trash, 1989, Hey Stoopid, 1991, The Last Temptation, 1994, Classicks, 1995, A Fistful of Alice, 1997, The Life and Crimes of Alice Cooper, 1999, Science Fiction, 2000, Brutal Planet, 2000, Take 2, Dragontown, 2001, The Eyes of Alice Cooper, 2003, Dirty Diamonds, 2005; singles include School's Out, 1972, Only Women Bleed, 1975, I Never Cry, 1976, You and Me, 1977, The Man Behind the Mask, 1986; actor (films) Sextette, 1978, Sgt. Pepper's Lonely Hearts Club Band, 1978, Roadie, 1980, Leviatán, 1984, Prince of Darkness, 1987, Freddy's Dead: The Final Nightmare, 1991, Wayne's World, 1992, Freakshow, 1999, The Attic Expeditions, 2001; host (radio shows) Nights with Alice Cooper, 2004-, The Breakfast Show, Planet Rock, London, 2006-. Recipient star on Hollywood Walk of Fame, 2003. Office: Alice Coopers'town 101 E Jackson St Phoenix AZ 85004-2445

COOPER, ALLEN DAVID, medical researcher, educator; b. NYC, Sept. 18, 1942; s. Samuel and Fay (Sussman) C.; m. Kristina Speer, 1997; children: Ian, Todd. BA, NYU, 1963; MD, SUNY Downstate Med. Ctr., NYC, 1967. Intern then resident Boston City Hosp., 1967-69; resident fellow in gastroenterology U. Calif., San Francisco, 1969-72; clin. asst. prof. medicine U. Tex. Med. Sch., San Antonio, 1972-74; asst. prof. medicine Stanford (Calif.) U., 1974-80, assoc. prof. medicine, 1980-89, courtesy assoc. prof. physiology, 1987-90, prof. medicine, 1990—, chief divsn. gastroenterology & hepathology, 2003—; dir. Palo Alto (Calif.) Med. Found. Rsch. Inst., 1986—2003. Sci. adv. bd. ChemTrak. Recipient Scholastic Achievement award Am Inst. Chem., 1963; Univ. fellow Stanford U., 1981-83, Andrew W. Mellon Found. fellow, 1977-79. Fellow ACP, Molecular Medicine Soc.; mem. Am. Soc. Clin. Investigation, Am. Soc. Biochemistry and Molecular Biology, Western Soc. Clin. Investigation (sec.-treas. 1988, pres. 1992), Am. Fedn. Clin. Rsch. (pres. 1974), South Beach Yacht Club, Single Handed Sailing Soc., Pi Lambda Xi, Alpha Omega Alpha. Avocation: sailing. Home: 88 King St Apt 325 San Francisco CA 94107-4026 E-mail: adc@stanford.edu.

COOPER, ANDERSON HAYS, news correspondent, cable news anchor; b. NYC, June 3, 1967; s. Wyatt Cooper and Gloria Vanderbilt. BA in Polit. Sci., Yale U., 1989; attended, U. Hanoi. Producer & chief internat. correspondent Channel One News; correspondent ABC News, ABC's World News Saturday/Sunday, ABC's World News Tonight; anchor ABC's World News Now, 2000—01; host The Mole, ABC, 2001; weekend anchor CNN, 2001—03, weekday anchor, 2003—; anchor, host Anderson Cooper 360, CNN, 2003—. Contr. editor Details mag. Author: Dispatches From the Edge: A Memoir of War, Disasters and Survival, 2006 (Publishers Weekly No. 1 Hardcover Bestseller). Recipient Emmy award, Silver Plaque, Chicago Internat. Film Festival, Bronze Telly, Bronze award, Nat. Ed. Film and Video Festival, GLAAD Media award for outstanding TV journalism. Office: CNN 10 Columbus Cir New York NY 10019

COOPER, APRIL HELEN, family practice nurse practitioner; b. Evergreen Park, Ill., Dec. 24, 1951; d. Frank and Anne (Mirocha) Stevens; m. Michael Dennis, June 20, 1970; children: Christine Michelle, Brian Michael, Jeannette Michelle. AAS, Ohio U., 1981, BSN, 1996; MS, Wright State U., 2000. RN Ohio; cert. family nurse practitioner, ANCC. Supr. home health care Med. Pers. Pool, Cambridge, Ohio, 1989-91; primary nurse pediat. home care Primary Care Nursing Svcs., Dublin, Ohio, 1989-91; case mgr. Buckeye Home Health Svc., Zanesville, Ohio, 1990-91; with home health svcs. Genesis Home Care, Zanesville, 1981-98; family nurse practitioner Bucyrus Cmty. Hosp., 2001—. Mem. ANA, Golden Key, Phi Kappa Phi, Sigma Theta Tau, Gamma Pi Delta. Republican. Methodist. Avocations: reading, travel. Home: 3172 Oak Dr Bucyrus OH 44820-9654

COOPER, ARNOLD COOK, management educator, researcher; b. Chgo., Mar. 9, 1933; s. Millard and Sarah Ellen C.; m. Jean Phillips Lord, Sept. 12, 1959; children: Katherine Lord, David Andrew BS in Chem. Engring., Purdue U., 1955, MS in Mgmt., 1957, PhD (hon.), 2005; D in Bus. Adminstrn., Harvard U., 1962. Engr. Proctor & Gamble, Cin., 1957-58; asst. prof. Harvard U., Cambridge, Mass., 1961-63; assoc. prof. Purdue U., West Lafayette, Ind., 1963-70, prof., 1970-84, Weil prof. mgmt., 1984—2005, emeritus, 2005—. Vis. assoc. prof. Stanford Univ., Palo Alto, Calif., 1967-68; vis. prof. Manchester Bus. Sch., Eng., 1972, IMEDE Mgmt. Devel. Inst., Lausanne, Switzerland, 1977-78, U. Pa., 1995; past dir. Grad. Profl. Programs, chmn. Mgmt. Policy Com., Purdue U., West Lafayette; mem. Ind. Employment Devel. Commn., 1982-89, Fed. Adv. Com. on Indsl. Innovation, 1978-79 Author: The Founding of Technologically Based Firms, 1971; co-author: Small Business Management, 1966, Technical Entrepreneurship: A Symposium, 1972, The Entrepreneurial Function, 1977, New Business in America, 1990, Entrepreneurial Strategies, 2006; contbr. numerous articles to profl. jours. and bus. publs.; mem. editorial bd. Stategic Mgmt. Jour., 1979-2006, Jour. of Bus. Venturing, 1985-2005, Acad. of Mgmt. Jour., 1978-84, Jour. High Tech. Mktg., 1986-87. 2nd lt. U.S. Army, 1956 Recipient Honeywell Master Tchr. award, 1990, Murphy Tchg. award, Disting. Scholar award, Internat. Coun. on Small Bus., 1987, Ten Year Author award, Babson Entrepreneurship Conf., 1990, Internat. award for Entrepreneurship and Small Bus. Rsch., 1997, John S. Day Disting. Alumni Acad. Svc. award, 2001. Mem. Acad. Mgmt. (chmn. bus. policy and strategy divsn. 1978-79, Outstanding Paper award Entrepreneurship Divsn. 1991, 92, Coleman Entrepreneurship Mentor award, 1993, Richard D. Irwin outstanding educator award, 1999, Internat. Coun. Small Bus., Strategic Mgmt. Soc. (bd. govs. 1984-86), Soc. of Fellows. Home: 616 Ridgewood Dr West Lafayette IN 47906-2367 Office: Purdue Univ Krannert Sch of Mgmt 1310 Krannert West Lafayette IN 47907-1310 Business E-Mail: coopera@mgmt.purdue.edu.

COOPER, ARTHUR WELLS, retired ecologist, educator; b. Washington, Aug. 15, 1931; s. Gustav Arthur and Josephine (Wells) C.; m. Jean Farnsworth, Aug. 30, 1953; children: Paul Arthur, Roy Alan. BA, Colgate U., 1953, MA, 1955; PhD, U. Mich., 1958. Asst. prof. botany N.C. State U., Raleigh, 1958-63, assoc. prof., 1963-68, prof., 1968-71, prof. forestry, 1976—2001, prof. emeritus, 2001—, head dept. forestry, 1980-94, faculty athletics rep., 1990-2001. Asst. sec. N.C. Dept. Natural and Econ. Resources, Raleigh, 1971-76; mem. N.C. Coastal Resources Commn., Raleigh, 1976-89, N.C. Environ. Mgmt. Commn., Raleigh, 1989-91; chmn. Com. Scientists for Nat. Forest Mgmt. Act, Washington, 1977-79, 82, Govs. Task Force on Forest Sustainability, 1995-96; bd. dirs. N.C. Environ. Def. Fund, 1987-90, So. Environ. Law Ctr., 1987-90. Trustee N.C. Nature Conservancy, Chapel Hill, 1977-87; mem. coun. NCAA, 1995-96, mem. Divsn. I mgmt. coun., 1996-2001. Recipient Am. Motors Conservation award, 1972, Sol Feinstone award SUNY Coll. Environ. Sci. and Forestry, Syracuse, 1982, Outstanding Svc. to Forestry award N.C. Forestry Assn., 2002; named Conservationist of Yr., N.C. Wildlife Fedn., 1982. Fellow AAAS, Soc. Am. Foresters (chmn. N.C. chpt. 1984, Appalachian Soc. 1990, Gifford Pinchot medal 1999); mem. Ecol. Soc. Am. (cert. sr. ecologist 1982-2005, v.p. 1974, pres. 1980-81, Disting. Svc. award 1984), N.C. Acad. Sci. (pres. 1979), Assn. Southeastern Biologists. Democrat. Home: 719 Runnymede Rd Raleigh NC 27607-3103 Office: NC State U Dept Forestry Raleigh NC 27695-8008 Personal E-mail: awcooper@earthlink.net. Business E-Mail: arthur_cooper@ncsu.edu.

COOPER, AUSTIN MORRIS, chemist, consultant, chemical engineer, researcher; b. Long Beach, Calif., Feb. 1, 1959; s. Merril Morris and Charlotte Madeline (Wittmer) C. BS in Chemistry with honors, Baylor U., 1981; BSChemE with honors, Tex. Tech U., 1983, MSChemE with honors, 1985. Solar energy researcher U.S. Dept. Energy, Lubbock, Tex., 1983-85; advanced mfg. and process engring. mgr. McDonnell Douglas Space Systems Co., Huntington Beach, Calif., 1986-87, chem.-process line mgr., 1987-89, prin. material and process engr., 1999—. Contbr. articles to profl. jours. Mem. AIChE, Am. Chem. Soc., Soc. Advancement of Materials and Process Engrs., SCV, SAR, Sigma Xi, Omega Chi Epsilon, Kappa Mu Epsilon, Beta Beta Beta.

COOPER, BILLY J., lawyer; b. Great Lakes, Ill., July 21, 1956; BA with high honors, Ohio No. Univ., 1978; JD, Univ. Okla., 1981. Bar: Okla. 1981, Va. 1989, Colo. 1992. Gen. counsel & mem. exec. com. Foster Wheeler Environ. Corp.; ptnr., Public Policy, Bus. Transactions practices, mem. mgmt. com., mng. ptnr. Denver office Patton Boggs LLP, Denver. Chmn. & legal liaison Product Stewardship Code Legal Adv. Group, 1992. Served to lt. comdr. JAGC USN, 1981—88. Decorated Commendation medal USN, Achievement medal (2), Sea Svc. Deployment medal, Meritorious Unit medal. Mem.: Colo. Bar Assn., ABA (vice chmn. Law of the Sea com. 1991). Office: Patton Boggs LLP Suite 1900 1660 Lincoln St Denver CO 80264-1901 Office Phone: 303-894-6326. Office Fax: 303-894-9239. Business E-Mail: bcooper@pattonboggs.com.

COOPER, BRETT D., mathematician, educator; b. Merriam, Kans., Oct. 4, 1976; s. Jean and Diann Cooper; m. Madonna Bockelman, July 22, 2006. BS in Math., U. Kans., Lawrence, 2000, MA in Math., 2003. Acad. coord., instr. Duke U. Talent Identification Program - Summer Studies Programs, Durham, NC, 2000—06; instr. ext. course U. Kans., Lawrence, 2003—; instr. math. William Jewell Coll., Liberty, Mo., 2005—. Scholar, U. Kans., 2000—03, U. Mo., Kans. City, 1995—97. Mem.: Nat. Coun. Tchrs. Math., Math. Assn. Am., Am. Math. Soc. Liberal. Home Phone: 913-334-1544. Personal E-mail: bdckbd@umkc.edu.

COOPER, BYRON STANLEY, internist, educator; b. Washington, May 21, 1947; s. Joseph David and Ruth (Zeidner) C.; m. Jane Ann Kanter, Feb. 5, 1978; children: Joseph, Allison. BA, Johns Hopkins U., 1969; MD, Washington U., St. Louis, 1973. Diplomate in internal medicine and pulmonary medicine Am. Bd. Internal Medicine. Clin. prof. George Washington U., Washington, 1981—. Fellow Am. Coll. Chest Physicians; mem. AMA (alt. del. 2000--), ACP, D.C. Thoracic Soc. (pres. 1994), Med. Soc. D.C. (pres. 1998-99). Avocations: photography, computers, running. Office: Capital Pumonary Internists 2440 M St NW Washington DC 20037-1404 Personal E-mail: bscooper547@hotmail.com.

COOPER, CHARLES BRADFORD, III, educational association administrator; b. Richmond, Va., Dec. 24, 1972; s. Charles Bradford Cooper, II and Virginia Irene Cooper; m. Sheila Davis, July 28, 1997; children: Charles Bradford IV, Erika Madelyn. BS, Palm Beach Atlantic U., West Palm Beach, Fla., 1995; Masters Cert. in Project Mgmt., Villanova U., Pa., 2005. Cert. profl. Microsoft Corp., 2001. Project mgr. fin. software devel. Northrop Grumman Newport News, Va., 2001—03; resource planning and control staff Northrop Grumman Integrated Systems, St. Augustine, Fla., 2004—05; bus. mgr. spl. programs ITT, Ft. Wayne, Ind., 2005—. Author: (novels) The Riddle of Common Sense, (poetry collection) Desperate Times (Best Poets of 2002). Pres. Holly Ridge Home Owners Assn., Ft. Wayne, 2006—07; officer Bunnell Lodge of Free and Accepted Masons, Fla., 2004—06; sponsoring mem. Cato Inst., Washington, 2002—05; active Rep. Nat. Com., Washington, 2003—06. 1st lt. US Army, 1997—2000. Decorated Commdg. Gens. award for Excellence US Army, TRADOC Safety award, Army Commendation medal, Purple Heart, Bronze Star. Mem.: Project Mgmt. Inst. (cert. project mgmt. profl.). Conservative. Home: 11433 Green Holly Cove Fort Wayne IN 46845 Home Phone: 260-602-9891; Office Phone: 260-451-1173. Personal E-mail: cb_cooper@hotmail.com.

COOPER, CHARLES DONALD, military association executive, editor, retired military officer; b. Exeter, NH, Dec. 19, 1932; s. Herbert Almon and Mildred (Pitcher) C.; m. Beverly Lorraine Hummel, May 18, 1957; children: Liane, Dale, Kristin. BS, Northwestern U., 1954; grad., Indsl. Coll. Armed Forces, Washington, 1975. Commd. 2d lt. USAF, 1954, advanced through grades to col., 1977, mem. ops. staff various AF bases, 1955-76; dep. chief pub. affairs USAF Fifth AF, Yokota Air Base, Japan, 1975-77; dep. chief community rels. USAF, Washington, 1977-78, dep. chief media rels., 1978-80, chief media rels., 1980-82, dir. internal info., 1982-83; vol. community svc. Springfield, Va., 1984-86; exec. editor The Ret. Officer Assn., Alexandria, Va., 1986-88, dir. publs., 1988-96. Contbr. articles to mags. and newspapers in field. Trustee Messiah United Meth. Ch., Springfield, 1985-96, mem. adminstrv. bd., 1998—2002, asst. treas., 1999—, mem. fin. com., 1999—, alt. del. Va. United Meth. Ch. Conf., 2003—. Decorated Meritorious Svc. Medal, D.F.C., Air medal with five oak leaf clusters, Legion of Merit. Mem. Mil. Officers Assn. Am., Am. Legion, Daedalians, Masons, Shriners. Avocations: gardening, skiing. E-mail: flyboyfifty6@netscape.net.

COOPER, CHARLES GILBERT, cosmetics executive; b. Chgo., Apr. 4, 1928; s. Benjamin and Gertrude Cooper; m. Miriam Meyer, Feb. 11, 1951 (dec. Oct. 17, 1983); children: Debra, Ruth, Janet, Benjamin; m. Nancy Cooper BS in Journalism, U. Ill., 1949. With sales promotion dept. Maidenform Co., NYC, 1949-51; with circulation promotion dept. Esquire mag., Chgo., 1951-52; with Helene Curtis Industries Inc., Chgo., 1953-96, pres. salon div., 1971-75, pres. consumer products div., 1975-82, corp. exec. v.p., 1982-85, exec. v.p., COO, 1985-93, sr. v.p., 1993-96; sr. ptnr. GCG Ptnrs. Adj. prof. Loyola U. With AUS, 1952-53. Office: 200 S Wacker Dr Ste 4000 Chicago IL 60606

COOPER, CHARLES GORDON, retired insurance company executive; b. Providence, May 31, 1927; s. Irving and Helen Christina (Skog) C.; m. Barbara Caroline Termohlen, June 17, 1950; 1 dau., Marie Suzanne. BA, Ohio Wesleyan U., 1949. C.L.U. Group rep. Washington Nat. Ins. Co., 1949-53, asst. mgr., 1953-58, mgr., 1958-63, dir. assn. field services, 1963-65, asst. sec., 1965-67, 3d v.p., 1967-72, 2d v.p., 1972-77, v.p., 1977-79, sr. v.p., 1979-83, exec. v.p. Evanston, Ill., 1983-85, dir., mem. exec. com., 1979-85; sr. v.p.-mktg. Washington Nat. Corp., parent co. Washington Nat. Ins. Co., Evanston, 1983-85, cons., 1985—; pres. Charles G. Cooper & Assocs., Inc., 1985—95. Dir. Washington Nat. Trust Co., 1974-85, chmn. exec. com., 1979-85; chmn., dir. Washington Nat. Fin. Services, Inc., 1979-85; pres., dir. Washington Nat. Equity Co., 1973-85, chmn. bd., 1983-85 Bd. dirs. North Shore Assn. for Retarded, Evanston, 1983—. Served with USNR, 1945-46, PTO. Mem. Am. Coll. Life Underwriters, Chartered Life Underwriters, Nat. Assn. Life Underwriters, Chgo. Life Underwriters Assn., Nat. Assn. Health Underwriters, Chgo. Health Underwriters Clubs: Ivanhoe (Ill.). Lodges: Masons, Shriners. Republican. E-mail: coop1151@comcast.net.

COOPER, CHARLES HOWARD, retired photojournalist, retired publishing executive; b. Clinton, NC, July 17, 1920; s. John Howard and Ella Jane (Bass) C.; m. Nell Elizabeth Slaughter, Jan. 2, 1943; children: Charles Howard II, John Phillip. Grad., U.S. Air Force Sch. Photography, 1943. Chief photographer, mgr. photo dept. Durham Herald Co. (N.C.), 1945-85; pub. Durham Morning Herald, 1945, Durham Sun, 1945-85. Chmn. Miss Nat. Press Photographer Pageant, 1952, 53, 55 Mem. Citizens Safety Com., Durham, 1961-71. Served with USAAF, 1942-45, ETO. Mem. Nat. Press Photographers Assn. (life, exec. dir. 1963-2000, exec. dir. emeritus 2001—,

Fellowship award, Joseph A. Sprague award 1961, Pres.'s medal 1964, 67, 2001, Merit award 1965, Joseph Costa award 1977, exec. dir. emeritus 1998, interim exec. dir. 2001), Carolinas Press Photographers Assn. (life, pres. 1952-54) Democrat. Baptist. Personal E-mail: chcscoop@verizon.net.

COOPER, CHARLES JUSTIN, lawyer, former federal agency administrator; b. Dayton, Ohio, Mar. 8, 1952; s. Robert Lee and Katherine (Thompson) C.; m. Debra Johnson; children: Paul Davis, Jay Daniel, McKinley Beth. BS in Fin., U. Ala.-Tuscaloosa, 1974; JD, U. Ala., Tuscaloosa, 1977. Bar: Ala. 1977, Washington, DC 1979, Ga. 1980. Law clk. to Hon. Paul Roney U.S. Ct. Appeals (5th Cir.), St. Petersburg, Fla., 1977-78; law clk. to Justice William H. Rehnquist U.S. Supreme Ct., Washington, 1978-79; assoc. Long Aldridge & Norman LLP, Atlanta, 1979-81; spl. asst., Civil Rights Divsn. US Dept. Justice, Washington, 1981-82, dep. asst. atty. gen., Civil Rights Divsn., 1982-85, asst. atty. gen., Office Legal Counsel, 1985-88; ptnr. McGuire Woods Battle & Boothe, Washington, 1988—90, Shaw Pittman Potts & Trowbridge, Washington, 1990—96; founding ptnr. Cooper & Kirk, PLLC (formerly Cooper & Carrin, PLLC), Washington, 1996—. Chmn. Nat. Sec. Coun. Policy Review & Planning Coordinating Groups, 1985—88, Pres. Working Group Federalism, 1986—89, Nat. Com. Responsibilities Financing Postsecondary Edn., 1991—94, Nat. Com. Jud. Discipline and Removal, 1991—93, Admin. Conf. US, 1991—94, Adv. Coun. Self-Determination and Federalism to Gov. George Allen, 1994—96, Standing Comt. Rules & Procedure Jud. Conf. US, 1998—. Named one of 75 Best Lawyers in Washington, Washingtonian survey mag., 2002. Mem. Ala. Bar Assn., D.C. Bar Assn., State Bar Ga., Am. Law Inst., Am. Assn. Appellate Lawyers, Federalist Soc. Office: Cooper & Kirk PLLC Ste 750 555 Eleventh St NW Washington DC 20004 E-mail: ccooper@cooperkirk.com.*

COOPER, CHRIS, actor; b. Kansas City, Mo., July 9, 1951; s. Charles and Mary Ann Cooper; m. Marianne Leone, July 1983; 1 child, Jesse Lanier (dec.). Student, U. Mo., Columbia, Stephens Coll. Actor: (films) Matewan, 1987, Thousand Pieces of Gold, 1990, Guilty by Suspicion, 1991, City of Hope, 1991, This Boy's Life, 1993, Pharaoh's Army, 1995, Money Train, 1995, Boys, 1996, Lone Star, 1996, A Time to Kill, 1996, Great Expectations, 1998, The Horse Whisperer, 1998, The 24 Hour Woman, 1999, October Sky, 1999, American Beauty, 1999, Me, Myself & Irene, 2000, The Patriot, 2000, Interstate 60, 2002, The Bourne Identity, 2002, Adaptation, 2002 (Acad. Award for Best Supporting Actor, 2003, Golden Globe award for Best Performance by an Actor in a Supporting Role, 2003), Seabiscuit, 2003, The Bourne Supremacy, 2004, Silver City, 2004, Capote, 2005, Jarhead, 2005, Syriana, 2005, Breach, 2007; (TV films) Journey Into Genius, 1988, To the Moon, Alice, 1990, A Little Piece of Sunshine, 1990, In Broad Daylight, 1991, Darrow, 1991, Bed of Lies, 1992, Ned Blessing: The True Story of My Life, 1992, One More Mountain, 1994, The Deliverance of Elaine, 1996, Breast Men, 1997, Alone, 1997, My House in Umbria, 2003; (TV series) The Equalizer, 1985, Miami Vice, 1984, Lifestories, 1990, Law & Order, 1990; (TV miniseries) Lonesome Dove, 1989, Return to Lonesome Dove, 1993. Address: Paradigm Talent Agy Ste 2500 10100 Santa Monica Blvd Los Angeles CA 90067*

COOPER, CORINNE, communications consultant, lawyer; b. Albuquerque, July 12, 1952; d. David D. and Martha Lucille (Rosenblum) Cooper. BA magna cum laude, U. Ariz., 1975, JD summa cum laude, 1978. Bar: Ariz. 1978, US Dist. Ct. Ariz. 1978, Mo. 1985. Assoc. Streich, Lang, Weeks & Cardon, Phoenix, 1978—82; asst. prof. U. Mo., Kansas City, 1982—86, assoc. prof., 1986—94, prof., 1994—2000, prof. emerita, 2000—; pres. Profl. Presence, Comm. Cons., Tucson, 2001—. Vis. prof. U. Wis., Madison, 1985, Madison, 91, U. Pa., Phila., 1988, U. Ariz., 1993, U. Colo., 1994. Author (with Bruce Meyerson): A Drafter's Guide to Alternative Dispute Resolution, 1991; actor: How to Build a Law Firm Brand, 2005; editor: The Portable UCC, 1993, 3d edit., 2001, 4th edit., 2004, Getting Graphic I, 1993, II, 1994, The New Article 9, 1999, 2d edit., 2000; editor in chief: Bus. Law Today, 1995—97; mem. editl. bd. ABA Jour., 1999—2005; author, editor: Attorney Liability in Bankruptcy, 2006; contbr. articles to profl. jours., chapters to books. Legal counsel Mo. for Hart campaign, 1984; dir. issues Goddard for Gov. campaign, 1990. Mem.: ABA (mem. editl. bd. Bus. Law Today 1991—97, mem. unifrom comml. code com., chmn. bus. sect. membership com. 1992—94, mem. coun. bus. sect. 1992—96, sect. bus. law pubs. 1998—2002, mem. standing com. strategic comm. 2001—03, coun. gen. practice sect. 2003—05), Mo. Bar Assn. (mem. comml. law com.), Ariz. Bar Assn., Am. Assn. Law Schs. (mem. comml. law 1982—2000), Am. Law Inst., Phi Beta Kappa, Order of Coif, Phi Kappa Phi. Democrat. Jewish. Office: Profl Presence 4558 N 1st Ave Tucson AZ 85718 Business E-Mail: c2@professionalpresence.com.

COOPER, DANIEL E., orthopedic surgeon; b. Newport News, Va., May 26, 1959; married; 3 children. BA in Biology (with the highest honors-magna cum laude), U. Tenn., 1980; MD, U. Tex. Southwestern Med. Sch., Dallas, 1984. Cert. Orthop. Surgery, Sports Medicine, Disorders of the Knee and Shoulder, Arthroscopic Surgery, lic. Tex. Intern, orthop. Bexar Co. Hosp., U. Tex. Health Scis. Ctr., San Antonio, 1984—85; resident, orthop. surgery U. Tex. Health Sci. Ctr., San Antonio, 1985—89; clin. instr., orthop. U. Tex. Health Scis. Ctr., Dallas; fellow, sports medicine, knew and shoulder Svc. Hosp. Spl. Surgery, Cornell U. Med. Ctr., NYC, 1989—90; hosp. appointment Baylor U. Med. Ctr., Dallas, attending physician, dept. orthop.; hosp. appointment Mary Shiels Hosp., Dallas, Presbyn. Hosp., Dallas; clin. assoc. prof., dept. orthop. U. Tex. Southwestern Med. Ctr., Dallas; attending orthop. surgeon Carrell Clinic, Dallas, 1990—. Med. staff NY Marathon, 1989, US Open Tennis Championships, 1989, World Cup Soccer, Dallas, 1994; physician NY Giants, 1989—90; asst. team physician St. John's U. Athletic Dept., 1989—90, So. Methodist U. Athletics, 1991—2000, Dallas Cowboys, 1991—2000, head team physician, 2000—, Dallas Stars Hockey Team, 1993—2005; previously affiliated with other intercollegiate athletics programs; mem. Dallas County Med. Soc. Fee Complaint Com., 1993, Baylor U. Med. Ctr. Trauma Com., 1993—94; mem. med. adv. bd. Transplant Svcs. Ctr. U. Tex. Southwestern Med. Ctr., Dallas, 1996; invited spkr. in field. Editl. reviewer Am. Jour. Sports Medicine, Jour. Arthroscopic Surgery, Jour. Bone and Joint Surgery; contbr. articles to profl. jours., chapters to books; co-editor: Review Sports Medicine and Arthroscopy. Adv. dir. to the bd. Leukemia Soc. Am., bd. trustee, North Tex. Chpt., 1996—; adv. dir. to the bd. Children's Cancer Fund of Dallas, bd. trustee, 1997—; dir. Chad Thomas Cooper Meml. Fund, 1992—; lifetime mem. Chancellor's Coun. U. Tex. Sys., Austin, 1995—. Named one of Best Doctor, 1998—99, 2001—07. Fellow: Arthroscopy Assn. N.Am., Am. Orthop. Soc. for Sports Medicine (Excellence in Rsch. award 1992), Am. Acad. Orthop. Surgeons; mem.: US Profl. Tennis Assn., Tex. Orthop. Assn., Tex. Med. Assn., U. Tex. Southwest Med. Sch. Alumni Assn. (life), State Orthop. Soc., State Med. Soc., Tex. Soc. Sports Medicine (pres. 1996), Nat. Hockey League Team Physician Soc., Nat. Football League Team Physician Soc., Alpha Omega Alpha. Achievements include being nationally recognized expert in the field of sports medicine, and treats all types of athletes-professionals, collegiate, high school and recreational; youngest physician in the history of both the Dallas Cowboys and Dallas Stars Hockey organizations to be given the position as head team physician. Avocation: golf. Office: Carrell Clinic Ctr 9301 N Central Expy Ste 400 Dallas TX 75231 Office Phone: 214-220-2468. Office Fax: 214-397-1534.*

COOPER, DANIEL L., federal agency administrator; BS, US Naval Acad., 1957; MPA, Harvard U., 1963. Commd. USN, 1959, advanced through grades to vice admiral, ret., 1991, served in amphibious force, with submarine svc. USS Trigger, 1959, on USS Haddo, exec. officer USS Simon Bolivar, comdg. officer USS Puffer, 1972—76, comdr. submarine squadron TEN New London, Conn., 1976—79, comdr. Atlantic fleet's submarine force, 1986—88; v.p., gen. mgr. nuclear svcs. divsn. Gilbert Commonwealth, Reading, Pa., 1991; mem. tech. adv. group Applied Physics Lab. Johns Hopkins U.; chmn. adv. bd. Applied Rsch. Lab. Pa. State U.; chmn. VA Claims Processing Task Force; under sec. for benefits US Dept. Veterans Affairs, Washington, 2002—. Bd. dirs. Exelon Corp., Chgo. Office: US Dept Veterans Affairs Vets Benfits Adminstrn 810 Vermont Ave NW Rm 520 Washington DC 20420

COOPER, DAVID R., neurosurgeon; b. Boston, Oct. 27, 1931; s. Herbert and Rose R. (Furman) Cooper; m. Sandra S. Rosenberg, Dec. 18, 1954; children: Ron H., Jane R. MD cum laude, Tufts U., Boston, 1956; BS in Med. Sci. magna cum laude, Boston U., 1975. Cons. Niagara Falls Meml. Hosp., NY, 1980—89, Mt. St. Mary's Hosp., Lewiston, NY, 1985—89. Contbr. articles to profl. jours. Mem. Environ. Mgmt. Coun., Niagara County, NY, 1986—, Environ. Commn., Lewiston, NY, 1999—; bd. dirs. Niagara Ednl. Found., Niagara Falls, 1980—2005. Lt. comdr. USNR, 1962—64. Mem.: Niagara Frontier Entomol. Soc. (founder, pres. 1993—). Home: 805 Carriage Ln Lewiston NY 14092

COOPER, DEBORAH ELLEN, lawyer; b. NYC, Mar. 30, 1953; d. Herman E. and Helen (Spector) C.; m. Daniel S. Sternberg, Oct. 10, 1981. BA, Radcliffe Coll., 1975; JD, Harvard Coll., 1978. Bar: N.Y. 1979, U.S. Dist. Ct. (so. dist.) N.Y. 1980, U.S. Dist. Ct. (ea. dist.) N.Y. 1983, U.S. Ct. Appeals (8th cir.) 1986, U.S. Ct. Appeals (10th cir.) 1986. Law clk. to presiding justice U.S. Dist. Ct. (so. dist.) N.Y., NYC, 1978-80; assoc. Gelberg & Abrams, NYC, 1980-82, Willkie, Farr & Gallagher, NYC, 1982-86, ptnr., 1987—; asst. sec. Cooke Ctr. For Learning & Devel. Vol. Lawyers Com. for Human Rights, N.Y.C., 1987—. Mem. Assn. of Bar of City of N.Y. Democrat. Jewish. Office: Cooke Ctr For Learning & Devel 475 Riverside Dr Ste 730 New York NY 10115 Office Phone: 212-280-4473.

COOPER, DONALD LEE, physician; b. Columbus, Kans., Aug. 11, 1928; s. Calvin M. and J. Pearl (Mullen) C.; m. Dona Faye Maddux, June 4, 1950; children: Donald Lee, Catherine Susan, Cheryl Lyn, Tad Houston. AB, Pittsburg State U., 1949; MD, U. Kans., 1953. Intern St. Mary's and Childrens Mercy hosps., Kansas City, Mo., 1953-54; pvt. practice medicine Manhattan, Kans., 1956-57; team physician, asst. dir. Health Center Kans. State U., 1957-60; dir. health service, team physician Okla. State U. Hosp. and Clinic, Stillwater, 1960-90, dir. athletic medicine, 1990-98, emeritus dir., 1998—. Vis. lectr. divsn. sportsmedicine, dept. orthopedic surgery Coll. Medicine U. Okla. Health Scis. Ctr., 1974—; liaison officer Am. Coll. Health Assn. to Nat. Athletic Trainers Assn., 1963—; Am. chmn. 1st Am.-Soviet Conf. on Student Health, Moscow, Russia, 1967; team physician U.S. Olympic Team, 1967-68; mem. Pres.'s Coun. Phys. Fitness and Sports, 1981-92, del. to Moscow to rev. phys. culture and olympic tng. sites in Russia, 1989; team physician U.S. Deaf Olympic Team, LA, 1985; elected chmn. Joint Commn. on Competitive Safegaurds and Med. Aspects of Sports, 1986. Author: (with others) Standard Nomenclature of Athletic Injuries, 1966; Contbr. (with others) articles med. jours. Served to capt. USAF, 1954-56. Recipient Pres.'s Challenge Sportsmedicine award Nat. Athletic Trainers Assn., 1974, Bill Coltrin Meml. award Western Athletic Conf. Sports Writers Assn., 1974, Edward Hitchcock award Am. Coll. Health Assn., 1975; named among 10 healthy American fitness leaders Nat. Jaycees, Pres.'s Coun. on Physical Fitness and Sports, Allstate Ins. Co., 1995; inductee Okla. Hall of Fame, 1998. Mem. AMA (chmn. com. med. aspects sports 1971-76, chmn. 1976-77, mem. coun. sci. affairs 1976-79), Nat. Collegiate Athletic Assn. (med. cons. to football rules com. 1969-75), Am. Coll. Health Assn. (past pres., exec. com.), Southwestern Coll. Health Assn. (past pres.), Nat. Athletic Trainers Assn., Alpha Omega Alpha, Nu Sigma Nu. Presbyterian (elder 1971—). Club: Lion. Home: 1001 W Liberty Ln Stillwater OK 74075-2113 Office: Okla State U Hosp & Clinic 1202 Farm Rd Stillwater OK 74078-0001 Office Phone: 405-744-7031. Office Fax: 405-744-6556. *We must realize and accept that life is neither fair nor unfair; one must accept it as a unique journey composed of all types of experiences. It is not so much what happens to us as we go along in life, it is how we react to what happens that is so very important.*

COOPER, EDWARD HAYES, lawyer, educator; b. Highland Park, Mich., Oct. 13, 1941; s. Frank Edward and Margaret Ellen (Hayes) C.; m. Nancy Carol Wybo, June 29, 1963; children: Lisa, Chandra. AB, Dartmouth Coll., 1961; LL.B., Harvard U., 1964. Bar: Mich. 1965. Law clk. Hon. Clifford O'Sullivan, U.S. Ct. of Appeals, 1964-65; practice law, Detroit, 1965-67; adj. prof. Wayne State U. Law Sch., 1965-67; assoc. prof. U. Minn. Law Sch., 1967-72; prof. law U. Mich. Law Sch., Ann Arbor, 1972-88, assoc. dean for acad. affairs, 1981-94, Thomas M. Cooley prof. of law, 1988—. Advisor Am. Law Inst. Restatement of the Law, 2d Judgments, 1976-80, Complex Litigation Project, Restatement of the Law, 3d Torts-Apportionment, Fed. Jud. Code Project, Transnational Procedure Project, Internat. Jurisdiction Judgment, Internat. Intellectual Property, Aggregation; reporter fed. state jurisdiction com. Jud. Conf. US, 1985-91; mem. civil rules adv. com., 1991-92, reporter, 1992—; reporter Uniform Transfer of Litigation Act, 1989-91. Author: (with C.A. Wright and A.R. Miller) Federal Practice and Procedure: Jurisdiction, Vols. 13-19, 1975-81, 2d edit., 1984-2002, 3d edit., 1999—; contbr. articles to law revs. Mem. ABA, Mich. Bar Assn., Am. Law Inst. (council). Office: U Mich 330 Hutchins Law Sch Ann Arbor MI 48109-1215 Home Phone: 734-663-7098; Office Phone: 734-764-4347. Business E-Mail: coopere@umich.edu.

COOPER, EDWARD SAWYER, cardiologist, internist, educator; b. Columbia, SC, Dec. 11, 1926; s. Henry Howard and Ada Crosland (Sawyer) Cooper; m. Jean Marie Wilder, Dec. 2, 1951 (dec. May 2006); children: Lisa Marie Cooper Hudgins, Edward Sawyer Jr.(dec.) , Jan Ada, Charles Wilder. AB, Lincoln U., Pa., 1946; MD, Meharry Med. Coll., Nashville, 1949; MS (hon.), U. Pa., 1972. Diplomate Nat. Bd. Med. Examiners, Am. Bd. Internal Medicine. Intern Phila. Gen. Hosp., 1949—51, resident in medicine, 1951—54, NIH fellow in cardiology, 1956—57, pres. med. staff, 1969—71, co-dir. Stroke Rsch. Ctr., 1968—74, chief med. svc., 1973—76; prof. Sch. Medicine U. Pa., 1976—96, prof. emeritus medicine Phila., 1996—. Bd. dirs. Independence Blue Cross. Bd. trustees Am. Heart Assn., pres.-elect, pres., chmn. Stroke Coun.; adv. com. NIH; trustee Am. Found. Negro Affairs, 1969—, Rockefeller U., 1992—, Hosp. of the U. of Pa., 2002—. Served to capt. USAF, 1954—56. Master: ACP; fellow: Phila. Coll. Physicians (coun.); mem.: Am. Heart Assn. (chmn., bd. dirs., past nat. pres.), Alpha Omega Alpha. Democrat. Methodist. Achievements include research in stroke and hypertension. Home: 6710 Lincoln Dr Philadelphia PA 19119-3155 Office: Univ Penn Hosp 3400 Spruce St Philadelphia PA 19104-4206 Personal E-mail: ecoopmdphila@aol.com.

COOPER, ELVA JUNE, artist; b. Wilmore, Ky., Mar. 18, 1933; d. Scott Combs and Rhoda Mae (Hundley) Bishop; m. Lowell Howard Cooper, Nov. 29, 1952; children: Lowell Scott, Linda Janet, Candace Lea, Connie Lynn, June Roxanne. Student, Georgetown Coll., 1952-53, Southwestern Jr. Coll., 1961, U. West Fla., 1994, Pensacola Jr. Coll., 1998. Owner June Bug Art and Gifts, Pensacola, Fla., 1973—2003, The Studio, Pensacola, Fla., 1986—. Cons. editor Church Recreation, 1993-95; contbr. articles to mags. Drama writer, dir. Myrtle Grove Bapt. Ch., Pensacola, Fla., 1977-96, artist in residence, 1973-96, discipleship tng. dir., 1973-79, 88-97; sec. Lillian (Ala.) First Bapt. Ch., 1984-95; writer Bapt. Sunday Sch. Bd., Nashville, Tenn., 1987-98; state recreation counselor Fla. Bapt. Conv., Jacksonville, 1994—; discipleship tng. dir. Pensacola Bay Bapt. Assn., 1994-96. Three time winner of Peggy award Popular Ceramics Mag., 1970; others; named to Internat. Soc. Poetry as Disting. Mem. Mem. Quayside Art Gallery (asst. publicity 1984, pub. rels. dir. 2005-07, bd. dirs. 2005-07), Art Study Club. Baptist. Avocations: porcelain doll making, sewing, flower arranging, stained glass artist.

COOPER, EUGENE BRUCE, speech pathology/audiology services professional, educator; b. Utica, NY, Dec. 20, 1933; s. Clements Everett and Beulah (Wetzel) C.; m. Crystal Silverman, Sept. 12, 1965; children: Philip Adam, Ivan Bruce. BS, SUNY, Geneseo, 1955; MEd, Pa. State U., 1957, DEd, 1962. Pathologist speech and lang. Franklin County Schs., Chambersburg, Pa., 1957-59; asst. prof. Ohio U., 1962-64, Pa. State U., 1964-66; program specialist U.S. Office Edn., 1966; exec. sec. sensory study sect., rsch. and demonstrations Rehab. Services Adminstrn., HEW, Washington, 1966-67; faculty U. Ala., Tuscaloosa, 1967-96, prof. speech-lang. pathology, 1969-96, chmn. dept. communicative disorders, dir. Speech and Hearing Ctr., 1967-96, prof., chair emeritus, 1996—; Disting. prof. comm. scis. and disorders Nova Southeastern U., 1997—. Chmn. Ala. Bd. Examiners Speech Pathology and Audiology, 1979; cons.-at-large Nat. Student Speech-Lang.-Hearing Assn., 1983-88. Author: Personalized Fluency Control Therapy, 1976, Understanding Stuttering: Information for Parents, 1979, revised edit., 1990; (with Crystal Cooper) The Cooper Personalized Fluency Control Therapy Program, 1985, 2d edit., 2003, Cooper Assessment for Stuttering Syndromes, 1995; contbr. articles to profl. jours. Fellow Am. Speech, Lang. and Hearing Assn. (legis. coun. 1971-72, 85-97), Divsn. Fluency and Fluency Disorders (steering com. 1993-99, divsn. coord. 1994-99), Am. Speech, Lang. and Hearing Found. (chmn. adv. and devel. bd. 1988-89, trustee 1989-94); mem. Coun. Exceptional Children (pres. divsn. children comm. disorders 1975-76), Nat. Coun. Grad. Programs in Speech, Lang. Pathology and Audiology (pres. 1978-80), Nat. Coun. State Bds. Examiners Speech-Lang. Pathology and Audiology (pres. 1980, 91, mem. exec. bd. 1988-91), Nat. Coun. Comm. Disorders (chmn. 1982), Nat. Alliance Prevention and Treatment on Stuttering (pres. 1985-86), Internat. Fluency Assn. (bd. dirs. 1991-96, pres. 2d world congress on fluency disorders 1997, chmn. specialty commn. on fluency disorders 1997-99). Office Phone: 954-385-1422. E-mail: ebcooper@msn.com.

COOPER, FRANK G., lawyer; b. Boston, Oct. 21, 1946; AB, George Washington U., 1968; JD, U. Pa., 1971. Bar: Pa. 1971, US Ct. Appeals (3rd cir.), US Dist. Ct. (ea. dist. Pa.), US Tax Ct., Supreme Ct. Pa. Assoc. Duane Morris, LLP, Phila., 1971—78, ptnr., 1978—, chair firm estates and asset planning group, 1994—, mem. ptnrs. bd. Bd. mem. William B. Dietrich Found. Named one of Top 100 Attys., Worth mag., 2005. Mem.: ABA, Phila. Bar Assn., Pa. Bar Assn. Office: Duane Morris LLP 30 S 17th St Philadelphia PA 19103-4196 Office Phone: 215-979-1906. Office Fax: 215-979-1020. E-mail: fgcooper@duanemorris.com.*

COOPER, GARY ALLAN, lawyer; b. Bristol, Va., Feb. 3, 1947; s. Earl Clarence and Reba Evelyn (Jenkins) C.; chidlren: Drew Kelsey, Gavin Morgan. BS in Journalism, U. Tenn., 1969, JD, 1972. Bar: Tenn. 1972, U.S. Dist. Ct. (ea. dist.) Tenn. 1972, U.S. Supreme Ct. 1979, Fla. 1981. Assoc. Luther, Anderson & Ruth, Chattanooga, 1972-76; ptnr. Luther, Anderson, Cleary, Luhowiak & Cooper, Chattanooga, 1976-79, Luther, Anderson, Cleary & Cooper, Chattanooga, 1979-80, Anderson, Cleary & Cooper, Chattanooga, 1981, Fleissner & Cooper, Chattanooga, 1982, Fleissner, Cooper & Marcus, Chattanooga, 1983-88, Fleissner Cooper Marcus & Steger, Chattanooga, 1988-89, Fleissner Cooper Marcus & Quinn, Chattanooga, 1990-97, Franklin, Cooper & Marcus, PLLC, Chattanooga, 1998—. Author: Tennessee Forms for Trial Practice, 1977, 5th edit., 1999, Tennessee Law Office Administration, 1977, Tennessee Forms for Trial Practice-Damages, 1997—. With USAR, 1972-79. Recipient Herman Hickman Postgrad. scholarship for Athletes U. Tenn., 1969. Mem. ABA, Chattanooga Bar Assn. (bd. dirs. 1984-86), Fla. Bar Assn. (mem. out-of-state practitioners com. 1983-86), Tenn. Bar Assn., Tenn. Def. Lawyers Assn. (chmn. amicus curiae com. 1987-89), Phi Delta Phi. Avocations: golf, reading, boating. Office: Franklin Cooper & Marcus PLLC 837 Fortwood St Chattanooga TN 37403-2313 Home Phone: 423-847-1305; Office Phone: 423-756-3596. Business E-Mail: gcooper@fcmlaw.net.

COOPER, GERALD RICE, clinical pathologist; b. Scranton, SC, Nov. 19, 1914; s. Robert McFadden and Viola Lavender Cooper; m. Lois Corrina Painter, Mar. 9, 1946; children: Annetta, Gerald Jr., Rodney. AB, Duke U., 1936, MA, 1938, PhD, 1939, MD, 1950. Cert. Am. Bd. Clin. Chemistry. Intern Atlanta VA Hosp., 1950-51, resident, 1951-52; rsch. assoc. Duke U. Sch. Medicine, Durham, NC, 1939-46; chief chemistry, hematology and pathology Ctrs. for Disease Control, Atlanta, 1952-72; rsch. med. officer Ctrs. for Disease Control, Nat. Ctr. Environ. Health, Atlanta, 1973—. Author (with others) books; contbr. articles to profl. jours. Col. USPHS. Decorated commendation medal, Superior Svc. award, Disting. Svc. medal, Asst. Sec. Health award for exceptional achievement; recipient Hektoen Silver medal AMA, 1954, Fulton County Med. Achievement award, 1954, Billings Silver medal, 1956, Sigma Xi Rsch. award, 1997, Lifetime Sci. Achievement award CDC, 2002 Disting. Alumnus awrd Duke U. Sch. Medicine, 2004. Mem. Am. Assn. for Clin. Chemistry (pres. 1984, bd. dirs. 1975-77, chmn. bd. editors of selected methods 1967-80, bd. editors Clin. Chemistry jour. 1970-76, Fischer award 1975, Dade Internat. award 1975, N.J. Gerulat award 1979, SE Sect. Meritorious Svc. award 1989, Outstanding Contbn. Clin. Chemistry award 1992), Internat. Fedn. Clin. Chemistry (apolipoprotein expert panel 1985), Am. Soc. Clin. Pathologists (chmn. clin. chemistry coun. 1974, Continuing Edn. award 1967, 77). Methodist. Home: 2165 Bonnevit Ct NE Atlanta GA 30345-4126 Office: Ctrs for Disease Control Chamblee 102/2319 F25 4770 Buford Hwy Atlanta GA 30341-3724 Office Phone: 770-488-7952. Business E-Mail: grcl@cdc.gov.

COOPER, GINNIE, library director; b. Worthington, Minn., 1945; d. Lawrence D. and Ione C.; m. Richard Bauman, Dec. 1995; 1 child, Daniel Jay. Student, Coll. St. Thomas, U. Wis., Parkside; BA, SD State U.; MLS, U. Minn. Tchr. Flandreau Indian Sch., SD, 1967-68, St. Paul Pub. Schs., 1968-69; br. libr. Washington County Libr., Lake Elmo, Minn., 1970-71, asst. dir., 1971-75; assoc. adminstr., libr. U. Minn. Med. Sch., Mpls., 1975-77; dir. Kenosha Pub. Libr., Wis., 1977-81; county libr. Alameda County Libr., Calif., 1981-90; dir. librs. Multnomah County Libr., Portland, Oreg., 1990—2003; exec. dir. Bklyn. Pub. Libr., 2003—06; chief libr. DC Pub. Libr., 2006—. Chair County Mgr. Assn.; county adminstr. Mayor's Exec. Roundtable. Mem. ALA (mem. LAMA, PLA and RASD coms., elected to coun. 1987, 91, mem. legis. com. 1986-90, mem. orgn. com. 1990—), Calif. Libr. Assn. (pres. CIL, 1985, elected to coun. 1986, pres. Calif. County Librs. 1986), Oreg. Libr. Assn., Pub. Libr. Assn. (pres. 1997-98). Office: DC Pub Libr 901 G St NW Washington DC 20001 Office Phone: 207-727-1101.

COOPER, GLORIA, editor, press critic; b. Oak Park, Ill., Jan. 8, 1931; c. Sam and Madelyn (Brandt) Glaser; m. Wallace J. Cooper, June 3, 1950; children— Alison, Julie BA summa cum laude, Briarcliff Coll., 1970; MA, Columbia U., 1974. From asst. editor to dep. exec. editor Columbia Journalism Rev., NYC, 1974—2007. Editor: Squad Helps Dog Bite Victim, 1980, Red Tape Holds Up New Bridge, 1987; contbr. articles, revs., editorials to Columbia Journalism Rev., 1974— Mem.: Ethical Soc. No. Westchester (pres. 2007—), Princeton Club (NYC). Home: 91 Long Hill Rd E Briarcliff Manor NY 10510-2611 E-mail: gc15@columbia.edu.

COOPER, GREGORY SCOTT, epidemiologist, gastroenterologist, educator; b. Newark, July 14, 1960; s. Murray and Frances Cooper; m. Cathy Lynne Cooper, Feb. 3, 1991; children: Marissa, Ryan, Nicole. BA, MA, U. Pa., 1982, MD, 1986. Diplomate Am. Bd. Internal Medicine. Intern, resident in internal medicine Univ. Hosps., Cleve., 1986-89, chief resident, 1991-92, fellow in gastroenterology, 1989-91, 92-93; instr. medicine Case Western Res. U., Cleve., 1991-93, asst. prof. medicine, 1993-96, asst. prof. medicine and epidemiology, 1996-98, dir. cancer epidemiology-health rsch., 2000—, assoc. prof. medicine and epidemiology, 1998—2005, prof. medicine and epidemiology, 2005—, staff investigator, 2000—05, leader prevention and control, 2005—. Tng. program dir. Case Western Res. U., 1997—; dir. disease mgmt. U. Hosps. Cleve., 1997-99. Contbr. chpts. to books, more than 100 articles to profl. jours. Grantee Nat. Cancer Inst., 1996—. Fellow ACP (med. sch. rep.), Am. Coll. Gastroenterology; mem. Am. Fedn. Med. Rsch. (midwest coun.), Am. Cancer Soc. (rsch. project grants 1997—). Avocation: long distance running. Office: Univ Hosps Cleveland 11100 Euclid Ave Cleveland OH 44106-5066 Home Phone: 216-591-1167; Office Phone: 216-844-5386. Business E-Mail: greg.cooper@case.edu.

COOPER, HAL, television director; b. NYC, Feb. 23, 1923; s. Benjamin and Adeline (Raichman) C.; m. Mary Patricia Meikle, Dec. 21, 1944 (div. 1971); children: Bethami, Pamela; m. Marta Lucille Salcido, June 26, 1971; 1 child, James Benjamin. BA, U. Mich., 1946. Ind. TV dir., writer, producer various prodn. cos., 1948—. Performer Big Bro.'s Rainbow House, Mut. Network, 1936-41, asst. dir. Dock Street Theatre, Charleston, S.C., 1946-48; writer, prodr. TV Babysitter, DuMont TV Network, 1948-52, The Magic Cottage, 1950-56; dir., prodr. various daytime TV shows including Search For Tomorrow, others, 1950-57; prodr. stage play The Troublemakers, London, 1952; dir. numerous TV shows (various episodes) including Death Valley Days, 1965-67, Dick Van Dyke Show, 1962, Gilligan's Island, 1966, I Dream of Jeannie, 1965-69, I Spy, 1966, That Girl, 1967-69, Courtship of Eddie's Father, 1968-71, The Odd Couple, 1970-72, Mary Tyler Moore, 1972, All in the Family, 1972, (pilots) Hot L Baltimore, 1974, One Day At a Time, 1975, All's Fair, 1976, Nancy Walker Show, 1976, The Time of Their Lives, 1987; dir., exec. prodr.: TV shows including Maude, 1972-78, Phyl and Mikky, 1980, Love, Sydney, 1982-83, Gimme a Break, 1983-87, Empty Nest, 1988-89, Dear John, 1989-92, The Powers That Be, 1992-93. Served to lt. (j.g.) USNR, 1943-46, PTO. Mem. Writers Guild Am., ASCAP, Screen Actors Guild, AFTRA, Actors Equity Assn., Dirs. Guild Am. (mem. dirs. council, nat. bd. dirs.). E-mail: halcoop@aol.com.

COOPER, HAL DEAN, lawyer; b. Marshall County, Iowa, Dec. 8, 1934; s. Truman Braton and Golda Frances (Chadwick) C.; m. Constance Bellinger Simms, Dec. 31, 1960; children: Shannon, Charles, Ellen. Student, Neb. U., 1952-54; BS in Mech. Engring., Iowa State U., 1957; JD with honors, George Washington U., 1963. Bar: Iowa 1963, Ohio 1963, U.S. Supreme Ct. 1971. Assoc., ptnr. Fay & Fay, Cleve., 1962-67; ptnr. Meyer, Tilberry & Body, Cleve., 1967-69, Yount, Tarolli, Weinshenker & Cooper, Cleve, 1969-72; trial judge U.S. Ct. Claims, Washington, 1972-75; ptnr. Jones, Day, Reavis & Pogue, Cleve., 1975-95, chmn. intellectual property sect., 1976—94; owner Halco Enterprises, Ltd., Austinburg, Ohio, 1995—; pvt. arbitrator, mediator, 1996—. Bd. trustees Ashtubula County Dist. Lib., 2004—, pres., 2005—. With AUS, 1957—59. Mem.: Ashtabula County Bar Assn., Cleve. Intellectual Property Law Assn., Rotary, Clifton Club, Rowfant Club. Episcopalian. Avocation: bookbinding. Home Phone: 440-275-1333. Personal E-mail: halcon@windstream.net.

COOPER, HELENE, editor; b. Monrovia, Liberia; naturalized, 1997. Reporter Providence (RI) Journal Bulletin, 1987—92; reporter, Washington, Atlanta bureaus Wall St. Journal, 1992—97, reporter, London bur., 1997—99, reporter, internat. econ., 1999—2002, asst. bur. chief Washington, 2002—04; asst. editl. page editor NY Times, NYC, 2004—, and editl. bd. mem., 2004—. Editor: (compilation of Daniel Pearl's writings) At Home in the World, 2002. Recipient Raymond Clapper award, 2000, Sandy Hume award, 2001, Mo. Lifestyle Journalism award, 2002. Office: Editorial Page NY Times 229 W 43rd New York NY 10036 Office Phone: 212-556-3768. Office Fax: 212-556-3815.

COOPER, J. MICHAEL, lawyer; BA, Swarthmore Coll., 1970; JD, Harvard U., 1973. Ptnr., mem. exec. com. Bryan Cave LLP, Washington, DC. Office: Bryan Cave LLP 700 Thirteenth Street NW Washington DC 20005 Office Phone: 202-508-6070. E-mail: wfbavinger@bryancave.com.

COOPER, JACQUELYN BARBER, librarian; b. Harrisburg, Pa., Jan. 7, 1940; d. John and Belinda (Weakley) Barber; m. Stephen T. Toy, Aug. 11, 1962 (div. 1972); 1 child, Deborah Lynne; m. Arthur Raymond Cooper, Jan. 10, 1987. BS magna cum laude, Susquehanna U., 1961; MLS, Kent State U., 1969. Tchr. music Tredyffrin-Eastern Schs., Berwyn, Pa., 1961-62; supr. music Alachua County Schs., Gainesville, Fla., 1962-66; reference libr. Providence (R.I.) Pub. Libr., 1969-73, br. libr., 1973-87, br. head, 1987-95, regional libr., 1995—2000, collection devel. mgr., 2000—03; ret. Sec. Mt. Hope Day Care Ctr. Inc., Providence, 1985-1998; substitute organist Providence Presbyn. Ch., 1989—, trustee, 1994-2000, deacon, 2006—. Pa. State Edn. Assn. scholar, 1957; recipient SAT scholar award Sigma Alpha Iota, 1961. Mem. ALA, New Eng. Libr. Assn. (exec. bd. 1982-92), R.I. Libr. Assn. (chmn. intellectual freedom com. 1980-82, Libr. of Yr. award 1992), Providence Pub. Libr. Staff Assn. (pres. 1971-72, 86-87, treas. 1987-89), Coalition Libr. Advs. (treas. 1994—96), Beta Phi Mu, Sigma Alpha Iota. Democrat. Presbyterian. Avocations: French horn, organ, natural history, sewing. E-mail: jackicr@hotmail.com.

COOPER, JAMES ALBERT, JR., electrical engineering educator; b. Columbus, Miss., Feb. 5, 1946; s. James Albert and Juanita (Perkins) C.; m. Barbara Crowder, Aug. 3, 1968; children: David Alan, Katherine Liann. BSEE, Miss. State U., 1968; MSEE, Stanford U., 1969; PhD, Purdue U., 1973. Mem. tech. staff Sandia Labs., Albuquerque, 1968-69; grad. rsch. asst. Sch. Elec. Engring. Purdue U., West Lafayette, Ind., 1970-72, prof., 1983—, dir. Purdue Optoelectronics Rsch. Ctr., 1986-89, Charles William Harrison prof., 2002—; mem. tech. staff Bell Labs., Murray Hill, NJ, 1973-83; co-dir. Birck Nanotech. Ctr., 2001—. Contbr. numerous articles to jours., chpts. to books; patentee in field. Fellow IEEE (assoc. editor Trans. on Electron Devices 1983-86). Republican. Mem. United Methodist Ch. Achievements include 13 patents in field; co-origination of the Time-of-Flight measurement technique for the study of high-field transport of electrons along semiconductor/insulator interfaces, design of Bell System's first microprocessor chip; co-development of first silicon carbide nonvolatile memory chips, first silicon carbide monolithic integrated circuits and first SiC DMOS power transistors. Office: Purdue U Birck Nanotech Ctr 1205 W State St West Lafayette IN 47907-2057

COOPER, JAMES D., lawyer; b. Whittier, Calif., Oct. 19, 1954; AB summa cum laude, Univ. Chgo., 1976; JD, Yale Univ., 1976. Bar: NY 1981. Assoc. Cravath, Swaine & Moore LLP, NYC, 1979—86, ptnr., corp., 1986—. Mem.: Phi Beta Kappa. Office: Cravath Swaine & Moore LLP Worldwide Plz 825 Eighth Ave New York NY 10019-7475 Office Phone: 212-474-1326. Office Fax: 212-474-3700. Business E-Mail: jcooper@cravath.com.

COOPER, JAMES HAYES SHOFNER (JIM COOPER), congressman, lawyer; b. Nashville, June 19, 1954; s. William Prentice Jr. and Hortense (Powell) Cooper; m. Martha Hays, 1985; children: Mary Argentine Adams, John James Audubon, Hayes Hightower. BA, U. NC, Chapel Hill, 1975; BA/MA, Oxford U., 1977; JD, Harvard Law Sch., 1980. Atty. Waller, Lansden, Dortch & Davis, Nashville, 1980-82; mem. US Congress from 4th Tenn. dist., 1983—94, mem. budget com., mem. energy and commerce com.; mem. US Congress from 5th Tenn. dist., 2003—, mem. armed svcs. com., mem. budget com.; mng. dir. Equitable Securities, 1995-99; founder, ptnr. & chmn. bd. Brentwood Capital Advs. LLC, 1999—2002. Adj. prof. Vanderbilt U. Owen Sch. Mgmt., 1995—2002. Bd. dirs. Resources for the Future, 1997—. Rhodes scholar, 1975, Morehead scholar, 1972. Mem.: Phi Beta Kappa. Democrat. Episcopalian. Mailing: US Ho Reps 1536 Longworth Ho Office Bldg Washington DC 20515-1535 also: Dist Office 706 Church St Ste 101 Nashville TN 37203 Office Phone: 202-225-4311.*

COOPER, JAMES MICHAEL, education educator; b. Steubenville, Ohio, July 29, 1939; s. James Stanley and Regina Marie (Coen) C.; m. Susan Callaway, Sept. 1, 1962 (div. June 1978); children: Jeffrey, Craig, Cynthia; m. Shamim Sisson, June 13, 1987. AB in History with distinction, Stanford U., 1961, AM in Edn., 1962, AM in History, 1966, PhD in Edn., 1967. Tchr. Jordan Jr. High Sch. of Palo Alto (Calif.) Unified Sch. Sys., 1961-63, Palo Alto High Sch., 1963-65; lectr. Stanford U. Sch. Edn., 1967; asst. prof. edn. U. Mass., Amherst, 1968-71; assoc. prof. U. Houston, 1971-74, prof., 1974-84; Commonwealth prof. U. Va. Curry Sch. Edn., Charlottesville, 1984—2004, dean, 1984-94, prof. emeritus, 2004—. Chmn. U. Houston faculty senate, 1982; exec. bd. dirs. Holmes Group, East Lansing, Mich., 1985-94; unit accreditation bd. Nat. Coun. Accreditation of Tchr. Edn., Washington, 1986-90 Co-author: Those Who Can, Teach, 11th edit., 2007; editor: Developing Skills for Instructional Supervision, 1984, Classroom Teaching Skills, 8th edit., 2006; co-editor: Kaleidoscope: Readings in Education, 11th edit., 2007. Recipient Florence B. Stratemeyer award Assn. for Student Teaching, Washington, 1967, Fulbright-Hays award Portugal Coun. Internat. Exch. Scholars, Washington, 1980, Outstanding Leader in Tchr. Edn. award Assn. Tchr. Educators, 1990. Mem.: ASCD, Raven Soc. (The Raven award 2001), Am. Assn. Colls. for Tchr. Edn. (bd. dirs. 1990—93), Am. Ednl. Rsch. Assn., Omicron Delta Kappa, Phi Delta Kappa. Democrat. Roman Catholic. Avocations: golf, travel. Office Phone: 434-977-5216. Business E-Mail: jimcooper@virginia.edu.

COOPER, JAMES NELSON, medical educator; b. SI, Aug. 6, 1938; s. Charles Sylvester and Ella (Sabine) C.; m. Carolyn Olverson; children: John Emerson, Charles Key, James Ashley, Catherine Quesenberry. BA, Columbia U., 1959; MD, NYU, 1963. Diplomate Am. Bd. Internal Medicine and Gastroenterology. Intern Georgetown U., Washington, 1963-65; resident Boston City Hosp., 1965-66; fellow gastroenterology U. Chgo., 1966-68; clin. assoc. prof. medicine Georgetown U., Washington, 1977-83, prof. medicine, 1983—2007, asst. dean Sch. Medicine, 1985—2005, dir. transitional residency program, 1985—2001; pres. med. staff Fairfax Hosp., Falls Church, Va., 1975-77, chief gastroenterology, 1971—82, chmn. dept. medicine, 1982—2005; prof. George Mason U., Fairfax, 2006—, dir. med. rsch. devel., 2006—; prof. medicine Va. Commonwealth U. Sch. Medicine, Richmond, 2003—. Cons. State Dept., Washington, 1970—74; dir. Inova Instn. Rsch. and Edn., 1991—2005; chmn. bd. mgrs. Theranostics Health, Rockville, Md., 2007—. Editor: Gastointestinal and Hepatic Complications In Pregnancy, 1986. Served to maj. USAR, 1964-71. Fellow ACP (Laureate award 1997), ACG; mem. Am. Gastroent. Assn., Am. Assn. Study Liver Diseases, No. Va. Acad. Internal Medicine (pres. 1975), Cosmos Club, Sigma Xi. Office: 10910 University Blvd MS4E3 Manassas VA 22010 Business E-Mail: jcoopera@gmu.edu.

COOPER, JAMES RUSSELL, retired law educator; b. New Kensington, Pa., July 21, 1928; s. John Edward and Isabella Bird (Bowen) C.; m. Carolyn Hocker, Sept. 21, 1953 (div. Dec. 1975); children: L. Rachel, Julia Anderoni, Evan Lloyd, Jennifer Meyer; m. Leigh Ann Brian, Feb. 25, 1995 (div. Nov. 1999). BS in Econs., U. Pa., Phila., 1952, JD, 1955. Bar: D.C., 1955, U.S. Supreme Ct., 1964; ordained to ministry Universal Brotherhood Movement, Inc., Meeting House for Aspiring Spirits. Pres., chmn. Radio WKPA-AM, WYDD-FM, New Kensington, 1959-64; urban renewal dir. Redevelopment Authority, New Kensington, 1964-68; assoc. prof. U. Ill., Champaign-Urbana, 1968-74; prof. legal studies Ga. State U., Atlanta, 1974-94, emeritus prof., 1994—. Author: Twilights Last Gleaming, 1992, Real Estate Investments, 3d edit. 1992. Sgt. U.S. Army, 1946-48. Mem. Fed. Bar Assn., D.C. Bar Assn., Am. Real Estate Soc. (founder, dir.). Home: 2822 Peavine Trail Lakeland FL 33810-2332 Office Phone: 863-838-5682, 863-859-7909. Personal E-mail: jrc@spiritsmeetinghouse.com.

COOPER, JANELLE LUNETTE, neurologist, educator; b. Ann Arbor, Mich., Dec. 11, 1955; d. Robert Marion and Madelyn (Leonard) C.; children: Lena Christine, Nicholas Dominic. BA in Chemistry, Reed Coll., 1978; MD, Vanderbilt U., 1986. Diplomate Nat. Bd. Med. Examiners; diplomate in neurology Am. Bd. Psychiatry and Neurology; registered med. technologist Am. Soc. Clin. Pathologists. Med. technologist Swedish Hosp. Med. Ctr., Seattle, 1978-80, U. Wash. Clin. Chemistry, Seattle, 1980-82, Vanderbilt U. Hosp., Nashville, 1983-84; intern medicine Vanderbilt U. Med. Ctr., Nashville, 1986-87, resident neurology, 1987-90; instr. neurology Med. Coll. Pa., Phila., 1990-91, asst. prof., clerkship dir., 1991—, mem. curriculum com., 1990-91, vis. asst. prof., 1991-95; neurologist Greater Ann Arbor Neurology Assocs., 1991-93; dir. neurol. svcs., med. dir. Indsl. Rehab. Program St. Francis Hosp., Escanaba, Mich., 1993-98; founder, dir. No. Neuroscis., Escanaba, 1993-98; pres. Holder Lady, Ltd., 1996—2005; chmn. dept. medicine St. Francis Hosp., Escanaba, Mich., 1998-99; dir. Affinity Health Sys., Oshkosh, Wis., 1998—, The Memory Ctr., Affinity Health Sys., Oshkosh, Wis., 1998—; med. dir. Memory Clinic of the Upper Peninsula, Escanaba, Mich., 1998—2000; chmn. dept. medicine Mercy Med. Ctr., 2002—04. ER physician Tenn. Christian Med. Ctr., 1989—90; physician MCP Neurology Assocs., Phila., 1990—91; neurologist Affinity Med. Group, Oshkosh, Wis., 1998—; presenter in field. Contbr. articles to profl. jours. Vol. Rape and Sexual Abuse Ctr., Nashville, 1988—90; mem. editl. bd. Nashville Women's Alliance, 1989—90; mem. adv. bd. Perspective Adult Daycare Ctr., 1996—99; founding dir. Memory Clinic of Upper Peninsula, 1998—2000; airport support network vol. Aircraft Owners and Pilots Assn.; mem. adminstrv. bd. Edgehill United Methodist Ch., Nashville; bd. dir. Upper Peninsula Physicians Network, 1995—98; mem. profl. adv. com. NE Wis. Alzheimer's Assn., 1999—. Recipient Svc. award for outstanding contbns. Rape and Sexual Abuse Ctr., 1990, Pres. award for Creativity Affinity Health Sys. 2006; epilepsy minifellow Bowman Gray U., 1995. Mem. AMA (physician's Recognition award 1989—), Am. Acad. Neurology (elected fellow 2006), Wis. State Med. Soc., Upper Peninsula Neuro Assn. (v.p. 1998-99, trustee 1998-99), Aircraft Owners and Pilots Assn., Women in Aviation Internat. (charter), National Association of Rocketry, Air Force Assn. (life patron), Assn. of US Army (life mem.). Methodist. Achievements include first synthesis of Difluoromethanedisulfonic Acid; research on neurobehavioral disorders; on effects of dietary lipids on the etiology of Alzheimer's disease; on the role of pantothenic acid in neurodegeneration; on virtual reality computer simulation for assessment of senior drivers clinical investigation trials for new medications for dementias. Home: 2819 Hughes St Oshkosh WI 54902-7158 Office: Memory Ctr Affinity Health Sys 2700 W Ninth Ave Ste 104 Oshkosh WI 54904-7863 Business E-Mail: jcooper@affinityhealth.org.

COOPER, JASON P., lawyer; b. Chipping Norton, Eng., May 30, 1966; BS in Mech. Engring., Purdue Univ., 1988; JD cum laude, Ind. Univ., 1992. Bar: NC 1992, registered: US Patent and Trademark Off. 1994. Product engr. Rexnord Corp.; ptnr., chmn., intellectual property mech. group Alston & Bird LLP, Charlotte, NC. Co-author: The Art and Science of Patent Law, 2004; frequent lectr., writer on patent law. Intellectual Property Adv. Bd. Ind. Univ. Law Sch. Mem.: Fed. Circuit Bar Assn., FICPI Commn. d'Étude et de Travail for Internat. Patents, US Sect., Fédération Internationale des Conseils en Propriété Industrielle (FICPI) (councilor). Office: Alston & Bird LLP Ste 4000 Bank of Am Plz 101 S Tryon St Charlotte NC 28280-4000 Office Phone: 704-444-1031. Office Fax: 704-578-1234. Business E-Mail: jcooper@alston.com.

COOPER, JAY LESLIE, lawyer; b. Chgo., Jan. 15, 1929; s. Julius Jerome and Grayce (Wolkenheim) Cooper; m. Darice Richman, July 30, 1970; children: Todd, Leslie, Keith. JD, De Paul U., 1951. Bar: Ill. 1951, Calif. 1953, U.S. Supreme Ct. 1965, N.Y. 1987. Ptnr. Cooper, Epstein & Hurewitz (and predecessors), Beverly Hills, Calif., 1955-93, Manatt, Phelps & Phillips, LA, 1993—2001; shareholder Greenberg Traurig, LLP, 2002—. Guest lectr. Advanced Profl. Program Legal Aspects of Music and Rec. Industry, U. So. Calif., 1968, 70, 75, Entertainment Industry Conf., 1971, Harvard Law Sch., 1985, Calif. Copyright Conf., 1967, 71, 73, 75, 77, 97, v.p., 1975, pres., 1976-77; co-chmn. annual program The Rec. Contract, UCLA, 1977—; lectr. Midem, 1977-95, 96-97; adj. prof. entertainment law Loyola U. Law Sch., LA, 1978-80; moderator UCLA Seminar, 1994. Profl. musician with, Les Brown, Charlie Barnet, Frank Sinatra, Los Angeles Philharm. others, 1945-55; editor: (with Irwin O. Spiegel) Record and Music Publishing Forms of Agreement in Current Use, 1971, Annual Program on Legal Aspects of Entertainment Industry, Syllabus, 1966-70; co-author: Talent in the New Millennium, 2001, The Work Made For Hire Conundrum, 2001. Recipient Tex. Star award for outstanding contbn. and achievement in entertainment law Tex. Bar, 2006; named Entertainment Lawyer of Yr. Billboard mag., 1975, Best of the Best, 2000, Entertainment Atty of Yr., Beverly Hills Bar Assn., 2003, So. Calif. Super Lawyers, L.A. Mag., 2004-05, Leading Business Lawyer, Chambers and Partners US Guide, Entertaiment Lawyer of Yr., Century City Bar Assn., 2005; named to Best Lawyers in Am., 1987—. Mem.: NARAS (chpt. pres. 1973—75, nat. pres. 1975—77), ABA (chmn. forum on entertainment and sports industries 1983—86), Internat. Assn. Entertainment Lawyers (exec. com.), LA Copyright Soc., Ill. Bar Assn., Calif. Bar Assn., LA County Bar Assn., Calif. Copyright Soc. (pres. 1976). Office: Greenberg Traurig LLP 2450 Colorado Ave #400 E Santa Monica CA 90404 Office Phone: 310-586-7888. Business E-Mail: cooper@gtlaw.com.

COOPER, JEAN SARALEE, retired judge; b. Huntington, NY, Mar. 7, 1946; d. Ralph and Henrietta (Halbreich) Cooper; stepchildren: Mitzi Concklin Prochnow, John Todd Concklin. BA, Sophie Newcomb Coll. of Tulane U., 1968; JD, Emory U., 1970. Bar: La. 1970, Ga. 1970, U.S. Dist. Ct. (ea. dist.) La. 1970, U.S. Ct. Appeals (5th cir.) 1972, U.S. Ct. Appeals (2d cir.) 1976, U.S. Ct. Appeals (4th cir.) 1977, U.S. Ct. Appeals (fed. cir.), U.S. Supreme Ct. 1974. Trial atty. Office of Solicitor, U.S. Dept. Labor, Washington, 1970-73, spl. projects asst., 1973, sr. trial atty., 1973-77; adminstrv. judge Bd. Contract Appeals, HUD, Washington, 1977—2003, acting chmn. and chief judge, 1980-81, vice chmn., 1983—2003; bd. dirs. Coalition Free Trade, 2003—07. Cons.; lectr. Contbr. articles to profl. jours. Recipient Moot Ct. award, Tulane Law Sch., 1968. Fellow: Am. Bar Found.; mem.: ABA (sec. jud. conf. 1979—, sec. jud. divsn. Nat. Conf. Adminstrv. Law Judges 1979—, standing com. on jud. selection, tenure and compensation, 1992—95, chair nat. conf. adminstrv. law judges jud. divsn. 1999—2000, standing com. on fed. jud. improvements 2000—01, adminstrn. law sect. vice chair debarment and suspension com. pub. contracts sect. 1992—97, vice chair alcohol beverage com., adjudication com., adminstrv. law sect.), Women for Winesense So. Ariz. chpt. (bd. dirs., cons.), Nat. Conf. Bd. Contract Appeals Mems., Prettyman-Leventhal Am. Inn of Ct. (past pres., master of bench 1989—2007), Am. Law Inst. (life), Am. Inns of Ct. Found. (trustee 1992—98, leadership com. 1998—), La. Bar Assn., Ariz. Opera League (v.p. 2007—). Republican. Home: 5878 N Bright Star Dr Tucson AZ 85718 Personal E-mail: jeansaralee@msn.com. *My approach to life has been "anything is possible." That removed the boundaries in my mind, so that I could move past the boundaries that might hold me back. I firmly believe in mentoring young people so that they, too, will see past boundaries real and imagined.*

COOPER, JEROME MAURICE, architect; b. Memphis, Jan. 24, 1930; s. Samuel and Bessie (Phillips) C.; m. Jean Kanter, Dec. 29, 1957; children: David Franklin, Samuel Randolph, Beth Lauren. BS, Ga. Inst. Tech., 1952, BArch, 1955; postgrad., U. Rome, Italy, 1956-57. Cert. Nat. Coun. Arch. Registration Bds. Fulbright fellow, Rome, 1956-57; pres. Cooper, Carry & Assocs., Inc., Atlanta, 1960—, chmn. Vis. artist Am. Acad. Rome. Prin. works include Coll. of Architecture bldg. Ga. Inst. Tech., Siemens Corp. Hdqrs., Nat. Svc. Industries Corp. Hdqrs., Adtraw Corp. Hdqrs., Huntsville, Ala., Sci. Atlanta Corp. Hdqrs, Lazarus Dept. Store, Pitts., Clin. Info. Mgmt. Ctr., Drake U. Med. Ctr., Sch. of Theology, Mercer U., Green Hill Mall (AIA design award), Heritage Village at Sea Pines, Underground Atlanta, C&P Hdqrs., No. Va., Rich's Dept. Store, Northpoint Mall, Atlanta, Jordan Marsh Dept. Store, Natick Mall, Boston. Trustee Nat. Bldg. Mus. Served to lt. (j.g.) USN, 1952-54. Recipient Rothschild medal, 1985, Silver medal Atlanta chpt. AIA, 1987. Fellow AIA (pres. chpt., nat. dir., task force on ethics, task force on certification, task force on long span buildings, Silver medal firm award Atlanta chpt. 1987), Nat. Jud. Coun. Home: 1070 Judith Way NE Atlanta GA 30324-2905 Office: Cooper Carry & Assocs Inc 3520 Piedmont Rd NE Ste 200 Atlanta GA 30305-1595

COOPER, JERROLD STEPHEN, historian, educator; b. Chgo., Nov. 24, 1942; s. Emanuel Cooper and Adele (Faberson) Smith; m. Elaine Abrams, Dec. 22, 1962 (div. 1969); children: Nina Lynn, Sari Jean; m. Carol Manson Bier, Nov. 18, 1982; 1 child, Jenny Alexandra. AB, U. Calif., Berkeley, 1963, MA, 1964; PhD, U. Chgo., 1969. Asst. prof. Johns Hopkins U., Balt., 1968-74, assoc. prof., 1974-79, prof., 1979—2003, W.W. Spence prof. semitic lang., 2003—, chmn. dept. Near Eastern Studies Balt., 1983-91; acting chmn. Near Eastern Studies, 1992-93; acting chmn. classics Johns Hopkins U., Balt., 1988-91. Vis. prof. UCLA, 1975, U. Calif., Berkeley, 1981, U. Padua, Italy, 1992, U. Rome, 1998, Venice Internat. U.,2006-07. Author: The Return of Ninurta, 1979, The Curse of Agade, 1983, Sumerian and Akkadian Royal Inscriptions, 1985; assoc. editor Jour. of Cuneiform Studies, 1972-89. NEH grantee, 1980-86, NSF grantee, 2002-2005. Mem. Am. Oriental Soc. (dir. 1982-85, v.p. 2007), Am. Schs. of Oriental Rsch. (trustee 1987-97), Internat. Assn. Assyriology (founding bd. mem. 2003-06). Avocation: early music. Office: Johns Hopkins U Dept Near East Studies Baltimore MD 21218 Office Phone: 410-516-7498. E-mail: anzu@jhu.edu.

COOPER, JOEL, psychologist, educator; b. NYC, Dec. 3, 1943; s. Samuel Cooper and Sarah Tobias; m. Barbara Orenstein, Dec. 17, 1966; children: Jason, Aaron, Grant. BS, CCNY, 1965; PhD in Social Psychology, Duke U., 1969. Asst. prof. psychology Princeton (N.J.) U., 1969-73, assoc. prof., 1973-78, prof., 1978—, chmn. psychology dept., 1985-92, dir. grad. studies dept. psychology, 1976-83. Chmn. Inst. Rev. Bd. Princeton U., 1974-81, 84-87, 96-99, com. appointments and advancements, com. on grad. sch.; sr. fellow East-West Population Inst., 1975. Author: Understanding Social Psychology, 1976, 1991, Social Psychology, 1999, Gender and the Computer: Understanding the Digital Divide, 2003; editor: Attribution Processes, Person, Perception, and Social Interaction: The Legacy of Edward E. Jones, 1998, Sage Handbook of Social Psychology, 2003; editorial bd.: Jour. Personality, Social Psychology Quar.; editor: Jour. Exptl. Social Psychology, 2006—. Office: Princeton U Dept Psychology Green Hall Princeton NJ 08544

COOPER, JOHN ALFRED, JR., community development company executive; b. Memphis, Sept. 13, 1938; s. John Alfred and Mildred (Borum) C.; m. Pat McInnis, Oct. 23, 1965; children: Mary Virginia, John Alfred III, Borum. Student, U. Ark., 1961. With Cherokee Village Devel. Co., Inc., 1962—, exec. v.p., 1967-68; pres. John A. Cooper Co., 1968-90, Cooper Communities Inc., 1972-90, vice chmn., 1990-91; chmn. Cooper Communities, Inc., 1991-97, pres., CEO, 1997—. Bd. dirs. 1st Nat. Bank of Sharp County, J.B. Hunt Transport Svcs., Inc. Mem.: Memphis Country, Little Rock Country. Office: Cooper Communities 903 N 47th St Rogers AR 72756-9615

COOPER, JOHN AMBROSE, management consultant, marketing professional; b. Freetown, Sierra Leone, Mar. 5, 1948; s. Daniel Philip and Nancy Etta Cooper; children: John Ambrose, Daniel Kalen. AA in Humanities, Onondaga C.C., SUNY, Syracuse, 1979; AA in Bus., Columbia Coll., Mo., 1984, BA in Individual Studies, 1986; MSc in Internat. Mktg., Syracuse U., 1988; BS in Indsl. Mgmt., Empire State Coll., SUNY, 1992; MBA, Syracuse U., 1996. Acct. gen. dept. City of Freetown, Sierra Leone, 1969-71; quality assurance insp., inventory control coord. Joseph Schlitz Brewing Co., Baldwinsville, NY, 1976-80; prin. clk. J.A. Jones Constrn. Co., Baldwinsville, 1980-82; mgmt. coord. Anheuser-Busch, Inc., Baldwinsville, 1982—. Mem. editing staff Baldwinsville (N.Y.) Eagle Newsletter. Tng. participant Resolve: A Ctr. for Dispute Settlement, Inc., Syracuse, 1982, Muscular Dystrophy Assn., Baldwinsville, N.Y. (lock-up fundraiser participant for children summer camp, 1996). Mem. Am. Mktg. Assn., Indsl. Rels. Rsch. Assn., West Indian Cultural Assn. (exec. com. 1990), Internat. Stars Soccer Orgn. (gen. sec., coach), Internat. Exhibitors Assn., Anheuser-Busch Employee Assn. (exec. bd. 1983), Hon Appointment to the rsch. bd Advisors, Am. Biographical Inst., Internat. Platform Assn., Soc. Competitive Intelligence Profls., Am. Mgmt. Assn., Eagle Club Crystal Cathedral Ministries. Roman Catholic. Avocations: competitive sports (soccer), debate, travel. Home: 111 Lafayette Rd Apt 625 Syracuse NY 13205-2936 also: One Busch Pl Saint Louis MO 63118

COOPER, JOHN ARNOLD, financial analyst; b. Detroit, Oct. 27, 1917; s. Gage Whitman and Helen Dorothy (Danger) Cooper; m. Sylvia Grace, Sept. 6, 1941 (div. 1977); 1 child, Maud Cooper Plumer; m. Virginia Bailey Svagr, Mar. 11, 1977 (dec. 1981); m. Anny Marion Van Dyke, Apr. 9, 1983. BA, Williams Coll., Williamstown, Mass., 1939; MBA, Mich. State U., 1968. CFA Inst. Chartered Fin. Analysts. Treas. Cooper Supply Co., Detroit, 1941-44, sec., 1944-56, pres., 1956-67; v.p. Texas Industries, Inc., Dallas, 1963-67; pres. Cooper, Van Dyke Assocs. Inc., Birmingham, Mich., 1970—2000; mem. Cooper, Van Dyke LLC, 2000—. Pres. Transit Mixed Concrete Inst. Met. Detroit, 1952—53, 1955—77, Constrn. Assn. Mich., 1967—68; assoc. prof. fin. Faculty Bus. Adminstrn. U. Windsor, Ont., Canada, 1977—83. Vice chair Oakland County Planning Commn., 1968—70; trustee Fin. Analysts Seminar, 1980—82; class agt. Williams Coll., 1989—94, 2007—; chmn. preservation fund drive Cmty. House, Birmingham, Mich., 1995—98, fin. com. mem., 1988—2001, bd. dirs., 1996—2000. Mem.: CFA Chpt. Detroit (pres. 1980—81, chmn. profl. conduct/ethics com. 1988—99), Inst. Chartered Fin. Analysts, Am. Trucking Assn. (bd. dirs. 1961—63), Mich. Trucking Assn. (bd. govs. 1958—63), Williams Club N.Y., Beta Gamma Sigma. Republican. Episcopalian. Avocations: photography, hiking, gardening, travel.

COOPER, JOHN MADISON, philosophy educator; b. Memphis, Nov. 29, 1939; s. Marion Armon and Bernardine (Sheehan) C.; m. Marcia Louise Coleman, Aug. 21, 1965; children: Stephanie Coleman, Katherine Alexander. AB magna cum laude, Harvard U., 1961, PhD, 1967; BPhil, Corpus Christi Coll., Oxford, Eng., 1963. Asst. prof. philosophy and the classics Harvard U., Cambridge, Mass., 1966-71; assoc. prof. U. Pitts., 1971-76, prof., 1976-81, chmn. philosophy dept., 1977-81; prof. Princeton U., NJ, 1981—, chmn. philosophy dept. NJ, 1984-92, Stuart prof. NJ, 1998—. Author: Reason and Human Good in Aristotle, 1976, Seneca: Moral and Political Essays, 1995, Plato: Complete Works, 1997, Reason and Emotion, 1999, Knowledge, Nature, and the Good, 2004; mem. editl. bd. Am. Philos. Quar., 1977-80, History of Philosophy Quar., 1983-86, The Monist, 1987—, Ratio, 1988, Archiv für Ges. d. Phil., 1994—; contbr. articles to profl. jours. Recipient Ctr. for Advanced Studies fellow U. Ill., 1969-70, NEH fellow, 1982-83, John Simon Guggenheim fellow, 1987-88, Ctr. for Advanced Study in the Behavioral Scis. fellow, 1992-93, Am. Coun. Learned Socs. fellow, 2002-03. Fellow Am. Acad. Arts and Scis.; mem. Am. Philos. Assn. (ea. divsn. exec. com. 1984-87, chmn. com. def. profl. rights 1983-88, ea. divsn. nominating com. 1991-94, chmn. ea. divsn. program com. 1980, v.p. 1998-99, pres. 1999-2000). Home: 182 Western Way Princeton NJ 08540-7208 Office: Princeton Univ Dept of Philosophy 1879 Hall Princeton NJ 08544-1006 E-mail: johncoop@princeton.edu.

COOPER, JOHNNIE EDWARD, JR., advocate; b. Plant City, Fla., Aug. 23, 1961; s. Johnnie E. and Dorothy L. Cooper. BA, Fla. Meml. Coll., 1989. Mem. Miami-Dade County (Fla.) Managed Care Ombudsman Com., 2004—05, UTD Legis. Action and Dem. Com., Miami, 2004—05. Libr. bd. mem. City of Opa-locka, Fla., 1996; Dem. nominee for state rep. Miami, 2003—. Mem.: So. Christian Leadership Conf (assoc.). Democrat. Home: PO Box 471234 Miami FL 33147 Home Phone: 305-877-6702. Personal E-mail: jecoope03@yahoo.com.

COOPER, JOSEPH, political scientist, educator; b. Boston, Sept. 10, 1933; s. Charles and Esther (Balder) Cooper; m. Frances Lorna Wollin, Aug. 24, 1965; children: Samuel Wollin, Meryl Charlotte. AB summa cum laude, Harvard U., 1955, AM, 1959, PhD, 1961. Asst. prof. govt. Harvard U., 1963-67; mem. faculty Rice U., Houston, 1967-91, prof. polit. sci., 1970-91, chmn. dept., 1967-72, Lena Gohlman Fox prof., 1978-89, dean Sch. Social Scis., 1979-88, Herbert S. Autrey prof. social scis., 1989-91, pres. Rice Inst. for Policy Analysis Sch. Social Scis., 1989-91; provost, v.p. for acad. affairs Johns Hopkins U., Balt., 1991-96, prof. dept. polit. sci., 1991—. Vis. Olin prof. polit. sci. Stanford U., 1988—89; staff dir. commn. adminstrv. rev. US Ho. Reps., 1976—78; vis. prof. govt. Harvard U., 1984—85; mem. acad. adv. coun. Ctr. Congress Ind. U.; mem. editl. bd. Baker Jour. Applied Pub. Policy, 2007, adv. bd., 07. Author: (book) The Origins of the Standing Committes and the Development of the Modern House, 1970, Congress and Its Committees, 1988; co-editor: Sage Yearbook on Electoral Studies, 1975—82; mem. bd. editors: Congress and the Presidency, Ency. of U.S. Congress, Legis. Studies Quar., 1987—90, 2001—03, assoc. editor: Ency. of Am. Legis. Sys., Congress of U.S. 1789-1989; contbr. articles to profl. jours. Mem. adv. com. Records of Congress U.S. Congress and Nat. Archives, 1995—2006; bd. dir. Balt. Hebrew U., 1994—2001, Dirksen Congl. Ctr., 1994—2000, 2002—05. Recipient Press award, Congl. Quar., 1989; Brookings Rsch. fellow, Harvard U., 1959—60, Sr. fwllow, NEH, 1973, grant, 2000. Mem.: D.C. Area Polit Sci. Assn. (mem. coun. 1993—94, v.p. 1994, pres. 1996), Midwest Polit. Sci. Assn., So. Polit. Sci. Assn., Southwestern Polit. Sci. Assn. (pres. 1977), Am. Polit. Sci. Assn. (sec. 1979, program chmn. 1985, nominations chmn. 1992, exec. com. legis. studies sect. 1999—2001, chair Rosenthal prize com. 2004—05), Asia Soc. (bd. dirs. 1990—92), Jefferson Davis Assn. (dir. 1980—91), Phi Beta Kappa, Sigma Xi. Office: Dept Polit Sci Johns Hopkins Univ Baltimore MD 21218-2685 Home Phone: 410-467-6063; Office Phone: 410-516-4879. Business E-Mail: jcooper@jhu.edu.

COOPER, JOSEPHINE SMITH, trade association and public affairs executive; b. Raleigh, NC, Aug. 2, 1945; d. Joseph W. and Marie (Peele) S. BA in Bus. and Econs., Meredith Coll., Raleigh, 1967; MS in Mgmt., Duke U., 1977. Program analyst Office of Air & Quality Planning and Stds. EPA, Rsch., Triangle Park, NC, 1968-78; environ. protection specialist Office of Rsch. and Devel., Washington, 1978-80; mem. profl. staff majority leader Howard H. Baker, Jr., U.S. Senate Com. on Environ. and Pub. Works, Washington, 1980-83; asst. adminstr. for external affairs EPA, Washington, 1983-85; asst. v.p. for environ. and health program Am. Paper Inst., Washington, 1985-86; sr. v.p. for policy Synthetic Organic Chem. Mfrs. Assn., Washington, 1986-88; sr. v.p., dir. environ. policy Hill & Knowlton, Inc., Washington, 1988-91; founder, dir. Capitoline Internat. Group, Ltd., Washington, 1991-92; v.p. environ. and regulatory affairs Am. Forest & Paper Assn., 1992-99; pres., CEO Alliance of Automobile Mfrs., Washington, 1999—2004; group v.p. for govt. and industry affairs Toyota Motor N.Am., 2004—. Treas. RTP Fed. Credit Union, 1969—72, pres., CEO, 1975; pres. Women's Coun. on Energy and Environment, 1986—88, Nat. Coun. on Clean Indoor Air, 1988—96; mem. nat. adv. environ. health scis. coun. NIH, 1990—94; mem. adv. com. EPA Clean Air Act, 1994—2005; liaison mem. trade and environ. policy adv. com. USTR, 1994—2002; chmn. bd. Nat. Urban Air Toxic Rsch. Ctr., 2003—; bd. dirs. Washington First Bank. Bd. visitors Duke U. Nicholas Sch. Environment, 1994—2002, Duke U. Fuqua Sch. Bus., 2004—; bd. dirs. Washington Performing Arts Soc., 2005—. Congl. fellow, 1979-80. Mem.: NAM (coun. bd. dirs. 2000—04), Orgn. of Internat. Auto Assn. (pres.), Orgn. d'Internationale Constructeurs d'Automobiles (chmn. 2003—04), Am. Soc. Assn. Execs. (bd. dirs. 2000—03), U.S. C. of C. (Com. of 100 2000—04), Women in Govt. Rels., Federally Employed Women (pres. 1972—77, treas.). Mem. Christian Ch. (Disciples Of Christ). Office Phone: 202-463-6830. Business E-Mail: jo_cooper@tma.toyota.com.

COOPER, JUDITH KASE, retired theater educator, playwright; b. Wilmington, Del., Dec. 13, 1932; d. Charles Robert and Elizabeth Edna (Baker) Kase; stepchildren: James, Elizabeth, John, Katherine, Ann, Patty, Doreen, Jeff. BA, U. Del., 1955; MA, Case Western Res. U., 1956. Tchr., dir. children's theatre Agnes Scott Coll., 1956, U. Tenn., 1957, U. Md., Germany, 1958-60, Denver Civic Theatre, Denver U., Kent Sch., 1960-61; dir. children's theatre U. N.H., Durham, 1962-69; dir. theatre resources for youth Somersworth, NH, 1966-69; assoc. prof. theatre U. South Fla., Tampa, 1969-74, assoc. prof. edn., 1975-83, prof., 1984—99, artistic dir. ednl. theatre, 1976—99, ret., 1999. Project dir. Hillsborough County Artists-in-Schs. Evaluation and Inservice Project, 1980—82; dir. Internat. Ctr. for Studies in Theatre Edn.; mem. Nat. Theatre Conf., Coll. Fellows Am. Theatre. Author: The Creative Drama Book: Three Approaches, other books; editor: Creative Drama in a Developmental Context; Children's Theatre, Creative Drama and Learning, Drama as a Meaning Maker, Introduction to Drama Teacher Resource Guide, Interconnecting Pathways to Human Experience, Teaching the Arts Across the Disciplines; contbr. articles to profl. jours.; pub. (plays) Snow White and The Seven Dwarfs, 1960, The Emperor's New Clothes, 1966, Southern Fried Cracker Tales, 1995. Bd. dirs. Fla. Alliance for Arts Edn., sec., 1976-77, vice-chmn., 1979-82, chmn., 1982-84; chmn. Wingspread Conf. on Theatre Edn., 1977; drama adjudicator Nat. Arts Festival, Ministry of Edn., Bahamas, 1975, 76, 79, 80; regional chmn. Alliance for Arts Edn., chmn. nat. adv. coun., mem. edn. adv. com., 1986—; trustee Children's Theatre Found.; bd. dirs. Coll. Fellows Am. Theatre of J.F. Kennedy Ctr. for Performing Arts, 1991-93, Fla. Assoc. Theatre Ed., exec. dir. 1995-99, Coll. Bus., 1993—; cons. S.E. Ctr. for Edn. in Theatre, 1995, Fla. Dept. Edn., 1994-96; cons. theatre edn. and prodn.; steering com. Arts for a Complete Edn., 1991-92; mem. curriculum writing com. Fla. Dept. Edn., 1994-96; active St. Marks Episcopal Parish, Tampa. Recipient Disting. Book of Yr. award, 1989, Arts Recognition award, Arts Coun. Hillsborough County, 1995. Mem. Children's Theatre Assn. Am. (pres.-elect 1975-77, pres. 1977-79, chmn. symposia 1981-85, spl. recognition citation 1984), Am. Theatre Assn. (chief divsn. pres.'s coordinating coun. 1977-78, commn. on theatre edn. 1982—, elected), Am. Alliance for Theatre and Edn. (dir. and project dir. theatre literacy collaborative study Internat. Ctr. for Studies in Theatre Edn., Presdl. award 1992), Speech Comm. Assn. (membership dir. 1961), Southeastern Theatre Confs. (Sara Spencer award 1980), Fla. Theatre Confs. (Disting. Career award), Nat. Theatre Conf., Internat. Assn. Theatres for Children and Youth, Internat. Amateur Theatre Assn. (N.Am. bd. dirs.), Fla. Assn. for Theater Edn. (Theatre Edn. of Yr. award 1986, exec. dir. 1994-99), Arts Coun. Hillsborough County (Arts Recognition award), Children's Theatre Found. Am. (trustee 1977-), Tampa Mus., Coterie Club. Republican. Episcopalian.

COOPER, KAREN RENÉ, health facility administrator, nursing administrator; b. Pleasanton, Calif., Oct. 15, 1957; d. Homer L. and Rosa B. (Upton) C.; m. Tommy Joe McCarty, Nov. 1, 1981. BSN, U. Ala., Birmingham, 1980. Cert. in profl. healthcare quality; healthcare cert. Bd. Nat. Commn. Certifying Agencies; cert. in profl. utilization rev.; cert. Interqual Nat. Registry; cert. chemotherapy, rehab. nurse, tissue therapy. Internship in SICU/MICU Cedars of Lebanon Hosp., Miami, Fla., 1980; mem. head injury/CVA and chronic pain team Spain Rehab. Ctr. U. Ala. Hosps., Birmingham, 1980-82, rheumatology charge nurse Spain Rehab. Ctr., 1982-88, staff nurse, 1988-90, coord. utilization rev./quality assurance med. care rev., 1990-91, coord. quality improvement med. care rev., 1991-93, sr. nurse coord. med. care rev., 1993, interim dir. med. care rev., 1993-94, sr. coord. dept. quality resources, 1994-2000; quality improvement coord. Dept. Joint Commn./ Regulatory Affairs, 2000—04, Dept. of Quality Resources, 2004—05; quality improvement coord. dept. quality U. Health Sys., Dept. Quality, Birmingham, 2005—06; dir. quality/risk mgmt. Physicians Carraway Med. Ctr., Birmingham, 2006—. Mem. Com. for Quality Improvement U. Ala. Birmingham Hosps., mem. Discharge Planning Com., Emergency Svcs. Quality Improvement, 1991-93, Key 100 Com., Med./Dental Staff Task Force, Mobile Med. ICU Quality Com. APACHE Study, 1990-92, Neurology Quality Com., 1990-92, Nursing Stds. Com., 1982-85, Nursing Task Force Com., 1984-88, Resuscitation Com., 1990-94, 98--, Skin Care/Tissue Therapy Com., 1986-89, Surg. Quality Improvement Com., 1991-93; mem. Arthritis Newsletter Com. U. Ala. Birmingham Multi-Purpose Arthritis Ctr., 1983-89; active Value Improvement Project of Birmingham Hosp. Network; participant, presenter numerous confs. and workshops in field. Contbr. articles to Arthritis Today and Arthritis Newsletter of U. Ala. Birmingham Multi-Purpose Arthritis Ctr., 1983-90. Pres. Coalnugget Ala. Mining Mus., 1987-89, chair literacy daycamp, 1990-92; participant Ala. State Fair Family Craft Divsn., 1975-94; co-chair AHPA Nat. Nursing Coun., 1986-88; vol. Children's Hosp., Dixie Wheelchair Assn. Regional Wheelchair Games, Goodwill Industries Doll Sale, Caring and Sharing Drive; troop leader Cahaba Coun. Girl Scouts Am., 1982—, POGO advisor, 1985-93, advisor outdoor interest group, 1995-98, mem. program operating unit, 1984-93, coun. trainer, 1984—, cons. svc. area events/programs, 1984-92, bd. dir., 1992-94, svc. area mgr. Upper 78 West, 1995-98, assn. chair, 1991-92, 2002-04, camp nurse, 1992—, mem. nominating com., 1993-95, facilities com., 1992-94, chair long-range property planning com., 1993, del. to nat. coun., 1993-99, life mem., 1993, mem. World of People Interest Group, 1997-98; mem. Ala. Assn. Healthcare Quality, Am. Juvenile Arthritis Orgn., 1982-88, Arthritis Found., 1982-90, liaison ACT Club support group, 1984-86; mem. UHC: Quality and Risk Mgmt. Com., 1993-2001, United Way/Benevolent Fund com. U. Ala. Birmingham Hosps., 1990, 2000-01; chair Honor the Children NA Festival, 2001—, Williamsburg Farm Fall NA Festival, 2003—, Blackwater Creek AI Fest., 2003—; coord. Hawks in Wind Family Clothing and Food Pantry, 1998—; bd. dirs. Am. Indian Scouting Assn., 2005—; bd. dirs. Walk of Faith Ministry, bd. sec., 2003—. Recipient Thanks award Girl Scouts Am. Cahaba Coun., 1989, Thanks II badge, 2005, Grey Wolf award Am. Indian Scouting Assn., 2004; fellow Girl Scouts U.S.A., 1976. Mem. NAFE, Nat. Assn. Healthcare Quality, U. Ala. Birmingham Alumni Assn. Avocations: painting, poetry, crafts. Home: 30 Scurlock Rd Dora AL 35062-4221 Office: Physicians Carraway Med Ctr 1600 Carraway Blvd Birmingham AL 35234 Home Phone: 205-648-8575. Business E-Mail: cooperk@carraway.com.

COOPER, KATHLEEN BELL, dean, former federal agency administrator; b. Dallas, Feb. 3, 1945; d. Patrick Joseph and Ferne Elizabeth (McDougle) Bell; m. Ronald James Cooper, Feb. 6, 1965; children: Michael, Christopher. BA in Math. with honors, U. Tex., Arlington, 1970, MA in Econs, 1971; PhD in Econs, U. Colo., 1980. Research asst. econs. dept. U. Tex., Arlington, 1970-71; corp. economist United Banks of Colo., Denver, 1971-79, chief economist, 1980-81; v.p., sr. fin. economist Security Pacific Nat. Bank, Los Angeles, 1981-83, 1st v.p., sr. economist, 1983-85, sr. v.p., economist, 1985-86, sr. v.p., chief economist, 1986-87, exec. v.p., chief economist, 1988-90; chief economist Exxon Corp., Irving, Tex., 1990-99, chief economist, mgr. econs. & energy divsn. corp. planning, 1999-2001; under sec. for econ. affairs & statistics adminstrn. US Dept. Commerce, Washington, 2001—05; dean Coll. Bus. Adminstrn. U. N. Tex., Denton, 2005—. Bd. dirs. The Williams Companies, Inc., 2006—. Trustee Scripps Coll., 1987-2001, Com. for Econ. Devel.1993-2001; mem. Coun. on Fgn. Rels., Internat. Women's Forum. Mem. Nat. Assn. Bus. Economists (past pres. Denver and L.A. chpts.; bd. dirs. 1975-78, pres. 1985-86), Nat. Bur. Econ. Rsch. (bd. dirs. 1987-2001, 05-, exec. com. 1999-2001, 06-), Am. Bankers Assn. (econ. adv. com. 1979-81, 86-90, chmn. 1989-90), U.S. Assn. Energy Econs. (pres. 1996), Am. Econ. Assn., Conf. Bus. Economists (tech. cons. to bus. coun. 1993-94).

COOPER, KEN ERROL, retired management educator; b. Bryan, Ohio, Mar. 10, 1939; s. George Wayne and Agnes Anibel (Fisher) C.; m. Karen Cremean, June 17, 1961; children: Kristin, Andrew. BS, Bowling Green State U., 1961; MBA, Miami U., Oxford, Ohio, 1962; PhD, U. Minn., 1984. Chartered fin. cons. Instr. Miami U., 1962-63; lectr. U. Minn., 1965-67, 84-86; group v.p. Land O'Lakes, Inc., Mpls., 1967-82; v.p. fin. and adminstrn. Hamline U., 1982-84; dean Coll. Bus., Ohio No. U., Ada, 1986-90, prof., 1990-2000; prof., post chair for ethics and professions Am. Coll., Bryn Mawr, Pa., 1994-95, ret., 1995; lectr. Ohio No. U., 2003—; now lectr. in philosophy. Vis. prof. (on leave) Coll. of St. Thomas, St. Paul, 1981-82; vis. prof. mgmt. U. San Diego, 2001-02, U. Evansville, 2002-03, Appalachian State U. 2006, We. New Eng. Coll., 2006—, Ashland U., 2007—. Trustee Westmar Coll., 1980-86; bd. dirs., sec.-treas. Acad. Mgmt., 1989-95; mem. Iowa Supreme Ct. Adv. Coun., 1972-75, North Ctrl. Devel. Found. Republican. Methodist. Office: Ohio No U Coll Bus Adminstrn Ada OH 45810

COOPER, KEVIN R., materials scientist; BS in Metals and Materials Engring., U. BC, 1992; PhD, U. Va., Charlottesville, 2001. Rsch. scientist Luna Innovations, Inc., Charlottesville, Va., 2001—04; prin. scientist Scribner Assocs., Inc., Southern Pines, NC, 2004—. Treas. nat. capitol sect. The Electrochem. Soc., Washington, 2002—03. Author: (technical, non-fiction) Experimental Methods and Data Analyses for Polymer Electrolyte Fuel Cells, articles in sci. jours. Recipient scholarship, U. BC, 1989, Charles A. and Jane C. Banks Found., 1989, Cy and Emerald Keyes scholarship in Metals and Materials Engring., 1990—91, scholarship, ISS Found., 1991, Thomas Beeching Scholarship Found., 1991, R. Randalf Bruce scholarship, 1991, award in Materials Engring., Assn. Profl. Engrs. and Geoscientists, Province of B.C., 1992, Student Travel award, Internat. Ion Chromatography Assn., 1998; fellow Tech. Ctr. Fellowship, Mobil Corp., 1997. Mem.: Nat. Assn. Corrosion Engrs. (Student Rschr. award 1994), The Electrochem. Soc. (Corrosion Divsn. Morris Cohen Grad. Student award 2002). Achievements include patents pending for Fiber Optic Strain Sensor for Asphalt. Office: Scribner Assocs Inc 150 E Connecticut Ave Southern Pines NC 28387 Office Phone: 910-695-8884.

COOPER, L.E., JR., banker, lawyer, counselor; b. Roanoke, Ala.; s. Leon Earl Sr. and Flora Evelyn (Bonner) C.; BS, U. Ala., 1965, JD, 1967; MBA, Harvard U., 1973. Bar: Ala. 1967; U.S. Tax Ct. 1993, U.S. Ct. Appeals (2nd and fed. cirs.) 1993, U.S. Supreme Ct. 1993; Patent atty. NASA, 1967; with Blyth Eastman Dillon & Co., Inc., N.Y.C., 1973-80, 80-; sr. v.p. Dean Witter Reynolds, Inc., N.Y.C., 1980-83, 83-; mng. dir.; counselor various govts. US, Eng., Japan, China, Saudi Arabia, 1984-; adv. Reagan, Bush 41 and Bush 43 administrns. of congress, fed res., and US Treas., UK Thacher, Maj. Blair, Brown Govts.; author: The Bush Family, China's U.S. Pres's., India's U.S. Pres's Capt. JAGC USAF, 1968-71. Mem. Jasons, Omicron Delta Kappa, Kappa Alpha. Office: 1140 Post Rd Fairfield CT 06824 Personal E-mail: kcofin2@aol.com.

COOPER, LEON N, physicist, researcher; b. NYC, Feb. 28, 1930; s. Irving and Anna (Zola) Cooper; m. Kay Anne Allard, May 18, 1969; children: Kathleen Ann, Coralie Lauren. AB, Columbia U., 1951, AM, 1953, PhD, 1954, DSc (hon.), 1973, U. Sussex, Eng., 1973, U. Ill., 1974, Brown U., 1974, Gustavus Adolphus Coll., 1975, Ohio State U., 1976, U. Pierre et Marie Curie, Paris, 1977. NSF postdoctoral fellow, mem. Inst. for Advanced Study, 1954—55; rsch. assoc. U. Ill., 1955—57; asst. prof. Ohio State U., 1957—58; assoc. prof. Brown U., Providence, 1958—62, prof., 1962—66, Henry Ledyard Goddard U. prof., 1966—74, Thomas J. Watson Sr. prof. sci., 1974—; dir. brain sci. program Inst. for Brain and Neural Sys., Providence, 1978—91; dir. Inst. for Brain and Neural Systems Brown U., Providence, 1991—. Spkr. in field; vis. prof. various univs. and summer schs.; cons. indsl., ednl. orgns.; sponsor Fedn. Am Scientists; mem. Def. Sci. Bd., 1989—93; assoc. Neuroscience Rsch. Program. Author: Introduction to the Meaning and Structure of Physics, 1968, Structure and Meaning, 1992, How We Learn, How We Remember: Toward an Understanding of Brain and Neural Systems, 1995, Memories and Memory: A Physicist's Approach to the Brain, 2000, Theory of Cortical Plasticity, 2004; contbr. articles to profl. jours. Recipient Nobel prize (with J. Bardeen and J.R. Schrieffer), 1972, award of Excellence, Grad. Faculties Alumni of Columbia U., 1974, Descartes medal, Acad. de Paris, U. Rene Descartes, 1976, John Jay award, Columbia Coll., 1985, award for Disting. Achievement, Columbia U., 1990, Alexander Hamilton award, Columbia Coll., 1995; fellow Alfred P. Sloan Found. rsch., 1959—66, John Simon Guggeinheim Meml., 1965—66. Fellow: AAAS, Am. Acad. Arts and Scis., Am. Phys. Soc.; mem.: NAS (Comstock prize with J.R. Schrieffer 1968), Internat. Neural Network Soc., Soc. Neurosci., Am. Philos. Soc., Sigma Xi, Phi Beta Kappa. Office: Dept Physics and Neurosci Brown U Box 1843 Providence RI 02912-1843 E-mail: leon_cooper@brown.edu.

COOPER, LYNN DALE, retired minister, retired navy chaplain; b. Aberdeen, Wash., Aug. 11, 1932; s. Lindsay Monroe and Mattie Ann (Cattron) Cooper; m. Doris Marlene Aydelott, June 2, 1956; children: Kevin Dale, Kathy Cooper O'Briant, Karen Cooper Holton. Student, Gray's Harbor Coll., 1950—51; BTh, Northwest Christian Coll., 1955; MDiv, Phillips U., 1961, D Ministry, 1977. Ordained to ministry Christian Ch., 1954. Commd lt. (j.g.) USN, 1965, advanced through grades to comdr., 1988, ret., 1988; assoc. pastor First Christian Ch., Olympia, Wash., 1955-57, min. Aline, Okla., 1957-61, Sumner, Wash., 1961-66; chaplain U.S. Navy, 1966-88; min. Cen. Christian Ch., Prosser, Wash., 1988-97. Bd. dirs. Jubilee Ministries, Prosser, Wash., 1988-96. Recipient many Navy and Marine Corps awards and medals; decorated Bronze Star medal. Mem. Mil. Chaplains Assn. U.S.A. (life), Disciples of Christ Hist. Soc. (life), Navy League of U.S. (life), Mil. Officers Assn. (life), Kiwanis (past pres. Prosser, Wash. chpt.), De Molay (past master councillor 1950—). Avocations: hiking, snowshoeing, kayaking. Home: 1818 Benson Ave Prosser WA 99350-1547

COOPER, MARC-ANTONIE, finance educator; s. LaVerne Cooper. B of Bus. Adminstrn., Davenport U., Dearborn, Mich., 1999; MBA, Keller Grad. Sch. Mgmt., Decatur, Ga., 2003, MPA, 2005. Gang crimes analyst Detroit Police Dept., 1994—99; dir. programming Cmtys. in Schs. Detroit, 1999—2001. Recipient Life Saving Valor medal, Detroit Police Dept., 1998, Medallon award, Bank of Am. Corp., 2004. Mem.: Nat. Assn. Black MBA's (assoc.), Phi Mu Alpha Sinfonia Profl. Music Frat. (assoc.), Kappa Alpha Psi Frat., Inc. (assoc.; vice-polemarch 2006, Achievement award 2006). Democrat-Npl. Nondenominational. Office: City Atlanta 23 Claire Dr Atlanta GA 30315 Home Phone: 770-879-1754; Office Phone: 404-622-7681. Office Fax: 404-622-0164. Personal E-mail: marcantcoop@bellsouth.net. Business E-Mail: macooper@atlantaga.gov.

COOPER, MARY LITTLE, judge; b. Fond du Lac, Wis., Aug. 13, 1946; AB in Polit. Sci. cum laude, Bryn Mawr Coll,, 1968; JD, Villanova U., 1972; LLD (hon.), Georgian Ct. Coll., 1987. Bar. N.J. 1972. Assoc. McCarter & English, Newark, 1972-80, ptnr., 1980-84; commr. N.J. Dept. Banking, Trenton, 1984-90; assoc. gen. counsel Prudential Property &

Casualty Ins. Co., Holmdel, NJ, 1991-92; judge U.S. Dist. Ct. N.J., 1992—. Chmn. bd. Pinelands Devel. Credt Bank. Bd. trustees Exec. Commn. Ethical Standards, Trenton, 1984-90, Corp. Bus. Assistance, Trenton, 1984-91, NJ Housing & Mortgage Fin. Agy., Trenton, 1984-90, NJ Cemetery Bd. Assn., 1984-90, NJ Hist. Soc., 1976-79., YMCA of Greater Newark, 1973-76; civil practice com. Supreme Ct. NJ, 1982-84, dist. ethics com., 1982-84 Fellow Am. Bar Found.; mem. John C. Lifland Am. Inn of Ct Office: US Courthouse 402 E State St Ste 5000 Trenton NJ 08608-1507 Office Phone: 609-989-2105.

COOPER, MATTHEW, journalist; b. NJ; m. Madeleine Grunwald, Nov. 29, 1997; 1 child, Benjamin. B, Columbia U., 1984. Writer & rschr. US Commn. Civil Rights, 1984—86; Washington corr. Thompson Newspapers, 1986—87; editor Washington Monthly; sr. editor US News & World Report, 1989—95, Atlanta bur. chief Ga., 1989—93, White House corr. Washington, 1993—95; sr. editor & columnist, White House Watch The New Republic, Washington, 1995—96; dep. Washington bur. chief & nat. corr. Newsweek, Washington, 1996—99; dep. Washington bur. chief Time mag., Washington, 1999—2003, White House corr., 2003—06; polit. editor Time.com, Washington, 2006—. Stand-up comedian, 1984—. Named Washington's Funniest Celebrity, DC Improv, 1998. Avocations: cooking, running, travel. Office: Time Mag 555 12th St NW Ste 600 Washington DC 20004

COOPER, MAX DALE, pediatrician, researcher; b. Hazlehurst, Miss., Aug. 31, 1933; s. Ottis Noah and Lily (Carpenter) Cooper; m. Rosalie Lazzara, Feb. 6, 1960; children: Owen Bernard, Melinda Lee Cooper Holladay, Michael Kane, Christopher Byron. Student, Holmes Jr. Coll., 1951—52, U. Miss., 1952—54; postgrad., U. Miss. Med. Sch., 1954—55; MD, Tulane U., 1957. Diplomate Am. Bd. Pediat. Intern Saginaw (Mich.) Gen. Hosp., 1957—58; resident dept. pediat. Tulane Med. Sch., New Orleans, 1958—60; house officer Hosp. for Sick Children, London, 1960, rsch. asst. dept. neurophysiology, 1961; allergy fellow dept. pediat. U. Calif. Med. Ctr., San Francisco, 1961—62; instr. Tulane Med. Sch., New Orleans, 1962—63; med. fellow specialist U. Minn., Mpls., 1963—64, instr., 1964—66; asst. prof. dept. pediat. U. Ala., Birmingham, 1967—71, assoc. prof. dept. microbiology, 1967—71, dir. rsch. Rehab. Rsch. and Tng. Ctr., 1968—70, prof. dept. microbiology, 1971—, dir. Cell. Identification Lab., 1987—90, dir. Ctr. Interdisciplinary Rsch. in Immunological Diseases, 1987—95, dir. Divsn. Devel./Clin. Immunology, 1987—, prof. dept. medicine, 1987—, investigator Howard Hughes Med. Inst., 1988—2006. Sr. scientist Comprehensive Cancer Ctr., U. Ala., Birmingham, 1971—, Multipurpose Arthritis Ctr., Birmingham, 1979—, Cystic Fibrosis Rsch. Ctr., Birmingham, 1981—; dir. Cellular Immunobiology Unit of Tumor Inst. U. Ala., Birmingham, 1976—87; vis. scientist, tumor immunology unit, dept. zoology U. Coll. London, 1973—74, Inst. D'Embryologie Nogent-Sur-Marne and Inst. Pasteur, Paris, 1984—85. Co-author: Acute Hemiplegia in Childhood, 1962, Ontogeny of Immunity, 1967, Immunologic Incompetence, 1971, Immunodeficiency in Man and Animals, 1975, numerous others; editl. bd. Immunology Today, 1986, Immunodeficiency Revs., 1987—94, Clin. Immunology and Immunopathology, 1987—90, Internat. Immunology, 1988—, assoc. editor Jour. Immunology, 1972—76, 1977—79, Arthritis and Rheumatism, 1985—90, Jour. Clin. Immunology, 1979—83, co-editor Seminars in Immunopathology, 1988—91, editor Current Topics in Microbiology and Immunology, 1981—; contbr. over 450 articles to profl. jours. Trustee Leukemia Soc. Am., 1983—88; faculty rsch. assoc. Am. Cancer Soc., 1966—71; bd. sci. advisors St. Jude Hosp., Memphis, 1981—84, 1991—, Becton-Dickinson Monoclonal Antibody Ctr., 1980—90; mem. med. adv. com. Immune Deficiency Found., 1981—99; bd. sci. counselors Nat. Cancer Inst., Bethesda, Md., 1982—86, Nat. Inst. Allergy and Infectious Diseases, 1978—82, 1990—95, Inst. Merieux, Lyons, France, 1985—90, Med. Biology Inst., La Jolla, Calif., 1986; mem. internat. sci. adv. bd. Basel (Switzerland) Inst. Immunology, 1987—91; mem NIH Immunobiology Study Sect., 1974—78. Recipient tchg. trainee award, Nat. TB Assn., 1962—63, Samuel J. Meltzer Founder's award, Soc. Exptl. Biology and Medicine, 1966, Life Scis. award, 3M, 1990, Sandoz prize for immunology, 1990, award for sci. leadership in immunology, Irvington Inst., 1999; fellow postdoctoral rsch., USPHS, 1964—66. Mem.: AAUP, AAAS, NAS, Ala. Healthcare (Hall of Fame 2002), Soc. Mucosal Immunology, Am. Acad. Arts and Scis., Inst. Medicine of NAS, Am. Acad. Scis., Clin. Immunology Soc. (Achieve. award 2004), Jefferson County Med. Assn., Ctrl. Soc. Clin. Rsch., So. Soc. Pediatric Rsch. (pres. 1975), Soc. Pediatric Rsch. (v.p. 1978), Soc. Francaise d'Immunologie (life Membre d'Honneur), Internat. Soc. Devel. and Comparative Immunology, Med. Assn. State Ala., Fedn. Am. Scientists, Am. Pediatric Soc., Am. Acad. Pediat., Am. Assn. Cancer Rsch., Am. Soc. Clin. Investigation, Am. Soc. Exptl. Pathology, Am. Assn. Microbiology (named one of Best Drs. in Am. 1992, Abbot Labs. award in Clin. and Diagnostic Immunology 2001), Am. Assn. Immunologists (chmn. membership com. 1974—77, councilor 1983—86, pres. 1988—89, Lifetime Achievement award 2000), Sigma Xi, Alpha Omega Alpha. Achievements include research in developmental immunobiology with emphasis on B cell and T cell differentiation; clinical immunology with emphasis on immunodeficiency diseases and lyhmphoid malignancies. Office: Univ Alabama Birmingham 507 SHEL 1530 3rd Ave S Birmingham AL 35294-2182 Office Phone: 205-934-3370. Business E-Mail: max.cooper@ccc.uab.edu.

COOPER, MICHAEL, journalist; Bur. chief reporter, govt., ct. appeals, Albany bur. The New York Times. Author: (articles) Tour boat victims were too frail to swim to shore, 2005. Office: New York Times 229 W 43rd St New York NY 10036

COOPER, MICHAEL ANTHONY, lawyer; b. Passaic, NJ, Mar. 29, 1936; BA, Harvard U., 1957; LLB, Harvard Law Sch., Cambridge, Mass., 1960. Bar: NY 1961, US Supreme Ct. 1969. With Sullivan and Cromwell, NYC, 1960, ptnr., 1968—2003, of counsel, 2004—. Pres. Legal Aid Soc., 1981—83; co-chair Lawyers Com. Civil Rights Under Law, 1993—95; dir. NYC Ballet, 1993—2001; bd. dirs. Vols. of Legal Svc., 1995—; chair, bd. dirs. Pro Bono Net, Inc., 2000—; trustee NYS Lawyers Assistance Trust, 2007—; mem. overseers vis. com. Harvard Law Sch., 2006—. Fellow: Am. Coll. Trial Lawyers (bd. regents 2000—, pres. 2005—06); mem.: ABA, NY County Lawyers Assn., Supreme Ct. Hist. Soc. (trustee 2004—), Am. Judicature Soc., Am. Law Inst., Fed. Bar Coun. (trustee 1994—2000), NYC Bar Assn. (pres. 1998—2000), NY State Bar Assn. Office: Sullivan & Cromwell LLP 125 Broad St New York NY 10004-2498 Home Phone: 212-717-6319; Office Phone: 212-558-3712. Business E-Mail: cooperm@sullcrom.com.

COOPER, MICHAEL JEROME, professional basketball coach and former player; b. LA, Apr. 15, 1956; Grad., U. N.Mex., 1978. Player LA Lakers, 1978—90, spl. asst. to gen. mgr. Jerry West, 1991—93, asst. coach, 1994—97, LA Sparks, 1999, head coach, 1999—2004, 2007—, NBA Devel. League Albuquerque Thunderbirds; asst. coach Denver Nuggets, 2004, interim head coach, 2004—05. Named to NBA All-Def. First Team, 1982, 84, 85, 87, 88; named NBA Defensive Player of Yr., 1987; co-recipient NBA Walter Kennedy Citizenship award, 1986., WNBA Coach of Yr. award, 2000. Achievements include being a member of five NBA Championship teams, 1980, 82, 85, 87, 88; led the Sparks to two WNBA Championships as head coach, 2001, 02. Office: LA Sparks 888 S Figueroa St Ste 2010 Los Angeles CA 90017*

COOPER, MICHAEL R., dean; b. Bklyn., Mar. 8, 1946; s. Sam and Shirley (Boris) C.; m. Ruth Mines, Sept. 7, 1969; children: Carolyn S., Jordan D. BA, Hofstra U, 1968; PhD, Ohio State U., 1972; grad. Owners and Pres. Mgmt. Program, Harvard U., 2001. Lic. psychologist, Mass.; diplomate Am. Bd. Adminstrv. Psychology. Sr. ptnr. The Hay Group, Phila., Washington, 1980-89; pres. Hay Rsch. for Mgmt., 1985-89, Hay Strategic Mgmt. Assocs., 1989—2000; chmn., CEO, bd. dirs. Opinion Rsch. Corp., Princeton, 1989—2000; prin. Cooper Interests LLC, Princeton, 1999—2001; pres., CEO Tempest Software, Inc., NYC, 2000; CEO Optimization Scis., San Francisco, 2001—02; dean Exec. Leadership Inst., Stevens Inst. Tech., Hoboken, NJ, 2002; CEO Market Optimization Tech., 2005—. Bd. dirs. Xlibis, Patient Passport, Trade Web Srs., N.Y. Pvt. Placement Exch. Trustee Mktg. Sci. Inst.; bd. dirs. European Info. Centre, Gordon Simmons Rsch. Group, Strategic Rsch. and Cons., Opinion Rsch. Corp.; mem. exec. bd. Senator Evan Bayh. Eisenhower Commn.; Consigned Full and Honorable Commn. by Pres. G. Ford, Pres. R. Reagan and Pres. G. Bush. Mem. Am. Psychol. Soc., Psychologists in Mgmt. (bd. dirs.). Office: Cooper Interests LLC 44 Coppervail Ct Princeton NJ 08540-7714 Office Phone: 609-466-9505. Business E-Mail: michael@cooper-interests.com.

COOPER, MICHAEL WAYNE, graphics designer; b. Salisbury, Md., Sept. 23, 1964; s. Jackie Samuel and Patricia Ann Cooper. BFA, Md. Inst. Coll. Art, Balt., 1982—86; MFA, Am. U., DC, 1987—89. Sr. graphic designer Salisbury U., Md., 1999—. Mem.: Intertel, Mensa, Internat. Soc. Philos. Enquiry (assoc.). Avocations: gardening, cooking, reading, exercise, travel. Home Phone: 410-749-4123.

COOPER, N. LEE, lawyer; m. Joy Clark; children: Clark, Catherine. BS, U. Ala., 1963, LLB, 1964. Pvt. practice, Birmingham, Ala., 1966—; founder Maynard, Cooper & Gale, P.C., Birmingham. Vice chair U.S. Congl. Commn. on Structural Alternatives for the Fed. Cts. of Appeals; dir. Lawyers Com. for Civil Rights. Articles and Notes editor Ala. Law Rev., 1962-64. Nat. bd. dirs. U. Ala.; trustee Ala. Law Sch. Found.; bd. overseers Rand Inst. for Civil Jusice. 1st lt. U.S. Army, 1964-66, capt. USAR. Fellow Am. Bar Found.; mem. ABA (chair, litig. sect. 1985-86, sec. litig. sect. 1976-78, Birmingham bar del. to ho. of deps. 1979-80, Ala. del. to ho. of dels. 1980-89, mem. drafting com. on model rules of profl. conduct 1982-84, mem. commn. on professionalism 1985-87, chair select com. on ho. of dels. 1989-90, chair ho. of dels. 1990-92, pres.-elect 1995-96, pres. 1996-97, chair Katrina task force 2005-06), Am. Judicature Soc. (dir.), Am. Bar Endowment (dir.), Am. Law Inst. (coun., advisor project on restatement of law governing lawyers), Ala. Bar Assn. (pres. young lawyers sect. 1974-75, Merit award 1976), Birmingham Bar Assn. (sec.-treas. 1972). Office: AmSouth Harbert Plz 1901 6th Ave N Ste 2400 Birmingham AL 35203-4604 Office Phone: 205-254-1000.

COOPER, NANCY E., computer software company executive; b. 1954; With IBM, 1976—98, dir. fin. mgmt. sys., pricing and fin. planning, 1982—92, CFO global industries divsn., asst. corp. controller, controller, treas.; ptnr. Gen. Atlantic Ptnrs., 1998; CFO Pitney Bowes Credit Corp., 1998—2000, Reciprocal, Inc., 2000—01; sr. v.p., CFO IMS Health Inc., 2001—06; exec. v.p., CFO CA, 2006—. Office: CA One CA Plz Islandia NY 11749

COOPER, NANNIE COLES, education educator, consultant; b. Washington, Oct. 25, 1930; d. Harry Willie and Lucy Jackson Coles; m. Clement Theodore Cooper; children: Patricia, Karen, Stephanie, Bridgette, Stacy. BS, D.C. Tchrs. Coll., 1964; M in Art of Tchg., Trinity Coll., Washington, 1973. Cert. nat. tchrs. exam. Elem. sch. tchr. D.C. Pub. Schs., 1964—77; reading and SAT preparation specialist Cromwell Acad., Washington, 1978—82; adj. prof. U. D.C., 1984—87; magnet sch. substitute tchr. Montgomery County (Md.) Pub. Schs., 1988—96; adj. prof. reading Am. English Lang. Program Montgomery Coll., Takoma Park, Md., 1986—2002; cons. prescriptive and diagnostic testing Washington, 2002—. Curriculum developer D.C. Pub. Schs., 1980—84, instr. SAT rev., 1984—86; instr. SAT preparation U. D.C., 1984—87; tutor writing and reading skills Montgomery Coll. Takoma Park campus, 2005—. Vol. Ward 4 Dem. race, Washington, 1996, Dem. Women, Washington, 1998—99; mem. choir Trinity Episcopal Ch., 1984—88. Named Outstanding Parent, Parent Tchrs. of Parochial Schs., Washington, 1985—87, Reading is Fundamental honoree, 1986. Mem.: Alpha Wives of D.C., Alpha Kappa Alpha. Avocations: reading, travel, writing. Home: 1220 East West Hwy Apt 821 Silver Spring MD 20910 Personal E-mail: ncooper760@aol.com.

COOPER, NORTON J. (SKY), liquor, wine and food company executive; b. Phila., Aug. 16, 1931; s. Maurice J. and Elsie (Goldstein) C.; m. Kim Muller, July 7, 2001; children from previous marriage: John Amos, Rob. BA, Cornell U., 1953. With Charles Jacquin et Cie Inc., Phila., 1955—, pres., CEO, prin. owner, 1979—, Doumen Canton Liquer Co. Ltd., Guandong, China, St. Dalfour et Cie, Marmande, France; pres. Pravda Vodka Factory, Bielsko-Biala, Poland. Author: off-Broadway prodn. Ballad of Jazz Street, 1959. Served to 1st lt. AUS, 1953-55. Decorated Ordre de Chevalier de Provence. Mem. Confrerie des Chevaliers du Tastevin. Business E-Mail: ncooper@jacquins.com.

COOPER, PAUL, retired mechanical engineer, director, researcher; b. Mt. Holly, NJ, May 21, 1934; s. Frederick and Katherine Lena (Sixt) C.; m. Therese Adams, Apr. 11, 1959; children: Margaret Mary, Gregory, Timothy Richard, Peter Dunstan. BSME, Drexel U., 1957; MSME, MIT, 1959; PhD in Engring., Case Western Res. U., 1972. Registered profl. engr., Ohio. Rsch. asst. MIT, Cambridge, 1957-59; instr. Case Western Res. U., Cleve., 1968, 72; fluids engring. specialist TRW Inc., Cleve., 1959-77; rschr., sr. staff Ingersoll-Rand Rsch., Inc., Princeton, NJ, 1977-85; dir. hydraulic tech. Ingersoll-Rand Co., Phillipsburg, NJ, 1986-87, dir. R & D Pump Group, 1987-92; dir. advanced tech. Ingersoll-Dresser Pump Co., Phillipsburg, NJ, 1992-99. Mem. adv. bd. Internat. Pump Symposium, Tex. A&M U., 1983-99; bd. dirs. R&D Coun. N.J., 1987-92. Co-editor: Pump Handbook, 3d edit., 2001; contbr. articles to profl. jours. Recipient George Stephenson Rsch. prize Instn. of Mech. Engrs., London, 1984. Fellow ASME (exec. com. fluids engring. divsn. 1982-87, fluid machinery design award 1992, Henry R. Worthington medal 1993, Robert Henry Thurston lectr. 1995, Fluids Engring. award 2002); mem. Soc. Petroleum Engrs., Sigma Xi, Pi Tau Sigma, Tau Beta Pi. Episcopalian. Achievements include patents relating to aircraft fuel pumps and commercial industrial pumps. Home and Office: 415 Pennington Titusville Rd Titusville NJ 08560-2012 Personal E-mail: paul.cooper@verizon.net.

COOPER, PAUL DOUGLAS, lawyer; b. Kansas City, Mo., July 22, 1941; s. W.W. and Emma Marie (Ringo) C.; m. Elsa B. Shaw, June 15, 1963 (div. 1991); children: Richard, Dean; m. Kay J. Rice, Aug. 30, 1992 (div. 2004); 1 child, Natanya BA in English, U. Mich., 1963; LLB, U. Calif., 1966. Bar: Colo. 1966, U.S. Dist. Ct. Colo. 1966, U.S. Ct. Appeals (10th cir.) 1967, U.S. Supreme Ct. 1979. Dep. dist. atty., Denver, 1969-71; asst. U.S. atty. Dist. of Colo., 1971-73; ptnr. Yegge, Hall & Evans, Denver, 1973-80; pres., dir. Cooper & Kelley PC, Denver, 1980-94, Cooper & Clough PC, Denver, 1994—. Faculty trial practice seminar Denver U. Law Sch., 1982; spl. asst. U.S. atty. Dist. of Colo., 1973-75; spl. prosecutor Mar. 1977 term, Garfield County Grand Jury; pres. Bow Mar Owners, Inc., 1976-77; mem. English adv. bd. U. Mich., 2000—. Mem. English adv. bd. Univ. Mich., 2000—. Recipient Spl. Commendation award for outstanding svc., 1972. Mem. ABA, Am. Bd. Trial Advocates, Colo. Bar Assn. (interprofl. com., bd. govs.), Denver Bar Assn. (trustee, 1st v.p. 1982-83), Colo. Med. Soc. (chmn. interprofl. com., Denver bar liaison com), Internat. Assn. Def. Counsel (exec. com. 1989-92). Republican. Home: 11571 Eliot Ct Westminster CO 80234-1665 Office: 1512 Larimer St Ste 600 Denver CO 80202-1610 Home Phone: 720-887-8066; Office Phone: 303-607-0077. Business E-Mail: pcooper@cooper-clough.com.

COOPER, PEGGY (MARY MARGARET), artist, educator, poet, composer, choreographer; b. Huntington, W.Va., Sept. 30, 1941; d. James Edwin and Lois Lucille (Sweeney) Hedger; m. Ralph Harold Gebhard, June 9, 1962 (div. July 1981); children: Stephan Marc, Timothy Michael, Peter Thomas, Christopher Todd; m. Earl Lee Cooper, Apr. 1, 1983. Student, Hamline U., St. Paul, 1960-63; BA cum laude, Drew U., Madison, NJ, 1965; MA, Pacific Oaks Coll., Pasadena, 1991; Waldorf Tchr. Cert., Antioch New Eng. Grad. Sch., 1996. Founding tchr. Creative Arts Workshop, Ill., 1968-75; artistic dir. Comedia Dance Co., 1968—84; artist-in-residence Colo. Coun. on Arts and Humanities, 1976-77; founding tchr. Holly/Lamar Sch. of the Arts, Colo., 1978-81; arts dir. Tom Sawyer, Pasadena, 1988-90; tutor Pasadena City Coll., 1984-90; founding tchr. Children's Garden, Madison , Wis., 1991—. Area coord. Joseph Chilton Pearce, So. Calif., 1986-91. Artist paintings: Goddess series, 1987 (Gallery award), Eternal Madonna, 1988; composer children's opera: singer Luminous Pearl, 2000; composer, poet: Singing the Spiral, 2001; poet, illustrator: Colors are Children of the Sun, 2002, Who Is One Year Old?, 2004, I Love, I Am, 2005, I Have a Sunrise Deep Inside, 2007; poet, illustrator, composer The Story of Mother Turtle, 2005; author, illustrator The Clay Pot, 2005, A Story of Winter, 2005, The Sunset Snails, 2005, Mother Earth and the Egg Cradles, Another Nut for Squirrel, 2006, Toto and Tute: A Story of Two House Rabbits, 2006. Audition com. Colo. Coun. on Arts and Humanities, Denver, 1978-80; vol. asst. Richards Inst. Ednl. Rsch., 1985-90; adv. bd. Chgo. Indian Village, 1972-75; gray lady ARC, 1958-70; vol. Children's Theater of Madison, 1993—, Elvhjem Mus. Art, 2000—; singer Madison Symphony Chorus, 1994—, Winds of So. Wis., 1998—; presenter Children's Mus. Peace Day, 1996-99; spkr., writer Waldorf Without Walls, 1996—; bd. dirs., singer Madison Chamber Choir, 1992—; singer, dancer Madison Early Music Festival, 2000—, Isthmus Vocal Ensemble, 2003—; mentor Oak Song Sch., Madison, Three Rivers Sch., La Cross, 2001-. Richards Inst. scholar, 1986, Pasadena Art Club scholar, 1988, Pasadena City Coll. scholar, 1988, recipient choral arts award, 1989; named Outstanding Young Woman, Colo., 1979. Democrat. Methodist. Avocations: gourmet cooking, gardening, felting, marionette craft, storytelling. Home and Office: 405 Stang St Madison WI 53704 Home Phone: 608-242-1471. Business E-Mail: elcooper@wisc.edu.

COOPER, REBECCA, art dealer; d. Frank N. Cooper and Bernice Silverstein; m. Michael J. Waldman, June 27, 1982. BA, MA, NYU; postgrad. Cert. appraiser. Owner Gallery Rebecca Cooper, Washington; pres. Rebecca Cooper Fine Art Tours, NYC, 1980—90; owner The Gallery in Sag Harbor, NY. Hon. chairperson N.Y. Women Bus. Owners Art Roundtable, 1981; lectr. Resources Coun., 1983, N.Y. Mayor's com. on interior design and furnishings, 1983; sec. bd. assocs. Am. Craft Mus., lectr. Collectors Circle; nat. patron Am. Fed. Art., Ind. Curators Inc. Patron, Mus. Modern Art; benefactor New Mus. Dirs. Forum; exhbn. mem. dirs. coun. Whitney Mus.; founder The Gallery in Sag Harbor, N.Y.; art tours, cons. Mem. Am. Appraisers Assn. (assoc.), Dame de la Chaine des Rotisseurs, Pvt. Art Dealers Assn., The Guild Hall of East Hampton, The Parish Art Mus. South Hampton, The Gallery in Sag Harbor, Women's 008 Investment Club, Nat. Arts Club, Lotos Club, Guggenheim Mus. (internat. cir.). Office Phone: 631-725-7707. Personal E-mail: rebeccacooperart@aol.com.

COOPER, REGINALD RUDYARD, orthopedic surgeon, educator; b. Elkins, W.Va., Jan. 6, 1932; s. Eston H. and Kathryn (Wyatt) C.; m. Jacqueline Smith, Aug. 22, 1954; children: Pamela Ann, Douglas Mark, Christopher Scott, Jeffrey Michael. BA with honors, W.Va. U., 1952, BS, 1953; MD, Med. Coll. Va., 1955; MS, U. Iowa, 1960. Diplomate Am. Bd. Orthopedic Surgeons (examiner 1968-70). Orthopedic surgeon U.S. Naval Hosp., Pensacola, Fla., 1960-62; assoc. in orthopedics U. Iowa Coll. Medicine, Iowa City, 1962-65, asst. prof. orthopedics, 1965-68, assoc. prof. orthopedics, 1968-71, prof. orthopedics, 1971—, chmn. orthopedics, 1973-99, prof. emeritus orthopaedics, 2003—. Rsch. fellow orthopedic surgery Johns Hopkins Hosp., Balt., 1964-65; exch. fellow to Britain for Am. Orthopedic Assn., 1969. Trustee Jour. Bone and Joint Surgeons, 1989-94, chmn. 1993-94. Trustee Nat. Easter Seals Rsch. Found., 1977-81, chmn., 1979-81. Served to lt. comdr. USN, 1960—62. Mem. Iowa, Johnson County Med. Socs., Orthopedic Rsch. Soc. (sec.-treas. 1970-73, pres. 1974-75), Am. Acad. Orthopedic Surgeons (Kappa Delta award for outstanding rsch. in orthopedics 1971), Can. Orthopedic Assn., Am. Orthopedic Assn., N.Y. Acad. Sci., Assn. Bone and Joint Surgeons, AMA, Am. Rheumatism Assn., Am. Acad. Cerebral Palsy, Am. Acad. Orthopedic Surgeons (chmn. exams. com. 1978-82, sec. 1982, 2d v.p. 1985-86, 1st v.p. 1986-87, pres. 1987-88, ortho residency rev. com. 1989-95, chmn. 1993-95). Avocations: travel, photography, anthropology, history. Home: 201 Ridgeview Ave Iowa City IA 52246-1625 Office: U Iowa Hosps & Clinics 450 Newton Rd Iowa City IA 52242

COOPER, RICHARD ALAN, lawyer; b. Hattiesburg, Miss., July 19, 1953; s. H. Douglas and Elaine (Reece) C. BA, BS, U. Ark., Little Rock, 1976; JD, Washington U., St. Louis, 1979. Bar: Mo. 1979, Ill. 1980, U.S. Dist. Ct. (ea. dist.) Mo. 1980, U.S. Dist. Ct. (so. dist.) Ill. 1988. Law clk. U.S. Dist. Ct., St. Louis, 1979-80; assoc. William R. Gartenberg, St. Louis, 1980-81, Davis, Reid, Murphy, Tobben & Cooper, St. Louis, 1983-87, ptnr., 1987-88, Law Office Terry Sharp, P.C., 1988-89; pvt. practice, 1989-90; ptnr. Danis & Boyce, 1990—93, Danis, Cooper, Cavanagh & Hartweger, LC, 1994—98; CFO MedCard Am., Inc., 1997-99; pvt. practice, 1999—. Liaison to Washington U. Sch. Law, Mo. Assn. Trial Attys., St. Louis, 1983-85; presenter in field. Bus. mgr. Urban Law Jour., 1978-79; editor Bankruptcy Law Reporter, 1983-88, co-mgr., editor, 1984-88; author: supplement to Missouri Desk Book Civil Procedure, 2000, 04; co-author numerous seminars; contbg. author: Missouri CLE Deskbook Civil Procedure on Rule 76, Executions; spkr. in field Recipient Milton F. Napier trial award Lawyers Assn. St. Louis, 1979, Outstanding Sr. Bus. Major award Wall St. Jour., 1976. Mem. Mo. Bar Assn., Boulder Yacht Club (commodore 1998-99), Commonwealth Yacht Club. Avocation: sailing. Office: Law Offices Richard Alan Cooper 2379 Cedar Dale Ct Maryland Heights MO 63043 Home Phone: 314-412-0261; Office Phone: 314-579-2422. Business E-Mail: richard@richardalancooperattorney.com.

COOPER, RICHARD ALAN, health policy consultant; b. Milw., Sept. 23, 1936; s. Peter and Annabelle (Schlomovitz) C.; m. Jaclyn Koppel, June 22, 1958 (dec.); children: Stephanie, Jonathan BS, U. Wis., 1958; MD, Washington U., St. Louis, 1961. Intern Harvard U. med. svcs. Boston City Hosp., 1961-63, resident in medicine, 1965-66, fellow in hematology Thorndike Meml. Lab., 1966-69; asst. prof. medicine Harvard U. Med. Sch., 1969-71; chief hematology divsn. Thorndike Meml. Lab. and Harvard Med. Svcs., Boston City Hosp., 1969-71; prof. medicine, dir. Cancer Ctr., chief hematology-oncology sect. U. Pa., Phila., 1971-85; prof. medicine, exec. v.p., dean Med. Coll. Wis., Milw., 1985-94, dir. health policy inst., 1992—2005; prof. medicine, sr. fellow Leonard Davis Inst. Health Econs., U. Pa., Phila., 2005—. Mem. editl. bd. Blood, 1979-84, Lipid Research, 1983-84. Served with USPHS, 1963-65. NIH grantee. Mem. Am. Soc. Hematology, Am. Fedn. Clin. Rsch., Am. Soc. Clin. Investigation, Assn. Am. Physicians, Am. Clin. Climatol. Assn., Phi Beta Kappa., Alpha Omega Alpha. Office: 3641 Locust Walk Philadelphia PA 19104-6218 Office Phone: 215-746-3173. Business E-Mail: cooperra@wharton.upenn.edu.

COOPER, RICHARD CASEY, lawyer; b. Tulsa, Jan. 20, 1942; s. Winston Churchill and Frances Margaret (Coppinger) Cooper; m. Ireen Lysbeth Evans, Nov. 24, 1965; children: Christopher Casey, Kimberly Ireen. BSBA, U. Tulsa, 1965, JD, 1967. Bar: Okla. 1967, U.S. Dist. Ct. (no., ea. and we. dists.) Okla. 1967, U.S. Ct. Mil. Appeals 1967, U.S. Ct. Appeals (10th cir.) 1972. Assoc. Boesche, McDermott & Eskridge, Tulsa,

1972-76, ptnr., 1977-92, mng. ptnr., 1990—2001, Cooper, McKinney & Woosley, Tulsa, 2001—. Editor-in-chief: Tulsa Law Jour., 1967. Counsel Tulsa Philharm. Orch., 1990—92; trustee Mervin Bovaird Found., Tulsa, 1991—, pres., 1995—; trustee Philbrook Mus. Art, 1997—, Tulsa Opera, 2000—06, Bacone Coll., 2001—. Lt. USNR, 1967—71, mil. judge JAGC USNR, 1970—71. Recipient Order of Curule Chair, 1967; Villard Martin scholar, U. Tulsa, 1967. Mem.: ABA, Tulsa County Bar Assn., Okla. Bar Assn., So. Hills Country Club. Republican. Avocations: fly fishing, travel. Home: 2923 E 58th St Tulsa OK 74105-7453 Office: Cooper McKinney and Woosley 401 S Boston Ave Tulsa OK 74103

COOPER, RICHARD F., lawyer; b. Jacksonville, Tex., 1951; BA, U. Ark., 1974, JD, 1977. Bar: Ark. 1977. Gen. counsel Ark. Best Corp., Ft. Smith, Ark., 1986—, sec., 1987—, v.p. risk mgmt., 1991—95, v.p. adminstrn., 1995—2004, sr. v.p. adminstrn., 2004—. Office: Ark Best Corp 3801 Old Greenwood Rd PO Box 10048 Fort Smith AR 72917-0048 Office Phone: 479-785-6130. Office Fax: 479-785-6124. E-mail: rcooper@arkbest.com.*

COOPER, RICHARD MELVYN, lawyer; b. Phila., Nov. 13, 1942; s. Arthur Martin and Sophia Phyllis (Gottlieb) C.; m. Sabina Abbe Karp, June 12, 1965 (div. 1978); children: Alexander, Stephanie; m. Judith Carole Areen, Feb. 17, 1979; children: Benjamin, Jonathan. BA summa cum laude, Haverford Coll., 1964; BA 1st class, Oxford U., 1966, MA, 1970; JD summa cum laude, Harvard U., 1969. Bar: D.C. 1970, U.S. Ct. Appeals (5th, 6th and 9th cirs.) 1988, U.S. Ct. Appeals (10th cir.) 1982, U.S. Ct. Appeals (11th cir.) 1984, U.S. Ct. Appeals (fed. cir.) 1985, U.S. Ct. Appeals (4th cir.) 1997, U.S. Supreme Ct. 1973. Law clk. to Justice William J. Brennan, Jr. U.S. Supreme Ct., Washington, 1969-70; sr. lectr. Law Devel. Ctr., Kampala, Uganda, 1970-71; assoc. Williams, Connolly & Califano, Washington, 1971-77; chief counsel FDA, Rockville, Md., 1977-79; ptnr. Williams & Connolly, LLP, Washington, 1980—; mem. exec. com. Williams & Connolly, Washington, 1983-84, 89-92. Sr. mem. Office Energy Policy and Planning, Exec. Office of Pres., Washington, 1977; adj. prof. Georgetown U. Law Ctr., Washington, 1987-92, 96; mem. Adminstrv. Conf. U.S., 1978-79, Jud. Conf. D.C., Washington, 1979; mem. Adv. Panel on Strategies for Med. Tech. Assessment, Washington, 1980-81; mem. coms. NAS, 1980-83, 87-90. Editor: Food and Drug Law, 1991; co-editor: Fundamentals of Law and Regulation, 1997; contbr. articles to profl. jours. Chief counsel credentials com. Dem. Nat. Conv., Washington and N.Y.C., 1976; adv. bd., Jelleff Boys and Girls Club, Washington, DC, 1993-2003; bd. mgrs. Haverford Coll., 1997—; Georgetown Univ. Law Ctr. Supreme Ct. Inst.; co-chmn. Finance Com., 2000-; bd. dir., Good Shepherd Ministries, Inc., Washington, DC, and member, Exec. Com., 2001-; Washington Shakespeare Co., 2004- Rhodes Trust scholar 1964; recipient FDA Award of Merit, 1979. Jewish. Office: Williams & Connolly 725 12th St NW Washington DC 20005-5901 E-mail: rcooper@wc.com.

COOPER, RICHARD NEWELL, economist, educator; b. Seattle, June 14, 1934; s. Richard Warren and Lucile (Newell) C.; m. Carolyn Jane Cahalan, June 5, 1956 (div. 1980); children: Laura Katherine, Mark Daniel; m. Ann Lorraine Hollick, Jan. 1, 1982 (div. 1994); m. Jin Chen, Oct. 13, 2000; children: William Chen, Jennifer. AB, Oberlin Coll., Ohio, 1956, LLD (hon.), 1978; MSc, London Sch. Econs., 1958; PhD, Harvard U., Cambridge, Mass., 1962; MA (hon.), Yale U., New Haven, Conn., 1966; D (hon.), U. Paris II, 2000. Sr. staff economist Coun. Econ. Advisers, 1961-63; asst. prof. econs. Yale U., 1963-65, prof., 1966-77, provost, 1972-74; dep. asst. sec. state internat. monetary affairs Dept. State, 1965-66, undersec. for econ. affairs, 1977-81; prof. econs. Harvard U., Cambridge, Mass., 1981—. Chmn. Fed. Res. Bank Boston, 1990-92; chmn. Nat. Intelligence Coun., 1995-97; bd. dirs. Inst. Internat. Econs., CNA Corp., Global Devel. Network; mem. Trilateral Commn. Author: Economics of Interdependence, 1968, Currency Devaluation in Developing Countries, 1971, Economic Policy in an Interdependent World, 1986, The International Monetary System, 1987, Economic Stabilization and Debt in Developing Countries, 1992; author: (with others) Boom, Crisis and Adjustment, 1993; author: Environmental and Resource Policies for the World Economy, 1994; editor, contbr.: A Reordered World, 1973, The International Monetary System under Flexible Exchange Rates, 1982, Can Nations Agree?, 1989, Trade Growth in Transition Economies, 1997, What the Future Holds, 2002; contbr. articles to profl. jours. Trustee Oberlin Coll., 1993-98. Named hon. prof., Beijing Normal U., 2007. Fellow Am. Acad. Arts and Scis.; mem. Am. Econ. Assn., Coun. Fgn. Rels. Office: Harvard U Weatherhead Ctr Internat Affairs 1737 Cambridge St Cambridge MA 02138-3016 Home Phone: 617-354-4933; Office Phone: 617-495-5076. Business E-Mail: rcooper@fas.harvard.edu.

COOPER, ROBERT ALFRED, electrical engineer; b. Rotherham, Yorkshire, England, Feb. 24, 1938; came to the U.S., 1983; s. Douglas Dentith and Ann (Duffy) C.; m. Carol Hawkhead, Aug. 12, 1961; children: Mark Anthony, Richard John. BS in Engring., RAF Coll., 1969; BA in Physics, Open U., 1979; postgrad., Cambridge U., 1971, postgrad., 1976. Commd. 2d lt. RAF, 1953, advanced through grades to squadron leader, 1977, ret., 1983; mgr. European programs mil. scis. group Sci. Applications Internat. Corp., McLean, Va., 1983-89, chief engr. space physics div. Washington, 1989-94; pres. Cooper Engring. Cons., Annapolis, Md., 1994-96; COO CSolutions LLC, 1996—; dir. NASA Inst. Advanced Aerospace Concepts, Allied Tech. Group, Lanham, Md., 1996—. Chmn. NASA Space Physics Tech. Panel, Washington, 1989-90; co-chmn. U.S./United Kingdom Space Assets Working Group, 1979-82. Author: Space Physics Handbook, 1991; editor: Engring. Coll. Jour., 1968. Flight safety officer CAP, Fairfax, Va., 1984—. Fellow British Interplanetary Soc.; mem. IEEE, AIAA, Inst. Elec. and Electronic Inc. Engrs. (North Am. rep. 1984—), Royal Yachting Assn., Rotary (dir. programs Dulles, Va. chpt. 1991). Roman Catholic. Avocations: yacht racing, shooting, swimming, stamp collecting/philately, astronomy. Home: 920 Yachtsman Way Annapolis MD 21403-3481

COOPER, ROBERT E., lawyer; b. Sept. 6, 1939; AB, Northwestern U., 1961; LLB, Yale U., 1964. Bar: Calif. 1965. Joined Gibson Dunn & Crutcher LLP, 1964—, now ptnr. litig. dept. LA. Bd. dir. Nat. Inst. of Transplantation Found., 1989; sec. Citizens Rsch. Found., 1980—90; mem. Calif. Law Revision Commn., 1996—99. Mem. Yale Law Jour., 1963—64, contbg. author Antitrust Advisor, 1971. Fellow: Am. Coll. Trial Lawyers; mem.: ABA, Los Angeles County Bar Assn. (vice-chmn., criminal practice and procedure com., antitrust law sect. 1984—86), US Courts for Ninth Cir., Phi Beta Kappa, Order of Coif. Office: Gibson Dunn & Crutcher LLP 333 S Grand Ave Los Angeles CA 90071-3197 Office Phone: 213-229-7179. Office Fax: 213-229-6179. Business E-Mail: rcooper@gibsondunn.com.

COOPER, ROBERT ELBERT, state supreme court justice; b. Chattanooga, Oct. 14, 1920; s. John Thurman and Susie Inez (Hollingsworth) C.; m. Catherine Pauline Kelly, Nov. 24, 1949; children: Susan Florence Cooper Hodges, Bobbie Cooper Martin, Kelly Ann Smith, Robert Elbert Jr. BA, U. N.C., 1946; JD, Vanderbilt U., 1949. Bar: Tenn. 1948. Assoc. Kolwyck and Clark, 1949-51; ptnr. Cooper and Barger, 1951-53; asst. atty. gen. 6th Jud. Ct. Tenn., 1951-53; judge 6th Jud. Circuit Tenn., 1953-60, Tenn. Ct. Appeals, 1960-70, presiding judge Eastern divsn., 1970-74; justice Tenn. Supreme Ct., 1974-90, chief justice, 1976-77, 84-85. Chmn. Tenn. Jud. Coun., 1967-90; chmn. Tenn. Code Commn., 1976-77, 84-85; mem. Tenn. Jud. Standards Commn., 1971-77. Mem. exec. bd. Cherokee coun. Boy Scouts Am., 1960-64; bd. dirs. Met. YMCA, 1956-65, St. Barnabas Nursing Home and Apts. for Aged, 1966-69. With USNR, 1941-46. Recipient Nat. Heritage award Downtown Sertoma Club, Chattanooga, 1989. Mem. Am., Tenn., Chattanooga bar assns., Conf. Chief Justices, Phi Beta Kappa, Order of Coif, Kappa Sigma, Phi Alpha Delta. Clubs: Signal Mountain Golf and Country, Masons (33 deg.), Shriners. Democrat. Presbyterian. Home and Office: 196 Woodcliff Cir Signal Mountain TN 37377-3147

COOPER, ROBERT ELBERT, JR., state attorney general; b. Chattanooga, Jan. 19, 1957; s. Robert Elbert and Catherine (Kelly) Cooper. BA in Economics magna cum laude, Princeton U., NJ, 1979; JD, Yale U. Law Sch., 1983. Reporter The Raleigh Times, NC, 1979—80; law clk. to Hon. Louis F. Oberdorfer US Dist. Ct., Washington, 1983—84; assoc. Bass, Berry & Sims, PLC, Nashville, 1984—90, ptnr., 1990—2003; legal counsel to Gov. Phil Bredesen State of Tenn., Nashville, 2003—06, atty. gen., 2006—. Adj. prof. Vanderbilt U. Law Sch., 1998—. Recipient Pres. award, Nashville Bar Assn., 1992. Mem.: ABA, Nashville Bar Assn., Tenn. Bar Assn. Office: Office of Atty Gen 500 Charlotte Ave Nashville TN 37243 Office Phone: 615-741-6474. Business E-Mail: bob.cooper@state.tn.us.

COOPER, ROGER MERLIN, information technology executive, school system administrator, federal agency administrator; b. Scottsbluff, Nebr., Feb. 25, 1943; s. Dean P. and Bette Jane (Ward) C.; children: Gregory Joseph, Lisa Jane. BS, U. Utah, 1964; MSA, George Washington U., 1970; MBA, U. So. Calif., 1970; grad., Fed. Execs. Inst. U. Utah, 1980, Harvard U. Kennedy Sch. Govt., 1984. Masters's lic. USCG. Mgr. sys. programming Larwin Group, Beverly Hills, Calif., 1973-74; chief teleprocessing sect. US CSC, Washington, 1974-76, chief info. tech. divsn., 1976-77; dir. Office Automated Sys. Devel., Macon, Ga., 1977-78; asst. dir. U.S. Office Pers. Mgmt., Washington, 1979-82; dir. med. info. resources mgmt. office VA, Washington, 1982-85; dep. asst. sec. for info. sys. US Dept. Treasury, Washington, 1985-88; dep. adminstr. Farmers Home Adminstrn., Washington, 1988-91; dep. asst. atty. gen. info. mgmt. US Dept. Justice, Washington, 1991-95; v.p. I-NET Inc., Bethesda, Md., 1995-96; dir. info. tech. Fairfax County Pub. Sch. Sys., Alexandria, Va., 1996—2002; CEO Cooper Group, Ltd., 2002—. CEO The Cooper Group, Ltd.; mem. Coun. of Prins., Nat. Comms. Systems, Coun. Sch. Networks; mem. adv. bd. FTS2000; chmn. Nat. Computer Security and Privacy Bd.; exec. bd. Inter-agy. Coun. on Info. Resources Mgmt., Fed. Micro Adv. Bd.; active Fed. Info. Ctr. Adv. Coun., Fed. Info. Rsch. Policy Coun., Fed. Data Ctrs. Dirs. Conf.; bd. dirs. Naval Liaison Office; mem. Consortium for Sch. Networking; mem. Dell Edn. Coun. Lt. USN, 1964-69; capt. USNR. Recipient Dept. Def. Joint Svc. achievment medal, 1988. Mem.: Armed Forces Comms. and Electronics Assn. (bd. dirs.). Avocations: sailing, skiing, tennis. Office Phone: 949-463-0018.

COOPER, RONALD STEPHEN, lawyer; b. Athens, Ga., Feb. 8, 1945; s. W. Roland and Frances (Wheeler) C.; m. Carolyn Joan Vardine, Sept. 17, 1966; children: Stephanie Joan, Jessica Kathleen. BA, U. Ga., 1966, JD, 1969. Bar: Ga. 1969, U.S. Ct. Appeals (5th and 8th cirs.) 1971, D.C., U.S. Dist Ct. D.C. 1972, U.S. Dist. Ct. (so. dist.) Ala. 1974, U.S. Supreme Ct. 1979, U.S. Dist. Ct. (ea. dist.) Mich. 1981, U.S. Ct. Appeals (10th cir.) 1982, U.S. Ct. Appeals (7th cir.) 1987. Law clk. to Hon. Walter P. Gewin US Ct. Appeals (5th Cir.), Tuscaloosa, Ala., 1969-70; staff atty. Office of Solicitor US Dept. Labor, Washington, 1970-72; assoc. Steptoe & Johnson LLP, Washington, 1972-76, ptnr., 1977—2006; gen. counsel US Equal Employment Opportunity Commn, Washington, 2006—. Adj. prof. Georgetown U. Law Ctr., Washington, 1981-90. Mem. ABA, Phi Beta Kappa, Phi Kappa Phi, Phi Eta Sigma; Fellow, Coll. Labor & Employment Lawyers, 1997- Democrat. Baptist. Office: US Equal Employment Opportunity Commn 1801 L St NW Rm 7001 Washington DC 20507

COOPER, ROY ASBERRY, III, state attorney general; b. Rocky Mount, NC, June 13, 1957; s. Roy Asberry Jr. and Beverly (Batchelor) Cooper; m. Kristin Bernhardt, Mar. 28, 1992; children: Hilary Godette, Natalie Rose, Claire Kristin. BA, U. NC, 1979, JD, 1982. Bar: NC 1982. Ptnr. Fields and Cooper, Rocky Mount, 1982—2001; atty. gen. State of NC, 2001—. Mem. NC Ho. Reps., 1987-91, chmn. jud. com., 1989-91; mem. NC Senate, 1991-2001, chmn. jud. com., 1991-2000. Morehead scholar U. NC, 1975-79. Democrat. Presbyterian. Office: Office of Atty General PO Box 629 Raleigh NC 27602 also: Office of Atty Gen Dept Justice PO Box 629 Raleigh NC 27602-0629 Office Phone: 919-716-6400.*

COOPER, RUSSELL JOHN, III, lawyer; b. East Orange, NJ, Mar. 2, 1942; s. Russell John and Cynthia Rhe (Runser) C.; m. Unni Irene Langaanes, June 20, 1964; children: Kirsten Elizabeth, R. John IV. AB, Amherst Coll., 1964; postgrad., U. Oslo, 1965; JD, Harvard U., 1968. Chief law clk. Supreme Jud. Ct. Mass., Boston, 1968-69; assoc. Cravath, Swaine & Moore, NYC, 1969-77; ptnr. Casey Lane & Mittendorf, NYC, 1977-82; gen. counsel video group Time Inc., NYC, 1982-84; exec. v.p., gen. counsel, sec. Young & Rubicam, Inc., NYC, 1984-94, also bd. dirs.; of counsel Hogan & Hartson, LLC, NYC, 1995-2000, 2004—; exec. v.p., gen. counsel, mng. dir. N.Am. hdqrs. Havas S.A., Paris, 2000—03. Bd. dirs. Dentsu Young & Rubicam Partnerships, NYC, Tokyo, DWD, Tokyo, Y&R Sovero, Moscow; pres. Interweave, 2003—. Editor: Cablespeech, 1983 Vestry Christ Ch., Short Hills, N.J., 1978-82, 99-02, lay min., 1980—; trustee N.J. Shakespeare Fest, 1986; chmn. Millburn-Short Hills Cable TV Com., 1986-94; prof. Salzburg Seminars, Austria, 1986; pres. Juniper Point Village Improvement Soc., Boothbay Harbor, Maine, 1997-99, Interweave, 2004—. Amherst Coll. fellow, Oslo, Norway, 1964-65 Mem. ABA (governing com., forum com. on sports and entertainment industries 1983-86), Assn. Bar City N.Y. (mem. antitrust and trade regulation com. 1982-84, corp. law depts. com. 1986-92), Am. Assn. Advt. Agys. (govt. rels. com. 1986-94), Short Hills (N.J.) Club, Boothbay Harbor Yacht Club (Maine), Harvard Club. Republican. Episcopalian.

COOPER, SHELDON MARK, immunologist, rheumatologist, educator, researcher; b. NYC, Dec. 5, 1942; s. Alex and Sylvia (Silverman) Cooper; m. Amy Diane Freedman, Nov. 23, 1966; 1 child, Jonas Eric. BS cum laude, Hobart Coll., 1963; MD, NYU, 1967. Diplomate Am. Bd. Internal Medicine, Am. Bd. Rheumatology. Intern, asst. resident in internal medicine King's County Hosp. Ctr., Bklyn., 1967-69; fellow rheumatic disease study unit NYU Med. Ctr., NYC, 1970-72; asst. prof. medicine U. So. Calif. Sch. Medicine, LA, 1974-80, assoc. prof., rsch. coord., 1980-82; assoc. prof. medicine, dir. rheumatology and clin. U. Vt. Coll. Medicine, Burlington, 1982-86, prof. medicine, dir. rheumatology and clin. immunology unit, 1986—. Mem. staff Los Angeles County U. So. Calif. Med. Ctr., 1974—82, Fletcher Allen Health Care, Burlington, 1982—. Contbr. articles to profl. jours. Mem. exec. com. Vt. chpt. Arthritis Found., Burlington, 1982—, chmn., trustee, 1990—; mem. panel gen. and plastic surgery devices FDA. Maj. USAF, 1972—73. Grantee, Nat. Cancer Inst., 1976, Nat. Inst. Arthritis Musculoskeletal and Skin Diseases, 1984—, NIH, 1984—; NIH fellow, 1971. Mem.: Union Concerned Scientists, Physicians Social Responsibility, Reticuloendothelial Soc., Am. Assn. Immunologists, Am. Fedn. Clin. Rsch., Am. Coll. Rheumatology. Democrat. Jewish. Avocations: tennis, swimming, travel, cinema. Home: Barstow Rd Shelburne VT 05482 Office: U Vt Given Bldg D301 Burlington VT 05405-0001 Office Phone: 802-656-2285. Business E-Mail: sheldon.cooper@uvm.edu.

COOPER, SIMON F., hotel executive; Pres. Delta Hotels & Resorts, Toronto, Ont., Canada, 1998, Marriott Lodging Can., Etobicoke, Canada, 1998, sr. v.p. New Eng. region, 2000; sr. v.p. Marriott Lodging Internat., Etobicoke, Canada, 1998; pres., COO Ritz-Carlton Hotel Co., Atlanta, 2001—. Mem.: Am. Hotel and Motel Assn. (fellow bd. trustees Ednl. Inst.). Office: The Ritz Carlton Hotel Co 3400 Peachtree Rd NE # 35 Atlanta GA 30326-1107 also: 4445 Willard Ave, Ste 800 Chevy Chase MD 20815*

COOPER, STEPHEN F., management consultant, corporate recovery executive; BA, Occidental Coll.; MBA, Univ. Pa., 1970. CPA. Ptnr. Touche Ross; co-founder, ptnr. Zolfo Cooper LLC, 1985—2002; chmn. Kroll Zolfo Cooper, NYC, 2002—; interim CEO Malden Mills Industries; vice chmn., chief restructuring officer Laidlaw Inc.; interim CEO Family Golf Ctr.; interim CEO, chief restructuring officer Enron Corp., Houston, 2002—; CEO Krispy Kreme Doughnuts Inc., Winston-Salem, NC, 2005—06, chief restructuring officer, 2006—; chmn. Collins & Aikman Corp., Troy, Mich., 2005—. Fellow: Am. Bankruptcy Inst.; mem.: Am. Inst. CPAs, NY State Soc. CPAs, Inst. Mgmt. Accountants, Turnaround Mgmt. Assn., Assn. Insolvency & Restructuring Advisors, Internat. Insolvency Inst. Office: Kroll Zolfo Cooper 6th Fl 900 Third Ave New York NY 10022

COOPER, STEPHEN HERBERT, retired lawyer; b. NYC, Mar. 29, 1939; s. Walter S. and Selma (Herbert) Cooper; m. Linda Cohen, Aug. 29, 1965 (dec.); m. Karen Gross, Sept. 6, 1981; 1 child, Zachary Noel. AB, Columbia U., 1960, JD cum laude, 1965. Bar: NY 1965. Assoc. Weil, Gotshal & Manges, LLC, NYC, 1966-73, ptnr., 1973—2005, ret., 2005. Lectr. Nat. Inst. Securities Regulation U. Colo., Boulder, 1985, Practicing Law Inst. 25th Annual Nat. Inst. Securities Regulation, NYC, 1993, Law Jours. Seminars, 1997—98; adj. prof. law Pace U. Law Sch., White Plains, NY, 2006—, NY Law Sch., NYC, 2003—05; bd. dirs. Hurco Cos. Inc., Advisen Ltd. Served to lt. USNR, 1960—62. Fellow: Am. Bar Found.; mem.: ABA (mem. com. fed. regulation securities 1990—2004). Office: Weil Gotshal & Manges LLC 767 5th Ave New York NY 10153-0119 Business E-Mail: stephen.cooper@weil.com.

COOPER, THOMAS ASTLEY, bank executive; b. Phila., July 19, 1936; s. Thomas Astley and Elmira (Betts) C.; m. Anita June Danenberger, Sept. 7, 1957; children: Aleta Cooper Bossert, Anita Cooper Barbato, Alane Cooper Inacker, Allison Cooper Cardona, Anne Cooper Fleming, Thomas Astley III. BA, Haverford Coll., 1957; BD, Drew U., 1960; postgrad., Pa. U., Wharton, 1972; Program for Mgmt. Devel., Harvard U., 1976. Pres. Girard Bank, Phila., 1978; vice chmn. Mellon Bank, Mellon Nat. Corp., Pitts., 1982; pres. Bank of Am., Bank Am. Corp., San Francisco, 1984; chmn. Investment Svcs. for America, Tampa, Fla., 1986-90; pres., CEO Goldome, Buffalo, 1986-90; prin. TAC Assocs., Buffalo, 1992-95; CEO Chase Fed. Bank, Miami, Fla., 1993-96; chmn. Flatiron Credit, Denver, 1997—2003. Dir. Dela. No. Cos., Buffalo, Rennaisance Reins., Bermuda, Wheeling Island Gaming, Inc.; CEO, TAC Assocs. Inc. Mem. Island Country Club, Brant Beach Yacht Club (N.J.). Office: 1291 Laurel Ct Marco Island FL 34145-2351

COOPER, THOMAS J., lawyer; b. Cambridge, Mass., Dec. 8, 1943; BA, George Washington U., 1966, MA in Internat. Affairs, 1971; JD, Tulane U., 1974. Bar: DC 1975, admitted to practice: US Ct. Appeals (DC Cir.). Minority counsel US House Adminstrn. Com., 1976—77; adminstrv. asst. to Congressman Matthew J. Rinaldo, 1979—82; exec. asst. to asst. sec. commerce Trade Adminstrn., 1983; asst. to dep. asst. sec. commerce Export Adminstrn., 1983—86; ptnr., Internat. Trade Dept. Venable LLP, Washington. Lectr. in field. Mem.: Phi Delta Phi. Office: Venable LLP 575 7th St NW Washington DC 20004 Office Phone: 202-344-4857. Office Fax: 202-344-8300. Business E-Mail: tjcooper@venable.com.

COOPER, THOMAS LOUIS, lawyer; b. Pitts., Mar. 16, 1938; s. Louis D. and Gertrude V. (Edmonds) C.; m. Leah Mary Meyers, Aug. 5, 1961; children: Marcia, Jeffrey, Daniel. BA, Dartmouth Coll., 1959; LLB, U. Pitts., 1962. Bar: Pa. 1962, U.S. Dist. Ct. (we. dist.) Pa. 1962, U.S. Ct. Appeals (3d cir.) 1962, U.S. Supreme Ct., 1962. Assoc. McArdle & McLaughlin, Pitts., 1962-69; ptnr. Gilardi & Cooper, Pitts., 1969—. Mem. civil procedural rules com. Pa. Supreme Ct., 1985-92, continuing legal edn. bd., 1992—, common pleas automation implementation team, 1990-92; adj. prof. U. Pitts. Sch. Law, 1986—. Contbr. articles to profl. jours. Fellow Am. Coll. Trial Lawyers; mem. Pa. Bar Assn. (v.p. 1989, pres.-elect 1990-91, pres. 1991-92, bd. govs., ho. of dels.), Allegheny County Bar Assn. (pres. 1984), Allegheny County Acad. Trial Lawyers (pres. 1982), Pa. Trial Lawyers Assn. (bd. govs.), Western Pa. Trial Lawyers Assn. (bd. govs.). Office: Gilardi Cooper & Lomupo 223 4th Ave Pittsburgh PA 15222-1717

COOPER, VALERIE GAIL, minister; b. Houston, May 30, 1962; d. Rev. M.C. and Mildred Chappel Cooper. BS in Pre-Medicine, Paul Quinn Coll., 1985; MDiv in Theology and Ministry, Interdenominational Theol. Ctr. Sem., 1998; D in Theology, Immauel Sch. Bible, 2000, DMin, 2005. Elder Full Gospel Bapt. Ch., 2001. Pastor Vistors Chapel African Meth. Episc. Ch., El Paso, Tex., 1998—2000; asst. pastor Morning Star Full Gospel Bapt. Ch., Houston, 2001—05; CEO, founder Faithful Anointed Victories Always with God Ministries, Houston, 2005—. Mem.: Sigma Gamma Rho. Home: 3805 Brill St Houston TX 77026 Personal E-mail: drvalcoop@yahoo.com. E-mail: favawithgod@yahoo.com.

COOPER, WILLIAM ALLEN, bank executive; b. Detroit, July 3, 1943; BS in Acctg., Wayne State U., 1967. CPA, Mich. With Touche, Ross & Co., Detroit, 1967-71; chm. Minn. Rep Party. Sr. v.p. Mich. Nat. Bank of Detroit, 1971-72; sr. v.p. Mich. Nat. Corp., 1971-78; exec. v.p. Huntington Nat. Bank, Columbus, Ohio, 1978-83, pres., 1983-84; pres., Am. Savs. & Loan Assn. of Fla., Miami, 1984-85 , also dir.; chmn. bd., chief exec. officer TCF Bank, FSB, Mpls., 1985—; chmn., TCF Fin. Corp., Mpls., from 1987, now chmn. bd., past chief exec. officer, bd. dirs. Mem. AICPA. Office: TCF Bank Office of Chmn Bd 801 Marquette Ave Minneapolis MN 55402-3475 also: Minn Rep Party 480 Ceder Street Ste 560 Castle Rock MN 55010

COOPER, WILLIAM EDWIN, former academic administrator; b. Balt., Mar. 20, 1951; s. William Daniel and Mildred (Hively) C.; m. Clarissa Holmes, July 5, 1984; children: Ashley, Courtney. AB magna cum laude, Brown U., 1973, AM, 1973; PhD, MIT, 1976. NIH postdoctoral fellow speech comm. group MIT Rsch. Lab. Electronics, Cambridge, 1976—78, rsch. affiliate, 1978—83; asst. prof. psychology Harvard U., Cambridge, 1978—81, assoc. prof. psychology, 1981—83; prof. psychology U. Iowa, Iowa City, 1983—89, assoc. dean R&D Coll. Liberal Arts, 1987—89; prof. psychology Tulane U., New Orleans, 1989—96, dean Coll. Arts and Scis., 1989—91, dean faculty liberal arts and sci., 1991—96; prof. linguistics and psychology Georgetown U., Washington, 1996—98, exec. v.p. main campus, 1996—98; pres. U. Richmond, Va., 1998—2007, pres. emeritus, 2007—. Fellow Newcomb Coll., 1989-96. Author: Speech Perception and Production: Studies in Selective Adaptation, 1979; co-author: Syntax and Speech, 1980, Fundamental Frequency in Sentence Production, 1981; editor: Cognitive Aspects of Skilled Typewriting, 1983; co-editor: Sentence Processing: Psycholinguistic Studies Presented to Merrill Garrett, 1979; contbr. articles to profl. jours. Recipient Harold Schlosberg Meml. award in psychology, 1973, Acoustical Soc. Am. Biennial award, 1986; NSF grad. fellow, 1973, John Simon Guggenheim fellow, 1983; Fulbright Sr. scholar U. Fed. de Minas Gerais, Belo Horizonte, Brazil, 1984. Mem. Phi Beta Kappa, Sigma Xi. Office: U Richmond 211 Weinstein Hall Richmond VA 23173 Office Phone: 804-289-8100. Business E-Mail: bcooper@richmond.edu.

COOPER, WILLIAM EWING, JR., retired army officer; b. Birmingham, Ala., June 19, 1929; s. William Ewing and Margaret (Tate) C.; m. Mary Jane Beers, Feb. 16, 1952; children: William Ewing III, Leslie Beers. BA in History, Citadel, 1951; MA in History, U. Miami, 1961; postgrad., Georgetown U., 1970-72, U.S. Army Command and Gen. Staff Coll., 1961-62, Armed Forces Staff Coll., 1966-67, Army War Coll., 1970-71. Commd. 2d lt. U.S. Army, 1951, advanced through grades to maj. gen., 1979, comdr. arty. group Darmstadt, Germany, 1972-73, sr. liaison officer to Brit. Army Germany, 1973-75, comdg. gen. arty. brigade Homestead AFB, Fla., 1976-79, chief of staff NORAD Peterson AFB, Colo., 1979-81, comdg. gen. 32d Army Air Def. Command Darmstadt, Fed. Republic Germany, 1981-83, dep. dir. Def. Intelligence Agy. Washington, 1983-85; ret., 1985; assoc. Burdeshaw Assocs. Ltd., Bethesda, Md., 1986-93; ret., 1993. Decorated D.S.M., Def. Superior Service medal with oak cluster, Legion of Merit, Bronze Star with V and 2 oak leaf clusters, Air medal with 3 oak leaf clusters, Army Meritorious Service medal; knights cross (Germany), Honor medal (Vietnam). Mem. Phi Alpha Theta, Phi Sigma Alpha Clubs: Fla. Citadel (v.p. 1976-78); Colo. Citadel (pres. 1980-81). Democrat. Presbyterian. Avocations: golf, skiing, hunting. Home: 5501 Dunrobin Dr Unit 3403 Sarasota FL 34238-8551 Personal E-mail: williamecooper@comcast.net.

COOPER, WILLIAM JAMES, JR., history professor; b. Kingstree, SC, Oct. 22, 1940; s. William James and Mamie (Mayes) C.; m. Patricia Holmes, Sept. 1, 1962; children: William James III, Michael Holmes. AB, Princeton U., 1962; PhD, Johns Hopkins U., 1966. Asst. prof. history La. State U., Baton Rouge, 1968-70, assoc. prof., 1970-78, prof., 1978—, dean Grad. Sch., 1982-89, Boyd prof., 1989—. Douglas Southall Freeman prof. U. Richmond, 2000. Author: The Conservative Regime: South Carolina 1877-1890, 1968, The South and the Politics of Slavery 1828-1856, 1978, Liberty and Slavery: Southern Politics to 1860, 1983, Jefferson Davis, American, 2000; co-author: The American South: A History, 1990, 3d edit., 2001; editor: Jefferson Davis, The Essential Writings, 2003, co-editor: A Master's Due: Essays in Honor of David Herbert Donald, 1985, Writing the Civil War: The Quest to Understand, 1998; editor: Social Relations in Our Southern States (Daniel Hundley), 1979, So. Biography Series, 1979-93; also articles. Served to capt. U.S. Army, 1966-68. Recipient Prize for Biography L.A. Times, 2001, Jefferson Davis award Mus. of Confederacy, 2001; sr. fellow Inst. So. History, Johns Hopkins U., 1971-72, rsch. fellow Charles Warren Ctr. Studies in Am. History, Harvard U., 1975-76, Guggenheim fellow, 1980-81, NEH fellow, 1988-89; named Disting. Rsch. Master La. State U., 1980. Fellow Soc. Am. Historians; mem. Am. Hist. Assn., Orgn. Am. Historians, So. Hist. Assn. Presbyterian. Home: 250 Amherst Ave Baton Rouge LA 70808-4603 Office: La State U Dept History Baton Rouge LA 70803-0001 Home Phone: 225-766-3871; Office Phone: 225-578-4495. Business E-Mail: wcooper@lsu.edu.

COOPER, WILLIAM S., retired state supreme court justice; b. Sept. 15, 1941; BA, U. Ky., 1963, JD with high distinction, 1970; attended, Nat. Jud. Coll., 1980, attended, 1983, attended, 1993. Law clerk Faurest, Collier, Arnett, Hensley & Coleman, 1968; ptnr. Collier, Arnett, Coleman & Cooper, 1970—79; judge Ky. 9th Judicial Cir., Div. 1, 1979—96; vice-regional judge Ky. Central Region, 1981—83, Ky. Green River Region, 1983—92, chief regional judge, 1992—96; justice Ky. Supreme Ct., Frankfort, 1996—2006; ret., 2006. Mem. Council for Higher Education Subcom. for Legal Education, 1983—85, U. Ky. Coll. of Law Visiting Com., 1986—, Ky. Evidence Rules Review Commn., 1995—2006, chair., 2000—06; chair Ky. Supreme Ct. Criminal Rules Com., 1997—2006; mem. Am. Law Inst., 2003—; CLE lecturer U. Ky., 1983—2004; lecturer U. Louisville, 1977—85, Murray State U., 1978, Northern Ky. U., 1986, Circuit Judges Jud. Coll., 1981—93, Dist. Judges Jud. Coll., 1992. Editor: Ky. Law Jour., 1969—70. Captain USAF, 1963—67. Recipient Community Service award, Knights of Columbus, 1991, Hall of Fame award, Elizabethtown-Hardin County Chamber of Commerce, 1997. Fellow: Ky. Bar Found. (life; bd. dirs. 1992—96, 2002—06); mem.: Circuit Judges Assn. (continuing education com. 1980—84, chair 1982—84), Ky. Bar Assn. (evidence rules com. 1987—92, chmn. com. jury instrns. 1991—93, mem. com. jury instrns. 1991—97, Publications com. 2007—, Ky. Bar Center award 1992, Outstanding Judge award 2004).

COOPER, WILLIAM SECORD, information science educator; b. Winnipeg, Man., Can., Nov. 7, 1935; m. Helen Clare Dunlap, July 22, 1964. BA, Principia Coll., 1956; MSc, MIT, 1959; PhD, U. Calif., Berkeley, 1964. Alexander von Humboldt scholar U. Erlangen, Germany, 1964-65; asst. prof. info. sci. U. Chgo., 1966-70; assoc. prof. info. sci. U. Calif., Berkeley, 1971-76, prof., 1976-94, prof. Grad. Sch., 1994-96, prof. emeritus, 1996—. Miller prof. Miller Inst., Berkeley, 1975-76. Hon. rsch. fellow Univ. Coll., London, 1977-78; ACM/SIGIR Triennial Rsch. award, 1994. Office: Univ Calif Sch Info Mgmt & Sys Berkeley CA 94720-0001 Office Phone: 510-642-4690. Business E-Mail: wcooper@calmail.berkeley.edu.

COOPER, WILLIAM THOMAS, natural history artist; b. Adamstown, NSW, Australia, Apr. 6, 1934; s. William and Coral (Bird) C.; m. Wendy Elizabeth Price, June 25, 1979. One-man shows include Artarmon Galleries, Sydney, 1973, 1980, City of Newcastle Art Gallery, 1973, Represented in permanent collections, Woodhall Art Found., Australian Nat. Libr., Papua New Guinea Govt., Newcastle Art Gallery, Rockhampton City Art Gallery; work represented in A Portfolio of Australian Birds, 1968, Parrots of the World, 1973, The Birds of Paradise and Bowerbirds, 1977, Australian Parrots, 1980, Kingfishers and Related Birds vol. I, 1983, vol. II, 1985, vol. III, 1987, vol. IV, 1993, vols. V & VI, 1995, Fruits of the Rainforest, 1995, The Turacos, 1997, The Cockatoos, 2001, illustrator Fierce Encounter, 1970, The Birds of Paradise, 1998, Cockatoos: A Portfolio of All Species, 2001, Fruits of the Australian Tropical Rainforest, 2004, designer (stamps), Papua, New Guinea, 1972, 1973; co-dir.:. Decorated Order of Australia, Australian Govt., 1994; recipient Gold medal Distinction, Natural History Art Acad. Natural Scis., Phila., 1992. Office: PO Box 314 Malanda 4885 Australia Fax: 07 40968 333.

COOPER, WILLIAM WAGER, economics, accounting and finance professor, dean; b. Birmingham, Ala., July 23, 1914; s. William Wager and Rae (Rossman) C.; m. Ruth Fay West, Sept. 11, 1944. AB, U. Chgo., 1938; postgrad., Columbia U., NYC, 1940—42; DSc (hon.), Ohio State U., Columbus, 1970; MA (hon.), Harvard U., Cambridge, Mass, 1976; DSc (hon.), Carnegie Mellon U., Pitts., 1982; D (hon.), U. Alicante, Spain, 1995. Asst. to comptroller TVA, 1938-40; prin. economist Bur. Budget, 1942-44; asst. prof. econs. U. Chgo., 1944-46; asst. prof. to prof. Carnegie-Mellon U., 1946-68; dean Carnegie-Mellon U. (Sch. Urban and Pub. Affairs), 1968-75, univ. prof. mgmt. sci. and pub. affairs, 1975-76, research prof. mgmt. sci. and pub. policy, 1976—; Arthur Lowes Dickinson prof. accounting Grad. Sch. Bus. Adminstrn., Harvard U., 1976-80; prof. mgmt. and acctg., mgmt. scis. and info. systems, Grad. Sch. Bus. Adminstrn. U. Tex., Austin, 1980-94; Foster Parker prof. fin. and mgmt. emeritus Grad. Sch. Bus. Adminstrn. U. Tex., Austin, 1994—; chmn. mgmt. sci. and info. systems dept. U. Tex., 1986-88. Vis. disting. internat. lectr. acctg. Am. Acctg. Assn., 1986, dir. pubs., chmn., pubs. com., exec. com., 1987-89; disting. IBM vis. prof. Aoyama Gakuin U., Tokyo, 1993. Author 28 books including; co-author (with A. Charnes): Management Models and Industrial Applications of Linear Programming; co-author: (with H. Leavitt, M.W. Shelly) New Perspectives in Organization Research; co-author: (with others) Studies in Budgeting; co-author: (with A. Charnes and R. Niehaus) Studies in Manpower Planning; co-author: (with Y. Ijiri) Eric Louis Kohler: Accounting's Man of Principles; co-author: (with A. Charnes, A. Lewin and L. Seiford) Data Envelopment Analysis: Theory, Methodology, Applications; co-author: (with A. Whinston) New Directions in Computational Economics; co-author: (with R.G. Thompson and R.M. Thrall) Extensions and New Developments in DEA: The Annals of Operations Research; co-author: (with L.M. Seiford and Kaoru Tone) Data Envelopment Analysis: A Comprehensive Text, 2000; co-author: (with L.M. Seiford and J. Zhu) Handbook of Data Envelopment Analysis, 2004; co-author: (with L.M. Seiford and Kaoru Tone) Introduction to Data Envelopment Analysis, 2005, 2nd edit., 2007; co-author: (with Piyu Yue) The Challenge of Muslim Countries: Present, Future and Past, 2008; editor: Auditing: A Jour. Practice and Theory, 1978—81; co-editor (with Y. Ijiri): Kohler's Dictionary for Accountants, 6th edit.; mem. editl. bd. Mgmt. Sci., 1954—74, Naval Rsch. Logistics Quar., 1957—74; contbr. over 500 articles to profl. jours. Co-recipient John Von Neumann theory prize, 1982; recipient award Am. Inst. Accts., 1945, Profl. Achievement citation U. Chgo. Alumni Assn., 1986, Outstanding Contbr. to Auditing award Am. Acctg. Assn., 1988, Outstanding Acctg. Educator award, 1990, Notable Contbns. to Lit. award in govtl. and non-profit acctg., 1991, Lifetime Contbns. to Mgmt. Acct. award, 2002, Gold medal award Soc. Multi-Criteria Decision Making, 2004; named to U. Tex. Coll. Bus. Adminstrn. Hall of Fame, 1990, Acctg. Hall of Fame, 1996, Internat. Operational Rsch. Hall Fame, 2006; Erskine fellow, U. Canterbury, New Zealand, 1991, fellow Inst. Ops. Rsch. and Mgmt. Sci., 2002 (Impact award, 2006). Fellow Econometric Soc., AAAS, INFORMS; mem. Inst. Mgmt. Sci. (1st pres.), Ops. Research Soc. Am. (editorial bd. 1957-68), Inst. of Operational Rsch. and Mgmt. Scis. Office: U Tex Austin Red McCombs Sch Bus 1 Univ Station 6B6500 Austin TX 78712-0212 Home: Apt 331 1034A Liberty Park Dr Austin TX 78746-6853 Business E-Mail: cooperw@mail.utexas.edu.

COOPER-CHEN, ANNE, journalism educator, researcher; b. Pitts., July 19, 1944; d. George Henry and Dorothy Louise (Pursley) Messerly; m. Charles Chin-tse Chen, July 12, 1986; stepchildren: Diana, Derek. AB, Vassar Coll., 1966; MA, U. Mich., 1969; MS, Va. Commonwealth U., 1979; PhD, U. N.C., 1984. Feature writer Daily News, V.I., 1963; writer, editor Asahi Evening News, Tokyo, 1966-68; editor, book pub. John Weatherhill, Inc., Tokyo, 1969-70; writer, columnist Sunday News, York, Pa., 1971-72; writer, editor Commonwealth mag., Richmond, Va., 1974-76; asst. prof. journalism So. Meth. U., Dallas, 1982-83, Mary Baldwin Coll., Staunton, Va., 1983-85; prof. Ohio U., Athens, 1985—. Miura Kohei prof. Chubu U., Japan, 2001. Author: Games in the Global Village, 1994, Mass Communication in Japan, 1997, Global Entertainment Media, 2005; co-author: Idols, Victims, Pioneers, 1976, contbg. author (chpt.) Global Journalism, Covering Africa, International Public Relations, Comics & Ideology; contbr. articles to profl. jours. Fulbright Sr. Rsch. scholar, Japan, 1992-93. Mem. Assn. for Edn. in Journalims and Mass Communications (various offices, disting. svc. award 2005), Intenat. Assn. Media & Comm. Rsch., Kappa Tau Alpha. Office: Ohio U Scripps Sch Journalism Scripps Hall Athens OH 45701 Home Phone: 740-594-3436; Office Phone: 740-593-2598. E-mail: acooper_chen@hotmail.com.

COOPERMAN, BARRY S., academic administrator, chemist, educator; b. NYC, Dec. 11, 1941; married, 1963; 2 children. BA, Columbia U., 1962; PhD in Chemistry, Harvard U., 1968. NATO fellow biochemistry Pasteur Inst., 1967-68; from asst. prof. to assoc. prof. dept. chemistry U. Pa., 1968-72, prof. bioorganic chemistry, 1977—, vice provost for rsch., 1982—95. Dir. French Inst., 1993-2001. Trustee Assoc. Univs., Inc., 1983—. chmn. bd., 1989-91; mem. policy governing bd. Advanced Tech. Ctr. S.E. Pa., 1984-88; bd. mgrs. Morris Arboretum, 1985-91; bd. dirs. Wistar Inst., 1987-2001; internat. sci. adv. bd. Max-Planck Inst. for Molecular Genetics, 2001—. Mem. Am. Soc. Biol. Chemists, Am. Chem. Soc. Achievements include research in mechanism of phosphoryl transfer enzymes; ribosomes; serum serine protease inhibitors; ribonucleotide reductase. Office Phone: 215-898-6330.

COOPERMAN, DANIEL, lawyer, computer software company executive; b. Perth Amboy, NJ, Nov. 27, 1950; s. Eli Louis and Dorothy (Salinger) C.; m. Linda Louise Schmidt, June 10, 1979; children: Jeffrey Eli, Justin Andrew. AB summa cum laude, Dartmouth Coll., Hanover, NH, 1972; JD, MBA, Stanford U., Calif., 1976. Bar: Calif. 1976. Cons. McKinsey & Co., San Francisco, 1976-77; atty. McCutchen, Doyle, Brown & Enersen, San Francisco, 1977-83, ptnr., 1983-97; sr. v.p., gen. counsel, sec. Oracle Corp., Redwood Shores, Calif., 1997—; sr. v.p., gen. counsel PeopleSoft Corp., 2004—. Sec., bd. dirs. Children's Discovery Mus., San Jose, Calif., 1993—; bd. advs. Cmty. Found. Santa Clara County, San Jose, 1994—. Mem. Santa Clara County Bar Assn. (chair bus. law sect. 1992-93), NASDAQ's Listing and Hearing Rev. Coun., ABA's Com. Corp. Gen. Counsel, Adv. Coun. Law, Sci. & Tech. Program Stanford Law Sch. Avocation: squash. Office: Oracle Corp 500 Oracle Pky Redwood City CA 94065-1675*

COOPERMAN, LEON G., investment company executive; b. NYC, Apr. 25, 1943; s. Harry and Martha (Rothenstein) C.; m. Toby F.; children: Wayne M., Michael S. BA, CUNY-Hunter Coll., 1964; MBA, Columbia U., 1967. Cert. fin. analyst. Quality control engr. Xerox Corp., Webster, NY, 1965-67; ptnr. Goldman, Sachs & Co., NYC, 1967-90, of counsel, 1990—; ltd. ptnr. Goldman Sachs Group, L.P., 1992—; chmn., chief exec. officer Goldman, Sachs Asset Mgmt., NYC, 1989-90, cons., chmn. profit-sharing and pension coms., 1992—; founder, chmn., CEO Omega Advisors, Inc., NYC, 1992—. Trustee United Jewish Appeal, N.J., 1980, St. Barnabas Hosp., Livingston, N.J.; bd. overseers Grad. Sch. Bus. Columbia U., bd. dirs., vice-chmn. finance and treasurer, Damon Runyon Cancer Rsch. Found.; global leadership coun. Building With Books. Mem. Fin. Analyst Fedn. (dir. 1980-), N.Y. Soc. Security Analysts (pres. 1980) Clubs: Atlantis Yacht (Monmouth Beach, N.J.). Office: Omega Advisors Inc 88 Pine St #31 New York NY 10005-1801 Office Phone: 212-495-5200. Office Fax: 212-495-5236.

COOPERMAN, SAUL, retired educational administrator; b. Newark, Dec. 18, 1934; s. Louis Frank and Lucille (Swarthberg) C.; m. Paulette Beth Koch, Aug. 17, 1958; children: Suzanne, Deborah, David. BS, Lafayette Coll., 1956; MEd, Rutgers U., 1964, EdD, 1969; DHL (hon.), Drew U., 1984. Tchr. North Plainfield H.S., NJ, 1960-64; prin. Belvidere H.S., NJ, 1964-68; rsch. asst. Rutgers U., New Brunswick, NJ, 1968-69; supt. schs. Montgomery Twp., NJ, 1969-74, City of Madison, NJ, 1974-82; commr. N.J. State Dept. Edn., Trenton, 1982-90. Pres. Educate Am., 1990—2000; chmn. edn. adv. panel New Am. Sch. Devel. Corp., 1990—97; sec., treas. New Am. Schs., 2000—05; founder, chmn. bd. dirs. Acad. for Tchg. and Leadership, 2004—. Author: How Schools Really Work: Practical Advice to Parents from an Insider; contbr. more than 60 articles to ednl. jours.; columnist (newspaper) Star Ledger, 1998—2003. Pres. 10,000 Mentors, Newark, 1996-2000. Served to rank of comdr. USNR, 1956—82. Avocations: reading, athletics, travel. Address: 181 Roundtop Rd Bernardsville NJ 07924-2106 Office Phone: 908-630-9900.

COOPER-RUSPOLI, ANNIE NATAF, psychiatrist, director; d. Victor and Arlette Nataf; m. Stephane Frank Ruspoli, June 9, 1997; 1 child, Jonathan Cooper. MD, U. Paris, 1975. Resident psychiatry Emory U. Sch. Medicine, Atlanta, 1975—78, fellow child psychiatry, 1978—79; med. dir. child and adolescent unit Ga. Regional Hosp. Atlanta, 1980—91; psychiatrist Piedmont Psychiat. Clinic, Atlanta, 1996—. Mem. Conseil Nat. de l'Ordre des Medecins, Paris, 1991—. Trustee Atlanta Internat. Sch., 1985—97, bd. dirs., 1997—2005; trustee Alliance Francaise d'Atlanta, 1992—95, Ga Casa, Atlanta, 1992—2001. Mem.: Atlanta Med. Assn., Ga. Med. Assn., Ga. Psychiat. Assn., Am. Psychiat. Assn. Independent. Office: Piedmont Psychiatric Clinic 1938 Peachtree Rd Ste 505 Atlanta GA 30309 Home Phone: 404-231-5516; Office Phone: 404-355-2914. Office Fax: 404-355-2917. Personal E-mail: acooperrus@aol.com.

COOPERSMITH, JEFFREY ALAN, real estate developer; b. NYC, Mar. 23, 1946; s. Jack J. and Anita S. (Selikoff) Coopersmith; m. Marjorie Myers, July 5, 1987; children: Jarred, Aubrey, Lorie, Julie. B in Mgmt. Engring., Rensselaer Poly. Inst., 1967; MBA, Ohio State U., 1979. Security arbitrage Arnhold and S. Bleichroeder, Inc., NYC, 1967-70; with Pfizer, Inc., NYC, 1970-72, asst. contr. Minerals, Pigments and Metals divsn.; with Distbn. Ctrs., Inc. subs. Distek, Inc., Westerville, Ohio, 1972-87, v.p., contr., 1975-77, v.p., treas., 1977-78, v.p. fin., 1978-80; exec.v.p. Distek, Inc., Westerville, 1980-83, pres., COO, 1983-87, also bd. dirs.; pres. Directel, Inc., 1981-93; pres., CEO Triplefin, Inc., 1993—2001, Core Properties LLC, Columbus, Ohio, 2002—. Mem.: JCCA Assn. (bd. dirs.), World Pres. Orgn. (bd. dirs. 2004, chmn. 2004), Columbus Jewish Found. (bd. dirs.), Columbus Jewish Fedn. (vice chmn.). Office: Core Properties LLC 1515 Lake Shore Dr #225 Columbus OH 43204

COOR, CAREN BARBARA, art educator; d. Chauncey Bryan and Cleo Barbara Coor. EdB, No. Ariz. U., Flagstaff, 1968; MA in Art and Art Edn., Ariz. State U., Tempe, 1970. Cert. Ariz. Std. Secondary Tchg. Cert. Ariz. Dept. Edn., Phoenix, 1968. Art tchr. Maryvale HS, 1968—70; mem. curriculum devel. bd. Phoenix Union HS Dist., 1968—70; art history guest lectr. Phoenix Coll., 1970—71; artist/ designer Tucson, 1973—80; graphic arts tchr. Arcadia HS, Scottsdale, Ariz., 1971—72; art tchr. Chinle HS, Ariz., 1973, 1999—; mem., sec. CUSD Fine Arts and Acad. Showcase com., Ariz., 1999—; mem. CUSD curriculum devel. bd., 2004—06; art tchr., curriculum developer, dir. fed. programs, counselor Hopi Tribe Edn. Dept., Kykotsmovi, Ariz., 1980—88; tchr., counselor, missionary Watchtower Soc., Guayaquil, Ecuador, 1987—94; comm. specialist Raychem Corp., Menlo Park, Calif., 1994—99. Mem.: NEA, Art Edn. Assn., Ariz. Edn. Assn., Ariz. Art Edn. Assn., Chinle Edn. Assn., Nat. Art Edn. Assn. Jehovah'S Witness. Avocations: reading, drawing, painting, flute, hiking. Office: PO Box 587 Chinle AZ 86503

COOR, LATTIE FINCH, university president; b. Phoenix, Sept. 26, 1936; s. Lattie F. and Elnora (Witten) C.; m. Ina Fitzhenry, Jan. 18, 1964 (div. 1988); children: William Kendall, Colin Fitzhenry, Farryl MacKenna Witten; m. Elva Wingfield, Dec. 27, 1994. AB with high honors (Phelps Dodge scholar), No. Ariz. U., 1958; MA with honors (Univ. scholar, Universal Match Found. fellow, Carnegie Corp. fellow), Washington U., St. Louis, 1960, PhD, 1964; LLD (hon.), Marlboro Coll., 1977, Am. Coll. Greece, 1982, U. Vt., 1991, No. Ariz. U., 2002. Adminstrv. asst. to Gov. Mich., 1961-62; asst. to chancellor Washington U., St. Louis, 1963-67, asst. dean Grad. Sch. Arts and Scis., 1967-69, dir. internat. studies, 1967-69, asst. prof. polit. sci., 1967-76, vice chancellor, 1969-74, univ. vice chancellor, 1974-76; pres. U. Vt., Burlington, 1976-89, Ariz. State U., Tempe, Ariz., 1990—2002, prof. pub. affairs, Ernest W. McFarland Ariz. Heritage chair in leadership and pub. policy, pres. emeritus, 2002—, chmn. leadership and pub. policy. Cons. HEW; spl. cons. to commr. U.S. Commn. on Edn., 1971-74; chmn. Commn. on Govtl. Rels., Am. Coun. on Edn., 1976-80; dir. New Eng. Bd. Higher Edn., 1976-89; co-chmn. joint com. on health policy Assn. Am. Univs. and Nat. Assn. State Univs. and Land Grant Colls., 1976-89; mem. pres. commn. NCAA, 1984-90, chmn. div. I, 1989; mem. Ariz. State Bd. Edn., 1993-98; chmn. Pacific 10 Conf., 1995-96; chmn., CEO Ctr. Future Ariz., 2002—. Trustee emeritus Am. Coll. Greece. Mem. Nat. Assn. State Univs. and Land Grant Colls. (chmn. bd. dirs. 1991-92), New Eng. Assn. Schs. and Colls. (pres. 1981-82), Am. Coun. on Edn. (bd. dirs. 1991-93, 2000-02), Kellogg Commn. on Future of State and Land-Grant Univs. Office: Ctr for Future of Ariz 541 E Van Buren Ave Ste B-5 Phoenix AZ 85004 Office Phone: 480-727-5005. Business E-Mail: Lattie.Coor@asu.edu.

COORS, JEFFREY H., technology manufacturing executive; b. Denver, Feb. 10, 1945; s. Joseph. B.Chem. Engring., Cornell U., 1967, M.Chem. Engring., 1968. With Coors Porcelain Co., 1968-70; with Adolph Coors Co., Golden, Colo., 1970-92, pres., 1985-89; chmn., chief exec. officer Coors Techs. Cos., Golden, 1989-92; pres. ACX Techs., Golden, 1992—2000; chmn., pres., CEO Graphic Packaging Corp., 2000—03; exec. chmn. bd. Graphic Packaging Internat., Inc., Golden, Colo., 2003—06.*

COORS, PETER HANSON, brewery company executive; b. Denver, Sept. 20, 1946; s. Joseph and Holly (Hanson) C.; m. Marilyn Gross, Aug. 23, 1969; children: Melissa, Christien, Carrie Ann, Ashley, Peter, David. BS in Idsl. Engring., Cornell U., 1969; MBA, U. Denver, 1970; PhD (hon.), Regis U., 1991; PhD, Wilberforce U., 1991, Johnson & Wales U., 1997. Prodn. trainee, specialist Adolph Coors Co., Golden, Colo., 1970-71, dir. fin. planning, 1971-75, asst. sec.-treas., 1974-76, dir. market research, 1975-76, v.p. self distbn., 1976-77, v.p. sales and mktg., 1977-78, sr. v.p. sales and mktg., 1978-82, div. pres. sales, mktg. and adminstrn., 1982-85, exec. v.p., 1991—93; pres. Coors Brewing Co. (formerly brewing div.), Golden, Colo., 1985—92; vice-chmn., CEO Coors Brewing Co., Golden, Colo., 1993—2002, chmn., 2002—05; vice chmn. Molson Coors Brewing Co., Golden, Colo., 2005—. Bd. dirs. U.S. Bancorp, Inc., H. J. Heinz Co., Energy Corp. of Am. Bd. dirs. Nat. Wildlife Fedn., 1978-81, Wildlife Legis. Fund, 1987—, Colo. Hosp., 2004-; hon. bd. dirs. Colo. Spl. Olympics Inc., 1978—; trustee Colo. Outward Bound Sch., 1978— , Adolph Coors Found., Pres.'s Leadership Com., U. Colo., 1978—; chmn. Nat. Commn. on the Future of Regis Coll., 1981-82, chmn. devel. com., 1983— , now trustee. Mem. Nat. Indls. Adv. Council, Opportunities Ctrs. of Am., Young Pres.' Orgn., Ducks Unlimited (nat. trustee 1979, sr. v.p., mem. mgmt. com., exec. com. 1982— , dir. Can. 1982— , pres. 1984-85, chmn. bd. 1986—) Clubs: Met. Denver Exec. (dir 1979, pres. 1981—). Office: Molson Coors Brewing Co PO Box 4030 Golden CO 80401*

COOVER, ANN E., lawyer; b. Sparta, Wis., Aug. 23, 1948; d. Orlin H. Runde and Kathleen Ann Dwyer; m. David M. Coover, July 22, 1972; 1 child, D. Marshall. BS, U. Wis., 1971; JD magna cum laude, U. Houston, 1975. Bar: Tex. 1975, U.S. Dist. Ct. (fed. dist.) 1975, U.S. Supreme Ct. 1978; bd. cert. family law Tex. Bd. Legal Specialization. Sr. law clk. to dist. judge U.S. Dist. Ct., Corpus Christi, Tex., 1976-78; ptnr. Coover & Coover, Corpus Christi, 1978—. Named one of Best Lawyers in Am., Tex. Super Lawyer, 2005—06. Mem.: State Bar Family Law Coun. Avocations: gardening, antiques, bridge. Office: Coover & Coover 921 N Chaparral St Corpus Christi TX 78401-2008 Office Phone: 361-882-2100. Business E-Mail: ann@cooverandcoover.com.

COOVER, HARRY WESLEY, manufacturing executive; b. Newark, Del., Mar. 6, 1919; s. Harry Wesley and Anna (Rohm) C.; m. Muriel Zumbach, Sept. 17, 1941; children: Harry Wesley, Stephen R., Melinda Coover Paul. BS in Chemistry (Southerland prize), Hobart Coll., Geneva, NY, 1941; MS, Cornell U., Ithaca, NY, 1942, PhD, 1944. Rsch. chemist Eastman Kodak Co., Rochester, NY, 1944-49; sr. rsch. chemist Tenn. Eastman Co., Kingsport, 1949-54, rsch. assoc., 1954-63, head polymers div., 1963-65, dir. rsch., 1965-73, v.p., 1970-73, exec. v.p., 1973-81; v.p. Eastman Kodak Co., Kingsport, 1981-84; internat. mgmt. cons. Kingsport, 1984-85; pres. New Bus. Devel. Loctite Corp., Newington, Conn., 1985-88, Mgmt. Cons., Kingsport, Tenn., 1988—. Bd. dirs. Reilly Industries Inc. Contbr. to sixty publs. in field. Named to, Nat. Inventors Hall of Fame, 2004. Mem. AAAS, Internat. Union Pure and Applied Chemistry, Am. Chem. Soc. (So. Chemist award 1960, Speaker of Yr. award N.E. Tenn. sect. 1962, Earle B. Barnes award 1985, Chem. Pioneers award 1986), Am. Inst. Chemists, Indsl. Rsch. Inst. (pres. 1981-82, medal award 1984, Holland award 1987, Achievement award 1999, Soc. Chem. Industry), Nat. Acad. Engrs. Presbyterian. Achievements include over 460 patents in field; discovery of cyanoacrylate adhesives. Office: PO Box 3866 Kingsport TN 37664-0866 Office Phone: 423-378-3733. Business E-Mail: drhw@coover.com.

COPE, JEANNETTE NAYLOR, minister; b. Corpus Christi, Tex., Feb. 9, 1956; d. Glen R. and Jeannine (Withington) N.; m. John R. Cope, May 22, 1993. BA in Psychology and Sociology, Trinity U., 1978; MDiv summa cum laude, Wesley Theol. Sem., Washington, 2007. Ordained Sacred Order of Deacons, Washington Nat. Cathedral, 2007. Asst. fin. dir. Jim Baker for Atty. Gen. Campaign, Houston, 1978; fin. dir. Rep. Party of Tex., Austin,

1979-81; regional Eagle rep. Rep. Nat. Com., Washington, 1981-83; devel. officer Nat. Endowment for the Arts, Washington, 1983-87; sr. project mgr. Internat. Skye Assocs., Washington, 1988; spl. asst. to Pres. of U.S. The White House, 1989-90, dep. asst. to Pres. of U.S., dep. dir. of presdl. pers., 1990-93; pres. J. Naylor Cope Co., Washington, 1994—2007. NEA liaison Pres.' Com. on Arts and Humanites, Washington, 1985-87; dir. Internat. Skye Advisor, Washington, 1988; bd. dirs. Bush/Quayle Alumni Assn., TransTech. Corp.; mem. Officer Pers. Mgmt.'s Task Force on Exec. and Mgmt. Devel., Washington, 1990; bd. dirs. Washington First Bank. Mem. Pres.'s Com. Arts and Humanities, 2001—; chmn. alumni admissions coun. Trinity U., Washington, 1986—87; mem. Bush Cheney Transition Team, 2001; vestrywoman St. John's Episcopal Ch., Washington, 1990—94, co-chmn. outreach com., 1991—94, chmn. search com. for 14th rector, jr. warden, 1994—97, sr. warden, 1998—2001; bd. dirs. The Compass Rose Soc. Anglican Communion, 1999—2005, exec. com., 2000—04; trustee Protestant Episcopal Cathedral Found., 2004—; asst. rector St. David's Episcopal Ch., Washington, 2007—; bd. dirs. Coop. Urban Ministry Ctr., Washington, 1987—89, Pennsylvania Ave. Devel. Corp., 1993—96, Decatur House, Washington, 1998—, exec. com., 2000—, vice-chmn., bd. dirs., 2001—03, chmn. bd. dirs., 2004—07; bd. visitors Kanuga Confs., 2001—. Scholar, Tex. Coun. of Ch. Related Colls., 1974. Mem. Am. Soc. Assn. Execs. (exec. recruiter), Tex. State Soc. (chmn. membership com. 1981), Nat. Trust for Hist. Preservation (bd. dirs. 2005—), Smithsonian Instn., Am. Film Inst., Mcpl. Art Soc. (N.Y.C.), 1925 F Street Club (chmn. mems. com.), Pres.'s Club, Columbia Country Club (Chevy Chase, Md.), Tex. Breakfast Club, Blue Key (sec. 1976-78), City Tavern Club, Chi Beta Epsilon (v.p. San Antonio coun. 1976). Republican. Episcopalian. Business E-Mail: jnc@jnaylorcopecompany.com.

COPE, JOHN R(OBERT), lawyer; b. San Angelo, Tex., May 30, 1942; s. Robert Lloyd and Meta (Young) C.; m. Jeannette L. Naylor; 1 child, Lloyd Chapman. BBA, U. Tex., Austin, 1964, JD, 1966; MTS summa cum laude, Wesley Theol. Sem., Washington, 2001; DMin, Seabury-We. Theol. Sem., Evanston, Ill., 2005. Bar: Tex. 1966, DC 1976. Ptnr. Bracewell & Giuliani Attys., Houston, 1966—76, Washington, 1976—, sr. ptnr., 1994—. Vice chmn. bd. dirs., gen. counsel Century Nat. Bank, Washington, 1982-2001; bd. dirs., gen. counsel Columbia Nat. Bank, Washington, 1987-90; bd. dirs., v.p., gen. counsel Century Bancshares, Washington, 1985-2001; mem. fed. savs. and loan adv. coun. Fed. Home Loan Bank Bd., Washington, 1980-81; chmn., lectr. Practicing Law Inst. Seminars on Energy Litig., Washington, 1980, 81; chief judge Wake Island Ct., Wake Island, North Pacific Ocean, 1989. Mem. exec. com., chmn. pers. and acad. affairs com. Wesley Theol. Sem., Washington, 1997-2003, bd.govs., 1997-2004; mem. devel. bd. Lon Morris Coll., Lake Jackson, Tex., 1974-76; mem. Southwest U. Spl. Edn. Found., San Marcos, Tex., 1973-76; v.p., dir. Harris County Easter Seal Soc., Houston, 1972-76; bd. dirs., sec. Nemours Wildlife Found., Yemassee, SC, 1995—; treas. Dem. Party Harris County, Houston, 1976-77; mem. nat. fin. coun. Dem. Nat. Com., Washington, 1976-80; vol. ESL tchr.; former cert. lay spkr. United Meth. Ch., former dist. dir. lay speaking Washington-Columbia Dist.; former mem. bd. visitors and former mem. program com. Kanuga Episcopal Conf. Ctr., Hendersonville, NC, Seabury Inst. adv. bd. Seabury-We. Theol. Sem., Evanston; mem. constn. and canons com. Episcopal Diocese of Washington; mem. Anglican Compass Rose Soc. Mem. ABA (litig. sect.), DC Bar Assn., Tex. Bar Assn., Houston Bar Assn. (gen. litig. sect.), Orton Soc. Republican. Office: 4449 Westover Pl NW Washington DC 20016 Personal E-mail: johnrcope@johnrcope.com.

COPE, KATHLEEN ADELAIDE, critical care nurse, parish nurse, educator; b. Bethlehem, Pa., Sept. 12, 1926; d. Harry Raymond and Mabel Eva (Newhard) Stine; m. Robert Clayton Cope, Aug. 9, 1951; children: Debra Kathleen Howard, Terry Faye Cicero. BA in Psychology summa cum laude, Belleville Coll., Nebr., 1972; diploma, St. Luke's Hosp., Bethlehem, 1951; student, Whitworth Coll., Spokane, 1989, Wash. State U., 1989. RN, Pa., Wash.; cert. nutrition support nurse; cert. critical care nurse, quality improvement, health promotion specialist. Pvt. duty nurse Exeter (N.H.) Hosp., 1957-60; nurse Red Cross Blood Mobile, Portsmouth area, N.H., 1961-65; staff nurse Clarkson Hosp., Omaha, 1966, asst. head nurse, 1966-67, head nurse, 1967-68, supr., organizer coronary care ctr., 1968-70; staff nurse ICU/critical care Sacred Heart Med. ctr., Spokane, 1973—; founder, dir. nutritional risk/identification network Health Improvement Partnership, Spokane, Wash., 1997—. Mem. adv. coun. edn. com. Nutrition Screening Initiative, Washington, 1992—, Nutrition Inst. La., New Orleans, 1993—; apptd. del. by U.S. Senate to White House Conf. on Aging, 1995; developer Body Mass Index awareness cmty. action project through Leadership Spokane Class, 1999; presenter Spokane's body mass index project U.S. Surgeon Gen.'s Inaugural Session on Obesity, 2001. Author: (manual) Malnutrition in the Elderly: A National Crisis, (resolution) Ensuring the Future of the Medicare Program presented to White House and Congress; contbr. articles to profl. jours. Apptd. Silver Senator by U.S. Senate for Wash. in Nat. Silver Haired Congress, 1997. Recipient Cmty. Leadership Recognition award, YWCA, Spokane, 1993, commendation for developing a model for nation from former U.S. Surgeon Gen. C. Everett Koop, 1999, Spl. Recognition award for contrbn. to malnutrition awareness, U.S. Adminstrn. on Aging, 2000. Mem. ANA, Wash. State Nursing Assn., Nat. Coun. on Aging, Am. Soc. for Critical Care Nursing (founding), Am. Soc. for Parenteral and Enteral Nutrition, U.S. apptd. Silver Senator for Wash. State in Nat. Silver Haired Congress, Sigma Theta Tau. Avocations: reading, walking, hiking, bicycling, cooking, crafts. Home: 8315 N Lucia Ct Spokane WA 99208-9654 Office Phone: 509-466-4514. Home Fax: 509-468-1026. Personal E-mail: kcope@mindspring.com.

COPE, KENNETH WAYNE, retail executive; b. Rifle, Colo., May 31, 1924; s. William Grant and Mary (Park) C.; m. Patricia Miller, Feb. 1, 1946; children: Kimberly Ann, Bradley Mark. BA, La Sierra Coll., Arlington, Calif., 1948; postgrad., U. Wash., 1948-50. CPA, Calif. From staff acct. to mgr. Price Waterhouse & Co., CPAs, LA, 1950-58, resident mgr. Phoenix, 1959-63; regional contr. Lucky Stores, Inc., San Leandro, Calif., 1963-68, v.p., corp. contr., 1968-83, sr. v.p. adminstrn., 1984-86, v.p. corp. affairs, 1986-87, ret., 1987. Served with AUS, 1943-46. Mem. AICPA, Calif. Soc. CPAs, Fin. Execs. Inst. Republican. Episcopalian.

COPE, LAURENCE BRIAN, financial, energy and strategic consulting executive; b. White Plains, NY, May 28, 1951; s. Lawrence Lyndon and Dorothea Anne (Herrick) C.; m. Ana Virginia (Ambrosini), June 7, 1986. BS in Bus., Fla. So. Coll., 1974; MS in Govt. and Pub. Adminstrn., So. Ill. U., Edwardsville, 1980; postgrad. in Econ., George Washington U., 1982. Mgr. cost estimating Potomac Electric Power Co., Washington, 1974—77, systems and tng. specialist, 1977—82, project mgr., 1982—84, mem. spkr. bur., 1978—84; project mgr., cons. Nat. Rural Utilities Coop. Fin. Corp., Herndon, Va., 1984—. Pres. Cope Assocs., LLC, Washington,2006—; trustee Cope Family Trusts; chmn. budget com. Oakton Condominium Assn., 1986-88. Contbr. articles to profl. jours. Co-chmn. Christian Young Adults Group, Washington, 1983. Mem. ASTD (reporter chpt. orgn. The Torch 1977, 78); Am. Soc. Pub. Adminstrn. (budget and fin. divsn.); Nat. Economists Club (rapporteur 1985—90); CFC Investment Club (pres. 1995). Roman Catholic. Office Phone: 301-718-9594.

COPE, LEWIS, journalist; b. Sweetwater, Tex., June 24, 1934; s. Millard L. and Margaret Wallace (Kilgore) C.; m. Betty Joan Ball, June 28, 1958; children— Margaret, Elizabeth, Mary Amelia. BA, Washington and Lee U., 1955. Reporter Greenville (Tex.) Herald-Banner, 1957-60; copy editor Richmond (Va.) Times Dispatch, 1960-62; copy editor, news editor San Antonio Express, 1962-66; sci. reporter Mpls. Star and Tribune, 1966-95; freelance science writer, newspaper cons., 1995—. Bd. dirs. Coun. Advancement of Sci. Writing, 1996—; writer-in-residence Nat. Cancer Inst., 1976. Author: Save Your Life, 1979, (with Victor Cohn) News and Numbers, 2001. Served as officer AUS, 1955-57. Recipient Merit award Am. Assn. Blood Banks, 1974, Journalism award Am. Acad. Family Physicians, 1976, 79, Penney award lifestyle reporting U. Mo., 1977, Nat. Media award Am. Cancer Soc., 1977, Blakeslee award Am. Heart Assn., 1979, Cecil award Arthritis Found., 1982, Harvey award Am. Med. Writers Assn., 1993; Sci. Writing fellow Columbia U. Grad. Sch. Journalism, 1963-64. Mem. Nat. Assn. Sci. Writers (exec. com. 1982-93, treas. 1985-88, v.p. 1989-90, pres. 1991-92), Sigma Delta Chi (pres. Minn. chpt. 1973-74, dep. regional dir. 1974-86). Episcopalian. Home: 5217 W 91st St Minneapolis MN 55437-1819 Personal E-mail: lcope02@comcast.net.

COPE, MELBA DARLENE, volunteer, photographer; b. Des Moines, Iowa, Feb. 16, 1944; d. Murray J. and Mary Lorena Van Hemert; m. Harvey J. Helgeland, 1964 (dissolved 1971); 1 child, Ingrid; m. Thom K. Cope, Nov. 8, 1980. Student, Nebr. Wesleyan U., Lincoln, 1975—76; BA in Women's Studies, U. Nebr., 1996. Bus. mgr. Williamson Olds/Honda, Lincoln, 1982—88; Granny Smith Washington Apple Commn., Wenatchee, Wash., 1999—2000; photographer Images by Melba, Tucson, 2002—. Photographer Habitat for Humanity Bldg. Project, Lincoln, Nebr., 1998. Contbr. chapters to books. Bd. dirs., sec., v.p. Rape Spouse Abuse Crisis Ctr., 1993—2002; active Older Women's League, 1998—2002, Bd. Friends Commn., 2000—01; mentor Women in Trades program YWCA, Lincoln, 1999; big sister Heartland Big Bros./Big Sisters Orgn., 2001—02; com. mem. Girls and Women in Sports and Fitness, 2001—02; co-chair Am. Cancer Soc. Annual Climb to Conquer Cancer, Tucson, 2005; bd. dirs. YWCA, 2001; bd. dirs., v.p. Women's Studies Adv. Coun., Tucson, 2004—06; commr., mem. exec. bd., v.p. Lincoln Lancaster Women's Commn., 1997—2001; bd. dirs. Coll. Arts and Scis. Alumni Assn. U. Nebr., 1997—2000; com. mem. Women in Transition, 1999; comms. com. Sunflower Cmty. Assn., Tucson, 2002—04. Recipient Elizabeth Kurtz Vol. award, Rape Spouse Abuse Crisis Ctr., Lincoln, Nebr., 2000, Outstanding Vol. award, United Way, Lincoln, 2000, Alice Paul award, Lincoln/Lancaster Women's Commn., Lincoln, 2001. Mem.: Sigma Alpha Iota (Sword of Honor award 1994), Phi Beta Kappa. Avocations: photography, hiking, reading, music, travel.

COPE, THOM K., account executive, lawyer; b. Bremen, Germany, Feb. 26, 1948; came to U.S., 1960; s. Ray and Gabriele E. (Meyer) C.; m. Melba D. Van Hemert, Nov. 8, 1980. BA with honors, Syracuse U., 1969; JD, U. Nebr., 1972. Bar: Nebr. 1972, Ariz. 2007, U.S. Dist. Ct. Nebr. 1972, U.S. Ct. Appeals (8th cir.) 1972, Calif. 1976, U.S. Dist. Ct. (no. dist.) Calif. 1976, U.S. Ct. Appeals (9th cir.) 1976, U.S. Supreme Ct. 1987, U.S. Claims Ct. 1988, U.S. Ct. Appeals (D.C. cir.) 1990., Fed. Dist. Ct. Ariz., 2007; lic. ins. agt., property, casualty, life and health. Agy. legal counsel Nebr. Workers' Compensation Ct., Lincoln, 1972-73; assoc. counsel Fireman's Fund Ins. Co., San Francisco, 1973-76; asst. gen. counsel Argonaut Ins. Co., Menlo Park, Calif., 1976-78; assoc. counsel Ins. Svcs. Office, NYC, 1978-82; assoc. atty. Tate & Assocs., Nebr., 1982-83, Bailey, Polsky, Cada & Todd, Nebr., 1983-84; ptnr. Bailey, Polsky, Cope & Knapp, Lincoln, 1984-97, Polsky Cope Shiffermiller Coe and Monzon and predecessors, Lincoln, 1997—2002; v.p. human resources Beaudry Motor Co., 2002—06; colonial supplemental life account exec., 2006—. Judge Nebr. Commn. of Indsl. Rels., 1986-91; mem. Nebr. Supreme Ct. Gender Bias Task Force; mem. Nebr. Motor Vehicle Industry Licensing Bd.; mem. Nebr. Atty. Gen. Odometer Fraud Task Force; mem. Fed. Practice Adv. Com.; lectr. in field. Author: Executive Guide to Employment Practices, 1985, 3d edit., 1999. Bd. dir. Friends of Elderly Found., Lincoln, 1986-90, Capital Humane Soc., Planned Parenthood Lincoln, 1997—, v.p., 1998, pres. 1999—2001; bd. dirs. Child Advocacy Ctr., 1995-97; bd. trustees Lincoln Bar Assn. Fellow Coll. Employment and Labor Law (cert. sr. profl. in human resources 2003); mem. Nat. Employment Lawyers Assn., Nebr. Bar Assn. (labor and employment sect., exec. com., sec.), Nebr. Trial Lawyers Assn., NOW (bd. dir. 1999), Soc. Human Resource Mgmt. Avocation: golf. Home and Office: HR Consultant 9343 N Sunflower Blossom Pl Tucson AZ 85743 Office Phone: 520-404-7521.

COPE, THOMAS FIELD, lawyer; b. Oak Park, Ill., Feb. 29, 1948; s. Benjamin Thomas and Myra Norma (Lees) C.; m. Ann Wattis, Mar. 21, 1970; children: Elizabeth Ann, Philip Thomas. BA, U. Denver, 1970, JD, 1974, MA, 1976; PhD, U. Chgo., 2001. Bar: Colo. 1974, Ill. 1978, Wyo. 1996, D.C. 2001. Assoc. Holme Roberts & Owen, Denver, 1974-78, 81-83, ptnr., 1984—2003, of counsel, 2003—. Instr. IIT Chgo.-Kent Coll. Law, 1980—81, Loyola U. Sch. Law, Chgo., 1980—81; chief of party ABA Ctrl. European and Eurasian Law Initiative, Moldova, 2002—03; adj. prof. U. Denver Coll. Law, 2003—04. Co-editor: Colorado Environmental Law Handbook, 1989, 4th rev. edit., 1996, Colorado Environmental Compliance Update, 1993-96; contbg. editor Oil & Gas Law and Taxation Rev., Oxford, Eng., 1987-93; mng. editor Shepard's Environ. Liability in Comml. Transactions Reporter, 1990-92; mem. bd. editors Denver Law Jour., 1972-74; contbr. articles to profl. jours. Bd. dirs. Colo. Fourteeners Initiative, 1996-2002, Colo. Mountain Club Found. (bd. dirs. 2006—). Mem. Am. Law Inst., Am. Soc. Legal History, Irish Legal History Soc., Selden Soc. (state corr. Colo. 1997—), Rocky Mountain Mineral Law Found. (mem. grants com. 1983-95, chmn. 1995-2002), Order St. Ives, Am. Alpine Club, Colo. Mountain Club (chair high altitude mountaineering sect. 2001-02). Democrat. Mem. Orthodox Ch. in Am. Avocations: mountain climbing, history. Home: 2800 S Univ Blvd 108 Denver CO 80210-6072 Office: Holme Roberts & Owen LLP 1700 Lincoln St Ste 4100 Denver CO 80203-4541 Office Phone: 303-866-0295. E-mail: thomas.cope@hro.com.

COPE, WENDY, poet; b. 1945; Tchr. Portway Jr. Sch., London, 1967-69, Keyworth Jr. Sch., London, 1969-73, Cobourg Primary Sch., 1973-81, Brindishe Primary Sch., 1984-86; writer, TV columnist The Spectator, London, 1986-90. Arts editor ILEA Contact Tchrs. Newspaper, 1982-84. Author: Across the City, 1980, Hope and the 42, 1984, Making Cocoa for Kingsley Amis, 1986, Poem from a Colour Chart of Housepaints, 1986, Men and Their Boring Arguments, 1988, Does She Like Word-Games?, 1988, Twiddling Your Thumbs, 1988, The River Girl, 1991, Serious Concerns, 1992, If I Don't Know, 2001; editor: Is That the New Moon?, Poems By Women Poets, 1989, The Orchard Book of Funny Poems, 1993, The Funny Side, 1998, The Faber Book of Bedtime Stories, 2000, Heaven on Earth: 101 Happy Poems, 2001; George Herbert: Verse and Prose (a selection), 2002. Recipient Cholmondeley award for poetry, 1987, Michael Braude award AAAL, 1995. Fellow Royal Soc. Lit. Office: Faber & Faber 3 Queen Sq London WC1N 3AU England

COPELAN, ANN HANSON, artist, psychologist; d. Jewell Joe and Emily Blanche (Peacock) Hanson; m. Thomas J. Phillips, Jr. (div.); children: Trae Phillips, Dean Phillips, Phoelicia Canup, Cindy McNally, Clay Phillips, David Phillips. Student, U. Ga., Athens, 1966—68; BS in Psychology, Ga. Coll. and State U., Milledgeville, 1981, MS in Psychology, 1986. Asst. to Curator U. Ga. Mus. Art, Athens, Ga., 1967—69; asst. dir., behavior specialist Putnam Jasper Support Svcs., Eatonton, Ga., 1984—; owner Ann H. Copelan Gallery, Greensboro, Ga., 1987—. Cons. Coliseum Psychiat. Hosp., Macon, Ga., 1986—88; mem. steering com. Putnam County Bicentennial, 2007, art dir., 07. One-woman shows include People's Bank, Eatonton, Ga., 1989, Little Acorn, Atlanta, 1989, Cathreen's Gallery, 1990—93, Ga. Coll. and State U. Blackbridge Hall Mus., Milledgeville, 1990, Left Bank Art Gallery, St. Simons Island, Ga., 1991, Sutton Galleries, New Orleans, 1992, 1996, Richard Guritz Antiques, Highlands, NC, 1993—94, Lawrence Charles Gallery, Tampa, Fla., 1993, Magnolia Gallery, Lake Oconee, Ga., 1999—2000, exhibited in group shows at People's Bank, Eatonton, 1987, Festival of the Arts, Moultrie, Ga., 1988, Buckhead Gallery, Atlanta, 1988, Winter Arts Festival, Macon, Ga., 1989, LA Art Expo., 1989, Ansley Inn, Atlanta, 1989, Left Bank Art Gallery, St. Simons, 1989—90, 1992, 1994—95, 1999, Cloister, Sea Island, Ga., 1989—96, 1998—2000, Art Expo., NY, 1990, Leon Loard Art Gallery, Montgomery, Ala., 1992, 1996, 1998, Little Acorn, Atlanta, 1992, 1994—97, 1999—2002, Magnolia Gallery, Lake Oconee, 2001, Harbor Club, 2003, represented in numerous pub. and pvt. collections. Founding bd. trustees John Milledge Acad., Milledgeville, Ga., 1972; bd. dirs. Eatonton-Putnam County Hist. Soc., Eatonton, Ga., 1986—88, Peoples Bank Found., Eatonton, 1988—. Named Outstanding Young Alumni, Ga. Coll. and State U., 1992. Mem.: Nat. Mus. Women in the Arts, Greene County Arts Alliance, Ga. Citizens for the Arts, Gamma Beta Phi. Republican. Baptist. Avocations: writing, reading, walking, painting, interior decorating. Home: Lake Oconee 1134 Harbor Ridge Dr Greensboro GA 30642

COPELAN, EDWARD A., medical educator; b. Phila., Pa., Oct. 28, 1951; s. Herbert W. and Ruth M. Copelan; m. Belinda Avalos-Copelan; children: Alex, Max, Olivia. BS, Muhlenberg Coll., Allentown, Pa., 1973; MD, Tufts U., Boston, 1977. Cert. internal medicine, hematology and oncology Nat. Bd. Med. Examiners. Fellow hematology/oncology Ohio State U., Columbus, 1980—82, dir. bone marrow transplantation, 1991—2005, prof. medicine, 1997—; vis. fellow bone marrow transplantation UCLA, 1982—83. Mem. cancer devel. com. Nat. Cancer Inst., Washington, 2000—; mem. exec. com. internat. bone marrow transplantation ctr. Ctr. for Internat. Bone Marrow Transplant Registry, Milw., 2000—06. Contbr. articles to profl. jours. Vol. Faith Mission, Columbus, 2003—. Mem.: ACP, Am. Soc. Hematology. Achievements include patents for inhibitors of Aspergillus fungal infection. Avocations: running, swimming. Home: 2001 Tremont Rd Columbus OH 43221 Office: Taussg Cancer Ctr 9500 Euclid Ave R35 Cleveland OH Office Phone: 216-445-5647. Fax: 614-293-6690. Business E-Mail: copela@ccf.org.

COPELAND, ANITA BOB, director, retired elementary school educator, senior consultant; b. Memphis, July 23; d. Bobbie and Margo Jewell; m. Bob Copeland, July 15, 1961; children: Cara Wynn, Robert Ryan. BS, Tex. Wesleyan U., Ft. Worth, 1964, MS. Classroom tchr. Arlington Ind. Sch. Dist., Tex.; ret., 2000. Twirling dir. Tex. Stars and Starlettes, Arlington, 1961—2005; tchr., judge Nat. Baton Twirling Assn., 1961—2005; asst. exec. sec. region 5 U. Interscholastic League, 2000—; sr. cons. Creative Memories, 2003—05; dir. Ignite Stream Energy, 2004—. Mem.: Ret. Tchrs. Assn. (historian dist. 11), Ret. Sch. Employees Arlington (historian), Arlington Women Rotary (pres. 1977—78, 1984—85, past pres.), Encore Club (officer 2000—, historian, publicity 2006—), Arlington Women's Club (officer 1979—). Home: 1811 Mossy Oak Arlington TX 76012 Personal E-mail: anita_copeland@yahoo.com.

COPELAND, BONNIE S., former school system administrator; b. Lima, Ohio, Nov. 27, 1949; BS, Miami U., 1971, MEd, 1972; PhD, St. Louis U., 1978. Supr. reading Lindburgh, Mo. Pub. Schools, 1972—78; exec. asst. supt. Anne Arundel Co. Pub. Schools, 1979—82; asst. state supt., dir. assessment ctr. program Md. State Dept. Edn.; assoc. supt. instr. Balt. Co. Pub. Schools; dept. state supt., acting supt. Md. State Dept. Edn., 1990—94; supt. Balt. Pub. Schools, 1994—2006. Exec. v.p. Greater Balt. Com., 1994—99; pres. Fund for Ednl. Excellence, 1999—. Named to Wapakoneta High Sch. Hall of Fame, 2002. Mem.: Balt. Ctr. Performing Arts (chmn. edn. com. 2001—). Office Phone: 410-396-8700.*

COPELAND, CHARLENE CAROLE, lawyer; b. Gloversville, NY, July 22; d. Joseph Frank and Marion (Dye) Born; children: Christopher, Todd, Tiffani. BS in Polit Sci., Lamar U.; JD, John Marshall U. Bar: Ill. 1991, U.S. Dist. Ct. (no. dist.) Ill. 1991, U.S. Ct. Appeals (7th cir.) 1993, Fed. Trial Bar, 1993. Assoc. Brenner, Mavrias & Alm, New Lenox, Ill., 1992-96; assoc. civil divsn. Will County State's Attys. Office, Joliet, Ill., 1997-1999; with Lehrer, Flaherty & Canavan, Wheaton, Ill., 2000—02; asst. atty. gen. Ill. Atty. Gen.'s office Indsl. Commn. Bur., 2002—. Mem. Will County Pro Bono Project; pres. Jaycettes, Port Authur, Tex., 1970-71; fin. chmn. League of Women Voters, 1971, pres. Joliet Region, 1979-81; area capt. March of Dimes Mothers' March, 1971; day chmn. George Bush for Senate Campaign, 1970; mem. Village of Shorewood Ad Hoc Com. on Ordinances, 1975, Fin. Com., 1976-78; pres. United Meth. Women of Grace Meth. Ch., 1980-81; crusade chmn. Shorewood Residential Cancer Crusade, 1982. Named Outstanding Pro Bono Vol., 1995. Mem. Ill. State Bar Assn., Will County Bar Assn., Will County Arbitration Panel, Will County Women's Bar Assn. (chmn. 1999), John Marshall Law Sch. Reunion Com. Home Phone: 815-744-6640; Office Phone: 312-814-3684. Business E-Mail: ccopeland@atg.il.state.us.

COPELAND, DOUGLAS ALLEN, lawyer; b. St. Louis, Mar. 22, 1956; s. William H. and Margaret J. (Wilson) C.; m. Amy Elizabeth Miles, May 18, 1985; children: Gregory Miles, Margaret Jane. BA, U. Mo., 1977; JD, St. Louis U., 1980. Bar: Mo. 1980, Ill. 1981, U.S. Dist. Ct. (ea. dist.) Mo. 1981, U.S. Ct. Appeals (8th cir.) 1987, U.S. Supreme Ct. 1988. Assoc. Brackman, Copeland, Oetting, Copeland, Walther & Schmidt, St. Louis, 1980-84, ptnr., 1985-86, Copeland, Gartner, Thompson & Jeep, St. Louis, 1987-88, Copeland, Gartner & Thompson, St. Louis, 1988-92, Copeland, Gartner, Thompson & Farris, St. Louis, 1993, Copeland Thompson Farris PC, St. Louis. Mem. ABA, NSBA (coun. sch. attys.), Mo. Bar Assn. (young lawyers sect., chmn. 1990-91, coun. mem. 1982-92, coun. sch. attys., pres.-elect 2004, pres. 2005), St. Louis County Bar Assn. (pres. 1988-89, exec. com. 1983-90, Outstanding Young Lawyer 1987), Bar Assn. of Met. St. Louis, Estate Planning Coun. of St. Louis, Nat. Health Lawyers Assn. Republican. Baptist. Avocations: tennis, softball, hunting. Office: Copeland Thompson Farris PC Ste 1220 231 S Bemiston Ave Saint Louis MO 63105*

COPELAND, EDWARD JEROME, lawyer; b. Chgo., Oct. 29, 1933; s. Harvey and Lilyan (Rubin) C.; m. Ruth Caminer, Sept. 2, 1962; children: Ellyn, Bradley. BA, Carleton Coll., 1955; JD, Northwestern U., 1958. Bar: Ill. 1959, N.Y. 1981. Mem. Ill. Ho. of Reps., Springfield, 1967-71; ptnr. Foss, Schuman, Drake & Barnard, Chgo., 1971-86, Wood, Lucksinger & Epstein, Chgo., 1986-88, Shefsky & Froelich, Ltd., Chgo., 1988-89, Schuyler, Roche & Zwirner, Chgo., 1989—. Chmn. Bank of North Shore, Northbrook, Ill., 1976-81. Mem. Ill. Bd. Edn., 1975-83, chmn., 1981-83. Mem. ABA, Ill. Bar Assn., Chgo. Bar Assn. Republican. Office: One Prudential Plaza Ste 3800 Schuyler Roche & Zwirner 130 E Randolph St Chicago IL 60601-6312 Office Phone: 312-565-8327. Business E-Mail: ecopeland@srzlaw.com.

COPELAND, EDWARD MEADORS, III, surgeon, educator; b. Augusta, Ga., Oct. 6, 1937; s. Edward Meadors Jr. and Louise (Leggitt) C.; m. Martha Patterson, Ar. 24, 1964; children: Edward Meadors IV, Catherine Leggitt. BA, Duke U., 1959; MD, Cornell U., 1963. Diplomate Am. Bd. Surgery (bd. dir. 1983-91, chmn. 1990-91). Intern in surgery U. Pa. Hosp., Phila., 1963-64, resident in gen. surgery, 1964-69; resident surg. oncology Anderson Hosp., Houston, 1971-72; asst. prof. to prof. U. Tex. Med. Sch., Houston, 1972-82, U. Tex. M.D. Anderson Hosp. and Tumor Inst., Houston, 1972-82; prof. U. Fla. Coll. Medicine, Gainesville, 1982—, chmn. dept., 1982—2003, disting. prof., 2004—. Project dir. Nat. Large Bowel Cancer Project, Nat. Cancer Inst., Houston, 1981-82; bd. dirs. Sun Bank North Ctrl. Fla. Maj. US Army, 1969-71, Vietnam. Decorated Bronze Star Rep. Vietnam; recipient Seale Harris award So. Med. Assn., 1984, Disting. Alumnus award M.D. Anderson Hosp. and Tumor Inst., 1987. Fellow Am. Surg. Assn., So. Surg. Assn. (pres. 1998-99); mem. ACS (chmn. bd. govs. 1995-96, bd. regents 1997—, vice chmn. 2002-03, chmn. 2004-05, pres.-elect 2005-06, pres. 2006-), Assn. Acad. Surgery (pres.

1978-79), Soc. Surg. Oncology (pres. 1998-99), Soc. Surg. Chmn. (pres. 1996-98), Halsted Soc. (pres. 1993), Southeastern Surg. Congress (pres. 2000-01), Soc. Univ. Surgeons, Gainesville Country Club. Avocations: fishing, golf, tennis. Home: 2605 NW 7th Rd Gainesville FL 32607-2600 Office: Univ Fla Coll Medicine Dept Surgery PO Box 100286 Gainesville FL 32610-0286 Home Phone: 352-373-9936; Office Phone: 352-265-0169.

COPELAND, EUGENE LEROY, lawyer, writer; b. Fairfield, Iowa, Mar. 5, 1939; BA, Parsons Coll., 1961; JD with distinction, U. Iowa, 1965. Admitted to Colo. bar, 1965, Iowa bar, 1965, U.S. Supreme Ct. bar, 1966. Individual practice law, Denver, 1965-66; sr. v.p., gen. counsel, sec. Security Life of Denver, Denver, 1966—; gen. counsel Nationale Nederlanden N.Am. Corp., Denver, 1986—. Lectr., speaker at legal and industry convs., seminars, meetings; participant contemporary issue program Today show NBC, 1980. Author: Preventive Law for Medical Directors and Underwriters, 1973; Underwriting in a New Age of Legal Accountability, 1978; Insurance Law, 1982; bd. editors Iowa Law Rev., 1965. Bd. dirs. Colo. Pub. Expenditures Coun., 1988—, Buffalo Mountain Met. Dist., Summit County, Colo., Friends Found. of Denver Pub. Libr., Denver Pub. Libr. Commn. Served with U.S. Army. Fulbright scholar (alt.). Mem. ABA, Colo. Bar Assn., Denver Bar Assn., Iowa Bar Assn., Assn. Life Ins. Council, Am. Council Life Ins. (state v.p. 1973-83, legis. com., reins. com., policyholder tax com., litigation com.), Colo. Life Conv. (pres. 1988-90, v.p. 1987-88, legis. chmn. 1973-86), Colo. Assn. Corp. Counsel, Denver Estate Planning Council, Colo. Assn. Life Underwriters (co-author learning guide 1978), Law Club Denver, Phi Kappa Phi. Unitarian Universalist. Office: Security Life Ctr 1290 Broadway Fl 6 Denver CO 80203-2122

COPELAND, FLOYD DEAN, insurance company executive, lawyer; b. Jackson, Miss., Apr. 11, 1939; s. Clyde Xenephon and Dorothy Russell (Dean) C.; m. Linda Gail Langston, Dec. 22, 1965; children: Albion Ehlers, Russell Braden. BA in history, U. Miss., 1961; BA in jurisprudence, U. Oxford, Eng., 1963; LLB, Yale U., 1965. Bar: Ga. 1967, Tenn. 1998. Assoc. Alston, Miller & Gaines, Atlanta, 1967-71; ptnr. Alston & Bird, Atlanta, 1972-97; exec. v.p., gen. counsel Provident Companies, Inc., Chattanooga, 1997-99; exec. v.p. legal and adminstrv. affairs, gen. counsel UnumProvident Corp., Chattanooga, 1999—2002, sr. exec. v.p., gen. counsel, 2002—, chief adminstrv. officer, 2003—. Bd. dirs. Atlanta Metro Boys and Girls Clubs, 1986-97; sec. State and Dist. Rhodes Scholarship Selection Committees, Atlanta, 1976-97. Capt. US Army, 1965—67. Rhodes scholar, 1961, Carrier scholar, 1957. Mem. Am. Law Inst. Presbyterian. Avocations: bicycling, reading, travel. Office: UnumProvident Corp One Fountain Sq Chattanooga TN 37402*

COPELAND, HENRY JEFFERSON, JR., former college president; b. Griffin, Ga., June 13, 1936; s. Henry Jefferson and Emory (Drake) C.; m. Laura Harper, Dec. 21, 1958; children: Henry Drake, Eleanor Harper. BA, Baylor U., 1958; PhD, Cornell U., 1966. Instr. Cornell U., Ithaca, NY, 1965-66; asst. prof. history Coll. Wooster, Ohio, 1966-69, assoc. dean, 1969-74, dean, 1974-77, pres., 1977-95, prof. history, 1995-98. Woodrow Wilson fellow, 1960 Presbyterian.

COPELAND, HUNTER ARMSTRONG, retired real estate company executive; b. Birmingham, Ala., Oct. 22, 1918; s. Miles Axe and Leonora (Armstrong) C.; m. Suzanne Curl, 1942 (div. 1954); children: Susan Diane, Hunter Armstrong; m. Patricia Ann McGregor, 1956 (div. 1976); children: John McGregor, Miles, Ann; m. Courteney Bass, May 27, 1978. Student, U. Ala., 1936-37; grad. advanced mgmt. course, Harvard U., 1952. Mortgage appraiser Prudential Ins. Co. Am., Birmingham, 1946-54; mortgage broker Huntoon-Paige, NYC, 1954-57; pres. Huntoon Copeland & Hedin, NYC, 1958-70; exec. dir. Hunter Copeland and Assocs., NYC, 1970-75; v.p. Colwell Co., NYC, 1970-75; pres. Copeland-Tresnan & Hornblower Inc., NYC, 1975-78, Hunter Copeland and Assocs., Birmingham, Ala., 1978—2002. Trustee Md. Realty Trust, Balt.; organizer, dir. New Canaan Bank & Trust Co., Conn.; mem. Ala. Cert. Bd. Alcoholism and Drug Counselors Mem. Am. Coun. on Alcoholism; exec. dir. Alcohol and Drug Abuse Coun. With inf. AUS, 1941-45; maj. USAF, 1952-54. Decorated Legion of Merit, Silver Star, Bronze Star with 4 oak leaf clusters, Purple Heart with oak leaf cluster., Legion of Merit, Croix du Combattant Voluntaire (France), War Cross Royal Yugoslav Army Peter II King of Yugoslavia, Medaille Commemorative Francaise, Medaille de France Liberee; named to Inf. Officers Hall of Fame, Ft. Benning, Ga., 1982. Mem. Mortgage Bankers Assn. Am., Mortgage Bankers Assn. N.Y. (pres. 1974-76, gov.), Am. Pub. Health Assn., Nat. Assn. Alcoholism and Drug Abuse Counselors, ASCD, Internat. Coun. Alcohol and Addictions, Vets. of Battle of the Bulge, Newcomen Soc., Commerce Exec. Soc. U. Ala., Chi Phi. Clubs: Kiwanis; Union League (N.Y.C.), Met. (N.Y.C.); Country of Birmingham. Address: PO Box 55912 Birmingham AL 35255

COPELAND, JACQUELINE TURNER, music educator; b. Birmingham, Ala., Mar. 22, 1939; d. Charles Smith and Julia (Northrop) Turner; m. William Edward Copeland, Apr. 20, 1962; children: Denise Arlene, Dawn Alane. B in Music Edn., Birmingham-So. Coll., 1960; M in Music Edn., Wichita State U., 1977. Cert. music tchr. grades K-12, Ala., Ga., Kans., La., Va. Music tchr. Jefferson County Bd. Edn., Birmingham, 1960-62, 63-64, DeKalb County Bd. Edn., Decatur, Ga., 1965-68; choral music tchr. Fairfax (Va.) County Bd. Edn., 1968-69, Derby (Kans.) Unified Sch. Dist. #260, 1977-80, Maize (Kans.) Unified Sch. Dist. #266, 1980-84; music tchr. Montgomery (Ala.) County Pub. Schs., 1984-85; instr. voice and piano Acad. Performing Arts, Montgomery, 1985-95, Studio of Jacqueline T. Copeland, Montgomery, 1995—. Accompanist County-Wide Music Festivals, Birmingham, 1960-65; sect. leader Dekalb Cmty. Chorus, Decatur, Ga., 1965-68; sect. leader, exec. bd. New Orleans Concert Choir, 1970-74; asst. dir., dir. chorale Wichita Choral Soc., 1974-84; dir. opening ceremony Bicentennial Fair, Wichita, 1976; mem. Montgomery (Ala.) Civic Chorale, 1984-87; musical dir. for theatre depts. Performing Arts Jr. High, Performing Arts H.S., Faulkner U., 1986—. Author: Music Teacher Handbook, 1967; editor, contbg. author: Teacher Advisement Handbook, 1980. Secret svc. wife White House Wives, Washington, 1968-70; leader, trainer, area chmn. Camp Fire Girls, New Orleans, 1970-74; leader, membership com., exec. bd. Camp Fire Girls, Wichita, 1974-82; elected ofcl. Citizens Participation Orgn., Wichita, 1984; area chmn. Am. Heart Assn., Montgomery, 1988-94; vol. DA Election, Montgomery, 1994. Recipient Groovey Tchr. award WQXI Radio, Atlanta, 1967, Gov.'s commendation Revolutionary Bicentennial Com., Wichita, 1976; named Outstanding Young Women of Am., New Orleans, 1971. Mem. NOW, AAUW, Music Tchrs. Nat. Assn., Ala. Music Tchrs. Assn., Montgomery Music Tchrs. Forum, Alpha Chi Omega (Montgomery chpt. treas. 1995-99, pres. 1999—), Alpha Chi Omega Alumnae (del. to 4 nat. convs., pres., v.p.). Democrat. Baptist. Avocation: searching for collectibles for country decor. Home: 6121 Bell Road Mnr Montgomery AL 36117-4362

COPELAND, JOHN HOWARD, communications executive, television producer; b. San Diego, Oct. 13, 1950; s. Glenn H. and Luella Louise (Schmid) C.; m. Shannon Gloria Casey, Nov. 20, 1987. BA, Chapman U., 1973. Asst. to exec. prodr. Evan Lloyd Prodns., London, 1974-76; mem. TV and audio visual staff Chapman U., Orange, Calif., 1977-78; asst. to prodr. Media Prodns., Inc., LA, 1978-79; post prodn. supr. Rattlesnake Prodns., Inc., LA, 1979-81, assoc. prodr., 1986-88, prodr., 1988-95; post prodn. supr. Walt Disney Pictures, Burbank, Calif., 1981-82; assoc. prodr. Walt Disney Pictures/Rattlesnake Prodns., Burbank, 1983-85; prodr., exec. v.p. Netter Digital Entertainment Inc., LA, 1995—, also sec. bd. dirs. Prodr. (TV documentaries) The Wild West, 1993 (Emmy nomination 1994), When Dinosaurs Roamed America, 2001, Dinosaur Planet, 2002, Secrets of Pearl Harbor, 2004, Red Flag: Thunder Over Hellis, 2005, Alien Planet, 2005, The Science of Star Wars, 2005, (TV shows) Babylon 5, 1993-98, The Real Flying Tigers, 2001, (TV movie) Siringo, 1994; co-prodr. (TV pilot) Babylon 5 - The Gathering, 1993; supervising prodr. (TV show) Hypernauts, 1995-96; prodr. (TV movies) Babylon 5: In the Beginning, 1997, Babylon 5: Third Space, Babylon 5: The River of Souls, 1998, Babylon 5: A Call to Arms; prodr. (TV series) Crusade, 1998-99; exec. prodr. (TV series) Voltron: The Third Dimension, 1998-99. Named Alumni of the Yr. Chapman U., Orange, 1996; recipient Hugo award World Sci. Fiction Soc., 1996, E. Pluribus Unum award Am. Cinema Found., 1997; recipient Hugo award World Sci. Fiction Soc., 1997, Best Cable Series award Acad. Sci. Fiction and Horror, 1999, Lifetime Achievement award in the arts Chapman U., 2005. Mem. NATAS (Emmy 1994, 95), Dir.'s Guild of Am. Office: Evergreen Films LLC 1515 Palisades Dr Ste N Pacific Palisades CA 90272

COPELAND, LOIS JACQUELINE, physician; b. Malden, Mass., Sept. 16, 1943; d. Arnold Alan and Ann Copeland; m. Richard A. Sperling, June 7, 1970; children: Mark Edward, Larissa Lynn, Lauren Anne, Lorraine Elizabeth. BA magna cum laude with distinction, Cornell U., 1964, MD, 1968. Intern N.Y. Hosp., NYC, 1968-69, resident, 1969-70, Bellevue Hosp., NYU Med. Ctr., 1970-72; tchg. asst. internal medicine NYU Med. Ctr., 1971—; attending physician Pascack Valley Hosp., Westwood, N.J., 1974—. Mem. courtesy staff Valley Hosp., Ridgewood, N.J., 1980—. Mem. secondary schs. com. Cornell U., 1978—; bd. dirs. Found. for Free Enterprise, 1994—; steering com. physicians coun. Heritage Found., 1993—; pres. Coun. Cornell Women, 1993-95 Mem. Assn. Am. Physicians and Surgeons (bd. dirs. 1991-99, pres. 1994), Assn. Liberty Choice and Self-Autonomy (pres. 1998—), Phi Beta Kappa, Phi Kappa Phi, Alpha Lambda Delta. Achievements include being originator and physician-plaintiff of landmark constitutional lawsuit Stewart v. Sullivan, which reaffirmed the right of senior citizens to contract privately with physicians, and Amicus in United Seniors v. Shalala for the right to pay privately for medical services. Home: 25 Sparrowbush Rd Upper Saddle River NJ 07458-1400 Office: 47 Central Ave Hillsdale NJ 07642-2118 Office Phone: 201-664-1212. Personal E-mail: loisjcope@aol.com.

COPELAND, MICHELLE, plastic surgeon; b. NYC, July 15, 1948; DMD magna cum laude, Harvard Dental Sch., 1977; MD, Harvard Med. Sch., 1980. Cert. Am. Bd. Plastic & Reconstructive Surgery. Oral maxillofacial surgery residency Mass. General Hospital, Boston, 1977—79; fellowship NY Hosp. Cornell Med. Ctr., NYC, 1980—82, Mt. Sinai Hospital, NYC, 1982—83, SUNY Downstate Med. Ctr., NYC, 1983—85; staff mem., div. plastic surgery Mount Sinai Med. Ctr.; former chief, div. plastic surgery City Hosp. Ctr., Elmhurst, NY; pvt. practice plastic surgery NYC; assist. prof. surgery Mount Sinai Sch. of Medicine, NYC; attending surgeon Mount Sinai Med. Ctr. & Manhattan Eye, Ear and Throat Hospital, NYC. Mem. med. advisory bd. Soc. for Advancement of Women's Health Rsch. Author: Beautiful Skin Workout, 2007; co-author: Change Your Looks, Change Your Life, 2002, 2d edit., 2003; commentator NBC Today Show, ABC Good Morning America; contbr. articles to newspapers, magazines & sci. pubs. Fellow: Am. Coll. Surgeons; mem.: Lipoplasty Soc., Am. Soc. for Laser Medicine and Surgery, Am. Med. Women's Assn., Am. Coll. of Maxillofacial Surgeons, Am. Soc. of Plastic & Reconstructive Surgeons, Am. Soc. for Aesthetic Plastic Surgery. Achievements include development of line of skin care products. Office: Cosmetic Plastic & Reconstructive Surgery 1001 Fifth Ave New York NY 10028 E-mail: mcopeland@drcopeland.com.

COPELAND, NEAL G., medical researcher; B in Biology, U. Utah, PhD in Biochemistry. Postdoctoral fellow Dana-Farber Cancer Ctr., Harvard Med. Sch.; assoc. staff scientist The Jackson Lab.; assoc. prof. microbiology and molecular genetics U. Cin. Coll. Medicine, Cin.; dir. Mammalian Genetics Lab. (as of 1999 renamed Mouse Cancer Genetics Program) ABL-Basic Rsch. Program (now Ctr. Cancer Rsch.), Nat. Cancer Inst., NIH, 1985—, also head Molecular Genetics of Oncogenesis Sect., 1985—. Office: Nat Cancer Inst Ctr Cancer Rsch Mouse Cancer Genetics Program Bldg 539 Rm 229 PO Box B Frederick MD 21702-1201 Office Phone: 301-846-1260. Office Fax: 301-846-6666. E-mail: ncopeland@imcb.a-star.edu.sg.

COPELAND, PATRICIA RUTH, elementary school educator; b. Columbus, Ohio, Apr. 14, 1948; d. George Ralph Jones and Dorothy Mae Ailiff; m. John Richard Copeland, July 10, 1993; m. Jerry Thomas Crouch (div.). BS in Sacred Lit., Circleville Bible Coll., Ohio, 1970; BA in Elem. Edn., Cedarville U., Ohio, 1976; MA in Early Childhood Edn., Tenn. Technol. U., Cookeville, 1984. Cert. career level III tchr. State of Tenn. Dept. of Edn. First grade tchr. Fentress County Schs., Jamestown, Tenn., 1977—. Ednl. workshop trainer Fentress County Schs., Jamestown, 1979—, substitute tchr. trainer, 1984—, chairperson first grade sys., 1984—99, parenting classes for sch. readiness trainer, 1986, tech. staff devel. trainer, 1993—. Mem. child abuse rev. team Dept. Human Svcs., Jamestown, 1986—2000. Recipient Nutrition Edn. grant, Tenn. Dept. Health, 1990; grantee Parenting Edn. grant, 1986, Goals 2000 Tech. grant, 2000. Mem.: NEA (assembly del. to Reps. Assembly 1984, 1988), Fentress County Edn. Assn. (sec. 1979—80, pres.-elect 1982—83, pres. 1983—84, contract chief negotiator 1984—88, 1994—), Tenn. Edn. Assn. (del. to Rep. Assembly 1978, 1979, 1983, 1984), Delta Kappa Gamma (chpt. pres. 1993—96), Kappa Delta Pi, Pi Lambda Theta. Methodist. Avocation: community choir. Home: 2803 Rugby Pike Jamestown TN 38556 Office: Allardt Elem Sch 220 Portland Ave Allardt TN 38504 Home Phone: 931-879-5390; Office Phone: 931-879-9515. Office Fax: 931-879-2702. Personal E-mail: copelandjp@twlakes.net. Business E-Mail: pcopeland@fentress.k12.tn.net.

COPELAND, PAUL MICHAEL, endocrinologist; s. Nathaniel and Beatrice Copeland; m. Maura Pepose, Sept. 4, 1988; children: Marnine Natalie, Daniel Ilan, Harry Samuel. BA, Yale U., New Haven, 1972, MPhil, 1977, MD, 1978. Diplomate Am. Bd. Internal Medicine, 1981, endocrinology and metabolism Am. Bd. Internal Medicine, 1983, cert. clin. densitometry Internat. Soc. Clin. Densitometry, 2003. Intern, resident Hosp. U. Pa., Phila., 1978—81; clin. affiliate medicine Mass. Gen. Hosp., Boston, 1984—; asst. clin. prof. of medicine Harvard Med. Sch., Boston, 1989—, Boston U. Sch. Medicine, 1990—; chief divsn. endocrinology North Shore Med. Ctr., Salem, Mass., 1994—. Baseball coach Swampscott Little League, Mass., 2006—07; bd. dirs., co-chmn. libr. com. Cohen Hillel Acad., Marblehead, Mass., 1998—2007. Named one of Top 3 Endocrinologists in Boston, Boston Mag., 1995, Best Doctors in Am., 2005, Top Ten Endocrinologists, Boston Mag., 2006; recipient Excellence in Tchg. award, Tufts U. Sch. Medicine, 1999; fellow, Mass. Gen. Hosp., 1981—84. Mem.: Endocrine Soc. (chmn. continuing med. edn. com. 2004—). Avocations: baseball, bicycling, cooking. Office: North Shore Medl Group 496 Lynnfield St Lynn MA 01904 Office Phone: 781-593-3400.

COPELAND, PHILLIPS JEROME, retired academic administrator, military officer; b. Oxnard, Calif., Mar. 22, 1921; s. John Charles and Marion (Moffatt) C.; m. Alice Janette Lusby, Apr. 26, 1942 (dec. April 1998); children: Janette Ann Copeland Bosserman (dec. Aug. 2000), Nancy Jo Copeland Briner; m. Joanne Barra Lankenau, July 9, 1999 (dec. June 2006). Student, U. So. Calif., 1947-49; BA, U. Denver, 1956, MA, 1958; grad., Air Command and Staff Coll., 1959, Indsl. Coll. Armed Forces, 1964. Commd. 2d lt. USAF, 1943, advanced through grades to col., 1964; pilot 8th Air Force, Eng., 1944-45; various flying and staff assignments, 1945-51; chief joint tng. sect. Hdqrs. Airsouth (NATO), Italy, 1952-54; asst. dir. plans and programs USAF Acad., 1955-58; assigned to joint intelligence Washington, 1959-61; plans officer Cincpac Joint Staff, Hawaii, 1961-63; staff officer, ops. directorate, then team chief Nat. Mil. command Ctr., Joint Chiefs of Staff, Washington, 1964-67; dir. plans and programs USAF Adv. Group, 1967-68; prof. aerospace studies U. So. Calif., LA, 1968-72, exec. asst. to pres., 1972-73, assoc. dir. office internat. programs, 1973-75, dir. adminstrv. svcs. Coll. Continuing Edn., 1975-82, dir. employee rels. LA, 1982-84. Advisor Vietnamese Air Force, Vietnam, 1967-68. Decorated D.F.C., Bronze Star, Air medal with 3 clusters, Medal of Honor (Vietnam). Mem. Air Force Assn., Order of Daedalians. Personal E-mail: gotcha3113@aol.com.

COPELAND, ROBERT BODINE, internist, cardiologist; b. Arab, Ala., Jan. 24, 1938; s. Haden Paul and Jimmie Alice (Bodine) Copeland; m. Virginia (Jenny) Ruth Trammell, June 26, 1960; children: Robert Theodore, Haden McTieyre. BS, Auburn U., 1960; MD, U. Ala., Birmingham, 1963. Diplomate Am. Bd. Internal Medicine, cert. internal medicine, cardiovasc. diseases and geriatrics. Intern then resident, clin. rsch. fellow in cardiology Mass. Gen. Hosp., Harvard Med. Sch., Boston, 1963-67; physician Clark Holder Clinic, LaGrange, Ga., 1967-77; founder, dir. Ga. Heart Clinic, LaGrange, 1972—2006; founder, pres. So. Cardiopulmonary Assocs., LaGrange, 1977—2003; clin. prof. med. U. Ala., Birmingham, 1980—2005, Emory U., Atlanta, 1980—. Bd. govs. Joint Commn. on Accreditation of Healthcare Orgns., Chgo., 1991—97, Am. Bd. Internal Medicine, Phila., 1980—86; trustee West Ga. Med. Sys., LaGrange. Contbr. Trustee LaGrange Coll.; chmn. bd. trustees ACP-ASIM Found., 1999—2002. Recipient Disting. Alumni award, U. Ala., Birmingham, 1985. Fellow: ACP (gov. Ga. chpt. 1987—91, Master 1993, regent 1993—99, chair bd. regents 1998—99), NAS Inst. Medicine, Am. Coll. Cardiology, Royal Coll. Physicians; mem.: Am. Clin. and Climatological Assn., Am. Heart Assn. (pres. Ga. affiliate 1985—86). Office: 1551 Doctors Dr Lagrange GA 30240-4139 Personal E-mail: rbcopelandmd@yahoo.com.

COPELAND, ROBERT GLENN, lawyer; b. San Diego, Mar. 15, 1941; s. Glenn Howard and Luella Louise (Schmid) C.; m. Harriet S. Smith, June 27, 1964 (div. Jan. 1977); children: Katherine Louise, Matthew Robert; m. Lynne Newman, Oct. 10, 1993; 1 child, Zachary Newman. AB, Occidental Coll., 1963; JD, U. So. Calif., 1966. Bar: Calif. 1966, U.S. Dist. Ct. Calif. (so. dist.), 1967. Ptnr. Gray, Cary, Ware & Freidenrich, San Diego, 1966-95, Luce, Forward Hamilton & Scripps, LLP, 1995—2004, Duane Morris LLP, 2004—. Mem. ABA, Calif. Bar Assn. Avocations: shooting, fly fishing, hiking, racquetball. Office: Duane Morris LLP 101 W Broadway Ste 900 San Diego CA 92101-3311 Office Phone: 619-744-2228. Business E-Mail: rcopeland@duanemorris.com.

COPELAND, ROBERT MARSHALL, music educator, department chairman; b. Douglas, Wyo., Jan. 30, 1945; s. Wilbur Clyde and Arvilla Estella (Walkinshaw) C.; m. Louise Margaret Edgar, June 10, 1966; children: Thomas Edgar, Anne Louise, Kathryn Elizabeth. BS, Geneva Coll., 1966; MM, U. Cin., 1970, PhD, 1974; postgrad., Westminster Choir Coll., 1981-82, Emory U., 1988. Asst. prof. to prof. music Mid-Am. Nazarene Coll., Olathe, Kans., 1971-81; prof. music, dir. choral activities Geneva Coll., Beaver Falls, Pa., 1981—, chmn. dept. music, 1981-99. Vis. lectr. U. Kans., Lawrence, 1977; trustee, sec. Ref. Presbyn. Theol. Sem., Pitts., 1981-93, vis. lectr., 1983-84; mem. Presbyn. and Ref. Joint Commn. on Chaplains and Mil. Pers., 1988-2002, sec., 1995-2002. Author: Spare No Exertions, 1986, Isaac Baker Woodbury: The Life and Works of an American Musical Populist, 1995; co-editor: The Book of Psalms for Singing, 1973; contbr. articles to profl. jours. Dir. music Internat. Covenanter Conf., Northfield, Minn., 1970, 76, 80, 84; ruling elder Ref. Presbyn. Ch., 1973—; moderator, Synod of the Ref. Presbyn. Ch. of N.Am., 1995-97; mem. Rep. County Com., 1992-2005. With AUS, 1966-68. NDEA fellow, 1968-71. Mem. AAUP (v.p. Kans. Conf. 1980-81), Am. Musicological Soc. (v.p. Allegheny chpt. 1987-89, 97-99, pres. 1989-91, 99-2001, coun. mem. 1992-95, 2001-04), Sonneck Soc. for Am. Music (founding mem., program com. 1982), Am. Choral Dirs. Assn. (co-editor Pa. Newsletter 1983-85, editor 1985-90), Soc. for Ethnomusicology, Huguenot Fellowship (bd. dirs. 1987—), Presbyn. and Ref. Joint Commn. on Chaplains and Mil. Pers. (sec. 1995-2002). Republican. Office: Geneva Coll 3200 College Ave Beaver Falls PA 15010-3557 Home: 116 Breezewood ct Beaver Falls PA 15010 Home Phone: 724-847-2759; Office Phone: 724-847-6665. Business E-Mail: rmc@geneva.edu.

COPELAND, SHARON, reporter; b. Cleve., Apr. 21, 1952; d. William James and Jessie Belle Copeland. BA, Cleve. State U., 1975. Freelancer, Cleve.; reporter Call & Post Newspaper, Cleve., Sta. KGIL Radio, LA; rschr. Sta. WERE Radio, Cleve.; news broadcaster Sta. WARO Radio, Cleve. Intake asst. San Fernando Valley Res. Mission; pub. asst. Fedn. Cmty. Planning. Recipient Grand award, LA Press Club, Best Documentary, San Fernando Valley Press Club. Mem.: Nat. Orgn. Women. Home: 12005 Craven Ave Cleveland OH 44105

COPELAND, SUZANNE JOHNSON, real estate company executive; b. Chgo., Aug. 01; d. John Berger and Eleanor (Dreger) Johnson; m. John Robert Copeland, Aug. 1, 1971 (div. June 1976). Assoc. French Lang. and Culture, Richland Coll., Dallas, 1974; BFA, Ill. Wesleyan U., Bloomington, 1965. Commercial artist Barney Donley Studio, Inc., Chgo., 1966-69; art dir. Levines Dept. Store, Dallas, 1970-74; creative dir. Titche-Goettinger, Inc., Dallas, 1974-78; catering mgr. Dunfey Hotel, Dallas, 1978-82; regional dir. corp. sales Rayburn Country Resort, Austin, Tex., 1982-84; real estate sales assoc. Henry S. Miller, Dallas, 1984-86; v.p. Exclusive Properties Internat., Inc., Dallas, 1986—. Cons. North Tex. Commn., Dallas, 1988. Acquisitions editor: Unser, An American Family Portrait, 1988. Mem. The Rep. Forum, Dallas, 1983-94; vol. Stars for Children, Dallas, 1988, Soc. for Prevention of Cruelty to Animals, Dallas, 1973-92, Preservation of Animal World Soc., 1986-92, Sedona Acad., 1996—, Sedona Humane Soc., 1996—. Sedona Women, 2001—; charter mem. P.M. League Dallas Mus. Art.; mem. Keep Sedona Beautiful, 1999—, Sedona Art Ctr., 2001—. Mem. Nat. Assn. Realtors, Tex. Assn. Realtors, Greater Dallas Assn. Realtors (com. chmn., Summit award 1984, 85), North Tex. Arabian Horse Club (bd. dirs. 1975-76, Pres.'s award 1978), Dallas Zool. Soc., Humane Soc. Dallas County (v.p. 1973-74), Humane Soc. U.S./Gulf States Humane Edn. Assn. (bd. dirs. 1990-91), Am. Montessori Soc., VASA Order of Am. (bd. dirs. Nordic Red Rocks Lodge 2004-), Delta Phi Delta, Phi Theta Kappa. Lutheran. Avocations: Arabian and thoroughbred horses, scuba diving. Office: Exclusive Properties PO Box 1973 Sedona AZ 86339 Office Phone: 928-203-9999. Personal E-mail: azmtnlion@aol.com.

COPELAND, TATIANA BRANDT, accountant; b. Dresden, Germany; came to U.S., 1959, naturalized, 1967; d. Cyril Alexander and Maria (von Satin) Brandt; m. Gerret van Sweringen Copeland, May 12, 1979. BS summa cum laude, UCLA, 1964; MBA, U. Calif., Berkeley, 1966. Sr. tax cons. Price Waterhouse & Co., LA, 1966-72; asst. tax mgr. Whittaker Corp., LA, 1972-75; mgr. internat. dept. E.I. Du Pont de Nemours, Wilmington, Del., 1975-80; pres. Tebec Assocs., Ltd., Wilmington, 1980—. Co-owner, CFO, Bouchaine Vineyards, Inc., Napa, Calif.; owner The Wine & Spirit Co., Greenville, Del.; co-owner, v.p. Rokeby Realty Co., Wilmington; pres. Napa Valley Holdings, Inc., Tebec Realty Internat. Co. Bd. dirs. Del. Symphony, Grand Opera House, Washington; mem. President's Adv. Com. for Trade Negotiations, 1982-87. Mem. AICPA, Am. Woman's Soc. CPA's, Am. Soc. Women Accts., Internat. Fiscal Assn., Del. Soc. CPA's, Phi Beta Kappa. Home: 175 Brecks Ln Wilmington DE 19807-3008 Office: PO Box 3662 Wilmington DE 19807-0662

COPENHAVER, CARL, physicist; b. NYC, May 18, 1929; s. Wilfred Monroe and Ethel Marker C.; 1 child, Sally Ann. BME, Columbia U., 1952, MME, 1954; MS in Physics, MIT, 1965; PhD in Physics, U. Tenn., 1976. Group leader Oak Ridge (Tenn.) Nat. Lab., 1954-60, also cons., 1966-69; group leader Mitre Corp., Bedford, Mass., 1962-64; reactor safety engr. Atomic Energy Commn., Oak Ridge, 1970-72; mem. staff Los Alamos (N.Mex.) Nat. Lab., 1984—. Instr. U. Tenn., Knoxville, 1971-74, mem. grad. council, 1975; vis. scientist Max-Planck-Institut fur Plasmaphysik, Garching, Fed. Republic Germany, 1977-79, Assn. EURATOM-CEA, Fontenay-aux-Roses, France, 1979-81; sci. specialist EG&G, Inc., Los Alamos, 1982-84; mem. faculty steering com. U. N.Mex., Los Alamos, 1972, adj. prof. physics, 1982-84. Contbr. articles to profl. jours; chpts. to books. Mem. Soc. Physics Students (councillor southwest region 1973), Am. Phys. Soc., AAAS, Sigma Xi, Tau Beta Pi, Sigma Pi Sigma. Office: Los Alamos Nat Scientific Lab PO Box 1663 # F641 Los Alamos NM 87544-0600

COPENHAVER, JOHN BARNS, not-for-profit executive, lawyer; b. Pearisburg, Va., Aug. 18, 1953; s. William Pierce and Jane Farrier Copenhaver; m. Diana Lynn Thompson, Dec. 10, 1994. BSc, Brown U., Providence, RI, 1975; JD, U. Ga., Athens, Ga., 1979. Bar: Ga. 1979; cert. bus. continuity profl. Disaster Recovery Inst., 1993. Geologist Texasgulf Inc., Houston, 1975—76; law clk. Ga. Ct. Appeals, Atlanta, 1980—81; regional dir. FEMA, Atlanta, 1981; pres. Disaster Recovery Inst. Internat., Atlanta, CEO. Bd. advisors Can. Ctr. Emergency Preparedness, Toronto, Ont., Canada, 2005—; bd. dir. Bus. Continuity Advancement Orgn., Tokyo. Co-author: A Legal Guide to Homeland Security and Emergency Preparedness for State and Local Governments; editor: Jane's Guide to Citizen Safety. Mem. Capital Campaign Com. U. Ga., Athens, 2005—06; founder, pres. Global Partnership Preparedness Found., Washington, 2004—; mem. Law Sch. Bd. Visitors U. Ga., 2002—05. Mem.: Buckhead Club, Commerce Club, Capital City Club, Kiwanis Club. Meth. Avocations: golf, travel, scuba diving. Office: Disaster Recovery Institute 1200 Abernathy Rd Suite 1700 Atlanta GA 30328 Home Phone: 770-552-8560; Office Phone: 770-350-2626. Business E-Mail: jcopenhaver@drii.org.

COPENHAVER, MARION LAMSON, retired state legislator; b. Andover, Vt., Sept. 26, 1925; d. Joseph Fenwick and Christine (Forbes) Lamson; m. John H. Copenhaver, June 30, 1946; children: John III, Margaret, Christine, Eric, Lisa. Student, U. Vt., 1945-46. Mem. N.H. Ho. of Reps., Concord, ranking Dem. health and human svcs. com., 1973-2000, mem. adminstrv. rules com., 1982-2000, mem. health and human svcs. oversight, 1990-2000; ret., 2000. Chair Grafton County Dems., 1986-91; assoc. supr. Grafton County Soil Conservation Dist., 1980-2002, supr., 2002—; supr. Hanover (N.H.) Dem. Town Com., 1992; mem.-at-large Dem. State Com., Concord, 1992; bd. dirs. Dartmouth Hitchcock Found., Hanover, 1991—; bd. incorporators Dartmouth Hitchcock Med. Ctr., Lebanon, N.H., 1984—; bd. dirs. Grafton County Sr. Citizens Coun., Inc., 1995-96, 2001, vice chair, Outreach House, an Assisted Living Facility, 2001—, Hanover, Friends of Norris Cotton Cancer Ctr., Women's Policy Inst. N.H. Named N.H. Legislator of Yr. N.H. Nurses Assn., 1989; recipient Meritorious award N.H. Women's Lobby, 1996, James A. Hamilton award N.H. Hosp. Assn., 1997. Mem. NOW, Bus. and Profl. Women's Club (Outstanding Mem. award 1990). Democrat. Unitarian Universalist. Avocations: golf, skiing. Home: 80 Lyme Rd 158 Hanover NH 03755 Home Phone: 603-643-5617. Personal E-mail: mlcope@valley.net.

COPENHAVER, W. ANDREW, lawyer; b. Roanoke, Va., Nov. 10, 1946; s. William Pierce and Jane Foote (Farrier) C.; m. Anne Phillips, July 7, 1973; children: William, Catherine, Andrew. BA, Duke U., 1969; cert. in internat. law, U. London, 1971; JD, U. N.C., 1972. Bar: N.C. 1972, U.S. Supreme Ct. 1981. Rsch. and teaching asst. Inst. Govt., 1970-72; assoc. Womble Carlyle Sandridge & Rice, Winston-Salem, N.C., 1972-77; ptnr. Womble, Carlyle, Sandridge & Rice, Winston-Salem, N.C., 1978-98, Washington, 1999—; head anti-trust and trade regulations sect. Womble Carlyle Sandridge & Rice, Winston-Salem, NC, 1992—2000. Mem. Fed. Bar Adv. Coun., N.C., 1992-98, chmn., 1994-95; permanent mem. Fourth Cir. Judicial Conf., 2000—. Bd. dirs. Winston-Salem Arts Coun., 1992-97, vice chmn., 1995-97; bd. dirs. U. N.C. Law Alumni Assn./Law Found., Inc., 1994-02, The Creel Found., 1998—, The Summit Sch., 1984-91, chmn., 1988-90; trustee Centenary United Meth. Ch., 1992-94. Fellow Am. Coll. Trial Lawyers, mem. Winston-Salem Rotary Club (bd. dirs. 1993-96), Old Town Club, Piedmont Club. Home: 1121 Arbor Rd Winston Salem NC 27104-1103 Office Phone: 336-721-3633. Personal E-mail: acopenhaver@wcsr.com.

COPES, MARVIN LEE, academic administrator; b. Connersville, Ind., Sept. 19, 1938; s. Kenneth Edward and Frances Gertrude (Bean) C.; m. Luretta Ann Grenard, Aug. 26, 1961; children: Bradley Alan, Brian Keith, Brent Lee. BS, Purdue U., 1961, MS, 1962, PhD, 1975; postgrad., Ind. State U., Terre Haute, 1967—68, Ind. U. Southeast, 1967—68. Cert. pub. mgr., Ky. Grad. asst. agrl. edn. Purdue U., West Lafayette, Ind., 1961—62, grad. instr., 1968—69; tchr. vocat. agriculture Tri-County Sch. Corp., Walcott, Ind., 1964—65; vocat. dir. Met. Sch. Dist. Vernon Twp., Crothersville, Ind., 1965—68; also dir. Ind. Vocat. Agr. Demonstration Ctr., 1965—68; asst. exec. sec. Kappa Delta Pi Hdqrs., West Lafayette, 1969—70; dir. Blue River Vocat.-Tech. Ctr., Shelbyville, Ind., 1970—79; nat. curriculum devel. coord. ITT Ednl. Svcs., Indpls., 1979—80, nat. dir. edn., 1980—82; dir. ITT Tech. Inst., Ft. Wayne, Ind., 1982—83, Indpls., 1983—86, Am. Coll., Mobile, Ala., 1986—89; nat. dir. edn. Am. Career Educators, Charlotte, NC, 1989, v.p. ednl. resources, 1989—91; pres. Treasure Wheel, Inc., Mobile, 1991—93; dean acad. affairs Phillips Jr. Coll., Mobile, 1992—96; v.p. acad. affairs Am. Inst. Commerce, Davenport, Iowa, 1993—96; dir. Ky. Tech. Jefferson State Campus, Louisville, 1996—98; pres. Jefferson Cmty. & Tech. Coll., 1998—2000, exec. dir. of occupl., tech. and apprenticeship programs, 2000—02, CEO Spl. Programs, 2001—02; dir. Heritage Inst., Falls Church, Va., 2002—03; edn., cmty. svc. AARP, Maylene, Ala., 2004—; ctr. mgr. Jefferson County WIA Career Ctr., Birmingham, 2004—05; dist. outreach coord. Employer Support the Guard and Reserve, 2004—; prin., owner Corp. Online Profile Employment Solutions, 2006—; job developer Jefferson County Office of Sr. Citizen Svcs., 2007—. Chmn. profl. devel. com. Ky. Postsecondary Tchr. Credentialing Adv. Bd.; mem. Welfare Reform Task Force, Ky.; bd. dirs. Pvt. Ind. Coun., Future Connections Sch. to Work; organizer Advanced Tech. Skills Acad., Advanced Welding Tech. Ctr.; pres. CopeSkills Cons., Power Ptnrs. cons.; columnist, Shelby County Reporter Newspaper, Sr. Living Newspaper. Author: A Curriculum Guide for Training in Agricultural Supply, 1968, Student Handbook for Cooperative Progress in Agricultural Occupations, 1968, A Predictability of Career Choices of High School Seniors, 1975, Personal Awareness Handbook, 1989, Retention Handbook, 1989, Placement Handbook, 1990, Vocational Adjustment Handbook, 1990, Train The Trainer Handbook, 1990, Instructor Certification Handbook, 1990, Administrative Certification Handbook, 1990, Master Teacher, 1990, Wheel of Fortune Enterprise Training Manual, 1991, Instructor Training Manual, 1993, Faculty Inservice Training Manual, 1993, Disaster Plan, 1993, Contract Training, 1994, School-to-Work Training, 1994, Assessment Planning, 1995, Welfare Reform, 1996, Guidelines for Apprenticeship Training, 2002, Guidelines for Corporate College, 2002, A Guide for Boomer and Business, 2007; mem. editl. bd. AARP/Ala.; columnist AgeTimes.com. Ops. coun. Met. Coll.; pres. Loper PTO, 1974-76; leader 4-H, 1964-68; advisor Future Farmers Am., 1964-70; cubmaster Boy Scouts Am., 1976-80, commr., bd. dirs. Shelbyville County, 1978-92; mem. vocat. gng. com. Futuring Project, NY State Dept. Edn.; bd. dirs. N.E. India Christian Mission, 1974, Kentuckiana Works; chmn. Shelby County Youth for Christ; mem. Nat. Curriculum Focus Group, 1993-96; bd. dirs., treas. Accrediting Coun. for Ind. Colls. and Schs., 1994; deacon area So. Bapt. Ch., 1995; mem. Kentukiana Edn. and Workforce Inst., Louisville Area Workforce Devel. Coun., School-to-Work Partnership Coun., Louisville/Jefferson County Redevel. Authority; bd. dirs. Career Resources One Stop Shop/Job Link, Pvt. Ind. Coun.; Louisville/Jefferson County Workforce investment bd., North Ctrl. Ky. Workforce Investment Bd.; mem. Louisville/Jefferson County Youth Coun., North Ctrl. Ky. Youth Coun., chmn.; mem. Immigrant/Refugee Task Force, Kentuckiana Works Skilled Trades Roundtable; mem. Leadership Louisville, 2000, Leadership Shelby County, 2005; sec., bd. dirs. Econ. and Indsl. Devel. Authority, Shelby County, 2006, edn. focus group, sr. vol. program, 2006; mem. Shelby County Transp. Task Force; mem. Ala. Rural Action Commn., 2007—. 1st lt. US Army, 1962-64. Recipient US Congrl. award, Dist. 6 Ala., Ala. Golden Eagle Journalism award, 2007. Mem. ASCD, Am. Vocat. Assn., Ind. Vocat. Assn., Nat. Coun. Local Adminstrs., Ind. Coun. Local Adminstrs., Bus. Profls. Am., Nat. Bus. Edn. Assn., Soc. Mfg. Engrs., Ky. Vocat. Assn. (pres. region 13), Robotics Internat., Network Iowa Svc. Learning, Ind. Assn. Pvt. Career Schs. (bd. dirs.), Future Farmers Am. Alumni Assn., Greater Shelby County C. of C., South Shelby County C. of C., Prichard C. of C. (bd. dirs.), Pershing Rifles, Gideons Internat., Metro Scholars, Davenport C. of C., Masons, Kiwanis, Order Ea. Star, Alpha Tau Alpha, Kappa Delta Pi, Phi Delta Kappa, Delta Pi Epsilon. Home: 108 Grande Club Dr Maylene AL 35114 Office Phone: 205-267-9304. Personal E-mail: mlcopes@charter.net. *Be a bridge for the life of others that they may cross on their life's journey. Education, motivation, goal setting and training are those bridges.*

COPES, PARZIVAL, economist, researcher; b. Nakusp, BC, Can., Jan. 22, 1924; s. Jan Coops and Elisabeth Catharina Coops-van Olst; m. Dina Gussekloo, May 1, 1946; children: Raymond Alden, Michael Ian, Terence Franklin. BA in Econs. & Polit. Sci., U. B.C., 1949, MA in Econs., 1950; PhD in Econs., London Sch. Econs., 1956; D in Mil. Sci. (hon.), Royal Roads Mil. Coll., 1991; D in Philosophy (hon.), U. Tromsö, 1993; DLitt (hon.), Meml. U. Newfoundland, 2004. Economist, statistician Dominion Bur. of Stats., Ottawa, Canada, 1953—57; from assoc. prof. to prof., head econs. dept. Meml. U. Nfld., St. John's, Canada, 1957—64; founding dir. econ. rsch. inst. Social and Econ. Rsch. Meml. U. Nfld., St. John's, 1961-64; prof. Simon Fraser U., Burnaby, B.C., Canada, 1964—91, founding head dept. econs. and commerce, 1964-69, chmn. dept. econs. and commerce, 1972—75, founding dir. Ctr. for Can. Studies, 1978—85, founding dir. Inst. of Fisheries Analysis, 1980—94, prof. emeritus, 1991—. Gov. Inst. Can. Bankers, Montreal, Que., 1967-71; dir. Can.-Fgn. Arrangements Project, Can. Govt. Dept. Environment, 1976; pres., chmn. Pacific Regional Sci. Conf. Orgn., 1977-85; spl. advisor to Minister of Fisheries, B.C., 1998; initiator, dir. collaborative rsch. and tng. agreement with Asian Fisheries Social Sci. Rsch. Network, 1989-94. Author: The Statistical Measurement of Morbidity Frequency, 1957, St. John's and Newfoundland: An Economic Survey, 1961, The Backward-Bending Supply Curve of the Fishing Industry, 1970, The Resettlement of Fishing Communities in Newfoundland, 1972, Factor Rents, Sole Ownership and the Optimum Level of Fisheries Exploitation, 1972, A Critical Review of the Individual Quota as a Device in Fisheries Management, 1986, The Extended Economics of an Innate Common Use Resource: The Fishery, 1998, Equity and the Rights Basis of Fishing in Iceland and Canada: Reflections on the Icelandic Supreme Court Decision, 1999, Sharing the Fishery Resources of the North Pacific for Mutual Advantage: Toward an International Management Regime, 1999, Aboriginal Fishing Rights and Salmon Management in British Columbia: Matching Historical Justice with the Public Interest, 2000, (with G Palsson) Challenging ITQs: Legal and Political Action in Iceland, Canada and Latin America, 2001, Fisheries Management Options: The Case for Limited Entry over ITQs, 2001, An Exploration of Fishery Access Rights and Community-Based Fishery Management for the Central and North Coast of British Columbia, 2003, A Vision for Community-Based Development of the Fisheries Sector on the Central and North Coast of British Columbia, 2003.(with A. Charles) Socio-Economics of Individual Transferable Quotas and Community-Based Fishery Management, 2004. With Netherlands Resistance Army, 1942—45, attached Can. Army, 1945—46, with Can. Officers Tng. Corps, 1946—49, lt. Can. Army, 1950—51, capt. 113 Manning Depot Can. Army Militia, 1953—57, capt. to maj. CO112 Manning Depot Can. Army Militia, 1957—63. Decorated officer Order of Can.; recipient Can. Forces Decoration, Can. Army, 1963. Fellow Acad. Natural Scis. of Russian Fedn. (fgn.); mem. Internat. Inst. Fisheries Econs. and Trade (exec. com. 1982-86, Disting. Svc. award 1996), Internat. Assn. for Study of Common Property, Can. Regional Sci. Assn. (pres. 1983-85), Can. Econs. Assn. (v.p. 1972-73), Assn. for Can. Studies, Western Regional Sci. Assn. (pres. 1977-78), Social Sci. Fedn. Can. (dir., v.p. 1979-83), Can. Assn. Univ. Tchrs., Internat. Arctic Sci. Com., Simon Fraser U. Faculty Assn. (life). Achievements include some of earliest research contributions to establish sub-discipline of fisheries economics; writing, speaking, research and international consulting in fisheries policy and resource management. Home and Office: 2341 Lawson Ave West Vancouver BC Canada V7V 2E5 Business E-Mail: copes@sfu.ca.

COPITHORNE, DAVID A., public relations executive; BS, Harvard U., 1975. CEO, co-founder Copithorne & Bellows (now Porter Novelli Convergence Group), Boston, 1988—2002; principal Aquarius Advisers, Newton Ctr., Mass., 2002—. Chief mktg. officer Outside the Classroom. Office: Aquarius Advisers 152 Homer St Newton Center MA 02459

COPLEY, DAVID C., newspaper publishing company executive; s. Helen K. and James S. Copley (Stepfather). BSBA, Menlo Coll., 1975. Pres., CEO, chmn. Copley Press, Inc., La Jolla, Calif., 1988—; chair, exec. com., chmn. sr. mgmt. bd. and bd. dir. The Copley Press, Inc., La Jolla, Calif.; pub. The San Diego Union-Tribune, 2001—, The Borrego Sun. Chair, pres. Copley N.W., Inc., Puller Paper Co.; pres. Copley News Svc.; trustee Copley Ohio Newspapers, The Peoria Jour. Star, Inc., The Gales. Print. and Publ. Co.; pres. Copley Northwest, Inc. and puller paper Co., others. Mem. editl. bd. San Diego Union-Tribune. Pres., trustee & pres. James S. Copley Found.; trustee Canterbury Sch., San Diego Crew Classic Found.; trustee emeritus La Jolla Playhouse, Am. Craft Coun., Mus. Photog. Arts; pres. assoc., pres. adv. com., exhibits com. Zool. Soc. San Diego; adv. bd. San Diego Automotive Mus.; pres. coun. Scripps Clinic and Rsch. Found., San Diego Kind Corp.; active Pres. Club U. San Diego, San Diego Aerospace Mus., San Diego Hall Sci., San Diego Maritime Mus., San Diego Coun. on Literacy. Named one of 400 Richest Americans, Forbes, 2005, 2006. Mem. Nat. Newspaper Assn., U.S. Humane Soc., San Diego Hist. Soc., San Diego Humane Soc., Bachelor Club San Diego. Office: The Copley Press Inc PO Box 1530 La Jolla CA 92038-1530 Office Phone: 858-454-0411.*

COPLEY, EDWARD ALVIN, lawyer; b. Memphis, Jan. 17, 1936; m. Connie James Patterson, Nov. 17, 1990; children: Julie, Ward, Drew, Kelly, Zeke. BA, So. Meth. U., 1957, JD, 1960. Bar: U.S. Dist. Ct. (no. dist.) Tex., U.S. Ct. Claims 1962, U.S. Supreme Ct. 1963, U.S. Tax Ct. 1966, U.S. Ct. Appeals (5th cir.) 1968. Atty. U.S. Dept. Justice, Washington, 1960-64, Ft. Worth, 1964-66; assoc. Akin, Gump, Strauss, Hauer & Feld, Dallas, 1966-67, ptnr., 1968—2001, sr. counsel, 2001—. Fellow Am. Coll. Probate Counsel; mem. Internat. Acad. Estate Trust Law, Dallas Bar Assn. (tax sect.), Dallas Estate Coun. (pres. 1975-76), So. Meth. U. Law Sch. Alumni Assn. (pres. 1978-79), Salesmanship Club, Order of Woolsac, Barristers, Dallas Country Club, Phi Alpha Delta. Avocations: racquetball, photography, hunting, fishing, reading. Home: 3711 Shenandoah St Dallas TX 75205-2120 Office: Akin Gump Strauss Hauer & Feld Ste 4100 1700 Pacific Ave Dallas TX 75201-4675 E-mail: ecopley@akingump.com.

COPMAN, LOUIS, radiologist; b. Phila., Jan. 17, 1934; s. Jacob and Eve (Snyder) C.; m. Avera Schuster, June 8, 1958; children: Mark, Linda. BA, U. Pa., 1955, MD, 1959. Diplomate Am. Bd. Radiology; Nat. Bd. Med. Examiners. Commd. ensign Med. Corps USN, 1958; advanced through grades to capt. M.C. USN, 1975; ret., 1975; asst. chief radiology dept. Naval Hosp., Pensacola, Fla., 1966—69; chief radiology dept. Doctors Hosp., Phila., 1969—73; radiologist Mercer Hosp. Ctr., Trenton, NJ, 1973—75; chmn. radiology dept. Naval Hosp., Phila., 1975—84; chief. radiology dept. Naval Med. Clinic, Pearl Harbor, Hawaii, 1984—89; pvt. practice radiologist Honolulu, 1989—92. Cons. Radiology Svcs., Wilmington, Del., 1978-84, Yardley (Pa.) Radiology, 1979-84. Author: The Cuckold, 1974. Capt. med. corps USN, 1958—89, ret., 1989. Recipient Albert Einstein award in Medicine, U. Pa., 1959. Mem. AMA, Assn. Mil. Surgeons U.S., Royal Soc. Medicine, Radiol. Soc. N.Am., Am. Coll. Radiology, Photographic Soc. Am., Sherlock Holmes Soc., Phi Beta Kappa, Alpha Omega Alpha. Avocations: photography, hang-gliding, scuba diving. Home: PO Box 384767 Waikoloa HI 96738-4767 Office: 68-1771 Makanahele Pl Waikoloa HI 96738-5128 Office Phone: 808-883-0059. Personal E-mail: louiscopman@earthlink.net. *Throughout one's life, one should choose his companions wisely.*

COPPA, FRANK JOHN, historian, educator; b. NYC, July 18, 1937; s. Peter Paul and Rafaella Coppa; m. Rosina Genovese, Aug. 7, 1965; children: Francesca, Melina. BA in History, Bklyn. Coll., 1960; MA in History, Cath. U. Am., Washington, 1962, PhD in History, 1966. Tchg. fellow Cath. U. Am., Washington, 1963—64; lectr. Bklyn. Coll., 1964; from instr. to assoc. prof. St. John's U., NYC, 1965—79, prof., 1979—. Guest spkr. Sta. WNBC-AM, NYC, 1972—73, Sta. WPAT-FM, NYC, 1972—73. Author: Economics and Politics in the Giolittian Age, 1971, Camillo di Cavour, 1973, Pope Pius IX, 1979, Cardinal Giacomo Antonelli and Papal Politics in European Affairs, 1990, The Origins of the Italian Wars of Independence, 1992, The Modern Papacy since 1789, 1998, The Papacy Confronts the Modern World, 2003, The Papacy, The Jews and The Holocaust, 2006; editor (with B. Bast and W. Griffin): From Vienna to Vietnam: War and Peace in the Modern World, 1969; editor: (with P. Dolce) Cities in Transition: From the Ancient World to Urban America, 1974; editor: Religion in the Making of Western Man, 1974; editor: (with T. Curran) The Immigration Experience in America, 1976; editor: Screen and Society: The Impact of Television upon Aspects of Contemporary Civilization, 1979; editor: (with R. Harmond) Technology in the Twentieth Century, 1983; editor: Dictionary of Modern Italian History, 1985, Studies in Modern Italian History: From the Risorgimento to the Republic, 1986, Italian History: An Annotated Bibliography, 1990, Controversial Concordats: The Vatican's Relations with Napoleon, Mussolini, and Hitler, 1999, Encyclopedia of the Vatican and Papacy, 1999, Great Popes Through History: An Encyclopedia, 2002, Encyclopedia of Modern Dictators: From Napoleon to the Present, 2006; editor: (assoc. editor) New Catholic Encyclopedia, 2007; contbr. articles to profl. jours.; lectr. (TV series) The Evolution of Cities: From the Village to Megalopolis and Beyond, 1972, acad. coord., participant (TV miniseries) The Immigrant in American Life, 1973, The Italian American-Experience: Past and Present, 1979. Fellow, KC, 1960—64; grantee, NEH, 1977, Banca Commerciate Italiana; Genoroso Pope scholar, 1956, Fulbright grantee, Italy, 1964—65, U.S. Ednl. Program Found. grantee, Belgium, 1965, Italian Ministry of Fgn. Affairs grantee, Columbia U., 1989. Mem.: Italian Hist. Soc. Am. (bd. dirs. 1991—), Interuniversity Ctr. European Studies, Instituto per la storia del Risorgimento, N.Y. State Assn. European Historians, Am. Cath. Hist. Soc. (mem. exec. coun. 1991—), Soc. Italian Hist. Studies, Am. Hist. Assn. Roman Catholic. Office: Saint Johns U Dept History Jamaica NY 11439 Office Phone: 718-990-6090. Business E-Mail: coppaf@stjohns.edu.

COPPEL, LAWRENCE DAVID, lawyer; b. Washington, July 3, 1944; s. Albert and Anne (Gold) C.; m. Arlene Cohen, Aug. 10, 1968; children: Jennifer, Allison. BA, U. Md., 1966, JD, 1969. Bar: Md. 1969, U.S. Dist. Ct. Md. 1971, U.S. Ct. Appeals (4th cir.) 1976, U.S. Ct. Appeals (3d cir.) 1983. Law clk. Md. Ct. Appeals, Annapolis, 1969-70; assoc. Gordon, Feinblatt, Rothman, Hoffberger & Hollander, LLC, Balt., 1970-77, mem., 1977—. Fellow Am. Coll. Bankruptcy; mem. ABA, Md. State Bar Assn., Bankruptcy Bar Assn. Dist. Md. (pres. 1988-89), Balt. City Bar Assn. Office: Gordon Feinblatt Rothman Hoffberger & Hollander LLC 233 E Redwood St Baltimore MD 21202-3332 Office Phone: 410-576-4000. E-mail: lcoppel@gfrlaw.com.

COPPER, JAMES ROBERT, manufacturing executive; b. St. Louis, Aug. 19, 1939; s. Charles Alva and Cora Imogene (Shifley) Copper; m. Patricia Leeper, Aug. 12, 1961; children: Susan, Robin, Julie. AB, Culver-Stockton Coll., 1961; MS, U. Tenn.-Knoxville, 1969. Tchr. Mo. Mil. Acad., Mexico, 1961-63; mgr. applications analysis Nuclear div. Union Carbide, Oak Ridge, Tenn., 1963-69; mgr. corp. mgmt. scis. Coca-Cola Co., Atlanta, 1969-76; v.p. strategic planning and analysis Pillsbury Co., Mpls., 1976-80; v.p. strategic planning IC Industries, Inc., Chgo., 1980-86, sr. v.p. corp. planning and devel., 1986-88; pres., COO Pet, Inc., St. Louis, 1988, pres., CEO, 1989—. Mem. Civic Progress; bd. dirs. YMCA Greater St. Louis, St. Louis area counc. Boy Scouts Am., United Way St. Louis, Boatmen's Nat. Bank of St. Louis, Christmas in St. Louis, St. Louis Variety Club, Culver-Stockton Coll. Mem. Mo. Athletic Club, St. Louis Club, Old Warson Country Club. Home: 5777 Gene Sarazen Dr Braselton GA 30517-4057

COPPERFIELD, DAVID (DAVID KOTKIN), illusionist, director, producer; b. Metuchen, NJ, 1956; Student, Fordham U., LHD (hon. doctorate with Sen. George Mitchell), 1999. Prof. magic NYU, 1974. Vanished a Jet Plane, 1981, levitated across Grand Canyon, 1984; walked through Great Wall of China, 1986; vanished Statue of Liberty, 1983; escaped from Alcatraz prison, 1987; survived bldg. implosion challenge, 1989; went over Niagara Falls, 1990; vanished Orient Express, 1991, introduced flying illusion, 1992 (flying in 8 years over 467 hours); escaped from burning ropes 13 stories above ground before 15,000 people, 1993; survived inside core of 2000 degree tornado of fire, 2001; performer, dir., producer, writer (TV spls.) The Magic of David Copperfield annually since 1978; presdl. command performance, 1980, 81, 82, 85, 87, 92, 97, 2002; performer (musical) Magic Man, 1974; appeared in film Terror Train, 1980; author: Tales of the Impossible, 1995, (with Ray Bradbury and Dean Koontz) Beyond Imagination, 1996. Creator, founder Project Magic (an internat. rehab. program now in 1000 hosps. in over 30 countries), 1982; nat. spokesperson at Olympics US Orgn. Disabled Athletes, Seoul, Republic of Korea, 1988; founder Internat. Mus. Library of the Conjuring Arts, 1992. Decorated chevalier Arts and Letters (France), Knighted, French Govt.; recipient 21 Emmy awards and/or nominations, 1979, 80, 81, 83, 84, 85, 86, 88, 89, 90, 91, 92, 2001, Golden Rose award Montreux Film Festival, 1987, Bambi award-European equivalent of Oscars, 1993; named Magician of Yr. Acad. Magical Arts, 1980, 87; named Entertainer of Yr. Am. Guild Variety Artists, 1981, City of Atlantic City, 1986, Nat. Assn. Campus Activities, 1987; named one of Ten Outstanding Young Men in Am. U.S. Jaycees, 1985; named one of Top Ten Entrepreneurs (age 30 or under) Young Entrepreneur Orgn., 1987; named America's Fastest Rising Star by Forbes Mag., 1993, Mardi Gras King, 1996, Magician of Millennium, Fedn. Internat. des Soc. Magiques, 2000, Magician of Century, Internat. Magician's Soc.; named a living legend Libr. of Congress, 2000, Magician of Century; recipient Bambi award, 1993, Golden Rose award, Montreux Film Festival, Millenium Merlin award Internat. Magician's Soc., Golden Ticket award Germany, 2005, 06; named to Forbes Highest Paid Celebrity List, 1997—. Achievements include being youngest magician to be inducted into the Soc. Am. Magicians at age 14, most awarded magician in history, Guinness Book of World Records, 2005, most amount of money earned by a magician, 2005, created world's largest magic collection/museum, 2005, highest total internat. TV audience for a magician, 2005, largest amount of shows per year, 2005, Am. producer to premiere Am. TV spl. in Peoples Republic of China, 1986; Broke box office attendance records Miami Knight Ctr., 1984, Warner Theater, Washington, 1985, Caesars Palace, Las Vegas, Nev., 1985, Taipei Sports and Cultural Stadium, 1987, Premier Theater, Mexico City, 1987, Coliseum, Hong Kong, 1988, World Trade Ctr., Singapore, 1988, Putra World Trade Ctr.,

Kuala Lumpur, 1988, Giganto Arena, Porto Allegre, Brazil, 1988, Fox Theatre, Detroit, 1989, 92; broke European attendance record Dortmond, Germany, 1993; Broadway record holder, Dreams and Nightmares with Francis Ford Coppola, 1997; Madame Tussaud's Waxworks, Flying Wax Copperfield, London, 1995; inducted Hollywood Walk of Fame, 1995; featured on postage stamps for 4 countries, 2000, record for largest total tickets sold worldwide for a solo entertainer, 2005; 1st living magician inducted into the Hollywood Walk of Fame; only living magician featured on US postage stamp.

COPPERMAN, STUART MORTON, pediatrician, educator; b. Bklyn., June 5, 1935; s. Irving and Anne (Reisfield) C.; m. Renee Stein, Aug. 17, 1958; children: Beth, Alan, Cara. BA cum laude, Bklyn. Coll., 1956; MD, SUNY-Bklyn., 1960. Diplomate Am. Bd. Pediatrics. Rotating intern. L.I. Jewish Hosp., New Hyde Park, NY, 1960-61, resident in pediat., 1961-63; practice medicine specializing in pediat. Merrick, NY, 1965-2000; sr. med. cons. Med. Advisers, P.C., 2001—02; mem. staff L.I. Jewish Hillside Med. Ctr., Schneider Children's Hosp., New Hyde Park, Nassau County Med. Ctr., East Meadow, Winthrop U. Hosp., Mineola, North Shore Univ. Hosp., Manhasset; clin. assoc. prof. pediat. SUNY Med. Sch., Stony Brook, 1972-2000; asst. prof. clin. health studies SUNY Sch. Allied Health, Stony Brook, 1977-2000; clin. instr. physicians asst. program Stony Brook Med. Ctr., 1972-2000; prof. pediat. St. George's Med. Coll., St. Vincent, W.I., acting chmn. pediat., 1979-80; healthcare security analyst, healthcare cons., 2000—02; medico-legal expert, 2000—04; physician exec. Health and Info. Svcs., 2001—02; pres. SMCMD, Ltd., 2003—; CEO Profl. Practice Brokers, 2002—; cons. Learning Dynamics, Inc., 2006—. Med. advisor Assn. Children with Downs Syndrome, 1971-98; mem. com. for handicapped Bellmore Sch. Dist., 1976-86; mem. ad hoc com. on cmty. as sch. Merrick-Bellmore Schs., 1976-90; bd. dirs. North Shore-L.I. Jewish I.P.O., L.I. Sch. Health Edn. Coalition, North Shore Physicians Orgn., North Shore - L.I. Jewish PHO; mem. Nassau County Sch. Health Edn. Commn., 1990-93; mem. ad hoc com. on prevention of birth defects March of Dimes; preceptor in pediat. Physicians Asst. Program, Cath. Med. Ctr.; mem. doctor's adv. com. Shaare Zedek Hosp., Jerusalem, 1974-98; med. cons. Matchbox Toys, 1985-88, Proctor & Gamble, 1988, Carnation Co., 1989-90, Disney Ednl. Svcs., 1990-95, vaccine divsn. Merck Corp., 1997—, Sepracor, 1999—; cons., mem. spkrs. bur. N.Y. State Med. Soc., N.Y. State Senate Com. Mental Hygiene, 1988—, Lederle Labs., 1989-95, Merck Labs., 1996—, Wallace Labs., 1996—, ucb Pharma, 1999—, Connaught, 1999—, Abbott Labs., 1996—, Pfizer, 1998—, Sepracor, 1999—; author, co-founder, pres., bd. dirs. Child Health Imagery Prodns.; founder, dir. brokerage website, 2002—. Author: Buying and Selling a Medical or Dental Practice, 2007; appearance TV shows on Downs Syndrome, learning disabilities, CPR, first aid, infant exercise programs, TV's effects on children, infectious disease, parent-infant bonding, immunizations, enuresis, toilet training, prevention of cigarette smoking among children, 1972—, also on HealthLinks (Life Time TV), 1990-93; mem. editl. adv. bd. Jour. Assn. for Physician Assts., 1987—; editl. cons. Jour. Pediat. Mgmt., 1991—; contbr. chpt. to Textbook Pediat. Sports Medicine; developer Babycise (infant parent interactive program in video tape and book form), 1985; rschr. on hetacillin, 1966, pyridoxine effect on serotonin level and performance in children with Down's Syndrome, 1970-75, Alice in Wonderland syndrome as presenting sympton of infectious mononucleosis, 1966-77, on transmission of group A Beta hemolytic strep infection from pet reservoirs to children, 1963-81; med. editor Air Fair Mag., 1991-93, L.I. Parent Mag., 1985-93, L.I. Family Mag., 1994-95; contbr. articles to profl. jours. Mem. sch. bd. Temple Beth Am., Merrick, 1972-78, mem. exec. com., 1973-74, chmn. com. Israel and World Affairs, 1976-78, mem. sch. com., 1976-78, mem. ritual com., 1976-93; mem. N.Y. State Senate com. on mental hygiene, 1990—; mem. profl. adv. bd. So. Shore divsn. YM-YWHA; benefactor Merrick Libr., 1992—. With U.S. Army, 1963-65. Recipient Physician Recognition award AMA, 1966—, testimonial dinner and plaque Assn. Children with Down Syndrome, 1972, Best Clin. Tchrs. of Pediat. award Nassau County Med. Ctr., 1981-82; named Merrick Profl. of Yr., 1994. Fellow Am. Acad. Pediat. (chmn. com. TV effects on children 1976—, mem. nat. com. comm. and pub. info. 1984-85, mem. nat. com. on substance abuse 1998-2001, media spokesperson 1988—, tobacco, alcohol and drug-free generation coord. 1988-98, chmn. substance abuse com. 1992—, N.Y. state chmn. substance abuse com. 1992-94, managed care com. chpt. 2 1993-95), Internat. Coll. Pediat.; mem. AMA, N.Y. State Med. Soc. (com. on alcohol 1997—), Nassau County Med. Soc. (com. on mental health 1980—, project assist 1992—, Nassau Acad. Medicine Pub. Health com. 1991—, libr. com. 1993—, chmn. pediat. sect. 1995—), Nassau Pediat. Soc. (mem. exec. bd. 1972—, chmn. com. on mental health 1972-88, v.p. 1994-95, pres. 1996-97). A Non-Smoking Generation Internat. (organizer, med. dir. Am. divsn.), Am. Lung Assn., Nassau-Suffolk Lung Assn. (life mem., dir. 1982-84), Am. Physicians Fellowship for Israel Med. Assn., Assn. Children with Learning Disabilities (mem. profl. adv. bd.), La Leche League, Latin Am. Parents Assn., L.I. Sch. Health Edn. Coun. (bd. dirs. 1989-92), Alpha Epsilon Pi (chancellor Phi Theta chpt. 1955-56), Phi Delta Epsilon (consul Zeta chpt. 1960), B'nai Brith. Office: 676 Balfour Pl Melville NY 11747 Home Phone: 631-367-3050; Office Phone. 516-698-3517. Personal E-mail: smcmd@aol.com. *No one person can do everything - but every person can do something. If you want something done, give it to a busy person. We must live for today with an eye toward tomorrow. I'd like my epitaph to read "While alive, he lived.".*

COPPERSMITH, SUSAN NAN, physicist, b. Johnstown, Pa., Mar. 18, 1957; d. Wallace Louis and Bernice Barbara (Evans) C.; m. Robert Daniel Blank, Dec. 20, 1981. BS in Physics, MIT, 1978; postgrad., Cambridge U., 1979; MS in Physics, Cornell U., 1981, PhD in Physics, 1983. Rsch. assoc. Brookhaven Nat. Labs., 1983-85; postdoctoral mem. tech. staff AT&T Bell Labs., Murray Hill, N.J., 1985-86, mem. tech. staff, 1987-90, disting. mem. tech. staff, 1990-95; prof. physics U. Chgo., 1995—2001, prof., chair dept. physics U. Wis., Madison, 2001—. Vis. lectr. Princeton U., 1986-87, vis. professorship for women NSF, 1986-87; gen. mem. Aspen Ctr. for Physics, 1991—2006; chancellor's disting. lectr. U. Calif., Irvine, 1991. Trustee Aspen Ctr. for Physics, 1993-96. Winston Churchill scholar, 1978-79, Bell Labs. GRPW fellow, 1979-83. Fellow AAAS, Am. Phys. Soc., Am. Acad. Arts and Scis. Office: Univ Wis Dept Physics 1150 University Ave Madison WI 53706 Office Phone: 608-262-8358. E-mail: snc@physics.wisc.edu.

COPPIE, COMER SWIFT, retired state official; b. Washington, Oct. 19, 1932; s. John Lee and Marion (Peck) C.; m. Judith Ann Wright, Apr. 29, 1961; children: Cynthia, Sean, Scott. AB, Hamilton Coll., 1955; M in Pub. Adminstrn., Syracuse U., 1959. Budget analyst Bur. of Budget, State of Md., Balt., 1958—62; exec. dir., trustee Md. State Colls., Balt., 1963—68; dep. budget dir. Govt. of D.C., Washington, 1968—69; dir. Office of Budget and Mgmt. Systems, Washington, 1969—78; exec. dir. N.Y. State Fin. Control Bd., NYC, 1978—86; CFO U.S. Postal Svc., Washington, 1986—92; 1st dep. compt. Office of State Compt., Albany, NY, 1993—99; ret., 1999. Past bd. dirs., past pres. Homeless and Travelers Aid Agy., Albany. Served with USN, 1955-57. Recipient Gold medal Fin. Officers Assn. of U.S. and Can., 1978. Mem. Cosmos Club (Washington). Episcopalian. Avocation: swimming. Personal E-mail: csc@aol.com.

COPPIN, CARYL MARY, retired librarian; b. Lakeview, Oreg., Dec. 24, 1917; d. Walter Herman and Edith Myron (Ogle) Leehmann; m. Cleve Woodrow Coppin, June 20, 1941 (dec.); children: Donald James, Michael John, Susan Edith. BS, Oreg. State U., Corvallis, 1940; postgrad., U. Oreg., Eugene, 1961, Portland State U., Oreg., 1961, Ea. Oreg. U., La Grande, 1962, postgrad., 1964. Cert. tchr. Oreg. Home demonstration agt. War Foods Adminstrn., Farm Security Adminstrn., Oreg., 1941—42; sch. libr. Joseph H.S., Oreg., 1964—66, Enterprise H.S., Oreg., 0196—1975; ret. Mem. Ea. Oreg. Tri County libr. bd. Oreg. State Libr., Enterprise, 1962—64; bd. chair Wallowa County Libr., Enterprise, 1964—72. Leader 4H, Joseph, 1954—65; bd. chmn., mem. Wallowa County Fair, Enterprise, 1985—99; bd. mem., chmn. Ea. Oreg. Devel. Coun., La Grand - Enterprise, Oreg., 1985—95; bd. dirs. Wallowa Mus. Named Woman of Yr., Beta Sigma Phi, 1981; recipient Unsung Hero award, Wallowa County C. of C., 1999. Mem.: PEO (pres. Enterprise chpt. 1984—85), Oreg. Ret. Tchr., Soroptimist Internat. (pres., sec. Wallowa County chpt. 1964—2006), Future Farmers Am. (hon.), Ea. Star (50 Yr. Pin for membership 2000). Avocation: painting. Home: 86439 Fort Rd Joseph OR 97846

COPPOCK, DORIS ELLEN, retired physical education educator, retired music educator; b. Chgo., May 18, 1927; d. Xury Landon and Martha Ellen (Evans) Coppock. AB, McPherson Coll., 1948; MA, U. Iowa, 1954, PhD, 1964. H.S. tchr. English, phys. edn., music, Hamilton, Kans., 1948—49; social worker Montgomery County Welfare Dept., Independence, Kans., 1949—50; from instr. to prof. McPherson (Kans.) Coll., 1950—92; ret., 1992. Tchr. Colo. State U., Gunnison, 1992; pres. Kans. Assn. Intercollegiate Athletics for Women, 1967—68, Ctrl. Assn. Phys. Edn. for Coll. Women, 1975—77. Active Meals on Wheels, McPherson, 1996—2000; ct. apptd. spl. advocate A Voice for Children, Inc., 2004—; ch. choir dir. Luth. Ch., McPherson, 1956—63, Presbyn. Ch., McPherson, 1964—77, Meth. Ch., McPherson, 1978—89; min. music Ch. of the Brethren, McPherson, 1993—2002. Named Coach of Yr. (Tennis), McPherson Coll., 1976, 1977, Woman of Yr., Soroptimist Internat. (McPherson, Kans. chpt.), 1977; named to Hall of Fame, Nat. Assn. Intercollegiate Athletics, 1993, Athletic Hall of Fame, McPherson Coll., 1999; recipient Honor award, Kans. Assn. for Health, Phys. Edn. and Recreation, 1980, Alumni Citation of Merit, McPherson Coll., 1993, Project Acclaim award, Nat. Assn. Girls and Women's Sports, 1996, Pathfinder award, 2004; grantee, NEH, 1987. Mem.: AAHPERD (life). Avocations: golf, music, reading, travel. Home: 1015 Darlow Dr Mcpherson KS 67460 E-mail: decop@sbcglobal.net.

COPPOCK, JANET ELAINE, mental health nurse; b. Tipton, Ind., June 2, 1954; d. Jack Donavon and Bonnie Ruth (Luse) Weismiller; divorced; children: Jonathan Andrew, Daniel Jason. Student, Ball State U., 1972—73; ASN, Ind. U. Kokomo, 1977. RN, Ind., Mich.; cert. psychiat./mental health nurse ANCC. RN charge staff and med.-surg. Tipton County Meml. Hosp., Ind., 1977—79; RN psychiat. staff Howard Cmty. Hosp., Kokomo, 1987—89; pvt. nurse Kokomo, 1989—95; RN psychiat. and addiction treatment, instr. Koala Hosp. & Counseling Ctr. Behavioral Healthcare Corp., Kokomo, 1995—98; RN psychiat. and addiction treatment Lafayette Behavioral Health System, Ind., 1998—99; RN psychiat. staff, patient care coord. Home Hosp. of Greater Lafayette Health Svcs., Inc., Lafayette, 1999—. Instr. parenting edn. Kinsey Youth Ctr., Kokomo, 1995-96; co-developer Koala Halfway House, Behavioral Healthcare Corp., Kokomo, 1996, house mgr., 1996-98. Author: Poetic Reflections, Expressions and Inspirations, 1986, Faithful Resolutions, 1993, Coming to Terms, 1998. Recipient Golden Poet award World Poetry Orgn., 1987, 88. Mem.: Nurses Svc. Orgn., Internat. Platform Assn, Ind. U. Alumni Assn. (life). Avocations: music, art, movies, basketball. Home: 2711 President Ln Kokomo IN 46902-3066

COPPOCK, RICHARD MILES, retired not-for-profit administrator; b. Salem, Ohio, Mar. 17, 1938; s. Guy Lamar and Helen Angeline (Johnston) Coppock; m. Rita Mae McArtor, June 20, 1961 (div. 1973); 1 child, Carole; m. Trelma Anne Kubacak, Nov. 21, 1973; children: James, Lori. BS, USAF Acad., 1961; MSME, U. Colo., 1969. Commd. 2d lt. USAF, 1961, advanced through grades to lt. col., 1983, ret., 1983; pres., CEO Assn. Grads. USAF Acad., Colo., 1983-99, ret., 1999. Decorated DFC (4), Air medal (29); named Outstanding Alumnus, Salem HS, 1980. Mem.: VFW (life), Mil. Officers Assn. Am., Elks, Am. Legion. Republican. Methodist. Avocations: music, history. Home: 2513 Mirror Lake Ct Colorado Springs CO 80919-3515

COPPOLA, FRANCIS FORD, film director, producer, writer; b. Detroit, Apr. 7, 1939; s. Carmine Coppola; m. Eleanor Neil; children: Gian-Carlo(dec.) , Roman, Sofia. BA, Hofstra U., 1958; Master of Cinema, UCLA, 1968. Pub. mag., San Francisco, 1975-76. Artistic dir. Zoetrope Studios.; dir. films including Dementia 13, 1964, You're a Big Boy Now, 1967, Finian's Rainbow, 1968, The Rain People, 1969, One from the Heart, 1981, Peggy Sue Got Married, 1986, Gardens of Stone, 1987, Tucker: The Man and His Dream, 1988, Bram Stoker's Dracula, 1992, The Rainmaker, 1997; writer films This Property Is Condemned, 1966, Reflections In a Golden Eye, 1967, The Rain People, 1969, Is Paris Burning, 1966, Patton, 1970, The Great Gatsby, 1974; co-writer, dir. The Cotton Club, 1984, Life Without Zoe (segment in New York Film Stories), 1990, writer, prodr., dir. The Godfather (Acad. awards for Best Screenplay and Best Picture, nominee for Best Dir., Film Dir.'s award Dirs. Guild Am, 1972), The Godfather, Part II, 1974 (Acad. awards for Best Screenplay, Best Dir. and Best Picture), The Conversation, 1974 (Golden Palm award Cannes Film Festival 1974), Apocalypse Now, 1979 (Golden Palm award Cannes Film Festival 1979), Rumble Fish, 1983, writer, dir. The Godfather: Part III, 1990, The Rainmaker, 1997, prodr., dir. (films) The Outsiders, 1983, Jack, 1996, The Rainmaker, 1997; prodr.: (films) THX 1138; 1971, The Escape Artist, 1982, The Black Stallion Returns, 1983, Lanai-Loa, 1998, The Florentine, 1999, The Virgin Suicides, 1999, Grapefruit Moon, 2000; exec. prodr.: Black Stallion, 1979, Hammett, 1983, Lionhart, 1987, The Secret Garden, 1993, Mary Shelley's Frankenstein, 1994, My Family/Mi Familia, 1995, Don Juan DeMarco, 1995, Buddy, 1997, The Third Miracle, 1999, Goosed, 1999, Sleepy Hollow, 1999, CQ, 2001, No Such Thing, 2001, Jeepers Creepers, 2001, Pumpkin, 2002, Jeepers Creepers II, 2003, Lost in Translation, 2003, Kinsey, 2004, Marie Antoinette, 2006; exec. prodr.: (films) The Good Shepherd, 2006; co-exec. prodr. Mishima, 1985; dir. TV Movie The People; prodr. (TV series) White Dwarf, 1995, First Wave, 1998; exec. prodr. TV movie Dark Angel, 1996, Outrage, 1998; exec. prodr.: (TV mini-series) The Odyssey, 1997, Moby Dick, 1998; dir. (play) Private Lives, opera The Visit; appeared in TV movie Marlon Brando: The Wild One, 1996. Mem.: Dirs. Guild Am. Inc.*

COPPOLA, MICHAEL N., former automotive parts executive; m. Dawn Coppola. BS in mktg., mgmt., Canisius Coll., Buffalo, 1970. Previously with Tops Friendly Markets, Buffalo, exec. v.p. mktg., 1991—97; sr. v.p. mdse. Advance Auto Parts Inc., Roanoke, Va., 2001—03, exec. v.p., COO, 2003—05, pres., CEO, 2005—07.

COPPOLA, NICOLAS See CAGE, NICOLAS

COPPOLA, SOFIA CARMINA, film director, film producer, scriptwriter; b. NYC, May 14, 1971; d. Francis Ford and Eleanor Coppola; m. Spike Jonze, June 26, 1999 (div. Dec. 9, 2003); 1 child, Romy. Intern with Karl Lagerfield Chanel; designer Milk Fed. Actor: (films) The Godfather, 1972, The Godfather: Part II, 1974, The Outsiders, 1983, Rumble Fish, 1983, The Cotton Club, 1984, Frankenweenie, 1984, Peggy Sue Got Married, 1986, Anna, 1987, The Godfather: Part III, 1990, Inside Monkey Zetterland, 1992, Star Wars: Episode I-The Phantom Menace, 1999, CQ, 2001; dir., prodr., screenwriter (films) Lick the Star, 1998, Lost in Translation, 2003 (Golden Athena, Athens Intl. Film Festival, 2003, Boston Soc. of Film Critics award for best dir., 2003, Nat. Bd. of Review award for special achievement, 2003, NY Film Critics Circle award for best dir., 2003, Toronto Film Critics Assoc. award for best screenplay, 2003, Golden Globe for best screenplay, 2004, Academy award for best screenplay, 2004), Marie Antoinette, 2006, dir., screenwriter The Virgin Suicides, 1999, host (TV series) Hi-Octane, 1994, segment writer N.Y. Stories, 1989, costume designer, 1989, series creator Platinum, 2003, writer, 2003; exec. prodr.: (TV series) Platinum, 2003; costume designer (plays) The Spirit of '76, 1990.*

COPPOLA, TALIA ROSE See SHIRE, TALIA ROSE

COPPOTELLI, BLAKE ALBERT, lawyer; s. James Vincent and Ilse Coppotelli; m. Cynthia Mary Houck, Oct. 24, 1987; children: Anna, Leah. BA, Wittenberg U., Springfield, Ohio, 1983; JD, St. John's U., Jamaica, NY, 1987. Bar: NY 1987. Asst. dist. atty. trial divsn. NY County Dist. Atty.'s Office, 1987—92; investigative trial atty. Manhattan Dist. Atty. Office, 1992—2001, sr. investigative counsel, 1996—97, chief labor racketeering unit, 1997—2001; chief construction industry strike force, intelligence and investigations Kroll Assocs. Inc., NYC, 2001—, mem. sr. mgmt. group, 2005—. Avocations: running, golf, tennis, reading. Office: Kroll Inc 900 3d Ave New York NY 10022

COPPS, MICHAEL JOSEPH, commissioner; b. Milw., Apr. 23, 1940; s. Edmund J. and Ruth E. (Klemm) C.; m. Elizabeth Miller, Sept. 5, 1970; children: Robert, Mary, Michael, William, Claire. BA, Wofford Coll., 1963; PhD, U. N.C., 1967. Asst. prof. history Loyola U., New Orleans, 1967-70; adminstrv. asst. to U.S. Sen. Ernest F. Hollings U.S. Senate, Washington, 1970-85; dir. govt. affairs Collins & Aikman Corp., Washington, 1985-89; sr. v.p. Am. Meat Inst., Washington, 1989-93; dep. asst. sec. for basic industries US Dept. Commerce, Washington, 1993-98, asst. sec. for trade devel., 1998-2001; commr. FCC, Washington, 2001—. Mem. Phi Beta Kappa, Pi Gamma Mu. Democrat. Avocations: reading, automobiles. Office: FCC Off of Comn 445 12th St SW Washington DC 20554 Business E-Mail: michael.copps@fcc.gov.

COPPS, SHEILA, former Canadian government official, political journalist, commentator; b. Hamilton, Ont., Can., Nov. 27, 1952; d. Victor Kennedy and Geraldine (Guthro) C.; m. Austin Thorne; 1 child, Danelle. BA in French, English with hons., U. Western Ont., London; postgrad., U. Rouen, France, McMaster U., Hamilton. Reporter Ottawa Citizen, 1974-76, Hamilton Spectator, 1977; asst. to Ont. Liberal leader Stuart Smith, Hamilton, 1977-81; mem. Legis. Assembly Ont., Toronto, 1981-84, House of Commons, Ottawa, 1984-97; apptd. dep. leader Liberal Party Can., Ottawa, Ont., 1990—; dep. prime min. Govt. of Can., Ottawa, 1993-97, min. environ., 1993-96, min. of Can. heritage, 1996—2003. Author: Nobody's Baby, 1986, Labattailleuse. Mem. Liberal Party. Office: Liberal Party Can 228 Bradford St Ottawa ON Canada K2B 5Z6 Office Phone: 613-355-0004. E-mail: copps@rogers.com.

COPSETTA, NORMAN GEORGE, real estate executive; b. Pennsauken, NJ, Mar. 11, 1932; s. Joseph J. and Mary P. (DeMello) C.; m. Patricia Fitzpatrick, Mar. 5, 1971 (dec.); children: Gregory, Margaret, Andrew, Norman G. Jr.; stepchildren: Samuel Sassano, James Sassano. Cert. real estate, Rutgers U., Camden, NJ, 1952; AA, Internat. Accts. Soc. Schl. Acctg., Chgo., 1968. Lic. title insurance agent, NJ. Settlement clk. Market Street Title Abstract Co., Camden, 1949-53; settlement administrator West Jersey Title & Guaranty Co., Camden, 1953; title examiner, abstract adminstr. Realty Abstract Co., Cherry Hill, NJ, 1954-64; mcpl. treas., tax collector Borough of Somerdale, NJ, 1961-65; title examiner, legal adminstr. Davis, Reberkenny & Abramowitz, Cherry Hill, 1974-97; pres., title officer Cooper Abstract Co., Cherry Hill, 1974-99, chmn. bd., 1997—. NJ fgn. commr. of deeds in and for Pa., 1959—2000; mem. faculty Title Acad. NJ, The Title Ins. Sch. Custodian of funds Somerdale Bd. Edn., 1960-64. Mem. NJ Title Ins. Agts. Assn., Haddonfield Hist. Soc., Camden County Hist. Soc. Avocation: local history. Office: Cooper Abstract Co 401 Cooper Landing Rd Ste C6 Cherry Hill NJ 08002-2598 Office Phone: 856-667-4800.

COPULOS, MILTON RUSSELL, energy executive; b. Chgo., Aug. 20, 1947; s. Aristides and Barbara Jean Copulos; m. Janet Ellen Babbitz, Aug. 26, 1978; 1 child, James Robert. BA, Am. U., DC, 1975—76. Dir. energy studies Heritage Found., 1976—. Mem. Nat. Petroleum Coun., Washington, 1980—93; dir. Nat. Def. Coun. Found., Alexandria, Va., 1982—2005; faculty mem. Am. Studies Salzburg Seminar, Austria, 1983—83; cons. US Dept. Energy, 1985—87, CIA, Langley, Va., 1987—87, White Ho., 1987—88; pres. Nat. Def. Coun. Found., Alexandria, 1988—2005. Author: (monograph) America's Achilles Heel. Host com. Environ. Inaugural Ball, Washington, 2004—05; mem. sculpture selection panel Vietnam Vets. Meml.; steering com. mem. Bush-Cheney 2004, 2003—04; founding dir. Alternative Energy Living Found., Chgo., 2005—05; dir. Found. Alternative & Complementary Therapies, Balt. Sgt. US Army, 1966—70, Vietnam. Decorated Civic Action Honor medal Rep. S. Vietnam, Vietnamese Cross Gallantry with Palm, Bronze Star medal US Army, Army Commendation medal; recipient Am. Hero award, Nat. Def. Coun. Found., 1981, Nat. Achievement award, Clean Fuels Edn. Found., 2004. Office: Nat Defense Coun Found 1220 King St Alexandria VA 21114 Home Phone: 301-261-6199. Business E-Mail: ndcf@erols.com.

COPUS, DAVID ALLEN, lawyer; b. Porterville, Calif., Feb. 19, 1942; s. Dale and Mildred Copus; m. Whitney Adams, Apr. 1, 1982; children: Taylor, Mclean. BA, Northwestern U., 1963; LLB, Harvard U., 1966. Bar: Tex. 1966, D.C. 1977. Atty. EEOC, Washington, 1966-71, dir. nat. programs divsn., 1971-77; atty. Pepper, Hamilton & Scheetz, Washington, 1977-80, Seyfarth, Shaw, et al., Washington, 1980-87; sr. atty. Jones, Day, Reavis & Pogue, Washington, 1987—. Author: Affirmative Action Manual for Government Contractors/Developing Goals and Timetables Pursuant to Executive Order 11,246, 1980, Affirmative Action Manual for Federal Contractors, 1984, Defending EEO Lawsuits, 1985, AIDS at Work, 1986, 2nd edit., 1988, Alcohol & Drug Abuse in the Workplace, 1986, Matters of Substance: Alcohol and Drugs in the Workplace, 1987, Defending the Public Employer, 1988, Alcohol and Drugs at Work: A Manual for Federal Contractors and Grantees, 1989, Model Human Resource Policies, 1989; co-author: The Complete Guide to Writing an Affirmative Action Plan, 1995; editor: OFCCP and Federal Contract Compliance, 1981; mem. adv. bd. NELI, 1989—, ADA Jour., 1991—.

COPUS, PHYLLIS LEE, retired federal agency administrator; b. Kansas City, Mo., Dec. 14, 1951; d. Jerry Lee and Lois Earline Yohe; m. Jimmy Dale Miller, Mar. 6, 1970 (dec. Oct. 30, 1994); 1 child, Jerry Dale Miller; m. Luster Gene Copus, Dec. 26, 1998. Student, East Ctrl. U., Ada, Okla., 1999—2001. Cert. vets. svc. officer Vietnam Vets. Am., 1996. Mem. Adm. Zumwalt's Com. Agt. Orange, Alexandria, Va., 1995—99; vets. svc. office Vets. Family Svcs., Oklahoma City, 1996—2002; ret., 2002. Vol. Friends Vietnam Vets., Washington, 1994—2000, Vietnam Moving Wall, Calif., 1994—98. Advised on what benefits veterans needed Clinton Presdl. Campaign, Oklahoma City, Okla., 1997—97. Recipient award, Vietnam Vets. Am. Avocations: genealogy, reading, travel. Home: 5436 South 163rd Road Brighton MO 65617 Home Phone: 417-467-4608. Personal E-mail: copusphyllis@yahoo.com.

COQUILLETTE, DANIEL ROBERT, lawyer, educator; b. Boston, May 23, 1944; s. Robert McTavish and Dagmar Alvida (Bistrup) C.; m. Judith Courtney Rogers, July 5, 1969; children: Anna, Sophia, Julia. AB, Williams Coll., 1966; MA Juris., U. Coll., Oxford U., Eng., 1969; JD, Harvard U., 1971. Bar: Mass. 1974, U.S. Dist. Ct. Mass. 1974, U.S. Ct. Appeals (1st cir.) 1974. Law clk. Mass. Supreme Ct., 1971-72; to chief justice Warren E. Burger U.S. Supreme Ct., 1972-73; assoc. Palmer & Dodge, Boston, 1973-75, ptnr., 1980-85; assoc. prof. law Boston U., 1975-78; dean, prof. Boston Coll. Law, 1985-93, prof., 1993-96, J. Donald Monan prof. law,

1996—. Vis. assoc. prof. law Cornell U., Ithaca, N.Y., 1977-78, 84; vis. prof. law Harvard U., 1978-79, 84-85, 94-2001, overseers com., Lester Kissel vis. prof., 2001—; reporter com. rules and procedures Jud. Conf. U.S.; mem. task force on rules of atty. conduct Supreme Jud. Ct. of Mass., 1996-97. Author: The Civilian Writers of Doctors Commons, London, 1988, Francis Bacon, 1993, Lawyers and Fundamental Moral Responsibility, 1995, Working Papers on Rules Governing Attorney Conduct, 1997, (with Basile, Beston, Donahue) Lex Mercatoria and Legal Pluralism, 1999, The Anglo-American Legal Heritage, 1999, 2d edit., 2004, (with McMorrow) Federal Law of Attorney Conduct, 2001, Real Ethics for Real Lawyers, 2005, (with York) Portrait of a Patriot, Political and Legal Papers of Josiah Quincy, 2005; editor: Law in Colonial Massachusetts, 1985, Moore's Federal Practice, 3d edit., 1997; bd. dirs. New Eng. Quar., 1986—; contbr. articles to profl. jours. Trustee, sec.-treas. Ames Found; bd. overseers vis. com. Harvard Law Sch., 1993-2003; propr., trustee emeritus Boston (Mass.) Athenaeum. Recipient Kaufman prize in English Williams Coll., 1966, Sentinel of the Republic prize in polit. sci. Williams Coll., 1965; Hutchins scholar, 1966-67, Fulbright scholar, 1966-68 Mem. ABA (com. on profl. ethics 1990-93), Am. Law Inst., Mass. Bar Assn. (task force on model rules of profl. conduct), Boston Bar Assn., Am. Soc. Legal History (bd. dirs. 1985-89), Mass. Soc. Continuing Legal Edn. (bd. dirs. 1985-89), Selden Soc. (state corr.), Colonial Soc. Mass. (v.p., mem. coun.), Anglo-Am. Cathedral Soc. (bd. dirs.), Mass. Hist. Soc., Am. Antiquarian Soc., Phi Beta Kappa. Democrat. Mem. Soc. Of Friends. Home: 12 Rutland St Cambridge MA 02138-2503 Office: Boston Coll Sch Law 885 Centre St Newton MA 02459-1148 Office Phone: 617-552-8650. E-mail: coquill@bc.edu.

COQUILLETTE, WILLIAM HOLLIS, lawyer; b. Boston, Oct. 7, 1949; s. Robert McTavish and Dagmar (Bistrup) C.; m. Mary Katherine Templeton, June 19, 1971 (div. Oct. 1984); 1 child, Carolyn Patricia; m. Janet Marie Weiland, Dec. 8, 1984; children: Benjamin Weiland, Madeline Marie, Elizabeth Charlotte. BA, Yale U., 1971, Oxford U., 1973; JD, Harvard U., 1975. Bar: Ohio 1976, Mass. 1976. Law clk. to presiding justice Mass. Supreme Ct., Boston, 1975-76; assoc. Jones Day, Cleve., 1976-83, ptnr., 1984—. Trustee, pres. Cleve. Foodbank. Mem. Kirtland Club, Yale Club (NYC), Yale Alumni Assn. Cleve. (trustee, pres.), Assn. Marshall Scholars, Union Club Cleve. (trustee, sec.), Skating Club, Rowfant Club (trustee, pres.), NY Yacht Club. Office: Jones Day 901 Lakeside Ave E Cleveland OH 44114-1190 Office Phone: 216-586-7137. Business E-Mail: whcoquillette@jonesday.com.

CORA, CAT, chef; b. Jackson, Miss. 1 child. BS in Exercise Physiology, Biology; grad., Culinary Inst. Am., Hyde Park, NY. Apprentice to George Blanc, France, Roger Verge, France; sous chef Old Chatham Shepherding Co., NYC; chef de cuisine Bistro Don Giovanni, Napa Valley; exec. chef Postino, East Bay. Co-host, Kitchen Accomplished Food Network, LA, 2004, co-host, Melting Pot, mem., Iron Chef Am., 2005—; ptnr. 3 Street Media; nutritional spokesperson UNICEF. Co-author (with Ann Kreuger Spivak): (cookbooks) Cat Cora's Kitchen, 2004; columnist Cooking from the Hip, Contra Costa (Calif.) Times; contbr. Bon Appetit Mag. Founding mem. Chefs for Humanity, 2004—. Mem.: SAG. Achievements include being named first female Iron Chef. Mailing: Food Network Ste 220 5757 Wilshire Blvd Los Angeles CA 90036*

CORACE, JOSEPH RUSSELL, automotive executive; b. Mt. Clemens, Mich., July 22, 1953; s. Joseph Anthony and Josephine (Coniglario) C.; m. Judith Agnes Cynowa, June 24, 1977; children: Christine Marie, Joseph R., Anthony Casmier. AA, Macomb Coll., 1973; BSME, Wayne State U., 1976; MBA, Mich. State U., 1980. Staff engr. GM Corp., Warren, Mich., 1976-81; mgr. Volvo Cars N. Am., Rockleigh, NJ, 1981-85; dir. Volvo Automated Sys., Sterling Heights, Mich., 1985-88; pres., CEO Inalfa Roof Sys., Auburn Hills, Mich., 1988-98; pres., CEO, owner Forum Motors Group, 1999—2003; COO, Cornerstone Schs., 2004—. Mem. Rockleigh Sch. Bd., 1986, Holy Name Ch., 1987; lector St. Fabian Ch. Recipient Disting. Engring. Alumnus award Wayne State U.; named to Wayne State U. Hall of Fame; Sloan fellow Volvo Cars N.Am., 1981. Mem. Soc. Automotive Engrs. (jour. contbr.), Soc. Mfg. Engrs., Young Pres. Orgn. (pres. East Mich. chpt. 1997, bd. dirs., officer), Legatus (bd. dirs., pres. Detroit chpt. 1998—), Oakland Hills Country Club, Engring. Soc. Detroit, Detroit Econ. Club, Am. Mgmt. Assn. (pres.'s coun.), Walnut Creek Country Club (bd. dirs., pres.), Rochester Racquet Club, Detroit Athletic Club, KC (officer Detroit 1979). Roman Catholic. Avocations: racquetball, golf, squash, harley davidson motorcycles, hunting.

CORAGGIO, JAMES THOMAS, educational researcher, measurement consultant; b. Clearwater, Fla., Nov. 7, 1966; s. Francis James Coraggio and Bonnie Sue Brzozowski; m. Penny Joy Klein, Nov. 30, 1996; children: Sydnie Paige, Allyson Belle. BA in Mass Comm., U. South Fla., 1994, MEd in Ednl. Measurement and Evaluation, 2003. Dir. of test devel., dir. of tech. devel. Schroeder Measurement Techs., Inc., Dunedin, Fla., 1997—2001; measurement and evaluation mgr. Eckerd Youth Alternatives, Inc., Clearwater, 2001—04; measurement cons. Coraggio Consulting, Clearwater, 2004—; assessment coord. for academic programs St. Petersburg Coll., Fla., 2006—. Presenter at confs. in field. Co-author: (book chpt.) Evidence of the effectiveness of an academic intervention using high stakes test results. Mem.: ASCD, Am. Soc. for Quality, Am. Statis. Assn., Nat. Coun. on Measurement in Edn., Am. Ednl. Rsch. Assn., Phi Kappa Phi, Beta Theta Pi. Avocations: Tae Kwon Do, travel. Home: 1122 Glenmoor Ct Clearwater FL 33764 Office: St Petersburg Coll PO Box 13489 Saint Petersburg FL 33733 Home Phone: 727-533-8866; Office Phone: 727-341-3084. Business E-Mail: coraggio.jesse@spcollege.edu.

CORAN, ARNOLD GERALD, pediatrician, surgeon; b. Boston, Apr. 16, 1938; s. Charles and Ann (Cohen) C.; m. Susan Myra Williams, Nov. 17, 1960; children: Michael, David, Randi Beth. AB, Harvard U., 1959, MD, 1963. Diplomate Am. Bd. Surgery, Am. Bd. Thoracic Surgery, Am. Bd. Pediat. Surgery. Intern in surgery Peter Bent Brigham Hosp., Boston, 1963-64, resident in general and thoracic surgery, 1964-69; resident in pediatric surgery Children's Hosp., Boston, 1966-68; chief pediat. surgery, assoc. prof. surgery U. So. Calif. Med. Sch., LA, 1972-74; chief pediat. surgery, prof. surgery U. Mich., Ann Arbor, 1974—2007; surgeon in chief C.S. Mott Childrens Hosp., Ann Arbor, 1981—2005. Contbr. articles to profl. jours. Lt. comdr. USN, 1970-72. Mem.: World Fedn. Pediat. Surgery (pres. 2005—07), Am. Pediat. Surg. Assn. (pres. 2001—02). Avocations: skiing, travel. Home: 505 E Huron St Apt 802 Ann Arbor MI 48104-1553 Office: CS Mott Childrens Hosp Rm F3970 Ann Arbor MI 48109-0245 Office Phone: 734-764-6482. Business E-Mail: acoran@umich.edu.

CORASH, MICHÈLE B., lawyer; b. May 6, 1945; BA, Mt. Holyoke Coll., 1967; JD cum laude, NYU, 1970. Legal advisor to chmn. FTC, 1970-72; dep. gen. counsel U.S. Dept. Energy, 1979; gen. counsel EPA, 1979-81; ptnr. Morrison & Foerster, San Francisco and L.A. Bd. editors Toxics Law Reporter; bd. advisors Jour. Environ. Law and Corporate Practice, Ecology Law Quarterly; mem. nat. editl. adv. bd. Prop 65 Clearingho. Bd. dirs. Calif. Counsel on Environ. and Econ. Balance, 1991—; mem. blue ribbon commn. Calif. Environ. Protection Agy. Unified Environ. Statute; mem. V.P. Bush Regulatory Task Force, 1981, mem. adv. council Environ. Curriculum Stanford Law Sch., bd. adv. Hastings West-Northwest Jour. Environmental Law & Practice. Named one of Best Lawyers in Am., Environ. Law, Corp. Counsel, Am. Lawyer, 2003, Top 50 Women Litigators in Calif., Daily Journal Extra, 2003, 100 Most Influential Lawyers in Calif., Daily Journal, 2002, 2005, Top 30 Women Litigators in Calif., 2002—05. Mem. ABA (mem. standing com. on environ. 1988-91, chair com. environ. crimes 1990), Inter-Pacific Bar Assn. (chair environ. law com.). Office: Morrison & Foerster 425 Market St San Francisco CA 94105-2482 Business E-Mail: mcorash@mofo.com.

CORASH, RICHARD, lawyer; b. NYC, Mar. 31, 1938; s. Paul and Mildred (Spanier) C.; m. Carol A. McKevitt, Dec. 11, 1966; children: Richard Jr., Sharon, Peter, Amy. BA, Harpur Coll., SUNY, Bingamton, 1959; MA, Bklyn. Law Sch., 1966; JD, Rutgers U., 1963. Bar: NY 1964, US Dist. Ct. DC 1964, US Supreme Ct. 1972. Pvt. practice, NYC, 1964-77; pres. Corash & Hollender, P.C., NYC, 1977—. Pres. NEFM Trading Co., NYC; chmn. North Eastern Fiscal Mgmt. Co., NYC; mng. mem. North Eastern Equities, LLC, co-mgr.; counsel Caywood Homeowners Assn. Mem. NY State Bar Assn. (real estate and trust and estates sects.), NY State Bar Assn. (chmn. grievance com.), Richmond County Bar Assn. Address: 81 Roxiticus Rd Far Hills NJ 07931-2225 Office Phone: 718-442-4897. Personal E-mail: rcorash@silawfirm.com.

CORBATO, CHARLES EDWARD, geology educator, academic administrator; b. LA, July 12, 1932; s. Hermenegildo and Charlotte Carella (Jensen) C.; m. Patricia Jeanne Ferg, May 18, 1957; children: Steven, Barbara, Susan. BA, UCLA, 1954, PhD, 1960. Instr. geology U. Calif., Riverside, 1959, Los Angeles, 1959-60, asst. prof., 1960-66; assoc. prof. Ohio State U., Columbus, 1966-69, prof., 1969-92, chmn. dept. geology and mineralogy, 1972-80, assoc. provost office of acad. affairs, 1987-92, prof., assoc. provost emeritus, 1992—. Geophysicist U.S. Geol. Survey, 1966-74; dir. State Postsecondary Rev. Entity, Ohio Bd. Regents, 1994-95, dir. info. svcs., 1995-99. Fellow: Geol. Soc. Am.; mem.: Am. Geophys. Union, Delta Tau Delta. Home: 2400 Buckley Rd Columbus OH 43220-4616 Office: Ohio State U 125 S Oval Mall Columbus OH 43210-1308 Personal E-mail: ccorbato@columbus.rr.com.

CORBET, KATHLEEN A., former financial information company executive; b. Feb. 22, 1960; m. Randy Corbet; children: Dylan, Ian. BS in Mktg. and Computer Sci., Boston Coll., 1982; MBA in Fin., NYU, 1989. Chmn. Alliance Capital, Australia, New Zealand, chief investment ops. and global trading, 1997—99; CEO Alliance Capital Ltd., London, 1998—2000; CEO fixed income divsn. Alliance Capital Mgmt., 2000—04; pres. Standard & Poor's, 2004—07; mem. CEO's coun. McGraw-Hill. Mem. bd. trustees Boston Coll. Recipient Australian Centenary Medal, 2003, Nicolas award, NYU Stern Sch. Bus., 2006. Mem.: New Caanan, Econ. Club NY, Coun. Fgn. Rels.*

CORBET, RICHARD HUGH, trade policy specialist, writer; b. Perth, Australia, Nov. 18, 1936; arrived in U.S., 1990; s. John Arthur and Freda Marian (Sherwood) Corbet; m. Rosalind Mary Willett Bevan, June 10, 1961 (div. Oct. 1978). BA, U. Adelaide, Australia, 1960; postgrad., U. Keele, Eng., 1990—93. Cert. journalist Brit. Inst. Journalists. Rsch. asst. Cazenove & Co., stockbrokers, London, 1961—62; rsch. asst. conservative backbench com. on European cmty. Brit. Ho. of Commons, London, 1962—63; econs. corr. Thomson Newspapers, London, 1963—65; specialist writer The Times, London, 1965—68; dir. Trade Policy Rsch. Ctr., London, 1968—89; mng. editor World Economy, Boston and Oxford, 1977—89; guest scholar Woodrow Wilson Internat. Ctr. for Scholars and the Brookings Inst., Washington, 1990—92; sr. fellow Manhattan Inst., NY and Washington, 1992—93; dir. trade policy program Sigur Ctr. for Asian Studies George Washington U., Washington, 1993—97; pres. Cordell Hull Inst., Washington, 1998—. Spl. advisor Opposition Spokesmen on Trade Brit. Ho. Commons, London, 1978—79; cons. on trade policy Internat. C. of C., Paris, 1979—83; mem. adv. com. on studies internat. trade policy U. Mich. Press, Ann Arbor, 1989—2006; mem. adv. bd. World Economy., Oxford and Boston, 1990—2001; cons. European Inst. Japanese Studies, Stockholm, 1994—97, Swiss-Asia Found., Lausanne, Switzerland, 1996—99. Author: Beyond the Rhetoric of Commodity Power, 1974; co-author: Trade Strategy for the Asia-Pacific Region, 1970, Opportunity of a Century to Liberalise Farm Trade, 2002; co-editor: Europe's Free Trade Area Experiment, 1970, Commonwealth Policy in a Global Context, 1971, In Search of a New World Economic Order, 1974, Reason vs. Emotion: Requirements for a Successful WTO Round, 1999; contbr. articles to profl. jours.

CORBETT, ALICE CATHERINE, investor; d. Marshal Richard and Coralyn Estelle Reckard; BS, U. Oreg., 1943. Tchr. Portland (Oreg.) Dept. Edn., 1944—47; mem. Oreg. Senate, Salem, 1950—58; commr. Multnomah County, Portland, 1964—68; investor Portland, 1964—. Mem.: Multnomah Club.

CORBETT, GORDON LEROY, minister; b. Melrose, Mass., Dec. 11, 1920; s. Winfield Leroy and Lalia Estey (Fiske) C.; m. Winifred Pickett, Sept. 7, 1946; children: Douglas Leroy, Christine, Patricia, Carolyn. AB, Bates Coll., 1943; MDiv, Yale U., 1948. Ordained to ministry Bapt. Ch., 1948. Pastor Montowese Bapt. Ch., North Haven, Conn., 1948-52; assoc. pastor First Presbyn. Ch., Glen Falls, N.Y., 1952-59; synod exec. Synod of Ky., Lexington, 1959-71; assoc. synod exec. for Alaska, 1971-84; interim synod exec. Synod of Lincoln Trails, Indpls., 1987-88; interim Presbyn. exec. Santa Barbara (Calif.) Presbytery, 1991-92. Trustee Appalachian Regional Hosps., Lexington, 1969-72, Sheldon Jackson Coll., Sitka, Alaska, 1972-84; chmn. chaplaincy com. Alaska Christian Conf., 1975-78, Alaska Pipeline Chaplaincy. Author: Thirteen Generations of Descendants of Robert Corbett, who died in Woodstock, Conn., 1695, 1995. Mem. San Jose Presbytery; chmn., bd. dirs. Encina Royale, Inc., 1997-98. Dist. chmn. Rep. Party, Anchorage, 1974-78. 1st lt. USAAF, 1944-45, China. Recipient Christian Citizenship award Sheldon Jackson Coll., 1984. *"Since we are surrounded by so great a cloud of witnesses. let us run with perserverance the race that is set before us". (Hebrews 12:1).*

CORBETT, JOHN, actor; b. Wheeling, W.Va., May 9, 1961; Actor: (films) Flight of the Intruder, 1991, Tombstone, 1993, Wedding Bell Blues, 1996, Volcano, 1997, Desperate But Not Serious, 1999, Dinner Rush, 2000, Serendipity, 2001, Prancer Returns, 2001, My Big Fat Greek Wedding, 2002, My Dinner with Jimi, 2003, Raising Helen, 2004, Elvis Has Left the Building, 2004, Bigger Than the Sky, 2004, Raise Your Voice, 2004, Bigger Than the Sky, 2005, Dreamland, 2006, The Messengers, 2007; (TV films) Innocent Victims, 1996, Don't Look Back, 1996, The Morrison Murders, 1996, The Warlord: Battle for the Galaxy, 1998, The Sky's On Fire, 1998, On Hostile Ground, 2000, Rocky Times, 2000, Private Lies, 2001, (voice only) The Griffin and the Minor Cannon, 2002, Hunt for Justice, 2005; (TV series) Northern Exposure, 1990—95, The Visitor, 1997—98, Sex and the City, 2000—03, Lucky, 2003; (TV miniseries) To Serve and Protect, 1999, (TV appearances) The Wonder Years, 1988, (voice only) Duckman: Private Dick/Family Man, 1996, Gary the Rat, 2003, (voice only) American Dad, 2006. Office: Creative Artists Agy 9830 Wilshire Blvd Beverly Hills CA 90212*

CORBETT, LENORA MEADE, mathematician, community college educator; b. Reidsville, NC, Aug. 1, 1950; children: Kenneth Russell Johnson, Ralph Nathaniel Brown. AAS in Electromechanics, Tech. Coll. of Alamance, 1985, AAS in Electronics, 1986; BS in Indsl. Tech., Electronics, N.C. A&T State U., 1996; candidate, World Acad. Letters, 2004. Cloth insp. Burlington (N.C.) Industries, 1971-74; electrician's helper Williams Electric, Greensboro, NC, 1978, Nobility Mobile Homes, Reidsville, NC, 1979; instr. math. and physics Alamance C.C., Graham, NC, 1985—2002, chmn. learning resources, 1993. Author: numerous poems. Sr. choir Jones Cross Rd. Ch., Reidsville, 1988-94, pastor's aide mem., 1988-90, jr. Sunday sch. tchr., 1989-91, asst. choir sec., 1988-94; bd. dirs. Nu Generation Enrichment Program, Nu Generation Enrichment Ctr., Teach Tolerance Nat. Campaign Tolerance, 2002-03 Nominee Poet of Yr., 2002, Internat. Poet of Merit, 2002, Noble Laureats, 2004, World Champion Amateur Poet; named Famous Poet, 1996, Poet of Yr., 2000, Best Love Poems from Sparrowgrass, 2001, Famous Poet, 2002, Poet of Yr., 2004, Outstanding Achievement in Poetry, 2004; named to Best Poets of 2000, 2000, Best Poems and Poets, 2001, Internat. Poetry Hall of Fame, 2003, Women's Internat. Hall of Fame; recipient Merit award, 1990, Golden Poet award, 1991, Merit award, 1992, Editor's Choice award, 1997, Recognition award, Famous Poets Soc., 1998, Famous Poet, 2000, Noble prize outstanding achievement and contbn. to soc., 2001. Mem. AAUP, AAUW, Alamance C.C. Alumni Assn., Golden Key, N.C. A&T State U. Alumni Assn. Baptist. Avocations: cooking, reading, poetry, drawing, singing.

CORBETT, LUKE R., former energy company executive; b. Feb. 11, 1947; m. Becky Corbett; 1 child, Carrie. Grad., U. Ga., 1969. Geophysicist Amoco Prodn. Co., Mitchell Energy, Aminoil; with Kerr-McGee Corp., 1985—, group v.p., 1992—95, pres., COO, 1995—97, chmn., CEO, 1997—99, CEO, 1999, chmn., CEO, 1999—2006. Mem. Nat. Petroleum Coun.; bd. dirs. Domestic Petroleum Coun., OGE Energy Corp., BOK Fin. Corp., Noble Corp., Integris Health, Inc.; bd. dir. Anadarko Petroleum Corp., 2006—. Trustee Okla. United Meth. Ch.; bd. dirs. Allied Arts Found., United Way. Mem.: Okla. Bus. Roundtable, Soc. Exploration Geologists, Am. Assn. Petroleum Geologists, Oklahoma City C. of C. (bd. dirs.). Office: Anadarko Petroleum Bd Directors 1201 Lake Robbins Dr Spring TX 77380

CORBETT, LUKE ROBINSON, lawyer; b. Pinehurst, NC, May 21, 1930; s. Paschal Butler and Delia Jane (McKenzie) C.; m. Joan Cole (div.); children: Steven, Rebecca, Laurie, Charles, Carolyn. AB in Polit. Sci., U. N.C., 1956, JD, 1959. Bar: Calif. 1959, U.S. Dist. Ct. (so. dist.) Calif. 1960. Assoc. Lindley, Scales & Patton, San Diego; ptnr. Scales, Patton, Ellsworth & Corbett, San Diego; shareholder, dir., pres. Lindley, Scales & Corbett and predecessor firm, San Diego; sr. counsel Butz, Dunn, DeSantis & Bingham, 2006—. 1st lt. USAF, 1951-55. Mem. ABA, San Diego County Bar Assn. (bd. dirs., treas., v.p. 1971-74), Am. Bar Found., San Diego County Bar Found. (bd. dirs.), State Bar Calif. (del., chmn. exec. com. conf. of dels. 1975-78), Am. Inns. of Ct. (master Louis F. Welch chpt. 1984), Assn. of Bus. Trial Lawyers (bd. dirs.). Office: Butz Dunn DeSantis & Bingham 101 W Broadway San Diego CA 92101 Home: 1937 Guizot St San Diego CA 92107 Office Phone: 619-233-4777. Business E-Mail: lrcorbett@butzdunn.com.

CORBETT, SIOBHAN AIDEN, surgeon; b. Aug. 11, 1959; BA, Princeton Univ., 1981; MD, UMDNJ Robert Wood Johnson Med. Sch., 1987. Diplomate Am. Bd. Surgery. Postdoctoral fellow Princeton (N.J.) U.; asst. prof. surg. scis. Robert Wood Johnson Med. Sch., New Brunswick, NJ, 1997—2004, assoc. prof. surg. sci. Recipient Clin. Sci. award Am. Heart Assn., 1995-96, Chmns. Fac. Rsch. award, Dept. Surgery UMDNJ, 1998. Mem.: Assn. Academic Surgery. Address: Clin Acad Bldg 125 Paterson St New Brunswick NJ 08901-1962 Office: 1 Robert Wood Johnson Pl New Brunswick NJ 08901-1928

CORBETT, THOMAS WINGETT, JR., state attorney general, lawyer; b. Phila., June 17, 1949; s. Thomas Wingett and Mary Bernadine (Diskin) C.; m. Susan Jean Manbeck, Dec. 16, 1972; children: Thomas Wingett III, Katherine. BA, Lebanon Valley Coll., 1971; JD, St. Mary's U., 1975. Bar: Pa., 1976, US Dist. Ct. (we. dist.) Pa., 1976, US Ct. Mil. Appeals, 1979, US Supreme Ct., 1984. Asst. dist. atty. Allegheny County, Pitts., 1976—80; asst. US atty. (we. dist.) Pa. US Dept. Justice, Pitts., 1980—83, US atty., 1989—93; assoc. Rose, Schmidt, Hasley & DiSalle, Pitts., 1983—86, ptnr., 1986—89; mem. US atty. gen.'s adv. com. We. Dist. Pa., Pitts., 1991—93, chmn., 1992—93; ptnr. Thorp, Reed & Armstrong, Pitts., 1993—95, 1997—98; atty. gen. State of Pa., Harrisburg, 1995—97, 2005—; asst. gen. counsel for govt. affairs Waste Mgmt. Inc., Pitts., 1998—2002; ptnr. Thomas Corbett & Assocs., 2002—05. Mem. Shaler Twp. Rep. Com., 1984-89, Allegheny County Rep. Com., 1985-89, 2002—, Gov. Tom Ridge's Partnership for Safe Children, 1995-2003, Pa. Weed and Seed Program, 1995-2003; chmn. Pa. Commn. on Crime and Delinquency, 1995—2003, del. Rep. Nat. Conv., 2000. Pres. St. Mary's Parent-Tchr. Guild, Glenshaw, Pa., 1983-85. Served in Pa Army Nat. Guard, 1971—84. Mem. ABA, Pa. Bar Assn., Allegheny County Bar Assn. (judiciary com.), NRA, Ancient Order Hibernians. Republican. Roman Catholic. Avocations: skiing, golf, reading. Office: Office of Atty General 1600 Strawberry Sq Harrisburg PA 17120*

CORBETT, WILLIAM JOHN, lawyer, public relations executive, minister, consultant; b. Bklyn., Mar. 15, 1937; s. John Joseph and Mildred (Bauer) Corbett; m. Ann Virginia Teplitz, June 25, 1966; children: William John, Spencer Thomas, Sally Ann. BA, Hobart Coll., 1959; JD, Fordham U., 1965; grad., New Sem., NYC, 2007. Bar: N.Y. 1966, U.S. Dist. Ct. (fed. dist.) 1968, Customs Ct. 1968, U.S. Supreme Ct. 1990; ordained to ministry 2007. Info. officer USAF, Greenville, SC, 1959-62; trial lawyer Nassau County Legal Aid Soc., Mineola, NY, 1966-67; asst. dist. atty. County of Nassau, 1967-68; corp. dir. pub. rels. Avon Products, Inc., NYC, 1968-84; v.p. comm. AICPA, NYC, 1984-90; chmn. Corbett Pub. Rels., Inc., Floral Park, NY, 1990—. Pros. atty. Inc. Village of Floral Park, NY, 1975—84, acting village justice, 1984—98; cons. status UN Office Info. and ECOSOC, NYC, 1979—84, NYC, 1990—93; pub. rels. advisor USIA, Washington, 1981—93; adj. asst. prof. Iona Coll. Grad. Sch. Comm., 1990—2000; selection com. Congrl. Acad., 1987—. Mem. adv. bd. Pub. Rels. News (Leadership award, 1984). Participant White House Conf. Indsl. World Ahead, 1972, White House Conf. Consumer Elderly, 1979, White House Conf. Small Bus., 1986, 1995, White House Conf. Librs. and Info. Svcs., 1991; staff mem. N.Y. State Senate, Albany, 1962—63. Capt. USAF, 1959—62. Named to Hall of Fame, U.S. Dept. Def. Info. Sch., 1990; recipient N.Y. State Conspicuous Svc. medal, 1970, Legion of Honor, Internat. Coun. Order DeMolay, 1982, Alumni award, Hobart Coll., 1984, Pinnacle award, 1990. Fellow: Internat. Pub. Rels. Assn. (bd. dirs. 1984—90, pres. 1990); mem.: Nassau County Bar Assn., NY State Bar Assn. (elder law, real estate, trusts sect.), Nassau County Magistrars Assn. (v.p., elder law, real estate, trusts sect.), Nat. Commn. Pub. Rels. Edn., Nat. Assn. Corp. Dirs. N.Y. (v.p. 1993—94), Pub. Affairs Coun., Ctr. Study Presidency (adv. bd.), Corp. Forum N.Y., Pub. Rels. Soc. N.Y. (past pres.), Pub. Rels. Soc. Am. (accredited, Fellow Pres. award 1985, 1988), Am. Legion (commdr. Floral Park chpt. 2001—02). Home: 102 Chestnut Ave Floral Park NY 11001-2421 Office: 111 S Tyson Ave Floral Park NY 11001-1822 Office Phone: 516-775-6849. E-mail: billcorbett@att.net.

CORBIN, BARRY, actor, writer; b. Lamesa, Tex., Oct. 16, 1940; s. Kilmer Blaine and Alma LaMerle (Scott) C.; m. Elyse Soap, 1966 (div. 1970); m. Susan James Berger, May 29, 1976 (div. 1993); children: James Barry, Christopher Clayton, Shannon Katy, Bernard Weiss. Student, Tex. Tech. U., 1959-64, U. Colo., summer 1964. Freelance actor, 1965—. Faculty N.C. State U., Raleigh, 1966-67. Playwright: Suckerrod Smith and the Cisco Kid, 1974 (Theater U.S.A. award 1974), Throckmorton, Tx., 76083, 1983; screenwriter The Wildcatters, 1986; films include Any Which Way You Can, 1980, Urban Cowboy, 1980, Dead and Buried, 1981, The Night the Lights Went Out in Georgia, 1981, Six Pack, 1982, The Best Little Whorehouse in Texas, 1982, Honkytonk Man, 1982, The Ballad of Gregorio Cortez, 1983, WarGames, 1983, The Man Who Loved Women, 1983, Hard Travelling, 1985, My Science Project, 1985, Nothing in Common, 1986, What Comes Around, 1986, Under Cover, 1987, Off the Mark, 1987, Permanent Records, 1988, Critters 2: The Main Course, 1988, It Takes Two, 1988, Who is Harry Crumb?, 1989, Short Time, 1990, Ghost Dad, 1990, The Hot Spot, 1990, Career Opportunities, 1991, Curdled, 1996, Solo, 1996, The Fanatics, 1997, The Gristle, 2001, Clover Bend,

2001, The Journeyman, 2001, No One Can Hear You, 2001, Race to Space, 2001, Waitin' to Live, 2002, Timequest, 2002, Dunsmore, 2003, Tin Can Shinny, 2003, Blackwater Elegy, 2003, Reiver's End, 2005, Yesterday's Dreams, 2005, Godless, 2005, The Dukes of Hazzard, 2005; TV series: Boone, 1983-84, Spies, 1987, Northern Exposure, 1990-95 (Emmy nomination, Supporting Actor - Drama, 1993, 94) The Big Easy, 1996, One Tree Hill, 2003-; mini-series: The Thorn Birds, 1983, Lonesome Dove, 1989, Moon Shot, 1994 (host); TV movies Rage, 1980, This House Possessed, 1981, The Killing of Randy Webster, 1981, Murder in Texas, 1981, Bitter Harvest, 1981, A Few Days in Weasel Creek, 1981, Fantasies, 1982, Prime Suspect, 1982, Travis McGee, 1982, Flight #90: Disaster on the Potomac, 1984, The Jesse Owens Story, 1984, Fatal Vision, 1984, Ratings Game, 1984, Death in California, 1985, The Defiant Ones, 1986, Firefighter, 1986, C.A.T. Squad, 1986, Warm Hearts, Cold Feet, 1987, LBJ: The Early Years, 1987, Secret Witness, 1988, Man Against the Mob, 1988, The People Across the Lake, 1988, Stranger on My Land, 1988, Red King, White Night, 1989, I Know My First Name Is Steven, 1989, Spooner, 1989, Last Flight Out, 1990, The Chase, 1991, Conagher, 1991, Siringo, 1994, Virus, 1995, Deadly Family Secretes, 1995, The Pandora Directive, 1996, My Son Is Innocent, 1996, Columbo: A Trace of Murder, 1997, Kiss and Tell, 1997, The Hired Heart, 1997, Judgement Day: The Ellie Nesler Story, 1998, A Face to Kill For, 1999, Sealed With a Kiss, 1999, Crossfire Trail, 2001, Monte Walsh, 2003, Hope Ranch, 2004, Alien Express, 2005, Hidden Places, 2006. Pvt. USMCR, 1962-64. Recipient Western Image award Dallas Apparel Mart, Buffalo Bill Cody award Nebraskaland Days, Wrangler award Nat. Cowboy Hall of Fame. Mem. Screen Actors Guild (bd. dirs. 1985, 87-90), Actors Equity Assn., AFTRA, Dramatists Guild, Acad. Motion Picture Arts and Scis. Avocations: cutting, cow penning, trail riding. Office: care Elkins Entertainment 8306 Wilshire Blvd # 438 Beverly Hills CA 90211-2382

CORBIN, DONALD L., state supreme court justice; b. Hot Springs, Ark., Mar. 29, 1938; BA, U. Ark., 1964, JD, 1966. Bar: Ark. 1966, U.S. Dist. Ct. (we. dist.) Ark. 1966. Atty. pvt. practice, DeQueen, Ark., 1966—67; lawyer Lewisville and Stamps, 1967-80; judge Ark. Ct. Appeals, 1981-87, chief judge, 1987-90; assoc. justice Ark. Supreme Ct., Little Rock, 1991—. State rep. Ark. Gen. Assembly, 1971-80. Served with USMC, 1955-59. Mem. ABA, Ark. Bar Assn., SW Ark. Bar Assn., Sigma Alpha Epsilon. Democrat. Avocation: duck hunting. Office: Supreme Ct Justice Bldg 625 Marshall St 120 Justice Bldg Little Rock AR 72201-1054*

CORBIN, FREDERIC H., plastic surgeon; BA with honors, Brown U., 1965; MD, NYU Sch. Medicine, 1969. Diplomate Am. Bd. Plastic & Reconstructive Surgery, cert. Am. Soc. Plastic & Reconstructive Surgeons, Inc., Continuing Med. Edn. Surg. intern U. Hosp. San Diego County, 1969—70, fellow in pulmonary-respiratory care, 1971—72; resident in surgery NYU Med. Ctr., NYC, 1970—71; resident in gen. surgery, chief resident Tufts-New Eng. Med. Ctr., Boston, 1974—77; instr. gen. surgery Tufts Med. Sch., Boston, 1976—77; resident in plastic surgery, chief resident Columbia Presbyn. Med. Ctr., NYC, 1977—79, tchg. fellow plastic surgery, 1979; resident in hand surgery Roosevelt Hosp. Littler-Eaton Hand Svc., NYC, 1979; clin. instr. plastic surgery U. Southern Calif., 1983—86, Western U. Health Sciences, Pomona, Calif., 1986—; pvt. practice Beverly Hills, Calif., Brea, Calif. Maj., staff surgeon US Army, 1972—74, Walson Army Hosp., Fort Dix, NJ. Mem.: AMA, Webster Soc. of Columbia Presbyn. Hosp., Orange County Med. Assn., LA Soc. Plastic Surgeons, Inc., LA County Med. Assn., Calif. Med. Assn., Am. Soc. Plastic & Reconstructive Surgeons, Am. Burn Assn., Woodmere Acad. Cum Laude Soc., Brown U. Cum Laude Soc., Sigma Xi. Office: 436 N Bedford Dr Ste 202 Beverly Hills CA 90210 also: 400 W Ctrl Ave Ste 101 Brea CA 92821 Office Phone: 310-284-8384, 714-671-3033. Office Fax: 714-671-1231. E-mail: fhcmd@aol.com.*

CORBIN, HERBERT LEONARD, public relations executive, director; b. Bklyn., Mar. 30, 1940; s. H. Dan and Lillian Corbin; m. Carol Heller, June 2, 1963; children: Jeffrey, Leslie Faith. BA, Rutgers U., 1961. Staff corr. Newark News, 1961—63; asst. dir. pub. rels. Rutgers U. News Svc., New Brunswick, NJ, 1963—65; account exec. A.A. Schechter Assocs., NYC, 1965—66; sr. account exec. Daniel J. Edelman, Inc., NYC, 1967—69; founder, chmn., mng. ptnr. KCSA Pub. Rels. Worldwide, NYC, 1969—. Mem. nat. bd. govs., chmn. pub. rels. com. Am. Jewish Com., White Plains Pub. Access Cable TV Commn.; mem. mktg. adv. com. United Jewish Appeal-Fedn. N.Y.; bd. gov. Pave the Way Found. Mem.: Pub. Rels. Soc. Am. (counsellors Acad.), Old Oaks Country Club (bd. dirs., sec., sec.). Home: 31 Hathaway Ln White Plains NY 10605-3610 Office: KCSA Pub Rels Worldwide 800 2nd Ave New York NY 10017-4709 Business E-Mail: hcorbin@kcsa.com.

CORBIN, MICHAEL, diplomat; b. NYC; m. Mary Ellen Hickey; 2 children. BA, Swarthmore Coll. Staff asst. Bur. Near Eastern and South Asian Afafirs US Dept. State, staff asst. UN Polit. Affairs Bur. Internat. Orgn. Affairs, with US Embassy in Tunis Tunisia, 1985—87, polit.-military affairs officer US Embassy in Kuwait, 1987—89, polit.-military affairs officer US Embassy in Cairo Egypt, 1994—97, dir. Counter-Narcotics Sect., US Embassy in Caracas Venezuela, 1997—2001, dep. dir. Office of Arabian Peninsula Affairs, 2001—03, minister counselor Economic and Polit. Affairs, US Embassy in Cairo Egypt, 2003—, chargé d'affaires in Cairo, 2005. Volunteer, agricultural extension officer Peace Corps, Mauritania, 1982—84. Fluent in French, Spanish and Arabic. Office: 7700 Cairo Pl Washington DC 20521-7700

CORBIN, ROSEMARY MACGOWAN, former mayor; b. Santa Cruz, Calif., Apr. 3, 1940; d. Frederick Patrick and Lorena Maude (Parr) MacGowan; m. Douglas Tenny Corbin, Apr. 6, 1968; children: Jeffrey, Diana. BA, San Francisco State U., 1961; MLS, U. Calif., Berkeley, 1966. Libr. Stanford (Calif.) U., 1966-68, Richmond (Calif.) Pub. Libr., 1968-69, Kaiser Found. Health Plan, Oakland, Calif., 1976-81, San Francisco Pub. Libr., 1981-82, U. Calif., Berkeley, 1982-83; mem. coun. City of Richmond, 1985-93, vice mayor, 1986-87, mayor, 1993—2001. Mem. Solid Waste Mgmt. Authority, 1985-2001, Contra Costa Hazardous Materials Commn., Martinez, Calif., 1987-2001, San Francisco Bay Conservation and Devel. Commn., 1987-2001; mem. League of Calif. Cities Environ. Affairs Com., 1994-2001; mem. energy and environ. com. U.S. Conf. Mayors and Nat. League of Cities, 1993-2001. Contbr. articles to profl. publs. Pres. Ujima Family Svcs.; chair Richmond Historic Preservation Com.; mem. Rosie the Riveter Trust Bd., San Francisco Bay Trail Bd.; bd. mem. Libr. Found., Inst. for Local Govt. Mem. LWV, NOW, Nat. Women's Polit. Caucus, Calif. Libr. Assn., Sierra Club. Democrat. Avocations: reading, hiking, golf, gardening, quilting. Home: 114 Crest Ave Richmond CA 94801-4031

CORBIN, SOL NEIL, lawyer; b. NYC, Apr. 16, 1927; s. Nathan I. and Sarah (Kaiser) Corbin; m. Tanya Jacobs, Aug. 7, 1963; 1 child, David J. BS, Columbia U., 1948; JD cum laude, Harvard U., 1951. Bar: N.Y. 1952. Pvt. practice, NYC, 1952—; law clk. Judge Charles D. Breitel, 1954-56; counsel Gov. of N.Y., 1962-65; ptnr. Corbin, Silverman & Sanseverino LLP, NYC, 1970—96, sr. counsel, 1997—2001, Taylor, Colicchio & Silverman, LLP, NYC, 2001—06. Chmn. N.Y. State Commn. Constl. Conv., 1966—67, N.Y. State Crime Control Planning Bd., 1974—75; mem. N.Y. State Banking Bd., 1969—76, N.Y. State Commn. Local Govt. Powers, 1971—73; mem. chief judge's com. to recruit state ct. adminstr., 1973; trustee bankruptcy Franklin N.Y. Corp., 1974—90; spl. counsel to v.p. U.S., 1975; apptd. counsel to trustee BCCI, 1990—97. Trustee N.Y. Pub. Libr., 1977—; mem. chief judge's com. availability legal svcs., 1988—90. With USNR, 1945—46. Mem.: ABA, Am. Law Inst., New York County Bar Assn., Assn. Bar City of N.Y., Lotos Club. Home: 1100 Park Ave New York NY 10128-1202

CORBIN, THEODORE J., JR., emergency physician; B., Lincoln U., Pa., 1990; MD, Med. Coll. Pa./Hahnemann U. Sch. Medicine, Phila., 1997. Cert. Emergency Medicine. Resident Howard U. Hosp., Washington; fellow Allegheny Gen. Hosp., Pitts.; emergency physician Thomas Jefferson U. Hosp., Phila., 2001—, asst. dir. residency program, 2004—. Clin. instr. emergency medicine Jefferson Med. Coll., Phila., 2001—. Recipient 40 Under 40 award, Phila. Bus. Jour., 2006; advocacy fellow, Inst. Medicine as a Profession, 2005. Mem.: Phila. Physicians for Social Responsibility. Office: Thomas Jefferson U Jefferson Medical Coll 239 Thompson Bldg Philadelphia PA 19107 also: Thomas Jefferson U Methodist Hospital 2301 S Broad St Philadelphia PA 19148 Office Phone: 215-955-6844, 215-952-9136. E-mail: theodore.corbin@jefferson.edu.

CORBIN, VERONICA L., secondary school educator, information scientist, consultant; BS in Chemistry, Va. Union U., 1999; MS in Computer Networking, Strayer U., 2003. Lab. specialist Dept. Gen. Svcs., Richmond, 1999—2001; educator Richmond Pub. Schs., 2001—05, Henrico County Pub. Schs., Richmond, Va., 2005—06; founder Platinum Networking Svs., Richmond, Va. Computer cons. Platinum Networking Svcs., Richmond, 1999—, Nehemiah Cmty. Ctr., Richmond, 2004—05.

CORBIN, WILLIAM R., wood products executive; BS in Forest Products, U. Wash., 1964; MS in Forestry, Yale U., 1956. Cons. forest products, Seattle, 1970's; v.p. ops. Vancouver Plywood Co., Inc.; v.p. So. timber and wood products Zellerbach Corp., 1974; sr. v.p. timber and wood products, group pres.; exec. v.p. wood products Weyerhaeuser Co., 1992-95, 98—, exec. v.p. timberlands and distbn., 1995-98. Bd. dirs. Weyerhaeuser Can. Ltd.; mem. mgmt. bd. World TimerFund. Trustee, mem. exec. com. Weyerhaeuser Co. Found., mem. policy com.; mem. adv. bd. U. Wash. Sch. Bus. Adminstrn. and Coll. Forest Resources, charter mem. internat. adv. bd. Inst. Environment and Natural Resoruce Rsch. and Policy; v.p., mem. exec. com. The Mountains to Sound Greenway Trust. Office: Weyerhaeuser PO Box 9777 Federal Way WA 98063-9777

CORBITT, DORIS ORENE, retired real estate agent, dietician; b. Warrior, Ala., Oct. 25, 1929; d. Olen J. and Begie Pernie (Motte) Florence; m. Wallace R. Cornett, Nov. 29, 1952 (div. 1980); children: Wallace R. Jr., Kris J., Brett T.; m. Weldon Plant Corbitt, Jr., Apr. 21, 1984 (dec. Mar. 8, 2006). BS in Dietetics, Maryville Coll., 1950; postgrad., Duke U., 1950-51. Registered dietitian. Asst. dir. dietary St. Mary's Hosp., Knoxville, 1952-53; dir. dietary Soldier and Sailor Sch. for Children, Bloomington, Ill., 1966-68; tchr. Nashville Area Vocat. Sch., 1971-73; dir. dietary Westside Hosp., Nashville, 1973-79, Meml. Hosp., Tampa, Fla., 1980-85; realtor assoc. Coldwell Banker, Tampa, 1986—2000; ret., 2000. Spkr. in field. Devel. original curriculum for Food Svc. Workers and Suprs., Tenn.; co-author first diet manual for Nashville Dietetic Assn. Sec. Galleria Homeowners Assn., Tampa, 1986-87; Sunday sch. tchr. Recipient Internat. Citizenship award, 1995; named The Honourable by Prince Kevin of Australia, 1996, Nobility status, 1996; named to 500 Notable Women Hall of Fame, 1998. Mem.: Red Hat Soc., Million Dollar Club. Republican. Mem. Ch. of Christ. Avocations: music, movies, reading, church work, walking. Home: 19410 Melody Fair Pl Lutz FL 33558-9216 Personal E-mail: wpcjrdoc@aol.com.

CORBITT, EUMILLER MATTIE, special education educator; b. Detroit, Jan. 07; d. Harrison and Arnetha (Tatum) Jones; m. Luther Corbitt (div. Dec. 1976); children: Tonya, Stephen. BS, Wayne State U., Detroit, 1969, MEd, 1976, EdS, 1995. Cert. elem. and secondary sch. tchr., cert. tchr. spl. edn. emotionally and mentally impaired, grades K-12, elem. secondary sch. and central office administration. Tchr. mentally impaired Detroit Pub. Schs., 1969-72, tchr. emotionally impaired, 1972-75, spl. edn. tchr. cons., 1975—, Title I tchr. math. and sci., summers 1993-96; mediator Spl. Edn. Mediation Svcs., Lansing, Mich., 1986-96, Spl. Edn. Mediation Svcs. State Project PL 94-142, Lansing, Mich., 1985—; spl. edn. hearing officer Mich. Dept. Edn., Lansing, 1985—. Developer at-risk program for emotionally impaired, socially maladjusted and ADHD students 12-17 yrs. Wolverine Human Svcs., Detroit, Mich. 1998—; mem. US del. educators and attys. to South Africa for evaluation of schs. and govtl. agys. under leadership of Nelson Mandella Citizen Amb. program People to People, Spokane, Wash., 1996; mem. citizens alliance to uphold spl. edn. study adv. com. Emotionally Impaired Children in Mich./Lansing, 1986; mem. North Ctrl. Assn. accreditation com. Grand Rapids Pub. Schs., Mich., 1981; presenter profl. devel. conf. Detroit Fedn. Tchrs. and Det. Pub. Sch. Adminstrs., 1996. Chair Met. Detroit chpt. March of Dimes, 1987; chair Women Who Dare to Care com. United Negro Coll. Fund, Detroit, 1987-89; gen. coord. Mus. African Am. History, Detroit, 1987; tutor, usher, chairperson Hartford Meml. Bapt. Ch., Detroit, 1979—. Recipient Mayor's award of merit for Cmty. Svc., City of Detroit, 1987, plaque and cert. March of Dimes, 1987; recognized as outstanding educator Detroit Tchr., Detroit Fedn. Tchrs., 1987, 94. Mem. Coun. for Exceptional Children (presenter nat. conv. 1983, cert. 1983), Soc. Profls. in Dispute Resolution, Wayne State U. Alumni Assn., Delta Sigma Theta (chairperson 1965—), Phi Delta Kappa (chairperson). Avocations: golf, poetry, racquetball, painting, reading. Office: Martin Luther King Jr Sr HS 3200 E Lafayette Detroit MI 48207 Home: 1249 Navarre Pl Detroit MI 48207 Personal E-mail: eumillercorbitt@aol.com.

CORBOY, JAMES MCNALLY, investment banker; b. Erie, Pa., Nov. 3, 1940; s. James Thomas and Dorothy Jane (Schluraff) C.; m. Suzanne Shaver, July 23, 1965; children: Shannon, James McNally. BA, Allegheny Coll., 1962; MBA, U. Colo., 1986. Mem. sales staff Boettcher & Co., Denver, 1964-70, Blyth Eastman Dillon, Denver and Chgo., 1970-74, William Blair & Co., Chgo., 1974-77; mgr. corp. bond dept. Boettcher & Co., Denver, 1977-79; ptnr. in charge William Blair & Co., Denver, 1979-86; first v.p. Stifel, Nicolaus & Co., Denver, 1986-88; pres., CEO SKB Corboy Inc., Denver, 1988-97, Century Capital Group Inc., 1997-98; ptnr. Corboy and Jerde, LLC, Englewood, Colo., 1999—, Deep Springs Capital Ptnrs., 2005—. With USMC, 1962—67. Republican. Presbyterian. Home: Castle Pines Village 870 Homestake Ct Castle Rock CO 80108 Office: 5350 S Roslyn St Ste 400 Greenwood Village CO 80111 Office Phone: 303-688-6767. Personal E-mail: jcorboy@yahoo.com.

CORBOY, PHILIP HARNETT, lawyer; b. Chgo., Aug. 12, 1924; s. Harold Francis and Marie (Harnett) C.; m. Mary A. Dempsey, Sept. 4, 1992; children from previous marriage: Philip Harnett, Joan Marie, John, Thomas. JD, Loyola U., 1949; student, U. Notre Dame; LLD (hon.), St. Ambrose Coll., 1978; LHD (hon.), Loyola U., 1996. Bar: Ill. 1949. Asst. corp. counsel City Chgo., 1949-50; individual practice, 1950-82; ptnr. Corboy & Demetrio, Chgo., 1982—. Contbr. articles to profl. jours. Trustee Roscoe Pound Found.; gen. counsel to Ill. Dem. Party, 1990-95. With AUS, 1943-45. Recipient Medal of Excellence award, Loyola U. Chgo. Sch. Law, 1967, The Lasallian award, Christian Brothers Midwest Province, 1972, Leonard Ring Lifetime Achievement award, Ill. Trial Lawyers Assn., 1995, Signum Fidei Honor, Chgo. Province Christian Brothers, 1995, Big Shoulders Humanitarian award, 1996, Champion of Justice award, Assn. Trial Lawyers Am., 1996, Freedom award, John Marshall Law Sch., 1998. Fellow Am. Coll. Trial Lawyers; mem. ABA. (chmn. litigation sect. 1979-80), Ill. Bar Assn., Chgo. Bar Assn. (pres. 1972-73), Law Sci. Acad., Am. Judicature Soc., Am. Trial Lawyers Assn., Ill. Trial Lawyer Assn. (pres. 1963-64), Nat. Inst. Trial Advocacy (vice chmn. 1971-72, chmn. 1985-86), Internat. Acad. Trial Lawyers, Internat. Soc. Barristers, Inner Circle Advs. Clubs: Evanston Golf, The Tavern, Mid-Am. Office: Corboy & Demetrio 33 N Dearborn St Fl 21 Chicago IL 60602-3102*

CORBUSIER, DRUE, apparel and home furnishings executive; Corp. exec. v.p., dir. Dillard's, Inc., Little Rock, 1998—; pres. Ft. Worth divsn. Office: Dillards Inc 4501 N Beach Fort Worth TX 76137

CORBY, FRANCIS MICHAEL, JR., business executive; b. Chgo., Feb. 2, 1944; s. Francis M. and Jean (Wolf) C.; m. Diane S. Orselli, Aug. 5, 1972; children: Francis Michael III, Brian A., Christopher S. BA, St. Mary of the Lake, 1966; MBA, Columbia U., 1969. With Chrysler Corp., 1969-80; treasury mgr. Chrysler Peru S.A., Lima, 1973-74; fin. dir. Chrysler Wholesale Ltd., London, 1974-76; mng. dir. Chrysler Comml. S.A. de C.V., Mexico City, 1976-77; v.p., treas. Chrysler Fin. Corp., Troy, Mich., 1977-80; treas. Joy Mfg. Co., Pitts., 1980-83, contr., 1983-86, v.p., 1984-86; sr. v.p. fin., CFO Harnischfeger Industries, Inc., Milw., 1986-94, exec. v.p. fin. and adminstrn., 1994-99; exec. v.p. Frederick & Co., 2000-2001; exec. v.p., CFO Guide Corp., Pendleton, Ind., 2001—04; sr. v.p., CFO GST Autoleather Inc., Hagerstown, Md., 2004—05; exec. v.p., CFO, Exide Techs., Alpharetta, Ga., 2005—. Bd. dirs. Magnasphere Corp. Mem.: Country Club of Naples. Office: 13000 Deerfield Pkwy Bldg 200 Alpharetta GA 30004 Business E-Mail: fran.corby@exide.com.

CORCORAN, ANDREW PATRICK, JR., lawyer; b. Frederick, Md., Nov. 20, 1948; s. Andrew Patrick and Beatrice Josephine (Poletti) C.; m. Margaret Cecila Boyle, July 3, 1971; children: Maureen Meredith, Andrew Patrick III. BA, Villanova U., 1970; JD, Seton Hall U., 1973. Bar: Pa. 1973, U.S Dist. Ct. (ea. dist.) Pa. 1974, U.S. Ct. Appeals (7th cir.) 1976, U.S. Ct. Appeals (3d cir.) 1977, U.S. Supreme Ct. 1982, Va. (corp. counsel) 2004. Atty. Pa. Cen. Transp. Co., Phila., 1973-75, sr. atty., 1975-79; asst. gen. atty. Consol. Rail Corp., Phila., 1979-82, sr. gen. atty., 1982-85, 1985-92, assoc. gen. counsel, 1992-99; gen. atty. Norfolk (Va.) So. Corp., 1999—2005, sr. gen. atty., 2005—. Mem.: Assn. of Am. R.R.'s (legal affairs com.). Republican. Roman Catholic. Home: 2433 Haversham Close Virginia Beach VA 23454-1157 Office: Norfolk So Corp Three Commercial Pl Norfolk VA 23510-9241 Office Phone: 757-664-5140. Business E-Mail: andy.corcoran@nscorp.com.

CORCORAN, BARBARA, real estate company executive; b. Edgewater, NJ; m. Dale Barlow, 1979 (div.); m. Bill Higgins, 1988; 1 child, Thomas. BA in English and Theology, St. Thomas Aquinas Coll.; D (hon.), Marymount Coll. Founder Corcoran Group, NYC, 1973, founder, chmn., 1980—2005, Barbara Corcoran Prodn., NYC, 2005—. Author: If You Don't Have Big Breasts, Put Ribbons in Your Pigtails, 2003, Use What You've Got: And Other Business Lessons I Learned From Mom, 2003, (newsletter) Corcoran Report, 1981—. Former chair NY chpt. Young Pres. Orgn.; former bd. govs. Real Estate Bd. NY. Recipient Harry B. Helmsley Disting. New Yorker award, 2006. Office: 1318 Madison Ave 4 New York NY 10128 also: 210 11th Ave 11th Fl New York NY 10001 Office Phone: 212-937-1000.

CORCORAN, CLEMENT TIMOTHY, III, lawyer, mediator, retired judge; b. Kansas City, Mo., Dec. 18, 1945; s. Clement T. and Bette Lou (Hohl) C. BA, U. N.C., 1967; JD, U. Va., 1973. Bar: Fla. 1973, U.S. Dist. Ct. (mid. dist.) Fla. 1973, D.C. 1974, U.S. Dist. Ct. (no. and so. dists.) Fla. 1975, U.S. Supreme Ct. 1979, U.S. Ct. Appeals (11th cir.) 1981; cert. cir. mediator Fla. Supreme Ct. Law clk. U.S. Dist. Ct., Tampa, Fla., 1973-75; assoc. Carlton, Fields, Ward, Emmanuel, Smith & Cutler, P.A., Tampa, 1975-78, ptnr., 1978-89; judge Bankruptcy Ct. (mid. dist.) Fla., Orlando, 1989-93, Tampa, 1993—2003. Dir. Bay Area Legal Svcs., Inc., Tampa, 1983-89, v.p., 1987, pres., 1988; bd. dirs. Fla. Coun. Bar Pres., 1982-88, pres., 1986-87; arbitrator Ct. Annexed Arbitration Program, U.S. Dist. Ct. (mid. dist.) Fla., 1984-89; counselor U. Tampa, 1981-86, fellow, 1986-89. Co-author: Conflicts of Interest, 1984; contbr. articles to legal jours. Lt. USNR, 1967-70. Mem. ABA (litigation sect., coun. mem. 1999-2002, co-chair comm. com. 1990-92, chair book pub. bd. 1992-98, 2007—, assoc. editor Litigation News 1982-87, mng. editor 1987, editor-in-chief 1988-90, 2002-04, co-dir. pubs. divsn. 2004-05, Nat. Conf. of Lawyers and Reps. of Media 1992-95, mem. adv. com. on nominations 1994-95, chair media-law roundtable 1994, chair sect. officers conf. com. on non-dues revenue 1995-96, mem. working group on ABA bus. plan for pub. 1995-96, standing com. on pub. oversight 1996-2002, ho. of dels. 2003-2005), Fla. Bar (chmn. voluntary bar liaison com. 1985-04, chmn. grievance com. 13-D 1986-88, chmn. legal edn. com. 1981-82, Most Productive Young Lawyer award 1981), Am. Judicature Soc., Hillsborough County Bar Assn. (Robert W. Patton Outstanding Jurist award 2002, Red McEwen award 1980, pres. 1982-83), Am. Inns of Ct. (Master of the Bench 1990-93, 96—). Roman Catholic. Office: 400 N Ashley Dr Ste 2540 Tampa FL 33602 Office Phone: 813-769-5020. Personal E-mail: ctcorcoran@mindspring.com.

CORCORAN, DAVID, newspaper editor; b. NYC, July 22, 1947; s. William and Ruth (Brody) Diebold; m. Karrie Olick; children: Thomas, Daniel, Katie. BA, Amherst Coll., Mass., 1969; fellow journalism, Stanford U., Calif., 1976-77. Tchr. Rockland Country Day Sch., Congers, NY, 1969-70; reporter Hackensack Record, NJ, 1969-73, from editl. writer to asst. editor NJ, 1973-77, editor editl. page NJ, 1977-87, chief news editor NJ, 1987-88; staff editor NY Times, 1988—2001, asst. sci. editor, 2001—. Trustee Ctr. Analysis of Pub. Issues, 1983-91. Mem. Am. Soc. Newspaper Editors, Nat. Conf. Editl. Writers, Soc. Profl. Journalists (dir. NJ chpt. 1980—, pres. NJ chpt. 1983-84). Home: 437 Wildwood Rd Northvale NJ 07647-1221 Office: NY Times 229 W 43rd St New York NY 10036-3959 Business E-Mail: corcoran@nytimes.com.

CORCORAN, ELIZABETH ANNE, journalist; d. John B. Corcoran and Virginia M. D.; m. George Charles Anders, Aug. 27, 1988; children: Matthew Corcoran Anders, Peter Corcoran Anders. BA in Economics, Georgetown U., Washington, 1984. Assoc. editor IEEE Spectrum, NYC, 1985—88; mem. bd. editors Sci. Am. mag., NYC, 1988—92; staff writer Washington Post, 1994—99; bur. chief Forbes mag. Silicon Valley bur., Burlingame, Calif., 1999—2002, contbg. editor, 2002—07; technology channel editor Forbes.com, Burlingame, Calif., 2007—. Knight journalism fellow MIT, Cambridge, Mass., 1993—94; radio and TV commentator Forbes on Fox, NYC, 1999—; frequent moderator and spkr. Named an Top Influencer, Mktg. Computers Media Report, 1999, 2000, 2002; recipient Feature Writing award, Computer Press Assn., 1991, News Reporting award, 1994. Mem.: Nat. Assn. Sci. Writers (Evert Clark award Nat. Press Found. 1993), US Masters Swimming Inc. Office: Forbes magazine 555 Airport Blvd Burlingame CA 94010

CORCORAN, JAMES B., bank executive; Sales exec. to sr. v.p. card mktg. European ops. Am. Express; head mktg. consumer bus. IBM; mng. dir. global sales Citigroup; pres. UK card bus. Bank One/First USA; mng. dir. retail distbn. Halifax Bank Scotland, 2000—06; pres. Retail Banking Washington Mut., Inc., 2006—. Office: Washington Mut Inc 1301 Second Ave Seattle WA 98101 Office Phone: 206-461-2000.*

CORCORAN, JOHN PAUL, lawyer, educator; b. Wilkes-Barre, Pa., Apr. 28, 1968; s. John Paul and Virginia M. Corcoran; m. Virginia Berlando, Mar. 4, 1995; 1 child, Gabrielle. JD, Duquesne U., Pitts., Pa., 1994. Bar: Pa. 1994. Ptnr. Jones, Gregg, Creehan and Gerace, Pitts., 1999—. Adj. prof. law Duquesne U., 2007—. Lt USN, 1994—98. Decorated Achievement medal USN. Office: Jones Gregg Creehan & Gerace 411 7th Ave Pittsburgh PA 15219 Home Phone: 412-261-6400; Office Phone: 412-261-6400. Business E-Mail: jpc@jgcg.com.

CORDANI, DAVID M., insurance company executive; BS, Tex. A&M U., College Station, 1988; MBA in Mktg., U. Hartford, Conn., 1994. Chartered fin. cons., CPA. With Coopers & Lybrand; contr. CIGNA Corp., v.p. corp. acctg. and planning, 2000—02; pres. SE Region CIGNA HealthCare, CFO field ops., sr. v.p. transformation and prog. mgmt., 2002, sr. v.p., CFO, 2002—04, pres. Health Segments, 2004—05, pres., 2005—. Bd. dirs. NAM. Office: CIGNA HealthCare 900 Cottage Grove Rd Bloomfield CT 06002 Office Phone: 860-726-6000.*

CORDARO, MATTHEW CHARLES, energy and utility executive, educator; b. NYC, July 25, 1943; s. Matteo C. and Josephine (Picone) C.; m. Janet Chick, June 24, 1967; children: Anne-Marie, Allison; m. Martha Warnock, July 18, 1987; 1 child, Marie Elena. BS, C.W. Post Coll., 1965; MS in Nuclear Engring., NYU, 1967; PhD in Engring. and Physics, Cooper Union, 1970. Asst. engr. L.I. Lighting Co., Hicksville, NY, from 1966, successively assoc. engr., nuclear physicist, sr. environ. engr., mgr. environ. engring., v.p. engring., 1978-84, v.p. engring. and adminstrn., 1984-85, sr. v.p. ops. and engring., 1985-88; pres. Long Lake Cogeneration Corp., Melville, NY, 1988-93; sr. v.p. Long Lake Energy Corp., NYC, 1988-93; pres. and CEO Nashville Electric Svc., 1993-99, Midwest Ind. Transmission Sys. Operator, 1999-2001; dean Coll. Mgmt., dir. Ctr. for Mgmt. Analysis, dir. Sch. Pub. Acctg., chair healthcare and pub. adminstrn. dept. Long Island U., Brookville, NY, 2001—. Cons. Bechtel, CMS, GE, Panhandle, Shoreham Project, 1992-93, R.J. Rudden Assocs., Hauppauge, N.Y.; guest rsch. assoc. Brookhaven Nat. Lab., 1968-71; adj. assoc. prof. nuclear engring. Poly. Inst. N.Y., 1979-80; adj. asst. prof. engring. C.W. Post Coll., 1968-72; former bd. dirs. ctr. for energy studies Adelphi U. Edtl. advisory bd. L.I. Business News, 2005-; contbr. articles to profl. jours. Mem. Coun. overseers C.W. Post Coll., 1968-72; former mem. campaign coun. L.I. U., cmty. adv. bd. Sta. WLIW Pub. TV, Garden City, N.Y., Nashville C. of C., bd. dirs., Nashville Urban League, Nashville BBB, Nashville Jr. Achievement, Nashville Heart Assn., Tenn. Mcpl. Elec. Power Assn., Tenn. Valley Pub. Power Assn., Nature Conservancy of Tenn., corp. bd. Nashville Bapt. Hosp., adv. com. Nashville Girl Scouts; chmn. Mid. Tenn. U.S. Savs. Bond campaign, 1995-97; trustee Elec. Power Rsch. Inst. 1997-2001. AEC fellow, 1965-66 Mem. Am. Pub. Power Assn. (bd. dirs. 1994-00). Office: Post Campus Long Island University Greenvale NY 11548-1300 Personal E-mail: mcsqd22@aol.com. *One must try with all their heart to achieve anything of value on this earth. The tragedy of life is not giving your full effort for fear of failure. Never give up, never give in.*

CORDDRY, ROB, comedian, actor; b. Weymouth, Mass., Feb. 4, 1971; m. Sandra Corddry, 2002; 1 child, Sloane Sullivan. Grad., U. Mass. Appeared with Third Rail Comedies, NYC, Naked Babies, NYC; performer, tchr. Uprights Citizen's Brigade Theater, NYC. Actor: (films) Old School, 2003, Blackballed: The Bobby Dukes Story, 2004, Failure to Launch, 2006, The Pleasure of Your Company, 2006, Unaccompanied Minors, 2006, The Ten, 2007, Blades of Glory, 2007; (TV series) Lake Night with Conan O'Brien, 1998—2002, The Daily Show with Jon Stewart, 2002—06, Upright Citizens Brigade, 1998—2002, The Winner, 2007. Office: The Daily Show 604R W 52nd St New York NY 10019-5013*

CORDEIRO, PETER GABRIEL, surgeon, plastic surgeon; b. Bombay, Feb. 10, 1958; MD, Harvard Med. Sch., 1983. Intern, gen. surgery New England Deacones, 1983—84, resident, plastic surgery, 1984—89; resident, micro surgery NYU Med. Ctr., 1989—91; fellow Meml. Sloan-Kettering Cancer Ctr., NYC, 1991, hosp. appt., plastic reconstructive surgery, 1992—, acting chief, plastic & reconstructive, 2001, chief, plastic & reconstructive svc., dept. surgery, 2001—; prof. surgery Cornell U., NYC. Lectr. in field. Author: several scientific papers and book chapters; mem. editl. bd. Annals Surgical Oncology, and others. Mem.: Internat. Acad. Oral Oncology. Achievements include being a leader in the area of oncologic reconstructive surgery at a national and international level. Office: Meml Sloan-Kettering Cancer Ctr 1275 York Ave New York NY 10021 Office Phone: 212-639-2521. Office Fax: 212-717-3677.*

CORDELL, LARRY KENNETH (L. KENNY), agricultural products executive; Mgmt. positions Rohm & Haas, 1979—89, BASF, 1989—92; dir. No. Am. agrl. products group FMC Agrl. Products, 1992—2001; joined United Agri Products Inc., 2001, pres., COO, 2002—03, pres., CEO, 2003—; pres. UAP Holding Corp., Greeley, Colo., 2003—04, pres., CEO, 2004—. Office: UAP Holding Corp 7251 W 4th St Greeley CO 80634*

CORDELL, LINDA S., anthropologist, educator, museum director; BA with distinction, George Washington U., 1965; MA, U. Oreg., 1967; PhD, U. Calif., Santa Barbara, 1972. Prof. anthropology Smithsonian Inst., 1963—65; tchg. asst. U. N.Mex, 1965; grad. tchg. asst. U. Calif., Santa Barbara, 1969—70; asst. prof. anthropology U. N.Mex, 1971—76, assoc. prof. anthropology, 1976—82, prof. anthropology, 1982—87, prof. and chair anthropology, 1983—87, acting v.p. rsch., 1986; vis. prof. Stanford U., 1990; Irvine curator anthropology, chair anthropology Calif. Acad. Sciences, 1987—93; dir. U. Colo. Mus. Nat. History, Boulder, 1994—; prof. anthropology U. Colo., Boulder, 1994—. Adv. bd. U. Press of Colo., 2003—, Chaco Digitization Project, 2002—; vis. scholar Santa Fe Inst., 2002; rsch. assoc. Maxwell Mus. Anthropology, 1994—, Am. Mus. Nat. History, 2001—. Editl. bd. Smithsonian Inst. Press, 1986—94, Pacific Discovery Mag., 1988—89, assoc. editor Jour. Anthrop. Rsch., 1987—89. Recipient Bryon S. Cummings award, Ariz. Archeol. and Hist. Soc., 2004. Fellow: AAAS; mem.: NAS, Southwestern Anthrop. Assn., Soc. Am. Archeol. (sec. elect. 2003—04, sec. 2005), N.Mex Archeol. Coun., Ariz. Archeol. Soc., Am. Anthrop. Assn., Albuquerque Archeol. Soc. Mailing: 3102 Gamow Ln Boulder CO 80301 Home Phone: 303-447-3724; Office Phone: 303-492-0666. E-mail: linda.cordell@colorado.edu.

CORDELL, PHILIP GRANVILE, music educator, musician; b. Urbana, Ohio, Sept. 12, 1959; s. Granville Ogden and Pauline Davis Cordell; life ptnr. Don W Roush, Jan. 1, 2003; 1 child, Athena Gambrina Doe. BMus in Piano Performance with Organ and Harpsichord Studies, Wittenberg U., 1981; MMus in Composition, Ohio U., 1982, MMus in Piano Performance/Pedagogy, 1984. Nat. cert. tchr. of music in piano, Permanent profl. tchg. cert. MTNA, 2006. Instr. The Ctr. for Musical Devel., Springfield, Ohio, 1977—86; accompanist dance dept. The Ohio State U., Columbus, 1987—89; lectr. Capital U., Bexley, Ohio, 1988—2001, instr., 2001—, orchestral pianist, theatre dept., 2003. Freelance musician, 1976—; pianist Ballet Met, Columbus, 1988—91; profl. accompanist Opera Columbus, 2001—02. Composer: (piano solos) Theme and Variation, 1979, Five Piano Preludes, 1980, Mini String Quartet, 1980, Work for Woodwinds, 1982, Three Sketches, 1996, The Wonder of Love, 1999, A Search for Peace, 2003, Christmas Piano Solo Arrangements, 2004—, Sacred Arrangements for Solo Piano and Solo Organ, (work for two violins) Dances for Two Violins; musician: (faculty rec.) Cmty. Music Sch. Faculty Concert, 1998, Conservatory of Music Faculty Concert, 1999; musician: (producer) (conservatory faculty concert) Conservatory Faculty Concert Rec., 2000. Super swimmer Ctrl. Ohio Diabetes Assn., Columbus, 1989—; organist New Life United Meth. Ch., Columbus, 1987—2003; organist, pianist St. Paul's Luth. Ch., Westerville, Ohio, 2003—. Mem.: Midwestern Keyboard Hist. Soc. (life), Coll. Music Soc. (life), Nat. Fedn. of Music Clubs (life; profl. adjudicator 1979—), Music Tchrs. Nat. Assn. (life; profl. adjudicator 1981—, dist. festival co-chmn. 1991, condr. for pianorama 1991—, dist. festival judge com. 2000—01, time keeper 2001, graves piano competition door monitor 2003, tchg. cert. 2006), Ctrl. Ohio Diabetes Assn. (life). Avocations: swimming, walking, playing electronic keyboard instruments. Office: Capital Univ 1 College and Main Columbus OH 43209

CORDERMAN, DOUGLAS GEORGE, retired non-profit organization executive; b. Ft. Sill, Okla., Sept. 3, 1931; s. W. Preston and Virginia (Sandt) C.; m. Joan Jaeckel, Nov. 30, 1974; children: Susan, David, Lisa, John, Jean, Daniel. AB, Dartmouth Coll., 1952; JD, Harvard U., 1955; DS (hon.), Fla. Inst. Tech., 1976. Contract adminstr. Gen. Dynamics Corp., Rochester, NY, 1958-60; mgr. contracts Dresser Industries, Houston, 1960-62; asst. mgr. adminstrn. McDonnell Aircraft Co., St. Louis, 1962-64; mgr. contracts Electronics and Space div. Emerson Electric Co., St. Louis, 1964-69, dir. adminstrn., 1969-71, v.p. adminstrn., 1971-78, sr. v.p., 1978-88; corp. dir. Product Liability, 1988-90; pres. US Nat. Sr. Sports Orgn., 1990-95; sr. warden Good Shepherd Episcopal. Ch., St. Louis, 1997—98. Contbr. articles to profl. publs. Mem. vestry Good Shepherd Episcopal Ch., St. Louis, 1995—98, St. James Episcopal Ch., Leesburg, Va., 2003-05, St. Timothy's Episcopal Ch., St. Louis, 1975-78, 81-83; mem. alumni coun. Dartmouth Coll., Hanover, NH, 1979-81; bd. dirs. West County YMCA, St. Louis, 1985-2000, US Olympic Com., 1990-95. Fellow Nat. Contract Mgmt. Assn. (nat. pres. 1975-77, Blanche Witte Meml. award 1970, hon. life mem.); mem. Am. Def. Preparedness Assn. (bd. dirs. St. Louis chpt. 1973-88, pres. 1981-82), Nat. Security Indsl. Assn. (hon. life mem., trustee 1980-90, exec. com. 1985-90, chmn. 1987-88), Navy League (hon. life mem.); Loudoun Golf and Country Club (Loudoun County, Va.). Republican. Avocations: running, skiing, swimming, triathlons. Personal E-mail: dgcorderma@aol.com.

CORDERO, FRANCISCO JAVIER, professional baseball player; b. Santo Domingo, Dominican Republic, May 11, 1975; Pitcher Detroit Tigers, 1999, Tex. Rangers, 1999—2006, Milw. Brewers, 2006—. Named to Am. League All-Star Team, Maj. League Baseball, 2004, Nat. League All-Star Team, 2007. Avocations: dominoes, billiards. Mailing: Milw Brewers One Brewers Way Milwaukee WI 53214-3652*

CORDERO, JOSE FERNANDO, pediatrician, dean; b. Camuy, PR, July 25, 1948; s. Fernando and Ana T. Cordero; m. Milagros J. Garcia, June 18, 1970; children: Jose F., Ana M., Joann M., Maria M. BS in Biology, U. P.R., Rio Piedras, 1969; MD, U. P.R., San Juan, 1973; MPH, Harvard U., 1979. Diplomate Nat. Bd. Med. Examiners, Am. Bd. Med. Genetics, Am. Bd. Pediatrics; lic. physician, Ga. Intern Boston City Hosp., 1973-74, jr. asst. resident dept. pediatrics, 1974-75; clin. and rsch. fellow pediatrics Mass. Gen. Hosp., 1975-77; pediatrican South End Cmty. Health Ctr., Boston, 1977-79; epidemiology intelligence svc. officer Bur. Epidemiology Ctrs. for Disease Control & Prevention, Atlanta, 1979-81, dep. chief birth defects and genetic diseases br., 1985-88, acting chief birth defects and genetic diseases bd., 1988-89, asst. dir. sci. divsn. birth defects and devel. disabilities, 1989-94, dep. dir. nat. immunization program, 1994—2001, dir. Nat. Ctr. on Birth Defects and Devel. Disabilities, 2001—06; asst. surgeon gen. USPHS, 1998—2006; dean U. P.R. Grad. Sch. Pub. Health, San Juan, 2006—. Clin. instr. pediatrics Children's Hosp., Boston, 1978-79; clin. asst. prof. pediatrics Emory U., 1982—. Co-editor jour. Teratology, 1983-86; mem. editl. bd. Birth Defects Ency., 1988; reviewer jours.; contbr. numerous articles and abstracts to publs. Mem. working group cancer chemotherapy Internat. Agy. Cancer Rsch., 1980; mem. task force on child health and related issues FDA, 1980-83; mem. rev. coms. NIH; coord. U.S. Govt. Task Force Premature Thelarche in P.R., 1982-85; trustee Calif. Birth Defects Monitoring Program, 1983-89; mem. adv. bd. TERIS, Seattle, 1986—, Fla. Teratogen Info. System, 1986-90; cons. WHO, Guatemala, 1990, 91, 92, Copenhagen, 1991; founding mem. Emmaus Community, 1992—; mem. troop 547 com. Boy Scouts Am., 1983-94. Recipient Arthur S. Flemming award, 1988, Physician's Recognition award AMA, 1980, 84, 88. Mem. APHA, Am. Soc. Human Genetics, Am. Bd. Med. Genetics, Am. Acad. Pediatrics (nutrition com. 1980, com. on drugs 1988-93, genetic com. 1985), Am. Epidemiology Soc., Mass. Med. Soc., Genetics Soc. Ga., Coalition of Spanish Speaking Mental Health and Human Svcs. Orgn., Teratology Soc., Soc. Pediatric Rsch. Roman Catholic. Avocations: bird watching, flying, painting, travel. Office: U PR Grad Sch Pub Health PO Box 365067 San Juan PR 00936-5067 Business E-Mail: jcordero@rcm.upr.edu.

CORDERO, VINCENT C., television network executive; b. 1971; BA in Philos., Polit. Sci., Chicano Studies, UCLA, 1996; JD, U. Chgo. Law Sch., 1999. Mem., Exec. Assoc. Prog. Univision Comm. Inc., 1999, v.p., bus. devel. and labor affairs; v.p., gen. mgr. Univision Television Grp., Chgo., 2005—. Mem. Chgo. Cmty. Trust, Mex. Fine Arts Mus. Office: Univision Television Group 541 N Fairbanks Ct 11 fl Chicago IL 60611 Office Phone: 312-670-1000. Office Fax: 312-494-6492.*

CORDES, BRETT MCCORMACK, otolaryngologist; s. Craig McCormack and Carole Vicknair Cordes; m. Katherine Diane Rippas, June 23, 2001; 1 child, Kevin Estuardo. BA summa cum laude, La. State U., Baton Rouge, 1999; MD with honors, La. State U., New Orleans, 2004. Cert. ACLS provider Am. Heart Assn., 2004, ATLS provider Am. Heart Assn., 2004. Resident physician dept. otolaryngology, head and neck surgery Baylor U. Coll. Medicine, Houston, 2004—. Seasonal vol. St. Andrew's Episcopal Ch., Pearland, Tex., 2005—07, Sunday sch. tchr., 2006—07. Recipient Young Investigator award, Emergency Medicine Rsch. Forum, 2004, J. Charles Dickson Clin. Rsch. award, 2007, Resident Tchg. award, 2007. Mem.: AMA (life), Otolaryngology-Head and Neck Surgery Soc. (life), Phi Beta Kappa, Alpha Omega Alpha (life). Achievements include research in molecular characteriazation of undifferentiated sinonasal tumors; inhibition of apoptosis in swine brain by hyperbaric oxygen therapy following cardiopulmonary arrest; medical research trial doxycycline sclerotherapy as primary treatment for head and neck lymphatic malformations. Avocations: exercise, religious association philanthropic activities.

CORDES, EUGENE HAROLD, retired pharmacy and chemistry educator; b. York, Nebr., Apr. 7, 1936; s. Elmer Henry and Ruby Mae (Hofeldt) C.; m. Shirley Ann Morton, Nov. 9, 1957; children: Jennifer Eve, Matthew Henry James. BS, Calif. Inst. Tech., 1958; PhD, Brandeis U., 1962. Instr. chemistry Ind. U., Bloomington, 1962-64, asst. prof., 1964-66, assoc. prof., 1966-68, prof., 1968-79, chmn., 1972-78; exec. dir. biochemistry Merck, Sharp and Dohme Research Labs., Rahway, NJ, 1979-84, v.p. biochemistry, 1984-87; v.p. R & D Eastman Pharms., Malvern, Pa., 1987-88; pres. Sterling Winthrop Pharms. Rsch. divsn. Sterling Winthrop Inc., Collegeville, Pa., 1988-94; prof. U. Mich., Ann Arbor, 1995—2002; chmn. bd. dirs. Vitae Pharma (formerly Concurrent Pharms.), 2002—06. Author: (with Henry Mahler) Biological Chemistry, 1966, 2d. edit., 1971, Basic Biological Chemistry, 1969, (with Riley Schaeffer) Chemistry, 1973; also articles. Recipient NIH Career Devel. award, 1966; Alfred P. Sloan Found. fellow, 1968. Mem.: AAAS, Am. Soc. Biol. Chemists. Home: 3603 Saint Davids Rd Newtown Square PA 19073-1410 Personal E-mail: cordeseh@aol.com.

CORDES, JILL, chef; m. Phil Johnston. Degree in Journalism, Penn State. News reporter NBC affiliate, Rapid City, SD, 1995, gen. assignment reporter Sioux Falls, SD, morning anchor Omaha; reporter WCCO, Mpls. Host (TV series) The Best Of, Food Network, My First Place, HGTV, host, co-prodr. Solutions With Jill; author: Food Network: Best Of the Best Of; prodr.: (films) Flightless Birds, 2004; guest appearances (TV series) Oprah. Avocations: scuba diving, yoga, running, reading.

CORDES, KATHLEEN ANN, retired physical education educator, director; d. Rita Ann and Edrick John Cordes. BS, Ind. U., Bloomington, 1972; MA, Ball State U., Muncie, 1973. Grad. asst., coach Ball State U., 1972—73; prof., coach Hanover Coll., Ind., 1973—75, U. Notre Dame, Ind., 1976—77; athletic dir. St. Mary's Coll., Notre Dame, 1977—79; prof. Whittier Coll., Calif., 1979—90; prof. emeritus, honors coord. Miramar Coll., San Diego, 1990—98. Interim exec. dir. AAHPERD, Reston, Va.; vis. prof. U. Zulia, Maracaibo, Venezuela, 1990—91, U. Andes, Merida, Venezuela, 1995; news dir. KSMK, Ariz., 1985. Author: America's National Historic Trails, 1999, America's National Scenic Trails, 2001, America's Millennium Trails: Pathways to the 21st Century, 2002, official project of the White House Millennium Council, 2001, 2002, Applications in Recreation, 3rd edit., 2002 (Chinese Transl., 2001), Parks, Recreation, and Leisure Service Management, 2002, Outdoor Recreation, 3d edit., 2007; editor: National Girls' and Women's Sports Tennis Guide, 1986. Mem. White House Millennium Trails Com., 1999—2001; v.p. YMCA, Whittier, 1988—90. Recipient Merit Svc. award, Am. Assn. Leisure and Recreation, 1997, Outstanding Achievement award, 2001, Dist. Svc. to Recreation award, CAHPERD, 1998, Past Pres. award of merit, 2005. Fellow: Am. Leisure Acad.; mem.: AAHPERD, Calif. Assn. Health, Phys. Edn., Recreation, and Dance Found. (v.p. recreation 1986—87, v.p. girl's and women sports 1995—96, bd. trustees 2006—, v.p.). Independent. Roman Catholic. Achievements include first woman to coach a varsity sport at the University of Notre Dame. Avocations: tennis, hiking, swimming, golf, gardening. Home: 3848 Flowerwood Ln Fallbrook CA 92028 Home Phone: 760-723-4044.

CORDES, MARY KENRICK, psychologist, retired; b. Flint, Mich., Aug. 6, 1933; d. Charles Fay and Margaret Lydia (Mitchell) Kenrick; m. John Cordes, July 30, 1955 (dec. 1970); children: James Charles, Mari Kenrick Cordes. BA, Denison U., 1955; MA, Oakland U., 1969. Ltd. lic. psychologist, Mich. Rsch. asst. Lafayette Clinic, Detroit, 1968; sch. psychologist Roseville (Mich.) Community Schs., 1968-93; assoc. Rochester (Mich.) Psychol. Clinic, 1970-82. Mem. State Licensure Bd. of Psychology, Lansing, Mich., 1978-81, Spl. Edn. Adv. Com., Lansing, 1984-88. Vol. counselor Crossroads-St. Paul's Cathedral, Detroit, 1982-90; singer Rochester Community Chorus, 1986—. Mem. APA (assoc.), Nat. Assn. Sch. Psychologists, Mich. Assn. Sch. Psychologists (regional bd dirs. 1973-77, Outstanding State Sch. Psychologist 1979), Macomb County Psychol. Assocs. (pres. 1972-73), Oakland County Dem. Party, Alternate State Dem. (exec. bd., 2004—, precinct del. 2003—). Avocation: travel. Home: 2452 Blockton Rd Rochester MI 48306-3902 Personal E-mail: mimicor@aol.com.

CORDOVA, BARBARA JOY, activities director; b. LA, Dec. 18, 1957; d. Joseph Cordova and Arlene Riesman; m. Robert Oliver Cordova, May 24, 1999. Student, Pierce Coll., 1975—77. Freelance art and jewelry sales, LA, 1986—93, Seattle, 1986—93; data processing staff Nationwide Title Clearing, LA, 1993—98; group activities dir. Celebrity Ctr. Internat. Ch. Scientology, Hollywood, Calif., 1998—. Author: (novels) Mission of the Artist, 2000; songwriter: music, 1998, writer: musical. Foudner Artists for a Better World; vol. min. dir. Ch. Scientology, Hollywood, event prodr. Avocations: hiking, swimming.

CÓRDOVA, FRANCE ANNE-DOMINIC, academic administrator, astrophysicist; b. Paris, Aug. 5, 1947; came to U.S., 1953; d. Frederick Ben Jr. and Joan Francis (McGuinness) C.; m. Christian John Foster, Jan. 4, 1985; children: Anne-Catherine Cordova Foster, Stephen Cordova Foster. BA in English with distinction, Stanford U., 1969; PhD in Physics, Calif. Inst. Tech., 1979; PhD (hon.), Loyola Marymount U., 1997. Staff scientist earth and space sci. div. Los Alamos Nat. Lab., 1979-89, dep. group leader space astronomy and astrophysics group, 1989; prof., head dept. astronomy and astrophysics Pa. State U., University Park, 1989—96; chief scientist NASA, Washington, 1993-96; vice chancellor for rsch., prof. physics U. Calif., Santa Barbara, 1996—2002, chancellor, disting. prof. physics and astronomy Riverside, 2002—07; pres. Purdue U., West Lafayette, Ind., 2007—. Mem. Nat. Com. on Medal of Sci., 1991-94; adv. com. for astron. scis. NSF, 1990-93, external adv. com. Particle Astrophysics Ctr., 1989-93; bd. dirs. Assn. Univs. for Rsch. in Astronomy, 1989-93; mem. Space Telescope Inst. Coun., 1990-93; mem. com. space astronomy and astrophysics Space Sci. Bd., 1987-90, internat. users com. Roentgen X-ray Obs., 1985-90, extreme ultraviolet explorer guest observer working group NASA, 1988-93, com. Space Sci. and Applications Group, NASA, 1991-93; mem. Hubble Telescope Adv. Camera Team, 1993; chair Hubble Fellow Selection Com., 1992. Guest editor Mademoiselle mag., 1969; editor: Multiwavelength Astrophysics, 1988, The Spectroscopic Survey Telescope, 1990; contbr. articles to profl. jours. including Astrophysics Jour., Nature, Astrophysics and Space Scis., Advanced Space Rsch., Astron. Astrophysics, Mon. Nat. Royal Astron. Soc., chpts. to books. Named One of Am.'s 100 Brightest Scientists under 40, Sci. Digest, 1984; grantee NASA, 1979; recipient Distinguished Svc. medal, NASA, Kilby Laureate, 2000. Mem. Internat. Astron. Union (US nat. com. 1990-93), Am. Astron. Soc. (v.p. 1993-96, chair high energy astrophysics divsn. 1990, vice chair 1989). Achievements include research in analysis of ultra-soft x-ray emission from active galactic nuclei; observations and modeling of the winds from accretion disks; studies of the interstellar medium using ultraviolet spectroscopy of nearby hot binary stars; observations and modeling of extended x-ray emitting regions in close binary systems; understanding the accretion geometry of magnetic binaries with accreting white dwarfs; coordinating radio and x-ray observations of x-ray binaries in an effort to find a unified model for correlated behavior; search for evidence of galactic magnetic monopoles by identifying a class of ultrasoft x-ray emitters; studying the multispectial emission from neutron stars; making observations of x-ray emitting pulsars and their associated supernova remnants in the radio and infrared; conceiving space instruments and data systems for imaging detectors (co-principal investigator for optical/UV Telescope launched 1999 on ESA's X-Ray Multi-Mirror mission); making multifrequency observations of high-energy sources. Office: Purdue U Office of Pres Hovde Hall 610 Purdue Mall West Lafayette IN 47907

CORDOVA, MARIA ASUNCION, dentist; b. Punta Arenas, Magallanes, Chile, May 14, 1941; came to U.S., 1972; d. Miguel Cordova and Maria Asuncion Requena; m. Carlos F. Salinas, July 27, 1963; children: Carlos M., Claudio A., Lola. DDS, U. Chile, Santiago, 1965; DMD, Med. U. S.C., 1986. From instr. to assoc. prof. physiology U. Chile, Valparaiso, 1965—72; postdoctoral fellow Johns Hopkins U., Balt., 1972-75; from instr. to asst. prof. dept. physiology Med. U. S.C., Charleston, 1975—86; pvt. practice Charleston, 1986—. Vis. scientist N.Y. Med. Coll., 1975. Contbr. articles to profl. jours. Pres. Circulo Hispanic Charleston; country specialist Amnesty Internat. U.S.A., Spoleto, Charleston, mem. outreach com.; past mem. Charleston C. of C. Hispanic Coun.; past bd. dir. Trident Urban League; former bd. dir. YWCA; bd. dir. Robert Ivey Ballet, S.C. Humanities Coun., 1996—2002. Mem. Acad. Gen. Dentists, Am. Dental Assn., Charleston Dental Assn., SC Dental Assn., Charleston Women's Network (pres. 1989-90), Circulo Hispano americano de Charleston (pres.). Roman Catholic. Office: 159 Wentworth St Charleston SC 29401-1731 Office Phone: 843-577-2898.

CORDOVA, RICHARD D., hospital administrator; b. Montebello, Calif. married; 3 children. BBA, Calif. State U., LA, 1972; MBA, Pepperdine U., 1984. With Dept. Health Svcs., County of LA, 1973—91, assoc. hosp. adminstr. of ops. Olive View Med. Ctr., 1978—86, adminstr. Gen. Hosp. LA County (LAC/USC Med. Ctr.), 1986—91; with Dept. of Pub. Health, City and County of San Francisco, 1991—98, CEO San Francisco Gen. Hosp., 1991—97, exec. adminstr. Cmty. Health Network, 1997—98; chief ops. officer Kaiser Permanente Health Plan, So. Calif., 1999—2002, pres. So. Calif. Region, 2002—04; pres., COO Childrens Hosp. LA, 2005—. Founding mem. San Francisco Pub. Health Authority, 1996—98; mem. Coun. on Grad. Med. Edn., 1996—98; bd. dirs. Inst. Diversity in Health Mgmt. Named one of Top 100 Hispanic Leaders, Hispanic Bus. Mag.,

2003; recipient Top 10 Latinos in Healthcare, LatinoLeaders mag., 2004. Mem.: Am. Coll. of Health Care Execs. (diplomat 1980—). Office: Childrens Hosp LA 4650 Sunset Blvd Los Angeles CA 90027

CORDOVA, RUBEN CHARLES, art historian, curator, photographer; s. Ruben Cordova and Rose (Martinez) Vollmer. BA in Semiotics, Brown U., Providence, 1980; PhD in Art History, U. Calif., Berkeley, 1998. Pub. rels. assoc. Am. Craft Coun. and Am. Craft Mus., 1986—87; curator Hershel B. Chipp collection, 1990—91; instr. of record U. Calif., Berkeley, 1994, 1995, 1996; curator Mexican Mus., San Francisco, 1996—97; asst. prof. U. Tex. Pan Am., Edinburg, 1998—99, U. Tex., San Antonio, 1999—2007. Cons. Arts and Entertainment Network, 1997; mem. art selection univ. libr. U. Tex Pan Am., 1998—99, mem. art exhbns. com., 1998—99; mem. faculty senate U. Tex., San Antonio, 2000—02, mem. univ. assembly, 2000—02; mem. adv. bd. NEH Rev. Com. San Antonio Mus. Art, 2000, A Ver: Revisioning Art History, UCLA, 2002; juror Henry Bonilla Congressional Art Competition, 2005; guest prof. Sarah Lawrence Coll., Bronxville, NY, 2007—. Author: (exhbn. catalogue) Arte Caliente: Selections from the Joe. A. Diaz Collection, 2004; exhibitions include Francisco Zúñiga, Mexican Mus., San Francisco, 1996—97, Trees of Life, 1996—97, Community Collects, 1997, Day of Dead, 1997—98, Fantastic Creatures, 1997—98, Arte Contemporaneo, Aztlán Cultural Ctr., San Antonio, 2004, Mestizaje, Arte Reyes, San Antonio, 2005, César Chávez Mordi, Inst. Tex. Cultures, 2006, Barrio Dogs, Arte Reyes, 2006, Jesse Almazan, 2007, Enrique Martinez, One 4 Zero 6 Gallery, 2007, Counterculture x3, Vtrue Art Space, 2007; contbr. chapters to books, articles to catalogues and profl. jours.; one-man shows include Inst. Texan Cultures, 2006, exhibited in group shows at Stella Haus Gallery Blue Star Art Complex, San Antonio, 2005, Ctrl. Libr. Art Gallery, 2005 (1st Pl. award, 07), 2007, Alameda Nat. Ctr. Latino Arts and Culture, 2005, i2i Gallery, 2005, 2006, Gallista Gallery, 2005, Aztlán Cultural Ctr., 2005, 2006, 2007, Casa Margarita Gallery, 2005, 2006, Finesilver Art Gallery, 2006, Bihl Haus Arts, 2006, 2007. Recipient Extending the Reach Instl. award, NEH, U. Tex.-San Antonio, 2001—02, rsch. award, U. Tex. San Antonio, 2000, 2003—04, 2005; fellow, Samuel H. Kress Found., 1995—96, U. Calif., Berkeley, 1998; grantee, 1996—97, Dean's Rsch. Asst. award, 1993—94, Tinker Found., 1994, Vice Chancellor Rsch. Fund award, U. Calif., Berkeley, 1994—95, McEnerny Fellowship for Innovation in Tchg., 1995—96, U. Calif., Berkeley, 1996, Judith Rothschild Found., Mexican Mus., 1997, William and Flora Hewlwtt Found., 1997; Katz Grad. fellow, U. Calif., Berkeley, 1995, Marian Hahn Simpson fellow, 1995. Mem.: MASA, Nat. Assn. Chicano Scholars, Am. Assn. Museums (mem. curators' com., mem. Latino network pub. interest com., mem. Native Am. and mus. collaboration network), Coll. Art Assn. (mem. assn. L.Am. art, mem. Am. soc. Hispanic art hist. studies). Avocations: art collecting, movie memorabilia. Office Phone: 914-395-2629. Personal E-mail: rubenccordova@gmail.com.

CORDRAY, RICHARD A., state legislator; b. Columbus, Ohio, May 3, 1959; s. Frank E. and Ruth E. Cordray; m. Margaret Meriwether, July 11, 1992; children Danny, Holly BA in Legal & Polit. Theory (summa cum laude), Mich. State U., 1981; MA with First Class Honours in Philosophy, Politics & Economics, Oxford U., 1983; JD with honors, U. Chgo. Law Sch., 1986. Legis. liaison Ohio Dept. Retardation, Columbus, 1978-81; law clk. U.S. Dept. Justice, Washington, 1986, U.S. Ct. Appeals, Washington, 1986; law clk. to Justice B. White U.S. Supreme Ct., Washington, 1987, law clk. to Justice A. Kennedy, 1988; atty. Jones, Day, Reavis & Pogue, 1989—93; lectr. on govt. Georgetown U., Washington, 1989; state rep. dist. # 3 Ohio Ho. of Reps., Columbus, 1991—93; state solicitor Ohio Atty. Gen. Office, 1993—94; Dem. nominee and candidate for Ohio Atty. Gen., 1998; Franklin county treas. Ohio, 2002; state treas. State of Ohio, 2006—. Adj. prof. law Ohio State U., Columbus, 1989-; mem. various coms. Ohio Ho. of Reps.; speaker Congrl. Youth Leadership Coun. on Close Up Found., 1988-89; mem. adv. bd. Ohio Community Corrections, Columbus, 1991-92. Mem. adv. bd. Friends of the Homeless, Columbus; cons. bd. mem. Hilltop YMCA. Mem. Friends of Turning Point, Southwestern Dem. Club, Ohio Hist. Soc., Oxford Soc., S.W. Sertoma, Vol. Ohio, Southside Jaycees, Westland Area Bus. Assn., Grove City C. of C. Achievements include being five-time undefeated winner on the "Jeopardy" TV game show in 1987 and a semifinalist in the Tournament of Champions. Avocations: reading, sports, travel, politics, family activities. Office: 30 E Broad St 9th Fl Columbus OH 43266-0421 Office Phone: 614-466-2160. Office Fax: 614-644-7313.

CORDRAY-VAN DE CASTLE, KAREN, elementary school educator; b. Key West, Fla., Dec. 20, 1953; d. Richard Palmer and Jzere Marlene Cordray; m. Lance Whitney Van de Castle, Aug. 6, 1983. AS, Northern Va. CC, Annandale, Va., 1973; BS in Ele. Edn., George Mason U., Fairfax, Va., 1975, EdM in New Profl. Studies, 2000. Cert. Va. Tchr. 5th grade Lightfoot Elem. Sch., Unionville, Va., 1977—80, Orange Elem. Sch., 1981; tchr. 6th grade Lightfoot Elem. Sch., Unionville, 1981—2003, Locust Grove Elem. Sch., 2003—. Mem. health com. Lightfoot Elem. Sch., Unionville, Va., 1981—84, mem. curriculum and instrn. com., 1998—2003; mem. county-wide sch. climate com. Orange County, Va., 2001—03; Md. testing program proctor, 2002—; new yr. tchr. mentor Locust Grove Elem. Sch., 2003—04, sci. club sponsor, 2003—04, mem. staff devel. com., 2003—04, mem. curriculum and instrn. com., 2003—, tchr. mentor, 2005—07, sci. dept. leader grades 6-8, 2005—06; presenter to profl. meetings and confs. Featured: film, 1985; contbr. articles to profl. jours. Mem. Humane Soc. of Madison Va., 1998—2002. Co-recipient Dedication to Learning and Cmty. award, George Mason U., 2000; named one of Nat. Sci. Tchrs. of Yr., Va., 1982; recipient recognition, Ho. Dels. Va. Gen. Assembly, 1998, Tchr. of Yr., Locust Grove Optimist Club, 2005; fellow, George Mason U., 2000; grantee, Orange County, Va., 1984—86. Avocations: environmental edn., conservation activities with students. Home: 583 Courtney Hollow Lane Madison VA 22727 Office: Locust Grove Mid Sch 31208 Constitution Hwy Locust Grove VA 22508-2631 Office Phone: 540-661-4444. Personal E-mail: kcordraylvdec@gemlink.com.

CORDY, ROBERT J., state supreme court justice; b. Manchester, Conn., May 18, 1949; married; 4 children. AB cum laude, Dartmouth Coll., 1971; JD, Harvard U., 1974. Def. atty. Mass. Defenders Com., 1974—78; spl. asst. atty. gen. Mass. Dept. Revenue, 1978—79; assoc. gen. counsel in charge of enforcement Mass. State Ethics Commn., 1979—82; asst. U.S. atty., 1982—87; ptnr. Burns & Levinson, Boston, 1987—91; chief legal counsel to Gov. William F. Weld, Boston, 1991—93; mng. ptnr. McDermott, Will & Emery, Boston, 1993—2001; assoc. justice Mass. Supreme Jud. Ct., 2001—. Lectr. Harvard Law Sch., 1987—96. Office: John Adams Courthouse 1 Pemberton Sq Ste 2200 Boston MA 02108-1735 Office Phone: 617-557-1000.*

CORELL, ROBERT WALDEN, science administrator, educator; b. Detroit, Nov. 4, 1934; s. George W. and Grace (Hagland) C.; m. Billie Jo Proctor, June 16, 1956; children: Robert Walden, David Proctor, Beth Anne. BSME, Case Inst. Tech., 1956; MS, MIT, 1959, PhD, 1964. Engr. GE, Cleve., 1955, program engr., Lynn, Mass., 1956-57; instr. U. N.H., 1957-58, asst. prof., 1959-60, assoc. prof., 1964-66, prof., 1966-90, chmn. dept. mech. engring., 1964-72, dir. marine program, 1975-87; asst. dir. geoscis. NSF, Arlington, Va., 1987-2000; sr. rsch. fellow Belfer Ctr. Sci. for Science and Internat. Affairs, 2000; sr. rsch. fellow Kennedy Sch. Govt. Harvard U., 2000—; sr. fellow Am. Meterol. Soc., Wash., 2000—. Rsch. engr. Huggins Hosp., Wolfeboro, N.H., 1957-60, Highland View Hosp., Cleve., 1960-64; vis. investigator Woods Hole Oceanographic Inst., 1965; rsch. assoc., vis. prof. Scripps Instn. Oceanography, 1971-72; vis. prof. U. Wash., 1985; chair U.S. Global Change Rsch. Com. of U.S. Govt., 1987-2000; sr. rsch. fellownumerous positions as chair of interagy. sci. coms. and internat. bodies. Contbr. articles to profl. jours. Founding chair Internat. Group of Funding Agencies for Global Change Rsch., 1988-90; chair Implementation Com. for Inter-Am. Inst. for Global Change Rsch., 1992-95; dir. White House Conf. on Sci. and Econs. to Global Change Rsch., 1990. Fellow Sr. Rsch. fellow, Harvard U., 2000—04. Fellow Am. Meteorological Soc.; mem. AAAS, Marine Tech. Soc., Adv. Group Sci. and Tech. Sustainable Devel. (ad hoc 2002-2004), Sigma Xi, Tau Beta Pi, Sigma Alpha Epsilon. Achievements include research in global change, climate and environmental research, medicine, medical engineering, ocean science and technology. Office: Am Meteorol Soc 1120 G St N W Ste 800 Washington DC 20005-737 E-mail: global@dmv.com.

CORELLI, JOHN CHARLES, physicist, researcher; b. Providence, Aug. 6, 1930; s. John Dominic Corelli and Immacolata (Caldarelli) C.; separated; children: Carolyn Margaret, John Joseph. BS in Physics, Providence Coll., 1952; MS in Physics, Brown U., 1954; PhD in Physics, Purdue U., 1958. Physicist Knolls Atomic Power Lab. GE, Schenectady, NY, 1958-61, cons., 1979-81; prof. nuclear engring. and engring. physics Rensselaer Poly. Inst., Troy, NY, 1962-96, prof. emeritus, 1997—. Rsch. program reviewer US Dept. State, 2007. Paper reviewer Sci. Jour. Internat., 2007; contbr. more than 100 articles to Jour. Applied Physics, Jour. Nuclear Materials, Phys. Rev., Jour. Vacuum Sci. and Tech. Spl. fellow NIH, Rochester Univ., N.Y., 1971., 1971. Mem. Am. Phys. Soc., Am. Nuclear Soc. Home: 11A Salem Ct Albany NY 12203-5932 Home Phone: 518-438-8068. Business E-Mail: corelj@rpi.edu.

CORETH, JOSEPH HERMAN, investment advisor; b. San Antonio, Jan. 14, 1937; s. Rudolph C. and Eltha (Zipp) C.; m. Margaret Nowell Graham, June 18, 1960; 1 child, Elizabeth Coreth Bowden. BS, U.S. Mil. Acad., 1959; MA, Cornell U., 1966; JD, George Washington U., 1989. Bar: Md. 1989, Tex. 1990, D.C. 1990, N.H. 1991, U.S. Supreme Ct. 1993; registered investment advisor. Commd. 2d lt. U.S. Army, 1959, advanced through grades to maj., 1967; assoc. prof. English U.S. Mil. Acad., West Point, NY, 1966—69; chief plans officer 4th Inf. Divsn., An Khe, Vietnam, 1969—70; resigned U.S. Army, 1970; exec. v.p. Nat. Mortgage Corp., Washington, 1970—78; pres. Stannard's, Inc., Silver Spring, Md., 1979—84; v.p., trust officer Riggs Bank NA, Washington, 1985—2002; v.p. Farr, Miller and Washington, LLC, Investment Counsel, Washington, 2002—. Past trustee, assoc. Grads. U.S. Mil. Acad.; mem. Order of St. John. Mem.: Chevy Chase Club (Md.), Met. Club (Washington). Avocations: golf, birding. Home: 5508 Park St Chevy Chase MD 20815-7107 Office: 1020 19th St NW Ste 200 Washington DC 20036

COREY, ELIAS JAMES, chemistry professor; b. Methuen, Mass., July 12, 1928; s. Elias and Tina (Hashem) Corey; m. Claire Higham, Sept. 14, 1961; children: David, John, Susan. BS, MIT, 1948, PhD, 1951; AM (hon.), Harvard U., 1959; DSc (hon.), U. Chgo., 1968, Hofstra U., 1974, Colby Coll., 1976, Oxford U., 1982, U. Liege, 1985, U. Ill., 1985, Kenyon Coll., 1989, Helsinki Coll., 1990, Ariz. U., 1990, Merrimac Coll., 1990, Hokkaido U., 1991, Rennselaer Polytechnic Inst., 1991, Boston Coll., 1992, Tex. A&M U., 1997, Nat. Chung Cheng U., 1999, U. Alicante, 1999, Cambridge U., 2000. From instr. to asst. prof. U. Ill., Champaign-Urbana, 1951—55, prof., 1955—59; prof. chemistry Harvard U., Cambridge, Mass., 1959—68, Sheldon Emory prof. of Chemistry, 1968—98, prof. emeritus, 1998—. Adv. bd. Microbia Scientific, 2002. Edtl. bd. mem. Jour. Organic Chemistry, 1962—65; contbr. articles to profl. jours. Recipient Intrasci. Found. award, 1968, Ernest Guenther award in chemistry, 1968, Centenary Medal, Chem. Soc. London, 1971, Harrison Howe award, 1971, Ciba Found. medal, 1972, Evans award, Ohio State U., 1972, Linus Pauling award, 1973, Dickson prize in sci., Carnegie Mellon U., 1973, George Ledlie prize in sci., Harvard U., 1973, Nichols medal, 1977, Buchman award, Calif. Inst. Tech., 1978, Franklin medal in sci., Franklin Inst., 1978, Sci. Achievement award, CCNY, 1979, J.G. Kirkwood award, Yale U., 1980, C.S. Hamilton award, U. Nebr., 1980, Chem. Pioneer award, Am. Inst. Chemists, 1981, Lewis S. Rosenstiel Award, Brandeis U., 1981, Medal of Excellence, U. Helsinki, 1982, Paul Karrer Award, U. Zurich, 1982, Tetrahedron Prize, 1983, Paracelsus Award, Swiss Chem. Soc., 1984, V.D. Mattia award, Roche Inst. Molecular Biology, 1985, Wolf prize in chemistry, Wolf Found., 1986, Silliman award, 1986, Japan prize, 1989, Nat. Med. Sci. award, 1988, Order of Rising Sun, Gold and Silver Star, Govt. Japan, 1989, Nobel prize in chemistry, 1990, Gold medal, AIC, 1990, Janot Medal, U. Paris, 1990, Messel Medallist, Soc. for Chem. Industry, 1994, Gold medal, AIC, 2003, Priestly medal, 2004; fellow, Swiss-Am. Exch., 1957, Guggenheim Found., 1957—58, 1968—69, Alfred P. Sloan Found., 1956—59, AAAS, 2000. Mem.: AAAS, Royal Soc. of London (foreign mem.), Inst. Medicine, Robert A. Welch Found. (mem. sci. adv. bd. 1968—), Franklin Inst., NAS (Award in Chem. Scis. 2002), Am. Acad. Arts and Scis., Soc. Synthetic Organic Chemistry (hon.), Pharm. Soc. Japan (hon.), Chem. Soc. Finland (hon.), Royal Soc. Chemistry (hon. Robert Robinson Medal 1988), Chem. Soc. Japan (hon.), Am. Chem. Soc. (hon. Pure Chemistry award 1960, Fritzche award 1968, award in synthetic chemistry 1971, Remsen award 1974, Arthur C. Cope award 1976, Willard Gibbs Award 1984, Madison Marshall award 1985, Roger Adams award organic chemistry 1993), Sigma Xi. Office: Harvard U Dept Chemistry Rm 319 12 Oxford St Dept Cambridge MA 02138-2902

COREY, GORDON RICHARD, financial advisor, former utilities executive; b. Osceola, Wis., Sept. 27, 1914; s. Ralph Watson and Bessie Mabel (Simpson) C.; m. Margarete Moeller, 1967; children by previous marriage: Eleanor Corey Tatge (dec.), Margaret Corey Amundson, Gordon Ralph, Martha Elizabeth. BA, U. Wis., 1936; MBA, Northwestern U., 1940. CPA, Ill. V.p. Commonwealth Edison Co., 1952-62, exec. v.p., 1962-64, chmn. fin. com., 1964-73, vice chmn., from 1973; now ret.; now pvt. fin. adv. Mem.: Wayfarers, Ridge and Valley Tennis. Home: Two Arbor Ln Apt 411 Evanston IL 60201-1970

COREY, JAMES WILLIAM, political scientist, educator; b. North Charleroi, Pa., Dec. 17, 1937; s. James William Corey and Elizabeth Marie Munch; m. Daria Ann Slentz, July 16, 1960; children: Kathleen Elizabeth Rhodes, Margaret Ann Buckwald, James Matthew, David Anthony. BS, Villanova U., 1959; PhD, Fla. State U., 1999. Commnd. ensign USN, Washington, 1959, advanced through grades to comdr., with, 1959—84; asst. prof. polit. sci. High Point U., NC, 1999—. Dir. Credit for Prior Learning Program High Point U., 2003—; participant Oxford Roundtable, 2005; bd. dirs. Hispanic Ctr., Piedmont Internat. Visitors Program. Author: Annotated U.S. Constitution, 2003; contbr. articles to profl. jours. Participant Cmty. Chorus, High Point, 2000—04; bd. dirs. Kids Vote; sec. NC Polit. Sci. Assn.; organizer candidate forums High Point U.; choir mem., lector Immaculate Heart Of Mary, High Point, 1999—2004. Mem.: Am. Polit. Sci. Assn. (assoc.), Phi Theta Kappa. Republican. Roman Catholic. Avocations: physical exercise, walking. Office: High Point U Montelieu Ave High Point NC 27262-3598 Office Phone: 336-841-4583. Business E-Mail: jcorey@highpoint.edu.

COREY, JUDITH ANN, retired elementary school educator; b. Peoria, Ill., Dec. 1, 1937; d. Lyle William and Eileen A. (Zigrang) Springston; m. Thomas W. Corey, Aug. 12, 1961; children: John William, Jeffrey Michael, Gregory Lyle, Mark Andrew. BA in Bus., English, Marycrest Coll., 1960; MA in Counseling, Bradley U., 1972. Lic. tchr. K-12, Ill.; lic. clin. profl. counselor. Tchr. Riverview Sch., Spring Bay, Ill., 1960-61, Lincoln Sch., East Peoria, Ill., 1963-64; counselor Bradley U., Peoria, 1972-73; clin. psychologist intern Zeller Zone Ctr., Peoria, 1973; dean students Morton (Ill.) High Sch., 1974-85; tchr. Jefferson Sch., Morton, 1985—2002; ret., 2002. Contbr. poem to Worlds Greatest Contemporary Poems, 1981 (Hon. Mention). Campaign work Grace Bunn Lievens Ill. Rep., 89th Dist. Ill., Morton, 1994; mem. exec. bd. Ill. State Deans' Assn., 1980-84, historian, 1980-82, membership com., 1982-84. Named to Outstanding Young Women in Am., 1973. Mem. NEA, Ill. Edn. Assn., Morton Edn. Assn. (newsletter editor 1987-90, mem. exec. com. and maj. negotiator, 1987-2000, v.p. 1993-95), Assn. Play Therapy, Phi Kappa Phi (life), Kappa Gamma Pi, Pi Lambda Theta. Roman Catholic. Avocations: reading, writing, photography, music, nature.

COREY, KENNETH EDWARD, urban planning and geography educator, researcher; b. Cin., Nov. 11, 1938; s. Kenneth and Helen Ann (Beckman) C.; m. Marie Joann Fye, Aug. 26, 1961; children: Jeffrey Allen, Jennifer Marie. BA with honors, U. Cin., 1961, MA, 1962, M of Cmty. Planning, 1964, PhD, 1969. Instr. U. Cin., 1962-65, asst. prof. cmty. planning, 1965-69, assoc. prof., 1969-74, prof., 1974-79, head grad. comty. planning and geography, 1969-78; assoc. prof. cmty. planning and geography U. R.I., 1966-67; prof. geography, planning, chmn. dept. geography, dir. urban studies U. Md., 1979-89; prof. geography and urban and regional planning Mich. State U., East Lansing, 1989—, dean Coll. Social Sci., 1989—99, sr. rsch. advisor to v.p. for rsch. and grad. studies, 1999—2004. Vis. prof. geography Un Wales, Aberystwyth, 1974-75, Peking U., 1986; chmn. Cin. Model Cities Bd., 1974; Fulbright rsch. scholar Inst. S.E. Asian Studies, Singapore, 1986, Fulbright group study abroad, Sri Lanka, 1983; trustee Met. Washington Housing Planning Assn., 1980-82. Author: The Local Community, 1968, Undergraduate Geography Students, 1973, The Planning of Change, 3d edit., 1976, Information Tectonics, 2000, Urban and Regional Planning Technology, 2006. Bd. dirs. Potomac River Basin Consortium, Washington, 1982-85. Recipient Svc. award Cmty. Chest and Coun. Cin., 1979; recipient Svc. award Planning Divsn., 1979, Svc. award Coalition of Neighborhoods, Cin., 1979, 83, medal of city Mayor of Seoul, South Korea, 1980. Fellow Royal Geog. Soc.; mem. Am. Inst. Cert. Planners, Am. Planning Assn., Assn. Am. Geographers (award spl. group on planning and regional devel. 1985), Assn. Asian Studies, Asia Soc., World Future Soc. Democrat.

COREY, LAWRENCE, medical educator; b. Detroit, Feb. 14, 1947; s. Aaron Corey; m. Amy Helaine Glasser, June 22, 1969; children: Leslie, Jordon, Daniel. AB with high distinction, U. Mich., 1967, MD, 1971. Diplomate Am. Bd. Internal Medicine. Intern U. Mich. Med. Ctr. Hosps., Ann Arbor, 1971-72, jr. asst. resident, 1972-73; epidemic intelligence svc. officer Ctr. for Disease Control, Atlanta, 1973-75; sr. fellow in medicine dept. internal medicine U. Wash., Seattle, 1975-77; attending physician internal medicine U. Washington Children's Hosp. and Med. Ctr., Seattle, 1977—; asst. prof. depts. lab. medicine, microbiology, immunology U. Wash., Seattle, 1977-81, assoc. prof. depts. lab. medicine and microbiology, 1981-84, prof. depts. lab. medicine and microbiology, 1984—, head diagnostic virology div., dept. lab. medicine; head, clin. rsch. divsn. program in infectious diseases Fred Hutchinson Cancer Rsch. Ctr., Seattle. Adj. asst. prof. depts. medicine and pediatrics U. Wash., Seattle, 1977-81; adj. assoc. prof. dept. medicine and pediatrics, 1981-84, adj. prof. depts. medicine and pediatrics, 1984—; cons. physician infectious diseases U. Wash. afiliated hosps., 1977—; chmn., co-chmn. course com. U. Wash., Seattle, 1986—; trustee-at-large U. Physicians, U. Wash., Seattle, 1992; acting dir. U. Wash. Ctr. for AIDS Rsch., 1989-90, head retrovirology core, 1989—; chmn. exec. com. clin. trials group NIAID AIDS, 1988-92; mem. program com. for 29th and 30th ICAAC, 1990-91; mem. subcom. IDSA/FDA guidlines for new anti-infective drugs, 1988-92; moderator panel on devel. of AIDS vaccines Inst. Medicine NAS, 1990, surrogate markers for licensing HIV compounds, 1989; mem. infectious diseases subspecialty com. Am. Coll. Physicians, 1988; mem. exec. com. Am. Venereal Disease Assn., 1988—; chmn. sci. adv. bd. Herpes Resource Ctr. Am. Social Health Assn., 1985—; mem. internat. bd. dirs. Internat. Soc. for Sexually Transmitted Disease Rsch., 1986-91; mem. bd. dirs. Am. Social Health Assn., 1986-90; cons. WHO, 1982. Author: (with others) Medical Microbiology: An Introduction to Infectious Diseases, 1984, Second Edition, 1990; editor: (with others) Medicine in a Changing Soc., Vol. I, 1972, Vol. II, 1977, Antiviral Chemotherapy: New Directions for Clinical Applications and Research, 1986, Second Edition, 1989, Third Edition, 1993, AIDS Dx/Rx, 1990; assoc. editor: Jour. Infectious Diseases, 1989—; editorial bd. numerous jours.; contbr. chpts. to books and articles to profl. jours. Recipient Spl. Svc. award Nat. Reyes Syndrome Found., 1983, Spl. Svc. award Nat. Insts. Allergy and Infectious Diseases, 1992, Pan Am. Soc. Clin. Virology award, Parran award, Am. Soc. for STD Rsch., U. Mich. Med. Sch. Disting. Alumnus award. Fellow Infectious Disease Soc. Am., Am. Coll. Physicians; mem. Internat. Immunocompromised Host Soc., Assn. Am. Physicians, Am. Soc. Clin. Investigation, Western Assn. Physicians, Western Soc. Clin. Investigation, Am. Fedn. Clin. Rsch. (councilor Western sect. 1978-81, nat. councilor 1982-83, nat. sec.-treas. 1983-86), Am. Venereal Diseases Assn. (exec. com. 1989—, Achievement award 1984), Acad. Clin. Lab. Physicians and Scientists, Am. Epidemiological Soc., Washington State Pediatric Soc. Office: Univ Wash Virology Div 1200 12th Ave S Rm 9301 Seattle WA 98144-2728 also: Fred Hutchinson Cancer Rsch Ctr 1100 Fairview Ave N Campus Box 358080 PO Box 19024 Seattle WA 98109 Office Phone: 206-667-6770. Office Fax: 206-667-4411. Business E-Mail: lcorey@u.washington.edu.*

COREY, MARK, historic site director; b. DeKalb, Ill., Aug. 3, 1950; BA, U. Miss., Oxford, 1972. Supt. Ocmulgee Nat. Park, Macon, Ga., 1988-92, Andrew Johnson Nat. Hist. Site, Greenville, Tenn., 1992—. Office: Andrew Johnson Nat Hist Site College and Depot Sts Greeneville TN 37743

CORGAN, BILLY (WILLIAM PATRICK CORGAN), musician; b. Elk Grove, Ill., Mar. 17, 1967; Founding mem., singer & guitarist Smashing Pumpkins, 1988—2000, 2006—. Albums with Smashing Pumpkins include Gish, 1991, Lull, 1992, Siamese Dream, 1993, Mellon Collie and the Infinite Sadness, 1995, Adore, 1998, Star Profiles, 1998, MACHINA/The Machines of God, 2000, Zeitgeist, 2007; other recordings include Rocket, 1994, Disarm, 1994, Pisces Iscariot, 1994, Bullet with Butterfly Wings, 1995 (Grammy award for Best Hard Rock Performance, 1996), Zero, 1996, Tonight, Tonight, 1996, The Aeroplane Flies High, 1996, The End is the Beginning is the End (Grammy award for Best Hard Rock Performane, 1997); solo albums include The Future Embrace, 2005; contbr. to compilations, Light Into Dark, 1988, 20 Explosive Dynamic Super Smash Hit Explosions!, 1991, Singles Soundtrack, 1992, No Alternative, 1993, No Toys for O.J., 1995, Ramson Soundtrack, 1996, Sweet Relief II, 1996, OnXRTOLive from the Archives Volume, 1996; composer (films) Stigmata, 1999, Graceful Swans of Never, 2001, The Heart is Deceitful Above All Things, 2004, When a Man Falls in the Forest, 2007, actor & composer Spun, 2002. Office: care Virgin Records 1790 Broadway Fl 20 New York NY 10019-1412*

CORIA, GUILLERMO, professional tennis player; b. Rufino, Argentina, Jan. 13, 1982; s. Oscar and Graciela Coria. Profl. tennis player ATP Tour, 2000—. Achievements include Winner of 9 singles titles: Vina del Mar, 2001, Basel, 2003, Hamburg TMS, 2003, Kitzbuhel, 2003, Sopot, 2003, Stuttgart, 2003, Buenos Aires, 2004, Monte Carlo TMS, 2004, World Championship UMAG, 2005. Office: c/o ATP Tour Internat Hdqs 201 ATP Tour Blvd Ponte Vedra Beach FL 32082*

CORIANO, IRMARIE, mathematics educator, department chairman; b. Mayaguez, PR, Aug. 27, 1970; d. Carlos D. Coriano and Myrna E. Torres. BA in Math. Edn., Interam. U. PR, San German, 1995. Cert. secondary math. tchr. HS and mid. sch. math. tchr. Caribe Christian Sch., Aguadilla, PR, Southwestern Ednl. Soc., Mayaguez, head math. dept. Office: Southwestern Ednl Soc PO Box 40 Mayaguez PR 00681

CORICH, EVELYN FRANCES, mathematics professor; m. John F. Corich, 1973; 4 children. BS, U. Mo., St. Louis, 1972; MA in Tchg.,

Webster U., St. Louis, 2000. Adj. faculty Webster U., St. Louis, 1994—2001; asst. prof. math. St. Louis C.C., 1999—. Volleyball coach jr. high sch. girls, St. Louis, 1988—; lansdcaping coord. Our Lady of Sorrows Cath. Ch., 2006; site chmn. Expand Your Horizons, 2006. Recipient Star award, Forest Park C.C., 1998. Mem.: Nat. Coun. Tchrs. Math. Office: St Louis Cmty Coll 5600 Oakland Ave Saint Louis MO 63110

CORIGLIANO, JOHN PAUL, composer; b. NYC, Feb. 16, 1938; s. John and Rose (Buzen) C. BA cum laude, Columbia U., 1959. Disting. prof. music Lehman Coll., NYC; mem. faculty Juilliard Sch. of Music, NYC, 1991—. Composer: Violin Sonata, 1963, Tournaments Overture, 1965, The Cloisters for Voice and Orch., 1965, Concerto for Piano and Orch., 1988, A Dylan Thomas Trilogy: A Choral Symphony, 1961-76, Concerto for Oboe and Orch., 1975, Etude Fantasy for Piano, 1976, Concerto for Clarinet and Orch., 1977, Promenade Overture, 1981, Summer Fanfare, 1982, Pied Piper Fantasy: Concerto for Flute and Orch., 1982, Fantasia on an Ostinato for Orch., 1985, The Ghosts of Versailles, 1987, Symphony # 1, 1991 (Grawemeyer award 1991), Troubadours (Variations for Guitar and Chamber Orch.), 1993, Fanfares to Music, 1993, Phantasmagoria for Cello and Piano, 1993, String Quartet, 1996, The Red Violin (chaconne for violin and orch., Acad. award for best original score 1999), 1997 (Genie award Best Original Score 1998), A Dylan Thomas Trilogy, rev. edit., 1998, Vocalise for Soprano, Orchestra and Electronics, 1999, Phantasmagoria for Orchestra, 2000, Mr. Tambourine Man: Seven Poems by Bob Dylan, 2000; film scores Altered States, 1981, Revolution, 1985, The Red Violin, 1998; commns. from N.Y. Philharm., Boston Symphony Orch., James Galway, Van Cliburn Found., Inc., Met. Opera Assn. Guggenheim fellow, 1968; nominee Acad. award and Grammy award for film score Altered States, 1981; recipient Anthony Asquith award for Best Film Score, Brit. Film Inst., 1985, Acad. Inst. Arts and Letters award, 1989, Grawemeyer award for Symphony Number 1, 1991, 2 Grammy awards for Symphony No. 1, 1992, Internat. Classical Music award Composition of Yr. The Ghosts of Versailles (opera), 1992; named Composer of Yr., Musical America, 1992, 2 Grammy awards for string quartet, 1996, Grammy for Symphony No. 1, 1996 (Classical CD of Yr.). Fellow: Am. Acad. Arts. and Scis.; mem.: ASCAP, Bohemian, Acad. Inst. Arts and Letters, Assn. Classical Music. Home: 365 W End Ave New York NY 10024-6511 Office: care G Schirmer Inc 257 Park Ave S 20th Fl New York NY 10010-7304

CORK, LINDA KATHERINE, veterinary pathologist, educator; b. Texarkana, Tex., Dec. 14, 1936; d. Albert James and Martine Sessions (Buntyn) Collins; m. P.S. Cork Jr., Mar. 1955 (div. 1965); children: Robin E., Jerald W. BS, Tex. A&M U., 1969, DVM, 1970; PhD, Wash. State U., 1974. Diplomate Am. Coll. Vet. Pathologists. Fellow Wash. State U., Pullman, 1970-74; asst. prof. U. Ga., Athens, 1974-76, Johns Hopkins U., Balt., 1976-82, assoc. prof., 1982-88, assoc. dir. rsch. Alzheimer's Disease Rsch. Ctr., 1985-93, prof., 1988-93; prof., chmn. Dept. Comparative Medicine Stanford U., 1994—. Coun. mem. NIH div. Rsch. Resources, Bethesda, Md., 1985-89; adv. bd. Registry Comparative Pathology, Bethesda. Grantee Nat. Inst. on Aging, 1985-89, Nat. Inst. Health, 1986-91, 86-93, 87-92. Mem. Inst. Medicine, Am. Assn. Neuropathologists (chmn. June 1988), Am. Assn. Pathology, U.S.-Can. Acad. Pathology. Methodist. Avocation: music. Office: Stanford Univ Dept Comparative Medicine MSOB Bldg Stanford CA 94305-5415

CORKEN, HEATHER MARIE, lawyer; b. Kalamazoo, May 12, 1969; d. Michael Rhodes and Karen Marie Fitzgerald; m. Kevin Robert Corken, May 14, 1994; children: Katherine Marie, Brittany Michelle, Margaret Alice, Elizabeth Ashley. BA, Rhodes Coll., Memphis, 1991; JD, Vanderbilt U. Sch. Law, Nashville, 1994. Bar: Tex. 1994. Assoc. Fulbright & Jaworski LLP, Houston, 1994—2005, ptnr., 2006—. Mem. United Way of Tex. Gulf Coast, mem. women's initiative steering com.; mem. Alexis de Tocqueville Soc.; mem. adv. coun. Houston Zoo. Mem.: ABA, Houston Bar Assn., DRI, State Bar Tex. Office: Fulbright & Jaworski LLP Fulbright Tower 1301 McKinney Ste 5100 Houston TX 77010 Office Phone: 713-651-8386. Office Fax: 713-651-5246. Business E-Mail: hcorken@fulbright.com.

CORKER, BOB (ROBERT PHILLIPS CORKER JR.), senator; b. Orangeburg, SC, Aug. 24, 1952; m. Elizabeth Corker, 1987; children: Julia, Emily. BS in Indsl. Mgmt., U. Tenn., 1974. Project mgr., constrn. supt., 1974—78; founder Bencor Corp., 1978—2001, Chattanooga Neighborhood Enterprise, 1986—; commr. fin. & adminstrn. State of Tenn., 1995—96; owner Osborne Bldg. Corp. & Stone Fort Land Co., 1999—; mayor City of Chattanooga, Tenn., 2001—05; US Senator from Tenn., 2007—. Bd. dir. U. Chattanooga Found., Chattanooga Housing Authority, Chattanooga CofC, Creative Discovery Mus., Southside Devel. Corp.; mem., exec. com. United Way. Mem.: Urban League, Rotary Club. Republican. Episcopalian. Office: US Senate B-40A Dirksen Senate Office Bldg Washington DC 20510*

CORKERN, DAVID E., music educator; b. Bogalusa, La., Feb. 28, 1950; s. Wilton Claude and Ruth (Tynes) Corkern; m. Mary Jess Sims, Dec. 30, 1972; children: Jessica Anne Woodworth, Jana Katherine. MusB Edn., La. State U., 1972, MusM Edn., 1975. Min. music First Bapt. Ch., Houma, La., 1978—83, Grass Valley, Calif., 1984—88, New Covenant Bapt. Ch., Grass Valley, 1989—95; pastor Penn Valley Bapt. Ch., Calif., 1996—98; asst. prof. music Hannibal-LaGrange Coll., Mo., 1999—. Adj. prof. music Sierra C.C., Grass Valley, 1998—99. Mem.: Coll. Band Dirs. Nat. Assn., Internat. Trumpet Guild, Music Educators Nat. Conf., Phi Mu Alpha, Phi Kappa Phi, Theta Xi. Baptist. Home: 1204 Walnut St Hannibal MO 63401 Office: Hannibal-LaGrange Coll 2800 Palmyra Rd Hannibal MO 63401 Home Phone: 573-221-7194; Office Phone: 573-221-3675 285. E-mail: dcorkern@hlg.edu.

CORKERY, JAMES CALDWELL, retired Canadian government executive, mechanical engineer; b. East Orange, NJ, June 23, 1925; S. Kirk James and Helen May (Caldwell) C.; m. Jane Woodruff, Sept. 19, 1953; children— Kirk, Candace BA Sc., U. Toronto, Ont., Can., 1948, MA Sc., 1950. Registered profl. engr., Ont. Plant mgr. Can. Gen. Electric, Montreal, Que., 1956-61, plant mgr. Oakville, Ont., 1961-68, mng. mfg. Toronto, 1968-70; regional gen. mgr. Can. Post, Toronto, 1970-77, dep. postmaster gen. Ottawa, Ont., 1977-82. Pres. Royal Can. Mint., Ottawa, 1982-86, chmn. bd., 1986-95; pres. Gold. Inst., 1986-88 Chmn. bd. Oakville Trafalgar Hosp., 1986-72; chmn. Easter Seal Campaign, Ottawa, 1985; chmn. bd. Ottawa Children Treatment Hosp., 1986-89. With RCAF, 1943-45. Mem. Profl. Engrs. Ont., Mint Dirs. Conf. (sec. 1984-86). Lodges: Rotary. Anglican. Avocations: furniture refinishing, antiques, gardening.

CORKINS, BOB, school system administrator; b. Jan. 25, 1961; m. Nancy Corkins; 2 children. BA, U. No. Iowa, 1983; JD, U. Kans., 1989. Exec. dir. Flint Hills Ctr., Wichita, Kans., 1998—2001, Kans. Legis. Edn. and Rsch., 2001—, Freestate Ctr. for Liberty Studies, 2001—; edn. commr. Kans. Dept. Edn., 2005—06. Office Phone: 785-296-3202. Office Fax: 785-296-7933. E-mail: bcorkins@ksde.org.

CORKRAN, VIRGINIA B., retired real estate agent; b. NYC, Feb. 13, 1924; d. Stuart H. and Bessie (Moses) Bowman; m. Sewell H. Corkran, Jr., June 15, 1946; children: Sewell H. III, Leslie C. Orloff. BA, Conn. Coll., 1945. Tchr. Low-Heywood Sch., Stamford, Conn., 1946—47; editor North Shore Calendar, Winnetka, Ill., 1955—59; real estate assoc. Lodge McKee Realty Inc., Naples, Fla., 1963—2001; ret., 2001. Mem. Naples City Coun., 1974-78; pres. Old Naples Assn., 1995-97; past bd. dirs. Big Cypress Nature Ctr., Naples, The Conservancy, Inc., Collier County LWV, Naples Garden Club, Collier Co. Audubon; hon. bd. dirs. S.W. Heritage, Inc., Naples, 2002 Recipient Guy Bradley award Collier County Audubon, ONA award Old Naples Assn., 1998.

CORLE, JAMES THOMAS, lawyer; b. Jay County, Ind., Dec. 28, 1927; s. Herbert R. and Mary M. (Reitenour) Corle; m. Jean Polhemus, July 16, 1950; children: James Thomas, Sarah Corle Thomas, Kenneth D. BS Engring. Law, Purdue U., 1955; JD, Ind. U., Bloomington, 1955. Bar: Ind. 1955, DC 1964. With E.I. DuPont de Nemours & Co., Wilmington, Del., 1955; patent counsel Washington, 1967—70; sr. supervising patent counsel, legal dept., 1970—85; corp. counsel, legal dept., 1986—92; intellectual property cons., 1993—. Lt. col. USAR, 1946—52. Mem.: Del. bar Assn., Phila. Patent Law Assn., Am. Patent Law Assn., ABA. Republican. Meth. Home Phone: 302-426-8489. E-mail: jimcorle@comcast.net.

CORLESS, DOROTHY ALICE, nursing educator; b. Reno, Nev., May 28, 1943; d. John Ludwig and Vera Leach (Wilson) Adams; children: James Lawrence Jr., Dorothy Adele Carroll. RN, St. Luke's Sch. Nursing, 1964. Clinician, cons., educator, grant author, adminstr. Fresno County Mental Health Dept., 1991—94; instr. police sci. State Ctr. Tng. Facility, 1991-94; pvt. practice, mental health cons., educator, 1970—; sr. assoc. guidance distbn. disaster svcs. ARC, 2003—04; mental health nurse Calif. Dept. Corrections and Rehabilitation, 2006—. Res. officer ARC, Disaster Mental Health Svcs., 1993-2003. Maj. USAFR, 1972-94. Mem. USAF Acad. Assn. Grads. (assoc. life), Forensic Mental Health Assn. Calif., Calif. Peace Officers Assn., Critical Incident Stress Found. Office: 1849 E Everglade Ave Fresno CA 93720 Home Phone: 541-991-7584; Office Phone: 559-325-9599. E-mail: dorothydmh@aol.com.

CORLEW, JOHN GORDON, lawyer; b. Dyersburg, Tenn., July 13, 1943; s. Emmett Atkins and Margaret Elizabeth (Swann) C.; m. Elizabeth Lee Scott, July 8, 1967; children: John Scott, William Heath, Carey Elizabeth. BA, U. Miss., 1965; JD, Vanderbilt U., 1968. Bar: Miss. 1968. Clk. to judge U.S. Dist. Ct. (so. dist.) Miss., 1968-69; assoc., then ptnr. Megehee, Brown, Williams & Corlew, Pascagoula, Miss., 1969-74; sole practice Pascagoula, 1975-78; ptnr. Corlew, Krebs & Hammond, Pascagoula, 1978-84, Watkins & Eager, Jackson, Miss., 1984. Mem. Miss. State Senate, 1974-80, chmn. appropriations com., 1979, chmn. constn. com., 1975-79, chmn. legis. audit com., 1978; chmn. Miss. State Bd. Pub. Welfare, 1980-84. Mem. ABA, Miss. Bar Assn., Hinds County Bar Assn., Miss. Bar Found., Order of Coif, Phi Delta Phi. Democrat. Methodist. Home: 2124 Eastover Dr Jackson MS 39211-6719 Office: Emporium Bldg 400 E Capitol St Jackson MS 39201-2610 Office Phone: 601-965-1944.

CORLEW, ROBERT EWING, history professor, academic administrator; b. Charlotte, Tenn., Mar. 24, 1922; s. Robert Corlew and Mary Ann Leech; m. Mary Saille Scott, June 16, 1950; children: Robert E. III, Daniel Scott, Mary Catherine. BS, Austin Peay State U., 1945; MA, Vanderbilt U., 1949; PhD, U. Ala., Tuscaloosa, 1954. Adj. prof. history Mid. Tenn. State U., 1990—95; prof. Bethel Coll., McKenzie, Tenn., 1946; prof. history Middle Tenn. State U., Murfreesboro, 1949—78, dean Sch. Liberal Arts, 1978—84, v.p. acad. affairs, 1984—90. Author: History of Tennessee, 1978. Chair Bi-centennial Commn. Rutherford County, Murfreesboro, Tenn., 1975—76; pres. Tenn. Hist. Soc., Nashville, 1985; mem. State Hist. Commn., Nashville, 1989—99; chmn. County Cultural Arts Commn., Murfreesboro, 1992—95, Tenn. Hist. Commn., 1996—99; trustee Bethel Coll., McKenzie, Tenn., 1948—60. Cpl. USAAF, 1943—45. Presbyterian. Home: 2685 Wilkinson Pike Murfreesboro TN 37129 Office: Middle Tenn State Univ Murfreesboro TN 37129

CORLEY, JENNY LYND WERTHEIM, elementary school educator; b. Lincoln, Ill., June 18, 1937; d. Robert Glenn and Nancy Lynd (Hoblit) Wertheim; m. William Gene Corley, Aug. 9, 1959; children: Anne Lynd Corley Baum, Robert William, Scott Elson. BS in Music Edn., U. Ill., 1959, MS in Music Edn., 1961; postgrad., U. Ill., Loyola U., 1985—2003. Tchr. choral music Mahomet (Ill.)/Seymour K-12, 1959-61; supr. music Fairfax County (Va.), 1961-63; tchr. music Highland Park (Ill.) 107, 1969, dir. gifted edn., 1969-70; tchr. music Glenview (Ill.) 34, 1981—2003, Corley Studio, 1959—. V.p. Corley Agroleum Properties, 1993—; water safety instr./trainer ARC; lifeguard instr./trainer Cmty. First Aid & Safety, 1995, instr. Northwestern U. Music Acad., Evanston, Ill., 2007—. Dir. mid-Am. bd. ARC, Chgo., 1980-86; mem. Chgo. Symhony Orch. Chorus, 1965-75. Recipient Heart of Gold United Way, 1992, Cmty. Svc. award Ill. Park & Recreation Assn./Ill. Assn. Park Dists., 1994, Disting. Svc. award Boys and Girls Swimming Ofcl., Ill. HS Assn., 1994, 25 yr. recognitiuon as swimming ofcl. Mem. Music Edn. Nat. Conf., North Shore Music Tchrs. Assn. (treas. 1987-90, pres. 2004—06), Ill. State Music Tchrs. Assn. (historian 2005—), Jr. League Chgo. (treas. 1978-81), Kappa Delta (house corp. pres. 2004—), Sigma Alpha Iota, Phi Delta Kappa (found. chmn. 1994-2006), U. Ill. Music Alumnae (pres. bd. dir. 1995-97). Presbyterian. Home: 744 Glenayre Dr Glenview IL 60025-4411 Personal E-mail: corley@corleywg.com.

CORLEY, JOHN D. W., career military officer; BS in Engring., USAF Acad., 1973; grad., Squadron Officer's Sch., 1978; MBA, U. of The Philippines, Manila, 1984; grad., Air Command and Staff Coll., 1985, Naval Command and Staff Coll., 1986; M in Nat. Security and Strategic Studies, 1986; grad., Army War Coll., 1993; grad. Russian & US Gen. Officer Exec. Program, Harvard U., 1999; grad. Program for Sr. Exec. in Nat. & Internat. Security, Harvard U., 2002. Commd. 2d lt. USAF, 1973, advanced through grades to gen., 2005; instr. pilot, flight examiner 64th Flying Tng. Wing, Reese AFB, Tex., 1974-78, 49th Tactical Fighter Wing, Holloman AFB, N.Mex., 1979-82; flight comdr. 26th Aggressor Squadron, chief Aggressor Ops., Clark Air Base, Philippines, 1982-85; analyst advanced tactical fighter Air Force Ctr. for Studies and Analyses, Washington, 1986-88; analyst comdr.'s action group Tactical Air Command, Langley AFB, Va., 1988-90; ops. officer 7th Fighter Squadron, comdr. 8th Fighter Squadron, 49th Fighter Wing, Holloman AFB, N.Mex., 1990-92; comdr. 33d Ops. Group, 33d Fighter Wing, Eglin AFB, Fla., 1993-95; chief Western Hemisphere divsn. Directorate of Strategic Plans and Policy, J-5 Joint Staff, 1995-97; comdr. 355th Wing, Davis-Monthan AFB, Ariz., 1997—99; dir. studies and analysis USAF Europe, Ramstein AFB, Germany, 1999—2000; dir. global power programs USAF, Washington, 2000—03, prin. dep. asst. sec. for acquisition, 2003—05; vice chief of staff, 2005—07; mil. dir. USAF Scientific Advisory Bd., 2003—05; comdr. Air Combat Command, Langley AFB, Va., 2007—. Decorated Def. Superior Svc. medal, Legion of Merit, Bronze Star medal, Def. Meritorious Svc. medal, Meritorious Svc. medal with 4 oak leaf clusters, Aerial Achievement medal with oak leaf cluster, Joint Svc. Commendation medal, Air Force Commendation medal, Joint Meritorious Unit award with oak leaf cluster, Combat Readiness medal, Southwest Asia Svc. medal with bronze star, Kosovo Campaign medal with bronze star, Global War on Terrorism Expeditionary medal, Kuwait Liberation medal (Govt. of Kuwait); recipient Lt. Gen. Glenn A. Kent Leadership award, 2007 Office: Air Combat Command 130 Andrews St Ste 202 Langley Afb VA 23665*

CORLEY, LARRY STEVEN, chemist; b. Johnson City, Tenn., June 17, 1954; s. Grady VanBuren and Kathleen Selma (Carmack) Corley; m. Stephanie Renee Johnson, June 23, 1996; children: Kendall Ann, Kelsey Renee. BS in Chemistry, King Coll., Bristol, Tenn., 1974; MS in Polymer Sci. and Engring., U. Mass., Amherst, 1976, PhD in Polymer Sci. and Engring., 1979. Rsch. chemist Shell Devel. Co., Houston, 1978-83, sr. rsch. chemist, 1983-87; staff rsch. chemist Shell Devel. Co./Shell Chem. Co., Houston, 1987-99, sr. staff rsch. chemist, 1999-2000, Resolution Performance Products, Houston, 2000—05, Hexion Specialty Chemicals, Houston, 2005—. Assoc. editor Progress in Polymer Sci., 1987-93, editl. bd. mem., 1994-98; contbr. chpt. to book and articles to profl. jours. Mem. Am. Chem. Soc. Achievements include over 55 US patents in epoxy, bismaleimide, bisbenzocyclobutene and other thermosetting resins chemistry; first discovery of optical activity (based on helicity only) in a solid polymer (polytrichloroacetaldehyde); developer of high-toughness, high-processability thermoset resin systems with very high heat resistance, industrial processes for epoxy resin and curing agent manufacture. Home: 8718 Chelsworth Dr Houston TX 77083-5656 Office: Hexion Specialty Chemicals WTC C-2150 3333 Highway 6 S Houston TX 77082-3101 Office Phone: 832-486-6624. Business E-Mail: steve.corley@hexion.com.

CORLEY, ROSE ANN MCAFEE, government official; b. Lawton, Okla., Aug. 21, 1952; d. Claude James and Mary Margaret (Holman) McAfee; m. Gary Michael Griffin, Feb. 14, 1973 (div. Oct. 1984); m. Terry Joe Corley, July 31, 1988 (div. Oct. 2002); stepson Troy Justin Corley. BS, Cameron U., Lawton, Okla., 1970; diploma, Army Command and Staff Coll., Ft. Leavenworth, Kans., 1989; MCJA, Oklahoma City U., 1990; cert., Army Mgmt. Staff Coll., Ft. Belvoir, Va., 1991. Cert. in distbn. mgt., Fed. Exec. Inst. Supply clk. Dept. of Army, Ft. Sill, Okla., 1972-80, supply mgmt. asst., 1980-82, supply systems analyst Ft. Lee, Va., 1982, supply tech. Ft. Sill, Okla., 1982-83, supr. inventory mgmt. specialist, 1983-86, manprint program mgr., 1986-91; weapon system advisor Def. Logistics Agy., San Antonio, 1991-96, customer svc. rep. Robins AFB, Ga., 1996-98; dir. supply mgmt. NIH, Rockville, Md., 1998—2002, dir. divsn. logistics svcs., 2002—05; deputy assoc. commr., publications and logistics Social Security Adminstrn., 2005—. Equal employment counselor USA Field Artillery Sch., Ft. Sill, Okla., 1976-82; mentor Fed. Women's Program, Kelly AFB, Tex., 1991-96. Active Md. Citizen Foster Care Rev. Bd., 1999-2001. Decorated Order of St. Barbara U.S. Army Arty. Sch., Ft. Sill; recipient cert. Appreciation, U.S. Sec. of Def., 1984, Directorate of Engring. and Housing, Ft. Sill, 1986; Excellence in Govt. Sr. fellow, Council for Excellence in Govt., 2001—. Mem. Fed. Women's Program, Soc. Logistics Engrs., Fed. Mgrs. Assn., Kelly Mgmt. Assn., World Affairs Coun. of San Antonio, Internat. City Mgmt. Assn., Tex. Corvette Assn. Avocations: auto racing, reading, golf, crafts. Office: Social Security Adminstrn 1540 Annex 6401 Security Blvd Baltimore MD 21235 also: SSA 1540 Annex 6401 Security Blvd Baltimore MD 21235 Home Phone: 301-694-2993; Office Phone: 410-965-9297, 410-965-9297. Personal E-mail: ra.corley@verizon.net. Business E-Mail: rose.ann.corley@ssa.gov.

CORLEY, WILLIAM EDWARD, hospital administrator; b. Pitts., Sept. 2, 1942; s. Robert Ray and Helen (Wise) C.; m. Angela Irvine Blose, Mar. 22, 1969; children: Laura, Matt BA in Bus. and Econs., Coll. of William and Mary, 1964; MHA in Hosp. Adminstrn., Duke U., Durham, 1966. Adminstrv. asst. Duke U., Durham, N.C., 1965-66; mgmt. cons. Booz, Allen & Hamilton, Chicago, 1968-71; assoc. hosp. dir. U. Ky., Lexington, 1971-75; hosp. dir. Milton S. Hershey Med. Ctr. of Pa. State U., Hershey, 1975-78; pres. Akron Gen. Med. Ctr., Ohio, 1978-84; pres., CEO Cmty. Health Network, 1984—. Bd. dirs. Vol. Hosps. Am. Tri-State, Indpls., Indpls. C. of C., Nat. City Bank, Indpls., Ind. Pro Health; tri-state chmn.; chmn. United Hosp. Svcs., Indpls., 1986-88; lectr. Ind. U.-Purdue U. at Indpls., 1984-98; high sch. basketball referee. Co-author: Ray E. Brown-A Manager's Manager: Lectures, Messages, Memoirs, 1990; contbr. articles to profl. jours. Chmn. United Hosp. Svc., 1986-88, Vol. Hosp. Am. Tri-State, 1989-91; bd. dirs. United Way. Named Sagamore of the Wabash, Gov. of Ind. Presbyterian. Avocations: photography, basketball, coaching, running. Home: 13570 N Gray Rd Carmel IN 46033-9708 Office: Cmty Health Network 1500 N Ritter Ave Indianapolis IN 46219-3095

CORLEY, WILLIAM GENE, engineering research executive; b. Shelbyville, Ill., Dec. 19, 1935; s. Clarence William and Mary Winifred (Douthit) C.; m. Jenny Lynd Wertheim, Aug. 9, 1959; children: Anne Lynd, Robert William, Scott Elson. BS in Civil Engring., U. Ill., Urbana-Champaign, 1958, MS in Structural Engring., 1960, PhD in Structural Engring., 1961. Lic. profl. engr., Ill.; registered profl. engr., Va., Wash., Miss., Fla., La., Pa., Ala., Tenn., Tex., Utah, Md., Mich., Mo., SD, SC, Kans., Ohio, NJ, NY, NC, Vt., W.Va.; registered civil engr., Calif., Hawaii; lic. structural engr., Ill.; chartered structural engr., UK. Devel. engr. Portland Cement Assn., Skokie, Ill., 1964-66, mgr. structural devel. sect., 1966-74, dir. engring. devel. divsn., 1974-86; sr. v.p. Constrn. Tech. Labs., Inc. (formerly Portland Cement Assn.), Skokie, 1986—. Adv. panels NSF.; prin. investigator, Bldg. Performance Study Okla. City Bombing; team leader, WTC Bldg. Performance Study. Contbr. articles to profl. jours. Pres. caucus Glenview Sch. Bd., Ill., 1971-72; elder United Presbyn. Ch., 1975-79; sec. bd. dirs. Assn. House, Chgo., 1976, treas., 1977, pres., 1978-79; chmn. bd. dirs. North Cook dist. ARC, bd. dirs. Mid-Am. chpt., chmn. North Region Coun., 1988-92; mem. Gov.'s Earthquake Preparedness Task Force, Ill. Recipient Wason medal, 1970, Martin Korn award Prestressed Concrete Inst., 1978, Authur J. Boase award Reinforced Concrete Rsch. Coun., 1986, Nat. Engring. award Am. Assn. Engring. Socs., 2007; named Tchr. of Yr., U. Ill., Chgo., Ill., 2004. Fellow: NSPE (Pres.'s award 2003), Inst. Structural Engrs.; mem.: NAE (award 2000), ASCE (hon. T.Y. Lin award 1979, lifetime achievement award 1994, Pres.'s award 2003, Lifetime Achievement in Design-OPAL award 2006, Chgo. Civil Engr. of Yr.), Am. Assn. Engring. Socs. (Nat. Engring. award 2006), Nat. Coun. Structural Engrs. Assns. (pres. 2007—08, Best Paper award 1999, Disting. Svc. award 1999), Post-Tensioning Inst., Nat. Coun. Examiners Engring. and Surveying (v.p., bd. dirs. 2002—04, Disting. Svc. award 2000), Am. Concrete Inst. (hon.; bd. dirs. 1994—97, Bloem award 1978, Reese Structural Rsch. award 1986, Henry C. Turner award 1988, Ferguson lectr. 1991, Henry Crown award 1997, Lindau award 1999, Alfred E. Lindau award 2000), Structural Engrs. Assn. Ill. (pres. 1986—87, meritorious publ. award 1993, 1997, John Parmer award 1997, meritorious publ. award 2003), Internat. Assn. Bridge and Structural Engring., Earthquake Engring. Rsch. Inst. (chpt. sec., treas. 1980—82, chmn. 1984—86), Reunion Internat. des Laboratoires d'Essais et Rsch. sur Materiaux Constrn., U. Ill. Alumni Assn. (Chgo. Illini of Yr. 2004), Bldg. Seismic Safety Coun. (vice-chmn. 1983—85, sec. 1985—87), Chgo. Com. High-Rise Bldgs. (vice-chmn. 1978—82, chmn. 1982—84). Presbyterian. Office: Constrn Tech Labs Inc 5400 Old Orchard Rd Skokie IL 60077-1030 Office Phone: 847-972-3060. Office Fax: 847-965-6541. E-mail: gcorley@ctlgroup.com.

CORLISS, DEANE KENWORTHY, lawyer; b. Phila., Oct. 18, 1945; d. Joseph Edmund and Edith Mae Kenworthy; m. David Alexander Corliss, June 22, 1968; 1 child, Jonathan David. BSN cum laude, Duke U., NC, 1967; MS in nursing, Ohio State U., 1970; JD summa cum laude, Cumberland Sch. Law, Birmingham, 1989. Bar: Ala. 1989, DC 1992, admitted to US Dist. Ct. for Northern Divsn. Ala.:. Staff nurse PeterBent Brigham Hosp., Boston, 1967—68; instr. sch. nursing Northeastern U., Boston, 1968—69, U. Ala., Birmingham, 1970—73, health edn. coord., ob/gyn, 1978—80, asst. prof. medicine dept. ob/gyn, 1983—86; nursing dir., pub. health area III Ala. Dept. of Pub. Health, Birmingham, 1980—83; assoc. Bradley Arant Rose & White LLP, Birmingham, 1989—95, ptnr., chair of health law practice group, 1996—. Adv. com. Samford U. Inst. for Healthcare Ethics and Law, Birmingham, 1999—2000. Bd. dirs. Unitarian Universalist Svc. Com., Boston, 1978—81; mem. Jefferson County Healthy Start Infant Mortality Adv. Com., 1994—95; bd. dirs. VSA Arts of Ala., Inc., Birmingham, 2003—; mem. adv. bd. UAB Palliative Care Ctr., Birmingham, Ala., 2005—. Named one of Top Health Care Leaders in Birmingham, Birmingham Bus. Jour., 2002, 2007. Mem.: Birmingham Bar Assn. (bd. dirs. women lawyers sect. 1999—, sec. treas. women lawyers sect. 2000—03, corr. sec. 2005), ABA Health Law Sect., Am. Health

Lawyers Assn., ABA. Avocations: scuba diving, jewelry making. Office: Bradley Arant Rose & White LLP 1819 5th Ave N Birmingham AL 35203 Office Phone: 205-521-8633. Office Fax: 205-488-6633. Business E-Mail: dcorliss@bradleyarant.com.

CORLISS, JOHN OZRO, zoology educator; b. Coats, Kans., Feb. 23, 1922; s. Clark L. and Catharine (Smith) C.; children: Susan Elizabeth, Joan Alison, Kimberley Ann, Jennifer Sara, Catharine Megan Corliss; m. Yuemei Geng, June, 1992. BS, U. Chgo., 1944; BA, U. Vt., 1947; PhD, NYU, 1951; DSc (hon.), Universite de Clermont, France, 1973. Postdoctoral fellow AEC, Coll. de France, Paris, 1951-52; instr. zoology Yale, 1952-54; asst. prof. to prof. zoology U. Ill., Urbana, 1954-64, prof., head dept. biol. scis. Chgo. Circle, 1964-69; dir. systematic zoology NSF, 1969-70; prof., chmn. dept. zoology U. Md., College Park, 1970-87, prof., 1987-89, emeritus prof., 1989—. Adj. prof. U. N.Mex., Albuquerque, 1988-96; hon. rsch. assoc. zoology Univ. Coll., London, 1960-61; vis. prof. zoology U. Exeter, Eng., 1961-62; vis. prof. protozoology, Shanghai, China, 1980, 86, Geneva, 1980; mem. panel systematic biology NSF, 1966-69; active Nat. Com. Internat. Biol. program, 1966-68; mem. Internat. Commn. on Zool. Nomenclature, 1972-96; mem. corp. Marine Biol. Lab., Woods Hole, Mass. Author: The Ciliate Protozoa, 1961, 2d edit., 1979; joint editor 5 books on protistology, 1984-91; contbr. articles on protozoology/protistology to profl. jours. Served to capt. USAAF, 1943-46. Fellow AAAS, Am. Inst. Biol. Scis., Am. Acad. Microbiology; mem. Soc. Protozoologists (past pres, mem. editl. bd., past editor), Am. Micros. Soc. (past editor, past pres.), Am. Zool. Soc. (hon.), French Zool. Soc. (hon.), Spanish Zool. Soc. (hon.), Mexican Zool. Soc. (hon.), Italian Zool. Soc. (hon.), Coun. Biology Editors (past chmn., CBE Meritorious award 1982), Am. Soc. Zoologists (past pres.), Soc. Systematic Zoology (past pres.), Am. Soc. Parasitologists, Am. Soc. Microbiology (U.S. Fedn. Culture Collections/J. Roger Porter award 1994), Internat. Congress Systematic and Evolutionary Biology (convenor 1970-74, 76-80), Internat. Union Biol. Scis. (chmn. U.S. nat. com. 1971-73), numerous others. Address: PO Box 2729 Bala Cynwyd PA 19004-6729 Home: 1211 Sandringham Rd Bala Cynwyd PA 19004-2024 Personal E-mail: jocchezmoi@aol.com.

CORMAN, JULIE ANN, producer, director; b. Omaha, June 22, 1942; d. Gordon Francis Halloran and Mary Julia (Corcoran) Halloran-Ferrier; m. Roger William Corman, Dec. 26, 1970; children: Catherine, Roger, Brian, Mary. BA, UCLA, 1964. V.p. New World Pictures, LA, 1971-83; exec. v.p. Concorde-New Horizons Pictures, Inc., LA, 1984—; pres. Trinity Pictures, Inc., LA, 1984—. Conf. chmn. UCLA Ext., 1991; chair grad. film and TV dept. NYU, 2000. Prodr.: (films) Boxcar Bertha, 1972, Crazy Mama, 1975, Lady in Red, 1976, The Dirt Bike Kid, 1985, DA, 1988, A Cry in the Wild (Silver medal Houston Internat. Film Festival, 1990); (TV films) Drop Out Mother, 1988, White Wolves series, 1990—95, Max is Missing, 1995, Legend of the Lost Tomb, 1996, The Westing Game, 1997. Mem. Air Resources Bd., Calif., Internat. Women's Forum, 1990. Named Prodr. of Yr. Acad. Family Film, 1996. Mem. Women in Film. Roman Catholic. Office: Trinity Pictures 11600 San Vicente Blvd Los Angeles CA 90049-5102

CORMAN, MARVIN LEONARD, surgeon, educator; b. Phila., Dec. 17, 1939; s. Joseph Mayer and Dorothy Frances (Stern) C.; children: John Mayer, Alexander Stern. BA, U. Pa., 1961, MD, 1965. Diplomate Nat. Bd. Med. Examiners, Am. Bd. Surgery, Am. Bd. Colon and Rectal Surgery; lic. surgeon, Calif., N.Y. Sr. registrar, vis. lectr. gen. infirmary, profl. surg. unit U. Leeds, Eng., 1968-69; surg. intern Boston City Hosp.-Fifth (Harvard) Surg. Svc., 1965, surg. resident, 1966-68, surg. resident, chief surg. resident, 1969-71; staff surgeon divsn. colon and rectal surgery, dept. surgery Lahey Clinic Med. Ctr., Boston, 1971-81, Sansum Med. Clinic, Santa Barbara, Calif., 1981-95; surgeon divsn. colon and rectal surgery UCLA, 1996-98; prof. surgery U. So. Calif. Sch. Medicine, 1998—2001; vice chmn. dept. surgery, assoc. surgeon-in-chief L.I. Jewish Med. Ctr., New Hyde Park, NY, 2001—04; prof. surgery Albert Einstein Coll. Medicine, 2001—05, SUNY, Stony Brook, 2004—. Instr. surgery Sch. Medicine Harvard U., Boston, 1972-77, clin. asst. prof. surgery, 1977-82, prof. surgery UCLA, 1996-98; co-dir. tng. program colon and rectal surgery Sansum Med. clinic, 1981-95, chmn. divsn. edn., 1983-90; credentials com. Santa Barbara Cottage Hosp., 1984-95, mem. libr. com., 1985-95, mem. com. on grad. med. edn., 1989-94, vice-chmn. dept. surgery, 1994-95; pres. alumni assn. Harvard Surg. Svc., Boston City Hosp., 1983-84; vis. prof. U. Tex. Health Sci. Ctr., San Antonio, 1982, Throckmorton Surg. Soc., Des Moines, 1985, Ogden (Utah) Surg. Soc., 1985, 20th ann. Surg. Congress Orange County Surg. Soc., Newport Beach, Calif., 1988, Royal Australasian Coll. Surgeons, Adelaide, Australia, 1989, Northwest Permanente Dept. Surgery, Portland, Oreg., 1990, Hahnemann U., Phila., 1991, El Colegio de Cirujanos Gererales de Mexicali, Mexico, 1991, Cleve. Clinic Fla., Ft. Lauderdale, Fla., 1992, Univ. Hosp. de Clinicas do Parana, Curitiba, Brazil, 1993; Ralph Coffey vis. prof. Sch. Medicine, U. Mo., Kansas City, 1988; Ralph B. Samson Meml. lectr. Grant Med. Ctr., Columbus, Ohio, 1991; Louis A. Buie vis. lectr. Mayo Med. Sch., Rochester, Minn., 1992; ann. vis. surgeon Queen Elizabeth Hosp. Ctr. of Montreal, Que., 1993; vis. prof. U. So. Calif. Sch. Medicine, L.A., 1995, U. Zurich., 2004, others; Neil Swinton vis. prof. Lahey Clinic, Burlington, Mass., 1997; del. leader Citizen Amb. Program Colon and Rectal Surgery Del. to Russia, Hungary and Czechoslovakia, 1992. Author: (textbook) Colon and Rectal Surgery, 1984, 89, 93, 99, 2005; assoc. editor: Diseases of the Colon and Rectum, 1977-92, Lahey Clinic Bull., 1972-81; contbr. numerous articles to profl. jours. Recipient Hoffman-LaRoche award, 1965, Piedmont Proctologic Soc. award, 1973, 1st prize of Med. Book award, 1985, John C. Goligher Meml. medal Assn. Coloproctology of Gt. Britain and Ireland, 1999, 25th Ann. award Crohn's and Colitis Found. Am., 2000. Fellow ACP; mem. ACS (So. Calif. chpt.), AMA (chmn. residency rev. com. for colon and rectal surgery 1985-86), Internat. Soc. Univ. Colon and Rectal Surgeons, Am. Soc. Colon and Rectal Surgeons (v.p. 1995-96), Am. Surg. Assn., Am. Med. Writers Assn. (hon.), Am. Coll. Gastroenterology, Assn. for Program Dirs. in Colon and Rectal Surgery, We. Surg. Assn., Pan Am. Med. Assn. (coun. sect. on colon and rectal surgery 1989—), Royal Australasian Coll. Surgeons (hon., sect. colon and rectal surgery 1989), New Eng. Surg. Soc., New Eng. Soc. Colon and Rectal Surgeons (sec.-treas. 1977-81), Boston Surg. Soc., Northeastern Soc. Colon and Rectal Surgeons, Soc. Surgery Alimentary Tract, N.Y. Surg. Soc., N.Y. Soc. Colon and Rectal Surgeons,Piedmont Proctologic Soc. (hon.), Argentine Soc. Coloproctology (hon.). Office: Dept Surgery SUNY Stony Brook HSC T 18-060 Stony Brook NY 11794-8191 Office Phone: 631-444-3431. Business E-Mail: marvin.corman@stonybrook.edu.

CORMAN, ROGER WILLIAM, film director; b. Detroit, Apr. 5, 1926; s. William and Anne C.; m. Julie Ann Halloran, Dec. 26, 1970; children: Catherine Ann, Roger Martin, Brian William, Mary Tessa AB, Stanford, 1947; postgrad., Oxford U., Eng., 1950; D in Fine Arts (hon.), Am. Film Inst., 1998. Founder, pres. New World Pictures, 1970-83, Concorde-New Horizons Corp., 1983—. Prodr. over 400 films, dir. over 50 films; films include; prodr.: (films) Dementia 13, 1963; prodr.: (films) Death Race 2000, 1975, I Never Promised You a Rose Garden, 1975, Hollywood Boulevard, 1976, Piranha, 1978, Avalanche, 1978, St. Jack, 1979, Rock 'n' Roll High School, 1979, Avalanche Alley, 2001; prodr., dir. (films) Five Guns West, 1955, Not of This Earth, 1957, Rock All Night, 1957, Machine Gun Kelly, 1958, Cry Baby Killer, 1958, A Bucket of Blood, 1959, Little Shop of Horrors, 1960, The Last Woman on Earth, 1960, The Intruder, 1961, Tales of Terror, 1962, The Haunted Palace, 1963, The Man with X-Ray Eyes, 1963, The Masque of the Red Death, 1964, The Tomb of Ligeia, 1965, The Wild Angels, 1966, The Trip, 1967, The St. Valentine's Day Massacre, 1967, The Fall of the House of Usher, 1960, The Pit & the Pendulum, 1961, The Premature Burial, 1962, The Raven, 1963, The Red Baron, 1971, Battle Beyond the Stars, 1980, Munchies, 1987, Crime Zone, 1988, The Terror Within, 1989, Carnosaur, 1993, The Fantastic Four, 1994, Black Scorpion, 1995, writer The Fast & the Furious, 1954, writer, co-prodr. Highway Dragnet, 1954, writer, dir., prodr. The Terror, 1963, Frankenstein Unbound, 1990, prodr., dir. Firefight, 2003, distbr. Cries & Whispers, Autumn Sonata, Amarcord, Small Change, The Tin Drum, Vacaza de Vaca, others; actor: (films) The Godfather: Part II, 1974, The Silence of the Lambs, 1991, Philadelphia, 1993, Apollo 13, 1995, Scream 3, 2000, Looney Tunes: Back in Action, 2003, The Manchurian Candidate, 2004; author: (autobiography) How I Made a Hundred Movies in Hollywood and Never Lost a Dime, 1998. Named to Nat. Film Registry; recipient Grand prize, Venice Film Festival, 1979, President's award, Acad. Sci. Fiction, Fantasy & Horror Films, 1984, Life Career award, 1988, Lifetime Achievement award, Raindance Film Festival, 1996, Fla. Film Festival, 1997, LA Film Critics Assn., 1997, Am. Film Market, 2001, Golden Eddie Filmmaker of Yr. award, Am. Cinema Editors, 1997, 1st Prodrs. of Century award, Cannes Film Festival, 1998, Independent Spirit award, UK Empire Awards, 2004, Governors award, Soc. Operating Cameramen, 2004, David O. Selznick Achievement award in Theatrical Motion Pictures, Prodrs. Guild Am., 2006, star on Hollywood Walk of Fame. Mem. Producers Guild Am., Dirs. Guild Am. Office: Concorde-New Horizons Corp 11600 San Vicente Blvd Los Angeles CA 90049-5102

CORMIE, DONALD MERCER, investment company executive; b. Edmonton, Alta., Can., July 24, 1922; s. George Mills and Mildred (Mercer) C.; m. Eivor Elisabeth Ekstrom, June 8, 1946; children: John Mills, Donald Robert, Allison Barbara, James Mercer, Neil Brian, Buce George, Eivor Emilie, Robert Ekstrom. BA, U. Alta., 1944, LLB, 1945; LLM, Harvard U., 1946. Bar: Alta. 1947. Queens Counsel, 1964; sessional instr. faculty law U. Alta., 1947-53; sr. ptnr. Cormie, Kennedy, Edmonton, Barristers, 1954-87; instr. real estate law Dept. of Extension, U. Alta., 1958-64; pres., bd. dirs. Collective Securities, Ltd., Cormie Ranch, Inc., Sea Investors Corp.; With Can. Mcht. Marine, 1943-44. Recipient Judge Green Silver medal in law. Mem. Dean's Coun. of 100 Ariz. State U., World Pres.'s Orgn., Chief Execs. Orgn. (bd. dirs. 1976-79), Can. Bar Assn. (mem. coun. 1961-76, chmn. adminstrv. law 1963-66, chmn. taxation 1972-82, v.p. Alta. 1968-69), Found. Legal Rsch. Can. (hon. life). E-mail: anchorsea@cox.net.

CORMIER, JOSEPH BOWMAN, private investigator, consultant; s. Pauline Jean and Pauline Jean Cormier; m. Mary Ann Henry, Apr. 27, 1968; children: Kellie Lynn Cormier Lanchey, Erick Bowman(dec.). BA in Mgmt. of Criminal Justice, Concordia U., Wis., 2002; grad., FBI Nat. Acad., Quantico, Va., La. State U. Law Enforcement Inst., Baton Rouge, La. State U. Traffic Mgmt. Inst. Comdr. criminal investigation divsn., chief detective, patrol officer Lafayette City Police Dept., La., 1968—87; cmty. rels./D.A.R.E. dep. Lafayette Parish Sheriff's Dept., 1989—93; criminal investigator La. Dept. Justice, Baton Rouge, 1996—. Founder (TV program) Criminal Justice and the Community. Vice chmn. La. Dept. Wildlife and Fisheries Commn. With USMC, 1963—68. Named Outstanding Office of Yr., So. Consumers' Edn. Found.; recipient Cert. Achievement, U. Va., Cert. Appreciation, Houston Fire Dept., Am. Women Lafayette, Cert. Commendation, Am. Legion Post #58. Mem.: Law Enforcement Inst. Alumni Assn. La. State U., Fraternal Order Police, La. Sheriffs Assn., LA Chpt. FBI Nat. Acad. Grads., Mcpl. Police Officer's Assn. La., Nat. Orgn. Black Law Enforcement Execs., La. Assns. Bus. and Industry, Magnolia State Peace Officers Assn. (pres., Outstanding Performance and Svc. award, Outstanding Office of Yr.). Avocations: racquetball, golf, volunteering. Office: C&S Unit LLC 402 S Pierce St Lafayette LA 70501

CORN, MILTON, dean, physician, consultant; b. Berlin, Jan. 17, 1928; came to U.S., 1934; m. Gilan Akbar Tocco; children: Stephanie, Sarah, Paul, Rhoya Tocco. BS with highest honors, Yale U., 1952, MD with highest honors, 1955. Diplomate Nat. Bd. Med. Examiners, Am. Bd. Internal Medicine, Am. Bd. Hematology. Intern then resident Peter Bent Brigham Hosp., Boston, 1955-58; fellow in hematology Johns Hospkins Sch. Med., Balt., 1958-60; asst. prof. medicine Seton Hall Coll. Medicine, 1960-63; from asst. to assoc. prof. medicine George Washington U., 1963-72, prof. medicine, 1972-73; chief of hematology D.C. Gen. Hosp. div. George Washington U., 1963-73, chief of medicine, 1970-73; dir. blood bank and emergency dept. Geogetown U., Washington, 1973-78; dir. clerkship jr. medicine, dir. med. residency tng. program Georgetown U., Washington, 1978-84, also vice chmn. medicine, 1978-84, assoc. dean hosp. liaison, 1984, med. dir. hosp., 1984-85; dean Sch. Medicine, Georgetown U., Washington, 1985-89; dir. Office of Clin. Informatics Georgetown U. Med. Ctr., Washington, 1989-90; spl. cons. to dir. Nat. Libr. Medicine, 1990—, assoc. dir. extramural programs, 1990—. Dir. med. edn., hematologist St. Michael's Hosp., Newark, 1960-63; cons. hematology FDA, 1978—; chief physician Cath. Relief Svcs. Refugee Capt, Thailand, 1981, 83; regional dir. rev. courses CX ACP, 1981-87; mem. UN Relief and Works Agy. Inspection Team for Palestinian Refugee Camps, 1984; guest lectr. U. Southampton, Eng., 1981; keynote speaker India Med. Soc., New Delhi, 1985. Co-editor Hematology Revs., 1984—; contbr. articles to profl. publs. Recipient Golden Apple award Georgetown U. Student Med. Assn., 1971, 83, Teaching award Kaiser Permanente, 1983, Maimonides award Anti Defamation League, 1989. Home: 6404 Goldleaf Dr Bethesda MD 20817-5830 Office: Nat Libr Medicine NIH Biomed Comms Bethesda MD 20894-0001 Home Phone: 301-229-3055; Office Phone: 301-594-4928. Personal E-mail: miltoncorn@comcast.net. Business E-Mail: cornm@mail.nih.com.

CORN, MORTON, environmental engineer, educator; b. NYC, Oct. 18, 1933; s. Julius and Sophie (Haber) C.; m. Jacqueline Karnell, Aug. 21, 1955; children: Matthew Irwin, Frederick Eliot. BS in Chem. Engring., Cooper Union, 1955; MS, Harvard U., 1956, PhD, 1961. Asst. san. engr. USPHS, Cin., 1956-58; rsch. assoc. Harvard, 1960-61; asst. prof. U. Pitts., 1962-65, assoc. prof., 1965-66, prof. Grad. Sch. Pub. Health and Sch. Engring., 1967-79; prof. and divsn. head environ. health engring. Sch. Hygiene and Public Health, Johns Hopkins U., Balt., 1980-97; prof. emeritus Johns Hopkins U., Balt., 1997—; pres. Morton Corn; Assocs., Cons. Engrs., 1977—. Cons. divsn. biology and medicine AEC, 1965—74; chmn. air pollution rsch. grants com. EPA, 1968—71, mem. sci. adv. bd., 1978—84; mem. com. no biol. effects air pollution NAS, 1971, mem. com. risk assessment, 1982—83; mem. expert panel occupl. health WHO, 1973—98; asst. sec. labor for occupl. safety and health U.S. Dept. Labor, 1975—77; mem. Allegheny County Air Pollution Adv. Com., 1967—72; mem. nat. adv. com. health vital stats. Dept. HHS, 1979—81; mine health rsch. adv. com. Nat. Inst. Occupl. Safety and Health, 1986—89, GM/UAW joint health and safety adv. com., 1988—92; chmn. OTA Commn. Preventing Injury and Illness in the Workplace, 1982—84; chmn. tech. adv. bd. Clean Sites, Inc., Alexandria, Va., 1984—87; trustee Assoc. Univ., Inc., 1991—93; mem. Hanford tank adv. panel DOE, 1993—99; cons. Health, Safety and Environment, 1993. Chmn. Gov. of Md.'s Toxic Coun., 1986-89. NSF postdoctoral fellow U. London, 1961-62; WHO fellow, 1970; Guggenheim fellow, 1972 Fellow APHA; mem. Am. Soc. Safety Engrs., Am. Indsl. Hygiene Assn. (bd. dirs. 2000-03), Am. Conf. Govt. Indsl. Hygienists (chmn. 1983-84). Home and Office: Morton Corn Assocs Inc 3208 Bennett Point Rd Queenstown MD 21658-1126 Office Phone: 410-827-3205. Personal E-mail: mjcorn@friend.ly.net.

CORN, WANDA MARIE, fine arts educator; b. New Haven, Nov. 13, 1940; d. Keith M. and Lydia M. (Fox) Jones; m. Joseph J. Corn, July 27, 1963. BA, NYU, 1963, MA, 1965, PhD, 1974. Instr. art history Washington Sq. Coll., NYU, 1965-66; lectr. U. Calif.-Berkeley, 1970, vis. asst. prof., 1976; lectr. Mills Coll., Oakland, Calif., 1970, vis. asst. prof., 1971, asst. prof., 1972-77, assoc. prof., 1977-80; assoc. prof. Stanford U., Calif., 1980-89, prof., 1989—, chair dept. art, 1989-91; Kress prof. Ctr. for Advanced Study in the Visual Arts, Nat, Gallery Art, 2006-07; acting dir. Stanford Mus., 1989-91; dir. Stanford Humanities Ctr., 1992-95; Clark prof. Williams Coll., 2004; vis. curator Fine Arts Mus., San Francisco, 1972, 73, 76; vis. curator Mpls. Inst. Arts, 1983-84, Grant Wood travelling exhbn. to Whitney Mus. Am. Art, N.Y.C., Art Inst. Chgo., Mpls. Inst. Arts, Fine Arts Mus. San Francisco; Kress prof. ctr. advanced study visual arts Nat. Gallery Art, 2006-07. Author: The Color of Mood, American Tonalism, 1880-1910, 1972; The Art of Andrew Wyeth, 1973; Grant Wood: The Regionalist Vision, 1983, The Great American Thing: Modern Art and National Identity 1915-35, 2000, The Great American Thing exhbn. Figge Art Mus., Davenport, Iowa, 2005, Tacoma Art Mus., 2006; contbr. articles to profl. jours. Commr. Smithsonian Am. Art Mus., 1988—95; bd. dirs. Terra Found. Am. Art, 1999—, Wyeth Found. for Am. Art, 2002—. Ford Found. fellow, 1966-70, Radcliffe Inst., 2003-04; recipient Graves award 1974-75; Smithsonian fellow, 1978-79; Woodrow Wilson fellow, 1979-80; Stanford Humanities Ctr. fellow, 1982-83, Regents fellow Smithsonian Instn., 1987; Am. Coun. Learned Socs. grantee, 1982, 86; rsch. assoc. Smithsonian Instn., 1983—; Phi Beta Kappa scholar, 1984-85. Mem. Coll. Art Assn. (bd. dirs. 1970-73, 1980-84, program chmn. ann. meeting, 1981, mem. numerous coms.), Women's Caucus for Art, Am. Studies Assn. (nat. coun. 1986-89), Assn. Historians of Am. Art. Office: Stanford U Dept Art and Art History Stanford CA 94305-2018

CORNABY, KAY STERLING, lawyer, retired state senator; b. Spanish Fork, Utah, Jan. 14, 1936; s. Sterling A. and Hilda G. Cornaby; m. Linda Rasmussen, July 23, 1965; children: Alyse, Derek, Tara, Heather, Brandon. AB, Brigham Young U., 1960; postgrad. law, Heidelberg, Germany, 1961-63; JD, Harvard U., 1966. Bar: NY 1967, Utah 1969, U.S. Patent and Trademark Office 1967. Assoc. Brumbaugh, Graves, Donahue & Raymond, NYC, 1966-69; ptnr. Mallinckrodt & Cornaby, Salt Lake City, 1969-72; sole practice Salt Lake City, 1972-85; mem. Utah State Senate, 1977-91, majority leader, 1983-84; shareholder Jones, Waldo, Holbrook & McDonough, Salt Lake City, 1985—. Mem. Nat. Commn. on Uniform State Laws, 1988-93; mem. adv. bd. U. Mich. Ctr. for Study of Youth Policy, 1990-93; mem. Utah State Jud. Conduct Commn., 1983-91, chmn., 1984-85; bd. dirs. KUED-KUER Pub. TV and Radio, 1982-88, adv. bd., 1990, bd. dirs. Salt Lake Conv. and Visitors Bur., 1985—2006. Mem. N.Y. Bar Assn., Utah Bar Assn., Utah Harvard Alumni Assn. (pres. 1977-79), Harvard U. Law Sch. Alumni Assn. (pres. 1995—). Office: Jones Waldo Holbrook & McDonough Ste 1500 170 S Main St Salt Lake City UT 84101-1644

CORNACCHIA, EUGENE JOHN, academic administrator, political science professor; b. Bronxville, NY, Aug. 3, 1954; s. Eugene and Marie (Consolazio) C.; m. Anne Marie, June 25, 1978; children: Lauren, Katherine. BA, Fordham Coll., 1976, MA, 1979, PhD, 1985. Adj. instr. dept. polit. sci. Iona Coll., 1981; rschr. dept. personnel City of NY, 1985; coord. social scis. Inst. for Advancement of Urban Edn., St. Peter's Coll., 1990-92; asst. prof. dept. polit. sci. St. Peter's Coll., Jersey City, 1985-90, assoc. prof., 1990, chmn. dept. polit. sci., 1985—2000, academic dean, dean faculty, 2000—02, provost, v.p. academic affairs, 2003—07, acting pres., 2007, pres., 2007—. Trustee Elmsford Bd. Edn., 1991, pres. 1996-2000; cons. in field. Contbr. articles to profl. jours. Mem. AAUP (pres. St. Peter's Coll. chpt.), Am. Polit. Sci. Assn., N.E. Assn. Prelaw Advisors. Home: 23 S Hillside Ave Elmsford NY 10523-3602 Office: St Peter's Coll Office of Pres 2641 John F Kennedy Blvd Jersey City NJ 07306-5943 Office Phone: 201-915-9241. E-mail: ecornacchia@spc.edu.*

CORNELISON, ALBERT OTTO, JR., (BERT CORNELISON), lawyer; b. NYC, Apr. 22, 1949; s. Albert O. and Margaret E. (Adams) C.; children: Adam Snow, Brendan Stover, Morgan Adams. BS cum laude, U. Santa Clara, 1971; JD, U. Calif., Davis, 1974. Bar: Calif. 1975, DC 1975, US Dist. Ct. (dist. DC) 1975, US Ct. Appeals (DC cir.) 1976, Md. 1989, Tex. 1992. Assoc. Howrey & Simon, Washington, 1974—82, ptnr., 1983—84; sr. assoc. counsel litig. Ogden Corp., NYC, 1984—86; v.p., gen. counsel Ogden Fin. Svcs., NYC, 1987—89; dep. gen. counsel Electronic Data Systems (EDS), 1990—93; staff v.p., assoc. gen. counsel litig. Dresser Industries, 1994—98; v.p., assoc. gen. counsel Halliburton Co., Houston, 1998—2002, v.p., gen. counsel, 2002, exec. v.p., gen. counsel, 2002—. Mem.: ABA, Assn. Gen. Counsels, State Bar of NY. Office: Halliburton 5 Houston Ctr 1401 McKinney Ste 2400 Houston TX 77010-4008

CORNELIUS, JAMES MILTON, pharmaceutical company executive; b. Kalamazoo, Oct. 28, 1943; s. Charles D. and Eleanor F. (Short) Cornelius; m. Kathleen McGovern; children: Andrew, Lindsay. BA magna cum laude in Acctg., Mich. State U., 1965, MBA in Fin., 1967; D (hon.), Marian Coll., 1996, U. Indpls., 1998, Mich. State U., 2001. Assoc. acct. Eli Lilly & Co., Indpls., 1967, fin. planning analyst, 1969—73, adminstr. corp. fin., 1973—75, mgr. econ. studies, 1975—78, initial dir. acquisitions, med. device and diagnostics divsn., 1978, dir. health care bus. planning, 1978—80, pres. IVAC Corp. subs. San Diego, 1980—82, corp. treas., 1982—83, v.p. fin., CFO, 1983—95; chmn. Guidant, 1994—2000, sr. exec., 1995—2000, non-exec. chmn., 2000—06, interim CEO, 2005—06, chmn. emeritus, 2006—; interim CEO Bristol-Myers Squibb Co., 2006—07, CEO, 2007—. Ind. dir. Given Imaging Ltd.; bd. dirs., chair bd. audit com. DirectTV Group, Inc.; bd. dirs. Chubb Corp., Bristol-Myers Squibb Co., 2005—, Hughes Electronic Corp., Am. United Mut. Ins. Holding Co., DowElanco, Ind. Nat. Bank, Ind. Bell Tel. Co., Compuserve, Nat. Bank Indpls. Corp., Leerink Swann & Co.; founder, mng. ptnr. Twilight Venture Ptnrs. Contbg. author: The CFO's Handbook, 1986. Treas. Noyes Found., Indpls., 1983; mem. adv. bd. bus. corp. Mich. State U., 1983; treas. bd. govs. Indpls. Mus. Art; trustee U. Indpls. Zool. Soc.; pres. Cornelius Family Charitable Found.; bd. dirs. Mcpl. Recreation, Inc., 1982, Cmty. Hosp. Found., 1991, Walker Rsch., 1991, United Way Ctrl. Ind. Served to 1st lt. Fin. Corps US Army, 1967—69. Recipient Man of Achievement award, Anti-Defamation League, 2003, Hoosier Heritage Lifetime Achievement award, 2005. Mem.: Pharm. Mfg. Assn. (past chmn. fin. sect.), Fin. Execs. Inst. Republican. Roman Catholic. Avocations: tennis, reading, jogging. Office: Bristol-Myers Squibb Co 345 Park Ave New York NY 10154*

CORNELIUS, RICHARD MEREDITH, literature and language professor; b. Phila., May 18, 1934; s. Frederick Meredith Cornelius and Elizabeth Marie Yahraes; m. Donna Jean Black, Aug. 15, 1959; children: Craig Alan, Crista Lynn. BA, William Jennings Bryan Coll., 1955; MA, U. Tenn., 1961, PhD, 1971. Tchr. Beulah Beal Elem. Sch., Jacksonville, Fla., 1957-58; prof. English William Jennings Bryan Coll., Dayton, Tenn., 1961-99, W.J. Bryan/Scopes trial liaison, archivist, 1978—, prof. emeritus English, 1999—. Adj. prof. Chattanooga State Tech. CC, 2000-01; chmn. English dept. William Jennings Bryan Coll., Dayton, 1962-76, 91-99, chair divsn. lit. and modern langs., 1974-76, 90-91, faculty chmn., 1979-80; co-chmn. Bryan Coll. 75th Ann. Plan Com., 2003-06; guest lectr. U. Tenn., Knoxville, 1991, The Citadel, Charleston, S.C., 1991, Natchez Nat. Lit. Celebration, Miss., 2000, Maryville Coll., Tenn., 1998, Conf. Am. Coll. Family Trial Lawyers, New Orleans, 1998, Cedarville U., Ohio, 2002, Jilin U., Changchun, China, 2002; exhibit designer U. Tenn. Theater, Knoxville, 2001, Cedarville Univ. Theater, 2002, Bryan Coll., 1986—; presenter and cons. in field. Author: Christopher Marlowe's Use of the Bible, 1984, Understanding William Jennings Bryan and the Scopes Trial: A Study Guide, 1998, (hist. supplement) Bryan Coll. 75th Anniversary Supplement of New American Standard Bible, 2004, Bryan William Jennings in American Conservatism: An Encyclopedia, 2006; editor: Dandilines, 12 vols., 1971-87, Legacy of Faith: The Story of Bryan College, 1995, Selected Orations of William Jennings Bryan, 1996, 2000; editor, author:

Impact: The Scopes Trial, 2000, Selected, Annotated Bibliography of William Jennings Bryan, the Scopes Trial, Creation, and Evolution, 1993, 4th edit., 2001; nat. TV appearances include The History Channel, 1998, Sta. WTCI-TV (PBS), 2001, Coral Ridge Ministries, 1988, 2005; contbr. articles to profl. publs. and chpts. to books. Co-founder, mem. Scopes Trial Festival Com., Dayton, 1988—; co-chmn. Scopes Trial Festival Symposia, Dayton, 1995-98, 2000, 02; dir. Scopes Trial Trail Markers Project, Dayton, 1995—; mem. bd. elders Grace Bible Ch., Dayton, 1962-99, 2000-03; mem. Southeastern Conf. on Christianity and Lit., 1979—, chmn., 1979-80; mem. Rhea County Hist. and Geneal. Soc., 2001—, bd. dirs. 2003—; chmn. Scopes Trial Mus. Com., 2003—, mem., vice chmn. planning com. Rhea County Heritage Mus., 2001—. Summer workshop grantee Christian Coll. Coalition/NEH, 1983, 88, 89, Tenn. Assn. Museums/Humanities Tenn., 2003. Mem. MLA, Nat. Coun. Tchrs. English, South Atlantic MLA, Am. Assn. State and Local History (Leadership in History award 2006), Tenn. Assn. Museums. Republican. Evangelical Christian. Avocations: creative writing, photography. Home: 311 Cedar Ln Dayton TN 37321-6234 Office: Bryan Coll 721 Bryan Dr Dayton TN 37321-7000 Office Phone: 423-775-7247. Business E-Mail: cornelri@bryan.edu.

CORNELIUS, WAYNE ANDERSON, electrical and computer engineering consultant; b. Russellville, Ky., Nov. 8, 1923; s. Eldon and Mabel Ruth (Gentle) C.; m. Elizabeth Grider (dec. Sept. 1946); children: Johanna Vastola, Keith, John(dec.); m. Linda Brady, Apr. 27, 1985; stepchildren: Pam Gondzur, Mark Smith, Todd Smith, Allison Stines. BS, U. Ky., 1953, EE, 1966; MS, U. Louisville, 1962; DEd, U. Cin., 1972. Elec. engr. U.S. Naval Ordnance Sta., Louisville, 1953-66, dir. engring. electronics lab., 1973-85; rsch. assoc. Pa. State U., State College, 1966-67; prof. engring. tech. Miami U., Oxford, Ohio, 1967-72; elec. engr. System Devel. Corp., Dayton, Ohio, 1972-73; chmn. dept. electronics tech. Ivy Tech. Coll., Sellersburg, Ind., 1985-90. Adj. prof. elec. engring. tech. Purdue U., New Albany, 1992-95, U. Louisville, 1976-84; adj. prof. math. Bellarmine Coll., Louisville, 1964-66, Ind. U., New Albany, 1990-91. With USN, 1942-45. Named to Honorable Order of Ky. Cols., 1963. Mem. NSPE, Am. Soc. for Engring. Edn., Phi Delta Kappa. Democrat. Presbyterian. Office: 9005 Lethborough Dr Louisville KY 40299-1437 Personal E-mail: waylin@insightbb.com.

CORNELL, BRIAN C., food service executive, retail executive; B, UCLA. Mgmt. positions Gallo Wine Co., Joseph E. Seagram Co., Tropicana Products; sr. v.p. mktg., European regional pres. PepsiCo Beverages Internat.; sr. v.p. sales & pres. N.Am. food svc. div. Pepsi Cola, 2003—04; exec. v.p. chief mktg. officer Safeway Inc., Pleasanton, Calif., 2004—07; CEO Michaels Stores Inc., Irving, Tex., 2007—. Bd. dir. OfficeMax Inc.; chmn. GroceryWorks Holdings Inc. Office: Michaels Stores 8000 Bent Branch Dr Irving TX 75063*

CORNELL, CHRIS (CHRISTOPHER JOHN CORNELL), singer, musician; b. Seattle, Wash, July 20, 1964; s. Ed and Karen (Cornell) Boyle; m. Susan Silver, Sept. 1990 (div. 2002); 1 child, Lillian Jean; m. Vicky Karayiannis, Mar. 2004; children: Toni, Christopher Nicholas. Musician Jones St. Band, Shemps, 1982-84; singer, drummer Soundgarden, 1984—97; singer Audioslave, 2001—07. Singer, musician (with Soundgarden): albums Ultramega OK, 1988, Louder Than Love, 1989, Screaming Life/Fopp, 1990, Badmotorfinger, 1991, Superunknown, 1994, Songs from the Superunknown, 1995, Down on the Upside, 1996, singer, musician (with Audioslave): albums Audioslave, 2002, Out of Exile, 2005, Revelations, 2006, singer (with various artists): albums Temple of the Dog, 1990; singer: (solo albums) Euphoria Morning, 1999, Carry On, 2007; prodr. (with Screaming Trees): (albums) Uncle Anesthesia, 1991; actor: (films) Singles, 1992. Recipient ASCAP Film & TV Music award, 2007. Office: c/o Suretone Records 2220 Colorado Ave Santa Monica CA 90404*

CORNELL, DEWEY GENE, psychologist; b. Louisville, June 22, 1956; m. Nancy Emily Trinka, Aug. 19, 1978; children: Cristina, Allison, Erin. AB, Transylvania U., 1977; MA, U. Mich., 1979, PhD, 1981. Lic. clinical psychologist. Intern U. Mich. Psychol. Clinic, Ann Arbor, 1979-81; postdoctoral scholar dept. psychiatry U. Mich., Ann Arbor, 1981-83; clin. psychologist Ctr. Forensic Psychiatry, Ann Arbor, 1983-86; asst. prof. Sch. Edn., U. Va., Charlottesville, 1986-91, assoc. prof., 1991-99, prof., 1999—, faculty assoc. Inst. Law, Psychiatry and Pub. Policy, 1986—. Dir. Va. Youth Violence Project, 1996—; asst. prof. psychology Mich. State U., East Lansing, 1985-86; pvt. practice, Charlottesville, 1986—. Author: Families of Gifted Children, 1984, Designing Safer Schools for Virginia, 1998; co-editor: Juvenile Homicide, 1989, Issues in School Violence Research, 2004; co-author: Recommended Practices in Gifted Education, 1991, Guidelines for Responding to Student Threats of Violence, 2006, School Violence: Fears versus Facts, 2006; contbr. articles to profl. jours. Fellow Internat. Soc. Rsch. Aggression; mem. APA, Am. Psychology Law Soc., Va. Psychol. Assn., Nat. Hon. Sch. Psychologists Avocations: Go, basketball, tennis. Office: U Va Sch Edn 405 Emmet St Charlottesville VA 22903 Office Phone: 434-924-0793. Business E-Mail: dcornell@virginia.edu.

CORNELL, ERIC ALLIN, physics professor; b. Palo Alto, Calif., 1961; s. Allin and Elizabeth (Greenberg) Cornell; children: Elixa, Sophia. BS in Physics with honors, Stanford U., 1985; PhD in Physics, MIT, 1990. Tchr. English as Fgn. Lang. Taichung YMCA, Taiwan, 1982; rsch. asst. Stanford (Calif.) U., 1982—85; tchg. fellow Harvard Ext. Sch., 1989; postdoctoral Rowland Inst., Cambridge, Mass., 1990; postdoctorate Joint Inst. Lab. Astrophysics, Boulder, Colo., 1990—92; asst. prof. adj. dept. physics U. Colo., Boulder, 1992—95; staff scientist Nat. Inst. Stds. and Tech., Boulder, 1992—; fellow JILA U. Colo and Nat. Inst. Stds. and Tech., Boulder, 1994—; prof. adj. dept. physics U. Colo., Boulder, 1995—. Contbr. over 30 articles to profl. jours.; patentee in field. Recipient Grad. fellowship, NSF, 1985—88, Undergrad. Rsch. award for Excellence, Firestone, 1985, Samuel Wesley Stratton award, 1995, Newcomb-Cleveland prize, 1995—96, Carl Zeiss award, 1996, Fritz London prize in low temperature physics, 1996, Gold medal, Dept. Commerce, 1996, Presdl. Early Career award in sci. and engring., 1996, I.I. Rabi prize in atomic, molecular and optical physics, Am. Phys. Soc., 1997, King Faisal Internat. prize in sci., 1997, Alan T. Waterman award, NSF, 1997, Benjamin Franklin Medal in Physics, 1999, The Nobel Prize in Physics, 2001. Fellow: Optical Soc. of Am., 2000 (R.W. Wood Prize, 1999); mem.: Am. Phys. Soc., 1997 (fellow), Royal Netherlands Acad. of Arts & Sci. (Lorentz Medal, 1998), NAS, 2000. Office: Univ Colo JILA Campus Box 440 Boulder CO 80309-0440

CORNELL, HENRY, lawyer; BA, Grinnell Coll., 1976; JD, New York Law Sch., 1981. Assoc. Davis Polk & Wardwell, NYC, 1981—84, Goldman Sachs & Co., NYC, 1984—94, ptnr., mng dir., 1994—. Trustee Asian Art Mus., San Francisco, Citizens Com. for NY, Whitney Mus. Am. Art; bd. dir. The Ping Ins. Co. of China, The Kookmin Bank of Korea, The Dusit Thani Group, Rajadamri Pub. Co. Ltd. Mailing: Whitney Mus Am Art 945 Madison Ave New York NY 10021

CORNELL, JOHN ROBERT, lawyer; b. Boston, Nov. 7, 1943; s. Robert Cole Cornell and Thelma Marjorie (Bassett) Strout; m. Susan Lindsay Jordan, June 11, 1966; children: Jared, Joshua, Alexandra, Margaret. AB, Colby Coll., 1965, MA, 1997; JD, Georgetown U., 1968; LLM in Taxation, NYU, 1972. Bar: NY 1969, Maine 1972, US Dist. Ct. Maine 1972, US Tax Ct. 1990. Assoc. Dewey Ballantine, NYC, 1968—72; from assoc. to ptnr. Drummond, Woodsum & MacMahon, Portland, Maine, 1972—81; ptnr. Jones Day, Cleve., 1981—98, Atlanta, 1998—2000, NYC, 2001—. Former chmn. employee benefits and exec. compensation practice sect. Jones Day; lectr. in field. Overseer Colby Coll., 1992-97, trustee, 1997-2003; trustee Cleve. San Jose Ballet, 1994-98, treas., 1995-98; mem. nat. coun. Atlantic Salmon Fedn., 2005-. Mem. ABA, Maine Bar Assn. (chmn. tax sect. 1980-81), Colby Coll. Alumni Assn. (chmn. 1979-82), Cleve. Yachting Club (Rocky River, Ohio), Anglers Club (NYC), Megantic Club (Eustis, Maine), DKE Club (NYC). Republican. Avocations: sailing, bicycling, skiing, fly fishing. Office: 222 E 41st St New York NY 10017 Home Phone: 212-977-0253; Office Phone: 212-326-8332. Business E-Mail: jrcornell@jonesday.com.

CORNELL, ROBERT ARTHUR, federal official; b. Mineola, NY, Sept. 8, 1936; s. Herbert and Clara (Lange) C.; m. Nadine E. Dittmer, May 4, 1962 (div. June 1993); children: Robert Arthur Jr., James E., Suzanne N.; m. Catherine Rescoussie, Aug. 29, 1995. AB, Columbia U., 1958, postgrad., 1965-66, Pacific Luth. U., 1960-61, Am. U., 1964-65; MBA, NYU, 1963. With Grace Nat. Bank, NYC, 1961-63, U.S. Govt., Washington, 1963-69, IBM World Trade Corp., 1970, S.J. Rundt & Assocs., NYC, 1970-71; dep. dir. Office Econ. Research U.S. Internat. Trade Commn., Washington, 1971-76, dir. Office Trade and Industry, 1976-77, dep. dir. ops., 1977-79; asst. dir. for stockpile trans. GSA, Washington, 1979-80; dep. asst. sec. for internat. trade and investment policy U.S. Treasury Dept., Washington, 1980-88; dep. sec.-gen. OECD, Paris, 1988-95; cons., writer, editor France, 1995—. Mem. faculty U. Md., 1968; pvt. cons. in econs. and fin. With USN, 1958-61. Recipient Arthur S. Flemming award, 1974. Mem. Am. Econ. Assn., Western Econ. Assn., Nat. Economists Club, Nat. Assn. Bus. Econs. Lutheran. E-mail: robert.cornell@orange.fr.

CORNELL, ROBERT WITHERSPOON, retired mechanical engineer; b. Orange, NJ, Aug. 16, 1925; s. Edward Shelton and Helen Lauretta (Lawrence) Cornell; m. Patricia Delight Plummer, June 24, 1950; children: Richard W., Delight W. Cornell Dobby, Elizabeth Cornell Wilkin, Roberta Shelton Wolfe. BSME, Yale U., New Haven, 1945, MSME, 1947, D in Engring., 1950. Registered profl. engr., Conn., N.Y. Instr. math. New Haven Jr. Coll., 1947-48; analytical engr. Pratt & Whitney Aircraft, East Hartford, 1947; with Hamilton Std., Windsor Locks, 1948—87, head stress analysis & vibration, 1961—63, chief applied mechanics and aerodynamics, 1963—87; instr. engring. Hillyer Coll., Hartford, 1955; pres. Cornell Cons., Hartford, 1973—2000, Cornell Enterprises, West Hartford, 1984—2000; ret., 2000. Adj. prof. Yale U., 1985, 90. Contbr. articles to profl. jours. Rep. state senatorial candidate 5th dist. State of Conn., 1988, 1994, state Rep. candidate 18th dist., 1990; bd. dirs., treas. Yale Sci. and Engring. Assn., 1969—2001, Conn. State Taxpayers Assn., Stratford, 1984—86; past pres., bd. dirs. West Hartford Taxpayers Assn., West Hartford, 1972—97, 2002—03; dir. Agawam Coun., 1993—99; mem. Svc. Corps. Ret. Execs., 1989—2002, chmn., 1998—2000. With USN, 1943—46. Fellow: ASME; mem.: Hartford Golf Club, Yale Club Hartford, Sigma Xi, Tau Beta Pi. Achievements include patents in field. Avocations: tennis, squash, jogging, swimming, gardening. Home: 80 Loeffler Rd Apt G404C Bloomfield CT 06002 Personal E-mail: cornellrp@aol.com.

CORNELL, SUSAN, medical educator; m. David Alan Cornell. PharmD, Midwestern U., Downers Grove, Ill., 2002. Cert. diabetes educator Nat. Cert. Bd. Diabetes Educators, 1999. Self-employed pharmacist diabetes educator cons., 2000—; asst dir., asst prof. Midwestern U., Downers Grove, 2003—. Mem. AADE, Chgo., 2004—07. Recipient Golden Apple Tchr. Yr., Midwestern U., 2005. Mem.: Ill. Pharmacist Assn (chair edn. com. 2003—06, Pharmacist Yr. 2003). Office: Midwestern Univ 555 W 31 St Downers Grove IL 60515 Home Phone: 630-515-6191; Office Phone: 630-515-6191. Business E-Mail: scorne@midwestern.edu.

CORNELL, WILLIAM DANIEL, mechanical engineer; b. Valley Falls, Kans., Apr. 17, 1919; s. Noah P. and Mabel (Hennessy) C.; m. Barbara L. Ferguson, Aug. 30, 1942; children: Alice Margaret, Randolph William. BS in Mech. Engring., U. Ill., 1942. Registered profl. engr., NY. Rsch. engr. Linde Air Products Co., Buffalo, 1942-48, cons. to Manhattan Dist. project, 1944-46; project engr. devel. of automatic bowling machine Am. Machine and Foundry, Buffalo, 1948-55; cons. Gen. Electric Co., Hanford, Wash., 1949-50; project engr. devel. of automatic bowling machine Brunswick Corp., Muskegon, Mich., 1955-59, mgr. advanced engring., 1959-72; mgr. advanced concepts and tech. Sherwood Med. Industries divsn. Am. Home Products Corp., St. Louis, 1972-85; mem. faculty Coll. Engring., U. Buffalo, 1946-47; cons. Cornell Engring., St. Louis, 1985—; mem. faculty Coll. Engring. Washington U., St. Louis, 1993-94. Patentee automatic golf and bowling game apparatus, med. instruments; developed new method of measuring hemoglobin, new method of counting platelets in whole blood Recipient Navy E award, 1945, Manhattan Project Recognition award, 1945, Merit award Maritime Commn., 1945. Republican. Presbyterian. Achievements include development of compensating i.v. flow controller; a self-powered rotary motion sensor; improved IV fluied flow controller. Home and Office: 907 Camargo Dr Ballwin MO 63011-1506

CORNELL, WILLIAM HARVEY, clergyman; b. Pitts., May 27, 1934; s. Floyd Anderson and Audrey Fern (Wasson) C.; m. Betty Jean Yates, July 24, 1954; children: Deborah Jean, William Mark, Darla Ruth. AA, Central Wesleyan Coll., SC, 1953; AB in Religion, Ind. Wesleyan U., 1956. Ordained to ministry Wesleyan Meth. Ch., 1958. Clergyman Wilgus Wesleyan Meth. Ch., Gypsy, Pa., 1956-59, Wolf Summit (W.Va.) Wesleyan Meth. Ch., 1959-63, Canal Wesleyan Meth. Ch., Utica, Pa., 1968-73, Greenville (Pa.) Wesleyan Meth. Ch., 1973-76, Salem (Ohio) Wesleyan Meth. Ch., 1976-78, Sagamore (Pa.) Wesleyan Meth. Ch., 1963-68, 78-95, Niles (Ohio) Wesleyan Meth. Ch., 1995-2000, ret., 2000—. Mem. mission bd. Allegheny Wesleyan Meth. Connection, 1965—2003, sec., 1973-98, editor ann. jour., 1973-98, mem. adv. bd., 1978-98; sec. N.W. Indian Bible Sch., Alberton, Mont., 1969—. Republican. Avocations: hunting, travel. Home and Office: PO Box 115 7695 Rte 85 Beyer PA 16211

CORNELSON, GEORGE HENRY, IV, retired textile company executive; b. Spartanburg, SC, July 12, 1931; s. George Henry Cornelson III and Elizabeth Marshall (Woodward) Cornelson; m. Ann Martin Shaw, Oct. 6, 1956; children: George Henry Cornelson V, Martin Shaw, Scott Montgomery, Elizabeth Woodward. Student, Davidson Coll., NC, 1949-51; BS in Textiles, NC State U., Raleigh, 1953; postgrad. in Bus. Adminstrn., Harvard U., Cambridge, Mass., 1953—54; DHL (hon.), Presbyn. Coll., Clinton, SC, 2003. With indsl. engring. dept. Clinton Mills, Inc., SC, 1954-55, 57-58, from v.p. to pres., 1958—86, CEO, 1985—86; v.p. Clinton Mills Sales Corp., NYC, 1958—86. Bd. dirs. Elastic Fabrics of Am., NC Textile Found., exec. com.; pres. Clinton Investment Co., 1985—86; bd. dirs. Clinton Mills of Geneva, past pres., dir.; vice chmn. bd. dirs. Bailey Fin. Corp., 1996—99; bd. dirs. Anchor Bank, Myrtle Beach, SC, 1999—2000, Carolina First Bank, Greenville, SC, 2000—03; mem. SC Gov.'s Trade Mission to Far East, Hong Kong, Singapore, 1979, Kuala Lumpur, 79, Taiwan, 79, Malaysia, 79. Trustee Presbyn. Coll., Clinton, 1959—68, 1994—2005, Davidson Coll., 1992—95, bd. visitors, 1986—91; trustee Ind. Coll. and Univs. S.C., 1971—92, life trustee, 1993—; trustee Thornwell Home for Children, Clinton, 1968—76, exec. com., 1973—74, sec. bd. trustees, 1974; organizing chmn. Greater Clinton Planning Commn., 1967—68; pres. Cmty. Chest and United Fund, 1963—64; chmn. Laurens County dist. Boy Scouts Am., 1973, exec. bd. Blue Ridge coun., 1974; chair adv. com. Bailey Found., 1969—; dir. SC State Mus. Found., 1986—89; expansion com. mem. Carolina's NFL, 1988—92; bd. dirs. Columbia Theol. Sem., Decatur, Ga., 1990—93; trustee Laurens County Health Care Sys., 1996—2000, chmn., 1997—99; deacon 1st Presbyn. Ch., Clinton, 1959—67, elder, 1967—73, 1976—81, 1983—87, 1988—93, elder emeritus, 2006. Officer USAF, 1955—57. Recipient Disting. Svc. award, Clinton Jr. C. of C., 1962, Outstanding Young Alumnus award, NC State U., 1965, Disting. Alumnus award, 1999, McCallie Sch., 1989. Mem.: SC Textile Mfrs. Assn. (bd. dirs. 1973—82, pres. 1979—80), Am. Textile Mfrs. Inst. (rsch. and tech. svcs. com. 1964—71, vice chmn. Crafted With Pride in USA com. 1985—87, vice chmn. edn. com. 1975—76, cotton com. 1981—82, safety amd health com. 1981—82), Clinton C. of C. (bd. dirs. 1959—61, 1966, v.p. 1968, pres. 1969), SC C. of C. (bd. dirs., exec. com. 1975—79), Musgrove Mill Golf Club (founder, bd. dirs.), Lions Club, Kappa Alpha, Phi Psi. Home: Merrie Oaks 1644 Hwy 56 S Clinton SC 29325

CORNETT, GREGG, publishing and computer company executive, editor; b. Dayton, Ohio, May 12, 1954; BA, U. Ark., 1985, MA, 1988; PhD in Computer Sci., Berkeley U., 1995. Pres. Computer Commuter, Batesville, Ark., 1982—87, Gregg Cornett Assocs., Batesville, Bald Knob, Searcy, Ark., 1984—; pub., editor Bald Knob Banner, 1987—; CEO G.C.A. Computer Svcs., 1993—; v.p. Wood Nursery, Inc., 1995—96; systems analyst Arkansas Pub., 1996—. Police photographer Bald Knob Police Dept., 1988—; computer cons. Gregg Cornett Assocs., 1984—, freelance journalist, Bald Knob, 1987—. Author (booklet) Neighborhood Crime Prevention, 1989; contbr. articles to newspapers. Area coord. City Crime Prevention, Bald Knob, 1988—; assoc. KARK-TV Community Network, Little Rock, 1990—; acting city clk. City of Bald Knob, 1991; rural community cons. City of Bald Knob, 1988—; founding bd. dirs. Rsch. Internat., Aruba; scoutmaster cub scout troop Boy Scouts Am., 2001—. Recipient Better Newspaper Advt. award Ark. Press Assn., 1988; Gregg Cornett Day proclaimed by City of Bald Knob, 1990. Fellow Rotary; mem. C. of C. (bd. dirs. 1988—). Avocations: writing, photography, electronics. E-mail: gcornett@bscn.com.

CORNETT, LLOYD HARVEY, JR., retired historian; b. Seminole, Okla., Aug. 29, 1930; s. Lloyd Harvey and Edna Lee (Walker) C.; children from previous marriage: Lloyd Harvey III, Rosemary Lynne, Carlton Wayne, Curtis Lee; m. Sarah Frances Missildine, Apr. 15, 1992. BA, U. Okla., 1951, MA, 1954; postgrad., U. N.Mex., 1965, Auburn U., 1977. Asst. dir. command history 2d Air Force, U.S. Air Force, 1955-57; historian Air Def. Command, 1957-58; asst. dir. command history Continental Air Def. Command, 1958-59; asst. dir. command history N.Am. Air Def. Command, 1959-61; ctr. historian Air Force Missile Devel. Ctr., 1961-70; historian Air Force Spl. Weapons Ctr., 1970-72; command historian Aerospace Def. Command, 1972-73; command historian Air Tng. Command, 1973-74; dir. U.S. Air Force Hist. Rschr. Ctr., Maxwell AFB, Ala., 1974-89; prin. Ind. Hist. Rsch./Adv. Svc., Montgomery, Ala., 1989—. Mem. Gov.'s Com. for Ala. Conf. on Libr. and Info. Svcs.; bd. advisors Ala. Hist. Commn. Co-editor: Alabama History: An Annotated Bibliography, Vol. of Am. Astronautical Soc. Hist. and (sch. text) Hist. of Ala., 1998; contbr. to hist. jours. Committeeman Boy Scouts Am., 1963-70, 75-79; mem. at large adminstrv. bd. Meth. Ch., 1978-81. Served with USMCR, 1951-53. Mem. AIAA (chmn. tech. com. on history 1983-96), Am. Astronautical Soc. Hist. Com., Western History Assn., Soc. for History in Fed. Govt. Democrat. Home and Office: 3751 Marie Cook Dr Montgomery AL 36109-1509

CORNETT, MICK, mayor; b. Oklahoma City, Oklahoma, 1958; m. Lisa Cornett; 3 children. Degree in journalism television news, Univ. of Oklahoma. Sportscaster and news anchor KOCO-5, 1981—97, city hall news anchor, 1997—99; pres. Mick Cornett Video Productions Inc., 1999—; ward 1 council mem. Oklahoma City Council, 2001—04; mayor Oklahoma City, 2004—. Chair urban econ. policy com. U.S. Conf. Mayors, trustee, 2007—. Office: 200 N Walker 3rd Floor Oklahoma City OK 73102 Business E-Mail: mayor@okc.gov.*

CORNETT, PATRICIA ANNE, oncologist, educator; b. Apr. 10, 1954; BS in Biology, Stanford U., Calif., 1976; MD, Med. Coll. Pa., 1980. Cert. Internal Medicine, Hematology, Med. Oncology. Intern, internal medicine Letterman Army Med. Ctr., San Francisco, 1980—81, resident, internal medicine, 1981—83, fellow, hematology/oncology, 1983—86, staff physician, 1986—91; asst. clin., prof. medicine U. Calif., San Francisco, 1991—97, dir., hematology/oncology fellowship, 1997—2001, assoc. clin. prof. medicine, 1997—2004, assoc. chair edn., dept. medicine, 2001—, clin. prof. medicine, 2004—; clin, chief, hematology/oncology Vet. Affairs Med. Ctr., San Francisco, 1991—. Mem. Vet. Affairs Bone Marrow Transplant Bd., 1996—. Contbr. articles to profl. jours. Named one of Golf Digest 2006 Top 250 Golfer Doctors in Am. Office: U Calif San Francisco Comprehensive Cancer Ctr Box 0128 UCSF San Francisco CA 94143-0128*

CORNFELD, DAVE LOUIS, lawyer; b. St. Louis, Dec. 24, 1921; s. Abraham and Rebecca (David) C.; m. Martha Herrmann, May 30, 1943; children: Richard Steven, James Allen, Lawrence Joseph. AB, Washington U., St. Louis, 1942, LLB, 1943. Bar: Mo. 1943. Practice law, St. Louis; ptnr. Husch & Eppenberger, 1954—2001, of counsel, 2001—. Adj. prof. Washington U., 1966-87. Co-author: Missouri Estate Planning, Will Drafting and Estate Administration, 2 vol., 1988, supplement, 2006; editor Law Quar. 1943. Bd. dirs. Jewish Fedn., St. Louis, 1977-80, 83-88, Jewish Ctr. for Aged, 1981-88; mem. adv. com. U. Miami Inst. Estate Planning, 1979—. Served with AUS, 1945-46. Disting. Alumnus award Washington U. Sch. Law, 2006. Mem. ABA (past chmn. com. taxation income estates and trusts, vice chmn. sect. taxation 1977-80, editor-in-chief Tax Lawyer 1977-80, sr. assoc. editor Probate and Property), St. Louis Bar Assn. (past chmn. taxation com), Am. Law Inst., Am. Coll. Trust and Estate Counsel (regent 1984-90), Am. Coll. Tax Counsel (regent 1980-88), Order of Coif. Jewish (trustee temple 1967-91). Club: Masons. Home: 834 Oakbrook Ln Saint Louis MO 63132-4812 Office: Husch & Eppenberger LLC 190 Carondelet Plz Ste 600 Saint Louis MO 63105-3441 Office Phone: 314-480-1616. E-mail: dcornfeld@charter.net, dave.cornfeld@husch.com.

CORNFELD, RICHARD STEVEN, lawyer; b. St. Louis, Aug. 21, 1950; s. Dave Louis and Martha (Herrmann) C.; m. Marcia Jackoway, Aug., 1, 1982; children: Lisa Sydney, Sarah Reva. AB, U. Mich., 1972; JD, Northwestern U., Chgo., 1975. Bar: Ill. 1975, U.S. Dist. Ct. (no. dist.) Ill. 1975, U.S. Dist. Ct. D.C. 1977, D.C. 1977, Mo. 1981. Assoc. Schwartz & Freeman, Chgo., 1975; law clk. to Hon. John F. Grady U.S. Dist. Ct. (no. dist.) Ill., Chgo., 1976; assoc. Bergson, Borkland, Margolis & Adler, Washington, 1976-80, Coburn, Croft & Putzell, St. Louis, 1980-83; ptnr. Thompson Coburn LLP and predecessor firms, St. Louis, 1983—, co-chair toxic tort practice group. Adj. prof. St. Louis U. Sch. Law, 2007—. Contbr. articles to profl. jours. Mem. ABA, Bar Assn. of Met. St. Louis, Mo. Bar, D.C Bar, Order of the Coif. Home: 21 Ladue Estates Dr Creve Coeur MO 63141-8321 Office: Thompson Coburn LLP One US Bank Plaza Saint Louis MO 63101-1693 Office Phone: 314-552-6023. Business E-Mail: rcornfeld@thompsoncoburn.com.

CORNFIELD, DANIEL BENJAMIN, sociology educator; b. Washington, Nov. 5, 1952; s. Melvin and Edith (Haas) C.; m. Hedy Merrill Weinberg, June 30, 1985. A.B., U. Chgo., 1974, A.M., 1977, Ph.D., 1980. Assoc. prof. sociology Vanderbilt U., Nashville, 1980—. Appearances on various TV and radio programs. Contbr. articles to profl. jours. Grantee Russell Sage Found., 1985, Nat. Council Employment Policy, 1980. Mem. Am. Sociol. Assn., So. Sociol. Soc., Indsl. Relations Research Assn. Democrat. Jewish. Avocations: guitar; clarinet; saxophone; piano; labor union organizing. Office: Dept Sociology Vanderbilt U Nashville TN 37203

CORNFIELD, MELVIN, lawyer, director; b. Chgo., June 5, 1927; s. Harry and Annabelle (Maltz) C.; m. Edith Pauline Haas, June 24, 1951; children: Daniel Benjamin, Deborah S. Cornfield Alexander. AB, U. Chgo., 1948, JD, 1951. Bar: D.C. 1951, N.Y. 1958. Atty. durable goods divsn. Office Price Stblzn., Washington, 1951-53; atty., advisor Chief Counsel's

Office IRS, Washington, 1953-58; assoc. Willkie, Farr, Gallagher, Walton & FitzGibbon, NYC, 1958-63; dir. taxes NBC, Inc., 1963-66; staff v.p. tax affairs RCA Corp., NYC, 1966-76, v.p., treas., 1976-82, v.p. tax affairs, 1982-85; dir. NYU Tax Inst., 1985-94. With USAAF, 1946-47. Home: 4703 Iselin Ave Bronx NY 10471-3323

CORNFORTH, SIR JOHN WARCUP, chemist; b. Sydney, Sept. 7, 1917; s. John William and Hilda (Eipper) Cornforth; m. Rita H. Harradence, Sept. 27, 1941; children: Brenda Osborne, John, Philippa Horder. BSc, U. Sydney, 1937, MSc, 1938; DPhil, Oxford U., 1941, DSc (hon.), 1976; DSc (hon.), E.T.H. Zurich, 1975, Trinity Coll., Dublin, Univs. Liverpool, Warwick, Aberdeen, Hull, Sussex, Kent and Sydney. Mem. sci. staff Med. Rsch. Coun., London, 1946—62; dir. Milstead Lab. Chem. Enzymology, Shell Rsch. Ltd., Sittingbourne, Kent, England, 1962—75; Royal Soc. rsch. prof. U. Sussex Sch. Chemistry and Molecular Scis., Brighton, Kent, England, 1975—82, prof. emeritus. Contbr. articles to profl. jours. Decorated comdr. Brit. Empire, knight, Companion of the Order of Australia; recipient Stouffer prize, 1967, Prix Roussel, 1972, Nobel prize in chemistry, 1975, Companion of the Order of Australia, 1991, Centenary of Federation medal, 2003. Fellow: Am. Chem. Soc. (Ernest Guenther award 1969), Royal Soc. Chemistry (Corday-Morgan medal 1953, Flintoff medal 1966), Royal Soc. (Davy medal 1968, Royal medal 1976, Copley medal 1982); mem.: NAS (assoc.), Netherlands Acad. Sci., Biochem. Soc. (CIBA medal 1966), Australian Acad. Sci. (corr.), Am. Soc. Biol. Chemists (hon.), Am. Acad. (hon.). Achievements include research in chemistry of penicillin, synthesis of steroids and other biologically active natural products, chemistry of heterocyclic compounds, biosynthesis of steroids, enzyme chemistry. Home: Saxon Down Cuilfail Lewes BN7 2BE England Office: U Sussex Sch Life Sci Falmer Brighton BN1 9QJ England

CORNGOLD, STANLEY ALAN, language educator, writer; b. Bklyn., June 11, 1934; s. Herman and Estelle (Bramson) C.; m. Marie Josephine Brettle, July 29, 1961 (div. May 1969); 1 child, Isabel Anna; m. Regine Schmidt-Ullner, Feb. 18, 1995. AB, Columbia U., 1957; postgrad., Sch. Oriental and African Studies-U. London, 1957-58; MA, Cornell U., 1963, PhD, 1969; postgrad., U. Basel, Switzerland, 1965-66. Instr. English U. Md. European div., 1959-62; teaching asst. English Cornell U., 1963-64; teaching asst. French Cornell U, 1964-65; asst. prof. German Princeton U., 1966-72, assoc. prof., 1972-79, assoc. prof. German and comparative lit., 1979-81, prof., 1981—, dir. grad. studies dept. German, 1979-82, 85, 93-95, 96-97. Vis. prof. Inst. Advanced Study, Princeton, 2003—04; disting. vis. scholar McMaster U., 2003; adj. prof. law Columbia U., 2006—. Author: The Commentators' Despair, 1973, The Fate of the Self, 1986, 2d edit., 1994, Franz Kafka: The Necessity of Form, 1988, Complex Pleasure: Forms of Feeling in German Literature, 1998, Literary Paternity, Literary Friendship: Essays in Honor of Stanley Corngold, 2002, Lambent Traces: Franz Kafka, 2004; co-author: Borrowed Lives, 1991; editor: Ausgewählte Prosa by Max Frisch, 1968, Aspekte der Goethezeit, 1975, Thomas Mann, 1875-1955, 1976; translator (editor): The Metamorphosis (Franz Kafka), 1972, Norton Critical Edition of The Metamorphosis (Franz Kafka), 1996, Norton Critical Edition of Kafka's Selected Stories, 2007; translator: Walter Benjamin, Selected Writings, 1996. Served with U.S. Army, 1955-57. Fellow Am. Coun. Learned Soc., 1965—66, NEH, 1973—74, Guggenheim Found., 1977—78; Fulbright fellow, 1986, Hölderlin Residence fellow, 1990, 1998, Literarisches Colloquium Berlin fellow, 1990, Princeton Honorific fellow, 2003, Internat. Forschungszentrum Kulturwissenschaften, Vienna, 2004. Mem. PEN, MLA (exec. com. divsn. on philos. approaches to lit. 1993-97, past chair, pub. com. 1993-95), Acad. Lit. Studies, N.Am. Nietzsche Soc., Kafka Soc. Am. (past pres.), Heidelberg Club Internat. Home: 51 Ridgeview Cir Princeton NJ 08544-7603 Office: Princeton U Dept German 219 E Pyne Bldg Princeton NJ 08544 Office Phone: 609-258-4137. Business E-Mail: corngold@princeton.edu.

CORNICK, MICHAEL F(REDERICK), accounting educator; b. Evansville, Ind., Apr. 15, 1940; s. Isadore John and Belle (Wigdor) C.; m. Charlotte Bozovich, Mar. 2, 1985; children: Elizabeth Ann, Ann Elliott. BS in Indsl. Mgmt., Purdue U., 1963; MBA, U.N.C., Chapel Hill, 1970, PhD, 1980. CPA, N.C. Stockbro. Thomson and McKinnon, Winston-Salem, N.C., 1965-68; bank officer 1 st. Nat. Atlanta, 1970-72; assoc. prof. acctg. U. N.C., Charlotte, 1985—2002, Winthrop U. , 2002—. Adv. Internat. Bus. Club, Charlotte, 1987—; leader Internat. Acctg. Overseas, Fed. Rep. Germany, London, 1988—. Author: Bank Accounting, 1984; contbr. articles to profl. jours. Mem. British Am. Bus. Coun. 1st lt. U.S. Army, 1963-65. Recipient cert. appreciation, Retarted Citizens Greensboro, 1983. Mem. AICPA, Inst. Mgmt. Accts. (dir. 1985-88), Am. Acctg. Assn., N.C. Soc. CPAs, Charlotte World Trade Assn. Avocations: reading, tennis, basketball. Home: 1409 Biltmore Dr Charlotte NC 28207-2556 Office: Winthrop Univ Rock Hill SC 29733 Home Phone: 704-331-9794; Office Phone: 803-323-4624. E-mail: cornickm@winthrop.edu.

CORNIES, LARRY ALAN, journalist, educator; b. Leamington, Ont., Can., Apr. 4, 1953; s. William Walter and Helen Louise (Rempel) C.; m. Jacquelyn Ann Brown, Aug. 17, 1974; children: Darryl, Graeme, Andrew, Natalie. BA in Religious Studies, U. Waterloo, 1975; postgrad., Wichita State U., 1981-84; MA in Journalism, U. Western Ontario, 1986. Comm. officer Conrad Grebel Coll., Waterloo, Ont., 1974-75; secondary sch. tchr. United Mennonite Ednl. Inst., Leamington, 1975-80; assoc. editor The Mennonite, Newton, Kans., 1980-84; comm. dir. Mennonite Ch. Hdqs., Newton, 1984-85; mng. editor London (Ont.) Mag., 1986-88; arts and entertainment editor The London Free Press, 1989-93, cluster editor, 1993-97, asst. city editor, 1997-98, Forum editor, 1998-2000, assoc. editor, 2000, editor, 2000—. Adj. prof. faculty info. and media studies U. Western Ont., 1987-97, 2004—; corr. World Report, Washington, 1983-85, Ecumedia News, N.Y.C., 1982-85; bd. govs. Conrad Grebel Coll., U. Waterloo, Ont., 1994-97; bd. dirs. Mennonite Pub. Svc., 2004—. Author: Essays in Journalism, 1986. Bd. dirs. divsn. gen. svcs. Gen. Conf. Mennonite Ch., Newton, Kans., 1995-2002. Recipient Derose-Hinkhouse award Religious Pub. Rels. Coun., 1985, Western Ont. Newspaper awards, 1997, 02; fellow Knight Ctr. Specialized Journalism, U. Md., 2001, 03. Mem. Coun. Ch. and Media (chmn. 1991-93), Assn. Opinion Page Editors (Best Series 2005). Avocations: music, baseball. Office: Globe and Mail 444 Front St W Toronto ON Canada M5V 2S9 Office Phone: 519-667-4549. E-mail: lcornies@lfpress.com.

CORNING, JOY COLE, retired state official; b. Bridgewater, Iowa, Sept. 7, 1932; d. Perry Aaron and Ethel Marie (Sullivan) Cole; m. Burton Eugene Corning, June 19, 1955; children: Carol, Claudia, Ann. BA, U. No. Iowa, 1954; degree (hon.), Allen Coll. Nursing. Cert. elem. tchr., Iowa. Tchr. elem. sch. Greenfield (Iowa) Sch. Dist., 1951-53, Waterloo (Iowa) Cmty. Sch. Dist., 1954-55; mem. Iowa Senate, Des Moines, 1984-90, asst. Rep. leader, 1989-90; lt. gov. State of Iowa, Des Moines, 1991-99. Past chmn. Nat. Conf. Lt. Govs. Bd. dirs. Inst. for Character Devel.; mem. policy bd. Performing Arts Ctr., U. No. Iowa, also trustee UNI Found.; bd. dirs. Nat. Conf. Cmty. and Justice, Des Moines Symphony, Planned Parenthood of Greater Iowa. Named Citizen of Yr., Cedar Falls C. of C., 1984; recipient ITAG Disting. Svc. to Iowa's Gifted and Talented Students award, 1991, Pub. Svc. award Iowa Home Econs. Assn., 1994, Friend of Math. award Iowa Coun. Tchrs. of Math., 1995, Iowa State Edn. Assn. Human Rights award, 1996, Govs. Affirmative Action award, Spl. Recognition award Nat. Foster Parent Assoc., Des Moines Human Rights Commn. award, Pub. Svc. award Coalition for Family and Children's Svcs in Iowa, Friends of Iowa Civil Rights, Inc. award, Martin Luther King Jr. Lifetime Svc. award, 1999, Svc. award Des Moines Area Religious Coun., 2002, NCCJ Brotherhood-Sisterhood award, 2003, Senator Barry Goldwater award Planned Parenthood Fedn. Am., 2003; recognized for Extraordinary Advocacy for Children of Iowa chpt. Nat. Com. for Child Abuse, award for leadership Early Care and Edn. Congress, Alumni Achievement award U. No. Iowa; named among YWCA Women of Achievement, 2000, Woman of Influence, Bus. Record, 2003; Nat. Conf. for Cmty. and Justice honoree, 2003; named to Iowa Women's Hall Fame, 2004. Mem. AAUW, LWV, PEO, Nat. Assn. for Gifted Children (mem. adv. bd. 1991-99), Rotary Club, Delta Kappa Gamma, Alpha Delta Kappa. Republican. Mem. United Ch. Of Christ. Home: 2880 Grand Ave No 406 Des Moines IA 50312 Personal E-mail: corningj@aol.com.

CORNING, NICHOLAS F., lawyer; b. Seattle, Nov. 8, 1945; s. Frank C. and Jessie D. (Weeks) Corning; m. Patricia A. Tomlinson, Dec. 14, 1968; children: Kristen Marie, Lauren Margaret. BCS cum laude, Seattle U., 1968; JD, U. Wash., 1972. Bar: Wash. 1972, U.S. Ct. Appeals (9th cir.) 1972, U.S. Dist. Ct. (we. dist.) Wash. 1973, U.S. Supreme Ct. 1976, U.S. Ct. Claims 1981. Assoc. Jennings P. Felix, Seattle, 1972-75; ptnr. Lagerquist, McConnell & Corning, Seattle, 1975-77; pres., ptnr. Treece, Richdale, Malone, Corning & Abbott, Inc., P.S., Seattle, 1977-99; atty. Corning Law Firm, Seattle, 1999—. Pres. Windemere Corp., Seattle, 1988, also bd. dirs. Recipient Am. Jurisprudence award in Criminal Law, U. Wash., 1971. Mem.: ATLA, Found. Wash. Cts. (v.p. 1999—), Am. Bd. Trial Advocacy, King County Bar Assn. (spkrs. bur. 1983—85, chmn. pub. info. com. 1985—87, chmn. judiciary and cts. com. 2001—), Wash. State Trial Lawyers Assn. (pres. 1994—95, bd. dirs.), Wash. State Bar Assn., Nat. Inst. Trial Advocacy, Ballard C. of C. (bd. dirs., pres. 1989—92), Beta Gamma Sigma (Key award 1968). Home: 5640 NE 55th St Seattle WA 98105-2835 Office: Corning Law Firm 720 Third Ave Ste 1400 Seattle WA 98104 Office Phone: 206-789-6503. E-mail: corninglawfirm@seanet.com.

CORNISH, BONITA CLARK, retired secondary school educator; b. Live Oak, Calif., Feb. 18, 1911; d. Cyrus Benito Clark and Anna Margretha Carstenbrook; m. Edwin Robert Cornish, July 23, 1935 (dec. Mar. 31, 1970); children: William Robert, Susan Margretha. AB, U. Calif., Berkeley, 1932, MA, 1933; postgrad., Fresno State U., 1944—2001, Coll. Pacific, 1956; EdD, Calif. Coast U., 2001. Life tchg. cert. Calif. Phys. edn., music and math. tchr., dean of girls Dunsmuir (Calif.) Internat. Union, 1934—38; pvt. music tchr. Yosemite Valley, Calif., 1943; asst. to prin. Fresno (Calif.) County Sys., 1944; spl. edn. tchr. Fresno City Sys., 1946—72; tchr. Bullard HS, Fresno, 1972, Roosevelt HS, Fresno, 1973—76; ret., 1976. Dramatics Calif. Ret. Tchrs. Assn., Fresno, 1976—2001; lectr. gerontology classes Fresno State U., 1990—2001; tchr. Elderhostel-Wonder Valley, Fresno, 1990—95. PTA pres. Coll. Elem., 1940—60; city coun. Assembly Woman, Calif., 1980—93; assembly-women Calif. Sr. Legis., 1980—86; bd. mem. YWCA, Fresno, 1985—90. Mem.: AARP, Fresno County Dem. Women's Club (pres. 1990), Order of Ea. Star (life; conductress 1937), Alpha Delta Kappa (Ca Xi cptr. charter pres. 1945). Avocations: camping, gardening, reading, folk art, cooking. Home: Apt 320E 9525 N Ft Washington Rd Fresno CA 93720-0681

CORNISH, EDWARD SEYMOUR, magazine editor; b. NYC, Aug. 31, 1927; s. George Anthony and Elizabeth Furniss (McLeod) C.; m. Sally Woodhull, Oct. 12, 1957 (dec. Mar. 1992); children: George Anthony, Jefferson Richard Woodhull, Blake McLeod. Diplome d'etudes, U. Paris, France, 1948; AB, Harvard U., Cambridge, Mass., 1950. Copy boy, cub reporter Evening Star, Washington, 1950-51; staff corr. U.P. Assn., Richmond, Va., 1951-52, Raleigh, NC, 1952-53, London, 1953-54, Paris, 1954-55, Rome, 1956; staff writer Nat. Geog. Soc., 1957-69; founder, pres. World Future Soc., Washington, 1966—2004; creator, editor The Futurist Mag., 1966—; editor World Future Soc. Bull., 1968-77. Cons. to govt., bus. and ednl. orgns. Author: The Study of the Future, 1977; editor: Resources Directory for America's Third Century, 1977, The Future: A Guide to Information Sources, 1977, 1979: The World of Tomorrow, 1978, Communications Tomorrow, 1982, Global Solutions, 1984, The Computerized Society, 1985, Careers Tomorrow, 1988, The 1990s and Beyond, 1989, Exploring Your Future: Living, Learning and Working in the Information Age, 1996, The Opportunity Society, 2000, Futuring: The Exploration of the Future, 2003; editl. cons. Nat. Goals Rsch. Staff, 1970, White House Report Toward Balanced Growth, 1970, Russian Acad. Forecasting, 1999—, UNESCO Coun. on the Future, 1999—. Bd. dirs. World Watch Inst., 1974-2000; adv. bd. Inst. for Alternative Futures. Mem.: Russian Future Studies Acad. (hon.). Home: 5501 Lincoln St Bethesda MD 20817-3723 Office: World Future Soc 7910 Woodmont Ave Bethesda MD 20814-3002 Office Phone: 301-656-8274. Business E-Mail: ecornish@wfs.org.

CORNISH, GEOFFREY ST. JOHN, golf course architect; b. Winnipeg, Man., Can., Aug. 6, 1914; came to U.S., 1947, naturalized, 1955; m. Carol Burr Gawthrop, Mar. 31, 1951 BSA., U. B.C., Can., 1935; MS, U. Mass., 1952, Dr. Sci. (hon.), 1987. Golf course architect Thompson-Jones & Co., Toronto, Ont., Canada, 1935-47; instr. U. Mass., 1947-52; pvt. practice golf course architecture Amherst, Mass., 1952—. Vis. lectr. U. Mass. Co-author: The Golf Course, 1981, rev. edit., 1987, The Architects of Golf, 1993, Golf Course Design, 1998, Eighteen Stakes on a Sunday Afternoon, 2002, Classic Golf Hole Design, 2002, Golf Course Design: An Annotated Bibliography, 2006; subject of Interview mag., Apr. 1987; contbr. articles to profl. jours. Served to maj. Can. Army, 1940-45 Recipient Disting. Svc. award Golf Course Supts. Am., 1981; named Can. Golf Hall of Fame, 1996. Mem. Am. Soc. Golf Course Architects (pres. 1975, Donald Ross award 1982), Brit. Assn. Golf Course Architects (hon.), Soil Sci. Soc. Am., Sigma Xi, Phi Kappa Phi Epsicopalian Home and Office: Fiddlers Grn 1030 S East St Amherst MA 01002-3078

CORNISH, JAY, JR., (THELBERT BERNARD), Internet company executive; b. Atlanta, Nov. 1, 1974; s. Thelbert Bernard Cornish and Kathleen Ross Henderson; stepfather, William L. Fentress; m. Marta Marie Rush, Apr. 22, 1996; children: Thelbert B. III, Solomon R., Jade B., Ashani L., Sophia K, Quincy L Student, N.C. State U., 1992—95; AA Bus. Admin., Strayer U., 2006, AS Computer Net/Internet, 2006. Cert. Apple server engr., svc. tech., solutions expert. Pres., CEO Eternal Computing, Inc., Raleigh, NC, 1997—2000, chmn., 2000—01; pres., CEO Subspace Wave Corp., Raleigh, 2000—01; ret., 2001; founder Cornish and Assocs., 2005, Cornish Inst. Innovation, Exch. and Policy, 2005. Musician, disc jockey radio broadcasting Underground 88, WKNC-FMN, 1995; asst. HS wrestling coach. NC Sch. Sci. Math., 2006-. Youth football coach Raleigh Parks and Recreation, 2005—; youth wrestling coach Dynamic Wrestling Club, 2004—. USAF scholar, 1991; N.C. Leadership fellow N.C. State U., 1992 Mem. Greater Raleigh C. of C., Coun. for Entrepreneurial Devel., Mensa. Achievements include development of one of IBM's first commercially avaliable OEM CHRP platform computing systems and pioneering the concept for the first contiguous national broadband wireless internet service and infrastructure. Avocations: reading, design, inventing, wrestling, computers. Office Phone: 919-360-2502. Business E-Mail: cornishassociatesllc@mac.com.

CORNISH, RICHARD POOL, lawyer; b. Evanston, Ill., Sept. 9, 1942; s. William A. and Rita (Pool) C.; children: William Darby, Richard Gordon. BS, Okla. State U., 1964; LLB, U. Okla., 1966. Bar: Okla. 1966, U.S. Dist. Ct. (ea. dist.) Okla. 1969, U.S. Supreme Ct. 1979. Ptnr. Baumert & Cornish, McAlester, Okla., 1967-71, Cornish & Cornish, Inc., McAlester, 1971-77; magistrate U.S. Dist. Ct. for Ea. Dist. Okla., McAlester, 1976—2000; prin. Richard P. Cornish, Inc., McAlester, 1977—. Bd. dirs. McAlester Boys Club, 1970-80, pres., 1974. Capt. JAGC, USAR, 1966-78. Mem. Okla. Bar Assn. (legal aid to servicemen com., legal specialization com.), Pittsburg County Bar Assn., McAlester C. of C. (bd. dirs. 1973-75). Roman Catholic. Home: 611 E Creek Ave Mcalester OK 74501-6929 Office: PO Box 1106 Mcalester OK 74502-1106 Office Phone: 918-423-5070. Business E-Mail: cornishrp@yahoo.com.

CORN-REVERE, ROBERT, lawyer; m. Sigrid Fry-Revere, 1984; children: Nathan Revere, Ian Revere, Jackson Revere, Lauren Revere. BA, Eastern Ill. U., 1977; MA, U. Mass., Amherst, 1980; JD, Catholic U. of Am., 1983. Bar: DC 1983, US Supreme Ct., US Ct. Appeals (D.C.) 2nd, 3rd, 4th, 6th & 10th circuits. Assoc. Steptoe & Johnson, 1983—85, Hogan & Hartson LLP, 1985—90, ptnr., 1994—2003, Davis Wright Tremaine LLP, Washington, 2003—; legal advisor to commr. James H. Quello FCC, 1990—94. Adj. prof. Columbus Sch. Law, Cath. U. of Am., 1987—2001. Bd. trustees Media Inst., 1997—2003; bd. mem. Freedom to Read Found., 2000—02. Office: Davis Wright Tremaine LLP 1919 Pennsylvania NW Washington DC 20006 Office Phone: 202-973-4225. Business E-Mail: bobcornrevere@dwt.com.

CORNWALL, DEBORAH JOYCE, management consultant, consulting firm executive; b. Wilmington, Del., Dec. 9, 1946; d. Samuel and Norma (Bram) Handloff; m. Barry Newland Cornwall, June 22, 1968; 1 child, Deborah Leigh. BA, Mount Holyoke, 1968; MBA, Boston U., 1975. Editor Houghton Mifflin Co., Boston, 1967-69, Harbridge House, Inc., Boston, 1969-73, cons., 1973-74, assoc., 1974-75, sr. assoc., 1975-77, prin., 1977-79, v.p., 1979-81, v.p., divsn. mgr., 1981-83, sr. v.p., divsn. mgr., 1983-90; founder and mng. v.p. Korn/Ferry Orgnl. Cons., Boston, 1991-96; founder and mng. dir. The Corlund Group, L.L.C., Boston, 1996—. Mem. mid. mgmt. excellence com. City of Boston, 1986. Bd. dirs. Mass. divsn. Am. Cancer Soc., 1994-97, New Eng. divsn., 2006-. Mem. Phi Beta Kappa, Beta Gamma Sigma. Office: The Corlund Group LLC 101 Federal St Boston MA 02110-1817 Office Phone: 617-423-9364.

CORNWALL, JOHN MICHAEL, physics professor, consultant; b. Denver, Aug. 19, 1934; s. Paul Bakewell and Dorothy (Zitkowski) Cornwall; m. Ingrid Linderos, Oct. 16, 1965. AB, Harvard U., 1956; MS, U. Denver, 1959; PhD, U. Calif., 1962. NSF postdoctoral fellow Calif. Inst. Tech., Pasadena, 1962-63; mem. Inst. Advanced Study, Princeton, NJ, 1963-65; prof. physics UCLA, 1965—. Vis. prof. Niels Bohr Inst., Copenhagen, 1968—69, Inst. Physique Nucléaire, Paris, 1973—74, MIT, 1974, 87, Rockefeller U., NYC, 1988; cons. Inst. Theoretical Physics, Santa Barbara, Calif., 1979—80; assoc. Ctr. Internat./Strategic Affairs UCLA, 1987—; dir.'s adv. com. Lawrence Livermore Labs., 1991—, chmn., 2002—; mem. Def. Sci. Bd., 1992—93, mem. task force, 1996; chmn. external rev. com. accelerator oper. and technol. divsn. Los Alamos Nat. Labs., 1995—97, rev. com. advanced hydrodynamics facility, 2001—; adv. bd. Los Alamos Neutron Scattering Ctr., 2000—01; chmn. external rev. com. Ctr. Internat. Security and Arms Control Stanford U., 1996; adv. commn. Accelerator Prodn. Tritium Project, 1997—2000; prof. sci. and policy analyis RAND Grad. Sch., 1998—; sci. and tech. panel Def. Threat Reduction Agy., 2000—02; rev. com. Advanced Accelerator Applications, 2001—02; mem. Missile Def. Agy. Countermeasures White Team, 2001—; tech. adv. group Integrative Grad. Edn. Rsch. and Tng. program in pub. policy and nuc. threat U. Calif., 2003—; chmn. predictive sci. panel Nat. Nuc. Security Adminstrn., Dept. Energy, 2004—; program rev. panel Nat. Ignition Facility Lawrence Livermore Labs., 2005; mem. study group quantification of margins and uncertainties NAS, 2007—; cons. in field. Author: (with others) Academic Press Ency. of Science and Technology, Union of Concerned Scientists Report on Nat. Missile Def., other encys. and books; contbr. numerous articles to profl. jours. With US Army, 1956—58. Grantee Dept. Energy, NSF, NASA, Dept. Edn.; pre and postdoctoral fellow NSF, 1960-63, A.P. Sloan fellow, 1967-71. Fellow: AAAS, Am. Phys. Soc.; mem.: NY Acad. Sci., Am. Geophys. Union. Avocations: jogging, bicycling, golf, bridge. Office: UCLA Dept Physics & Astronomy Los Angeles CA 90095-0001 Business E-Mail: cornwall@physics.ucla.edu.

CORNWELL, DAVID GEORGE, biochemist, educator; b. San Rafael, Calif., Oct. 8, 1927; s. John Nevius and Nora (Jonasen) C.; m. Normagene Coon, Mar. 14, 1959; children: Karen Sue, David Andrew. BA (hon.), Coll. Wooster, 1950; MA, Ohio State U., 1952; PhD, Stanford U., 1955. NRC fellow Harvard U., 1954-56; faculty Ohio State U., 1956-92, prof. molecular and cellular biochemistry, 1963-92; part-time prof., 1993—; chmn. dept. medical biochemistry Ohio State U., 1965-80, assoc. dean acad. affairs Coll. Medicine, 1979-92, prof. and assoc. dean emeritus, 1992—; mem. nutrition study sect. NIH, 1966-70, nutrition sci. tng. rev. sect., 1970-73; hon. prof. Tongji Med. U., Wuhan, China, 1993—. Mem. editl. bd. Jour. Lipid Rsch., 1962-66, 88-95, Jour. Nutrition, 1969-72; mem. adv. bd. Jour Lipid Rsch., 1974-78, Chem. Abstracts, 1979-84; contbr. articles to profl. jour. Trustee Children's Hosp. Rsch. Found., Columbus, 1982-93. With AUS, 1946-47. Co-recipient hon. mention for rsch. 6th Internat. Congress Hematology, 1956. Mem. Am. Chem. Soc., Am. Soc. Biol. Chemists, Am. Oil Chemists Soc., Am. Inst. Nutrition, Alpha Omega Alpha, Sigma Xi. Presbyterian (elder). Home: 2290 Middlesex Rd Columbus OH 43220-4646 Office Phone: 614-292-7411. Business E-Mail: cornwell.1@osu.edu.

CORNWELL, EDWARD E., III, surgeon; b. Washington, Nov. 30, 1956; s. Edward E. Cornwell, II and Shirley Cornwell; m. Maggie Burdette Covington, June 24, 1989; 1 child, Michael Elijah. BA, Brown U., 1978; MD, Howard U., 1982. Asst. prof. surgery Howard U., Washington, 1989—93, U. So. Calif., LA, 1993—97, assoc. prof. surgery, 1998, Johns Hopkins U., Balt., 1998—, assoc. prof. surgery and critical care medicine, 1999—. Chief editor: Multi-Disciplinary Critical Care Knowledge Assessment Program, 1996—98. Pres. Hopkins Injury Prevention and Cmty. Outreach Collaboration, 2000—; Bd. dirs. Police Athletic League, Balt., 1998—; bd. dirs. New Song Cmty. Learning Ctr., Balt., 2001—. Grantee Am. Trauma Soc., 2001, Ctr. for Disease Control and Prevention, 1996, Agy. for Healthcare Policy Rsch., 1993. Mem.: ACS, Soc. Univ. Surgeons, Am. Assn. for Surgery of Trauma, Nat. Med. Assn. (invited William H. Sinkler lectr. 1995, invited William E. Matory lectr. 1997, pres. surg. sect. 2002—), Soc. Black Acad. Surgeons (pres. 2001—), Alpha Omega Alpha. Office: Johns Hopkins Hosp CSIER 625 600 N Wolfe St Baltimore MD 21287

CORNWELL, GIBBONS GRAY, III, retired internist, educator; b. West Chester, Pa., Jan. 17, 1933; s. Gibbons Gray and Eva Chambers (Parke) C.; m. Mary Helen Fortmiller, Sept. 13, 1958; children: Gibbons Gray IV, Heidi Cornwell Trout, Holly Fortmiller. BS, Yale U., 1954; MD, U. Pa., 1963; MA (hon.), Dartmouth Coll., 1993. Diplomate Am. Bd. Internal Medicine, Am. Bd. Hematology. Resident in medicine Hosp. U. Pa., Phila., 1963-64, 65-66; research fellow Cambridge U., England, 1964-65; hematology fellow Hosp. U. Pa., Phila., 1966-68; biochemistry fellow Dartmouth Med. Sch., Hanover, NH, 1968-70, asst. prof. medicine, 1971-74, assoc. prof., 1974-80, prof., 1980-95, prof. pathology, 1990-95, prof. emeritus medicine and pathology, 1995—, assoc. dean student and acad. affairs, 1973-76, chmn. sect. hematology-oncology, 1977-84. Vis. prof. Inst. Immunology, Oslo, 1976-77; dir. clin. rsch. Norris Cotton Cancer Ctr., Hanover, 1978-91; bd. dirs. Cancer and Leukemia Group B, Boston, 1978-91; trustee, chmn. Hitchcock Found., Hanover, 1978-90; staff bd. govs. Mary Hitchcock Meml. Hosp., Hanover, 1981-88; vis. scientist Inst. Pathology/Swedish Med. Rsch. Coun., Uppsala, Sweden, 1987. Contbr. articles to profl. jours. Bd. dirs. Upper Valley Hospice, Lebanon, N.H., 1980; mem. sch. bd. Town of Lyme, N.H., 1973-76, health officer, 1970-74, mem. conservation com., 1970-74, budget com., 1996—; trustee Lyme Found., 1998—, chmn., 2000—. Lt., jet fighter pilot USAF, 1955-59. Clin. rsch. grantee NIH, 1978-91. Fellow ACP; mem. Am. Fedn. Clin. Rsch.

(emeritus), Am. Soc. Hematology, N.H. Med. Soc. Republican. Episcopalian. Avocations: bicycling, stamp collecting/philately, whale watching, computer animation, scuba. Home: 1 Orfordville Rd Lyme NH 03768-3305

CORNWELL, PATRICIA DANIELS, writer; b. Miami, Florida, June 9, 1956; d. Sam and Marilyn Daniels; m. Charles Cornwell, 1980 (div. 1989). BA in English, Davidson Coll., 1979. Police reporter Charlotte Observer, NC, 1979-81; tech writer to computer analyst Office Chief Med. Examiner, Richmond, Va., 1984—90. Author: A Time for Remembering: The Story of Ruth Bell Graham, 1983 (Medallion award), Life's Little Fable, 1999, Food to Die For, 2001, Portrait of a Killer: Jack the Ripper, Case Closed, 2002, (novels) Postmortem, 1990 (only novel ever to simultaneously win Edgar, Creasey, Anthony and Macavity awards), Body of Evidence, 1991, All That Remains, 1992, Cruel and Unusual, 1993, The Body Farm, 1994, From Potter's Field, 1995, Cause of Death, 1996, Hornet's Nest, 1997, Unnatural Exposure, 1997, Point of Origin, 1998, Southern Cross, 1998, Scarpetta's Winter Table, 1998, Black Notice, 1999, The Last Precinct, 2000, Isle of Dogs, 2001, Blow Fly, 2003, Trace, 2004, From Potter's Field, 2005, At Risk, 2006 (No. 1 Publishers Weekly Hardcover Bestseller List, 2006). Vol. police officer. Address: ICM 40 W 57th St Fl 16 New York NY 10019-4001 Office: Cornwell Enterprises 2260 High Bush Cir Glen Allen VA 23060-2258

CORNYN, JOHN, senator; b. Houston, Feb. 2, 1952; s. John and Gale Cornyn; m. Sandra Hansen; children: Danley, Haley. BA in Journalism, Trinity U., 1973; JD, St. Mary's U., 1977; LLM, U. Va., 1995. Cert.: Tex. Bd. Legal Specialization (personal injury trial law), bar: Tex. 1977, US Dist. Ct. We. Dist. Tex. 1980. Assoc., ptnr. Groce, Locke & Hebdon, San Antonio, 1977—84; judge 37th Dist. Ct., Bexer County, 1985—90; presiding judge 4th Adminstrv. Jud. Region, 1989—92; justice Supreme Ct. Tex., Austin, 1991—97; atty. Thompson & Knight; atty. gen. State of Tex., Austin, 1999—2002; US Senator from Tex., 2002—. Bd. vis. Trinity U., Pepperdine U. Sch. Law; Tex. Supreme Ct. liaison Bd. Law Examiners, 1991—, Gender Bias Task Force, 1993—95; lectr. CLE programs; mem. com. armed services US Senate, com. budget, com. judiciary, com. small business and entrepreneurship, joint econ. com. Recipient Outstanding Tex. Leader award, John Ben Shepperd Public Leadership Forum, 2000, James Madison award, Freedom Information Found. Tex., 2001, Award Manufacturing Legis. Excellence, Nat. Assn. Manufacturers, 2004, Champion for Healthcare in Rio Grande Valley, Valley Baptist Med. Ctr., Tex., 2004, Congressional Partnership award, Nat. Assn. Development Orgn., 2004, Friend of Farm Bur., Am. Farm Bur. Fedn., 2004, Friend of Rural Water award, Tex. Rural Water Assn., 2004, Hero of Taxpayer award, Am. Tax Reform, 2004, Statesman of Yr. award, Tex. Asian Republican Conf., 2004. Fellow: San Antonio Bar Found., Tex. Bar Found.; mem.: Tex. Bar Assn., ABA, Robert W. Calvent Inn of Ct. (pres. 1994—95), William Sessions Inn of Ct. (master bencher 1988—90, pres. 1989—90), Am. Law Inst. Republican. Office: US Senate 517 Hart Senate Office Bldg Washington DC 20510 also: District Office Ste 1530 221 West Sixth St Austin TX 78701-3403 Office Phone: 202-224-2934, 512-469-6034. Office Fax: 202-228-2856, 512-469-6020.

CORONA, JOSEPH ANTHONY, operations research analyst, mathematician, educator; b. North Miami, Fla., Apr. 28, 1973; s. John Victor and Elizabeth Vance Corona. AA, Broward C.C., 1997; BS with hons. in Math., Fla. Atlantic U., 2000; MS in Ops. Rsch., Fla. Inst. Tech., 2003. Math tutor Broward C.C., Davie, Fla., 1996—98; tchg. asst. Fla. Atlantic U., Boca Raton, Fla., 1998—99; math tutor Palm Beach C.C., Boca Raton, 1999—2000; ops. rsch. analyst TRADOC Analysis Ctr., Fort Lee, Va., 2001—. Mem. math. team Broward C.C., Davie, Fla., 1997. With US Army, 1992—94. Decorated Achievement medal U.S. Army. Mem.: Math. Assn. Am. (assoc.), Golden Key Nat. Honor Soc. (assoc.), Phi Kappa Phi (assoc.). Independent. Avocations: travel, concerts, reading, stained glass art. Office Phone: 804-765-1814. Personal E-mail: coolio1729@hotmail.com. E-mail: joseph.corona@us.army.mil.

CORONEL, VICTOR FELIPE, engineering educator; s. Simon Coronel and Teresa Chauca; m. Cecilia F. Moreno, Mar. 18, 1977. PhD, Columbia U., NYC, 1978—83. Prof. engring. and physics SUNY Rockland, Suffern, NY, 1990—; tech. expert, med. image processing IAEA, Lima, Peru, 1996—2004. Contbr. scientific papers. Achievements include research in magnetomechanical damping. Office: SUNY Rockland 145 College Rd Suffern NY 10901 Business E-Mail: vcoronel@sunyrockland.edu.

CORONITI, FERDINAND VINCENT, physics and astronomy professor; b. Boston, June 14, 1943; s. Samuel Charles and Ethel Marie (Havlik) C.; m. Patricia Ann Smith, Aug. 30, 1969; children: Evelyn Marie, Samuel Thomas. AB, Harvard U., 1965; PhD, U. Calif.-Berkeley, 1969. Rsch. physicist UCLA, 1967-70, asst. prof. physics, 1970-74, assoc. prof., 1974-78, prof. physics and astronomy, 1978—. Cons. TRW Systems Contbr. articles to sci. jours. NASA grantee, 1974, NSF grantee, 1974—. Fellow Am. Geophys. Union, Am. Phys. Soc.; mem. Am. Astron. Soc., Internat. Union Radiol. Sci. Home: 10475 Almayo Ave Los Angeles CA 90064-2301 Office: UCLA Dept Physics & Astronomy 405 Hilgard Ave Los Angeles CA 90095-1547 Office Phone: 310-825-3923. E-mail: coroniti@astro.ucla.edu.

COROTIS, ROSS BARRY, civil engineer, educator, academic administrator; b. Woodbury, NJ, Jan. 15, 1945; s. A. Charles and Hazel Laura (McCloskey) C.; m. Stephanie Michal Fuchs, Mar. 19, 1972; children: Benjamin Randall, Lindsay Sarah. SB, MIT, Cambridge, 1967, SM, 1968, PhD, 1971. Lic. profl. engr., Ill., Md., Colo., structural engr., Ill. Asst. prof. dept. civil engring. Northwestern U., Evanston, Ill., 1971-74, assoc. prof. dept. civil engring., 1975-79, prof. dept. civil engring., 1979-81, Johns Hopkins U., Balt., 1981-82, Hackerman prof., 1982-83, Hackerman prof., chmn. dept. civil engring., 1983-90, Hackerman prof., assoc. dean engring., 1990-94; dean Coll. Engring. and Applied Sci. U. Colo., Boulder, 1994-2001, Denver Bus. Challenge prof., 2001—, Mem. bldg. rsch. bd. Nat. Rsch. Coun., Washington, 1985-88; lectr. profl. confs. Editor in chief Internat. Jour. Structural Safety, 1991-2000; contbr. articles to profl. jours. Mem. Mayor's task force City of Balt. Constrn. Mgmt., 1985. Recipient Engring. Tchg. award Northwestern U., 1977, Disting. Engring. Alumnus award U. Colo. Coll. Engring. and Applied Scis., 2000, U. Colo. Boulder Faculty Assembly award, 2006; named Md. Engr. of Yr., Balt. Engrs. Week Coun., 1989; Rsch. grantee NSF, Nat. Bur. Stds., US Dept. Energy, 1973-96; Jefferson Sci. fellow, 2007—. Fellow: ASCE (chmn. safety bldgs. com. 1985—89, v.p. Md. chpt. 1987—88, pres. 1988—89, chmn. tech. adminstrv. com. structural safety and reliability 1988—92, chmn. probabilistic methods com. 1996—98, editor Jour. Engring. Mechanics 2004—, Walter L. Huber rsch. prize 1984, Civil Engr. of Yr. award Md. chpt. 1987, Outstanding Educator award Md. chpt 1992); mem.: NAE (natural disasters roundtable steering com. 2002—05, fin. and budget com. 2003—06, civil engring. sect. sec. 2003—06, nominating com. 2004, vice chair 2007—), Nat. Inst. Bldg. Scis. (mem. multihazard mitigation coun. 2002—, affiliate), Nat. Inst. Stds. and Tech. (bd. on assessment 1999, chair panel on bldg. and fire rsch. lab. 2002—07), Am. Nat. Stds. Inst. (chmn. live loads com. 1978—84), Am. Concrete Inst. (chmn. structural safety com. 1986—88), Am. Soc. Engring. Edn. (mem. pub. policy com. 1998—2001, mem. deans exec. bd. 1998—2001), Internat. Assn. Structural Safety and Reliability (chair exec. bd. 1998—2001, Sr. Rsch. prize 2005, Jefferson Sci. fellow 2007—). Office: U Colo Coll Engring & Applied Sci PO Box 428 Boulder CO 80309-0428 Home Phone: 303-449-1235; Office Phone: 303-735-0539.

CORPORON, JOHN ROBERT, broadcast executive; b. Arcadia, Kans., Mar. 1, 1929; s. George William and Portteus (Stephens) C.; m. Harriett Sloan; children: John Robert Jr., David Sloan. BS in Journalism, U. Kans., 1951, MA in Polit. Sci., 1953. Reporter Pitts. Sun, 1950, UP, New Orleans, 1955, bur. chief Baton Rouge, 1956, New Orleans, 1956-58; correspondent Sta. WDSU-TV, New Orleans, Washington, 1958-60, La. and Miss., 1960-62; news dir. Sta. WDSU-TV-AM, New Orleans, 1962-66; v.p., news dir. Sta. WNEW-TV, Metromedia, NYC, 1967; v.p. news Metromedia TV, NYC, Los Angeles, Washington and Kansas City, 1967-68; v.p., gen. mgr. Sta. WTOP-TV, Washington, 1968-71; exec. prodr. Newsweek Broadcast Svc., 1971-72; v.p., news dir. Sta. WPIX, NYC, 1972-83, sr. v.p., 1983-96. Founding pres. Ind. TV News Assn., 1980; co-founder Ind. Network News, 1980. Spl. reporter London Economist, Washington Post, 1960's. Mem. Park Slope Civic Assn.; trustee William Allen White Found., U. Kans., 1994—; mem. adv. bd. Pew Charitable Trust Project, 1997—; v.p. Overseas Press Club Found., 2000—. Served with U.S. Army, 1953-55. Recipient Nat. Emmy award Acad. Arts and Scis., 1965. Mem. N.Y. State Associated Press Broadcasters (bd. dirs. 1984-96, pres. 1986-87), Radio TV News Dirs. Assn. (bd. dirs. 1988-91), Nat. AP Broadcasters (bd. dirs. 1989-2000, pres. 1995-97), Deadline Club, Overseas Press Club (pres. 1996-98). Democrat. Avocations: jogging, swimming, reading. Home: 671 10th St Brooklyn NY 11215-4501 Office: Overseas Press Club 40 W 45th St New York NY 10036-4202 E-mail: jhcorpny@aol.com.

CORR, EDWIN GHARST, ambassador; b. Edmond, Okla., Aug. 6, 1934; s. E.L. and Rowena C.; m. Susanne Springer, Nov. 24, 1957; children: Michelle Ruth, Jennifer Jean, Phoebe Rowena. BS, U. Okla., 1957, MA, 1961, U. Tex., 1969. Fgn. svc. officer Dept. State, Wash., 1961-62; assigned to Mex., 1962-66; Peace Corps dir. Cali, Colombia, 1966-68; Panama desk officer Dept. State, 1969-71; program officer Inter Am. Found., 1971; exec. asst. to amb. Am. Embassy, Bangkok, 1972-75, counselor polit. affairs Quito, Ecuador, 1976, dep. chief of mission, 1977-78; dep. asst. sec. internat. narcotics matters Dept. State, 1978-80; U.S. Amb. to Peru Lima, 1980-81; U.S. Amb. to Bolivia La Paz, 1981-85; U.S. Amb. to El Salvador San Salvador, 1985-88; Dept. State diplomat-in-residence U. Okla., Norman, Okla., 1988—90, prof. polit. sci., 1990—96; dir. Energy Inst. Ams. U. Okla., 1996—2002; assoc. dir. Internat. Programs Ctr. U. Okla., 1996—2007, sr. rsch. fellow, 2007—. Author: The Political Process in Colombia, 1971; co-editor: Low-Intensity Conflict: Old Threats in a New World, 1992, The Middle East Peace Process: Vision vs. Reality, 2002, The Search for Israeli-Arab Peace, 2007; co-author: The Search for Security: The U.S. Grand Strategy in the 21st Century, 2003; contbr. to books and profl. jours. Mem. bd. dirs., chair Meml. Inst. for Prevention of Terrorism, Bd. Med. Assistance Programs Internat. Served to capt. USMC, 1957-60. Mem. Am. Fgn. Service Assn. Home: 1617 Jenkins Ave Norman OK 73072-6508 Office Phone: 405-325-1396. E-mail: ecorr@ou.edu.

CORR, JAMES VANIS, furniture manufacturing executive, accountant; b. Selma, Ala., June 28, 1922; s. Mark Stroud and Julia (Dozier) C.; m. Judith Ann Hackney, Feb. 3, 1971; children by previous marriage: James Jr., William V., Emily S., Julia D. BS, U. Ala., 1948, LLB, 1951. CPA, Ala., Ga. Ptnr. Dent & Corr, CPA's, Birmingham, Ala., 1954-61; exec. v.p. Buck Creek Industries, Inc., Atlanta, 1961-70, pres., 1970-77, also bd. dirs.; v.p. Sperry & Hutchinson Co., NYC, 1976-78, group v.p. furnishings divsn. Atlanta, 1976-78. Pres. JVC Enterprises, Inc., Atlanta, 1978—; speaker tax clinic U. Ala., 1954—. Bd. dirs. Met. YMCA, Birmingham. With AC, USMCR, 1944-46 Decorated D.F.C., Air medal with 2 oak leaf clusters. Mem. Ala. Soc. CPAs (past chmn. Birmingham chpt.), Ga. Soc. CPAs, ABA, Ala. Bar Assn., Am. Inst. CPAs, Ala. Textile Assn., Ga. Textile Assn., Exch. Club (Birmingham), Mountain Brook (Ala., past pres.). Home: 545 River Chase Pt NW Atlanta GA 30328-3555

CORRADA DEL RIO, BALTASAR, lawyer, retired former state supreme court justice; b. Morovis, PR, Apr. 10, 1935; s. Romulo and Ana Maria (del Rio) Corrada del R.; m. Beatrice Betances, Dec. 24, 1959; children: Ana Isabel, Francisco Javier, Juan Carlos, Jose Baltasar. BA in Social Scis., U. PR, 1956, JD, 1959. Bar: PR, 1959. Ptnr. McConnell Valdes Sifre & Ruiz Suria, San Juan, 1959-75; atty., chmn. Civil Right Commn., PR, 1970-72; mem., resident commr. from PR 95th-98th Congress; mayor City of San Juan, 1985-89; atty. Baltasar Corrada Law Office, 1989-92; sec. of state Govt. of PR, 1993-95; assoc. justice PR Supreme Ct., 1995—2005, ret., 2005; of counsel The Law Firm of McConnell Valdés, San Juan, 2005—. Pres. New Progressive Party, 1986-89. Pres. editl. bd. PR Human Rights Rev., 1971-72. Bd. dirs. PR Teleradial Inst. Ethics. Recipient Great Cross of Civil Merit of Spain King Juan Carlos I, 1987. Mem. ABA, Fed. Bar Assn., PR Bar Assn., Exch. Club, San Juan Rotary. Roman Catholic. Office: The Law Firm of McConnell Valdés PO Box 36 4225 San Juan PR 00936-4225 Home Phone: 787-268-4648; Office Phone: 787-250-5693. Business E-Mail: bcr@mcvpr.com.

CORREA, ADOLFO, epidemiologist, educator; s. Adolfo Correa and Estela Villaseñor; m. Ana I. Castro, June 2, 1978. BS, San Diego State U., 1969; MS, U. Calif., La Jolla, 1970, MD, 1974; MPH, Johns Hopkins U., Balt., 1981, PhD, 1987. Diplomate Am. Bd. Pediat., 1981, Am. Bd. Preventive Medicine, 1983. Assoc. prof. Johns Hopkins U., Balt., 1987—98; med. epidemiologist CDC, Atlanta, 1998—. Adj. assoc. prof. Johns Hopkins U., Balt., 1998—; adj. prof. Emory U., Atlanta, 2004—. Recipient Sec.'s award for Disting. Svc., Dept. HHS, 2000, 2004. Fellow: Am. Coll. Epidemiology; mem.: Am. Diabetes Assn., Teratology Soc., Soc. Epidemiologic Rsch., Soc. Pediatric and Epidemiologic Rsch., Delta Omega. Achievements include research in genetic and environmental risk factors of major cardiovascular malformations; Reye's syndrome and medication use. Avocations: philosophy, classical guitar. Office: CDC 1600 Clifton Rd MS E-86 Atlanta GA 30333 Home Phone: 404-625-3917; Office Phone: 404-498-3811. Office Fax: 404-498-3040. Business E-Mail: acorrea@cdc.gov.

CORREA, DANIEL, energy executive, physics engineer; b. NYC, Dec. 9, 1964; s. Maria Rodriguez. MS, St. Johns U., NY, 1998. Registered profl. engr., NY and Fla., 1999. Physics engr., CEO Oil & Gas Petroleum Corp., NYC, 2001—; analytical devel. Dept. Energy, Washington. Physics engr., CEO InterNef teGaz & PetroGas SA, Russia. Lt. comdr. USN, 1990—2000. Mem.: Soc. Petroleum Engrs. (life). Home and Office: Oil & Gas Petroleum Corp 244 5th Ave G222 New York NY 10001 Home Phone: 212-222-1900. Business E-Mail: ceo@oilgaspetroleum.com.

CORREA-DE-ARAUJO, ROSALY LIA, medical researcher, medical educator; arrived in U.S., 1990; d. Creighton Correa-de-Araujo and Maria Rosa Lia de Araujo. MD, Fed. U. Bahia, Salvador, Bahia, Brazil, 1980; MS in Human Pathology, U. São Paulo, Ribeirão Preto, São Paulo, Brazil, 1986, PhD in Morphology & Cell Biology, 1988. Assoc. prof. and chmn. dept. anatomic pathology and forensic medicine, chief univ. hosp. autopsy sect. Sch. Medicine Triangulo Mineiro, Uberaba, Minas Gerais, Brazil, 1986—93; vis. assoc. Nat. Heart, Blood and Lung Inst., Bethesda, Md., 1990—92; fellow cardiovasc. pathology Armed Forces Inst. Pathology, Washington, 1992—94; program dir. for geriat. and med. info. specialist US Pharmacopeia, Rockville, Md., 1994—2000; program dir. geriat. and internat. health Am. Soc. Cons. Pharmacists, Alexandria, Va., 2000—02; dir. women's health and gender-based rsch. Agy. for Healthcare Rsch. and Quality, U.S. Dept. HHS, Rockville, 2002—. Mem. and chair bd. pharm. sciences' pub. policy com. Internat. Pharm. Fedn., Hague, Netherlands, 2000—04; adj. assoc. prof. anatomy Sch. Medicine, George Washington U., Washington, 1993—; clin. asst. prof. experiential learning program Sch. Pharmacy, U. Md., Balt., 2002—. Contbr. chapters to books, articles to profl. jours.; mem. editl. bd.: Jour. Women's Health, 2005—. Recipient Dirs. Merit award, Agy. for Healthcare Rsch. and Quality, 2004, Dirs. Citation for Outstanding Performance, 2003, 2004, 2005, Commissioner's Spl. Citation, FDA, 2004, Bd. Trustees Performance award, US Pharmacopeia, 1995—2000, Carlos Chagas award, Nat. Acad. Medicine, Brazil, 1986. Mem.: Acad. Health (mem. and chair gender health interest group 2002—), Am. Med. Dirs. Assn. (mem. and chair medication mgmt. in long-term care com. 2000—), Am. Geriatrics Soc. Democrat-Npl. Roman Catholic. Achievements include expanding the Women's Health Program at the Agy. for Healthcare Rsch. and Quality to encompass gender-based rsch. and analysis; research in gender differences in drug use and expenditures in a privately insured population of order adults; gender differences across racial and ethnic groups in the quality of care for acute myocardial infarction and heart failure associated with comorbidities; gender differences across racial and ethnic groups in the quality of care for diabetes. Avocations: reading, arts and decoration, jewelry making, travel, classical music, jogging. Home Phone: 240-632-2809; Office Phone: 301-427-1550. Office Fax: 301-427-1562.

CORREA-PEREZ, JUAN RAMON, andrologist, embryologist, researcher; b. San Juan, May 3, 1968; s. Juan Antonio Correa-Matos and Isabel Perez-Marquez; m. Nirma Aixa Corchado-Pastor, Dec. 19, 1998; 1 child, Fernando Juan Antonio Correa-Corchado. BS cum laude, U. Puerto Rico-Mayaguez Campus, 1991; MS, U. Ky., 1994, PhD, 1997. Cert. lab. dir. Am. Assn. Bioanalysts, 2004, lab. dir. in andrology and embryology Am. Bd. Bioanalysis, 2006, high-complexity lab. dir. Am. Bd. Bioanalysis, 2006. Rsch. asst., reproductive physiology U. Ky., Lexington, Ky., 1991—96, post-doctoral fellow, reproductive physiology-medicinal chemistry pharm., 1994—97; andrology lab. dir. Centro de Fertilidad del Caribe, Rio Piedras, PR, 1998—99, sci. dir., 1999—2005; assoc. prof. physiology/pathology San Juan Bautista Sch. Med, Caguas, PR, 2004—; pres., co-founder Andrology Consultants, Inc., Caguas, 2004—; lab. dir. Infertility & IVF Ctr., St. Louis, 2006—, Procreative Cryobank, St. Louis, 2006—. Ad hoc reviewer Theriogenology, Gainesville, Fla., 1997—, Mid. East Fertility Soc., Cairo, Fertility and Sterility, 2005, Jour. Men's Health and Gender, 2006, mem. ad hoc editl. bd., 06; assoc. mem., instl. animal care and use com. (IACUC) San Juan Bautista Sch. Med., 2004—, pres. instnl. rev. bd., 2005—; columnist-male reproductive health Bus. PR Mag., San Juan, 2004—, El Vocero Newspaper, San Juan, 2004—; founder Andrology Cons., Inc., Caguas, PR, 2004, develop. support groups-male issues, 2004—; lect. PR Urol. Assn., San Juan, 2005—; lectr. Endometriosis Support Group-Ponce Sch. Medicine, 2005—, Coll. Med. Technologists-Puerto Rico, Guaynabo, 2005—; mem. editl. bd. Sci. World Jour. -Urology, 2006; profl. mem. fertile HOPE Am. Fertility Assn. Consortium Improvement in Erectile Dysfunction. Mem.: Fedn. Am. Socs. for Exptl. Biology, Soc. Male Reproduction and Urology, Internat. Soc. Andrology, Soc. for Study of Reproduction, Am. Assn. Bioanalysts (life), Am. Assn. Bioanalysts' Coll. Reproductive Biology (life), Reproductive Lab. Technologists Profl. Group-American Soc. for Reproductive Medicine (life), Soc. Assisted Reproductive Tech. (life), Am. Soc. Reproductive Medicine (life; mem. reproductive biologists profl. group, mem. fertility preservation spl. interest gorup, mem. genetic counseling spl. interest group, mem. sexuality spl. interest group), NY Acad. Sciences (life), Am. Soc. Andrology (life), Ky. Cols. (life), Golden Key Nat. Honor Soc. (life), Gamma Sigma Delta (life). Roman Catholic. Achievements include research in Development and adaptation of a physiological test for frozen-thawed sperm membrane based on swelling of the sperm tail; Development of vaginal contraceptives based on spermicides consisting of nonoxynol-9 and iodine with anti-HIV properties; Development of tablet/capsule delivery systems for vaginal contaceptives consisting of spemicides with anti-HIV properties; Development of standardized methods for sperm processing based on the swim-up effect; Methods for increasing the quantity and quality of human semen for purposes of infertility therapy; Incorporation of the colloid osmotic pressure effect to improve the selection of healthy spermatozoa for use in invitro fertilization; Assessment of factors contributing to the occurrence of epididymal necrospermia-a condition characterized by high levels of dead sperm in semen; development of new methods to improve/maximize the recovery, processing and cryopreservation of retrograde ejaculates from male diabetec patients for use in assisted reproduction. Avocations: basketball, astronomy, reading, movies, history. Office: Infertility and IVF Ctr Ste 359-C 3009 N Ballas Rd Saint Louis MO 63131 Home: PO Box 410173 Saint Louis MO 63141-0173 Office Phone: 314-872-9200. Personal E-mail: dr_jrcorrea@hotmail.com. Business E-Mail: dr_andrologo@yahoo.com.

CORREDOR, MARY B., director, language educator; b. Fairbury, Ill. d. Agnes K. Runyon; 1 child, Erik. MA, Ill. State U., 1976; MA TESOL, Am. U., Washington, 1996. Lectr. Spanish, ESL, and pedagogy Sul Ross State U., Alpine, Tex., 1996-98; dept. chair ESL Austin (Tex.) C.C., 1998—. Freelance translator, Austin, 1999—. Mem. TESOL, Austin Translators and Interpreters Assn., Am. Assn. Tchrs. of Spanish and Portuguese. Office: Austin CC-Rio Grande Campus 1212 Rio Grande Austin TX 78701 Home: 2702 Deeringhill Dr Austin TX 78745-5112 E-mail: mcorredo@austin.cc.tx.

CORRELL, ALSTON DAYTON, JR., (PETE), forest products company executive; b. Brunswick, Ga., Apr. 28, 1941; s. Alston Dayton and Elizabeth (Flippo) Correll; m. Ada Lee Fulford, June 23, 1963; children: Alston Dayton, Elizabeth Lee. BSBA, U. Ga., 1963; MS in Pulp and Paper Tech., U. Maine, 1966, MS in Chem. Engring., 1967. Tech. svc. engr. Westvaco, 1963—64; instr. U. Maine, Orono, 1964—67; various pulp and paper mgmt. positions Weyerhaeuser Co., 1967—77; pres. paperboard divsn. Mead Corp., Dayton, Ohio, 1977—80, group v.p. paperboard, 1980, group v.p. paper, 1981, group v.p. forest products, 1981—83, sr. v.p. forest products, 1983—88; sr. v.p. pulp and printing paper Ga.-Pacific Corp., Atlanta, 1988—89, exec. v.p. pulp and paper, 1989—91, COO, 1991—93, pres., 1991—2002, CEO, 1993—2005, chmn., 1993—2006, advisor, chmn. emeritus, 2006—. Bd. dirs. SunTrust Banks, Atlanta, SunTrust Banks, Inc., SunTrust Banks Ga., Inc., Mirant Corp., Norfolk Southern Corp.; chmn. Inst. Paper Sci. and Tech., Inc.; bd. councilors The Carter Coun. Trustee U. Ga. Found., Robert W. Woodruff Arts Ctr.; mem. Atlanta coun. Boy Scouts Am.; mem. Atlanta Action Forum; mem. exec. com. Nat. Coun. Paper Industry for Air and Stream Improvement, Inc., past chmn. bd.; bd. dirs. Miami Valley (Ohio) Boy Scouts, Nature Conservancy, Keep Am. Beautiful Inc.; Ga. Rsch. Alliance; chmn. United Negro Coll. Fund, vice chmn. Atlanta Campaign; bd. dirs. Ctrl. Atlanta Progress, chmn., 1995—97. Named CEO of Yr., Atlanta Bus. League, 1998, Exec. Papermaker of Yr., PaperAge, 1999, 2005; named one of 100 Most Influential Georgians, Ga. Trend Mag., 1994, 1995, 25 Most Influential Georgians, 1996, 1997, 1998; named to Bus. Hall of Fame, Ga. State Univ. J. Mack Robinson Coll. of Bus., 2005, Junior Achievement Atlanta Bus. Hall of Fame, 2005; recipient Nat. Brotherhood award, 1991, Disting. Alumnus award, U. Ga., Terry Coll. Bus., 1994, Salute to Greatness award, The King Ctr., 1999, Atlanta Urban League Disting. Cmty. Svc. award, 2001, Brit. Am. Bus. Group — Oglethorpe Sword, 2002, Nat. Multiple Sclerosis Soc. Silver Hope award, 2003, CEO of Yr., Business to Business Mag., 2004, Paperloop, 2005. Mem.: Am. Forest and Paper Assn. (bd. dirs., forest resource product group exec. com.), Atlanta C. of C. (bd. dirs., Forward Atlanta Policy Group, chmn. 1997—98), Ga. C. of C. (bd. dirs.), Commerce Club (bd. dirs. Atlanta chpt.). Republican. Presbyterian.

CORRELL, DONALD L., water services company executive; BS, Pa. State Univ.; MBA, NYU. CPA NY. Positions through sr. v.p. & CFO, then chmn., pres., CEO United Water Resources, Harrington Park, NJ, 1978—2003; pres., CEO Pennichuck Corp., Merrimack, NH, 2003—06, American Water, Vorhees, NJ, 2006—. Commr. NJ Water Supply Authority; mem. environ. fin. adv. bd. U.S. EPA; bd. dir. HealthSouth Corp., Interchange Fin. Services Corp.; bd. mem. Nat. Assn. Water Companies. Office: American Water 1025 Laurel Oak Rd Voorhees NJ 08043

CORRENTE, ROBERT CLARK, prosecutor; BA, Dartmouth Coll., 1978; JD, NYU, 1981. Mng. ptnr. Corrente, Brill & Kusinitz, Providence, 1985—98; ptnr. Hinckley, Allen & Snyder, Providence, 1998—2004; US atty. dist. RI US Dept. Justice, 2004—. Chair RI Judicial Nom. Commn., 1998—2000; ethics adv. bd. RI Supreme Ct., 1997, chair, 2000. Office: US Attys Office Fleet Ctr 50 Kennedy Plz 8th Fl Providence RI 02903*

CORRIGAN, BRIAN JAY, literature educator, writer; b. Kansas City, Mo., Feb. 19, 1957; s. David Vincent Corrigan and Constance Joan Bernstein, Sheldon Bernstein (Stepfather); m. Damaris Moore. BA, U. Mo., Kansas City, 1983; JD, Tulane U., New Orleans, 1986, PhD, 1989. Sr. prof. Renaissance lit. N. Ga. Coll. and State U., Dahlonega, 1990—. Founder, artistic dir. N. Ga. Shakespeare Festival, Dahlonega, 1990—99; co-founder, chmn. Dahlonega Lit. Festival, 2004—; programming com. mem. Decatur (Ga.) Book Festival, 2006—; judge O, Georgia! Writing Contest, Cumming, 2003—04. Author: (novels) The Poet of Loch Ness (Ga. Author of the Yr., 2006), (Josiah W. Bancroft Lit. prize, 2001), (book) Playhouse Law in Shakespeare's World, The Misfortunes of Arthur: a critical, old-spelling edition, (ency.) The Continuum Encyclopedia of British Literature, (CD-ROM) The Compendium of Renaissance Drama. Named Rookie of the Yr., N. Ga. Coll. Student Govt. Assn., 1991, Keynote spkr., Internat. Shakespeare Assn., 2003, Fla. First Coast Writers Conf., 2005, 2007, Tchg. Excellence/Prof. of the Yr., Ga. Bd. Regents, 2005; recipient Bicentennial Play Writing Contest, Lincoln U., 1975, Achievement in Writing, Maritime Lawyer prize, Tulane U. Law Sch., 1984, Commencement address, N. Ga. Coll. and State U., 2005; grantee, Ga. Bd. Regents, 2003; Bing fellow, Huntington Libr., 1989. Master: Atlanta Writers Club; mem.: Renaissance Soc. Am., Internat. Shakespeare Assn., Shakespeare Assn. Am., Ga. Writers Assn. Avocations: dressage, fencing, sculpting, gardening, landscape design. Home Phone: 706-864-2253. Personal E-mail: bcorrigan@ngcsu.edu.

CORRIGAN, CAROL A., state supreme court justice; b. Stockton, Calif., Aug. 16, 1948; d. Arthur Jospeph and Genevieve Catherine (Green) C. BA, Holy Names Coll., 1970; postgrad., St. Louis U., 1970-72; JD, U. Calif., San Francisco, 1975. BAr: Calif. 1975, U.S. Dist. Ct. Calif. 1975. Dep. dist. atty. Office Dist. Atty. Alameda County, Oakland, Calif., 1975—85; adj. prof. law U. Calif. Hastings Coll. Law, San Francisco, 1981-87, 89, U. Calif., Berkeley, 1984-87, U. San Francisco, 1987—89; sr. dep. dist. atty. Office Dist. Atty. Alameda County, Oakland, 1985-87; mcpl. ct. judge Oakland, Piedmont and Emeryville Jud. Dist., Oakland, 1987-91; judge Alameda County Superior Ct, 1991-94; assoc. justice Calif. Ct. Appeals, 1994—2006, Calif. Supreme Ct., San Francisco, 2006—. Adj. prof. sociology and polit. sci. Holy Names Coll., Oakland, 1976-80; vis. prof. law U. Puget Sound Sch. Law, Tacoma, 1981; spl. cons. Pres.'s Task Force on Victims of Crime, Washington, 1982, White House Conf. on Drug Free Am., 1988; mem. Pres.'s Commn. on Organized Crime, Washington, 1983-86; mem. faculty, cons. Nat. Inst. Trial Advocacy, South Bend , Ind., 1982—, Alaska Dept. Law, Fairbanks, 1983, Hawaii Dist. Atty. and Pub. Def.'s Office, Honolulu, 1981-83, Nat. Coll. Dist. Attys., Houston, 1984-87; trustee Holy Names Coll., 1987—. Author: Report Task Force on Victims of Crime, 1982, book chpts.; contbr. articles to profl. jours.; editor Point of View, 1981-84. Bd. dirs. Goodwill Industries of East Bay, Oakland, 1984-87, St. Vincent's Day Home, Oakland, 1984—; mem. adv. bd. St. Mary's Community Ctr. for Elderly, Oakland, 1985-87; trustee Holy Names Univ., Oakland, 1988—, chair, 1990-95. Mem. ABA, Calif. State Bar Assn., Alameda County Bar Assn., Asia Found. (advisor 1987), Calif. Dist. Attys. Assn. (bd. dirs.). Roman Catholic. Office: Calif Supreme Ct 350 McAllister St San Francisco CA 94102*

CORRIGAN, E(DWARD) GERALD, diversified financial services company executive; b. Waterbury, Conn., June 13, 1941; BS, Fairfield U.; MA, PhD, Fordham U. Group v.p. mgmt. and planning Fed. Res. Bank NY, 1976-80; spl. assignment to chmn. bd. govs. Fed. Res. Sys., 1979-80; pres. Fed. Res. Bank Mpls., 1981-84, Fed. Res. Bank NY, NYC, 1985-93; chmn. internat. advisors Goldman, Sachs & Co., NYC, 1994-96; mng. dir. The Goldman Sachs Group, Inc. (formerly Goldman, Sachs & Co.), NYC, 1997—. Chmn. Basel Com. on Banking Supervision, 1991—93; co-chair The Bretton Woods Com., The Per Jacobsson Found., The Group of Thirty, The Inst. for Fin. Stability, Bank for Internat. Settlements, The Trilateral Commn., Aspen Inst. Program on the World Economy, Internat. Adv. Panel of Monetary Authority of Singapore. Mem. Aspen Inst. (co-chmn.), Econ. Club of N.Y. Office: The Goldman Sachs Group Inc 85 Broad St New York NY 10004-2456*

CORRIGAN, FAITH, journalist, educator, historian; b. Cleve., Oct. 16, 1926; d. William John and Marjorie (Wilson) C.; m. Sigvald Matias Refsnes, Sept. 18, 1957 (dec. Feb. 1994); children: Marjorie Refsnes, Sunniva Collins, Stephen Refsnes. BA, Ohio State U., 1948; MAT, Kent State U., 1987. Cert. tchr. English, reading, Ohio. Staff writer women's news N.Y. Times, NYC, 1953-57; investigative reporter Cleve. Plain Dealer, 1962-66; dir. pub. info. Cuyahoga County Bd. Commrs., Cleve., 1966-69; dir. news, publs. Huron Rd. Hosp., East Cleveland, Ohio, 1970-73; lectr. II U. Akron, Ohio, 1990-91; adj. prof. Kent State U., North Canton, Ohio, 1996-97, Ashtabula br. Kent State U., Geauga/Twinsburg, Ohio, 1999—2005, Willoughby Hills br. Bryant and Stratton Coll., 2005—. Lectr. Fordham U., N.Y.C., 1956; expert witness U.S. Senate Medicare Hearings, Cleve., 1965; mgr. Cuyahoga County Welfare Levy Campaign, Cleve., 1966; owner Willoughby Antiques Pub Author: First Generation, 2002, Bread Glass and History, 2003; contbr. articles to newspapers. TESOL, Lit. Vols. Am.; mem. bd. mgrs. Eleanor B. Rainey Meml. Inst., Cleve., 1966-78; officer, trustee Lake County Cmty. Svcs. Coun., 1984-90; mem. adv. bd. Lake Geauga Legal Aid Soc., Painesville, Lake County, 1984-87; chair Initiative Petition Campaign on Environ. Waste Plant Issue, Willoughby, Ohio, 1991; officer, founder Ohio State U. chpt. Am. Newspaper Guild, 1947-48; del. rep. assembly N.Y. Newspaper Guild, 1954-57; poll judge Lake County Bd. Elections, 1984-2006; field rep. U.S. Census Bur., 1989—; recruiter, crew leader U.S. Census 2000. Recipient award of achievement Press Club of Cleve., 1964, Pulitzer nominee Cleve. Plain Dealer, 1964, 1st in state Ohio Newspaper Women's Assn., 1964, 1st in state Pub. Contest of Am. Heart Assn., 1972, 1st pl. publs. award Internat. Assn. Bus. Communicators, 1971-72. Mem. VFW (Ladies Aux.), Willoughby Hist. Soc. (trustee, v.p. 1997-2002, Heritage chmn. 2003-), Ohio Bicentennial Hist. Markers Rsch., Early Am. Pattern Glass Soc. Democrat. Roman Catholic. Avocations: expert on American china, glass, american labor history. Home: 37550 Euclid Ave Willoughby OH 44094-5622

CORRIGAN, HELEN GONZÁLEZ, retired cytologist; b. San Diego, Tex., Sept. 30, 1922; d. Rodrigo Simon and Eva Ruby (Corrigan) Gonzalez. BS, Our Lady of Lake, San Antonio, 1943. Registered cytologist Internat. Acad. Cytology. Tchr. San Diego H.S., 1943-45; microbiologist Nix Hosp. Profl. Lab., San Antonio, 1952-59; med. technologist Tucson Med. Ctr., 1959-60; cytologist in charge Jackson-Todd Cancer Detection Ctr., San Antonio, 1961-64; cytologist in charge cytology sect. Pathology Lab. 4th and 5th US Army Ref. Area Lab., Ft. Sam Houston, Tex., 1964-78; instr. trouble shooters, quality control analyst cytology sect. Brooks Med. Ctr., Fort Sam Houston, 1978-81; owner Corrigan Enterprises, San Diego, 1981-91; ret., 1997. Cytologist Waco Med. Lab. Svc., Waco, Tex., 1988—89, Nat. Health Lab., San Antonio, 1989—90, Internat. Cancer Screening Lab., San Antonio, 1990—91; head cytologist Dr. R. Garza & Assocs., Weslaco, Tex., 1992—. Adv. bd. mem. EEO, Ft. Sam Houston, 1972—74. Mem.: NAFE, Am. Soc. Clin. Pathologists (assoc. registered cytologist, registered med. technologist), Greater San Antonio Women's C. of C. Republican. Roman Catholic. Avocations: fishing, hunting, tennis, skiing, dance. Home: 147 Perry Ct San Antonio TX 78209-6211

CORRIGAN, JAMES JOHN, JR., pediatrician, educator, dean; b. Pitts., Aug. 28, 1935; BS, Juniata Coll., Huntingdon, Pa., 1957; MD, U. Pitts., 1961. Diplomate Am. Bd. Pediats. (hematology-oncology). Intern, then resident in pediat. U. Colo. Med. Ctr., 1961-64; trainee in pediat. hematology-oncology U. Ill. Med. Center, 1964-66; assoc. in pediat. Emory U. Med. Sch., 1966-67, asst. prof. Atlanta, 1967-71; mem. faculty U. Ariz. Coll. Medicine, Tucson, 1971-90, prof. pediat., 1974-90; chief sect. pediat. hematology-ongology, also dir. Mountain States Regional Hemophilia Ctr., U. Ariz., Tucson, 1978-90; chief of staff U. Med. Ctr. U. Ariz., Tucson, 1984-86; prof. pediat., vice dean for acad. affairs Tulane U. Sch. Medicine, New Orleans, 1990-93, interim dean, 1993-94, dean, 1994-2000, v.p., 2000—02, prof. emeritus pediat., 2002—; clin. prof. pediat. U. Ariz. Coll. Medicine, Ariz., 2003—. Assoc. editor Am. Jour. Diseases of Children, 1981-89, 90-93, interim editor, 1993; contbr. numerous papers to med. jours. Grantee NIH, Mountain States Regional Hemophilia Ctr., Ga. Heart Assn., GE, Am. Cancer Soc. Mem. Am. Acad. Pediatrics, Am. Soc. Hematology, Soc. Pediatric Rsch., Western Soc. Pediatric Rsch., Am. Heart Assn. (coun. thrombosis), Internat. Soc. Thrombosis and Haemostasis, Am. Pediatric Soc., World Fedn. Hemophilia, Pima County Med. Soc. (v.p., 1986—, pres. 1988—), Alpha Omega Alpha. Republican. Roman Catholic. Office: Univ Ariz Health Scis Ctr Dept Pediatrics 1501 N Campbell Ave Tucson AZ 85724 Business E-Mail: jcorrig@tulane.edu.

CORRIGAN, JANET M., health science association administrator; MBA, U. Rochester, M in Cmty. Health; M in Indsl. Engring., U. Mich., PhD in Health Svcs. Orgn. and Policy. V.p. planning and devel. Nat. Com. for Quality Assurance, 1991-95; prin. rschr. Ctr. for Studying Health Sys. Change Robert Wood Johnson Found., 1995—98; exec. dir. consumer protection and quality in health care industry Pres.'s Advisory Commn., 1998; dir. Health Care Svcs. Bd. Inst. Medicine of Nat. Academies, 1998—. Office: Inst Medicine Nat Acad Scis Health Care Svcs 500 5th St, NW, Rm 760 Washington DC 20418-0007 Fax: 202-334-1463. E-mail: jcorriga@nas.edu.

CORRIGAN, JOHN EDWARD, JR., retired banker, lawyer; b. Chgo., Sept. 26, 1922; s. John Edward and Veronica (Mulvey) C.; m. Eileen Williams, Nov. 4, 1950 (div. 1979); m. Sylvia Dennison McElin, Sept. 24, 1983. BA, Harvard U., 1943, JD, 1949. Bar: Ill. 1950. With First Nat. Bank Chgo., 1949-79, asst. atty., 1954—59, asst. v.p., 1960-61, v.p., 1961-72, sr. v.p., 1972-79; prin. Hedberg, Tobin, Flaherty & Whalen P.C., Chgo., 1980-87; of counsel Hedberg, Tobin, Flaherty & Whalen Inc., Chgo., 1988-92. With AUS, 1943-46, 51-52. Home: 560 Greenwood Ave Kenilworth IL 60043-1024 Personal E-mail: jscorrigan@comcast.net.

CORRIGAN, KARINA HELEN HILTJE, museum administrator; b. Boston, Sept. 1, 1970; d. Donald Anthony and Sharon Huisman Corrigan. BA, Wellesley Coll., Mass., 1993; MS in Historic Preservation, U. Pa., Phila., 1995; MA in Early Am. Culture, U. Del., Newark, 2001. Asst. curator Peabody Essex Mus., Salem, Mass., 1997—2001, assoc. curator Asian export art, 2001—. Trustee Hamilton Hall, Inc., Salem, 2005—. Trustee Friends Nalamdana, Mt. Vernon, Wash., 2005—. Democrat. Episcopalian. Office: Peabody Essex Mus East India Sq Salem MA 01970

CORRIGAN, MAURA DENISE, state supreme court justice; b. Cleve., June 14, 1948; d. Peter James and Mae Ardell (McCrone) Corrigan; m. Joseph Dante Grano, July 11, 1976 (dec.). BA with hon., Marygrove Coll., 1969; JD with hon., U. Detroit, 1973; LLD (hon.), No. Mich. U., 1999, Mich. State U., 2003; JD (hon.), Mercy Law Sch., 2002, Ea. Mich. U., 2004, Schoolcraft Coll., 2005. Bar: Mich. 1974. Jud. clk. Mich. Ct. Appeals, Detroit, 1973—74; asst. prosecutor Wayne County, Detroit, 1974—79, asst. U.S. atty., 1979—89, chief appellate divsn., 1979—86, chief asst. U.S. Atty., 1986—89; ptnr. Plunkett & Cooney PC, Detroit, 1989—92; judge Mich. Ct. Appeals, 1992—98, chief judge, 1997—98; justice Mich. Supreme Ct., Detroit, 1999—, chief justice, 2001—04; mem. Family Support Coun. MIch. Vice chmn. Mich. Com. to formulate Rules of Criminal Procedure, Mich. Supreme Ct., 1982-89; mem. Mich. Law Revision Commn., 1991-98; mem. com. on standard jury instrns., State Bar Mich., 1978-82; lectr. Mich. Jud. Inst., Sixth cir. Jud. Workshop, Inst. CLE, ABA-Cin. Bar Litigation Sects., Dept. Justice Advocacy Inst.; v.p. Conf. Chief Justices, 2003-04; bd. dirs. Vista Maria. Co-author: book on civil procedure; contbr. chpt. to book, articles to legal revs. Vice chmn. Project Transition, Detroit, 1976-92; mem. citizens Adv. Coun. Lafayette Clinic, Detroit, 1979-87; bd. dirs. Detroit Wayne County Criminal Advocacy Program, 1983-86; pres., bd. dirs. Rep. Women's Bus. and Profl. Forum, 1991; mem. Pew Commn. on Children in Foster Care, 2003-05. Named disting. Alumna, Marygrove Coll., 2003, U. Detroit Mercy Law Sch., 2004, Detroit News Michiganian of Yr., 2005, Vista Maria Child Advocate of Yr., 2005, Angel in Adoption, Congl. Coalition on Adoption, 2005, Jurist of Yr., Police Officers Assn. Mich., 2006, Outstanding Judge, Spectrum Human Svcs., 2006; recipient award of merit, Detroit Commn. on Human Rels., 1974, Dir.'s award, Dept. Justice, 1985, Outstanding Practitioner of Criminal Law award, Fed. Bar Assn., 1989, award, Mich. Women's Commn., 1998, Grano award, 2001, Disting. Svc. award, HHS, 2002, disting. Alumna, St. Joseph Acad., 2004. Mem. Mich. Bar Assn., Detroit Bar Assn., Fed. Bar Assn. (pres. Detroit chpt. 1990-91), Inc. Soc. Irish Am. Lawyers (pres. 1991-92, Achievement award 2001), Federalist Soc. Office: Mich Supreme Ct 8-500 3034 W Grand Blvd Detroit MI 48202 Office Phone: 313-972-3232.

CORRIGAN, ROBERT ANTHONY, academic administrator; b. New London, Conn., Apr. 21, 1935; s. Anthony John and Rose Mary (Jengo) C.; m. Joyce D. Mobley, Jan. 12, 1975; children by previous marriage: Kathleen Marie, Anthony John, Robert Anthony; 1 stepdau., Erika Mobley. AB, Brown U., 1957; MA, U. Pa., 1959, PhD, 1967; LHD (hon.), 1995; DFA (hon.), Golden Gate U., 2007. Rschr. Phila. Hist. Commn., 1957—59; lectr. Am. civilization U. Gothenburg, Sweden, 1959-62, Bryn Mawr Coll., 1962-63, U. Pa., 1963-64; prof. U. Iowa, 1964-73; dean U. Mo., Kansas City, 1973-74; provost U. Md., 1974-79; chancellor U. Mass., Boston, 1979-88; pres. San Francisco State U., 1988—. Author: American Fiction and Verse, 1962, 2d edit., 1970, also articles, revs.; editor: Uncle Tom's Cabin, 1968. Vice chmn. Iowa City Human Rels. Commn., 1970-72, Gov.'s Commn. on Water Quality, 1983-84; mem. Iowa City Charter Commn., 1972-73; chmn. Md. Com. Humanities, 1976-78, Assn. Urban Univs., 1988-92; mem. Howard County Commn. Arts, Md., 1976-79; bd. dir. John F. Kennedy Libr.; trustee San Francisco Econ. Devel. Corp., 1989-92, Adv. Coun. Calif. Acad. Scis., Calif. Hist. Soc., 1989-92; chmn., bd. dir. Calif. Compact, 1990—; mem. exec. com. Campus Compact, 1991—, chmn., 1995-2004; Mayor's Blue Ribbon Commn. on Fiscal Stability, 1994-95; chmn. Pres. Clinton's Steering Com. Coll. Pres. for Am. Reads and Am. Counts, 1996-2000. Smith-Mundt prof., 1959-60; Fulbright lectr., 1960-62; grantee Std. Oil Co. Found., 1968, NEH, 1969-74, Ford Found., 1969, Rockefeller Found., 72-75, Dept. State, 1977; recipient Clarkson Able Collins Jr. Maritime History award, 1956, Pa. Colonial Soc. Essay award, 1958, 59, William Lloyd Garrison award Mass. Ednl. Opportunity Assn., 1987, Cmty. Svc. award Anti-Defamation League, 2007; Disting. Urban Fellow Assn. Urban U., 1992. Mem. Am. Assn. Colls. and Univs. (chmn. 2006—07), San Francisco C. of C. (bd. dirs., chmn. 2006-08), San Francisco World Affairs Coun. (bd. dirs.), Pvt. Industry Coun. (bd. dirs.), Boston World Affairs Coun. (1983-88), Greater Boston C. of C. (v.p. 1987-89), Fulbright Alumni Assn. (bd. dirs. 1978-80), Univ. Club, St. Francis Yacht Club, Bankers Club, Commonwealth Club (bd. dirs. 1995-99), Phi Beta Kappa. Democrat. Office: San Francisco State U 1600 Holloway Ave San Francisco CA 94132-1722 Office Phone: 415-338-1381. Business E-Mail: corrigan@sfsu.edu.

CORRIGAN, WILFRED J., computer company executive; b. 1938; Divsn. dir. Motorola, Phoenix, 1962-68; pres. Fairchild Camera & Instrument, Sunnyvale, Calif., 1968-80; CEO LSI Logic Corp., Milpitas, Calif., 1980—2005, chmn., 1980—2005, non-exec chmn., 2005—. Bd. dir. Silicon Power Corp., FEI Co., Lucas Film Entertainment Co. Recipient Robert N. Noyce award, Semiconductor Industry Am., 1998. Fellow: London's City and Guild Inst., Imperial Coll., Royal Acad. Engring. Office: LSI Logic Corp 1621 Barber Ln Milpitas CA 95035

CORRIGAN, WILLIAM THOMAS, retired broadcast news executive; b. Bridgeport, Conn., Sept. 18, 1921; s. Thomas F. and Anna M. (Callan) C.; m. Harriett Bell, Sept. 1, 1951; children: Kevin, Brian. BS, Am. U., 1948. Reporter Bridgeport Herald, sports broadcaster sta. WUST, Washington, 1947; writer, reporter, prodr. NBC News, 1948-51; prodr., editor NBC-TV (newsreel), 1951-52; assignment editor NBC-TV News, 1952-53; Washington mgr. CBS Newsfilm, Washington bur. chief, 1953-59; dir. news and pub. affairs Sta. KNXT-TV, West Coast bur. chief CBS TV News, 1959-61; Am. Networks prodr./editor Eichmann Trial, Jerusalem, Israel, 1961; mgr. Washington bur. NBC News, 1962; prodr. Huntley Brinkley Report, Wash., 1963-65; dir. news ops. NBC, NYC, 1965-68; gen. mgr. ops. NBC News, NYC, 1968-73, gen. mgr., 1973-79, dir. broadcast svc., 1979-81. Staff sgt. USAAF, 1943—45, WWII. Decorated D.F.C., Air medal. Mem.: Soc. Profl. Journalists, Nat. Press Club, Radio-TV Corrs. Assn., White House Photographers Assn., Radio-TV News Dirs. Assn., Bath Club (Nokomis), Phi Sigma Kappa. Achievements include flying 35 combat missions over Japan as a B29 Tail Gunner. Home: Apt 125 5248 Manz Pl Sarasota FL 34232 Personal E-mail: harbil4@juno.com.

CORRIPIO, ARMANDO BENITO, retired chemical engineering professor; b. Mantua, Cuba, Mar. 6, 1941; came to U.S., 1961; s. Bernardo Manuel and Maria Teresa (Pedraja) C.; m. Consuelo Lucia Careaga, June 9, 1962; children: Consuelo T., Bernardo M., Mary A., Michael G. B of Chem. Engring, La. State U., 1963, M of Chem. Engring., 1967, PhD, 1970. Registered profl. engr., La. Systems engr. Dow Chem. Co., Plaquemine, La., 1963-68; instr. La. State U., Baton Rouge, 1968-70, asst. prof., 1970-74, Disting. Faculty fellow, 1974, assoc. prof., 1974-81, prof. dept. chem. engring., 1981-98, Jay Affolter prof., 1998—2007; prof. emeritus, 2007—. Pvt. cons., 1968—; vis. engr. MIT, Cambridge, 1978-79. Author: Tuning of Industrial Control Systems, 1990, 2d edit., 2000, Design and Application of Industrial Control System, 1998; co-author: Automatic Process Control, 1985, 3d edit., 2005; contbr. numerous articles to profl. jours. Chmn. St. George Bd. Edn., Baton Rouge, 1975-77; lector St. Aloysius Cath. Ch., Baton Rouge, 1989—. Recipient Excellence in Instrn. award Exxon Co., 1986, Excellence in Tchg. award Dow Chem. Co., 1989, Faculty Professionalism award La. Engring. Found., 1997. Fellow Am. Inst. Chem. Engrs. (instr. 1977-87, chmn. Baton Rouge sect. 1990, Charles E. Coates Meml. award with Am. Chem. Soc. 1990); mem. Instrument Soc. Am. (sr., instr. 1977—), Tau Beta Pi, Phi Lambda Upsilon, Phi Kappa Phi. Avocations: sailing, swimming, reading, duplicate bridge. Home: 9344 Bermuda Ave Baton Rouge LA 70810-1121 Office: La State Univ Dept Chem Engring Baton Rouge LA 70803-7303 Business E-Mail: corripio@lsu.edu.

CORROTHERS, HELEN GLADYS, criminal justice official; b. Montrose, Ark., Mar. 19, 1937; d. Thomas and Christene (Farley) Curl; m. Edward Corrothers, Dec. 17, 1968 (div. Sept. 1983); 1 child, Michael Edward. AA in Liberal Arts magna cum laude, Ark. Bapt. Coll., 1955; BS in Bus. Adminstrn. Mgmt., Roosevelt U., 1965; grad. officer leadership sch., WAC Sch., 1965; grad, Inst. Criminal Justice, Exec. Ctr. Continuing Edn., U. Chgo., 1973; postgrad., Calif. Coast U., 1981—. Enlisted U.S. Army, 1956, advanced through grades to capt., 1969, chief mil. pers. Ft. Meyer, Va., 1965-67; dir. for housing Giessen Support Ctr., Germany, 1967-69; resigned, 1969; social interviewer Ark. Dept. Corrections, Grady, 1970-71, supt. women's unit Pine Bluff, 1971-83; commr. U.S. Parole Commn., Burlingame, Calif., 1983-85, U.S. Sentencing Commn., Washington, 1985-91; fellow U.S. Dept. Justice, Washington, 1992-95; criminal justice cons., 1996—. Instr. women and crime U. Md., College Park, 1994; instr. corrections U. Ark.-Pine Bluff, 1976-79; mem. bd. visitation Jefferson County Juvenile Ct., Pine Bluff, 1978-81; bd. dirs. Vols. in Cts., 1979-83, Vols. Am., 1985-94; mem. Am./Can. study team Mex. penal system Am. Correctional Assn., Islas Marias, Mex., 1981; mem. Ark. Commn. Crimes and Law Enforcement, 1975-78; mem. U.S. Atty. Gen.'s Correctional Policy Study Team, 1987. Mem. Ark. Commn. on Status of Women, 1976-78; bd. dirs. Com. Against Spouse Abuse, 1982-83; mem. nat. adv. bd. dept. criminal justice Xavier U., Cin., 1993-97; bd. dirs. Bapt. Mission Found. of Md./Del., Columbia, Md., 1993-98. Recipient Ark, Woman of Achievement award Ark. Press Women's Assn., 1980, Human Rels. award Ark. Edn. Assn., 1980, Outstanding Woman of Achievement award Sta. KATV-TV, Little Rock, 1981, Correctional Svc. award Vols. Am., 1984, William H. Hastie award Nat. Assn. Blacks in Criminal Justice, 1986, Outstanding Victim Advocacy award Nat. Victim Ctr., 1991, Appreciation cert. Dept. Justice Office for Victims of Crime, 1994; recipient testimonial for svc. to fed. judiciary Adminstrv. Office of Cts., 1991. Mem.: NAFE, Nat. Orgn. Hispanics in Criminal Justice, Am. Soc. Criminology, Nat. Coun. on Crime and Delinquency, Ark. Law Enforcement Assn., N.Am. Assn. Wardens and Supts., Am. Correctional Assn. (treas. 1980—86, v.p. 1986—88, pres. 1990—92, mem. Del. Assembly 1993—, chmn. rsch. coun. 1997—2000, mem. past pres. coun. 1998—, chmn. Correctional awards com. 2001—05, chmn. retirees com. 2005—07, mem. pres.'s field adv. task force 2005—07, mem. ethics com. 2003—, E.R. Cass Correctional Achievement award 1993), Ark. Sheriff's Assn. (hon.), Delta Sigma Theta (local sec. 1976—79, local parliamentarian 1983). Baptist. Avocations: reading, music. Office: Am. Correctional Assn. 206 N Wash St Ste 200 Alexandria VA 22314

CORRY, ALINE LAHUSEN, art educator; d. Alfred Gustave Lahusen and Marianna Posey; m. Henry Cecil Corry, Apr. 23, 2004; children: Christa, Amy 1 stepchild, Elaine. BA, U. La., Lafayette, 1973, MEd, 1980. Tchr. secondary sch. art St. Landry Parish, Opelousas, La., 1975—85; tchr. elem. sch. art Houston Ind. Sch. Dist., 1986—88; tchr. mid. sch. art Galena Park Ind. Sch. Dist., 1988—89, 1997—98; tchr. elem. art Katy Elem. Sch. Dist., 1989—93; tchr. art Ft. Bend Ind. Sch. Dist., Sugarland, 1993—97; tchr. elem. sch. art Clear Creek Ind. Sch. Dist., League City, 1999—. Cons. Transdesigns, Atlanta, 1983—85; instr. Art Alliance Ctr., Nassau Bay, Tex., 2004—. Sponsor Youth Art Coun. Am., La., 1976—81, Gifted Talented Conv., Baton Rouge, 1981; vol. Houston Art Educators Assn., 1987. Mem.: Houston Art Educators Assn., Phi Delta Kappa. Avocations: painting, drawing, sailing. Office Phone: 281-284-6300.

CORRY, CHARLES ELMO, geophysicist, not-for-profit developer; b. Salt Lake City, May 15, 1938; s. Elmo Leigh Corry and Sylvia Birch; children: Christopher Charles, Matthew Lee. BS in Geology, Utah State U., 1970; MS in Geophysics, U. Utah, 1972; PhD in Geophysics, Tex. A&M U., 1976. Electronic missile checkout GD Convair-Astronautics, San Diego, 1960-64; rsch. assoc. Scripps Inst. Oceanography, La Jolla, Calif., 1965-68, Woods Hole (Mass.) Oceanographic Inst., 1968; mgr. geophys. rsch. AMAX, Golden, Colo., 1977-82; v.p. Nonlinear Analysis, Inc., Bryan, Tex., 1982-84; vis., adj., assoc. prof. geophysics Tex. A&M U., College Station, 1983-87; assoc. prof. geophysics U. Mo., Rolla, 1984-89; coord. world ocean circulation experiment Woods Hole Oceanographic Inst., 1990—95; database cons. Denver and Colorado Springs, 1995—2001; pres. Equal Justice Found., 2001—. Author: Laccoliths, Mechanics of Emplacement and Growth, 1988, Geology of the Solitario, Trans-Pecos Texas, 1990, Domestic Violence Against Men, 1999 (award); contbr. articles and conf. procs. to profl. jours. With USMC, 1956—59. Fellow: Geol. Soc. Am.; mem.: Soc. Exploration Geophysicists, Am. Geophys.

Union, Marine Corps League. Republican. Buddhist. Achievements include overturning of paradigm that had existed for over 150 years regarding galvanic current flow in ore bodies; discovery that ore minerals are commonly ferroelectrics and that ore bodies behave as a polarized dielectric medium, or solid plasma, in electrical surveys; development of controlled source audiomagnetotelluric method for electrical exploration; relational database design and data modeling; civil liberties, voting rights and prevention of election fraud; research in field and theoretical studies of magmatic intrusions; terrestrial heat flow studies in the North Pacific; intimate partner violence; coordination of hydrographic program of World Ocean Circulation Experiment. Home: 455 Bear Creek Rd Colorado Springs CO 80906-5820 Business E-Mail: ccorry@ejfi.org.

CORRY, DALILA BOUDJELLAL, internist, educator; b. El-Arrouch, Algeria, July 7, 1943; came to U.S., 1981; MD, U. Algiers, 1974. Diplomate in internal medicine and nephrology Am. Bd. Internal Medicine. Intern Hosp. Mustapha Algiers, 1972-73; resident Hosp. Tenon, Paris, 1975-79; fellow in nephrology UCLA, 1981-83; chief renal divsn. Olive View-UCLA Med. Ctr., Sylmar, Calif., 1983—; from asst. prof. to prof. clin. medicine UCLA, 1993, prof. clin. medicine, 2001—. Fellow Am. Heart Assn. Office: Olive View-UCLA Med Ctr Dept Medicine 2B182 14445 Olive View Dr Sylmar CA 91342-1437 Office Phone: 818-364-3205. Business E-Mail: dbcorry@ucla.edu.

CORRY, STEVE, chef; b. 1970; m. Michelle Corry. Grad., New England Culinary Inst., Vt., 1999—2001. Brewmaster San Francisco Brewing Com., Mammoth Lakes Brewing Com., Harpoon, Boston; chef Domaine Chandon, Napa, Calif.; sous chef Grissinis Restaurant; co-owner, exec. chef Five Fifty-Five, Portland, Maine, 2003—. Named one of Best New Chefs, Food and Wine Mag., 2007. Avocation: beer brewing. Office: Five Fifty-Five 555 Congress St Portland ME 04101 Office Phone: 207-761-0555.*

CORS, JEANNE MARIE, lawyer; b. Bowling Green, Ohio, Jan. 7, 1968; BA in French, Marquette U., 1989, BA in German, 1989, BA in Polit. Sci., 1989; MA in Polit. Sci., U. Mich.; JD, Georgetown U. Law Ctr., 1999. Bar: Ohio 1999. Legis. asst. Senator Herb Kohl; assoc. Taft, Stettinius & Hollister LLP, Cin., mem., Women's Resource Grp. Named one of Ohio's Rising Stars, Super Lawyers, 2005, 2006; named to Leading Lawyers list, Cincy Bus. Mag., 2006. Mem.: Ohio State Bar Assn. (mem., Bd. Governors, Antitrust Sect.). Office: Taft Stettinius & Hollister LLP 425 Walnut St Ste 1800 Cincinnati OH 45202-3957 Office Phone: 513-381-2838. Office Fax: 513-381-0205.

CORSARO, FRANK ANDREW, theater director; b. NYC, Dec. 22, 1924; s. Joseph and Marie (Quarino) C.; m. Mary Cross Bonnie Lueders, May 30, 1971; 1 child, Andrew. Grad. in Drama, Yale, 1947. Tchr. pvt. acting class for singers and actors; artistic dir. Actors' Studio and Julliard Opera Ctr., Julliard Sch. Head music drama div. opera/music theatre Inst. N.J.; trustee Nat. Opera Inst. Dir.: Broadway prodn. A Hatful of Rain, 1955-56, The Night of the Iguana, 1961-62, Treemonisha, 1975, Cold Storage, 1978, Whoopee, 1979, Knockout, 1979, It's So Good to be Civilized, 1987; off-Broadway prodn. Master Class, 1986; dir.: N.Y.C. Opera, 1958—, Washington Opera Soc., 1970-74, St. Paul Opera, 1971, Houston Grand Opera, 1973-77, assoc. artistic dir., 1977—, Glyndebourne Festival, 1982-85, Deutsches Opera, Berlin, 1983, Chgo. Lyric Opera, 1984, 96, Covent Garden, 1984, Met. Opera, 1984, Spitalfields Festival, London, 1985, Den Norske Opera, Oslo, 1985, Australian Opera, 1986; appeared in: Broadway prodn. Mrs. McThing, 1951; film Rachel, Rachel, 1967; author: adaptation L'Histoire du Soldat, 1974, Memoir Maverik, 1978, Love for Three Oranges Glyndebourne Version, 1985, (novel) Kunma, 2003, (libretto) Frau Margot, 2007; dir. (double bill) Where the Wild Things Are, Higgeldy Piggelby Pop, 1985, Los Angeles Opera, 1986, Amsterdam Netherlanders Opera, 1986, Montreal Opera, 1986 Ravel: L'enfant et les Sortileges, L'heure Espagnol, Glyndebourne Festival, 1987, Hansel and Gretel, Houston Can. Opera Co., Rigoletto, 2001, Traviata, 2003; (libretto) Heloise and Abelard. Mem. Dirs. Guild Am., Soc. Stage Dirs., Choreographers, Am. Guild Mus. Artists. Home: 33 Riverside Dr New York NY 10023-8012 Office Phone: 212-799-5000 ext 261.

CORSIGLIA, ROBERT JOSEPH, retired electrical construction company executive; b. Chgo., Jan. 22, 1935; s. John Robert and Marie Virgina Corsiglia; m. Patricia Ann Ryan, Jan. 26, 1960 (div. Jan. 1984); children: Nancee, Thomas, Karen; m. Emilie Clementz, Sept. 10, 1989. BSEE, Ill. Inst. Tech., Chgo., 1963. Registered profl. engr., Ill., Ind., Calif., Tex., Fla. CEO, pres. Hyre Electric Co. Ind., Highland, 1970-90, JWP/Hyre Electric Co. Ind., Highland, 1990—2004; CEO Midwestern region JWP Mech./Elec. Svcs. Inc., Oak Brook, Ill., 1991-93; chmn. C & H Engring. Co., Inc., Highland, 1984-90; sec.-treas. Adventures in Travel, Highland, 1984-95; ret., 2004. Bd. dirs. Bank One, Highland. Bd. dirs. No. Ind. Arts Assn., Munster, 1989-93, v.p. devel., 1990; bd. dirs. N.W. Ind. United Way, Highland, 1985, Chgo. Engring. Found., 1991-97; bd. dirs. IIT Alumni Bd., Chgo., 1985, v.p. adminstrn., 1986; mem. IIT Pres.' Coun., 1985—; mem. Legacy Found. Inc. Lake County, Griffith, Ind., 1993—; mem. exec. bd. Boy Scouts of Am. Calumet Coun., 1993—; pres. Nat. Elec. Contractors Assn., 1975, 76, 77. Served with U.S. Army, 1964-70. Mem. Internat. Brotherhood of Elec. Workers (hon.), Chgo. Pres. Orgn., Young Pres. Orgn., World Pres. Orgn., Union League Club. Republican. Roman Catholic. Avocations: collecting, golf. Home: 8701 Northcote Ave Munster IN 46321-2726 Home Phone: 219-923-6077; Office Phone: 219-923-6100. Personal E-mail: rjcorsig@sbcglobal.net.

CORSO, FRANK MITCHELL, lawyer; b. NYC, July 28, 1928; s. Joseph and Jane (DeBenedetto) C.; m. Dorothy G. McVeety, Apr. 7, 1951; chldren: Frank, Elaine, Patricia, Dorothy LLB, St. John's U., 1952. Bar: N.Y. 1954, D.C. 1981, U.S. Ct. Mil. Appeals 1954, U.S. Supreme Ct. 1960. Ptnr. Corso & Fertig, 1957—61, Corso & Petito, 1966—69, Corso & Landa, Jericho, NY, 1971—73, Corso & Engelberg, 1973—82; sr. ptnr. Frank Mitchell Corso, P.C., Westbury, NY, 1982—. Bd. dirs. UN Devel. Corp. by N.Y. Gov., N.Y. Mcpl. Bond Bank Agy.; lectr. St. John's U. Sch. of Law; candidate U.S. Congress, N.Y.; trustee WLIW Pub. TV channel Contbr. articles to legal jours.; TV commentator legal topics With U.S. Army, 1951-53 Decorated Knight of Holy Sepulchre (Vatican City); named Man of Yr. Am.-Italians of L.I., 1966 Mem. ABA, ATLA, N.Y. State Bar Assn., Nassau Bar Assn., Internat. Bar Assn., World Assn. Lawyers (founder) Home: 1 Southdown Ct Huntington NY 11743-2548 Office: 350 Jericho Tpke Jericho NY 11753-1317 Office Phone: 516-333-9500. Personal E-mail: fmc28@aol.com.

CORSO, JOHN ANTHONY, management consultant, educator; s. Vero R. and Rita Jane Corso; m. Maria Lourdes Cano, Sept. 8, 1990; children: Sara Susan children: Mary Bridget, Bernadette Jane. BS, U. Md., 1980; MS in Adminstrn., Ctrl. Mich. U., 1991; MPA, DPA, U. So. Calif., LA, 2001. Cert. charter cert. Myers-Briggs type indicator profl. Consulting Psychologists Press, 2001, profl. contracts mgr. Nat. Contract Mgmt. Assn., 1995. Mgmt. cons. Booz, Allen, & Hamilton, McLean, Va., 1992—92; contract specialist U.S. Dept. Vet. Affairs, Washington, 1992—97, sr. procurement analyst, 1997—99, mgmt. and program analyst, 1999—2004, mgr. program Mgmt. Analysis Bus. Process Reengring., 2004—. Program dir., adj. prof. Georgetown U. Ctr. for Profl. Devel., Washington, 2001—. Contbr. articles to profl. jours. Extraordinary min. holy communion St. Raphael's Cath. Parish, Rockville, Md., 1996—2002. Lt. USN, 1983—92, Various, ret. comdr. USNR, 2002. Decorated Navy Expeditionary Medal USN, Navy Commendation Medal. Mem.: ASPA, Leadership VA Alumni Assn., Soc. Cath. Social Scientists, Secular Franciscan Order, KC (outside guard 1976—76). Roman Catholic. Home: 12601 Orchard Brook Terr Potomac MD 20854 Office: US Dept Vets Affairs 810 Vermont Ave NW Washington DC 20420 Personal E-mail: corsojohn@aol.com.

CORSO, LEE, former football coach, football analyst; b. Jan. 22, 1944; BA in Phys. Edn., Fla. State U., 1957, M in Adminstrn. and Supervision, 1958. Coach U. Louisville, 1969-72, India. U., 1973-83, No. Ill. U., 1984-85, Orlando Renegades, 1985; gen. mgr. Orlando Thunder, 1991; analyst Coll. Football Assn. telecasts ESPN and ABC, 1987-88, football analyst, studio analyst Coll. GameDay, 1987—. Office: care ESPN 935 Middle St # 2 Bristol CT 06010-1001

CORSON, THOMAS HAROLD, retired manufacturing executive; b. Elkhart, Ind., Oct. 15, 1927; s. Carl W. and Charlotte (Keyser) C.; m. Dorthy Claire Scheide, July 11, 1948; children: Benjamin Thomas, Claire Elaine. Student, Purdue U., 1945-46, Rennsselaer Poly. Inst., 1946-47, So. Meth. U., 1948-49. Chmn. bd. dirs. Coachmen Industries, Inc., Elkhart, 1965-97, chmn. emeritus, dir., 1997—2005, ret., 2005. Bd. dirs. R.C.R. Sci. Inc., Goshen, Ind., Micrology Labs., Inc., Goshen, Elkhart County Econ. Devel. Corp., Elkhart, Ind.; chmn., sec. Greenfield Corp., Middlebury. Adv. coun. U. Notre Dame; past trustee Ball State U.; dir., past trustee, past vice chmn. Interlochen Arts Acad. and Nat. Music Camp., Mich. With US Naval Air Force, 1945-47. Mem. Ind. Mfrs. Assn. (past dir.), Elkhart C. of C. (past bd. dirs.), Ind. C. of C. (past bd. dirs.), Ind. Hist. Soc. (past dir.), Royal Poinciana Golf Club, Elcona Club (past bd. dirs.), 33 Degrees, Mason, Shriners. Methodist. Home and Office: PO Box 340 Middlebury IN 46540-0340

CORT, JULIA, television director, television producer, scriptwriter; Prodr., writer, dir. WGBH Ednl. Found., Boston. Prodr.: Horizon, 2003, (also writer): Elegant Universe, 2003, NOVA, 2001—. Recipient AAAS Sci. Journalism award, 1998, 2001, 2006. Office: WGBH Ednl Found 125 Western Ave Allston MA 02134

CORTES, ENRIC, marine biologist; b. Barcelona, Aug. 2, 1958; arrived in U.S., 1991; s. Enrique Cortes and Consuelo Perez; m. Kristen Edwards, Mar. 2, 1991; 1 child, Ariane. BSc, U. Barcelona, 1981; MSc, U. Miami, 1987; PhD, U. Barcelona, 1991. Post-doctoral rschr. Mote Marine Lab., Sarasota, Fla., 1992—97; rsch. assoc. Fla. State U., Panama City, Fla., 1997—98; rsch. fishery biologist Nat. Oceanographic and Atmospheric Adminstrn., Nat. Marine Fisheries Svc., Panama City, 1998—. Spanish astronaut candidate European Space Agy., Ministry Industry and Energy; cons. in field; presenter in field; shark specialist Internat. Union for the Conservation of Nature, 1998—. Co-author 4 book chpts.; contbr. over 50 articles to profl. jours. Recipient Employee of Yr. award, Nat. Marine Fisheries Svc., 2002; fellow, Ministry Edn. and Sci., Spain, 1992—94, Govt. Catalonia, Spain, 1994—95; scholar, Fulbright-La Caixa, 1984—86, U.S. Joint Com. for Cultural and Ednl. Cooperation, 1986—87; Reitmeister fellowship, U. Miami, 1986. Mem.: Fisheries Soc. Brit. Isles, Deutsche Elasmobranchier Gesellschaft, Soc. Brasileira Estudio de Elasmobranquios, Ecol. Soc. Am., Soc. Conservation Biology, Am. Fisheries Soc., Am. Elasmobranch Soc. (bd. dirs. 1996—2005). Office: NOAA NMFS 3500 Delwood Beach Road Panama City FL 32408 Office Phone: 850-234-6541.

CORTÈS, LUIS, religious organization administrator; b. 1958; m. Damaris Flores-Cortés; 2 children. BA Sociology, City Coll. of New York; MDiv, Union Theological Seminary; MS Econ. Devel., New Hampshire Coll. Vice-chmn. Federal Home Loan Bank Board of Pittsburgh; founder, exec. dir. Hispanic Clergy of Philadelphia; pres., CEO Esperanza USA. Author: (novels) Repare su crédito ahora (How to Fix Your Credit) (Serie Esperanza), 2006, There Is an Answer: How to Prevent and Understand HIV/AIDS (Esperanza), 2006, How to Buy a Home, 2006. Mem. Pennsylvania Minority Business Devel. Authority, Workforce Investment Bd. Named one of 25 Most Influential Evangelicals in Am., Time mag., 2005. Baptist. Achievements include being one of the founders of United Bank, the first African-American owned commercial bank in Pennsylvania. Office: Esperanza USA 4261 North 5th St Philadelphia PA 19140 Office Phone: 215-324-0746. Office Fax: 215-324-2542.*

CORTÉS, PEDRO A., state official; b. 1966; m. Lissette Lizardi-Cortés; 1 child, Gabriela Paola. BS in Hotel, Restaurant and Travel Adminstrn., U. Mass.; M in Pub. Adminstrn., Pa. State U.; JD, Dickinson Sch. Law. Cert. in Pub. Sector Human Resources Mgmt. Penn State Univ. Exec. dir. PA Govs. Adv. Commn. on Latino Affairs; served with PA State Civil Service Commn., PA Dept. of Pub. Welfare; sec. commonwealth Commonwealth of Pa., Harrisburg, 2003—. Actively involved Latino Luncheon, Inter-Agency Taskforce on Civil Tension, PA Commn. on Crime and Delinquency's Disproportionate Minority Confinement Subcommittee, PA Minority Bus. Devel. Authority, PA Small Bus. Coalition, PA Statewide Latino Coalition, PA Supreme Ct. Com. on Racial and Gender Bias in the Judicial Sys. and State Sys. of Higher Education's Diversity Plan, Neighborhood Dispute Settlement, Coun. for Utility Choice, Kutztown Univ. Small Bus. Devel. Ctr. Democrat. Office: Office of Sec of Commonwealth 302 N Capitol Bldg Harrisburg PA 17120 Office Phone: 717-787-8727. Office Fax: 717-787-1734.*

CORTESE, ALFRED WILLIAM, JR., lawyer, consultant; b. Phila., Apr. 2, 1937; s. Alfred William and Marie Ann (Coccio) C.; m. Rosanna S. Zimmerman, Aug. 18, 1962 (div. Aug. 1981); children: Aline Elizabeth, Alfred William III, Christina Nicole; m. Diana P. Nowezki, May 16, 2003. BA cum laude, Temple U., 1959; JD, U. Pa., 1962. Bar: Pa. 1963, U.S. Supreme Ct. 1972, D.C. 1977. Assoc., ptnr. Pepper, Hamilton & Scheetz, Phila., 1962-71; asst. exec. dir. FTC, Washington, 1972-73; assoc. Dechert, Price & Rhoads, Phila., 1974-76; ptnr. Clifford & Warnke, Washington, 1977-81; chmn., CEO Cortese & Loughran Inc., Washington, 1982-84; ptnr. Kirkland & Ellis, Washington, 1985-94, Pepper Hamilton, LLP, Washington, 1994-98; mng. mem. Cortese PLLC, Washington, 1999—. Cons. Gen. Motors Corp., Detroit, 1985—2003. Lt. U.S. Army, 1959-60. Mem.: Pa. Bar Assn., Lawyers for Civil Justice, D.C. Bar Assn., Am. Law Inst. Avocations: vintage automobile racing and restoration, art & antique collecting, cooking. Office: 113 3rd St NE Washington DC 20002-7313 Business E-Mail: awc@corteseplic.com.

CORTESE, DENIS A., healthcare executive, medical educator; b. Phila., Feb. 27, 1944; MD, Temple U., 1970. Cert. Nat. Bd. Med. Examiners, diplomate Am. Bd. Internal Medicine, in pulmonary disease Am. Bd. Internal Medicine, cert. Am. Bd. Laser Surgery. Intern Mayo Clinic, Rochester, Minn., 1970—71; resident in internal medicine Mayo Grad. Sch. Medicine, Mayo Clinic, Rochester, 1970—72, resident in thoracic medicine, 1972—74; fellow in thoracic diseases and bronchoscopy Mayo Clinic, 1976, pulmonary medicine specialist, 1976; prof. medicine Mayo Med. Sch.; pres., CEO Mayo Clinic, Rochester, 2003—. Mem. Ctr. Corp. Innovation. Bd. trustees Healthcare Leadership Coun.; mem. Harvard/Kennedy Sch. Healthcare Policy Group; bd. govs. Mayo Clinic, Rochester, 1987—92, trustee, 1990—94, 1997—, chair bd. govs. Jacksonville, 1999—2002; bd. dirs. St. Luke's Hosp., Jacksonville, 1999—2002, chair exec. com., 2002. Fellow: Royal Coll. Physicians London; mem.: Inst. Medicine. Office: Mayo Clinic 200 1st St SW Rochester MN 55905 Office Phone: 507-284-2663.

CORTESE, EDWARD, marketing and public relations executive; BS in English and Journalism, Fordham U., 1949. Tchr. English Tulane U.; mktg., advt. exec. Loew's-MGM; sr. v.p. mktg. Levitt and Sons; sr. v.p. mktg. and pub. rels. Lefrak Orgn Inc, NYC. With USN, 1950—54. Office: Lefrak Orgn Inc 40 West 57th St New York NY 10019

CORTESE, RICHARD ANTHONY, computer company executive; b. New London, Conn., Dec. 4, 1942; s. Anthony John and Winifred Silvia (Beebe) Cortese; m. Cindy Sue Folsom, Feb. 9, 1983; children: Cynthia Ann, Jennifer Lynn; m. Susan Louise Turner, Feb. 13, 1965 (div. 1973). BS, U. So. Calif., 1965, MBA, 1967. Fin. dir. Nat. Semiconductor Corp., Santa Clara, Calif., 1973-78; fin. control dir. TRW Corp., LA, 1978-79; v.p. fin. No. Telecom Sys. Corp., Minn. and Calif., 1979-80; v.p., gen. mgr. Gen. Automation Inc., Anaheim, Calif., 1980-82; pres., CEO Alpha Microsystems, Santa Ana, Calif., 1982-87, also bd. dirs.; pres., CEO Hugin Sweda, Pine Brook, NJ, 1987-89; pres., CEO, vice-chmn. BOD, 1990-96; pres., CEO Racotek, Burnsville, Minn., 1990-96; pres. RMB Assocs., Durango, Colo., 1996—. Active Young Pres.'s Orgn., N.J. Named All-Am. in track and field NCAA, 1964, All-Am. in track and field AAU, 1964. Mem. Computer Communication Industry Assn. (mem. exec. com. 1983—), SoCal 10 (founding mem., bd. dirs. 1983—). Clubs: Chancellor's. Avocation: reading.

CORTÉS-VÁZQUEZ, LORRAINE, state official; b. Oct. 18, 1950; m. Louis M. Vázquez; 1 child, Michael. BA, Hunter Coll., 1975; MA, Robert F. Wagner Grad. Sch. Pub. Svc., NYU, 1983. Dir. Sr. Citizen Peer Counseling Program Experimental & Bilingual Inst., 1976—77; dir. Bur. Program & Resource Devel. NYC Dept. Aging, 1979—92; exec. dir. ASPIRA, 1992—96; chief of staff to Assemblyman Roberto Ramirez NY State Assembly, 1996—98; pres. Hispanic Fedn., 1998—2004; v.p. govt. & pub. affairs Cablevision Systems Corp., 2004—06; sec. state State of NY, Albany, 2007—. Mem. NY State Bd. Regents, 2001—07. Office: Office Sec State 41 State St Albany NY 12231*

CORTEZ, RICARDO LEE, investment management executive; b. NYC, Mar. 9, 1950; s. Eddie Adam and Marian Ruth (Lee) C.; children: Vanessa, Natalie, Rebecca; m. Harriet Anne Howard, Jan. 16, 1993. BA cum laude, CUNY, 1971; postgrad., Columbia U., 1971—73. Sr. stock market analyst Merrill Lynch, NYC, 1971-76; exec. v.p. Trident Investment-Grace Capital, NYC, 1976-78; pres. Liberty Capital Mgmt., NYC, 1978-84, Cortez Capital Mgmt., NYC, 1984-89; v.p., dir. fixed income Summit (NJ) Trust Co., 1985-86; 1st v.p., dir. programs and comm. Prudential Securities, NYC, 1989-96, nat. sales dir. investment mgmt. svcs., 1996—; No. divsn. dir. Prudential Investments, 1998—, nat. dir. investment mgmt. svcs. divsn.; v.p. global multi-mgr. strategies, mgr. Goldman Sachs, NYC, 2000, program mgr., v.p., 2000—01; pres. pvt. client group Torrey Assocs., NYC, 2001—. Lectr. stock market analysis NY Inst. Fin., NYC, 1973—75; bd. advisors Investment Mgmt. Cons. Assn., 1998—; guest lectr. Harvard U., 2004—, U. Pa., 2004—, U. Calif., Berkeley, 2006—. Author: (with Edson Gould) Industry and Stock Forecast, 1976. Named Spkr. of Yr., Mcpl. Treas.'s Assn. Calif., 1981. Office: Torrey Assocs 505 Park Ave New York NY 10022 Office Phone: 212-644-7800. Business E-Mail: rcortez@thetorreyfunds.com.

CORTINA, BETTY, magazine editor; BJ, U. Fla., 1992. City hall reporter Miami Herald; LA staff corr. People Weekly, 1995—96; assoc. editor People En Espanol, 1996—99; sr. writer Entertainment Weekly, 1999; founding news editor O, the Oprah mag., 1999—2001; editl. dir. Latina mag., 2001—. Adv. coun. Journalism Dept., U. Fla. Mem.: Am. Soc. Mag. Editors (bd. dirs. 2007—). Office: Latina Mag 1500 Broadway Ste 700 New York NY 10036 E-mail: betty@latina.com.

CORTNER, HANNA JOAN, retired political scientist, researcher; b. Tacoma, Wash., May 9, 1945; d. Val and E. Irene Otteson; m. Richard Carroll Cortner, Nov. 14, 1970. BA in Polit. Sci. magna cum laude with distinction, U. Wash., 1967; MA in Govt., U. Ariz., 1969, PhD in Govt., 1973. Grad. tchg. and rsch. asst. dept. govt. U. Ariz., Tucson, 1967-70, rsch. assoc. Inst. Govt. Rsch., 1974-76, rsch. assoc. forest-watershed and landscape resources divsns. Sch. Renewable Natural Resources, 1975-82, adj. assoc. prof. Sch. Renewable Natural Resources, 1983-89; exec. asst. Pima County Bd. Suprs., 1985-86; adj. assoc. prof. renewable natural resources, assoc. rsch. scientist Water Resources Rsch. Ctr. U. Ariz., Tucson, 1988-89, prof., rsch. scientist Water Resources Rsch. Ctr., 1989-90, prof., rsch. scientist, dir. Water Resources Rsch. Ctr., 1990-96, prof., rsch. scientist Sch. Renewable Resources, 1997-2000; rsch. prof., assoc. dir. Ecol. Restoration Inst. No. Ariz. U., Flagstaff, 2001—04; ret. Program analyst USDA Forest Svc., Washington, 1979-80; vis. scholar Inst. Water Resources, Corps of Engrs., Ft. Belvoir, Va., 1986-87; com. arid lands AAAS, 1986-89; com. natural disasters NAS/NRC, 1988-91, com. on planning and remediation of irrigation-induced water quality impacts, 1994-95; rev. com. nat. forest planning Conservation Found., Washington, 1987-90; chair adv. com. renewable resources planning techs. for pub. lands Office of Tech. Assessment U.S. Congress, 1989-91; policy coun. Pinchot Inst. Conservation Studies, 1991-93, bd. dirs. 2005-; co-chair working party on evaluation of forest policies Internat. Union Forestry Rsch. Orgns., 1990-95, chair working party on forest instns. and forestry adminstrn., 1996; vice-chair Man and the Biosphere Program, Temperate Directorate, US Dept. State, 1991-96; cmtys. com. steering com., Am. Forest Congress, 1996-2004, rsch. com., 1996-97; sci. adv. com. Consortium for Environ. Risk Evaluation, 1996-97; cons. Greeley and Hansen, Cons. Engrs., US Army Corps Engrs., Ft. Belvoir, US Forest Svc., Washington, Portland, Oreg., Ogden, Utah. Assoc. editor Society and Natural Resources, 1992-94; book reviewer We. Polit. Sci. Quar., Am. Polit. Quar., Perspectives, Natural Resources Jour., Climatic Change, Society and Natural Resources, Jour. of Forestry, Environment; mem. editl. bd. Jour. Forest Planning, 1995—, Forest Policy and Econs., 1999-2002; co-author: The Politics of Ecosystem Management, 1999, George W. Bush's Healthy Forests, 2005; co-editor: The State and Nature, 2002; contbr. articles to profl. jours. Bd. dirs. Planned Parenthood So. Ariz., 1992-94, planning com., 1992, bd. devel. and evaluation com., 1994; bd. dirs. N.W. Homeowners Assn., 1982-83, v.p., 1983-84, pres., 1984; vice chmn., chmn. Pima County Bd. Adjustment Dist. 3, 1984; active Tucson Tomorrow, 1984-88; water quality subcom. Pima Assn. Govts., 1983-84, environ. planning adv. com., 1989-90, chmn., 1984, mem. Avra Valley task force, 1988-90; bd. dirs. So. Ariz. Water Resources Assn., 1984-86, 87-95, sec., 1987-89, mem. com. alignment and terminal storage, 1990-94, CAP com., 1988-92, chair, 1989-90, basinwide mgmt. com., 1983-86, chair, 1992-93; active Ariz. Interagy. Task Force on Fire and the Urban/Wildland Interface, 1990-92; wastewater mgmt. adv. com. Pima County, 1988-92, subcom. on effluent reuse Joint CWAC-WWAC, 1989-91, citizens water adv. com. Water Resources Plan Update Subcom., 1990-91; bd. dirs. Ctrl. Ariz. Water Conservation Dist., 1985-90, fin. com., 1987-88, spl. studies com., 1987-88, nominating com., 1987; mem. Colo. River Salinity Control, 1989-90; chair adv. com. Tucson Long Range Master Water Plan, 1988-89; water adv. com. City of Tucson, 1984. Travel grantee NSF/Soc. Am. Foresters; Rsch. grantee US Geol. Survey, US Army Corps of Engrs., USDA Forest Svc., Soil Conservation Svc., Utah State U., Four Corners Regional Commn., Office of Water Rsch. & Tech.; Sci. & Engring. fellow AAAS, 1986-87; recipient Copper Letter Appreciation cert. City of Tucson, 1985, 89, SAWARA award, 1989. Mem. Am. Water Resources Assn. (nat. award com. 1987-90, statues and bylaws com. 1989-90, tech. co-chair ann. meeting 1993), Am. Forests Assn. (forest policy ctr. adv. coun. 1991-95), Soc. Am. Foresters (task force on sustaining long-term forest health and productivity 1991-92, com. on forest policy 1994-96, sci. and tech. bd. 2001-04), Am. Polit. Sci. Assn., Western Polit. Sci. Assn. (com. on constrn. and bylaws 1976-80, chair 1977-79, exec. coun. 1980-83, com. on profl. devel. 1984-85, com. on status of women 1984-85), Nat. Fire Protection Assn. (tech. com. on forest and rural fire protection 1990-94), Phi Beta Kappa. Democrat. Achievements include research in political and socio-economic aspects of natural resources policy, administration, and planning, water resources management, ecosystem management, wildland fire policy and management. Home: 6064 E Mountain Oaks Flagstaff AZ 86004-7222 Personal E-mail: hannacortner@aol.com.

CORTRIGHT, BARBARA JEAN, public relations executive, writer; b. Oxford, Miss., Dec. 29, 1927; d. Lewis Stephen and Lucile (Chevalier) Grandy; m. Lem R. Cortright, Aug. 19, 1946 (dec. Oct. 2002); children: Lewis Stephen, Clyde Kenneth, Eric Allen, Barbara Edith. BFA with honors, Ariz. State U., 1949, MA in Humanities, 1977, MA in German Lang., 1979; PhD in Art History, U. N.Mex., Albuquerque, 1993. Instr. in art history Scottsdale (Ariz.) Coll., 1974-78; newsletter editor Heard Mus., Phoenix, 1978-79; lectr. in non-fiction Ariz. State U., Tempe, 1979-80; publicist O.K. Harris West Gallery, Scottsdale, 1981-84. Author: The Reach of Solitude, 1984; contbr. articles to profl. jours. NEA fellow, 1976. Mem. Phi Kappa Phi, Alpha Mu Gamma. Democrat. Episcopalian. Home: 516 E Erie Dr Tempe AZ 85282-3713 Personal E-mail: GreenPer@aol.com.

CORTS, PAUL RICHARD, educational association and former federal agency administrator; b. Terre Haute, Ind., Sept. 15, 1943; s. Charles H. and Hazel Corts; m. Diane Stevens, May 29, 1965; children: Kenneth Stevens, Daniel Paul, Susan Diane. BA, Georgetown Coll., 1965; MA, Ind. U., 1967, PhD, 1971. Assoc. prof. speech communication Western Ky. U., Bowling Green, 1968-78, dir. internat. edn., 1973-76, dir. univ. honors program, 1972-78, asst. dean for instrn., 1973-78, assoc. v.p. for instrn., 1978; exec. v.p., chief adminstrv. officer Okla. Bapt. U., Shawnee, 1978-83; pres. The Corts Co., Shawnee, 1983, Wingate (N.C.) Coll., 1983-91, Palm Beach Atlantic U., West Palm Beach, Fla., 1991—2002; asst. atty. gen. justice mgmt. divsn. Dept. Justice, 2002—06; pres. Coun. Christian Colleges & Universities, Washington, 2006—. Cons. bd. govs. U. N.C., Chapel Hill, 1987-88; mem. president's mgmt. coun., coun. chief fin. officers, enduring constl. govt. coordinating coun., exec. bd. internat. cooperative adminstrv. support svcs. Dept. of State, strategic mgmt. coun., sr. exec. rev. bd.; bd. dirs. Fed. Prisons Industries; designated agency ethics ofcl., chief procurement officer, chmn. exec. coun. justice prisoner and alien transp. sys. Co-author: Fundamentals of Effective Group Communication, 1979, Let's Talk Business, 1983. Pres. coun. pres.' Carolinas Intercollegiate Athletic Conf., 1986-88; mem. edn. com. Bapt. World Alliance, McLean, Va., 1990—; bd. dirs. United Way Cen. Carolinas, Monore and Charlotte, 1984-91. Mem. Am. Assn. Pres. Ind. Colls. and Univs. (bd. dirs., pres. 2000-01), Charlotte Area Ednl. Consortium (pres. 1987-88), Am. Coun. Edn., Ind. Colls. and Univs. Fla. (chmn. 2000—), Williamsburg Pres. Colloquy (chmn. 1990), Palm Beach Lit. Soc. (pres. 1992-2000), Coun. Christian Colls. and Univs. (bd. dirs. 1999—, pres. 2006-), Fla. Coun. 100, Gov.'s Club (bd. dirs. 2000-), Good Samaritan Med. Ctr. (gov. bd. 2002-), Rotary. Office: Coun Christian Colls & Univs 321 8th St NE Washington DC 20002 Office Phone: 202-546-8713 ext. 320. Office Fax: 202-548-5205. E-mail: pcorts@cccu.org.*

CORTS, THOMAS EDWARD, academic administrator; b. Terre Haute, Ind., Oct. 7, 1941; s. Charles Harold and Hazel Louise (Vernon) C.; m. Marla Ruth Haas, Feb. 15, 1964; children: Jennifer Ruth Corts Fuller, Rachel Anne Corts Wachter, Christian Haas BA, Georgetown Coll., Ky., 1963; MA, Ind. U., 1968, PhD, 1972; DLitt (hon.), Georgetown Coll., Ky., 1991; DHL (hon.), Campbell U., 1995, U. Ala., 2002; DD (hon.), Judson Coll., 2006. Asst. to pres. Georgetown Coll., 1963-64, 67-69, asst. prof., 1967-69, exec. dean, 1969-73, exec. v.p. Ky., 1973; coord. Higher Edn. Consortium, Lexington, Ky., 1973-74; pres. Wingate Coll., NC, 1974-83, Samford U., Birmingham, Ala., 1983—2006, pres. emeritus, 2006—; interim chancellor Ala. Coll. Sys., Ala. Dept. Postsecondary Edn., 2006—. Bd. dirs. Samford U. Found., 1990—2006, Found. Ind. Higher Edn., 1988-92; chmn. Ala. Commn. on Sch. Performance and Accountability, 1993-94. Contbr. articles to profl. jours. Bd. dirs. Birmingham chpt. ARC, 1983-89, Ala. Citizens for Constl. Reform, 2000-05; mem. adv. bd. Salvation Army, 1987-97; mem. exec. coun. Boy Scouts Am., Birmingham, 1984-2005; bd. dirs. Leadership Birmingham, 1984-95; mem. exec. com. Birmingham Better Bus. Bur., 1996—2006, Birmingham Summerfest, 1984-95, Birmingham Area Consortium on Higher Edn., Ala. Poverty Project, Inc.; mem. gen. coun. Baptist World Alliance, 1996-; mem. Pub. Affairs Rsch. Coun. Ala. Recipient Outstanding Alumnus award Georgetown Coll., 1987, Jefferson award Downtown Action Com., Birmingham, 1988, Outstanding Educator award Ala. Assn. Coll. and Univs.-Ala. Assn. Women, Birmingham, 1989, Good Shepherd award Assn. Bapt. for Scouting, 1990, Citizen of Yr., 1990, Most Supportive Pres. award Am. Assn. Colls. for Tchr. Edn., 1991, Charles D. Johnson Disting. Sc. award Internat. Assn. Bapt. Colls. and Univs., 2006; named to Birmingham Bus. Hall of Fame, 2005, U. Ala. Comms. Hall of Fame, 2005. Mem. Am. Assn. Pres. of Ind. Colls. and Univs. (v.p. 1990-92, pres. 1992-95, bd. dirs. 1989-2002, 04-06), Coun. for Advancement of Pvt. Colls. in Ala. (past pres.), Ala. Assn. Ind. Colls., Nat. Fellowship Bapt. Educators (pres. 1988-89), Assn. So. Bapt. Colls. and Schs. (v.p. 1988-89, pres. 1990-91, bd. dirs. 2004-), So. Assn. Colls. and Schs. (trustee 1991-98, mem. commn. on colls., vice chmn. 1991, chmn. exec. coun. 1992-94, pres. 1996, Disting. Leadership award 2001), Coun. Higher Edn. Accreditation (bd. dirs. 1995-97), Assn. Governing Bds. (pres.'s commn., chmn. 2003-04), Birmingham Area C. of C. (bd. dirs. 2000-04), Ala. Acad. Honor. Democrat.

CORTY, ANDREW P., publishing executive; b. Wilmington, Del., June 16, 1952; s. Claude and Susanne Corty; m. Betty L. Wallace, Apr. 30, 1983; children: Robert Wallace, Edward Wallace. AB, Harvard U., 1974; MBA, Stanford U., 1978. Copy editor The Morning News, Wilmington, 1974—75; reporter The Record, Havre de Grace, Md., 1975—76; asst. to pub. The St. Petersburg (Fla.) Times, 1978—80; pub. Fla. Trend mag., St. Petersburg, 1981—85; gen. mgr. Washington Post mag., 1985—89; mktg. dir. St. Petersburg Times, 1989—91; v.p., sec., bd. dirs. Times Pub. Co., St. Petersburg, 1991—; vice chmn. Congrl. Quar., Inc., Washington, 1991—; pres. Fla. Trend, St. Petersburg, 1991—. Trustee Salvador Dali Mus., St. Petersburg, Fla. Office: St Petersburg Times PO Box 1121 Saint Petersburg FL 33731-1121

CORUN, RONALD LEWIS, asphalt refining executive; b. Balt., Nov. 17, 1952; s. John Grebe and Cleo Hazel (Cornwell) C.; m. Mary Ann Hack, July 9, 1977; children: Mary Frances, Ronald Lewis. BSCE, U. Md., 1974. V.p., gen. mgr. Corun & Gatch, Inc., Fallston, Md., 1965—94; v.p. T.C. Simons, Inc., Fallston, 1994—96; mgr. tech. support Citgo Asphalt Refining Co., Blue Bell, Pa., 1997—; pres. RLC Cons., Inc., Fallston, 1997—. Mem. Harford County Environ. Adv. Bd., Bel Air, Md., 1982-95. Recipient Sheldon G. Hayes award Nat. Asphalt Pavement Assn., 1994. Mem. Assn. Asphalt Paving Techs. Republican. Lutheran. Avocations: golf, skiing, fishing. Office: Citgo Asphalt PO Box 3220 Ocean City MD 21843 Office Phone: 410-952-4020. Personal E-mail: roncorun@msn.com. E-mail: rcorun@citgo.com.

CORVINO, BETH BYSTER, lawyer; b. Dec. 8, 1956; m. John Corvino. BA, Ind. U.; JD with honors, DePaul U. Assoc. Katten Muchin Zavis Rosenman, 1982—83; various positions Am. Hosp. Supply Corp., Staley Continental Inc., 1983—89; asst. gen. counsel Whitman Corp., 1989—92; with Gen. Instrument Corp., 1992—98; v.p., gen. counsel, corp. sec. Chas. Levy LLC, 1998—2004; exec. v.p., gen. counsel, corp. sec. Laidlaw Internat. Inc., 2004—. Office: Laidlaw Internat Inc 55 Shuman Blvd Ste 400 Naperville IL 60563 Office Fax: 630-848-3167. Business E-Mail: bcorvino@laidlaw.com.

CORWELL, ANN ELIZABETH, public relations executive; b. Battle Creek, Mich. d. James Albert Corwell and Marion Elizabeth (Petersen) Shertzer. BA, Mich. State U., 1971, MBA, 1981; cert. fin., Wharton Sch., 1986. Sr. publicist City of Dearborn, Mich., 1972-76; sr. assoc. GM, Detroit, 1976-77, media coord. NYC, 1977, mgr. cmty. rels. Pontiac, Mich., 1977-81, mgr. internal comm., 1981-82; dir. pub. rels. Pillsbury Co., Mpls., 1982-85, Avon Products Inc., NYC, 1985-87; exec. v.p. MECA Internat., Flat Rock, Mich., 1987-95; v.p. coll. rels. William Tyndale Coll., Farmington Hills, Mich., 1995—. Dir. Mich. State U. Nat. Alumni Bd. Mem. Pub. Rels. Soc. Am., Women In Comm., Oakland County C. of C. (dir. 1988-91), Dearborn C. of C. (dir. 1989-91). E-mail: acorwell@williamtyndale.edu.

CORWIN, BERT CLARK, optometrist; b. Rapid City, SD, Oct. 4, 1930; s. Meade and Adeline (Clark) C.; m. Lydia M. Forehand; children: B. Clark II, Kelley Linette Fromm. AS, S.D. State U., 1952; BS, Ill. Coll. Optometry, Chgo., 1956, OD, 1957. Pvt. practice, Rapid City, 1957—. Projects chmn. S.D. Lions Sight and Svc. Found., 1964; chmn. med. adv. com. to S.D. Dept. Pub. Welfare, 1968-76; mem. S.D. Adv. Coun. for Regional Med. and Health Planning, 1971; cons. S.D. Dept. Human Svcs., 1989—; adv. bd. S.D. Dept. of Svc. to Visual Impaired; bd. dirs. Super 8 Motel Developers, Rapid City Regional Airport, v.p., 1999-2000, pres., 2000—; chmn. bd. dirs. Transaction Network, Inc., 1997—; mng. ptnr. Tight Line Lake, 1999-2002. Contbr. articles to profl. jours. Pres. Cleghorn PTA, Rapid City, 1968-70; bd. dirs. Am. Optometric Found., 1989-90, v.p., 1990-94, pres., 1994-96; chmn. bd. dirs. Terry Peak Condominiums, 2001—. Recipient Presdl. medal of honor Pres. of Ill. Coll. of Optometry, 1999, 2002, Spl. honor Am. Optometric Found. Fellow Am. Acad. Optometry (diplomate contact lens sect., sec.-treas. 1985-86, pres.-elect 1987-88, pres. 1988-90, chmn. 1st internat. meeting 1992, nom. com. 2000-02); mem. Am. Optometric Assn. (exec. com. 1974-76, Am. Optometrist of the Yr. 1993), S.D. Optometric Soc. (pres. 1970-71), North Ctrl. State Optometric Conf. (bd. dirs. 1970-71), Black Hills Optometric Soc. (sec.-treas. 1958-69), S.D. State Bd. Examiners (pres. 1982-85), Nat. Acad. Practice Optometry (sec.-treas. 1990-94, Disting. Practitioners award, co-chmn. 1994-96). Clubs: Black Hills Water Ski (pres. 1963). Lodges: Masons, Elks, Lions (pres. Rushmore chpt. 1961-62, Robert Tyler award 1998). Republican. Methodist. Avocations: skiing, water-skiing, hunting, piloting, public speaking. Home: 5048 Carriage Hills Dr Rapid City SD 57702 Office: 2800 3rd St Rapid City SD 57702-2520 Office Phone: 605-718-2303. Personal E-mail: bc.corwin@juno.com.

CORWIN, CAROLYN F., lawyer; b. Mpls., July 27, 1950; AB, Oberlin Coll., 1971; MSLS, Cath. U. of Am., 1972; JD, Yale U., 1977. Bar: DC 1977. Law clk. to Judge Caleb M. Wright U.S. Dist. Ct. Del., 1977-78; asst. to solicitor gen. U.S. Dept. Justice, Washington, 1982-85; ptnr. Covington & Burling, Wash., DC, 1985—. Mem. Am. Law Inst., ABA, Energy Bar Assn., Georgetown U. Law Ctr. Supreme Ct. Inst. (adv. bd. mem.), Transp. Industry Com. (ABA antitrust law sect., chair and vice chair) 2001-06. Office: Covington & Burling 1201 Pennsylvania Ave NW Washington DC 20004 Office Phone: 202-662-5338. Business E-Mail: ccorwin@cov.com.

CORWIN, DANNY WILLARD, rehabilitation services professional, director; b. Ann Arbor, Mich., Jan. 23, 1959; s. Willard Milo and Nancy Jean Corwin; m. Marcela L. Lumayog, Nov. 27, 1999; children: Dustin J., Tiffanie Mara. Correctional Cert., Kellogg C.C., Battle Creek, Mich., 1995. Registered rep. Security Exch. Commn., 1987. Gen. mgr. Corwin Oil Co., Coldwater, Mich., 1977—83; registered rep. John Hancock Fin. Svcs., Kalamazoo, 1986—88; regional sales mgr. Putnam Hitch Products USA, Bronson, Mich., 1998—2003; nat. sales mgr. K & W Mfg., Bronson, 2003—05; exec. placement profl. Angola Pers. Svcs., Inc., Ind., 2006—07; exec. dir. Hope Ho., Jonesville, Mich., 2007—. Bd. dirs. Coldwater Jaycees, 1982—86. Named Chmns. Planning Guide of Yr., Mich. Jaycees, 1982, Outstanding Young Men of Am., 1983, 1984, 1985, 1986; recipient Outstanding Sales Achievement award, Putnam Hitch Products USA, 1998, 1999. Mem.: Am. Mensa Ltd. (assoc.), The Mind Soc. (life). Home: 22 Lilly St Coldwater MI 49036 Office: Hope Ho 401 W Chicago Rd Jonesville MI 49250 Office Phone: 517-849-2330. Office Fax: 517-849-2906.

CORWIN, GREGG MARLOWE, lawyer; b. Mpls., May 4, 1947; s. Gerald Sidney Corwin and Shirley Mae (Nathenson) Nadler; m. Frances Gail Shapiro, mar. 21, 1971; children: Mitchell, David. BA summa cum laude, U. Minn., 1969, JD cum laude, 1972. Bar: Minn. 1972, U.S. Dist. Ct. Minn. 1972, U.S. Ct. Appeals (8th cir.) 1976, U.S. Supreme Ct. 1977. Assoc. Fred Burstein Law Firm, Mpls., 1972-77; ptnr. Cortlen Cloutier, Mpls., 1977-78; pvt. practice, Mpls., 1978—. Capt. USAF. Mem. ABA, Minn. Bar Assn., Hennepin County Bar Assn., Phi Beta Kappa. Democrat. Jewish. Avocations: reading, music, sports. Office: 1660 Hwy 100 Ste 508 E Minneapolis MN 55416-1534 Office Phone: 952-544-7774. Business E-Mail: GCorwin@GCorwin.com.

CORWIN, JEFF, biologist, anthropologist, television host; m. Natasha Corwin; 1 child, Maya Rose. BS in Biology, Bridgewater State Coll., BS in Anthropology, degree (hon.) in pub. edn., 1999; grad., U. Mass. Co-founder Emerald Canopy Rainforest Found.; mem. environ. program UN. Co-creator, prodr., host: (TV series) Going Wild With Jeff Corwin, Disney Channel, 1997—99; exec. prodr. The Jeff Corwin Experience, Animal Planet, 2000—; host (TV series) Corwin's Quest, Animal Planet, —, Into Alaska With Jeff Corwin, Travel Channel, 2007—. Recipient Emmy award for best performer in a children's series, 2004. Office: Discovery Comm Inc 1 Discovery Pl Silver Spring MD 20910*

CORWIN, NORMAN, scriptwriter, film producer, film director; b. Boston, May 3, 1910; s. Samuel H. and Rose (Ober) C.; m. Katherine Locke, Mar. 1947; children: Anthony, Diane. Student, Boston, also Winthrop, Mass.; LittD, Columbia Coll., 1967, LHD, 1978; D in Lit. Arts, Lincoln Coll., 1990; LHD (hon.), Calif. Luth. U., 1996. Writer, producer, dir. CBS; vis. prof. U. So. Calif., 1981—; Patten Meml. lectr. Ind. U., 1981. Dir. creative writing Idyllwild (Calif.) Sch. Music and Art, 1970—86; mem. LaGuardia One World Meml. Commn. to Europe, 1948; trustee L.A. Internat. Film Expn.; film adv. bd. L.A. County Mus. Art; adv. bd. Inst. for Readers Theatre, Poetry Therapy Inst.; lectr. in field. Wrote, produced radio broadcasts; commemorative broadcasts: We Hold These Truths, on 150th anniversary of Am. Bill of Rights, 1941, Bill of Rights: 200, 1991; chief spl. projects, UN Radio; wrote films for, RKO, MGM, 20th-Century Fox, UN; writer, dir., prod.: 26 By Corwin, 1941, This is War, 1942, An American in England, 1942, Columbia Presents Corwin, 1944-45; writer, dir.: (stage plays) The Hyphen, The Rivalry, The World of Carl Sandburg, Together Tonight--Jefferson, Hamilton and Burr; writer for: films Scandal at Scourie, Lust for Life (Oscar nominee), The Blue Veil, The Story of Ruth; producer, host: TV series Norman Corwin Presents for Westinghouse Group W, 1972; author: TV spl. The Ct. Martial of the Tiger of Malaya, 1974; writer, host: TV series Academy Leaders, 1979, radio series More by Corwin, 1996-97. Author: They Fly Through the Air With the Greatest of Ease, 1939, Thirteen by Corwin, 1942, More by Corwin, 1944, On a Note of Triumph, 1945, Untitled and Other Dramas, 1945, Dog in the Sky, 1952, The Plot to Overthrow Christmas, 1952, The World of Carl Sandburg, 1961, Overkill and Megalove, 1963, Prayer For the 70s, 1969, Jerusalem Printout, 1978, Holes in a Stained Glass Window, 1978, Greater than the Bomb, 1981, A Date with Sandburg, 1981, Trivializing America, 1988, Years of the Electric Ear, 1994, Norman Corwin's Letters, 1994; plays Cervantes, 1973; stage play The Rivalry (produced as Hallmark TV spl.); contbr. articles to mags.; writer: text of Human Rights Cantata, Yes Speak Out Yes (commd. by UN), text CONartist (cartoons of Paul Conrad), 1993; Norman Corwin's Letters, 1993, Years of the Electric Ear, 1994; subject of documentary film, 2006. Recipient Page One award Am. Newspaper Guild, 1944-45, award UCLA Ctr. Aging, 2001, Ray Bradbury award, 2001, Distinguished Merit award NCCJ, 1945, UCLA Icon award, 2001, Calif. Hist. Soc. Cmty. Enrichment award, 2003, Human Nuturance award, Ashley Montague Inst., 2005; Unity award Interracial Film and Radio Guild, 1945; citation Nat. Council Tchrs. English, 1945; citation Assn. Tchrs. Social Studies of N.Y., 1945; award Am. Schs. and Colls. Assn., 1946; first place in nat. poll radio editors Billboard mag., for On a Note of Triumph, 1946; co-winner 1st prize Met. Opera awards for new Am. opera, The Warrior, produced Jan. 1947; Freedom award telecast Between Americans, 1951; hon. grant Am. Acad. Arts and Letters; Valentine Davies award Writers Guild Am., 1972; Artists award U. Judaism, 1972; Pacific Pioneer Broadcasters' Carbon Mike award, 1974; Preceptor's award San Francisco State U., 1979; PEN award for body of work, 1986, Friends of Old Time Radio award, 1990, Byron Kane medal SPERDVAC, 1990, Gold medal Internat. Radio Festival, 1992, Lifetime Achievement award N.Y. Festival, 1992, Lifetime Achievement award League of Women Voters, 1993, Alfred I. duPont-Columbia U. award for 50 Yrs. after 14th Aug. commemorating surrender of Japan, 1997. Fellow Radio Hall of Fame; mem. Acad. of Motion Picture Arts and Scis. (chmn. documentary awards com. 1967-82, 85-92, co-chmn. scholarship com., bd. govs. 1979-86 , 1st v.p. acad. 1988, sec. Acad. Found. 1983-88), Aspen Film Conf. (steering com.), Authors League Am., Dramatists Guild, Writers Guild Am. (dir.), Dirs. Guild Am., ASCAP, Internat. Documentary Assn. (bd. dirs.), Soc. Preservation of Radio Drama, Variety and Comedy. Wendell Willkie One World Flight award (flew around world, recording speeches leaders of state, artists and scientists, June-Oct. 1946), first award Inst. for Edn. by Radio, 1946; prod. and narrated One World Flight, 1947; being the subject of two film documentaries. Home: 1840 Fairburn Ave Los Angeles CA 90025-4958 Personal E-mail: corwin@usc.edu.

CORWIN, STANLEY JOEL, book publisher; b. NYC, Nov. 6, 1938; s. Seymour and Faye (Agress) C.; m. Donna Gelgur; children: Alexandra, Donna, Ellen. AB, Syracuse U., 1960. Dir. subsidiary rights, v.p. mktg. Prentice-Hall, Inc., Englewood Cliffs, NJ, 1960-68; v.p. internat. Grosset & Dunlap, Inc., NYC, 1968-75; founder, pres. Corwin Books, NYC, 1975; pres., pub. Pinnacle Books, Inc., LA, 1976-79; pres. Stan Corwin Prodns. Ltd., 1980—; pres., CEO Tudor Pub. Co., NYC and L.A., 1987-90. Lectr. Conf. World Affairs U. Colo., 1976, U. Denver, 1978, Calif. State U., Northridge, 1980, Learning Annex; participant Pubmart Seminar, NYC, 1977, UCLA, 1985, 93, 98; guest lectr. U. So. Calif., 1987—, iVillage Internet Chat Room, Bestseller Seminars, 1999—; columnist Buddhascape Internet Network; expert witness nat. media trials. Author: Where Words Were Born, 1977, How to Become a Best Selling Author, 1984, 3rd edit., 1999, The Creative Writer's Companion, 2001; contbr. articles L.A. Times, N.Y. Times, short stories to Signature mag. and Silent Voices Lit. mag.; prodr.: (films) Remo Williams-The Adventure Begins, 1986, (video) How to Golf with Jan Stephenson, 1987; exec. prodr.: The Elvis Files TV Show, 1991, The Marilyn Files, 1993; pub.: The Movie Script Libr., 1994. Mem. Pres. Carter's U.S. Com. on the UN, 1977. Served with AUS, 1960. Nat. prize winner short story contest Writers' Digest, 1966 Mem. Assn. Am. Pubs., PEN. Home and Office: 9309 Burton Way Beverly Hills CA 90210

CORY, CYNTHIA STRONG, mathematics professor; b. Rochester, Ind., Nov. 11, 1954; d. Clair Eugene and Betty Jane Strong; m. Timothy James Cory, Aug. 6, 1983; children: Bettina Jane, Kevin Scott, Nicholas David, Christopher Steven. BS, Purdue U., 1973—77; MBA, Morehead U., Ky., 2000—03. Teacher Certification Ind. U. Purdue U. at Indpls., Indpls., IN, 1989. Math. instr. Hazard Cmty. and Tech. Coll., Hazard, 2000—, challenger learning ctr. of Ky., 1999—2000; math. tchr. Perry County Schools, Hazard, Ky., 1996—99; fin. officer US Army Reserves, 1983—89, US Army, 1977—83. Dir., soapbox derby Kiwanis Club of Hazard, 2001—07; parish planners Mother of Good Counsel Cath. Ch., Hazard, 2003—07. Capt. US Army, 1977—83, Korea, Fort Harrison, Fort Knox. Decorated Parachutist Badge US Army, Army Commendation medal; recipient, 1982, Coach of the Yr., Ky. Track and Cross Country Coaches Assn., 2003, 2004, Unsung Hero award for Volunteerism, US Army, Ft. Ord, Calif., 1992, 1993. Mem.: Math. Assn. of Am., Nat. Coun. of Teachers of Math., Kiwanis Club of Hazard, Phi Kappa Phi, Delta Mu Delta. Avocations: gardening, candle making, glass blowing. Home: PO Box 472 Dwarf KY 41739 Office: Hazard Cmty and Techl Coll 1 Community College Drive Hazard KY 41701 Home Phone: 606-378-7474; Office Phone: 606-436-5721. Personal E-mail: ccory1234@msn.com. Business E-Mail: cynthia.cory@kctcs.edu.

CORY, WALLACE NEWELL, retired civil engineer; b. Olympia, Wash., Mar. 10, 1937; s. Henry Newell and Gladys Evelyn (Nixon) C.; m. Roberta Ruth Matthews, July 4, 1959; children: Steven Newell, Susan Evelyn Cory Carbon. BS in Forestry, Oreg. State U., 1958, BSCE, 1964; MSCE, Stanford U., 1965. Registered profl. engr., Idaho, Oreg. Asst. projects mgr. CH2 M/Hill, Boise, Idaho, 1965-70; environ. mgr. Boise Cascade Corp., 1970-78, dir. state govt. affairs, 1978-82; dir. indsl. group JUB Engrs., Boise, 1982-84; chief engr. Anchorage Water & Wastewater, 1984-90; dir. pub. works City of Caldwell, Idaho, 1990-92; prin. engr. Montgomery Watson, Pasadena, Calif., 1992-95; adminstr. Idaho Divsn. Environ. Quality, Boise, 1995-98; planning and assessment leader Alexandria Wastewater Project Chemonics Internta., 1998-99. Precinct committeeman Idaho Rep. Com., Boise, 1968-72, region chmn., 1973-77. Capt. USAF, 1958-62. Fellow ASCE; mem. NSPE, Idaho Soc. Profl. Engrs. (pres. 1976-77, Young Engr. of Yr. award 1971), Air Pollution Control Assn. (chmn. Pacific N.W. sect. 1977-78), Idaho Assn. Commerce and Industry (chmn. environ. com. 1974-75). Avocations: hunting, fishing, shooting. Home: 7247 Cascade Dr Boise ID 83704-8635

CORYELL, GLYNN HEATH, financial services executive; b. Lexington, Ky., May 8, 1929; s. Glynn Lawrence Coryell and Allie May (Heath) C.; m. Diane Garnett Dobyns, Dec. 27, 1955 (div. Aug. 1981); children: Heather Diane, Holly. Grad., Culver Summer Cavalry Sch., Ind., 1947; AB, Harvard U., 1951; student, Harvard Law Sch., 1951-52, 54-55; MBA, Northwestern U., 1957. Supr. cost acctg. Procter & Gamble Co., Cin., 1957-60; sr. fin. analyst Socony Mobil Oil Corp., NYC, 1961-62; dir. corp. profit planning, corp. economist Libby, McNeill & Libby, Chgo., 1962-67; treas. Lyntex Corp., NYC, 1968-69; asst. treas. Std. Brands, Inc., NYC, 1969-71; v.p. adminstr. and ops. Std. Brands Foods Co., NYC, 1971-73; fin. v.p. Grand Union Co., Elmwood Park, NJ, 1973-76; exec. v.p., CFO, dir. Cramer Electronics, Inc., Newton, Mass., 1976-79; sr. v.p., CFO, dir. Kuhn's-Big K Stores Corp., Nashville, 1979-81; v.p. fin. and adminstrn., sec. Sunmark, Inc., St. Louis, 1981-83; corp. fin. cons. Lemoyne, Pa., 1984-88; pres. Glynn H. Coryell & Assocs. Inc. doing bus. as Travel Agts. Internat., Falls Church, Va., 1988-94; corp. fin. cons. Alexandria, Va., 1994—2004. Mem. Rep. Nat. Com., John Harvard Soc. With Intelligence US Army, 1953—54. Mem.: Indiana Soc. of Washington, Ky. Soc. of Washington, Culver Edn. Found., Civil War Preservation Trust, Ky. Hist. Soc., Ind. Hist. Soc., Korean War Vets. Assn., Alumni Assn. Kellogg Grad. Sch. Mgmt. Northwestern U. Republican. Baptist. Home and Office: Garnett Hall 200 Masonic Home Dr Apt 110 Masonic Home KY 40041 also: 11108 Fairfax Sta Rd Fairfax Station VA 22039 Office Phone: 502-259-5392.

CORYELL, SANDRA KAY, music educator; d. Levi Ward and Anna Grace (Blesie) Deaton; m. James Robert Coryell. BM, U. Iowa, 1974, MFA, 1977. Undergrad. accompanist, assistantship U. Iowa, Iowa City, 1972—74, grad. rsch. asst., 1978—79, grad. tchg. asst., 1979; adj. instr. preparatory piano Millikin U., Decatur, Ill., 1977—83, adj. asst. prof. music and preparatory dept., 1983—96, adj. instr. preparatory piano dept., 1996—. Preparatory honors recital coord. Millikin U., Decatur, 1998—2004, preparatory recital coord., 2002—04. Active YMCA, 1993—; dir. bell choir Westminster Presbyn. Ch., Decatur, Ill., 2003—04, deacon, 2005—. Grantee, Music Tchrs. Nat. Assn. Found., 1997, 1998,

Archer Daniels Midland Corp., 1999, Decatur Area Arts Coun. and Ill. Arts Coun., 2001, 2002; scholar, Sigma Alpha Iota, U. Iowa. Mem.: PEO (Chpt. CJ), Am. Coll. Musicians Nat. Guild Piano Tchrs. (Decatur audition site chmn. 1992, 1993, 1996—, judge 1997), Decatur Area Music Tchrs. Assn. (treas. 1990—92, vice chmn. 1993—95, treas. 1994—95, sec. 1995—96, pres. 1996—98, treas. 1998—2001, 2002—, grantee), Ill. State Music Tchrs. Assn. (East dist. chair 1998, 2006), Music Tchrs. Nat. Assn. (grantee 1999), Humane Soc. Decatur-Macon County, Mortar Bd. Avocations: walking, piano, playing with dogs. Office: Millikin Univ Perkinson Music Ctr 1184 W Main Decatur IL 62522 Office Phone: 217-424-6390.

CORZINE, JENNIFER JEAN, music educator; b. Evanston, Ill., Apr. 2, 1946; d. Raymond Alfred and Majorie Palmer; children: Christopher, Lindsay, Erin. MusB with hon., Wis. State U., 1968; MA, U. Hawaii, 1970; MS, Fla. State U., 1991, MSW, 1994. Cert. tchr. NY , Fla. Vocal music tchr. Tomorrow River Sch., Amherst, Wis., 1968—69, Greece Ctrl. Sch. Dist., Rochester, NY, 1970—71; instrumental music tchr. Pittsford Ctrl. Sch., NY, 1971—72; gen. music tchr. Evansville-Vanderburgh Sch. Corp., Ind., 1972—73; instrumental music tchr. Maclay Sch., Tallahassee, 1973—. Vol. choir mem. various ch., 1970—85; vol. family counselor Family Living Ctr., Tallahassee, 1986; vol. Am. Heart Assn., 1999—2005; vol. supr. social work interns Maclay Sch., 2002—06. Mem.: Fla. Bandmasters Assn., Fla. Music Educators Assn., Music Educators Nat. Conf. Achievements include established instrumental music program at Maclay School. Avocations: travel, reading, gardening. Office: Maclay Sch 3737 N Meridian Rd Tallahassee FL 32312 Office Phone: 850-893-2138. Business E-Mail: jcorzine@maclay.org.

CORZINE, JON STEVENS, governor, former senator; b. Taylorville, Ill., Jan. 1, 1947; s. Roy Allen and Nancy June (Hedrick) C.; m. Joanne Dougherty, Sept. 8, 1968 (div. 2003); children: Jennifer, Joshua, Jeffrey. BA, U. Ill., 1969; MBA, U. Chgo., 1973; LLD, Rutgers U., 2006. Bond officer Continental Ill. Nat. Bank, Chgo., 1970-73; asst. v.p. BancOhio Corp., Columbus, 1974-75; with Goldman, Sachs & Co., NYC, 1975—99, v.p., 1977, pntr., 1980, mem. mgmt. com., 1985-94, co-head fixed income divsn., ptnr., 1985-94, chmn., CEO, 1994-99; US Senator from NJ, 2001—06; mem, fgn. rels. com.; gov. State of NJ, Trenton, 2006—. Bd. dirs. NJ Performing Arts Ctr., 1993-94, chmn. coun. trustees, 1995-, NY Philharmonic, 1996, Overlook Hosp., Summit, NJ; dir. Family Services, Summit, NJ; co-chaired the Summit area YMCA's Second Century Campaign; trustee Kennedy Ctr. for the Performing Arts in Washington, DC, U. Chgo., NY Univ. Child Study Ctr. Reserve USMC, 1969—75. Mem. Pub. Securities Assn. (vice chmn. 1985, chmn. 1986) Democrat. Office: Office of Governor PO Box 001 Trenton NJ 08625 Office Phone: 609-292-6000. Office Fax: 609-777-2922.*

CORZO, MIGUEL ANGEL, academic administrator; b. Mex. City, Mar. 2, 1942; came to U.S., 1985; s. Miguel A. and Josefina (Melgar) C.; m. Liliane Maunier, June 13, 1964; children: Liliane, Alexandre, Xavier Edward; m. Allison Sampson, Sept. 17, 2000. BS, UCLA, 1967; MS, Nat. U. Mexico, Mexico City, 1970; DSc, Tech. U. Munich, Germany, 1974. Prof. Nat. U., Mexico City, 1967-74; dean acad. affairs Met. U., Mexico City, 1974-77; spl. adviser Mexican Ministry Urban Devel., Mexico City, 1977-80; sec. tourism Mexican Ministry Tourism, Mexico City, 1980-82; pres. Friends Arts of Mex., LA, 1988-91; dir. spl. projects Getty Conservation Inst., LA, 1986-88, dir., 1991—2000; pres. U. Arts, Phila., 2000—. Mem. Cultural Property Adv. Com., 1995. Author: Engineering Design, 1971, Human Settlements, 1979 (gold award 1979); editor over 20 books. Fulbright fellow Harvard U., 1979. Office: U Arts 320 S Broad St Philadelphia PA 19102

COSAR, EDIZ FERGÜN, pathologist, researcher; b. Igdir, Turkey, July 16, 1964; s. Ergün and Sevgi (Cölkesen) C.; m. Elifce Özlem (Koca) Cosar, July 27, 1990. MD, Cukurova U., Adana, Turkey, 1988. Cert. anatomic and clin. pathologist 2002. Pathologist, clin. prof. Cukurova U., Adana, Turkey, 1995—97; resident Cukurova U. Sch. Med., Adana, Turkey, 1989—95, Ill. Masonic Med. Ctr., Chgo., 1998—99, Loyola U. Med. Ctr., Maywood, Ill., 1999—2002, fellow in molecular genetic pathology, 2002—03, U. Mass. Meml. Med. Ctr., 2003—04. Editor (book): Cancer Incidence in Turkey, 1994; contbr. articles to profl. jours. Mem. European Soc. Pathology, Friends and Alumni of Armed Forces Inst. Pathology, U.S., Turkish Assn. Cancer Rsch. and Control, Cukurova Pathology Soc., US and Can. Acad. Pathology, Am. Assn. Cancer Rsch., Assn. Molecular Pathology, Coll. Am. Pathologists. Avocations: tennis, swimming. Office: U Mass Meml Med Ctr Dept Pathology 55 Lake Ave North Worcester MA 01655-0002

COSBY, BILL, actor, television producer; b. Phila., July 12, 1937; s. William Henry and Anna C.; m. Camille Hanks, Jan. 25, 1964; children: Erika Ranee, Erinn Chalene, Ennis William (dec.), Ensa Camille, Evin Harrah. Student, Temple U.; MA, U. Mass., 1972, EdD, 1976; MusD (hon.), Berklee Coll. Music, 2004. Pres. Rhythm and Blues Hall of Fame, 1968—. Appeared in numerous night clubs, including The Gaslight, N.Y.C., Hungry I, San Francisco, Shoreham Hotel, Washington, Basin St. East, N.Y.C., Hilton, Las Vegas, Nev., Harrah's Lake Tahoe; guest appearances on numerous TV shows, including The Electric Co., 1971-72, Capt. Kangaroo, Touched by an Angel, 1997, 99, King of Queens, 1999, Everybody Loves Raymond, 1999, Becker, 1999, Tonight Show with Jay Leno, 2005, ABC News Nightline, 2005, Dr. Phil, 2005; co-star: TV show I Spy, 1965-68;star (TV show) The Team That Changed the World, 2005, Hey Hey Hey: Behind the Scenes of 'Fat Albert', 2004; star (TV series) The Bill Cosby Show, 1969-71, The New Bill Cosby Show, 1972-73, (host, voices) Fat Albert and the Cosby Kids, 1972-79, Cos, 1976, (host, voices) The New Fat Albert Show, 1979-82, The Cosby Show, 1984-92, The Cosby Mysteries, 1994-95, Cosby, 1996-2000; host, TV game show You Bet Your Life, 1992-93, Kids Say the Darndest Things, 1998-2000, Jack Paar "As I Was Saying.", 1997; interviewee 4 Little Girls (TV), 1997; exec. prodr. TV show A Different World, 1987-93, Here and Now, 1992-93; TV movies include I Spy Returns, 1994, The Bill Cosby Mystery Movies, 1994; recs. include: Revenge (Grammy award Nat. Acad. Performing Arts and Scis. 1967), To Russell, My Brother, With Whom I Slept, 1968 (Grammy award), Why Is There Air, 1965 (Grammy award), Wonderfulness, 1966 (Grammy award), It's True, It's True, Bill Cosby is a Very Funny Fellow.Right, 1963, I Started Out as a Child, 1964 (Grammy award), Reunion, 1982, Bill Cosby.Himself, 1983 (dir., prodr.), Those of You With or Without Children, You'll Understand, (jazz albums) Where You Lay Your Head, 1990, My Appreciation, 1991, Hello Friend: To Ennis With Love, 1997; films include Hickey and Boggs, 1972, Man and Boy, 1972, Uptown Saturday Night, 1974, Let's Do It Again, 1975, Mother, Jugs and Speed, 1976, A Piece of the Action, 1977, California Suite, 1978, (voice) Aesop's Fable, 1978, Devil and Max Devlin, 1979, Bill Cosby.Himself, 1985, Leonard: Part VI, 1987, Ghost Dad, 1990, The Meteor Man, 1993, Jack, 1996; exec. prodr., writer Fat Alber, 2004; co-exec. prodr., writer (TV series) Fatherhood, 2004; recipient 4 Emmy awards 1966, 67, 68, 69, 8 Grammy awards, named number 1 in comedy field Top Artists on Campus Poll (album sales) 1968; author: The Wit and Wisdom of Fat Albert, 1973, Bill Cosby's Personal Guide to Power Tennis, Fatherhood, 1986, Time Flies, 1988, Love and Marriage, 1989, Childhood, 1991. Served with USNR, 1956-60. Named to Hall of Fame, Acad. TV Arts and Scis., 1994, NAACP Image Awards Hall of Fame, 2007; recipient Bob Hope Humanitarian award, Academy of Television Arts & Sciences, 2003. Achievements include setting concert attendance record Radio City Music Hall, 1986.*

COSBY, RITA KAREN, newscaster; b. Bklyn., Nov. 18, 1964; d. Richard Roger and Adda Otilia (Arenfeldt) C. Honors degree, Conn. Sch. Broadcasting, 1983; BA in Broadcast Journalism, Spanish, U. S.C., 1989. Nat. sales mgr. Basic Wallpaper, Inc., Stamford, Conn., 1983-86; bus. cons. Lin-Gor, Inc., Clifton, NJ, 1986-89; announcer, control operator Sta. WACH-TV, Columbia, SC, 1989; intern, asst. CBS Evening News, NYC, 1989; anchor, reporter Sta. KERO-TV, Bakersfield, Calif., 1989-92, Sta. WBTV-CBS, Charlotte, NC, 1992-95; sr. corr. Fox News, Washington, 1995—2001, host Foxwire with Rita Cosby, 2002—05; primetime host, spl. correspondent MSNBC, 2005—. News anchor S.C. Pub. Radio, Columbia, 1988-89; host, interviewer, prodr. Bus. and Fin. Shows, Bakersfield, 1989-92; host, interviewer Community Affairs Show, Bakersfield, 1989-92, Take One Prodns., N.Y.C., 1989—, Spanish Cable TV Show, Charlotte, 1993-95. News editor (newspaper) The Gamecock, 1987-89; writer (newspaper) The State, 1988-89; columnist (Hispanic newspaper) El Progreso Hispano, 1993—. Mem. adv. bd. Youth Involvement Coun., Charlotte, 1992-95; host, fundraiser United Negro Coll. Fund, Charlotte, 1993-95, Children's Miracle Network Telethon, Charlotte, 1993-95, Muscular Dystrophy Assn., Bakersfield, 1990-92; spkr., reader Charlotte-Mecklenburg Schs., Charlotte, 1992-95; vol., spkr. Girl Scouts U.S., 1989—; motivational spkr. anti-drug program DARE. Recipient Outstanding Sr. award U. S.C., 1989, Best Reporting award Kern County Press Club, 1991. Mem. NATAS (Emmy 1992, 95, listed as Outstanding Young Am. 1989, mem. nominating bd. 1997—), L.Am. Coalition (spkr. 1993—), L.Am. Women's Assn. (spkr. 1994—), Soc. Profl. Journalists (student pres. 1987—), Alpha Epsilon Rho (pub. info. officer 1987-89), Omicron Delta Kappa. Avocation: foreign languages. Office: MSNBC News One MSNBC Plz Secaucus NJ 07094 Office Phone: 201-583-5000.

COSCIA, ANTHONY R., state agency administrator, lawyer; b. Paterson, NJ, Sept. 9, 1959; BSFS, Georgetown U., 1981; JD, Rutgers U., 1984. Bar: NJ 1984, NY 1985. Ptnr. Corp. and Securities, Fin. Transactions and Real Estate Practice Groups Windels Marx Lane & Mittendorf, LLP, New Brunswick, NJ, mem. Exec. Com. Chmn. NJ Econ. Devel. Authority (NJEDA), 1992—2003, NJ Schs. Construction Corp. (NJSCC), 2002—03; chmn. bd. commrs. Port Authority of NY & NJ, 2003—; dir. Interchange Fin. Svcs. Corp. Trustee NJ Network Found., Cerebral Palsy of North Jersey; mem. Gov.'s Jobs and Econ. Growth Commn., New Capital Sources Partnership; adv. bd. mem. Fannie Mae Regional Partnership. Mem.: Phi Beta Kappa. Office: Windels Marx Lane & Mittendorf, LLP 120 Albany St Plaza New Brunswick NJ 08901 also: Port Authority of NY & NJ 225 Park Ave S New York NY 10003 Office Phone: 732-846-2120. Office Fax: 732-846-8877. E-mail: acoscia@windelsmarx.com.

COSELL, BERNARD, retired computer systems architect; b. NYC, Aug. 28, 1946; s. Bernard Delfy and Julia Cocozziello; m. Lynn Karyl Marquardt, Sept. 7, 1968. MS in Math., Northeastern U., 1977. Sr. systems arch. Bolt Beranek and Newman, Cambridge, Mass., 1965—92. Mem. adj. faculty Va. Western C.C. Treas., bd. dirs. Triangle Ruritan, Pearisburg, Va., 1996—2005. Achievements include development of the modern notion of network management and implementation of the first network management system; participation on the team that implemented the original switching software for the ARPAnet network node; help in development and operational deployment of the first dialup terminal access system for the ARPAnet; design of the will/wont, do/dont machinery for the ARPAnet telnet protocol. Avocation: shepherding. Home Phone: 540-921-2358. Personal E-mail: bernie@fantasyfarm.com.

COSENTINO, BARBARA, counseling administrator; d. John and Anna Adamczuk; m. Michael Cosentino, Jan. 6, 1970. BA, U. Ill., Chgo., 1996; MA in Counseling Psychology, St. Xavier U., 2000. Lic. profl. counselor Ill., 2001. Placement specialist Roosevelt U., Chgo., 1999—2000; asst. dir. placement Northeastern Ill. U., Chgo., 2001—. Bd. mem. Govt. Coll. Rels. Coun., Chgo., 2002—, pres., 2005—; mem. Chgo. Career Professionals Network, 2005—. Author: (bi-weekly career column) Lerner Newspapers Job Hunter. Mem.: Midwest Assn. Colleges & Employers, Nat. Career Devel. Assn. Liberal. Roman Catholic. Avocations: writing, travel. Office: Northeastern Illinois U 5500 N St Louis Ave B-119 Chicago IL 60625 Home Phone: 630-963-1690; Office Phone: 773-442-4686. Office Fax: 773-442-4690. Business E-Mail: b-cosentino@neiu.edu.

COSENTINO, MARY JANE, retired science educator; d. Joseph and Rose Cosentino. B in Edn, Bowling Green State U., Ohio, 1942; MS, Purdue U., West Lafayette, Ind., 1968. Permanent secondary tchr. Ohio, 1969. Sci. and math. tchr. Milan H.S., Ohio, 1943—45; sci. tchr. Sandusky Jr. H.S., 1945—46; tchr. grade 6 Rosary Cathedral Sch., Toledo, 1946—51; sci. tchr. St. Gerard H.S., Lima, 1951—53; tchr. grade 6 St. Thomas Sch., Toledo, 1953—56, 1960—61; tchr. biology and physics Mary Manse Sch., 1956—58; tchr. biology and English Lima Ctrl. Cath., Ohio, 1958—61; tchr. biology and anatomy Calvert H.S., Tiffin, 1961—64, St. Ursula Acad., Toledo, 1964—2004; ret., 2004. Sci. dept. chair St. Ursula Acad., Toledo, 1964—2004; mem. planning com. Ohio Acad. Sci., 1970—95, mem. office com. state sci. day, Columbus, 1980—95; presenter Nat. Assn. Biology Tchrs. Conv., New Orleans, 1979. Named Northwest Dist. Outstanding Sci. Tchr., Ohio Acad. Sci., 1973, Outstanding Secondary Tchr., NEA, 1974, Outstanding H.S. Sci. Tchr., Sigma Xi, Toledo, 1991; recipient Gov.'s Youth Sci. Excellence award, Ohio Acad. Sci., 1985—92, Outstanding Lifetime Work award, Nat. Cath. Edn. Assn., Canada, 1990, Purdue U., 1964—67; grantee, Marquette U., 1960. Mem.: Nat. Assn. Biology Tchrs. (Ohio Biology Tchr. 1978). Roman Catholic. Avocations: stamp collecting/philately, African violets, reading. Home: 4025 Indian Rd Toledo OH 43606

COSGRAVE, PAUL J., commissioner; BS, MS, Rensselaer Polytechnic Inst. Chmn., pres., CEO Claremont Tech. Group; chief info. officer IRS, 1998—2001; exec. v.p. Crown Consulting, Inc., 2001—06; commr. Dept. Info. Tech. and Telecom., NYC, 2006—. Office: Dept Info Tech and Telecom 75 Park Pl 9th Fl New York NY 10007 Office Phone: 212-788-6633. Office Fax: 212-788-8130.

COSGRIFF, JAMES ARTHUR, physician; b. Lamberton, Minn., Mar. 18, 1924; s. James Arthur and Elsie Ann (Forster) C. BS summa cum laude, Coll. St. Thomas, 1944; MD, U. Minn., 1946. Intern St. Mary's Hosp., Duluth, Minn.; pvt. practice Olivia, Minn., 1949—. With USN, 1947-49. Fellow Am. Acad. Family Physicians; mem. Minn. Acad. Family Physicians (pres. 1963, Merit award 1964), Alpha Omega Alpha. Roman Catholic. Avocations: travel, photography, reading, music. Home: 802 E Park Ave Olivia MN 56277-1361 Office: Olivia Clinic 619 E Lincoln Ave Olivia MN 56277-1349 Office Phone: 320-523-2131.

COSGROVE, DANIEL JOSEPH, biology educator; b. Westover AFB, Mass., Sept. 15, 1952; s. Alfred Kevin and Irene B. (Roullier) C.; m. Leandra Throughton, Sept. 29, 1979; 1 child, Kevin. BA, U. Mass., 1974; PhD in Biol. Sci., Stanford U., 1980. Vis. scientist Kernforschunganlage, Jülich, West Germany, 1980-81; postdoctoral assoc. botany dept. U. Wash., Seattle, 1981-82; asst. prof., assoc. prof. biology dept. Pa. State U., University Park, 1983-91, prof., 1991—. Contbr. articles to profl. jours. Named Presdl. Young Investigator, NSF, 1984, 89; recipient award McKnight Found., 1986, 89, Sr. Prof. award Fulbright/Hayes Commn., 1989-90, Alexander von Humboldt award, 1996; J.S. Guggenheim Found. fellow, 1989. Fellow AAAS; mem. Am. Soc. Plant Biologists (formerly Am. Soc. Plant Physiologists) (pres. 2000-01, Charles Albert Shull award 1991), Am. Soc. Gravitational and Space Biology (governing bd. 1993-96), Am. Soc. Photobiology (councillor 1987-90), NAS. Office: Pa State U Biology Dept 208 Mueller Lab University Park PA 16802-5301 Office Phone: 814-863-3892. E-mail: dcosgrove@psu.edu.

COSGROVE, DELOS M. (TOBY COSGROVE), health facility administrator, surgeon; b. Watertown, NY, July 28, 1940; s. Delos M. and Margaret C.; m. Anita Desiderio, May 8, 1976; children: Nicole Ashley, Britt Lindsey. BA, Williams Coll., Williamstown, Mass., 1962; MD, U. Va., 1966. Diplomate Am. Bd. Surgery, Am. Bd. Thoracic Surgery. Intern Strong Meml. Hosp., Rochester, NY, 1966-67, resident in surgery, 1967-68, Mass. Gen. Hosp., Boston, 1970-72, sr. resident in cardiac surgery, 1973-74; registrar in cardiac surgery Brook Gen. Hosp., London, 1972-73; chief resident Boston Children's Hosp., 1974; assoc. staff dept. thoracic and cardiovascular surgery The Cleve. Clinic, 1975-76, profl. staff, 1976—, chmn. dept. thoracic and cardiovascular surgery, 1990—, CEO, 2004—, chmn., bd. governors, 2004—. Bd. trustees Healthcare Leadership Coun. Contbr. articles to profl. jours. Mem. Am. Assn. Thoracic Surgery (pres. 2000), Internat. Soc. Cardiovascular Surgery, Am. Coll. Cardiology, Am. Coll. Chest Physicians, ACS, Am. Heart Assn., AMA, Am. Surg. Assn., Cleve. Surg. Soc., Ohio State Med. Assn., Ohio Thoracic Soc., Cleve. Acad. Medicine, Soc. Thoracic Surgeons, Soc. for Thoracic Surg. Edn. (chmn. membership com. 1985-87), Peruvian Coll. Angiology (hon.), Chilean Soc. Cardiology (hon.), Dominican Republic Soc. Cardiology (hon.), Argentine Coll. Cardiology (hon., mem. editorial bd. The Annals of Thoracic Surgery). Avocation: sailing. Office: Cleve Clinic Surgery 9500 Euclid Ave Cleveland OH 44195-0001

COSGROVE, GARTH REES, neurosurgeon; b. Montreal, Canada, Sept. 22, 1956; s. James Bert Cosgrove and Alison Mabel Chown; m. Karen Ann Roche, Feb. 26, 1983; children: Kathryn, Priscilla, Martha. MD, Queen's U., Kingston, Ontario, 1980. Intern Royal Victora Hosp., McGill U., 1980—81; resident Montreal Neurol. Inst., 1981—86; instr. surgery Harvard Med. Sch., Boston, 1986—89, asst. prof. surgery, 1989—90, assoc. prof. surgery, 1992—96; asst. prof. neurology U. Va., Charlottesville, 1990—92; prof. neurosurgery Tufts U. Sch. Medicine, Boston, 2005—. Vis. asst. prof. neurol. surgery U. Va. Sch. Medicine, 1992—. Fellow: Royal Coll. Surgeons Can. Office: Lahey Clinic 41 Mall Rd Burlington MA 01805 Home Phone: 781-721-0291; Office Phone: 781-744-1990. E-mail: g.rees.cosgrove@lahey.org.

COSGROVE, HOWARD EDWARD, JR., utilities executive; b. Phila., Apr. 12, 1943; s. Howard Edward and Margaret C. (May); m. Roberta Joyce Olewine, Apr. 19, 1965; children: Pamela Joyce, Susan Ann. BS in Mech. Engring., U. Va., 1966; MBA, U. Del., 1970. Registered profl. engr., Del. With Delmarva Power Co., Wilmington, Del., 1966—, mgr. fin., 1979, v.p., chief fin. officer, 1979—, exec. v.p., 1984-92, chmn., CEO, 1992—2002; now chmn., pres. & CEO Conectiv, Wilmington, Del.; chmn. NRG Energy, 2003—. Mem.: Nat. Soc. Profl. Engrs. Home: PO Box 197 Rockland DE 19732-0197

COSGROVE, JOHN FRANCIS, lawyer, mayor; b. Coral Gables, Fla., July 1, 1949; s. Francis Freheil and Vivian Adair (Rafferty) C.; m. Bernardine Elizabeth Cosgrove, Dec. 19, 1981; children: Michael, Tiffany, Colleen. AA, U. Fla., 1969, BS in Journalism, 1971; JD, Cumberland Sch. Law, 1975. Bar: Fla., U.S. Dist. Ct. (so. dist.) Fla., U.S. Ct. Appeals (5th cir.), U.S. Supreme Ct. Assoc. Hall & Hedrick, Miami, Fla., 1975-80; sole practice Miami, 1980—. Mem. Fla. Ho. of Reps., 1981-84, 1986—; gen. counsel Biscayne Coll.; columnist Miami Rev.: Juris Conspectus, 1975—; chair Nat. Conf. State Legislatures Com. on Commerce and Comm.; chair property and casualty com., mem. exec. com. Nat. Conf. Ins. Legislatures. Chmn. Coral Gables Code Enforcement Bd.; mem. Coral Gables Econ. Devel. Bd.; mem. Jr. Orange Bowl Com.; chmn. Metro-Dade Econ. Devel. Bd., Miami Budget Rev. Com.; mem. South Miami Hosp. Assocs. Mem. ABA, Fla. Bar Assn. (Jud. Selection, Adminstrn. and Tenure Com., vice chmn. jud. nominating com.), Dade County Bar Assn. (3d v.p.), Am. Judicature Soc., ATLA, Pvt. Industry Coun. Dade County, Emerald Soc. South Fla., Miami Springs-Hialeah C. of C., Coral Gables C. of C., Grtr. Miami C. of C., Blue Key, Serra Club, Viscayans Civic Club, Le Lega Civic Club, Grtr. Miami Leadership Prayer Breakfast Club, KC (grand knight Coral Gables; pres. Dade County chpt.), Kiwanis, Knight of Malta, Phi Kappa Tau. Democrat. Roman Catholic (chmn. Cath. Svc. Bur.-50th anniversary). Home: 8230 SW 192nd St Miami FL 33157-8013 Office: 18320 SW 97th Ave Miami FL 33157 Office Phone: 305-373-5313. Personal E-mail: jfc7149esq@aol.com.

COSGROVE, JOHN PATRICK, editor; b. Pittston, Pa., Sept. 25, 1918; s. Raymond Patrick and Alice (Gilroy) C.; m. Patricia Ellen O'Hara, Mar. 26, 1951. Student pub. schs., Pa. Reporter, Wilkes-Barre (Pa.) Record, 1936-37, AP, Washington, 1938-40; writer, research Nat. Republican Congl. Com., Washington, 1940; exec. asst. U.S. Senator Hiram W. Johnson, 1941-42; free lance writer, 1946-48; dir. publs. Broadcasting Publs., Inc. (pubs. Broadcasting Businessweekly, Television monthly, Broadcasting Yearbook), Washington, 1948-68. Author: The Gendreau Story: War History of DE 639; editor: SHRDLU-An Affectionate Chronicle of the first fifty years of the Nat. Press Club, 1959. Publicity dir. Honor Am. Day Celebration, 1970; exec. dir. Am. Hist. and Cultural Soc., Inc., 1970-88; sec. Nat. Christmas Pageant of Peace, 1974—2006, v.p., 1985—2006, mem. com. to light nat. Christmas tree; Washington rep. Nat. Com. Neurol. Disorders and Stroke, 1972-78, R.R. Task Force for Northeast Region, 1973-75; bd. dirs. Am. Irish Found., 1967-87, pres., 1971-73; bd. dirs. Washington chpt. Nat. Multiple Sclerosis Soc., 1962-70, Am. Ireland Fund, 1987—2001; mem. bd. dirs. USN Meml. Found., Washington, 1986—, sec. and chmn. dedication com., 1987-; bd. dirs. Ellis Island Restoration Commn., N.Y., 1989—, Destroyer-Escort Hist. Mus., 1993—; vice chmn. Am. Fedn. Irish Heritage, 1988—; bd. dirs. Internat. Svc. Agys., 1992-99, mem. bd. govs. Internat. Grad. U., 2003-. Served with USNR, 1942-46; assigned Office Censorship, Washington 1942; U.S.S. Gendreau 1944-46. Named Gael of Yr., Washington D.C. St. Patrick's Parade, 1999. Mem. VFW (life), White House Corrs. Assn. (hon.), Soc. Profl. Journalists, Destroyer-Escort Sailors Assn. (life, bd. dir. 1981-96), Nat. Press Club (bd. govs. 1956-59, v.p. 1960, pres. 1961, chmn. awards com. 1974, chmn. election com. 1978, comdr. post no. 20, 1999-2005), Am. Legion (life), Soc. Friendly Sons of St. Patrick (life, bd. dir. 1976-82), Nat. Headliners Club (Atlantic City), Circus Saints and Sinners Club (exec. v.p., dir. P.T. Barnum tent 1973-89, pres. 1989-91), Army, Navy and Air Force Vets. of Can. Roman Catholic. Home: 7906 Jensen Pl Bethesda MD 20817-4671 Office: 1124 National Press Building Washington DC 20045-2101 Office Phone: 202-628-3400.

COSGROVE, THERESA MARGARET, museum director; d. William C. and Agnes T. Wegner; m. Steven W. Cosgrove, June 6, 1981; 1 child, Shannon M. BFA, U. Wis., Eau Claire, 1972; MA in Music Adminstrn., JFK U., San Francisco, 1983. Cert. Music Mgmt. Inst., U. Calif., 1981. Mus. & arts specialist US Fed. Govt., 1983—2004; mus. dir. Bainbridge Island Hist. Mus., Wash., 2005—. Lectr. US Dressage Fedn., Lexington, Ky., 2004. Parent tchr. bd. mem. Bainbridge Island Pub. Sch., 2000—. Grantee Travel grant, Nat. Endowment Humanities, 1980, MMI scholarship, 1981; Grad. fellowship, Rotary Internat. Found., 1978—79. Achievements include design of museum exhbt. Home: 6850 NE Day Rd Bainbridge Island WA 98110

COSIER, RICHARD A., dean, finance educator; b. Jackson, Mich., May 18, 1947; s. Roy A. and Wilma M. (Braund) C.; m. Rae L. Pettelle, June 14, 1969 (div. Feb. 1985); children: Jeffrey R., Nathan R.; m. Lynn M. Hays, Aug. 30, 1986; children: Courtney M., Kelsey L. BS, Mich. State U., 1969; MBA, Loyola U., 1972; PhD, U. Iowa, 1976. From asst. to assoc. prof. mgmt. Ind. U., Bloomington, 1976-86, prof. mgmt., 1986-92, chairperson, prof. mgmt., 1983-90, assoc. dean for acads., prof. mgmt., 1990-92; dean, Fred E. Brown chair U. Okla., Norman, 1993-99; Leeds prof. mgmt. Purdue U., 1999—, dean Krannert Grad. Sch. Mgmt. and Sch. Mgmt.,

1999—, dir. Burton D. Morgan Ctr. Entrepreneurship, 2002—05; with faculty U. Notre Dame. Bd. dirs. Kite Realty Group Trust, Roll Coater, Inc., AACSB Internat.; cons. in field. Contbr. over 75 articles and book chpts. to profl. jours.; co-author mgmt. textbook; contbr. book chpts.; inventor patented packaging technique. Active with United Way Am.; mem. exec. com. Greater Lafayette Comty. Devel. Corp., 2001; chmn. United Way campaign Purdue U., 2003—. Fellow Richard D. Irwin. Mem.: Acad. Mgmt. Republican. Office: Krannert Sch Mgmt Rm 122 Purdue U West Lafayette IN 47907-1310 Office Phone: 765-494-4366. E-mail: rcosier@purdue.edu.

COSING, ARTHUR PAUL, JR., writer, artist; b. Miami, Fla., May 11, 1926; s. Arthur Paul Cosing Sr. and Ruby Myrtledean Ogorek; m. Shirley Mae Baumann, Oct. 16, 1954 (dec. June 7, 1997); 1 child, Arthur Paul III. BS, U. Md., 1950. Artist Washington Post, Washington, 1950—52; visual info. specialist NIH, Bethesda, Md., 1952—55, pub. info. specialist, 1955—60; speech writer Office Surgeon Gen. USPHS, Washington, 1960—63; pub. info. officer Bur. Family Svcs. HEW, Washington, 1963—67; asst. chief Office Comm. NIMH, Rockville, Md., 1967—78, chief tech. svcs., 1978—88; ret. Contbr. articles to profl. jours. and lit. publs.;, co-author paperback book of humor. With US Army, 1944—45, ETO. Decorated Combat Badge, Purple Heart, Bronze Star; recipient award, NIH, 1958, HHS, 1985. Mem.: Omicron Delta Kappa, Pi Delta Epsilon, Theta Chi. Avocations: sketching, writing, travel, golf. Home: 3693 Persimmon Cir Fairfax VA 22031 Personal E-mail: apcosing@cox.net.

COSLER, STEVEN DOUGLAS, diversified financial services company executive; b. Indpls., July 17, 1955; s. Robert Douglas Cosler and Ruth (Beasley) Pape; m. Lynne Ulbrich, Jan. 14, 1978; children: Stephanie Lynne, Robert Louis. BS in Indsl. Mgmt., Purdue U., 1977. Sales engr. Ross Gear div. TRW, Lafayette, Ind., 1977-78; mktg. rep. IBM Corp., Louisville, 1978-83, regional mktg. staff Cin., 1983-84, mktg. mgr. Indpls., 1984-87, bus planning mgr. Chgo., 1987-88, br. mgr. Indpls., 1989—; v.p. 1st Benefit Corp., Anderson, Ind., 1992—96; sr. v.p., gen. mgr. Priority Healthcare Svcs. (subs. Bindley We. Industries), 1996—97; exec. v.p., pharmacy svcs. Priority Healthcare, Lake Mary, Fla., 1997—2000, exec. v.p., 2000—01, COO, 2000—02, pres., 2001—, CEO, 2002—. Mem. bd. advisors 1st Benefit Corp., 1990-92. Mem. state bd. dirs. Fellowship of Christian Athletes, Indpls., 1985—, nat. bd. dirs., Orlando, Fla., 1989—; chmn. sub. com. NCAA Championships, Indpsl., 1991, PGA Championship, 1993, U.S. Women's Open, 1993; deacon E 91st St. Christian Ch., Indpls., 1989-90. Mem. Highland Golf and Country Club, Gold Coats of Purdue U., Rotary. Avocations: golf, travel, sports, reading. Office: Priority Healthcare 250 Technology Pk Lake Mary FL 32746

COSMAN, FRANCENE JEN, former government official; b. Windsor, Ont., Can., Jan. 14, 1941; d. John Douglas and Dorothy Mae (Machel) McCarthy; m. David Killam Cosman, July 25, 1964 (div.); children: Lara Machel, Andrea Leigh; m. Aza Avramovitch, June 27, 1998 (dec.). Diploma in Nursing, St. John Gen. Hosp., NB, 1962; postgrad. diploma, Margaret Hague Hosp., Jersey City, 1963. RN Can., cert. healing touch practitioner. Various nursing positions, 1963-68; county councillor County of Halifax, N.S., 1976-79; mayor Town of Bedford, N.S., 1979-82; pres. Adv. Coun. on Status of Women, N.S., 1982-86; exec. dir. N.S. Liberal Party, 1989-93; mem. Legis. Assembly, House of Assembly of N.S., Halifax, 1993-99, dep. spkr., min. comty. svcs., 1997—99; ret. Chair Sr. Citizens Secretariat, 1997—99; min. responsible administrn. Adv. Coun. Status Women Act, 1997-99; min. Cmty. Svcs., 1997-99; min. responsible Disabled Persons Commn. Act, 1997-99; mem. Healing Touch Ministry, 2000—. Contbr. numerous reports, briefs, documents to provincial and fed. levels of govt.; opinion col. writer Chronicle Herald Newspaper, 1987-88. Liberal. Mem. United Ch. Avocations: artist, poetry, swimming, healing touch practitioner. E-mail: fjc@eastlink.ca.

COSPOLICH, JAMES DONALD, electronics executive, consultant; b. New Orleans, Dec. 19, 1944; s. Clarence James and Olga Marie C.; m. Shirley Patricia Knipper, Feb. 4, 1967; children: Brian James, Jeffery Donald, Stephen William. BEE, La. State U., 1967, MEE, 1972. Registered profl. engr., La., Calif., Tex. Geophysicist Pan Am. Petroleum Corp. subs. AMOCO, New Orleans, 1967; elec. engr. Waldemar S. Nelson & Co., New Orleans, 1967, asst. v.p., elec. engring., 1974—83, v.p., mgr. elec. engring., 1983—85, sr. v.p. ops., 1985—91, exec. v.p., 1991—. Mem. Nat. Elec. Code Panel 14. Mem. Rep. Nat. Com., Washington, 1988; v.p. Ormond Civic Assn., Destrehan, La., 1985, pres., 1986; mem. representing St. Charles Parish, New Orleans Internat. Airport Noise Abatement Com. With USCGR, 1964-72. Mem. NFPA (nat. elec. code com.), IEEE, NSPE, Instrument Soc. Am. (sr., com. mem. 1975—), Am. Petroleum Inst. (com. recommended practice stds.), Gas Processors Assn., La. Engring. Soc., Ormond Country Club, The Am. Legion. Republican. Roman Catholic. Avocations: fishing, tennis, golf, skiing, boating, woodworking. Home: 61 Rosedown Dr Destrehan LA 70047-2529 Office: Waldemar S Nelson & Co Inc 1200 Saint Charles Ave New Orleans LA 70130-4334 Office Phone: 504-593-5293. Personal E-mail: jim.cospolich@wsnelson.com.

COSS, BARBARA SUE, humanities educator; d. James Harvey and Margaret Iola Coss; children: Shannon James Madison, Katherine Chelsea Allison. BA in English, Philosophy, CIS, Western Mich. U., Kalamazoo, 1989, M in Mid. Sch. Edn., 1998. First grade classroom tchr. Kalamazoo Acad., 1990—91; mid. sch. humanities tchr. Kalamazoo Country Day Sch., 1991—. Student coun. advisor Kalamazoo Country Day Sch., 1992—. Office: Kalamazoo Country Day School 4221 E Milham Kalamazoo MI 49002 Home Phone: 269-349-3162; Office Phone: 269-329-0116 214. Business E-Mail: bcoss@kalamazoocountryday.org.

COSS, DAVID, mayor; s. Ron and Millie Coss; m. Carol Rose Coss; children: Celedina, Dylan, Molly. BS, N.Mex. State U.; MS, So. Ill. U., 1981. Surface water scientist City of Santa Fe, mgr. environ. protection divsn., dir. pub. works dept., 1995—96, city mgr., 1996, environ. protection mgr. state land office, mem. city coun., 2002—06, mayor, 2006—. Mem. Regional Planning Authority, Buckman Direct (Water) Diversion Bd.; chmn. Water Conservation Com. Office: 200 Lincoln Santa Fe NM 87501 Office Phone: 505-955-6590. Office Fax: 505-955-6695. E-mail: mayor@santafenm.gov.

COSS, STEPHEN K., lawyer; b. 1969; BA, Duke U.; JD, U. Va. Gen. counsel Sonic Automotive Inc., Charlotte, NC, 2000—04, sr. v.p., gen. counsel, 2004—. Mem.: ABA, 1994. Office: Sonic Automotive 6415 Idlewild Rd Ste 109 Charlotte NC 28212 Office Phone: 704-566-2420.*

COSSÉ, STEVEN A., lawyer, oil industry executive; b. Dec. 2, 1947; m. Andree D. Cossé. BA, Southeastern La. U., Hammond; JD, Loyola U. Bar: La. 1975. Gen. counsel Murphy Oil Corp., El Dorado, Ark., 1991—, v.p., 1993—94, sr. v.p., 1994—2005, exec. v.p., 2005—. Office: Murphy Oil Corp PO Box 7000 El Dorado AR 71731-7000 Office Phone: 870-862-6411. Office Fax: 870-864-6373. E-mail: steve_cosse@murphyoilcorp.com.*

COSTA, DANIEL LAWRENCE, architect; b. Providence, Feb. 16, 1953; s. Dimas and Laurinda (Diogo) C.; m. Shepley Patterson Metcalf, May 31, 1980 (div. Mar. 1988); 1 child, Hilary Metcalf. AB, Brown U., 1974; MArch, Harvard U., 1980. Architect Archtl. Resources Cambridge (Mass.), Inc., 1980-87, Shepard/Quraeshi Assocs., Watertown, Mass., 1987-88; prin. Costa/Flenniken Assocs., Boston, 1988-90, Dan Costa AIA, Boston, 1990—. Mem. Somerville (Mass.) Design Rev. Bd., 1988; bd. dirs. Somerville Hist. Preservation Commn., 1991-96. Recipient Home of Yr. award Met. Home Mag., 1997, Best in Am. Living award Profl. Builder Mag., 1995, Southern Home award So. Living Mag., 1995. Mem. AIA, Boston Soc. Architects. Office: 355 Congress ST Boston MA 02210 Office Phone: 617-451-5898. Personal E-mail: dancosta@earthlink.net.

COSTA, FRANCISCO, fashion designer; b. Brazil, 1966; Studied, Hunter Coll., Fashion Inst. Tech. Asst. Oscar de la Renta, NYC; designer Gucci, Paris, Calvin Klein, NYC, lead designer, 2003—. Recipient Womenswear Designer of the Yr. award, Coun. of Fashion Designers of Am., 2006. Office: Phillips-Van Heusen Corpn 200 Madison Ave New York NY 10016

COSTA, GUSTAVO, Italian studies scholar; b. Rome, Mar. 21, 1930; came to U.S., 1961; s. Paolo and Ida (Antonangelo) C.; m. Natalia Zalessow, June 8, 1963; 1 child, Dora L. Maturità Classica, Liceo Virgilio, Rome, 1948; PhD cum laude, U. Rome, 1954. Asst. Istituto di Filosofia, Rome, 1957-60; instr. Italian Univ. de Lyon, Lyons, France, 1960-61, U. Calif., Berkeley, 1961-63, asst. prof., 1963-68, assoc. prof., 1968-72, prof., 1972-91, prof. emeritus, 1991—, chmn. dept. Italian, 1973-76, 88-91. Vis. prof. Scuola di Studi Superiori, Naples, 1984, Inst. Philosophy, U. Rome La Sapienza, 1992, Scuola Europea di Studi Avanzati, Naples, 2003, Inst. Italiano per Gli Studi Filosofici, Naples, 2004; reviewer RAI Corp., Rome, 1982-89 Author: La leggenda dei secoli d'oro nella lett. ital., 1972, Le antichità germaniche nella cultura italiana, 1977, Il sublime e la magia da Dante a Tasso, 1994, Vico e l'Europa: Contro la boria delle nazioni, 1996, Malebranche y Vico, 1998, Vico e l' Inquisizione, 1999, Malebranche e Roma, 2003, La Santa Sede Di Fronte a Locke, 2003, La Congregazione dell'Indice e Jonathan Swift, 2004, Thomas Burnet e la censura pontificia, 2006; mem. editl. bd. Nouvelles de la République des Lettres, New Vico Studies, Cuadernos sobre Vico. Inst. Italiano Studi Storici fellow, Naples, Italy, 1954-57, Guggenheim Meml. Found. fellow, N.Y.C., 1977; grantee French Govt., Paris, 1956, Belgian Govt., Brussels, 1956, Targa d'oro Apulia, Italy, 1990. Mem. Am. Assn. Tchrs. Italian, Am. Soc. for Eighteenth-Century Studies, Renaissance Soc. Am., Dante Soc. Am. Avocations: gardening, stamp collecting/philately. Office: U Calif Dept Italian Studies Berkeley CA 94720-2620 Office Phone: 510-642-5055.

COSTA, JIM, congressman; b. Fresno, Calif., Apr. 13, 1952; BA Polit. Sci., Calif. State U., Fresno, 1974. Spl. asst. to Congressman John Krebs, 1975-76; adminstrv. asst. Assembly Mem. Richard Lehman, 1976-78; mem. Calif. Assembly, 1978-94, Calif. State Senate, 1994—2004, chmn. agr. and water resources com., housing and land use com., mem. fin., investment and internat. trade com., transp. com.; mem. US Congress from 20th Calif. dist., 2005—; mem. Agriculture com., Resources com. and Sci. com. Senate rep. Calif. World Trade Commn., 1995-2004; pres. Nat. Conf. State Legislatures, 2000-01. Mem. Fresno County Farm Bur., I.D.E.S. Men's Lodge, Fresno Cabrillo Club. Democrat. Roman Catholic. Office: US Ho Reps 1004 Longworth Ho Office Bldg Washington DC 20515-0520 Office Phone: 202-225-3341.*

COSTA, KATHY, retired librarian; b. Montgomery, Minn., July 28, 1933; d. John Egan and Bozena Rose (McKeon) Grathwol; m. Alfredo Costa, Aug. 5, 1957 (div. 1973) BA, Coll. St. Catherine, 1955; MLS, U. Ariz., 1975. Libr. St. Paul Pub. Libr., 1961—72, U. N.Mex., Albuquerque, 1973—74, 1976—79, Gallup, N.Mex., 1975—76; children's coord. Santa Fe Pub. Libr., 1979—94, youth outreach libr., 1994—2003; ret., 2003. Fulbright Travel grantee U.S. Govt., 1955-56; recipient French Govt. Tchg. Assistantship, 1955-56, Econo-Clad Lit. Program award Assn. Libr. Svc. Children, 1996, Celebrate Literacy award Internat. Reading Assn., 1987 Mem. ALA, AAUW, Nat. Assn. for Perpetuation and Preservation of Storytelling Roman Catholic. Avocations: storytelling, singing, travel.

COSTA, LAIS ROSA RODRIGUES, veterinarian, educator, medical researcher; arrived in US, 1989; d. Carlos Rodrigues Costa and Mercedes Therezinha Sammarco Rodrigues Costa; m. Matthew Enrico Baur, Apr. 3, 1993; 1 child, Markus Henrick Baur-Costa. DVM, São Paulo State U., Botucatu, Brazil, 1987; MS, U. Ky., Lexington, 2004; PhD, La. State U., Baton Rouge, 2005. Diplomate in large animal internal medicine Am. Coll. Vet. Internal Medicine, 1999, in equine practice Am. Bd. Vet. Practitioners, 2006, cert. vet. acupuncturist Internat. Vet. Acupuncture Soc., 2001. Intern in large animal medicine Sch. Vet. Medicine La. State U., Baton Rouge, 1990; rsch. asst. U. Ky., Lexington, 1991—94; clin. and rsch. fellow Sch. Vet. Medicine U. Calif., Davis, 1994—96; resident in equine medicne Sch. Vet. Medicine La. State U., Baton Rouge, 1996—99, doctoral fellow, clin. instr., 1999—2006; asst. prof. large animal medicine Sch. Vet. Medicine Tufts U., North Grafton, Mass., 2006—. Recipient Horacio Passos award, Rotary, 1987; grantee, Sigma Xi, 2001. Mem.: AVMA, Am. Bd. Vet. Practitioners, La. Bd. Vet. Medicine, Am. Assn. Equine Paractitioners, Vet. Comparative Respiratory Soc. (Joan A. O'Brien award 1999, 2002), Am. Coll. Vet. Internal Medicine (Young Investigator Rsch. award 1998, 1999), Gamma Sigma Delta, Phi Zeta (First pl. Best Clin. Rsch. 1998, 2d pl. Best Clin. Rsch. 1999). Office: Sch Vet Medicine Tufts Univ 200 Westboro Rd North Grafton MA 01536 Home Phone: 508-529-4236; Office Phone: 508-839-5395. Business E-Mail: lais.costa@tufts.edu.

COSTA, MARY, soprano; b. Knoxville, Tenn. Student, L.A. Conservatory of Music; PhD (hon.), Hardin-Simmons U., 1973. Film voice of Aurora Disney's Sleeping Beauty, 1959; appeared TV commls., 1955—57; debut LA Opera, 1958; appeared Glyndebourne Opera House, 1958; v.p. Calif. Inst. Arts; in La Boheme, San Francisco Opera, 1959; recorded "La Boheme" for RCA Victor from the stage of Rome Opera Ho., 1961; soloist John F. Kennedy Meml. Svc. at Sports Arena, LA, 1963; as Violetta in La Traviata Met. Opera, NYC, 1964; appeared Royal Opera House Covent Garden, Teatro Nacional de San Carlos, Grand Theatre de Geneve, Vancouver, Lisbon, Kiev, Leningrad, Tbilisi, Boston, Cin., Hartford, Newark, Phila., San Antonio, Seattle; toured US with Bernstein's Candide; appeared English prodn. Candide; tour Soviet Union, 1970; Bolshoi debut in La Traviatta, 1970; revival Bernstein's Candide at John F. Kennedy Ctr. for Performing Arts, 1971; starring role motion picture The Great Waltz, 1972; v.p. Hawaiian Fragrances, Honolulu, 1972; appeared internat. recitals, orchs.; command performance at the White House, 1974; Met. Opera hist. tour of Japan as Musetta in La Boheme, 1975. Named Woman of Yr., LA, 1959, Tenn. Woman of Distinction, Am. Lung Assn., 2000; recipient DAR Honor medal, 1974, Tenn. Hall of Fame award, 1987, Women of Achievement award, Northwood Inst., Palm Beach, Fla., 1991, So. Birmingham Coll., 1993, Tenn. Achievement award, Gov. of Tenn., 1998, Disney Legends award, 1999, Disting. Verdi performances of 20th Century, Met. Opera Guild, 2001; Mary Costa Scholarship established at U. Tenn., 1979. Achievements include apptd. by Pres. to serve on Nat. Coun. on the Arts, 2003; featured artist at Hollywood Bowl tribute to "Walt Disney: 75 Years of Music", 2004.

COSTA, PAUL JOSEPH, psychologist; b. Allison Park, Pa., Mar. 9, 1968; s. Ralph Felix and Therese Marie Costa; m. Rashida Stacy-Ann Campbell, Apr. 16, 2004. BS cum laude Biology, Wofford Coll., 1990; MS summa cum laude Gen. Psychology, Carlos Albizu U., 1996, PsyD summa cum laude Clin. Psychology, 2001. Cert. residential counselor Comprehensive Alcoholism Rehab. Programs, Inc., lic. psychologist Fla. Dept. Health, 2002. Staff psychologist Ctr. Clin. and Forensic Psychology, Inc., Plantation, Fla., 2002—; designated mental health authority Eckerd Youth Devel. Ctr., Okeechobee, Fla., 2004—06; residential counselor Comprehensive Alcoholism Rehab. Programs Inc., West Palm Beach, Fla., 2006—. Lab. and tchg. asst. Wofford Coll., Spartanburg, SC, 1987—90, Spartanburg, 1987—90; psychotherapist Goodman Psychol. Svcs. Ctr., Miami, Fla., 1996—97; psychol. evaluator PsychSolutions, Coral Gables, Fla., 1998; clin. psychology intern Atlantic Shores Hosp., Fort Lauderdale, Fla., 1999—2000; neuropsychol. resident Cognitive Rehabilitative Assoc. South Fla., Inc., Miami, 2001—02; clin. neuropsychologist Ctrs. Psychol. Growth, Inc., Miami, 2002—03; spkr. in field. Musician: The Invertebrates; author: (short stories) Waiting for the Furnace to Kick On (Nat. Honors, Scholastic Writing Awards, 1986), Visions of Terror (Nat. Honors, Scholastic Writing Awards, 1986); composer (musician): (film soundtrack) Frustration; musician: (musical) Grease: The Musical. Benjamin Wofford scholar, Wofford Coll., 1986—90. Mem.: APA, Fla. Psychol. Assn. Roman Catholic. Avocations: singing, naturalist, music, writing. Office: Ctr Clin and Forensic Psychology Inc 6830 SW 16th St Plantation FL 33325 Home: 3608 Moon Bay Cir Wellington FL 33414 Office Phone: 954-584-6155. Personal E-mail: zepplication@yahoo.com.

COSTA, WALTER HENRY, architect; b. Oakland, Calif., July 2, 1924; s. Walter H.F. and Mamie R. (Dunkle) C.; m. Jane Elisabeth Ledwich, Aug. 28, 1948; 1 dau., Laura. BA, U. Calif., Berkeley, 1948, MA, 1949. Designer Mario Corbett (architect), San Francisco, 1947-48, Ernst Born (architect), San Francisco, 1949; draftsman Milton Pflueger, San Francisco, 1950-51; designer Skidmore, Owings & Merrill, San Francisco, 1951-57, participating assoc., then assoc. prtnr., 1957-69, gen. prtnr., 1969-89, ret., 1990. Bd. dirs. East Bay Regional Park Dist., 1977-87, pres., 1984-85; mem. city council, Lafayette, Calif., 1972-76, mayor, 1973. Served with USSNR, 1943-46. Mem.: AIA. Home: 2130 Cactus Ct #2 Walnut Creek CA 94595

COSTA-GAVRAS, (CONSTANTIN GAVRAS), film director, writer; b. Athens, Greece, Feb. 13, 1933; naturalized French citizen; m. Michele Ray, Sept. 12, 1968; children: Alexandre, Helene, Romain. Student, U. Sorbonne, Paris; DFA (hon.), Simon Fraser U., Vancouver, 2006. Diplomate Inst. Higher Cinematic Studies. Ballet dancer, Greece; asst. to film dirs. Yves Allegret, Jacques Demy, Rene Clair, Rene Clement, Jean Giorno. Pres. Festival Paris-Cinema, 2003—, Cinematheque francaise, 2007—. Dir., screenwriter films: The Sleeping Car Murders, 1964; Z, 1969 (Acad. awaard for best fgn. lang. film, 70, Jury prize, Cannes Film Festival, 69, Raoul-Levy prize, 69, Golden Globe award, 70); Missing, 1982 (Golden Palm award Cannes, 82, Acad. Award for best screenplay, 82); dir.: (films) Un Homme de Trop, 1966 (Moscow Film Festival prize), L'Aveu, 1970 (The Confession), State of Siege, 1973 (Cannes Film Festival award, 75), Special Section, 1975, Madame Rosa (also actor), 1978, Clair de Femme, 1979, Hanna K, 1983, Conseil de Femme, 1986, Betrayed, 1988, Music Box, 1990 (Golden Bear award Berlin film festival, 90), Little Apocalypse, 1992, Mad City, 1996, The Parthenon, 2004; prodr, dir., writer: The Ax, 2004; dir.: (Operas) Il Mondo Dela Luna (Joseph Haydn), 1994, Mad City, 1997; co-dir.: A Propos de Nice, 1995; Lumiere and Compagnie, 1995; Amen, 2001 (named Best European movie, 2002, Globo D'oro Assn. Fgn. Press, 2002); dir.: (theater musical show) All Around is Light, 2003; writer, prodr.: (films) Mon Colonel, 2006. Named Best Dir., Cannes Film Festival 1975, Officier Ordre National du Merite; decorated Comdr. Arts and Letters, France, Chevalier Legion d'Honneur; recipient Life Achievement award De l'Academie Francaise, 1998, Gold medal of Bellas Artes King of Spain. Office Phone: 331-44411373. Personal E-mail: kg@kgproduection.fr.

COSTAGLIOLA, FRANCESCO, retired government official; b. Cranston, RI, Aug. 24, 1917; s. Luigi and Rose (Lubrano) C.; m. Agnes Mary Ross, June 14, 1952 (dec.); children: Francesca Danieli (dec.), Marisa Costagliola, Antonia Burns, Roseanne Rubin. Student, U. R.I., 1935-37; BSEE, U.S. Naval Acad., 1941; postgrad., Naval Postgrad. Sch., 1946-47, MIT, 1947-49, Cath. U. Am., 1967-71; MBA, Am. U., Washington, 1974. Commd. ensign USN, 1941, advanced through grades to capt., 1960, served in U.S.S. Phoenix in 24 ops. PTO, 1941-46; comdg. officer U.S.S. Halsey Powell, Republic of Korea, 1951-52; various positions naval sea and shore assignments involving atomic energy USN, 1952-64; mil. asst. to asst. to Sec. Def. for atomic energy, 1964-67; ret., 1968; commr. AEC, 1968-69; engr. RCA, 1974-76; staff mem. Joint Congl. Com. on Atomic Energy, Washington, 1967-68, 69-71, 76-77, Office of Sec. of Senate, Washington, 1977-86. Mem. Md. Radiation Control Adv. Bd., 1973-81. Contbr. articles to profl. jours. Treas. Class of '41 U.S. Naval Acad., 1997—. Decorated Bronze Star with Combat V (2). Mem. AAAS, Inst. Ops. Rsch. and Mgmt. Scis., Am. Nuc. Soc., U.S. Naval Inst., Pearl Harbor Survivors Assn. (pres. No. Va. chpt. 1991-1993, 2003-04), Naval Acad. Alumni Assn., Mil. Order World Wars, Mil. Order Carabao, Army and Navy Club (Washington). Roman Catholic. Home: 307 Gibbon St Alexandria VA 22314-4129 Personal E-mail: costagliola@comcast.net.

COSTANDI, WISAM EMILE, application developer, biomedical researcher, consultant; b. Aley, Lebanon, May 24, 1975; arrived in US, 1992; s. Emile Costandi and Afaf Maasri Costandi; m. Elodie Mancel, Sept. 29, 1997. BSc in Biomed. Engring., Northwestern U., 1996; MS in Biomed. Engring., U. Calif., Davis, 2001, MBA in Tech. Mgmt., 2001. Dir., tech. support GDI, Orlando, Fla., 1996—98; sr. cons. Deloitte and Touche LLP, San Francisco, 2001—03; ptnr. CIL, LLC, Berkeley, Calif., 2003—06. Contbr. articles to profl. jours. Recipient The Duke of Edinburgh award, 1992;, NIH fellow, 1998. Mem.: Healthcare Info. and Mgmt. Sys. Soc., Northwestern U. Alumni Admissions Coun., Math. Assn. Am., Mensa. Achievements include research in optical detection of particles within microdroplets using immunoassay methodologies. Office Phone: 510-868-1044. E-mail: wisam@costandi.com.

COSTAS, BOB (ROBERT QUINLAN COSTAS), sportscaster; b. Queens, NY, Mar. 22, 1952; s. John George and Jayne (Quinlan) C.; m. Carole Randall Krummenacher, June 24, 1983; children: Keith Michael, Taylor. Student, Syracuse U., NY, 1970-74. Sportscaster Sta. KMOX-AM, St. Louis, 1974-81; sportscaster, host sports programs NBC Sports, NYC, 1980—; radio host Costas Coast to Coast, 1986—96; substitute anchor Larry King Live, 2005. Announcer: (TV series) Game of the Week, 1982—89; host Later with Bob Costas, 1988—94; TV and film appearances include: Diamonds on the Silver Screen, 1992; Cheers: Last Call, 1992; The Drew Carey Show, 1999; NewsRadio, 1996; ESPN Sports Century, 2000—04; host: (TV series) On the Record with Bob Costas, 2001—05; CostasNow, 2005—; host Inside the NFL, 2002—; TV and film appearances include: Baseketball, 1998; Coach Carter, 2005; Cars, 2006; author: (books) Costas on Sports, 1997, Costas on Baseball, 1999, Fair Ball: A Fan's Case for Baseball, 2000; co-author: Clearing the Bases: The Greatest Baseball Disputes of the;Last Century, 2002. Recipient 15 Sports Emmy awards, 8 for outstanding sports broadcaster, 2 Emmy awards for writing, 1 Emmy award for interview show, 1996, one for play-by-play braodcast of 1997 World Series; named Nat. Sportscaster of Yr., Nat. Sportscasters and Sportwriters Assn., 1985, 87, 88, 91, 92, 95, 97. Office: CostasNow HBO 1100 Ave of the Americas New York NY 10036*

COSTA-ZALESSOW, NATALIA, foreign language educator; b. Kumanovo, Macedonia, Dec. 5, 1936; arrived in US, 1951; d. Alexander P. and Katarina (Duric) Z.; m. Gustavo Costa, June 8, 1963; 1 child, Dora. BA in Italian, U. Calif., Berkeley, 1959, MA in Italian, 1961, PhD in Romance Langs. and Lits., 1967. Tchg. asst. U. Calif., Berkeley, 1959—63; instr. Mills Coll., Oakland, Calif., 1963; asst. prof. San Francisco State U., 1968—74, assoc. prof., 1974—79, prof., 1979—98, coord. Italian program, 1992—98, prof. emerita, 1998—. Author: Scrittrici italiane dal XIII al XX secolo, Testi e critica, 1982; editor: Anima, 1997; transl.: Her Soul, 1996; contbr. articles to profl. jours. Sidney M. Ehrman scholar U. Calif., Berkeley, 1957-58, Gamma Phi Beta scholar U. Calif., Berkeley, 1958, Herbert H. Vaughan scholar U. Calif., Berkeley, 1959-60, Advanced Grad. Traveling fellow in romance lang. and lit. U. Calif., Berkeley, 1964-65.

Mem. MLA, Am. Assn. Tchrs. Italian, Renaissance Soc. Am., Dante Soc. Am., Croatian Acad. Am. Roman Catholic. Avocations: swimming, hiking, opera. Office: San Francisco State U Dept Fgn Lang and Lit San Francisco CA 94132

COSTELLO, CHRISTINE ANN, fine arts director, church organist; b. Webster, Mass., Sept. 13, 1966; d. Robert Ashmore Cozzens and Joyce Alice Redlitz-Cozzens; m. James J. Costello, Dec. 10, 1988; 1 child, Jonathan Ashmore. BA in Music, Mount Holyoke Coll., 1988; MA in Music, U. Conn., 2000. Lic. tchr. Mass. Dept. Edn., cert. dir. fine arts Fitchburg State Coll., 2002, fine arts administration Fitchburg State Coll., Mass., 2002. Dir. vocal music Southbridge Pub. Schs., Mass., 1993—99; middle sch. music specialist Auburn Pub. Schs., Mass., 1999—2001; dir. fine arts Tantasqua Regional/Union 61 Schools, Fiskdale, Mass., 2001—. Mem. Music Educators Nat. Conf., 1993—. Mem.: Assn. Supervison and Curriculum Devel., Nat. Art Educators Assn. Luth. Avocation: gourmet cooking. Home: 77 Vinton Rd Holland MA 01521 Office: Tantasqua Regional Schools 320B Brookfield Rd Fiskdale MA 01518 Office Phone: 508-347-7381 x28. Business E-Mail: costelloc@tantasqua.org.

COSTELLO, DANIEL BRIAN, lawyer, consultant; b. Arlington, Va., Apr. 23, 1950; s. James Russell and Hazel Virginia (Caudle) C.; m. Margaret Ruth Dow, June 13, 1970; children: James Brian, Rebecca Ruth, Kathleen Marie. BA, U. Va., 1972; JD, Coll. of William and Mary, 1975. Bar: Va. 1975, U.S. Dist. Ct. (ea. dist.) Va. 1979, U.S. Ct. Appeals (4th cir.) 1979, U.S. Bankruptcy Ct. (ea. dist.) Va. 1979, D.C. 1984. Reporter Globe Newspapers, Vienna, Va., 1965-68; freelance journalist Williamsburg, Va., 1972-73; news dir. Sta. WMBG, WBCI-FM, Williamsburg, 1973-76; spl. asst. atty. gen. Commonwealth of Va., Suffolk, Va., 1976-78, asst. atty. gen. Richmond, Va., 1978-80; ptnr. Dameron, Costello & Hubacher, Alexandria, Va., 1980-89, Costello & Hubacher, Alexandria, 1989-99; pvt. practice Springfield, 1999—2004; dist. Right of Way and utilities mgr. Va. Dept. Transp., 2004—; corp. sec., gen. counsel Olivares U.S.A., Inc., Fairfax, Va., 1999-2000, pres., 2000—03. Press rels. cons. Va. Bar Assn.; spl. commr. in chancery Alexandria Cir. Ct. Author: Land Use Planning and Eminent Domain, 1997, 2d edit. 1999, Foreclosure in Virginia, 1991; co-editor, co-author The Layman's Guide to Virginia Law, 1977; editor night news Sta. WINA, 1969-72; contbr. articles to profl. jours. Mem. Va. State Bar, D.C. Bar, Soc. Alumni Coll. of William and Mary, U. Va. Alumni Soc., Rolling Hills Club. Presbyterian. Avocations: hunting, fishing, coin collecting/numismatics. Office: VDOT-R/W 14685 Avion Pky Ste 230 Chantilly VA 20151 Office Phone: 703-383-2174. Business E-Mail: brian.costello@vdot.virginia.gov.

COSTELLO, ELLEN M., bank executive; b. 1955; BBA, St. Francis Xavier U.; MBA, Dalhousie U., Canada. Account officer BMO Fin. Grp., 1983, sr. positions in corp. banking and treasury, 1983—93, leadership positions in derivatives and as regional treasurer Hong Kong, 1993—95, sr. v.p., dep. treas., 1995—97, exec. v.p., global treasury grp., 1997—2000, head of securitization and credit investment mgmt., 2000—03; head BMO Capital Markets, NYC, 2003—06; CEO Harris Bankcorp, Inc., 2006—. Mem. bd. dirs. United Way of Met. Chgo., Chgo. Pub. Edn. Fund, After Sch. Matters, Chgo. Cmty. Trust, Bd. of Governors of St. Francis Xavier U. Named one of 25 Women to Watch, Crain's Chgo. Bus., 2007. Mem.: Fin. Services Roundtable, Econ. Club of Chgo., Executives Club of Chgo., The Chgo. Club, Civic Com. of the Commercial Club of Chgo., Chgo. Network. Office: Harris Bankcorp Inc 111 W Monroe St Chicago IL 60603*

COSTELLO, ELVIS (DECLAN PATRICK MCMANUS), musician, songwriter, singer; b. London, 1954; s. Ross McManus; m. Cait O'Riordan, 1986; m. Diana Krall, Dec. 2003; children: Dexter Henry Lorcan, Frank Harlon James; 1 child from previous marriage. Composer: (songs) Alison, 1977, Watching the Detectives, 1977, (I Don't Want To Go To) Chelsea, 1979, Radio Radio, 1978, 1978;: (songs) Crawling to the USA, 1978, Radio Radio, 1978, Stranger in the House, 1978, Girls Talk, 1979, Oliver's Army, 1979, Boy With a Problem, 1982, Every Day I Write the Book, 1983; musician: (albums) My Aim is True, 1977, This Year's Model, 1978, Armed Forces, 1979, Get Happy!!, 1980, Trust, 1980, Almost Blue, 1981, Imperial Bedroom, 1982, Punch the Clock, 1983, Goodbye Cruel World, 1984, The Best Of, 1985, Blood and Chocolate, 1986, King of America, 1986, Spike, 1989, Girls, Girls, Girls, 1990, Mighty Like a Rose, 1991, (with Steve Nieve, Pete Thomas, Bruce Thomas and Nick Lowe) Brutal Youth, 1994, (with the Brodsky Quartet) The Juliet Letters, 1993 (Dutch Edison award), The Very Best of Elvis Costello and the Attractions, 1994, Kojak Variety, 1995, All This Useless Beauty, 1996, Extreme Honey, 1997, Terror & Magnificence, 1997, Painted From Memory, 1998 (Grammy, 1999), When I Was Cruel, 2002 (nominated for 3 Grammy awards), Cruel Smile, 2002, North, 2003, Il Sogno, 2004, The Delivery Man, 2004, Marian McPartland's Piano Jazz Radio Broadcast, My Flame Burns Blue, 2006; musician: (with Allen Toussaint) Hot As Pistol, Keen As a Blade, 2006, The River In Reverse, 2006; appears in concert U.S. and Eng., 1978—, appeared in film Americathon, 1979—; actor(appeared in): Austin Powers 2: The Spy Who Shagged Me, 1999; recorded with Burt Bacharach: I'll Never Fall in Love Again, The Sweetest Punch: The Songs of Costello and Bacharach, 1999. Nominee for an Oscar for Best Song 'The Scalet Tide', for Cold Mountain, co-written with T Bone Burnett, 2004; recipient Ivor Novello awards for songwriting (two), Nordoff-Robbins Silver Clef award, BAFTA for music written with Richard Harvey for TV series G.B.H., Founder's award, ASCAP, 2003; inducted into, Rock and Roll Hall of Fame, 2003.*

COSTELLO, FRANCIS WILLIAM, lawyer; b. Cambridge, Mass., Apr. 16, 1946; s. Frank George and Anna M. (Sinnott) C. BA, Columbia U., 1968, JD, 1973. Bar: NY 1974, Calif. 1977. Assoc. Whitman & Ransom, NYC, 1973-74, Anderson, Mori & Rabinowitz, Tokyo, 1974—76, Whitman & Ransom, LA, 1976-82, ptnr., 1982-93, Whitman, Breed, Abbott & Morgan, LA, 1993-2000, Holland & Knight, LLP, LA, 2000—. Bd. dirs. Hattori Found., LA, Hamazawa Investment Co., LA, Japan Travel Bur. Internat., LA; dir. com. Holland & Knight, LLP., LA, Calif., 2001-04. Served with US Army, 1968-70, Vietnam. Mem. ABA, State Bar Calif., State Bar NY, LA County Bar Assn., Pumpkin Ridge Golf Club (Oreg.), Wilshire Country Club (LA), Calif. Club (LA). Home: 415 Knight Way La Canada Flintridge CA 91011-2725 Office Phone: 213-896-2452. Business E-Mail: fcostell@hklaw.com.

COSTELLO, JEFFREY, apparel designer; Grad., Parsons Sch. of Design. Co-owner, designer (with Robert Tagliapietra) Costello Tagliapietra, 2004—. Work featured in Metropolitan Museum of Art's Costume Inst., Vogue, Elle, Bazaar, Style.com, Gloss, Maxim, Black Book. Recipient Ecco Domani Fashion Found. award, 2005. Office: Costello Tagliapietra 97 Second Pl 3Fl Brooklyn NY 11231

COSTELLO, JERRY F., JR., congressman, former county official; b. Sept. 25, 1949; m. Georgia Jean Cockrum; children: Jerry, Gina, John. AA, Bayeville Area Coll., 1971; BA, Maryville Coll. of Sacred Heart, 1973. County bd. chmn. St. Clair County, Ill.; dir. ct. svcs. and probation 20th Jud. Cir. Campaign; chmn. Heart Assn., Belleville, Ill., 1983; vice chmn. Ill. div. United Way, 1984, chmn., 1985; mem. U.S. Congress from 21st (now 12th) Ill. Dist., 1988—; former mem. budget com.; mem. transp., infrastructure and sci. coms. Bd. dirs. Ill. Ctr. for Autism; active St. Clair County Big Bros./Big Sisters, Belleville Women's Crisis Ctr., Children's Ctr. for Behavioral Devel.; helped establish St. Clair County chpt. Vets. Outreach Info. Ctr.; mem. East St. Louis Econ. Opportunity Commn., Ill.; vice chmn. Southwestern Ill. Bus. Devel. Fin. Corp., 1985—; bd. dirs. So. Ill. Leadership Council; pres. Urban Counties Council of Ill. Recipient cert. of Appreciation, Bus. and Profl. Women's Assn., 1985; honored Citizens League for Adequate Social Services; 1985 AAHMES Court #84, Daus. ISIS Ann. Humanitarian award, Gene Hughes award Ill. Ct. Services and Probation Assn. Democrat. Office: US Ho of Reps 2454 Rayburn House Off Bldg Washington DC 20515-1312*

COSTELLO, JOHN H., III, business and marketing executive; b. Akron, Ohio, June 2, 1947; s. John H. Jr. and Lia Costello; children from previous marriage, Michael, Jeffrey, Matthew. BS in Indsl. Mgmt., Akron U., 1968; MBA, Mich. State U., 1970. Mktg. dir. Procter & Gamble Co., Cin., 1971—84; sr. v.p. Pepsi-Cola USA, Purchase, NY, 1984—86; exec. v.p. Wells, Rich, Greene, Inc., NYC, 1986—88; pres., chief oper. officer Nielsen Mktg. Rsch. U.S.A., Chgo., 1988—93; sr. exec. v.p. Sears, Roebuck & Co., Hoffman Estates, Ill., 1993—98; pres. Auto Nation, Inc., Ft. Lauderdale, Fla., 1999—; CEO MVP.com, 1999—2001; chief global mktg. officer Yahoo!, 2001—02; exec. v.p., chief mktg. officer Home Depot, 2002—05. Sr. mktg. execs. panel Conf. Bd., NYC, 1985-87; industry speaker on bus. trends and issues, 1985—; bd. dirs. The Quaker Oats Co, Sears Can., Bombay Co. Mem. exec. bd. N.E. Ill. coun. Boy Scouts Am., 1993-97; trustee Multiple Sclerosis Soc., Chgo., 1990—, vice chmn., 1995—; bd. dirs. Nat. Multiple Sclerosis Soc., 1989—, chair fundraising, 1990-94, mem. exec. com., 1990-94, chair nominating com., 1996—; trustee Ga. Acquarium, 2006. Mem. Am. Film Inst. (trustee 2005—), Assn. Nat. Advertisers (bd. dirs. 1995—, vice chmn. 1998, chmn. 1999), Direct Ad Coun. (bd. dirs. 1996—, vice chmn. 1998), Direct Retail Advt. and Mktg. Assn. (bd. dirs. 1995—, Retail Mktg. Hall of Fame 1997), Econ. Club Chgo., Conway Farms Golf Club, Congl. Country Club. Episcopalian. Avocations: skiing, golf, travel, fly fishing. Office: Home Depot 2455 Paces Ferry Rd Atlanta GA 30339-5000 Home: 4716 Northside Dr NW Atlanta GA 30327-4552 Home Phone: 404-497-0628. Personal E-mail: jhc860@yahoo.com.

COSTELLO, JOHN WILLIAM, lawyer; b. Chgo., Apr. 16, 1947; s. William John and June Ester (O'Neill) C.; m. Maureen Grace Matthews, June 13, 1970; children— Colleen, William, Erin, Owen. BA, John Carroll U., 1969; JD, DePaul U., 1972. Bar: U.S. Dist. Ct. (no. dist.) Ill. 1982. Assoc. Arvey, Hodes, Costello & Burman, Chgo., 1972-76; ptnr., 1976-90, ptnr. Wildman, Harrold Allen & Dixon, 1990—. Co-author: (manual) The Bankrupcy Reform Act of 1978, 1981. Served to capt. U.S. Army, 1972-73. Mem. ABA (bus. bankruptcy com., jurisdiction and venue and secured creditors subcoms.), Ill. State Bar Assn. (former vice chmn., chmn. comml. banking and bankrupcy law sect. 1979-81), Am. Bankruptcy Inst., Turnaround Mgmt. Assn. (former bd. dirs. Midwest sect.). Democrat. Roman Catholic. Office: Wildman Harrold Aller & Dixon 225 W Wacker Dr Chicago IL 60606-1224 Office Phone: 312-201-2971.

COSTELLO, THOMAS JOSEPH, retired bishop; b. Camden, NY, Feb. 23, 1929; s. James G. and Ethel A. (Dupont) C. Lic. in Sacred Theology, Cath. U. Am., 1954, JCB, 1960. Ordained priest Roman Cath. Ch., 1954. Sec. Diocesan Tribunal, Diocese of Syracuse, 1958; supt. schs. Cath. Diocese of Syracuse, 1960—75; pastor Our Lady Lourdes Ch., Syracuse, NY, 1975—78; aux. bishop Syracuse, 1978—2004. Roman Catholic. Home: 1515 Midland Ave Syracuse NY 13205-1447 Office: PO Box 511 240 E Onondaga St Syracuse NY 13201 Office Phone: 315-470-1460. E-mail: costello@syracusediocese.org.

COSTES, NICHOLAS CONSTANTINE, aerospace scientist, educator, retired government agency administrator; b. Athens, Greece, Sept. 20, 1926; came to U.S., 1948, naturalized, 1959; s. Constantine Nicholas and Anna (Papadopoulou) C.; m. Polytime Andros, Nov. 22, 1958; children: Constantine Nicholas, Anna Amalia, Christina Smaragtha. Diploma, Sci. Sch., Athens Coll., 1945; student, Athens Nat. Tech. U, 1945-48; AB, Darthmouth Coll., 1950, MSC.E. (George W. Davis scholar), 1951; A.M., M.E.N., Harvard U., 1962; MS, N.C. State U., 1955, PhD (Ford Found. fellow), 1965. Registered profl. engr., N.C., Ill. Teaching fellow dept. civil engrng. N.C. State U., Raleigh, 1951-53, instr., 1962-63; materials engr. N.C. State Hwy. and Pub. Works Commn., Raleigh, 1953-56; research civil engr. U.S. Army Cold Regions Research and Engrng. Lab., Hanover, NH, 1956-62; sr. research scientist space sci. lab Marshall Space Flight Center, NASA, Huntsville, Ala., 1965-98, team leader Apollo II Soil Mechanics Investigation Sci. Team, co-prin. investigator Apollo 12, 13 Lunar Geology Experiment, Apollo 14-17 Soil Mechanics Expt., 1991—, prin. investigator, co-investigator, project scientist Mechanics of Granular Materials Microgravity Expt., 1991—. Cons. geotech. engrng., 1965—; adj. prof. U. Colo., Boulder, 1998. Contbr. articles and tech. reports to profl. jours. Recipient Dartmouth Soc. Engrs. prize, 1951; recipient NASA awards including cert. of appreciation, 1970, Group Achievement award Lunar Roving Vehicle Team, 1971, invention award, 1971, Astronauts' Silver Snoopy award, 1972, dirs. commendation achievement, 1973, Group Achievemnt award Flow Process Modeling Space Shuttle Main Engine, 1985, Group Achievement awards Environs Definition of Space Shuttle Solid Rocket Motor Team, Challenger Incident, 1986, Mechanics of Granular Materials (MGM) Microgravity Expt. Fellow ASCE (life, Norman medal 1972, chmn. program com. aerospace council 1973-75, exec. com. aerospace div. 1976-82, chmn. 1980-81, profl. coordination com. 1982—), AIAA (assoc. fellow, dir. Ala./Miss. sect. 1976-79, Outstanding Aerospace Engr. award 1976, Martin Schilling award 1979, Herman Oberth award 1998); mem. NSPE, AAAS, Am. Geophys. Union, Dartmouth Soc. Engrs., Soc. Harvard Engrs. and Scientists, Assn. Civil Engrs. Greece (hon.), N.Y. Acad. Scis., Am. Men and Women of Sci., Sigma Xi, Phi Kappa Phi, Chi Epsilon Greek Orthodox. Office: PMB 190 Ste 30 4800 Whitesburg Dr S Huntsville AL 35802-1600 E-mail: nccostes@hotmail.com.

COSTIGAN, CONSTANCE FRANCES, artist, educator; b. Hoboken, NJ, July 3, 1935; d. Charles Francis and Joan Aletta C.; m. John Francis Christian, June 6, 1959 (div. 1972); m. Michael Krausz, May 14, 1976. BS, Simmons Coll. and Boston Mus. Sch. Fine Arts, 1957; MA, Am. U., 1965; postgrad., U. Calif.-Berkeley, 1971, U. Va.-Fairfax, 1968-69, U. D.C., 1972-73. Cert. tchr. Va. Designer Smithsonian Instn., Washington, 1957-59, mus. svcs. staff mem., 1962-68, drawing and design instr., 1971-76; art and crafts instr. Arlington County (Va.) Pub. Schs., 1970-75; prof. fine arts George Washington U., Washington, 1976—2002, prof. fine arts emeritus, 2003—; curator Arlington Art Ctr., Va., 1980; disting. vis. prof. Am. U. in Cairo, 1980-81; vis. prof. in drawing Haystack Mt. Sch. Crafts, Deer Isle, Maine, 1990. Jurist and judge art show D.C. area, 1975, 76, 90, 82, area show Del. Ctr. for Contemporary Arts, 1985; judge art show Sussex County Arts Coun. Mems. Show, 1991; mem. adv. bd. So. Del. Ctr. for the Arts and Humanities, 2003—; panelist Del. Divsn. of the Arts, 2004— Author: Leonardo, 1982, Elements of Art: Line, 1980; one-woman shows Hodson Gallery, Hood Coll. Frederick, Md., 2005, Visual Arts Gallery, Habitat Ctr. for the Arts, Dehli India, 2003, Lavinia Ctr., Milton, Del., 2003, Soho 20 Gallery, N.Y.C., 1997, Hampshire Coll. Gallery Hampshire Coll., Amherst, Mass., 1996, Dimock Gallery, George Washington U., 1987, Franz Bader Gallery, Washington, 1985, 90, No. Va. C.C., Alexandria, 1983, Barbara Fiedler Gallery, Washington, 1979, 82, Phillips Collection, Washington, 1977, Gulbenkian Gallery, U. Kent, Canterbury, Eng., 1975, Talbot Rice Arts Ctr., Edinburgh, Scotland, 1974, Design Ctr. Gallery, Cleve., 1974, Annenburg Arts Ctr., Phila., 1973; represented pub. collections Hirschhorn Mus. and Sculpture Garden, Washington, Phillips Collection, Washington, U. Iowa Mus., Iowa City, Dimock Gallery, George Washington U., Del. Mus. Art, others; included in numerous pvt. collections USA and abroad Sec. steering com. Del. chpt. Nat. Mus. for Women in the Arts, Newark, 1997-2001; mem. adv. bd. So. Delaware Ctr. for the Arts and Humanities, 2003-; bd. mem. Rehoboth Art League, Delaware, 2006-. Named to Nat. Mus. for Women in Arts to represent Del., 1998; recipient Jurors award, Del. Ctr. Contemporary Arts, Wilmington, 2006; fellow, Macdowell Colony, 1977, Ossabaw Island project, 1980; grantee, Lester Hereward Cooke Found., 1978—79, GSAS Facilitating Fund, 1990. Fellow Royal Soc. Arts. Home: 210 NE Market St Lewes DE 19958-1574 Office: 210 NE Market ST Lewes DE 19958-1574 Business E-Mail: cfc@gwu.edu.

COSTIGAN, EDWARD JOHN, retired investment banker; b. St. Louis, Oct. 31, 1914; s. Edward J. and Elizabeth Keane; m. Sara Louise Guth, Mar. 30, 1940 (dec. Nov. 6, 1988); children: Sally, Edward, John, James(dec.) , Betsy, Robert, David, Louise; m. Mildred F. Fabick, Dec. 27, 1995. AB, St. Louis U., 1935; MBA, Stanford U., 1937. Analyst, v.p. Whitaker & Co., St. Louis, 1937-43; ptnr. Edward D. Jones & Co., 1943-72; sr. v.p. Stifel Nicolaus & Co. Inc., St. Louis, 1972-74, pres., 1974-79, vice chmn., 1979-83, emeritus, 1983. Gov. Nat. Assn. Securities Dealers, 1967-70, Investment Bankers Assn., 1968-69, Midwest Stock Exch., Chgo., 1962-64; bd. dirs. 12 cos. Trustee Cath. Cemeteries Arch Diocese St. Louis, 1956—. Mem. St. Louis Soc. Fin. Analysts (pres. 1956), Harvard Club St. Louis (pres. 1955), Bellerive Country Club, Mo. Athletic Club, Old Warson Country Club, Noonday Club. Republican. Roman Catholic. Office: 501 N Broadway Fl 8 Saint Louis MO 63102-2102

COSTIGAN, RICHARD, III, lawyer; BA, U. Ga., 1988; JD, Cumberland U., 1991. Prin. cons. budget com., appropriations com. Calif. State Assembly, chief of staff, office of minority leader, chief of staff Assembly Rep. Caucus; sr. advisor Manatt, Phelps & Phillips, LLP; v.p. govt. rels. and chief policy advocate Calif. C. of C.; dep. chief of staff, legis. affairs sec. to Gov. Arnold Schwarzenegger State of Calif., 2003—06; co-mng. dir. McKenna Long & Aldridge LLP, Sacramento, 2006; sr. dir., state govt. and affairs Manatt, Phelps & Phillips LLP, Sacramento, 2007—. Office: Manatt Phelps & Phillips LLP 1215 K St Ste 1900 Sacramento CA 95814 Office Phone: 916-552-2370. Office Fax: 916-552-2323. E-mail: rcostigan@manatt.com.*

COSTIKYAN, EDWARD N., lawyer; b. Weehawken, NJ, Sept. 14, 1924; s. Mihran Nazar and Berthe (Muller) C.; m. Frances Holmgren, 1950 (div. 1975); chldren: Gregory, Emilie; m. Barbara Heine, Mar. 6, 1977. AB, Columbia U., 1947, LLB, 1949. Bar: NY 1949, US Dist. Ct. (so. dist.) NY 1950, US Ct. Appeals (2d cir.) 1950, US Supreme Ct. 1964. Law sec. to judge Harold R. Medina US Dist. Ct., NYC, 1949-51; ptnr. Paul, Weiss, Rifkind, Wharton & Garrison, NYC, 1960-93, of counsel, 1994—. Spl. advisor to mayor on sch. and borough governance City of NY, 1994-96, chairperson mayor's investigative commn. on sch. safety, 1995-96; mem. Commn. on Integrity in Govt., NYC, 1986, mem. joint com. on jud. adminstrn., 1985-92; adj. fellow Ctr. for Edn. Innovation, 1997—. Author: Behind Closed Doors: Politics in the Public Interest, 1966, How to Win Votes: The Politics of 1980, 1980, What Happened to the Body Politic, 2005, Commentaries, 2005; co-author: Re-Structuring the Government of New York City, 1972, New Strategies for Regional Cooperation, 1973; rsch. editor Columbia Law Rev.; mem. editl. bd. City Jour., 1992—; mem. bd. editors NY Law Jour., 1976—; contbr. articles on legal and polit. subjects to profl. publs. Chmn. NY State Task Force on NYC Juristiction and Structure, 1971-72; vice chmn. State Charter Revision for NYC, 1972-77; county leader New York County Dem. Com., 1962-64; Dem. presdl. elector, 1964, 88; trustee, mem. exec. com., chmn. alumni adv. bd. Columbia U., 1981-93, trustee emeritus, 1993—; bd. dirs., mem. coun. Mcpl. Art Soc., 1993-98; chmn. bd. dirs. NY Found. for Sr. Citizens, 1993—. 1st lt. inf. US Army, 1943-46. Recipient William J. Brennan Jr. award for Outstanding Cont. to Pub. Discourse, 1997. Fellow Am. Coll. Trial Lawyers; mem. Assn. of Bar of City of NY (mem. exec. com. 1986-90), Century Club. Unitarian Universalist. Home: 50 Sutton Pl S New York NY 10022-4167 Office: Paul Weiss Rifkind Wharton & Garrison Ste 12J 1285 Avenue Of The Americas Fl 21 New York NY 10019-6028 Office Phone: 212-688-0829.

COSTIN, JOSEPH LAURENCE, JR., information services executive; b. Chgo., Mar. 14, 1941; s. Joseph Laurence and Maribel (Cummings) Costin; m. Joan Gayley, June 20, 1964 (dec. June 1998); children: Jennifer, Michael. BA, U. Chgo., 1966. Divsn. mgr. Marshall Field and Co., Chgo., 1967—81; sr. v.p. Seligman and Latz, Inc., NYC, 1981—83; exec. v.p. CCC Info. Svcs., Inc., Chgo., 1983—93, vice-chmn., 1993—. Bd. dirs. CCC Info. Svcs. Inc. Lifetime trustee emeritus ICAR Edn. Found.; trustee Omega chpt. Psi Upsilon Fraternity; active Irish Angels Network, U. Notre Dame, 2006—; bd. dirs. Chgo. Youth Symphony Orch., 2005—. With Ill. Army N.G., 1963—69. Mem.: Contemporary Arts Coun., East Bank Club, Westmoreland Country Club. Roman Catholic. Avocations: golf, art, history. Office: World Trade Ctr Chgo 444 Merchandise Mart Plz Chicago IL 60654-1005

COSTLEY, GARY EDWARD, food company executive; b. Caldwell, Idaho, Oct. 26, 1943; s. Donald Clifford and Verna C.; m. Cheryl J. Zesiger, Dec. 21, 1963; children: Angela I., Chad D. BS, Oreg. State U., MS, PhD in Nutrition-Biochemistry. Formerly dir. nutrition, dir. public affairs, v.p. public affairs, v.p. and asst. to pres. Kellogg Co., sr. v.p. corp. devel., sr. v.p. sci. and quality, exec. v.p. sci. and tech., exec. v.p.; pres. Kellogg USA Inc.; area dir. Kellogg N.Am., to 1994; chmn., pres., CEO Internat. Multifoods, Mpls., 1997—2004; dean Grad Sch. Mgmt. Wake Forest U., 1995-97. Bd. dirs. Candlewood Inc., Pharmacopeia, Inc., ecFood.com. Trustee Miller Found, Battle Creek, Youth for Understanding Internat. Exch., Am. Health Found., Sarah W. Stedman Ctr.-Duke U. Med. Sch. Mem. Am. Inst. Nutrition. Lutheran. Home: 257 Barefoot Beach Blvd 404-202 Bonita Springs FL 34134-8594

COSTNER, KEVIN, actor; b. Lynwood, Calif., Jan. 18, 1955; s. Bill and Sharon Costner; m. Cindy Silva, Mar. 5, 1978 (div. Dec. 12, 1994); children: Annie, Lily, Joe, Liam; m. Christine Baumgartner, Sept. 25, 2004; 1 child, Cayden Wyatt Degree in mktg., Calif. State U., Fullerton, 1978. Owner prodn. co. TIG Prodns. Actor: (films) Sizzle Beach U.S.A., 1974, Shadows Run Black, 1981, Chasing Dreams, 1981, Frances, 1982, Night Shift, 1982, Testament, 1983, Table for Five, 1983, Stacy's Knights 1983, The Gunrunner, 1983, The Big Chill, 1983, American Flyers, 1985, Fandango, 1985, Silverado, 1985, The Untouchables, 1987, No Way Out, 1987, Bull Durham, 1988, Field of Dreams, 1989, JFK, 1991, The Bodyguard, 1992, A Perfect World, 1993, The War, 1994, Tin Cup, 1996, For Love of the Game, 1999, Play It to the Bone, 1999, 3000 Miles to Graceland, 2001, Dragonfly, 2002, The Upside of Anger, 2005, Rumor Has It., 2005, The Guardian, 2006, Mr. Brooks, 2007; actor, dir., prodr.: (films) Dances with Wolves, 1990 (Acad. Award for Best Dir. 1991, Acad. Award for Best Picture, 1991, Best Dir. Feature Film, Dir. Guild Am. 1991), The Postman, 1997, Open Range, 2003; actor, prodr.: (films) Revenge, 1990, Robin Hood: Prince of Thieves, 1991, Wyatt Earp, 1994, Waterworld, 1995, Message in a Bottle, 1999, Thirteen Days, 2000; actor: (TV appearances, Amazing Stories, 1985; host, exec. prodr. (TV series) 500 Nations; co-prodr. China Moon, 1993; exec. prodr. Rapa Nui, 1994. Named Hasty Pudding Man of Yr., Harvard U., 1990; recipient Star of Tomorrow award, Nat. Assn. Theatre Owners, 1987.*

COSTON, WILLIAM DEAN, lawyer; b. Ann Arbor, Mich., Oct. 9, 1950; s. Dean Walter and Kathryn (Moran) C.; m. Barbara Ellen Carney, Aug. 18, 1973; children: Elizabeth, Nicholas. BA with highest honors, U. Mich., 1972; JD cum laude, Harvard U., 1975. Bar: Mass. 1976, DC 1979, US Supreme Ct. 1979, DC Ct. Appeals, US Ct. Appeals (Fed. cir.) 1997, US Dist. Ct. Mich., US Dist Ct. Ariz., US Dist. Ct. Md., US Dist. Ct. DC, US Ct. Appeals (2nd cir.) 1997, US Ct. Appeals (3rd cir.), admitted to practice: US Ct. Appeals (4th Cir.), bar: US Ct. Appeals (5th cir.), US Ct. Appeals (6th cir.), US Ct. Appeals (7th cir.), US Ct. Appeals (8th cir.), US Ct. Appeals (9th cir.), US Ct. Appeals (10th cir.). Law clk. Ct. Appeals MIch., Detroit, 1975-76; atty. U.S. Dept. Justice Antitrust div., Washington,

1976-79; spl. asst. U.S. atty. U.S. Atty's Office, Alexandria, Va., 1979; assoc. and ptnr. Peabody, Rivlin, Lambert & Meyers, Washington, 1979-84; ptnr. Bishop Cook Purcell & Reynolds, Washington, 1984-90; ptnr. intellectual property litig. Venable LLP, Washington, 1990—. Recipient Atty. Gen. Spl. Achievement Awards, 1977—78. Fellow: Am. Coll. Trial Lawyers; mem.: Am. Intellectual Property Law Assn., ABA (Antitrust Sect., Litig. Sect., Intellectual Property Sect.), Phi Beta Kappa. Avocations: swimming, gardening. Office: Venable lLP 575 7th St NW Washington DC 20004 Office Phone: 202-344-4813. Office Fax: 202-344-8300. Business E-Mail: wdcoston@venable.com.

COSTRELL, ROBERT MICHAEL, economist; b. Washington, Apr. 10, 1950; s. Louis and Esther (Klaiman) C.; m. Rochelle Myrna Ryman, Dec. 17, 1983; children: Sarah Anne, Benjamin David. BA, U. Mich., 1972; PhD, Harvard U., 1978. Asst. prof. U. Mass., Amherst, 1978—85, assoc. prof., 1985—92, prof., 1992—2006; prof. edn. reform and econs., endowed chair edn. accountability U. Ark., Fayetteville, 2006—. Vis. asst. prof. U. Toronto, 1982-84; adj. assoc. prof. Brandeis U., Waltham, Mass., 1986; cons. panel on tech. and employment NAS, Washington, 1986, joint econ. com. U.S. Congress, 1987-88; vis. scholar Boston U., 1993-94; dir. R&D Mass. Exec. Office for Adminstrn. and Fin., 1999-2002, chief economist, 2003-06; edn. advisor Mass. Gov. Mitt Romney, 2005-06; steering com. Econ. Framework and Specifications, Nat. Assessment of Ednl. Progress, 2001-02, Mass. Sch. Bldg. Authority, 2005-06. *Professor Costrell has contributed to the theory and practice of education reform. His academic career has featured seminal publications on the theory of educational standards and influential writings on school finance. As Education Advisor to Massachusetts Governor Romney, he helped craft comprehensive education reform proposals, and as Chief Economist, he led the state's reforms of district and charter funding formulas. His extensive expert testimony in the landmark Hancock school finance case proved critical to the successful defense of Massachusetts' education reform program. As endowed chair at the University of Arkansas, Costrell's current research interests include student achievement, teacher pensions, and school finance.* Contbr. articles to profl. jours. Pres. Brookline Com. for Quality Edn., 1990-95; gov. appointee Mass. Tax Alternatives Commn., 1997-98; adv. coun. on edn. stats. US Dept. Edn., 2001-02; gov.'s designee Pub. Employee Retirement Adminstrn. Commn. 2001-2003 Mem. Am. Econ. Assn., Phi Beta Kappa. Home: 3683 W Howard Nickell Rd Fayetteville AR 72704 Office: U Ark 201 Grad Edn Bldg Fayetteville AR 72701 Home Phone: 479-442-5199; Office Phone: 479-575-5332. E-mail: costrell@uark.edu.

COTA, LISA FOLEY, secondary school educator; b. Hartford, Conn., Feb. 14, 1955; d. Francis Joseph and Carol Castle Foley; m. Mark Steven Guglielmo, Apr. 22, 1958; children: Steven Samuel, Nicolas Joaquin Guglielmo, Samantha Carol. AA, Broward C.C., Pompano Beach, Fla., 1975; B in Secondary Edn., Fla. Atlantic U., Boca Raton, 1977; EdM, Ariz. State U., Tempe, 1982. Cert. std. secondary edn. grade 7-12 Ariz. Dept. Edn., 2001, Ariz. C.C. regular A.1.a State Bd. Dirs. for Cmty. Colleges, Ariz., 1999. Social studies/reading tchr. Apollo H.S., Glendale, Ariz., 1978—81; social studies tchr. Deer Valley H.S., Glendale, 1981—. Mentor tchr. Deer Valley H.S., Glendale, 1999—, dept. chairperson for social studies, 2004—; social studies tchr. Deer Valley Charter Sch., Glendale, 2003—. Mem. Tchg. Tolerance/Wall of Tolerance, Washington, 2001—06; youth counselor Upward Bound, Shawnee, Okla., 1974; Spirit Squad club sponsor Deer Valley H.S., Glendale, 1983—93; summer missionary North Am. Mission Bd., Albuquerque, 1973—74. Scholar, Okla. Bapt. U., 1973, 1974. Mem.: Nat. Coun. for Social Studies (assoc.). Republican. Avocations: travel, camping. Home: 6033 W Kings Ave Glendale AZ 85306 Office: Deer Valley High School 18424 N 51 Ave Glendale AZ 85308 Home Phone: 602-896-8244; Office Phone: 602-467-6871. Personal E-mail: classy310@cox.net. Business E-Mail: lisa.cota@dh.dvusd.org.

COTAYO, CHARLES, journalist, film producer, writer, critic; Degree, Fla. State U., Tallahassee, 1982—86. Journalist El Nuevo Herald, Miami, Fla., 1998—. Dir.(producer, screenwriter, art director): (motion picture) Decapolis II; author: (screenplays) The Prince and Sister Wrath, Experimental Involvement, Mother Goes to Mars, The Price of Greatness, The Count, (play) Jacob's Well, (novel) Salvation. Recipient Phi Eta Sigma Freshman Award for Academic Excellence, Phi Eta Sigma Chpt. of The Fla. State U., 1983, awards, Nat. Assn. Hispanic Publs., 2000—. Achievements include expert in art and business of motion pictures and the Hispanic market. Office: El Nuevo Herald One Herald Plaza 6th Fl Miami FL 33132 Office Phone: 305-376-4652. Personal E-mail: cotahay@aol.com. Business E-Mail: ccotayo@herald.com.

COTCHETT, JOSEPH WINTERS, lawyer, writer; b. Chgo., Jan. 6, 1939; s. Joseph Winters and Jean (Renaud) C.; children— Leslie F., Charles P., Rachael E., Quinn Carlyle, Camilla E. BS in Engring., Calif. Poly. Coll., 1960; LLB, U. Calif. Hastings Coll. Law, 1964. Bar: Calif. 1965, DC 1980. Ptnr. Cotchett, Pitre & McCarthy, Burlingame, Calif., 1965—. Mem. Calif. Jud. Coun., 1975-77, Calif. Commn. on Jud. Performance, 1985-89, Commn. 2020 Jud. Coun., 1991-94; select com. on jud. retirement, 1992—. Author: (with R. Cartwright) California Products Liability Actions, 1970, (with F. Haight) California Courtroom Evidence, 1972, (with A. Elkind) Federal Courtroom Evidence, 1976, (with Frank Rothman) Persuasive Opening Statements and Closing Arguments, 1988, (with Stephen Pizzo) The Ethics Gap, 1991, (with Gerald Uelmen) California Courtroom Evidence Foundations, 1993; contbr. articles to profl. jours. Chmn. San Mateo County Heart Assn., 1967; pres. San Mateo Boys and Girls Club, 1971; bd. dirs. U. Calif. Hastings Law Sch., 1981-93. With Intelligence Corps, U.S. Army, 1960-61; col. JAGC, USAR, ret. Named one of Top Ten Lawyers in Bay Area, San Francisco Chronicle, 2003. Fellow Am. Bar Found., Am. Bd. Trial Advs., Am. Coll. Trial Lawyers, Internat. Acad. Trial Lawyers, Internat. Soc. of Barristers, Nat. Bd. Trial Advs. (diplomate civil trial adv.), State Bar Calif. (gov. 1972-75). Clubs: Commonwealth, Press (San Francisco). Office: 840 Malcolm Rd Burlingame CA 94010-1401 also: 9454 Wilshire Blvd Ste 907 Beverly Hills CA 90202

COTE, DAVID EDWARD, state legislator; b. Nashua, NH, Oct. 28, 1960; s. Edward David and Dorothy Eliza (Soucy) C. Mem. N.H. Ho. of Reps., Concord, 1982-88, 89—, asst. Dem. whip, 1991-92, dep. Dem. whip, 1992-96, mem. Ho. Dem. Leadership, 1996—2003, chair judiciary com., 2007—. Del. NH Constl. Conv., 1984, NH Dem. Convs., 1982—; mem. platform com. NH Dem. Com., 1984; vice chmn. Nashua City Dem. Com., 1985-86; chair NH House Judiciary Com., 2007—; active various Dem. campaigns. Home: 96 W Hollis St Nashua NH 03060-3146 Office: NH Ho of Reps N State St Rm 306 Concord NH 03301-3229 Business E-Mail: david.cote@leg.state.nh.us.

COTE, DAVID M., diversified technology and manufacturing company executive; BS in Bus. Adminstrn., 1976, LLD (hon.) Pepperdine U., 2001. With GE, 1974—99, corp. sr. v.p., and pres., CEO appliances divsn., 1996—99; chmn., pres., CEO TRW, Cleve., 1999—2002; pres., CEO, chmn. Honeywell Internat. Inc., 2002—. Appointed mem. Nat. Security Telecommunications Adv. Com.; bd. dir. JPMorgan Chase & Co., 2007—. Office: 101 Columbia Rd Morristown NJ 07962*

COTE, MICHAEL RICHARD, bishop; b. Sanford, Maine, June 19, 1949; Student, Our Lady of Lourdes Sem., Cassadaga, NY, St. Mary's Sem. Coll., Balt., Gregorian U. Rome, Cath. U. Washington; JCL, Cath. U., 1981. Ordained priest Roman Cath. Ch. 1975. Asst. SS Athanasius & John, Rumford, Maine, 1975—78; assoc. Holy Rosary, Caribou, 1978—79; notary Vice-Officialis Diocesan Tribunal, Portland, 1980—89; sec. Apostolic Nunciature, Washington, 1989—94; pastor Sacred Heart, Auburn, Maine, 1994—95; titular bishop Diocese of Cebarades, 1995—; aux. bishop Diocese of Portland, 1995—2003; bishop Diocese of Norwich, Conn., 2003—. Office: 274 Broadway Norwich CT 06360-4353

COTE, RICHARD JAMES, pathologist, researcher; b. LA, May 10, 1954; s. Richard Patrick and Kathrine C.; m. Anne L. Foxen, Feb. 8, 1992; children: Nicholas Foxen, Juliet Anne, Grace Elizabeth. BS in Biology, U. Calif., Irvine, 1976, BA in Chemistry, 1976; MD, U. Chgo., 1980. Diplomate Am. Bd. Pathology. Intern in surgery U. Mich. Hosp., Ann Arbor, 1980-81; rsch. fellow, immunology Meml. Sloan-Kettering Cancer Ctr., NYC, 1981-83; rsch. assoc., immunology Meml. Sloan-Kettering Hosp., NYC, 1983-85, fellow, pathology, 1987-88, chief fellow, pathology, 1988-90; resident, pathology Cornell U. Med. Ctr., NYC, 1985-87; asst. prof., pathology Keck Sch. Medicine, U. So. Calif., LA, 1990-95, assoc. prof., 1995-99, prof., 1999—; dir. genitourinary program Keck Sch. Medicine, U. So. Calif./Norris Cancer Ctr., 1997—; chair biomed nanosci. initiative U. So. Calif., 2005—; attending pathologist Kenneth Norris Cancer Ctr., 1990—, dir. lab. immuno and molecular pathology, 1991—. Founder, dir. IMPATH, Inc., NYC, 1987—2003; chief med. officer Chromavision Med. Sys. (now Clarient Inc.), 2004—05; mem. numerous nat. and internat. adv. bds.; sci. cons. MD Anderson Cancer Ctr., Houston, 2001—, Roche Molecular Sys., 2002—. Author: Immunomicroscopy, 1994, 2005; editor Modern Surg. Pathology; assoc. editor Applied Immunohistochemistry; mem. editl. bd. Jour. Clin. Oncology, 2007—; contbr. articles to profl. jours., book chpts. Patentee in field. Am. Cancer Soc. fellow, 1988; named one of Best Doctor's in Am., 2005—, Am's. Top Doctor's, 2001—; recipient rsch. grants, awards NIH, ACS, others, 1981—. Mem.: Am. Assn. Cancer Rsch., Phi Beta Kappa. Office: U So Calif Keck Sch Medicine 1441 Eastlake Ave Los Angeles CA 90089-0112 Home Phone: 360-474-6542; Office Phone: 323-865-0212. Business E-Mail: cote_r@ccnt.usc.edu.

COTHERMAN, AUDREY MATHEWS, educational association administrator, management consultant; b. St. Paul, May 20, 1930; d. Anthony Joseph and Nina Grace (Harmon) Mathews; m. Richard Louis Cotherman, Dec. 30, 1950 (div. 1973); children: Steven, Michael, Bruce, Gen Elizabeth. BA, Hamline U., 1952; MA, U. Wyo., 1973, EdD, 1977. Comm. coord. Natrona Sch. Dist., Casper, Wyo., 1968—69; hostess TV program KTWO-TV, Casper, 1970—71; exec. dir. United Way, Casper, 1971—73, Wyo. Coun. Humanities, Laramie, 1973—79; dep. state supt. pub. instrn. Wyo. Dept. Edn., Cheyenne, 1979—90; devel. officer Coll. Edn. U. Wyo., Laramie, 1990—91; pres. Connections: Mgmt. and Policy Cons., Casper, 1991—96; spl. asst. U.S. Dept. Edn. Region VIII, 1996—99; asst. dir. U. Wis. Comprehensive Ctr., 1999—2006; dir. North Ctrl. Comprehensive Ctr., 2006—07; prin., owner Once Again Antiques, Casper, Wyo., 2006. Exec. sec. Wyo. Bd. Edn., 1979-90; dir. cmty. programs HSS, Cheyenne, 1986-90; cons. Wyo. Atty. Gen., Cheyenne, 1990; dealer Profiles, Internat.; dir. Casper Civic Auditorium, 2006-07. Dem. precinct chair, Laramie, 1986—90; campaign dir. Casper Civic Auditorium, 2006—, bd. dirs. Wyo., dir., 2007—. State exec. policy fellow U.S. Dept. Edn., 1985. Mem. LWV (past pres. local chpts., Wyo. chpt.), Am. Assn. Pub. Adminstrs. (pres. 1987-88), Wyo. Assn. Pub. Adminstrs. (Pub. Adminstr. of Yr. 1982), Phi Delta Kappa. Presbyterian. Avocations: writing, reading, antiques, politics. Home: 704 E 11th Casper WY 82601 Personal E-mail: amcotherman@bresnan.net.

COTHORN, JOHN ARTHUR, lawyer; b. Des Moines, Dec. 12, 1939; s. John L. and Marguerite (Esters) C.; m. Connie Cason, Aug. 6, 1996; children: Jeffrey, Judith. BS in Math., U. Mich., 1961, BS in Aero. Engring., 1961, JD, 1980. Bar: Mich. 1981, U.S. Dist. Ct. (ea. dist.) Mich. 1981, U.S. Ct. Appeals (6th cir.) 1981, U.S. Dist. Ct. (we. dist.) Mich. 1986, U.S. Supreme Ct. Exec. U.S Govt., 1965-78; asst. prosecutor Washtenaw County, Ann Arbor, Mich., 1981-82; ptnr. Kitch, Saurbier, Drutchas, Wagner & Kenney P.C., Detroit, 1982-94, Meganck & Cothorn P.C., Detroit, 1994-97, Meganck, Cothorn & Stanczyk P.C., Detroit, 1997-98, Cothorn & Stanczyk, P.C., Detroit, 1998-2000, Cothorn & Braceful, Detroit, 2000—02, Cothorn & Assocs., P.C., Detroit, 2002—04, Cothorn & Mackley, P.C., 2004—. Served to capt. U.S. Army, 1961-65. Mem. ABA, Nat. Bar Assn. (numerous fed. and state coms.), Soc. Automotive Engrs., Assn. Def. Trial Counsel, Phi Alpha Delta. Republican. Avocations: bridge, golf. Office: 535 Griswold St Ste 530 Detroit MI 48226-3696 Office Phone: 313-964-7600. Business E-Mail: jcothorn@comcast.net.

COTHRAN, ANNE JENNETTE, academic administrator; b. Buffalo, Nov. 28, 1952; d. Raymond John and Thelma Lorraine C. BA in English, Gordon Coll., 1975; MBA in Specialization Mktg., U. Chgo., 1989; MEd, Loyola U., Chgo., 2000, EdD, 2004. Mgr. 1776 House, Salem, Mass., 1974-75; dept. mgr. Goldblatt's Dept. Store, Chgo., 1975-77; sales rep. Sta. WWMM, Arlington Heights, Ill., 1977-79, Sta. WYEN, Des Plaines, Ill., 1979-81; coop. mgr. Southtown Economist Newspapers, Chgo., 1981-83, div. sales mgr., 1983-88; retail advt. mgr. Lansing (Mich.) State Jour., 1988-90; advt. & mktg. dir. Herald-Bulletin Newspapers, Anderson, Ind., 1990-92; mgr. Dealer Network Advt. Sys. Newspaper Assn. of Am., Chgo., 1993-94; pub. dir. Standard Rate and Data Svc., Chgo., 1994—95; exec. dir. Sylvan Learning Systems, Contract Svcs. Divsn., Balt., 1996-98; tchr. Chgo. Pub. Schs., 1998-2000; dean J. Sterling Morton H.S. Dist. 201, 2000—02; sys. dir. Sch. Dist. 201, 2002—. Bd. dirs. Cabrini Green Legal Aid Clinic, Chgo., 1981-83. Mem.: ASCD, Internat. Tech. Edn. Assn., Internat. Reading Assn., Nat. Mid. Sch. Assn., Am. Ednl. Rsch. Assn., U. Chgo. Women's Bus. Group (bd. dirs. chpt. devel., chair 1987), Ikebana Internat., Rotary (v.p. Anderson suburban chpt. 1992—93). Avocations: theater, ikebana, gardening.

COTHRON, TONY L., career military officer; b. Greenbrier, Tenn. Grad., Middle Tenn. State U., 1977, Aviation Officer Candidate Sch., Armed Forces Staff Coll.; M in Nat. Security and Strategic Studies, Naval War Coll. Advanced through grades to Rear Admiral USN, various operational tours aboard USS America, USS Theodore Roosevelt, USS George Washington, served in Operation Desert Storm, Operation Provide Comfort Iraq, various tours ashore including submarine analyst and watch stander, Fleet Ocean Surveillance Intelligence Ctr. Detachment Atlantic Fleet, sr. watch analyst, pacific and strategic forces divsn. head Navy Operational Intelligence Command, dir. fleet intelligence for comdr., Fleet Forces Command, comdr. U.S. European Command Joint Analysis Ctr. RAF Molesworth, England, 2001—03, comdr. nat. level, operational intelligence and sci. and intelligence analysis ctr. Office Naval Intelligence, 2004—06, dir. naval intelligence, 2006—. Decorated Def. Superior Svc Medal, Legion of Merit (3 awards), Bronze Star, Def. Meritorious Svc. Medal, Meritorious Svc. Medal (2 awards), Navy Commendation Medal (six awards). Office: USN Office Naval Intelligence 200 Navy Pentagon Washington DC 20350*

COTHRUN, THOMAS KEITH, secondary school educator; b. Miami, Ariz., Mar. 9, 1959; s. Milton James and Nadine L. (Thomas) Cothrun. BA in Edn., U. Ariz., 1982; MA in German Studies, U. N.Mex., 1993. Tchr. German, Alamogordo (N.Mex.) H.S., 1983-86, Las Cruces (N.Mex.) H.S., 1986—2007; assoc. dir. world lang. cultures The Coll. Bd., Duluth, Ga., 2007—. Dir. German Weekend, N.Mex., 1985-89, 99-01; mem. task force Nat. Stds. in Fgn. Lang., Yonkers, N.Y., 1993-96; cons. Coll. Bd., NY, 1993-2006. Co-author: German-American Partnership Program Handbook, 1993; contbr. articles to profl. jours. Trustee Am. Southwest Theatre Co., 2005—, pres., 2006—07. Named Tchr. of Yr., Las Cruces Pub. Schs., 1995, Walt Disney Am. Tchr. award honoree, 1995; fellow U.S. Holocaust Meml. Mus. Mandel, 1999-2000; recipient award for excellence in tchg., Am. Couns. for Internat. Edn., 1999, Friedrich Gerstäcker award Checkpoint Charlie Found., 2001. Mem. ASCD, NEA, Am. Assn. Tchrs. German (v.p., pres.-elect 1994-95, pres. 1996-97, cert. of merit 1993, Outstanding German Educator 2001), Am. Coun. on Tchg. Fgn. Langs. (pres.-elect 2003, pres. 2004), S.W. Conf. on Lang. Tchg., N.Mex. Orgn. Lang. Educators (Creativity in Tchg. award 1993, Tchr. of Yr. 2002), Nat. Bd. for Profl. Tchg. Stds. (fgn. lang. stds. chair 1998-01, bd. dirs. 2002—). Office: The Coll Bd 3700 Crestwood Pkwy Ste 700 Duluth GA 30096

COTRONE, JANICE LYNNE, nursing consultant; b. Arlington, Va., Sept. 11, 1956; d. James Franklin and Ferne Smith Cooper; m. Mitchell John Cotrone, July 6, 1996; children: Philip Joseph, Joshua John, Francia Marie. BSN, Ind. Wesleyan U., 1978, MS in Cmty. Health Nursing, 1995. RN Va. Charge nurse Shenandoah County Meml. Hosp., Woodstock, Va., 1978—79; asst. head nurse Arlington Hosp., 1979—81; staff nurse, cardiac ICU Fairfax (Va.) Hosp., 1981—84; dir. mission clinic Petit Goave, Haiti Wesleyan World Missions, Indpls., 1981, missionary nurse to Haiti, 1984—94, 1997—2001; nurse case mgr. Samaritan Bethany Home Health Agy., Rochester, Minn., 1995—96; RN cons. Hope Wesleyan Ch., Naples, Fla., 2002—. Dir. mission clinic in Haiti Wesleyan World Missions, Indpls., 1981, adminstr. La Gonave (Haiti) Wesleyan Hosp., 1984—94, prof. nursing La Gonave (Haiti) Wesleyan Hosp., 1985—88, med. dir. Wesleyan Ch. Haiti, 1986—88, DON Wesleyan Hosp. La Gonave, 1984—94, dir. surgery Wesleyan Hosp. La Gonave, 1984—94, mission sta. mgr. Wesleyan Mission Haiti, 1991—94, mission/hosp. bookkeeper and acct. Wesleyan Mission Haiti, 1985—2001; spkr. seminars, confs., retreats, and convs. Author: (book) Nutritional Assessment of American School-Age Children; contbr. articles to mags.; featured on radio and TV interviews regarding work in Haiti. Transl., cons. local health dept., physician's and dentist's offices, local nursing homes, Naples, 2002—05; vol. liaison Am. and Haitian comty., 2002—05; poll worker, poll inspector, Creole transl. for 2004 presdl. election, 2004; English tchr. to Haitian nurses Wesleyan Mission to Haiti, Petit Goave and La Gonave, 1981—2001, vol. meal server to 9 Haitian sch. children La Gonave, 1984—94, funded sch. for 15 Haitian children, 1984—2004; field dir. child-sponsorship program World Hope Internat., Haiti, 1997—2001. Recipient Continuing Edn. scholarship, Ind. Wesleyan U., 1994. Mem.: Wesleyan Women (work dir. 2004—05), Wesleyan Med. Fellowship (Continuing Edn. scholarship 1994), Sigma Theta Tau. Republican. Avocations: knitting, travel, composing music and writing lyrics, piano, tutoring school students. Home: 1740 45th St SW Naples FL 34116 Office: Hope Wesleyan Ch 4445 17th Ct SW Naples FL 34116 Home Phone: 239-354-1140; Office Phone: 239-455-1825.

COTRUBAS, ILEANA, opera singer, retired lyric soprano; b. Galati, Romania; d. Vasile C. and Maria C. m. Manfred Ramin, 1972. Student, Scoala speciala de Musica, Bucharest, Ciprian Porumbescu Conservatory, Musikakademie, Vienna, Austria. Tchr. master-classes, interpretation and operatic roles. Debut as Yniold in Pelleas et Melisande, Bucharest Opera, 1964; appeared with Frankfurt (Fed. Republic Germany) Opera, 1968-71, Staatsoper, Vienna, 1970—, Covent Garden, London, 1971—, Staatsoper, Munich, 1973—, Lyric Opera Chgo., 1973-75, 83—, Opera Paris, 1974—, La Scala, Milan, 1975—, Met. Opera, N.Y.C., 1977—, San Francisco Opera, 1978, Ehrenmitglied Vienna Staatsoper, 1991; major roles include: Zerlina, Susanna, Pamina, Norina, Gilda, Violetta, Elisabetta (Don Carlos), Mimi, Tatyana, Micaela, Manon, Antonia, Melisande; ret., 1990; author: Truth About Opera, 1998. Recipient 1st prize Internat. Singing Competition, Hertogenbusch, Netherlands, 1965; 1st prize Munich Radio Competition, 1966; Kammersängerin Vienna Staatsoper, 1981; Great Officer of the Order Sant' Iago da Espada, Portugal, 1990, Great Officer of Star of Romania, 2000.

COTRUVO, JOSEPH ALFRED, water, environmental and public health consultant; b. Toledo, Aug. 3, 1942; s. Nicholas and Angela (Campanale) C.; m. Karen Shrum, June 18, 1983; 1 child, Joseph Alfred Jr. BS in Chemistry, U. Toledo, 1963; PhD, Ohio State U., 1968; postgrad., U. Bologna, Italy, 1969. Mgr. R & D ChemSampCo, Columbus, Ohio, 1970-72; programs analyst EPA, Washington, 1973-76, dir. drinking water criteria and stds. divsn., 1976-90, dir. health and environ. rev. divsn., 1990-92; dir. risk assessment divsn., 1992-96; sr. regulatory exec. NSF Internat., Washington, 1996-98. V.p. environ. health scis. NSF Internat., 1998—2000; coun. pub. health cons. Nat. Sanitation Found., Ann Arbor, Mich., 1980—96; dir. NSF Internat./WHO Collaborating Ctr. Water Safety and Tech., 1996—2006; adj. prof. environ. scis. Am. U., 1997; mem. sci. adv. bd. Santa Ana River Water Quality and Health; mem. rsch. adv. bd. Nat. Water Rsch. Inst., Ground Water Replenishment Study; ind. adv. bd. Tampa Water Resource Reuse Panel, 1997—98; pres. J. Cotruvo & Assocs. LLC; mem. sci. adv. bd. Cal-Fed Delta Water Quality Project; rsch. adv. bd. Water Reuse Found.; sci. panel on water sys. security rsch. NAS, 2003, Heterotrophic Plate Counts, 2003, Emerging Pathogen, 2004; mem. San Diego Water Reuse Adv. Com., 2004—; vis. prof. environ. sci. Tech. U. Bari, 2005. Co-editor: Ozone/Chlorine Dioxide, 1978, Water Chlorination, 1983, Procs. Safe Drinking Water in Small Sys.: Tech., Ops. and Econs., 1999; chmn., editor: NATO/CCMS Drinking Water Pilot, 1980; co-editor: Emerging Pathogens in Drinking Water, Bromate Health Rsch. Strategy, Toxicology and AWWARF, 2005; mem. editl. bd. Am. Water Works Assn. Jour., 1987-90; contbr. articles to jours. in field. Bd. dirs. D.C. Water and Sewer Authority, 2006—. Recipient Environ. Leadership award Nat. Sanitation Found., Ann Arbor, 1988, Donald R. Boyd award Assn. Met. Water Agys., 1990; named Meritorious Exec., Pres. U.S., 1983. Mem. Internat. Desalination Assn., Am. Chem Soc., Am. Water Works Assn. (hon. life), InterAm. Assn. Sanitary and Environ. Engring. (dir. at large 2000-02, v.p. 2003, pres. 2007-). Roman Catholic. Avocations: woodworking, light construction. Office Phone: 202-362-3076. Personal E-mail: joseph.cotruvo@verizon.net.

COTSAKIS, PATRICIA JOAN, music educator; d. Henry Louis Hering and Mamie May Jones; m. William John Catsakis; children: Frederick Joseph, Daniel John. BA, Elmhurst Coll., Ill., 1975. Pvt. tchr. music, 1948—; chapel pianist Elmhurst Coll., 1949—51; organist, children's choir St. Paul's Ch., Franklin Park, Ill., 1952—65; organist, dir. adult and children's choir Palatine Presbyn. Ch., Ill., 1965—. Substitute tchr. music Dist. 211, Palatine, 1992—. Mem.: Evanston Music Club, North Shore Musicians Club. Home: 1653 S Garden St Palatine IL 60067

COTSAKOS, CHRISTOS MICHAEL, retired internet financial services company executive; b. Paterson, NJ, July 29, 1948; s. Michael John and Lillian (Scoulikas) C.; m. Hannah Batami Fogel, July 1, 1973; 1 child, Suzanne Renee. BA in Communications and Polit. Sci., William Paterson Coll., 1972; MBA, Pepperdine U., 1984. Tour guide Universal Studios, Burbank, Calif., 1973; courier Fed. Express Corp., Burbank, 1973-74, sales rep. Long Beach, Calif., 1974, sta. mgr. San Jose, Calif., 1974, we. dist. mgr., 1974, region engring. mgr. Denver, 1975, mng. dir. Chgo., 1975-80, v.p. Sacramento, 1980-92; pres., COO Nielsen, Europe, Middle East, Africa, 1992-93; pres., CEO Nielsen Internat., 1993-95; pres., co-CEO, COO, dir. A.C. Nielsen, Inc., 1995-96; CEO, chmn. E*TRADE Group, Inc., Palo Alto, Calif., 1996—2003. Instr. Consumers River Coll., Placerville, Calif., 1985-86; bd. dirs. Airlifeline, Sacramento, Nat. Processing, Inc., Louisville, Forté Software, Inc., Oakland, 4th Comms. Network, San Jose, Datacard, Mpls. Author: (book) It's Your Money: The E*Trade Step by Step Guide to Online Investing, 2000. Served as sgt. U.S. Army, 1967-70, Vietnam. Decorated Bronze Star, 1967, Purple Heart, 1967. Mem. World Econ Forum (Davos, Switzerland), Sutter Club, Comstock Club.

COTSARELIS, GEORGE, dermatologist, educator; MD, U. Pa.; BA, U. Pa, 1983. Cert. Dermatology. Intern Geisinger MC, Danville, Pa., 1987—88; resident U. Pa., Phila., 1989—92; instr. Hosp. U. Pa., Phila., 1992—96; asst. prof. U. Pa. Med. Sch., Phila., 1996—2004, assoc. prof., 2004—. Contbr. articles to profl. jours. Named a Top Docs Issue, Phila. Mag., 2004, 2005, 2007. Office: U Pa 422 Curie Blvd Philadelphia PA 19104 also: U Pa Dermatology Dept 3400 Spruce St Philadelphia PA 19104 Address: Pa Medicine Radnor 250 King of Prussia Rd Radnor PA 19087 E-mail: cotsarel@mail.med.upenn.edu.*

COTTAM, KEITH M., librarian, educator, administrator; b. St. George, Utah, Feb. 13, 1941; s. Von Bunker and Adrene (McArthur) Cottam; m. Laurel Springer, June 16, 1961 (div. Feb. 4, 2000); children: Mark Patrick, Lisa Diane, Andrea Jill, Brian Lowell, Heather Dawn; m. Mary Bultena Albertson, Oct. 5, 2001. BS, Utah State U., 1963; MLS, Pratt Inst., 1965. Trainee Bklyn. Pub. Libr., 1963—65, asst. instr. reading improvement program, 1964—65, adult services libr., 1965; asst. social scis. libr., instr. So. Ill. U., Edwardsville, 1965—67; head, social sci. libr., instr. asst. prof. Social Scis. Libr., Brigham Young U., Provo, Utah, 1967—72; supr., inst. Libr. Technician Program Brigham Young U., Provo, Utah, 1969—72; head undergrad. libr., assoc. prof. U. Tenn., Knoxville, 1972—75, asst. dir. librs., assoc. prof., 1975—77; asst. dir. for pub. svcs. and employee rels. Vanderbilt U. Libr. (formerly Joint Univ. Librs.), Nashville, 1977—80, assoc. dir., 1980—82, acting dir., 1982—83; dir. libraries, prof. U. Wyo., Laramie, 1983—2000, dean univ. librs., 2001; assoc. dean outreach sch., dir. U. Wyo./Casper Coll. Ctr., Casper, 2001—05, emeritus prof., 2005—. Cons. tng. program Assn. Rsch. Librs., 1979—80; mem. Leadership Wyo. Tng. Program, 2002—03; bd. dirs. Casper Area C. of C., 2004—, Platte River Pkwy. Trust, 2004—, ServeWyo. (formerly Wyo. Commn. Nat. and Cmty. Svc.), 2003—. Author: Writer's Research handbook, 1977, 2d edit., 1978; editor Utah Libraries jour., 1971-72; mem. editl. bd. RQ jour., 1980-84; contbr. articles to profl. jours. Fellow Coun. Libr. Resources, 1975-76; sr. fellow UCLA Grad. Sch. Libr. Info. Sci., 1985-86. Mem.: ALA, Wyo. Libr. Assn. (pres. 1998—99), Phi Kappa Phi, Beta Phi Mu. Republican. Mem. Ch. of Jesus Christ of Latter-day Saints. Avocations: bicycling, racing and touring, free-lance writer, gardening. Business E-Mail: kcottam@uwyo.edu.

COTTEN, ANNIE LAURA, psychologist, educator; b. Oxford, NC, Nov. 18, 1923; d. Leonard F. and Laura Estelle (Spencer) Cotten; children: Hollis W., Rebecca Ann, Laura Cotten. Diploma, Hardbarger Bus. Coll., 1944; AB, Duke U., 1945; MEd, U. Hartford, Conn., 1965; PhD, The Union Inst., 1979. Diplomate Am. Bd. Sexology, lic. Am. Assn. Marriage & Family Therapists, 1987. Asst. to pres. So. Meth. U., 1953; rsch. asst. Duke U., 1947-49; exec. sec. Ohio Wesleyan U., 1955-56, Conn. Coun. Chs., 1958-60; adj. prof. U. Hartford, 1976-78, 1976-78; clin. pastoral counselor Hartford Hosp., 1962-65; asst., then assoc. dir. social svcs. Hartford Conf. Chs., 1965-67; tchg. fellow U. NC, 1970-71; assoc. prof. Ctrl. Conn. State U., New Britain, 1967-93, adj. prof., 1994—2002. Adj. prof. St. Joseph Coll., 1986-96; clin. intern Montefiore Med. Ctr., 1995; dir. elderhostel programs Ctrl. Conn. State U., 1989-93, organizer ctr. adult learners, 1991-93; cons. Somers Correctional Ctr., Conn., 1980-81, instr./rschr., 1980-81; cons. Conn. Life Ins. Mktg. Rsch., 1981-1982; amb. to China, spring, 1986; presenter 3d Internat. Interdisciplinary Cong. on Women, 1987; vis. prof., scholar Duke U., 1989; adj. prof. health and human svcs. Ctrl. Ch. St. U., 1995-2002; vis. prof. Conn. Coll., New London, 1990; mem. clin. faculty, Am. Bd. Sexology, 1994; land developer NC Triangle, 1995—. Author: Comparisons of Gender Differences in Sexuality 1970s/1990s; cons. editor: Jour. Feminist Family Therapy, 2000—, reviewer: Contemporary Sexuality, 2003, Sexual and Relationship Jour., 2005. Fellow; Am. Acad. Clin. Sexologists (clin. faculty 1994—, founder), Nat. Coun. Family Rels.; mem.: APA (chair divsn. 1987—91), AAUW, Soc. Sci. Study of Sexuality (presenter ann. meeting 2003), Conn. Assn. Marital and Family Therapists (clin.) (bd. dirs. 2000—02), Sex Info. and Edn. Coun. of Conn. (bd. dirs. 1994—2002, Human Sexuality Leader of Yr. 1997), Conn. Psychol. Assn., Am. Assn. Sex Educators Counselors and Therapists (supr. sex therapy 2005—, sex therapy cert. com. 2005, Disting. Svc. award 1998), Hartford Women's Network. Personal E-mail: anniecotten@nc.rr.com.

COTTEN, SAMUEL RICHARD, fisheries consultant, former state legislator, consultant; b. Juneau, Alaska, July 16, 1947; s. Samuel L. Cotten and Kathryn Russell; m. Martha Tillion, June 16, 1984; children: Samuel Tillion, Augustus O'Dwyer Russell. AA, U. Alaska, 1971. Rep. Alaskan Ho. of Reps., Juneau, 1975-82, 85-91, speaker, 1989-91; senator Alaska State Senate, Juneau, 1991-93; chmn. Alaska Pub. Utilities Commn., 1995—99; fisheries cons., 1999—. Spl. advisor Intergovtl. Consultative Com. to North Pacific Fisheries Adv. Bd., 1989-92; advisor Internat. North Pacific Fisheries Commn., 1984-90; apptd. by US sec. commerce North Pacific Fisheries Mgmt. Coluon., 2007—; bd. dir. Fire Lake Recreational Ctr., Eagle River, Alaska. Co-chmn. Alaska Criminal Code Revision Commn., Juneau, 1976; mem. Anchorage Planning and Zoning Commn., 1983-84; candidate for Gov. Alaska, 1994—. Recipient Nat. Def. award Vietnam Svc. (2); named Outstanding Vietnam Vet. No Greater Love Found., 1976. Mem. Cook Inlet Seiners Assn., Navy League, Elks, VFW (life), Anchorage Ski Club. Democrat. Avocations: fishing, skiing, bowling. Home: PO Box 770296 Eagle River AK 99577-0296 Home Phone: 907-696-2581. E-mail: samc.er@qci.net.

COTTER, GEORGE R., retired information scientist; Former chief Office Corp. Assessments, spl. asst. to dep. dir. Nat. Security Agy., Md., former dir. info. tech., chief info. officer. Former mem. adv. bd. Def. Intelligence Agy.; former sr. Nat. Security Agy. rep. Fed. Info. Tech. Working Group. Mem.: NAE. Home: 193 Southdown Rd Edgewater MD 21037-1622 Home Phone: 410-956-6019.*

COTTER, HOLLAND, art critic, writer; b. Canaan, Conn., Apr. 9, 1947. BA, Harvard U., 1970, MA City U. NY, 1990, MPhil, Columbia U., 1992. Editor New York Arts Jour., NYC, 1976-80; writer Arts Mag., NYC, 1976—, Flash Art, Milan, Italy, 1984—; contbg. editor Art in Am.; editl. assoc. Artnews; art critic NY Times. Home: 91 Payson Ave Apt 6E New York NY 10034-2756 Office: NY Times Culture Desk 229 W 43rd St New York NY 10036 Office Phone: 212-556-4225. Office Fax: 212-556-1516. Business E-Mail: cotter@nytimes.com.

COTTER, JOSEPH FRANCIS, retired bank executive, hotel executive; b. Brockton, Mass., May 18, 1927; s. Joseph and Sarah (Thornell) C.; m. Catherine Florence Sullivan, 1950 (dec.); m. Barbara Tribou Salter, 1986. BS cum laude, Boston Coll., 1949. CPA, Mass., N.Y. Accountant Price Waterhouse & Co., NYC, 1949-67; v.p., contr. Howard Johnson Co., Braintree, Mass., 1967-70; exec. v.p., comptr., dir. Sheraton Corp., Boston, 1970-85, exec. v.p. planning and devel., 1985-87; ret., 1987-89; exec. Bank of Boston, 1989-95; ret., 1995. Former vice chmn. bd. trustees Boston Coll.; former chmn. bd. dirs. Greater Boston YMCA.; former v.p., bd. dirs. Greater Boston C. of C.; trustee for life Dana-Farber Cancer Rsch. Inst.; former bd. dirs. United Way of Mass. Bay; adv. bd. Holy Cross Sch., So. Portland. Mem. AICPA, N.Y. Soc. CPAs, Mass. Soc. CPAs, Boston Coll. Alumni Assn. (past pres.), Purpoodock Club. Avocation: golf. Home: 11 Running Tide Rd Cape Elizabeth ME 04107-2933

COTTER, JUNE ANN, special education educator; b. Kingston, Pa., July 28, 1968; m. Terry James Cotter, Feb. 14, 1992; children: Matthew Berton Brown-Linn, T.J. John. MS in Edn., U. Kans., Lawrence, 1998; postgrad., U. Alaska, Fairbanks, 2001—. Cert. spl. edn. cognitive impairments Kk-25 Mich., 2004, reading edn. Mich., 1990, reading Mich., 2004. Intensive resource tchr. Fairbanks North Star Borough Sch. Dist., North Pole, Alaska, 1999—2004; functional skills tchr. Marquette Area Pub. Sch., Mich., 2004—07. Adj. instr. U. Alaska, Alaska, 2001—. Treas. Cub Scouts, Fairbanks, 1999—2004. Sgt. US Army, 1986—93. Decorated Soldier of Month US Army, Soldier of Quarter, Soldier of Yr. Mem.: Assn. Persons With Severe Handicaps, Order of Ea. Star (sec. 2007). Democrat-Npl. Methodist. Avocations: reading, four wheel off roading. Home: E5452 Curtis Dr Au Train MI 49806 Office: Marquette Area Pub Sch 1201 W Fair Marquette MI 49855 Home Phone: 906-892-8557; Office Phone: 906-250-4219. Personal E-mail: juneac@charter.net.

COTTER, MICHAEL WILLIAM, retired ambassador; b. Madison, Wis., Aug. 1, 1943; s. Patrick William and Lois Katherine (Schaus) Cotter; m. Joanne Marie Miller, Aug. 30, 1974. BSFS, Georgetown U., 1965; JD, U. Mich., 1968; MS, Stanford U., 1976. Polit.-mil. affairs officer Am. Embassy, Ankara, Turkey, 1980-82; sr. Turkish desk officer U.S. Dept. State, Washington, 1982-84; polit. officer Am. Embassy, Kinshasa, Zaire, 1984-86, polit. counselor, 1986-88; mgmt. analyst sec. of mgmt. U.S. Dept. State, 1988-90, office dir. politico-military affairs, 1990-92; dep. chief of mission Am. Embassy, Santiago, Chile, 1992-95; U.S. amb. to Turkmenistan, 1995-98; internat. cons. Washington, 1999-2001; lectr. Chapel Hill, NC, 2001—. V.p., assoc. publ. Am. Diplomacy Publs., Chapel Hill, NC, 2001—. Mem.: Am. Fgn. Svc. Assn. (secy 1989—91, bd govs 1988—89). Home and Office: 685 Fearrington Post Pittsboro NC 27312-8523 E-mail: mwcotter@hotmail.com.

COTTER, PATRICIA O'BRIEN, state supreme court justice; b. South Bend, Ind., 1950; m. Michael W. Cotter, 1979; 2 children. BS in Polit. Sci. and History with honors, We. Mich. U, 1972; JD, Notre Dame, 1977. Pvt. practice, South Bend, 1977—83, Great Falls, Mont., 1984; ptnr. Cotter & Cotter, Great Falls, 1985—2000; justice Mont. Supreme Ct., 2001—. Chair lawyer representatives Ninth Circuit Judicial Conf., 1996—98, exec. com., 1998; mem. commn. on judicial conduct Mont. Supreme Ct. Mem.: Mont. Trial Lawyers Assn. (chair amicus com. 1993—99, Public Service award 1992, 1998). Office: Rm 323 PO Box 203003 Helena MT 59620*

COTTER, PATRICK LINNAE, lawyer; b. Rochester, Minn., Aug. 20, 1974; BA cum laude, Coll. St. Thomas, 1997; JD, William Mitchell Coll. Law, 2002. Bar: Minn. 2002, US Dist. Ct. (dist. Minn.) 2003. Pros. atty. Burnsville & Eagan; atty. Cotter Law Office, P.L.L.C., Mendota Heights, Minn., 2005—. Named a Rising Star, Minn. Super Lawyers mag., 2006; recipient Pub. Svc. award, Minn. Justice Found. Mem.: Minn. Assn. Criminal Def. Lawyers, Minn. Trial Lawyers Assn., Assn. Trial Lawyers of Am., Minn. State Bar Assn., Ramsey County Bar Assn., Dakota County Bar Assn., Vol. Lawyers Network, Delta Theta Phi. Office: Cotter Law Office PLLC 750 S Plz Dr Ste 218 Mendota Heights MN 55120 Office Phone: 651-686-5347. E-mail: pcotterlaw@gmail.com.*

COTTER, ROBERT F., hotel executive; b. Brockton, Mass. married; 3 children. BA in Philosophy, Boston Coll., 1973. With, 1973—; various sales and mktg. positions Sheraton Hotels, L.A., Honolulu, area dir. mktg. Hawaii, 1980-82, v.p. dir. advt. Hawaii, Japan & Far East divsn., 1983-85, sr. v.p., dir. mktg. Hawaii-Japan divsn., 1985-88, dir., hotel mktg., 1988—89, v.p., hotel mktg., 1989—91, sr. v.p., mktg. & product mgmt., 1991—93, exec. v.p., mktg. & product mgmt., 1993—94, pres., COO Europe Brussels, 1994-99; pres. internat. ops. Starwood Hotels & Resorts Worldwide, Inc., 1999, COO White Plains, NY, 2000—03, pres., 2003—05, Kerzner Internat., Ltd., 2007—. Named One of the 25 most influential execs. in the travel industry. Fellow Inst. of Cert. Travel Agts., Am. Hotel and Motel Assn. (mktg. com.)

COTTER, WILLIAM RECKLING, foundation administrator; b. Detroit, Mar. 9, 1936; s. Fred Joseph and Esther Jean (Reckling) C.; m. Linda Jane Kester, June 14, 1959; children: David Andrew, Deborah Anne, Elizabeth Anne. BA in Polit. Sci. magna cum laude, Harvard U., 1958, JD cum laude, 1961; LHD (hon.), Bowdoin Coll., 1987, West Brook Coll., 1995, U. New Eng., 2000, Colby Coll., 2000, Thomas Coll., 2003. Bar: N.Y. 1962, U.S. Supreme Ct. 1965. Law clk. to U.S. Fed. Judge, NYC, 1961-62; MIT fellow in Africa Nigeria, 1962-63; assoc. firm Cahill, Gordon, Sonnett, Reindell & Ohl, NYC, 1963-65; White House fellow Washington, 1965-66; Ford Found. rep. to Colombia and Venezuela, 1966-70; pres. African-Am. Inst., NYC, 1970-79, Colby Coll., 1979-2000, Oak Found., Boston and Geneva, Switzerland, 2000—05, chair adv. com., 1997—2007; cons. Robertson Found., 2005—. Contbr. articles on fgn. policy and edn. to profl. jours. Bd. dirs. Pvt. Agys. Collaborating Together, 1975-81, Waterville ARC, 1980-87, Kennebec Valley Regional Health Agy., 1982-88, Mid-Maine Econ. Devel. Corp.; chmn. bd. trustees Oyster Bay-East Norwich (N.Y.) Pub. Libr., 1975-79; trustee African-Am. Inst., 1970-2001; bd. dirs. Maine Pub. Broadcasting, 1979-2000; chair bd. dirs. Waterville Regional Arts and Cmty. Ctr., 1996-2000; chmn. bd. visitors Baxter Sch. for the Deaf, 1982-87; chmn. com. for study ct. structure, probate and family law matters, 1985; bd. advisors Carrabassett Valley Acad., 1981-91; chair com. on pub. disclosure New Eng. Assn. Schs. and Colls., 1987; trustee Westbrook Coll., 1986-92; past mem. exec. com. South African Edn. Program; past mem. commn. on govt. rels. Am. Coun. on Edn.; commr. State of Maine Edn. Commn.; mem. Nat. Commn. on Responsibilities for Financing Postsecondary Edn., 1991-93; bd. visitors U. Maine Sch. Law; past chair and dir. Nat. Assn. Ind. Colls. and Univs.; trustee Colby Coll., 1979—; trustee Olin Coll., 2002—, Mass. Hist. Soc., 2004—; chmn. Robertson Scholars Program, Duke U., U. NC, 2004-. Named Educator of Yr. The Washington Ctr., 1993, Leader of Yr. Equity Inst. Maine, 1996, Disting. Citizen Waterville C. of C., 1998. Mem. Nat. Assn. Ind. Colls. and Univs. (past chair and dir.), Coun. Fgn. Rels., Harvard Club (NYC), Harvard Club (Boston).

COTTING, JAMES CHARLES, manufacturing executive, director; b. Winchester, Mass., Oct. 15, 1933; s. Edward L. and Mary Ellen (Worrell) C.; m. Marjorie A. Kirsch, Feb. 8, 1963; children: James Charles, Steven Robert, Brenda Ann-Marie. BA cum laude, Ohio State U., 1955. Acctg. supr. U.S. Steel Corp., Pitts., 1959-61; mgr. profit analysis Ford Motor Co., Dearborn, Mich., 1961-63; mgr. devel. planning A.O. Smith Corp., Milw., 1963-66; asst. contr. Gen. Foods Corp., White Plains, NY, 1966-71; v.p. planning Internat. Paper Co., NYC, 1971-76, v.p., contr., 1976-79; sr. v.p. fin. and planning, CFO Navistar Internat. Corp., Chgo., 1979-82, exec. v.p. fin., 1982-83, vice chmn., CFO, 1983-87, chmn., CEO, 1987-95, chmn. bd., 1995-96. Mem. Pres. Reagan's Task Force on Mkt. Mechanisms; bd. dirs. USG Corp.; former dir. Asarco Inc., Interlake Corp., Chgo. Stock Exchange. Dir. Jr. Achievement of Chgo.; trustee Adler Planetarium. Lt. USN, 1955-58. Mem. Chgo. Coun. on Fgn. Rels., Comml. Club Chgo., Econ. Club Chgo., Montclair Golf Club, Barrington Hills Country Club, Chgo. Club, Phi Beta Kappa, Alpha Tau Omega.

COTTINGHAM, RICHARD SUMNER, paper company executive; b. Columbus, Ohio, May 7, 1941; s. Robert E. and Lee Alice (Gasaway) C.; m. Sheila L. Robertson, Dec. 20, 1980. BA in History, Ohio State U., 1964. Pres. Cottingham Paper Co., Columbus, 1968—. Bd. dirs. Network Svcs. Co., 1984-90, chmn., 1986-88. Served as lt. (j.g.) USN, 1964-67, Vietnam. Recipient Ernst & Young Master Entrepreneur of Yr. award for Columbus and Ctrl. Ohio, Bus. First Newspaper, 1998, Bus. First Fast Fifty award, 2001, 02; named among Columbus Bus. First Fast Fifty Cos., 2001, 02; named Family Firm of Distinction, Weatherhead Sch. Mgmt., 2001. Mem. Nat. Paper Trade Assn. (young exec. com. 1976), Am. Mgmt. Assn., Nat. Assn. Wholesale Distbrs., Internat. Sanitary Supply Assn., Chief Exec. Bds. Columbus, Econ. Club Columbus, Columbus C. of C., Worthington Country Club. Republican. Address: Cottingham Paper Co 324 E 2d Ave PO Box 163579 Columbus OH 43216-3579 E-mail: rcottingham@cottinghampaper.com.

COTTINGHAM, ROBERT, artist; b. Bklyn., Sept. 26, 1935; s. James G. and Aurelia Ann C.; m. Jane Marie Weismann, Dec. 23, 1967; children: Reid Ann, Molly Jane, Kyle Annie Bliss. Student, Pratt Inst., Bklyn., 1959-64; AA, Pratt Inst., 1962. Art dir. Young & Rubicam Advt., Inc., NYC, 1959-64, LA, 1964-68; tchr. Art Ctr. Coll. Design, LA, 1969-70. One man shows include Molly Barnes Gallery, Los Angeles, 1968, 69, 70, O.K. Harris Gallery, N.Y.C., 1971, 74, 76, 78, Aldrich Mus., Ridgefield Conn., 1979, Galerie de Gestlo, Cologne, Fed. Republic Germany, 1979, Delta Gallery, Rotterdam, Netherlands, 1979, Getler-Pall Gallery, N.Y.C., 1979, Thomas Segal Gallery, Boston, 1980, Ball State U., 1980, U. Bridgeport (Conn.), 1980, Fendrick Gallery, Washington, 1981, 84, Mattatuck Mus., Waterbury, Conn., 1981, Swain Sch. Design, New Bedford, Mass., 1981, Coe Kerr Gallery, N.Y.C., 1982, 84, Signet Arts, St. Louis, 1983, 86, Wichita Art Mus., Kans., 1983, Springfield Art Mus., Mo., 1984, retrospective exhbn., 1986-88; numerous group shows including Abilene Christian U., Roger Ramsay Gallery, Chgo., Reynolds House Mus. Am. Art, Winston-Salem, N.C., Ark. Arts Ctr., Little Rock, Fendrick Gallery; represented in numerous permanent collections including Whitney Mus. Am. Art, N.Y.C., Cleve. Art Mus., Detroit Mus. Art, Phila. Mus. Art, Harvard, Honolulu Acad. Art, Carnegie Inst., Pitts., U. Iowa, Long Beach (Calif.) Mus. Art, Indpls. Mus. Art, Dartmouth Coll., Mus. Modern Art, N.Y.C., Guggenheim Mus., N.Y.C., Detroit Inst. Arts, Hirshhorn Mus. and Sculpture Garden, Washington, Library of Congress, Washington, Nat. Mus. Am. Art, Washington, Princeton U., Yale U., Met. Mus. Art, N.Y.C., Mus. City of N.Y., Art Inst. Chgo., others, including numerous European museums; commns. include 12 enamel panels One Union Pl., Hartford, Conn. With U.S. Army, 1955-58. Nat. Endowment Arts grantee, 1974-75; named Artist of Yr., Fairfield C. of C., 1988. Address: Blackman Rd PO Box 604 Newtown CT 06470-0604 Office Phone: 203-426-4072.

COTTINGHAM, TRACY THOMAS, III, lawyer; b. Fayetteville, NC, July 17, 1947; s. Tracy Thomas and Frances (Godwin) C.; m. Gloria Jean Schmidt; children: Tracy Thomas, Christopher Todd. BA, Davidson Coll, NC, 1969; JD, Cornell U., 1976. Bar: Ala. 1976, U.S. Dist. Ct. (no. dist.) Ala. 1976, U.S. Dist. Ct. (mid. dist.) Ala. 1987, U.S. Dist. Ct. (so. dist.) Ala. 1988, U.S. Ct. Appeals (5th cir.) 1976, U.S. Ct. Appeals (11th cir. 1981), N.C. 1989. Assoc., then ptnr. Burr & Forman, Birmingham, Ala., 1976—98; ptnr., litig., intellectual property, antitrust, office managing ptnr., head of firm's security practice group Hunton & Williams LLP, Charlotte, NC, 1998. Served to capt. U.S. Army, 1969-73, Vietnam. Decorated Bronze Star. Mem. ABA (litigation sect.), N.C. Bar Assn., Birmingham Bar Assn., Ala. Def. Lawyers Assn., Def. Research Inst. Avocations: running, history, wildlife. Office: Hunton & Williams LLP Bank of Am Plz Ste 3500 101 S Tryon St Charlotte NC 28280 Office Phone: 704-378-4714. Office Fax: 704-378-4890. Business E-Mail: tcottingham@hunton.com.

COTTLE, RICHARD WARREN, retired operations research educator; b. Chgo., June 29, 1934; s. Charles Albert and Rachel Cottle; m. Suzanne Cottle, June 21, 1959; children: Corinne, David. AB, Harvard U., Cambridge, Mass., 1957, AM, 1958; PhD, U. Calif., Berkeley, 1964. Tchr. math. Middlesex Sch., Concord, Mass., 1958—60; mem. tech. staff Bell Labs, Holmdel, NJ, 1964—66; prof. Stanford U., Calif., 1966—2005; prof. emeritus, 2005—. Author: Stanford Street Names, 2005; co-author: The Linear Complementarity Problem, 1992; editor: The Basic George B. Dantzig, 2003. Recipient Lanchester prize, Inst. Ops. Rsch. and Mgmt. Sci., 1994; U.S. Sr. Scientist, Alexander von Humboldt Found., 1977. Mem.: Math. Assn. Am., Am. Math. Soc., Math Programming Soc. Avocations: woodworking, gardening, photography. Office: Stanford Univ Mgmt Scis and Engring Dept Stanford CA 94305 Office Phone: 650-725-0558. E-mail: rwc@stanford.edu.

COTTON, SALLY JEAN, retired music educator; b. East St. Louis, Ill., July 5, 1955; d. Clifford Leroy and Shirlee Ruth Corbier; children: Daniel Joseph, Julie Ann. BS Edn., Grand Canyon U., 1992; MEd, No. Ariz. U., Flagstaff, 1999, postgrad. Yamaha Sch. of Music, 2000. Conductor piano ensemble ASMTA, MTNA, Phoenix, 1982—2000; music tchr. piano, voice, guitar self-employed, Glendale, Ariz., 1982—; music tchr. Glendale Elem. Sch., Ariz., 1992—2001. Co-author: (pamphlet) Ascending and Descending Melodic Intervals in Song, 1985. Singer Cactus Country Singers Sweet Adelines; pres. Phoenix chpt. Nat. Jr. Fedn. Music Clubs, 1989—2000. Grantee Technology in Music, 1993. Mem.: NEA (rep 1987—), Music Educators Nat. Conf. (co-conductor 1992—2000), Music Tchrs. Nat. Assn. (spkr. 1997), Ariz. State Music Tchrs. Assn. (sec. 1987—88). Democrat. Nazarene. Home: 5747 W Missouri Ave #37 Glendale AZ 85301 Office Phone: 602-290-5299.

COTTON, W(ILLIAM) PHILIP, JR., architect; b. Columbia, Mo., July 11, 1932; s. William Philip and Frances Barbara (Harrington) C. AB, Princeton U., 1954; MArch, Harvard U., 1960. Registered architect, Mo., Ill. Pvt. practice architecture, St. Louis, 1964—. Author: 100 Historic Buildings in St. Louis County, 1970. Treas. New Music Circle, St. Louis, 1968-96, Pub. Revenue Edn. Coun., St. Louis, 1977—; v.p. Music Diversions Soc., St. Louis, 1993—2005; pres. Collegium Vocale, 1999—. Recipient St. Louis AIA/CPC Urban Design Merit award, 2002, Pres.'s award, Landmarks Assn. St. Louis. Fellow AIA (Ctrl. States Spl. Honor award 1981, Rozier award for Hist. Preservation 1991); mem. Valley Sailing Club (commodore 1985). Roman Catholic. Home: 5145 Lindell Blvd Saint Louis MO 63108-1221 Office: W Philip Cotton Jr Architect 1221 Locust St Ste 1410 Saint Louis MO 63103-2364

COTTON, WILLIAM ROBERT, retired dentist; b. Miami, Fla., Nov. 29, 1931; s. Robert Lee and Mamie Bell (Daniel) Cotton; m. Marye Ruth Hartz; children: Caroline Ruth Vance, William Robert Jr., David Michael, Lynn Cathryn Tavel. DDS, U. Md., 1955; MS, Northwestern U., Chgo., 1963; MA, Roosevelt U., 1973; EdS, George Washington U., 1980. With USN, 1955-81, commd. capt., 1973, ret., 1981; asst. dental officer Marine Corps Schs. and USS F.D. Roosevelt CVA 42, Quantico, Va. and Mayport, Fla., 1957-61; head exptl. pathology div. Naval Med. Rsch. Inst., Bethesda, Md., 1963-67; dental officer USS Fulton AS-11, New London, Conn., 1967-69; chief histopathology div. Naval Dental Rsch. Inst., Great Lakes, Ill., 1969-72, exec. officer, 1972-73, dep. comdg. officer, 1973-76; chmn. dental scis. dept. Naval Med. Rsch. Inst., Bethesda, Md., 1976-79; dir. Casualty Care Rsch. Program Ctr., Naval Med. Rsch. Inst., Bethesda, Md., 1979-81; assoc. prof. dept. operative dentistry Temple U., Phila., 1981-83; prof., chmn. dept. operative dentistry Georgetown U., Washington, 1983-90; pvt. practice Rockville, Md.; ret., 1999; dentist Mission of Mercy, Frederick, Md., 2001—. Adv. com. dental tech. program So. Ill. U., Carbondale, 1976—85; cons. Naval Dental Rsch. Inst., Great Lakes, 1981—85, Dentsply Internat., York, Pa., 1984—88; mem. spl. study sect. NIH, Washington, 1984, Washington, 87; clin. dentist Mission of Mercy, Brunswick, Md., 2001—; adj. clin. prof. dept. restorative dentistry U. Md. Dental Sch., Balt., 2004—. Contbg. author: book Biology Dental Caires, 1968, Dental Clinics of North America, 1986, editl. bd.: Jour. Dental Rsch., 1976—86, 1988, Jour. Operative Dentistry, 1986—92. Elder Presbyn. Ch. Fellow: Internat. Coll. Dentists (life), Am. Coll. Dentists (life); mem.: ADA (life), D.C. Dental Soc. (life; bd. dirs. 1986—89). Democrat. Home: 11816 Winterset Ter Potomac MD 20854-2846 Personal E-mail: wmrc@comcast.net.

COTTON-COBB, ROBIN LEEANNE, music educator; b. Flagstaff, Tex., Jan. 4, 1966; d. Peter Robin Cotton and Linda Ann Minasi; children: Christina Michele Dawson, Daniel Cobb. BA in Psychology, U. Tex., Austin, 1987, MusM in Vocal Performance and Pedagogy, 1990, postgrad., 1992—94. Pvt. voice instr. Klein Ind. Sch. Dist., 1999—; vocal instr., choral dir. Christian Arts Acad., Houston, 2000—03; adj. lectr. music San Houston State U., Huntsville, Tex., 2003—. Pvt. voice instr. Spring Ind.

Sch. Dist., 2000—03, Austin Ind. Sch. Dist., Tex., 1994—96. Singer various recitals, (Operas) Austin Lyric Opera, Opera North, Cimmaron Cir. Opera. Mem.: Nat. Assn. Tchrs. Singing (2d pl. Texoma region 1989, 5th pl. 1990). Avocations: skiing, soccer.

COTTONGAME, W. BRICE, lawyer; b. Ft. Worth, June 4, 1958; s. William Robert and Nelda Ree Cottongame; m. Elizabeth Cramer, Jan. 9, 1992; children: Kate, Will. BA in Polit. Sci., U. Tex., 1980; JD, S. Tex. Coll. Law, 1984. Bar: Tex., 1984, U.S. Dist. Ct. (no. and so. dists.) Tex., U.S. Ct. Appeals (5th cir.), U.S. Supreme Ct.; bd. cert. personal injury trial law Tex. Bd. Legal Specialization. Atty. Wallace Craig & Assocs., Ft. Worth, 1980-95, Henderson Haksell & Cottongame, Ft. Worth, 1995-98, Law Office W. Brice Cottongame & Assocs., Ft. Worth, 1998—. Fellow State Bar Tex., Tarrant County Bar Found.; Mem. Tex. Trial Lawyers Assn. (assoc. dir. 1986-90, dir. 1990-95), Tarrant County Trial Lawyers Assn. (dir. 1989-93, pres. 1994), Tarrant County Bar Assn. Democrat. United Methodist.

COTTRELL, G. WALTON, manufacturing executive; b. Auburn, NY, Sept. 26, 1939; s. George H. and Eleanor H. (Day) C.; m. Jean H. Springer, June 15, 1963; children: Lisa, Lori. BSME, Cornell U., 1962, MBA, 1963. Various positions Owens-Ill., Inc., Toledo, 1965-85, treas., 1980-83, v.p. corp. planning, 1984-85; dir. fin. Europe Owens-Ill. Internat., Geneva, 1976-80; v.p. fin. The Allen Group, Inc., Melville, NY, 1986; v.p., treas. Squibb Corp., Princeton, NJ, 1987-88; sr. v.p. fin., CFO Carpenter Tech. Corp., Reading, Pa., 1989-2001, sr. v.p. strategic planning, 2001; ret., 2001. Dir. Andersen Labs., Inc., Bloomfield, Conn., 1992-98. Bd. dirs. Jr. Achievement N.W. Ohio, Toledo, 1980-86, Planned Parenthood N.W. Ohio, Toledo, 1982-86, United Way Berks County, 1990-97, Berks County Cmty. Found., 1999-03, Sciencenter Discovery Mus., 2004-; mem. coun. Cornell U., 1985-95. Lt. USNR, 1963-65. Mem. Fin. Execs. Inst. (bd. dirs. 1982-85), Nat. Assn. Corp. Treas. (pres. 1997-98, chair bd. dirs. 1998-99). Republican. United Ch. of Christ. Home: 15 Windjammers Way Ithaca NY 14850 Personal E-mail: cottrellgw@aol.com.

COTTRELL, JAMES E., anesthesiologist, medical educator; b. Charleston, W.Va., Nov. 9, 1942; m. Geraldine Kincaid. BS, Morris Harvey Coll., 1961; MD, W.Va. U., 1968. Diplomate Am. Bd. Anesthesiologists. Asst. prof. NYU Sch. of Medicine, 1974-78, assoc. prof., 1978-79; prof., chmn. SUNY Downstate Med. Ctr., Bklyn., 1979—. Editor books; contbr. articles to profl. jours. Mem. Am. Soc. of Anesthesiologists (v.p. 2001, pres. 2003), N.Y. State Soc. of Anesthesiologists, Assn. of Univ. Anesthesiologists, Soc. of Acad. Anesthesia Chmn., World Congress in Anesthesiology. Office: SUNY Downstate Med Ctr 450 Clarkson Ave Brooklyn NY 11203-2056 E-mail: jcottrell@downstate.edu.

COTTRELL, JAMES RAY, lawyer; b. Norton, Va., Aug. 9, 1952; BA, Va. Mil. Inst., 1974; JD, U. Richmond, 1976. Bar: Va. 1977, DC 1979. Ptnr. Gannon & Cottrell, P.C., Alexandria, Va., 1977—. Mem.: ATLA, ABA (mem. family law sect.), Fairfax Bar Assn., Alexandria Bar Assn., DC Bar, Va. Trial Lawyers Assn., Va. State Bar (sec. 1987—88, vice chmn. 1988—89, chmn. 1989—90, bd. govs. family law sect.), Phi Delta Phi. Office: Gannon and Cottrell PC PO Box 1286 Alexandria VA 22313-1286*

COTTRELL, JEANNETTE ELIZABETH, retired librarian; b. Buffalo, Dec. 10, 1923; d. Benjamin Birch and Mary Jeannette (Ashdown) Milnes; m. William Barber Cottrell, Jan. 21, 1944 (dec.); children: Karen Jean, Susan Marie, William Milnes, Scott Barber, Stephen Ashdown. BA in Sociology, U. Tenn., 1970, MS, 1976; student, Alfred U., 1940-43. Cert. tchr. libr., Tenn. Nursery sch. tchr. Concord Meth. Ch., Knoxville, Tenn., 1964-65; libr. City Sch. Sys., Knoxville, Tenn., 1971-84, ret., 1984. Author: (with husband) An American Family in the 20th Century, 1987; recorder textbooks for the blind, 1983—. Libr. Concord United Meth. Ch., Knoxville, 1975—, reading chair Suzanna Wesley Circle. Mem. DAR, Phi Kappa Phi, Beta Phi Mu. Republican. Methodist. Avocations: singing, bridge, cooking, travel, reading. Home: 308 Camelot Ct Knoxville TN 37922-2076

COTTRELL, MARY-PATRICIA TROSS, bank executive; b. Seattle, Apr. 24, 1934; d. Alfred Carl and Alice-Grace (O'Neal) Tross; m. Richard Smith Cottrell, May 17, 1969 (dec. 1995). BBA, U. Wash., 1955. Sys. svc. rep. IBM, Seattle, Endicott, NY, 1955-58, customer edn. instr. Endicott, 1958—65; cons. data processing Stamford, Conn., 1965-66; asst. treas. Union Trust Co., Stamford, 1967-68, asst. v.p., 1969-76, v.p., 1976-78, v.p., head corp. svcs., 1978-83; v.p. corp. fin. svcs. Citytrust, Bridgeport, Conn., 1983-90, sr. v.p. cash mgmt. svcs., 1990-91; v.p. cash mgmt. Chase Manhattan Bank Conn., N.A., 1991-92, Centerbank, New Haven, 1992-95; v.p. corp. svcs. Lafayette Am. Bank, Bridgeport, 1995-97; sr. v.p. corp. svcs. Union Savs. Bank, Danbury, Conn., 1997—. Bd. dirs. Family and Children's Agy., 1982—; trustee Norwalk Seaport Assn., 1997—2001; bd. dirs. New Eng. Network, Inc., Bank Mktg. Assn., 1988—91, Bridgeport Housing Svcs., 1985—91, Danbury Cemetery Assn., 2002—04, Gaylord Hosp., 1986—92, 1998—2004, vice chmn., 1991, chmn., 2003—04, chmn. develop. com., 1992—2004; chmn. Family and Children Agy., 1986—87; bd.dirs. Stamford Rehab Ctr., 1996—2004, chmn., 2003—04. Mem.: Danbury Vis. Nurse Assn. (bd. dirs. 2003—, pres. 2006—07), New Eng. Automated Clearing House Assn. (bd. dirs. 1995—97), Fairfield County Bankers Assn. (dir., pres. 1984—85), Electronic Funds Transfer Assn. (chmn. bd. dirs. 1983—84, vice chmn., bd. dirs.), Phi Beta Kappa, Beta Gamma Sigma. Republican. Roman Catholic. Office Phone: 203-830-6927. Business E-Mail: mcottrell@unionsavings.com.

COUCH, DANIEL MICHAEL, healthcare executive; b. Chgo., July 1, 1937; s. Arthur Daniel and Helen Margret (Kreamer) C.; m. Marilee Hermon, Sept. 12, 1958; children: Laura Ann, Mark Allen, Kristina Lynn, Michelle Louise, Daniel Michael Jr. BS in Bus., Ind. U., 1958; MBA, Butler U., 1977. Field examiner Ind. State Bd. Accounts, Indpls., 1959-61; controller Community Hosp., Anderson, Ind., 1961-67; field rep. Am. Hosp. Assn., Chgo., 1967-68; treas./controller Health & Hosp. Corp. of Marion County, Indpls., 1968-71; assoc. adminstr. Winona Meml. Hosp., Indpls., 1971-78; pres. Huntington (Ind.) Meml. Hosp., 1978-80; dep. exec. dir. Truman Med. Ctr., Kansas City, Mo., 1980-99; CFO Health Care Found. Greater Kansas City, 2005—. Bd. dirs. Nat. Pub. Health and Hosp. Inst., Washington, 1987-90, chmn., 1989. Bd. dirs, mem. exec. com. Labor-Mgmt. Coun., Kansas City, Mo., 1982—2006, co-chmn, 1991—97; bd. dirs. Greater Kansas City Mental Health Found., 1984—93, pres., 1992—93; bd. dirs. Kansas City Care Ctr., 1990—, treas., 1999—; bd. dirs. Resource Devel. Inst., Kansas City, 1998—2005, pres., 2002—04; bd. dirs. Vis. Nurse Home Care Svcs., Kansas City, 1991—98, chmn., 1993—98; bd. dirs. A Rising Tide-The Greater Kansas City Healthcare Found., 2003—05. 1st lt. USAR, 1958—67. Fellow Am. Coll. Healthcare Execs. (life fellow, nominating com. 1995-99); mem. Am. Hosp. Assn. (ho. of dels. and Regional Policy Bd. 7 1989-92, governing coun. sect. met. hosps. 1990-93, chmn. 1993), Nat. Assn. Pub. Hosps. (bd. dirs. 1981-99, chmn. 1989), Kansas City Area Hosp. Assn. (bd. dirs. 1990-96), Greater Kansas City C. of C. (various coms. 1985-99), Healthcare Fin. Mgmt. Assn. (advanced), Kansas City Care Network (bd. dirs. 1995-99, pres. 1995-99), Family Health Ptnrs. (bd. dirs. 1995-99), Found. Fin. Officers Group, Masons, Rotary. Episcopalian. Avocations: golf, bowling, reading. Office Phone: 816-241-7006. E-mail: dcouch@healthcare4kc.org. *While into life a little rain must fall, I like to dwell on the fact that into every life a little joy must come.*

COUCH, JESSE WADSWORTH, retired insurance company executive; b. Atlanta, Mar. 2, 1921; s. Jesse Newton and Laura (Day) W.; m. Charlotte Lucretia Collins, Jan. 13, 1945 (dec.); children: Robert Collins (dec.), Laura W.; m. Charlotte H. Gran, Oct. 17, 1997. AB, Princeton, 1947. With 1st Nat. Bank Houston, 1947-51; assoc. Wray Assocs., Houston, 1951-60; ptnr. Wray, Couch & Elder, Houston, 1960-69; v.p. Marsh & McLennan, Inc., 1969-83; pvt. cons., 1983-95. Mem. exec. bd. Episcopal Diocese of Tex., 1965-67, 68-71; trustee St. Luke's Episcopal Hosp., 1971-76; bd. dirs. Houston-Harris County YMCA, 1969-74, Houston Soc. Prevention Cruelty to Animals, 1974—2004; Bd. dirs. Tex. divsn. Am. Cancer Soc., mem. exec. com., 1982-91; chmn. Am. Cancer Soc. Greater Houston, 1981-83; trustee Mus. Fine Arts, Houston, 1970-74. Served to capt. USAAF, 1943-46. Mem.: Houston C. of C. (aviation com. 1965—75), Allegro Club, Bayou Club, Houston Country Club, Rod & Gun Club, Eagle Lake. Home: 6015 Pine Forest Rd Houston TX 77057-1431 Personal E-mail: jcouch@pdq.net.

COUCH, KATRINA DENISE, elementary school educator; b. Grand Rapids, Mich., Oct. 26, 1972; d. Kathy L. (Couch) Matthews-Walker and James Lee Couch; 1 child, Trevian Javon. BS, Oakwood Coll., Ala., 1995; MS (hon.), Walden U., 2005. Profl. Ednl. Cert. Mich., 2005. Wyo. pub. schs. diversity com. Diversity Coun. for the Wyo. Pub. Schs., Wyoming, Mich., 1996—2005; climate com. leader Taft Elem., 2004—. Singles ministry leader Bethel Seventh-day Adventist Ch., 2002—03, women's ministries leader Grand Rapids, Mich., 2003—05; music ministries dir. Bethel SDA, 2006. Recipient Least Restrictive Environment award, Wyoming Pub. Sch., 2000. Office: Taft Elem 2700 Taft SW Wyoming MI 49519 Home Phone: 616-301-3915; Office Phone: 616-249-7627 4542. Business E-Mail: couchk@wyoming.k12.mi.us.

COUCH, ROBERT BARNARD, physician, medical researcher, microbiologist, immunologist, educator; b. Guntersville, Ala., Sept. 25, 1930; s. Ezekiel Harvey and Frances Jane (Barnard) C.; m. Katherine Frances Klein, Apr. 23, 1955; children: Robert Steven, Leslie Ann, Colleen Frances, Elizabeth Lee. BA, Vanderbilt U., 1952, MD, 1956. Diplomate Am. Bd. Internal Medicine. Intern Vanderbilt U. Hosp., Nashville, 1956—57, resident in medicine, 1959—60, chief resident in medicine, 1960—61; clin. assoc. NIH, Washington, 1957—59, sr. investigator, 1961—65, head clin. virology sect., 1965—66; assoc. prof. Baylor Coll. Medicine, Houston, 1966—71, dir. influenza rsch. ctr., 1974—91, prof. microbiology, immunology and medicine, 1971—2000, Disting. prof., 1995—, head infectious diseases sect. medicine, 1987—92, chmn. dept. microbiology and immunology, 1989—2000, dir. acute viral respiratory diseases unit, 1991—96, dir. respiratory pathogens rsch. unit, 1996—, dir. Ctr. for Infection and Immunity Rsch., 1999—, prof. molecular virology, microbiology and medicine, 2000—. Mem. rsch. rev. panels infectious diseases; cons. NIH, Dept. Def., FDA, various others. Contbr. articles to profl. jours. Served to sr. surgeon USPHS, 1957-66. Mem. ACP, AAAS, Soc. Exptl. Biology and Medicine, Am. Soc. Microbiology, Infectious Diseases Soc. Am., Am. Assn. Immunologists, Am. Fedn. Clin. Rsch., Am. Soc. Clin. Investigation, So. Soc. Clin. Investigation, Am. Assn. Physicians, Am. Soc. Epidemiology, Am. Soc. Virology. Office: Baylor Coll Medicine MS 280 One Baylor Plaza Houston TX 77030 Office Phone: 713-798-4474. Business E-Mail: rcouch@bcm.edu.

COUCH, ROBERT M., lawyer, federal agency administrator; b. Apr. 3, 1957; m. Anne E. Couch; children: Mary Stuart, Frances. BS, Washington & Lee U., 1978, JD, 1982. Bar: 1984. Law clk. to Hon. John F. Wisdom US Ct. Appeals (5th Cir.); law clk. to Hon. Lewis F. Powell, Jr. US Supreme Ct.; gen. counsel, CFO First Comml. Bancshares, Inc., Birmingham, Ala.; chmn. Mortgage Bankers Assn., 2003—04, mem. blue ribbon task force; pres., CEO New South Fed. Savings Bank, Birmingham, Ala.; mng. dir. Collateral Mortgage, Ltd.; pres. Govt. Nat. Mortgage Assn. (Ginnie Mae), Washington, 2006—07; gen. counsel, chief legal officer US Dept. Housing & Urban Devel., Washington, 2007—. Past pres. Mortgage Bankers Assn. Ala.; mem. thrift industry adv. coun. Fed. Reserve. Office: US Dept Housing & Urban Devel 451 Seventh St SW Rm 10110 Mail Stop C Washington DC 20410*

COUCHMAN, ROBERT GEORGE JAMES, foundation executive; b. Toronto, Ont., Can., Feb. 21, 1937; s. Robert George and Mary (Bigelow) C.; m. Jane Barker (div. 1985); children: Barbara, Stephen, Michael. BA, Queen's U., Kingston, Ont., 1965; MEd, U. Toronto, 1969. Tchr. Scarborough (Ont.) Bd. Edn., 1957-63; dir. student svcs. Etobicoke (Ont.) Bd. Edn., 1963-74; exec. dir. Family Svc. Assn. Met. Toronto, 1974-89; pres. Donner Can. Found., Toronto, 1989-93; assoc. Re Think Group, 1993; dir. Terra Nova, 1995-97; chmn. Outward Bound Can., 1990—94. Co-chmn. UN Can. Com. Internat. Yr. of Family, 1993-94; patron Outward Bound Can., 1995-99; mem. nat. adv. com. Fed. Minister of Health on Rural Health. Author: Reflections on Canadian Character, 2003; contbr. 40 articles to profl. jours Chmn. Outward Bound Wilderness Sch., 1987-88, Outward Bound Can., 1990-94; pres. Can. Mental Health Assn., Ont., 1971-73; dir. White Ribbon Found. of Can.; bd. dirs. Addiction Rsch. Found., Ont., 1980-86, Metro Toronto Housing Co., 1982-88, United Way Metro Toronto, 1994-96; vice chmn. Vanier Inst. of the Family, 1988-90; chmn. Atlin Big Water Soc.; gov., Grey Owl Nature Trust, 1997-2000, advisor Can. Arctic Resources Com.; exec. dir. PQR Found., 1993—. Mem.: Yukon Family Svcs. Assn. (exec. dir. 1999—2001), Ont. Assn. Profl. Social Workers (hon.), Rotary (com. chmn.). United Church. Office: 137 Wilson Dr Whitehorse YT Canada Y1A 5R2 Office Phone: 867-393-2398. Personal E-mail: bcouchman@northwestel.net.

COUDERT, DALE HOKIN, real estate executive, marketing consultant; b. Chgo., Nov. 29, 1941; d. Sidney and Ruth (Brower) Manowitz; m. Frederic R. Coudert (div.); children Dana, Alexandra. BA, Northwester U., 1964. V.p. Cross & Brown, NYC, 1975-86; dir., sec. First Women's Bank, NYC, 1980-87; head bus. devel., office of pres. 1st N.Y. Bank for Bus., 1988-91; mktg. dir. Lafer Mgmt., NYC, 1993-94; pres., CEO Coudert Assocs. Ltd., NYC, 1991—; broker Brown Harris Stevens Palm Beach Real Estate, Pal, 1999—; founder, pres. Coudert Inst., 2001—. Dir. Hosp. Tak Co., LI, NY, 1979—98; creator, chmn., CEO Coudert Inst. at Villa Dei Fiori, Palm Beach, Fla., 2001—. Pub., editor: (book) Business and Pleasure, 1986-87. Bd. dirs. Women's Rep. Club, N.Y.C., 1994, N.Y. Drama League, N.Y.C., 1975—; mem. nat. bd. dirs. Aspen Art Mus., Kennedy Ctr., 1996-98; trustee, treas. Zoo of the Palm Beaches at Dreker Park, 1996-98, bd. dirs., 1996—; regent St. John the Divine, N.Y.C., 1988. Fellow Aspen Inst. (life); mem. Internat. Womens Forum, Met. Opera Club, Women's Forum Fla. Avocations: piano, voice, dance, golf, tennis. also: Brown Harris Stevens Palm Beach Real Estate Ste 329 340 Royal Poinciana Plz Palm Beach FL 33480-4048 Home: 163 Seminole Ave Palm Beach FL 33480-3732 E-mail: dal1129@aol.com.

COUGAR, JOHN See **MELLENCAMP, JOHN**

COUGHENOUR, JOHN CLARE, federal judge; b. Pittsburg, Kans., July 27, 1941; s. Owren M. and Margaret E. (Widner) C.; m. Gwendolyn A. Kieffaber, June 1, 1963; children: Jeffrey, Douglas, Marta. BS, Kans. State Coll., 1963; JD, U. Iowa, 1966. Bar: Iowa 1963, D.C. 1963, U.S. Dist. Ct. (we. dist.) Wash. 1966. Ptnr. Bogle & Gates, Seattle, 1966-81; vis. asst. prof. law U. Washington, Seattle, 1970-73; judge U.S. Dist. Ct. (we. dist.) Wash., Seattle, 1981—, chief judge, 1997—2005. Recipient William L. Dwyer Outstanding Jurist award, King County Bar Assn. Mem. Iowa State Bar Assn., Wash. State Bar Assn., Ninth Cir. Dist. Judges' Assn. (past pres.). Office: Dist Judge Ste 16229 700 Stewart St Seattle WA 98101-1271 Home: 700 Stewart St Seattle WA 98101-1271

COUGHENOUR, KAVIN LUTHER, career officer, military historian; b. New Kensington, Pa., Mar. 1, 1947; s. Roy Edgar and Anna Louise (Coleman) C.; m. Kathryn Mary Domurat, May 17, 1969; 1 child, Stacey Anne Aldrich. BA in Social Scis., Ind. U. of Pa., 1969; MA in Pers. Mgmt., Ctrl. Mich. U., 1979; diploma, U.S. Army War Coll., 1990. Commd. 2d lt. U.S. Army, 1969, advanced through grades to col., 1991, adj. Ft. Meade, Md., 1973-75, adj. gen. 79th Res. Command Willow Grove, Pa., 1976-79, adj. 5th Spl. Forces Group Ft. Bragg, NC, 1979-82, adj. gen. 3d Armored Divsn. Frankfurt, Germany, 1985-86, commdg. officer U.S. Mil. Entrance Processing Sta., Dept. Defense Chgo., 1986-88, tng. officer Spl. Forces Sch. Ft. Bragg, 1988-89, spl. forces br. chief Pers. Command Alexandria, Va., 1990-92, dep. comdr. Ctr. Mil. History Washington, 1992-95; lic. battlefield guide Gettysburg (Pa.) Nat. Mil. Park, 1995—. Decorated Legion of Merit; recipient Gold medal, Nat. Hon. Soc. Pershing Rifles, 1968, Supts. award of Excellence, Gettysburg Nat. Mil. Park, 2001, Eagle Scout. Mem. Spl. Forces Assn., Soc. Mil. History, U.S.A. War Coll. Assn., Philmont Staff Assn., Assn. Lic. Battlefield Guides. Republican. Methodist. Avocation: civil war history. Home: Lake Heritage 964 Johnson Dr Gettysburg PA 17325-8970 Office Phone: 717-476-1015. Personal E-mail: kavinc@aol.com.

COUGHLAN, GARY PATRICK, pharmaceutical executive; b. Fresno, Calif., Feb. 14, 1944; s. Edward Patrick and Elizabeth Claire (Ryan) C.; m. Mary Cary Kelley, Dec. 21, 1967; children: Christopher, Sarah, Laura, Claire, Moira. BA, St. Mary's Coll., 1966; MA in Econs., UCLA, 1967; MBA, Wayne State U., 1971. Sr. fin. analyst Burroughs Corp., Detroit, 1969-72; with Dart Industries, LA, 1972-81, group v.p. field services, 1978-81, v.p. ops. services, 1981, Dart & Kraft Inc., Northbrook, Ill., 1981-82, v.p. fin., contr., 1984-85, sr. v.p. fin. affairs, 1985-86, sr. v.p., CFO, 1986; v.p. fin. retail food group Kraft Inc., Glenview, Ill., 1982-84, sr. v.p., CFO, 1986-88; sr. v.p. fin. Kraft Gen. Foods, Glenview, 1989-90; sr. v.p. fin., CFO Abbott Labs., Abbott Park, Ill., 1990-2001, ret., 2001. Instr. prof. fin. ext. program UCLA, 1974—80; bd. dirs. Arthur J. Gallagher, Itasca, Ill., Hershey (Pa.) Corp., Chgo. Hort. Soc., Glencoe, Ill.; mem. adv. coun. Coun. Fgn. Rels., Chgo. Com. Mem. Fin. Execs. Inst. Republican. Roman Catholic. Home: 1135 Central Rd Glenview IL 60025-4432 Office: Ste 306 1200 Central Ave Wilmette IL 60091 Office Phone: 847-920-1677. Personal E-mail: gcoughlan@earthlink.com.

COUGHLAN, KENNETH L., lawyer; b. Chgo., July 8, 1940; BA, U. Notre Dame, 1962; JD, Northwestern U., Chgo., 1966. Bar: Ill. 1967. Trust officer Am. Nat. Bank & Trust Co., Chgo., 1969-72; sec. bd., sr. v.p., gen. counsel, cashier Ctrl. Nat. Bank., Chgo., 1972-82; sec., gen. counsel Ctrl. Nat. Chgo. Corp., 1976-82; sr. v.p., gen. counsel Exch. Nat. Bank, Chgo., 1982-83; gen. counsel Exch. Internat. Corp., Chgo., 1982-83; chmn. bd., pres. Union Realty Mortgage Co., Inc., Chgo., 1981-83; shareholder DeHaan & Richter P.C., 1983—2000; mem. Kelly, Olson, Michod, DeHaan & Richter, L.L.C. Capt. U.S. Army, 1966-68. Fellow Ill. Bar Found.; mem. ABA, Ill. State Bar Assn. (chmn. sect. on comml., banking and bankruptcy law 1981-82), Chgo. Bar Assn. (chmn. fin. instns. com. 1980-81, chmn. comml. fin. com. 1979-80), Lawyers Club (Chgo.).

COUGHLAN, PATRICK CAMPBELL, lawyer, mediator; b. Orange, NJ, May 28, 1940; s. Gerald Noel and Carter (Van Schaick) C.; m. Joyce Miskuf; children: Kimberly Campbell,Devon Gerald, Carter Turner. BA, Duke U., 1962, JD, 1965. Bar: Fla. 1965, U.S. Supreme Ct. 1968, Calif. 1974, Maine 1985. Assoc. Alley, Maass, Rogers & Lindsay, Palm Beach, Fla., 1969-72, ptnr., 1972-74; judge Mcpl. Ct., Ocean Ridge, Fla., 1970-72; assoc. firm Richards, Watson & Gershon, Los Angeles, 1974-75, ptnr., 1975-84; city atty. City of Rancho Palos Verdes, Calif., 1975-82, City of San Fernando, Calif., 1977-82, City of Seal Beach, Calif., 1978-84, City of La Habra Heights, Calif., 1979-84, Avalon, Calif., 1981-84, Rolling Hills, Calif., 1981-84, Westlake Village, Calif., 1981-84; chair bd. appeals Raymond, Maine, 1985-98; pres. Kingsley Pines, Inc.; prin. Coughlan Assoc., 1987-88; pres. Resolve Disputes, Inc. N.Am., Portland, Maine, 1989-92, Conflict Solutions, Portland, Maine, 1992—, Naples, Fla., 1992—. Ptnr. Atlanean Ptnrs. LLC. Author: Why Mediation, Taking the Leap of Faith. Pres. No. Pines, Inc., 1980-86; trustee, sec. Gulf Stream Sch. Found., Inc., 1970-85; bd. dirs. Mountains Restoration Trust, 1981-82; trustee North Yarmouth Acad., 1984-93, pres., 1985-89; treas., trustee Natural Resources Coun. Maine, 1989-93; pres. parish coun. Our Lady of Perpetual Help, 1983-85; pres. World Affairs Coun. of Maine, 1986-89, trustee, 1985-93; trustee Portland Stage Co., 1989-93, sec., 1990-91, v.p., 1991-92; trustee Maine Youth Camps Assn., 1989-96, sec., 1990, v.p., 1990-93, pres., 1993-95; trustee Susan Curtis Found., 1991-96; dir. Pvt. Adjudication Ctr. Duke U., 1994-2002, mediator 1998-2002; dir. The Club at La Peninsula, 1997-98, Adms. Watch at Windstar, 2004-2005. Capt. USAF, 1965-68. Fellow Internat. Acad. Mediators (bd. dirs. 1999—, v.p. 2001-2005); mem. ABA, State Bar Calif., Fla. Bar, Maine State Bar, Soc. Profls. in Dispute Resolution, Am. Acad. Civil Trial Mediators, Maine Assn. Dispute Resolution Profls. (pres. 1990-92), Windstar Country Club (Naples, Fla.). Roman Catholic. Home: 1540 Star Pointe Lane Naples FL 34112 Office: 112 Plains Rd Raymond ME 04071 Personal E-mail: coglan@aol.com. Business E-Mail: pat@conflictsolutionsinc.com.

COUGHLIN, CATHY M., telecommunications industry executive; b. St. Louis, 1958; BA Econ., Northwestern U.; MA Fin., Saint Louis U. Joined SBC Midwest, 1979; v.p. Consumer and Bus. Mktg., SBC Ops.; sr. v.p. Mktg., Southwestern Bell Yellow Pages; pres. Consumer Markets, SBC Ameritech, Midwest Bus. Comm. Services; pres., CEO AT&T Midwest, 2005—. Mem. bd. dirs. Mus. of Sci. and Industry, Coll. of DuPage Found., Jr. Achievement Inc., Civic Cons. Alliance, United Way of Met. Chgo. Named one of 25 Women to Watch, Crain's Chgo. Bus., 2007; recipient Luminary Award, Girl Scout's, 2006. Mem.: The Commercial Club and The Chgo. Network, The Civic Com., Econ. Club of Chgo. Office: AT&T Inc 175 E Houston San Antonio TX 78205

COUGHLIN, CHRISTOPHER J., financial executive; With Ernst & Young (formerly Arthur Young), Sterling Winthrop, Inc., 1982-96, CFO, bd. dirs., 1993-96; exec. v.p., CFO Nabisco Internat., 1996—98, Pharmacia & Upjohn, Inc., Peapack, NJ, 1998—2003; COO Interpub. Group Cos., Inc., NYC, 2003—; exec. vice-pres., CFO Tyco Internat. Ltd. Office: Interpub Group Cos Inc 1271 Ave of Americas New York NY 10020

COUGHLIN, FRANCIS RAYMOND, JR., surgeon, educator, lawyer; b. NYC, Feb. 22, 1927; s. Francis Raymond and Isabel (Archibald) C.; m. Barbara Ann Blunt, June 9, 1951; children: Hilary, Mary, Patricia, Christopher Francis, Geoffrey Blunt, Daniel Taylor, Isabel, David Carleton. BS, Fordham U., Bronx, NY, 1948; MD, Yale U., New Haven, Conn., 1952; MS, McGill U., Montreal, Que., Can., 1955, diploma in surgery, 1959; JD, U. Bridgeport, Conn., 1988. Bar: N.Y., Conn., D.C., U.S. Supreme Ct.; diplomate Am. Bd. Surgery, Am. Bd. Thoracic Surgery. Intern N.Y. Hosp., NYC, 1952-53; resident McGill U. Teaching Hosp., Montreal, 1953-57, Overholt Thoracic Clin., Boston, 1958-60; mem. staff Stamford (Conn.) Hosp., 1960—; practice medicine specializing in thoracic surgery Stamford, 1960—88; medico-legal cons., 1988—. Dir. thoracic and vascular surgery St. Josephs Hosp., Stamford, 1970-73, 80-85, assoc. chief surgery, 1971-73, chief surgery, 1973-77; assoc. prof. clin. surgery N.Y. Med. Coll., 1981-2002; mem. staff Norwalk Hosp., 1965-89; vice chair Conn. State Commn. Medicolegal Investigations, 1990-2002. With U.S. Maritime Svc., 1945-46. Recipient Encaenia award Fordham U., NYC, 1958; Teaching fellow Harvard U., 1958. Fellow ACS (sec.-treas. Conn. chpt. 1966-70), Royal Coll. Surgeons (Can.), Am. Coll. Cardiology, Am. Coll. Chest Physicians, Royal Soc. Medicine; mem. Soc. Thoracic Surgeons (founding mem.), NY Acad. Medicine, Conn. Heart Assn. (dir. 1961-64), Conn. Lung Assn. (dir. and exec. com. 1963-69, v.p. 1967-69),

Lung Assn. So. Fairfield County (pres. 1963-68, dir. 1960-70), Soc. Med. Jurisprudence (v.p. 1992-93, pres. 1995-97), English-Speaking Union, Scottish-Am. Found., Can. Soc. NY, Yale Club NY, Army Navy Club (Washington), Yale Med. Sch. Alumni Assn. (v.p. 1999-01, pres. 2001-03, Disting. Alumni Svc. award 2006, trustee Yale Med. Sch. Whitney Cushing Libr. 2004-). Republican. Office: 20 Mead St New Canaan CT 06840-5701 Office Phone: 203-966-2197. E-mail: fcoughlinmd@att.net.

COUGHLIN, JACK, printmaker, sculptor, art educator; b. Greenwich, Conn., Feb. 19, 1932; s. John J. and Gabrielle S. (Jones) Coughlin; m. Joan M. Hopkins, July 5, 1958; children: Maura, Molly. Student, Art Students League, NYC, 1950-52; BFA, R.I. Sch. Design, 1954, MS, 1961. Asst. prof. art U. Mass., Amherst, 1964-68, assoc. prof., 1968-73, prof., 1973-94, prof. emeritus, 1994—. Hendriks Gallery, Dublin, Ireland, 1971, one-man shows include, 1974, 1976, 1978, 1980, 1983, 1987, Harvard U., 1974, Associated Am. Artists, N.Y.C., 1977, Dublin Writers Mus., 1993, Brandeis U., 1995, Springfield Coll., 2004, exhibited in group shows at 17th Biennial Am. Printmaking, Bklyn., 1970, Davidson Nat. Print Show, 1973, NAD, 1974—, Represented in permanent collections Met. Mus. Art, N.Y.C., Mus. Modern Art, Nat. Collection Arts, Washington, commd. regularly, The New Republic. With US Army, 1954—56. Recipient numerous awards, prizes for work, Nat. Inst. Arts and Letters, 1969, prize for drawing 158th Nat. Exhbn., NAD, 1983, 33d N.D. Print and Drawing Ann., 1991, 34th Nat. Pring Exhbn., Hunterdon Art Ctr., NAD prize, 2005, 2007. Mem.: NAD (academician), Soc. Am. Graphic Artists. Office Phone: 413-367-2469. E-mail: jackjr@art.umass.edu.

COUGHLIN, JAMES PATRICK, mathematician, educator; s. Patrick and Mary Ellen (Duffy) Coughlin. BS, Fordham Coll., 1960; MA, Columbia U., 1961; PhD, U. Colo., 1973. Instr. Arlington (Tex.) State Coll., 1962, Rockhurst Coll., Kans. City, Mo., 1962—63, Regis Coll., Denver, 1963—65; prof. math. Towson (Md.) U., 1979—. Physicist U.S. Naval Surface Weapons Lab., Dahlgren, Va., 1960—83. Co-author: Neural Computation From The Hopfield Net To The Boltzmann Machine, 1995. Mem.: Math. Assn. Am., Sigma Xi. Avocations: history, cryptography, bridge. Office: Mathematics Dept Towson 8000 York Road Towson MD 21252

COUGHLIN, JEANNINE MARIE, music educator; b. Midland, Mich., May 30, 1969; d. Jeremiah Thomas and Marciann Coughlin. BA in Music Edn., Saginaw Valley State U., 1992, postgrad., 1996, postgrad., 2003. Instrumental music tchr. Saginaw Pub. Schs., Mich., 1993—. Tennis coach Saginaw HS, 1998—2000, softball coach, 2001—; dir. Herter Band Camp, 1995—, Mich. HS All Star Band, 2001—; cons., presenter Reading and Writing in the Arts, Bay City, Mich., 2001, Success of Baldridge in the Classroom, Saginaw, Bay City, 2001—03. Co-author: (anthology) Reflections: Threads-Words that Bind Us, 2001. Leader Arenac County 4-H Club, Standish, Mich., 1999—. Named Saginaw Valley Tchr. of the Yr., Mich. H.S. Athletic Assn., 2000, Saginawian of Yr., 2006; recipient Excellence in Edn. award, Mich. Edn. Assn., 1996. Democrat. Roman Catholic. Avocations: reading, writing, sports, music. Home: 2640 Midland Rd Saginaw MI 48603 Office: Saginaw High Sch 3100 Webber St Saginaw MI 48601

COUGHLIN, NATALIE, Olympic swimmer; b. Vallejo, Calif., Aug. 23, 1982; d. Jim and Zennie Coughlin. Grad., U. Calif., Berkeley, 2004. Mem. US Olympic Swim Team Athens Olympic Games, 2004. Co-author (with Michael Silver): Golden Girl: How Natalie Coughlin Fought Back, Challenged Conventional Wisdom, and Became America's Swimming Champion, 2006. Named Nat. HS Swimmer of Yr., 1998, NCAA Swimmer of Yr., 2001, 2002, 2003, Female Swimmer of Yr., Swimming World Mag., 2002. Achievements include holding the world record for 100m backstroke (first woman under one minute - 59.58); world record-holder in the 100m and 200m backstroke (short course); first US woman to break 54 seconds in 100m freestyle (long course) - 53.99; gold medal, 100m backstroke, 800m freestyle relay, World Championships, 2001; Am. record-holder in over 10 events, including the 50m, 100m and 200m backstroke (long course); won 9 NCAA Titles, University of California-Berkeley, 2001-03; gold medal, 100m backstroke, 4x200m freestyle relay, Silver medal, 4x100m freestyle relay, 4x100m MR, Bronze medal, 100m freestyle, Athens Olympic games, 2004; won two national titles 100m freestyle and 100m backstroke at the 2005 World Championship Trials; won the gold medal in 100m backstroke at the 2007 World Championships. Office: c/o USA Swimming One Olympic Plz Colorado Springs CO 80909*

COUGHLIN, SHAUN R., research scientist; BS, MS, MIT, 1976, PhD, 1981; MD, Harvard Med. Sch., 1982. Intern, resident Mass. Gen. Hosp., 1982—84; postdoctoral asst. rsch. cardiologist, clin. fellow Cardiovascular Rsch. Inst., U. Calif., San Francisco, 1984—86, dir., 1997—; asst. prof. U. Calif., San Francisco, 1986—91, assoc. prof., 1991—96, prof. medicine, 1996—, prof. cellular and molecular pharmacology, 1997—. Dir. Millennium Pharm., Inc. Recipient Jeffrey M. Hoeg award, Am. Heart Assn., 2000, Freedom to Discover award for Disting. Achievement in Cardiovascular Rsch., Bristol-Myers Squibb, 2004. Mem.: Inst. Medicine, NAS. Office Phone: 415-476-6174. Office Fax: 415-476-8173. Business E-Mail: coughlin@cvrimail.ucsf.edu.

COUGHLIN, TOM, professional football coach; b. Waterloo, NY, Aug. 31, 1946; m. Judy Coughlin; children: Keli, Katie, Tim, Brian. BA Educ., Syracuse U.; MA Educ. Grad. asst. Syracuse U., 1969; head coach Rochester Inst. Tech., 1970-73; offensive backfield coach Syracuse U., 1974-76, offensive coord., 1977-80, Boston Coll., 1981-83; wide receivers coach Philadelphia Eagles, 1984-85; receivers coach Green Bay Packers, 1986-87, N.Y. Giants, 1988-90; head coach Boston Coll., 1991-93, Jacksonville Jaguars, 1994—2002, N.Y. Giants, 2004—. Founder The Jay Fund Found., 1996—. Named AFC Coach of the Year, 1996. Avocations: reading, running, golf. Office: c/o NY Giants Giants Stadium East Rutherford NJ 07073

COUGHRAN, WILLIAM M., JR., information technology executive, researcher; s. William M. Coughran, Sr. and Marianne Coughran; m. Bridget A. McGuire, Sept. 2, 1972; children: Megan J., Brendan W. BS, MS, Calif. Inst. Tech., 1975, Stanford U., 1977, PhD, 1980. V.p. Computing Scis. Rsch. Ctr., Bell Labs, Murray Hill, NJ, 1996—99; sr. v.p. Bell Labs Rsch. Silicon Valley, Palo Alto, Calif., 1998—2000; CEO, founder Entrisphere, Inc., Santa Clara, Calif., 2000—02; prin. Coughran Consulting, Palo Alto, 2003; v.p. engring. Google, Mountain View, Calif., 2003—. Bd. dirs. nSolutions, Inc., Santa Clara, Calif., Teneo Systems Inc.; mem. tech. adv. bd. Hammerhead Systems, Inc., Mountain View, Calif., 2002—. Office: Google Inc 1600 Amphitheatre Pkwy Mountain View CA 94043-1351 Personal E-mail: bill@coughran.net.

COUGILL, ROSCOE MCDANIEL, retired military officer; b. Charleston, Ill., Oct. 24, 1941; s. Oral Wilson and Malora Emaline (Vaughn) C.; m. Sallie Anne Carrow, Feb. 15, 1969; children: Christopher McDaniel, Andrew Ashby. BS in Edn., Ea. Ill. U., 1963; MS in Guidance and Counseling, Troy State U., Ala., 1976; postgrad., Air Command and Staff Coll., Maxwell AFB, Ala., 1976, Army War Coll., Carlisle, Pa., 1981. Commd. 2d lt. USAF, 1964, advanced through grades to brig. gen., 1989, ret., 1992; staff and exec. officer Hdqrs. USAF, Washington, 1976-80, dir., 1985-86, dep. asst. chief staff, 1988-89; comdr. 2179th Command Group, Patrick AFB, Fla., 1981-83; exec. officer internat. mil. staff NATO, Brussels, 1983-85; chief staff Air Force Comm. Command, Scott AFB, Ill., 1986-88; dir. command and control, comm. and computer sys. Hdqrs. U.S. Cen. Command, MacDill AFB, Fla., 1989-92; mayor City of Charleston, Ill., 1993—2005. Decorated DSM, Legion of Merit, Def. Superior Svc. medal.

COUKIS, PETER GEORGE, musician, composer; b. Waterbury, Conn., Jan. 15, 1955; s. George Peter and Antoinette (Kachulis) C.; m. Lucrecia Monje, Aug. 20, 1998; 1 child: George Joshua. BA, Western Conn. State U., 1978; AS, Mattatuck C.C., Waterbury, 1987. Musical arranger, composer Waterbury Children's Found., 1977-78; arranger, songwriter Youth Theatre Ensemble, Watertown, Conn., 1985-87; prodr., performer Laurel Cablevision, Litchfield, Conn., 1988-91; solo recording artist Waterbury, Wallingford, Conn., 1990—; founder Blue Plum Records, 1993—, Weird Garden Records. Composer, keyboardist The Nutmeg Ballet, Torrington, Conn., 1988; songwriter World Star Prodns., New Haven, 1988; keyboardist South Mich. Ave, Wolcott, Conn., 1980-86; synthesizer player Angels and Co. (Nunsense), N.Y.C. and Waterbury, 1989; artist, prodr. cable In Performance, 1988, Repertoire, 1989 (Laurel award 1989), Kaleidoscope, 1991, 13-week cable series, 1991, cable spl., 1992; released cassette single Girl, 1992; rec. artist Stick Bride, 1994, Strange Beauty, 1995, Believe in Me, 1995, Midgetmajority, 1997, Tournament, 1997, Stephania in Orange, 1997, Blossoms of Beauty, 1999, (15 CD set) Archive of Tracks, 2000, The Orchard, 2001, Harp, 2001, Curtains of Autummn, Organ Symphony No. 1, 2002, Songs for Eluthera, 2003, Orchestral Suit for John Paul II, 2005, Mystery Disc; Daughter of Cacophony, 2005, Peter Coukis Black Album, 2006, Poetique: The Bodineau Family; Piano Sonata No. 3, 2006, Piano Sonatas No. 4-8, 2007, Organ Sonata No. 2, 2007, several instrumental suites and sets of piano music, 2004. Talk show guest Barbara Davitt's Coffee Break, Sta. WATR, Waterbury, 1990; feature guest Lifestyles with Dr. Kotler, Sta. WCAT-13, Waterbury, 1990. Mem. NARAS, Am. Composers Forum, Conn. Songwriters Assn. (3-yr. award 1985, 5-yr. award 1987). Democrat. Avocations: reading, travel, outdoors, environmental awareness. Office Phone: 203-597-8163. Personal E-mail: weirdgardenrecords@juno.com.

COULLARD, CHAD, information systems specialist; b. Bridgeport, Conn., Oct. 23, 1947; s. John B. and Elizabeth F. (Orfanello) C. BSc, Syracuse U., 1969; postgrad., U. Md.; MBA, Nichols Coll., 1986. Sys. analyst Am. Chem. Soc., 1969-73; sr. programmer analyst Amherst (Mass.) Coll., 1973-77; programmer analyst, sys. analyst Spalding Divsn. Questor Corp., 1977-79; spl. projects coord. Gerber Sci., Inc., Hartford, Conn., 1979-98; info. tech. mgr. Barco, Inc., South Windsor, Conn., 1998—2002. Mem. Assn. Computing Machinery. Business E-Mail: chadcoullard@peoplepc.com.

COULSON, ELIZABETH ANNE, physical therapist, educator, state representative; b. Hastings, Nebr., Sept. 8, 1954; d. Alexander and Marilyn (Marvel) Shafernich; m. William Coulson, Feb. 14, 1986. Student, Wellesley Coll., 1972-73; BS in Edn., U. Kans., 1976; cert. in phys. therapy, Northwestern U., Chgo., 1977; MBA, Keller Grad. Sch. Mgmt., 1985; postgrad., U. Ill., 1991. Lic. phys. therapist, Ill. Assoc. prof. dept. phys. therapy Chgo. Med. Sch., North Chicago, Ill., chmn. dept. phys. therapy, 1993-96. Contbr. articles to profl. jours. Trustee Northfield Twp., Ill., 1993-97; Ill. state rep. 17th dist., 1997—. Mem. APHA, Am. Phys. Therapy Assn. (Ill. del. 1986-93, chief del. 1991-93), Ill. Phys. Therapy Assn. (chmn. jud. com. 1989-91). Home: 1701 Sequoia Tr Glenview IL 60025-2022 Office Phone: 847-724-3233.

COULSON, ROBERT, retired professional society administrator, arbitrator, writer; b. New Rochelle, NY, July 24, 1924; s. Robert Earl and Abby (Stewart) C.; m. Cynthia Cunningham, Oct. 16, 1961; children: Cotton Richard, Dierdre, Crocker, Robert Cromwell, Christopher. BA, Yale U., 1949; LLB, Harvard U., 1953; DSc in Bus. Adminstrn. (hon.), Bryant U., 1985; LLD (hon.), Hofstra U., 1987. Bar: NY 1954, Mass. 1954. Assoc. Whitman, Ransom & Coulson, NYC, 1954-61; ptnr. Littlefield, Miller & Cleaves, NYC, 1961-63; exec. v.p. Am. Arbitration Assn., NYC, 1963-71, pres., 1971-94; ret., 1994. Cons. N.Y. State Div. Youth, 1961-63; pres. Youth Consultation Service of N.Y., 1970 Author: How to Stay Out of Court, 1968, Labor Arbitration: What You Need to Know, 1973, Business Arbitration: What You Need to Know, 1980, The Termination Handbook, 1981, Fighting Fair, 1983, Arbitration in Schools, 1985, Business Mediation, 1987, Alcohol and Drugs in Arbitration, 1988, Empowered at Forty, 1990, Police Under Pressure, 1993, ADR in America, 1994, Family Mediation, 1996; editor: Racing at Sea, 1958; contbr. articles to profl. jours. Bd. dirs. Fedn. Protestant Welfare Agys., pres., 1982-84, chmn. 1985-87; adv. com. Internat. Coun. for Comml. Arbitration. Mem. N.Y. Yacht Club, Cruising Club Am., Riverside Yacht Club. Avocations: sailing, travel, writing. Home: 9 Reginald St Riverside CT 06878-2522 Personal E-mail: coulfamily@aol.com.

COULSON, WILLIAM ROY, lawyer; b. Waukegan, Ill., Oct. 5, 1949; s. Robert E. and Rose (Stone) C.; m. Elizabeth A. Shafernich, Feb. 14, 1986. AB, Dartmouth Coll., Hanover, NH, 1969; JD, U. Ill., 1972. Bar: Ill. 1972, US Dist. Ct. (no. dist.) Ill. 1974, US Supreme Ct. 1976. Law clk. to judge US Dist. Ct., East St. Louis, Ill., 1972-74, Chgo., 1975; asst. US atty. US Dept. Justice, Chgo., 1975-88, supr. criminal divsn., 1980-88; mng. ptnr. Cherry & Flynn, Chgo., 1988-99, Gold & Coulson, 1999—. Faculty Atty. Gens. Adv. Inst., Washington, 1980-88, Ill. Inst. for Continuing Legal Edn., Springfield, 1983-88, Fed. Law Enforcement Tng. Ctr., Glynco, Ga., 1983-86; co-chmn. U.S. Magistrate Merit Selection Panel, 1989-91; bd. dirs. Regional Transp. Authority, Chgo., dir., 2007-. Author: Federal Juvenile Law, 1980; contbg. author Animation mag., 1993—. Served to 2d lt. Ill. N.G., 1965-66. Finalist US Senate Jud. Selection Panel, 1996. Mem. ABA, Chgo. Bar Assn. (jud. evaluation com. 1987-89, vice chair 1990-91), Fed. Bar Assn. (pres. 1991-92), Dartmouth Club. Office: 11 S La Salle St Chicago IL 60602-2590

COULSON, ZOE ELIZABETH, retired consumer marketing executive; b. Sullivan, Ind., Sept. 22, 1932; d. Marion Allan and Mary Anne (Thompson) C. BS, Purdue U., 1954; AMP, Harvard Bus. Sch., 1983. Asst. dir. home econs. Am. Meat Inst., Chgo., 1954-57; acct. exec. J. Walter Thompson Co., Chgo., 1957-60; creative consumer dir. Leo Burnett Co., Chgo., 1960-64; mag. editor-in-chief Donnelley-Dun & Bradstreet, NYC, 1964-68; food editor Good Housekeeping, NYC, 1968-75; sr. editor, dir. G H Inst., 1975-81; corp. v.p. Campbell Soup Co., Camden, N.J., 1981-91. Bd. dirs. RubberMaid Inc.; mktg. cons. Internat. Exec. Svc. Corp., Russia, 1998-99. Author: Good Housekeeping Cookbook, 1972, Good Housekeeping Illustrated Cookbook, 1980. Trustee Cooper Hosp./Univ. Med. Ctr., 1982-91; elder Old Pine Presbyn. Ch., 1992-96. Named Disting. Alumni Purdue U., 1971. Mem. Women's Econ. Bus. Alliance (bd. govs. 1987-91), Food and Drug Law Inst. (food bd. dirs. 1979-81), Soc. Hill Towers Owners Assn. (mem. coun. 1996-99), Harvard Bus. Sch. Club (Phila. v.p. budget 1994-95, chmn. program com. 2003-04, bd. dirs. 2001—), Purdue Club Phila. (pres. 1999-), Friends Old Pine (bd. dirs. 1995-, chmn. awareness com. 2005—), Kappa Alpha Theta (pres. house corp. Beta Eta chpt. 1991-2000). Republican. Avocation: Meso-Am. archaeology. Home: 220 Locust St Apt 18B Philadelphia PA 19106-3931 Home Fax: 215-922-4233. Personal E-mail: zcoulson@aol.com.

COULTER, ANN, writer, political columnist, lawyer; b. New Caanan, Conn., Dec. 8, 1961; d. John V. and Nell Martin Coulter. BA cum laude, Cornell U., 1985; JD, U. Mich. Law Sch., 1988. Law clk. to Hon. Pasco Bowman II US Ct. Appeals (8th cir.), Kansas City, 1989; atty. US Dept. Justice Honors Program for outstanding law sch. grads.; corp. lawyer, pvt. practice NYC; handled crime and immigration issues for Senator Spencer Abraham Senate Judiciary Com., Mich., 1994—96; polit. commentator MSNBC, 1996; litigator Ctr. Individual Rights, Wash., DC; legal affairs corr. Human Events. Writer syndicated column, Universal Press Syndicate; guest appearances Politically Incorrect, Larry King Live, Hannity and Colmes, The O'Reilly Factor, Am. Morning with Paula Zahn, Crossfire, "This Week", ABC, Good Morning Am., The Leeza Show. Author: High Crimes and Misdemeanors: The Case Against Bill Clinton, 1998, Slander: Liberal Lies About the American Right, 2002, Treason: Liberal Treachery From the Cold War to the War on Terrorism, 2003, How to Talk to a Liberal (If You Must), 2004, Godless: The Church of Liberalism, 2006; editor: The Mich. Law Review. Named one of Time Mag. 100 Most Influential People, 2005. Office: Human Events One Mass Ave NW Washington DC 20001

COULTER, CHARLES ROY, lawyer; b. Webster City, Iowa, June 10, 1940; s. Harold L. Coulter and Eloise (Wheeler) Harrison; m. Elizabeth Bean, Dec. 16, 1961; 1 child, Anne Elizabeth. BA in Journalism, U. Iowa, 1962, JD, 1965. Bar: Iowa 1965. Assoc. Stanley, Bloom, Mealy & Lande, Muscatine, Iowa, 1965-68; v.p. Stanley, Lande & Hunter, Muscatine, 1969—, also bd. dirs. County fin. chmn. Leach for Congress, 1980-96. Fellow Coll. of Law Practice Mgmt. (dir. 1994-2004, pres. 2001-04), Am. Bar Found., Iowa State Bar Found., Am. Coll. Trust and Estate Counsel; mem. ABA (mem. coun. law practice mgmt. sect. 1984-88, sec. 1988-89, vice chair 1989-90, chair 1991-92, chair coord. commn. legal tech. 1994-97, mem. standing com. on tech. and info. sys. 1997-98), Iowa Bar Assn., Muscatine County Bar Assn., Thirty-Three Club (pres. 1981), Rotary, Order of Coif. Episcopalian. Avocation: tennis. Office: Stanley Lande & Hunter 2201 E Grantview Dr Ste 200 Coralville IA 52241 Office Phone: 319-248-9000. Business E-Mail: chuckcoulter@slhlaw.com.

COULTER, DAVID A., investment banker; b. Pitts. BA in Math., Carnegie-Mellon U., MA in Indsl. Adminstrn. Chmn., CEO BankAmerica, 1996—98; CEO Bank of Am. NT&SA, 1996—98; ptnr. Beacon Group LP, 2000; pres. Chase Fin. Svcs., 2000—01; vice chmn. investment bank, private equity, asset & wealth mgmt. JP Morgan & Chase Co., NYC, 2001—04, chmn. West Coast Ops., 2005; mng. dir. and sr. adv. Warburg Pincus LLC, NYC, 2005—. Bd. dirs. PG&E, 1996—, Pub. Policy Inst. Calif., 1997—, Coors Tek, Internat. Inst. Fin., Joint Venture Silicon Valley Network; mem. adv. coun. Fed. Res. Bank N.Y. Bd. trustees U. So. Calif., Carnegie-Mellon U., U. Calif., San Francisco, 1997—2000. Recipient Global Bus. Leader award, Com. of 100, 2003. Office: Warburg Pincus LLC 466 Lexington Ave New York NY 10017*

COULTER, FERN GOSHEN, retired secondary school educator; b. Zanesville, Ohio, Jan. 29, 1916; d. Charles Manderson and Janey W. (Miller) Goshen; m. George E., Sr. Coulter, July 10, 1944 (dec.); children: George (Skip) E. Jr., Christine E., Margaret A. Nelson. BA, Greenville Coll., Ill., 1938; MA, U. Mich., Ann Arbor, 1943; postgrad., Kent State U., Ohio. Cert. tchr. English, Latin, biology. Tchr. Orrville Pub. Schs., Ohio, 1938—44, El Paso Pub. Schs., 1944—45, El Paso Tech. HS, 1947—48, Canton So. HS, North Industry, Ohio, 1940—41, Plain Ctr. Jr. HS, North Canton, 1947—48; tchr., guidance counselor Marlington HS, Alliance, Ohio, 1961—71; guidance counselor Lousville Jr. HS, Louisville, Ohio, 1971—74; ret., 1974. Contbr. articles to mags. Rep. Nat. Hist. Preservation, Zoar, Ohio, 1975—84; bd. dirs. Salvation Army, Louisville, 1971—74; vol. counselor, youth leader Orrville Meth. Ch., 1938—44; tchr. Bible Study Group, 1997—. Recipient mounted emblem, Salvation Army, 2005. Republican. Avocations: antiques, reading. Home: 3010 OConner Ct Helena AL 35080

COULTER, JACK BENSON, JR., financial planner; b. Louisville, Jan. 30, 1947; s. Jack Benson and Mary Belle (Roby) C.; m. Mary Llew Browne, July, 1977. BS, Fla. State U., 1967, MBA, 1969. CPA, Fla. Staff acct. Arthur Andersen & Co., Miami, Fla., 1971-73; sales rep. Commerce Clearing House, Inc., Miami, 1973-80; pres. First Fin. Planners, North Palm Beach, Fla., 1980-92, Coulter Fin. Advisors, Inc., Juno Beach, 1992—. Capt. U.S. Army, 1969-71. Mem. Inst. CFPs (nat. bd. dirs. 1986-89), Fla. Assn. CFPs (chmn. 1989-91), Fin. Planning Assn., Fla. Inst. CPAs. Republican. Office Phone: 561-627-6992. E-mail: ben@coulterfinancial.com.

COULTER, KATHLEEN MARIE, psychotherapist, consultant; b. Norristown, Pa., July 19, 1970; d. David George and Maryann Gullick; m. Michael Patrick Coulter, Sept. 13, 1997; children: Shawn Cullin, Aiden Kheil. BS in Psychology, U. Mary Washington, 1992; MSc, Hahnemann U., 1996. Lic. Profl. Counselor Pa., 2003, cert. Masters' Level Psychologist PA, 2003, Elementary School Counselor Pa., 2005. Tng. coord., specialist United Human Svcs., North Wales, Pa., 1995—97; behavior specialist, mobile therapist Northwestern Human Svcs., Lansdale, 1997—2000; neurodevelopmentalist Nat. Assn. Child Devel., West Chester, 2000—01; individual, group psychotherapist, clin. supr. Creative Health Svcs., Pottstown, 2001—04; individual, group psychotherapist Psychology & Counseling Assocs., P.C., Pottstown, 2004—. Parent and cmty. trainer, cons. Goddard Sch., Sanatoga, 2003; spkr. in field, Pa., 2003—. Youth group leader Mary Mother of Redeemer Cath. Ch., North Wales, 1996—97. Mem.: ACA. Avocations: volunteerism, coaching, reading. Office: Psychology Counseling Assocs PC 2091 E High St Pottstown PA 19464 Home Phone: 610-287-2469; Office Phone: 484-686-4855.

COULTER, MYRON LEE, retired academic administrator; b. Albany, Ind., Mar. 21, 1929; s. Mark Earl and Thelma Violet (Marks) C.; m. Barbara Bolinger, July 21, 1951; children: Nan and Benjamin (twins). BS, Ind. State Tchrs. Coll., 1951; MS, Ind. U., 1956, EdD, 1959; HLD (hon.), Coll. Idaho, 1982. Tchr. English Reading (Mich.) Pub. Schs., 1951-52; tchr. elem. grades Bloomington (Ind.) Pub. Schs., 1954-56; instr. edn. Ind. U., Bloomington, 1958-59; asst. prof. Pa. State U., 1959-64, asso. prof., 1964-66; vis. prof. U. Alaska, Fairbanks, 1965; asso. dean edn., prof. edn. Western Mich. U., Kalamazoo, 1966-68, v.p. for adminstrn., prof. edn., 1968-76, interim pres., 1974; pres. Idaho State U., Pocatello, 1976-84; chancellor Western Carolina U., Cullowhee, NC, 1984-94, chancellor emeritus, 1994—. Del. Israeli Univs., 1976, Am. Assn. State Colls. and Univs. to People's Republic of China, 1981, Swaziland Coll. Tech., 1985, People's Republic China, 1985, 87, 88, 90, Jamaica, 1986, 89, 91, 94, Thailand, 1987, 90, The Netherlands, 1991; mem. US Panama Canal Treaty Com., 1977-79 Author school textbooks. Bd. dirs. Kalamazoo C. of C., 1975-76, Pocatello Jr. Achievement; bd. dirs., chair NC Arboretum, 1994-98; bd. dirs. WNC Pub. Radio, WNC Devel. Assn., WNC Tomorrow, Joint PVO/Univ. Rural Devel. Ctr., WNC Comm. Found., Friends of Great Smoky Mountain Nat. Park, 1994—, Inter-Regional Ctr., 2001—; lay leader Kalamazoo Meth. Ch., 1971-74; mem. Gov.'s Task Force on Aquaculture, 1988, NC Bd. Sci. and Tech., 1993—, Commn. for Competitive NC, 1993—; chair NC Indian Gaming Cert. Commn., 1994-; trustee Bronson Hosp., Kalamazoo, 1975-76, NC Ctr. Advancement Tchg., C.J. Harris Cmty. Hosp.; chmn. Cherokee Preservation Found., 2001-05; chair devel. com. Givens Estates, CCRD, 2005—. With US Army, 1952-54. Named Disting. Alumnus, Ind. State U., 1975, Ind. U., 1994; recipient award Western Mich. U. Alumni Assn., 1974, resolution of tribute Mich. State Legislature, 1976, NC Order of the Long Leaf Pine, 1994. Mem. Internat. Reading Assn., Am. Assn. State Colls. and Univs. (bd. dirs. 1981-84, exec. com. 1981-84, sec.-treas. 1984-87, found. bd. dirs. 1987—, chmn. 1988-89), Nat. Soc. Study of Edn., NC Assn. Colls. and Univs. (bd. dirs.), Western Coll. Assn., Pocatello C. of C. (bd. dirs. 1977-80), Asheville C. of C. (bd. dirs. 1985-86), Cherokee Hist. Assn., Ind. U. Coll. Edn. Alumni Assn. (Disting. Alumnus award 1994), Phi Delta Kappa, Omicron Delta Kappa, Phi Kappa Phi, Beta Gamma Sigma. Office: Western Carolina Univ Office Chancellor Emeritus 278 Belle Cullowhee NC 28723 Business E-Mail: coulter@email.wcu.edu.

COULTER, WILLIAM KIRK, lawyer; b. Wilmington, Del., May 31, 1946; s. George R. and Jane (Jernee) C.; m. Mary Susan Pearson, Feb. 14, 1972; children: Michael William, Kathryn Amanda BA cum laude, Franklin & Marshall Coll., 1968; JD with honors, U. Pitts., 1971; cert. Internat. bus., Univ. Va.; cert. Govt. Contracting, William & Mary Univ. Bar: Pa. 1972, D.C. 1972. Deputy atty. gen. Del. Atty. Gen. Office, Wilmington, 1970; assoc. Richards, Layton & Finger, Wilmington, 1971—; v.p., gen. counsel, dir. COMSAT Internat. Corp., Washington, 1988-94; ptnr. Baker, Donelson, Bearman & Caldwell, Washington, 1994-95; sr. v.p., internat. trade & new ventures COMSAT, Washington, 1995—98; ptnr. Coudert Bros. LLP, Washington, 1998—, head Tech., Media & Telecom. practice, 2005—. Com. counsel to U.S. Sen. Howard Baker, Washington, 1993—98; mem. legal adv. com. U.S. State Dept., Washington; rep. Nat. Security Comm. Working Group, U.S. Dept. Def., Washington; founding mem. Internat. Telecom. Union Legal Symposium; gen. counsel Global Mobile Satellite Users Assn., World Teleport Assn., Worldwide Internet Forum. Author: Earth Station Ownership Worldwide. Mem. Fed. Comm. Bar Assn. (internat. chmn. 1988-92), sust. mem. Pac. Telecom. Council. Office Phone: 202-775-5100. Office Fax: 202-775-1168. Business E-Mail: coulterw@coudert.com.

COUMOU, DAVID J., electrical engineer, consultant; b. New Hyde Park, NY, Dec. 26, 1968; s. David Vincient and Lynda Jane Coumou; m. Kimberly A. Brennan, Aug. 19, 1995; children: Ashley Christine, Lindsey Kathleen, David Justin. BSEE in Tech., Rochester Inst. Tech., NY, 1992, MSEE, 2001. Elec. engr. Bell Engring., Rochester, 1993—94, Morrison Knudsen Corp., Hornell, 1994—95, Gen. Dynamics - Electric Boat Divsn., Groton, Conn., 1995—97, Spectronic Instruments Inc., Rochester, 1997—98; sr. elec. engr. Alstom Signaling Inc, 1998—99; prin. engr. MKS ENI Products, 1999—2005, 2007—; dsp cons. D3 Engring., LLC, 2004—07. Contbr. articles to profl. jours., chapters to books; author: various funding proposals for US Dept. Defense. Co-chmn. image processing workshop We. NY, 2004—07; com. mem. Acad. Excellence Com. Cath. Sch. Diocese Monroe Country, Rochester, 2004—05; youth coach Webster Soccer Assn., 2004—07, Webster Softball Assn., 2005—07, Webster Baseball Assn., 2004—04. Grantee, US Dept. Def., 2006, SBA, 2007. Mem.: IEEE (co-chair We. NY Image Processing workshop 2004—07, chpt. officer 2004—06). Roman Catholic. Achievements include patents for RF metrology characterization for field installation and serviceability; broadband design of a probe analysis system; RF power probe head with a thermally conductive bushing; method and apparatus for radio frequency (RF) metrology; adaptive plasma characterization system; multirate processing for metrology of plasma RF source; patents pending for distortion Correction for RF metrology of RF plasma source; frequency and phase tracking control for RF plasma source; sub-pixel accuracy using a least squares solution; watermark synchronization system and method for embedding in features tolerant to errors in feature estimates at receiver; high reliability RF generator architecture; multipoint voltage and current probe system. Home: 852 Arlberg Cir Webster NY 14580 Office: MKS ENI Products 100 Highpower Rd Rochester NY 14623 Home Phone: 585-787-8896; Office Phone: 585-292-7561. Office Fax: 585-292-8828. Personal E-mail: davidcoumou@ieee.org. Business E-Mail: david_coumou@mksinst.com.

COUNCE, DIANE RYDER, neurologist, researcher; d. Robert Hessey and Mary (Barnum) Ryder; m. Steven Earl Counce, Dec. 31, 1994; children: Rachel, Andrew. BS in Biology summa cum laude, Delta State U., Cleveland, Miss., 1991; MD, U. Miss., Jackson, 1996. Resident in neurology U. Ala., Birmingham, 1996—2000, chief neurophysiology fellow, 2000—01; neurologist Simon-Williamson PC, Alabaster, Ala., 2001—. Clin. rschr. Clin. Rsch. Cons., Hoover, Ala. Contbr. articles to profl. jours. Mem.: Am. Assn. Neuromuscular and Electrodiagnostic Medicine, Am. Headache Soc., Am. Acad. Neurology, Phi Eta Sigma, Omicron Delta Kappa, Phi Kappa Phi, Alpha Epsilon Delta. Office: Simon-Williamson PC 10221st St N Ste 400 Alabaster AL 35007

COUNCIL, JAMES BRAXTON, JR., school system administrator; b. Aug. 13, 1944; BE, Atlantic Christian Coll., Wilson, NC, 1966; MEd, George Mason U., Fairfax, Va., 1974. Post-grad. profl. cert. Va. Tchr. Prince William County Public Sch., Manassas, Va., 1966—80, prin., 1980—91, supr. music, art, phys. edn., 1991—99. Contbr. articles to profl. jours. Mem.: Nat. Assn. Secondary Sch. Prin., Am. Guild Organists. Home: 119 W College St Whiteville NC 28472 Personal E-mail: jbc81344@aol.com.

COUNCIL, THOMAS MAURICE, music educator; b. Pt. Arthur, Tex., Apr. 18, 1961; s. Max and Mary Elizabeth Council; m. Mitzi H. Council, Aug. 8, 1981; children: Philip, Aaron, Jessica, Jacob. MusB, Toccoa Falls Coll., 1983; MusM, Samford U., 1985; PhD in Music Edn., Auburn U., 2000. Music tchr. Briarwood Christian Sch., Birmingham, Ala., 1984—90, Parkway Christian Acad., Birmingham, 1990—94; assoc. prof. Southeastern Bible Coll., Birmingham, 1994—2000; dir., sch. music Toccoa Falls Coll., Toccoa, Ga., 2000—; part time min. music Antioch Bapt. Ch., Mt. Airy, Ga., 2004—. Condr. Toccoa Symphony Chorus, 2004—; guest condr. Carnegie Hall, NYC, 1996—, Lincoln Ctr., NYC, 2002. So. Bapt. Avocation: fishing. Home: P O Box 800744 Toccoa Falls GA 30598 Office: Toccoa Falls Coll 325 Chapel Dr Toccoa Falls GA 30598

COUNELIS, JAMES STEVE, education educator; b. Streator, Ill., June 26, 1927; s. Steve and Mary (Drivas) C.; m. Anna Catherine Marakas, Nov. 25, 1962; children: Steven George, George James. AA, Chgo. City Jr. Coll., 1948; AM, U. Chgo., 1951, PhD, 1961. Cert. high sch., jr. coll. tchr., pub. sch. principal, Ill. High sch. tchr. Chgo. Pub. Schs., 1951-55; asst. prof. history and social scis. Chgo. City Jr. Coll., Woodrow Wilson br., 1955-62, dir. evening program, 1962-64; asst. prof. edn. Chgo Tchrs. Coll., 1964-66; assoc. prof. edn. Pa. State U., University Park, 1966-67; sr. adminstrv. analyst U. Calif., Berkeley, 1968-70; prof. edn. U. San Francisco, 1970-98, prof. emeritus in edn., 1998—, dir. instl. studies and mgmt. info. systems, 1971-75, coord. evaluation Sch. Edn., 1986-90, chmn. orgn. and leadership program, 1989-91. Author, editor: To Be A Phoenix: The Education Professoriate, 1969; author: Higher Learning and Orthodox Christianity, 1990, Inheritance and Change in Orthodox Christianity, 1995; contbr. articles, revs. and papers to profl. publs. Pres., trustee Greek Orthodox Cathedral of the Ascension, Oakland, Calif., 1973; pres. Hellenic Am. Profl. Soc., San Francisco, 1974, 75; trustee tenure Hellenic Coll./Holy Cross, 1951-53, trustee, 1982-86; mem. Calif. Council on Criminal Justice (recipient bronze plaque for svc. 1998), 1987; bd. dirs. Paul Wattson Lecture series, 1989. Served with Signal Corps, U.S. Army, 1946-47. Recipient Archon Chartoularius (honoris causa) award Ecumenical Patriarchate Constantinople and New Rome, 1976, Norbert Wiener award The World Orgn. Gen. Systems and Cybernetics, 1978, Scholar U. Chgo., 1951-52, 60-61, Pacific Sch. Religion, 1958; U. Calif. grantee, Berkeley, 1962; Coolidge Rsch. fellow Andover-Newton Theol. Sch., 1985, Wayne J. Doyle Rsch. award, 1986, Hellenic Coun. on Edn. award for scholarship and univ. teaching, 1991. Mem. AAAS, Am. Assn. Artificial Intelligence, Am. Assn. Higher Edn., Am. Assn. Instnl. Rsch., Am. Ednl. Rsch. Assn., Am. Ednl. Studies Assn., Internat. Soc. System Scis., Hellenic Am. Profl. Soc. (Axion award 1982), Hellenic Coun. on Edn. (award for Scholarship and University Teaching 1991), Orthodox Theol. Soc. Am., U. San Francisco Faculty Assn., Mensa, Gold Key, Phi Delta Kappa (U. San Francisco chpt. v.p. for programs 1990-91, pres. 1991-92). Avocations: travel, photography, reading, music. Home: 109 Casa Vieja Pl Orinda CA 94563-3832 Fax: 925-254-2845.

COUNTRYMAN, DAYTON WENDELL, lawyer; b. Sioux City, Iowa, Mar. 31, 1918; s. Cleve and Susie (Schaeffer) Countryman; m. Ruth Hazen, Feb. 2, 1941 (dec.); children: Karen, Joan, James, Kay. BS, Iowa State Coll., 1940; LLB, State U. Iowa, 1948, JD, 1969. Bar: Iowa 1948. Practiced in, Nevada; ptnr. Hadley & Countryman, Nevada, Iowa, 1949-64; mem. Countryman & Zaffarano P.C., 1984-87, Dayton Countryman Law Offices, P.C., 1987—; county atty. Story County, Iowa, 1950-54; atty. gen. State of Iowa, 1954-56. Candidate for U.S. Senate, 1956, 1960, 68. Air Force Res. pilot USAAF, 1941—46. Mem. ABA, Iowa Bar Assn., Story County Bar Assn., VFW, Am. Legion, Iowa State U. Alumni Assn. (pres. 1970-71), Iowa 2B Jud. Dist. Assn., Masons, Lions (pres. 1975-76). Methodist. Office: PO Box 28 Nevada IA 50201-0028 Office Phone: 515-382-2605.

COUNTRYMAN, EDWARD FRANCIS, historian, educator; b. Glens Falls, NY, July 31, 1944; s. Edward Francis and Agnes (Alford) C.; m. Evonne von Heussen, 1987; children: Karon Samantha, Kirstein Dawn; 1 son from previous marriage, Samuel Robert. BA, Manhattan Coll., 1966; MA, Cornell U., Ithaca, NY, 1969; PhD, Cornell U., 1971; LHD, Manhattan Coll., 1999. Lectr. in history U. Canterbury, N.Z., 1970-74; lectr. U. Warwick, Eng., 1975-83, sr. lectr., 1983-88, reader, 1988-91; prof. So. Meth. U., Dallas, 1991-99, disting. prof., 1999—. Vis. lectr. U. Cambridge, Eng., 1979-80, Mellon vis. sr. scholar, 1999; vis. scholar NYU, N.Y.C., 1980-81; Cardozo vis. prof. Yale U., spring 1989; coun. mem. Omohundro Inst. Early Am. History and Culture, 1999—. Cons. editor Radical History Rev., 1982—; author: A People in Revolution, 1981 (Bancroft prize 1982), The American Revolution, 1985, rev. edit. 2003; (video) American Independence 1776, 1989, Americans: A Collision of Histories, 1996; co-author: Who Built America, 1990, Shane, 1999; editor: How Did American Slavery Begin?, 1998, What Did the Constitution Mean to Early Americans?, 1998; co-author: The Empire State, 2001. Active civil rights movement, U.S., 1965-68; spokesperson Anti-War Movement, N.Z., 1970-73; active Campaign for Nuclear Disarmament, Eng., 1981—. Woodrow Wilson fellow, 1966-67, Danforth fellow, 1966-71, Samuel Foster Haven fellow, 1983; Mellon vis. sr. scholar U. Cambridge, 1998. Home: 5454 Anita St Dallas TX 75206-5336 Office: So Meth U Dept History Dallas TX 75275-0001 E-mail: ecountry@mail.smu.edu.

COUNTRYMAN, GARY LEE, retired insurance company executive; b. South Bend, Wash., July 30, 1939; s. William T. and Vernela K. (Stewart) C.; m. Sally Ann Mathews, Aug. 16, 1958; children: Christopher John, Susan Michelle, Sherry LeeAnn, Stefanie May. BS, U. Oreg., 1961, MS, 1963. With Liberty Mut. Ins. Co., Boston, 1963—, pres., 1981-86, pres., chief exec. officer, 1986-91, chmn., pres., CEO, 1991-92, chmn., 1992-99, CEO, 1998; pres. Liberty Fin. Co., Inc., Boston, 1999-2000, chmn., pres., CEO, 2000—01, chmn emeritus, 2001—. Bd. dirs. Liberty Mut. Ins. Group, Bank of Boston Corp., 1st Nat. Bank Boston, Boston Edison Co., Harcourt Gen., Inc., Alliance Am. Insurers, CBS Corp., 2007-; chmn. bd. dirs. Boston Mgmt. Consortium, Inc. Bd. dirs. Inst. Civil Justice, Jobs for Mass., Inc., Com. for Econ. Devel.; trustee Northeastern U., U. New Eng., Mus. Sci., Sudbury Valley Trustees; chmn. bd. Dana-Farber Cancer Inst.; bd. overseers Mass. Gen. Hosp. H.T. Miner fellow, 1962-63 Mem. NAM, Am. Inst. Property and Liability Underwriters (bd. dirs.), Algonquin Club.

COUNTS, STANLEY THOMAS, retired military officer, retired electronics executive; b. Okfuskee County, Okla., July 3, 1926; s. Claud Curtley and Thelma (Thomas) C.; m. Bettejan Heft, Nov. 18, 1949; children:Ashlie Heft Jenkins. BS, U.S. Naval Acad., 1949; BS in Elec. Engring, U.S. Naval Postgrad. Sch., 1954, MS in Elec. Engring, 1955. Commd. ensign U.S. Navy, 1949, advanced through grades to rear adm., 1972; comdg. officer USS Bronstein, 1963-64; comdg. officer USS Towers, 1966-68; project mgr. NATO Seasparrow Surface Missile System, 1968-70; comdg. officer USS Chgo., 1970-71; dir. ships, weapons, electronics and asso. systems Office Asst. Sec. Def. for Installations and Logistics Washington, 1971-73; dep. comdr. Naval Ordnance Systems Command, 1973-74; designated Naval ordnance engr., 1974; comdr. (Naval Ordnance Systems Command), 1974; vice comdr. Naval Sea Systems Command, 1974-76; comdr. Cruiser-Destroyer Group 5 San Diego, 1976-78; ret., 1978; exec. Hughes Aircraft Co., Fullerton, Calif., 1979-89; ret., 1989; aerospace cons., chief exec. officer Bjan Enterprises, La Jolla, Calif., 1989-99. Chmn. Seasparrow steering com. NATO, 1973-76. Bd. dirs. San Diego chpt. Freedoms Found. at Valley Forge, 1992-94, 97-98; bd. dirs. Greater La Jolla Meals on Wheels, Inc., 1998—, pres., 2000-04 Decorated Legion of Merit with three oak leaf clusters, Bronze Star with combat distinguishing device. Mem. VFW, Surface Navy Assn. (life, bd. dirs. 1985-93), U.S. Naval Inst. (life), DAV (life), Ret. Officers Assn. (life), Navy League, USNA Alumni Assn. (life), Am. Legion, Rest and Aspiration Club San Diego. Home: 856 La Jolla Rancho Rd La Jolla CA 92037-7408 Personal E-mail: radmstc1949@aol.com.

COUNTY, JANIS EMERSON, school counselor; b. Seattle, Mar. 17, 1950; d. Raymond Roger and Wanda Maxine Emerson; m. William Walter County, Aug. 17, 1974; children: Brandon Emerson, Trevor William. BS in Edn., U. Akron, Ohio, 1973; MEd in Counseling, Cleve. State U., 1987. Cert. sch. counselor Ohio, tchr. Ohio, nat. cert. counselor Nat. Bd. Cert. Counselors, Inc., nat. cert. sch. counselor Nat. Bd. Cert. Counselors, Inc. Tchr. Elyria Schs., Ohio, 1981—88, counselor, 1988—2007. Trainer Polly Barrett and Associates, Westlake, Ohio, 1994—97, Love and Logic, Inc., Golden, Colo., 2003—, aha!Process, Inc., Highlands, Tex., 2005—. Co-author: (behavior management) Goal System for Behavior Management (Copyright, 2006). Mediator Chadwick Garden Apartments, Elyria, 1993—94, Oberlin Cmty. Mediation, Ohio, 1995—96. Recipient Recognition award, Ohio Commn. Dispute Resolution and Mgmt., 1994; grantee Mediation Tng. Grant, Nord Family Found., 1990-1992, Safe and Drug Free Schs., 2000—03; Jennings scholar, Martha Holden Jennings Found., 1999—2000. Mem.: NEA, Am. Sch. Counselor Assn., Assn. Play Therapy, Inc. (registered play therapist). Avocations: gardening, jazz, fitness. Home Phone: 440-774-3611.

COUPE, JAMES WARNICK, lawyer; b. Utica, NY, Mar. 3, 1949; s. J. Leo and Helen Carbery (Brennan) C.; m. Andrea Jean Schaaf, Nov. 26, 1983; children: Helen Shriver, Benjamin Warnick, Charlotte Fitzgerald. AB, Hamilton Coll., 1971; JD, Vanderbilt U., 1974. Bar: N.Y. 1975, Calif. 1981, Tenn. 1995, U.S. Dist. Ct. (so. and ea. dists.) N.Y. 1975, U.S. Ct. Appeals (2d cir.) 1975. Law clk. to judge U.S. Dist. Ct. (so. dist.) N.Y., NYC, 1974-75; assoc. Donovan, Leisure, Newton & Irvine, NYC, 1975-79, Phillips, Nizer, Benjamin, Krim & Ballon, NYC, 1979-81; sr. atty. Atlantic Richfield Co., LA, 1981-86; chief counsel Beverly Enterprises, Inc., Pasadena, Calif., 1986-88; gen. counsel Completion Bond Co., Inc., Century City, Calif., 1988-93; exec. Sullivan Curtis Monroe Ins. Brokers, Pasadena, Calif., 1993-95; v.p. bus. & legal affairs Cinema Completions Internat. Inc., LA, 1995-97; sr. v.p. bus. and legal affairs Cinema Completions Internat., 1997—2002; atty. pvt. practice, 2002—. Mem. L.A. County Bar Assn., State Bar Calif. Republican. Roman Catholic. Office: Law Offices of James W Coupe 777 S Figueroa St Ste 4700 47th Fl Los Angeles CA 90017 Office Phone: 213-406-1171. Business E-Mail: barrister74@msn.com.

COUPEY, SUSAN MCGUIRE, pediatrician, educator; b. Montreal, Que., Can., June 29, 1942; came to U.S., 1978; d. Clarence Herbert and Paulette (Lefevre) McGuire; m. Pierre M.L. Coupey, July 1964 (div. 1981); children: Marc M.R., Ariane S.; m. James R. English III, Nov. 23, 1988. BA, Queen's U., Kingston, Ont., Can., 1962; postgrad., McGill U., Montreal, 1962-63; MD, U. B.C., Vancouver, Can., 1975. Diplomate Am. Bd. Pediatrics, subboard in adolescent medicine. Devel. chemist Merck, Sharp & Dohme, Ltd., Montreal, 1963-64; rotating intern Montreal Gen. Hosp., 1975-76; resident in pediatrics Montreal Children's Hosp., 1976-78; fellow in adolescent medicine Montefiore Med. Ctr., Bronx, NY, 1978-79, attending pediatrician, 1980—; rsch. asst. Cancer Rsch. Ctr., U. B.C., 1967-72; instr., asst. prof. pediatrics Albert Einstein Coll. Medicine, Bronx, 1979-85, assoc. prof., 1985-93, prof., 1993—, assoc. dir. div. adolescent medicine, 1984—2001, course dir. introduction to clin. medicine, 1989—2007, mem. faculty senate, 1983-84, 88-90, co-chair divsn. edn., 2000—07, chief adolescent medicine, 2002—. Attending pediatrician North Ctrl. Bronx Hosp., 1979-97; cons. in adolescent medicine Flushing (N.Y.) Hosp. and Med. Ctr., 1982-96; Maricopa-Pima vis. prof. U. Ariz., 1989; vis. prof. Children's Hosp. Ea. Ont., U. Ottawa and Ea. Can. chpt. Soc. for Adolescent Medicine, 1990; vis. prof. Philippine Children's Med. Ctr., U. Philippines Coll. of Medicine, 1997; chmn. health svcs. adv. com. Children's Aid Soc., 1985—, bd. trustees, 1993—; mem. adv. bd. Office Substance Abuse Ministry, Archdiocese of N.Y., 1983-85; spkr. Hosp. Italiano, Buenos Aires, Argentina, 1999, Israeli Soc. Adolescent Medicine, Jeruseleum, Israel, 2000, Greek Soc. Adolescent Med., Athens, Greece, 2000. Editor: Primary Care of Adolescent Girls, 2000; assoc. editor Adolescent Medicine Clinics, 1990—; assoc. editor Jour. Devel. & Behavioral Pediatrics, 1992-96, editl. bd., 1996-00; assoc. editor Jour. Pediat. & Adolescent Gynecology, 1992-98, editl. bd. 1998—; editl. bd. Jour. of Youth and Adolescence, 1998-04; contbr. articles to med. jours., also chpts. to books and monographs. Fellow Am. Acad. Pediatrics (exec. com. sect. on adolescent health 1993-96, Adele Dellenbaugh Hofman award for excellence in adolescent health, 2005); mem. Soc. for Adolescent Medicine (nominations com. 1984-85, chmn. jour. adv. com. 1987-97, program com. 1991-93, awards com. 1992-95, bd. dirs. 1997-2000), Am. Pediat. Soc. (abstract review com. 1999—2001), Soc. for Behavioral Pediatrics, N.Am. Soc. Pediat. and Adolescent Gynecology (bd. dirs. 1993-96, sec. 1996-2001, chair publs. com. 1996-2001, pres.-elect 2001-02, pres. 2002-03), Sex Info. and Edn. Coun. U.S., Am. Acad. on Comm. in Healthcare, Albert Einstein Coll. Medicine Alumni Assn. (v.p. pediatrics 1983-84, pres. 1984-85), Alpha Omega Alpha (Kappa chpt. councilor, Harry F. Gordon award for outstanding clin. tchg. at Albert Einstein Coll. Medicine, 2002). Office: Albert Einstein Coll Medicine Montefiore Med Ctr 111 E 210th St Bronx NY 10467-2401 Office Phone: 718-920-6781. Business E-Mail: scoupey@montefiore.org.

COUPLAND, DOUGLAS CAMPBELL, writer; b. Baden Söllingen, Germany, Dec. 30, 1961; s. Douglas Charles Thomas and C. Janet (Campbell) C. Student, Emily Carr Coll. Art and Design, Vancouver, Can., 1984. Author: (fiction) Generation X: Tales for an Accelerated Culture, 1991, Shampoo Planet, 1992, Life After God, 1994, Microserfs, 1995, Girlfriend in a Coma, 1997, Miss Wyoming, 1999, God Hates Japan, 2001, All Families Are Psychotic, 2001, Hey Nostradamus!, 2003, Eleanor Rigby, 2005, jPod, 2006; (non-fiction) Polaroids from the Dead, 1996, City of Glass, 2000, Souvenir of Canada, 2001, School Spirit, 2002, Souvenir of Canada 2, 2004; (plays) September Tenth, 2004; contbr. articles to periodicals including The New Republic, The New York Times, Saturday Night, Artforum. Office: c/o Harper Collins 10 E 53rd St New York NY 10022-5244

COUPLES, FREDERICK STEVEN, professional golfer; b. Seattle, Oct. 3, 1959; m. Thais; 2 children: Gigi, Oliver. Student, U. Houston. Mem. U.S. Ryder Cup golf team, 1989, 91, 93, 95, 97; mem. nat. teams USA vs. Japan, 1984, Asahi Glass Four Tours World Championship of Golf, 1990, 91, Dunhill Cup, 1991, 92, 93, 94, World Cup, 1992, 93, 94, 95, Pres.'s Cup, 1994, 96, 98. Founder Millie Medin Violet Sobich Couples Fund. Named All-Am., 1978, 79; winner numerous skins games, golf tournaments and internat. tournaments (and over 15 PGA events) including Kemper Open, 1983, Tournament Players Championship, 1984, Byron Nelson Golf Classic, 1987, French PGA, 1988, Nissan L.A. Open, 1990, 92, Tournoi Perrier de Paris, 1991, B.C. Open, 1991, Federal Express St. Jude Classic, 1991, Johnnie Walker World Championship, 1991, Nestle Invitational, 1992, The Masters, 1992, (with Jan Stephenson) J.C. Penney Classic, 1983, (with Mike Donald) Sazale Classic, 1990, (with Raymond Floyd) RMCC Invitational, 1990, Buick Open, 1994, World Cup, 1994, Dubai Desert Classic, 1995, Johnnie Walker Classic, 1995, The Player's Championship, 1996, Bob Hope chrysler Classic, 1998, Memorial Tournament, 1998; Shell Houston Open, 2003; recipient Vardon trophy, 1991, 92; named PGA Player of Yr. Golf World Mag., 1991, 92, Golf Writers Assn., 1991, 92, PGA Tour Player of Yr, 1993, 94. Achievements include being the leading money winner PGA, 1992. Address: c/o PGA Tour 100 Ave of The Champions PO Box 109601 Palm Beach Gardens FL 33410

COURANT, PAUL NOAH, university librarian, economist, educator; b. Ithaca, NY, Jan. 5, 1948; s. Ernest David and Sara (Paul) Courant; m. Katherine Olive Johnson, Sept. 21, 1969 (dissolved 1984); children: Ernest Mendel, Noah Albert; m. Marta Anne Manildi, Jan. 30, 1988; 1 child, Samuel Robinson Manildi. BA, Swarthmore Coll., 1968; MA, Princeton U., 1972, PhD, 1973. Jr. economist Coun. Econ. Advisers, Washington, 1969—70, sr. economist, 1979—80; asst. prof. econs., pub. policy U. Mich., Ann Arbor, 1973—78, assoc. prof., 1978—84, prof. econs. and pub. policy, 1984—, dir. Inst. Pub. Policy Studies, 1983—87, 1989—90, chmn. econs. dept., 1995—97, assoc. provost, 1997—2001, provost, exec. v.p. acad. affairs, 2002—05, Harold T. Shapiro collegiate prof. pub. policy Gerald R. Ford Sch. of Pub. Policy, Arthur F. Thurnau prof. econs., prof. info., univ. libr., dean Univ. Librs., 2007—. Mem. task force long-term econ. growth State of Mich., 1983—84; cons. Mich. Dept. Commerce, Lansing, 1984—85, Congl. Budget Office, Washington, 1988—89; bd. dirs. Mich. Future. Author: (book) America's Great Consumption Binge, 1986; co-author: Economics, 12th edit., 1999; contbr. articles to profl. jours. Bd. dirs. Ctr. Watershed and Cmty. Health, Eugene, Oreg., 1997—. Grantee, NSF, 1976—77, 1979—81, 1994—97, Rockefeller Found., 1985—87, Nat. Cancer Inst., 1992—95. Mem.: Nat. Tax Assn., Assn. Pub. Policy Analysis and Mgmt. (mem. policy coun. 1994—98), Am. Econ. Assn. Avocations: sailing, skiing, tennis, hiking, clarinet. Office: U Mich 818 Hatcher Grad Libr S Ann Arbor MI 48109-3091 Office Phone: 734-764-9356. E-mail: pnc@umich.edu.

COURIC, KATIE (KATHERINE ANNE COURIC), newscaster, journalist; b. Arlington, Va., Jan. 7, 1957; d. John and Elinor; m. John Paul (Jay) Monahan III, 1989 (dec. Jan. 24, 1998); children: Elinor Tully Monahan, Caroline Couric Monahan. BA in Am. Studies, U. Va., 1979. Desk asst. ABC News, Washington, 1979; prodr. news show CNN, Atlanta, 1980; reporter, WTVJ NBC, Miami, 1984—86, reporter, WRC-TV Washington, 1987—89, Pentagon reporter, 1989; nat. corr. NBC News Today (The Today Show), Washington, 1990—91, co-anchor, 1991—2006; anchor, mng. editor CBS Evening News, 2006—. Contbg. anchor Dateline NBC, 1994—2006; co-host Macy's Thanksgiving Day Parade, 1991—, Summer Olympics, Barcelona, 1992; contbr. 60 Minutes, 2006—. Anchor: (documentaries) Everybody's Business: America's Children, 1995; author: The Brand New Kid, 2000, The Blue Ribbon Day, 2004; actor: (films) Austin Powers in Goldmember, 2002, Shark Tale (voice only), 2004; guest appearances Murphy Brown, 1992, Cheers, 1993, Will & Grace, 2002, and several others. Co-founder Nat. Colorectal Cancer Rsch. Alliance (NC-CRA), 1999. Named News Person Yr., TV Guide, 2001; named one of 25 Most Intriguing People, People mag., 2001, 100 Most Powerful Women, Forbes mag., 2005—06, 100 Most Influential People, Time Mag., 2006; recipient six Emmys, Associated Press award, Nat. Headliner award, Sigma Delta Chi award, Nat. Soc. Profl. Journalists, Matrix award, Gracie Allen award, Peabody award, 2001, Julius B. Richmond award, Harvard Sch. Pub. Health, 2003, Golden Plate award, Acad. Achievement, 2006. Achievements include being the first woman sole anchor of a major US network evening newscast in 2006 (CBS Evening News). Office: CBS Evening News 524 W 57th St New York NY 10019

COURSON, JOHN EDWARD, state legislator, insurance company executive; b. Aug. 21, 1944; s. James W. and Mary C. (Harris) C.; m. Elizabeth Poinsett Exum, Apr. 1973; children: James Poinsett, Elizabeth Boykin, Harris Russell. BA, U. S.C., 1968. Sr. v.p. Keenan & Suggs. Field dir. S.C. Republican Party, 1969—75, sec., 1976—80; nat. committeeman for S.C. Rep. Nat. Committee, 1980—88; chmn. campaign '80 for S.C.; Presdl. elector Rep., 1980, 1984; chmn. edn. com. SC Senate; co-chmn., treas. Re-elect Thurmond Com., 1990—95. With USMCR, 1968—74. Named Young Agt. of Yr., Ind. Ins. Agts. S.C., 1981; recipient Mounted Gold Elephant, S.C. Republican Party, 1975, 1980, 1982, Order of Palmetto. Mem.: Am. Legion, Marine Corps League, Palmetto Club, Columbia Ball Club, Forest Lake Club, Tarantella Club, Sigma Chi. Episcopalian. Avocations: tennis, politics. Office: 402 Gressette Senate Office Bldg PO Box 142 Columbia SC 29202 Office Phone: 803-212-6250. E-mail: siv@scsenate.org.

COURSON, MARNA B.P., public relations executive; b. Waynesboro, Pa., Feb. 22, 1951; d. Eugene Perry and Charlotte Mae (Sherman) Roschli; m. Sydney E. Courson, May 24, 1982 (dec. 1999); 1 child, Sydney Alexandra. BA, Franklin and Marshall Coll., 1973; postgrad., U. Kans., Kansas City. Reporter Beach Haven Times/The Beacon, Manahawkin, N.J., 1973-74, Dailey Observer Newspaper, Toms River, N.J., 1974-76; comm. mgr. Frick India Ltd., New Delhi, 1976-77; reporter, dictationist UPI, Washington, 1978-80, reporter Richmond, Va.; reporter, editor AP, Balt., 1980-84; comm. coord. St. Luke's Hosp. Found., Kansas City, Mo., 1986-88; exec. v.p. pub. rels. Spaw and Assocs., Inc., Overland Park, Kans., 1988-89; exec. v.p. CCI Pub. Rels. & Mktg. Comm., Inc., Shawnee Mission, Kans., 1990-92, pres. Kansas City, Mo., 1992—. Former bd. dirs. Wonderscope Children's Mus.; active Kansas City Downtown Coun.; bd. mem. Notre Dame de Sion; bd. dirs. Platte County Citizens Coalition, mem. exec. com.; mem. econ. devel. coun. Platte County; former bd. dirs., former exec. com. Mid Am. Youth Aviation Assn.; bd. dirs. Met. Ensemble Theatre. Recipient Prism award for Fund Raising, numerous awards and honors for reporting, 1973—80, pub. rels. awards, 1988—2006. Mem.: Platte County Econ. Devel. Coun., Nat. Assn. Women Bus. Owners, Pub. Rels. Soc. Am. (Pres.'s award with GKC), Internat. Assn. Bus. Communicators, World Futurists Soc., Olathe Kans. C. of C., Greater Kansas City C. of C., Northland Regional C. of C. Office: CCI Pub Rels and Mkgt Comms 601 Walnut St Ste 200 Kansas City MO 64106 Home Phone: 816-746-0556; Office Phone: 816-471-2900. Business E-Mail: marna@cci-pr.com. *Every step in my career has been building on my accumulated experience skill and knowledge, providing the basis for creativity and learning for the next stage. In every case, I've found that for me the process is as important as achieving the goal.*

COURT, LEONARD, lawyer, educator; b. Ardmore, Okla., Jan. 11, 1947; s. Leonard and Margaret Janet (Harvey) C.; m. JoAnn Dilleshaw, Sept. 2, 1967; children: Chris, Todd, Brooke. BA, Okla. State U., 1969; JD, Harvard U., 1972. Bar: Okla. 1973, U.S. Dist. Ct. (we. dist.) Okla. 1973, U.S. Dist. Ct. (no. dist.) Okla., 1978, U.S. Dist. Ct. (ea. dist.) Okla. 1983, U.S. Ct. Appeals (10th cir.) 1980, U.S. Ct. Mil. Appeals 1973. Assoc. Crowe & Dunlevy, Oklahoma City, Okla., 1977-81, shareholder, dir., 1981—. Adj. prof. Okla. U. Law Sch., Norman, 1984-85, 88-89, 99-00, Okla. City U. Law Sch., 1998—; planning com. Ann. Inst. Labor Law, S.W. Legal Found., Dallas, 1984-2004. Contbg. author: (supplement book) The Developing Labor Law, 1978, Corporate Counsel's Annual, 1974, Labor Law Developments, 1993, Employment Discrimination Law, Supplement, 1998, 2000, Winning Legal Strategies for Employment Law, 2005. Chmn. bd. elders Meml. Christian Ch., Oklahoma City, 1980, 98-2000; cubmaster Last Frontier coun. Boy Scouts Am., 1984, co-chmn. sustaining fund raising drive Oklahoma City Downtown YMCA, 1989, mem. bd. mgmt., 1994-96; participant Leadership Oklahoma City, 1987-88, bd. govs. Okla. State U. Found., 1990-2002; Oklahoma City Ronald McDonald House, 1990-93, mem. exec. com. 1991-93; co-chmn. ann. teleparty fundraising drive Am. Heart Assn., Okla. City, 1996-98, bd. dirs., 1996-98. Capt. USAF, 1973-77. Recipient Leadership in Law award, Okla. Jour. Record, 2007. Fellow Am. Coll. Labor and Employment Lawyer; mem. Am. Employment Law Coun., U.S. C. of C. (mem. labor rels. com. 1997—, chmn. fair labor stds. act subcom. 1999—, mem. steering com. 1999—), Oklahoma City C. of C. (mem. sports and recreation com. 1982-85, indsl. devel. com. 1986), Okla. State U. Alumni Assn. (nat. bd. dirs. 1989—, nat. exec. com., 1992-97, pres. 1995-96, chmn. alumni ctr. task force 1998—, Disting. Alumni award 1998, Hall Fame 2006), Okla. County Alumni Assn. (bd. sec. 1987-88, treas. 1988-89, v.p. 1989-90, pres. 1990-91), Harvard Law Sch. Assn., ABA (labor and employment law sect. com. on devel. of law under Nat. Labor Rels. Act, com. on EEO law, lititgation sect./employment and labor rels. law com.), Okla. Bar Assn. (labor and employment law sect. coun. 1978-83, 85-87, chmn. 1986), Okla. County Bar Assn., Fed. Bar Assn., U.S. Tennis Assn. (life). Office: Crowe & Dunlevy Mid America Tower 20 N Broadway Ave Ste 1800 Oklahoma City OK 73102-8273 Office Phone: 405-235-7700. E-mail: courtl@crowedunlevy.com.

COURTAUD, BERNARD JEAN-JACQUES, human resource consulting executive; b. Massy, France, June 22, 1945; s. Paul and Simone (Mustel) C.; children: Sebastien, Alexandre, Stanilas, Paul Engring. degree, Ecole Centrale, Paris, 1968; MBA, Insead, Fontainebleau, France, 1972. Cons. Commissariat a l'energie Atomique, 1968—72; cons. Port N.Y. Authority, NYC, 1970—71, Peat Marwick Mitchell & Co., 1972—74; chmn. Groupe Courtaud, Paris, 1974—98; founder H.R. Cons. Network, 1998—2005; with Hestia Ptnrs., Paris, 2005—. Chmn. Insead Alumni Assn., France, 1983-88 Office: Hestia Ptnrs 23 Rue D'Anjou 75008 Paris France Office Phone: 33 0 607011617. E-mail: courtaud@hestiapartner.com.

COURTEAU, GIRARD ROBERT, retired prosecutor; b. St. Paul, Aug. 21, 1942; s. Robert William and Laura Gertrude Courteau; m. Mary Linda Lucas, Apr. 3, 1964 (div. May 1997); m. Susan Frances DeBaca, Aug. 8, 1997; children: Steven, Girard, Devin, Heather. AA, Coll. Marin, 1965; BA, U. Calif., Berkeley, 1967; JD, U. Calif., 1970. Bar: Calif. 1971, U.S. Dist. Ct. (ctrl. dist.) Calif. 1971, U.S. Dist. Ct. (no. dist.) Calif. 1983. Dep. dist. atty. Monterey County, Calif., 1971, Marin County, San Rafael, Calif., 1972-2001; ret., 2001. Mem. editl. bd. Hasting's Law Jour., 1970; editor Marin Law Enforcement Newsletter, 1974-89. Named Prosecutor of the Yr., Marin County Dist. Attys. Office, San Rafael, Calif., 1987. Mem. Order of the Coif, Thurston Soc., Corvettes of Sonoma County, Palm Springs Corvettes Team ZR-1, Nat. Corvette Restorers Soc. Roman Catholic. Avocations: gardening, reading, corvettes. Home: 4550 Hall Rd Santa Rosa CA 95401 Personal E-mail: courvettes@sbcglobal.net.

COURTEAU, JOANNA, foreign language educator; d. Ryszard Wojtowicz; m. Richard Courteau (div. Sept. 1976); two children: m. Charles Gratto, June 29, 1977; four stepchildren. BA cum laude, U. Minn., Mpls., 1960; MA, U. Wis., Madison, 1965, PhD, 1970. Lab. technician dept. anatomy U. Minn., Mpls., 1958-60; NDEA grad. fellow U. Wis., Madison, 1960-63, 66-67; instr. Sullins Coll., Bristol, Va., 1963-65; asst. prof. U. Ark., Fayetteville, 1967-71; asst., assoc., full prof. Iowa State U., Ames, 1971-99, univ. prof., 1999—. Dir. summer riding acad. Rimrock Sch. Horsemanship, Elkins, Ark., 1972-76; vis. prof. U. Warsaw, Poland, 1979; presenter in field. Author: The Poetics of Rosalia de Castro's Sombra Negra, 1995; editor: Mujer, Sexo y Poder en la Literatura Femenina del S. XIX, 1999; assoc. editor Hispania, 1992-2002; contbr. numerous articles and writings on modernist writers, feminist studies, and nat. identity to profl. jours. and essay collections. Activist Amnesty Internat., Ames, 1976—, Iowans Against the Death Penalty, Ames, Des Moines, 1995—; pres. Planned Parenthood, Ames, 1981-83, UN Assn. Am., Ames, 1999-2001; del. county, dist., state and nat. convs. (alternate, 1996), mem. rules com. county and state Dem. Party. Recipient Fish award City of Ames, 1985, Human Rels. Recognition award City of Ames, 1989, Wilton Park Internat. award, 1997, Univ. Prof. award Iowa State U., 1998, Travel award, Gulbenkian Found., Portugese Found. Devel., Camões Found, City of Ames Humanitarian award, 2007; fellow Ford Found., São Paulo and Rio de Janeiro, 1967, fellow Gulbenkian Found., Lisbon, Portugal, 1988, 93. Mem. AAUP (exec. bd. 1993-96), MLA, NOW, Am. Portuguese Studies Assn. (founder, pres. 1996-98, past pres., recognition as founder/rschr. 2006), Am. Assn. Tchrs. Spanish and Portuguese (exec. bd. 1992-95), Internat. Assn. Lusitanists (exec. bd. 1987-93), Women's Studies Assn., Women's Internat. League Peace and Freedom, Archie C. and Nancy A. Martin Found. (founder, pres. 2000-05, exec. bd. 2005—), Beyond Welfare (exec. bd. 2006—). Office: PO Box 1158 Ames IA 50014 Office Phone: 515-294-2306. Business E-Mail: courteau@iastate.edu.

COURTENAY, WILLIAM JAMES, historian, educator; b. Neenah, Wis., Nov. 5, 1935; s. Walter Rowe and Emily (Simpson) C.; children: Elizabeth Spire, William Todd. AB, Vanderbilt U., 1957; STB, Harvard U., 1960, PhD, 1967. Instr. history Stanford (Calif.) U., 1965-66; asst. prof. U. Wis., Madison, 1966-69, assoc. prof., 1969-71, prof., 1971—, C.H. Haskins prof., 1988—, Hilldale prof., 1998. Vis. scholar Am. Acad. in Rome, 1995, 97, 98. Author: Adam Wodeham, 1978, Covenant and Causality, 1984, Schools and Scholars in 14th Century England, 1987, Capacity and Volition. A History of the Distinction of Absolute and Ordained Power, 1990, Parisian Scholars in the Early Fourteenth Century: A Social Portrait, 1999; editor: Rotuli Parisienses. Supplications to the Pope from the University of Paris, vol. I: 1316-1349, 2002, vol. II: 1352-1378, 2003; also over 100 scholarly articles; co-editor (4 vols.) Gabriel Biel, Canonis Misse Expositio, 1963-67; mem. editl. bd. Jour. the History Ideas, 1976—, Vivarium, 1990—, Medieval Acad. Am., 1978-82; sr. editor series: Education and Society in the Middle Ages and Renaissance, 1990- Recipient Younger Scholar award NEH, Washington, 1968-69, 83; fellow Alexander von Humboldt Stiftung, Germany, 1975-76, 79-80, Guggenheim Found, 1980, NEH, Newberry Libr., Chgo., 1983, Humboldt Preis, 1988, Inst. for Advanced Study, Princeton, N.J., 1989, Herzog August Bibliothek fellow, 1997, 2002, 2003, Am. Coun. Learned Socs. fellow, 1995-96. Fellow Medieval Acad. Am. (mem. coun. 1974-77, 2001-04), Am. Acad. Arts and Scis., Royal Hist. Soc. (London); mem. Am. Soc. Ch. History (councillor 1982-85, pres. 1988), Internat. Soc. for the Study of Medieval Philosophy (assesseur de bureau), Univ. Club. Avocation: sailing.

COURTER, JAMES A. (JIM), communications executive, retired congressman; b. Montclair, NJ, Oct. 14, 1941; s. Joseph A. and Madeleine C.; m. Carmen McCalmen, Dec. 5, 1970; children: Donica, Katrina. BA, Colgate U., 1963; JD, Duke U., 1966. Vol. U.S. Peace Corps, Venezuela, 1967-69; asst. corp. counsel City of Washington, 1969-70; atty. Union County Legal Services, Plainfield, N.J., 1970-71; 1st asst. prosecutor Warren County, 1973-77; mem. 96th-101st Congresses from 12th N.J. Dist., 1979—91; chmn. President's Defense Base Closure and Realignment Commission, 1991—94; ptnr. Verner, Liipfert, Bernhard, McPherson & Hand, 1994—96; vice-chmn., pres. IDT Corp., Newark, 1996—2001; vice chmn., CEO IDT Corp, Newark, 2001—. Adjunct professor NJIT. Mem. civic adv. council Hackettstown Community Hosp.; bd. dirs. Warren County Legal Services; Rep. candidate for Gov. of N.J., 1989 Mem. Nat. Dist. Atty.'s Assn., County Prosecutors N.J. Assn., N.J. Fedn. Planning Ofcls., N.J. Inst. Mcpl. Attys., N.J. Trial Attys. Assn., N.J. Bar Assn., Am. Bar Assn., Warren County Bar Assn., Washington Bar Assn. Clubs: Hackettstown Rotary (past pres.). Office: c/o IDT Corp 520 Broad St Newark NJ 07102*

COURTÉS, JOSEPH JEAN-MARIE, humanities educator, writer; b. Hérault, France, Feb. 6, 1936; s. Jean and Marthe (Carles) C.; m. Annie Joullié, June 22, 1974; children: Sophie, Jean-Noël, Benoît. Lic., Paris U., 1964, doctorate, 1965, doctorate, 1971, doctorate, 1983. Dir. Internat. Ctr. Semiotics and Linguistics, Urbino, Italy, 1971-73; asst. prof. Ecole de Hautes Études en Scis. Soc., Paris, 1973-84; prof. semiotics Toulouse U., France, 1985—2005. Pres. of commn. of semiotics and linguistics Toulouse U., 1986-92, 98-2005; emeritus prof. of French U., internat. cons. EHESS, 1985-2005; mem. Sci. Coms. of Revs., France, 1986-2005; emeritus prof. Univs. Author: Lévi-Strauss et les contraintes de la pensée mythique, 1973, Introduction à la sémiotique narrative et discursive, 1976, Sémiotique, dictionnaire raisonné de la théorie du langage, vol. I, 1979, vol. II, 1986, Le conte Populaire: poétique et mythologie, 1986, Sémantique de l'énoncé, 1989, Sémiotique du discours: de l'énoncé à l'énonciation, 1991, Du signifié au signifiant, 1992, Sémiotique narrative et discursive, 1993, Du lisible au visible: analyse sémiotique d'une nouvelle de Maupassant, d'une bande dessinée de B. Rabier, 1995, Éthnolittérature, rhétorique et sémiotique, 1995, Stratégies d'écriture et instabilité du sens, 1996, Des motifs ethno-litteraires aux topoi, 1997, L'énonciation comme acte sémiotique, 1998, Sémiotique du langage, 2003, 05, Plan de l'expression et perception, 2007. Mem. Assn. for Devel. Semiotics (pres. 1988—), Semio-Linguistics Soc. Ctr. (pres. 1991-93). Home Phone: 33 05 61 56 37 55. Personal E-mail: joseph.courtes@wanadoo.fr.

COURTNAY, WILIAM GERARD, osteopathic physician; b. Guthrie, Okla., Aug. 22, 1962; s. Clarence Clive and Patricia Ann (Pike) C.; m. Sandra Louise Ferrell, June 4, 1994. BS, U. Ctrl. Okla., Edmond, 1986; DO, Okla. State U., Tulsa, 1994. Emergency dept. technician Midwest City (Okla.) Meml. Hosp., 1979-88; med. examiner investigator Office of Chief Med. Examiner, Oklahome City, 1988-90; intern Hillcrest Health Ctr., Oklahome City, 1994-95; physician in pvt. practice Moore, Okla., 1995—. Vol. med. examiner Office of Chief Med. Examiner, Oklahoma City, 1995; dir. Mercy Health Network. Mem. AMA, Am. Osteo. Assn., Grady County Med. Soc. Republican. Roman Catholic. Avocations: percussion/music, woodworking, forensic sciences. Office Phone: 405-840-4456.

COURTNEY, CAROLYN ANN, school librarian; b. Plainview, Tex., Aug. 1, 1937; d. John Blanton and Geneva Louise (Stovall) Ross; m. Moyland Henry Courtney, Aug. 17, 1957; 1 child, Constance Elaine. BA summa cum laude, Wayland Bapt. Coll., 1969; MEd, W. Tex. State Coll., 1976; MLS, U. North Tex., 1990. Cert. elem., secondary, libr. tchr. 5th grade tchr. Hale Ctr. (Tex.) Ind. Sch. Dist., 1970-77, libr., 1977—. Bd. dirs. Plainvierw Cmty. Concerts, 2000—. Mem. LWV (bd. dir. 1970-75), DAR (Good Citizen chair 1981-85), Tex. State Tchs. Assn. (life), Tex. Classroom Tchrs. Assn. (sec. 1983-85), Tex. Libr. Assn., Delta Kappa Gamma (rsch. chair 1975-77, publs. chair 1984-86, pres. 2002-, scholarship 1975), Plainview Country Club. Methodist. Avocations: genealogy, travel. Home: 209 S Floydada St Plainview TX 79072-6665 Office: Hale Center Ind Sch Dist PO Box 1210 Hale Center TX 79041 E-mail: ccourtlibr@hotmail.com.

COURTNEY, EDWARD, retired classics educator; b. Belfast, Northern Ireland, Mar. 22, 1932; came to U.S., 1982; s. George and Kathleen (Nicholson) C.; m. Brenda Virginia Meek, Dec. 18, 1962; children: Richard Marcus, Adam Matthew. BA, Trinity Coll., Dublin, Ireland, 1954; MA, Oxford U., 1957. Research lectr. Christ Ch., Oxford, 1955-59; lectr. in classics King's Coll., London, 1959-70, reader in classics, 1970-77, prof. Latin, 1977-82; prof. classics Stanford U., Calif., 1982-93, Ely prof. humanities Calif., 1986-93; Gildersleeve prof. classics U. Va., Charlottesville, Va., 1993—2002, prof. emeritus, 2002—. Author: Commentary on the Satires of Juvenal, 1980, The Poems of Petronius, 1991, The Fragmentary Latin Poets, 1993, 2d edit., 2003, Musa Lapidaria, A Selection of Latin Verse Inscriptions, 1995, Archaic Latin Prose, 1999, A Companion to Petronius, 2002; editor: Valerius Flaccus, Argonautica, 1970, Juvenal, The Satires, A Critical Text, 1985, Statius, Silvae, 1990; joint editor: Ovid, Fasti, 1978, 4th edit., 1997. Mem. Am. Philol. Assn. Avocation: chess. Personal E-mail: edcourt2@cs.com.

COURTNEY, EUGENE WHITMAL, computer company executive; b. East St. Louis, Ill., Jan. 3, 1936; s. Eugene and Goldie Genell (Mitchell) C.; m. Barbara Ann Beckwith, Aug. 1, 1959; children: Kevin Eugene, Kyle Patrick. BSEE, Princeton U. with honors, 1957. Exec. v.p., gen. mgr., dir. Digital Sci. Corp., San Diego, 1970-75, pres., CEO, 1975-79; dir. Digital Sci./Europe, 1975-79; v.p. corp. devel. Topaz, Inc., San Diego, 1979, Nat. Computer Sys., Mpls., 1980-81, v.p., gen. mgr. scanning divsn., 1981-83, group v.p., 1983-88; exec. v.p., COO, dir. HEI Inc., Victoria, Minn., 1988-90, pres., CEO, 1990-99; dir., 1989-2000; prin. and dir. Triangle Industries, Inc., 1988—; pres., CEO RSI Sys., Edina, Minn., 1999-2001; prin. E.W. Courtney & Assocs., 2001—. Dir., chmn. Datakey, Inc., Mpls., 1995-2005; mem. Minn. Software Tech. Com., 1985-86; dir. Waters Instruments, Inc., Mpls., 2003—. Contbr. articles to profl. jours. Trustee, v.p. engring. San Diego Hall of Sci., 1974-79; mem. State of Calif. gov.'s task force on edn. and industry, 1977-78; mem. Rancho Santa Fe (Calif.) Park and Recreation Bd., 1978; mem. tech. adv. bd. Minn. Dept. Corrections, Shakopee, 1985-86. Mem. Am. Electronics Assn. (nat. bd. dirs., chmn. San Diego coun. 1976-79, chmn. Minn. coun. 1993-96), Princeton Club (N.Y.C.). Avocation: print collecting. Home: 509 Holly Ave Saint Paul MN 55102 also: Courtaparteen Kinsdale County Cork Ireland

COURTNEY, JOE (JOSEPH D. COURTNEY), congressman; b. Hartford, Conn., Apr. 16, 1953; s. Robert Edward and Dorothy (Kane) Courtney; m. Audrey Courtney; children: Robert, Elizabeth. BA, Tufts U., 1975; JD, U. Conn., 1978. Asst. pub. defender Rockville Superior Ct., 1979—81; mem. Conn. Gen. Assembly from 56th dist., 1987—95; ptnr. Courtney, Boyan & Foran, LLC.; town atty. Vernon, Conn.; mem. US Congress from 2nd Conn. dist., 2007—. Conn. coord. John Edwards campaign, 2004. Named Most Conscientious, Conn. Mag., 1994, Dem. Most Admired by Republicans, 1994. Democrat. Office: PO Box 1372 Vernon Rockville CT 06066 Home Phone: 860-871-7693; Office Phone: 860-577-8283. Office Fax: 860-896-0153.*

COURTNEY, WILLIAM HARRISON, security firm executive; b. Balt., July 18, 1944; s. Wilbur Harry Courtney and Mary Lee (Mitchell) Fleming; m. Laryssa Lapychak; children: William Jr., Mary Alison. BA in Econs., W.Va. U., 1966; PhD in Econs., Brown U., 1980. Fgn. svc. officer Dept. State, Washington, 1972-99; dep. exec. sec. NSC, The White House, Washington, 1987-88; dep. U.S. negotiator U.S.-Soviet Def. and Space Talks, Geneva, 1988-91; amb. Nuc. Testing and Nuc. Weapons Safety, Security, and Dismantlement, ACDA, Washington, 1991-92, Kazakhstan, 1992-95, Georgia, 1995-97; spl. asst. to Pres. for Russia, Ukraine and Eurasia, White House, Washington, 1997-98; sr. advisor Fgn. Affairs Reorgn. U.S. Dept. State, Washington, 1998-99; sr. advisor U.S. Commn. Security & Coop. Europe, 1999; sr. v.p. nat. security programs DynCorp, Alexandria, Va., 2000—04; dir. strategy and devel. Computer Scis. Corp., Falls Church, Va., 2004—. Mem.: Coun. Fgn. Rels. Home: 3722 48th St NW Washington DC 20016-3213 Office: 3110 Fairview Park Dr Falls Church VA 22042 Office Phone: 202-215-4243. Personal E-mail: courtneywmh@gmail.com. Business E-Mail: wcourtney@csc.com.

COURTOIS, BERNARD ANDRE, communications executive; BA, U. Mont., 1965, LLB, 1968. Bar: Que. 1969, Ont. 1984. Various regulatory, legal and exec. roles Bell Can., Ottawa, Ont., Canada, 1991—2003; pres., CEO, Info. Tech. Assn. Can., Ottawa, 2004—. Bd. dirs. Info. Tech Assn. Can., Ottawa, 1999—. Dir., treas. Nat. Gallery of Can. Found. Mem.: Internat. Inst. Comm. (pres. 2001—05). Office: Info Tech Assn Can Ste 1120 220 Laurier Ave W Ottawa ON Canada K1P 5Z9 Office Phone: 613-238-4822. Business E-Mail: bcourtois@itac.ca.

COURTOIS, JEAN-PHILIPPE, information technology executive; DECS, The Ecole Superieure de Commerce, Nice, France. Product mgr. Memsoft; channel sales rep. Microsoft France, 1984—86, So. Europe sales mgr., head mktg. dept., 1986—89, gen. mgr., 1989—91, gen. mgr. sales and mktg., 1991—94, gen. mgr., 1994—98; v.p. Worldwide Customer Mktg., Microsoft Corp., Redmond, Wash., 1998—2000, sr. v.p., 2000—, pres., Europe, Mid. East & Africa Redmond, Wash., 2000—03, CEO, Microsoft Europe, Mid. East & Africa, 2003—, sr. v.p., 2005—; pres. Microsoft Internat., 2005—. Office: Coeur Defense Tour B La Defense 4 100 Esplanade du Gen de Gau 92932 Paris France Office Phone: 00 33 17099 10 00.

COURTOIS, MICHAEL G., biology educator; s. George A. and Mary P. Courtois; m. M. Kathleen Hamel, Aug. 16, 1986; children: Mary Elizabeth, Patrick M., Kathleen P. BA, Coll. of Holy Cross, Worcester, Mass., 1977—81; M of Natural Scis., Worcester Poly. Inst., Mass., 1986—90. Profl. Educator N.H. Dept. Edn., 1981. Biology tchr. Salem HS, NH, 1981—, student coun. advisor, 1984—. Exec. dir. N.H. Assn. Student Councils, 2002—. Recipient Advisor of Yr., N.H. Assn. Student Councils, 1994. Mem.: NEA, Nat. Assn. State Student Coun. Exec. Dirs., Salem Edn. Assn. (chief negotiator 1998). Roman Catholic. Avocations: music, sports, reading. Office: Salem HS 44 Geremonty Dr Salem NH 03079 Home Phone: 603-890-9195; Office Phone: 603-893-7069 292. Office Fax: 603-893-7087. Business E-Mail: mcourtois@salem.k12.nh.us.

COURVILLE, ARTHUR F., lawyer; b. Jan. 5, 1959; BA, Stanford U., 1981; MBA, JD, U. Calif., 1987. Bar: Calif. 1987. Atty. Gibson, Dunn & Crutcher, 1987—92; with Symantec Corp., Cupertino, Calif., 1993—, dir. legal dept., 1994—97, dir. product mgmt. Internet tools bus. unit, 1997, dir. legal dept., 1998, v.p., gen. counsel, 1999—. Bd. dirs. Bus. Software Alliance; trustee Software Patent Inst. Office: Symantic Corp 20330 Stevens Creek Blvd Cupertino CA 95014-2132 Office Phone: 408-517-8000. Office Fax: 408-517-8186. E-mail: artcourv@symantec.com.*

COURY, ROBERT J., pharmaceutical executive; BS in Indsl. Engring., U. Pitts., 1984. Founder, CEO, prin. owner Coury Cons., L.P., Pitts., 1989—2002; dir., vice-chmn. of bd., CEO Mylan Labs. Inc., Canonsburg, 2002—. Mem. Allegheny Conference on Community Develop. Office: Mylan Labs Inc 1500 Corp Dr Ste 400 Canonsburg PA 15317 Office Phone: 724-514-1800.

COUSER, WILLIAM GRIFFITH, nephrologist, academic administrator, educator; b. Lebanon, NH, July 11, 1939; s. Thomas Clifford and Winifred Priscilla (Ham) C. BA, Harvard U., 1961, MD, 1965; BMS, Dartmouth Med. Sch., 1963. Diplomate Am. Bd. Internal Medicine. Intern Moffitt Hosp./U. Calif. Med. Ctr., San Francisco, 1965-66, 66-67; resident Boston City Hosp., 1969-70; asst. prof. medicine U. Chgo., 1972-73; asst. prof. Boston U., 1972-77, assoc. prof., 1977-82; prof., head divsn. nephrology U. Wash., Seattle, 1982—2002, Belding Scribner prof. medicine, 1995—2004, affiliate prof. medicine, 2004—. Mem. sci. adv. bd. Kidney Found. Mass., Boston, 1974—82; mem. rsch. grant com. Nat. Kidney Found., NYC, 1981—86; mem. rev. bd. for nephrology VA, Washington, 1981—84; mem. exec. com. Coun. on Kidney in Cardiovasc. Disease, Am. Heart Assn., Dallas, 1982—85; mem. pathology A study sect. NIH, chmn., 1988—89; subsplty. bd. in nephrology Am. Bd. Internal Medicine, 1988—92; dir. George M. O'Brien Kidney Rsch. Ctr. U. Wash., 1993—2003. Co-editor: Immunologic Renal Diseases, 1997, 2d edit. 2001; contbr. numerous articles, chpts., abstracts to profl. publs.; mem. editl. bd. Kidney Internat., 1982-96, Am. Jour. Kidney Diseases, Am. Jour. Nephrology, Jour. Am. Soc. Nephrology, editor-in-chief, 2001-07. Served to capt. U.S. Army, 1967-69, Vietnam. Recipient Rsch. Career Devel. award NIH, 1975-80, Method to Extend Rsch. in Time award, 1991-97; fellow Nat. Kidney Found., 1971, NIH, 1973; grantee, 1974-2004. Fellow: ACP, AAAS, Am. Heart Assn., Royal Coll. Physicians, Western Assn. Physicians (coun.), Am. Assn. Exptl. Pathology, Internat. Soc. Nephrology (coun. 1999, v.p. 2001—03, pres.-elect 2003—05, pres. 2005—07), Am. Soc. Nephrology (coun. 1991—98, pres. 1996), Am. Assn. Physicians, Am. Soc. Clin. Investigation (v.p. 1983—84). Mailing: 16050 169th Ave NE Woodinville WA 98072 Office Phone: 425-990-4542. Business E-Mail: wgc@u.washington.edu.

COUSINO, JOE ANN, sculptor; b. Toledo, Nov. 17, 1925; d. George Carl and Lucille Caroline (Kocher) Bux; m. (div.); children: Paula Rene, Richard Nils. BA in Art, U. Toledo, 1947; student, U. Mex., 1948, U. So. Ill., 1953; attended, Internatl. Wkshp., Pietra Santa, Italy, 1980. Art tchr. Ctrl. YMCA & YWCA, Toledo, 1945-47; sculpture tchr. U. Tex. Jr. Coll., Gainesville, 1965, Defiance (Ohio) Coll., 1970, Bowling Green (Ohio) State Univ., 1971; instr. sculpture Sch. Art and Design Toledo Mus. Art, 2003—; sculpture workshop Toledo Botanical Gardens Conf. Ctr., 2005—. Founder, pres. Toledo Potters Guild, 1951—55; Ohio rep. Am. Craft Coun., NYC, 1960—62; pres. Fed. Art Socs. North Ohio, 1965—67, trustee, 1963—; co-chair midwest Kefauver com. Art in the Embassies Program, Dept. State, Washington, 1966; guest sculptor U. So. Calif., Berkley, 1981; judge Crosby Festival Arts at Toledo Bot. Gardens, 2006, 07. One-woman shows include Toledo Mus. Art, Frank Ryan Gallery, Chgo., Forsythe Gallery, Mich., Mount St. Joseph Gallery, Cin., Arndt Mus. Art, Elmira, N.Y., Button Gallery Ltd., Saugatuck, Mich., Bowling Green State U. Grad. Ctr. Gallery, Ohio State Gallery, Kent State U. Gallery, Toledo Mus. Westgate Gallery, 2003, Exhbn. Bangkok, 1990; prin. sculptures include Ency. Britannica Hdqs., Rome, 1960, Scerbo Assocs., Cairo, 1960, Rio de Janeiro Brazil Dept. Commerce, 1963, John Leslie Stevens Meml., Oak Harbor, Ohio, Mame Gordon Meml., United Ch., Sylvania, Ohio, Greek Orthodox Holy Cathedral, Christ the King Ch., Toledo Hosp., Riverside Hosp., Toledo, Mercy Hosp., Toledo, Med. U. Ohio, Toledo, Toledo Bot. Gardens, U. Toledo Student Union Bldg., 1994, Way Libr., Perrysburg, Ohio, 1986, U. Toledo McMaster Astronom Bldg., 1989, Sister of St. Francis Mother House, Tiffon, Ohio, 1999, Toledo Opera Sculpture Honor Opera Condrs., Shedell Gardens, Elmira, Ohio, City Port Clinton, Ohio; Presentation, 1999, Schedel Arboretum and Gardens, Elmore, Ohio, 2001, Eagle Pitcher Bearing divsn. Bunting Brass of U.S.A., Engring. Soc. Ohio, Lillian Gish Mus., Bowling Green U., Ohio, 2007, Swiss Air Office, Cairo, First Fed. Bank, Toledo; (in film) Folks, 20th Century Fox, Push Point: Sculpture, 1982 (Bronze medal); works featured in mags. and jours. including The Blade Newspaper, Toledo, 2000, Chgo. Tribune Newspaper, Ceramics Monthly Internat., 1965, U. Toledo Alumni Mag., 2002. Featured spkr. UNICEF, Madras, India, 1984; bd. dirs. Toledo Arts Commn., 1978-84, Rare Books Ctr., U. Toledo, 1965-66; pres. Toledo Women's Art League, 1950-51. Recipient Outstanding Svc. in Field of Art award Fedn. of Arts, Toledo, 1967, Woman of Toledo Civic award, 1987, Touchstone nomination award Press Club of Toledo, 2000, Lifetime Achiever award, 2000; named Outstanding Intellectual of 21st Century, Internat. Biog. Ctr., London, 2001. Mem.: Internat. Sculpture Ctr., Pan Pacific S.E. Asia Women's Assn., Scandinavian Club of Toledo. Episcopalian. Avocations: travel, folk dancing, jazz, photography. Home and Studio: 3717 Indian Rd Toledo OH 43606-2408

COUSINS, ROBERT JOHN, nutritional biochemist, educator; b. NYC, Apr. 5, 1941; s. Charles Robert and Doris Elizabeth (Sifferlen) C.; m. Elizabeth Anne Ward, Jan. 25, 1969; children: Sarah, Jonathan, Allison. BA, U. Vt., 1963; PhD, U. Conn., 1968. NIH postdoctoral fellow biochemistry U. Wis., 1968-70; asst. prof. nutrition Rutgers U., 1971-74, assoc. prof., 1974-77, prof. nutritional biochemistry, 1977-79, prof. II (disting. Prof.), 1979-82, dir. grad. program in nutrition, 1976-82, mem. grad. programs in biochemistry, nutrition and toxicology; Boston family prof. human nutrition and biochemistry U. Fla., Gainesville, 1982—, eminent scholar chair, 1982—; dir. Nutritional Sci. Ctr., U. Fla., 1987—, grad. coun., 1990-93. Mem. nutrition study sect. NIH, 1980-84; mem. USDA Expt. Sta., dir. subcom. on human nutrition, 1987-01; J.L. Pratt vis. prof. Va. Poly. Inst. and State U., 1980; Wellcome vis. prof. Auburn U., 1986; C. Malcolm Trout vis. scholar Mich. State U., 2003; mem. NAS, Inst. of Med. Commn. on opportunites in nutrition and food scis., 1991-93, Food and Nutrition Bd., 1997-02, Dietary Reference Intakes Sci. Evaluation Commn., 1999-01, Ad Hoc Bionutrition Commn., NIH, 1993; Mary Short lectr. U. Md., 1989, James Waddell lectr. U. Wis., Madison, 1989, Stars in Nutrition lectr. Pa. State U., 1990, Hans Fisher lectr. Rutgers U., 1995, Lucille Hunley lectr. U. Calif., Davis, 1997, Eric Underwood lectr. Evian, France, 1999; Disting. spkr. biochemistry U. Wis., Milw., 1989; Mary Shoub lectr. U. Md., 1989; James Waddell Meml. lectr. U Wis., Madison, 1989, Eric Underwood lectr., Evian, France, other lectureships. Assoc. editor Jour. Nutrition, 1990-96; mem. editl. com. Ann. Revs. Nutrition, 1985-90, 96-99, assoc. editor, 1999-04, editor, 2005-; contbg. editor Nutrition Revs., 1980-88; mem. editl. bd. FASEB Jour., 1994-99, Biol. Trace Element Rsch. 1982-03; contbr. articles in nutritional biochemistry to profl. jours., chpts. to books Recipient Mead Johnson award in nutrition, 1979, Osborne and Mendel award for basic rsch. in nutrition, 1989, U. Conn. Disting. Alumnus award, 1991, Merit award NIH, 1992, USDA Sec.'s Honor award, 2000, Am. Coll. Nutrition Rsch. award, 2003, Bristol-Myers Squibb/Mead Johnson award for disting. achievement in biomed. rsch., 2003; Future Leader grantee Nutrition Found., Inc., 1973, NIH grantee, 1972—, Am. Coll. Nutrition Rsch. award, 2003. Mem. AAAS, NAS (elected mem. 2000), Am. Soc. Biochem. and Molecular Biology, Am. Soc. Nutrition Sci. (chmn. nominating com. elected officers 1983, coun. 1986-89, pres.-elect 1995-96, pres. 1996-97), Soc. Exptl. Biology and Medicine (edit. bd. Proc. 1980-86), Am. Chem. Soc., Soc. Toxicology, Fedn. Am. Socs. Exptl. Biology (vice chmn. summer conf. 1985, chmn. summer conf. 1989, bd. dirs. 1989—, v.p. 1990-92, pres., chmn. bd. 1991-92, chmn. subcom. consensus conf. biomed. funding 1991-94, chmn. pub. affairs exec. com. 1992-93), Sigma Xi, Phi Kappa Phi, Gamma Sigma Delta (U. Conn. Disting. Alumni). Home: 8454 NW 64th Ln Gainesville FL 32653 Office: U Fla Ctr for Nutritional Sciences 201 Food Sci & Human Nutr Bldg Gainesville FL 32611 Home Phone: 252-377-5271; Office Phone: 352-392-2133. Business E-Mail: cousins@ufl.edu.

COUTANT, MARY MCELWEE, retired editor; b. Charleston, Ill., Oct. 14, 1919; d. William Willard Merritt and Mary Emma Turman; m. Laurence Allen McElwee (dec.); m. Thurmond Ingram Adams (dec.); m. Albert Syze Coutant. Cert., Utterback's Bus. Coll., 1943. Catalog editor Ea. Ill. U., Charleston, 1967—86; ret., 1986. Active Coles County Tax Payers Assn.; bd. dirs. Coles County Farm Bureau. Named to Wall of Tolerance, Nat. Campaign for Tolerance, 2002, Legion of Honor., NRA. Mem.: AARP, Ill. Sheriff's Assn., Coles County Taxpayers Assn., Kaskaskia Archeol. Soc., Ea. Ill. U. Found., Ea. Ill. U. Annuitants Assn., Coles County Hist. Assn. (v.p. 1992—98), Nat. Assn. Ednl. Office Personnel (life), Ill. Assn. Ednl. Office Personnel (life), Nat. Arbor Day Found., Smithsonian Instn., Nat. Audubon Soc., Ea. Ill. U. Alumni Assn., Defenders of Wildlife, Coles County Arts Coun., M.J. Hummel Club, Epsilon Sigma Alpha. Republican. Methodist. Home: 9228 N County Rd #1840 Charleston IL 61920

COUTIFARIS, CHRISTOS, gynecologist, research scientist; b. NYC, Sept. 30, 1953; s. Basil Coutifaris and Lina Tsakyris-Coutifaris; m. Deborah Anne Driscoll, Oct. 24, 1987; children: Basil, Paulina. AB, Amherst Coll., Mass., 1976; MD, U. of Pa., Phila., 1982, PhD, 1984. Diplomate Nat. Bd. of Med. Examiners, lic. ob-gyn. Am. Bd. of Ob-Gyn., reproductive endocrinology and infertility Am. Bd. of Ob-Gyn. Asst. prof. ob-gyn. U. of Pa., Phila., 1987—94, assoc. prof. ob-gyn., 1994—2004, prof. ob-gyn., 2004—. Dir. divsn. of reproductive endocrinology and infertility and of Pa. Fertility Care U. of Pa., Phila., 1997—. Named J.H. Rudolph Vis. Prof., U. of Rochester, 1996, Isadore Forman Vis. Prof., Temple U., 1999, Mortel Visting Prof., Pa. State U., 2002; recipient Lindback Award for Disting. Tchg., Lindback Nat. Soc., 1992, rsch. grants, NIH, 1991—. Fellow: ACOG (exec. bd. mem. 2004—06), Alpha Omega Alpha; mem.: Soc. for Reproductive Endocrinology and Infertility (pres. 2004—05), Am. Soc. for Reproductive Medicine (exec. bd. mem. 2004—05). Achievements include research in Understanding human embryo implantation, human follicular development and have contributed to the development of diagnostic and therapeutic modalities related to human reproduction. Avocations: travel, reading, sports, classical music, opera. Office Fax: 215-349-5512. Business E-Mail: ccoutifaris@obgyn.upenn.edu.

COUTO, C. DOUGLASS, state agency administrator; s. Edward D. and Darlene D. (Douglass) C.; m. Katharine E. Couto, Aug. 18, 1973 (div.). BBA in Indsl. Relations, U. Iowa, 1972; MSA in Govtl. Adminstrn., George Washington U., 1976, MBA, 1983. Commd. USAF, 1972, chief of base adminstrn. communications Langley AFB, 1972-75, comdr. squadron sect., 1975-77, exec. support officer hdqrs. Washington, 1977-81, asst. prof. aerospace studies Howard U., 1981-84, hdqrs. squadron commdr., chief of staff Thule Air Base, Greenland, 1984-85, dir. adminstrn. hdqrs. strategic communications div. Offutt AFB, Nebr., 1985-88, exec. officer hdqrs. strategic communications div., 1988-89, dir. info. mgmt. electronic security command San Antonio, 1989-91, dir. info. mgmt. Air Force Intelligence Command, 1991, ret., 1994; chief info. officer State of Iowa, 1995—97; named chief info. officer Mich. Dept. Transp., 1997—2001; now info. officer Mich. Dept. Info. Tech. Instr. bus. adminstrn. Park Coll., Hampton, Va., 1977-79; instr. mgmt. No. Va. Community Coll., Alexandria, 1978-81; instr. exec. writing program, Pentagon, Washington, 1979-81; adj. faculty public adminstrn. Western Mich. U., Lansing, 2002-05; chair info. sys. tech. com. Transportation Rsch. Bd., 2004-. Founder, editor The Air Force Adminstr., 1977-81; speaker, lectr. on mgmt. and leadership. Advisor Andrew D. Turner Squadron Arnold Air Soc., Washington, 1983-84; mem. speakers' bur. Presdl. Inaugural Com., Washington, 1981. Recipient Disting. Award of Merit, Boy Scouts Am., 1976; named one of the Premier 100 IT Leaders, Computerworld, 2005. Mem. Air Force Assn., Eagle Scout Alumni Assn., Am. Legion (Americanism award 1977), Toastmasters Internat. (area gov., div. lt. gov., 2d. lt. gov., adminstrv. lt. gov. dist. 36 Nat. Capitol area, dist. gov. dist. 24 State of Nebr. 1989-90, Disting. Toastmaster award 1981, bd. dirs. 1992-94), Armed Forces Comms. Electronics Assn. (life; bd. dirs. Greater Omaha chpt. 1988-89), Alpha Phi Omega. Avocations: tennis, travel, reading. Office: Mich Dept Info Tech Van Wagoner Bldg 3rd Fl 425 West Ottowa St Lansing MI 48909 Office Phone: 517-241-2899. Office Fax: 517-335-4239.

COUTTS, LAWRENCE ROBERT, publisher; b. La Crosse, Wis., Oct. 9, 1948; s. Robert Samuel and Margaret Yvonne (Hougen) C.; m. Linda Lee Florio, May 23, 1970; children: Melissa, Marcia, Michelle, Michael. BS in political science, Carroll Coll., Waukesha, Wis., 1970; MBA, U. Wis., Milw., 1976. Advt. mgr. The Ansul Co., Marinette, Wis., 1970; mgr. comm. and advt. Will Ross Inc., Milw., 1970—74; advt. specialist GE Med. Sys. divsn., Waukesha, Wis., 1974—77; mgr. advt. and promotion Pfizer Med. Sys. Inc., Columbia, Md., 1977—78; mktg. svcs. dir. Extrocorporeal Med. Spec., King of Prussia, Pa., 1978—80; pres. Coutts Enterprises LLC, Scottsdale, Ariz., 1980—; pub. Nephrology News and Issues and Hematology Oncology News and Issues, Scottsdale, Ariz., 1986—; co-founder, pres. Med. News & Issues, Inc., Medicalnews.com., Inc., HON&I, Inc. and NN&I, Inc., 2001—. Chmn. dialysis mktg. subcom. Health Industry Mfrs. Assn., Washington, 1979-80; patient advocacy task force, Am. Kidney Fund, 2000-03; pubs. adv. com., BPA Internat., Inc., 2001—. Recipient Bell Ringer award with direct mail campaign Bus./Profl. Advt. Assn. Milw., 1978, NKF Pub. Svc. award, 1988, 90. Republican. Lutheran. Avocations: golf, tennis, bridge, gardening, horseback riding. Home: 7335 East Quail Track Rd Scottsdale AZ 85262 Office: Medical News & Issues 13880 N Northsight Blvd Ste 101 Scottsdale AZ 85260-3666 Home Phone: 480-595-2121; Office Phone: 480-443-4635. E-mail: larry@medicalnews.com.

COUTTS, ROBERT B., aerospace transportation executive; b. Westbury, NY; BSME, Tufts U.; advanced management courses, Harvard Univ. With General Electric Corp. (merged w/ Martin Marietta), 1972—93; v.p., Material Acquisition and Subcontract Management Martin Marietta (merged w/ Lockheed Martin), 1993—94, pres., Aero & Naval Systems, 1994—95; pres., Gov. Electronic Systems Lockheed Martin Corp., 1995—98, pres., COO electronics sector, 1998—99, exec. v.p., Systems Integration, 1999—2003, exec. v.p. electronic systems, 2003—07, spl. assignment to CEO, 2007—. Bd. dirs. Lockheed Martin. Former bd. dirs. local YMCAs, County United Way; bol. Greater Cin. and No. Ky. Area Boy Scout Coun.; bd. dirs. Balt. Symphony Orchestra; trustee Maryvale Prep. Sch.; bd. govs. Wesley Theol. Seminary. Mem. ASME, Tau Beta Pi. Office: Lockheed Martin Corp 6801 Rockledge Dr Bethesda MD 20817-1836*

COUTU, RONALD ARMAND, JR., electrical engineer, program manger; b. Framinghanm, Mass., May 28, 1966; s. Ronald Armand, Sr. and Bonnie Jean Coutu; m. Suzanne Marie LaCasse, Dec. 12, 1987; children: Joseph Thomas, Kevin Ronald. BS in Elec. Engring., U. Mass., Amherst, 1993; MS in Elec. Engring., Calif. Poly. State U., San Luis Obispo, 1995; PhD in Elec. Engring., Air Force Inst. Tech., Wright-Patterson AFB, Ohio, 2004. Cert. Profl. Engr., Calif., 1997. Flight test engr. Air Force Flight Test Ctr., Edwards AFB, Calif., 1997—2001; mems. rschr. Air Force Rsch. Lab., Wright-Patterson AFB, 2004—06; program mgr. Aero. Sys. Ctr., 2006—. Adj. asst. prof. Air Force Inst. Tech., Wright-Patterson AFB, 2005—. Maj. USAF, 1984. Decorated Air Force Achievement medal USAF, Air Force Commendation medal, Aerial Achievement medal, Meritorious Svc. medal. Mem.: IEEE, Eta Kappa Nu (sect. pres.), Tau Beta Pi (life; sect. pres.). Conservative. Roman Catholic. Achievements include research in novel MEMS microswitch electric contact materials. Avocations: Tae Kwon Do, reading, running. Office: Aeronautical Sys Ctr Dayton OH 45433 Home Phone: 937-429-9689; Office Phone: 937-255-9373. Personal E-mail: rscoutu@earthlink.net. Business E-Mail: ronald.coutu@wpafb.af.mil.

COUTURE, SISTER DIANE RHEA, sister, artist, educator; b. Hartford, Conn., Jan. 8, 1952; d. Rheal Paul Couture and Mary O'Shea. BA, Flagler Coll., 1979; student, U. North Fla., 1979—80; student in Pastoral Studies, Baptist Hosp., 1981—82; student in Spiritual Direction, San Pedro Ctr., 1989—92; student in Painted Glass, Klopfenstein Studios, 1995—98; student in Glass Painting, Millard Studio, 2002—03. Sister St. Joseph of St. Augustine, Fla., 1973. With Pine Hills Bike & Mower Shop, Orlando, Fla., 1968—72, Senco of Fla., Orlando, Fla., 1972—73; psych. counselor Flagler Hosp., St. Augustine, Fla., 1975—76; pastoral asst. St. Catherine Labouere Manor, Jacksonville, Fla., 1979—83; counselor Oncology Unit Mercy Hosp., Miami, Fla., 1983—87; youth minister St. Agnes Cath. Ch., Key Biscayne, Fla., 1987—89; dir. social svcs. Fla. Manor Nursing Home, Orlando, 1989—94; dir. Sisters of St. Joseph Archl. Stained Glass Studio, Orlando, 1992—99, Sisters of St. Joseph Stained Glass Studio, Orlando, 2000—. Adj. art prof. Flagler Coll., St. Augustine, Fla., 2000—05; spkr. in field. Prin. works include Meml. Window for 9/11 Victims, N.Y., Meml. Window, St. Francis of Assisi Nat. Shrine, Meml. Window for bay, St. Louis, recovery team for stained glass destroyed by Hurrican Katrina, New Orleans. Recipient Nat. Leadership award, Pres. U.S., 2003. Mem.: Stained Glass Assn. Am. Roman Catholic. Avocations: fishing, hiking. Office: SSJ Stained Glass 2745 Industry Ctr Rd 6 Saint Augustine FL 32084 Office Phone: 904-823-1918. Business E-Mail: LiteArt@aol.com.

COUTURE, JEAN GUY, bishop; b. Quebec, Can., May 6, 1929; s. Odilon and Eva (Drolet) C. BA, PhB, Laval U., Quebec, 1949, L.Theol., 1953, L.Sc.Phys., 1959. Ordained priest Roman Cath. Ch., 1953. Prof. math. and scis. St. Georges H.S. and Coll., Beauce, Que., 1953-65, adminstr. coll., 1961-68; mem. adminstrn. Roman Cath. Diocese Quebec, 1968-75; bishop of Hauterive Que., 1975-79; bishop of Chicoutimi Que., 1979—2004; bishop emeritus of Chicoutimi Que., 2004—. Mem. Order of Can., Order of Red Cross (officer). Roman Catholic. Home: 4864 050 Ch St Éloi Jonquière PQ Canada G7X 7V4 E-mail: jeanguyc@sympatico.ca.

COUTURE, JON N., bank executive; B in Mgmt., So. Ill. U.; M in Instrnl. and Performance Tech., Boise State U., Idaho; D in Human Performance at Work, U. So. Calif., LA. Cert. sr. profl. in human resources Soc. Human Resources Mgmt. Mem. human resources exec. com. Siemens N. Am. Siemens Bus. Svcs., Inc., sr. v.p. human resources Norwalk, Conn.; with Nat. City Corp., Cleve., 2004—, sr. v.p. corp. human resources. Adj. prof. human resources Fordham U., NY. Served in USAF. Mem.: Soc. Human Resources Mgmt. Office: Nat City Corp Nat City Ctr 1900 E Ninth St Cleveland OH 44114-3484 Office Phone: 216-222-2000.*

COUTURE, RONALD DAVID, art association administrator, web site designer, consultant; b. Ware, Mass., Dec. 1, 1944; s. Roy and Thelma Mary (Ledger) C.; m. Sandra Elaine Sharpe, Sept. 28, 1968; children: David, Meredith. Diploma, Butera Sch. Art, Boston, 1966. Graphic designer Sta. WGBH-TV Ednl. Found., Cambridge, Mass., 1970-73; promotion art dir. The Boston Globe, 1973-74, editl. design dir., 1974-77; asst. mng. art dir. N.Y. Times, 1977-78, assoc. mng. art dir., 1978-79, mng. art dir., 1979-84, dep. dir./editl. art, 1984-86, mng. dir./editl. art, 1986-88; owner, pres. Newsvision Inc., Mt. Kisco, NY, 1988-95. Owner Riverbend Design, 1996-2002, Riverbend Gallery and Workshop, 2003—; design cons. for Web and corp. pub.; design cons. Met. Cultural Alliance, Boston, 1972-77, IBM Corp. Pubs., 1991-93; guest lectr. Boston U. Sch. Comm., 1977; judge 62d and 64th Ann Exhibit, The Art Dirs. Club of N.Y., 1983; internat. editl. design Internat. Editl. Design Forum, N.Y.C., 1983. Contbr. articles in field to profl. jours. Mem. Westborough Planning Bd., Mass., 1977; apptd. regional rep. Ctrl. Mass. Regional Planning Bd., Westborough, 1977; apptd. chmn. Archtl. Rev. Bd., Mount Kisco, N.Y., 1978, 81, 84, 86, 89, 92, 95; mem. task force Labor Market Info. Network of N.Y. Labor Dept. and N.Y.C. Dept. Employment, 1979; bd. dirs. Blanchard Means Found., 1997—; mem. Brookfield Hist. Commn., 1999—. Recipient Gold medal set design New England Theater Conf., 1974, Gold medal newspaper design Soc. Newspaper Design, 1980; Lucy Stone Cmty. Svc. award, 2005. Mem. Soc. Newspaper Design (Gold medal chart design 1981, bd. dirs., nat. conf. dir. 1987-90), Art Dirs. Club N.Y., Am. Inst. Graphic Artist, Art Dirs. Club Boston, Nat. Computer Graphics Assn., Soc. Publ. Design Roman Catholic. Home: 44 Lake Rd Brookfield MA 01506-0537 Office: PO Box 537 9 S Maple St Brookfield MA 01506-0537 E-mail: riverbendpainter@verizon.net.

COUTURIER, DARREL J., art dealer, director; s. Robert A. and Marion B. Couturier. MA, Montclair State Coll., NJ, 1970. Gallery owner, dir. Couturier Gallery, LA, 1987—. Co-founder, pres. LA Art Galleries, 1992—97. Office: Couturier Gallery 166 N La Brea Ave Los Angeles CA 90036-2912 Business E-Mail: info@couturiergallery.com.

COUVILLION, DAVID IRVIN, federal judge; b. Simmesport, La., Oct. 27, 1934; s. J. Forest Couvillion and Leontine Rabalais. BS, La. State U., 1956, JD, 1959; LLM, Georgetown U., 1973. Bar: La. 1959. Pvt. practice, Marksville, La., 1959-67; adminstrv. asst. US Congressman Speedy O. Long, Washington, 1967-72; assoc. McCollister, McCleary, Fazio and Holliday, Baton Rouge, 1974-85; spl. trial judge US Tax Ct., Washington, 1985—. Mem. ABA, La. State Bar Assn. Office: US Tax Ct 400 2nd St NW Washington DC 20217-0002 Home Phone: 703-323-5410; Office Phone: 202-521-3344.

COVALT, EDNA IRENE, retired medical/surgical nurse; b. May 3, 1935; married; 5 children. Grad., Sch. Nursing, Blackwell, Okla., 1957; AS in Nursing, Grayson State U., 1971; BSN, Wichita State U., 1979. Charge nurse Blackwell Gen. Hosp., 1957—71, Madill (Okla.) Hosp., 1957—71; dir. nursing Christ Villa Nursing Home, 1974—79, Seneca Manor, 1979—83; contract nurse Nebr., Kans., Tex., Okla., 1983—98; ret. Nurse med. pers. pool, 1974—79. Sec. First Christian Ch., Lamont, Okla., 1998-99. Home: PO Box 213 302 S Walnut Lamont OK 74643 E-mail: Landpub@yahoo.com.

COVALT, ROBERT BYRON, chemicals executive; b. Chgo., Nov. 8, 1931; s. Byron L. and Thelma A. (Adams) C.; m. Virginia, Aug. 17, 1952; children: Karen Elizabeth Clark, David Byron. BSChemE, Purdue U., 1953, DEng (hon.), 1992; MBA, U. Chgo., 1967. Devel. engr. B.F. Goodrich Chem. Co., Avon Lake, Ohio, 1953-54; with Morton Chem. div. Morton Thiokol, Inc., 1956—, v.p. engring. and mfg. Chgo., 1973-78, group v.p., 1978-79, pres., 1979-87; pres. specialty chems. group, group v.p. Morton Thiokol, Inc., 1987-89; pres. splty. chems. group, group v.p. Morton Internat. Inc., 1989-90, exec. v.p., 1990-94; chmn., pres. and CEO Sovereign Specialty Chems., Inc., 1994—2002, dir., 1994—2004; pres. RBC Assocs., Inc., Chgo., 2004—. Bd. dirs. CFC Internat. Served as 1st lt. USAF, 1954-56. Recipient Disting. Engring. Alumnus award Purdue U. Mem. AIChE, Am. Chem. Soc. Office: RBC Associates Inc 10 S Riverside Plz Ste 1800 Chicago IL 60606 *Success in business is truly based upon teamwork and the accomplishment of all members working in concert toward a common goal. In the end, it is the result of what you do with your people, not what you do to your people.*

COVASSIN, TRACEY, athletic training educator; b. Mississauga, Ont., Canada, Mar. 25, 1972; d. Gino and Joyce Covassin. PhD, Temple U., Phila., 2003. Asst. prof. Shippensburg U., Pa., 2003—05; asst. prof., program dir. undergraduate athletic tng. Mich. State U., East Lansing, 2005—. Contbr. articles to profl. jours. Mem.: Am. Psychology Assn., Assn. for Advancement Applied Sport Psychology, Am. Coll. Sports Medicine, Nat. Athletic Trainers' Assn. (cert., grantee 2002). Home Phone: 517-699-0390; Office Phone: 517-353-2010.

COVAULT, CRAIG, editor; b. Dayton, Ohio, 1949; BS in Journalism, Bowling Green State U., 1971. Writer Urbana Citizen, 1971—72; sr. space editor Aviation Week & Space Tech., Washington, 1972—92, chief Paris bur., 1992—96, sr. editor, 1996—. Mailing: Aviation Week & Space Technology 1200 G St Washington DC 20005

COVELL, RUTH MARIE, medical educator, academic administrator; b. San Francisco, Aug. 12, 1936; d. John Joseph and Mary Carolyn (Coles) Collins; m. James Wachob Covell, 1963 (div. 1972); 1 child, Stephen; m. Harold Joachim Simon, Jan. 4, 1973; 1 child, David. Student, U. Vienna, Austria, 1955-56; BA, Stanford U., 1958; MD, U. Chgo., 1962. Clin. prof. and assoc. dean sch. medicine U. Calif. San Diego, La Jolla, 1969—; dir. Acad. Geriatric Resource Ctr. Bd. dirs. Calif. Coun. Geriatrics and Gerontology, Beverly Found., Pasadena, Alzheimer's Family Ctr., San Diego, San Diego Epilepsy Soc., Devel. Svcs. Inc., San Ysidro Health Ctr., NIH SBIR Stude Sect. Geriatrics; cons. Agy. Health Care Po licy and Rsch.; chair Calif. Ctr. Access to Care Adv. Bd. Contbr. articles on health planning and quality of med. care to profl. jours. Mem. AMA (sect. on med. schs. governing coun.), Am. Health Svcs. Rsch., Assn. Tchrs. Preventive

Medicine, Am. Pub. Health Assn., Assn. Am. Med. Colls. Group on Instl. Planning (chair 1973-74, sec. 1983-84), Phi Beta Kappa, Alpha Omega Alpha. Home: 1604 El Camino Del Teatro La Jolla CA 92037-6338 Office: U Calif San Diego Sch Medicine La Jolla CA 92093-0602

COVENEY, RAYMOND MARTIN, JR., geology educator; b. Marlboro, Mass., Oct. 15, 1942; s. Raymond Martin and Rita Marie (Brani) C.; m. Anne Marie Keating, Feb. 22, 1965; children: Christine, Maureen, David. BS in Geology, Tufts U., 1964; MS in Geology, U. Mich., 1968, PhD in Geology, 1972. Asst. geologist N.J. Zinc Co., Hanover, N.Mex., 1968; geologist Dickey Exploration Co., Alleghany, Calif., 1969-70; grad. tchg. asst. U. Mich., Ann Arbor, 1966-70; from asst. prof. to prof. dept. geosci. U. Mo., Kansas City, 1971—, interim dean Coll. Arts and Scis., 1992-93, chair dept. geoscis., 1996—2005, dir. environ. studies, 1998—2004. Cons. ProSoCo., Inc., Kansas City, 1986-92, Midwest Rsch. Inst., Kansas City, 1986-91, Woodward Clyde, Kansas City, 1981, Hunt Midwest, 1997; review panel Earth and Environ. Sci. Finnish Acad., 2004. Contbr. articles to profl. jours. Lt. (j.g.) USNR, 1964-66. Rackham Predoctoral Rsch. fellow, U. Mich., 1970-71; NSF Rsch. grantee, 1981-85, 90-93, 95-98; recipient N.T. Veatch award, 1988. Fellow Geology Soc. Am., Soc. Econ. Geologists (councilor 1993-96, trustee 1992-96, chair pubs. com. 1995-2001); mem. AAAS, Geol. Soc., Am. Geophys. Union. Roman Catholic. Achievements include research in metal-rich black shales and related deposits of molybdenum, zinc, platinum. Home: 5405 Locust St Kansas City MO 64110-2443 Office: U Mo 5100 Rockhill Rd Kansas City MO 64110-2481 Office Phone: 816-235-2980, 816-523-3492, 816-235-1334. Business E-Mail: coveneyr@umkc.edu.

COVENSKY, EDITH, language educator, poet; b. Bucharest, Romania, Apr. 14, 1945; arrived in U.S., 1965, naturalized; d. Moshe Friedrich Michaeli and Gizy Heinish Michaeli Bizaoui; m. Harvey Covensky, June 26, 1969; children: Jeffrey, Laurice. BA, MA, Wayne State U., 1971, PhD qualifications, 1980. Tchr. Congregation Shaarey-Zedek, Southfield, Mich., 1968—75; instr. Hebrew Wayne State U., Detroit, 1987, lectr. Hebrew, 1998—. Author: Other Words, 1985, Syncopations, 1987, Night Poems, 1992, An Anatomy of Love, 1992, Partial Autobiography, 1993, Origins, 1994, Synesis, 1995, Jerusalem Poems, 1996, Poetics, 1997, After Auschwitz, 1998, Metamorphosis and Other Poems, 1999, Steps, 2000, Electrifying Love, 2000, Collage, 2002, Zohar, 2002, Anatomy of Love: Selected Poems, 1992-2002, 2005; contbr. poetry to numerous publs. Scholarship chair Hillel Found. of Met. Detroit, 2000—, bd. dirs., 1991—. Sgt. comm. corps Israeli Army, 1963—65. Finalist, Nat. Libr. Poetry, 1995; recipient Editor's Choice award, 1995, Internat. Poet of Merit award, 1996. Mem.: Internat. Soc. Poets (disting., nominee Poet of Yr. 1996). Avocations: reading, running, music, tennis. Home: 3816 Columbia Bloomfield Hills MI 48302 Office: Wayne State U 455 Manoogian Hall Detroit MI 48202 Office Phone: 313-577-6267. Home Fax: 248-865-9242. E-mail: edithpoet@aol.com.

COVERDALE, JOHN HOWARD, psychiatrist; b. Auckland, New Zealand, Aug. 26, 1954; s. Howard Vincent and Margaret Evelyn Coverdale; m. Mary Bakht Coverdale, Sept. 2, 1991; children: Sara, Thomas, Emma. MB, BChir, U. Otago, New Zealand, 1980, MD, 2004; MEd, U. Houston, Houston, 2004. Lic. physician Tex. Assoc. prof. psychiatry and med. ethics Baylor Coll. Medicine, Houston, 2000—. Editor: Academic Psychiatry, 2002—; contbr. articles to profl. jours. Recipient Fullbright and Jaworski Disting. Educator award, Baylor Coll. medicine, 2003—04, McGovern Disting. Tchr. awrd, Baylor Coll. Medicine, 2006. Achievements include research in medical ethics. Office: Menninger Dept Psychiatry One Baylor Plz Houston TX 77030

COVERT, EUGENE EDZARDS, aerospace engineer, aeronautics professor; b. Rapid City, SD, Feb. 6, 1926; s. Perry and Eda (Edzards) C.; m. Mary Solveig Rutford, Feb. 23, 1946; children: David H., Christine J., Pamela M., Steven P. BS, U. Minn., 1946, MS, 1948; ScD, MIT, 1958. Registered profl. engr., Mass.; chartered engr., U.K. Preliminary design group USNADC, Johnsville, Pa., 1948-52; mem. staff MIT Aerophysics Lab., 1952-63, assoc. dir., 1963-75, assoc. prof. aeronautics and astronautics, 1963-68, prof., 1968—97, T. Wilson prof. aeronautics, 1993-96, head dept. aeronautics and astronaut., 1985-90; T. Wilson prof. of aeronautics emeritus, 1997—. Chief scientist USAF, 1972—73, mem., chmn. sci. adv. bd., 1975—86, 1990—94; mem. panel Naval Aeroballistic Adv. Com., 1965—75; mem. aeronautical adv. com. NASA, 1985—89, 2006—, mem. adv. com., 2006—; mem. Aeronautics and Space Engring. Bd., 1986—92, chmn., 1992; chmn. power, energy and propulsion panel adv. group aerospace R&D NATO, 1982—86, aero. policy com. office sci. and tech. policy, 1976—92; mem. commn. investigation space shuttle accident Pres. US; cons. in field. Mem. Blue Ribbon Com. on the Osprey, 2001; mem. nonadvocate rev. NASA Aeronautics Program, 2004. With USNR, 1943—47. Recipient Exceptional Civilian Sci. award USAF, 1973, 86, 94, Univ. Educator of Yr. award, Am. Soc. Aerospace Edn., 1980, Tech. Leadership award U. Minn. Alumni Assocs., 1993, Pub. Svc. award NASA, 1991, von Karman medal Adv. Group for Aerospace R&D, 1980, Wright Bros. Lectureship Aeronautics AIAA, 1997, Guggenheim medal, 2005, Outstanding Achievement award U. Minn., 2007. Fellow AAAS, Royal Aero. Soc., AIAA (hon.; bd. dirs., Ground Testing award 1990, W.F. Durand lectr. for pub. svc. 1992, Wright Bros. lectr. 1997); mem. NAE, N.Y. Acad. Scis., Sigma Xi. Office: MIT 77 Massachusetts Ave Rm 9-335 Cambridge MA 02139-4307

COVERT, SUSAN JANE, rehabilitation services professional, director; b. St. Augustine, Fla., Aug. 9, 1956; d. Orland H. and Helen Mary Covert; 1 child, Joshua Dobson. AS, Stark Tech. Coll., Canton, Ohio, 1998; AA in Gen. Studies, Kent State U., Canton, Ohio, 1998, BA in Gen. Studies, 2000; MA in History, Youngstown State U., Ohio, 2004. Lic. physical therapist. Dir. rehab. Therapy Ptnrs., Wooster, Ohio; program mgr. Paul Kroh Inc., Canton; physical therapy asst. Arbor Rehab., Smithville, Ohio; program dir. Siffrin, Inc., Canton, Mary Thomas Residential, Akron; physical therapy asst. Blick Clin., Akron, Stark Co. Bd. Edn., Canton. Spkr. preservation Rotary, Stark Libr., Canton, Ohio, 2004—05; cons. to nominate bldg. Nat. Registry List, Canton, 2005. Mem.: Canton Preservation Soc. (edn. com. 2003—06), Ohio Acad. History, Ohio Acad. Med. History, Ohio Hist. Soc. (history day judge 2002—06), Phi Alpha Theta. Home: 1124 Brant Ave NW Canton OH 44708

COVEY, DANA CURTIS, military officer, orthopaedic surgeon; b. Woodland, Calif., Mar. 27, 1951; s. Dale Curtis and Marjorie Lee Covey; m. Lynn Suzanne Bachofer, May 18, 1985; children: Ashley Lane, Chelsea Elizabeth, Lauren Michelle, Matthew Curtis. BS, US Naval Acad., 1973; MSc, U. Idaho, 1980; MD, U. Wash., 1984. Diplomate Nat. Bd. Med. Examiners, 1985, Am. Bd. Orthopaedic Surgery, 1992; Surface Warfare Officer USN, 1976, Surface Warfare Medical Officer USN, 1992. Commd. ensign USN, 1969, advanced through grades to capt., 1997, midshipman Annapolis, Md., 1969—73, divsn. officer, officer of the deck and command duty officer USS STEIN (FF-1065) San Diego, 1974—76, asst. prof. naval sci. U. Idaho Moscow, 1977—80; intern in orthop. surgery La. State U. Med. Ctr., 1984—85, resident in orthop. surgery, 1985—89; fellow in orthop. surgery U. Pa., 1989—90; orthopaedic surgeon USN, Comideastfor, Bahrain, 1989, staff orthopaedic surgeon Naval Hosp. Phila., 1990—91, orthopaedic surgeon Fleet Hosp. Fifteen and EOD Group One Det. A Saudi Arabia, Kuwait, Iraq, 1991, chief orthopaedic surgery Naval Hosp. Bremerton, Wash., 1991—97, dir. surg. svcs. Naval Hosp., 1998—2000; dir. surg. svcs. Fleet Hosp. Six USN and UN, Velika Gorica, Croatia, 1994; exec. officer Fleet Hosp. Five and med. officer (j-7) USSPTGP-Haiti USN, Port-au-Prince, Haiti, 1997, officer-in-charge Operation Brava Colombo, Sri Lanka, 1998, dir. surg. svcs. U.S. Naval Hosp. Chatan, Okinawa, Japan, 2001—04, officer-in-charge Operation Brava Hanoi, Vietnam, 2003—03; commdg. officer Naval Res. Naval Hosp. USNR, Shreveport, La., 1987—89; officer-in-charge, forward resuscitative surg. sys.-3 USMC, Al Anbar, Iraq, 2004, orthopaedic surgeon Bravo Surg. Co. Camp Al Asad, Al Anbar, Iraq, 2005—. Asst. prof. naval sci. U. Idaho, Moscow, 1977—80; clin. asst. prof. orthopaedic surgery U. Pa., Phila., 1991—96; asst. prof. surgery Uniformed Services U. Sch. Medicine, Bethesda, Md., 1998—; dir. Soc. Mil. Orthopaedic Surgeons, San Antonio, 1998—2006; oral bd. examiner Am. Bd. Orthopaedic Surgery, Chapel Hill, NC, 2003—; presenter in field. Contbr. articles to profl. jours. Decorated Navy Achievement medal USN, Navy Commendation medal, Navy Achievement medal, Combat Action ribbon, Legion of Merit, Meritorious Svc. medal, Navy Commendation medal, Meritorious Svc. medal USMC, Bronze Star; recipient Outstanding Rsch. prize, Seattle Gynecol. Soc., 1983, 1984; grantee, Population Coun. Ctr. for Biomedical Rsch., 1977—80, Navy Med. Dept., 1992, Naval Health Rsch. Ctr., 1995, Fisher Found., 1998—, Naval Med. R & D Command; Wilson Found. Academic scholar, U. Wash., 1981. Fellow: ACS, Am. Acad. Orthopaedic Surgeons; mem.: Orthopaedic Trauma Assn., Am. Orthopaedic Assn., Soc. Med. Consultants to the Armed Forces, U.S. Naval Acad. Alumni Assn. (life). Achievements include invention of Mobile Shipboard Surgical Suite. Home: 5212 Pacific Grove Pl San Diego CA 92130-3702 Office: Naval Medical Center 34800 Bob Wilson Dr San Diego CA 92134-5000 Home Phone: 858-509-7932; Office Phone: 619-532-8427. Office Fax: 619-532-8467. Personal E-mail: dccovey@aol.com. Business E-Mail: dccovey@nmcsd.med.navy.mil.

COVEY, LIRIO S., research scientist; b. Manila, Oct. 24, 1943; came to U.S., 1965; d. Carlos Cruz and Hortensia (Agudo) Sobrevinas; m. Michael H. Covey, June 15, 1968; children: William, Michael L. BS, St. Theresa's Coll., 1964; MA in Psychology, Columbia U., 1967; PhD in Psychology, CUNY, 1983. Rsch. asst. Am. Health Found., NYC, 1970-72, epidemiologist, 1973-74; rsch. assoc. CUNY, 1976; adj. instr. psychology Damavand Coll., Tehran, Iran, 1977-78; sr. epidemiologist Am. Health Found., 1979-82; rsch. scientist N.Y. State Psychiat. Inst., 1987—; asoc. rsch. scientist Columbia U., NYC, 1987-92. Editor: Helping the Hard-Core Smoker: A Clinician's Guide; contbr. articles to profl. jours. including Jour. Nat. Cancer Inst., Am. Jour. Epidemiology, Annals of Behavior Medicine, Tobacco Control, Drugs, Jour. AMA, Internat. Acad. Biomed. Drug Rsch., Am. Jour. Pub. Health, Am. Jour. Psychiatry, Jour. Clin. Psychiatry. Com. chair Sci. and Tech. Coun. Philippine Consulate, N.Y.C., 1990-94. Named one of 10 Outstanding Students of The Philippines, 1964; NIH-Nat. Inst. Mental Health fellow, 1984-87; NIH-Nat. Inst. Mental Health trainee, 1974-77. Mem. APHA, Soc. Behavioral Medicine, Soc. Rsch. in Nicotine/Tobacco, Soc. for Epidemiologic Rsch. Achievements include development of scale to measure nicotine dependence; research in lung cancer in women; environmental factors in cancer of the larnyx; smoking habits and occupational status; nicotine and major depression; future trends in pharmacological treatment of smoking cessation. Office: NY Psychiat Inst 722 W 168th St New York NY 10032-2603

COVEY, MICHAEL J., forest products and real estate executive; b. Mont. B in Forestry, Univ. Mont.; MBA, Univ. Oreg. Various positions to exec. v.p. Plum Creek Timber Co., Atlanta, 1982—2005; pres., CEO Potlatch Corp., Spokane, Wash., 2006—. Bd. dir. Potlatch Corp., 2006—. Office: Potlatch Corp Ste 1100 601 W Riverside Ave Spokane WA 99201 Office Phone: 509-835-1516. Office Fax: 509-835-1559.*

COVEY, RICHARD OSWALT (DICK COVEY), aerospace transportation executive, former astronaut; b. Fayetteville, Ark., Aug. 1, 1946; s. Charles D. Covey; m. Kathleen Allbaugh; 2 children. B in Engring. Scis., USAF Acad., 1968; M in Aeronautics and Astronautics, Purdue U., 1969. Astronaut NASA, 1978—94; dep. prog. mgr. space ops. Unisys, Houston, 1994—96; divsn. dir. McDonnell Douglas' Houston Ops. Boeing Co., 1996; dep. prog. dir. ops. Boeing's NASA Consolidated Space Ops. Contract, 1998; v.p. Boeing Houston Ops.; pres. Boeing Svc. Co., Colorado Springs, Colo.; exec. v.p., COO United Space Alliance, 2006—. Co-chmn. Return-to-Flight Task Grp., 2003—05. Test force dir., test pilot, operational fighter pilot USAF. Decorated 2 DSMs, 5 DFCs; co-recipient Goddard Trophy, Nat. Space Club, 1994; named to Astronaut Hall of Fame, 2004; recipient Disting. Pub. Svc. medal, NASA. Fellow: AIAA; mem.: Assn. Space Explorers, Soc. Exptl. Test Pilots, Air Force Assn., USAF Acad. Assn. Grads., Order of Daedalians. Avocations: golf, water sports, photography, skiing, volleyball. Office: United Space Alliances 1150 Gemini Houston TX 77058*

COVEY, STEPHEN MERRILL RICHARDS, business consultant, speaker, author; b. Provo, Utah, Apr. 25, 1962; s. Stephen Richards and Sandra Renee (Merrill) C.; m. Jerolyn Shae Hutchings, Apr. 26, 1985; children: Stephen Hutchings, McKinlee Louise. BA magna cum laude, Brigham Young U., Provo, Utah, 1985; MBA, Harvard U., 1989. Leasing agt. Trammell Crow Co., Dallas, 1985-87; summer assoc. First Boston Corp., NYC, 1988; pres., CEO Covey Leadership Ctr. (now FranklinCovey Co.), Provo, 1989, also bd. dirs.; now co-chairman FranklinCovey Co. Author: Seven Habits of Highly Effective People, 1990, Principle-Centered Leadership, 1991, First Things First, 1994, Seven Habits of Highly Effective Families, 1997, Living the Seven Habits, 1999, Seven Habits of Highly Effective Teens, 1998, Beyond the Seven Habits, 2003, The Eighth Habit, 2004, translations into multiple languages, numerous audio books. Recipient Mc-Feely award for significant contributions to mgmt. and edn., Internat. Mgmt. Coun., Thomas More Coll. Medallion for svc. to humanity. Mem. Lds Ch. Avocations: travel, reading, sports. Office: FranklinCovey Co 2200 W Parkway Blvd Salt Lake City UT 84119 Office Phone: 801-975-1776. Office Fax: 801-817-8313.

COVEY, STEVEN K., lawyer; b. Chgo., Aug. 5, 1951; Bachelors, U. Ill., 1973; JD, DePaul U., 1977. Corp. sec. Navistar Internat. Corp., Warrenville, Ill., 1990—2000, dep. gen. counsel, 2004, sr. v.p., gen. counsel, 2004—; v.p. gen. counsel Navistar Fin. Corp., Warrenville, Ill., 2000—04. Office: Navistar Internat Corp 4201 Winfield Rd Warrenville IL 60555*

COVIELLO, ROBERT FRANK, retail executive; b. Hartford, Conn., Dec. 20, 1941; s. James Joseph Coviello and Ann Frances (Links) Leary; m. Anne Elizabeth Lomasney, Oct. 22, 1966; 1 child, Michael James. Student, U. Conn., 1960-61, U. Madrid, 1961-62; grad., Machine Accts. Tng., 1963; student, Northeastern U., Boston, 1969. Data processing mgr. Chadwick-Miller, Inc., Boston, 1964-66; systems design analyst nat. accts. KeyData Corp., Watertown, Mass., 1969-70, systems designs mgr. NYC, 1970-72, western regional mgr. Chgo., 1972-73; pres. Gallery of Gifts Shoppes, Inc. (doing bus. as Kitchen Etc.), Hampton, NH, 1973-93; co-founder, exec. v.p. merchandising Kitchen Etc., NH, 1993-95; pres., founder Housewares Tabletop Internat., 1995—; founder, pres. HTI Buying Group, Inc., NH, 1998—. Chmn. Downtown Bd. of Trade, Dover, N.H., 1975-77, 82-83; pres. Merchants Assn. of Lilac Mall, Rochester, N.H., 1982-83. Dir. C. of C., Dover, 1983-86. With U.S. Army, 1966-68. Recipient Buyer's award of recognition Housewares Club New Eng., 1986, Potter's Club award Pfaltzgraff Co., 1986, 89. Mem. Retail Mchts. Assn. N.H. (past pres. 1985-87, dir. 1980-96, named Retailer of Yr. 1988), Am. Mgmt. Assn. (pres.'s Assn divsn. club), Gift Assn. Am. (dir. 1981-95), World Cup (St. Paul). Avocations: cooking, travel, flying, railroads, deep sea sports fishing. Office: HTI 47 Charles St Rochester NH 03867-2927 Office Phone: 888-484-3380. Personal E-mail: htibuying@verizon.net, rfcoviello@yahoo.com.

COVIN, DAVID L., retired political science professor; b. Chgo., Oct. 3, 1940; s. Odell Jerry and Lela Jane (Clements) Johnson; m. Judy Bentinck Smith, May 7, 1965; children: Wendy, Holly. BA, U. Ill., 1962; MA, Colo. U., 1966; PhD, Wash. State U., 1970. From asst. prof. to assoc. prof. govt. and Pan African studies Calif. State U., Sacramento, 1970—79, prof., 1979—, assoc. dean gen. studies, 1972-74, acting dir. Pan African studies, 1979-81, dir. Pan African studies, 1986—2004, ret., 2006. Commr. Edn. Mgmt. and Evaluation Commn., 1977—81; trustee Congl. Black Caucus, Washington, 1977—92; adj. prof. Union Grad. Sch., 1979—82; mem. Criminal Justice Brain Trust; co-dir. Race and Democracy in Ams. Project, 1999—. Author: (novel) Brown Sky, 1987 (Best New Novel 1987 Calif. Black Faculty and Staff Assn. News), Axe: The Unified Black Movement in Brazil, 1978-2000, 2006, short stories; contbr. articles to profl. jours.; mem. bd. editors Jour. Pan African Studies. Active Sacramento Black Area Caucus, 1972—, Com. Fair Adminstrn. Justice, Sacramento, 1985—; edn. co-chmn. Sacramento Black Cmty. Activist Com., 1985—90; founder, bd. dirs. Black Sci. Resource Ctr.; bd. dirs. Women's Civic Improvement Ctr.; co-chmn. Nat. Black Ind. Polit. Party, Sacramento, 1981—85. Recipient Cmty. Svc. award, Sacramento Area Black Caucus, 1976, Omega Psi Phi, 1982, All African People's Revolutionary Party, 1986, John L. Livingston Disting. Faculty Lecture award, 1992, medal of honor, Cooper Woodson Coll., 1998, Walter R. Bremond Cmty. Svc. award, Sacramento Black United Fund, 1998, Sacramento Observer medallion for edn., 2003, Cmty. Svc. award, Coll. Social Scis. and Interdisciplinary Studies, 2004. Mem.: Assn. Caribbean Studies, Western Polit. Sci. Assn. (mem. com. status blacks), Nat. Conf. Black Polit. Scientists (pres. 2003—05), Nat. Coun. Black Studies. Avocations: fishing, skiing, reading. Home: 4131 44th St Sacramento CA 95820-2829 Office: Calif State U 6000 J St Sacramento CA 95819-2605 Home Phone: 916-456-4981. Business E-Mail: covindl@csus.edu.

COVINGTON, ALEC C., retail executive; Div. pres. Wetterau Inc.; pres., COO Houchens Industries Inc., Richfood Inc.; exec. v.p., pres. COO distbn. co. div. SuperValu Inc., 2000—01; CEO AmeriCold Logistics LLC, 2001—04; pres., CEO Tree of Life Inc., 2004—06, Nash Finch Co., Edina, Minn., 2006—. Mailing: Nash Finch Co PO Box 355 Minneapolis MN 55440-0355 Office: Nash Finch Co 7600 France Ave S Edina MN 55435*

COVINGTON, ANN K., lawyer, former state supreme court justice; b. Fairmont, W.Va., Mar. 5, 1942; d. James R. and Elizabeth Ann (Hornor) Kettering; m. James E. Waddell, Aug. 17, 1963 (div. Aug. 1976); children: Mary Elizabeth Waddell, Paul Kettering Waddell; m. Joe E. Covington, May 14, 1977. BA, Duke U., 1963; JD, U. Mo., 1977. Bar: Mo. 1977, U.S. Dist. Ct. (we. dist.) Mo. 1977. Asst. atty. gen. State of Mo., Jefferson City, 1977-79; ptnr. Covington & Maier, Columbia, Mo., 1979-81, Butcher, Cline, Mallory & Covington, Columbia, Mo., 1981-87; justice Mo. Ct. Appeals (we. dist.), Kansas City, 1987-89, Mo. Supreme Ct., 1989—2001, chief justice, 1993-95; ptnr. Bryan Cave, St. Louis, 2001—. Bd. dirs. Mid Mo. Legal Services Corp., Columbia, 1983-87; chmn. Juvenile Justice Adv. Bd., Columbia, 1984-87. Bd. dirs. Ellis Fischel State Cancer Hosp., Columbia, 1982-83, Nat. Ctr. for State Cts., 1998—; chmn. Columbia Indsl. Revenue Bond Authority, 1984-87; trustee United Meth. Ch., Columbia, 1983-86, Am. Law Inst., 1998—. Recipient Citation of Merit, U. Mo. Law Sch., 1993, Faculty-Alumni award U. Mo., 1993; Coun. of State Govt. Toll fellow, 1988. Fellow Am. Bar Found.; mem. ABA (jud. adminstrv. divsn., mem. adv. com. on Evidence Rules, U.S. Cts.), Mo. Bar Assn., Boone County Bar Assn. (sec. 1981-82), Am. Law Inst., Acad. Mo. Squires, Order of Coif (hon.), Mortar Bd. (hon.), Phi Alpha Delta, Kappa Kappa Gamma. Office: Bryan Cave One Metropolitan Sq 211 N Broadway Ste 3600 Saint Louis MO 63102-2750

COVINGTON, EILEEN QUEEN, secondary school educator; b. Washington, May 25, 1946; d. Louis Edward and Evelyn (Travers) Q.; m. Norman Francis Covington; children: Norman, Marina, Deanna, Trena. BS, D.C. Tchrs. Coll., 1971; postgrad., George Washington U., 1978-81. Tchr., coach Evan Jr. High Sch., D.C. Pub. Schs., Washington, 1971, Woodrow Wilson H.S., Washington, 1971-95, chmn. phys. edn. dept., 1971-75, 77-81, 1984-87, athletic dir., 1988-95, Anacostia Sr. H.S., Washington, 1995—, chmn. dept. health and phys. edn., tchr. health/phys. edn., 1995—, swim coach, 1996, softball coach, 1996—, student activities dir., 1995. Cons. Coaches Assn., Washington, 1973-76; athletic dir. Woodrow Wilson H.S., 1988-95; pres. DCAA Athletic Dir. Assn., 1997—; sports chmn. in field. Named Coach of Yr., Ea. Bd. Ofcls., 1977, Nat. Coaches Assn. 2d Region, 1982, 86, Nat. Fedn. State H.S. Assns., 2000, Winningest Coach Washington Coaches Assn., 1982, Coach of Yr. U.S., 1986, Coach of Yr. Washington Post, 1987, Athletic Dir. of Yr., 1989, Volleyball All-Interhigh Coach, 1989; recipient Billie Jean King award Women Sports and Am. Fedn. Coaches, 1980-81, Disting. Women award D.C. Polit. Women Com., 1996, D.C. Women's Bd. Affiliated Chs., 1996; inducted into Nat. High Sch. Athletic Coaches Assn. Hall of Fame, 2000. Mem. NAFE, Nat. High Sch. Athletic Coaches Assn. (bd. dirs., named to Hall of Fame 2000, regional dir. region II), D.C. Coaches Assn. (3rd v.p., v.p. volleyball 1981-83, softball coach 1990, Athletic Dir. of Yr. 1992, pres. 1993-96, chmn. crew coun. 1994, Regional Softball Coach of the Yr. 1993, Coach of the Yr. in Volleyball and Softball 1993, Softball Coach of Yr. 1994, 95, Coach/Athletic Dir. of Yr. 1988), NIAAA and D.C. Coaches Assn. (named Athletic Dir. of Yr. 1998, mem. dir.), Assn. Health, Phys. Edn. Athletics, D.C. High Sch. Coaches Club, Women's Sports Found., DCIAA (pres. athletic dir. 1997—). Home: 7601 Ingrid Pl Landover MD 20785-4624 Office: Anacostia Sr HS 16 & R Sts SE Washington DC 20020 Office Phone: 202-698-2173. Personal E-mail: ecovin@hotmail.com.

COVINGTON, GEORGE MORSE, lawyer; b. Lake Forest, Ill., Oct. 4, 1942; s. William Slaughter and Elizabeth (Morse) C.; m. Shelagh Tait Hickey, Dec.28, 1966 (div. May 1995); children: Karen Morse, Jean Tait, Sarah Ingersoll Covington; m. Barbara Schilling Trentham, Dec. 19, 1998. AB, Yale U., 1964; JD, U. Chgo., 1967. Assoc. Gardner, Carton & Douglas, Chgo., 1970-75, ptnr., 1976-95; atty. pvt. practice, Lake Forest, Ill., 1995—. Lectr. in field. Contbr. articles to profl. jours. Active Grant Hosp. of Chgo., 1974-95, chmn. of bd. 1990-95; bd. dirs. Grant Healthcare Found., 1995—, chmn. 1999—2001; trustee Chgo. Acad. Sci., 1974-85, pres., 1980-82; trustee, chmn. Ill. chpt. Nature Conservancy, Chgo., 1974-88; bd. dirs. Latin Sch Chgo., 1979-80, Open Lands Project, Chgo., 1972-86, Chgo. Farmers, 1994-96; bd. dirs., sec. Lake Forest Open Lands Assn., 1984—; bd. dirs., sec., treas. Les Cheneaux Found., 1978—; bd. dirs. Student Conservation Assn., 1996-2005, vice chmn., 1999-2002, chmn., 2002-04; bd. dirs. Little Traverse Conservancy, 1998-2007; mem. Bd. Fire and Police Commrs., Village of Lake Bluff, Ill., 1991-2005. With U.S. Army, 1967-69. Mem. ABA, Ill. Bar Assn., Lake County Bar Assn., Chgo. Bar Assn., Univ. Club (bd. dirs. 1985-88), Commonwealth Club, Lawyers Club, Shoreacres (Lake Bluff, Ill.), Les Cheneaux Club (Cedarville, Mich.), Lambda Alpha. Office: 500 N Western Ave Ste 204 Lake Forest IL 60045-1955 Personal E-mail: gcovington@sbcglobal.net.

COVINGTON, JAMES EDWIN, government agency administrator, psychologist; b. Wadesboro, NC, June 26, 1943; s. James Edwin and Louise (Memory) C.; m. Linda Doreen Davis, May 31, 1971 (div. Feb. 1982); children: James Edwin III, Bradley Davis; m. Lisa Marie Rygleewicz, June 26, 2004. BA, Duke U., 1965; MSc, N.C. State U., 1977, PhD, 1981. Lic. psychologist, N.C. Commd. 2d lt. U.S. Army, 1967, advanced through grades to col., 1989, ret., 1992; spl. advisor for arms control and chem. demilitarization Dept. of Def. Washington, 1993—2001, chief Chem. Biol. Def. Divsn. Army Acquisition Office, 2001—. Psychol. cons., Alexandria, Va., 1992—; first prof. mil. sci. Duke U., Durham, N.C., 1983; primary planner for retrograde U.S. Chem. Weapons from Germany, 1990; del. 1st U.S. visit to former Soviet Chem. Weapons Sites in Russia, 1990; mem. U.S. delegation for negotiation of worldwide Chem. Weapons Conv., Geneva, 1992; advisor U.S. Delegation to Chem. Weapons Preparatory Commn., The Hague, 1993. Decorated Def. Superior Svc. medal, Purple Heart with oak leaf cluster, Bronze Star, Air Medal with 7 oak leaf clusters, Army Commendation Medal with valor device, 5 oak leaf clusters, others; decorated for heroism at Hamburger Hill, Vietnam, 1969. Mem. APA, Va. Psychol. Assn. Methodist. Avocations: history, music, exercise. Home: 5909 Dawes Ave Alexandria VA 22311-1116 Office: Office of Asst Sec of the Army Acquisition Logistics and Tech 2511 Jefferson Davis Hwy Arlington VA 22202-3926 Office Phone: 703-604-7270. Personal E-mail: nedcovington@aol.com. Business E-Mail: james.e.covington@us.army.mil.

COVINGTON, ROBERT NEWMAN, law educator; b. Evansville, Ind., Sept. 9, 1936; s. George Milburn and Roberta (Newman) C.; m. Paula Anne Hattox, July 29, 1972. BA, Yale U., 1958; JD, Vanderbilt U., 1961. Bar: Tenn. 1961. Asst. prof. law Vanderbilt U., Nashville, 1961-64, assoc. prof., 1964-69, prof., 1969—. Chair faculty senate Vanderbilt U., 1988-89; vis. prof. U. Mich., 1971, U. Calif., Davis, 1975-76, U. Tex., 1983; adminstrv. law officer Calif. Agrl. Labor Rels. Bd., 1975-76; cons. Tenn. Dept. Labor, 1972, Tenn. Law Libr. Commn., 1965-75. Author works in field. Mem. ABA, Tenn. Bar Assn., Am. Arbitration Assn., Tenn. Employment Rels. Rsch. Assn. (pres.-elect 2000-01, pres. 2001-02), Order of Coif, Univ. Club (Nashville), Phi Beta Kappa. Democrat. Episcopalian. Home: 907 Estes Rd Nashville TN 37215-1008 Office: Vanderbilt U Sch Law 21st Ave S Nashville TN 37203 Office Phone: 615-322-0036. Business E-Mail: robert.covington@law.vanderbilt.edu.

COVITZ, CARL D., investment company executive, federal and state official; b. Boston, Mar. 31, 1939; s. Edward E. and Barbara (Matthews) C.; m. Aviva Habert, May 15, 1970; children: Philip, Marc. BS, Wharton Sch., U. Pa., 1960; MBA, Columbia U., 1962. Product mgr. Bristol-Myers Co., NYC, 1962-66; dir. mktg. Rheingold Breweries, NYC, 1966-68; nat. mktg. mgr. Can. Dry Corp., NYC, 1968-70; v.p. mktg., dir. corp. devel. ITT/Levitt & Sons, Lake Success, NY, 1970-73; owner, pres. Landmark Communities, Inc., Beverly Hills, Calif., 1973-87, pres., 1989-91; dep. sec. HUD, Washington, 1987-89; sec. bus., transp. and housing State of Calif., Sacramento, 1991-93; pres. Landmark Capital, Inc. (formerly Landmark Communities, Inc.), 1993—; chmn. bd. Century Housing Corp., 1995-2000. Bd. dirs. Arden Realty Group, chmn. acquisition com., Molina Healthcare, Inc., 2002-03; chmn. bd. Fed. Home Loan Bank, San Francisco, 1989-91; trustee SunAmerica Annuities Funds, 2000—, Phoenix Kane Anderson Mut. Funds, 2000-05 Exec. com. Presl. Commn. Cost Control and Efficiency (Grace Commn.); co-chmn. Dept. Def. Task Force; past chmn. ops. com. Mus. Contemporary Art LA; chmn. LA County Delinquency and Crime Commn.; dir. Columbia U. Grad. Bus. Sch. Alumni Assn. Mem. Young Pres. Orgn.; chmn. LA Housing Authority Commn., 1989-91. Office: 9595 Wilshire Blvd Beverly Hills CA 90212-2512 Office Phone: 310-273-7320. Business E-Mail: cdc@landmarkcapital.com.

COVUCCI, GEORGE E., lawyer; b. Aug. 15, 1951; BA, CCNY, 1972; JD, Georgetown Univ., 1976. Bar: Va. 1976, D.C. 1977. Ptnr., Real Estate Practice Group Arnold & Porter LLP, Washington. Contbr. articles to profl. jours. Mem.: ABA, Va. State Bar, D.C. Bar. Office: Arnold & Porter LLP 555 Twelfth St NW Washington DC 20004-1206 Office Phone: 202-942-5026. Office Fax: 202-942-5999. Business E-Mail: george.covucci@aporter.com.

COWAN, ANDREW GLENN, television writer, producer, performer; b. Phila., Dec. 24, 1951; s. Raymond Harold and Audrey Rene (Federman) C. BA in Psychology, The Am. U., 1973; MS in Broadcasting, Boston U., 1975. News reporter, writer Sta. WLYH-TV, Lancaster, Pa., 1975; announcer, news reporter Sta. WHUM, Reading, Pa., 1975; comedy performer various clubs, nationwide, 1976-81; talent coord., writer, performer, segment prodr. The Merv Griffin Show, Paris, L.A., NYC, Atlantic City, and Las Vegas, 1981-86; freelance writer TV series Cheers Paramount, LA, 1985-87; host, writer L.A. Singles, Group W Cable, LA, 1985-86; freelance writer TV series Throb Taft Entertainment, LA, 1986; story editor TV series Take Five Imagine Entertainment, CBS, LA, 1987; freelance writer TV series Family Ties Paramount, LA, 1988; staff writer, performer The Pat Sajak Show, CBS, LA, 1988-90; staff writer Into the Night ABC, 1990; staff writer My Talk Show Second City Entertainment, 1990; freelance writer for Jay Leno The Tonight Show, NBC, LA, 1990; Walt Disney Prodns., 1991; creator, writer TV pilot Howie Republic Pictures, LA, 1991; staff writer TV pilot Only Human CBS Entertainment, 1991-92; freelance writer TV series Seinfeld Castle Rock Entertainment, LA, 1994, then program cons., 1994-95; story editor TV series Double Rush Shukovsky-English Entertainment, LA, 1994; exec. cons. TV series 3rd Rock from the Sun Carsey-Werner Co., LA, 1995-96; exec. prodr., co-creator, writer, host tv pilot Evening Stew, 1996-97; writer, tv pilot Barely Fitz, 1999, Outer Child, 2000, Howie, 2001; writer JackFM Radio Network, 2007. Vocalist various clubs and venues, L.A., 1987—; vocalist pilot theme song Life As We Know It, Second City Entertainment, 1990; voice-over announcer Aerospace Ednl. Svcs., L.A., 1985-89, Cutler Prodns., CBS Morning Zoo, L.A., 1990; host, writer, prodr., co-dir. video short Six Minutes, Showtime, The Movie Channel, Bravo, PBS, 1989-91. Voice-over actor Seinfeld, 1994, 3rd Rock from the Sun, 1995, Best Damn Sports show Period, 2002, Time-Warner Audio Books, Lucas Films, Star Wars-Dark Empire, The Audio Drama, 1994, Star Wars-Dark Empire 2, 1995; writer, co-host (on internet) Up & Down Guys, 2000; contbr. columns to mags., radio shows and cartoons; contbr. articles to profl. jours. Recipient CableAce award for best short-form programming spl., 1991; named one of 50 Creatives to Watch, Variety, 1996. Mem. AFTRA, Writers Guild Am. West. Avocations: cartooning, playing keyboards. *You're better off creating your own opportunities, rather than waiting for someone to create them for you. Ignore the naysayers. And if you listen to conventional wisdom, develop a serious case of amnesia afterwards.*

COWAN, BARRY W., lawyer; b. Tulia, Tex., Dec. 23, 1961; BA with honors in Mgmt. Info. Systems and Fin., Tex. Tech U., 1984; JD, South Tex. Coll. Law, 1988. Bar: Tex. 1988. Shareholder, chair Employee Benefits Practice Winstead, Sechrest & Minick, P.C., Dallas. Adj. prof. law, taxation of deferred compensation So. Meth. U. Sch. Law. Named a Tex. Super Lawyer, Tex. Monthly, 2003—06; named one of 40 Under 40, Tex. Lawyer, 2001, Best Lawyers in Dallas, D Mag., 2003, 2005, Top 200 Lawyers, Am. Lawyer, 2003, Best Lawyers in Am., 2007. Mem.: Nat. Assn. Stock Plan Profls., ABA, S.W. Benefits Assn., Tex. Bar Assn., Tarrant County Bar Assn., Dallas Bar Assn. (past chair Employee Benefits Sect.). Office: Winstead Sechrest & Minick PC 5400 Renaissance Tower 1201 Elm St Dallas TX 75270-2199 Office Phone: 214-745-5715. Office Fax: 214-745-5390. E-mail: bcowan@winstead.com.*

COWAN, BARTON ZALMAN, lawyer; b. Cleve., Mar. 3, 1934; s. Milton Jerome and Clara (Umans) Cowan; m. Teri Anne Thomas, June 25, 1961; children: Pamela B., Cynthia R. Stewart, Susan L. Kraft. BA (hon.), U. Mich., 1955; JD cum laude (hon.), Harvard U., 1958. Bar: Ohio 1958, Pa. 1962, U.S. Dist. Ct. (we. dist.) Pa., U.S. Ct. Appeals (3d, 4th, and DC cir.), U.S. Supreme Ct. Assoc. Eckert, Seamans, Cherin, and Mellott, Pitts., 1961—67; mem. Eckert, Seamans, Cherin, and Mellott, LLC, Pitts., 1968—99, sr. counsel, 2000—05, of counsel, 2006—. Chmn. lawyers com., mem. policy com. Atomic Indsl. Forum, Washington, 1981—87; chmn. lawyers com. Nuc. Mgmt. and Resource Coun., Washington, 1988—90; vis. prof. Coll. Law W. Va. U., 2001—. Pres. Hebrew Inst. Pitts., 1987—91; bd. dirs. Union for Reform Judaism, 2002—; life trustee, past pres., past chmn. Pitts. chpt. Am. Jewish Com.; life trustee, past pres. Rodef Shalom Congregation, Pitts.; mem. bd. of mgmt. Internat. Nuc. Law Assn., 2003—; mem. bd. overseers Hebrew Union Coll. Jewish Inst. Religion, 1986—2003, mem. bd. govs., 1992—2000; bd. dirs. ARZA World Union N.Am., 1998—. 1st lt. USAF, 1958—61. Recipient Clyde A. Lilly Award, Atomic Indsl. Forum, Inc., 1985, Leadership Award, Hebrew Inst. Pitts., 1991, Dedication and Commitment to Jewish Edn. Award, Jewish Edn. Inst., 1992, Am. Jewish Com. Human Rels. Award, 1996, Bonds Award, State of Israel, 2002. Fellow: Allegheny County Bar Found.; mem.: Pitts. Symphony Soc. (bd. dirs. 1992—2000, 2005—), ABA (chmn. energy resources law com. tort and ins. practice sect. 1986—87), Internat. Nuc. Law Assn., Allegheny County Bar Assn., Pa. Bar Assn., Duquesne Club. Republican. Office: Eckert Seamans Cherin and Mellott LLC 600 Grant St Ste 44th Pittsburgh PA 15219-2702 Home Phone: 412-682-5105. Personal E-mail: teribart61@aol.com. Business E-Mail: bcowan@eckertseamans.com.

COWAN, BRYAN D., medical educator, department chairman; b. Brush, Colo., Jan. 19, 1949; m. Harriette L. Hampton. MD, U. Colo. Sch. Medicine, Denver, 1971—75. Cert. Reproductive Endocrinology Sub-Specialty Am. Bd. Ob-Gyn., 1983. Prof., chmn. U. Miss. Med. Ctr., Jackson, 2002—06. Lt. comdr. USN, 1975—83. Office: Univ Miss Med Ctr 2500 N State St Jackson MS 39216-4505 Office Phone: 601-984-5300. Office Fax: 601-984-6904.

COWAN, DALE HARVEY, internist, lawyer; b. Cleve., Jan. 25, 1938; s. Milton Jerome and Clara (Umans) C.; m. Deborah Wolowitz, Jan. 28, 1967; children: Rachel, Morris Benjamin, William Ezra. AB, Harvard U., Cambridge, Mass., 1959, MD, 1963; JD, Case Western Res. U., Cleve., 1981. Diplomate Am. Bd. Internal Medicine with subspecialty cert. in hematology and med. oncology. Bar: Ohio 1981. Intern Cleve. Met. Gen. Hosp., 1963-64, resident, 1964-65, 67-70; practice medicine specializing in internal medicine, hematology and oncology; dir. hematology and oncology Marymount Hosp., Cleve., 1982-2001; asst. prof. medicine Case Western Res. U., Cleve., 1970-75, assoc. prof., 1975-84, clin. prof. environ. health scis., 1985—; assoc. Health Sys. Mgmt. Ctr., 1982-90; of counsel Burke, Haber & Berick, 1984-86; pres. med. staff Parma Cmty. Gen. Hosp., Ohio, 1997-98; med. dir. Cmty. Oncology Group Cleve. Clinic Found., Cleve., 1999—2006; dir. dept. regional oncology Cleve. Clinic Cancer Ctr., 2006—07. Spl. cons. President's Commn. on Bioethics, Washington, 1981-82; nat. adv. coun. Nat. Heart Lung and Blood Inst., Bethesda, Md., 1982-85. Author: Preferred Provider Organizations, 1984; co-editor: Human Organ Transplantation, 1987; contbr. articles to profl. jours. Bd. dirs. Bur. Jewish Edn., 1977-87, Northeast Ohio affiliate Am. Heart Assn., 1982-86; pres. Ohio/W.Va. Oncology Soc., 1990-94; trustee No. Ohio Cancer Resource Ctr., 1998-2001, chmn. 1999-2001. Lt. comdr. USPHS, 1965-67. Recipient David J. Greenburg Service Award, Am. Health Lawyers Assn., 1995. Fellow ACP, Am. Coll. Legal Medicine (bd. govs. 2001-07, sec., mem. exec. com., 2007—); mem. Am. Soc. Hematology, Am. Soc. Clin. Oncology, Am. Assn. Cancer Rsch., Am. Health Lawyers Assn. (bd. dirs. 1988-94), Am. Soc. Law and Medicine, Acad. Medicine Cleve. (pres. 1997-98), Cleve. Med. Libr. Assn. (pres. 2004-05), Greater Cleve. Bar Assn. Office: 6100 W Creek Rd Ste 15 Cleveland OH 44131-2133 Home: 6806 Hidden Lake Tr Brecksville OH 44141 Office Phone: 216-524-7979. Business E-Mail: cowand@ccf.org.

COWAN, DIANE, research scientist, educator; PhD, Boston U. Marine Program, 1992. Asst. prof. Bates Coll., 1992—94; founder, exec. dir., sr. scientist The Lobster Conservancy, Friendship, Maine, 1996—, also v.p. bd. dirs.; chief lobster biologist State Maine Dept. Marine Resources, 1998—99, leader, divsn. biol. monitoring for the lobster, shrimp, herring and urchin fisheries, 1998—99; marine policy fellow Woods Hole Oceanographic Institution, 1999—2000, sr. rsch. fellow, 2005. Prin. investigator Lobster Sonar Tracking Project and Juvenile Lobster Monitoring Program. Presdl. U. Grad. Fellow, Boston U. Marine Program, 1992. Office: The Lobster Conservancy PO Box 235 Friendship ME 04547 Office Phone: 207-832-8224. Business E-Mail: dcowan@lobsters.org.*

COWAN, EDWARD, journalist, editor; b. Bklyn., Nov. 14, 1933; s. Marcy Hamilton and Jennie (Taleisnik) C.; m. Ann Louise Wrubel, July 1, 1962; children: Jeffrey Wrubel, Emily Martha, Rachel Jennifer. BA, Columbia Coll., 1954; MA in Econs., Johns Hopkins U., 1960. With UPI, 1957-62; with N.Y. Times, 1962-86, banking reporter, 1963-65, Benelux corr. Brussels, 1965-66, corr. London bur., 1966-67, corr. Toronto (Can.) Bur., 1967-72, Washington corr., 1972-83, Washington econs. editor, 1983-86; Washington mgr. Ried, Thunberg and Co., Inc., 1986-99; assoc. editor Am. Enterprise Inst., 2000—02; pres. Editorial Svc., 2003—. Instr. econs. Johns Hopkins, 1956-57; cons. U.S. Bur. Budget, 1963, Nat. Inst. Standards and Tech. 2001, Congl. Budget Office, 2003, World Bank, 2004, Dawson Assocs., 2004—, Hudson Inst., 2006—; co-founder Chronicle, Barton, Vt., 1974; vol. tutor, D.C. Pub. Schs., 2000-03. Author: Oil and Water: The Torrey Canyon Disaster, 1968; contbr. to The Economist, 1977-90, op-ed pages Washington Post, Washington Times, L.A. Times, New Eng. Regional Rev., Jour. Commerce, Indonesnian Daily News, Jakarta Post, Milw. Jour. Sentinel, Edn. Week, Coos County (N.H.) Democrat, Littleton (N.H.) Courier, and Barton (Vt.) Chronicle. Dir. and treas. Anne Frank Ho., 1987—90; bd. dir. Cmty. Coun. Homeless, 2005—. With US Army, 1954—56. Fellow Knight Internat. Press; recipient Chanler Hist. Essay prize Columbia, 1954, Gerald R. Loeb Found. award for fin. reporting, 1971. Mem. Nat. Econs. Club (v.p. programs 1989-90, pres. 1990-91, chmn. 1991-93, bd. govs. 2003-05). Home: 3924 Harrison St NW Washington DC 20015

COWAN, ERIC WARD, lawyer; b. Boston, Nov. 26, 1957; s. Frederick S. and H. Ellen (Glazer) Cowan. BLS, Boston U., 1981; JD, Cath. U. Am., 1987. Bar: Pa. 1987, Mass. 1988, Md. 1989. Atty. State Mut. Cos., Worcester, Mass., 1987-88; assoc. Frank Bernstein Conaway & Goldman, Balt., 1988—; ptnr., bus. dept. Thelen Reid & Priest LLP, Washington. Bd. dir. Nat. Found. for Ileitis & Colitis, Boston, 1980—82. Mem.: ABA. Democrat. Jewish. Office: Thelen Reid And Priest Llp 701 8th St Nw Washington DC 20001-3721 Office Phone: 202-508-4309. Office Fax: 202-829-2284. Business E-Mail: ecowan@thelenreid.com.

COWAN, FAIRMAN CHAFFEE, lawyer; b. Wellesley Hills, Mass., Apr. 22, 1915; s. James Franklin and Hortense Victoria (Fairman) C.; m. Martha Logan Allis, Apr. 24, 1943; children: Douglas Fairman, Frederick Allis, Leonard Chaffee. AB magna cum laude, Amherst Coll., Mass., 1937; LLB, Harvard U., Cambridge, Mass., 1940; AMP, Harvard Bus. Sch., Cambridge, Mass., 1963. Bar: Mass. 1940. Assoc. Goodwin, Procter & Hoar, Boston, 1940-41, ptnr., 1952—54; gen. counsel, clk., sec., v.p., dir. Norton Co., 1955-79; counsel Bowditch & Dewey, Worcester, Mass., 1979-90. Mem. Citizen Plan E Assn. Worcester, 1957-87; vice chmn. Worcester Civic Ctr. Commn., 1977-79; chmn. Pvt. Industry Coun., Worcester Area CETA Consortium, 1979-83; bd. dirs. Legal Assistance Corp. of Ctr. Mass., 1982-86, Social Svc. Planning Corp., 1975-88, Worcester Mcpl. Rsch. Bur., Inc., 1986—, Mass. Job Tng. Inc., 1983-92, Elder Home Care Svcs. of Worcester, Inc., 1987-92, Daybreak, Inc., 1993-96; incorporator Alliance for Edn., 1986—2003, Worcester Dynamy, Inc., 1992—, Worcester YWCA, 2001—, Worcester Hist. Mus., 1995—, YOU, Inc., 1983—, ARC Ctrl. Mass., 2000—; mem. State Job Tng. Coordinating Coun., 1985-87, Worcester Housing Partnership, 1986-93; trustee Clark U., 1964-76, 79—, Meml. Hosp., Worcester, 1967-86, United Way Ctrl. Mass., 2000—; mem. bd. overseers Planned Parenthood League Mass., 1992-2001, mem. adv. bd. Mass. Coastal Resource Bd., 1992-2000. Lt. USNR, 1942-45. Co-recipient Worcester State Coll. Cmty. Svc. award; recipient Isaiah Thomas award, 1995, Great Guy award, Worcester YWCA, 2005, Good Guys award, Mass. Women's Polit. Caucus, 2007. Mem. Am. Antiquarian Soc., Mass. Civic League (v.p. 1947), Worcester Club, Worcester Com. on Fgn. Rels., Phi Beta Kappa, Alpha Delta Phi. Home: 48 Berwick St Worcester MA 01602-1443 Personal E-mail: fcowan1059@aol.com.

COWAN, FREDERIC JOSEPH, judge; b. NYC, Oct. 11, 1945; s. Frederic Joseph Sr. and Mary Virginia (Wesley) C.; m. Linda Marshall Scholle, Apr. 28, 1974; children: Elizabeth, Caroline, Allison. AB, Dartmouth Coll., 1967; JD, Harvard U., 1978. Bar: Ky. 1978, U.S. Dist. Ct. (we. dist.) Ky. 1979, U.S. Ct. Appeals (6th cir.) 1984, U.S. Supreme Ct. 1989. Vol. Peace Corps, Ethiopia, 1967-69; assoc. Brown, Todd & Heyburn, Louisville, 1979-83; ptnr. Rice, Porter, Seiller & Price, Louisville, 1983-87; atty. gen. Commonwealth of Ky., 1988-92; counsel Lynch, Cox, Gilman & Manan P.S.C., 1992—2006; judge Jefferson Cir. Ct., Ky., 2007—. Ky. State Rep., 32d legis. dist., 1982-87; chair Ky. Child Support Enforcement Commn., 1988-91, Ky. Sexual Abuse and Exploitation Prevention Bd., 1988-91; bd. dirs. Ky. Job Tng. Coordinating Coun., Frankfort, Louisville Bar Found., 1986; chmn. bd. dirs. The Family Pl., 2005-06. Vice chmn. judiciary criminal com. Ky. Ho. of Reps., 1985-87; chmn. budget com. on justice Judiciary and Corrections Ky. Ho. of Reps., 1985-87, Leadership Ky., 1985; U.S. del. election mission to Namibia Nat. Dem. Inst. for Internat. Affairs, 1989; U.S. del. dem. instns. seminar Nat. Dem. Inst. for Internat. Affairs, Slovenia, 1992; electoral supr. Orgn. for Security and Cooperation in Europe, Bosnia and Herzogovina, 1996; adv. com. Samara Oblast, Russia, 2001. Mem. ABA (adv. com. east european law initiative 2001), Ky. Bar Assn., Louisville Bar Assn., Ky. Acad. Trial Attys. Methodist. Home: 1747 Sulgrave Rd Louisville KY 40205-1643 Office: Jefferson Cir Ct Jud Ctr 700 W Jefferson St Louisville KY 40202 Office Phone: 502-595-3011.

COWAN, GEORGE ARTHUR, chemist, bank executive, director; b. Worcester, Mass., Feb. 15, 1920; s. Louis Abraham and Anna (Listic) C.; m. Helen Dunham, Sept. 7, 1946. BS, Worcester Poly. Inst., 1941, DSc (hon.), 2002; DSc, Carnegie-Mellon U., Pitts., 1950, DSc and Tech. (hon.), 2002; DHL (hon.), Coll. Santa Fe, N.Mex., 2003. Rsch. asst. Princeton U., 1941-42, U. Chgo., 1942-45; mem. staff Columbia U., NYC, 1945; mem. staff, dir. rsch., sr. fellow Los Alamos Sci. Lab., N.Mex., 1945-46, 49-88, sr. fellow emeritus, 1988—; tchg. fellow Carnegie Mellon U., Pitts., 1946-49. Chmn. bd. dirs. Trinity Capital Corp., Los Alamos, 1974-95; pres. Santa Fe Inst., 1984-91; mem. The White House Sci. Coun., Washington, 1982-85, cons., 1985-90, Air Force Tech. Applications Ctr., 1952-88; chmn. Los Alamos Nat. Bank, 1965-94, dir., 1995-2006, dir. emeritus, 2006—. Contbr. sci. articles to profl. jours. Bd. dirs. Santa Fe Opera, 1964-79; treas. Santa Fe Opera Found., 1970-79; regent N.Mex. Inst. Tech. Socorro, 1972-75; pres. The Delle Found.; bd. dirs. Adv. Bd. Ctr. Neural Basis Cognition, Carnegie-Mellon U. Recipient E.O. Lawrence award, 1965, Disting. Scientist award N.Mex. Acad. Sci., 1975, Robert H. Goddard award Worcester Poly. Inst., 1984, Enrico Fermi award, Presdl. Citation, Dept. Energy, 1990; disting. fellow Santa Fe Inst., Los Alamos Nat. Lab. medal, 2003. Fellow AAAS, Am. Phys. Soc., Am. Acad. Arts and Scis.; mem. Am. Chem. Soc., N.Mex. Acad. Sci., Sigma Xi. Avocations: skiing, fly fishing. Home: 721 42nd St Los Alamos NM 87544-1804 Office: Santa Fe Inst 1399 Hyde Park Rd Santa Fe NM 87501-8943 Business E-Mail: gac@santafe.edu.

COWAN, JOHN JAMES, physicist, astronomer, educator; b. Washington, Apr. 3, 1948; s. John Robert and Anna V. Cowan; m. Linda Elaine Demetry, May 24, 1971. BA, George Washington U., 1970; MS, Case Inst. Tech., 1972; PhD, U. Md., 1976. Postdoctoral fellow Harvard U., Cambridge, Mass., 1976—79; asst. prof. U. Okla., Norman, 1979—84, assoc. prof., 1984—89, prof. physics and astronomy, 1989—, S.R. Noble Presdl. prof., 1998—2002, David Ross Boyd prof., 2002—; rsch. fellow U. Tex., 2002. Mem. rev. panel NASA, Washington, 1987; vis. rsch. assoc. Harvard U., Cambridge, 1987—88; vis. prof. Columbia U., NYC, 1991—92; mem. com. visitors NSF, Washington, 2002; lectr. in field. Reviewer: Astrophys. Jour., 1976—; contbr. articles to profl. jours. Recipient Kinney-Sugg Outstanding Prof. award, U. Okla., 2004; grantee, NASA, 1994—, NSF, 1997—. Mem.: Am. Astron. Soc., Phi Beta Kappa. Achievements include co-discoverer of gold in one of the oldest stars in the universe. Avocations: racquetball, physical fitness. Office: Univ Okla 440 W Brooks St Norman OK 73019 Office Phone: 405-325-3961. Business E-Mail: cowan@nhn.ou.edu.

COWAN, JOYCE A., lawyer; BA in Polit. Sci. cum laude, U. Wash., 1983; JD with honors, George Washington U., 1986. Ptnr. Epstein Becker & Green, Washington, Sonnenschein Nath & Rosenthal LLP, Washington, 2004—. Mem.: ABA (mem. health law sect.), Am. Health Lawyers Assn. Office: Sonnenschein Nath & Rosenthal LLP Ste 600, E Tower 1301 K St NW Washington DC 20005 Office Phone: 202-408-3239. Office Fax: 202-408-6399. Business E-Mail: jcowan@sonnenschein.com.

COWAN, KEITH O., telecommunications industry executive; b. Hartford, Conn., 1956; BA, Univ. NC, Chapel Hill, 1978; JD, U. Va., 1982. Atty. Alston & Bird, 1982—90, ptnr., 1990—96; from exec. officer to pres. mktg. and product mgmt. BellSouth Corp., Atlanta, 1996—2005, pres. mktg. and product devel., 2005—07; exec. v.p. Genuine Parts Co., 2007; pres. strategic planning, corp. initiatives & new product develop. Sprint Nextel, Reston, Va., 2007—. Former mem. adminstrv. com., chmn. securities practice group, chmn. continuing legal edn. com. Alston & Bird; bd. dirs. Atlanta Landmarks, Inc. Mem. bd. dirs. Metro Atlanta YMCA, VSA Arts of Ga. Mem.: Atlanta Bar Assn. (former bd. dirs., chmn. bus. and fin. law sect., chmn. continuing legal edn. com.). Office: Sprint Nextel 20001 Edmund Halley Dr Reston VA 20191*

COWAN, MARIE JEANETTE, dean, nurse, educator; b. Albuquerque, July 20, 1938; d. Adrian Joseph and Leila Bernice (Finley) Johnson; m. Samuel Joseph Cowan, Aug. 14, 1961; children: Samuel Joseph, Kathryn Anne, Michelle Dionne. Diploma, Mary's Help Coll., 1961; BS, U. Wash., 1964, MS, 1972, PhD, 1979. Charge nurse Herrick Meml. Hosp., Berkeley, Calif., 1961-62; staff nurse ICU Univ. Hosp., Seattle, 1966-68; asst. prof. Seattle U., 1972-75; from asst. prof. to prof. nursing U. Wash., Seattle, 1979-97, assoc. dean rsch., 1985-96; dean UCLA Sch. Nursing, 1997—. Rsch. grant reviewer Am. Heart Assn. Wash., Seattle, 1977-82, divsn. rsch. grants reviewer nursing study sect., 1987-90; chair CVN AHA, 1989-91. Mem. editl. bd. Am. Rev. Nursing Rsch., Rsch. in Nursing and Health, Nursing Rsch.; contbr. articles to profl. jours. Grantee, NIH, 1977, 1981, 1984, 1985, 1991, 1996, 2000. Fellow: Am. Acad. Nursing; mem.: ANA, AACN, Wash. State Nurses Assn., Calif. State Nurses Assn. Roman Catholic. Office: UCLA Sch Nursing PO Box 951702 Los Angeles CA 90095-1702

COWAN, RACHEL, rabbi; m. Paul Cowan (dec.); 2 children. Grad., Hebrew Union Coll.-Jewish Inst. Religion. Cert. ordained Rabbi Hebrew Union Coll.-Jewish Inst. Religion, 1989. Program dir., Jewish Life Nathan Cummings Found., 1990—2003; dir. outreach 92nd St YMHA; dir. Inst. Jewish Spirituality. Bd. dir. Synagogue 3000. Named one of The Top 50 Rabbis in America, Newsweek Mag., 2007. Office: The Inst Jewish Spirituality Ste 1401 330 7th Ave New York NY 10001 Office Phone: 212-774-3608.*

COWAN, ROBERT RANDALL, science educator; s. Robert B. and Yoland V. Cowan; m. Donna R. McBrian, June 20, 1970; children: Jeffrey S., Christa M. BA in Biology, So. Ill. U., 1970, MS, 1976. Cert. tchr. secondary edn. Ill., 1972, athletic adminstr. Nat. Interscholastic Athletic Adminstrs. Assn., 2002, in gen. adminstrn. Ill., 2004. Sci. tchr. Madison Jr. HS, Ill., 1971—72; math tchr. Ctrl. Jr. HS, Granite City, 1972—73;

baseball, football coach Granite City HS, 1972—85, sci. club sponsor, 1973—78, biology, sci. tchr., 1973—85, anatomy, physiology tchr., 1993, asst. athletic dir., 1993, sci. dept. chmn., 1996; biology, anatomy, health instr. Southwestern Ill. Coll., Belleville, GraniteCity, Ill., 1985—93. Bd. mem. Granite City Sports Hall of Fame, 2000. Mem.: Ill. Fedn. Tchrs. (assoc.; bldg. rep.), Nat. Interscholastic Athletic Adminstrs. Assn. (assoc.), Ill. Athletic Dirs. Assn. (assoc.; state conf. com. chmn., exec. bd. mem. 1999—), Nat. Assn. Biology Tchrs. (assoc.). Office: Granite City HS 3101 Madison Ave Granite City IL 62040 Home Phone: 636-441-9532; Office Phone: 618-451-5808 ext. 2522. Office Fax: 618-451-6296.

COWAN, STUART MARSHALL, lawyer; b. Irvington, NJ, Mar. 20, 1932; s. Bernard Howard and Blanche (Hertz) C.; m. Marilyn R.C. Toepfer, Apr., 1961 (div. 1968); m. Eleanor Schmerel, June, 1953 (dec.); m. Jane Alison Averill, Feb. 24, 1974 (div. 1989); children: Fran Lori, Robin L., Michael L., Catherine R.L., Erika R.L., Bronwen P.; m. Victoria Yi, Nov. 11, 1989. BS in Econs., U. Pa., 1952; LLB, Rutgers U., 1955. Bar: N.J. 1957, Hawaii 1962, U.S. Supreme Ct. 1966. Atty. Greenstein & Cowan, Honolulu, 1961—70; counsel Cowan & Frey, Honolulu, 1970—89; pvt. practice, 1989—; of counsel Price Okamoto Himeno & Lum, 1993—. Arbitrator Fed. Mediation & Conciliation Svc., Honolulu, 1972—, Am. Arbitration Assn., Honolulu, 1968—, Hawaii Pub. Employee Rels. Bd., 1972—. Pres. Hawaii Epilepsy Soc., 1984-86, 2004—; acquisition chair Hawaii Family Support Ctr., 1995-97; bd. dirs. Hawaii Epilepsy Found. Lt. USN, 1955-61. Mem. ABA, ATLA (state committeeman for Hawaii 1965-69, bd. gov. 1972-78), Hawaii Bar Assn., Am. Judicature Soc., Consumer Lawyers Hawaii, Hawaii Trial Lawyers Assn. (v.p. 1972-78), Japan-Hawaii Lawyers Assn., Soc. Profls. in Dispute Resolution, Inter Pacific Bar Assn., Honolulu Symphony Soc. (bd. dirs. 1989-99), Royal Order of Kamehameha, Order of St. Stanislas, Sovereign Order of St. John of Jerusalem Knights Hospitallers, Mil. Order of Temple at Jerusalem, Queen's Club, Mil. Order of World Wars, Waikiki Yacht Club, St. Francis Yacht Club, Royal Hawaiian Ocean Racing Club, Hawaii Scottish Assn. (chieftain 1983-88), St. Andrews Soc., Caledonian Soc. (vice chieftain 1983-85), Honolulu Pipes and Drums (sec. treas. 1985-90), Celtic Pipes and Drums Honolulu, New Zealand Police Pipe Band, Masons (York Rite, Scottish Rite No. and So. jurisdictions), 33d deg., Aloha Shrine, Salaam Shrine, Grand Lodge Hawaii (grand orator 1992, 2007, sr. grand steward 1993, jr. grand warden 1994, sr. Grand Warden 1995 grand Master 1997), Red Cross of Constantine, Royal Order Scotland, Pearl Harbor (master 1971, 2001-04), Lodge Progres de l'Oceanie, Masonic Kilties NJ, Azure-Masada (#51 NJ), USS Missouri Meml. Assn., Nat. Sojourners (pres. 2005—06), Chinese Acacia Club, Royal Hawaiian Ocean Racing Club. US Coast Guard Aux., Navy League of U.S. (nat. dir. 2004-07). Jewish. Home: 47-339 Mapumapu Rd Kaneohe HI 96744-4922 Office: Ste 728 Ocean View Ctr 707 Richards St Honolulu HI 96813-4616 also: 47-653 Kamehameha Hwy # 202 Kaneohe HI 96744-4965 Office Phone: 848-538-1113. Personal E-mail: stuartgm@juno.com.

COWAN, WALLACE EDGAR, retired lawyer; b. Jersey City, Jan. 28, 1924; s. Benjamin and Dorothy (Zunz) C.; m. Ruth Daitzman, June 8, 1947; children: Laurie, Paul, Judith. BS magna cum laude, NYU, 1947; JD cum laude, Harvard U., 1950. Ptnr. Stroock, Stroock & Lavan, NYC, 1950—93; ret., 1993. Dir. Ametek, Inc., Paoli, Pa., 1982-93, sec., 1969-93, sec. H.S. Stuttman, Inc., Westport, Conn., to 1996; adv. bd. Hackensack River Greenway, Teaneck, NJ. Mem. Teaneck Adv. Bd. on Parks, Playgrounds and Recreation, 1966—2006, chmn., 1974-06, vice chmn., 2005—; pres. No. Valley Commuters Assn.; past pres., life trustee Congregation Beth Sholom, Teaneck; forum adv. bd. Sch.-Based Youth Svcs. Project, 1998-2003. 1st lt. USAF, 1942-45, ETO. Decorated Air medal with silver cluster; recipient Vol. in the Parks award Bergen County, N.J., 1993, Disting. Svc. award Bergen County, N.J., 1994, Disting. Achievement award Bergen County, N.J., 2001. Mem. Beta Gamma Sigma. Home: 499 Emerson Ave Teaneck NJ 07666-1927

COWART, JAMES D., psychologist; b. Dallas, Dec. 24, 1944; s. Marlin Young Cowart and Jessie Ruth McGlothlin; m. Lynne Eve Frankel, Nov. 21, 1967; children: Jason Samuel, Emily Sung Eun. BS, East Tex. State U., Commerce, 1967; MSW, U. Mich., Ann Arbor, 1972; PhD, Western Mich. U., Kalamazoo, 1982. Lic. psychologist Mich.; LCSW Mich. Sch. social worker Kalamazoo Regional Ednl. Svc. Agy., 1973—84; sr. therapist mental health Health Cir., Kalamazoo, 1984—85, dir. mental health, 1985—87; mgr. Delano Southside Clinic, Borgess Med. Ctr., Kalamazoo, 1987—90; dir. Delano Outpatient Clinic, Borgess Med. Ctr., Kalamazoo, 1990—2000; clinical psychologist Pvt. Practice, Portage, Mich., 2000—. Pres. Profl. Consultants Clinicians, Kalamazoo, 2006—. Co-author: (audiotape package) Guided Instruction for Coping with Anxiety and Stress, 1996. Vol. VISTA, Kettleman City, Calif., 1967—68; donor Save the Children, 1990—. Mem.: Assn. Behavioral and Cognitive Therapies. Democrat. Avocations: sailing, birdwatching, horseracing, theater, reading. Office: 5100 Lovers Ln Portage MI 49002

COWART, RICHARD G., lawyer; b. Bourne, Mass., 1954; BSBA magna cum laude, Univ. Southern Miss., 1975; JD with honors, Univ. Miss., 1978. Ptnr., chmn. health law pub. policy dept. Baker Donelson Bearman Caldwell & Berkowitz PC, Nashville. Articles editor Miss. Law Jour., 1977—78, health law columnist Medical News Inc. Mem.: ABA, Miss. Bar, Tenn. Bar Assn., Am. Health Lawyers Assn. (pres. 2004—05, bd. dir.), Phi Delta Phi, Omicrom Delta Kappa, Phi Kappa Phi. Office: Baker Donelson Bearman PC Commerce Ctr Ste 1000 211 Commerce St Nashville TN 37201 Office Fax: 615-726-5660. Business E-Mail: dcowart@bakerdonelson.com.

COWART, T(HOMAS) DAVID, lawyer; b. San Benito, Tex., June 12, 1953; s. Thomas W. Jr. and Glenda Claire (Miller) C.; children: Thomas Kevin, Lauren Michelle, Megan Leigh; m. Greta E. Gerberding, Aug. 12, 1995. BBA, U. Miss., 1975, JD, 1978; LLM in Taxation, NYU, 1979. CPA Tex., Miss.; bar: Miss. 1978, Tex. 1979. Assoc. Dossett, Magruder & Montgomery, Jackson, Miss., 1978; ptnr., assoc. Strasburger & Price, Dallas, 1979-87; shareholder Johnson & Gibbs, Dallas, 1988-90, Jenkens & Gilchrist, Dallas, 1991—2007, Sonnenschein Nath & Rosenthal, Dallas, 2007—. Adj. prof. law So. Meth. U. Sch. Law, 1988; mem. key dist. adv. coun. IRS, Dallas, 1989—95, chmn., 1990—93; mem. Coll. State Bar Tex.; lectr. in field. Mem. editl. bd.: Flexible Benefits, 1993—, 401k Advisor, 1994—, COBRA, 1996—. Mem. adv. com. Goals for Dallas, 1984-85; vol. Children's Med. Ctr., 1992-96. Named Best Lawyer in Am., 2001—06, Best Lawyer in Dallas, 2003—07, Tex. Super Lawyer, 2003—07; recipient Best Lawyer award, Corp. Coun., 2003. Mem.: ABA (health care task force 1991—98, sect. 83 issues task force, chmn. health plan designs issues subcom. 1992—95, sect. taxation, employee benefit com., vice-chmn. 1995—98, chmn.-designate joint com. on employee benefits 1997—98, chmn. 1998—99, chmn. joint com. employee benefits 1999—2000), Dallas Bar Found., Am. Law Inst., Phi Alpha Phi, Dallas Benefits Soc. (co-moderator 1991—92, bd. dirs. 1991—93), S.W. Benefits Assn. (bd. dirs. 1994—97), Dallas Bar Assn. (lectr. 1985—, coun. mem. employee benefits sect. 1989—92, treas. 1992, sec. 1993, v.p. 1994, pres. 1995), State Bar Tex. (fed. legislation, regulations and revenue rulings subcom. 1986—87, chmn. fiduciary stds. for trustees subcom. 1987—88, sect. taxation, com. compensation and employee benefits), Am. Coll. Employee Benefits Counsel (bd. govs. 2000—, 1st chair, charter mem.), Beta Alpha Psi, Omicron Delta Kappa. Office: Sonnenschein Nath & Rosenthal LLP 1717 Main St Ste 3400 Dallas TX 75201-7395 Office Phone: 214-259-0906. Business E-Mail: dcowart@sonnenschein.com.

COWELL, SIMON, television personality, music producer; b. London, Oct. 7, 1959; s. Eric and Julie Cowell. Mail room clerk EMI Music Pub., with, 1977—82; founder, co-owner Fanfare Records, 1982—89; A&R cons. BMG records, London, 1989—; founder, co-owner S Records, 2001—03. Judge (TV series) Pop Idol, 2001—02, American Idol, 2002—; exec. prodr.: (TV series) Cupid, 2003; exec. prodr.: (TV series) America's Got Talent, 2006—; prodr.: (albums) Sonia, 1991, Robson & Jerome, 1995, 5ive: The Album (5ive), 1998, Invincible, (5ive), 1999, Westlife, 1999, Coast to Coast (Westlife), 2000, World of Our Own (Westlife), 2001;, prodr. many others; guest appearance (film) Scary Movie 3, 2003; author: I Don't Mean to Be Rude, But.:Backstage Gossip from American Idol & the Secrets that Can Make You A Star, 2003. Named one of 100 Most Powerful Celebrities, Forbes.com, 2007. Office: BMG Records UK Ltd BMG Enterprises Bedford house 69-79 Fulham High St London SW6 3JW England Office Phone: 020 7384 7520. Office Fax: 020 7371 8987.*

COWEN, CARL C., mathematics professor; b. Madison, Ind., Nov. 15, 1945; s. Carl and Janet Catherine (Craig) C.; m. Janice Ann Wheater, Aug. 15, 1970; children: Carol, Craig. AB, Ind. U., 1967, MA, 1971; PhD, U. Calif., Berkeley, 1976; postgrad., U. Warwick, Coventry, Eng., 1967-68. Instr. math. Ind. U., Richmond, 1969-72; vis. asst. prof. U. Ill., Urbana, 1976-78; prof. math. Purdue U., W. Lafayette, Ind., 1978—2004; prof. Ind. U. Purdue U. Ind., 2004—. Dean Sch. Sci. Ind. U. Purdue U. Ind., 2004—06. Contbr. articles to profl. jours. Co-chair Ind. Resolve, Lafayette, 1980-82. Mem. Am. Math. Soc., Math. Assn. Am. (chair Ind. sect. 1989-90, pres. 2006-07). Avocation: hiking. Home: 707 Crestview Pl West Lafayette IN 47906-2313 Office: IUPUI Dept Math 402 N Blackford Indianapolis IN 46202 Office Phone: 317-278-8846. Business E-Mail: ccowen@iupui.edu.

COWEN, EDWARD S., lawyer, consultant; b. NYC, Mar. 3, 1936; s. Michael and Edith (Cohen) C.; m. Lesley J. Hoffman, Nov. 16, 1958; children: Adrienne Zammiello, Justine Bons. BS, Syracuse U., 1957; JD, NYU, 1961. Bar: NY 1962, US Dist. Ct. (so. dist.) NY 1965, US Dist. Ct. (ea. dist.) NY 1979, US Ct. Appeals (2d cir.) 1965, US Supreme Ct. 1967. Law clk. to judge U.S. Dist. Ct. (so. dist.) N.Y., 1961-62; ptnr. Seligson & Morris, NYC, 1963-69, Robinson, Silverman, Pearce, Aronsohn & Berman, NYC, 1975-90, Kirkland & Ellis, NYC, 1991-96; of counsel Pillsbury Winthrop, LLP, NYC, 1996—2001. Cons. Poorman-Douglas Corp., 2002—; mem. faculty Practicing Law Inst. Author: Bankruptcy in Joint Venture Partnerships, Practicing Law Institute, 1985, Enforcing Liens Postpetition, Bankruptcy Strategist, 1998. With USAF, 1958. Named Honoree Lawyer of Yr. Fedn. NY Lawyers Divsn. Mem. ABA, NY State Bar Assn., Assn. Bar City NY (chmn. bankruptcy and corp. reorganization). Office: 1400 S Ocean Blvd Boca Raton FL 33432 Office Phone: 212-628-6500. Personal E-mail: ecowen@verizon.net.

COWEN, EUGENE SHERMAN, broadcast executive; b. NYC, May 2, 1925; s. Jacob M. and Shirley (Sherman) C.; m. Phyllis L. Wallach, Jan. 29, 1948; children: James Sherman, Stephanie Jane. BA magna cum laude, Syracuse U., 1949, MA, 1954. Reporter Syracuse Herald-Jour., 1948-52, Newhouse News Bur., Washington, 1952-53; press sec. Rep. Frances P. Bolton, Washington, 1953-56; info. officer HEW, Washington, 1956-58; v.p. Standard Pub. Rels., Washington, 1958-59; chief staff Senator Hugh Scott, 1959-69; spl. asst., dep. asst. to pres. White House, 1969-71; v.p.-Washington Capital Cities/ABC, Inc., 1971-90; cons. in field Washington, 1990—. Author: (book) My Life, A Novel, 2003. Legis. affairs dir. Svc. Corps Ret. Execs. With USAAF, 1943-46. Decorated Air medal. Mem. Phi Beta Kappa. Home: 8100 Connecticut Ave Apt 809 Chevy Chase MD 20815-2816

COWEN, JOHN EDWIN, education educator; b. Jersey City , Sept. 3, 1940; s. John E. Cowen Sr. and Edna May O'Donnell; m. Jay Totten Miesegaes, June 28, 1964; children: Jill Totten, Juliet Totten. Student, St. Peter's Coll., 1962; MA, N.J. City U., 1965; profl. diploma, Columbia U., 1971, EdD, 1973. 8th grade lang. arts and reading tchr. Pinellas Park Jr. H.S., Fla., 1962-63; lang. arts, speech and drama tchr. Benjamin Franklin Jr. H.S., 1963-65; instr. directed studies dept. St. Petersburg Jr. Coll., Fla., 1966-67; English tchr. Teaneck (N.J.) H.S., 1967-71; project dir., spl. edn. tchr. comms. workshop Teaneck Bd. Edn., 1971-84, asst. supt. curriculum and instrn., 1984-95; assoc. prof. reading and edn. Peter Sammartino Sch. Edn. Fairleigh Dickinson U., Teaneck and Madison, NJ, 1995—. Coord. N.J. State reading specialist cert. program, grad. elem. edn. MA in Tchg. program, 1995—; adj. prof. U. South Fla., 1967, N.J. City U., 1968-69, William Paterson U., 1974, Fairleigh Dickinson U., 1980-82; reading instr. NYU Reading Inst., 1965-73; pub., mng. editor Bravo—The Poet's Mag., 1980-97, pub., editor, 1998—; judge Teaneck Poetry Anthology, 1983. Author: (non-fiction) Human Reading Strategies that Work, 1979, English Teacher's Portfolio of Multicultural Activities, 1996, A Balanced Approach to Beginning Reading Instruction: A Synthesis of Six Major U.S. Research Studies, 2003; co-author (with V. Cohen): (nonfiction) Literacy for Children in an Information Age: Teaching Reading, Writing, and Thinking, 2007; editor: (non-fiction) Teaching Reading Through the Arts, 1980, (poetry) José Garcia Villa's Parlement of Giraffes-Poems for Children Eight to Eighty; editor: (pub.) Introducing Mr. Vanderborg, 1977, Appassionata-Poems in Praise of Love by José Garcia Villa, 1977; co-editor: (non-fiction) The Anchored Angel-Selected Writings by José Garcia Villa, 1999; editl. adv. bd. (jour.) Jour. Reading, 1986—88; editor (editor-in-chief): (jour.) Reading Instn. Jour., 1980—83; contbr. numerous poems and essays to profl. jours., lit. mags., anth. Lit. trustee Estate of Jose Garcia Villa, 1997—. Recipient Nat. Validation award Nat. Dept. Edn. Nat. Diffusion Network, 1978, 1st prize for poem Parnassus Lit. Jour., 1993, Outstanding Tchr. award Fairleigh Dickinson U., 2004-2005. Mem. ASCD, N.J. ASCD, UN Soc. Writers, Acad. Am. Poets, E.E. Cummings Soc., Am. Lit. Assn., Bergen County Poets, Internat. Reading Assn. (Best Received World Congress Presenter award 1980), N.J. Reading Assn. (pres. 1984-85, Spl. Svc. award 1985, Pres.' award for spl. svc. 1984, Citation of Membership Prestigious Pres.' Club 1985), Nat. Coun. Tchrs. English, Assn. Tchr. Educators. Office: Fairleigh Dickinson U 1000 River St T-BH 2-01 Teaneck NJ 07666 Office Phone: 201-692-2000. Business E-Mail: cowtra@aol.com.

COWEN, ROBERT E., federal judge; b. Newark, Sept. 4, 1930; s. Saul and Lillie (Selzer) C.; m. Toby Cowen, Dec. 21, 1973; children: Shulie, Eve. BS, Drake U., 1952; LLB, Rutgers U., 1958. Bar: NJ. Assoc. Schreiber, Lancaster & Demos, Newark, 1959—70; asst. prosecutor Essex County, NJ, 1970—71; dep. atty. gen. organized crime Criminal Justice Dept., NJ, 1971—73; dir. Div. Ethics and Profl. Svcs. Adminstrv. Office of Courts, NJ, 1973—78; magistrate US Dist. Ct. NJ, Newark, 1978-85, judge Trenton, 1985-87, US Ct. Appeals (3d cir.), Trenton, 1987-98, sr. judge, 1998—. Pvt. practice, Newark, 1961-69. Office: US Courthouse Rm 207 402 E State St Trenton NJ 08608-1507*

COWEN, ROY CHADWELL, JR., language educator; b. Kansas City, Mo., Aug. 2, 1930; s. Roy Chadwell and Mildred Frances (Schuetz) Cowen; m. Hildegard Bredemeier, Oct. 6, 1956 (dec.); 1 child, Ernst Werner (dec.). BA, Yale U., 1952; PhD, U. Gottingen, Federal Republic of Germany, 1960. Instr. U. Mich., Ann Arbor, 1960-64, asst. prof., 1964-67, assoc. prof., 1967-71, prof., 1971—, chmn. dept. Germanic langs., 1979-85. Author: (book) Christian Dietrich Grabbe, 1972, Naturalismus Kommentar zu einer Epoche, 1973, Hauptmann Kommentar zum dramatischen Werk, 1981, Poetischer Realismus: Kommentar zu einer Epoche, 1985, Das deutsche Drama im 19. Jahrhundert, 1988, Christian Dietrich Grabbe-Dramatiker ungeloester Widersprueche, 1998. With USN, 1952—56. Decorated Sr. Officer's Cross Federal Republic of Germany; recipient Williams Tchg. award, U. Mich., 1967; fellow Sr., NEH, 1972—73. Mem.: MLA, Internationale Vereinigung fur Germanistik. Democrat. Methodist. Home: 2874 Baylis Dr Ann Arbor MI 48108-1764 Office: U Mich Dept Germanic Langs/Lits Ann Arbor MI 48109 Business E-Mail: rcowen@umich.edu.

COWEN, SCOTT S., academic administrator; m. Marjorie Cowen; 4 children. BS, U. Conn., 1968; MBA, George Washington U., 1972, DBA in Fin., 1975. Asst. prof. mgmt. Bucknell U., 1974—76; faculty Case Western Res. U., Cleve., 1976—98, dean, Albert J. Weatherhead III prof. mgmt., 1984—98; Seymour S Goodman Meml. prof. bus. A.B. Freeman Sch. Bus. Tulane U., 1998—, prof. econs. Faculty of Liberal Arts and Scis., 1998—, pres., 1998—. Eleanor F. and Philip G. Rust vis. prof. Colgate Darden Grad. Sch. Bus. Adminstrn., U. Va., 1982—83; bd. dirs. Newell Rubbermaid, Inc., Am. Greetings Corp., Jo-Ann Stores, Inc., Forest City Ent., Inc.; cons. in field. Co-author: Introduction to Business: Concepts and Applications, 1981, Information Requirements of Corporate Boards of Directors, 1983, Accounting Today: Principles and Applications, Innovation in Professional Education: Steps on a Journey From Teaching to Learning, 1995; contbr. articles to profl. jours. Bd. dirs. New Orleans Bus. Coun., Com. for a Better New Orleans, New Orleans Bldg. Corp. With US Army, 1968—71. Co-recipient award of Achievement in Edn., No. Ohio Live Mag., 1991; named Disting. Alumni, George Washington U., 1998—99; named to, Sch. Bus. Adminstrn. Hall of Fame U. Conn.; recipient Torch of Learning, Hebrew U., Torch of Liberty, Anti-Defamation League, Leadership Cleve. award, Greater Cleve. Growth Assn., 1987—88; fellow, Ernst & Whitney, Cleve., 1978, 1979. Mem.: Nat. Assn. Ind. Colls. and Univs., Am. Coun. Edn. (bd. dirs.), Am. Assembly of Collegiate Schs. Bus. (pres.). Office: Tulane University Tech Srvcs 1555 Poydras St Ste 1400 New Orleans LA 70112-5406 Office Phone: 504-865-5210. Office Fax: 504-865-5202. Business E-Mail: scowen@tulane.edu.

COWEN, TYLER, economics professor; b. Jan. 21, 1962; BS Econ., George Mason U., 1983; PhD. Econ., Harvard U., 1987. Asst., assoc. prof. econ. U. Calif., Irvine, 1987—89; prof. econ. George Mason U., 1989—, Holbert C. Harris Chair of Economics, 2000—. Gen. dir. Mercatus Ctr., 1998—, James M. Buchanan Ctr. for Polit. Econ., 1998—; co-owner Marginal Revolution Economics Blog. Editor: (novels) The Theory of Market Failure: A Critical Examination, 1988, Public Goods and Market Failures: A Critical Examination, 1991; co-author Explorations in the New Monetary Economics, 1994; author Risk and Bus. Cycles: New and Old Austrian Perspectives, 1998, co-editor So. Econ. Jour.; author: (novels) In Praise of Commercial Culture, 1998; editor Econ. Welfare, 2000; author What Price Fame?, 2000; co-editor New Theories of Market Failure, 2002; author Creative Destruction: How Globalization is Changing the World's Cultures, 2002, Markets and Culture Voices:Liberty vs. Power in the Lives of the Mexican Amate Painters, 2005, Good & Plenty: The Creative Successes of American Arts Funding, 2006; contbr. articles to profl. jours.; author: (novels) Discover Your Inner Economist: Use Incentives to Fall in Love, Survive Your Next Meeting, and Motivate Your Dentist, 2007; contbr. articles Economic Scene column, NY Times. Office: James M Buchanan Ctr George Mason U MSN 1D3 Carow Hall Fairfax VA 22030 Office Phone: 703-993-2312. Office Fax: 703-993-4910. E-mail: tcowen@gmu.edu.*

COWGER, GARY L., automotive executive; b. Kansas City, Kans., 1947; m. Kay Cowger; 2 children. BS in Industrial Engring., General Motors Inst., 1970; MS in Mngmnt., MIT, 1978. Plant superintendent General Motors Corp., Kansas City, variety of engring. & mfr. positions, 1965—79, general superintendent Oldsmobile Division Lansing, Mich., 1979—80, production manager GM Assembly Division St. Louis, 1981—82, plant manager GM Assembly Division Wentzville, Mo., 1982—85, complex manager Lordstown Assembly facilities, 1985—87, mfr. mgr. Cadillac Motor div., 1987—90, exec. dir. adv. mfr. engring. GM Tech. Ctr. Warren, Mich., 1990—92, exec.-in-charge NAO Mfr. Ctr., 1993, pres. & mng. dir. Mexico div., 1994—98, v.p., 1994—; v.p. mfr. General Motors Europe, 1998; chmn. & mng. dir. Adam Opel AG, 1998; v.p. & group exec. Labor Relations, N.A. Internal Comm. General Motors Corp., 1998—2001, v.p. mfr. & labor relations, 2001, pres. General Motors N. Am., 2001—05. Co-chmn. fin. com. Mo. Gov.'s Com. on Sci. Tech. Vice chmn. bd. mgrs. St. Charles YMCA. bd. dirs. Mo. C. of C.; exec. com. St. Louis Regional Commerce and Growth Assn.; Gov.'s Hawthorn Found.; bd. dirs. Career Productivity Inst. of Lindenwood Coll., Mo. Incu Tech. Found.; adv. bd. dirs. St. Charles County Council of Chambers; pub. mem. Blue Cross Corp. Assembly; bd. trustees Lindenwood Coll.; pres.'s council St. Louis U. Office: Buick Oldsmobile Cadillac Group PO Box 444 Wentzville MO 63385-0444

COWGER, SHARI ANN, music educator; d. Richard Paul and Janet Leatrice Negley; m. Jerry W. Cowger, Sept. 18, 1999; children: Savannah Paige Boggess, Kylie Glen Boggess, Noah Paul Boggess. BS in Edn., N.W. Mo. State U., Maryville, 1980; MEd, U. of Idaho, Moscow/Boise, 2006. Classified sales mgr. The Daily Tribune, Ames, Iowa, 1986—90; advt. sales KMVT TV, Twin Falls, Idaho, 1990—98; elem. music tchr. Twin Falls Sch. Dist., 1998—. Pvt. music instr. Magic Valley Sch. of Performing Arts, Twin Falls, 2002—. Sunday sch. tchr. Twin Falls Ref. Ch., Twin Falls, 2000—02, pianist, 2005. Mem.: Nation Orff Orgn. R-Conservative. Office: Oregon Trail Elementary School 660 Park Ave Twin Falls ID 83301 Home Phone: 208-736-7397; Office Phone: 208-733-8480. Home Fax: None. E-mail: cowgersh@tfsd.k12.id.us.

COWGILL, DONALD FRANKLIN, physicist; b. Springfield, Mo., Apr. 6, 1942; s. Donald Olen and Mary Strain Cowgill; m. Dorothy Annette Rickette (div.); children: Jeffrey Glenn, Christine Marie; m. Maris Ann Rabel Loftus, Mar. 30, 1983. BS in Physics and Math., Wichita State U., 1965, MS in Physics, 1966; PhD in Physics, Washington U., 1971. Physicist Hewlett-Packard Labs., Palo Alto, Calif., 1972—74, Sandia Nat. Lab., Albuquerque, 1974—87, prin. physicist Livermore, Calif., 1987—. Contbr. articles to profl. jours. Recipient Award of Excellence, U.S. Dept. Energy, 2001. Mem.: Sigmam Xi. Achievements include patents in field. Avocations: restoring MG cars, home remodeling, hiking, skiing. Home: 2714 Farnsworth Dr Livermore CA 94551 Office: Sandia Nat Lab PO Box 969 Dept 8758 Livermore CA 94551 Business E-Mail: dfcowgi@sandia.gov.

COWGILL, URSULA MOSER, biologist, educator, environmental consultant; b. Bern, Switzerland, Nov. 9, 1927; came to U.S., 1943, naturalized, 1945; d. John W. and Mara (Siegrist) Moser. AB, Hunter Coll., 1948; MS, Kans. State U., 1952; PhD, Iowa State U., 1956. Staff MIT, Lincoln Lab., Lexington, Mass., 1957-58; field work Doherty Found., Guatemala, 1958-60; research assoc. dept. biology Yale U., New Haven, 1960-68; prof. biology and anthropology U. Pitts., 1968-81; environ. scientist Dow Chem. Co., Midland, Mich., 1981-84, assoc. environ. cons., 1984-91; environ. cons., 1991—. Environ. measurements adv. com. Sci. Adv. Bd. EPA, 1976-80; Internat. Joint Commn., 1984-89. Contbr. articles to profl. jours. Trustee Carnegie Mus., Pitts., 1971-75. Grantee NSF 1960-78, Wenner Gren Found., 1965-66, Penrose fund Am. Philos. Soc., 1978; Sigma Xi grant-in-aid, 1965-66 Mem. AAAS, Am. Soc. Limnology and Oceanography, Internat. Soc. Theoretical and Applied Limnology. Achievements include research in ecology, biology and mineralogy. Home and Office: PO Box 1329 Carbondale CO 81623-1329 E-mail: ucowgill@sopris.net, ucowgill@direcway.com.

COWHER, BILL (WILLIAM LAIRD COWHER), sportscaster, former professional football coach; b. Pitts., May 8, 1957; s. Laird and Dorothy Cowher; m. Kaye Cowher; children: Meagan Lyn, Lauren Marie, Lindsay Morgan. BS in Edn., N.C. State, 1979. Profl. football player Phila. Eagles,

1979, 1983-84, Cleve. Browns, 1980-82, spl. teams coach, 1985-86, secondary coach, 1987-88; def. coord. Kans. City Chiefs, 1988-91; head coach Pitts. Steelers, 1992—2007; studio analyst NFL Today, CBS, 2007—. Named NFL Coach of Yr., AP, 1992, Sporting News, 1992, 2004, Pitts. Man of the Yr., Dapper Dan Club, Best Coach, Espy award, 2006. Achievements include being the youngest head coach to lead his team to the Super Bowl, 1995; head coach for the Super Bowl XL champions, 2006.*

COWHILL, WILLIAM JOSEPH, retired naval officer, consultant; b. Bklyn., May 29, 1928; s. Joseph Henry and Lucy Rose (Foppiano) C.; m. Jennifer Jackson, Apr. 16, 1955; children Robin, Joseph, Beth, Michael, Douglas. BS, Northwestern U., 1950. Commd. ensign USN, 1950, advanced through grades to vice adm., 1979, comdg. officer USS Dace and USS Will Rogers, 1965-68, PCO instr., div. Naval Reactors, AEC, 1968-70, comdg. officer USS Holland, Rota, Spain, 1970-72, nuclear power program mgr. Bur. Naval Personnel, 1972, comdr. tng. command, U.S. Atlantic Fleet, 1973-75, asst. dep. chief naval ops. for submarine warfare, Office Chief Naval Ops., Washington, 1975-77, comdr. submarine force, U.S. Pacific Fleet, 1977-79, dep. chief ops. for logistics, office chief naval ops., 1979-83, dir. logistics, joint chiefs of staff, 1983-85, ret.; pvt. cons. Washington, 1985—. Decorated Def. D.S.M., Navy D.S.M., Legion of Merit. Home and Office: 9428 Vernon Dr Great Falls VA 22066

COWIN, JUDITH ARNOLD, state supreme court judge; b. Boston, Apr. 29, 1942; m. William I. Cowin, 1965; 3 children. BA, Wellesley Coll., 1963; LLD, Harvard U., 1970. Asst. legal counsel Mass. Dept. Mental Health, 1971—72; legal counsel for chief justice Mass. Dist. Ct., 1972—79; asst. dist. atty. Norfolk County, 1979—91; judge Mass. Superior Ct., 1991—99; justice Mass. Supreme Jud. Ct., Boston, 1999—. Clinical field supervisor Harvard Law Sch., 1980. Office: Mass Supreme Judicial Ct One Pemberton Sq #2 Boston MA 02108

COWIN, STEPHEN CORTEEN, biomedical engineering educator, consultant; b. Elmira, NY, Oct. 26, 1934; s. William Corteen and Bernice (Reidy) C.; m. Martha Agnes Eisel, Aug. 10, 1956; children: Jennifer Marie, Thomas Burrows. BCE, Johns Hopkins U., 1956, MCE, 1958; PhD in Engring. Mechanics, Pa. State U., 1962. Registered profl. engr., La. Prof. mech. engring. Tulane U., 1969-77, prof. mechanics dept. biomed. engring., 1977-85, adj. prof. orthopedics, 1978-88, prof.-in-charge Tulane-Newcomb Jr. Yr. Abroad program, 1974-75, chmn. applied math. program, 1975-79, prof. applied stats., 1979-88, Alden J. Laborde prof. engring., 1985-88; disting. prof. CUNY, 1988—, chmn. dept. biomed. engring., 2002—03; dir. NY Ctr. for Biomed. Engring., 2000—. Sci. Rsch. Coun. Gt. Brit. sr. vis. fellow U. Strathclyde, 1974, 80; vis. research prof. Instituto de Matematica, Estatistica e Ciencia de Computanao, Universidade Estadual de Campinas, Brazil, 1978; adj. prof. orthopaedics, Mt. Siani Sch. Medicine, NY, 1989; participant U.S. Nat. Acad. Scis. interacad. exch. program with Bulgaria, 1983; fellow Japan Soc. for the Promotion Sci., 1987; sr. internat. Fogarty fellowship, Nederlandse Organisatie voor Wetenschappelijk Onderzoek fellowship, Vrije U., Amsterdam, 1996-97; mem. bd. advisors in biomedical engring., Tulane U., 2001-. Editor: (with M. Satake) Continuum Mechanical and Statistical Approaches in the Mechanics of Granular Materials, 1978, Mechanics Applied to the Transport of Granular Materials, 1979, (with M.M. Carroll) The Effects of Voids on Material Deformation, 1976, Bone Mechanics, 1988, Bone Mechanics Handbook, 2001, (with J. Humphrey) Cardiovascular Soft Tissue Mechanics, 2001, (with S. Doty) Tissue Mechanics, 2006; assoc. editor: Jour. Applied Mechanics, 1974-82, Jour. Biomech. Engring., 1982-88; editl. adv. bd. Handbook of Materials, Structures and Mechanics, 1981—, Handbook of Bioengineering, 1981, Acta Biomechanica, 1986—; editl. bd. Annals Biomed. Engring., 1985—, Mechanics Rsch. Comm., 2005—; editl. cons. Jour. Biomechanics, 1988— Served to capt. U.S. Army, 1957-64 Recipient Maurice A. Biot medal ASCE, 2004; grantee NSF, NIH, NASA, U.S. Army Rsch. Office, Edward G. Schlieder Found.; fellow Fogarty Internat. Ctr., Amsterdam, 1996-97, Johns Hopkins U., 1958; Md. state scholar, Ambrose Howard Carner scholar. Fellow AAAS, ASME (Melville medal 1993, H.R. Lissner medal 1999), Am. Inst. Med. and Biol. Engring., European Soc. Biomechanics (Rsch. award 1994), Am. Acad. Mechanics; mem. Nat. Acad. Engring., Orthopedic Rsch. Soc., Soc. Rheology, Soc. Natural Philosophy (treas. 1977-79), Soc. Engring. Sci., Math. Assn. Am., NY Acad. Scis., Sigma Xi. Home: 2166 Broadway Apt 12D New York NY 10024 Office Phone: 212-650-5208. Personal E-mail: scowin@earthlink.net.

COWING, CHARLES OGDEN, talent agency executive; b. Boston, Aug. 10, 1954; s. Robert Harlan and Margaret Ogden Cowing; m. Evianne Muller, June 27, 1982; 1 child, Grayson Muller. BA, Colby Coll., Waterville, Maine, 1977. Cert. franchised talent agt. SAG, AFTRA, 1985. Actor, dir. Mabou Mines, NYC, 1978—82; voice-over talent agt. J. Michael Bloom & Assoc., NYC, 1983—89, head voice-over dept., 1989—99; pres. Access Talent, NYC, 1999—. Chmn. Elisha Kent Kane Hist. Soc., NYC, 1996—; bd. dirs. Wilderness Rsch. Found., Inc., NYC, 1999—. Master: Masons (life); mem.: Am. Polar Soc. (corr.), Arctic Inst. N.Am. (corr.), Players Club (assoc.), Union League Club (assoc.), Explorers Club (assoc.). Avocations: skiing, photography, sailing. Office: Access Talent 171 Madison Ave # 910 New York NY 10016 Home Phone: 917-549-0187; Office Phone: 212-331-9600 609.

COWLES, CHARLES, art dealer; b. Santa Monica, Calif., Feb. 7, 1941; s. Gardner and Jan (Streate) C. Student, Stanford, 1963. Assoc. pub. Artforum mag., San Francisco, 1964-65; pub., pres. Artforum, Inc., Los Angeles, 1965-67, pub., pres., chmn. NYC, 1967-75, pres., chmn., 1975-79; chmn. Collegiate Press, NYC, 1968-71; curator modern art Seattle Art Mus., 1975-79; pres. Charles Cowles Gallery, NYC, 1980—. Mem. Fine Arts Council Fla., 1972-75; Trustee Studio Mus. in Harlem, N.Y.C., 1967-75, Miami Art Ctr., 1973-75, San Francisco Art Inst., 1978-80, Cowles Charitable Trust, 1983—; mem. internat. council Mus. Modern Art, N.Y.C., 1967-79. Mem. Seattle Arts Commn., 1976-79; trustee Wolfsonian F.I.U., Miami Beach, 1995—, Laueier Sculpture Pk. St. Louis, 1996—, Am. Fedn. of the Arts, N.Y., 2000—, Alliance for the Arts, 2001--; trustee N.Y. Studio Sch., 1985-2003, chmn., 1987-95; trustee com. for librs. Mus. of Modern Art, N.Y., 2000—. With USCG, 1962—63, with USCGR, 1963—70. Mem.: Art Dealers Assn. Am. (bd. dirs. 1988—90, 1993—96). Office: Charles Cowles Gallery 537 W 24th St New York NY 10011-1104 Fax: 212-925-3501. E-mail: charlie@cowlesgallery.com.

COWLES, FREDERICK OLIVER, lawyer; b. Steubenville, Ohio, Oct. 18, 1937; s. Oliver Howard and Cornelia Blanche (Regal) C.; m. Christina Monica Muller, Sept. 9, 1961; children: Randall, Eric, Gregory, Cornelius. AB magna cum laude, Yale U., 1959; JD, Harvard U., 1962. Bar: R.I. 1963, Mich. 1967, Ill. 1969, N.Y. 1998, Conn. 1998. Assoc. Hinckley, Allen, Salisbury & Parsons, Providence, 1962-67; internat. atty. Upjohn Co., Kalamazoo, 1967-69; chief internat. atty. Am. Hosp. Supply Crp., Evanston, Ill., 1969-71; internat. atty. Kendall Co., Boston, 1971-73; chief internat. counsel Colgate Palmolive Co., NYC, 1973-86, assoc. gen. counsel, asst. sec., 1986-90, assoc. gen. counsel, asst. sec., v.p. legal ops., 1990-94, sr. assoc. gen. coun., asst. sec., v.p. legal ops., 1994-97, multinat. estate planning, 1997—2003; ret., 2003. Dir. various cos. Co-founder Internat. House R.I. Inc.; group leader Operation Crossroads Africa, Gambia. Mem. ABA, Internat. Bar Assn., Yale Alumni Assn. Westchester, Internat. Lawyers Assn., Phi Beta Kappa. Home: 111 Oscaleta Rd South Salem NY 10590-1003

COWLES, JIM E., lawyer; b. Wichita Falls, Tex., Mar. 3, 1934; BBA, U. Tex., 1958, LLB, 1961. Bar: Tex. 1961, US Supreme Ct., US Dist. Ct. (we. and no. dists. Tex.) 1962, US Dist. Ct. (ea. dist. Tex.) 1964, US Ct. Appeals (5th cir.) 1968, US Dist. Ct. (so. dist. Tex.) 1979. Founder to shareholder Cowles & Thompson, P.C., Dallas, 1978—. Served in JAG USNR. Named one of Best Lawyers in Am., Am. Lawyer, 1995—2007, Best Lawyers in Dallas, D Mag., 1997, 2001, 2003, 2005, 2007, Top 100 Super Lawyers in Tex., Tex. Monthly and Law & Politics Mag., 2003—07, Top 10 Lawyers in Tex., 2005. Mem.: Patrick E. Higginbotham Am. Inn Ct., Am. Bd. Trial Advs., Def. Rsch. Inst., Coll. State Bar Tex., Intern. Assn. Def. Coun., Tex. Assn. Def. Coun. (Pres.'s award 1993), Dallas Assn. Def. Coun., State Bar Tex., Dallas Bar Assn. (Trial Lawyer of Yr. Award 2005), ABA. Office: Cowles & Thompson PC 901 Main St Ste 4000 Dallas TX 75202-3793 Office Phone: 214-672-2101. Office Fax: 214-672-2301. E-mail: jcowles@cowlesthompson.com.

COWLES, JOE RICHARD, biology professor; b. Edmonson County, Ky., Oct. 29, 1941; s. Otis Wilson and Mamie E. (Rountree) C.; m. Barbara Sutton, June 5, 1965; children: Richard William, Daniel Morgan. BS, Western Ky. U., 1963; MS, U. Ky., 1965; PhD, Oreg. State U., 1968. Postdoctoral fellow Purdue U., West Lafayette, Ind., 1968-69, U. Ga., Athens, 1969-70; asst. prof. U. Houston, 1970-75, assoc. prof., 1976-81, chmn. biology dept., 1981-90, prof., 1982-90; head biology Va. Tech. U., Blacksburg, 1990—2002, prof., 1990—. Contbr. more than 40 articles to profl. jours. Grantee NASA, NSF, Dept. Energy, USDA. Mem. Am. Soc. Plant Physiology, Sigma Xi. Democrat. Baptist. Avocation: sports. Office: Virginia Tech U Dept Biology Blacksburg VA 24061 E-mail: cowlesjr@vt.edu.

COWLES, JOHN, JR., publishing executive, women's sports promoter, philanthropist; b. Des Moines, May 27, 1929; s. John and Elizabeth (Bates) C.; m. Jane Sage Fuller, Aug. 23, 1952; children: Tessa Sage Flores, John, Jane Sage, Charles Fuller. Grad., Phillips Exeter Acad., 1947; AB, Harvard U., 1951; LittD (hon.), Simpson Coll., 1965. With Cowles Media Co. (formerly Mpls. Star and Tribune Co.), 1953-83, v.p., 1957-68, editor, 1961-69, pres. or chmn., 1968—83, dir., 1956-84; pres. Harper's Mag., Inc., 1965-68, chmn. bd., 1968-72; dir. Harper & Row, Pubs., Inc., NYC, 1965-81, chmn., 1968-79. Dir. Des Moines Register & Tribune Co., 1960-84, Farmers & Mechanics Savs. Bank, Mpls., 1960-65, Cowles Comms., Inc., NYC, 1960-65, Equitable Life Ins. Co. Iowa, Des Moines, 1964-66, 1st Bank Systems, Inc., Mpls., 1964-68, A.P., NYC, 1966-75, Midwest Radio-TV, Inc., Mpls., 1967-76; fitness instr. Sweatshop Fitness Ctr., St. Paul, 1989-93; guest artist Bill T. Jones/Arnie Zane & Co., 1990-92; vice chmn. Women's Pro. Softball League LLC, Denver, 1994-02, chmn. Nat. Pro Fastpitch LLC, 2002-04; ptnr. St. Anthony Films LLC, 1998-04, "Herman USA", 2001; investor Block E Hotel Capital LLC, 2000—. Mem. adv. bd. on Pulitzer Prizes, Columbia U., 1970-83; campaign chmn. Mpls. United Fund, 1967; bd. dirs. Guthrie Theatre Found., 1960-71, pres., 1960-63, chmn., 1964-65, arch. selection com., 2000-01, endowment campaign steering com., 1987-91; trustee Phillips Exeter Acad., 1960-65; bd. dirs. Walker Art Ctr., 1960-69, 87-92, Minn. Civil Liberties Union, 1956-61, Urban Coalition Mpls., 1968-70, Mpls. Found., 1970-75, German Marshall Fund U.S., 1975-78; bd. dirs. Am. Newspaper Pubs. Assn., 1975-77; mem. govt. affairs com., 1976-79; mem. Woodhill Country Club, 1954-84, Century Assn., 1967-92, Coun. on Foreign Rels., 1969-92, Minn. Bus. Partnership, 1977-83, Minn. Project Corp. Responsibility, 1977-83, Trilateral Commn., 1978-82. Served to 2d lt. US Army, 1951-53. Hill fellow Humphrey Inst. U. Minn., 2005-06; named one of Ten Outstanding Men of Yr. U.S. Jr. C. of C., 1964, 200 Rising Leaders in Am. Time Mag., 1974; recipient John Phillips award Exeter, 1977, US Bank Sally Ordway Irvine award, St. Paul, 2000, Regents award U. Minn., 2004. Mem. Greater Mpls. C. of C. (dir. 1978-81, chmn. stadium site task force 1977-82), Mpls. Club, Mill Reef Club (Antigua), A.D. Club at Harvard, Signet Assn. at Harvard (pres. 1950-51). Home: 700 S 2nd St Loft 91 Minneapolis MN 55401 Office: 155 Fifth Ave S Ste 1000 Minneapolis MN 55401-2550 Office Phone: 612-359-9449.

COWLES, ROBERT LAWRENCE, lawyer; b. Jacksonville, Fla., Feb. 5, 1942; m. Barbara Bearden; children: Robert L., Kelli R. McMullin. BS, U. N.C., 1964; JD, Emory U. Law Sch., 1969. Bar: Fla. 1969, Ga. 1969. Claims adjuster, supr. Travelers Ins. Co., Jacksonville, Atlanta, N.Y.C., 1964-68; assoc. Neely, Freeman & Hawkins, Atlanta, 1968-69, Swift, Currie, McGhee & Hiers, Atlanta, 1969-71; dir. Howell, Kirby, Montgomery, D'Aiuto, Dean & Hallowes PA, Jacksonville, 1971-76; pres. Cowles, Coker & Myers, Jacksonville, 1976-83, Cowles, Coker, Myers, Schickel & Pierce PA, Atlanta, 1982-83, Cowles, Hayden, Facciolo, McMorrow & Barfield PA, Jacksonville, 1984-87; judge Fourth Jud. Cir. Ct., Atlanta, 1987-90; comdr. Legler, Werber, Dawes, Sadler & Howell PA, Jacksonville, 1990-91; pvt. practice Law Offices of Robert L. Cowles, 1991-93; ptnr. Cowles & Shaughnessy PA, Jacksonville, 1993-2000; pvt. practice The Cowles Law Firm, Jacksonville, 2000—01; assoc. Wood Atter & Assocs., Jacksonville, 2001—03; pvt. practice Robert L. Cowles, 2003—. Bd. dirs. Boys Home of Jacksonville, 1989—. Mem. Am. Bd. Trial Advocacy, Fla. Bar Assn. (chmn. bd. cert. civil trial lawyers com. 1998-00, chmn. 1998-99), State Bar Ga. Avocations: golf, gardening, travel. E-mail: rlc@cowleslawfirm.com.

COWLES, ROGER E., computer consultant; b. Boston, Feb. 9, 1950; s. S. Edwin C. and Irene M. Woodard. BA in Internat. Econs. with honors, Ohio Wesleyan U., 1974. Network cons. LAN Sys., Inc., NYC, 1988-91, Network Alternatives, Inc., Washington, 1991-92; dir. network sys. Quad Microsys. Inc., Southampton, Pa., 1992-93; network cons. Integrated Microcomputer Sys., Inc., Rockville, Md., 1993-95; sys. cons. Emtec, Inc., Mt. Laurel, NJ, 1995—; prin., owner DINET Corp., 1998—. Cons. World Bank, Washington, 1992, Judge Tech. Svcs., Bala Cynwyd, Pa., 1997; sr. cons. Chem. Bank, N.Y.C., 1995-96; sr. network cons. Arco Chem. Co., 1998—; founder Transcend Media Corp., 1998, Di-Net.Corp., 1998. Mem. IEEE, Assn. Sys. Mgmt. Avocations: reading, politics, economics, sports, travel. Personal E-mail: rcowles@earthlink.net.

COWLES, WILLIAM STACEY, newspaper publisher; b. Spokane, Wash., Aug. 31, 1960; s. William Hutchinson 3rd and Allison Stacey C.; m. Anne Cannon, June 24, 1989. BA in Econs., Yale Coll., 1982; MBA in Fin., Columbia U., 1986. With The Spokesman Rev., Spokane, Wash., 1989—, pres., pub., 1992—. Office: Cowles Publishing Co PO Box 2160 Spokane WA 99210-2160 Office Phone: 509-459-5217. Business E-Mail: staceyc@spokesman.com.

COWLEY, ALLEN WILSON, JR., physiologist; b. Harrisburg, Pa., Jan. 21, 1940; m. Theresa Ann Malinoski BA, Trinity Coll., Hartford, Conn., 1961; MS, Hahnemann Med. Coll., Phila., 1965, PhD, 1968. Instr. physiology and biophysics U. Miss. Med. Ctr., Jackson, 1968-69, asst. prof. physiology and biophysics, 1969-72, assoc. prof. physiology and biophysics, 1973-75, prof. physiology and biophysics, 1975-80; prof. physiology, chmn. physiology dept. Med. Coll. Wis., Milw., 1980—; chmn. dept. physiology Marquette U., Milw., 1990—. Lectr. and invited spkr. in field; organizer various confs. Mem. editl. bd. Clin. and Exptl. Hypertension, 1977—, Am. Jour. Physiology: Circulation Sect., 1979-83, Hypertension, 1980-91, 93—, Am. Jour. Physiology: Regulatory, Integrative and Comparative Physiology, 1984-88, Internat. Jour. Cardiology, 1985—, Am. Jour. Physiology: Heart and Circulatory Physiology, 1987-89, Clin. Exptl. Pharmacology Physiology, 1993-96, Jour. Hypertension, 1993-96, Physiol. Revs., 1997—, News in Physiol. Scis., 1997—, assoc. editor 1988-91; guest editor Hypertension, Ann. Supplement Procs. Coun. for High Blood Pressure Rsch., 1981-84; contbr. 30 chpts. to books and symposia, over 180 articles to profl. jours. and conf. procs. Recipient numerous NIH rsch. grants, 1971—; recipient Established Investigatorship award Am. Heart Asnsn., 1973-78, Alumnus of Yr. award Hahnemann Med. Coll., 1975, MERIT award NIH, 1996. Fellow Am. Heart Assn. Coun. High Blood Pressure Rsch. (chmn. publs. com. 1982-84, mem. various coms., Disting. Achievement award 1996, Novartis award 1997), Am. Heart Assn. Coun. on Circulation (various coms.), Am. Physiol. Soc. Cardiovasc. Sect.; mem. Am. Physiol. Soc. (various coms., pres.-elect 1996-97, pres. 1997—, Ernest H. Starling Disting. lectureship 1996, Wiggers award 1997), Internat. Soc. Hypertension, Am. Soc. Nephrology, Microcirculation Soc., Assn. Chairmen Depts. Physiology (various offices and coms., pres. 1990), Hungarian Physiol. Soc. (hon.), Brazilian Acad. Sci. (hon.), Sigma Xi. Office: Med Coll Wisconsin Dept Physiology 8701 W Watertown Plank Rd Milwaukee WI 53226-3548

COWLEY, ROBERT WILLIAM, editor, writer, consultant, lecturer; b. NYC, Dec. 16, 1934; s. Malcolm and Muriel (Maurer) C.; m. Blair Phillips (div.); children: Elizabeth Blair Roberts, Miranda Phillips Heller; m. Edith Pray Lorillard, June 24, 1978; children: Olivia Wassenaar, Savannah Caroline Lorillard. AB, Harvard U., 1956. Assoc. editor Am. Heritage, NYC, 1956-64; mng. editor Sky, NYC, 1964; asst. editor The Reporter, NYC, 1965-66; articles editor, mng. editor Horizon, NYC, 1966-72; co-editor The Saturday Review of the Arts, NYC and San Francisco, 1972-73; sr. editor, exec. editor Houghton Mifflin, Boston, 1973-77; sr. editor Random House, NYC, 1977-84, Henry Holt, NYC, 1984-88; founding editor, editor-in-chief MHQ: The Quarterly Jour. of Military History, NYC, 1988-98; cons. Smithsonian Books, 2004—06, Random House, 2006—. Author: The Rulers of Britain, 1982; editor, contbr.: Experience of War, 1992, The Great War, 2003, The Cold War: A Military History, 2005; co-editor: (with Malcolm Cowley) Fitzgerald and the Jazz Age, 1966; (with Geoffrey Parker) The Reader's Companion to Military History, 1996; (with Thomas Guinzburg) West Point: Two Centuries of Honor and Tradition, 2002; contbg. author: A Weekend with the Great War: Proceedings of the Fourth Annual Great War Inter-Conf. Sem., 1997, To the Best of My Ability: The American Presidents, 2000, What Might Have Been, 2004, I Wish I'd Been There, 2006; editor, contbr. What If?: The World's Foremost Military Historians Imagine What Might Have Been, 1999, The Collected What If?, 2004; editor: No End Save Victory, 2001, With My Face to the Enemy, 2001, What If? 2, 2001, What Ifs? of American History, 2003. Fellow Soc. Am. Historians; mem. Soc. Mil. History. Democrat. Episcopalian. Avocations: jazz collecting, military archaeology. Home: PO Box 268 Sherman CT 06784-0268 Personal E-mail: cowleyrw219@aol.com.

COWLEY, SAMUEL C., lawyer, transportation services executive; BA in Econs., Brigham Young U., Provo, Utah; JD, Cornell Law Sch. Bar: NY, Ariz. Atty. Reid & Priest, NYC, Snell & Wilmer LLP, Phoenix, 1990—2005; exec. v.p., gen. counsel Swift Transp. Co., Inc., Phoenix, 2005—, also dir., 2005—. Office: Swift Transp Co Inc 2200 S 75th Ave Phoenix AZ 85043 Office Phone: 602-269-9700.*

COWLING, TERIANNE, medical researcher; d. Delta Ray and Madge Faye Cowling. BA, U. Tex., 1988; student, U. NC, 2006—. Rsch. analyst Baylor U. Med. Ctr., Dallas, 1994—96, rsch. assoc., 1996—2006; rsch. analyst Inst. for Health Care Rsch. and Improvement, Dallas, 2006—. Contbr. articles to profl. jours., chapters to books. Office: Inst for Health Care Rsch and Improvement Ste 500 LB81 8080 N Central Expressway Dallas TX 75206 Office Phone: 214-265-3677. Business E-Mail: teric@baylorhealth.edu.

COWLISHAW, MARY LOU, government educator; b. Rockford, Ill., Feb. 20, 1932; d. Donald George and Mildred Corinne (Hayes) Miller; m. Wayne Arnold Cowlishaw, July 24, 1954; children: Beth Cowlishaw McDaniel, John, Paula Cowlishaw Rader. BS in Journalism, U. Ill., 1954; DHL, North Ctrl. Coll., 1999; DHL (hon.), Benedictine U., 2000. Mem. editorial staff Naperville (Ill.) Sun newspaper, 1977-83; mem. Ill. Ho. of Reps., Springfield, 1983—2003, chmn. elem. and secondary edn. com., 1995—97, vice-chmn. pub. utilities com., 1995—2003, mem. joint Ho.-Senate edn. reform oversight com., 1985—97; assoc. Ctr. for Govtl. Studies No. Ill. U., 2003—; adj. prof. North Ctrl. Coll., Naperville, Ill., 2003—. Mem. Ill. Task Force on Sch. Fin., 1990-96; vice chmn. Ho. Rep. Campaign Com., 1990—; co-chair Ho. Rep. Policy Com., 1991-2003; chmn. edn. com. Nat. Conf. State Legislatures, 1993-97; mem. Joint Com. Adminstrv. Rules, 1992-2003; commr. Edn. Commn. of the States, 1995-2002; chair, Ill. Women's Agenda Task Force, 1994—; mem. Nat. Edn. Goals Panel, 1996—, bd. govs. Lincoln Series for Excellence in Pub. Svc., 1996—. Author: This Band's Been Here Quite a Spell, 1983; columnist Ill. Press Assn., 2003—. Mem. Naperville Dist. 203 Bd. Edn., 1972-83; co-chmn. Ill. Citizens Coun. on Sch. Problems, Springfield, 1985-2003. Recipient 1st pl. award Ill. Press Assn., 1981, commendation Naperville Jaycees, 1986, Golden Apple award Ill. Assn. Sch. Bds., 1988, 90, 92, 94, Outstanding Women Leaders of DuPage County award West Suburban YWCA, 1990, Activator award Ill. Farm Bur., 1996, 98, Bd. of Dirs. award Little Friends, Inc., 1998, Honor award Ill. Math. and Sci. Acad., 2002, Pub. Svc. award West Suburban Higher Edn. Consortium, 2002; named Best Legislator, Ill. Citizens for Better Care, 1985, Woman of Yr., Naperville AAUW, 1987, Best Legislator, Ill. Assn. Fire Chiefs, 1994, Outstanding Edn. Adv. Indian Prairie Sch. Dist. 204, 1994, Legislator of Yr., Ill. Assn. Pk. Dists., 1995; commr. Edn. Commn. of the States, 1994-2002; Mary Lou Cowlishaw Elem. Sch. named in her honor, 1997, Legislator of Yr., Ill. Assn. Mus., 1998. Mem. Am. Legis. Exch. Coun., Conf. Women Legislators, Nat. Fedn. Rep. Women, DAR, Naperville Rep. Women's Club (pres. 1994—). Methodist. Avocation: the violin. Home: 924 Merrimac Cir Naperville IL 60540-7107 Office: North Central Coll 30 N Brainard St Naperville IL 60540-4690

COWPER, STEPHEN CAMBRELENG, international business consultant, former governor; b. Petersburg, Va., Aug. 21, 1938; s. Marion Cowper and Stephanie Smith; m. Michael Margaret Stewart; children: Katherine, Grace, Wade. BA, U. N.C., 1960, JD, 1963. Pvt. practice, Norfolk, Va.; asst. dist. atty. State of Alaska, Fairbanks, 1968-70; ptnr. Cowper & Madson, Fairbanks, 1971-84; mem. legislature Alaska Ho. of Reps., Fairbanks and Juneau, 1974-78; chmn. Alaska Permanent Fund Corp., Juneau, 1983-84; Gov. State of Alaska, Juneau, 1986-90; ptnr. Tradelink Alaska, Fairbanks, 1990—. Columnist Alaska newspapers, 1979-80, 85; author: (documentary film) A Trail to Break-A History of Alaska Lands, 1979. Mem. Alaska Native Brotherhood Klawock Camp, Eielson Area Grange, Fairbanks. With U.S. Army, 1960. Mem. Sundawgs Rugby Club. Democrat. Episcopalian. Avocations: banjo, rugby, scuba diving, reading.*

COWPERTHWAIT, LINDLEY MURRAY, lawyer; b. Abington, Pa., Mar. 13, 1933; s. Lindley Murray Cowperthwait and Ruth Bronde Nicholas; m. Suzanne Dewees, Nov. 26, 1955 (div. July 1976); children: Murray, Mary Ruth, Edward, Linda, Tom, Suzanne; m. Karin Schmid Cowperthwait, Apr. 1, 1989. BA, Calif. State U., 1957; LLB, U. Pa., 1960, JD, 1970. Bar: Pa. 1961, Md. 2005. Assoc. Wisler, Pearlstine, Talone Craig & Garrity, Norristown, Pa., 1960-68, ptnr., 1968-80; pvt. practice Norristown, 1980-96; of counsel High, Swartz, Roberts & Seidel, LLP, Norristown, 1997—2002, Law Offices of Thomas N. Yeager, Chestertown, Md., 2002—. Prodr., author, dir. (video) Medicine for Lawyers, 1980-93; author: Damages-Delay and Punitive 1999, 2000, 01, 04, HIPPA-A Thorn in the side of the Legal Profession, 2004, Scrivener Med-Leg Code of Ethics, 1960, 75, 94, 2001, 04 Bd. dirs. ARC, Norristown, 1993-95, Big Bros./Big Sisters, Norristown, 1985-92. Recipient Citizenship award Big Bros./Big Sisters, 1992, Comm. award Montgomery County Med. Soc., 2002. Mem. Pa. Trial Lawyers Assn. (pres. 1974-75), Montgomery County Trial Lawyers (founder, sec. 1965-74, Trial Lawyer of Yr. 2003), Assn. Trial

Lawyers of Am., Pa. Bar Assn., Md. Bar Assn., Am. Coll. Legal Medicine (invited mem., litigator cons., counselor), Pa. Soc., Md. State Bar Assn., Kent County State Bar Assn. Republican. Episcopalian. Avocation: sailing.

COWSER, DANNY LEE, lawyer, mental health specialist; b. Peoria, Ill., July 7, 1948; s. Albert Paul Cowser and Shirley Mae (Donaldson) Chatten; m. Nancy Lynn Hatch, Nov. 11, 1976; children: Kimberly Catherine Hatch Cowser, Dustin Paul Hatch Cowser. BA, No. Ill. U., 1972, MS, 1975; JD, DePaul U., 1980. Bar: Ill. 1980, Wis. 1981, U.S. Dist. Ct. (no. dist.) Ill. 1981, U.S. Ct. Appeals (7th cir.) 1983, U.S. Dist. Ct. (ea. and we. dists.) Wis. 1984, U.S. Supreme Ct. 1984, Ariz. 1985, U.S. Ct. Appeals (9th cir.) 1987, U.S. Dist. Ct. Ariz. 1989, U.S. Tax Ct. 1990, U.S. Ct. Claims 1990, Colo. 2000. Adminstr. Ill. Dept. Mental Health, Elgin, 1972-76, psychotherapist, 1976-79; assoc. Slaby, Deda & Henderson, Phillips, Wis., 1982-83; ptnr. Slaby, Deda & Cowser, Phillips, 1983-86; asst. atty. City of Flagstaff, Ariz., 1986-88; pub. defender Coconino County, Flagstaff, 1988-89; pvt. practice Flagstaff, 1989-97. Atty. City Park Falls, Wis., 1982-86; spl. dep. Mohave County capital def., 1989-90; instr. speech comms. No. Ariz. U., 1992-93; adminstrv. law judge Ariz. Dept. Econ. Security, 1997—. Bd. dirs. DeKalb County (Ill.) Drug Coun., 1973-75, Counseling and Personal Devel., Phillips, 1985-86. Reginald Heber Smith fellow, 1980-81; C.J.S. legal scholar, 1979. Mem. Ariz. Bar Assn., State Bar Ariz. (cert. specialist in criminal law 1993-98), State Bar Wis. Democrat. Avocations: skiing, photography, bicycling.

COWSIK, RAMANATH, physics professor; b. Nagpur, Madhya, India, Aug. 29, 1940; came to U.S., 1970; s. Ramakrishna K. and Saraswati C. (Ayyar) C.; m. Shyamala Balasubrahmanian, Aug. 20, 1979 (div. Feb. 1989); 1 child, Siddhartha. BS, Mysore U., Bangalore, India, 1958; MS in Physics, Karnatak U., India, 1960; PhD, Bombay U., 1968. Jr. rsch. assoc. Tata Inst. Fundamental Rsch., Bombay, 1961—, reader, 1975—, assoc. prof., 1977—, prof., 1984—, disting. prof.; asst. prof. U. Calif., Berkeley, 1970-73; vis. scientist Max-Planck Inst. Extension Physik, Munich, 1973-74; dir. Indian Inst. for Astrophysics, Bangalore, dir. emeritus, Vainu Bappu disting. prof.; prof. physics Washington U., St. Louis. Vis. prof. Washington U., St. Louis, 1987—. Contbr. articles to Jour. Physics Rev., Astrophys. Jour. Recipient Sarabhai award Hari om Soc./Phys. Rsch. Lab., 1981, Group Achievement award NASA, 1986. Fellow Indian Acad. Scis., Indian Nat. Sci. Acad. (Bhatnagar award 1984); mem. Am. Phys. Soc. (life), Internat. Astron. Union (life), NAS (fgn. assoc.). Achievements include development of the theory that weakly interacting particle relicts from the big bang are the constituents of dark matter and set the upper bound on the sum of their masses, in particular of neutrinos; recognized the cosmological significance of the hard x-ray background; derived the leaky box and nested leaky box models for cosmic rays; research in high energy astrophysics of nonthermal emissions from quasars and supernova remnants and in astroparticle physics and experimental gravitation; measurement of the double beta decay life-time of the tellurium-128 nucleus as 7.7x10 24 years the longest, implying the Majorana mass of the neutrino to be less than 1 eV. Office: Washington U Dept Physics Campus Box 1105 One Brookings Dr Saint Louis MO 63130-4899

COX, ALBERT HARRINGTON, JR., retired economist; b. St. Louis, Oct. 13, 1932; s. Albert Harrington and Hildegarde (Raab) C.; m. Frances Marie French, Apr. 12, 1960; children: Cynthia, Bruce Harrington. BBA, U. Tex., 1954, MBA, 1956; PhD, U. Mich., 1965. Asst. prof. finance So. Meth. U., Dallas, 1959; economist First Nat. City Bank, NYC, 1960-61; sec. research com. Am. Bankers Assn., NYC, 1962-64; v.p., economist First Nat. Bank, Dallas, 1965-68; spl. asst. to chmn. Pres.'s Council Econ. Advs., Washington, 1969-70; exec. v.p., chief economist, dir. Lionel D. Edie & Co., NYC, 1970-75; sr. econ. adv. Merrill Lynch, Pierce, Fenner & Smith, Inc., NYC, 1970-75; pres. Merrill Lynch Econs., Inc., NYC, 1976-81, chmn., 1982-84; chief economist Merrill Lynch & Co., 1976-81; ret., 1984. Mng. dir. Merrill Lynch Capital Markets Group, Merrill Lynch Capital Fund; mem. econ. adv. bd. Dept. Commerce, 1974-76; dir., sr. econ. adviser BIL Trainer, Wortham Inc. (Bank in Liechtenstein, A.G.), 1985-90; sr. econ. adviser Trainer Wortham, Inc., 1991; portfolio cons. Seibels Bruce Ins. Cos., Columbia, SC, 1993-94, dir., 1994-97; mem. Pres.'s Inflation Policy Task Force, 1980; disting. lectr. bus. and econs. U. SC, Hilton Head, 1988-90; dir. Nestor, Inc., 2003-06. Author: Regulation of Interest Rates on Bank Deposits, 1966; contbg. economist Coast Business, 1997-99, Bankers Monthly mag., 1970-88; bus. columnist Hilton Head News, 1990-98; contbr. articles to profl. jours. Mem. Nat. Assn. Bus. Economists (past dir.), Securities Industries Assn. (chmn. econ. adv. com. 1979-80), Am. Econ. Assn., Beta Gamma Sigma, Beta Theta Pi, Phi Eta Sigma. Republican. Mem. Reformed Ch. Home and Office: 5485 Villa Lake Ct Suwanee GA 30024 Office Phone: 678-513-0626. Personal E-mail: albertfrances@bellsouth.net.

COX, ALBERT REGINALD, retired dean, retired cardiologist; b. Victoria, BC, Can., Apr. 18, 1928; s. Reginald Herbert and Marie Christina (Fraser) C.; m. Margaret Dobson, May, 1954; children: Susan Margaret, David John, Steven Fraser. BA, U. B.C., 1950, MD, 1954. Intern Vancouver Gen. Hosp., 1954-55, resident, 1955-59; fellow in cardiology U. Wash., 1959-61; asst. prof. medicine U. B.C., 1962-65, assoc. prof., 1966-69; prof., chmn. medicine Meml. U., St. John's, Nfld., Canada, 1969-74, dean medicine, 1974-87, v.p. Health Scis. and Profl. Sch., 1988-90, v.p. acad., pro-vice chancellor, 1990-91; ret., 1991. Decorated mem. Order of Can. Fellow ACP, Royal Coll. Physicians and Surgeons Can., Am. Coll. Cardiology; mem. Nfld. Med. Assn., Can. Med. Assn., Can. Soc. Clin. Investigation, Assn. Can. Med. Colls. (pres. 1980-81), Coun. of Royal Coll. Physicians and Surgeons (v.p. medicine 1990-91), Alpha Omega Alpha. United Ch. Home: 1275 Campbell Rd Cobble Hill BC Canada V0R 1L6

COX, ALLAN JAMES, management consultant; b. Berwyn, Ill., June 13, 1937; s. Brack C. and Ruby D. C.; m. Jeanne Begalke, 1961 (div. 1966); 1 child, Heather; m. Bonnie Lynne Welden, 1966 (div. 1990); 1 child, Laura; m. Cheryl Patric, 1991. BA, No. Ill. U., 1961, MA, 1962; postgrad., McCormick Theol. Sem., Chgo., 1962-63, postgrad., 1973—75, Alfred Adler Inst. of Chgo., 1965-67, Gestalt Inst. of Chgo., 1994-96. Instr. Wheaton (Ill.) Coll., 1963-65; assoc. Case and Co., Inc., Chgo., 1965-66, Spencer Stuart & Assos., Inc., Chgo., 1966-68; v.p. Westcott Assos., Inc., Chgo., 1968-69; founder, pres. Allan Cox & Assocs., Inc., 1969—; chmn. Berryman Comm. Co., Chgo., 1994-98; chmn. of the bd. Amateur Baseball, Inc., Chgo., 1992-96, CEO, 1996-98; chmn., CEO Assn. for Internat. Youth Sports, Inc., Chgo., 1998-99. Adj. staff Ctr. for Creative Leadership, Greensboro, NC, 1985-90; mem. vis. com. U. Chgo. Div. Sch., 1996-2005; mem. San Diego Regional Econ. Devel. Corp Author: Confessions of a Corporate Headhunter, 1973, Work, Love and Friendship, 1974, The Cox Report on the American Corporation, 1982, The Making of the Achiever, 1985, The Achiever's Profile, 1988, Straight Talk for Monday Morning, 1990, Redefining Corporate Soul: Linking Purpose and People, 1996, Your Inner CEO, 2007; columnist LA Times Syndicate, 1986-90; contbr. articles to profl. jours. Chmn. bd. Ctr. for Ethics and Corp. Policy, 1987-92; Elder Fourth Presbyn. Ch. of Chgo. Mem.: N.Am. Soc. Adlerian Psychology, Corp. Dirs. Forum, Nat. Assn. Corp. Dirs., Chgo. Club, Alpha Kappa Delta. Presbyterian. Office: 45 East Bellevue Pl Chicago IL 60611-1133 Office Phone: 312-337-8010. Business E-Mail: allan@allancox.com.

COX, ANA MARIE, writer, former political blogger; b. 1972; m. Chris Lehmann. Grad., U. Chgo., 1994. Editor Mother Jones, The Chronicle of Higher Edn., The American Prospect; with Feedmag.com, inside.com; sr. editor In These Times; former exec. dir. Suck.com; founding editor, polit. blog Wonkette.com, 2003—06, wonkette emerita, 2006; Washington editor Time.com, 2006—. Author: Dog Days, 2006; contbg. writer, Ana Log Time Mag. online, 2006—, maintains personal website anamariecox.com, guest appearances Scarborough Country, 2006, Fox News Channel, 2006, MSNBC, 2006. Office: Time online 555 12th St NW Washington DC 20004 Office Phone: 202-861-4000. E-mail: dogdaysgirl@gmail.com.*

COX, ANNA LEE, retired administrative assistant; b. Knoxville, Tenn., Feb. 18, 1931; d. Carter Calloway and Fairy Belle (Byers) Bayless; m. William Smith Cox, Sept. 4, 1952; 1 child, Catherine Anne Cox Faust. Grad. high sch., Knoxville. Sec. Am. Mut. Liability Ins. Co., Knoxville, 1948-53; flight procedures clk. FAA, Atlanta, 1963-66; legal sec., paralegal U.S. Atty.'s Office for Dist. S.C., Greenville, 1972-79; sec. criminal investigation div. IRS, Knoxville, 1981-84; sec., adminstrv. asst. CIA, Knoxville, 1984-88; adminstrv. asst. U.S. Dept. Def., Knoxville, 1988-91, ret., 1991. Tutor Greenville Literacy Assn., 1977-79; founder, dir. NATO Womens Chorus, Izmir, Turkey, 1969-71; choir dir., pres. United Meth. Women, Stephenson Meml. United Meth. Ch., Greenville, 1972-79; bd. dirs. Fountainhead Conservatory Music, Knoxville, 1983-85, 92-95, sec. of bd. dirs., 1994-95; singer Knoxville Choral Soc., 1955-56, Atlanta Symphony Chorus, 1971, Greenville Civic Chorale, 1973-79; vol. Farragut Folklife Mus., Concord United Meth. Ch. Republican. Avocations: music, drama. Home: 619 Farragut Commons Dr Knoxville TN 37934-1673 Personal E-mail: annaleecox@aol.com.

COX, ARCHIBALD, JR., investor; b. Framingham, Mass., July 13, 1940; s. Archibald and Phyllis (Ames) C.; m. Judy G. Cox; children: Suzanne, Archibald III, Christopher. BA in Econs. cum laude, Harvard Coll., Cambridge, Mass., 1962; MBA with distinction, Harvard Bus. Sch., Allston, Mass., 1964. Assoc. and mng. dir. Morgan Stanley, NYC, 1964—88, London, 1964—88; pres., CEO The First Boston Corp., NYC, 1990-93; chmn. Sextant Group, Inc., NYC, 1993—; pres., CEO Magnequench, Inc., Indpls., 1995—2005; chmn. Precision Magnetics Singapore Pte. Ltd., Singapore, 2004—, Neo Materials Technologies, Toronto, Canada, 2005—06; dir. Hutchinson Tech. Inc., 1996—, Builders Info. Group, 2004—, Micell Tech. Inc., 2007—. Bd. dirs. Claremont McKenna Coll., 1992-97. Mem.: Bucks Harbor Yacht Club, Links Club NYC, NY Yacht Club. Independent. Episcopalian. Avocations: bicycling, sailing, hiking, rowing. Office: Sextant Group Inc 60 High Oaks Dr Watchung NJ 07069 Office Phone: 908-822-2211. Business E-Mail: acox5005@aol.com.

COX, BEULAH ELIZABETH, violinist, music educator; b. Newport News, Va., Mar. 15, 1955; d. Willis Franklin and Rosemary Christian Coates Cox. BA, Coll. of William and Mary, 1973—77. Violinist Colonial Williamsburg Found., Williamsburg, Va., 1975—78, Hudson Valley Philharm., Poughkeepsie, NY, 1984—95, The Greenwich Symphony, Conn., 1984—; violinist/founder The Ambrosia Trio, NYC, 1990—; violin soloist Allegro Chamber Ensemble, New York, NY, 1991, Virtuoso Strings, NYC, 1992, Doansburg Chamber Ensemble, Brewster, NY, 1993; violinist Nat. Chorale, NYC, 1994—; violin soloist Buglisi/Foreman Dance Co., NYC, 1996. Violinist Joseph Fuchs Chamber Music Inst., Alfred, NY, 1976—83, Grand Teton Music Festival, Teton Village, Wyo., 1984, Am. Inst. of Musical Studies, Graz, Austria, 1985, Banff Chamber Music, Banff, Canada, 1995; adj. prof. of violin Fordham U., Bronx, NY, 2000—; string tchr. Ethical Culture Sch., NYC, 1997—; violin and piano tchr. Riverdale YM-YWHA - Rhoda Grundman Sch. of Music, Bronx, 1999—; violin tchr. Bronx Arts Ensemble Sch., Bronx, 2000—05. Musician: (recording) Peter and the Wolf, 1999, Baroque Sonatas and Trios, 1975, Berlioz Te Deum - Voices of Ascension, 1996, Meet The Ambrosia Trio!, 1997, The Ambrosia Trio Close Up, 2000. Mem.: Am. Fedn. of Musicians, Chamber Music Am.

COX, BOBBY (ROBERT JOE COX), professional baseball manager; b. Tulsa, Okla., May 21, 1941; m. Pamela Cox; children: Kami, Keisha, Skyla. Student, Reedley Jr. Coll., Calif. Player Calif. League, Reno, 1960, Northwest League, Salem, Oreg., 1961-62, Texas League, Albuquerque, 1963-64, Pacific Coast League, Salt Lake City, 1965, Tacoma, 1966, Internat. League, Richmond, Va., 1967, New York Yankees, NYC, 1968-69, Internat. League, Syracuse, NY, 1970, Fla. State League, Ft. Lauderdale, 1971, mgr., 1971, Ea. League, West Haven, Conn., 1972, Internat. League, Syracuse, 1973-76; 1st base coach New York Yankees, NYC, 1977; mgr. Atlanta Braves, 1978-81, Toronto (Ont., Can.) Blue Jays, 1982-85, Atlanta Braves, 1990—. Named Am. League Mgr. Yr., 1985, Major League Baseball Writers Assn.; Nat. League Mgr. Yr., 1991, 2004-05 Achievements include coaching World Series Champion Atlanta Braves, 1995; being the ninth manager in MLB history to win 2,000 games, 2004. Office: care Atlanta Braves PO Box 4064 Atlanta GA 30302-4064

COX, BRIAN, actor; b. Dundee, Scotland, June 1, 1946; m. Caroline Burt, 1968 (div. 1986); children: Alan, Margaret; m. Nicole Ansari, 2002; 2 children. Actor: (films) Nicholas and Alexandra, 1971, In Celebration, 1975, Manhunter, 1986, Hidden Agenda, 1990, Deceptions, 1992, Iron Will, 1994, Prince of Jutland, 1994, Rob Roy, 1995, Bravehart, 1995, Chain Reaction, 1996, The Glimmer Man, 1996, The Long Kiss Goodnight, 1996, Kiss the Girls, 1997, The Boxer, 1997, Merchants of Venus, 1998, Desperate Measures, 1998, Rushmore, 1998, The Minus Man, 1999, The Corruptor, 1999, For Love of the Game, 1999, The Invention of Dr. Morel, 2000, Complicity, 2000, Mad About Mambo, 2000, The Green Man of Knowledge (voice only), 2000, A Shot at Glory, 2000, L.I.E., 2001, Super Troopers, 2001, Saltwater, 2000, The Legend of Loch Lomond, 2001, The Affair of the Necklace, 2001, Strictly Sinatra, 2001, The Rookie, 2002, The Bourne Identity, 2002, The Ring, 2002, Adaptation, 2002, 25th Hour, 2002, X2: X-Men United, 2003, The Reckoning, 2003, Troy, 2004, The Bourne Supremacy, 2004, Get the Picture, 2004, Match Point, 2005, Red-Eye, 2005, The Ringer, 2005, The Flying Scotsman, 2006, Running with Scissors, 2006, Zodiac, 2007; (TV films) The Year of the Sex Olympics, 1968, She Stoops to Conquer, 1971, The Changeling, 1974, The Cantor of St. Thomas's, 1984, King Lear, 1984, Pope John Paul II, 1984, Florence Nightingale, 1985, The Deliberate Death of a Polish Priest, 1986, The Fourth Floor, 1986, Shoot for the Sun, 1986, Beryl Markham: A Shadow on the Sun, 1988, Murder by Moonlight, 1989, Secret Weapon, 1990, The Lost Language of Cranes, 1991, Six Characters in Search of an Author, 1992, The Cloning of Joanna May, 1992, Sharpe's Eagle, 1993, Sharpe's Rifles, 1993, Grushko, 1994, The Negotiator, 1994, Witness Against Hitler, 1996, Food for Ravens, 1997, Poodle Springs, 1998, Longitude, 2000, The Biographer, 2002, Blue/Orange, 2005, The Strange Case of Sherlock Holmes & Arthur Conan Doyle, 2005; (TV miniseries) Out, 1978, The Devil's Crown, 1978, Therese Raquin, 1980, Red Fox, 1991, Shakespeare: The Animated Tales (voice only), 1992, The Big Battalions, 1992, Nuremberg, 2001 (Emmy award Oustanding Supporting Actor in Miniseries, 2001); dir.: (plays) The Man with a Flower in His Mouth, 1973; stage appearances include: As You Like It, 1966—67; In Celebration, 1969; Danton' Death, 1982; Strange Interlude, 1984; Rat in the Skull, 1984 (Laurence Olivier Theatre award Best Actor in a New Play, 1985); Titus Andronicus, 1988 (Laurence Olivier Theatre award Best Actor in a Revival, 1989); Frankie and Johnnie in the Clair-de-Lune, 1989; St. Nicholas; Skylight, 1997; Art, 1998; Dublin Carol, 2000; others; actor: (TV appearances) Thirty-Minute Theatre, 1969, Z Cars, 1969, Doomwatch, 1970, Sutherland's Law, 1974, Target, 1977, Hammer House of Horror, 1980, Minder, 1982, Perfect Scoundrels, 1990, Van der Valk, 1992, Inspector Morse, 1993, Great Composers (voice only), 1997, Red Dwarf, 1997, Superman, 1997, Frasier, 2002, Danny Phantom, 2005. Recipient comdr., Order. Brit. Empire, 2002, London Critics Circle Theatre award, 1984, 1987. Office: IFA Talent Agency 8730 Sunset Blvd Ste 490 Los Angeles CA 90069*

COX, CARRIE, pharmaceutical executive; b. 1957; m. Ken Cox; 2 children. BS, Mass. Coll. Pharmacy and Health Sci., 1981. With Sandoz Pharm., 1982—92; v.p. women's healthcare Wyeth-Ayerst; sr. v.p. & head global bus. mgmt. Pharmacia & Upjohn, 1997, exec. v.p., 1999; exec. v.p., pres. global perscription Pharmacia, 2002; pres. global pharm. Shering-Plough, 2003—, also exec. v.p., 2003—. Mem. bd. dir., audit com. Texas Instruments, 2004—. Named Healthcare Businesswoman of Yr., Healthcare Businesswomen's Assn., 2001; named one of 50 Most Powerful Women in Bus., Fortune mag., 2005, 2006, 10 Most Powerful Women in NJ Bus., Star-Ledger, 2006. Office: Shering-Plough Corp Headquarters 2000 Galloping Hill Rd Kenilworth NJ 07033-0530 Office Phone: 908-298-4000.*

COX, CATHY, academic administrator, former state official; b. Bainbridge, Ga., July 18, 1958; d. Walter Cox; m. Mark Dehler. A.Agr., Abraham Baldwin Agrl. Coll., 1978; ABJ summa cum laude, U. Ga., 1980; JD magna cum laude, Mercer U., 1986. Newspaper reporter The Gainesville Times, Gainesville, 1980-82, Post-Searchlight, Bainbridge, 1982-83; atty. Hansell & Post, Atlanta, 1986-88, Lambert, Floyd & Conger, Bainbridge, Ga., 1988-95; mem. Ga. Gen. Assembly from dist. 160, 1993-96; asst. sec. state State of Ga., Atlanta, 1996-98, sec. state, 1999—2007; pres. Young Harris Coll., Ga., 2007—. Carl E. Sanders polit. leadership scholar U. Ga. Sch. Law, Athens, 2007—. Editor Mercer U. Law Rev. Named Conservation Legislator of Yr., Ga. Wildlife Fedn., 1994, Woman of Courage award, Woman's Policy Group, 1995, Woman of Yr., Ga. Commn. on Women, 2000, named one of 11 Pub. Officials of Yr., Governing Mag., 2002. Democrat. Methodist. Office: Young Harris College PO Box 98 Young Harris GA 30582 Office Phone: 706-379-5137. Office Fax: 706-379-4319. Business E-Mail: ccox@yhc.edu.

COX, CHAPMAN BEECHER, retired lawyer, charitable organization and aerospace executive; b. Dayton, Ohio, July 31, 1940; s. Charles Benjamin and Jewel Lorene (Nicholson) C.; m. Jeannette Gail Korody, Aug. 28, 1964; children: Charles Benjamin, Andrew David. BA, U. So. Calif., 1962; JD, Harvard U., 1965. Bar: Calif. 1966, Colo. 1972, U.S. Ct. Mil. Appeals 1966, U.S. Supreme Ct. 1986. Assoc. Adams, Duque & Hazeltine, Los Angeles, 1968-72, Sherman & Howard, Denver, 1972-74, ptnr., 1974-80, mng. ptnr., 1980-81, ptnr., 1987-90; dep. asst. sec. U.S. Dept. Navy, Washington, 1981-83, asst. sec., 1983-84; gen. counsel Dept. Def., Washington, 1984-85, asst. sec., 1985-87; pres., CEO United Svc. Orgns., Inc., 1990-96; sr. v.p. Lockheed Martin IMS, 1996-2000; ret., 2000. Vis. lectr. U. Colo. Sch. Law, Boulder, 1977-78; def. policy bd. US Dept. Def., 1988-90; comml. space transp. adv. com. US Dept. Transp., 1989-91; chmn. Colo. Commn. Space Sci. and Industry, 1988-90. Gen. counsel Colo. Reps., Denver, 1977-81; del. U.S. Dept. State cultural exch. mission to Syria and Jordan, 1979; ruling elder Presbyn. Ch., 1976—; bd. dirs. United Svc. Orgns., 1985-96, Colorado Springs Symphony Orch., 1988-90, MicroLithics Corp., 1989-91, Presbyn. Ch. U.S.A. Found., 1990-99, Freedoms Found., 1994-99, Fund for Am. Studies, 1995-00, New Covenant Trust Co., 1996-99, Presbyn. Lay Com., 1997-00, Alliance Def. Fund, 2002-, chmn., 2007—, Manhattan Initiative, Inc., 2005-; bd. govs. Army-Navy Club Washington, 1998-2000. Col. USMCR, 1962-93, ret. Fellow: Am. Coll. Trust and Estate Counsel; mem.: ABA (standing com. law and nat. security 1988—2002), Colo. Bar Assn. (bd. govs. 1977—79, chmn. probate and trust law sect. 1978—79), Calif. Bar Assn., Army-Navy Club of Washington. Personal E-mail: chapmancox@att.net.

COX, CHARLES C., economist; b. Missoula, Mont., May 8, 1945; m. Monica Lewis, 1984. BA magna cum laude, U. Wash., 1967; AM, U. Chgo., 1970, PhD, 1975. Asst. prof. econs. Ohio State U., Columbus, 1972-80; nat. fellow Hoover Instn., 1977-78; asst. prof. mgmt. Tex. A&M U., College Station, 1980-82; chief economist SEC, Washington, 1982-83, commr., 1983-89, acting chmn., 1987; prin., sr. v.p. Lexecon, Inc., Chgo., 1989—. Nat. fellow Hoover Institution, 1977-78. Mem. Am. Econ. Assn., United Shareholders Assn. (chmn. 1990-93), Mt. Pelerin Soc., Phi Beta Kappa. Office: Lexecon Inc 332 S Michigan Ave Ste 1300 Chicago IL 60604-4397

COX, CHARLES SHIPLEY, oceanography researcher, educator; b. Paia, Hawaii, Sept. 11, 1922; s. Joel Bean and Helen Clifford (Horton) C.; m. Maryruth Louise Melander, Dec. 23, 1951; children: Susan (dec.), Caroline, Valerie, Ginger, Joel. BS, Calif. Inst. Tech., 1944; PhD, U. Calif., San Diego, 1955. From asst. rschr. to prof. U. Calif., San Diego, 1955—. Rschr. in field. Fellow AAAS, NAS (Alexander Agassiz medal 2001), Am. Geophys. Union (Maurice Ewing medal 1992), Royal Astron. Soc. Democrat. Office: U Calif San Diego Scripps Inst Oceanography La Jolla CA 92093-0213 E-mail: cscox@ucsd.edu.

COX, (CHARLES) CHRISTOPHER, federal agency administrator, former congressman; b. St. Paul, Oct. 16, 1952; s. Charles C. and Marilyn A. (Miller) C.; m. Rebecca Gernhardt; children: Charles, Kathryn, Kevin. BA magna cum laude, U. So. Calif., 1973; MBA with honors, Harvard Bus. Sch., 1977; JD with honors, Harvard Law Sch., 1977. Bar: Calif. 1978, D.C. 1980. Law clk. to Hon. Herbert C. Choy U.S. Ct. Appeals (9th cir.), 1977—78; assoc. Latham & Watkins LLP, Newport Beach, Calif., 1978-82, ptnr., 1984-86; lectr. bus. adminstrn. Harvard U., 1982-83; sr. assoc. counsel to Pres. Ronald Reagan The White House, Washington, 1986-88; mem. U.S. Congress from 48th dist. Calif. (formerly 47th), Washington, 1989—2005, mem. energy and commerce com., steering com., mem. fin. svcs. com.; chmn. house Rep. policy com., 1994—2005, house com. on homeland security, 2003—05; mem. Bipartisan Commn. on Entitlement and Tax Reform, Washington, 1994—95; mem. leadership steering com.; chmn. SEC, Washington, 2005—. Prin., co-founder Context Corp., St. Paul, 1984-86. Editor Harvard Law Rev., 1975-77. Former mem. adv. bd. U. Calif., Irvine, Brain-Imaging Ctr.; mem. bd. dirs. Nat. Endowment Democracy, Washington. Named a Taxpayer Fighter, Nat. Limitation Com., Hero of the Taxpayer, Americans for Tax Reform, Super Friend of Seniors, 60/Plus Assn., Guardian of Small Bus., Nat. Fedn. Ind. Bus.; recipient People of the Year award, PR Computing mag., 1999, Founders Circle award, TechNet, 2002, Friend of Small Bus. award, Nat. Fedn. Ind. Bus., Friend of the Consumer award, Consumer Alert, Golden Bulldog award, Watchdogs of the Treasury, Hero to the Taxpayer award, Citizens Against Govt. Waste, Taxpayers Friend award, Nat. Taxpayers Union. Republican. Roman Catholic. Office: SEC 100 F St NE Washington DC 20549 Office Phone: 202-942-8088.*

COX, CLAIR EDWARD, II, urologist, medical educator; b. Lawrenceville, Ill., Sept. 2, 1933; s. Clair Edward and May E. (Judy) C.; m. Clarice Wicks, Aug. 23, 1958; children— Clair Edward III, Daniel Paul, Kevin Christopher, Kenneth Harold. Student, U. Mich., 1951-54, MD, 1958. Diplomate Am. Bd. Urology. Intern U. Colo. Med. Center, Denver, 1958-59, surg. resident, 1959-60; resident urology U. Cal. Med. Center at San Francisco, 1960-63; mem. faculty Bowman Gray Sch. Medicine, Wake Forest U., Winston Salem, NC, 1963-72, assoc. prof., 1967-70, prof. urology, 1970-72; prof., chmn. dept. urology U. Tenn. Med. Sch., Memphis, 1972—. Contbr. profl. jours. Fellow ACS; mem. AMA, Am. Assn. Genito-Urinary Surgeons, Am. Urol. Assn., Internat. Soc. Urology, N.Y. Acad. Scis., Infectious Disease Soc. Am., Soc. Univ. Urologists, Am. Assn. Med. Colls., Am. Soc. Microbiology. Achievements include research in urinary tract infectious disease. Home: 6011 Sweetbriar Cv Memphis TN 38120-2514

COX, CLIFFORD ERNEST, information systems consulting executive, former academic administrator; b. Chgo., Apr. 28, 1942; s. Clifford Ernest and Beulah May (Lynn) C.; m. Scenobia Butler, June 20, 1964; children: Clifford, Fred, Sean. BA, U. Chgo., 1964, MBA, 1966; postgrad., No. Ill.

U., 1988—. Cert. in data processing. Sr. systems engr. IBM, Chgo., 1966-69; v.p. MIS Golden Fifty Pharm., Chgo., 1969-71; sr. mgr. Arthur Andersen & Co., Chgo., 1971-79; pres. Cenox Systems, Inc., Chgo., 1979-81, 97—; chief info. officer Chgo. Pub. Schs., 1981-92; deputy supt. Detroit Pub. Schs., 1992-97; pres. Cenox Sys. Am., Cleve., 1998—. Lectr. Keller Grad Sch. Mgmt., 1986-89; del. Ill. Regional White House conf., 1990. Contbr. articles to profl. jours. Bd. dirs. Assn. House, Chgo., 1991; mem. Chgo. Assembly. Office: Cenox Sys 4289 Stoddard Rd West Bloomfield MI 48323 Home Phone: 248-539-0295; Office Phone: 248-626-4861. E-mail: cliffcox@cenox.com.

COX, COURTLAND, minority business administrator; b. NYC, Jan. 27, 1941; married; 1 child. Student, Howard U. Co-owner, mgr. Drum and Spear Bookstore, Drum and Spear Pubs.; spl. asst. to dep. mayor for econ. devel. D.C. Govt., dir. Minority Bus. Opportunity Commn., dir. Office of Internat. Bus.; spl. asst. to dep. asst. sec. for Africa, Near East and South Dept. of Commerce, Washington, 1993, dir. Office of Civil Rights, 1994, dir. Minority Bus. Devel. Agy., 1998—. Bus. con. drafting D.C. Small, Minority and Disadvantaged Bus. Legislation.

COX, DARLENE BETH, secondary school educator; b. Cin., Oct. 28, 1952; d. Kenneth and Ruth Janet Cox. BS, U. N.Mex., Albuquerque, 1996. Cert. level two tchr. N.Mex. Dept. Edn., 1999, lab. animal tech. Am. Assn. for Lab. Animal Sci., 1982, radiation protection tech. U. N.Mex., 1982. Lab. animal tech. U. N.Mex., Albuquerque, 1977—91; h.s. sci. tchr. Moriarty Mcpl. Schs., N.Mex., 1996—. Chmn. regional exam. bd. #19 Am. Assn. for Lab. Animal Sci., Albuquerque, 1991—92. Primary contbr.: Training Manual Series, American Association for Laboratory Animal Science. Dream Fund grantee, Ctr. for Tchg. Excellence, Ea. N.Mex. U., 1999, 2000. Mem.: NSTA, World Class Tchrs. Network, N.Mex. Sci. Tchrs. Assn., SW Dairy Goat Assn., Am. Goat Soc., Am. Dairy Goat Assn. (life), SW Nigerian Dwarf Dairy Goat Club (bd. mem. 2003—05), Golden Key Nat. Honor Soc., Phi Beta Kappa. Independent. Avocation: showing and breeding of Nigerian dwarf dairy goats. Home: 27 Nizhoni Ln Tijeras NM 87059 Office: Moriarty HS 2000 Center St Moriarty NM 87031 Home Phone: 505-286-8533; Office Phone: 505-832-4254. Personal E-mail: caprinz@aol.com.

COX, DAVID ARCHIBALD, mathematics professor; b. Washington, Sept. 23, 1948; s. John Tatum Cox, Jr. and Shirley Elizabeth (Barker) Cox; m. Elaine Louise Brighty, Jan. 17, 1981; children: Kevin Charles, Laura Elizabeth. BA, Rice U., 1970; PhD, Princeton U., 1974. Lectr., asst. prof. Rutgers U., New Brunswick, NJ, 1975—79; prof. of math. Amherst (Mass.) Coll., 1979—. Vis. asst. prof. Haverford (Pa.) Coll., 1974—75; mem. editl. bd. pure and applied math. John Wiley & Sons, Inc., Hoboken, NJ, 1993—2004, cons. editor, 2005—. Author: (textbook) Primes of the Form x2 + ny2, Ideals, Varieties and Algorithms, Using Algebraic Geometry, (monograph) Mirror Symmetry and Algebraic Geometry, (textbook) Galois Theory. Mem.: Math. Assn. of Am. (mem. 2d. pl. team Putnam Exam 1970), Am. Math. Soc. (coun. mem. 1991—94). Office: Amherst Coll Dept Math and Computer Sci Amherst MA 01002 Home Phone: 413-243-2173; Office Phone: 413-542-2082.

COX, DAVID JACKSON, biochemistry professor; b. NYC, Dec. 22, 1934; s. Reavis and Rachel (Dunaway) C.; m. Joan M. Narbeth, Sept. 6, 1958 (dec. Oct. 8, 1982); children: Andrew Reavis, Matthew Bruce, Thomas Jackson; m. Tamara L. Compton, Nov. 26, 1983. BA, Wesleyan U., 1956; PhD, U. Pa., 1960. Instr. biochemistry U. Wash., 1960-63; asst. prof. chemistry U. Tex., 1963-67, assoc. prof., 1967-73; prof., head dept. biochemistry Kans. State U., 1973-89; prof. chemistry Ind. U./Purdue U., Ft. Wayne, 1989-2000, prof. emeritus, 2000—. Vis. prof. U. Va., 1970-71; dean arts scis. Ind. U./Purdue U., Ft. Wayne, 1989-96. NSF predoctoral fellow, 1956-59; NSF sr. postdoctoral fellow, 1970-71 Mem. Am. Soc. Biochemistry, Molecular Biology Soc., Am. Chem. Soc., Phi Beta Kappa, Sigma Xi. Democrat. Presbyterian. Home: 309 Crown Ln Bellingham WA 98229-5929 Personal E-mail: comcox@yahoo.com.

COX, DAVID LEON, telecommunications industry executive; b. Lima, Ohio, Sept. 8, 1952; s. Leon Hamiln and Mildred Marie (Johnson) C.; m. Carolle Marie Mallette, July 17, 1978; children: Paul David, Elizabeth Christine. BS in Chemistry, Mich. State U., 1975, BS in Computer Sci., 1976; MBA in Telecomms., Parkwood U., London, 2001. Registered profl. engr., Va. 76asst. v.p. engrng. KollMorgan Corp., Newburgh, NY, 1975; staff mgr. AT&T, Bedminster, N.J., 1976-79; asst. v.p. Satellite Bus. Systems, McLean, Va., 1979-83; devel. mgr. MCI, Washington, 1983-84; chief engr. Harris Corp., Melbourne, Fla., 1984-95; asst. dir. GTE, Rockville, Md., 1997-2000, dir. Irving, Tex., 1998-2000; exec. dir. engrng. Parsons Brinkerhoff, Dallas, 2000; dir. Sprint PCS, Flower Mound, Tex., 2001—04; exec. engr. mgr. Rockwell-Collins Govt. Sys., Richardson, Tex., 2004—. Mem. Pres.'s Commn. on Crit. Infrastructure Protection, advisor, 1996—2002 Pres.'s Nat. Security Telecomms. adv. com., cons., 1995-2002; bd. dirs. GTE, Irving, Tex. Contbr. articles to profl. jours. Active Friends of the Palm Bay (Fla.) Libr., Space Coast Sci. Ctr., 1000 Friends of Fla., Tallahassee, Turkey Creek Homeowners Assn., Turkey Creek Santuary Bd., Palm Bay PTA; vice chmn. pub. rels. Boy Scouts of Am., 1991-95, dist. com. mem., 1991-95, unit commr., 1990-95, troop com. mem., 1992-95, park com. mem., 1987-95; mem. Comprehensive Plan Com., Palm Bay, Fla., 1986-87. Mem. IEEE, Am. Chem. Soc., Am. Inst. Plant Engrs., Mensa, Assn. for Computing Machinery, N.Y. Acad. Sci., Nat. Fire Protection Assn., Building Industry Cons. Svc. Internat., Am. Radio Relay League, Nat. Eagle Scout Assn. (life), Nat. Coun. Boy Scouts of Am., Mich. State U. Alumni Assn., Lyman Briggs Coll. Alumni Assn., Mason (3d deg.), Orlando Scottish Rite (32nd deg., Master of Royal Secret), Alpha Phi Omega (Beta Beta chpt.). Republican. Presbyterian. Achievements include 7 patents in integrated svcs. digital network tech., signaling system 7, and surveillance technologies. Home: 6000 Grand Meadow Ln Flower Mound TX 75028-4830 Office: Rockwell Collins 3200 E Renner Rd Richardson TX 45082 Office Phone: 972-705-3070. Fax: 214-513-8413. E-mail: coxdl@gte.net.

COX, DONALD CLYDE, electrical engineering educator; b. Lincoln, Nebr., Nov. 22, 1937; s. Elvin Clyde and C. Gertrude (Thomas) C.; m. Mary Dale Alexander, Aug. 27, 1961; children: Bruce Dale, Earl Clyde. BS, U. Nebr., 1959, MS, 1960, DSc (hon.), 1983; PhD, Stanford U., 1968. Registered profl. engr., Ohio, Nebr. With Bell Tel. Labs., Holmdel, NJ, 1968-84, head radio and satellite systems rsch. dept., 1983-84; mgr. radio and satellite systems rsch. divsn. Bell Comm. Rsch., Red Bank, NJ, 1984-91, exec. dir. radio rsch. dept., 1991-93; prof. elec. engrng. Stanford (Calif.) U., 1993—, Harald Trap Friis Prof. Engring., 1994—, dir. telecomms., 1993-99. Em. commns. U.S. nat. com. Internat. Union of Radio Sci.; participant enbanc hearing on Personal Comm. Sys., FCC, 1991; mem. rsch. visionary bd. Motorola Labs., 2002-03. Contbr. articles to profl. jours.; patentee in field. 1st lt. USAF, 1960-63. Recipient Guglielmo Marconi prize in Electromagnetic Waves Propagation, Inst. Internat. Comm., 1983, Alumni Achievement award U. Nebr., 2002; Johnson fellow, 1959-60. Fellow IEEE (Morris E. Leeds award 1985, Alexander Graham Bell medal 1993, Millenium medal 2000), AAAS, Bellcore 1991, Radio Club Am.; mem. NAE, Comm. Soc. of IEEE (Leonard G. Abraham Prize Paper award 1992, Comms. Mag. Prize Paper award 1990), Vehicular Tech. Soc. of IEEE (Paper of Yr. award 1983), Antennas and Propagation Soc. of IEEE (elected mem. adminstrn. com. 1986-88), Sigma Xi. Achievements include rsch. in wireless communication systems, cellular radio systems, radio propagation. Home: 924 Mears Ct Stanford CA 94305-1029 Office: Stanford U Dept Elec Engring Packard 361 Stanford CA 94305-9515 Home Phone: 650-813-1716; Office Phone: 650-723-5443. Business E-Mail: dcox@spark.stanford.edu.

COX, DOUGLAS LYNN, management consultant, researcher; b. Des Moines, Dec. 13, 1945; s. Carol Eugene and Maribelle (Harter) C.; m. Janice C. Kuchka, Nov. 15, 1969; children: David Michael, Kristen Anne. BS, U. Pa., 1968, MBA, 1973. With IU Internat. Corp., Phila., 1974-88, treas. assoc. long-term fin., 1974-76, sr. treas. assoc. internat. fin., 1976-77, mgr. internat. fin., 1977-79, dir. treas. planning, 1979-80, asst. treas., 1980-85, v.p., treas., 1985-88; sr. v.p. fin., CFO Elf Atochem N.Am., Phila., 1988-98; exec. v.p., CFO Opinion Rsch. Corp., Princeton, 1998—. Class gift chmn. U. Pa.; bd. dirs., treas. Big Bros./Big Sisters; treas. Old Pine St. Presbyn. Ch.; bd. govs. Pa. Econ. League; trustee Friends Select Sch., pres. bd. trustees; bd. dirs. Pa. Bus. Roundtable. With USCG, 1969-72. Decorated Gallantry Cross (Vietnam). Mem. Phila. Racquet Club, TPC Jasna Polana, Phi Kappa Sigma. Home: 1220 Rodman St Philadelphia PA 19147-1130 Office: Opinion Rsch Corp PO Box 183 Princeton NJ 08542-0183 Office Phone: 908-281-5100. E-mail: dcox@prn.opinionresearch.com.

COX, EMMETT RIPLEY, federal judge; b. Cottonwood, Ala., Feb. 13, 1935; s. Emmett M. Jr. Cox and Myra E. (Ripley) Stewart; m. Ann MacKay Haas, May 16, 1964; children: John Haas, Catherine MacKay. BA, U. Ala., 1957, JD, 1959. Bar: Ala. 1959, US Ct. Appeals (5th, 8th and 11th cirs.), US Supreme Ct. Assoc. Mead, Norman & Fitzpatrick, Birmingham, Ala., 1959—64; assoc. then ptnr. Gaillard, Wilkins, Smith & Cox, Mobile, Ala., 1964—69; ptnr. Nettles, Cox & Barker, 1969—81; judge US Dist. Ct. (so. dist.) Ala., Mobile, 1981—88, US Ct. Appeals (11th cir.), Mobile, 1988—2000, sr. judge, 2000—. Mem. def. svcs. com. Jud. Conf. US, 1992—98, chair, 1995—98, mem. jud. br. com., 2001—05. Mem.: Maritime Law Assn. US, Fed. Bar Assn., Mobile Bar Assn., Ala. Bar Assn., Alpha Tau Omega (past pres.), Phi Delta Phi, Omicron Delta Kappa. Office: US Courthouse 11th Circuit 113 Saint Joseph St Ste 433 Mobile AL 36602-3624 also: 56 Forsyth St NW Atlanta GA 30303*

COX, FREDERICK MORELAND, retired dean, social worker; b. LA, Dec. 8, 1928; s. Frederick Alfred Edward and Ethel (Moreland) C.; m. Gay Campbell, June 1951 (dec. June 1991); children: Lawrence, Elizabeth, Sherman. BA, UCLA, 1950, MSW, 1954; DSW, U. Calif., Berkeley, 1968. Caseworker child welfare L.A. Bur. Public Assistance, 1952-53; mental health counselor L.A. Superior Ct., 1953; caseworker Family Service Bur., Oakland, Calif., 1954-57; program dir. Easter Seal Soc., Oakland, 1957-60; asst. prof. to prof. social work U. Mich., Ann Arbor, 1964-76; prof., dir. Sch. Social Work, Mich. State U., East Lansing, 1976-80; prof., dean Sch. Social Welfare, U. Wis., Milw., 1980-89, ret., 1989. Author: As We See It: Men's Stories About Their Experiences with Prostate Cancer, 1999; sr. co-editor: Cmty.-Action Planning Development, A Casebook, 1974, Tactics and Techniques of Community Practice, 1977, 2d edit., 1984, Strategies of Community Organization, 4th edit, 1987; co-editor: Families in Trouble (5 vols.), 1988. Pres. Wis. Coun. Human Concerns, 1985-86. Spl. Rsch. fellow NIMH, 1960-63. Mem. NASW (v.p. Wis. chpt. 1984-86), Acad. Cert. Social Workers, Nat. Deans and Dirs. Schs. Social Work (sec.-treas. 1985-87), Coun. Social Work Edn. (bd. dirs. 1985-89). Home: 11300 First Ave NE # 221 Seattle WA 98125-6038 Personal E-mail: fredmcox@hotmail.com.

COX, GARY WALTER, political science professor; b. Patuxent River, Md., Sept. 23, 1955; s. Dale William and Patricia Broadway Cox; m. Diane Christine Lin, June 18, 1988 (dec. Jan. 1999); 1 child, Dylan Gregory; m. Karen J. Cox, Oct. 4, 2003;. BS, Calif. Inst. Tech., 1978, PhD, 1982. From asst. prof. to assoc. prof. U. Tex., Austin, 1982-86; assoc. prof. U. Calif., La Jolla, 1986-90, prof. polit. sci., 1990—. Author: (books) The Efficient Secret, 1987 (George Hallet prize 2002), Making Votes Count, 1997 (Woodrow Wilson Found. award 1998; co-author: (books) Legislative Leviathan, 1993 (Fenno prize 1994), Elbridge Gerry's Salamander, 2002. Guggenheim fellow, 1995, Am. Acad. Arts and Scis. fellow, 1996, NAS fellow, 2005. Mem.: NAS. Business E-Mail: gcox@ucsd.edu.

COX, HEADLEY MORRIS, JR., lawyer, educator; b. Mt. Olive, NC, July 25, 1916; s. Headley Morris and Frank (English) C.; m. Irene Todd, June 26, 1940; children: John Morris, Deborah English, Thomas Headley; m. Elizabeth Shelton Smith, Dec. 30, 1994. AB, Duke, 1937, AM, 1939; postgrad., U. Colo., 1944-45; PhD, U. Pa., 1958; JD, U. S.C., 1984. Successively instr., asst. prof., assoc. prof., prof. English Clemson (S.C.) U., 1939-82, head dept., 1950-69, dean Coll. Liberal Arts, 1969-80; of counsel Olson, Smith, Jordan & Cox, P.A., 1984—. Sr. Fulbright lectr. in Am. lit. Universitat Graz, Austria, 1958-59 Served with USNR, 1944-46. Mem. Phi Beta Kappa. Methodist. Address: 213 Riggs Dr Clemson SC 29631-1427

COX, HEIDI PINKERTON, pediatric surgeon; b. New Brunswick, NJ, Aug. 23, 1967; d. Harvey Charles and Gail Joanne Sarner; m. Jordy Charles Cox, Sept. 11, 2005. BS cum laude, UCLA, 1989; MD with highest distinction, U. So. Calif., LA, 1994. Bd. cert. gen. surgery Am. Bd. Surgery, Pa., bd. cert. pediat. surgery Am. Bd. Surgery, Pa. Gen. surgeon Gt. Lakes Naval Hosp., Great Lakes, Ill., 2000—01; asst. prof. of surgery U. of Tex., San Antonio, 2003—05; chief of pediat. surgery Wilford Hall Med. Ctr., San Antonio, 2003—05; pediat. surgeon Ea. Maine Med. Ctr., Bangor, 2005—06, Ariz. Children's Surgery, P.C., Mesa, 2006—. Maj. USAF, 2003—05. Decorated Expeditionary Svc. Ribbon USAF, Global War on Terrorism Expeditionary medal, Nat. Def. Svc. medal, Air Force Tng. Ribbon; recipient AMA ERF award for top student in class, AMA, 1994, Achievement Citation, Am. Med. Women's Assn., 1994, Dept. Honors in Cybernetics, UCLA, 1989, Spl. Task Force Citation, USAF, 2003, 2005, Health Professions scholarship, 1992, pediat. surgery fellowship, 2001, Golden Scalpel award for best tech. surgery resident, Med. Coll. of Wis., 2000, U. So. Calif. Dept. of Surgery Excellence in Tchg. award, 1995. Fellow: ACS (life), Am. Assn. Pediats. (life); mem.: Internat. Pediatric Endosurgery Group (life), Am. Pediat. Surg. Assn. (life), Alpha Omega Alpha (life). Avocations: rock climbing, international travel, music. Office: Ariz Children's Surgery PC Ste 301 1432 S Dobson Rd Mesa AZ 85202 Home Phone: 480-250-2140; Office Phone: 480-464-9400. Office Fax: 480-464-9401; Home Fax: 480-464-9401. Personal E-mail: hpink23@hotmail.com.

COX, HENRY, engineer, researcher; b. Phila., Mar. 7, 1935; s. Henry Robert and Helen (Kane) C.; m. Mary Ann Shaw, Sept. 3, 1960 (dec.); children: James, Daniel, Michael, Diane. BS, Coll. Holy Cross, 1956; ScD, MIT, 1963. Analyst Office Sec. of Def., 1970-72; research assoc. Scripps Instn. Oceanography, LaJolla, Calif., 1972-73; officer in charge Naval Underwater Systems Ctr., New London, Conn., 1973-76; div. dir. Def. Advanced Research Projects Agy., 1976-78; project mgr. Naval Electronic Systems Command, Arlington, Va., 1978-81; divisional v.p. BBN Systems and Tech. Corp., Arlington, 1981-91; chief tech. officer, sr. v.p. Orincon Corp., Arlington, 1991—2003; chief tech. officer Lockheed Martin Orincon Def., Arlington, 2003—05; sr. fellow Lockheed Martin, Arlington, 2005—. Contbr. articles to tech. jours. Served to capt. USN, 1956-81. Decorated Legion of Merit; decorated Meritorious Service medal, Navy Commendation medal; recipient Def. Superior Service medal Dept. Def., 1978 Fellow Acoustical Soc. Am., IEEE (Disting. Tech. Achievement award Oceanic Engring. Soc. 1991); mem. Am. Soc. Naval Engrs. (hon. Gold medal), Nat. Acad. Engring., U.S. Naval Inst. Roman Catholic. Home: 6513 Waterway Dr Falls Church VA 22044-1328 Office: Lockheed Martin 4350 Fairfax Dr Arlington VA 22203-1695 Home Phone: 703-354-7684; Office Phone: 703-351-4440. Business E-Mail: harry.cox@lmco.com.

COX, HOWARD ELLIS, JR., venture capitalist; b. NYC, Feb. 1, 1944; s. Howard Ellis and Anne Delafield (Finch) C BA, Princeton U., 1964; JD, Columbia U., 1967; MBA, Harvard U., 1969. Bar: NY 1967. Ptnr. Greylock, Boston, 1971—. Bd. dir. Greylock Mgmt. Corp., Boston, Stryker, Kalamazoo, In-Q-Tel, Washington; bd. dirs. TT&W, Atlanta; mem. investment com. Ptnr. Healthcare. Bd. dir. Nat. Venture Capital Assn., Washington, 1997—, chmn., 2002; trustee Dana Farber Cancer Inst., 1987—; pres. Assn. Relief of the Elderly, NYC; overseer Mus. Fine Arts; mem. bd. fellow Harvard Med. Sch. Capt. US Army, 1969-71. Mem.: Coun. Fgn. Rels., Bus. Assoc. Club Boston (pres. 1979—80), New Eng. Venture Capital Assn. (pres. 1986—88), Comml. Club Boston. Episcopalian. Office: Greylock 880 Winter St Ste 300 Waltham MA 02451 Office Phone: 781-622-2244.

COX, J. ARTHUR, minister; b. Utica, NY, Aug. 5, 1940; s. James F and Margaret (Craig) Cox; m. Mahaillie Tillson, Dec. 29, 1962; children: Deborah Jean, James Andrew. AAS, Mohawk Valley C.C., 1961; BTh, Concordia Sem., 1975; D Ministry, Faith Sem., Tacoma, 1991. Cert. Ordained to ministry Luth Ch-Mo Synod, 1975. Pastor Grace Luth. Ch., Bradford, Pa., 1975-2000; pres. devel. leaders for ministry Mo. Synod., 2000—. Del. Synodical Conv., Dallas, 1977; counselor Cattaraugus Ctr., Bradford, 1982; chmn. Dist Open House, Bradford, 1982, Dist. Ext. Fund, Buffalo, 1982—85; chmn. ea. dist., bd. dirs. mission svcs. Alive in Christ, 1982—88, mem. evangelism com. ea. dist., 1992—97, bd. dirs.; chmn. dist. bd. Congl. Svcs., 1997—2002; counselor Cattanaugus Ct., 2002—03. Chmn. bd. Excell Personnel Svcs., Inc., 1999—; bd dirs Evergreen Hylands, 1979, Am Cancer Soc, 1980, Vis Nurse Assn., 1980—86, Bradford Hosp, 1985—; bd. dirs. Bradford Area Sch. Dist., 2004—. Mem.: Pennhills Country Club (bd. dirs.), Rotary (bd dirs 1978—82, pres 1982—83). Republican. Home: 465 Interstate Pky Bradford PA 16701-2733 Office Phone: 814-362-3244. E-mail: jacox@penn.com. *Life is a sequence of God-given opportunities to serve Him and His people. The excitement is derived from accepting His call to service and experiencing His magnificent power working through you to accomplish His purpose.*

COX, JACK RONALD, JR., finance educator; b. Houston, Aug. 29, 1964; s. Jack Ronald Sr. and Peggy Lou (Mitchell) C. BS, Park U., 1997; MS, Lesley Coll., 1998; PhD, Capella U., 2001. Spl. weapons & tactics cert. 1988; cert. law enforcement Fla. 1988; cert. advanced peace officer Tex. 1990; advanced EMT; basic EMT. Patrolman USAF, Woodbridge, UK, 1992-93, sr. patrolman, program mgr. Incirlik, Turkey, 1993-94, program mgr. personal readiness Cheyenne, Wyo., 1994-97, Songtan, South Korea, 1997-98, program mgr. Tercierra, Azores, 1999—; faculty criminal justice, bus., mgmt. U. Md., Tercierra, Portugal, 2000—. Vol. Wyo. Emergency Mgmt. Assn., 1994—97, ARC, New Philadelphia, Ohio, 1983—86, numerous fire depts., Nelsonville, Ohio, 1984—90; asst. fire chief Normagee Vol. Fire Dept., 2003; mem. coun. Leon County Govt., Tex.; bd. dirs. Jewett EMS, 2004—. E-5 SSgt USAF, 1991—2001. Mem. Acad. Mgmt., VFW. Avocations: historical research, music collection. Home: 849 Eskridge Ln Normangee TX 77871 Office Phone: 972-279-6511. Personal E-mail: drjcox@tconline.net. Business E-Mail: jcox@amberton.edu.

COX, JAMES D., law educator; b. 1943; JD, U. Calif. Hastings Sch. Law, 1969; LL.M., Harvard U., 1971; D in Mercature (hon.), U. South Denmark, 2001. Bar: Calif. 1970. Atty.-adv. Office Gen. Counsel FTC, Washington, 1969-70; teaching fellow Boston U., 1970-71; asst. prof. U. San Francisco, 1971-74; assoc. prof. U. Calif. Hastings Sch. Law, 1974-75; vis. assoc. prof. Stanford U., 1976-77; prof. U. Calif. Hastings Sch. Law, 1977-79; vis. prof. Duke U. Sch. Law, spring 1979, prof., 1979-2000, Brainerd Currie prof. law, 2000—. Com. on corps. State Bar Calif., NC bus. corp. act. draft com., NC nonprofit corp. draft com.; E.T. Bost rsch. prof., 1980, 96; legal adv. com. NY Stock Exch., 1995—; legal adv. bd. NASD, 1999—; mem. ABA com. corporate laws, 2006-. Author: Financial Information, Accounting and the Law, 1980, Quick Review of Corporations, 4th edit., 2004, (with Hillman and Langevoort) Securities Regulation: Cases and Materials, 5th edit., 2006; (with Hazen) Corporations, 2d edit., 2003. Sr. Fulbright Rsch. fellow, Australia, 1989. Mem. Am. Law Inst., Order of Coif, Phi Kappa Phi Office: Duke U Sch Law Durham NC 27708-0360 Office Phone: 919-613-7056. Business E-Mail: cox@law.duke.edu.

COX, JAMES D., radiologist; b. Steubenville, Ohio, 1938; AB (magna cum laude), Kenyon Coll., 1960; MD with honors, U. Rochester Sch. Medicine and Dentistry, 1965; DSc (hon.), Kenyon Coll., Gambier, Ohio, 1997. Diplomate Am. Bd. Radiology, Therapeutic Radiology, Nat. Bd. Med. Examiners. Intern U. Chgo., Pritzker Sch. Medicine, 1965-66; resident, therapeutic radiology Penrose Cancer Hosp., Colo. Springs, 1966-69, fellow, clin. oncology & therapeutic radiology, 1963—64; fellow, dept. radiotherapy Therapeutic Radiology Inst., Gustave-Roussy Villejuif, France, 1969-70; asst. prof. radiology, dir. therapeutic radiology Georgetown U. Sch. Medicine; assoc. prof. radiology, head divsn. therapeutic readiology Med. Coll. Wis., Milw., 1973—77, prof. radiology, 1977—82, founding chair dept. radiation oncology, 1982—84, founding dir., Cancer Ctr., 1984; prof. with tenure, chair, dept. radiation oncology Columbia U. Coll. Physicians and Surgeons; dir. radiation oncology Presbyterian Hosp., NYC; prof. radiotherapy, physician-in-chief U. Tex. MD Anderson Cancer Ctr., Houston, 1988—92, Hubert L. and Olive Stringer Disting. Chair in Oncology, 1992, head, divsn. radiation oncology, 1995—, chair, dept. radiation oncology, prof., radiation oncology. Mem. bd. scientific counselors, divsn. cancer treatment Nat. Cancer Inst., Dept. Health and Human Svcs., 1987—91; principle investigator, chair Radiation Therapy Oncology Group (RTOG), 1987—97; chair Com. of Cooperative Group Chairs, Cancer Therapy Evaluation Program, Divsn. Cancer Treatment, Nat. Cancer Inst., 1990—93; invited lectr. in field. Author of scientific publications; editor-in-chief Internat. Jour. Radiation Oncology, Biology and Physics. Vis. dir. bd. dir. Radiation Effects Rsch. Found., 2004. Maj. US Army. Named one of Top Doctors, Inside Houston Mag., 1998, Top Doctors for Women, Good Housekeeping, 1999, America's Top Doctors, 2001; recipient Gold medal, del Regato Found., 1994, French Soc. for Oncologic Radiotherapy, 1997, Medaille Antonie Baclere of the French Radiology Cmty., 1997, Clin. Rsch. award, Assn. Cmty. Cancer Ctrs., Seattle, Wash., 1998, Charles A. LeMaistre, M.D., Outstanding Achievement award in Cancer, 2003, Gold medal, Tex. Radiology Soc., 2004; Robert Fowler Fellow, Anti-Cancer Coun. Victoria, Australia, 1984. Fellow: Am. Coll. Radiology (chancellor, Gold medal 1997); mem.: Am. Radium Soc. (past pres.), Intersociety Coun. Radiation Oncology (past chair), Royal Acad. Medicine Belgium (fgn.) (corr.), European Soc. for Therapeutic Radiology and Oncology (hon.), Belgian Assn. for Radiation-Oncology (hon.), Spanish Assn. Radiotherapy and Oncology (hon.), Soc. of Chmn. of Academic Radiation Oncology Programs (past pres.), Am. Soc. for Therapeutic Radiology and Oncology (ASTRO) (pres. 1995, Gold medal 1997), Alpha Omega Alpha (U. Rochester Sch. Medicine), Phi Beta Kappa. Office: U Tex MD Anderson Cancer Ctr 1515 Holcombe Blvd # Houston TX 77030 Office Phone: 713-563-2316. Office Fax: 713-563-2368.*

COX, JAMES ELMER, medical educator, department chairman; m. Marta Katrina Leonhardt, Dec. 31, 1983. MD, Georgetown U., DC, 1979—83. Diplomate Am. Bd. Internal Medicine, 1987. Chief cons. internal medicine AFMOA, Bolling AFB, 2000—02; chairmen dept. medicine MGMC, Andrews AFB, Md., 2003—06. Katrina recovery vol. St. Paul's United Meth. Ch., Kensington, Md., 2006—. Col. USAF. Fellow: ACP. Home Phone: 301-588-7012. Personal E-mail: appliedhealthsci@aol.com.

COX, JAMES SIDNEY, physician; b. Homer, La., Nov. 17, 1950; s. Sidney and Rita (Haynes) C.; m. Judy Katherine Vickers, Oct. 21, 1984; children: Shannon Ruth, Sarah Anne, Megan Elizabeth. Student, La. State

U., 1968-71; MD, Tulane U., 1971-75. Diplomate Am. Bd. Family Practice, Am. Bd. of Emergency Medicine. Intern, resident in family practice John Peter Smith Hosp., Ft. Worth, 1975-78; city health officer family practice City of Athens, Tex., 1978-84; pvt. practice Athens, 1978-84, Ft. Worth, 1984—; mem. staff Henderson County Meml. Hosp., Athens, vice chief med. staff, 1981-82; mem. staff Lakeland Med. Ctr., Athens, chief med. staff, dir., 1983-84; vice chief emergency medicine dept. Harris Meth. Hosp., Ft. Worth, 1988-91, dir. occupational medicine, 1989—, chief emergency dept. Ft. Worth, 1992-93, 98-2000, sec. med. staff, 1994-95, sec. emergency medicine divsn., 1996-97. Pres., chmn. bd. dirs. Occuhealth Physicians Group, P.A., Ft. Worth; mem. faculty U. Tex. Health Sci. Ctr.-Dallas Cmty. Medicine Dept., John Peter Smith Hosp., Ft. Worth, 1978-96, course dir. ACLS, 1989-1998, mem. affiliate faculty ACLS, 1991-95, med. rev. officer for urine drug testing; med. bd. Harris Meth. Hosp., 1992-95, 98-2000; team chmn. emergency dept. redesign Rochester Inst. Tech. Coll. Bus., 1996; v.p. for physician affairs Emergency Medicine Cons., 1998-2005, exec. dir., 2005-06, cief adminstrv. officer, 2006—; assoc. med. dir. Harris Meth., Ft. Worth, 2000-2007; med. dir. ACLS, Campbell Health Sys., 1997-98. Author: Intestinal Obstruction: A Programmed Text, 1975. Recipient Quality Cup award of Excellence, USA Today, 1996. Fellow Am. Acad. Family Physicians, Am. Coll. Emergency Physicians; mem. AMA (Physician's Recognition award), Am. Coll. Occupl. and Environ. Medicine, Tex. Med. Assn. (alt. del. 1994-96, 2003—), Tarrant County Med. Soc. (bd. dirs. 1994-96, 2003—), Rotary (bd. dirs. Athens chpt. 1983-84), Alpha Epsilon Delta. Presbyterian. Avocations: reading, skiing, bonsai, horticulture, astronomy. Home: 3458 Lantern Holw Fort Worth TX 76109-2411 Office: Emergency Medicine Cons 6451 Brentwood Stair Rd Ste 200 Fort Worth TX 76112-3200 Office Phone: 817-496-9700. Personal E-mail: jimcoxem@charter.net. Business E-Mail: jcox@emdocs.com.

COX, JAMES TALLEY, lawyer; b. Temple, Tex., Sept. 22, 1921; s. George Allan and Jane (Talley) Cox; m. Alice Tarver, Jan. 12, 1945; children: Martha Cox Daniels, Louise Cox McGuire, Anne, Allan. BBA, U. Tex., 1943; LL.B., 1947. Bar: Tex. 1947, U.S. Supreme Ct. 1951. Spl. atty. Justice Dept., Washington, 1947-48; staff atty. Tax Ct. U.S., Washington, 1948-50; trial atty. Treasury Dept., Phila., 1950-51; tax counsel Schlumberger Well Services, Houston, 1951-65; ptnr. Hoover, Cox & Shearer, Houston, 1965-86; sole practice Houston, 1986-90; pres. James T. Cox, P.C., Houston, 1990—, Advent Trust Co., 1991-99. V.p., bd. dirs. Westchase Travels, Inc., 1972-82; bd. dirs. Paradigm Valve Svcs. Inc., Embedded Sys. Products Inc. Contbr. articles to profl. publs. Bd. dirs. Houston Met. YMCA, 1972-78, Pin Oak Charity Horse Show Assn., 1972—, Retina Rsch. Found., 1977—. Served to lt. USNR, 1943-46. Mem. Am., Tex., Houston Bar Assns., Tax Rsch. Assn. (exec. com. 1950-67), Delta Theta Phi, Phi Kappa Psi. Republican. Presbyterian. Home: 11701 Forest Glen St Houston TX 77024-6433 Office: 11701 Forest Glen Houston TX 77024 E-mail: alicetcox@yahoo.com.

COX, JOE BRUCE, lawyer; b. Ft. Smith, Ark., Dec. 4, 1939; s. Bruce McKinley and Allie Delisca (McCalman) C.; children from a previous marriage: Jennifer Lynn, Lindsay Lambert; m. Justyna Ford, Aug. 12, 1995. BA, Okla. State U., 1963; JD, U. Tulsa, 1966; LLM in Estate Planning, U. Miami, 1976. Bar: Okla. 1966, US Ct. Appeals (10th cir.) 1967, Fla. 1976, US Ct. Appeals (5th and 11th cirs.) 1977, US Tax Ct. 1978, cert.: Fla. Bar (estate planning and adminstrn. and taxation). Atty. Sanders & McElroy, Tulsa, Okla., 1966-70; v.p., trust officer F & M Bank & Trust Co., 1970-75; atty. Cummings and Lockwood, Naples, Fla., 1976; ptnr. Cox & Nici, Naples, Fla. Contbr. articles to profl. publs. Vice chmn., bd. mem. Naples Cmty. Hosp., 1985; v.p. Cmty. Found., Naples, 1982; chmn., bd. mem. Naples Civic Assn., 1980-84; chmn. YMCA Endowment Fund, Naples, 1984-86; chmn. Citizens for Excellence in Govt. Polit. Action Com., Naples, 1985; chmn. Friends of Connie Mack, US Senator, 1989. Named one of Top 100 Attys., Worth mag., 2005. Fellow Am. Coll. Trust & Estate Counsel; mem. ABA, Fla. Bar Assn., Okla. Bar Assn., Collier County Bar Assn., Fla. C. of C. (bd. dirs., mem. exec. com., chmn. legis. coun., sec., chmn. Fla. chamber found., fed. jud. selection com.), Port Royal Club (Naples), Naples Bath and Tennis Club, SAR. Republican. Methodist. Office: Cox & Nici 1185 Immokalee Rd Ste 110 Naples FL 34110 Office Phone: 239-254-0706.*

COX, JOHN CURTIS, health facility administrator; b. Lovington, N.Mex., July 27, 1947; s. Samuel Spurgeon and Monah LaJoyce (Perry) King; m. Mary Margaret King, May 27, 1967; children: Melissa Lynn Ewing, Melinda Leanne Field. BBA, Hardin-Simmons U., Abilene, Tex., 1969; MHA, Baylor U., 1978; PhD, Tex. A&M U., 1988. Commd. 2d lt. U.S. Army, 1969, advanced through grades to lt. col.; chief Ft. Hood Health Facility Project Office, Office Surgeon Gen., 1978-85; assoc. dir., mgr. field office, health facilities planning U.S. Army Med. Command, Stuttgart, Germany, 1988-89, dir. health facilities planning Heidelberg, Germany, 1989-90; chief programming div. Def. Med. Facilities Office, Office Asst. Sec. Def., Washington, 1990-91; ret. U.S. Army, 1991; adminstrv. asst. Garland (Tex.) Ind. Sch. Dist., 1991-93, exec. dir. sch. facilities, 1993-95; planning & cons. coord. HED Baylor Health Care Sys., 1995-98; adminstrv. dir. support svcs. Baylor Med. Ctr., Grapevine, Tex., 1997-98; project dir. Med. Cities Inc., Dallas, 1998-2001. Owner Cox Cons., 2001—. Editl. adv. bd. Facility Care; contbr. articles to profl. jours. Trustee Belton (Tex.) Ind. Sch. Dist., 1981-84; mem. pub. sch. bd. mems. adv. com. Tex. State Bd. Edn., 1982-84; fund raiser Garland br. Dallas YMCA, 1992-94. Decorated Legion of Merit, Bronze Star medal, Meritorious Svc. medal with 2 oak leaf clusters, Army Commendation medal, others; recipient Svc. Citation award Tex. Fellow Am. Coll. Healthcare Execs., Am. Soc. Healthcare Engrs., Phi Kappa Phi, Alpha Chi. Baptist. Avocations: woodworking, antiques, exercise.

COX, JOHN FRANCIS, retired cosmetic company executive; b. Chgo., Sept. 25, 1929; s. Roland Francis and Vera Pauline (Paisley) C.; m. T. Joanne Brown, Nov. 27, 1954 (dec.); children: James O., Thomas B., Paul A. BJ, U. Ill., 1951; MS in English and Edn., Western Ill. U., 1954. Reporter Galesburg (Ill.) Register Mail, 1954-56; staff writer pub. rels. United Airlines, Chgo., 1956-58; press rels. mgr. Kiekhaefer Corp., Fond du Lac, Wis., 1958-60, Internat. Minerals and Chems. Corp., Skokie, Ill., 1960-67, Heublein Inc., Hartford, Conn., 1967-69, v.p. pub. affairs Farmington, Conn., 1981-83; v.p. pub. rels. and advt. Warner Nat. Corp., Cin., 1969-72; v.p. franchising and pub. rels. Ky. Fried Chicken, Louisville, 1972-81; group dir. pub. rels. R. J. Reynolds Industries, Inc., Winston-Salem, NC, 1983-84; sr. v.p. comm. Avon Products, Inc., NYC, 1984-91. Staff sgt. US Army, 1951—53. Mem.: Soc. Profl. Journalists. E-mail: johnfcox@aol.com.

COX, JOHN THOMAS, JR., lawyer; b. Shreveport, La., Feb. 9, 1943; s. John Thomas and Gladys Virginia (Canterbury) C.; m. Tracey L. Tanquary, Aug. 27, 1966; children: John Thomas, III, Stephen Lewis. BS, La. State U., 1965; JD, 1968. Bar: La. 1968, U.S. Dist. Ct. (we., mid. and ea. dist.) La., U.S. Dist. Ct. (ea. dist.) Tex., U.S. Ct. Appeals (5th and 8th cir.), U.S. Tax Ct., U.S. Supreme Ct. Assoc. Sanders, Miller, Downing & Keene, Baton Rouge, 1968-70, Blanchard, Walker, O'Quin & Roberts, Shreveport, La., 1970-71; ptnr., 1971—. Tchr. bus. law Centenary Coll. La., La. State U., Shreveport. Lt. USAR, 1963—69. Recipient George Washington Honor medal Valley Forge Freedoms Found. Mem. ABA, La. Bar Assn., Shreveport Bar Assn., Am. Assn. Def. Counsel, La. Assn. Def. Counsel, Com. of 100, Shreveport Club. Presbyterian. Address: 555 Dunmoreland Dr Shreveport LA 71106-6124 Office Phone: 318-221-6858. Business E-Mail: jcox@bwor.com.

COX, JOHN W., federal agency administrator; m. Sally Cox; 1 child, Kate. BA, Tex. A&M U. CPA Tex. With Ernst & Young LLP, Houston, 1984—89; mgr. taxation BMC Software, Inc., 1989—91, mgr. investor rels., 1991—98, v.p., 1998—, chief acctg. officer, controller, 1999—2006; CFO US Dept Housing & Urban Devel, Washington, 2006—. Mem. coll. liberal arts devel. coun. Tex. A&M U.; bd. dirs. Benchmark Electronics, Inc., 2003—06. Office: US Dept Housing & Urban Devel 451 7th St SW Washington DC 20410

COX, KAREN MICHELLE, finance educator, computer company executive; b. Drexel Hill, Pa., Oct. 16, 1963; d. Robert Harold and Margaret Ellen (O'Brien) Cox; div.; children: Joshua Robert, Philip Christopher. BSBA, Drexel U., 1985; MBA, Villanova U., 1994. Fin. analyst Spectacor, Wynnewood, Pa., 1987-89; project mgmt. analyst Wyeth Ayerst Labs., Radnor, Pa., 1990-95; prof. mktg. Villanova (Pa.) U., 1995—. Cons. on advt. Mercia Grassi Assocs., Phila., 1984; cons. on strategy Villa St. John Hosp., Downingtown, Pa., 1992; cons. on new bus. devel. IBM, Wayne, Pa., 1995—. Mem.: NAFE, Am. Mktg. Assn., Beta Gamma Sigma. Avocations: photography, collecting sea shells, travel, hiking, design. Home and Office: 612 Thorncroft Dr West Chester PA 19380-6442 E-mail: karenmcox@yahoo.com.

COX, KATHY, school system administrator; m. John Hamilton Cox Jr.; children: John, Alex. BA, Emory U., Atlanta, MA in Polit. sci. Tchr. social studies McIntosh H.S., Fayette County Bd. Edn., Atlanta, 1987—2002; rep. Ga. Ho. of Reps., Atlanta, 1998—2003; supt. of edn. State of Ga., Atlanta, 2003—. Supporter Boy Scouts Am. Cub Scout Pack 201, Boy Scout Troop 275. Mem.: Kiwanis, Phi Beta Kappa. Meth. Office: Ga Dept Edn 2066 Twin Towers East 205 Jesse Hill Jr Dr SE Atlanta GA 30334*

COX, KENNETH ALLEN, retired lawyer, communications executive, consultant; b. Topeka, Dec. 7, 1916; s. Seth Leroy and Jean (Sears) C.; m. Nona Beth Fumerton, Jan. 1, 1943; children— Gregory Allen, Jeffrey Neal, Douglas Randall. BA, U. Wash., 1938, LLB, 1940; LLM, U. Mich., 1941; LLD, Chgo. Theol. Sem., 1969. Bar: Wash. 1941. Law clk. Wash. Supreme Ct., 1941-42; asst. prof. U. Mich. Law Sch., 1946-48; with firm Little, LeSourd, Palmer, Scott & Slemmons (and predecessor), Seattle, 1948-61, partner, 1953-61; spl. counsel com. interstate and fgn. commerce charge TV inquiry U.S. Senate, 1956-57; chief broadcast bur. FCC, Washington, 1961-63, commr., 1963-70; counsel to comm. law firm Haley, Bader & Potts, 1970-99; sr. v.p., dir. MCI Comm. Corp., 1970-87; ret, 1980; cons. MCI, 1987—2000. Lectr. U. Washington Law Sch., part-time 1954, 60; adj. prof. Georgetown U. Law Center, 1971, 72. Vice pres. Municipal League Seattle and King County, 1960, Seattle World Affairs Council, 1960; pres. Seattle chpt. Am. Assn. UN, 1957; chmn. one of five citizen subcoms. Legis. Interim Com. Edn., 1960; Bd. dirs. Nat. Pub. Radio, 1971-80; bd. dirs. Nat. Advt. Rev. Bd., 1971-74, chmn. bd., 1976-96. Served to capt. Q.M.C. AUS, 1943-46, 51-52. Recipient Alfred I. duPont award in broadcast journalism Columbia U., 1970; Everett C. Parker award, the Minortiy Media and Telecommunications Coun., 2003. Mem. Am., Fed. Communications, Wash. State, D.C. bar assns., Order of Coif, Phi Beta Kappa, Phi Delta Phi. Democrat. Congregationalist. Home: 5836 Marbury Rd Bethesda MD 20817-6076 Personal E-mail: nkcox@verizon.net.

COX, KERMITT L., insurance company executive; B in Math., Iowa State U., Ames; grad. student in Actuarial Sci., U. Nebr. Tchr.; with Mut. of Omaha Ins. Co., ALFAC Inc., 1987—, v.p., asst. corp. actuary, sr. v.p., corp. actuary, 1998—. Served in USAF. Mem.: Southeastern Actuarial Club, Internat. Actuarial Assn., Am. Acad. Actuaries, Soc. Actuaries. Office: AFLAC Inc 1932Wynnton Rd Columbus GA 31999 Office Phone: 706-323-3431.*

COX, L. KEVIN, human resources specialist; With rsch. and devel. labs. Pepsi Bottling Group, 1989—92, dir. human resources Atlantic Coast bus., 1992—94; dir. orgnl. capability and sales devel. Pepsi-Cola Co., 1994—96, v.p. orgnl capability, 1996; sr. v.p. human resources Pepsi-Cola Bottling Co., 1997—98, sr. v.p., chief personnel officer, 1998—2004, exec. v.p., 2004—05; exec. v.p. human resources Am. Express, 2005—, mem. global mgmt. team, 2005—, bd. dirs. compensation and benefits com., 2005—. Office: Am Express Co World Fin Ctr 200 Vesey St New York NY 10285 Office Phone: 212-640-2000.*

COX, LARRY, human rights organization executive; BA in History, Mt. Union Coll. Various positions including press officer, comm. dir., and first dep. dir. Amnesty Internat. USA, head program to abolish death penalty, 1976—84; dep. sec. gen. Amnesty Internat., London, 1985—90; exec. dir. Rainforest Found., 1990—95; sr. program officer human rights unit Ford Found., NYC, 1995—2006; exec. dir. Amnesty Internat. USA, NYC, 2006—. Office: Amnesty Internat USA 5 Penn Plz New York NY 10001 Office Phone: 212-573-5000. Office Fax: 212-351-3677.

COX, LINDA SMOAK, real estate broker; b. Yonges Island, SC, Sept. 5, 1943; d. Ryan Lanier Smoak and Frances Lapish Bock. Grad., Kings Coll., Charlotte, NC, 1962. Lic. real estate broker, relocation specialist, new homes specialist. Exec. sec. Charlotte Observer Transp. Co., 1963-65; various positions Eastern Airlines, Charlotte, 1965-88; real estate salesperson Allen Tate Realtors, Charlotte, 1990—. Program dir. Delta Investment, Charlotte, 1984-88; mem. Bd. Realtors, Charlotte, 1990—; mem. Bd. Realtors, Rock Hill, SC, 1993—. Troop leader Girl Scouts US, Charlotte, 1964; mem., vol. US Humane Soc., Charlotte, 1964, 96—; co-founder, vol. Midway Meth. Ch. Libr., Kannapolis, NC, 1958; mem. coun. River Hills Cmty. Ch., Lake Wylie, SC, 1980-82, chair fellowship com., 1979-80, mem. edn. com., 1984-85, bd. trustees, 2002—; founding mem., vol. Stowe Bot. Gardens, Belmont, NC, 1994—. Mem.: SC Realtors Assn., Charlotte Regional Realtor Assn., NC Assn. Realtors. Avocations: water sports, snow ski race team, sailing, gardening. Office Phone: 704-367-7217, 888-364-6401 ext 7217. Personal E-mail: lindacox1@aol.com.

COX, LINDA SUSAN, allergist, immunologist; b. Oakland, Calif., Aug. 17, 1955; d. James Lee Dolan and Nancy Jane (Christie) C.; m. Robert Louis Wolfgram Jr.; children: Mary Elizabeth Cox, Christopher Alexander Cox-Wolfgram. BA cum laude, Boston U., 1978; postgrad., Harvard U., 1978-79, Hahnemann Med. Coll., 1979-80; MD, Northwestern U., 1985. Diplomate Am. Bd. Internal Medicine, Am. Bd. Allergy and Immunology. Intern in internal medicine Jackson Meml. Hosp., U. Miami, Fla., 1985-88; emergency room physician North Ridge Med. Ctr., Ft. Lauderdale, Fla., 1988-89; fellow in allergy and immunology Nat. Jewish Hosp., Denver, 1989-91; pvt. practice Allergy, Asthma and Clin. Immunology Ctr., Miami, Fla., 1991-92, Adult and Pediat. Allergy and Immunology, Ft. Lauderdale, 1992—; emergency rm. physician Imperial Point Med. Ctr., 1997—. Part-time emergency room physician Fitzsimmons Med. Ctr., Aurora, Colo., 1989-91, Palmetto Gen. Hosp., 1992—; rschr. U. Miami Sch. Medicine Dept. Clin. Immunology, 1987, U. Colo. Sch. Medicine Dept. Allergy and Clin. Immunology, 1990-91; asst. clin. prof. medicine U. Miami Sch. Medicine, 1996—, also bd. dirs.; asst. clin. prof. medicine Nova Southeastern U. Ortho. Sch. Medicine. Fellow Am. Coll. Allergy and Immunology, ACP; mem. Am. Acad. Allergy and Immunology, Am. Coll. Chest Physicians, Fla. Allergy and Immunology Soc. (mem. exec. com. 1998—, sec. practice std. com., mem. edn. com.), Broward County Med. Assn. (bd. dirs. 1996—). Episcopalian. Avocations: ballet, skiing. Home: 5802 Poinsettia Ave West Palm Beach FL 33407-2536 Office: 5333 N Dixie Hwy Ste 210 Fort Lauderdale FL 33334-3454

COX, M. CAROLYN, lawyer; b. June 10, 1949; BA, Agnes Scott Coll., 1971; JD, Yale Univ., 1974. Bar: Ala. 1975, DC 1976. Law clk. Judge Frank M. Johnson, US Dist. Ct., Middle Dist. Ala., 1974—75; ptnr., Corp. dept., chmn. Ethics com. Wilmer Cutler Pickering Hale & Dorr, Washington. Dir. Yale Barristers Union. Office: Wilmer Cutler Pickering Hale & Dorr 1801 Pennsylvania Ave NW Washington DC 20006 Mailing: Wilmer Pickering Hale & Dorr 1875 Pennsylvania Ave NW Washington DC 20006-3642 Office Phone: 202-663-6645. Office Fax: 202-663-6363. Business E-Mail: carolyn.cox@wilmerhale.com.

COX, MARLINA R., social studies educator; d. Willie M. and Pecolia Cox. AAS in Archtl. Drafting, East Ctrl. C.C., Decatur, Miss., 1997; BS in Secondary Edn. and Social Studies, Miss. State U., 2001. Social studies tchr. Bettye Mae Jack Mid. Sch., Morton, Miss., 2003—. Co-sponsor Jr. Beta Club, Morton, Miss., 2005. Dean's Scholar, Miss. State, 1999, 2000, Pres's Scholar, 2000. Mem.: Nat. Coun. Social Studies, Miss. Profl. Educators, Kappa Delta Pi. Avocations: traveling, drawing, reading, singing, shopping. Home: 7541 Mudline Rd Lake MS 39092 Office: Bettye Mae Jack Mid Sch PO Box 500 Morton MS 39117 Office Phone: 601-732-6977.

COX, MARSHALL, lawyer; b. Cleve., Nov. 17, 1932; s. Marshall H.C. and Mary (Bateman) Mills; m. Nancy Huntley, Aug. 3, 1957 (div. Oct. 1994); 1 child, Vanessa; m. Nathalie Menapace, Jan. 3, 1997. BA, Vanderbilt U., 1954; JD, Ohio State U., 1958. Bar: D.C. 1974, N.Y. 1959. Assoc. Cahill Gordon & Reindel, NYC, 1959-67, ptnr., 1968-97. Served to 1st. lt. U.S. Army, 1955-57, Korea. Republican. Episcopalian.

COX, MELVIN MONROE, lawyer; b. Omaha, Jan. 31, 1947; s. Monroe M. Cox and Wilma Grace (Prickett) McPherson. BA with high honors, U. Wyo., 1969; JD, Harvard U., 1972. Bar: Pa. 1972, US Dist. Ct. (we. dist.) Pa. 1972, NJ 1987, US Dist. Ct. (NJ) 1987. Assoc. Rose, Schmidt & Dixon, Pitts., 1972-78; atty. Chgo. Pneumatic Tool Co., NY, 1978-81, asst. sec. NYC, 1981-88; asst. gen. counsel Sun Chem. Corp., Ft. Lee, NJ, 1989-93, asst. gen. counsel, asst. sec., 1993-97, v.p., gen. counsel, sec., 1997—2004, sr. v.p., gen. counsel, sec., 2004—. Adj. prof. engring. law The Cooper Union, NYC, 1984—91; asst. sec. DIC Ams., Inc., Ft. Lee, NJ, 1993—97; mng. dir. Sun Chem. B.V., Soest, Netherlands, 1996—2004; bd. visitors U. Wyoming, Coll. Arts and Scis., 1997—, vice chmn., 1998—2001. Bd. dirs. Good Shepherd Cmty. Svcs., Inc., Ft. Lee, 1999-2001, Wyo. Art Mus., 2007—; trustee U. Wyoming Found., 2001-; mem. collections com. U. Wyo. Art Mus, 2004-; chair, mem. exec. com. pub. responsibility com. 2004-06, chair devel. com., 2006. Recipient Outstanding Alumnus award, U. Wyo., 2002. Mem.: ABA, Am. Corp. Counsel Assn., Phi Beta Kappa, Phi Kappa Phi. Office: Sun Chem Corp 35 Waterview Blvd Parsippany NJ 07054

COX, MIKE (MICHAEL A. COX), state attorney general; b. 1961; s. John and Rita Cox; m. Laura M. Cox; 4 children. BA with distinction in Polit. Sci., U. Mich., 1986, JD, 1989. Asst. pros. atty. Office Pros. Atty. Oakland County, Pontiac, Mich., 1989—90; asst. pros. atty. spl. crimes sect. Office Pros. Atty. Wayne County, Detroit, 1990—2001, dep. chief homicide unit, 2001—03; atty. gen. State of Mich., Lansing, 2003—. With USMC, 1980—83. Mem.: Inc. Soc. Irish/Am. Lawyers, State Bar Mich. (criminal law sect.), Pros. Attys. Assn. Mich. (instr. Basic Sch.). Republican. Office: G Mennen Williams Bldg 7th Fl PO Box 30212 525 W Ottawa St Lansing MI 48909-0212 Office Phone: 517-373-1110.*

COX, MITCHEL NEAL, editor; b. Portsmouth, Ohio, Sept. 8, 1956; s. Walter Eugene and Mary Agnes (Orlett) Cox; m. Lisa Renee LaLonde, Sept. 8, 1979 (dec. May 2001); children: Harmony, Leigh Ann, Katie. BS in Journalism, Ohio State U., 1985. Mng. editor The Puller, Columbus, Ohio, 1984-87; editor Bicycles Today, Columbus, 1985-87, Fur-Fish-Game, Columbus, 1987—. Mem. Outdoor Writers Assn. Am. Office: Fur-Fish-Game 2878 E Main St Columbus OH 43209-2698 Office Phone: 614-231-9585. E-mail: ffgcox@ameritech.net.

COX, NANCY JANE, microbiologist; b. Emmetsburg, Iowa, July 21, 1948; d. Emmett Stanley and Verna Lucille (Olson) Cox; B.S. with honors, Iowa State U., 1970; Ph.D., Cambridge, (Eng.) U., 1975; m. M. Evan Lindsay, Apr. 11, 1981; 1 child, Julia Claire Lindsay. Postdoctoral fellow Muscular Dystrophy Assn., Balt. and Atlanta, 1975-77; staff fellow Centers for Disease Control, Atlanta, 1978-80, research chemist, 1980—, now dir. Influenza Divsn. Recipient Marshall Scholarship for study abroad, 1970; postdoctoral fellow Muscular Dystrophy Assn. Am., 1975. Nmed one of 100 Most Influential People, Time Mag., 2006. Mem. AAAS, Am. Soc. Virology, Am. Soc. Microbiology, Sigma Xi. Methodist. Contbr. articles to profl. jours. and books. Office: Div Viral Diseases 7-111 Centers for Disease Control 1 600 Clifton Rd Atlanta GA 30316-2228

COX, PAUL ALAN, ethnobotanist, educator; b. Salt Lake City, Oct. 10, 1953; s. Leo A. and Rae (Gabbitas) C.; m. Barbara Ann Wilson, May 21, 1975; children: Emily Ann, Paul Matthew, Mary Elisabeth, Hillary Christine, Jane Margaret. BS, Brigham Young U., 1976; MSc, U. Wales, 1978; AM, Harvard U., 1978, PhD, 1981; DSc (hon.), U. Guelph, Can., 2000. Teaching fellow Harvard U., Cambridge, Mass., 1977-81; Miller research fellow Miller Inst. Basic Research in Sci., Berkeley, Calif., 1981-83; asst. prof. Brigham Young U., Provo, Utah, 1983-86, assoc. prof., 1986-91, prof., 1991—98, dean gen. edn. and honors, 1993-97; King Gustav XVI prof. environ. sci. Swedish Biodiversity Ctr., 1997—98; dir. Nat. Tropical Botanical Garden, Kalaheo, Hawaii, 1998—2004, Inst. for Ethnomedicine, Provo, 2004—. Disting. prof. Brigham Young U., Hawaii, 2000—; ecologist Utah Environ. Coun., Salt Lake City, 1976; project ecologist Utah MX Coordination Office, Salt Lake City, 1981. Mem. editl. bd. Pacific Studies. Recipient Bowdoin prize, The Goldman Environ. prize, 1997; Danforth Found. fellow, 1976-81, Fulbright fellow, 1976-77, NSF fellow, 1977-81, Linnean Soc. fellow, named NSF Presdl. Young Investigator, 1985-90, Hero of Medicine, Time Mag., 1997, Rachel Carson award, 1999. Mem. AAAS, Brit. Ecol. Soc., Internat. Soc. Ethnopharmacology (former pres.), Am. Soc. Naturalists, Assn. Tropical Biology, Soc. Econ. Botany (former pres.), Seacology Found. (founder and chmn.), AIDS Rsch. Alliance (bd.), Ctr. for Plant Conservation (bd.). Mem. Lds Ch. Office: Inst for Ethnomedicine PO Box 3464 Jackson WY 83001 Office Phone: 801-375-6214.

COX, PETER, artist; b. NYC, 1942; Grad., Phoenix Sch. Design, Parsons Sch., Holy Cross Coll. V.p. Nat. Arts Club, 1986—97; instr. Arts Students League, 1984—, NY Acad. Art, 1994—2000, Nat. Acad. of Design Mus. Sch., 2002—; represented Caravaggio Studios Inc. Exhibitions include, Carolyn Hill Gallery, 1989—91, Joseph Keiffer Inc., 1992, Louis Newman Galleries, 1993, CFM Galleries, 1994, Gallery Dai, 1996, M B Modem, 1997, 1998, exhibited in group shows, Artists of Am., 1981—92, John Pence Gallery, 1991—92, In Collaboration Gallery, 1992, Arnot Mus., 1993, Allan Stone Gallery, 1995—96, Nat. Arts Club, 1997, Survey of the Am. Figure in Painting, 1820-Present Babcock Galleries, 2000, Represented in permanent collections, Ark. Art Ctr., Arnot Mus., Redding Mus., Nat. Acad. of Design. Named to National Acad., 2002; recipient John Gordon Mem. Award, Soc. of the Four Arts, 1986, Gold Medal, Pastel Soc. of Am., 1987, Cert. of Merit, Nat. Academy of Design, 1988, Gold Medal, Nat. Arts Club, 1988, 1997, Gary Melchers Award, Artist Fellowship, 1998. Office: c/o Caravaggio Studios Inc 315 West 39th Suite #506 New York NY 10018 Home Phone: 917-414-4362; Office Phone: 212-736-6635. Personal E-mail: petercox@verizonmail.com.

COX, REBECCA GERNHARDT, air transportation executive; m. Christopher Cox. BA, DePauw U., Greencastle, Ind., 1976; JD, Cath. U., Washington. Asst. sec. govt. affairs US Dept. Transp.; chairperson Interagency Com. for Women's Bus. Enterprises; asst. to the pres., dir. Office of Pub. Liaison White House; staff v.p. govt. affairs Continental Airlines, Inc., 1989, v.p. govt. affairs, 1990—2003, sr. v.p. govt. affairs, 2003—. Office: Continental Airlines Inc 1350 I St NW Ste 1250 Washington DC 20005

COX, RICHARD HORTON, civil engineering executive; b. Paia, Hawaii, Oct. 10, 1920; s. Joel B. and Helen Cliford (Horton) C.; m. Hester Virginia Smith, Dec. 12, 1942 (dec. Aug. 12, 1995); children: Millicent, Janet, Lydia, Evelyn, David, Samuel (dec.). BS, Calif. Inst. Tech., Pasadena, 1942, MS, 1946. Registered profl. engr., surveyor, Hawaii. Supr. rocket range Calif. Inst. Tech., Pasadena, 1942—46; civil engr. McBryde Sugar Co., Eleele, Hawaii, 1946—56; land mgr. Alexander & Baldwin, Honolulu, 1956—71, v.p., 1971—86; engring. cons. Honolulu, 1986—. Mem. State Commn. on Water Resource Mgmt., 1987-94, 95-99. Fellow: ASCE; mem.: NSPE, AAAS, Am. Geophys. Union. Mem. Soc. Of Friends. Home and Office: 1951 Kakela Dr Honolulu HI 96822-2156

COX, RICHARD JAMES, information science educator; b. Balt., Feb. 9, 1950; s. Richard Theodore Cox and Shirley Clarice (Aikens) Brown; m. Lynn Wilson, Jan. 11, 1975; 1 child, Emma Greer. BA, Towson State U., 1972; MA, U. Md., 1978; PhD, U. Pitts., 1992. Curator of manuscripts Md. Hist. Soc., Balt., 1973-78; city archivist City of Balt., 1978-83; head archives and records Ala. Dept. Archives and History, Montgomery, Ala., 1983-86; assoc. archivist N.Y. State Archives, Albany, 1986-88; lectr. U. Pitts., 1988-92, asst. prof. library & info. sci., 1992-96, assoc. prof., 1996—. Author: American Archival Analysis: The Recent Development of the Archival Profession in the United States, 1990 (Leland Soc. of Am. Archivists award 1991), Managing Institutional Archives: Foundational Principles and Practices, 1992, The First Generation of Electronic Records Archivists in the United States: A Study in Professionalization, 1994, Documenting Localities, 1996, Closing an Era: Historical Perspectives on Modern Archives and Records Management, 2000, Managing Records as Evidence and Information, 2000, Vandals in the Stacks? A Response to Nicholson Baker's assault on Libraries, 2002, Flowers After the Funeral: The Implications of 9/11 in the Digital Era, 2003, No Innocent Deposits: Rethinking Archival Appraisal, 2004 (Leland Soc. of Am. Archivists award 2005), Lester J. Cappon and the Relationship of History, Archives, and Scholarship in the Golden Age of Archival Theory, 2004, A Minor Nuisance Spread Across the Organization: Factors Leading to the Establishment and Support of Records and Information Management Programs, 2005, Archives and Archivists in the Information Age, 2005, Understanding Archives & Manuscripts, 2006; co-editor (with David Wallace) Archives and the Public Good: Accountability and Records in Modern Society, 2002 Fellow Soc. Am. Archivists (coun. mem. 1986-89, editor Am. Archivist 1992-95). Presbyterian. Avocation: golf. Office: U Pittsburgh Sch Info Sci 614 LIS Bldg 135 N Bellefield Ave Pittsburgh PA 15260 E-mail: rcox@sis.pitt.edu.

COX, ROBERT, retired landscape company executive; b. Nambour, Queensland, Australia, June 23, 1939; arrived in US, 1984; s. Leslie Gordon and Margaret Mary Cox; m. Mary Ann Craig, Dec. 27, 2003. Student, Sydney Missionary and Bible Coll., Australia, 1960—63, Auckland Tech. Inst., New Zealand, 1978—82. Cert. in commerce New Zealand Authority Advanced Vocat. Awards. Mgr. Woolworths (Australasia), Sydney and Auckland, 1971—79; acct. mgr. Aerosol Products, 1979—83; owner Ariz. Gardens, Siera Vista, 1994—2006; ret., 2006. Mem.: Mensa (life; regional vice chmn. 1989—93, 1998—2002, nat. sight coord. 2002—, Owl award 1997). Avocations: birdwatching, theater, travel.

COX, ROBERT C., insurance company executive; BS in Bus. Mgmt. and Fin., San Jose State U., Calif. Fin. instns. underwriter The Chubb Corp., San Francisco, 1981, ea. zone underwriting mgr. dept. fin. instns., 1986, worldwide mgr. dept. fin. instns., 1996, COO Chubb Splty. Ins., 2001—, mng. dir. Chubb & Son, Inc., 2003, sr. v.p. Chubb & Son, Inc., 2003, exec. v.p. Chubb & Son, Inc. Office: The Chubb Corp 15 Mountain View Rd Warren NJ 07059 Office Phone: 908-903-2000. Office Fax: 908-903-2027.*

COX, ROBERT HAMES, chemist, consultant; b. Toronto, Can., Mar. 23, 1923; came to U.S., 1951; s. Giffard and Lavinia Sarah (Hames) C.; m. Dora Maria Forstrom, Sept. 5, 1953; children: William H., Frederick G., Irene M. B of Pharmacy, U. Toronto, 1946; BS in Pharmacy, U. Sask., Saskatoon, Can., 1948, MSc, 1950; PhD in Medicinal Chemistry, U. Mich., 1954. Lic. pharmacist, Ont. Head dept. pharm. chemistry U. B.C., Vancouver, Canada, 1949-51; asst. to mgr. product devel. Mallinckrodt Chem. Works, St. Louis, 1954-56; tech. dir. Vick Internat. divsn. Richardson-Merrell, NYC, 1956-60, assoc. dir. tech. svcs., 1960-64, v.p. rsch. and devel. Walker Labs. Mt. Vernon, NY, 1964-66; dir. new products Winthrop Labs. divsn. Sterling Drug, NYC, 1966-75; co-founder, pres. New Eng. Pharms., Inc., Randolph, Mass., 1978-82; pres. Robert H. Cox & Co., Scarsdale, NY, 1975—, Cox & Fay, Inc., Scarsdale, 1991—. Cons. Drug Enforcement Adminstrn., Washington, 1976-78, Nat. Cancer Inst., Bethesda, Md., 1980-81, Indonesian Govt., Jakarta, Java, 1991—. Co-editor-in-chief: Medicinal Chemistry, Vol. III, 1956, Vol. IV, 1959. Leader Jamaica Mission, UN Adv. Svcs., 1988; mem. U.S. Exchs. del. to China, 1990. With Royal Can. Air Foirce, 1942-45. Recipient Roberts medal Ont. Coll. Pharmacy, 1955, George E. Parke medal, 1957. Fellow Am. Inst. Chemists (pres. N.Y. 1986-87, leader sci. del. to China 1986, co-leader to USSR 1989); mem. Am. Chem. Soc. (treas. medicinal chemistry divsn. 1962-63), Parenteral Drug Assn., Ctrl. Atlantic States Assn. Food and Drug Ofcls., Chemists Club (trustee). Episcopalian. Achievements include patents for drugs (sympatholytics/cycloplegics) and medical devices including hemodialysis; conducted practical synthesis of suberone precursor of early antihypertensive, guanethidine; early evaluation (1940s) of oxidized cholesterols in etiology of experimental atherosclerosis. E-mail: bcox@snet.net.

COX, RODY P(OWELL), internist, educator; b. New Brighton, Pa., June 24, 1926; s. Raymond James and Hazel (Powell) C.; m. Jane Beverly Birks, Sept. 5, 1953 (dec. Apr. 1995); children: Shelley Lea, Rody Powell, Sue Ellen; m. LaVaun Jeanne Sears, Mar. 1, 1997. Student, Franklin and Marshall Coll., 1946-48; MD, U. Pa., 1952. Diplomate Am. Bd. Internal Medicine. Intern U. Mich., 1952-53, resident in medicine, 1953-54, U. Pa., Phila., 1953-57, asst. prof. medicine, 1957-60; rsch. assoc. U. Glasgow, Scotland, 1960-61; prof. medicine NYU, NYC, 1961-79, prof. pharmacology, 1972-79, chief div. human genetics, 1972-79; prof., vice chmn. dept. medicine Case-Western Res. U., Cleve., 1979-88; chief med. svc. VA Med. Ctr., Cleve., 1979-88; dean Med. Sch. U. Tex. Southwestern Med. Ctr., Dallas, 1988-89, prof. internal medicine, 1988—. Mem. metabolism study sect. NIH, 1970-74, chmn. genetics study sect., 1978-79, chmn. mammalian genetics study sect., 1979-81; mem. panel on clin. scis. NRC, 1976-86. Editor: Cell Communication, 1974; co-editor: Epithelial Cell Culture, 1981; contbr. articles to profl. publs. Sgt. U.S. Army, 1944-46, NATOUSA. Fellow ACP; mem. Am. Soc. Clin. Investigation (emeritus), Assn. Am. Physicians, Ctrl. Soc. Clin. Rsch., John Morgan Soc. U. Pa., Harvey Soc., Am. Clin. Climatol. Assn., Am. Soc. Human Genetics, Interurban Clin. Club, Alpha Omega Alpha (councillor NYU chpt. 1970-76). Home: 5 Connaught Ct Dallas TX 75225-2459 Office: U Tex Southwestern Med Ctr 5323 Harry Hines Blvd Dallas TX 75390-8889 Home Phone: 214-363-4329; Office Phone: 214-648-7805. Business E-Mail: rcox@mednet.swmed.edu.

COX, ROGER FRAZIER, lawyer; b. Phila., Sept. 11, 1939; s. Roger Newcomb and Ethel May (Frazier) Cox; m. Lucy Jakstas, June 24, 1967. BA, Amherst Coll., 1962; LLB, U. Pa., 1966. Bar: DC 1967, Pa. 1967, Calif. 1970. Law clk. to presiding judge US Dist. Ct., NYC, 1966-67; asst. dist. atty. Phila. Dist. Atty.'s Office, 1967-69; staff atty. Alameda County Legal Aid Soc., Oakland, Calif., 1969-71; from assoc. to ptnr., of counsel Blank Rome LLP, Phila., 1971—. Mem.: ABA, Phila. Bar Assn., Pa. Bar Assn., Am. Judicature Soc., Order of Coif. Home: 303 Delancey St Philadelphia PA 19106-4208 Office: Blank Rome LLP One Logan Sq Philadelphia PA 19103-6998 Office Phone: 215-569-5601. Business E-Mail: cox@blankrome.com.

COX, SANFORD CURTIS, JR., lawyer; b. El Paso, Tex., July 31, 1929; s. Sanford Curtis Sr. and Iva M. (Richardson) C.; m. Helen A. Thurston, Sept. 27, 1958; children: Sanford Curtis III, Christopher Thurston. BA, Tex. Western Coll., 1951, MA, 1952; LLB, U. Tex., 1957. Bar: Tex. 1957, U.S. Dist. Ct. (we. dist.) Tex. 1960, U.S. Ct. Appeals (5th cir.) 1964, U.S. Ct. Appeals (D.C. cir.) 1975. Assoc. Andress, Lipscomb, Peticolas & Fisk, El Paso, 1957-61; ptnr. Lipscomb, Fisk & Cox, El Paso, 1961-74, Fisk & Cox, El Paso, 1974-79; sole practice El Paso, 1979-81; pres./shareholder Sanford C. Cox Jr. P.C., El Paso, 1981-93, mem., 1993—. Mem. bd. editors U. Tex. Law Rev. Mem. adv. bd. Booth Meml. Home, 1963-79, Pleasant View Home, 1979-91. Served with U.S. Army, 1952-54. Mem. ABA, Tex. Bar Assn. (admissions com. 17th dist. 1976), El Paso Bar Assn. (ethics com. 1965-69, fee arbitration com. 1973-75), Order of Coif, Phi Delta Phi. Republican. Episcopalian. Office: 6006 N Mesa St El Paso TX 79912-4659 Home Phone: 915-584-1574; Office Phone: 915-581-3477.

COX, SEAN F., federal judge; b. Detroit, Sept. 24, 1957; B. Gen. Studies, U. Mich., 1979; JD, Detroit Coll. Law, 1983. Bar: Mich. 1983. Law clk. James Flynn, PC, 1983; assoc. Kitch, Saurbier, Drutchas, Wagner & Kenney, 1984—89, Bloom & Kavanaugh, 1989—90; ptnr. Cummings, McClorey, Davis & Acho, PC, 1990—96; judge 3rd Mich. Jud. Cir. Ct., 1996—2006, US Dist. Ct. (Ea. dist.) Mich., Detroit, 2006—. Office: US Dist Ct 5th Fl 231 W Lafayette Detroit MI 48226 Office Phone: 313-234-2650.*

COX, THOMAS A., lawyer; b. Johnson City, Tenn., July 28, 1951; BS with high honours, U. Tenn., 1973; JD cum laude, Harvard U., 1976. Bar: Ga. 1976. Mem. Sutherland, Asbill & Brennan, Atlanta; of councel Weekes & Candler, LLP, Decatur, Ga. Adj. prof. of Law Emory U., 2004. Mem. Phi Beta Kappa, Ga. Office: Weekes & Candler LLP 1 Decatur Town Ctr 150 E Ponce de Leon PO Box 250 Decatur GA 30030 Office Phone: 404-378-4300. Office Fax: 404-378-3617.

COX, WALTER THOMPSON, III, lawyer, federal judge, educator; b. Anderson, SC, Aug. 13, 1942; s. Walter Thompson and Mary (Johnson) C.; m. Victoria Grubbs, Feb. 8, 1963; children: Lisa, Walter. BS, Clemson U., 1964; JD, U. S.C., 1967. Bar: S.C., 1967, U.S. Dist. Ct. S.C., 1967, U.S. Ct. Appeals (4th cir.), 1976, U.S. Ct. Appeals for Armed Forces, 1984, U.S. Supreme Ct., 1987. Commn. capt. U.S. Army, 1964, atty., 1964-73; ptnr. Jones, McIntosh, Threlkeld, Newman & Cox, Anderson, SC, 1973-78; trial judge 10th cir. State S.C., Anderson, 1978-84; judge US Ct. Appeals for the Armed Forces, Washington, 1984-95, 1999—2000, chief judge, 1995-99, sr. judge, 2000—; sr. lecturing fellow Duke U. Law Sch., Durham, NC; of counsel Nelson Mullins Riley & Scarborough, LLP, Charleston, SC, 2003—. Adj. prof. Charleston Sch. Law, 2005. Mem. ABA, FBA, Judge Adv.'s Assn., S.C. Bar Assn. (del.), Wild Dune Golf and Racquet Club. Episcopalian. Office: Nelson Mullins Riley & Scarborough LLP 151 Meeting St St 600 Charleston SC 29401 Office Phone: 843-853-5200. Business E-Mail: wcox@law.duke.edu.*

COX, WARREN JACOB, architect; b. NYC, Aug. 28, 1935; s. Oscar Sydney and Louise Bryson (Black) C.; m. Claire Christie-Miller, July 1, 1975; children: Alexandra Louise, Samuel Oscar. BA magna cum laude, Yale U., 1957, MArch, 1961. Ptnr. Hartman-Cox Architects, Washington, 1965—. Vis. archtl. critic Yale, 1966, Cath. U. Am., 1967, U. Va., 1976; lectr. in field. Works include master plan, dormitory and chapel, Mt. Vernon Coll., EURAM bldg. Nat. Perm. Bldg., Folger Shakespeare Libr. addition, Washington, Immanuel Presbyn. Ch. Va., Nat. Humanities Ctr., Raleigh, Am. Embassy, Malaysia, HEB corp. hdqrs., San Antonio, Chrysler Mus. remodeling, Norfolk, Dumbarton Oaks remodeling, Monroe Hall and McIntire Sch. Commerce, U. Va., Charlottesville, Sumner Sq., 1001 Pa. Ave., Market Sq., Franklin Sq., Georgetown U. Law Ctr. Libr. and Residence Hall, Washington, John Carter Brown Libr. addition, Providence, Winterthur New Exhbn. Bldg., Wilmington, Del., Tulane Law Sch., New Orleans, Law Sch. Libr. U. Conn., Hartford, Law Sch. Washington U., St. Louis, Libr. Case We. Res. U., Cleve., Fed. Courthouse, Corpus Christi, Tex., Concert Hall remodeling Kennedy Ctr. for Performing Arts, Washington, New Dist. and Cir. Courthouses, Lexington, Kennedy Warren Apts. addition, Lincoln and Jefferson Memls. restoration, Patent Office Bldg. renovation, Nat. Archives Bldg. renovation, Washington, Jefferson Libr., Monticello and spl. collections libr., U. Va., Charlottesville, Div. Sch. addition Duke U. Divinity Sch., Durham, NC. Mem. Georgetown Commn. Fine Arts, 1971-75; chmn. Friends of Folger Shakespeare Libr., 1987-88; bd. dirs. Ctr. for Palladian Studies in Am., 1982-, D.C. Preservation League, 1987-89. Recipient History of Art prize Yale U., 1957, Henry Adams prize 1961, more than 115 nat. and regional design awards including Louis Sullivan Prize (1972). Fellow: AIA (Archtl. Firm award 1988, Arthur Ross award for arch. 2006, Centennial award DC chpt. 2006, six Nat. Honor awards). Home: 3111 N St NW Washington DC 20007-3420 also: PO Box 1 Church Hill MD 21623-0001 Office: Hartman Cox Architects 1074 Thomas Jefferson St NW Washington DC 20007-3832

COX, WILFORD DONALD, retired food company executive; b. Marion, Ill., Sept. 5, 1925; s. James Roy and Mamie (Stahlhut) C.; m. Helen Eunice Turner, Sept. 8, 1945; 1 child, James Dexter. Grad. high sch., Crab Orchard, Ill. Asst. plant mgr. Std. Brands Inc., San Antonio, 1956-60; plant mgr. Dallas, 1960-64; asst. div. mgr. Kansas City, Mo., 1964-70; div. mgr., 1972-78; v.p. procurement NYC, 1978-81; v.p. Cal-Maine Foods, Jackson, Miss., 1970-72; v.p. commodities Nabisco Brands Inc., East Hanover, N.J., 1981-84; v.p. oil procurement Kraft Inc., Glenview, Ill., then Memphis, 1984-90, ret., 1990. Mem. Nat. Inst. Oilseed Processors, Nat. Soybean Processors Assn., Nat. Assn. Purchasing Mgrs., Colonial Country Club (Memphis). Republican. Avocation: golf. Office Phone: 901-682-8085. Personal E-mail: jchcmtw@bellsouth.net.

COX, WILLIAM ANDREW, cardiovascular thoracic surgeon; b. Columbus, Ga., Aug. 3, 1925; s. Virgil Augustus and Dale Jackson C.; m. Nina Recelle Hobby, Jan. 1, 1948; children: Constance Lynn Cox Rogers, Patricia Ann Cox Brown, William Robert, Janet Elaine Cox Sidewater. Student, Presbyn. Coll., Clinton, SC, 1942, Harvard U., Cambridge, Mass., 1944-45, Cornell U., Ithaca, NY, 1945; BS, Emory U., Atlanta, 1950, MD, 1954; MS in Surgery, Baylor U., Waco, Tex., 1961. Diplomate Am. Bd. Surgery, Am. Bd. Thoracic Surgery. Active duty USN, 1943-46; lt. (j.g.) USNR, 1946-54; commd. 1st lt. MC US Army, 1954, advanced through grades to col., 1969; intern Brooke Army Med. Ctr., San Antonio, 1954-55, resident gen. surgery, 1956-60; resident cardiovasc. thoracic surgery Walter Reed Army Med. Ctr., Washington, 1960-62, staff cardiothoracic surgeon, 1962; asst chief cardiothoracic surgery Letterman Gen. Hosp., San Francisco, 1962-65; performed first Star Edwards mitral valve replacement at Letterman Gen. Hosp. Presidio San Francisco, 1964; chief dept. surgery and cardiothoracic surgery 121 Evaculation Hosp. Seoul, Korea, 1965-66; cons. cardiothoracic surgery Korean Theatre, 1965-66; asst. chief cardiothoracic surgery Brooke Army Med Ctr., 1966-69, chief, 1969-73, performed first triple coronary artery bypass graft at Brooke Gen. Hosp. San Antonio, 1969, bd. dirs. thoracic surgery residency programs, 1966-73, ret., 1973. Brooke Tower, on call for Pres. Lyndon B. Johnson when he visited his Tex. Ranch, 1967-72; clin. prof. cardio-thoracic surgery U. Tex. Sch. Medicine, San Antonio, 1971—; practice specializing in cardiovasc. thoracic surgery, Corpus Christi, Tex., 1973-93; cons. cardio-thoracic surgery Brooke Army Med. Ctr., San Antonio, 1977—; chief staff Meml. Med. Ctr., 1980; dir. disaster med. care region 3A Tex. State Dept. Health, 1973-88; mem. Coastal Bend Coun. Gov.'s Emergency Med. Svc. Commn., 1979-88; adv. bd. on congenital heart disease Tex. Dept. Health, 1980-88; participant joint confs. on cardiovasc. surgery and thoracic surgery Am. People Amb. Program, Leningrad, Moscow, Bucharest, Romania, Belgrade, Yugoslavia, Prague, Czechoslovakia, 1987; del. Vanderbilt U. Joint conf. vascular surgery Dublin, Ireland, Edinburgh, Scotland, London, 1986; participant joint confs. cardiovasc. surgery and thoracic surgery Am. Amb. People to People Program, Singapore, Kuala Lumpur, Malaysia, Hanoi, Vietnam, DaNang, Vietnam, Hue, Vietnam, Saigon, Vietnam, Hong Kong, 1992, People to People Am. Amb. Program, Eng., Scotland, Wales, 1996, 13th worldwide conf., Chester, England, 1998, 14th worldwide conf., Hong Kong, 2000, Denton A. Cooley Cardiovasc. Surgery Soc. mtg. Coeur d'Alene, Idaho, 2000; spkr. symposium Controversies in Cardiology, Dr. Willis Hurst, Holland Am. Lines Veendam, 1997; invited spkr. on open heart surgery 780 Bomb Squadron, Gainesville, 2001 Contbr. over 40 articles to profl. jours.; 4 profl. articles were selected for publication in the Yearbook of Surgery by editor Michael DeBakey. Ruling elder Presbyn. Ch., 1960—. Decorated Legion of Merit, Army Commendation medal; recipient A Prefix award Surgeon Gen. US Army, commendation Surgeon Gen. South Korea, commendation Eighth US Army Commdg. Gen. for Emergency Surgery on Adm. Blackburn US Negotiator for Peace, Pan mun jom, North Korea; named hon. citizen Phila. by Mayor Edward G. Rendell, 1995; recipient Tex. Med. Assn. Mem. Recognition 50 Yrs. award 1954-2004, 2004. Fellow Am. Coll. Chest Physicians (emeritus); mem. AMA, Soc. Thoracic Surgeons, Denton A. Coley Cardiovasc. Surgery Soc., Tex. Med. Assn. (del. conf. infectious diseases Bangkok, Hong Kong, Beijing, Shanghai, 1983), So. Thoracic Surgery Assn., Nueces County Med. Soc., Corpus Christi Surg. Soc., 38th Parallel Med. Soc., U.S. Power Squadron, People to People Internat., Internat. Platform, USN League (life), Ret. Officers Assn. (life), Navy Meml. Yacht Club (past commodore presidio San Francisco), T-Bar-M Racquet Club, Corpus Christi Country Club, Corpus Christi Athletic Club, Corpus Christi Town, Ft. Sam Houston Officers Club. Republican. Office Phone: 361-728-7091.

COX, WILLIAM JACKSON, retired bishop; b. Valeria, Ky., Jan. 24, 1921; s. Robert Lee and Ora Ethel (Lawson) C.; m. Betty Drake, Dec. 20, 1941; children: Sharon Lee, William Richard, Michael Colin Student, U. Cin., 1939-40, George Washington U., Washington, 1945-46, U. Md. overseas extension, London, 1951-53, Va. Theol. Sem., Alexandria, 1957, D.Div. (hon.), 1974, Episcopal Theol. Sem. Ky., Lexington, 1980. Ordained priest Episcopal Ch., 1957. Pres., gen. mgr. McCook Broadcasting Co., McCook, Nebr., 1947-49; rector Church of the Holy Cross, Cumberland, Md., 1957-72; suffragan bishop of Md. Episcopal Ch., Frederick, Md., 1972-80, asst. bishop Okla. Tulsa, 1980—88; ret., 1988. Pres. Appalachian Peoples Service Orgn., Blacksburg, Va., 1974-80; chmn. Standing Com. on the Church in Small Communities, N.Y.C., 1976-82 Pres., Nursing Home Bd. of Allegany County, Cumberland, Md., 1965-72; pres. Episcopal Ministries to the Aging, Balt., 1973-80. Served to lt. col. U.S. Army, 1942-46, 1949-54; ETO. Episcopalian. Avocation: flying. Home: 3701 N Cincinnati Ave #7 Tulsa OK 74106-1533 E-mail: bpcox@cox.net.

COX, WILLIAM MARTIN, lawyer, educator; b. Bernardsville, NJ, Dec. 26, 1922; s. Martin John and Nellie (Fotens) Cox; m. Julia Sebastian, June 14, 1952; children: Janice Cox Trautman, William Martin, Joann Cox Cahoon, Julieann Cox Allen. AB, Syracuse U., NY, 1947; JD, Cornell U., Ithaca, NY, 1950. Bar: NJ 1950, US Dist. Ct. 1950. Mem. Dolan & Dolan, Newton, NJ, 1950—; mem. faculty, tchr. zoning admintrn. Rutgers U., New Brunswick, NJ, 1968—98. Gen. counsel NJ Planning Ofcls., 1967—93, gen. counsel emeritus, 1998—; pres. NJ Inst. Mcpl. Attys., 1982—84; mem. Land Use Law Drafting Com., 1970—, chmn., 1993—98; dir. emeritus Equip, Inc., Marion, NC; bd. dirs. Newton Cemetery Co., v.p., 2000—. Author: Zoning and Land Use Adminstrn. in New Jersey, 2007. With US Army, 1943—45. Named Citizen Yr., Town Newton, 2002; recipient Resolution Appreciation award, NJ Senate Gen. Assembly, 1994, Pres.'s Disting. Svc. award, NJ League Municipalities, 1999, Excellence Land Use Law award, NJ Inst. Mcpl. Attys., 1999, Professionalism Law award, Sussex County NJ State Bar Assn., 2003, Michael A. Pane award integrity local govt., 2003, Newton Pride Found. award, 2004. Mem.: NJ Bar Assn., Sussex County Bar Assn., NJ Planning Ofcls., Am. Planning Assn., Non-Commd. Officers Assn., VFW, Rotary (pres. 1978—79, Vocat. award 1996), Monarchist League, Am. Legion. Baptist. Office: 1 Legal Ln Newton NJ 07860-1827 Business E-Mail: wcox@dolanlaw.com.

COX, WILLIAM VAUGHAN, arbitrator, lawyer; b. Jersey City, Nov. 12, 1936; s. Walter Miles and Emily (McNenney); divorced; children: Millicent S., Jennifer V. BA, Princeton U., 1958; LLB, Yale U., 1964. Bar: Colo. 1965, N.Y. 1974. Law clk. Holland & Hart, Denver, 1963; atty. Conoco Inc., Denver, 1966-72, asst. to v.p., gen. counsel Stamford, Conn., 1972-73; v.p., gen. counsel Stromberg-Carlson Corp., Rochester, N.Y., 1974-78; mng. ptnr. Bader & Cox, Denver, 1979—86, of counsel, 1986—88; pres. Law Office of William V. Cox, Denver, 1988—2007, bd. dirs.; project and planning dir. Interwest Comm. Corp., 1995-97. Pres. New West Indies Trading Co., Denver, 1984-2005, bd. dirs.; pres. Coll. Football Ltd., Denver, 1990-2005; arbitrator Arbitration Alternative Inc., Denver, 2005—. Sportswriter/editor: Colorado Springs Free Press, 1960-61. Football coach Cheyenne Mountain H.S., Colorado Springs, 1961; founder, bd. dir., v.p., com. chmn., editor Colo. chpt. Nat. Football Found., 1992-2001; mem. adv. bd. Downtown Denver Dist., 1991-93; bd. dir., com. chmn. Downtown Denver Residents, 1990-93; pres., bd. dir. Barclay Towers Condominiums, Denver, 1990-92, sec., bd. dir., 1998-99, pres. bd. dir., 1999-2000, 2001-2003, sec. bd. dir., 2000-2001, 2003-2007; dist. capt. Rep. Com., Cherry Hills, Colo., 1980-85; bd. dir. Monroe County Humane Soc., Rochester, 1975-78. With inf., intelligence USAR, 1959—65. Mem.: Am. Arbitration Assn. (arbitrator 2002—), Denver Bar Assn., Colo. Bar Assn., Law Club Denver (com. chmn. 1971), Princeton Rocky Mountain Club (com. chmn. 1970—71), Univ. Club Denver (bd. dirs. 1997—2000), Am. Legion, Corbey Ct., Phi Delta Phi. Roman Catholic. Avocations: running, politics, history, animal rights. Office: 1999 Broadway Ste 2400 Denver CO 80202 Business E-Mail: wvcsq@citynetdsl.com.

COX ARQUETTE, COURTENEY, actress; b. Birmingham, Ala., June 15, 1964; d. Richard L. Lewis and Courteney Bass-Copland; m. David Arquette, June 12, 1999; 1 child, CoCo. Attended, Mt. Vernon Coll. Spokesperson Kinerase skin care products, 2005—; co-founder Coquette Prodns., 2003—. Appearances include (music video) Bruce Springsteen's Dancing in the Dark, 1984, The Rembrandts I'll Be There For You, 1995; (TV series) As The World Turns, 1984, Murder, She Wrote, 1984, Misfits of Science, 1985-86, Family Ties, 1987-88, Dream On, 1990, Seinfeld, 1990, The Larry Sanders Show, 1992, The Trouble with Larry, 1993, Friends, 1994-2004; (TV pilots) Sylvan in Paradise, 1986; (TV films) If It's Tuesday, It Still Must Be Belgium, 1987, A Rockport Christmas, 1988, Roxanne: The Prize Pulitzer, 1989, Judith Krantz's Till We Meet Again, 1989, Curiosity Kills, 1990, Morton and Hays, 1991, Topper, 1992, Sketch Artist II: Hands That See, 1995; (films) Down Twisted, 1986, Masters of the Universe, 1987, Cocoon: The Return, 1988, Mr. Destiny, 1990, Blue Desert, 1990, Shaking the Tree, 1992, The Opposite Sex (and How to Live with Them), 1993, Ace Ventura, Pet Detective, 1994, Scream, 1996,

Commandments, 1996, Scream 2, 1997, The Runner, 1999, Scream 3, 2000, 3000 Miles to Graceland, 2001, The Shrink Is In, 2001 (also exec. prodr.), Get Well Soon, 2001, Alien Love Triangle, 2002, November, 2004, The Longest Yard, 2005, Alpha Dog, 2006, (voice) Barnyard: The Original Party Animals, 2006, Zoom, 2006, The Tripper, 2006; exec. prodr. TV Series Mix It Up, 2003; actor, exec. prodr. Dirt, 2006. Office: Brillstein Grey Entertainment 9150 Wilshire Blvd Beverly Hills CA 90212*

COXE, HENRY M., III, lawyer; b. 1948; m. Mary Coxe; children: Katie, Matson, Anne English. BA in Polit. Sci., U. of South, Tenn., 1969; JD, Washington and Lee U., 1972. Bar: Va. 1972, Fla. 1973, US Supreme Ct. 1995, US Ct. Appeals (5th Cir.) 1975, US Ct. Appeals (11th Cir.) 1981, US Dist. Ct. (Mid. Dist. Fla.) 1975. Dir. felony divisions & spl. prosecution divsn. Fla. State Atty. Office, 1973; mgr. pvt. law firm, 1981—96; ptnr. Bedell Dittmar DeVault Pillar & Coxe PA, Jacksonville, Fla., 1996—. Bd. dirs. Jacksonville Area Legal Aid; chmn. disciplinary grievance com. US Dist. Ct. (Jacksonville); mem. judicial nom. commn. Fourth Judicial Cir., 1987—91, First Dist. Ct. Appeal, 1994—96; charter mem. Fla. Bench/Bar Commn. Named Lawyer of Yr., Financial Daily News; recipient Justice for All award, Jacksonville Area Legal Aid, 2004, Pro Bono award, City of Jacksonville, Pres. award, Am. Bd. Trial Advocates, 2004. Master: Chester Bedell Inn of Ct.; fellow: Am. Coll. Trial Lawyers; mem.: Va. State Bar, Fla. Bar (bd. gov. 1995—, pres. 2006—07, Pres. Pro Bono Svc. award, Pres. Award of Merit), Jacksonville Bar Assn. (pres. 1995—96, bd. gov. 1992—96). Office: Bedell Dittmar DeVault Pillan & Coxe PA Teh Bedell Bldg 101 E Adams St Jacksonville FL 32202-3303 Office Phone: 904-353-0211. Office Fax: 904-353-9307.

COY, CRAIG P., airport terminal executive; Degree, U.S. Coast Guard Acad.; MBA, Harvard U. Various sr. level positions Fed. Govt., 20 yrs; v.p., gen. mgr. Lear Siegler Svcs. Inc., 1992-97; CEO HR Logic, Waltham, Mass., 1997—2001, Mass. Port Authority, 2001—. Past bd. dirs. White House Fellows Assn., U.S. Coast Guard Acad. Office: Mass Port Authority One Harborside Drive Ste 200S East Boston MA 02128-2909 E-mail: info@hrlogic.com.

COYE, MARY P., counselor; b. NC; m. Stephen Coye; children: Candace, Ashley. AAS with honors, Ctrl. Carolina CC, Sanford, NC, 1992; BAS, Campbell U., Buies Creek, NC, 1994; MA, Campbell U., 1999. Lic. sch. counselor (k-12) NC. Dep. clk. of ct. Adminstrv. Office of the Cts., Raleigh, NC, 1978-83; computer lab. asst., news reporter Campbell U., 1992-94, asst. to curriculum materials coord., 1994-95; tutorial coord. Ctrl. Carolina CC, 1995-96; data entry staff N.C. Dept. Environ. Health, Raleigh, 1997; counseling intern North Harnett Elem. Sch., Angier, NC, 1997-98. Interviewer, counselor Employment Security Commn., 1998-2000; admissions counselor Campbell U., 2000-01, sch. counselor, 2001—. Mem. Cape Fear Friends of the Fine Arts, Sch. Counselor's Assn., Grange. Recipient All Am. Scholar award, US Achievement Acad. award. Mem. Omicron Delta Kappa, Delta Kappa Pi. Democrat. Baptist. Avocations: reading, singing, horseback riding, photography, piano. Home: PO Box 36 Glenmont NY 12077 Personal E-mail: coye_m@yahoo.com.

COYLE, DIANE BONANOMI, special education educator; b. Phila., Apr. 26, 1950; d. Fernand Joseph Bonanomi and Alice Mabel Pooler; m. James Edward Coyle Jr., Oct. 10, 1981; children: Kathryn Janine, Susan Elizabeth, Caryn Marie. BS in Elem. Edn., Gwynedd Mercy Coll., Pa., 1972; MEd, Lehigh U., Bethlehem, Pa. Cert. elem. edn. tchr. Pa., tchr. socially and emotionally disturbed Pa., spl. edn. tchr. Pa. 2nd grade tchr. St. Stanislaus Sch., Lansdale, Pa., 1969—72, resource rm. tchr., 1972—76; learning disabilities cons. READS, Montgomery County, Pa., 1976—78; spl. edn. tchr. New Hope-Solebury Jr./Sr. HS, New Hope, Pa., 1978—83; acting spl. edn. supr. New Hope - Solebury Sch. Dist., New Hope, 1983—88; 4th grade and spl. edn. tchr. New Hope - Solebury Elem. Sch., New Hope, 1990—. Math and reading tutor, Bucks County, Pa., 1982—; multisensory lang. tchr. Wilson Reading Sys., Bucks County, 2000—; tchr. Confraternity of Christian Doctrine Queen of Universe Parish, St. John the Evangelist Parish, Levittown/Yardley, Pa., 1990—95. Leader Girl Scouts USA, Bucks County, 1986—96; asst. children's summer theater Ocean Grove Youth Assn., NJ; costume dir. Drama Works, Yardley, 1997—2000; mem., co-chmn. costume com.Youth Club, Morrisville Presbyn. Ch., Pa., 2000—06, chmn. youth bd., 2004—06; jr. Christian Youth Orgn. bd. St. John the Evangelist Parish, Morrisville, 1993—97, chmn. social concerns com., 2005—07, mem. peace and justice com., 2000—05. Recipient Apple award, New Hope Solebury Upper Elem. Sch., 2005. Mem.: New Hope-Solebury Edn. Assn. (pres. 2000—02), Coun. Exceptional Children (assoc.). Democrat. Roman Catholic. Avocations: reading, swimming, gardening, travel, sewing. Home: 300 Hollow Branch Ln Yardley PA 19067 Office: New Hope Solebury Sch Dist 180 W Bridge St New Hope PA 18938 Business E-Mail: dcoyle@nhsd.org.

COYLE, DOROTHY, government agency administrator; Grad., Marquette U., Milw., Northwestern U. Kellogg Sch. Mgmt., 2001. Dir. Chgo. Office of Tourism, 1999—. Bd. dirs. Visit Ill. Named one of Top 40 Under 40, Crain's Chgo. Bus., 2006. Office: Chgo Office of Tourism Chgo Cultural Ctr 78 E Washington St 4th Fl Chicago IL 60602-4801 E-mail: dcoyle@cityofchicago.org.*

COYLE, JOSEPH THOMAS, psychiatrist; b. Chgo., Oct. 9, 1943; s. Joseph Thomas and Mercedes (Sartor) Coyle; m. Genevieve Sansoucy, Aug. 19, 1968; children: Andrew, Peter, David. AB, Coll. of the Holy Cross, Worcester, Mass., 1965; MD, Johns Hopkins U., Balt., 1969; MA (hon.), Harvard U., Cambridge, Mass., 1991. Diplomate Am. Bd. Psychiatry and Neurology. Asst. prof. pharmacology Johns Hopkins Sch. of Medicine, Balt., 1974—76, asst. prof pharmacology and psychiatry, 1976—78, assoc. prof pharmacology and psychiatry, 1978—80, prof of neurosci., psychiatry and pharmacology, 1980—91, dir. divsn. child psychiatry, 1982—91, Disting. Svc. prof. of child psychiatry, 1985—91; Eben S. Draper prof. of psychiatry and neurosci. Harvard U., Boston, 1991—; chair consol. dept. psychiatry Harvard Med. Sch., Boston, 1991—2001. Co-dir. outpatient pharmacotherapy clinic Johns Hopkins Hosp., Balt., 1977—82; mem. sci. adv. bd. Pfizer Scholars Program, NYC, 1989—94, John F. Merck Found., Boston, 1990—2000, Abbott Pharms., North Chicago, Ill., 1990—, Guilford Pharms., Balt., 1992—98. Contbr. articles to profl. jours.; editor: Archives of General Psychiatry, 2002—. Mem. adv. bd. NIMH, Washington, 1990—94. Recipient AE Bennett award, 1978, Gold Medal award, 1991, EA Strecker award, Inst. Pa. Hosp., 1993, Thomas Salmon lecture, NY Acad. Medicine, 1993, Passarow Found. award, 1997, Lieber award, Nat. Alliance Rsch. Schizophrenia and Depression, 2004, Sanctae Crucis award, Coll. Holy Cross, 2006. Fellow: Am. Acad. of Arts and Scis., Am. Psychiat. Assn. (Found. Fund prize 1985, Adolph Meyer award 1994, Kemp Fund award 1996); mem.: Inst. of Medicine of the Nat. Acad. Sci., Am. Soc. Pharmacology and Exptl. Therapeutics (John Jacob Abel award 1979), Am. Acad. Child and Adolescent Psychiatry, Am. Coll. Neuropsychopharmacology (pres. 2001, Effron award 1982), Soc. Neurosci. (pres. 1991—92, Spl. Achievement award 2001). Avocations: reading, fishing. Office: Harvard Med Sch Dept Psychiatry 115 Mill St Belmont MA 02478-1041 Office Phone: 617-855-2101. Business E-Mail: joseph_coyle@hms.harvard.edu.

COYLE, LINDA MARIE, elementary school educator; d. Francis Thomas and Mary Anita Flynn; m. Michael Coyle, May 24, 1986. AAS, Scottsdale C.C., Scottsdale, Ariz., 1992; BS, Ea. Mich. U., Ypsilanti, Mich., 1978; MA, Ariz. State U., Tempe, Ariz., 1989. Sci. tchr. Paradise Valley Unified Sch. Dist., Phoenix, Ariz., 1980—, sci. program area coord., 1997—2004. Cmty. mem. representing sci. edn. Paradise Valley Learning Connections, Phoenix, Ariz., 2002—04. Recipient Greenway Mid. Sch. Tchr. of the Yr., Ctrl. Ariz. Mid. Level Tchg. Assn., 1999, Sch. Bus. Partnership, Grand Canyon Nat. Pk.-Revegetation, 1995-1999; grantee Environ. Edn. Rsch. Grant, Ariz. Adv. Coun. on Environ. Edn., 2001, Project Resource Grant for Environ. Edn., Salt River Project, 1995-1997. Mem.: NEA, NSTA, Paradise Valley Edn. Assn., Ariz. Sci. Coord. Assn., Ariz. Sci. Tchrs. Assn. Independent. Achievements include Ariz. Sci. Tchr. of the Yr; Crescordia Award for Environl. Edn.- Valley Forward Assn. Avocations: horseback riding, hiking, reading, travel. Office: Mountain Trail Mid Sch 2323 E Mountain Gate Pass Rd Phoenix AZ 85024 Home Phone: 623-465-0266; Office Phone: 480-538-7100.

COYLE, MARTIN ADOLPHUS, JR., lawyer; b. Hamilton, Ohio, June 3, 1941; s. Martin Adolphus and Lucille (Baird) C.; m. Sharon Sullivan, Mar. 29, 1969 (div. Dec. 1991); children: Cynthia Ann, David Martin, Jennifer Ann; m. Linda J. O'Brien, July 31, 1993 (div. July 1996); m. Sandra C. Lund, July 1998. BA, Ohio Wesleyan U., 1963; JD summa cum laude, Ohio State U., 1966. Bar: N.Y. 1967, Ohio 1966. Assoc. Cravath, Swaine & Moore, NYC, 1966-72; chief counsel securities and fin. TRW Inc., Cleve., 1972-73, sr. counsel, asst. sec., 1973-75, asst. gen. counsel, asst. sec., 1976, asst. gen. counsel, sec., 1976-80, v.p., gen. counsel, sec., 1980-89, exec. v.p., gen. counsel, sec., 1989-97, exec. v.p., 1997-99. Sec. TRW Found., 1975-80, trustee, 1980-98. Pres. Judson Retirement Cmty., 1986-88, trustee, 1986-90; trustee Berea Coll. 1989—, Chautauqua Found., 1999-2003, Chautauqua Inst., 1990-2000, Ohio Wesleyan U., 1992-2001, Gebbie Found., 2001—; vice chair Berea Coll., 2006—. Mem. ABA, Am. Soc. Corp. Secs. (pres. Ohio regional group 1978-80, nat. dir. 1981-87, nat. chmn. 1985-86), Assn. Gen. Counsel (exec. com. 1992-99, pres. 1995-97). Home Phone: 707-996-3552. E-mail: m3865232@mac.com.

COYLE, MICHAEL LEE, lawyer; b. Mechanicsburg, Pa., Oct. 2, 1944; s. Patrick G. and Bertha M. C.; m. Kathleen J. West, July 15, 1967; children: Patrick M., Darren W. BS in Acctg., Utica Coll., 1966; JD, Syracuse U., 1971; LLM in Taxation, Georgetown U., 1975. Bar: N.Y. 1972, Conn. 1975, U.S. Tax Ct. 1975. Acct. Peat, Marwick, Mitchell & Co., Syracuse, NY, 1966, tax acct., 1969-71; atty., adviser interpretive div. Office Chief Counsel IRS, Washington, 1971-73; atty. adviser to judge U.S. Tax Ct., Washington, 1973-75; mem. firm Reid & Riege, P.C., Hartford, Conn., 1975—. Trustee U. Hartford Tax Inst., 1982-86; bd. dirs. adv. coun. Nat. Inst. State & Local Taxation, Old Lyme, Conn., 1987—. Mem., v.p., pres. St. Paul's Luth. Ch. Coun., Wethersfield, Conn., 1976-82, 87-92, 97-2000; bd. dirs. Children's Home Cromwell, Inc., Conn., 1980-88; mem. leadership Greater Hartford, 1978, Conn. Task Force Corp. Taxation; pres. Wethersfield Bus. & Civic Assn., 1978-80. With U.S. Army, 1966-68. Named one of Best Lawyers in Am., 1987—. Mem. ABA (chmn. sales and fin. transaction com., tax sect. 1983-85), Conn. Bar Assn. (tax exec. com., ltd. liability subcom. 1991—), Conn. Bus. & Industry Assn. (tax com. 1987—), Hartford Tax Study Group, Tax Club Hartford (pres.). Avocations: tennis, reading. Home: 144 Stonehill Dr Rocky Hill CT 06067 Office: Reid & Riege PC 1 Financial Plaza Fl 2100 Hartford CT 06103-3185 E-mail: mcoyle@reidandriege.com.

COYLE, PAT, professional basketball coach; Grad., Rutgers U., 1982. Asst. coach U. Miami, 1983—85, Rutgers U., 1985—89, St. Joseph's U., 1989—92; head coach Loyola Coll., Md., 1992—98; asst. coach NY Liberty, 1998—2004, head coach, 2004—. Asst. coach WNBA Ea. Conf. All-Star Team, 2000, 01. Named to Rutgers U. Basketball Hall of Fame, 1993. Office: NY Liberty 2 Penn Plz 14th Fl New York NY 10121*

COYLE, ROBERT EVERETT, federal judge; b. Fresno, Calif., May 6, 1930; s. Everett LaJoya and Virginia Chandler C.; m. Faye Turnbaugh, June 11, 1953; children— Robert Allen, Richard Lee, Barbara Jean BA, Fresno State Coll., 1953; JD, U. Calif., 1956. Bar: Calif. Ptnr. McCormick, Barstow, Sheppard, Coyle & Wayte, 1958-82; chief judge U.S. Dist. Ct. (ea. dist.) Calif., 1990-96, sr. judge, 1996—. Former chair 9th Cir. Conf. of Chief Dist. Judges, chair 9th Cir. space and security com., mem. com. on state and fed. cts. Mem. Calif. Bar Assn. (exec. com. 1974-79, bd. govs. 1979-82, v.p. 1981), Fresno County Bar Assn. (pres. 1972). Office: US Dist Ct 5116 US Courthouse 1130 O St Fresno CA 93721-2201 Office Phone: 559-498-7318.

COYNE, BRIAN J(OSEPH), pharmaceutical researcher; b. Belfast, No. Ireland, Dec. 5, 1961; s. Edward Anthony and Mary H. Coyne; m. Katharine Brunner, Apr. 11, 1992; children: Patrick Michael, Caroline Genevieve. BA, Ctrl. Conn. State U., New Britain, 1987; MA, Montclair State U., Upper Montclair, NJ, 1995; MPA, Seton Hall U., South Orange, NJ, 2002. Cert. med. rep. Cert. Med. Rep. Inst., 1992, Coun. Accreditation Pharm. Mfrs. Reps. Can. Coun. Continuing Pharm. Edn. Can., 1997, mem. Med. Rep. Inst. of Ireland, 2000, clin. rsch. assoc. Assn. Clin. Rsch. Profls., 2005, med. investigator Am. Coll. Forensic Investigators, 2003. Country study mgr. The Clin. Resource Network, NYC, 2003—04; sr. clin. rsch. scientist Novartis Pharmaceuticals Corp., East Hanover, NJ, 2004—05, Forest Labs. Inc., Jersey City, 2005—. Mgr. clin. rsch. Knoll Pharm. Co., Mount Olive, NJ, 1988—2000, Cordis Corp., Warren, 2001—02; study mgr. North Am. ops. Aventis Pharmaceuticals Inc., Bridgewater, 2000—01; mgr. clin. ops. U.S. clin. rsch. assoc. Hemosol Inc., Parsippany, 2002—03. With USN, 1981—85. Decorated Battle E Ribbon U.S. Navy, Expeditionary medal, Rifle and Pistol Marksmanship medals, others; Fellowship, Royal Acad. Medicine, Ireland, 2002. Fellow: Royal Soc. Antiqueries Scotland; mem.: AMVETS, VFW, Am. Coll. Forensic Examiners (juris pro expert witness), Assn. Mil. Surgeons US, Royal Soc. Medicine, Am. Coll. Clin. Pharmacology, Mil. History Soc. Ireland, Soc. Mil. History, US Naval Inst., Am. Legion, Friendly Sons St. Patrick, Naval Order US. Avocations: running, weightlifting, history, scuba diving, reading. Home Phone: 973-584-7929.

COYNE, CHARLES COLE, lawyer; b. Abington, Pa., Dec. 3, 1948; s. James Kitchenman Jr. and Pearl (Black) Coyne; m. Paula J. Latta, May 15, 1976; 1 child, Anna Elizabeth. BS in Econs., U. Pa., 1970; JD, Temple U., 1973. Bar: Pa. 1973, US Supreme Ct. 1982, NJ 1985. Intern Gen. Svcs. Adminstrn., Washington, 1971; of counsel Obermayer Rebmann Maxwell & Hippel, LLP, Phila., 2007—. Bd. dirs. George S. Coyne Chem. Co., Inc., Croydon, Pa., sec., 1973—; dir. Kitchenman Terminal Co. LLC; mng. dir. Cygnet Leasing Co. LLC; vis. prof. Szczecin U., Poland, 2006—; fellow Ctr. Internat. Legal Studies, 2006—. Assoc. editor: Temple Law Rev., 1972—73, columnist: Life in the Country, Ledger Newspaper Group, 1993—99. Chester County rep. Delaware Valley Regional Planning Commn., Pa., 1982—2003; mem. Chester County Health and Edn. Facilities Authority, 1982—, chmn., 1996—2000; bd. suprs. East Fallowfield Twp., Chester County, 1982—83; mem. panel US Bankruptcy Trustees, 1991—93; mem. Chester County Pk. and Recreation Bd., 1998—2005; mem. racing com. Pa. Hunt Cup, 1992—; amb. People to People, Brazil, 2004; chmn. Greater Phila. Young Reps., 1975—76; Rep. candidate Pa. State Legislature, 1976; Phila. Rep. City Policy Com., 1975—77; chief counsel Jim Coyne for Congress Com., 1980, Re-Election Com., 1982. Recipient Disting. Young Rep. award, 1976; AIESEC scholar, U. Melbourne, 1968. Mem.: ABA, S.R. (bd. mgrs. 2000—03), Nat. Steeplechase Assn., Phila. Bar Assn., Pa. Bar Assn., Pa. Soc., U. Pa. Gen. Alumni Soc. (mem. alumni leadership coun., pres. class of 1970), Temple Law Sch. Alumni Assn., Quaker City Farmers Club, Union League, Lawyers Club Phila., Masons (master), Kappa Alpha Soc. Home: Sycamore Run Farm PO Box 155 Unionville PA 19375-0155 Office: Obermayer Rebmann Maxwell & Hippel LLP One Penn Ctr 19th Fl 1617 JFK Blvd Philadelphia PA 19103-1895 Office Phone: 215-665-3000. Business E-Mail: charles.coyne@obermayer.com.

COYNE, EDWARD JAMES, SR., international business educator; b. St. Louis, Sept. 25, 1930; s. Horace John and Bessie (Stinebaker) C.; m. Kathleen (Hayman), Sept. 9, 1952 (dec. April 1985); children: Edward James, Kevin Patrick, Shawn Thomas, Colin Mark, Kathleen Patrice (dec. Feb. 1968); m. Beulah (Shelton), April 19, 1986. BS, La. State U., 1952; MBA, Nova U., 1992; PhD, Bradford U., Eng., 1994; LHD (hon.), Nova U., 1980. Gen. mgr., dir. Comalco Products, Pty., Sydney, Australia, 1966-73; pres. Kaiser Bauxite Co., Discovery Bay, Jamaica, 1974—86; v.p., gen. mgr., Rod, Bar, Wire Kaiser Aluminum & Chem., Oakland, Calif., 1986-90; exec., residence Nova U., Ft. Lauderdale, Fla., 1991-93; dir. MIBA program Nova Southeastern U., Ft. Lauderdale, 1993-96; acad. dean Am. Coll. Dublin, Dublin, 1997-98; vis. prof. Samford U., Birmingham, Ala., 1999—; CFO Connexxia, LLC, 2001—04; ptnr. Kevin Coyne ptnrs., Inc., 2006—. Adv. bd. Inst. Internat. Edu., Southeastern Region, 1983-86, Ctr. Internat. Bus., U. Leeds, U.K., 1995-2001; vis. fellow U. Bradford, U.K., 1996-98. Author: Targeting the Foreign Direct Investor, 1995; co-author: Human Resources: Caregiving Career Progression, and Gender. 2004; contbr. chpt. to book, articles to profl. jours. Vice-chmn. Agr. Mktg. Corp., Jamaica, 1981-86; chmn. Discovery Bay Water Co., Jamaica, 1974-80; vice-chmn. Aboukir Edu. & Industl. Inst., Jamaica, 1976-85; adv. bd. World Trade Council Ft. Lauderdale, 1995-96. Recipient Comdr. Order of Distinction, Govt. Jamaica, 1980; Sports Hall of Fame, Jackson-Madison County, Tenn., 1997. Mem. Acad. Internat. Bus., HR Devel. Internat. Jour. Republican. Roman Catholic. Avocations: reading, travel, teaching. Home: 2752 Berkeley Dr Birmingham AL 35242-4105 Office: Sch Bus Samford U 800 Lakeshore Dr Birmingham AL 35229-0001 Office Phone: 205-726-2041. Personal E-mail: ebcoyne@aol.com.

COYNE, JERRY ALLEN, ecologist, educator; BS summa cum laude with highest honors in Biology, Coll. William & Mary, 1971; summer student in Tropical Ecology, Univ. Costa Rica, 1974; PhD in Biology, Harvard Univ., 1978. Med. tech. Cornell Univ. Med. Sch., 1971—72; rsch. assoc., Mus. Comparative Zoology Harvard Univ., 1978—79; NIH post-doctoral fellow, dept. genetics Univ. Calif., Davis, 1979—82; asst. prof., zoology Univ. Md., College Park, 1982—86, assoc. prof., 1986; assoc. prof., ecology, evolution Univ. Chgo., 1986—91, prof., 1991—. Grantee John Simon Guggenheim Found. Fellowship, Paris, 1989. Fellow: Am. Acad. Arts & Scis.; mem.: Phi Beta Kappa. Office: Dept Ecology and Evolution Univ Chgo 1101 E 57th St Chicago IL 60637 Office Phone: 773-702-1105. Office Fax: 773-702-9740. Business E-Mail: j-coyne@uchicago.edu.*

COYNE, JOHN F., computer company executive; B Mech. Engring., Univ. Coll., Dublin, 1971. Mgmt. positions Western Digital Corp., Ireland, 1983—97, Malaysia, 1997—2000, sr. v.p. worldwide ops. Lake Forest, Calif., 2000—05, exec. v.p., COO, 2005—06, pres., COO, 2006—07, pres., CEO, 2007—. Office: Western Digital Corp 20511 Lake Forest Dr Lake Forest CA 92630-7741*

COYNE, PATRICK IVAN, physiological ecologist; b. Wichita, Kans., Feb. 26, 1944; s. Ivan Lefranz and Ellen Lucille (Brown) C.; m. Mary Ann White, Aug. 22, 1964; children: Shane Barrett, Shannon Renee. BS, Kans. State U., 1966; PhD, Utah State U., 1970. R & D coord. U.S. Army Cold Regions Rsch. and Engring. Lab., Hanover, NH, 1970-72; asst. prof. forestry U. Alaska, Fairbanks, 1973-74; plant physiologist, environ. scientist Lawrence Livermore (Calif.) Nat. Lab., 1975-79, cons., 1980—; rsch. plant physiologist USDA/ Agrl. Rsch. Svc., Woodward, Okla., 1979-85; prof., head Agrl. Rsch. Ctr. Kans. State U., Hays, 1985-94, prof., head Western Kans. Agrl. Rsch. Ctrs., 1994—2006, prof. Agrl. Rsch. Ctr., 2006—. Mem. adv. coun. Kans. Geol. Survey, Lawrence, 1986-91. Contbr. 33 articles to profl. jours. Capt., U.S. Army, 1970-72. Mem. Am. Soc. Agronomy, Soil Sci. Soc. Am., Crop Sci. Soc. Am., Soc. Range Mgmt., Hays Area C. of C. (bd. dirs. 1988-90). Republican. Mennonite Brethren Ch. Home and Office: Kans State U Agrl Rsch Ctr 1232 240th Ave Hays KS 67601-9228

COYNE, PATRICK JOSEPH, lawyer; b. Harrisburg, Pa., Mar. 9, 1956; s. Joseph R. and Louise A. (Blewitt) C.; m. Nancy S. Lazear, Oct. 20, 1984. BS in Civil Engring. with high distinction, U. Va., 1979, JD, 1982. Bar: DC 1982, US Claims Ct. 1982, US Dist. Ct. DC 1983, US Ct. Appeals (fed. cir.) 1983, US Patent & Trademark Office 1984, US Ct. Appeals (1st, 3rd, 4th, 5th, and 9th cirs.) 1987, US Supreme Ct. 1987. Rsch. assoc. Planning Rsch. Corp., McLean, Va., 1979; law clk. Finnegan, Henderson, Farabow, Garrett & Dunner, Washington, 1981-82, ptnr., 2003—; law clk., tech. adv. to Hon. Edward S. Smith US Ct. Appeals (fed. cir.), Washington, 1982-84; assoc. Collier, Shannon, Rill & Scott, Washington, 1984-89; ptnr. Collier, Shannon Rill & Scott, 1990—2003. Commr. Under Six Divsn., coach Sports on the Hill, 1991—. Mem. ABA, Fed. Bar. Assn., Fed. Cir. Bar Assn. (chmn. patent litig. com. 2005-06, bd. govs. 2006-), Am. Intellectual Property Law Assn. (chmn. antitrust law com. 2003-05, mem. amicus com. 2006-), Internat. Trademark Assn., Copyright Soc. US, Tau Beta Pi, Chi Epsilon. Democrat. Roman Catholic. Avocations: travel, cooking, reading, photography, snowboarding, scuba diving. Home: 805 E Capitol St SE Washington DC 20003-1347 Office: Finnegan Henderson Farabow Garrett & Dunner LLP 901 New York Ave NW Washington DC 20001-4413 Business E-Mail: patrick.coyne@finnegan.com.

COYNE, THOMAS JOSEPH, economics and finance professor; b. Dec. 24, 1933; s. Thomas Joseph and Mary Germaine (Fox) C.; m. Patricia Anne Smith, June 8, 1957 (div. June 1986); children: Kathleen, Karen, Kevin, Kenneth, Thomas. BBA, Marshall U., 1958; MBA, Kent State U., 1961; PhD, Case Western Res. U., 1967; postgrad., U. Chgo., 1968, U. Mich., summers, 1972-73. With B.F. Goodrich Co., Akron, Ohio, 1959-61, Robinson Clay Products Co., Akron, Ohio, 1961-63, C&O-B&O Ry., Cleve., 1963-65; instr. econs. Kent State U., Ohio, 1963-67, instr. money and fin. mgmt., 1967—; asst. prof. econs., chmn. dept. Marshall U., Huntington, W.Va., 1967-69; prof. bus. econs. U. Akron, 1969-81; prof. fin. John Carroll U., Cleve., 1981-95. Owner The Coyne Trust, 1986-91; pres. Coyne & Assocs., Akron, 1980—, Coyne Pub. Co., 1991—; pub. The Coyne Quar., 1990—; corp. valuations, acquisitions; cons. in field; presenter seminars in fin. engring. and mgmt., Zagreb, Croatia Stock Exch., 1993; leader 1st del. in fin. to USSR, 1989; arbitrator Am. Arbitration Assn., Fed. Mediation and Conciliation Svc., 1968—, pres. 1979-81; mem. Nat. Mediation Bd., Washington, 1999—; pres. Summit Petroleum Corp., Akron; founder, pres. Cosntn. Endl. Assn., Inc., 2000—. Author: Understanding Managerial Economics, 1975, Managerial Economics: Analysis and Cases, 5th edit., 1984, Readings in Managerial Economics, 5th edit., 1992, License To Lie, 1997, 2000, How to Take Charge of Yourself, Your Money, Your Government, 1999; also articles and monographs; host half-hour weekly radio show, 1994; host one hour weekly radio show, 2001-2004; pub. (econ. commentaries) Coyne Quar., Online. V.p. rsch. Akron Regional Devel. Bd., 1975-78, chmn. taxation and legis. com., 1975-78, spkr. in field; candidate U.S. Senate, Ohio, 1994—. Served with inf., U.S. Army, 1952-54, Korea. Nat. City Bank Cleve. fellow, 1963-65; candidate Office of Gov., W. Va., 2004 Mem. Sigma Phi Epsilon. Home: PO Box 834 Bath OH 44210-0834 Office Phone: 330-836-0563. Business E-Mail: tom@coyne-assoc.com. *When God has given you a great deal, He expects a great deal of you. If you achieve everything you set out to achieve, you probably did not set out to achieve enough in the first place.*

COYNE, WAYNE, musician; b. Jan. 13, 1961; Founder & guitarist The Flaming Lips, 1983—, lead singer & songwriter, 1985—; co-founder Lovely Sorts of Death music label, 1985. Musician: (albums) The Flaming Lips, 1985, Hear It Is, 1986, Oh My Gawd!!!.The Flaming Lips, 1987, Telepathic Surgery, 1989, In a Priest Driven Ambulance, 1990, Hit to Death in the Future Head, 1992, Transmissions from the Satellite Heart, 1993,

Clouds Taste Metallic, 1995, Zaireeka, 1997, The Soft Bulletin, 1999, Yoshimi Battles the Pink Robots, 2002 (Grammy award, Best Rock Instrumental Performance, 2003), At War with the Mystics, 2006 (2 Grammy awards: Best Rock Instrumental Performance, Best Non-Classical Engineered Album, 2007), Spider-Man 3 soundtrack, 2007; writer, dir., actor (films) Christmas on Mars, 2005. Office: c/o Scott Booker Hellfire Enterprises Ltd 1208 Chowning Ave Edmond OK 73034 Office Phone: 405-715-0600. Office Fax: 405-715-0632. E-mail: SDBMKTG@hellfireltd.com.*

COYNE, WILLIAM J., retail executive, former member house representatives; b. Chgo., Aug. 10, 1956; m. Maryann C. Coyne, May 28, 1983; children: Patrick, Jonathan, Robert. BS in Fin./Econs., U. Ill., 1978; JD, U. So. Calif., 1981. Bar: Calif. 1981, Minn. 1989, U.S. Dist. Ct. (so., ctrl., ea. and no. dists.) Calif., U.S. Ct. Appeals (9th cir.). Assoc. Overton, Lynan & Prince, LA, 1981-85, Diepenbrock, Wulff, Plant & Hannegan, Sacramento, 1985-89, ptnr., 1990-97; gen. counsel Raley's, Sacramento, 1997—2002; COO Raley's, Inc., Sacramento, 2002, pres., COO, 2002—. Office: Raleys 500 W Capitol Ave West Sacramento CA 95605-2696

COYNE, WILLIAM JOSEPH, former congressman; b. Pitts, Aug. 24, 1936; s. Phillip and Mary (Ridge) C. BS, Robert Morris Coll., 1965. Mem. Pa. Ho. of Reps., 1970-72; mem. Pitts. City Council, 1973-80, U.S. Congress from 14th Pa. dist., Washington, 1981—2002; mem. budget com.; mem. ways and means com. With AUS, 1955-57. Democrat. Roman Catholic.

COZBY, RICHARD SCOTT, electronics engineer, military officer; b. Las Cruces, N.Mex., Apr. 13, 1961; s. Scott Dempsey and Elizabeth Ann (Carroll) Cozby; m. Maria (Jo) Blackwell, Dec. 28, 1984; children: Brenton Blackwell, Bradford Carroll. B in Engring., Vanderbilt U., Nashville, Tenn., 1983; diploma, US Army Command Coll., 1994; MSA, Ctrl. Mich. U., Mt. Pleasant, 2002; diploma, Def. Sys. Mgmt. Coll., 2002. Commd. USAR, advanced through grade to lt. col.; comm. engr. US Army Signal Corps, 1983—; electronics engr., chief, simulation and tech. divsn. Army Testing and Evaluation Command, Aberdeen Proving Ground, Md., 1988—, chief tech. mgmt. divsn., 1998—2006; asst. dir. Army Future Combat Sys., 2006—. US Army prin. Mutli-Svc. Test Investment Rev. Com., Washington, 1990—95; bd. dirs. N.E. Md. Tech. Coun. Author: (book) Army GPS Test Results, 1984, Aquilla RPV Test Results, 1985. Chmn. Hickory Recreation Coun., Bel Air, 1998—; mem. outreach com. St. Margaret Parish, Bel Air, Md., 1989—95. Recipient Analyst of Yr., Army Rsch. Lab., 2003. Mem.: IEEE, Internat. Testing and Evaluation Assn. (chpt. pres. 1993, chpt. dir. 1994—), Harford Leadership Alumni Assn. (bd. dirs. 1996—, v.p. 1997—). Roman Catholic. Avocation: stamp collecting/philately. Office: CSTE-DTC-TT-M Aberdeen Proving Ground MD 21005 Personal E-mail: rcozby@verizon.net.

COZEN, STEPHEN ALLEN, lawyer; b. Phila., Aug. 13, 1939; s. Samuel D. and Jean (Orlofsky) C.; m. Sandra Wexler, June 7, 1961; children: Sheri L., Lori S., Cathi A. BA with honors, U. Pa., 1961, LLB with honors, 1964. Bar: Pa. 1964, U.S. Dist. Ct. (ea., mid. and we. dists.) Pa. 1984, U.S. Ct. Appeals (3d and 9th cirs.) 1984, U.S. Ct. Claims 1984, U.S. Supreme Ct. 1984. Founder, chmn. Cozen and O'Connor, Phila., 1970—. Lectr. U. Pa.; bd. dirs. 1st Exec. Bank. Gen. editor: Insuring Real Property, 1989; contbr. numerous articles to profl. jours. Bd. dirs. Arthritis Ctr., Hahnemann U., Police Athletic League; trustee Fedn. Jewish Agys. Recipient Torch of Learning award Am. Friends of Hebrew U., 1984, Peace medal, 1991, State of Israel. Fellow Am. Bar Found., Am. Coll. Trial Lawyers; mem. ABA (vice chmn. ins. law com.), Pa. Bar Assn., Phila. Bar Assn., Am. Judicature Soc., Def. Rsch. Inst., Pa. Def. Inst., Pa. Bar Inst. (bd. dirs.), Fedn. Ins. and Corp. Counsel. Home: 1230 Mt Pleasant Rd Villanova PA 19085-2107 Office: Cozen and O'Connor The Atrium 1900 Market St Philadelphia PA 19103-3527

CRABB, BARBARA BRANDRIFF, federal judge; b. Green Bay, Wis., Mar. 17, 1939; d. Charles Edward and Mary (Forrest) Brandriff; m. Theodore E. Crabb, Jr., Aug. 29, 1959; children: Julia Forrest, Philip Elliott. AB, U. Wis., 1960, JD, 1962. Bar: Wis. 1963. Assoc. Roberts, Boardman, Suhr and Curry, Madison, Wis., 1962-64; legal rschr. Sch. Law, U. Wis., 1968-70, Am. Bar Assn., Madison, 1970-71; US magistrate US Dist Ct. (we. dist.) Wis., Madison, 1971-79; judge U.S. Dist. Ct. (we. dist.) Wis., Madison, 1979—, chief judge, 1980-96, 2002—. Mem. Gov. Wis. Task Force Prison Reform, 1971-73 Membership chmn., v.p. Milw. LWV, 1966-68; mem. Milw. Jr. League, 1967-68. Mem. ABA, Nat. Assn. Women Judges, State Bar Wis., Dane County Bar Assn., U. Wis. Law Alumni Assn. Office: US Dist Ct PO Box 591 120 N Henry St Madison WI 53701-0591

CRABB, KENNETH WAYNE, obstetrician, gynecologist; b. Glendive, Mont. s. Kenneth Willard and Marjorie Jane C.; m. Gwen Aldean Wendelschafer; children: Kenneth Wendel, Richard David. BS in Biochemistry with honors, U. Iowa, 1971, MD, 1975. Diplomate Am. Bd. Ob-Gyn. Intern, then resident in ob-gyn St. Paul Ramsey Med. Ctr., 1975-79; practice medicine specializing in ob-gyn St. Paul, 1979—; obstetrician, gynecologist, pres. Advanced Specialty Care for Women, St. Paul, 1980—. Clin. asst. prof. ob.-gyn. U. Minn., Mpls., 1981-89, clin. assoc. prof., 1989-2003, adj. prof., 2003—; vice-chmn. dept. ob.-gyn. United Hosp., St. Paul, 1984-86, 91-93, pharm. and therapeutics com., 1980-84, oncology com., 1995-2000; preceptor family practice resident St. John's Hosp., St. Paul, 1979—, maternal health com., 1979-88, cancer com., 1984-85; quality assurance com. St. Joseph's Hosp., St. Paul, 1981-83; mem. Med. Affairs Coun. for Health One, 1989-93; chmn. bd. dirs. ParaNatal Svcs., Inc., 1990-94; bd. dirs. Preferred One Physicians Assn., pres. 1994-96, Prefered One PPO, 1987-98, Preferred One Mgmt. Co., 1994-96, Peak Adminstrv. Svcs., PACE Ins. Co., 1996-99; physician advisor Medtrac. Health Mark, StratisHealth; adv. bd. Washington County Pub. Health, Minn., 2000-2003, chmn. 2003; mem. Med. Resource Corp., 2005—. With Actors Theatre of St. Paul, 1980-90, bd. dirs. 2d v.p., 1984-85; bd. trustees Minn. Med. Found., 1997-2005; mem. coun. Grace Luth. Ch., 1984-87; chmns. cabinet Northstar coun. Boy Scouts Am., 1986—, coun. advancement chair, 1996-2000, North Star Scouting Mus., 2002—. Named one of Minn.'s 100 Most Influential Health Care Leaders, Minn. Physician; recipient Appreciation award, Am. Acad. Family Physicians, 1979—90, Silver Beaver award, Indianhead Coun. Boy Scouts Am., 2002, Cmty. Svc. award, Minn. Med. Assn., 2003. Fellow: Am. Soc. Reproductive Medicine, Am. Coll. Ob-Gyn. (jr. fellow adv. coun. 1978—80, chmn. higher edn. loan program com. 1989—91, adv. coun. Minn. sect. 1996—98, jr. fellow dist. chmn. 1978-79, chmn. 1989 Dist. VI meeting, Appreciation award 1978—79); mem.: AMA (alt del. 1997—2002, del. 2002—, Physicians Recognition award 1985, 88, 90, 93, 96, 99), Am. Coll. Physician Execs. Strategic Health, Assn. Profs. Ob-Gyn., Ramsey Med. Soc. (trustee 1993-94, med. practice com. 1982-87, del. 1983, 85-87, fin. com. 1984-89, med. svc. com. 1986-88, nominating com. 1992-93, polit. action com. 1988-94, pres.-elect 1995, pres. 1996), Minn. Obstet. and Gynecologic Soc. (program com. 1984), Minn. Med. Assn. (del. 1983—, 1985—87, nominating com. 1986—87, legis. com. 1988—94, vice chmn. 1989—96, 1989—96, del. 1994—, med. practice and planning com. 1995—96, legis. com. 1997—), Am. Assn. Gynecologic Laparoscopists, Am. Soc. Colposcopy and Cervical Pathology, Ctrl. Assn. Obstetricians and Gynecologists, Toastmasters, Rotary (dist. gov. 2004—05, com. chmn. 1983-84, 87-88, bd. dirs. 1984-86, 89-91, v.p. 1991-92, pres. 1992-93, sgt. at arms 1986-87, asst. dist. gov. 2000-2002, internat. pres. rep. 2006), Phi Beta Phi, Omicron Delta Kappa, Phi Beta Sigma. Avocations: volleyball, skiing, theater, science fiction, sailing. Office: Advanced Specialty Care for Women 280 Smith Ave N Ste 460 Saint Paul MN 55102 Office Phone: 651-224-4897.

CRABBS, ROGER ALAN, publishing executive, director, small business owner, military officer, educator; b. Cedar Rapids, Iowa, May 9, 1928; s. Winfred Wesley and Faye (Woodard) C.; m. Marilyn Lee Westcott, June 30, 1951; children: William Douglas, Janet Lee Crabbs Turner, Ann Lee Crabbs Menke. BA in Sci., State U. Iowa, 1954; MBA, George Washington U., 1965, DBA, 1973; M Christian Leadership, We. Sem., 1978. Commd. 2nd lt. USAF, 1950, advanced through grades to lt. col., 1968, Ret., 1972; prof. mgmt. U. Portland, Oreg., 1972-79; prof. bus. George Fox Coll., Newberg, Oreg., 1979-83; pres. Judson Bapt. Coll., The Dalles, Oreg., 1983-85. Pres. Host Pubs. Inc., pres., chmn. various corps., 1974-86; past chmn. nat. adv. bd. Travelhost, Inc.; pres. Crabbs and Co., 2005-; cons. in field. Author: Employee Motivation in the Panama Canal Company, 1973, The Infallible Foundation for Management-The Bible, 1978, The Secret of Success in Small Business Management-Is in the Short Range, 1983; co-author: The Storybook Primer on Managing, 1976. Past pres. English Speaking Union, 1994-96, bd. dir., 1994-97; bd. dir. Christ Cmty. Ch., Portland Oreg. Vis. Assn., Conv. and Vis. Bur. of Washington County, 1986-2001, Oakhills Townhouse Assn., v.p., 1991-95. Decorated Air Force Commendation medal with oak leaf cluster, Meritorious Service medal Dept. Def.; proclaimed Am. for Peace, Rep. of Korea, 2007; rated Command Air Force Missileman; recipient Jack Rosenberg Cmty. Svcs. award, 2000, regional, dist. and nat. awards SBA, Bonnie Hays Tourism award, 2001. Mem.: Soc. Advancement of Mgmt., Svc. Corps Ret. Execs., Am. Arbitration Assn., Acad. Mgmt., Assn. Atomic Vets., 51st Fighter Interceptor Wing Assn., Air Force Assn., Lang Syne Soc. of Portland, Portland Officers Club, Rotary (past pres.), Masons, Phi Mu Alpha, Delta Epsilon Sigma, Alpha Kappa Psi. Republican. Personal E-mail: leecrabbs@everdream.com. *A positive attitude, sincere interest in others and a sense of humility have been the building blocks of my personal philosophy. They have served me well through my three careers - professional military, university professor and publisher.*

CRABTREE, BEN C., neuromuscular therapy clinic director; b. Las Vegas, Sept. 11, 1964; s. Ben C. and Jaynelle (Felix) C.; m. Virginia Kathryn Vance, Feb. 7, 1988 (div. Nov. 1989); m. Tania Oylan Tason, May 5, 1992; children: Greta, Bryan. AS, Panama Canal Coll., La Boca, Rep. of Panama, 1993, Austin Peay State U., 1995; BBA, Our Lady of the Lake U., 1995. Cert. firearms instr.; registered massage therapist; cert. neuromuscular therapist; lic. massage therapy instr.; cert. neuromuscular therapy instr. Software tech., adminstr. asst. Ace Personal Health Care, Inc., San Antonio, 1994-95; dir. info. systems River City Fin. Health Group/Home Health Care Solutions, San Antonio, 1995; chief fin. officer, alt. adminstr. A&E Quality Home Health Care, San Antonio, 1996-99; pres. Oylan, Inc., San Antonio, 1997-99; pres., owner Antonian Bodyworks, 1999-2001; instr. neuromuscular therapy Neuromuscular Therapy Ctr. N.Mex., 2000—. Profl. adv. com. Silver Days Home Health Care, San Antonio, 1996-97, Responsive Health Svcs., 1997-99. Mem. Dist. 128 State Budget Adv. Com., San Antonio, 1995. Ssgt. U.S. Army, 1984-92. Mem.: Soc. Ortho-Bionomy Internat., Internat. Massage Assn., Tex. Action Shooting Club, U.S. Practical Shooting Assn. Avocations: practical shooting, web page design. Office: San Antonio Neuromuscular Therapy Ctr 11120 Wurzbach Ste 200 San Antonio TX 78230 E-mail: 4info@massagebyben.com.

CRABTREE, BEVERLY JUNE, retired dean; b. Lincoln, Nebr., June 22, 1937; d. Wayne Uniack and Frances Margaret (Wibbels) Deles Dernier; m. Robert Jewell Crabtree, June 1, 1958; children: Gregory, Karen. BS in Edn., U. Mo., 1959, MEd, 1962; PhD, Iowa State U., 1965. Tchr. home econs. area pub. schs., Pierce City and Sarcoxie, Mo., 1959-61; mem. faculty home econs. Mich. State U., East Lansing, 1964-67; assoc. prof. U. Mo., Columbia, 1967-72, coord. home econs. edn., 1967-73, prof., 1972-73, assoc. dean home econs., dir. home econs. extension programs, 1973-75; dean Coll. Home Econs. Okla. State U., Stillwater, 1975-87; dean Coll. Family and Consumer Scis. Iowa State U., Ames, 1987-97, ret., 1997. Mem. faculty Family Impact Seminar Inst. Ednl. Leadership, George Washington U., 1976-82, Cath. U. Am., 1982-87; mem. nat. panel cons. for Vocat. Ednl. Pers. Devel., 1969-70; mem. nat. com. on future of coop. extension USDA and Nat. Assn. State Univs. and Land Grant Colls., 1982; mem. joint coun. on food and agrl. scis., 1987-91. Contbr. articles in field to profl. jours. Gen. Foods fellow, 1963-64; recipient Centennial Alumni award Coll. Home Econs. Iowa State U., 1971, Alumni Citation of Merit, Coll. Home Econs. U. Mo., 1976, Profl. Achievement award Iow State U., 1983. Mem. Am. Home Econs. Assn. (pres. 1977-78, chmn. adv. coun. Ctr. for Family 1982-83, mem. coun. profl. devel. 1980-83, a leader to commemorate 75th anniversary 1984, pres. found. 1987-88, chair Coun. for Certification 1991-92, chair Coun. for Accreditation 1997-98, Disting. Svc. award 1993), Okla. Home Econs. Assn. (Profl. Achievement award 1983), Nat. Assn. State Univs. and Land Grant Colls. (mem. commn. home econs. 1981-84), Assn. Tchr. Educators, Home Econs. Edn. Assn., Nat. Coun. of Adminstrs. of Home Econs., Am. Ednl. Rsch. Assn., Am. Assn. Higher Edn., Nat. Assn. Tchr. Educators for Home Econs. (pres. 1969), Nat. Coun. on Family Relations, Mortar Bd., Golden Key, Omicron Nu, Phi Upsilon Omicron, Phi Delta Kappa, Omicron Delta Kappa, Pi Lambda Theta, Phi Kappa Phi, Gamma Sigma Delta. Methodist. Home: 3113 Rosewood Cir Ames IA 50014-4589

CRABTREE, DAVIDA FOY, minister; b. Waterbury, Conn., June 7, 1944; d. Alfred and Davida (Blakeslee) Foy; m. David T. Hindinger Jr., Aug. 28, 1982; stepchildren: Elizabeth Anne, David Todd. BS, Marietta Coll., 1967; MDiv, Andover Newton Theol. Sch., 1972; D of Ministry, Hartford Sem., 1989. Ordained to ministry United Ch. of Christ, 1972. Founder, exec. dir. Prudence Crandall Ctr. for Women, New Britain, Conn., 1973-76; min., dir. Greater Hartford (Conn.) Campus Ministry, 1976-80; sr. min. Colchester (Conn.) Federated Ch., 1980-91; bd. dirs. Conn. Conf. United Ch. of Christ, Hartford, 1982-90; conf. min. So. Calif. Conf., United Ch. of Christ, Pasadena, 1991-96, Conn. Conf., United Ch. of Christ, Hartford, 1996—. Rsch. assoc. Harvard Div. Sch., Cambridge, Mass., 1975—76. Author: The Empowering Church, 1989 (named one of Top Ten Books of Yr. 1990); editorial advisor Alban Inst., 1990-98. Bd. dirs. Hartford region YWCA, 1979-82, Christian Conf. of Conn., 1997—; trustee Cragin Meml. Libr., Colchester, 1980-91, Hartford Sem., 1983-91, Sch. of Theology at Claremont, 1993-96, Andover Newton Theol. Sch., 1997—; founder Youth Svcs. Bur., Colchester, 1984-89; pres. Creative Devel. for Colchester Inc., 1989-91; coun. Religious Leaders of L.A., 1991-96; v.p. Hope in Youth Campaign, 1992-96; dir. UCC Ins. bd., 1993-2000, 06—; bd. dirs. Amistad America, 1998—; trustee UCC Cornerstone Fund, 2000-04; chair Coun. of Conf. Mins., United Ch. of Christ, 2004-06. Named one of Outstanding Conn. Women, UN Assn., 1987; recipient Antoinette Brown award, Gen. Synod, United Ch. of Christ, 1977, Conf. Preacher award, Conn. Conf. United Ch. of Christ, 1982, Woman in Leadership award, Hartford region YWCA, 1987, Pres.'s award, Conn. Coalition Against Domestic Violence, 1997, Somos Uno award, United Neighborhood Orgn., 1995, award, Vet. Feminists Am., 2005. Mem. Nat. Coun. Chs. (bd. dirs. 1969-81), Christians for Justice Action (exec. com. 1981-91). Mem. United Ch. Of Christ. E-mail: dfc@ctucc.org.

CRABTREE, JACQUELYNN KAY, elementary school educator; d. Jack Kennith Jones and Laura Catherine Crabtree, adopted d. Gary Joe Crabtree; 1 child, Brian Colten Liles-Crabtree. AA, Rich Mountain C.C., Mena, Ark., 1988; BS in Psychology, U. So. Colo., Pueblo, 1994. Cert. elem. tchr. Colo., 1999. Summer reading tchr. Cotopaxi Sch., Colo., 1999—2005, 2d grade tchr., 1999—2005, reading tchr., 2005—. Playground com. - vol. recruitment Parent Tchr. Club, Cotopaxi, Colo., 2003; bldg. leadership team Reading First, Cotopaxi, Colo., 2005—; jr. high sponsor Cotopaxi Sch. Dist., Colo., 2004—05, student intervention team, 2005—, freshmen sponsor, 2005—06. Mem.: Nat. Coun. Tchrs. English, Assn. Supervision and Curriculum Devel., Collegiate Peaks Reading Coun. (pres. 2000—07, treas. 2007—), Colo. Coun. of Internat. Reading Assn. (Outstanding Svc. award 2001), Internat. Reading Assn., Cotopaxi Lions Club (bd. dirs. 2006—). Alpha Chi. Avocations: reading, crocheting, travel, camping, fishing. Home Phone: 719-942-3417; Office Phone: 719-942-4131.

CRABTREE, JOHN DAVID, manufacturing company executive; b. Evansville, Ind., Apr. 13, 1947; s. George B. and Lucille (Barnhart) C.; m. Teresa Jean Whitsitt, June 15, 1968; children: John David Jr., Katherine Suzanne. BS in Indsl. Econs., Purdue U., 1969. Tool and die engr. Willow Run Hydramatic, Ypsilanti, Mich., 1974—75, foreman, 1975—77, gen. foreman plant 3, 1977—78, upt. plant 3, 1978—80, gen. supt. mfg., 1980—83, gen. supt. maintenance and process engring., 1983—85; plant mgr. Toledo Powertrain divsn. GM Corp., Buffalo, 1985—91, plant mgr. Flint V8 engine, 1991—99, plant mgr. Flint Engine South, 1999—2005, plant mgr. Tonawanda Engine Plant, 2005—06. Mem. governing bd. Edison Indsl. Systems Ctr., Toledo 1987-88; coun. advisors ctr. for bus. and industry U. Toledo, 1988. Constable Saline Twp., 1985-88, mem. bd. tax rev., 1985-88; bd. dirs. Jr. Achievement, Toledo, 1986-88, Genesee County Econ. Growth Alliance, 2004-05; governing bd. Working Coun. for Employee Involvement, NW Ohio, 1989, mem., 1990-91; regional chair United Way of Genesee County, 2003-05. Mem. Soc. Automotive Engrs., The Forum (Toledo), Toledo Leadership (com. of 100 1990-93), Am. Legion, Kiwanis. Republican. Methodist. Avocations: flying, private pilot. Home: 2423 Pepperidge Trl Brighton MI 48114-8956 E-mail: john.crabtree@gm.com.

CRABTREE, LOREN WILLIAM, academic administrator, history professor; b. Aberdeen, SD, Sept. 2, 1940; s. Benjamin Forrest and Harriet Caroline (Zempel) C.; m. Sheila Ann Volz, Aug. 25, 1961 (div. May 1987); children: Christopher, Kathryn, Paul; m. Monica Sue Christen, 1987. BA, U. Minn., 1961, MA, 1965, PhD, 1969. Instr. Bethel Coll., St. Paul, 1965-67; from instr. to prof. history Colo. State U., Ft. Collins, 1967—, dean Coll. Liberal Arts, 1991-97, provost, acad. v.p., 1998-2001; v.p. and provost U. Tenn., Knoxville, 2001—03, chancellor, 2003—. Vis. assoc. prof. U. Colo., Boulder, 1980; vis. prof., dean semester at sea program U. Pitts., 1986, 91; faculty affiliate Nat. Faculty, Atlanta, 1988—. Author: The Lion and the Dragon, 1970; co-author: Civilizations: A Cultural Atlas, 1994; contbr. articles to profl. publs. Trustee Am. Bapt. Ch., Ft. Collins, 1970-74; bd. deacons First Christian Ch., Ft. Collins, 1984-86. NDFL Chinese Lang. fellow Harvard U., 1964. Mem. Assn. for Asian Studies (pres. western conf. 1983-84), Coun. Colls. of Arts and Scis., Golden Key, Mortar Board, Phi Beta Kappa, Phi Alpha Theta. Democrat. Avocations: hiking, mountain climbing, court sports, furniture building. Office: Chancellor 527 Andy Holt Tower Univ Tenn Knoxville TN 37996 Home: 523 Cumberland Ridge Dr Knoxville TN 37922 Office Phone: 865-974-3265. Business E-Mail: lcrabtrl@utk.edu.*

CRABTREE, ROBERT HOWARD, chemistry professor, consultant; b. Apr. 17, 1948; came to U.S., 1977, naturalized, 1985; s. Arthur and Marguerite (Vaniere) C. BA, Oxford U., 1970; PhD, Sussex U., Eng., 1973, DSc (hon.), 1985. Attache of rsch. Nat. Ctr. Sci. Rsch., Paris, 1975-77; asst. prof. chemistry Yale U., New Haven, Conn., 1977-83, assoc. prof., 1983-85, prof., 1985—. Home Phone: 203-393-1890; Office Phone: 203-432-3925.

CRABTREE, VICKI GAIL, musician; b. Willmar, Minn., Mar. 30, 1952; d. Roger Duane and Ruth Elaine Anderstrom; m. Samuel William Crabtree, Aug. 4, 1973; children: Dawn Joy, Mandi Gail, Aryn Gail, Jordan Gera. B, St. Cloud U., 1974. Music instr. Hayti Pub. Sch., Hazel, SD, 1974—81; music dir. Brookings Wesleyan Ch., Brookings, SD, 1981—97; organist Asbury Meth. Ch., Mpls., 2001—02; music instr. LA Musique Studios, Minnetonka, Minn., 2000—. Performer: (albums) I Will Follow the Son, 1971, The Son Seekers, 1972. Mem.: Nat. Piano Tchrs. Guild. Baptist. Home: 1800 13th Ave South Minneapolis MN 55404

CRABTREE-IRELAND, DUNCAN, lawyer; b. 1972; life ptnr. John Crabtree-Ireland; 1 child, Watson. BS in Fgn. Svc., Georgetown U., 1994; JD, U. Calif., Davis, 1998. Dep. dist. atty. LA County; counsel SAG, LA, 2000—02, asst. gen. counsel, 2002—05, dep. gen. counsel, 2005—06, interim gen. counsel, 2006, gen. counsel, 2006—. Lectr. law U. So. Calif.; judge pro tem, ct. apptd. arbitrator LA Superior Ct. Mem.: Lesbian and Gay Lawyers Assn. LA (treas.), LA County Bar Assn. (chair del. Conf. of Dels. of Calif. Bar Assns.). Avocations: sailing, reading, movies, travel. Office: SAG 5757 Wilshire Blvd Los Angeles CA 90036-3600 Office Phone: 323-549-6627. Office Fax: 323-395-5997. E-mail: direland@sag.org.

CRACCHIOLO, JAMES M., diversified financial services company executive; BS, MBA, NYU. CPA. With Am. Express, 1982—2005; pres. Am. Express Travel Related Svcs. Internat., 1998—2003; group pres. Am. Express Global Fin. Svcs., 2000—05; chmn. Am. Express Bank Ltd., 2000—05; pres., CEO Am. Express Financial, 2000—05; chmn., CEO Am. Express Fin. Advisors, 2001—05, Ameriprise Fin. Inc., Mpls., 2005—. Bd. dirs. Tech Data Corp., 1999—. Mem. bd. adv. March of Dimes. Office: Ameriprise Financial Inc 243 Ameriprise Fin Ctr Minneapolis MN 55474*

CRACKEL, THEODORE JOSEPH, historian; b. Urbana, Ill., Sept. 10, 1938; s. Orville Lee and Aleta (Smith) C.; m. Kay Knight, Sept. 2, 1961 (div. 1972); children: Todd, Dana; m. Mai Thi Nguyen, Oct. 14, 1972 (div. 1991); children: John, Robert; m. Mary-Jo Kline, May 23, 1998. BA, U. Ill., 1962; MA, Rutgers U., 1971, PhD, 1985. Commd. 2nd lt. U.S. Army, 1962, advanced through grades to lt. col., 1978, tank unit comdr. Germany, 1963-66, advisor Vietnam, 1966-67, 71-72; weapons sys. analyst Combat Devels. Command, Ft. Knox, Ky., 1967-69; asst. prof. history U.S. Mil. Acad., West Point, NY, 1972-75, 78-81; instr. Dept. Strategy U.S. Army Command and Gen. Staff Coll., 1975-77; dir. mil. history and strategy studies U.S. Army War Coll., Carlisle Barracks, Pa., 1981-83, ret., 1983; sr. fellow The Heritage Found., Washington, 1983-85; sr. cons. GE Co., Washington, 1985-87; exec. dir. Papers of the Comdg. Gens., 1988-93; dir., editor Papers of the War Dept. 1784-1800, 1993—2004; prof. U. Va., Charlottesville, Va., 2004—, editor-in-chief The Papers of George Washington, 2004—. Vis. prof. history dept. US Mil. Acad., West Point, NY, 2001-02. Author: The Army Additional Duty Guide, 1970, Mr. Jefferson's Army, 1987, The Illustrated History of West Point, 1991, History of the Civil Reserve Air Fleet, 1993, West Point: A Bicentennial History, 2002; contbr. articles to profl. jours. Mem. Assn. Documentary Editors, Orgn. Am. Historians, Soc. Historians of Early Am. Republic, Army and Navy Club (Washington), Chi Psi. Office: Papers George Washington U Va PO Box 400117 Charlottesville VA 22904-4117

CRADDOCK, BANTZ JOHN (JOHN CRADDOCK), career military officer; b. Doddridge County, W.Va., 1949; m. Linda Craddock; children: Zachary, Amanda. BS, W.Va. U., 1971; M of Mil. Arts and Sci., Army Command Gen. Staff Coll., 1984; graduate, US Army War Coll., 1993. Commd. Armor officer US Army, 1971, advanced through grades to gen., 2006; initial tour of duty 3d Armored Divsn., Germany; armor test officer US Army Armor and Engr. Bd., Ft. Knox, Ky.; tank comdr. 1st bn., 32d Armor, 3d Armored Divsn., Friedberg, Germany; systems analyst Engring divsn., Office of Program Mgr. Abrams Tank Sys., Warren, Mich., 1981, exec. officer to program mgr., 1982-85; exec. officer 4th Bn. 69th Armor 8th Infantry Divsn., Germany; dep. G-3, Ops. 8th Infantry Divsn. Hdqs.; comdr. 4th bn., 64th Armor 24th Infantry Divsn., Ft. Stewart, Ga., 1989; asst. chief of staff, G-3, Ops. 24th Infantry divsn., Ft. Stewart, Ga., 1991-93; comdr. 194th Separate Armored Brigade, Ft. Knox, 1993-95; asst. chief of staff, G-3 III Corps, Ft. Hood, Tex., 1995-96; asst. dep. dir. in J-5 Jt. Staff, Pentagon, 1996-98; asst. divsn. comdr. for maneuver 1st Infantry

Divsn., Germany, 1998; comdr. US Forces for initial entry operation into Kosovo; commdg. gen. 7th Army Training Command, US Army Europe, 1999; comdr. 1st Infantry Divsn., 2000; sr. mil. asst. to sec. US Dept. Def., Washington, 2002—04; comdr. US So. Command (USSOUTHCOM), Miami, 2004—06, US European Command (USEUCOM), Stuttgart, 2006—; supreme allied comdr. NATO, Europe (SACEUR), Brussels, 2006—. Decorated Valorous Unit award, Def. Disting. Svc. Medal, Disting. Svc. Medal, Silver Star, Def. Superior Svc. Medal with 1 Oak Leaf Cluster, Legion of Merit with 2 Oak Leaf Clusters, Bronze Star. Mem.: US Army Armor Assn. Office: NATO Hdqs Blvd Leopold III 1110 Brussels Belgium also: US European Command (USEUCOM) Unit 30400 Patch Barracks APO AE 09131 Stuttgart-Vaihingen Germany*

CRADLER, JUDITH A., science educator; d. Robert E. and Ruth H. Keller; m. Burton C. Cradler, Dec. 22, 1973; children: Christopher, Tyler. BA, SUNY, Geneseo, 1968; MEd, U. Buffalo, NYC, 1973; postgrad., U. Mass., Amherst. Cert. tchr. biology, social studies N.Y., tchr. sci. Mass. Sci. tchr. Lew-Port Ctrl. Sch., Youngstown, NY, 1968—70; sci. tchr. grade 7 Starpoint Ctrl. Sch., Lockport, NY, 1970—74; sci. tchr. grades 7 and 9 Worcester Pub. Schs., Mass., 1994—. Design team mem. New Eng. Small Sch. Network, Worcester, 2001; rep. U.S. People to People, Beijing, 2005. Contbr. articles to profl. jours. Mem. Northbor Jr. Woman's Club, 1998—; chmn bd. Boy Scout Am., Southboro, Mass., 1992—96. Named Tchr. of the Yr., Worcester Pub.Schs., 2000. Mem.: ASCD, NEA, Edn. Assn. Worcester, Mass. Edn. Assn., Nat. Assn. of Rsch. in Sci., Nat. Sci. Tchrs. Assn. Avocations: gardening, reading, American revolution history. Home: 78 Indian Meadow Dr Northborough MA 01532

CRAFORD, M. GEORGE, physicist, research administrator; b. Sioux City, Iowa, Dec. 29, 1938; BA, U. Iowa, 1961; MS, U. Ill., 1963, PhD in Physics, 1967. Mem. staff Monsanto, St. Louis, 1967-74, Palo Alto, Calif., 1974-79; mgr. R&D optoelec. divsn. Hewlett Packard, San Jose, Calif., 1979—2001; chief tech. officer Lumileds Lighting, San Jose, Calif., 2001—. Recipient Nat. Medal Technology, US Dept. Commerce, 2002. Fellow IEEE; mem. Nat. Acad. Engring. Achievements include development of visible light emitting diodes; nitrogen-doped GaAsP technology; first to develop AlInGaP LED's, AlGaAs and GaN products. Office: Lumileds Lighting LLC 370 W Trimble Rd San Jose CA 95131

CRAFT, CHERYL MAE, neurobiologist, anatomist, researcher; b. Lynch, Ky., Apr. 15, 1947; d. Cecil Berton and Lillian Lovelle C.; m. Laney K. Cormney, Oct. 14, 1967 (div. Sept. 1980); children: Tyler Craft Cormney, Ryan Berton Cormney (dec.); m. Richard N. Lolley (dec.). BS in Biology, Chemistry and Math., Valdosta State Coll., 1969; cert. in Tchg. Biology and Math., Ea. Ky. U., 1971; PhD in Human Anatomy and Neurosci., U. Tex., San Antonio, 1984. Undergrad. rsch. asst. Ea. Ky. U., Richmond, 1965-67; tchg. asst. dept. cell-structural biology U. Tex. Health Sci. Ctr., San Antonio, 1979-84; postdoctoral fellowship lab. devel. neurobiology NICHD and LMDB/NEI, Bethesda, Md., 1984-86; instr. dept. psychiatry U. Tex. Southwestern Med. Ctr., Dallas, 1986-87, asst. prof., 1987-91; dir. lab. Molecular Neurogenetics Schizophrenia Rsch. Ctr., VA Med. Ctr., Dallas, 1988-94; dir. Lab. Molecular Neurogenetics Mental Health Clinic Rsch. Ctr., U. Tex. Southwestern Med. Ctr., 1990-94; assoc. prof. U. Tex. Southwestern Med. Ctr., 1991-94; Mary D. Allen chair Doheny Eye Inst. U. So. Calif. Keck Sch. Medicine, LA, Calif., 1994—, founding chmn. dept. cell and neurobiology, 1994—2004. Ad hoc reviewer NEI/NIH, Bethesda, 1993—; reviewer Molecular Biology, NSPB Fight for Sight Grants, 1991-94; STAR-sci. adv. bd. U. So. Calif./Bravo Magnet H.S., L.A., 1995—. Contbr. author: Melatonin: Biosynthesis, Physiological Effects, 1993; exec. editor Exptl. Eye Rsch. jour., 1993—; editor Molecular Vision. Recipient Merit award for rsch. VA Med. Ctr., 1992, 93, 94, nomination for Women in Sci. and Engring. award Dallas VA, 1992, 93; NEI fellow, 1986, NICHD/NIH fellow, 1986. Mem. AAAS, AAUW, Assn. for Rsch. in Vision and Ophthalmology (chair program planning com. 1991-94), Am. Soc. for Neurochemistry (Jordi Folch Pi Outstanding Young Investigator 1992), Sigma Xi (sec./treas. 1986-93, pres. 1993-94). Avocations: reading, travel. Office: U So Calif Keck Sch Medicine 1355 San Pablo St Rm 405 DVRC Los Angeles CA 90033 Office Phone: 323-442-6694. Personal E-mail: eyesightresearch@hotmail.com. Business E-Mail: ccraft@usc.edu.

CRAFT, DOUGLAS DURWOOD, artist; b. Greene, NY, Oct. 20, 1924; s. Harry Benjamin and Phoebe (Hotchkiss) C.; m. Elizabeth Louise Harms, Sept. 8, 1951. BFA, U. Chgo. and Art Inst. Chgo., 1950; MA in Painting, U. N.Mex., 1953. Grad. asst. U. N.Mex., 1951-52; assoc. prof. fine arts Sch. Art Inst., Chgo., 1957-65, Carnegie-Mellon U., Pitts., 1966-69; prof. fine arts Coll. New Rochelle, NY, 1970-91. Vis. artist in residence U. Ky., 1964, Cooper Union, N.Y.C., 1969-71, Sch. Visual Arts, N.Y.C., 1988; 1st Am. exch. prof., artist in residence Royal Coll. Art, London, 1964-65; guest artist curator Selected Women, Painters Castle Gallery, Coll. New Rochelle (N.Y.), 1982, Of Paper, Pigment and Glass, Castle Gallery, New Rochelle, 1987. One-man shows include Kasha Heman Gallery, Chgo., 1963, 61, U. N.Mex., 1964, 52, U. Ky., 1964, Travers Festival Gallery, Edinburgh, Scotland, 1965, Royal Coll. Art, London, 1964, Carnegie Mellon U., 1968, Mus. Art, Carnegie Inst., Pitts., 1968, Fischbach Gallery, N.Y.C., 1973, Jersey City Mus., 1978, 55 Mercer Gallery, N.Y.C., 1980, Bratton Gallery, Inc., N.Y.C., 1989, Coll. Ctr. Art Gallery, Coll. New Rochelle, 1989, Rosefsky Studio Art Gallery SUNY, Binghamton, 1993, retrospective Butler Inst. Am. Art, Youngstown, Ohio, 1993, Paul McCarron Gallery, N.Y.C., 1995, Delaware Valley Arts Ctr., Narrowsburg, 1996, retrospective traveling exhbn. Makee Gallery, Canton, Mo., Gray Gallery, Quincy, Ill., Keokuk Art Ctr., Iowa, 1997, Paul McCarron Gallery, N.Y.C., 1996, 98, Del. Valley Arts Ctr., Narrowsburg, 2001, 2004, Gorshow Arch., N.Y.C., 2000, Mesaros Galleries, Butler Inst. Am. Art, Youngstown, 2005, others; exhibited in group shows at Rose Fried Gallery, N.Y.C., 1968, Montclair (N.J.) Art Mus., 1984, Traverse Gallery, Edinburgh, 1984, Studio K, Long Island City, N.Y., 1985, Castle Gallery, New Rochelle, N.Y., 1985-86, Jersey City Mus., 1987, Montclair Art Mus., 1987, Robeson Gallery, Rutger's U., Newark, 1987, N.A.M.E. Gallery, Chgo., 1988, Bratton Gallery, Inc., N.Y.C., 1988-89, Schick Art Gallery Skidmore Coll., 1995, Del. Arts Ctr. Gallery, 1995, Pavel Zoubok Gallery, N.Y.C., 2001-02, others; represented in permanent collections Smithsonian Instn., Washington, Art Inst. Chgo., U. Ky., Mus. Modern Art, N.Y.C., Whitney Mus. Am. Art, N.Y.C., U. N.Mex., Gill Libr. Coll. New Rochelle, Butler Inst. Am. Art, Youngstown, Ohio, Meml. Art Gallery, U. Rochester, N.Y., others; corp. collections; pvt. collections in U.S.A, Can., Eng. Scotland, France, Saudi Arabia, Japan. With USNR, 1943—46. Recipient Logan bronze medal Art Inst. Chgo., 1966, Harry Allison Logan meml. award Chautauqua Art Assn., 1963, jury award in painting Carnegie Inst., 1968; Carr scholar U. Iowa, 1942-43; Carl Loeb fellow Syracuse U., 1950; grantee Richard A. Florsheim Art Fund, 1993. Home: PO Box 245 Jeffersonville NY 12748-0245 Studio: 21 Jefferson Ave Jeffersonville NY 12748 Office Phone: 845-482-3438.

CRAFT, EDMUND COLEMAN, retired manufacturing executive; b. Plainfield, NJ, Dec. 23, 1939; s. Edmund Coleman and Ruth Irene (Morrell) C.; m. Gail Christensen; children: Edmund Coleman III, Elisabeth Gordon, William Todd. BS, Lycoming Coll., 1963; postgrad., Syracuse U., 1963-64; grad. exec. program, U. Minn., 1984. With Borg-Warner Corp., Detroit, adminstrv. asst. to chmn. Chgo., 1969-70; with Borg-Warner Ltd., Letchworth, Hertfordshire, Eng., 1970-75; v.p. hydraulics div. Borg-Warner, Wooster, Ohio, 1975-79; dir. hydraulics div. Donaldson Co. Inc., Mpls., 1979-83, v.p., 1983-2000; sr. advisor Global Aftermarket, 2000-2001; ret., 2001. Bd. dirs. Jr. Achievement of Upper Midwest Inc., 1993-2000, mem. exec. com., 1994-2000; divsn. chmn. United Way, Wooster, 1974. Mem. Automotive Filter Mfrs. Coun. (vice chmn. 1985-89, chmn. 1989-91, bd. dirs. 1991-2000), Dataw Island Club, Dataw Island Yacht Club. Republican. Presbyterian. Avocations: golf, boating. E-mail: craft@islc.net.

CRAFT, MARY FAYE, public relations executive, consultant, television producer, poet; b. Glennville, Ga., Jan. 20, 1936; d. James Levy Durrence and Mary Frances (Merritt) Thompson; widow; children: James P. Craft, Joseph A. Craft. DD, Calvary Grace Bible Inst., Rillton, Pa., 1975; cert. of journalism arts, CNS Internat., Willow Springs, Mo., 1991; D of Phil. in Film and Video, LaSalle U., Mandeville, La., 1995. Cert. tchr., Protocol Sch. of Washington, D.C., 1993. Dist. mgr. Family Record Plan, Honolulu, 1963-64; acct. exec. Heirloom Inc., Honolulu, 1964-65; pres. Durracraft Advt. and Photography, Cocoa Beach, Orlando, Fla., 1965-71; CEO Western American Corp., Orlando, 1971-73; pres. MF Craft & Assoc. Travel, Orlando, 1972-73, Mary Faye Craft & Assocs., Washington, 1977—; prodr., host FCAC Ch. 10, Fairfax, Va., 1990—; editor MFDC Rev., Springfield, Va., 1992—; pres. Facets, Inc., Savannah, Ga., 2003—. Owner, mgr. Gallery Unique, Alexandria, Va., 1974-75. Author: Poems of Perception, 1984, Gifts of Poetry, 1986, Poems by Mary Faye Craft, 1988, Poems A to Z, 1997, MFDC Rev. Millennium edit., 1999, Christmas Poems and Songs, 2000, The Legend of Tattnall Count and other Poems, 2001, MFDC Rev. edit., 2002, True to the Red White and Blue, 20 Facets of Life, 2003, Life is a Poem, 2005; composer, performer music album Facets of Music, 1989 (Mid Atlantic Contest winner 1990). Bd. dirs. Jacksonville Sister's City Assn., 1996—; active Nursing Home Ministries, 1985—, Homeless Ministries, 1989—. Recipient Paul E. Garber award, Grover Loening award, Gill Robb Wilson award Civil Air Patrol, Maxwell AFB, Ala., 1982, 83, Golden Poets award, World of Poetry, Las Vegas, 1987, Tattnal County Bicentennial Poet Laureate award, 2001. Mem. AAUW, Nat. Press Club, Nat. Space Club, C. of C., Garden Club, Mil. Officers Assn., Air Force Assn., Marine Corps Assn., Rotary (Paul Harris fellow), Phi Theta Kappa. Republican. Roman Catholic. Avocations: photography, television production. Home: PO Box 220 Glennville GA 30427 Office Phone: 202-737-2249. Personal E-mail: mfctv@aol.com.

CRAFT, RANDAL ROBERT, JR., lawyer; b. Greenwood, Miss., Sept. 14, 1941; s. Randal Robert and Elizabeth (Nelson) C.; m. Irene Tichenor, Nov. 27, 1971; children: Elizabeth Napton, Sarah Nelson. BS in Aerospace Engring., U. Tex., 1964; JD, Georgetown U., 1968. Bar: Va. 1968, NY 1969, US Dist. Ct. (so. and ea. dists.) NY 1971, U.S. Ct. Appeals (2d cir.) 1975, US Supreme Ct. 1976, US Ct. Appeals (8th cir.) 1985, US Ct. Appeals (5th cir.) 1989, US Ct. Appeals (6th cir.) 1993. Assoc. Haight, Gardner, Poor & Havens, NYC, 1968-76, ptnr., 1976-97, chmn. litig. dept., 1995-97; ptnr. Holland & Knight, NYC, 1997—2005. Gen. counsel AIAA, 1984-91; gen. counsel, bd. dirs., exec. com. NYC Ballet, 1978—. Author: (with others) Management of Complex Mass Tort Litigation, 1986, Aircraft Crash Litigation, 1984; co-author: The Government Contractor Defense, 1986; contbr. articles to profl. jours. Moderator Judson Meml. Ch., 1975-76; bd. dirs. NYC Ctr. Music and Drama, 1991—, U. Tex. Engring. Adv. Bd., 2002—. Mem. ABA, Assn. of Bar of City of NY, Lawyers Alliance for NY (co-founder, chmn. 1970-71), Wings Club (bd. dirs. 1989-92, gen. counsel 1992—), Delta Upsilon. Republican. Baptist. Avocations: tennis, music. Office: Holland & Knight 195 Broadway 24th Fl New York NY 10007-3189 Office Phone: 212-513-3411.

CRAFT, ROBERT HOMAN, JR., lawyer; b. NYC, Sept. 24, 1939; s. Robert Homan and Janet Marie (Sullivan) C.; m. Margaret Jamison Ford, Feb. 6, 1971; children: Robert H. III, Gerard Ford. AB, Princeton U., 1961; BA, Oxford U., 1963; LLB, Harvard U., 1966. Bar: NY 1973, US Dist. Ct. (so. and ea. dists.) NY 1977, US Ct. Appeals (DC cir.) 1977, US Dist. Ct. DC 1978, US Ct. Appeals (2nd cir.) 1974, US Supreme Ct. 1977. Assoc. Sullivan & Cromwell, NYC, 1966-74; spl. asst. to under sec. of state for security assistance U.S. Dept. State, Washington, 1974-76; exec. asst. to chmn. SEC, Washington, 1976; ptnr. corp. and fin. Sullivan & Cromwell LLP, Washington, 1977—, mng. ptnr. DC office, v.p. gen counsel. Bd. trustees Washington Nat. Opera, 1978—, pres. 1998-2002; dir. Coun. for Excellence in Govt., 1989—, Harvard Law Sch. Fund (nat. chair, 1997-99) Mem. ABA, DC Bar Assn., NY State Bar Assn., Assn. Bar City of NY, Am. Soc. Internat. Law, Met. Club (Washington), Chevy Chase (Md.) Club. Office: Sullivan & Cromwell LLP 1701 Pennsylvania Ave NW Washington DC 20006-5866 Office Phone: 202-956-7500. Office Fax: 202-293-6330. Business E-Mail: craftr@sullcrom.com.

CRAFT DAVIS, AUDREY ELLEN, writer, educator; b. Vanceburg, Ky., June 9, 1926; d. James Elmer and Lula Alice (Vance) Gilkison; m. Vernon Titus Craft, Nov. 5, 1943 (dec. Aug. 1979); children: James Vernon Craft, Alice Ann Craft Schuler; m. Louis Amzie Davis, Oct. 22, 1986 (dec.). PhD, Ohio U., 1964; Dr. of Metaphysics, Coll. Divine Metaphysics, 1968; DD, Ohio U., 1971; postgrad., St. Petersburg Jr. Coll., 1975; DD (hon.), Assoc. Minister, Coll. Metephysical Studies, 1998. Owner beauty salon Audrey Craft Enterprises, Tampa Bay, Fla., 1970-83, owner cosmetic co. Portsmouth, Ohio, 1958-70; owner, distbr. Nightingale Motivation, Tampa Bay, 1960—; tchr., counselor Bus. Coll. U., Tampa Bay, 1965—; ins. staff Investors Heritage & Wabash, Portsmouth, 1967-70; ins. broker Jackson Nat. & Wabash, Tampa Bay, 1971-91; pres. The Gardens 107, Inc., Tampa Bay, 1987—. Travel writer, counselor Cruises/Travel & Etc., Fla., 1981—. Author: (poetry) Pathways, 1990, Metaphysical Techniques That Really Work, 1994, (Spanish translation), 2nd edit., 2002, Metaphysical Encounters, 1992, How to Stay Secure in a Chaotic World, 1993, Metaphysics Encounters of a Fourth Kind, 1995, How to Safeguard Your World and Avoid Becoming a Target, 1996, Angel Trails, 2003, Hidden Truths and Unusual Events of the Bible, 2002, Making Love with God, 2006, Metaphysical Encounters of a 4th Kind, An Exciting Science, 2006, Magnificent Journey Into Prosperity Consciousness; contbr. articles to profl. jours. Bd. dirs. The Gardens Domicurculums Cmty. Coun., 1987—, bd. dirs. State Bd. Cosmetology, Columbus, Ohio, 1962-63, Bus. and Profl. Women, Portsmouth, 1967-69, Sci. Rsch., Portsmouth, 1965-69, Tampa Bay, 1972-74. Recipient Key to Miami, Office of Mayor Claude Kirk, 1969, Million Dollar trophy Lt. Gov. John Brown Ohio; commd. Ky. Col. by Gov. Edward T. Breathitt, 1968, Gov. Wendell Ford, 1969. Mem. AARP, S.E. Writers Assn., Christian Writers Guild, Writers Digest Book Club, Nat. Assn. Retired Fed. Employees (assoc.), Am. Heart Assn. (chmn. Seminole area 1994). Democrat. Avocations: writing, lectures, counseling, travel, meditation. Home and Office: 12 Saint Petersburg Dr W Oldsmar FL 34677-3620 E-mail: audreyedavis@msn.com.

CRAFTON-MASTERSON, ADRIENNE, real estate company executive; b. Providence, Mar. 6, 1926; d. John Harold and Adrienne (Fitzgerald) Crafton; m. Francis T. Masterson, May 31, 1947 (div. Jan. 1977); children: Mary Victoria Masterson Bush, Kathleen Joan, John Andrew, Barbara Lynn Harrison. Student, No. Va. C.C., 1971—74; A in Biblical Studies, Christ to World Bible Inst., Jacksonville, Fla., 1992; A in Pastoral Leadership, Calvary Bible Inst., Jacksonville, Fla., 1993. Mem. staff Senator T.F. Green of R.I., Washington, 1944-47, 54-60, with U.S. Senate Com. on Campaign Expenditures, 1944-45; asst. chief clk. Ho. Govt. Ops. Com., 1948-49; clk. Ho. Campaign Expenditures Com., 1950; asst. appointment sec. Office of Pres., 1951-53; with Hubbard Realty, Alexandria, Va., 1962-67; owner, mgr. Adrienne C. Masterson Real Estate, Alexandria, 1968-82; pres. Adrienne Investment Real Estate (AIRE) Ltd., Alexandria, 1982-91; devel. staff writer Calvary Internat., Jacksonville, Fla., 1992-93; Adrienne Crafton-Masterson Real Estate, Winchester, Va., 1993-94, owner, prin., broker Haymarket, Va., 1994—. Pres. AIRE-Merkli developers, 1988-92; founder AIHRE USA, Inc., 1993—. Mem. adv. panel Fairfax County (Va.) Coun. on Arts, 1987-88; founder, pres. Mt. Vernon/Lee Cultural Ctr. Found., Inc. 1984-92; mem. Haymarket (Va.) Hist. Commn., 1994-95, 97-2001, chmn., 1999-2001. Fellow Internat. Biog. Ctr. (dep. dir. gen.); mem. Internat. Orgn. Real Estate Appraisers (sr.), Nat. Assn. Realtors, No. Va. Assn. Realtors (chmn. comml. and indsl. com. 1982-83, cmty. revitalization com. 1983-84, pres. land comml. indsl. mems. 1985, v.p. land comml. and indsl. mems. 1989), Fairfax Affordable Housing Inc. (sec. 1990-91), Haymarket-Gainesville (Va.) Busl. and Profl. Assn. (bd. dirs. 1996-99, sec. 1998-99), Alexandria C. of C., Mt. Vernon/Lee C. of C., Friends of Kennedy Ctr. (founder), Optimist Club Gainesville-Haymarket (charter, bd. dirs. 1997-99). Office: PO Box 305 Haymarket VA 20168 Office Phone: 703-754-1166. Personal E-mail: aihrecraft@earthlink.net. E-mail: aihrenet@taconic.net.

CRAGER, GINNY LEE, gifted and talented educator; b. Parker Valley, Idaho, Oct. 29, 1941; d. John Loren Wingler and Isabel Sylvia Parker-Wingler; m. J.L. Crager, Apr. 21, 1963; children: Raven Jennifer Barkley, Brenny Gail, Latika Black Horse Hope. BA, U. So. Miss., Hattiesburg, 1975, MS, 1982, D of Adminstrn., 1984. Log comptr. Martin Bros. Container Corp, Oakland, Oreg., 1960—64, Ga. Pacific Corp, Coos Bay, 1964—68; instr. gifted elem. Buckatunna Elem. Sch., Miss., 1988—96; instr. gifted art history Wayne County H.S., Waynesboro, 1996—. Design cons. Neshtas Creations, Waynesboro, 1999—, Raven Clothiers, Inc., 1994—; v.p. C & C Agy. Inc., 2002—. Singer: (Operas) Madam Butterfly (Lead Singer, 1960). Chair Am. Cancer Soc., Waynesboro, 1998—2006, luminaria chair relay life, 1998—2006. Recipient Tchr. of Yr., Oak Grove, 1976—77, Outstanding Tchr., Buckatunna Parent Org, 1994, Golden Apple award, WDAM TV/ Alfa Ins., 1994, Allen R. Barton award, Miss. Power, 1995; fellow, 1996; grantee, Hewlett Packard, 2002. Mem.: Miss. Profl. Educators (hon.; legis. del. 1987—2006). Independent. Baptist. Achievements include design of Native American clothing. Avocations: landscape painting, jewelry designing, leather work, horseback riding, swimming. Home: POBox 833 Waynesboro MS 39367 Office: Wayne County High School 1325 Azalea Drive Waynesboro MS 39367 Office Phone: 601-735-2405. Office Fax: 601-671-8944; Home Fax: 601-671-8944. Personal E-mail: ladyelvis1941@hotmail.com.

CRAGIN, CHARLES LANGMAID, lawyer; b. Portland, Maine, Oct. 9, 1943; s. Charles Langmaid and Ruth (Meriam) C.; m. Maureen Patricia Ford, Oct. 8, 1994; children: Christine, Jean, Cathleen. BS, U. Maine, 1967, JD, 1970. Bar: Maine 1970, U.S. Dist. Ct. Maine 1970, U.S. Supreme Ct. 1974, U.S. Ct. Appeals (DC cir.) 1989, U.S. Ct. Appeals (Vet.) 1997. Assoc. Verrill & Dana, Portland, Maine, 1970-74, ptnr., 1974-90; chmn. US Bd. of Vet.'s Appeals, Washington, 1991-97; counselor to undersec. US Dept. VA, 1997, prin. dep. asst. sec. of def., Res. affairs, 1997-98, acting asst. sec. of def., res. affairs, 1998-2001; prin. dep. under sec. defense, personnel & readiness US Dept. Defense, 1998-2001, acting under sec. def., personnel and readiness, 2001; ptnr. Blank Rome LLP, Washington, 2001—03; sr. v.p. nat. intelligence, security and response Sys. Planning Corp., Arlington, Va., 2003—06, sr. adv. to CEO, 2006—. Sr. govt. affairs counselor Maine St. Solutions, LLC, Augusta, Maine, 2006—, Washington, 2006—. Contbr. articles to legal publs. Rep. candidate for gov. Maine, 1982; bd. dirs., v.p. Margaret Chase Smith Found., Skowhegan, Maine, 1986—, Potomac divsn. AAA, 1992—; chmn. budget com. Rep. Nat. Com., 1984-90; mem. MaineCommn. on Govt. Ethics and Elections, 1986-88, Def. Adv. Com. on Women in Svcs.,1986-88; bd. dirs. U.S. Navy Meml. Found., 1989-2004, vice chmn., 2002-04. Capt. USNR; ret. Decorated Legion of Merit; named Outstanding Young Man Maine, Maine Jaycees, 1976; recipient Disting Svc. award U. So. Maine Alumni Assn., 1986, Exceptional Svc. award U.S. Dept. Vets. Affairs, 1997, Disting. Pub. Svc. award USCG, 2000, Nat. Pres.'s award Naval Res. Assn., 2000, Minuteman award Res. Officers Assn., 2000, Outstanding Svc. award Nat. Mil. Family Assn., 2000, Disting. Svc. medal DC Nat. Guard, 2000, Disting. Pub. Svc. medal Dept. Def., 2001, Decoration for Exceptional Civilian Svc., USAF, 2001, U.S. Army, 2001, Disting. Pub. Svc. medal U.S. Navy, 2001. Fellow Am. Acad. Hosp. Attys. (bd. dirs. 1979-82); mem. ABA, Maine Bar Assn. (Disting. Svc. award 1986), DC Bar Assn., Capitol Hill Club (Washington), Army and Navy Club (Washington), Officers' and Faculty Club (US Naval Acad.). Roman Catholic. Avocations: skiing, wine collecting, amateur radio, gardening. Office: Maine St Solutions LLC 45 Memorial Cir Augusta ME 04332-5307 also: 400 N Capitol St Ste 585 Washington DC 20001-7432 Office Phone: 207-622-7432. Business E-Mail: ccragin@mainestreetsolutions.com.

CRAGNOLINO, GUSTAVO ADOLFO, research scientist; b. Marcos Juarez, Cordoba, Argentina, July 23, 1940; arrived in US, 1976; s. Roberto Clemente and Maria Antonia (Ferrer) Cragnolino; m. Aida Apter, Aug. 16, 1966; children: Ana, Ernesto. Licenciado in Chem. Scis., U. Buenos Aires, 1966, D in Chem. Scis., 1975. Rsch. assoc. Atomic Energy Commn., Buenos Aires, 1968—76; rsch. scientist Ohio State U., Columbus, 1976—86; assoc. scientist Brookhaven Nat. Lab., Upton, NY, 1986—88; sr. rsch. scientist Atomic Energy Commn., Buenos Aires, 1988—90; prin. scientist S.W. Rsch. Inst., San Antonio, 1990—95, staff scientist, 1995—2003, inst. scientist, 2003—05, tech. advisor, 2005—. Lectr., adv. Internat. Atomic Energy Agy., Vienna, 1994; presenter in field. Co-editor: Accelerated Corrosion Tests for Service Life Prediction of Materials, 1994, Scientific Basis for Nuclear Waste Management XXV, 2002, Corrosion Resistant Materials in Extreme Environments, 2005; co-author: ASME Handbook on Water Technology for Thermal Power Systems, 1998; contbr. articles to profl. jours. Fellow: Nat. Assn. Corrosion Engrs. Internat. (chmn. tech. com. 1996—98); mem.: Rsch. Com. ASTM Internat., Am. Nuc. Soc., Electrochem. Soc. Office: SW Rsch Inst 6220 Culebra Rd San Antonio TX 78238-5166 Office Phone: 210-522-5539. Business E-Mail: gcragno@swri.org.

CRAHALLA, JACQUELINE R., state representative; b. Phila., Oct. 8, 1940; m. Benjamin R. Crahalla; children: Benny, Richie(dec.). BA in English, Gwynedd-Mercy Coll. Supr. Lower Providence Twp.; twp. liaison Lower Providence Sewer Authority, Pa. state rep., 2002—06. Mgr. corp. contbn. AstraZeneca; human health divsn. Merck & Co., Inc. Feature writer, weekly corr. (newpaper) Today's Post. Republican. Lutheran.

CRAHAN, ELIZABETH SCHMIDT, librarian; b. Cleve., Oct. 6, 1913; d. Edward and Margaret (Adams) Schmidt; m. Kenneth Acker, 1938 (div. 1968); children: Margaret Miller, John Acker, Steven Acker, Charles Acker; m. Marcus E. Crahan, Dec. 16, 1968. Student, Wellesley Coll., Mass., 1931—32; BArch, U. So. Calif., 1937, MLS, 1960. Reference libr. Los Angeles County Med. Assn., L.A. 1960—61, head reference libr., 1961—67, asst. libr., 1967—78, dir. libr. svcs., 1978—90. Mem.: Fletcher Soc., Am. Assn. History Medicine, George Dock Soc. History of Medicine, Med. Libr. Assn., Friends of the UCLA Libr. (pres. 1977—79, sec. 1978—97), Zamorano Club. Personal E-mail: escrahan@mcn.org.

CRAHAN, JACK BERTSCH, retired manufacturing executive; b. Peoria, Ill., Aug. 24, 1923; s. John F. and Ann B. (Bertsch) C.; m. Peggy Furey, Sept. 9, 1944; children: Patrick Michael, Colleen Mary, Kevin Furey. BS, U. Minn., 1948. With Flexsteel Industries, Inc., Dubuque, Iowa, 1948—50, plant mgr., 1950-54, gen. mgr., v.p., 1955-70, exec. v.p., 1970-84, pres., 1985-89, vice-chmn., COO, 1989-90, chmn., CEO, 1990-99; ret., 1999. Trustee United Steel Workers Am. Pension Fund, 1960—99; dir. Pres.'s Coun. for Phys. Fitness in Industry, 1970—74, Dubuque Bank & Trust, 1970—94; bd. dirs. Dubuque Racing Assn., 1987—2000. Bd. regents Loras Coll., 1967-80; bd. dirs. Xavier Hosp., 1969-78, Boys Club Am., 1981-99. Served with USNR, 1942-43, with USMC, 1943-46, 53-54. Decorated DFC, Air medals (3). Mem. Am. Furniture Assn. (bd. dirs. 1967-74). Republican. Roman Catholic. Home: 1195 Arrowhead Dr

Dubuque IA 52003-8594 Office: Flexsteel Industries Inc Brunswick Indsl Block PO Box 847 Dubuque IA 52004-0847 Office Phone: 563-556-7730. Business E-Mail: jzemann@flexsteel.com.

CRAIB, KENNETH BRYDEN, research and development company executive, physicist, economist; b. Milford, Mass., Oct. 13, 1938; s. William Pirie and Virginia Louise (Bryden) C.; m. Gloria Faye Lisano, June 25, 1960; children: Kenneth Bryden, Judith Diane, Lori Elaine, Melissa Suzanne, Brandi Lynn. BS in Physics, U. Houston, 1967; MA in Econs., Calif. State U., 1982; postgrad., Harvard U., 1989. Aerospace technologist NASA, Houston, 1962-68; staff physicist Mark Sys., Inc., Cupertino, Calif., 1968-69; v.p. World Resources Corp., Cupertino, 1969-71; dir. resources devel. divsn. Aero Svc. Corp., Phila., 1971-72; dir. ops. Resources Devel. Assocs., Los Altos, Calif., 1972-80; pres., CEO Diamond Springs, Calif., 1980-85; owner Sand Ridge Arabians, 1980-98; chmn., dir. Resources Devel. Assocs., Inc., 1982-86, Devel. Support Internat. Inc., Placerville, Calif., 1981-86; pres., chn., dir. RDA Internat., Inc., 1985-96, chmn., CEO, dir., 1995—2000; mgr. acad. affairs U. Phoenix, Sacramento, 2001—02, chmn. Coll. Undergrad. Bus. and Mgmt. Ft. Lauderdale, Fla., 2002—, prof., 2002—06; prof., dir. acad. affairs, chief acad. officer U. Phoenix, Savannah, Ga., 2006—. Adj. prof. Sacramento City Coll., 1996—2001; prof. U. Phoenix, Sacramento, 1997—2002. Contbr. articles to profl. jours. Served with USAF, 1957-61. Recipient Sustained Superior Performance award NASA, 1966; NASA grantee, 1968. Mem. Am. Soc. Photogrammetry, Soc. Internat. Devel., Agrl. Rsch. Inst., Calif. Select Com. Remote Sensing, Internat. Assn. Natural Resources Pilots, Remote Sensing Soc. (coun.), Am. Soc. Oceanography (charter), Aircraft Owners and Pilots Assn., Gulf and Cribbean Fisheries Inst., Placerville C. of C., Harvard Alumni Assn., Exptl. Aircraft Assn., Asian Fisheries Soc. Mailing: 121 Companion Way Savannah GA 31419 Office: U Phoenix Savannah Campus 8001 Chatham Center Dr STe 200 Savannah GA 31405 Office Phone: 912-232-0531. *What you do is not as important as how you do it, and the people whose lives you touch in the process.*

CRAIG, ALBERT M., history professor, researcher; b. Chgo., Dec. 9, 1927; s. Albert Morton and Adda (Clendenin) C.; m. Teruko Ugaya, July 10, 1953; children: John, Paul, Sarah. BS, Northwestern U., 1949; postgrad., Universite de Strasbourg, 1949-50, Kyoto U., 1951-53, Tokyo U., 1955-56; PhD, Harvard, 1959. Instr. U. Mass., 1957-59; instr. Harvard U., Cambridge, Mass., 1959-60, asst. prof., 1960-63, assoc. prof., 1963-67, prof., 1967—99, Harvard-Yenching prof. history, 1999—2005, Harvard-Yenching rsch. prof. history, 1999—2005, prof. emeritus, 2005—; dir. Harvard-Yenching Inst., 1976-87. Author: Choshu in the Meiji Restoration, 1961, 2000, The Heritage of Chinese Civilization, 2001, 06, The Heritage of Japanese Civilization, 2003, (with others) East Asia: The Modern Transformation, 1965, East Asia: Tradition and Transformation, 1973, 3d edit., 1989, The Heritage of World Civilizations, 1986, 7th edit., 2005; editor: Japan, A Comparative View, 1979; co-editor: Personality in Japanese History, 1970. Served with AUS, 1946-47. Home: 172 Goden St Belmont MA 02478-2951 Office: 9 Kirkland Pl Cambridge MA 02138-2020 E-mail: acraig@fas.harvard.edu.

CRAIG, ANN, library director; b. 1962; m. Paul Knox; 3 children. BA, Northern Ill. U., M in Libr. and Info. Studies. Libr. Founders Meml. Libr., Northern Ill. U.; with Ill. State Libr., 1989—, coord. pub. services, assoc. dir., libr. automation and tech., dir., 2005—; network coord., reference libr. Ill. Libr. Info. Network/Online Computer Libr. Ctr. Office: Ill State Library Gwendolyn Brooks Bldg 300 S 2nd St Springfield IL 62701-1796 Office Phone: 217-782-2994. Business E-Mail: acraig@ilsos.net.*

CRAIG, CHARLES SAMUEL, marketing educator; b. Atlantic City, May 6, 1943; s. Charles Hays and Catherine Sara (McMullen) C.; m. Elizabeth Anne Coyne, Aug. 10, 1985; children: Mary Catherine, Caroline Elizabeth. BA, Westminster Coll., 1965; MS, U. R.I., 1967; PhD, Ohio State U., 1971. Mktg. rep. IBM, Providence, 1966—68; asst. dir. Mechanized Info. Ctr., Columbus, 1971—73; asst. prof. lib. adminstrn. Ohio State U., Columbus, 1971—73, asst. prof. mktg., 1972—74; asst. prof. mktg. Grad. Sch. Bus. and Pub. Adminstrn. Cornell U., Ithaca, NY, 1974—77, assoc. prof., 1977—79; from assoc. prof. mktg. Stern Sch. of Bus. to prof. NYU, 1979—, assoc. dean academic affairs, 1984—88, chair mktg. dept., 1990—98, dir. entertainment, media and tech. program, 1999—, Catherine and Peter Kellner prof., 2001—, deputy chair mktg. dept., 2005—. Bd. dirs. P&R Pub. Co., Phillipsburg, NJ; mem. exec. bd. Jour. Retailing, 1985—. Co-author: Consumer Behavior: An Information Processing Perspective, 1982; International Marketing Research, 1983, 3d edit., 2005, Global Marketing Strategy, 1995; co-editor: Personal Selling: Theory, Research and Practice, 1984, The Development of Media Models in Advertising, Repetition Effects over the Years, The Relationship of Advertising Expenditures to Sales, 1986; mem. editl. bd. Jour. Mktg. Rsch., 1978-85, Jour. Retailing, 1980-85, Jour. Advt. Rsch., 1994—, Internat. Jour. of Advt., 1997—, Jour. Internat. Mktg., 2007—; contbr. articles to profl. jours. Bd. dir. NY Chpt. Am. Marketing Assn., 2005—. NDEA fellow, 1969-71. Mem. Am. Mktg. Assn., Assn. Consumer Rsch., Acad. Internat. Bus., Phi Kappa Phi, Omicron Delta Epsilon, Psi Chi. Presbyterian. Home: 100 Bleecker St Apt 28D New York NY 10012-2207 Office: NYU 40 W 4th St New York NY 10012-1106

CRAIG, CONSTANT PETER, retired military officer, military analyst, consultant; arrived in US, 1958; s. Guy Constant and Nelva May Craig; m. Dawn Eloise Howard, Aug. 18, 1982; children: Heather D., Johnathan C. BS in Bus. Adminstrn., U. Fla., Gainesville, 1976; MS in Mgmt., Colo. Internat. U., Colorado Springs, 2005. 2nd lt. USMC, 1976, commd. officer, 1976, advanced through grades to maj., 1988, ret., 1996; asst. project mgr. AST Inc., Anniston, Ala., 1996—98; program mgr. IEM Inc., Ft. Leonard Wood, Mo., 1998—2005, Tetra Tech EM Inc., Ft. Leonard Wood, 2005—06; sr. analyst Northrop Grumman, Ft. Leonard Wood, 2006—. Cons. Internat. Inst. Policy Studies, Washington, 2004—06, ERTS Inc., Salem, Ala., 2005—06. Candidate City Coun., Lebanon, Mo., 2005. Decorated Meritorious Svc. medal USMC; recipient Employer Recognition award, Nat. Guard Assn., 2005, Outstanding Alumni award, Colo. Tech. Inst., 2006. Mem.: VFW, Nat. Def. Industry Assn., US Naval Inst. Avocations: reading, flying, politics. Home: 2416 Copperwood Dr Lebanon MO 65536 Office: Northrop Grumman 192 Replacement Ave Ste 100 Fort Leonard Wood MO 65473

CRAIG, DANIEL, actor; b. Chester, Eng., Mar. 2, 1968; m. Fiona Loudon, 1992 (div. 1994); 1 child. Grad., Guildhall Sch. Music and Drama. Actor: (films) The Power of One, 1992, A Kid in King Arthur's Court, 1995, Saint-Ex, 1996, Obsession, 1997, Love and Rage, 1998, Elizabeth, 1998, The Trench, 1999, I Dreamed of Africa, 2000, Some Voices, 2000, Lara Croft: Tomb Raider, 2001, Road to Perdition, 2002, Occasional, Strong, 2002, The Mother, 2003, Sylvia, 2003, Enduring Love, 2004, Layer Cake, 2004, The Jacket, 2005, Fateless, 2005, Munich, 2005, (voice) Renaissance, 2006, Infamous, 2006, Casino Royale, 2006, The Invasion, 2007; (TV films) Genghis Cohn, 1993, Sharpe's Eagle, 1993, Kiss and Tell, 1996, The Fortunes and Misfortunes of Moll Flanders, 1996, The Ice House, 1997, Shockers: The Visitor, 1999, Copenhagen, 2002, Archangel, 2005.*

CRAIG, EDWARD VINCENT, orthopedic surgeon, educator; b. Bklyn., May 5, 1947; s. Edward Vincent and Lorraine (Youngkin) C.; m. Kathryn Ann Davis, July 4, 1982. BA, Princeton U., 1969; MD, Columbia U., 1973. Diplomate Am. Bd. Orthopaedic Surgery. Intern Columbia-Presbyn. Med. Ctr., NYC, 1973-74, resident in internal medicine, 1975-76, resident in orthopaedic surgery, 1977-80, fellow in shoulder surgery, 1980-81, fellow in hand surgery, 1981-82; attending surgeon U. Minn. Hosp., Mpls., 1982-94, Hosp. Spl. Surgery, NYC, 1994—, New York Hosp., NYC, 1994—; prof. clin. surgery Cornell Med. Coll., NYC, 1994—. Cons., designer Biomet Atlas Total Shoulder Replacement Sys., Warsaw, Ind., 1985—; cons. Minn. Twins Baseball Club, 1993-94. Author: The Shoulder, 1995, Clinical Orthopaedics, 1999, The Unstable Shoulder, 1999, An Atlas of Replacement Surgery, 2006, Shoulder, Replacement Surgery, 2007; contbr. articles to profl. jours. Bd. dirs. Waveny Day Care Ctr., New Canaan, Conn., 1996, New Canaan Country Sch., 2002, Juvenile Diabetes Found. Fairfield County, New Canaan Basketball Assn. Fellow Am. Acad. Orthopaedic Surgeons; mem. AMA, Am. Shoulder and Elbow Surgeons (pres. 1985—), Am. Orthopaedic Soc. for Sports Medicine (rsch. grantee 1995), Am. Soc. Surgery of the Hand, Am. Orthopaedic Assn. (ABC Traveling fellow 1980). Republican. Roman Catholic. Avocations: piano, skiing, golf, tennis, running. Office: Hosp Spl Surgery 535 E 70th St New York NY 10021-4872 also: 143 Sound Beach Ave Old Greenwich CT 06870 Home Phone: 203-966-0045; Office Phone: 212-606-1966. Business E-Mail: craige@hss.edu.*

CRAIG, ELIZABETH COYNE, marketing executive; b. NYC, Jan. 7, 1956; d. John Thomas and Mary Ellen (O'Sullivan) Coyne; m. Charles Samuel Craig, Aug. 10, 1985; children: Mary Catherine, Caroline Elizabeth. BS in Occupl. Therapy, NYU, 1980, MBA, 1986. Occupl. therapist Jacobi Hosp., NY, 1980-81, St. Vincent's Hosp., NY, 1981-85; mktg. intern worldwide consumer banking Citibank US, Europe Consumer Bank, Citicorp Ins., NYC, 1985-86, mgmt. assoc., 1986-87, asst. mgr., 1987-88, mktg. mgr. new product devel., 1988-90, asst. v.p. life acquisitions, relationship mktg., 1990-93, v.p. life, health acquisitions, relationship mktg., 1993-94, v.p. 3d party direct response, retail ins. sales pilots, 1994-96, v.p. annuity product mgmt., 1996-99; sr. v.p. e-commerce investment and ins., product mgr. Citi fi Interactive Fin. Network, LI, NY, 1998-99; v.p., internet customer relationship mgr. Citibank, 1999—2001, v.p. protection products credit cards, 2001—05, sr. v.p. Rona enhancement svcs. Sr. v.p. enhancement svcs. Citibank, Rona. Mem. Fin. Women's Assn., Direct Mktg. Assn. Avocations: antiques, bicycling, skiing. Office: Citibank 153 E 3d Ave New York NY 10021 Office Phone: 212-559-5276. Business E-Mail: elizabeth.craig@citigroup.com.

CRAIG, GEORGE DENNIS, economics professor, consultant; b. Sept. 14, 1936; s. George S. and Alice H. (Childs) C.; m. Lelah Price, Aug. 21, 1984; children: R. Price Coyle, R. Nolan Coyle, Deborah L. Craig, W. Sean Coyle. BA, Wheaton Coll., 1960; MS, U. Ill., 1962, PhD, 1968. Asst. prof. econs. La. State U., Baton Rouge, 1965-69; assoc. prof. sch. bus. No. Ill. U., DeKalb, 1969-82; prof. econs., chmn. Oklahoma City U., 1982—. Cons. AT&T, Oklahoma City, 1984—. Contbr. articles to profl. jours. Mem. Am. Econs. Assn., So. Econs. Assn., Nat. Assn. Bus. Economists, Internat. Inst. Forecasting. Avocations: duplicate bridge, tennis. Home: 6915 Avondale Ct Oklahoma City OK 73116-5008 Office: 6421 Avondale Dr Ste 208 Oklahoma City OK 73116-6429 Home Phone: 405-842-6724; Office Phone: 405-842-8925. Personal E-mail: craigg784@aol.com.

CRAIG, GREGORY BESTOR, lawyer; b. Norfolk, Va., Mar. 4, 1945; s. William Gregory and Lois (Bestor) C.; m. Margaret Davenport Noyes, July 27, 1974; children: William Eliot, Eliza Noyes, Margaret Bestor, Mary Duncan, James Gregory. AB magna cum laude, Harvard Coll., 1967; diploma in historical studies, Cambridge U., 1968; JD, Yale U., 1972. Bar: D.C. 1972, U.S. Ct. Appeals (D.C., 2d, 3d, 4th, 6th, 7th and 11th cirs.), U.S. Supreme Ct. Assoc. Williams Connolly & Califano, Washington, 1972-74; asst. fed. pub. defender U.S. Dist. Ct. Conn., 1974-76; assoc. Williams & Connolly, Washington, 1977-78, ptnr., 1979-84; sr. advisor on fgn. policy and def. Sen. Edward M. Kennedy, Washington, 1984-88; ptnr. Williams & Connolly, Washington, 1989-97; dir. Office of Policy and Planning Dept. of State, 1997—98, asst. to pres. and spl. counsel, 1998—99; ptnr. Williams & Connolly, Washington, 1999—. Tchr. trial practice Yale Law Sch., 1975-76, Harvard Inst. Trial Advocacy, 1980-84; chmn. Internat. Human Rights Law Group, 1989-96. Trustee Overseas Devel. Coun., 1993-96; vice chmn. Carnegie Endowment for Internat. Peace, 1990-97, 1999-2007, Robert F. Kennedy Meml., 1989-97, 99—, Fgn. Student Svc. Coun., 1990-96, Mexican-Am. Legal Def. and Edn. Fund, 1995-97. Recipient John Harvard Scholar, Emmanuel Coll. Cambridge U., 1967—68. Fellow: Am. Coll. Trial Lawyers; mem.: ABA, Phi Beta Kappa. Avocations: mountain climbing, hiking. Office: Williams & Connolly 725 12th St NW Washington DC 20005-5901 Home Phone: 202-686-2820; Office Phone: 202-434-5506. Business E-Mail: gcraig@wc.com.

CRAIG, HAROLD KENT, mechanical contracting executive, systems analyst; b. Columbus, Ohio, Nov. 21, 1956; s. Harold Harding and Mildred Annie (King) C.; m. Cathy M. Preslar, Nov. 19, 1979 (div. Sept. 2000); 1 child, Brian Scagel; m. Liann Craig Tabor, Oct. 24, 2000 (div. Dec. 2004); m. Kristi Linn Servies Rigg, May 14, 2005. Student, Goddard Coll., 1979. Lic. plumbing, boiler making, air conditioning, forced warm air heating; spl. elec. lic.; cert. exam proctor. V.p., project mgr. Craig Plumbing Co., Inc., Raleigh, N.C., 1972-95; v.p., project mgmt., sys. analyst Confluence Tech., Raleigh, NC, 1976—; sr. sys. analyst Datasonix Inc., Smithfield, NC, 1980—83; heating, ventilation, air cond., plumbing and mech. cons. Valley Constrn. Co., Inc., Koslusco, Miss., 1985-86; chief, sr. project mgr., estimator Sneeden Mechanical Contractors, Inc., Wilmington, NC, 1986-88; U.S. bus. agent The Circle Group, Arusha, Tanzania, 1974—; sr. estimator, sr. project mgr. Bay Mech. Inc., Raleigh, 1996—97; sr. project mgr., estimator Atlantic Coast Mech., Inc., Raleigh, 1997-98; sr. estimator, project mgr. Superior Plumbing & Mech., Inc., Wilson, NC, 1998—2003; sr. project mgr., estimator Raleigh office Goldstar Mech., Charlotte, NC, 2003—06; mgr. comm. divsn. Goldstar Mech. Svcs., Inc., 2003—06. Sys. cons. Consulting, Tech., and Design, Inc., Research Triangle Park, NC, 1988-94; bd. dirs. NC Bldrs. Inst., Durham, NC. Author: Yes, the Sun Will Rise, 1979; editor Joe's Bozart mag., 1978; mem. editl. bd. In the Steps, 1976-81; contbr. articles to profl. jours.; contbg. editor, Contractor mag., 1998—. Mem. bd. adjustments Town of Cary (N.C.), 1981; mem. bd. Raleigh Artists' Cmty., 1974-79 Mem.: Am. Humanists Assn. (Humanists N.C. chpt. bd. dirs. 1974—81, editor The Tarheel Humanist newsletter 1975—78, named Humanist Adv. 1979). Mailing: PO Box 4153 Cary NC 27519-4153 Office Phone: 919-386-5587. Business E-Mail: kent@hkentcraig.com.

CRAIG, JAMES HICKLIN, fine arts consultant; b. Chester, SC, July 23, 1937; s. John Edward and Una Bee (Martin) C. Student, U. S.C., 1955-56, Cin. Coll. Conservatory Music, 1956-59, Juilliard Sch. Music, 1960, Paris, 1960. Curator decorative arts N.C. Dept. Archives & History, Raleigh, 1962-64; grantee writing book on N.C. decorative arts Mus. So. Decorative Arts, 1964-65; prin. James Craig Fine & Decorative Arts, 1965-69; pres. Craig & Tarlton, Inc., Raleigh, 1969-85; fine arts cons. Independence, Va., 1985—. Bd. dirs. Sparta Mus. Project, Raleigh Chamber Music Soc., NYC Chamber Opera Theater, Mint Mus. of Art, Charlotte, trustee 2000—; cons. NC Gov.'s Mansion bd.; mem. acquisitions com. Author: The Arts and Crafts in North Carolina 1699-1840, 1965 (listed by Montgomery as part of 100 best in field). Bd. dirs. Sparta (N.C.) Mus. Project. Avocations: art, antiques, gardening. Office: James Craig Fine Arts PO Box 397 Independence VA 24348-0397 Personal E-mail: jim@jcraigart.com.

CRAIG, JAMES LYNN, physician, health services administrator; b. Columbia, Tenn., Aug. 7, 1933; s. Clifford Paul and Maple (Harris) Craig; m. Suzanne Anderson, July 20, 1957; children: James Lynn, Margaret; m. Roberta Annette Craig, May 17, 1980. Student, Mid. Tenn. State U., 1953; MD, U. Tenn., 1956; MPH, U. Pitts., 1963. Diplomate Am. Bd. Preventive Medicine. Intern U. Tenn. Meml. Hosp., Knoxville, 1957; resident in occupl. medicine U. Pitts., 1962-64, TVA, Chattanooga, 1964-65, physician, 1966-69, chief med. officer, 1969-74; corp. med. dir. Gen. Mills Corp., Mpls., 1974-76, v.p. corp. med. dir., 1976-80, v.p., dir. health and human svcs., 1980-98; adj. clin. prof. U. Minn., Mpls., 1979—, chmn. cmty. adv. com. Ctr. for Environ. and Health Policy, 1994-97, mem. adv. coun. health in scis., 1992-95, chmn. adv. bd. Ctr. for Environ. and Health Policy, 1994-97; pres. Family and Preventive Health Svcs., Inc., Mpls., 1998—. Clin. instr. U. Tenn., Memphis, 1970—74, Meharry Med. Sch., Nashville, 1972—74; mem. adv. bd. to dir. Ctr. Disease Control and Prevention, 1996—99; nat. adv. bd. Internat. Health and Media Awards, 1996—2006. Contbr. articles to profl. jours. Bd. dirs. Mpls. Blood Bank, 1976—88, Minn. Safety Coun., 1981—90, Minn. Heart Assn., Mpls., 1976—87, Children's Heart Fund, 1976—88, Meth. Hosp. Found., 1979—87, Park Nicolett Med. Found., 1987—93, Altcare, 1983—95, Meth. Hosp. Health Assn., 1987—93, Minn. Wellness Coun., 1986—91, Health Sys. Minn. Assocs., 1993—94, Health Sys. Minn. Inst. Rsch. and Edn., 1996—2000, chmn., 1997—2000, Park Nicollet Inst., 2000—01; trustee Minn. Med. Found., 2001—, Crossroads Coll., Rochester, 2007—; bd. dirs. Minn. Bible Coll., Rochester, 1978—83. Named Legacy Laureate, U. Pitts., 2000; recipient Cmty. Svc. award, Park Nicolett Med. Ctr., 1995, Knudsen award in occupl. medicine, Am. Coll. Occupl. and Environ. Medicine, 2000. Fellow: Am. Acad. Family Practice, Am. Acad. Occupl. Medicine (treas. 1982—83, sec. 1983—84, v.p. 1984—85, pres. 1986—87), Am. Occupl. Medicine Assn. (bd. dirs. 1974—78); mem.: AMA (alt. del. Ho. Dels. 1990—92, del. 1992—96, Recognition award 1975, 1978, 1981, 1985, 1989, 1993, 1996, 1999, 2002, 2005), Minn. Med. Found. (bd. dirs. 2001—), Emergency Physicians Assn. (bd. dirs. 1984—92), Mpls. Acad. Medicine (sec. 1983—85, pres. 1985—86), Minn. Acad. Medicine, North Ctrl. Occupl. Medicine Assn. (pres. 1977), Occupl. Health Inst. (chmn. 1983—84), Mpls. Kiwanis Club (trustee 2004—). Home: 10008 S Shore Dr Minneapolis MN 55441-5011 Office: PO Box 270330 Minneapolis MN 55427-6330 Office Phone: 612-669-3847. Personal E-mail: jimlcraig@aol.com. *My goals and objectives are based on a proper balance between quality and acceptance.*

CRAIG, JENNY, human services manager; b. New Orleans; d. James Yoric Guidroz and Gertrude Acosta; m. Sid Craig, 1979; children: Denise, Michele. Worked for Silhouette/Am. Health gym; owner Healthetic gym; from mgr. to nat. dir. ops. Body Contour, Inc.; co-founder Jenny Craig Inc., Australia, 1983—, entered US marketplace in LA, 1985, sold company, 2002. Achievements include providing a comprehensive weight mgmt. prog. designed by registered dietitians, psychologists and a med. adv. bd. to grow into one of the largest weight mgmt. cos. in the world; only weight mgmt. co. listed on N.Y. Stock Exch. Office: Jenny Craig Inc 5770 Fleet St Carlsbad CA 92008-4700

CRAIG, JOHN BRUCE, former ambassador, air transportation executive; BS, American U. With Sr. Fgn. Svc., dep. chief of mission Syria, Colombia, with Bur. Near Eastern Affairs Washington, dir. jr. officer divsn. Bur. of Pers., dir. Office of Arabian Peninsula Affairs, amb. Sultanate of Oman, 1998—2001; spl. asst. to Pres., mem. Nat. Security Council, sr. dir. for combating terrorism White House, Washington, 2001—03; v.p., Middle East internat. rels. Boeing Co., 2003—. Office: Boeing Company 100 N Riverside Plz Chicago IL 60606-1596

CRAIG, JOHN TUCKER, economist, consultant; b. Bklyn., June 17, 1926; s. Clarence Tucker and Rena (Stebbins) C.; m. Ruth Doris Weiler, Aug. 5, 1950; children: Daniel, Thomas, Andrew, Paul. BA, Oberlin Coll., 1948; MPA, Princeton U., 1950; postgrad., Tufts U., 1966-67. With AID, 1950-80, program officer Tunis, Tunisia, 1967-68, Kathmandu, Nepal, 1968-71, internat. rels. officer Latin Am. Bur. Washington, 1971-74, program officer Port-au-Prince, Haiti, 1974-78, asst. dir. Georgetown, Guyana, 1978-80; cons. Silver Spring, Md., 1980-83; economist for agr. survey U. Md./Rwanda Agrl. Ministry, Kigali, Rwanda, 1983-86; chief party Assocs. in Rural Devel., Proje Sove Te, Burlington, Vt. and Camp Perrin, Haiti, 1988-90; cons. Washington, 1986—. Part-time fgn. affairs officer Freedom of Info., Dept. State. Editor: Haiti: Development Assistance Program, 1976, Guyana: Country Development Strategy Statement, 1980. With USN, 1944—46. Recipient Superior Honor Award, AID, 1980. Mem.: Am. Econ. Assn. Methodist. Avocations: hiking, swimming. Home and Office: Apt 502 4200 Massachusetts Ave NW Washington DC 20016-4752 Personal E-mail: johntcraig1@comcast.net.

CRAIG, L. CLIFFORD, lawyer; b. Ohio, Aug. 29, 1938; Student, Stanford U., 1957-59; BA, Duke U., 1961, LLB, 1964. Bar: Ohio. Ptnr. Taft, Stettinius & Hollister, Cin., 1971—. Fellow Am. Coll. Trial Lawyers; mem. ABA, Ohio Bar Assn., Cin. Bar Assn. Office: 425 Walnut St Ste 1800 Cincinnati OH 45202-3957 Office Phone: 513-381-2838. Business E-Mail: craig@taftlaw.com.

CRAIG, LARRY EDWIN, former senator; b. Council, Idaho, July 20, 1945; m. Suzanne Thompson; 3 children. BA in Polit. Sci. and Agr. Economics, U. Idaho, 1969; postgrad, George Washington U., 1970. Farmer, rancher, Midvale area, Idaho; mem. Idaho State Senate, 1974-80, US Congress from 1st Idaho dist., 1981—91; US Senator from Idaho, 1991—2007. Chmn. Idaho Rep. State Senate Races, 1976-78; mem. Nat. Congressional Coun., Nat. Found. Defense Analysis; mem. com. appropriations US Senate, com. energy and natural resources, com. veterans affairs, spl. com. aging. Pres. Young Rep. League Idaho, 1976-77; mem. Idaho Rep. Exec. Com., 1976-78; chmn. Rep. Ctrl. Com. Washington County, 1971-72; advisor vocat. edn. in pub. schs. HEW, 1971-73; mem. Idaho Farm Bur., 1965-79. Served with US Army, 1970—72. Recipient Disting. Svc. award, Am. Legion, 2000. Mem. NRA (bd. dirs. 1983—), Future Farmers of Am. (v.p. 1966-67). Republican. Methodist.*

CRAIG, NANCY L., molecular biologist, educator, geneticist; BS in Biology and Chemistry, Bryn Mawr Coll.; PhD in Biochemistry, Cornell Univ.; postdoctoral fellow, NIH. Assoc. prof., microbiology and Immunology, biochemistry and biophysics Univ. Calif., San Francisco; investigator Howard Hughes Med. Inst., 1991—; prof., molecular biology, genetics Johns Hopkins Univ., Balt. Fellow: AAAS, Am. Acad. Microbiology, Am. Acad. Arts & Scis. Office: Molecular Biology & Genetics Johns Hopkins Univ 502 PCTB 725 N Wolfe St Baltimore MD 21205 Office Phone: 410-955-3933, 410-955-2731. Business E-Mail: ncraig@jhmi.edu.*

CRAIG, PAMELA J., management consulting firm executive; married; 2 children. B in Econs., Smith Coll., 1979; MBA, NYU. CPA. With Accenture Ltd., NYC, 1982—, ptnr., 1991—, positions in media & entertainment practice Comm. & High Tech oper. group., group. dir. bus. ops. & services, sr. v.p. fin., 2004—06, CFO, 2006—. Bd. dirs. Comprehensive Devel. Inc., NYC, Avanade Inc. Named one of Top 100 Women in Corp. Am. Mem.: C200. Office: Accenture Ltd 1345 Ave of the Americas 6th Fl New York NY 10105*

CRAIG, PAUL MAX, JR., retired lawyer; b. Munich, Aug. 8, 1921; came to US, 1941; naturalized, 1944; s. Paul Max and Helen A. Craig; m. Leonie R. Hildebrand, June 26, 1962: children: Anthony P., Claudine A., Stephen P. BS in Elec. Engring., Worcester Poly. Inst., Mass., 1946; LLB, Georgetown U., 1950; LLM, George Washington U., 1952. Bar: DC 1950. Patent examiner U.S. Patent Office, Washington, 1946-50; patent advisor Office Chief Ordnance, Dept. Army, Washington, 1950-52; pvt. practice Washington, 1952—; ptnr. Craig & Antonelli (and predecessor firm), Washington, 1967-82, Craig & Burns, Washington, 1982-86, Barnes & Thornburg, Washington, 1986-88, Paul M. Craig, P.C., Washington, 1989-97; of counsel Dow, Lohnes & Albertson, 1989-92, affiliated with, 1992-95; of counsel Birch, Stewart, Kolasch & Birch, Falls Church, Va., 1995-97; pvt. practice Silver Spring, Md., 1998—; ret., 2005—. With

USNR, 1944-46. Mem. Am., Inter-Am. bar assns., Am. Patent Law Assn., Licensing Execs. Soc., Am. Soc. Internat. Law, Assn. Trial Lawyers Am. Home: 207 Quaint Acres Dr Silver Spring MD 20904-2715 Personal E-mail: pmcraig@starpower.net.

CRAIG, STEVE A., lawyer; m. Mary Craig. BA, Ohio State U., Columbus, 1973, JD, 1976. Bar: Ohio, US Dist. Ct. Ohio. Pvt. practice, Hilliard, Ohio, 1976—. Pres. Hilliard C. of C., Ohio, 1983—86, Hilliard Conv. and Visitors Bur., 1994—. Recipient John W. Galbreath award, 1986, commendation, Ohio House Reps., 1986. Avocation: walking. Office: 5251 Norwich St Hilliard OH 43026

CRAIGHEAD, HAROLD GENE, physicist, educator; BS with high honors in Physics, U. Md., College Park, 1974; PhD in Physics, Cornell U., 1980. Mem. tech. staff device physics rsch. dept. Bell Labs., Holmdel, NJ, 1979-84; rsch. mgr. quantum structures rsch. grp. Bell Comm. Rsch., Red Bank, NJ, 1984-89; prof. sch. applied and engring. physics Cornell U., Ithaca, NY, 1989—, dir. Sch. Applied and Engring. Physics, 1998—2000, dir. Naniobiotechnology Ctr., 2000—01, 2006—, co-dir. Naniobiotechnology Ctr., 2002—06, interim dean engring., 2001—02, Charles W. Lake, Jr. prof. engring. Dir. Nat. Nanofabrication Facility, Cornell U., 1989-95. Contbr. articles to profl. jours. Mem.: NAE. Achievements include patents in field. Office: Sch Applied and Engring Physics Cornell U 212 Clark Hall Ithaca NY 14853 Office Phone: 607-255-8707. Business E-Mail: hgc1@cornell.edu.

CRAIGHEAD, JOHN EDWARD, pathology educator; b. Pitts., Aug. 14, 1930; s. Samuel Judson and Madeleine Rose (Schmalz) C.; m. Dorothy Ellen Ford, July 29, 1957 (div. July 1992); 2 children; m. Christina Ann Canon, Aug. 29, 1992; 7 children. BS, U. Utah, 1952, MD, 1956. Diplomate Am. Bd. Pathology, Nat. Bd. Med. Examiners (mem. pathology com. 1978-81). Intern ward med. svc. Barnes Hosp., St. Louis, 1956-57; jr. asst. resident in pathology Peter Bent Brigham Hosp., Boston, 1960-61, sr. asst. resident, 1961-62, chief resident, 1962-65, assoc. in pathology, 1965-68; asst. prof. pathology Harvard U. Med. Sch., Boston, 1963-66, assoc. prof., 1966-68, U. Vt. Coll. Medicine, Burlington, 1968-69, prof., 1969-72, chmn. dept. pathology, 1974-90. Attending physician Med. Ctr. Hosp. Vt., Burlington, 1970-94, Fletcher Allen Health Care, Burlington, 1995—; Harry B. Harding meml. lectr. Evanston (Ill.) Hosp., 1981; 4th ann. Karl Sohlberg lectr. U. Ill., 1981; Finlayson seminar lectr. McGill U., Montreal, Que., Can., 1987; George Hoyt Whipple lectr. U. Rochester, N.Y., 1989; assoc. mem. Commn. Viral Infections, Armed Forces Epidemiol. Bd., 1966-68; mem. adv. com. on infectious diseases Nat. Inst. Allergy and Infectious Diseases, 1971-75; mem. pathology A study sect. NIH, 1984-86, mem. nat. adv. environ. health scis. coun., 1985-89; mem. adv. com. Registry Comparative Pathology, Armed Forces Inst. Pathology, 1993-96; mem. Vt. Regional Cancer Ctr., 1988-91; mem. med. sci. adv. bd. Juvenile Diabetes Found., 1978-80; mem. residency rev. com. for pathology Accreditation Coun. for Grad. Med. Edn., 1979-83, vice chmn., 1982-84; dir. sci. program, chmn. environ. pathology task force Univs. Assoc. for Rsch. and Edn. in Pathology, 1991-98; mem. pulmonary panel Am. Registry Pathology, 1992-98. Editor: The Pathology of Environmental and Occupational Disease, 1995; mem. editl. bd. Lab. Investigation, Archives Pathology and Lab. Medicine, Human Pathology, Am. Jour. Pathology, 1980-92; contbr. numerous articles and abstracts to med. jours., chpts. to books. Surgeon USPHS, 1957-60. Recipient David Rumbough sci. award, U. Ill., 1976, Moses Barron award, Twin Cities Diabetes Assn., 1977; spl. fellow NIH, 1963; travel fellow Royal Soc. Medicine, 1971. Mem. AAAS, AMA (mem. coun. sci. affairs, mem. adv. panel on asbestos related diseases, chmn. 1982-83), Am. Acad. Pathology, Am. Assn. for Cancer Rsch., Am. Assn. Pathologists, Am. Soc. Clin. Pathologists (mem. basic sci. rsch. symposium com. 1978-82, H.P. Smith Meml. award 1987), Am. Thoracic Soc., Assn. Pathology Chairmen (past sec.-treas., v.p., pres. 1981-82), Internat. Acad. Pathology (councillor 1980-84), Coll. Am. Pathologists (mem. environ. resource com. coun. on pathology practice 1980-81), Am. Soc. for Virology, New England Soc. Pathologists (pres. 1980-81), Mass. Soc. Pathologists (mem. exec. com. 1967), Vt. Med. Soc., Chittenden County Med. Soc. Avocation: horticulture. Office Phone: 802-425-3465.

CRAIGHEAD, OWEN LINDSAY, writer; b. Cross River, NY, Aug. 30, 1934; d. Robert Feuchter Craighead and Alice Wilson; m. Janice Lee Rankin, Jan. 23, 1954; children: Carol Lee Yugovich, Thomas Wilson, Lauren Lindsay Maxwell, William Owen. Owner Craighead Kennels, Cross River, NY; radio talk show host WGHQ, Kingston, NY; author and owner Crunk Publishing, Lubbock, Tex.; editor and founder Tom's E-zine for Am. Awareness. Author: (book) Skydivers Flying with their Pants, 1999, The Way It Is, Is, 2002, One of God's Salesmen, 2003, (advisory pamphlet) Home Buyer, Be Aware, 2003; prodr.(and dir.): (video) Skydiving, The New Frontier, 2003; author: (book) The Lethal Liberal Society in America, 2004. Vol. fireman South Salem Fire Dept., 1952—89, chmn., bd. fire commn., 1984—89; founder Lewisboro Vol. Ambulance Corp., 1977, pres., 1977—79, Lewisboro Lions Club, 1975—76; zone chmn. Saugerities Lions Club, 1992—93; sec. South Plains Lions Club, 2000—01; bulletin editor Lubbock Habitat for Humanity, 1999—2004; rep. candidate Lewisboro Town Bd., 1972; committeeman Lewisboro Rep. Com., 1977—85. Recipient Citizen of the Yr., Lewisboro C. of C., 1984, Lion of the Yr., Lewisboro Lions Club, 1984, Appreciation award, US Army Parachute Team Golden Knights, 1999. Mem.: Lewisboro Vol. Ambulance Corp. (life), South Salem Fire Dept. (life), Lions Internat. (life). Home: 8114 Temple Ave Lubbock TX 79401

CRAIGIE, JAMES R., consumer products and former sports equipment apparel company executive; With General Foods and Kraft divsn. Phillip Morris, exec. v.p., pres. Beverage and Desserts divsn.; pres., CEO Spalding Sports Worldwide, Chicopee, Mass., 1998—2003, Church & Dwight Co., Inc., Princeton, NJ, 2004—07, chmn., pres., CEO, 2007—. Mem. bd. dirs. Graham-Windham, 1997—, World Kitchens, 2003—, Acosta, 2003, Church & Dwight Co., 2004—, GMA, 2004—, Meredith Corp., 2005—. Office: Church & Dwight Co Inc 469 N Harrison St Princeton NJ 08543-5297

CRAIGLOW, JAMES HAWKINS, academic administrator; b. Harrisburg, Pa., Nov. 21, 1941; s. James Hawkins and Jeanette (Sweeney) C.; m. Elizabeth Blatz, Aug. 31, 1964 (div. Nov. 1978); children: Alison, Hilary; m. Shelley Whittier, Aug. 22, 1981; 1 child, Brittany. BA, Lafayette Coll., 1963; MEd, Antioch N.E Grad. Sch., Keene, NH, 1977. Secondary tchr. social studies Walton (N.Y.) Ctrl. Sch., 1963-66; elem. tchr. Transfiguration Day Sch., Freeport, NY, 1966-70; dept. chmn., adminstrv. intern Emma Willard Sch., Troy, NY, 1970-77; assoc. dean Antioch New Eng. Grad. Sch., 1977-86, pres., CEO, 1986—2002; chancellor Antioch U., 2002—. Mgmt. cons.; presenter numerous confs. Contbr. numerous articles to profl. jours. Bd. dirs. Monadnock Children's Mus., Keene, 1987-91, Monadnock United Way, 1989-98, Monadnock Family Svcs., 1989-98, MonadNet Corp., 1994—; chair cmty. goals com. Mayor's Ct.; chair Ashuelot Park Adv. Bd. Mem. Nat. Assn. Coll. and Univ. Bus. Officers, Coun. for Adult and Experimental Edn., Coun. for the Advancement and Support Edn. (vice chair, exec. com. N.H. Campus Compact), Greater Keene C. of C. (bd. dirs. 1988-91). Avocations: antique collecting, reading, baseball.

CRAIK, MARY BERNICE, artist, art gallery owner; b. Louisville, Ky. d. Huse and Grace Wilhite; m. James Craik Jr. (dec.); children: Earl Richard Wilhelm, Jr., Stephen, Juliet. AA, Armstrong Jr. Coll., Savannah, Ga., 1953; BA in Tchg., U. Tex., El Paso, 1960, MA, 1963; PhD, U. Iowa, Iowa City, 1968. Lic. tchr. Tex., 1960. Tchr. Bowie H.S., El Paso, Tex., 1960—62; instr., rschr. U. Tex., El Paso, Tex., 1962—64; instr. U. N.Mex., Silver City, N.Mex., 1965; prof. St. Cloud (Minn.) State U., 1968—83; freelance artist Louisville, 1997—; prin., owner Mary Craik Gallery, Louisville, 2004—. Numerous one-woman shows including most recently, one-woman shows include Makeready Gallery, Montclair, N.J., 2004, Ekstrom Libr., U. Louisville, 2004, Meidinger Tower Lobby Show, Louisvill, 2004, Baer's Gallery, Louisville, Ky., 2005, Portland Mus., 2005, Numerous group exhibitions including most recently, exhibitions include Ky. Mus. Art and Craft, Louisville, 2000—06, Louisville (Ky.) Pub. Libr., 2006, Thrust Theater, Louisville, Ky., 2006. Named to Hall Fame, Shawnee H.S., 1997; recipient Outstanding Svc. to Univ. Women award, Inter Faculty Orgn., 1984, Sex Equity Policy award, Women Educators Nat. Orgn., 1984, Achievement award, Women's Equality Group, 1985, Ednl. Equity award, 1995, Salute to Seven Sisters Star award, The Plaiades Theater Co., 2005, Women Leaders in Edn. Tower award, Presentation Acad., 2000, numerous art awards, 2001—06, Lucy Friebert award, Project Women, U. Louisville; grantee, Ky. Found. Mem.: Louisville (Ky.) Arts Coun., Alliance Am. Quilts, Am. Quilters Soc., Louisville (Ky.) Artisans Guild, Louisville (Ky.) Visual Arts Assn., Louisville (Ky.) Area Fiber and Textile Artists, Artcentric, Nat. Mus. Women in Arts.

CRAIN, ALAN RAU, JR., lawyer, oil industry executive; b. Washington, June 20, 1951; s. Alan Rau Crain and Florence Carol (Clemmer). BS in Mgmt. Engring., Rensselaer Poly. Inst., 1973, MS, 1973; MBA, Syracuse U., JD, 1976. Bar: DC, Md., Tex. 1977, US Dist. Ct. (so. dist. Tex.) 1980, US Ct. Appeals (5th cir.) 1983, US Ct. Internat. Trade 1983, US Supreme Ct. 1983. Assoc. Glaser, Fletcher & Johnson (now Gardner, Carton & Douglas), Washington, 1975—76; counsel to sr. counsel to prin. counsel The El Paso LNG Co., Houston, 1976—81; sr. atty. Pennzoil Co., Houston, 1981—88; v.p., gen. counsel Union Tex. Petroleum Holdings Inc., Houston, 1988—98; adj. prof. internat. law U. Houston Law Sch., Houston, 1989—99; exec. v.p., gen. counsel, sec. Crown Cork Seal & Co., 1999—2000; v.p., gen. counsel Baker Hughes Inc., Houston, 2000—07, sr. v.p., gen. counsel., 2007—. Mem.: State Bar Tex. (chmn. 1989—90, corp. counsel 1996—97), Houston Bar Assn. (chmn. internat. law sect. 1987—88), Tex. Bar Assn., Internat. Bar Assn., Briar Club. Houston. Office: Baker Hughes 3900 Essex Ln Ste 1200 Houston TX 77027-5177 Office Phone: 713-439-8600. Office Fax: 713-439-8699. E-mail: alan.crain@bakerhughes.com.*

CRAIN, JOHN WALTER, historian, educator; b. Amarillo, Tex., July 11, 1944; s. John Clyde and Roma (McDowell) C.; m. Mary Hemingway, Aug. 18, 1973; children: John Matthew, Sarah Hemingway, Margaret Aileen. BA, U. Tex., Austin, 1966; MA, S.W. Tex. State U., 1970; cert. arts adminstrn., Harvard U., 1975; cert. mus. mgmt., U. Calif.-Berkeley, 1979. Dir. Star of the Republic Museum, Washington-on-the-Brazos, Tex., 1971-76, Dallas Hist. Soc., 1976-90; chmn. Dallas County Hist. Commn., 1993-95. Cons. in field. Exec. dir. Summerlee Commn. on Tex. History, 1990-91; v.p., bd. dirs. program History Summerlee Found., Tex., 1990—, pres., 2004-; bd. dirs. Dallas County Hist. Found., Friends of Gov.'s Mansion; mem. adv. bd. Clements Ctr., So. Meth. U. Mem. Tex. State Hist. Assn. (hon., coun. 1994, exec. com., pres.), Conf. of S.W. Founds. (bd. dirs.), Tex. Map Soc. (bd. dirs., pres.), Philos. Soc. Tex. Methodist. Office: 5956 Sherry Ln Ste 610 Dallas TX 75225-8017

CRAIN, MARY ANN, elementary school educator; b. Dallas, Sept. 5, 1951; d. Robert Lee and Mary Ann (T.) Crain. MusB in Edn., Fla. State U., 1973; MusM, Ohio State U., 1974; EdS, U. Ga., 1998. Cert. tchr. T-6, music, early childhood edn., mid. grades, ednl. leadership Ga. First clarinet Vienna Kursalon Orch., Vienna, 1975—77; band dir. Sch. Bd. of Broward County, Ft. Lauderdale, Fla., 1977—78; teller Fla. Coast Bank, Coral Springs, Fla., 1978—79; strings tchr., grades 6-7 DeKalb County Bd. Edn., Decatur, Ga., 1979—82, band tchr., grades 6-7, 1982—86, classroom tchr., grades 4-7, 1986—96, math. specialist, grades 2-5, 1996—2000, early intervention math. and reading specialist, grades 2-5, 2000—02; math. specialist, grades K-5 Bethesda Elem. Sch., Lawrenceville, Ga., 2002—06; math specialist, grades K-5 Benefield Elem. Sch., Lawrenceville, Ga., 2006—. Mem.: Phi Delta Kappa (chpt. v.p. for membership 2005—07, chpt. pres. 2007—). Office: Benefield Elem Sch 970 McElvaney Ln SW Lawrenceville GA 30044 Personal E-mail: corkgrease@msn.com.

CRAIN, RUSSELL JON, lawyer; b. Dallas, June 20, 1973; s. Joe Crain and Beverly Keller; m. Sarah Williams, Sept. 20, 1997; children: Lauren Nicole, William Charles, Katherine Elizabeth, Brandon Allen. BS in Aerospace Engring., U. Tex., 1996; MBA, JD, So. Meth. U., 2004. Cert. engr., Tex. Bd. Profl. Engrs., 1996; bar: Tex. 2004, U.S. Dist. Ct. (no. dist.) Tex. 2004. Rsch. asst. Inst. Advanced Tech., Austin, Tex., 1995—96; engr. Northrop Grumman, Dallas, 1997—2000, Vought Aircraft, Dallas, 2000—04; atty. Baker Botts LLP, Dallas, 2004—. Editor: So. Meth. Law Rev. Counselor vol. income tax assistance program IRS, Dallas, 2004; counselor Crowne Fin. Ministries, Dallas, 2006. Scholar, So. Meth. U., 2000—04, Jour. Air Law and Commerce, 2003, Dallas Lawyer's Aux., 2004; Summerfield G. Roberts scholarship, So. Meth. U., 2000—04. Mem.: Dallas (Tex.) Assn. Young Lawyers, Dallas Ft. Worth (Tex.) Intellectual Property Law Assn., Dallas (Tex.) Bar Assn., Beta Gamma Sigma, Phi Delta Phi, Order of Coif. Achievements include research in hypervelolcity physics; design of human-powered helicopter; development of 3D laser inspection systems; statistical analysis systems for use in manufacturing. Office: Baker Botts LLP 2001 Ross Ave Dallas TX 75201 Office Phone: 214-953-6803.

CRAINE, THOMAS KNOWLTON, not-for-profit developer; b. Utica, NY, Apr. 19, 1942; s. Donald Holmes and Marjorie (Knowlton) C.; m. Susan Lynda Moseley, Dec. 21, 1966; children: Matthew Moseley, Tish Marjorie. BA, U. Rochester, 1964; MEd, SUNY, Buffalo, 1966, EdD, 1972. Dir. architecture and planning SUNY, Buffalo, 1968-72, asst. to pres., 1972-76, clin. assoc. prof., 1975-83, asst. v.p. acad. affairs, 1976-79; exec. v.p., assoc. prof. D'Youville Coll., Buffalo, 1979-83; pres. Loretto Heights Coll., Denver, 1983-88; v.p instl. advancement and planning Iliff Sch. Theology, Denver, 1988-98; pres./CEO YMCA Met. Denver, 1998—2002, pres. emeritus, 2002—03; dir. N. Am. Urban Group of YMCA, 2003—. Interim COO YMCA of USA; evaluator North Cen. Assn. Instns. Higher Edn., 1984—, Assn. Theol. Schs., 1993—; cons. in strategic planning, bd. devel., fund raising. Mailing: YMCA of the USA 101 N Wacker Dr Chicago IL 60606 E-mail: tom.craine@ymca.net.

CRAKES, GARY MICHAEL, economics professor; b. Southington, Conn., July 2, 1953; s. Harry Fremont and Frances Katherine (Koth) C.; m. Deborah Jean MacArthur, Aug. 14, 1976; children: Andrew David, Jeffrey Alan, Timothy Scott. BA in Econs., Ctrl. Conn. State U., 1975; MA in Econs., U. Conn., 1976, PhD in Econs., 1984. Rsch. asst. Health Ctr. U. Conn., Farmington, 1976-79, vis. prof. Health Ctr., Sch. Dental Medicine, 1988, instr. Hartford, 1979-80; asst. prof. So. Conn. State U., New Haven, 1980-85, assoc. prof., 1985-89, prof., 1989—, chmn. dept. econs. and fin., 1991-96. Pres. Maher, Crakes & Assocs., Cheshire, Conn., 1987—; econ. expert witness. Contbr. articles to profl. jours. Mem. State of Conn. Sr. Economist Exam. Com., Hartford, 1987. Richard D. Irwin fellow Irwin Publ. Co., Homewood, Ill., 1983-84, U. Conn. fellow, 1983; recipient Univ. Tchr. of the Yr. award, 1987, Schs. of Bus. Outstanding Tchg. award, 1998; honored for pro bono work on behalf of World Trade Ctr. victim families, Assn. of Trial Lawyers of Am., 2004. Mem. AAUP, Am. Econ. Assn., Ea. Econ. Assn. Nat. Assn. Forensic Econ., Omicron Delta Epsilon. Democrat. Avocations: golf, fishing. Home: 860 Ward Ln Cheshire CT 06410-3363 Office: So Conn State U 501 Crescent St New Haven CT 06515-1330 Home Phone: 203-272-5178. Personal E-mail: gmcrks@aol.com.

CRAMB, CHARLES W., cosmetics executive; BA, Dartmouth Coll., 1968; MBA, U. Chgo., 1970. With The Gillette Co., Boston, 1970—2005, various fin. positions European ops., 1976-81, controller internat. ops. Boston, v.p. fin. and strategic planning Gillette North Atlantic, asst. controller, 1984, v.p. fin., planning and adminstrn. diversified group, 1991, v.p., corp. controller, 1995-97, sr. v.p. fin., CFO, 1997—2005; exec. v.p. fin. and tech., CFO Avon Products Inc., NYC, 2005—. Bd. dirs. Tenneco Automotive Inc., Idenix Pharmaceuticals. Bd. visitors Northeastern U. Sch. Bus., Lawrence Acad., Groton, Mass. Office: Avon Products Inc 1345 Ave of the Americas New York NY 10105*

CRAMER, ALFRED WILLIAM, musician, educator; b. Austin, Tex., Mar. 29, 1965; s. Owen Carver and Rebecca Lowrey Cramer; m. YouYoung Kang, June 7, 1997. BA, Yale U., New Haven, Conn., 1983—87; PhD, U. Pa., Phila., 1988—97. Violinist Colo. Springs Symphony Orch., 1981—83; freelance violinist various orchestras, New Haven, 1986—88, freelance violinist, baroque violinist Phila., 1989—95; instr. Pomona Coll., Claremont, Calif., 1995—97, asst. prof., 1997—2003, assoc. prof., 2003—. Contbr. articles to profl. jours. Commn. on ch. and soc. Claremont United Meth. Ch., Calif., 1998. Recipient Outstanding Publ. award, Soc. Music Theory, 2004. Mem.: Am. Musicological Soc., Soc. Music Theory. D-Liberal. Methodist. Achievements include research in musical implications of literacy, psychology and ideas about sound in the 19th and early 20th centuries. Office: Pomona Coll Music Dept 340 College Ave Claremont CA 91711 Home Phone: 909-399-5159. Business E-Mail: alfred.cramer@pomona.edu.

CRAMER, ALLAN P., lawyer; b. Norwich, Conn., Mar. 8, 1937; s. E.L. and Dorothy N. (Pasnik) Cramer; children: Peter Alden, Alison Jane. BA cum laude, U. Pa., 1958; JD, U. Conn., 1964. Bar: Conn. 1964, US Dist. (Conn.) 1965, US Ct. Appeals (2d cir.) 1965. Atty. HEW, Wash., 1964—65; ptnr. Cramer and Ahern, Westport, Conn., 1966—. Chmn. Westport Dem. Town Com., 1972—73; J.P. Town of Westport, 1973—77; bd. dirs. Westport Pub. Libr., 1975—82; mem. Westport Zoning Bd. Appeals, 1984—88. Mem.: Westport Bar Assn., Conn. Bar Assn. Home: Yankee Hill Rd Westport CT 06880 Office: Cramer & Ahern 38 Post Rd W Westport CT 06880-4207 Office Phone: 203-222-7000.

CRAMER, DALE LEWIS, retired economics professor; b. Dixon, Ill., June 25, 1924; s. Ray C. and Rebecca (Levan) C.; m. Hula Jean Bond, Aug. 30, 1946; children: Becky Cramer McCarn, Craig Alan, Randall Scott. BS, Bradley U., 1949, MA, 1951; PhD, La. State U., 1958. Asst. prof. econs. La. State U., 1953-54, U. Tex.-El Paso, 1955-57, assoc. prof., 1957-58; assoc. prof. econs. U. Ala., 1958-63, prof., 1963-88, prof. emeritus econs., 1988—, head dept., 1968-72, acting head dept., 1981-82. Contbr. articles to profl. jours., books. Served with AUS, 1943-46. Earhart Found. fellow, 1954-55 Mem. Am., So. econ. assns., AAUP, Omicron Delta Epsilon, Beta Gamma Sigma. Home: 103 Riverdale N Tuscaloosa AL 35406-1818

CRAMER, DOUGLAS SCHOOLFIELD, broadcasting executive; b. Louisville, Aug. 22; s. Douglas Schoolfield and Pauline (Compton) C.; m. Joyce Haber, Sept. 25, 1966 (div. 1973); children: Douglas Schoolfield, III, Courtney Sanford. Student, Northwestern U., 1949-50, Sorbonne, Paris, 1951; BA, U. Cin., 1953; MFA, Columbia U., 1954. Prodn. asst. Radio City Music Hall, NYC, 1950-51; with script dept. Metro-Goldwyn-Mayer, 1952; mng. dir. Cin. Playhouse, 1953-54; instr. Carnegie Inst. Tech., 1955-56; TV supr. Procter & Gamble, 1956-59; broadcast supr. Ogilvy, Benson & Mather, 1959-62; v.p. program devel. ABC, 1962-66, 20th Century-Fox-TV, LA, 1966-68; exec. v.p. in charge prodn. Paramount TV, 1968-71; ind. producer, pres. Douglas S. Cramer Co., 1971—; exec. v.p. Aaron Spelling Prodns., 1976-87, vice-chmn., 1988-90. Exec. prodr.: Star Trek, 1968-69, Bridget Loves Bernie, CBS-TV, 1972-73, QB VII, 1973-74, Dawn: Portrait of a Teenage Runaway, NBC-TV, 1976, Danielle Steel's Fine Things, 1990, Kalediscope, 1990, Changes, 1991, Daddy, 1991, Palomino, 1990-91, Secrets, 1991, Heart Beat, 1992, Star, 1993, Message to Nam, 1993, Vanished, 1995, Family Album, 1994, Perfect Stranger, 1994, No Greater Love, 1995, Mixed Blessings, 1995, Zoya, 1995, Family of Cops I & II, CBS-TV, 1995-96, The Ring, 1996, Remembrance, 1996, Full Circle, NBC-TV, 1996, Family of Cops III, 1999; co-exec. prodr.: Love Boat, ABC, 1977-86, Vegas, ABC, 1978-81, Wonder Woman, ABC, 1975-77, CBS, 1977-78, Dynasty, 1981-89, Hotel, 1983-87, Trade Winds, 1993; prodr.: (feature film) Sleeping Together, 1995; author: (plays) Call of Duty, 1953, Love Is A Smoke, 1957, Whose Baby Are You, 1963, Last Great Dish, 1994, Lust For Murder, 1995. Pres. Mus. Contemporary Art, LA, 1990-93, 1st vice-chair, 1993-96: bd. trustees, 1983-96; Internat. Coun. Mus. Modern Art, NYC, 1993—; pres., bd. trustees Douglas S. Cramer Found., 1993—; trustee MOMA NY, 1993—. Named one of Top 200 Collectors, ARTnews Mag., 2004. Mem. Univ. Club of NYC, Beta Theta Pi. Avocation: collector of contemporary art, especially 1960s & 1980s Am. Address: PO Box 713 Lakeville CT 06039-0713 Office: 160 E 72d St New York NY 10021

CRAMER, EDWARD MORTON, lawyer, music company executive; b. NYC, May 27, 1925; s. Israel and Elsie (Neuman) C.; m. Henrietta Pantel, 1973 (div.); children: Evin Joyce, Marjorie Sue, Charles Harris; m. Ethel Metzger, June 13, 1982. BA, Columbia U., 1947; LLB with distinction, Cornell U., NY, 1950; LLM, NYU, 1953; HHD (hon.), Lincoln Coll., Ill., 1982; LHD (hon.), Five Towns Coll., NY, 1998. Bar: N.Y. 1950, U.S. Supreme Ct. 1953. Teaching fellow NYU Sch. Law, 1950-51; assoc. Rosenman & Colin, NYC, 1951-58; ptnr. Cramer & Hoffinger, NYC, 1958-68; pres., CEO Broadcast Music, Inc. (BMI), 1968-86; pvt. practice NYC, 1986—. Treas. Copyright Soc. US, 1963-68, 78-79, bd. editors bull., 1953-63; former mem. Peabody Awards Selection Com.; editor Cornell Law Quar. Trustee Congregation Adas Emuno; former trustee Tony Martell Found., Ford's Theater. Jr. grade lt. USNR, 1943—46. Recipient Spl. award Songwriters Guild Am., 1986, Spl. award Am. Composers Alliance, 1987, Spl. Peabody award, 1991; named Personality of Yr. Nat. Arts Club, 1972; Ed Cramer Day named in his honor, NYC, 1979. Mem.: ABA (copyright com.), Nat. Acad. Popular Music (trustee, bd. dirs. 1969—93, founding mem. Songwriters Hall of Fame, adv. com.), Internat. Confedn. Authoral Socs. (adminstrv. coun.), Broadcast Pioneers (pres. 1984, officer, bd. dirs. 1984—97), Nat. Music Coun. (v.p. 1968—86), Assn. Bar City NY (copyright com.), B'nai B'rith (pres. 1989—90, trustee, officer, pres. music and performing arts unit, Man of Yr. award 1979), Order of Coif. Jewish. Home: 254 Chestnut St Englewood NJ 07631-3134 Office: 110 E 59th St New York NY 10022-1304 Office Phone: 212-421-3350. E-mail: emcramer.law@verizon.net. *I'm not a creatively talented person but working with people who are, has given me a sense that I have shared their accomplishments.*

CRAMER, GAIL LATIMER, economist; b. Walla Walla, Wash., Sept. 27, 1941; s. Lawrence Theodore and Myrtle Pauline (Latimer) C.; m. Marilyn Jean Karlenberg, Aug. 31, 1963; children: Karilee, Bruce. BS, Wash. State U., Pullman, 1963; MS, Mich. State U., East Lansing, 1964; PhD, Oreg. State U., Corvallis, 1968. Asst. prof. Mont. State U., Bozeman, 1967-72, assoc. prof., 1972-76, prof., 1976-86; L.C. Carter prof. U. Ark., Fayetteville, 1987-2000; prof., dept. head La. State U., 2000—. Vis. prof. Harvard U., Cambridge, 1974-75, Winrock Internat., Morrilton, Ark., 1980-81, U. Calif. Berkeley, 1993, Ohio State U., Columbus, 1994; bd. dirs. Internat. Agrl. Mgmt. Assn. Co-author: Grain Marketing, 1993, Agricultural, Economics and Agribusiness, 1997; editor Am. Agrl. Econs. Assn. Jour., 1999-2002. Bd. dirs. ARC, Bozeman, 1982-83, Bozeman Kiwanis Club, 1972-86 (Disting. Pres. 1983); mem. White House Agrl. commn. Washington. Recipient E.G. Nourse award, Am. Inst. Coop., Washington, 1968, Communication award, Am. Agrl. Econs. Assn., 1980, Rice Rsch. award, Tech. Workers, Little Rock, 1992, 1998, SAEA Lifetime

Achievement award, 2002. Fellow: IAMA; mem.: Nat. Assn. Agrl. Econ. Administrators (pres. 2004—), Gamma Sigma Delta Internat. (Dist. Achievement Agrl. award). Avocations: basketball, running, writing. Office: La State U Dept Agrl Econs Baton Rouge LA 70808 Home: 13735 Clarendon Dr Baton Rouge LA 70810-3584 Business E-Mail: gcramer@agcenter.lsu.edu.

CRAMER, HAROLD, lawyer; b. Phila., June 16, 1927; s. Aaron Henry and Blanche (Greenberg) Cramer; m. Geraldine Hassuk Cramer, July 14, 1957; 1 child, Patricia Gail. AB, Temple U., 1948; JD cum laude, U. Pa., 1951. Bar: Pa. 1951. Law clk. to judge Common Pleas Ct. No. 2, 1953; mem. law faculty U. Pa., 1954; assoc. firm Shapiro, Rosenfeld, Stalberg & Cook, 1955-56, ptnr., 1956-67, Meslrov, Gelman, Jaffe & Levin, 1967-74, Mesirov, Gelman, Jaffe & Cramer, Phila., 1974-77, Mesirov, Gelman, Jaffe, Cramer & Jamieson, Phila., 1977-89, of counsel, 1996-2000; ret. ptnr. Schnader, Harrison Segal & Lewis, 2000—; CEO Grad. Health System, Phila., 1989-96. Instr. Nat. Inst. Trial Advocacy, 1970-78; pres. Jewish Exponent, 1987-89, Times., 1987-89; bd. dirs. Penn Nat. Gaming Inc. Co-author: Trial Advocacy, 1968; contbr. articles to profl. jours. Chmn. bd. Eastern Pa. Psychiat. Hosp., 1974-81, Grad. Hosp., 1975-91; trustee Fedn. Jewish Agys., Jewish Publ. Soc., pres., 1996-98, chmn., 1998-2001. 1st lt. U.S. Army, 1951-53. Decorated Bronze Star. Fellow Am. Bar Found., Phila. Coll. Physicians; mem. ABA, Am. Law Inst., Pa. Bar Assn. (ho. of dels. 1966-75, 1978-2006, bd. govs. 1975-78), Phila. Bar Found. (pres. 1988, trustee, pres. elect), Phila. Bar Assn. (bd. govs. 1967-69, chmn. 1969, vice chancellor 1970, chancellor 1972, editor The Shingle 1970-72, medal for extraordinary svc. to the bar 2003), U. Pa. Law Alumni Soc. (bd. mgrs. 1959-64, pres. 1968-70), Order of Coif (past chpt. pres., nat. exec. com. 1973-76), Tau Epsilon Rho (chancellor Phila. grad. chpt. 1960-62), Philmont Country Club, Pyramid Club, Greate Bay Golf Club. Office: Schnader Harrison Segal & Lewis 1600 Market St Ste # 34 Philadelphia PA 19103-7501 Home: 1520 Spruce St Apt 1200 Philadelphia PA 19102-4509 Office Phone: 215-751-2312. Business E-Mail: hcramer@schnader.com.

CRAMER, HOWARD ROSS, geologist, environmental consultant; b. Chgo., Sept. 17, 1925; s. Don William and Esther Natalia (Johnson) C.; m. Ardis V. Lahann, Dec. 15, 1950 (dec. 1980); m. Themis Poulos, Dec. 5, 1982 BS (with honors), U. Ill., 1949, MS, 1950; PhD, Northwestern U., 1954. Registered geologist, Ga. Mem. faculty Franklin and Marshall Coll., 1953-58; asst. prof. geology Emory U., Atlanta, 1958-62, assoc. prof., 1962-76, prof., 1976-87, chmn. dept., 1981-87; cons. geology Ga. State U., Atlanta, 1988-91. Chmn. Ga. Bd. Registration Geologists, 1977-79; mem. Ga. Natural Areas Council, 1968-72. Contbr. articles to profl. jours., chapters to books. Served with AUS, 1943-46, to lt. USAR, 1948-53. Decorated Bronze Star; recipient Holgate prize Northwestern U., 1953, Cert. Commendation, Am. Assn. State and Local History, 1974, Honor award Am. Fedn. Mineralogy and Lapidary Socs., 1986. Fellow Geol. Soc. Am.; mem. Am. Assn. Petroleum Geologists, Nat. Assn. Geology Tchrs. (pres. Southeastern sect. 1971-73), Ga. Acad. Sci. (pres. 1964-65), Lambda Chi Alpha. Lodges: Ahepa. Greek Orthodox. Home: 2047 Deborah Dr NE Atlanta GA 30345-3917 Personal E-mail: hcramer@emory.edu.

CRAMER, JACKIE RAE, information technology executive; b. Ladysmith, South Africa, Aug. 7, 1965; arrived in US, 1972; d. Selwyn David Goodwin and Marita Helena Malan; children: Elizabeth Rae, Jackson Hart, Isabella Malan. BS in MIS, U. Ariz., Tucson, 1991. Analyst NationsBanc Capital Markets, Richmond, Va., 1993—96; pres. MedData Corp., Richmond, 1996—, CEO, 1996—. Home: 826 Ewell Rd Richmond VA 23235 Office: MedData Corp 210 N Robinson St Richmond VA 23220

CRAMER, JAMES DALE, physicist, scientific company executive; b. Canton, Ohio, Aug. 4, 1937; s. Dale and Vera Arlene (Lindower) C.; m. Geraldine M. Bendoski, July 20, 1957; children: Karen Lynn, Eric James. BS, Calif. State U., Fresno, 1960; MS, U. Oreg., 1962; PhD, U. N.Mex., 1969. Mem. tech. staff U. Calif., Los Alamos, 1962-70; v.p. Davis-Smith Corp., San Diego, 1970-73; mem. tech. staff Sci. Applications, Inc., LaJolla, Calif., 1970-73, group v.p. Albuquerque, 1973-80, dir., 1974-80; pres. Sci. & Engring. Assocs., Inc., Albuquerque, 1980—. Cons. in field; pres. Albuquerque Mus. Found., 1981-83. Contbr. articles to profl. publs. Mem. Am. Phys. Soc., IEEE.

CRAMER, JAMES PERRY, management strategist, architectural author, educator; b. Aberdeen, SD, Aug. 7, 1947; s. Harry John and Carol B. (Bickel) C.; m. Corinne M. Aaker, Dec. 21, 1969; children: Ryan James, Austin Michael. BS, No. State U., Aberdeen, 1969; MA, St. Thomas U., St. Paul, 1974; planning cert., U. Minn., Mpls., 1976; bus. mgmt. cert., Wharton Sch. Bus., U. Pa., 1987. Dir., teaching faculty U. Minn., Mpls., 1974-76; dir. St. Louis Park Community Svcs., Minn., 1976-78; exec. v.p. Minn. Soc. Architects, Mpls., 1978-82; pres., chief exec. officer AIA Svc. Corp., Washington, 1982-86, also bd. regents; pres. Greenway Comms. Inc., 1994—. Pres. Am. Archtl. Found. and Octagon Mus., Washington, 1986-89; CEO AIA, Washington, 1989-94; group pub. Architecture Mag., 1982-88, pub. chmn., 1990-94; with Archtl. Tech. Mag., 1983-89; chmn. The Greenway Group; pres. Greenway Comm. Inc., 1994—; adj. prof. U. Hawaii Sch. Arch., 1999—. Pres. Coun. Archtl. Components, Washington, 1980-81; pres. Greenway Civic Assn., McLean, Va., 1986-88; trustee Nat. Bldg. Mus., Washington, 1989-94; chmn. Washington div. United Way Assn., 1992; White House liaison, 1988-95. Recipient Disting. Alumnus award No. State U., 1992, medal of Distinction, U. Minn., 1994; Richard Upjohn fellow; leadership fellow Western Behavioral Scis. Inst., 1998-. Mem. AIA (hon.; chmn. 1981-82, CEO 1989—, Spl. award 1982), Am. Soc. Assn. Execs. (cert. assn. exec.), Mag. Pubs. Am., Octagon Soc. (life hon.), Am. Archtl. Found. (life; pres. 1986-89, regent 1981-82, 86—), Am. Design Coun. (founder, bd. dirs. 1988-95), Soc. Archtl. Historians (bd. dirs. 1994-97), Design Futures Coun. (chmn. 1994—). Avocations: gardening, tennis, antiquarian books, design. Home: 2320 Littlebrooke Dr Dunwoody GA 30338-3156 Office: 30 Technology Pkwy S Ste 200 Norcross GA 30092-2925

CRAMER, JIM (JAMES J. CRAMER), financial information executive; b. Wyndmoor, Pa., Feb. 10, 1955; m. Karen Cramer; 2 children. B in Govt., Harvard U., 1977; JD, Harvard Law Sch., 1984. Reporter Tallahassee (Fla.) Democrat, LA Herald-Examiner, Am. Lawyer, 1979-83; broker Goldman, Sachs & Co., NYC, 1984-87; founder Cramer, Berkowitz, & Co. (formerly Cramer & Co.), NYC, 1987—2000; co-founder thestreet.com, NYC, 1996—, dir., market commentator, adv. to CEO, 2001—. Market's commentator CNBC's Squawk Box; co-host Am. Now; co-founder Smart-Money mag.; former co-host, Kudlow & Cramer CNBC, host, Mad Money, 2005—; columnist NY Mag.; radio show host WOR. Contbr. to NY mag.; author: Confessions of a Street Addict, 2002, You Got Screwed! Why Wall Street Tanked and How You Can Prosper, 2002, Jim Cramer's Real Money: Sane Investing in an Insane World, 2005; co-author (with Cliff Mason): Mad Money: Watch TV, Get Rich, 2006. Office: thestreet.com 14 Wall St 15th Fl New York NY 10005 Business E-Mail: jjcletters@thestreet.com.*

CRAMER, JOHN MCNAIGHT, lawyer; b. Lewistown, Pa., Sept. 23, 1941; s. John Mumma and Elaine Elizabeth (McNaight) C.; m. Susan Oakman, Nov. 26, 1966 (div. Mar. 1989); children: Natalie, Daniel, Melinda; m. Kay Stephenson, Apr. 8, 1989; children: Julia, Maria. AB, Juniata Coll., 1963; LLB, Harvard Law Sch., 1966. Bar: Pa. 1968. Law clk. U.S. Dist. Ct. So. Dist. N.Y., 1966-67; assoc. Reed Smith Shaw & McClay, Pitts., 1967-76, ptnr., 1976—2002, of counsel, 2002. Advocacy fellow Dickinson Sch. Law, Pa. State U., Carlisle, 1987-2002. Mem. editl. staff Harvard Law Rev. Trustee Juniata Coll., Huntingdon, Pa., 1981—, sec., 1983—96, vice chair, 1996—97, chair, 1997—2001; bd. dirs. Ctrl. Pa. Food Bank, 1996—2001. Democrat. Home: Box 17 205 Mill St New Buffalo PA 17069 E-mail: crmfrm@earthlink.net.

CRAMER, OWEN CARVER, classics educator, department chairman; b. Tampa, Fla., Dec. 1, 1941; s. Maurice Browning and Alice (Carver) C.; m. Rebecca Jane Lowrey, June 23, 1962; children: Alfred, Thomas, Ethan, Benjamin AB, Oberlin Coll., 1962; PhD, U. Tex., 1973. Spl. instr. U. Tex., Austin, 1964-65; instr. in classics Colo. Coll., Colorado Springs, 1965-69, asst. prof. classics, 1969-75, assoc. prof. classics, 1975-84, M.C. Gile prof. classics, 1984—, dir. comparative lit., 1993—2002, Bemis humanities chair, 2006—. Cons. humanist Colo. Humanities Program, Denver, 1982-83; vis. prof. U. Chgo., 1987-88; reader Advanced Placement Latin Exam., 1995-99; summer faculty Wyo. Humanities Coun. program, 2004. Editorial asst. Arion, 1964-65; contbr. papers, articles on Greek lang. and lit. to profl. publs., 1974—; contbr. classical music revs. to Colorado Springs Sun, 1984-86. Chorus tenor Colo. Opera Festival, Colorado Springs, 1976-82; mem. El Paso County Dem. Ctrl. Com., Colo., 1968-88; ordained elder Presbyn. Ch., 1992; mem. alumni coun. Oberlin Coll., 1992-02, 2006-. Recipient Boettcher Faculty Excellence award Colo. Coll., 2005; Hon. Woodrow Wilson fellow, 1962, fellow U. Tex., Austin, 1962-64. Mem. Am. Philol. Assn. (campus adv. svc. 1989, chmn. com. on smaller depts. 1979-80), Am. Comparative Lit. Assn., Classical Assn. Middle West and South, Modern Greek Studies Assn., Colo. Classics Assn., Round Table (Colorado Springs) Club., Phi Beta Kappa. Home: 747 E Uintah St Colorado Springs CO 80903-2546 Office: Colo Coll Dept Classics Colorado Springs CO 80903 Home Phone: 719-634-3392; Office Phone: 719-389-6443. Business E-Mail: ocramer@coloradocollege.edu.

CRAMER, PHEBE, psychologist; b. San Francisco, Dec. 30, 1935; children: Mara, Julia. BA, U. Calif., Berkeley, 1957; PhD, NYU, 1962. Clin. psychologist Malmonides Hosp., Bklyn., 1962-63; asst. prof. Psychology Barnard Coll., NYC, 1963-65; vis. asst. prof. Psychology U. Calif., Berkeley, 1965-70; assoc. prof. Psychology Williams Coll., Williamstown, Mass., 1970-73, prof. Psychology, 1973—. Pvt. practice in clin. psychology, Williamstown, 1970—; chief psychologist Berkshire Mental Health Ctr., Pittsfield, Mass., 1978-86. Author: Word Association, 1968, Understanding Intellectual Development, 1972, The Development of Defense Mechanisms, 1991, Story-telling, Narrative, and the Thematic Apperception Test, 1996, Protecting the Self, 2006; mem. editl. bd. Jour. of Personality, 1987-96, assoc. editor, 1991-96; mem. editl. bd. Jour. of Personality Assessment, 1989—, European Jour. Personality, 2000—, Jour. Rsch. Personality, 2003—. Judge U.S. Figure Skating Assn., 1989—. Mem.: APA, Soc. Personality and Social Psychology, Soc. for Personality Assessment. Office: Williams Coll Dept Psychology Bronfman Sci Ctr Williamstown MA 01267 Home: 20 Forest Rd Williamstown MA 01267-2029 Office Phone: 413-597-2463. Business E-Mail: phebe.cramer@williams.edu.

CRAMER, ROBERT E., JR., (BUD CRAMER), congressman, lawyer; b. Huntsville, Ala., Aug. 22, 1947; 1 child, Hollan. BA in English, U. Ala., 1969, JD, 1972. Former prof. U. Ala. Sch. of Law; asst. dist. atty. Madison County, Ala., 1973—75, dist. atty., 1981—91; mem. U.S. Congress from 5th Ala. dist., 1991—. Mem. appropriations com. U.S. Ho. of Reps., subcom. on HUD, VA and IA, on the Interior, NASA. Mem. Nat. Legal Resource Cr. for Child Advocacy & Protection; co-founder Nat. Children's Advocacy Ctr.; adv. bd. mem. Nat. Ctr. for Missing and Exploited Children. Served in US Army, 1972, served in USAR, 1976—78. Mem.: ABA, Ala. Dist. Atty. Assn. Democrat. Methodist. Office: US Ho of Reps 2368 Rayburn Ho Office Bldg Washington DC 20510-0105 Office Phone: 202-225-4801. Office Fax: 202-225-4392.*

CRAMER, ROBERT VERN, retired college administrator, consultant; b. Fayetteville, Ark., Jan. 6, 1933; s. Paul and Fern (Way); m. M. Joan Sullivan, Sept. 6, 1953; children: Paula Jo, Melinda Kay, John Aaron. BA, Monmouth Coll., Ill., 1954; MA, U. Conn., 1964, PhD, 1965; LHD (hon.), Ill. Coll., 1985, Carroll Coll., 1988. Tchr. Monmouth Jr. HS, 1954—56; prin. Vandalia Elem. Sch., Ill., 1956—57; dir. publicity and publs. Monmouth Coll., 1957—59; dir. publs. and pub. info., also instr. journalism Millikin U., Decatur, Ill., 1959—61; v.p. Old Sturbridge Village, Mass., 1961—64; asst. dean, instr. Sch. Edn., U. Conn., 1964—65; v.p. Hanover Coll., Ind., 1965-68; pres. Northland Coll., Ashland, Wis., 1968—71, Carroll Coll., Waukesha, Wis., 1971—88, pres. emeritus, 1988—. Pres. Brunswick Pub. Charitable Found., Inc., Skokie, Ill., 1985-88; v.p. Wis. Found. Ind. Colls., 1969-71, pres., 1971-73, treas., 1973-76, sec., 1979-83; commr. Commn. Instns. Higher Edn., North Central Assn., 1972-76; v.p. Wis. Assn. Ind. Colls. and Univs., 1973-75, pres., 1985-87; bd. dirs. Payco Am. Corp., 1988-91; Council Ind. Colls, sec. 1979-81, vice chmn., 1981-83, chmn. 1983-85. Contbr. articles to profl. jours. Bd. dirs. Waukesha United Way, 1975-78, Waukesha Symphony, 1972-76, Waukesha Meml. Hosp., 1973-82, Lad Lake Residential Treatment Ctr. for Emotionally Disturbed Boys, 1974-78, Wis. Coun. on Econ. Edn., 1976-79; bd. dirs. Milw. chpt. ARC, 1973-81, vice chmn., 1978-80; mem. nexus com. Presbyn. Coll. Union, 1973-83; bd. dirs. Am. Coun. Edn., 1985-88; sec. Presbyn. Coll. Union, 1977-79, pres., 1979-81; trustee Columbia Coll. of Nursing, 1983-88, Hist. Preservation Soc. Durham, 1993-94; active Durham County Nursing Home Adv. Com., 1991-95, commr. Durham Hist. Preservation Com., 1992-97, Glaxo Welcome Instnl. Animal Care and Use Com., 1992-99. Recipient Outstanding Young Alumnus award Monmouth Coll., 1968, Disting. Alumnus award, 1980; named Ky. Col., 1975. Mem. Wis. Assn. Higher Edn. (exec. com., sec. 1972-73, pres. 1973-74), Delta Sigma Nu, Phi Delta Kappa, Theta Chi. E-mail: rvc-mjc@webtv.net.

CRAMER, STEVEN CRAIG, neurologist, educator; BA in Neurology, U. Calif., Bekeley, 1983; MD, U. So. Calif. Sch. Medicine, LA, Calif., 1988; Master's in Med. Scis., Harvard Med. Sch., Boston, 1997. Resident, internal medicine UCLA Ctr. for Health Scis., 1988—91; resident, neurology Mass. Gen. Hosp., 1992—95, fellow, cerebrovascular disease, 1995—97; staff neurologist Seattle VA, Seattle, 1997—98; asst. prof., neurology U. Wash., Seattle, 1997—2002, affiliate asst. prof., neurology, 2002—; asst. prof., neurology U. Calif., Irvine, 2002—05, dir., neuroimaging core, Gen. Clin. Rsch. Ctr., 2003—, asst. prof., anatomy and neurobiology, 2003—05, assoc. clin. dir., Stem Cell Rsch. Ctr., 2006—, assoc. prof., neurology, anatomy & neurobiology, 2005—; co-dir., clin. stroke svc. U. Calif. Med. Ctr., Irvine, 2003—. Mem.: Soc. for the Neural Control of Movement, Am. Heart Assn. Stoke Coun., Nat. Stroke Assn., Am. Acad. Neurology, Organization for Human Brain Mapping. Office: U Calif Irvine Med Ctr 101 The City Dr S Bldg 53 Rm 203 Orange CA 92868-4280 Office Phone: 714-456-6876. Office Fax: 714-456-8805. Business E-Mail: scramer@uci.edi.*

CRAMER, WILLIAM ANTHONY, biochemistry and biophysics researcher, educator; b. NYC, June 11, 1938; s. Robert and Sylvia (Blumstein) C.; m. Hanni Aebersold, Sept. 11, 1964; children: Rebecca, Jean-Marc, Gabrielle, Nicholas. BS, MIT, 1959; MS, U. Chgo., 1960, PhD, 1965. NSF post doctoral fellow U. Calif., San Diego, 1965-67, rsch. assoc., 1967-68; asst. prof. dept. biol. scis. Purdue U., West Lafayette, Ind., 1968-73, assoc. prof., 1973-78, prof., 1978—, assoc. head dept., 1984-86, Henry Koffler prof. biol. scis. West Lafayette, Ind., 1995-2001, Henry Koffler Disting. prof. biol. scis., 2001—. Head panel predoctoral fellowships in biophysics and biochemistry NSF, 1979, mem. molecular biology panel, 1980-82, mem. cellular biochemistry panel, 1989-91; mem. panel competitive grants USDA, 1983-84; chmn. Gordon Confs. on Photosynthesis, 1990, Bioenergetics, 2001; mem. phys. biochemistry study sect. NIH, 1991-95. Author textbook on bioenergetics; editor: Archives Biochemistry and Biophysics, 1979—91, Biochim. Biophys. Acta, 1983—2003, Photosynthesis Rsch., 1989—98, Jour. Bioenergetics Biomembranes, 1991—, Biophys. Jour., 1999—2005, Biochem. Jour., 2001—04, Jour. Biol. Chemistry, 2002—; contbr. articles to profl. jours. Recipient Rsch. Career Devel. award, NIH, 1970—75, Charles F. Kettering award, Am. Soc. Plant Physiologists, 1996, H.N. McCoy award for sci. achievement, Purdue U., 1988; sr. EMBO fellow, U. Amsterdam, 1974—75, Alexander von Humboldt fellow, Max-Planck Inst., Frankfurt, 1992, John Simon Guggenheim fellow, 1992—93. Fellow: Biophys. Soc. (chmn. bioenergetics subgroup 1989—92, program chair 40th ann. meeting 1996, coun. 1997—2001, exec. coun. 1999—2001, pub. policy com. 1999—); mem.: AAAS, Am. Soc. Biochemistry and Molecular Biology. Office: Purdue U Dept Biol Sci Lilly Hall Life Scis 915 W State St West Lafayette IN 47907 Business E-Mail: waclab@purdue.edu.

CRAMES, MICHAEL J., lawyer; b. NYC, Apr. 20, 1935; s. Paul and Regina (Haicken) C.; m. Elinor Weintraub, July 14, 1957; children: Michele Zenkel, Stefanie Solomon, Leslie Rainer. BA, Amherst Coll., 1956; JD, NYU, 1961. Ptnr. Levin & Weintraub, Crames & Edelman, NYC, 1961-90, Kaye Scholer LLP, NYC, 1991—2005, mng. ptnr., 1993—97, chmn. exec. com., 1993—97; with Peter J. Solomon Co., NYC. Spkr. at seminars in field. Author: Fundamentals of Bankruptcy and Corporate Reorganization, 1998; contbr. articles to profl. jours. Recipient Judge Learned Hand Human Rels. award Am. Jewish Com., 1992; named Benjamin Wientraub lectr. Hofstra U. Sch. Law, 1985; honoree Bankruptcy and Reorgn. Group Lawyers Divsn. UJA Fedn., 1993. Mem. Assn. of Bar of City of NY (sec. 1969-71, chmn. bankruptcy and corp. reorgn. com. 1972-75), Fed. Bar Coun., Nat. Bankruptcy Conf. (exec. com. 1981-83), NY County Lawyers Assn., NY State Bar Assn., Westchester County Bar Assn., Am. Coll. Bankruptcy. Avocations: golf, bicycle riding, hiking, reading. Office: Peter J Solomon Co 520 Madison Ave New York NY 10022-3506 Office Phone: 212-508-1626. Business E-Mail: mcrames@pjsolomon.com.

CRAMP, JOHN FRANKLIN, retired lawyer; b. Ridley Park, Pa., Mar. 14, 1923; s. Alfred Charles and Mildred Frances (Cummins) C.; m. Suzanne Surrick, Sept. 15, 1951 (div.); children: John F., Catherine T., David B., Andrew H., Daniel E.; m. Gloria C. Maddox, Jan. 29, 1972. BS, Pa. Mil. Coll. (now Widener U.), 1943; LLB, Dickinson Sch. Law, 1948. Bar: Pa. 1949, US Dist. Ct. (ea. dist.) Pa. 1951, US Ct. Appeals (3d cir.) 1951. Assoc. Hodge, Hodge & Balderston, Chester, Pa., 1949-53; ptnr. Hodge, Hodge & Cramp, Media, Pa., 1953—56; sr. ptnr. Cramp & D'Iorio, 1956—70; pres. Cramp, D'Iorio, McConchie & Forbes, P.C., 1970—90; founding counsel Beatty, Cramp, Kauffman & Lincke, 1996—2003; ret., 2003. Gen. counsel, bd. dirs. Bryn Mawr Group (name now Dixon Ticonderoga Inc.), 1965-79, pres. 1973-74; gen. counsel Widener U., 1968-91; bd. dirs. Phila. Subtransp. Co. Trustee Williamson Sch., 1968-91; bd. dirs., chmn. Crozer Chester Med. Ctr.; Elwyn Inst.; bd. dirs. Chester Hosp., Crozer-Keystone Health System; chmn. bd. dirs. Am. Inst. Mental Studies, Jerusalem Elwyn, Can. Friends of Elwyn; Rep. county chmn., 1957-61; del. Rep. Nat. Conv., 1960; state chmn. Citizens for Scranton, 1962. Mem. ABA, Del. County Bar Assn., Pa. Bar Assn., Internat. Soc. Barristers, Nat. Assn. Coll. and Univ. Attys., Def. Rsch. Inst., Vasari Country Club, Masons. Episcopalian.

CRAMPON, JEAN ELAINE, librarian; m. William Jacques Crampon, Aug. 5, 1972; 1 child, Michael William. BA, San Diego State U., 1969; MS in LS, U. N.C., 1971. Libr. San Diego Pub. Libr., 1971—73, So. Ill. U. Sch. Medicine, Springfield, 1974-87, instr., 1974-81, asst. prof., 1981-87; head libr. Hancock Libr. Biology and Oceanography, U. So. Calif., LA, 1987-98, curator Hancock Meml. Mus., 1997-98, Sci. and Engring. Team Libr., 1998—. Author: Station Logs of the Velero IV, 2005; contbr. articles to profl. jours. Elder Presbyn. Ch. USA, Long Beach, Calif., 1994-98, deacon, 2002-04. Recipient cert. of recognition Midwest Health Sci. Libr. Network, Chgo., 1981, 82. Mem. PEO, Spl. Librs. Assn. (editor, treas. biol. and life scis. divsn. 1983-98, sect. chmn. info. tech. divsn. 1998-99, v.p., pres., treas., exec. or adv. bds. So. Calif. chpt. 1993-95, 98-2001, 2003—04, mem. chair leadership and mgmt. divsn. 2004-07, Billie Connor award, Southern Calif. Chpt., 2007), Internat. Assn. Aquatic and Marine Sci. Librs. and Info. (resource sharing com. 1999-2001, mentoring com. 2002-04). Office: U So Calif Sci and Engring Libr 910 Bloom Walk SSL303-A Los Angeles CA 90089-0481 Office Phone: 213-740-4421. Office Fax: 213-821-4214. Business E-Mail: crampon@usc.edu.

CRAMPTON, STUART JESSUP BIGELOW, physicist, researcher; b. NYC, Nov. 3, 1936; s. Henry Edward and Harriet Elizabeth (Jessup) Crampton; m. Susan Harris, Dec. 29, 1961; children: David Stuart Jessup, Rebecca Lynn, Alexandra Lee. BA, Williams Coll., 1958; BA with honors, Worcester Coll., Oxford U., Eng., 1960, MA, 1965; PhD, Harvard U., 1964. NSF postdoctoral fellow Harvard U., 1964-65; mem. faculty Williams Coll., 1965—, prof. physics, 1975—, Barclay Jermain prof. natural philosophy, 1979—, chmn. dept. physics, 1970-77, chmn. dept. physics and astronomy, 1977-80; dir. Bronfman Sci. Ctr., 1988-90. Vis. prof. U. Paris VI, 1982—83; cons. Hughes Rsch. Labs., Sherman Fairchild Sci. Equipment Program; vice chair Coun. Undergrad. Rsch., 1988—89, chair, 1989—90, pres., 1990—91; mem. bd. assessment physics lab. Nat. Inst. Stds. and Tech., 1994—99; provost Williams Coll., 1995—99; bd. dirs. Rsch. Corp., chmn. bd. dirs. Author: paper in field. Recipient NSF Faculty Profl. Devel. award, 1977—78; grantee, Nat. Bur. Stds., NSF, Office Naval Rsch., NASA; Alfred P. Sloan Rsch. fellow, 1967—69, NATO Sr. Postdoctoral Rsch. fellow, 1975. Fellow: Am. Phys. Soc. (councilor-at-large 1989—92, award for rsch. undergrad. instn. 1989); mem.: Sigma Xi, Sigma Phi. Episcopalian. Home: 54 Grandview Dr Williamstown MA 01267-2528 Office: Williams Coll Bronfman Sci Ctr 18 Hoxsey St Williamstown MA 01267-2518 Home Phone: 413-458-8558; Office Phone: 413-597-2247. Business E-Mail: scrampto@williams.edu.

CRAMTON, ROGER CONANT, lawyer, educator; b. Pittsfield, Mass., May 18, 1929; s. Edward Allen and Dorothy Stewart (Conant) C.; m. Harriet Cutter Haseltine, June 29, 1952; children: Ann, Charles, Peter, Cutter. AB, Harvard U., 1950; JD, U. Chgo., 1955; LLD, Nova U., 1980; MA (hon.), Oxford U., 1987. Bar: Vt. 1956, Mich. 1964, N.Y. State 1979. Law clk. to Hon. S.R. Waterman U.S. Ct. of Appeals (2d cir.), 1955-56; law clk. to assoc. justice Harold H. Burton U.S. Supreme Ct., 1956-57; asst. prof. U. Chgo., 1957-61; assoc. prof. U. Mich. Law Sch., 1961-64, prof., 1964-70; chmn. Adminstrv. Conf. of U.S., 1970-72; asst. atty. gen. Justice Dept., 1972-73; dean Cornell U. Law Sch., Ithaca, NY, 1973-80, Stevens prof., 1982—2002, Stevens prof. emeritus, 2002—. Mem. U.S. Commn. on Revision Fed. Ct. Appellate Sys., 1973-75; bd. dirs. U.S. Legal Svcs. Corp., 1975-79, chmn. bd., 1975-78; mem. U.S. Commn. on Jud. Discipline and Removal, 1991-93. Co-author: Conflict of Laws, 5th rev. edition, 1993, Law and Ethics of Lawyering, 4th rev. edit., 2005, Reforming the Court - Term Limits for Supreme Court Justices, 2006; editor Jour. Legal Edn., 1981-87; contbr. articles to profl. jours. Guggenheim fellow, 1987-88; recipient Rsch. award Am. Bar Found., 2000. Mem. ABA, Am. Law Inst. (council mem.), Assn. Am. Law Schs. (pres. 1985), Am. Acad. Arts and Scis., NY State Bar Assn. (Ethics award), Order of Coif, Phi Beta Kappa. Congregationalist. Office: Cornell Law Sch Myron Taylor Hall Ithaca NY 14853-4901 Home: 475 Savage Farm DR Ithaca NY 14850-6508 Business E-Mail: rcc10@cornell.edu.

CRANCH, LAURENCE E., lawyer, investment company executive; BA cum laude, Amherst Coll.; JD cum laude, Univ. Pa. Atty., mng. ptnr. Rogers & Wells, 1973—99; ptnr. Clifford Chance, 1999—2004; exec. v.p., gen.

counsel Alliance Capital Mgmt., NYC, 2004—. Mem.: Internat. Bar Assn., Assn. Bar City of NY, Order of the Coif. Office: Alliance Capital Management 1345 Ave of the Americas New York NY 10105

CRANDALL, ALBERT EARL, retail executive, accountant, entrepreneur; b. Balt., May 21, 1943; s. Albert Earl and Ethel (Geren) C.; m. Carolyn Jane Carlock, Aug. 31, 1968; children: Ian Kelby, Jeb Stafford. BS, Am. U., 1969. Diplomate Am. Bd. Forensic Acctg.; CPA, Md. Sr. acct. Main Lafrentz & Co., Washington, 1968-73; controller King Pontiac Co., Gaithersburg, Md., 1973-78; controller, treas. Capitol Cadillac, Washington, 1980; owner, mgr. Crandall Assocs., Gaithersburg, 1981-85; owner, operator Warehouse Beer & Wine Co., Gaithersburg, 1981-89; pres. Field Grade Products Inc., Gaithersburg, 1982-85, The Crandall Group, Inc., 1987-90; v.p. ops. King Pontiac-GMC, Inc., Gaithersburg, Md., 1990-92; pres. Pockets of Frederick, Inc., 1992-96, Pockets, Inc., 1992-96, Capitol Easyriders, 1995-98. Chmn. bd. Office Boy Inc.; mem. faculty Montgomery Coll., 1982; CFO Gentry & Assocs., 1999-. Treas., Greater Laytonsville Civic Assn., 1982. Served with U.S. Army, 1961-64. Mem. AICPAs, NRA, Am. Coll. Forensic Examiners, Heritage Found., Izaak Walton League, Rotary (Paul Harris fellow). Republican. Baptist.

CRANDALL, BLANE MITCHELL, obstetrician, gynecologist; b. Atlanta, Ga., Dec. 4, 1970; s. Blane Milton and Doshie Ruth Crandall; m. Montese Marie Miller, June 12, 1993; children: Greyson Marie, Scarlett Cay. MD, U. Of South Fla., 1993—98. Diplomate Am. Bd. Ob-Gyn. Ob-gyn. resident U. Chgo., 1998—2000, Northshore U., 2000—02; pvt. practice Blane M. Crandall, MD, Clinton, Okla., 2002—06, Naples, Fla., 2006—. Featured spkr. Symposium On Metal Ions In Biology And Medicine, Barcelona, 1996; vis. rschr. Royal Free Hosp., London, 1996; adj. prof. Southwestern Okla. State U., 2003—. Contbr. articles to profl. jours. Active mem. Noon Lions Club, Clinton, Okla., 2002—06; vol. dr. Clinton Free Clinic, Okla., 2002—06; bd. mem. Sunnyside Therapeutic Riding Ctr., Clinton, Okla., 2002—06. Recipient Most Humanistic Resident, U. Of Chgo. Hospitals, 1999, Outstanding Tchg. award, 2000, Humanism And Excellence In Tchg. award, Arnold P. Gold Found., 2000, Physician's Recognition award, AMA, 2001, 2002, 2003. Fellow: Am. Coll. Of Obstetricians And Gynecologists; mem.: AMA, Fla. State Med. Assn. Collier County Med. Soc., Soc. Of Med. Educators, Am. Assn. Of Gynecologic Laparoscopists, Nat. Assn. Of Doctors. Avocations: travel, golf, boating. Office: 1660 Med Blvd St 101 Naples FL 34110-1415

CRANDALL, ELIZABETH WALBERT, retired home economics professor; b. Columbus, Kans., Jan. 18, 1914; d. Stanley Giltner and Edna Maude (Daniel) Walbert; m. Robert Dalton Crandall, Aug. 3, 1946 (dec. Sept. 1999). BS, Kans. State Coll., 1935, MS, 1939; EdD, Boston U., 1962. Tchr. Cedar Point (Kans.) H.S., 1935-36, Ellsworth (Kans.) H.S., 1936-38; instr., asst. prof. home econs. Mich. State Coll., East Lansing, 1939-46; instr., asst. prof., assoc. prof. home econs. R.I. State Coll., Kingston, 1946-62; prof. home econs., dept. chair U. R.I., Kingston, 1962-73, acting dean, Coll. Home Econs., 1973-76, dean, Coll. Home Econs., 1976-77, prof. emerita, 1977—. Vice chair R.I. Consumer Adv. Com., Office Price Stabilization, Providence, 1952-53; mem. adv. com. R.I. Office Vocat. Rehab., Providence, 1962-64, Cmty. Homemaker Svcs. R.I., Inc., Providence, 1965-79; mem. various coms., U. R.I., 1961-77. Co-author (coll. textbooks): Home Management in Theory and Practice, 1946, Management for Modern Families, 1st edit., 1954, 2d edit., 1963, 3d edit., 1973, 4th edit., 1980. Mem. So. Poverty Law Ctr., Montgomery, Ala., 1974—, Equal Rights for Maine Coalition, Augusta, 1984; citizen lobbyist, Maine Women's Lobby and Women's Devel. Inst., Hallowell, 1989—; legis. chair Maine Home Econs. Assn., rep. Women's Legis. Agenda Coalition, Augusta, 1984-93, rep. Maine Choice Coalition, Augusta, 1990-93; mem. campaign com. for Hon. Sophia Pfeiffer's election to Maine Ho. of Reps., 1990; adv. com. Bath-Brunswick Child Care Svcs., Inc., 1994-95; various other civic activities. Recipient Presdl. award for courage, svc. and integrity, Maine Lesbian/Gay Polit. Alliance, Augusta, 1987; recipient Maine Women's Hall of Fame award Maine Fedn. Bus. & Profl. Women's Clubs and U. Maine, 1996. Mem. AAUW (hon. life mem.; pres. R.I. divsn. 1977-79, rep. New England Energy Task Force 1978-79, 79-81, mem. exec. bd. 1982-90, 92-95, chair legis. program 1984-86, chair women's issues com. 1986-88, chair legal advocacy fund 1992-95; Elizabeth "Liz" W. Crandall Rsch. & Projects Endowment, AAUW of Maine, 1996), LWV (exec. bd. Brunswick, Maine league 1981-93, pres. 1983-85), NOW, Family Planning Assn. Maine, Phi Kappa Phi, Phi Upsilon Omicron, Omicron Nu (nat. editor 1953-55, nat. pres. 1957-59). Democrat. Episcopalian. Avocations: philanthropy, feminism, physical fitness, social action, wildflowers.

CRANDALL, IRA CARLTON, electrical engineer, consultant; b. South Amboy, NJ, Oct. 30, 1931; s. Carlton Francis and Claire Elizabeth (Harned) C.; m. Jane Leigh Ford, Jan. 29, 1954; children— Elizabeth Anne, Amy Leigh, Matthew Garrett BS in Radio Engring., Ind. Inst. Tech., 1954, BS in Elec. Engring., 1958; BS in Electronics Engring., U.S. Naval Postgrad. Sch., 1962; PhD, U. Sussex, 1964; MA, Piedmont U., 1967, DSc (hon.), 1968; LLB, Blackstone Sch. Law, 1970; DLitt, St. Matthew U., 1970; EdD, Mt. Sinai U., 1972; Assoc. Bus., LaSalle U., 1975, B in Computer Sci., 1986; D. Internat. Rels., Australian Inst. for Coordinated Rsch., 1991. Tchr. Madison Twp. Pub. Schs., NJ, 1954-55; commd. ensign U.S. Navy, 1955, advanced through grades to lt. comdr., 1965, released to inactive duty, 1972; engring. cons. Concord, Calif., 1972—. Pres. 7C's Enterprises, Concord, 1972-96; v.p. Dickinson Enterprises, Concord, 1972-77, Williamson Engring., Inc., Walnut Creek, Calif., 1974-82; pres., chmn. bd. I.C. Crandall and Assocs., Inc., Concord and Westminster, Calif., Tigard, Oreg., 1976-82; pres. Internat. Rsch. Assocs., Concord, 1982-98; v.p. Gayner Engring. Inc., San Francisco, 1982-92; sr. engr. Ajmani Assoc., San Francisco, 1992-99, Syska and Hennesy, L.A., 1999-02. Vice pres. PTA, Concord, 1969; tribal organizer Mt. Diablo YMCA Indian Guide Program, 1971-74; pres. Mt. Diablo Unified Schs. Interested Citizens. Decorated Vietnamese Cross of Valor. Fellow Am. Coll. Engrs.; mem. IEEE, U.S. Naval Inst. Am. Naval Assn., Assn. Elec. Engrs., Am. Inst. Tech. Mgmt. (sr.), Soc. Am. Mil. Engrs., Nat. Model Ry. Assn., Assn. Old Crows, Concord Homeowners Assn., Concord Chamber Singers, Concord Blue Devils, Scottish-Am. Military Soc., Am. Legion, Order of the Knights (knight), Templar of Jerusalem, Lofsensic Ursinius Order (knight commdr. 1991—), Pi Upsilon Eta, Gamma Chi Epsilon, Alpha Gamma Upsilon Republican. Methodist (adminstrv. bd. ch. 1971-76). Clubs: Navy League, Century. Lodge: Optimists (pres.) Home and Office: 5754 Pepperridge Pl Concord CA 94521-4821 Personal E-mail: crcandall@yahoo.com.

CRANDALL, JOHN ALFRED, corporation official; s. John Wilson and Dorothea Lucas Crandall. Student, Valley Forge Mil. Acad., Wayne, Pa., U. Pitts. Reporter Syandard & Poors Corp., NYC. Active Human Rights Campaign, Washington. With US Army, 1956—58. Decorated Good Conduct medal US Army. Mem.: Order of the Founders and Patriots of Am. (assoc.), Magna Charta Barons (life; Somerset chpt.), Mensa (life). Democrat. Episcopalian.

CRANDALL, JOHN LYNN, retired insurance company executive, consultant; b. Chgo., Apr. 17, 1927; s. Paul Bertram and Olga (Bleich) C.; m. Irene Anze Ruenne, Dec. 26, 1973; children by previous marriage: Deborah Crandall Kulchar, Jeffrey, Lynne Crandall Blais; stepchildren: George Ruenne, Helgi Ruenne. BS in Fire Protection Engring., Ill. Inst. Tech., 1951. CPCU; cert. in gen. ins. Highly protected risk insp. FIA, Chgo., 1951-53, asst. engr. supr., 1953-56, engring. supr., 1956-59, underwriting supr., spl. agt., 1959-65; HPR engr., underwriter Kemper Group, Chgo., 1965-67, HPR sales specialist, 1967-71; asst. to dir. underwriting Protection Mut. Ins. Co., Park Ridge, Ill., 1971-73, v.p. underwriting, 1973-78, v.p., dir. underwriting, 1978-90; cons. Served with USN, 1945-46. Mem. Soc. Fire Protection Engrs. (charter), Soc. CPCU (chpt. pres. 1980-81, nat. dir. 1987-90, ethics com. 1990-97, sr. resource com. 1997-2000, chmn. sr. rsch. com. 2000-02, v.p. ch. coun. 1992-95, mem. sr. rsch. com. 2002—). Home: 811 Young St Galena IL 61036-1414 also: 9216 Spatterdock Ct Lakeland FL 33810-2344 Personal E-mail: jlc913@sbcglobal.net.

CRANDALL, ROGER W., insurance company executive; BA in Econs., U. Vt., Burlington; MBA, U. Pa., Phila. CFA. With MassMutual Fin. Group, 1988—, exec. v.p., chief investment officer Mass. Mut. Life Ins. Co., 2005—, co-COO Mass. Mut. Life Ins. Co., 2007—; vice chmn., mng. dir., head corp. securities Babson Capital Mgmt. LLC (subs. of MassMutual Fin. Group), 2000, head corp. bond mgmt., pub. bond trading and instl. fixed income units, chmn., 2005—, pres., CEO, 2006—. Office: MassMutual Fin Group 1295 State St Springfield MA 01111-0001 Office Phone: 800-767-1000.*

CRANDALL, STEPHEN HARRY, engineering educator; b. Cebu, Philippines, Dec. 2, 1920; s. William Harry and Julia Josephine (Kuenemann) C.; m. Patricia Estelle Stickel, Jan. 21, 1949; children: Jane S., William S. M.E., Stevens Inst. Tech., 1942; PhD, MIT, 1946. Registered profl. engr. Mem. staff radiation lab MIT, Cambridge, 1942-43, instr. math, 1944-46, asst. prof. mech. engring., 1947-51, assoc. prof., 1951-58, prof., 1958—, Ford prof. engring., 1975-91, prof. emeritus, 1991—, head div. applied mechanics, 1957-59, 61-67, head. div. mechanics and materials, 1968-71. Vis. prof. Marseille, France, 1960, U. Nat. Autonoma Mex., Mexico City, 1967, Ecole Nat. Superieure de Mecanique, Nantes, France, 1978, Fla. Atlantic U., 1993, Korean Advanced Inst. Sci. and Tech., 1996; exch. prof. Imperial Coll., London, 1949; NSF sci. faculty fellow, vis. scholar U. Calif., Berkeley, 1964-65; hon. rsch. assoc. Harvard U., 1971-72; Lady Davis vis. prof. Technion, Israel, 1987. Author: Engineering Analysis, 1956, Random Vibration in Mechanical Systems, 1963, (with others) Dynamics of Mechanical and Electromechanical Systems, 1968; editor: Random Vibration vol. 1, 1958, Random Vibration vol. 2, 1963, (with others) Mechanics of Solids, 1959, author (with others), 3d edit., 1978; contbr. artcles to profl. jours. Recipient ASCE Von Karman medal, 1984, Freudenthal medal, 1996, Alexander von Humboldt sr. U.S. scientist award, 1989; Fulbright fellow, London, 1949. Fellow AAAS, ASME (Worcester Reed Warner medal 1971, v.p. 1978-80, hon. mem. 1988, Timoshenko medal 1990, Den Hartog award 1991), Am. Acad. Arts and Scis., Am. Acoustical Soc. (Trent-Crede medal 1978), Am. Acad. Mechanics (pres. 1997, Disting. Svc. medal 1993); mem. NAS, NAE, NSPE, Soc. Indsl. and Applied Math., Am. Math. Soc., Am. Soc. for Engring. Edn., Internat. Union Theoretical and Applied Mechanics (chmn. U.S. del. 1974), Russian Acad. Engring. (fgn. mem.). Home: 25 Tabor Hill Rd Lincoln MA 01773-2905 Office: MIT/3-360 Dept Mech Engring Cambridge MA 02139 Office Phone: 617-253-2244. Personal E-mail: crandall@mit.edu.

CRANDELL, KENNETH JAMES, management consultant, entrepreneur; b. Ajax, Ont., Can., July 12, 1957; s. James Bauder Butterill and Barbara Joy Gillard; m. Christine Josephine McElhenney, July 28, 1984. B in Adminstrn. and B in Commerce, U. Ottawa, 1980; MBA, Fla. Atlantic U., 1982. CPA, Fla., Calif. Assoc. dir. entrepreneurial svcs. div. Ernst & Young, Ft. Lauderdale, Fla., 1982-88; founder, chmn., CEO NBS Cons. Group, Inc. dba New Bus. Strategies, Los Gatos, Calif., 1988—. Guest lectr. State Univ. System. Writer, co-producer TV series Florida Business Advisor, 1988; contbr. articles to mags. Recipient Up and Comer award, 1988. Mem. AICPA, Fin. & Adminstrn. Mgmt. in Entertainment, Fla. Inst. CPAs, Calif. Soc. CPAs, Am. Assn. Accts. (MAS divsn. 1980-93), Inst. Mgmt. Accts. (bd. dirs. Ft. Lauderdale 1983—, pres. 1988-89, bus. planning com. 1987-89), Can.-Am. C. of C. (co-founder), U. Miami Venture Coun. Forum, Gold Coast Venture Capital Club (v.p., bd. dirs. 1987-91, treas. 1987-88, co-editor newsletter 1987-89), Ft. Lauderdale C. of C. (chmn. venture capital activities 1986-88, small bus. coun. 1985-90), others. Avocations: ice hockey, published songwriter, reading. Office: NBS Cons Group Inc PMB #J 245 Mount Hermon Rd Ste M Scotts Valley CA 95066-4045 Office Phone: 954-946-2600. Personal E-mail: james.crandell@newbizs.com.

CRANDLEMERE, ROBERT WAYNE, engineering executive; b. South Weymouth, Mass., Mar. 5, 1947; s. Robert Winton and Elizabeth Mildred (Smith) C.; m. Cynthia Robin Stoddard, May 18, 1980; children: Donna Marie, Raina Lee. A.E. in Chem. Tech., Franklin Inst. Boston, 1967; BS in Chemistry, Suffolk U., 1970, MS in Analytical Chemistry, 1975. V.p., chief chemist, lab. dir., dir. Briggs Engring. & Testing Inc., 1973-83; founder, prin., pres., CEO Cert. Engring. & Testing Co., Weymouth, Mass., 1983-92, R.W. Crandlemere & Assocs., Inc., Weymouth, Mass., 1993—2002; sr. mgr. Green Environ., Inc., Quincy, Mass., 2002—03; mgr. R.W. Crandlemere, LLC, Holbrook, Mass., 2003—. Former instr. environmental and phys. chemistry Suffolk U. Contbr. articles to profl. jours. Memm. ASTM (com. E50 on envrion. assessment, risk mgmt. and corrective action), Nat. Inst. Bldg. Scis. (com. on asbestos ops. and mgmt. programs). Home: 423 S Franklin St Holbrook MA 02343-1855 Office: 423 South Franklin St Holbrook MA 02343 Office Phone: 781-767-9490. Personal E-mail: rwaynecrandlemere@comcast.net.

CRANE, BARBARA BACHMANN, photographer, educator; b. Chgo., Mar. 19, 1928; d. Burton Stanley and Della (Kreeger) Bachmann; children: Elizabeth, Jennifer, Bruce. Student, Mills Coll., 1945-48; BA in Art History, NYU, 1950; MS in Photography, Inst. Design, Ill. Inst. Tech., 1966. Prof. photography Sch. Art Inst. Chgo., 1967-93, prof. emeritus, 1993—; vis. prof. Phila. Coll. Art (now Univ. of the Arts), 1977, Sch. Mus. Fine Arts, Boston, 1979, Cornell U., Ithaca, NY, 1983; represented by Stephen Daiter Gallery, Chgo., Flatfile Photography Gallery, Chgo., Francoise Paviot Gallery, Paris. Vis. prof. Bezalel Acad. Art and Design, Jerusalem, 1987. Author: (retrospective monograph) Barbara Crane: 1948-80, (exhibn. catalog) Barbara Crane: The Evolution of a Vision, 1983, Barbara Crane: Chicago Loop, 2002, Barbara Crane Urban Anomalies: Chicago, 2002, Barbara Crane Still Lifes: Natures Mortes, 2004, Barbara Crane: Grids, 2005. Named Disting. Artist, Union League Club Chgo., 2006, Brown U., 2006; grantee, Polaroid Corp., 1979—95, Ill. Arts Coun., 1985, 2001; Photography fellow, NEA, 1975, 1988, Guggenheim Meml. fellow in photography, 1979—80. Mem.: Soc. Photog. Edn. (Nat. Honored Educator award 1993). Studio: 1017 W Jackson Blvd 1A Chicago IL 60607-2918 *Many of my photographic ideas have grown from chance or accident, both visually and technically, or from the subject matter itself. I welcome any unaccountable occurrence stemming from combinations of shutter speed, subject changes, technical happenings, or my mistakes. When such unpredictable pictures appear, I try to harness the visual episode by taking pictures that will allow the new experience to happen with intent. Fortunately, this way of working seems to expand my ideas and to continuously generate new visual experiences.*

CRANE, BARRY D., former federal agency administrator; Grad., USAF Acad.; PhD in Physics, U. Ariz. With Air Force Studies and Analyses Chief Tactical Br. USAF, 1983—86; specialist for electronic sys. Office of the Dir. of Def. Rsch. and Engring., 1987—91; project leader operational evaluation divsn. Inst. for Def. Analysis; dep. dir. for supply reduction Office Nat. Drug Control Policy Exec. Office of the Pres., Washington, 2002—04. Col. USAF, 1991.

CRANE, BENJAMIN FIELD, lawyer; b. Holden, Mass., May 5, 1929; s. Frederick Turner and Gertrude (Stange) C.; m. Sarah Anne Molloy, Feb. 8, 1959; children: Michael Turner, Elizabeth Loring, Susan Field. BA, U. Iowa, 1951; LL.B., NYU, 1954. Bar: N.Y. 1955. Assoc. Cravath, Swaine & Moore, NYC, 1954-63, ptnr., 1963-94. Served with U.S. Army, 1946-47. Mem. Assn. of Bar of City of N.Y. Office: Cravath Swaine & Moore LLP Worldwide Plz 825 8th Ave New York NY 10019-7475

CRANE, CHARLES GRANT, financial analyst; b. Akron, Ohio, Nov. 22, 1959; s. Grant and Phyllis (Hamilton) C.; m. Leisa Beth Suhayda, July 2, 1983. AB, Dartmouth Coll., 1981, MBA, 1983. V.p. Oppenheimer and Co., Inc., NYC, 1983-86, Prudential Bache Securities, NYC, 1986-88, first v.p., 1988; dir. rsch. Spears Benzak Salomon & Farrell, NYC, 1988—97, ptnr., 1989—2004; chief market strategist Key Asset Mgmt., 1997—2000; mng. ptnr., chief investment officer Victory SBSF Capital Mgmt. (formerly Spears Benzak Salomon & Farrell and Key Asset Mgmt.), 2000—04; co-founder Scotsman Capital Mgmt. LLC, 2004—. Spkr. in field. Author: (newsletter) The Corner of Wall and Madison, 1984-88. Former trustee HealthCare Chaplaincy, NY; dir. Habitat for Humanity, Portland, Maine; mem. MBA adv. bd. Amos Tuck Sch., Hanover, NH; treas. Pool Assoc., Biddeford, Maine; mem. bd. advisors James M. Allwin Initiative Corp. Citizenship, Hanover; former dir. Housing Works, NY. Edward Tuck scholar Amos Tuck Sch., Hanover, NH, 1983; named to All-Am. Rsch. Team Instl. Investor; recipient Spirit of Humanity award Habitat for Humanity Greater Portland (now called Charlie and Leisa Crane Spirit of Humanity award, 2003), 2003. Mem. Univ. Club, Abenakee Club, Union Club, Phi Beta Kappa. Republican. Greek Orthodox. Avocations: golf, sea Kayaking, cooking, travel. Office: Scotsman Capital Mgmt 10 Rockefeller Plz 16th Fl New York NY 10020-1903 Office Phone: 212-713-7613.

CRANE, CHARLOTTE, law educator; b. Hanover, NH, Aug. 30, 1951; d. Henry D. and Emily (Townsend) C.; m. Eric R. Fox, July 5, 1975; children: Hillary, Teresa. AB, Harvard U., 1973; JD, U. Mich., 1976. Bar: N.H. 1976, Ill. 1978. Law clk. to presiding judge U.S. Ct. Appeals (6th cir.), Detroit, 1976-77; law clk. to presiding justice U.S. Supreme Ct., Washington, 1977-78; assoc. Hopkins & Sutter, Chgo., 1978-82; asst. prof. Northwestern U., Chgo., 1982-86, assoc. prof., 1986-90, prof., 1990—. Contbr. articles to profl. jours. Mem. U.S. Women's Nat. Crew Team, 1976. Mem. ABA, Chgo. Tax Forum. Office: Northwestern U Sch Law 357 E Chicago Ave Chicago IL 60611-3059 Office Phone: 312-503-4528. Business E-Mail: ccrane@law.northwestern.edu.

CRANE, CHRISTOPHER M., utilities executive; Student, NH Tech. Coll. Cert. sr. reactor operator. Site v.p. TVA Browns Ferry Nuc. Plant, Ala.; v.p. boiling water reactor ops. Exelon Corp., 1998—99, sr. v.p. nuc. ops., 1999, COO Exelon Nuc., 2003, sr. v.p., pres. and chief nuc. officer Exelon Nuc., pres. and CEO AmerGen. Mem. exec. rev. group Inst. Nuc. Power Ops.; mem. steering com. Nuc. Energy Inst. Nuc. Strategic Issues Adv. Com. Office: Exelon Corp 10 S Dearborn St 37th Fl PO Box 805398 Chicago IL 60680-5398*

CRANE, CONRAD C., history professor; b. Jan. 22, 1952; BS, US Mil. Acad.; MA, PhD, Stanford U.; grad., US Army Command and Gen. Staff Coll., US Army War Coll. Prof. history US Mil. Acad.; mem. Strategic Studies Inst. US Army War Coll., Carlisle, Pa., 2000—, dir. Mil. History Inst. Carlisle Barracks, 2003—. Author: Bombs, Cities, and Civilians: American Airpower Strategy in World War II, 1993, American Airpower Strategy in Korea, 1950-1953, 1999, Landpower and Crises: Army Roles and Missions in Smaller-Scale Contingencies During the 1990s, 2001; co-author (with W. Andrew Terrill): Reconstructing Iraq: Insights, Challenges, And Missions For Military Forces In A Post-conflict Scenario, 2004; co-author: Field Manual 3-24, Counterinsurcency, 2006. Office: US Army Mil History Inst 950 Soldiers Dr Carlisle PA 17013 Office Phone: 717-245-4483. Business E-Mail: Conrad.crane@us.army.mil.

CRANE, DAVID, producer; b. Phila., Aug. 13, 1957; With Bright-Kauffman-Crane Prodns., Burbank, Calif. Creator, prodr. Dream On, 1990-96 (Cable Ace award); creator, exec. prodr. Friends, 1994-2004 (Emmy nominee 1995, 96), The Class, 2006-; writer, prodr. Couples, 1994; creator, exec. producer Veronica's Closet, 1997-2000; exec. prodr. Jesse, 1998-2000; co-writer (with Marta Kauffman) book and lyrics for the musical Personals (Outer Critics award, Drama Desk nomination). Office: Bright Kauffman Crane Prodns 4000 Warner Blvd Bldg 160 Burbank CA 91522-0001

CRANE, DAVID MICHAEL, prosecutor, former judge advocate, educator; b. Santa Monica, Calif., May 29, 1950; s. John Richard and Iris Joan (Nord) C.; m. Judith Anne Ponder, June 17, 1972; children: Katherine Carol, David Lewington. BGS summa cum laude, Ohio U., 1972, MA, 1973; JD, Syracuse U., 1980; postgrad., U. Va., 1985. Bar: N.D. 1981, U.S. Ct. Mil. Appeals 1981, U.S. Supreme Ct. 1985. With U.S. Army, 1972—96; sr. inspector gen., nat. security systems US Dept. Def, 1997—2002; chief prosecutor, Spl. Ct. for Sierra Leone UN, Freetown, 2002—05; Disting. prof. law Syracuse U., NY, 2005—. Contbr. articles to profl. jours. Mem. ABA, Assn. Trial Lawyers Am., Phi Alpha Theta, Omicron Delta Kappa. Democrat. Presbyterian. Avocations: running, reading. Office: Syracuse U Coll Law Syracuse NY 13244 Office Phone: 315-443-9541. Personal E-mail: dmcrane@law.syr.edu.

CRANE, DAVID W., energy executive; BA, Princeton Univ.; JD, Harvard Univ. V.p. Asia-Pacific region ABB Energy Ventures; sr. v.p. global power group Lehman Bros., 1996—2000; COO Internat. Power PLC, 2000—02, CEO, 2003; pres., CEO, dir. NRG Energy, Princeton, NJ, 2003—. Sec. Elec. Power Supply Assn. Office: NRG Energy 211 Carnegie Ctr Princeton NJ 08540*

CRANE, EDWARD HARRISON, III, academic administrator, financial analyst; b. LA, Aug. 15, 1944; s. Edward Harrison Jr. and Mary Barbara (Greene) C.; m. Kristina Knall; children: Geoffrey Harrison, Kathleen Wilder, Mary Adams. BS, U. Calif., Berkeley, 1967; MBA, U. So. Calif., 1968. Chartered fin. analyst. Portfolio mgr. Scudder, Stevens & Clark, Los Angeles, 1969-73; v.p. Alliance Capital Mgmt. Corp., San Francisco, 1973-75; nat. chmn. Libertarian Party, Washington, 1974-77; pres. Cato Inst., Washington, 1977—. Bd. Nat. Taxpayers Legal Fund, 1978-82; chmn. Ctr. Competitive Politics, 2006—. Pub. Inquiry mag., 1977-81, Regulation mag., 1990—; editor: Beyond the Status Quo, 1984, An American Vision, 1988, Market Liberalism, 1993; contbr. articles to profl. jours. Bd. dirs. Inst. Rsch. on Econs. of Taxation, 1988-92, Inst. Rsch. in Exptl. Econs., U.S. Term Limits, 1993—, Ams. for Ltd. Govt., 2006-; bd. advisors Am. Inst. of Bus. and Econs. in Moscow. Inst. Chartered Fin. Analysts, Mont Pelerin Soc., Sigma Chi. Avocation: rowing. Office: Cato Inst 1000 Massachusetts Ave NW Washington DC 20001-5400 Home: 3239 Juniper Ln Falls Church VA 22044 Business E-Mail: ecrane@cato.org.

CRANE, EDWARD M., lawyer; b. Chgo., 1957; BS, DePaul U., 1979, JD, 1982. Bar: Ill. 1982, US Dist. Ct. (no., ctrl. & so. dists. Ill.), US Ct. Appeals (4th, 5th, 7th & 11th cirs.). Ptnr. Skadden, Arps, Slate, Meagher & Flom, Chgo. Mem.: Product Liability Adv. Coun., Def. Rsch. Inst., Internat. Assn. Def. Counsel, Chgo. Bar Assn., Ill. State Bar Assn., ABA. Office: Skadden Arps 333 W Wacker Dr Chicago IL 60606 Office Phone: 312-407-0522. Office Fax: 312-407-8503. E-mail: ecrane@skadden.com.*

CRANE, FREDERICK BARON, retired music educator; b. Mount Pleasant, Iowa, Mar. 4, 1927; s. Baron Dana and Ruth Marie Crane; m. Lois Ann Zanger, Feb. 12, 1971; 1 child, Susan stepchildren: Mark, Reed, Robert; m. Lois Irene Russell, Aug. 15, 1956; 1 child, Elizabeth. BA, Carleton Coll., Northfield, Minn., 1949; MA, U. Iowa, Iowa City, 1956, PhD, 1960. From tchg. asst. to prof. emeritus U. Iowa, Iowa City,

1957—94, prof. emeritus, 1994—; instr. Minot (N.D.) State Coll., 1957—58, SUNY, Binghampton, NY, 1960—63; asst. prof. La. State U., Baton Rouge, 1967—68. Author: Materials for the Study of the Fifteenth Century Basse Danse, 1968, Extant Medieval Musical Instruments: A Provisional Catalog by Types, 1972, Medieval Music: An Outline, 1974, A History of the Trump in Pictures: Europe and America, 2003; editor: The Jew's Harp Jour. VIM, 1982—2003, Jour. of the Internat. Jew's Harp Soc., 2003—; contbr. articles to profl. jours. With USN, 1945—46, with USN, 1951—52. Mem.: Soc. am. Music (program com. 1987, Lowens award com. 1989, chmn. program com. 1992, Lowens award com. 1997), Am. Musicological Soc. (sec., treas. Gulf States chpt. 1965—67, mem. coun. 1977—79, program com. Midwest chpt. 1982—83), Am. Musical Instrument Soc. (bd. dirs. 1976—79, chmn. program 1977, chmn. nominating com. 1986), Internat. Jew's Harp Soc. (hon. pres. for life). Home: 601 N White St Mount Pleasant IA 52641 E-mail: fcrane@iowatelecom.net.

CRANE, HUGH WINGATE, railroad executive; b. Evergreen Park, Ill., Dec. 25, 1941; s. Hugh B. and Grace May (Wesche) C.; m. Kathy Ann Jent, Sept. 27, 1975; children: Steven Henry, Katie R. Student, DeVry, 1964, Milw. Sch. Engring., 1969. Tchr., mem. faculty Milw. Sch. Engring., 1966-71; engring. instr. Control Data Tech. Inst., Chgo., 1971-72; founder, chmn. bd., pres., chief engring. officer Crab Orchard & Egyptian R.R. (CO & E R.R.), Marion, Ill., 1972—; mem. bd. dirs. Regional Econ. Devel. Corp., Marion, Ill. Guest lectr. transp. and freight So. Ill. U., Carbondale, 1980. Author: (workbook) Engineering Descriptive Geometry, 1968, (textbook) Engineering Descriptive Geometry/Theory and Application, 1970. V.p. Lake Egypt Assn. Property Owners, Creal Springs, Ill., 1996-97. With ROTC, 1958-59. Recipient Sam Walton Cmty. Bus. Leader award, Marion, 1998; named Industrialist of Yr., Marion C. of C., 1993, Cert. of Appreciation, N.G. of Ill., 1995; transp. achievements recognized in U.S. congl. record U.S. Senator Paul Simon, 1994. Mem. Am. Rlwy. Engring. Assn., Am. R.R. Devel. Assn., Rotary. Avocations: boating, building large scale steam powered models. Office: CO & E RR 514 N Market St Marion IL 62959 also: REDCO 2305 W Main St Marion IL 62959

CRANE, JAMES R., delivery service executive; Grad., Ctrl. Mo. State U., 1976. Founder, chmn., CEO EGL, Inc., Houston, 1984—. Bd. dir. HCC Ins. Holdings. Bd. dir. Houston Mus. Natural Sci. Office: Intercontinental Airport 15350 Vickery Dr Houston TX 77032*

CRANE, LANSING E., paper company executive; b. Dalton, Mass., Oct. 12, 1945; m. Katie Crane, Dec. 7, 2002; 2 children. Grad., Yale U., New Haven; JD, Boston U., 1970. Former lawyer, New Haven; bd. dirs. Crane & Co., Inc., Dalton, Mass., 1985, pres., CEO, 1995—. Former faculty mem. psychiatry and law Yale U., New Haven. Bd. dirs. Colonial Theatre, Pittsfield, Mass.; bd. trustees Austen Riggs Ctr., Stockbridge, Mass.; bd. mem. Norman Rockwell Mus., Stockbridge, Mass. Named one of VIP 23, Berkshire Eagle, 2003. Achievements include running the company that has been supplying almost all of the paper used for US currency since 1879. Avocations: swimming, golf, hiking, skiing, reading. Office: Crane & Co Inc 30 South St Dalton MA 01226*

CRANE, LAURA JANE, retired chemist; b. Middletown, Ohio, Nov. 2, 1941; d. David R. and Frances T. (Watkins) Scott; m. Robert K. Crane, Apr. 13, 1972. BS, Carnegie Inst. Tech., 1963; MS, Harvard U., 1964; PhD, Rutgers U., 1972. Postdoctoral fellow Roche Inst. Molecular Biology, 1972-74, rsch. assoc., 1974-75; analytical chemist Eastman Kodak Co., Rochester, NY, 1962; asst. scientist Warner-Lambert Co., Morris Plains, NJ, 1965, 67-68; English tchr. Am. Sch., Manila, 1966; assoc. scientist W.R. Grace & Co., Clarksville, Md., 1969; sr. scientist diagnostic enzymology Warner-Lambert Co., 1975, group leader coagulation rsch., 1976-79; mgr. lab. products rsch. J.T. Baker Inc., Phillipsburg, NJ, 1979, asst. dir. R&D, 1980-85, dir. R&D, 1986-92; sr. dir. new product innovation Schering-Plough Health Products, Inc., Memphis, 1992-93, sr. dir. adv. products rsch. and new product innovation, 1993—2003, rsch. fellow, 2003—04, ret., 2004. Mem. faculty Seton Hall U., 1979; participant profl. symposia; mem. R&D coun. N.J., state sci. adv. coun. Rutgers U.; pres. Am. Clerical Soc. Memphis Section, 2005-; cons. in field. Contbr., editor sci. articles and books. Mem. Memphis Symphony Chorus, 2006—. US Dressage Federation Bronze Medalist, 2003, Armco Corp. scholar, 1959-63; Women's Dormitory Coun. scholar; William Connelly scholar: nat. Merit scholar; NSF fellow; DuPont fellow; NDEA fellow, 1969-72, others. Mem. AAAS, Am. Chem. Soc. (pres. Memphis chpt. 2005), U.S. Dressage Fedn. (judge), Delta Dressage Assn. (pres. 2005—, judge 2005—), Arabian Horse Registry Assn., Al Khamsa Arabian Horse Breeders Assn. (pres.). Office: Schering-Plough Health Products Inc 3030 Jackson Ave Memphis TN 38112-2020 Personal E-mail: ljcrane@bellsouth.net.

CRANE, SIR PETER ROBERT, botanist, geologist, paleontologist, educator; b. Eng., July 18, 1954; came to U.S., 1981; m. Elinor Margaret Hamer, 1986; c. Sam and Emily. BSc in Botany with honors, U. Reading, Eng., 1975, PhD in Botany, 1981. Lectr. dept. botany U. Reading, 1978-81; postdoctoral rsch. scholar dept. biology U. Ind., Bloomington, 1981-82; asst. curator paleobotany dept. geology Field Mus. Natural History, Chgo., 1982-85, assoc. curator paleobotany dept. geology, 1985-90, curator paleobotany dept. geology, 1990-92, chmn. dept. geology, 1991-92, v.p. acad. affairs, 1994—, dir., 1995—99, Royal Botanical Garden, Kew, England, 1999—2006; Marion and John Sullivan Univ. Prof. Dept. Geophysical Sci. U. Chgo., 2006—. Lectr. Com. on Evolutionary Biology, U. Chgo., 1984—; vis. prof. Botanischer Garten and Inst. Systematische Botanik, U. Zurich, Switzerland, 1987, Dept. Botany, U. Mass., Amherst, 1989; vis. rsch. fellow Dept. Botany The Natural History Mus., London, 1990-93; Mac Arthur curator The Field Mus., Chgo., 1992-94; sr. Mellon fellow, Smithsonian Instn., Washington, 1993-95; prof. dept. geophys. scis., U. Chgo., 1992—; chmn. dept. botany, Field Mus., 1993-96, dir. Ctr. for Evolutionary and Environ. Biology, Field Mus., 1994—, A Watson Armour III Curator, The Field Mus., Chgo.; mem. edtl. bds. Rev. of Palaeobotany and Palynology, Internat. Jour. Plant Sci., Plant Systematics and Evolution. Co-author: (with P. Kenrick) The Origin and Early Diversification of Land Plants, 1997; co-editor: (with others) The Origins of Angiosperms and Their Biological Consequences, 1987, The Evolution, Systematics and Fossil History of the Hamamelidae (Vols. I and II, 1989, Fifth North American Paleontological Convention, Abstract and Program, 1992; contbr. articles to profl. jours.; assoc. editor Botnical Jour. Linnean Soc., 1983-90; co-editor Paleobiology, 1984-86; mem. Rev. Panel, Kew Bull., 1987-91; editor Internat. Jour. Plant Scis. Grantee: NSF, 1984, 87, 88, 90, 91, 93, 96, Am. Chem. Soc., 1990. Fellow Royal Soc.; mem. Linnean Soc. London (Bicentenary medal 1984), Paleontological Soc. (pres. 1998—, Schuchert award 1993). Office: Univ Chicago Hinds Geophysical Sciences 201 5801 South Ellis Chicago IL 60637 Office Phone: 773-702-1789. E-mail: pcrane@uchicago.edu.

CRANE, ROBERT KENDALL, engineering educator, researcher, consultant; b. Worcester, Mass., Dec. 9, 1935; s. Kendall Buck and Marjorie Armitage C.; m. Emma Ruth, June 15, 1957; children: Garry Robert, Susan Emma Crane Jennings, Katherine Anne Crane Kulas, Cynthia Elizabeth. BSEE, Worcester Poly. Inst., 1957, MSEE, 1959, PhD, 1970. Staff engr. MITRE Corp., Bedford, Mass., 1959-64; staff mem. Lincoln Lab. MIT, Lexington, 1964-76, cons., 1976-88; divsn. sr. scientist, dep. divsn. mgr. Environ. Rsch. and Tech., Inc., Concord, Mass., 1976-81; rsch. prof. Thayer Sch. Engring. Dartmouth Coll., Hanover, NH, 1981-91; prof. meteorology, elec. engring. Coll. Geoscis. U. Okla., Norman, 1992-2000, prof. emeritus meteorology, elec. engring., 2000—. Cons. Raytheon Corp., Sudbury, Mass., 1981-87, Tech. Svc. Corp., Silver Spring, Md., 1988, Norden Sys., Melville, NY, 1988, Globalstar, San Jose, Calif., 1995-97, Applied Data Trends, Inc., 1996—2000, Teledesic Corp., 1997-99, Triton Network Sys., Inc., 1999, Hughes Network Sys., 1999-2000, Boeing Satellite Sys., 2001, Jet Propulsion Lab., 2004-07. Author: Electromagnetic Wave Propagation Through Rain, 1996, Propagation Handbook for Wireless Communication System Design, 2003; contbr. over 100 tech. papers, reports to profl. jours. and other publs. Webmaster New London Conservation Commn., NH, 2005—, AMC Cold River Camp, 2007—. Fellow IEEE (life, Disting. lectr. Antenna and Propagation Soc. 1988-91, adminstrv. com. 1985-87, wave propagation stds. com. 1971-92, assoc. editor Trans. Antennas and Propagation 1972-74), Internat. Sci. Radio Union (chmn. commn. F. 1987-90, vice comm. F. 1984-87), US Nat. Com. Internat. Sci. Radio Union (chmn. 1985-87); mem. Am. Meterorol. Soc. (cert. cons. meterorologist, com. on radar meteorology 1981-83), Am. Geophys. Union, Sigma Xi, Eta Kappa Nu. Avocations: hiking, skiing, photography. Home: 315 Forest Acres Rd New London NH 03257 also: 337 Lovewell Pond Rd Fryeburg ME 04037 E-mail: bcrane@ou.edu.

CRANE, ROBERT MEREDITH, health facility administrator; b. 1947; m. Susan Crane, May 5, 1973; 1 child, Alexis Meredith. BA, Coll. of Wooster, 1969; M Pub. Adminstrn., Cornell U., Ithaca, NY, 1971. Health planning specialist U.S. Dept. Health, Edn. and Welfare, Rockville, Md., 1971-73, tech. assistance bur. chief, 1973-76, regulatory methods bur. chief, 1976-77; sr. staff assoc. U.S. Ho. of Reps., Washington, 1977-79; dep. commr. N.Y. State Health Dept., Albany, 1979-82; dir. N.Y. State Office Health Sys. Mgmt., Albany, 1982-83; v.p. govt. rels. Kaiser Found. Health Plan, Oakland, Calif., 1983-88, sr. v.p. nat. accts. and pub. rels., 1988-92, sr. v.p. quality mgmt., 1992-94, sr. v.p., chief adminstrv. officer, 1994-99, sr. v.p., rsch. and policy devel., dir. Inst. for Health Policy, 1999—2007; pres. Kaiser Permanente Internat., Oakland, 2004—. Bd. dirs. Acad. Health Svcs. Rsch. and Health Policy, 2000—; mem. Nat. Acad. Social Ins., 2000-03. Campaign cabinet United Way Bay area, 1989-90; steering com. Bay Area Econ. Forum, 1988-94, Bay Area Coun., 1991—; selection judge, preceptor Coro Found., San Francisco, 1985-86; chmn. bd. Alpha Ctr., 1992-98; co-chair conf. bd. Coun. of Shared Bus. Svcs. Execs., 1996—; trustee Employee Benefits Rsch. Inst. Sr. exec. fellow Harvard U., 1981. Mem. APHA (chmn. cmty. health planning sect. 1983-84, bd. govs. 1979-81), Am. Health Planning Assn. (bd. dirs. 1986-92). Presbyterian. Avocations: tennis, golf. Office: Kaiser Found Health Plan 1 Kaiser Plz Oakland CA 94612-3610

CRANE, ROGER RYAN, JR., lawyer; b. Washington, Mar. 28, 1946; s. Roger Ryan Crane and Jeanette (Hurlbut) Rosar. AB, Coll. of Holy Cross, 1968; JD, Fordham U., 1973; LLM, NYU, 1980. Bar: N.Y. 1974; U.S. Dist. Ct. (so. and ea. dist.) N.Y. 1974; U.S. Ct. Appeals (2nd cir.) 1974, (1st cir.) 1994. Assoc. Dunnington Bartholow & Miller, NYC, 1973-79, Trubin Sillcocks Edelman, NYC, 1979-81, ptnr., 1981—84; ptnr., head litig. dept. Bachner Tally Polevoy & Misher, NYC, 1984-2000; co-mng. ptnr. N.Y. office McCarter & English, NYC, 2000—02; ptnr. Nixon Peabody LLP, NYC, 2002—. Author: The Last Confession, 2007; contbr. articles to profl. jours. Mem. N.Y.C. Bar Assn. (prof. discipline com. 1996-99), Univ. Club N.Y., Tuxedo Club. Avocations: golf, tennis, fly fishing, riding. Office: Nixon Peabody 437 Madison Ave New York NY 10022 Office Phone: 212-940-3190. Personal E-mail: rcrane@nixonpeabody.com.

CRANE, RON G., state official; b. Nampa, Idaho; m. Cheryl Crane; 6 children. Founder Crane Alarm Svc., 1980—; state legislator Idaho, 1982—98, state treas., 1998—. Mem. Idaho Nat. Guard, 1971—77. Named Soldier of the Year, Idaho, 1975. Mem.: Nat. Assn. State Auditors, Controllers and Treas. (exec. com.), Nat. Assn. State Treas. (exec. com.). Republican. Office: Idaho State Treas 700 W Jefferson Rm 102 PO Box 83720 Boise ID 83720-0091 Office Phone: 208-334-3200. Office Fax: 208-332-2960. Business E-Mail: rgcrane77@cableone.net.*

CRANE, STEPHEN CHARLES, medical association executive; b. Waterbury, Conn., Oct. 4, 1946; s. Homer and Edna Crane; children: Russell, Elizabeth. BA, Princeton U., NJ, 1969; MPH, U. Mich., 1973, PhD, 1981. Legis. analyst, mgmt. intern Office of the Dir., NIH, Bethesda, Md., 1969; project dir. Columbia Rsch. Assocs., Inc., Cambridge, Mass., 1970; program analyst Office Asst. Sec. for Planning & Evaluation US Dept. Health, Edn. and Welfare, 1972; grad. rsch. fellow Program Health Planning U. Mich. Sch. Pub. Health, 1973, sr. rsch. assoc., rsch. assoc., grad. rsch. fellow, 1973-79, lectr. program and bur. hosp. adminstrn., 1979-80, asst. prof., lectr. dept. med. care orgn., 1980-83; asst. prof. Sch. Pub. Health Boston U., 1984-93, dep. chief health svc. sect. Sch. Pub. Health, 1988, asst. acad. v.p. for health affairs, 1986-88, dir. ednl. programs Health Policy Inst., 1983-90; v.p. Assn. for Health Svc. Rsch. & Found. for Health Svc. Rsch., Washington, 1990-93; program dir. Robert Wood Johnson Found. Investigator Awards in Health, 1992-93; exec. v.p. Am. Acad. Physician Asst., Alexandria, Va., 1993—2007; exec. dir. Am. Thoracic Soc., NYC, 2007—. Investigator and presenter in field. Contbr. articles to profl. jours. Staff Mich. Pub. Health Statue Revision Project, 1975-78; cons. Spkr.'s Office, Mich. Ho. of Reps., Lansing, 1975-81; mem. adv. com. Mercy Coll. Physician Asst. Program, Detroit, 1979-83, Western Mich. Physician Asst. Program, Kalamazoo, 1981-85; staff Boston Mayor's Com. on Access to Health Care, 1984-86; mem. task force on access to health care Divsn. Alcoholism, Mass. Dept. Pub. Health, 1985-86; health care cons. Mass. Com. for the Medically Uninsured, 1985-86; cons. Gen. Assembly Task Force on Health Cost/Policies, Nat. Presbyn. Ch., 1985-91; corporator Milton Med. Ctr., 1988-90; mem. Commn. on Future of U. Detroit/Mercy. McConnell fellow Woodrow Wilson Sch., Princeton U., 1968; USPH Svc. fellow, 1972-73; Grad. Rsch. fellow Bur. Hosp. Adminstrn., Sch. Pub. Health, U. Mich., 1973-74; hon. fellow Mich. Acad. Physician Assts., 1977; recipient commendation Pub. Health Statue Revision Commn., 1979; Faculty Devel. grantee Ctr. for Rsch. on Learning and Teaching, U. Mich., 1982, John H. Romani Disting. Alumni award Mich. Sch. Pub. Health, 1996. Office: Am Thoracic Soc 61 Broadway New York NY 10006-2755 Office Phone: 212-315-8600. Office Fax: 212-315-6498.*

CRANER, LORNE WHITNEY, not-for-profit institute executive, former federal agency administrator; b. Bitburg AFB, Fed. Republic Germany; came to U.S., 1960; s. Robert Roger and Audrey Evelyn Craner. BA, Reed Coll., 1982; MA, Georgetown U., 1986. Staff asst. Congressman John McCain, Washington, 1983-84; legis. asst. Congressman Jim Kolbe, Washington, 1985, Congressman John McCain, Washington, 1986-87; staff Senate Cen. Am. observer Group, Washington, 1987-89; dep. asst. sec. for legis. affairs US Dept. State, Washington, 1989—92; dir. Asian Affairs NSC, Washington, 1992—93; v.p. prog. Int. Rep. Inst., Washington, 1993—95, pres., 1995—2001, 2004—; asst. sec. for democracy, human rights and labor U.S. Dept. State, Washington, 2001—04. Staff asst. George Bush for Pres., Alexandria, Va., 1980; mem. campaign staff John McCain for Senate, Phoenix, 1986. Mem.: Coun. on Fgn. Rels. Republican. Office: Internat Rep Inst 1225 Eye St NW Ste 700 Washington DC 20005

CRANFILL, VIRGINIA MAY, retired nursing administrator; b. Winfield, Kans., Jan. 28, 1931; d. Archie Lewis and Eva Dell (Martin) Fisher; m. B. Charles Smith, Aug. 3, 1949 (div. Nov. 1978); children: Charles David Smith, Terry Lee Smith (dec.), Bruce Wayne Smith, Nancy Ann Smith Barnhurst; m. Bert D. Cranfill, Oct. 1, 1981. Grad. with honors, Hinsdale Hosp., Ill., 1964; student, South Fla. C.C., Avon Park, 1971—73; AS with honors, Polk C.C., Winter Haven, Fla., 1975; student, Fla. So. Coll., Lakeland, 1983—84. Diplomate coord. Am. Bd. Quality Assurance Utilization Rev. Physicians, Inc., cert. case mgr. Am. Bd. Quality Assurance Utilization Rev. Physicians, Inc.; RN Fla., Ga., Tenn., Calif., LPN III, Tenn., Fla., cert. profl. healtcare quality, Nat. Assn. Health Care Quality; vegetarian cooking, vegetarian food instr. Emergency rm. nurse Hinsdale (Ill.) Hosp., 1964—65; office receptionist, dental asst. Dr. J.C. Trivett, DDS, Madison, Tenn., 1965—66; charge nurse Little Creek Sanitarium and Hosp., Concord, Tenn., 1966—68; nurse and surg. tech. Walker Meml. Hosp., Avon Park, Fla., 1968—73, circulating surg. nurse, 1975—76, charge nurse and head nurse, 1979—86, house supr., 1982—86; office nurse Dr. S.A. King, Gen. Practice, 1973—75; asst. DON Hillcrest Nursing Home, Avon Park, 1975; charge nurse med./surg. unit Smyrna (Ga.) Hosp., 1976; insvc. dir. and asst. DON Jellico (Tenn.) Cmty. Hosp., 1976—77; charge nurse maximum security infirmary Avon Park Correctional Instn., 1978—79; charge nurse med./surg./orthop. unit Med. Ctr. Hosp., Punta Gorda, 1979; circulating surg. nurse St. Helena Hosp., Deer Park, Calif., 1981-82; DON Lake Wales (Fla.) Convalescent Ctr., 1987-88; nursing quality assurance coord. Fla. Hosp. Heartland Divsn., 1988—92, med. staff quality assurance, 1988—92, asst. dir. and coord. case mgmt., 1992—93, physician liaison, 1993—95, part-time internal auditor, 1996—97; ret., 1997; part-time nurse Ctr. Wound Care Fla. Hosp. Heartland Divsn., 2004—05. Past mem. adv. bd. Home Health Agy., Sebring, Fla.; asst. to physicians regarding rules and guidelines of Fed. Govt. Health Care Fin. Adminstrn., 1990-1996; participant profl. seminars and workshops. Author: Our Heavenly Messenger, 2001. Cmty. instr. ARC; past vol. EMT and nurse Jellice Ambulance Svc., vol. Fla. Hosp. Heartland Divsn.; spiritual mentor Walker Meml. Jr. Acad.; deaconess, hostess, active in evangelism outreach Walker Seventh-Day Adventist Ch., parish nurse, 2000, coord. health clinic and lectr. Philippines mission, 2004. Recipient Outstanding Achievement in Nursing, Lakeland (Fla.) Hosp., 1984. Mem.: Am. Bd. Quality Assurance Utilization Rev. Physicians, Inc, Fla. Utilization Rev. Assn., Fla. Assn. Health Care Quality, Assn. Seventh-Day Adventist Nurses (bd. dir., pres.-elect), Nat. Assn. Health Care Quality, Case Mgmt. Soc. Republican. Avocations: church activies, reading, crafts, sewing, music. Home: 1417 W Avon Blvd Avon Park FL 33825-9511 E-mail: vcran@tnni.net.

CRANFORD, JAMES MICHAEL, lawyer; b. Washington, Jan. 26, 1946; s. Jack and Wanda C.; m. Teresa, July 23, 1994; children: William Bodie, James Michael, Heather, Christopher. BA, Mercer U., 1978; JD, Woodrow Wilson U., 1984. Atty. pvt. practice, Macon, Ga., 1985—. Mem. Macon City Coun., 1995—99, 2004—. Mem. Ga. Bar Assn., Ga. Trial Lawyers Assn., Ga. Assn. Criminal Defense Lawyers, Macon Bar Assn., Macon Assn. Criminal Defense Lawyers, Middle Ga. Trial Lawyers Assn. Episcopalian. Avocations: motorcycle racing, scuba diving, boxing, fishing. Home: 1842 Williamson Rd Macon GA 31206-3342 Office: 913 Washington Ave Macon GA 31201-6720 Home Phone: 478-788-5323; Office Phone: 478-746-0704.

CRANFORD, PAGE DERONDE, lawyer; b. West Chester, Pa., Nov. 20, 1935; s. Joseph D. and Dorothy (Griffith) C.; m. Virginia Langen, Nov. 21, 1965; children: Elizabeth, Courtenay. BS, Washington and Lee U., 1958; JD, George Washington U., 1964; postgrad. in banking, Rutgers U., 1981. Bar: Md. 1964, D.C. 1965, Va. 1974, U.S. Ct. Appeals (D.C. cir.) 1965. Asst. v.p. Nat. Bank Washington, 1958-65; staff counsel U.S. Comptr. of Currency, Washington, 1965-66, regional adminstr. nat. banks Richmond, Va., 1966-72; sr. v.p., sec., gen. counsel Fidelity Am. Bank, Lynchburg, Va., 1972-75; assoc. Boothe, Prichard & Dudley, Fairfax, Va., 1975-76; corp. gen. counsel Va. Nat. Bankshares, Norfolk, Va., 1976-89; exec. v.p., gen. counsel Sorvan Fin. Corp, Norfolk, 1989-90, sr. exec. v.p., gen. counsel, 1990-91; sr. exec. v.p., gen. counsel, sec. C&S/Sovran Corp., Norfolk and Atlanta, 1990-92; ptnr. McGuire Woods Battle & Boothe, Norfolk, 1992-99, ptnr. in charge, 1992-96; of counsel McGuire Woods LLP, Norfolk, 2000—. Adj. prof. Sch. Law Regent U., Va. Beach, 1995-99, Sch. Law Coll. William and Mary, Williamsburg, Va., 1997-98. Trustee Richmond Montessori Sch., 1970-72, Lynchburg Montessori Sch., 1972-75, James River Day Sch., Lynchburg, 1973-75, Va. Symphony, Norfolk, 1984—. Served to capt. U.S. Army, 1958-66 Recipient Arthur S. Fleming award Jaycees, 1972 Mem. ABA (banking law subcom, corp. counsel subcom., bus. law sect.), Va. Bar Assn., Md. Bar Assn., D.C. Bar Assn., Town Point Club (Norfolk). Republican. Episcopalian. Office: McGuire Woods LLP 9000 World Trade Ctr 101 W Main St Ste 9000 Norfolk VA 23510-1655

CRANG, RICHARD FRANCIS EARL, botanist, writer, research scientist; b. Clinton, Ill., Dec. 2, 1936; s. Richard Francis and Clara Esther (Cummins) Crang; m. Linda L. Crang, Aug. 10, 1958 (div.). BS, Ea. Ill. U., 1958; MS, U. S.D., 1962; PhD, U. Iowa, 1965. Asst. prof. biology Wittenberg U., 1965—69; assoc. prof. biol. sci. Bowling Green State U., 1969—74, prof., 1974—80; prof. plant biology U. Ill., Urbana-Champaign, 1980—2002, assoc. head dept. plant biology, 1995—97, faculty fellow in acad. adminstrn., 1997—99, dir. Ctr. Elec. Microsci., 1980—92, prof. emeritus, 2002—. Adj. prof. anatomy Med. Coll. Ohio, 1974—80; summer rsch. prof. Lehman Coll., CUNY, Bronx, vis. prof. biol. sci., 1999—2006; vis. scientist Cambridge U., England, 1978—79, Komarov Bot. Inst., 1980—92, Warsaw U., Poland, 1993; rschr., collaborator in fungal adhesion Kaohsiung Med. Coll., Taiwan, China, 1988—90; lectr. in field. Author: (with A. Vassilyev) CD-ROM Text on Plant Anatomy, 2003; contbr. numerous articles to profl. jours. Mem. Statewide Democratic Support Group, Ill. Recipient Outstanding Faculty Rsch. Recognition award Bowling Green State U., 1973, 75; grantee Paint Rsch. Inst., 1976-83, NSF, 1981-83, EPA, 1984-86, USDA, 1986-89, Internat. Plant and Pollution Lab., 1993-98; lifetime assoc. fellow Clare Hall, Cambridge, Eng. Mem. AAAS, Bot. Soc. Am., Internat. Soc. Environ. Botanists (advisor, life, inaugurated 1st internat. meeting, Lucknow, India 1996), Microscopy Soc. Am. (nat. chmn. cert. bd. 1982-89, dir. U.S.A. local affiliates 1990-93, Disting. Svc. award 1994, Cecil Hall award 1994), Sigma Xi. Achievements include development of asynchronous learning techs. at college level by means of networked computers on world wide web and other educational technologies. Office: U Ill Plant Biology 505 S Goodwin Ave 665 Morrill Hall Urbana IL 61801-3707 Home: 576 Selborne Rd Riverside IL 60546-1669 Business E-Mail: r-crang@life.uiuc.edu.

CRANGLE, ROBERT D., lawyer, management consultant, entrepreneur; b. Putnam, Conn., May 5, 1943; s. Dale E. and Libbie S. (Krepela) C.; m. S. Jeanne Rose, June 6, 1968; children: Rob, Scott, Elenor, Bill, Kimball, Susan, Sara, Paul, Hally. BS in Nuclear Engring., Kans. State U., 1966; JD, Harvard U., 1969. Bar: Mass. 1969, Ill. 1974, Kans. 1987, U.S. Dist. Ct. Kans. 1987; cert. mgmt. cons. 1980. Sr. v.p. Harbridge House, Inc., Boston, 1969-84; pres., dir. Rose & Crangle, Ltd., Lincoln, 1984—; dir. Helisys Inc., LA, 1985-99; ptnr. Metz and Crangle, Chartered, Lincoln, Kans., 1987—2003; elected Lincoln County Atty., 1997—2001; atty. Crangle Law Office, Lincoln, 2003—. Mem. faculty Bus. Sch., Ill. Inst. Tech., Chgo., 1984-87; dir. IIT Ctr. Rsch. on Indsl. Strategy and Policy, Chgo., 1984-87. Bd. dirs. Lake Bluff Sch. Bd., Ill., 1982-87, Farmers Nat. Bank, 1992-2004, Midwest Cmty. Bank, 2004—, adv. bd.; mem. Kans. Sci. and Tech. Coun., 1992-96; mem. Natural History Mus. Bd., 1995-98, Kans. Geol. Survey Adv. Com., 1995-2002. Recipient Meritorious Pub. Svc. award NSF, 1985. Fellow AAAS (sect. officer 2006—); mem. Kans. Bar Assn. (officer bus. law sect. 1993-97), N.W. Kans. Bar Assn., co-organizer Kans. Math and Sci. Edn. Coalition. Republican. Mem. Soc. Of Friends. Avocations: science policy, oil painting, entrepreneurship. Office: Crangle Law Office Chtd 117 N 4th PO Box 285 Lincoln KS 67455-0285: PO Box 285 117 N 4th St Lincoln KS 67455-0285 Office Phone: 785-524-5050. Business E-Mail: rcltd@nckcn.com.

CRANK, PATRICK J. (PAT CRANK), state attorney general; m. Anna Crank; children: Abbigail, Jerry, Zachary, Noah. BA, U. Wyo., 1982, JD, 1985. With Wyo. Atty. Gen. Office, 1985—86, Natrona County Dist. Atty. Office, 1987—90, US Atty. Office for Dist. Wyo., 1990—2002; atty. gen. State of Wyo., Cheyenne, 2003—. Democrat. Avocations: hunting, fishing, camping. Office: Atty Gens Office 123 Capitol 200 W 24th St Cheyenne WY 82002*

CRANMER, SCOTTY, professional trick bike rider; b. Jackson, NJ, 1990; Profl. sponsored bike rider Felt Bikes, Tylenol, Fox clothes, Vans Shoes, Unbound Energy Drink. Achievements include first place finishes Roots Jam, Orlando, Fla., 2003, Vans Let it Ride, Las Vegas, 2005; silver medal in BMX Freestyle, ESPN X Games, 2006. Office: c/o Felt BMX 20372 Hermana Cir Lake Forest CA 92630

CRANMER, THOMAS WILLIAM, lawyer; b. Detroit, Jan. 13, 1951; s. William Eugene and Betty Lee (Orphal) C.; children: Jacqueline, Taylor, Chase. BA, U. Mich., 1972; JD, Ohio No. U., 1975. Bar: Mich. 1975, U.S. Dist. Ct. (ea. dist.) Mich. 1978, U.S. Ct. Appeals (6th cir.) 1978, U.S. Supreme Ct. 1982, U.S. Tax Ct. 1986. Asst. pros. atty. Oakland County, Mich., 1975-78; asst. atty. U.S. Dist. Ct. (ea. dist.) Mich., 1978-80, asst. chief criminal div., 1980-82; assoc. Miro, Miro & Weiner, Bloomfield Hills, Mich., 1982-84, ptnr., 1984—; prin. Miller, Canfield, Paddock & Stone PLC, 2005—. Mem. faculty Atty. Gen's. Adv. Inst., Washington, 1980-82, Nat. Inst. Trial Adv., Northwestern Chicago, Ill., 1987—, trial adv. workshop Inst. Continuing Legal Edn., 1988—, local rules adv. com. U.S. Dist. Ct. (ea. dist.) Mich., 1989-92; hearing panelist Atty. Discipline Bd., 1987—. Fellow Am. Coll. Trial Lawyers, Am. Bar Found., Oakland County Bar Found. (charter, trustee 1994—, pres. 2002-03), Mich. State Bar Found., Internat. Acad. Trial Lawyers, Internat. Soc. Barristers; mem. ABA (chair litigation sect., Detroit graphic subcom. of com. on complex crimes litigation 1990), FBA (exec. bd. dirs. Detroit chpt. 1988-96, pres. 1995-96, Leonard R. Gilman award 1995), Am. Bd. Trial Advocates, Am. Arbitration Assn. (mem. hearing panel 1990), State Bar Mich. (rep. assembly 1986-92, mem. grievance com. 1990—, chair 1993-97, bd. commrs. 1998—, treas. 2001-02, sec. 2002-03, v.p. 2003-04, pres.-elect 2004-05, pres. 2005-06), Oakland County Bar Assn. (chair CLE com. 1992, bd. dirs. 1994-03, Disting. Svc. award 1996, chair membership com. 1997), Am. Bar Found. Republican. Presbyterian. Office: Miller Canfield Paddock & Stone PLC Ste 2500 150 W Jefferson Ave Detroit MI 48226 Home: 4739 Sandpiper Ln West Bloomfield MI 48323-2063 Home Phone: 248-682-0589; Office Phone: 248-267-3381. Business E-Mail: cranmer@millercanfield.com.

CRANNEY, MARILYN KANREK, retired lawyer; b. Bklyn., June 18, 1949; d. Sidney Paul and Aurelia (Valice) Kanrek; m. John William Cranney, Jan. 22, 1970 (div. June 1975); 1 child, David Julian. BA, Brandeis U., Waltham, Mass., 1970; MA in History, Brigham Young U., Provo, Utah, 1975; JD, U. Utah, Salt Lake City, 1979; LLM in Tax Law, NYU, 1984. Bar: N.Y. 1980, U.S. Dist. Ct. (so. and ea. dists.) N.Y. 1992, U.S. Supreme Ct., 2006. Assoc. Cravath Swaine & Moore, NYC, 1979-81; 1st v.p., asst. gen. counsel Morgan Stanley Investment Advisors Inc., NYC, 1981—2005; pvt. practice Bklyn., 2005—. Mem. Order of the Coif. Democrat. Jewish. Avocations: travel, reading.

CRANSTON, HOWARD STEPHEN, lawyer, management consultant; b. Hartford, Conn., Oct. 20, 1937; s. Howard Samuel and Agnes (Corvo) C.; m. Karen Youngman, June 16, 1962; children: Margaret, Susan. BA cum laude, Pomona Coll., 1959; LLB, Harvard U., 1962. Bar: Calif. 1963. Assoc. MacDonald & Halsted, LA, 1964-68; ptnr. MacDonald, Halsted & Laybourne, LA, 1968-82, of counsel, 1982-86; pres. Knapp Comm., LA, 1982-87, S.C. Cons. Corp., 1987—. Author: Handbook for Creative Managers, 1987. 1st lt. US Army, 1962—64. Republican. Episcopalian. Office: 1613 Chelsea Rd # 252 San Marino CA 91108-2419 Personal E-mail: hscran@earthlink.net.

CRANSTON, JOHN WELCH, historian, educator; b. Utica, NY, Dec. 21, 1931; s. Earl and Mildred (Welch) C. BA, Pomona Coll., 1953; MA, Columbia U., 1964; PhD, U. Wis., 1970. Asst. prof. history West Tex. State U., 1970-74, U. Mo., Kansas City, 1970, Rust Coll., Holly Springs, Miss., 1974-80, assoc. prof., 1980-83; historian U.S. Army Armor Ctr., Ft. Knox, Ky., 1983-95; ret., 1995. Adj. prof. history and govt. Elizabethtown C.C., Ft. Knox, 1988-2002. Contbr. history articles to profl. lit. With U.S. Army, 1953-55. NEH fellow, summers 1976, 81. Mem. Am. Hist. Assn., Orgn. Am. Historians. Democrat. Episcopalian. Home: 900 E Harrison Ave Apt D-61 Pomona CA 91767

CRANSTON, MARY BAILEY, lawyer; b. Palo Alto, Calif., Dec. 29, 1947; d. James Alfred and Bettye (Luhnow) Bailey; m. Harold David Cranston, Aug. 15, 1970; children: Susan Anne, John David. AB in polit. sci., Stanford U., 1969, JD, 1975; MA in psychology, UCLA, 1970. Bar: Calif. 1975. Assoc. atty. Pillsbury, Madison & Sutro, San Francisco, 1975-82, ptnr., 1983—2001, firm chair, 1999—2001; (Pillsbury, Madison & Sutro merged with Winthrop, Stimson, Putnam & Roberts, 2001); ptnr. Pillsbury Winthrop LLP, San Francisco, 2001—, firm chair, 2001—04; (Pillsbury Winthrop LLP merged with Shaw Pittman LLP, 2005); firm chair Pillsbury Winthrop Shaw Pittman LLP, San Francisco, 2005—06, sr. ptnr., 2007—. Faculty The Rutter Group, 1984—, Calif. Continuing Edn. of the Bar, 1985—, Nat. Inst. Trial Advocacy, San Francisco, 1986—; bd. dirs. GrafTech Internat. Ltd., 1999—, Bay Area Coun., 1999—; editl. bd. Nat. Law Jour., 2004—. Contbr. articles to profl. journals. Trustee San Francisco Ballet, 1996, Stanford U., 2000—; mem. The Yosemite Fund; mem. nat. centennial com. Girl Scouts USA, 2001; bd. dirs. Legal Services for Children, San Francisco, 1983—87, San Francisco C. of C., 1999—2001; bd. dirs. hist. soc. US Dist. Ct. No. Dist. Calif., 2001—; bd. mem. Episcopal Charities, 2003—; exec. com. bd. visitors Stanford Law Sch., 1977—80, 1996—, chair bd. visitors, 2001; chair bd. advisors we. region Catalyst, 2004—; bd. governors Commonwealth Club of Calif. Named one of The 100 Most Influential Lawyers in Calif., LA Daily Jour., 1999—2002, The 50 Most Influential Bus. Women in the Bay Area, San Francisco Bus. Times, 1999—2003, The 100 Most Influential Lawyers in Am., Nat. Law Jour., 2000, The 2 Best Law Firm Leaders in the US, Of Counsel, 2002; recipient Stanford Associates Award for disting. svc., Stanford U., 1999, Disting. Jurisprudence Award, Anti-Defamation League, 2000, Award of Merit, Bar Assn. San Francisco, 2002, Athena Award, 2004. Fellow: Am. Coll. Trial Lawyers; mem.: Assn. Bus. Trial Lawyers (bd. dirs. 1993—97), Calif. State Bar (mem. com. on women 1986—89, chair sect. of antitrust and trade regulation 1998—99), ABA (mem. commn. on women 1993—2000, coun. mem. antitrust sect. 1994—97, officer antitrust sect. 1997—2000), Am. Law Inst., Stanford Alumni Assn. (bd. dirs. 1986—93, 2001—, pres. 1990), Cap & Gown (Stanford) (treas. 1974—75). Avocations: reading, sports. Office: Pillsbury Winthrop Shaw Pittman 50 Fremont St Ste 1474 San Francisco CA 94105 Office Phone: 415-983-1621. Office Fax: 415-983-1200. Business E-Mail: mary.cranston@pillsburylaw.com.*

CRANSTON, STEWART E., career officer; BA in Math., U. So. Calif., 1966; MBA, Auburn U., 1979; Grad., Air Command and Staff Coll., 1979; Diploma, Indsl. Coll. of Armed Forces, 1986; postgrad., Carnegie-Mellon U., 1989. Commd. 2d lt. USAF, 1966, advanced through ranks to lt. gen., 1997; various assignments to dep. chief of staff, test and opers. Hdqtrs. Air Force Material Command, Wright-Patterson AFB, Ohio, 1992-93; comdr. Air Force Devel. Test Ctr./Air Force Material Command, Eglin AFB, Fla., 1993-97; vice-comdr. Hdqtrs. Air Force Material Comman, Wright-Patterson AFB, Ohio, 1997—. Decorated Disting. Svc. medal, Legion of Merit, Disting. Flying Cross, Meritorious Svc. medal with four oak leaf clusters, Air medal with 15 oak leaf clusters, Air Force Commendation medal with oak leaf cluster, Republic of Vietnam Gallantry Cross with Palm, Vietnam Svc. medal with four svc. stars, others. Office: AFMC/CV 4375 Chidlaw Rd Ste 1 Wright Patterson Afb OH 45433-5066

CRANZ, GALEN, architecture educator, sociologist; b. Seattle, Apr. 7, 1944; d. Richard F. and Phyllis (Whitaker) Cranz. BA, Reed Coll., 1966; PhD, U. Chgo., 1971. Vis. asst. prof. Ill. Inst. Tech., 1969—71; asst. prof. Princeton (N.J.) U., 1971—75, U. Calif., Berkeley, Calif., 1975—81, assoc. prof. dept. arch., 1981—87, prof. dept. arch., 1987—. Juror Progressive Arch. Design awards, 1980, Penn Yards Design Charrette, NYC, 1991, Todos Santos Pla., Concord, Calif., 1987; cons. in field. Author: User Based Evaluation of Housing for the Elderly, 1975, Politics of Park Design: A History of Urban Parks in America, 1982, What Arthur Park Tells Us About Our Time, 1988, The Chair: Rethinking Culture, Body & Design, 1998, paperback edit., 2000. Fellow, NIMH, 1966—68, USPHS, 1968—69, Kellogg Nat., 1981—84; grantee, Graham Found., 1973—78, 1997—2000. Mem.: Orgn. Women Archs., Women's Study Group Environ. Issues in China, Environ. Design Rsch. Assn., Am. Sociol. Assn. Office: U Calif Dept Arch Berkeley CA 94720-0001 Office Phone: 510-658-9330. Business E-Mail: galen@berkeley.edu.

CRAPARO, JOHN S., information technology executive; b. NYC, Sept. 3, 1959; s. Francis Xavier Craparo, Jane Constance Licciardi. BA, Iona Coll., New Rochelle, NY, 1981; MS in Mgmt., Poly. U., Bklyn., 1990. Sr. v.p., chief tech. officer GE Capital Corp., Stamford, Conn., 1989—98; v.p. global info. tech. ops. Dell Computer Corp., Round Rock, Tex., 1998; CIO Dell Fin. Svcs., Round Rock, 2002; sr. v.p. global telecom, network transformation and HP Labs IT HP, 2006—. Assoc. prof. Pace U., White Plains, NY, 1990—; chancellor Continental U., Lemmon, SD, 1999—. Editor: (jour.) Journal of Continuing Professional Development, 1999; author: (book and software program) Trunkalculator: the telecommunications management tool, 1989. Torchbearer Salt Lake City Olympic Games, 2002; bd. dirs. and mentor Jr. Achievment of Ctrl. Tex., Austin, 1990—; mem. adv. bd. Pace U., White Plains, NY, 1997—; bd. dirs. ARC Ctrl. Tex.; ofcl. U.S. agt. U. of South Africa, Pretoria, Gauteng, South Africa, 1998—; mem. Catholic Hospitalier Order of the the Knights of Malta - Brotherhood of the Blessed Gerard, Mandeni, South Africa, 1998—. Capt. USAF Aux. Fellow Internat. Mgmt. Ctrs., 1999, N.Y.C. Sci. Found. fellow, Medgar Evers Coll. of CUNY, 1986—89; scholar N.Y. State Regent's scholar, SUNY, 1977—81. Fellow: Royal Soc. Arts; mem.: Assn. of Computing Machinery. Republican. Roman Catholic. Office: HP 3000 Hanover St Palo Alto CA 94304-1185

CRAPO, MICHAEL DEAN, senator, former congressman, lawyer; b. Idaho Falls, May 20, 1951; s. George Lavelle and Melba (Olsen) C.; m. Susan Diane Hasleton, June 22, 1974; children: Michelle, Brian, Stephanie, Lara, Paul. BA in Polit. Sci., summa cum laude, Brigham Young U., 1973; postgrad., U. Utah, 1973-74; JD cum laude, Harvard U., 1977. Bar: Calif. 1977, Idaho 1979. Law clk. to Hon. James M. Carter US Ct. Appeals (9th cir.), San Diego, 1977-78; assoc. atty. Gibson, Dunn & Crutcher, LA, 1978-79; atty. Holden, Kidwell, Hahn & Crapo, Idaho Falls, 1979-92, ptnr., 1983-92. mem. Idaho State Senate from 32A Dist., 1985—93, asst. majority leader, 1987—89; pres. Pro Tempore, 1989-92; congressman U.S. House of Reps., 2d Idaho dist., Washington, 1993—99; mem. commerce com., new mem. leader 103rd Congress, sophomore class leader 104th Congress, co-chair Congl. Beef Caucus, dep. whip western region U.S. House of Reps., Washington, vice chair energy and power subcom., strategic planning leader House Leadership 105th Congress, mem. house resources com., mem. commerce com., mem. resources com.; US Senator from Idaho, 1999—; dep. whip 108th congress US Senate. Precinct committeeman Dist. 29, 1980-85; vice chmn. Legislative Dist. 29, 1984-85; Mem. Health and Welfare Com., 1985-89, Resources and Environ. Com., 1985-90, State Affairs Com., 1987-92; Rep. Pres. Task Force, 1989; mem. com. agr., nutrition and forestry US Senate, com. banking, housing and urban affairs, com. budget, com. fin., com. Indian affairs. Leader Boy Scouts Am., Calif., Idaho, 1977-92; mem. Bar Exam Preparation, Bar Exam Grading; chmn. Law Day.; Bonneville County chmn. Phil Batt gubernatorial campaign, 1982. Named one of Outstanding Young Men of Am., 1985; recipient Cert. of Merit Rep. Nat. Com., 1990, Guardian of Small Bus. award Nat. Fedn. of Ind. Bus., 1990, 94, Cert. of Recognition Am. Cancer Soc., 1990, Idaho Housing Agy., 1990, Idaho Lung Assn., 1985, 86, 89, Friend of Agr. award Idaho Farm Bur., 1989-90, medal of merit Rep. Presdl. Task Force, 1989, Nat. Legislator of Yr. award Nat. Rep. Legislators Assn., 1991, Golden Bulldog award Watchdogs of the Treas., 1996, Thomas Jefferson award Nat. Am. Wholesale Grocers Assn.-Ind. Food Distbrs. Assn., 1996, Spirit of Enterprise award US C. of C., 1993, 94, 95, 96, Watchdogs of Treasury Golden Bulldog award Am. Frozen Food Inst., 2000, Ground Water Protector award Nat. Ground Water Assn., 2002, Best and Brightest award Am. Conservative Union, 2003. Mem. ABA (antitrust law sect.), Idaho Bar Assn., Rotary. Republican. Mem. Lds Ch. Avocations: sports, backpacking, hunting, skiing. Office: US Senate 239 Dirksen Senate Ofc Bldg Washington DC 20510-0001 also: District Office Ste 205 251 East Front St Boise ID 83702-7312 Office Phone: 202-224-6142, 208-334-1776. Office Fax: 202-228-1375, 208-334-9044.*

CRAPOL, EDWARD P., history professor; b. Buffalo, Sept. 29, 1936; s. Paul H. and Emmi H. (Klinger) C.; m. Jeanne Zeidler, Aug. 1, 1973; children: Heidi, Jennifer, Paul, Andrew. BA, SUNY, Buffalo, 1960; MS, Univ. Wis., 1964, PhD, 1968. Tchr. Amherst Ctrl. Jr. High Sch., Amherst, NY, 1961-63; instr. history Wis. State Univ., Eau Claire, Wis., 1966-67; asst. prof. history Coll. William and Mary, Williamsburg, Va., 1967-71, assoc. prof. history, 1971-77; exchange prof. history Univ. Exeter, Exeter, England, 1976-77; prof. history dept. Coll. William and Mary, Williamsburg, Va., 1978—, chmn. history dept., 1981-84, acting chmn. history dept., 1986-87, prof. history, 1994—2004, prof. emeritus, 2004—. Vis. faculty Utah State U., summer, 1972; reviewer grant proposals NEH, 1983—95; lectr. in field. Author: James G. Blaine: Architect of Empire, 1999, John Tyler, The Accidental President, 2006, America for Americans: Economic Nationalism and Anglophobia in the Late Nineteenth Century, 1973; editor: Women and American Foreign Policy: Lobbyists, Critics, and Insiders, 1987, 1992; reviewer manuscripts for Diplomatic History, Journal of the Early Republic, Alfred A. Knopf, Scholary Recources, Greenwood Press, Kent State Univ. Press, D.C. Health, Univ. N.C. Press. Va. Found. for Humanities and Pub. Policy grant, 1983, NEH grant, 1984, 1986, Internat. Studies Curriculum Devel. grant Coll of William and Mary, 1987; U. Humanities fellow Coll. William and Mary, 1988; recipient Thomas A. Graves Jr. award William and Mary Coll., 1991, Thomas Jefferson award Coll. William and Mary, 1992 Mem. Soc. Historians Am. Fgn. Rels., Orgn. Am. Historians, Am. Hist. Assn., Soc. Historians Early Am. Republic. Home: 148 Mimosa Dr Williamsburg VA 23185-4004 E-mail: edpcal@wm.edu.

CRAPON DE CAPRONA, COUNT NOËL FRANÇOIS MARIE, retired senior United Nations official; b. Chambery, Savoie, France, May 23, 1928; s. Denys and Eleanor Worthington (Mather) Crapon de Caprona; m. Barbro Sigrid Wenne, 1954; children: Guy, Yann. BA, Coll. St. Martin, Pontoise, France, 1946; LLB, U. Paris, 1952; diploma, Inst. Comparative Law, 1951; postgrad., Sch. Polit. Scis., 1952—54. Asst. mgr. Sta. Catalina Estancias, Argentina, 1947—48; editor dept. gen. affairs and info. FAO, UN, Rome, 1954—57; liaison officer for UN and various orgns. FAO Office Dir. Gen., 1957—65, chief reports and records, 1966—72, chief conf. ops. br., 1972—74; sec. gen. FAO Conf. and Coun., 1974—78; dir. FAO Conf., Coun. and Protocol Affairs, Rome, 1974—83. Author: The Longobards, A Tentative Explanation, 1995. Served with French Army, 1944. Recipient 25 Years of Svc. award, Silver medal, FAO, 1979, Medal of Honor, City of Salon de Provence, 1992. Mem.: Soc. in France of SAR, Alumni Assn. Ecole des Sciences Politiques, Alumni Assn. Coll. St. Martin. Roman Catholic. Achievements include research in early medieval history, especially Longobards. Address: Palais Hadrien Pl dei Tres Mast 83600 Port-Fréjus France also: 73-75 Lojovägen S-18147 Lidingö Sweden

CRARY, MINER DUNHAM, JR., lawyer; b. Warren, Pa., Sept. 8, 1920; s. Miner D. and Edith (Ingraham) C.; m. Mary Chapman, Jan. 23, 1943; children: Edith Crary Howe, James G., Laura Crary Hall, Harriet Crary, Miner A. BA, Amherst Coll., 1942; MA, Harvard U., 1943, LLB, 1948. Bar: N.Y. 1949. Assoc. Curtis, Mallet-Prevost, 1949-61, ptnr., 1961-96, coun., 1996—. Trustee Am. U. in Cairo, 1959—, Heckscher Art Mus., Huntington, N.Y., 1968-85; trustee Sterling and Francine Clark Art Inst., Williamstown, Mass., 1974—; bd. dirs. Robert Sterling Clark Found., N.Y.C., 1972—; chmn. exec. com. alumni coun. Amherst Coll., 1961-68; chmn. Huntington Bd. Edn. and Ctrl. Sch. Dist. 2, 1961-67; acting village justice Village of Asharoken, Northport, N.Y., 1987-2002. Lt. USNR, 1942-45. Mem. ABA (real property and probate com.), N.Y. State Bar Assn. (taxation and estate com. 1973), Assn. of Bar of City of N.Y. (surrogate ct. com. 1969-73), Union League Club, Century Assn. Club. (N.Y.C.), Huntington Country Club. Office: Curtis Mallet-Prevost Colt 101 Park Ave Fl 38 New York NY 10178-0061 Office Phone: 212-696-6006. E-mail: mdcrary@aol.com, mcrary@cm-p.com.

CRASEMANN, BERND, physicist, researcher; b. Hamburg, Germany, Jan. 23, 1922; came to U.S., 1946, naturalized, 1955; s. Pablo Joaquin and Hildegard Carlota (Vorwerk) C. AB, UCLA, 1948; PhD, U. Calif.-Berkeley, 1953. With Lavadora de Lanas S.A., Viña del Mar, Chile, 1941-46; asst. prof. physics U. Oreg., Eugene, 1953-58, assoc. prof., 1958-63, prof., 1963-89, prof. emeritus, 1989—, chmn. dept., 1976-84, dir. Chem. Physics Inst., 1984-87. Guest assoc. physicist Brookhaven Nat. Lab., Upton, N.Y., 1961-62; vis. prof. U. Calif., Berkeley, 1968-69, Université Pierre et Marie Curie, Paris, 1977; vis. scholar Stanford U., 1983; cons. Lawrence Radiation Lab., 1954-68, physicist, 1968-69; mem. com. on atomic and molecular sci. NRC/Nat. Acad. Scis., 1976-82; vis. scientist NASA Ames Rsch. Ctr., 1975-76; mem. panel on radiation rsch. NRC, 1985-87, chair bd. on assessment of NIST programs panel on atomic molecular and optical physics, 1989-90; chair exec. com. Advanced Light Source Users, 1984-88, sci. policy bd., 1989-92; chair adv. bd. Basic Energy Scis. Synchrotron Radiation Ctr. Argonne Nat. Lab, 1991-93; mem. U. Chgo. Review Com. for Argonne Nat. Lab. Physics Divsn., 1993-98; U.S. advisor in physics U.S.-Mex. Found. for Sci., 1994-97. Author (with J.L. Powell): Quantum Mechanics, 1961; editor: Atomic Inner-Shell Processes, 1975, Atomic Inner-Shell Physics, 1985, Phys. Rev. A, 1992—2006; mem. editl. bd.: Phys. Rev. C, 1978, Atomic Data and Nuc. Data Tables, 1982—, mem. publs. bd.: Am. Inst. Physics, 1992—2000; contbr. articles to sci. jours. Mem. region XIV selection com. Woodrow Wilson Nat. Fellowship Found., 1959-61, 62-68. Recipient Ersted award for distinguished teaching U. Oreg., 1959; NSF research grantee, 1954-64; U.S. AEC grantee, 1964-72; NASA grantee, 1972-79; AFOSR grantee, 1979-86; NSF grantee, 1986-95. Fellow AAAS, Am. Phys. Soc. (chmn. div. electron and atomic physics 1981-82, councillor 1983-86, mem. com. on internat. sci. affairs 1997-2000, chmn. 2000); mem. ACLU, Am. Assn. Physics Tchrs. (pres. Oreg. sect. 1956-57), Croatian Acad. Scis. and Arts (corr. mem.), Sierra Club, Phi Beta Kappa. Office: U Oreg Dept Physics Eugene OR 97403-1274 Home Phone: 541-485-3372; Office Phone: 541-346-4754. Business E-Mail: berndc@uoregon.edu.

CRASWELL, RICHARD, law educator; b. 1954; BA in Econs. with high honors, Mich. State U., 1974; JD cum laude, U. Chgo., 1977. Atty. office policy planning FTC, 1977—81, atty. bur. competition and bur. economics, 1982, atty.-advisor to commr. David A. Clanton, 1982—83; asst. prof. U. So. Calif. Law Ctr., 1983—85, assoc. prof., 1985—88, prof. law, 1988—94, Carolyn Craig Franklin prof., 1991—94, assoc. dean, 1988—90; prof. law U. Chgo. Law Sch., 1994—98, Stanford Law Sch., 1998—, William F. Baxter - Visa Internat. prof. law, 2002—; assoc. dean, 1999—2001. Adj. prof. Georgetown U. Law Ctr., 1983; vis. prof. U. Chgo. Law Sch., 1987—88, Stanford Law Sch., 1993. Victor H. Kramer Fellow, Yale Law Sch. and Yale Instn. for Social & Policy Studies, 1981—82. Office: Stanford Law Sch Crown Quadrangle 559 Nathan Abbott Way Stanford CA 94305-8610 Office Phone: 650-725-8542. Office Fax: 650-723-8230. Business E-Mail: rcraswel@stanford.edu.

CRATER, TIMOTHY ANDREWS, internist; b. Winston-Salem, NC, Aug. 27, 1966; s. John Lee Crater and Nancy Denton Crater; m. Debra Marie Schuh, Feb. 14, 1992; children: Reed Brooks, Zoe Emerson, Grace Warren, Isabelle Holton. BA in History magna cum laude, Wake Forest U., 1989; student field arty. officers basic course, Ft. Sill Arty. Sch., Okla., 1990; officer's tng., U.S. Army Airborne Sch., Ft. Benning, Ga., 1990, 1st Infanty Divsn., 1991; MD, U. Kans., 1998. Commd. 2d lt. US Army, 1989, advanced through grades to 1st lt., 1992, fire support officer hdqs. battery 1/5 field arty. Ft. Riley, 1990-91, fire direction officer bravo battery 1/5 field arty., 1991-92, targeting officer hdqs. battery 1/5 field arty., 1992-93; resigned, 1993; resident in internal medicine U. Ala. Birmingham Hosp., 1998-2001; staff physician internal medicine Hutchinson Clinic, Kans., 2001—, bd. dirs., 2004—; asst. med. dir. Odyssey Hospice, 2006; clin. asst. prof. internal medicine U. Kans. Sch. Medicine, Wichita, 2002—; asst. med. dir. Reno County Hospice, 2003—04; vice chief of staff Hutchinson Hosp., 2005—, chmn. utilization rev., 2005—07, chief of staff, 2007—. Bd. dirs. Hutchinson Hosp., 2005—. Bd. dirs. New Beginnings, 2005—. Decorated Bronze Star medal, Army Commendation medal, Army Achievement medal with oak leaf cluster; fellow, Am. Coll. Physicians; History of Medicine grantee, U. Kans., 1995. Fellow ACP; mem. AMA, VFW (life), Kans. Soc. SAR, Am. Mensa, Am. Legion (life), Officers of the 1st Divsn., U. Kans. Med. Hon. Soc., Rotary (Hutchinson bd. dirs., Paul Harris fellow Rotary Internat.), Phi Beta Kappa, Phi Alpha Theta, Alpha Omega Alpha. Republican. Avocation: reading. Home: 3504 Thunderbird Dr Hutchinson KS 67502 Office: Hutchinson Clinic PA 2101 N Waldron Hutchinson KS 67502 Office Phone: 620-694-4225. Personal E-mail: cratermd@aol.com. Business E-Mail: cratert@hutchclinic.com.

CRAVATH, JAY LEWIS, cultural educator; b. Bozeman, Mont., Mar. 15, 1951; s. John Lewis and Margaret Lee Cravath; children: Chloe Ann Moore, Jeffrey William. BA in Music and Psychology, Rocky Mountain Coll., 1973; MA in Humanities Edn., Ariz. State U., 1990, PhD in Curriculum and Instrn., 2002. Spkr., scholar Ariz. Humanities Coun., Phoenix, 1989—2006; cultural educator Colo. River Indian Tribes, Parker, Ariz., 2002—. Mng. editor Jour. Am. Indian Edn. Ariz. State U. Ctr. for Indian Edn., Tempe, 1998—2006. Author: (nonfiction) North American Indian Music, 2002, The Humanities-Based Classroom, 2002; composer: (music album) Songs for Ancient Days, 1996, (overture) The Wickenburg Way. Bd. dirs. Poston Project, preservation and mus. at former Japanese Am. Internment Camp; vol. Habitat for Humanity, Wickenburg, Ariz., 2005—06; mem. Four Nations Cmty. Sch. Bd.; music dir. Epiphany Episcopal Ch., Tempe, 1994—2002. Named 1992 Citizen of Yr., Ariz. Cable TV Assn., 1992, Ariz. Scholar of Yr., Ariz. Humanities Coun., 1994, Faculty Mem. of Yr., Maricopa County Cmty. Colleges, 1996; Bilingual fellow, Ariz. State U., 2000—02. Mem.: Ariz. Coun. for Social Studies (pres. 1999—2000, bd. dirs.), Ariz. Humanities Coun. (assoc.; speakers bur. 1989—2006). Home: PO Box 1284 Parker AZ 85344 Office: Colorado River Indian Tribes Rt 1 Box 23-B Parker AZ 85344 Home Phone: 928-231-9754; Office Phone: 928-669-8831. Office Fax: 928-669-8732. Personal E-mail: cravath@gmail.com.

CRAVATS, MONROE, science educator; b. NYC, June 8, 1930; s. Max and Ethel Cravats. BA, Bklyn. Coll., 1951; MA, Columbia U., NYC, 1955, PD, 1964, EdD, 1968. Sci. tchr. NYC Bd. Edn., 1951—68; prof. CUNY, 1968—96; ret. Cons. biology Rutgers U., Newark, 1988. Co-author: Course of Study - Biology, 1965, 1969. Chmn., vol. Am. Cancer Soc., NYC, 1969—81.

CRAVCENCO, LUDMILA, academic administrator; b. Balts, Moldova, Oct. 16, 1963; arrived in U.S., 1998; d. Klaudia Rozneritsa; m. Sergei Cravcenco, Nov. 20, 1987; 1 child, Egor Cravcenco. BE, Balts State U., 1985; MEd, Kent State U., 1995, PhD in Higher Edn. Adminstrn., 2004. Adminstr., tchr. English Balts High Sch., Moldova, 1985—87; tchr. English Balts Spl. English Sch., 1987—91; asst. prof. Balts State U., 1991—97; tng. coord. USAID, 1996—97; translator, intepretor, analyst Internat. Monetary Fund, 1997—98; rschr., grad. tchg. asst. Kent State U., Ohio, 1998—2004, adj. prof., 2004—05. Mem.: Nat. Assn. Fgn. Student Advisors, Am. Edn. Rsch. Assn., Am. Soc. Higher Edn., Phi Beta Delta. Avocations: hiking, dance, reading. Home: 9121 Ranch Rd #1301 Streetsboro OH 44241 Office Phone: 330-672-2580. Business E-Mail: lcravce1@sbcglobal.net.

CRAVEN, DONALD EDWARD, epidemiologist, researcher; b. Omaha, Jan. 13, 1944; s. Orvin William and Florence (Waite) Craven; m. Margaret McClave, July 21, 1966 (div. 1971); m. Dianne Munson, Sept. 10, 1983 (div. 1994); children: Natalie, Hillary; m. Kathleen Walsh Steger, Apr. 1, 1995; children: David, Jenny, Kristina. BA, Wesleyan U., Middletown, Conn., 1966; MD, Union Coll., Barbourville, Ky., 1970. Rsch. assoc. NIH Bur. Biologics, Bethesda, Md., 1976-79; hosp. epidemiologist Boston City Hosp., 1979-87, dir., AIDS Pub. Health, 1987-89, dir., AIDS program, 1989—; asst. prof. Boston U. Sch. Medicine and Pub. Health, 1979-84; assoc. prof. Boston U. Sch. Medicine, 1984—2001, prof. medicine, microbiology, epidemiology and biostatics, 1989—; prof. medicine Tufts U. Sch. Medicine, 2001—; chmn. infectious diseases Lahey Clinic Med. Ctr., Burlington, Mass. Mem. adv. bd. AIDS Action Com., 1988-90, mem. hosp. infection control practices adv. com., 1991-95, Ctrs. for Disease Control, 1991, Best Drs. Am., 1992-2006, Am.'s Best Educators. Contbr. 200 articles on hosp. epidemiology and AIDS to med. jours. Sr. surgeon USPHS, 1976-79. Recipient Gov. Recognition award for AIDS Rsch., 1987. Fellow ACP, Royal Coll. Physicians, Am. Coll. Chest Physicians, Infectious Disease Soc.; mem. Soc. Health Care Epidemiologists (pres. 1993), Mass. Hosp. Assn. (mem. adv. bd. for AIDs 1988-93). Home: 20 Clifford St Wellesley MA 02482-6041 Office Phone: 781-744-8608.

CRAVEN, GEORGE W., lawyer; b. Louisville, Mar. 11, 1951; s. Mark Patrick and Doris Ann Craven; m. Jane A. Gallery, Aug. 16, 1980; children: Charles, Francis. Student, Sophia U., Tokyo, Japan, 1970-71; BA, U. Notre Dame, 1973; JD, Harvard U., 1976. Bar: Ill. 1976, U.S. Dist. Ct. (no. dist.) Ill. 1976, U.S. Tax Ct. 1977. Assoc. Sidley & Austin, Chgo., 1976—80; ptnr. Ogden & Robertson, Louisville, 1980—81; assoc. Mayer, Brown, Rowe & Maw, Chgo., 1981—82, ptnr., 1983—. Sec., United Way, Chgo., 1997—2003, gen. counsel 2003-. Mem. ABA (sect. taxation), Coun. on Global Affairs (Chgo. com. 1996—), Econ. Club Chgo. Roman Catholic. Office: Mayer Brown Rowe & Maw LLP 71 S Wacker Dr Chicago IL 60606-4637 Office Phone: 312-701-7231. E-mail: gcraven@mayerbrown.com.

CRAVEN, PAMELA F., lawyer; b. Bloomfield, NJ, 1953; m. Bill Craven; 2 children. BA in English, U. Pa., 1974, JD, 1977; LLM in taxation, NYU, 1981. Bar: 1977. Assoc. McCarter & English, 1977—79, Coudert Brothers, 1979—82; asst. gen. counsel, asst. sec. NCR Corp., 1982—92; atty. AT&T, 1992—96; v.p. law Lucent Technologies Inc., Murray Hill, NJ, 1996—2000, sec., 1999—2000, v.p., gen. counsel, sec. Enterprise Networks Group, 2000; v.p., gen. counsel, sec. Avaya Inc., Basking Ridge, NJ, 2000—02, sr. v.p., gen. counsel, sec., 2002—. Bd. overseers U. Pa. Law Sch., 2004—; bd. managers U. Pa. Law Alumni Assn.; chair cmty. adv. bd. NJ Network. Recipient Alumni Award of Merit, U. Pa. Law Alumni Soc. Office: Avaya Inc 211 Mount Airy Rd Basking Ridge NJ 07920*

CRAVEN, WES, film director; b. Cleve., Aug. 2, 1939; m. Bonnie Broecker, 1964 (div. 1969); children: Jonathan, Jessica; m. Mimi Craven, July 25, 1982 (div. 1987); m. Iya Labunka, Nov. 27, 2004. Co-owner prodn. co. Craven/Maddalena Films. Writer, editor, dir. (films) Last House on the Left, 1972, The Hills Have Eyes, 1977; 2d editor You've Got To Walk It Like You Talk It or You'll Loose That Beat, 1973; dir. (films) Deadly Friend, 1986, The Serpent and the Rainbow, 1988, Vampire in Brooklyn, 1995, Music of the Heart, 1999, Cursed, 2005, Red Eye, 2005, (TV films) A Stranger in Our House, 1978, Invitation to Hell, 1984, Chiller, 1985; actor: (films) The Fear, 1995, The Cutting Edge: The Magic of Movie Editing, 2004, (TV films) Shadow Zone: The Undead Express, 1996; actor, dir.: (films) Scream, 1996, Scream 2, 1997, Scream 3, 2000; writer: (films) A Nightmare on Elm Street 2: Freddy's Revenge, 1985, A Nightmare on Elm Street 4: The Dream Master, 1988, A Nightmare on Elm Street: The Dream Child, 1989, Freddy's Dead: The Final Nightmare, 1991, Freddy vs. Jason, 2003, Pulse, 2006; writer, dir. (films) Deadly Blessing, 1981, Swamp Thing, 1982, A Nightmare on Elm Street, 1984; writer, prodr.: (films) The Hills Have Eyes II, 2007; exec. prodr. (films) A Nightmare on Elm Street 3: Dream Warriors, 1987, Shocker, 1989, Night Visions, 1990, The People Under the Stairs, 1991, New Nightmare, 1994, The Outpost, 1995, Wishmaster, 1997, Carnival of Souls, 1998, Dracula 2000, Feast, 2005, (TV films) Laurel Canyon, 1993, Don't Look Down, 1998, They Shoot Divas, Don't They?, 2002, (TV series) Nightmare Cafe, 1992, Hollyweird, 1998, author: (novel) The Fountain Society. Mem. Dirs. Guild Am. Avocation: birdwatching.*

CRAVENS, GARY DEAN, information scientist, physician; b. Phila., Oct. 18, 1953; s. Robert Walker and Mary Edna Cravens. BA, Ind. U., 1975, MS, 1979, MS, 1984, MS, 1992, MD, 1997. Computer programmer analyst Naval Surface Warfare Ctr., Crane, Ind., 1984—85; mathematician USAF Sch. Aerospace Medicine, San Antonio, 1985—87; advanced discipline specialist Vanguard Tech. Corp., Crane, 1987—88; resident Mayo Clinic, Rochester, Minn., 1999—2000; sr. informaticist Ingenix Health Intelligence, Eden Prairie, 2000—02; bioinformaticist Ind. U., Indpls., 2002—04; physician U. Pitts. Med. Ctr., 2004—05; informaticist Ind. U., Indpls., 2005—. Contbr. articles to profl. jours. 2d lt. USAF, 1975-77. Med. Informatics fellow Ind. U., 1997-99. Mem. Am. Med. Informatics Assn. (reviewer 1998-99), World Future Soc., Alpha Omega Alpha. Avocations: travel, reading. Office: Indiana Univ Sch Informatics 535 W Michigan St IT 468 Indianapolis IN 46202 Personal E-mail: gcravens@iupui.edu.

CRAVER, CHARLES HENRY, illustrator; b. Eldon, Mo., Dec. 6, 1909; s. Charles Henry and Sylvia (John) C.; m. Nadia Aileen Palmer, Nov. 5, 1950. Student, St. Louis Sch. Fine Art, 1927-30, 34-36; AB, Washington U., 1933. Freelance mag. illustrator Capper Publs., Topeka, 1933-36, So. Agriculturist, Nashville, 1936-42, Christian Bd. of Publ., St. Louis, 1945-1948; staff artist Mo. Dept. Health, Jefferson City, 1948—2002, bur. chief, 1957, Mo. Dept. Health Edn., Jefferson City, 1959; instr. art dept. Lincoln U., Jefferson City, 1991-94. Works include mural at Christian Ch., 1937, Bapt. Ch., 1945, exhibit at Am. Pub. Health, 1955 (2 awards), Mo. state seal, 1949, numerous landscapes, 1950-97. Mem. Capital City Coun. on the Arts, Jefferson City; advisor Nichols Ctr., Jefferson City. Staff Sgt. U.S. Air Corps, 1942-45, Africa. Recipient presdl. citation Mo. Pub. Health Assn., Jefferson City, 1984. Mem. St. Louis Artists Guild, Co. of Mil. Historians, Soc. for Army Hist. Rsch., Mil. Hist. Soc. Republican. Mem. Christian Ch. (Disciples Of Christ). Home: 1305 Moreland Ave Jefferson City MO 65101-3734 E-mail: nadapc@aol.com.

CRAVER, EARLENE, historian, educator; b. Fresno, Calif., Jan. 8, 1940; d. Earl H. Craver and Rose K. Gregorian; m. Axel Leijonhufvud, June 18, 1977; stepchildren: Gabriella Leijonhufvud, Christina Leijonhufvud. BA summa cum laude, Fresno State Coll., 1960; PhD, U. So. Calif., 1972. Instr. U. Calif., Riverside, 1968—70; asst. prof. U. Ky., Lexington, 1970—74; lectr. Calif. State U., Northridge, 1983, UCLA, 1983; vis. prof. U. Trento, Italy. Contbr. articles to profl. jours. Fellow, Nat. Def. Edn. Act, 1960—64, NEH, 1987—88. Mem.: Orgn. Am. Historians, Soc. Italian Hist. Studies, Am. Hist. Assn., Phi Kappa Phi.

CRAVER, JAMES BERNARD, lawyer; b. Morristown, NJ, July 20, 1943; s. Herbert Seward and Anne (Brady) C.; m. Elinor Ladd, Aug. 27, 1966; children: Elisabeth Ladd, Amy Richmond Nightingale. AB cum laude, Harvard U., 1965; JD, U. Pa., 1970. Bar: N.Y. 1970, Mass. 1974, Ohio 1980. Assoc. Sullivan & Cromwell, NYC, 1970-73; asst. counsel, asst. sec. Mass. Fin. Svcs. Co., Boston, 1973-76; gen. counsel, sec. Anchor Corp., Elizabeth, NJ, 1976-79; sec., sr. corp. counsel B.F. Goodrich Co., Akron, Ohio, 1979-84; ptnr. Baker & Hostetler, Columbus, 1984-90; sr. v.p., gen. coun. Signature Fin. Group, Inc., Boston, 1991-95; mng. dir. Eagle Instl. Fin. Svcs., Inc., Dover, Mass., 1995-2000; ptnr. Burns & Levinson, Boston, 2000—05; of counsel Seyfarth Shaw, Boston, 2005—07; gen. counsel Medder Fin., Inc., 2007—. Mem. N.Y. State Bar Assn., Mass. Bar Assn., Ohio Bar Assn., Boston Bar Assn., Sakonnet Golf Club (Little Compton, R.I.), Harvard Club of Boston, Harvard Club of Akron, Dedham (Mass.) Country and Polo Club. Home: PO Box 811 Dover MA 02030-0811 Office Phone: 617-345-0007. Business E-Mail: craverjim@comcast.net.

CRAWFORD, BRETT A., lawyer; BA in Journalism, La. State U., 1988; MBA, Dartmouth Coll., 1994; JD, Georgetown U., 2004, PhD candidate, 2006. Bar: Md. Cons. World Bank, Washington, 1989; assoc. coord. higher edn. transition team for Gov.-elect Mike Foster, La., 1995; co-owner, prin. cons. The Sequoia Group LLC, Baton Rouge; exec. dir. LA. Econ. Devel. Corp., 1996—97; undersec. revenue State of La., 1998—99, sec. revenue, 1999—2000; assoc. Sonnenschein Nath & Rosenthal LLP, Washington. Office: Sonnenschein Nath & Rosenthal LLP Ste 600, E Tower 1301 K St NW Washington DC 20005 Office Phone: 202-408-9238. Office Fax: 202-408-6399. Business E-Mail: bcrawford@sonnenschein.com.

CRAWFORD, BRUCE EDGAR, advertising executive; b. West Bridgewater, Mass., Mar. 16, 1929; s. Harry Ellsworth and Nancy (Morrison) C.; m. Christine Amelung, Feb. 1, 1958; 1 son, Robert Bosworth. BS in Econs., U. Pa., 1952. With Benton & Bowles, Inc., NYC, 1954-58; v.p. Ted Bates & Co., NYC, 1958-61; advt. dir. Chesebrough Ponds Inc., NYC, 1961-63; with Batten, Barton, Durstine & Osborn, Inc., NYC, 1963-85, pres., from 1978, BBDO Internat., NYC, 1975-83, chief exec. officer, 1977-85, chmn., 1985; dir. Met. Opera Assn., from 1976, v.p., 1981, pres., 1984-85, gen. mgr., 1986-88; pres., chief exec. officer Omnicom Group, NYC, 1989-97; chmn. Omnicom Group, Inc., NYC, 1995—, Lincoln Center for the Performing Arts, NYC, 2002—05. Served with U.S. Army, 1947-48. Mem.: Racquet and Tennis (N.Y.C.); Turf and Field. Republican.*

CRAWFORD, CAROL GLORIA, mathematician, educator; b. Wilkes-Barre, Pa., Dec. 8, 1951; d. Harry H. and Gloria P. Crawford. BA in Math., Misericordia Coll., 1973; MA in Math., Georgetown U., 1975, PhD in Math., 1979. Prof. math. LeMoyne Coll., Syracuse, NY, 1979—81, U.S. Naval Acad., Annapolis, Md., 1981—. Mem. rev. panels NSF, 1997—99, 2003; v.p. faculty senate U.S. Naval Acad., 2001—03; presenter in field. Author: Math Without Fear, 1981; contbr. articles to profl. jours.; assoc. editor Am. Math. Monthly, 1984—86. Named rsch. fellow, USN, 1982, NASA, 1984; recipient Civilian Meritorious Svc. award and medal, USN, 1998; fellow, Inst. for Combinatorics, Winnipeg, Can., 1990; grantee, FBI, 1994—96, Office of Naval Rsch., 1994—96, NASA, 1994—96, David Taylor Rsch. Ctr., 1994—96, Carderock Divsn., 1994—96, Naval Air Warfare Ctr. Mem.: Math. Assn. Am. (regional chair, vice chair 1998—2000). Office: US Naval Acad Dept Math Annapolis MD 21402 Business E-Mail: cgc@usna.edu.

CRAWFORD, CAROL TALLMAN, law educator; b. Mt. Holly, NJ, Feb. 25, 1943; m. Ronald Crawford; children: Timothy, Jeffrey, Richard. BA, Mt. Holyoke Coll., 1965; JD magna cum laude, Washington Coll. Law, Am. U., 1978. Bar: Va. 1978, DC 1979. Legis. asst. to Senator Bob Packwood, Washington, 1969-75; assoc. firm Collier, Shannon, Rill & Scott, Washington, 1979-81; exec. asst. to chmn. FTC, Washington, 1981-83, dir. bur. consumer protection, 1983-85; assoc. dir. Office of Mgmt. & Budget, Washington, 1985-89; asst. atty. gen. legis. affairs U.S. Dept. Justice, Washington, 1989-90; commr. U.S. Internat. Trade Commn., 1991-2000; disting. vis. prof. law George Mason U., Arlington, Va., 2000-01. Bd. dirs. European Inst., Ind. Women's Forum, Smithfield Foods, Inc. Trustee Barry Goldwater Chair of Am. Instns., Ariz. State U., Phoenix, 1983—; chair internat. trade and investment subcom. Federalist Soc., 1998—99, chair internat. and nat. security sect., 1999—2003; adv. com. NAFTA Labor Agreement, 2002—; bd. trustees Torray Fund, 2006—. Republican.

CRAWFORD, CLAIRE CRESSMAN, volunteer, educator; d. Robert Leonard and Edna Mae Finkle Cressman; m. William Gentry Crawford, Jr., July 28, 1990. AA, Broward CC, Fort Lauderdale, Fla., 1968; BA, Fla. State U., Tallahassee, 1971; cert. in arts adminstrn., Harvard U., 1973; MFA, Fla. State U., Tallahassee, 1974; DPA, Nova Southeastern U., Ft. Lauderdale, 1989; cert. in fund raising mgmt., Ind. U., 2007. Exec. dir. Tallahassee CC Found., 1987—88; fed. rels. officer Fla. Dept. State, Tallahassee, 1979—81, chief bur. statewide programs, 1982—86; adj. prof. Fla. Atlantic U., Ft. Lauderdale, 1997—2006. Editor: (mag.) Act 1. Trustee Tallahassee Arts Coun., 1972—85; mem. Broward Cultural Coun., Ft. Lauderdale, 1989—2007, chair, 2004, 2005; chair fund devel. Ft. Lauderdale Hist. Soc., 2000—06, trustee, 2006—07. Recipient Hist. Commr.'s award, Broward County Hist. Commn., 2002, Cultural Leadership, Broward Cultural Coun., 2004, 2005, Joseph Leavitt award for Dedication to the Arts, Fla. Youth Orch., 2005. Mem.: Assn. Fund Raising Profls., Rev. Club. Roman Catholic. Avocations: reading, philanthropic fund raising. Home: 2409 N E 7th Pl Fort Lauderdale FL 33304 Home Fax: 954-563-7910.

CRAWFORD, CLINTON, art historian, educator; b. Georgetown, Demerara, Guyana, July 26, 1952; s. Muriel Crawford and Berkley Saltus Williams; m. Reba Joyce Ashton, Aug. 15, 1992. MFA, U. Calif., Santa Barbara, 1986, M in Edn., 1988; EdD, Columbia U., N.Y.C., 1992. Prof. Medgar Evers Coll., CUNY, Bkyln., 1993—. Dir. John Henrik Clarke-CLR James African World Rsch. Inst., Bklyn., 1999—; lectr. and presenter in field. One-man shows include Casa de la Rasa, Santa Barbara, 1986, U. Calif., 1987, Tchrs. Coll. Columbia U., NYC, 1991, Medgar Evers Coll., CUNY, Bklyn., 2000; author: Recasting Ancient Egypt in the African Context: Toward a Model Curriculum Using Art and Language, 1996; editor: Ebonics and Language Education of African Anecestry Studies, 2001; mem. editl. bd.: Cmtyl. Rev. CUNY Faculty Scholarly Jour., 1995—. Supporter Elephantine Island Sch., Aswan, Egypt, 2002—07. Mem.: Harlem Writers Guild, Coll. Composition and Comm., Nat. Conf. Tchrs. English (life; Black Caucus 1995—). Office: Medgar Evers Coll CUNY 1650 Bedford Ave Brooklyn NY 11225 Home Phone: 718-756-8904. Personal E-mail: sankofawp@netscape.net. Business E-Mail: crawford@mec.cuny.edu.

CRAWFORD, DAVID L., astronomer; b. Tarentom, Pa., Mar. 2, 1931; s. William Letham and A. Blanche (Livingstone) C.; m. Mary Louise Mueller, Aug. 16, 1940; children: Christine, Deborah, Lisa. PhD, U. Chgo., 1958. Rsch. asst. Yerkes Obs., Chgo., 1953-57; asst. prof. Vanderbilt U., Nashville, 1957-59; staff astronomer Kitt Peak Nat. Obs., Tucson, 1960-96, emeritus astronomer, 1997—. Rsch. asst. McDonald Obs., 1955-57; project mgr. Kitt Peak Nat. Obs., 1963-73, assoc. dir. rsch., 1970-73, head office univ. rels., 1984-85, head office of tech. transfer, 1993-95; exec. dir. Internat. Dark-Sky Assn., 1987—, pres. bd. dirs. GNAT, Inc., 1993—. Recipient outstanding svc. award Astron. League, 1992. Fellow AAAS (coun. 1986-89, com. on coun. affairs 1986-88), Illuminating Engring. Soc. N.Am. (roadway lighting com., outdoor environ. lighting impact com., sports lighting com.); mem. Am. Astron. Soc. (coun. 1972-75, Van Briesbrock award 1997), Astron. Soc. Pacific (bd. dirs. 1970-76, nominating com., publs. com.), Internat. Astron. Union (active numerous commns., exec. coms., past chmn. working group on amateur/profl. rels.). Avocations: travel, reading, teaching, trout fishing, photography. Office: IDA 3225 N First Ave Tucson AZ 85719 Office Phone: 520-293-3198. E-mail: crawford@darksky.org, ida@darksky.org.

CRAWFORD, DENISE F., lawyer; BS, Calif. Polytechnic Univ., 1999; JD, Univ. San Diego, 2002. Bar: Calif. 2002. Assoc., criminal defense Law Offices of Jennifer L. Keller, Irvine, Calif. Named a Rising Star, So. Calif. Super Lawyers, 2006. Office: Law Offices of Jennifer L Keller Ste 560 18500 Von Karman Ave Irvine CA 92612-1043 Office Phone: 949-476-8700. Office Fax: 949-476-0900.

CRAWFORD, DONALD WESLEY, philosophy educator, university official; b. Berkeley, Calif., July 30, 1938; s. Arthur Loyd and Josephine (Gareffa) C.; m. Sharon Dee Messenger, Nov. 5, 1960; children: Kathryn, Alison. BA, U. Calif., Berkeley, 1960; PhD, U. Wis., 1965. From tchg. asst. to dean U. Wis., Madison, 1962—89, dean Coll. Letters and Sci., 1989-92; asst. prof. U. Sask., Saskatchewan, Canada, 1965-68; vice chancellor acad. affairs U. Calif., Santa Barbara, 1992-93, exec. vice chancellor, 1993-98, prof., 1992—2004, prof. emeritus, 2004—, dir. London Ctr. for Edn. Abroad program, 1998-2000, dep. assoc. provost, 2001—. Author: Kant's Aesthetic Theory, 1974; editor Jour. Aesthetics and Art Criticism, 1989-93. Bd. dirs. Meriter Hosp., Madison, 1989-92, Santa Barbara Bot. Garden, 1993-98, U. Calif. Santa Barbara Found., 1992-98, U. Calif. Trust (U.K.), 2000—. NEH fellow, 1974. Mem. Am. Soc. for Aesthetic, Brit. Soc. for Aesthetic. Office: U Calif Dept Philosophy South Hall Santa Barbara CA 93106 E-mail: crawford@philosophy.ucsb.edu.

CRAWFORD, DOROTHY HILL, retired secondary school educator, art educator, artist; b. Kirk, Colo., July 29, 1922; d. Arthur John and Daisy Goldus Hill; m. Carroll Knight Crawford, Dec. 24, 1948; 1 child, Mardi Eileen; m. Dennie Greene (div.); 1 child, Thane Verlyn Greene. BFA, U. No. Colo., Greeley, 1948, MFA, 1964, post grad., 1965. Cert. life tchg. Colo. Tchr. North Sch., Ft. Morgan, Colo., 1948—49; secondary tchr. Kirk Sch., 1949—50, 1954—55, Liberty Sch., Kirk, Colo., 1955—82; ret., 1982. Pvt. piano tchr., 1984—89. Mem. Habitat Humanity, Public Citizen, Common Cause, NOW; contr. U. No. Colo. Visual Arts, Rocky Mountain PBS, Drug Policy Alliance, So. Povery Law Ctr., Nat. Breast Cancer Coalition. Mem.: Union Concerned Scientists, Nat. Women's History Mus., Nat. Mus. Women in Arts (charter 1988). Avocations: piano, interior decorating, cats. Home: 1901 CR H Joes CO 80822

CRAWFORD, FRANKLIN DAVID, publishing executive; b. Denver, Aug. 9, 1928; s. Clifford Theodore and Sarah Ann (Fergeson) C.; m. Ruth Emilia Dallenbach, Oct. 19, 1957; children: Mark Franklin, Grant Robert. BA, Alma White Coll., 1953. Retail exec. Saks Fifth Av., NYC, 1954-56, Federated Dept. Stores, NYC, 1956-58, Allied Stores Corp., NYC, 1958-61, J.C. Penney Corp., NYC, 1961-63; owner, pres. Princeton Microfilm Corp., NJ, 1963—. Pres. Nat. Library Service Co., Princeton, 1974—. Chmn. bd. US Hist. Documents Inst., Washington, 1970—; cons. Alma White Coll., Zarephath, NJ; v.p., bd. dirs. Weaver Found., St. Louis, 1966—; mem. Internat. Tennis Found. and Hall of Fame, Inc. Served with USAF, 1946-49, 53-54. Mem.: Nassau, Beadensbrook, West Side Tennis. Republican. Home: PO Box 7006 Princeton NJ 08543-7006 Office: PO Box 2073 Princeton NJ 08543-2073 Home Phone: 609-845-2066; Office Phone: 800-257-9502. E-mail: fdc@princetonmicro.com.

CRAWFORD, FRED ALLEN, JR., cardiothoracic surgeon, educator; b. Columbia, SC, Oct. 17, 1942; s. Fred Allen and Susan Valery Floyd C.; m. Mary Jane Dantzler, June 11, 1966; children: Fred Allen III, Mary Elizabeth. MD, Duke U., 1967. Diplomate Am. Bd. Surgery, Am. Bd. Thoracic Surgery. Intern Duke U. Med. Ctr., Durham, NC, 1967-68, resident in surgery, 1971-76, instr. surgery, 1975-76; asst. prof. surgery, chief divsn. cardiac surgery U. Miss., Med. Ctr., Jackson, 1976-79; prof. surgery pediat., chief divsn. cardiothoracic surgery Med. U. of S.C., Charleston, 1979—, chmn. dept. surgery, 1988—. Contbr. numerous articles to profl. jours. Maj. U.S. Army, 1969-71. Decorated Bronze Star. Mem. ACS, Am. Surg. Assn., Charleston County Med. Soc., S.C. State Med. Assn., Soc. Thoracic Surgeons, So. Surg. Assn., So. Thoracic Surg. Assn., Am. Heart Assn., Am. Assn. Thoracic Surgery (pres. 2003), Am. Bd. Thoracic Surgery (bd. dirs. 1991-2002, chmn., 2001), Am. Coll. Cardiology, Phi Beta Kappa, Alpha Omega Alpha. Presbyterian. Office: 96 Jonathan Lucas St Rm 409 Charleston SC 29425-0001 Home Phone: 843-884-0361; Office Phone: 843-792-5897. Business E-Mail: crawfrdf@musc.edu.

CRAWFORD, HUNT DORN, JR., retired military officer, educator, diplomat; b. Louisville, Dec. 25, 1948; s. Hunt Dorn Sr. and Carrol Frank (Watson) C.; m. Kate Kerr Delano, Aug. 1, 1970; children: Scott Holden, Carolyn Hunt. BS, U.S. Mil. Acad., 1970; MA and MS, Stanford U., Palo Alto, Calif., 1978; MPh, Columbia U., 1980; MMAS, Command & Gen. Staff Coll., 1985. Commd. 2d lt. U.S. Army, 1970, advanced through grades to lt. col., 1987; staff officer, comdr. 1st Inf. Div. Forward, Augsburg, Germany, 1970-73; staff officer Hdqrs. III Corps, Ft. Hood, Tex., 1974-75; from instr. to asst. prof. U.S. Mil. Acad., West Point, NY, 1978-81; staff prin. 1st Inf. Div. Forward, Goppingen, 1981-84; instr. Command & Gen. Staff Coll., Ft. Leavenworth, Kans., 1985-88; strategic analyst U.S. Army Concepts Analysis Agy., Bethesda, Md., 1988-91; ret. U.S. Army, 1992; polit./mil. affairs advisor U.S. Arms Control & Disarmament Agy., Washington, 1991-99, U.S. Dept. of State, Washington, 1999—. Mem. NATO arms control analysts group SHAPE Tech. Ctr., Hague, Netherlands, 1988-90; mem. conv. arms control work group Ctr. for Strategic and Internat. Studies, Washington, 1989-90; mem. arms control ad hoc study group Carnegie Endowment for Internat. Peace, Washington, 1990-92; mem. conventional arms control project Ford Found., 1993-96; adj. prof. polit. sci. U. Louisville, 1995—. Author: Conventional Armed Forces in Europe (CFE): A Review and Update of Key Treaty Elements, ann. 1991—; contbr. articles to profl. jours. and books. Decorated ACDA Meritorious honor award, Def. Superior Svc. medal, 5 M.S.M. awards. Mem. AAAS, Am. Polit. Sci. Assn., Acad. Polit. Sci., Internat. Inst. Strategic Studies, Internat. Studies Assn., Mil. Ops. Rsch. Soc. (bd. dirs. 1991-98, exec. coun. 1995-98), Inst. Ops. Rsch. and Mgmt. Scis., Phi Kappa Phi. Republican. Episcopalian. Avocations: bicycling, racquetball, aquaria. Home: 932 Audubon Pkwy Louisville KY 40213-1365 Office: US Dept of State 2201C St NW Washington DC 20520 Office Phone: 202-647-9407. E-mail: crawforddo@t.state.gov, dorncrawford@aol.com.

CRAWFORD, J. BROOKS, ophthalmologist, educator; b. San Francisco, Aug. 2, 1933; s. Joseph William Crawford and Ora Amanda Brooks; m. Christine Mayne, Sept. 12, 1964; children: Catherine Helene Crawford Bradford, Peter Brooks. B Engring, Yale U., New Haven, 1955; MD, U. Calif. San Francisco, 1960. Diplomate Am. Bd. Ophthalmology. Intern Columbia Presbyn. Med. Ctr., NYC, 1960—61; resident ophthalmology U. Calif. Med. Ctr., San Francisco, 1961—64; clin. assoc. NIH, Bethesda, Md., 1964—66; NIH Spl. fellow eye pathology Armed Forces Inst. Pathology, Washington, 1966—67; chief ophthalmology Children's Hosp., San Francisco, 1978—92; clin. prof., dir. eye pathology U. Calif., San Francisco, 1992—; pvt. practice ophthalmology San Francisco, 1967—. Asbury lectr. U. Cin., 2004; guest lectr. Japanese Ophthalmic Pathology

Soc., Osaka, 1998, European Ophthalmic Pathology Soc., Stockholm, 2003; bd. dirs. That Man May See, San Francisco; dir. Eye Pathology Lab. Dept. Ophthalmology U. Calif. Sch. Medicine, San Francisco, 1972—. Contbr. articles to profl. jours. Bd. trustees Town Sch. Boys, San Francisco, 1976—85; bd. dirs. Am. Bd. Ophthalmology, 1976—93, chmn., 1993; bd. dirs. No. Calif. Soc. Prevention Blindness, pres., 1992—93. Lt. cmdr. USPHS, 1960—66. Recipient Charlotte Baer Meml. award, U. Calif. San Francisco, 1995, Crowell Beard award Dept. Ophthalmology, 1995. Fellow: ACS; mem.: Beard-Quickert Soc., Cordes Eye Soc. (pres. 1981—82, Hogan lectr. 1992), Verhoeff Soc. (pres. 1988), Am. Assn. Ophthalmic Pathologists, Am. Ophthalmol. Soc. (editor Trans. 1997, pres.-elect 2003—04, pres. 2004—05), Am. Acad. Ophthalmology (assoc. sec. 1993—97, Zimmerman lectr. 2000), Armed Forces Inst. Pathology Alumni Assn., Pacific Union Club, Bhemian Club, Gold Headed Cane Soc., Tau Beta Pi, Alpha Omega Alpha, Sigma Xi. Office: 3838 California St San Francisco CA 94118

CRAWFORD, JACKIE R., retired federal agency administrator; m. Frances Lindsey; children: Jessica, Andrea, Katrina. BBA, Fla. State U., 1967; M in Acctg., Bowling Green State U., 1974; postgrad., Fed. Exec. Inst., Charlottesville, Va., 1988, Harvard U., 1991. CPA, Fla. Auditor Air Force Audit Agy., Eglin AFB, Fla., 1967-72, audit mgr. Wright-Patterson AFB, Ohio, 1972-77, supr. auditor L.A. AFB, 1977-79, Robins AFB, Ga., 1980-82, assoc. dir. weapon sys. audits Wright-Patterson AFB, Ohio, 1982-86, assoc. dir. acquisition, 1986-87, asst. auditor gen. acquisition and logistics audits, 1988-93; dir. acquisition support programs Dept. Def., Arlington, Va., 1987-88; auditor gen. of the Air Force The Pentagon, Washington, 1993—2001. Home: 233 Sweetwater Run Niceville FL 32578

CRAWFORD, JAMES DEE, chemical distribution executive; b. Boise, Idaho, June 23, 1950; s. Glen E. and Beverly J. (Thomas) C.; m. Diane E. Crawford (Ball), July 8, 1994. BBA, Boise State U., 1972. CPA, Idaho. Staff acct. J.R. Simplot Co., Boise, 1972-75, corp. acctg. mgr., 1975-79, asst. contr. Caldwell, Idaho, 1979-80; treas. SimCal Chem. Co., Fresno, Calif., 1980-83; dir. fin services J.R. Simplot Co., Boise, 1983-85, treas., 1995—97; CFO Wilbur-Ellis Co., San Francisco, 2000—; v.p., contr. J.R. Simplot Co., Boise, 1997—2000. Bd. dirs. Micron Tech., Inc., Boise, Investors Fin. Corp., Boise. Com. chmn. St. Alphonsus Found., Boise, 1985. Named one of Outstanding Young Men Am., Jaycees, 1974. Mem. AICPA, Idaho Soc. CPAs, Nat. Assn. Corp. Treas. Clubs: Crane Creek Country (Boise), City Club of San Francisco. Republican. Episcopalian. Avocation: golf.

CRAWFORD, JAMES DOUGLAS, lawyer; b. Phila., May 31, 1932; s. James A. and Katharine M. (Evenson) C.; m. Judith N. Dean, Apr. 29, 1977; 1 child, Christopher Anne Crawford Samson. AB, Haverford Coll., 1954; LLB, U. Pa., 1962. Bar: Pa. 1963, DC 1979, US Supreme Ct. 1968. Assoc. Montgomery, McCracken, Walker & Rhoads, Phila., 1962-66; asst. dist. atty. Phila., 1966-68; dep. dist. atty., chief appeals divsn., 1968-72; gen. counsel Redevel. Authority of City of Phila., 1972-74; ptnr. Schnader, Harrison, Segal & Lewis, Phila., 1974-97, sr. counsel, 1998—. Mem. adv. com. on appellate rules Pa. Supreme Ct., 1985-92; lectr. in law U. Pa., 1971-73; bd. dirs. Na. Assn. Law Placement, 1978-79; nat. chmn. ann. giving U. Pa. Law Sch., 1985-87. Editor in chief U. Pa. Law Rev., 1961-62. Mem. exec. com. Friends Phila. Mus. Art, 1980—86, fin. sec., 1981—82, co-chmn., 1982—84, mem. prints and drawing com., 1987—; treas. Hist. Soc. US Ct. Appeals for 3d Cir., 1994—2000, pres., 2000—; bd. dirs. ACLU, 1978—, v.p., 1985—, bd. dirs. Pa. chpt., 1962—, v.p., 1980—85, pres., 1985—; bd. dirs., mem. exec. com. ACLU Greater Phila., 1972—, v.p., 1983—85; bd. dirs. Pub. Interest Law Ctr. Phila., 1980—90, mem. adv. bd., 1991—; bd. dirs. Citizens Crime Commn. Phila., 1986—96, Samuel S. Fleisher Art Meml., 1984—, pres., 1998—; bd. dirs. Print Club Phila., 1983—85, v.p., 1984—96, mem. adv. coun., 1997—. With US Army, 1955—57. Fellow Am. Bar Found., Am. Coll. Trial Lawyers, Am. Acad. Appellate Lawyers; mem. Phila. Bar Assn. (gov. 1973-75, chmn. com. of censors 1972), Phila. Bar Found. (trustee 1987-93, sec. 1988-92), Am. Law Inst., Defender Assn. Phila. (bd. dirs. 1975—), Athenaeum Club, St. Andrews Soc., Order of Coif, Phi Beta Kappa. Republican. Presbyterian. Office: Schnader Harrison et al 1600 Market St Ste 3600 Philadelphia PA 19103-7287 also: 68 Renme Ct 11 Upper Ground London SE1 9NZ England Personal E-mail: cd2018@aol.com Business E-Mail: jcrawford@schnader.com.

CRAWFORD, JAMES LEROY, minister, retired theology studies educator; b. Tonkawa, Okla., Aug. 22, 1935; s. Leroy Jefferson and Beulah Lucille Crawford; m. Sammye Helen Henson, Jan. 26, 1957; children: James Jr., Joyce E. McCartney, Janet K. Austin. BA, Okla. Bapt. U., 1956, M Div., Southwestern Bapt. Theol. Sem., 1965, ThM, 1967, ThD, 1970. Ordained min. Bapt. Ch. Pastor S.E. Bapt. Ch., Muskegee, Okla., 1959—60, 1st So. Bapt. Ch., Rock Falls, Ill., 1960—61, Immanuel Bapt. Ch., Poteau, Okla., 1961—65, Mt. Gilead Bapt. Ch., Keiler, Tex., 1965—67, 1st Bapt. Ch., Alba, Tex., 1967—69; prof., ch. planter Internat. Mission Bd., So. Bapt. Conv., Richmond, Va., 1964—2001; ret., 2001; prof. ext. Southwestern Bapt. Theol. Sem., Ft. Worth; pastor Iglesia Bautista El Olivar Spanish congregation of Olivet Bapt. Ch., Oklahoma City, 2005—06. Adj. prof. Okla. Bapt. U., Shawnee, 2001—04, Okla. Bapt. U., MTI Ctr., Oklahoma City, 2001—, Southwestern Bapt. Theol. Sem. Ctr., Shawnee, 2006; prof. Spanish Bible Inst. Golden Gate Sem., Oklahoma City, 2004—; prof. Bapt. Theol. Sem., Los Teques, Venezuela, 1971—80, Los Teques, 1985—2000, pres., 1980—85, pres. emeritus, 1996. Author: (guide) Study Guide for the Old Testament, 1974, Biblical Introduction, 1996, (commentary series) Exegisis of the Book of Leviticus (in Spanish), 1998. Mem.: History Channel Club. Avocation: scroll sawing. Home: 5800 Melton Dr Oklahoma City OK 73132 E-mail: jlcrawford1@cox.net.

CRAWFORD, JAMES WELDON, psychiatrist, educator, administrator; b. Napoleon, Ohio, Oct. 27, 1927; s. Homer and Olga (Aderman) C.; m. Susan Young, July 5, 1955; 1 child, Robert James AB, Oberlin Coll., 1950; MD, U. Chgo., 1954, PhD, 1961. Intern Wayne County Hosp. and Infirmary, Eloise, Mich., 1954-55; resident Northwestern U., Chgo., 1958-59, Mt. Sinai Hosp./Chgo. Med. Sch., 1959-60; practice medicine specializing in occupational, individual and family psychiatry Chgo., 1961—. Mem. staff St. Lukes-Presbyn. Med. Ctr.; clin. assoc. prof. dept. psychiatry Sch. of Medicine, U. Ill. at Chgo., 1970—; chair and assoc. prof. dept. psychiatry Ravenswood Hosp. Med. Ctr., 1973-79; chmn. J.W. Crawford Assocs., Inc., 1979-82; assoc. prof. depts. behavioral scis. and psychiatry Rush Med. Co. Contbr. articles to profl. jours. Bd. dirs. Pegasus Players, Chgo., 1978—96, chmn. bd. dirs., 1979-84; bd. dirs. Bach Soc., 1985-98; adv. Ill. Masonic Med. Ctr.; health adv. com. Cook County (Ill.) Commr., 2003—; del. to Russia and the Ukraine with People-to-People Internat., 1993, del. to Kenya, 1995, del. to China, 1998. NIH Inst. Neurol. Diseases postdoctoral fellow, 1955-59. Fellow Am. Psychiat. Assn. (life, dist. mem.), Am. Orthopsychiat. Assn.; mem. AAAS, Am. Soc. Psychoanalytic Physicians, Nat. Coalition Mental Health Profls. and Consumers, Ill. Coalition Mental Health Profls. and Consumers (steering com.), Ill. Psychiat. Soc., Chgo. Assn. for Psychoanalytic Psychology, Nat. Coun. on Family Rels., Rotary (com. mem. profl. rep.), Sigma Xi. Achievements include research in identified field and EEG. Home and Office: 2418 Lincoln St Evanston IL 60201-2151 Office Phone: 847-869-3108. Personal E-mail: sjcrawf@aol.com.

CRAWFORD, JEFFREY C., oncologist, educator; children: Matt, Andy. BA, Wesleyan U., Ohio, 1970; MD, Ohio State U., 1974. Cert. Internal Medicine, Med. Oncology, Hematology. Intern, medicine Duke Med. Ctr., Durham, NC, 1974—75, resident, hematologic oncology, 1975—77, 1977—80, fellow, 1977—78, 1979—81; prof., med. oncology Duke U. Med. Ctr., Durham, NC, 1997—, chief, divsn. med. oncology, 2004—; assoc. dir., clin. rsch. Duke Comprehensive Cancer Ctr., Durham, NC. Contbr. articles to profl. jours. Office: Duke U Med Ctr Morris Bldg DUMC 3476 Durham NC 27710 Office Phone: 919-681-9509, 919-684-5621. Office Fax: 919-681-9599, 919-681-5864. E-mail: crawf006@mc.duke.edu.*

CRAWFORD, JOE JAY, real estate company executive; b. Nagoya, Honsu, Japan, Oct. 27, 1954; came to U.S., 1954; s. Charles B. and Betty K. (Wilson) C.; m. Kimberly R. Glover, Aug. 13, 1977; children: Taylor Garrett, Kimberly Faith. BBA in Econ. and Finance, Baylor U., 1976; MBA in Finance, U. Tex., 1978. Comml. credit analyst InterFirst Bank Dallas, 1979, banking officer, 1979-80, asst. v.p., 1980-83, CitiCorp Real Estate, Dallas, 1983-85, v.p., area dir., 1985-90, v.p., sr. banker, team leader, 1990-93; sr. exec. officer Amstar Group, Ltd., Dallas, 1993-98, COO, 1998—. Cons. in field; bd. dirs. Nat. Multi-Housing Coun., Sycor Internat., Inc. Adult choir pres. 1st Bapt. Ch., Mesquite, Tex., 1984, Sunday sch. dir., tchr., 1986-87, chmn. budget com., 1986-88, deacon, 1982-89, vice chmn. deacons, 1984; dir., tchr. Sunday sch. Lakeridge Bible Ch., Mesquite, 1991-93. Named Outstanding Young Men of Am., U.S. Jaycees, 1980. Mem. Dallas Young Mortgage Bankers Assn. (sec.-treas. 1983), Sigma Phi Epsilon (life), Alpha Kappa Psi (treas., v.p. 1973-76, nat. conv. del. 1975, life 1976—), Omicron Delta Epsilon. Republican. Avocations: fly fishing, golf, hunting, camping, auto restoration. Office: Amstar Group Ltd 1050 17th St Ste 1220 Denver CO 80265-1050

CRAWFORD, JOHN EDWARD, retired geologist, consultant; b. Richmond, Va., June 6, 1924; s. James Henry and Loretta Ellen (Bankerd) C.; m. Mary Elizabeth Ayres, May 15, 1948; children: Michelle Lorraine, Caprice Lizette. BA, Johns Hopkins, 1947. Reg. geologist, Calif. Geologist uranium exploration program U.S. Geol. Survey, 1948-51; nat. stockpile materials specialist Munitions Bd., Office Sec. Def., 1951-53; prodn. engr. AEC, 1953-54; specialist on source, feed, fissionable materials Bur. Mines, 1954-57, nuclear tech. adviser to dir., 1957-60, chief nuc. engr. for atomic rsch. programs, 1960-63; dir. Marine Mineral Tech. Ctr., Tiburon, Calif., 1963-66; pres., founder Crawford Marine Specialists, Inc., San Francisco, also Suva, Fiji, 1966-76; pres. Earth Tech. Corp., San Rafael, 1973-77; mgr. geothermal rsch. programs and Salton Sea sci. drilling project U.S. Dept. Energy Ops. Office, Oakland, Calif., 1977-89; mgr. ops. and prin. geologist Western Geologic Resources, Inc., San Rafael, Calif., 1989-90; cons. geothermal and environ. affairs, 1990—; assoc., regional mgr. Western Ops. Earth Resources Internat., L.C., Carson City, Nev., 1994-2000; ret., 2007. Author: Facts Concerning Uranium Exploration and Production, 1956; contbr. articles to govt. and profl. jours., Leaders in Am. Sci. Vol. VIII, 1968-69. Mem. Calif. Gov.'s Commn. Ocean Resources, 1966-67, Calif. Gov.'s Small Hydro Task Force, 1981-82. Served with AUS, 1943-46. Mem. Internat. Marine Minerals Soc. (Moore medal for excellence in devel. of marine minerals 1998), Geol. Soc. Am., Marine Tech. Soc. (past chmn. marine mineral resources com., past chmn. marine resources div.), Delta Upsilon. Home and Office: 1510 Valencia Ct Carson City NV 89703-2333 Home Phone: 775-884-3735; Office Phone: 707-884-3735.

CRAWFORD, KENNETH CHARLES, retired academic administrator; b. Nokomis, Ill., Oct. 31, 1918; s. Charles Bryant and Blanche Dora (Gates) C.; m. Madge Marie Douglas, Aug. 23, 1942; 1 son, James Douglas. BA, Ill. Coll., 1946, SJD (hon.), 1970; JD, U. Va., 1951; grad., Command and Gen. Staff Coll., 1957, Army War Coll., 1962; MA, George Washington U., 1962. Bar: Va. 1951, Ga. 1967, Korean 1965, U.S. Supreme Ct. 1970, D.C. 1977. Commd. 2d lt. U.S. Army, 1942, advanced through grades to col., 1962; served in (F.A. and JAG Corps); tchr. legal subjects U. Md., U. Ga., Ga. State U., Nat. U., Washington, 1957-67; comdr. JAG Sch., 1967-70; ret., 1970; pres., CEO Ken Crawford Ednl. Inst., Inc., 1986-89. Editor: Laws of the Republic of Korea, 1964. Assoc. dir. edn. Southwestern Legal Found., Dallas, 1970-71, Atty. at Law, 1990-92; dir. edn. and tng. Fed. Jud. Ctr., Washington, 1971-86; cons. Fed. Jud. Ctr., 1986-87. Decorated Legion of Merit with 2 oak leaf clusters, Soldiers medal, Bronze Star, Belgian Fourragere, Disting. Citizen citation Ill. Coll., 1993. Mem. State Bar Va., Korean Bar, Order of Coif. Home Phone: 210-677-2709.

CRAWFORD, KYLE A., industrial engineer; b. Amarillo, Tex., Aug. 20, 1960; s. Alvin G. and Bonnie J. Crawford; children: Megan A., Cameron P., Bryce K. BS in Indsl. Engring., Wichita State U., Kans., 1984, MS in Engring. Mgmt. Sci., 1989; M Engring. in Mech. Engring., Ga. Inst. Tech., Atlanta, 1999, postgrad., 1999—. Cert. quality engr., Am. Soc. Quality, 1988. Engr. Kans. Gas and Electric, Wichita, 1984—89; sr. engr. Westinghouse, Aiken, SC, 1989—95; supply chain mgr. BellSouth Telecom., Atlanta, 1995—97; sr. rsch. engr. Ga. Tech Rsch. Inst., Atlanta, 1997—2006; project mgr. inComm, Atlanta, 2007—. Vol. Big Bros. Big Sisters, Wichita, Kans., 1982—84, United Way, Augusta, Ga., 1992, Am. Diabetes Assn., Atlanta, 2006—07. Recipient Total Quality Achievement award in mgmt., Westinghouse, 1993, Total Quality Achievement award in engring., 1994. Mem.: IEEE, Ga. Tech Alumni Assn., Mensa Soc., Alpha Pi Mu (life). Achievements include invention of methodolgy for certification: leak before break analysis; knowledge-based system for aiding the procurement process; research in knowledge-based system for assuring nuclear material quality. Home: 251 10th St NW Apt A223 Atlanta GA 30318-5600 Home Phone: 404-206-3223; Office Phone: 678-528-7607. Office Fax: 404-601-1000. Personal E-mail: gt6165b@mail.gatech.edu. Business E-Mail: kcrawford@incomm.com.

CRAWFORD, LENEIDA MARIE, singer, educator; d. Charles Dewey and Noreta M. Crawford; m. Lewis H. Ziska, Jan. 3, 1987. BS, Va. Commonwealth U., Richmond, 1975; MA, Calif. State U., Fresno, 1987; Dr. of Mus. Arts, U. of Md., 1996. Adj. prof. Prince George's C.C., Largo, Md., 1987—96; assoc. prof. Towson U., Towson, Md., 1996—, asst. chmn. dept. music, 2005—. Mem.: Nat. Assn. of Tchrs. of Singing. Democrat-Npl. Avocations: snorkeling, travel, white-water rafting. Office: Towson University/Department of Music 8000 York Rd Towson MD 21252 Home Phone: 410-233-6585; Office Phone: 410-704-2818. Office Fax: 410-704-2841. Personal E-mail: leneida@comcast.net. E-mail: lecrawford@towson.edu.

CRAWFORD, LESTER MILLS, JR., former federal agency administrator; b. Demopolis, Ala., Mar. 13, 1938; s. Lester Mills and Susan Doris (Mitchell) C.; m. Catherine Walker, July 27, 1963; children: Catherine Leigh, Mary Stuart. DVM, Auburn U., Montgomery, Ala., 1963; PhD in Pharmacology, U. Ga., Athens, 1969; MDV (hon.), Budapest U., Hungary, 1987. Pvt. practice vet. medicine, Meridian, Miss. and Birmingham, Ala., 1963-64; R & D staff agrl. divsn. Am. Cyanamid Co., Princeton, NJ, 1964-66, cons.; assoc. dean Coll. Vet. Medicine, U. Ga., 1970-75, head dept. physiology-pharmacology, 1980-82; dir. Ctr. Vet. Medicine, FDA, Dept. Health and Human Svcs., Rockville, Md., 1978—80, 1982—85; assoc. adminstr. food safety and inspection svc. USDA, Washington, 1986-87, adminstr., food safety and inspection svc., 1987-91; exec. v.p. sci. affairs Nat. Food Processors Assn., Washington, 1991-93; exec. dir. Assn. Am. Vet. Med. Colls., Washington, 1993—97, 2001—02; dir. Ctr. Food and Nutrition Policy, Georgetown U., Washington, 1997-2001; dir. Ctr. Food and Nutrition Policy Va. Tech., 2001—02; dep. commr. FDA, US Dept. Health & Human Services, Rockville, Md., 2002—04, acting commr., 2004—05, commr., 2005; sr. counsel Policy Directions Inc., Washington, 2006—. Cons. pharm. industry, agribus. FDA, WHO; mem. Health Professions Commn., Pew Meml. Trust, 1990-93; bd. dir. Cary Pharm. and Immunobiosciences; mem. sci. adv. bd. Inst. Food Tech., 1999-2002; chmn. dept. physiology-pharmacology, U. Ga. Contbr. sci. articles to profl. jours. Vice chmn. Codex Alimentarius Commn., 1991-93; bd. dir. Food and Drug Law Inst., 1988-2002; expert advisor food safety WHO. Recipient A.M. Mills award, 1979, K.F. Meyer award, 1980, U.S. Presdl. Rank award of Meritorious Exec., 1988, Disting. Alumnus award, Auburn U., 1989, Wooldridge Meml. medal, Brit. Vet. Assn., 1991, Commrs. Spl. citation FDA, award of merit, 1983. Fellow: Internat. Acad. Food Sci. and Tech., Royal Soc. Medicine (U.K.); mem.: WHO (mem. expert adv. panel food safety), AVMA, AAAS, NAS Inst. Medicine, Fedn. Am. Sch. Health Professions (pres. 1997), French Acad. Vet. (hon.), Nat. Acad. Practice, Cosmos Club (Washington), Phi Kappa Phi, Phi Zeta, Sigma Xi. Republican. Office: Policy Directions Inc 818 Connecticut Ave NW Ste 950 Washington DC 20006 *I have always predicated my own life on the certain knowledge that God is still at work in the world. I believe that every person carries a divine spark, and that the function of leadership is to ignite that spark. I furthermore believe that a Franciscan love of and respect for animals is a prerequisite for membership in the human race. And I believe that the true rewards in life are to be found in communion with family, friends and colleagues.*

CRAWFORD, LINDA SIBERY, lawyer, educator; b. Ann Arbor, Mich., Apr. 27, 1947; d. Donald Eugene and Verla Lillian (Schenck) Sibery; m. Leland Allardice Crawford, Apr. 4, 1970; children: Christina, Lillian, Leland. Student, Keele U., 1969; BA, U. Mich., Ann Arbor, 1969; postgrad., SUNY, Potsdam, 1971; JD, U. Maine, 1977. Bar: Maine 1977, U.S. Dist. Ct. Maine 1982, U.S. Ct. Appeals (1st cir.) 1983. Tchr. Pub. Sch., Tupper Lake, N.Y., 1970-71; asst. dist. atty. State of Maine, Farmington, 1977-79, asst. atty. gen. Augusta, Maine, 1979-95; prin. Linda Crawford and Assoc., 1985—. Litigation Consulting Firm, NYC, 1986—. Legal adv. U. Maine, Farmington, 1975; legal counsel Fire Marshal's Office, Maine, 1980-83, Warden Svc., Maine, 1981-83, Dept. Mental Health, 1983-90, litigation divsn. 1990-95; tchg. team trial advocacy Law Sch., Harvard U., 1987—; lectr. Sch. Medicine Harvard U., 1991, 2004—; counsel to Bd. of Registration in Medicine, 1994-95; chmn. editl. bd. Mental and Physical Disability Law Reporter, 1993-95; arbitrator Am. Arbitration Assn., 1995—; facilitator Nat. Constrn. Task Force, St. Louis, 1995. Contbg. editor: Med. Malpractice Law and Strategy, 1997—, Managed Care Law Strategist, 1999—2002. Bd. dirs. Diocesan Human Rels. Coun., Maine, 1977-78. Arthritis Found., Maine, 1983-88; atty. expert commn. experts UN War Crime Investigation in the former Yugoslavia, 1994. Named one of Outstanding Young Women of Yr., Jaycees, 1981. Mem. ABA (com. on disability 1992-95), Nat. Assn. State Mental Health Attys. (treas. 1984-86, vice chmn. 1987-89, chmn. 1989-91), Nat. Health Lawyers Assn. Office: 150 Orleans St PH 1 East Boston MA 02128 also: 45 Rockefeller Plz Fl 20 New York NY 10111-2099 Office Phone: 800-208-6117. Business E-Mail: crawford@lcandassociates.com.

CRAWFORD, (EDWIN) MAC, pharmaceutical company executive; b. 1949; m. Linda Crawford; children: Andrew, Ellen. BS, Auburn U., 1971. CPA. With Arthur Young & Co., 1971—77, 1978—81, Salem Nat. Corp., 1977—78, GTI Ltd., 1981—85, 1986, Oxylance Corp., 1985—86, Mulberry St. Investment Co., 1986—90; exec. v.p. hosp. ops. Charter Med. Corp., Atlanta, 1990—92; pres., COO Magellan (formerly Charter Med. Corp.), Atlanta, 1992—93, chair., pres., CEO, 1993—97; pres., CEO MedPartners, Inc., Birmingham, 1997—98; chmn., pres., CEO Caremark Rx, Inc. (formerly MedPartners), Birmingham, 1998—2007; chmn. CVS Caremark Corp., Woonsocket, RI, 2007—. Bd. dirs. Nashville Healthcare Coun., 2003—04, Pharm. Care Mgmt. Assn.; bd. trustees Healthcare Leadership Coun. Office: CVS Caremark Corp 1 CVS Dr Woonsocket RI 02895*

CRAWFORD, MARC, professional hockey coach; Hockey player Vancouver Canucks; head coach Quebec Nordiques, 1994-95, Colo. Avalanche, 1995-97, Vancouver Canucks, 1998—2006, LA Kings, 2006—. Head coach Team Can. Nagano Olympic Games, 1998. Recipient Louis A.R. Pieri Meml. award, 1992-93, Jack Adams award, 1994-95; named NHL Coach of Yr. The Sporting News, 1994-95. Achievements include coach, Stanley Cup Champion Colo. Avalanche, 1996. Office: LA Kings 1111 S Figueroa St, Suite 3100 Los Angeles CA 90015

CRAWFORD, MARIA LUISA BUSE, geology educator; b. Beverly, Mass., July 18, 1939; d. William Theodore Buse and Barbara (Kidder) Aldana; m. William A. Crawford, Aug. 29, 1963. BA, Bryn Mawr Coll., 1960; postgrad., U. Oslo, 1960-61; PhD, U. Calif., 1965. Asst. prof. Bryn Mawr (Pa.) Coll., 1965-73, assoc. prof., 1973-79, prof., 1979-92, prof. environ. studies and sci., 1992—2006, William R. Kenan Jr. prof., 1985-92, chmn. dept. geology, 1976—88, 1998—2005; mem. U.S. Nat. Com. Geology, 1994-97. Chmn. women geoscientists com. Am. Geol. Inst., 1976-77; mem. U.S. Nat. Com. Geochemistry, 1980-82; organizing com. 28th Internat. Geol. Cong., 1987-89. MacArthur fellow, 1993-98; grantee NASA, 1973-76, NSF, 1967—. Fellow Geol. Soc. Am. (councillor 1982-85), Mineral Soc. Am. (councillor 1989-92); mem. Mineral Assn. Can. (councilor 1985-87), Am. Geophys. Union, Norwegian Geol. Soc., Phila. Geol. Soc., Assn. Women in Sci. Office: Bryn Mawr Coll Dept Geology Bryn Mawr PA 19010 Office Phone: 610-526-5111. Business E-Mail: mcrawfor@brynmawr.edu.

CRAWFORD, MARK E., chemist; s. Robert and Margaret Crawford. BS, U. Wis., Madison, 2000. Chemist U. Wis., 2000—05; applications chemist Gilson, Inc., Middleton, Wis., 2005—. Contbr. articles to profl. jours. Home: 821 Ctr St Baraboo WI 53913 Office: Gilson Inc 3000 Parmenter St Middleton WI 53562 Home Phone: 608-235-3121; Office Phone: 608-828-3273. Personal E-mail: mcrawford@gilson.com.

CRAWFORD, MICHAEL HOWARD, cardiologist, educator, researcher; b. Madison, Wis., July 10, 1943; s. William Henry and A. Kay (Keller) C.; m. Janis Raye Kirschner, June 23, 1968; children: Chelsea Susan, Dinah Jaye, Stuart Michael. AB, U. Calif., Berkeley, 1965; MD, U. Calif., San Francisco, 1969. Diplomate in internal medicine and cardiovasc. disease Am. Bd. Internal Medicine. Med. resident U. Calif. Hosps., San Francisco, 1969-71, sr. med. resident Beth Israel Hosp., Boston, 1971-72; tchg. fellow Harvard Med. Sch., Boston, 1971-72; cardiology fellow U. Calif. Hosps., San Diego, 1972-74; asst. prof. medicine U. Calif. Sch. Medicine, San Diego, 1974-76, U. Tex. Health Sci. Ctr., San Antonio, 1976-78, assoc. prof. medicine, 1978-82, prof. medicine, 1982-89; Robert S. Flinn prof. cardiology U. N.Mex. Sch. Medicine, Albuquerque, 1989—2001; prof. medicine Mayo Med. Sch., Minn., 2001—03, U. Calif., San Francisco, 2003—, Lucie Stern chair cardiology, 2005—. Asst. dir. Ischemic Heart Disease Specialized Ctr. Rsch., San Diego, 1975—76; adj. scientist S.W. Found. Biomedical Rsch., San Antonio, 1980—89; co-dir. div. cardiology U. Tex. Health Sci. Ctr., San Antonio, 1983—89; chief div. cardiology U. N.Mex. Sch. Medicine, Albuquerque, 1989—2001; cons. cardiovasc. diseases Mayo Clinic, Scottsdale, Ariz., 2001—03; chief clin. cardiology U. Calif. San Francisco Med. Ctr., 2003—07; chief divsn. cardiology U. Calif., San Francisco, 2007—. Editor: Current Diagnosis and Treatment in Cardiology, 1995, 2d edit., 2004, Cardiology, 2001, 2d edit., 2003; editor Clin. Cardiology Alert newsletter, 1990—; cons. editor (periodical) Cardiology Clinics, 1989-; mem. editl. bd. Circulation Jour., 1990-99, Jour. Am. Coll. Cardiology, 1992-95, 2003-. Pres. Am. Heart Assn., San Antonio, 1981, Austin, Tex., 1987, chmn. coun. clin. cardiology, Dallas, 1989, pres., Albuquerque, 1995-96. Recipient Paul Dudley White award, Assn. Mil. Surgeons of U.S., 1981; Merit Review grantee, Dept. VA, 1985—91, Rsch. Tng. grantee, Nat. Heart Lung Blood Inst., 1993—2004. Fellow: ACP, Am. Heart Assn., Am. Coll. Cardiology (bd. trustees 1998—2003); mem.: Western Assn. Physicians, Assn. Univ. Cardiologists (pres. 2005—06), So.

Soc. Clin. Investigation, Am. Soc. Echocardiography (bd. dirs. 1980—83). Avocation: skiing. Home: 4104 Shelter Bay Ave Mill Valley CA 94941 Office: U Calif 505 Parnassus Ave Box 0124 San Francisco CA 94143-0124 Office Phone: 415-502-8584.

CRAWFORD, MURIEL LAURA, lawyer, educator, writer; d. Mason Leland and Pauline Marie (DesIlets) Henderson; m. Barrett Matson Crawford, May 10, 1959; children: Laura Joanne, Janet Muriel, Barbara Elizabeth. BA with honors, U. Ill., 1973; JD with honors, Ill. Inst. Tech., 1977; cert. employee benefit splst., U. Pa., 1989. Bar: Ill. 1977, Calif. 1991, U.S. Dist. Ct. (no. dist.) Ill. 1977, U.S. Dist. Ct. (no. dist.) Calif. 1991, U.S. Ct. Appeals (7th cir.) 1977, U.S. Ct. Appeals (9th cir.) 1991; CLU; chartered fin. cons. Atty. Washington Nat. Ins. Co., Evanston, Ill., 1977-80; sr. atty., 1980-81; asst. counsel, 1982-83; asst. gen. counsel, 1984-87; assoc. gen. counsel, sec., 1987-89; cons. employee benefit splst., 1989-91; assoc. Hancock, Rothert & Bushoft, San Francisco, 1991-92. Author: (with Beadles) Law and the Life Insurance Contract, 1989, (sole author) 7th edit., 1994, Life and Health Insurance Law, 8th edit., 1998; co-author: Legal Aspects of AIDS, 1990; contbr. articles to profl. jours. Recipient Am. Jurisprudence award Lawyer's Coop. Pub. Co., 1975, 2nd prize Internat. LeTourneau Student Med.-Legal Article Contest, 1976, LOMA FLMI Ins. Edn. award, 1999. Fellow Life Mgmt. Inst.; mem. Ill. Inst. Tech./Chgo.-Kent Alumni Assn. (bd. dirs. 1983-89, Bar and Gavel Soc. award 1977), Daughters of the Am. Revolution (registrar Anne Loucks Chpt., Nat. Soc., 2006-). Democrat.

CRAWFORD, NORMAN CRANE, JR., academic administrator, consultant; b. Newark, Oct. 30, 1930; s. Norman Crane and Anna (Wares) C.; m. Garnette Bell, June 25, 1955; children: Sally Jean, Ellen Ann. BS in Edn., Rutgers U., 1951, MEd, 1957; PhD, Northwestern U., 1966. Dir. scholarships Nat. Merit Scholarship Corp., Evanston, Ill., 1957-62; asst. dean arts and sci., asst. to provost U. Del., 1962-66, 67-70; acting dir. exams. Coll. Entrance Exam. Bd., NYC, 1966-67; pres. Salisbury (Md.) State Coll., 1970-80, Drury Coll., Springfield, Mo., 1981-83; v.p. ops. Council for Advancement and Support Edn., Washington, 1985-87; interim pres. U. Maine, Farmington, 1987-88; v.p. pub. affairs Thomas A. Edison State Coll., 1989-91; cons. higher edn. Berlin, 1992—. Lt. j.g. USN, 1951-55. Joint recipient Higher Edn. Leadership award Gov. Del., Gov. Md., Gov. Va., 1974; named hon. trustee Ward Found. Wildfowl Art Museum, 1977. Mem. Phi Delta Kappa. Episcopalian. Home and Office: 108 Ocean Pkwy Ocean Pines MD 21811-1644 E-mail: nccrawford@salisbury.edu.

CRAWFORD, PAUL FLEMING, historian; b. Toronto, Ontario, Can., July 20, 1961; arrived in US, 1965; s. Charles Mervyn and Paula Ruth Crawford; m. Ardella Mae Lacy, Oct. 6, 1984. AS, Lamar CC, Colo., 1982; BA, Peru State Coll., Nebr., 1984; MA, U. Wis., Madison, 1993, PhD, 1998. Game designer Adventure Learning Sys., Colorado Springs, 1984; computer sci. instr. Lamar CC, Colo., 1985—90; adj. faculty history U. Wis., Milw., 1996, 1998—99, lectr. history Oshkosh, 1999—2001; asst. prof. history Alma Coll., Alma, Mich., 2001—06, Calif. U. of Pa., California, 2006—. Cons. Weller-Grossman (History Channel), 1999, Lion TV (History Channel), 2004—05, Atlantic Prodns. (History Channel), 2005—06, Nat. Geographic TV, 2005—; co-founder online reference ORB; appearance History's Mysteries: The Children's Crusade (History Channel), 2000, The Crescent and the Cross (History Channel), 2005, Lost Worlds: The Knights Templar (History Channel), 2006. Translator: The Templar of Tyre: Pt. III of the Deeds of the Cypriots, 2003; contbr. chapters to books. Fellow, Alma Coll., 2005—06; Heckman fellow, Hill Monastic Manuscript Libr. St. John's U. Minn., 1997, 1998, E.B. Fred fellow, U. Wis. Madison, 1991. Mem.: Am. Hist. Assn., Soc. Study of Crusades and the Latin East. Avocations: reading, fencing, horseback riding. Office: Calif U of Pa 250 Univ Ave California PA 15419-1394 Office Phone: 724-938-6054. Business E-Mail: crawford_p@cup.edu.

CRAWFORD, R. GEORGE, investment company executive, educator, filmmaker; b. Mpls., Oct. 30, 1943; s. Robert John and Agnes C.; m. M. Holly Shissler, May, 17, 1980; 1 child, Katherine Barnes. BA, Harvard U., 1965, JD, 1968. Bar N.Y. 1974, DC 1970, Calif. 1972, Ohio, 1969. Law clk. to Hon. Byron R. White U.S. Supreme Ct., Washington, 1968—69; staff asst. to Pres. Washington, 1970—72; v.p. Archon, Inc., LA, 1972—74; chair pvt. capital sect. Jones Day Reavis & Pogue, LA, 1974—93; pres. Ilex Group, NYC, 1997—; prof. Stanford U., Calif., 1993—2001. Author: Derivatives for Decision Makers, 1996; prodr., dir.: (documentary) The Healing Within-Stress Reduction for Cancer and Heart Disease, 2006; contbr. articles to profl. jours. Pres. Fiduciary Found., N.Y., N.Y., 1992—; mem. supr. coun. Internat. Ctr. Not-for-Profit Law, Washington, 1998—; mem. adv. bd. Wealth Trust, Nashville, 2006—. Home: 152 Woodlands Rd Harrison NY 10528 Business E-Mail: gc@iinc.us.

CRAWFORD, RANDY M., lawyer; b. Memphis, July 3, 1972; s. Hubert Crawford Jr. and Gloria Dean Crawford; m. Shalana Monique Alexander, June 19, 2004; 1 child, Taylor D. BA, U. Ark., Fayetteville, 1993—2003; JD, U. Mo., Kansas City, 1997. Asst. prosecutor Jackson County Mo. Pros. Attys. Office, Kansas City, 1997—99; trial atty. Allstate Ins. Co. Staff Coun., Kansas City, 1999—2003, lead counsel, 2003—06; lawyer Rasmussen, Willis Dickey, & Moore LLC, Kansas City, Mo., 2006—. Cmty. prosecutor Jackson County Mo. Pros. Attys. Office, Kansas City, 1998—99. V.p. of bd. dirs. Aviation Youth Acad., Lee's Summit, Mo., 2004; trustee Ebenezer AME Ch., Kansas City, 2006. Maj. US Army N.G., 1989—, Olathe, Kans. Decorated Brigage Co. Grade Officer Yr. 69th Brigade, Kans. Army N.G., Officer Tng. scholar US Army, Parachutist badge US Army Airborne, Achievement medal US Army N.G., Res. Components Achievement medal (4th award), Nat. Def. Svc. medal (2nd award), Commendation medal (4th award) US Army N. G., Gobal War Terrorism medal US Army, Overseas Svc. Ribbon, Bronze Star medal, Svc. Ribbon; recipient Individual Svc. Award, Allstate Ins. Co., 2001. Mem.: ABA (assoc.), Kans. Bar Assn. (assoc.), Mo. Bar Assn. (assoc.), Kans. City Met. Bar Assn. (assoc.). Achievements include community service: working with under-privileged children to help them see that their current circumstances do not define their destinies. Office: Rasmussen Willis Dickey & Moore LLC 9200 Ward Parkway Ste 310 Kansas City MO 64114 Office Phone: 816-360-1746. Office Fax: 816-960-1669. Business E-Mail: rcrawford@rwdmlaw.com.

CRAWFORD, RAYMOND MAXWELL, JR., management consultant; s. Raymond Maxwell and Mary Elizabeth (Bates) C.; m. J. Denise LeDuc, Mar. 10, 1951; children: Denis, Michael, Deborah, Peter, Elizabeth. BS, Wayne State U., 1958, MS, 1960; PhD, UCLA, 1969. Registered profl. engr., 1978. Instr. Wayne State U., 1960-63; asst. prof. Calif. State U., Northridge, 1963-66; mem. tech. staff Atomics Internat., 1969-71; nuc. engr. Argonne Nat. Lab., Ill., 1971-74; assoc. and asst. head nuc. safeguards and licensing divsn. Sargent & Lundy, Chgo., 1974-80; v.p. Sci. Applications, Inc., Oak Brook, Ill., 1980-83; engring. dir. Nutech, Chgo., 1983-86; pres. Engring. Rsch. Group, Naperville, Ill., 1986—; mgr. spl. projects Fluor Daniel, Inc., 1988—2003; cons. Longenecker & Assocs., 2004—. Tech. cons. Atomic Power Devel. Assn., 1962-63; summer fellow NASA Lewis Rsch. Ctr., 1965-66. Contbr. articles to profl. jours. Scoutmaster, counsellor Boy Scouts Am., 1963—66; active YMCA, 1966—69, Recs. for Blind, 1964—65. Recipient numerous awards. Mem. Am. Nuclear Soc., Am. Inst. Chem. Engrs., Am. Chem. Soc., Nat. Soc. Profl. Engrs., Ill. Soc. Profl. Engrs. Republican. Presbyterian. Home: 1005 Kennebec Ln Naperville IL 60563-1413

CRAWFORD, RICHARD BRADWAY, biologist, biochemist, educator; b. Kalamazoo, Feb. 16, 1933; s. Kenneth and Alma (Smith) C.; m. Betty J. Jacobs, Jan. 30, 1954; children: Kathleen, Christine, Kevin, Nancy. AB, Kalamazoo Coll., 1954; PhD in Biochemistry, U. Rochester, 1959. Post-doctoral fellow U. Rochester, NY, 1959; instr. to assoc. prof. U. Pa., 1959-67; assoc. prof. to prof. biology Trinity Coll., Hartford, Conn., 1967-98, prof. emeritus, 1998—, chmn. dept., 1978-87, resuming chmn., 1996-97. Asst. dir., trustee Mt. Desert Island Biol. Lab., Salsbury Cove, Maine, 1966-82; vis. scientist Jackson Lab., Bar Harbor, Maine, 1988; vis. prof. biology U. Warwick, Eng., 1988; vis. prof. marine biology U. Calif. San Diego, 1974; vis. prof. U. Edinburgh, 1996; mem. faculty and curriculum com. Acadia Sr. Coll., 2000—, v.p. bd. dirs. Contbr. articles to profl. jours. Mem. Inlands, Wetlands and Water Courses Commn., Wethersfield, Conn., 1976-81, Wethersfield Conservation Commn., 1995-98; bd. dirs. Mt. Desert Island Hist. Soc., sec., 2001—; v.p. bd. dirs. Acadia Sr. Coll., 2003-. Mem. Beatrix Farrand Soc. (bd. dirs. 2006—), Rotary Club Hartford (pres. 1994-95), Mount Desert Island Rotary. Democrat. Congregationalist. Home: PO Box 826 Mount Desert ME 04660-0826

CRAWFORD, RICHARD EBEN, JR., retired investment advisor; b. Lake Forest, Ill., Dec. 24, 1930; s. Richard Eben Crawford and Alice B. (Appleton) Smith; m. Caroline Hellen Kelley, June 20, 1952 (div. 1980); children: Wes, John, J.D., Lindsay, Richard; m. Debbie Sum Chan, Feb. 1, 1985; children: Alexandra, Jessica. BA, Trinity Coll., Hartford, Conn., 1953; MBA, U. Pa., 1976. Various positions Minn. Natural Gas Co., St. Louis Park, Minn., 1957-69, pres., chief exec. officer, 1969-74; pres. Minn. Natural div. Minn. Gas Co., St. Louis Park, 1974-77; underwriter Conn. Gen. Life Ins. Co., Mpls., 1978-79; pres. Crawford Assocs., Tucson, 1980—85, Crawford Meml. Cemetery, Emlenton, Pa., 1986; founder Crawford Entrepreneurial Studies, LLC, 2002. Co-author: The Crawfords from Venango County, Pennsylvania, 1999. Area and state judge Career Devel. Conf. Ariz. Distbv. Edn. Clubs Am., 1986; vol. Mobile Meals program, Tucson, 1984-90; trustee St. Andrews Presbyn. Ch., Tucson, 1992-93, pre-sch. adv. bd., 1993; chartered mem. Presbyn. Ch. Am., 1998—; Rep. committeeman, 1992-94; chmn. Ariz. Advocacy Group for the US Pres. Line Item Veto, co-founder, 2004, 05. Capt. USAF, 1955-57. Mem. SAR (treas. Tucson chpt. 1991, 2d v.p. 1992, 1st v.p. 1994), Tuscon C. of C. (com. mil. affairs 1983-90), Pres.'s Club U. Ariz. Found., Skyline Country Club (tennis com. 1988-90), Wharton Club Ariz. (founder, pres. 1986-90), Greater Tuscon Econ. Coun. (agy. com. 1992-95), Toastmasters (pres. Aztec club 1984, 92, area gov. 1986-87, chmn. speechcraft com. 1987-88, Disting. Toastmaster, Catalina Foothills H.s. youth leadership pub. spkg. counselor 1995-96), Rotary (dist. treas. 1988-89, chmn. various coms.), Alpha Delta Phi. Avocations: genealogy, tennis, fishing. Personal E-mail: richardcrawford30@comcast.net.

CRAWFORD, ROBERT F., lawyer; 2 children. BA, U. N.D., 1970; JD, Ariz. State U., 1973, MBA, 1983. Bar: Ariz. 1973, N.D. 1973, Minn. 1973, U.S. Dist. Ct. Ariz. 1975. Asst. prosecutor City of Phoenix, Phoenix, 1974—84, asst. city counsel Civil divsn., 1984—85, ct. adminstr. mcpl. ct., 1985—86; pvt. practice Scottsdale, Ariz., 1986—. Mem. Ariz. Com. on Profl. Responsibility, 1984—94. Pres. Broadmor PTA, Tempe, Ariz., 1993—95; mem. budget adv. com. Tempe Elem. Sch. Dist., Tempe, 1999. Mem.: ABA, Scottsdale Bar Assn., Maricopa County Bar Assn. (Vol. of Month Vol. Lawyer Program 2002), State Bar Ariz. Assn., Ariz. Bar Found. Avocations: coaching youth softball, coaching youth baseball. Office: 7509 E First St Scottsdale AZ 85251 Office Phone: 480-946-4300.

CRAWFORD, ROBERT JOHN, credit company executive; b. Cleve., Mar. 8, 1942; s. Robert John and Jean (Holmes) C.; m. Edna Jean Parker, June 14, 1975. AA, U. Alaska, Fairbanks, 1967, BE, 1971; HHD (hon.), London Inst. of Applied Rsch., 1975; BA/BS, SUNY, 1978. Pres. World Credit Corp., Wilmington, Del., 1972—; rep. in U.S. Hillcrest Worldwide Devel. Corp., S.A., Panama, 1988—; mediator Summit Ct. Sys., Akron, Ohio, 1994—; judge Summit Ct. Bd. Elections, 2006—. With US Army, 1961—64. Mem. Mensa, Intertel, Internet Corp. Assigned Names and Numbers. Libertarian. Avocations: computers, real estate. Home: 74 Maplewood Ave Akron OH 44313-6898 Home Phone: 330-836-5250; Office Phone: 330-836-5250. E-mail: A@att.net.

CRAWFORD, ROBERT LAWRENCE, mathematics professor; b. Washington, May 9, 1968; s. Robert Percy Crawford and Eileen Elizabeth; m. Jessica Gabriel Barnes; children: Ian, Matthew; m. Kelly Lynn (div.); children: Joshua, Daniel. BS, Howard U., 1991; MA in Philosophy, U. Calif., Davis, 1993, MA in Math., 1997. Cert. adult edn. credential. Mental health worker Pine Tree Gardens, Davis, 1998—2000; math. prof. Sacramento (Calif.) City Coll., 1998—; math. and physics prof. Cosumnes River Coll., Sacramento, 1998—; math. prof. Woodland (Calif.) C.C., 2000—01; adult edn. instr. Washington Adult Sch., West Sacramento, Calif., 2001—04, substitute tchr., 2001—04; prof. math., learning skills Sacramento State U. Vol. ministry to the homeless, Sacramento, 1998—. Recipient Cool, Calm and Collected award, Washington Alternative Schs., 2003. Mem.: Math. Assn. Am. Avocations: astronomy, geology, poetry, unicycling, athletics. Office: Solano Hall Calif State U Sacramento CA Office Phone: 916-278-3776. E-mail: rlcrawdaddy@hotmail.com, crawford@crc.lostrios.edu.

CRAWFORD, ROBERT W., JR., furniture rental company executive; b. Yonkers, NY, Oct. 19, 1938; BS, Dickinson Coll., 1960; MBA, U. Pa., 1963. Founder, chmn., CEO Brook Furniture Rental, Inc., Lake Forest, Ill. Trustee Field Mus. Inductee Chicagoland Entrepreneurial Hall of Fame, 1998. Mem. Nat. Recreation Found. (chmn., trustee), Internat. Furniture Rental Assn. (chmn., bd. dirs.), Chicagoland C. of C. (chmn. bd. dirs.), The Chgo. Club, The CEO Club, Execs. Club Chgo., Comml. Club Chgo., Econ. Club Chgo., Phi Kappa Sigma (Alumnus of Yr. award). Office: Brook Furniture Rental Inc 100 Field Dr Ste 220 Lake Forest IL 60045 E-mail: rwc@bfr.com.

CRAWFORD, ROY EDGINGTON, III, lawyer; b. Topeka, Dec. 23, 1938; s. Roy E. and Ethel Trula (Senne) C.; children: Michael, Jennifer. BS, U. Pa., 1960; LL.B., Stanford U., 1963. Bar: Calif. 1964, U.S. Ct. Mil. Appeals 1964, U.S. Tax Ct. 1969, U.S. Dist. Ct. (no. dist.) Calif. 1971, U.S. Ct. Claims 1974, U.S. Supreme Ct. 1979. Assoc. Brobeck Phleger & Harison, San Francisco, 1967-73, ptnr., 1973—2003; spl. counsel Heller Ehrman LLP, San Francisco, 2003—. Contbr. chpts. to books; bd. editors: Stanford U. Law Rev., 1962-63. Served to capt. AUS, 1964-67. Recipient award of merit U.S. Ski Assn., 1980. Mem. ABA (chmn. com. on state and local taxes 1979-81), Calif. State Bar Assn., San Francisco Bar Assn., Calif. Trout (bd. dirs. 1970-1992, v.p. 1975-94, sec.-treas. 1994-2001), The Nature Conservancy of Idaho (bd. dirs. 1994-2003), Yosemite Inst. (bd. dirs. 1997-2007), Beta Gamma Sigma. Office: Heller Ehrman LLP 333 Bush St San Francisco CA 94104 Office Phone: 415-772-6705. Business E-Mail: roy.crawford@hellerehrman.com.

CRAWFORD, SANDRA KAY, lawyer; b. Sept. 23, 1934; d. Obie Lee and Zilpha Elizabeth (Ash) Stalcup; m. William Walsh Crawford, Dec. 21, 1968; children: Bill, Jonathan, Constance, Amelia, Patrick. BA, Wellesley Coll., 1957; LLB, U. Tex., 1960. Bar: Tex. 1960, U.S. Supreme Ct. 1965, Colo. 1967, Ill. 1974. Asst. v.p.-legal Hamilton Mgmt. Corp., Denver, 1966—68; v.p., gen. counsel, sec. Transamerica Fund Mgmt. Corp., LA, 1968; cons. to law dept. Met Life Ins. Co., NYC, 1969—71; counsel Touche Ross & Co., Chgo., 1972—75; v.p., assoc. gen. counsel Continental Ill. Bank, Chgo., 1975—83; sr. div. counsel Motorola, Inc., Schaumburg, Ill., 1984; sr. counsel, asst. sec. Sears Roebuck & Co., 1985—90. Mem.: ABA, Tex. Bar Assn., Colo. Bar Assn., Ill. State Bar Assn., Beach Club (Palm Beach), Everglades Club. Home: 100 Royal Palm Way Apt G5 Palm Beach FL 33480-4270

CRAWFORD, SHEILA JANE, librarian, reading specialist; b. Beckley, W.Va., Mar. 1, 1943; d. Roger and Ruth (Ashworth) Crawford; m. Lloyd E. Johnston, June 4, 1966 (dec.); 1 child, Jacqueline; m. Troy Thomason, June 28, 2000. BA, Tenn. Tech. U., 1963; MA in Christian Edn., Seabury Western Theol. Sem., 1965; MS in Curriculum and Instrn., U. Tenn., Martin, 1989; EdD in Instrn. and Curriculum Leadership, U. Memphis, 1994; postgrad., San Jose State U., U. Calif., Berkeley, U. Utah, Tex. Woman's U. Cert. tchr. Tenn. Dir. Christian edn. St. Luke's Episcopal Ch., Rochester, Minn., 1965-66; elem. tchr. Santa Catalina Sch. Girls, 1967-69, Rowland-Hall St. Mark's Sch., Salt Lake City, 1968-69, Union City (Tenn.) Christian Sch., 1984-87; libr. Dept. Edn. U. Tenn. at Martin, 1987-89; rsch. asst. U. Memphis, 1989-92, adj. prof., 1996; prof., edn. dept. chair Lane Coll., Jackson, Tenn., 1992-94; reading tchr., drama club sponsor Ashland (Miss.) Mid. Sch., 1994-95; ednl. cons. Delta Faucet of Tenn. divsn. Masco Corp., Jackson, 1995—; homebound tchr. Jackson-Madison County Schs., 1996-97; instr., libr. LaGrange-Moscow (Tenn.) Sch., 1997-99; libr. Lauderdale Sch., Memphis. Mem. campus All Stars, Honda, Jackson, Tenn., 1992—93; cons., presenter in field. Contbr. articles to profl. jours. Mem. AAUW, DAR, Nat. Libr. Assn., Internat. Reading Assn., Sch. Libr. Assn. (instr. storyteller workshops), Ch. and Synagogue Libr. Assn., Tenn. Assn. Sch. Librs., Order Eastern Star (worthy matron 1980-81), Sigma Tau Delta, Kappa Delta Pi Anglican. Achievements include research in the effect of chess on predicting and summarizing skills. Office: Denver Elem Sch 1940 Frayser Blvd Memphis TN 38122 Home Phone: 901-365-4863; Office Phone: 901-416-3936. Personal E-mail: crawfords444@bellsouth.net.

CRAWFORD, STEPHEN, national association executive; b. Doylestown, Pa., Nov. 22, 1942; m. Liliane Pasquale Floge; 1 child, Pascal Hoang. BA, Cornell U., 1964; MBA, Wharton Bus. Sch., U. Pa., 1971; PhD, Columbia U., 1987. Former exec. dir. Gov.'s Work Force Investment Bd., State of Md., Balt., Ctr. Internat. and Security Studies, U. Md., Albert Einstein Instn., Cambridge, Mass.; former v.p., treas. Nat. Policy Assn., Washington; dir. Social, Econ. and Workforce Programs Divsns. Nat. Govs. Assn., Washington, 2002—. Author: Technical Workers in an Advanced Society, 1989. Dem. nominee for U.S. House 6th dist., Md., 1996; former mem. Frederick County (Md.) Bd. of Edn. From pvt. to 1st lt. US Army, 1964—67. Decorated Bronze Star, Cross of Gallantry with Gold Star; recipient 2 Fulbright rsch. awards. Home: 7100 Panorama Dr Derwood MD 20855 Personal E-mail: scrawford123@comcast.net.

CRAWFORD, STEPHEN S., investment banker; b. May 20, 1964; BA, U. Va., 1986. With mgmt. investment banking divsn. Morgan Stanley Dean Witter, NYC, 1986-98, mng. dir., 1998—2000, chief strategic and adminstrv. officer, 2000—01; pres., CFO Morgan Stanley, 2001—04, exec. v.p., chief adminstrv. officer, 2004—05, co-pres., 2005, mem. bd. & mgmt. com. with joint responsibility Institutional Securities Group, Individual Investor Group and Investment Mgmt., 2005; founding ptnr. Centerview Partners LLC, NYC, 2006—. Bd. dirs. Morgan Stanley, 2005. Bd. dirs. Nat. Ctr. for Learning Disabilities, New York Philharmonic. Mem.: The Ctr. for Excellence in Acctg. and Security Analysis, Columbia Bus. Sch. (adv. bd. mem. 2003—).

CRAWFORD, SUSAN, library director, educator, editor, writer; b. Vancouver, BC, Can. d. James Y. and S. Young; m. James Weldon Crawford, July 5, 1955; 1 son, Robert James. BA, U. B.C., 1948; MA, U. Toronto, 1950, U. Chgo., 1954, PhD, 1970. With bur. libr. and indexing svc. ADA, 1954-56; with office exec. v.p. AMA, Chgo., 1956-60, dir. divsn. libr. and archival svcs., 1960-81; assoc. prof. Sch. Libr. Sci., Columbia U., NYC, 1972-75; prof., dir. Sch. Medicine Libr. and Biomed. Comm. Ctr. Washington U., 1981-92; adj. prof. dept. psychiatry U. Ill., Chgo., 1994—; rsch. asst. Northwestern U. Kellogg Sch. Mgmt., 2005—06. Internat. steering com. Royal Coll. Physicians and Surgeons. Mem. internat. steering com. Universal Guide Sci. Publs.; mem. editl. bd. Med. Socioecon. Rsch. Sources, Index to Sci. Revs., Jour. Am. Soc. Info. Sci., Med. Libr. Assn. News, Health and Info. Librs., Budapest, Health Librs. Rev., London, Health Info. and Librs. Jour., Oxford, Eng., 2003—; assoc. editor Jour. Am. Soc. Info Sci., 1979-82; editor Med. Info. Sys., 1988-90; editor-in-chief Jour. Med. Libr. Assn., 1982-88, 91-92; author of books; contbr. aticles to profl. jours.; mem. editl. bd. of 9 scientific jours. Bd. regents Nat. Libr. Medicine, NIH, 1971-75; mem. bd. overseers for univ. librs. Tufts U., 1988-89; cons. for grants rev., Nat. Sci. Found., Nat. Libr. Medicine Recipient Eliot award for scientific pubs.; Janet Doe hon. lectr., 1983; Disting. Alumni award U. Toronto, 1987; Grad. medal U. Toronto, 1989; McGovern award, Med. Libr. Assn., 1986; recipient of grants NIH, Inst. for Scientific Info., Majors Scientific Publications, St. Louis Metro. Med. Soc., St. Louis Sch. Dental Medicine. Fellow AAAS (chmn. coms.), Med. Libr. Assn. (life, Eliot award 1976, chmn. com. on surveys and stats. 1966-75, publs. panel 1977-80, chmn. consulting editors panel 1981-88, 91-92, spl. award to editor of bull. 1988, Noyes award 1992, Pres.'s award 1992, Centennial award), Med. Libr. Assn. (100 Most Notable 1998); mem. ALA, Soc. Social Studies Sci., Am. Soc. Info. Sci. and Tech. (chmn. med. info. sys. 1987-88, outstanding splty. group award 1988, 89, edn. com., publications com., bd. and program chair Chgo. chpt. 1993-95), Am. Med. Informatics Assn., Acad. Health Info. Profls. (disting. mem.), European Assn. Health and Info. Librs. (U.S. rep. 1989-94), Sigma Xi (chmn. coms.). Achievements include research in scientific and biomed. comm., statis. surveys, info. sys. Home: 2418 Lincoln St Evanston IL 60201-2151 Office Phone: 847-869-3108. Personal E-mail: sjcrawf@aol.com.

CRAWFORD, SUSAN JEAN, federal judge; b. Pitts., Apr. 22, 1947; d. William Elmer Jr. and Joan Ruth (Bielau) C.; m. Roger W. Higgins; 1 child, Kelley S. BA, Bucknell U., 1969; JD, New Eng. Sch. Law, 1977. Bar: Md. 1977, DC 1980, US Ct. Appeals for Armed Forces 1985, US Ct. Appeals (4th cir.) 2003, US Supreme Ct. 1993. Tchr. history, coach Radnor (Pa.) HS, 1969-74; assoc. Burnett & Eiswert, Oakland, Md., 1977-79; ptnr. Burnett, Eiswert and Crawford, Oakland, 1979-81; prin. dep. gen. counsel Dept. Army, Washington, 1981-83, gen. counsel, 1983-89; insp. gen. US Dept. Def., Arlington, Va., 1989-91; judge US Ct. Appeals for the Armed Forces, Washington, 1991-99, 2004—06, chief judge, 1999—2004, sr. judge, 2006—; convening authority, Office Mil. Commissions US Dept. Def., Washington, 2007—. Asst. states atty. Garrett County, Md., 1978-79; instr. Garrett County C.C., 1979-81. Del. Md. Forestry Adv. Commn., Garrett County, 1978-81, Md. Commn. for Women, Garrett County, 1980-83; chair Rep. State Cen. Com., Garrett County, 1978-81, Bucknell U., 1988—, chair bd. trustees, 2003—; trustee New Eng. Sch. Law, 1989—. Mem. FBA, Md. Bar Assn., DC Bar Assn., Edward Bennett Williams Am. Inn of Ct. Presbyterian. Office: US Ct Appeals Armed Forces 450 E St NW Washington DC 20442-0001*

CRAWFORD, VICTOR L., consumer products company executive; BS in Acctg., Boston Coll. With PriceWaterhouse, Fed. Mogul Corp., Mich.; various fin. and sales positions Pepsi-Cola Bottling Co., Mich., 1990—98; v.p., gen. mgr. Greater Chgo. Divsn. Pepsi-Cola Gen. Bottlers, Inc., 1998; sr. v.p. Distbn. Svcs. Marriott Internat., 2000—01, exec. v.p., gen. mgr. Distbn. Svcs., 2001—05, sr. v.p., chief ops. officer Ea. region, 2005; sr. v.p., gen. mgr. Mid-Atlantic Bus. Unit Pepsi Bottling Group, Inc., 2005—06, sr. v.p. worldwide ops., 2006—. Office: Pepsi Bottling Group Inc 1 Pepsi Way Somers NY 10589-2201 Office Phone: 914-767-6000.*

CRAWFORD, WILLIAM DAVID, real estate broker, consultant; b. Abbeville County, SC, Aug. 13, 1945; s. Jesse David and Elizabeth Virginia (Ashley) C.; m. Gail Eileen Watkins, June 9, 1967 (div. Aug. 1985); 1 child, Merritt Caitlin; m. Dawn P. Lantz, June 10, 1995; stepchildren: Chelsea Lantz-Cashman, Devon Lantz-Cashman. BA, Wofford Coll., 1967; MS, Tex. A&M U., 1974; MBA, U. New Orleans, 1977. Lic. real estate broker, S.C., N.C., Ga., Tex., Tenn.; lic. comml. aircraft pilot; cert. comml.

investment mgr. Comml. Investment Real Estate Inst.; cert. internat. property specialist, Comml. Investment Real Estate Inst. Gen. mgr. Ramada Inn, New Orleans, 1973-74; rschr. divsn. bus. and econ. rsch. U. New Orleans, 1975-77; exec. asst. to pres. LaSalle Properties, New Orleans, 1977-81; v.p. Doerring Devel. Co., Austin, Tex., 1981-84; project mgr. Street-Martin Cos., Austin, 1984; pres. TriSource Corp., San Antonio, 1985-86; v.p. Merritt Properties, Inc., Greenville, SC, 1986—87; pres. Crawford Associates, Inc., Greenville, 1986—. Author: Louisiana Business Survey, 1977, Application of Travel Economic Impact Model to New Orleans, 1977. Chmn. Paris Mountain Water Dist., Greenville, 1990—. Capt. C.E., U.S. Army, 1968-71. Mem. Comml. Investment Real Estate Inst., Nat. Assn. Real Estate Cons. (cert.), Nat. Assn. Realtors, Greenville Bd. Realtors, Comml. Bd. Realtors, Greenville C. of C., Gamma Sigma Delta, Beta Gamma Sigma. Mem. Unity Ch. Avocations: hiking, skiing, scuba diving, flying. Home: 2 Persimmon Ln Greenville SC 29609-6511 Office: PO Box 3625 Greenville SC 29608-3625 Office Phone: 864-235-7855. Business E-Mail: will@crawfordassociates.com.

CRAWFORD, WILLIAM EDWARD, law educator; b. Key West, Fla., Dec. 15, 1927; s. John Felder and Elizabeth (Cooper) C.; m. Sandra Holmes Shuler, June 30, 1962; children: William, Jr., John F. II, Andrew. BA, La. State U., 1951, JD, 1955. Bar: La. 1955, U.S. Dist. Ct. (ea. dist.) La. 1955, U.S. Ct. Appeals (5th cir.) 1958. Pvt. practice, New Orleans, 1955-65; asst. dean, assoc. prof. La. State U. Law Sch., Baton Rouge, 1966-69, assoc. prof., 1969-71, prof., 1971—; dir. La. State Law Inst., Baton Rouge, 1978—. Spl. master U.S. Dist. Ct., Baton Rouge, 1973-76; cons. La. Assn. Bus. & Industry, Baton Rouge, 1988-92; cons. Gov. Foster, State of La., Baton Rouge, 1996-06. Author: (book) La. Tort Law, 2000; editor: La. Code of Civil Procedure, 1982—2006, Stone, Tort Doctrine, 1982—2003, West La. Formulary, 2003—06; translator: La Nouvelle Code de Procedure Civile, 1978. With USAF, 1951-53. Named James J. Bailey Professor, La. State U. Ctr., 1987, named La. Bar Foundation Disting. Prof. of 2003. Fellow, La. Bar Found.; mem. La. State Bar Assn. (sec. 1960-62). Avocations: fishing, golf. Home: 7052 Highland Rd Baton Rouge LA 70808-6632 Office: LSU Law Ctr La State U Baton Rouge LA 70803-0001 Office Phone: 225-578-0204. E-mail: crawfordw@lsli.org.

CRAWFORD, WILLIAM WALSH, retired consumer products company executive; b. Clearwater, Fla., Oct. 7, 1927; s. Francis Marion and Frances Marie (Walsh) C. BS, Georgetown U., 1950; LL.B., Harvard, 1954. Bar: N.Y. 1955, Ill. 1972. Assoc. Sullivan & Cromwell, NYC, 1954-58; counsel Esso Standard Oil, NYC, 1958-60; ptnr. Alexander & Green, NYC, 1960-71; v.p., gen. counsel Internat. Harvester Co., Chgo., 1971-76, v.p., gen. counsel, sec., 1976-80; sr. v.p. gen. counsel Kraft, Inc., Glenview, Ill., 1980-81; sr. v.p., gen. counsel, sec. Dart & Kraft, Inc., 1981-86, Kraft, Inc., 1986-88, sr. v.p., sec., 1988-89, ret., 1989. Mem. ABA, Ill. Bar Assn., Assn. Bar City N.Y., Am. Judicature Soc., Am. Law Inst., Assn. Gen. Counsel, Chgo. Club, Beach Club, Everglades Club, Old Guard Soc. Palm Beach Golfers.

CRAWFORD-MASON, CLARE WOOTTEN, television producer, journalist; b. Durham, NC, July 22, 1936; d. Charles Thomas and Clare (Erly) Wootten; m. Robert Watts Mason; children: Victor Lawrence Crawford Jr., Charlene Elizabeth Crawford; stepchildren: John Mason, Robert Mason 3d. BA, U. Md., College Park, 1958. Reporter, columnist Washington Daily News, 1961-72; columnist Washington Star News, 1972-74; Washington bur. chief People mag., 1974-82; reporter, sr. prodr. NBC-TV, 1969-80; pres. CC-M Prodns. Inc., Washington, 1981—, managementwisdom.com. Prodr. 1st network documentary on spouse abuse NBC-TV, 1975 (blue ribbon San Francisco Film Festival), 1st network documentary on child sexual abuse NBC, TV, 1977, People of the Year (CBS), 1982, If Japan Can, Why Can't We, 1980 (Dupont award Columbia U. Sch. Journalism), It's Up to the Women, 1984, The Issues Hit Home, 1986, Windows on Women, 1986, How To Fix Up a Little Old American Town, 1987, Work Worth Doing, 1987 (Golden Eagle award Coun. on Internat. Non-theatrical Events), The Deming Library: Vols. I-27, Implementing Deming, vols. 1-4; co-author: Thinking About Quality, Progress, Wisdom and the Deming Revolution, 1995; prodr., dir. documentary series Quality of Else, 1991, W. Edwards Deming: The Prophet of Quality, 1994; co-author: Quality or Else: The Revolution in World Business, 1991, The Nun and the Bureacrat: How They Found an Unlikely Cure for America's Sick Hospitals, 2006; prodr., dir. How Everyone Wins: Joy, Meaning and Profit in the Workplace, 1997, The Enneagram Nine Paths to a Productive and Fulfilling Life, 1999, Good News: How Hospitals Heal Themselves, 2006. Recipient Bill Pryor Meml. award, 1st prize Washington Newspaper Guild, 1966, Disting. Pub. Affairs Reporting award Am. Polit. Sci. Assn., 1967, Nat. Assn. Broadcasters award, 1971, 2 Emmy awards Nat. Acad. TV Arts and Scis., 1972, award for broadcast investigative reporting AAUW, 1972, award for investigative reporting Chesapeake Press Assn., 1971, Douglas Southall Freeman award for pub. service Va. Assn. Press Broadcasters, 1972, Washington Newspaper Guild award, 1974, Blue Ribbon Am. Film Festival, 1977, 1st place award Nat. Edn. Film Festival, 1985, documentary award Am. Women in Radio and TV, 1986, Golden Eagle award, 1986, 87, Excellence award Soc. Tech. Communication, 1988, Bronze plaque Columbus Instn. Film & Video Festival, 2006. Mem. AFTRA, SAG. Democrat. Roman Catholic. Office: 7755 16th St NW Washington DC 20012-1460 Office Phone: 202-882-7430.

CRAWLEY, CHERYL K., school system administrator; b. Stanley, Wis., Aug. 14, 1943; d. Donald Arthur and Margaret Banderob Schultze; m. Edward Todd Marckx, Mar. 23, 1996; 1 child, Damara Leanne Crawley Griffith. BS, Mont. State U., Bozeman, 1965; MA, Calif. State U., Hayward, 1976; CPhil, U. Calif., Berkeley, 1983. Cert. K-12 supt. Oreg., Mont. Dir. programs Hardin-Crow Agency-Ft. Smith Schs., Mont., 1978—82; asst. supt. Hardin-Crow Agency Ft. Smith Schs., Mont., 1983—86; dir. student svcs. Salem-Keizer Sch. Dist., Oreg., 1986—94; supt. Pub. Schs., Joseph, Oreg., 1994—97; supt. schs. The Dalles, Oreg., 1997—2004, Ross Valley, Marin County, Calif., 2004—07, Great Falls Pub. Schs., Mont., 2007—. Mem. gov.'s task force Devel. Disabilities Svcs., Oreg., 1987—88; keynote spkr. Mont. Assn. for Bilingual Edn., 1987; mem. Horace Mann Soc. Pub. Edn., 1995—; chmn. resolutions com. Confederation Oreg. Sch. Adminstrs., 2002—03; bd. dirs. numerous non-profit orgns. Sr. examiner Baldridge Nat. Quality Award, Dept. Commerce, Washington, 2001—; fellow Leadership Am., Washington, 1997—, Leadership Mid-Columbia, Columbia Gorge, Oreg., 1998; govt. affairs com. C. of C., The Dalles, Oreg., 1999—2004; Oreg. econ. summit Oreg. Bus. Coun., 2002—03. Named Woman of Distinction, The Dalles Chronicle, 2001; recipient various grants, 1978—86. Mem.: NAFE, Am. Anthropol. Assn., Am. Assn. Sch. Adminstrs., Rotary (The Dalles pres. 1998—99, Dist. 5100 area rep. 2001—04, Paul Harris fellow 2002, Presdl. Citation 1999). Avocations: photography, travel, environment, child advocacy. Office Phone: 406-268-6001. Business E-Mail: cheryl_crawley@gfps.k12.mt.us.

CRAWLEY, EDWARD FRANCIS, aerospace engineering educator; b. Boston, Sept. 7, 1954; s. Edward George and Dorothy Marie (Horgan) C. Student, Leningrad U., Russia, 1975; BS, MIT, 1976, MS, 1978, ScD, 1980. Asst. prof. MIT, Cambridge, 1980-86; aerospace engr. Johnson Space Flight Ctr., Houston, 1981; assoc. prof. MIT, Cambridge, 1986-90, dir. Space Engring. Rsch. Ctr., 1988-96, prof., 1990—, MacVicar faculty fellow dir. Sys. Design & Mgmt. Program, 1992—, dept. head, 1996—; co-exec. dir. Cambridge-MIT Inst. Vis. scholar Stanford U., Palo Alto, Calif., 1988; pres., CEO Sugarbush Soaring Assoc., Vt., 1987-90; chmn. Active Control Experts, 1992—. Assoc. editor Jour. of Intelligent Material Systems and Structures, 1988-95; author: over 50 jour. publs. Mem. presdl. adv. com. space sta. redesign, 1993, tech. and commercialization adv. com., NASA. NSF Presdl. Young Investigator, 1986. Fellow AIAA (assoc., assoc. editor Handbook of Astronautics 1988-92); mem. ASME (past chmn.), NAE (adv. space sta. com. 1987), Soaring Soc. Am. (chmn. structures materials panel). Office: Mass Inst Tech 77 Massachusetts Ave Bldg 33-207 Cambridge MA 02139 E-mail: crawley@mit.edu.

CRAWLEY, VERNON OBADIAH, academic administrator; b. Oct. 22, 1936; s. Joseph and Ruth (Adkins) C.; m. Betty W. Wood, July 9, 1966; children: V. Alan, Vonda, Keith. BS in Chemistry, Va. State U., 1958; postgrad., Coll. William and Mary, 1962, Am. U., 1964; MEd, U. Va., 1965; EdD, Pa. State U., 1971. Chemist Stuart Products Co., Richmond, Va., 1958-61; tchr. sci. and math. Ruthville (Va.) High Sch., 1961-64; asst. prof. sci. dept. Morgan State U., Balt., 1965-69; instr. phys. sci. Towson State Coll., Balt., 1969; assoc. prof. chemistry, chmn. sci., math. and technologies Dundalk C.C., Balt., 1971-74; assoc. dean acad. affairs Mercer County C.C., Trenton, N.J., 1974-78; pres. St. Louis C.C. at Forest Park, 1978-91, Moraine Valley C.C., Palos Hills, Ill., 1991—. Acting dean James Kerney campus Mercer County C.C., Trenton, 1976-77; adminstrv. specialist in sci. NASA, Washington, summer 1966, 67, 68; cons. N. Cen. Assn., Coro Found. Adv. bd. mem. St. Francis Hosp., Blue Island, Ill.; fin. adv. com. mem. Ill. C.C. Bd.; chmn. Ill. Coun. C.C. Pres.; bd. dirs. Southwest YMCA, Alsip, Ill. Recipient Outstanding Svc. to Williams Cmty. Sch. award 8th Dist. Police Cmty.Youth Network Com., 1990, Assistance with Minority Tchr. Recruitment Program award St. Louis Area Pers. and Place Adminstrs., 1989, Outstanding Leadership award Nat. Coun. Black Am. Affairs, 1987, Citizenship award Wellston Sch. Dist., 1983, NSF Acad. Yr. award, 1964-65, Southern fellowship, 1965. Mem. League for Innovation in C.C. (bd. dirs.), Expanding Leadership Opportunities for Minorities in C.C. (nat. adv. group), Am. Assn. C.C. (bd. dirs., exec. bd.), Nat. Coun. on Black Am. Affairs (bd. dirs.), Econ. Devel. Corp. for Southwest Suburbs (bd. dirs.), Rotary Club Oak Lawn, Moraine Valley C.C. Found. (bd. dirs.), Mo. Assn. Community and Jr. Colls. (bd. dirs.), Mo. Coun. C.C. Pres./Chancellors (chmn. 1986-87, v.p. 1985-86, sec. treas. 1984-85), Sigma Xi, Phi Theta Kappa. Avocations: travel, reading, gardening. Home: 7841 Sioux Rd Orland Park IL 60462-1894 Office: Moraine Valley CC 10900 S 88th Ave Palos Hills IL 60465-2175

CRAWSHAW, RALPH, psychiatrist; b. NYC, July 3, 1921; AB, Middlebury Coll., Vt., 1943; MD, NYU, 1947. Diplomate: Nat. Bd. Med. Examiners, Am. Bd. Psychiatry and Neurology. Intern Lenox Hill Hosp., NYC, 1947-48; resident Menninger Sch. Psychiatry, Topeka, 1948-50, Oreg. State Hosp., Salem, 1950-51; practice medicine specializing in psychiatry Washington, 1954; staff psychiatrist C.F. Menninger Meml. Hosp., Topeka, 1954-57; asst. chief VA Mental Hygiene Clinic, Topeka, 1957-60; staff psychiatrist Community Child Guidance Clinic, Portland, Oreg., 1960-63; founder, clinic dir. Tualatin Valley Guidance Clinic, Beaverton, Oreg., 1961-67; pvt. practice medicine, specializing in psychiatry Portland, 1960—2001; mem. staff Holladay Park Hosp., 1961—73. Lectr. dept. child psychiatry Med. Sch. U. Oreg., 1961-63, clin. prof. dept. psychiatry, 1976; lectr. Sch. Social Work, Portland State U., 1964-67; founder Banjamin Rush Found., 1968, pres., 1968—; founder Friends of Medicine, 1969, Ct. of Man, 1970, Club of Kos, 1974, Oreg. Health Decisions, 1983, Am. Health Decisions, 1989, Health Vol. Overseas, 1984; Sonian Machanic vis. prof. South African Coll. Medicine, 1993. Contbr. editor: AMA Jour. of Socio-Econs, 1972-75; Columnist: Prism mag, 1972-76, The Pharos, 1972— , Portland Physician, 1975, Western Jour. Medicine, 1980—; Contbr. articles to med. jours. Cons. Bur. Hearings and Appeals, HEW, 1964-90; cons. Albina Child Devel. Center, Portland, 1965-75, HEW Region 8 Health Planning, 1979; mem. Inst. Medicine, Nat. Acad. Sci., 1978, Oreg. Health Coordinating Council, 1979; Mem. Gov.'s Adv. Com. on Mental Health, 1966-72; ad hoc com. Nat. Leadership Conf. on Am. Health Policy, 1976, Gov.'s Adv. Com. on Med. Care to Indigent, 1976—; trustee Millicent Found., 1964-67, Multnomah Found. for Med. Care, 1977; pres. Bull Run Heritage Found., 1996; vis. scholar Center for Study Democratic Instns., 1969; Jack Murdock Charitable Trust, 1977, U.S.-USSR exchange scholar, 1973; founder Bull Run Heritage Found., 1996. Served with AUS, 1943-46; to lt., M.C. USN, 1951-54. Named Oreg. Dr./Citizen of Yr., 1978; U.S.-USSR rsch. scholar, 1973, 79; recipient I.N. Piragou medal for humanitarian Svcs., Russian Govt., 1992; Ralph Crawshaw Ann. Lectr. in Civic Medicine named in honor by Oreg. Found. for Med. Excellence, 1987. Fellow Am. Psychiat. Assn.; mem. AMA, APA, AAAS, Nat. Med. Assn., Oreg. Med. Assn. (trustee 1972—), Multnomah County Med. Soc. (pres. 1975), Royal Soc. Medicine, Inst. of Medicine of NAS, North Pacific Soc. Neurology and Psychiatry, Soc. for Psychol. Study Social Issues, Western European Assn. Aviation Psychology, Am. Med. Writers Assn., Portland Psychiatrists in Pvt. Practice (pres. 1971), Russian Acad. Natural Scis. (fgn. mem.), Alpha Omega. Home: 2884 NW Raleigh Portland OR 97210 E-mail: rckos@imagina.com.

CRAY, BENJAMIN A., mechanical engineer; s. Douglas W. and Barbara P. Cray; m. Karen M. Markin, June 6, 1987; 1 child, Colleen S. BSME, Tufts U., 1983; MSME, Yale U., 1986; PhD, NC State U., Raleigh, 1992. Mech. engr. Naval Undersea Warfare Ctr., Newport, RI, 1983—. Named Scientist of Yr., Naval Sea Sys. Command, 1999. Mem.: Acoustical Soc. Am. Office: Naval Undersea Warfare Ctr 1176 Howell St Newport RI 02841-1708 Office Phone: 401-832-8454. Business E-Mail: crayba@npt.nuwc.navy.mil.

CRAYBAS, JILL, professional tennis player; b. Providence, July 4, 1974; d. Norbert and Camille. Degree in telecom., U. Fla., 1996. Profl. tennis player, 1996—. Recipient Ranked #8 in U.S. 18s, 1992, NCAA Champion, 1996, Ranked #97, WTA, Ranked #14 Among U.S. Players, Highest Season Ending Singles Rank #57, 2002, 1WTA Tour Singles Title, Japan, 2002, 1 WTA Tour Doubles Title, Madrid, 2003, 2 ITF Women's Circuit Tour Titles, 8th Place Wimbledon, 2005. Office: WTA Tour Corporate Headquarters One Progress Plz Ste 1500 Saint Petersburg FL 33701

CRAYPO, CHARLES, labor economics professor; b. Jackson, Mich., Jan. 3, 1936; s. Norman Laverne and Ann Marie (Bogdan) C.; m. Mary Louise Vaclavik, Sept. 6, 1958; children: Jack, Carrie, Susan. BA in Econs., Mich. State U., 1959, MA in Econs., 1961, PhD in Econs., 1966. Asst. prof. econs. U. Maine, Orono, 1966-67; assoc. prof. Mich. State U., East Lansing, 1967-72, Pa. State U., University Park, 1972-78, U. Notre Dame, Ind., 1978-82, prof. Ind., 1984-2000, prof., chmn. dept. econs. Ind., 1984-93; prof. Cornell U., Ithaca, NY, 1982-84. Bd. dirs. Bus. Devel. Com., South Bend, Ind.; dir. Bur. Workers Edn., U. Maine, Orono, 1966-67, Higgins Labor Rsch. Ctr., U. Notre Dame, 1993; mem. acad. evaluating com. Labor Studies Ctr., Empire State Coll., SUNY, 1980; mem. labor studies dept. Ramapo Coll., 1981; mem. indsl. rels. dept. LeMoyne Coll., Syracuse, N.Y., 1983, Bur. of Labor Edn., U. Maine, Orono; external rev. mem. Divsn. Labor Studies Ind. U., 1998-99; mem. Labor Rsch. Adv. Coun., Bureau Labor Statistics, U.S. Dept. Labor, 2000; lectr. in field; expert witness. Author: Economics of Collective Bargaining, 1986, Grand Designs, 1993; mem. editl. bd., bus. mgr. Labor Studies Jour., 1976-80, chmn. editl. bd., 1980-85; mem. editl. bd. Contbns. to Labor Studies, 1989-97; internat. mem. editl. bd. Indsl. Rels. Jour., 1989-2002; contbr. articles to profl. jours. Mem. acad. adv. com. Divsn. Labor Studies Ind. U., 1978-82, 84-92, 95-96. Served with USMC, 1953-55. Recipient Lilly Endowment, 1992, D. Dority Labor Rsch. Fund, Ganey Rsch. award, 2002; grantee NEH, 1981, Rsch. grant, Dept. Commerce, 1984. Mem.: Indsl. Rels. Rsch. Assn. Home: 50600 Sorrel Dr Granger IN 46530-8506 Office Phone: 574-631-6934. E-mail: craypo.3@nd.edu.

CRAYTON, ARNELL, secondary school educator; b. Galveston, Tex., Jan. 25, 1949; s. Arnell and Careline Crayton. BS, Tex. Christian U., 1971. Cert. educator Tex. Dir. planning and evaluation Gulf Coast Regional Mental Health and Mental Retardation Ctr., Galveston, 1972—74; acctg. supr. Allstate Ins. Co., Englewood, Colo., 1974—79; retail mgr. J C Penney, Houston, 1980—91, Dillards Dept. Stores, Houston, 1992—2003; tchr. Bellaire H.S., Bellaire, Tex., 2003—. Participant Park City Math. Inst., Inst. Advanced Sci., 2005; mem. textbook adoption com. Houston Ind. Sch. Dist. Stats., 2007. Parish social min. St. Vincents De Paul, Houston, 2004. Named Area Sales Mgr. of Quarter (8), Dillards Dept. Stores, 1994—2003; fellow Woodrow Wilson Found., 1971; Sherer Math. scholar, Tex. Christian U., 1970. Mem.: ASCD, Nat. Coun. Tchrs.Math. (life). Democrat. Roman Catholic. Avocations: music, reading, biblical studies. Home: 6824 Linden Houston TX 77087 Office: Bellaire HS 5100 Maple Bellaire TX 77401 Home Phone: 713-928-6382; Office Phone: 713-294-3704. Office Fax: 713-294-3704; Home Fax: 713-928-6382. Personal E-mail: a.crayton@worldnet.att.net.

CREA, VIVIEN S., career military officer; BA, U. Tex.; MS, Mass. Inst. Tech.; MA, Ctrl. Mich. U. Advanced through grades to vice admiral USCG, 2006, chief office of programs, Coast Guard Hdqs., commdg. officer Air Station Clearwater, exec. asst. to commandant, commdg. officer Air Station Detroit, ops. officer Air Station Borinquen PR, coast guard aide to Pres. Reagan, comdr. First Coast Guard Dist., chief info. officer, comdr. Coast Guard Altantic Area, comdr. U.S. Maritime Def. Zone, 2004—06, vice comdt., 2006—. Decorated Legion of Merit, Def. Superior Svc. Medal, Coast Guard Commendation Medal; Sloan Fellow. Office: USCG US Dept Homeland Security 2100 2d St SW Washington DC 20593

CREAGER, JOE SCOTT, geology and oceanography educator; b. Vernon, Tex., Aug. 30, 1929; s. Earl Litton and Irene Eugenia (Keller) C.; m. Barbara Clark, Aug. 30, 1951 (dec.); children: Kenneth Clark, Vanessa Irene; m. B. J. Wren, Sept. 5, 1987 (dec.); m. Eva R. Milligan, Mar. 18, 2001 (div.); m. Joanne L. Thronson, Aug. 7, 2004. BS, Colo. Coll., 1951; postgrad., Columbia, 1952-53; MS, Tex. A&M U., 1953, PhD, 1958. Asst. prof. dept. oceanography U. Wash., Seattle, 1958-61, assoc. prof., 1962-66, prof. oceanography, 1966-91, prof. geol. scis., 1981-91, prof. emeritus, 1991—, asst. chmn. dept. oceanography, 1964-65, assoc. dean arts and scis. for earth and planetary scis., 1966-95, assoc. dean for rsch., 1966-91, divisional dean emeritus, 1995—; program dir. for oceanography NSF, 1965-66; chief scientist numerous oceanographic expdns. to Arctic and Sub-arctic including Leg XIX of Deep Sea Drilling project, 1959-91. Vis. geol. scientist Am. Geol. Inst., 1962, 63, 65; U.S. Nat. coord. Internat. Indian Ocean Expedition, 1965-66; vis. scientist program lectr. Am. Geophys. Union, 1965-72; Battelle cons., advanced waste mgmt., 1974; cons. to U.S. Army C.E., 1976, U.S. Depts. Interior and Commerce, 1975; exec. sec., exec. com., chmn. planning com. Joint Oceanographic Insts. Deep Earth Sampling, 1970-72, 76-78; mem. evaluation com. Northwest Assn. Schs. and Colls., 1989-99. Mem. editorial bd. Internat. Jour. Marine Geology, 1964-91; assoc. editor Jour. Sedimentary Petrology, 1963-76; asst. editor Quaternary Research, 1970-79; contbr. articles to profl. jours. Skipper Sea Scout Ship, Boy Scouts Am., Bryan, Tex., 1957; coach Little League Baseball, Seattle, 1964-71, sec., 1971; cons. sci. curriculum Northshore Sch. Dist., 1970; mem. Seattle Citizens Shoreline Com., 1973-74, King County Shoreline Com., 1980. Served with U.S. Army, 1953-55. Colo. Coll. scholar, 1949-51; NSF grantee, 1962-82; ERDA grantee, 1962-64; U.S. Army C.E. grantee, 1975-82; Office of Naval Research grantee; U.S. Dept. Commerce grantee; U.S. Geol. Survey grantee. Fellow Geol. Soc. Am., AAAS; mem. Internat. Assn. Quaternary Research, Am. Geophys. Union, Internat. Assn. Sedimentology, Internat. Assn. Math. Geologists, Soc. Econ. Paleontologists and Mineralists, Marine Tech. Soc. (sec.-treas. 1972-75), Sigma Xi, Beta Theta Pi, Delta Epsilon. Home: 7449 NE 118th Pl Kirkland WA 98034 Office: U Wash PO Box 353765 Seattle WA 98195-3765 Personal E-mail: bjnjoe@att.net.

CREAMER, PAULA, professional golfer; b. Mountain View, CA, Aug. 5, 1986; Golfer LPGA Tour, 2004—. Named Amateur of the Yr., Golf Digest, 2004, Golfweek, 2004, Player of the Yr., Am. Junior Golf Assoc., 2003; recipient Louise Suggs Rolex Rookie of the Year award, 2005. Achievements include being the first amateur to win the LPGA Final Qualifying Tournament, 2004; being youngest person to win the LPGA Final Qualifying Tournament, 2004; winning three career LPGA tour events; winning 19 national championships, 11 American Junior Golf Association tournaments. Office: Ladies Professional Golf Association 100 International Golf Drive Daytona Beach FL 32124*

CREAMER, ROBERT ALLAN, lawyer; b. Sept. 25, 1941; m. Joy A. Blakslee. BA, Northwestern U., 1963; LLB, Harvard U., 1967. Bar: Ill. 1967, U.S. Dist. Ct. (no. dist.) Ill. 1967, U.S. Ct. Appeals (7th cir.) 1969, U.S. Supreme Ct. 1976. Assoc. Keck, Mahin & Cate, Chgo., 1967—73, ptnr., 1974—94; v.p., loss prevention counsel Attys.' Liability Assurance Soc., Inc., Chgo., 1994—2006; pvt. practice Evanston, Ill., 2006—. Adj. prof. John Marshall Law Sch., Chgo., 1969—75, Northwestern U. Sch. Law, Chgo., 2000—. Mem.: ABA, Am. Law Inst., Ill. Bar Assn. (chmn. standing com. profl. conduct 1990—91, 1997—98), Chgo. Bar Assn., Northwestern U. Alumni Assn. (pres. 1990—94), Univ. Club (Chgo.), Cliff Dwellers Club (Chgo.), Lawyers Club Chgo. Democrat. Episcopalian. Home: 1500 Oak Ave Evanston IL 60201-4279 Office: PO Box 5170 Evanston IL 60204-5170 Office Phone: 847-328-2490. Personal E-mail: rac914@msn.com.

CREAN, MAUREEN ROSE, educational consultant; b. Rockville Centre, NY, Oct. 8, 1949; d. Patrick Joseph and Drusilla (Donnelly) C. AAS, Hudson Valley C.C., Troy, NY, 1977; AB, Radcliffe Coll./Harvard U., 1979; MBA, U. Albany, NYC, 1988. Dir. instl. planning Hudson Valley C.C., Troy, 1988-92; assoc. dir. C.D. Edni. Opportunity Ctr., Troy, 1992-94; dir. instl. planning Regents Coll., Albany, 1994-96. Pres. Productivity Ptnrs., Niskayuna, N.Y., 1990—96; pres. Savoy Girls, Hermosa Beach, Calif., 1996-; founder, publisher Distinctively Diva. Co-author: I am Diva, Every Woman's Guide to Outrageous Living, 2003. Pres., bd. dirs. Niskayuna Cmty. Daycare, 1995—, Girls, Inc., 1996; vol. Farano House, Albany, 1992—; bd. dirs. Our Bros. Keepers Found., Rsch. for Rett, Inc. JTPA grantee, 1991; N.Y. Sci. and Tech. Found. grantee, 1990. Mem. Harvard Club of Northeastern N.Y., Soc. Coll. and Univ. Planners, Harvard Bus. Sch. Alumni Assn. S.C. Address: 904 1st St Apt 2 Hermosa Beach CA 90254-5312 Office: PO Box 3735 Redondo Beach CA 90277 E-mail: maureen@savvgirls.com.

CREAN, PETER THOMAS, lawyer; b. NYC, Feb. 14, 1955; s. Thomas D. and Dorothy (Barry) C.; m. Stefanie Lewand, May 26, 1979; children: T.R., Patrick, Rosemary. AB in Politics, U. Mass., 1977; JD, Fordham U., 1981. Bar: N.Y. 1982, U.S. Dist. Ct. (ea. and so. dists.) N.Y. 1982, U.S. Supreme Ct. 1995. Ptnr. Martin, Clearwater & Bell, NYC, 1981—. Bd. trustees St. Agnes Hosp., White Plains, NY. Mem. N.Y. State Bar Assn., Assn. Bar City N.Y., Def. Rsch. Inst., Am. Health Lawyers Assn., Assn. Healthcare Risk Mgrs. Office: Martin Clearwater & Bell 220 E 42nd St New York NY 10017-5806

CREASEY, F. CLAY, retail executive; married; 2 children. BS, MBA, Stanford Univ. CPA. Actuarial analyst Fireman's Fund, 1971—73; v.p., corp. lending officer Crocker Bank, 1975—81; fin. mgmt. positions Lucky Stores, 1981—92, Mervyn's (subs. Target Corp.), 1992—2000, sr. v.p., CFO, 2000—05; CFO Zoom Systems, San Francisco, 2005—06; exec. v.p., CFO Toys "R" Us Inc., Wayne, NJ, 2006—. Office: Toys "R" Us Inc 1 Geoffrey Way Wayne NJ 07470*

CREASEY, GRAHAM HAROLD, surgeon, researcher; b. Luanshya, Zambia, Mar. 26, 1948; MB, ChB, Edinburgh Med. Sch., Scotland, 1972; BSc in Med. Sci., U. Edinburgh, Scotland, 1970. Attending physician MetroHealth Med. Ctr., Cleve., 1993—, VA Med. Ctr., Cleve., 1999—; med. dir. Advanced Platform Tech. Ctr., Cleve, 2005—. Assoc. prof. Case Western Res. U., Cleve., 2001—. Contbr. articles to profl. jours. Recipient Advanced Rsch. Career Devel. award, Dept. Vet. Affairs, 1999—2002; fellow, Wellcome Trust, 1974—75, Internat. Spinal Rsch. Trust, 1983, Winston Churchill Trust, 1985, Burroughs Wellcome Trust, 1999—2001, Macy Found., 2001; scholar, Anglo Am. Corp., 1966—72. Fellow: Royal Coll. Surgeons Edinburgh (mem. audio-visual com. 1987—88); mem.: Internat. FES Soc., Am. Spinal Injuries Assn. (mem. neurol. classification com. 1992—95), Groupe d'Etude NeuroUrologique de la Langue Francaise, Internat. Med. Soc. Paraplegia (mem. editl. bd. 1986—90), Biol. Engrng. Soc. UK (sec. rehab. engrng. group 1984—86). Achievements include patents for implantable medical electronic devices. Office: Advanced Platform Tech Ctr Rm BC-301 VAMC 10700 East Boulevard Cleveland OH 44106 Home Phone: 216-295-0451; Office Phone: 216-791-3800 3802. Office Fax: 216-707-6420. Business E-Mail: graham.creasey@case.edu.

CREASIA, JOAN CATHERINE, dean, nursing educator; b. Burlington, Vt., Aug. 14, 1941; d. Ramon J. and Marjorie E. (Rising) LaBelle; m. Donald A. Creasia, June 29, 1963; children: Karen, Tracey. BSN, U. Vt., Burlington, 1964; MSN, U. Tenn., 1978; PhD, U. Md., 1987. Staff nurse psychiat. unit Mass. Mental Health Ctr., Boston, 1964-65; instr. D'Youville Sch. Nursing, Cambridge, Mass., 1965-66; staff nurse Boston Lying-In Hosp., 1966-67; staff nurse med. surg. units Norwood Hosp., Mass., 1967-70; staff nurse, nursing supr. Oak Ridge Hosp., Tenn., 1971-74; staff nurse, supr. Frederick Meml. Hosp., Md., 1977-78, 86-92; instr. in nursing U. Tenn., Knoxville, 1974-77; rsch. asst. U. Md., Balt., 1980-83; instr., coord., asst. prof. med. surg. nursing Frederick (Md.) C.C., 1978-80, 81-83; asst. prof., coord. RN-BSN program U. Md. Sch. Nursing, Balt., 1983-90, assoc. prof., chair RN-BSN/MS programs, 1990-94, dir. statewide programs, 1991-94; assoc. dean for acad. programs and interim dean Med. U. SC Coll. Nursing, Charleston, 1994-95; dean, Coll. Nursing, U. Tenn., Knoxville, 1995—. Cons. in field. Author: Conceptual Foundations of Professional Nursing Practice, 1991, 96 (Book of Yr. award Am. Jour. Nursing 1992), Conceptual Foundations: The Bridge to Professional Nursing Practice, 2001, 4th edit., 2006; contbr. articles to profl. jours. and books. Bd. dirs. Tenn. Ctr. for Nursing. Recipient Outstanding Achievement in Indirect Nursing Rsch. award, 1987, Nat. Rsch. Svc. award, 1982, 83, Profl. Nurse Traineeship award, 1981, Outstanding Leadership award Md. Nurses Assn., 1990, Excellence in Nursing Leadership award Tenn. Orgn. Nurse Execs., Knoxville Coun., 2006. Mem.: ANA, Am. Assn. Colls. Nursing (bd. dirs.), Nat. League Nursing, Phi Kappa Phi, Sigma Theta Tau. Home: 605 Scotswood Cir Knoxville TN 37919-7457 Office Phone: 865-974-7583. Personal E-mail: joan.creasia@comcast.net. Business E-Mail: jcreasia@utk.edu.

CREATH, CURTIS JANSSEN, pediatric dentist; b. Lynwood, Calif., Mar. 10, 1958; s. Ronald J. and Madelyn W. (Chryst) C.; m. Deborah Ann Lipari, June 23, 1990; 1 child, Andrew. Student, UCLA, 1976-81; DMD, Oral Roberts U., 1985; MS, U. Ala., 1988. Asst. prof. Sch. Dental Medicine SUNY, Stony Brook, 1988-91, Sch. Dentistry U. Ala., Birmingham, 1991-94; staff pediat. dentist Family Cental Care Assocs., Cin., 1994-95; pvt. practice Milford, Ohio, 1995—. Team leader dental mission trips to Mex., Jamaica, Peru, 1982-84. Contbr. chpt. to: Special and Medically Compromised Patients in Dentistry, 1989, Clark's Clinical Dentistry, Vol. 2, 1994; contbr. articles, revs. on tobacco control, pediat. dentistry, and preventive medicine to profl. jours. Mem. ADA, Am. Acad. Pediat. Dentistry (mem. edn. com.), Am. Assn. Dental Schs. (v.p. 1986-88), Ala. Soc. Pediat. Dentistry (sec.-treas. 1992-94), Christian Med. and Dental Soc., Omicron Kappa Upsilon. Republican. Presbyterian. Avocations: vocal music, preaching, missionary work, woodworking, gardening. Home: 6514 Tulip Ct Liberty Township OH 45044-9726 Office: 1106-C Main St PO Box 267 Milford OH 45150-0267 Personal E-mail: curtjcre@aol.com.

CREAVEN, PATRICK JOSEPH, pharmacologist; b. Eng., Jan. 31, 1933; MB, BS, St. Mary's Hosp. Med. Sch., U. London, 1956, PhD, 1964. House surgeon Bedford Gen. Hosp.; also house physician Barnet Gen. Hosp., Eng., 1956-57; asst. lectr. biochemistry U. London, St. Mary's Hosp. Med. Sch., 1963-64, lectr., 1964-66; chief biochemistry Tex. Rsch. Inst. Mental Sci., 1966-69; head, pharmacology lab. Nat. Cancer Inst., VA Med. Oncology Br., 1969-75; assoc. chief, cancer rsch. clinician Roswell Park Meml. Inst. (now Roswell Park Cancer Inst.), Buffalo, 1975-79, chief cancer rsch. clinician, 1979—, chmn. dept. clin. pharmacology and therapeutics, 1979-89, chief div. clin. pharmacology and therapeutics, Dept. Medicine, 1989-91, sr. investigator dept. investigational therapeutics, 1991—; dir. Phase I Program Roswell Park Cancer Inst., 2001—; rsch. prof. medicine dept. medicine SUNY Med. Sch., Buffalo, 1994—. Contbr. articles to profl. jours. Fellow Am. Coll. Clin. Pharmacology, Royal Soc. Health; mem. Am. Assn. Cancer Rsch., Am. Soc. Clin. Oncology, Am. Soc. Pharmacology and Exptl. Therapeutics, Am. Soc. Clin. Pharmacology and Therapeutics. Office: Roswell Park Cancer Inst Elm And Carlton St Buffalo NY 14263-0001 Office Phone: 716-845-7614. Business E-Mail: patrick.creaven@roswellpark.org.

CREBBIN, ANTHONY MICEK, retired lawyer, military officer; b. Columbus, Neb., Sept. 10, 1952; s. Harry and Donna Mae (Micek) C. BA, Rockhurst Coll., 1974; JD, St Louis U., 1977; LLM, JAG Sch., 1989; M in Jud. studies, U. Nev., Reno, 2000. Bar: Mo. 1977, U.S. Ct. Mil. Appeals 1980, Hawaii 1987, U.S. Supreme Court 1989. Commd. 2d lt. USMC, 1978, advanced through grades to maj., 1986, trial counsel Cherry Point, NC, 1979, officer legal assistance, def. counsel, 1980, chief trial counsel, 1982, chief def. counsel Kaneohe Bay, Hawaii, 1986-87, chief legal assistance, 1987-88, staff judge adv. marine amphibious unit, 1980—81, 1984—85, mil. judge Camp Pendleton, Calif., 1989-92; dep. staff judge adv. Camp Pendleton, Calif., 1992-95; judge adv. 3d Marine Air Wing, Miramar, Calif., 1995-97; law clk. to Hon. John A. Borron, Jr., Probate Ct., Jackson County, Mo., 2000—03. Mem. ABA, Mo. Bar Assn., Hawaii Bar Assn. Democrat. Roman Catholic. Avocations: marathoning, scuba diving, skiing.

CRECELIUS, DANIEL NEIL, history professor; b. St. Louis, Jan. 15, 1937; s. Wilson John and (Imhof) R.; m. Anahid Tashjian, July 21, 1963; 1 child, Gia Maria. BA, Colo. Coll., 1959; MA, Princeton U., 1962, PhD, 1967. From asst. prof. to prof. emeritus Calif. State U., LA, 1964—2001, assoc. prof., 1968-73, prof. emeritus, 2001—, chairperson, 1980-83, 98-01. Vis. lectr. UCLA, 1966-67, Colo. Coll., 1990, Cairo U., 1992. Author 2 books, editor 16 books; contbr. numerous articles to profl. jours., chpts. to 15 books. Recipient Outstanding Prof. award Calif. State U., L.A., 1974; Trustees' scholar Colo. Coll., 1955-59; Woodrow Wilson Nat. fellow, 1959-60, Princeton U. Near East fellow, 1961-62; grantee U. Mich., 1960, Princeton U., 1961, Fulbright Found., 1962-63, 91-92, 92, 95-96, 96, Nat. Def. Fgn. Lang. grantee, 1963-64, Am. Rsch. Ctr., 1972, 79, 96, Am. Philos. Soc., 1975, 80, 89, Social Sci. Rsch. Coun., 1973, Dept. HEW Office Edn., 1973, Calif. State U., L.A., 1975, NEH, 1980-82, 83-84, 87, 91-92, 92, Calif. State U. L.A. Found., 1979, 81, others; Joseph P. Malone fellow, 1998. Mem. Mid. East Studies Assn., Mid. East Inst., Turkish Studies Assn., Am. Rsch. Ctr. Egypt, Phi Beta Kappa, Pi Gamma Mu, Phi Kappa Phi Lutheran. Avocations: travel, hiking, bird watching. Address: 9268 Wintergreen Cir Fountain Valley CA 92708-1448 Office Phone: 323-343-2020. Personal E-mail: DNCrecelius@aol.com.

CREECH, JOHN LEWIS, botanist, consultant; b. Woonsocket, RI, Jan. 17, 1920; s. Edward and Bessie (Faulkner) C.; m. Amy Elizabeth Wentzel, Feb. 14, 1942 (dec. Apr. 1984); children: Diane, Victoria, John; m. Elaine E. Godden Innes, July 10, 1984 (dec. July 2003). BS in Horticulture, U. R.I., 1941; MS in Horticulture, U. Mass., 1947; PhD in Botany, U. Md., 1953. Instr. horticulture U. Mass., Amherst, 1946-47; horticulturist Office Plant Exploration, Agrl. Rsch. Svc. USDA, 1947-50, asst. chief new crops rsch. br. Agrl. Rsch. Svc., 1958-66, chief br. Agrl. Rsch. Svc., 1966-72, scientist nat. program staff Agrl. Rsch. Svc., 1972-73; dir. U.S. Nat. Arboretum, Washington, 1973-80, N.C. Arboretum, 1987-88. Sr. adviser Internat. Bd. for Plant Genetic Resources; negotiator Bicentennial gift of Nat. Bonsai Collection from people of Japan; developer Nat. Herb Garden; program dir. for conservation of plant genetic materials Internat. Biol. Program, NAS; mem. panel FAO, 1966-74; preparer U.S. position paper for Stockholm Conf. on the Environment; adj. prof. biology U. N.C., Asheville; bd. dirs. N.C. Arboretum, Asheville, interim dir., 1986-87; U.S. judge Internat. Flower & Garden Expo, Japan, 1990; leader 9 plant expeditions Japan, China, Taiwan, USSR, Nepal, 1955-78; co-chmn. Genetic Resource Team, China, 1974; rev. nat. gen. resource program USDA, NAS, 1988-92; cons. Time-Life Books for Children, 1993; cons. in horticulture; leader hort. tours; mem. sci. & edn. com. Internat. Dendiology Soc. Author: The Bonsai Saga, 2001; co-author: Brocade Pillow, 1984, Garden Shrubs and Their Histories, 1992. Capt. U.S. Army, 1941-45, prisoner of war, ETO. Decorated Silver Star, Bronze Star; recipient Gold medal Scott Found., Gold medal Garden Club Am., Gold Seal medal Nat. Coun. State Garden Clubs, Thomas Roland medal Mass. Hort. Soc., Silver medal FAO-UN, Hort. medal Fedn. Garden Clubs N.Y., Norman J. Colman award Am. Nurserymans Assn., Hutchinson medal Chgo. Bot. Garden/Chgo. Hort. Soc., 1987, Gold medal and cert. of merit City of Kurume, Japan, 1988, Veitch Meml. medal Royal Hort. Soc., U.K., 1992, Award of Merit, Am. Assn. Bot. Gardens and Arb., 2000, Pres. award U. R.I., 2002, Disting. Svc. award Azalea Soc. Am., 2006; grantee Merrill Found., 1976, Nat. Geog. Soc., 1978, Japan Found., 1982; selected to give Morrison Meml. lecture. Mem. Am. Genetics Assn. (bd. dirs., Meyer medal), Am. Hort. Soc. (pres. 1954-56, profl. citation, Liberty Hyde Bailey medal 1989), Internat. Dendrology Soc. (v.p. 1989—), NC Arboretum (life, bd. dirs.), Sigma Xi, Phi Kappa Phi, Pi Alpha Xi. Republican. Episcopalian. Achievements include introduction of several plant varieties. Fax. Personal E-mail: jlcreech@teleplex.net.

CREED, ROBERT PAYSON, SR., retired literature educator; b. Phila., Apr. 22, 1925; s. Edward E. and Blanche H. (Southerland) Creed; m. Catherine Hilton, Oct. 9, 1987; children from previous marriage: Mary Louise, Robert Payson. BA, Swarthmore Coll., Pa., 1948; MA, Harvard U., Cambridge, Mass., 1949, PhD, 1956. Instr. Smith Coll., Northampton, Mass., 1952-56; from asst. prof. to assoc. prof. Brown U., Providence, 1956—65; assoc. prof. SUNY, Stony Brook, 1965-67, prof., 1967-69; prof. English U. Mass., Amherst, 1969-97, prof. emeritus, 1997—, dir. grad. studies in English, 1969-72, prof. English and comparative lit., 1980-90, chmn. comparative lit. dept., 1980-85. Cons. G&C Merriam Co., Springfield, Mass., 1955—56; featured storyteller Ann. Nat. Storytelling Festival, Jonesborough, Tenn., 1985, Jonesborough, 92; nat. vis. prof. Paul Valery U., Montpellier, France, 1987; disting. faculty lectr. U. Mass., Amherst, 1993—94. Writer, chief performer Beowulf, Sta. WNYC pub. radio, 1979 (award Corp. Pub. Broadcasting); author: (book) Reconstructing the Rhythm of Beowulf, 1990; featured performer Asheville (N.C.) Poetry Festival, 1994. Pres. bd. dirs. Arcadia Players Baroque Orch., Chorus and Chamber Ensemble, Northampton, Mass., 1995—98; bd. dirs. Hampshire Shakespeare Co., 2005—, Friends of Qualtin, 2005—; mem. Corp. Boston Early Music Festival, 2002—. With USNR, 1943—46, served to lt. (j.g.) USNR, 1949. Grantee, Am. Coun. Learned Soc., 1978; John Simon Guggenheim fellow, 1962—63, NEH fellow, Yugoslavia, 1976, Inst. Advanced Studies Humanities fellow, Edinburgh U., 1976. Mem.: AAAS, MLA (life), Archaeol. Inst. Am. (exec. coun. Western Mass. Soc. 1996—2006), European Soc. Study Cognitive Sys., Lang. Origins Soc., Nat. Storytelling Assn., N.Y. Acad. Scis., Internat. Soc. Anglo-Saxonists. Home: 5 Kinder Ln Shutesbury MA 01072-9762 Personal E-mail: creed@english.umass.edu. *Though a professor of literature, I have become more and more deeply concerned with oral traditions. Behind surviving traditions-indeed, behind literature-lie tens of thousands of years of what we may call Memorable Speech, some of which survives embedded in early texts. Back of Memorable Speech lies the origin of human language. Through the study of (sound-) patterned Memorable Speech, I am trying to work back towards the beginning of language, our most adaptive and humanizing invention.*

CREEDON, GERALDINE, state legislator; b. Springfield, Mass., Sept. 26, 1945; m. Robert Stanton Creedon Jr.; children: Jennifer, Robert S. BA, Emmanuel Coll., 1967. Vice chair edn. Mass. Ho. of Reps., Boston, mem. house ways and means com., mem. election laws, mem. Dist. 11, 1995—. Mem. Brockton (Mass.) City Coun., 1992-95, pres., 1995; bd. dirs. Charity Guild, 1990-97; mem. Dem. City Com. Roman Catholic. Office: Mass State Legis Rm 473G State House Boston MA 02133 Home Phone: 508-584-1975; Office Phone: 617-722-2070.

CREEL, HAROLD JENNINGS, JR., federal commission administrator, lawyer; b. Florence, SC, July 1, 1957; s. Harold Jennings Sr. and Dorothy Louise (Fenters) C. BA in Polit. Sci., Wofford Coll., 1979; JD, U. S.C. Law Sch., 1982. Bar: La. Assoc. Courtenay, Forstall, Grace & Hebert, New Orleans, 1982-83; atty./advisor NOAA, Washington, 1983-89; sr. counsel subcom. of com. on commerce, sci. and transp. U.S. Senate - Mcht. Marine Subcom., Washington, 1989-94; commr. Fed. Maritime Commn., Washington, 1994-96, chmn., 1996—2002, commr., 2002—. Nominee Fed. Maritime Comm., U.S. Pres. Mem. La. State Bar Assn. Democrat. Avocations: fishing, gardening. Office: Fed Maritime Commn 800 N Capitol St NW Washington DC 20211-0001

CREEL, LUTHER EDWARD, III, lawyer; b. Huntsville, Ala., Sept. 23, 1937; s. Luther Edward and June (Oldacre) C.; m. Nan Dee McHalek, Apr. 11, 1974; children by previous marriage: Scott Mitchell, Todd Oldacre. AB in Psychology, George Washington U., 1959; JD, So. Methodist U., 1963. Bar: Tex. 1963. Pvt. practice, Dallas, 1963—; chmn. Creel & Atwood (and predecessors), Dallas, 1971-96; of counsel Malouf, Lynch, Jackson, Kessler & Collins, Dallas, 1996-98; chmn. Creel, Sussman & Moore, Dallas, 1998—2002; ptnr. Creel & Moore, 2002—. Pres., chmn. The Pines Camp, 1999—2001; lectr. in bankruptcy and reorgn. law. Contbr. articles to profl. jours. Chmn. Ford Debtor Assistance Program, 1995-98. Mem. Dallas Bar Assn. (chmn. bankruptcy sect. 1972), Henderson County Bar Assn., State Bar Tex. (cert. bus. bankruptcy specialist 1989-2003, chmn. bankruptcy com. 1979-81, exec. com. bankruptcy sect. 2002—), Am. Bankruptcy Inst. (co-founder, pres. 1982-87, vice-chmn. 1987-96, bd. dirs. 1982-2000, chmn. 1996-98, chmn. emeritus 1998-2000), Am. Coll. Bankruptcy (co-founder, fellow, pres. 1996-97), John C. Ford Inn of Ct. (master, exec. com. 1999-2004), GTG Tex. Longhorn Assn. (pres. 1998-2000), Internat. Tex. Longhorn Assn. (bd. dirs.). Republican. Baptist. Home: 20487 Marimac Rd Trinidad TX 75163 Office: Creel & Moore 8235 Douglas Ave Ste 1100 Dallas TX 75225-6011 Office Phone: 214-378-8270. Personal E-mail: creel3@aol.com.

CREEL, MICHAEL ALLEN, energy executive; b. Lake Charles, La., Dec. 27, 1953; s. Harold Lee and Reba (Harkens) Creel; m. Kathy Roberts, Nov. 26, 1977; children: Michael Andrew, Matthew Robert. BS in Acctg., McNeese State U., 1975. CPA Tex. Contr. Guaranty Fed. Savs. Loan Assn., Lake Charles, 1973-76, Houston 1st Am. Savs., 1976-80; mgr. cash adminstrn. Coastal Corp., Houston, 1980—81, mgr. cash control, 1981-82, project leader corp. fin., 1982-84, mgr. fin. planning, 1984-86, dir. fin. planning, 1986-91; dir. corp. fin. Enron Corp., Houston, 1991-93, gen. mgr. corp. fin., 1994-95; v.p., treas. NorAm Energy Corp., Houston, 1995-97; sr. v.p. fin. Tejas Energy LLC, Houston, 1997, sr. v.p., CFO, 1998-99; sr. v.p. Enterprise Products Co. Ptnrs. LP, Houston, 1999—2001, CFO, 2000—01, exec. v.p., CFO, 2001—07; dir., pres., CEO Enterprise Products Co. Partners L.P., Houston, 2007—; pres., CEO Enterprise GP Holdings LP, 2005—07. Mem.: AICPA, Fin. Execs. Internat., Tex. Soc. CPAs, Nat. Eagle Scout Assn. Office: Enterprise Products Co PO Box 4324 Houston TX 77210-4324 E-mail: mcreel@eprod.com.

CREEL, SUE CLOER, retired secondary school educator; b. Columbus, Miss., July 4, 1943; d. Cornelius Ducler Cloer and Sara Verna (Shackelford) Cloer Mackie; children: Ricky (dec.), Ronny. BA, Harding U., 1982, MEd, 1986; grad., Jackson State U., 1996. Nat. bd. cert. Adolescent and Young Adult English Lang. Arts, 2000. Tchr. 8th grade English Alfh Jr. H.S., Searcy, Ark., 1982-87; part-time editor, writer for neurosurgery Miss. Med. Ctr., Jackson, 1987-89; adminstrv. asst. to dean of nursing U. Miss. Med. Ctr., Jackson, 1988-89; tchr. advanced placement English and creative writing Jackson Pub. Schs., 1990—2006, sponsor, editor student lit. mag. Post Script, 1999—2003; adj. instr. world lit. and Brit. lit. Holmes C.C.; ret., 2006. Adj. prof. Holmes C.C., 1999-2000; adj. instr. English Hinds C.C., Raymond, Miss., 1987-89; cons. Nat. Writing Project, 1985, Univ. Ctrl. Ark., Conway, Ark., Nat. Writing Project; session chair Writing-Across-the-Curriculum K-12, Charleston, S.C., 1997; tchr. long distance learning interactive video ETV, 1998-99, 2000-2001; presenter Nat. Coun. Tchrs. English, 2001; instr. U.S. Army, 2006. Contbg. poet: Moments in the Garden, 1998, Miss. Musings, Miss. Poetry Soc., 1997, The Drifting Sands, 1999. With USN, 1962—63. Grantee Entergy, Jackson, 1994-96; fellowship Jackson (Miss.) State U., 1996; recipient 3 Editor's Choice awards, Beyond Call of Duty award JPSD, 1999; named tchr. excellence Calloway H.S., 2000; finalist Sharp Wave award U.S. Army, 1962. Mem. Nat. Coun. Tchrs. English, Miss. Poetry Soc. (v.p. ctrl. br. 2002-), The Poetry Guild (poetry included Best Poems of the 90s, 1998), Phi Kappa Phi, Beta Sigma Phi (v.p. XI chpt. 2002—, pres. 2003, Valentine Ball Queen 2003, mem. Internat. Queen's Ct. 2003), Alpha Chi, Kappa Delta Pi, Sigma Tau Delta, Phi Alpha Theta, Phi Kappa Phi. Mem. Ch. Of Christ. Avocations: reading, writing, theater, gardening, competitions. Home: 625 Choctaw Rd Jackson MS 39206-5325

CREEL, THOMAS LEONARD, lawyer; b. Kansas City, Mo., June 21, 1937; s. Thomas Howard and Elizabeth Alberta (Sharon) C.; m. Carol M. Plaisted, Nov. 26, 1992; children: Charles, Andrew, Andrea, Thomas, Joseph, Lauren. BS, U. Kans., 1960; LLB, U. Mich., 1963. Bar: Mich. 1963, N.Y. 1967, D.C. 1983, U.S. Supreme Ct. 1973, Ct. Mil. Appeals, 1964, U.S. Patent and Trademark Office 1965. Assoc. Kenyon and Kenyon, NYC, 1966-74, ptnr., 1974-92, Kaye, Scholer, Fierman, Hayes & Handler, NYC, 1992—2001, Goodwin Procter LLP , NYC, 2001—. Faculty lectr. Columbia U. Sch. Law, N.Y.C., 1984-2001. Editor: Guide to Patent Arbitration, 1987. Capt., U.S. Army, 1963-66. Mem. ABA, N.Y. Intellectual Property Law Assn. (past pres.), Am. Intellectual Property Assn. Office: Goodwin Procter LLP 599 Lexington Ave New York NY 10022 Home Phone: 212-715-0851; Office Phone: 212-813-8866. Business E-Mail: tcreel@goodwinprocter.com.

CREEM, CYNTHIA STONE, state legislator, lawyer; BSBA, JD, Boston U. Mem. Mass. Senate, Boston, 1998—, chair revenue com., vice chair pub. health com., mem. ways and means com., bonding capital expenditures com., telecomm. com., mem. judiciary com. Mem. Newton Bd. Aldermen, Gov.'s Coun. Fellow Women's Bar Assn.; mem. Mass. Bar Assn. Democrat. Office: Mass State Senate State House Rm 416B Boston MA 02133 E-mail: cynthia.creem@state.ma.us.

CREENAN, KATHERINE HERAS, lawyer; b. Elizabeth, NJ, Oct. 7, 1945; d. Victor and Katherine Petervary; m. Edward James Creenan; 1 child, David Heras. BA, Kean Univ., 1968; JD, Rutgers U., 1984. Bar: N.J. 1984, Maine 1996, N.Y. 2005, U.S. Dist. Ct. N.J. 1984, U.S. Ct. Appeals (3d cir.) N.Y., 2005. Various tchg. positions including, Union and Stanhope, NJ, 1968-81; law clk. to presiding judge NJ Appellate divsn. Superior Ct., Newark, 1984-85; assoc. Lowenstein, Sandler, Kohl, Fisher & Boylan, Roseland, NJ, 1985-88, Kirsten, Simon, Friedman, Allen, Cherin & Linken, Newark, 1988-89, Whitman & Ranson, Newark, 1989-93, Skadden, Arps, Slate, Meagher & Flom LLP, Newark, 1999—2004; sr. atty. Whitman Breed Abbott & Morgan LLP, Newark, 1993-99; sr. staff assoc. Skadden, Arps, Slate, Meagher & Flom LLP, NYC, 2004—07; pvt. practice Elizabeth, NJ, 2007—. Mem. ABA, N.J. State Bar Assn. Office Phone: 908-355-5151. Business E-Mail: kcreenan@creenanlaw.com.

CREER, THOMAS LASELLE, psychologist, educator, writer; b. Lund, Idaho, Nov. 2, 1934; s. Laselle Lewis Creer and Naomi Johanna Jones; m. Patricia J. Plummer, July 7, 1961; children: Jennifer, Matthew. BS, Brigham Young U., 1956; Master's, Utah State U., 1961; PhD in Psychology, Fla. State U., 1967. Lic. psychologist Colo. Prof. psychology Ohio U., Athens, 1980—96; pres. Creer Sys., Inc., Provo, Utah, 1995—2002. Co-exec. dir. Nat. Asthma Ctr., Denver, 1977—80. Author: Chronically Ill and Handicapped Children, 1976, Asthma Therapy: A Behavioral Health Care System for Respiratory Disorders, 1979, Self-Management of Chronic Disease, 1986, Psychology of Adjustment, 1997, Respiratory Disorders and Behavioral Medicine, 2002, others; contbr. 200 articles, revs., writings and chpts. in field. Bd. dirs. Am. Lung Assn. Ohio, Columbus, 1983—93, Am. Lung Assn. Utah, 2002—; pres. Am. Lung Assn., Utah, 2004—05. With US Army, 1956—58. Recipient Pre-doctoral Internship award, VA, 1966—67; fellow Pre-doctoral fellow, U.S. Pub. Health Svc., 1963—66. Liberal. Avocation: reading. Home: 144 E 4620 N Provo UT 84604 Personal E-mail: tcreer@comcast.net.

CREEVY, WILLIAM R., orthopedist, surgeon, educator; b. 1960; MD, Boston U., 1985; MS in Health Care Mgmt., Harvard U., 2001. Cert. Am. Bd. Orthopaedic Surgery, 1995. Resident gen. surgery U. Pa., Grad. Hosp., Phila., 1985—87, fellow sports medicine, 1992—93; resident orthopaedic surgery Boston U. Sch. Medicine, 1988—92, vice chmn., Dept. Orthopaedic Surgery, asst. prof. Contbr. articles to med. jours. Named one of Top 250 Golfer Doctors in Am., Golf Digest, 2006; recipient Annual Award for Academic Excellence, Phila. Orthopaedic Soc. for Sports Medicine, 1993. Office: Boston Med Ctr 818 Harrison Ave, Dowling 2 N Boston MA 02118 Office Phone: 617-414-5212. Office Fax: 617-414-7957. E-mail: william.creevy@bmc.org.*

CREGAN, FRANK ROBERT, financial executive, consultant; b. Jersey City, July 27, 1940; s. Frank Vincent and Maurie Geraldine (Kennedy) C.; m. Joan Marie Swancer, July 19, 1969; children: Christina Eileen, Darren Michael, Keith Francis. BBA, Manhattan Coll., 1962; MBA, St. John's U., Jamaica, NY, 1972. CPA, N.Y. Supr. KPMG Peat Marwick, NYC, 1962-68; dir. taxes DuPont Glore Forgan, Inc., NYC, 1968-73; v.p. taxes Marsh & McLennan Cos., Inc., NYC, 1973-78; ptnr. Deloitte & Touche, Parsippany, N.J., 1978-83; v.p. fin. Madison Resources, Inc., NYC, 1983-86; v.p., treas. WSGP Internat., Inc., Morristown, N.J., 1986-89; mng. dir. William E. Simon & Sons, L.L.C., Morristown, 1989—. Fin. planning cons., Morristown, N.J., 1962—. Fundraiser, United Way of Essex and West Hudson Counties, Newark, 1978, Morristown-Beard Sch., 1990-92, Colonial Touchdown Club, Morristown, 1991-94; bd. dirs. Better Bus. Bur. Greater Newark, 1981-83; team mgr. Morristown Nat. Little League, 1982-86; leader Boy Scouts Am., Morristown, 1984-95, fin. advisor Morris/Sussex coun., Denville, N.J., 1991-92; mem. adv. bd. St. Joseph Sch., Bronx, N.Y., 1991—, Resurrection Sch., N.Y.C., 1996—; treas. Morristown H.S. Booster Club, 1992-94; beautification com. Twp. of Morris, 1998-2003, Kiwanis Club of Morristown, 1998-2002. Mem.: Coun. N.J. Grantmkers,

Fin. Execs. Inst., N.J. Soc. CPAs, AICPA, Friendly Sons of St. Patrick of Morris County. Avocation: golf. Office: William E Simon & Sons LLC PO Box 1913 Morristown NJ 07962-1913 Home Phone: 908-835-7972; Office Phone: 973-898-0290. Business E-Mail: fcregan@wesandsons.com.

CREGER, DAVID LEE, financial planner, insurance executive; b. Bristol, Tenn., Mar. 20, 1957; s. Bobby Gene and Mary Nell (Goodman) C.; children: Joshua A., Sarah R. Student, Va. Highlands C.C., Abingdon, Va., 1975-76. Life Underwriter Tng. Coun. fellow; cert. agt./continuing edn. instr. Tenn., Va., registered fin. cons. Ins. agt. Home Beneficial Life Ins. Co., Bristol, Va., 1984-85, staff sales mgr., 1985-89; personal producing gen. agt./owner The David L. Creger Co., Bristol, 1989-91; agt. and mktg. svcs. mgr. Settlers Life Ins. Co., Bristol, 1991-96; pres. Pinnacle Fin. Svcs., Inc., Bristol, 1994—; v.p., gen. mgr. Ally-ance Mktg. Group, Inc., Bristol, 1996-97. Disability income ins. course moderator Life Underwriter Tng. Coun., 1989-90; mem. adj. faculty Va. Highlands C.C., 1999—; lectr. in field. Contbr. articles to profl. jours. Pres. Bristol affiliate Am. Heart Assn., 1993-95, chmn. bd., 1995-96, chmn. Queen of Hearts Fundraiser, 1992, 93; vol. Appalachia region March of Dimes, 1992-93; account exec. United Way of Bristol, 1992-93, team capt., 1994, bd. dirs., 1995-2000, treas., chair fin. com., 1996-97, investment com. chmn., 1996-97, v.p., pres.-elect 1998; chmn. Profl. Div. Campaign Chmn. 1998—, Small Bus. Divsn. Campaign, 1999; pres. bd. dirs. 1999, immediate past pres., 2000; bd. dirs., The Janie Hammitt Meml. Children's Home, 1997; trustee, treas. Janie Hammitt Meml. Inc., 1998; mem. Tri-Cities Estate Planning Coun., 1998—; chmn. TALU Edn. Found. Com., 1997-98. Recipient Ernest E. Cragg Amb. award Life Underwriting Tng. Coun., 1994; named to Tri-Cities Bus. Jour. Regional 40 Under Forty, 1995, United Way of Bristol Vol. of Yr., 1996; named one of Outstanding Young Men of Am., 1998. Mem. Nat. Assn. Ins. and Fin. Advisors (polit. action com. 1989—), Tenn. Assn. Ins. and Fin. Advisors (N.E. Tenn. regional v.p. 1992-95, chair state profl. devel. com. 1994-95, sec. 1995-96, pres.-elect 1996-97, pres. 1997-98, past pres. 1998-99, state nat. committeeman 1999-2000), Bristol Assn. Ins. and Fin. Advisors (bd. dirs. 1985—, Queen of Hearts program com. 1986-97, pres. 1989-90, chair edn. com. 1991-93, exec. sec. 1993-94, chair state law and legis. com. 1993-95, 99-2001, Louis I. Dubin Pub. Svc. award 1989-90, Robert L. Rose Edn. and Assn. Achievment awards), Bristol C. of C. (VA legis. com. chair 1994, fed. issues com. chair 1995, govtl. rels. coun. vice-chair 1996, vice chair cmty. and govtl. rels. coun. 1997, exec. com. 1997, chmn. govtl. rels. divsn. 1998), vice-chmn. presdl. appointment bd. dirs. exec. com., 1999, Assn. Health Ins. Advisors (charter), Fin. Planning Assn. (charter), Nat. Assn. Ins. and Fin. Advisors (charter), Registered Fin. Planners Inst., Tri-Cities Estate Planning Coun., Tri-Cities Regional Chamber Coalition (bd. dirs. 1998), Bristol C. of C. (bd. dirs. 1995-2000), Rotary (Tenn.-Va. Sustaining Paul Harris fellow, bd. dirs.). Republican. Avocations: reading, computers, billiards. Office: PO Box 16008 Bristol VA 24209-6008 E-mail: dlreger@pinnacledreams.com.

CREGG, HUGH ANTHONY See LEWIS, HUEY

CREGG, ROGER A., construction executive; b. Peabody, Mass., Apr. 5, 1956; BS in Acctg., Northwestern U., M in Mgmt. CFO Sweetheart Cup Co.; exec. v.p., CFO Zenith Electronics Corp.; sr. v.p., CFO Pulte Homes Corp., Bloomfield Hills, Mich., 1998—2003, exec. v.p., CFO, 2003—. Mem. Detroit bd. dirs. Chgo. Fed. Res. Bank, 2004—. Mem.: Fin. Execs. Internat. Office: Pulte Homes Corp Ste 300 100 Bloomfield Hills Pky Bloomfield Hills MI 48304*

CREGO, MARY, lawyer; b. Seattle, June 23, 1975; BA magna cum laude, Univ. Alaska, Anchorage, 1997; JD magna cum laude, Univ. Wash., 2001. Bar: Wash. 2001. Civil litig. atty. Hillis Clark Martin & Peterson, Seattle, 2001—. Contbr. articles to numerous profl. jours. Named Seattle Rising Star, SuperLawyer Mag., 2006. Mem.: King Co. Bar Assn., Wash. State Bar Assn. Office: Hillis Clark Martin & Peterson 500 Galland Bldg 1221 Second Ave Seattle WA 98101-2925

CREHAN, JOSEPH EDWARD, lawyer; b. Detroit, Dec. 8, 1938; s. Owen Thomas and Marguerite (Dunn) C.; m. Sheila Anderson, Nov. 6, 1965; children: Kerry Marie, Christa Ellen. AB, Wayne State U., Detroit, 1961; JD, Ind. U., 1965. Bar: Ind. 1965, Mich. 1966, U.S. Supreme Ct. 1984. Pvt. practice, Detroit, 1966-68; assoc. Louisell & Barris (P.C.), 1968-72; ptnr. Fenton, Nederlander, Dodge, Barris & Crehan (P.C.), 1972-74, Barris & Crehan (P.C.), 1975-88; pvt. practice Bloomfield Hills, Mich. and Naples, Fla., 1977—. Mem. Am. Trial Lawyers Assn. Roman Catholic. Home and Office: 827 Bentwood Dr Naples FL 34108-8204

CREHORE, CHARLES AARON, lawyer; b. Lorain, Ohio, Sept. 15, 1946; s. Charles Case and Catherine Elizabeth Crehore; 1 child, Charles Case II. BA, Wittenberg U., 1968; postgrad., U. Mich., 1968—69, Cleve. State U., 1972—73; JD, U. Akron, 1976; diploma mgmt. mgrs. program, Pa. State U., 1983. Bar: US Patent Office 1975, Ohio 1976, US Dist Ct (no dist) Ohio 1976, US Ct Appeals (DC cir) 1977, US Tax Ct 1977, US Supreme Ct 1980, US Ct Appeals (fed cir) 1982. Assoc. chemist B.F. Goodrich Co., Akron, 1969-70, chemist, 1970-72, sr. chemist, 1972, patent atty. trainee, 1972-74, sr. patent atty. trainee, 1974-75, patent assoc., 1975-76, patent atty., 1976-79; atty. regulatory affairs The Lubrizol Corp., Wickliffe, Ohio, 1979-81, corp. counsel environment, health and safety, 1981-85, sr. corp. counsel, 1985-94, counsel, 1994-99; patent atty. Hudak and Shunk Co., L.P.A., 2000; of counsel Ulmer & Berne, LLP, 2000—06, sr. counsel, 2006—. Guest lectr. moot ct judge Case Western Res Univ. 1983—; spkr. Calif Inst Bus Law, Ohio, 1991, Northeast Ohio Software Asn, 2001—, Lakeland Cmty. Coll., 2001—, Media Profls. Conf., 2002—; adv bd applied environ mgmt program Lake Erie Col, 1991—94. Grantee, Kennedy Found, 1968—69; scholar, Delta Sigma Phi Found, 1968—69. Mem.: ABA, Cleve. Bar Assn., Ohio State Bar Assn., Cleve. Intellectual Property Law Assn., Am. Intellectual Property Law Assn., Greater Cleve. Internat. Lawyers Group, Phi Alpha Delta. Home: PO Box 466 Wickliffe OH 44092-0466 also: 1660 W 2nd St Cleveland OH 44113-1454 Office Phone: 216-583-7070. E-mail: ccrehore@aol.com.

CREIGH, JAMES CAREY, lawyer; s. Thomas Creigh, Jr. and Dorothy Weyer Creigh; m. Victoria L. Creigh, Aug. 18, 1990; children: Alexandra, Thomas, James. AB, U. Nebr., 1990; JD, MBA, Georgetown U., Washington, 1995. Assoc. Foley & Lardner, Milw., 1995—97, Wilson Sonsini Goodrich & Rosati, Palo Alto, Calif., 1997—2003; ptnr. Blackwell Sanders Peper Martin LLP, Omaha, 2003—06; v.p., strategic bus. devel. West Corp., Omaha, 2006—. Contbr. articles to profl. jours. Pres. Creigh Family Found., Omaha, 2003—; bd. dirs. Nebr. State Hist. Soc. Found.; trustee Hastings Coll. Nat. Merit scholar, 1986. Office: West Corp 11808 Miracle Hills Dr Omaha NE 68154 Office Phone: 402-963-1200.

CREIGHTON, DONALD LOUIS, mechanical engineer, consultant; b. Hays, Kans., Jan. 3, 1932; s. Alexander Quinn and Marigold Frances (Allen) Creighton; m. Monica Ann Price, Nov. 27, 1953; 1 child, Christopher Price. BSME, Univ. Kans., Lawrence, Kans., 1954, MSME, 1961; PhD, U. Ariz., 1964. Asst. instr. U. Kans., Lawrence, 1953—54, instr., 1959—61; engr. Gen. Elec., Kansas City, Mo., 1954; R & D engr. Aero Divsn., Mpls. Honeywell, Mpls., 1957; engr. rocket test Rocketdyne N.Am. Aviation, Neosho, Mo., 1958—59; instr. U. Kans., Lawrence, 1959—61; asst. prof. U. Mo., Columbia, 1964—68, assoc. prof., 1968—78, prof., 1978—89, prof. emeritus, 1989—. Owner Donald L. Creighton, PhD, P.E., Columbia, Mo., 1965—; cons. in field. Contbr. articles pub. to profl. jour. Lt. JG USN, 1954—57, Korea. Fellow Ryan Aeronautical Found., U. Ariz., 1961—63; John Morse Found. Fellowship, Univ. Kans., 1951—53. Mem.: ASME, Am. Welding Soc., Soc. of Automotive Engrs., Am. Soc. for Agrl. Engrs., Am. Soc. for Metals, Pi Tau Sigma, Sigma Tau, Tau Beta Pi, Sigma Xi. Home: 651 Covered Bridge Rd Columbia MO 65203 Office Phone: 573-817-3232. Personal E-mail: aanddcreighton@aol.com.

CREIGHTON, JOANNE VANISH, academic administrator; b. Marinette, Wis., Feb. 21, 1942; d. William J. and Bernice Vanish; m. Thomas F. Creighton, Nov. 9, 1968; 1 child, William. BA with honors, U. Wis., 1964; MA, Harvard U., 1965; PhD, U. Mich., 1969. From instr. to prof. English Wayne State U., Detroit, 1968—85, assoc. dean liberal arts, 1983—85; dean arts and scis., prof. English U. N.C., Greensboro, 1985—90; v.p. acad. affairs, provost, prof. English Wesleyan U., Middletown, Conn., 1990—94, interim pres., 1994—95; pres., prof. English Mt. Holyoke Coll., South Hadley, Mass., 1995—. Author: William Faulkner's Craft of Revision, 1977, Joyce Carol Oates, 1979, Margaret Dabble, 1985, Joyce Carol Oates: Novels of the Middle Years, 1992. Grantee, Am. Coun. Learned Socs. Mem.: Phi Kappa Phi, Phi Beta Kappa. Home: 45 College St South Hadley MA 01075-1403 Office: Mount Holyoke Coll Office of Pres 50 College St South Hadley MA 01075-1423 Office Phone: 413-538-2500. Office Fax: 413-538-2391.*

CREIGHTON, JOHN WALLIS, JR., writer, former management educator, consultant, small business owner; b. Yeung Kong, China, Apr. 7, 1916; s. John Wallis and Lois (Jameson) C.; m. Harriet Harrington, June 30, 1940; childrn: Carol (Mrs. Brian LeNeve), Joan (Mrs. Robert Nielsen). Student, Wooster Coll., 1933-36; BS in Forestry, U. Mich., 1938; AB, Hastings Coll., 1939; PhD in Wood Tech. and Indsl. Engring., U. Mich., 1954. Operator, sawmill, Cuyahoga Falls, Ohio, 1939—41; mem. staff US Bd. Econ. Warfare, Ecuador, 1942—45; asst. gen. mgr. R.S. Bacon Veneer Co., Chgo., 1945—46; gen. mgr., v.p. Bacon Lumber Co., Sunman, Ind., 1945—46; faculty Mich. State U., Lansing, 1946—54, prof. wood tech., 1946—54; asst. to gen. mgr., v.p. Baker Furniture Inc., Grand Rapids, Mich., 1954—58; pres. Creighton Bldg. Co., Santa Barbara, Calif., 1958—65; prof. mgmt. Colo. State U., Ft. Collins, 1965—67, US Naval Post grad. Sch., Monterey, Calif., 1967—86, chmn. dept., 1967—71, dir. fed. exec. mgmt. program, 1974—82, emeritus prof., 1986; wrtier, publ., owner Quail Valley Books, 1988—. Cons. in field. Assoc. editor, co-founder Jour. Tech. Transfer, 1975-88; fiction writer, 1986-; author: Waring's War, 2001, Aira in Red, 2002, Among Spies, 2004; contbr. articles to profl. jours. Former mem. Forestry Commn., Carmel, Calif., 1986-95. Recipient numerous Rsch. grants. Mem. Tech. Transfer Soc., Writer's Internat. Network, Calif. Writer's Club. Presbyterian. Home: 8065 Lake Pl Carmel CA 93923-9514 Office Phone: 831-625-3071.

CREIGHTON, PEGGY MILAM, media specialist, writer; b. Richmond, Va., Sept. 8, 1953; d. Robert Charles and Nola Maxine (Brisentine) Squier; married; children: Ryan Wesley Milam, Sara Kristen Milam. BS in Elem./Spl. Edn., Ga. State U., 1975, postgrad., 1999; MEd in Early Childhood, Mercer U., 1992; EdS in Media/Inst. Tech., State U. West Ga., 2002. Cert. libr. media specialist Nat. Bd. Cert., 2003. Tchr. 6th grade lang. arts Newton County Bd. Edn., Covington, Ga., 1975—76, Gwinnett County Bd. Edn., Lawrenceville, Ga., 1976—80; elem. tchr. Mt. Vernon Presbyn. Sch., Atlanta, 1986—99; from dir. media svcs. to coll. dean Interactive Coll. Tech., Chamblee, Ga., 1999—2001; libr. media specialist Cobb County Bd. Edn., Marietta, Ga., 2001—. Mem. Media Leadership Team, Marietta, 2001—05; tchr. support specialist, 2005—; presenter in field. Author: Infoquest: A New Twist on Information Literacy, 2002, National Board Certification in Library Media: A Candidates Journal, 2005; contbr. articles to profl. jours. New tchr. mentor Mighty Mentors, 2000—01; relay for life fundraiser Am. Cancer Soc., Atlanta, 2000—; amb. People to People: Spl. Needs Delegation to China, 2006. Named Most Outstanding Specialist in Media, State U. West Ga., 2003; recipient Extra Mile award, Interactive Coll. Tech., 2000. Mem.: ASCD, ALA, Ga. Assn. Sch. Libr. Media Specialists, Cobb County Assn. Libr. Media Specialists (pres.-elect 2004—05, pres. 2005—06), Internat. Soc. for Tech. in Edn. (sec. 2004—, pres. 2007—), Pi Lambda Theta. Avocations: reading, writing, sewing, quilting. Office: Compton Elem Sch 3450 New Macland Rd Powder Springs GA 30127 Personal E-mail: peggymilam@hotmail.com.

CREIGHTON, ROBERT EMMETT, retired language educator, retired chaplain; b. Chgo., July 19, 1935; s. Matthew Eugene and Mary Cecilia Creighton; m. Mary Ellen Creighton, Aug. 10, 1968; 1 child, Robert Matthew. AB in Latin, Xavier U., Cin., Ohio, 1958; MA in Classical Studies, Loyola U., Chgo., 1968. Cert. tchr. H.S. Latin Ill., 2007, tchr. elem. sch. Latin Ill., 2007, tchr. K-9 Ill., 2007. Tchr. Archdiocesan Schs., Chgo., 1963—69; asst. prof. Ctrl. Meth. Coll., Fayette, Mo., 1969—72; itinerant Latin tchr. Sch. Dist. Phila., 1972—78; substitute tchr. Chgo. Pub. Schs., 1979—82, tchr. latin, 1983—97; chaplain Alexian Rehabilitaion Hosp., Elk Grove Village, Ill., 1997—2006. Eucharistic min. St. Gerald's Ch., Oak Lawn, Ill., 1986—93, St. Edmund's Ch., Oak Park, Ill., 1994—, Oak Pk. Hosp., 2006—; co-founder Latin Olympics Chgo. Pub. Schs. Recipient Outstanding Tchr. K-6 Latin award, Bur. Fgn. Langs., Chgo. Bd. of Edn., 1989. Mem.: Assn. Clin. Pastoral Edn. (clin. mem.), Assn. Profl. Chaplains (affiliate), Nat. Assn. Cath. Chaplains (affiliate). Home: 1029 DesPlaines 101 Forest Park IL 60130

CRELLIN, ALAN W., air transportation executive; married; 2 children. Mgmt. positions Pacific S.W. Airlines (acquired by US Airways Inc.), 1971—88; joined US Airways, Inc., Arlington, Va., 1988—95, v.p. ground svcs., 1995—2000, sr. v.p. customer svc., 2000—02, exec. v.p. ops, 2002—. Police officer, LA. With USMC. Office: US Airways 111 West Rio Salado Pkwy Tempe AZ 85281

CREMEANS, JAMES L., minister; b. Rayland, Ohio, Dec. 22, 1939; s. Leroy and Waneda (Montgomery) C.; m. Mary McCormick, Oct. 4, 1956; children: James, David, Jeffery, Diane, Janet. DD (hon.), Internat. Bible Sem., 1985. Ordained to ministry lst Tabernacle Ch., Ironton, Ohio, 1967. Pastor City Mission Ch., Ironton, 1967—; exec. dir. City Welfare Mission, Ironton, 1967—. Dir. corr. sch. Evangelistic Outreach, Pedro, Ohio, 1982—, v.p., 1975—, also bd. dirs. Mem. Lawrence County (Ohio) Welfare Adv. Bd., 1980-82, Home Health Care Bd., Ironton, 1980—, Lawrence County Youth Coun., 1988—; mem. bd. biomed. ethics River Valley Hosp., 1998—; bd. dirs. Ironton/Lawrence County Cmty. Action Orgn., 2002. Named Citizen of Yr., Cmty. Betterment Club, Lawrence County, 1979, Ironton Tribune, 1993. Mem. Lawrence County Ministerial Assn. (chmn. radio and TV 1975-80, sec.-treas. 1995—, chmn. chaplancy com. 1993—). Home: 365 Township Road 150 Pedro OH 45659-8928 Office: City Mission Ch 710 N 5th St Ironton OH 45638-1306 Personal E-mail: jimmaryc@peoplepc.com.

CREMEENS, JOANNE, medical researcher; BS in Psychology, U. Warwick, England, 2000; PhD in Psychology, U. Sheffield, England, 2004. Lead clin. rsch. assoc. St. Jude Children's Rsch. Hosp., Memphis, 2004—.

CREMER, LEON E., retired federal agency administrator, lawyer; b. Cin., Dec. 30, 1945; s. Walter H. and Beatrice (Campbell) C. BS, Calif. State U., 1973; MA, George Wash. U., Washington, DC, 1976; JD, Rutgers U., 1982. Bar: Pa. 1982. Officer US Secret Svc., Washington, 1975-77; spl. agt. US Bur. Alcohol Tobacco and Firearms, Phila., 1977—83, FBI, 1983—2003; ret., 2003. Served in US Army, 1968-69. Mem. ABA, FBI Agts. Assn., Am. Mensa Soc. Avocations: boating, aviation, skiing, running, motorhoming. Personal E-mail: leoncremer@msn.com.

CREMINS, JAMES SMYTH, lawyer; b. Washington, June 11, 1921; m. Mary Louise Gallagher (dec.); 5 children. AB with honors, U. Mo., Columbia, 1943; JD, U. Va., 1949. Asst. gen. counsel CSX Corp., Richmond, Va., 1980-85. Treas. Dem. Party Va., 1977-89. Contbr. articles to profl. jours. Lay min. St. Mary's Ch., Richmond, 1968-85; bd. visitors U. Va., 1984-88, Pres.'s Roundtable JMU, 1985-90; mem. adv. bd. St. Gertrude H.S., Richmond, 1984-88; past instnl. rep. Robert E. Lee coun. Boy Scouts Am.; mem. fin. coun. Richmond Cath. Diocese, 1978—; trustee Commonwealth Cath. Charities, 1981—; bd. dirs. Maymont Found., 1976-89; mem. State Dem. Steering Com., 1972-89, State Dem. Ctrl. Com., 1972-89. Lt. USNR, 1943-46. Recipient Brotherhood award, Nat. Conf. Christians and Jews, 1985. Fellow: Am. Bar Found.; mem.: KC (4th degree) (knight equestrian Order of Holy Sepulcher of Jerusalem 1998), ABA, Am. Judicature Soc. (bd. dirs. 1973—77), Richmond Bar Assn. (chmn. corp. counsel sect. 1964—65), Va. Bar Assn., Ancient Order Hibernians (charter mem. Maj. James Dooley divsn. 1), Nat. Soc. SAR (trustee 1989—90), Navy League U.S. (Judge adv. Richmond coun. 1985—89), Va. Soc. SAR (pres. 1988—89), Phi Delta Phi, Omicron Delta Kappa (hon.), Alpha Tau Omega.

CREMINS, WILLIAM CARROLL, lawyer; b. Virginia Beach, Va., Nov. 13, 1957; s. James Smyth and Mary Louise (Gallagher) C.; m. Kelly Robin Knapp, July 6, 1985; children: William Carroll Jr., Robert Gallagher. BA, BJ, U. Mo., 1980; JD, St. John's U., 1984. Bar: Tenn. 1984, NY 1985, US Dist. Ct. (ea. dist.) Tenn., US Ct. Appeals (6th cir.). Assoc. Law Offices of J.D. Lee, Knoxville, Tenn., 1984-85; pvt. practice, Knoxville, 1986—. Dep. nat. organizer Ancient Order of Hibernians in Am., Inc., Tenn., 1985, pres. James Dardis divsn., 1997-98; bd. dirs. Florence Crittenton Agy. of Knoxville, Inc., 1989-96, 2002—, pres., 1995; Little League baseball coach, 1993-97, football coach, 1987, 1993-94, soccer coach, 1992, 1995. Recipient Pro Bono award Knoxville Bar Assn. Vol. Legal Assistance Program, 1992. Mem. ATLA (Advocate recognition 1994), ABA, Tenn. Bar Assn., Knoxville Bar Assn., Tenn. Trial Lawyers Assn. Roman Catholic. Home: 710 Saint John Ct Knoxville TN 37922-1556 Office: 810 Henley St Knoxville TN 37902-2901 Office Phone: 865-546-7124. Office Fax: 865-546-7151. Personal E-mail: wmcremins@aol.com.

CRENNEL, ROMEO, professional football coach; b. Lynchburg, Va. m. Rosemary Crennel; 3 children. BA physical Ed., Western Kentucky Univ. MA. Grad. asst. Western Kentucky Univ., 1970, defensive line coach, 1971—74; defensive asst. Texas Tech Univ., 1975—77; defensive ends coach Univ. of Miss., 1978—79; defensive line coach Ga. Tech Univ., 1980; special teams, defensive asst. coach NY Giants, 1981—82, spl. teams coach, 1983—89, defensive line coach, 1990—92, New England Patriots, 1993—96, NY Jets, 1997—99; defensive coordinator, line coach Cleve. Browns, 2000; defensive coordinator New England Patriots, 2001, 2004, defensive coordinator, defensive line coach, 2002—03; head coach Cleve. Browns, 2005—. Achievements include being a member of Super Bowl Champion New York Giants, 1986, 1990, New England Patriots, 2001, 2003, 2004. Office: c/o Cleveland Browns 76 Lou Groza Blvd Berea OH 44017

CRENSHAW, ALBERT BURFORD, journalist; b. Lexington, Va., Oct. 4, 1942; s. Ollinger and Marjorie (Burford) C.; m. Margaret Alice Price, Aug. 11, 1973; children: David Ollinger, Caroline Abbey. AB, Harvard U., 1964; MS, U. Va., 1966; MS in Journalism, Columbia U., 1967. Reporter Washington Daily News, 1969-71, asst. city editor, 1971-72; asst. nat. editor Washington Post, 1972-76, night nat. editor, 1977-82, real estate editor, 1982-85, asst. fin. editor, 1985-88, fin. reporter, columnist, 1988—. Served with U.S. Army, 1967-69 Mem.: Harvard (N.Y.C.); Nat. Press (Washington). Home: 321 E Capitol St SE Washington DC 20003-3808 Office: Washington Post 1150 15th St NW Washington DC 20071-0002

CRENSHAW, ANDER, congressman, lawyer; b. Jacksonville, Fla., Sept. 1, 1944; m. Kitty, 1971; children: Sarah, Alex. BA, U. Ga., 1966; JD, U. Fla., 1970. Mem. Fla. Ho. of Reps., 1972—78; candidate Fla. Sec. of State, 1978, US Senate, 1980; mem. Fla. State Senate, Fla., 1986—94, Rep. leader, 1990—92, pres., 1993; sr. v.p. Donaldson, Lufkin and Jenrette, 1990—95, William R. Hough & Co., 1995—; mem. U.S. Congress from 4th Fla. Dist., 2001—. Mem. Congressional com. Armed Svcs., 2003—Budget, 2001—, Appropriations, Veterans' Affairs, Rep. policy; subcom. Mil. Rsch. and Devel., Mil. Installations and Facilities, Mil. Quality of Life, Foreign Ops., Homeland Security, Health, Benefits; appt. Asst. Majority Whip; rep. to House of GOP leadership. Mem. Fla. Ethics com., Fla. Constitution Revision com. Republican. Episcopalian. Office: US Ho of Reps 127 Cannon House Office Bldg Washington DC 20515-0904*

CRENSHAW, BEN, professional golfer; b. Austin, Tex., Jan. 11, 1952; m. Julie Ann; children: Katherine Vail, Claire Susan, Anna Riley. Grad., U. Tex. Mem. U.S. World Amateur Cup Team, 1972; mem. U.S. Ryder Cup, 1981, 83, 87, 95; profl. golfer, 1973—; U.S. team capt. Kirin Cup, 1988; team capt. Ryder Cup Team, 1999. Winner San Antonio Open, 1973, Western Amateur open match and medal plan champion, 1973, Bing Crosby Nat. Pro-Am., Ohio Kings Island Open, Hawaiian Open, 1976, Colonial Nat. Invitational, 1977, NCAA Championship, 1971, 72, 73, Irish Open, 1976, Phoenix Open, 1979, Walt Disney World Team Championship, 1980, AnheuserOBusch Classic, 1980, Tex. State Open winner, 1980, Ryder Cup, 1981, 83, 87, Byron Nelson Classic, 1983, Masters tournament, 1984, PGA Sr. Event Jeremy Ranch Shoot-Out teameed with Miller Barber, 1985, Buick Open, 1986, Vantage Championship, 1986, USF&G, 1987, Doral Ryder Open, 1988, World Cup, 1988, Western Open, 1992, Masters winner Augusta Nat. Golf Club, 1995, Masters Tournament, 1995, Ryder Cup, 1999, admitted to World Golf Hall of Fame, 2002. Mem. Profl. Golfers Assn. Am. Office: PO Box 50568 Austin TX 78763-0568

CRENSHAW, EDWARD LEE, SR., aviation electronics technician; b. Shelby, NC, Oct. 31, 1946; s. William and Ida Mae Crenshaw; m. Linda F. Yates, June 15, 1986; children: Edward Lee Jr., Kevin William, Bryant E. Yates. Lic. airframe and powerplant FAA/FCC. Airline servicer, customer svc. agt. aviation maintenance tech, aviation electronic tech. Eastern Air Lines Inc., United Air Lines Inc., Miami, San Francisco, Seattle, 1970—. Dir. BWI Chess Club, Balt., 1979—83. Author: (novels) ATC Emergency Code 7700 (10th Ann. Writers Digest Participation Cert., 2001), Deadly Satellites, 2004. Tchr. Local Union 141 Chess Club, San Francisco, 1992—96. Lt. cpl. USMC, 1964—68. Decorated Sharpshooter, Nuc. Biol. Chem. specialist USMC. Mem.: Assn. Writers and Writing Programs, Writers Cir. Home: 110 Sw 313th St Federal Way WA 98023 Office: United Air Lines Inc Seattle Tacoma Internat Airport Seattle WA 98158 Office Phone: 253-946-4549. Business E-Mail: EL@fictionwritersplus.com.

CRENSHAW, FRANCIS NELSON, retired lawyer; b. Washington, Dec. 9, 1922; s. Russell Sydnor and Sally Nelson (Robins) C.; m. Jane Elizabeth Treadwell, Aug. 20, 1949 (dec. June 1993); children: Elizabeth, Page, Marian; m. Anne Alfriend Abbitt, July 12, 1997. Grad., St. George's Sch., 1939; BA, U. Va., 1943, LLB, 1948. Bar: Va. 1948. Ptnr. Baird, White & Lanning, Norfolk, 1952-55, Baird, Crenshaw & Lanning, Norfolk, 1955-60, Baird, Crenshaw & Ware, Norfolk, 1960-68, Crenshaw, Ware & Johnson, Norfolk, 1968-89, Crenshaw, Ware & Martin, Norfolk, 1989-99; ret., 1999. Mem. Va. Bd. Bar Examiners, 1973-90, pres., 1983-90. Mem. Norfolk City Sch. Bd., 1955-64, chmn., 1962-64; bd. visitors Old Dominion U., 1968-76, rector, 1972-76; mem. bd. commrs., Ea. Va. Med. Authority, 1966-68. Served with USNR, 1943-46. Decorated Bronze Star. Fellow ABA, Va. Law Found.; mem. Va. Bar Assn. (chmn. exec. com. 1988-89), Va. State Bar (chmn. sr. lawyers sect. 1998-99; editor sr. lawyers newsletter 1999-2002), Norfolk-Portsmouth Bar Assn. (pres. 1967), Maritime Law Assn. Home: One Colley Ave Unit 400 Norfolk VA 23510

CRENSHAW, HORACE, JR., military officer; b. Meridian, Miss., Dec. 6, 1970; s. Horace Cremshaw Sr. and Sarah R. Crenshaw; m. Trina Lavorn Johnson (div.); 1 child, Nilah Iman; m. Rhonda Latrice Crenshaw, Sept. 25, 2004. BA Polit. Sci., Tuskegee U., Ala., 1994; MA Internat. Rels., Webster U., St. Louis, 1999. Mgr. Red Lobster, Jackson, Miss., 1995—96; commd U.S. Army, 1993, advanced through grades to capt., 1995, supply and svcs. officer 329th q.m. bn. St. Louis, 1996—99; student Combined Logistics Capts., Fort Lee, Va., 1999—2000; ops. officer 361st Q.M. Bn, Montgomery, Ala., 2000—02; company commdr. 233rd q.m. co. (PS), Phila., 2002—04; planner/ team chief Army Material Command, Ft. Belvoir, Va., 2004—. Mem.: Mil. Officers Assn., Masons, Kappa Alpha Psi. Avocations: basketball, golf, reading, running. Office: US Army Material Command Bldg 464 6000 6th St Fort Belvoir VA 22060 Office Phone: 703-806-4405 4750. Fax: 703-806-2078. E-mail: armynupe6@msn.com.

CREPET, WILLIAM LOUIS, botanist, educator; b. NYC, Aug. 10, 1946; s. Louis Henry and Adaire Elaine (Richardson) C.; m. Laura Marie Stewart, July 29, 1972 (div. 1978); m. Ruth Chadab, July 27, 1980. BA, Harpur Coll., SUNY, Binghamton, 1969; MPh (Wadsworth fellow), Yale U., 1972, PhD (Cullman fellow), 1973. Cons. to Grad. Sch. U. Tex., Austin, 1972-73; lectr. Ind. U., 1973-75; asst. prof. U. Conn., 1975-78, assoc. prof., 1979-84, prof., 1985—, head dept., 1985-90; chmn., prof. Bailey Hortorium Cornell U., Ithaca, NY, 1990—, and chair, dept. plant biology. Mem. bd. trustees Paleontological Rsch. Inst., 2005. N.Y. State Regents scholar SUNY, 1969. Fellow Explorers Club; mem. Bot. Soc. Am. (chmn. paleobotany sect. 1979-80, Paleobot. award 1972), Am. Inst. Biol. Scis., Beta Chi Sigma. Achievements include research in Mesozoic and Tertiary genera. Office: Cornell U LH Bailey Hortorium 462 Mann Library Ithaca NY 14853-4301 Office Phone: 607-255-2131. Business E-Mail: wlc1@cornell.edu.

CRESANTI, ROBERT CHARLES, federal agency administrator; s. Sam and Christa Cresanti; m. Colleen Cresanti; children: Katja, Kristin. BA, Austin Coll.; JD, Baylor U. Legis. asst. to Congressman Paul Gillmor of Ohio; counsel to Senator Robert Bennett of Utah; staff dir. US Senate Spl. Com. on Yr. 2000 Tech. Problem, Subcommittee of Fin. Svcs. and Tech., US Senate Banking Com.; sr. v.p., gen. counsel Info. Tech. Assn. Am., 2000; v.p. pub. policy Bus. Software Alliance; under sec. of commerce for tech. US Dept. Commerce, Washington, 2006—. Mem. Edn. and Training, Internat. Sci., Engring., and Tech., Nat. Security and Tech. Coms. Pres.'s Nat. Sci. and Tech. Coun. Office: US Dept Commerce 1401 Constitution Ave, NW Washington DC 20230 Office Phone: 202-482-1575. Office Fax: 202-501-2595.

CRESPO DE SANABIA, MARÍA MILAGROS, retired education educator; b. Mayaguez, Puerto Rico, June 5, 1948; d. Osvaldo J. Crespo Salas and Joaquina Reyes Rivera; m. Aníbal Sanabia, June 24, 1972; children: Aníbal Iván Sanabia Crespo, Aníbal Osvaldo Sanabia Crespo. MA in Edn., U. Phoenix, PR, 1996. Sci. tchr. Dept. Edn., Río Piedras, 1978—2001; asst. project dir. Ednl. Linkages Demonstration Project, Bronx, 1999—2001; coord. PR Statewide Systemic Initiative, San Juan, 1994—2000; ednl. cons. Evans Newton Inc., Scottsdale, Ariz., 2004—06; prof. (part time) Universidad del Este, Carolina, 2006—. Coord. profl. devel. program Evans Newton Inc., 2005—06. Recipient Tchr. of Yr., Dept. of Edn. - Converse, Sci. Tchr. of P. R., Dept. of Edn., 1992. Mem.: NSTA (assoc.), ASCD (assoc.). Achievements include design of profl. devel. programs; acad. for new tchrs. of sci. and math. Avocations: travel, craftman, reading, exercise. Home: Colinas de Fair View 202 St 4E-#26 Trujillo Alto PR 00976 Home Phone: (787)760-7229. Personal E-mail: maria_s@prw.net.

CRESSEY, BRYAN CHARLES, venture capitalist; b. Seattle, Sept. 28, 1949; s. Charles Ovington and Alice Lorraine (Serry) C.; m. Christina Irene Petersen, Aug. 19, 1972; children: Monique Joy, Charlotte Lorraine, Alicia Lin. BA, U. Wash., 1972; MBA, JD, Harvard U., 1976. Bar: Wash. 1976, Ill. 1977. Sr. investment mgr. First Chgo. Investment Corp., Chgo., 1976-80; prin. Golder, Thoma, Cressey, Fauner, Inc., Chgo., 1980—; prnt. Thoma, Cressey Equity Ptnrs., 1998—. Chmn., bd. dirs. Cable Design Techs., Inc.; bd. dirs. Am. Habilitation, Inc., Houston, Assistive Tech., Ill., Clarion tech., Ill., Select Med., Harrisburg, Pa., Boston. Author: (theatrical play) Explosions. Bd. dirs. Infant Welfare Soc., Chgo., 1984—, Jr. Achievement, Chgo. Inductee Entrepreneurial Hall of Fame, 1998. Home: 500 W County Line Rd Barrington IL 60010-9629 Office: Thoma Cressey Equity Partners 9200 Sears Tower Chicago IL 60606

CRESSLER, JOHN DAVID, electrical engineering educator; b. Chattanooga, Sept. 18, 1961; s. Charles W. and Elizabeth (Bolling) C.; married; children: Matthew J., Christina E., Joanna M. BS in Physics, Ga. Inst. Tech., 1984; MS in Applied Physics, Columbia U., 1987, PhD in Applied Physics, 1990. Mem. staff rsch. divsn. IBM Thomas J. Watson Rsch. Ctr., Yorktown Heights, NY, 1984-92; prof. Auburn U., Ala., 1992—2002; Byers prof. elec. and computer engring. Ga. Inst. Tech., 2002—. Co-author (with Guofu Niu) Silicon-Germanium Heterojunction Bipolar Transistors, 2003; author Reinventing Teenagers: the Gentle Art of Instilling Character in Our Young People, 2004; editor (book) Silicon Heterostructure Handbook: Materials, Fabrication, Devices, Circuits, and Applications of SiGe and Si Strained-Layer Epitaxy, 2006; contbr. articles to profl. jours. Recipient Auburn U. Alumni Engring. Coun. Rsch. award, 1996, Auburn U. Birdsong Merit Testing award, 1998, Auburn U. Alumni Undergraduate Tchg. Excellence award, 1999. Fellow IEEE (sr. mem., assoc. editor Jour. of Solid-State Circuits 1998-2001, guest editor for Transactions on Nuclear Sci. 2002-05, assoc. editor Transactions on Electron Deveices, 2005-; mem. tech. program com. Internat. Solid-State Circuits Conf., 1992-98, 1999-2001, Bipolar/BiCMOS Circuits and Tech. Mtg., 1995-99, Internat. Electron Devices Mtg., 1996-97, Nuclear and Space Radiation Effects Conf., 2000, 2002-06, Internat. Reliability Physics Symposium, 2005; tech. program chair, Internat. Solid-State Circuits Conf., 1998; conf. co-chair 2004 Topical Mtg. on Silicon Monolithic Integrated Circuits in RF Systems, Internat. advisor European Workshop on Low Temperature Electronics; mem. technical program com. Internat. SiGe Tech. and Device Mtg.; mem. exec. com. ECS Symposium on SiGe: Materials, Processing, and Devices; IEEE Electron Device Soc. Disting. Lectr., 1994-; recipient Millennium medal, 2000); mem. Eta Kappa Nu (C. Holmes MacDonald award 1996). Office: Ga Inst Tech Sch Elec and Computer Engring 777 Atlantic Dr NW Atlanta GA 30332-0250 Office Phone: 404-894-5161. Office Fax: 404-894-4641. Business E-Mail: cressler@ece.gatech.edu.

CRESWELL, DOROTHY ANNE, computer consultant; b. Burlington, Iowa, Feb. 6, 1943; d. Robert Emerson and Agnes Imogene (Gardner) Mefford; m. John Lewis Creswell, Aug. 28, 1965. AA, Burlington CC, 1963; BA in Math., U. Iowa, 1965; MS in Math., We. Ill. U., 1970; postgrad., Iowa State U., 1974. Computer programmer Mason & Hanger, Silas Mason Co., Inc., Burlington, 1965—74; sys. programmer Contractor's Hotline, Ft. Dodge, Iowa, 1974; dir. data processing Iowa Ctrl. CC, Ft. Dodge, 1975—80; mgr. sys. programming Norand Corp., Cedar Rapids, Iowa, 1980—82; mgr. spl. svcs. Pioneer Hi-Bred Internat., Inc., Cedar Rapids, 1982—87; owner, pres. D.C. Cons., Inc., Ankeny, Iowa, 1987—2003. Computers-in-edn. del. to China People to People Internat., Kansas City, Mo., 1987. Contbr. articles, papers to profl. publs. Mem.: Ind. Computer Cons. Assn. (editl. bd. 1989—96, chpt. pres.-at-large 1993—95), DEC Users Group (v.p. Ea. Iowa chpt. 1981—82), Hawkeye Pers. Computer Users, Assn. Computing Machinery, Adminstrv. Mgmt. Soc. (sec. 1985—86, v.p. 1986—90, Merit award 1987), Data Processing Mgmt. Assn. (bd. dirs. 1986—87, v.p. 1988, 1991—93, pres. 1993—94). Democrat. Methodist. Avocations: jogging, travel.

CRESWELL, JULIE, reporter; BA, Iowa. Reporter Fortune mag., writer-reporter, 1999—2000, writer, 2000, regular contbr.; contbg. writer CNN/Money; banking reporter NY Times. Office: NY Times 229 West 43rd St New York NY 10036 Office Phone: 212-556-1474. Office Fax: 212-556-1448.

CRETAN, DONNA, neonatal nurse, lactation consultant; b. Mpls., May 18, 1939; d. Howard Robert and Frances E. (Warner) Bjerke; m. Nestor Nicholas Cretan, Jan. 24, 1959; children: Colette, John, Christopher, Bernadette. ADN, Contra Costa Coll., 1973; BSN, Sacred Heart U., Fairfield, Conn., 1986. RN Conn. Nurse mgr., cons. St. Joseph Med. Ctr., Stamford, Conn., 1974-89; staff nurse Cmty. Hosp., Santa Rosa, Calif., 1989-93, Greenwich (Conn.) Hosp., 1993—2002, Mark Twin St. Joseph Hosp., San Andreas, Calif., 2002—. ESL tutor LVA, 1997—. Host parent A Better Chance, New Canaan, Conn., 1982-84, Am. Field Svc., 1983-84, Calif., 1991-93, Cultural Homestay, Cohasset, Mass., 1991-95, People Link, Petaluma, Calif.; sec. Hist. Soc., Sebastopol, Calif., 1989-92; vol. nurse Americares Free Clinic Norwalk, 1994—; literacy vol. ESL Inst., 1997-98. Mem.: ANA, Internat. Lactation Cons. Assn. (cert.), Neonatal Network, Obstetrics and Neonatal Nurses, Assn. Women's Health. Avocations: lactation promotion, photography. Office: Mark Twain St Joseph Hosp San Andreas CA Home: 22865 Northrup Ct Columbia CA 95310-9419

CRETARA, DOMENIC ANTHONY, artist, educator; b. Chelsea, Mass., Mar. 29, 1946; s. Anthony Mario and Carmella (Addivinola) C.; m. Elizabeth Tarquinio, June 20, 1970; children: Jeanette, Anthony. BFA magna cum laude, Boston U., 1968, MFA, 1970. Chmn. fine arts dept. Art Inst. Boston, 1972-78, instr. painting and drawing, 1970-83, assoc. prof. painting, 1983-86; prof. painting Calif. State U.-Long Beach, 1986—. One man shows: Art Inst. Boston, 1976, Boston U., 1977, Camargo Found., Cassis, France, 1979, Helen Bumpus Gallery, Duxbury, Mass., 1980, Coll. William and Mary, 1980, U. Mass., 1980, Duxbury Art Complex Mus., 1981, First St. Gallery, N.Y.C., 1983, Segal Gallery, N.Y.C., 1984, 85, Koplin Gallery, L.A., 1987, Victor McNeil Gallery, N.Y.C., 1988, Alon Gallery, Brookline, Mass., 1989, 91, 95, John Thomas Gallery, Santa Monica, Calif., 1991-93, Brenda Taylor Gallery, N.Y.C., 1995-96, Mulligan-Shanosky Gallery, San Francisco, 1997, Frye Art Mus. Seattle, 2001, Schomberg Gallery, Santa Monica, 2002; group shows: Fitchburg (Mass.) Art Mus., 1973, Am. Embassy, Rome, 1975, Inst. Internat. Edn., N.Y.C., 1978, Boston Cyclorama, 1980, Drawing Ctr., N.Y.C., 1983, Weatherspoon Art Gallery, Greensboro, N.C., 1983, Sherry French Gallery, N.Y.C., 1987, L.A. Internat. Arts Fair, 1975, 86, 88, 96, Riverside (Calif.) Art Mus., 1989, Triton Mus. Art, Santa Clara, Calif., 1990, 94, Callery 84, N.Y.C., 1994, Mulligan-Shanosky Gallery, San Francisco, 1995, Las Vegas Art Mus., 1997, Wright State U., 2000, Koplin Gallery. L.A., 2000, 02, (traveling exhbn.) Frye Art Mus. Seattle, Art Mus. S.Tex., Corpus Christi, Laguna Art Mus., 2001, others; (retrospective) Las Vegas Art Mus, 1998; represented in permanent collections: Boston U., Art Inst. Boston, Met. Mus., Triton Art Mus., Duxbury Art Ctr. Mus., Riverside Art Mus., Calif.; contbr. articles to The Artist's Mag., 1990, 91, 93, Am. Artist, 1995.; contbg. artist The Delirium, 2001-03, The Millstone, 2002, The Pomngranite, 2003. Fulbright-Hays grantee, Italy, 1974-75; resident painter Camargo Found., Cassis, France, 1978-79; Boston-Padua Sister Cities grantee, 1984; fellow Pub. Corp. for Art, 2001; recipient Disting. Faculty Tchg. award Calif. State U.-Long Beach, 1994, Disting. Scholarly Creative Ach. award Calif. State U. Long Beach, 1998, Outstanding Prof. award, 2003. Mem. Coll. Art Assn. Drawings and paintings reproduced in: Figure Drawing, 1976; The Art of Responsive Drawing, 1977, American Artist, 1992, Oil Highlights, 1995; Painting: Visual and Technical Fundamentals, 1979. Video: Domenic Cretara Painting Circumstantial Evidence (Best Shot Video Bronxville, N.Y. 1997). Office Phone: 562-985-4383.

CREUTZ, EDWARD CHESTER, physicist, museum director; b. Beaver Dam, Wis., Jan. 23, 1913; s. Lester Raymond and Grace (Smith) C.; m. Lela Rollefson, Sept. 13, 1937 (dec. Feb. 1972); children: Michael John, Carl Eugene, Ann Jo Carmel Creutz Cosgrove; m. Elisabeth B. Cordle, Oct. 5, 1974. BS, U. Wis., 1936, PhD, 1939. From rsch. assoc. to instr. physics Princeton U., 1939-41; physicist NDRC, 1941-42; physicist metall. lab. U. Chgo., 1942-44; physicist Manhattan Project, Los Alamos, 1944-46; assoc. prof. Carnegie Inst. Tech., Pitts., 1946—48, prof., head dept. physics, dir. Nuc. Rsch. Ctr., 1948—55; dir. John Jay Hopkins Lab. for Pure and Applied Sci., 1955-59; dir. rsch. Gen. Atomic Divsn. Gen. Dynamics Corp., San Diego, 1955-59, v.p. R&D, 1959-67, Gulf Gen. Atomic, San Diego, 1967-70; asst. dir. NSF, Washington, 1970-77, acting dep. dir., 1976-77; dir. Bernice Pauahi Bishop Mus., Honolulu, 1977-84, cons., 1984—. Mem. sea water conversion com. Water resources Ctr., U. Calif.-Berkeley, 1958-68; adv. com. office Sci. Pers. NRC, 1960-63; mem. exec. coun. Argonne Nat. Lab. (1946-51); cons. NSF, 1950-68; scientist-at-large Project Sherwood divsn. rsch. AEC, 1955-56; mem. com. sr. reviewers Dept. Energy, 1972-79, fusion power coordinating com., 1971-79; cons. Oak Ridge Nat. Lab., 1946-58; adv. panel gen. scis. Dept. Def., 1959-63; rsch. adv. com. electrophysics NASA, 1964-71, tech. adv. com., 1971-77; adj. prof. physics and astronomy U. Hawaii, 1977-87; adj. prof. physics U. Calif., San Diego, 1987—. Co-editor: Handbuch der Physik, vols. 14, 15; mem. editl. bd. Ann. Rev. Nuclear Sci., 1961-66, 72-75, Handbook of Chemistry and Physics, 1961-71; mem. editorial bd.: Interdisciplinary Science Reviews, London, 1976—; editl. adv. com. ann. revs.: Nuclear Sci. and Engring., 1959-72. Bd. dirs. San Diego Hall Sci. and Planetarium, v.p., 1956-70; v.p. San Diego Industry-Edn. Coun., 1956-65; mem. adv. coun. Dept. Edn. San Diego County. Fellow AAAS, Am. Phys. Soc. (NRC rep. 1956-57), Am. Nuclear Soc.; mem. NAS, Am. Assn. Physics Tchrs., Phys. Soc. Pitts. (pres. 1949), Am. Inst. Physics (dir.-at-large bd. govs. 1965-68) Home: PO Box 2757 Rancho Santa Fe CA 92067-2757 Home Phone: 858-756-4980; Office Phone: 858-756-4980.

CREW, SPENCER, museum administrator; b. Poughkeepsie, NY, Jan. 7, 1949; s. R. Spencer and Ada Lee (Scott) C.; m. Sandra Lorraine Prioleau, June 19, 1971; children: Alika, Adom. BA, Brown U., 1971; MA, Rutgers U., 1973, PhD, 1979. Asst. prof. U. Md. Baltimore County, Catonsville, 1978-81; historian Nat. Mus. Am. History, Smithsonian Instn., Washington, 1981-87, curator, 1987-89, chmn. dept. social and cultural history, 1989-91, dep. dir., acting dir., 1991-94, dir., 1994—2001; pres., CEO Nat. Underground R.R. Freedom Ctr., 2001—07. Mem. Md. Commn. on Afro-Am. History and Culture, Annapolis, 1990—96; hist. cons. Nat. Civil Rights Mus., Memphis, 1987-91; cons. Civil Rights Inst., Birmingham, Ala., 1991-94; bd. dirs. Nat. History Day, 1994—98. Exhbns. include Field to Factory: Afro-Am. Migration, 1915-40, 1987 (award 1988), Go Forth and Serve: Black Land Grant Colls., 1990, The American Presidency, 2000. Trustee Brown U., 1995-2001, 07—; adult leader Bapt. Youth Fellowship, St. John Ch., Columbia, Md., 1989-91. Recipient Osceola award Delta Sigma Theta, 1988, Cert. award Smithsonian Instn., 1989, 90, 91, 92, Svc. award Assn. for Study of African Am. Life and History, 1994, Robert A. Brooks award Smithsonian Instn., 1994. Mem. African Am. Mus. Assn. (2d v.p. 1989-91, Lifetime Achievement award 2002), Orgn. Am. Historians (editl. bd. 1989-92), Am. Assn. Mus. (bd. dirs. 1991-96, 2004—), Nat. Coun. History Edn. (trustee 1995-2007), Am. Hist. Assn. (exhibit rev. co-editor 1990-95), Oral History in Mid Atlantic Region (exec. bd. 1987-90). Office: Nat Underground RR Freedom Ctr 50 E Freedom Way Cincinnati OH 45202

CREWDSON, JOHN MARK, journalist, writer; b. San Francisco, Dec. 15, 1945; s. Mark Guy and Eva Rebecca (Doane) C.; m. Prudence Gray Tillotson, Sept. 11, 1969; children: Anders Gray, Oliver McDuff. AB in Econs. with gt. distinction, U. Calif., Berkeley, 1970; postgrad. studies in politics, Oxford U., Eng., 1971-72. Reporter N.Y. Times, Washington, 1973-77, nat. corr. Houston, 1977-82; nat. news editor Chgo. Tribune, 1982-83, met. news editor, 1983-84, west coast corr. LA, 1984-90, nat. corr. Washington, 1990-96, sr. writer, 1996—2002, sr. corr., 2002—07, assoc. Washington editor, 2007—. Author: The Tarnished Door, 1983, By Silence Betrayed, 1988, Science Fictions, 2002. Recipient Bronze medallion Sigma Delta Chi, 1974, Goldberg award N.Y. Deadline Club, 1977, Page One award N.Y. Newspaper Guild, 1977, Pulitizer prize for nat. reporting, 1981, Silver Gavel award ABA, 1981, Polk award for med. reporting L.I. U., 1990, William H. Jones award for investigative reporting, 1990, 95, 97, Peter Lisagor award Chgo. Headline Club, 1997, Edward Scott Beck award fgn. reporting, 1998. Office Phone: 202-824-8261. Business E-Mail: jcrewdson@tribune.com.

CREWE, ALBERT VICTOR, physicist, researcher, artist; b. Bradford, Yorkshire, Eng., Feb. 18, 1927; came to U.S., 1955, naturalized, 1961. s. Wilfred and Edith Fish (Lawrence) C.; m. Doreen Blunsdon, Apr. 9, 1949; children: Jennifer, Sarah, Elizabeth, David. BS in Physics, U. Liverpool, Eng., 1947, PhD, 1951; degree (hon.), Lake Forest Coll., 1972, U. Mo., 1972, Elmhurst Coll., 1972, U.Liverpool, 2001. Asst. lectr. U. Liverpool, Eng., 1950-52, lectr., 1952-55; rsch. assoc. U. Chgo., 1955-56, asst. prof., 1956-58, assoc. prof., 1958-63; prof. dept. physics Enrico Fermi Inst., 1963-71, dean phys. scis. divsn., 1971-81; also William Wrather Disting. Svc. prof. physics, 1958-61; emeritus, 1996—; dir. particle accelerator divsn. Argonne Nat. Lab., 1958-61, dir., 1961-66; pres. Orchid One Corp., 1987-90. Chmn. Chgo. Area R&D Coun. Recipient Outstanding Local Citizen in Field of Sci. award Chgo. Jr. Assn. Commerce and Industry, 1961; Outstanding New Citizen of Year award Citizenship Coun. Chgo., 1962; award for outstanding achievement in field of sci. Immigrant's Service League, 1962; Man of Year in Rsch. award Indsl. Rsch., Inc., 1970; Michelson medal Franklin Inst., 1977; Duddell medal Inst. of Physics, 1980. Fellow Am. Phys. Soc., Royal Microscopical Soc. (hon.), Chinese Electron Microscope Soc. (hon.); mem. NAS, Sci. Rsch. Soc. Am., Electron Microscopy Soc. Am. (Disting. Svc. award 1976), N.Y. Microscope Soc. (Abbe award 1979), Am. Acad. Arts and Scis., Palette and Chisel Acad. (artist mem.). Achievements include research on electron optics, design of electron microscopes, first images of single atoms. Home: 8 Summitt Dr Chesterton IN 46304-1024 E-mail: crewe@midway.uchicago.edu.

CREWE, NANCY MOE, retired psychologist; b. Mpls., Aug. 27, 1939; d. Arnold O. and Ruby V. Moe; m. James C. Crewe (div.); 1 child, Laurel; m. John Pond. BA, U. Minn., 1961, MA, 1964, PhD, 1967. Lic. psychologist, Mich. Staff psychologist Am. Rehab. Found., Mpls., 1966-69, Robbinsdale (Minn.) Sch. Dist., 1969-71; asst. prof. psychology U. Minn., Mpls., 1971-78, assoc. prof. psychology, 1978-87; postdoctoral fellow New England Rehab. Hosp., Boston, 1985-86; prof. Mich. State U., East Lansing, 1987—2006, ret., 2006. Co-author: Employment After Spinal Cord Injury, 1978, Psychology of Disability, 2004; co-editor: Independent Living for Disabled People, 1983. Bd. dirs. Accessible Space, Mpls., 1980-82, Met. Ctr. for Ind. Living, Mpls., 1983-85; bd. dirs., chairperson Comprehensive Svcs. for Disabled Citizens, Mpls., 1980-87, Capital Area Ctr. for Ind. Living, 2000-05. Recipient Disting. Faculty award, Mich. State U., 1997. Fellow: APA (pres. divsn. 22 1987—88, Disting. Contbns. to Rehab. Psychology award 1993, Roger Barker Disting. Career award 2001); mem.: ACA, Nat. Coun. Rehab. Edn. (Disting. Career in Rehab. Edn. award 2004), Nat. Rehab. Assn., Am. Rehab. Counseling Assn., Am. Assn. Spinal Cord Injury Psychologists and Social Workers (bd. dirs. 1995—98, Disting. Svc. award 1990), Am. Congress Rehab. Medicine (Licht award 1981, Disting. Mem. award 1990), Phi Beta Kappa. Avocations: glass blowing, jewelry making. Office: Mich State Univ 443 Erickson Hall East Lansing MI 48824-1034 Business E-Mail: ncrewe@msu.edu.

CREWS, FREDERICK CAMPBELL, humanities educator, writer; b. Phila., Feb. 20, 1933; s. Maurice Augustus and Robina (Gaudet) C.; m. Betty Claire Peterson, Sept. 9, 1959; children: Gretchen Detre, Ingrid Márquez. AB, Yale U., 1955; PhD, Princeton U., 1958. Faculty U. Calif., Berkeley, 1958—, instr. in English, 1958-60, asst. prof., 1960-62, assoc. prof., 1962-66, prof., 1986-94, vice-chair for grad. studies, 1988-92, chair dept., 1992-94; prof. emeritus, 1994—. Mem. study fellowship selection com. Am. Coun. Learned Socs., 1971-73; mem. selection com. summer seminars Nat. Endowment for Humanities, 1976-77; Ward-Phillips lectr. U. Notre Dame, 1974-75, Dorothy T. Burstein lectr. UCLA, 1984; Frederick Ives Carpenter vis. prof. U. Chgo., 1985; Lansdowne visitor U. Victoria, 1987-88; John Dewey lectr., 1988, Nina Mae Kellogg lectr. Portland (Oreg.) State U., 1989; mem. exec. com. bd. dirs. Mark Twain Project, 1984-94; faculty rsch. lectr. U. Calif., Berkeley, 1991-92; David L. Kubal Meml. lectr. Calif. State U., L.A., 1994; mem. sci. and profl. adv. bd. False Memory Syndrome Found., 1994—; mem. exec. coun. Com. for Sci. Investigation of Claims of the Paranormal, 2000—. Author: The Tragedy of Manners, 1957, E.M. Forster: The Perils of Humanism, 1962, The Pooh Perplex, 1963, The Sins of the Fathers, 1966, The Patch Commission, 1968, The Random House Handbook, 1974, 6th edit., 1992, Out of My System, 1975, Skeptical Engagements, 1986, 2000, The Critics Bear it Away, 1992, Postmodern Pooh, 2001, Follies of the Wise, 2006; co-author: The Borzoi Handbook for Writers, 1985, 3d edit., 1993; prin. author: The Memory Wars, 1995; editor: The Red Badge of Courage (Crane), 1964, Great Short Works of Nathaniel Hawthorne, 1967, Starting Over, 1970, Psychoanalysis and Literary Process, 1970, The Random House Reader, 1981, Unauthorized Freud, 1998; mem. contbg. bd. editors The Common Review, 2000—. Recipient Essay prize Nat. Endowment Arts, 1968, Disting. Tchg. award U. Calif., Berkeley, 1985, Spielvogel Diamonstein PEN prize, 1992; named Fulbright lectr. Turin, Italy, 1961-62; fellow Am. Coun. Learned Socs., 1965-66, Ctr. for Advanced Study in Behavioral Scis., 1965-66, Guggenheim Found., 1970-71, Am. Acad. Arts and Scis., 1992. Fellow: Com. for Sci. Medicine and Mental Health (mem. exec. coun., mem. com. skeptical inquiry). Home: 636 Vincente Ave Berkeley CA 94707-1524 Personal E-mail: fredc@berkeley.edu.

CREWS, KENNETH DONALD, law educator, consultant, dean; b. Fairborn, Ohio, Feb. 14, 1955; s. Ralph Wilson and Betty Jo (Anderson) C.; m. Elizabeth Dellvera St. Clair, July 24, 1982; 2 children: Veronica St. Clair Crews, Arthur Wilson Crews. BA, Northwestern U., 1977; JD, Washington U., 1980; PhD, UCLA, 1990. Bar: Calif. 1980. Pvt. practice, LA, 1980—90; legal cons., 1990—; assoc. prof. bus. law San Jose State U., 1990—94; assoc. prof. law, libr. and info. sci. Ind. U., 1994—2000, prof., 2000—; assoc. dean faculties Ind. U.-Purdue U. Indpls., 1994—, Samuel R. Rosen prof. of law, 2003—. Exec. dir., co-founder Los Angeles Venture Assn., 1984-85; visitor Max Planck Inst., Munich, 2001, Munich Intellectual Property Law Ctr., 2003-. Author: Edward S. Corwin and the American Constitution, 1985, University Copyright Policies, 1987, Copyright, Fair Use, and the Challenge for Universities, 1993, Copyright Law and Graduate Research, 2000, Copyright Law for Librarians and Educators, 2000, 2d edit., 2006; editor: Corwin's Constitution, 1986. Counsel Wesley Found. Serving UCLA, 1983-90. Disting. scholar UCLA Alumni Assn., 1986; Assn. Coll. Rsch. Libraries Dissertation fellow 1989; Faculty Study grantee German Acad. Exchange Svc., 2000; recipient Dissertation award Assn. for the Study of Higher Edn., 1990. Mem. ABA, ALA (Patterson Copyright award, 2005), Calif. Bar Assn. (chmn. history of law com. 1985-86), Am. Assn. Law Librs. Avocations: camping, hiking, bicycling, architecture. Office: Indiana Univ Sch Law 530 W New York St Indianapolis IN 46202-3225 Office Phone: 317-274-4400.

CREWS, TERRELL K., agricultural products executive; BS in Acctg., Freed Hardeman U.; M in Mgmt., Kelloggs Exec. M Program. Cost analyst acctg., bus. analysis lead Latin Am. Monsanto, controller Latin Am., fin.

lead Asia Pacific - Singapore, gen. auditor, global fin. lead, exec. v.p., CFO, 2000—. Bd. trustees Freed Hardeman U.; bd. dirs. Jr. Achievement of Miss. Valley, Inc.; nat. council John M. Olin Sch. Bus., Washington U. Office: Monsanto 800 N Lindbergh Blvd Saint Louis MO 68167*

CREWS, WILLIAM ODELL, JR., religious organization administrator; b. Houston, Feb. 8, 1936; s. William O. Sr. and Juanita (Pearson) C.; m. Wanda Jo Ann Cunningham; 1 child, Ronald Wayne. BA, Hardin Simmons U., 1957, HHD, 1987; BDiv, Southwestern Bapt. Theol. Sem., 1964; DD, Calif. Bapt. Coll., 1987; DMin, Golden Gate Bapt. Theol. Sem., 2000. Ordained to ministry Bapt. Ch., 1953. Pastor Grape Creek Bapt. Ch., San Angelo, Tex., 1952-54, Plainview Bapt. Ch., Stamford, Tex., 1955-57, 1st Bapt. Ch., Sterling City, Tex., 1957-60, 7th St. Bapt. Ch., Ballinger, Tex., 1960-65, Woodland Heights Bapt. Ch., Brownwood, Tex., 1965-67, Victory Bapt. Ch., Seattle, 1967-72, Met. Bapt. Ch., Portland, Oreg., 1972-77; dir. comm. N.W. Bapt. Conv., Portland, 1977-78; pastor Magnolia Ave Bapt. Ch., Riverside, Calif., 1978-86; pres. Golden Gate Bapt. Theol. Sem., Mill Valley, Calif., 1986—2003, chancellor, 2003—. Pres. N.W. Bapt. Conv., Portland, 1974-76, So. Bapt. Gen. Conv. Calif., Fresno, 1982-84. Trustee Fgn. Mission Bd., Richmond, Va., 1973-78, Golden Gate Bapt. Theol. Sem., 1980-85, Marin Cmty. Hosp. Found., 1992-95; bd. dirs. Midway Seatac Boys Club, Des Moines, 1969-72, Marin Gen. Hosp., 1998-2004, North Bay Coun., 1998—. Mem. Marin County C. of C. (bd. dirs. 1987-95), Midway C. of C. (bd. dirs. 1968-72), Rotary (bd. dirs. San Rafael chpt. 1992—, pres. Portland club 1975-76, pres.-elect Riverside club 1984-85). Baptist. Home: 3505 NW 9th Ave Camas WA 98607 Office: Golden Gate Bapt Theol Sem 3200 NE 109th Vancouver WA 98632 Business E-Mail: billcrews@ggbts.edu.

CREWSON, WENDY JANE, actress; b. Hamilton, Ontario, Canada, May 9, 1956; d. Robert Binnie and June Doreen (Thomas) C.; m. Michael George Murphy, Mar. 7, 1988; children: Margaret Mary, Branton. BA, Queen's U., 1977; postgrad., Weber-Douglas Acad. Drama, London, England, 1979. Actor: (films) Skullduggery, 1983, The Sight, 1985, Mark of Cain, 1985, The Doctor, 1991, I'll Never Get to Heaven, 1992, Folks!, 1992, The Good Son, 1993, Corrina, Corrina, 1994, The Santa Clause, 1994, To Gillian on Her 37th Birthday, 1996, Air Force One, 1997, Gang Related, 1997, Sleeping Doges Lie, 1998, At the End of the Day: The Sue Rodriguez Story, 1998, Escape Velocity, 1998, The Eighteenth Angel, 1998, Where's Marlowe?, 1998, Better Than Chocolate, 1999, Question of Privilege, 1999, Bicentennial Man, 1999, Mercy, 2000, What Lies Beneath, 2000, The 6th Day, 2000, Suddenly Naked, 2001, Between Stangers, 2002, Perfect Pie, 2002, The Santa Clause 2, 2002, The Clearing, 2004, Niagara Motel, 2005, Eight Below, 2006, The Covenant, 2006, Away from Her, 2006, Who Loves the Sun, 2006, The Santa Clause 3: The Escape Clause, 2006, (TV films) War Brides, 1980, Mazes and Monsters, 1982, Heartsounds, 1984, The Guardian, 1984, Murder: By Reason of Insanity, 1985, My Father, My Rival, 1985, Murder in Space, 1985, Whodunit, 1986, Perry Mason: The Case of the Shooting Star, 1986, Covert Action, 1987, A Hobo's Christmas, 1987, Getting Married in Buffalo Jump, 1990, Lives of Girls & Women, 1994, Spenser: The Judas Goat, 1994, Spenser: A Savage Place, 1995, Ebbie, 1995, Summer's End, 1999, Love and Murder, 2000, Deadly Appearances, 2000, The Wandering Soul Murders, 2001 A Colder Kind of Death, 2001, The Many Trials of One Jane Doe, 2002, Verdict in Blood, 2002, An Unexpected Love, 2003, Jack, 2004, Hunt for Justice, 2005, The Man Who Lost Himself, 2005; (TV series) Keep the Home Fires Burning, 1981-85 (Best Actor award 1985), Night Heat, 1985, Hard Copy, 1987, Studio 5-B, 1989, The Beast, 2001, Crimes of Passion, 2006, TV guest appearances include Adderly, 1986, Street Legal, 1990, Due South, 1997, Black Harbour, 1997, 24, 2003. Recipient Lorne Greene award Queen's U., 1977.*

CRICHLOW, DAVID A., lawyer; b. Oct. 2, 1963; BA, Hofstra U., 1985; JD, U. Pa., 1989. Bar: NY 1990, U.S. Dist. Ct. (so. and ea. dist.) NY 1991, DC 1992, U.S. Dist. Ct. DC 1994, U.S. Dist. Ct. Md. 1994. Law clk. to Hon. Clifford Scott Green U.S. Dist. Ct. (ea. dist.) Pa., 1992—93; assoc. Winthrop Stimson Putnam & Roberts (now Pillsbury Winthrop Shaw Pittman LLP, NYC, 1989—2000, ptnr., 2000—06, mng. ptnr., 2006—. Mem.: ABA (mem. litig. sect.), Nat. Bar Assn. (mem. comml. litig. divsn.), DC Bar Assn., Assn. Bar. City of NY. Office: Pillsbury Winthrop Shaw Pittman LLP 1540 Broadway New York NY 10036-4039 Office Phone: 212-858-1640. Office Fax: 212-858-1500. E-mail: david.crichlow@pillsburylaw.com.

CRICHTON, FLORA CAMERON, volunteer, foundation administrator; b. Waco, Tex. d. William Waldo and Helen Emelyn (Miller) Cameron; m. John H. Crichton, 1989; children: Ike Simpson Kampmann III(dec.) , Megan Cameron Kampmann. Dir., mem. exec. com. Certain-Teed Corp., 1971—78; exec. com. San Antonio World's Fair, 1968. Mem. Pres.'s Mission to Latin Am., 1969; U.S. del. Inter-Am. Commn. Women, 1969—72; mem. nat. adv. coun. Georgia O'Keefe Mus.; mem. citizens stamp adv. commn. U.S. Postal Svc., 1969—71; cons. Bur. Inter-Am. Affairs, Dept. State, 1972—75; pres. Flora Cameron Found.; trustee Trinity U., San Antonio, 1965—2005, chmn., 1976—78; trustee Sweet Briar Coll., 1969—78; mem. Pres.'s Commn. German-Am. Tricentennial, 1983—84; bd. govs. East-West Ctr., Honolulu, 1989—92; vice chmn. exec. com. Tex. Rep. Party, 1958—60; del. Rep. Nat. Conv., 1960, 1964, alt. del., 1968, sec. platform com., 1960; former mem. Rep. Nat. Fin. Com., 1965—, pres., chmn., 1976—78; vice chmn. nat. fin. com. George Bush for Pres., 1987—88; mem. Tex. Rep. Nat. Com., 1960—65; former mem. bd. dirs. San Antonio Art Inst., Sch. Am. Rsch., Santa Fe; former mem. nat. coun. Met. Opera. Mem.: San Antonio Jr. League, Colonial Dames Am. Home: 315 Westover Rd San Antonio TX 78209-5653 Office: 5701 Broadway St San Antonio TX 78209-5722

CRICHTON, MICHAEL (JOHN MICHAEL CRICHTON), writer, film director; b. Chgo., Oct. 23, 1942; AB summa cum laude, Harvard U., 1964, MD, 1969. Postdoctoral fellow Salk Inst., La Jolla, Calif., 1969-70. Vis. writer MIT, Cambridge, 1988; vis. lectr. Cambridge U., 1965; creator, co-exec. prodr. TV show ER, 1994. Author: The Andromeda Strain, 1969, Five Patients, 1970 (Writer of the Year award Assn. American Medical Writers 1970), The Terminal Man, 1972, The Great Train Robbery, 1975 (Edgar award Mystery Writers of America 1979), Eaters of the Dead, 1976, Jasper Johns, 1977, Congo, 1980, Electronic Life, 1983, Sphere, 1987, Travels, 1988, Jurassic Park, 1990, Rising Sun, 1992, Disclosure, 1994, The Lost World, 1995, Airframe, 1996, Timeline, 1999, Prey, 2002, State of Fear, 2004 (Publishers Weekly bestseller list), Next, 2006; (as Jeffrey Hudson) A Case of Need, 1968 (Edgar award Mystery Writers of America 1968); (as John Lange) Odds On, 1966, Scratch One, 1967, Easy Go, 1968, Venom Business, 1969, Zero Cool, 1969, Grave Descend, 1970, Drug of Choice, 1970, Binary, 1972; co-author (with Douglas Crichton) Dealing: Or, The Berkeley to Boston Forty-Brick Lost-Bag Blues, 1971; dir. (films) Pursuit, 1972, Physical Evidence, 1989 screenwriter, dir. (films) Westworld, 1973, Coma, 1978, The Great Train Robbery, 1979, Looker, 1981, Runaway, 1984; co-screenwriter (films) Jurassic Park, 1993, Rising Sun, 1993; co-screenwriter, co-writer (films) Twister, 1996; co-prodr. (films) Disclosure, 1994, Sphere, 1998, 13th Warrior, 1999, Timeline, 2003; creator, co-exec., prodr. (TV series) ER, 1994 Mem. bd. overseers Harvard U. Recipient George Foster Peabody award ER, 1995, Emmy Best Dramatic series ER, 1996, Best Long Form Television Script for ER, Writer's Guild Am., 1995, Acad. Motion Pictures Arts and Scis. Tech. Achievement award for pioneering computerized motion picture budgeting and scheduling, 1995, Journalism award, Am. Assn. Petroleum Geologists, 2006; Henry Russell Shaw traveling fellow, 1964-65. New ankylosaur named in honor Crichtonsaurus bohlini, 2003. Mem. Authors Guild (coun. 1995—), Writers Guild Am. West, Dirs. Guild Am., PEN Am. Ctr., Acad. Motion Picture Arts and Scis.; bd. dirs. Internat. Design Conf. at Aspen, 1985-91, Western Behavioral Scis. Inst., La Jolla, 1986-91; Phi Beta Kappa. Avocation: computer games. Office: Constant C Prodns Ste 433 2118 Wilshire Blvd Santa Monica CA 90403

CRICHTON, THOMAS, IV, lawyer; b. Shreveport, La., Dec. 2, 1947; BS, La. State U., 1969, JD, 1972. Bar: Tex. 1972, La. 1972, D.C. 1988. Mem. Vinson & Elkins, LLP, Dallas, co-head Tax Law Sect. Adj. prof. sch. law U. Houston, 1978-86. Mem. Order of Coif, Beta Alpha Psi, Beta Gamma Sigma, Omicron Delta Kappa, Phi Kappa Phi. Office: Vinson & Elkins LLP 3700 Trammell Crow Ctr Dallas TX 75201-2975 also: Vinson & Elkins LLP 2500 First City Tower 1001 Fannin St Ste 3300 Houston TX 77002-6706 also: Vinson & Elkins LLP 1455 Pennsylvania Ave NW Fl 7 Washington DC 20004-1008 Office Phone: 214-220-7984. Business E-Mail: tcrichton@velaw.com.

CRIDER, ROBERT AGUSTINE, international financier, protective services official; b. Washington, Jan. 3, 1935; s. Rana Albert and Terasa Helen (Dampf) C.; m. Debbie Ann Lee, Feb. 1960. Student, U. Md., 1959-63. Police officer Met. Police Dept., Washington, 1957-67; substitute tchr., bldg. trades instr. Maries R-1 Sch., Vienna, Mo., 1968-70; vets. constrn. tng. officer VA Dept. Edn., Mo., 1968-70; constrn. mgr. Tectonnics Ltd., Vienna, 1970-79; owner, dir. R-A Crider & Assocs., St. Louis, 1979—. Bd. dirs. TI-CO Investment Corp., Langcaster Corp. With USAF, 1952-56. Mem. Assn. Ret. Policemen, Internat. Conf. Police, Internat. Assn. Chiefs of Police, Nat. Police Assn., World Future Soc., Internat. Platform Assn., Mo. Police Chiefs Asn., Mo. Sheriff's Assn., Am. Correctional Assn., Law Enforcement Intelligence Assn., Internat. Drug Enforcement Assn., Nat. Assn. Fin. Cons., Internat. Soc. Financiers, Am. Legion, St. Louis Honor Guard, Lions, K.C. (4th degree). Roman Catholic. Home: PO Box 109 Vienna MO 65582-0109 Office: R-A Crider & Assocs 2644 Roseland Ter Saint Louis MO 63143-2304 Personal E-mail: racriderassoc@aol.com.

CRIDER, RUDYARD LEE, psychotherapist; b. Abilene, Kans., Oct. 16, 1942; s. Clarence A. and Myrtle (Cox) C.; m. Doris Elaine Heisey, Aug. 3, 1962; 1 child, Michele Renee. BA, Messiah Coll., 1971; MS, Shippensburg U., 1978. Cert. clin. mental health counselor; nat. cert. counselor; cert. diplomate in psychotherapy; lic. profl. counselor. Mental health worker King's View Hosp., Reedley, Calif., 1966-68; crisis intervention counselor Holy Spirit Hosp. Mental Health, Camp Hill, Pa., 1974-78, sr. psychotherapist, 1978—, asst. coord. outpatient svcs., 1989—2001, program supr. behavioral health svcs., 2001—06, clin. supr. behavioral health svcs., 2006—; pvt. practice psychotherapy, 1992—. Sr. peer reviewer Holy Spirit Hosp. Mental Health, Camp Hill, 1990-96, quality assurance com., 1990—, clin. site supr., 1983—, mem. extended mgmt. team, 1994—. Recipient Recognition for Outstanding Svc. award Cumberland Perry County Mental Health-Mental Retardation Program, 1993. Mem. Acad. Clin. Mental Health Counselors, Am. Counseling Assn., Am. Mental Health Counselors Assn., Am. Psychotherapy Assn., Pa. Counselors Assn., Pa. Psychol. Assn. Lutheran. Avocations: photography, bicycling, hiking, drawing, backpacking. Home: 438 Parkside Rd Camp Hill PA 17011-2127 Office: Holy Spirit Hosp 21st St Camp Hill PA 17011

CRIER, CATHERINE, newscaster; b. Dallas; BA in Polit. Sci., Univ. Tex.; JD, So. Meth. Univ., Dallas. Asst. dist. atty., felony chief prosecutor Dallas Co. Dist. Atty. Off., 1978—81; civil litig. atty. Dallas, 1982—84; former judge 162nd Dist. Ct. Tex., 1984-89; anchor Cable News Network, 1989-92; corr. ABC 20/20, 1993-95; news corr. ABC News, 1995—96; anchor Crier Report Fox News, 1996—99; exec. show host and editor legal news spls. Courtroom TV Network LLC, 1999—, host Catherine Crier Live, 2001—. Author: The Case Against Lawyers, 2002 (NY Times bestseller), Contempt-How the Right is Wronging American Justice, 2005 (Number One NY Times bestseller, 2005); co-author (with Cole Thompson): A Deadly Game: The Untold Story of the Scott Peterson Investigation, 2005 (Number One NY Times bestseller). Named one of the Dynamic Dozen, TV Guide Mag., 1990, Twenty Young Lawyers Who Make a Difference, ABA Barrister Mag., 1990; recipient Outstanding Young Tex. Ex award, Univ. Tex., Austin, 1990, Les Femmes du Monde award, Dallas Coun. on World Affairs, 1996, Emmy award, 1996, duPont-Columbia award, 2001, two Gracie Allen awards, Found. Am. Women in Radio and TV. Avocations: golf, scuba diving, raising, training Arabian horses. Office: Courtroom TV Network LLC Frnt 2 600 3rd Ave New York NY 10016 Business E-Mail: info@criercommunications.com.

CRILE, SUSAN, artist; b. Cleve., Aug. 12, 1942; d. George Jr. and Jane (Halle) C.; m. Joseph S. Murphy, May 18, 1984. Student, NYU; BA, Bennington Coll., 1965. Mem. faculty Fordham U., NYC, 1972-76, Princeton U., NJ, 1974-76, Sarah Lawrence Coll., Bronxville, NY, 1976-79, Sch. Visual Arts, NYC, 1976-82, Barnard Coll., NYC, 1983-86, Hunter Coll., NYC, 1983—. Travelling rep. to Hungary and Portugal with exhbn. Am. Paintings in the Eighties, Internat. Comm. Agy., Washington, 1981; resident-in-painting Am. Acad. in Rome, 1990. One-woman shows include Kornblee Gallery, NYC, 1971-73, Fischbach Gallery, NYC, 1974-75, 77, Brooke Alexander Gallery, NYC, 1975, Phillips Collection, Washington, 1975, New Gallery, Cleve., 1977, Ctr. Gallery Bucknell U., Lewisburg, Pa., 1978, Droll Kolbert Gallery, NYC, 1978, 80, Ivory Kimpton Gallery, San Francisco, 1981, 84, 88, Van Straten Gallery, Chgo., 1983, Lincoln Ctr. Gallery, NYC, 1983, Cleve. Ctr. for Contemporary Art, 1984, Nina Freundenheim Gallery, Buffalo, NY, 1980, 84, Graham Modern, NYC, 1985, 87-88, 90, Adams Middleton Gallery, Dallas, 1986, Gloria Luria, Bay Harbor Island, Fla., 1987-88, 90, St. Louis Art Mus., 1994, Blaffer Gallery- U. Houston, 1994, Univ. Art Mus. U. So. Calif., Long Beach, 1994, Fed. Reserve Bd., Washington, 1995, Herbert Johnson Mus. Cornell U., Ithaca, NY, 1995, Middlebury Coll. Mus. Art, Vt., 1995, James Graham & Sons, NYC, 1995, 98, 2001, Nat. Coun. for Culture, Art and Letters, Kuwait City, Kuwait, 1996, U. Ariz. Mus. Art., Tucson, 2003, James Graham and Sons, NYC, 2004, Bertha and Karl Leubsdorf Gallery, Hunter Coll., 2006, Michael Steinberg Fine Art, NYC, 2006; exhibited in group shows at Whitney Mus. Art, NYC, 1972, 82, Indpls. Mus. Art, 1972, 74, Kent State U., 1972, Art Inst. Chgo., 1972, Corcoran Gallery Art, Washington, 1973, Va. Mus. Fine Arts, 1975, USI.A., 1979, Grey Art Gallery, NYC, 1979, 83, Janie C. Lee Gallery, Houston, 1979, Meml. Art Gallery, U. Rochester, 1980, Bklyn. Mus., 1980-81, 83, Carnegie Inst., Pitts., 1981, Inst. Contemporary Art, 1981, Am. Acad. Arts and Letters, 1983, 94, 99, Weatherspoon Gallery, Greensboro, NC, 1984, Columbus Mus. Arts and Sci., Ga., 1985, Queens Mus., 1986, Portland Mus. Art, Maine, 1986, Mus. Fine Arts, Boston, 1986, Cleve. Mus. Art, 1987, Mt. Holyoke Coll. Art Mus., South Hadley, Mass., 1987, Hudson River Mus., 1988, Bowdoin Coll. Mus. Art, Brunswick, Maine, 1992, Denver Art Mus., 1993-94, Am. Acad. Arts & Letters, NYC, 1994, Fla. Internat. U., Miami, 1995, James Graham & Sons, NYC, 1997, 99, 2003, Times Sq. Gallery, NYC, 2000, Art in Gen., NYC, 2000, U. Ariz. Mus. Art, Tempe, 2001, Smith and Eds, Palo Alto, Calif., U. Colorado Springs, Colo., 2002, Lehman Coll. Art Gallery, NYC, 2004, MOCA, Cleve., 2005, Detroit Mus. Art, 2005; poster commn.: Il Museo di Roma at Teastevere, Rome, 2007, Live from Lincoln Ctr., NYC, 1980, Mostly Mozart, 1985, IBM Gallery Aci. & Art, NYC, 1989, Nat. Gallery Art, Washington, 1989, Detroit Inst. Art, 1991, Nat. Mus. Women in the Arts, Washington, 1991, William Proctor Art Gallery, Bard Coll., Annandale-on-Hudson, NY, 1992, Bowdoin Coll. Mus. Art, Brunswick, Maine, 1992, Andre Emmerich Gallery, NYC, 1992, Denver Art Mus., 1993, Cleve. Ctr. for Contemporary Art, 1993; represented in permanent collections Albright-Knox Art Gallery, Buffalo, Bklyn. Mus., Mus. Art Carnegie Inst., Pitts., Guggenheim Mus., NYC, Hirshhorn Mus., Washington, Met. Mus. Art, NYC, Phillips Collection, Washington, Cleve. Mus. Art, Libr. Congress, Washington, Denver Mus. Art, Middlebury Coll. Mus. Art, Ariz. State U. Art Mus., Tempe, Bowdoin Coll. Mus. Art, Brunswick, Fed. Res. Bd., Washington, Portland Mus., Weatherspoon Art Gallery, Greensboro. Trustee Bennington Coll., 1979-81; active Yaddo Corp., 1986—, bd. dirs., 1991—. Resident grantee Yaddo, 1970-71, 74-75, 78, MacDowell Colony, 1972, grantee Ingram Merrill Found., 1972; fellow Nat. Endowment for Arts, 1982, 89-90; grant, Rockefeller Found., residency at Bellagio Study and Rsch. Ctr., Italy, 2007. Home: 168 W 86th St New York NY 10024-4033 E-mail: scrile@rcn.com.

CRIM, FORREST FLEMING, JR., chemist, educator; b. Waco, Tex., May 30, 1947; s. Forrest Fleming Sr. and Almanor Adair (Chapman) C.; m. Joyce Ann Wileman, June 21, 1969 (div.); 1 child, Tracy F. BS, Southwestern U., 1969; PhD, Cornell U., 1974. Staff mem. Engring. Rsch. Ctr. Western Electric Co., Princeton, NJ, 1974-76; postdoctoral staff mem. Los Alamos (N.Mex.) Sci. Lab., 1976-77; from asst. prof. to assoc. prof. Dept. Chemistry U. Wis., Madison, 1977-84, prof. Dept. Chemistry, 1984—. Mem. rev. panel, Dept. of Energy Combustion Rsch. Facility, 1983-85, chmn., 1985, review com., Chemistry Dept., Brookhaven Nat. Lab., 1989; mem. Nat. Rsch. Coun. Workshop on the Chemistry Dept. of the Future, 1987; chmn. Gordon Rsch Conf. on Atomic and Molecular Interactions, 1988; external adv. com. of the Chemical and Laser Scis. Divsn., Los Alamos Nat. Lab., 1990—; rev. com. Associated Univs. Chemistry Dept., Brookhaven Nat. Lab., 1990—; mem. Nat. Rsch. Coun. Panel on Future Opportunities in Atomic, Molecular, and Optical Sci., 1991—. Editorial bd. internat. revs. Phys. Chemistry, 1990—, editorial adv. bd. Ency. of Applied Physics, 1989—, Jour. Phys. Chemistry, 1987-93; contbr. articles to profl. jours. Fellow Alfred P. Sloan Rsch., 1981-83, fellow AAAS, 1995, fellow Am. Acad. Arts and Scis., 1998; named Camille and Henry Dreyfus Tchr.-Scholar, 1982, Helfaer Prof. Chemistry, 1985-91, Robert A. Welch Foun. lectr., 1989, Bayer-Mobay lectr., U. N.H., 1991, Malcolm Dole Disting. lectr., Northwestern U., 2000; recipient Alexander von Humboldt Sr. U.S. Scientist award, 1986, Southwestern Univ. Alumni Assn. Citation of Merit, 1987, Max Planck award Alexander von Humboldt Soc., 1993. Fellow Am. Phys. Soc. (Earl K. Plyler Prize Selection Com. 1992—, Earle K. Plyler Molecular Physics prize 1998); mem. AAAS, NAS, Am. Chem. Soc. (chmn. Symposium on State-to-State Chemistry 1986, vice-chmn. Phys. Chemistry Div. 1986-87, chmn.-elect 1987-88, chmn. 1988-89, chmn. Task Force to Monitor Jour. of Physical Chemistry 1990-91, Irving Langmuir award in Chemical Physics, 2006), Optical Soc. of Am. (Quantum Electronics and Laser Scis. com. 1990-91). Office: Univ Wis Dept Chemistry 1101 University Ave Madison WI 53706-1322

CRIMINALE, WILLIAM OLIVER, JR., applied mathematics professor; b. Mobile, Ala., Nov. 29, 1933; s. William Oliver and Vivian Gertrude (Sketoe) C.; m. Ulrike Irmgard Wegner, June 7, 1962; children: Martin Oliver, Lucca. BS, U. Ala., 1955; PhD, Johns Hopkins U., 1960. Asst. prof. Princeton (N.J.) U., 1962-68; asso. prof. U. Wash., Seattle, 1968-73, prof. oceanography, geophysics, applied math., 1973—, chmn. dept. applied math., 1976-84. Cons. Aerospace Corp., 1963—65, Boeing Corp., 1968—72, AGARD, 1967—68, Lenox Hill Hosp., 1967—68, ICASE, NASA Langley, 1990—2003; guest prof., Canada, 1965, 2001, France, 1967—68, Germany, 1973—74, Sweden, 1973—74, Scotland, 1985, 89, 91, England, 90, 91, Stanford U., 1990, Brazil, 92, 2001, Italy, 1999, Crete, 2005; Nat. Acad. exch. scientist USSR, 1969, 72. Author: Stability of Parallel Flows, 1967, Theory and Computation in Hydrodynamic Stability, 2003; contbr. articles to profl. jours. Served with U.S. Army, 1961-62. Boris A. Bakmeteff Meml. fellow, 1957-58, NATO postdoctoral fellow, 1960-61, Alexander von Humboldt Sr. fellow, 1973-74, Royal Soc. fellow, 1990-91. Fellow Am. Phys. Soc.; mem. Am. Acad. Mechanics, Am. Geophys. Union, Fedn. Am. Scientists. Home: 1635 Peach Ct E Seattle WA 98112-3428 Office: U Wash Dept Applied Math Box 352420 Seattle WA 98195-2420 Office Phone: 206-543-9506. Business E-Mail: lascala@amath.washington.edu.

CRIMLISK, JANE THERESE, probation officer; b. Boston, Dec. 2, 1945; d. Herbert Leo and Grace Beatrice (McGilvray) C. AS, Aquinas Coll., Newton, Mass., 1968; BA in Sociology cum laude, Boston Coll., 1974; MS in Bus. Edn., Suffolk U., Boston, 1978; MEd in Rehab. Counseling, U. Mass., 1991, Cert. of Advanced Grad. Study, 1995. Tchr. religious edn., 1965-88, 93—; legal sec. Hale, Sanderson, Byrnes & Morton, Boston, 1968-69; sec. Boston Coll. Law Sch., Chestnut Hill, 1969-74, Life Resources, Inc., Boston, 1974-75; tchr. Archbishop Williams High Sch., Braintree, Mass., 1975-78; exec. sec. Cramer Electronics, Newton, Mass., 1978-79; jud. sec. Com. of Mass. Ct. Systems, Boston, 1979-95; probation officer Probate and Family Ct., Boston, 1995—; tchr. adult edn. Aquinas Coll., Milton, 1989—. Vol. counselor Pregnancy Help, Brighton, Mass., 1992, Arthur Clark for U.S. Congress campaign, Newton, 1980, Marian Walsh for State Senate campaign, 1992, 94, Mass. Citizens for Life. Mem. Boston Coll. Alumni Assn. (bd. dirs. 1982-84), Boston Coll. Evening Coll. Alumni Assn. (bd. dirs., past pres.), Aquinas Coll. Alumni Assn. Democrat. Roman Catholic. Avocations: swimming, ice skating, crewel, cross stitch, music. Home: 416 Belgrade Ave Apt 25 West Roxbury MA 02132-1540 Office: Probate and Family Ct Dept 24 New Chardon St Boston MA 02114-4703

CRIMMINS, PHILIP PATRICK, retired metallurgical engineer, lawyer; b. Poughkeepsie, NY, Aug. 1, 1930; s. Philip Patrick and Eva (Booth) C.; m. Janet E. Ballou, Feb. 14, 1953; children: Lisa Jane, Philip Patrick, Michael Mathew. BS, MIT, Cambridge, Mass., 1952; MS, Wayne State U., Detroit, 1959; JD, U. Pacific, Sacramento, Calif., 1972. Registered profl. metall. engr. Metall. engr. Ford Motor Co., Livonia, Mich., 1954-58; dir. engring. Aerojet Space Boosters, Sacramento, 1958—95; ret., 1995. Served with AUS, 1952-54. Recipient William Sparagen award Am. Welding Soc., 1968 Calif. Fellow Am. Inst. Chemists; mem. Am. Soc. Metals, Fed., Am., Calif. bar assns. Home: 9113 Rosewood Dr Sacramento CA 95826-4526

CRINION, GREGORY PAUL, lawyer; b. Eau Claire, Wis., Feb. 19, 1959; s. Harlan D. and Shirley P. (Paff) C. BBA cum laude, U. Wis., Eau Claire, 1981; MBA, U. Minn., 1982; JD cum laude, U. Wis., 1985. Bar: Wis. 1985, Tex. 1985, U.S. Dist. Ct. (we. dist.) Wis. 1985, U.S. Dist. Ct. (so. dist.) Tex. 1985, U.S. Ct. Appeals (5th cir.) 1985, U.S. Dist. Ct. (ea. dist.) Tex. 1986, U.S. Ct. Appeals (7th cir.) 1986, D.C. 1987, Colo. 1994, U.S. Supreme Ct. 1989, U.S. Dist. Ct. (no. dist.) Tex. 1990, U.S. Dist. Ct. (we. dist.) Tex. 2004. Atty. Exxon Co., U.S.A., Houston, 1985-87, Exxon Corp., NYC, 1987; from assoc. to ptnr. Jackson Walker, LLP (and predecessor firms), Houston, 1987-97; ptnr. Citti & Crinion, LLP, Houston, 1997-99, Ashby Crinion LLP, Houston, 1999—. Bd. dirs., pres. Innovative Alternatives, Inc., 2000-02, 2005. Apptd. NORM (Naturally Occurring Radioactive Material) Adv. Com., 1996-99, sign ordinance rev. com. City of Friendswood, 1996-98, cmty. and econ. devel. com., 2000-06, chair, 2002-04, vice chair, 2004-06; mem. Galveston County Mediation Svcs. Bd., 2000-02; mem. Leadership Friendswood Class I, 2001-02. Recipient Scroll of Appreciation U.S. Army, Europe, 1984. Mem. ABA, Bay Area Houston Econ. Partnership, Friendswood C. of C. (bd. dirs. 2003—, vice-chair, exec. bd. 2005-06, chair 2007—). Office: Ashby Crinion LLP 17040 El Camino Real Ste 200 Houston TX 77058-2601

CRINO, MARJANNE HELEN, anesthesiologist; b. Rochester, NY, Aug. 18, 1933; d. Michael Jay and Helen Barbara (Kennedy) C.; m. Michael Anthony La Iuppa, Nov. 12, 1960 (dec. Feb. 1996); children: James Michael, Barbara Helen, John Christopher. BS, Coll. St. Teresa, 1955; MD, Marquette U. Sch. Medicine, 1959; MA in Theology, St. Bernard's Inst., 1991. Diplomate Nat. Bd. Med. Examiners. House staff Genesee Hosp., Rochester, 1959—61; perinatal mortality rsch., resident in anesthesiology Jackson Meml Hosp.-U. Miami, 1962—65; attending staff in anesthesiology Genesee Hosp., Rochester, 1969—2000, mem. exec. com., med. staff sec., 1980, Rochester, 1982, acting chmn. dept. anesthesiology, 1989, 1991, chmn. pain control com., 1989—95; clin. instr. anesthesiology U. Rochester Sch. Medicine, 1983—99; ret., 1999. Cons. anesthesiology Rochester Psychiat. Ctr., 1975-85; instr. anesthesiology U. Miami Sch. medicine, 1966, 67; attending staff anesthesiology Jackson Meml. Hosp., Miami, 1966, 67. Mem. adv. bd. Isaiah House Hospice, 1994-2000, com. Pittsford Rep. Party, NY, 1970's-80's; vol. chaplain Genesee Hosp. Mem. NY State Soc. Anesthesiologists (bd. dirs., vice spkr. 1983-86, del. 1971-82, 87-2002), Am. Soc. Anesthesiologists (del. 1979-86, 97), AMA, NY State Med. Soc., Med. Soc. County of Monroe, Rochester Acad. Medicine, Cath. Physicians Guild Rochester (bd.dirs., pres. 1988-89), Margaret Roper Guild (pres. 1975-76), Cath. Women's Club (Diocese of Rochester). Roman Catholic. Avocations: reading, gardening, music. *Whether you are dealing with a large group, a small gathering or a single person, don't worry about the impression you are making or how uncomfortable you are. Try to find some way to make the others comfortable. You will never go wrong.*

CRIPE, FREDERICK F., insurance company executive; BS, Manchester Coll. Actuarial & pricing rsch. positions Allstate Ins. Co., Northbrook, Ill., 1979—90, asst. v.p. auto pricing rsch., mktg., urban & ethnic markets, gen. mgr. specialty lines, 1990—2000, v.p policy & pricing, 2000—03, v.p. prod. ops., 2003—06, sr. v.p. prod. ops., 2006—. Bd. dir. Highway Loss Data Inst. Fellow: Casualty Actuarial Soc.; mem.: Am. Acad. Actuaries. Office: Allstate Corp 2775 Sanders Rd Northbrook IL 60062*

CRIPPEN, JOHN RAYMOND, museum director; b. Worthington, Minn., Nov. 17, 1967; s. Gary L. and Nancy K. (Eigeman) Crippen; m. Sheila M. Stuhlman, Sept. 21, 1991; 1 child, Audrey M. BA, U. Minn., Mpls., 1990; MA, SUNY, Oneonta, 1994. Hist. sites adminstr. Minn. Hist. Soc., St. Paul, 1994—2001, head metro hist. sites, 2001—04, dir. Mill City Mus., Mpls., 2004—. Sec. St. Anthony Falls Heritage Bd., Mpls., 2004—. Mem. Mpls. Heritage Preservation Commn., 2007—. Recipient Academic Achievement award, Cooperstown Grad. Program, 1994; Louis C. Jones fellow, 1992—94. Mem.: Am. Assn. State and Local History, Nat. Grange, Phi Beta Kappa. Office: Minn Hist Soc Mill City Museum 704 South 2nd St Minneapolis MN 55401 Office Phone: 612-341-7648. Office Fax: 612-341-7001. Business E-Mail: john.crippen@mnhs.org.

CRIPPS, DEREK J., dermatologist, educator; b. Sept. 17, 1928; s. Edmund James and Susan Ann (Mayell) C.; m. Eileen Wright, Dec. 21, 1963; children: Andrew, Alasdair, Annabelle, Amanda. MB BS, U. London, 1953, MD, 1965; MS, U. Mich., 1961. Diplomate Am. Bd. Dermatology. Resident in dermatology U. Mich., 1959-62; asst. prof. medicine U. Wis., Madison, 1965-68, assoc. prof. medicine, 1968-72, prof., head dermatology, 1972-2000, emeritus prof. medicine, 2001—; pvt. practice Advanced Dermatology, Inc., Madison, 2006—. Cons. for sunscreens FDA, 1974-85; lectr. in field. Author: Royal Navy Ships, Captains, and Stations Vol. I 1773-1972, 2003, Vol. II 1793-1800, 2003, Steel's List of the Royal Navy Ships Commanders and Stations: 1793-1805, 2004; conbr. over 100 articles to profl. jours. Mem. Great Brit. Nat. Swimming Team, 1950-51; surgeon lt. Royal Navy, 1954-58. Recipient Merit award AMA, 1968; grantee EPA, Porphyria in Turkey, 1979-84, NIH, 1965-84, Action spectra and Biochemistry of Photodermatoses. Fellow ACP; mem. Am. Acad. Dermatology (photobiology com., pres. 1976, Exhibit Gold award 1975), Brit. Dermatologic Assn., Ctrl. Soc. for Clin. Rsch., Soc. for Investigative Dermatology, Royal Soc. of Medicine, Wis. Dermatological Soc. (pres. 1976). Avocations: swimming, travel. Office: UW Health Dept Derm One South Park 7th Fl Madison WI 53715 Home Phone: 608-244-1712; Office Phone: 608-287-2620. Personal E-mail: drdjc727@aol.com.

CRIQUI, ROBERT J., sports association executive; Grad., Fairleigh Dickinson U., Madison, NJ, 1976. Mgr. Ernst & Young, 1976—83; contr. NBA, NYC, 1983—89, v.p., 1989—97, sr. v.p., 1997—2004, exec. v.p. fin., 2004—. Office: NBA 450 Harmon Meadow Blvd Secaucus NJ 07094*

CRISCI, MATHEW G., financial consultant, writer; b. NYC; s. Mathew Anthony and Frances (Coscia) C.; m. Mary Ann, Nov. 14, 1968; children: Mathew Joseph, Mark David, Mitchell Justin. BS, Iona Coll., New Rochelle, NY. Sr. v.p. Young & Rubicam, Inc., NYC and Sydney, Australia, 1968—82; exec. v.p., COO, bd. dirs. Integrated Barter Internat., NYC and LA, 1982—85; sr. v.p., gen. mgr., bd. dirs. Chiat/Day Advt. Inc., San Francisco, 1986—90; exec. v.p., mng. dir. Lowe Lintas Worldwide, NYC, 1991—97; exec. v.p., chief mktg. officer Alton Entertainment Co., LA, 1997—2001, also bd. dirs.; chief mktg. officer, sr. v.p., ptnr. Asset Mktg. Sys., San Diego, 2001—, also bd. dirs. Author: Observations of a Kind, 1998, Bittersweet, 2003, This Little Piggy, 2005, Harrassment, 2006, Mary Died Today, 2007. Office Phone: 760-390-2055, 760-804-7360. Business E-Mail: mattcrisci@roadrunner.com.

CRISCIMAGNA, NED HENRY, engineer; b. Madison, Wis., Dec. 24, 1942; s. Frank Salvatore and Grace Mary Rose (Stancampiano) C.; m. Sandra Anne Kratina, June 19, 1965; children: Christine Marie Brent, Matthew Sean. BSME, U. Nebr., 1965; MS in Sys. Engring., Air Force Inst. Tech., 1970. Cert. reliability engr., profl. logistician. Apprentice engr. Henningson, Durham & Richardson, Omaha, 1965; commd. 2d lt. USAF, 1965, advanced through grades to lt. col., 1981, ret., 1985; staff prin. engr. ARINC Rsch. Corp., Annapolis, Md., 1985-93; sci. adv. IIT Rsch. Inst., Lanham, Md., 1993—2003, Alion Sci. & Tech., Lanham, Md., 2003—06, Criscimagna Consulting, LLC, 2006—. Co-author: Product Reliability, Maintainability, and Supportability Handbook, 1995. Treas. Homeowners Assn., Annapolis, 1995-98, v.p., 2006-; mem. Annapolis Chorale, 1990—, mem. bd. dirs.; mem., lector St. Anne's Episcopal Ch., Annapolis, 1987—. Mem. Internat. Soc. Logistics (sr., cert.), Am. Soc. Quality (cert. reliability engr.), Soc. Automotive Engrs., Order Sons of Italy in Am. (v.p. 1997-99). Avocations: college football, coin and stamp collecting, photography, music, computer simulation games. Home and Office: 307 S Cherry Grove Ave Annapolis MD 21401-4234 Personal E-mail: nhc_llc@comcast.net, ned_criscimagna@comcast.net.

CRISE, ROBERT D., JR., mathematics professor; s. Robert D. and Fran Crise. BS in Math., U. Calif., 1977; MA in Math., Calif. State U., 1985. Assoc. prof. math. Crafton Hills Coll., Yucaipa, Calif., 2000—. Mem.: AMA, Math. Assn. Am., Am. Math. Assn. of Two Yr. Colls., Calif. Math. Counsel of CC's South (student liaison 2004). Office: Crafton Hills Coll 11711 Sand Canyon Rd Yucaipa CA 92399-1799 Office Phone: 909-389-3382.

CRISER, MARSHALL M., lawyer, retired academic administrator; b. Rumson, NJ, Sept. 4, 1928; s. Marshall and Louise (Johnson) C.; m. Paula Porcher, Apr. 27, 1957; children: Marshall III, Edward, Mary, Glenn, Kimberly, Mark. BSBA, U. Fla., 1951, LLB, 1951 (replaced by J.D., 1967). Bar: Fla. 1951. Pvt. practice, Palm Beach, 1953-84; ptnr. Gunster, Yoakley, Criser & Stewart, 1955-84; atty. Palm Beach County Sch. Bd., 1958-64; pres. U. Fla., Gainesville, 1984-89, pres. emeritus, 1989—; shareholder Mahoney, Adams & Criser, Jacksonville, Fla., 1989-97; of counsel McGuire Woods, LLP, Jacksonville, 1998-2000, ret. ptnr., 2000—. Dep. chmn. Rinker Group Ltd., 2003—; chmn. bd. dirs. Rinker Materials, Corp., 1989-2002; mem. pres.'s coun. NCAA, 1986-87; chmn. Installment Land Sales Bd., 1963-64, chmn. Acad. Task Force rev. tort and ins. law, Fla., 1986-88, The Emerald Funds; chmn. bd. trustees Emerald Fund, 1997-98; mem. Scripps Fla. Funding Corp., 2004-06, chmn., 2004-06. Bd. dirs. Univ. Med. Ctr., Jacksonville, 1989-96, Shands at Jacksonville Hosp., 1999-2002, M.E. Rinker Found., 1998—; bd. dirs. Shands Tchg. Hosp., Gainesville, Fla., pres., 1984-89, bd. dirs., 1996-2001; bd. govs. Good Samaritan Hosp., West Palm Beach, pres., 1979-84; mem. Fla. Bd. Regents, 1965, 71-81, chmn., 1974-77, Bus.-Higher Edn. Forum, 1987-89; trustee Collins Ctr., 1989-99; pres., chmn. Alliance for World Class Edn., Duval County, 1998-2001; chmn. Fed. Crt. Adv. Group Mid. Dist. of Fla., 1991-96; trustee U. Fla., 2001-03, chmn., 2001-03; mem. Fla. Fed. Jud. Nominating Com., 2001-05; mem. Gov.'s Med. Malpractice Task Force, 2002—03. With U.S. Army, 1951-53. Fellow Am. Bar Found.; mem. Fla. Coun. 100 (chmn. 1979-80), ABA (ho. dels. 1968-72), Fla. Bar (gov. 1960-68, pres. 1968-69), Fla. Blue Key, Phi Delta Phi, Sigma Nu. Office: 100 NW 20th St Gainesville FL 32603 Business E-Mail: mcriser@uff.ufl.edu.

CRISHAM, THOMAS MICHAEL, lawyer; b. Chgo., June 7, 1939; s. John and Ellen (Moore) C.; m. Catherine Marie Schaab, Oct. 2, 1965; children: Catherine Marie, Megan, Maura. BBA, Loyola U., 1962, JD cum laude, 1965. Bar: Ill. 1965, U.S. Dist. Ct. (no. dist.) Ill. 1965, U.S. Supreme Ct. 1971, U.S. Ct. Appeals (7th cir.) 1978. Ptnr. Hinshaw & Culbertson, Chgo., 1965-95; sr. ptnr. Quinlan & Crisham, Ltd., Chgo., 1996—2001, Crisham & Kubes, Ltd., Chgo., 2001—. Mem. editl. bd. Ins. Outlook, Colorado Springs, Colo., 1990; pres. Def. Rsch. and Trial Lawyers Inst., Chgo., 1989, chmn. bd., 1990; mem. advisors Expert Evidence Reporter, Colorado Springs, 1990. Contbg. author: Abortion and Social Justice, 1973, Human Life: Our Legacy and Our Challenge, 1975, Architect and Engineer Liability: Claims Against Design Professional, 1987, Prosecuting and Defending Insurance Claims, 1989. Bd. dirs. Wendy Will Case Cancer Rsch. Found., Boys' Hope Scholars. Cpl., USMCR, 1959-60. Fellow Am. Coll. Trial Lawyers, Internat. Soc. Barristers; mem. ABA, Advocate Am. Bd. Trial Advs., Internat. Assn. Def. Counsel, Ill. Bar Assn., Trial Lawyers Club Chgo. (pres. 1975-76), Soc. Trial Lawyers Ill., Appellate Lawyers Assn., Assn. Def. Trial Lawyers, Am. Inns of Ct., Chgo. Bar Assn. Roman Catholic. Office: Crisham & Kubes Ltd 30 N Lasalle St Ste 2800 Chicago IL 60602-2511 Office Phone: 312-917-8460. Business E-Mail: tcrisham@crishamlaw.com.

CRISMAN, MARY FRANCES BORDEN, librarian; b. Tacoma, Nov. 23, 1919; d. Lindon A. and Mary Cecilia (Donnelly) Borden; m. Fredric Lee Crisman, Apr. 12, 1975 (dec. Dec. 1975). BA in History, U. Wash., 1943, BA in Librarianship, 1944. Asst. br. libr. in charge work with children Mottet br. Tacoma Pub. Libr., 1944-45, br. libr., 1945-49, br. libr. Moore br., 1950-55, asst. dir., 1955-70, dir., 1970-74, dir. emeritus, 1975—; mgr. corp. libr. Frank Russell Co., 1985-96, ret., 1997. Chmn. Wash. Cmty. Libr. Coun., 1970-72. Hostess program Your Libr. and You, Sta. KTPS-TV, 1969-71. Active Highland Homeowners League, Tacoma, 1980-04, incorporating dir. 1980, sec., registered agt., 1980-82; active Denham West Condominium Assn., Sun City, Ariz., 1995—, chair by laws com., 1999, sec., 2002-07. Mem. ALA (chmn. mem. com. Wash. 1957-60, mem. nat. libr. week com. 1965, chmn. libr. adminstrn. divsn. nominating com. 1971, mem. ins. for librs. com. 1970-74, vice chmn. libr. adminstrn. divsn. personnel adminstrn. sect. 1972-73, chmn. 1973-74, mem. com. policy implementation 1973-74, mem. libr. orgn. and mgmt. sect. budgeting acctg. and costs com. 1974-75), Am. Libr. Trustee Assn. (legis. com. 1975-78, conf. program com. 1978-80, action devel. com. 1978-80), Pacific N.W. (trustee divsn. nominating com 1976-77), Wash. Libr. Assn. (exec. bd. 1957-59, state exec., dir. Nat. Libr. Week 1965, treas., exec. bd. 1969-71, 71-73), Urban Librs. Coun. (editl. sec. Newsletter 1972-73, exec. com. 1974-75), Ladies Aux. to United Transp. Union (past pres. Tacoma), Friends Tacoma Pub. Libr. (registered agt. 1975-83, sec. 1975-78, pres. 1978-80, bd. dirs. 1980-83), Smithsonian Assocs., Nat. Railway Hist. Soc., U. Wash. Alumni Assn., U. Wash. Sch. Librarianship Alumni Assn. Clubs: Quota Internat. (sec. 1957-58, 1st v.p. 1960-61, pres. 1961-62, treas. 1975-76, pres. 1979-80) (Tacoma). Home: 9054 N 109th Ave Sun City AZ 85351-4676

CRISMOND, LINDA FRY, public relations executive; b. Burbank, Calif., Mar. 1, 1943; d. Billy Chapin and Lois (Harding) Fry; m. Donald Burleigh Crismond, 1965 (dec.). BS, U. Calif.-Santa Barbara, 1964; M.L.S., U. Calif.-Berkeley, 1965. Cert. county libr., Calif., assn. exec. Reference libr., EDP coordinator San Francisco Pub. Library, 1965—72; head acquisition San Francisco Pub. Libr., 1972-74; asst. univ. libr. U. So. Calif., LA, 1974-80; chief dep. county libr. L.A. County Pub. Libr., LA, 1980-81, county libr. Downey, 1981-89; exec. dir ALA, Chgo., 1989-92; v.p. public rels. Profl. Media Svc. Corp., Chgo., 1992-98; v.p. pub. rels. Follett Media Distbn., Crystal Lake, Ill., 1999—2003; nat. media cons. BWI, Lexington, Ky., 2003—07; pres. Frugal Dougal's Golf Cart Accessories, 2007—. Western rep. quality control council Ohio Coll. Libr. Ctr., Columbus, 1977-80; mem. Am. Nat. Standards Inst., N.Y.C., 1978-80; bd. councillors U. So. Calif. Sch. Libr. and Info. Mgmt., 1980-83; adv. bd. mem. UCLA Libr. Sch., 1981-89; chmn. bd. dirs. L.A. County Pub. Libr. Found., 1982-85; mem. OCLC Users Coun., 1988-89; mem. exec. com. L.A. County Mgmt. Coun., 1986-88, pres., 1988; cons. libr. Trinity Coll., 1995-99; prin. The Charleston Group, Inc., 1996—. Author: Directory of San Francisco Bay Area, 1968, Against All Odds, 1994; editor: Urban Librs. Coun. Exch., 1994-2005, The Charleston Report, 1996-99 Bd. dirs. So. Meth. U. Libr., 1992-98. Named Staff Mem. of Year San Francisco Pub. Libr., 1968 Mem. ALA , Calif. Libr. Assn. (council 1980-82), Calif. County Libr. Assn. (pres. 1984), L.A. County Mgmt. Assn. (pres. 1988). Home: 303 Mariner Dr Tarpon Springs FL 34689-5840

CRISP, COCO (COVELLI CRISP), professional baseball player; b. LA, Nov. 1, 1979; Minor league baseball player St. Louis Cardinals Farm Sys.; outfielder Cleve. Indians, 2002—05, Boston Red Sox, 2005—. Office: Boston Redsox 4 Yawkey Way Boston MA 02215

CRISPELL, BRIAN LEWIS, history professor; b. Rochester, NY, Apr. 5, 1964; s. Elmer Lyle and Florence Louise Crispell; m. Jean Ann Thomas, Feb. 3, 1990; children: Thomas Riley, Conner Francis, Sarah Katherine. BS in Social Studies Edn., Fla. State U., Tallahassee, 1990, MA in History, 1993, PhD in History, 1996. Tchr. Thomas County Schs., Thomasville, Ga., 1990—2000; adj. prof. U. South Fla., Tampa/Sarasota, 2000—05; prof. Fla. Coll., Temple Terrace, 2000—. Author: (book) Testing the Limits-George Smathers and Cold War America, 1999. Sgt. USAF, 1982—87. Nominee Bancroft prize, Columbia U., 1999—2000; recipient Top Lecturing Prof. award, Fla. Coll., 2001—05. Mem.: Hist. Soc., So. Hist. Assn. Republican. Mem. Ch. Of Christ. Avocations: hiking, baseball, travel. Office: Fla Coll 119 N Glen Arven Ave Temple Terrace FL 33617 Office Phone: 813-899-6842. Business E-Mail: crispell@floridacollege.edu.

CRISPIN, ANDRE ARTHUR, diversified financial services company executive; b. Brussels, Aug. 23, 1923; came to U.S., 1947; naturalized Am. citizen; m. Sylvia Clevenger; 5 children. Student, U. Louvain, Belgium, 1943. V.p. Am. Supply and Equipment Co., Houston, 1947-48; chmn. Crispin Co., Houston, 1949—; hon. consul-gen. Belgium; ret. hon. consul-gen. Past chmn. bd. trustees so. region Inst. Internat. Edn.; mem. Citizens Environ. Coalition; past pres. Music Guild Houston; past chmn. bd. trustees Awty Internat. Sch. With Belgian Army, 1940, 44-46; chmn. emeritus Houston Counsular Ball, mem. Senate of Internat. Jr. C. of C. Decorated officier Ordre de Leopold II, Civic Cross 1st class, officier Ordre de Leopold Ier (Belgium); chevalier Legion d'Honneur (France), Commdr.'s Cross Order of the Crown (Belgium), 1997; named one of 5 Outstanding Young Texans, 1953; recipient Houston Internat. Svc. award, 1986, medal of City of Bordeaux, Disting. Consul award Pres. George H. Bush. Mem. Nat. Assn. Steel Pipe Distbrs. (past pres., bd. dirs.), Academie Internationale du Vin, Alliance Française de Houston (past pres., dir., exec. com.), Commanderie de Bordeaux d'Amerique (grand maitre emeritus, gov.), Commanderie de Bordeaux du Texas à Houston (founder, past maitre, commandeur), Commanderie du Bontemps, de Medoc et de Graves (France, commandeur d'honneur), German Wine Soc., Prodhomme, Jurade de St. Emilion Stylobate, Piliers Chablisiens, Compagnon de Loupiac, Echevin, Lussac Puisseguin St. Emilion, Lalande de Pomerol, Hospitaliers de Pomerol, Downtown Houston Assn., Belgian-Am. C. of C. (past bd. dirs.), French-Am. C. of C. (past pres. Houston chpt., dir.), Houston C. of C. (now named Greater Houston Partnership, bd. dirs. world trade divsn., internat. bus. com., past chmn.), Jr. C. of C. (internat. senator 2001), World Trade Assn. (past pres., dir.), Petroleum Club of Houston (past dir., past 1st v.p.). Home: One Crestwood Dr Houston TX 77007 Office: 57 Bering Ste 300 Houston TX 77007 Office Phone: 713-224-8000, 713-974-8814. E-mail: andrecris@crispinco.com.

CRISPIN, JAMES HEWES, engineering and construction company executive; b. Rochester, Minn., July 23, 1915; s. Egerton Lafayette and Angela (Shipman) C.; m. Marjorie Holmes, Aug. 5, 1966. AB in Mech. Engring., Stanford U., 1938; MBA, Harvard U., 1941; grad., Army Command & Gen. Staff Sch., 1943. Registered profl. mech. engr., Calif. With C.F. Braun & Co., Alhambra, Calif., 1946-62; treas. Bechtel Corp., San Francisco, 1962-73, v.p., mem. fin. com., 1967-75, mgr. investment dept., 1973-75; retired, 1976. Investment cons., Santa Barbara, Calif., 1978—. Trustee Santa Barbara Mus. Art, 1979-91, 97-98, pres., 1986-88, life. hon. trustee, 1992—. Lt. col. Ordnance Corps, AUS., 1941-46. Decorated Army Commendation medal with oak leaf cluster. Mem. Mil. Order World Wars, S.R., Soc. Colonial Wars, Colonial Wars Calif., Baronial Order Magna Carta, Mil. Order Crusades, Am. Def. Preparedness Assn., World Affairs Coun. No. Calif. (trustee 1968-75), Calif. Hist. Soc. (trustee 1979-86), Valley Club of Montecito (pres. 1987-90, bd. dirs. 1981-91), Calif. Club L.A., World Trade Club San Francisco (pres. 1977-78, bd. dirs. 1971-78), Santa Barbara Club (pres. 1995-96, bd. dirs. 1991-96), Pacific Union Club, San Francisco, Beta Theta Pi. Republican. Office: La Arcada Bldg 1114 State St Ste 220 Santa Barbara CA 93101-6712 Office Fax: 805-966-2081; Home Fax: 805-565-9077.

CRISSMAN, KATHERINE KOLB, counseling administrator; b. Jamestown, NY, Sept. 8, 1979; d. Harry Herb, Jr. and Stephanie Viola (Stowell) Kolb; m. Jason Earl Crissman, Aug. 11, 2001. BA, Messiah Coll., Grantham, Pa., 1997—2001; MEd, Ind. U. Pa., 2001—02, Ednl. Specialist Cert. in Sch. Psychology, 2002—04. Cert. sch. psychologist NASP, 2004, Commonwealth of Pa., 2004, Dept. Pub. Instrn. N.C., 2004. Sch. psychology intern Greater Latrobe Sch. Dist., Pa., 2003—04; sch. psychologist Gaston County Sch. Dist., Gastonia, NC, 2004—. Assessment adminstr. PsychCorp, San Antonio, 2004—. Vol. youth advisor Locust Grove Ch. of the Brethren, Johnstown, Pa., 2001—04; vol. group leader, Friday Night Kids New Day Corp., Johnstown, Pa., 2003—04; vol. youth group advisor First Wesleyan Church, Gastonia, 2005—; vol. Cruiser Ministry, Gastonia, NC, 2005—. Named Gaston County Sch. Psychologist of Year, 2006—07. Mem.: NASP, Phi Kappa Phi. Office: Gaston County Sch Dist 730 W Garrison Blvd Gastonia NC 28052

CRIST, CHARLIE (CHARLES JOSEPH CRIST JR.), governor, former state attorney general; b. Altoona, Pa., July 24, 1956; s. Charles Joseph and Nancy Crist; m. Amanda Morrow, 1979 (div. 1980). Student, Wake Forest U., 1974-76; BA in Govt., Fla. State U., 1978; JD, Samford U., 1981. Gen. counsel Nat. Assn. Profl. Baseball Leagues, 1982—87; atty. Wood & Crist, 1987—; mem. Fla. State Senate, Tallahassee, 1992—98; dep. sec. Fla. Dept. Bus. and Profl. Regulation, 1999—2000; edn. commr. State of Fla., Tallahassee, 2000—02, atty. gen., 2003—07, gov., 2007—. Mem. subcommittee D Criminal Justice Ways and Means Com., 1996-98, Judiciary Com., 1996-98, Govtl. Reform and Oversight Com., 1996-98, Criminal Justice Com., 1996-98; chmn. Exec. Bus., Ethics and Elections Com., 1996-98; former state dir. US Sen. Connie Mack; chmn. anti-trust adv. com. Sen. Connie Mack's Baseball Anti-Trust Adv. Com.; mem. Sen. Connie Mack's Fed. Jud. Adv. Com., 1989-92; mem. ethics com. Fla. Bar. Mem. Pinellas County Rep. Exec. Com., Area Agy. on Bay Mgmt.; mem. adminstrv. bd. First United Meth. Ch.; mem. Booster Fla. State U.; bd. dirs. Found. for Fla.'s Future, Op. PAR, Police Athletic League; mem. adv. com. Tampa Bay MDA. Recipient Phil Piton award for svc. Major League Baseball, Leadership St. Petersburg, Roll Call award Fla. C. of C., 1993, PACE award, 1993, Legis. award Pinellas Sch. Adminstrs., 1993, Fla. Assn. Sch. Adminstrs., 1993, Fla. Sheriffs Assn., 1994, 96, Govt. award Urban League, 1995, Senatorial Leadership award Fla. Pros. Attys. Assn., 1995, Legis. Conservation award Fla. Conservation Assn., 1996, Disting. Legislator award Fla. Police Benevolent Assn., 1996; named Conservationist Legislator of Yr. Fla. Wildlife Fedn., 1995, Legislator of Yr. Police Benevolent Assn., 1995, Hon. Sheriff, 1995. Fellow Am. Swiss Assn.; mem. ABA, Am. Lung Assn. (mem. pres.'s coun. Pinellas County), Fla. Conservation Assn., St. Petersburg C. of C., Pinellas Pk. C. of C., Hillsborough Bar Assn., St. Petersburg Bar Assn., Rep. Nat. Lawyers Assn. (bd. govs.), Suncoasters Civic Club, Rotary, Suncoast Tiger Bay Club (bd. dirs., True Grit award). Republican. Methodist. Avocations: water-skiing, reading, jogging. Office: Office of Gov The Capitol 400 S Monroe St Tallahassee FL 32399*

CRIST, CHRISTINE MYERS, consulting executive; b. Harrisburg, Pa., Feb. 5, 1924; d. John Eyster and Eunice Horton (Ingham) Myers; m. Robert Grant Crist, June 25, 1949; children: Catherine Ingham Crist Marcson, Jessica Rogers Crist, Robert Jeffrey Myers Crist. BA, Dickinson Coll., 1946. Reporter The Patriot, Harrisburg, Pa., 1946-49; editor West Shore Times, Lemoyne, Pa., 1964-65; adminstr. arts in edn. Pa. Dept. Edn., Harrisburg, 1974-77, dir. leadership in arts edn., 1977-79; press sec. gov.'s office Pa. Commn. for Women, Harrisburg, 1980-83, dir. Gov.'s Commn. for Women, 1983-87; exec. dir. com. for women Evang. Luth. Ch. in Am., Chgo., 1987-90; ptnr. Crist and Crist, Cons., Camp Hill, Pa., 1990—. Mem. State Employees Retirement Bd., 1986-88; state coord. We the People Edn. Program. Editor: Song As A Measure of Man, 1975 (excellent pub. 1975). Mem. Camp Hill (Pa.) Sch. Bd., 1967-73, Capital Area Intermediate Bd., Lemoyne, Pa., 1970-73; pres. Camp Hill (Pa.) Civic Club, 1970-72, women's orgn. Trinity Lutheran Ch., 1999; chair Ch. in Society, Lower Susquehanna Synod, Evang. Lutheran Ch. in Am.; mem. coun. Trinity Congregation, 1991-94; mem. Harrisburg Choral Soc., Dickinson Alumni Coun., 1992—; bd. dirs. Women's Polit. Network Pa., Camp Hill Cmty. Found., 1996—; mem. candidacy bd. Luth. Ch., 1992—; Pa. bd. Common Cause, 1997—; mem. Envision Capital Region Task Force, 2000-02; mem. Nat. Assn. Comms. for Women, 1987. Recipient Women in Comms. Freedom of Info. award, 1982, Great Commicators award, 1985, Pa. Women's History award, Pa. Com. for Women, 2003, Women Inventing Future award, Cumberland County, 2003. Mem. Monday Club, Cumberland County Fedn. Women's Clubs (pres. 1996—), Coll. Club Harrisburg (pres. 2004—). Lutheran. Home and Office: Crist and Crist 1915 Walnut St Camp Hill PA 17011-3854 Personal E-mail: camcrist@paonline.com.

CRIST, JUDITH, film and drama critic; b. NYC, May 22, 1922; d. Solomon and Helen (Schoenberg) Klein; m. William B. Crist, July 3, 1947 (dec. Apr. 1993); 1 son, Steven Gordon. AB, Hunter Coll., 1941; tchg. fellow, State Coll. Wash., 1942-43; MSc in Journalism, Columbia, 1945; DHL (hon.), SUNY, New Paltz, 1994. Civilian instr. 3081st Army AFB Unit, 1943-44; reporter N.Y. Herald Tribune, 1945-60, editor arts, 1960-63, assoc. theater critic, 1957-63, film critic, 1963-66; film, theater critic NBC-TV Today Show, 1963-73; film critic World Jour. Tribune, 1966-67; critic-at-large Ladies Home Jour., 1966-67; contbg. editor and film critic TV Guide, 1966-88; founding film critic N.Y. mag., 1968-75; film critic The Washingtonian, 1970-72, Palm Springs Life, 1971-75; contbg. editor, film critic Saturday Rev., 1975-77, 80-84, N.Y. Post, 1977-78, 50 Plus, 1978-83, L'Officiel/USA, 1979-80; arts critic Sta. WWOR-TV, 1981-87; critical columnist for Coming Attractions, 1985-93; contbg. editor Hollywood Mag., 1985-93; contbg. editor Columbia Mag., 1993-95. Instr. journalism Hunter Coll., 1947, Sarah Lawrence Coll., 1958-59; assoc.

journalism Columbia Grad. Sch. Journalism, 1958-62, lectr. journalism, 1962-64, adj. prof., 1964—; host Judith Crist Film Weekends at Tareytown House, NY, 1971-2006. Author: The Private Eye, The Cowboy and the Very Naked Girl, 1968, Judith Crist's TV Guide to the Movies, 1974, Take 22: Moviemakers on Moviemaking, 1984, rev. edit., 1991; contbr. articles to popular mags. Trustee Anne O'Hare McCormick Scholarship Fund. Named to 50th Anniversary Honors List, Columbia Grad. Sch. Journalism, 1963, Hunter Alumni Hall of Fame, Hunter Coll., 1973; recipient Page One award, NY Newspaper Guild, 1955, George Polk award, 1950, Newswomen's Club of NY award, 1955, 1959, 1963, 1965, 1967, Edn. Writers Assn. award, 1952, Alumni award, Columbia Grad. Sch. Journalism, 1961, 50th Anniversary Award, 1965, Centennial Pres.'s medal, Hunter Coll., 1970, Hall of Fame award for outstanding profl. achievement, 2003, Grad. Sch. Journalism's Faculty and Alumni award, Columbia U., 1998, Univ. Alumni Fedn. medal for conspicuous svc., 2003. Mem.: Soc. of the Silurians, Columbia Journalism Alumni Exec. Com. (pres. 1967—70), Sigma Tau Delta. Office: 180 Riverside Dr New York NY 10024-1048 *Care about people-not things.*

CRIST, PAUL GRANT, lawyer; b. Denver, Sept. 9, 1949; s. Max Warren and Marjorie Raymond (Catland) C.; m. Christine Faye Clements, June 4, 1972; children: Susan Christine, Benjamin Warren, John Willis. BA, U. Nebr., 1971; JD cum laude, NYU, 1974. Bar: Ohio 1974, US Ct. Mil. Appeals 1975, Calif. 1976, US Dist. Ct. (no. dist.) Ohio 1979, US Ct. Appeals (6th cir.) 1982, US Dist. Ct. (no., ea., so. and ctrl. dists.) Calif. 2003, US Ct. Appeals (9th cir.) 2003. Assoc. Jones, Day, Reavis & Pogue, Cleve., 1974, 78-83, ptnr., 1984—. Rsch. editor NYU Law Rev., 1972-74. Elder Grace Presbyn. Ch. Capt. JAGC USAF, 1974—78. Decorated Meritorious Svc. medal. Fellow Am. Coll. Trial Lawyers; mem. Cleve. Bar Assn., State Bar Calif., Order of Coif. Democrat. Presbyterian. Avocations: golf, reading. Office: Jones Day North Point 901 Lakeside Ave Cleveland OH 44114 Office Phone: 216-586-7139. Business E-Mail: pgcrist@jonesday.com.

CRIST, RICHARD LE ROY, voice educator; b. Harrisburg, Pa., Oct. 21, 1947; s. Robert Elsworth, sr. and Mildred Cesil Crist; m. Yvonne Marie Brennan, Mar. 3, 1992; children: Tanya Lynne, Patrick Raymond, Daniel Owen. BS in Music Edn., Messiah Coll., Pa., 1970; MusM in vocal performance, New Eng. Conservatory, Boston, 1972; Spl. student in Opera Theater, Curtis Inst., Phila., 1980; diploma, Goldovsky Opera Inst., NYC, 1981. Voice instr. Smith Coll., North Andover, Mass., 1996—97, Messiah Coll., Grantham, Pa., 1997—2000, Elizabethtown (Pa.) Coll., 1998—99; asst. prof. opera, artist in residence Arkansaw U., Fayetteville, 2000—02; asst. prof. voice Okla. U., Norman, 2002—05; artist, tchr. voice, dir. opera theater Ohio U., Athens, 2005—. Prin. artist Opera Co. of Boston, 1971—91; soloist Cleve. Orch., 1978—83, Pitts. Symphony, 1979—85, Minn. Orch., Mpls., 1980—89; prin. artist Bolshoi Opera, Moscow, 1981—93; soloist Phila. Orch., 1982—88; prin. artist San Francisco Opera, San Francisco, 1983—84; soloist Am. Symphony Orch., NYC, 1984—2000; prin. artist Opera de Lyon, Lyon, France, 1984—85, Phila. Opera, 1984—86, Met. Opera, NYC, 1985—88, Hamburg State Opera, Germany, 1985—87; soloist N.Y.C. Opera, 1996—98. Singer: (Operas) (recordings) Die Liebe der Danae with Am. Symphony, TELARC, (TV series) PBS Great Performances Queen of Spades, Verdi Requiem, Haydn Creation with Oklahoma City Philharm., Masterwork Chorale, 2001—04, Beethoven Ninth with Wyo. Symphony, 2004; singer: (soloist) Sarah Caldwell Meml. Svc., Boston, 2006. Recipient First Pl., Ea. Region of U.S., Nat. Assn. Tchrs. of Singing, 1969, Second Pl., Opera Co. of Boston, 1973, Finalist Rosa Poncel Contest, Balt. Opera, 1978; scholar Music Edn. award, Theodore Presser Co., 1968—70, Grad. Studies award, New Eng. Conservatory, 1970—72, Opera Study award, Goldovsky Opera Inst., 1978—81. Mem.: Am. Guild Musical Artists, Coll. Music Soc., Nat. Assn. Teachers of Singing. Office: Ohio Univ 381 Robert Glidden Hall Athens OH 45701 Office Fax: 740-593-4234. Business E-Mail: cristr@ohio.edu.

CRIST, WILLIAM MILES, dean, pediatrician, educator; b. Florence, SC, July 21, 1943; s. Harry Brogan and Rosemary (Reid) C.; m. Helen Lucille Valle, June 5, 1971; 1 child, Brian. BA cum laude, Cen. Meth. Coll., 1965; MD, U. Mo., 1969. Intern in pediatrics Mott Children's Hosp., Ann Arbor, Mich., 1969-70; resident fellow in pediatrics and pediatric hematology St. Louis Children's Hosp., 1971-72; trainee Nat. Cancer Inst. Wash. U. Sch. Medicine, St. Louis, 1974-75; asst. prof. pediatrics U. Ala., Birmingham, 1975-78; assoc. scientist Comprehensive Cancer Ctr. U. Ala., Birmingham, 1975-78; acting dir., then dir. hematology/oncology Children's Hosp. U. Ala., Birmingham, 1976-85; prof. pediatrics, dir. pediatrics, hematology/oncology U. Tenn., Memphis, 1985—2000; chmn. dept. hematology/oncology St. Jude Children's Rsch. Hosp., Memphis, 1985—94, dep. dir., 1994—97; chair dept. pediats. and adolescent medicine Mayo Clinic, Rochester, 1997—2000; dean U. of Missouri-Columbia Sch. of Med., 2000—, Hugh E. & Sarah D. Stephenson dean, 2004—. Mem. Children's Oncology Group, 1976—. Maj. USAF, 1972-74. Mem. Am. Soc. Hematology, Sigma Epsilon Pi, Omicron Delta Kappa. Office: U Missouri Columbia Sch Med One Hospital Dr Columbia MO 65212

CRISTESCU, NICOLAIE DAN, engineering educator; b. Chelmenti, Romania, Feb. 17, 1929; married (dec.); 1 child. Diplomat, Bucharest U., Romania, 1951, docent, 1967; PhD, Romanian Acad., 1955. Asst. prof. U. Bucharest, Romania, 1951-55, lectr., 1955-57, assoc. prof., 1957-66, prof., 1966-92, dept. chmn., 1982-90, pres., 1990-92; vis. grad. rsch. prof. U. Fla., 1970-76, grad. rsch. prof. dept. aerospace engring. mechanics and engring. sci. Gainesville, 1992—. Vis. prof. Johns Hopkins U., Balt., 1968-69, Drexel U., Phila., 1969; lectr. in field. Author: Dynamic Problems in Theory of Plasticity, 1958, The Mechanics of Extensible Strings, 1964, Dynamic Plasticity, 1967, 70 (in Japanese), Introduction to Rate-Dependent Plasticity (A Dynamic Approach), 1971, Rock Mechanics, 1983, 2d edit., 1984, supplemental 1988, Mechanics of Composite Materials, 1983, Rock Rheology, 1989, Rock Mechanics-Rheology Aspects, 1990, Rock Viscoplasticity, 1992, Viscoplasticity of Geomaterials, 1994, (with I. Suliciu) Viscoplasticity, 1976, 82, (with S. Cleja-Tigoiu) Theory of Plasticity with Application to Metal Working, 1985, (with U. Hunsche) Time Effects in Rock Mechanics, 1998, (with E.M. Craciun and E. Soos) Mechanics of Elastic Composites, 2004, (with H.R. Hardy, Jr. and R.O. Simionescu) Basic and Applied Salt Mechanics, 2002, Dynamic Plasticity, 2007; contbr. articles to profl. jours.; sr. editor: Internat. Jour. Plasticity; mem. editl. bd. Internat. Jour. Mechanical Sci., Mechanics Rsch. Comm., Mechanics of Cohesive-Frictional Materials and Structures, others. Fellow Romanian Acad., Acad. Europaea; mem. ASME (Arpad L. Nadai award 1995), Soc. Scholars, Internat. Soc. Interaction of Mechanics and Maths. (founder), Am. Rock Mechanics Assn. (founder), Am. Acad. Mechanics, Soc. Exptl. Stress Analysis, Group Français de Rheology, Internat. Assn. Computer Methods and Advances in Geomechanics, Internat. Soc. Rock Mechanics, Tau Beta Pi, Sigma Xi. Achievements include research in mechanics of solid deformable bodies, theory of plasticity, rheology, rock and soil mechanics, mechanics of powder-like materials. Office: U Fla 231 Aerospace Bldg PO Box 116250 Gainesville FL 32611-6250 Office Phone: 352-392-6747. Office Fax: 352-392-7303. Business E-Mail: cristesc@ufl.edu.

CRISTOFER, MICHAEL, actor, writer, playwright, scriptwriter; s. Joseph Peter and Mary (Muccioli) Procaccino. Student, Catholic U. Am., 1962-66, Am. U., Beirut, 1968-69. Repertory actor Arena Stage, Washington, 1967-68, Theatre of Living Arts, Phila., 1968, Beirut Repertory Co., 1968-69, N.Y. Shakespeare Festival, 1970, Mark Taper Forum, L.A., 1972-75; stage performance in Chinchilla, 1979, No End of Blame, 1983, Hamlet, 1993; TV appearances in The Entertainer, 1975, The Last of Mrs. Lincoln, 1975, Knuckle, 1976; film appearance in Die Hard III, 1995, Enemy of The People, 1976, Little Drummer Girl, 1983; author plays The Mandala, 1967, Rienzi, 1968, Dorian, 1969, Plot Counter Plot, 1971, Americomedia, 1972, The Shadow Box, 1972 (L.A. Drama Critic award for best play 1975, Pulitzer prize drama 1977, Antoinette Perry award 1977, Tony award, 1977), Ice, 1974, Black Angel, 1976, The Lady and the Clarinet, 1980, C.C. Pyle and the Bunyan Derby, 1978, Breaking Up, 1986, Casablanca (adaption), 1985, Love Me or Leave Me, 1990, Amazing Grace, 1993; screenplays include Falling in Love, 1984, Witches of Eastwick, 1987, Bonfire of The Vanities, 1990, Mr. Jones, 1993, Breaking Up, 1997, Casanova, 2005; author screenplay, dir.: (HBO original movie) Gia, 1998 (Dirs. Guild Am. award), Original Sin, 2001. Recipient Theatre World award for performance, 1977, L.A. Drama Critics award for acting, 1973, OBIE award for acting, 1979. Office: ICM 8942 Wilshire Blvd Beverly Hills CA 90211

CRISTOL, A. JAY, federal judge; b. Fountain Hill, Pa., Feb. 25, 1929; s. Samuel and Mae (Stein) C.; m. Eleanor Rubin; children: Stephen Michael, David Alan. BA, U. Miami, 1958, LLB, 1959, PhD, 1997. Bar: Fla. 1959. Spl. asst. to Atty. Gen. of Fla., Tallahassee, 1959-65; sr. ptnr. Cristol, Mishan, Sloto, Miami, 1959-85; judge U.S. Bankruptcy Ct., Miami, 1985-93, chief judge, 1994-99, chief judge emeritus, 1999—. Adj. prof. U. Miami Law Sch.; bd. govs. 11th cir. Nat. Conf. Bankruptcy Judges; bankruptcy rules adv. com. Jud. Conf. of U.S., 1995-2001; bankruptcy com. U.S. Ct. Appeals (11th cir.), 1996-2002; tchr. bankruptcy law to judges in Czech Republic, Slovenia, Thailand, Russia, India, Malaysia, Hong Kong, South Africa. Bd. trustees U. Miami, 1988-90, Coral Gables; bd. dirs. ARC, Miami, 1989—, Wings Over Miami Aviation Mus., 2001—. Capt. USNR, 1951-89. Fellow Am. Coll. Bankruptcy; mem. ABA, Am. Bankruptcy Inst., Nat. Conf. Bankruptcy Judges, Bankruptcy Bar Assn. (so. dist. of Fla.), Fla. Bar Assn., Dade County Bar Assn. Avocations: water-skiing, windsurfing, flying, reading. Office: US Bankruptcy Ct 1412 Fed Bldg 51 SW 1st Ave Miami FL 33130-1669 Office Phone: 305-714-1770. Business E-Mail: a_jay_cristol@flsb.nscourts.gov.

CRISTOL, STANLEY JEROME, retired chemistry professor; b. Chgo., June 14, 1916; s. Myer J. and Lillian (Young) C.; m. Barbara Wright Swingle, June 1957; children: Marjorie Jo, Jeffrey Tod, Kurt W. Swingle, Sharon S. Metcalf, Larry M. Swingle. BS, Northwestern U., 1937; MA, UCLA, 1939, PhD, 1943. Rsch. chemist Std. Oil Co., Calif., 1938-41; rsch. fellow U. Ill., 1943-44; rsch. chemist U.S. Dept. Agr., 1944-46; asst. prof., then assoc. prof. U. Colo., 1946-55, prof., 1955—, Joseph Sewall Disting. prof., 1979—, chmn. dept. chemistry, 1960-62, grad. dean, 1980-81. Vis. prof. Stanford U., summer 1961, U. Geneva, 1975, U. Lausanne, Switzerland, 1981; with OSRD, 1944-46; adv. panels NSF, 1957-63, 69-73, NIH, 1969-72 Author: (with L.O. Smith, Jr.) Organic Chemistry, 1966; editorial bd., Chem. Revs., 1957-59, Jour. Organic Chemistry, 1964-68; contbr. rsch. articles to sci. jours. Guggenheim fellow, 1955-56, 81, 82; recipient James Flack Norris award in phys.-organic chemistry, 1972, Alumni Merit award Northwestern U., 1987. Fellow AAAS (councilor 1986-92); mem. NAS, AAUP, Am. Chem. Soc. (chmn. organic chemistry div. 1961-62, adv. bd. petroleum rsch. fund 1963-66, coun. policy com. 1968-73), Colo.-Wyo. Acad. Sci., Royal Soc. Chemistry, Phi Beta Kappa, Sigma Xi, Phi Lambda Upsilon. Home: 1638 W 3d Ave Durango CO 81307 E-mail: stanleycristol@durango.net.

CRISWELL, CHARLES HARRISON (HARRY), analytical chemist, environmental and forensic consultant, executive; b. Springfield, Mo., Jan. 9, 1943; s. John Philip and Elba Anne (Denton) C.; m. Joyce LaVonne Louth, Apr. 26, 1968; 1 child, Christina Rachel. AB in Chemistry and Biology, Drury Coll., 1967; postgrad., U. Mo., 1967-68. Cert. hazardous materials and waste specialist, environ. health profl., hazardous material emergency response trainer, profl. chemist, qualified environ. profl., hazardous materials emergency responder-ops./tech./specialist levels; registered hazardous substances profl. Dir. Water Pollution Control Labs City of Springfield, 1968-72, chief Water Pollution Sect., 1972-80; pres., chmn. bd. dirs. Cons. Analytical Svcs. Internat., Springfield, 1979—98; assoc. Environ. Planning Assocs., Inc., 1985—; adj. faculty, spl. instr. in environ. law and hazardous materials chemistry Drury U.; prin., mng. mem. Criswell Cons., LLC, Springfield, 1999—; exec. dir., CFO Spl. Events Mktg., Inc., 2004—. Apptd. by gov. mem. Mo. Hazardous Waste Mgmt. Commn., 1978; mem. Mo. Joint Commn. on Hazardous Waste Mgmt. Legis., statewide ad-hoc Com. on Regulations; mem. curriculum adv. com. Environ. Resource Ctr., Crowder Coll.; tech. advisor S.W. Mo. Household Hazardous Waste Project; tech. advisor, chem. emergency specialist for hazardous materials response City of Springfield, Mo. Fire Dept., Logan-Rogersville Tri-County Fire Dist., expert courtroom testimony, spkr. in field, nationwide. Contbr. more than 120 papers, presentations, articles to profl. jours. Active Springfield Employees Activities Club, Thirteen Gallon Club of ARC, Friends of Zoo; judge Southwest Mo. Regional Sci. Fair; vice chmn., 1990-93, chair 1993-98, mem. numerous subcoms. Greene County Local Emergency Planning Com.; ruling elder 1st and Calvary Presbyn. Ch., elected for life, 1973, elected clk. of session, 1996-2000, deacon, sr. high sch. youth advisor, active numerous coms.; mem. permanent jud. commn. John Calvin Presbytery, 1977-85, 93—99, treas., 1974—2003; mem., moderator 12 spl. adminstrv. commns. to ordain and install pastors, 4 Presbytery Synod Gen. Assembly Inter-judicatory Consultations on Long Range Ch. Fin., moderator com. on nominations, 1996-2001, presbytery moderator, 1999-2000, interim presbytery exec., 2001-02, commr. to gen. assembly, 1998-99, mem. fin. affairs com., 1996-2001, mem. com. on nominations, 2000-01, Synod of Mid-Am., stated clk. and other offices; mem. gen. assembly Presbyterian Ch. (USA), 1998-99; alumni bd. dirs. Greenwood Lab. Sch., 1992—, pres., 1993—, chmn. bd., 1993—; ofcl. WEF rep. to bd. trustees Inst. Profl. Environ. Practice, 1996-99. Recipient Gift of Time award for cmty. svc. Springfield Area Coun. Chs., C. of C., others; named Pheresis Donor of Yr., ARC, 1988. Fellow Am. Inst. Chemists; mem. ASTM (mem. subcom. on environ. assessment of real estate), Am. Inst. Biol. Scis., Am. Chem. Soc. (mem. com. on environ. analytical methodology, charter mem. Ozarks sect.), Nat. Assn. Safety Health Profls., nat. Assn. Environ. Profls., Nat. Environ. Health Assn., Internat. Union Pure and Applied Chemistry (affiliate), Assoc. Industries Mo. (mem. environ. com., mem. hazardous waste task group), Mo. Acad. Sci., Mo. Waste Control Coalition, Mo. Rural Water Assn., Mo. Water and Sewerage Conf. (sect. pres. 1975), Mo. Water Enrivon. Assn. (pres., mem. exec. com. 1977-83, chmn. 1979-80, newsletter assoc. editor, chmn. numerous coms. and confs., award of merit 1991, 92, 93), Nat. Environ. Tng. Assn., Hazardous Materials Control Resources Inst., Inst. Profl. Environ. Practice (mem. internat. bd. trustees), Assn. Ofcl. Analytical Chemists, Analytical Lab. Mgrs. Assn., N.Am. Hazardous Materials Mgmt. Assn. (internat. bd. dirs.), Water Environ. Fedn. (chmn./asst. chmn. nat. confs., mem. indsl. wastes com. 1975-81, 87-90, govt. affairs com. 1977-83, 86-91, 92-96, tech. practices com. 1978-80, 90-95, 96-98, program com. 1979, 88-93, hazardous wastes com. 1992-97, membership com. 1987-98, vice chmn. 1992-95, chmn. 1995-97, GAC nat. task group on permits and monitoring 1978-82, chmn. 1987-80, IWC nat. subcom. to study changes in indsl. analytical protocols chmn. 1980-82, chmn. GAC nat. task group on maximum contaminant levels in water 1988-89, chmn. MC nat. subcom. on expansion of membership base into toxics and hazardous waste mgmt. disciplines, 1987-90, chmn. IWC nat. subcom. liaison with mem. assns. and with other orgns., 1988-90, mem. indsl. wastes steering com. 1988-90, exec. com. nat. task group on orgnl. name change 1990-91, mem. exec. com. nat. task group on profl. environ. credentials 1995-99, Arthur Sidney Bedell award), Mensa (life), Springfield Area C. of C. (mem. environ. com., chairperson emergency preparedness and cmty. right to know subcom.), Beta Beta Beta, Phi Mu Alpha, Gamma Alpha. Republican. Avocations: music, tennis, other sports. Office: Criswell Cons LLC 1437 S Summer Pl Springfield MO 65809-2247 Office Phone: 417-224-4357.

CRISWELL, ELEANOR CAMP, psychologist; b. Norfolk, Va., May 12, 1938; d. Norman Harold Camp and Eleanor (Talman) David; m. Thomas L. Hanna (dec. 1990). BA, U. Ky., 1961, MA, 1962; EdD, U. Fla., 1969. Asst. prof. edn. Calif. State Coll., Hayward, 1969; prof. psychology, former chair Calif. State U., Sonoma, 1969—. Faculty adviser Humanistic Psychology Inst., San Francisco, 1970-77; dir. Novato Inst. Somatic Rsch. and Tng.; editor Somatics jour.; cons. Venturi, Inc., Autogenic Sys., Inc.; clin. dir. Biotherapeutics, Kentfield Med. Hosp., 1985-90; founder Humanistic Psychology Inst. (now Saybrook Grad. Sch.), 1970. Author: How Yoga Works, 1987, Biofeedback and Somatics, 1995; co-editor: Biofeedback and Family Practice Medicine, 1983; patentee optokinetic perceptual learning device. Mem. APA (past pres. divsn. 32), Biofeedback Soc. Calif. (past pres.), Assn. for Humanistic Psychology (past pres.), Somatic Soc. (pres.), Equine Hanna Somatics (founder), Internat. Assn. Yoga Therapists (v.p.). Office: Novato Inst 1516 Grant Ave #212 Novato CA 94945 Home Phone: 415-897-6044; Office Phone: 415-897-0336. Business E-Mail: ecriswel@ix.netcom.com.

CRISWELL, STEPHEN, astronomer; Program mgr. Fred Lawrence Whipple Obs., Amada, Ariz. Project mgr. Very Energetic Radiation Imaging Telescope Array Sys. (VERITAS), a collaboration which pioneered the Imaging Atmospheric Cherenkov Technique for the detection of very high energy (VHE) gamma rays. Mailing: Fred Lawrence Whipple Obs PO Box 6369 Amado AZ 85645-6369 Office: Fred Lawrence Whipple Observatory 670 Mt Hopkins Rd Amado AZ 85645 E-mail: scriswell@cfa.harvard.edu.

CRITCHFIELD, ALISON, education educator; b. Plainfield, NJ, Mar. 30, 1951; d. John A. and Barbara A. Doby; m. Tom L. Critchfield, Sept. 29, 1974; 1 child, Julie Anna. BA in Elem. Edn., U. Ky., Lexington, 1978, MS in Family Studies, 1985. Cert. tchr. Ky. Presch., lab. sch. tchr. U. Ky., Lexington, 1983—84; child care cons. Child Car Coun., Lexington, 1985—88; dir. latchkey program Maxwell Presbyn. Ch., Lexington, 1986—87; presch. lab. tchr., dir. Midway Coll., Ky., 1989—92, prof., 1992—. Advisor student program Ky. Edn. Assn., 2000—. Recipient Trustee award tchg. excellence, Midway Coll., 1998, Outstanding Educator award, 2006, Outstanding Advisors award, Ky. Edn. Assn., 2006—. Mem.: Nat. Coun. Tchrs. English, Internat. Reading Assn., Phi Upsilon Omicron. Office: Midway Coll 512 E Stephens St Midway KY 40347

CRITCHLOW, BRYAN DOUGLAS, music educator; b. Haxton, Colo., Nov. 3, 1959; s. Earl Douglas and M. Yolanda Critchlow; m. Judith Ann Laux, May 3, 1987. MusB Edn., U. No. Colo., Greeley, 1982; MA Tchg., Colo. Coll., Colorado Springs, 1995. Tchr. music Pawnee Sch. Dist., Grover, Colo., 1982—83, Kiowa County Schs., Eads, Colo., 1983—85; tchr. instrumental music Cheyenne Mountain Sch. Dist. 12, Colorado Springs, 1985—88; tchr. music Ellicott Sch. Dist., Colo., 1988—92; tchr. instrumental music Woodland Park Schs. RE-2, Colo., 1992—. Chmn. Pikes Peak Music Educators, Colorado Springs, 1998—2001; mem. Woodland Park Wind Symphony, 1994—, Pikes Peak Civic Orch., Colorado Springs, 1992—98; founding mem. Little London Winds, Colorado Springs, 1991—. Named to Who's Who Among Am. Tchrs., 2002, 2006. Mem.: Woodland Park Edn. Assn. (v.p. 2003—06), Colo. Music Educators Assn. (8th grade band performed at conv. 2000). Avocations: skiing, travel, house building, stained glass, G scale railroading. Office: Woodland Park Mid Sch 600 E Kellys Rd Woodland Park CO 80866

CRITCHLOW, CHARLES HOWARD, lawyer; b. Morristown, NJ, Nov. 23, 1950; s. George F. and Florence Critchlow; m. Mary Ellen Donnelly (dec.); children: Katharine F., Mary E.G.; m. Cecil S. Hanft. BA, Yale U., 1972; JD, Columbia U., 1975. Bar: N.Y. 1976, U.S. Dist. Ct. (so. and ea. dists.) N.Y. 1976, U.S. Ct. Appeals (2d cir.) 1982, U.S. Ct. Appeals (3d and 10th cirs.) 1991, U.S. Supreme Ct. 1993, U.S. Ct. Appeals (5th cir.) 1994, U.S. Ct. Appeals (4th cir.) 1995, U.S. Ct. Internat. Trade 1996, U.S. Ct. Appeals (Fed. Cir.) 1996. Assoc. Lord, Day & Lord, NYC, 1975-85, ptnr., 1985-86, Coudert Bros. LLP, NYC, 1986—2005, Baker & McKenzie LLP, NYC, 2005—. Contbr. to Antitrust Law Developments; contbr. articles to profl. jours. Active Yale Alumni Fund; mem. Yale Alumni Schs. Com. Mem.: ABA. Office: Baker & McKenzie LLP 1114 Avenue of the Americas New York NY 10036-7703 Home Phone: 718-852-2972; Office Phone: 212-626-4496. Business E-Mail: charles.h.critchlow@bakernet.com.

CRITCHLOW, RICHARD H., lawyer; b. Pitts., Mar. 28, 1947; s. John Park and Ruth Lauderbaugh C.; m. Deirdre Lynn Flower, Feb. 18, 1979; children: Courtney Leigh, Caitlin Anne. BA in Polit. Sci., Union Coll., 1969; JD, U. Miami, 1973. Bar: Fla., 1973, U.S. Supreme Ct., 1976, U.S. Tax Ct., 1978, U.S. Dist. Ct. (ea. dist.) La. 1980, U.S. Dist. Ct. (so. dist.) Fla. 1973, U.S. Dist. Ct. (mid. dist.) Fla. 1978, U.S. Ct. Appeals (5th and 11th cirs.) 1973. Assoc. Tew, Tew, Rosen & Murray, Miami, Fla., 1973-76; ptnr. Tew & Tew, Miami, Fla., 1976-77, Tew, Critchlow, Sonberg, et al, Miami, Fla., 1977-82, Finley, Kumble, Wagner, Underberg, Manley & Casey, Miami, Fla., 1982-88; mng. ptnr. McDermott, Will & Emery, Miami, Fla., 1988-91; ptnr. Kenny, Nachwalter, Seymour, Arnold & Critchow, Miami, Fla., 1991—. Arbitrator Nat. Assn. Securities Dealers, Miami, 1988—. Active United Way of Miami, 1991. Mem. ABA (vice-chmn. TIPS 1985-87), Fla. Bar Assn. (chmn. grievance com. 1987-90). Republican. Congregationalist. Office: Kenny Nachwalter Seymour Arnold & Critchow 201 S Biscayne Blvd Miami FL 33131-4332

CRITELLI, MICHAEL J., manufacturing executive, lawyer; b. 1948; m. Joyce Critelli; 3 children. BA, U. Wis., 1970; JD, Harvard U., 1974. Bar: Ill. 1974, NY 1982. Assoc. Ross & Hardies, Chgo., 1974-76, Schwartz & Freeman, Chgo., 1976-79; counsel Pitney Bowes, Inc., 1979-83, sr. counsel, 1983-84, asst. gen. counsel, 1984-86, assoc. gen. counsel, 1986-88, v.p., sec., gen. counsel, 1988, chief pers. officer, 1990-94, vice chmn., 1994—, chmn., CEO, 1996—2007, exec. chmn., 2007—. Office: Pitney Bowes Inc 1 Elmcroft Rd Stamford CT 06926-0700*

CRITELLI, NICHOLAS, lawyer, barrister; b. Des Moines, Iowa, Feb. 15, 1944; BA, Drake U., 1966, JD, 1967. Bar: Iowa 1967, US Supreme Ct. 1971, NY 1990, Eng. and Wales (Barrister Mid. Temple) 1991. Founder, ptnr. Law Chambers of Nicholas Critelli PC, Des Moines, IA, and London, Eng., 1967—. Adj. prof. trial law and practice Drake U., 1980—89. Mem. Civil Justice Reform Act com. US Dist. Ct., 1990—97; mem. adv. com. rules of evidence Iowa Supreme Ct. Recipient InnovAction award, Coll. of Law Practice Mgmt., 2004. Fellow: Soc. Advanced Legal Studies (London), Iowa Criminal Def. Assn. (bd. gov. 1997), Am. Acad. Trial Lawyers, Internat. Soc. Barristers; mem.: Honorable Soc. Blackstone Inn of Ct. (pres. and master of the bench), Honourable Soc. Mid. Temple Inn of Ct. (London), Am. Bd. Trial Advocates, Am. Arbitration Assn., Internat. Bar Assn., ABA (mem. litig. sect., torts and ins.sect., and internat. law sect.), NY State Bar Assn. (mem. litig. sect., mem. internat. law sect.), Iowa Acad. Trial Lawyers (gov. 1981, pres. 1986—87), Iowa State Bar Assn. (chmn. litig. legis. com. 1988—90, chmn. spl. com. on fgn. practice 1989—95, chmn. professionalism com. 1989—96, pres. 2004). Avocation: amateur radio. Office: Critelli Law Ste 950 317 Sixth Ave Des Moines IA 50309-4128 also: Barrister's Chambers 9 Stone Bldgs Lincoln's Inn London WC2A 3NN England*

CRITES, CARL D., auditor; b. Cushing, Oklahoma, Aug. 13, 1956; s. Paul W. and Anna F. Crites; m. Sue B. Britton, Dec. 20, 1986; 1 child, Courtney B. BS in Elec. Engring. Tech., Okla. State U., 1986; MS in Mgmt., So. Nazarene U., 1994; MBA, Okla. City U., 1998. Audio visual technician White Ho. Comm. Agy., Washington, 1975—78; sound technician Tele Hifi, Tulsa, 1980—84; sr. assoc. systems engr. E-Systems, ETAG, Fairfax, Va., 1987—89; systems engr., paws support team leader Eagle Tech., Fairfax, 1989—92; v.p. Okla. ops. Potomac Systems Engring., Okla. City, 1992—95; staff engr. BDM Internat., Okla. City, 1995—97; yr. 2000 project mgr. U. Okla., Norman, 1997—99; sr. assoc. PriceWaterhouseCoopers, Okla. City, 1999—2001; info. systems audit supr. The Hertz Corp., Okla. City, 2001—; sr. info. sys. auditor Kerr-McGee Corp., 2003—05; sr. assoc. Grant Thornton LLP, Oklahoma City, 2006—. Bd. dirs. Mid. Earth Child Devel. Ctr., Norman, Okla., 1996—99, mem. fund raising com., 2000—05; info. systems audit cons., Okla. City, 2002—03. Served in US Army, 1975—78. Mem.: Inst. Internal Auditors (cert. internal auditor), Info. Systems Control and Audit Assn. (cert. info. sys. auditor). Democrat. Avocation: auto racing. Home: 1608 Old Farm Rd Norman OK 73072 Office: Grant Thorton LLP 211 N Robinson Ste 1200 Oklahoma City OK 73102 Office Phone: 405-218-2887. Business E-Mail: carl.crites@gt.com.

CRITES, RICHARD RAY, financial planner, finance company executive, investment advisor; b. Rapid City, SD, Aug. 29, 1952; s. Charles Dayton and Marcia Ann (Heil) C.; m. Randel E. Golobic, Dec. 27, 1980 (div. May 1988); m. Ellen L. Edmondson, Mar. 13, 1998. B of Liberal Studies, U. Okla., 1975; MS, Stanford U., 1978; cert. sr. security checker, Advanced Orgn. L.A., 1987, cert. false purpose rundown auditor, 1988. Cert. staff status II, exec. status I, Am. St. Hill Orgn., exec. dir. full hat course Celebrity Ctr. Internat., 1992; cert. in ins.: series 7 securities lic., series 63, series 24 gen. securities principal lic., series 66 investment adv. rep. lic.; cert. life and disability ins., Fla.; lic. mortgage broker, Fla. From nat. sales trainer to regional sales mgr. Continental Mktg. Corp., Detroit, 1975—80; pres., CEO Retail Packaging Specialists, Inc., San Mateo, Calif., 1982-86; owner, CEO Miracle Method of San Mateo, Inc., 1985-87, Miracle Method of Beverly Hills, Inc., LA, 1987-90, Miracle Method of So. Calif., Inc., LA, 1986-92, Miracle Method of No. Calif., Inc., LA, 1988-89; v.p., treas., chmn. bd. Miracle Method of the U.S., Inc., LA, 1988-92; pres., chmn. bd. Internat. Miracle Method Appearance Ctrs. Pacific, Inc., LA, 1988-92, Internat. Miracle Method Ctrs. Equip. & Supply, Inc., LA, 1989-92; pres., chmn. bd. dirs. Miracle Method of the U.S., Inc., LA, 1992-96; gen. mgr. Stellar Mgmt. Co., LA, 1993-96; mng. mem. Stellar Mgmt. LLC, 1996—; securities prin. WMA Securities, Inc., Norcross, Ga., 1996—2002; mgr. br. office Graham Group Mortgage Corp., 2001—; registered rep., br. office supr., investment advisor rep. CapWest Securities, 2002; investment adv. rep., registered rep. SAL Fin. Svcs., Inc., Birmingham, Ala., 2002—04; securities prin., br. office mgr. Equity Leadership Securities Group, Inc., 2004—07; securities prin., br. mgr. First Founders Securities, Inc., 2007—. Trustee New Civilization Found., 1996—. Author: First Founders Financial New Associate Training Course and Resource Manual, 2007. Mem. Citizen's Commn. on Human Rights, Citizens for an Alternative Tax System. Mem. Internat. Assn. Scientologists (sponsor), Assn. for Better Living Through Edn. Republican. Scientologist. Avocations: skiing, jazz vocal music, tennis, camping, flying. Office: Stellar Mgmt LLC 600 Bypass Dr Ste 106 Clearwater FL 33764 Office Phone: 727-726-2447. Office Fax: 727-726-7338.

CRITTENDEN, DANIELLE ANN, writer, journalist; b. Toronto, Ont., Can., Apr. 20, 1963; d. Maxwell John Crittenden and Yvonne Ann (Wilson) Worthington; m. David Jeffrey Frum, June 26, 1988; children: Miranda Ann, Nathaniel Saul. Reporter Toronto Sun, 1983-86; founding editor Women's Quar., Arlington, Va., 1994-99; columnist The Nat. Post, NYC, 1999; contbr. Nat. Pub. Radio; contbr. blogger The Huffington Post, 2005—. Author: What Our Mothers Didn't Tell Us: Why Happiness Eludes the Modern Woman, 1999, Amanda Bright@home, 2003. Jewish. Office: c/o William Morris Agency 1325 Avenue of the Americas New York NY 10019 E-mail: danielle@daniellecrittenden.com.

CRITTENDEN, GARY LEWIS, diversified financial services company executive; b. Ogden, Utah, July 13, 1953; s. Charles Lee and Ruth Emily (Fowers) C.; m. Catherine Jean Cox, Dec. 19, 1975; children: KelliAnn, Stephanie, Spencer. BS, Brigham Young U., 1976; MBA, Harvard U., 1979. V.p. Bain & Co., Boston, 1979—90; exec. v.p. Filene's Basement, Wellesley, Mass., 1990—94; CFO Melville Corp., Rye, NY, 1994—95, Sears Roebuck & Co., 1996—98; sr. v.p., CFO Monsanto Co., 1998—2000; exec. v.p., CFO Am. Express Co., NYC, 2000—07, head Global Network Services unit, 2005—07; CFO Citigroup Inc., NYC, 2007—. Mem. Lds Ch. Avocation: running. Office: Citigroup Inc 399 Park Ave New York NY 10043*

CRITTENDEN, JOHN CHARLES, engineering educator; b. Nov. 12, 1949; BS in Chem. Engring., U. Mich., 1971, MS in Civil and Environ. Engring., 1972, PhD in Civil and Environ. Engring., 1976. Sr. v.p. Limno-Tech, Inc., Ann Arbor, Mich., 1975-77; asst. prof. civil and environ. engring. Wash. State U., Pullman, 1977-78; asst. prof. civil engring., environ. engring. sect. U. Ill., Urbana, 1978-79, Mich. Tech. U., Houghton, 1979-81, assoc. prof. civil engring., environ. engring. sect., 1981-84, adj. prof. chem. engring., 1981-84, prof. civil and environ. engring., 1984—. Dir. Ctr. for Clean Indsl. and Treatment Techs., Houghton, 1992—; presdl. prof. civil engring. CenCITT Mich. Tech. U., 1988—. Mem. AIChE, ASCE (Rudolph Hering award 1980, Walter L. Huber rsch. prize 1991), Am. Acad. Environ. Engrs., Water Pollution Control Fedn., Internat. Soc. Humic Substances, Assn. Environ. Engring. Profs., Am. Water Works Assn. (publs. award 1989), Am. Chem. Soc. Achievements include patents in field. Office: Mich Tech U Dept Civil & Environ Engr 1400 Townsend Dr Houghton MI 49931-1200

CRNKOVICH, RUTH ANNE, art appraiser, museum director; b. Dayton, Ohio, Aug. 31, 1967; d. Donald Paul and Odette Maria Burks; children: Maxwell Thomas, Trevor Paul. AA in Art, South Suburban Coll., 1989; BA in Art, Governors State U., 1992, MA in Art History, 1997. Cert. Appraisers Assn. Am., NYC, 2004, Appraisers Assn. Am., NYC, 2002. Curator Brauer Mus. Art, Valparaiso U., Ind., 1998—99; dir. exhbns. No. Ind. Arts Assn., Munster, 2000—04; founder and pres. CRN Fine Art Svcs., Chgo., 2002—; exec. dir. Nat. Vietnam Veterans Art Mus., Chgo., 2004—, Tall Grass Arts Assn., Park Forest, Ill., 2006. Cons. No. Ind. Arts Assn., Munster, 2004—, Shimmery Gallery, Munster, 2004—; fundraising chair Bridge Mag., Chgo., 2004—. Dir., curator (exhibitions) That 70s Show: The Age of Pluralism in Chicago, Karamu: Remnants of Ritual, Imagined Vistas: Paintings By Paul Sierra, Children of War, Valor: The Warsaw Uprising, Emergence: Women Artists in the New Millennium, Relections in Silver, Sideshow of the Absurd, Celebration in Glass, Emergence: Women Artists in the New Millennium, Beyond Icons: Contemporary Art in Armenia, prodr., curator Semper fidelis: How I Met My Father. Vol. FRIENDS of Braur Mus. Art, Valparaiso, Ind., 2002—04; mem. Columbia Coll. Photography Mus. Auxillary Bd., Chgo., 2004—05. Scholar, Governors State U., 1995-1997. Mem.: AAM (assoc.), Appraisers Assn. Am. (assoc.), Aumni Assn. Governors State U. (assoc.), Soc. Contemporary Art (assoc.), Am. Craft (assoc.), Arts Club of Washington DC (assoc.). Home: 10033 Gettler St Dyer IN 46311 Home Phone: 219-365-7350; Office Phone: 219-313-9960. Personal E-mail: info@crnart.com.

CROAN, ROBERT JAMES, music critic; b. NYC, Apr. 30, 1937; s. Sydney Joseph and Sylvia (Zorn) C. BA, Columbia U., 1958, MA, 1959; PhD, Boston U., 1968. Prof. voice Duquesne U. Sch. of Music, Pitts., 1962-2000, chmn., 1983-2000; ret. Pitts. Post-Gazette, 1999, music critic, 1964-99, sr. editor, 1999—. Mem. Music Critics Assn. N.Am. (chmn. ednl. activities 1978-90, pres. 1997-2001), Nat. Assn. Tchrs. of Singing. Democrat. Avocations: travel, culinary arts. E-mail: rcroan@lycos.com.

CROCE, ANNE LALLY, nurse, commissioner; b. Staten Island, NY, Mar. 7, 1926; d. Austin and Anne (McStravick) Lally; m. James P. Croce Jr., June 9, 1951; children: Patricia L. Balcom, James Peter III, Kathleen Kampmann. Diploma, Bayonne Hosp. Sch. Nursing, 1949; postgrad., Polyclinic Med. Sch. and Hosp., 1950, Osaka U., Japan, 1951. Sch. nurse Friends Acad., Long Island, NY; pub. sch. nurse, day care nurse Roslyn Pub. Schs., LI; sch., camp nurse Doug Pierce/Price County Day Sch., LI; commr., ombudsman Town of North Hempstead, Manhasset, NY, 1989—. Pub. educator on blood pressure, CPR, diet; featured on local TV and in local newspaper. Bd. dirs. Roslyn Little League (Women of the Year award), Community Mammography and Breast Cancer Screening, Local Emergencies Planning Com., SARA III Program, Community Plus Program for Srs., Free Flu Shots Program; liason Town North Hempstead Civic Assn., Martin Luther King Edn., L.I. Heart Coun. (Gold Madalion award). Recipient Women of the Year award Roslyn Rotary Club., Roslyn Kiwanis Club. Mem. N.A.A.C.P. Office: Town North Hempstead 220 Plandome Rd Manhasset NY 11030-2399

CROCE, ARLENE, critic; b. Providence, May 5, 1934; d. Michael Daniel and Louise Natalie (Pensa) C. Student, Women's Coll., U. N.C., 1951-53; BA, Barnard Coll., 1955. Founder, editor Ballet Rev., 1965-78; dance critic New Yorker mag., 1973-98. Dance panelist Nat. Endowment for Arts, 1977-80. Author: The Fred Astaire & Ginger Rogers Book, 1972, Afterimages, 1977, Going to the Dance, 1982, Sight Lines, 1987, Writing in the Dark, Dancing in the New Yorker, 2000. Recipient AAAL award 1979, award of Honor for Arts and Culture Mayor N.Y.C., 1979, Janeway prize Barnard Coll., 1955; Hodder fellow Princeton U., 1971; Guggenheim fellow, 1972, 86, NEH fellow 1992, Nat. Arts Journalism Program sr. fellow, 1999. Office: New Yorker Mag 4 Times Sq New York NY 10036-6561 Office Phone: 212-286-2860.

CROCKER, CHESTER ARTHUR, diplomat, federal agency administrator; b. NYC, Oct. 29, 1941; s. Arthur M. and Clare V.; m. Saone Baron, Dec. 18, 1965; children: Bathsheba, Karena, Rebecca. BA, Ohio State U., 1963; MA in Internat. Studies, Johns Hopkins U., 1965, PhD, 1969. News editor Africa Report, 1968-69; lectr. Am. U., 1969-70; staff officer NSC, 1970-72; dir. M.S. in Fgn. Svc. program Georgetown U., Washington, 1972-78, dir. African studies Ctr. for Strategic-Internat. Studies, 1976-81, disting. prof. diplomacy Sch. Fgn. Svc., 1989-98, James R. Schlesinger prof. strategic studies Sch. Fgn. Svc., 1998—; asst. sec. state African affairs, 1981-89. Cons. in strategy and negotiation; chmn. Africa working group Reagan campaign, 1980; coord. for Africa Bush campaign; bd. dirs. A.S.A. Ltd., Good Governance Group Ltd., Henry-Dunant Ctr. for Humanitarian Dialogue, Nat. Def. U., U.S. Inst. Peace, Universal Corp., First Africa Group, Ltd. Author: High Noon in Southern Africa, 1992, Managing Global Chaos, 1996, Herding Cats: Case Studies in International Mediation, 1999, Turbulent Peace: The Challenges of Managing International Conflict, 2001, Taming Intractable Conflicts: Mediation in the Hardest Cases, 2004, Grasping the Nettle: Analysing Cases of Intractable Conflict, 2005, Leashing the Dogs of War: Conflict Management in a Divided World, 2007, others; contbr. articles to profl. jours. Mem. adv. cmty. democratic promotion Dept. State; bd. dirs. housing HIV Found.; bd. dirs. Friends of South African Inst. Race Relations. Recipient Disting. Svc. award Sec. State, 1988, Presdl. Citizen's award, 1989 Mem. Coun. Fgn. Rels., Internat. Inst. Strategic Studies, Am. Acad. Diplomacy, Cosmos Club, Tahawus Club. Republican. Office: Georgetown U Sch Fgn Svc Intercultural Ctr Rm 801 Washington DC 20057-0001 Office Phone: 202-687-5074. Business E-Mail: crockerc@georgetown.edu.

CROCKER, JOHN C., chemical and biomolecular engineer, educator; AB in Physics, U. Chgo., 1990, AM in Physics, 1992, PhD in Physics, 1996. Skirkanich asst. prof. innovation in chem. engring. and chem. and biomolecular engring. U. Pa., Phila. Contbr. articles to sci. jours. Named one of Brilliant 10, Popular Sci. mag., 2005. Office: U Pa Chem and Biomolecular Engring 349 Towne Bldg 220 S 33rd St Philadelphia PA 19104-6393 Office Phone: 215-898-9188. Office Fax: 215-573-2093. E-mail: jcrocker@seas.upenn.edu.*

CROCKER, RAY DEAN, musician, musical director; b. Ft. Worth, Nov. 1, 1949; s. Ben Raglin and Nancy Mahota (Potts) C.; m. Emily Janice Holt. Student, Tex. Christian U., 1967-69; MusB, North Tex. State U., 1974, MusM, 1977. Pianist Casa Manana Musicals, Ft. Worth, 1979-83; mus. asst. Opera Theatre U. North Tex. (formerly North Tex. State U.), Denton, 1980-81, instr. music, 1983-84; staff accompanist Tex. Womans's U., Denton, 1982-85; mus. dir. Surflight Summer Theatre, Beach Haven, NJ, 1984-85; asst. condr. 42nd St., nat. tour, 1985-86; mus. dir. Dallas Repertory Theatre, 1986-89, Sacramento Music Circus, 1988-90, Oscar's Place Dinner Theatre, Milw., 1990, 42d St. European Tour Co., 1991-97, Great Lake Opera, Milw., 1992. Bd. dirs. Paint It Yellow Prodns., Inc., pres., 1999-2004 Composer: Twas the Night Before Christmas, 1983, Frosty the Snowman, 1985, others; condr.: Dreamgirls, 1988 Mem. ASCAP, Am. Fedn. Musicians, Dramatists Guild, Phi Mu Alpha, Kappa Kappa Psi, Alpha Psi Omega. Home: 2764 N 90th St Milwaukee WI 53222-4609 E-mail: dcrocker@operamail.com.

CROCKER, RYAN CLARK, ambassador; b. Spokane, Wash., June 19, 1949; m. Christina Barnes. BA, Whitman Coll., 1971; postgraduate student, Univ. Coll., Dublin, Ireland. Fgn. svc. officer US Consulate, Khorramshahr, Iran, 1972—74; econ. comml. officer Am. Embassy, Doha, Qatar, 1974—76, chief econ. /comml. sect. US interests sect. Baghdad, 1978—81, chief polit. sect. Beirut, 1981-84; dep. dir. Office Israel and Arab-Israeli Affairs US Dept. State, Washington, 1985-87; polit. counselor Am. Embassy, Cairo, 1987-90; US amb. to Lebanon US Dept. State, Beirut, 1990-93, US amb. to Kuwait Kuwait City, 1994-97, US amb. to Syria Damascus, 1998—2001, interim envoy to Afghanistan Kabul, 2002, dep. asst. sec. for Near Eastern Affairs Washington, 2001—03; dir. governance Coalition Provisional Authority, Baghdad, Iraq, 2003; internat. affairs adv. Nat. War Coll., 2003—04; US amb. to Pakistan US Dept. State, Islamabad, 2004—07, US amb. to Iraq Baghdad, 2007—. Office: Executive Office APO AE 09316

CROCKER, SAONE BARON, lawyer; b. Bulawayo, Zimbabwe, Jan. 11, 1943; came to U.S., 1963; d. Benjamin and Rachel (Joffe) Baron; m. Chester Arthur Crocker, Dec. 18, 1965; children: Bathsheba Nell, Karena Wynne, Rebecca Masten. BA, U. Cape Town, 1961, BA with honors, 1962; MA, Johns Hopkins U., 1966; JD cum laude, Georgetown U., 1983. Bar: DC 1983, U.S. Ct. Appeals (DC cir.) 1985, U.S. Dist. Ct. DC 1990, U.S. Supreme Ct. 1990, U.S. Ct. Appeals (7th cir.) 1991, U.S. Ct. Appeals (4th cir.) 1998. Adminstr. Guinea program African Am. Inst., Washington, 1965-66, author Africa Report, 1966; writer fgn. affairs divsn. Am. U., 1967—68; freelance writer, 1968—80; atty. firm Wilmer, Cutler & Pickering, 1983—84; clk. to judge U.S. Ct. Appeals for DC Circuit, 1984—85; atty. firm O'Melveny & Myers, 1985—90, Beveridge & Diamond, 1990—92, Wright & Talisman, P.C., 1992—2001; pvt. practice, 2001—. Contbg. author: Zambia Handbook, 1967. AAUW fellow, 1963-65; Fulbright fellow, 1963; Johns Hopkins U. fellow, 1964-65; recipient Lawyers Coop. Pub. Co. awards, 1980. Mem. ABA, AAUW (state pres. 1992-94), Fulbright Assn. Home Phone: 202-265-3366; Office Phone: 202-256-3366. Personal E-mail: saonec@aol.com.

CROCKER, SUZANNE, painter; m. Peter Crocker; children: Travis, Hayden. BA in History of Art cum laude, U. Pa., 1987; student, Montserrat Coll. Art, 1997—2000; studied with, Wolf Kahn and Cynthia Packard. One-woman shows include Hamilton Pub. Libr., Mass., 2000, Conomo Cafe, Essex, Mass., 2001, Copley Soc., Boston, 2004—05, Woodstock Folk Art, Vt., 2005—07, Powers Gallery, Acton, Mass., 2007, exhibited in group shows at Wenham Mus., Mass., 2000, Northshore Art Assn., 2001—04, Lyme Art Assn., Conn., 2002, 2004, Boltax Gallery, N.Y., 2002—05, Mingo Gallery, Mass., 2002, Nat. Arts Club Galleries, N.Y., 2002, River Gallery, Mass., 2002—03, Newburyport Art Assn., 2002—05, Michael Price Gallery, 2003, Copley Soc. Art, 2003—, Powers Gallery, Mass., 2004—07, Woodstock Folk Art, Vt., 2005—, This Old House Designer Showhouse (PBS TV), Mass., 2005, Green Mountain Cultural Ctr., Vt., 2005, Rocky Neck Art Gallery, Mass., 2005, Trinity Ch., 2005, Bennett St. Gallery, Atlanta, 2006—07, Gardner Colby Gallery, Martha's Vineyard, 2006—07, Left Bank Gallery, Wellfleet, Mass., 2006. Named Copley Artist, 2005; fellow, Vt. Studio Ctr., 2002, 2005. Mem.: Artists' Fellowship, Inc., Copley Soc. Art, Audubon Artists (assoc.), Allied Artists Am. (assoc.). Independent. Home Phone: 978-468-7842.

CROCKER, THOMAS DUNSTAN, economics professor; b. Bangor, Maine, July 22, 1936; s. Floyd M. and Gloria F. (Thomas) C.; m. Sylvia Fleming, Dec. 31, 1961 (div. Sept. 1986); children: Sarah Lydia, Trena Elizabeth; m. Judith Powell, Sept. 9, 1989. AB, Bowdoin Coll., 1959; PhD, U. Mo., 1967. Asst. prof. econs. U. Wis., Milw., 1963-70; assoc. prof. U. Calif., Riverside, 1970-75; prof. U. Wyo., Laramie, 1975-2001, chairperson dept. econs. and fin., 1991-93, dir. Sch. Environment and Natural Resources, 1993-98, J.E. Warren distng. prof of Energy and Environment, 1997—, disting. prof. emeritus, 2001—. Sr. rsch. assoc. U. Calif., Berkeley, 1973, Pa. State U., 1974; mem. sci. adv. bd. EPA, Washington, 1973—76, mem. panel, 1974, 75, 78, 81, 95, 97, 2001—02, 2004—06, NSF, 1977—80, 2002—03; cons. Asarco, Inc., 1985—89, Mathtech, Inc., Princeton, NJ, 1987—88, Princeton, 1999—2001, Shea and Gardner, Washington, 1989, Arco, Inc., 1992, A. Coors Co., 1992, Eastern Rsch. Group, 1997, Indsl. Econs., Inc., Cambridge, Mass., 1998—99; mem. panel on long range transport issues U.S. Congress, Washington, 1981; mem. Gov.'s Competition Rev. Com., State of Wyo. Co-author: Environmental Economics, 1971; author, editor: Economic Perspectives on Acid Deposition Control, 1984; editorial coun. Jour. Environ. Econs. and Mgmt., 1973-88, 95-99; contbr. articles to profl. jours. Mem. com. impacts pollution on agriculture Orgn. for Econ. Cooperation and Devel., Paris, 1987-88. Grantee, NSF, 1968, 1973, 1981, EPA, 1971, 1976—85, 1997—2005; scholar, Fulbright Found., 2001—06. Mem.: European Assn. Environ. Resource Econs., Assn. Environ. Resource Econs. (contributed papers com. 1989, Rsch. of Enduring Quality award 2002), Am. Econ. Assn. (mem. awards structure com. 1981—83), The Nature Conservancy. Republican. Avocations: skiing, bicycling, travel, trekking, rafting. Office: Univ Wyo Dept Econs Laramie WY 82071 Home Phone: 307-742-5169; Office Phone: 307-766-6423. Business E-Mail: tcrocker@uwyo.edu.

CROCKER, THOMAS EDWARD, lawyer; b. Washington, June 9, 1949; s. Thomas Edward and Miriam (Hedges) C.; m. Elizabeth Jane Lichte, Apr. 7, 1990; children: Edward Day Hedges, Thomas Paul August AB, Princeton U., 1971; JD, Columbia U., 1974. Bar: D.C. 1976, U.S. Ct. Appeals (D.C. cir.) 1976. Assoc. Hunton & Williams, Washington, 1974-76; fgn. svc. officer U.S. Dept. of State, 1976-81; assoc. Quarles & Brady, Washington, 1981-83; atty. Shaw, Pittman, Potts & Trowbridge, Washington, 1983—96; ptnr., co-chmn., internat. trade and regulatory group Alston & Bird LLP, Washington, 1996—. Contbr. articles to profl. jours. Mem. ABA, DC Bar, Met. Club, Chevy Chase Club Episcopalian. Avocations: reading, history, writing, squash. Office: Alston & Bird LLP 950 F St NW Washington DC 20004-1404 Office Phone: 202-756-3318. Office Fax: 202-756-3333. Business E-Mail: tcrocker@alston.com.

CROCKER, WILLIAM HENRY, ethnologist, researcher; b. San Francisco, Aug. 20, 1924; s. William Willard and Ruth (Hobart) C.; m. Roma Dillon Smyth, Apr. 11, 1969 (div. Nov. 1983); 1 child, Myles Hobart; m. Jean Galloway Thomas, Dec. 19, 1987. BA, Yale Coll., 1950; MA, Stanford U., 1953; PhD, U. Wis., 1962. Curator Smithsonian Inst., Washington, 1962-93, emeritus curator, 1993—. Author: The Canela: An Ethnographic Introduction, 1990; co-author: The Canela: Kinship, Ritual and Sex in an Amazonian Tribe, 2004. Trustee World Learning, Inc., Brattleboro, Vt., 1974-92. Cpl. U.S. Army, 1943-46. Mem. Bohemian Club, Cosmos Club. Democrat. Avocation: photography. Home: 4 Chalfont Ct Bethesda MD 20816-1805 Office: Smithsonian Inst Dept Anthropology MRC 112 Washington DC 20560-0112

CROCKETT, ANDREW DUNCAN, bank executive; b. Mar. 23, 1943; s. Andrew and Sheilah (Stewart) C.; m. Marjorie Hlavacek, 1966; 3 children. Student, Queens' Coll., Cambridge U., Eng., Yale U. Staff member Internat. Monetary Fund, 1972-89; exec. dir. Bank of England, London, 1989—93; gen. mgr. Bank Internat. Settlements, Basel, Switzerland, 1994—2003; pres. J.P. Morgan Chase Internat., NYC, 2003—. Chmn. Fin. Stability Forum, 1999-2003, Per Jacobsen Found., Internat. Counsel China Banking Regulatory Commn. Contbr. articles to profl. jours. Avocations: reading, golf, tennis. Office: JP Morgan Chase Internat 15th Fl 277 Park Ave New York NY 10017-2014

CROCKETT, DODEE FROST, brokerage house executive; b. Oklahoma City, Oct. 19, 1956; d. Carl S. Frost and Mikki (Matheny) Marcus; m. Billy Crockett. M in Theol. Studies, So. Meth. U., Dallas, 2003. Chartered advisor in philantropy 2005, cert. divorce fin. analyst 2006. 1st v.p., wealth mgmt. advisor Merrill Lynch Pvt. Client, Dallas, 1980—. Bd. dirs. Ronald McDonald House of Dallas, 1992—, Dallas Social Venture Ptnrs., 2003—, chair of bd., 2005; trustee Dallas Opera, 1991—; exec. bd. Perkins Sch. Theology, So. Meth. U., Dallas, 2003-; found. adv. bd. Dallas Found.; pres. Cir. Shared Housing Ctr., Dallas. Mem. Nat. Assn. Securities Dealers (gen. securities prin., mcpl. securities rulemaking bd. prin., registered options prin., bd. arbitrators), NYSE (com. mem.), Merrill Lynch Dirs. Cir. Office: Merrill Lynch Pierce Fenner and Smith 2000 Premier Pl 5910 N Central Expy Ste 2000 Dallas TX 75206-5152

CROCKETT, DONALD HAROLD, composer, music educator; b. Pasadena, Calif., Feb. 18, 1951; s. Harold Brown and Martha Amy C.; m. Karen Anne Gallagher Crockett, Nov. 11, 1972 (div. 1986); 1 child: Katherine Jane Crockett; m. Vicki Lyn Ray, June 6, 1988. MusB, U. So. Calif., 1974, MusM, 1976; PhD, U. Calif., Santa Barbara, 1981. Composer-in-residence Pasadena Chamber Orch., 1984-86, L.A. Chamber Orch., 1991-97. Asst. prof. U. So. Calif., L.A. 1981-84, assoc. prof., 1984-94, prof. 1994—; music dir., condr. U. So. Calif. Contemporary Music Ensemble, L.A., 1984—, Xtet, 1992-; sr. composer-in-residence Chamber Music Conf. and Composers Forum of the East, 2002—. Composer: Celestial Mechanics oboe and string quartet, 1990, Array string quartet number 1, 1987, Roethke Preludes for Orchestra, 1994, Concerto for Piano and Wind Ensemble, 1988, Scree for cello, piano and percussion, 1997, Island for concert band, 1998, The Falcon's Eye for solo guitar, 2000, Cascade for orchestra, 2001, Blue Earth for orchestra, 2002, The Ceiling of Heaven for piano quartet, 2004, Fanfares and Laments for orchestra, 2005. Recipient Friedheim award Kennedy Ctr., Washington, 1991, Aaron Copland award Copland House, 1998, Sylvia Goldstein award Copland House, 2003; Goddard Lieberson fellow Am. Acad. Arts and Letters, N.Y.C., 1994; Nat. Endowment for the Arts grantee, Washington, 1993; artists' fellow Calif. Arts Coun., 1999; Guggenheim fellow, 2006; Bogliasco fellow, 2006.

Mem. BMI, Am. Music Ctr., Am. Composers Forum, Phi Kappa Phi. Avocations: reading, backpacking, skiing. Office: Univ Southern Calif Thornton School Of Music Los Angeles CA 90089-0851 E-mail: dcrocket@usc.edu.

CROCKETT, FRANK MCCLUNG, retired arts and music educator; b. Jonesville, Va., July 25, 1921; s. Frank McClung Crockett and Elizabeth Wynn; m. Wanda Hill, Dec. 28, 1983; m. Betty Jean Weldon (dec.); 1 child, Lisa. BS Violin, Juilliard, NYC, 1949; MM, U. Tex., Austin, Tex., 1952; EdD Music Edn., U. Ill., Urbana, Ill., 1960. Cert. T7 Tchg.at doctoral level Ga., 1986. Instr. of violin and viola Edinboro State Teachers Coll., Edinboro, Pa., 1949—50; coord. string project U. Tex., Austin, Tex., 1950—52; coord. string instrn. U. Miss., Oxford, Miss., 1952—54; assoc. prof. music U. So. Miss., Hattiesburg, Miss., 1954—58; coord. arts and humanities Ga. Dept. of Edn., Atlanta, 1958—86. Pres. So. Divsn. Music Tchrs. Nat. Assn., 1960—62; chmn. Nat. Interscholastic Activities Commn. of Music Educators, 1957—60; chmn. nat. com. on music tchg. Music Tchrs. Nat. Assn., 1964—67; exec. sec. Ga. Music Coun., Ga., 1960—86; organizer, condr. South Miss. Youth Orch.; guest faculty, conductor U. Tex., U. Mich., U. Ala., U. Fla. State., Va. Music Camp, Nat. Music Camp Interlochen, Mich. Author: Organizing String Programs; contbr. Ga. Govs. Honors Program, scientific papers. Mem. Philharmonic Orch., Erie, Pa., 1949—50; vol. Atlanta Symphony Orch., 1995—2004; pres. Atlanta Music Club, 1991—94. T-5 US Army, 1943—46, European Theater. Recipient Disting. Career Award, Ga. Music Educators Assn., Bicentennial Award, Ga. C. of C., 1974 1975 1976, Disting. Svc., Atlanta Music Club; Danforth Tchr. Study Grant, Danforth Found. Mem.: Am. String Tchrs. Assn. (pres. 1991—94), Music Educators Nat. Conf., Ga. Music Educators Assn. (Disting. Career Award 1999). Achievements include development of music program for Ga. Govs. Honors Program. Avocations: travel, music, coaching chamber music. Home: 2553 Rivermont Cir Kingsport TN 37660 Home Phone: 423-245-1481.

CROCKETT, JOAN M., insurance company executive; B in Polit. Sci., John Carroll Univ., 1972. Underwriter, various positions in human resources Allstate Ins. Co., 1973—94, sr. v.p. human resources, 1994—. Bd. dirs. INROADS; adv. bd. Univ. Ill. Chgo. Internat. Student Exchange Program; ptnr., bd. dirs. Ctr. for Human Resource Mgmt. Univ. Ill., gov. coun. Good Shepherd Hosp., Barrington, Ill. Named Human Resource Exec. of Yr., Human Resource Exec. mag., 1997. Mem.: Nat. Acad. Human Resources. Office: Allstate Corp 2775 Sanders Rd Northbrook IL 60062-6127 Office Phone: 847-402-5000. Office Fax: 847-326-7519.*

CROCKETT, KRISTEN MICHELLE, director; b. Washington, Dec. 12, 1976; d. Michael Anthony and Janet Gray Crockett. BA in Comm., Loyola U., New Orleans, 1998; MA in Film/Video, Am. U., Washington, 2000; JD, George Washington U., Washington, 2003. Bar: DC 2004. Youth devel. facilitator Coll. Summit, Washington, 2000—; dir. programs Thurgood Marshall Acad., Washington, 2005—. Mem.: ABA. Home: 1343 Locust Rd NW Washington DC 20012 Home Phone: 202-487-6697; Office Phone: 202-563-6862. Personal E-mail: kristen_crockett@yahoo.com.

CROFFIE, JOSEPH M., gastroenterologist, educator; b. Lawra, Ghana, Mar. 16, 1953; s. William Aloysius and Monica Ama Croffie; m. Grace Irene Dadzie, Feb. 28, 1981; children: Joseph William, Jeremy Sylvanus, Samantha Danielle. BS, Ctrl. State U., Edmond, Okla., 1979; MPH, U. of Okla. Health Sci Ctr., Oklahoma City, 1980; MD, U. of Liberia, Monrovia, 1985. Diplomate Am. Bd. of Pediat. with subspecialty in pediat. gastroenterology, 1991. Resident in pediat. James Whitcomb Riley Hosp. for Children, Ind. U. Sch. of Medicine, Indpls., 1988—91, fellow in pediat. gastroenterology, 1991—94; staff pediat. gastroenterologist James Whitcomb Riley Hosp. for Children, 1994—; assoc. prof. of clin. pediat. Ind. U. Sch. of Medicine, Indpls., 2001—. Dir. of gastrointestinal motility lab. James Whitcomb Riley Hosp. for Children, 1995—. Co-author (with others): (textbook) Idiopathic Constipation in Children, 2004; contbr. articles to profl. jours. Recipient WoW! award for care in delivery of health care, Deaconness Hosp., Evansville , Ind., 2006. Fellow: Am. Acad. of Pediat., Am. Coll. of Gastroenterology; mem.: Gastroenterology Rsch. Group, Am. Motility Soc., N. Am. Soc. of Pedia. Gastroenterology, Hepatology and Nutrition. Achievements include research in in pediatric gastroenterology. Office: James W Riley Hospital for Children 702 Barnhill Dr Indianapolis IN 46202 Office Phone: 317-274-3774. Office Fax: 317-274-8521. E-mail: jcroffie@iupui.edu.

CROFT, CANDACE ANN, psychology professor, academic administrator, small business owner; b. Lancaster, Wis., Jan. 14, 1957; d. Wilford Stanley and Myrna Viola Croft. BA, St. Olaf Coll., 1979; MS, U. Ariz., 1980; PhD, Pa. State U., 1984. Psychotherapist Forrester Clinic, Chgo., 1984-86; dir. rsch. on child and adolescent health Am. Acad. Ped., Elk Grove Village, Ill., 1986-92; dir. rsch. and sci. affairs Am. Acad. Orthop. Surgeons, Rosemont, Ill., 1992-94; sr. program assoc. Aon Found., Chgo., 1994-95; dir. Strong Spirit Wellness Ctr., Chgo., 1995-96; adj. prof. DePaul U., Chgo., 1993-96; assoc. prof. psychology, chmn. dept. psychology Clarke Coll., Dubuque, Iowa, 1996—2003, chair instl. rev. bd., 2000—03; dean health and human svc. occupations SW Tech. Coll., Fennimore, Wis., 2003—06; pres. Tabankhu, LLC, 2005—; dean Kaplan U., 2007—. Textbook reviewer McGraw-Hill, 1998-2003; media contact Clarke Coll.-Fox-40, Dubuque, Iowa, TV Sta. KWWL, Dubuque, Nat. Coun. Family Rels., St. Paul, 1998—, state policy liason, 2006—; adv. Clarke Coll.; owner Heart Light Shining; aromatherapist, appreciative inquiry facilitator. Author: Annalia's Simply Splendid, 2003, Growing Good Hearts: The Rooting Years, 2005, The Tao of the Magician, 2005; contbr. articles to sci. and profl. jour.; exec. prodr. film Heart of the Matter, 1991 (bronze award Houston Internat. Film Festival 1991); contbr. Living With Heart, 2002—. Mem. liturg. ministry St. Mary's Ch., Platteville, Wis., 1999—2001. Mem. Nat. Coun. Family Rels. (cert. family life educator), Assn. Humanistic Psychology, Inst. Noetic Scis., Assn. for Transpersonal Psychology, Phi Kappa Phi, Omicron Nu. Avocations: writing, music, aerobics, swimming, photography. Home and Office: 119 North Monroe Lancaster WI 53813 Office Phone: 877-252-8454. Personal E-mail: cacroft@chorus.net.

CROFT, GEORGE T., physicist; b. Washington, Sept. 29, 1926; s. William Thomas and Georgietta (Lyon) C.; m. Geraldine Frizzel (div. Feb. 1995); children: Linda Marie, David Thomas, John Frizzell Croft; m. Nancy Mitchell, Aug. 14, 1996. BS in Physics, Western Md. Coll., Westminster, 1948; PhD in Physics, U. Pa., 1953. Rsch. physicist McGraw-Edison, West Orange, N.J., 1953-58; dir. R&D and staff engrng. Pitney Bowes, Stamford, Conn., 1958-70; v.p. corp. R&D and staff engrng. Addressograph-Multigraph, Cleve., 1970-76; v.p. R&D Am. Optical, Southbridge, Mass., 1976-80; pres. Technol. Resources Mgmt. Group, Hilton Head Island, S.C., 1980-87; dir. Coll. of Hilton Head U. S.C., Hilton Head Island, 1983-85; instr. physics and math. Savannah (Ga.) Tech. Inst., 1987-95; asst. adj. prof. physics U. S.C., Beaufort, 1995—. Pres. Intellectual Resources Group, Inc., 1992—; mem. adv. coun. to dean engrng. U. Mass., Amherst, 1978-83; mem. R&D coun. Am. Mgmt. Assn., 1975-1980; mem. corp. assoc. adv. com. Am. Phys. Soc., 1977-80. Author: Three Dimensional Analytic Geometry, 2000, Applications of Three Dimensional Analytic Geometry, 2002; contbr. articles to profl. jours. Served with USNR, 1945-46, PTO. Mem. IEEE, Am. Phys. Soc. Achievements include staffing and organizing 3 research and development labs and establishing product development and related research programs in them; product development in office equipment and optical equipment industries; patents on safe hand gun locks. Home: 22 Coventry Ct Bluffton SC 29910-5706 E-mail: geotomirg@aol.com.

CROFT, HARRY ALLEN, psychiatrist; b. Houston, July 2, 1943; s. Louis and Ida (Kaplan) C.; m. Benay Bleacher, Dec. 27, 1964; children: Jamie Sue, Bradley Lane, Chasen Ashley. BS, So. Meth. U., 1964; MD, U. Tex. at Galveston, 1968. Intern Brackenridge Hosp., Austin, 1968-69; resident in obstetrics and gynecology U. Tex. Med. Br., 1969-70, resident in psychiatry, 1970-73; dir. methadone program Galveston County, Tex.; dir. sex therapy program U. Tex., Galveston, 1972-73; commd. capt. U.S. Army, 1973, advanced through grades to maj., 1975; chief (Mental Hygiene Service, Brooke Army Med. Center), Houston, 1973-76; pvt. practice, 1976—; med. dir. San Antonio Psychiat. Rsch. Ctr., 1988—. Clin. asst. prof. psychiatry and ob-gyn. Med. Sch. San Antonio, 1973-75; columnist San Antonio Express-News, 1975-76; weekly contbr. Sta. KMOL-TV (NBC) newscast, also KENS TV, 1988-90, KMOL TV, 1990-92; dir. rsch. and edn. Covenant Behavioral Health. Contbr. articles to profl. jours. Recipient physician's recognition award AMA, 1974, awards for med. TV work Nat. Healthcare Assn., 1988, Women in Comm., 1988; Meritorious Svc. medal U.S. Army, 1976, Ware 1st place audio-visual award Dept. Army, 1976, Gov.'s award State of Tex., 1991, award City of San Antonio, award Acad. Radio and TV Health Comm., Jules Bergman award-Broadcaster of Yr. award, 1995, Best Radio Show In U.S., Nat. Mental Health Assn., 1996; named Honoree, Am. Heart Assn., 2003. Mem. Am. Psychiat. Assn. (award 1991), Tex. Med. Assn. (award 1988), Am. Soc. Sex Educators, Counselors and Therapists, Am. Soc. Addiction Medince (cert. addictionist). Home: 12738 Hunters Chase St San Antonio TX 78230-1930 Office: 8038 Wurzbach Rd Ste 570 San Antonio TX 78229-3815 Home Phone: 210-602-9418; Office Phone: 210-692-1222. E-mail: hacmd@aol.com.

CROFT, JANET BRENNAN, academic librarian; b. Pitts., May 5, 1961; d. Earl David and Marian (Maxwell) Brennan; m. Duane Shiffler, Aug. 11, 1984; 1 child, Sarah Gail. BA in English & Classical Civilization, Ind. U., 1982, MLS, 1983. Libr. Jenner and Block Law Firm, Chgo., 1983-84, Carnegie Libr. Pitts., 1985, Sewickley (Pa.) Pub. Libr., 1985-88, Moon Twp. Pub. Libr., Coraopolis, Pa., 1988-89, 90; libr. dir. Martin Meth. Coll., Pulaski, Tenn., 1993-2000; head access svcs. U. Okla. Libr., 2001—. Author: War and the Works of J.R.R. Tolkien, 2004, Legal Solutions in Electronic Reserves and Electronic Delivery of Interlibrary Loan, 2004; editor: Tolkien on Film, 2004, Tolkien and Shakespeare, 2006; editor jour. Mythlore, 2006-; editor (newsletter): Okla. Libr., 2006-; contbr. articles to profl. jours. Mem.: ALA, Popular Culture Assn., Mythopoeic Soc. (Inklings Scholarship award 2005). Office: U Okla Bizzell 104NW 401 W Brooks St Norman OK 73019-6030 Office Phone: 405-325-1918. Business E-Mail: jbcroft@ou.edu.

CROFT, JOSEPH DAVID, medical educator; s. Joseph D. and Julia Croft; m. Betty Jane Grubb, Sept. 3, 1960; children: Joseph D., Julia Croft Peterson. BA cum laude, Princeton U., Cornell, Md., 1958; MD, Cornell U., NYC, 1962. Lic. rheumatologist DC, 1969; NY, 1964, Md., 1973. Intern, resident, chief med. resident, rheumatology fellow Strong Meml. Hosp., U. Rochester, NY, 1962—67; clin. assoc. Nat. Cancer Inst., NIH, 1967—69; private practice rheumatology, 1969—. Clin. prof. medicine, rheumatology Georgetown U. Med. Sch., Washington, 1989—; pres. Am. Coll. Rheumatology, Atlanta, 1999—2000. Contbr. articles to profl. jours. Recipient Maters award, Am. Coll. Rheumatology, 2002. Office: Arthritis and Rheumatism Assocs 5530 Wisconsin Ave Chevy Chase MD 20815 Office Phone: 240-497-0230. Office Fax: 240-497-0233. Personal E-mail: jdcroft@aol.com.

CROFT, KATHRYN DELAINE, social worker, consultant; b. Eastover, SC, Jan. 13, 1944; d. Randolph and Ethel (Williams) Lloyd; m. Daniel Marranzini, June 26, 1987. BS, Wilberforce U., 1965; MS, Columbia U., 1982, New Sch. for Social Rsch., 1988. Cert. social worker, N.Y. Exec. dir. Family Dynamics, Inc., NYC, 1987—92; asst. provost Columbia U., NYC, 1992—94; commr. N.Y.C. Child Welfare Adminstrn., NYC, 1994—96; dir. ops. Just One Break, Inc., NYC, 1997—2000, exec. dir., 2000—02; chief program officer ARC Greater N.Y.C., 2002—04; adminstrv. dir. supported housing and real property Women-in-Need, Inc., 2004—. Cons. various nonprofit orgns., N.Y.C., 1996—. Bd. dirs. Artsgenesis, N.Y.C., 1993—, chmn., 1996-99; bd. dirs. Ackerman Inst., N.Y.C., 1997-2000. Recipient scholarships New Sch. for Social Rsch., 1985-88, Columbia U., 1978-82. Mem. NAFE, Assn. Black Women in Higher Edn. Avocations: travel, reading, photography. Office: 115 W 31st St New York NY 10001

CROFT, TERRENCE LEE, lawyer, mediator, arbitrator; b. St. Louis, Apr. 13, 1940; s. Thomas L. and Anita Belle Croft; m. Merry Patton, July 9, 1977; children: Michael, Shannon, Kimberly, Kristin, BethAnn, Katherine. AB, Yale U., 1962; JD with distinction, U. Mich. Law Sch., 1965. Bar: Mo. 1965, Ga. 1970, Fla. 1970, US Ct. Appeals (5th, 8th and 11th cirs.), US Supreme Ct. Assoc. Coburn, Croft & Kohn, St. Louis, 1965—69, Hansell, Post, Brandon & Dorsey, Atlanta, 1969—73; ptnr. Huie, Sterne & Ide, Atlanta, 1973—78, Kutak, Rock & Huie, Atlanta, 1978—83; shareholder Griffin, Cochrane & Marshall, Atlanta, 1983—93; ptnr. King & Croft LLP, Atlanta, 1994—. Mediator Henning Mediation & Arbitration Svc., Atlanta, 1996—. Fellow Am. Coll. Civil Trial Mediators; mem. ABA (ho. of dels. 1993-99), State Bar Ga. (bd. govs. 2002-, chair alt. dispute resolution sect.), Atlanta Bar Assn. (pres., sec., treas. bd. dirs. 1986-99, chmn., bd. dirs. litig. sect. 1982-86, pres. Alt. Dispute Resolution Lawyers sect. 1996-97, Charles Watkins award 1996, Distinguished Svc. award 2007), Atlanta Coll. Arbitrators and Mediators (founder), Atlanta Bar Found. (pres. 1998-2003), Ga. Trial Lawyers Assn., Lawyers Club Atlanta, Old War Horse Lawyers Club. Episcopalian. Avocations: hiking, shooting, motorcycling, reading. Home: 2580 Westminster Heath NW Atlanta GA 30327-1449 Office: King & Croft LLP 707 The Candler Bldg 127 Peachtree St NE Atlanta GA 30303-1810 Home Phone: 404-609-9011; Office Phone: 404-577-8400. Office Fax: 404-577-8401. Business E-Mail: tlc@king-croft.com.

CROFTS, ANTONY RICHARD, biochemistry and biophysics educator; b. Harrow, Eng., Jan. 26, 1940; came to U.S., 1978; s. Richard Basil Iliffe and Vera Rosetta (Bland) C.; m. Paula Anne Hinds-Johnson, June 7, 1969 (div. 1981); 1 child, Charlotte Victoria Patricia; 1 adopted child, Rupert Charles; m. Christine Thompson Yerkes, Dec. 23, 1982; children: Stephanie Boynton, Terence Spencer. BA, U. Cambridge, Eng., 1961, PhD, 1965. Asst. lectr. dept. biochemistry U. Bristol, Eng., 1964-65, lectr., 1966-72, reader, 1972-78; prof. biophysics U. Ill., Urbana-Champaign, 1978—, prof. microbiology, 1992-99, chmn. biophysics divsn., 1978-91, assoc. dean Coll. Liberal Arts & Scis., 1996-98, prof. biochemistry, 1998—. Mem. organizing com. 4th Internat. Congress Photosynthesis, Reading, Eng., 1977, 7th Internat. Congress Photosynthesis, Providence, 1986, Table Ronde, Rousel-UCLA Forum, Paris, 1985; vis. prof. Coll. de France, 1983; Lans Ernster Meml. Lecture, Stockholm U., 2005; lectr. in field. Contbr. numerous articles, revs., etc., in area of biophysics, photosynthesis and bioenergetics; mem. editl. bd. Biochem. Jour., U.K., 1971-72, Biochimica Biophysica Acta, Holland, 1972-77, jour. Bacteriology, 1979-83, Archives Biochemistry and Biophysics, 1980-85. Major scholar nat. sci. U. Cambridge, 1958-61, U. Ill. scholar, 1989-92; grantee U.S. Dept. Energy, 1982-96, Guggenheim Found., 1985, NSF, NIH, U.S. Dept. Agr., 1979—. Fellow AAAS; mem. Biophys. Soc., Am. Soc. Biochemistry and Molecular Biology, Am. Soc. Plant Physiologists (Charles F. Kettering award 1992). Avocations: windsurfing, skiing, fishing, sailing, philosophy. Office: U Ill Dept Biochemistry 419 Roger Adams Lab Box B4 600 S Mathews Ave Urbana IL 61801-3602 Office Phone: 217-333-2043. Business E-Mail: a-crofts@life.uiuc.edu.

CROGNALE, MICHAEL ANTHONY, medical educator, neuroscientist, consultant; b. Ft. Rucker, Ala., Aug. 4, 1958; s. Joachim Crognale and Patricia Olivia King; m. Holly Ann Herzog, Sept. 12, 1993; children: Samuel Dante, Alana Rose. BA in Psychology, U. Calif., San Diego, 1982; PhD in Psychology, U. Calif., Santa Barbara, 1989. Lic. flight instr. instrument rating FAA, 1997. Lab. asst. U. Calif., San Diego, 1982—83, rsch. asst., 1983—89, rsch. scientist, 1989—90, post doctoral fellow Berkeley, 1990—94; rsch. asst. prof. U. Wash. Children's Hosp., Seattle, 1994—98; prof. U. Nev., Reno, 1998—. Dir. cognitive brain scis. psychology program U. Nev., Reno, 2003—; cons. SeeAero Ltd., Reno, 2006—; mem. editl. bd. Visual Neuroscience, Cambridge. Contbr. scientific papers to profl. jours. Martial arts instr. High Sierra Jujitsu Am. Judo and Jujitsi Fedn., Reno, 2004—06. Grantee Royalty Rsch. Fund Grant, U. Wash. Seattle, 1997, Sanford Ctr. Aging, 2000—01, 2005—06, U. Nev. Reno, 2000—01, NIH and Nat. Inst. Aging, 2001—02, NASA/Ames, 2002—05, 2005—06, FAA, 2003—06, 2005—06; Pub. Health Svc. Rsch. fellow, NIH and Nat. Eye Inst., 1992—94. Mem.: AAAS, Optical Soc. Am., Nat. Assn. Flight Instructors, Internat. Soc. Clin. Electrophysiology of Vision, Internat. Rsch. Group Color Vision Deficiencies, Assn. Rsch. in Vision and Ophthalmology, Am. Phys. Soc., Aerospace Med. Assn., Vision Sciences Soc., Soc. Neurosci., Aerospace Lighting Inst. Achievements include contributions to the studies of vision and human factors; research in comparative vision; human color vision deficiencies; human factors in aviation. Avocations: martial arts, skiing, flying, percussionist, scuba diving. Office: U Nev Reno Dept Psychology 296 Reno NV 89557 Home Phone: 775-746-4774; Office Phone: 775-682-8690.

CROHN, MAX HENRY, JR., lawyer; b. Asheville, NC, Feb. 4, 1934; s. Max Henry and Edith Pearl (Hoffman) C.; m. Barbara Jean Morris, Jan. 28, 1960; children: David Michael, Edith Ann, Randal Morris. BA in Polit. Sci, U. N.C., 1955; LL.B., Georgetown U., 1961. Bar: D.C. 1961, N.C. 1977, N.Y. 1986. Practiced in, Washington, 1961-68; trial atty. Bur. Restraint of Trade, 1963-65; atty. adviser to chmn. FTC, 1965-66; asso. mem. firm Arnold & Porter, Washington, 1966-68; asso. counsel R.J. Reynolds Industries, Inc., Winston-Salem, NC, 1968-75, asst. gen. counsel, 1975-78; sec. R.J. Reynolds Tobacco Co., 1971-81, gen. counsel, 1978-81; ptnr. Jacob, Medinger and Finnegan, 1981-95. Former chmn. bd. dirs. Forsyth County Econ. Devel. Corp., 1975-78. Served to lt. (j.g.) USNR, 1955-58. Mem. ABA. Home: 517 Redbud Rd Chapel Hill NC 27514-1710

CROISETIERE, JACQUES M., chemicals executive; m. Marthe Croisetiere. BS in Fin., U. Montreal, 1985. Fin. staff Master Card divsn. Bank of Montreal; dir. fin. Canadelle, Inc., 1983—90; from v.p. fin. Can. Salt to v.p., gen. mgr. plastic additives, biocides and sealants Morton Internat., Inc., 1990—98; v.p. Rohm and Haas Co., Phila., 1999—2003, v.p., CFO, 2003—07, exec. v.p., CFO, 2007—. Office: Rohm and Haas Co 100 Independence Mall W Philadelphia PA 19106-2399*

CROLAND, BARRY I., lawyer; b. Paterson, NJ, Jan. 11, 1938; s. Louis L. and Rae R. (Levine) C.; m. Joan Kohlreiter, Dec. 20, 1958; children: Richard, Heidi, Lizabeth, Jennifer. BA, Middlebury Coll., 1959; JD, Rutgers U., Newark, 1961. Bar: NJ 1962, NY 1983, US Ct. Appeals (3d cir.) 1973. Law clk. to Hon. John Grimshaw NJ Superior Ct., 1961, law clk. to Hon. Morris Pashman, 1961-62; assoc. Cole, Berman & Garth, Paterson, 1962-63, Shavick, Thevos, Stern, Schotz & Steiger, Paterson, 1963-68; ptnr. Shavick, Stern, Schotz, Steiger & Croland, Paterson, 1968-79, Stern, Steiger, Croland, Tanenbaum & Schielke, Paterson, 1979-95, Shapiro & Croland, Hackensack, NJ, 1995—. Asst. bar examiner State of NJ, 1965-68; mem. Fed. Ethics Com., Dist. of NJ, 1975; lectr. Inst. for Continuing Legal Edn., 1975—, faculty Trial Advocacy Inst., U. Houston Law Ctr., 2004-2006; sec. Dist. II Ethics Com. for Bergen County, 1980-81; mem. com. on civil practice NJ Supreme Ct., 1965, matrimonial litig. com. 1980, family ct. com., 1982, family practice com., 1983-87, 2002—06. Mem. bd. editors Rutgers Law Rev., 1959-61, case editor, 1960-61; sr. editor NJ Family Lawyer, 1981-2002. Fellow Am. Bar Found., Am. Acad. Matrimonial Lawyers (NJ bd. mgrs.); mem. ABA (family law sect., instr. 2004—), ATLA (matrimonial trial lawyers sect. emeritus bd. 2002—), Am. Coll. Family Trial Lawyers (diplomate 1994—), Am. Inns of Ct. (master Morris Pashman 1990-95, pres.-master NJ family law 1995-99), NJ State Bar Assn. (mem. exec. com. family law sect. 1981-95), Bergen County Bar Assn. (chmn. jud. and prosecutorial appts. com. 1983-95, chmn. jud. performance com. 1999-2001, 2007—), Matrimonal Lawyers Alliance. Home: 243 Myrtle St Haworth NJ 07641-1137 Office: Shapiro & Croland 411 Hackensack Ave 6th Fl Hackensack NJ 07601-6365 Office Phone: 201-488-3900. Business E-Mail: bcroland@shapiro-croland.com.

CROLL, TONY, cinematographer, television director; Cinematographer: (films) The Journey Of Jared Price, 2000, Down and Out with the Dolls, 2001, Kid Bang, 2002; (TV series) Survivor: Marquesas, 2002, (Ultimate Albums, 2002, Survivor: Thailand, 2002, My Life Is a Sitcom, 2004, Next Action Star, 2004; cinematographer, dir.: (TV series) The Surreal Life, 2003, Average Joe: Hawaii, 2004, Average Joe: Adam Returns, 2004; dir., dir.: (TV series) Outback Jack, 2003, Three Wishes, 2005— (DGA Award for Outstanding Directorial Achievement in Reality Programs, 2005); prodr., prodr.: (TV series) Outback Jack, 2003, Hell's Kitchen, 2005; camera operator (TV series) Fear Factor, Ultimate Albums, 2002, The Bachelor, 2002, Meet My Folks, 2002, Operation Junkyard, 2002, The Bachelorette, 2003, Survivor: The Amazon, 2003, The Family, 2003, The Apprentice, 2004. Office: c/o caa 9830 Wilshire Blvd Beverly Hills CA 90212

CROMAR, MICHAEL EARL, information and finance executive, distribution and transportation, oil and gas exploration and production executive; b. Salt Lake City, July 2, 1947; s. Earl B. and Mary L. (Peterson) C.; m. Nancy E. Maher, Feb. 5, 1972 (div. Oct. 1984); children: Matthew M., Martha E.; m. Robin A. McMullen, May, 1985 (div. Dec. 1987). BS in Bus., U. Utah, 1972. CPA, Calif. Asst. contr. Natomas Co., San Francisco, 1980-82; contr. Am. Pres. Lines, Oakland, Calif., 1982-84; v.p., contr. Computerland Corp., Oakland, 1984; v.p. Royal Viking Line, San Francisco, 1984-85; contr. Am. Pres. Cos., Oakland, 1985-86, dir. info. resources, 1986-88; sr. v.p. fin. and info. Gearbulk Ltd., Bergen, Norway, 1988—92; supr. CFO Harper Group, 1992—94; sr. v.p., CFO GATX Capital Corp., San Francisco, 1994—99; v.p. bus. transformation IBM Global Financing, Armonk, 1999—2003; exec. v.p., CFO Core Logic Sys., Sacramento, 2004—. Capt. inf. U.S. Army, 1966-69, Vietnam. Mem. Am. Inst. CPA's, San Francisco Yacht Club (Belvedere, Calif.). Libertarian. Avocations: small yacht racing, skiing, woodworking.

CROMARTIE, J. VERN, humanities educator; b. Screven, Ga., Oct. 17, 1954; s. Jimmie Lee Cromartie and Julia Frazier; m. Cassaundra Marie Lang; children: Aliya Julia-Lucy, Jamil Antar. AA in Social Sci., Coll. Alameda, Calif., 1982; AA in Psychology & English, Coll. Alameda, 1983; BS in Human Rels. & Orgnl. Behavior, U. San Francisco, 1983; MA in Sociology, Calif. State U., Hayward, 1985; MA in Humanities, Calif. State U., 1987; EdD in Orgn. & Leadership, U. San Francisco, 1991; MS in Counseling, Calif. State U., Hayward, 1995. Social worker Alameda County Social Svcs. Agy., Oakland, Calif., 1993—2003; prof. sociology Contra Costa Coll., San Pablo, Calif., 2000—. Author: (poetry book) Red Sun Songs, (book) Attitudes of University of California and California State University Tenured Sociologists Toward an Ethnic Studies General Education Requirement. Mem. Los Medanos Healthcare Dist., Pitts., Calif., 2004; bd. dirs. Los Medanos Cmty. Healthcare Dist., San Pablo, 2004—. E-5 USN, 1981, DC. Recipient Gil Scott-Heron Poetry Contest award, Arista Record Co. & KRE Radio Sta., 1979. Mem.: Pacific Sociol.

Assn. (com. on cmty. colls. chmn. 2007), Calif. Sociol. Assn. (gov. coun. mem. 2004). Office: Contra Costa Coll 2600 Mission Bell Dr San Pablo CA Personal E-mail: jusfrazier@yahoo.com.

CROMARTIE, WILLIAM JAMES, medical educator, researcher; b. Garland, NC, May 19, 1913; s. Robert Samuel and Mary Blanche (Jester) C.; m. Josephine Colter Rule, Nov. 19, 1945; children: William James, Robert Colter, Mary Blanche, John Benjamin, Martha Anne. Student, Presbyn. Jr. Coll., 1929-30, U. N.C., 1931, U. Ala., 1931-33; MD, Emory U., 1937. Diplomate Am. Bd. Internal Medicine. Intern Emory U. divsn. Grady Hosp., Atlanta, 1937-38; resident Vanderbilt U. Hosp., Nashville, 1938-40; instr. pathology Vanderbilt U., 1939-41; asst. prof. bacteriology and medicine U. Minn., Mpls., 1949-50, assoc. prof., 1950-51; assoc. prof. bacteriology and medicine U. N.C., Chapel Hill, 1951-59; chief divsn. infectious diseases, dept. medicine N.C. Meml. Hosp., Chapel Hill, 1952-65, chief of staff, 1967-72; prof. microbiology-immunology-medicine U. N.C., Chapel Hill, 1959-85, prof. emeritus, 1985—. Mem. adv. panel microbiology Office Naval Rsch., Washington, 1950-55; mem. Nat. Bd. Med. Examiners, Phila., 1966-68; mem. infectious disease adv. com. NIH, Bethesda, Md., 1971-75. Mem. bd. govs. Capital Health Planning Agy., Durham, N.C.; mem. exec. com. Regional Med. Program N.C., 1972-76; mem. intelligence mission investigating German rsch. on biol. warfare. Maj. U.S. Army, 1942-46, ETO. Decorated Legion of Merit; named Alumni Disting. Prof. U. N.C., 1980 Fellow ACP, Am. Acad. Microbiology (chmn. bd. govs. 1974-75); mem. Soc. Am. Microbiologists (mem. coun. 1974-75), Am. Assn. Pathologists, Infectious Disease Soc. Am., U. N.C. Med. Alumni Assn. (Disting. Faculty award 1983, Disting. Svc. award 1989). Democrat. Home: 437 Cedar Club Cir Chapel Hill NC 27517 Office: U NC Sch Medicine Dept Microbiology and Immunology 804 FLOB 23L-H Chapel Hill NC 27514

CROMBIE, DOUGLASS DARNILL, aerospace communications system engineer; b. Alexandra, New Zealand, Sept. 14, 1924; arrived in U.S., 1962, naturalized, 1967; s. Colin Lindsay and Ruth (Darnill) C.; m. Pauline L.A. Morrison, Mar. 2, 1951. BSc, Otago U., Dunedin, New Zealand, 1947, MSc, 1949. New Zealand nat. rsch. fellow Cavendish Lab., Cambridge, England, 1958-59; head radio physics divsn. New Zealand Dept. Sci and Indsl. Rsch., 1961-62; chief spectrum utilization divsn., chief low frequency group Inst. Telecom. Scis., Dept. Commerce, Boulder, Colo., 1962-71, dir. inst., 1971-76; dir. Inst. Telecom. Scis., Nat. Telecom. and Info. Adminstrn., Boulder, 1976-80; chief scientist Nat. Telecom. and Info. Agy., 1980-85; sr. engrng. specialist Aerospace Corp., LA, 1985—. Served with New Zealand Air Force, 1943-44. Recipient Gold medal Dept. Commerce, 1970, citation, 1972. Fellow IEEE; mem. NAE. Home: 524 Standard St El Segundo CA 90245-3039 Office: The Aerospace Corp PO Box 92957 Los Angeles CA 90009-2957

CROMER, DONALD L., aerospace and electrical engineer; b. Grand Junction, Colo., Jan. 23, 1936; BS in Engring., U.S. Naval Acad., 1959; MSEE, U. Denver, 1969. Commd. 2d lt. USAF, advanced through grades to lt. gen., 1988; mem. staff Project Gemini NASA; mem. staff Satellite Data Systems program office; directorate of space Hdqrs. USAF; sec. Air Force Spl. Projects Office; responsible for payloads on space shuttle Dept. Def., 1984—86; comdr. Space and Missile Test Orgn., Vandenberg AFB, 1986—88, Space Sys. Divsn., 1988—91; v.p. Hughes Electronics; pres. Hughes Space and Comms. Co. Bd. dirs. Draper Labs., Aerospace Corp., Global Crossings, Universal Space Networks. Recipient Schriever award. Mem.: AIAA, Internat. Acad. Aeronautics, Calif. Space Authority (bd. dirs.), Air Force Assn. (life).

CROMIE, WILLIAM J., urologist; b. Corinth, NY, Mar. 25, 1943; m. Cynthia Polk Skinner, Aug. 23, 1968; children: Daniel, John, Clare, Virginia, William Jr. BS, Fordham U., NYC, 1964; MD, St. Louis U. Med. Sch., 1968; MBA, Rensselaer Poly. Inst., Troy, NY, 1990. Lic. urologist Am. Bd. Urology, 1978. Asst. surgeon, urology Children's Hosp., Phila., 1977—79; assoc. prof. surgery and pediats. Albany Med. Ctr., 1979—85, prof. surgery, pediats., 1985—94, U. Chgo., 1994—2001, vice chmn., dept. surgery, 1995—2001. Bd. mem. Capital Trust Bank, Albany, Little Sisters of Poor, Latham, NY, Saratoga Performing Arts Ctr., NY, Ronald McDonald Ho., Albany. Exec. com. mem. NY State Bus. Coun., Albany, Ctr. Econ. Growth, Albany, Am. Health Ins. Plans, Washington. Comdr. Nat. Naval Med. Ctr., 1975—76, Bethesda. Recipient Gift Life award, Nat. Kideny Foun., 2007, Rsch. award, Am. Acad. Pediats., 1989, Silver Scalpel award, Albany Med. Coll., 1992, Exec. of Yr., Capital Dist. Bus. Rev., 2002, Scout of Yr., Boy Scouts Am., 2004, Your Heart Our Work award, Salvation Army, 2006; scholar, MacLean Ctr. MEd. Ethics, 1995. Mem.: Ft. Orange Club. Independent. Roman Catholic. Avocations: bicycling, canoeing, hiking, archery. Office: 500 Patroon Creek Blvd Albany NY 12206

CROMLEY, ALLAN WRAY, retired journalist; b. Topeka, Apr. 11, 1922; s. Frank George and Elsie May (Leedom) C.; m. Marian Minor, Jan. 30, 1949; children: Kathleen, Janet, Carter. BS in Journalism, U. Kans., 1948. Reporter Kansas City Kansan, 1948-49, Oklahoma City Times, 1949-53; Washington bur. chief Daily Oklahoman and Oklahoma City Times, 1953-87; sr. corr. Washington bur. Daily Oklahoman, 1987-95; ret., 1995. Sec. standing com. corrs. House and Senate Galleries, 1961. Bd. visitors U. Okla., 1970-72; trustee William Allen White Found. U. Kans., 1978-90; bd. dirs. Nat. Press Found., 1987-99, Battle of the Bulge. With AUS, 1943-45, ETO. Mem.: Nat. Gridiron Club (pres. 1978), Nat. Press Club (pres. 1968). Home: 3320 Stoneybrae Dr Falls Church VA 22044-1222 Personal E-mail: alcromley@aol.com.

CROMLEY, BRENT REED, lawyer, state senator; b. Great Falls, Mont., June 12, 1941; s. Arthur and Louise Lilian (Hiebert) C.; m. Dorothea Mae Zamborini, Sept. 9, 1967; children: Brent Reed Jr., Giano Lorenzo, Taya Rose. AB in Math., Dartmouth Coll., 1963; JD with honors, U. Mont., 1968. Bar: Mont. 1968, U.S. Dist. Ct. Mont. 1968, U.S. Ct. Appeals (9th cir.) 1968, U.S. Supreme Ct. 1978, U.S. Ct. Claims 1988, U.S. Ct. Appeals (D.C. cir.) 1988. Law clk. to presiding justice U.S. Dist. Ct. Mont., Billings, 1968-69; assoc. Hutton & Sheehy and predecessor firms, Billings, 1969-77, ptnr., 1977-78, Moulton, Bellingham, Longo & Mather, P.C., Billings, 1979—, also bd. dirs.; mem. Mont. Ho. of Reps., 1991-92, Mont. Senate, 2003—; pres. State Bar Mont., 1998-99. Contbr. articles to profl. jours. Mem. Yellowstone Bd. Health, Billings, 1972—; chmn. Mont. Bd. Pers. Appeals, 1974-80. Mem. ABA (appellate practice com.), ACLU, Internat. Assn. Def. Counsel, State Bar Mont. (chmn. bd. trustees 1995-97, trustee 1991—, pres. 1998-99), Yellowstone County Bar Assn. (various offices), Internat. Assn. Def. Counsel, Christian Legal Soc., Internat. Brotherhood of Magicians, Kiwanis. Avocations: running, magic. Home: 235 Parkhill Dr Billings MT 59101-0660 Office: Moulton Bellingham Longo & Mather PC 27 N 27th St Ste 1900 Billings MT 59101-2399 E-mail: Cromley@moultonlawfirm.com.

CROMLEY, JON LOWELL, lawyer; b. Riverton, Ill., May 23, 1934; s. John Donald and Naomi M. (Mathews) C. JD, John Marshall Law Sch., 1966. Bar: Ill. 1966. Real estate title examiner Chgo. Title & Trust Co., 1966-70; pvt. practice Genoa, Ill., 1970—; mem. firm O'Grady & Cromley, Genoa, 1970-96. Bd. dirs. Citizen's First Nat. Bank, 1984-92, Kingston Mut. Ins. Co., Genoa Main St., Inc. Mem.: ABA, DeKalb County Bar Assn., Chgo. Bar Assn., Ill. State Bar Assn. Home: 130 Homewood Dr Genoa IL 60135-1260 Office Phone: 815-784-5895.

CROMWELL, ADELAIDE M., sociology educator; b. Washington, Nov. 27, 1919; d. John Wesley Jr. and Yetta Elizabeth (Mavritte) Cromwell; 1 child, Anthony C. Hill. AB, Smith Coll., 1940; MA, U. Pa., 1941; cert. in Social Work, Bryn Mawr Coll., 1943; PhD, Radcliffe Coll., 1952; LHD (hon.), U. Southwestern Mass., 1972, George Washington U., 1989, Boston U., 1995. Mem. faculty Hunter Coll., 1942—44, Smith Coll., 1945—46, Boston U., 1951—85, prof. sociology, 1971—85, dir. Afro-Am. studies, 1969—88, prof. emerita sociology, 1985—; mem. faculty Harvard U. Ext., 1965—66. Mem. adv. com. vol. fgn. aid AID, 1964-80; mem. NEH, 1968-70; adv. com. corrections Commonwealth Mass., 1955-68; mem. commn. instns. higher edn., 1973-74; adv. com. to dir. IRS, 1970-71, to dir. census, 1972-75. Bd. dirs. Wheelock Coll., 1971-74, Nat. Ctr. Afro-Am. Artists, 1971-80, African Am. Scholars Coun., 1971—, Nat. Fellowship Fund, 1974-75, Mass. Hist. Commn., 1993—; bd. dirs. Sci. and Tech. for Internat. Devel., 1984-86; mem. exec. com. Am. Soc. African Culture, 1967. Mem. AAAS, African Studies Assn. (bd. dir. 1966-68), Am. Acad. of Arts and Scis., Am. Sociol. Assn., Coun. on Fgn. Affairs (bd. fgn. scholarships 1980-84), Mass. Hist. Soc., Phi Beta Kappa. Home: 51 Addington Rd Brookline MA 02445-4519

CROMWELL, FLORENCE STEVENS, occupational therapist; b. Lewistown, Pa., May 14, 1922; d. William Andrew and Florence (Stevens) Cromwell. BS in Edn., Miami U., Oxford, Ohio, 1943; BS in Occupl. Therapy, Washington U., St. Louis, 1949; MA, U. So. Calif., 1952; cert. in health facility adminstrn., UCLA, 1978. Mem. staff, then supervising therapist Los Angeles County Gen. Hosp., 1949—53; occupl. therapist Goodwill Industries, LA, 1954—55; staff therapist Vis. Nurse Assn., Phila., 1955—56; rsch. therapist United Cerebral Palsy Assn., LA, 1956—60; dir. occupl. therapy Orthopaedic Hosp., LA, 1961—67; coord. occupl. therapy Rsch. and Tng. Ctr. U. So. Calif. Med. Sch., LA, 1967—70; assoc. prof. U. So. Calif., LA, 1970—76, acting chmn. dept. occupl. therapy, 1973—76; mem. adv. bd. project SEARCH, Sch. Medicine, 1969—72; founding editor Occupl. Therapy in Health Care jour., 1984—88, editor emerita, 1988—. Assoc. dir. L.A. Job Corps Ctr., 1977—78; cons. in edn. and program devel., 1976—95; freelance editor, 1986—. Author: Manual for Basic Skills Assessment, 1960; contbr. articles to profl. jours. Mem. scholarship com. L.A. March of Dimes, 1963—70; mentor U. Tex.-Galveston Class 1990 Occupl. Therapy; bd. dirs. Am. Occupl. Therapy Found., 1965—69, v.p., 1966—69; bd. dirs. Nat. Health Coun., 1975—78. Served to lt. (j.g.) WAVES USNR, 1943—46. Recipient Disting. Alumni award, Washington U., 1978, Disting. Lectr., Calif. Occupl. Therapy Found., 1986. Fellow: Am. Occupl. Therapy Assn. (pres. 1967—73, Pres.'s WLWest commendation AOTA-AOTF 1999); mem.: Assn. Schs. Allied Health Professions (dir. 1973—74), Coalition Ind. Health Professions (chmn. 1973—74), So. Calif. Occupl. Therapy Assn. (pres. 1950—51, 1975—76), Inst. Medicine NAS (emerita 2002), Cwen, Kappa Kappa Gamma, Kappa Delta Pi, Mortar Bd. Personal E-mail: fscromwell@aol.com.

CROMWELL, JAMES, actor; b. LA, Jan. 27, 1940; s. John Cromwell and Kay Johnson; m. Anne Ulvestad, Nov. 27, 1976 (div. 1986); 3 children; m. Julie Cobb, May 29, 1986. Attended, Carnegie Inst. Tech. Actor (films) Murder by Death, 1976, The Cheap Detective, 1978, The Man with Two Brains, 1983, Tank, 1984, Revenge of the Nerds, 1984, Oh, God! You Devil, 1984, The House of God, 1984, Explorers, 1985, Revenge of the Nerds II: Nerds in Paradise, 1987, The Rescue, 1988, The Runnin' Kind, 1989, Pink Cadillac, 1989, The Babe, 1992, Romeo is Bleeding, 1993, Babe, 1995 (Oscar award nominee for best supporting actor), Star Trek: First Contact, 1996, Eraser, 1996, Owd Bob, 1997, The People vs. Larry Flynt, 1996, The Education of Little Tree, 1997, L.A. Confidential, 1997, Snow Falling on Cedars, 1998, Deep Impact, 1998, Species II, 1998, Babe: Pig in the City, 1998, Winter, 1998, The General's Daughter, 1999, The Green Mile, 1999, Space Cowboys, 2000, Spirit: Stallion of the Cimarron (voice), 2002, Sum of All Fears, 2002, The Nazi, 2002, Blackball, 2003, The Snow Walker, 2003, I, Robot, 2004, The Longest Yard, 2005, Dante's Inferno, 2006, The Queen, 2006, Becoming Jane, 2007, Spider-Man 3, 2007; (TV series) All in the Family, 1971, Hot L Baltimore, 1975, The Nancy Walker Show, 1976, The Last Precinct, 1986, Easy Street, 1986, Mama's Boy, 1988, Walking After Midnight, 1999, Citizen Baines, 2001, Six Feet Under, 2004-05; (TV miniseries) Once an Eagle, 1976, Dream West, 1986, Fail Safe, 2000, The Magnificent Ambersons, 2002, RFK, 2002, A Death in the Family, 2002, Angels in America, 2003; (TV films) The Girl in the Empty Grave, 1977, Deadly Game, 1977, A Christmas Without Snow, 1980, The Rainmaker, 1982, Spraggue, 1984, Alison's Demise, 1987, China Beach, 1988, Christine Cromwell: Things That Go Bump in the Night, 1989, Miracle Landing, 1990, In a Child's Name, 1991, Revenge of the Nerds III: The Next Generation, 1992, The Shaggy Dog, 1994, Revenge of the Nerds IV: Nerds in Love, 1994, RKO 281, 1999, Fail Safe, 2000, The Magnificent Ambersons, 2002, Salem's Lot, 2004, Pope John Paul II, 2005, Avenger, 2006; (TV guest appearances) The Rockford Files, 1974, All in the Family, 1974, Barney Miller, 1977, 1979, 1981, M*A*S*H, 1977, Three's Company, 1977, Eight is Enough, 1979, Little House on the Prairie, 1980, Dallas, 1984, 1985, Hardcastle and McCormick, 1985, Scarecrow and Mrs. King, 1986, Star Trek: the Next Generation, 1990, 1993, Home Improvement, 1994, Picket Fences, 1995, The Client, 1996, ER, 2001, Enterprise, 2001, 05, The West Wing, 2004.*

CROMWELL, OLIVER DEAN, investment banker; b. Cleve., Sept. 19, 1950; s. Oliver and Mildred Jeanette (Galko) C.; m. Sheila Lea Terry, May 19, 1984; children: Ashley Melissa, Oliver Spencer. AB, Brown U., Providence, 1972; MBA, Harvard U., Cambridge, Mass., 1976. CFA. Trust adminstr. Bankers Trust, NYC, 1973-74; assoc. Donaldson, Lufkin & Jenrette, NYC, 1976-79, v.p., 1980-84, sr. v.p., 1985-87, Oppenheimer & Co. Inc., NYC, 1987-88; 1st v.p. Paine Webber, NYC, 1988-90; founder, pres. Bentley Assocs. L.P., NYC, 1990—; pres. Bentley Securities Corp., NYC, 1991—. Co-author: Leading Investment Bankers: The Art & Science of Investment Banking, 2002. Co-chmn. NY met. area com. Brown Campaign, 1992—94; class '72 v.p. Brown U., 1997—2002, 2002—07, 1997—; exec. com. Harvard Bus. Sch. 30th Reunion, 2005—06; exec. com. ann. fund Riverdale County Sch., 2000—03, co-chmn. parents com. Upper Sch., co-chair Sr. Parents Gift Com., 2006—07; co-chmn. Upper Sch. Parents Com., 2006—07; co-head class agent annual fund Brown U., 1983—87. Recipient Alumni Svc. award Brown U., 1990. Mem.: Assn. Corp. Growth, Securities Industry Assn. NY (exec. com. 1987—90), NY Soc. Security Analysts, Assn. for Investment Mgmt. and Rsch., Assn. Alumni Brown U. (exec. com., bd. dirs. 1985—87, steering com. 5 yr. reunion fund 1985—87, co-chmn. 20 yr. reunion fund 1991—92, exec. com. ann. fund 1991—93, co-chmn. 25 yr. reunion fund 1996—97, bd. govs. 1997—98, co-chmn. 30 yr. reunion fund 2001—02, exec. com. ann. fund leadership coun. 2004—07, co-chmn. 35th yr. reunion fund 2006—07), Bentley Drivers Club (UK), Aston Martin Owners Club-East, Rolls Royce Owners Club (bd. dirs. 1992—93), Maserati Club Am., Harvard Bus. Sch. Club NY, Brown U. Club NYC (bd. dirs. 1983—95, treas. 1984—89, v.p. 1989—91, pres. 1991—93). Home: 4 Eastway Bronxville NY 10708-4302 Office: Bentley Assocs LP 360 Lexington Ave New York NY 10017 Office Phone: 212-972-8700. Business E-Mail: odcromwell@bentleylp.com.

CRON, KENNETH D., information technology executive; BA in Psychology, U. Colo. Pres. publishing CMPMedia Inc. (now CMP Media LLC), Manhasset, NY, 1978—99; chmn., CEO Uproar Inc. (later acquired by Flipside), NYC, 1999—2001; CEO Flipside Network (div. of Vivendi Universal Games, Inc.), NYC, 2001; chmn., CEO Vivendi Universal Games, Inc. (div. of Vivendi Universal, S.A.), LA, 2001; interim COO Vivendi Universal Entertainment, NYC, 2002; bd. dirs. Computer Associates Internat., Inc., Islandia, NY, 2002—, interim CEO, 2004—05; chmn. Midway Games, Inc., Chgo. Office: Computer Assoc Internat Inc One Computer Plaza Islandia NY 11749 also: Midway Games Inc 2704 W Roscoe St Chicago IL 60618

CRONCE, PAUL CALVIN, retired dermatologist; b. Trenton, NJ, Dec. 25, 1931; s. Paul I. and Rachie Cathryn (Allen) C.; m. Nancy Elizabeth Dorrien, Aug. 27, 1960 (div. Aug. 1979); children: Paul Allen, Charles Scott, Thomas Taylor. BA summa cum laude, Duke U., Durham, NC, 1954; postgrad., Duke U. Grad. Sch. Arts & Scis., Durham, NC, 1954—55; MD, Duke U. Sch. Medicine, Durham, NC, 1960. Diplomate Am. Bd. Dermatology, 1965. Rotating med. intern USPHS Hosp., Boston, 1960-61; acting dermatology resident USPHS Hosp., Staten Island, 1961—62, dermatology resident, 1962—65, asst. chief dermatology, 1965—66; vis. fellow in dermatology Columbia-Presbyn. Med. Ctr., NYC, 1964-65; ptnr. Alden & Cronce Dermatology, Atlanta, 1966-73; pres. and treas. Alden Dermatology Assocs., P.A., Atlanta, 1973-99; ret., 1999. Instr. medicine, dermatology Emory U. Sch. Medicine, 1967-71, asst. clin. prof. dermatology, 1971-78, assoc. clin. prof. dermatology, 1978-89, clin. prof. dermatology, 1989-2001, prof. emeritus dermatology, 2001-. Contbr. articles to profl. jours. Fellow Am. Acad. Dermatology; mem. Southeastern Dermatological Assn., Ga. Soc. Dermatologists (vice chmn. 1971), Med. Assn. Ga., Internat. Soc. Dermatologic Surgery, Atlanta Dermatological Assn. (sec.-treas. 1967, pres. 1968), Med. Assn. Atlanta, Phi Beta Kappa, Alpha Omega Alpha. Republican. Presbyterian. Avocations: travel, gardening.

CRONE, ANNA LISA, Russian literature educator; b. Bklyn., June 9, 1946; d. James Clarence Jr. and Ethel Margaret (Donnelly) C.; m. Vladimir Donchik, July 12, 1982; 1 child, Liliana Donchik. BA in Russian Lit., Goucher Coll., 1967; MA in Russian Lang. and Lit., Harvard U., 1969, PhD in Russian Lang. and Lit., 1975; LHD (hon.), Goucher Coll., 1988, DHC (hon.), 1998. From instr. to asst. prof. Russian and Russian lit. Goucher Coll. Johns Hopkins U., Balt., 1971—74; tchr., translator Associated Jewish Charities, Balt., 1974—75; rschr. Radcliffe Inst., Harvard U., Cambridge, Mass., 1975—76; from asst. prof. to prof. Slavic langs. and lits. U. Chgo., 1977—. Hon. vis. fellow Slavonic Inst. U. London, 1998—; internat. lectr. on Russian topics. Author: (scholarly study) Rozanov and the End of Literature, 1978; author: The Daring of Derzhavin, 2001, My Petersburg/Myself, 2004; editor, contbr.: New Studies in Russian Language and Literature, 1986; mem. editl. bd. Russian Lang. Jour., Ency. of Russian Literature, Ency. of the Essay; contbr. articles to profl. jours. Mem. Univ. Senate U. Chgo., 1992-95. Nat. Def. Fgn. Lang. fellow, 1967-71, Woodrow Wilson fellow, 1967; recipient Quantrell Tchr. of Yr. award, U. Chgo., 1985, Best Grad. Tchr.award, 2000, Barbara Heldt prize for scholarship and mentoring in Slavic studies, 2004, Main Nat. Lifetime Achiev. award for woman in the Slavic field. Mem. Am. Assn. Tchrs. of Slavic and East European Langs. (Best Grad. Prof. award 2000), Am. Assn. Advancement of Slavic Studies, Stochastic Soc. (pres. 1991-92, 96-97), Phi Beta Kappa. Democrat. Avocations: music, travel, intellectual history, history of culture, amateur acting. Office: U Chgo Slavic Dept 1130 E 59th St Chicago IL 60637-1539 Personal E-mail: liscron@yahoo.com. Business E-Mail: acrone@midway.uchicago.edu.

CRONE, EUGENE N., addictions specialist, retired educator; b. Newton Falls, Ohio., Apr. 17, 1929; s. Clarence Bennet and Violet Richards Crone. BM, Youngstown U., 1954; MA, Columbia U., 1958; PhD, Nat. U. Grad. Studies, Dallas, 1974. Cert. addiction profl., MAC-master addiction counselor, nat. cert. addiction counselor II, internat. cert. alcohol and drug counselor. Tchr., prof. various pub. schs. and colls., 1952—78; dir. addictions Horizon Psychiatric Hosp., Clearwater, Fla., 1978—95, Nat. Deaf Acad., Mt. Dora, Fla., 1995—, La Amistad Health Svcs., Maitland, Fla., 1999—2003; with Nat. Deaf Acad., Mt. Dora, Fla., 2003—. Presenter in field. Author: They Hear Through Their Eyes, 2003, To Russia With Hope, 2006; contbr. articles to profl. jours. PFC US Army, 1950—52. Named one of 10 addiction profls. to tour Russian Addiction Treatment Centers in Moscow and St. Petersburg, 2005; recipient Profl. of Yr. Nat. award, NAADAC Nat. Conv., 1997, Profl. of Yr. award, Fla. NAADAC, 1996. Mem.: NAADAC, Addiction Profls. of Fla., Internat. Cert. Alcohol & Drug Counselors (presenter). Methodist. Home: 1001 Bristol Lake Rd #212 Mount Dora FL 32757 Office: Nat Deaf Acad 19650 US Hwy 441 Mount Dora FL 32757 Personal E-mail: ecrone17@msn.com.

CRONENBERG, DAVID, film director; b. Toronto, Ont., Can., Mar. 15, 1943; Student, U. Toronto. Dir.: (films) Stereo, 1969, Crimes of the Future, 1970, Shivers, 1975, They Came From Within, 1976, Rabid, 1977, The Brood, 1979, Fast Company, 1979, Scanners, 1981 (Internat. Fantasy Film award for Best Film), Videodrome, 1983 (Best Sci. Fiction Film), The Dead Zone, 1983, The Fly, 1986, Dead Ringers, 1988, Naked Lunch (NSFC award, NYFCC award), 1992, M. Butterfly, 1993, eXistenZ, 1998 (Silver Berlin Bear 1999), Camera, 2000, Spider, 2002, A History of Violence, 2005 (Best Dir. award, Nat. Soc. Film Critics, 2006); dir.: (TV films) Tourettes, 1971, Letters From Michelangelo, 1971, Winter Garden, 1972, Scarborough Bluffs, 1972, Lakeshore, 1972, In the Dirt, 1972, Fort York, 1972, Don Valley, 1972; dir., writer, prodr., actor: Crash, 1997 (Cannes Jury Spl. prize); actor: Into the Night, 1985, Nightbreed, 1990, Blue, 1992, Trial by Jury, 1994, Boozecan, 1994, Henry & Verlin, 1994, To Die For, 1995, Blood and Donuts, 1995, Extreme Measures, 1996, The Stupids, 1996, Last Night, 1998, Resurrection, 1999, The Judge, 2001, Jason X 2001. Recipient Billy Wilder award for excellence in directing, Nat. Bd. Rev., 2005. Office: William Morris Agy c/o John Burnham 151 S El Camino Dr Beverly Hills CA 90212-2775

CRONENWETT, JACK LEMOYNE, vascular surgeon educator; b. Ludington, Mich., Dec. 13, 1946; s. Jack L. and K. Marie (Grundmark) C.; m. Linda R. Houk, 1969 (div. 1980); children: Sara, Molly; m. Debra A. Cote, Sept. 26, 1981. BS, U. Mich., 1969; MD, Stanford U., 1973. Diplomate in gen. surgery and vascular surgery Am. Bd. Surgery. Resident in gen. surgery U. Mich., Ann Arbor, 1973-79; resident in vacsular surgery U. Tenn., Memphis, 1979-80; asst. prof. surgery U. Mich., Ann Arbor, 1980-84; assoc. prof. surgery Dartmouth Coll., Hanover, NH, 1984-89, prof. surgery, 1989—. Editor Jour. Vascular Surgery, 2003—. Mem. Am. Surg. Assn., New Eng. Soc. Vascular Surgery (sec. 1991-96, pres. 1997-98), Soc. Vascular Surgery (recorder 1996-2001, pres. 2002-03), Soc. Univ. Surgeons, Ea. Vascular Soc., Midwestern Vascular Soc., Assn. Program Dirs. in Vascular Surgery (sec.-treas. 1993-97, pres. 2000-02). Office: Dartmouth-Hitchcock Med Ctr 1 Medical Center Dr Lebanon NH 03756-0002 Home Phone: 603-448-1886; Office Phone: 603-650-8670. Business E-Mail: j.cronewett@hitchcock.org.

CRONENWETT, LINDA HOUK, dean, nursing educator; BSN, U. Mich., 1966, PhD in nursing, 1983; MSN in maternal-child nursing, U. Washington, 1970. Dir. profl. nursing, dir. nursing rsch. and edn. Mary Hitchcock Meml. Hosp., Lebanon, NH, Dartmouth-Hitchcock Med. Ctr., Lebanon; mem. faculty U. Mich., U. N.H., Dartmouth U.; with U. N.C., Chapel Hill, 1998—, dean Sch. Nursing, 1999—. Mem. editl. bd. Jour. Nursing Measurement; contbr. articles to profl. hours. With USN. Recipient Disting. Profl. Svc. award Assn. Women's Health, Obstetric and Neonatal Nurses, 1993, Disting. Scholar Nursing award NYU, 1997, NH Nursing Leadership Award. Fellow Am. Acad. Nursing, Nat. Academies of Practice. Office: U NC Sch Nursing CB 7640 Carrington Hall Chapel Hill NC 27599-0001 Office Phone: 919-966-7460.

CRONIN, ANNE, editor; Asst. met. editor NY Times. Office: NY Times Metropolitan Desk 229 West 43rd St New York NY 10036 Office Phone: 212-556-1533. Office Fax: 212-556-3690. E-mail: ancron@nytimes.com.

CRONIN, BONNIE KATHRYN LAMB, museum director; b. Mpls., Mar. 11, 1941; d. Edwin Rector and Maude Kathryn (MacPherson) Lamb; m. Barry Jay Cronin, Jan. 23, 1963 (div. Feb. 1972); 1 son, Philip Scott. BA, U. Mo., 1963, BS, 1964; MS, Ill. State U., 1970. Copywriter Neds & Wardlow Advt., Columbia, Mo., 1962-64; tchr. Columbia Sch. Sys., 1964-68, Normal (Ill.) Sch. Sys., 1968-69; asst. gen. mgr. Sta. WGLT, Normal, 1969-70; dir. devel. Radio Sta. WBUR, Boston, 1970-71, program dir., 1971-75, gen. mgr., 1975-78; dir. pub. rels. Joy of Movement Ctr., 1978-80; dep. scheduler Anderson for Pres., 1980; scheduler Spaulding for Gov., 1980-81; dir. scheduling John Kerry Campaign, 1982; dir. of scheduling Mass. Lt. Gov.'s Office, dir. ops., 1983-84; dep. campaign mgr. Kerry for Senate Com., 1984; dir. ops. Senator John Kerry, Washington, 1985-86, dir. constituency outreach Boston, 1986-92, exec. asst., 1992-95; chief staff to Senator John Kerry Boston, 1995-97; dir. devel. and pub. affairs Working Capital, 1997-2001; dir. found. rels. USS Constn. Mus., 2001—. Chair Mass. Micro Enterprise Coalition, 2000-01. Commr. Melrose Human Rights Commn., Mass., 2004—; active Melrose Econ. Devel. Coun., 2002—04. Mem.: Mass. Broadcasters Assn. (dir. 1973—78, chair scholarship com., pub. svc. com., adminstrv. oversight com.), Polymnia Choral Soc. (pres. 2002—04), Nat. Pub. Radio (dir. 1974—77, chairperson devel. com.). Office: Box 1812 Boston MA 02129 Personal E-mail: bonniemelrose@aol.com.

CRONIN, DANIEL ANTHONY, emeritus archbishop; b. Boston, Nov. 14, 1927; s. Daniel George and Emily Frances (Joyce) Cronin. STL, Gregorian U., 1953, STD summa cum laude, 1956; LLD, Suffolk U., Boston, 1969, Stonehill Coll., North Easton, 1971. Ordained priest Roman Catholic Ch., 1952. Attache Apostolic Internunciature, Addis Ababa, Ethiopia, 1957—61, Secretariat of State, Vatican City, 1961—68; named Monsignor by His Holiness Pope John XXIII, 1962; named titular bishop of Egnatia and aux. bishop of Boston, 1968—70; Episcopal ordination from Archbishop of Boston Richard Cardinal Cushing, 1968; pastor St. Raphael Ch., Medford, Mass., 1968—70; bishop Fall River, Mass., 1970—92; archbishop of Hartford Conn., 1992—2003; archbishop emeritus of Hartford, 2003—. Mem.: KC (Father Michael J. McGivney award 1999). Office: 469 Bloomfield Ave Bloomfield CT 06002

CRONIN, DOREEN, writer, former lawyer; b. Queens, NY; m. Andrew Cronin. Grad., Pa. State U., St. John's U. Former comml. and civil litigation atty., NY; children's book author, 2000—. Author: Click, Clack, Moo: Cows That Type, 2000 (Caldecott Honor, 2000, Red Clover award, N.Y. Times best-seller, Cuffie award, Simington Black Honor, BookSense Honor, The Bill Martin Jr. award Kans. Reading Assn., 2003, The Charlotte award NYSRA, 2002, The Md. Sunflower award, 2002, The Smart award, 2002), Giggle, Giggle, Quack, 2000, Diary of a Worm, 2003, Duck for President, 2004 (Book Sense Book of Yr. for children's illustrated book, 2005). Office: Simon & Schuster Childrens Pub 1230 Ave of the Americas New York NY 10020

CRONIN, JAMES WATSON, physicist, researcher; b. Chgo., Sept. 29, 1931; s. James Farley and Dorothy (Watson) Cronin; m. Annette Martin, Sept. 11, 1954; children: Catheryn, Emily, Daniel Watson. AB, So. Methodist U., 1951; PhD, U. Chgo.; D (hon.), U. Paris, 1995, U. Leeds, 1996, Univ. Pierre & Marie Curie, 1994; DSc (hon.), U. Leeds, 1996. Asst. physicist Brookhaven Nat. Lab., 1955—58; asst. prof. Princeton, 1958—65, prof. physics, 1965—71; prof. physics and astronomy to prof. emeritus U. Chgo., 1971—. Loeb lectr. physics Harvard U., 1967; participant early devel. spark chambers; co-discoverer CP-violation, 64; lectr. Nashima Found., 1993; rschr. Internat. Ctr. Sci. Rsch. Contbr. articles to sci. jours. Decorated chevalier Legion of Honor (France); recipient Rsch. Corp. Am. award, 1967, John Price Wetherill medal, Franklin Inst., 1976, E.O. Lawrence award, ERDA, 1977, Nobel prize for Physics, 1980, Nat. medal of Sci., 1999; fellow Guggenheim, 1982—83; Sloan fellow, 1964—66, Guggenheim fellow, 1970—71. Mem.: NAS (coun. mem.), Royal Soc. UK (fgn.), Russian Acad. Sci. (fgn.), Am. Phys. Soc., Am. Acad. Arts and Scis., Am. Philos. Soc. Achievements include showing that in rare instances subatomic particles called K mesons violate CP symmetry during their decay. Office: U Chgo Enrico Fermi Inst 5630 S Ellis Ave Chicago IL 60637-1433 E-mail: jwc@uchep.uchicago.edu.*

CRONIN, JEROME JOSEPH, JR., marketing educator, consultant; b. Springfield, Ohio, Apr. 27, 1952; s. Jerome Joseph Cronin and Edith E. Markley; m. Karen Sue Westerberg, Oct. 9, 1976 (div. Aug. 1980). BS in Mktg., Wright State U., 1974; MBA, U. Dayton, 1976; PhD in Mktg., The Ohio State U., 1981. Vis. asst. prof. Ohio State U., Columbus; asst. prof. U. Ky., Lexington, 1982—86, Fla. State U., Tallahassee, 1986—88, 1988—94, assoc. prof. to prof., 1994—2002, co-dir. Mktg. Inst., 1997—, Carl DeSantis Prof. Bus. Adminstrn., 2002—. Co-dir. Mktg. Inst., 1997—; prin. Tedsson & Assocs. Mem. editl. rev. bd.: Journal of Business Research, International Journal of Service Industry Management, Journal of Marketing Management, Journal of Management Research, Managing Service Quality, Health Marketing Quarterly; contbr. articles to profl. jours. Nominee Univ. Tchg. award, 2001, 2002, 2005; named Tchg. Assoc. of Yr., Ohio State U., 1979—81; fellow, Albert Haring Symposium, 1980, German Marshall Fund, 2001. Mem. Soc. Mktg. Advances, Am. Mktg. Assn., Acad. Mktg. Sci. Democrat. Roman Catholic. Avocations: baseball, travel, photography. Home: 3701 Sally Ln Tallahassee FL 32312 Office: Fla State Univ Coll of Business Tallahassee FL 32306 Office Phone: 850-644-7858. Personal E-mail: tedsson@comcast.net. Business E-Mail: jcronin@fsu.edu.

CRONIN, KEVIN STEWART, historian, educator; b. Cranston, RI, Dec. 3, 1953; s. James Michael and Brita Welch Cronin; m. Margie Elaine Hazel, Dec. 18, 1974; children: Kevin Stewart II, Catherine Elaine. AAS in Tech., C.C. of Air Force, Montgomery, AL, 1987; BS in Bus. Mgmt., U. Md., 1989; MEd in Bus. Edn., Valdosta State U., 1998, MA in History, 2001. Enlisted USAF, 1972, advanced through grades to tech. sgt., 1992; adj. instr. Ctrl. Tex. Coll., Misawa AFB, Japan, 1989; owner Crown Enterprises, Valdosta, Ga., 1992—96; substitute tchr. Valdosta City Sch. Sys., Ga., 1996—98; coord. dept. social scis. Ga. Mil. Coll., Valdosta, 2001—05, assoc. prof. history, 2001—. Adj. instr. Ctrl. Tex. Coll., Misawa AFB, Japan, 1989, Valdosta State U., 2001—03, 2007; faculty advisor Phi Theta Kappa, Valdosta, Ga., 2002—; mem. promotion bd. Ga. Mil. Coll., Valdosta, 2005—07. Vol. Boy Scouts of Am., Las Vegas, 1980—95, Japan's Red Feather, Misawa, Tohoku, 1986—88, Habitat for Humanity, Valdosta, Ga., 2003—05, Operation Teddy Bear, Valdosta, Ga., 2004—05, L.D.S. Helping Hands, 2004—07. Decorated Commendation medal USAF, Achievement medal, Meritorius medal; named one of Outstanding Young Men of Am., 1987; recipient Red Feather Vol. award, Misawa Red Feather Orgn., 1988. Mem.: Orgn. Am. Historians, Assn. So. Historians, Profl. Assn. Ga. Educators, Air Force Assn. (life), Am. Legion, Phi Alpha Theta, Omicron Delta Kappa. Mem. Lds Ch. Avocations: reading, wargaming, building historical models, restoring historical home. Home: 1804 Slater St Valdosta GA 31602 Office: Ga Mil Coll 4201 N Forrest St Valdosta GA 31605 Office Phone: 229-293-6019. Business E-Mail: kcronin@gmc.cc.ga.us.

CRONIN, PHILIP MARK, lawyer; b. Boston, July 21, 1932; s. Herbert Joseph and Elizabeth Ann (Sullivan) C.; m. Paula Cook Budlong, June 8, 1957; children: Thomas B., Philip S. AB, Harvard U., 1953, LLB, 1956. Bar: Mass. 1956. Sr. ptnr. firm Withington, Cross, Park & Groden, Boston, 1956-89, Peabody & Arnold, Boston, 1989—. Pres., pub. Harvard mag., 1971-78; city solicitor, Cambridge, Mass., 1968-72. Mng. editor: Mass. Law Rev, 1976-81; editor-in-chief, 1981-90; editor Mass. Legal History Jour., 1996—. Trustee Harvard Crimson, 1972—; pres. Cambridge Homes, 1991-94; overseer Mass. Supreme Jud. Ct. Hist. Soc., 1994—, editor jour., 1995—. Home: 3 Lincoln Ln Cambridge MA 02138-3351 Office: 30 Rowes Wharf Boston MA 02110-3339 Office Phone: 617-951-2100.

CRONIN, ROBERT LAWRENCE, painter; b. Lexington, Mass., Aug. 10, 1936; s. Daniel Augustus and Eileen Ursula (Keating) C.; m. Constance Marie Nelson, June 27, 1964 (div. 1974). BFA, R.I. Sch. Design, 1959; MFA, Cornell U., 1962. Tchr. Mich. State U., East Lansing, 1965-66, Bennington (Vt.) Coll., 1967-68, Brown U., Providence, 1969-71; tchrs. Sch. Worcester (Mass.) Art Mus., 1972-80. One-man shows Mus. Art Carnegie Inst., Pitts., 1981, Sculpture Ctr. Gallery, N.Y.C., 1981, Gimpel Fils Gallery, London, 1982, Gimpel & Weitzenhoffer Gallery, N.Y.C., 1982, 84, 87, 89, Watson de Nagy Gallery, Houston, 1983, 86, Gimpel-Hanover Galerien, Zurich, 1983, Clark Gallery, Lincoln, Mass., 1983, 85, 87, Janet Steinberg Gallery, San Francisco, 1985, Galerie Esperanza, Montreal, 1985, 87, Klonaridis Gallery, Toronto, 1984, 85, 87, 88, 89, Galerie Keeser-Bohbot, Hamburg, Germany, 1987, 89, Alice Simsar Gallery, Ann Arbor, Mich., 1988, Yoh Art Gallery, Osaka, 1989, Gallery Hiro, Tokyo, 1989, Helander, Gallery, Palm Beach, Fla., 1990, Fitchburg (Mass.) Art Mus., 1990, Munson Gallery, New Haven, 1991, Sound Shore Gallery, Stamford, Conn., 1992, Virginia Lynch Gallery, Tiverton, R.I., 1996, 98, Dillon Gallery, N.Y.C., 1996, 99, Tremaine Gallery, Hotchkiss Sch., Lakeville, Conn., 1999, Joseph Rickards Gallery, N.Y.C., 2001, Dillon Gallery, Oyster Bay, N.Y., 2002, Brown U. Hillel, Providence, 2004, Kouros Gallery, N.Y.C., 2004; represented in permanent collections Bklyn. Mus., Mus. Fine Arts, Boston, Mus. Art, U. Okla., Mus. Art, Carnegie Inst., Mus. Art, R.I. Sch. Design, Nat. Air and Space Mus., Mus. Fine Arts, Springfield, Worcester Art Mus., Worcester Polytech. Inst., De Cordova Mus., Nat. Acad. Design, N.Y.C Recipient 1st prize for painting Boston Fine Arts Festival, 1963; recipient awards Mass. Artists Found., 1975, 79; individual support grantee Adolph and Esther Gottlieb Found., 1991. Mem. Nat. Acad. Design. Home: PO Box 74 Falls Village CT 06031-0074

CRONIN, TIMOTHY CORNELIUS, III, computer manufacturing executive; b. Manchester, NH, Sept. 26, 1927; s. Timothy Cornelius and Ann Frances (Meaney) C.; m. Gloria Mara, June 8, 1949 (dec. Sept. 1984); children: Gloria Ann, Constance, Timothy, Barbara, Mary, Thomas; m. A. Jeanine Wallis, June 15, 1991; children: Erik Wallis, Dana Wallis. BS, U.S. Mil. Acad., 1949; MBA, Ohio State U., 1952. Commd. 2d lt. USAF, 1949, advanced through grades to capt., 1956, resigned, 1956; mgr., v.p. Honeywell, Inc., Mpls. and Wellesley, Mass., 1956-71; v.p. Addressograph Multigraph, Cleve., 1971-74; chmn., CEO Inforex, Inc., Burlington, Mass., 1974-79; cons. in field Waltham, Mass., 1980-82; v.p. Wang Labs., Lowell, Mass., 1983-87; pres., CEO Wang Fin. Info. Svcs. Corp., NYC, 1987-90, Digitran, Inc., Englewood Cliffs, N.J., 1990-91; ret., pvt. investor, 1991. Decorated Legion of Merit. Mem. Computer Industries Assn. (exec. com. 1975-79), Assn. Industries Mass. (bd. dirs. 1976-79). Republican. Roman Catholic. Home: 31 Shaw Dr Bedford NH 03110-6050

CRONK, LEONARD, management consultant; b. Paterson, NJ, Apr. 19, 1943; s. Leonard and Ruth (Brewer) Cronk; m. Martha Fanning, Aug. 21, 1965 (div. 1998); children: Catherine Cronk Clifford, Martha Brewer; m. Hisayo Arikawa, Oct. 25, 1998. BS in Indsl. Engring., Cornell U., 1965, M in Indsl. Engring., 1966, MBA, 1967. Cert. mgmt. cons., mgmt. acctg., securities registrations. Mem. ops. rsch. staff Mobil Corp., NYC, 1967-69; from cons. to sr. mgr. Price Waterhouse, NYC, 1969-79; mgr. fin. systems Kennecott Corp., Stamford, Conn., 1979-82; v.p. Kidder, Peabody, NYC, 1982-87, Merrill Lynch, NYC, 1987-91; mgmt. cons. Rowayton, Conn., 1991—; v.p. Manley Mktg., Greenwich, Conn. Adv. bd. Belle Haven Land Assn., Greenwich, Conn., 1983-85, bd. dirs., 1986-89; bd. dirs. Belle Haven Club, Greenwich, 1990-94. Mem.: Wilson Cove Yacht Club (bd. govs. 2004—05). Republican. Episcopalian. Avocations: playing trumpet, tennis. Home: 110 Leroy Ave Darien CT 06820 Office Phone: 203-655-3961. E-mail: leonardcronk@sbcglobal.net.

CRONKITE, WALTER, radio and television news correspondent; b. St. Joseph, Mo., Nov. 4, 1916; s. Walter Leland and Helen Lena Cronkite; m. Mary Elizabeth Maxwell, Mar. 30, 1940 (dec. Mar. 15, 2005);; children: Nancy Elizabeth, Mary Kathleen, Walter Leland III. Student, U. Tex., 1933—35; LLD (hon.), Rollins Coll., 1966, Bucknell U., Syracuse U.; LHD (hon.), Ohio State U.; degree (hon.), Am. Internat. Coll., Harvard U. News writer, editor Scripps-Howard, also UP, Houston, Kansas City, Dallas, Austin, El Paso; UP war corr., 1942—45; fgn. corr., reopening burs. in Amsterdam, Brussels, chief corr. Nuremberg war crimes trials, bur. mgr., Moscow, 1946—48; lectr., mag. contbr., 1948—49; CBS-News corr., 1950—81; spl. corr., 1981—; mng. editor CBS Evening News with Walter Cronkite, 1962—81. Chmn. The Cronkite Ward Co., 1993—; host spl. Universe, CBS, The Holocaust: In Memory of Millions, The Discovery Channel, 1993; anchor for TV news spls. Vietnam: A War That is Finished, 1975, In Celebration of US, 1976, Our Happiest Birthday, 1977, The President in China, 1975, Solzhenitsyn: 1984 Revisited. Author: Eye on the World, 1971, The Challenges of Change, 1971, A Reporter's Life, 1996, Around America, 2002; co-author: South by Southeast, North by Northeast, Westwind; prodr.(host): The e Reports (12 episode series for Discovery Channel), 1994—96, Cronkite Remembers (8 part series for CBS and Discovery Channel), 1996. Recipient Cable Ace award for best program interviewer, 1993, Peabody award, 1962, 1981, Emmy awards, William A. White award for journalistic merit, 1969, George Polke Journalism award, 1971, Gold medal, Internat. Radio and TV Soc., 1974, Alfred I. DuPont-Columbia U. award in broadcast journalism, 1978, 1981, Presdl. medal of Freedom, 1981. Mem.: Assn. Radio News Analysts, Acad. Arts and Scis. (pres. nat. acad. N.Y. chpt. 1959, Gov.'s award 1979), Bohemian Club, N.Y. Yacht Club, Nat. Press Club, Overseas Press Club, Explorers Club, Chi Phi. Avocation: sailing. Office: CBS Inc 51 W 52nd St Ste 1934 New York NY 10019-6119

CRONON, WILLIAM, history professor; b. New Haven, Sept. 11, 1954; m. Nancy Elizabeth Fey. BA in History, English with honors, U. Wis., 1976; MA in Am. History, Yale U., New Haven, Conn., 1979, M of Philosophy in Am. History, 1981, PhD in Am. History, 1990; DPhil in Brit. History, Oxford U., 1981; degree (hon.), Northland Coll., Ashland, Wis., 2006. Asst. prof. history Yale U., New Haven, 1981-86, assoc. prof., 1986-91, prof., 1991-92, mem. studies in environment program creation com., 1983-84, co-chair studies environment program, 1989-92, dir. grad. studies, history dept., 1990-92; Frederick Jackson Turner chair of history, geography, and environ. studies U. Wis., Madison, 1992—, dir. honors program Coll. Letters and Sci., 1996-98, Frederick Jackson Turner and Vilas rsch. prof. history, geography and environ. studies, 2003—; found. fac. dir. Chadbourne Residential Coll., 1997-2000. Asst. Am. sec. Rhodes Scholarship Trust, 1978-80, Wis. state sec., 1993-98; cons. in field; adv. bd. The History Tchr., 1986-2000. Rhodes Dist. chmn., 2002-. Author: Changes in the Land: Indians, Colonists and the Ecology of New England, 1983 (Valley Forge honor cert. 1984, Soc. Colonial award citation of honor 1984, Francis Parkman prize 1984), Nature's Metropolis: Chicago and the Great West, 1991 (Chgo. Tribune Heartlaand prize 1991, Bancroft prize 1992, George Perkins Marsh prize 1993); editor: (with Miles and Gitlin) Under an Open Sky: Rethinking America's Western Past, 1992, Uncommon Ground: Rethinking the Human Place in Nature, 1995; mem. bd. editors Forest and Conservation History, 1986-91; also articles; gen. editor Weyerhaeuser Environ. Books, U. Wash. Press, 1993—. Bd. dirs. Conn. Fund for Environ., 1986-91, v.p., 1987-89; adv. bd. TV series Am. Experience Sta. WGBH-TV; trustee Conn. Nature Conservancy, 1989-91; bd. dirs., mem. com. on problems and policy Social Sci. Rsch. Coun., 1991-96, chmn. com. on problems and policy, 1994-96. Rhodes scholar Oxford U., 1976-78; fellow Danforth Found., 1976-82, Newberry Libr., 1980, Mellon Found., 1982-83, Morse fellow Yale U., 1985-86, MacArthur Found., 1985-90, Whitney Humanities Ctr., 1987-89, fellow U. Calif. Humanities Rsch. Inst., 1994, Guggenheim fellow, 1995. Fellow AAAS, Wis. Acad. Sci., Arts and Letters; mem. Am. Hist. Assn. (Robinson prize com. 1990), Am. Philos. Soc. (v.p. profl. divsn. 2002—), Orgn. Am. Historians (chmn. Curti prize com. 1987-88), Forest History Soc. (bd. dirs.), Econ. History Assn., Agrl. History Soc., Ecol. Soc. Am., We. Hist. Assn. (conv. program com. 1987, chmn. 1991-92), Assn. Am. Geographers, Am. Studies Assn., Am. Anthrop. Assn., Wilderness Soc. (gov. coun. 1995—), Am. Soc. for Ethnohistory, Chgo. Hist. Soc., Am. Antiquarian Soc., Soc. Am. Historians, Phi Beta Kappa (William C. DeVane award Yale chpt. 1988), Phi Kappa Phi, Phi Eta Sigma; fellow Am. Acad. Arts & Sciences Office: U Wis Dept History 3211 Humanities 455 N Park St Madison WI 53706-1405 Home: 2027 Chadbourne Ave Madison WI 53726-4046 Office Phone: 608-265-6023. Business E-Mail: wcronon@wisc.edu.

CRONQUIST, ROBERT LEE, conductor; b. Chgo., June 10, 1929; s. Floyd Lee and Pearl Matilda Cronquist; m. Nancy Anne Konker (dec.); 1 child, Robert Jr.; m. Joan Debra Ferst, Sept. 22, 1995. Student, Ariz. State U., 1947—49; BS, Western Res. U., 1952, MA, 1956. Music dir., condr. Mansfield (Ohio) Symphony, 1954—76; music dir., condr., mgr. Lakeside (Ohio) Symphony, 1970—; mgr. Ohio Chamber Orch., Cleve., 1988—90; music dir., condr. Cleve. Women's Orch., 1990—. Asst. prof. West Liberty (W.Va.) Coll., 1958—59; dir. Harvard E. Branch, Cleve. Music Settlement, 1977—88; French horn player Phoenix Symphony, Cleve. Orch., Youngstown Symphony, Canton Symphony, Akron Symphony; guest condr. Ind. Chamber Orch., Ft. Wayne, Ind., Opera in Canton, Ohio. Scholar, Ariz. State Coll., 1947—49. Mem.: Cleve. Fedn. Musicians (life). Home: 2691 Country Club Blvd Rocky River OH 44116 Office: Womens Cleve Orch 2315 Warrensville Center Rd Cleveland OH 44118

CRONSON, ROBERT GRANVILLE, lawyer; b. Chgo., Dec. 23, 1924; s. Berthold A. and Ethel (Larson) C.; m. Agnes L. Diaz; children from previous marriage: Karen, Christopher, Keelyn, Morgan, Seth. AB in Econs., Dartmouth Coll., 1947; JD, U. Chgo., 1950. Bar: Ill. 1950. Atty. Daily, Dines, Ross & O'Keefe, Chgo., 1951-53; ptnr. DeBoice, Greening, Ackerman & Cronson, Springfield, Ill., 1957-60; asst. sec. of state of Ill. Springfield, 1958-64; sr. vp., sec. The Chgo. Corp., Chgo., 1965-73; assoc. prof. pub. adminstrn. Roosevelt U., 1973-74; adj. prof. adminstrn. Sangamon State U., 1983-87; auditor gen. State of Ill., 1974-92; retired, 1992. Mem. exec. com. post audit sect. Nat. Conf. State Legislatures, 1976-85, Nat. Assn. State Auditors, Comptrs. and Treasurers, 1979-81, and Nat. Intergovtl. Audit Forum, 1974-76; mem. Midwest Intergovtl. Audit Forum, 1974-92; adv. com. govt. acctg. standards Govt. Acctg. Stds. Bd. 1984-85. Chmn. Midwest Vehicle Proration Compact, 1959-61, Ill. Securities Adv. Com., 1964-73; chmn. William H. Chamberlain Scholarship Fund, Sangamon State U., 1972-85. Cpl. USMCR, 1942-46. Recipient Fin. Mgmt. Improvement (Scantlebury) award, U.S. Govt., 1980. Mem. Midwest Securities Commrs. Assn. (chmn. 1959-64), Securities Industry Assn. Am. (chmn. state legislation com. 1970-72), Nat. State Auditors Assn. (pres. 1980-81), Pi Alpha Alpha (hon.), Phi Kappa Psi. Republican. Congregationalist. Office Phone: 217-546-1330. Personal E-mail: jsnoopus@warpnet.net.

CROOK, CHARLES SAMUEL, III, lawyer; b. Des Moines, Iowa, Oct. 24, 1944; s. Charles Samuel, Jr. and Gertrude A. (Nichols) Crook; children: Donald, Michael, Brian, Nicole. BA, Drake U., 1969, JD, 1971. Bar: Iowa 1971. Law clk. to chief dist. judge U.S. Dist. Ct. (so. dist.), Iowa, 1971—73; pros. atty. Polk County Atty.'s Office, Des Moines, 1973—76; ptnr. Beving, Swanson & Forrest, P.C., Des Moines, 1976—83; pvt. practice Des Moines, 1983—. Lectr. Des Moines Area CC, 1979; assoc. prof. med. jurisprudence U. Osteo. Health Scis. Contbr. articles to profl. jours. Leader Cub Scouts Am., Des Moines. With US Army, 1963—66. Mem.: ABA, Nat. Bd. Trial Advocacy (cert. 1981—86), Polk County Bar Assn., Iowa Bar Assn. Democrat. Roman Catholic. Home: PO Box 721 Des Moines IA 50303-0721 Office: Fleming Bldg 218 6th Ave Ste 1100 Des Moines IA 50309-4005

CROOK, ROBERT WAYNE, retired portfolio manager; b. Hartford, Conn., Apr. 6, 1936; s. William Gregor and Laura Foster (Keenan) C.; m. Leslie C. Rischer, Oct. 22, 1988; children from previous marriage: Robert Wayne, Laura Sigrid. AB, Harvard U., 1959; postgrad., U. Va. Sch. Law, 1962. With White, Weld & Co., Inc., Boston, 1961—78, v.p., 1971—75, 1st v.p., 1975—78; pres., dir. White Weld Money Market Fund, Boston, 1974—78, White Weld Govt. Fund, Boston, 1977—78; with Merrill Lynch Asset Mgmt., Inc., Boston, 1978—2001, v.p., 1981—89, sr. v.p., 1989—2001; v.p. Merrill Lynch Funds Distbr., Inc., 1978—89, sr. v.p., 1989—2001; pres., trustee Merrill Lynch Funds for Instns. Series, Boston, 1978—2001, Merrill Lynch Tax-Exempt Fund, 1983—2001; mng. dir. Merrill Lynch Investment Mgrs., 1997—2001; ret., 2001. Served with U.S. Army, 1960. E-mail: jeyhue99@comcast.net.

CROOKE, ROBERT ANDREW, media consultant, writer, educator; b. Bklyn., Apr. 17, 1947; s. Henry A. and Theresa E. (Dougherty) C.; m. Angela Keller Lynch, Sept. 13, 1969; 1 child, Sean Peter. BA in English, Providence Coll., 1969; MA in English, Fordham U., 1974. Sports reporter, columnist L.I. Press, Jamaica, N.Y., 1969-75; profl. radio, TV, ednl. film script writer NYC, 1976-79; assoc. editor Mag. Age, NYC, 1979-81; reporter, contbg. editor L.I. Bus. Newsweekly, Ronkonkoma, N.Y., 1981-86; sr. acct. exec. Howard J. Rubenstein, NYC, 1986-87; dir. media rels. Reuters Am., Inc., NYC, 1987-94; v.p. comm. Reuters New Media, NYC, 1994-96; v.p. media rels. Reuters Am. Holdings, Inc., NYC, 1996-2000; mng. dir. Broadgate Consultants Inc., NYC, 2000-01; media cons. Makinson Cowell (US) Ltd., 2001—. Adj. instr. English Suffolk County C.C., Selden, N.Y., 1972-76; lectr. Sch. Journalism, U. Nebr., 1998-99, Sch. Journalism, U.S.C., 2000, U. Conn., 2006; adj. prof. pub. affairs NYU, 1998-2000. Author: (history) Between Ocean and Empire, 1985; (poetry) West Hills Rev., 1986, 87; (fiction) American Family, 2004. Office: PO Box 392 334 Main St S Bridgewater CT 06752-1537 Personal E-mail: rcrooke@msn.com.

CROOKE, STANLEY THOMAS, pharmaceutical executive; b. Indpls., Mar. 28, 1945; m. Nancy Alder (dec.); 1 child, Evan; m. Rosanne M. Snyder. BS in Pharmacy, Butler U., 1966; PhD, Baylor Coll., 1971, MD, 1974. Asst. dir. med. rsch. Bristol Labs., NYC, 1975-76, assoc. dir. med. rsch., 1976-77, assoc. dir. R&D, 1977-79, v.p. R&D, 1979-80, Smith Kline & French Labs., Phila., 1980-82; pres. R&D Smith Kline French, Phila., 1982-88; chmn. bd., CEO ISIS Pharms., Inc., Carlsbad, Calif., 1989. Chmn. bd. dirs. GES Pharms., Inc., Houston, 1989-91; adj. prof. Baylor Coll. Medicine, Houston, 1982, U. Pa., Phila., 1982-98; chmn. bd. dirs. GeneMedicine, Houston, 1996-98; bd. dirs. Calif. Healthcare Inst., 1993-2003, Indsl. Biotech. Assn., Washington, Idun Pharms., San Diego 1997-2002, Epix Med., Cambridge, Mass., 1996-2005, BIO, Washington, 1993-94; mem. sci. adv. bd. SIBIA, La Jolla, Calif. 1992-99; adj. prof. pharmacology UCLA, 1991, U. Calif. San Diego, 1994; bd. dirs. Synsorb Biotech Inc., Calgary, Can., 1999-2002; bd. dirs. Axon Instruments, Inc., Foster City, Calif. 1999-2004, Valentis, Inc., Burlingame, Calif., 1999-2002, Antisense Therapeutics Ltd., Toorak, Victoria, Australia, 2002-06, Applied Molecular Evolutions, Inc., San Diego, Calif., 2001-02, Biocom/San Diego, Calif., 2003—; mem. arts and scis. adv. coun. No. Ariz. U., 2002- Mem. editl. adv. bd. Molecular Pharmacology, 1986-91, Jour. Drug Targeting, 1992; editl. bd. Antisense Rsch. and Devel., 1994; sect. editl. bd. for biologicals and immunologicals Expert Opinion on Investigational Drugs, 1995. Trustee Franklin Inst., Phila., 1987-89; bd. dirs. Mann Music Ctr., Phila., 1987-89; children's com. Children's Svcs., Inc., Phila., 1983-84; adv. com. World Affairs Coun., Phila. Recipient Julius

Stermer award, Phila. Coll. Pharmacy and Sci., 1981, Outstanding Lectr. award, Baylor Coll. Medicine, 1984, Disting. Prof. award, U. Ky., 1986. Mem. AAAS, Am. Assn. for Cancer Rsch. (state legis. com.), Am. Soc. for Microbiology, Am. Soc. Pharmacology and Exptl. Therapeutics, Am. Soc. Clin. Pharmacology and Therapeutics, Am. Soc. Clin. Oncology, Indsl. Biotech. Assn. (bd. dirs. 1992-93). Achievements include numerous patents in field. Office: ISIS Pharms Inc 1896 Rutherford Rd Carlsbad CA 92008-7208 E-mail: scrooke@isisph.com.

CROOKS, NEIL PATRICK, state supreme court justice; b. Green Bay, Wis., May 16, 1938; s. George Merrill and Aurelia Ellen (O'Neill) C.; m. Kristin Marie Madson, Feb. 15, 1964; children: Michael, Molly, Kevin, Kathleen, Peggy, Eileen. BA magna cum laude, St. Norbert Coll., 1960; JD, U. Notre Dame, 1963. Bar: Wis. 1963, U.S. Supreme Ct. 1969. Assoc. Cohen and Parins, Green Bay, 1963; ptnr. Cohen, Grant, Crooks and Parins, Green Bay, 1966-70; sr. ptnr. Crooks, Jerry, Norman and Dilweg, Green Bay, 1970-77; judge Brown County (Wis.) Ct., 1977-78, Brown County (Wis.) Cir. Ct., 1978-96; justice Wis. Supreme Ct., Madison, 1996—. Instr. bus. law U. Wis., Green Bay, 1970-72; mem. faculty Wis. Jud. Coll., 1982. Editor Law Rev. Notre Dame, 1962-63. Pres. Brown County United Way, 1976-78; chmn. Brown County Legal Aid, 1971-73; mem. Northeast Criminal Justice Coord. Coun., 1973-85; pres. St. Joseph Acad. Sch. Bd., 1987-89. Capt. U.S. Army, 1963-66. Recipient Human Rights award Baha'i Community of Green Bay, 1971, Disting. Achievement award in Social Sci. St. Norbert Coll., 1977 award of Yr. U. Notre Dame, 1978, Brown County Vandalism Prevention Assn. award, 1982, W. Heraly MacDonald award Brown County United Way, 1983, Community Svc. award St. Joseph Acad., 1989, Alma Mater award St. Norbert Coll., 1992, Disting. Alumnus of Yr. award Notre Dame Acad., 2002; named Wis. Trial Judge of the Year Wis. Chpt. Am. Bd. of Trial Advocates, 1994. Mem. ABA (law sch. evaluator legal edn. and admissions sect.), FBA, State Bar Wis., Brown County Bar Assn. (pres. 1977), Wis. Acad. Trial Lawyers, Wis. Law Found. (bd. dirs., mem. exec. com.), Assn. of Women Lawyers for Brown County, Dane County Bar Assn., James E. Doyle Am. Inn of Ct., Wis. Jud. Coun., Notre Dame Law Assn. (dir.). Roman Catholic. Office: PO Box 1688 State Capitol 16 E Madison WI 53701 Home Phone: 608-222-6568; Office Phone: 608-266-1883. E-mail: patrick.crooks@wicourts.gov.

CROOKS, ROSELYN JUNE, artist, writer; b. Lancaster, Ohio, Sept. 15, 1924; d. Ralph E. and Mildred Cecelia (Lutz) Sieber; m. J. Robert Crooks, Apr. 7, 1951 (dec. Dec. 1988); children: John R., Kimberly K. BFA, Ohio State U., Columbus, 1946, postgrad., 1947. Illustrator Curtiss-Wright Corp., Columbus, 1944; advt.-display mgr. Hickle's Dept. Store, Lancaster, Ohio, 1947—48; pvt. practice Tucson, 1951—. Spkr. in field. Author: (short story) Ariz. Daily Star, 2007; one-woman shows include Skyline Country Club Gallery, Tucson, Ariz., 1980, 1982, 1983, 1986, 1999, 2001 (Pima County Art Competition for painting, 2005), 2005, exhibited in group shows at Tucson Mus. Art, Ariz., 1970, 1972, So. Ariz. Watercolor Guild, 1994, 1998, Skyline Country Club Gallery, 1984, 1986, 1987, 1992, 1992, 1995, 1995, 1998, 2000, 2002, 2004, 2006, 2007. Mem.: Skyline Art Group (founder 2004), So. Ariz. Watercolor Guild, Soc. Southwestern Authors (assoc.), Tucson (Ariz.) Mus. Art. Avocations: crossword puzzles, reading, travel. Home: 5822 N Placita Bacanora Tucson AZ 85718 Home Phone: 520-299-9230. Personal E-mail: roselynjc@aol.com.

CROOKSTON, R. KENT, agronomy educator; b. Magrath, Alta., Can., Mar. 8, 1943; s. Bryan Grant and Lisadore (Brown) C.; m. Gayle Loraine Jones, June 22, 1966; children: Rebecca, Casey, Polly, Daniel, Elizabeth, Emily, Sadie. BS, Brigham Young U., 1968; MS, U. Minn., 1970, PhD, 1972. Postdoctoral fellow Agr. Can., Lethbridge, Alta., 1972; rsch. assoc. Cornell U., Ithaca, NY, 1972-74; from asst. prof. to prof. U. Minn., St. Paul, 1974—82, dir. sustainable agr. program Coll. Agr., 1988-92, head dept. agronomy, 1990-98. Adj. prof. Inst. Agronomique Et Veterinaire Hassan II, Rabat, Morocco, 1984—; dean Coll. Biology and Agr., Brigham Young U., Provo, Utah, 1998-2005. Author rsch. manuscripts. With Can. armed forces, 1962. Fellow Am. Soc. Agronomy, Crop Sci. Soc. Am.; mem. Coun. Agrl. Sci. and Tech. Avocations: painting, woodworking, writing, photography. Home: 1055 N 1100 E Orem UT 84097-4390 Office: College of Biology and Agriculture 301 WIDB Brigham Young Univ Provo UT 84602-5250 Office Phone: 801-422-9142. Business E-Mail: kent_crookston@byu.edu.

CROOM, FREDERICK HAILEY, academic administrator, mathematician, educator; b. Lumberton, NC, Aug. 6, 1941; s. Robert DeVane and Anna Rosalyn (Currie) Croom; m. Henrietta Brown, Aug. 17, 1963 (div. May 2000); children: Elizabeth Bonner, Frederick Hailey; m. Nancy Mishoe Brennecke, June 1, 2002; children: Alexander McMillan, Augustus Brennecke. BS, U. N.C., 1963, PhD, 1967. Asst. prof. math. U. Ky., Lexington, 1967-71. U. of the South, Sewanee, Tenn., 1971-74, assoc. prof., 1974-81, prof., 1981—, dir. Summer Sch., 1980-88, assoc. dean, 1984-88, provost, 1989-2001. Author: (book) Basic Concepts of Algebraic Topology, 1978, Principles of Topology, 1989. Pres. Tenn. Coll. Assn., 1999—2000; bd. dirs. St. Andrews-Sewanee Sch., 1981—86, Tenn. Found. Ind. Colls., 1996—99; trustee U. of the South, 1983—85. Fellow Woodrow Wilson, 1963, NSF, 1963—67. Mem.: AAUP, Mat. Assn. Am., Am. Math. Soc., Sigma Xi. Episcopalian. Office: U South University Ave Sewanee TN 37383-0001 Office Phone: 931-598-3385. Business E-Mail: fcroom@sewanee.edu.

CROPSEY, JOSEPH, retired political science professor; b. NYC, Aug. 27, 1919; s. Gustave and Margaret Cropsey; m. Lillian Crystal Levy, Nov. 4, 1945 (dec.); children: Seth, Rachel Cropsey Simons. AB, Columbia U., 1939, A.M., 1940, PhD, 1952; DHL (hon.), Colo. Coll., 1989. Tutor, asst. prof. CCNY, 1946-57; instr. polit. sci. New Sch. Social Rsch., NYC, 1949-54; asst. prof. U. Chgo., 1958-64, assoc. prof., 1964-70, prof., 1970-85, Disting. Svc. prof., 1985-89, prof. emeritus, 1989—; ret., 1989. Author: Polity and Economy, 1957, Political Philosophy and the Issues of Politics, 1977, Plato's World, 1995; editor: Ancients and Moderns, 1964; co-editor, co-author: History of Political Philosophy, 1963 Served to 1st. lt. U.S. Army, 1941-46, PTO, ETO Office: U Chgo 5828 S University Ave Chicago IL 60637-1515

CRORY, ELIZABETH LUPIEN, retired state legislator; b. Gardner, Mass., Sept. 12, 1932; d. James Quaiel and Mary (Reilly) Lupien; m. Frederick E. Crory, Aug. 21, 1954; children: Thomas, David, Ellen, Ann, Edward, Stephen. AB, U. Mass., 1954; MALS, Dartmouth Coll., 1975. Tchr. Amherst (Mass.) Schs., 1954, Lyme (N.H.) Schs., 1972-76; mem. N.H. Ho. of Reps., 1977-87, 92-96, mem. commerce/consumer affairs com., 1977-87, 93-96, mem. spl. com. on med. malpractice, 1984; exec. dir. Children's Ctr. of Upper Valley, 1986-90. Bd. dirs. Mascoma Savs. Bank. Mem. character and fitness com. N.H. Supreme Ct., 1998-2005; chair N.H. Health Svcs. Planning and Rev. Bd., 1999-2005; bd. dirs. Kendal at Hanover, 2001—. Roman Catholic. Home: 40 Rip Rd Hanover NH 03755-1614 Personal E-mail: elizabethcrory@verizon.net.

CROSBY, DEBORAH BERRY, artist; b. Gulfport, Miss., Oct. 9, 1930; d. Thomas Davis and Deborah Bennett (Hewes) Berry; m. Charles E. McHale Jr., Nov. 23, 1950 (div. 1952); 1 child Deborah Bennett McHale; m. Hueston T. Fortner, Jr., Mar. 17, 1957 (div. 1963); 1 child, Hueston G. Fortner; m. Richard Louis Crosby, Dec. 27, 1981. BA, Sophie Newcomb Coll., 1951; MA, Ind. State U., 1968; postgrad., Utah State U., 1969, Tulane U., 1979; BA (hon.), U. New Orleans, 1984. Educator Wesleyan Coll., Rocky Mt., NC, 1969-70; prof. Spanish, Bay de Noc Coll., Escanaba, Mich., 1970-72; instr. yoga, Spanish, U. So. Miss.-Gulf Park Campus, Long Beach, 1972-78, Miss. Gulf Coast Jr. Coll. Dist., Keesler AFB Ctr., 1972-78; instr. reading, English, Miss. Gulf Coast Jr. Coll. Dist.-Jefferson Davis Campus, Keesler AFB Ctr., 1972-78; freelance artist Metairie, La., 1988—. Vis. artist at various galleries. One-woman shows include Dixie Art Co., Jefferson, La., 1990, World Trade Ctr., New Orleans, 1993—, Reginelli's Eating Gallery, 1994, Marceline Bonorden Fine Arts Gallery, 1998, 1999, Agora Gallery, Soho, N.Y.C., 2000, Movie Pitchers, 2000—01, Ambassador Hotel, New Orleans, 2002—04, Leahy Gardens, Covington, La., 2005, exhibited in group shows at Artists Showroom Gallery, 1993—95, Rivertown Art Gallery, Kenner, La., Slidell Cultural Ctr., La. State Archives, Baton Rouge, La., Martin Hall, U. of Mobile, Ala., George E. Ohr Arts and Cultural Ctr., Biloxi, Miss., Stamford (Conn.) Mus., Havre de Grace (Mich.) Mus., West Wind Gallery, Casper, Wyo., Jefferson SQ, Klamath Falls, Oreg., Destrehan (La.) Plantation, Lexington (Ky.) Mus., Falls River Mills, Calif., Our Lady of the Rosary Gallery, NOLA Pitot Historic Ho., New Orleans, Marceline Bonorden Fine Arts Gallery, The Purple Mullet Gallery, Ala., Serenity Gallery, The Artisan Mkt., Riverview Gallery, Zigler Art Mus., Jennings La., Amsterdam Whitney Internat. Fine Arts Gallery, Inc., NYC, 2002—, Regional Art Ctr., Hammond, La., 2004—, New Orleans Mus. Art, New Orleans Art Assn. Fine Arts Festival, Blue Bonnet Libr., Baton Rouge, 2007 (1st place), St. Charles Art Assn. (1st place), Metairie Art Guild, 1996 (1st place), Oil Met. Art Guild (1st place), Grumbacher (1st, 2d and 3d place, 2002), Rivertown Gallery, Kenner, La., 2005, La. Archives, Baton Rouge, 2006—, Riverstone Gallery, New Orleans, 2004—05, Represented in permanent collections World Trade Ctr., prin. works include Juvenile Diabetes Assn., 2001, Exhibited in group shows at WTC, New Orleans, 1995—2001; designer, executor (cover chess book) The Art of Bisguier, 2003; coloring book for Children's Life on a Louisiana Plantation, 2006. Chmn. auction Heart Ambs., 1995; mem. Ladies Leukemia League, 1994-, program chmn., 1996; mem. Goodwill Industries VS, 1995-2002, BRAVO Ballet, 1995—; Spring Fiesta hostess Napoleon's Home, Spring Fiesta Assn., 2002, 05, Bourbon Street Home, 2007; bd. dirs. Profl. Women's Adv. ABI, Inc., 2003, East Jefferson Hosp. Aux., 2005—, historian, 2004-07; active Contemporary Arts Ctr. NOLA, 2003, 05, New Orleans Arts Coun., 2003—; art chmn. East Jefferson Gen. Hosp., 2007—. Named Sweetheart, Local Br. Am. Heart Assn. Heart Ambs., 2001; recipient Superior Performance award, USAF, Keesler AFB, 1955, 1956, Lyricist award, U. New Orleans, 1984, Spl. Painting award, Winsor-Newton, 1994, Great Lady award, New Orleans Met. area by East Jefferson Hosp. Aux., 2000, Spl. award for lyricist for, Archbishop Hannan Sch. Song, New Orleans, 2006. Mem. Nat. League Am. Pen Women (chaplain 1996—, v.p. 1998-2000), New Orleans Art Assn. (v.p. 1995-98), Le Petit Art Guild (program chair 1995-97, Le Grand chair, 1995-2003, officer 1995-97), St. Charles Art Assn. (pres. 1994-95, Artist of Yr. award 1991-92), Nat. Mus. Women in the Arts, Newcomers Club. Avocations: yoga, community activist, languages, travel, songwriting. Home: 5600 Kawanee Ave Metairie LA 70003-1414 Office Phone: 504-455-1275.

CROSBY, EDWARD GEORGE, psychologist; b. Trenton, Mich., Aug. 28, 1970; s. Edward George Crosby Sr. and Carlotta Ann Gilbert; m. Bernadette Ann Itle, May 16, 1998; 1 child, Megan Elaine. BS, Marywood Coll., Scranton, Pa., 1992; MA, Boston Coll., Chestnut Hill, Mass., 1994; PhD, Pa. State U., University Park, 2004. Cert. sch. psychologist Pa. Dept. Edn., 2000, lic. psychologist State Bd. Psychology, Pa., 2007. Sch. psychologist Tuscarora Intermediate Unit 11, McVeytown, Pa., 2001—. Contbr. articles to profl. jours. Recipient award, Ednl. Comm. Scholarship Found., 1993, Rose Drexel Edn. award, Pa. State U., 1998. Mem.: APA (Early Career scholar 2005), NASP, Assn. Sch. Psychologists Pa., Phi Kappa Phi, Pi Lambda Theta, Phi Delta Kappa, Kappa Gamma Pi, Delta Epsilon Sigma. Roman Catholic. Office: Tuscarora Intermediate Unit 11 2527 US Hwy 522 South Mc Veytown PA 17051-9717 Office Phone: 814-644-9018 104. Business E-Mail: ecrosby@tiu11.org.

CROSBY, FRED MCCLELLAN, retail executive; b. Cleve., May 17, 1928; s. Fred Douglas and Marion Grace (Naylor) Crosby; m. Phendalyne D. Tazewell, Dec. 23, 1958; children: Fred, James, Llionicia. Grad. HS. V.p. Seaway Flooring & Paving Co., Cleve., 1959-63; chmn., CEO Crosby Furniture Co., Inc., Cleve., 1963—. Vice chmn. bd. dirs. First Bank Nat.; bd. dirs. Budget Rent-A-Car Sys., Surveyors Telecom., Inc.; bd. dirs., chmn. First Intercity Banc Corp. Commr. Nat. Small Bus. Adv. Coun., 1980; bd. dirs. Forest City Hosp. Found., Cleve. State U. Found., Greater Cleve. Growth Assn., 1971—90, 1993—, Coun. Smaller Enterprise, 1973—80, Goodwill Industries, 1973—80, 1997—, Woodruff Hosp., 1975—82, Cleve. Devel. Found., Pub. TV, Sta. WVIZ-TV, Cleve.-Cuyahoga Port Authority, 1986—90; bd. dirs., treas. Urban League Cleve., 1971—78; chmn. Minority Econ. Devel. Corp., 1972—83; chmn. bd. dirs. Glenville YMCA, 1973—76; dir. adv. coun. Ohio Bd. Workmen's Compensation, 1974—82; trustee Cleve. Play House, 1979—87, Eliza Bryant Health Care Ctr., 1984—86, Cleve. Small Bus. Incubator, 1986—90, Better Bus. Bur., 1995—, Ohio Motorist, 1993—, Murtis H. Taylor Mental Health, Metro Hosp. Sys. Found.; mem. adv. coun. Small Bus. Assn.; mem. adv. bd. Salvation Army, 1980; commr. Ohio State Boxing Commn., 1984—94, Pvt. Industry Coun., 1985; county commrs. appointee Cmty. Adv. Bd.; mem. Cleve. Opera Coun., 1987—89; Gov. Voinovich appointee to minority devel. fin. adv. bd., 1996—; bd. advs. Antioch Coll. With US Army, 1950—52. Named Family of the Yr., Cleve. Urban League, 1971; recipient award bus. excellence, Dept. Commerce, 1972, Presdl. award, YMCA, 1974, Gov. Ohio award cmty. action, 1973, 1st Class Leadership, Cleve., 1977. Mem.: NAACP (v.p. Cleve. 1969—78, exec. dir.), Ohio Home Furnishings and Appliance Assn. (pres. 1981—87), Ohio Coun. Retail Mchts. (chmn. 1991—93), Am. Auto Assn. (corp. mem.), Cleve. C. of C., Univ. Club (Cleve.), Braternahl Club, Harvard Bus. Sch. Club, Mid-Day Club, Rotary, Clevelander, Exec. Order Ohio Commodore. Office: 12435 Saint Clair Ave Cleveland OH 44108-2013 Home Phone: 216-752-5678; Office Phone: 216-541-5040. Personal E-mail: phendaly@aol.com.

CROSBY, GLENN ARTHUR, chemistry professor; b. Youngwood, Pa., July 30, 1928; s. Edwin Glenn and Bertha May (Ritchey) C.; m. Jane Lichtenfels, May 29, 1950; children: Brian, Alan, Karen. BS, Waynesburg Coll., 1950; PhD, U. Wash., 1954. Rsch. assoc. Fla. State U., Tallahassee, 1955-57, vis. asst. prof. physics, 1957; asst. prof. chemistry U. N. Mex., Albuquerque, 1957-62, assoc. prof. chemistry, 1962-67; prof. chemistry and materials sci. Wash. State U., Pullman, 1967—2001, chmn. chem. physics program, 1977-84, prof. emeritus, 2001—. Mem. adv. com. Rsch. Corp., Tucson, 1981—88, 1990—92; vis. prof. phys. chemistry U. Tubingen, Germany, 1964; vis. prof. physics U. Canterbury, Christchurch, New Zealand, 1974; Humboldt sr. scientist, vis. prof. phys. chemistry U. Hohenheim, Germany, 1978—79; mem. commn. on life scis. NRC, 1991—96, com. on programs for advanced study math and sci. in U.S. h.s., 1999—2001. Author: Chemistry: Matter and Chemical change, 1962; also numerous sci. and sci.-related articles Recipient U.S. Sr. Scientist award Humboldt Found., Fed. Republic Germany, 1978-79, Catalyst award Chem. Mfrs. Assn., 1979, Disting. Alumnus award Waynesburg Coll., 1982, Wash. State U.Faculty Excellence award in instrn., 1984, Wash. State U. Faculty Excellence award for pub. svc., 1989, Disting. Prof. award Wash. State U. Mortar Bd., 1990, Wash State U. Legacy Excellence award, 2006, Pres.'s medallion Waynesburg Coll. for disting. lifetime sci. and ednl. achievement, 1998; named Prof. of Yr., U. N.Mex., 1967; NSF fellow U. Wash., Seattle, 1953-54; Rsch. Corp. Venture grantee, 1960; Fulbright fellow, 1964. Fellow: AAAS, Wash. Sci. Tchrs. Assn. (Outstanding Coll. Sci. Tchr. award 1975), Inter-Am. Photochem. Soc.; mem.: Am. Inst. Chemists (Chem. Pioneer award 2006), Nat. Sci. Tchrs. Assn., Am. Phys. Soc., Am. Chem. Soc. (numerous activities including chmn. divsn. chem. edn. 1982, chmn. com. on edn. 1990—91, bd. dirs. 1994—2002, Western Conn. sect. Vis. Scientist award 1981, Nat. award in chem. edn. 1985, Harry and Carol Mosher award Santa Clara Valley sect. 1998, Divsn. Chem. Edn. Outstanding Svc. award 2003), Sigma Xi, Sigma Pi Sigma, Phi Kappa Phi. Home: 1208 E Excelsior Rd Spokane WA 99224-9257 E-mail: gac@wsunix.wsu.edu.

CROSBY, JACQUELINE GARTON, newspaper editor, journalist; b. Jacksonville, Fla., May 13, 1961; d. James Ellis and Marianne (Garton) Crosby. ABJ, U. Ga., 1983; MBA, U. Cen. Fla., 1987. Staff writer Macon Telegraph & News, Ga., 1983-84; copy editor Orlando Sentinel, Fla., 1984-85; dir. spl. projects Ivanhoe Communications, Inc., Orlando, Fla., 1987-89; producer spl. projects Sta. KSTP-TV, Mpls., 1989-94; asst. news editor Star Tribune Online, Mpls., 1994—2003, reporter, 2003—. Recipient award for best sports story Ga. Press Assn., 1982; award for best series of yr. AP, 1985, Pulitzer prize, 1985 Mem. Quill Avocations: competing in triathlons, playing electric bass, tutoring, reading. Home: 5348 Drew Ave S Minneapolis MN 55410-2006 Office: Star Tribune 425 Portland Ave Minneapolis MN 55488-0001

CROSBY, JOHN BARTLETT, lawyer, health science association administrator; b. South Bend, Ind., Mar. 25, 1947; s. John Strong and Dorothy (Bartlett) C.; m. Mary Jo Knaup, Dec. 27, 1969; children: Lara, Patrick, Anne. BA in History, Washington U., St. Louis, 1969; JDS cum laude, Ohio State U., 1972. Assoc. Thompson & Mitchell, St. Louis, 1972-77; adminstrv. asst. Congressman Richard A. Gephardt, Washington, 1977-81; dir. Project Hope Ctr. for Health Info., Millwood, Va., 1982-83; sr. v.p. and gen. counsel Nat. Assn. of Ind. Insurers, Des Plaines, Ill., 1983-89; sr. v.p. health policy AMA, Chgo., 1989-97; exec. dir. Am. Osteo. Assn., Chgo., 1997—. Bd. dirs. Chgo. Health Policy Rsch. Coun., 1993-2000, Health Care Quality Alliance, 1993-99, Nat. Health Coun., 2004-06. Mem. ABA, Mo. State Bar Assn. Office: Am Osteopathic Assn 142 E Ontario St Chicago IL 60611 Office Phone: 312-202-8001. E-mail: jcrosby@osteopathic.org.

CROSBY, JOHN GRIFFITH, investment banker; b. Bayshore, NY, Feb. 10, 1943; s. Gordon Josiah and Ruth Louise (Plante) C.; m. Joan Louise Kelly, July 10, 1965; children: Bruce, Brian, David. BA with distinction, Lafayette Coll., 1965; MBA, Harvard U., 1969. V.p., stockholder, dir. Kidder, Peabody & Co. Inc., NYC, 1969-80; mng. dir. Merrill Lynch & Co., NYC, 1980-90; ptnr. The Lodestar Group, 1990-93; mng. dir. LSG Advisors, 1993-95; chmn., pres. Madison Ptnrs., Inc., 1995—. Author: Private Placement Market Review, 1975-81. Class fund mgr. Lafayette Coll., 1969-90, mem. leadership coun., 1997-2001; bd. deacons Presbyn. Ch., Madison, N.J., 1972; campaign chmn. Madison YMCA, 1975; coach Little League, 1977-84; treas. troop 125 Boy Scouts Am., 1984-87; bd. dirs. asst. treas. Am. Coun. Arts, 1987-90; pres. PTO, 1979-80. 1st lt. U.S. Army, 1965-67, Vietnam. Decorated Bronze Star medal. Mem.: Orchid Island Golf and Beach Club (bd. govs.). Home (Winter): 534 White Pelican Cir Vero Beach FL 32963-9561 Home (Summer): 5972 Lake Shore Dr Bolton Landing NY 12814-4521 Personal E-mail: nuinweh@aol.com.

CROSBY, MARENA LIENHARD, retired academic administrator; b. Shreveport, La., Mar. 2, 1948; d. John Joseph and Clara Curtis (Lawton) L.; m. H.W. Patrick Obrien, Sept. 23, 1977; m. John L. Crosby, Nov. 23, 1997. MEd, U. New Orleans; JD, Loyola U., New Orleans. Bar: La. 1971; lic. profl. counselor, La.; diplomate Am. Coll. Profl. Mental Health Practitioners. Instr. Delgado C.C., New Orleans, 1973-80, counselor, 1980-86, coord. testing, 1986-88, dir. admissions, 1988-90, dir. counseling and mktg., 1990-93, dir. degree audit program, 1993-97, asst. to v.p. student affairs, 1997-98, ret., 1998. Mem. DAR, FBA, ACA, Internat. Assn. New Sci., Assn. Rsch. and Enlightenment, Am. Psychotherapy Assn., Am. Mental Health Counselors Assn., Inst. Noetic Scis., Theosophical Soc. Am., Family Mediation Coun., La. Bar Assn., La. Notary Assn., La. Assn. Spiritual and Religious Values in Counseling, New Orleans Bar Assn., New Orleans Womens Opera Guild, New Orleans Mus. Art, Colonial Dames, Magna Charta Dames. Republican. Avocations: reading, piano. Home: 811 Rue Royal Metairie LA 70005 Personal E-mail: cmloc18@aol.com.

CROSBY, MICHAEL P., science administrator; BS, Old Dominion U., MS with honors; PhD in Marine-Estuarine-Environ. Sci., U. Md. Various sci. positions Nat. Marine Fisheries Svc., U.S. Army Corps Engrs., Nat. Cancer Inst., NIH; numerous faculty positions U. S.C., Coastal Carolina U., U. Charleston, Salisbury State U.; exec. dir. nat. sci. bd. Nat. Oceanic and Atmospheric Adminstrn., nat. rsch. coord. ocean and coastal resource mgmt., chief scientist sanctuaries and reserves, sr. adv. internat. sci. policy under sec. office internat. affairs; sr. sci. adv. marine and coastal ecosystems U.S. Agency Internal Devel.; exec. officer, office dir. Nat. Sci. Bd., 2003—. Mem. numerous nat. and internat. sci. panels and adv. coms. Panelist, reviewe: numerous sci. jours.; editor: numerous books and manuals on marine protected areas and coral reefs. Grantee NSF, Nat. Oceanic and Atmospheric Adminstrn., EPA, DOD, USAID, others. Fellow: Royal Linnean Soc. London; mem.: AAAS, Pacific Congress Marine Sci. and Tech., Sci. Rsch. Soc., Estuarine Rsch. Fedn., Nat. Shellfisheries Assn., Coastal Soc., Nat. Areas Assn., Sigma Xi. Office: Nat Sci Bd 4201 Wilson Blvd Arlington VA 22230 Office Phone: 703-292-7000. E-mail: mcrosby@nsf.gov.

CROSBY, NATHANIEL HOWARD, elementary school educator; b. Milo, Maine, July 3, 1949; s. Luthan Albert and Patricia Cousins Crosby; m. Elaine Marie Martin, Dec. 27, 1977; children: Nathaniel, Marita, Derrick, Kyle, Nyssa, Desmond, Brianna, Jordanna. BS, U. Maine, Fort Kent, 1971. Cert. tchr. U. Maine, 1971. Tchg. asst. Fort Kent Elem. Sch., 1971, tchr., 1972—84; labor-mgmt. rep., auditor State of Maine, 1984—88, command logistics officer, 1988—90; tchr. Chelsea Elem. Sch., Maine, 1990—. Sec., v.p. Greater Augusta Fed. Employee Assn., 1985—89; acad. team leader Chelsea Elem. Sch., 1991, student assistance team-leader, 1995—2005. Active Maine Army N.G., Augusta, 1984—90. Capt. US Army, 1971—90, comdr. svc. battery and battalion S-4 US Army, 1980—84. Recipient 12 Svc. award, Fort Kent Elem. Sch., 1985. Republican. Avocations: hunting, fishing, writing. Home: 396 Pond Rd Wayne ME 04284 Office: Chelsea Elem Sch 566 Togus Rd Augusta ME 04330 Personal E-mail: nathaniel_crosby@yahoo.com.

CROSBY, NORMAN LAWRENCE, comedian; b. Boston, Sept. 15, 1927; s. John and Ann (Lansky) C.; m. Joan Crane Foley, Nov. 1, 1966; children: Daniel Joseph, Andrew Crane. Student, Mass. Sch. Art, Boston. Ind. comedian, entertainer, 1947—. Nat. spokesman Anheuser-Busch Natural Light Beer. Began work as comedian in New Eng. clubs, frat. and polit. dinners, numerous civic and charity functions; N.Y.C. debut Latin Quarter; several appearances London Palladium, regular appearances at all major hotels in Las Vegas, numerous other night clubs, concert halls, theaters, TV variety and panel shows; host: (syndicated TV series) Norm Crosby's Comedy Shop; nat. co-host on Jerry Lewis Muscular Dystrophy Assn. Telethon. Nat. hon. chmn. better Hearing Inst., Washington; trustee Hope for Hearing Found., UCLA; sponsor Norm Crosby Ann. Celebrity Golf Tournament benefitting City of Hope. With USCG, 1945-46. Recipient Jack Benny Comedy award Authors and Celebrities, 1981, Star on Hollywood (Calif.) Walk of Fame, Hollywood C. of C., 1982, Lifetime Achievement award in Entertainment, Touchdown Club, Washington, 1988, Victory award, Kennedy Ctr. Pres. George Bush, 1991; honored by USO and given privilege of laying wreath at tomb of Unknown Soldiers, Washington, 2001; named Internat. Variety Clubs Man of Yr., 1986; recipient Lifetime Achievement award in Comedy, Emerson Coll., Boston Comedy Festival. Mem. Friars Club (N.Y.C., L.A.; 20th term Internat. Amb. of Good Will for City of Hope), Masons, Shriners. Jewish. Personal E-mail: jonoprod@webtv.net.

CROSBY, PETER ALAN, management consultant; b. Santa Barbara, Calif., Oct. 20, 1945; s. Harold Bartley and Margaret Maida (Peterson) C.; m. Stephanie Jay Ellis, Dec. 20, 1969; children: Kelly Michelle, Michael Ellis. BS in Engring., U. Calif., Berkeley, 1967; MS in Ops. Rsch., Stanford U., 1969; ED, Stanford Bus. Sch., 1971. Cert. mgmt. cons. Logistics inventory analyst Ford Motor Co., Palo Alto, Calif., 1967-71; corp. ops. planning analyst FMC Corp., San Jose, Calif., 1972; assoc. mgmt. cons. A.T. Kearney, Inc., San Francisco, 1972-75; mgr. materials mgmt. cons. svcs. Coopers & Lybrand, Los Angeles, 1976-78; ptnr. gen. cons. unit (Case & Co.) Towers Perrin Forster & Crosby, LA, 1978-81; prin. Crosby, Gustin, Rice & Co. (CGR Mgmt. Cons.), 1981—. Dir. Carbide Products Internat. Co. Mem. adv. bd. dirs. Stanton Chase. Mem. Coun. Logistic Mgmt., Inst. Mgmt. Cons. (past pres.), Food Cons. Group, Assn. for Corp. Growth, Phi Gamma Delta. Office: CGR Mgmt Consultants Ste 1900 1901 Avenue Of The Stars Los Angeles CA 90067-6020 Office Phone: 310-553-6837. Personal E-mail: crosbycgr@cs.com. Business E-Mail: petecrosby@cgrmc.com.

CROSBY, RALPH WOLF, communications executive; b. Annapolis, Md., Dec. 16, 1933; s. Raymond Thomas and Lillian Sylvia (Wolf) C.; m. Carlotta Stafford, June 16, 1958; children: Laura Crosby Avallone, Raymond, Belinda Crosby Butler. BS in Journalism, U Md., 1956. Reporter, editor Balt. News-Am., 1956-60; bur. editor Iron Age Mag., Washington, 1960-65, Med. Econs. mag., Washington, 1966-67; assoc. editor Kiplinger's Changing Times, Washington, 1967-70; exec. v.p. Annapolis Harbour House, Inc., 1970-86; chmn., CEO Crosby Mktg. Comm., Annapolis, 1972—. Bd. dirs. Annapolis Bank and Trust Co. Editor (book) Person to Person Management, 1966; contbr. articles to numerous mags. including N.Y. Times Mag. Bd. govs. U. Md. Coll. Journalism, 2005—. Recipient Jesse H. Neal editorial award, 1966. Mem. Md. Direct Mktg. Assn., Advt. Assn. Balt., Greater Annapolis C. of C. (pres. 1975-76, hall of fame 2005), Annapolis Bus. Coalition (pres. 1983-84), Nat. Press Club, Annapolis Touchdown Club (pres. 1976), U. Md. Coll. Journalism (bd. govs., 2005—), U. Md. Dean's First Edit. Club (chmn. 1986—, named Cool. of Journalism Alumnus of the Yr. 2005), Annapolitan Club. Democrat. Avocation: tennis. Home: 139 Wallace Manor Rd Edgewater MD 21037-1205 Office: Crosby Mktg Comms 705 Melvin Ave Ste 200 Annapolis MD 21401-1544 Office Phone: 410-626-0805.

CROSBY, SAMUEL NEIL, lawyer; b. Evanston, Ill., July 13, 1951; BA, U. Va., 1973; JD, U. Ala., 1978. Bar: Ala. 1978, US Dist. Ct. (So. Dist. Ala.) 1979. Mcpl. judge, Loxley, Ala., 1989—94; ptnr. Stone, Granade & Crosby PC, Daphne, Ala. Adj. prof. U. South Ala.; editl. bd. Ala. Lawyer, 1987—88, Addendum. Author: (short stories) The Sleeping Juror, 2002. Trustee U. Ala. Law Sch. Found., mem. law sch. exec. com.; mem. Chief Justice's Commn. on Professionalism, Ala. Law Inst., Ala., 2005. Ret. JAG Corps US Naval Res. Fellow: Ala. Law Found. (life); mem.: Baldwin County Bar Assn. (pres. 1987—88), Ala. State Bar Assn. (pres.-elect 2006—07, pres. 2007). Office: Stone Granade & Crosby PC 7133 Stone Dr Daphne AL 36526 Office Phone: 251-626-6696. Office Fax: 251-626-2617.

CROSBY, SIDNEY, professional hockey player; b. Cole Harbor, Nova Scotia, Can., Aug. 7, 1987; Center Rimouski Oceanic (QMJHL), Canada, 2003—05, Pitts. Penguins, 2005—, capt., 2007—. Center Team Canada, World Junior Championships, Helsinki, Finland, 2004, Grand Forks, ND, 05. Named Rookie of the Yr., Can. Hockey League, 2004, Player of the Yr., 2004, 2005, NHL Player of Yr., Sporting News, 2007, Best NHL Player, ESPY awards, 2007; named to NHL All-Star Game, 2007, First All-Star Team, NHL, 2007; recipient Mark Messier Leadership Award, 2007, Art Ross Trophy, 2007, Hart Trophy, 2007, Lester B. Pearson Award, 2007. Achievements include being the only player under the age of 18 to play for the Canadian Junior Hockey Team, 2004; being the first overall draft pick in NHL entry draft, 2005; leading the CHL in scoring, 2004, 2005; being a member of Gold Medal Team Canada, World Junior Championships, 2005; being the youngest captain in NHL history. Office: c/o Pittsburgh Penguins 66 Mario Lemieux Pl Pittsburgh PA 15219*

CROSBY, WILLIAM DUNCAN, JR., lawyer; b. Louisville, Sept. 1, 1943; s. William Duncan and Lucille (Edwards) C.; m. Constance Elaine Frederick, June 2, 1973; children: William Duncan III, Lelia Margaret. BA, Yale U., 1965; JD, Columbia U., 1968. Bar: Ky. 1968, U.S. Dist. Ct. D.C. 1971, U.S. Supreme Ct. 1977. Rep. chief counsel Com. on Rules U.S. Ho. of Reps., Washington, 1972-94, chief counsel Com. on Rules, 1995-99; v.p., COO The Solomon Group, Washington, 1999—2001; exec. dir. The Livingston Solomon Group, LLC, Washington, 2002—03; prin. The Livingston Group, LLC, Washington, 2003—05, cons., 2005—; pres. The Crosby Group, LLC, Washington, 2005—. Chmn. Dranesville Dist., Fairfax County (Va.) Rep. Party, 1987-89; mem. Fairfax County Rep. Com., 1981—, chmn. fin. com., 2003—04. Lt. (j.g.) USNR, 1968-71. Mem. ABA, FBA, Ky. Bar Assn., D.C. Bar, The Federalist Soc., Columbia Law Sch. Alumni Assn. of Washington (pres. 1987-89). Republican. Baptist. Avocation: swimming. Home: 920 Mackall Ave Mc Lean VA 22101-1618 Office: The Livingston Group LLC 499 S Capitol St SW Ste 600 Washington DC 20003 Office Phone: 202-289-9881. Personal E-mail: billcrosby1@aol.com. Business E-Mail: bcrosby@livingstongroupdc.com.

CROSKELL, MADELON BYRD, music educator, classical vocalist; b. Ardmore, Okla., Nov. 16, 1937; d. Lyndall Rae Byrd and Avis Madeline Bradshaw; m. Henry Croskell, July 24, 1955; children: Maralyn Lee and Mark Henry Student, U. N.Mex., Albuquerque, 1955, Southeastern State U. Okla., Durant, 1956—58; MusB cum laude, U. Mo., St. Louis, 1979. Nat. cert. tchr. music - piano and theory. V.p. Ind. Piano Tchrs. Guild, Indpls., 1964—69, Okla. Music Tchrs. Assn., Bartlesville, 1969—72, St. Louis Area Music Tchrs. Assn., 1974—89; tchr. music, dir. choir Parkway Ctrl. Jr. H.S., St. Louis, 1979—80. Performed 32 oratories with Indpls. Symphonic Choir, St. Louis Symphony; contbr. articles to Mo. Music Tchrs. Notes, 1980-89 Vol. sr. tour guide Mo. Bot. Garden, St. Louis, 1978-89 Mem. Nat. Fedn. Music Clubs (jr. counselor), Music Tchrs. Nat. Assn., Tex. Music Tchrs. Assn., Dallas Music Tchrs. Assn. (bd. dirs., founder Playathon 2004), Richardson Music Tchrs. Assn. (bd. dirs., pres. 1989-2007, founder Playathon 1995-2007), St. Louis Area Music Tchrs. Assn. (founder Music Masters 1984-2007), Sigma Alpha Iota (Sword of Honor award St. Louis chpt., pres. alumnae chpt. 1974-89) Republican. Presbyterian. Avocations: gardening, horseback riding, swimming, reading. Office Phone: 972-233-9990. Personal E-mail: madelonbc88k@earthlink.net.

CROSLEY, DAVID RISDON, chemical physicist; b. Webster City, Iowa, Mar. 4, 1941; s. Carlton Whitley and Helen Elizabeth (Mingle) C.; m. Barbara DeVries, Sept. 7, 1963 (div. 1985); 1 child, Stephen Risdon. BS, Iowa State U., 1962; MA, Columbia U., 1963, PhD, 1966. Postdoctoral fellow Joint Inst. Lab. Astrophysics, Boulder, Colo., 1966-68; prof. U. Wis., Madison, 1968-75; rsch. chemist Ballistic Rsch. Lab., Aberdeen, Md., 1975-79; program mgr. SRI Internat., Menlo Park, Calif., 1979-88, assoc. lab. dir., 1988-95, lab. dir., 1995—2001, sr. staff scientist, 2001—. Cons. Battelle, Columbus, Ohio, 1975-81, Sci. Applications Internat. Corp., La Jolla, Calif., 1982-86, NASA, Washington, 1984-89; vis. prof. Ruhr U., Bochum, Fed. Republic of Germany, 1988, U. Paris, Orsay, France, 1989, U. Bielefeld, Germany, 1997, U. Leeds, Eng., 2004. Editor: Laser Probes of Combustion Chemistry, 1980; contbr. over 190 articles to sci. jours. NSF grad. fellow, 1964-66. Fellow Am. Phys. Soc., AAAS; mem. Am. Chem. Soc., Combustion Inst., Am. Geophysical Union, Pi Mu Epsilon, Phi Lambda Upsilon, Sigma Chi. Democrat. Achievements include research in laser-induced fluorescence spectroscopy, quantum state specific collisional energy transfer, gas-phase reaction kinetics and laser-based diagnostic techniques, environmental monitoring and applications to small molecules important in the chemistry of combustion, the atmosphere and materials processing. Office: SRI Internat Molecular Physics Lab Menlo Park CA 94025 Home Phone: 650-494-8727; Office Phone: 650-859-2395. Business E-Mail: david.crosley@sri.com.

CROSMAN, CHRISTOPHER BYRON, museum director; b. Chgo., June 25, 1946; s. John Byron and Leila (Pomeroy) C.; m. Janet Thomas, Dec. 28, 1968; 1 child, Anne. BA, Washington and Lee U., 1968; postgrad., Oberlin Coll., 1970-72. Educator Albright-Knox Gallery, Buffalo, 1972-84; dir. Heckscher Mus., Huntington, N.Y., 1984-88, Farnsworth Art Mus., Rockland, Maine, 1988—. Panelist N.Y. State Coun. on Arts, N.Y.C., 1982-85; mem. adv. coun. adult learning, N.Y. Dept. Edn., Albany, 1982-85; bd. dirs. Gallery Assn. N.Y. State, Hamilton, 1986-88, Maine Coast Artists, Rockport, 1988—; treas. L.I. Mus. Assn., 1987-88. Co-author: From Museums, Libraries and Galleries: Artists on Tape, 1984; contbr. articles to profl. jours.; co-producer video documentaries, 1974-84; curator exhbns. Mem. Am. Assn. Mus., Maine League Hist. Socs. and Mus., Rotary. Office: Farnsworth Art Mus 16 Museum St Rockland ME 04841-0466

CROSMER, JANIE LYNN, insurance company executive; b. Sioux City, Iowa, Nov. 8, 1969; d. William J. and Penny Lou Crosmer; m. Scott Thomas Clifford, Feb. 14, 1971. BS, Iowa State U., Ames, 1993; MS, Tex. Woman's U., Denton, 2000, MBA, 2006, post grad., 2002—. Cert. cmty. health edn. specialist The Nat. Commn. Health Edn. Credentialing, Inc., 1997, gen. lines agent Tex. Dept. Ins., 2000. Managed care technician Medicap Pharmacies, Inc., West Des Moines, Iowa, 1993—94; mktg. coord., fitness dir. SportsRidge Athletic Club, Richardson, Tex., 1994—95; response Coord., profl. rels. and customer svc. rep. PCA Health Plans Tex., Dallas, 1995—97; sr. client svc. specialist UnitedHealth Group, Plano, Tex., 1997—99; account exec. Waldman Bros., Dallas, 1999—2001; dental strategic account exec. UnitedHealth Group, Plano, Tex., 2001; strategic account exec. Optum, 2006—. Tchg. asst. Tex. Woman's U., Denton, Tex., 2002—. Treas. bd. dirs. Grand Park Estates Homeowners Assn. Named Outstanding Sr. in Cmty. Health Edn., Iowa State U., 1993; recipient Top Dental Sales Achievement award, UnitedHealthcare Dental, 2004, United-Healthcare Pinnacle award, 2001; scholar, Iowa State U., 1992. Mem.: Am. Alliance for Health, Phys. Edn., Recreation and Dance, DFW Cyclone Club, Iowa State Alumni Assn. (ambassador). Methodist. Avocations: swimming, exercise, piano, reading. Home: 2021 Cartwright Ct Flower Mound TX 75028 Office: Optum PO Box 9472 Minneapolis MN 55440-9472 Home Phone: 972-539-9194; Office Phone: 972-874-2062. Home Fax: 972-355-0487. Personal E-mail: jlcrosmer@verizon.net. Business E-Mail: janie_l_crosmer@uhc.com.

CROSS, ALVIN MILLER (AL CROSS), journalist; b. Knoxville, Tenn, Apr. 24, 1954; s. Perry Martin and Winnie Cook (Miller) C.; m. Patricia Hodges, June 19, 1976. BA in Mass Comm., Western Ky. U., 1978; postgrad., Poynter Inst. Media Studies, 1999. Sports reporter Clinton County News, Albany, Ky., 1965—71; announcer WANY Radio, Albany, 1968-75; advt. mgr., reporter, editor College Heights Herald, Bowling Green, Ky., 1973-74; editor and gen. mgr. The Reporter, Monticello, Ky., 1974-75; asst. mng. editor Logan Leader & News-Democrat, Russellville, Ky., 1975-77; editor Leitchfield Gazette, Grayson County News-Gazette, Ky., 1977-78; reporter Courier-Journal, Louisville, 1978-88, polit. writer, 1989—2004, polit. columnist, 1999—; dir. Inst. for Rural Journalism and Cmty. Issues U. Ky., Lexington, 2004—. Contbg. author: Campaigns and Elections: Contemporary Case Studies, 2002, Kentucky Governors, 2004, Kentucky 24/7, 2004. Rep. acad. coun. Associated Student Govt. We. Ky. U., 1972-73; bd. dirs. Sigma Delta Chi Found, 2001—. Recipient Founder's award Foothills Festival Inc., Albany, 1989, Outstanding Print Journalist in Ky. and Adjoining States award journalism dept. Western Ky. U., 1995, Deadline Reporting award Metro Louisville Journalism, 1989, 92, Column Writing award, 1989, 2004, Continuing Coverage award, 1992, 95. Mem. Soc. Profl. Journalists (regional dir. 1987-89, v.p. Louisville chpt. 1983-84, pres. 1984-85, chmn. nat. com. Project Watchdog 1995-99, nat. sec.-treas. 1999-2000, pres.-elect 2000-01, pres. 2001-02, Outstanding Newspaper in Region 5 award 1974, Outstanding Ky. Journalist 2005), Ky. Hist. Soc., Appalachian Studies Assn., Filson Hist. Soc, Com. Concerned Journalists, Internat. Soc. Weekly Newspaper Editors, Assn. for Edn. in Journalism and Mass. Comm., Nat. Newspaper Assn., Western Ky. U. Alumni Assn. Baptist. Avocations: reading, gardening, boating, touring. Home: 123 W Todd St Frankfort KY 40601-2825 Office: U Ky 122 Grehan Bldg Lexington KY 40506-0042 Office Phone: 859-257-3744. E-mail: al.cross@uky.edu.

CROSS, AUREAL THEOPHILUS, geology and botany educator; b. Findlay, Ohio, June 4, 1916; s. Raymond Willard and Myra Jane (Coon) C.; m. Christina Aleen Teyssier, Mar. 11, 1945; children: Timothy Aureal, Christina Avonne Cross Collier, Jonathan Ariel, Cheryl Aleen (Mrs. Richard M. Bowman), Christopher Charles. BA, Coe Coll., 1939; MS in Botany, U. Cin., 1941, PhD in Botany and Paleontology, 1943. Instr. to asst. prof. U. Notre Dame, 1942—46; NRC fellow in geology, 1943—44; paleobotanist; with Ctrl. Expt. Sta., U.S. Bur. Mines, Pitts., 1945; asst. prof. dept. geology U. Cin., 1946—49, asst. prof. dept. botany, 1948—49; part-time geologist Geol. Survey Ohio, 1946—51; coal geologist and paleobotanist W.Va. Geol. and Econ. Survey, 1949—57; assoc. prof. to prof. dept. geology U. W.Va., 1949—57; sr. rsch. engr. Pan Am. Petroleum Corp. Rsch. Center, Tulsa, 1957—61, supr. tech. group and rsch. group, 1959—61; prof. dept. geology Mich. State U., East Lansing, 1961—86, prof. dept. botany and plant pathology, 1961—86, prof. emeritus East Lansing, 1987—. Prof. ecology U. Alaska, 1971; rsch. palynologist U. So. Calif., 1972; Morton vis. prof. Ohio U., Athens Ohio, 1981; Nathaniel S. Shaler Disting. lectr. U. Ky., 1991; UNESCO adviser U. grants commn. India Coal Programs, 1983; Calcutta adviser geology dept. Jadavpur U., India, 1983. Editor: Palynology in Oil Exploration, 1964, Compte Rendu 9th Internat. Congress Carboniferous Stratigraphy and Geology, vol. 4, Econ. Geology: Coal, Oil and Gas, 1985; co-editor: Coal Resources and Research in Latin America, 1978, World Class Coal Deposits, Internat. Jour. Coal Geology, 1993; assoc. editor: Fossil Spores and Pollen, 55 vols. 1956-87; contbr. articles to profl. jours. Chmn. citywide rally Fellowship Christian Athletes, Tulsa, 1960; nat. council U.P. Men, 1966-68, 74-84; active Boy Scouts Am., YMCA, others. Named Seward Meml. lectr. Sahni Inst. Palaeobotany, 1985, J. Sen Meml. lectr., 1985, Disting. lectr. Am. Assn. Petroleum Geologists, 1964, Outstanding Educator, Am. Assn. Petroleum Geologists Ea. Sect., 1987, 2005; recipient Gordon H. Wood Jr. Meml. award, 1993, John T. Galey medal, 1995. Mem. Am. Assn. Stratigraphic Palynologists (hon.; medal of Excellence in Edn. 1999), Bot. Soc. Am. (chmn. paleobotany sect. 1953, 77, grantee 1954, Disting. Svc. Paleobotany award 1985), Geol. Soc. Am. (Gilbert H. Cady Coal Geology award 1987, chmn. coal geology divsn. 1966, chmn. North Ctrl. sect. 1969-70, exec. sec. sect. 1971-80, grantee 1951), Soc. Econ. Paleontologists and Mineralogists (chmn. rsch. com. 1961-62, councillor in paleontology 1971-73), Soc. Organic Petrology (John Castano hon. membership award 2005), Am. Assn. Petroleum Geologists (Grover E. Murray Disting. Educator award, 2005), numerous other internat., nat. and regional profl. assns. Presbyterian. Home: 529 N Harrison Rd East Lansing MI 48823-3015 Office: Mich State Univ Dept Geol Scis East Lansing MI 48824 Office Phone: 517-355-4630. Office Fax: 517-353-8787. Business E-Mail: cross1@msu.edu.

CROSS, BEVERLY JEAN, music educator; b. Cumberland, Md., Mar. 2, 1946; d. Floyd Carl and Noami Ruth Boor; 1 child, Catherine Elizabeth. BA in Music magna cum laude, SUNY, Geneseo, 1973; MusM with distinction, SUNY, Potsdam, 1991. Pvt. piano tchr., Potsdam, 1976—91; piano tchr. Aladdin Music Inst., Tampa Bay, Fla., 1997—. Mem.: Fla. State Music Assn., Nat. Piano Guild (regional chmn. auditions 1984—91, evaluator regional auditions 1988—, judge 1984—). Democrat. Avocation: art. Home: 2623 Seville Blvd # 311 Clearwater FL 33764 Personal E-mail: bcross20032000@yahoo.com.

CROSS, BRUCE MICHAEL, lawyer; b. Wash., Jan. 30, 1942; AB magna cum laude, Dartmouth Coll., 1964; JD magna cum laude, Harvard U., 1967. Bar: Wash. 1967. Law clk. to Hon. Frank P. Weaver Supreme Ct. Wash., 1967-68; mem. Perkins Coie LLP, Seattle, 1969—. Office: Perkins Coie LLP 1201 3rd Ave Fl 40 Seattle WA 98101-3099 Home Phone: 206-270-9215; Office Phone: 206-359-8453. Business E-Mail: bcross@perkinscoie.com.

CROSS, CHRISTOPHER T., educational association administrator, consultant; b. Lakewood, Ohio, May 30, 1940; s. Sterling Leonard and Virginia Mae (Taylor) C.; m. Constance Heatherly Woods, Aug. 26, 1961 (div. 1981); children: H. Allyson (dec.), Dana M., Charles M.B.; m. Diane Stricklan DeRoche, June 11, 1982; 1 child, Charles. BA in Polit. Sci., Whittier Coll., Calif., 1962; MA, Calif. State Coll., 1969. With Dept. HEW, Washington, 1969-70, dep. asst. sec. for legislation, 1970-73; sr. ednl. cons. U.S. Ho. of Reps., Washington, 1973-77, Rep. staff dir., com. on edn. and labor, 1977-78; dir. Washington Office ops. Abt Assoc., Inc., 1978-80; mktg. mgr. fed. govt. Westinghouse Info. Svc., Washington, 1980-82, mgr. fed. svc., 1982-83; pres., COO Univ. Rsch. Corp., Chevy Chase, Md., 1983-89; asst. sec. for ednl. rsch. and improvement U.S. Dept. Edn., Washington, 1989-91; dir. Am. Inst. Rsch., 1993—; chmn. Cross & Joftus, LLC, 2004—. Exec. dir., edn. initiative The Bus. Roundtable, 1991-94; pres. Coun. for Basic Edn., 1994-2001; mem. Nat. Edn. Commn. on Time and Learning, 1992-94; mem. Md. State Bd. Edn., 1993-97, pres. 1994-97. Contbr. articles to profl. jours. Trustee Whitter Coll., 1999—; chair Nat. Coun. Edn. & Human Devel. George Washington U., 2000-02. Mem. Profl. Svc. Coun. (exec. com. 1981-86, trustee), Coun. Excellence in Govt. Congregationalist. Home: 109 Sunhaven Rd Danville CA 94506 Office Phone: 925-314-1863. Business E-Mail: chris@edstrategies.net.

CROSS, CLINTON FERGUSON, lawyer; b. Waco, Tex., Mar. 2, 1939; s. Clinton Janes Heath and Mary Augusta Cross; m. Nellie Cross, 1973 (div. 1976); children: Joyce, Roberta. BA, Pomona Coll., 1962; LLB, U. Tex., 1968. Bar: Tex. 1968, US Dist. Ct. (no. dist.) Tex. 1972, US Ct. Appeals (5th cir.) 1986, US Dist. Ct. (we. dist.) Tex. 1987. Staff atty. El Paso Legal Assistance Soc., 1969-73; asst. atty. Tex. Atty. Gen.'s Office, El Paso, 1973-76; dir. Tex. Legal Svcs. Ctr., Austin, Tex., 1977-85; asst. county atty. El Paso County Atty.'s Office, 1985-86, 96—. Instr. El Paso CC, 1974-76, 89-92. Bd. dirs. El Paso Legal Assistance Soc., 1973-76, Nat. Legal Aid and Defender Assn., Washington, 1980-83. With USMCR, 1962-68. Mem. ABA, State Bar Tex (chmn. com. on legal svcs. to indigent in civil matters 1977-80), El Paso Bar Assn. (chmn. consumer law com. 1991-92, chmn. legal aid lawyer referral com. 1993-94, bd. dir. 2004-07). Democrat. Episcopalean. Avocations: swimming, chess. Office: El Paso County Atty El Paso County Courthouse 500 San Antonio St El Paso TX 79901 Home: 500 Thunderbird Dr Apt 105 El Paso TX 79912-3345 Office Phone: 915-546-2050. Personal E-mail: ccross39@aol.com.

CROSS, DOROTHY ABIGAIL, retired librarian; b. Bangor, Mich., Sept. 9, 1924; d. John Laird and Alice Estelle (Wilcox) C. BA, Wayne State U., 1956; MA in Libr. Sci., U. Mich., 1957. Jr. libr. Detroit Pub. Libr., 1957-59; adminstrv. libr. U.S. Army, Braconne, France, 1959-61, Poitiers, France, 1961-63, area libr. supr., 1963, asst. commd. libr. Kaiserslautern, Germany, 1963-67, acquisitions libr. Aschaffenburg, Germany, 1967, Munich, 1967-69, sr. staff libr. specialist, 1969-72, commd. libr. Stuttgart, Germany, 1972-75, dep. staff libr. Heidelberg, Germany, 1975-77; chief libr. 18th Airborne Corps and Ft. Bragg, N.C., 1977-79; chief ADP sect. Pentagon Libr., Washington, 1979-80, chief readers svcs. br., 1980-83, dir., 1983-91. Mem. ALA, U. Mich. Alumni Assn., Delta Omicron. United Methodist. Home: 6511 Delia Dr Alexandria VA 22310-2609 E-mail: dacross@starpower.net.

CROSS, EASON, JR., architect; b. Bisbee, Ariz., Nov. 14, 1925; s. Eason and Olive (Hardwick) C.; m. Diana Johnson, June 17, 1950; children: Ben, Becca, Amy, Susan. BA, Harvard U., 1949, MArch, 1951. Assoc. Charles M. Goodman, Washington, 1952-59, Keyes, Lethbridge & Condon, 1959-61; ptnr. Cross & Adreon, Arlington, Va., 1961-87; pres. Va. Architects Accord P.C., Alexandria, 1989—; prin. Cross Assocs., Alexandria, Va., 1987—. Patentee fastenings and furniture. Pres. Hollin Hills Cmty. Assn., 1978; chmn. Fairfax County Appeals Bd., 1970-80; pres. Old Dominion DESA, 1997-98, Purysburg Preservation Found., 1998-2007. With USNR, WWII. Recipient Ware prize, 1950, Washington Bd. Trade design award, 1965, Bethesda-Chevy Chase C. of C. design awards, 1966, 67; House and Home awards AIA, 1965-66; Mid-Atlantic Region design awards, 1967, 69; Nat. Honor award, 1968; Nat. Honor award Am. inst. Steel Constrn., 1967; 4 awards HUD-Washington Ctr. Urban Studies furniture competition, 1971; Frameworks Home Design Merit award, 1995; Fairfax County Exceptional Design award 1985, 87, N.V. CAA Design award 1999. Fellow AIA, Housing Competition ADPSR winner 1993; mem. Va. Soc. AIA (Energy award 1979, Design award 1986, Noland medal 1994), Harvard Club, Fox Club, Ga. Salzburger Soc. Purysburg Found., Ricochet Club. Episcopalian. Home: 2309 Glasgow Rd Alexandria VA 22307-1821 Personal E-mail: easonc@verizon.net.

CROSS, GEORGE ALAN MARTIN, biochemistry professor, researcher; b. Cheadle, Cheshire, Eng., Sept. 27, 1942; s. George Bernard and Beatrice Mary (Horton) C.; 1 child, Julia Elizabeth. BA, Cambridge U., Eng., 1964, PhD, 1968. Scientist Med. Rsch. Coun., Cambridge, 1970-77; dept. head Wellcome Found. Rsch. Labs., Kent, Eng., 1977-82; Andre and Bella Meyer prof. molecular parasitology Rockefeller U., NYC, 1982—, dean grad. and postgrad. studies, 1995-99. Cons. Wellcome Found., Eng., 1982-87, World Health Orgns., Geneva, 1983-87, New Eng. Biolabs., Beverly Mass., 1985-99. Contbr. articles to profl. jours. Recipient Paul Ehrlich prize, 1984, Chalmers medal Royal Soc. of Tropical Medicine, 1983; named Fleming Lectr. Soc. for Gen. Microbiology, 1978. Fellow The Royal Soc. (Leeuwenhoek Lectr. 1998). Office: The Rockefeller Univ 1230 York Ave New York NY 10021-6399 E-mail: gamc@mail.rockefeller.edu.

CROSS, J. BRUCE, lawyer; b. Sharon, Pa., Oct. 6, 1949; s. John Lantz and Agnes (Bruce) C.; m. Joy Cross; children: Lantz Davis, Heather Lynn. BA, U. Notre Dame, Ind., 1971; JD, U. Ark., Fayetteville, 1974. Bar: Ark. 1974, US Ct. Appeals (8th cir.) 1979, US Supreme Ct. 1980. Ptnr. House, Holmes and Jewell, Little Rock, 1974-90, Cross and Gunter, P.A., Little Rock, 1990, McGlinchey Stafford Lang, Little Rock, 1991-97, Cross, Gunter, Witherspoon & Galchus, P.C., Little Rock, 1997—. Chpt. atty. Ark. Subcontractors Assn., Little Rock, 1987-90; mem. young execs. coun. Associated Gen. Contractors, 1989. Contbr. to profl. publs. Active Big Bros. Ark., Little Rock, 1976-87; pres., bd. dirs. Ark. divsn. Nat. Soc. to Prevent Blindness, 1987-90; bd. dirs. Urban League Ark., 1989, Ark. Constrn. Edn. Found., Boy Scouts Am., 2004-07, Single Parent Scholarship Fund of Pulaski County, 2004-07, pres., 2007; nat. bd. dirs. Associated Builders and Contractors Am., 1999-2001; active Leadership Hot Springs, Habitat for Humanity, Youth Home; bd. dirs. Single Parent Scholarship Fund, 2005-06, Boy Scouts Am., 2004-05, Mus. of Discovery, 2005-07, exec. com., Jr. Achievement Ark., 2005-07, exec. com. Recipient Pres.'s award Nat. Soc. to Prevent Blindness. Mem. Ark. Hospitality Assn. (bd. dirs. 1988-89), Ark. Subcontractors Assn., Assoc. Bldrs. and Contrs. (pres. 1999-2000), Ark. Bar Assn. (past chmn. labor sect.), Ark. Ready Mixed Concrete Assn., Little Rock C. of C. (ptnrs. in edn. com. 1989-90), ABA (sect. labor and employment law com. on labor arbitration and the law of collective bargaining agreements 1981-99, com. on devel. of the law under the NLRA 2000—), Greater Hot Springs C. of C., Notre Dame Club Ark. (pres.). Roman Catholic. Office: Cross, Gunter, Witherspoon & Galchus PC 500 President Clinton Ave Ste 200 Little Rock AR 72201-1747 Business E-Mail: jbcross@cgwg.com.

CROSS, JAMES EDWARD, electrical engineering educator; b. Hampton, Va., May 29, 1937; s. Julia Ann-Cross Morgan; m. Velta Rose Jones, Dec. 1, 1965; children: Michael Levi, Andre Lene, Michelle Monique-Cross Brown. Diploma in radio, TV and electronics, DeVry Tech. Inst., 1956; BE sci. in Elec. Engring., Johns Hopkins U., 1960; MSEE, La. State U., 1967; postgrad. in elec. engring., U. of Fla., 1972; student in Elec. Engring., La. State U., 1973; BTh, Christian Bible Coll., Baton Rouge, La., 1982, ThM, 1984, ThD, 1987. Asst. prof. in elec. engring. So. U., Baton Rouge, 1962—64, chmn. elec. engring. dept., 1964—91, assoc. prof. of elec. engring., 1991—. Mem. tech. staff Western Electric Co., Allentown, Pa., 1970, GE Rsch. Ctr., Schenectady, NY, 1971, Westinghouse Corp., Youngwood, Pa., 1965, Western Electric Co., Atlanta, 1966, Autonetics divsn. N.Am. Rockwell, Anaheim, Calif., 1968, Radiation Inc., Melbourne, Fla., 1969; tchg. assoc. U. Fla., Gainesville, 1971—72; vis. lectr. La. State U., Baton Rouge, 1972—73, rsch. asst., 1973; NASA/ASEE summer faculty fellow Langley Rsch. Ctr., Hampton, Va., 1974; mem. tech. staff Bell Labs., Holmel, NJ, 1979, IBM, Charlotte, NC, 1981, Caterpillar, Inc., Peoria, Ill., 1990; rschr. Air Force Rsch. Lab., Wright-Patterson AFB, Ohio, 2002; reviewer , evaluator of proposals NSF, Washington, 1987—. Co-author tech. papers to confs. Mem. Baton Rouge Coun. on Human Rels., La., 1969—; mem., sec. Christian Bible Coll., La., 1964—2001; mem. deacon bd. Mt. Pilgrim Bapt. Ch., Baton Rouge, 1964—; mem. La. Coun. on Human Rels., Lafayette, La., 1990—. Capt. res. Army Corp of Engrs., 1960—62, Heidelberg, Germany. Grantee, Air Force Rsch. Lab., 1996—99, La. Bd. of Regents, 1989—90, Raytheon Co., 2000—02. Mem.: AAUP (pres. of local chpt. 1969—71), IEEE (life), Am. Soc. for Engring. Edn., Early Risers Kiwanis Club, Am. Legion, Masons (sec., Hon. Worshipful Master, Twilight Lodge # 166). Democrat. Baptist. Home: 13608 Alba Dr Baker LA 70714 Office Phone: 225-775-4153. Personal E-mail: cross4153@aol.com.

CROSS, KATHRYN PATRICIA, education educator; b. Normal, Ill., Mar. 17, 1926; d. Clarence L. and Katherine (Dague) C. BS, Ill. State U., Normal, 1948; MA, U. Ill., Urbana, 1951, PhD, 1958; LLD (hon.), Ill. State U., 1970; DS (hon.), Northeastern U., Boston, 1975; HHD (hon.), Grand Valley State Colls., Mich., 1975; D in Pedagogy (hon.), Our Lady of Lake U., Tex., 1977; LHD (hon.), Hood Coll., Md., 1979; DS (hon.), Loyola U., Chgo., 1980; LHD (hon.), Marymount Manhattan Coll., NY, 1982, Coll. St. Mary, 1985, De Paul U., Chgo., 1986, Thomas Jefferson U., Pa., 1987; LittD (hon.), SUNY, 1988; DHL (hon.), Open U., The Netherlands, 1989; LHD (hon.), Rider Coll., NJ, 1992, U. Mass., Lowell, 1995, Coll. Lifelong Learning, NH, 1999. Math. tchr. Harvard (Ill.) Community High Sch., 1948-49; rsch. asst. dept. psychology U. Ill., Urbana, 1949-53, asst. dean of women, 1953-59; dean of women then dean of students Cornell U., Ithaca, N.Y., 1959-63; dir. coll. and univ. programs Ednl. Testing Svc., Princeton, N.J., 1963-66; rsch. educator Ctr. R&D in Higher Edn. U. Calif., Berkeley, 1966-77; rsch. scientist, sr. rsch. psychologist, dir. univ. programs Ednl. Testing Svc., Berkeley, 1966-80; prof. edn., chair dept. adminstrn., planning & social policy Harvard U., Cambridge, Mass., 1980-88; Elizabeth and Edward Conner prof. edn. U. Calif., Berkeley, 1988-94, David Pierpont Gardner prof. higher edn., 1994-96. Mem. sec. adv. com. on automated personal data sys. Dept. HEW, 1972-73; del. to Soviet Union, Seminar on Problems in Higher Edn., 1975; vis. prof. U. Nebr., 1975-76; vis. scholar Miami-Dade CC, 1987; trustee Berkeley Pub. Libr., 1998-2002; spkr., cons. in field; bd. dirs. Elderhostel, 1999-; nat. adv. bd. Ctr. for First-Year Experience, 2000-. Author: Beyond the Open Door: New Students to Higher Education, 1971 (Sch. and Soc. Outstanding Books in Edn. award, 1971); author: (with S. B. Gould) Explorations in Non-Traditional Study, 1972; author: (with J. R. Valley and Assocs.) Planning Non-Traditional Programs: An Analysis of the Issues for Postsecondary Education, 1974; author: Accent on Learning, 1976 (Am. Coun. Edn. Borden medal, 1976), Adults as Learners, 1981; author: (with Thomas A. Angelo) Classroom Assessment Techniques, 1993; author: (with Mimi Harris Steadman) Classroom Research, 1996; author: (with Elizabeth Barkley and Claire Major) Collaborative Learning Techniques: A Handbook for College Faculty, 2005; contbr. articles, monographs to profl. publs., chapters to books; mem. editl. bd. several ednl. jours., cons. editor (ednl. mag.) Change, 1980—. Active Nat. Acad. Edn., 1975—, Coun. for Advancement of Exptl. Learning, 1982-85; trustee Bradford Coll., Mass., 1986-88, Antioch Coll., Yellow Springs, Ohio, 1976-78; nat. adv. bd. Nat. Ctr. of Study of Adult Learning, Empire State Coll., Okla. Bd. Regents; higher edn. rsch. program Pew Charitable Trusts; vis. com. Harvard Grad. Sch. Edn., 1998—; bd. dirs. Elderhostel, 1999—; trustee Berkeley Pub. Libr., 1999—, Carnegie Found., 1999—. Named to Hall of Fame, Internat. Adult and Continuing Edn., 1997; recipient Leadership award, Assn. Continuing Higher Edn., 2000, Lifetime Contbns. to Learning Assistance and Devel. Edn. award, Am. Coun. Devel. Edn., 2000, Morris Keeton award, Coun. For Adult Exptl. Learning, 2005, Tchrs. Coll. medal, Columbia U., 2006, Fellow League for Innovation in CC (nat. adv. bd. Learning Coll. Project 2000-); mem. Am. Assn. Higher Edn. (bd. dirs. 1987—, pres. 1975, chair 1989-90), Am. Assn. Comty. and Jr. Colls. (vice chair commn. of future comty. colls.), Carnegie Found. Advancement of Tchg. (adv. com. on classification of colls. and univs., trustee 1998-), Nat. Ctr. for Devel. Edn. (adv. bd.), New Eng. Assn. Schs. and Colls. (commn. on instns. higher edn. 1982-86), Am. Coun. Edn. (commn. on higher edn. and adult learner 1986-88). Home Phone: 510-527-9020. Business E-Mail: patcross@berkeley.edu.

CROSS, KIM L., engineer, sales executive; b. Charlotte, NC, Sept. 2, 1953; s. Benjamin and Betty (Deaton) Cross; m. Abby Aro, May 23, 1983; children: Kyle, Celia. AS, Ctrl. Piedmont, Charlotte, 1974; BS, Va. Tech., Blacksburg, 1976. Jr. engr. Duke Power Co., Charlotte; sr. project mgr. Eastside Delta, Atlanta; v.p. constrn. Wallace Mech., Atlanta; sales engr. Dan McNeil Co., Atlanta; regional sales mgr. Victaulic Co., Easton, Pa.; nat. sales mgr. Flo-Pak, Atlanta, Patterson Pump, Toccoa, Ga. Recipient God and Country award, Boy Scouts Am., 1969, Eagle Scout award, 1970. Mem.: ASHRAE, ASPE. Office: Patterson Pump 2921 Ayersville Rd Toccoa GA 30577

CROSS, LESLIE ERIC, electrical engineering educator; b. Leeds, Eng., Aug. 14, 1923; came to U.S., 1961; s. Charles Eric and Alice Emily (Plant) C.; m. Lorna Lucilla Fish, Apr. 1, 1950; children: Peter Charles, Matthew John, Daniel Eric, Rebecca Lorna, Rachel Jean, Elizabeth Mary. B.Sc., PhD, Leeds U.; D.Sc. (hon.), Xian Jiaotong U. ICI fellow Leeds U., 1951—54; rsch. scientist Elec. Rsch. Assn., Eng., 1954—61; sr. rsch. asst. Pa. State U., University Park, 1961—64, assoc. prof. solid state engring., 1964—66, prof. solid state sci., 1966—68, prof. elec. engring., 1968—85, dir. materials rsch. lab., 1985—89, Evan Pugh prof. elec. engring., 1985—99, Evan Pugh prof. emeritus, 1999—. Recipient John Jeppson medal, 1984; Ross Coffin Purdy award, 1985, MRS medal, 1992. Fellow IEEE, Am. Ceramics Soc. (Electronics award 1968), Optical Soc. Am., Am. Phys. Soc.; mem. Japan Phys. Soc., US Nat. Acad. Engring. Office: Pa State U Materials Rsch Inst Rm 187 University Park PA 16802 Home: 305 Windmere Dr Apt 322 State College PA 16801-7687 Business E-Mail: lec3@psu.edu.

CROSS, MARCIA, actress; b. Marlborough, Mass., Mar. 25, 1962; d. Mark and Janet Cross; m. Mahoney Tom Cross, June 24, 2006; children: Eden, Savannah. Grad., Julliard Sch., NYC; M in Psychology, Antioch U., LA, Calif. Actress (TV series) The Edge of Night, 1984, One Life to Live, 1986—87, Another World, 1986, Knots Landing, 1991—92, Melrose Place, 1992—93, 1994—97, Everwood, 2003—04, Desperate Housewives, 2004— (Screen Actors Guild Award for outstanding performance by an ensemble in a comedy series, 2005, 2006), (TV films) Brass, 1985, The Last Days of Frank and Jesse James, 1986, Pros & Cons, 1986, Almost Grown, 1988, Storm and Sorrow, 1990, M.A.N.T.I.S, 1994, All She Ever Wanted, 1996, Target Earth, 1998, Eastwick, 2002, (TV miniseries) George Washington II: The Forging of a Nation, 1986, (films) Bad Influence, 1990, Ripple, 1995, Female Perversions, 1996, Always Say Goodbye, 1996, Dancing in September, 2000, Living in Fear, 2001, Bank, 2002, The Wind Effect, 2003; performer: (plays) La Ronde, Twelfth Night, Gentleman of Verona; guest appearances Tales From the Darkside, 1986, Cheers, 1989, 1990, Booker, 1989, "Who's the Boss?", 1989, Doctor Doctor, 1989, Quantum Leap, 1990, Jake and the Fatman, 1991, Murder, She Wrote, 1992, Herman's Head, 1992, Raven, 1993, Ned and Stacey, Burke's Law, 1995, Seinfeld, 1997, The Outer Limits, 1999, Boy Meets World, 1999, Touched by an Angel, 1999, Profiler, 2000, Spin City, 2000, Ally McBeal, 2000, Strong Medicine, 2001, CSI: Crime Scene Investigation, 2001, The King of Queens, 2002, 2003, Life & Style, 2004, "Corazón, Corazón", 2005. Address: Desperate Housewives Touchstone Television 100 Universal City Plaza Bldg 2128 Ste G Universal City CA 91608

CROSS, MEREDITH B., lawyer; b. Oct. 14, 1957; BA cum laude, Duke Univ., 1979; JD, Vanderbilt Univ., 1982. Bar: Ga. 1983, DC 1998. Law clk. Judge Albert J. Henderson, US Ct. Appeals (11th cir.); atty. fellow Div. Corp. Fin., SEC, Washington, 1990—92, chief counsel, 1992—94, assoc. dir., Internat. Corp. Fin. & Small Bus. sect., 1994, dep. dir., 1994—98; ptnr. Wilmer Cutler Pickering Hale & Dorr, Washington, 1998—, co-chmn. Corp. dept. Frequent speaker at securities law conferences. Mem.: Order of the Coif. Office: Wilmer Cutler Pickering Hale & Dorr 1899 Pennsylvania Ave NW Washington DC 20006 Office Phone: 202-663-6644. Office Fax: 202-663-6363. Business E-Mail: meredith.cross@wilmerhale.com.

CROSS, MILTON H., lawyer; b. Phila., July 28, 1942; s. Sidney B. and Edythe Cross; m. Joyce Volchok, June 4, 1966; children: Brian, Jonathon. BS, U. San Francisco, 1965; JD, Villanova U., Pa., 1968. Bar: Pa. 1968. Corp. counsel AEL, Inc., Phila., 1968-75; assoc. Cohen, Verlin, Sherzer & Porter, Phila., 1975-78; pvt. practice Phila., 1978-79; ptnr. Monteverde & Hemphill, Phila., 1980-96, Spector, Gadon & Rosen, Phila., 1996—. Adj. prof. Phila. Coll. Textiles and Sci., 1970-73. Chmn. Cheltenham Twp. Sch. Bd. Authority. Mem. ABA (sect. corp., banking and bus. law, named a Pa. Super Lawyer of Yr. 2005, 06, 07), Pa. Bar Assn., Phila. Bar Assn. Home: 251 Ironwood Cir Elkins Park PA 19027-1315 Office: Spector Gadon & Rosen 7 Penn Ctr Fl 7 Philadelphia PA 19103-2200 Office Phone: 215-241-8811. Business E-Mail: mcross@lawsgr.com.

CROSS, RICHARD JOHN, bank executive; b. Denver, May 22, 1929; s. Arthur Chester and Gertrude Eva (Ryan) C.; m. Mildred Louise Mouton, Jan. 19, 1957; children: John Charles, Carolyn Louise, Paul Arthur. BS, U. Colo., 1950; M.B.A, Wharton Sch. Finance U. Pa., 1955. With Lloyds Bank Calif., 1962-81, exec. v.p., 1974-81; mng. ptnr. Cross Investment Co., 1971—. Dir. bus. program Woodbury U., L.A., 1985-87; adj. prof. fin. and mgmt., 1987-97; chmn. bd. Highland Fed. Bank; adv. bd. Archdiocese of L.A. Dept. Detention Ministries, 1991-97; bd. dirs. Atwater Park Ctr., treas. 2001—, chmn., 2004—. Mem. bd. councilors U. So. Calif. Andrus Gerontology Ctr., 2001—. With USN, 1950—53. Fellow Royal Soc. Arts; mem. Calif. Bankers Assn., So. Calif. Trust Officers Assn., Knight Holy Sepulcher Jerusalem, Delta Tau Delta, Phi Epsilon Phi., Sutter Club, Jonathan Club, Oakmont Country Club. Democrat. Roman Catholic. Home: 1430 Greenbriar Rd Glendale CA 91207-1256 Personal E-mail: richjcro@yahoo.com.

CROSS, ROBERT CLARK, journalist; b. Cheboygan, Mich., May 12, 1939; s. Warren Clark and Meryle M. (Allaire) Cross; m. Juju Lien; children: Gabriel Francis, Amy Lien. BA in Journalism, Wayne State U., 1962. Writer, researcher Newsweek mag., 1962; reporter, editor Chgo. Tribune, 1962-66, 67-82, assoc. editor mag., 1973-82, writer, 1982—; reporter Newsday, 1966-67; travel writer, 1992—. Recipient Gold and Silver Lowell Thomas awards Soc. of Am. Travel Writers, 1995, 2000, 04. Office: 435 N Michigan Ave Chicago IL 60611-4066 Business E-Mail: bcross@tribune.com.

CROSS, ROBERT LOUIS, retired realtor, landscape architect, land use planner, writer, real estate appraiser; b. Alton, Ill., Aug. 9, 1937; s. Louis William and Marion (Hanna) C.; m. Paula Sutton, June 8, 1958 (div. June 1970); children: Britomart, Christopher, Amoret; m. Carolee Sharko, May 5, 1990. BA, U. Kans., Lawrence, 1959, MA, 1961, grad., UCLA, 1969, Realtors Inst., LA, 1980. Lectr. English lang. U. Kans., Lawrence, 1959-60; Washburn U., Topeka, 1960-61; editorial-mktg. rep. Prentice-Hall, Inc., Englewood Cliffs, N.J., 1962-64; dir. pub. info. Forest Lawn Meml. Pk., Glendale, Calif., 1964-68; account exec. pub. rels. J. Walter Thompson, LA, 1968-70; sr. account exec. pub. rels. Botsford Ketchum, LA, 1970-71, Harsh, Rotman & Druck, LA, 1971-72; pres. Crossroads Combined Comm., LA, 1973-80; real estate agt. Carmel (Calif.) Bd. Realtors, 1979—2005; gen. ptnr. Crossroads Design Ltd., Big Sur, Calif., 1990—2005; co-owner Crossroads Pacific, Kapaau, Hawaii, 2004—, Big Sur Properties. Cons. Watts Mfg. Corp., L.A., 1970-73, U.S. Office Edn., Washington, 1971, U.S. Dept. Interior, Washington, 1972, Calif. State Coastal Commn., San Francisco, 1980-85; land use advisor Puakea Bay Ranch, Hawaii, dir., 2005—. Author: Henry Miller: The Paris Years, 1991; assoc. editor Calif. Life Mag., 1976; contbr. IN Monterey Mag., 1977, Big Sur Mag., 2004; real estate editor Monterey Life Mag., 1978. Pres., dir. Big Sur Hist. Soc., 1980-90, Coastlands Mut. Water Co., Big Sur, 1984—2004; v.p., dir. Puakea Bay Ranch, 2005—; co-founder Dialogue for Big Sur, 1984; dir. Big Sur Natural History Assn., 1984-86, founding docent Dept. Pks. and Recreation, Pt. Sur Historic State Park, Big Sur, 1987; active ARC Disaster Svcs.; founder Big Sur Cmty. Action Team. With U.S. Army, 1961-63 Mem. Agora Internat. Press Corps, Archeol. Inst. Am., Nat. Assn. Realtors, Am. Soc. Landscape Architects, Nat. Assn. Real Estate Appraisers (cert.), Calif. Assn. Realtors, Monterey County Assn. Realtors (Multiple Listing Svc. Sales award 1980), Carmel Multiple Listing Svc., Big Sur Grange, Coast Property Owners Assn., Environ. Assesment Assn. (cert.). Avocations: art, travel, automobiles, music, reading.

CROSS, ROBERT WILLIAM, lawyer, venture capitalist; b. Balt., Oct. 9, 1937; s. Rosamond and Mildred (Fowler) C.; m. Deanna Louise Deerr, Feb. 7, 1965; children Ann Elizabeth, Robert William II. BSBA, Washington U., St. Louis, 1962; JD, Washington U., 1964. Bar: N.Y. 1964. Assoc Winthrop, Stimson, Putnam & Roberts, NYC, 1964-68; gen. counsel Electronic Data Systems Corp., Dallas, 1968-69; pres. R.W. Cross & Co., Dallas and NYC, 1970-90; chmn., CEO Cross Tech. Inc., NYC, also Solebury, Pa., 1990—; pres., CEO Nanophase Tech. Corp., Romeoville, Ill., 1993-98; pres., COO Vcapital Inc., Chgo., 1999—2002; pres., CEO Vcapital Securities, Chgo., 2000—02; chmn., CEO DigitalWork, Inc., Chgo., 2003—05; chmn. Patron Sys., Inc., 2005—; mng. prin. Batterson Cross Zakin Venture Ptnrs., 2005—. Mem. adv. bd. Apex Venture Fund V, 2003—. With USMC, 1957—63. Mem.: Bus. Execs. for Nat. Security, Marine Corps Assn., Union League Club Chgo., Univ. Club NY, Omicron Delta Kappa. Republican. Home: PO Box 200 Solebury PA 18963-0200 Office: Cross Tech Inc 6475 Upper York Rd Solebury PA 18963 Business E-Mail: rcross@crosstechnologiesUS.com. E-mail: bobcross99@aol.com.

CROSS, TERRY M., career military officer; m. Susan Dufort; children: Sean, Shannon. BS in Engring., Coast Guard Acad., 1970; M in Indsl. Adminstrn., Purdue U.; grad., Nat. War Coll. Advanced through grades to vice admiral USCG, various staff and operational positions including deck watch officer, chief of staff, comdr., ops. officer, dir. ops. policy Coast Guard Hdqs., comdr. 11th and 17th Coast Guard dists., asst. comdt. ops., comdr. Pacific area, vice comdt., 2004—. Office: USCG US Dept Homeland Security 2100 2d St SW Washington DC 20593

CROSS, THEODORE LAMONT, publisher, author; b. Newton, Mass., Feb. 12, 1924; s. Gorham Lamont and Margaret Moore (Warren) C.; m. Sheilah Burr Ross, Sept. 16, 1950 (div. 1972); children: Amanda Burr, Lisa Warren; m. Mary Warner, 1974. Grad., Deerfield Acad., 1942; AB, Amherst Coll., 1946; LLB, Harvard U., 1950. Bar: Mass. 1950, N.Y. 1953. With Hale and Dorr, Boston, 1950-52; chmn. bd., CEO Warren, Gorham & Lamont, Inc., 1980-83; chmn. Faulkner & Gray, Pubs., 1985-92, Hanover Pub., Inc., 1985—; editor in chief Bus. and Soc. Rev., 1971—; editor Jour. of Blacks in Higher Edn., 1993—. Cons. HEW, Fed. Office Econ. Opportunity, 1964-69; pub. gov. Am. Stock Exchange, 1972-77; bd. dirs. Inst. for Sci. Info., 1988—; lectr. on inner city econs. and minority econ. devel. Harvard, Cornell U., U. Va. Author: Black Capitalism: Strategy for Business in the Ghetto (McKinsey Found. book award 1969), (with Mary Cross) Behind the Great Wall, 1979, The Black Power Imperative, 1984, Birds of the Sea, Shore and Tundra, 1989; founder: Atomic Energy Law Jour., 1959; editor Harvard Law Rev., 1948-50. Trustee Amherst Coll., chmn. investment com., 1976-88; trustee Folger Shakespeare Libr., Princeton U. Press, Inst. Advanced Study, Nat. Humanities Ctr., John Simon Guggenheim Meml. Found.; mem. Coun. Fgn. Rels.; dir. Legal Def. Fund, NAACP, Century Assn., N.Y.C. With USNR, 1945-46. Mem. Coun. on Fgn. Rels. (treas.), Am. Philos. Soc. Home: 1 Campbelton Cir Princeton NJ 08540 Office: 200 W 57th St New York NY 10019-3211

CROSS, WALTER THOMAS, investment company executive; b. Knoxville, Tenn., Sept. 1, 1949; s. Joseph Eugene and Wanda (Price) C.; children: Joseph, Victoria; m. Pamela M. BS, U. Tenn., 1971; CLU, Am. Coll., Bryn Mawr, Pa., 1983; ChFC, Am. Coll., 1987. Sales rep. John Hancock Fin. Svcs., Knoxville, 1971-72, sales mgr., 1972-78, regional supr. Washington, 1978-79, agy. mgr. Appleton, Wis., 1979-84, Memphis, 1984-95; sr. v.p. product distbn. Securities Am., Inc., Omaha, 1995—; pres. Fin. Dynamics Am., Inc., Omaha, 1997—. Chair troop com., scoutmaster Boy Scouts Am., Germantown, Tenn., 1991-95. Mem. Am. Soc. CLU and ChFC (bd. dirs. 1992-95), Am. Health Ins. Assn., Gen. Agts. and Mgrs. Assn. (pres. Appleton chpt. 1977-78, pres. Memphis chpt. 1988-89, pres. 1993-94), Memphis Life Underwriters (bd. dirs. 1985-88). Avocations: golf, scouting. Office: Securities Am Inc 7100 W Center Rd Ste 500 Omaha NE 68106-2798 Office Phone: 402-399-9111. Business E-Mail: tcross@saionline.com.

CROSS, WILLIAM DENNIS, lawyer; b. Tulsa, Nov. 7, 1940; s. John Howell and Virginia Grace (Ferrell) C.; m. Peggy Ruth Plapp, Jan. 30, 1982; children: William Dennis Jr., John Frederick. BS, U.S. Naval Acad., 1962; JD, NYU, 1969. Bar: N.Y. 1970, U.S. Dist. Ct. (so. and ea. dists.) N.Y. 1970, U.S. Ct. Appeals (2d cir.) 1970, U.S. Supreme Ct. 1974, Calif. 1977, U.S. Dist. Ct. (ctrl. dist.) Calif. 1977, U.S. Ct. Appeals (9th cir.) 1977, U.S. Ct. Appeals (5th, 10th and 11th cirs.) 1981, Mo. 1982, U.S. Dist. Ct. (we. dist.) Mo. 1982, U.S. Ct. Appeals (8th cir.) 1989, U.S. Ct. Appeals (fed. cir.) 1992, U.S. Dist. Ct. Ariz. 1997, U.S. Dist. Ct. Colo. 1997, U.S. Dist. Ct. Kans. 1998. Commd. ensign USN, 1962, advanced through ranks to lt., 1965, resigned, 1966; assoc. Cravath, Swaine & Moore, NYC, 1969-76, Lillick, McHose & Charles, LA, 1976-77; asst. gen. counsel FTC, Washington, 1977-82; of counsel Morrison & Hecker, Kansas City, Mo., 1982-83, ptnr., 1983—2002, Stinson Morrison Hecker, 2002—07. Staff mem. NYU Law Rev., 1967-69, editor, 1968-69; assoc. editor Antitrust Mag. Mem. ABA, Calif. Bar Assn., Mo. Bar Assn., Assn. Bar City N.Y., Kansas City Bar Assn., Lawyers Assn. Kansas City. Office: Stinson Morrison Hecker LLP 1201 Walnut St STe 2800 Kansas City MO 64106-2150 Home: 5835 Cherokee Dr Mission KS 66205-3315 Office Phone: 816-691-2708. Business E-Mail: dcross@stinsonmoheck.com.

CROSSAN, JOHN ROBERT, lawyer; b. Buckhannon, W.Va., May 31, 1947; s. Thomas Benjamin Jr. and Margaret Windsor (Hicks) C.; m. Monique Margaretha Scheen, Dec. 22, 1973; children: Ashley Margaret, Aubry Kelly. BS with honors, U. Va., 1969; JD, U. Chgo., 1974. Bar: Ill. 1974, U.S. Dist. Ct. (no. dist.) Ill. 1974, (ctrl. dist.) Ill. 1998, U.S. Ct. Appeals (4th and 10th cirs.) 1978, U.S. Ct. Appeals (7th cir.) 1979, U.S. Ct. Appeals (fed. cir.) 1983, U.S. Supreme Ct. 1985, U.S. Ct. Appeals (6th cir.) 1989. Staff atty. Ill. Task Force N.E. Ill. Pub. Transp., Chgo., 1972-73; assoc. Hill, Van Santen, Steadman, Chiara, Chgo., 1973-77; assoc., then ptnr. Cook, Wetzel and Egan, Ltd., Chgo., 1978-88; counsel Willian, Brinks, Hofer, Gilson and Lione, Chgo., 1989-90; ptnr. Brinks, Hofer, Gilson & Lione, Chgo., 1991-97, Chapman and Cutler, LLP, Chgo., 1998—, Vp. Va. Engring. Found., 1998—2000, pres., 2000—02. Author: Quick Guide to the Patent Law, 1994; contbr. articles to profl jours. Pres. aux. bd. Chgo. Architecture Found., 1983-85. Mem. ABA, Am. Intellectual Property Lawyers Assn., Chgo. Yacht Club. Home: 2825 N Cambridge Ave Chicago IL 60657-6018 Office: Chapman and Cutler, LLP 111 W Monroe St Ste 1700 Chicago IL 60603-4080 Home Phone: 773-348-7458; Office Phone: 312-845-3420. Personal E-mail: jrcrossan@hotmail.com. Business E-Mail: crossan@chapman.com.

CROSSELY, MARY A., dean, law educator; BA in History, U. Va., Charlottesville, 1984; JD, Vanderbilt U., Nashville, 1987. Bar: Tenn. 1987, Conn. 1989, Calif. 1990. Jud. clk. Hon. Harry W. Wellford, U.S. Ct. of Appeals (6th Cir.), Memphis, 1987—88; assoc. Wiggin & Dana, New Haven, 1988—89, Shartsis, Friese & Ginsburg, San Francisco, 1990—91; asst. prof. Hastings Coll. Law, U. Calif., 1991—94, asst. prof., 1994—97, prof., 1997—2000, assoc. academic dean, 1998—2000; vis. prof. Fla. State U. Coll. Law, 2000—01, Fla. Bar Health Law Sect. Prof. Law, 2001—05; prof. law U. Pittsburgh Sch. Law, 2005—, dean, 2005—. Courtesy faculty mem. Fla. State U. Coll. Medicine, 2002—. Mem.: Am. Soc. of Law, Medicine and Ethics, State Bar of Calif., Am. Bar Assn., Phi Beta Kappa, Order of the Coif. Office: University of Pittsburgh School of Law Barco Law Building 3900 Forbes Street Pittsburgh PA 15260 Office Phone: 412-648-1401. Business E-Mail: crossley@law.pitt.edu.

CROSSER, CARMEN LYNN, marriage and family therapist, social worker, consultant; b. Iowa Falls, Iowa, Jan. 17, 1970; d. Gary Laverne Sr. and Karen Dorothy (Ulrich) C. AA, Ellsworth C.C., 1990; BS, Iowa State U., 1993; MSW, U. Iowa, 1995; PhD, U. Chgo., 2006. Lic. clin. social worker, marriage and family thrapist, Ill.; ACSW. Grad. teaching asst. U. Iowa, Iowa City, 1994-95; mental health therapy intern Mid-Eastern Cmty. Mental Health Ctr., Iowa City, 1994-95; clin. social worker Sinnissippi Ctrs., Inc., Dixon, Ill., 1995-97; family therapist Ctr. for Counseling, DeKalb, Ill., 1997—2005; pvt. practice DeKalb, 2005—, St. Charles, Ill., 2005—. Cons. sexual abuse svcs. Sinnissippi Ctrs. Inc., 1997—98; rsch. asst. U. Chgo., 1998—2000, tchg. asst., 1999—2001; revs. asst. Jour. of Marital and Family Therapy, 1999—2000; adj. prof. Dominican U., River Forest, Ill., 2002—. Am. Family Therapy Acad., 2003—. Mem. Dekalb Area Women's Ctr., 1997—2000; mem. instnl. rev. bd. No. Ill. U., DeKalb, 1997—2000. All-Am. scholar, 1995. Mem. ACA, NASW, NOW, Am. Soc. Prevention Cruelty Animals (voting mem.), Am. Assn. Marriage and Family Therapy (clin. mem.), Am. Coll. Counselors, Internat. Assn. Marriage and Family Counselors, Ill. Soc. Clin. Social Work, Assn. Play Therapy, Nat. Fedn. Socs. for Clin. Social Work, Golden Key, Phi Kappa Phi, Phi Alpha. Office: 400 E Hillcrest Dr Ste 100A Dekalb IL 60115 Office Phone: 630-845-1529. Business E-Mail: c-crosser@uchicago.edu.

CROSSLEY, FRANK ALPHONSO, retired metallurgical engineer; b. Chgo., Feb. 19, 1925; s. Joseph Buddie and Rosa Lee (Brefford) C.; m. Elaine J. Sherman, Nov. 23, 1950 (dec. 1996); 1 child, Desne Adrienne. BSChemE, Ill. Inst. Tech., Chgo., 1945, MS in Metall. Engring, 1947, PhD in Metall. Engring, 1950. Instr. Ill. Inst. Tech., Chgo., 1948-49; prof. foundry engring., head dept. foundry engring. Tenn. Agrl. and Indsl. State U., 1950-52; sr. scientist Ill. Inst. Tech. Rsch. Inst., 1952-66; sr. mem. rsch. lab. Lockheed Missiles & Space Co., Palo Alto, Calif., 1966-74, mgr. dept. producibility and standards, 1974-78, mgr. dept. missile body mech. engring., 1978-79, cons. engr. missile systems div. Sunnyvale, Calif., 1979-86; dir. rsch. propulsion materials Aerojet Propulsion Rsch. Inst., 1986-87, rsch. dir. materials applications, 1987-90; tech. prin. Aerojet Propulsion div. GenCorp, Sacramento, 1990-91; ret., 1991. Contbr. articles to metall. jours. and symposia. Served to ensign (D)L USNR, 1944-46, PTO. Recipient GenCorp Aerojet 1990 R.B. Young Tech. Innovation award. Fellow Am. Soc. for Metals Internat.; mem. AIAA (mem. materials tech. com. 1979-81), Minerals, Metals and Materials Soc. of AIME (chmn. titanium com. 1974-75), Sigma Xi. Congregationalist. Achievements include patent on Transage titanium alloys and grain refiner for titanium alloy castings; research in titanium alloys; diffusion bonding of metals and alloys. Home: 44 Goodnow Ln Framingham MA 01702-5505 Personal E-mail: dac9fac78@aol.com. *Choose well how your time is spent. Time spent doing one thing is time that cannot be spent doing something else.*

CROSSLEY, NANCY RUTH, retired federal agency administrator; b. San Jose, Feb. 2, 1944; d. Edward and Ruth Flesher Crossley. Grad., San Francisco Bus. Sch., 1964. Adminstr. U.S. Geol. Survey, Menlo Park, Calif., 1965—88, internat. program specialist Reston, Va., 1988—89, Menlo Park, Calif., 1989—97, ret., 1997. Sec. Nat. Heart Inst., Taipei, Taiwan, 1962—63. Vol. Lee Meml. Health Sys., Cape Coral, Fla., 2001—02. Avocations: travel, swimming, games, puzzles. Home Phone: 239-267-8368.

CROSSMAN, WILLIAM WHITTARD, retired wire cable and communications executive; b. Mineola, NY, Aug. 10, 1927; s. Homer Danforth and Emily May (Whittard) C.; m. Mary DeJesu, Dec. 6, 1952; children: William Whittard Jr., Lindsay Maria, Michael DeJesu. BS in Engring. Sci., U. Miami, 1949. West coast mgr., gen. mgr. HiTemp Wires div. Simplex Wire & Cable Co., 1955-69; pres. surprenant divsn. ITT Corp., 1969-74, pres. royal electric divsn. Pawtucket, RI, 1974-77, group gen. mgr. NYC, 1977-85, v.p., 1979-87, chmn. and group exec. comm. and info. svcs. Secaucus, NJ, 1985-88, sr. v.p., 1987-88, ret., 1988. With USNR, 1945-46, USAF, 1951. Mem.: San Remo Club, Owls Head Harbor Club. Republican. Episcopalian. Home: 24 White Oak Shade Rd New Canaan CT 06840

CROSSON, FREDERICK JAMES, retired dean, humanities educator; b. Belmar, NJ, Apr. 27, 1926; s. George Leon and Emily (Bennett) Crosson; m. Mary Patricia Burns, Sept. 5, 1953; children: Jessica, Christopher, Veronica, Benedict, Jennifer. BA, Cath. U. Am., 1949, MA, 1950; postgrad., U. Paris, 1951-52; PhD, U. Notre Dame, 1956. From instr. to assoc. prof. U. Notre Dame, Ind., 1953—66, prof., 1966—, O'Hara Disting. prof. philosophy, 1976-84, Cavanaugh Disting. prof. humanities, 1984—98, dean Coll. Arts and Letters, 1968-76. Author: (book) The Modeling of Mind, 1963, Philosophy and Cybernetics, 1967, Science and Contemporary Society, 1967; editor: Review of Politics, 1976—83. With USN, 1943—46. Mem.: North Ctrl. Assn. (exec. commr. 1984—89), Am. Cath. Philos. Assn. (pres. 1990—91), Am. Philos. Assn., Phi Beta Kappa (senator 1982—2000, v.p. 1994—97, pres. 1997—2000). Home: 51997 Heather Cv South Bend IN 46635-1074 Office: Coll Arts and Letters U of Notre Dame Notre Dame IN 46556

CROSTHWAITE, RACHEL ANSPACH, editor; b. Colfax, Iowa, Sept. 28, 1922; d. William Earl and Rachel Mae (Sykes) Anspach; m. Richard Maurice McCarthy (div.); children: Deborah McCarthy, Sarah McCarthy, Carrell McCarthy, Kate McCarthy, Richard McCarthy; m. Noel Crosthwaite, 1971 (dec.). Studied, U. Southern Calif., LA, 1946; BA, U. Iowa, 1942. Editor Bangkok World Newspaper, 1968—70, Femina Mag., Bangkok, 1970—72; owner Impress Pub. Relations, Bangkok, 1970—75; ret., 1975. Co-mgr. Bangkok Music Group, 1967—75; mem. Siam Soc., 1965—75. Mem.: PEO. Avocations: writing, sculpting, gardening, travel. Home: 433 Ashlar Dr Napa CA 94558

CROTHERS, DANIEL J., state supreme court justice; b. Fargo, ND, Jan. 3, 1957; BA, U. ND, 1979, JD, 1982. Bar: N.Mex. 1982, ND 1983. Law clk. NM Ct. Appeals, 1982—83; asst. states atty. Walsh County, ND, 1983; former ptnr. Nilles, Hansen & Davies Ltd., Fargo; justice ND Supreme Ct., 2005—. Adj. real estate law Moorhead State U., 1986—89, natural resources law, 1988. Staff mem. Univ. ND Law Rev., 1980—82. Mem.: ND Bar Assn. (pres. 2001—02). Office: ND Supreme Ct State Capitol Bismarck ND 58505-0530

CROTTS, CAROLYN PEARL, school librarian; b. Dodge City, Kans., Nov. 3, 1935; d. Ed LaVerne and M. Pearl (Suiter) DeVore; m. Johnny LaVelle Hager, Mar. 27, 1955 (dec. Sept. 1958); children: Diane, Johnny, Jeffrey; m. Robert Gene Crotts, Aug. 25, 1960; children: Roseanne, Sandra, Sharon, David. BA, Ft. Hays Kans. State Coll., 1961; MLS, Emporia U., Kans., 1995. Cert. tchr. English, elem. edn., libr., Kans. Elem. libr. Unified Sch. Dist. 351, Macksville, Kans., 1967—69; h.s. libr., tchr. 8th grade lang. arts Unified Sch. Dist. 371, Montezuma, Kans., 1965—66, tchr. 6th grade, 1969—72, h.s. and elem. libr., 1972—87; h.s. libr. Unified Sch. Dist. 102, Cimarron, Kans., 1987—98; cons. Cimarron City Libr., 1998—. Substitute tchr. Cimarron Unified Sch. Dist. 102, 1998—2004. Mem. choral union Dodge City C.C., 2004—. Mem. ALA, NEA, Kans. Nat. Edn. Assn.-Cimarron-Ensign (treas. 1992-97), Kans. Libr. Assn., Kans. Assn. Sch. Librs. (asst. dir. Dist. V 1995-96, dist. dir. 1996-97), Lambda Iota Tau Mem. Christian Ch. Avocations: reading, sewing, round dancing, church choir.

CROTTY, ROBERT BELL, retired lawyer; b. Dallas, Aug. 16, 1951; s. Willard and Betty (Bell) C.; m. Sarah (Smith), Mar. 8, 1980; children: Robert Edwin, Rebecca Bell. BA, Va. Mil. Inst., 1973; JD, U. Tex., 1976. Bar: Tex., 1976; US Dist. Ct. (no., so. and ea. dists.) Tex., 1977; US Ct. Appeals (5th cir.), 1978. Assoc. Akin, Gump, Strauss, Hauer, and Feld, Dallas, 1976-82, ptnr., 1983-92, hiring ptnr., 1988-91; prin. McKool Smith, P.C., Dallas, 1992-94; ptnr. Crotty & Johansen, LLP, Dallas, 1995—2005; pvt. practice Crotty Law Firm, Dallas, 2006—07; men's equipping dir. Watermark Cmty. Ch., Dallas, 2007—. Vis. bd. Va. Mil. Inst., 1995-99. Mem. Leadership Dallas, 1981; dir. Salesmanship Club, 1989—90, 1994—95, 2001—02, 2005—, pres., 2005—06; dir. Va. Mil. Inst. Alumni Assn., 1991—95, Highland Pk. Ind. Sch. Dist. Edn. Found., 1991—97, 2004—, pres., 1997—2000; chmn. bd. dir. Salesmanship Club Youth & Family Ctr., Inc., 2001—02; chmn. G.T.E. Byron Nelson Classic, 1995; bd. dir. Goodwill Industries of Dallas, Inc., 2002—; pres. Dallas Bus. League, 1983, Big Bros. Big Sisters Met. Dallas, 1987—88. First lt. US Army, 1976, first lt. USAR, 1973—81. Fellow Tex. Bar Found. (sustaining life), Dallas Bar Found. (sustaining life, pres. fellows 1999-2000); mem. Dallas Bar Assn., Tex. Law Rev. Assn. (life), State Bar Tex., Northwood Club (pres. 2003). Avocations: golf, reading, hunting, cycling. Office: Watermark Cmty Ch 7540 LBJ Freeway Dallas TX 75251 Office Phone: 214-922-7555. Personal E-mail: robertbcrotty@gmail.com. Business E-Mail: bcrotty@crottylawfirm.com.

CROUCH, J.D. (JACK DYER CROUCH II), former federal official, former ambassador; b. July 1, 1958; m. Kristin Crouch; children: Lara, Jake. BA in Internat. Relations, U. So. Calif., MA, Ph.D, U. So. Calif. Advisor for U.S. Del. to Nuclear and Space Arms Talks U.S. Arms Control and Disarmament Agy., 1985—86; mil. legis. asst. to Sen. Malcolm Wallop US Senate, 1986—90; assoc. prof. dept. def. & strategic studies S.W. Mo. State U., Springfield, Mo., 1993—2001; dep. asst. sec. for internat. security policy US Dept. Def., Washington, 1990—92, asst. sec. for internat. security policy, 2001—03; US amb. to Romania US Dept. State, Bucharest, 2004—05; asst. to the Pres. The White House, Washington, 2005—; asst. to the Pres. & dep. asst. for nat. security affairs NSC, Washington, 2005—07. Co-founder PalmGear.com.*

CROUCH, PETER E., engineering educator; b. Newcastle upon Tyne, Eng. BSc in Engring. Sci., U. Warwick, Eng., 1973, MSc in Control Theory, 1974; PhD in Applied Scis., Harvard U., 1977. Lectr. in control theory dept. elec. engring. U. Warwick, England, 1977—85, acting dir. Control Theory Ctr., 1983—84; rsch. assoc. divsn. applied sciences Harvard U., 1982; vis. assoc. prof. dept. math. Ariz. State U., 1984—85, assoc. prof. dept. elec. and computer engring., 1985—88, prof. dept. elec. engring., 1988—, acting chair dept. elec. and computer engring., 1988—89, dir. Ctr. for Systems Sci. and Engring., 1989—95, chair dept. elec. engring., 1992—95, dean, Ira A. Fulton Sch. Engring., 1995—. Assoc. editor Jour. of Math. Control and Info., 1984—, Systems and Control Letters, 1988—93, Math. of Control, Signals and Systems, 1989—, Jour. of Dynamical and Control Systems, 1994—; mem. bd. Internat. Performance Conf. on Computers and Comm., 1995—; mem. bd. advisors Inst. Systems & Robotics, Portugal, 1995—. Author: numerous papers and jour. articles. Recipient Hartree Premium Award, Instn. Elec. Engineers, 1982; Frank Knox Meml. Fellowship, 1974—76. Fellow: IEEE (assoc. editor Transactions on Automatic Control 1986—88, assoc. editor at large 1995—); mem.: Ariz. Soc. Profl. Engineers, Am. Soc. Engring. Edn., Soc. Indsl. and Applied Math., Am. Math. Soc. Office: Ariz State U Ira A Fulton Sch Engring PO Box 875506 Tempe AZ 85287-5506

CROUCH, RICHARD EDELIN, lawyer; b. Arlington, Va., Dec. 3, 1940; s. Howard Fairfax and Helen Nora (Edelin) Crouch; m. Mary Blake French, Feb. 6, 1965; children: John Howard, Virginia Elizabeth. AB, Coll. William and Mary, 1962, JD, 1964. Bar: Va. 1964, U.S. Ct. Mil. Appeals 1965, U.S. Dist. Ct. (ea. dist.) Va. 1970, U.S. Ct. Appeals (DC cir.) 1970, U.S. Supreme Ct. 1970, U.S. Ct. Appeals (4th cir.) 1972. Assoc. Crouch & Crouch, Arlington, 1964; editor U.S. Law Week & Criminal Law Reporter, Washington, 1968-74; prin. Crouch & Crouch, Arlington, 1974—. Cons. editor legal svcs. Bur. Nat. Affairs, Inc., Washington, 1981—84. Mng. editor: Family Law Reporter, 1974—81; author: The Rights of Homemakers in Virginia, 1977, Interstate Custody Litigation, 1981, Brandy Station: A Battle Like None Other, 2002. Capt. US Army, 1964—68. Mem.: SCV (judge advocate Va. divsn. 2006—), ABA, Loudoun County Preservation Soc., Fairfax County Hist. Soc., Arlington Hist. Soc., King and Queen County Hist. Soc., Am. Acad. Matrimonial Lawyers, Internat. Acad. Matrimonial Lawyers, Va. State Bar (chmn. 10th dist. disciplinary com. 1988—89, bd. govs. family law sect. 1988—92). Episcopalian. Home: 2624 18th St N Arlington VA 22201-4049 Office: 2101 Wilson Blvd Ste 950 Arlington VA 22201-3051 Home Phone: 703-528-4623; Office Phone: 703-528-6700.

CROUCH, STANLEY, writer, musician; b. LA, Dec. 14, 1945; Playwright, actor under Jayne Cortez, 1965-67; drummer with pianist Raymond King, 1966; drummer, bandleader with Quartet, Black Music Infinity, 1967—; instr. Claremont Coll., Calif., 1969-75. Columnist L.A. Free Press, The Cricket, SoHo Weekly News; jazz critic Village Voice; contbg. editor New Republic, 1990—; co-founder, artistic dir. Lincoln Ctr. jazz program. Author: Ain't No Ambulances for No Nigguhs Tonight, 1972, Notes of a Hanging Judge: Essays and Reviews, 1979-1989, 1990, The Artificial White Man: Essays on Authenticity, 2004; composer: Future Sallie's Time, Chicago for Bobby Seale, The Confessions of Father None, Flying Through Wire, Attica in Black September, Noteworthy Lady; albums include Now Is Another Time, Past Spirits. MacArthur grantee, 1993; recipient Jean Stein award Am. Acad. Arts and Letters, 1993. Office: Lincoln Ctr for Performing Arts Jazz Program 70 Lincoln Center Plz New York NY 10023-6548

CROUGHAN, MARY, medical educator; BS in Cmty. Health, U. Calif., Davis, 1982; PhD in Epidemiology, Johns Hopkins U. Sch. Hygiene and Pub. Health, 1987. Asst. rsch. epidemiologist dept. family and cmty. medicine U. Calif., San Francisco, 1987—88, hon. postdoctoral fellow Pew health policy prog. at Inst. Health Policy Studies, 1987—89, asst. adj. prof. depts. family and cmty. medicine and epidemiology and biostatistics, 1989—96, assoc. prof., 1996—, prof., 2002—04, prof. dept. ob-gyn. and reproductive scis. and epidemiology and biostatistics, 2004—. Vice chair dept. family and cmty. medicine U. Calif., San Francisco, 1999—2004. Contbr. articles to profl. jours. Recipient RESOLVE No. Calif. Vol. of Yr. award, 1998. Office: Comprehensive Cancer Ctr U Calif San Francisco Box 1793 San Francisco CA 94143-1793 E-mail: mary.croughan@ucsfmedctr.org.

CROUSE, CAROL K. MAVROMATIS, elementary school educator; d. George and Helen Mavromatis; m. David Crouse (dec. Dec. 1998). BS in Edn., Temple U., 1972, MEd in Curriculum and Instrn., 1981. Elem. tchr. grades 1, 3, 4, 5, Upper Darby (Pa.) Sch. Dist., 1974—, mem. Sci. Curriculum Writing Commn., 1974—99. Mem. excellence edn. team Hillcrest Elem. Sch., Pa., 1987; cert. NASA Lunar Rock and Meteorite Edn. Program, 1993—; tchr. adv. bd. Phila. Zoo, 1995—; mem. writing and evaluation team Schuykill Valley Nature Ctr., 1993—94; mem. Highland Park Elem. Sch. Learn and Serve Cmty. Svc. Ctr., Kids Care Club, 2000—02, Safety Patrol Advisor, 2002—. Recipient Howard W. McComb award, Temple U. Phi Delta Kappa, 1981. Mem.: NSTA, ASCD, Upper Darby Recreation Tennis Players (First Serve Tennis Racket stringer 1981—, tournament co-dir. 1983—92, supr. summer camp 2004—). Home: 122 Crestview Rd Upper Darby PA 19082

CROUSE, FARRELL R., lawyer; b. Portsmouth, Va., Dec. 23, 1963; s. Farrell Rondall and Grace Alice (Kenworthy) C. BA in History and Sociology, Bucknell U., Lewisburg, Pa., 1986; JD, Widener U., Wilmington, Del., 1989, LLM in Taxation, 1992. Bar: N.J. 1989, Pa. 1989, U.S. Dist. Ct. N.J. 1989. Assoc. Law Offices John William Neef, Carneys Point, NJ, 1990-91; pvt. practice Woodstown, NJ, 1991—99, Sewell, NJ, 1999—. Mem.: ABA, Pa. Bar Assn., NJ Bar Assn. Avocations: auto racing, travel, collecting auto racing books and memorabilia. Home and Office: 36 Crimson Ct East Sewell NJ 08080-2608

CROUSE, JERRY K., energy company executive; b. Jan. 1964; m. Ann Crouse. Former v.p., contr. Tenaska Energy, Omaha, CFO, 2003—. Office: Tenaska Energy 1044 N 115th St Ste 400 Omaha NE 68154 Office Phone: 402-691-9500. Office Fax: 402-691-9575. E-mail: power@tenaska.com.*

CROUT, J(OHN) RICHARD, pharmacologist, researcher; b. Portland, Oreg., Dec. 30, 1929; s. John and Georgia Crout; m. Carol Keith, June 19, 1954; children: Linda, Keith, Andrew. AB, Oberlin Coll., 1951; MD, Northwestern U., 1955, MS, 1956; DMed (hon.), U. Uppsala, Sweden, 1977. Intern Passavant Meml. Hosp., Chgo., 1955-56; asst. resident in internal medicine VA Rsch. Hosp., Chgo., 1956-57; clin. assoc. Nat. Heart Inst., Bethesda, Md., 1957-60; asst. resident in Medicine NYU-Bellevue Med. Ctr., NYC, 1960-61; USPHS fellow, instr. pharmacology Harvard U., 1961-63; asst. prof. pharmacology and internal medicine U. Tex. Southwestern Med. Sch., Dallas, 1963-65, assoc. prof., 1965-70; prof. pharmacology and medicine Mich. State U., 1970-71; dep. dir. Bur. Drugs FDA, Rockville, Md., 1971-72, dir. office sci. evaluation Bur. Drugs, 1972-73, dir. Bur. Drugs, 1973-82; dir. Office of Med. Applications of Rsch. NIH, 1982-84; v.p. med. and sci. affairs Boehringer Mannheim Pharms., 1984-94; scholar in residence Inst. Medicine, 1994-95; pres. Crout Cons., Bethesda, 1994—. Mem. drug resch. bd. NAS-NRC; cons. WHO, 1974—84; trustee U.S. Pharmacopeia, 1985—95; mem. coms. Inst. Medicine, 1990, 1992—93, 1998, 2000; bd. dirs. Trimeris. Contbr. articles to profl jours. Served to sr asst surgeon USPHS, 1957—60, asst surgeon gen USPHS, 1976—84. Recipient Dist Serv Award, USPHS, 1977, Spec Citation, Comnr FDA, 1981, 1982, Distinguished Career Award, Drug Info Asn, 1994, Oscar B Hunter Award in Therapeutics, Am Soc Clin Pharmaceutical and Therapeutics, 1997; scholar Burroughs Wellcome, 1965—70. Fellow: ACP; mem.: Soc. Clin. Trials, Am. Soc. Clin. Pharmacology and Therapeutics, Am. Soc. Clin. Investigation, Am. Soc. Pharmacology and Exptl.Therapeutics, Alpha Omega Alpha, Phi Beta Kappa. Home and Office: 5300 Alta Vista Rd Bethesda MD 20814-1629 E-mail: jrcrout@aol.com.

CROUTHAMEL, THOMAS GROVER, SR., editor, consultant; b. Berkeley, Calif., Sept. 10, 1930; s. Martin Luther and Elizabeth (Grover) C.; m. Madalene Donati, Sept. 6, 1954; children: Thomas Grover Jr., Annalise. BS, Thiel Coll., 1953. Sr. drug investigator FDA, L.A. and Edison, N.J., 1958-81; pres. Thomas G. Crouthamel, Inc., Bradenton, Fla., 1981—; ptnr. Crouthamel & Crouthamel, Bradenton, 1983-93; treas. Crouthamel Enterprises, Inc., Liberty Hill, Tex., 1986-92; sr. editor Keystone Press, Bradenton, 1982—. Author: Auditing EtO, 1982, It's OK, 1986, A History of Trailer Estates, 1987; When the Unthinkable Happens, 1995; contbr. articles to profl. jours. Cubmaster Boy Scouts Am., Pomona, Calif., 1963, committeeman, Spotswood, N.J., 1968-76, adult adviser Explorer Post, 1976-79; trustee Spotswood Libr. Bd., 1970-79; co-leader Compassionate Friends, Sarasota, Fla., 1984-90, chpt. advisor, facilitator, Englewood, Fla., 1989-91. With U.S. Army, 1953-55. Mem. Internat. Narcotics Officers Assn., The Authors Guild, Toastmasters (pres. 1969-71), Masons (high priest local chpt. 1967), FDA Alumni Assn., T.E. Masonic Square Club (pres. 2002, 03), Am. Legion, VFW. Avocations: travel, reading, fishing. Office: PO Box 6163 Bradenton FL 34281-6163

CROVITZ, LOUIS GORDON, publishing executive, journalist, lawyer; b. Durham, NC, Aug. 22, 1958; s. Herbert Floyd and Elaine Sandra (Kobrin) C. BA, U. Chgo., 1980; MA, Oxford U., 1982; JD, Yale U., 1986. Editor, founder Chgo. Jour., 1976-79; rsch. assoc. Lexecon, Inc., Chgo., 1979-80; editl. writer Wall St. Jour., NYC, 1980-82, editl. page editor Brussels, 1982-84, editl. writer, mem. editl.bd. NYC, 1984-86, asst. editl. page editor, 1986-92; with Dow Jones & Co., NYC, 1980—, editor, Far Eastern Econ. Rev. (subs.), 1992—97; mng. dir. Dow Jones Markets Asia, Hong Kong, 1997; v.p., planning and development Dow Jones & Co., NYC, 1997—98, sr. v.p., pres. electronic pub., 1998—2006, exec. v.p., 2006—, pres. consumer media group, 2006—, pub. Wall St. Jour. franchise, 2006—. Dir. Review Pub. Co. Ltd.; mng. dir. Dow Jones Markets Asia, 1997, dir., Downtown-Lower Manhattan Assn., Rhodes Scholar Selection Com. Editl. commentary contbr. Barron's, 1989-92; editor Far Eastern Econ. Rev., 1992-97, editor and pub., 1993-97, co-editor, The Fettered Presidency, 1989. Rhodes scholar, 1980-82; recipient Disting. Alumni award Durham Acad., 1984, Gerald Loeb award for bus. commentary, 1990; named one of top 10 bus. innovators NY Exec. Coun., 2004. Mem. Federalist Soc., Coun. Fgn. Rels., Phi Beta Kappa. Jewish. Office: Dow Jones and Co 200 Liberty St Fl 11 New York NY 10281-1099*

CROW, HAROLD EUGENE, physician, educator; b. Farber, Mo., Jan. 17, 1933; s. Leslie J. and Laura L. (Sparks) C.; m. Mary Kay Krenke, July 5, 1974; children: Janet L., Jason P. MD, U. Mo., 1963. Diplomate Am. Bd. Family Practice, Am. Bd. Med. Examiners. Intern E.W. Sparrow Hosp., Lansing, Mich., 1963-64; pvt. practice medicine specializing in family practice Lansing, 1964-70; dir. family practice residency E.W. Sparrow Hosp., Lansing, Mich., 1970-82; chmn. dept. family and community medicine Sch. Medicine, U. Nev., Reno, 1982-87, dir. office Rural Health Sch. Medicine, 1984-87; med. dir. S.W. Med. Assocs., Reno, 1987-88; dir. Lynchburg (Va.) Family Practice Resident Program, 1988-96; patient advocate Cons. for Caring, Sun City Center, Fla., 1996—98; dir. Outer Banks Edn. and Program Devel. Project, East Carolina U. Sch. Medicine, Nags Head, NC, 1999—. Dir. Outer Banks Edn. and Program Devel. Project. Developer non-rotational residency model for family practice tng., tng. model for rural med. practice; innovator computerized health info. systems for family physicians. Numerous civic activities. With U.S. Army, 1955-57. Mem.: Am. Coll. Physician Exec. Presbyterian. Home: 408 Stoneham Dr Sun City Center FL 33573-5841 E-mail: hecrow@pol.net. *Not being hampered by Dogma, but being freed up by curiousity. Not being a heavy handed teacher, but a caring helper of learning; that's the essense of a successful innovator and educator.*

CROW, JAMES FRANKLIN, retired genetics educator; b. Phoenixville, Pa., Jan. 18, 1916; s. H. Ernest and Lena (Whitaker) C.; m. Ann Crockett, Aug. 9, 1941; children: Franklin, Laura, Catherine. AB, Friends U., 1937; PhD, U. Tex., 1941; DSc. (hon.), U. Chgo., 1991. Instr., then asst. prof. zoology Dartmouth U., 1941-48; faculty U. Wis., 1948—, prof. genetics, 1954-86, chmn. dept. med. genetics, 1958-63, 65-71, acting dean sch. medicine, 1963-65, prof. emeritus, 1986—. Chmn. genetics study sect. NIH, 1965-68 Author: Genetics Notes, 8th edit, 1983, Introduction to Population Genetics Theory, 1970, Basic Concepts in Population, Quantitative and Evolutionary Genetics, 1986, also articles. Chmn. mammalian genetics study sect. NIH, 1985-88. Mem. Nat. Acad. Scis. (chmn. com. genetic effects atomic radiation 1960-63, 70-72, chmn. com. chem. environ. mutagens 1980-83), Japan Acad. (fgn. mem.), Genetics Soc. Am. (pres. 1960), Am. Soc. Human Genetics (pres. 1963), Royal Soc. (fgn. mem.). Home: 24 Glenway St Madison WI 53705-5206 Office Phone: 608-263-4438. E-mail: jfcrow@wisc.edu.

CROW, JUDSON LEWIS, plastic surgeon; b. Brinkley, Ark., Apr. 16, 1936; s. Judson Lawrence and Lorene Louise (Gibson) C.; m. Barbara Elizabeth Hulme, Oct. 22, 1964; children: Sarah, Melanie, Elizabeth. MD, U. Ark, 1961. Diplomate Am. Bd. Gen. Surgery, Am. Bd. Plastic Surgery. Intern Flower Hosp., Toledo, 1961-62; med. officer USN, Antarctica, New Zealand, Japan, 1962-66; resident in gen. surgery Naval Hosp., Portsmouth, Va., 1966-70, med. officer Danang, Vietnam, 1965-66, staff surgeon Camp Lejune, N.C., 1970-72; plastic surgery resident U. Tex., San Antonio, 1972, U. Tenn. and City of Memphis Hosps., 1973-75; pvt. practice in plastic surgery, 1975—; plastic surgeon Grand Forks (N.D.) Clinic, 1986—. Tutor specialist in plastic surgery, Auckland, New Zealand, 1975-76. Comdr. USN, 1962-72. Fellow ACS; mem. Am. Soc. Plastic and Reconstructive Surgeons, Am. Soc. Aesthetic Plastic Surgeons. Avocation: gardening. Office: Red River Plastic Surgery Clinic 1408 Ctrl Ave NE East Grand Forks MN 56721 Office Phone: 281-773-1390. Business E-Mail: jcrow@rivervigahealth.org.

CROW, LYNNE CAMPBELL SMITH, insurance company representative; b. Buffalo, Oct. 13, 1942; d. Stephen Smith and Jean Campbell (Ruggles) Hall; m. William David Crow II, Apr. 16, 1966 (div. Dec. 1989); children: William David III, Alexander Fairbairn, Margaret Campbell. BA, Sweet Briar Coll., Va., 1964; postgrad., The Am. Coll., Bryn Mawr, Pa., 1986. CLU; ChFC; registered rep. Claims rep. Liberty Mut. Ins. Co., Bklyn. and NYC, 1964-66; with McGraw-Hill Corp., NYC, 1966-67; claims rep. Liberty Mut. Ins. Co., East Orange, N.J., 1967-68; sales assoc. Realty World/Allsopp Realtors, Millburn, N.J., 1981-82; field rep. Guardian Life Ins. Co., 1982—; registered rep. Park Ave. Securities. Bd. dirs. Jr. League Oranges and Short Hills, Millburn, 1979-80, 95-96, Millburn LWV, 1979-80, Cheshire Homes, 2004-05; campaign chair, bus. chair, bd. dirs. United Way Millburn/Short Hills, 1981-88, 90-96, sec., 1990-91; adult planning chair Cora Hartshorn Arboretum, 2000-03, bd. dirs., trustee, 2000-04, sec., 2003-04; bd. dirs. Cheshire Homes, 2005—. Named Life Underwriter of Yr., 1996. Mem. AAUW, Nat. Assn. Ins. and Fin. Advisors (Nat. Quality award 1988, 91, 95, Nat. Health Achievement award 1988,

90), Nat. Assn. Health Underwriters, Am. Soc. Fin. Svc. Profls. (bd. dirs. 1994-99), NJ Assn. Ins. and Fin. Advisors (dir. region II 1993-95, sec. 1998-99, 2d v.p. 1999-2000, 1st v.p. 2000-01, pres. 2001-02, health chair 2006), Newark Assn. Life Underwriters (bd. dirs. 1986-94, sec. 1987-88, treas. 1988-89, 3d v.p. 1989-90, 2d v.p. 1990, pres.-elect 1991-92, pres. 1992-93, health chair 1995-98, Life Underwriter of Yr. 1986), Nat. Assn. Ins. and Fin. Advisors (governance com. 2003-04, com. on assns. 2004-06), Women in Fin. Svcs., Leader's Recognition Soc., Million Dollar Round Table (life, capt. focus session on non-core products and investments 1999-2000, chair spl. events 2000-01, asst. dir. program gen. arrangements 2006, asst. dir. registration 2007), Million Dollar Round Table Found. (trustee 2002-05, platinum knight, trusteeship com. 2003-04, mem. nominating com. 2007-08, Inner Cir., 2007), Assn. Health Ins. Advisors, Nat. Assn. Security Dealers, Chatham (Mass.) Beach and Tennis Club. Republican. Episcopalian. Avocations: travel, sailing, reading, hiking, photography. Home: 22 Winding Way Short Hills NJ 07078-2530 Office: Cert Fin Svcs LLC 52 Forest Ave Paramus NJ 07652 Office Phone: 201-843-7700 x358. Personal E-mail: lscrow22ww@aol.com. E-mail: lcrow@glic.com.

CROW, MICHAEL M., academic administrator; m. Sybil Francis; 3 children. BA in Polit. Sci. and Environ. Studies, Iowa State U., 1977; D in Pub. Adminstrn., Syracuse U. Exec. vice provost Columbia U., prof. sci., tech. policy; prof. tech. mgmt. Iowa State U., dir., inst. phys. rsch. & tech; pres. Ariz. State U., Tempe, 2002—. Co-author: Limited by Design, 1998, Synthetic Fuel Technology Development in the United States, 1998; contbr. articles to profl. jours.;, editor numerous books. Fellow: Nat. Acad. Pub. Adminstrn. Avocations: hiking, mountain biking. Office: Ariz State Univ 300 E Univ ASU Fulton Ctr 4th Fl PO Box 877705 Tempe AZ 82587-7705

CROW, MICHAEL P., lawyer; b. Ft. Sill, Okla., Jan. 22, 1945; BA, Baker Univ., Kans., 1967; JD, Washburn Univ., Topeka, 1973. Ptnr. Crow, Clothier and Associates, Leavenworth, Kans., 1974—. Law clerk Hon. Arthur J. Stanley Jr., U.S. Dist. Ct., 1974—75; lectr., judicial process Wichita State Univ., 1976—77; mcpl. judge, Basehor, Kans., 1976—79, Linwood, Kans., 1977—79; atty. Delaware Twp., Kans., 1977—79; city atty. Tonganoxie, Kans., 1977—2004; state rep. Kans. Ho. of Reps., 1978—82; atty. Leavenworth Civil Svc. Commn., Kans., 1988. Lt. US Army, 1967—70. Mem.: Assn. of Trial Lawyers of Am., Kans. Trial Lawyers Assn. (bd. dir. 1989—, treas. 1995—96), Am. Bar Assn., Leavenworth County Bar Assn. (pres. 1981—82, bd. dir. 1990—94), Kans. Bar Assn. (bd. gov. 1995—, sec. 2001—02, v.p. 2002—03, pres. 2004—05), Phi Alpha Delta. Office: Crow Clothier & Assocs 302 Shawnee PO Box 707 Leavenworth KS 66048*

CROW, NANCY REBECCA, lawyer; b. Ridgecrest, Calif., Nov. 3, 1948; d. Edwin Louis and Eleanor Elizabeth (Gish) C.; 1 child, Rebecca Ann Carr; m. Mark A.A. Skrotzki, Apr. 4, 1987. BA, Antioch Coll., 1970; JD, U. Colo., 1974; LLM in Taxation, NYU, 1977. Bars: Colo. 1974, Calif. 1977. Atty., advisor IRS, NYC, 1975-77; assoc. Brawerman & Kopple, Los Angeles, 1977-80; prof. Sch. Law, U. Denver, 1980-81; of counsel Krendl & Netzorg, Denver, 1981-84; shareholder Krendl & Krendl, Denver, 1984-92, Pendleton, Friedberg, Wilson & Hennessey, P.C., Denver, 1992—. Editor estate and trust forum Colorado Lawyer, 1992-93, bd. editors, 1993-2000; contbr. chpts. to books. Mem. alumni bd. Antioch Coll., 2000—; bd. dirs. Philharmonic Orch., 1998—2001; bd. trustees Denver Philharmonic Found., 2001—. Fellow Am. Coll. Trust and Estate Counsel; mem. ABA (chmn. Welfare Benefits subcom. of personal svcs. orgns. com. com., tax sect. 1987-92), Colo. Bar Assn. (exec. coun. tax sect. 1990-93, sec. tax sect. 1993-94, chair-elect 1994-95, chair 1995-96, bd. govs. 1996-98), Colo. Women's Bar Assn. (chair pub. policy com. 1982-83, trustee 2005—), Denver Bar Assn., Denver Tax Assn., Denver Tax Inst. Planning Com., Alliance of Profl. Women, Women's Estate Planning Coun. (bd. dirs. 1996-98), U.S.-Mex. C. of C. (bd. dirs. Rocky Mountain chpt., sec. 1998-2001), Sierra Club. Democrat. Unitarian Universalist. Avocations: skiing, backpacking, cello, running. Home: 1031 Marion St Denver CO 80218-3016 Office: Pendleton Friedberg Wilson & Hennessey PC 1875 Lawrence St 10th Fl Denver CO 80202 Home Phone: 303-861-1068; Office Phone: 303-839-1204. Business E-Mail: ncrow@penberg.com.

CROW, PAUL ABERNATHY, JR., retired minister; b. Birmingham, Ala., Nov. 17, 1931; s. Paul Abernathy and Beulah Elizabeth (Parker) C.; m. Mary Evelyn Matthews, Sept. 11, 1955; children: Carol Ann, Stephen Paul, Susan Margaret. BS, U. Ala., 1954; BD, Lexington Theol. Sem., 1957; STM, Hartford Sem. Found., 1958, PhD, 1962; postdoctoral studies, Oxford U., 1967-68, U. Geneva, Ecumenical Inst. Bossey, 1981-87; DD, Phillips U., 1983, Bethany Coll., 1983, Yale U., 1986, Va. Theological Sem., 1987; DHL, Lynchburg Coll., 1997. Ordained to ministry Disciples of Christ, 1957. Minister in various Disciples congregations, Ala., Ky., 1953—57; min. First Congl. Ch., Hadley, Mass., 1957-61; assoc. prof. ch. history Lexington Theol. Sem., 1961-66, prof., 1966-68; Am. Assn. Theol. Schs. vis. fellow Oxford U., 1967-68; gen. sec. Consultation on Ch. Union, Princeton, NJ, 1968-74; pres. Coun. on Christian Unity, Indpls., 1974-98; affiliate prof. Christian Theol. Sem., 1974—; Tillard prof. ecumenical theology Pontifical U. St. Thomas Aquinas, Rome, 2006—07. Vis. lectr. Princeton Theol. Sem., 1968-78, Ecumenical Inst. World Coun. Churches, Switzerland, 1983, 1987; affiliate prof. Christian Theol. Sem., 1974-; mem. ctr. com. World Coun. Chs., exec. com., faith and order plenary commn., 1975-98; vice moderator Faith and Order Commn., 1992-98; del. faith and order confs., St. Andrews, Scotland, 1960, Montreal, Que., Can., 1963, Bristol, Eng., 1967, Louvain, Belgium, 1971, Accra, Ghana, 1974, Bangalore, India, 1978, Lima, Peru, 1982, Stavanger, Norway, 1985, Budapest, Hungary, 1989, Santiago de Compostela, Spain, 1993, Moshi, Tanzania, 1996, Kuala Lumpur, Malaysia, 2004; del. World Coun. Chs. assembly Uppsala, Sweden, 1968, Nairobi, Kenya, 1975, Vancouver, Can., 1983, Canberra, Australia, 1991, Harare, Zimbabwe, 1998; del. ch. union confs., Limuru, Kenya, 1970, Toronto, Ont., Can., 1975, Colombo, Sri Lanka, 1981, Potsdam, German Democratic Republic, 1987, Ocho Rios, Jamaica, 1995, WCC World Missionary Conf., San Antonio, Tex., 1989; mem. exec. com. Consultation on Ch. Union; chmn. Disciples of Christ del., 1974-98, mem. exec. com., mem. gen. bd. Nat. Coun. Chs., 1974-98; moderator of bd. Ecumenical Inst. Bossey, Céligny, Switzerland, 1974-83; co-chmn. Disciples of Christ-Roman Cath. Internat. Bilateral, 1977-2002; co-chmn. Disciples-Russian Orthodox Internat. Bilateral, 1987-98, Disciples-Reformed Internat. Bilateral, 1987-98, Disciples-Finnish Luth., 1996-98; gen. sec. Disciples Ecumenical Consultative Coun., 1975-98; vis.prof. Lexington Theol. Sem., 2001-; lectr. in field. Author: Where We Are in Church Union, 1965, The Ecumenical Movement in Bibliographical Outline, 1965, No Greater Love: The Gospel and Its Imperatives, 1967, Church Union at Mid-Point, 1972, Christian Unity: Matrix for Mission, 1982, The Anatomy of a Nineteenth Century United Church, 1983, The Vision of Christian Unity: Essays in Honor of Paul A. Crow, Jr., 1997; author: (with James Duke) The Church for Disciples of Christ, 1998; contbr. over 300 articles to maj. scholarly jours. and ency.; editor: Mid-Stream: An Ecumenical Jour., 1974—99; associate editor: The Journal of Ecumenical Studies, 2006—. Trustee Disciples of Christ Hist. Soc. Recipient Disting. Alumni award Hartford Sem. Found., 1986, Ecumenical Svc. award Nat. Workshop on Christian Unity, 1998, Focolare Internat. Luminos (Light) of Christian Unity award, 1998, Ecumenism award Washington Theol. Consortium, 2004; Jacobus fellow Hartford Sem. Found., 1958-60. Mem. Nat. Assn. Ecumenical Officers (pres. 1988-93), Am. Soc. Ch. History, North Am. Acad. Ecumenists, Societas Oecumenica, Fellowship of St. Alban and St. Sergius, Nassau Club (Princeton, N.J.), Indianapolis Athletic Club, Omicron Delta Kappa, Theta Phi, Pi Kappa Phi. Democrat. Home: 7215 Vauxhall Rd Indianapolis IN 46250-2737 Personal E-mail: paulcrowjr@aol.com.

CROW, SAM ALFRED, judge; b. Topeka, May 5, 1926; s. Samuel Wheadon and Phyllis K. (Brown) Crow; m. Ruth M. Rush, Jan. 30, 1948; children: Sam A., Dan W. BA, U. Kans., 1949; JD, Washburn U., 1952, LLD (hon.), 2006. Ptnr. Rooney, Dickinson, Prager & Crow, Topeka, 1953—63, Dickinson, Crow, Skoog & Honeyman, Topeka, 1963—70; sr. ptnr. Crow & Skoog, Topeka, 1971—75; part-time U.S. magistrate, 1973—75; U.S. magistrate, 1975—81; judge U.S. Dist. Ct. Kans., Wichita, 1981—92, Topeka, 1992—96, sr. judge, 1996—. Bd. rev. Boy Scouts Am., 1960—70, cubmaster, 1957—60; chmn. Kans. March of Dimes, 1959, bd. dirs., 1960—65, Topeka Coun. Chs., 1960—70; mem. Kans. Hist. Soc., 1960—; pres., v.p. PTA; bd. govs. Washburn Law Sch. Alumni Assn., 1993—99; mem. Shawnee County Hist. Soc., Kans.; mem. vestry Grace Episcopal Ch., Topeka, 1960—65. Col. JAGC USAR, ret. Named to, Topeka H.S. Hall of Fame, 2000; recipient Washburn U. Sch. Law Disting. Svc. award, 2000. Fellow: Kans. Bar Found.; mem.: ABA (del. Nat. Conf. Spl. Ct. Judges 1978), Topeka Lawyers Club (sec. 1964—65, pres. 1965—66), Wichita Bar Assn., Topeka Bar Assn. (chmn. jud. reform com., chmn. bench and bar com., chmn. criminal law com., Disting. Svc. award 2000), Nat. Assn. U.S. Magistrates (com. discovery abuse), Kans. Trial Lawyers Assn. (sec. 1959—60, pres. 1960—61), Kans. Bar Assn. (chmn. mil. law sect. 1965, 1967, 1970, trustee 1970—76, chmn. mil. law sect. 1972, 1974, 1975), Shawnee Country Club, Shriners (Shriner of Yr. 2005), Am. Legion, Sigma Alpha Epsilon, Delta Theta Phi. Office: US Dist Ct 444 SE Quincy St Topeka KS 66683

CROW, SHERYL, singer, songwriter, musician; b. Kennett, Mo., Feb. 11, 1962; 1 adopted child, Wyatt Steven. Degree in classical piano, U. Mo., 1984; Ph.D (hon.), S.E. Mo. St. U. Backup singer Bad tour Michael Jackson, 1987; backup singer The End of the Innocence tour Don Henley, 1989; also backup singer George Harrison, Joe Cocker, Stevie Wonder, Rod Stewart. Singer: (albums) Tuesday Night Music Club, 1993, Sheryl Crow, 1996, The Globe Sessions, 1998, Sheryl Crow and Friends: Live in Central Park, 1999, C'mon, C'mon, 2002 (Grammy award best female rock vocal performance, 2003), Live at Budokan, 2003, The Very Best of Sheryl Crow, 2003, Wildflower, 2005, (songs) Leaving Las Vegas, 1994, All I Wanna Do, 1994 (Grammy awards for Record of Year and Female Pop Vocal, 1995), Strong Enough, 1994, Can't Cry Anymore, 1995, Everyday Is a Winding Road, 1996, If It Makes You Happy, 1996, My Favorite Mistake, 1998, Anything But Down, 1999, Soak up the Sun, 2002, The First Cut Is the Deepest, 2003; singer: (with Kid Rock) Picture, 2001; participant Lilith Fair, 1998, 1999. Co-recipient Vocal Event of Yr. award, Acad. Country Music, 2007; recipient Grammy award for Best New Artist, 1995, Favorite Female Artist award Pop or Rock, Am. Music Awards, 2004, Favorite Artist award Adult Contemporary Music, 2004, Golden Plate award, Acad. Achievement, 2006.*

CROW, STEVEN D., educational association administrator; BA in Hist., Lewis and Clark Coll., Oreg.; MA in Hist., PhD in Hist., U. Wis., Madison; cert. in Bus. Adminstrn. for Not-for-Profit Mgmt., U. Ill., Chgo. Adminstr., tchr. Kalamazoo Coll., Bates Coll., Vanderbilt U., Bowdoin Coll.; with Higher Learning Commn. of North Ctrl. Assn. Colls. and Schs., Chgo., 1982—, mem. critical issues com., mem. com. on orgnl. effectiveness and future directions, exec. dir, Chgo. Contbr. articles to profl. publs. Office: Higher Learning Commn 30 N LaSalle St Ste 2400 Chicago IL 60602-2504 Office Phone: 800-621-7440 ext. 102. E-mail: scrow@hlcommission.org.*

CROW, TIM, consumer products company executive; Retail mgmt. positions Sears Roebuck, KMart; v.p. performance systems Home Depot, Atlanta, 2002—05, sr. v.p. talent, org. & performance systems, 2005—07, exec. v.p. HR, 2007—. Office: Home Depot 2455 Paces Ferry Rd Atlanta GA 30339-4024*

CROWDER, BARBARA LYNN, judge; b. Mattoon, Ill., Feb. 3, 1956; d. Robert Dale and Martha Elizabeth (Harrison) C.; m. Lawrence Owen Taliana, Apr. 17, 1982; children: Paul Joseph, Robert Lawrence, Benjamin Owen. BA, U. Ill., Urbana-Champaign, 1978, JD, 1981. Bar: Ill. 1981. Assoc. Louis E. Olivero, Peru, Ill., 1981—82; asst. state's atty. Madison County, Edwardsville, Ill., 1982—84; ptnr. Robbins & Crowder, Edwardsville, 1985—87, Robbins, Crowder & Bader, Edwardsville, Ill., 1987—88, Crowder, Taliana, Rubin, and Buckley, Edwardsville, 1988—98; assoc. judge 3d Jud. Cir. Madison County, Edwardsville, 1999—2006, cir. judge, 2006—. Spkr. Ill. Inst. CLE seminars Family Law Update, 1993—2006; co-chair 3d. Jud. Cir. Family Violence Coord. Coun., 1999—, chair ct. com., 1999—; presiding judge Family divsn. 3d Jud. Cir., Edwardsville, 2000, 2003—04, 2005—06; spkr. edn. Conf. Adminstrn. Office Ill. Ct., 2002—06; mem. spl. com. child custody issues Supreme Ct., Ill., 2002—; peer review com. on edn. Ill. Jud. Conf., 2007—; spkr. in field. Co-author chpts. in ISBA Family Law Handbook, 1995, Maintenance Chapter Ill. Family Law Ill. Inst. CLE, 1998, supplement, 2001; contbr. articles to profl. jours Chmn. City of Edwardsville Zoning Bd. Appeals, 1986-87; committee woman Edwardsville Dem., Precinct 15, 1986-98; mem. City of Edwardsville Planning Commn., 1985-87; bd. dirs. Madison-Bond County Workforce Devel. Bd., 1995-96, 96-97, Ill. Judges Found., 2007—. Named Best Oral Advocate, Moot Ct. Bd., 1979, Outstanding Young Career Woman, Dist. XIV, Ill. Bus. and Profl. Women, 1986; recipient Alice Paul award Alton-Edwardsville NOW, 1987, Woman Achievement YWCA, 1996; recipient Athena award Edwardsville/Glen Carbon C. of C., 1991, V-Day Warrior Phoenix Crisis Ctr. and U.S. Women of Steel, 2006, Ptnrs. in Peace award 3d Cir. Family Violence Coordinating Coun., 2006, Civic Svc. award, NAACP, 2007. Mem. Ill. Bar Assn. (family law coun. sect. 1990-99, chair 1997-98, co-editor Family Law newsletter 1993, vice chair 1996-97, Bench and Bar sect. coun. 2002—, sec. 2004-2005, vice chair, 2005-2006, chair Bench and Bar sect. coun. 2006-07), Ill. Judges' Assn. (bd. dirs. 2002-07), Nat. Assn. Women Judges, Ill. Fedn. Bus. and Profl. Women (parliamentarian dist. XIV 1991-92, Outstanding Working Woman Ill. 1988-89), Women Lawyers Assn. Met. East (pres. 1986), Edwardsville Bus. and Profl Women's Club (pres. 1988-89, 95-96, treas. 1989-90, Woman of Achievement award 1985, Jr. Svc. award 1987), U. Ill. Alumni Assn. (v.p. met.-east club 1994-95, bd. dirs. 1995-97, alumni bd. vis. 2005-), Ill. Judges Assn Found. (1st v.p., 2007—). Democrat. Office: Madison County Cthse 155 N Main St Edwardsville IL 62025-1955 Home Phone: 618-692-0866; Office Phone: 618-296-4411. Business E-Mail: blcrowder@co.madison.il.us.

CROWDER, MARJORIE BRIGGS, lawyer; b. Shreveport, La., Mar. 26, 1946; d. Rowland Edmund and Marjorie Ernestine (Biles) Crowder; m. Ronald J. Briggs, July 11, 1970 (div. Nov. 2000); children: Sarah Briggs, Andrew Briggs. BA, Carson-Newman Coll., 1968; MA, Ohio State U., 1969, JD, 1975. Bar: Ohio 1975, U.S. Ct. Appeals (6th cir.) 1983, U.S. Ct. Claims 1992, U.S. Supreme Ct. 2001. Asst. dean of women Albion Coll., Mich., 1969-70; dir. residence hall Ohio State U., Columbus, 1970-71, acad. counselor, 1971-72; assoc. Porter, Wright, Morris, Arthur, Columbus, 1975—83, ptnr., 1983-2000; AmeriCorps atty. Southeastern Ohio Legal Svs., Portsmouth, Ohio, 2000—02, staff atty., 2002—03; domestic violence team leader Legal Aid Soc. Columbus, 2003—04; supr. legal rsch. Franklin Co. Mcpl. Ct., 2005—07; program mgr. children, families and cts. Supreme Ct. Ohio, 2007—. Legal aide Cmty. Law Office, Columbus, 1973—74. Co-author: (book) Going to Trial, A Step-By-Step Guide to Trial Practice and Procedure, 1989. Trustee, pres. Epilepsy Assn. Ctrl. Ohio, Columbus, 1977—84; bd. dirs. Scioto County Domestic Violence Task Force, 2001—04, v.p., 2001—; bd. dirs. Action Ohio Coalition Battered Women, 2002—, Columbus Speech & Hearing, 1977—82. Fellow: Columbus Bar Found. (trustee 1993—95); mem.: Scioto County Bar Assn., Columbus Bar Assn. (com. chmn. 1979—83, docket control task force 1989—91, editor 1981—83), ABA (mem. gavel awards com. 1989—96, gen. practice sect. 1983—, chair litig. com. 1987—89, mem. exec. coun. 1989—93, dir. bus. com. group 1990—91, chair program com. 1991—93, torts and ins. practice sect. 1993—, vice chair health ins. law com. 1993—96), Ohio Bar Assn. (mem. joint task force gender fairness 1991—93), Scioto County Bar Assn. Office: 209 E Pacemont Rd Columbus OH 43202 Office Phone: 614-387-9385. Business E-Mail: crowderm@sconet.state.oh.us.

CROWDER, RICHARD MORGAN, pilot; b. Wurzburg, Bavaria, Germany, July 22, 1963; (parents Am. citizens); s. Richard Thomas and Margaret Taylor (Rainey) C. BS, U. Minn., 1986; postgrad., U. Colo., 1995-96. Capt., pilot Classic Aviation, Mpls., 1985-87; pilot Air South, Homestead, Fla., 1987, AVAir, Raleigh, NC, 1987-88, Am. Eagle, Dallas, 1988-89, USAir, Arlington, Va., 1989-92, United Airlines, Chgo., 1992—. Republican. Presbyterian. Avocations: reading, running, bible study, trap shooting, foreign travel.

CROWDER, RICHARD THOMAS, ambassador; b. Baskerville, Va., Aug. 3, 1939; s. George Thomas and Estelle (Morgan) C.; m. Margaret Rainey, Sept. 4, 1960; children: Richard, Matthew. BS, Va. Poly. Inst. and State U., 1960, MS, 1962; PhD, Okla. State U., 1967. Staff economist Exxon USA, Houston, 1966-68; dir. econ. analysis Wilson & Co., Inc., Oklahoma City, 1968-75; sr. v.p. The Pillsbury Co., Mpls., 1975-89; under sec. for internat. affairs and commodity programs USDA, Washington, 1989—92; exec. v.p., gen. mgr. Armour Swift-Eckrich (divsn. of ConAgra), 1992—94; sr. v.p., internat DEKALB Genetics Corp., 1994—99; ind. cons., 1999—2002; pres., CEO Am. Sneed Trade Assn., Alexandria, Va., 2002—05; chief agrl. negotiator Office US Trade Rep., Washington, 2005—. Advisor Spl. Trade Representation, Washington, Office of Tech. Assessment, Washington; exec. v.p. Pillsbury Restaurant Group, 1987-89. Rep. precinct vice chmn. Hennepin County. Capt. U.S. Army, 1962-64. Mem. Am. Agrl. Econs. Assn. (bd. dirs. 1975-78, assoc. editor 1983-86). Methodist. Avocations: running, tennis, bridge, reading. Office: Office US Trade Rep 600 17th st NW Washington DC 20508

CROWDER-PAGANO, LINDA LOUISE, special education educator; b. Queens, NY, Apr. 9, 1956; d. Roy Miller Crowder and Edith Elizabeth Sisson Crowder; m. Theodore Joseph Pagano, Apr. 26, 1996; children: David Theodore, Christopher Alexander, Jeffrey Joseph. BA in Edn., Dowling Coll., 1978; MSc in Spl. Edn., Adelphi U., 1981, MSW, 1993. Cert. sch. social worker NJ; elem. tchr. NY, tchr. handicapped NJ, tchr. psychology NJ, hypnotherapist Nat. Assn. Cert. Hypnotherapists. Tchr. spl. edn. Saxton Jr. H.S., NY; tchr. Patchogue-Medford Sch. Dist.; tchr. resourse and self contained Ocean Ave. Elem. Sch., Middleton, NJ, 1988—. Freelance tutor, NY, NJ. Recipient Tchr. of Yr. award, Gov., 1992. Mem.: Psi Chi. Avocations: antiques, tennis, music, writing. Home: 14 Boxwood Dr Colts Neck NJ 07722 Office Phone: 732-787-0092.

CROWDUS, GARY ALAN, film company executive; b. Lexington, Ky., Jan. 2, 1945; s. Charles Dallas and Bess May (Rice) C. BFA, NYU Inst. Film and TV, 1969. Founding editor Cineaste mag., NYC, 1967—; assoc. editor Film Society Review, NYC, 1968-72; v.p. Tricontinental Film Ctr., NYC, 1972-79, Unifilm Inc., NYC, 1979-80; gen. mgr. The Cinema Guild, Inc., NYC, 1981—2004; dir. mktg. and publicity First Run/Icarus Films, Inc., Bklyn, 2004—. Mem. U.S. Conf. on Alternative Cinema, N.Y.C., 1978-79; mem. internat. adv. com. Internat. Documentary Film Week, 1989. Co-author: (with others) Quinze and de Cinema Mondial, 1975, The Documentary Tradition, 1979, The Cineaste Interviews, 1983, New Challenges for Documentary, 1988, Film and Politics in the Third World, 1988, Celluloid Power: Social Film Criticism from The Birth of a Nation to Judgement at Nuremberg, 1992, The Political Companion to American Film, 1994, The Cineaste Interviews, Vol. 2, 2002. Mem. Assn. Ind. Video and Filmmakers, Internat. Documentary Assn. Home: 116 Saint Marks Pl Apt 8 New York NY 10009-5856 Office: Cineaste Mag Art Politics Cinema 235 Fifth Ave # 706 New York NY 10016 also: FirstRun/Icarus FilmsI 32 Court St 21st Fl Brooklyn NY 11201 Office Phone: 212-366-5720, 718-488-8900. Business E-Mail: cineaste@cineaste.com.

CROWE, CAMERON, screenwriter, film director; b. Palm Springs, Calif., July 13, 1957; m. Nancy Wilson, July 27, 1986; 2 children. Student, Calif. State U., San Diego. Writer Rolling Stone mag., NYC. Author: (book) Fast Times At Ridgemont High, 1981; scripts include Fast Times at Ridgemont High, 1982, The Wild Life, 1984; screenwriter, dir.: Say Anything, 1989, Singles, 1992, Jerry Maguire, 1996; writer, prodr., dir. Almost Famous, 2000, Vanilla Sky, 2001, Elizabethtown, 2005; actor: American Hot Wax, 1978; creative cons.: (TV series) Fast Times, 1986. Office: c/o Robert Bookman Creative Artists Agy 9830 Wilshire Blvd Beverly Hills CA 90212

CROWE, CAMERON MACMILLAN, chemical engineering professor; b. Montreal, Que., Can., Oct. 6, 1931; s. Ernest Watson and Marianne (Macmillan) C.; m. Jean Margaret Gilbertson, Feb. 15, 1969. Student, Royal Mil. Coll., 1948-52; B.Eng., McGill U., 1953; PhD, Cambridge U., Eng., 1957. Sr. devel. engr. DuPont of Can., Maitland, Ont., 1957-59; mem. faculty dept. chem. engring. McMaster U., Hamilton, Ont., 1959—, assoc. prof., 1964-70, prof., 1970-96, prof. emeritus, 1996—, chmn. dept., 1971-74. Author: (with others) Chemical Plant Simulation, 1971; Assoc. editor: Canadian Jour. Chem. Engring, 1975-81. C.D. Howe Meml. fellow Rice U., Houston, 1967-68; Athlone fellow, 1953-55 Fellow Chem. Inst. Can.; mem. Am. Inst. Chem. Engrs., Can. Soc. Chem. Engring. (bd. dirs. 1984-87, v.p. 1990-91, pres. 1991-92). Home: 821 Glenwood Ave Burlington ON Canada L7T 2J8 Office: Chem Engring Dept McMaster U Hamilton ON Canada L8S 4L7

CROWE, JAMES JOSEPH, lawyer; b. New Castle, Pa., June 9, 1935; s. William J. and Anna M. (Dickson) C.; m. Joan D. (Verba), Dec. 26, 1959. BA, Youngstown State U., 1958; JD, Georgetown U., 1963. Bar: Va. 1963, Ohio 1966. Atty. SEC, Washington, 1964-65, Gen. Tire and Rubber Co., Akron, Ohio, 1965-68; sr. atty. Eaton Corp., Cleve., 1968-72; sec. gen. counsel U.S. Shoe Corp., Cin., 1972-95, v.p., 1975-95; ptnr. Kepley, Gilligan, and Eyrich, Cin., 1996-2000; counsel Thompson Hine LLP, Cin., 2001—07. Chmn. divsn. Fine Arts Fund, 1976; trustee Springer Edn. Found., 1978-84, Cin. Music Festival Assn., 1980-86, 96-2003; group chmn. United Way, 1980; mem. pres. coun. Coll. Mt. St. Joseph, 1985-88; trustee Tennis for Charity Inc., 1986—. Playhouse in the Park, 1990-96, Greater Cin. Ctr. for Econ. Edn., 1992-96, Leadership Cin., Class XIV, 1990-91; trustee Cin. Nature Ctr., 1993-2000, chmn. 1996-98; bd. visitors U. Cin. Coll. Law, 1993-2002; trustee Invest in Neighborhoods, 1982-89, pres. 1984-86; trustee Cin. Hort. Soc., 1996-2002, World Piano Competition, 1999-2005. 2d lt. U.S. Army, 1958-59. Mem. Cin. Country Club, Queen City Club, Met. Club. Home Phone: 513-871-8928. Personal E-mail: jcrowe7246@aol.com.

CROWE, JAMES QUELL (JIM), communications executive; b. Camp Pendleton, Calif., July 2, 1949; s. Henry Pierson and Mona (Quell) C.; m. Pamela L. Powell, June 20, 1986; children: Sterling, Angela, James Michael. BS in Mech. Engring., Rensselaer Poly. Inst., 1972; MBA, Pepperdine U., 1982. Project engr. Cozzolino Constrn. Co., Port of Albany, NY, 1971-73; ind., cons. engr. Albany, 1973-74; engr. Morrison-Knudsen, Saratoga, NY, 1974-75, project engr. Washington, 1975-76, project mgr. various cities, 1976-80, v.p. ops. Boise, 1980-83, group v.p. power, 1983-86; pres. Kiewit Indsl. Co., Omaha, 1986—91; pres., CEO MFS Communications, 1993—97, Level 3 Communications, Broomfield, Colo., 1997—2000, CEO, 2000—. Chmn., CEO MFS Comms. Co., Inc., Omaha,

1988-97; chmn. WorldCom, Inc., 1997; bd. dir. Level 3 Comms., Inc., 1993—; dir. RCN Corp., Commonwealth Tel. Mem. NAE, Am. Nuclear Soc. Office: Level 3 Comm Inc 1025 Eldorado Blvd Broomfield CO 80021*

CROWE, JOHN T., lawyer; b. Cabin Cove, Calif., Aug. 14, 1938; s. J. Thomas and Wanda (Walston) C.; m. Marina Protopapa, Dec. 28, 1968; 1 child, Erin Aleka. BA, U. Santa Clara, 1960, JD, 1962. Bar: Calif. 1962, U.S. Dist. Ct. (ea. dist.) Calif. 1967. Ptnr. Crowe, Mitchell & Crowe, 1974—85; gen. coun. Sierra Wine, 1986—96; lawyer Visalia, Calif., 1964—. Bd. dirs. Willson Ranch Co., pres. 1997—; referee State Bar Ct., 1976-82. Bd. dirs. Mt. Whitney Area coun. Boy Scouts Am., 1966-85, pres., 1971, 1972; bd. dirs. Visalia Associated In-Group Donors (now United Way Tulare County), 1973-81, pres., 1978-79; bd. dirs. Tulare County Libr. Found., 2000-06, Mineral King Dist. Assn., 2001—; mem. Visalia Airport Commn., 1982-90; Army Res. Forces Policy Com., 1995-99, chmn., 1997-99. 1st lt. U.S. Army, 1962-64, maj. gen. Res., 1960-62, 1964-99. Decorated DSM with oak leaf cluster, Legion of Merit with oak leaf cluster, Meritorious Svc. medal with 3 oak leaf clusters, Army Commendation medal; recipient Silver Beaver award Boy Scouts Am., 1983, Rudder medal Assn. U.S. Army, 1999; named Young Man of Yr., Visalia, 1973, Senator, Jr. Chamber Internat., 1970; named to Sr. Army Res. Comdrs. Assn. Hall of Fame, 2003. Mem. ABA, Tulare County Bar Assn., Nat. Assn. R.R. Trial Counsel, State Bar Calif., Assn. U.S. Army (bd. dirs. 2000-06, No. Calif. state pres. 2001—), Visalia C. of C. (pres. 1979-80), Rotary (pres. 1980-81), Visalia Country Club. Republican. Roman Catholic. Home: 3939 W School Ave Visalia CA 93291-5514 Office Phone: 559-734-0747.

CROWE, ROBERT WILLIAM, lawyer, mediator; b. Chgo., Aug. 20, 1924; s. Harry James and Miriam (McCune) C.; m. Virginia C. Kelley, Mar. 25, 1955 (dec. Feb. 1976); children: Robert Kelley, William Park; m. Elizabeth F. Roenisch, Oct. 22, 1977. AB, U. Chgo., 1948, JD, 1949. Bar: Ill. 1949. Practice in Chgo., 1949-57; with R.R. Donnelley & Sons Co., Chgo., 1957-83, sec., 1965-83, v.p., 1970-83; chmn. Resolve Dispute Mgmt. Inc., Chgo., 1983-92; pres. Dearborn Inst. for Conflict Resolution, Chgo., 1992-94. Dir. Peoria Jour. Star, Inc., 1972-95. Bd. dirs. Chgo. Child Care Soc., 1963—; trustee Christian Century Found., 1966—; vis. com. U. Chgo. Divinity Sch. Served to 1st lt. USAAF, 1943-45. Decorated Air Medal with 5 oak leaf clusters. Mem. ABA, Chgo. Bar Assn., Lawyers Club Chgo., Econ. Club (Chgo.), Univ. Club (Chgo.). Presbyterian. Home and Office: 1228 Westmoor Rd Winnetka IL 60093-1845 Home Phone: 847-446-2553; Office Phone: 847-446-7054. Personal E-mail: rwcrowe@sbcglobal.net. *Cultivate a sense of gratitude as an approach to all of life, for the gift of life itself and for the potential for finding something joyful, empowering or at least instructive in every circumstance. These are the seeds for sharing the best of one's life with others.*

CROWE, RUSSELL, actor; b. Wellington, New Zealand, Apr. 7, 1964; m. Danielle Spencer, Apr. 7, 2003; children: Charles Spencer, Tenyson Spencer. Actor: (plays) Grease, Rocky Horror Picture Show; (films) The Crossing, 1993, The Quick and the Dead, 1995, Proof, 1995, Romper Stomper, 1995, Rough Magic, 1995, Virtuosity, 1995, Under the Gun, 1995, Heaven's Burning, 1997, Breaking Up, 1997, L.A. Confidential, 1997, Mystery Alaska, 1999, The Insider, 1999 (Nat. Soc. of Film Critics award for best actor, 2000, Acad. Award nomination for best actor, 2000), Gladiator, 2000 (Academy award for best actor, 2002, Blockbuster Entertainment award, 2001, Broadcast Film Critics Assoc. award, 2001, Empire award, 2001, London Critics Circle award, 2001, Santa Fe Film Critics Circle award for best actor, 2001), Proof of Life, 2000, A Beautiful Mind, 2001 (Acad. award nomination for best actor, 2002, Golden Globe for best actor in a drama, 2002, SAG award for best actor, 2002, BAFTA Film award for best actor, 2002), Master and Commander: The Far Side of the World, 2003 (Golden Globe nomination for best actor in a drama, 2004), Cinderella Man, 2005; dir.: 60 Odd Hours in Italy, 2002; dir., prodr.: Texas, 2002; singer: 30 Odd Foot of Grunts. Named one of 50 Most Powerful People in Hollywood, Premiere mag., 2004—06; recipient Global Achievement award, Australian Film Inst., 2001. Address: c/o Shirley Pearce Bedford & Pearce Mgmt Paty Ltd 2/263-269 Alfred St PO Box 171 Cammeray North Sydney 2062 Australia also: William Morris Agency 151 El Camino Dr Beverly Hills CA 90212

CROWE, STEPHEN J., comptroller; b. Calif., Oct. 1947; BBA, U. Calif., Berkeley, 1969, MBA, 1970. Analyst Chevron Corp., San Ramon, Calif., 1972—90, asst. comptr., 1990—92, v.p. fin., 1992—96, v.p., comptr., 1996—2000, corp. v.p., 2000—01; v.p., comptr. Chevron Texaco Corp., San Ramon, Calif., 2001—05; v.p., CFO Chevron Corp., San Ramon, Calif., 2005—. With USN. Mem.: Conf. Bd.'s Contr.'s Coun., World Affairs Coun., Am. Petroleum Inst. Office: Chevron Texaco Corp 6001 Bollinger Canyon Rd San Ramon CA 94583-2324*

CROWE, THOMAS LEONARD, lawyer; b. Amsterdam, NY, Aug. 3, 1944; s. Leonard Hoctor and Grace Agnes (O'Malley) C.; m. Barbara Ann Hauck, Aug. 2, 1969; children: Patrick, Brendan. AB, Georgetown U., 1966, JD, 1969. Law clk. to chief judge U.S. Dist. Ct. (no. dist.), Elkins, W.Va., 1969-70; trial atty. U.S. Dept. Justice, Washington, 1970-72; asst. U.S. atty. Balt., 1973-78; chief of criminal divsn. U.S. Atty.'s Office, Balt., 1977-78; ptnr. Cable, McDaniel, Bowie & Bond, Balt., 1979-91, McGuire, Woods, Battle & Boothe, Balt., 1991-95; of counsel Monshower & Miller, LLP, Columbia, Md., 1996-98; pvt. practice Balt., 1998—. Mem. jud. conf. U.S. Ct. Appeals for 4th Cir. Recipient John Adams award, US Dist. Ct., 2007. Fellow Md. Bar Found.; FBA (pres. Balt. chpt. 1981-82), Md. Bar Assn., Barristers Club (pres. 1990-91),. Democrat. Roman Catholic. Home: 11 Osborne Ave Baltimore MD 21228-4935 Office: Law Offices of Thomas L Crowe 1622 The World Trade Ctr 401 E Pratt St Baltimore MD 21202-3117 Home Phone: 410-747-8369; Office Phone: 410-685-9428. Personal E-mail: tom.crowe@verizon.net.

CROWE, WILLIAM JAMES, JR., former Chairman of the Joint Chiefs of Staff, international consultant; b. La Grange, Ky., Jan. 2, 1925; s. William James and Eula (Russell) C.; m. Shirley Mary Grennell, Feb. 14, 1954; children: William Blake, James Brent, Mary Russell. BS, U.S. Naval Acad., 1946; MA in Edn., Stanford U., 1956; PhD in Politics (Harold W. Dodds fellow), Princeton U., 1965. Advanced through grades to adm USN, 1960, ret., 1989, Commd. ensign, 1946, comdg. officer U.S.S. Trout, 1960—62; comdr. Submarine Div. 31 San Diego, 1966-67; sr. adviser Vietnamese Navy, 1970-71; dep. to Pres.'s Spl. Rep. for Micronesian Status Negotiations, 1971-73; dep. dir. strategic plans CNO Staff, 1973-75; dir. East Asia and Pacific region Office of Sec. of Def. Washington, until 1976; comdr. Middle East Force Bahrain, 1976-77; dep. chief naval ops. plans and policy Washington, 1977-80; comdr.-in-chief Allied Forces So. Europe, 1980-83; comdr.-in-chief Pacific, 1983-85; chmn. Joint Chiefs of Staff, 1985-89; prof. geopolitics U. Okla., Norman, 1989-94; chmn. Fgn. Intelligence Adv. Bd., Washington, 1993-94; U.S. amb. to U.K. US Dept. State, London, 1994-97. Counselor Ctr. for Strategic and Internat. Studies, Washington, 1989-94; prof. U. Okla., 1989-94. Author: Line of Fire, 1993; co-author: Reducing Nuclear Danger: The Road Away from the Brink, 1993; author supr. ops. plan for repatriation of U.S.S. Pueblo crew. Trustee Princeton U., 1995-2000; dir. USNA Found., 1998—. Decorated Defense DSM with three oak leaf clusters (Dept. Def.), Navy DSM with two oak leaf clusters (USN), DSM (U.S. Army, USAF, USCG), Legion of Merit, Bronze Star with combat V, Air medal with six oak leaf clusters, Presdl. Medal of Freedom. Mem. U.S. Naval Inst., Am. Polit. Sci. Assn., Internat. Studies Assn., Coun. on Fgn. Rels., Washington Inst. Fgn. Affairs, Phi Gamma Delta, Phi Delta Phi. Office: Global Options 1615 L St NW Ste 300 Washington DC 20036-5655

CROWE, WILLIAM JOSEPH, librarian; b. Boston, Feb. 27, 1947; s. William J. and Mary (Dawley) C.; children: Katherine. BA in European History with highest honors, Boston State Coll., 1968; MLS, Rutgers U., 1969; PhD in Adminstrn. Acad. Librs., Ind. U., 1986. Cataloger Boston Pub. Libr., 1969-70, asst. to acquisitions libr., 1970-71; coord. processing Ind. U. Librs., Bloomington, 1971-76, asst. to dean univ. librs., 1977-79; mgmt. intern U. Mich. Libr., Ann Arbor, 1976-77; asst. to dir. librs. Ohio State U., Columbus, 1979-83, asst. dir. librs. adminstrn. and tech. svcs., 1983-90; dean librs. U. Kans., Lawrence, 1990-96, vice chancellor, dean, 1996-99, libr. Spencer Rsch. Libr., 1999—. Trustee Online Computer Lit. Ctr., 1996—. Contbr. articles to profl. jours. Sr. fellow UCLA, 1991. Mem. ALA, Kans. Libr. Assn., Beta Phi Mu, Phi Alpha Theta. Home: 910 E 850th Rd Lawrence KS 66047-9578 Office: U Kans Spencer Rsch Libr Lawrence KS 66045-7616 Office Phone: 785-864-4970. Business E-Mail: wcrowe@ku.edu. *We must work to expand the next generation's opportunity for education--to foster greater equality of intellectual privilege.*

CROWELL, CRAVEN H., JR., retired federal agency administrator; b. Nashville, Aug. 27, 1943; s. Craven H. and Addie Ailene (Cooper) Crowell; m. Fredricka Friedli, Nov. 27, 1970; 1 child, Stephanie Kaye. BA, Lipscomb U., 1965. Reporter, city editor Nashville Tennessean, 1964-77; press sec. Senator Jim Sasser, 1977-80, chief of staff, 1989-93; dir. info. Tenn. Valley Authority, Knoxville, 1980-87, v.p. govtl. and pub. affairs Nashville, 1987-89, chmn. bd. dirs., 1993-2001; ret., 2001. Mem. exec. com. Nuc. Energy Inst.; past chmn. bd. dirs., mem. exec. com., mem. bd. adv. coun. Electric Power Rsch. Inst.; bd. dirs. EPRI Worldwide. Hon. pres. Hohai U., China, 1997. With USMC, with USNR. Named Alumnus of the Yr., Lipscomb U., 1995; recipient Nat. Headliner award, 1969. Mem.: Econ. Club N.Y., Pi Delta Epsilon. Democrat. Mem. Ch. Of Christ. Office Phone: 865-671-3398. Personal E-mail: cravencrowell@aol.com.

CROWELL, GREGORY F., musician, director; b. Garmisch, Partenkirchen, Germany, Apr. 7, 1958; s. Steven S. and Elizabeth Crowell. MusB, New Eng. Conservatory, Boston, 1980; MusM, U. Cin., 1985, PhD in Musical Arts, 1992. Music dir. Trinity Unified Meth. Ch., Grand Rapids, Mich., 1995—; organ & harpsichord artist faculty Grand Valley State U., Mich., 1999—; dir. publs. Organ Hist. Soc., Richmond, Va., 2004—. Lectr. in field. Bd. mem. Grand Rapids Bach Festival, 1997—; program com. mem. Internat. Clavichord Symposium, Magnano, Italy, 2003—, Grantee Scholar-in-residence, Rikkyo U., 2000; Rsch. grant, San Francisco AGO, 1992. Mem.: Midwestern Hist. Keyboard Assn. (sec. 1999—2004, pres. 2004—). Home: 736 Ethel SE Grand Rapids MI 49506

CROWELL, JOHN B., JR., lawyer, former government official; b. Elizabeth, NJ, Mar. 18, 1930; s. John B. and Anna B. (Trull) C.; m. Rebecca Margaret McCue, Feb. 13, 1954; children: John P., Patrick E., Ann M. AB, Dartmouth Coll., 1952; LL.B., Harvard U., 1957. Bar: NJ bar 1958, Oreg. bar 1959. Law clk. to Judge Gerald McLaughlin U.S. Ct. Appeals, Newark, 1957-59; atty. Ga.-Pacific Corp., Portland, Oreg., 1959-72; gen. counsel La.-Pacific Corp., Portland, 1972-81; asst. sec. for natural resources and environment Dept. Agr., Washington, 1981-85; ptnr. Lane Powell Spears Lubersky, Portland, 1986-98, of counsel, 1998—. Served with USN, 1952-54. Mem. Am. Ornithologists Union, Wilson Ornithol. Soc., Cooper Ornithol. Soc., Soc. Am. Foresters, Soil Conservation Soc. Am. Clubs: Univ. (Portland). Republican. Presbyterian. Home: 1185 Hallinan Cir Lake Oswego OR 97034-4970 Office: Lane Powell 601 SW 2nd Ave Ste 2100 Portland OR 97204-3154 Office Phone: 503-778-2172. Business E-Mail: crowellj@lanepowell.com.

CROWELL, JOHN C(HAMBERS), geology educator, researcher; b. State College, Pa., May 12, 1917; s. James White and Helen Hunt (Chambers) C.; m. Betty Marie Bruner, Nov. 22, 1946; 1 child, Martha Lynn Crowell Bobroskie. BS in Geology, U. Tex., 1939; MA in Oceanographic meteorology, Scripps Inst. Oceanography UCLA, 1946; PhD in Geology, UCLA, 1947; DSc (hon.), U. Louvain, Belgium, 1966. Geologist Shell Oil Co., Inc., Ventura, Calif., 1941-42; from instr. to prof. geology UCLA, 1947-67, chmn. dept., 1957-60, 63-66; prof. geology U. Calif., Santa Barbara, 1967-87, prof. emeritus, 1987, rsch. geologist Inst. for Crustal Studies, 1987—. Chmn. Office of Earth Scis., NRC, Nat. Acad. Scis., 1979-82. Served to capt. U.S. Army USAAF, 1942-46. Fellow AAAS, Geol. Soc. Am. (Penrose medal 1995), Am. Acad. Arts and Scis.; mem. Am. Assn. Petroleum Geologists, Am. Geophys. Union, Nat. Acad. Scis. Achievements include special research in structural geology, tectonics, interpretation sedimentary rocks, studies of San Andreas fault system, California tectonics, ancient glaciation, continental drift. Office: 300 Hot Springs Rd Apt 99 Santa Barbara CA 93108 Office Phone: 805-969-8218. E-mail: crowell@geol.ucsb.edu.

CROWL, JOHN ALLEN, retired publishing company executive; b. Winchester, Va., Aug. 10, 1935; s. John Decatur and Cora Elizabeth (LLoyd) C.; m. Dana Jane Bernasek, Aug. 27, 1960 (div. 1986); 1 son, Patrick Joseph; m. Gaal Shepherd, Feb. 10, 1988. BA, U. Md., 1957, MA, 1961; LhD (hon.), Lebanon Valley Coll., 1993. Instr. Staunton (Va.) Mil. Acad., 1958-59; asst. dir. pub. rels. Johns Hopkins U., Balt., 1961-64; assoc. dir. Editl. Projects for Edn., Inc., Balt. and Washington, 1964-75, v.p., 1975-78; assoc. editor Chronicle of Higher Edn., Washington, 1966-72, mng. editor, 1972-79, pub., 1978-91, v.p., 1979-92. Founder Thistle Hill Publs., 2000—. Contbg. editor: Vt. Mag., 1995—2001; mem. editl. adv. bd. Vt. Life mag., 2002—; dir.: Vt. Pub. Radio, 2004—. Trustee Vt. Folklife Ctr., 1994-99, Vt. Arts Coun., 1994-98; trustee Planned Parenthood of No. New Eng., 1994-2000, chair 1997-99. With U.S. Army, 1958. Recipient Edn. Writers award AAUP, 1971. Home: Thistle Hill North Pomfret VT 05053 Office Phone: 802-457-2050. Personal E-mail: crowl1@earthlink.net.

CROWL, ROBERT B., bank executive; B in Psychology, U. Richmond, Va., 1985, MBA, 1990. Various positions in trust, control and asset/liability mgmt. depts. Crestar Bank, Richmond, 1986—98; mgr. asset/liability and securitization Nat. City Corp., Cleve., 1998, sr. v.p., corp. comptr. Office: Nat City Corp Nat City Ctr 1900 E Ninth St Cleveland OH 44114-3484 Office Phone: 216-222-2000.*

CROWL, SAMUEL RENNINGER, former university dean, English language educator, author; b. Toledo, Oct. 9, 1940; s. Lester Samuel and Margaret Elizabeth (Renninger) C.; m. Susan Richardson, Dec. 29, 1963; children: Miranda Paine, Samuel Emerson. AB, Hamilton Coll., 1962; MA, Ind. U., 1969, PhD, 1970. Resident lectr. Ind. U., Indpls., 1967-69; asst. prof. English, Ohio U., Athens, 1970-75, assoc. prof., 1975-80, prof., 1980—, dean Univ. Coll., 1981-92, trustee prof. Eng., 1992—; cons. NEH, Washington, 1980—; observer Royal Shakespeare Co. Mem. Ohio Humanities Coun., 1985-91, Ohio Student Loan Commn., 1985-88. Author: Shakespeare Observed: Studies in Performance on Stage and Screen, 1992, Shakespeare at the Cineplex, 2003, The Films of Kenneth Branagh, 2006; co-author: Ohio University's Educational Plan, 1977-78; contbr. articles to profl. and Shakespearean jours. Recipient O'Bleness award for pub. broadcasting Ctr. Telecommunications, Ohio U., 1976, several awards disting. teaching. Fellow Royal Soc. Arts (London); mem. Nat. Assn. Univ. and Gen. Coll. Deans (pres. 1991—), Nat. Humanities Faculty, Ohio Shakespeare Assn. (founding mem.), Ohio U. Alumni Assn. (hon.), Univ. Club (Chgo.), Phi Kappa Phi. Avocations: Royal Shakespeare Co., Detroit Tigers. Office: Ohio U Eng Dept Ellis Hall Athens OH 45701 Office Phone: 740-593-2838. Business E-Mail: Crowl@ohio.edu.

CROWL, STEVEN CRAIG, aerospace engineer; b. Davenport, Iowa, Oct. 13, 1951; s. Robert Morris and Marilyn Joyce Crowl. BS in Aerospace, Iowa State U., Ames, 1974, independent grad. study in Engring., 1976. Ind. aero-space engr., rschr., Davenport, 1980—. Mem.: IEEE (nuclear & plasma scis. soc. & computer soc. 2001—), Math. Assn. Am., Am. Math. Soc., Nat. Soc. Profl. Engrs., Am. Inst. Aeronautics & Astronautics (sr.). Avocations: computers, walks. Personal E-mail: sccrowl@netscape.com.

CROWLEY, ARTHUR EDWARD, JR., lawyer; b. Rutland, Vt., Oct. 18, 1928; s. Arthur Edward and Mildred (Gilfeather) C.; m. Marcia Colby Smith, July 29, 1961 (div. 1984); children: Robert, David, Andrew, Christopher; m. Mary Roemmele, Feb. 21, 1987. Student, Boston U., 1947-50, student, 1953-56. Bar: Vt. 1958. Pvt. practice, Rutland, 1959; dep. atty. gen. State of Vt., Montpelier, 1960-61; state's atty. Rutland County, 1961-65; ptnr. Bishop & Crowley, 1965-77, Keyser Crowley, 1977-84. Corp. counsel City of Rutland, 1965-67. Mem. Vt. Rep. State Com., 1961-71, chmn. exec. com., 1963-67; chmn. Rutland County Rep. Party, 1961-71; alderman City of Rutland, 1987-95, sch. commr., 2000-03; trustee Vt. State Colls., 1979-85, Coll. St. Joseph, 1987-92. Served with AUS, 1951-53. Mem. Rutland County Bar Assn. (pres. 1983-84), Vt. Bar Assn., Am. Legion, Rutland Region C. of C. (dir. 1967-71). Office: 56 1/2 Merchants Row Ste 310 Rutland VT 05701-5907

CROWLEY, BOB, scenic designer, costume designer, director; b. Cork, Ireland; Assoc. Royal Shakespeare Co., Royal Nat. Theatre. Scenic designer, costume designer (Broadway Shows) Les Liaisons Dangereuses, 1987, Carousel, 1994—95 (Tony Award for best scenic design of a musical, 1994), Racing Demon, 1995, The Capeman, 1998, The Judas Kiss, 1998, Twelfth Night, 1998, The Iceman Cometh, 1999, Amy's View, 1999, Putting It Together, 1999—2000, Aida, 2000—04 (Tony Award for best scenic design of a musical, 2000), The Invention of Love, 2001 (Drama Desk award outstanding set design of a play, 2001), Sweet Smell of Success, 2002, dir., scenic designer, costume designer Tarzan, 2006—, designer The History Boys, 2006— (Tony Award for best scenic design of a play, 2006), The Coast of Utopia, 2007 (Outer Critics Cir. award outstanding set design, 2007, Drama Desk award outstanding set design of a play, 2007, Tony award best scenic design of play, 2007), Mary Poppins, 2007 (Drama Desk award outstanding set design of a musical, 2007, Tony award best scenic design of musical, 2007), (Operas) La Traviata, (ballets) Anastasia. Recipient Laurence Olivier Award for Designer of Yr., 1990, Royal Designer to Industry Award.*

CROWLEY, CYNTHIA WARNER JOHNSON, secondary school educator; b. Summit, NJ, June 28, 1930; d. Theodore Eames and Frances Lysett (Wetmore) J.; m. Robert J. Crowley, Sept. 6, 1952 (dec.); children: David Cochrane II, Cynthia Wetmore BA, U. Pa., 1952; MA, Fairleigh-Dickinson U., 1980. Cert. English tchr., NJ. Tchr. econs. and reading St. Mary's Sch., Peekskill, NY, 1952—53; tchr. humanities Henry Hudson Regional Sch., Highlands, NJ, 1969—92, coord. gifted program, 1983—92. Pres. Associated Ednl. Svcs.; with N.J. Curriculum Revision Project; adv. bd. mem. N.J. Coun. U.S. Congl. Awards Program; ednl. cons.; cons., lectr. creative writing workshops; mem. secondary sch. admissions com. U. Pa Prodr. TV Tutor Series for Home and Schs. Former mem. Atlantic Highlands Bd. Edn., also past pres.; mem. adv. bd. Women's Athletic bd. U. Pa., 1992—, chair, 1999—; former mem. exec. com. Monmouth County Sch. Bds. Assn. Team Room named in her honor U. Pa., Palestra, 1997; named to Hall of Fame, U. Pa., 1998; recipient U. Pa. Alumni award, 1997, Alumni Merit award U. Pa., 2004 Mem. ASCD, Nat. Coun. Tchrs. English, NATAS (N.Y. chpt.), Gifted Educators (exec. com. 1986—), Alumni Pres.'s Coun. Ind. Secondary Schs. (life, past pres.), Phi Delta Kappa, Kappa Alpha Theta Home and Office: 245 Shore Rd Westerly RI 02891-3707 Office Fax: 401-322-8379.

CROWLEY, DANIEL FRANCIS, JR., transportation and logistics executive; b. Yonkers, NY, Oct. 23, 1949; s. Daniel F. and Margaret M. (Murphy) C.; m. Karen E. Williams, Dec. 18, 1982; children: Daniel, Ryan. BA in Lit., Columbia U., 1971, MBA in Fin., 1973. Mem. audit staff Arthur Andersen & Co., NYC, 1973-78, audit mgr. London, 1978-81; dir. internal audit IMS Internat. Inc., London, 1981-82, contr. pharmacy svcs. divsn., 1982-83; exec. v.p., bd. dirs. Pharmassist, Inc., Dallas, 1983-84; sr. mgr. Coopers & Lybrand, NYC, 1985-90; v.p. audit Grand Met. Food Sector, Mpls., 1990-91; v.p., contr. Grand Met./Green Giant USA, Mpls., 1991-92; v.p., ops. contr. Grand Met./Pillsbury, Mpls., 1992-93, v.p. reengring., 1993-95; v.p., contr. food sector Grand Met, London, 1995; dir. Pearle Vision, Inc., 1995-97; sr. v.p., CFO, Pearle Vision/Grand Met, Dallas, 1995-97; v.p. planning Frito-Lay Internat., Plano, Tex., 1997-98; exec. v.p., CFO BAX Global/Pittston, 1998—. Bd. dirs. Pearle Vision, Inc., 1995-97; treas. Grand Met/Pearle Found., Dallas, 1995-97. Treas. Grand Met/Pillsbury Found., Mpls., 1991-93. Mem. AICPA. Home: 3815 Vista Azul San Clemente CA 92672-4543 Office: BAX Global 440 Exchange Irvine CA 92602-1309

CROWLEY, JAMES PATRICK, hematologist, medical educator, immunologist; b. Birmingham, Eng., Oct. 13, 1943; came to U.S., 1947; s. Francis Michael and Rose Ann (Donaghy) C.; m. Carol Ann Crowley, Dec. 6, 1943; children: Jason W.F., James M. AB, Providence Coll., 1965; MD, Georgetown U., 1969; MA, Brown U., 1981. Intern Boston City Hosp./Harvard Med. Sch., 1969, resident, 1970, Mass. Gen. Hosp., Boston, 1971, Peter Bent Brigham Hosp., Boston, 1974; instr. medicine Harvard Med. Sch., Boston, 1974; asst. prof. medicine Brown U., Providence, 1975-81, assoc. prof., 1981-92, prof., 1992—2006, prof. emeritus, 2006—; dir. hematology R.I. Hosp./Brown U., Providence, 1992-2000; chief hematology/oncology Meml. Hosp. of R.I., Pawtucket, 2000—; dir. Cancer Ctr. Meml. Hosp. of R.I., 2003—06. Bd. dirs. Providence Ambulatory Health Care Found., Inc.; cons. Naval Blood Rsch. Program, USN, 1977—; adj. prof. medicine Tufts U. Sch. Vet. Medicine, 1986—1996. Author: Principles of Transfusion Medicine, 2nd edit., 1995; contbr. articles to profl. jours. Mem. Retirement Bd. City of Providence, 1993—; physician Camp Yawgoog Boy Scouts Am., 1992—. Capt. USNR, 1971-95, ret. Recipient Transfusion Medicine Acad. award NIH, 1984-89, award R.I. Blood Banking Soc., 1986. Mem. Am. Soc. Hematology, R.I. Med. Soc. (pres. 1992-93), Providence Med. Assn., (pres. 1992-92), Mt. Tom Club (v.p. 1994). Democrat. Roman Catholic. Achievements include important contbns. to the devel. of successful system for freezing blood and deglycerolizing blood for transfusion on Navy hosp. ships, successful demonstration that erythropoeitin could enhance autologous pre-donation prior to orthopedic surgery and the immunosuppressive effects of passenger leukocytes during allogeneic transfusion. Office: Cancer Ctr Meml Hosp RI 111 Brewster St Pawtucket RI 02860 Office Phone: 401-729-2241. Business E-Mail: james_crowley@mhri.org.

CROWLEY, JAMES WORTHINGTON, retired lawyer, investor, financial consultant; b. Cookville, Tenn., Feb. 18, 1930; s. Worth and Jessie (Officer) C.; m. Laura June Bauserman, Jan. 27, 1951; children: James Kenneth, Laura Cynthia; m. Joyce A. Goode, Jan. 15, 1966; children: John Worthington, Noelle Virginia; m. Carol Golden, Sept. 4, 1981. BA, George Washington U., 1950, LLB, 1953. Bar: D.C. 1954. Underwriter, spl. agt. Am. Surety Co. of N.Y., Washington, 1953-56; adminstrv. asst., contract adminstr. Atlantic Rsch. Corp., Alexandria, Va., 1956-59, mgr. legal dept., asst. sec., counsel, 1959-65, sec., legal mgr., counsel, 1965-67, Susquehanna Corp. (merger with Atlantic Rsch. Corp.), 1967-70; pres., dir. Gen. Communication Co., Boston, 1962-70; v.p., gen. counsel E-Systems, Inc., 1970-95, sec., 1976-95; ret., 1995; ind. cons. bus. and fin., investor Dallas, 1995—. V.p., asst. sec., dir. Cemco, Inc.; v.p., dir. TAI, Inc., Serv-air, Inc., Greenville, Tex., Engring. Rsch. Assocs., Inc., Vienna, Va., HRB Systems,

Inc., State Coll., Pa.; mem. adv. bd. sec. Internat. and Comparative Law Ctr.; v.p., sec., dir. Advanced Video Products, 1992-95; v.p., sec., gen. counsel E-Systems Med. Electronics, Inc., 1992-95. Mem. Am. Soc. Corp. Secs. (pres. Dallas regional group 1988-89, nat. dir. 1989-92), Inf. Mus. Assn., Nat. Security Indsl. Assn., Mfrs.' Alliance for Productivity and Innovation (mem. law coun.), Omicron Delta Kappa, Alpha Chi Sigma, Phi Sigma Kappa. Republican. Baptist. Avocations: classical music, piano, French horn. Home and Office: 16203 Spring Creek Rd Dallas TX 75248-3116 Personal E-mail: jwcrowle@ix.netcom.com.

CROWLEY, JOHN CRANE, real estate developer; b. Detroit, June 29, 1919; s. Edward John and Leah Helen (Crane) C.; m. Barbara Wenzel Gilfillan, Jan. 12, 1945; children: F. Alexander, Leonard, Philip, Eliot, Louise, Sylvia. BA with high honors, Swarthmore Coll., 1941; MS, U. Denver, 1943. Asst. dir. Mcpl. Fin. Officers Assn., Chgo., 1946-48; So. Calif. mgr. League Calif. Cities, Los Angeles, 1948-53; mgr. City of Monterey Park, Calif., 1953-56. Founder, exec. v.p. Nat. Med. Enterprises, L.A., 1968; pres. Ventura Towne House (Calif.), 1963-96; mem. faculty U. So. Calif. Sch. Pub. Adminstrn., 1950-53; bd. dirs. Regional Inst. of So. Calif., The L.A. Partnership 2000, Burbank-Glendale-Pasadena Airport Authority; commr. Bob Hope Airport. Trustee Pacific Oaks Friends Sch. and Coll., Pasadena, 1954-57, 92-98, Swarthmore Coll., 1987—; bd. dirs. Pasadena Area Liberal Arts Ctr., 1962-72, pres., 1965-68; bd. dirs. Pacificulture Found. and Asia Mus., 1971-76, pres., 1972-74; bd. dirs. Nat. Mcpl. League, 1986-92, AAF Rose Bowl Aquatics Ctr., 1997—; chmn. Pasadena Cultural Heritage Commn., 1975-78; city dir. Pasadena, 1979-91; mayor City of Pasadena, 1986-88; bd. dirs. Western Justice Ctr., 1992—, v.p., 1995—, LA County Commn. on Efficiency and Economy, 1994—; mem. L.A. County Commn. on Local Govt., 2000—. Sloan Found. fellow, 1941-43; recipient Arthur Nobel award City of Pasadena. Mem. Am. Soc. Pub. Adminstrn. (local chpt., Winston Crouch award 1990), Internat. City Mgmt. Assn., Nat. Mcpl. League (nat. bd. 1980-92, Disting. Citizen award, 1984), Inst. Pub. Adminstrn. (sr. assoc.), Phi Delta Theta. Democrat. Unitarian Universalist. Home: 615 Linda Vista Ave Pasadena CA 91105-1122 Office Phone: 626-795-8221. E-mail: jccrowley@charter.net.

CROWLEY, JOHN FRANCIS, III, university dean; b. New Haven, Jan. 29, 1945; s. John Francis Jr. and Anna Cecil (Elliott) C.; m. Alice Ann Kennedy, Dec. 26, 1970; children: John Francis IV, Sarah Ann. MA in Regional and City Planning, U. Okla., 1973, PhD in Urban Geography, 1977. Dir. planning Seminole, Okla.; chief planner Okla. State Parks, 1973—74; asst. prof. environ. design U. Ga., Athens, 1974—78, prof., dean Coll. Environ. and Design, 1996—; exec. dir. Tulsa Metro Area Planning Commn., 1978—80; v.p., devel. Williams Realty Corp., Tulsa, 1980—87; pres. Urbantech Inc., Tulsa, 1987—; dir. Okla. Dept. of Transp., Oklahoma City, 1993—95. Bd. dirs. Athens Classic Ctr. Authority, 1983-89; chmn. Sales Tax Overview Com., Tulsa, 1988-90; sec. bd. trustees Tulsa County Pub. Facilities Authority, 1983-96. 1st lt. U.S. Army, 1965-69 Sara Moss faculty fellow U. Ga., 1976. Fellow Am. Inst. Cert. Planners; mem. Am. Soc. Landscape Architects, Am. Planning Assn., Nature Conservancy, Urban Land Inst., Transp. Rsch. Bd. Democrat. Roman Catholic. Avocations: art, sports, travel. Home: 335 Crystal Ct Athens GA 30606-3245 Business E-Mail: jcrowley@uga.edu.

CROWLEY, JOHN WILLIAM, literature and language professor; b. New Haven, Dec. 27, 1945; s. John Adam and Mary T. (McKenna) C.; m. Sheila A. Myers, Mar. 17, 1967 (div. 1977); children: Matthew, Anne; m. Susan Wolstenholme, May 27, 1978 (div. 2001); children: Raphael, Mary; m. Emily T. Smith, Nov. 23, 2001. BA, Yale U., 1967; MA, Ind. U., 1969, PhD, 1970. Asst. prof. English Syracuse (N.Y.) U., 1970-74, assoc. prof., 1974-79, prof., 1979—2002, dir. humanities doctoral program, 1985—88, 1996—2002, dir. grad. studies, 1986-89, chair, 1989—92; prof. U. Ala., Tuscaloosa, 2002—, chair dept., 2002—03. Author: George Cabot Lodge, 1976, The Black Heart's Truth, 1985, The Mask of Fiction, 1989, The White Logic, 1994, The Dean of American Letters, 1999, Bill W. and Mr. Wilson, 2000; co-author: Drunkard's Refuge, 2004; editor: New Essays on Winesburg, Ohio, 1990, Chinese edit., 2006, Genteel Pagan, 1991, The Sunnier Side, 1996, The Rise of Silas Lapham, 1996, Drunkard's Progress, 1999; co-editor: The Haunted Dusk, 1983. Hon. Woodrow Wilson fellow, 1967; NDEA fellow, 1967-70; Nat. Endowment for Humanities summer stipend, 1975 Mem.: Phi Beta Kappa. Democrat. Office: Dept of English U Ala Tuscaloosa AL 35487-0244 Home: 463 High Field Rd Tuscaloosa AL 35405 Office Phone: 205-348-8522. Business E-Mail: jcrowley@english.as.ua.edu.

CROWLEY, JOSEPH, congressman; b. Elmhurst, NY, Mar. 16, 1962; m. Kasey Nilson; 3 children. BA in Polit. Sci. and Comm., Queens Coll., 1985. Mem. NY State Assembly, 1987-98, US Congress from 7th NY dist., 1999—, mem. fgn. affairs com., ways and means com., chief dep. whip, 2003—, co-chair Congl. caucus on Bangladesh. Del. Am. Inst. Free Labor Devel. observers of Nicaragua election, 1990. Recipient YMCA Congl. Champion award, YMCA of U.S.A., 2003. Mem. Armagh Assn., Cavan Men's Assn., Hudson Coun., VFW, KC Democrat. Roman Catholic. Office: US House Reps 312 Cannon House Office Bldg Washington DC 20515 Address: 74-09 37th Ave Ste 306B Jackson Heights NY 11372-6303 Office Phone: 718-779-1400, 202-225-3965.*

CROWLEY, JOSEPH NEIL, political science professor, former academic administrator; b. Oelwein, Iowa, July 9, 1933;. James Bernard and Nina Mary (Neil) C.; m. Johanna Lois Reitz, Sept. 9, 1961; children: Theresa, Neil, Margaret, Timothy. BA, U. Iowa, 1959; MA, Calif. State U., Fresno, 1963; PhD (Univ. fellow), U. Wash., 1967. Reporter Fresno Bee, 1961-62; asst. prof. polit. sci. U. Nev., Reno, 1966-71, asso. prof., 1971-79, prof., 1979—, chmn. dept. polit. sci., 1976-78, pres., 1978-2000, pres. emeritus, regents prof., 2001—, interim pres., 2005—06, San Jose State U., 2003—04. Bd. dirs. Citibank Nev., 1985-2006; policy formulation officer EPA, Washington, 1973-74; dir. instl. studies Nat. Commn. on Water Quality, Washington, 1974-75. Author: Democrats, Delegates and Politics in Nevada: A Grassroots Chronicle of 1972, 1976, Notes From the President's Chair, 1988, No Equal in the World; An Interpretation of the Academic Presidency, 1994, The Constant Conversation: A Chronicle of Campus Life, 2000, In the Arena: The NCAA's First Century, 2006; editor: (with R. Roelofs and D. Hardesty) Environment and Society, 1973. Chair Nev. Rhodes Scholar Comm., 1988—2000, mem., 2002—04; mem. coun. NCAA, 1987—92, mem. pres.' commn., 1991—92, pres., 1993—95; bd. dirs. Nat. Consortium for Acads. and Sports., 1992—; bd. dirs. campaign chmn. No. Nev. United Way, 1985; bd. dirs. campaing chmn., 1997—2002; bd. dir. Collegiate Women Sports Awards, 1994—; mem. Commn. on Colls., 1980—87; mem. adv. commn. on mining and minerals rsch. U.S. Dept. Interior, 1985—91; mem. humanities commn. Nev., 2004—. Recipient Thornton Peace Prize U. Nev., 1971, Humanitarian of Yr. award NCCJ, 1986, Alumnus of Yr. award Calif. State U., Fresno, 1989, ADL Champion of Liberty award, 1993, Disting. Alumni award U. Iowa, 1994, Giant Step award Ctr. for Study of Sport in Soc., 1994, William Anderson award AAHPERD, 1998, Lifetime Achievement award Nat. Consortium for Acads. and Sports, 2001, Nev Arts and Humanities award for pub. svc., 2000, Nev. Edn. Hall of Fame, 2003; Nat. Assn. Schs. Pub. Affairs and Adminstrn. fellow, 1973-74. Mem.: Nat. Assn. State Univs. and Land Grant Colls. (bd. dirs. 1998—2000). Office: U Nev Mail Stop 310 Reno NV 89557 Home Phone: 775-747-3605; Office Phone: 775-784-1500. Business E-Mail: crowley@unr.edu.

CROWLEY, JUANITA A., lawyer; b. Jan. 11, 1953; BA, Trinity Coll., 1974; JD, Georgetown Univ., 1977. Bar: DC 1977. Law clk. Judge Herbert F. Murray, US Dist. Ct. (Md. dist.), 1977—78; ptnr., co-chmn. Litigation dept. Wilmer Cutler Pickering Hale & Dorr, Washington. Prof. Nat. Inst. Trial Advocacy, Boulder, Colo. Editor (exec.): Georgetown Law Jour. Mem.: ABA, Phi Beta Kappa. Office: Wilmer Cutler Pickering Hale & Dorr 2445 M St NW Washington DC 20037 Office Phone: 202-663-6207. Office Fax: 202-663-6363. Business E-Mail: juanita.crowley@wilmerhale.com.

CROWLEY, ROSA QUINONEZ, literature and language educator; b. Quininde, Ecuador, July 1, 1966; d. Victor Edilfonso Quininez and Maria Reneira Quinonez; m. Frederic C. Crowley, Apr. 25, 2001. Degree in edn., U. Guayaquil, Ecuador, 1992; BA in Spanish, RI Coll., Providence, 2002. Tchr. Spanish Aida Lara Sch., Guayaquil, 1992—98, St. Mary Acad., Riverside, RI, 2002—03, Ctrl. Falls High Sch., 2004, Woonsocket High Sch., 2003—. Elected mem. Cumberland Sch. Com., RI, 2004—. Mem.: ASCD, RI Fgn. Lang. Assn. (bd. dirs. 2003—), Am. Coun. Tchg. Fgn. Langs., Am. Assn. Tchrs. Spanish and Portuguese. Avocations: travel, writing, reading, gardening, soccer. Home: 15 Liberty St Cumberland RI 02864 Office: Woonsocket High Sch 777 Cass Ave Woonsocket RI 02895

CROWLEY, WILLIAM C., retail executive; BS in Psychology, Yale U., 1979. Mem. staff to mng. dir. mergers and acquisitions dept. Goldman Sachs, 1986—99; pres., COO ESL Investments, Inc., 1999—2003; sr. v.p. fin., bd. dirs. Kmart Corp., 2003—05; exec. v.p., chief adminstrv. officer Sears Holdings Corp., 2005—. Bd. dirs. AutoNation, Inc., 2002—. Office: Sears Holdings Corp 3333 Beverly Rd Hoffman Estates IL 60179

CROWLEY, WILLIAM FRANCIS, JR., endocrinologist, educator; b. Meriden, Conn., Dec. 28, 1943; s. William Francis and Kathryn (Kiernan) C.; m. Nancy Marie Colwell; children: William Francis III, Sean Timothy, Regan Elizabeth, Colin Colwell. BA (honors curriculum), Holy Cross Coll., Worcester, Mass., 1965; MD, Tufts U., Medford, Mass., 1969. Diplomate Am. Bd. Internal Medicine. Intern Mass. Gen. Hosp., Boston, 1969-70, asst. resident in medicine, 1970-71, sr. resident in medicine, 1973-74, clin. and rsch. fellow in endocrinology, 1974-76; instr. medicine Harvard Med. Sch., Mass. Gen. Hosp., 1976-80; asst. prof. medicine Harvard Med. Sch., Boston, 1980-84, assoc. prof., 1984-92, prof. medicine, 1992—. Chief reproductive endocrine unit Mass. Gen. Hosp., 1984—, attending physician, 1988—; dir. clin. rsch., 1996—; dir. Vincent Rsch. Labs., 1987-90, dir. Harvard Reproductive Endocrine Sci. Ctr. 1991—; adv. bds. NIH, FDA, 1979—; lectr. in sci. writing, Harvard U., 1974-76; vis. prof. Yale U., 1982, Duke U., 1983, N.Y. Obstet. Soc., 1983, George Washington U., 1985, U. Miami, 1989; Endocrinology Trust vis. prof. in Eng., 2006; Goldfarb lectr., Vanderbilt U., 1989; Leathem lectr., Rutgers U., 1981; Israel Mackler lectr. Albert Einstein Coll. Medicine, 1982; lectr. Mayo Clinic, 1990, U. Chgo., 1990, U. Va., 1994, Northwestern U., 1995; invited speaker Laurentian Hormone Conf., 1984, 90; Winkler Meml. lectr. U. Buffalo, 1989; cons. Study Sect., Ctr. for Population, 1979-80, Contract Adv. Bd. Contraceptive Devel. Br., Nat. Inst. Child Health and Human Devel., NIH, 1979—; dir. Mass. Gen. Hosp. Reproductive Endocrine Scis. Ctr.-NIH Ctrs. of Reproductive Excellences, 1991, Nat. Ctr. Infertility Rsch., Mass. Gen Hosp., 1991—2002, NIH Tng. Grant in Reproductive and Devel. Biology, 1991—; mem. sci. adv. bd. PRACIS Pharm. Co., 1996—98, Ligand Pharm. Co., 1997-2000. Editor: (with J.G. Hofler) The Episodic Secretion of Hormones, 1987; contbr. articles to profl. jours.; mem. editorial bds. numerous profl. and sci. jours. including Jour. Clin. Endocrinology and Metabolism, 1983-87, Neuroendocrinology, 1987—, Acta Endocrinologica, 1983—, Internat. Jour. Fertility, 1985—, Annals Internal Medicine, 1986—, Endocrinology, 1988—, Molecular and Cellular Neuroscis., 1989—. Mem. Union of Concerned Scientists, Planned Parenthood, RESOLVE (physicians' bd.); founder Acad. Health Ctr. Clin. Rsch. Forum, 1996. Lt. USNR, 1971-73. Recipient Mentoring award Women in Endocrinology, 2000; Daland fellows Am. Philos. Soc., 1975-78; NIH grantee, 1979—. Fellow Royal Coll. Physicians (hon.); mem. ACP, Am. Fedn. Med. Rsch., Soc. for Study Reprodn., Am. Soc. Clin. Investigation, Assn. Am. Physicians, Endocrine Soc. (pres. 2000-01, Presdl. lectr. 1996, pres. 2001, Clin. Investigator award 2000, Fred Conrad Koch award 2005), Peripatetic Soc., Interurban Club, Mass. Med. Soc., Am. Fertility Soc., Am. Fedn. Clin. Rsch., Inst. Medicine (clin. rsch. roundtable 2000—), N.Y. Acad. Scis., Hyannisport Country Club (Mass.). Avocations: tennis, skiing, walking, reading, golf. Office: Mass Gen Hosp Reproductive Endocrine Scis Ctr Bartlett Hall Ext 5 Boston MA 02114 Office Phone: 617-726-5390.

CROWN, DAVID ALLAN, criminologist, educator; b. Long Beach, NY, Sept. 13, 1928; s. John and Florence (Coe) Crown; m. Maria Brami, Feb. 13, 1954; children: Ingrid, Eric. BS, Union Coll., 1948; M in Criminology, U. Calif., 1960, D in Criminology, 1969. Spl. agt. CIC, 1951-53; asst. dir. San Francisco Indentification Lab., U.S. Postal Inspection Service, 1957-67; dir. Questioned Document Lab., Records Analysis Group, Dept. Army, Washington, 1967-72, Questioned Documents Staff, INR/DDC, U.S. Dept. State, Washington, 1972-77; chief Questioned Documents Lab., Office of Tech. Services, 1977-82. Lectr. Chabot Coll., Hayward, Calif., 1966—67; adj. prof. Am. U., Washington, 1971—80; lectr. Georgetown U., Washington, 1973, professorial lectr., 1973—77, Antioch Sch. Law, 1977—81; guest lectr. FBI Acad., Quantico, Va.; pres. Crown Forensic Labs., Inc. Author: The Forensic Examination of Paints and Pigments, 1968; co-author: Forensic Science, 1982, Legal Medicine, 1985, Forensic Handwriting Examination, 1993; contbr. articles to profl. publs.; mem. editl. bd. Jour. Forensic Scis., 1971—73, Internat. Jour. Forensic Document Examiners; book rev. editor:, assoc. editor:. Pres. Temple Bat Yam, Sanibel, Fla., 1996—98. Mem.: ASTM (chmn. questioned document com. 1970—71, vice chmn. 1972), Forensic Sci. Found. (dir. 1971—72, trustee 1973—75), Am. Soc. Questioned Document Examiners (chmn. accreditation com. 1969—70, sec.-treas. 1976—78, pres. 1980—82), Am. Acad. Forensic Scis. (chmn. questioned document sect. 1969—70, mem. exec. com. 1970—74, pres. 1974—75, chmn. recert. com.), Mil. Officers Assn. Am. Home: 3344 Twin Lakes Ln Sanibel FL 33957-5528 Office Phone: 239-395-1900. Personal E-mail: davidcrown120840@aol.com.

CROWN, ERIC J., information systems executive; BSc in Bus. Computer Info. Sys., Ariz. State U., 1984. Chmn., CEO, founder Insight Enterprises, Tempe, Ariz., 1988—. Office: Insight Enterprises 6820 S Harl Ave Tempe AZ 85283-4318 E-mail: ecrown@insight.com.

CROWN, JAMES SCHINE, investment company executive; b. Chgo., June 25, 1953; s. Lester and Renée (Schine) Crown; m. Paula Anne Hannaway, June 27, 1985; children: Victoria, Hayley, William Andrew, Summer Olivia. BA, Hampshire Coll., 1976; JD, Stanford U., 1980. Bar: Ill. 1980. V.p. Salomon Bros. Inc., NYC, 1980-85; gen. ptnr. Henry Crown and Co., Chgo., 1985—2003, pres., 2003—. Bd. dirs. Gen. Dynamics Corp., Falls Church, Va., JPMorgan Chase & Co., Sara Lee Corp. Chmn. bd. U. Chgo.; Trustee Mus. Sci. and Industry, Chgo., Orchestral Assn., Chgo. Mem.: Ill. State Bar Assn. Office: Henry Crown and Co 222 N La Salle St Chicago IL 60601-1003

CROWN, LESTER, manufacturing executive; b. Chgo., June 7, 1925; s. Henry and Rebecca (Kranz) C.; m. Renee Schine, Dec. 28, 1950; children: Steven, James, Patricia, Daniel, Susan, Sara, Janet. BS in Chem. Engring., Northwestern U., 1946; MBA, Harvard U., 1949. Instr. math. Northwestern U., 1946-47; v.p., chem. engr. Marblehead Lime Co., 1950-56, pres., 1956-66, also bd. dirs.; v.p. Material Svc. Corp. subs. Gen. Dynamics Corp., Chgo., 1953-66, pres., 1970-83; chmn. Material Svc. Corp., Chgo., 1984—2006, also bd. dirs.; pres. Henry Crown & Co., Chgo., 1969—2002, chmn., 2002—, also bd. dirs. Ptnr. Yankee Global Enterprise, 1973-; chmn. Comml. Club Chgo., 2005-. Trustee, vice chmn. Aspen Inst. Humanistic Studies, Northwestern U.; bd. dirs. Lyric Opera Corp., Children's Meml. Med. Ctr., Jewish Theol. Sem., Jerusalem Found.; mem. bd. govs. Weizmann Inst. of Sci./Tel Aviv U.; chmn. Chgo. Coun. Global Affairs, 2004—. Mem. Am. Acad. Arts and Scis., Lake Shore Country Club, Northmoor Country Club, Old Elm Club, Standard Club, Econ. Club (dir. 1972), Chgo. Club, Comml. Club, John Evans Club of Northwestern U., Tau Beta Pi, Pi My Epsilon, Phi Eta Sigma. Office: Henry Crown and Co 222 N LaSalle #2000 Chicago IL 60601

CROWN, MICHELE FLEURETTE, lawyer; b. NYC, Nov. 16, 1943; d. Louis and Sophia C.; m. Norman R. Williams, Dec. 2, 1972; children: Zachary Crown Williams, Oliver Crown Williams. BA, Queens Coll., CUNY, 1965; JD, Brooklyn Law Sch., 1967. Bar: N.Y. 1968, D.C. 1969. Trial atty. FTC, Washington, 1967-72, 1975-79; gen. counsel Am. Meat Inst., Washington, 1979-82; of counsel Perito, Duerk & Pinco, Washington, 1982-84, Olsson, Frank & Weeda, Washington, 1984—, Venable LLP, Washington, 2001—. Author reports to Congress; contbr. articles to profl. jours. Mem. ABA, FDLI (mem. academic oversight com.), Pi Sigma Alpha. Office: Venable LLP 575 7th St NW Washington DC 20004 Office Phone: 202-344-4778. Office Fax: 202-344-8300. Business E-Mail: mfcrown@venable.com.

CROWN, ROBERTA, artist, educator; b. N.Y.C., Sept. 9, 1946; d. Louis and Sophia (Siegal) C. BA, Queens Coll., MA, 1970. Art tchr. N.Y. Bd. Edn., N.Y.C., 1969—. One-woman shows include Harbor Sq., Washington, 1970, Andalusia Arts, Inc. Gallery, N.Y.C., 1974, Women's Studio Workship Gallery, Rosendale, N.Y., 1988, Queens Coll. Art Ctr., Flushing, N.Y., 1989, Dag Jammaraskjold Tower, N.Y.C., 1997, Uniproperty Gallery, N.Y.C., 1998; group shows include Air Naval Res. Show (1st prize oils, 3d prize watercolors), 1969, East Meadow Outdoor Show, N.Y.C., 1970, Aorta, East Hampton, N.Y., 1971, United Art Group, N.Y.C., 1976, WIA Gallery, N.Y.C., 1978-80, Bklyn. Coll. (2d prize oils), 1978, One Hundred Artists Show, N.Y.C., 1979, Picture Show Gallery, N.Y.C., 1979, Contemporary Arts Ctr., 1980, Fed. S.I. Artists, Lever House, N.Y.C., 1980, Fine Arts Gallery Ocean County Coll., 1980, Panassus Gallery, Woodstock, N.Y., 1980, Gallery 14, Copenhagen, 1980, Newhouse Gallery, 1981, Queens Mus., 1981, 84, Off the Wall Show, 1982, Cork Gallery, 1983-84, 86-87, Nugent Gallery, Marymount Manhattan Coll., 1983, 84, Garcia Gallery, Bronx, N.Y., 1983, City Gallery, N.Y.C., 1984, Franklin Furnace, N.Y.C., 1984, Lehigh U., Bethlehem, Pa., 1984, Chgo. Gallery, U. Ill., 1984, Tokyo Met. Mus., 1984, Arsenal Gallery, 1984, 86, Art and Design HS, N.Y.C., 1985, Janco-Dada Mus., Ein-Hod, Israel, 1985, Passaic CC, Patterson, N.J., 1986, Todd Capp Gallery, N.Y.C., 1986, Castillo Gallery, N.Y.C., 1987, WRIC Ctr., 1987, Appalachian State U., Boone, N.C., 1988, Transco Energy Gallery, Houston, 1988, Rice Gallery, 1991, Sotherby's, 1991, Nat. Mus. Women in Arts, 1991, NAWA Traveling Show, 1992, Tesori Gallery, 1993, Queens Coll., 2005, Broome Street Gall, 2005. Mem. Women in the Arts Found., Inc. (exec. coord. 1980—), Women Caucus in Art, NY State Assn. Tchrs. Art. Studio: 365 Canal St New York NY 10013

CROWN, TIMOTHY A., computer technology company executive; BS in Bus. and Computer Sci., U. Kans., 1986. Adminstrv. analyst NCR Corp., 1986-87; various positions to pres. Insight Enterprises, Tempe, Ariz., 1988-89, co-CEO, co-chmn., 1994—, now chmn. Ind. computer bus. cons., 1987-88. Office: Insight Enterprises 6820 S Harl Ave Tempe AZ 85283

CROWNOVER, MIKE, energy executive; BBA in Acctg., U. Tex., Arlington. With Halliburton Energy Svcs., 1977—97; corp. compensation mgr. to corp. human resources mgr. to corp. human resources dir. to exec. dir. employee rels. and retail human resources Valero Energy Corp., 1997—2002, v.p. human resources, 2002—. Bd. mem. S.W. Mental Health Ctr. Office: Valero Energy Corpn 1 Valero Way San Antonio TX 78292-0500

CROWSON, HENRY LAWRENCE, mathematician, educator; b. Okeechobee, Fla., Apr. 16, 1927; s. Ernest Hubbard and Mary Elizabeth Crowson; m. Betty Mae George, June 16, 1951; children: Lawrence George, James Maxwell, Timothy David. BChemE, U. Fla., Gainesville, 1953, MS in Math., 1955, PhD in Math., 1959. Cert. engr. in tng., Fla. Asst. prof. U. Fla., Gainesville, 1958-60; advisory mathematician IBM Corp., Gaithersburg, Md., 1960-72; sr. mathematician CACI Corp., Arlington, Va., 1975-77; assoc. prof. U. P.M., Saudi Arabia, 1977-79, U. Houston, 1982-86, TIEC/MUCIA, Shah Alam, Malaysia, 1986-89, Tex. A&M Internat. U., Laredo, 1990-98. Cons. Bell Labs., CACI, Vitro Labs., Cornell U., others, 1955—. Reviewer books and math. texts, 1965-68. Mem. Am. Math. Soc., Sigma Xi, Pi Mu Epsilon. Republican. Avocations: reading, music, composing poetry. Home: 10127 Falls Rd Potomac MD 20854-4107

CROWSON, WATIE DEE, foundation administrator, poet, lyricist; b. Vian, Okla., Aug. 29, 1953; s. Harvey and Gussie B. Crowson; m. Sandra G. Brewster, Aug. 26, 1972 (div. June 1974); m. Sharon K. Moody, Mar. 27, 1979 (div. Aug. 1979); life ptnr. Alice F. Allen; 1 child, Regina Lea. Student, Carl Albert U. Former welder, iron worker, home builder, power plant operator, lakes and park ranger asst.; legis. chmn. DAV, Sallisaw, Okla., 1998—. Second vice comdr. Disabled Am. Vets. Chpt. 83, Post 27; With USN, 1974-75. Mem. Am. Legion (Honor Guard, legis. chmn.), USS Kitty Hawk Assn, Marble City Citizen Bank, Seyquayah county Hist. Soc., VFW. Independent. Avocations: guitar, gardening, cooking, reading, landscaping. Home: Apt E 210 N Walnut Sallisaw OK 74955

CROWSTON, KEVIN GHEN, information scientist, educator; b. Toronto, Ontario, July 4, 1962; s. Wallace Bruce Stuart and Taka Crowston; life ptnr. Marie Frances Williams. AB, Harvard Coll., Cambridge, Mass., 1980—84; PhD, MIT, Cambridge, 1984—91. Asst. prof. U. Mich. Sch. Bus., Ann Arbor, 1991—96; prof. Syracuse U. Sch. Info. Studies, NY, 1996—. Office: Syracuse Univ Hinds Hall 348 Syracuse NY 13244

CROXTON, JACK SANDERS, director, consultant; b. Auburn, Ind., Aug. 3, 1949; s. Jack Anderson and Virginia Sanders Croxton; m. Mary Martha Miller, Dec. 31, 1973; children: Jessica Loring, Jennifer Allison, Joshua Benjamin. BS in Gen. Bus., Miami U., Oxford, Ohio, 1971, MS in Psychology, 1976, PhD in Social Psychology, 1979. Rsch. psychologist Nat. Inst. Occupl. Safety and Health, Cin., 1978—79; asst. prof. dept. psychology SUNY, Fredonia, NY, 1979—85, assoc. prof. dept. psychology, 1985—93, prof. dept. psychology, 1993—, chair dept. psychology, 2002—, dir. office campus assessment, 1999—2002, interim dean Coll. Natural and Social Scis., 2005—06, dir. office student rsch. and creative activity, 2005—. External program reviewer SUNY, Albany, 2002—03; cons. Chautauqua County Sch. to Work Consortium, Jamestown, 1996—2000; instr. Burgas Free U., Bulgaria, 2001; vis. assoc. prof. Princeton U., NJ, 1987—88. Contbr. articles to profl. jours. Sch. bd. mem. Fredonia Ctrl. Schs., 1996—97. Recipient Rsch. Opportunity award, NSF, 1987, Pres.'s award Excellence in Tchg., SUNY, Fredonia, 1991; fellow, Princeton U., 1987—88; Fulbright fellow, 2001. Mem.: Midwestern Psychol. Assn., Ea. Psychol. Assn., Sigma Xi, Beta Gamma Sigma, Phi Beta Kappa. Avocations: travel, kayaking, hiking. Home: 22 Gillis St Fredonia NY 14063 Office: SUNY Thompson Hall Fredonia NY 14063 Home Phone: 716-679-1774; Office Phone: 716-673-3129. Office Fax: 716-673-3332. Personal E-mail: jackcroxton@hotmail.com. E-mail: jack.croxton@fredonia.edu.

CROYLE, BARBARA ANN, health facility administrative executive; b. Knoxville, Tenn., Oct. 22, 1949; d. Charles Evans and Myrtle Elizabeth (Kellam) C. BA cum laude in Sociology, Coll. William and Mary, 1971; cert. corp. tax and securities law, Inst. Paralegal Tng., 1971; JD, U. Colo., 1975; cert. program mgmt. devel., Colo. Women's Coll., 1980; MBA, U. Denver, 1983. Bar: Colo. 1976. Paralegal Holland & Hart, Denver, 1972-73; law clk. Colo. Ct. Appeals, Denver, summer 1976; assoc. firm

Shaw Spangler & Roth, Denver, 1976-77; mgr. acquisitions/lands Petro-Lewis Corp., Denver, 1977-85; mgr. strategic planning Westinghouse, Transp. Divsn., Denver, 1985-87; mng. dir. Benefit Resource Mgmt. Group subs. Blue Cross We. Pa., 1987-92; COO, v.p. D.T. Watson Rehab. Hosp., 1992-93; v.p. ambulatory care svcs., compliance officer Franciscan Med. Ctr., Dayton campus, Ohio, 1994-2000; exec. dir. Swedish Am. Ctr. for Complementary Medicine, Rockford, Ill., 2000—02; v.p., legal advisor Peninsula United Meth. Homes, Inc., Hockessin, Del., 2003—. Tchr. oil and gas law Colo. Paralegal Inst., 1978, 79; arbitrator Am. Arbitration Assn.; mediator Dayton Mediation Ctr. Mem. ABA, Del. Bar Assn., Inst. Noetic Scis., Am. Coll. Healthcare Execs. Home: 150 Mercer Mill Rd Landenberg PA 19350 Office: Peninsula United Meth Home 726 Loveville Rd Hockessin DE 19807 Home Phone: 610-274-8439; Office Phone: 302-235-6823. Personal E-mail: bcroyle@earthlink.net.

CROYLE, ROBERT T., federal agency administrator, psychologist, educator; b. Seattle, Jan. 19, 1956; s. William R. and Elcena (Torrance) C.; m. Carol Jackson, Aug. 8, 1981; children: Kaitlin, Thomas. BA in psychology, U. Wash., 1978; MA in psychology, Princeton U., 1981, PhD in social psychology, 1985. Asst. prof. psychology Williams Coll., Williamstown, Mass., 1983-86; vis. investigator Cancer Prevention Rsch. Program Fred Hutchinson Cancer Rsch. Ctr., Seattle, 1987—89; asst. prof. psychology U. Utah, Salt Lake City, 1989—91, assoc. prof., 1991—98, prof., 1998—99, mem. Huntsman Cancer Inst., 1994—98, head social psychology program, 1992—95, acting chair dept. psychology, 1994; assoc. dir. behavioral rsch. program, Divsn. Cancer Control & Population Sciences Nat. Cancer Inst., 1998—2002; acting dir. Divsn. Cancer Control & Population Sciences, Nat. Cancer Inst., 2002—03, dir., 2003—. Co-editor: (books) Mental Representation in Health and Illness, 1991; editor: Psychosocial effects of screening for disease prevention and detection, 1995. Recipient NIH Merit Award, 1999, 2002, NIH Dir.'s Award, 2000. Fellow: Soc. Behavioral Medicine; mem.: APHA, Soc. Pub. Health Edn., NY Acad. Sciences, Soc. Exptl. Social Psychology, Am. Psychol. Assn., Am. Soc. Preventive Oncology, Acad. Behavioral Medicine Rsch. Office: Nat Cancer Inst Divsn Cancer Control and Popluation Sci 6130 Executive Blvd Executive Plz N Rockville MD 20852 Office Phone: 301-594-6776. Office Fax: 301-594-6787. E-mail: croyler@mail.nih.gov.

CROZIER, SCOTT A., lawyer; b. 1950; BA, Ariz. State U., 1975, JD, 1978. Bar: Ariz. 1978. Asst. counsel Talley Industries, Inc., 1980-87; sr. counsel, dir. environ. svcs. dept. Phelps Dodge Corp., 1987-90, assoc. gen. counsel, dir., 1990-91, v.p., gen. counsel, 1991—99; sr. v.p., gen. counsel PetSmart, Inc., 1999—, corp. sec., 2000—, chief compliance officer, 2005—. Former enforcement atty. securities div. Ariz. Corp. Commn.; former special asst. atty. gen. Ariz. Atty. General's Office. Office: PetSmart Inc 19601 N 27th Ave Phoenix AZ 85027*

CRUDEN, JOHN CHARLES, lawyer; b. Topeka, Feb. 23, 1946; s. George Harry and Agnes (Telban) C.; m. Sharon Lynn Holland, June 15, 1968; children: Kristen, Heather. BS, U.S. Mil. Acad., 1968; JD, U. Santa Clara, 1974; MA, U. Va., 1975; grad., Gen. Staff Coll., 1982. Bar: Calif. 1975, DC 1979, U.S. Supreme Ct. 1979. Commd. 2d lt. U.S. Army, 1968, advanced through grades to col., 1987, with airborne, ranger, spl. forces Germany, Vietnam, 1968—71, clk. Calif. Supreme Ct., 1974, prosecutor Germany, 1975—76, chief litig. br. Hdqrs. Europe, 1976—78, sr. trial atty. comml. br. litig. divsn., 1978—79, gen. counsel Def. Nuc. Agy., 1979—80; prof., chief Adminstrv. and Civil Law divsn. Judge Adv. Gen.'s Sch., Charlottesville, Va., 1982—85; staff Judge Adv. Europe, 1985—87; spl. counsel to asst. atty. gen. civil divsn. U.S. Dept. Justice, 1987—88; chief legis. counsel Dept. Army, 1988—91; chief environ. enforcement sect. Environ. & Natural Resource divsn. U.S. Dept. Justice, Washington, 1991—95, dep. asst. atty. gen., 1995—2001, acting asst. atty. gen., 2001—02, dep. asst. atty. gen., 2002—. Contbr. articles to profl. jours. Decorated Legion of Merit, Bronze Star medal, Air Medal with Oak Leaf Clusters, Defense Meritorious Svc. award, Vietnamese Cross of Gallantry with Silver Star; recipient Younger Fed. Lawyer award, FBA, 1981, Disting. Alumni award, Santa Clara Law Sch., 2006, Presdl. Rank award, 1999, 2002; fellow, Army War Coll., 1988. Mem.: ABA (adv. com., standing com. on law and nat. security 1988—94, vice chmn. fed. legis. com. 1989—92, coun. sect. on environment, energy and resources 2002—06, ho. of dels. 2004—06, vice chmn. environment and natural resources sect. 2007—, Oustanding Govt. Svc. Lawton award 2006), Calif. Bar Assn., Nat. Conf. Bar Pres. (coun. 2006—), DC Bar Assn. (bd. govs. 2001—, pres.-elect 2004—05, pres. 2005—06), JAG Sch. Alumni Assn. (pres. 1982—85). Office: US Dept Justice Environment and Natural Resources Divsn 950 Pennsylvania Ave Washington DC 20530-0001 Home Phone: 703-764-3286; Office Phone: 202-514-2718. Business E-Mail: john.cruden@usdoj.gov.

CRUDEN, ROBERT WILLIAM, botany educator; b. Cleve., Mar. 18, 1936; m. Diana Benedict Loeb, Dec. 21, 1967; children: Nathalie Rebecca, Lyda Marie; m. Diana Ruth Gannett, July 1996. AB, Hiram Coll., Ohio, 1958; MS, Ohio State U., Columbus, 1960; PhD, U. Calif., Berkeley, 1967. Asst. prof. U. Iowa, Iowa City, 1967-71, assoc. prof., 1971-78, prof., 1978-99, prof. emeritus, 1999—. Acting dir. Iowa Lakeside Lab., Wahepton, 1989-94, past asst. dir.; adj. prof. U. Mich, Ann Arbor, 2001- Editor Ecol. Soc. Am., 1983-86; editl. bd. Madrono; contbr. numerous articles to profl. jours. Mem. pres.'s coun. on sci. initiatives Hiram Coll., 1994-2007. Recipient J.J. Turner award Hiram Coll., 2001. Fellow Iowa Acad. Sci.; mem. AAAS, Am. Soc. Plant Taxonomists, Bot. Soc. Am., Ecol. Soc. Am., Iowa Acad. Sci., Soc. for the Study of Evolution, Assn. for Tropical Biology, New Eng. Bot. Soc. Home: 550 Woodhill Dr Saline MI 48176 Home Phone: 734-429-4355. Personal E-mail: robert-cruden@uiowa.edu.

CRUESS, DEAN, psychologist, educator; s. Donald and Vera Cruess; m. Stacy Wagner, May 29, 1999; 1 child, Zachary. PhD and MS, U. Miami, 1998; BA, U. Conn., 1993. Lic. Psychologist Pa, 2001. Asst. prof. U. Pa, Phila., 2000—; postdoctoral fellow U. Miami, Coral Gables, Fla., 1998—2000; psychology intern Brown U., Providence. Mem.: APA, Am. Psychosomatic Soc. (Scholar award 1999), Soc. of Behavioral Medicine. D-Conservative. Roman Catholic. Avocations: tennis, basketball. Office: University Of Penn Psychology Dept 3814 Walnut St Philadelphia PA 19104-3605 Office Phone: 215-573-4801. E-mail: dcruess@psych.upenn.edu.

CRUESS, RICHARD LEIGH, orthopedic surgeon, dean; b. London, Ont., Can., Dec. 17, 1929; s. Leigh S. and Martha A. (Peever) C.; m. Sylvia Crane Robinson, May 30, 1953; children: Leigh S., Andrew C. BA, Princeton U., 1951; MD, Columbia U., 1955; DSc (hon.), U. Laval, 2004. Diplomate Am. Bd. Orthopedic Surgery. Intern Royal Victoria Hosp., Montreal, Que., 1955-56, resident surgery, 1956-57, N.Y. Orthopedic Hosp., 1959-60, asst. resident orthopedic surgery, 1960-61, resident orthopedic surgery, 1961-62, Annie C. Kane fellow orthopedic surgery, 1961-62; research asso. depts. orthopedic surgery and biochemistry Columbia U., NYC, 1962-63; John Armour Travelling fellow, 1962-63; Am.-Brit.-Can. Travelling fellow, 1967; practice medicine specializing in orthopedic surgery Montreal, 1963-95; orthopedic surgeon Royal Victoria Hosp., orthopedic surgeon-in-charge, 1968-81, asst. surgeon-in-chief, 1970-81; chief surgeon Shriner's Hosp. for Crippled Children, Montreal, 1970-82; prof. surgery McGill U., Montreal, 1970—, chmn. div. orthopedic surgery, 1976-81, dean faculty medicine, 1981-95, prof. Ctr. for Med. Edn., 1995—. Hon. cons. orthopedic surgery Queen Elizabeth Hosp., 1972-95; mem. clin. grants com. Med. Rsch. Coun., 1972-75, mem. coun., 1980-86, mem. exec., 1983-86. Contbr. articles on surgery to profl. jours.; mem. editl. bd. Jour. Internat. Orthopedics, 1976-85, Jour. Bone and Joint Surgery, 1977-83, Current Problems in Orthopedics, 1977-83, Jour. Orthopaedic Rsch., 1986-88. Served to lt. M.C., USN, 1957-59. Decorated mem. and officer Order of Can., officer Order of Que. Fellow Royal Coll. Physicians and Surgeons Can. (chief examiner orthopedic surgery 1970-72), ACS, Am. Acad. Orthopedic Surgeons, Royal Soc. Can.; mem. Can. Orthopedic Assn. (sec. 1971-76, pres. 1977-78), Can. Orthopedic Rsch. Soc. (pres. 1971-72), Am. Orthopedic Rsch. Soc. (pres. 1975-76), Am. Orthopedic Assn., Ann. Orthopedic Surgeons Province Que. (treas. 1971-72), Société Française de Chirurgie Orthopedique (hon.), McGill Osler Reporting Soc., Assn. can. Med. colls. (pres. 1987-89). Home: Apt 903 2333 Sherbrooke St W Montreal PQ Canada H3H 2T6 Office: McGill U 1110 Pine Ave W Montreal PQ Canada H3A 1A3 Home Phone: 514-732-0670; Office Phone: 514-398-7331. E-mail: richard.cruess@mcgill.ca.

CRUICKSHANK, JOHN DOUGLAS, publishing executive; b. Toronto, Ont., Can., Apr. 7, 1953; s. Norman and Jean (McPherson) C.; m. Jennifer Hunter; children: Simone, Noah. BA with honors, U. Toronto, 1975. Reporter The Kingston Whig-Standard, Ont., Canada, 1977-79, The Montreal Gazette, 1979-81; edn. writer The Globe & Mail, Toronto, 1981-82, Queen's Park writer, 1982-85, bur. chief Vancouver, 1985-88, editorial writer Toronto, 1988-90, assoc. editor, 1990-92, mng. editor, 1992-95; editor-in-chief The Vancouver Sun, 1995-2000; v.p. editl. Chgo. Sun-Times, 2000—03, pub., 2003—; COO Sun-Times News Group (formerly Hollinger Internat. Inc.), 2003—. Office: Chicago Sun Times 350 N Orleans St Ste 1270 Chicago IL 60654-2148*

CRUIKSHANK, JOHN W., III, insurance agent; b. Sharon, Pa., Aug. 22, 1933; s. John W. and Jeannette Sprague (Lane) C.; m. Myrna Jean Wright, Nov. 25, 1960; children: Nancy Lynn, David Wright. BA, Princeton U., 1955. CLU. Group ins. sales rep. Conn. Gen. Life Ins. Co., Hartford, also Chgo., 1955-56; spl. agt. Northwestern Mut. Life Ins. Co., Chgo., 1959—, pres. Spl. Agts., Inc., 1983-84, faculty advanced planning sch. Northbrook, Ill., 1978-97; pres. Assn. of Agts. Northwestern Mut. Life, 1994-95. Pres. Million Dollar Round Table Found., 1988—89; divisional v.p. Million Dollar Round Table, 1976—77, 1986—87, 1992—93, exec. com., 1994—98, pres., 1996—97; trustee Life Underwriter Tng. Coun., 1997—2001. Bd. dirs. Life and Health Ins. Found. for Edn., 1997—2003, chmn., 2002; bd. dirs. North Shore Sr. Ctr., 2001—, sec., mem. exec. com., 2006—; mem. gov. bd. Super Sibs!, 2007—; trustee Pikeville (Ky.) Coll., 1969—75, The Am. Coll., 2001—02; pres. Nat. Coun. United Presbyn. Men, 1971—72; elder United Presbyn. Ch. in U.S.A., 1975—, mem. gen. assembly mission coun., 1972—78; chmn. mission divsn. Presbytery of Chgo., gen. coun., 1966—67, 1980—84; bd. dirs. Vocation Agy., Presbyn. Ch. in U.S.A., 1982—87. Named one of Most Outstanding Life Underwriters in the U.S. for decade of 1990s, Leaders Mag., 1999; recipient Cir. of Life award, Million Dollar Round Table Found., 1998, Huebner Scholar award, Am. Soc. CLU and ChFC, Chgo., 1995, Disting. Citizen award, Ill. St. Andrew Soc., 1998, Grauer Disting. Svc. award, Chgo. Chpt. Fin. Svc. Profls., 2000. Home: 1412 Ridge Rd Northbrook IL 60062-4628

CRUIKSHANK, THOMAS HENRY, energy services and engineering executive; b. Lake Charles, La., Nov. 3, 1931; s. Louis James and Helene L. (Little) Cruikshank; m. Ann Coe, Nov. 17, 1955; children: Thomas Henry Jr., Kate Martin, Stuart. BA, Rice U., 1952; postgrad., U. Tex., 1952—53, U. Houston, 1953—55. CPA Tex.; bar: Tex. Accountant Arthur Andersen & Co., Houston, 1953-55, 58-60; mem. firm Vinson & Elkins, Houston, 1961—69; v.p. Halliburton Co., Dallas, 1969—72, sr. v.p., 1972—80, exec. v.p., 1980, pres., CEO subs. Otis Engring. Corp., 1980—81, pres., 1981—83, pres., CEO, 1983-89, chmn., CEO, 1989—95, dir., 1977—95. Former bd. dirs. Williams Cos., Goodyear Tire and Rubber Co.; former mem. Nat. Petroleum Coun.; policy com. Bus. Roundtable; dir. Lehman Bros. Holdings, Inc. Trustee Calif. Inst. Tech., 1991—95; nat. bd. dirs. Jr. Achievement, 1976—95, chmn., 1989—90; bd. dirs. Up With People, 1998—2000; Pres. Jr. Achievement, Dallas, 1974—76, chmn., 1976—78. Lt. (j.g.) USNR, 1955—58. Mem.: Am. Petroleum Inst., Tex. Bar Assn., ABA, Pine Valley Golf Club, Eldorado Country Club (Calif.), Grandfather Golf and Country Club (N.C.), Dallas Country Club.

CRUISE, TOM (THOMAS CRUISE MAPOTHER IV), actor; b. Syracuse, NY, July 3, 1962; s. Thomas C. III and Mary Lee Mapother; m. Mimi Rogers, May 9, 1987 (div. Feb. 4, 1990); m. Nicole Kidman, Dec. 24, 1990 (div. Aug. 8, 2001); adopted children: Isabella Jane Kidman, Connor Antony Kidman; m. Katie Holmes, Nov. 18, 2006; 1 child, Suri. Grad. H.S., Glen Ridge, NJ. Cofounder (with Paula Wagner) Cruise/Wagner Productions, 1993—, prodr., ptnr. Actor: (films) Endless Love, 1981, Taps, 1981, The Outsiders, 1983, Losin' It, 1983, Risky Business, 1983 (Golden Globe nomination for best actor in a motion picture comedy/musical, 1984), All the Right Moves, 1983, Legend, 1985, Top Gun, 1986, The Color of Money, 1986, Cocktail, 1988, Rain Man, 1988, Born on the Fourth of July, 1989 (Golden Globe award for best actor in a motion picture drama, 1990, Acad. award nomination for best actor, 1990), Far and Away, 1992, A Few Good Men, 1992 (Golden Globe nomination for best actor in a motion picture drama), The Firm, 1993, Interview with the Vampire, 1994, Jerry McGuire, 1996 (Golden Globe award for best actor, 1997, Acad. Award nomination for best actor, 1997), Eyes Wide Shut, 1998, Magnolia, 1999 (Golden Globe award for best supporting actor in a motion picture, 2000, Acad. Award nomination for best supporting actor, 2000), Minority Report, 2002, Collateral, 2004, War of the Worlds, 2005; actor, prodr.: (films) Mission Impossible, 1996, Mission Impossible II, 2000, Vanilla Sky, 2001, The Last Samurai, 2003 (Golden Globe nomination for best actor, 2004), Mission Impossible III, 2006; actor, writer: (films) Days of Thunder, 1990; prodr.: (films) Without Limits, 1998; exec. prodr.: (films) The Others, 2001, Narc, 2002, Shattered Glass, 2003. Co-recipient Nova award for outstanding achievement by new or emerging prodr. in theatrical motion pictures, Producer's Guild, 1997; named one of 50 Most Powerful People in Hollywood, Premiere mag., 2004—06, The 10 Most Fascinating People of 2005, Barbara Walters Special, The 100 Most Powerful Celebrities, Forbes.com, 2006—07; recipient Star on the Hollywood Walk of Fame, John Huston Award for Artists Rights, The Artists Rights Found., 1998.*

CRULL, JAN, JR., lawyer, investment banker, consultant; b. The Netherlands; s. Jan Crull and Frederika Minderop. Grad., Lake Forest Acad.; student, Northwestern U., Evanston, Ill.; BA with honors, Dalhousie U., Can., 1975; MA, Purdue U., 1977, U. Chgo., 1984; JD, Tulane U. La., New Orleans, 1990. Intern GGvA, NYC, 1973—74; tchg. asst., grad. instr. Purdue U., 1975—76; asst. to OOTC, NYC, 1978; asst. to chpt. pres. Ramah Navajo Reservation, Pinehill, N.Mex., 1979—80; profl. staff mem. US Ho. of Reps., Washington, 1981; asst. money mgr. Gulf and Occidental Investment Co. SA, Geneva, 1982, 1985—86, 1989, counsel, advisor, 1990—91; counsel, co-prin. SandCru, Inc., Chgo., 1992—; pres., gen. counsel Vigil Film Prodn. Co., LA and Sacramento, 1993—97; dir./counsel Von Quesar Holdings, OHG, Vienna, 1994—98, Beeltsnijder KG, Berlin, 1995—97. Adv. LFFE, Ltd., Hebei, China, 2004—. Developer (films) What About My Friend's Children, 1973, Not in Fiction Only: There and Here Also, 1974, A Free People, Free to Choose, 1992—93, AIDDS: American Indians' Devastating Dilemma Soon, 1993, To Mute Them Once Again, 1994, Indian Buckaroos, 1996. Author provisions for First Reauthorization of Tribally Controlled Cmty. Coll. Assistance Act 97th US Congress; author spl. provisions for Native Ams. in Libr. Svcs. Constrn. Act 97th - 98th US Congress. Nominee Rockefeller Pub. Svc. award, 1981. Mem.: Chgo. Coun. Global Affairs, Chgo. Bar Assn., 1781 Club Netherlands Antilles, Quadrangle Club Chgo., Phi Kappa Psi. Mem. Protestant Dutch Reformed Ch. Office: Shangbat TEH PO Box 0492 Chicago IL 60690-0492

CRUM, ALBERT B., psychiatrist, consultant; b. Omaha, Nov. 17, 1931; s. J. Rufus and Alberta (McCreary) C.; m. Rosa Maria Hennessy y Sinclair; children: Rosa Maria Crum O'Brien, Elsie Crum McCabe, Alberta Crum Fousek. BS, U. Redlands, Calif., 1953, DSc (hon.), 1974; MD, Harvard U., 1957; MS, NYU, 1987. Diplomate Am. Bd. Forensic Medicine, in Psychotherapy Am. Psychotherapy Assn., Am. Bd. Forensic Examiners. Med. intern Columbia U. divsn. Bellevue Med. Ctr., NYC, 1957—58; rsch. fellow, psychiat. resident Creedmoor Inst. for Psychobiol. Studies, Queens Village, NY, 1958—59; chief, neuropsychiatric svcs. Continental Air Command Hdqs. 2500 USAF Hosp., 1959-61; psychiat. resident Columbia U. Psychiat. Inst. of Columbia-Presbyn. Hosp., NYC, 1961—63; pvt. practice Brooklyn Heights, NY, 1963—. Co-chmn. US Coordinating Commn. for Nomination of His Holiness the Dalai Lama of Tibet for the Nobel Peace Prize, Brooklyn Heights, 1986; chmn. Human Behavior Found., Bklyn. Heights, 1968—; chmn. selection com. Human Behavior Found.'s Albert Schweitzer Humanitarian Award, Bklyn. Heights, 1986—; expert Nat. Forensic Ctr.; pres. Stress Watchers, Inc., The ProImmune Co., LLC., Y.F. One/NY, Ltd., 1991—; advisor Office of Tibet, NYC, 1984—; clin. prof. mgmt. sci., adj. prof. anatomy and neuroanatomy NYU, 1987-2002. Author: The 10-Step Method of Stress Relief: Decoding the Meaning and Significance of Stress, CRC Press, 2000; contbr. articles and abstracts to profl. jours. Bd. dirs. Albert Schweitzer Fellowship, NYC, 1982—2002, Burdick Internat. Ancestry Library, Sarasota, Fla., 1985—; mem., chmn., adv. bd. NYU's Coll. of Dentistry, 1988-96; mem. Bklyn. Heights Assn., 1970-96; class agent Harvard Med. Sch. Class of 1957; pres. Stress Watchers, Inc. Capt. USAF, 1959-61. Recipient Disting. Svc. award Bklyn. Jr. C. of C., 1966, Bicentennial award Nat. Jogging Assn., 1976; Citizen of Yr. award, Achievements in Medicine and Human Understanding, Bklyn. Philharm., 1986; named Disting. Lectr., NYU Coll. Dentistry, Omicron Kappa Upsilon lectr., 1986. Fellow Royal Coll. Physicians and Surgeons in Psychiatry; mem. Sci. Rsch. Soc. (life), Am. Acad. of Forensic Scis. (assoc.), Nat. Bd. Med. Examiners, Med. Coun. of Can., Am. Physicians Art Assn., Harvard Med. Soc., Harvard Club of N.Y., MENSA (life, nat. coord. 1980-84), Phi Beta Kappa (councillor 1981-84), Sigma Xi (life). Achievements include patents for nutritional or therapeutic composition; nutritional or therapeutic supplement and method. Avocations: jogging, studying world religions, history. Home and Office: 64 E Market St Rhinebeck NY 12572 Office Phone: 845-876-3222. Personal E-mail: albertbcrum@aol.com.

CRUM, CHRISTOPHER PAUL, pathologist, educator; b. Newport News, Va., Nov. 26, 1948; s. Blaine Cecil and Mercedes Smith Crum; m. Tucker Anne Roane, May 20, 1974; children: Emily Foster Day, Amanda Tucker Gibson. MD, U. Va., Charlottesville, 1974. Cert. Am. Bd. Pathology, 1980. Dir. women's and perinatal pathology Brigham and Women's Hosp., Boston, 1990—. Grantee Physician Scientist award, NIH, 1985. Mem.: Am. Soc. Investigative Pathologists, Am. Soc. Colposcopy and Cervical Pathology, Soc. Gynecologic Oncology, US and Can. Acad. Pathology (pres. 2006—07). Office: Brigham and Women's Hosp 75 Francis Boston MA 02115 Home Phone: 617-732-5481; Office Phone: 617-732-7530.

CRUM, JOHN KISTLER, management consultant; b. Brownsville, Tex., July 28, 1936; s. John Mears and Mary Louise (Kistler) C. BS, U. Tex., 1960, PhD, 1964; grad. Advanced Mgmt. Program, Harvard U., 1975. Research fellow Robert A. Welch Found., 1962-64; asst. editor Am. Chem. Soc., Washington, 1964-65, assoc. editor, 1966-68, mng. editor, 1969-70, group mgr. jours., 1970, dir. books and jours. div., 1971-75, treas., chief fin. officer, 1975-80, dep. exec. dir. and chief operating officer, 1981-82, exec. dir., 1983—2003; pres., CEO Quinta Assocs., LLC, 2004—. Chmn. bd. Centcom Ltd., 1983-2003, Sci. Info. Internat., Ltd., 1995-2003; chmn. governing bd. Chem. Abstracts Svc., 1991-1996, ACS publs., 1997-2003; mem. U.S. nat. com. Internat. Union Pure and Applied Chemistry; sr. mem. Con. Bd.; mem. Bretton Woods Com., 2002—; bd. dirs. Consumers Union of U.S., 1991-93. Contbr. articles to profl. jours. Fellow Washington Acad. Scis.; mem. Royal Chem. Soc. (London), Am. Chem. Soc., Am. Soc. Assn. Execs., Coun. Engring. and Sci., Soc. Execs., Assn. Sci. Soc. Editors, N.Y. Acad. Scis., Chem. Soc. Washington, Cosmos Club, City Club, Univ. Club (Washington), Chemists Club (N.Y.), Sigma Xi, Phi Theta Kappa. Republican. Home: PO Box 780 Cobbs Creek VA 23035 Home Phone: 804-725-0331; Office Phone: 703-528-0321.

CRUMB, GEORGE HENRY, composer, educator; b. Charleston, W.Va., Oct. 24, 1929; s. George Henry and Vivian (Reed) C.; m. Elizabeth May Brown, May 21, 1949; children: Elizabeth Ann, David Reed, Peter Stanley. BMus, Mason Coll., 1950; MMus, U. Ill., 1952; postgrad. (Fulbright fellow), Hochschule für Musik, Berlin, Germany, 1955-56, Berkshire Music Center, Tanglewood, Mass., summer 1955; DMus Arts, U. Mich., 1959. Instr. theory Hollins Coll., Va., 1958-59; asst. prof. composition and piano U. Colo., 1959-64; creative asso. composition State U. N.Y. at Buffalo, 1964-65; asst. prof. composition U. Pa., Phila., 1965-66, asso. prof., 1966-71, prof., 1971—, Annenberg prof., 1983—. Composer: String Quartet, 1954, Sonata; for solo violoncello, 1955; Variazioni; for large orch., 1959; Five Pieces; for piano, 1962, Night Music I; for soprano, keyboard and percussion, 1963; Four Nocturnes Night Music II; for violin and piano, 1964; Madrigals, Books I and II; for solo voice and instruments, 1965; Eleven Echoes of Autumn; for violin, alto flute, clarinet and piano, 1966; Echoes of Time and the River, 1967 (Pulitzer prize 1968); for orch. Songs, Drones and Refrains of Death for baritone and electric instruments; U. Iowa commn., 1968, Madrigals, Books III and IV; for soprano and instruments, 1969; Night of the Four Moons; for alto and instruments, 1969; Black Angels (Thirteen Images from the Dark Land); for electric string quartet, U. Mich. commn., 1970; Ancient Voices of Children; for soprano and instruments, Coolidge Found. commn., 1970; Vox Balaenae; for electric flute, electric cello and electric piano, 1971; Lux Aeterna; for soprano, sitar, bass flute and two percussionists, 1971; for amplified piano Makrokosmos, Vol. I, 1972, Vol. II, 1973; Makrokosmos, Vol. I Music for a Summer Evening; for 2 amplified pianos and percussion, Fromm Found. commn., 1974; Dream Sequence; for violin, cello, piano, percussion and glass-harmonica, 1976; Star-Child: A Parable; for Solo Soprano, Antiphonal Children's Voices, Bell Ringers and Large Orch., Ford Found. Commn., 1977; Celestial Mechanics, Cosmic Dances; for Amplified Piano, 4-Hands, 1979; Apparition; elegiac songs and vocalises for soprano and amplified piano, 1979; A Little Suite for Christmas, A.D. 1979, 1980, Gnomic Variations for Piano, 1981, Pastoral Drone for Organ, 1982, Processional for piano, 1983, A Haunted Landscape for Orchestra, 1984, The Sleeper for Soprano and Piano, 1984, An Idyll for the Misbegotten for Flute and Drums, 1985; Federico's Little Songs for Children for Soprano, Flute and Harp, 1986, Zeitgeist for two amplified pianos, 1987, Easter Dawning for Carillon, 1991; also commns. Koussevitzky Found., 1964, Bowdoin Coll., 1965, U. Chgo., 1966; Quest, 1994 for guitar and chamber ensemble, Mundus Canis for Guitar and Percussion, 1997, for amplified piano, Eine Kleine Mitternachtmusik, 2002, Unto the Hills, 2002 for voice, percussion quartet and amplified piano, Otherworldly Resonances, 2002, A Journey Beyond Time, 2003, The River of Life, 2003, The Winds of Destiny, 2004 for voice, percussion quartet and amplified piano, Yesteryear, 2005 for soprano and three instruments, Voices from a Forgotten World, 2006 for solo male and female voices, percussion quartet and amplified piano. Edward MacDowell Colony medal, Peterborough, 1995. Mem. B.M.I., Nat. Inst. Arts and Letters, German Acad. Arts (hon.), Bavarian Acad. Fine Arts, Am. Acad. Arts and Scis., Pi Kappa Lambda, Phi Mu Alpha. Office: U Pa Music Bldg Philadelphia PA 19104

CRUMBLEY, DONALD LARRY, accounting educator, writer; b. Kannapolis, NC, Jan. 18, 1941; s. Carl Donald and Velvia (Kelly) C.; m. Donna Darlene Loflin, Aug. 31, 1963; children: Stacey Lynn, Dana Lea, Heather

Ann. BS cum laude, Pfeiffer U., 1963; MS, La. State U., 1965, PhD, 1967. CPA NC, cert. forensic acct.; diplomate Am. Bd. Forensic Accts.; cert. fraud deterrence. Grad rsch. asst. La. State U., Baton Rouge, 1963-65, tchg. asst., 1965-66; asst. prof. acctg. Pa. State U., State College, 1967-69; staff acct. Arthur Andersen & Co., NYC, 1969-70; adj. asst. prof. NYU Grad. Sch. Bus., 1970; faculty resident Laventhol & Horwath, 1972; assoc. prof., dir. M. Bus. Taxation program U. So. Calif., LA, 1973-74, U. Fla., Gainesville, 1970-73, 74-75; prof. Tex. A&M U., College Station, 1975-97, Shelton prof. taxation, 1984-97; KPMG endowed prof. La. State U., Baton Rouge, 1997—. Newspaper and mag. columnist; creator Soc. for a Return to Acad. Stds., 1993—. Author: Financial Management of Your Coin-Stamp Estate, 1978, Practical Guide to Preparing a Federal Gift Tax Return, 1981, Readings in Selected Tax Problems of the Oil Industry, 1982, Handbook of Accounting for Natural Resources, 1986, Handbook of Estate Planning, 1988, Handbook of Governmental Accounting and Finance, 1988, 1992, Handbook of Financial Management for Banks, 1988, The Ultimate Rip-off: A Taxing Tale, 1999, Accosting the Golden Spire, 1989, Handbook on Financial Aspect of Divorce and Separation, 1989, Keys to Understanding the Financial News, 2000, Keys to Estate Planning and Trusts, 1989, Keys to Personal Financial Planning, 1991, Keys to Surviving a Tax Audit, 1991, Handbook of Natural Gas Accounting, 1991, Keys to Understanding Social Security Benefits, 1992; co-author: Donate Less to the IRS, 1981, Readings in Oil Industry Accounting, 1980, Estate Planning: A Guide for Advisers and Their Clients, West's Federal Taxation, 4 vols., Trap Doors and Trojan Horses, 1991, Financial Analysis, 1994, How To Manage Corporate Cash, 1994, Costly Reflections in a Midas Mirror, 1995, Barron's Guide to Tax Terms, 1995, Activity Based Costing, 1995, Deadly Art Puzzle: Accounting for Murder, 1996, The Bottom Line is Betrayal, 1995, Non-profit Sleuths: Follow the Money, 1997, Simon the Incredible: A Novel, 1998, Chemistry in Whispering Caves, 1998, Computer Encryptions in Whispering Caves, 1999, The Big R: An Internal Auditing Action Adventure, 2000, U.S. Master Auditing Guide, 2d edit., Forensic and Investigating Accounting, 2003, 2d edit., 2005; contbr. chpts. to books, articles to profl. jours.; editor Oil, Gas & Energy Quar., 1977—, Jour. Forensic Acctg., 1999—; co-editor Tex. Tax Services, 1983—; cons. editor Lawyers and Judges Pub. Co., Tucson; contbg. editor Hard Facts and Tax Angles; mem. editl. bd. Jour. Petroleum Acctg., Jour. Managerial Issues, Jour. East-West Bus., Forensic Examiner, Acctg. Educators' Jour., Acctg. Rev.; mem. editl. adv. bd. Advances in Acctg. Named to Alumni Hall of Fame, A.L. Brown H.S., 1972; recipient Contbn. to Cmty. award Sta. WRUF, 1972; Coll. Bus. Adminstrn. Rsch. award Tex. A&M U., 1982; Ford Found. grantee, 1966-67; Disting. Alumni award Pfeiffer Coll., 1972; Arthur Young Rsch. grant, 1984-85. Mem. Am. Taxation Assn. (pres. 1974-75, trustee 1975-77, founder), Am. Inst. CPA's, Am. Acctg. Assn., Nat. Taxation Assn., Am. Tax Assn. (founding pres.), Govt. Fin. Officers' Assn., Tex. Soc. CPA's, La. Soc. CPA's, Numis. Lit. Guild, Order of Sundial, Phi Kappa Phi, Beta Gamma Sigma, Beta Alpha Psi. Methodist. Office: La State U Dept Acctg 3101 CEBA Bldg Baton Rouge LA 70803-0001 Office Phone: 225-578-6231. Business E-Mail: dcrumbl@lsu.edu.

CRUMBLEY, ESTHER HELEN KENDRICK, retired real estate agent, retired secondary school educator, councilman; b. Okeechobee, Fla., Oct. 3, 1928; d. James A. and Corrine (Burney) Kendrick; m. Chandler Jackson, Oct. 24, 1949 (dec.); children: Pamela E., Chandler A., William J. BS in Math. Edn., Ga. So. Coll., 1966; M in Math., Jacksonville U., Fla., 1979. Cert. secondary edn. tchr., Ga. Secondary edn. tchr. Camden County Bd. Edn., St. Mary's, Ga., 1958-92, ret.; realtor Watson Realty, St. Mary's, 1985-98, ret., 1998. Dept. chairperson Camden H.S., St. Mary's, 1966-72. Reporter: for hometown newspaper. Councilwoman City of St. Mary's, 1979-86, mayor pro tem, 1981-86. Mem. Camden Ga. Assn. Educators (pres. 1976, sec.-treas. 1977-78, star tchr. 1972), PAGE (biog. com. rep. 1984-92, 1992 retired, named outstanding 8th dist. bldg. rep.), Camden Gen. Mcpl. Assn. (pres., sec.-treas. 1979-88), fin. and budget coms.), Math. Assn., Internat. Platform Assn. Internat. Dictionary Ctr., ABI. Republican. Baptist. Avocations: reading, art. Home: RR 3 Box 810 Folkston GA 31537-9729 *Hard work, perseverance and determination will get you to any goal in life. Put God first, country and family in that order. Can't should not be in your vocabulary.*

CRUMLEY, DAVID OLIVER, publishing executive, writer, corporate executive; b. New Orleans, May 18, 1949; s. David Shiffer III and Martha Ann (Carey) C BA, Tulane U., 1974. Sec., editor The Social Dir. of Greater New Orleans, Inc., 1975—77, pres., pub., 1977—92. Pres. Laser Documentation Inc Author, historian: Reflection of Life in New Orleans: Architecture & Interior Decoration as Historical, Social & Cultural Commentary, 1970; pub., author: Mardi Gras in New Orleans 1971, 1971; rschr. Town & Country, 1979 Historian hist. marker Ashland Plantation, 1969, La Maison Blanche Plantation, 1974; co-founder Soc. Huguenot A Nouvelle, New Orleans, 1973, Grand Priory of South, Mil. and Hospitaller Order St. Lazarus of Jerusalem, New Orleans, 1976; vestry Mt. Olivet Episc. Ch., 1971-90, jr. warden vestry, 1976-88, sr. warden vestry, 1989 Internat. Rels. scholar Tulane U., 1974 Mem. Sons of Revolution (genealogist La chpt. 1974-88), Societe Huguenot A Nouvelle Orleans (bd. dirs.), Soc. War of 1812 (vice-genealogist La. chpt. 1974-80), Royal Soc. St. George (bd. dirs. New Orleans chpt. 1974-76), Soc. Colonial Wars (dep. genealogist La. chpt. 1974-77, 79-88, genealogist La. chpt. 1977-79), SAR (genealogist George Washington chpt. 1986-87), La. Hist. Soc., Masons Avocation: reading. Home and Office: 3200 Rue Parc Fontaine Ste 3510 New Orleans LA 70131 Office Phone: 504-391-9300.

CRUMLEY, JAMES ROBERT, JR., retired bishop; b. Bluff City, Tenn., Mar. 30, 1925; s. James Robert and Ida Frances (Fine) C.; m. Sara Annette Bodie, May 26, 1950; children: Frances Crumley Holman, James Robert, Jeanne Crumley Lindemann. BA, Roanoke Coll., 1948, DD (hon.), 1973; MDiv, Luth. Theol. So. Sem., Columbia, SC, 1951; DD (hon.), Newberry Coll., SC, 1971, Augustana Coll., 1982, Muhlenberg Coll., Allentown, Pa., 1983; LLD (hon.), Susquehanna U., Selinsgrove, Pa., 1977; LHD (hon.), Lenoir-Rhyne Coll., Hickory, NC, 1979; LittD (hon.), Bethany Coll., 1981; LHD (hon.), Manhattan Coll., 1984, U. S.C., 1987. Ordained to ministry Luth. Ch., 1951. Pastor chs. in, Greenville and Oak Ridge, Tenn., Savannah, Ga., 1951-74; sec. Luth. Ch. in Am., NYC, 1974-78, bishop, 1978-88. Vis. prof. ecumenism Luth. Theol. So. Sem., Columbia, S.C., 1988, ret., 1993. Lutheran. Home: 108 Castle Church Rd Roanoke VA 24036 Personal E-mail: jcrum362@aol.com.

CRUMLEY, JOHN WALTER, lawyer; b. Ft. Worth, July 20, 1944; s. Frank E. and Mary Cecilia (Gaudin) C.; m. Paulette Gavin, July 25, 1970; children: John Gavin, Brian Christopher. BS, Springhill Coll., 1967; JD, So. Meth. U., 1970, M of Comparative Law, 1973. Bar: Tex. 1970, U.S. Dist. Ct. (no. dist.) Tex. 1976, U.S. Ct. Appeals (5th cir.) 1981, U.S. Tax Ct. 1988. Assoc. McBryde & Bogle, Ft. Worth, 1973-75; ptnr. Crumley, Murphy & Shrull, Inc., Ft. Worth, 1975-85, Tracy, Crumley & Holland, Ft. Worth, 1985-92; prin. John W. Crumley, P.C., Ft. Worth, 1992—. Mem. bd. dirs. Goodrich Ctr. for the Deaf, 1995—, pres., 1998-2002; vice chair Bingo Advisor Com., 1995-96; mem. bd. dirs. Wings of Hope Equitherapy, 2006-. Mem. steering com. Tarrant County Vol. Guardianship, Ft. Worth, 1986-87; bd. dirs. Camp Fire, Ft. Worth, 1985-87, Cath. Social Svcs., Ft. Worth, 1985-86. Capt. U.S. Army, 1970-72. Mem. State Bar Tex., Tarrant County Bar Assn., Tex. Assn. Def. Counsel, Tex. Assn. Diocesan Attys., U.S. Conf. Diocesan Attys. Assn., Serra Club (pres. Ft. Worth club 1985-86), KC (state adv. 1986-91, 95-96). Office: 501 University Ctr 1300 S University Dr Fort Worth TX 76107-5737 Home Phone: 817-732-7539; Office Phone: 817-334-0291. Personal E-mail: crumley1@airmail.net.

CRUMLEY, MARTHA ANN, charity fundraising executive; b. New Orleans, Aug. 8, 1910; d. Mark Oliver and Mary Elizabeth (Schroder) Carey; m. David Shiffer Crumley III, May 7, 1947; 1 child, David Oliver Pres., CEO Westbank Acad., Gretna, La., 1953—68; sr. v.p. The Social Directory Greater New Orleans, Inc., 1975—82, pres., 1992—94. Pres. Algiers Little Theatre, New Orleans, 1930; tchr. speech and drama YWCA, New Orleans, 1938-39, prodr., dir. plays, 1938-39; pres. Krewe of Aparamest, New Orleans, 1938; chmn. fundraising New Orleans Philharm. Symphony, 1967; mem. women's vol. com. New Orleans Mus. Art, 1967-68; dir. sr. and jr. choir Mt. Olivet Episcopal Ch., New Orleans, 1922-83, mem. altar guild, 1922-83; pres. Mt. Olivet's Women Aux., New Orleans, 1950; mem. women's guild New Orleans Philharm Mem. DAR, English Speaking Union, La. Landmark Soc., Friends of Cabildo, Children of Am. Revolution (sr. prs. 1969), Colonial Dames XVII Century (pres. La. chpt. 1977)

CRUMLEY, ROGER LEE, surgeon, educator, otolaryngologist; b. Perry, Iowa, Oct. 8, 1941; s. Dwight Moody and Helen Ethelwyn (Anderson) C.; m. Janet Lynn Conant, Nov. 13, 1987; children: Erin Kelly Helen, Danielle Nicole. BA, Simpson Coll., 1964; MS, U. Iowa, 1975, MD, 1967; MBA, U. Phoenix, 1999. Diplomate Am. Bd. Otolaryngology (dir. 1992—2004). Intern L.A. County Gen. Hosp., 1967-68; resident in surgery Highland-Alameda Hosp., Oakland, Calif., 1968-69; bn. surgeon 1st Marine Div., Vietnam, 1968-69; resident in otolaryngology U. Iowa, Iowa City, 1971-75; chief otolaryngology San Francisco Gen. Hosp., 1975-81; assoc. prof., then prof. U. Calif., San Francisco, 1981-87, prof., chief otolaryngology-head and neck surgery Irvine, 1987—. Guest prof. Humboldt U., East Berlin, 1982, M.S. McLeod vis. prof. S. Australian Postgrad. Edn. Ctr., Adelaide, 1988; treas., pres. Am. Acad. Facial Plastic Surgeons, 1994-95, Triological Soc., 2002-03; McBride lectr. U. Edinburgh, 1998. Contbr. articles and book chpts. to profl. pubs. With USN, 1969-71, Vietnam. Recipient Alumni Achievement award Simpson Coll., 1984. Fellow ACS, Am. Acad. Otolaryngology (bd. dirs. 1988—, award 1989); mem. Soc. Univ. Otolaryngologists, Triological Soc. (pres. 2002-), Bohemian Club (San Francisco), Center Club (Costa Mesa, Calif.). Republican. Methodist. Avocations: music, piano, jazz flügelhorn, running, skiing. Office: U Calif-Irvine Med Ctr Dept Otolaryngology Head & Neck 101 The City Dr S Orange CA 92868-3201 Home Phone: 714-289-0253; Office Phone: 714-456-5750. Business E-Mail: rcrumley@uci.edu.

CRUMLISH, JANE C., pediatrician; b. Camden, NJ, Apr. 8, 1940; d. Henry Stanley and Frances Anita (née Laurie) Cushing; m. Paul William Crumlish, Dec. 5, 1998; m. Patrick McCaffrey (div.); children: Laurie née McCaffrey, Kevin McCaffrey. BA, Cornell U., Ithaca, 1962; MD, U. Md., Balt., 1966. Cert. pediats. Am. Bd. Pediats., 1971, devel. and behavioral pediats. Am. Bd. Pediats., 2002. Resident U. Md., Balt., 1966—69, clinical instr. pediats., 1969—73; pediatrician Pvt. Practice, Geneva, NY, 1973—; fellow devel. behavioral pediats. U. Rochester Med. Sch., NY, 1996—98; developmental pediatrician Rochester Gen. Hosp., 2003—04. Pediat. cons. Head Start Health Adv. Bd., Geneva, 1975—; chief med. staff Geneva Gen. Hosp., 2001—03. Bd. mem. Finger Lakes Symphony Orch., Newark, NY, 1995—, Success for Geneva's Children, Geneva, 2000—. Recipient Athena award, Geneva C. of C., 2006. Fellow: Am. Acad. Pediats.; mem.: Soc. Devel. and Behavioral Pediats. Democrat. Avocations: music, French horn, sailing. Office: Finger Lakes Med Assocs 200 N St Ste 101 Geneva NY 14456

CRUMM, MAX (AARON MAXIMILLIAN CRUMM), actor; b. Pasadena, Calif., Oct. 8, 1985; Actor: (plays) The Grinch, A Midsummer Night's Dream, Lysistrata, Sound of Music, The Wizard of Oz, Into the Woods, You're a Good Man, Charlie Brown, Anything Goes, Hello Dolly, Titanic, Damn Yankees, Grease, Beyond Therapy, PS Your Cat is Dead, Once in a Lifetime, Prisoner of Second Avenue; actor & writer (plays) SWAY-Z GREY, SakeBombers; actor: (Broadway plays) Grease, 2007. Achievements include winning the role of Danny Zuko in Broadway production of Grease through competition on NBC Grease: You're the One That I Want. Mailing: c/o Jessica Rose - Grease East Bldg Ste 202 7800 Beverly Blvd Los Angeles CA 90036*

CRUMMETT, ALLAN WARREN, psychologist; b. Midland, Mich., Jan. 13, 1953; s. Warren Berlin and Elizabeth Ann Crummett; m. Carrie Ann Bristow, Aug. 21, 1992; children: Warren Luke, Autumn Leah. BS, Western Mich. U., 1976, MA, 1978, specialty program in alcohol and drug abuse, 1979, EdD, 1991. Substance abuse therapist Mercy Hosp., Muskegon, Mich.; pvt. practice Affiliated Psychol. Svcs., Muskegon, Assessment Ctr., Muskegon, Day Spring Counseling, Muskegon, Alpha Psychol., Muskegon. Mem.: APA (assoc.), Marriage and Family Network, Peace and Safety in the Christian Home, Soc. Christian Psychology, Psychology of Religion (divsn. 36), Internat. Soc. for the Study Personality Disorders, Am. Assn. Christian Counselors, Christian Assn. for Psychol. Studies (life). Republican. Avocations: music, theology, reading. Home: 2699 Scenic Dr Muskegon MI 49445 Office: Alpha Psychol Svcs Western Mich PLLC 1804 Oak Muskegon MI 49442 Office Phone: 231-773-8093. Personal E-mail: allanwcrummett@aol.com.

CRUMMETT, WARREN BERLIN, analytical chemistry consultant; b. Moyers, W.Va., Apr. 4, 1922; s. Elmer and Virginia Maude (Smith) C.; m. Elizabeth Ann Stathers, Feb. 28, 1948; children: Allan Warren, Daniel David. BA, Bridgewater Coll., Va., 1943; PhD, Ohio State U., 1951. Control chemist Solvay Process Co., Hopewell, Va., 1943-46; chemist Dow Chem. Co., Midland, Mich., 1951-55, lab. supr., 1955-61, asst. lab. dir., 1961-71, rsch. scientist, 1971-84, rsch. fellow, 1984-88; cons. chemist, Midland, 1988—. Mem. sci. adv. bd. EPA, Washington, 1976-78, cons., 1980; cons. USAF, Washington, 1981. Author: Decades of Dioxin, 2002; contbr. articles to sci. jours. Recipient H.H. Dow medal, 1980, Disting. Alumnus award Bridgewater Coll., 1983. Mem. Am. Chem. Soc. (chmn. analytical divsn. 1983, Midland sect. award 1987), Rsch. Soc. Am., N.Y. Acad. Scis. Achievements include research on hypothesis of trace chemistries of fire. Home and Office: 808 Crescent Dr Midland MI 48640-3434

CRUMMIE, ANN VAUGHN, mental health services professional; d. Edward McDonald Vaughn and Ruth Leila Vaugh-Martin; m. Robert Gwinn Crummie, Nov. 21, 1990; children: Robin, Ruby, Rebecca, Robert, Ryan, Rhett, Reid, Virginia; m. Nolan Paul Clark (div.); children: Jennifer, Scotty, Glenn, Carolyn. BS in Biology and Chemistry, Methodist Coll., Fayetteville, NC; MA in Edn., NC State U., MS in Psychology; PhD in Psychology, Union Univ. APA, NCMFT, AAMFT, LPC, NAADAC, CCAS, SAP. Profl. dancer, NYC; operator, instr. Ann Clark Schs. of Dance, Fayetteville, Elizabethtown, Clinton, NC; psychology instr. Meth. Coll. Ft. Bragg Edn. Ctr. Pembroke (N.C.) Univ.; mental health profl. Raintree Clinic, Rutherfordton, NC. Recipient Ronald Reagan award, 2004, 2005. Home: 236 Charlotte Rd Rutherfordton NC 28139-2914 Home Phone: 828-286-0505; Office Phone: 828-287-8861. E-mail: dravc@bellsouth.net.

CRUMP, FRANCIS JEFFERSON, III, lawyer; b. Alexandria, Va., Dec. 4, 1942; s. Ross Gault and Pauline C.; m. Nancy Jo Burkle, Aug. 20, 1966; children: Tom, Laura, Elizabeth. BS in Math., Va. Mil. Inst., 1964; JD, Ind. U., 1967. Bar: Ind. 1967, U.S. Dist. Ct. (so. dist.) Ind. 1967. Gen. ptnr. Jewell, Crump, Angermeier & Prall, Columbus, Ind., 1971—. Pres. First Nat. Corp.; mem. Columbus Fit, LLC, 2003—; bd. dirs., sec., treas. Hawpatch Corp. Past pres., bd. dirs. Columbus Boys' Club; past pres., bd. dirs., v.p., treas. Found. for Youth, Inc.; dir., sr. v.p. Babe Ruth Baseball, Inc., 1983-88; deacon First Presbyn. Ch. Columbus, 1972-75, elder 1977-79, 2000-03; bd. dirs. Ecumenical Assembly Barth County Chs., Inc., dir., 1999—, v.p., 2001, pres., 2002-03; dir. Presbyn. Found. Columbus, Ind., Inc., 2002—, Hoosier Hills Estate Planning Coun., 2000-2004, Love Chapel Found., Inc., 2007. Mem. Ind. State Bar Assn., Bartholomew County Bar Assn., Inc. (pres. 1983-84, treas., dir. 2001-07), Rotary, Phi Alpha Delta. Republican. Home and Office: PO Box 1061 Columbus IN 47202-1061 Office Phone: 812-376-9751. Personal E-mail: fjc@iquest.net.

CRUMP, GERALD FRANKLIN, retired lawyer; b. Sacramento, Feb. 16, 1935; s. John Laurin and Ida May (Banta) C.; m. Glenda Roberts Glass, Nov. 21, 1959; children: Sara Elizabeth, Juliane Kathryn, Joseph Stephen. AB, U. Calif., Berkeley, 1956; JD, U. Calif., 1959; MA, Baylor U., 1966. Bar: Calif. 1960. Dep. county counsel L.A. County, 1963-73, legis. rep., 1970-73, chief pub. works div., 1973-84, sr. asst. county counsel, 1984-85, chief asst. county counsel, 1985-97; ret., 1997. Lectr. Pepperdine U., 1978, U. Calif., 1982. Former v.p. San Fernando Valley Girl Scout Coun. Served to capt. USAF, 1960-63; to maj. gen. USAFR, 1963-95, ret.; mobilization asst. to the JAG. Decorated DSM, Legion of Merit. Mem. ABA, State Bar Calif., L.A. County Bar Assn. (past chmn. trustee govtl. law sect., past mem.exec. com. litig. sect.), Air Force Assn., Res. Officers Assn., Phi Alpha Delta, Delta Sigma Phi. Home: 4020 Camino De La Cumbre Sherman Oaks CA 91423-4522

CRUMP, JOHN, lawyer; Exec. dir. Nat. Bar Assn., Washington. Office: Nat Bar Assn 1225 11th St NW Washington DC 20001-4217

CRUMP, LINDA R., lawyer; b. NYC; BS in Biology, City Coll. NY; JD, U. Nebr., 1990. Teacher biology, gen. sci., physical sci. and physics Lincoln High Sch., Nebr.; asst. to chancellor equity, access & diversity programs U. Nebr., Lincoln. Co-chair Nebr. Minority Justice Com.; mem. Nebr. Commn. on Women, Homestead Girl Scout Coun.; mem. cmty. adv. bd. Nebr. Pub. Radio; bd. dirs. Sr. Ctr. Found., Lincoln Cmty. Found., Legal Services of Southeast Nebr.; mem. instl. rev. bd. Harris Lab.; bd. dirs. West Gate Bank, Planned Parenthood Nebr. Mem.: Nebr. State Bar Assn. (house of delegates 1992, chair 2000, pres. 2006—07). Office: Univ Nebraska Lincoln 128 Canfield Administration Lincoln NE 68588-0437 Office Phone: 402-472-3417.

CRUMP-CAINE, LYNN, food service executive; b. Aug. 11, 1956; Mgmt. trainee McDonald's Corp., Oakbrook, Ill., 1975—77, various regional dept. head positions Norfolk, Nashville, S. Fla., 1977—85, head worldwide restaurant systems and U.S. restaurant systems, 1985—97, regional v.p. Atlanta region Oakbrook, 1997—2001, exec. v.p. worldwide ops. and systems, 2001—04; CEO OutsideIn Consulting, 2004—. Bd. dirs. Krispy Kreme Doughnuts Corp., 2007—. Mem. adv. bd. Women Looking Ahead News Magazine; bd.dirs. Goodman Theater, Chgo. Recipient Outstanding Bus. and Profl. award, Dollars and Sense, 1991. Mem.: NAFE, McDonald's Black Employee Network. Office: OutsideIn Consulting Concourse Ctr 5 Concourse Pkwy Ste 3000 Atlanta GA 30328*

CRUMPLER, ALGE, professional football player; b. Greenville, NC, Dec. 23, 1977; s. Charleston Crumpler; m. Jenn Crumpler; 1 child, Kendal. BA in Comm., U.N.C., Chapel Hill, 2001. Tightend Atlanta Falcons, 2001—. Vol. Falcons Rush for Reading, 2001—. Named to All-ACC Team, 1998—2000, NFC Pro Bowl Team, 2005—07. Office: Atlanta Falcons 4400 Falcon Pkwy Flowery Branch GA 30542

CRUMPTON, CHARLES WHITMARSH, lawyer; b. Shreveport, La., May 29, 1946; s. Charles W. and Frances M. (McInnis) C.; m. Rebecca Woodland; children: Kim, Ian. BA, Carleton Coll., Northfield, Minn., 1968; MA, U. Hawaii, 1974, JD, 1978. Bar: Hawaii 1978, US Dist. Ct. Hawaii 1978, US Ct. Appeals (9th cir.) 1982. Tchr. dept. edn. State of Hawaii, Honolulu, 1972—73, 1975—77; Fulbright prof. U. Can Tho, Vietnam, 1973—75; assoc. John S. Edmunds, Honolulu, 1978—80, Ashford & Wriston, Honolulu, 1980—85, David W. Hall, Honolulu, 1985—88; dir. Hall & Crumpton, Honolulu, 1988—93; dir., shareholder Clay Chapman Crumpton Iwamura & Pulice, Honolulu, 1993—. Pres./dir. Internat. Law Found., 1996—; barrister Am. Inn of Ct. IV, Honolulu, 1985-87; arbitrator Court-Annexed Arbitration program 1st Cir. Ct. State of Hawaii, 1987—; arbitrator, mediator Am. Arbitration Assn., 1988—, Arbitration Forums, 1990—, Mediation Specialists, 1994—, Dispute Prevention & Resolution, 1995—; mem. com. on lawyer professionalism Hawaii State Jud. Conf., 1988-89; prof. Hawaii Pacific U., 1995—; faculty/spkr. on ins. law, employment law, alternative dispute resolution, civil litigation, 1993—. Asst. dir. youth vols. Am. Cancer Soc., Honolulu, 1972-73. Recipient Lawyer as Problem Solver award Mediation Ctr. of Pacific, 2005; named one of Best Am. Alternative Dispute Lawyers Woodward/White, 2005-; Fulbright grantee US Dept. State, 1973-75. Fellow Am. Coll. Civil Trial Mediators; mem. ATLA, ABA (torts and ins. practice sect., litig. sect., alt. dispute resolution sec.), Hawaii Bar Assn. (arbitrator, mediator fee disputes com. 1990—, jud. adminstrn. com. 1990—, jud. performances com. 1992-94, chair alt. dispute resolution sect. 1997), Inter-Pacific Bar Assn. Avocations: sports, guitar. Office: Clay Chapman Crumpton Iwamura & Pulice 700 Bishop St Ste 2100 Honolulu HI 96813-4120 Home: 1251 Heulu St Apt 1001 Honolulu HI 96822-3087 Home Phone: 808-521-4212; Office Phone: 808-535-8400. E-mail: crumpton@paclawteam.com.

CRUMPTON, HENRY A. (HANK CRUMPTON), former federal agency administrator; b. Athens, Ga., 1957; s. Dan and Charlene Crumpton; married; 3 children. BA in Polit. Sci., U. of New Mex.; MA in Internat. Pub. Policy, John Hopkins U. Dep. chief internat. terrorism ops. FBI US Dept. Justice, Washington, 1998—99; dep. chief counter terrorism ctr., spl. ops. CIA, 1999—2002, chief nat. resources divsn., 2003—05; amb. at large, coord. counter terrorism dept. US Dept. State, 2005—07. Contb. author Transforming U.S. Intelligence, 2005. Recipient George H.W. Bush award for excellence in counter terrorism, Sherman Kent award, Donovan award, others. Avocations: backpacking, fishing, hunting.

CRUNDWELL, DUNCAN JAMES, electronics executive; b. Maidstone, Kent, Eng., Mar. 18, 1957; arrived in US, 1995; s. James Stanley and June Crundwell; m. Bridgette Grieve, Dec. 24, 1983 (div. Jan. 1995); 1 child, Ben; m. Natasha Shankova, May 12, 1995. BSME, Brunel U., London, 1979; MBA, Henley Mgmt. Coll., Eng., 1996. Charterd engr. Student engr. Dowty Group, Cheltenham, Eng., 1975-79; chief engr. Yamco, London, 1979-80; tech. mgr. Bandive, London, 1980-84; custom projects mgr. Solid State Logic, Oxford, Eng., 1984-86, systems mgr., 1986-88, product group mgr., 1988-90; mng. dir. Solid State Logic Organ Systems, Brandon, Eng., 1990-95, CEO, pres. Detroit, 1995—2002, 1602 Group LLC, Alexandria, Va., 2002—; founding ptnr. People Going Global LLC, 2000—. Tchr. Opening Windows Engring., Oxford Schs., 1988—91; client, project mgr. new hdqs. bldg. Solid State Logic. Prodr.: (radio program) Glad to Be Gay or Not?, 1977 (UK Local Radio award, 1977). Recipient award, Royal Inst. Brit. Archs., 1989, Dir. Gen.'s cert., Engring. Coun., London, 1990. Mem.: Instn. Mech. Engrs. (chmn. YM panel 1988—89, sec. 1987—88, Outstanding Project Work award 1979). Anglican. Achievements include inventor in field. Avocations: photography, architecture, music, fine art. Office: 1602 Group LLC 4900 Seminary Rd Ste 560 Alexandria VA 22311-1009 Home: 4900 Seminary Rd Ste 560 Alexandria VA 22311-1811

CRUSE, JULIUS MAJOR, JR., pathologist, educator; b. New Albany, Miss., Feb. 15, 1937; s. Julius Major and Effie (Davis) C. BA, BS with honors, U. Miss., 1958; DMS with honors, U. Graz, Austria, 1960; MD, U. Tenn., 1964, PhD in Pathology (USPHS fellow), 1966. USPHS postdoctoral fellow, 1964-67; DD (hon.), Gen. Theol. Sem., NYC, 1999. Prof. immunology and biology Grad. Sch. U. Miss., 1967—74, prof. pathology, 1974—, assoc. prof. microbiology, 1974—, dir. grad. studies program in pathology, 1974—, dir. clin. immunopathology, 1978—, dir. immunopathology sect., 1978—, dir. tissue typing lab., 1980—, assoc. prof. medicine, 1989—, disting. prof. history medicine Med. Sch., 2003—, Guyton disting prof., 2004—. Lectr. pathology U. Tenn. Coll. Medicine, 1967-74; adj. prof. immunology Miss. Coll., 1977-92; mem. NIH study section on transplantation immunology, 1992; mem. sci. adv. bd. Immuno Tech. Corp., LA; active FDA Expert Panel on Alternatives to Silicone Breast Implants, 1994—. Author: Immunology Examination Review Book, 1971, rev. edit., 1975, Introduction to Immunology, 1977, Principles of Immunopathology, 1979; editor-in-chief Immunologic Rsch., 1981—, Pathology and Immunopathology Rsch., 1982-90, Concepts in Immunopathology, 1985—, The Year in Immunology, 1984—, Pathobiology: Jour. Immunopathology, Molecular and Cellular Biology, 1990-98, Exptl. & Molecular Pathology, 1999—, Transgenics: Biological Analysis Through DNA Transfer, 1992-; immunology cons.: Dorland's Illustrated Medical Dictionary, 1967-1994; contbns. to Microbiology and Immunology; editor Immunomodulation of Neoplasia, Antigenic Variation: Molecular and Genetic Mechanisms of Relapsing Disease, 1987, Autoimmunoregulation and Autoimmune Disease, 1987; The Year in Immunology, vol. 1, 1984-85, vol. 2, 1985-86, The Year in Immunology, vol. 3, 1987, The Year in Immunology, vols. 4, 5, 1988, vol. 6, 1989-90, Genetic Basis of Autoimmune Disease, 1988, Cellular Aspects of Autoimmunity, 1988, Therapy of Autoimmune Diseases, 1989, B Lymphocytes: Function and Regulation, Conjugate Vaccines, 1989, Molecules and Cells of Immunity, 1990, Immunoregulation and Autoimmunity, 1986, Organ-Based Autoimmune Diseases, 1985, Autoimmunity: Basic Concepts, Systemic and Selected Organ-Specific Diseases, 1985, Clinical and Molecular Aspects of Autoimmune Diseases, 1990, Immunoregulatory Cytokines and Cell Growth, 1989, Complement Profiles, 1992; co-editor: Self-Nonself Discrimination in the Immune System, 1992, Complement Profiles, vol. 1, 1992, Illustrated Dictionary of Immunology, 1995, 2d edit., 2003, Atlas of Immunology, 1998, 2d edit., 2003, Immunology Guidebook, 2004, Historical Atlas of Immunology, 2005, T.S. Eliot Bibliography, 2003, Historical Atlas of Immunology, 2005; editor-in-chief: Experimental and Molecular Pathology, 1999—; mem. editl. bd. Human Immunology, 2007-; contbr. chpts. to books and articles to profl. jours. Recipient Pathologists award in continuing edn. Coll. Am. Pathologists-Am. Soc. Clin. Pathologists, 1976; Julius M. Cruse collection in immunology established in his honor Middleton Med. Libr., U. Wis., Madison, 1979, Julius M. Cruse collection of T.S. Eliot's works, St. Mark's Libr., Gen. Theol. Sem. (Episcopal), NYC, Julius M. Cruse collection in history of immunology Rowland Med. Libr., U. Miss. Med. Ctr., 2004; Wilson Found. grantee, 1990-95, 93-94, 95-98, 99-2003; B.S. Guyton lectr. on history of medicine, 1998; Fulbright scholar U. Graz, Austria, 1958-60. Fellow AAAS, Royal Soc. Medicine, Royal Soc. Promotion Health, Am. Acad. Microbiology, Am. Soc. for Histocompatibility and Immunogenetics (chmn. publs. com. 1987-95, councillor 1997-99, historian 2000—), Intercontinental Biog. Assn.; mem. AMA (Physicians Recognition award 196-75), Clin. Immunology Soc., Am. Inst. Biol. Scis., Am. Soc. Clin. Pathologists, Can. Soc. Microbiologists, NY Acad. Scis. Exptl. Biology and Medicine, Am. Diabetes Assn., Soc. Francaise d'Immunologie, Reticuloendothelial Soc., Transplantation Soc., Electron Microscopy Soc. Am., Am. Assn. History Medicine, The Paul Ehrlich Soc., Am. Soc. Investigative Pathology, Am. Assn. Pathologists, Am. Chem. Soc., Brit. Soc. Immunology, Can. Soc. Immunology, Am. Soc. Microbiology, Internat. Acad. Pathology, Am. Assn. Immunologists (historian 1990—), T.S. Eliot Soc., Soc. of Mary, Mariological Soc. Am., Sigma Xi, Phi Kappa Phi, Phi Eta Sigma, Alpha Epsilon Delta, Gamma Sigma Epsilon, Phi Chi. Anglican Catholic. Office: U Miss Med Ctr Dept Pathology 2500 N State St Jackson MS 39216-4500 Office Phone: 601-984-1565. Business E-Mail: jcruse@pathology.umsmed.edu.

CRUSTO, MITCHELL FERDINAND, lawyer, educator; b. New Orleans, Apr. 22, 1953; BA magna cum laude, Yale U., 1975; BA, Oxford U., Eng., 1980, MA, 1985; JD, Yale U., 1981. Bar: La. 1982, Mo. 1984, Ill. 1985. Law clk. to Hon. John M. Wisdom U.S. Ct. Appeals (5th cir.), New Orleans, 1981-82; assoc. Jones, Walker, Waechter, Pointevent, Carrere & Denegre, New Orleans, 1982-84; sr. v.p., gen. counsel, asst. corp. sec. Stifel, Nicolaus & Co., Inc., St. Louis, 1984-88; CEO Crusto Capital Resources, Inc., St. Louis, 1988-89; assoc. dep. adminstr. for fin., investment and procurement U.S. Small Bus. Adminstrn., Washington, 1989-91; dir. corp. environ. policy Monsanto Co., St. Louis, 1991-93; sr. mgr. Arthur Andersen Environ. Svcs., Chgo., 1993-95; prof. Loyola Sch. Law, New Orleans, 1995—. Vis. prof. Vt. Law Sch., summers 2000-2003, Washington U. Sch. Law, summer 1999; mem. faculty Washington U., St. Louis, 1985-89, St. Louis U. Law Sch., 1987-88, Webster U., St. Louis, 1986; securities advisor to sec. of state State of Mo., 1986-89; lectr. legal divsn. Securities Industry Assn., 1986-88; mem. Pres. Clinton transition team natural resource cluster EPA, 1992; owner Angelic Asset Mgmt., 1998—. Contbr. articles in newspapers, mags., jours. Mem. ABA, La. Bar Assn., Mo. Bar Assn., Ill. Bar Assn., Middle Temple (London). Office: Loyola U Sch Law 7214 Saint Charles Ave # 901 New Orleans LA 70118-3538 Home: PO Box 410648 Saint Louis MO 63141-0648 Office Phone: 504-861-5743. Business E-Mail: mfcrusto@loyno.edu.

CRUTCHER, MICHAEL BAYARD, lawyer, retired consumer products company executive; b. Seattle, Apr. 7, 1944; s. M. Bayard and Marjorie (Sandstrom) C.; m. Judith Johnston, Aug 26, 1967; children: Alexandra, Andrew, Charles. BA, Yale U., 1966; JD, Harvard U., 1969. Bar: Wash. 1969, Ky. 1990. Assoc. Preston, Thorgrimson, Ellis & Holman, Seattle, 1969-73, ptnr., 1974-89; sr. v.p., gen. counsel, sec. Brown-Forman Corp., Louisville, 1989—2003, vice chmn., gen. counsel, sec., 2003—07. Bd. dirs. Distilled Spirits Coun. U.S., 1991-99, chmn., 1992-94; chmn. Internat. Ctr. Info. on Beverage Alcohol, 1994-95, Internat. Ctr. Alchohol Policy, 1996-97, Louisville Fund for Arts, 2004-; trustee Bellarmine U., 2003-. Republican. Home Phone: 502-459-5763; Office Phone: 502-774-7631. E-mail: michael_crutcher@b-f.com.*

CRUTCHER, RONALD ANDREW, academic administrator, music educator; b. Cin., Feb. 27, 1947; s. Andrew James and Burdella (Miller) C.; m. Betty Joy Neal, Nov. 24, 1979; 1 child, Sara Elizabeth. BM, Miami U., 1969; M in Musical Arts, Yale U., 1972; Diploma, State Acad. Music, Frankfurt, Germany, 1976; D in Musical Arts, Yale U., 1979. Cello instr. Bonn Sch. Music, Germany, 1973-76; asst. prof., head string program Wittenberg U. Sch. of Music, Springfield, Ohio, 1977-79; asst. prof. U. NC, Greensboro, 1979-84, assoc. prof., coord. string area, 1984—88, acting asst. vice chancellor academic affairs, 1988-89, assoc. vice chancellor academic affairs/faculty devel. and instrn., 1989-90; v.p. academic affairs, dean of conservatory, mem. chamber and cello music faculties Cleve. Inst. Music, 1990-94; dir. Sch. of Music U. Tex., Austin, 1994—99, Marie and Joseph D. Jamail Sr. Regents Prof. in Fine Arts, 1994—98, Florence Thelma Hall Chair in Music, 1998—99; provost, exec. v.p. academic affairs, prof. music Miami U., Ohio, 1999—2004; pres. Wheaton Coll., Norton, Mass., 2004—. Bd. dirs. Chamber Music Am., NY, 1993—01, v.p., 1994-96, pres., 1996-2000; bd. dirs. Fulbright Assn., 1998-2002, OhioLINK, 1999-; bd. dirs. Assn. Am. Colls. and Univs., 2000- , mem. exec. com., 2003- , chair, 2005—; mem. coun. acad. affairs Nat. Assn. State Univs. and Land Grant Colls., 2001-04, vice chair 2004-05, chair 2005-; bd. dirs. Cin. Opera Assn. 2001-04; mem. commn. on accreditation Nat. Assn. Schs. Music, Reston, Va., 1993—99; mem. adv. coun. Chgo. Civic Orch., 1994—96; mem. exec. com. Austin Symphony Orch., 1994—99; trustee Cavani Quartet, 1994-; trustee Musical Arts Assn./Cleve. Orch., 1993—96, internat. trustee, 1996-. Contbr. articles to jours. in field; Carnegie Hall debut, 1985; cellist The Klemperer Trio, 1980—. Bd. dirs. Am. Coun. Edn., 2007—; alumni adv. coun. Yale Sch. Music, 2000—02; bd. dirs. Posse Found., 2006—. Recipient Outstanding Svc. to Strings award, NC Chpt. Am. String Tchrs. Assn., 1983, Cultural Excellence award, Cleveland Music. Sch. Settlement, Cert. Merit, Yale Sch. Music Alumni Assn., 2000, Father of Yr. award, Boston, 2006; Woodrow Wilson fellow, 1969, Ford Found. fellow, 1969, Lucy G. Moses fellowship, Yale U., 1971-72, Fulbright fellow, Germany, 1972-74. Mem. Philos. Soc. Tex., Cum Laude Soc., Phi Beta Kappa (pres. 1987-89), Pi Kappa Lambda (pres. 1988-90), Phi Kappa Phi (Centennial Excellence Award, 1997), Sigma Pi Phi, Gamma Gamma Boulé, Alpha Phi Alpha. Avocations: fitness, cooking, bicycling, travel. Office: Wheaton Coll 115 Park Hall E Main St Norton MA 02766-2322 Home Phone: 508-622-1306; Office Phone: 508-286-3485. Business E-Mail: rcrutcher@wheatonma.edu.

CRUTCHFIELD, GEORGE THOMAS, journalism educator; b. Sutton, W.Va., Sept. 11, 1933; s. Harry Lee and Grace Rae (Gibson) C.; m. Carmen Rhodes, Aug. 28, 1955 (dec. Oct. 30, 1966); children: Lisa Susan, Laurence Steven; m. Frances Bailey, May 6, 1995; 1 stepchild, Henry Ruffin Broaddus. BS, Fla. So. Coll., 1955, DHL (hon.), 1990; MS, Fla. State U., 1959; postgrad., Syracuse U., 1959—63. Writer, editor Braxton Dem., Sutton, 1953-55; dir. pub. rels. Athens (Ala.) Coll., 1955-57; writer AP, Tallahassee, 1957-59; copy editor Syracuse (N.Y.) Post-Std., 1959-63; dir. coll. rels. Emory (Va.) & Henry Coll., 1963-65; asst. prof. U. S.C., Columbia, 1965-70; prof., dir. Sch. Mass. Comms. Va. Commonwealth U., Richmond, 1970-99; disting. prof., endowed chair in mass comms. Fla. So. Coll., Lakeland, 1999—2001. Educator-in-residence Richmond Newspapers, Inc., 1989-90. Bd. dirs. Better Bus. Bur., Richmond, 1991-2001, Va. Inst. Pastoral Care, Richmond, 1997—; bd. dirs. Tuckahoe Little League, Richmond, 1972-92, pres., 1978-79; bd. govs. Va. Home for Boys, Richmond, 1998—; exec. dir. N.Y. State Soc. Newspaper Editors, Syracuse, 1960-63, S.C. Scholastic Press Assn., Columbia, 1965-68; mem. exec. bd. Heart of Virginia coun. Boy Scouts Am., 1989—, v.p., 1989-2004. Recipient Communicator of Achievement award Va. Press Women, 1992, Disting. Alumnus award Fla. So. Coll., 1992, Silver Antelope award Boy Scouts Am., 1999; named to Va. Comms. of Fame, 1990. Mem. Soc. Profl. Journalists (George Mason award 1982), Fine Creek Club, Kappa Tau Alpha (nat. pres. 1986-88). Episcopalian. Avocations: camping, backpacking. Home: 1196 Huguenot Tr Midlothian VA 23113 Personal E-mail: oldscouts2@aol.com.

CRUTCHFIELD, JAMES N., publishing executive; b. McKeesport, Pa., Dec. 7, 1947; m. Cynthia L. Parish; 1 child. BA in Journalism, Duquesne U., 1992. Reporter Pitts (Pa.) Press, 1968-71; pub. info. officer Pitts. Model Cities Program., 1971; reporter Pitts. Post-Gazette, 1971-76, Detroit Free Press, 1976-79; press. sec. for U.S. Sen. Carl Levin of Mich., 1979-81; chief of bur. Free Press., Lansing, Mich., 1981-83; asst. city editor, dep. city editor, dept. mng. editor Free Press, Lansing, Mich., 1983-89; mng. editor Akron (Ohio) Beacon Jour., 1989—93; exec. editor Press-Telegram, Long Beach, Calif., 1993—98; gen. man. Akron (Ohio) Beacon Journal, 1999—2001, pres., 2001—, pub., 2001—. Bd. dirs. Duquesne U. Mem. accrediting coun. Edn. Journalism and Mass Comm.; bd. trustees Found. Am. Comm.; mem. bd. John S. and James L. Knight Found., United Way Summit County. Mem.: Ohio Newspaper Assn., Asian Am. Journalists Assn., Nat. Assn. Minority Media Execs., Nat. Assn. Black Journalists, Am. Soc. Newspaper Editors.

CRUTCHFIELD, MARJORIE ALICE, retired elementary school educator, director; 2 children. BE in Music and Edn., Fresno State Coll., Calif., 1943; MEd, Loyola U. LA, 1964; EdD in Elem. and Curriculum Edn., UCLA, 1970. Life credential in elem. edn., elem. adminstrn., reading specialist. Elem. tchr. Bakersfield City Sch. Dist., Calif., 1943—44, Broward County Sch. Dist. Pompano Sch., Ft. Lauderdale, Fla., 1944—45, Hawthorne City Sch. Dist., Calif., 1946—49, 1951—52, Fresno Unified Sch. Dist., Calif., 1949—51, Manhattan Beach City Sch. Dist., Calif., 1952—63, elem. prin., 1963—66, 1969—73, dir. compensatory edn., 1966—68, dir. reading and spl. projects, 1968—69; part-time asst. prof. edn. Calif. State U. Dominguez Hills, 1973; asst. prof. edn., dir. early childhood edn. Loyola Marymount U., LA, 1973—80; ret., 1980. Per diem cons. in reading Ency. Britannica Ednl. Corp., Chgo., 1967—70; vis. asst. prof. Loyola U. LA, 1972. Author: The Kindergarten Teacher's Handbook, 1973, Individualized Reading: A Guide for Teaching Word Analysis Skills, 1975, Elementary Social Studies. An Interdisciplinary Approach, 1978. Chairperson Manhattan Beach Sister Com. Inc., 1971, 1981, 1995, 1996; neighborhood watch block capt. Manhattan Beach Lions Club, 2001—02, pres., 2001—02, 2002—03; zone chairperson dist. 4-L3 so. region zone B Lions Internat., 2003—04, region chairperson dist. 4-L3 so. region zone B, 2006—07; coordinating coun. bd. mem. Manhattan Beach, 1965—75; bd. mem. US/Mex. Sister Cities Assn., 1975; bd. mem. So. Calif. chpt. Sister Cities Internat., 1975; mem. Soroptimist Internat., 1970—75, Quota Club Internat., 1986—91, Calif. Agrl. Literacy Fair Found.; mem. bd. dirs. South Bay Aux. to Children's Hosp., 1999—2002; life mem. PTA, 1973. Named Citizen of Yr., Manhattan Beach Lions Club, 1983, Lion of Yr. award, 2006; recipient and honoree, LA County Older Ams., 2001, honored with Recognition Day outstanding vol. svc., Pres.'s cert. of appreciation, Lions Internat., 2003. Mem.: NEA (life), Lions Club Internat. (Melvin Jones fellow), Lions Club (Excellence award 2007).

CRUTCHFIELD, SUSAN RAMSEY, neurophysiologist; b. Pasadena, Calif., Oct. 7, 1941; d. Henry Colwell Ramsey and Rowena Ruth (Lockett) Banning; m. Ralph L. Crutchfield, Sept. 26, 1964 (div. Sept. 1973); children: Pamela Montague, Ashley Noland. AA, Pine Manor Coll., 1961; student, Sorbonne U., Paris, 1961-62; BA, George Washington U., 1964; MA, U. Calif., San Diego, 1978; PhD, Aston U., Birmingham, Eng., 1986. Rsch. assoc. U. Calif. Med. Ctr., San Diego, 1978-80, rschr., 1986-89, clin. instr. dept. pediats. divsn. neonatology, 1989-94, asst. clin. prof. depts. ophthalmology and pediat., 1994-98, clin. prof. dept. pediat., 1998—; rschr. Birmingham U., England, 1980-86. Owner Daisy's Bookstore and the Ute Theater, LLC. Mem. AAAS, NY Acad. Scis., European Neurosci. Soc., Internat. Soc. Clin. Electrophysiology Vision, Assn. Rsch. Vision and Ophthalmology, Brit. Soc. Neurophysiology, La Jolla Beach and Tennis Club, Univ. Club (San Diego). Avocations: camping, horseback riding, hiking, photography, gardening. Office: Univ Calif San Diego Pediat Divsn San Diego CA 92103-0831 Home: PO Box 190 Embudo NM 87531 Home Phone: 505-579-4697; Office Phone: 303-818-5180. Personal E-mail: daisyute@earthlink.net.

CRUTCHFIELD, WILLIAM GAYLE, JR., retail executive; b. Charlottesville, Va., Oct. 14, 1942; s. William Gayle and Theresa F. (Saltzsieder) Crutchfield; m. Jana Kay Heischman, Dec. 5, 1981 (div. 2004); children: Jennifer Anne, William Gayle III; m. Scheline Thornton, Sept. 23, 2006. BS in Commerce, U. Va., 1965. Asst. to pres. Ridge Electronics Corp., Charlottesville, 1972—75; sec.-treas. Haight Engring. Co., Inc., Charlottesville, 1972—75; pres. Crutchfield Corp., Charlottesville, 1974—. Vis. lectr. Darden Grad. Bus. Sch. U. Va.; participant Carter Ctr.'s Consultation Competitiveness, 1988. Bd. visitors U. Va., 1997—2005; mem. ops. bd. U. Va. Med. Ctr., 2002—05; chmn. adv. bd. McIntire Sch. Commerce U. Va., 1981—85; mem. Gov.'s Commn. on Efficiency and Effectiveness, 2002; exec.-in-residence McIntire Sch. Commerce U. Va., 1992. Capt. USAF, 1966—70. Decorated Air Force Commendation medal; named Ctrl. Va. Marketer of Yr., Am. Mktg. Assn., 1983; named to Dealerscope Hall of Fame, 2001, Hall of Fame, Consumer Electronics Assn., 2007; recipient award, SBA, 1980, Entrepreter of Yr. for Va., Ernst & Young, 1999. Mem.: Chief Exec. Orgn., World Presidents Orgn., Va. Strategic Coun., Raven Soc., Young Pres. Orgn., SC Yacht Club, Farmington Country Club, Beta Gamma Sigma. Republican. Home: 2406 Northfield Rd Charlottesville VA 22901-1728 Office: 1 Crutchfield Park Charlottesville VA 22911 Home Phone: 434-975-3085; Office Phone: 434-817-1000. E-mail: bcrutchfield@crutchfield.com.

CRUTHIRD, BRANDY K., gym owner and fitness instructor; BS in Communications and Pub. Rels., James Madison Univ., Harrisonburg, VA. Former mktg. rep. Reebok Internat., Inc.; founder, owner, pres. Body by Brandy Fitness, Boston, 1996—. Contbr. articles to profl. online jours. Fitness demonstrator YWCA Breast Cancer Awareness Day, Af. Am. Women on Tour Convention; co-organizer Everybody Walk Your Body Fitness and Health Fair, Boston, 1997—. Named Rookie Yr., NCAA Women's Basketball; named one of 40 Under 40, Boston Bus. Jour., 2005; recipient Girl Scout's Leading Women award, 2001, Rebecca Lee award, Harvard Univ., 2002. Home: Body by Brandy 2181 Washington St Roxbury MA 02119

CRUVER, SUZANNE LEE, communications executive, writer; b. Indpls., Mar. 24, 1942; d. William Edward and Margaret Rosetta (McArtor) Ozzard; m. Donald Richard Cruver, June 9, 1963 (div. Feb. 1989); children: Donald Scott, Kimberly Sue, Brian Richard. BA in English, Rutgers U., 1964; postgrad., Rice U., 1990—. Asst. dir. pub. rels. dept. Upsala Coll., East Orange, N.J., 1964-65; asst. planner, pub. editor N.J. Divsn. State & Regional Planning, Trenton, 1967-68; realtor Vonnie Cobb Realtors, Houston, 1979-81; owner Sugar Land Comm., 1980-94; exec. v.p., mktg. mgr. Photoflight Aviation Corp., Sugar Land, Tex., 1982; exec. v.p., artist mgr. H. McMillan Orgn., Inc., Sugar Land, 1983-85; account exec. Mel Anderson Comm., Inc., Houston, 1986; exec. dir. Ft. Bend Arts Coun., Sugar Land, 1986-87; dir. resource devel., vol. svcs., pub. info. Richmond (Tex.) State Sch., Tex. Dept. Mental Health/Mental Retardation, 1987-93; dir. corp. and found. giving Meml. Found., Meml. Healthcare Sys., Houston, 1993-94; owner SLC Comms., Houston & Englewood, Fla., 1994-2000; mktg. coord., pub. info. officer Gulf Coast Workforce Bd. Houston-Galveston Area Coun., 2000—. Mem. adv. bd. Ft. Bend Regional Coun. on Alcoholism and Drug Abuse, Rosenburg, Tex., 1989—. Writer, editor: PATCH Handbook: A Parent to Parent Guide to Texas Children's Hospital, 1983, Ft. Bend mag., 1985-86; book editor, contbg. writer: Fort Bend County, Texas - A Pictorial History, 1996. Pres. Ft. Bend Arts Coun., Ft. Bend County, Tex., 1987-89; founding dir. PATCH, Tex. Children's Hosp., Houston, 1982; mem. adv. bd. Challenger Ctr. of Ft. Bend; committeeman Houston Livestock Show & Rodeo, 1996—; co-coord. 25th Anniversary of lunar landing celebration and internat. space expo, Houston, 1994; bd. dirs. United Way South Sarasota County. Mem. NAFE, Nat. Soc. Fundraising Execs., Women in Comm., Ft. Bend Profl. Women, Pub. Rels. Soc. Am., Houston (Tex.) Advt. Fedn., Houston World Trade Assn., Ft. Bend C. of C., Rosenberg/Rich C. of C., Leadership Tex. Alumni Assn., Exch. Club of Sugar Land, Ft. Bend Exch. Club (charter bd. mem.). Republican. Presbyterian. Avocations: travel, scuba diving, golf, dance, photography. Business E-Mail: sue.cruver@theworksource.org.

CRUZ, DENIS J., elementary school educator; b. Waterloo, Iowa; Tchg. cert. Calif. State Univ.-Long Beach. Lang. arts. tchr. Whittier (Calif.) Elem. Sch. Named Calif. Tchr. of Yr., 2006. Mem.: Whittier Elem.Tchr. Assn. Office: Katherine Edwards Mid Sch 6812 S Norwalk Blvd Whittier CA 90606 E-mail: cruzin5@mylifeline.net.*

CRUZ, JOSE BEJAR, JR., engineering educator; b. Bacolod City, Sept. 17, 1932; came to U.S., 1954, naturalized, 1969; s. Jose P. and Felicidad (Bejar) C.; m. Stella E. Rubia; children by previous marriage: Fe E. Cruz Langdon, Ricardo A., Rene L., Sylvia C. Cruz Loebach, Loretta C. Cruz Spray. BSEE summa cum laude, U. Philippines, 1953; MS in Elec. Engring., MIT, Cambridge, Mass., 1956; PhD in Elec. Engring., U. Ill., 1959. Lic. profl. engr., Ill., Ohio. Instr. elec. engring. U. Philippines, Quezon City, 1953-54; rsch. asst. MIT, Cambridge, 1954-56, vis. prof., 1973; from instr. to assoc. prof. U. Ill., Urbana-Champaign, 1956-65, prof. elec. engring., 1965-86, assoc. mem. Ctr. Advanced Study, 1967-68; rsch. prof. Coordinated Sci. Lab., 1965-86; prof. dept. elec. and computer engring. U. Calif., Irvine, 1986-92, chmn. dept., 1986-90; prof. elec. engring. Ohio State U., Columbus, 1992—2004, dean Coll. Engring., 1992-97, Howard D. Winbigler chair in engring., 1997—2004, dist. prof. engring., 2004—. Vis. assoc. prof. U. Calif., Berkeley, 1964-65; vis. prof. Harvard U., 1973; pres. Dynamic Sys.; theory com. Am. Automatic Control Coun., 1967; gen. chmn. Conf. on Decision and Control, 1975; mem. profl. engring. exam. com. State of Ill., 1984-86; mem. Nat. Coun. Engring. Examiners, 1985-86; project adv. group on engring. and sci. edn. project Dept. Sci. and Tech., Republic of The Philippines, 1993-98. Author: (with M.E. Van Valkenburg) Introductory Signals and Circuits, 1967, (with W.R. Perkins) Engineering of Dynamic Systems, 1969, Feedback Systems, 1972, translated into Chinese, 1976, Polish, 1977, System Sensitivity Analysis, 1973, (with M.E. Van Valkenburg) Signals in Linear Circuits, 1974, translated into Spanish, 1978; Assoc. editor: Jour. Franklin Inst, 1976-82, Jour. Optimization Theory and Applications, 1980—; series editor Advances in Large Scale Systems Theory and Applications; contbr. articles on network theory, automatic control systems, system theory, sensitivity theory of dynamical systems, large scale systems, dynamic games and dynamic scheduling in mfg. systems to sci., tech. jours. Recipient Purple Tower award Beta Epsilon U., Philippines, 1969, Diamond award, 1999, Curtis W. McGraw Rsch. award Am. Soc. for Engring. Edn., 1972, Halliburton Engring. Edn. Leadership award, 1981, Most Outstanding Alumnus award U. of the Philippines Alumni Assn. Am., 1989, Most Outstanding Overseas Alumnus Coll. Engring., U. of the Philippines Alumni Assn., 1990, Richard E. Bellman Control Heritage award Am. Automatic Control Coun., 1994, others Fellow AAAS (sect. com. for sect. on engring. 1991-94, sec. 1998-2003, chmn.-elect 2003-04, chmn. 2004-05, ret. chair 2005-06, mem. coun. 2005-06) Am. Soc. Engring Edn. (awards policy com., Terman awards com.), IEEE (chmn. linear sys. com., group on automatic control 1966-68, assoc. editor Trans. on Circuit Theory 1962-64), Internat. Fedn. Automatic Control (chmn. theory com. 1981-84, vice-chmn. tech. bd. 1984-87, policy com. 1987-93, vice-chmn. 1993, 99, chmn. 1996, congress internat. program com.); mem. Control Sys. Soc. (adminstrv. com. 1966-75, 78-80, v.p. fin. and adminstrv. activities 1976-77, pres. 1979, chmn. awards com. 1973-75, ednl. activities bd. 1973-75, editor Trans. on Automatic Control 1971-73, tech. activities bd. 1979-83, chmn. 1982-83, v.p. tech. activities 1982-83, edn. med. com. 1977-79, dir. 1980-85, vice-chmn. publs. bd. 1981, chmn. 1984-85, chmn. panel of tech. editors 1981, chmn. TAB periodicals com. 1981, chmn. PUB. Soc. publs. com. 1981, v.p. publ. activities 1984-85, exec. com. 1982-85, Richard M. Emberson award 1989), Philippine Engrs. and Scientists Orgn., US Nat. Acad. Engring. (peer com. for electronics engring. 1982, 2000-04, vice-chmn. 2002-03, chmn. 2003-04, com. on nat. agenda for career-long edn. for engrs. 1986-88, membership com. 1987-90, 2003-07, acad. adv. bd. 1994-97, com. on diversity in engring. workforce 1999-2001), Nat. Acad. for Sci. and Tech. (corr.), Philippine-Am. Acad. Sci. and Engring. (founding mem. 1980, pres. 1982, chmn. bd. dirs. 1998-2000, Founders Lecture award 2001), Philippine Engrs. and Scientists Orgn., Sigma Xi, Phi Kappa Phi, Eta Kappa Nu. Roman Catholic. Achievements include introduction of concept of comparison sensitivity in dynamical feedback systems, of leader-follower strategies in hierarchical engineering systems; development of synthesis methods for time-varying systems. Office: Ohio State Univ Dept Elec & Computer Engring 2015 Neil Ave Columbus OH 43210-1272 Office Phone: 614-292-1588. Personal E-mail: jbcruz@ieee.org. Business E-Mail: cruz@ece.osu.edu.

CRUZ, JUAN-CARLOS, chef; married. Grad., Calif. Culinary Acad., 1993. Apprentice Amillios Restaurant, San Francisco; pastry chef Stanford Park Hotel, 1994—96; pastry sous chef Hotel Bel Air, 1996—2001; founder, exec. pastry chef Pastrydude.com, LA, 2001—; owner, exec. chef Calorie Commando Catering, LA; tchr. Chefs Inc. School of Culinary Arts, LA. Appearances on (TV series) Body Challenge, Discovery Health Network, Body Challenge 2, Body Challenge 3, Soap Center, Soap Opera Network, The Modern Girls Guide to Life, Style Network, Cooking School

Stories, Food Network, (TV specials) Countdown to the Academy Awards, E!, Celebrity Diets, VH1, host (TV series) Calorie Commando, Weighing In, Food Network, Take It Off, 2005—. Vol. Love on 4 Paws, LA Children's Hospital. Office: TV Food Network GP 1180 Ave of Americas 11th Fl New York NY 10036*

CRUZ, MICHAEL W., lieutenant governor, surgeon; s. Miguel de Gracia and Rosalinda Quinata Cruz; m. Jennifer Rosario Cruz; children: Shaunn, Mika'ele, Christine, Christian Payumo. BS in Biology, Walla Walla Coll.; MD, Loma Linda U. Sch. Med., 1984. Surgeon, Guam; med. dir. Guam Meml. Hosp.; senator Territory of Guam, 2004—07, chmn. Com. on Health and Human Svcs., vice chmn. Com. on Natural Resources, Utilities and Micronesian Affairs, Com. on Aviation, Immigration, Labor and Housing, lt. gov., 2007—. Contbr. articles to profl. jours. Pres. Ayuda Found. Col. Guam Army Nat. Guard. Decorated Bronze Star Medal; recipient Nat. Govs. Award, 2004. Fellow: Am. Coll. Surgeons; mem.: Guam Med. Soc. Office: Office of Lt Gov PO Box 2950 Hagatna GU 96932 Office Phone: 671-475-9380. Office Fax: 671-477-2007. E-mail: ltgov@mail.gov.gu.*

CRUZ, NELSON XAVIER, healthcare executive; b. NYC, June 30, 1950; s. Jaime and Angela (Vega) C.; m. Asuncion Rosado, July 10, 1971 (div. 1976); children: Celena, Jasmin; m. Lydia Cordero, 1987; 1 child, Lauren A. BA, Hunter Coll., 1974; MS, Herbert H. Lehman Coll., 1978; MBA, Manhattan Coll., 1985; JD, Rutgers U., 1998. CLU, ChFC. Recreation therapist Bronx (N.Y.) Children's Psychiat. Hosp., 1974-78; dir. rehab. svc. Rockland Children's Psychiat. Hosp., Orangeburg, NY, 1978-79; dir. mkgt. Fordham-Tremont Community Mental Health Ctr., Bronx, 1979-83; adminstr. dept. emergency Woodhull Hosp., Bklyn., 1983-85, assoc. dir. quality assurance, 1985-86; dir., fin. CFO Promesa, Inc., Bronx, 1986-87; adminstr. ambulatory care network Bronx-Lebanon Hosp. Ctr., 1987-92; exec. dir. United Cmty. Health Plan/United Hosps. Med. Ctr., Newark, 1992-95; dir. network devel. PruCare HMO, Prudential Life Ins. Co. of Am., Iselin, NJ, 1995-97; v.p., COO Universal Inst., Inc., Livingston, NJ, 1997-98; mgr. St. Mary's Hosp. Family Health Ctr., 1998-2000; pres., CEO Henry J. Austin Health Ctr., Inc., Trenton, NJ, 2001—04; dir. Hurtado Health Ctr., Rutgers U. Health Svcs., New Brunswick, NJ, 2000-01; CEO Jewish Renaissance Med. Ctr., 2004—. Project coord., cons. Inst. Puerto Rican Hispanic Elderly, N.Y.C., 1983; account exec. Medi-Scan, Inc., Worcester, Mass., 1983; healthcare mktg. cons. BSquared Comm., Inc., 1999-2000. Adv. bd. Bronx Legal Aid Soc.; bd. dirs. Community Planning Bd. 6, 1981-82; mem. Bronx-Boro-Wide Mental Health Svcs. Com., 1979-81. Leadership Mgmt. Urban Execs. Inst. fellow, Rutgers U., 1996; Leadership N.J. fellow, 1994—; Hispanic Leadership Opportunity Program fellow, 1993-94. Fellow Am. Managed Care and Rev. Assn. (cert.); mem. Am. Coll. Healthcare Execs. (diplomate, cert. health care exec.), Assn. Healthcare Execs. of N.J., Med. Group Mgmt. Assn., Am. Coll. Med. Practice Execs., Group Health Assn. Am., Am. Coll. CLUs and ChFCs, N.J. Med. Group Mgmt. Assn., Am. Coll. Healthcare Mktg., Hispanic Assn. Health Svcs. Execs. (mktg. cons. 1986-87), N.Y. Assn. Ambulatory Care, Health Adminstrs. Assn. N.Y., Acad. Health Svcs. Mktg., Nat. Assn. Health Svcs. Execs. Democrat. Roman Catholic. Avocations: running, squash, swimming, music. Office: Jewish Renaissance Med Ctr 149 Kearny Ave Perth Amboy NJ 08861 Office Phone: 732-293-0135. Personal E-mail: nelxav@aol.com. Business E-Mail: nelsonxaviercruz@comcast.net.

CRUZ, PENELOPE, actress; b. Madrid, Apr. 28, 1974; d. Eduardo and Encarna Cruz. Studied classical ballet, Nat. Conservatory, Madrid. Actor: (films) El Laberinto griego, 1991, Belle époque, 1992, Jamón, jamón, 1992, La Ribelle, 1993, La Celestina, 1996, Más que amor, frenesí, 1996, Et Hjørne af paradis, 1997, Carne trémula, 1997, Abre los ojos, 1997, Don Juan, 1998, The Man with Rain in His Shoes, 1998, Talk of Angels, 1998, La Niña de tus ojos, 1998, The Hi-Lo Country, 1998, Todo sobre mi madre, 1999, Volavérunt, 1999, Woman on Top, 2000, All the Pretty Horses, 2000, Blow, 2001, Captain Corelli's Mandolin, 2001, Sin noticias de Dios, 2001, Vanilla Sky, 2001, Waking Up in Reno, 2002, Masked and Anonymous, 2003, Fanfan la tulipe, 2003, Gothika, 2003, Noel, 2004, Head in the Clouds, 2004, Sahara, 2005, Chromophobia, 2005, Bandidas, 2006, Volver, 2006 (Hollywood Actress of the Yr. award, Hollywood Awards, 2006, Best Actress, European Film Awards, 2006, Runner-up, Best Actress award, LA Film Critics Assn., 2006); (TV films) Framed, 1992. Founder Sabera Found. Named a Knight in Order of Arts and Letters, France, 2006. Office: Creative Artists Agy 9830 Wilshire Blvd Beverly Hills CA 90212*

CRUZ, TED, lawyer; s. Rafael Bienvenido and Eleanor Elizabeth (Darragh) Cruz; m. Heidi Suzanne Nelson, May 27, 2001. AB cum laude, Princeton U., Princeton, NJ., 1992; JD magna cum laude, Havard Law Sch., Cambridge, Mass., 1995. Bar: Tex. 1997, D.C. 1998. Law clk. U.S. Ct. Appeals 4th Cir., Washington, 1995—96, U.S. Supreme Ct., Washington, 1996—97; atty. Cooper, Carvin, and Rosenthal, Washington, 1997—99; domestic policy advisor Bush - Cheney 2000, Austin, Tex., 1999—2000; assoc. dep. atty. gen. U.S. Dept. of Justice, Washington, 2001; dir. of policy Fed. Trade Comm., Washington, 2001—03; solicitor gen. of Tex. Austin, Tex., 2003—; adj. prof. U. Tex. Sch. of Law, 2004—. Bd. dirs. Criminal Justice Legal Found. Editor: (primary) Harvard Law Rev., 1995, (exec.) Harvard Jour. of Law and Pub. Policy, 1995, (co founding) Harvard Latino Law Rev. Dept. Justice Coord. Bush Cheney Transition Team, Washington, 2001; atty. Bush Cheney Presdl. Recount, Fla., 2000; poineer Bush-Cheney '04; found. dir. Tex. Mavericks. Named Traphagen Disting. Alumnus, Harvard Law Sch.; named one of 20 Young Hispanics to Watch, Newsweek Mag., 1999, 50 Most Influential People in Politics, George Mag, 2001, Litigation's Rising Stars, Am. Lawyer, 2007, 100 Most Influential Hispanics, Hispanic Business Mag.; recipient Best US Supreme Ct. Merits Brief award, Nat. Assn. Attys. Gen., 2003, 2004, 2005. Mem.: Tex. Rev. of Law and Politics (steering com.), Tex. Lyceum (dir., v.p.), Tex. Hispanic Alliance Progress (chmn.). Republican. Office: Office of Atty Gen PO Box 12548 Austin TX 78711 Office Phone: 512-936-1700.

CRUZ, WILHELMINA MANGAHAS, critical care physician, educator; b. Bulacan, Philippines, July 20, 1942; d. Rectorino Bernardo and Mercedes Correa (Mangahas) C.; m. Antonio I. Lee, May 28, 1977; children: Richard Anthony, Alexander Victor. AA, U. Santo Tomas, The Philippines, 1960, MD, 1965. Diplomate in internal medicine and critical care medicine Am. Bd. Internal Medicine; diplomate Am. Bd. Nephrology. Intern Meml. Hosp., Albany, NY, 1967-68; resident in internal medicine Coney Island Hosp., Bklyn., 1968-71; fellow in nephrology VA Hosp., Bronx, 1971-72, SUNY Downstate Med. Ctr., Bklyn., 1972-73; staff physician King's County Hosp. Ctr., Bklyn., 1973-76; coord. in medicine Kingsbrook Jewish Med. Ctr., Bklyn., 1976—. Assoc. med. dir. ICU Drs. Cmty. Hosp., Lanham, Md., 1977-99; med. dir. Critical Care Svcs., 1999—; clin. asst. prof. SUNY Downstate Med. Ctr., 1977—. Mem. ACP, Med. and Chirurg. Soc. Md., Prince George's Med. Soc., Soc. Critical Care Medicine, Philippine Med. Assn. Washington. Roman Catholic. Office: PO Box 34534 Bethesda MD 20827 Office Phone: 301-552-5693.

CRUZ, ZOE, diversified financial services company executive; b. Feb. 2, 1955; m. Ernesto Cruz. BA in Literature, Harvard U., 1977, MBA, 1982. With Morgan Stanley, 1982—, v.p., 1986—88, prin., fixed income, 1988—90, mng. dir., fixed income, 1990—93, co-chief, fgn. exch., 1993—2000, head of worldwide fixed income, fgn. exch. and commodities, 2000—05, acting pres., 2005—06, co-pres., 2005, 2006—, bd. dirs., 2005—. Named one of Most Powerful Women, Forbes mag., 2005—06, 50 Women To Watch, Wall St. Jour., 2005, 2006, 50 Most Powerful Women in Bus., Fortune mag., 2006. Office: Morgan Stanley 1585 Broadway New York NY 10036*

CRUZ-CONNERTON, MAYRA, elementary school educator; d. Louis Cruz and Maria Christina Quiñones-Cruz; m. Christopher Charles Connerton, Aug. 29, 1998; children: Isabella Maria Connerton(dec.) , Julian Christopher Connerton, Gabriel Ryan Connerton. BA in English Lit., Georgian Ct. Coll., 1993, postgrad., 1994—. Tchr. Atlantic City (N.J.) Bd. Edn., 1997—. Adj. prof. Atlantic Cape C.C., NJ, 2006. Author: When Children Go to Heaven, 2004. Named Gov.'s Tchr. of Yr., State of N.J., 1998—99. Democrat. Roman Catholic. Avocations: reading, writing.

CRUZ-ROMO, GILDA, soprano; b. Guadalajara, Jalisco, Mexico; came to U.S., 1967; d. Feliciano and Maria del Rosario (Diaz) C.; m. Robert B. Romo, June 10, 1967. Grad., Coll. Nueva Galicia, Guadalajara, 1958; student, Nat. Conservatory of Music of Mexico, Mexico City, 1962-64. Tchr. voice U. Tex., Austin, 1990—. Assoc. prof., coach, voice tchr. U. Tex., Austin, 1990—. With, Nat. and Internat. Opera, Mexico City, 1962-67, toured, Australia, N.Z., S.Am., with, Dallas Civic Opera, 1966-68, N.Y.C. Opera, 1969-72, Lyric Opera Chgo., 1975, Met. Opera debut as Madama Butterfly, 1970, leading soprano, 1970—, appeared in U.S. and abroad including Covent Garden, La Scala, Vienna State Opera, Rome Opera, Paris Opera, Florence Opera, Torino Opera, Verona Opera, Portugal, Buenos Aires, others, concert appearances in U.S., Can., Mexico; U.S. rep. World-Wide Madama Butterfly Competition, Tokyo, 1970; La Scala rep. in: Aida, USSR, 1974; appeared on radio, TV; filmed and recorded: Aida, with Orange Festival, France, 1976; roles include Aida, Madama Butterfly, Suor Angelica, Tosca, Odabella in Attila; Manon Lescaut, Leonora in Il Trovatore; Norma; Maddelena in Andrea Chenier; Desdemona in Otello; Donna Anna in Don Giovanni; Santuzza in Cavalleria Rusticana; (title role) La Gioconda; Adriana Lecouvreur; Luisa Miller; Elisabetta in Don Carlo; Margherite in Faust; Venus in Tannhauser; Giorgetta in Il Tabarro; also roles in Macbeth, Turnadot, Norma, Medea. Named Winner Met. Opera Nat. Auditions, 1970, Best Singer, 1976—77, honoree, Opera Guild of San Antonio, 2003; recipient Critics award, Union Mexicana de Cronistas de Teatro y Musica, 1973, Minerva al Arte award, Mexico, 1991, Silver Bird award, Govt. of Jalisco, Mexico, 1998, season Cronistas de Santiago de Chile, 1976, Baccarat 2001 award, The Licia Albanese-Puccini Found., 2001, Lifetime Achievement award, Nat. Opera Assn., 2003, Pedro Sarquis Merrewe Found., 2004, Gold medal fine arts, Bellas Artec, Mex., 2006. Personal E-mail: bobgilda2@sbcglobal.net.

CRYE, HAROLD, real estate company executive; married; 3 children. BBA, Ark. State U., 1967; ed., Quartermaster Sch., US Army, Ft. Lee, Va., 1968; ed. in Fundamentals of Real Estate, Memphis State U., 1973. Cert. Grad. Realtors Inst., 1974, Cert. Residential Specialist, 1978, Cert. Real Estate Brokerage Mgr., 1981. Mgmt. trainee Container Corp. Am., 1970—73; sales mgr. The Sterling Co., 1973—76; cofounder, mng. ptnr. Crye-Leike, Memphis, 1977, founder, pres. Nashville, 1992, Chattannooga, 1997, Johnson City, 2000, Little Rock, 2002; pres. Crye-Leike Ins. Agy.; chmn. Realty Alliance, Dallas. Bd. dirs. First Trust Bank, Realty Title & Escrow Inc, Realty Alliance, 1997—2000, Homestore.com, Inc.; bd. dirs. and vice chmn. Relo Internat., 2002—. Bd. dirs. Memphis Better Bus. Bur.; pres. Chickasaw Coun. Boy Scouts of Am., 1991—92; mem. Youth Villages, United Way. Served as officer US Army, 1967—69. Named one of Real Estate's 25 Most Influential Thought Leaders, Realtor Mag., 2006; recipient Silver Beaver award, Nat. and Chickasaw Coun. Boy Scouts of Am., Disting. Alumni award, Ark. State U. Coll. Bus., 1986, Chairman's award, Carnival Memphis Bus. & Industry Salute to Real Estate, 2003. Mem.: Soc. Entrepreneurs (mem. 1994—), Memphis Area Assn. Realtors (pres. 1991, Realtor of Yr. 1992, Life Mem. Million Dollar Club), Germantown Exchange Club (charter pres.), Germantown Jaycees (charter pres.). Baptist. Avocations: sports, reading, travel. Office: Crye-Leike Inc 6525 N Quail Hollow Rd #100 Memphis TN 38120-1325*

CRYER, PHILIP EUGENE, endocrinologist; b. El Paso, Ill., Jan. 5, 1940; s. Clifford Eugene and Carol Ruth (Cherry) C.; m. Susan Odette Shipman, Dec. 23, 1963 (div. May 1990); children: Philip Clifford, Justine Laurel; m. Carolyn Elizabeth Havlin, Sept. 16, 1994. BA, Northwestern U., 1962, MD, 1965; MD (hon.), U. Copenhagen, 2000. Diplomate Am. Bd. Internal Medicine, diplomate Am. Bd. Endocrinology and Metabolism. Intern, resident Barnes Hosp., St. Louis, 1965-67; fellow in endocrinology Barnes Hosp./Washington U., 1967-68, resident in medicine, 1968-69, 71-72; investigator Naval Med. Rsch. Inst., Bethesda, Md., 1969-71; from instr. to assoc. prof. Washington U. Sch. Medicine, St. Louis, 1971-80, prof., 1981—, Irene E. and Michael M. Karl prof. endocrinology/metabolism, 1995—, dir. gen. clin. rsch. ctr., 1978—2006, dir. divsn. endocrinology, diabetes and metabolism, 1985—2002. Connaught-Novo lectr. Can. Diabetes Assn., 1987; Pimstone lectr. Soc. Endocrinology, Metabolism and Diabetes, South Africa, 1989; Kellion lectr. Australian Diabetes Soc., 1992; Plenary lectr. Japan Diabetes Soc., 1994, plenary lectr. Argentine Diabetes Assn., 1998, plenary lectr. Asean Fed. Endocrine Socs., 1999. Author: Diagnostic Endocrinology, 1976, Diagnostic Endocrinology, 2d edit., 1979, Hypoglycemia, 1997; editor: Diabetes; mem. edit. bd.: Jour. Clin. Investigation, Am. Jour. Physiology; contbr. 82 chapt. to books, over 325 articles to profl. jours. Lt. comdr. M.C. USNR, 1969—71. Recipient Rorer Clin. Investigator award Endocrine Soc., 1988, Rumbaugh Sci. award Juvenile Diabetes Found., 1989, Banting medal Am. Diabetes Assn., 1994, Excellence in Clin. Rsch. award NIH, 1994, Claude Bernard medal European Assn. Study Diabetes, 2001, Merit award NIH, 2001.; grantee Am. Diabetes Clin., 1988-, NIH, 1980—; named Disting. Alumnus, Northwestern U. Med. Sch., 2006. Fellow ACP; mem. Am. Fedn. Clin. Rsch. (councilor 1979-80), Am. Soc. Clin. Investigation (v.p. 1985-86), Assn. Am. Physicians, Am. Diabetes Assn. (pres. 1996-97), Phi Beta Kappa, Alpha Omega Alpha. Office: Washington U Sch Medicine 660 South Euclid Ave Box 8127 Saint Louis MO 63110 Home Phone: 314-752-7201; Office Phone: 314-362-7635. Business E-Mail: pcryer@wustl.edu.

CRYER, THEODORE HUDSON, ophthalmologist, educator; b. Chgo., May 8, 1946; s. Arthur William and Maxine (Ritter) Cryer; children: Timothy Hudson, Jordan Tinley, Megan Elizabeth, Rebecca Jeanne. AB in Chemistry, Taylor U., 1968; MD, U. Md., 1972. Diplomate Am. Bd. Ophthalmology. Straight med. intern South Balt. Gen. Hosp., 1972-73, jr. asst. resident, 1973-74; asst. resident U. Md. Hosp., Balt., 1974-76, resident, 1976-77; pvt. practice Waynesboro, Pa., 1977—, Westminster, Md., 1977-85. Instr. U. Md. Sch. Medicine, 1979—91, clin. asst. prof. ophthalmology, 1991—; chmn. com. ethics Waynesboro Hosp., 1984, trustee, 1991—97, chmn. com. quality assurance, 1996—97, v.p. mem. staff, 1988—89, 1999, pres., 1990—91, 2000—01, treas. med. staff, 2001—03, chmn. com. credentialing, chmn. bylaws com., 2003—, chief of surgery, 1992—96, 2004—07. Clk. session Westminster Reformed Presbyn. Ch., 1980—83; trustee Christ United Meth. Ch., 1997—2000. Fellow: ACS, Am. Acad. Ophthalmology; mem.: AAAS, AMA, Opthal. Assn. Rsch. to Prevent Blindness, Nat. Soc. to Prevent Blindness (charter mem.), Pa. Acad. Otolaryngology and Ophthalmology, Md. Eye Physicians and Surgeons, Franklin County Med. Soc., Pa. Med. Soc. Republican. Methodist. Office: 1647 E Main St Waynesboro PA 17268-1874 Home Phone: 717-765-9271; Office Phone: 717-762-1158. Office Fax: 717-762-8858.

CRYSTAL, BILLY, actor, comedian; b. Long Beach, NY, Mar. 14, 1947; s. Jack and Helen Crystal; m. Janice Goldfinger; children: Jennifer, Lindsay. Student, Marshall U., Nassau Community Coll; BFA in TV & Film Direction, N.Y.U., 1970. House mgr. for play You're a Good Man Charlie Brown, 1971; mem. group 3's Company; later solo appearances as stand-up comedian; exec. prodr., writer Midnight Train to Moscow, 1989 (Emmy award outstanding writing 1989), Sessions, 1991; actor (films) Rabbit Test, 1978, (voice only) Animalympics, 1979, This Is Spinal Tap, 1984, Running Scared, 1986, The Princess Bride, 1987, Goodnight Moon, 1987, Throw Momma from the Train, 1987, (also prodr., co-screenwriter) Memories of Me, 1988, When Harry Met Sally.., 1989, Forget Paris, 1995, Hamlet, 1996, Father's Day, 1997, Deconstructing Harry, 1997, My Giant, 1998, Analyze This, 1999, The Adventures of Rocky & Bullwinkle, 2000, America's Sweethearts, 2001, (voice only) Monsters, Inc., Mike's New Car, 2002, Analyze That, 2002, (voice only) Howl's Moving Castle, 2004; actor, dir., prodr, writer (films) City Slickers ((Golden Globe nomination best actor 1991, Am. Comedy award 1991), 1991, Mr. Saturday Night, 1992, City Slickers II: The Legend of Curley's Gold, 1994; actor (TV movies) SST-Death Flight, 1977, Human Feelings, 1978, Breaking Up Is Hard to Do, 1979, Enola Gay, The Men, The Mission, The Atomic Bomb, 1980; dir., prodr. (TV movies) 61, 2001; actor (TV series) Soap, 1977-81, The Billy Crystal Comedy Hour, 1982, Saturday Night Live, 1984-85; theatre performances include 700 Sundays, 2005 (Outer Critics Cir. award, outstanding solo performance, 2005, Tony award for best spl. theatrical event, 2005, Drama Desk award, outstanding solo performance, 2005); host (HBO) Comic Relief, 1986, (TV host) Grammy Awards, 1988, 89, Acad. Awards, 1990-93, 96-98, 2000, 2004 (Emmy award outstanding performance in special events, 1989, Emmy award outstanding writing, 1991, Emmy award outstanding indiv. performance, 1991, 98), Saturday Night Live: 25th Anniversary, 1999, AFI's 100 Years, 100 Laughs: America's Funniest Movies, 2000; author: I Already Know I Love You, 2004, 700 Sundays, 2005, Grandpa's Little One, 2006; co-author (with Dick Schaap) Absolutley Mahvelous, 1986; recordings You Look Mahvelous, 1985.*

CRYSTAL, J. SCOTT, publishing executive; BS in Psychology, SUNY, Binghamton. Mktg., sales mgmt. NY Times Co., USA Today, Hearst Corp., 1982—92; western advt. dir. Nat. Geog. Soc., Inc., 1992—94, v.p., pub. dir., 1994—2000; exec. v.p., pub. dir. Consumer Mag. Group, Ziff Davis Media, Inc., 2000—01; pres., CEO Gruner & Jahr USA Bus. Innovator Group, 2001—02; pub./sr. v.p. Gemstar - TV Guide Internat. Inc., NYC, 2002—05, pres. TV Guide Mag., 2005—. Named to Advt. Hall of Achievement, Am. Advt. Fed. Office: Gemstar TV Guide Internat Inc 4th Floor 1211 Ave of Americas 28th Fl New York NY 10036-8701 Office Phone: 212-853-7310. Office Fax: 212-852-7323.*

CRYSTAL, JAMES WILLIAM, insurance company executive; b. NYC, Oct. 9, 1937; s. I. Frank and Evelyn G. Crystal; m. Jean Crystal; children: James F., Sanford F., Jonathan F. BS, Trinity Coll., 1958. With Royal Globe Ins. Group, NYC, 1956; underwriter Home Ins. Co., NYC, 1957, spl. agt. San Francisco, 1958-59; chmn., CEO Frank Crystal & Co. Inc., NYC, 1960—. Chmn. bd. F.F.H. Ins. Co., N.E. Ins. Co.; bd. dirs. Atlantic Internat. Ins. Co., Auto Resources, Inc., Blockbuster L.L.C., Stewart & Stevenson, LLC, Banco di Caribe NV, Ennia Caribe Holding NV. Vice chmn. Mt. Sinai Med. Ctr.; trustee Mt. Sinai NYU Health Orgn., NYC, Mt. Sinai Med. Sch. Mem.: Nat. Assn. Casualty and Surety Agts., Wings Club NY, Century Country Club, India House Club NY, Harmonie Club. Republican. Home: 875 Park Ave New York NY 10021-0341 Office: Frank Crystal & Co 32 Old Slip New York NY 10005 Office Phone: 212-504-5999. Business E-Mail: jwc@fcrystal.com.

CSAKI, CSABA, physicist; b. Budapest, Hungary, Dec. 13, 1969; arrived in US, 1993; s. Csaba and Borbala (Munkacsi) Csaki; m. Zsuzsanna Tonkovics, Sept. 19, 1992; children: Agnes, Zoltan. BSc, Eotvos U., Budapest, 1993; PhD, MIT, 1997. Miller Rsch. fellow U. Calif., Berkeley, 1997—99; J.R. Oppenheimer fellow Los Alamos Nat. Lab., N.Mex., 1999—2001; asst. prof. physics Cornell U., Ithaca, NY, 2002—07, assoc. prof. physics, 2007—. Author over 60 jour. articles, over 3000 citations of articles. Named Outstanding Jr. Investigator, US Dept. Energy, 2001; recipient 1st prize ann. essay competition, Gravity Rsch. Found., 2001, 3d prize Physics Olympics, Bad Ischl, Austria, 1988. Mem.: Am. Phys. Soc. Office: Cornell U Dept Physics Ithaca NY 14853 Office Phone: 607-254-8935. Business E-Mail: csaki@lepp.cornell.edu.

CSAR, MICHAEL F., lawyer; b. Chgo., May 26, 1950; s. Frank J. and Rosaria (Motto) C.; children: Cordelia, Christian. BA summa cum laude, Yale U., 1972; MA, Kings Coll., Cambridge, 1974; JD, Yale U., 1977. Bar: Ill. 1977, U.S. Dist. Ct. (no. dist.) Ill. 1977. Assoc. Wilson & McIlvaine, Chgo., 1977-83; ptnr. Quarles & Brady (formerly Wilson & McIlvaine), Chgo., 1983-98, Gardner Carton & Douglas LLC, Chgo., 1998—, Drinker Biddle & Reath, Chgo. Mem. Bldg. Owners and Managers Assn., Nat. Assn. Real Estate Investment Trusts. Mem.: ABA, Lambda Alpha Internat. Office: Drinker Biddle & Reath 191 N Wacker Dr Ste 3700 Chicago IL 60606 Office Phone: 312-569-1223. Office Fax: 312-569-3000. Business E-Mail: michael.csar@dbr.com.

CSERE, CSABA, editor-in-chief; b. Cleve., June 16, 1951; s. Zoltan and Theresa (Balazs) Csere; m. Mary Patricia O'Brien, July 6, 1975; 1 child, Madeline Christine. BS, MIT, 1975. Design engr. Data Gen. Corp., Southboro, Mass., 1975—77, Ford Motor Co., 1978—80; tech. editor Car and Driver mag., 1980—87, tech. dir., 1987—93, editor-in-chief, 1993—. Mem.: Am. Soc. Mag. Editors, Soc. Automotive Engrs. Office: Car and Driver Hachette Filipacchi Mags Inc 2002 Hogback Rd Ann Arbor MI 48105-9795 Office Phone: 734-971-3600. Office Fax: 734-971-9188.

CSERR, ROBERT, psychiatrist, physician, hospital administrator; b. Perth Amboy, NJ, May 29, 1936; s. Frank Joseph and Helen (Bodzany) C.; m. Helen Fitzgerald, May 28, 1962; 1 dau., Ruth. AB magna cum laude, Harvard U., 1958, MD, 1962. Med. intern U. Va. Hosp., 1962-63; resident fellow in psychiatry Mass. Gen. Hosp., Harvard Med. Sch., 1963-66; alcohol coordinator Mass. Gen. Hosp., 1967-68, clin. assoc. psychiatry 1968—; asst. supt. Medfield State Hosp., Harding, Mass., 1968-70, supt., 1970-74, area program dir., 1970-74; dir. Outlook Psychiat. Facility, Hampstead, NH, 1974-76; med. dir. Charles River Hosp., Wellesley, Mass. 1976-80, psychiatrist-in-chief, 1980-87, Hahnemann Hosp., Boston, 1982—; med. dir. Taunton Hosp. and Regional Svc. Ctr., 1990-92; assoc. med. dir. psychiatry PHCS, Lexington, Mass., 1991-93, v.p., med. dir. mental health svcs. Waltham, Mass., 1993-96. V.p. clin. affairs Cmty. Care Systems Inc., 1979-86, sr. cons., 1986—; asst. clin. prof. psychiatry Boston U. Sch. Medicine, 1968-74, assoc. clin. prof., 1979—; asst. psychiatrist Beth Israel Hosp., 1970—; lectr. in psychiatry Harvard Med. Sch., 1972-89; cons. Med. Mgmt. Managed Care Programs, 1986—. Pres. Medfield Found.; bd. overseers Mt. Desert Island Biol. Lab. Served with AUS, 1966-68. Mem. Am. Coll. Mental Health Adminstrs., Mass. Med. Soc., BCN Med. Soc. Office: 707 Green Acres North Dighton MA 02764

CSIKAI, GYULA, physicist, researcher; b. Tiszaladany, Hungary, Oct. 31, 1930; s. Miklós P. and Zsuzsanna (Bay) C.; m. Margit Buczkó, July 22, 1957; children: Gyula, Attila. Maturity, Calvinist Coll., Debrecen, Hungary, 1949; tchr. in math. and physics, Kossuth U., Debrecen, Hungary, 1953; DSc (hon.), Acad. of Sci., Budapest, Hungary, 1966. Kiev Nat. U., 2001—. Cert. high sch. tchr. Head neutron physics dept. Atomki, Debrecen, 1956-67; head Inst. of Exptl. Physics, Debrecen, 1967-95. Dep. min. Ministry of Culture and Edn. Hungary, Budapest, 1987, prof. 1967-2000, prof. emeritus, 2001—; dean 1972-75, rector 1981-86 Kossuth U., Debrecen; expert Internat. Atomic Energy Agy. UN, Vienna, 1968—. Author: Fast Neutron Generators, 1987, Neutrons and Paleosciences, 1987, Nuclear Act Data 1987, 2002, 03; contbr. over 270 articles to profl. jours. Recipient State award Govt. Hungary 1983, Disting. Leadership award ABI 1986; named Hon. Freeman of Tiszaladany, 2000-; named one of Leading Educators of World IBC, 2006. Mem. Internat. Union Pure and Applied Physics, Commn. Nuclear Physics (sec. 1993-96—), Hungarian Acad. Sci. (v.p. dept. math. and physics, Brody prize 1957, first prize 1967, Eotvos medal 1980, Szilard prize, 2004, Wigner prize, 2005), N.Y. Acad. Sci., European Phys. Soc. (coun. mem. 1978—), Acad. Europe, Phys. Soc.

Hungary (pres. 1980-85, hon. pres. 1995—). Avocations: music, photography, travel. Office: Inst Exptl Physics Bem ter 18/a H-4026 Debrecen Hungary Office Phone: 36 52 415 222. Business E-Mail: csikai@delfin.unideb.hu.

CSIKSZENTMIHALYI, MIHALY, psychology professor; b. Fiume, Italy, Sept. 29, 1934; came to U.S., 1956; s. Alfred and Edith (Jankovich) C.; m. Isabella Selega, Dec. 30, 1961; children: Mark, Christopher. BA, U. Chgo., 1960, PhD, 1965. Reporter European News Service, Rome, 1952-56; free-lance artist Rome, 1954-56; translator U.S.A. Pubs., Chgo., 1958-64; prof. sociology Lake Forest (Ill.) Coll., 1965-70; prof. psychology human devel., edn. U. Chgo., 1971—. Adv. bd. Ency. Britannica, Chgo., 1985—, J.P. Getty Mus., Malibu, Calif., 1985—. Author: Beyond Boredom and Anxiety, 1975, Flow: The Psychology of Optimal Experience, 1990, The Evolving Self, 1993, Creativity, 1996, Finding Flow in Everyday Life, 1997, Good Business, 2003; (with others) The Creative Vision, 1976, The Meaning of Things, 1981, Being Adolescent, 1984, Optimal Experience, 1988, Television and the Quality of Life, 1990, The Art of Seeing, 1990, Talented Teenagers, 1993, Creating Worlds, 1994, Becoming Adult, 2000, Good Work, 2001, A Life Worth Living, 2006, Experience Sampling, 2006. Fulbright Sr. scholar, 1984, 1990, Fellow Ctr. for Advanced Studies in the Behavioral Sci., 1994-95. Fellow Am. Acad. Arts and Scis., Am. Acad. Edn., Am. Acad. Leisure Scis., Am. Acad. Polit. and Social Scis.; mem. Quadrangle Club. Avocations: mountain climbing, reading, art, chess. Home: 700 Alamosa Dr Claremont CA 91711 Office: 1021 N Dartmouth Ave Claremont CA 91711 Home Phone: 909-621-7345. Business E-Mail: miska@cgu.edu.

CSONKA, PAUL L., theoretical physicist, educator; b. Budapest, Hungary, Aug. 10, 1938; came to U.S., 1957; s. Pal Csonka and Margit Warga; m. Martha E. C.; children: Emese C., Paul J., Livia M. PhD, Johns Hopkins U., 1963. Postdoctoral fellow Lawrence Livermore (Calif.) Nat. Lab., 1964-66; NSF postdoctoral fellow CERN Labs., Geneva, Switzerland, 1966-68; prof. physics U. Oreg., Eugene, 1968—, dir. Robert D. Clark Honors Coll., 1997-2000. NORDITA vis. prof. to Scandinavia, 1972-73; dir. Inst. of Theoretical Sci., U. Oreg., 1977-79. Alfred P. Sloan fellowship, 1970-72; recipient Fulbright Sr. Rsch. award Budapest, Hungary, 1993, 94. Office: U Oreg Dept Physics Eugene OR 97403 Business E-Mail: pcsonka@oregon.uoregon.edu.

CSÖRGÖ, MIKLÓS, mathematics and statistics educator; b. Egerfarmos, Hungary, Mar. 12, 1932; arrived in Can., 1957, naturalized, 1962; s. Miklos and Ilona (Veres) Csörgö; m. Anna Eszter Toth, Aug. 10, 1957; children: Adria, Lilla. BA, Karl Marx U. Econs., Budapest, Hungary, 1955; MA, McGill U., 1961, PhD, 1963. Instr., postdoctoral fellow Princeton U., NJ, 1963—65; asst. prof. McGill U., Montreal, Que., Canada, 1965—68, assoc. prof., 1968—71; vis. prof. U. Vienna, 1969—70; assoc. prof. math. and stats. Carleton U., Ottawa, Ont., Canada, 1971—72, prof., 1972—, co-dir. Lab. for Rsch. in Stats. and Probability, 1983—. Vis. prof. U. Utah, 1991—92. Author (with P. Révész): Strong Approximations in Probability and Statistics, 1981; author: Quantile Processes with Statistical Applications, 1983; author: (with others) An Asymptotic Theory for Empirical Reliability and Concentration Processes, 1986; author: (with L. Horváth) Weighted Approximations in Probability and Statistics, 1993; author: (with L. Horvath) Limit Theorems in Change-Point Analysis, 1997; assoc. editor The Annals of Probability, 1979—81, mem. editl. bd. Stats. and Decisions, 1981—2002, Jour. Multivariate Analysis, 1986—87. Fellow, Can. Coun., 1969—70, 1976—77, Killam sr. rsch. fellow, 1978—79, 1979—80. Fellow: Inst. Math. Stats., Royal Soc. Can.; mem.: Hungarian Acad. Sci. (external mem.), Internat. Statis. Inst., Bernoulli Soc., Statis. Soc. Can., Can. Math. Soc., Am. Math. Soc. Office: Carleton U Lab Rsch in Stats 1125 Colonel By Dr Ottawa ON Canada K1S 5B6 Office Phone: 613-520-2128. E-mail: mcsorgo@math.carleton.ca.

CUADRA, CARLOS ALBERT, library and information scientist, consultant; b. San Francisco, Dec. 21, 1925; s. Gregorio and Amanda (Mendoza) C.; m. Gloria Nathalie Adams, May 3, 1947; children: Mary Susan Cuadra Nielsen, Neil Gregory, Dean Arthur. AB in Psychology with highest honors, U. Calif., Berkeley, 1949, PhD in Psychology, 1953. Staff psychologist VA, Downey, Ill., 1953-56; with Sys. Devel. Corp., Santa Monica, Calif., 1957-78, mgr. libr. and documentation sys. dept., 1968-70, mgr. edn. and libr. sys. dept., 1971-74; gen. mgr. SDC Search Svc., 1974-78; founder Cuadra Assocs., LA, 1978—. Founder, editor: Ann. Rev. of Info. Sci. and Tech., 1964—75; contbr. articles to profl. jours. Mem. Nat. Commn. Librs. and Info. Sci., 1971-84. Served with USN, 1944-46. Recipient Merit award Am. Soc. Info. Sci., 1968, Best Info. Sci. Book award Am. Soc. Info. Sci., 1969, Miles Conrad award Nat. Fedn. Abstracting and Info. Svcs., 1980, Roger Summit award Assn. Ind. Info. Profls., 2001; named Disting. Lectr. of Yr., Am. Soc. Info. Sci., 1970, hon. fellow Nat. Fedn. Abstracting and Info. Svcs., 1997. Mem. Info. Industry Assn. (bd. dirs., Hall of Fame award 1980), Chem. Abstracts Soc. (governing bd. 1991-96), Am. Chem. Soc. (governing bd. pub. 1997-2000), Phi Beta Kappa. Home: 13213 Warren Ave Los Angeles CA 90066-1750 Office: Cuadra Associates 11835 W Olympic Blvd Ste 855 Los Angeles CA 90064-5001

CUALING, HERNANI DEL MUNDO, physician, researcher; s. Pablo Mateong and Flor Del Mundo Cualing; m. Rawia Salem Yassin, Dec. 20, 1989; children: Kareem Yassin Khozaim, Phillip, Andrew. BS, U. Philippines, 1974, MD, 1978. Diplomate Am. Bd. of Pathology, 1991, Am. Bd. of Hematology, 1992. Chief resident Nassau County U. Med. Ctr., East Meadow, NY, 1990—91; fellow dept. pathology Ind. U. Med. Ctr., Indpls., 1991—92; asst. prof. U. Cin. Med. Ctr., 1992—2002; assoc. prof. dept. pathology U. Cin., 2002—02; assoc. prof. U. South Fla./Moffitt Cancer Ctr., Tampa, 2002—. Consulting hematopathology staff VA Med. Ctr., Cin., 1993—2002; med. dir. U. Cin. Med. Ctr., 1993—96, Diagnostic Immunology and Flow Cytometry Interpretation of Leukemias and Lymphomas, Diagnostic Flow Cytometry by Health Alliance, 2000—02; med. dir. immunohistochemistry/histology Moffitt Cancer Ctr. and Rsch. Inst., Tampa, Fla., 2002—. Period furniture, Queen Anne Desk; contbr. articles to profl. jours. Mem. Clin. Cytometry Soc., 2002—03; pres. Med. Student Soc., 1977. Recipient First prize Paper, Fla. Soc. Pathologists, 2004, Tchr. of Yr., U. South Fla. Pathology Residents, 2004, Internat. Rschr. award, U.P. Med. Alumni, 2003; grantee Biomedical Engring. of Leukemia/Lymphoma, Whitaker Found., 1997-2000; Pioneering grant, U. Cin. Biomed. Engring., 1994. Fellow: Internat. Acad. Pathologists/Coll. Am. Pathologists (assoc.); mem.: Coun. Health Care Advisors (assoc.), Am. Soc. Hematologists (assoc.). R-Liberal. Catholic. Achievements include invention of computerized virtual flow cytometry of immunostained cells. Avocations: woodworking, sailing, fishing, history. Home: 18804 Chaville Rd Lutz FL 33558 Office Phone: 813-979-3914. Business E-Mail: cualinhd@moffitt.usf.edu.

CUARÓN, ALFONSO, film director, film producer; b. Mexico City, Mex., Nov. 28, 1961; Student, Cooperative Universataria Edigtrice Cagliaritana, Mex. 1st asst. dir.: (films) Gaby, A Love Story, 1987; Romero, 1989; dir.: Cuarteto para el fin del tiempo, 1983, Solo Con Tu Pareja, 1991 (Best Original Screenplay, Mexican Acad. Awards), A Little Princess, 1995 (L.A. Film Critics New Generation award), Great Expectations, 1998, Harry Potter and the Prisoner of Azkaban, 2004, (TV episode) Fallen Angels, 1993 (CableACE award), Cita Con La Muerte, 1989; prodr.: (films) Me La Debes, 2001, The Assassination of Richard Nixon, 2004; dir., prodr. (films) Love in the Time of Hysteria, 1991, dir., prodr., writer Y Tu Mama Tambien, 2001 (Best Screenplay award Venice Film Festival, L.A. Film Critics award, Ind. Spirit award for Best Fgn. Film), dir., writer The Children of Men, 2002 (Rave award for Film, WIRED Mag., 2007), Pan's Labyrinth, 2006 (Film Not in the Eng. Lang. award, Brit. Acad. Film and TV Arts, 2007).*

CUARTAS, BEATRIZ H., humanities educator; b. Bucaramanga, Santander, Colombia, June 9, 1977; arrived in US, 1992, naturalized, 1999; d. Sergio Leon Cuartas and Clotilde Jaimes-Duran; life ptnr. Hans-Filip Jorgen Fex; 1 child, Ulysses Del Mar Chaslus. BA in Internat. Affairs & Polit. Sci., U. Maine, Orono, 1999; DEA in Comparative Polit. Sci., Polit. Sci. Inst., France, 2002. Cert. notary pub. Tex. Sec. State, Dallas, 2004. ESOL instr. Colombo-Am. Alliance, Bucaramanga, Colombia, 1993—94; rsch. intern OAS, Washington, 1999; exec. asst. Inter-Am. Devel. Bank, 2002—03; French, Spanish instr. Pk. U., El Paso, Tex., 2003—04; analyst US Govt. Accountability Office, Dallas, 2004—05; govt. instr. El Paso CC, 2005—. Writer Norton Pub. Co., NYC, 2005—; faculty coord., sen. El Paso CC, 2005—. Vol. dep. registrar Tex. Sec. State, El Paso, 2005; moderator El Paso CC Candidate Awareness Debate; vol. Get Out the Vote. Recipient Vol. of Yr. award, 2003, Cmty. Svc. award, Socorro Head Start, 2003. Mem.: El Paso CC Faculty Senate, Upper Rio Grande Econs. Assn., Pi Sigma Alpha. Independent. Roman Catholic. Avocations: swimming, sports, reading, writing, travel. Office: El Paso CC PO Box 20500 El Paso TX 79998-0500 Office Phone: 915-831-5215. Office Fax: 915-831-5122; Home Fax: 915-831-5122. Business E-Mail: bchaslus@epcc.edu.

CUATRECASAS, PEDRO MARTIN, research biochemist, pharmaceutical executive; b. Madrid, Sept. 27, 1936; came to U.S., 1947, naturalized 1954. s. Jose and Martha C.; m. Carol Zies, Aug. 15, 1959; children: Paul, Lisa, Diane, Julia. AB, Washington U., St. Louis, 1958, MD, 1962; DSc honoris causa, U. Barcelona, 1984, Mt. Sinai Sch. Medicine, 1985, U. Buenos Aires, 1990, U. Naples, Italy, 1990. Intern, then resident in internal medicine Osler Svc. Johns Hopkins Hosp., 1962-64, asst. physician, 1972-75; clin. asso., clin. endocrinology br. Nat. Inst. Arthritis and Metabolic Diseases, NIH, 1964-66; spl. USPHS postdoctoral fellow Lab. Chem. Biology, 1966-67, med. officer, 1967-70; professorial lectr. biochemistry George Washington U. Med. Sch., 1967-70; assoc. prof. pharmacology and exptl. therapeutics, assoc. prof. medicine, dir. div. clin. pharmacology, Burroughs Wellcome prof. clin. pharmacology Johns Hopkins U. Med. Sch., 1970-72, prof. pharmacology and exptl. therapeutics, assoc. prof. medicine, 1972-75; v.p. rsch., devel. and med. Wellcome Rsch. Labs.; dir. Burroughs Wellcome Co., Research Triangle Park, NC, 1975-86; sr. v.p. R&D Glaxo Inc., 1986-89; also bd. dirs. Glaxo Inc., Glaxo Internat. Rsch., Ltd., London, 1986-89; pres. pharm. rsch. divsn., and co. v.p. Warner-Lambert Co., Ann Arbor, Mich., 1989-97; ind. pharm. rsch. cons. San Diego, 1997—; prof. dept. medicine & pharm. U. Calif., San Diego, 1997—. Adj. prof. Duke U. Med. Sch., 1975-89; adj. prof., mem. adv. com. cancer rsch. program U. N.C. Med. Sch., 1975-90; adj. prof. dept. pharm. and medicinal chemistry, U. Mich., 1990-97; bd. dirs. Alliance Pharms.; mem. FDA sci. bd., 1994-98. Editor: Receptors and Recognition Series, 1975-98, Jour. Solid-Phase Biochemistry, 1975-80, Handbook of Experimental Pharmacology, 1984-99, Internat. Jour. Biochemistry, 1973, Molecular and Cellular Endocrinology, 1973-77, Biochimica Biophysica Acta, 1973-79, Life Scis., 1978-88, Neuropeptides, 1979-99, Jour. Applied Biochemistry, 1978-91, Cancer Research, 1980-81, Jour. Applied Biochemistry and Biotech., 1980—98, Toxin Revs., 1981-90, Biochem. Biophys. Rsch. Comms., 1981-94; contbr. articles to profl. jours. Active Am. Diabetes Assn., 1972-97, PMA Commn. on Drugs and Rare Diseases, 1982-89; bd. dirs. Burroughs Wellcome Fund, 1975-86. Recipient John Jacob Abel prize, 1972, Laude prize Pharm. World, 1975, Beerman award Soc. Investigative Dermatology, 1981, Isco award U. Nebr., 1985, Dupont Splty. Diagnostics award Clin. Ligand Assay Soc., 1986, Alumni Achievement award Washington U. Sch. Medicine, 1987, Wolf Found. prize in medicine, 1987, N.C. Gov.'s medal award in sci., 1988, Achievement award Soc. for Biomolecular Screening, 1999, Johns Hopkins U. Disting. Alumnus award, 2000; FDA Commr.'s Spl. citation, 1997, City of Medicine award (disting. achievement in medicine), 1998; inducted into Johns Hopkins Soc. Scholar, 1990. Fellow Am. Acad. Arts and Scis.; mem. Am. Soc. Biol. Chemists, Nat. Acad. Scis., Inst. Medicine of Nat. Acad. Scis. (governing council 1988-96), Am. Soc. Pharmacology and Exptl. Therapeutics (Goodman and Gilman award 1982), Am. Soc. Clin. Investigation, Am. Soc. Clin. Rsch., Spanish Biochem. Soc., Md. Acad. Scis. (Outstanding Young Scientist of Year 1970), Am. Cancer Soc., Endocrine Soc., Am. Chem. Soc., Am. Diabetes Assn. (Eli Lilly award 1975), Am. Diabetes Assn., Sigma Xi. Personal E-mail: pedrocuatrecasas@znet.com.

CUBA, STANLEY L., government official; b. Denver, Apr. 30, 1948; s. Frank L. (Czuba) Cuba and Wanda Helen Kugaczewska; m. Ewa Zofia Galkowska, Sept. 18, 1998. BA in Polit. Sci., Europe-Columbia U., 1970; cert. in East European studies, Inst. on East Cen., 1972; MA in History, Columbia U., 1978. Assoc. conf. coord. Polish Inst. Arts and Scis., NYC, 1970-72; asst. to pres. Kosciuszko Found., NYC, 1972-79; assoc. dir. Andre Zarre Gallery, NYC, 1980-82; transl. Denver, 1983-90; ct. clk. II Denver County Ct., 1986-90; cert. investigator Mayor's Office of Contract Compliance, Denver, 1990-2000; prevailing wage investigator auditor's office Denver Internat. Airport, 2000—. Mayor's Office of Contract Compliance liaison to Asian C. of C., Denver, 1993-2000; presenter in field. Author: (exhbn. catalogs) Stefan Mrozewski (1894-1975) Wood Engravings: A Posthumous Exhibition, 1976, Jozef Pankiewicz (1886-1940): A Loan Exhibition of Oils, Watercolors, Sketches and Graphics, 1978, Hussars and the Crescent: The Polish Relief of Vienna, 1983, The Art of Jozef Bakos: An Early Modernist, 1891-1977, 1988, Colorado Women Artists, 1859-1950: An Unprecedented Exhibition of Women Artists Living or Working in Colorado from 1859 to 1950, 1989, Jan Sawka: A Selected Retrospective, 1990, The Art of Jozef Bakos: Selections from the Estate of Jozef Gabryel Bakos, 1992, Olive Rush: A Hoosier Artist in New Mexico, 1992, John F. Carlson and Artists of the Broadmoor Art Academy, 1999; co-author: (book) Great Drawings of the 20th Century, 1981, The Colorado Book, 1993, The Art of Charles Partridge Adams, 1993, (exhbn. catalogs) George Luks: An American Artist, 1987, Pikes Peak Vision: The Broadmoor Art Academy, 1919-1945, 1989, Hayes Lyon: A Colorado Regionalist (1909-1987), 1991; contbr. to Allgemeines Kunstler Lexikon, 1998-99, also to exhbn. catalogs and mags. Mem. Denver Cath. Archdiocesan Adv. Coun., 1999-2002, photo/art acquisitions com. We. History Dept. Denver Pub. Lib.; mem. Denver Cath. Archdiocesan Due Process Panel, 2003-; mem. mus./gallery com. Arvada Ctr. for Arts and Humanities, Colo., 1990-2002. Recipient Bicentennial Recognition of Exhbn. Curated on History of Polish Cmty. in Colo., 1859-1876, Colo. Bicentennial Commn./Denver Mayoral Bicentennial Commn., 1976; Interpreter grantee Ford. Found./Citizens Exch. Corps, 1969, Polonian Rsch. Ctr. grant Jagiellonian U., Krakow, 1980. Mem. Polish Nat. Alliance (lodge 134, v.p. 1990-96, fin. sec. 1996-98), Polish Am. Hist. Assn. (mem., chmn. award com. 1979-83, Rev. Joseph Swastek prize 1984), Polish Inst. Arts & Scis., Kosciuszko Found. Democrat. Roman Catholic. Avocations: travel, art, concerts, theater, films. Home: 2643 Utica St Denver CO 80212-3007 Office Phone: 303-342-2710. Personal E-mail: s.cuba@worldnet.att.net.

CUBAN, MARK, professional sports team owner, Internet company executive; b. Pitts., July 31, 1958; m. Tiffany Stewart, Sept. 21, 2002; 1 child. BA in Bus. Adminstrn., Ind. U., 1981. Founder MicroSolutions (sold to CompuServe), 1983-90; pres. Radical Computing; co-founder Audionet (became broadcast.com in 1998 (acquired by Yahoo!), 1995—99; owner, mng. ptnr. Dallas Mavericks, 2000—; co-founder, pres., chmn. HDNet and HDTV Cable Network, 2001—; chmn., co-owner Magnolia Pictures, Landmark Theaters; chmn., majority owner Rysher Entertainment; co-owner 2929 Entertainment. Owner IceRocket; ptnr. RedSwoosh; investor Weblogs, Inc., Brondell, Inc., Goowy Media Inc.; spkr. in field. Exec. prodr.: (films) Godsend, 2004; exec. prodr.: (films) Criminal, 2004, The War Within, 2005, One Last Thing.., 2005, Bubble, 2005, Good Night and Good Luck, 2005, The Jacket, 2005, Akeelah and the Bee, 2006, The Architect, 2006, Diggers, 2006, Fay Grim, 2006, Turistas, 2006, Black Christmas, 2006, Fast Track, 2006; exec. prodr.: (films) Broken English, 2007; exec. prodr.: (films) We Own the Night, 2007; (documentaries) Searching for Debra Winger, 2002, Enron: The Smartest Guys in the Room, 2005, Herbie Hancock: Possibilities, 2006; (TV series) The Mark Cuban Show, 2002; exec. prodr.: (TV series) Geek to Freek with Dennis Rodman, 2007; co-exec. prodr. (TV series) Star Search, 2002—04; actor: (films) Talkin About Sex, 1994, Lost at Sea, 1995; (TV series) Walker, Texas Ranger, 2000, (video) Like Mike 2: Streetball, 2006; (TV films) 20 on 20, 2007; host, prodr.: (TV series) The Benefactor, 2004; maintains (blog site, Blogmaverick.com); performer: Dancing With the Stars, 2007. Founder Mark Cuban Found., The Fallen Patriot Fund, 2003—. Named a WIRED Renegade, WIRED Rave Awards, 2006; nominee WIRED Rave award-Blogs, 2005; named one of Forbes 400 Richest Ams., Forbes Mag., 2000—06; recipient Webby Entrepreneur of Yr., Internat. Acad. Digital Arts and Scis., 2006. Office: Dallas Mavericks The Pavillion 2909 Taylor St Dallas TX 75226*

CUBBAGE, BOBBIE DANIELLE, pre-school administrator, educator; d. Robert Carter and Dorothy June Norman; m. Samuel Junior Cubbage II, May 4, 2002. BA in Journalism and Comm., Point Pk. U., Pitts., 1996. On air talent WPGR Radio 1080am, Pitts., 1999—2000; on air talent, pub. svc. dir., promotions asst. WGBN 1150 am Radio, New Kensington, Pa., 1999—2004. Co-founder Revelation the Gospel Newsletter, Pitts., 2000—. Author: (children's book) A Bedtime Story for Annika, short stories. Preschool tchr. Fox Chapel Presbyn. Ch. Recipient Trailblazers award, Rennasance Newspaper, 1996, Am. Fitness award, Am. Coun. Fitness Profls., 1990, 1991, 1993, 1995; scholar Coll. Students in Broadcasting, CBS Found., 1996. Mem.: Alpha Angels (pres. 1990—91). Avocations: fitness, spinning, cooking, weightlifting, travel. Office: Fox Chapel Presbyterian Church 384 Fox Chapel Rd Pittsburgh PA 15238 Home Phone: 412-826-8383; Office Phone: 412-963-8243. Personal E-mail: angeloftheairwaves1@yahoo.com. Business E-Mail: cubbageb@foxchapelpresby.com.

CUBELL, HOWARD ALAN, lawyer; b. Brookline, Mass., Dec. 23, 1948; s. Robert and Mildred (Sugarman) C.; m. Ivy Beth Wiener, May 2, 1972; children: Michael and Daniel (twins). BA, U. Mich., 1970; JD, Boston, 1973; postgrad., NYU, 1973-76. Bar: N.Y. 1973, Mass. 1975. Assoc. Skadden, Arps, Slate, Meagher & Flom, NYC, 1972-73, Debevoise & Plimpton, NYC, 1973-75; ptnr. Goodwin Procter LLP (formerly Goodwin, Procter & Hoar), Boston, 1975—; chair, tax practice group Goodwin Procter LLP, Boston. Editor articles Boston U. Law Rev., 1972-73. Mem. ABA (tax sect.), Internat. Bar Assn., Boston Bar Assn. (co-chmn. internat. tax subcom. tax sect.). Office: Goodwin Procter LLP Exchange Pl 53 State St Boston MA 02109-2803 Office Phone: 617-570-1560. Office Fax: 617-523-1231. Business E-Mail: hcubell@goodwinprocter.com.

CUBIN, BARBARA LYNN, congresswoman; b. Salinas, Calif., Nov. 30, 1946; d. Russell G. and Barbara Lee (Howard) Sage; m. Frederick William Cubin, Aug. 1; children: William Russell, Frederick William III. BS in Chemistry, Creighton U., 1969. Chemist Wyo. Machinery Co., Casper, Wyo., 1973-75; social worker State of Wyo.; office mgr. Casper, Wyo.; mem. Wyo. Ho. Reps., 1987-92, Wyo. Senate, 1993-94; pres. Spectrum Promotions and Mgmt., Casper, 1993-94; mem.-at-large US Congress from Wyo., Washington, 1995—, mem. resources com., energy and commerce com. Mem. steering com. Exptl. Program to Stimulate Competitive Rsch. (EPSCOR); mem. Coun. of State Govts.; active Gov.'s Com. on Preventive Medicine, 1992; vice chmn. Cleer Bd. Energy Coun., Irving, Tex., 1993—; chmn. Wyo. Senate Rep. Conf., Casper, 1993—; mem. Wyo. Rep. Party Exec. Com., 1993; pres. Southridge Elem. Sch. PTO, Casper, Wyo. Toll fellow Coun. State Govts., 1990, Wyo. Legislator of Yr. award for energy and environ. issues Edison Electric Inst., 1994. Mem. Am. Legis. Exch. Coun., Rep. Women. Republican. Avocations: bridge, golf, singing, reading, hunting. Office: US House of Reps 1114 Longworth House Office Bldg Washington DC 20515-5001 also: Dist Office 100 East B St Ste 4003 Casper WY 82601*

CUBITTO, ROBERT JOHN, lawyer; b. Globe, Ariz., Aug. 1, 1950; s. Claude A. and Arizona C. (DiMario) C. BA, U. Ariz., 1972, BSBA, 1974; JD, Harvard Law Sch., 1976. Bar: Mass. 1977, N.Y. 1979, U.S. Dist. Ct. (so. and ea. dists.) N.Y. 1979, U.S. Tax Ct. 1979. Cons. Boston Cons. Group, 1976-78; assoc. Debevoise & Plimpton LLP, NYC, 1978-84, ptnr., 1985—. Bd. dirs. Met. Opera, 2005—. Mem. ABA, NY State Bar Assn. (exec. com. tax sect. 1987-88), Assn. of Bar of City of NY, Harvard Club NYC (asst. treas. 1985-89, bd. mgrs. 1990-93), The Club of Turtle Bay (treas. 1994-97, pres. 1998—), The Met. Opera (bd. dirs. 2005-). Office: Debevoise & Plimpton LLP 919 3rd Ave New York NY 10022-3916 Office Phone: 212-909-6338.

CUCCO, ULISSE P., retired obstetrician, gynecologist; b. Bklyn., Aug. 19, 1929; s. Charles and Elvira (Garafalo) C.; m. Antoinette DeMarco, Aug. 31, 1952; children— Carl, Richard, Antoinette Marie, Michael, Frank, James BS cum laude, L.I. U., 1950; MD, Loyola U., Chgo., 1954. Diplomate Am. Bd. Ob-Gyn. Intern Nassau County Hosp., Hempstead, NY, 1954-55; resident in ob-gyn Lewis Meml. Mercy Hosp., Chgo., 1955-58; practice medicine specializing in ob-gyn Des Plaines, Ill., 1960—2001. Past pres. med. staff, chmn. dept. ob-gyn. Holy Family Hosp., Des Plaines, Ill.; clin. asst. prof. Stritch Sch. Medicine, Loyola U. Contbr. articles to med. jours. Mem. ACS, Am. Fertility Soc., Ctrl. Assn. Ob-Gyn., Ill. Med. Soc., Chgo. Med. Soc., Chgo. Gynecol. Soc. (past pres.), Chgo. Inst. Medicine, Sunset Ridge Country Club. Roman Catholic. Home: 665 Midfield Ln Northbrook IL 60062-5507

CUCIN, ROBERT LOUIS, plastic surgeon, lawyer; b. NYC, Apr. 17, 1946; s. Robert and Julia C. BA magna cum laude, Cornell U., 1967, MD, 1971; JD, Fordham U., 1985; MBA, Columbia U., 2003. Bar: N.Y. 1983, N.J. State Sureme Ct., Washington Ct. of Appeals; bd. cert. legal medicine, diplomate Am. Bd. Surgery, Am. Bd. Plastic Surgery, lic. physician NJ, N.Y. State, Calif., Va., gen. socs. prin.; securities license series 4, 7, 24, 27 and 63. Intern Cornell-N.Y. Hosp., NYC, 1971-72, resident in gen. surgery, 1972-76, resident in plastic surgery, 1977-79; fellow in surgery Meml.-Sloan Kettering Found., 1972-76, 77-79; practice medicine specializing in plastic surgery Columbia MBA, NYC, 1979—; instr. surgery Cornell U. Med. Coll., 1980—; asst. attending plastic surgeon Beth Israel North, N.Y. Downtown Hosp., 1979—, N.Y. Hosp., 1980—, Drs. Hosp., 1987—. Pres. Esquire Cadillac Limousine Svc. Inc., 1977—93, Beaux Arts Holdings, 1979—, Rocin Labs., Inc., 1981—; pres., CEO Biosculpture Tech., Inc., 2001—. Author: The Kindest Cut, Keeping Face, Medical Malpractice: Handling Plastic Surgical Cases; contbr. articles to profl. jours. Mem. N.Y. County Health Svc. Rev. Orgn., 1976—; founder dir Rocin Found. for Plastic Surg. Rsch., 1979—; Maj. M.C., USAF, 1976-77; Japan. Fellow: ACS, Am. Coll. Legal Medicine, Internat. Coll. Surgeons; mem.: ABA, ATLA, AMA (Physicians Recognition award 1978, 1981), N.Y. Acad. Scis., N.Y. County Med. Soc. (health systems, pub. rels., peer rev. coms.), N.Y. State Med. Soc., Royal Soc. Medicine, Am. Soc. Plastic and Reconstructive Surgery, Am. Mensa, Cornell Club, N.Y. Athletic Club, Le Club, Phi Beta Kappa. Republican. Office: 40 Central Park South New York NY 10019-1560 Office Phone: 212-586-9500.

CUCULLU, SANTIAGO, artist; b. Buenos Aires, 1969; BFA, Hartford Art Sch., 1992; MFA, Mpls. Coll. Art & Design, 1999. One-man shows include Solo Show, Boom Gallery, Mpls., 1999, Art Houston, Barbara

Davis Gallery, Houston, 2002, Wiyya To Hell Owwa That, Julia Friedman Gallery, Chgo., 2003, Art Basel Miami: Art Statements, Barbara Davis Gallery, Houston, 2003, Arco: Madrid Project Room, Julia Friedman Gallery, Chgo., 2004, Mori Art Mus., Tokyo, 2004, Hammer Mus., LA, 2004, exhibited in group shows, Escacio de Pensamiento, Bueno Aires, Argentina, 1995, Dumb & Evil, Calhoun Sq. Gallery, Mpls., 1998, Push, Pull Pop, 1999, XL, Weinstein Gallery, Mpls., 2000, 13 From Mpls., Mpls., 2002, Fresh-The Altoids Collection, Mus. Contemporary Art, NY, 2003, Works on Paper, Blum & Poe Gallery, LA, 2003, How Latitudes Become Forms, Walker Art Ctr., Mpls., 2004, Whitney Biennial, Whitney Mus. Am. Art, 2004. Jerome Emerging Artist Fellowship, Mpls. Coll. Art & Design, 2000. Office: c/o Perry Rubenstein Gallery 527 W 23rd St New York NY 10011

CUDAHY, RICHARD D., federal judge; b. Milw., Feb. 2, 1926; s. Michael F. and Alice ((Dickson)) Cudahy; m. Ann (Featherston), July 14, 1956 (dec. 1974); m. Janet (Stuart), July 17, 1976; children: Richard D., Norma K., Theresa E., Daniel M., Michaela A., Marguerite L., Patrick G. BS, U.S. Mil. Acad., 1948; JD, Yale U., 1955; LLD, Ripon Coll., 1981, DePaul U., 1995, Wabash Coll., 1996, Stetson U., 1998. Bar: Conn. 1955, D.C. 1957, Ill. 1957, Wis. 1961. Commd., 2d. lt. US Army, 1948, 1st. lt., 1950; law clk. to presiding judge US Ct. Appeals (2d cir.), 1955—56; asst. to legal adv. Dept. State, 1956—57; assoc. Isham, Lincoln, and Beale, Chgo., 1957—60; pres. Patrick Cudahy, Inc., Wis., 1961—71, Patrick Cudahy Family Co., Wis., 1968—75; ptnr. firm Godfrey and Kahn, Milw., 1972; commr., chmn. Wis. Pub. Svc. Commn., 1972—75; ptnr. Isham, Lincoln, and Beale, Chgo. and Washington, 1976—79; judge US Ct. Appeals (7th cir.), Chgo., 1979—94, sr. judge, 1994—. Lectr. law Marquette U. Law Sch., 1962—66; vis. prof. law U. Wis., 1966—67; prof. lectr. law George Washington U., Washington, 1978—79; adj. prof. DePaul U. Coll. Law, 1995—. Commr. Milw. Harbor, 1964—66; pres. Milw. Urban League, 1965—66; trustee Environ. Def. Fund, 1976—79; chmn. DePaul U., Human Rights Law Inst., 1990—98; mem. adv. com. Ctr. for Internat. Human Rights, Northwestern U., 2000—; mem. vis. com. U. Chgo. Div. Sch.; chmn. Wis. Dem. Party, 1967—68; Dem. candidate for Wis. Atty. Gen., 1968. Mem.: ABA (spl. com. on Energy Law 1978—84, pub. utility sect. coun. group), Internat. Aviation Law Inst. of DePaul U., DC Cir. Apptd. Ind. Counsel (spl. divsn. 1998—2002), Ill. Bar Assn., DC Bar Assn., Am. Inst. for Pub. Svc. (bd. selectors 1973—98), Fed. Judges' Assn. (bd. dirs. 1993—96), Chgo. Bar Assn., Wis. Bar Assn., Am. Law Inst., Cath. Theol. Union, Lawyers Club, Chgo. (pres. 1992—93). Office: US Ct Appeals 219 S Dearborn St Ste 2648 Chicago IL 60604-1874*

CUDAK, GAIL LINDA, lawyer; b. Bellville, Ill., July 13, 1952; d. Robert Joseph and Margaret Lucille Cudak; m. Thomas Edward Young, Sept. 15, 1979. BA, Kenyon Coll., 1974; JD, Case Western Res. U., 1977, MBA, 1991. Bar: Ohio 1977, U.S. Dist. Ct. (no. dist.) Ohio 1977, U.S. Ct. Appeals (6th cir.) 1977, U.S. Ct. Appeals (fed. cir.) 1989. Assoc. Fuerst, Leidner, Dougherty & Kasdan, Cleve., 1977-79; staff atty. The B.F. Goodrich Co., Akron, Ohio, 1979-84, sr. corp. counsel Independence, Ohio, 1985-89, divsn. counsel Brecksville, Ohio, 1990-98, group counsel, 1998-99; counsel ops. Eaton Corp., Cleve., 1999—. Trustee Great Lakes Theater Festival, 1992—, mem. exec. com. Mem.: ABA, Assn. Corp. Counsel (trustee N.E. Ohio chpt. 2006—), Cleve. Internat. Lawyers Group, Cleve. Bar Assn. (past chair corp. sect.), Ohio State Bar Assn. Home: 12520 Edgewater Dr Apt 1405 Lakewood OH 44107-1639 Office: Eaton Corp 1111 Superior Ave E Cleveland OH 44114-2507

CUDDIHY, ROBERT VINCENT, JR., finance and marketing executive; b. Rochester, NY, July 15, 1959; s. Robert Vincent Sr. and June Marie (Tuck) C.; m. Michele Pittenger; children: Brendan, Shea, Tara. BA in Acctg., Franklin and Marshall Coll., Lancaster, Pa., 1981. CPA N.Y. Sr. mgr. KPMG Peat Marwick, NYC, 1981-87; pres., CFO, COO, sec. HMG Worldwide Corp., NYC, 1987-2001, bd. dirs., 1988—2001, chief oper. officer, 1989-2000, pres., 1990-93, chief info. officer, 2000-01; CFO, treas., sec. iDNA, Inc. (formerly Nat. Auto Credit, Inc.), 2001—; pres. Shannon Hill Assocs., 2001—. Cons. in field. Bd. dirs., pres. Bridgewater Bears Hockey Assn., 2001—06; del. Mid-Atlantic Women's Hockey Assn., 2004—06. Mem. Am. Inst. CPAs, N.Y. State Soc. CPAs, Nat. Assn. Accts. Republican. Avocations: home improvements, hockey, reading.

CUDDY, DANIEL HON, bank executive; b. Valdez, Alaska, Feb. 8, 1921; s. Warren N. and Lucy C.; m. Betty Puckett, Oct. 6, 1947; children: Roxanna, David, Gretchen, Jane, Lucy, Laurel. BA, Stanford U., 1946; LLD (hon.), U. Alaska, 2000. Bar: Alaska 1948. Pvt. practice, Anchorage, 1948-53; pres. First Nat. Bank Anchorage, 1951—, chmn. bd.; consul for the Netherlands, 1975—85. With U.S. Army, World War II, ETO. Named a William A. Egan Outstanding Alaskan, Alaska State C. of C., 2006; named Alaskan of Yr., 2002. Office: First Nat Bank 101 W 36th Ave Anchorage AK 99503-5904

CUDNEY, ELIZABETH A.F., industrial engineer; d. John S.W. Fargher, Jr. and Eleanor J. Fargher; m. Brian J. Cudney, Apr. 18, 1998; children: Caroline E., Joshua C. BS in Indsl. Engring., NC State U., Raleigh, 1996; M of Mech. Engring., U. Hartford, Conn., 2000, MBA, 2002; PhD in Engring. Mgmt., U. Mo., Rolla, 2006. Postdoctoral fellow U. Mo., 2006—07, asst. prof., 2007—. Grad. rsch. asst. U. Mo., 2003—06; adj. prof. U. Hartford, 2000—03; mfg. mgr., quality engr. Jacobs Vehicle Systems, Bloomfield, Conn., 1998—2003; indsl. engr. Dana Corp., Whitsett, NC, 1996—98. Contbr. articles to profl. jours. Recipient Outstanding Young Mfg. Engr. award, Soc. Mfg. Engrs., 2006, Outstanding Grad. Tchg. Asst. award, UMR Engring. Mgmt. and Systems Engring. Dept., 2004. Mem.: DAR (sec. 2006—), ASME, Soc. Automotive Engineers, Am. Soc. Quality, Inst. Indsl. Engrs. (pres. lean divsn. 2005—07), Rotary (bd. dirs. 2006—07), Omicron Delta Kappa, Tau Beta Pi. Office: U Mo 112A Engring Mgmt Rolla MO 65409 Business E-Mail: elizabeth.cudney@umr.edu.

CUELLAR, HENRY, congressman, lawyer; b. Laredo, Tex., Sept. 19, 1955; s. Martin and Odilia (Perez) Cuellar. AA, Laredo CC, Tex., 1976; BS cum laude in Fgn. Svc., Georgetown U., 1978; JD, U. Tex., Austin, 1981; MA in Internat. Trade, Tex. A&M Internat. U., 1982; PhD in Govt., U. Tex., Austin, 1998. Bar: Tex., US Dist. Ct. (so. dist. Tex.), US Ct. Appeals (5th cir.), US Ct. Internat. Trade. Atty. Henry Cuellar Law Office, Laredo, Tex., 1981—; customs broker Laredo, Tex., 1983—; mem. Tex. State Ho. Reps., 1987—2001; sec. state Tex., 2001; mem. US Congress from 28th Tex. dist., 2005—, mem. agr. com., mem. budget com. Adj. prof. internat. comml. law Laredo State U., 1984-86; instr. state and nat. govt. Laredo Jr. Coll., 1982-86; speaker in field. Pres. bd. dirs. Laredo Legal Aid Soc. Inc., 1982-84, Laredo Vol. Lawyers Prog. Inc., 1982-83, Internat. Good Neighbor Coun., 1984-85; treas., bd. dirs. Stop Child Abuse and Neglect, 1982-83, adv. bd., 1984—; state legal adv. Am. GI Forum Tex., 1986-88; bd. dirs. United Way. 1982-83. Named Laredo Pro Bono Atty. of Yr., 1985; named one of Outstanding Young Men Am., 1982, 1986. Mem.: ABA, Inter-Am. Bar Assn., Tex. Bar Assn., Laredo Young Lawyers Assn. (pres. 1982—83), Kiwanis (bd. dirs. 1982—83). Democrat. Roman Catholic. Avocations: reading, karate, football, weightlifting. Office: US Ho Reps 1404 Longworth Ho Office Bldg Washington DC 20515-4328 Office Phone: 202-225-1640.

CUENDET, MURIEL, research scientist; b. Lausanne, Vaud, Switzerland, July 20, 1970; d. Marc-Henri Emile and Marlyse Cuendet; m. Alejandro Licea, June 28, 2003; 1 child, Amanda Noemi Licea. PharmD, U. Lausanne, Switzerland, 1994, PhD, 1999. Rsch. asst. prof. U. Ill., Chgo., 2002—05; vis. asst. prof. Purdue U., West Lafayette, Ind., 2005—06; rsch. scientist Gerald P. Murphy Cancer Found., West Lafayette, 2007—. Leader Scouts, Lausanne, 1988—99. Mem.: Assn. Women Sci., Am. Assn. Cancer Rsch. Achievements include research in study of natural inhibitors of carcinogenesis. Avocation: flute. Office: Gerald P Murphy Cancer Found 3000 Kent Ave West Lafayette IN 47906 Home Phone: 765-497-2679; Office Phone: 765-775-1034. Business E-Mail: cuendet@purdue.edu.

CUERO, RAUL G., microbiologist, researcher, educator; BSc in Biology with honors, Heidelberg Coll., 1971; MSc in Plant Pathology, Ohio State U., 1974; PhD, U. Strathclyde, 1986. Biologist U. Valle, Cali, 1965—69, prof., rschr. microbiology, cons. FAO-UN fish microbiology project, 1975—80, cons. FAO-UN fish microbiology project, 1976—77, internat. cons. sci.-tech. industry and govts.; biology lab. asst. Heidelberg Coll., Tiffin, Ohio, 1970—71; rsch. lab asst. Ohio State U., 1971—74, Agrl. Rsch. Devel. Ctr., Wooster, Ohio, 1971—74; mem. planned staff Faculty Former DAG Hammarskhold Coll., Md., 1974; rsch. assoc. US grain mktg. rsch. lab. USDA, Manhattan, Kans., 1980; rsch. assoc. USDA-ARS So. Regional Rsch. Ctr., New Orleans, 1986—87; rsch. scientist Prairie View A&M U., 1987—, disting. hon. prof., 2000; rsch. microbiologist Coop. Agrl. Rsch. Ctr., Prairie View (Tex.) A&M U., 1988—. Vis. scientist USDA-ARS So. Regional Rsch. Ctr., New Orleans, 1982, Volcani Rsch. Ctr., Israel, 1993; coord. US Govt. Nutrition and Health Program for Migrant Workers, Ohio, 1971; project evaluator Tex. Internat. Edn. Consortium, 1994; sci. evaluator nat. projects on environ. biology EPA, 1995—96; sci. project evaluator SBIR/USDA, 1995—; sci.-tchg. project evaluator Tex. Dept. Edn. Agy., 1997; presenter, cons., lectr. in field; internat. sci. lectr. nat. and internat. presentations. Author: (autobiography) Between Triumph and Survival, 2005; mem. editl. bd.: Jour. Food Chemistry and Agrl. Bioengring. and Biotech.; contbr. articles to profl. jours., to more than 90 sci. publs., chapters to books. Rsch. mentor Prairie View A&M U., 1995. Nominee Tech. Brief Monetary award, NASA; named Outstanding Student, UNESCO, Eng., 1983, Disting. Rsch. Scientist, Prairie View A&M U., 1989, Outstanding Mentor, 1995; named one of The Best Basketball Players, History of Colombia, 1965—79, Colombian Outstanding Scientist Oversea, Diners Club, 1994; recipient Outstanding Recognition award, Prairie View A&M U., 1989, 1992, 1993, 1994, Tech. award, NASA, 2003, Colombia Honor medal, Colombian Congress, 2003, Simon Bolivar Honor medal, The Gov. State of Valle, Colombia, 2005; grantee, OMO Co., 2004, NASA, 2005; scholar, Heidelberg Coll., 1970—71, Ohio State U., 1971—74; Synthetic Biology grantee, NSF, 2006. Mem.: Am. Phytopathol. Soc., Internat. Soc. for Molecular Microbe-Plant Interactions, Internat. Commn. on Natural Health Products, Colombian Soc. for Phytopathology, Am. Soc. Phytopathology, Am. Mus. Nat. History, Am. Chitosci. Soc., Soc. for Gen. Microbiology (Gt. Britain), Sigma Xi. Achievements include patents for fungal biocontrol in plant and food; patents pending for enhancement of purification of crude oil, reduction of sulfur, increase of combustion and control of oil contamination, removal of radio-nuclear and heavy metal pollutants using a martian simulant material; invention of cost effective oil bioremediation method, semi scale pilot sys. to study bioremediation of chemicals and oil, recovery and flocculation of toxic metals chromium, lead, zinc and copper; antifungal and antibacterial bioactive glass; using maritan simulant soil to remove toxic and/or radionuclide metals; research in in antimicrobial and environmental technology; biogenesis; discovery of of latest scientific paradigm which is extra-terrestial microscopic life is between inorganic and organic. Avocations: piano, writing, reading, tennis. Mailing: PO Box 685 Prairie View TX 77446 Personal E-mail: olimpa@aol.com.

CUERVO-CAZURRA, ALVARO, finance educator; PhD in Bus. Econ., U. Salamanca, Spain, 1997; PhD in Mgmt., MIT, Cambridge, Mass., 1999. Asst. prof. internat. bus. Carlson Sch. Mgmt., U. Minn., Mpls., 1999—2005, Moore Sch. Bus., U. S.C., Columbia, 2005—. Mem. editl. bd.: Orgn. Studies, 2003—, Mgmt. Rsch., 2003—, Economia y Administracion, 2005—, Globalization, Competitiveness and Govt., 2007—; contbr. articles to profl. jours. Mem.: Strategic Mgmt. Soc. (rep. at large 2006—07), Am. Econ. Assn., Acad. Internat. Bus., Acad. Mgmt. (comm. exec. com., internat. mgmt. divsn. 2006—07). Office: Moore Sch Bus Univ SC 1705 College St Columbia SC 29208 Office Phone: 803-777-0314. Office Fax: 803-777-3609. Business E-Mail: acuervo@moore.sc.edu.

CUETO, ROCHELLE E., elementary school educator; b. Chgo., Nov. 19, 1949; d. Morris and Marsha L. (Rotman) Federman; m. Fernando J. Cueto, Sept. 13, 1979 (div. Aug. 1987); children: Steven, Jennifer; children: Eric Raymond, Laura Raymond. BA in Spl. Edn., Northeastern Ill. U., 1974, MA in Spl. Edn., 1980. Cert. tchr. Ill., spl. edn., lang. arts cert./endorsement, mid. sch. endorsement, sci. endorsement, cert. family life coord., Golden Tchr. coach. Tchr. elem. Jordan Cmty. Sch. Chgo. Pub. Schs., 1975—. Judge Chgo. Bd. Elections, 1977. Mem.: NSTA, Ill. Sci. Tchrs. Assn. Jewish. Avocations: needlepoint, reading, gardening. Home: 7233A N Campbell Ave Chicago IL 60645 Office: Jordan Cmty Sch 7414 N Wolcott Ave Chicago IL 60626 Office Phone: 773-534-2220.

CUETTER, ALBERT CAYETANO, neurologist; b. Cartagena, Colombia, Aug. 7, 1938; MD, Med. U. Cartagena, Colombia, 1963. Diplomate Am. Bd. Neurology, Bd. of Electrodiagnostic Medicine. Intern Hosp. Santa Clara, Cartagena, Colombia, 1963-64; resident in neurology Northwestern U., 1965-68, fellowship in electromyography, 1968-69; prof. neurology Tex. Tech U. Health Scis. Ctr., El Paso, 1990—. Office Phone: 915-545-6703. Personal E-mail: albert.cuetter@ttuhsc.edu.

CUFF, VIRGINIA EVELYN, architectural firm executive, consultant; d. Raymond and Dorothy Edwina Williams; m. Elliott Cuff, Dec. 9, 1989. MPA, Baruch Coll., NY, 1998. Founding exec. dir. Family & Life Ctr. Mt. Ararat, Bklyn., 1994—2004; exec. asst. to exec. commr. NYC Human Resources Adminstrn., 1996—97; cons., pres. Virgelli-Snu, Inc., Mason, Ohio, 2006—; archtl. adminstr. DHArchitects, Inc., Fairfield, 2006—. Bd. mem. Scholarship Found. Mt. Ararat, Bklyn., 1995—2004; vp bus. devel. Greater Cin. C. of C., Cin., 2004—05; mem. bd. Help, USA, Bklyn., 2003—04; treas. Northridge Village Assn., Mason, 2006; adv. bd. mem. universal pre-kindergarten fed. initiative Dept. Edn., Dist. 23, 1998—2002. Recipient DAR Good Citizenship award, DAR, Va. Chpt., 1982, Disting. Leadership award, 2001, Ezra award Excellence, Mt. Ararat, 1999, Vigorous Spririt award, Elon Cosmetics, 2005; fellow, Nat. Urban and Rural Fellows, Inc., 1996—98. Mem.: Golden Key Nat. Honor Soc. Baptist. Achievements include development of Music & Arts Academy Serving inner-city children; Assisted in developing an economic development corporation for African American families in the inner-city; Summer Cultural Camp for inner-city children; School-Age program for inner-city children; School with an emphasis on Early Childhood Education for inner-city children. Avocations: tennis, golf, travel, reading, writing. Office: Virgelli-Snu Inc PO Box 132 Mason OH 45040 Home Phone: 513-398-7137; Office Phone: 513-258-8137. E-mail: consulting@virgelli-snu.com.

CUFFEY, KURT M., geophysicist, geochemist, educator; PhD, U. Wash., 1999. Asst. prof. to prof. depts. geography and earth and planetary scis. U. Calif., Berkeley. Contbr. articles to sci. jours. Named one of Brilliant 10, Popular Sci. mag., 2004; recipient Macelwane medal, Am. Geophys. Union, 2003. Office: Dept Geography U Calif Berkeley 507 McCone Hall Berkeley CA 94720-4740 Office Phone: 510-643-1641. Office Fax: 510-642-3370. E-mail: kcuffey@berkeley.edu.*

CUGGINO, MICHAEL JOSEPH, financial executive; b. Cambridge, Mass., Feb. 9, 1963; s. Joseph Anthony Jr. and Christine Adele (Dabrowski) C. Student, Bentley Coll., 1985. CPA, Mass., Calif.; CISA. With Ernst & Young, LLP, 1985-91; pvt. practice acctg., 1991—2002; founder, pres., CEO, Pacific Heights Asset Mgmt., LLC, 2002—. Treas. Permanent Portfolio Family of Funds, Inc., 1993-07, bd. dirs., 1998—, pres., 2003—, sec., 2007—; treas. World Money Securities, Inc., 1993-96, Bullion Security Corp., 1993-02, Passport Fin., Inc., 1993-02. Mem. AICPA (pvt. cos. practice sect., mgmt. cons. practice sect., pers. fin. planning practice sect., tax practice sect.), Mass. Soc. CPAs, Calif. Soc. CPAs, EDP Auditors Assn. Home: 2201 Pacific Ave Apt 703 San Francisco CA 94115-1440 Office: Transam Ctr 600 Montgomery St 27th Fl San Francisco CA 94111-2702

CUI, HONGLIANG, engineering company executive, researcher; b. Hegang, Heilongjiang, China, July 7, 1965; arrived in U.S., 1999; s. Guanglin Cui and Jinyu Wang; m. Junxiu Zhu, May 15, 1965; 1 child, Weiqi. BS, Northwestern Poly. U., 1986; MS, Beijing U. Aeros. and Astronautics, 1991; PhD, U. Tokyo, 1999, Stevens Inst. Tech., 2006. Dir., engr. Shenyang Aircraft Rsch. Inst., Liaoning, China, 1986—95; with Inst. of Space and Aero. Sci. / U. Tokyo, Shagamihara, Kanagawa Ken, Japan, 1996—99; rschr. ABB Robotics, Windsor, Conn., 2000—04; exec. mgr. NDT, East Windsor, Conn., 2004—. Mem.: AIAA, ASME, Sigma Xi. Christian. Achievements include development of China fighter structure design; composite aircraft structure design; research in kinematics and error modeling of parallel robot; patents in field of six degrees of freedom measuring system. Home Phone: 860-233-8853. Office Fax: 860-627-9476; Home Fax: 860-233-8853. Personal E-mail: hcuids@gmail.com. Business E-Mail: hcui@ndt-us.com.

CUIFFO, FRANK WAYNE, lawyer; b. Houston, Oct. 13, 1943; s. Richard and Helen (Giaco) C.; m. Barbara Joyce Streeter, Nov. 26, 1966; children: Karen, Deborah, Richard, Steven. BS, U. Notre Dame, 1964; JD, Fordham U., 1967. Bar: N.Y. 1967. Assoc. Pennie & Edmonds (formerly Pennie, Edmonds, Morton, Taylor & Adams), NYC, 1967-69; sr. assoc. Emmet, Marvin, & Martin, NYC, 1969-74, Golenbock & Barell, NYC, 1974-78; mng. ptnr. Carro, Spanbock, Kaster & Cuiffo, NYC, 1978-93; chmn. real estate dept., exec. com. Donovan, Leisure, Newton & Irvine, NYC, 1993-98; ptnr. McDermott, Will & Emery, NYC, 1998—. Mem. ABA, U.S. Patent Bar, N.Y. State Bar, Siwanoy Country Club, South Seas Club. Office: McDermott Will & Emery LLP 340 Madison Ave New York NY 10017 Home Phone: 914-337-4704. Personal E-mail: fcuiffo@mwe.com.

CULBERSON, GARY MICHAEL, hotel manager; b. Jackson, Miss., Sept. 16, 1955; s. William James and Peggy Ann (Pickett) C.; m. Mary Lee Yadron, May 8, 1986; children: Ashley Victoria, Brent Michael. Student, Miss. State U., 1973-78. Cert. hotel adminstr. Resident mgr. Kingston Plantation, Myrtle Beach, SC; exec. asst., mgr. Brown Palace Hotel, Denver; mng. dir. Tremont Hotel, Chgo., 1991; gen. mgr. Embassy Suites Hotel, Denver, 1996-97; hotel mgr. Casino Magic Hotel, Biloxi, Miss., 1997—2002; v.p. Beau Rivage Resort, Biloxi, 2002—05; owner Mellow Mushroom Restaurant, 2005—. Mem.: So. Innkeepers (v.p. 2001—), Miss. Hotel and Lodging Assn. (v.p. 2001—02, pres. 2002—03, Gen. Mgr. of Yr. 2002), Miss. Gulf Coast Hotel and Motel Assn. (v.p. 1998—99, pres. 2000—02), Confrerie de la Chaine des Rotisseurs (Maitre of Table Restaurateur 1991—92), Mensa. Avocations: skiing, golf. Office: 3903 Cabildo Pl Ocean Springs MS 39564 Office Phone: 228-818-5581. E-mail: mellowmushroom@cableone.net.

CULBERSON, JOHN ABNEY, congressman, lawyer; b. Houston, June 24, 1956; m. Belinda Burney, Dec. 1989; 1 child: Caroline Virginia. BA in hist., So. Meth. U., Dallas, 1981; JD, South Tex. Coll. Law, 1988. Oil rig mud logger, 1978—81; polit. advt. agy. employee, 1981—85; sr. assoc. civil def. atty. Lorance & Thompson, Houston, 1985; mem. Tex. State Ho. Reps., 1986-2000, US Congress from 7th Tex. dist., 2001—, mem. appropriations com. Co-recipient Outstanding Young Houstonian award, Houston Jaycees, 1994; recipient Leader of Excellence award, Free Market Assn., 1993, Friend of the Taxpayer award, Tex. Citizens for a Sound Economy, 2000, Hero of the Taxpayer award, Ams. for Tax Reform, 2002, Spirit of Enterprise award, US C. of C., 2002, Award for Mfg. Legis. Excellence, Nat. Assn Mfrs., 2005, Brighter Vision award, Seniors Coalition, 2005. Mem. United Meth. Church. Office: US Ho Reps 1728 Longworth Ho Office Bldg Washington DC 20515-4307 Office Phone: 202-225-2571.*

CULBERT, DAVID HOLBROOK, historian, educator, editor, writer; b. San Antonio, July 7, 1943; s. Robert William Culbert and Dorothy Fairfax Kift; m. Lubna Araki, May 26, 1979. Student, Mozarteum, Salzburg, Austria, 1963-64; BA, Oberlin Coll., 1966; MusB, Oberlin Conservatory Music, 1966; PhD, Northwestern U., 1970. Asst. prof. history Yale U., New Haven, 1970-71, La. State U., Baton Rouge, 1971-76, assoc. prof. history, 1976-84, prof. history, 1984—, John L. Loos prof. history, 2005—. Author: News for Everyman, 1976, Mission to Moscow, 1980; editor-in-chief: Film and Propaganda in America, 5 vols., 1990—93; editor (with John Chambers): World War II, Film and History, 1996; editor: (with Nicholas Cull and David Welch) Propaganda and Mass Persuasion: A Historical Encyclopedia (1500 to the Present), 2003; editor: (with K. R. M. Short) Cambridge Studies in the History of Mass Communications, 1999—; editor: (with David Welch) Studies in Propaganda, 1999—; editor: Hist. Jour. Film, Radio and TV, 1992—; contbr. articles to profl. jours.; dir. hist. rsch., assoc. prodr.: (films) Huey Long, 1985; co-prodr.: Television's Vietnam: The Impact of Media, 1986; hist. cons.: Die Macht der Bilder: Leni Riefenstahl, 1993; sr. cons.: (TV miniseries) Dawn of the Eye, 1998. Organist-choirmaster St. James Episcopal Ch., Baton Rouge, 1981—. Fellow, Woodrow Wilson Ctr. Scholars, 1976—77, Nat. Humanities Inst., Yale U., 1977—78; Vis. fellow, Inst. Advanced Study, 1995. Mem.: Internat. Assn. Media and History (coun., pres. 1987—89), Am. Hist. Assn. (chmn. John O'Connor Prize com. 2000—01), Orgn. Am. Historians (1st chmn. com. radio-TV-film media, 1st chmn. Erik Barnouw Prize com. 1981—84), Grolier Club, City Club Baton Rouge, Phi Beta Kappa, Pi Kappa Lambda. Republican. Home: 2933 Reymond Ave Baton Rouge LA 70808 Office: Dept History La State U 224 Himes Hall Baton Rouge LA 70803 Office Phone: 225-578-4471. Personal E-mail: dhculbert@aol.com.

CULBERTSON, FRANCES MITCHELL, psychology professor; b. Boston, Jan. 31, 1921; d. David and Goldie (Fishman) Mitchell; m. John Mathew Culbertson, Aug. 27, 1947; children: John David, Joanne, Lyndall, Amy. BS, U. Mich., 1947, MS, 1949, PhD, 1955. Diplomate Am. Bd. of Profl. Psychology; lic. psychologist, Wis. Clin. child psychologist Wis. Diagnostic Ctr., Madison, 1961-65; chief clin. psychologist dept. child psychiatry U. Wis., Madison, 1965-66; resident rsch. psychologist NIMH, Berkeley, Calif., 1966-67; psychologist Madison Pub. Schs., 1967-68; prof. psychology U. Wis., Whitewater, 1968-88, prof. emeritus, 1988—; psychologist Mental Health Assocs., Madison, 1987—2003. Clin. psychologist Counseling and Psychotherapy Assn., Madison, 1982-87; clin. hypnotherapy cons. Family Achievement Ctr., Oconomowoc, Wis., 1984-89; cons. Wis Disability Determination Bur., 2001—. Author: Voices in International School Psychology, 1985; contbr. chpts. to books, articles to profl. jours. Mem. Dane County Mental Health Bd., Madison, 1980-82. Fellow: APA (bd. conv. affairs 1990—94, pres. sect. clin. psychology women 1991—92, coun. rep. liaison and bd. mem. internat. psychology divsn. 52 1997—97, chmn. membership com., coun. rep. psychol. hypnosis divsn. 1998—99, coun. rep. internat. psych. divsn., coun. mem. 1999—2003, bd. dirs. internat. psych. divsn. 2003—, bd. dirs. divsn. 52 2003—07, accreditation rev. com. 2005—, Contbn. award for internat. achievement 1994, Divsn. 1 Eminent Woman in Psychology award 1999, Divsn. 52 Career award for outstanding contbns. to internat. psychology 1999); mem.: Madison Hypnotherapy Soc. (pres. 1986—94), Brazilian Soc. Clin. Psychology (hon. pres. 1979), Wis. Psychol. Assn. (pres. divsn. psychol. hypnosis 1991—99), Internat. Coun. Psychologists (pres. 1979), Internat. Soc. Clin. Psychology (founding co-chair 1997—98, treas.

1997—), Internat. Assn. Applied Psychology Divsn. Applied Gerontology (pres.-elect 1994—98, exec. bd. mem. 1995—, pres. 1998—2003, past pres. 2003—), Phi Kappa Phi, Pi Lambda Theta, Sigma Xi. Avocations: skiing, walking, hiking, reading, gardening. Home: 8301 Old Sauk Rd Apt 323 Middleton WI 53562-4394 Office: Capitol Assoc LLC 440 Science Dr #200 Madison WI 53711 Office Phone: 608-238-5176. Personal E-mail: franculb@aol.com.

CULBERTSON, JACK ARTHUR, education educator; b. Nickelsville, Va., July 16, 1918; s. Otto Cecil and Lola Kate (Fuller) C.; m. Mary Virginia Pond, Aug. 12, 1952; children: Karen Anne Hasselo, Margaret Lynn. AB in Edn., Emory and Henry Coll., Va., 1943; MA in German, Duke U., Durham, NC, 1946; PhD in Ednl. Adminstrn., U. Calif., Berkeley, 1955. Cert. tchr., sch. adminstr., Va., Calif. Tchg. prin. Scott County Sch. Sys., Gate City, Va., 1937—41, Jewell Ridge (Va.) Sch. Sys., 1941—42, Tazewell (Va.) County Sch. Sys., 1947—49; H.S. tchr. Mineral Springs (N.C.) Sch. Sys., 1943—44; tchr. jr. H.S. El Centro (Calif.) Sch. Sys., 1949—51; sch. supt. Ellwood Sch. Dist., Goleta, Calif., 1951—53; prof. U. Oreg., Eugene, 1955—59; exec. dir. Univ. Coun. for Ednl. Adminstrn., Columbus, 1959—81; prof. Ohio State U., Columbus, 1981—86, emeritus prof., 1986—. Cons. W.K. Kellogg Found., Battle Creek, Mich., 1968, Ford Found., N.Y.C., 1967; advisor Edn. Commn. States, Denver, 1967, Pan Am. Union, Washington, 1968; founder 1st Internat. Intervisitation Program in Ednl. Adminstrn., 1966; spkr. OAS, Brasilia, Brazil, 1968, Australian Coun. for Ednl. Rsch., Sydney, 1967, German Assn. for Tng. Sch. Adminstrs., 1975. Author: Building Bridges, 1995; co-author: Administrative Relationships, 1960, Preparing Educational Leaders for the Seventies, 1969. Recipient Commonwealth Fellow award Commonwealth Coun. for Ednl. Adminstrn., 1978, Roald F. Campbell Lifetime Achievement award Univ. Coun. for Ednl. Adminstrn., 1993. Mem. Am. Ednl. Rsch. Assn. (v.p. 1964-66), Am. Assn. Sch. Adminstrs. (adv. commn. 1974-76), Nat. Coun. for Profs. of Ednl. Adminstrn. (exec. com. 1957-60, Living Legends award 1999-2000), Nat. Soc. for Study of Edn. (co-editor yearbook 1986). Avocations: reading, television, card playing. Home: 145 Montrose Way Columbus OH 43214-3634

CULBERTSON, JANE YOUNG, statistician; b. Phila., Sept. 9, 1917; d. Samuel Lemon Young and Jennie Goddard Harper; m. Harry Edward Jr. Culbertson (dec.); children: Karen Ruth Corbin, Harry Edward III. BS in Edn., Temple U., Phila., 1938. Statistician Farm Jour., Phila., 1937—42; sec. to supt. DuPont, Phila., 1945—50. Soloist Local churches in NJ and Pa.; pres., treas. Free Pub. Libr., 1990—92. Recipient Citizen of Yr., Sentinel Ledger, Ocean City, NJ, 1998, Libr. Citation, Ocean City C. of C., 2000. Mem.: MENSA, Ocean City Gardens Civic Assn., Ocean City Hist. Mus. Republican. Presbyterian. Avocations: bridge, crossword puzzles, Scrabble. Home: 416 W Surf Rd Ocean City NJ 08226

CULBERTSON, JANET LYNN, artist; b. Greensburg, Pa., Mar. 15, 1932; d. Joseph F. and Helen C. (Moore) Culbertson; m. Douglas I. Kaften, Sept. 30, 1964. BFA, Carnegie Inst. Tech., 1953; MA, NYU, 1963. Instr. art Pace Coll., NYC, 1964-68, Pratt Art Inst., Bklyn., 1973; assoc. prof. Southampton Coll., 1976; drawing instr. Parrish Art Mus., 1979. Exhibited one-woman shows 20th Century West Gallery, N.Y.C., 1967, Molly Barnes Gallery, L.A., 1970, Midtown Gallery, Atlanta, 1971, Lerner-Misrachi Gallery, N.Y.C., 1971, Lerner-Heller Gallery, N.Y.C., 1973, 75, 77, Tower Gallery, Southampton, N.Y., 1976, Benson Gallery, Bridgehampton, N.Y., 1978, 81, 89, Interart Gallery, N.Y.C., 1979, Harriman Coll., N.Y., 1980, Nardin Gallery, N.Y.C., 1981, Aronson Gallery, Atlanta, 1982, Harrisburg State Mus. Pa., 1988, Women Artists Series Rutgers U., N.J., 1988, Carnegie Mellon U., Pitts., 1991, Acme Art Co., Columbus, Ohio, 1992, Islip (N.Y.) Mus., 1992, Suffolk Coll., Riverhead, N.Y., 1996, Stone Quarry Art Park, Cazenovia, N.Y., 1996, Wave Hill, Bronx, N.Y., 1997, Atelier A/E Gallery, N.Y.C., 1997, U. Alaska, Anchorage, 1997, Nat. Acad. Scis., Washington, 1998, Hoyt Mus., New Castle, Pa., 1998, U. Nebr., Omaha, 2002, Huntington Arts Coun. Gallery, N.Y., 2002-03, Cambridge Multicultural Arts Ctr., 2003, Nat. Mus. of Women in the Arts, Washington, 2004, Nassau County Mus., Hewlett-Woodmere Gallery, 2004, Ill. Ctrl. Coll., Ohio, 2005, Seton Hill U., Greensburg, Pa., 2006, deCordora Gallery, Greenfort, N.Y., 2006; two-women shows Women's Art Ctr., San Francisco, 1975; four-women show Heckscher Mus., Huntington, N.Y., 1980; numerous group exhbns.from 1953 to present including most recently Parrish Art Mus., Southampton, N.Y., 2000, N.J. Ctr. Visual Arts, Summit, 2000, Toxic Landscapes, Puffin Found. traveling exhib., Morning, Noon and Night, The Long Island Mus. of Stony Brook, N.Y., Earth 2002, U. Miami Coral Gables, Denise Bibro Fine Art, N.Y.C., 2002, Soho Photo, N.Y.C., 2002, Savannah Coll. Art and Design, Ga., 2002, Long Beach Found. for Arts, NJ, 2002, Antioch Coll., Ohio, 2004, Telfair Mus., Savannah, Ga., Silverpoints, 2006, Hunterdon Mus., Clinton, N.J., 2006, Space 301, Mobile, Ala., 2007, Coll. NJ, Ewing, 2007, others; contbr. collage to Attica Book, 1972; contbr. articles to profl. jours., prodr. and contbr. Heresies #13 mag. Creative Artists Pub. Svc. grantee, 1979. Recipient Shirk Meml. award for oil painting Nat. Assn. Women Artists, Inc., 1993, first place award Notorious L.I. exhibit Hillwood Art Mus., Brookville, N.Y., 1994, Purchase award Hoyt Art Inst., 1995, Purchase award Nassau County Mus. Art, 1997, Print Ctr. Excellence award, Phila., 2001, Pollock-Krasner award, 2007, Best in Show award East End Arts Coun., Riverhead, NY, 2007; fellow Ossabaw Found., 1981, Dorland, 1983, Ucross Found., 1989, 99, Blue Mt. Found., 1991, 94, 96, 2000, 02, VCCA Ctr. Found., Ragdale Found., 1984, 2001; David and Julia White Colony, Costa Rica, 2003, 05, Ludwig Vogelstein grantee, 2004, Puffin grantee, 2004, Pollock/Krasner grantee, 2007. Home: PO Box 455 Shelter Island Heights NY 11965 Personal E-mail: jan@janetculbertson.net.

CULBERTSON, LESLIE S., computer company executive; B, Lewis and Clark U., 1971. Cost mgr. British Petroleum/Standard Oil Ohio; acctg. mgr., controller Intel, Santa Clara, Calif., 1979—98, dir. corp. fin., 1997—, v.p., co-dir. materials orgn., 1998—2000, v.p., gen. mgr. sys. mfg., 2000—. Office: Intel 2200 Mission Coll Blvd Santa Clara CA 95052

CULBERTSON, RICHARD ALLEN, healthcare educator, health facility administrator; b. Fremont, Ohio, Aug. 13, 1946; s. Raymond Clark and Ruth Elizabeth Culbertson; m. Linnea VanDyne, July 11, 1970 (div. Dec. 1981); m. Susan Mary Leary, May 3, 1986. BA, Lawrence U., 1967; MDiv, Harvard U., 1970; M in Health Adminstrn., U. Minn., 1973; PhD, U. Calif., San Francisco, 1993. Cert. healthcare exec. Am. Coll. Health Execs. Asst. prof. U. Minn., Mpls., 1976—78; dep. dir. and COO St. Paul-Ramsey Med. Ctr., 1978—84; hosp. dir. and CEO Kaiser Found. Hosp., LA, 1984—87; dir. adminstrn. U. Calif. San Francisco Med. Group, 1987—92; assoc. dean and vice chancellor U. Wis., Madison, 1992—95; assoc. prof. and dir. Ind. U., Indpls., 1995—97; assoc. prof. Tulane U., New Orleans, 1997—. Chmn. bd. dirs. Aurora HealthCare Inc., Milw., 1994—; spl. asst. to pres. for NCAA cert. Tulane U., New Orleans, 1999—2002, chmn. gen. faculty sch. pub. health, 2005—, chair senate com. on intercollegiate athletics, 2002—05, chair sch. pub. health and tropical medicine faculty, 2005—07; cert. site reviewer NCAA, Indpls., 2001—; mem. governing bd. Touro Infirmary, New Orleans, 2004—. Contbg. author The Nation's Health, 6th edit., 2001; contbr. articles to profl. jours. Mem. Mardi Gras Krewe of Mid-City; pres. Humane Soc. Ramsey County, St. Paul, 1981—84; bd. dirs. Touro Found., New Orleans, 2004—, Wis. Profl. Rev., Madison, 1994—95, Eldercare Dane County, Madison, 1994—95. Named Emerging Leader in Healthcare, Healthcare Forum, San Francisco, 1986; recipient Spurgeon award for cmty. svc., Explorer Scouts, St. Paul, 1983; Nat. Leader fellow, W.K. Kellogg Found., 1985—88. Mem.: Am. Hosp. Assn. Chgo. (governance com. 2006—), U. Minn. Pres. Club, Harvard Club (La.), Delta Omega Soc. (Eta chpt.), Phi Beta Kappa (La. Alpha chpt.), Beta Theta Pi. Avocations: swimming, intercollegiate athletics, dance organizations patron, Tae Kwon Do. Office: Tulane Univ Sch Pub Health 1430 Tulane Ave SL-29 New Orleans LA 70112 Office Phone: 504-988-6247. Business E-Mail: rculber@tulane.edu.

CULBERTSON, RICHARD DONNELL, oil industry executive, lawyer; b. July 26, 1945; BA, Tex. Christian U., Ft. Worth, 1967, MA, 1970; PhD, U. Tex., Arlington, 1999. Bar: Tex. 1970; cert. tchr. Tex. Asst. atty. gen. Tex. State Atty. Gen. Office, Ft. Worth, 1985—86; v.p. Corvette Oil Corp., Ft. Worth, 1984—; prof. history Tarrant County Coll., Hurst, Tex., 2000—04. Author: Society and Politics of Hispanics in Tarrant County, Texas, 1970-2004, 2004. Mem.: Tex. State Hist. Assn., Tex. Bar Assn., Am. Anthropol. Assn., Am. Hist. Assn. Home: 6428 Arthur Dr Fort Worth TX 76134

CULBRETH, JAMES HAROLD, JR., lawyer; b. Durham, NC, Nov. 12, 1953; s. James Harold and Florence Rittenhouse C.; m. Kate Dickson Banks, Oct. 24, 1981; children: Julia Fairbairn, Duncan Banks. BA in Psychology, Wake Forest U., 1977; JD, George Washington U., 1980. Bar: D.C. 1981, Va. 1982, N.C. 1984. Assoc. Baylinson Kudysh & Greenberg, Washington, 1981-84; trust officer, asst. v.p. Ctrl. Carolina Bank & Trust Co., Durham, 1984-90; assoc. McGuire Woods Battle & Boothe, Richmond, Va., 1990-93, Wishart Norris Henninger & Pittman, Burlington, N.C., 1993-95; ptnr. Helms, Mulliss & Wicker, PLLC (formerly Smith Helms Mulliss & Moore LLP), Charlotte, NC, 1995—. Lectr. employee benefits Am. Bankers Assn. Nat. Trust Sch., 1987—. Chair stewardship com. and fin. com. University City United Meth., Charlotte, 1998—. Democrat. Avocations: tennis, bicycling, camping, writing. Office: Helms Mulliss & Wicker LLP 201 N Tryon St Charlotte NC 28202-2146

CULBRETH, LUCRETIA JOY, science educator; d. Dewey N. and Ruth A. (Hughes) Walls, Josephine M. (Bennett) Walls (Stepmother); m. Larry McCoy Culbreth; children: Lauren Nicole (Culbreth) Duty, Lance McCoy. BS in Mid. Grades Edn., North Ga. Coll. and State U., Dahlonega, 1965; MS in Mid. Grades Edn., Columbus Coll. and State U., Ga., 1984; EdS in Curriculum, Instrn., Mgmt., Adminstrn., NOVA Southeastern U., Ft. Lauderdale, Fla., 2003. Cert. elem. tchr. with ednl. specialist degree Ga., 2003. Tchr. sci. Ft. Benning Dependent Sch. Sys., Ga., 1982—85, Coweta County Sch. Sys., Newnan, Ga., 1985—. Chair dept. sci. Madras Mid. Sch., Newnan, Ga., 2001—04, 7th grade tean leader, 2002—03. Recipient Tchr. of Month award, Madras Mid. Sch. Faculty, 2005. Avocations: collector, crochet. Office: Madras Mid Sch 240 Edgeworth Rd Newnan GA 30263 Home Phone: 770-463-3002; Office Phone: 770-254-2744. E-mail: lucretia.culbreth@cowetaschools.org.

CULCASI, KAREN, geographer, researcher; Degree, U. Vt., 1998; postgrad., Syracuse U., NY, 2001—07. Tchg. assoc. Syracuse U., 2001—04, rsch. fellow, 2005—. Rsch. fellow Am. U., Cairo, 2005. Big sister Big Brother Big Sisters, Madison, Wis., 2006—07. Fellow, Maxwell Sch. Citizenship and Pub. Affairs, 2005—06, Syracuse U., 2006—07; scholar, Maxwell Sch. Citizenship and Pub. Affairs, 2005; Summer grantee, 2003, Goekjian fellow, Moynihan Ctr. Global Affairs, 2004. Mem.: Mid. East Studies Assn., Assn. Am. Geographers, Am. Acad. Surveying and Mapping (scholar 2007).

CULHANE, JOHN JOSEPH, lawyer, food products executive; b. Yonkers, NY, Apr. 24, 1945; s. John Jospeh and Anna Rita (Merrins) Culhane. BS with honors, St. Peters Coll., 1968; JD with honors, Fordham U., 1973. Bar: NJ 1973, Wis. 1975, US Ct. Appeals (7th cir.). Chief prosecutor, Weehawken, NJ, 1973—75; ptnr. Howard, Peterman & Eisenberg, Milw., 1975-80; dep. gen. counsel Schlitz Brewing Co., Milw., 1980—82; assoc. gen. counsel, asst. sec. Stroh Brewing Co., Detroit, 1982-83; v.p., gen. counsel Pabst Brewing Co., Milw., 1983—86; sr. fin. counsel Coca-Cola Co., Atlanta, 1986—92, gen. counsel N.Am. group, 1992—98; gen. counsel, corp. sec. Coca-Cola HBC, London, 1998—2001, Coca-Cola Bottlers' Sales and Svcs. Co., 2001—04; spl. counsel Coca-Cola Enterprises Inc., 2001—04, interim gen. counsel Atlanta, 2004, sr. v.p., gen. counsel, 2004, exec. v.p., gen. counsel, 2004—. Dir. US Brewers Assn., 1983—85, Future Milw. Com., 1983—85. Mem.: Milw. Bar Assn., Wis. Bar Assn., NJ Bar Assn., ABA. Roman Catholic. Office: Coca-Cola Enterprises Inc 2500 Windy Ridge Pky Atlanta GA 30339*

CULHANE, STEPHEN (DAVID STEPHEN KING CULHANE), lawyer; s. David M. Culhane and Jennifer King Curran; m. Susannah Churchill Drake, Aug. 21, 1993. AB cum laude, Princeton U., 1986; MPhil, U. Oxford Magdalen Coll., 1988; JD, NYU Sch. Law, 1993. Fin. analyst Baring Bros. & Co., NYC, 1989—90; assoc. Coudert Bros., NYC, 1993—94, Akin Gump Strauss Hauer & Feld LLP, NYC, 1994—97; v.p. & asst. gen. counsel Goldman, Sachs & Co., NYC, 1997—99, legal dir. pvt. equity group, 1999—2004, assoc. gen. counsel, 2002—04; ptnr. pvt. equity & investment funds group King & Spaulding, NYC, 2004—06; ptnr. investment mgmt. practice Linklaters, NYC, 2006—. Office: Linklaters 1345 Ave of the Americas New York NY 10105 Office Phone: 212-903-9000. E-mail: stephen.culhane@linklaters.com.

CULICK, FRED ELLSWORTH CLOW, engineering and physics professor; b. Wolfeboro, NH, Oct. 25, 1933; s. Joseph Frank and Mildred Beliss (Clow) C.; m. Frederica Mills, June 11, 1960; children: Liza Hall, Alexander Joseph, Mariette Huxham. Student, U. Glasgow, Scotland, 1957-58; SB, MIT, 1957, PhD, 1961. Rsch. fellow Calif. Inst. Tech., Pasadena, 1961-63, asst. prof., 1963-66, assoc. prof., 1966-70, prof. mech. engrng. and jet propulsion, 1970-97, Richard L. and Dorothy M. Hayman prof. mech. engrng., 1997—, prof. jet propulsion, 1997—. Cons. to govt. agys. and indsl. orgns. Fellow AIAA, Internat. Acad. Astronautics; mem. Internat. Fedn. Astronautics, Am. Phys. Soc. Home: 1375 Hull Ln Altadena CA 91001-2620 Office: Calif Inst Tech Caltech 205-45 207 Guggenheim Pasadena CA 91125 Office Phone: 626-395-4783. Business E-Mail: fecfly@caltech.edu.

CULKIN, CHARLES WALKER, JR., retired trade association administrator; b. Aug. 22, 1947; s. Charles Walker and Helen Elizabeth (Wilson) C.; m. Carolyn DeWayne Franklin, Apr. 5, 1974; children: David Laurence Franklin, Kimberly Anne Franklin A in Bus. Adminstrn., Benjamin Franklin U., Washington, 1968, BA in Comml. Sci., 1970. Asst. auditor United Va. Bank, Vienna, 1967—70; sr. asst. dir. US GAO, Washington, 1970—97; exec. dir. Assn. Gov. Accts., Washington, 1997—2003; ret., 2003. Chmn. Pacific Emerging Issues Conf., Honolulu, 1982; spkr. confs. and seminars; founder, incorporator Reston Commuter Bus., Inc., 1971, treas., dir., 1971-78 Pub. The Jour. Govt. Fin. Mgmt., 1997-2003; contbr. articles to profl. jours Recipient RCB Bd. Dirs. award 1978, Outstanding Achievement award Fairfax County Bd. Suprs., Va., 1978, Nat. Pres. award Am. Soc. of Mil. Comptr., 1999, 2003 Mem. Am. Assn. for Budget Program Analysis, Inst. Internal Auditors (sec. no. Va. chpt. 1984-86), Assn. Govt. Accts. (dir. Hawaii chpt. 1981-84, conf. mgr. fed. leadership conf. 1994, No. Va. chpt. 1991—, Nat. AGA Spl. Recognition award 1988, 90, 93, Pres.'s award 1992, 95-96, Outstanding Mem. award 1983, nat. treas.-elect, 1995-96, nat. treas. 1996-97, Edn. award 1994, Robert W. King Meml. award 2006), Nat. Assn. Accts. (no. Va. chpt. dir. 1977-78, v.p. 1979-80), Benjamin Franklin U. Alumni Assn. (pres. 1988-92, Outstanding Leadership award 1991, Bd. Govs. Svc. award 1992, Disting. Alumni award, 1995), George Washington U. Gen. Alumni Assn. (dir. 1991-92, Vol. of Yr. award 1992), KC (Coun. #3358 dep. grand knight 2004-2005, grand knight 2005-07, Knight Yr., 2004-2005). Roman Catholic. Home: 5351 Fox Run Rd Sarasota FL 34231-7348 Personal E-mail: cinandchas@comcast.net.

CULKIN, DANIEL JOSEPH, urologist, educator, department chairman; s. Lawrence Francis and Madeline Culkin; m. Jane Marie Graham, July 10, 1951; children: Matthew Lawrence, Daniel James. BS, Creighton U., Omaha, Nebr., 1968—72, MD, 1975—79; MS, Loyola U., Chgo., 1972—75; MBA/HCM, U. Phoenix, 2003—05. Lic. dr. Okla. State Bd. Med. Licensure, 2006, La. State Med. Licensure Bd., 2006, Ill. State Med. Bd., 2006. Fellow endourology and neurourology Loyola U. Med. Ctr., Maywood, Ill., 1982—85, urology instr., 1985—87; asst. prof. urology La. State U. Med. Ctr., Shreveport, La., 1987—88, assoc. prof. urology, 1988—91, prof. urology, 1991—94; chief urology Shreveport Va. Med. Ctr., 1987—88; prof., chair dept. urology Okla. U. Health Sci Ctr., Okla. City, 1994—, Pres.'s Assoc. Presdl. prof., 2006. Mem. SW Oncology Group, San Antonio, 1991—2006. Mem.: AMA (assoc.), Soc. U. Urology (pres. 2003—04), Am. Paraplegic Soc. (dir. 1988—91). Catholic. Avocations: water sports, golf, fishing. Home: 6104 LaQuinta Dr Edmond OK 73003 Office: Univ Okla Health Sci Ctr PO Box 26901 Oklahoma City OK 73190 Home Phone: 405-341-6762. Office Fax: 405-271-3118; Home Fax: 405-271-3118. Business E-Mail: daniel-culkin@ouhsc.edu.

CULKIN, MACAULAY, actor; b. NYC, Aug. 26, 1980; s. Christopher "Kit" and Pat Culkin; m. Rachel Miner, June 21, 1998 (div. Aug. 5, 2000). Student, St Joseph's Sch. of Yorkville, NYC, George Balanchine's Sch. of Ballet. Film appearances include Rocket Gibraltar, 1988, Uncle Buck, 1989, See You In The Morning, 1989, Jacob's Ladder, 1990, Home Alone, 1990, My Girl, 1991, Only the Lonely, 1991, Home Alone 2: Lost In New York, 1992, The Good Son, 1993, George Balanchine's The Nutcracker, 1993, Getting Even With Dad, 1994, The Pagemaster, 1994, Richie Rich, 1994, Party Monster, 2003, Saved!, 2004; (TV movies)The Midnight Hour, 1985; (TV series) Wishkid (voice only), 1991-92; (TV appearances) The Equalizer, 1988, Frasier, 1994, Will & Grace, 2003, Robot Chicken (voice only, 2005; appeared in Michael Jackson's Black or White video, 1991; author: (novels) Junior, 2006.

CULLARI, SALVATORE SANTINO, clinical psychologist, educator, writer; b. Caroniti, Calabria, Italy, Apr. 1, 1952; came to US, 1955; s. Carmelo and Carmela (Cullari) C.; m. Kathryn Plesce, Apr. 26, 1985; children: Catherine, Dante. BA, Kean Coll., 1974; MA, Western Mich. U., Kalamazoo, 1976, PhD, 1981. Lic. psychologist, Pa., W.Va. Dir. psychology White Haven Ctr., Pa., 1982—83; psychologist Danville State Hosp., Pa., 1983—84; coord. of psychology Harrisburg State Hosp., Pa., 1984—86; prof., chair dept. psychology Lebanon Valley Coll., Annville, Pa., 1986—2003, prof. emeritus, 2003—; founder, owner Cullari Vineyards and Winery, Hershey, Pa., 2005—. Cons. Bur. Disability Determination, Harrisburg, 1987—. Author questionaire acad. social evaluation scales, 1990, Treatment Resistance, 1996; editor Found. of Clin. Psychology, 1998, Counseling and Psychotherapy, 2001; contbr. numerous articles to profl. jours. Mem. APA, Assn. Advancement of Behavior Therapy, Pa. Psychol. Assn. (pres. 2005-, Psychology in the Media award 2003), Pa. Psychol. Found. (pres. 2005-06), Pa. Psychology Licensing Bd., Soc. for the Exploration of Psychotherapy Integration. Office Phone: 717-533-8985. Personal E-mail: scullari@sprynet.com.

CULLEN, CHARLES THOMAS, historian, librarian; b. Gainesville, Fla., Oct. 11, 1940; s. Spencer L. and Blanche J. Cullen; m. Shirley Harrington, June 13, 1964; children: Leslie Lanier, Charles Spencer Harrington. BA, U. of South, 1962; MA, Fla. State U., 1963; PhD, U. Va., 1971; HHD (hon.), Lewis U., 1987; DLitt (hon.), U. South, 1994; LLD (hon.), John Marshall Law Sch., 1995; DHist (hon.), Lincoln Coll., 2000. Asst. prof. history Averett Coll., 1963-66; assoc. editor Papers of John Marshall Inst. Early Am. History and Culture, Williamsburg, Va., 1971-74, co-editor, 1974-77, editor, 1977-79; lectr. history Coll. William and Mary, 1971-79; sr. research historian, editor Papers of Thomas Jefferson Princeton (N.J.) U., 1979-86; pres., libr. Newberry Library, Chgo., 1986—2005, pres., libr. emeritus, 2005—. Mem. N.J. Hist. Commn., 1985-86, Nat. Hist. Publs. and Records Com., 1990—; mem. adv. bd. Abraham Lincoln Presdl. Libr. and Mus., 2002-04. Trustee Thomas Jefferson Found., 2004—. Nat. Hist. Publs. and Records Commn. fellow, 1970-71. Mem. Assn. Documentary Editing (pres. 1982-83), Orgn. Am. Historians, Am. Hist. Assn., Am. Antiquarian Soc., Heartland Lit. Soc. (pres. 1994—), The Poetry Found. (vice chmn. 1998-2005), Ind. Rsch. Librs. Assn. (pres. 2000—03), Caxton Club, Grolier Club. Office: Newberry Libr 60 W Walton St Chicago IL 60610-7324

CULLEN, EDWARD PETER, bishop; b. Phila., Mar. 15, 1933; Student, St. Charles Borromeo Sem., Overbrook, Pa.; MSW, U. Pa., 1970; M in Edn., LaSalle U., 1971; MDiv, St. Charles Borromeo Sem., 1974. Ordained priest Roman Cath. Ch. 1962. Asst. pastor St. Maria Goretti Ch., Hatfield, St. Bartholomew Ch., Phila.; chaplain to Sisters of Mercy Merion Motherhouse; chaplain St. Edmond's Home for Children, See of Allentown; titular bishop Diocese of Paria, Proconsolare, 1994—; aux. bishop Diocese of Phila., 1994—99; bishop Diocese of Allentown, Pa., 1998—. Mem. Cath. Social Svcs. Named Hon. Prelate to His Holiness Pope John Paul II, 1982. Office: Diocese of Allentown PO Box F Allentown PA 18105-1538

CULLEN, JACK JOSEPH, lawyer; b. Sept. 20, 1951; s. Helen Cullen; children: Cameron, Katherine. BA, Western Wash. State Coll., 1973; JD, U. Puget Sound, 1976. Bar: Wash. 1977, U.S. Dist. Ct. (we. dist.) Wash. 1977, U.S. Dist. Ct. (ea. dist.) Wash. 1977, U.S. Tax Ct. 1984, U.S. Ct. Appeals (9th cir.) 1980. Staff atty. Wash. State Bar Assn., Seattle, 1977-79; assoc. Hatch & Leslie, Seattle, 1979-85, mng. ptnr., 1985-91; ptnr. Foster Pepper & Shefelman, Seattle, 1991-96, mng. ptnr., 1996—2002, mng. chair, 1991—. Spkr. in field. Co-author: Prejudgment Attachment, 1986. Active Frank Lloyd Wright Bldg. Conservancy, 1989—; trustee Seattle Repertory Theater, 1999-2002. Mem. ABA (bus. law sect.), Am. Bankruptcy Inst., Wash. State Bar Assn. (creditor-debtor sect., chair exec. 1982-90, spl. dist. counsel 1988—, hearing officer 1990), Seattle-King County Bar Assn. (bankruptcy rules subcom. 1988-90), Vancouver-Seattle Involvency Group (charter mem. 1990—), U.S. Sport Parachuting Team (nat. and world champions 1976, instrument rated pilot). Office: Foster Pepper & Shefelman PLLC 1111 3rd Ave Ste 3400 Seattle WA 98101-3299 E-mail: jc@foster.com.

CULLEN, JAMES D., lawyer; b. St. Louis, May 18, 1925; s. James and Frances C. Cullen; m. Joyce Marie Jackson, Aug. 19, 1950 (div.); children: Mary Lynn Cullen Walsh, James D., Michael Parnell, Carol Cullen Bernstein. LLD, St. Louis, 1948. Bar: Mo. 1948. Pvt. practice law, St. Louis. Bd. dirs. Gen. Protestant Children's Home, Richard Greene Co. 1st lt. USAF, 1943—45. Mem.: ABA, Lawyers Assn. St. Louis, St. Louis Bar Assn., Mo. Bar Assn. Roman Catholic. Office: 16 Berkshire Saint Louis MO 63117 Office Phone: 314-277-2334.

CULLEN, JAMES G., telecommunications industry executive; b. 1942; Married. BA, Rutgers U., 1964; Postgrad., M.I.T. With NJ Bell Tel. Co., Newark, 1964, pres., CEO, 1989—93; pres. Bell Atlantic Corp., 1993—95, vice chmn., 1995—98, pres., COO, 1998—2000. Bd. dir. Nuestar Inc., Johnson & Johnson Inc., Prudential Life Ins. Co.; dir., non-exec. chmn. Agilent Technologies Inc.*

CULLEN, MARK RICHARD, medical educator; b. Phila., Feb. 25, 1950; AB with honors, Harvard Coll., 1971; MD, Yale U., 1976. Resident Yale-New Haven Hosp., 1976-79, chief resident, 1979-80; dir. Yale-New Haven Occupl. and Environ. Medicine program Yale U. Sch. Medicine, 1980—, asst. prof. medicine, 1980-85, assoc. prof. medicine and epidemiology, 1985-93, prof. medicine and pub. health, 1993—. Vis. prof. U. Zimbabwe Faculty Medicine, 1988; cons. in field. Author: Clinical

Occupational Medicine, 1986, Occupational Medicine: State of the Art Reviews, 1987, Textbook of Clinical Occupational and Environmental Medicine, 2004; contbr. articles to profl. jours., chpts. to books. Mem. Assn. Occupl. and Environ. Clinics (interim bd. dirs. 1986-88), Inst. Medicine, Inst. Medicine Bd. Health Sci. Policy. Office: Yale Occupl & Environ Medicine Program Yale U Sch Medicine 135 College St Ste 3D New Haven CT 06510-2483 Home Phone: 203-245-0547; Office Phone: 203-785-6434. E-mail: mark.cullen@yale.edu.

CULLEN, PAUL, medical educator; b. Oak Park, Ill., Aug. 6, 1968; BS, U. Ill., Champaign-Urbana, 1990; PhD, Wash. U., 1997. Asst. prof. SUNY, Buffalo, 2004—. Grantee, Am. Heart Assn., 2004—07. Achievements include discovery of signal transduction pathways in cells; signaling molecules in cell biology. Office: SUNY 627 Cooke Hall Buffalo NY 14260-1300 Office Phone: 716-645-2363 200.

CULLEN, SHAWN PAUL, emergency physician, military officer; b. Ellsworth AFB, SD, Nov. 27, 1976; s. William Patrick and Margie E. Cullen; m. Edith Mae Berngen, Dec. 28, 2002. BS in Biology, St. Louis U., 1999, MD, 2003. Emergency medicine resident St. Francis Hosp., Peoria, Ill., 2003—05, emergency medicine chief resident, 2005—06; emergency medicine physician USAF, Keesler AFB, Miss., 2006—. Disaster team physician Regional Emergency Med. Response Team, Peoria, 2003—06; tactical physician Spl. Tactical Assitance Trauma Team, Peoria, 2004—06, Tactical Response Team, Keesler AFB, 2006—. Capt. USAF, 2000—06. Mem.: AMA, Emergency Medicine Resident Assn., Am. Coll. Emergency Physicians. Avocations: scuba diving, music, movies.

CULLER, DAVID ETHAN, computer science educator; b. Santa Barbara, Calif., Nov. 12, 1959; s. Glen Jacob and Susanne (Kreith) C.; m. Sara Chie Mayeno, May 20, 1983; children: Ethan, Jeremy. BA, U. Calif., Berkeley, 1980; MS, MIT, 1985, PhD, 1989. Programmer Culler-Harrison Inc., Santa Barbara, 1976, UCSD Chemistry Dept., La Jolla, Calif., 1976-78; logic designer CHI Systems Inc., Santa Barbara, 1979; math. programmer Lawrence Berkeley Lab., Berkeley, 1980; systems programmer Nat. Magnetic Fusion Energy Computer Ctr., Livermore, Calif., 1980-82; rsch. asst. MIT Lab. Computer Sci., Cambridge, 1982-89; co-founder, chief systems architect A.I. Architects Inc., Cambridge, 1986-88; assoc. prof. U. Calif., Berkeley, 1989, prof. computer sci.; co-founder, CFO, Arch Rock Corp, 2005—. Inventor, patentee in field. Named NSF Presdl. Young Investigator, 1990, Presdl. faculty fellow, 1992; jr. faculty rsch. grantee, 1990; regents jr. faculty fellow, 1990. Fellow IEEE, NAE; mem. Assn. Computing Machinery, Sigma Xi. Avocations: racquet sports, skiing, building. Office: U Calif Computer Sci Divsn # 1776 627 Soda Hall Berkeley CA 94720-1776 Office Phone: 510-643-7572. Office Fax: 510-643-7352. E-mail: culler@cs.berkeley.edu.

CULLETON, JAMES FREDERICK, neurologist; b. Sewickley, Pa., Apr. 6, 1918; s. James and Jessie (Scragg) C.; m. Flora McDonald Stuart Brown, Mar. 22, 1943; four children. BS, U. Pitts., 1940, MD, 1943. Diplomate Am. Bd. Psychiatry and Neurology. Intern, resident in pathology U. Pitts. Med. Ctr., 1943-44; fellow in neuropsychiatry Inst. Living, Hartford, Conn., 1947-49; resident in neurology Neurol. Inst. N.Y.C., 1949-51, attending neurologist, 1951-84; assoc. in neurology Columbia-Presbyn. Med. Ctr., NYC, 1951-84; dir. EEG and Neurology, New Rochelle Hosp. Med. Ctr., 1954-82; cons. in neurology Miami VA, 1984-95. Maj. M.C. US Army, 1944—47. Mem. AMA, Am. Acad. Neurology, N.Y. State Med. Soc., Westchester County Med. Soc., Westchester Acad. Medicine, Scottish Rite, Masons. Home: 87 Chase Point Rd Mirror Lake NH 03853-6152 Office Phone: 603-569-2472. E-mail: jimflo1@adelphia.net.

CULLETON, JAMES J., lawyer, former prosecutor; b. Sept. 27, 1948; JD, Fordham U., 1973. Asst. dist. atty. Bronx, NY, 1973—85; pvt. practice Culleton, Marinaccio & Foglia, 1985—. Office: Culleton Marinaccio & Foglia 245 Main St White Plains NY 10601 Office Phone: 914-761-0707.

CULLIGAN, JOHN AUSTIN, thoracic surgeon; b. St. Paul, Oct. 21, 1926; s. John Maurice and Margaret McGovern Culligan; m. Sheila Spriggs Culligan, Dec. 27, 1952; children: John, Kathleen, Sheila, Thomas, Elizabeth, Shannon, Paul. BS, Notre Dame U., 1946; MB, MD, U. Minn., 1950. Diplomate Am. Bd. Surgery, Am. Bd. Thoracic Surgery. Pvt. practice, St. Paul, 1960—90; clin. prof. surgery U. Minn., 1968—90; surgeon Mayo Clinic, Ariz., 1990—96; ret., 1996. With USNR, 1951—54. Roman Catholic. Home: 25832 Primo Cir Rio Verde AZ 85263

CULLIGAN, PATRICK JOHN, obstetrician, urogynecologist, surgeon, researcher; s. Thomas Michael and Lois Fern Culligan; m. Kimberly D Dovey, May 20, 1995; children: Molly Elizabeth children: Brian Thomas, Clare Dovey. BS, Ga. Inst. of Tech., 1989; MD, Mercer U., 1993. Diplomate Am. Bd. of Obstetrics and Gynecology, 2001. Resident ob-gyn. Greenville (S.C.) Hosp. Sys., 1993—97; fellow urogynecology and reconstructive pelvic surgery Northwestern U. Med. Sch., Evanston, Ill., 1997—99; asst. prof. of ob-gyn. U. of Louisville (Ky.) Health Scis. Ctr., 1999—, assoc. prof. of ob-gyn., 2002—; v.p. U. OB-GYN Assocs., PSC, Louisville, 2002. Cons. Domain Associs., LLC, Princeton, NJ, 1994—; bd. dirs. U. OB-GYN Found., Inc. Co-author: Urogynecology and Reconstructive Pelvic Surgery, 2002; contbr. articles to profl. jours. Bd. dir. Girls on the Run, Louisville, 2001. Recipient Thompson A Gailey award for academic achievement, Greenville Hosp. Sys. Dept. of OB-GYN, 1997, Faculty Devel. award, Berlex Found., 2002. Fellow: ACS (assoc.), Am. Coll. of Ob-Gyn. (assoc. grantee 1999); mem.: Am. Urogynecologic Soc. (assoc.; pub. rels. com. mem. 2001—02), Soc. of Gynecologic Surgeons (assoc.), Young President's Org. Republican. Roman Catholic. Avocations: tennis, skiing, bicycling, travel. Office Phone: 502-629-2184. Business E-Mail: culligan@mybladdermd.com.

CULLIGAN, THOMAS M., electronics executive; b. Aug. 1951; BS, MS, Fla. State U. Legis. dir. Fla. Congressman Earl Hutto, Fla.; chief of staff Fla. Sec. of State; exec. McDonnell Douglas; pres. govt. ops. Allied Signal, 1994—96, v.p. mktg., sales and svc., 1996—99; v.p., gen. mgr. def. and space Honeywell Internat., Inc., 1999—2001; CEO Raytheon Internat., Inc., 2001—; exec. v.p., bus. develop. Raytheon Co., Arlington, Va., 2001—. Office: Raytheon Co 1100 Wilson Blvd Arlington VA 22209-3978*

CULLIN, ROB, librarian; BS in Elec. Engring. Tech., Purdue U., 1995. Co-founder, co-owner E-vanced Solutions, 2002—. Co-author: Technology Made Simple: An Improvement Guide for Small and Medium Libraries, 2006; contbr. Named one of the Movers & Shakers, Libr. Jour., 2007. Office: E-Vanced Solutions Inc 712 Willow Pointe North Dr Plainfield IN 46168 Fax: 888-519-5770.

CULLINAN, BERNICE ELLINGER, education educator; b. Hamilton, Ohio, Oct. 12, 1926; d. Lee Alexander and Hazel (Berry) Dees; m. George W. Ellinger, June 5, 1948 (div. 1966); children: Susan Jane Ellinger, James Webb Ellinger; m. Paul Anthony Cullinan, June 9, 1967 (div. 1994); m. Kenneth Seeman Giniger, Apr. 13, 2002. BS, Ohio State U., 1948, MA, 1951, PhD, 1964. Cert. elem. educator Ohio, NY. Tchr. Maple Pk. Elem. Sch., Middletown, Ohio, 1944-46, Trotwood Elem. Sch., Ohio, 1946-47, Columbus Pub. Schs., Ohio, 1948-50, Upper Arlington Pub. Schs., Ohio, 1950-52; instr. Ohio State U., Columbus, 1959-64, asst. prof., 1964-67, Ohio State U./Charlotte Huck prof. children's lit., 1997; assoc. prof. NYU, NYC, 1967-72, prof. reading, 1972-97, prof. emeritus, 1998—; editor-in-chief Wordsong Books, Honesdale, Pa., 1990—. Chair selection com. Ezra Jack Keats New Writer award, 1984—2000; exec. sec. English Stds. Project, 1993—94. Author (with Lee Galda): Literature and the Child, 1989, 6th edit., 2006; author: Children's Literature in the Classroom: Weaving Charlotte's Web, 1989, 2d edit., 1994, Read to Me: Raising Kids Who Love to Read, 1992, 3d edit., 2006, Let's Read About: Finding Books They'll Love to Read, 1993; author: (with Brod Bagert) Helping Your Child Learn to Read, 1993; author: (with Dorothy Strickland and Lee Galda) Language Arts: Learning and Tchg., 2003; author: (with L. Galda and D. Strickland) Language, Literacy and the Child, 1993; author: 3d edit., 2002; author: (with Marilyn Scala and Virginia Schroder) Three Voices: Invitation to Poetry Across the Curriculum, 1995; author: 75 Authors and Illustrators Everyone Should Know, 1994; author: (with David Harrison) Poetry Lessons That Dazzle and Delight, 1999; editor: Children's Literature in the Reading Program, 1987, Invitation to Read: More Children's Literature in the Reading Program, 1992, Black Dialects and Reading, 1974, Fact and Fiction: Literature Across the Curriculum, 1993, Children's Voices, 1993, Pen in Hand, 1993, A Jar of Tiny Stars, 1996; editor: (with Diane Person) The Continuum Encyclopedia of Children's Literature, 2003; editor: (with Bonnie L. Kunzel and Deborah A. Wooten) The Continuum Encyclopedia of Young Adult Literature, 2005; author (with M. Jerry Weiss): Books I Read When I Was Young, 1980; author: (with Carolyn Carmichael) Literature and Young Children, 1977; author: Children's Literature in the Classroom: Extending Charlotte's Web, 1993; mem. editl. bd. Nat. Coun. Tchrs. English, Champaign, Ill., 1973—76, New Adv., 1987—99, Ranger Rick Mag., 1992—; contbr. articles to profl. jours. Adv. bd. Reading Rainbow, 1979—, Sta. WGBH-TV, 1989—; mem. selection com. Caldecott award ALA, Chgo., 1982—83; trustee Highlights Children Found., 1993—. Named Outstanding Educator in Lang. Arts, Nat. Coun. Tchrs. English, 2003; named to Ohio State U. Coll. Edn. Hall of Fame, 1995; recipient Ind. U. Citation for outstanding contbn. to literacy, 1995. Mem.: Reading Hall of Fame (pres. 1998—99, inducted 1989), Internat. Reading Found. (trustee 1984—91, Jeremiah Ludington award 1992), Internat. Reading Assn. (bd. dirs. 1979—84, pres. 1984—85, chair Tchrs. Choices 1988—91, chair spl. svc. award selection com. 2005—07, Arbuthnot award for outstanding tchr. children's lit. 1989), Ch. Club NY, Century Assn., Alpha Chi Omega. Avocations: tennis, reading for pleasure, poetry. Home: 1045 Park Ave Apt 6A New York NY 10028 Office: 3 Tudor Ln Sands Point NY 11050-1104 Office Phone: 212-369-7899. Personal E-mail: bernicecullinan@verizon.net.

CULLINAN, MARY PATRICIA, academic administrator, literature and language professor; BA, U. Pa., 1972; MA, U. Wis., 1973, PhD in English Lit., 1978. Writing cons. MBA Program U. Calif., Berkeley, 1980—81; lectr. Dept. Mktg. Calif. State U., Hayward, 1981—87, assoc. prof., dir. Composition Program, 1987—91, prof. Dept. English, 1992, interim dean Sch. Arts, Letters and Social Scis., 1992—93, dir. Office of Faculty Devel. and Faculty Ctr. for Excellence in Tchg., 1994—96, dean Coll. Arts, Letters and Scis. Stanislaus, 1996—2003; provost, v.p. Academic Affairs, prof. English Stephen F. Austin State U., 2003—06; pres. So. Oreg. U., Ashland, 2006—. Author: Susan Ferrier, Business Communication: Principles and Processes, Business English for Industry and the Professions; co-editor: American Women Writers: Diverse Voices in Prose Since 1845. Office: So Oreg U Office of Pres 1250 Siskiyou Blvd Ashland OR 97520-5032 E-mail: cullinanm@sou.edu.*

CULLINEY, JOHN JAMES, radiologist, educator; b. NYC, Oct. 17, 1955; s. Michael and Marion (Dakowski) C.; m. Margaret Mary Steinhardt, Oct. 11, 1986. BS, Rutgers U., 1977, MS, 1981; MD, U Medicine and Dentistry N.J., 1984. Diplomate Am. Bd. Radiology, Nat. Bd. Med. Examiners. Intern physician Med. Coll. of Pa. Hosp., Phila., 1984-85; resident physician U. Medicine & Dentistry N.J., Newark, 1985-89, asst. prof. clin. diagnostic radiology, chief uroradiology, 1990-92; fellow body imaging, instr. diagnostic radiology Hahnemann U. Hosp., Phila., 1989-90; clin. instr. diagnostic radiology, chief cross-sect. imaging Mercy & Moses Taylor Hosps. affiliates Temple Med. Sch., Scranton, Pa., 1992-2001; pres. Radiol. Cons. Inc., 1999-2001; radiologist and radiation safety officer Kauai Med. Clinic, Hawaii, 2001—, chmn. dept. radiology, 2004—, vice chmn. dept. radiology, 2002—03, bd. dirs., 2002—06; mem. KMC Physicians Adv. Group, 2005; bd. dirs. Wilcox Hosp., 2007—. Bd. dirs. Radiol. Cons., Inc., Dunmore, Pa., 1994-2001; co-dir. Phoenix Vascular Lab.; dir. radiology Mercy Hosp. Scranton, Clin. Vascular Lab.; bd. dirs. Wilcox Meml. Hosp., 2007—. Mem. AMA, AAUP, Am. Coll. Radiology, Am. Soc. Breast Imagers, Roentgen Soc. N.Am., KC. Roman Catholic. Avocations: amateur radio, skiing. Home: 2940 Kanani St Lihue HI 96766 Office: Kauai Med Clinic 3-3420 Kuhio Hwy Ste B Lihue HI 96766 E-mail: culliney@aol.com.

CULLINS, ROBERT CARLTON, academic administrator; s. Robert Carlton and Josephine (Thomas) Cullins; m. Melinda Mills, Sept. 15, 1990; children: Carlton Rob, Luke Wallace. AAS, AAE, Tyler Jr. Coll., Tex., 1968; BS, Northwestern State U. La., 1970, MEd, 1974. Registrar, dir. instl. rsch., counselor Tyler Jr. Coll., 1974—90; dir. admissions and records Westark C.C., Fort Smith, Ark., 1990—94; registrar Sul Ross State U., Alpine, Tex., 1994—. Sgt. E-5 US Army, 1971—73. Recipient Legacy Lion, Dist. 2T3 Lions (West Tex.), 2004, Presdl. Achievement award, Lions Club Internat., 2006; Jack Weich Fellow, Tex. Lions Camp for Crippled Children, 1998. Mem.: Tex. Assn. Collegiate Registrars and Admissions Officers (various com. chairs 1985—2006), Ft. Smith Downtown Sertoma Club, Alpine Lions Club (sec./treas. 1996—2006, Lion of Yr. 1966, 1997, 2002, Disting. Svc. award 1999, 2003), Frontier Lodge 766. Office: Sul Ross State University SRSU Box C-108 Alpine TX 79832 Office Fax: 432-837-8431. E-mail: rcullins@sulross.edu.

CULLITON, BARBARA J., publishing executive; b. Buffalo, May 2, 1943; Grad., Vassar Coll. Founder, dep. editor and head editl. ops. N.Am. Nature Publs. Nature Medicine, Structural Biology, Nature Genetics., 1991—99; founder, sci. comm. and exec. editor GeneWire.com Celera Genomics, 1999—2001; v.p. for pub. The Inst. for Genomic Rsch., Rockville, Md., 2001—; editor-in-chief Genome News Network, Rockville, 2001—. Times Mirror vis. prof. and dir. Writing About Sci. The Writing Seminars, Johns Hopkins U., Balt., 1990—98; advisor Am. Bd. Internal Medicine; adv. com. Knight Journalism Fellows, MIT, Cambridge; journalism advisor Fulbright Scholars program; advisor Sound Print, the radio series; panelist Sci. Jour., a Pub. Broadcasting prodn. Editor (founding editor-in-chief): Nature Genomics, Nature Structural Biology, Nature Medicine. Bd. overseers Darmouth Med. Sch. Co-recipient George Polk award for journalism. Mem.: Coun. for Advancement of Sci. Writing (pres. 1985—89, bd. dirs.), Nat. Assn. Sci. Writers (pres. 1981—82), Inst. of Medicine of NAS (mem. governing coun.), Italian Soc. for Molecular Medicine (hon.), Sigma Xi (hon.). Episcopalian.

CULLMAN, HUGH, retired tobacco company executive; b. NYC, Jan. 27, 1923; s. Howard S. and Elsie (Gottheil) C.; m. Nan Alva Ogburn, May 12, 1951; children: Katherine Victoria, Hugh Jr., Alexandra Miriam. BS, U.S. Naval Acad., 1945. With Benson & Hedges, 1949-54, mgr. research, 1952-54; with Philip Morris Inc., 1954—, treas., 1959-60, v.p., asst. chief ops., 1960-64, exec. v.p. ops., 1966—, also bd. dirs.; exec. v.p. Philip Morris Internat., 1965, pres., 1967-78, also bd. dirs.; group exec. v.p. Philip Morris Inc., 1978-84; chief exec. officer Philip Morris U.S.A., 1978-84; vice chmn. Philip Morris Cos. Inc., 1985-88. Sr. trustee U.S. Coun. for Internat. Bus.; emeritus mem. Tyron Palace Commn.; bd. dirs. Carteret County Cmty. Found. Lt. USN, 1945—47, PTO, Lt. USN, 1951—52, Europe. Address: 821 Front St Beaufort NC 28516-2230

CULLMAN, LEWIS B., philanthropist; b. 1919; m. Dorothy Cullman. Founder and CEO Cullman Ventures Inc.; dir. Gen. Am. Investors Co., Inc. Mem. leadership coun. New Am. Found. Author: (memoir) Can't Take It With You -- The Art of Making and Giving Money, (booklet) How to Succeed in Fundraising by Really Trying. Chmn. Chess-in-the-Schools, NYC; founder Dorothy and Lewis B. Cullman Child Devel. Ctr., Sidney, NY. Recipient NYC Mayor's award arts and culture. Mem.: Am. Acad. Arts and Sci. Mailing: New America Foundation 7th Floor 1630 Connecticut Ave NW Washington DC 20009*

CULLOM, WILLIAM OTIS, retired trade association executive; b. Huntsville, Ala., Mar. 20, 1932; s. Otis McKinley and Elna (Reese) C.; m. Caryl James, May 26, 1956; children: Cheryl Ann Cullom Stewart, Jennifer James Cullom Barksdale. BS, Fla. State U., 1958. Finger-print expert FBI, 1950-52; asst. bus. mgr. Fla. State U., 1954-64; with Ryder Truck Rental Inc., Miami, Fla., 1964-79, exec. v.p. mktg., 1979, ret., 1979; pres., COO Jartran, Inc., Coral Gables, Fla., 1979-81; pres. Greater Miami C. of C., 1981—2004; founder WOC Consulting Co., 2004—, ret., 2005; pvt. practice Burnsville, 2005—. V.p. Orange Bowl Com., 1992—. Sec., bd. dirs. Miami-Dade Coll. Found.; mem. cabinet exec. com. Beacon Coun. United Way, Miami, 1974-80; trustee Bethune Cookman Coll., Daytona Beach, Fla., Barry U., St. Thomas U., Miami-Dade C.C. Found.; past chmn. bd. trustees Fla. State U; chmn. adminstrv. bd. Kendall Meth. Ch.; mem. pres.'s adv. com. Fla. Meml. Coll., Miami; bd. dirs. Bapt. Hosp. Found., Coconut Grove Playhouse, Goodwill Industries, Salvation Army; v.p. Orange Bowl Com.; chmn. bd. trustees Fla. State U. Found., 1994-95; chmn. Greater Miami Chamber Coalition. With U.S. Army, 1952-54. Recipient Miami Black Bus. Cmtys. Econ. Unity award, 1984, Anti Defamation League Human Rels. award, 1992, Disting. Cmty. Svc. award, 1998, Cedars Found. Concern award, 1994, NCCJ Humanitarian award, 1995, Silver Medallion award Greater Miami NCCJ, Citizen of Yr. award Greater Miami Rotary Club, Club at Dornal award, Life Achievement award Nat. PTA, Sand in My Shoes award, 2003, Carrfour Supportive Housing highest award, 2003, Lifetime Achievement award Human Svcs. Coalition, 2003, Daily Point of Light award, Pres. George Sr. and George W. Bush, 2004; named South Fla. Scout of Yr., Scouts Internat. in South Fla., 1997. Mem. Am. Trucking Assn., Truck Leasing and Renting Assn. (pres. Fla. chpt. 1972-73), Fla. State U. Nat. Alumni Assn. (pres.), Miami Hist. Assn., Brickell Club, Univ. Club, Riviera Country Club, City Club, Bankers Club, Ocean Reef Yacht Club, Gov.'s Club (Tallahassee), Dearing Bay Yacht Club, Biscayne Bay Yacht Club, Mountain Air Country Club (Burnsville, NC), Rotary, Doral Country Club (mem. of. bd. Doral Golf Championship), Democrat. Meth. Home and Office: 55 Cullom Chapel Rd Burnsville NC 28714 Office Phone: 828-682-6379.

CULLUM, JOHN, actor, singer; b. Knoxville, Tenn., Mar. 2, 1930; m. Emily Frankel; 1 child, John David. BA, U. Tenn. Former tennis player and real estate salesman. N.Y. debut with Shakespearewrights, 1957; joined N.Y. Shakespeare Festival, 1960; Broadway debut in Camelot, 1962; played Laertes in Hamlet, 1964; other Broadway appearances include On A Clear Day You Can See Forever, 1965 (Theatre World award 1965), Man of La Mancha, 1966, 1776, 1969, Vivat! Vivat Regina, 1972, Shenendoah, 1975 (Tony award as best actor 1975), The Trip Back Down, 1977, On the Twentieth Century, 1978 (Tony award as best actor in musical 1978), Deathtrap, 1979, Whistler, 1981 (Drama Desk award), Private Lives (with Richard Burton and Elizabeth Taylor), 1983, Doubles, 1985, The Boys in Autumn (with George C. Scott), 1986, Urinetown, 2002, Purlie, 2005, The Other Side, 2005, 110 in the Shade, 2007; other leading roles include plays Hamlet, Cyrano de Bergerac; film appearances include: All the Way Home, 1963, Hawaii, 1966, 1776, 1972, The Prodigal, 1982, Sweet Country, 1985, Marie, 1985, The Boys in Autumn (with George C. Scott), 1986, Ricochet River, 1998, Held Up, 1999, Blackwater Elegy, 2003, Candide, 2005, The Night Listener, 2006; concert readings include The Golden Apple, 2005; appeared in TV films A Man Without a Country, 1973, The Day After, 1984, Shootdown, 1988, With a Vengeance, 1992, Inherit the Wind, 1999, also public TV films Summer, 1980, Carl Sandburg, 1981; TV series include: Buck James, 1987-88, Northern Exposure, 1990-95 (Emmy nomination, Supporting Actor - Comedy, 1993), ER, 1994, To Have & To Hold, 1998; TV appearance in All My Children, 1997; spokesman for arts and entertainment cable TV, Victorian Days. Served with U.S. Army.*

CULLUM, LEE BROOKS, journalist; b. Dallas, Mar. 18, 1939; d. Charles Gillespie and Garland Chapman Cullum; m. James Howard Clark Jr., June 29, 1962 (div. June 1976); 1 child, James Howard Cullum Clark. Student, Sweet Briar Coll.; BA, So. Meth. U., 1961; DHL (hon.), Monterey Inst. Inter. Studies, 1997, U. Puget Sound, 2002. Reporter, then exec. prodr. and on-air moderator Newsroom Sta. KERA-TV, Dallas, 1970-76, v.p. program devel., 1976-81; account exec. Hill & Knowlton, Dallas, 1981-82; editor D Mag., Dallas, 1982-85; dir. client svcs. Hill & Knowlton, Dallas, 1985-86; editor editl. page Dallas Times Herald, Dallas, 1986-91; commentator Newshour with Jim Lehrer (formerly Macneil-Lehrer Newshour), Washington, 1988—2001; contbg. columnist Dallas Morning News, Dallas, 1992—; commentator All Things Considered Nat. Pub. Radio, 1994—2000; commentator Morning Edition, NPR affiliate KERA-FM, Dallas-Ft. Worth, 2000—; host, CEO PBS affiliate KERA-TV, Dallas-Ft. Worth, 2007—. Bd. dirs. Pacific Coun. Internat. Policy, LA, Sammons Dallas Found., Social Sci. Found. benefitting Grad. Sch. Internat. Studoes U. Denver, Dallas Com. on Fgn. Rels. Author: Genius Came Early: Creativity in the Twentieth Century, 1999; host CEO KERA-TV, 2007—. Bd. dirs. S.W. Legal Found., Dallas, 1995-99, Coun. on Fgn. Rels., 1996-2006, The Hockaday Sch., Dallas, 1997-2003; bd. visitors Internat. Programs Ctr., Okla. U., 1997—; mem. Am. Coun. on Germany; mem. Nat. Com. on US-China Rels., InterAm. Dialogue; mem. Trilateral Commn. Dallas Inst. for Humanities and Culture fellow; recipient Matrix award Women in Comms., 1977, 85, J. B. Marryatt award Dallas Press Club, 1996. Mem.: Nat. Conf. Editl. Writers. Episcopalian. Avocations: the arts, travel, books. Personal E-mail: lcullum@swbell.net.

CULLY, JOSEPH ANDREW, hazard substance scientist; b. Inglewood, Calif., Apr. 29, 1961; s. Russell Alexander Cully and Ruth Joanne Hosick. BS, Pepperdine U., 1982; MPH, Loma Linda U., 1985. Registered Environmental Health Specialist State of Calif. Environ. health specialist Imperial County Health Dept., El Centro, Calif., 1986—88; hazardous substance scientist Enivron. Protection Agy., Cypress, Calif., 1988—. Mem.: Am. Indsl. Hygiene Assn. (sec. elect 2006—). Avocations: singing, ballroom dancing. Home: 1911 Upland St Rancho Palos Verdes CA 90275 Office: Dept Toxic Substances Control 5796 Corporate Ave Cypress CA 90630 Office Phone: 714-484-5473.

CULMO, TOM A., lawyer; b. Miami, Fla. m. Elisabeth; 4 children. BA, U. Pa., 1984; JD, Mercer U., 1988. Bd. cert. specialist in civil trial practice: Fla. Bar and Nat. Bd. Trial Advocates, bar: Fla. 1988, US Dist. Ct. Ptnr. Alters, Boldt, Brown, Rash & Culmo, PA. Lectr. in field. Active numerous profl., cmty., civic orgns.; mem. bd. dir. Mercer Univ. Coll. of Law Alumni Assn. Achievements include represented clients in virtually every type of personal injury matter, business dispute, and insurance claim; jury verdicts in 15 different Florida counties, and recoveries in excess of one million dollars in over 50 cases.

CULNON, SHARON DARLENE, special education educator, reading specialist; b. Balt., Apr. 20, 1947; d. Clayton Claude and Ann (McIntyre) Legg; m. Allen William Culnon, July 9, 1975. BA in Elem. Edn., U. Mich., 1972; MAT in Reading Edn., Oakland U., 1980; cert. Learning Disabilities, Ariz. State U., 1983. Cert. K-8 edn., K-12 reading specialist, K-12 learning disabilities specialist. Tchr. Mt. Morris Consolidated Schs., Mich., 1972—77; reading specialist Paradise Valley Schs., Phoenix, 1978—87, learning disabilities specialist, 1987—90, tchr., 1990—2000. Mem. Kachina Jr. Women's Club, Phoenix, 1980-83, sec., 1981-82. Recipient Learning Leader/dist. award Paradise Valley Bd. of Edn., Phoenix, 1986. Mem. Phi Delta Kappa (historian 1987-88). Presbyterian. Avocations: travel, wildlife viewing and study, reading, pets, photography. Home: 9035 N Concho Ln Phoenix AZ 85028-5318

CULOTTA, VINCENT ANTHONY, JR., obstetrician, gynecologist; b. New Orleans, Aug. 2, 1949; s. Vincent Anthony and Ethel Chachere Culotta; m. Aurelie F. Culotta, June 20, 1975; children: Christine, Melissa, Trey, Jason. BS, La. State U., Baton Rouge, 1970, MD, 1974; M Health Svc. Adminstrn., Coll. St. Francis, 1993. Diplomate Am. Bd. Ob-Gyn. Pvt. practice, New Orleans, 1977—97; physician Lakeside Women's Spec. Ctr., Metairie, La., 1997—2001, Jefferson Ob-Gyn, Metairie, 2001—. Chmn. coun. LSMS, Baton Rouge. Fellow: ACOG, ACS (McCain fellow in govt. regulation). Roman Catholic. Avocations: electronics, photography. Home: 6301 Bertha Dr New Orleans LA 70122

CULP, GORDON LOUIS, consulting engineer, management consultant; b. Topeka, Dec. 30, 1939; s. Russell Louis and Dorothy Marion (Wilson) C.; m. Rosemary Anne Smith, Apr. 7, 1990. BS in Civil Engring., U. Kans., 1961, MS in Environ. Health Engring., 1962; MA in Applied Psychology, U. Santa Monica, 1991. Registered profl. engr., Calif., Nev., Wash., Oreg.; cert. Myers Briggs practitioner MBTI Cert. Program, Gainsville, Fla. San. engr. USPHS, Cin., 1962-64, CH2M/Hill Engrs., Corvallis, Oreg., 1964-66; rsch. engr. Neptune Microfloc, Corvallis, 1966-70; rsch. mgr. Battelle N.W., Richland, Wash., 1970-71; regional mgr. CH2M/Hill Engrs., Reston, Va., 1971-73; pres. Culp, Wesner Culp (acquired by HDR Engring. 1986), Cameron Park, Calif., 1973-93, Smith Culp Consulting, Las Vegas, Nev., 1993—. Author: New Concepts in Water Purification, 1974, Handbook of Advanced Wastewater Treatment, 1978, 2d edit., 2001, Managing People (including Yourself) for Project Success, 1991,The Lead Dog Has the Best View: Leading Your Project Team to Success, 2005, others. Named one of four Outstanding Graduates in Hist. of Civil Engrg. Program, U. Kans. Mem. ASCE, Am. Water Works Assn., Water Environment Fedn., Am. Acad. Environ. Engrs., Assn. Psychol. Type, Rotary (pres. 1977-78). Office: Smith Culp Consulting 653 Ravel Ct Las Vegas NV 89145-8628 Office Phone: 702-360-1120. Business E-Mail: gordon@smithculp.com.

CULP, H. LAWRENCE, manufacturing executive; BA in Econs., Wash. Coll., 1985; MBA, Harvard U., 1990. Product mgr. Veeder-Root, 1990, v.p. mktg. and sales, pres., 1993—95; group exec., corp. officer Danaher Corp., 1995—99, exec. v.p., 1999—2000, COO, 2000—01, CEO, pres., 2001—. Office: 2099 Pennsylavania Ave NW Washington DC 20006-1813*

CULP, JOE C(ARL), electronics executive; b. Little Rock, July 23, 1933; s. Charles Carl and Doris Evelyn (Jackson) C.; m. Norma Carol Kennan, Jan. 26, 1954; 1 dau., Karen Gay Culp Ashorn. BSEE, U. Ark., 1955. Staff asst. to exec. v.p. Collins Radio, Dallas, 1967—68; with Rockwell Internat., Dallas, 1968—88, dir. data sys. mktg., 1968—71, dir. mktg. transmission sys. divsn., 1971—78, v.p. Latin-Am. divsn., 1978—80, v.p., gen. mgr. transmission sys. divsn., 1980—82, pres. telecom. group, 1982—88; pres., CEO Lightnet, Rockville, Md., 1988—89; exec. v.p. Comm. Transmission Inc., Austin, Tex., 1989—90. Pres. Culp Comm. Assocs., Austin, 1990—; bd. dirs. Brecon Ridge Mfg. Sys. Chmn. engring. bd. advisors U. Tex., Arlington, 1984; bd. advisors Coll. Engring. U. Ark., Fayetteville, 1982. Named Disting. Grad., Coll. Engring. U. Ark., 1981, Disting. Engr., U. Tex., Arlington, 1984. Mem. Electronic Industry Assn. (bd. govs. 1984-88), U.S. Tel. Suppliers Assn. (dir. 1984-88), Ind. Tel. Pioneers. Republican. Methodist. Office: Culp Comm Assocs Inc 2305 Barton Creek Blvd #20 Austin TX 78735

CULP, KRISTINE ANN, dean, theology studies educator; B in Gen. Studies with distinction, U. Iowa, 1978; MDiv, Princeton Theol. Sem., 1982; PhD in Religion, U. Chgo., 1989. Vis. instr. theology St. Paul Sch. Theology, Kansas City, Mo., 1985-86, instr. theology, 1986-89, asst. prof. theology, 1990-91; dean Disciples Div. House U. Chgo., 1991—, sr. lectr. theology Div. Sch., 1991—. Contbr. articles to profl. jours. Office: U Chgo Disciples Divinity House 1156 E 57th St Chicago IL 60637-1536 also: The Divinity Sch-U Chgo Swift Hall S-406 1025 E 58th St Chicago IL 60637-1509

CULP, MICHAEL BRONSTON, investor, writer, publisher; b. NYC, June 17, 1952; s. Robert Walter and Ann Lee (Filtzer); m. Deborah T. Bronston. BA in Econs. cum laude, CUNY, 1973; CFA, U. Va., 1979. Securities analyst Standard & Poor's, NYC, 1974—79; v.p., securities analyst E. F. Hutton & Co., Inc., NYC, 1979—82; v.p., sr. securities analyst Prudential Securities Inc., NYC, 1982-86, sr. v.p., mng. dir. rsch., 1986-94, sr. v.p., dir. global rsch., 1994-97, bd. dirs., 1986-91, oper. coun., 1991-97, chmn. stock selection com., 1989-97, chmn. equity devel. com., 1991-97, equity transactions bd., 1994-97, investment banking com., 1994-97; mem. investment com. Roman Arch Fund, 1996-97; mng. dir., dir. rsch., mem. oper. com. PaineWebber Inc., NYC, 1997-2000, also bd. dirs., 1997-2000; pres. Michael Culp & Co., Inc., NYC, 2000—01, Mecox Bay Press LLC, 2002—05; dir., mem. audit com. The Nat. Rsch. Exch., 2004—. Author: Conflicted, A Novel, 2003. Mem.: Mensa, Assn. for Investment Mgmt. and Rsch., Inst. CFAs, Internat. Soc. Fin. Analysts, Fin. Analysts' Fedn., N.Y. Soc. Security Analysts, Pubs.' Mktg. Assn., Omicron Delta Epsilon, Phi Beta Kappa. Home: 11 Jule Pond Dr Southampton NY 11968 also: 350 East 79th Street New York NY 10021

CULP, MILDRED LOUISE, corporate financial executive; b. Ft. Monroe, Va., Jan. 13, 1949; d. William Whitfield and Winifred Louise (Stilwell) C. BA in English Lit., Knox Coll., Galesburg, Ill., 1971; MA in Religion and Lit., U. Chgo., 1974, PhD Com. on History of Culture, 1976. Faculty, adminstr. Coll., 1976—81; dir. Exec. Résumés, Seattle, 1981—; pres. Exec. Directions Internat., Inc., Seattle, 1985—2000, Clive, Iowa, 2000—03, Crete, Ill., 2003—. Mem. MBA mgmt. skills adv. com. U. Wash. Sch. Bus. Adminstrn., 1993; spkr. in field; contract rschr. U.S. Army Recruiting Command, 1997. Author: Be WorkWise: Retooling Your Work for the 21st Century, 1994; columnist Seattle Daily Jour. Commerce, 1982-88; writer Singer Media Corp., 1991-98, Worldwide Media, 1999-2002, Globalvision, Inc., 2002-06, WorkWise syndicated column, 1994—, Universal Press Syndicate, 1997-01, WorkWise Interactive syndicated column, 2004-, WorkWise Advice column, 2004-; WorkWise Internet audio program, 2000—; featured on TV and radio; contbr. articles to profl. jours.; presenter WorkWise Report, Sta. KIRO, 1991-96. Admissions counselor U. Chgo., 1981—, vol. Jeff Metcalf Fellow Program, 2006—; mem. Nat. Alliance Mentally Ill, 1984-91; life mem. Alliance Mentally Ill Hamilton County, 1984—; founding mem. People Against Telephone Terrorism and Harassment, 1990; co-sponsor WorkWise award, 1999-2000. Recipient Alumni Achievement award Knox Coll., 1990, 9 other awards; named Hon. Army Recruiter. Mem.: U. Chgo. Puget Sound Alumni Club (bd. dir. 1982—86), Knox Coll. Alumni Network. Personal E-mail: culp@workwise.net.

CULPEPPER, DAUNTE, professional football player; b. Ocala, Fla., Jan. 28, 1977; Quarterback Minn. Vikings, 1999—2006, Miami Dolphins, 2006—07. Named to Nat. Football Conf. Pro-Bowl, 2000, 2003—04; recipient Sammy Baugh Trophy, 1998, Breakthrough Athlete of the Yr. award, ESPY, 2000, Ed Block Courage award, 2001, Korey Stringer Good Guy award, 2003—04. Achievements include setting NCAA record for single season completion percentage (.736), 1998; drafted by MLB NY Yankees, 1995.

CULPEPPER, GUY LEE, physician; b. Dallas, June 14, 1957; s. Pat McPherson; m. Deborah Mills, Oct. 4, 1986; children: Dillon, Justin, Logan. MD, U. Tex., Houston, 1984. Lic. dr. Am. Bd. Family Medicine, 1984. Pres. Bent Tree Family Physicians, Dallas, 1987—; CEO Jefferson Physician Grp., Dallas, 1995—. Found. bd. Dallas County Cmty. Coll., 2003—07. Fellow: AAFP. Home: 5353 Spanish Oaks Dr Frisco TX 75034 Office: Bent Tree Family Physicians 3550 Parkwood Blvd #600 Frisco TX 75034 Office Fax: 972-377-8808. Personal E-mail: glcdlc@aol.com.

CULPEPPER, MARY KAY, editor; Exec. editor Weight Watchers; exec. dir. Coastal Living, 2000—01; exec. editor Cooking Light Mag., editor-in-chief, 2001—, v.p., 2002—. Office: Cooking Light Magazine 2100 Lakeshore Dr Birmingham AL 35209 Office Phone: 205-445-6600. Office Fax: 205-445-6600.*

CULTON, PAUL MELVIN, retired counselor, educational administrator, professor, interpreter; b. Council Bluffs, Iowa, Feb. 12, 1932; s. Paul Roland and Hallie Ethel Emma (Paschal) C. AB, Crossroads Coll., 1955; BS, U. Nebr., Omaha, 1965; MA, Calif. State U., Northridge, 1970; EdD, Brigham Young U., 1981. Cert. tchr., Iowa. Tchr. Iowa Sch. for Deaf, Council Bluffs, 1956-70; ednl. specialist Golden West Coll., Huntington Beach, Calif., 1970-71, dir. disabled students, 1971-82, instr., 1982-88; counselor El Camino Coll., Via Torrance, Calif., 1990-93, acting assoc. dean, 1993-94, counselor, 1994-97, lectr., 1997—2006; prof. First Global C.C., Nong Khai, Thailand, 2006. Interpreter various state and fed. cts., Iowa, Calif., 1960-90; asst. prof. Calif. State U., Northridge, Fresno, Dominguez Hills, 1973, 76, 80, 87-91, L.A., 1999—; vis. prof. U. Guam, Agana, 1977; prof. First Global C.C., NongKhai, Thailand, 2006; mem. allocations task force, task force on deafness, trainer handicapped students Calif. C.C.s, 1971-81 Editor: Region IX Conf. for Coordinating Rehab. and Edn. Svcs. for Deaf proceedings, 1970, Toward Rehab. Involvement by Parents of Deaf conf. proceedings, 1971; composer Carry the Light, 1986. Bd. dirs. Iowa NAACP, 1966-68, Gay and Lesbian Cmty. Svcs. Ctr., Orange County, Calif., 1975-77; founding sec. Dayle McIntosh Ctr. for Disabled, Anaheim and Garden Grove, Calif., 1974-80; active Dem. Cent. Com. Pottawattamie County, Council Bluffs, 1960-70; del. People to People N.Am. Educators Deaf Vis. Russian Schs. & Programs for Deaf, 1993. League for Innovation in Community Coll. fellow, 1974. Mem. Calif. Assn. Postsecondary Edn. and Disability (founding v.p.), Registry of Interpreters for Deaf, Am. Sign Lang. Tchrs. Assn., Nat. Assn. Deaf. Mem. Am. Humanist Assn. Avocations: vocal music, languages, community activism, travel, politics. E-mail: pmculton@joimail.com.

CULTON, SARAH ALEXANDER, psychologist, educator; b. Burwell, Nebr., Nov. 12, 1927; d. James Claude and Frances Ann (Evans) Alexander;m. Verlen Ross Culton, June 19, 1949; children: James Verlen, Sarah Ann. BA in Edn., Ea. Wash. U., 1953, MA in Edn., 1956; EdD in Psychology, U. Idaho, 1966. Tchr. pub. schs., Kennewick, Northport, Wash., Potlatch, Idaho, 1946-56; prof. Lewis-Clark U. of Idaho, Lewiston, 1956-59, North Idaho Jr. Coll., Coeur d'Alene, 1961-66; sch. psychologist Sch. Dist. 81, Spokane, Wash., 1966-67; prof. psychology Spokane Falls Community Coll., 1967-88; author Colville, Wash., 1988—; sch. psychologist Adna (Wash.) Spl. Edn. Coop., 1994; mid. sch. counselor Soda Springs (Idaho) Sch. Dist., 1994-98; sch. psychologist Canyon-Owyhee Spl. Svc. Agy., Caldwell, Idaho, 1998—. Sch. psychologist, sch. counselor vol. Northport Schs., 1989-92; presenter convs. in field. Author: Psychology of Stress and Nutrition, 1992, Documentary of the Scotch-Irish Alexander Family History, 2002, 3d edit., 2005; contbg. editor: Gen Weekly, 2004—05. Doctoral fellow Wash. State U., 1959, U. Idaho, 1964; recipient Faculty Achievement award Burlington No. Found., 1988. Fellow Am. Inst. Stress; mem. NEA, APA, Internat. Coun. Psychologists, Internat. Stress Mgmt. Assn. (newsletter editor), Nat. Stroke Assn., Western Psychol. Assn., Am. Counseling Assn. (writer invitation 1992), Nat. Assn. Sch. Psychologists, Internat. Soc. Family History Writers and Editors, Alpha Delta Kappa. Baptist. Achievements include design of Alexander family history website www.houseofalexander.com. Avocations: travel, painting, photography, genealogy, writing. Mailing: 717 Prouty Corner Loop Rd Colville WA 99114-9208 Home Phone: 509-684-2070; Office Phone: 509-684-2070. Personal E-mail: versar@theofficenet.com.

CULVER, CATHERINE MARIE, secondary school educator; d. David Larry Culver, Sr. and Mary Ann Culver. BS in Edn., Calif. U. of Pa., California, 2001; postgrad., Morgan State U., Balt., 2006—. Cert. tchr. Pa., 2001, Md., 2002, athletic trainer Nat. Athletic Trainers' Assn. Bd. of Certification, 2002. Records clk. Howrey, Simon, Arnold, & White LLP, Washington, D.C. / Largo, Md., 2001—02; 9th, 10th, and 12th grade English tchr. Charles County Pub. Schs., La Plata / Waldorf, Md., 2002—05, athletic trainer, 2002—05; 8th grade English tchr. Anne Arundel County Pub. Schs., Annapolis / Millersville, Md., 2005—, athletic trainer, 2005—. Mem.: Edn. Assn. Charles County (gen. counsel 2003—04, bldg. rep. 2002—05, co-chair new educators voice com. 2003—05), Tchrs. Assn. of Anne Arundel County, Mid-Atlantic Athletic Trainers Assn., Md. Athletic Trainers Assn., Nat. Athletic Trainers Assn. (home course study reviewer bd. cert. 2004—), Nat. Coun. Tchrs. English, Md. State Tchrs. Assn. (new mem. task force 2003—05). D-Liberal. Roman Catholic. Avocations: creative writing, swimming, hiking, reading. Office: Old Mill Middle School South - AACPS 620 Patriot Ln Millersville MD 21401 Office Phone: 410-969-7000.

CULVER, CHET (CHESTER JOHN CULVER), governor; b. Washington, Jan. 25, 1966; s. John and Ann (Cooper) Culver; m. Mariclare Thinnes Culver; 2 children. BA in Polit. Sci., Va. Poly. Inst. and State U., Blacksburg, 1988; MA in Tchg., Drake U., 1994. Tchr. govt. and hist., coach Roosevelt HS and Hoover HS, Des Moines; investigator Atty. Gen.'s Office; sec. state State of Iowa, Des Moines, 1999—2007, gov., 2007—. Established Iowa Student Polit. Awareness Club; elder mem. Ctrl. Presbyn. Ch. Mem.: Iowa State Edn. Assn. (Fulbright Meml. Fund Tchrs. scholarship 1997), Coun. State Govts., Elections Task Force, New Millenium Youth Initiative, Presdl. Caucuses and Primaries Com., Elections and Voter Participation Com., Nat. Assn. Secs. State, State Records Mgmt. Com., State Voter Registration Commn. (chmn.), Exec. Coun. (chmn.). Democrat. Presbyterian. Office: Office of Gov State Capitol Bldg Des Moines IA 50319 Office Phone: 515-281-8993. Office Fax: 515-242-5952.*

CULVER, CURT S., diversified financial services company executive; BA in Real Estate with honors, Univ. Wis., Madison, MS in Urban Land Econ. with honors. Joined Mortgage Guaranty Ins. Corp. (subs. MGIC Investment Corp.), Milw., 1982, COO, 1996—99, pres., 1996—, CEO, 1999—; also pres. MGIC Investment Corp., Milw., 1999—, CEO, 2000—, chmn., 2005—. Named one of Most Powerful People in Am., Forbes mag. Office: MGIC 250 E Kilbourn Ave Milwaukee WI 53202 Office Phone: 414-347-6480.

CULVER, DAN LOUIS, federal agency administrator; b. Savannah, Ga., Dec. 7, 1957; s. Louis and Jean Culver. BS in Mktg., U. Tenn., 1981; postgrad., Air Force Acad., 1982, Cornell U., Ithaca, NY, 1985; BS in Edn. and Tng., U. West Fla., Pensacola, 1995, MEd in Orgnl. Devel. and Leadership, 1998. Cert. tchr. Fla. Logistics support officer USAF, Ft. Walton Beach, Fla., 1982-86; mgmt. assoc. Barnett Bank, Ft. Walton Beach, Fla., 1987-89; program adminstr. disaster relief SBA, Atlanta, 1989—. Diplomatic observer UN, NYC; promoter lectrs., entertainers and authors; disaster recovery expert and cons. Pioneered automation of airforce support ops., 1982—84. Vol. disaster relief for victims of Hurricane Hugo, Charleston, SC, 1989, Hurricane Andrew, Miami, Fla., 1992, Miss. River flood, 1993, L.A. earthquake, 1994, World Trade Ctr. destruction, NYC, 2001, Hurricanes Charley and Ivan, 2004, Hurricane Katrina, Biloxi, Miss., 2005; bd. dirs. non-profit orgns. Recipient Comdr.-in-Chief's Spl. Recognition for Excellence award, Pres. Ronald Reagan, 1986. Mem.: Asia Soc., Internat. Parliament Safety and Peace, Maison Internat. des Intellectuels, Internat. Platform Assn., Order of Knight Templars. Avocations: flying, skiing, sailing. Mailing: 2045 Mt Zion Rd #120 Morrow GA 30260

CULVER, GREGORY K., science educator; b. Murray, Ky., Aug. 4, 1954; PhD, So. Ill. U., Carbondale, 2000. Instr. U. So. Ind., Evansville, 2000—. Home: PO Box 38 Calvert City KY 42029 Office: Univ So Indiana 8600 Univ Blvd Evansville IN 47712 Home Phone: 270-395-4624; Office Phone: 812-461-5203.

CULVER, JENNIFER LYNN, secondary school educator; b. Pontiac, Ill., Sept. 7, 1970; d. John Murray Lehman and Lynn Elizabeth Payette, Lois Jane Lehman (Stepmother) and Jay Payette (Stepfather); m. Richard Bruce Culver; children: John Raven McCarthy, Catharine Elizabeth Falka 1 stepchild, Richard Heinrich. BA, Tex. Woman's U., Denton, 1996; post-grad., U. North Tex., Denton, 2004—. Cert. tchr. Tex. English tchr., gifted and talented and creative writing tchr. Hebron HS, Carrollton, Tex., 2002—. Curriculum advisor Tex. Edn. Agy., Austin, 2005—; nat. writing project mentor U. North Tex., 2005—; dist. writing/literacy project mentor Lewisville Ind. Sch. Dist., Flower Mound, Tex., 2002—; presenter in field. Vol. Habitat for Humanity, Plano, Tex., 2004—06. Grantee, NEH, 2004. Mem.: Mortar Bd., Sigma Tau Delta (v.p. 1994—96). Home: 5520 Rutledge The Colony TX 75056 Home Phone: 972-625-7863; Office Phone: 972-862-1600. Personal E-mail: ferrrr@msn.com. Business E-Mail: culverjl@lisd.net.

CULVER, MICHAEL PATRICK, music educator, composer; b. Memphis, Oct. 24, 1948; s. Charles Lawrence and Ruth Enid (Boone) Culver; m. Linda Marie Szymanski, Dec. 17, 1966; children: Erik-Jon, Ezra Charles, Soren Bernard. A Music, Ulster County C.C., 1975; BA Music Composition, Empire State Coll., 1989; MFA Music Composition, Bard Coll., 1993. Tutor, evaluator Empire State Coll., New Paltz, NY, 1992—96; pvt. practice Bloomington, NY, 1975—96. Composer: Dadaloop, for magnetic tape, 1979, Ontic Emanations: music for piano, 1980—87, 2 Etudes for Electronic Sound Sources, 1990, Four Georgics for String Quartet, 1991, Medium of Exchange, for flute, cello, piano, 1992, Her Sleeping Form Shifting, for oboe, viola, piano, 1994, Stevedores, for violin, bass clarinet, piano, 1996, Pronaos: Structural Trio for Seven Instruments, 1998, Occasional Chairs: 10 trio sonatas, 2002, Non Liquet, for String Quartet, 2004, Itinerary, for tape recorder and piano, 2004, Lontano Series for tape recorder and piano, 2007. Home: 166 Apple Hill Rd Hurley NY 12443 Home Phone: 845-338-3652; Office Phone: 845-338-3652.

CULVER, MILTON LAWRENCE, historian, educator; b. Birmingham, Ala., Jan. 30, 1972; s. Milton Lawrence Culver and Rosemary Walker Tenney. BA in History and English, U. Montevallo, Ala., 1994; MA in History, Utah State U., 1997; PhD in History, UCLA, 2004. Tchg. asst. dept. history Utah State U., Logan, 1995—97, asst. prof., 2004—; tchg. assoc. dept. history UCLA, 1999—2001, tchg. fellow, 2002—03. Rsch. assoc. Autry Nat. Ctr., LA, 2003—04, rsch. asst., 2001—03; archival intern Buffalo Bill Hist. Ctr., Cody, Wyo., 1997. Contbr. articles to profl. jours., chapters to books. Recipient Rsch. award, Mountain West Ctr. for Regional Studies, 1997, Haynes Found. Rsch. award, Hist. Soc. So. Calif., 2001, 2004, 2005, 2006, 2007, Excellence in Instrn. award, Utah State U., 2007; Summer Rsch. fellow, Autry Mus. Western Heritage, 2001, Dissertation Yr. fellow, UCLA, 2003—04, New Faculty Rsch. grantee, Utah State U., 2005, Martin Ridge fellow, Huntington Libr., 2005, Mellon fellow, 2006. Mem.: Western History Assn., Am. Soc. Environ. History (Rachel Carson prize for best dissertation 2005), Am. Hist. Assn. Avocations: reading, travel, camping, hiking. Office: Utah State Univ Dept History 0710 Old Main Hill Logan UT 84322-0710 Office Phone: 435-797-3101. Business E-Mail: lawrence.culver@usu.edu.

CULVER, VICKY, art gallery director, artist; b. Aug. 31, 1948; BSc in Graphic Design, Photography and Comm., Manchester Met. U., Eng., 1969. With Longman Ednl. Publishers, Harlow, England, 1974—79; with Dept. Industry, Trade and Commerce, Can. Govt., Ottawa, 1974—79; with Banfield Advt., Ottawa, Canada, 1981—84; freelance graphic designer Ottawa, Canada, 1984—87; dir. Guild Creative Art, Shrewsbury, NJ, 2000—. One-woman shows include Navesink Libr. Theater, Middletown, NJ, 2003, Metuchen Libr., 2003, Music and Art Acad., Marlboro, NJ, 2003, Tratto'ria, Metuchen, Germany, 2004, Powys Gallery, 2004, Monmouth Beach Cultural Ctr., 2005, West Long Br. Pub. Libr., 2005, Small World Coffee, Princeton, NJ, 2006, Guild of Creative Art Studio, 2006, Georgian Ct. U., 2006, McKay Imaging Gallery, Red Bank, NJ, 2007, Monmouth Mus., Lincroft, NJ, 2007, Main Ave. Gallery, Ocean Grove, NJ, 2007, Guild of Creative Art, Shrewsbury, NJ, 2007, exhibited in group shows, 2003, Art Alliance of Monmouth County, Red Bank, NJ, 2002, Guild of Creative Art, Shrewsbury, NJ, 2002, Asbury Park, NJ, 2001, Poricy Pk. Nature Ctr., Middletown, NJ, 1998, Little Silver Borough Hall, NJ, 1998, PNC Bank, Howell, NJ, 1997, Art and Attic Gallery, Red Bank, NJ, 1997; contbr. articles to profl. jours. Recipient 1st Pl. in Photography, Art Soc. Momouth County Ruth Crown Meml. Art Show, 2007, 2d Pl. for Photography, Art Soc. Monmouth County Ann. Art Show, 2007, 1st Pl. for Photography, Monmouth Art Gallery, 2001, 3d Pl. Mixed Media, Monmouth Arts Gallery, 2002, 3d Pl. in Photography, 2003, 2004, 2d Pl. Mixed Media, Freehold Art Soc., 1997—98, Judge's awards, 1999—2000, 2002—03, numerous hon. mentions, 1997—2007. Home: 39 Forrest Hill Dr Howell NJ 07731-2160

CULVERWELL, ALBERT HENRY, historian; b. Portland, Oreg., Jan. 28, 1913; s. John Albert and Nettie L. (Kingery) C.; m. Ethel E. Klein, Aug. 17, 1941 (dec.); children: Cheryl Evelyn, John Albert; m. Eleanor M. Liere, May 6, 1986 (dec.). Scholarship student in stagecraft, color and design, Cornish Sch., Seattle, 1935-36; BA, U. Wash., Seattle, 1936, MA, 1941; postgrad., Am. U., Washington, DC, Wash. State U., Pullman. Mem. faculty Whitworth Coll., Spokane, Wash., 1941-42, 46-50; civilian US Naval Air Sta., Seattle, 1942-45; safety engr., asst. dir. personnel Pacific Car & Foundry Co., Renton, Wash., 1945-46; instr. social sci. Wash. State U., Pullman, 1949-50; asst. prof. history Western Wash. State Coll., Bellingham, 1950-53; historian, supr. interpretation Wash. State Parks, Olympia, 1953-62; chief br. interpretive services Region 4, U.S. Forest Service, Ogden, Utah, 1962-68; dir. Eastern Wash. State Hist. Soc. Mus., Spokane, 1968-82; pres. Wash. Art Consortium, 1979-82. Mem. Wash. Archives Adv. Bd., 1977-82, Adv. Coun. Preservation of Hist. Sites and Bldgs., 1968-78, com. to develop Hist. Interpretive Ctr., Wash. State Capitol Bldg., 1983-84; mem. design com. Main St. Program, San Jacinto, Calif., 1988-91; vol. art assoc. in support and adminstrn. Fine Arts Gallery, Mt. San Jacinto Coll., 1988-98; vol. history assoc. in preservation and interpretation of Estudillo Mansion in San Jacinto, 1993-98, pres. Resident Coun. SunWest Village, Hemet, Calif., 1998-99. Author articles in field, also, film and TV scripts. Elder United Presbyn. Ch. U.S.A., 1942—; adminstrv. adv. com. Sheldon Jackson Jr. Coll., Sitka, Alaska, 1961-63; bd. dirs. Westminster Found., 1961-62; mem. Woodway Planning Commn., Wash., 1961-63, Wash. Gov.'s Adv. Coun. on Observance Civil War Centennial, 1961; Gov. Wash. Coun. Boundary Survey Centennial, 1961. Recipient cert. of commendation Am. Assn. State and Local History, 1965 Mem. Am. Assn. Museums (pres. Western regional conf. 1969-71), Orgn. Am. Historians, Pacific N.W. Hist. Soc., Idaho Hist. Soc., Utah Hist. Soc., Westerners, Phi Sigma Kappa, Pi Sigma Alpha. Clubs: Rotary. Home: 973 Sunwest Dr Hemet CA 92545-1626 *In my life I have striven to achieve something positive in whatever I have done. Success depends on faith in myself as well as in someone greater than I, and, to an extent, with those* *with whom I have worked. This has brought a measure of patience to me which has made it possible to accept setbacks which make achievement slow. But when one has gained confidence and patience, success is often achieved.*

CULWELL, CHARLES LOUIS, retired manufacturing executive; b. Putnam, Tex., Apr. 26, 1927; s. Willie and Ila Alberta (Crosby) C.; m. Virginia Green, June 10, 1949; children: Andrew Scott, Perry Neal, Curtis Austin, Travis Lee. BSEE, U.S. Naval Acad., 1949; MS in Mgmt., U.S. Naval Postgrad. Sch., 1969. Commd. ensign U.S. Navy, 1949, advanced through grades to capt., 1969; service in Korea and Vietnam; comdg. officer Naval Supply Center, Oakland, Calif., 1975-76; ret., 1976; asst. to pres., then v.p. Purex Corp., 1976-79; group v.p., gen. mgr. indsl., instl. and comml. products Purex Industries, Inc., Lakewood, Calif., 1979-84, v.p., asst. to CEO Carson, Calif., 1984-86, Purex Industries Liquidation, Carson, Calif., 1986-87, ret., 1987. Decorated Legion of Merit, Bronze Star with combat V, Meritorious Svc. medal. Mem. U.S. Naval Acad. Alumni Assn. Baptist. Personal E-mail: chasvaculw@aol.com.

CULY, STEVEN WAYNE, application developer, physicist; b. New Castle, Ind., Mar. 2, 1961; s. Ralph Richard and Martha Faye Culy. BSc in Physics, Ind. U., Bloomington, 1983; PhD in Physics, U. Colo., Boulder, 1993. Software engr. Affinity Software, Englewood, Colo., 1993—96, Distbn. Resources, Englewood, 1996—98; sr. software engr. Visual Numerics, Boulder, 1998—2000; software arch. Athene Software, Boulder, 2000—01; software engr. NSA Geotechnical Svcs., Golden, Colo., 2003—04, Amazon.com, Seattle, 2004—. Mem.: IEEE (assoc.), Am. Phys. Soc. (assoc.), Assn. Computing Machinery (assoc.), Am. Mensa (assoc.), Am. Canoe Assn. (assoc.), Phi Beta Kappa (assoc.). Avocation: kayaking. Home Phone: 425-427-8298. Personal E-mail: sculy@charcware.com.

CULYER, RICHARD C., III, education educator, consultant; b. Balt., Md. s. Richard C. and Virginia F. Culyer Jr.; m. Gail J. Blake; 1 child, Virginia Gail. BS, Appalachian State U., Boone, NC, 1959, MA, 1963; PhD, Fla. State U., Tallahassee, 1973; postgrad., U. SC, Columbia, U. NC, Charlotte, Converse Coll., Spartanburg, SC, Citadel, Charleston, SC. Cert. elem. tchr., prin., curriculum and instrn. specialist, spl. edn. tchr. NC, SC. Tchr. Kings Mountain Schs., NC, 1959—66, reading cons., 1966; tchr. Appalachian State U., 1966—72; tchr. fellow Fla. State U., 1972—73; asst. dir. Right to Read State of Fla., Tallahassee, 1973—74; prof. edn. Coker Coll., Hartsville, SC, 1976—2003; freelance reading cons. Hartsville, 1974—. Curriculum specialist, reading specialist, spkr. in field, 1966—. Contbr. articles to profl. newspapers and jours. including: Messenger Newspaper and Hartsville News Jour.; co-author (with Edwin Smith): Teaching Reading To Adults, 1975; co-author: (with Gail B. Culyer) Preventing Reading Failure: A Practical Approach, 1987; co-author: (with Ed Ebert) School: An Introduction to Education, 2008; co-author: (with Aimee Galloway) (children's book) Disaster Hits Dogville Elementary, 1994, author monographs in field. Organizer, chmn. Patrick Sawyer Meml. Bike Safety Com., Hartsville, 1988—2003. Grantee, Leadership Learning Acad. Polk County, Fla.; Project Improving Reading Instr. Statewide award, NC Dept. Edn. Wesleyan. Avocations: writing, genealogy, reading, piano. Home: 401 Gandy Dr Hartsville SC 29550 Office: Vineyard Press 6220 Pekin Rd Mount Gilead NC 27306

CUMMING, IAN M., holding company executive; b. 1940; BA, U. Kans., 1964; MBA, Harvard U., 1970. Chmn., CEO Leucadia Nat. Corp., NYC, 1978—; chmn. Finova Group, 2001—, Barbados Power & Light, WilTel Comm. Group, interim pres., CEO, 2002. Bd. dir. Skywest Inc., 1986—, Allcity Ins., 1988—, HomeFed Corp., 1999—, Carmike Cinemas, 2002—. Office: Leucadia National Corp 315 Park Ave S New York NY 10010-3686

CUMMING, ROBERT EMIL, editor, writer; b. Lincoln, Nebr., June 2, 1933; s. Eugene Earl and Christiana (Jensen) C. Student, U. Nebr., 1955; Music Ed. (Presser Found. scholar), Nebr. Wesleyan U., 1956. With Music Jour. mag., NYC, 1958-75, editor in chief, 1964-75; with Weekly Reader Corp. (formerly Xerox Edn. Publs. and Field Publs.), 1977-97; founder, pres. Conn. Singers Agy., 1997—. Theater editor Middlesex mag., 1995-97, The Trumpeter, 1997-99, critic Hometown News Pubs., 1999—2002; critic, condr., singer, stage dir. Village Light Opera Group, Hunter Coll., N.Y.C., Cmty. Opera, Little Orch. Soc.; founder-mem. Singing Editors, nationally concertized, 1974-76; toured U.S. and Can. as stage dir. Naughty Marietta, Little Orch. Concerts, 1976; compiler, editor: The Power of Music by Dmitri Shostakovich, 1968, They Talk About Music, 1971-72; editor Spl. Librs. Assn. Bull., Publ. Divsn., 1989-91, Life is a Poem, 1999; composer children's operettas Rumplestiltskin, 1952, Song of Andorra, 1953; songs: God Is My Salvation, 1954, How Sly, 1954, Ya Gotta Have Love, 1955, The Hills of Sand, 1969; ann. music report for Living History of the World, 1967-68; contbr. articles to profl. jours. Mem. East Haddam Hist. Soc., 1977—, pres., 1998—2004, exec. dir., 2005—; dir. U. Conn. Gilbert and Sullivan Summer Prodns., 1985—88, East Lyme Arts Coun., 1990—93; bd. dirs. Middletown Found. for the Arts, 2005—07. Named Arts Advocate of 2005, Middletown Commn. on the Arts. Mem. N.Y. Gilbert and Sullivan Soc. (pres. 1967-69), Conn. Gilbert and Sullivan Soc. (founder, dir. 1980—), Conn. Sinfonia Soc. (founder), So. Conn. Libr. Coun. (bd. dirs. 1986-89), Conn. Critics Circle. Episcopalian. Home: PO Box 196 East Haddam CT 06423-0196 Office: PO Box 294 Moodus CT 06469-0294 Personal E-mail: singers.agency@snet.net. *I have developed an awareness of the need for: enough strength to overcome loneliness; enough ego to communicate well; enough vision to perceive the need; enough ambition to overcome laziness; enough drive to complete what is begun; enough compassion to wish to help; enough insight to grow humility; enough talent to be grateful; enough intelligence to remain practical; enough wisdom to be open; enough sensitivity to be myself; enough pain to keep in balance; enough pleasure to retain my humor; enough culture to be knowing; enough honesty to admit ignorance; enough love to appreciate symbols; enough religion to sense God.*

CUMMING, ROBERT HUGH, artist, photographer; b. Worcester, Mass., Oct. 7, 1943; s. Robert H. and Evelyn (Schold) C. B.F.A., Mass. Coll. Art, 1965; M.F.A., U. Ill., 1967. Lectr. UCLA Extension, 1974-77, Otis Art Inst., Los Angeles, 1975-76, Calif. Inst. Arts, Valencia, 1976-77; asst. prof. U. Calif.-Irvine, 1977-78; assoc. prof. U. Hartford, West Hartford, Conn., 1978-86. Juror, cons. U.S. Eye Exhibit Winter Olympics, Lake Placid, N.Y., 1979; vis. artist Polaroid Corp., Cambridge, Mass., 1979, traveling retrospective through Australian Gallery Dirs. Coun., Sydney, Australia, 1979 Exhibited retrospective show, Friends of Photography, Carmel, Calif., 1979, Travelling retrospective show, Brisbane, Sydney, Melbourne, Adelaide, and Burney, Australia, 1979, one man shows, Castelli Gallery, N.Y.C., 1982, 85, 86, 88, 91, Werkstatt fur Photographie, Berlin, 1982, Whitney Mus. Am. Art, 1986, Hirshhorn Mus., Washington, 1988; retrospective exhbns. include San Diego Mus. of Contemporary Art, Boston Mus. of Fine Arts, Houston Contemporary Arts Mus., 1993-94. Recipient Awards in Visual Arts, Winston-Salem, N.C., 1984, Creative Arts award Brandeis U., 1985; grantee Nat. Endowment for Arts, 1972, 75; John S. Guggenheim fellow, 1980; fellow Japan-U.S. Friendship Commn., 1981

CUMMING, THOMAS ALEXANDER, brokerage house executive; b. Toronto, Ont., Can., Oct. 14, 1937; s. Alison A. and Anne B. (Berry) C.; m. E. Mary Stevens, Mar. 12, 1965; children: Jennifer, Allison, Katy. BAS, U. Toronto, 1960. Registered profl. engr., Can. With Bank of Nova Scotia, 1965-88; spl. rep. Toronto, 1965-68; br. mgr. Dublin, 1969-71, London, 1971-75; v.p. Calgary, Alta., Canada, 1975-80; sr. v.p. Calgary, Alta., Canada, 1980-85, Toronto, 1986-88; pres., CEO Alta. Stock Exchange, Calgary, 1988-99. Bd. dirs. Pengrowth Energy Trust; chair Canadian Investor Protection Fund, Balancing Pool. Mem. Assn. Profl. Engrs., Calgary C. of C. (pres. 1991), Calgary Golf and Country Club, Calgary Petroleum Club. Home and Office: 2906 10th St SW Calgary AB Canada T2T 3H2

CUMMINGS, ALEXANDER B., JR., food products executive; b. Liberia; BS in Fin. and Econs., No. Ill. U.; MBA in Fin., Atlanta U. Joined The Pillsbury Co., 1982, v.p. fin., 1993—97; deputy region mgr. Nigeria The Coca-Cola Co., 1997, region mgr. Nigeria, 1998, pres. North and West Africa divsn., 2000, pres., COO Africa Group, 2001—, exec. v.p. corp., 2002—. Chmn. The Coca-Cola Africa Found.; mem. Ctr. for Global Devel. Commn. on U.S. Policy toward Low-Income Poorly Performing States; bd. dirs. Africa-Am. Inst., Corp. Coun. on Africa, U.S.-Egypt Bus. Coun.; past bd. dirs. Sabathani Cmty. Ctr., Mpls. Office: The Coca-Cola Co PO Box 1734 Atlanta GA 30301

CUMMINGS, ANDREA J., lawyer; b. 1967; BA in Polit. sci., BS in Journalism, Boston U., 1990; JD, U. Va., 1995. Bar: Tex. 1995, Calif. 1999, Ill. 2000. With Locke Purnell Rain Harell, Tex., 1995—97, Weil, Gotshall Manges LLP, 1997—98, Nomura Asset Capital Corp., 1998—99, Gray Cary Uare Freidenrich, 1999—2000, Sidley Austin LLP (formerly Sidley Austin Brown & Wood LLP), Chgo., 2000—, ptnr., 2003—. Office: Sidley Austin LLP 1 S Dearborn Chicago IL 60603 Office Phone: 312-853-2107. Office Fax: 312-853-7036. Business E-Mail: acummings@sidley.com.*

CUMMINGS, ANTHONY WILLIAM, lawyer, educator, banker; b. Port Jefferson, NY, Dec. 3, 1962; s. Leonard and Annie (Earl) C. Student, Tulane U., 1980-81; BS in Applied Econs., Hofstra U., 1985, JD, 1988; MBA, U. N.C., 1997. Bar: N.Y. 1988, D.C. 1990, U.S. Dist. Ct. (ea. and so. dists.) N.Y. 1990, U.S. Ct. Mil. Appeals 1990, U.S. Ct. Appeals (2d, 11th and fed. cirs.) 1991, U.S. Tax Ct. 1991, U.S. Supreme Ct. 1992, N.C. 1995; diplomate Am. Bd. Forensic Examiners. Assoc. Ronald J. Rosenberg, Garden City, NY, 1988—89; of counsel Costa & Bernsten, Hauppauge, NY, 1989—92; contract atty. Bernsten & Newman, Hauppauge, 1990—93; pvt. practice Patchogue, NY, 1990—94, Raleigh, NC, 1994—97; assoc. Fin. Instns. Group, 1997—99, First Union Securities, Inc., Charlotte, NC, 1999—2000; v.p. Hales & Co., NYC, 2000—01; pvt. practice Melville, NY, 2001—, Staten Island, 2002—03, Great Neck, 2003—05, Manhattan, 2005—. Adj. instr. law Suffolk County C.C., Selden, NY, 1992—94; coord. adminstrv. svcs. N.C. Biotech. Ctr., Research Triangle Park, NC, 1994—95; adj. instr. bus. Wake Tech. C.C., Raleigh, 1995—97; coord., lectr. CLE programs Suffolk Acad. Law, 1989—94; co-chmn. appellate practice com. Suffolk County Bar Assn.; judge Jessup Internat. Law Moot Ct. Competition, 1990—91; pres. Cummings Capital Advisors LLC, 2001—; adj. prof. law Hofstra U. Zarb Sch. Bus., 2001—; adj. prof. forensic exam. Touro Coll. Sch. Health Scis., 2002—. Editor-in-chief Hofstra Property Law Jour., 1988; assoc. editor Jour. Suffolk Acad. Law, 1992-94. Pres. U. N.C. MBA Student Assn., 1996-97. Recipient award of recognition Suffolk County Bar Assn., 1991, cert. of disting. merit Suffolk Acad. Law, 1991. Mem. ABA, Am. Coll. Forensic Examiners, N.C. State Bar Assn., D.C. Bar Assn., N.Y. State Bar Assn., Hofstra U. Alumni Orgn. (exec. coun. 1990-94), Scabbard and Blade, Phi Eta Sigma. Office: 105 Maxess Rd Ste 124 S Melville NY 11747 Address: 247 W 38th St New York NY 10018 Office Phone: 212-391-2193. Business E-Mail: anthonyc@touro.edu, acummings@cummingslawofficepc.com.

CUMMINGS, CANDACE S., lawyer, apparel company executive; b. New London, Conn., Apr. 11, 1947; BA in Econs., Middlebury Coll., 1969; MD, U. Va., 1972. Assoc. to sr. bus. ptnr. Dechrt, Price & Rhoads, Phila., 1972-94; v.p., gen. counsel VF Corp., Greensboro, NC, 1994-96, v.p. adminstrn., gen. counsel, 1996—, sec., 1997—. Address: VF Corp PO Box 21488 Greensboro NC 27420 Office Phone: 336-424-6000. Office Fax: 336-424-7668.*

CUMMINGS, CHARLES WILLIAM, otolaryngologist, educator; b. Boston, Nov. 16, 1935; s. Harry Blanchard and Madge (Frey) C.; m. Jane Drake Cummings, July 1, 1983; children: Charles William, Lee Blanchard, Evelyn Howard. AB, Dartmouth Coll., 1957; MD, U. Va., 1961. Intern Mary Hitchcock Meml. Hosp., Hanover, NH, 1961-62; resident otolaryngology Harvard U. Med. Sch., 1965-68; assoc. prof. otolaryngology Upstate Med. Sch., SUNY, Syracuse, 1976-78; prof., chmn. dept. otolaryngology-head and neck surgery U. Wash. Med. Sch., Seattle, 1978-91, Johns Hopkins Hosp. and Med. Ctr., Balt., 1991—93; disting. svcs. prof., med. dir. Johns Hopkins Internat., Balt., 2003—05. Chief staff Johns Hopkins Hosp., 1996-98; bd. dirs. Am. Bd. Otolaryngology Author: Atlas of Laryngeal Surgery; co-author: Comprehensive Text of Otolaryngology-Head and Neck Surgery; contbr. sci. articles to profl. jours. Served to capt., M.C. USAF, 1963-65. Mem. ACS (chmn. adv. coun.), Soc. Head and Neck Surgeons, Am. Soc. for Head and Neck Surgery (sec., pres.), Soc. Univ. Otolaryngologists, Assn. Acad. Depts., Otolaryngology (past pres.), Triological Soc., Laryngological Soc., Bronchoesophagological Soc. (past pres.), Am. Acad. Otolaryngology-Head and Neck Surgery (bd. dirs., past pres.). Episcopalian. Office: Johns Hopkins U Dept Otolaryngology/Head/Neck/Surgery 601 N Caroline St Baltimore MD 21287-0006 Home Phone: 410-833-4458; Office Phone: 410-955-7400. Business E-Mail: ccumming@jhmc.edu.

CUMMINGS, DAVID WILLIAM, artist, retired educator; b. Okmulgee, Okla., July 15, 1937; s. Harold Raymond and Mildred Delores (Smith) C.; m. Marcia Mills Laging, June 20, 1964 (div. 1970); m. Beatrice M. Mady, Oct. 2, 1981. BFA, Kansas City Art Inst., 1963; MFA, U. Nebr., 1967. Prof. SUNY, New Paltz, 1964-70, CUNY, 1971-89; adj. instr. Wagner Coll., SI, NY, 1970-71; adj. prof. St. Peter's Coll., Jersey City, 1985—2003; adj. faculty Parson School of Design, New School U., 2004—06; adj asst. prof. Raritan Valley Coll., Somerville, NJ, 2004; ret. Vis. prof. NYU, 1980-82, SUNY, Purchase, 1984, Rochester (N.Y.) Inst. Tech., 1983, U. N.D., Grand Forks, 1982, Colo. Mountain Coll., Vail, 1975-84. One-man shows include Katz Galleries, N.Y.C., 1970, Henri Gallery, Washington, 1969-70, Allan Stone Gallery, N.Y.C., 1974-77, Gallery Alexandra Monett, Brussels, 1975, 77, 78, Sebastian/Moore Gallery, Denver, 1978, Ericson Gallery, N.Y.C., 1981, U. N.D., Grand Forks, 1981, Shahin Requicha Gallery, Rochester, N.Y., 1983, La Petite Galeria, Bayonne, N.J., 1986, Gallery Jupiter, Little Silver, N.J., 1987, A.M.B. Galleries, Hoboken, N.J., Cabrillo Coll. Gallery, Aptos, Calif., 1991, Clin. Ctr. Galleries, NIH, Bethesda, Md., 1993, Rabbet Gallery, New Brunswick, N.J., 1996, St. John's U., Jamaica, N.Y., 1999, Johnson and Johnson Galleries, New Bruswick, N.J., 2001. Served with U.S. Army, 1957-59. Wood Found. fellow, 1966-67, N.J. State Coun. of Arts fellow, 1985, 91; Ford Found. grantee, 1963.

CUMMINGS, ELIJAH E., congressman; b. Balt., Jan. 18, 1951; BS, Howard U., 1973; JD, U. Md., 1976. Bar: Md. 1976. Atty. priv. practice, 1980—96, Md. Gen. Assembly, 1982; mem. Md. Ho. of Dels., Annapolis, 1983—96, vice chmn. constl. and adminstrv. law com., 1987—96, chmn. com. econ. devel., 1996, vice chmn. house econ. matters com., 1994—96, speaker pro tempore, 1995—96; mem. transp. subcom. for coast guard and maritime transp., mem. transp. subcom. for water resources and environ. US Congress from 7th Md. dist., 1996—; mem. govt. reform com. and transp. infrastructure com. Chmn. Md. Legis. Black Caucus; chmn. Gov.'s Commn. on Black Males, 1990—; pres. Bancroft Lit. Soc., Congressional Black Caucus Found. (first vice chmn., bd. dirs., now chair) 1998, chmn., 2003-. Named Outstanding U.S. Student Govt. Leader Royal Arts Soc. of London; named one of Most Influential Black Americans, Ebony mag., 2006 Mem.: Md. Bar Assn. Democrat. Office: US Ho of Reps 2235 Rayburn Ho Office Bldg Washington DC 20515-2007 Office Phone: 202-225-4741. Office Fax: 202-225-3178.*

CUMMINGS, FRANK, lawyer; b. NYC, Dec. 11, 1929; s. Louis and Florence (Levine) Cummings; m. Jill Schwartz, July 6, 1958; children: Peter Ian, Margaret Anne. BA, Hobart Coll., 1951; MA, Columbia U., NYC, 1955, LLB, 1958. Bar: NY 1959, DC 1963. Adminstrv. asst. to US Senator Jacob Javits, 1969-71; minority counsel com. labor and pub. welfare US Senate, Washington, 1965-67, 71-72; assoc. Cravath, Swaine & Moore, NYC, 1958-63, Gall, Lane & Powell, Washington, 1967-68, ptnr., 1972-75, Marshall, Bratter, Greene, Allison & Tucker, Washington, 1976-85, Nossaman, Keurger & Knox, 1982-83, Cummings & Cummings, P.C. and predecessor firm, 1983-86, LeBoeuf, Lamb, Greene & MacRae, LLP, Washington, 1986-2000, of counsel, 2000—. Lectr. law Sch. Law Columbia U., 1970—74, U. Va., 2000—; adj. prof. Sch. Law Georgetown U., 1983—86; adj. prof. law Sch. Law NYU, 2005—; chmn. Am. Law Inst.-ABA Ann. Course ERISA Litigation, 1989—, Employment and Labor Rels. Law for Corp. Coun. and Gen. Practitioner, 1978—; mem. pub. adv. coun. employee welfare and pension benefit plans Dept. Labor, 1972—74; mem. adv. bd. Pension Reporter Bur. Nat. Affairs. Author: Capitol Hill Manual, 1976, Capitol Hill Manual, 2d edit., 1984, Pension Plan Terminations-Single Employer Plans, 4th edit., 2007, Multiemployer Plans, 2d edit., 1986; articles editor: Columbia U. Law Rev., 1957—58. Fellow Am. Coll. Employee Benefits Counsel; mem. ABA (chmn. com. pension, welfare and related plans 1976-79), Am. Law Inst. (advisor to restatement of employment law 2002—), Bar Assn. DC (chmn. com. labor rels. law 1972-73), Cosmos Club, Phi Beta Kappa. Home: 800 25th St NW Washington DC 20037 Office: LeBoeuf Lamb Greene & MacRae LLP 1101 New York Ave NW Washington DC 20005-4213 Office Phone: 202-986-8022. Business E-Mail: fcumming@llgm.com.

CUMMINGS, JAMES WILLIAM, poet; b. Bangor, Maine, Mar. 9, 1960; s. Donald Ernest and Marjorie May (Condon) C. Grad., Nokomis Regional H.S., Newport, Maine, 1978. With Cianbro Corp., Pittsfield, Maine, 1979, Stinson Seafood Co., Belfast, Maine, 1987—2001, Little River Apparel, 2001—. Contbg. author (anthologies) Treasured Poems of America, 1990—92, Memories of Tomorrow, 2000, Stars and Stripes, 1991, songwriter See You that Manger, After the Storm, Lights of the City, creator audiotape (poetry) Caliburn, A Sidney Family, A Death in Loudon, 2000, A Respectable Man: Captain Abiel Lovejoy, 2001; author: For My Grandmother's Hundredth Birthday, 2002, Visions of the Maine Coast, 2002, The Brothers Maguire, 2003 (named Poet of Merit, 2003, Outstanding Achievement in Poetry award, 2003), Poetry.com, Ode to the Muses, 2003, Mothers Make the World, 2003, A Surfer, 2003, A Soldier, 2003, Darlington, 2004, The Two Fishermen, 2004, (poetry) The Coming Age and Other Poems, 2007; contbr. articles to periodicals. Recipient Editor's Choice award, 2005. Mem.: Gen. Medieval Web List, Libr. of Congress (charter), Smithsonian Instn., Poetry Guild, Sparrowgrass Poetry Forum, Internat. Soc. of Poets (various anthologies 1993—), History Channel Club (life). Home: 56 Masonic Rd Dixmont ME 04932-3543 E-mail: jwc1870@aol.com.

CUMMINGS, JAN NORMAN, interior designer, educator; d. Max E. and Reba ImaJean Norman; m. Ranald I. Cummings II, Jan. 15, 1977; children: Ranald I. III, Leigh N. BS, William Woods U., Fulton, Mo., 1972; MS, Kans. State U., Manhattan, 1984. Owner, interior designer Jan Cummings Interiors, Overland Park, Kans., 1982—2006; chair interior design program Johnson County C.C., 1982—. Recipient Burlington No. Faculty Achievement award, Burlington No. and JCCC, 1999, 2004, Disting. Svc. award, Johnson County C.C., 2003. Mem.: Interior Design Educators Coun., Phi Kappa Phi, Phi Delta Kappa. Presbyterian. Avocations: travel, photography. Office: Johnson County Community College 12345 College Blvd Overland Park KS 66210 Home Phone: 913-888-1268; Office Phone: 913-469-8500 3941. Business E-Mail: janc@jccc.edu.

CUMMINGS, JOAN E., health facility administrator, educator; BA, Trinity Coll., 1964; MD, Loyola U., 1968. Diplomate Am. Bd. Internal Medicine, Geriatric Medicine. Med. intern St. Vincent Hosp., Worcester, Mass., 1968-69; med. resident Hines VA Hosp., Hines, Ill., 1969-71, sr. resident in nephrology, 1971-72, ambulatory care svc. chief gen. med. sect., 1971-84, med. dir., hosp. based home care, 1972-87, chief, intermediate care svc., 1984-87, assoc. chief of staff, extended care and geriatrics, 1987-90, med. dir., extended care center, 1987-90, dir., 1990—; asst. prof. clin. medicine U. Ill., 1976-82, Loyola U., 1983-91, assoc. prof. clin. medicine, 1991—; network dir. Dept. Vet. Affairs, Hines, Ill., 1995—2005. Ad hoc com. on primary care U. Ill., 1980-82, coll. edn. policy com. U. Ill., 1980-82, State Ill. Emergency Med. Svc. Coun., 1981-83, Comprehensive Health Ins. Plan Bd. State Ill., 1990—, Med. Licensing Bd. State Ill., 1992—, exec. com. Chgo. Fed. Exec. Bd. State Ill., 1992—; program dir. Loyola/Hines Geriatric Fellowship Program, 1987-90; bd. trustees Rosalind Franklin U. Medicine and Sci., 2005-; bd. dirs. Ismie Mutual Ins. Co., 2003-. Contbr. to profl. mags. and jour. Recipient Disting. Svc. award Abraham Lincoln Sch. Med. Univ. Ill., 1979, 81, Leadership award VA, 1980, Certificate of Appreciation award VA, 1980, Laureate award Am. Coll. Physicians, 1990. Fellow ACP; mem. AMA (Ill. delegation 1985—, vice speaker ho. of dels. 1987-89), Chgo. Med. Soc. (pres. Hines-Loyola br. 1982-83), Ill. State Med. Soc. (trustee 1984—, chmn. com. on Ill. med., 1988—, spkr. ho. of dels. 1989-91, exec. com., 1989-91, policy com., 1989—), Chgo. Geriatric Soc., Am. Geriatric Soc. Office: 772 St Charles Rd Glen Ellyn IL 60137 Home Phone: 630-858-7716. Personal E-mail: joanecum@msn.com.

CUMMINGS, JOHN PATRICK, lawyer; b. Westfield, Mass., June 28, 1933; s. Daniel Thomas and Nora (Brick) C.; m. Dorothy June D'Ingianni, Dec. 27, 1957 (div. May 1978); children: John Patrick, Mary Catherine, Michael Brick, Kevin Andrew, Colleen Elise, Erin Christine, Christopher Gerald; m. Marilyn Ann Welch, May 23, 1980. BS, St. Michael's Coll., 1955; PhD, U. Tex., 1969; JD, U. Toledo, 1973, MCE, 1977. Bar: Ohio 1973, U.S. Mil. Appeals 1974, U.S. Dist. Ct. (no. dist.) Ohio 1979. Mgr. Hamilton Mgmt., Inc., Austin, Tex., 1962-68; scientist Owens Ill., Toledo, 1968-73, risk mgr., 1974-76, staff atty., 1977-80, mgr. legis. affairs, 1981-84; pres. Hansa World Cargo Svc., Inc., Oakland, Calif., 1984-86; in-house counsel Brown Vence & Assocs., San Francisco, 1987-88; gen. counsel Pacific Mgmt. Co., Sacramento, 1986-88; pres. John P. Cummings & Assoc., Fremont, Calif., 1988—. Cons. Glass Packaging Inst., Washington, 1970-83, EPA, Washington, 1970-74. Contbr. articles to profl. jours. With USAF, 1955-62, 68-69, 75-76, 84-85, col. ret. 1986. USPHS fellow, 1963-66. Fellow Royal Chem. Soc.; mem. ABA, VFW, ASTM (chmn. 1979), Am. Ceramic Soc. (chpt. chmn. 1973), Am. Indsl. Hygiene Assn., Am. Chem. Soc., Res. Officers Assn. (legis. chmn. 1979-85), Am. Legion, KC (4th degree), Amvets. Roman Catholic. Achievements include patents in field. Avocations: reading, travel, coin and stamp collecting. Home: 843 Barcelona Dr Fremont CA 94536-2607 Office: PO Box 2847 Fremont CA 94536-0847 Office Phone: 510-505-0722. Personal E-mail: epigeneint@aol.com.

CUMMINGS, JOHN W., diversified financial services company executive; BA in Econs., Fairfield U. Joined Merrill Lynch & Co., Stamford, Conn., 1981, COO global tech. and svcs. NYC, 2001, CEO, 2002—03, sr. v.p., 2002—, head global tech. & svcs., 2003, COO global pvt. client, head corp. and diversified fin. svcs. grp. Bd. dirs. Depository Trust & Clearning Corpn., Merrill Lynch Fin. Data Scvs, Inc.; adv. bd. master of sci. in tech. mgmt. prog. Columbia U. Office: Merrill Lynch & Co 4 World Fin Ctr 250 Vesey St New York NY 10080

CUMMINGS, JOSEPHINE ANNA, writer, consultant, advertising executive; b. Gainesville, Fla., July 12, 1949; d. Robert Jay and Marcella Dee (Mount) Cummings. ABJ./Design cum laude, U. Ga., Athens, 1971; MA, NYU, 1999. Copywriter William Cook, Jacksonville, Fla., 1971-73;

creative dir. Leo Burnett, Chgo., 1973-76; sr. v.p., group creative dir. D. D. B. Needham, Chgo., 1976-84; sr. v.p., creative dir. Saatchi-Saatchi, NYC, 1984; sr. v.p., sr. creative dir. Ted Bates, NYC, 1984; exec. v.p., chief creative officer Tracy-Locke, Dallas, 1985-87; exec. v.p., exec. creative dir. Bozell, Chgo, 1989; exec. v.p., creative dir. Y&R, NYC, 1990-92; pres. The Joey Co., NYC, 1992—. Author: (play) Azaleas, 1988, (short story collection) Crimes of Passion, 1988, (childrens' book) The Hospital is a Funny Place, 1988, (short film) Night Magic, 1989. Named as creator One of Hundred Best TV Commls. Advt. Age, 1978-79, one of Advt. 100 Best Advt. Age, 1986, one of People to Watch Fortune mag., 1986, Ad Age one of Best and Brightest, N.Y. Mem. Amelia Earhard, Ninety Niners Club, N.Y. Women in Film. Avocations: reading, writing, golf. Office: The Joey Company Ste 632 45 Main St Brooklyn NY 11201 Business E-Mail: joey@thejoeycompany.com.

CUMMINGS, MARTIN MARC, physician, educator, academic administrator; b. Camden, NJ, Sept. 7, 1920; s. Samuel and Cecelia (Silverman) Cummings; m. Arlene Sally Avrutine, Sept. 27, 1942; children: Marc Steven, Lee Bernard, Stuart Lewis. BS, Bucknell U., 1941, DSc, 1969; MD, Duke U., 1944, DSc (hon.), 1985; DHL (hon.), Georgetown U., 1976; DSc (hon.), U. Nebr., Emory U.; MD (hon.), Karolinska Inst., 1972, U. Lvov, 1975. Diplomate Am. Bd. Microbiology. Intern, resident Boston Marine Hosp., 1944—46; resident Tb Grasslands Hosp., Valhalla, NY, 1946—47; dir. Tb evaluation lab. Communicable Disease Ctr., USPHS, Atlanta, 1947—49; instr. medicine Emory U. Sch. Medicine, 1948—50, assoc. medicine, 1950—52, asst. prof., 1953; chief Tb sect., also dir. Tb rsch. lab. VA Hosp., Atlanta, 1949—53; dir. rsch. svcs. VA Ctrl. Office, Washington, 1953—59; prof. microbiology, chmn. dept. Okla. U. Sch. Medicine, 1959—61; chief Office Internat. Rsch., NIH, USPHS, 1961—63; dir. Nat. Libr. Medicine, 1964—84, dir. emeritus, 1984—; cons. Coun. on Libr. Resources, 1984—, chmn., bd. dirs., 1994—96. Assoc. dir. rsch. grants NIH, 1963—64; chmn. com. med. rsch. Nat. Tb Assn., 1958—59; chmn. panel Sarcoidosis NRC-NAS, 1958—60; dist. prof. cmty. medicine Georgetown U. Sch. Medicine, 1986—90. Author (with Dr. H.S. Willis): Diagnostic and Experimental Methods in Tuberculosis, 1952, The Economics of Research Libraries, 1986; editor: Influencing Change in Research Libraries, 1989; contbr. chpt. on Tubercle Bacilli Diagnostic Procedures and Reagents, 1950. With AUS, 1943—44. Recipient Exceptional Svc. award, VA, 1959, Disting. Svc. award, HEW, 1968, Rockefeller Pub. Svc. award, 1973, Disting. Achievement award, Modern Medicine, 1976, Disting. Svc. award, Am. Coll. Cardiology, 1978, John C. Leonard award, Assn. Hosp. Med. Edn., 1979. Fellow: AAAS, Phila. Coll. Physicians, Med. Libr. Assn., Royal Soc. Medicine, N.Y. Acad. Medicine (hon.); mem.: NAS, Inst. Medicine, Am. Fedn. Clin. Rsch., Am. Soc. Clin. Investigation (sr.). Home: 700 John Ringling Blvd Apt 1407 Sarasota FL 34236-1555 Personal E-mail: martincummings@comcast.net.

CUMMINGS, NANCY, library director; b. Reno; BA, U. Nev., Las Vegas; MLS, San Jose State Coll., Calif. Sys. adminstr. Clark County Libr. Sys., Las Vegas; dir. Yuma County Libr. Dist., Ariz., Washoe County Libr. Sys., Reno, 1995—. Mem. Peace Corps, Philippines. Named Libr. of Yr., Ariz. Libr. Assn., 1988; recipient Disting. Svc. award, 1994. Office: Washoe County Libr Sys 301 S Center St Reno NV 89501-2102 Office Phone: 775-327-8340. Office Fax: 775-327-8393. E-mail: ncummings@washoecounty.us.

CUMMINGS, NICHOLAS ANDREW, psychologist; b. Salinas, Calif., July 25, 1924; s. Andrew and Urania (Sims) C.; m. Dorothy Mills, Feb. 5, 1948; children: Janet Lynn, Andrew Mark. AB, U. Calif., Berkeley, 1948; MA, Claremont Grad. Sch., 1954; PhD, Adelphi U., 1958. Chief psychologist Kaiser Permanente No. Calif., San Francisco, 1959-76; pres. Found Behavioral Health, San Francisco, 1976—; chmn., CEO Am. Biodyne, Inc., San Francisco, 1985-93, Kendron Internat., Ltd., Reno, 1992-95; chmn. Nicholas & Dorothy Cummings Found., Reno, 1994—; chmn., pres. UK Behavioural Health, Ltd., London, 1996-98; Disting. prof. U. Nev., 1997—; chmn., CEO DynaMed Integrated Care, Inc., 1998—. Co-dir. South San Francisco Health Ctr., 1959-75; pres. Calif. Sch. Profl. Psychology, LA, San Francisco, San Diego, Fresno campuses, 1969-76; chmn. bd. Calif. Cmty. Mental Health Ctrs., Inc., LA, San Diego, San Francisco, 1975-77; pres. Blue Psi, Inc., San Francisco, 1972-80, Inst. for Psychosocial Interaction, 1980-84; mem. mental health adv. bd. City and County San Francisco, 1968-75; bd. dirs. San Francisco Assn. Mental Health, 1965-75; pres., chmn. bd. Psycho-Social Inst., 1972-80; dir. Mental Rsch. Inst., Palo Alto, Calif., 1979-80; pres. Nat. Acads. of Practice, 1981-93. Served with U.S. Army, 1944-46. Fellow APA (dir. 1975-81, pres. 1979); mem. Calif. Psychol. Assn. (pres. 1968). Office: Nicholas & Dorothy Cummings Found 4781 Caughlin Pkwy Reno NV 89509 Office Phone: 775-526-3311. Personal E-mail: cummfound@aol.com.

CUMMINGS, ROBERT See ZOMBIE, ROB

CUMMINGS, ROGER HOLT, lawyer; b. Dearborn, Mich., Jan. 22, 1949; s. Richard H. and Cynthia (Holt) C.; m. Elizabeth Gail Knudsen, June 3, 1972; children: David Michael, Julia Anne, Jessica Lynn, Amanda Susan. BA summa cum laude (hon.), Amherst Coll., 1971; JD magna cum laude (hon.), Harvard U., 1974. Bar: NY 1975, US Dist. Ct. (so. and ea. dists.) NY 1975, Mich. 1981, US Dist. Ct. (ea. dist.) Mich. 1981. Law clk. to J. Edward Lumbard US Ct. of Appeals (2nd cir.), 1974—75; assoc. Cravath, Swaine & Moore, NYC, 1975-80, Dykema, Gossett, Spencer, Goodnow & Trigg, Detroit, 1981, ptnr., 1982-83; v.p. Energy Conversion Devices Inc., Troy, Mich., 1983-85; of counsel Dickinson, Wright, Moon, Van Dusen & Freeman, Detroit, 1985-87, ptnr., 1988; mem. Dickinson Wright PLLC, Bloomfield Hills, Mich. Editor (with David Goldsweig): (Book) International Joint Ventures: A Practical Approach to Working with Foreign Investors in the US and Abroad, 2nd edit., 1990. Mem., bd. trustee Garrett-Evangelical Theol. Sem., Evanston, Ill. Mem. ABA, Detroit Bar Assn. Avocations: family, sports, church involvement, detroit compact tutor. Office: Dickinson Wright PLLC 38525 Woodward Ave Ste 2000 Bloomfield Hills MI 48304 Office Phone: 248-433-7551. Office Fax: 248-433-7274. Business E-Mail: rcummings@dickinsonwright.com.

CUMMINGS, SANDRA EILEEN, medical products executive; d. Edwin T. Cummings and Regina E. DeVecchis; m. Richard S. Surwit; children: Daniel Surwit, Sarah Surwit. BA, Wake Forest U., 1973; MA, Middlebury Coll., 1978; MBA, U. N.C., 1983. Mktg. mgmt. Nortel Networks, Research Triangle Park, NC, 1983—96; pres. ZyCare, Inc., Chapel Hill, NC, 1996—. Chairperson Sch. Governance Coms., Chapel Hill, 1993—2003, 2006—07. Small Bus. Innovation and Rsch. Fast Track grant Nat. Heart and Lung Inst., NIH, 2001—04. Achievements include patents for computer programs for remote managment of patients with chronic conditions; research in The CoagCare Anticoagulation Management System. Office: ZyCare Inc 3804 Sweeten Creek Rd Chapel Hill NC 27514 Office Phone: 919-419-7228.

CUMMINGS, STEPHEN EMERY, investment banking executive; b. Atlanta, May 27, 1955; s. Robert Emery and Catherine Brierly (Longyear) C.; m. Karen Lee Ludwick, Feb. 21, 1981; children: William Ludwick, Stephen Clifton, Caroline Margret, Russell Ludwick, Lee Wyman. BA in Adminstrv. Sci., Colby Coll., Waterville, Maine, 1977; MBA, Columbia U., NYC, 1979. V.p. Kidder, Peabody & Co., Inc., NYC, 1979-85; with Bowles Hollowell Conner & Co. (merged with First Union), Charlotte, 1985—98, chmn., CEO, 1993—98; Managing Director and Head of Mergers and Acquisitions First Union Corp. (now Wachovia Corp.), 1998—99, Managing Director, Co-Head Investment Banking Group, 1999—2000; sr. exec. v.p., co- head Corporate and Investment Banking division Wachovia Corp., 2000—04, sr. exec. v.p., head Corporate and Investment Banking division, 2004—. George F. Baker scholar Colby Coll., 1977. Mem. Beta Gamma Sigma. Republican. Episcopalian. Office: Wachovia Corp 1 Wachovia Ctr Charlotte NC 28288*

CUMMINGS ROCKWELL, PATRICIA GUILBAULT, psychiatric nurse; b. Ludlow, Mass., June 22, 1939; d. Lee Allen and Mavis Isabella (White) Guilbault; m. Philip W. Cummings, Oct. 23, 1960 (dec. Jan. 1978); children: Sharon Ellen Timmons, Geoffrey Scott Cummings, Susan Mavis Lornitzo, Lee Millett Cummings, Mary Rockwell Thon; m. William Leonard Rockwell Jr., Aug. 18, 1990. ADN, Vt. Coll., 1982; BSN, Norwich U., 1987. RN, Vt. Staff nurse Ctrl. Vt. Hosp. Nursing Home, Berlin, 1982-84, 87—; staff psychiat. nurse Va. Hosp. Ground East, White River Junction, Vt., 1987-94; owner Globe Travel, Bradford, Vt., 1988-94; rschr. Norwich U., Northfield, Vt., 1988—. Nurse-entrepeneur Globe Travel, 1988—. Tchr. adult edn. ARC, Bradford, Vt., 1988, 89; bd. dirs. Fedn. of Vt. Lakes and Ponds, Inc.; v.p. Vale Hospice Internat.; dir. Fedn. Vt. Lakes and Ponds Inc. Mem. ANA (nat. and Vt. chpts.), AAUW, New Eng. Hist. Geneal. Soc. Avocations: writing, travel, medical genealogy, genetics and geneology. Home: 307 Godfrey Rd East Thetford VT 05043-9517 Office Phone: 802-785-4812. Personal E-mail: patsy@together.net.

CUMMINS, BUD, former prosecutor; b. Enid, Okla., 1959; BS, U. Ark., 1981, JD, 1989. Clk. US Dist. Judge Stephen Reasoner, US Magistrate John Forster Jr.; chief legal counsel Gov. Mike Huckabee; atty. Little Rock; US atty. (ea. dist.) Ark. US Dept. Justice, 2001—06. Republican.*

CUMMINS, CHARLES FITCH, JR., lawyer; b. Lansing, Mich., Aug. 19, 1939; AB in Econs., U. Mich., 1961; LLB, U. Calif., Hastings, 1966. Bar: Calif. 1966, Mich. 1976. Assoc. Hall, Henry, Oliver & McReavy, San Francisco, 1966-70, ptnr., 1971-75, Cummins & Cummins, Lansing, Mich., 1976-82, Pitto & Ubhaus, San Jose, Calif., 1982-85; prin. Law Offices Charles F. Cummins Jr., San Jose, 1985-87; ptnr. Cummins & Chandler, San Jose, 1987-92; prin. Law Offices of Charles F. Cummins, Jr., San Jose, 1992—. Bd. dirs., officer various civic orgns., chs. and pvt. schs. Lt. USNR, 1961-63. Office Phone: 408-872-0203. Personal E-mail: cfclaw@ix.netcom.com.

CUMMINS, CHRISTOPHER C., chemistry professor; b. Boston, Feb. 28, 1966; AB, Cornell U., 1989; PhD, MIT, 1993. Prof. chemistry, rschr. MIT, Cambridge, Mass. Contbr. articles to profl. publs. Recipient Alan T. Waterman award, NSF, 1998, F. Albert Cotton award in synthetic inorganic chemistry, Am. Chem. Soc., 2007. Achievements include research in new methods for inorganic synthesis; the synthesis, isolation and characterization of unusually reactive transition metal and actinide complexes of unique design and construction; the activation of ubiquitous small molecules including dinitrogen; the assembly of novel functional groups containing both transition metals and main group elements; development of new reagents for organic systhesis. Office: MIT Dept Chemistry Rm 2-227 77 Massachusetts Ave Cambridge MA 02139-4301 Office Phone: 617-253-5332. Office Fax: 617-259-5700. E-mail: ccummins@mit.edu.*

CUMMINS, DELMER DUANE, academic administrator, historian; b. Dawson, Nebr., June 4, 1935; s. Delmer H. and Ina Z. (Arnold) C.; m. Darla Sue Beard, Oct. 6, 1957; children: Stephen Duane, Cristi Sue, Caroline Renee. BS, Phillips U., Enid, Okla., 1957; MA, U. Denver, 1965; PhD, U. Okla., 1974; LLD, William Woods Coll., 1979; HHD (hon.), Phillips U., 1983; DLitt (hon.), Chapman U., 1996. Tchr., Jefferson County Pub. Schs., Denver, 1956-67; mem. faculty Oklahoma City U., 1967-77, Darbeth-Whitten prof. history, 1974-77, curator George Shirk Collection, 1977. Chmn. dept. history Oklahoma City U., 1969—72; dir. Robert A. Taft Inst. Govt., 1972—77; pres. Bethany (W.Va.) Coll., 1988—2002, pres. emeritus, 2002—; pres. Brite Div. Sch., 2002—03; vis. scholar in history Johns Hopkins U., 2002—. Author: The American Frontier, 1968, Origins of the Civil War, 1971;: 2d edit., 1978, The American Revolution, 1968, Contrasting Decades, 1920's and 1930's, 1972;: 2d edit., 1978, Consensus and Turmoil, 1972, William R. Leigh: Biography of a Western Artist, 1980, A Handbook for Today's Disciples, 1981, 3d edit., 2003; author (with D. Hohweller) An Enlisted Soldier's View of the Civil War, 1981, 3d edit., 2003; author: (with others) Seeking God's Peace in a Nuclear Age, 1985; author: The Disciples Colleges: A History, 1987, The Search for Identity, Disciples of Christ-The Restructure Years, 1987, Dale Fiers: Twentieth Century Disciple, 2003, Biography of Kenneth L. Teegarden, 2007; editor: The Disciples Theol. Digest, 1986—88, Biography of Alexander Campbell, 2004, Vol. II, 2007; contbr. articles to profl. jours. and encys. Active Pitts. Opera Bd., 1996—2001; moderator, active multiple nat. bds. and task forces Christian Ch., 1993—95; bd. dirs. Disciples of Christ Hist. Soc., pres., 2004—05; pres. divsn. higher edn. Christian Ch., 1978—88; trustee Culver-Stockton Coll., 1978—88, Tougaloo Coll., 1978—88, vice chmn., 1985—88; bd. trustees Phillips Theol. Sem., 2005—; Danforth assoc., 1976—78. Mem. Okla. Humanities Coun.(grantee 1974), Phillips U. Alumni Assn. (pres. 1975-76), Nat. Assn. Ind. Colls. and Univs. (secretariat, policy commn. 1990-94), chair pres.'s athletic conf. 1990-92), W.Va. Assn. Ind. Colls. (chair 1994-97, chair east ctrl. coll. consortium 1997-98), Co. Ind. Colls. (bd. dirs. 1998-01). Home: 255 Sears Ln Swanton MD 21561 Personal E-mail: d_cummins@gcnetmail.net. Business E-Mail: d.cummins@mail.bethanywv.edu.

CUMMINS, HERMAN ZACHARY, physicist; b. Rochester, NY, Apr. 23, 1933; s. Louis H. and Rhoda Edith (Kitay) Kominz C.; m. Marsha Z. Hirsch, Aug. 18, 1963. BS, MS, Ohio State U., 1956; Diplome d'Etudes Superieures, U. Paris, 1957; PhD, Columbia U., 1963; D honoris causa, U. P. et M. Curie, 1999. Rsch. assoc. Columbia U., NYC, 1963-64; asst. prof. physics Johns Hopkins U., Balt., 1964-67, assoc. prof., 1967-69, prof., 1969-71; prof. physics NYU, 1971-73; disting. prof. physics City Coll., CUNY, 1973—2004, prof. emeritus, 2004—. Guggenheim fellow, 1984-85; Sloan fellow, 1969-72; recipient von Humboldt Sr. Rsch. award, 1998. Fellow Am. Phys. Soc., N.Y. Acad. Scis., Am. Assn. Adv. Sci.; mem. NAS, Am. Acad. Arts and Scis. Achievements include research in laser light scattering physics; phase transitions and critical phenomena; laser Doppler velocimetry; solid state and biophysics; liquid-glass transition; alloy solidification and pattern-forming instabilities. Office: City Coll CUNY Dept Physics New York NY 10031 Office Phone: 212-650-6921. E-mail: cummins@sci.ccny.cuny.edu, hzcummins@aol.com.

CUMMINS, JAMES DUANE, retired news correspondent; b. Cedar Rapids, Iowa, Mar. 11, 1945; s. Dewey Homer and Dorothy Marie (Colgan) Cummins; m. Constance Marie Driscoll; children: Kimberly, Christine, Douglas, John, Molly, Bill. BS in journalism, Northwestern U., 1967, MS in journalism, 1968. News reporter Sta. KGLO-TV, Mason City, Iowa, 1969-70, Sta. WOOD-TV, Grand Rapids, Mich., 1970-73, Sta. WTMJ-TV, Milw., 1973-75, Sta. WMAQ-TV, Chgo., 1975-78; corr. NBC News, Chgo., 1978-89, corr./bur. chief Dallas, 1989—2007. Corr. (news reports) Iranian Hostage Crisis, 1979, Civil War-El Salvador, 1981, Korean Airline Disaster, 1983, Tylenol Murders, 1982, Hurricane Hugo, 1989, Waco Standoff, 1993, Iowa Floods, 1993, Calif. Earthquake, 1994, Okla. City Bombing, 1995, Oklahoma Tornadoes, 1998, Fla. Presdl. Recount, 2000, Shuttle Disaster, 2003, California Wildfires, 2003. Nominee Nat. News Emmy award, Oklahoma Tornadoes, 2000, Shuttle Disaster, 2003; named to, Iowa HS Basketball Hall of Fame, 1982; recipient HS 2nd Team All-Am., Parade Mag., 1963, Emmy award, Chgo. TV Acad., 1976, Nat. News Emmy award for "Floods", 1993, 1st place award, Nat. Assn. Black Journalists, 2000, Nat. News Emmy award, Hurricane Katrina, 2006. Mem. Northwestern U. Sch. Journalism Alumni Assn., Northwestern U. N Men's Club, Elfun Soc., Sigma Delta Chi. Avocations: reading, swimming, golf, boating. Home: 5815 Flintshire Ln Dallas TX 75252-5132 E-mail: cumminstrue@gmail.com.

CUMMINS, NANCYELLEN HECKEROTH, electronics engineer; b. Long Beach, Calif., May 22, 1948; d. George and Ruth May (Anderson) Heckeroth; m. Weldon Jay Cummins, Sept. 15, 1987; children: Tracy Lynn, John Scott, Darren Elliott. Student, USMC, Memphis, 1966-67. From tech. publ. engr. to engring. instr. Missile and Space divsn. Lockheed Corp., Sunnyvale, Calif., 1973-77; test engr. Gen. Dynamics, Pomona, Calif., 1980-83; quality assurance test engr. Interstate Electronics Co., Anaheim, Calif., 1983-84; quality engr., certification engr. Rockwell Internat., Anaheim, 1985-86; sr. quality assurance programmer Point 4 Data, Tustin, Calif., 1986-87; software quality assurance specialist Lawrence Livermore Nat. Lab., Yucca Mountain Project, Livermore, Calif., 1987-89, software quality mgr., 1989-90; from sr. constrn. insp. to sr. quality assurance engr. EG&G Rocky Flats, Inc., Golden, Colo., 1990-91, engr. IV software quality assurance, 1991-92, instr., developer environ. law and compliance, 1992-93; software, computer cons. CRI, Dabois, Wyo., 1993-97; contractor Dept. of Energy, Golden, Colo., 1997-98; test mgr. Keane Inc., Lakewood, Colo., 1998, project officer, 1998—. Customer engr. IBM Gen. Sys., Orange, Calif., 1979; electronics engr. Exhibits divsn. LDS Ch., Salt Lake City, 1978; electronics repair specialist Weber State Coll., 1977-78. Author: Package Area Test Set, 6 vols., 1975, Software Quality Assurance Plan, 1989. Vol., instr. San Fernando (Calif.) Search and Rescue Team, 1967-70; instr. emergency preparedness and survival, Claremont, Calif., 1982-84, Modesto, Calif., 1989; mem. Lawrence Livermore nat. Lab. Employees Emergency Vols., 1987-90, EG&G Rocky Flats Bldg. Emergency Support Team, 1990-93, Dubois Search and Rescue, 1995-97. Mem. NAFE, NRA, Nat. Muzzle Loading Rifle Assn., Am. Soc. Quality, Job's Daus. (majority mem.), Ea. Starr. Republican. Avocations: history, weapons, camping, native American crafts. Office Phone: 406-882-4513. E-mail: whiltierna@fortinedsl.net, fallingleafcircle@fortinedsl.net.

CUMMINS, WILMA JEANNE, actress, comedienne; b. Guthrie, Okla., Sept. 25, 1927; d. Chauncey Dewitt and Etta (Marshall) Anderson; m. Joseph Sylvester Cummins, May 24, 1952; children: Jeanetta Kay Arnold, Bunny Gail Cline, Mary Jo Stoops, Susan Dee. BA, Phillip's U., 1948; MA, U. Tulsa, Okla., 1980. Cert. tchr., lic. real estate broker. Ops. base payload control United Air Lines, Denver, 1948-50; lab. tech. Barnes Hosp., St. Louis, 1950, Coffeyville, Kans., 1951—53; elem. tchr. Kansas City, Mo., 1951-53; actress Gaslight Dinner Theatre, Tulsa, 1984, Discoveryland's Okla., Prattville, 1985; tchr. Tulsa Pub. Schs., 1970-78; part time tchr. Tulsa Jr. Coll., 1987-89; freelancer in TV and radio SAG, AFTRA, Dallas, Tulsa, 1991—. Real estate broker, Tulsa, 1981—93. Performer: (radio) Grasso's Barn Dance Festival, 1950, Mayfest, 2003, (plays) Whales of August, 2005; actor: (films) The Ripper, 1985, UHF, 1988, Christmas Child, 2003; (TV series) Rosie O'Donnell Show, 1997, America's Funniest People, 1991, Howie Mandel Show, 1999, Tonight Show with Jay Leno, 2001, 30 Seconds to Fame, 2002, Lawrence Welk Champagne Theatre, 1997, Spotlight Theatre, 1983—, (commercial) Tex. Transp. Inst., 2002. Pres. Christian Women's Fellowship First Christian Ch., Tulsa, 1983; vol. Gilcrease Mus., Tulsa, 1995—2002; pres. Internat. Club, Tulsa, 1996, Pan-Am. Round Table, Tulsa, 1990—92, Altrusa Club, Tulsa, 1985, Conversing Couples, Toastmasters Internat., 1986, Pro-Am., 2001—02. Recipient 1st pl. monologue, Internat. Platform Assn., 1989, 2d pl., 1991, 1st pl., Srs. Take Ctr. Stage, Welk Resort, 2000. Republican. Methodist. Avocations: theater, commercials. Office Phone: 918-628-1359. Personal E-mail: wilmajeannecummins@sbcglobal.net.

CUMMIS, CLIVE SANFORD, lawyer; b. Newark, Nov. 21, 1928; s. Joseph Jack and Lee (Berkie) C.; m. Ann Denburg, Mar. 24, 1956; children: Andrea, Deborah, Cynthia, Jessica. AB, Tulane U., 1949; JD, U. Pa., 1952; LL.M., N.Y. U., 1959. Bar: N.J. 1952. Law sec. Hon. Walter Freund, Appellate Div., Superior Ct., 1955-56; partner firm Cummis & Kroner, Newark, 1956-60; chief counsel County and Mcpl. Law Revision Commn., State of N.J., Newark, 1959-62; partner firm Schiff, Cummis & Kent, Newark, 1962-67, Cummis, Kent, Radin & Tischman, Newark, 1967-70; sr. v.p., dir. Cadence Industries, NYC, 1967-70; dir. Plume & Atwood Industries, Stamford, Conn., 1969-71; chmn., chmn. emeritus Sills Cummis Epstein & Gross, P.C., Newark, 1970—; exec. v.p. law and corp. affairs, sec. Park Place Entertainment corp., Las Vegas, Nev., 1999—2001; vice chmn. bd. dirs. Caesars Entertainment, Inc., Las Vegas, Nev., 2000—05. Dir. Essex County State Bank, Financial Resources Group; instr. Practising Law Inst. Chief counsel County and Mcpl. Revision Commn., 1959-62, N.J. Pub. Market Commn., 1961-63; counsel Bd. Edn. of South Orange and Maplewood, 1964-74, Town of Cedar Grove, 1966-70, Bd. Edn. of Dumont, 1968-72; mem. com. on rules and civil practice N.J. Supreme Ct., 1975-78. Assoc. editor NJ. Law Jour., 1961—. Trustee Newark Beth Israel Med. Ctr., 1965-75, Northfield YM-YWHA, 1968-70, U. Medicine and Dentistry NJ, 1980-84, Newark Mus., NJ Performing Arts Ctr., Blue Cross and Blue Shield NJ, 1983-93, Found. U. Medicine and Dentistry NJ, 1999—; gen. coun. NJ Turnpike Authority, 1990-94; bd. overseers U. Pa. Law Sch., 1991-96; bd. govs. Daus. Israel Home for Aged, 1968-70; active NJ Commn. on Statue of Liberty; pres.'s coun. Tulane U., 1992—; pres. bd. dirs. Tulane Assocs., 1994-96; Pres.'s commn. on White House Fellows, 1993-2001; dir. NJ Regional Planning Assn., Horizon Found., NJ, 2004—, Flame of Charity Found., 2005—. Recipient 1st Ann. Judge Learned Hand award Am. Jewish Com., 1994, First Ann. Disting. Citizen award N.J. Med. Sch., 2002. Fellow Am. Bar Found.; mem. ABA, Am. Law Inst. (life, bd. dirs.), Am. Judicature Soc. (dir.), U. Pa. Law Sch. Alumni Soc. (pres.), NJ Bar Assn., Essex County Bar Assn., NY Athletic Club (NYC), Greenbrook County Club (North Caldwell, NJ), Stockbridge Golf Club (Mass.). Democrat. Jewish. Office: Sills Cummis Epstein & Gross PC One Riverfront Pl Newark NJ 07102 Home Phone: 973-736-5505; Office Phone: 973-643-5499. Business E-Mail: ccummis@sillscummis.com.

CUNARD, DEREK, academic administrator; s. Tom Cunard and Rose Marie Winesett; life ptnr. Aaron M. Wische, Aug. 27, 2004. Cert. facilitator AchieveGlobal customer svc. Tex., facilitator 7 habits workshops UT, facilitator TimeQuest UT, facilitator JCAHO stds., HIPAA and Critical Care Workshops Fla. Dir. tng. and univ. WellCare Health Plans, Tampa, Fla., 2003—04; v.p. OD and culture HPS of Am., Tampa, 2004—. Dir. univ. Prudential Corp. Asia, Hong Kong. Mem.: ASTD. Personal E-mail: derekcunard@aol.com.

CUNDIFF, EDWARD WILLIAM, retired marketing educator; b. Long Beach, Calif., Sept. 28, 1919; s. Harry Thomas and Martha Magdalene (Koltes) C.; m. Margaret Wallace Stroud, Sept. 8, 1956; children: Richard Wallace, Gregory Edward, Geoffrey William. BA, Stanford, 1940, MBA, 1942; EdD, 1952; Ford Fellow, Harvard Sch. Bus. Adminstrn., 1956. Retailing exec., 1946-48; instr. mktg. San Jose State Coll., 1949-52; asst. prof., later asso. prof. mktg. Syracuse U., 1952-58, asst. dean, 1954-58; prof. mktg., chmn. dept. mktg. adminstrn. U. Tex., 1958-73, assoc. dean Grad. Sch. Bus., 1973-76; L.J. Buchan distinguished vis. prof. U. Tex. at San Antonio, 1976-77; Charles C. Kellstadt prof. mktg. Emory U., 1977-87; John A. Beck Centennial prof. comm. U. Tex., Austin, 1987-94, John A. Beck emeritus prof. comm. dept. advt., 1994-96, emeritus prof. mktg., 1996—; ret., 1994. Vis. prof. mktg., Fontainebleau, France, Palermo, Sicily, 1960-61. Author: (with R.R. Still) Sales Management: Decisions, Policies and Cases, 5th edit, 1988, Basic Marketing: Concepts, Environment, and Decisions, 1964, rev. edit., 1970, Essentials of Marketing, 1966, 3d edit., 1986, (with R.R. Still and N.A.P. Govoni) Fundamentals of Modern Marketing, 3d edit, 1980, (with Marye Hilger) Marketing in the International Environment, 2d edit., 1988; editor: Jour. Mktg, 1973-76. Served to lt. (s.g.) USNR, World War II. Mem. Am. Mktg. Assn. (v.p. 1980—), So. Mktg. Assn. (pres. 1967-68), Beta Gamma Sigma, Delta Sigma Pi, Theta Chi. Home: # 1281 4100 Jackson Ave Apt 229 Austin TX 78731-6038 Office: U Tex Coll Communication Austin TX 78712 Personal E-mail: edcundiff@sbcglobal.net.

CUNDIFF, LOU WILLIE, artist, sculptor, writer; b. Nashville, Mar. 20, 1926; d. John Melvin and Bertha Agnes (Johnson) Gibson; m. James Howard Cundiff, Sept. 16, 1944; children: Billie June, James Howard, Jr., Michael Douglas. Diploma, Howard H.S., Nashville. Typist clk. City of Nashville Ct., 1944; sales asst. mgr. Spartan Dept. Store, Nashville, 1966-70; credit clk. Woolco Credit Office, 1970-72; sec. H.D. Lee, Nashville, 1972-75; exec. sec. Red Kap Industries, Nashville, 1972-75; vol. Art judge AT&T Pioneers of Am., Nashville, 1990, Cheatham County H.S., Ashland City, Tenn., 1993, 94, 95. Maury County, Columbia, Tenn., 1994; Tenn. Art League Sch. Auctions, Tenn. Art League Gallery, Nashville, 1990-96. Author, illustrator: Miss Cundiff Speaking, 1975; editor, illustrator: Tennessee Art League Cookbook, 1995-96; compiler, illustrator: Word and Image Guild Manual, 1995-96; writer, compiler, illustrator: Steps of Time Chapbook, 1995. Speaker, artist 55 Health Fair Symposiums, Two Rivers Bapt. Ch., 1991; sec., scrapbook host Christian Women Club, Internat. Soc. Poets, Nashville; TV interview CT 39 TV, Murfreesboro, Tenn., 1993, WAGG Channel 3, Franklin, Tenn., 1987-90. Recipient 1st Oil 1982, 85, 92, Tenn. State Fair, Nashville, CASE Parthenon Ctrl. South Art Exhbn., Nashville, 1991, Solo 1992 Show Cheekwood Art Ctr., Pineapple Rm., Nashville, 1992, Ornament 1991 Trees nat. Mus. Women in Arts, Washington, 1991. Tenn. Art League Gallery, Tenn. Art League Gallery, Word and Image Guild, Friends of Tenn. Art League Gallery, Hendersonville Artists Guild. Mem. Two Rivers Baptist Ch. Avocations: bowling, reading, creative writing, sculpting, computers. Home: 909 Drummond Dr Nashville TN 37211-2730

CUNDIFF, VICTORIA ANNE, lawyer; d. Jerome W. and Anne C. BA summa cum laude, U. Denver, 1977; JD, Yale U., 1980. Bar: N.Y. 1981, U.S. Dist. Ct. (so. and ea. dists.) N.Y. 1981, U.S. Ct. Appeals (2nd cir.) 1984, U.S. Ct. Appeals (3rd cir.) 1988, U.S. Supreme Ct. 1991, U.S. Ct. Appeals (11th cir.). Assoc. Breed Abbott & Morgan, NYC, 1980-82, Milgrim Thomajan & Lee, P.C., NYC, 1982-87, mem., 1987-92; ptnr. Paul, Hastings, Janofsky & Walker, NYC, 1992—. Intellectual property adv. bd. mem. Practicing Law Inst. Author: Maximum Security: How to Prevent Departing Employees From Putting Your Trade Secrets to Work for Your Competitors, 1992, Trade Secrets and the Internet: Preventing the Internet from Being an Instrument of Destruction, Strategic Planning for Strategic Alliances: An Intellectual Property Perspective, How to Hire Your Competitor's Employee: A Trade Secret's Perspective, What you Need to Know About Economic Espionage act, The New York Law of Trade Secrets: A Practical Guide; contbg. editor Intellectual Property Law. Bd. dirs. Yale Law Sch. Fund, 1990-95, Yale Law Sch. Alumni Assn., NYC; Practicing Law Inst. Intellectual Property Adv. Bd. 2000—. Fellow: ABA (mem. com. on intellectual property litigation 1988-93, chairperson subcom. on trade secrets litigation 1990-93, lectr. ABA Nat. Inst. on Corp. Litigation); mem. N.Y. State Bar Assn. (chair intellectual property sect. 2000-02, co-chair com. trade secrets 1992-2006, exec. com. intellectual property sect. 2003—), Assn. of Bar of City of N.Y. (mem. com. on sci. and law, 1991-93, com. trademarks and unfair competition 1987-90, chair PLI program on trade secret protection and litigation 1992, 2002), Intellectual Property Owners Assn. (com. trade secrets 2005—). Avocations: art history, historic preservation. Office: Paul Hastings Janofsky & Walker LLP Park Avenue Tower 75 E 55th St, 1st Fl New York NY 10022 Office Phone: 212-318-6030. Office Fax: 212-230-7643. Business E-Mail: victoriacundiff@paulhastings.com.

CUNDY, KENNETH CHARLES, pharmaceutical executive; s. John Thomas and Patricia Ivy Cundy; m. Doris Chen Cundy, Mar. 25, 2000; children: Evelyn Victoria, Rebecca Isabel. BPharm, U. Manchester, Eng., 1980; PhD, U. Ky., Lexington, 1874. MRPharmS Royal Pharm. Soc. Eng., 1981. Postdoctoral fellow U. Calif., Berkeley, 1984—88; prin. rsch. investigator Sterling Rsch. Group, Great Valley, Pa., 1988—92; sr. dir. biopharmaceutics Gilead Sciences, Inc., Foster City, Calif., 1992—2000; sr. v.p. preclinical devel. XenoPort, Inc., Santa Clara, Calif., 2000—. Contbr. articles to profl. jours. Recipient Regent award for Meritorious Work, U. Manchester, 1980; scholar Nat. Rho Chi scholar, Rho Chi Soc. for Academic Honors in Pharmacy, 1983—84. Mem.: Controlled Release Soc. (assoc.), Am. Soc. Microbiology (assoc.), Am. Assn. Pharm. Scientists (assoc.), Am. Coll. Clin. Pharmacology (assoc.), Royal Pharm. Soc. (assoc.). Achievements include invention of Viread(R) for treatment of HIV; nanocrystal technology for drug delivery; 19 patents in field. Avocations: writing, painting, travel, genealogy. Office: XenoPort Inc 3410 Central Expressway Santa Clara CA 95051 Home Phone: 650-365-4277; Office Phone: 408-616-7307. Personal E-mail: ken_cundy@xenoport.com.

CUNEO, DENNIS CLIFFORD, automotive company executive; b. Ridgway, Pa., Jan. 12, 1950; s. Clifford Francis and Erma Theresa (Nissel) C.; m. Bonnie Frances Mish, Aug. 18, 1972; children: Corinne, Kyle, James. BS, Gannon U., 1971; MBA, Kent State U., 1973; JD, Loyola U., New Orleans, 1976. Bar: D.C. 1977. Trial atty. U.S. Dept. Justice, Washington, 1976-80; assoc. Arent, Fox, Kintner, Plotkin & Kahn, Washington, 1980-84; gen. counsel New United Motor Mfg. Inc. joint venture GM-Toyota, Fremont, Calif., 1984-88, v.p. legal and govt. affairs, 1988-90, v.p. corp. planning and legal affairs, 1990-92, v.p. corp. planning and external affairs, corp. sec., 1992-96; sr. v.p. legal, environ., external affairs Toyota Motor Mfg. N.Am., 1996-2000, sr. v.p., 2000—. Chmn. Calif. Workside Rsch. Com., Sacramento, 1988—96; lectr. exec. program U. Calif., Davis, 1988—95; lectr. internat. motor vehicle program MIT, Berlin and Beijing, 1994; mem. Gov. Pete Wilson Trade Mission to Asia, 1993; bd. dirs. Toyota Motor Corp. Svcs., Inc., 1996—99; mem. Cin. Bus. Com.; mem. gov.'s econ. adv. com., Frankfort, Ky., 2001—. Campaign chmn. United Way, Alameda County, 1993-95, No. Ky. United Way, 2000; co-chmn. Blue Ribbon com. to Save the Oakland A's, 1994; vice chmn. Alameda County Econ. Devel. Bd., Oakland, 1990-96, Team Calif., Sacramento, 1994; bd. visitors Loyola Law Sch., 1987-95; mem. Calif. Select Com. on Jud. Retirement, 1993; mem. steering com. Bay Area Coun., San Francisco, 1990-95, Bay Area Dredging Coalition, San Francisco, 1991-96; mem. Statewide Pupil Assessment Rev. Panel, Sacramento, 1996-97; bd. dirs. Oakland-Alameda County Coliseum, 1995-97, Cin. United Way, 1997—, Bay Area Regional Tech. Alliance, Oakland, 94-96; mem. flood relief cabinet ARC, 1997; mem. Gov.'s Task Force on Child Devel., Frankfort, Ky., 1999—. Mem.: ABA, Calif. Mfrs. Assn. (vice chmn. 1994—99, pres. Calif. manufactures svcs. corp. 1996—97), Nat. Mfrs. Assn. (chmn. human resources policy group 1999—, bd. dirs., exec. com.), Oakland Football Mktg. Assn. (pres. 1995—96), Greater Cin. C. of C. (bd. dirs. 1998—), No. Ky. C. of C. (bd. dirs. 1997—98), Assoc. Industries Ky. (bd. dirs. 1999—), Cin. Club, Metro. Club (bd. dirs. 1999—). Avocations: skiing, model trains. Office: Toyota Motor Mfg NAm 25 Atlantic Ave Erlanger KY 41018-3188

CUNEO, DONALD LANE, lawyer, educator; b. Alameda, Calif., Apr. 19, 1944; s. Vernon Edmund and Dorothy (Lane) c.; m. Frances Susan Huze, Aug. 8, 1981; children: Kristen Marie, Lane Michael. BA, Lehigh U., 1966; JD, MBA, Columbia U., 1970. Bar: N.Y. 1971, D.C. 1992, U.S. Claims Ct. 1972, U.S. Tax Ct. 1972, U.S. Dist. Ct. (so. dist.) N.Y. 1973, U.S. Dist. Ct. (no. dist.) 1978, U.S. Dist. Ct. D.C. 1992, U.S. Ct. Appeals (2nd cir.) 1979, U.S. Ct. Appeals (D.C. cir.) 1992, U.S. Ct. Internat. Trade 1979, U.S. Ct. Appeals (fed. cir.) 1979, U.S. Supreme Ct. 1979. Assoc. Shearman & Sterling, NYC, 1971-79, ptnr., 1979-93; pres., CEO Internat. House, 1993—. Sec., trustee Internat. House, N.Y.C., 1977-93; pres. Morningside Area Alliance, N.Y.C., 2000—03. Author: (with others) Prevention and Prosecution of Computer and High Technology Crime, 1988; contbr. articles to profl. jours. Reginald Heber Smith Cmty. Lawyer fellow U.S. Govt., 1970-71. Mem. Coun. Fgn. Rels. Avocations: sports, travel. Home and Office: Internat House 500 Riverside Dr New York NY 10027-3916 E-mail: dcuneo@ihouse-nyc.org.

CUNG, THIEP H., architectural firm executive; Lic. Calif. With Warner Group Archs., Inc., Santa Barbara, Calif., 1995—, pres., 1999—2005, CEO, 2005—. Prin. works include Milken Residence, Lake Tahoe, Monterey Peninsula Country Club. Bd. mem. State St. Ballet, Santa Barbara. Mem.: AIA. Office: Warner Group Archs Inc 1250 Coast Village Rd Ste J Santa Barbara CA 93108 Office Phone: 805-969-5074. Office Fax: 805-565-3797.*

CUNHA, MARK GEOFFREY, lawyer; b. Lexington, Mass, Sept. 26, 1955; s. John Henry and Dolores (DeRosas) C.; children: Celine Yvonne, Nicholas Brian. AB magna cum laude, Cornell U., Ithaca, NY, 1977; JD, Stanford U., Calif., 1980. Bar: NY 1981, US Dist. Ct. (so. and ea. dists.) NY 1981, US Ct. Appeals (2nd cir.) 1991, US Ct. Appeals (3d cir.) 2001, US Ct. Appeals (4th cir.) 2006, US Tax Ct. 1992, US Supreme Ct. 1996. Intern The White House, Washington, 1979-80; assoc. Simpson Thacher & Bartlett, NYC, 1980-88, ptnr., 1989—. Mediator comml. divsn. NY State Supreme Ct., NY County, 1996—; vice chair bd. dirs. legal svc. for NYC, 1997-. Bd. dirs. NY Lawyers for Pub. Interest, 1989-2004; trustee Inst. for Ednl. Achievement, 1995—, Lycee Francais NY, 1998—. Recipient Outstanding Vol. Lawyers award Legal Aid Soc., 1990, Pro Bono award NY County Lawyers Assn., 1991, Chevalier de l'Order Des Palmes Academique, Govt. France, 1997. Mem.: Assn. Bar City NY (v.p., chmn. exec. com., chmn. com. on legal assistance, chmn. del. to NY State Bar Assn. Ho. of Dels., steering com. on legal assistance), NY State Bar Assn. (exec. com. on comml. and fed. litigation sect.), Internat. Bar Assn., ABA, Phi Beta Kappa. Democrat. Home: 1150 Fifth Ave Apt 3A New York NY 10128-0724 Office: Simpson Thacher & Bartlett 425 Lexington Ave New York NY 10017-3954 Office Phone: 212-455-3475. Business E-Mail: mcunha@stblaw.com.

CUNNINGHAM, ALICE WELT, law and mathematics educator; b. Washington, Aug. 18, 1949; d. Samuel Louis and Beatrice (Boxer) Welt; m. Daniel Paul Cunningham, Aug. 10, 1975; adopted children: Stephen Paul, Philip James 1 child, Samuel Paul (dec.). BA summa cum laude, Yale U., New Haven, 1971; JD, Harvard U., Cambridge, Mass., 1974; MA in Math. Edn., Columbia U., NYC, 2001, MPhil, 2006, PhD in Math. Edn., 2007. Bar: N.Y. 1975, Calif. 1975, U.S. Dist. Ct. (no. dist.) Calif. 1975, U.S. Ct. Appeals (fed. cir.) 1980, U.S. Tax Ct. 1976. Assoc. Shearman & Sterling, NYC, 1974-75, Heller Ehrman, White & McAuliffe, San Francisco, 1975-78, Debevoise & Plimpton, NYC, 1978-83; assoc. prof. N.Y. Law Sch., NYC, 1983-86. Contbr. articles to profl. jours. Mem.: ABA, Assn. Bar City N.Y., N.Y. State Bar Assn., Kappa Delta Pi, Phi Beta Kappa. Personal E-mail: acunnin167@aol.com.

CUNNINGHAM, ANDREA LEE, public relations executive; b. Oak Park, Ill., Dec. 15, 1956; d. Ralph Edward and Barbara Ann C.; m. Rand Wyatt Siegfried, Sept. 24, 1983. BA, Northwestern U., 1979. Feature writer Irving-Cloud Pub. Co., Lincolnwood, Ill., 1979-81; account exec. Burson-Marsteller Inc., Chgo., 1981-83; group account mgr. Regis McKenna Inc., Palo Alto, Calif., 1983-85; founder, owner, pres. Cunningham Communication Inc., Santa Clara, Calif., 1985—. Mem. Am. Electronics Assn., U.S. C. of C., Young Pres.' Orgn., Software Pubs. Assn., Boston Computer Soc., Leadership Calif., U.S. Cambridge C. of C. Republican. Avocations: running, roller skating, aerobics, racquetball.

CUNNINGHAM, ANTHONY WILLARD, lawyer; b. Lakeland, Fla., Nov. 10, 1931; s. Elmo and Anna Catherine Cunningham; m. Kathleen, 1960 (div. 1974); children: Matthew, Tracy, Melisse, Megan, Joshua, Alexandra; m. Robin Richards, Nov. 22, 1980. LLB, U. Fla., 1962. Bar: Fla. 1963, U.S. Dist. Ct. (mid. dist.) Fla. 1964, U.S. Ct. Appeals (5th cir.) 1964, U.S. Supreme Ct. 1975. Assoc. Fishback, Davis, Dominick & Troutman, Orlando, Fla., 1962-64, Nichols, Gaither, Beckham, Colson, Spence & Hicks, Miami, Fla., 1964-65, Orlando and Tampa, Fla., 1965-67; prin. Wagner, Cunningham, Vaughan & McLaughlin, P.A., Tampa, 1967-92, Cunningham Law Group, P.A., Tampa, 1992—. 1st lt. fighter pilot USAF, 1951—56. Mem. ATLA (bd. govs. 1979—, 90, 95), Trial Lawyers Pub. Justice (bd. dirs. 1986—, pres. elect 1990-91, pres. 1991-92), Acad. Fla. Trial Lawyers (bd. dirs., past pres. 1971—). Democrat. Avocations: boating, fishing, skiing. Office: Cunningham Law Group 100 S Ashley Dr Ste 280 Tampa FL 33602-5348 Home Phone: 813-814-2244; Office Phone: 813-223-1700. E-mail: carrie@cunninghamlawgroup.com.

CUNNINGHAM, ATLEE MARION, JR., aeronautical engineer; b. Corpus Christi, Tex., Aug. 17, 1938; s. Atlee Marion and Carlos Dean (Shepherd) Cunningham; m. Diana Wahl Bonelli, July 17, 1976; children from previous marriage: Christopher Atlee Acie, Scott Patrick, Sean Michael. BSME, MSME, U. Tex., 1961, PhD, 1966. Rsch. scientist Def. Rsch. Lab., Austin, Tex., 1965; engrng. staff specialist Gen. Dynamics Corp., Ft. Worth, 1965—93, Lockheed Corp., Ft. Worth, 1993—95, Lockheed Martin, 1995—, sr. prin. rsch. engr., sr. tech. fellow, 2002—. Vis. indsl. prof. So. Meth. U. Inst. Tech., Dallas, 1969—70; vis. assoc. prof. aero. engrng. U. Tex., 1978—; lectr. in aeroelasticity Nat. Cheng Kung U., Taiwan, 1984, U. Tex., Arlington, 1990—; mem. tech. teams NATO-RTO; cons. NASA, USAF, USN, U. Tex.; cons. on aeroelastic and vibration issues for Lockheed Martin F-16, C-130J, F-22 and F-35 aircraft. Contbr. articles to profl. jours. V.p. Tex. Fine Arts Assn., Ft. Worth, 1972. With USN, 1962—64. Recipient NASA Cert. of Recognition for tech. publ., 1980, Achievement award, Gen. Dynamics, 1980, 1983, 1989; Welding Rsch. Assn. fellow, 1961—62. Fellow: AIAA (assoc.; tech. reviewer jours.); mem.: Sigma Xi. Achievements include innovations in subsonic, transonic and supersonic steady and oscillatory aerodynamics method; major contributions to aeroelastic developments and improvements for Gen. Dynamics/Lockheed Martin F-16 and F-111 aircraft, F-22 and F-35 aircraft; development of new methods for predicting high angle of attack aerodynamics in subsonic and supersonic flows; steady and unsteady force testing techniques for aerodynamic investigations using water tunnels, new concepts and methods for nonlinear aeroelasticity; pioneered new technology development for unsteady separated flows and buffeting on aircraft maneuvering at high angle of attack involving support of Air Force; Navy; NASA; Nat. Aerospace Lab. (Netherlands); Lockheed Martin; U. Tex., Austin; patents in field. Home: 4932 Black Oak Ln Fort Worth TX 76114-2936

CUNNINGHAM, BILL, state supreme court justice; b. Ky. m. Paula Cunningham; 5 children. BA, Murray State U., 1962; JD, U. Ky. Coll. Law. City atty., Eddyville, Ky., 1974—91; pub. defender Ky. State Penitentiary, 1974—76; commonwealth atty. 56th Jud. Dist., 1976—88; hearing officer Ky. Bd. Claims, 1981—85; trial commr. Lyon County Dist. Ct., 1989—92; cir. ct. judge 56th Jud. Cir., Ky., 1991—2007; assoc. justice for 1st Supreme Ct. dist. Ky. Supreme Ct., 2007—. US Army, Vietnam, Korea, Germany. Recipient Outstanding Commonwealth Atty. of Ky. Office: Ky Supreme Ct 700 Capital Ave Rm 235 Frankfort KY 40601 Office Phone: 502-564-5444.*

CUNNINGHAM, BILLIE M., accounting educator; b. Joliet, Ill., Apr. 2, 1946; d. William Morgan and Mildred Jane (Watson) Klett; m. Robert T. Cunningham, Feb. 27, 1971; 1 child, Dana Marie. BBA, North Tex. State U., 1968, MBA, 1975, PhD, 1980. Applications programmer Burroughs Corp., Dallas, 1969-71; software programmer USAA, San Antonio, 1971-72; asst. prof. Tex. Christian U., Ft. Worth, 1980-85; prof. Collin County C.C., Plano, Tex., 1986-93; Disting. lectr. U. North Tex., Denton, 1993-94; adj. asst. prof. U. Mo., Columbia, 1994—2004, adj. assoc. prof., 2004—. Mem. reaffirmation com. So. Assn. Colls. and Schs., West Palm Beach, Fla., 1991, DeKalb Coll., Decatur, Ga., 1992, Brevard CC, Cocoa, Fla., 1993; mem. acctg. edn. workshop planning com. Tex. Tech. U., Lubbock, 1992; acctg. adv. bd. Brookhaven Coll., Dallas, 1993; ad hoc reviewer Issues Acctg. Edn., Sarasota, Fla., 1993; breakout leader lyceum Fedn. Schs. Accountancy/Ernst & Young, Vero Beach, Fla., 1993; grant reviewer KMPG Peat Marwick, Montvale, NJ, 1994; spkr. in field. Author: Accounting: Principles and Applications, 5th edit., 1986, Financial Accounting, Principles and Applications, 5th edit., 1986, Accounting: Basic Principles, 5th edit., 1986, Accounting Information for Business Decisions, updated 2d edit., 2007; mem. editl. bd. Advances in Acctg., Edn., 1995—2001, Issues in Acctg. Edn., 2001—; contbr. articles to profl. jours. Chair pedagogical resources com. Fedn. Schs. Accountancy, St. Louis, 1995—96, mem. ednl. rsch. com., 1996—2001; mem. second century breakfast com. U. N. Tex., 1991—92, mentor Cmty. Mentors Program, 1991—93. Recipient Nat. Tchg. Excellence award, Nat. Inst. Staff and Orgnl. Devel., 1989, Exemplary Acctg. Educator award, Mo. Assn. Acctg. Educators, 1995, Raymond F. and Mary A. O'Brien Excellence in Tchg. award, U. Mo., 2005—06, Teaching Excellence award in accountancy, Williams-Keepers LLC, 2007; Rsch. grantee, Tex. Christian U., 1981—82. Mem.: AICPA (pre-cert. edn. exec. com. 2000—03, chair core competency framework best practices task force 2000—04, virtual grassroots panel 2003—07), Acctg. Historians (mem. edn. com. 1990—94), Am. Acctg. Assn. (sec.-editor 2-yr. coll. sect. 1989—90, mem. program adv. com. 1990—91, vice-chair 2-yr. coll. sect. 1990—91, coun. 1991—92, chair 1991—92, coord. regional reps./officer at large 1991—92, mem. acctg. edn. adv. com. 1992—94, mem. curriculum revision com. 1993—94, v.p. 1994—96, vice-chair tchg. and curriculum sect. 1996—97, chair 1997—98, mem. exec. com. 1998—99, mem. by-laws com. 2000—01, 2000—, mem. outstanding educator award com. 2005—06), Beta Alpha Psi, Alpha Kappa Psi, Phi Delta Kappa, Gamma Phi Beta. Avocations: tennis, golf, skiing, weight-lifting. Office: U Mo Columbia Sch Accountancy 349 Cornell Hall Columbia MO 65211-6100 Business E-Mail: cunningham@missouri.edu.

CUNNINGHAM, FRANCIS, artist; b. NYC, Jan. 18, 1931; s. Francis de Lancey and Marcia (Davis) C.; m. Katharine Spalding, Sept. 18, 1954; children: Marcia, Katharine. AB, Harvard Coll., 1953; student, The Art Students League, 1955-59. Tchr. CCNY, 1962-65, Bklyn. Mus. Art Sch., 1962-80, The Art Students League N.Y., 1980-83; founder, co-dir. The New Bklyn. Sch. Life Drawing, Painting & Sculpture, 1980-83; founder, co-dir. N.Y. Acad. Art, 1983-85. One man shows include Waverly Gallery, N.Y.C., 1964, Harry Salpeter Gallery, N.Y.C., 1966, The Berkshire Mus., Pittsfield, Mass., 1969, Distelheim Galleries, Chgo., 1970, Michelson Gallery, Washington, 1971, Welles Gallery, Lenox, Mass., 1971, Hirschl & Adler Galleries, N.Y.C., 1967, 70, 75, New Bklyn. Sch. Life Drawing, Painting and Sculpture, N.Y.C., 1982, Danish Consulate, N.Y.C., 1987, Marsh Gallery U. Richmond, Va., 1989, Gallerihuset, Copenhagen, Denmark, 1995, First St. Gallery, N.Y.C., 1995, Pro Persona Gallery, Stockholm, Sweden, 1998, Laurel Tracey Gallery, 2000, 02, 03, 04, 06, 07; exhibited in group shows at Nat. Acad. Design, The Tel Aviv Museum of Art, 1999, Fedn. Modern Painters, N.Y.C., 2001, Art Students League of N.Y., 2001, Galerie Susanne Ho/Jriis, Copenhagen, Denmark, 2002, numerous others. Capt. USMCR, 1953-57. Recipient Purchase award Berkshire Mus., 1968, Peebles award, 1965, Benjamin West Clinedinst medal Exceptional Artistic Merit Artists' Fellowship, 2004; Louis Comfort Tiffany Found. grantee, 1973; artist in residence The Sense of Place, Manhattan, Kans., 1974; named Nat. Academician, Nat. Acad. Design, 1994; fellow, Bogliasco Found., 1997. Mem. Audubon Artists (bd. dirs. 1988—, Salmagundi award 1973, Minnie Stern award 1977, cert. of merit 1980, Joseph Raskin award 1985), Century Assn. Home and Office: 789 W End Ave New York NY 10025-5469

CUNNINGHAM, GARY ALLEN, lawyer; b. Seattle, July 4, 1940; s. Chester Martin and Elsie Annette (Peterson) C.; m. Marilyn Phyllis Thunman, June 13, 1964. B in Engring., Yale U., 1962; JD, U. Wash., 1965. Bar: Wash. 1965, US Dist. Ct. (we. dist.) Wash. 1965, US Ct. Appeals (9th cir.) 1967, US Supreme Ct. 1993. Dep. prosecutor Office King County Pros. Atty., Seattle, 1965-67; ptnr. Bishop, Cunningham & Andrews, Inc., P.S., Bremerton, Wash., 1967—. Bd. dirs. Hood Canal Environ. Coun., Seabeck, Wash., 1970—, pres., 1974, 78; bd. dirs., sec. Olympic Peninsula Kidney Ctr., Bremerton, 1980—; bd. dirs. Kitsap Land Trust, Bremerton, 1989-2000, pres., 1993-2000; bd. dirs. Great Peninsula Conservancy, 2000—, pres., 2000-02; pres. Kitsap County Estate Planning Coun., 1985. Mem.: Kitsap County Bar Assn. (pres. 1975—76), Wash. State Bar Assn., Kitsap Golf and Country Club, Bremerton Rotary Club. Avocations: golf, hiking, skiing, foreign travel. Home: 8411 Sunset Ln NW Seabeck WA 98380-9529 Office: PO Box 5060 Bremerton WA 98312-0469 Home Phone: 360-830-5091; Office Phone: 360-377-7691. Business E-Mail: cunningham@bcalawyers.com.

CUNNINGHAM, GARY H., lawyer; b. Grand Rapids, Mich., Jan. 11, 1953; s. Gordon H. and Marilyn J. (Lookabill) C.; children: Stephanie M., Gregory H. B.Gen. Studies, U. Mich., 1975, MA, 1977; JD, Detroit Coll. Law, 1980. Bar: Mich. 1980, U.S. Dist. Ct. Mich. 1983, U.S. Ct. Appeals (6th cir.) 1986, U.S. Ct. Appeals (Fed. cir.) 1990, U.S. Supreme Ct. 2004. Law clk. and estate adminstr. U.S. Bankruptcy Ct., Ea. Dist. Mich., Detroit, 1980-83; assoc./ptnr. Schlussel, Lifton, Simon, Rands, Galvin & Jackier, Southfield, Mich., 1983-90; ptnr./shareholder Kramer Mellen, P.C., Southfield, Mich., 1990-95; prin. shareholder Strobl Cunningham & Sharp, P.C., Bloomfield Hills, Mich., 1995—2006, Cox, Hodgman & Giarmarco, Troy, Mich., 2006—. Sr. staff mem. Detroit Coll. of Law Rev., 1978-80; contbr. articles to profl. jours. Mem. ABA (bus. law sect.), Fed. Bar Assn. (chmn. bankruptcy sect. 1989-91), Oakland County Bar Assn. (bus. law com.), State Bar of Mich. (mem. corp., fin. and bus. law sect.), Am. Bankruptcy Inst. (sponsor), Comml. Law League of Am., Detroit Econ. Club, Detroit Inst. Arts, Delta Theta Phi. Avocations: sailing, skiing, tennis. Home: 3399 Roxbury Dr Troy MI 48084-2613 Office: Cox Hodgman & Giarmarco 101 W Big Beaver Rd Troy MI 48084-5280 Office Phone: 248-457-7000. Business E-Mail: gcunningham@chglaw.com.

CUNNINGHAM, GORDON ROSS, finance company executive; b. Toronto, Nov. 15, 1944; s. Wendell Carson and Catherine Ann C.; m. Patricia Dorothy Westheuser, Dec. 22, 1966; children: Kristyn Catherine, Kaleigh Ann, James Gordon. BA, U. Toronto, 1966, JD, 1969; LLD (hon.), U. Victoria, 1995. Bar: Ont. 1971. With Tory, Tory, DesLauriers & Binnington, Toronto, 1971-76; ptnr. Toronto, 1977-84; exec. v.p., COO Trilon Fin. Corp., Toronto, 1984-88, pres., COO, 1988-89, bd. dirs.; pres., CEO London Life Ins. Co. and London Ins. Group Inc., 1989-96; pres. Cumberland Pvt. Wealth Mgmt. Inc., 1997—. Pres., dir. Fairmoor Holdings Inc.; bd. dirs. Intertape Polymer Group, Inc., Allied Properties Real Estate Investment Trust. Former nat. corp. campaign chmn. Diabetes Can. Mem. Can. Bar Assn., Can. Life and Health Ins. Assn. (past chmn.), Upper Can. Law Soc., Rosedale Golf Club, Univ. Club, Devil's Glen Ski Club, Mad River Golf Club, Portmarnock Golf Club (Dublin), Ristigouche Salmon Club. Avocations: golf, squash, fishing, tennis, skiing. Office: Cumberland Asset Mgmt Corp M99 Yorkville Ave Toronto ON Canada M5R 3K5 Office Phone: 916-929-1090.

CUNNINGHAM, GUNTHER, professional football coach; m. Rene Cunningham; children: Natalie, Adam. BS in Gen. Sci., U. Oreg., 1969. Football coach U. Oreg., 1969-71, U. Kar., 1972, Stanford (Calif.) U., 1973-76, U. Calif., 1977-80; coach defensive line, linebackers CFL's Hamilton Tiger Cats, 1981; defensive line coach Balt. Colts, 1982-84; mentor defensive line San Diego Chargers, 1985-90; coach linebackers Oakland (Calif.) Raiders, 1991, defensive coord., 1992-93, defensive line, 1994; defensive coord. Kansas City (Mo.) Chiefs, 1995-98, head coach, 1999—2001, defensive coord., 2004—; coach linebackers Tenn. Titans, Nashville, 2002—04. Office: c/o Kansas City Chiefs One Arrowhead Dr Kansas City MO 64129

CUNNINGHAM, JACQUELINE LEMMÉ, psychologist, educator, researcher; b. Biddeford, Maine, Apr. 22, 1941; d. S. James and Alice (Fréchette) Lemmé; m. Seymour Cunningham II, Dec. 16, 1960 (dec. 1987); children: Macklin Todd, Danielle, Alyssa. BA in Psychology cum laude, U. Maine, Orono, 1963; MS in Psychology, U. South Ala., Mobile, 1983; PhD in Ednl. Psychology, U. Tex., 1994. Tchr. Mobile Pub. Schs., Ala., 1976—81; psychology intern Devereux Found., Devon, Pa., 1988-89; fellow in developmental disabilities Children's Hosp. Harvard Med. Sch., Boston, 1990; prof. U. SD, Vermillion, 1994-95; fellow in pediat. neuropsychology Children's Nat. Med. Ctr., George Washington U. Med. Ctr., Washington, 1995—97; psychologist pvt. practice, Wilmington, Del., 1997—2000, Children's Hosp. of Phila., Phila., 2000—. Cons. in field. Contbr. articles to profl. jours., chapters to books. Mem. Am. Psychol. Assn. (outstanding dissertation of yr. award 1994), Internat. Neuropsychol. Soc., Nat. Acad. Neuropsychology, Soc. History Behavioral Scis., Phila. Neuropsychology Soc. (bd. dirs. 1998-2002), Phi Kappa Phi. Avocations: travel, writing. Office: Children's Hosp of Phila 34th St & Civic Ctr Blvd Philadelphia PA 19104 Business E-Mail: cunningham@email.chop.edu.

CUNNINGHAM, JAMES BLAIR, ambassador; b. Allentown, PA, Sept. 2, 1952; s. Blair and Julia Katherine C.; m. Leslie Ann Genier, Aug. 9, 1975; children: Emma Julianne, Abigail Kathleen. B of Polit. Sci. and Psychology cum laude, Syracuse U., 1974. Staff asst. to the amb., polit. officer fgn. svc. U.S. Embassy, Stockholm, 1975-77; dep. Spanish affairs officer U.S. State Dept., Washington, 1977-79, sec. affairs, 1979-81; polit.-mil. affairs officer U.S. Embassy, Rome, 1981-85; U.S. mission NATO, 1985-88; dir. pvt. office of NATO sec. gen. Manfred Woerner Brussels, 1988-90; dep. polit. counselor U.S. mission to UN US Dept. State, Washington, 1990-92, dep. dir. office of European security and polit. affairs, 1992-93, dir. office of European security and polit. affairs, 1993-95; dep. chief of mission U.S. Embassy, Rome, 1996—99; amb., dep. U.S. rep. to UN US Dept. State, NYC, 2001—05, acting permanent rep. to UN, 2001, consul gen. Hong Kong & Macau Spl. Adminstrv. Regions, 2005—. Recipient Pres. Meritorious Svc. award, Nat. Performance Review Hammer award. Office Phone: 852-2841-2445.

CUNNINGHAM, JAMES GERALD, JR., transportation company executive; b. Morristown, NJ, Aug. 5, 1930; s. James Gerald and Kathryn Virginia (Cannon) C.; m. Marilyn Swanson, Sept. 22, 1956; children: Kathleen, Jean Marie, Barbara, James Gerald, III, Carl. BSCE, Newark Coll. Engring., 1952. Civil engr. Pa. R.R., 1952-54; trainmaster Erie-Lackawanna R.R., 1956-62; divsn. mgr., dir. transp. Consol. Freightways, Menlo Park, Calif., 1962-69; sr. v.p., dir. REA Express, Inc., NYC, 1969-75; also dir. REA Holding Corp.; pres., dir. Gateway Transp. Co., La Crosse, Wis., 1976-78; gen. mgr. intermodal ops. Consol. Rail Corp., Phila., 1978-79; pres., CEO PTL Truck Line LLC, Phila., 1980—. Served with Transp. Corps AUS, 1953-55. Mem. Am. Trucking Assn. (chmn. met. planning orgn. task force, exec. com.), Equipment Interchange Assn. (exec. com., past pres.), Intermodal Transp. Assn. (exec. com., past pres.), White Manor Country Club. Home: 3505 Saint Davids Rd Newtown Square PA 19073-1417 Office: PTL Truck Line LLC 320 King of Prussia Rd Radnor PA 19087 Personal E-mail: msclpwr1@verizon.net.

CUNNINGHAM, JANIS ANN, lawyer; b. Seattle, May 13, 1952; d. Luvern Victor and Anna Jane Rieke; m. D. John Cunningham, June 10, 1972; children: Emily Jane, Laura Christine. BS with honors, U. Wis., Milw., 1973; JD, U. Wash., 1976. Bar: Wash. 1976, U.S. Dist. Ct. (we. dist.) Wash. 1976, U.S. Ct. Appeals (9th cir.) 1976. Law clk. to Hon. Eugene A. Wright U.S. Ct. Appeals (9th cir.), Seattle, 1976-77; assoc. Karr, Tuttle, & Campbell, Seattle, 1977-84; ptnr. Karr, Tuttle, Koch, Campbell, Mawer & Sax, Seattle, 1984-89; ptnr., Personal Planning Area Perkins Coie LLP, Seattle, 1989—. Lectr. community property law U. Wash., Seattle, 1984, mem. estate planning coun. adv. bd., 1984-85. Co-author: Washington Practical Probate, 1982, 5th rev. edit., 1988; editor in chief U. Wash. Law Rev., 1975-76. Mem. estate plnning com. Am. Heart Assn., Seattle, 1978; bd. dirs. Community Services for the Blind, Seattle, 1977-79. Fellow Am. Coll. Trust and Estate Counsel; mem. Wash. State Bar Assn. (Real Property, Probate & Trust Section, exec. com. 1988-95, chmn. 1993-94), Seattle Estate Planning Coun., King County Bar Assn. (Real Property, Probate & Trust Section, pres 1986-87), Order of Coif. Avocations: hiking, canoeing. Office: Perkins Coie LLP 1201 3rd Ave 48th Fl Seattle WA 98101-3029 Office Phone: 206-359-8607. Office Fax: 206-359-9607. Business E-Mail: jcunningham@perkinscoie.com.

CUNNINGHAM, JESSIE JEROME, real estate investor, import/export company executive, entrepreneur, small business owner; b. Miami, Fla., Oct. 10, 1963; s. Jesse James and Racheal Mae Cunningham. Student, Morristown Coll., 1989—91, Knoxville Coll., 1992—93. CEO, founder Cunningham Family Enterprises and subs. The Midnight Mail Order Almanac Co., Gregareo Koustodia Maranatha Ministries, Cunningham Ventures and Realty, Twilight Prime HDDT TV Motion Picture Studios of Burbank, Calif., Phila., 1993—. Author: (novels) The Flame of Silence Jones Book One/Ever Prevailing Enemy!, 2001, Insights for Our Days and Time, 2002, Trilogy of the Gods, 2002. Mem.: Internat. Traders, Phi Beta Lambda (Omega Lambda chpt.). Avocations: running, travel, painting, sculpting, acting. Office Phone: 877-362-6101. Business E-Mail: jessie87@prepaidlegal.com.

CUNNINGHAM, JOEL LUTHER, academic administrator; b. Mooresville, NC, Jan. 11, 1944; s. Elbert Claxton and Ruth Morton (Journey) Cunningham; m. Trudy Bender, June 12, 1965; children: Nancy Elizabeth, Susan Ruth. BA, U. Tenn., Chattanooga, 1965; MA, U. Oreg., 1967, PhD, 1969. Asst. prof. math. U. Ky., Lexington, 1969—74; dean continuing edn. U. Tenn., Chattanooga, 1974—79; acad. v.p. Susquehanna U., Selinsgrove, Pa., 1979—84, pres., 1984—2000; vice-chancellor, pres. U. South, Sewanee, Tenn., 2000—. Chmn. Nat. Assn. Coll. and U. Commn. Policy Analysts, 1996—98, with, 1998—99, 2002—; treas. Tenn. Ind. Coll. Assn., 2005—, Appalachian Coll. Assn., 2005—; trustee Assn. of Episcopal Coll., 2000—, chair, 2002—; bd. dirs. Sunbury (Pa.) Hosp., 1992—98; mem. nat. adv. com. Woodrow Wilson Fedn., 1995—; pres. Sunbury (Pa.) Hosp., 1998—2000, Coll. and U. Anglican Commn., 2001—, treas., 2002—; mem. St. Mary's Conf. Ctr., 2000—. Fellow Woodrow Wilson fellow, 1965, Am. Coun. on Edn. fellow, 1976—77. Mem.: Soc. for Values in Higher Edn. (bd. dirs. 1992—99, v.p. 1994—95, pres. 1995—99), Am. Assn. for Higher Edn., Math. Assn. Am., Am. Math. Soc., Sigma Chi (chmn. bd. leadership tng. 1977—87, treas. 1987—89, v.p. 1989—91, pres. 1991—93, Internat. Balfour award 1965), Sigma Xi. Episcopalian. Home: PO Box 3326 Sewanee TN 37375 Office: U South Office VC & Pres 735 University Ave Sewanee TN 37383 Office Phone: 931-598-1101. E-mail: jcunning@sewanee.edu.

CUNNINGHAM, JOHN EDWARD, retired geologist, educator; b. Malone, NY, Apr. 18, 1931; s. Felix Patrick and Beth Milicent (Sornberger) Cunningham; m. Paula Marie Ratcliffe, Dec. 18, 1959; children: John Andrew, Moira Kathleen, Patrick Hollis, Kristen Gil. BA, Darmouth Coll., NH, 1953; PhD, U. Ariz., Tucson, 1965. Asst. prof. Eastern N.Mex U., Portales, 1962—63; asst. prof. to prof. Western N.Mex. U., Silver City, 1964—94; geologist Bureaus of Mines, Summers, N.Mex., 1956—90; field dir. U. Ga. Summer Honors Field Geology Course, Athen, Ga., 1990—91; prof. emeritus, 1994. Author: (geologic mapping) Silver City Quadrangle, 1974, Circle Mesa Quadrangle, 1995. Battalion Comdr. N.Mex. Defense Force, Silver City, 1990—2002. Sgt. US Army, 1953—55, Tokyo. Recipient Presdl. Tchg. award, Western N.Mex. U., 1984. Mem.: N.Mex. Geological Soc. (pres. 1980, 1992), Am. Legion (comdr. 1996—2000, 2001—02). Independent. Catholic. Avocation: bagpipes. Home: 9 Crestway Dr Silver City NM 88061 Personal E-mail: rockdoc53@msn.com.

CUNNINGHAM, JOHN RANDOLPH, project manager; b. Alexandria, La., July 17, 1954; s. John Adolphus and Zelma Audrey (Cox) C.; m. Teresa Ellen Toms, Jan. 22, 1977. BS in Computer Sci., La. Tech. U., 1976; masters cert. in project mgmt., George Washington U., 1999; MBA in Technology Mgmt., U. Phoenix, 2006. Cert. project mgmt. profl. Customer support specialist South Ctrl. Bell Tel. Co., New Orleans, 1977-81; data comm. designer Weyerhaeuser, Tacoma, 1981-87, acct. rep., 1987-89, planning mgr., 1989-92, EDI project leader, 1992-2000, capacity planning mgr., 2001—05, SAP cutover analyst, 2005—07, SAP change mgmt. lead, 2007—; project mgr. Vision Compass, Inc., Seattle, 2000, Network Commerce, Seattle, 2000-01. Adv. bd. U. Wash., Seattle, 1989-94; spkr. fin. EDI confs. Contbr. articles to profl. jours. Vol. Big Bros., Tacoma, 1989—99, Wash. State First Responder, 1989—2000; instr. CPR, 1999—2000; instr. neighborhood emergency tng., 1999—2000; instr. emergency first aid, 2001—06. Mem. NRA, Computer and Automated Systems Assn. (treas. 1991-95, pres. 1995-99), Project Mgmt. Inst., Indsl. Computing Soc., Instrument Soc. Am., Toastmasters Internat., Upsilon Pi Epsilon. Republican. Baptist. Home: 319 SW 328th St Federal Way WA 98023-5645 Business E-Mail: randy.cunningham@weyerhaeuser.com.

CUNNINGHAM, JUDY MARIE, lawyer; b. Durant, Okla., Sept. 7, 1944; d. Rowe Edwin and Margaret (Arnott) C. BA, U. Tex., 1967, JD, 1971; postgrad., Schiller Coll., Heidelberg, Fed. Republic Germany, 1976. Bar: Tex. 1972. Quizmaster U. Tex. Law Sch., Austin, 1969-71; rschr. Tex. Law Rev., Washington, 1970; staff atty. Tex. Legis. Coun., Austin, 1972-75; adminstrv. law judge, dir. sales tax div., assoc. counsel Comptr. of Pub. Accounts, Austin, 1975-85; owner, editor J.C. Law Publs., Austin, 1986—; pvt. practice Austin, 1986—. Author: (with others) Texas Tax Service, 1985; pub., editor, contbr. (newsletter) Tex. State Tax Update, 1986—; contbr. articles to Revenue Adminstrn.; assoc. editor Tex. Law Rev., 1968-71. State del. Dem. Party, Ft. Worth, 1990, county del., Austin, 1972, 88, 90, 92; vol. numerous Dem. campaigns, Austin, 1972-90. Mem. Industry Practitioners Liaison Group (comptr. pub. accts.), State Bar Tex. (taxation sect.), Austin (Tex.) Bar Assn. (bus. corp. and taxation sect.), Tex. Taxpayers and Rsch. Assn. Avocations: travel, cooking, reading mysteries, photography, swimming. Office: 4905 W Park Dr Austin TX 78731-5535 Office Phone: 512-459-3810. Personal E-mail: judymcunningham@earthlink.net.

CUNNINGHAM, JULIA WOOLFOLK, author; b. Spokane, Oct. 4, 1916; d. John George and Sue (Larabie) C. Grad., St. Anne's Sch., Charlottesville, Va., 1933. Author: (juveniles): The Vision of Francois the Fox, 1960, Dear Rat, 1961, Macaroon, 1962, Candle Tales, 1964, Dorp Dead, 1965 (Children's Spring Book Festival award), Violet, 1966, Onion Journey, 1967, Burnish Me Bright, 1970, Wings of the Morning, 1971, Far in the Day, 1972, The Treasure Is the Rose, 1973, Maybe, A Mole, 1974, Come to the Edge, 1977 (Christoper award 1978), Tuppenny, 1978, A Mouse called Junction, 1980, Flight of the Sparrow, 1980 (Commonwealth Club Calif. award, Honor Book award Boston Globe), The Silent Voice, 1981, Wolf Roland, 1983, Oaf, 1986, (with Betsy Hearne) Dorp Dead, 2002; (poetry) Shadow Heart, 1999, The Stable Rat and Other Christmas Poems, 2001, Cicada, 2001. Mem. Authors Guild. Home: 4310 Ramsey Aave Austin TX 78756-3207 E-mail: office@mcunninghamphd.com.

CUNNINGHAM, KATHY, artist, educator; b. New Brunswick, NJ, Oct. 12, 1947; d. John Christopher and Josephine Wilkens; m. Robert Edward Cunningham, Jan. 19, 1985; children: Kevin, Darren; m. Stephen Dennis Lane (div.). BS in Art Edn., St. John's U., Jamaica, NY, 1974; MS in Art Edn., C.W. Post, LI U., Greenvale, NY, 1978. Cert. art tchr. K-12 NY, elem. tchr. N-6 NY. Art tchr. K-6 South Huntington Pub. Schs., NY, 1974—75, North Merrick Pub. Schs., NY, 1977—81, 1987—, kindergarten tchr., 1981—86, art tchr., 1986—; art tchr. 5-12 Tapei Am. Sch., Taipei, Taiwan, 1975—76. Developed and taught tchr. workshops Art for Classroom Teachers, North Merrick, 2005, North Merrick, 06. One woman show, West Islip (N.Y.) Pub. Libr., 2002, 2006; contbr. articles to Arts and Activities mag., Sch. Arts mag. Mem.: Am. Press Assn., L.I. Art Tchrs., NY State Art Tchrs. Avocations: running, reading, drawing. Home Phone: 631-422-6459; Office Phone: 516-379-3732.

CUNNINGHAM, KIMBERLY ELLEN, medical transcriptionist; b. Parkersburg, W.Va., Dec. 17, 1965; d. James and Louella Adkins; m. Eric Kent Cunningham, Feb. 21, 1987; children: Ericka, Cherith, Blake. Degree in med. lang. and transcription studies, At Home Professions, Ft. Collins, Colo., 2000. Stenographer I, receptionist W.Va. Dept. Hwys., Charleston, 1984—86, stenographer II, 1986—90; med. transcriptionist Medquist Inc., Mount Laurel, NJ, 2000—. Youth dir. Kelly's Creek Bapt. Ch., 2000—, sec., 2005—. Mem.: Am. Assn. for Med. Transcription (practitioner 2005—). Republican. Avocations: line dancing, scrapbooks, photography, travel, four-wheeling. Home and Office: Route 4 Box 214-3 Charleston WV 25312 E-mail: meandmyteen@aol.com.

CUNNINGHAM, LEEANN, assistant prosecutor; b. Denville, NJ, Nov. 18, 1961; d. William Thomas and Patricia Carole Cunningham; m. Keith Henry Melofchik; children: Megan Patricia Melofchik, Carleigh Joan Melofchik. BA in Polit. Sci., Pa. State U., 1984; JD, Vt. Law Sch., 1987. Bar: N.J. 1987, U.S. Dist. Ct. N.J., U.S. Ct. Appeals (3d cir.) 2001. Legal intern Hon. Donald G. Collester, Jr., and Hon. Herbert S. Friend, Morristown, NJ, 1986; legal intern, mem. ho. and senate judiciary coms. Legis. Coun. Vt. Legislature, Montpelier, 1987; jud. clk. Hon. Paul Bangiola, J.S.C., Morristown, 1987—88; litigating atty. James, Wyckoff, Vecchio & Pitman, Denville, NJ, 1988—90, Gebhardt & Kiefer, Clinton, NJ, 1991—94; atty. Law Office of LeeAnn Cunningham, Esq., Long Valley, NJ, 1994—2000; asst. prosecutor Warren County Prosecutor's Office, Belvidere, NJ, 2000—05, Essex County Prosecutor's Office, Newark, 2005—. Contbg. author (legal treatise) New Jersey Practice, Family Law and Practice sect., 1999. Leader troop 518 Morris Area Girl Scouts, Long Valley, NJ, 2003—05; elder Long Valley Presbyn. Ch., 1998—2000. Mem.: Nat. Dist. Attys. Assn., Pa. State U. Alumni Assn. (life). Methodist. Avocations: hiking, skiing, tennis. Office: Essex County Prosecutor's Office 50 West Market St Newark NJ 07102 Office Phone: 973-621-4409. Office Fax: 973-621-4669. Business E-Mail: leeann.cunningham@njecpo.org.

CUNNINGHAM, MARK ALAN, surgeon; s. Michael James and Gloria Faye Cunningham; m. LeeAnn Toshie Cunningham; children: Lauren Sumiko, Maxwell Kazuo. BA in Anthropology, San Jose Stae U., 1983, MA in Cell Biology, 1987; MD, St. Louis U., 1991. Diplomate Am. Bd. Surgery, Am. Bd. Surg. Critical Care. Intern Valley Med. Ctr./U. Calif., San Francisco, resident; asst. prof. surgery U. Calif. San Francisco, Fresno, Calif., 1997—2003; ptnr. Valley Surg. Specialists, Fresno, 2005—. Recipient Kaiser award for Tchg., U. Calif. San Francisco, 2000. Office: Valley Surg Specialists 7202 N Millbrook Ave #105 Fresno CA 93720 Office Phone: 559-450-3901.

CUNNINGHAM, MARY ANN MICHAEL, secondary school educator; b. Jackson, Pa., Mar. 5, 1947; d. Chester Benjamin and Wanda Mae (Plew) Michael; m. Donald Lewis Cunningham, Apr. 16, 1976; children: Courtney A., Donald M. AA, Keystone Coll., LaPlume, Pa., 1967; BS, Bloomsburg U., Pa., 1969; MA, U. Scranton, Pa., 1971; post grad, 1971—. Faculty Montrose Area Sch. Dist., Pa., 1969—2006. Chair and fund raiser Sunshine Club, Montrose, Pa., 1977—2003, exch. tchr.; advisor Key Club, 1992—2002; adj. instr. Luzerne C.C., Wilkes-Barre, 1998—; exch. tchr. Northeastern Ill. U. Sponsor Big Brothers Big Sisters Susquehanna County, Montrose, 1990—94. Named Woman of Distinction, Alpha Alpha State; recipient Cmty. Svc. citations (4), Susquehanna County Commrs., 1994—98, Fundraising award, March of Dimes, Svc. award, Garden Club Montrose, Laurel award. Mem.: Montrose Edn. Assn. (dir. activities 1969—), Delta Kappa Gamma (pres. 1990—92, Beta Rho chpt.), Phi Alpha Theta, Phi Theta Kappa. Republican. Avocations: gardening, reading, nature, travel. Home: RD2 177B New Milford PA 18834

CUNNINGHAM, MARY ELIZABETH (MARY CUNNINGHAM-LUSBY), physician; b. Newark, Apr. 21, 1931; d. William Rutherford and Mary Agnes Veronica (Harvey) C.; m. Perry Minor Lusby, Nov. 30, 1996. AB, Mount Holyoke Coll., 1953; MS, U. Ill., 1957; PhD, U. Oregon, 1964; MD, U. Conn., 1982. Diplomate Am. Bd. Emergency Medicine. Sr. physicist Lawrence Livermore Nat. Lab., Livermore, Calif., 1964-78; residency in emergency medicine Mich. State U. Affiliated Hosp., 1982—85, chief resident, 1984—85; sr. physician The Permanente Med. Group, Sacramento, 1985—96, ret., 1996, vol. physician, 1996—. Cons. emergency medicine King Faisal Specialist Hosp. and Rsch. Ctr., Jeddah, 2000-01. Contbr. articles to profl. jours. Physician Flying Samaritans-Mother Lode chpt., Sonoma, Calif., 1991—. Fellow Am. Coll. Emergency Physicians (life); mem. AMA, Am. Phys. Soc., Calif. Chpt. Am. Coll. Emergency Physicians, Calif. Med. Assn., NY Acad. Scis., Phi Beta Kappa, Sigma Xi (grant-in-aid-of-rsch. award 1963-64). Roman Cath. Office: Kaiser Permanente Med Ctr 6600 Bruceville Rd Sacramento CA 95823-4671

CUNNINGHAM, MERCE, performing company executive, dancer; b. Centralia, Wash. Student, Cornish Sch.; PhD (hon.), U. Ill.; DFA (hon.), Wesleyan U., 1995. Own dance co., 1953—; tchr. Sch. Am. Ballet, 1948-51; propr. own dance sch. NYC, 1959—. Dancer with company on world tour, 1964, S.Am. tour, 1968, numerous tours including U.S., Europe, Far East, Australia, South Am., others, choreographer The Seasons, 1947, Sixteen Dances for Soloist and Company of Three, 1951, Septet, 1953, Minutiae, 1954, Suite for Five, 1956, Nocturnes, 1956, Rune, 1959, Crises, 1960, Aeon, 1961, Story, 1963, Winterbranch, 1964, Variations V, 1965, How to Pass, Kick, Fall and Run, 1965, Place, 1966, Canfield, 1969, Tread, 1970, Second Hand, 1970, Signals, 1970, Landrover, 1972, Changing Steps, 1975, Solo, 1975, Un Jour ou Deux, 1973, Sounddance, 1975, Rebus, 1975, Torse, 1976, Squaregame, 1976, Travelogue, 1977, Inlets, 1977, Fractions, 1977, Exchange, 1978, Locale, 1979, Duets, 1980, Channels/Inserts, 1981, Trails, 1982, Quartet, 1982, Coast Zone, 1983, Roaratorio, 1983, Pictures, 1984, Doubles, 1984, Phrases, 1984, Native Green, 1985, Arcade, 1985, Points in Space, 1986, Fabrications, 1987, Shards, 1987, Five Stone Wind, 1988, Cargo X, 1989, August Pace, 1989, Polarity, 1990, Neighbors, 1991, Trackers, 1991, Beach Birds, 1991, Loosestrife, 1991, Change of Address, 1992, Touchbase, 1992, Enter, 1992, Doubletoss, 1993, CRWDSPCR, 1993, Ocean, 1994, Ground Level Overlay, 1995, Windows, 1995, Rondo, 1996, Installations, 1996, Scenario, 1997, Pond Way, 1998, BIPED, 1999, Interscape, 2000, Way Station, 2001, Loose Time, 2002, Fluid Canvas, 2002, Split Sides, 2003, Views on Stage, 2004, eyespace, 2006—07. Decorated comdr. Order of Arts and Letters Legion of Honor (France); recipient Gold medal, Internat. Festival Dance, 1966, Grand prix, Belgrade Internat. Theatre Festival, 1972, Creative Arts award, Brandeis U., 1973, Capezio award, 1977, Samuel H. Scripps/Am. Dance Festival award, 1982, Mayor's award of honor for arts and culture, N.Y.C., 1983, Kennedy Ctr. honors, 1985, Laurence Olivier award, 1985, Meadows award for Excellence in Arts, So. Meth. U., 1987, Nat. Medal of Arts, 1990, Digital Dance Premier award, 1990, Wexner prize, Wexner Ctr. for Arts, Columbus, Ohio, 1993, Golden Lion award, Venice Biennale, 1995, Nellie Cornish Arts Achievement award, Cornish Coll. of Arts, Seattle, 1996, Medal of Distinction, Barnard Coll., 1997, Grand Prix, SACD, France, 1997, Belknap award in Humanities, Princeton U., 1998, Key to City, Montpellier, France, 1999, Established Artists award, Bagley Wright Fund, Seattle, 1998, Isadora Duncan award for Lifetime Achievement in Dance, Nat. Dance Week, San Francisco, 1999, Premio Tani, Rome, 1999, Handel Medallion, N.Y.C., 1999, Nijinsky Spl. prize, Monaco, 2000, Dorothy and Lillian Gish prize, 2000, Praemium Imperiale award (Theatre/Film), Japan Art Assn., 2005; MacArthur Found. fellow, 1985. Mem.: Am. Acad. and Inst. Arts and Letters (hon.). Office: Cunningham Dance Found 55 Bethune St New York NY 10014-2010 Office Phone: 212-255-8240. E-mail: info@merce.org.*

CUNNINGHAM, MICHAEL, lawyer; b. 1961; m. Jane Whittendale; children: Spencer, Austin. BS in Applied Math. & Statistics, SUNY Stony Brook, 1983; JD magna cum laude, Order of the Coif, U. Pa. Law Sch., 1988. Engr. Sperry Def. Electronics (now Unisys Corp.), 1983—85; with Dechert LLP, 1988—94; ptnr. & assoc. gen. counsel PricewaterhouseCoopers, 1994—2002; assoc. gen. counsel IBM Bus. Consulting Svc. Divsn., 2002—04; gen. counsel Red Hat, Inc., Raleigh, NC, 2004—. Mem.: ABA (Bus. Law sect.), Computer Law Assn., Order of the Coif. Office: Red Hat Varsity Dr Raleigh NC 27606 Office Phone: 919-754-3700.

CUNNINGHAM, MICHAEL GERALD, composer, writer, music educator emeritus; b. Warren, Mich., Aug. 5, 1937; s. Edmund John and Mary Ann (Etienne) C. MusB, Wayne State U., 1959; MusM, U. Mich., 1961; MusD, Ind. U., 1973. Accompanist, music dir. dance dept. Wayne State U., Detroit, 1961, 64-67, instr. music dept., 1967-69; teaching asst. Ind. U. Sch. Music, Bloomington, 1969-71; lectr. music theory U. Kans. Sch. Fine Arts, Lawrence, 1972; asst. prof. Conservatory Music, U. Pacific, Stockton, Calif., 1973; prof. music theory and composition U. Wis., Eau Claire, 1973—2006. Author: The Inner World of Traditional Theory, 1989, The Romantic Century, 2000, Progressive Bach, 2001, A Musician's Primer, 2002, Divisional Counterpoint, 2004, Form and Articulation in Music, 2006, Concert Band Arranging in Six Lessons, 2007, Renaissance Counterpoint, 2007, Technique for Composers, 2007; composer: numerous compositions. With U.S. Army, 1962-63. Mem. ASCAP (ann. stipend 1969—), Wis. Alliance Composers, Sigma Alpha Iota. Office Phone: 715-836-4172. Business E-Mail: cunninmg@uwec.edu.

CUNNINGHAM, MILAMARI ANTOINELLA, retired anesthesiologist; b. Cody, Wyo., Oct. 4, 1949; d. Milo Leo and Mary Madeline (Haley) Olds; m. Michael Otis Webb, June 4, 1970 (div. Feb. 1971); m. James Kenneth Cunningham, June 14, 1975. BA with honors, U. Mo., 1971, MD, 1975. Diplomate Am. Bd. Anesthesiologists. Intern and resident U. Mo., Columbia, 1975—78; jr. ptnr. Anesthesiologist, Inc., 1979—82, ptnr., 1982—86; owner Cunningham Anesthesia, 1986—2003; dir. anesthesia dept. Ellis Fischel Cancer Ctr., 1991—92; acting chief anesthesia Harry S. Truman Meml. Vets. Hosp., 1994—95; instr. U. Mo. Columbia Anesthesia Dept. Mem. med. staff U. Mo. Hosp. and Clinics, Columbia; vice chair Mo. Health Facilities Rev. Com., 2004—05. Mem. editl. bd.: Mo. Medicine Jour., 2001—06; contbg. editor, 2007—. Active Mo. Med. Polit. Action Com., 1991-2000, Friends of Music, Friends of Libr., Boone County Fair, 1978-94, with ham breakfast divsn., 1978-85, with draft horse and mule show, 1986-88; Mo. bd. dirs. A Call to Serve, 1996-2007, program mgr., 2004-07. Named Lifetime Senator, World Nations Congress, 2003; recipient Disting. Svc. award, U. Mo. Med. Alumni Assn., 2007; fellowship, Am. Coll. Anesthesiologists, 1977, 1977. Mem.: AMA (life Physicians Recognition award 1978, 1985, 1987, 1991, 1995), Vis. Nurses Assn. (bd. dirs. 1982—89, adv. bd. 1989—93), Am. Soc. Anesthesiologists (alt. dir. dist. 17 2003, Mo. dist. dir. 2003—05), Mo. State Med. Assn. (commn. econs. 3d party payors 1986—89, del. 1996—2004), Boone County Med. Soc. (sec. treas. 1996, bd. dirs. 1996—99, pres. 1998), Mo. Soc. Anesthesiologists (membership chair 1982—94, v.p. 1986—87, pres. 1988—89, spkr. ho. dels. 1992—2002, bd. dirs. 1996—99), Phi Beta Kappa. Home and Office: 8202 S Bennett Dr Columbia MO 65201-9178 E-mail: mila@tranquility.net.

CUNNINGHAM, PAUL GEORGE, minister; b. Chgo., Aug. 27, 1937; s. Paul George Sr. and Naomi Pearl (Anderson) C.; m. Constance Ruth Seaman, May 27, 1960; children: Lori, Paul, Connie Jo. BA, Olivet Nazarene U., 1960; BDiv., Nazarene Theol. Sem., 1964; DD, Mid Am. Nazarene Coll., 1975. Sr. pastor Coll. Ch. of the Nazarene, Olathe, Kans., 1964-93; gen. supt. Internat. Ch. of the Nazarene, 1993—. Adv. bd. Kansas City Dist. Ch. of the Nazarene, Overland Park, Kans., 1971-93; trustee Mid Am. Nazarene Coll., Olathe, 1971—; chmn. book com. Nazarene Pub. House, Kansas City, Mo., 1974-90; pres. gen. bd. Internat. Ch. of the Nazarene, Kansas City, 1985-93. Police chaplain Olathe (Kans.) Police Dept., 1975-93; adv. bd. Good Samaritan Ctr., Olathe, 1990—. Recipient Disting. Svc. award Jaycees, Olathe, 1967, Paul Harris fellow Rotary Internat., Olathe, 1989. Mem. Nat. Assn. Evangs., Rotary. Mem. Ch. Of The Nazarene. Home: 12543 S Hagan Ln Olathe KS 66062-6075 Office: Ch of the Nazarene 6401 Paseo Blvd Kansas City MO 64131-1213 Business E-Mail: pcunningham@nazarene.org.

CUNNINGHAM, PAULA DIANE, bank executive, former academic administrator; b. Akron, Ohio, 1949; d. David Samuel and Mattie Pauline (Mason) Marsh; m. Darius Lee Cunningham, Aug. 29, 1970; children: Darius Lee II, Dana Leigh. BA in Journalism, Mich. State U., 1981, M in Labor and Indsl. Rels., 1991. Legis. asst. Mich. State Capitol, Lansing, 1975; exec. dir. Profl. Devel. Ctr., Lansing, 1985-86; owner, mgr. Mason Hills Golf Course; assoc. prof. bus. Lansing CC, 1985-92, dir. pub. info., 1994, dir. profl. devel., 1992-94, pres., 2000—06, Capitol Nat. Bank, Lansing, 2006—. Cons. to Kellogg Found., Battle Creek, Mich., 1991—, Lansing Bd. Water and Light, 1993—; spkr. in field. Bd. dirs. Capitol Area United Way, Lansing, 1995—, Impression and Sci. Mus., Lansing, 1994—, Martin Luther King Holiday Commn., 1995—; mem. com. ARC, 1995—. Recipient Master Tchr. award U. Tex., 1992. Mem. Nat. Mktg. and Pub. Rels. Assn., Nat. Inst. for Staff and Orgnl. Devel., Pub. Rels. Soc. Am., Am. Soc. Staff and Orgnl. Devel. Avocations: golf, jogging, reading, cross country skiing, travel. Office: Capitol Bancorp Ctr 200 Washington Sq N Lansing MI 48933*

CUNNINGHAM, PIERCE EDWARD, lawyer, city planner; b. Cin., Aug. 18, 1934; s. Francis E. and Adelaide (Kraus) C.; m. Roberta Roche, Sept. 6, 1958; children: Pierce E., Jr. James M., Sarah Ellen, Anna C. BA, Coll. Holy Cross, 1956; LLB, Georgetown U., 1959. Bar: Ohio 1960, U.S. Supreme Ct. 1977. Atty. Hartford Accident and Indemnity Co., Cin., 1960-61; pvt. practice Hamilton, Ohio, 1961-62; asst. atty. gen. Ohio State Atty. Gen.'s Office, Columbus, 1963-70; prin. Pierce E. Cunningham and Assocs., Cin., 1964-75; ptnr. Clark & Eyrich, Cin., 1975-81, Frost & Jacobs, Cin., 1981-97; of counsel Baker Hostetler, Cleve., 1997—2002; Hamilton County spl. prosecutor, 2002—. Spl. counsel to Hamilton County Mcpl. Ct. judges, 1995; chmn. Riverfront Adv. Commn., Cin., 1970-72, Zoning Bd. Appeals, Cin., 1970-72; mem. Urban Design and Rev. Bd., Cin. 1970-72, City Planning Com., Cin., 1968-73, chmn. 1970-73; founder Thomas H. Crush Dispute Resolution Forum, Cin., N.Y.C., Chgo., 2005. Contbr. articles to profl. jours. Vol. Lawyers for the Poor; mem. May Festival Com., Cin., 1972—74; bd. trustees Cin. Symphony Orch., 2002—, bd. dirs., 2002—. Named Lawyer of Yr. Cin. Bar Assn. Vol. Lawyers for Poor, 1982-83. Mem.: Inner Cir. U.S. Senate, Potter Stewart Inn of Ct., Cin. Country Club (bd. govs. 1996—), Cin. Tennis Club, Am. Arbitration Assn. (midwest region adv. coun., large complex litigation panelist), Cin. Bar Assn. (panel of neutrals CPR 1998—), Ohio Bar Assn. (faculty cont. legal edn.), Am. Bd. Trial Advs. Avocations: tennis, sailing. Office: Deters Benzinge & LaVelle 3500 Carew Tower Cincinnati OH 45202 Home: 1201 Edgecliff 1053 Cincinnati OH 45206 Home Phone: 513-281-8099; Office Phone: 513-361-0100. E-mail: pcunningham@fuse.net.

CUNNINGHAM, RICHARD ANTHONY, science administrator; b. Farnborough, Kent, England, Mar. 7, 1975; s. Richard John and Theresa Anne Cunningham; m. Rosina Carlota Menicucci, Feb. 18, 2006. BA with honors, Leeds U., England, 1997; MBA, U. Edinburgh, Scotland, 2000. Fin. journalist, editor Buenos Aires Herald, Argentina, 1998—99; cons. Merial, Lyon, Rhone, France, 2001—02, sr. mgr. strategic devel. Duluth, Ga., 2002—05, dir. corp. strategy & competitive intelligence, 2005—. Office: Merial 3239 Satellite Blvd Duluth GA 30096 Home Phone: 678-296-8473; Office Phone: 678-638-3572. E-mail: richard.cunningham@merial.com.

CUNNINGHAM, ROBERT DEL, librarian; s. Ronald Ray and Linda Ann Cunningham; m. Jennifer Corin Lighthouse, June 27, 1998; children: Morgan, Moria. BA, Houghton Coll., NY, 1998; MLS, U. Buffalo, 2005. Pub. libr. prof. cert. NY. Libr. asst. Houghton Coll., 1996—98; archivist, data storage specialist Data Vault, Rochester, 1999—2001; tech. svcs. asst. Appellate Divsn. 4th Dept. Law Libr., Rochester, 2000—. Picture framer Chase-Pitkin, Rochester, 1999—2006. Author: Ne-Ho-Ga-Gis-Da-Yen-Duk- Origins of the Seneca Reservation at Caneadea, 1998. Chair adv. bd. NY State Archives Documentary Heritage Program-Rochester Region, 2004—06; asst. scoutmaster Troop 320 Boy Scouts Am., Rochester, 1994—, archivist Otetiana Coun., 2001—, asst. cubmaster pack 321, 2007—; archivist, historian Latta Rd. Bapt. Ch., Rochester, 1993—2007, libr., 2001—07. Grantee, Lindley Family/Houghton Coll., 1997. Mem.: Order of the Arrow (assoc. advisor, Founder's award 2003). Avocations: local history and archives, collecting Boy Scout memorabilia, camping, hiking. Office: NY State Supreme Ct Appellate Divsn 4th Dept 50 East Ave Ste 100 Rochester NY 14604 Office Phone: 585-530-3265. Office Fax: 585-530-3272. E-mail: rcunnin@courts.state.ny.us.

CUNNINGHAM, ROBERT JAMES, lawyer; b. Kearney, Nebr., June 27, 1942; m. Sara Jean Dickson, July 22, 1967. BA, U. Nebr., 1964; JD, NYU, 1967, LLM in Taxation, 1969. Bar: N.Y. 1967, Ill. 1969, U.S. Dist. Ct. (no. dist.) Ill. 1969, U.S. Ct. Claims 1970, U.S. Tax Ct. 1970, U.S. Ct. Appeals (D.C. cir.) 1972, U.S. Ct. Appeals (9th cir.) 1975, U.S. Ct. Appeals (7th cir.) 1979, U.S. Ct. Appeals (fed. cir.) 1982. Instr. law NYU, NYC, 1967-69; assoc. Baker & McKenzie LLP, Chgo., 1969-74, ptnr., 1974—. Spkr. in field. Contbr. articles to profl. jours. Mem. ABA, Ill. Bar Assn., Chgo. Bar Assn. Office: Baker & McKenzie LLP One Prudential Plz 130 E Randolph Dr Ste 3900 Chicago IL 60601-6342 Office Phone: 312-861-2931. Business E-Mail: robert.j.cunningham@bakernet.com.

CUNNINGHAM, RONNIE WALTER, venture capitalist; b. Creston, Iowa, Mar. 16, 1932; s. Walter Wilfred and Gladys (Backen) C.; m. Dorothy League, Dec. 27, 1997; children: Brian Keith, Kimberly Ann. BS in Physics, UCLA, 1960, MA, 1961; advanced mgmt. program, Harvard Grad. Sch. Bus., 1974. Rsch. asst. Planning Rsch. Corp., Westwood, Calif., 1959-60; physicist RAND Corp., Santa Monica, Calif., 1960-64; astronaut NASA, 1964-71; crew member of first manned Apollo spacecraft Apollo 7; chief, Skylab br., 1968-71; sr. v.p. Century Devel., 1971-74; pres. Hydrotech Devel. Co., Houston, 1974-76; sr. v.p. 3D/Internat., Houston, 1976-79; founder The Capital Group, Houston, 1979-86; mng. ptnr. Genesis Fund, 1986-98. Bd. dirs. numerous tech. based cos.; mem. adv. bd. Nat. Renewable Energy Lab.; lectr. in field. Author: The All American Boys, 1977; host radio talk show Lift-Off to Logic, 1998—. Judge Rolex awards for enterprise, 1984. With USNR, 1951-52, fighter pilot USMCR, 1952-74, col. ret. Recipient NASA Exceptional Service medal, also; Haley Astronautics award; Profl. Achievement award UCLA Alumni, 1969; Spl. Trustee award Nat. Acad. Television Arts and Scis., 1969; medal of valor Am. Legion, 1975; Outstanding Am. award Am. Conservative Union, 1975, George Haddaway award, 2000; named to Internat. Space Hall of Fame, Houston Hall of Fame, Astronaut Hall of Fame, 1997. Fellow Am. Astronautical Soc.; mem. Soc. Exptl. Test Pilots, Am. Inst. Aeros. and Astronautics, Assn. Space Explorers-U.S.A., Am. Geophys. Union, Sigma Pi Sigma.

CUNNINGHAM, STANLEY LLOYD, lawyer; b. Durant, Okla., Feb. 7, 1938; s. Stanley Ryan and Hazel Dell (Dillingham) C.; m. Suzanne Yerger, Sept. 18, 1960; children: Stanley William, Ryan Yerger. BS in Geology, U. Okla., 1960, LLB, 1963. Bar: U.S. Dist. Ct. (we. dist.) Okla. 1963; U.S. Ct. Appeals (10th cir.) 1965; U.S. Supreme Ct. Okla. 1963. Atty. Phillips Petroleum Co., Oklahoma City, 1963-64, Bartlesville, Okla., 1964-71; counsel McAfee, Taft, et al., Oklahoma City, 1971—. Lectr. U. Okla. Coll. Law, Norman, 1977, 79, S.W. Legal Found., Dallas, 1986, 89. Contbr. articles to profl. jours. Layreader All Souls' Episcopal Ch., Oklahoma City, 1972-75. 1st lt. USAFR, 1963-72. Harry J. Brown scholar, U. Okla., 1960—63. Mem. ABA, Fed. Energy Bar Assn., Am. Soc. Internat. Law, Geological Soc. Am., Alumni Adv. Coun., U. Okla. Assoc., Oklahoma City Golf & Country Club, Order of Coif, Phi Alpha Delta, Sigma Gamma Epsilon. Republican. Episcopalian. Avocations: golf, reading. Office: McAfee & Taft 2 Leadership Sq Fl 10 Oklahoma City OK 73102 Office Phone: 405-235-9621.

CUNNINGHAM, STEVE, orthopedic surgeon; b. Kingston, NY, May 11, 1943; BA, Northwestern U., Evanston, Ill., 1965; MD, U. Nebr., Omaha, 1970. Diplomate Am. Bd. Orthopedic Surgery. Pvt. practice orthopedic surgery, Reno, 1977—. Dir. arthroplasty svcs. Renown Med. Ctr., Reno, 2004—. Maj. US Army, 1975—77. Fellow: N.Am. Spine Soc., Am. Acad. Orthopedic Surgeons (bd. councilors 1997—2003). Office: Alpine Bone & Joint Clinic 845 Aitken St Reno NV 89502

CUNNINGHAM, TERENCE THOMAS, III, hospital administrator; b. Bell, Calif. BS in Microbiology, Calif. State U., Long Beach; MA in Hosp. Adminstrn., George Washington U., Washington, 1974. Commd. 2d lt. USAF, advanced through grades to col., 1989; adminstrv. resident MacDill Hosp., Tampa, Fla., 1973-74; adminstr. Rhein-Main Clinic, Frankfurt, Germany, 1974-79; hosp. cons. Air Force Med. Inspection Ctr., San Bernardino, Calif., 1979-81; CFO, David Grant Med. Ctr., Fairfield, Calif., 1981-82; CEO, Torrejon Hosp., Madrid, 1982-85; COO, CFO, materials officer Office Command Surgeon, Hdqrs. Mil. Airlift Command, Bellville, Ill., 1985-87; CEO, Wright Patterson Med. Ctr., Dayton, Ohio, 1987-92; adminstr. Wilford Hall Med. Ctr., San Antonio, 1992-94; v.p. adminstrn. Johns Hopkins Hosp., Balt., 1994-2000; CEO Ben Taub Gen. Hosp., Houston, 2000—06, Shriners Hosps. Children, LA, 2006—. Instr. grad. program health care adminstrn. Chapman Coll., Calif., 1981—82; preceptor grad. students in hosp. and health care adminstrn. Xavier U., Cin., 1987—, Baylor U., San Antonio, 1988—, George Washington U., Washington, 1995—, Johns Hopkins U., Balt., 1995—; asst. clin. prof. Wright State U. Sch. Medicine, Dayton, Ohio, 1990—; assoc. prof. dept. health policy and mgmt. Johns Hopkins U. Sch. Pub. Health and Hygiene; clin. instr. Baylor Coll. Medicine, 2001; adj. prof. Grad. Sch. Mgmt. Rice U., Houston, 2003—; cons. to Surgeon Gen. USAF, 1986—. Book reviewer: Hosps. and Health Svcs. Adminstrn., Jour. Quality Assurance, Mil. Medicine; mem. editl. bd. Frontiers Health Svcs. Mgmt., Health Adminstrn. Press. Bd. dirs. Am. Red Cross, Houston. Fellow: Am. Coll. Healthcare Execs. (mem. various coms., regent to USAF); mem.: Assn. Mil. Surgeons US (Young Fed. Healthcare Adminstr. of the Yr. 1983, Fed. Healthcare Adminstr. of the Yr. 1989, Sr. Fed. Healthcare Adminstr. of the Yr. 1992), Tex. Hosp. Assn. (mem. edn. com., mem. disaster readiness task force), Greater Dayton Area Hosp. Assn. (bd. dirs.), Hosp. Assn. So. Calif., Ohio Hosp. Assn. (chmn. accreditation com.), Interagy. Inst. Fed. Health Care Alumni Assn. Avocations: bicycling, photography, sailing, reading.

CUNNINGHAM, THOMAS JUSTIN, lawyer; b. Hinsdale, Ill., Feb. 27, 1968; s. Thomas J. and Diane (Carlton) C.; m. Paula J. Friant, Sept. 9, 1989; children: Thomas Justin, Nicholas Joseph. BS, Ariz. State U., 1989; JD, DePaul U., 1993. Bar: Ill. 1993, U.S. Dist. Ct. (no. dist.) Ill. 1993, U.S. Ct. Appeals (7th cir.) 1993, U.S. Dist. Ct. (ctrl. dist.) Ill. 1996, U.S. Dist. Ct. (we. dist.) Mich. 2002, U.S. Supreme Ct. 1996, Trial bar 1997. Dep. clk. U.S. Bankruptcy Ct., Chgo., 1989—90; law clk. Burke, Smith & Williams, Chgo., 1990—93; assoc. Smith, Lodge & Schneider, Chgo., 1993—98, Hopkins & Sutter, Chgo., 1998—2001; ptnr. Lord, Bissell & Brook, Chgo., 2001—. Contbr. articles to profl. jours. Pres. Ill. Dist. 58 Bd. Edn. Mem. Chgo. Bar Assn. (chair moot ct. com. 1995, co-editor in chief YLS jour.). Republican. Presbyterian. Avocations: hunting, fishing. Home: 5220 Benton Ave Downers Grove IL 60515-5037 Office: Lord Bissell & Brook 111 S Wacker Dr Chicago IL 60606 Office Phone: 312-443-1731. Business E-Mail: tcunningham@lordbissell.com.

CUNNINGHAM, TOM ALAN, lawyer; b. Houston, Nov. 5, 1946; s. Warren Peek and Ellen Ardelle (Benner) Cunningham; m. Jeanne Adrienne Moran, July 21, 1972; 1 child, Christopher Alan. BA, U. Tex., 1968, JD, 1974. Bar: Tex. 1974, U.S. Dist. Ct. (so. dist.) Tex. 1976, U.S. Dist. Ct. (no. dist.) Tex. 1982, U.S. Dist. Ct. (we. dist.) Tex. 1984, U.S. Ct. Appeals (5th and 11th cirs.) 1981, U.S. Ct. Appeals (8th cir.) 1991, U.S. Supreme Ct. 2007. Ptnr. Fulbright & Jaworski L.L.P., Houston, 1974—98; founding ptnr. Cunningham Darlow, LLP (formerly Cunningham, Welsh, Darlow, Zook & Chapoton, LLP), Houston, 1998—. Bd. trustee Children's Charity Fund, Houston, 1983—88; active South Tex. Ctr. Legal Responsibility; mem. exec. com., bd. dirs. Assn. for Cmty. TV. Lt. (j.g.) USNR, 1969—72. Fellow: Houston Bar Found., Am. Bd. Trial Advs., Am. Coll. Trial Lawyers, Am. Bar Found., Tex. Bar Found. (life; chmn. bd. trustees, adv. bd., chair 1995—, chair bd. trustees 1995—, chair Lola Wright com., adv. bd., new fellows com., awards com., pub. com., bd. dirs., ct. ruels com.); mem.: ABA (arbitration com. 1995—, litigation sect., discovery com., forum com. constrn. industry, alternate dispute resolution com.), CPR Inst. for Dispute Resolution, Resolution Forum, Inc. (pres.), Tex. Empowerment Network (bd. dirs.), Tex. Ctr. Legal Ethics and Professionalism, Tex. Bd. Legal Specialization, State Bar Tex. (chmn. spl. com. on lawyer adt. and solicitation 1982, chmn. dist.4H grievance com. 1982—88, bd. dirs. 1989—92, chair bd. dirs. exec. com. 1991—92, chair com. for lawyer discipline 1992—94, chair gen. counsel adv. com., exec. com., ct. rules com., Pres.'s award 1983, Pres.'s citation for meritorious svc. 1991, Pres.'s spl. recognition for meritorious svc. 1993, 1994, nominee Outstanding Young Lawyer 1981), Houston Bar Assn. (professionalism com., chmn. constn. bicentennial com., arbitration com., membership com., Pres.'s award 1988), Am. Arbitration Assn. (panel of arbitrators), Houston Club, Coronado Club, Phi Delta Phi. Home: 10811 Pine Bayou St Houston TX 77024-3018 Office: Cunningham & Darlow LLP 909 Fannin St Ste 3700 Houston TX 77010 Office Phone: 713-255-5500. Business E-Mail: tcunningham@cunninghamdarlow.com.

CUNNINGHAM, VALERIE S., historic preservationist, researcher; b. Portsmouth, NH, May 31, 1941; d. Clarence Woodrow and Augusta Serena Ragland Cunningham; children: Bradley D. Randolph, Kirby A. Randolph. B of Gen. Studies, U. Sys. N.H., 1988. Rschr., writer, lectr. and cons. African Am. Resource Ctr., Portsmouth, 1988—. Mem., former trustee Strawbery Banke Mus., Portsmouth, 1996—2002; mem., past sec. New Eng. chpt. Afro-Am. Hist. & Genealogical Soc., Bedford, Mass., 1998—2000; exec. bd. Seacoast African Am. Cultural Ctr., Portsmouth, 2000—05; founder, pres. Portsmouth Black Heritage Trail, Inc., 1995—2005; co-founder, past pres., exec. bd. Blues Bank Collective, Inc., 1985—2005; co-founder Chichester Connections/N.H. Cir. Friends; mem. commn. status women N.H., 2005—. Co-author: (book) Black Portsmouth: Three Centuries of African-American Heritage, Portsmouth Black Heritage Trail Resource Book; contbr. articles to profl. jours., essays to enycs. Apptd. N.H. Commn. Status of Women, 2005. Named Outstanding Woman N.H., Keene State Coll., 2004; recipient Achievement award, U. N.H. Commn. Status Women, 1991, Cmty. Svc. award, N.H. Coalition MLK Holiday, 1991, Pres.'s award Excellence, U. N.H., 1992, Race Amity award, Seacoast Area Baha'i Cmty., 1994, Spirit Seacoast award, Cmty. Resource Network, 1997, Jefferson award, Am. Inst. Cmty. Svc., 1999, A. J. Gerrier award History, Portsmouth Advocates, 2000, Am. History award, Ranger chpt. DAR, 2001, Robert Frost Contemporary Am. award, Plymouth State U., 2005. Mem.: Schomburg Ctr. Rsch. African-Am. Life and Culture, N.H. Hist. Soc., Nat. Trust Hist. Preservation, Mus. African-Am. History, New Eng. Hist. Assn., Am. Assn. State and Local History, N.H. Preservation Alliance, Assn. Black Women Historians, Afro-Am. Hist. and Geneal. Soc. (New Eng. chpt.), Portsmouth Athenaeum, Nat. Ctr. Black Philanthropy. Unitarian-Universalist. Avocations: travel, jazz, movies. Office: Portsmouth Black Heritage Trail Inc PO Box 5094 Portsmouth NH 03802 Home Phone: 603-431-2768; Office Phone: 603-862-3520, 603-431-2768. Personal E-mail: nhblackhistory@aol.com. Business E-Mail: pbhtrail@aol.com. E-mail: vc@unh.edu.

CUNNINGHAM, WILLIAM FRANCIS, JR., literature and language professor, academic administrator; b. Holyoke, Mass., Feb. 9, 1931; s. William Francis and Constance Emma (Cox) C.; m. Eleanor Mary Bissonette, Dec. 27, 1956; children— Margaret Ann, William John, Mary Elizabeth. AB, Holy Cross Coll., 1954; MA, Boston Coll., 1956; PhD, U. Pitts., 1961; DHL honoris causa, Le Moyne Coll., 1994. Asst. prof. English, Duquesne U., 1955-63; prof. Le Moyne Coll., 1963-78; prof. English Creighton U., 1978—, dean Coll. Arts and Scis., 1978-87, acting v.p. for acad. affairs, 1986-87, v.p. acad. affairs, 1987-93, spl. asst. to pres., 1993-96; dean emeritus, 1994—; ret., 1997. Danforth assoc., 1974—. Contbr. articles on 18th-century Brit. lit. to profl. jours. Mem. Coll. Bd. (coun. on coll.-level svcs., exec. com. Midwestern regional assembly 1980-84), Am. Soc. 18th-century Studies.

CUNNINGHAM, WILLIAM HENRY, retired food products executive; b. Oxnard, Calif., Dec. 2, 1930; s. William Henry and Carrie Edna (Wilson) C.; m. Carmen Nelson Alden, Jan. 19, 1957; children: Nelson, Clifford, Cynthia. BA, U. Calif., Santa Barbara, 1952; B of Foreign Trade, Am Grad. Sch. Internat. Mgmt., 1958. With Colgate-Palmolive Internat., NY and Colombia, El Salvador, 1958-63; mktg. cons. Anderson, Clayton Co., Mexico City, Buenos Aires and Lima, 1963-66; mgr. consumer divsn. Cyanamid, Buenos Aires, 1966-69; dir. mktg. and sales Alimentos Kraft, Caracas, Venezuela, 1969-74; gen. mgr. Panama and Cen. Am. Panama and Ctrl. Am. Kraft Foods, Inc., 1974-80; pres. Alimentos Kraft Alimentos Kraft Foods, Inc., Venezuela, 1980-86; v.p., dir. Kraft Foods, Inc. Kraft Gen. Foods, Walt Disney World, Fla., 1986-92. V.p., dir. The Land, Epcot Ctr., Walt Disney World, Fla. Stewareship chmn. St. Lukes Meth. Ch., Windermere, Fla., 1991-92; vol. Inter Exec. Svc. Corp. for assignment in L.Am. to help local industry, 1993, assignment to Bogota Colombia, 1994, Ctrl. Russia, 1996; vol. Second Helping; Spanish transl. Free Clinic, Deep Well; pres. Hosp. Aux., Hilton Head, S.C. 2002-03. Recipient Tribute Appreciation award U.S. State Dept., 1980, Order of Vasco Nunez de Balboa, Govt. Panama, 1980, First Class Work Merit award Govt. Venezuela, 1985, Jonas Mayer Disting. Alumni award Thunderbird Grad. Sch. for Internat. Mgmt., 1997, Friendship award US-Panimian Bus. Coun., 2006, Citizen's Honor award Hilton Head, 2003. Mem. Am. C. of C. (pres., founder Panama City chpt. 1979, sec. Caracas 1986), Am. Soc. (pres. Panama City chpt. 1977), Walt Disney World Participant Assn. (pres. 1990-91), U. Calif. Alumni Assn. (bd. dirs. Santa Barbara 1992-98, chair awards, Lifetime Achievement award 2006, Friendship award 2006), Bear Creek Golf Club, Hilton Head. Democrat. Methodist. Avocations: golf, tennis. Home: 11 Bear Creek Dr Hilton Head Island SC 29926-1904 Personal E-mail: CarmenAC@adephia.net.

CUNNINGHAM, WILLIAM HUGHES, retired academic administrator, marketing professional, educator; b. Detroit, Jan. 5, 1944; married; 1 child BA, Mich. State U., 1966, MBA, 1967, PhD, 1971, LLD (hon.), 1993. Mem. faculty U. Tex., Austin, 1971—, assoc. prof. mktg., 1973-79, prof., 1979—, assoc. dean grad. programs, 1976-82, Foley/Sanger Harris prof. retail merchandising, 1982-83, acting dean Coll. Bus. Adminstrn. and Grad. Sch. Bus., 1982-83, dean, 1983-85, pres., 1985-92, Centennial Chair Bus. Edn. Leadership, 1983-85, Regents Chair Higher Edn. Leadership, 1985-92, Lee Hage and Joseph D. Jamail Regents Chair Higher Edn. Leadership, 1992-2000, James L. Bayless Chair for Free Enterprise, 1988—; chancellor U. Tex. Sys., Austin, 1992-2000. Bd. dirs. Lincoln Nat. Corp. (formerly Jefferson-Pilot Corp.), John Hancock Funds, S.W. Airlines Co., Introgen Therapeutics, Hayes Lemmerz Internat., LIN TV; mem. corp. Conf. Bd. Author: (with W.J.E. Crissy and I.C.M. Cunningham) Selling: The Personal Force in Marketing, 1977, 2d edit. (with D.W. Jackson and Cunningham), 1988, Effective Selling, 1977, Spanish edit., 1980, (with S. Lopreato) Consumers' Energy Attitudes and Behavior, 1977, (with Cunningham) Marketing: A Managerial Approach, 1981, 2d edit. (with Cunningham and C. Swift), 1988, (with R. Aldag and C. Swift) Introduction to Business, 1984, 3d edit. (with R. Aldag and S. Block), 1992, 4th edit. (with R. Aldag and M. Stone), 1995, (with B. Verhage and Cunningham) Grondslagen van het Marketing Management, 1984, (with R. Aldag and S. Block) Business in a Changing World, 1992, also monographs and articles; editor Jour. Mktg., 1981-84. Bd. dirs. Houston Area Rsch. Coun., 1984; mem. Mental Health/Mental Retardation Legis. Oversight Com., 1984; mem. adv. bd. Found. for Cultural Exch./The Netherlands-U.S.A.; bd. dirs. Lyndon Baines Johnson Found. Recipient Tchg. Excellence award U. Tex. Coll. Bus. Adminstrn., 1972, Alpha Kappa Psi, 1975, Hank and Mary Harkins Found., 1978, Disting. Scholastic Contbn. award Coll. Bus. Adminstrn. Found. Adv. Coun., 1982, Disting. Alumnus award Coll. and Grad. Sch. Bus., Mich. State U., 1983, 93, Tree of Life award Jewish Nat. Fund, 1992, U. Tex. Austin Presdl. citation, 2005; named among top 20 profs. Utmost Mag., 1982; Rsch. grant Univ. Rsch. Inst., 1971-73, Latin Am. Inst., 1972, So. Union Gas Energy, 1975-76, ERDA, 1976 Mem. Am. Inst. for Decision Scis., Am. Mktg. Assn., Assn. Consumer Rsch., So. Mktg. Assn., S.W. Social Sci. Assn., Phi Kappa Phi, Omicron Delta Kappa Office: U Tex PO Box E Austin TX 78713 Business E-Mail: connie@po.utexas.edu.

CUNNINGHAM-RUNDLES, CHARLOTTE, physician, educator; b. Ann Arbor, Mich., July 12, 1943; d. R. Wayne Rundles and Mary Alice (Cunningham) Cunningham-Rundles; m. James B. Bussel, Nov. 13, 1982; 1 child, A. Christine. BS, Duke U., 1965; MD, Columbia U., 1969; PhD, NYU, 1974. Diplomate Am. Bd. Internal Medicine. Intern Bellevue Hosp., NYU, NYC, 1969-70, resident, 1970-72; with dept. immunology NYU Med. Ctr., 1972-74; assoc. Sloan Kettering Inst., NYC, 1974-86, dir. biochem. immunology, 1982-86; assoc. attending physician Meml. Hosp., NYC, 1978-86, adj. assoc., 1986—; prof. biochemistry, medicine and pediatrics Mt. Sinai Med. Ctr., NYC, 1986—, assoc. prof. Immunobiology Inst., 1986—; prof. Immunology Inst., 1994—. Bd. dirs. Immunodeficiency clinic; speaker various nat. and internat. mtgs. on immunology, program dir., Allergy Immunology Fellowship, 2001-, mem. blood safety adv. com. FDA, 2002-04; bd. med. advisors Primary Immunodeficiency Found., 1988—, Modell Found., 1989—; adv. NASA Contbr. numerous articles to sci. and med. jours., chpts. to books. Recipient Lifetime Achievement award Modell Found.; grantee NIH, Nat. Cancer Inst., Am. Cancer Soc., Nat. Found. March of Dimes, Multiple Sclerosis Soc. Fellow ACP; mem. Am. Fedn. Clin. Rsch., Am. Assn. Immunologist, Mucosal Immune Soc., Clin. Immunology Soc. (pres. 2003-04), The Harvey Soc. Episcopalian. Avocations: painting, drawing, computer graphics. Office: Mt Sinai Med Ctr 1 Gustave L Levy Pl New York NY 10029-6500

CUNO, JAMES, museum director; b. St. Louis, Apr. 6, 1951; married; 2 children. BA in History, Willamette U., 1973; MA in Art History, U. Oreg., 1978; MA in Fine Arts, Harvard U., 1980, PhD in Fine Arts, 1985. Asst. curator prints Fogg Art Mus., Harvard U., Cambridge, Mass., 1980-83; asst. prof. dept. art Vassar Coll., Poughkeepsie, NY, 1983-86; dir. Grunwald Ctr. for Graphic Arts, UCLA, 1986-89; dir. Hood Mus. Art, Dartmouth Coll., Hanover, NH, 1989-91; dir. Univ. Art Mus. Harvard U., Cambridge,

Mass., 1991—2003; dir. Courtauld Institute of Art, London, 2003—04; pres., Eloise W. Martin dir. Art Inst. of Chgo., 2004—. Trustee Wadsworth Atheneum; panelist NEH, NEA; mem. pub. grant adv. com. Getty Grant Program, 1991-96; mem. vis. com. J. Paul Getty Mus. Author, editor exhbn. catalogues (with others) Foirades/Fizzles: Echo and Allusion in the Art of Jasper Johns, 1987, Politics and Polemics: French Caricature and the Revolution, 1789-1799, 1988, Scenes and Sequences: Recent Monotypes by Eric Fischl, 1990, Jonathan Borofsky: Prints and Multiples, 1982-91, 1991, The Popularization of Images: Visual Culture Under the July Monarchy, 1994; contbr. articles to profl. jours. Mem. Assn. Art Mus. Dirs. (trustee, pres.). Office: Art Inst of Chgo 111 S Michigan Ave Chicago IL 60603-6110

CUOMO, ANDREW MARK, state attorney general, former secretary of housing and urban development; b. Queens, NY, Dec. 6, 1957; s. Mario M. and Matilda (Raffa) Cuomo; m. Kerry Kennedy, June 9, 1990 (div.); children: Cara, Mariah, Michaela. BA, Fordham U., 1979; JD, Albany Law Sch., 1982. Asst. dist. atty. Dist. Atty's Office, Manhattan; ptnr. Blutrich, Falcone and Miller, NYC, 1985—88; chmn. NYC Commn. on the Homeless, 1991-93; asst. sec. cmty. planning and devel. US Dept. Housing & Urban Devel., Washington, 1993-97, sec., 1997-2001; atty. gen. State of NY, Albany, 2007—. Pub. spkr. The Allen Agy.; vis. fellow Inst. of Politics, Harvard U. Editor: Crossroads: The Future of American Politics, 2003. Campaign mgr. Mario M. Cuomo for Gov. NY, 1982; founder, pres. H.E.L.P., 1986, founder Genesis, 1992. Recipient Good Neighbor award ARC, Outstanding Cmty. Svc. award Latin Soul, 1988, Man of Yr. award Coalition of Italian Am. Orgns., 1988, Ed Sulzberger award, Our Town newspaper, 1989, Pub. Svc. award Coun. Jewish Orgns., 1989, Disting. Cmty. Svc. award NYU, 1991, Bard award, 1992, Albert Einstein award, 1993, Encore Heart to Heart award, 1994, Innovation Am. Govt. award John F. Kennedy Sch. Govt. Harvard U., 1996. Roman Catholic. Office: Dept Law The Capitol 2nd Fl Albany NY 12224*

CUOMO, CHRIS(TOPHER), newscaster, lawyer; b. Queens, NY, Aug. 9, 1970; s. Mario and Matilda Raffa Cuomo; m. Cristina Greeven, Nov. 24, 2001. BA, Yale U., 1992; JD, Fordham U. Polit. policy analyst CNBC, MSNBC, CNN; polit. policy analyst , corr. Fox News Channel; reporter Fox Files Fox Broadcast Network, 1998—99; corr. ABC News, 1999—, corr., co-anchor 20/20 Downtown, 2002, co-anchor Primetime, 2004—, sr. legal corr., 2005—07; anchor, analyst, host Politics Live ABC News Now; news anchor Good Morning Am., ABC News, 2006—. Recipient Emmy award, Gerald Loeb Award, 2005. Office: Good Morning America ABC News 7 W 66th St New York NY 10023

CUOMO, MARIO MATTHEW, lawyer, former governor; b. Queens County, NY, June 15, 1932; s. Andrea and Immacuiata (Giordano) Cuomo; m. Matilda Raffa, June 5, 1954; children: Margaret Cuomo Maier, Andrew, Maria Cuomo Cole, Madeline Cuomo O'Donoghue, Christopher. BA summa cum laude, St. John's Coll., 1953; LLB cum laude, St. John's U., 1956. Bar: NY 1956, U.S. Dist. Ct. (no. dist.) NY 1957, U.S. Dist. Ct. (so. dist.) NY 1998, U.S. Supreme Ct. 1960, U.S. Dist. Ct. (ea. dist.) NY 1962, U.S. Ct. Appeals (2d cir.) 1967. Confidential legal asst. to Hon. Adrian P. Burke, NY State Ct. Appeals, 1956—58; assoc. Corner, Weisbrod, Froeb and Charles, Bklyn., 1958—63; ptnr. Corner, Cuomo & Charles, 1963—75; sec. of state State of NY, Albany, 1975—79, lt. gov., 1979—83, gov., 1983—94; of counsel Wilkie Farr & Gallagher LLP, NYC, 1995—. Mem. faculty St. John's U. Sch. Law, 1963—73; counsel to cmty. groups, including Corona Homeowners, 1966—72; charter mem. First Ecumenical Commn. of Christians and Jews for Bklyn. and Queens, NY. Author: Forest Hills Diary: The Crisis of Low-Income Housing, 1974, Diaries of Mario M. Cuomo, The Campaign for Governor, 1982, More Than Words: The Speeches of Mario Cuomo, 1993, The New York Idea: An Experiment in Democracy, 1994, Reason to Believe: A Keen Assessment of Who We Are: An Inspiring Vision of What We Could Be, 1995; co-author: The Blue Spruce, 1999; co-author: (with Harold Holzer) Why Lincoln Matters: Today More Than Ever, 2004; co-editor: Lincoln on Democracy, 1990; contbr. articles to legal publs. Spkr. keynote address Dem. Nat. Conv., San Francisco, 1984, nominating address Dem. Nat. Conv., NYC, 1992. Recipient Rapallo award, Columbia Lawyers Assn., 1976, Dante medal, Italian Govt.-Am. Assn. Tchrs. Italian, 1976, Silver medallion, Columbia Coalition, 1976, Pub. Adminstr. award, C.W. Post Coll., 1977, Theodore Roosevelt award, Internat. Platform Assn., 1984. Mem.: ABA, Am. Judicature Soc., Assn. of Bar of City of NY, Queens County Bar Assn., Nassau Bar Assn., Bklyn. Bar Assn., NY State Bar Assn., Cath. Lawyers Guild of Queens County (pres. 1966—67), St. John's U. Alumni Fedn. (chmn. bd. 1970—72), Skull and Circle. Home: 50 Sutton Pl S New York NY 10022-4167 Address: Wilkie Farr & Gallagher LLP 787 7th Ave Rm 203 New York NY 10019-6018 E-mail: mcuomo@wilkie.com.

CUOMO, RIVERS, singer, songwriter; b. NYC, June 13, 1970; m. Kyoko Ito, June 18, 2006. BA, Harvard Coll., 2006. Band member Avant Garde, 1989—90; singer, songwriter, guitarist Weezer, 1992—. Performer: (albums) Weezer (The Blue Album), 1994, Pinkerton, 1996, Weezer (The Green Album), 2001, Maladroit, 2002, Make Believe, 2005, (singles & videos include) Undone, 1994, Buddy Holly, 1994 (4 MTV Music Video awards), Say It Ain't So, 1994, Hash Pipe, 2001, Island in the Sun, 2001, Beverly Hills, 2005, Perfect Situation, 2005. Hindu. Avocation: meditation. Mailing: c/o Karl Koch PO Box 733 Derby NY 14047

CUOZZO, STEVEN DAVID, newspaper editor; b. NYC, Jan. 17, 1950; s. Joseph and Lillian (Picini) C.; m. Jane Hershey, Nov. 29, 1980 BA in English, SUNY, Stony Brook, 1971. Arts and leisure editor NY Post, NYC, 1978-80, asst. mng. editor features, 1980-91, mng. editor, 1991-93, exec. editor, 1993—, also food critic. Author: It's Alive: How America's Oldest Newspaper Cheated Death and Why It Matters, 1996. Office: NY Post 10th Fl 1211 Avenue Of The Americas New York NY 10036 E-mail: scuozzo@nypost.com.

CUPP, ANETA JOAN, music educator; b. Bonham, Tex., Dec. 30, 1940; d. Emmett Morgan and Hattie Fay (Taylor) Northcutt; m. Charles Daniel Cupp, Mar. 8, 1980; 1 son, Daniel Emmett, B.Mus., North Tex. State U., 1963; M.Ed., U. Houston, 1983. Sec. health workshop North Tex. State U., Denton summer 1963; sec. to recreation music dir. Parks and Recreation Dept. Houston, summers 1964, 65, 66, 68; tchr. elem. itinerant music Houston Ind. Sch. Dist., 1963-96; substitute tchr. H.I.S.D. and Meml. Hall Sch., 1996-2002, Meml. Hall Sch., 2002—. Named Tchr. of Yr., Houston Ind. Sch. Dist., 1976, named to Hall of Honor, 1984; Jim Collins scholar Corsicana Sr. H.S., 1959. Mem. Congress Houston Tchrs. Lutheran. Home: 1237 Althea Dr Houston TX 77018-5230 Office: Memorial Hall Sch 3721 Dacoma Houston TX 77092

CUPP, B. GARLAND, computer company executive; Dir. bus. services McDonnell Douglas Automation Co.; with Am. Express Corp., 1978—95, exec. v.p., TRS Technologies, CIO, travel related services divsn.; bd. dir. BMC Software, Inc., Houston, 1989—, chmn. bd. dir., 2001—. Chmn. compensation com. and CEO succession planning BMC Software, Inc., Houston; chmn. Apex Mortgage Co.; bd. dir. Edmond Bank and Trust. Office: BMC Software Inc 2101 City West Blvd Houston TX 77042-2827 Office Phone: 713-918-8800. Office Fax: 713-918-8000.

CUPP, DAVID FOSTER, photographer, journalist; b. Derry Twp., Pa., Feb. 4, 1938; s. Foster Wilson and Elizabeth (Erhard) C.; m. Catherine Lucille Lum, Nov. 20, 1965; children: Mary Catherine, David Patterson, John. BA in Journalism, U. Miami, 1960. Staff photographer Miami News, 1960-63, Charlotte (N.C.) Observer, 1963-66; photographer, writer Inter-nat. Harvesters, Chgo., 1966-67; picture editor Nat. Geog. Mag., Washington, 1967, photographer, 1967-69; picture editor Detroit Free Press, 1969; writer, photographer Denver Post, 1969-77; freelance writer, photographer, 1977-88; dir. photography Press-Enterprise, Riverside, Calif., 1988-90; instr. photojournalism, dept. journalism U. Mo., Columbia, 1990; instr. Sch. Vis. Communication Ohio U., Athens, 1991-92; working book author Cupp Design, Inc., Atlanta, 1993; graphics editor Ft. Lauderdale (Fla.) Sun-Sentinel, 1993-94; freelance writer & photographer Hilliard, Ohio, 1994—; pres., creative dir. Photos Online, Inc., Hilliard, 1995—; pres. Half Moon Pub., LLC, Hilliard, 2003—. Tchr. jr. and sr. h.s.-adult classes, including Journalist-in-the-schs., pilot program, Aurora, Colo., 1974-76, Nat. Endowment Arts poet-in-residence 5 Colo. schs.; photography aboard Voyager Spacecraft Co-author Search and Rescue Dogs, 1988; contbg. author: Nat. Geog. books; co-author: Cindy, a Hearing Ear Dog, The Animal Shelter, All Wild Creatures Welcome; contbr. article, photographs to popular mags. Bd. dirs. Friends of Children of Vietnam, adoption agy., 1973. Mem. Nat. Press Photographers Assn. (named Nat. runner-up Photographer of Year 1965, 72, named Regional Photographer of Year 1974, 2d Pl. News Picture Story award 1974, 3rd Pl. Sports Picture Story award 1974, McWilliams award for picture story 1974, McWilliams award for single picture 1974-75, 2d Home, Family Picture Story award 1972, co-chmn. nat. conv.), Colo. Press Photographers Assn. (v.p.), Am. Soc. Mag. Photographers. Home: 4508 Swenson St Hilliard OH 43026-3811 Personal E-mail: pol@columbus.rr.com. *I don't think it's possible to sum life up in a few sentences, life is too complex, but if I were to try, I would have to say that I try to live my life in such a way that my children have pride in me, what I do, and how I do it. I don't feel I can tell my children to be honest, then I be dishonest, or tell them to have compassion, while I have none. I cannot punish a child for doing something at night, that I do during the day. In short, I try to be the person that I would want my children to be.*

CUPP, LUCY PASCHALL, retired elementary school educator, minister; b. Portsmouth, Va., Sept. 18, 1949; d. John Robert Paschall and Frances Wright Pridgen; m. Daniel Lee Cupp, Aug. 17, 1968; children: Jeannie Kay, Paul Daniel. BS in Elem. Edn., Old Dominion U., 1970, MS in Edn. Adminstrn./Supervision, 1980; MA in Counseling, Liberty U., 1987; postgrad., various instns. Cert. elem. tchr., 1-7, elem. prin., elem. supr., elem. counselor, Va; ordained minister, 1999. Tchr. elem. edn. Norfolk (Va.) Pub. Schs., 1970-86, 90-92, tchr. regular elem. edn., 1986-90, SPIRAL educator, 1990—. Vol. edni. adminstr. Ingleside Bapt. Ch., Norfolk, Va., 1990-92; assoc. pastor, sch. adminstr. Bayview Baptist Ch., 1999-2001; vol. guidance counselor Ryan Acad., 2004-06. Recipient Sch. Bell award, Norfolk Pub. Schs., Honor Citation, AWANA Clubs Internat., Meritorious Achievement award. Mem. AACD, Am. Assn. Elem. Sch. Guidance Counselors, Am. Sch. Counselor Assn., Am. Assn. Christian Counselors. Personal E-mail: funcupp@aol.com.

CUPP, ORVILLE SHAWN, military officer; s. Wayne Wine and Susan Auville Cupp; m. Kimberly Teagle, June 27, 1987; 1 child, Kayla Christine. BS in Agr. Edn., Va. Tech, 1985, MS in Vocat. Edn., 1986; M in Mil. Art and Sci., US Army Command and Gen. Staff Coll., 2002. Asst. prof. US Army Command and Gen. Staff Coll., Ft. Leavenworth, Kans., 2001—05. Contbr. articles to profl. jour. including US Army Profl. Jour. Adult leader Girl Scouts, Ft. Leavenworth, Kans., 2002—04. Lt. col. US Army, 1986—2005, US, Germany, Desert Shield/Desert Storm, Korea, Kosovo, combined joint task force mem., Operation Enduring Freedom, Horn of Africa, Djibouti, Africa. Mem.: VFW (assoc.), US Army Ordnance Corps Assn. (assoc.). Office: US Army Command & Gen Staff Coll 1 Reynolds Ave Fort Leavenworth KS 66027 Home Phone: 913-758-1363; Office Phone: 913-684-2983. Personal E-mail: orville.cupp@leavenworth.army.mil.

CUPP, ROBERT ERHARD, golf course architect, land use planner; b. Lewistown, Pa., Dec. 27, 1939; s. Foster Wilson and Elizabeth (Erhard) C.; m. Glenda Dell, Aug. 26, 1962 (div. 1983); children: Robert E. II, Caren E., Laura G.; m. Pamela Patricia Amy, Dec. 27, 1986. BA, U. Miami, Coral Gables, Fla., 1962; MA, U.S. Army, Anchorage, 1966. Art dir. Jefferson, Inc., Miami, 1966-67; golf profl. Colonial Palms Country Club, Miami, 1967-68, Crooked Creek Country Club, Miami, 1968-69; pvt. practice golf course architect Miami, 1969-72; golf course architect Golden Bear Enterprises, North Palm Beach, Fla., 1972-86; pvt. practice golf course architect Atlanta, 1984—. Sr. designer Jack Nicklaus Design, North Palm Beach, 1972-86; pres. Cupp Design, Inc., Atlanta, 1984—. Designed East Sussex (Eng.) Nat. Golf Club, site of 1993-94 European Open Championship (Best New Golf Course, Golf Monthly), Pumpkin Ridge Golf Club, Portland, Oreg., Site of 1996 U.S. Amateur Championship, 1992 & 2003 U.S. Women's Open Championship, 2000 U.S. Boys and Girls Nat. Championship, Old Waverly Golf Club, West Point, Miss. (Top 100 Golf Course in U.S., Golf Digest, Site of U.S. Women's Open Championship), Settindown Creek Golf Club, Atlanta, (site of U.S. Nike Tour Championship, 1995, 96, and U.S. Women's Amateur Championship 2005), Pumpkin Ridge, Ghost Creek, 1992 (Best New Course, Golf Digest), Western Gales, Osceola, Mich., 1993, Indianwood, Lake Orion, Mich., 1988 (Runner up Best New Course, Golf Digest), Pumpkin Ridge, Witch Hollow, Portland, 1992, Old Waverly, West Point, 1989, Big Sky Country Club, Pemberton, B.C., Can., 1994, Crosswater Golf Club, Sunriver, Oreg., 1995 (Best New Course 1995), Hawks Ridge, Atlanta, 2000 (Best New Course runner up Golf Digest), others. Served to capt. U.S. Army, 1963-66. Named Golf World/Golf Digest Designer of Yr., 1992, Top 100, Golf Digest. E-mail: cuppdsgn@aol.com.

CUPP, ROBERT RICHARD, state supreme court justice, former state senator, attorney; b. Bluffton, Ohio, Nov. 9, 1950; s. William Henry and Pearl Margaret (Keifer) C.; m. Lisbeth Ann Cochran, July 29, 1978; children: Matthew R., Ryan W. BA, Ohio Northern U., 1973, JD, 1976. Bar: Ohio. Commnr. Allen County, Ohio, 1981-84, 2001—02; prosecutor, asst. city law dir. City of Lima, Ohio, 1976-80; ptnr. Cupp and Smith, Attys., Lima, 1983-86; mem. Ohio Senate, 1985-2000; ptnr. Cupp and Jenson, Attys., Lima, 1986-93; judge Ohio Ct. Appeals, 3rd Appellate Dist., 2003—06, adminstrv. judge, 2004—05, presiding judge, 2005—06; assoc. justice Ohio Supreme Ct., 2007—. Pres. Bd. County Commrs., Allen County, Ohio, 1981, 82, 84; chmn. Gilmor Commn. Sch. Funding, 1987-88; commerce and labor com. chmn. Ohio Senate 1989-94; com. chmn. Fin. Instns. Ins. and Commerce, 1995-96; majority whip Ohio Senate, 1995-96, pres. pro tem, 1997-2000; vis. prof. applied politics Ohio Northern U., 2001—; mem. Ohio Commn. Dispute Resolution & Conflict Mgmt. Co-author: Ethics and Discipline in Ohio, 1977 Co-chmn. Midwest Fedn. Coll. Reps., 1974; pres. exec. bd. Black Swamp coun. Boy Scouts Am.; chmn. League of Coll. Republican Clubs, 1972-73; bd. trustees Nat. Communication Assn. Higher Learning Commn. Recipient Ohio 4-H Alumni award, Robert E. Hughes Meml. award, Ohio Assn. Elected Officials. Mem.: Ohio State Bar Assn. (Disting. Svc. award), Allen County Bar Assn. Methodist. Office: Ohio Supreme Ct 65 S Front St Columbus OH 43215-3431 Office Phone: 614-387-9000.*

CUPPLES, STEPHEN ELLIOT, lawyer; b. St. Louis, Feb. 20, 1955; children: Christina, James, Catherine, Stephanie, Alex. AB summa cum laude, U. Mo., 1976, JD summa cum laude, 1979. Bar: Mo. 1979, U.S. Dist. Ct. (ea. dist.) Mo. 1979, U.S. Ct. Appeals (8th cir.) 1980, U.S. Tax Ct. 1981, U.S. Claims Ct. 1985. Assoc. Peper, Martin, Jensen, Maichel and Hetlage, St. Louis, 1979-84; ptnr. Cupples & Cupples, P.C., St. Louis, 1985, Cupples, Edwards, Cooper & Singer, St. Louis, 1985-86, Lashly & Baer, P.C., St. Louis, 1987-95, Thompson Coburn LLP, St. Louis, 1995—. Bd. dirs. Estate Planning Coun. of St. Louis, 1992-, pres. 2002-03. Fellow Am. Coll. Trust and Estate Coun.; mem. ABA, Mo. Bar Assn., Bar Assn. Met. St. Louis (chmn. taxation sect. 1988-89), Young Lawyers Tax Club (chmn. 1983-87), Phi Beta Kappa, Phi Kappa Phi. Office: Thompson Coburn LLP One US Bank Plaza Ste 2600 Saint Louis MO 63101-1693 Office Phone: 314-552-6027. Business E-Mail: scupples@thompsoncoburn.com.

CURA, MARCO ANTONIO, interventional radiologist, educator; s. Jorge and Martha Cura; m. Natalia Martinez. MD, Cordoba Cath. U., Argentina, 1990—95. Lic. radiologist Am. Bd. Radiology, 2003. Intern Lincoln Med. Ctr., Bronx, NY, 1998—99; resident Mt. Sinai Med. Ctr., Miami Beach, Fla., 1999—2003; clin. instr. Columbia U., NYC, 2003—04; asst. prof. U. Tex. Health Sci. Ctr. San Antonio, 2005—. Mem.: Radiology Soc. N.Am. Office: U Tex Health Sci Ctr San Antonio 7703 Floyd Curl Dr San Antonio TX 78229 Home Phone: 210-842-8938. Business E-Mail: curam@uthscsa.edu.

CURATOLA, DANIEL L., retired sales executive; b. Oct. 26, 1919; BA, Moravian Coll., Bethlehem, Pa., 1948. Pressman Times Pub. Co., Bethlehem, 1939—42; proofreader Bethlehem Globe Times, 1948—49; sr. sales asst. Bethlehem Steel Corp., 1950—81; ret., 1981. Served US Army, 1942—47. Decorated 3 Bronze stars, Purple Heart; recipient Presdl. citation. Mem.: Sons of Italy in Am. (fin. sec. Bethlehem chpt. 1947—).

CURB, JESS DAVID, medical educator, researcher; b. Raton, N.Mex., Dec. 29, 1945; s. Leslie Calvin and Evelyn Lula (Lindley) C.; m. Beatriz Lorenza Rodriquez; children: Jess Calvin, William Noa, Maria Lorenza, Isabel Alani. BA, U. Colo., 1967; MD, U. N.Mex., Albuquerque, 1971; MPH, U. Tex., Houston, 1974. Diplomate, cert. geriatric medicine Am. Bd. Internal Medicine. Intern Harlem Hosp., Columbia U., NYC, 1971-72; rsch. assoc. U. Tex. Sch. Pub. Health and Medicine, Houston, 1973-76, asst. prof., 1978-80; resident internal medicine Northwestern U. Sch. Medicine, Chgo., 1976-78; asst. prof. Baylor Coll. Medicine, Houston, 1980-83; assoc. prof. U. Hawaii, Honolulu, 1983-85, prof., 1985-87; assoc. dir. Nat. Inst. on Aging, Bethesda, Md., 1986-89; prof. geriatric medicine, chief Divsn. Clin. Epidemiology U. Hawaii, Sch. Medicine, Honolulu, 1989—; CEO, med. dir. Pacific Health Rsch. Inst., 1995—2003, pres., 2003—07. Contbr. articles to profl. jours. Grantee Honolulu Heart Program, Nat. Heart, Lung and Blood Inst., Honolulu, 1989-2003, Hawaii Asia Aging Study, Nat. Inst. on Aging, Honolulu, 1994-2002, Women's Health Initiative, NIH, Honolulu, 1994—, Family Blood Pressure Program, 1995—. Fellow ACP, Am. Heart Assn. (coun. on epidemiology); mem. Am. Geriatric Soc. Office: U Hawaii 347 N Kuakini St Honolulu HI 96817 Business E-Mail: curb@hawaii.edu.

CURBEAM, ROBERT L., JR., astronaut; b. Balt., Md., Mar. 5, 1962; m. Julie Dawn Lein; 2 children. BSc in Aerospace Engring., U.S. Naval Acad., 1984; MSc in Aero. Engring., Naval Postgraduate Sch., 1990, degree in Aero. & Astronautical Engring., 1991. Commd. 2d lt. USN, 1984, advanced through grades to comdr.; sta. on USS Forrestal, 1986—91; project officer Strike Aircraft Test Directorate, 1991—94; instr. U.S. Naval Acad., 1994—95; astronaut NASA, Houston, 1995—. Spacecraft communicator (CAPCOM) relaying all voice comm. between mission control and crews aboard the Space Shuttle and Internat. Space Station; CAPCOM branch chief and payloads group chief; dep. assoc. adminstr. for safety and mission assurance NASA Hdqs., Washington, 2002; safety branch chief for astronaut office; astronaut space mission (STS-85), 1997, space mission (STS-98), 2001; lead spacewalker, crew mem. STS-116 Mission (Discovery), 2006. Mem.: U.S. Naval Acad. Alumni Assn., Assn. Old Crows. Achievements include setting a record for most spacewalks (4) during a single shuttle mission STS-116 Mission (Discovery) in 2006. Avocations: weightlifting, bicycling, family activities, backpacking. Office: Astronaut Office CB NASA Johnson Space Center Houston TX 77058*

CURCI, PAULA, counseling educator, poet, radio personality; b. Bklyn., Oct. 11, 1962; d. Michael C. and Angela (Surace) Curci; m. Emilio Squillante III, Dec. 4, 2005. BA, Adelphi U., 1984; MEd, L.I. U., 1986, profl. diploma in sch. adminstrn., 2006. Cert. sch. counselor, sch. adminstr. N.Y. Sch. counselor L.I. Luth. HS, 1986—88, Sewanhaka HS, 1988—. Talk show host WRHU Radio Hofstra U., Hempstead, NY, 2000—; founder Acoustic Poets Network, 2004—. Author (prodr.): (book and CDs) Letters Never Sent, 1998, Emissary, 2000, Bittersweet, 2005. Chair Drug Free Sch. Com., Sewanhaka, 2005—. Named Best Poet, Vault Artist Cmty., 2000, 2004; recipient Guardian Angel award, Hope for the Children Found., 2005, Golden Apple award, March of Dimes, 2006. Office: Sewankala HS 500 Tulip Ave Floral Park NY

CURCIO, CHRISTOPHER FRANK, deputy director; b. Oakland, Calif., Feb. 3, 1950; s. Frank William and Virginie Theresa (Le Gris) C. BA in Speech/Drama, Calif. State U., Hayward, 1971; MBA in Arts Adminstrn., UCLA, 1974; MPA in Pub. Policy, Ariz. State U., 1982. Intern John F. Kennedy Ctr. for Arts, Washington, 1973; gen. mgr. Old Eagle Theatre, Sacramento, 1974-75; cultural arts supr. Fresno Parks and Recreation Dept., 1975-79; supr. cultural and spl. events Phoenix Parks and Recreation Dept., 1979-87, budget analyst, 1987, mgmt. svcs. adminstr., 1987-97, dep. dir., 1997—2006; dep. exec. dir. Valley Metro RPTA, Phoenix, 2006—. Mgmt. and budget analyst City of Phoenix, 1985; grants panelist Phoenix Arts Commn., 1987, Ariz. Commn. on Arts, 1987-88; voter Zony Theatre Awards, 1991-92; freelance theater critic, 1987-89; theater critic Ariz. Republic, 1990-98, 2004—, PHX Downtown, 1997-98, CityAZ, 1997-98, Ariz. Foothills Mag., 1998-2002, Sunday Showtunes Broadway's Biggest Hits, 1998-2000, In Theater Mag., 1999-2000, Variety, 1995—, KBAQ-FM Radio, 1999—, Broadway's Biggest Hits, 2000—, Ariz. Producton Assn., 2002—, Curtain Up, Phoenix, 2004-. Active Valley Leadership Program, Phoenix, 1987—, Valley Big Bros./Big Sisters, 1980-94; chair allocation panel United Way, 1990-92; sec. Los Olivos Townhome Assn., Phoenix, 1986-92. Mem. Am. Soc. Pub. Adminstrn., Nat. Recreation and Park Assn., Am. Theatre Critics Assn., Internat. Theater Critics Assn., Ariz. Park and Recreation Assn. Republican. Avocations: theater, writing, reading, cooking. Office: Valley Metro RPTA 302 N First Ave Ste 700 Phoenix AZ 85003 Office Phone: 602-534-0734. Personal E-mail: criticrep@aol.com. Business E-Mail: chris.curcio@phoenix.gov.

CURET, MYRIAM JEANETTE, surgeon, educator; b. San Juan, PR, Jan. 25, 1957; AB magna cum laude, Bryn Mawr Coll., Pa., 1978; MD, Harvard Med. Sch., Boston, 1982. Cert. Am. Bd. Surgery, lic. Calif., N.Mex. Gen. surgery internship U. Chgo. Hosps., 1982—85, Charles E. Culpepper rsch. fellowship, rsch. assoc. dept. surgery, 1985—87, gen. surgery residency, 1987—89; dep. clin. dir., chief gen. surgery and surg. svcs. Gallup Indian Med. Ctr., N.Mex., 1989—93; instr. surgery U. N.Mex./VA Med. Ctr., 1993—94; chief gen. surgery team A, dir. Minimally Invasive Surgery Ctr. U. N.Mex., 1995—2000; dir. minimally invasive surgery program Stanford U. Med. Ctr., 2000—. Commd. officer Indian Health Svc., 1989—94; comdr. Pub. Health Svc., 1989—94; mem. various hosp. coms. Gallup Indian Med. Ctr., 1989—94; surg. endoscopy fellow U. N.Mex., Albuquerque, 1993—94, asst. prof. surgery, 1994—99, mem. various ednl. and hosp. coms., 1994—2000, assoc. prof. surgery, 1999—2001, vis. prof., 2004, U. Va., 2003, U. Tex., San Antonio, 2003; clin. assoc. prof. surgery Stanford U. Med. Ctr., 2000—02, chief sect. minimally invasive surgery, 2001—; site dir. med. student surgery rotation Stanford U., 2001—, assoc. program dir. gen. surgery residency program, 2001—, mem. gen. surgery residency exec. com., 2001—, mem. task force HIPAA, 2002—03, mem. ethic com., 2002—03, at-large senator med. faculty senate, 2002—03, dir., founder Surg. Edn. Grand Rounds, 2002—, assoc. prof. surgery, 2002—, mem. com. performance assessment and advising, 2003—, co-developer On-line Clerkship Evaluator's Tutorial, 2004, chair working group on student assessment, 2004—, mem. pediats.

chair search com., 2005, dir. clerkship edn., 2005—, co-dir. intro. to surgery course, 2005, course dir. applied biomed. scis., 2005—, mem. com. courses and curriculum, 2005—, assoc. dean med. edn., 2006; presenter in field. Contbr. articles to profl. jours. Named Physician of Yr., Gallup Svc. Unit, 1990; recipient Charles E. Culpepper Fellowship award, U. Chgo. Hosps. and Clinics, 1985—86, Ann. Residents' Competition award, Am. Acad. Pediats., 1985, Achievement award, USPHS, 1991, Excellence award, Navajo Area Indian Health Svc., 1993, Faculty Tchg. Excellence award, U. N.Mex., 1999, Khatali Tchg. Excellence award, 2000, Med. Student Tchg. award, Stanford U., 2001, 2002, 2005, John Austin Collins Meml. award, 2003, Henry J. Kaiser award, Stanford U. Sch. Medicine, 2003, Tchg. Excellence award, 2004, 2005, Leadership in Edn. award, 2005, Best Fellow Presentation award, Am. Soc. Bariatric Surgery, 2005. Mem.: ACS (mem. applicants com. N.Mex. chpt. 1994—2000, sec.-treas. N.Mex. chpt. 1998—2000, mem. resident edn. com. 2000—, vice-chair resident edn. com. 2001—04, mem. med. student edn. com. 2001—, chair diversity issues com. 2002—04, mem. diversity issues com. 2002—, mem. objective structured clin. examination working group 2003—, chair resident edn. com. 2004—, surgeons as educators course faculty 2006, Best Resident Presentation award N.Mex. chpt. 2000), Greater Albuquerque Med. Assn. (sec. 1999—2000), Western Surg. Assn., Southwestern Surg. Congress (vice-councilor N.Mex. 1996—2000), Soc. Univ. Surgeons (mem. com. 2003—), Soc. Surgery of Alimentary Tract, Soc. Am. Gastrointestinal Endoscopic Surgeons (resident edn. com. 2000—02, resident rsch. com. 2002—), Pacific Coast Surg. Assn., Assn. Women Surgeons (chair laparoscopic rsch. grant com. 1995—2000, coun. mem. 1996—99, v.p. 1999—2000, pres.-elect 2000—01, pres. 2001—02), Assn. Surg. Edn. (mem. awards com. 2001—05, chair awards com. 2003—04, mem. program com. 2004—, Mater Tchr. award 2006). Office: Stanfod Hosps and Clinics Dept Surgery H3680 300 Pasteur Dr Stanford CA 94305 Business E-Mail: mcuret@stanford.edu.*

CURETON, CLAUDETTE HAZEL CHAPMAN, retired biology professor; b. Greenville, SC, May 3, 1932; d. John H. and Beatrice (Washington) Chapman; m. Stewart Cleveland Cureton, Dec. 27, 1954; children: Ruthye, Stewart II, S. Charles, Samuel. AB, Spelman Coll., Atlanta, 1951; MA, Fisk U., Nashville, Tenn., 1966; DHum (hon.), Morris Coll., Sumter, SC, 1996. Tchr. North Warren H.S., Wise, NC, 1952-60; tchr. Sterling H.S., Greenville, 1960-66, Wade Hampton H.S., Greenville, 1967-73; instr. Greenville Tech. Coll., 1973-95, ret., 1995. Bd. dirs. State Heritage Trust, 1978-91; commr. Basic Skills Adv. Program, Columbia, 1990—; mem. adv. bd. Am. Fed. Bank, NCNB Bank, Greenville, 1991—; mem. Higher Edn. S.C. Com. for Selection Prof. of Yr., 1995 Mem. Greenville Urban League, NAACP, SC Curriculum Congress; v.p. Woman's Bapt. E.& M. Conv. of SC; mem. SC Commn. on Higher Edn. Com. for Selection of the 1995 Gov.'s Prof. of the Yr., Gov.'s Task Force on Juvenile Crime, SC, Best Chance Network Task Force of Am. Cancer Soc., 1995-, Gov.'s Juvenile Justice Youth Coun., SC, 1996—, Gov.'s Juvenile Justice Task Force, 1997, SC, Piedmont Mental Health Bd., Simpsonville, SC, 2006; bd. dirs. Sisters Saving Sisters, Roper Mountain Sci. Ctr., 2003-. Recipient Presdl. award Morris Coll., 1987, 91, Svc. award SC Wildlife and Marine Dept., 1986, Outstanding Jack and Jill of Am. citation, 1986, Excellence in Tchg. award Nat. Inst. for Staff and Orgnl. Devel., U. Tex., Austin, 1992-93, Educator of Yr. award Greenville chpt. Am. Cancer Soc., 1994, Outstanding Svc. award Best Chance Network/Am. Cancer Soc., 1994, Citation SC Ho. of Reps., 1995, Outstanding Svc. award Reedy River Bapt. Assn., 2001; named Unsung Hero of the Cmty. for Outstanding Svc. to Humankind Greenville Tech. Coll., 1999. Mem. AAAS, AAUW, Nat. Assn. Biology Tchrs., SC Curriculum Congress, Nat. Coun. Negro Women, Inc., Delta Sigma Theta (past v.p. Greenville chpt. alumnae). Home: 501 Mary Knob Ct Greenville SC 29607-5242

CURETON, GLEN, pharmaceutical executive; b. Santa Cruz, Calif., Mar. 29, 1938; s. Eugene Nehf Cureton and Frances Alice Larson; m. Virginia Layton Goldsmith (dec.); 1 child, Paul D.; m. Virginia Young, Aug. 10, 1985; children: Joan K. Meyer, Jon D. Meyer. Degree in pre-pharmacy, U. Calif., Berkeley, 1958; PharmD, U. Calif., San Francisco, 1962; MBA, Harvard U., Boston, 1964. Registered pharmacist Calif., Nev., Tenn. Adminstrv. asst. to gen. mgr. life scis. Stanford Rsch. Inst., Menlo Park, Calif., 1964—67; dir. new products Chattem Drug and Chem. Co., Chattanooga, 1967—72; dir. R&D Barnes-Hind Pharm., Sunnyvale, Calif., 1972—76; dir. comml. devel. Cutter Labs. (Bayer A.G.), Berkeley, 1976—84; v.p. bus. devel. Calif. Biotech., Mountain View, Calif., 1984—86; v.p. Applied Immune Scis., Menlo Park, 1986—88; sr. cons. SRI Internat., Menlo Park, 1988—95. Mem. adv. bd. Repro, Inc., Chattanooga, 1968—72; cons. in field. Contbr. articles to profl. jours. Cubmaster, asst. scoutmaster Boy Scouts Am., Los Altos, Calif., 1972—90. Mem.: U. Calif. San Francisco Pharmacy Alumni Orgn. (pres. 1975—77). Achievements include patents for pharmaceutical container, squeeze bottle for inhalation. Avocations: gardening, snorkeling, skiing, water-skiing, hiking. Home: 4545 N Rodeo Gulch Rd Soquel CA 95073 Personal E-mail: gng@cruzio.com.

CURFMAN, FLOYD EDWIN, retired engineering educator; b. Gorin, Mo., Nov. 16, 1929; s. Charles Robert and Cleo Lucille (Sweeney) C.; m. Eleanor Elaine Fehl, Aug. 5, 1950; children: Gary Floyd, Karen Elaine. BSCE, U. Mo., 1958; BA in Math. Edn., Mt. Mary Coll., 1988. Registered profl. engr., Wis., Mo.; cert. tchr. Wis. Forest engr. US Forest Svc., Rolla and Harrisburg, 1958-70, engring. dir. Milw., 1970-84, chief tech. engr. Washington, 1984-86; tchr. Wauwatosa HS, Wis., 1987-89, Our Lady of Rosary, Milw., 1989-96; ret., 1996. Author: (booklet) Forest Roads-R-9, 1973; co-author: (tng. manual) Transportation Roads, 1966. Co-leader Boy Scouts Am., Harrisburg, 1958-62; activities coord. Cmty. Action Com., Brookfield, 1970-76; bike and hiking trails com. City of Brookfield (Wis.), 1982-83; program chair Math Counts, 1982. With U.S. Army, 1952-54. Mem. ASCE (program chair, Letter Nat. award 1970), NSPE (coms. 1970-86), Nat. Coun. Tchrs. Math., Wis. Soc. Profl. Engrs. (pres. Milw. chpt. 1982-83, State Recognition award 1983). Avocations: travel, reading. Home: 1755 N 166th St Brookfield WI 53005-5114

CURIE, CHARLES G., former federal agency administrator; b. Ind., July 22, 1955; m. Candace Curie. Grad., Huntington Coll., 1977; MA, U. Chgo., 1979. Cert. Acad. Cert. Social Workers. Exec. dir., CEO Sandusky Valley Ctr., Tiffin, Ohio; pres., CEO Helen H. Stevens Cmty. Mental Health Ctr., Carlisle, Pa., 1988—90; dir. risk mgmt. services Henry S. Lehr Inc., Bethlehem, Pa., 1990—95; dep. sec. for mental health and substance abuse services Dept. Pub. Welfare, State of Pa., 1995—2001; adminstr. Substance Abuse and Mental Health Services Adminstrn. US Dept. Health & Human Services, Rockville, Md., 2001—06. Named Alumnus of Yr., Huntington Coll., 1996; recipient McGovern Award for Leadership in Drug Abuse Prevention, Inst. for Behavior and Health, 2005. Mem.: Rotary Internat.

CURIE, ROGER KENT, adult education educator, consultant; b. Brownwood, Tex., Feb. 4, 1943; s. Kent R. and Ethna Ruth Curie. BA, Columbia Pacific, Calif., 1984; MBA, Columbia Pacific U., Calif., 1986; PhD in criminal justice (summa cum laude), Middleham U., Eng., 1988. Capt. U.S. Army, 1961—81; pres., owner Sentinel Guard Spetene, LA, 1982—92; guest lectr., 1993—. Commr. Internat. Bridges, El Paso, Tex.; mem. steering com. Cmty. Devel. Mem.: Nat. Assn. Chiefs of Police, ASIS, MENSA. Home: 3409 War Arrow Pl El Paso TX 79936-1212 Personal E-mail: rkcurie243@aol.com.

CURIEL, CAROLYN, former ambassador; b. Hammond, Ind. BA in Radio-TV-Film, Purdue U., 1976. Chief Caribbean Divsn. UPI; editor Late Editions Fgn. Desk N.Y. Times, NYC, Washington Post; writer, prodr. ABC News Nightline, 1992; spl. asst. to pres., sr. presdl. speechwriter White House, Washington; U.S. amb. to Belize Dept. State, 1997. Sr. fellow Pew Hispanic Ctr.; editl. bd. NY Times, 2002—. Recipient Disting. Alumni award, Purdue Univ., 2005. Office: Editl Bd NY Times 229 W 43rd St New York NY 10036

CURIEL, JUDITH REA, language educator; d. Ed and Betty Foreman; m. Harvey Harr, Aug. 4, 1996. BS, West Chester U., 1977; MA, Immaculata Coll., Pa., 1981; PhD, Berne U., Vt., 1998. Cert. Spanish K-12 Pa., 1977, elem. edn. Pa., 1977, English Pa., 2005, ESL Pa., 2005. Tchr., Spanish Del. County CC, Exton, Pa., 2000—02; tchr. Spanis, ESL Octorara High, Atglen, Pa., 1986—. Vol. Tails Tundra Siberian Husky Rescue, Lansdale, Pa., 2001—. Recipient DELE Certification, Spanish Embassy, 1996. Office: Octorara High 226 Highland Rd Atglen PA 19310 Home Phone: 610-873-9332; Office Phone: 610-593-8254. Personal E-mail: jcuriel@mac.com. Business E-Mail: jcuriel@octorara.org.

CURL, LAYTON SETH, psychologist, consultant, educator; b. Batesville, Ark., Apr. 3, 1976; s. Eric Lynn and Rita Kay Curl. Diploma in Asian studies, Kansai Gaidai U., Japan, 1997; BA in Psychology, Lyon Coll., Batesville, AR, 1998; MA in Exptl. Psychology, U. Miss., Oxford, 2000, PhD in Social and Cross-Cultural Psychology, 2002. Instr. English Kansai Gaidai U., Kyoto, 1996—97; instr. psychology U. Miss., Oxford, 1998—2002; mng. editor Internat. Jour. Intercultural Rels., Hilo, Hawaii, 2000—02; prof. cross-cultural psychology Hobart and William Smith Colleges, Geneva, NY, 2002—04; prof. social psychology Met. State Coll. Denver, 2004—. Mem. Human Rights Campaign, New York City, 2000. Scholar, Dept. of Higher Edn. & Century Tube Corp., 1996. Fellow: Internat. Assn. Intercultural Rels. (assoc.); mem.: Asian Assn. Social Psychologists, Internat. Assn. Cross-Cultural Psychology. Democrat. Home: 855 Pennsylvania St #206 Denver CO 80203 Office: Dept Psychology Metropolitan State Coll Denver Campus Box 54 PO Box 173362 Denver CO 80217-3362 Office Phone: 303-556-3025. Business E-Mail: lcurl@mscd.edu.

CURL, ROBERT FLOYD, JR., chemistry professor; b. Alice, Tex., Aug. 23, 1933; s. Robert Floyd and Lessie (Merritt) Curl; m. Jonel Whipple, Dec. 21, 1955; children: Michael, David. BA, Rice U., 1954; PhD, U. Calif., Berkeley, 1957; D (hon.), U. Buenos Aires, 1997; D, U. Littoral, 2002. Rsch. fellow Harvard U., Cambridge, Mass., 1957—58; from asst. prof. chemistry to prof. Rice U., Houston, 1958—2003, Kenneth S. Pitzer-Schlumberger prof. natural scis., 2003—05, Kenneth S. Pitzer-Schlumberger prof. natural scis. emeritus, 2005—; master Lovett Coll., 1968—72, univ. prof., 2003—05, prof. emeritus, 2005—, rsch. prof. chemistry, 2005—. Vis. rsch. officer NRC Can., 1972—73; vis. prof. Inst. Molecular Sci., Okazaki, Japan, 1977, U. Bonn, 1985; Erskine fellow U. Canterbury, 1999; hon. prof. USTC, 2002—, Xiamen U., 2006—. Contbr. articles to profl. jours. Co-recipient Nobel prize in Chemistry, 1996; named to, Tex. Sci. Hall of Fame; recipient Clayton prize, Instn. Mech. Engrs., London, 1958, Internat. New Materials prize, Am. Phys. Soc., 1992, Alexander von Humboldt sr. U.S. scientist award, 1984, Order of Golden Plate, 1997, Achievement award, Am. Carbon Soc., 1997, Tex. Disting. Scientist award, 1997, Johannes Marcus Marci award in spectroscopy, 1998, Madison Marshall award, 1998, Space Act award, 1998, Centenary medal, Royal Soc. Chemistry, 1999, Forschungspreis Chemie, U. Bochum, 2004; fellow NSF, Alfred P. Sloan, 1961—63, NATO postdoctoral, 1964. Fellow: Am. Acad. Arts and Scis., Am. Optical Soc., Royal Soc. of New Zealand (hon.); mem.: NAS, European Acad. Scis., Arts and Letters (titulaire mem.), Am. Chem. Soc., Sigma Xi, Phi Beta Kappa. Methodist. Home: 1824 Bolsover Rd Houston TX 77005-1728 Office: Rice University PO Box 1892 6100 Main St Houston TX 77005-1892 Office Phone: 713-348-4816. E-mail: rfcurl@rice.edu.

CURL, SAMUEL EVERETT, retired dean, agriculturist, consultant; b. Ft. Worth, Dec. 26, 1937; s. Henry Clay and Mary Elva (Watson) C.; m. Betty Doris Savage, June 6, 1957 (div.); children: Jane Ellen, Julia Kathleen, Karen Elizabeth; m. Mary Behrends Reeves, Sept. 11, 1993; stepchildren: Ryan Andrew, Shelly Lyn. Student, Tarleton State Coll., 1955-57; BS, Sam Houston State U., 1959; MS, U. Mo., 1961; PhD, Tex. A&M U., 1963. Mem. faculty Tex. Tech U., Lubbock, 1961, 63-76, 79-97, tchr., rschr. animal physiology and genetics, 1963-76, asst., assoc. and interim dean Coll. Agrl. Sci., 1968-73, assoc. v.p. acad. affairs, prof., 1973-76, dean Coll. Agrl. Scis. and Natural Resources, prof., 1979-97; pres. Phillips U., Enid, Okla., 1976-79; agrl. cons., 1964-76, 2004—; dean and dir. divsn. agrl. scis. and natural resources Okla. State U., Stillwater, 1997—2004, ret., 2004; past pres. So. Assn. Agrl. Scientists. Bd. dirs. Am. Distance Edn. Consortium, Okla. Sci. and Tech. R&D Bd., Food and Agr. Ednl. Info. Sys., Okla. Youth Expo.; past chmn. So. Region Adminstrv. Heads, So. Region Adminstrv. Heads Liaison to Coun. on Agrl. Rsch., Ext. and Tchg.; mem. adminstrv. com. Okla. State U. Sch. Internat. Studies; former bd. dirs. Mid Am. Internat. Agrl. Consortium, 1997—2002, past chmn., 1998—99, 2001—02; mem. Gov.'s Task Force on Agrl. Devel. in Tex., 1982—83, 1988, Tex. Crop and Livestock Adv. Com., 1985—91, Tex. Agrl. Resources Protection Authority, 1989—97, Tex. Agribus. Rsch. Promotion Coun., 1995—97, Okla. State Com., Exptl. Program to Stimulate Competitive Rsch.; del. Eisenhower Consortium for Western Environ. Forestry Rsch., 1979—84; mgmt. com. S.W. Consortium on Plant Genetics and Water Resources, 1984—97, chmn., 1989—95; mem. USDA Nat. Planning Com. on Hispanic Minority Recruitment, 1988—93; trustee Consortium for Internat. Devel., 1979—97, mem. exec. com., 1981—84, 1986—87, 1989—90; former mem. High Plains Rsch. Coord. Bd., So. Regional Coun., U.S. Joint Coun. Food and Agrl. Scis.; former trustee Water Inc.; chmn. agrl. and natural resources program rev. task force Sam Houston State U., 1982—83; mem. adv. com. Sch. Agr. Angelo State U., 1989—95; mem. 1995 farm bill task force Tex. Dept. Agr., 1994—95; chair agrl. team Okla. Govs. EDGE project; adj. faculty mem., outreach coord. Tarleton State U., Stephenville, Tex., 2005—06, exec. asst. to provost, 2006—; cons. in field. Author: (with others) Progress and Change in the Agricultural Industry, 1974, Food and Fiber for a Changing World, 1976, 2d edit., 1982; contbr. 95 articles to profl. jours. Pres. Lubbock Econ. Coun., 1982; bd. dirs. Market Lubbock Econ. Devel. Corp., 1995-97; former mem. bd. overseers Ranching Heritage Assn.; mem. Goals for Lubbock: A Vision into the 21st Century Com., 1995-96; elder Westminster Presbyn. Ch., Lubbock, 1994-97; mem. First United Meth. Ch., Stillwater, 1997-2005; mem. adminstrv. coun. First United Meth. Ch., Acton, Tex., 2005—; 2d lt. U.S. Army, 1959, capt. USAR. Danforth Assn. fellow, 1964-76, Am. Coun. Edn. fellow, 1972-73; recipient Disting. Alumnus award, Faculty-Alumni Gold medal U. Mo., 1975, Outstanding Agr. Alumnus award Sam Houston State U., 1986, Disting. Alumnus award, 1993, Tex. Citation for Outstanding Svc. award Tex. 4-H Found., 1987, Tex. 4-H Alumni award, 1993, Disting. Svc. award Vocational Agrl. Tchrs. Assn. Tex., 1987, Blue and Gold Meritorious Svc. award Tex. Future Farmers of Am., 1988, Tex. State degree Future Farmers Am., 1988, Area Disting. Svc. award Vocat. Agr. Tchrs., 1987, Okla. Hon. State degree Future Farmers Am., 2002. Mem.: Profl. Agrl. Workers Tex. (bd. dirs., Disting. Svc. to Tex. Agr. award 1984), Coun. Adminstrv. Heads of Agr., Nat. Assn. State Univs. and Land-Grant Colls. (exec. com. bd. agr. 1994—97, 1998—2001), Assn. U.S. Univ. Dirs. Internat. Agrl. Programs, Am. Assn. Univ. Agrl. Adminstrs., Am. Soc. Animal Sci. (program com. Biennial Symposium on Animal Reprodn. 1972—76, reviewer Jour. Animal Sci.), Lubbock C. of C. (chmn. agr. task force, chmn. rsch. com. 1981—86, bd. dirs. 1988—92, water com., legis. affairs com., agr. com., gubernatorial appointments task force), West Tex. C. of C. (former bd. dirs., chmn. agrl. and ranching com.), Century Club, Tex. Tech. U. Centennial Rotary (hon.), Okla. State U. Alumni Assn., Lubbock Rotary Club (bd. dirs., 1st v.p.), Sirloin Club Okla., Sigma Xi, Gamma Sigma Delta, Phi Kappa Phi, Omicron Delta Kappa, Farmhouse Frat. (assoc.). Methodist. Home: 8703 Claremont Dr Pecan Plantation Granbury TX 76049 Office Phone: 817-776-1285. Personal E-mail: samcurl@charter.net.

CURLAND, DAVID JOSEPH, retired language educator; b. L.A., Dec. 1, 1926; s. Jack and Rae (Zeitlin) Curland; m. Agnes Camilla Jung, Jan. 5, 1950; children: Susan, Matthew, Martin. BA in Arts and Scis., UCLA, 1950; MA in Spanish, U. Oreg., Eugene, 1963. Cert. secondary tchr. Spanish Oreg. Spanish tchr. Willamette H.S., Eugene, Oreg., 1960—66; Spanish instr. Oreg. Pub. Broadcasting Sys., Eugene, 1965—66; sr. instr. U. Oreg., Eugene, 1966—92, sr. instr. emeritus, 1992—. Creater Coll. Bd. Achievement Tests, 1967—72; co-founder Yamada Lang. Ctr. U. Oreg., dir. summer programs Romance langs., Spain, 1969, Spain, 77; project dir. NEH, Mexico, 1971, 75, Eugene, 85, Eugene, 87, Eugene, 92, Eugene, 94, Eugene, 95. Author: (Spanish video) La Catrina, 1997, El Ultimo Secreto, 1998, En Busca de la Verdad, 2005. Founder Fgn. Lang. Day U. Oreg., Eugene, 1983. With US Army, 1943—45. Recipient Fulbright award, Fulbright Commn., 1972—73, 1977—78, Outstanding Contbn. to Fgn. Lang. Edn. in Oreg., Confederation Fgn. Lang. Tchrs., 1986; Orgn. Am. States fellow, U. Mexico, 1965. Mem.: Am. Coun. Fgn. Lang. Tchrs., Am. Assn. Spanish Tchrs. Avocation: swimming. Home: 1905 Cleveland Ave Santa Barbara CA 93103

CURLANDER, PAUL JOSEPH, technology executive; b. Balt., Dec. 15, 1952; BSEE, U. Colo., 1974; MSEE, MIT, 1977, PhDEE, 1979. Elec. engr. gen. products divsn. IBM, Boulder, 1974—78, staff printer tech. group office product divsn., 1978—85, product mgr. laser printers, 1985-86, product mgr. letter quality printers info. products divsn., 1986-89, dir. printer products, 1989-91; gen. mgr. Lexmark Printer Bus., 1991-93; v.p., gen. mgr. printing sys. bus. Lexmark Internat., Lexington, Ky., 1993-95, exec. v.p. ops., 1995-97, pres., COO, 1997-98, pres., CEO, 1998—, chmn., 1999—. Contbr. articles to profl. jours.; patentee in field. Office: Lexmark Internat Inc 740 W New Circle Rd Lexington KY 40550*

CURLE, ROBIN LEA, computer company executive; b. Denver, Feb. 23, 1950; d. Fred Warren and Claudia Jean (Harding) C.; m. Lucien Ray Reed, Feb. 23, 1981 (div. Oct. 1984). BS in Bus. Comm., U. Ky., 1972. Systems analyst 1st Nat. Bank, Lexington, Ky., 1972-73, SW BancShares, Houston, 1973-77; sales rep. Software Internat., Houston, 1977-80; dist. mgr. UCCEL, Dallas, 1980-82; v.p. and gen. mgr. Southeastern region Info. Sci., Inc., Atlanta, 1982-83; v.p. sales and mktg. TesserAct, San Francisco, 1983-86, Foothill Rsch., San Francisco, 1986; pres., founder Curle Cons. Group, San Francisco, 1986-89; mgr. strategic mktg. MCC, Austin, Tex., 1989-90; founder, exec. v.p. Evolutionary Tech., Inc., Austin, 1991-99; pres., CEO Journée Software, Austin, 1999-2000; founder, mng. dir. CEO Partnerships, Austin, 2000—02; pres., CEO Zebra Imaging, 2002—06; pres. J. B. Goodwin Co., 2006—. Bd. dirs. Evolutionary Techs. Internat., Austin Software Coun., Tex. Property and Casualty, Zebra Imaging, Govs. Bus. Coun.; adv. bd. 360 Summit; dir. adv. bd. U. Tex. Engring. Sch. Mem. bus. adv. com. Rep. Party, Austin. Recipient Ma Ferguson award Exec. Women Internat. 1997, Grad of Yr. award Nat. Bus. Incubator Assn. 1996, Profiles in Power award, 1999, Entrepreneur of Yr. award 360 Summit Adv. Bd.; feature in Forbes Mag., 1996, Entrepreneur Mag., 1997; named top 50 most prestigious people Digital South; profile documentary Entrepreneurial Revolution, 1997, Inc 500 List, 1997, 98. Mem. U. Ky. Alumni Assn., Women in Tech., Women of Austin, Software Exec. Com., Inc. 500 Cos., Austin C. of C. (bd. dir.), Delta Gamma (pres. 1969). Avocations: scuba diving, running, skiing, cooking. Home: 7009 Quill Leaf Cv Austin TX 78750-8306 Office: 3933 Steck Austin TX 78750 Office Phone: 512-633-3011. E-mail: robin@robincurle.com.

CURLEE, F. LYNN, illustrator; b. High Point, NC, Oct. 9, 1947; s. J. Sherwood and Dorothy Anderson Curlee. BA, U. NC, Chapel Hill, 1969; MA, U. Pa., Phila., 1971. Gallery artist various galleries, 1973—2000. Author, illustrator, 1991—. Horses with Wings, 1993; author (illustrator): Ships of the Air, 1996, Into the Ice, 1998, Rushmore, 1999, Liberty, 2000, Brooklyn Bridge, 2001 (Seibert Honor Book, 2001), Seven Wonders of the Ancient World, 2002, Capital, 2003, Parthenon, 2004, Ball Park, 2005, Skyscraper, 2007. Independent. Office: PO Box 699 Jamesport NY 11947 Business E-Mail: flcurlee@aol.com.

CURLER, JEFFREY H., packaging manufacturing executive; Various positions Bemis Co., Inc., Mpls., 1973—, pres., 1995—98, pres., COO, 1998—2000, pres., CEO, 2000—05, chmn., pres., CEO, 2005—. Office: Bemis Co Inc 222 S 9th St Ste 2300 Minneapolis MN 55402-4099*

CURLEY, EDWIN MUNSON, philosophy educator; b. Albany, NY, May 1, 1937; s. Julius Edwin and Gertrude E.; m. Ruth Helen Snyder, Dec. 12, 1959; children: Julia Anne, Richard Edwin. BA, Lafayette Coll., 1959; PhD, Duke U., 1963. Asst. prof. philosophy San Jose State Coll., 1963-66; research fellow Australian Nat. U., Canberra, 1966-68, fellow, 1968-72, sr. fellow, 1972-77; prof. philosophy Northwestern U., 1977-83, U. Ill.-Chgo., 1983-93, U. Mich., 1993—. Author: Hellenistic Philosophy, 1965, Spinoza's Metaphysics, 1969, Descartes Against the Skeptics, 1978, The Collected Works of Spinoza, vol. 1, 1985, Behind the Geometrical Method, 1988, A Spinoza Reader, 1994, Hobbes' Leviathan, 1994; Am. co-editor Archiv für Geschichte der Philosophie, 1979-95; contbr. articles to profl. jours. Fellow AAAS; mem. Am. Philos. Assn. (v.p. ctr. divsn., 1989-90, pres. 1990-91). Democrat. Home: 2645 Pin Oak Dr Ann Arbor MI 48103-2370 Office: U Mich Dept Philosophy 2215 Angell Hall Ann Arbor MI 48109 Office Phone: 734-764-6285. Business E-Mail: emcurley@umich.edu.

CURLEY, ELMER FRANK, librarian; b. Florence, Pa., Jan. 13, 1929; s. Augustus Wolfe and Bessie (Andrews) C. BA, U. Pitts., 1961; MLS, Carnegie Mellon U., Pitts., 1962; Adv. Cert., U. Pitts., 1964; postgrad., U. Nev., 1996—. Ref. libr. U. Pitts., 1962-64; head ref. dept. SUNY-Stony Brook, 1964-67; head pub. svcs. U. Nev.-Las Vegas, 1967-76, asst. dir. libr. svcs., 1976-81, ref. bibliographer, 1981-94, ret., 1994.

CURLEY, JOHN FRANCIS, JR., mutual fund executive; b. Wollaston, Mass., July 24, 1939; s. John Francis and Ann (Omar) C.; m. Loretta Mae O'Keeffe, Oct. 20, 1962; children: William Laurance, Edward Reid, David Neil. Grad., Phillips Acad.; AB, Princeton U., 1960; MBA, Harvard U., 1962. With Paine, Webber, Jackson & Curtis, Inc., NYC, 1964—, gen. ptnr., 1969-72, exec. v.p., 1972-77, pres., 1977-80, chmn. fin. com., 1980-82; vice-chmn. bd. Legg Mason, Inc., Balt., 1982-98, Legg Mason Wood Walker, Inc., Balt., 1982-98. Chmn. bd. dirs. Legg Mason Mutual Funds, 1982-; bd. govs. Investment Co. Inst., ICI Mut. Ins. Co., 1994-98, Sellinger Sch. Bus., 1995-98. 1st lt. AUS, 1962-64. Mem. Securities Industry Assn. (dir., exec. com. 1978-80), Investment Assn. N.Y. (past pres.). Office: Legg Mason Wood Walker Inc 100 Light St Baltimore MD 21202-1099

CURLEY, ROBERT AMBROSE, JR., lawyer; b. Boston, June 5, 1949; s. Robert Ambrose and Terese M. (O'Hara) C.; m. Kathleen M. Foley, June 10, 1972; children: Christine, Elizabeth, Margaret. AB cum laude, Harvard U., 1971; JD, Cornell U., 1974. Bar: Mass. 1974, U.S. Dist. Ct. Mass. 1975, U.S. Ct. Appeals (1st. cir.) 1976. Prin. Curley & Curley, P.C., Boston, 1974—, pres. Lectr. Mass. Continuing Legal Edn., Mass. Def. Attys., Mass. Acad. Trial Attys., Flaschner Jud. Inst., Nat. Bus. Inst.; dir. IADC Found., 2003—, v.p., 2004—. Fellow Am. Coll. Trial Lawyers; mem. ABA, ATLA (assoc.), Internat. Assn. Def. Counsel (dir. found. 2003—), Def. Trial Acad., Mass. Bar Assn. (lectr., chmn. civil trial practice sect., civil litig. com. 1990-91, mem. ho. of dels. 2001-2002), Mass. Def. Lawyers Assn.

(co-chmn. products liability sects. 1994-96, bd. dirs., sec. 1998-99, treas., v.p. 1999-2000, pres. 2001-2002, Def. Lawyer of Yr. 2004), Nat. Bus. Inst., Def. Rsch. Inst. (state rep. 2002—), Harvard Club (Hingham, treas. 1983-84, v.p. 1984-85, pres. 1985-86), Clover (Boston). Roman Catholic. Office: Curley & Curley PC 27 School St Ste 600 Boston MA 02108-4391 Home Phone: 781-749-2527; Office Phone: 617-523-2990. Business E-Mail: rac@curleylaw.com.

CURLEY, THOMAS, newspaper executive; b. Easton, Pa., July 6, 1948; s. John Joseph and Emily Dixon (Sprague) Curley; m. Marsha Stanley, Sept. 14, 1974; children: Laura Stanley, Melinda Burke. BA in Polit. Sci., La Salle U., 1970; MBA, Rochester Inst. Tech., 1977. Reporter The News Tribune, Woodbridge, NJ, 1967, 1968, reporter, copy editor, 1970—72; night city/suburban editor The Times-Tribune, Rochester, NY, 1972—76; dir. info. Gannett Co., Inc., Rochester, 1976—80, dir. rsch., 1980—82; editor Norwich (Conn.) Bulletin, 1982—83; pub. The Courier-News, Bridgewater, NJ, 1983—85; exec. v.p. USA Today, Washington, 1985—86, pres., 1986—89, pres., COO, 1989—91, pres., pub., 1991—2003; sr. v.p. Gannett Co., Inc., 1998—; pres., CEO The Associated Press, NYC, 2003—. Trustee LaSalle U., Phila., 1987—, Rochester Inst. Tech., Ronald McDonald House Charities; former chmn. Am. Advertising Fed. Hall of Fame; mem. exec. bd. Ad Council. Pres. Ctrl. Jersey C. of C., Plainfield, NJ, 1984—85; exec. v.p. United Way Somerset Valley, Bridgewater, 1985; bd. dirs. Assn. for Retarded Citizens, Manville, NJ, 1983—85. Recipient Alumnus of Yr. award, Rochester Inst. Tech., 1986; Pub. Opinion Rsch. fellow, Northwestern U., 1976. Office: The Associated Press 50 Rockefeller Plz Flr 7 New York NY 10020-1605

CURLEY, WALTER JOSEPH PATRICK, diplomat, investment banker; b. Pitts., Sept. 17, 1922; s. Walter Joseph and Marguerite Inez (Cowan) C.; m. Mary Walton, Dec. 18, 1948; children: Margaret Cowan, Walter Joseph, Patrick III, John Walton (dec. 2003), James Mellon (dec. 1994). BA, Yale U., 1944; cert., U. Oslo, 1948; MBA, Harvard U., 1948; LLD (hon.), Trinity Coll., Dublin, Ireland, 1976. Mgr. Caltex Oil Co., India, 1948-52, Italy, 1952-55, NYC, 1955-57; v.p. San Jacinto Petroleum, 1957-60; ptnr. J.H. Whitney Co., 1961-75. Commr. pub. events, chief protocol City of N.Y., 1973-74; amb. to Ireland, 1975-77, amb. to France, 1989-93; prin. W.J.P. Curley, 1978—; pres. Curley Land Co., Pitts., 1993—; chmn. internat. adv. bd. Sotheby's, 1999—. Author: Letters From The Pacific, 1965, Monarchs in Waiting, 1974, Vanishing Kingdoms, 2004. Trustee Buckley Sch., 1960-75, Miss Porter's Sch., Farmington, Mass., 1965-74, Barnard Coll., 1966-75, N.Y. Pub. Libr., 1972-75, The Frick Collection, 1993-2004; hon. chmn. French-Am. Found., N.Y., 1993—. Decorated Bronze Star; Cloud and Banner (Republic of China); comdr. French Legion of Honor. Mem. Coun. Fgn. Rels., Yale Club, Knickerbocker Club, Links Club, Racquet and Tennis Club, Rolling Rock Club (Ligonier, Pa.), Kildare St. Club (Dublin), Bedford Golf and Tennis Club, Traveller's Club (Paris). Office: 645 Fifth Ave 18th Fl New York NY 10022 E-mail: curleywjp@aol.com.

CURLOOK, WALTER, management consultant; b. Coniston, Ont., Can., Mar. 14, 1929; s. William and Stephanie (Acker) C.; m. Jennifer Burak, May 28, 1955; children: Christine, William Paul, John Michael, Andrea. BA in Sci., U. Toronto, 1950, MA in Sci., 1951, PhD, 1953, DEng (hon.), 2002; DSc (hon.), Laurentian U., 1983. Postdoctoral fellow Imperial Coll. Sci. and Tech., London, 1954; rsch. metallurgist Inco, Sudbury, Ont., Canada, 1954-59, supr. rsch. sta. Port Colborne, Ont., Canada, 1959-60, supr. rsch. Copper Cliff, Ont., Canada, 1960-64, asst. to gen. mgr., 1964-69, v.p. adminstrv. and engring. svcs., 1973-74, v.p. NYC, 1974-77; dir. tech. COFIMPAC, Paris, 1969-72; sr. v.p. prodn. Inco Metals Co., Toronto, 1977-80, pres., chief exec. officer, 1980-82; exec. v.p. Inco Ltd., Toronto, 1982-91, vice chmn., 1991-94, dir., 1989-94; pres. Inco Gold Co., Toronto, 1987-89; pres. commr. P.T. Inco, Indonesia, 1990-93; pres., dir. gen. Goro Nickel, S.A., Noumea, New Caledonia, 1992-97. Disting. adj. prof. U. Toronto, 1999—; mem. Nat. Adv. Com. Mining Industry, 1980-94; mem. Premier's Coun. Econ. Renewal, 1991-94. Patentee in field. Bd. dirs. Cambrian Found., Sudbury, 1983; first chmn. bd. Cambrian Coll. Applied Arts and Tech., Sudbury, Ont., 1967. Named to Can. Mining Hall of Fame, 1997; recipient McCharles prize, U. Toronto, 1989, Charles F. Rand medal, AIME, 2002. Fellow Can. Acad. Engring.; mem. Assn. Profl. Engrs. of Ont., Metall. Soc. of Can. Inst. Mining and Metallurgy (Airey award 1979, Platinum medal 1994), Mining Assn. Can. (bd. dir. and past chmn.), Sci. North (hon. life Sudbury chpt. 1988), Ont. Mining Assn. (past pres.), Order of Can. Home and Office: 25 Cluny Dr Toronto ON Canada M4W 2P9 Home Phone: 416-934-1048; Office Phone: 416-934-1048.

CURNUTTE, MARY E., artist; b. Valera, Tex., Dec. 15, 1920; d. Robert Franklin and Mary Elizabeth (Walker) Line; m. James Richard Curnutte, Oct. 14, 1950 (dec. Feb. 1972); 1 child, Sandra Elizabeth Curnutte; m. Robert Frederick Furman, Apr. 27, 1985 (dec. Apr. 2003). Bookkeeper, sec. drug stores, 1942-49, NCO Club, Goodfellow AFB, San Angelo, Tex., 1949-51; bookkeeper Boyce Hardware and Fuel Oil, Portsmouth, Va., 1953; artist/logs/filing Christian Broadcasting Network, Portsmouth, 1972-73; tchr. art Frederick Mil. Acad., Portsmouth, 1978-82, Alliance Christian Sch., Portsmouth, 1981-85; artist and pvt. tchr. art and music, restorer of art Portsmouth, 1959-89; artist Winter Haven, Fla., 1989—. Recipient Silver Cup award Alliance Christian Sch., 1984. Mem.: DAV Aux., Nat. Assn. Ret. Fed. Employees, Nat. Mus. Women in the Arts (charter), Nat. Ret. Tchrs. Assn. Baptist. Avocations: photography, reading, fishing, music, travel.

CURPHEY, THOMAS JOHN, chemist, researcher; b. NYC, Oct. 7, 1934; s. Theodore Joscelyn and Aies Curphey; m. Marilyn Gomulka, Aug. 2, 1959; children: Linda Lee, Alison. AB, Harvard U., 1956, PhD, 1960. Rsch. assoc. U. of Wis., Madison, Wis., 1960—62; instr. in chemistry Yale U., New Haven, 1962—64; asst. prof. of chemistry St. Louis U., St. Louis, 1964—68, assoc. prof. of chemistry, 1968—73, prof. of chemistry, 1973—74; adj. prof. of chemistry Dartmouth Coll., Hanover, NH, 1974—2003; sr. rsch. assoc. Dartmouth Med. Sch., Hanover, NH, 1974—80, rsch. assoc. prof. of pathology, 1980—85, rsch. prof. of pathology, 1985—2003, rsch. prof. pathology emeritus, 2003—. Cons. Crime Lab, St. Louis Met. Police, St. Louis. Contbr. articles to profl. jours. Grantee More than 30, NIH, NSF, 1962 - 2002. Mem.: Am. Chem. Soc. (treas. St. Louis sect. 1971—72, dir. 1974—75, chmn. organic tropical group 1966—67). Home: 12 Dresden Rd Hanover NH 03755 Office: Dartmouth Med Sch Hanover NH 03755 Office Phone: 603-650-1972. Business E-Mail: tjcu@dartmouth.edu.

CURRAN, CHARLES EDWARD, theology studies educator, priest; b. Rochester, NY, Mar. 30, 1934; s. John F. and Gertrude (Beisner) C. BA, St. Bernard's Coll., 1955; Licentiate in Sacred Theology, Pontifical Gregorian U., Rome, 1959, STD, 1961, Acad. Alfonsiana, 1961; PhD (hon.), U. Charleston, 1987, Concordia Coll., Portland, 1992. Ordained priest Roman Cath. Ch., 1958. Prof. moral theology St. Bernard's Sem., Rochester, 1961-65; from asst. prof. to prof. Cath. U. Am., Washington, 1965-87; vis. Kaneb prof. Cath. studies Cornell U., Ithaca, NY, 1987-88; vis. Brooks prof. Religion U. So. Calif., LA, 1988-89, vis. Firestone prof. Religion, 1989-90; vis. Goodwin-Philpott eminent scholar in Religion Auburn (Ala.) U., 1990-91; Elizabeth Scurlock U. prof. of human values So. Meth. U., Dallas, 1991—. External examiner in Christian ethics U. W.I., 1982-86; lectr. in field. Author: Christian Morality Today, 1966, A New Look at Christian Morality, 1968, Contemporary Problems in Moral Theology, 1970, Catholic Moral Theology in Dialogue, 1972, The Crisis in Priestly Ministry, 1972, Politics, Medicine and Christian Ethics: A Dialogue with Paul Ramsey, 1973, New Perspectives in Moral Theology, 1974, Ongoing Revision: Studies in Moral Theology, 1976, Themes in Fundamental Moral Theology, 1977, Issues in Sexual and Medical Ethics, 1978, Transition and Tradition in Moral Theology, 1979, Moral Theology: A Continuing Journey, 1982, American Catholic Social Ethics: Twentieth Century Approaches, 1982, Critical Concerns in Moral Theology, 1984, Directions in Catholic Social Ethics, 1985, Directions in Fundamental Moral Theology, 1985, Faithful Dissent, 1986, Toward an American Catholic Moral Theology, 1988, Sexualitat und Ethik, 1988, Tensions in Moral Theology, 1988, Catholic Higher Education, Theology, and Academic Freedom, 1990, The Living Tradition of Moral Theology, 1992, The Church and Morality: An Ecumenical and Catholic Approach, 1993, History and Contemporary Issues: Studies in Moral Theology, 1996, The Origins of Moral Theology in the U.S.: Three Different Approaches, 1997, Moral Theology at the End of the Century, 1999, The Catholic Moral Tradition Today: A Synthesis, 1999, Catholic Social Teaching 1891-Present: A Historical, Theological, and Ethical Analysis, 2002, The Moral Theology of Pope John Paul II, 2005, Loyal Dissent: Memoir of a Catholic Theologian, 2006; also articles; (with others) Dissent In and For the Church: Theologians and Humanae Vitae, 1969, The Responsibility of Dissent: The Church and Academic Freedom, 1969; editor: Absolutes in Moral Theology?, 1968, Contraception: Authority and Dissent, 1969, Moral Theology: Challenges for the Future, 1990; co-editor book series: (with Richard A. McCormick) Readings in Moral Theology: No. 1: Moral Norms and Catholic Tradition, 1979, No. 2: The Distinctiveness of Christian Ethics, 1980, No. 3: The Magisterium and Morality, 1982, No. 4: The Use of Scripture in Moral Theology, 1984, No. 5: Official Catholic Social Teaching, 1986, No. 6: Dissent in the Church, 1988, No. 7: Natural Law and Theology, 1991, No. 8: Dialogue About Catholic Sexual Teaching, 1993, Feminist Ethics and the Catholic Moral Tradition: Readings in Moral Theology No. 9, 1996, John Paul II and Moral Theology: Readings in Moral Theology No. 10, 1998, The Historical Development of Fundamental Moral Theology in The United States: Readings in Moral Theology No. 11, 1999, The Catholic Church, Morality, and Politics: Readings in Moral Theology No. 12, 2001, Change in Official Catholic Moral Teachings: Readings in Moral Theology No. 13, 2003, Conscience Readings in Moral Theology No. 14, 2004 Am. Assn. Theol. Schs. fellow, 1971; Georgetown U. Kennedy Ctr. for Bioethics scholar, 1972; named ABC-TV person week, 1986. Mem. Cath. Theol. Soc. Am. (pres. 1969-70, John Courtney Murray award 1972), Soc. Christian Ethics (pres. 1971-72, mem. editorial bd. Ann. 1991—), Am. Theol. Soc. (pres. 1989-90), Coll. Theology Soc. (Pres. award, 2003). Avocations: golf, swimming, reading. Home: 4125 Woodcreek Dr Dallas TX 75220-5074 Home Phone: 214-352-8974; Office Phone: 214-768-4073. Business E-Mail: ccurran@smu.edu.

CURRAN, DANIEL J., academic administrator, sociologist, educator; b. Phila. m. Claire M. Renzetti; children: Sean, Aidan. B in Sociology, St. Joseph's U., Phila., 1973; M in Sociology, Temple U., 1978; PhD in Sociology, U. Del., 1980. Joined St. Joseph's U., Phila., 1979, faculty positions dept. sociology, chair dept. sociology, 1988—92, dean Coll. Arts and Scis., 1994—97, v.p. acad. affairs, 1997—2002, exec. v.p., 1999—2002; pres., prof. sociology U. Dayton, Ohio, 2002—. Concurrent professorship Nanjing (China) U.; mem. task force on sports wagering NCAA, 2004—; mem. Ohio Aerospace and Def. Adv. Coun.; bd. dirs. Dayton Devel. Coalition. Author: Dead Laws for Dead Men, 1993; co-author (with Claire M. Renzetti): Social Problems: Society in Crisis Women, Men and Society, Contemporary Societies: Problems and Prospects Criminology, Living Sociology, Theories in Crime. Bd. dirs. St. Joseph's Carpenter Soc. Recipient Eternal Flame award for Holocaust edn., 2002; Fulbright Sr. scholar, U. Melbourne, Australia, 1990. Mem.: Dayton Area C. of C. (mem. exec. com.). Office: Univ Dayton 300 College Pk Dayton OH 45469 E-mail: Daniel.Curran@notes.udayton.edu.*

CURRAN, DARRYL JOSEPH, photographer, educator; b. Santa Barbara, Calif., Oct. 19, 1935; s. Joseph Harold and Irma Marie (Schlagel) C.; m. Doris Jean Smith, July 12, 1968. AA, Ventura Coll., 1958; BA, UCLA, 1960, MA, 1964. Designer, installer UCLA Art Galleries, 1963-65; mem. faculty Los Angeles Harbor Coll., 1968-69, UCLA Ext., 1972-79, Sch. Art Inst. Chgo., 1975; prof. art Calif. State U., Fullerton, 1967-2001, chmn. art dept., 1989-99; curator various shows, 1971—. Bd. dirs. Los Angeles Center Photog. Studies, 1973-77, pres., 1980-83; juror Los Angeles Olympics Photog. Commns. Project, 1983. One-man shows include U. Chgo., 1975, U. R.I., 1975, Art Space, L.A., 1978, Photoworks Gallery, Richmond, Va., 1979, Alan Hancock Coll., Santa Maria, Calif., 1979, G. Ray Hawkins Gallery, L.A., 1981, Portland (Maine) Sch. Art, 1983, Grossmont Coll., San Diego, 1982, (retrospective) Chaffey Coll., Alta Loma, Calif., L.A. Ctr. for Photog. Studies, 1984, U. Calif. Ext. Ctr., San Francisco, 1986, Cuesta Coll., San Luis Obispo, Calif., 1992, Cypress Coll., 1993, Tex. Woman's U., Denton, 1997, Irvine Valley Coll., 1997, Ellen Kim Murphy Gallery, Santa Monica, 2000, William Marten Gallery, Rochester, N.Y., 2001, No. Ky. U., 2002, Carnegie Art Mus., Oxnard, Calif., 2003; two-person show No. Ky. U., 1995; group exhbns. include Laguna Mus. Art, San Francisco, 1992, Friends of Photography, San Francisco, 1993, U.S. Info. Agy. Empowered Images, 1994—, USIA, Jan Abrams Gallery, L.A., 1995; group exhbns. include Mt. St. Mary's Coll., 1997, Ranch Santiago Coll., 1997, Norton Simon Mus., Pasadena, 2006, Pasadena Mus. California Art, 2006, U. Ky., 2006; represented in permanent collections Mus. Modern Art, Royal Photog. Soc., London, Nat. Gallery Can., Ottawa, Mpls. Inst. Art, Oakland Mus., U. N.Mex., UCLA, Seagram's Collection, N.Y.C., Mus. Photog. Arts, San Diego, Phila. Mus. Art, J. Paul Getty Mus., Phila. Mus. Art, San Francisco Mus. Art. Bd. dirs. Cheviot Hills Home Owners Assn., 1973. Served with U.S. Army, 1954-56. Recipient Career Achievement award Calif. Mus. Photography, 1986; NEA Photographers fellow, 1980; Honored Educator award Soc. Photographic Edn., 1996. Mem. Soc. Photog. Edn. (dir. 1975-79, honored educator 1996). Home: 10537 Dunleer Dr Los Angeles CA 90064-4317 Personal E-mail: localdj@mindspring.com. *I am an artist with abstract expressionist sympathies who chooses to use the photographic medium in its broadest definition.*

CURRAN, EMILY KATHERINE, museum director; b. Boston, Mar. 27, 1960; d. George Morton and Gloria Rose (Martino) C.; m. John Vincent Callahan, Oct. 8, 1989; 1 dau., Clara Huiru. AB in Fine Arts, Bard Coll., 1982; MS in Mus. Leadership, Bank Street Coll., 1992. Sr. developer The Children's Mus., Boston, 1982-88; dir. edn. The Old South Meeting House, Boston, 1988-92, exec. dir., 1992—. Vis. cmty. artist Great George's Project, Liverpool, Eng., 1983. Author: Science Sensations, 1989, An Architectural History of the Old South Meeting House, 1995. Bd. dirs. Freedom Trail Found., Boston, 1992-97; elected mem. Colonial Soc. Mass., 1996—; mem., exec. com. mem. cmty. adv. bd. WGBH, Boston, 1996-99, vice chair, 1998-99. Mus. edn. fellow Bank Street Coll., 1989-91. Fellow Mass. Hist. Soc.; Mem. Am. Assn. Mus., Am. Assn. State and Local History, New Eng. Mus. Assn., Boston Mus. Educators' Roundtable (chair steering com. 1989-91). Office: Old South Meeting House 310 Washington St Boston MA 02108-4616

CURRAN, J. JOSEPH, JR., former state attorney general; b. West Palm Beach, Fla., July 7, 1931; s. J. Joseph Sr. and Catherine (Clark) Curran; m. Barbara Marie Atkins, 1959; children: Mary Carole, Alice Ann, Catherine Marie, J. Joseph III, William A.(dec.). LLB, U. Balt., 1959. Bar: Md. 1959, U.S. Dist. Ct. Md., U.S. Supreme Ct. 1987. Mem. Md. House of del., 1958—63; State senator from Md., 1963—82; lt. gov. State of Md., 1983—87, atty. gen. Balt., 1987—2007. Mem. Md. Regional Planning Coun., 1963—82. Mem.: Balt. Bar Assn., Md. Bar Assn. Democrat. Mailing: 5203 Springlake Way Baltimore MD 21212*

CURRAN, JAMES W., epidemiologist, educator, dean; b. Monroe, Mich., Sept. 16, 1944; married; 2 children. BS, U. Notre Dame, 1966; MD, U. Mich., 1970; MPH, Harvard U., 1974. Rsch. instr. dept. preventive and cmty. medicine U. Tenn. Med. Sch., 1971—73; career devel. tng. Ctr. Disease Control, USPHS, 1973—75; asst. commr. health med. svc. Columbus (Ohio) City Health Dept., 1975—78; chief oper. rsch. br. Venereal Disease Control Ctr. Disease Control and Prevention, 1978—82; dir. Acquired Immune Deficiency Syndrome Activ, 1982—84; chief AIDS br. Divsn. Viral Diseases, Ctr. Infectious Diseases, 1984—85; dir. WHO Referal Ctr. AIDS & Retroviruses, 1985—92; assoc. dir. human immunodeficiency virus/AIDS Ctr. Disease Control and Prevention, 1992—95; dean Rollins Sch. Pub. Health Emory U., Atlanta, 1995—. L. Vernon Scott lectr. U. Okla. Health Sci. Ctr., 1985; Verna & Mars lectr. Baylor Coll. Medicine, 1988; Oliver Cope lectr. Mass. Gen. Hosp., 1988; clin. rsch. investigator Venereal Disease Br., Ctr. Disease Control, 1971—73; med. dir. Influenza Immunization Program, Franklin County, 1976—77; clin. rsch. investigator, coord. Oper. Rsch. Bd., Venereal Disease Control Divsn., Ctr. Disease Control, 1975—78; clin. asst. prof. dept. preventive ve and cmty. medicine Coll. Medicine, Ohio State U., 1976—79; John Forbes fellow infectious disease Fairfield Hosp., Melbourne, Australia, 1985; vis. prof. Coll. Medicine, U. Ill., 1988; asst. surgeon gen. USHPS, 1991. Recipient William C. Watson Jr. award, 1987. Fellow: Am. Epidemiol. Soc., Am. Coll. Preventive Medicine, Infectious Disease Soc. Am.; mem.: AAAS, Am. Venereal Disease Assn., Inst. Medicine-NAS, Sigma Xi. Office: Emory U Rollins Sch Pub Health 1518 Clifton Rd NE Rm 1820 Atlanta GA 30322-4201

CURRAN, JOSEPH PATRICK, lawyer; b. Providence, Apr. 25, 1951; s. Joseph Patrick and Susan (Donohue) C.; m. Sheila Jane McGowan, July 14, 1974; children: Christopher, Peter. BA, Holy Cross Coll., 1973; MA, London Sch. Econs., 1974; JD, U. Mich., 1978. Bar: R.I. 1978. Spl. asst. to gen. counsel Office of Sec. USN, Washington, 1978-81; assoc. Hinckley, Allen & Snyder, Providence, 1981-86; ptnr. Hinckley, Allen & Snyder, Providence, 1986—. Editor U. Mich. Law Rev., 1976-78. Lt. USN, 1978—81. Mem. ABA, R.I. Bar Assn., Order of Coif. Home: 232 Taber Ave Providence RI 02906-3351 Office: Hinckley Allen Snyder 50 Kennedy Plz Providence RI 02903 Home Phone: 401-861-2278; Office Phone: 401-274-2000. E-mail: jcurran@haslaw.com.

CURRAN, LEIGH, actress, playwright; b. Santa Barbara, Calif., Dec. 5, 1943; d. John Van Benschoten and Barbara (Hansl) Griggs; m. Edward Herrmann, Sept. 9, 1978. Grad., Am. Mus. and Dramatic Acad., 1964. Mem. L.A. Women's Shakespeare Co., 1992—. Actress: (Broadway debut) How Now, Dow Jones, Lunt-Fontanne Theatre, 1968, (stage prodns.) The Lunch Girls, 1977 (also author), 'night, Mother, 1985, Stitchers and Starlight Talkers, 1986, Walking The Blonde, 1989 (also author), The 52nd Street Project, 1987-91, (feature films) I Never Promised You a Rose Garden, 1977, Reds, 1981, (TV series) Adam's Rib, 1974, St. Elsewhere, 1985, Another World, 1986, L.A. Law, 1991, West Wing, 2002, Judging Amy, 2002 author: (play) Alterations, Useful Trash, Zone 13 Hair, Michelle Hammer, Girl Detective, Destiny, Destiny, Destiny, Pressed Against Strangers; (teleplays) The Paper Chase, St. Elsewhere; founder, artistic dir. The Virginia Avenue Project, 1991—. Mem. AFTRA, Actors' Equity Assn., Screen Actors Guild, Writers Guild, Dramatists Guild, Women in Film. Office: Va Ave Project 3000 W Olympic Blvd Santa Monica CA 90404 Office Phone: 310-264-4224.

CURRAN, LISA M., environmental scientist, educator; AB with honors in Anthropology, Harvard U., 1984; PhD in Ecology and Evolutionary Biology, Princeton U., 1994. Mercer postdoctoral fellow Harvard U., 1994—96; asst. prof. ecol. sustainability dept. biology U. Mich., 1996—2001; assoc. prof. tropical resources Sch. Forestry and Environ. Studies Yale U., 2001—06, prof., 2006—. Bd. mem. Tropical Forest Found., 1999—; vis. rsch. fellow ecosystems and governance prog. East West Ctr., Honolulu, 2001—02; John Musser dir. Yale U. Tropical Resource Inst., 2001—; external faculty Santa Fe Inst., 2003—; cons. Contbr. articles to profl. jours.; mem. editl. bd.: Environ. Rsch. Letters, 2006—. MacArthur fellow, John D. and Catherine T. MacArthur Found., 2006. Mem.: Soc. Conservation Biology, Internat. Soc. Tropical Foresters, Assn. Tropical Biologists, Am. Geophys. Union, AAAS, Ecol. Soc. Am. (Aldo Leopold Leadership Program fellow 2004—). Office: Sch Forestry & Environ Studies Yale U 370 Prospect St New Haven CT 06511 E-mail: lisa.curran@yale.edu.

CURRAN, LOUIS JEROME, JR., choral master; b. Meriden, Conn., June 13, 1934; s. Louis Jerome and Gertrude Marie (Frederick) C. Mus.B. (H.B. Jepson scholar), Yale U., 1956, postgrad., 1959-62, New Eng. Conservatory Music, 1956-57, Oxford U., 1963-65; Mus.M., U. Tulsa, 1963. Organist, master of choristers Cathedral Ch. St. Mary, Fall River, Mass., 1956-57; dir. music 1st Congl. Ch., Wallingford, Conn., 1960-62; asso. prof. music N.E. Mo. State U., Kirksville, 1965-66; dir. music Central Congl. Ch., Worcester, Mass., 1966-67, Grace Episcopal Ch., Amherst, Mass., 1967-68; dir. music, master of choristers Ch. of St. Peter, Worcester, 1970-82, Ch. of Notre Dame, Worcester, 1982-85; founding full prof. dept. music Worcester Poly. Inst., 1966—2005. Also European and Am. concert tours including Cathedrals of Canterbury, Worcester, Chichester, Wells, Westminster Abbey, Notre Dame, Paris, Basilica, Madrid, St. Peter's Basilica, Rome, St. Francis Basilica, Assisi, Italy, Nat. Radio TV, Brussels. Mem. Worcester Cultural Commn., 1978-80. Served with AUS, 1958-59. Recipient Beacon prize Universalist Unitarian Ch., 1993; Fulbright scholar Oxford U. Mem. Orgn. Hist. Soc., Intercollegiate Mus. Council (nat. bd. 1977-80), Am. Guild Organists, Am. Musical Soc., Coll. Music Soc., Am. Choral Dirs. Assn. Democrat. Episcopalian. Home: 141 Main St S Meriden CT 06451-5120 Address: 12335 Oak Brook Ct Fort Myers FL 33908

CURRAN, MARY, lawyer; b. NYC, Aug. 29, 1947; d. Philip Joseph and Catherine Mary (Galvin) C.; m. John Michael Quigley, Feb. 4, 1978; children: Oliver, Jane-Claire. AB, Fordham U., 1969; JD, Yale U., 1981; PhD, Columbia U., 1992. Bar: Calif. 1981, U.S. Dist. Ct. (no. and ctrl. dists.) Calif. 1981, 90. Asst. prof. Yale U., New Haven, 1975-79; assoc. McCutchen, Doyle, Brown & Enersen, San Francisco, 1981-84; sr. atty. Dean Witter Reynolds, Inc., San Francisco, 1984-85, v.p., 1985-87, asst. gen. counsel, 1987-92, sr. v.p., assoc. gen. counsel, 1992-97; gen. counsel, sr. v.p. Morgan Stanley Dean Witter Online, San Francisco, 1997—2002; mng. dir., gen. counsel Sutton Place Mgmt., LLC, San Francisco, 2002—. Mem. ABA, State Bar Calif., Bar Assn. San Francisco (cert. of commendation 1990-91). Office: Sutton Place Mgmt LLC 433 California St 11th Fl San Francisco CA 94104 Business E-Mail: mcurran@forwardmgmt.com.

CURRAN, MAURICE FRANCIS, lawyer; b. Yonkers, NY, Feb. 20, 1931; s. James F. and Mary (O'Brien) C.; m. Deborah M. Dee, May 7, 1960; children: James, Maurice, Amy, Bridget, Ceara, Sara. Student, Cathedral Coll., 1950; BA in Philosophy, St. Joseph Coll. and Sem., 1952; LLB, Fordham U., 1958. Bar: N.Y. 1958, U.S. Dist. Ct. (so. and ea. dists.) N.Y. 1960, U.S. Ct. Appeals (2d cir.) 1982, U.S. Supreme Ct. Assoc. Kelley, Drye, Newhall & Maginnes, NYC, 1958-60, Wilson & Bave, Yonkers, 1960-65; divsn. counsel Merck & Co., Rahway, N.J., 1965-67; asst. gen. counsel E.R. Squibb & Sons, Inc., NYC, 1967-70; corp. counsel, chief law dept. City of Yonkers, 1970-72; ptnr. Bleakley, Platt, Schmidt & Fritz, White Plains, N.Y., 1972-83, Banks, Curran & Schwam, LLP, Mt. Kisco, NY, 1983—2005; counsel Banks, Curran, Schwamm & Squirrell, LLP, Mt. Kisco, NY, 2005—. Past trustee, vice chmn. Westchester CC. Capt. USMCR, 1952-58. Mem. Fed. Bar Coun., Assn. Bar City N.Y. Roman Catholic. Home: 388 Bronxville Rd Bronxville NY 10708-1233 Office: 61 Smith Ave Mount Kisco NY 10549-2813 Home Phone: 914-337-3511; Office Phone: 914-666-2161.

CURRAN, MICHAEL J., finance company executive; Grad., Collgate U. Sr. v.p. Fleet Bank, 1993—99; dir. global svcs. FleetBoston Fin. Corp., 1999—. Mem. Fleet's Adv. Group, Fleet's Corp. Diversity Coun., Fleet's eCatalyst Exec. Panel.

CURRAN, MICHAEL J., stock exchange executive; BA in economics, Dickinson Coll., Carlisle, Pa., 1976. Sys. engr. Electronic Data Sys., 1977; mgr. info. sys. Peat, Marwick, Mitchell & Co.; mgr. data processing and strategic planning Apollo Computer; mgr. to ptnr. Coopers & Lybrand, 1986—93; CIO Scudder Stevens & Clark, 1994—96; pres. Kemper Svc. Co., 1998—2000; COO internat. mutual funds Scudder Kemper Investments, 2000—01; pres. Scudder Can., 2000—01; CIO Boston Stock Exch., 2001—03, COO, 2003—04, CEO, 2004—, acting chmn., 2004, now chmn. Adv. bd. Hickory Hill Ventures LLC; bd. mem. Midwest ISO. Office: Boston Stock Exch 100 Franklin St Boston MA 02110 Office Phone: 617-235-2000. Office Fax: 617-235-2200.*

CURRAN, MICHAEL WALTER, management scientist; b. St. Louis, Dec. 6, 1935; s. Clarence Maurice and Helen Gertrude (Parsons) Curran; m. Jeanette Lucille Rawizza, Sept. 24, 1955 (div. 1977); children: Kevin Michael, Karen Ann, Kathleen Marie(dec.) , Kimberly Elizabeth; m. Mary Jane Lemanek, Aug. 18, 1981. BS, Washington U., St. Louis, 1964. With Monsanto Co., St. Louis, 1953-65, supervisory positions dept. adminstrv. services, 1956-64, rsch. technician inorganic chems. divsn., 1964-65; sr. ops. rsch. analyst Pet Inc., St. Louis, 1965-68; CEO, dir. Decision Scis. Corp., St. Louis, 1968—, chmn. bd., 2007—. Former mem. adv. bd. Entrepreneurial Bus. Ctr., U. Mo., St. Louis; judge Tech. Excellence Awards, St. Louis, 2002—04. Co-author: (book) Handbook of Budgeting, 1981, Handbook of Budgeting, 4th edit., 1999, Effective Project Management Through Applied Cost and Schedule Control, 1996; editor: Professional Practice Guide to Risk, Vols. 1-3, 1998; contbr. articles to profl. jours. Adviser Jr. Achievement, St. Louis, 1958—59; active United Way, 1958—62. Fellow: Assn. Advancement Cost Engring. (chmn. risk mgmt. com. 1991—, mem. editl. adv. com. 1997—, Tech. Excellence award 2000); mem.: Soc. Cost Estimating and Analysis, Project Mgmt. Inst., Ops. Rsch. Soc. Am., Inst. Mgmt. Scis. (chmn. St. Louis chpt. 1971—72), Intertel, Mensa, Alpha Sigma Lambda, Sigma Xi. Achievements include development of theories of bracket budgeting and range estimating; theories of risk established value, value-based risk management and bubble management; provoke-to-evoke data elicitation methodology. Office: Decision Scis Corp PO Box 28848 Saint Louis MO 63123-0048 Office Phone: 314-739-2662.

CURRAN, PATRICIA A., retail executive; Positions from hourly assoc. through regional v.p. & div. mdse. mgr. Wal-Mart Stores Inc., Bentonville, Ark., 1983—2003, sr. v.p. store ops., 2003—05, exec. v.p. store ops., 2005—07, exec. v.p. people, 2007—. Mem. Coca-Cola Retailing Rsch. Council, Ctr. for Retailing Excellence, Sam M. Walton Coll. Bus., Univ. Ark. Mem. Single Parent Scholarship Fund Wash. County. Named one of 50 Most Powerful Women in Bus., Fortune mag., 2006, 50 Women to Watch, Wall St. Jour., 2006. Mem.: Network of Exec. Women. Office: Wal-Mart Stores Inc 702 SW Eighth St Bentonville AR 72716*

CURRAN, ROBERT BRUCE, lawyer; b. Charleston, W.Va., July 2, 1948; s. Bruce Frederick and Hazel Viola (Hoy) C.; children: Michael Robert, Laura Elizabeth, Emily Ann. BA, U. Del., 1971; JD, U. Md., 1974. Bar: Md. 1974. Ptnr. Frank, Bernstein, Conaway & Goldman, Balt., 1974-92, Whiteford Taylor & Preston, Balt., 1992—. Co-author: Tax Planning Forms for Businesses and Individuals, 1985. Mem. Md. Bar Assn. (sec. and treas. taxation sect. 1985-86, chmn. taxation sect. 1987-88). Office: Whiteford Taylor & Preston 7 Saint Paul St Baltimore MD 21202-1626 Home Phone: 410-821-7320; Office Phone: 410-347-9472. Business E-Mail: rcurran@wtplaw.com.

CURRAN, WARD SCHENK, economist, educator; b. Springfield, Ill., June 26, 1935; s. Nathaniel Buckmaster and Clara Marguerite (Schenk) C.; m. Kathleen Marie Jannett, Nov. 25, 1963; children: Andrea Jannett, Colleen Thayer. AB, Trinity Coll., Hartford, Conn., 1957; MA, Columbia U., 1958, PhD, 1963. Mem. faculty Trinity Coll., Hartford, 1960—, prof. econs., 1971—, George M. Ferris prof. corp. fin. and investments, 1981—2005, Ward S. Curran disting. prof. econs., 2006—. Vis. prof. Yale U., Wesleyan U., Middletown, Conn.; mem. Gov. Conn. Commn. Higher Edn.; cons. adv. in field. Author: An Economic Approach to Regulation of the Corporate Securities Market, 1976, Principles of Financial Management, 1970, Principles of Corporate Finance, 1988; also articles, revs. Mem. Am. Econ. Assn., Am. Fin. Assn., Fin. Mgmt. Assn. Office: Trinity Coll Dept Econs 300 Summit St Hartford CT 06106-3100 Office Phone: 860-297-2489.

CURRAN, WILLIAM P., lawyer; b. Mpls., Feb. 27, 1946; s. William P. and Margaret L. (Killoren) C.; m. Jean L. Stabenow, Jan. 1, 1978; children: Patrick, Lisa, John. BA, U. Minn., 1969; JD, U. Calif., Berkeley, 1972. Law clk. Nev. Supreme Ct., Carson City, 1973-74, state ct. adminstr., 1973-74; assoc. Wiener, Goldwater & Galatz, Las Vegas, Nev., 1974-75; chief dept. dist. atty. Clark County Dist. Atty.'s Office, Las Vegas, 1975-79; county counsel Clark County, Las Vegas, 1979-89; pvt. practice Las Vegas, 1989-94; ptnr. Curran & Parry, Las Vegas, 1994; now ptnr., real estate dept, mng. ptnr., Las Vegas, Ballard Spahr Andrews & Ingersoll LLP, Las Vegas. Co-author: Nevada Judicial Orientation Manual, 1974. Mem. Nev. Gaming Commn., 1989-99, chmn., 1991-99. Recipient Educator Yr. award UNLV Internat. Gaming Inst., 1998. Mem. ABA (state del. 1994-, bd. govs., 2004-), Internat. Assn. Gaming Regulators (chmn. 1992-94), Nat. Assn. County Civil Attys. (pres. 1984-85), State Bar Nev. (pres. 1988-89). Democrat. Roman Catholic. Office: Ballard Spahr Andrews & Ingersoll LLP BOA Plz Ste 1201 300 S Fourth St Las Vegas NV 89101 Office Phone: 702-471-7000. Business E-Mail: curranb@ballardspahr.com.

CURRERI, PETER WILLIAM, health facility administrator, consultant; b. Milw., Sept. 2, 1936; s. Anthony Rudolph and Dorothea Christiana (Heubsch) C.; m. Patricia Ann Egry, Aug. 14, 1958 (div. 1975); children: Charles Anthony, James Bradley, Regina Dawn. BA, Swarthmore Coll., 1958; MD, U. Pa., 1962. Intern Hosp. of U. Pa., 1962-63, resident in surgery, 1963-68; asst. prof. surgery U. Tex., Southwestern Med. Ctr., Dallas, 1971-74; assoc. prof. surgery U. Wash. Med. Sch., Seattle, 1974-77; prof. surgery Cornell U. Med. Ctr., NYC, 1977-81; prof., chmn. surgery U. South Ala. Med. Sch., Mobile, Ala., 1981—88; chmn. Strategem of Ala., Inc., Daphne, 1988—. Mem. surgery anesthesiology and trauma study sect. NIH, Washington, 1980-84, chmn., 1986-88; commr. Physician Payment Rev. Commn., Washington, 1988-97; mem. Medicare Payment Adv. Com., 1997-99. Contbr. articles to profl. jours. Lt. col. U.S. Army, 1968-71. Decorated Meritorious Svc. medal; recipient Rsch. Career Devel. award NIH, 1972, Curtis P. Artz award Am. Trauma Soc., 1989. Mem. Am. Assn. for Surgery of Trauma (pres. 1989-90), Am. Burn Assn. (pres. 1983-84), Am. Coll. Surgeons (sec. bd. govs. 1987-89), Halstead Surg. Soc. (pres. 1988-89), Soc. Univ. Surgeons (pres. 1980-81), Assn. Acad. Surgery (recorder 1972-74). Baptist. Avocations: golf, walking. Office: Strategem Inc 26064 Capital Dr Ste A Daphne AL 36526-6166 Office Phone: 251-625-2205. Personal E-mail: curcur@msn.com.

CURREY, CECIL BARR, retired history professor; b. Clarks, Nebr., Nov. 29, 1932; s. Cecil Chalmers Currey and Edith Estelle Barr; m. Laura Gene Hewett, Aug. 14, 1952; children: Samuel Bowman, Anne Estelle, Laura Alise. BA, Ft. Hays State U., 1958, MS, 1959; PhD, U. Kans., 1965. From asst. to assoc. prof. history Nebr. Wesleyan U., Lincoln, 1964—67; prof. mil. history U. So. Fla., Tampa, 1967—2001, prof. emeritus, 2002—. Vis. prof. U. Nebr., 1966-67; vis. prof. mil. history U. Hawaii, Honolulu, summers 1991, 92; ednl. cons., 1967-98; mil. analyst Desert Shield/Desert Storm, various T.V. stas., 1990-91; invited spkr. Viet Nam Fgn. Ministry, Hanoi, 1988. Author: Road to Revolution: Benjamin Franklin in England, 1765-1775, 1968, Code Number 72, 1973, Follow Me and Die: The Destruction of an American Division in World War II, 1984, Edward Lansdale: The Unquiet American, 1989, Victory at Any Cost: The Genius of Viet Nam's General Vo Nguyen Giap, 1996 (Pulitzer nomination 1997), Long Binh Jail: An Oral History of the U.S. Army's Notorious Prison in Viet Nam, (novel) Innocence Dies, 1999, (novel) A Time to Remember, 2004; works translated into 6 langs.; contbr. to books, encys., and dictionaries, over 25 articles to profl. publs. Col. USAR, 1953-92. Grantee U. So. Fla. Rsch. Found., 1988, 89; recipient Disting. Alumni award Ft. Hays State U., 1975. Mem. Assn. 3d World Studies (book prize 1997). Avocation: travel. Home: 3330 Crenshaw Lake Rd Lutz FL 33548 Personal E-mail: cbcthor123@aol.com.

CURREY, THOMAS ARTHUR, ophthalmologist; b. Itawamba County, Miss., July 9, 1933; s. Charles Edward and Anna L. (Williams) C; m. Carol Ann Clabough, Nov. 7, 1959; children: Thomas A. Jr., C. Russell. Degree, U. Miss., 1955; MD, U. Tenn., 1958. Diplomate Am. Bd. Ophthalmology. Intern City of Memphis Hosps., 1958-59; resident in ophthalmology U. Tenn., Memphis, 1962-65; pvt. practice Memphis, 1965—; mem. staff St. Francis Hosp., 1965—, pres. med. staff, 1985. Assoc. instr. ophthalmology dept. family practice, 1990—, asst. clin. instr. ophthalmology U. Tenn., 1965—. Fellow ACS; mem. Tenn. Med. Assn. (v.p. 1987), Tenn. Acad. Ophthalmology (pres. 1975), Memphis & Shelby County Med. Soc. (treas. 1983-86). Office: Eye Specialists Assoc PC 1900 Kirby Pky Memphis TN 38138-3690 Office Phone: 901-754-0930. Personal E-mail: tcurrey901@aol.com.

CURRIE, BARBARA FLYNN, state legislator; b. LaCrosse, Wis., May 3, 1940; d. Frank T. And Elsie R. (Gobel) Flynn; m. David P. Currie, Dec. 29, 1959; children: Stephen Francis, Margaret Rose. AB cum laude, U. Chgo., 1968, AM, 1973. Asst. study dir. Nat. Opinion Rsch. Ctr., Chgo., 1973-77; part time instr. polit. sci. DePaul U., Chgo., 1973-74; mem. Ill. Ho. of Reps., 1979—, chmn. House Dem. Study Group, 1980-83, asst. majority leader, 1993, asst. minority leader, 1995, majority leader, 1997. V.p. Chgo. LWV, 1965-69; mem. Ind. Voters of Ill., Ill. Conf. Women Legislators, Ind. Precinct Orgn., Hyde Park Coop. Named Legislator of Yr., NASW, 1984, 1997, Ill. Women's Substance Abuse Coalition, 1984, Illinoisan of Yr., Ill. News Broadcasters Assn., 2001; recipient awards, Welfare Rights Coalition of Orgns., Ill. Pub. Action Coun., Chgo. Heart Assn., BEST BETS award, Nat. Ctr. Policy Alternatives, 1988, Svc. award, Nat. Ctr. for Freedom of Info. Studies, 1989, Beautiful Person award, Chgo. Urban League, 1989, Friend of Labor award, Ill. AFL-CIO, 1990, Ill. Maternal and Child Health Coalition award, 1990, Ill. Hunger Coalition award, 1991, cert. of appreciation, SEIU Local 880, 1989, March of Dimes, 1988, Chgo. Tchrs. Union, Ill. Hosp. Assn., Ptnr. Vision award, Families' and Children's AIDS Network, Woman of Vision award, Women's Bar Assn. Ill., 1997, Nat. Elected Pub. Ofcl. award, NASW, 1997, Outstanding Working Woman of Ill. award, Ill. Fedn. Bus. and Profl. Women, Dist. Pub. Health Legislator award, Am. Pub. Health Assn., 1999, Legis. award, Ill. Primary Health Care Assn., 2002, Ill. Press Assn., 2003, Legis. of Yr. award, Access Living, 2003, others, Environment Leadership award, Ill. Environ. Coun., 2005, Outstanding Elected Ofcl. award, Campaign for Better Health Care, 2006. Mem.: LWV, ACLU (bd. dirs. Ill.). Office: Ill Gen Assembly 300 State House Springfield IL 62706-0001 Office Phone: 773-667-0550.

CURRIE, BRUCE, artist; b. Sac City, Iowa, Nov. 27, 1911; s. Malcolm and Clara Mabel (Austin) C.; m. Ethel Magafan, June 30, 1946; 1 dau., Jenne Magafan. Student, Northwestern U., 1930-32, U. Chgo., 1932-33. One-man shows include Am. Embassy, Athens, Greece, 1952, Ganso Gallery, NYC, 1953, 54, Roko Gallery, 1958, 60, Albany Inst. History and Art, 1958, Ulster County CC, Kingston, NY, 1967, Joseloff Gallery, U. Hartford, 1968, Schenectady Mus., 1970, Jacques Seligmann Galleries, NYC, 1978, Midtown Galleries, NYC, 1980, 83, retrospective exhbns. Woodstock (NY) Artists Assn., 1993, Windham (NY) Fine Arts, 2004, Twentieth Century Contemporaries Gallery, Hudson, NY, 2005; represented in permanent collections SUNY-Albany, Dwight Art Meml., Mt. Holyoke Coll., Colorado Springs Fine Arts Ctr., Butler Inst. Am. Art, Kalamazoo Inst. Arts, N.A.D., Ulster County CC, Kingston, Berkshire CC. Served with USAAF, 1942-45, ETO. Decorated European - African - Middle Ea. Theater ribbon with 1 Silver and 1 Bronze Battle Star; recipient Purchase award Henry Ward Ranger Fund, N.A.D., 1964, 75, Clarke prize, 1966, Benjamin Altman figure prize, 1979, Gold medal of honor Nat. Arts Club, 1964; Albany Inst. History and Art award, 1967, Berle award Berkshire Art Assn., 1967, purchase award, 1973, Soletsky award Nat. Soc. Painters in Casein and Acrylic, 1973, Grumbacher award, 1974, John J. Newman Meml. award, 1976, Wallach Meml. award, 1980, Wright Meml. prize Cooperstown Art Assn., 1978, grand prize, 1981, also others. Mem. NAD (acad.), Audubon Artists (life, Medal of Honor 1963, 82, 98, Joseph Raskin Meml. award 1987, Ralph Fabri Medal of Honor 1989, Emily Lowe award 1990, Silver medal 1998Richeson award 2000, Salmagundi award 2002), Am. Watercolor Soc. (Silver medal 1958, Emily Lowe award 1968, Whitney award 1975, Winsor-Newton award 1981, Mario Cooper award 1985, Elsie and David WU Ject-Key Meml. award 1997), Adirondack Nat. Exhbn. of Am. Watercolors (Martin award 1988, Smith Packing Co. award 1990), Conn. Acad. Fine Arts (prize for Painting, 1965, Charles Noel Flagg Meml. prize 1968). Home: 72 Boggs Hill Rd Woodstock NY 12498-2706 Office Phone: 845-679-2170.

CURRIE, CAMERON MCGOWAN, federal judge; b. 1948; BA, U. S.C., 1970; JD with honors, George Washington U., 1975. Tchr. Moultrie H.S., Mt. Pleasant; law intern to magistrate judge Hon. Arthur L. Burnett U.S. Dist. Ct. D.C., 1973-74; atty. Arent, Fox, Kintner, Plotkin & Kahn, Washington, 1975-78; asst. U.S. Atty. Office U.S. Atty., Washington, 1978-80, Columbia, S.C., 1980-84; magistrate judge U.S. Dist. Ct. S.C., Columbia, 1984-86; pvt. practice Columbia, 1986-89; chief dep. atty. gen. Office Atty. Gen., State of S.C., Columbia, 1989-94; judge U.S. Dist. Ct. S.C., Columbia, 1994—. Adj. prof. in trial advocacy Sch. Law U. S.C., 1986-89. Assoc. editor SEC No Action Letters Index, 1972-73. Bd. dirs. Wings, Inc., 1986-94, sec., 1992-94. Mem. S.C. Bar, D.C. Bar, S.C. Women Lawyers Assn., Fed. Judges Assn., John Belton O'Neall Inn of Ct. Office: US Dist Ct 901 Richland St Columbia SC 29201

CURRIE, CHARLES LEONARD, educational association administrator; b. Phila., July 9, 1930; s. Charles Leonard and Elizabeth Katherine (Harper) C. AB, Boston Coll., 1955, MA, 1956; PhL, Weston Coll., 1956; PhD, Cath. U. Am., 1961; STB, Woodstock Coll., 1962, STL, 1964; DSc (hon.), Bethany Coll., 1975; LLD (hon.), W.Va. Wesleyan Coll., 1982; DLitt (hon.), U. Cin., 1984; DSc (hon.), St. Thomas Inst., 1984; DHL (hon.), Hebrew Union Coll., 1986. Joined S.J., Roman Cath. Ch., 1950; vis. scientist Nat. Bur. Stds., Washington, 1961—62, NRC, Ottawa, Canada, 1963—65; postdoctoral rsch. fellow Cambridge U., Eng., 1965—66; asst. prof. chemistry Georgetown U., Washington, 1966—72, dir. bicentennial, 1986—90; pres. Wheeling Coll., W.Va., 1972—82, Xavier U., Cin., 1982—86; sr. fellow Woodstock Theol. Ctr., Washington, 1990—91; rector Jesuit cmty. St. Joseph's U., Phila., 1991—97, prof. Theology and Sci.; pres. Assn. Jesuit Colls. and Univs., Washington, 1997—. Bd. dirs. Coll. Holy Cross, St. Peter's Coll., U. Scranton, St. Joseph's U., Oak Knoll Sch., Summit, NJ, Linsly Inst., St. Joseph's Prep, W.Va. Found.; chmn. W.Va. Bd. Miner Tng. Contbr. articles to profl. jours. V.p., bd. dirs. United Way Upper Ohio Valley. Recipient Sci. and Theology award, Templeton Found., 1995. Mem. Am. Chem. Soc., Chem. Soc. (London), NY Acad. Scis., Washington Acad. Scis., AAUP. Am. Assn. Univ. Adminstrs., Sigma Xi, Am. Coun. Edn. (bd. dirs.), Assn. Jesuit Colls. and Univs., Assn. Ind. Colls. and Univs. of Ohio, Ohio Coll. Assn., W.Va. Assn. Pvt. Colls., W.Va. Assn. Coll. and Univ. Pres., W.Va. C. of C., Comml. Club, Cin., Queen City Club, Cin. Clubs: Rotary; Univ., Pitts. Office: Assn Jesuit Colls and Univs One Dupont Cir Ste 405 Washington DC 20036 Office Phone: 202-862-9893. Office Fax: 202-862-8523.*

CURRIE, DAVID PARK, law educator; b. Macon, Ga., May 29, 1936; s. Gillette Brainerd and Elmyr (Park) C.; m. Barbara Suzanne Flynn, Dec. 29, 1959; children: Stephen Francis, Margaret Rose. BA, U. Chgo., 1957; LLB, Harvard U., 1960. Bar: Ill. 1963. Law clk. to Hon. Henry J. Friendly U.S. Ct. Appeals (2d cir.), NYC, 1960-61; to Hon. Felix Frankfurter U.S. Supreme Ct., Washington, 1961-62; asst. prof. law U. Chgo., 1962-65, assoc. prof., 1965-68, prof., 1968—, Edward H. Levi Disting. Svc. prof., 1991—2006, prof. emeritus, 2006—. Vis. prof. Stanford (Calif.) U. Law Sch., 1965, U. Mich. Law Sch., Ann Arbor, 1964, 68, U. Hanover, Germany, 1981, U. Frankfurt, Germany, 1986, U. Heidelberg, Germany, 1989, U. Tubingen, Germany, 1996, U. Aix-Marseille, France, 1998; coord. environ. quality State of Ill., Chgo., 1970; chmn. Ill. Pollution Control Bd., Chgo., 1970-72. Author: Cases and Materials on Federal Courts, 1968, 4th edit., 1990, On Pollution, 1975, On Conflict of Laws, 1968, 6th edit., 2001, Federal Jurisdiction in a Nutshell, 1976, 81, 90, 99, Air Pollution: Federal Law and Analysis, 1981, Constitution in the Supreme Court, 2 vols., 1985, 1990, Constitution of the Federal Republic of Germany, 1994, Constitution in Congress, 4 vols., 1997, 2001, 05. Mem. Am. Acad. Arts and Scis. Office: U Chgo Law Sch 1111 E 60th St Chicago IL 60637-2776 Business E-Mail: david_currie@law.uchicago.edu.

CURRIE, EDWARD JONES, JR., lawyer; b. Jackson, Miss., May 23, 1951; s. Edward J. and Nell (Branton) C.; m. Barbara Scott Miller, June 26, 1976; children: Morgan E., Scott E. BA, U. Miss., 1973, JD, 1976. Bar: Miss. 1976, U.S. Dist. Ct. (no. and so. dists.) Miss. 1976, U.S. Ct. Appeals (5th cir.) 1978, U.S. Supreme Ct. 1979. Assoc. Wise, Carter, Child, Steen & Caraway, Jackson, 1976—80; ptnr. Steen, Reynolds, Dalehite & Currie, Jackson, 1980—94, Currie Johnson Griffin Gaines & Myers, P.A., Jackson, 1994—. Adj. prof. Miss. Coll. Sch. Law, Jackson, 1977-81, 84-86. Bd. dirs. Miss. chpt. Am. Diabetes Assn., Jackson, 1980—82, 2004—. Named a Super Lawyer of Mid South, 2006; named one of The Best Lawyers in Am., 2005, 2006. Mem. Fed. Bar Assn. (pres. Miss. chpt. 1989, adv. com. Miss. rules of civil procedure), Internat. Assn. Def. Coun. (trial acad. faculty 1992), Nat. Inst. Trial Advocacy, Nat. Lawyers Assn. (chmn. ins. sect. 1998-99), Fedn. Def. and Corp. Counsel, Nat. Lawyers Assn. Found. (bd. dirs. 1998-00), Miss. Jud. Coll. (model civil jury instrn. com. 1991), Miss. Def. Lawyers Assn. (bd. dirs. 2000-2003, v.p., pres. 2005), Miss. Bar Assn. (bd. dirs. young lawyers sect. 1981-82, chmn. litigation/gen. practice sect. 1992, mem. MDP Task Force 2000), Jackson Young Lawyers (bd. dirs. 1980-81), Hinds County Bar Assn., Miss. Bar Found., Phi Delta Phi, Sigma Alpha Epsilon (pres. Ctrl. Miss. alumni 1981), Omicron Delta Kappa. Presbyterian. Home: 50 Moss Forest Cir Jackson MS 39211-2905 Office: Currie Johnson Griffin Gaines & Myers PA PO Box 750 Jackson MS 39205-0750

CURRIE, FRANCIS SPARRE, lawyer; b. NYC, Apr. 12, 1950; s. Francis and Teresita (Sparre) C.; m. Christine Lachaze, Aug. 26, 1978; children: Katherine, Caroline, Elizabeth. BA magna cum laude, Harvard U., 1972, JD, 1975; attended, Inst. d'Etudes Politiques, Paris. Bar: Calif. 1975. Ptnr. Pillsbury, Madison & Sutro, San Francisco, 1975-84, Wilson, Sonsini, Goodrich & Rosati, Palo Alto, Calif., 1984—, Davis Polk & Wardwell, Menlo Park, Calif., 1999—. Mem. State Bar Calif. Democrat. Roman Catholic. Office: Davis Polk & Wardwell 1600 El Camino Real Menlo Park CA 94025 Office Phone: 650-752-2002. Office Fax: 650-752-3602. Business E-Mail: frank.currie@dpw.com.

CURRIE, JOHN THORNTON (JACK CURRIE), retired investment banker; b. Houston, Aug. 4, 1928; s. John Felix and Irma Lillian (Haxthausen) C.; m. Dorothy Lee Peek, May 30, 1959; children: Harriss Thornton, Laura Graef. BA, U. Tex., 1949, BBA, 1950. Salesman Harris, Upham & Co., NYC and Houston, 1950-52; ptnr. Moreland, Brandenberger & Currie, Galveston, Tex., 1955-60; pres., bd. dirs. Moroney, Beissner & Co., Inc., Houston, 1960-74; sr. v.p., bd. dirs. Rotan Mosle Inc., Houston, 1974-81, chmn., 1981-83; vice chmn. Rotan Mosle Fin. Corp., Houston, 1984; mng. dir. Mason Best Co., Houston, 1984-86. Bd. dirs. family mut. funds managed by Am. Nat. Ins. Co., Galveston, Artspace Inc., Mpls., Minn., Internat. Exec. Svc. Corps.; rep. Muslim Comml. Bank, Karachi, Pakistan, 1992, Govt. of Lithuania, Vilnius, 1993, Capital Ptnrs., Bratislava, Slovakia, 1997. Trustee Holly Hall, Houston, 1968-73, Harris and Eliza Kempner Fund, Galveston, Tex., 1975—03; mem. devel. bd. U. Tex. Health Sci. Ctr., Houston, 1978-89, U. Tex. Med. Br., Galveston, 1992—; mem. Chancellor's Coun. U. Tex. System; established Mary Tucker Currie Professorship, Tex. A&M U.; 1st lt. U.S. Army, 1952-54. Mem.: Krewe of Momus Galveston, Galveston Artillery Club, Houston Country Club. Republican. Episcopalian. Avocations: sailing, hunting, history. Home: 323 Longwoods Ln Houston TX 77024-5615 Office: 520 Post Oak Blvd Ste 125 Houston TX 77027-9495 *The acquisition of material goods makes life comfortable. Love received and given is the only real hallmark of a successful life.*

CURRIE, MALCOLM RODERICK, aerospace and automotive executive, research scientist; b. Spokane, Wash., Mar. 13, 1927; s. Erwin Casper and Genevieve (Hauenstein) C.; m. Sunya Lofsky, June 24, 1951; children: Deborah, David, Diana; m. Barbara L. Dyer, Mar. 5, 1977. AB, U. Calif., Berkeley, 1949, MS, 1951, PhD, 1954. Rsch. engr. Microwave Lab., U. Calif. at Berkeley, 1949-52; elec. engring. faculty microwave lab. U. Calif., Berkeley, 1953-54; lectr. UCLA, 1955-57; rsch. engr. Hughes Aircraft Co., 1954-57, v.p., 1965-66; head electron dynamics dept. Hughes Rsch. Labs., Culver City, Calif., 1957-60, dir. physics lab. Malibu, Calif., 1960-61, asso. dir., 1961-63, v.p., dir. rsch. labs., 1963-65, v.p., mgr. R & D divsn., 1965-69; v.p. R & D Beckman Instruments, Inc., 1969-73; undersec. rsch. and engring. dept. Office Sec. Def., Washington, 1973-77; pres. missile sys. group Hughes Aircraft Co., Canoga Park, Calif., 1977-83, exec. v.p., 1983-88, CEO, chmn. bd. dirs., 1988—, also bd. dirs.; pres., CEO Delco Electronics Corp., 1986-88. Chmn., CEO Hughes Aircraft Co., 1988—92, chmn. emeritus, 1992—; CEO Currie Techs. Inc., 1997—2003; bd. dirs. Innovative Micro Techs., Regal One, Enova Sys. Corp., Real Spirit; bd. overseers Keck Med. Sch., U. So. Calif.; trustee U. So. Calif., 1989—, chmn., 1995—2000, Real Spirit USA, Inc. Contbr. articles to profl. jours.; patentee in field. Mem. adv. bd. U. Calif., Berkeley, UCLA, Galaxy Edn. Inst., Calif. Coun. Sci. and Tech.; former chmn. bd. trustees U. So. Calif., 1989; trustee Howard U., 1989-92, UCLA Found.; bd. dirs. western region United Way, 1987; coord., head U.S. Savs. Bond Dr., So. Calif., 1991. With USNR, 1944-47. Decorated comdr. Legion of Honor France; named Nation's Outstanding Young Elec. Engr. Eta Kappa Nu, 1958, one of 5 Outstanding Young Men of Calif. by Calif. Jr. C. of C., 1960; recipient Nat. Achievement medal Am. Elec. Assn. 1992, Goddard Astronautics award AIAA, Chester Nimitz award U.S. Navy League, 192, Thomas White award USAF, 1992, President's Medal, U. So. Calif., Space Hall Fame. Fellow IEEE (Founders award 1995), AIAA (pres. 1994, Goddard Astronautics award), AAAS, Royal Aeronautic Soc., AAAS; mem. NAE, Am. Phys. Soc., Berkeley Fellow, Commn. on Competitiveness, Calif. Coun. on Sci. and Tech. (co-chair project Calif.), Cosmos Club, Phi Beta Kappa, Sigma Xi, Lambda Chi Alpha. Home: 28780 Wagon Rd Agoura Hills CA 91301-2732 Office Phone: 818-707-8652. Personal E-mail: mrcurrie@sbcglobal.net.

CURRIE, MICHAEL J., military officer; b. Boston, Mass., May 25, 1971; s. Matthew and Nancy Currie; m. Stacey Nicole Currie; 1 child, Gracelyn. BS, Bridgewater State Coll., Mass., 1998. US army truck platoon leader 1166th Truck Co., Ware, Mass., 2002—05; brigade logistics officer US Army N.G., Devens, Mass., 2005—. Operation challenge program coord. Mass. N.G., Milford, Mass., 1998—2001. Capt. Quartermaster US Army, 1990—2007, Devens, MA. Decorated Commendation medal US Army, Commander's award for Civilian Excellent Mass. Army N.G., Army Achievement medal US Army. Mem.: Mil. Officer's Assn. Am. (assoc.), Assn. Quartermasters (assoc.), Nat. Def. Transp. Assn. (assoc.), N.G. Assn. MA (assoc.), Assn. US Army (assoc.). Democrat-Npl. Buddhist. Achievements include development of secure web presence of 26th Infantry Brigade. Avocations: hiking, mountain biking, music, saxaphone. Home: 91 Hill St Winchendon MA 01475 Office: 26th (YANKEE) Brigade Combat Team 9 Charlestown St Devens MA 01434 Home Phone: 978-297-5044; Office Phone: 508-233-7913. Office Fax: 508-233-7955. Personal E-mail: curriemj@mindspring.com.

CURRIE, NANCY JANE, astronaut; b. Wilmington, Del., Dec. 29, 1958; m. David W. Currie; 1 child. BA in Biol. Scis., Ohio State U., 1980; MS in Safety, U. So. Calif., 1985; D in Indsl. Engring., U. Houston, 1997. Neuropathology rsch. asst. Ohio State U. Coll. Medicine; commd. 2nd lt. U.S. Army, 1981, helicopter instr. pilot, sect. leader, platoon leader, brigade flight standardization officer, master army aviator; flight simulation engr. shuttle tng. aircraft NASA Johnson Space Ctr., Houston, 1987, astronaut, 1991, flight crew rep. for crew equipment, lead for remote manipulator sys., spacecraft communicator, flight engr. mission specialist on STS-57, 1993, flight engr. mission specialist on STS-70, 1995, flight engr. mission specialist on STS-88, 1998, flight engr. mission specialist on STS-109, 2002, chief asstronaut office robotics br. Mem. Army Aviation Assn. Am., Ohio State U. and ROTC Alumni Assns., Inst. Indsl. Engrs., Human Factors and Ergonomics Soc., Phi Kappa Phi. Avocations: weightlifting, running, swimming, scuba diving, skiing. Office: NASA Lyndon B Johnson Space Ctr Houston TX 77058

CURRIE, ROBERT, communications executive; b. Plainfield, NJ, July 30, 1959; s. Ashton Markoe and Evelyn Margaret (Gautreau) C.; m. Suzanne Jean Morris, Oct. 18, 1987; 1 child, Claire MacPherson Currie; 1 stepchild, Hilary Buchanan Boller. BS in Mktg. cum laude, Fairleigh Dickinson U., 1981, MA in Corp. and Orgnl. Comms., 1996. Journalist Foster Pubs., Scotch Plains, NJ, 1979-81; internat. specialist Hoechst Celanese Corp., Bridgewater, NJ, 1981-89, mktg. coord. Summit, NJ, 1989—96; dir. global comms. GAF Corp., Wayne, NJ, 1996—98; v.p., chief commn., pub. affairs officer J.M. Huber Corp., Edison, NJ, 1998—. V.p. HCC Sci. and Tech. Co., Inc., Bridgewater, 1989-92. Producer/dir. film: Trade Secrets and Technology, 1991 (Disting. Achievement award Am. Soc. Indsl. Security); editor (book): With Sword and Harp, 1992, (website) clancurrie.com; writer/dir. films: Winning Strategies, 1993 (Bronze medal N.Y. Festival, Bronze plaque Columbus Internat. TV Festival), The Pipes of Christmas, 2002, 03, 05 (Telly award); prodr. Tartan Day on Ellis Island, 2002—, The Crafter's Song (documentary short film); prodr. exhbn. The Life and Legacy of John Muir, 2005. Pres. Clan Currie Soc. Summit, N.J., 1990—; dir. Bonnie Brae Scottish Games, Millington, N.J., 1985-88, U.S. Equestrian Team - Horse Trials, Gladstone, N.J., 1990-91; chmn. Ethnic Adv. Coun. State N.J., 1993—2000; hon. plankowner USS John Paul Jones, Scottish Heritage U.S.A.; chmn. NJ Nat. Tartan Day.; bd. dirs. Save Ellis Island! Found.; mem. N.J. Gov.'s Adv. Com. on Preservation and Use of Ellis Island, 1998-2000. Recipient James S. Cogswell Outstanding Indsl. Secruity Achievement award Dept. Def., 1992, World Pairs Driving Championship, Gladstone, N.J., 1993, 11 Telly awards for broadcast and non-broadcast TV programming, 1993-2002, Outstanding Ethnic Leader of NJ award, 1999, Communicatior of Yr. award Internat. Assn. Buc. Communicators, 2005. Fellow Soc. Antiquaries, Friends of Order of the Garter; mem. St. Andrew's Soc. of N.Y., Coun. Comm. Mgmt., Pub. Rels. Soc. Am., Nat. Investor Rels. Inst., Am. Soc. Media Photographers, Finlaggan Trust. Avocations: golf, photography, genealogy, music. Home: PO Box 541 Summit NJ 07902-0541 Office: JM Huber Corp 333 Thornall St Edison NJ 08837-2220 E-mail: clancurrie@mail.com.

CURRIE, ROBERT EMIL, retired lawyer; b. Jackson, Tenn., Oct. 10, 1937; s. Forrest Edward Currie and Mary Elizabeth (Nuckolls) Empson; m. Brenda Ray Eddings, July 2, 1960; children: Cheryl Lynn, Forrest Clayton, Kristin Emil. BS with distinction, U.S. Naval Acad., 1959; LLB cum laude, Harvard U., 1967. Bar: Calif. 1967, U.S. Ct. Appeals (9th cir.) 1970, U.S. Supreme Ct. 1979. Assoc. Latham & Watkins, LA, 1967-75, ptnr. Costa Mesa, Calif., 1975—2003, mng. ptnr., 1993—96; ret., 2003. Dir. Constl. Rights Found., Orange County, Calif., 1986-91; lawyer rep. 9th Cir. Jud. Conf., 1991-93. Mem. exec. com. Orange County coun. Boy Scouts Am., Costa Mesa, 1982-95. Capt. USNR, 1955-83. Recipient Silver Beaver award Boy Scouts Am., Orange County coun., 1991. Fellow Am. Coll. Trial Lawyers; mem. Orange County Bar Assn. (dir. 1984-91), U.S. Supreme Ct. Hist. Soc. (chmn. So. Calif. 1992-93), Orange County Bar Found. (dir. 1999—). Home: 24 Pinehurst Ln Newport Beach CA 92660 Business E-Mail: robert.currie@lw.com.

CURRIE, STEVEN RAY, artist; b. Flint, Mich., Sept. 1, 1954; s. Richard Lee and Gwen Laurie (Cummings) C.; m. Annette Marie Davidek, July 27, 1985. BFA, U. Mich., 1977; MFA, Yale U., 1984. One man shows include Borgenicht Gallery, N.Y.C., 1988, 90, 92, 93, Ctr. Contemporary Art, Chgo., 1989, 91, Weatherspoon Art Gallery, Greensboro, N.C., 1995, Revolution Gallery, Detroit, 1995, J.P. Slusser Gallery at U. Mich., 1996, Littlejohn Contemporary, N.Y.C., 1997, Elizabeth Harris Gallery, N.Y.C., 2006; group shows include Boise (Idaho) Art Mus., 1994, Faulconer Gallery, Grinnell (Iowa) Coll., 2001, 80 Washington Sq. East Galleries, NYU, N.Y., 2002; represented in various mus. collections including Bklyn. Mus., Modern Art Mus. Ft. Worth, Walker Art Ctr., Mpls., Met. Mus. Art, N.Y.C., Albright-Knox Art Gallery, Buffalo, Orange County Mus. Art, Newport Beach, Calif. NEA fellow, 1988, N.Y. Found. Arts fellow, 1990, 97.

CURRIE, WILLIAM G., forest products executive; b. Youngsville, NY, 1947; Degree, Hope Coll., 1969. With Universal Forest Products, Inc., Grand Rapids, Mich., 1971—, pres., 1983—90, pres., CEO, 1990—2000, vice chmn., CEO, 2000—06, exec. chmn., 2006—. Office: Universal Forest Products Inc 2801 E Beltline NE Grand Rapids MI 49525*

CURRIER, BRADFORD LEONARD, spine and orthopedic surgeon; s. Malcolm and Evelyn Currier; m. Nancy Romness Currier; children: Sarah, Michael, Thomas. BS in Biology, Emory U., 1977; MD, Georgetown U., 1981. Diplomate Am. Acad. Orthop. Surgeons, lic. Fla., Minn. Intern in gen. surgery Mayo Grad. Sch. Medicine, Rochester, Minn., 1981—82, resident in orthop. surgery, 1984—88; fellowship in spine surgery U. Miami, Fla., 1988—89; spine/orthop. surgeon Mayo Clinic, Rochester, Minn., 1989—, prof. orthop., 2006—, vice chmn. practice dept. orthop., 2003. Dir. spine fellowship Mayo Clinic, 1993—. Contbr. numerous articles to profl. jours. Mem.: AMA, Am. Orthop. Assn., Zumbro Valley Med. Soc., N.Am. Spine Soc., Minn. Orthop. Soc., Minn. Med. Soc., Mid-Am. Orthop. Assn., Cervical Spine Rsch. Soc. (pres. 2004—05), Am. Acad. Orthop. Surgeons, Sigma Xi. Office: Mayo Clinic 200 First St SW Rochester MN 55905 Office Phone: 507-284-0412. Office Fax: 507-266-4234.

CURRIER, MIKE, elementary school educator, writer; b. Omaha, June 21, 1943; s. Melvin Ellis and Margaret (Morris) Currier; m. Linda K. White, Sept. 3, 1999; children: Melanie E. McQueen, Kjirsten L. Wellman, Marshall E., Merrill P. BS Elem. Edn. in Humanities, U. Omaha, 1965, MS in Edn. in Reading, 1968; PhD in Edn., U. Nebr., 1977. Cert. elem. tchr. Tex., reading, English, social studies tchr. Tex., ESL Tex., mid. mgmt. adminstr. Tex. 6th grade tchr. Coun. Bluffs (Iowa) Cmty. Schools, 1965—67, reading clinician, 1969—70; reading cons. Ednl. R & D Ctr., Pipestone, Minn., 1968; assoc. prof. elem. edn. Peru (Nebr.) State Coll., 1970—73; ednl. specialist: rural edn. Edn. Svc. Unit #2, Fremont, Nebr., 1973—74; assoc. prof. of early childhood edn. Ft. Hays (Kans) State U., 1974—83; tng. devel. , presenter Performance Learning Systems, Inc, Arlington, Tex., 1983—93; spl. edn. and preschool cons. Region XI Ednl. Svc. Ctr., Fort Worth, 1994—96; curriculum specialist Castleberry Ind. Sch. Dist., Fort Worth, Tex., 1996—99; classroom tchr. Springtown (Tex.) Intermediate Sch., 1999—; faculty Weatherford Coll., Tex. Ednl. cons., trainer State Departments Edn., 1969—2005; pres. Nebr. State Reading Assn., Omaha, 1976—77. Author: 5 Fingers: Games to Motivate the Growing Reader, Creating Effective Classroom Environments, (text) The Unordinary Classroom, Kindergarten: A Lily Pad or a Launching Pad, Teaching with M-powerment, The Write way to Teach Penmanship. Mem.: Nat. Assn. Edn. for Young Children (bd. dirs. Kans. chpt. 1979—84), Nat. Coun. Tchrs. English, Internat. Reading Assn. Republican. Baptist. Avocations: 1st century biblical history, etymology, computers, pottery, gardening. Home: 7344 Chambers Ln Fort Worth TX 76179-2960 Home Phone: 817-236-1730; Office Phone: 817-236-1730. Personal E-mail: curierm@charter.net.

CURRIER, NATHAN K., composer, educator; b. Dec. 22, 1960; B, Peabody Conservatory, Balt., 1984; M, Juillard Sch., NY, 1986, D, 1989. Piano faculty Queens NY Sch. Music, 1988—89; adj. faculty Mercy Coll., 1990; faculty Juilliard Sch., NY, 1991—2002; lectr. U. Va., Charlottesville, 2002—. Recipient Rome prize, Am. Acad. Rome, 1995—96, Lifetime Achievement Acad. award, Am. Acad. Arts & Letters, NY, 1999; grantee, Fromm Found., Harvard U., 1991; fellowship, Guggenheim Found., NY, 1993, Composer fellowship, Nat. Endowment for Arts, Washington, 1993. Mem.: ASCAP (award 1988, 1989).

CURRIS, CONSTANTINE WILLIAM, educational association administrator; b. Lexington, Ky., Nov. 13, 1940; s. William C. and Mary (Kalpakis) C.; m. Roberta Jo Hern, Aug. 9, 1974; children: Robert Alexander and Elena Diane. BA, U. Ky., 1962; MA, U. Ill., 1965; EdD, U. Ky., 1967. V.p., dean of faculty Midway Coll., Ky., 1965—68; dir. ednl. progs. W.Va. Bd. Edn., Charleston, 1968—69; dean student pers. progs. Marshall U., Huntington, W.Va., 1969—71; v.p., dean of faculty W.Va. Inst. Tech., Montgomery, 1971—73; pres. Murray State U., Ky., 1973—83, U. No. Iowa, 1983—95, Clemson U., 1995—99, Am. Assn. State Colls. and Univs., 1999—. Chmn. emeritus Am. Humanics Inc. Trustee Midway Coll., Allen Coll. Nursing, Sigma Chi Found.; charter mem. adv. coun. Nat. Small Bus. Devel. Ctr. Recipient Algernon S. Sullivan medallion U. Ky., 1962; named Outstanding Young Man in Ky., Jaycees, 1974, U. Ky. Alumni Hall of Fame, 2000. Mem. Phi Beta Kappa, Omicron Delta Kappa. Greek Orthodox. Office: Am Assn State Colls and Univs 1307 New York Ave NW Washington DC 20005 Office Phone: 202-293-7070. *I am very grateful for what America has given me. As the son of a Greek immigrant who possessed neither education nor a command of the English language, I am keenly aware of the opportunities a government of and for the people affords its citizens. If there is any quality to which I attribute what success I have achieved it would be that of an abiding devotion to the "public interest" rather than allowing my decisions to be determined by vested or parochial interests.*

CURRIVAN, JOHN DANIEL, lawyer; b. Paris; s. Gene and Rachel Currivan; m. Patrice Salley; children: Christopher, Melissa. BS with distinction, Cornell U.; MS, U Calif.-Berkeley; MS, U. West Fla.; JD summa cum laude, Cornell Law Sch., 1978. Bar: Ohio 1978. Mng. ptnr. S.W. Devel. Co., Kingsville, Tex., 1971-76; note editor Cornell Law Rev., Ithaca, NY, 1977-78; prosecutor Naval Legal Office, Norfolk, Va., 1978-79, chief prosecutor, 1979-81; sr. atty. USS Nimitz, 1981-83; trial judge Naval Base, Norfolk, 1983-84; tax atty. Jones Day, Cleve., 1984-88, ptnr., 1989—, coord. tax practice (Cleve. br.), 2006—. Adj. prof. law Case Western Res. U. Sch. Law, 1997—2003; chmn. Cleve. Tax Inst., 2005. Author: (with Rickert) Ohio Limited Liability Companies, 1999. Comdr. USN, 1969-84. Recipient Younger Fed. Lawyer award FBA, 1981. Mem. ABA, Nat. Assn. Bond Lawyers, Order of Coif, Tau Beta Pi, Eta Kappa Nu, Phi Kappa Phi. Home: 12700 Lake Ave Ste 2105 Lakewood OH 44107-1506 Office: Jones Day 901 Lakeside Ave E Cleveland OH 44114-1190 Office Phone: 216-586-7262. Business E-Mail: jdcurrivan@jonesday.com.

CURRY, ALAN CHESTER, actuary; b. Columbus, Ohio, Oct. 15, 1933; s. Harold E. and Martha (Dew) C.; children: Diane, Thomas, Timothy, Jeffrey. Student, U. Ill., 1951-52; EdB, Ill. State U., 1957. Various actuarial positions State Farm Mut. Automobile Ins. Co., Bloomington, Ill., 1952-70, v.p., actuary, 1970-97. Fellow Casualty Actuarial Soc. (dir. 1970-73, 87-90); mem. Am. Acad. Actuaries (dir. 1977-80), Midwestern Actuarial Forum (pres. 1972-73), Shriners, Pi Gamma Mu, Pi Omega Pi, Kappa Delta Pi. Home and Office: 7 Canterbury Ct Bloomington IL 61701-3401 Office Phone: 309-662-8689.

CURRY, ANN, correspondent, anchor; b. Agana, Guam, Nov. 19, 1956; d. Robert Paul and Hiroe (Nagase) Curry; m. Brian Wilson Ross, Oct. 21, 1987; children: Anna McKenzie, William Walker. Student, U. Oreg., 1974—78. Reporter Sta. KTVL-TV, Medford, Oreg., 1978—81; reporter, weekend anchor Sta. KGW-TV, Portland, Oreg., 1981—84; reporter Sta. KCBS-TV, LA, 1984—90; corr., anchor NBC News at Sunrise NBC News, NYC, 1991—96; news anchor Today Show, 1997—. Nominee Emmy award, 1985, 1986, 1987, 1988; recipient Golden Mike award, RTNA, 1986, 1987, 1989, Cert. Excellence award, AP, 1987, 1988, Greater L.A. Press Club, 1987, Superior Reporting award, NAACP, 1989, Emmy award, Acad. TV Arts and Scis., 1987, 1989, Nat. award, AAJA, 2000, AmeriCares Humanitarian Medial award, 2002. Avocation: art history. Office: NBC News 30 Rockefeller Plz # 374E New York NY 10112-0002

CURRY, BOYKIN (RAVENEL BOYKIN CURRY IV), investment manager; s. Ravenel Boykin and Beth Curry; m. Cecilia Lacoste Kemble, Mar. 12, 2005. B. in Economics, Yale U., 1988; MBA, Harvard U., 1994. Sr. assoc. Advisory Bd. Co.; with asset mgmt. group Morgan Stanley; with Kingdon Capital, 1997; mng. ptnr. Eagle Capital Mgmt. LLC. Co-editor (with Brian Kasbar): Essays That Worked: 50 Essays From Successful Applications to the Nation's Top Colleges, 1986. Founder Democrats Edn. Reform, Young Friends MTC, Girls Prep. Democrat. Office: Eagle Capital Mgmt LLC 499 Park Ave New York NY 10022

CURRY, CARLTON E., broadcast and waterworks executive, councilman; b. Lizton, Ind., Mar. 4, 1935; m. Ann Merritt, 1957. BS, Purdue U., 1958. Registered profl. engr., Ind., cert. profl. logistician. Program adminstr. Allison Gas Turbine divsn. GM, 1966-79, staff systems analyst, 1979-83, mgr. mktg. program, 1983-85, dir. logistics support, 1985-90; cons., 1990-93; pres. SaniServ, Inc., 1990-96, Curry Inc., 1997—. Chmn. Cable Franchise Bd., 1996-2002. City councilman, Indpls., 1983-99; bd. dirs. Dept. of Waterworks, 2002; dir. contracts & ops. Dept. of Waterworks, 2002—; presdl. elector, 1988. With USN, 1958-66, USAR, 1956-63. Mem. AIAA, Am. Water Works Assn., Soc. Logistics Engrs., Lions, Kiwanis. Republican. Baptist. Office Phone: 317-264-7739. Personal E-mail: accurry2@comcast.net.

CURRY, DANIEL FRANCIS MYLES, filmmaker; b. NYC, Sept. 22, 1946; s. John Joseph Curry Jr. and Florence Cecelia (Rattler) Curry; m. Ubolvan Chaiwatana, July 27, 1972; children: Devin, Daniel. BA in Fine Arts, minor in Theatre, Middlebury Coll., 1968; MFA in Film and Theatre, Humboldt State U., 1979. Vol. cmty. devel. U.S. Peace Corps, Khon Kaen, Thailand, 1969—71; writer-dir. ednl. TV Ministry of Edn., Govt. of Thailand, Bangkok, 1971—72; freelance filmmaker/artist/designer various clients Bangkok, 1972—74; instr. fine arts Cape Cod Community Coll., West Barnstable, Mass., 1974—77; instr. film and theatre Humboldt State U., Arcata, Calif., 1977—79; visual effects artist Universal Studios Hartland Facility, North Hollywood, Calif., 1979—80; art dir. Modern Film Effects, Hollywood, Calif., 1980—85; v.p., dir. creative svcs. Cinema Rsch. Corp., Hollywood, 1985—88; visual effects producer-dir. Star Trek, the Next Generation, Paramount Pictures, Hollywood, 1987—; pres. O.M.R. Prodns., Manhattan Beach, Calif., 1989—. Supr., title designer: Star Trek IV; Top Gun; Flash Dance; Fatal Attraction; Cujo; The Blob; Rocky IV; Cobra; Staying Alive; Tootsie; Risky Business; Amadeus; The Right Stuff; Mommie Dearest; Uncommon Valor; Pure Luck; Back to School; Raging Bull; Class; Cool World; Captured; Christine; Body Double; Flashpoint; Tiger Town; Invasion U.S.A.; Fast Forward; Bolero; Wild Thing; Pray for Death; Days of Thunder; Indian Jones & The Temple of Doom; Star Trek, Generations; visual effects prodr.: 6th Season Star Trek, The Next Generation (best spl. visual effects Emmy award, 1992); Star Trek Deep Space Nine, 1993—; Star Trek Voyager, 1995— (Emmy award). Nominee Emmy award, 1989, 1990; recipient Emmy award for spl. visual effects, Acad. TV Arts and Scis., 1992, 1994, Internat. Monitor award, 1996. Mem.: Am. Soc. Cinematographers, Am. Film Inst., Soc. Motion Picture and TV Engrs., Acad. TV Arts and Scis. Fluent in Thai and Lao.

CURRY, ESTELLA ROBERTA, education educator, school psychologist, consultant; d. John Henry and Grace Gannon; m. Carl Alton Curry, Apr. 7, 1950 (dec. Feb. 1986); children: John, Carl, Carla, David. BS cum laude, Ohio U., 1968, postgrad., 1973—2002; MA, Marshall U., 1969, postgrad., 1971—73. Cert. elem. tchr. Ohio, 1961, sch. counselor Ohio, 1969, sch. psychologist Ohio, 1973. Middle sch. tchr. South Point (Ohio) Local Schs., 1961—64, elem. sch. tchr., 1964—68, elem. guidance counselor, 1969—72; grad. asst. Marshall U., Huntington, W.Va., 1968—69; sch. guidance counselor Fairland Local Schs., Proctorville, Ohio, 1972—73; G.E.D. adminstr., coordinator of psychological svcs., sch. psychologist/counselor Lawrence County Ednl. Svc. Ctr., Ironton, Ohio, 1973—. Therapist, clin. supr. Prestera Mental Health Ctr., Huntington, 1991—96; instr. Ohio U., Ironton, 1999—; ednl. cons. Oakridge Treatment Ctr., Ironton, 1999—. Mem.: Sch. Psychology Assn. South Ea. Ohio, Ohio Sch. Psychologist Assn., Coun. for Exceptional Children. Avocations: reading, travel, cooking, art collecting, gardening. Home: 3964 County Rd 15 South Point OH 45680 Office: Lawrence County Ednl Svc Ctr 111 S 4th St Ironton OH 45638 Office Phone: 740-532-4223. Personal E-mail: ecurry3600@aol.com.

CURRY, GOLDIE, elementary school educator; b. St. Paul, May 25, 1952; d. Immanuel and Eileen Goldie; m. David Risser (div.). BA in Child Devel., Calif. State U., Northridge, 1978; MA in Human Devel., Pacific Oaks Coll., Pasadena, Calif., 1980; MA in Adminstrn., San Francisco State U., 2006. Cert. spl. edn. tchr., multiple subject tchr. Calif., 1980. Spl. edn. tchr. Marvin Ave. Elem. Sch., LA, 1981—83, Culver HS, Culver City, Calif., 1983—84, Marin County Dept. Edn., San Rafael, Calif., 1997, Fairmont Elem. Sch., San Francisco, 1997—99; 2d grade tchr. Hamilton Elem. Sch., Novato, Calif., 1999—; case mgr., classroom tchr. New Vistas, Santa Fe, 1987—90; ednl. therapist San Fernando Child Guidance Clinic, Northridge, 1986. Mem. faculty Santa Fe CC, 1989; cons. in field. Named Golden Bell Outstanding Tchr., Marin County Office Edn., 2004; recipient Tchr. Recognition award, Rotary Club, Novato, 2003, Hon. Svc. award, Hamilton Elem. Sch. PTA, 2004, 2005, Artistic Achievement award, Novato Unified Sch. Dist. Youth in Arts, 2005; grantee, Marin County Office Edn., 2002, Redwood League, 2004—06, Marin County Office Edn., 2004, Yosemite Nat. Insts., Headlands INst., 2004—05, Novato Unified Sch. Dist., 2004. Mem.: ASCD, Calif. Fedn. Tchrs., Am. Fedn. Tchrs., Assn. Calif. Sch. Adminstrs. Democrat. Jewish. Avocations: dance, hiking, gardening, travel.

CURRY, JANE LOUISE, writer; b. East Liverpool, Ohio, Sept. 24, 1932; d. William Jack and Helen Margaret (Willis) C. Student, Pa. State U., University Park, 1950-51; BS, Ind. U. of Pa., 1954; postgrad., UCLA, 1957-59; AM, Stanford U., Calif., 1962, PhD, 1969. Tchr. art East Liverpool schs., 1955, L.A. schs., 1956-59; teaching asst. dept. English Stanford U., 1959-61, 64-65, acting instr., 1967-68, instr., 1983-84, lectr., 1987. Storyteller, 1962—. Author: Down from the Lonely Mountain, 1965, Beneath the Hill, 1967, The Sleepers, 1968, The Change-Child, 1969, The Daybreakers, 1970, Mindy's Mysterious Miniature, 1970, Over the Sea's Edge, 1971, The Ice Ghosts Mystery, 1972, The Lost Farm, 1974, Parsley Sage, Rosemary and Time, 1975, The Watchers, 1975, The Magical Cupboard, 1976, Poor Tom's Ghost, 1977, The Birdstones, 1977, The Bassumtyte Treasure, 1978, Ghost Lane, 1979, The Wolves of Aam, 1981, Shadow Dancers, 1983, The Great Flood Mystery, 1985, The Lotus Cup, 1986, Back in the Beforetime, 1987, Me, Myself and I, 1987, The Big Smith Snatch, 1989, Little Little Sister, 1989, What the Dickens?, 1991, The Great Smith House Hustle, 1993, The Christmas Knight, 1993, Robin Hood and his Merry Men, 1994, Robin Hood in the Greenwood, 1995, Moon Window, 1996, Dark Shade, 1998, Turtle Island, 1999, A Stolen Life, 1999, The Wonderful Sky Boat, 2001, The Egyptian Box, 2002, Hold Up the Sky, 2003, Brave Cloelia, 2004, The Black Canary, 2005. Scholar Fulbright Scholar, U. London, 1961—62; Leverhulme Fellow, 1965—66. Office: Simon & Schuster Children's Publ Divsn 1230 Ave of Ams New York NY 10020

CURRY, JOHN MICHAEL, investment banker; b. Buffalo, Dec. 30, 1942; s. John Vincent and June (Eisele) C.; m. Thea Adrian KIrk, July 12, 1969 (div. 1982); children: John Adrian, James Prescott; m. Margaretta Buckley, Mar. 17, 1990; 1 child, Michael Jeremiah. BA, U. San Francisco, 1968; MBA, Harvard U., Cambridge, Mass., 1970; postgrad., Suffolk U., Boston, 1971. Cert. property mgr.; registered rep. and gen. securities rep.; registered fiduciary and investment adviser, registered securities prin. Developer Devel. Corp. Am., Boston, 1970-73; founder, chmn. APT Fin. Svcs., Inc., Boston, 1977—, Am. Securities Team, Inc., Boston, 1992—, Am. Properties Team, APT Asset, Boston, 1987—; chmn. Am. Devel. Team, 1985-92, Am. Realty Team, Fla., 1994—, Infrastructure Repair Technologies, 1998—. Bd. dirs. six corps.; Boston rep. Taylor Woodrow PLC, London, 1983-85. Vol. various fed., state, local polit. orgns. and campaigns. Sgt. US Army, 1961-64. Recipient Modernization award Building Mag., 1980-81, Outstanding Restoration award Lowell C. of C., 1981, Nat. Jewish Life award, 1987. Mem. Harvard Club (Boston), various securities firms orgns. Avocations: scuba diving, Karate, golf. Personal E-mail: jcurry1@adelphia.net. Business E-Mail: jcurry@aptfin.com.

CURRY, JOHN PATRICK, insurance company executive, management consultant; b. Logan, W.Va., May 3, 1934; s. Albert Bruce and Mary Naomi (Shugert) C.; m. Patricia Jean Blessington, Oct. 26, 1956; children: Joseph Patrick, Mary Patricia, Kathleen Anne, Carmen Frances, John Gregory. Student, St. Charles Coll., Catonsville, Md., 1949-52; BA, U. Notre Dame, 1956; MS in Ops. Rsch., Western Mich. U., 1976. Lic. prof. cons., Mich. Agt. Conn. Mut. Life Ins. Co., 1959-65; gen. agt. Occidental Life Ins. Co., LA, 1965-66; pres. Investment Assocs. Inc., LA, 1966-69; gen. agt. Fed. Life Ins. Co., Peoples Home Life Ins. Co. and Home Assurance Cos., 1969-71; actuarial cons. Am.-Brit. Ins. & Annuity Co. Ltd. (Bermuda), Battle Creek, Mich., 1979-87, mgmt. cons., 1971-88; owner, mgr. Nat. Search Cons., exec. search firm, Kalamazoo; owner, operator Curry Supply

Co., Portage, Mich., 1978-83; pres. The Consulting Group Inc. (Del.), Kalamazoo, 1985—93, JPC Holding, Inc., 1993—. Pres. The Pilot Co., Turks and Caicos Islands, 1985-90; dir. Anglo-Am. Ins. Co., Ltd. (Bermuda), 1979-87. With US Army, 1957—59. U. Notre Dame scholar, 1952-56; Pat O'Brien scholar, 1956. Mem.: Rep. Pres.'s Round Table, Sertoma Club (charter dir. Kalamazoo club 1961—64). Republican. Roman Catholic. Home: 7226 Rockford St Portage MI 49024-4122 Office: The Consulting Group Kalamazoo MI 49024 Office Phone: 269-978-0824. E-mail: jpcurry@charter.net, jpchinc@hotmail.com.

CURRY, NANCY ELLEN, psychologist, psychoanalyst, educator; b. Brockway, Pa., Jan. 26, 1931; d. George R. and Mary F. (Covert) C. BA, Grove City Coll., 1952; MEd, U. Pitts., 1956, PhD, 1972; grad., Pitts. Psychoanalytic Inst., 1988, grad. child analytic program, 1992. Lic. psychologist, Pa. Tchr. public schs., East Brady and Oakmont, Pa., 1952-55; presch. demonstration tchr. Arsenal Family and Children's Center, U. Pitts., 1955-79, assoc. dir., 1971-79; from instr. in psychiatry to prof. child devel. Sch. Social Work, U. Pitts, 1957-93; prof. emeritus Sch. Social Work, U. Pitts.; also mem. faculty U. Pitts Sch. Medicine, Sch. Edn., Sch. Health Related Professions.; pvt. practice in psychoanalysis and psychotherapy; ret., 2000. Supr., cons.; Fulbright exchange tchr. North Oxford Nursery Sch., Oxford, Eng., 1957-58; vis. prof. Oreg. State U., summer, 1964, Ariz. State U., summer, 1969; assoc. dir. early childhood project Edn. Professions Devel. Act, U.S. Office of Edn., 1970-74; cons. in field. Co-producer 12 films on children's play; co-author Beyond Self-esteem, 1990; editor The Feeling Child; author numerous articles on child devel. Adv. bd. Fred Rogers Ctr; bd. mem. Family Commn. Mem. APA, Assn. Child Psychoanalysis Home: 149 Shadow Ridge Dr Pittsburgh PA 15238-2133 Personal E-mail: NCU149@comcast.net.

CURRY, RAYMOND HOWARD, physician; b. Lexington, Ky., June 5, 1956; s. Howard Jr. and Venita (Dawson) C. AB, U. Ky., 1977; MD, Washington U., St. Louis, 1982. Diplomate Am. Bd. Internal Medicine. Resident in internal medicine McGaw Med. Ctr. Northwestern U., Chgo., 1982-85; internist Northwestern Med. Faculty Found., Chgo., 1985—; instr. Northwestern U. Med. Sch., Chgo., 1985-89, asst. prof., 1989-96, assoc. prof., 1996—2002, prof., 2002—, dir. undergrad. edn. dept. medicine, 1992—98, dean for edn., 1998—; mem. staff Northwestern Meml. Hosp., Chgo., 1985—; pres. McGaw Med. Ctr. NW U., 2004—. Mem. ACP, Soc. Gen. Internal Medicine, Am. Acad. Physician and Patient, Phi Beta Kappa. Office: Northwestern U Feinberg Sch of Medicine 303 E Chicago Ave Chicago IL 60611

CURRY, ROBERT LEE, III, lawyer; b. New Orleans, Sept. 29, 1931; s. Robert Lee Jr. and Lydia (Sporl) C.; m. Courtney Davis, June 11, 1955; children: Robert Lee IV, Cynthia Curry Alexander, Thomas Davis, Kevin Courtney. BS, JD, La. State U., 1954; LLM in Taxation, NYU, 1958. Bar: La. 1954, U.S. Ct. Appeals (5th cir.) 1961, U.S. Supreme Ct. 1958. Judge advocate USAF, Wichita, Kans., 1954-56; teaching fellow NYU Sch. of Law, 1956-57; atty. advisor U.S. Tax Ct., Washington, 1957-60; atty. Theus, Grisham, Davis & Leigh, Monroe, La., 1960—. Coun. mem. La. Law Inst. Coun., Baton Rouge, 1978—, pres., 1995-98. Fellow Am. Coll. Trust and Estate Counsel, Am. Coll. Tax Counsel; mem. Internat. Acad. Estate and Trust Law. Episcopalian. Office: Theus Grisham Davis & Leigh 1600 Lamy Ln Monroe LA 71201-3736 Home Phone: 318-388-0871; Office Phone: 318-388-0100. Business E-Mail: rcurry@theuslaw.com.

CURRY, THOMAS J., federal and former state agency administrator; Grad. summa cum laude, Manhattan Coll.; JD, New Eng. Sch. Law. Bar: Mass., Conn. Atty. Mass. Sec. of State's Office, 1982; asst. gen. counsel Commonwealth of Mass.-Divsn. Banks, 1986—87, first dep. commr. banks, 1987—94, acting commr. banks, 1994-95, commr. banks, 1995—2003. Mem. state liaison com. Fed. Fin. Instn. Exam. Coun., 1996—2003; chmn. regulatory com. Conf. of State Bank Suprs., 2000—03; mem., bd. dirs. FDIC, Washington, 2004—. Mem. Phi Beta Kappa. Office: FDIC 550 17th St NW Rm 6098 Washington DC 20429-9990 Office Phone: 202-898-3957.

CURRY, TIM, actor; b. Grappenhall Cheshire, Eng., Apr. 19, 1946; s. James and Patricia Curry. Grad., U. Birmingham, Eng. Stage performances include A Mid-Summer Night's Dream, The Rocky Horror Show, Amadeus, The Pirates of Penzance, Me and My Girl, My Favorite Year; films The Rocky Horror Picture Show, 1975, The Shout, 1980, Times Square, 1980, Annie, 1982, The Ploughman's Lunch, 1984, Clue, 1985, Legend, 1986, Pass the Ammo, 1988, The Hunt for Red October, 1990, Oscar, 1991, (voice) Ferngully.The Last Rainforest, 1992, Passed Away, 1992, Home Alone 2: Lost in New York, 1992, Loaded Weapon 1, 1992, The Three Musketeers, 1993, The Shadow, 1994, Congo, 1995, Lovers' Knot, 1995, (voice) The Pebble and the Penguin, 1995, Muppet Treasure Island, 1996, McHale's Navy, 1997, (voice) Rugrats Movie, 1998, The Titanic Chronicles, 1999, Jackies Back, 1999, Pirates of the Plain, 1999, Charlie's Angels: The Movie, 2000, Sorted, 2000, Lion of Oz, 2000, Four Dogs Playing Poker, 2000, (voice) Rugrats in Paris: The Movie Rugrats II, 2000, Ritual, 2000, Scary Movie 2, 2001, The Scoundrel's Wife, 2002, (voice) The Wild Thornberrys Movie, 2002, (voice) I, Crocodile, 2002, (voice) Rugrats Go Wild, 2003, Kinsey, 2004, Baily's Billion$, 2005, (voice) Valiant, 2005, The Chosen One, 2006, Garfield: A Tale of Two Kitties, 2006; TV appearances Oliver Twist, 1982, Stephen King's It, 1990, (voice) Peter Pan and the Pirates, 1991 (Emmy award), Family Affair, 2002-03; numerous voices in TV series including Fish Police, 1992, Tales From the Crypt (Death of Some Salesman), 1993 (Emmy nomination, Guest Actor - Drama, 1994), Earth 2, 1994, (voice) Superhuman Samurai Syber-Squad, 1994, Aaahh!! Real Monsters, 1994, The Mask, 1995, Toonstruck, 1996, Story of Santa Claus, 1996, Quack Pack, 1996, Mighty Ducks, 1996, Bruno the Kid, 1996-97, Jumanji, 1996-99, Lexx: The Dark Zone, 1997, The Wild Thornberrys, 1998, The Net, 1998, Mattimeo: A Tale of Redwall, 2000; albums: Read My Lips, 1978, Fearless, 1979, Simplicity, 1981, The Best of Tim Curry, 1989. Office: William Morris Agency c/o Elyse Scherz 151 S El Camino Dr Beverly Hills CA 90212-2775

CURRY, VIRGINIA FRANCES, retired language educator; b. Kansas City, Kans., Feb. 20, 1922; d. Garfield Allen and Pauline Charlton Curry. AB, U. Kans., Lawrence, 1943, MA, 1944; PhD, Ind. U., Bloomington, 1947. Tchr. Langston U. Coll., Okla., 1949—50, Spelman Coll., Atlanta, 1950—52, Tex. So. U., Houston, 1953—57, Fla. A&M U., Tallahassee, 1958—60; tchr., dept. head Fayetteville State U., NC, 1961—92; ret., 1992. Scholar, Ford Found., Kansas City, 1939. Mem.: NAACP, Phi Sigma Iota, Pi Lambda Theta, Phi Beta Kappa. Home: 1846 Broadell Dr Fayetteville NC 28301

CURRY, WILLIAM SIMS, management consultant; b. Mt. Vernon, Wash., Feb. 6, 1938; s. Eli Herbert Curry and Winona Geraldine Davis; m. Kirsten Ingeborg Arms, May 20, 1971; children: William II, Kevin, Randal, Kim Cannova, Derek. BS in Bus. Mgmt., Fla. State U., Tallahassee, 1967; MBA, Ohio State U., 1968. Cert. profl. contracts mgr. Asst. purchasing officer Stanford Linear Accelerator Ctr., Calif., 1977-80; subcontract adminstr. Lockheed Missiles & Space Co., Sunnyvale, Calif., 1980-81; materials mgr. Altus Corp., San Jose, Calif., 1981-86; purchasing mgr. Litton Electron Devices, San Carlos, Calif., 1986-95, Comms. & Power Industries, Palo Alto, Calif., 1995-97; contracts mgr. Landacorp, Chico, Calif., 1998; purchasing svcs. mgr. Butte County, Oroville, Calif., 1998-01, dep. adminstrv. officer, 2001—07, gen. svcs. dir., 2001—07; cons. WSC Cons., Chico, Calif., 2007—. Bd. dirs. Industry Coun. for Small Bus. Devel., Sunnyvale, 1992-97, v.p. programs, 1992-93, exec. v.p., 1994-95, pres., 1995-97. Contbr. articles to profl. jours. Capt. USAF, 1955-77. Decorated Meritorious Svc. medal with one oak leaf cluster, USAF, 1977. Fellow Nat. Contract Mgmt. Assn.; mem. Calif. Assn. Pub. Purchasing Officers, Am. Mensa, Beta Gamma Sigma. Republican. Avocations: chess, writing, bicycling. Home and Office: 17 Northwood Commons Pl Chico CA 95973-7213 Home Phone: 530-899-8436; Office Phone: 530-899-8436. Personal E-mail: bnkcurry@sbcglobal.net.

CURRY SCOTT, SHIRLEY GOODMAN, retired director; b. Perry, Fla., Nov. 14, 1935; d. Hezekiah and Vivian Inez Goodman; children: Gherry Monte Rolle, Veleta Inez Roberson. BS in Phys. Edn., Health, Fla. A&M U., Tallahassee, 1961, MEd in Guidance, 1969. Phys. edn. tchr. Taylor County Sch. Bd., Perry, Fla., 1961—74, dean, 1975—82, 1988—90, dir. student svcs., 1983—87, 1991—97; ret., 1997. Bd. dirs. Big Bend Hospice, Perry, 1994—, United Way of Big Bend, Perry, 2004—. Coun. mem. City of Perry, 1992—2000, mayor, 1995, vice mayor, 1996; Sunday sch. supt. Stewart Meml. AME Ch., 1995—2005, Sunday sch. tchr., 2005—06, steward pro tem, 2002—. Named to Wall of Tolerance, So. Poverty Law Ctr., 2005. Mem.: Taylor County Ret. Tchrs. Assn., Taylor County FAMU Alumni Chpt., Vogue XIII, Inc. (life; pres. 1982—2000). Methodist. Achievements include First woman elected to serve as council member, vice mayor, and mayor of the City of Perry, Florida; first African American inducted into the Taylor County Educator's Hall of Fame. Avocations: reading, travel. Home Phone: 850-584-2404.

CURSON, THEODORE, musician; b. Phila., June 3, 1935; s. Leroy and Reava (Paige) Curson; m. Marjorie N. Goltry, Apr. 1, 1967; children: Charlene, Theodore II. Student, Mastbaum Sch., Granoff Music Conservatory, Phila., 1952-53. Mem. Charles Mingus' Jazz Workshop, 1959-60. Guest instr. U. Vt. Festival Contemporary Music, 1968; instr. music Warsaw U.; pres. Nosruc Pub. Co., 1961—. Trumpeter: with Max Roach, Philly Joe Jones, Cecil Taylor, Eric Dolphy, 1960—63; musician: appeared on radio, TV, clubs, jazz festivals include Riga, Latvia, Tallinn, Estonia, Vienna, France, NorthSea, The Hague, Nice, Jazz Yatra, India, Antibes, Aix en Provence, Lugano, Bologna, Macerata, Prague, Bled, Warsaw, Molde, Kongberg, Ahus, Laren, Pori, Caracas, Amsterdam, 1964, featured on AllTomorrow's Parties Festival, 2005, U.S. festivals New Music Across America, Birdland, Newport/N.Y., Newport Rebels Festival, univ. concerts include Princeton U., U. Wis., Baton Rouge, Columbia U., N.Y.U., Hobart Coll., We. Wash. Coll., Grinnell Coll., U. Calif., Santa Monica and Berkeley, U. Vt., toured India, Middle East and N. Africa for State Dept., 1980, toured Siberia, 1996; guest soloist Norddeutscher Rundfunk TV, star PBS TV show Jazz Set, 1972, star, with NOS Dutch TV (jazz video) Last Date; composer: Nosruc Waltz, 1960, Flatted Fifth, 1960, The Leopard, 1964, Straight Ice, 1965, Typical Ted, 1970, Reava's Waltz, Airi's Tune, Searchin for the Blues, Lost Her, 1987; musician: (recording) Plenty of Horn, 1961, Fire Down Below, 1963, Tears for Dolphy, 1976, 1994, New Thing and Blue Thing, 1965, Urge, 1966, Ode to Booker Ervin, 1970, Pop Wine, 1972, Quicksand, 1975, Jubilant Power, 1976, Blue Piccolo, 1976, Flip Top, 1977, Typical Ted, 1977, The Trio, 1979, I Heard Mingus, 1980, Snake Johnson, 1981, Round Midnight, 1990, Cattin' Curson, 1993, Traveling On, 1997, Sugar'n Spice, 1999, Pori Jazz, 2001, Face to Face, 2002, Ted Curson with Voices, Ted Curson in Paris, 2007, (films) Teorema, 1968, Notes for a Film on Jazz, 1968, The Brown Bunny, 2003; dir.: Blue Note Open Jam, 1984—93, Trumpets Open Jam, 2003—06. Named New Star, Monterey Jazz Festival, 1962, winner, Trumpet sect. Down Beat Internat. Critics Poll, 1966, Down Beat Reader's Poll, 1978, New Jazz Artist, Jazz Podium, Germany; recipient LI Musicians Soc. award, 1970, Pori City Std., Finland, 1978, Keys to City, 1998, Paul Robeson Cmty. Arts award, Jersey City Pub. Libr., 1994. Mem.: Am. Fedn. Musicians.

CURT, ALAN SANDMAN, neuroscientist, educator; s. Carl E. and Violet E. Sandman; m. Jennifer L. Barron, Sept. 21, 1985; children: Sandra K. Sandman, Kelli S. Sandman Hurley, Erinn E. Johnson, Camerin L. Barron-Sandman. PhD, La. State U., Baton Rouge, 1971. Lic. clinical psychologist Calif., 1979. Prof. psychology Ohio State U., Columbus, 1971—79; prof. psychiatry and human behavior U. Calif. Irvine, Orange, Calif., 1979—. Chief rsch. State of Calif., Fairview, Costa Mesa, 1979—2006; chmn. Winter Neuropeptide Conf., 1983—2007. Contbr. articles to profl. jours. Grantee, NIH, 1985—2006. Achievements include research in role of prenatal stress on human development. Office: Univ Calif Irvine 333 City Drive Blvd W Orange CA 92868 Home Phone: 949-497-6217; Office Phone: 714-940-1924.

CURT, DENISE MORRIS, painter, photographer; b. New Haven, Nov. 15, 1936; d. Bertrand and Anna Geraldine (Fiak) Rocheleau; m. John Morris, Oct. 4, 1954 (dec.); children: Tyler John, Cynthia Leigh Morris Bell; m. Albert A. Curt, 1973 (div. 1981). Student of Louis Crescenti, Orange, Conn., 1950—52; student, Whitney Sch. Art, New Haven, 1950, Luchetti Sch. Art, 1951, Paier Sch. Art, Hamden, Conn., 1951. Interior designer State of Conn., Hartford, 1972—75; dir. Meet The Artists and Artisans, Milford, 1962—. One-woman shows Gull Gallery, Provincetown, Mass., Chapelle Jean Cocteau, Villefranche Sur Mer, France, Garfield Galleries, Orange, Yale U., Stratford Gallery, Stevenson (Md.) Galleries; represented in numerous pvt. and pub. collections throughout world; contbr. artwork to The Conn. Limner. Lectr. to numerous civic orgns.; mem. Vis. Artists in Schs., 1970—; commr. Conn. Commn. on Arts, 1974-79; photography chmn. Milford Fine Arts Coun., New Haven Arts Coun.; bd. dir. Milford Hosp. Aux.; mem. Literacy Vols., Milford. Recipient award Mystic Art Festival, 1969, Sterling House Art Show, 1985, Glastonbury Art Guild, 1988 Mem. Guilford Art League (bd. dir. 1975-80), Nat. League Am. Pen Women (category painting, bd. dirs. Fairfield chpt., art chair), Conn. Classic Arts, Milford Hist. Soc., Yale U. Gallery, Met. Mus. Art., Milford C. of C. (amb. 2005—). Republican. Congregationalist. Avocations: art, antiques, travel, classical music. Home and Studio: The Connecticut Limner 41 Green St Milford CT 06460-4709 Home Phone: 203-874-5672; Office Phone: 203-874-5672. E-mail: ctlimner@snet.net.

CURTIN, BRIAN JOSEPH, retired ophthalmologist; b. NYC, July 25, 1921; s. James Joseph and Julia Margaret (Smith) C.; m. Claire Margaret Flood, June 18, 1955; children: Edward Brian, James Martin, Thomas Hayes, Deirdre Claire. BS, Fordham U., NYC, 1942; MD, NYU, 1945. Intern St. Vincent's Hosp., NYC, 1945-46; resident surgeon Manhattan Eye, Ear and Throat Hosp., 1950-53, asst. attending surgeon, asso. attending surgeon, 1953-74, surgeon dir., 1974-89, surgeon dir. emeritus, 1990—, pres. med. bd., 1977-79, vice chmn. dept. ophthalmology, 1983-89, med. dir., 1989-91; attending ophthalmologist, chief svc. Misericordia-Lincoln Affiliated Hosps., 1958-79; attending ophthalmologist N.Y. Hosp., 1969-84; assoc. attending ophthalmologist Columbia Presbyn. Med. Ctr., 1985-92; asst. prof. clin. ophthalmology NYU, 1954-70; assoc. prof. clin. ophthalmology Cornell Med. Coll., 1970-84, Columbia U. Coll. Physicians and Surgeons, 1985-98; pvt. practice NYC. Med. adv. bd. Eye Bank for Sight Restoration, N.Y.C., 1978-90, chmn., 1988-90; attending ophthalmologist, chmn. dept. St. Clare's Hosp. and Health Ctr., 1978-81. Author: The Myopias: Basic Science and Clinical Management, 1985; mem. editorial bd. Cornea, 1981-85; contbr. chpts. to textbooks, articles to med. jours. With U.S. Navy, 1946-48. Recipient Achievement award Fordham U., 1976. Mem. ACS, AMA, AAAS, Am. Ophthalmol. Soc., N.Y. State Med. Soc., N.Y. County Med. Soc., N.Y. Acad. Medicine, N.Y. Acad. Scis., Am. Acad. Ophthalmology, N.Y. Ophthal. Soc. (v.p. 1981-82, pres. 1982-83), Am. Eye Study Club. Home: 4402 Theall Rd Rye NY 10580-1480 Personal E-mail: bcurti85@hotmail.com.

CURTIN, CONSTANCE O'HARA, language educator, writer; b. NYC, Mar. 11, 1927; d. V. Winthrop and Belle Callum O'Hara; m. David Yarrow Curtin, July 1, 1950; children: Susan M., David F., Jane C. Jones. AB, Mt. Holyoke Coll., Mass., 1948; MA in Chemistry, Columbia U., 1950, PhD in Chemistry, 1953; MAT in Russian, U. Ill., Urbana, 1966. Author of cyrillic alphabet lesson PLATO (Programmed Logic for Automatic Tchg. Ops.), U. of Ill., Urbana, Ill., 1966—89; author of Russian reading program PLATO U. Ill., 1966—89, author of lab. material Slavic 101-104 PLATO, 1966—82, tchr. of Russian U. H.S., 1966—89; ret. Project dir. Apple Edn. Found., Urbana. Author: (cd) Russian Alphabet Program for TRS80, Apple II and IBM PC, Language Review Packets for Apple II and IBM, Conversations Around the World: in French, German, Russian, Spanish. Recipient Outstanding Tchr. of Russian, Ill. Fgn. Lang. Assn., 1986, Achievement award, Mt. Holyok Coll. Alumnae Assn., 1989; NEH grant, Apple Edn. Found. Mem.: Am. Assn. of Tchrs. Slavic and East European Langs. (sec., treas., v.p., pres. 1980—85), Phi Beta Kappa. Home: 12114 Lakewood Court Fort Myers FL 33908 Home Phone: 239-481-1035.

CURTIN, DAVID YARROW, chemist, educator; b. Phila., Aug. 22, 1920; s. Ellsworth Ferris and Margeretta (Cope) C.; m. Constance O'Hara, July 1, 1950; children— Susan McLean, David Ferris, Jane Yarrow. AB, Swarthmore Coll., 1943; PhD, U. Ill., 1945. Pvt. asst. Harvard, 1945-46; instr., then asst. prof. chemistry Columbia U., 1946-51; mem. faculty U. Ill., Urbana, 1951—, prof. chemistry, 1954-86, Fuson prof. emeritus, 1988—, head div. organic chemistry, 1963-65. Vis. lectr. Inst. de Quimica, Mexico, summer 1955, U. Tex., 1959; Reilly lectr. U. Notre Dame, 1960 Mem. editorial bd.: Organic Reactions, 1954- 64; adv. bd., 1965—; mem. bd. editors: Jour. Organic Chemistry, 1962-66. Einstein fellow Israel, 1982. Mem. Am., Brit., Swiss chem. socs., Nat. Acad. Sci., Am. Crystallographic Assn. Achievements include special research organic reaction mechanisms, stereochemistry, exploratory organic chemistry, reactions in solid state. Home: 12114 Lakewood Ct Fort Myers FL 33908

CURTIN, JANE THERESE, actress, writer; b. Cambridge, Mass., Sept. 6, 1947; d. John Joseph and Mary Constance (Farrell) C.; m. Patrick F. Lynch, Apr. 31, 1975; 1 child, Tess. AA, Elizabeth Seton Jr. Coll., 1967; student, Northeastern U., 1967-68. Appeared in plays The Proposition, Cambridge and N.Y.C., 1968-72, Last of the Red Hot Lovers touring co., 1973; Broadway debut in Candida, 1981; author, actress Off-Broadway mus. rev. Pretzels, 1974-75; star TV series NBC Saturday Night Live, 1975-79, Kate & Allie, 1984-88, Working It Out, 1990, 3rd Rock from the Sun, 1996-2001 (Golden Satellite for best actress 1996), Crumbs, 2006-; appeared in films including Mr. Mike's Mondo Video, 1979, How to Beat the High Cost of Living, 1980, O.C. and Stiggs, 1987, Coneheads, 1993, Antz, 1998, Geraldine's Fortune, 2004, Brooklyn Lobster, 2005, The Shaggy Dog, 2006; TV films include Divorce Wars-A Love Story, 1982, Suspicion, 1988, Maybe Baby, 1988, Common Ground, 1990, Tad, 1995, Christmas in Washington, 1996, Catch a Falling Star, 2000, Our Town, 2003, The Librarian: Quest for the Spear, 2004; TV guest appearance Recess, 1997. Recipient Emmy nomination, 1977, 87; Emmy awards for outstanding actress in comedy series, 1984, 85 Mem. Screen Actors Guild, Actors Equity, AFTRA. Office: ICM care Boaty Boatwright 40 W 57th St Fl 16 New York NY 10019-4098

CURTIN, JOHN JOSEPH, JR., lawyer; b. Englewood, NJ, Mar. 12, 1933; s. John Joseph and Marion (Walsh) C.; m. Mary Daly, Sept. 27, 1958; children: Kevin Joseph, Catherine Mary, Joseph Patrick, Ann Mary, Daniel Joseph. AB magna cum laude, Boston Coll., 1954, JD, 1957; LLM, Georgetown U., 1959. Bar: Mass. 1957, DC 1959, US Supreme Ct. 1961. Atty. US Dept. Justice, Washington, 1957-59; assoc. firm Hogan and Hartson, Washington, 1959-61; atty. Office of U.S. Atty., Boston, 1961-64; chief civil divsn., 1963-64; assoc. then ptnr. Bingham McCutchen LLP (formerly Bingham, Dana & Gould), Boston, 1964—2005, of counsel, 2005—. Instr. Boston Coll. Law Sch., 1965—; lectr. Harvard U. Law Sch., 1977-82; bd. dirs. Nat. Consumer Law Ctr., 1994—. Trustee Regis Coll., 1977-83, Newton Coll. Sacred Heart, 1973-75; mem. local govt. adv. com. Commonwealth of Mass., 1978; mem. Town Mtg., Wellesley, Mass., 1970-79, moderator, 1979-84, chmn. adv. com., 1974-75, chmn. town improvements coordinating com., 1977-79, chmn. capital budgeting and investment com., 1979-80; chmn. bd. advisors Boston Coll. Law Sch., 1997—; mem. bd. govs., exec. com. mem. Ctr. for Public Resources, 1994—. Recipient Lifetime Achievement award, Am. Lawyer mag., 2005 Mem. ABA (chmn. sect. litigation 1984-85, pres. 1990-91, chmn. working group state justice initiatives, 1994-97, chmn. coalition for justice 1997—), Boston Bar Assn. (pres. 1979-81, chmn. task force profl. fulfillment, 1996—), Am. Bar Found., Am. Law Inst., Greater Boston Legal Svcs. (bd. dirs. until 1990), Boston Coll. Alumni Assn. (v.p., pres. 1975-76), Nat. Consumer Law Ctr., Mass. Assn. Town Fin. Fin. Com. (pres. 1978), Nat. Assn. Pub. Interest Law, Fellowships for Equal Justice (pres. 1992-95), Nat. Legal Aid and Defender Assn. (bd. dirs. 1990-95). Office: Bingham McCutchen LLP 150 Federal St Fl 15 Boston MA 02110-1745 E-mail: jjcurtin@bingham.com.

CURTIN, JOSEPH, violinmaker; Attended, U. We. Ontario, 1971—73, U. Toronto, 1974—77. Founder, prin., violinmaker Joseph Curtin Studios, 1997—. Co-dir. acoustic workshop Violin Soc. America, Oberlin Coll.; trustee, contbg. editor Catgut Acoustical Soc. Named MacArthur fellow, John D. and Catherine T. MacArthur Found., 2005. Achievements include research in integrating acoustic science and nontraditional materials and structures with traditional violinmaking methods to improve an instrument's sound and response. Office: Joseph Curtin Studios 3493 West Delhi Ann Arbor MI 48103

CURTIN, LAWRENCE N., lawyer; b. Glen Ridge, NJ, Apr. 29, 1950; BS with honors, Fla. State U., 1972; JD with honors, Fla. State U. Coll. Law, 1976. Bar: Fla. 1976, U.S. Dist. Ct. (No. Dist.) Fla., U.S. Ct. Appeals (4th, 5th, 11th and D.C. cirs.). Law clerk to Hon. William Stafford U.S. Dist. Ct. (No. dist.) Fla., 1976-78; exec. ptnr. Holland & Knight, Tallahassee. Mem. Law Review, 1975-76; co-author: Surface Water Pollution Control, vol. 1, 1986-96; contbr. articles to profl. jours. Mem. ABA (litig., corp., bus. and banking sects.), Fla. Bar (chmn. energy law com. 1983-84, mem. adminstrv. and environ. and land use law sect., natural resources law), Tallahassee Bar Assn., Beta Gamma Sigma, Sigma Iota Epsilon. Office: Holland & Knight LLP PO Drawer 810 315 S Calhoun St Ste 600 Tallahassee FL 32301-1897 Office Phone: 850-224-7000, 850-425-5678. E-mail: larry.curtin@hklaw.com.

CURTIN, MICHAEL FRANCIS, publishing executive; b. Columbus, Ohio, Oct. 23, 1951; s. Robert Edward and Marie (Cummins) C.; m. Sharon Rhodes, May 26, 1976; children: Matthew, Christy. BA in Journalism, Ohio State U., 1973. Reporter The Columbus (Ohio) Dispatch, 1973-85, pub. affairs editor, 1985-94, exec. mng. editor, 1994-95, editor, 1995-99, assoc. pub., 1998—; pres. The Dispatch Printing Co., 1999—2002, COO, 2002—, vice chmn., 2005—. Bd. dirs. The Columbus Dispatch, Ohio Mag. Author: (book) The Ohio Politics Almanac, 1996, 2006. Bd. dirs. YMCA, Columbus, 1996-97, Prevent Blindiness/Ohio, Columbus, 1997, Greater Columbus C. of C., Mt. Carmel Health Sys., Columbus Met. Libr. Found., Cath. Found. of Columbus Diocese. Mem. Soc. Profl. Journalists, Ohio Newspaper Assn., Athletic Club. Roman Catholic. Office: The Columbus Dispatch 34 S 3rd St Columbus OH 43215-4241 Office Phone: 614-461-5069. E-mail: mcurtin@dispatch.com.*

CURTIN, PETER J., lawyer; b. Cin., Sept. 18, 1967; BA summa cum laude, U. Cin., 1988; JD magna cum laude, Georgetown U., 1991. Bar: DC 1991, US Ct. of Appeals (4th cir.) 1993, US Ct. of Appeals (fed. cir.) 2002, US Dist. Ct. Md. 1998, US Dist. Ct. DC 2004, US Dist. Ct. (ea. dist.) Wis. 2005. Former mil. prosecutor; former spl. asst. US atty. 6th Mil. Jud. Cir., Ea. Dist., NC; ptnr., intellectual property litigation Venable LLP, Washington, 2001—. Capt. US Army, 1992—95. Mem.: ABA (mem. litigation and intellectual property sects.), Am. Intellectual Property Law Assn., Federal

Circuit Bar Assn., DC Bar Assn. Office: Venable LLP 575 7th St NW Washington DC 20004 Office Phone: 202-344-8187. Office Fax: 202-344-8300. Business E-Mail: pjcurtin@venable.com.

CURTIN, PHYLLIS, music educator, dean, vocalist; b. Clarksburg, W.Va. d. E. Vernon and Betty R. (Robinson) Smith; m. Eugene Cook, May 6, 1956 (dec.); 1 child, Claudia Madeleine. BA, Wellesley Coll., 1943. Prof. Yale Sch. Music, New Haven, 1974-83; master Branford Coll. Yale U., New Haven, 1979-83; dean Coll. Fine Arts, prof. music Boston U., 1983-91, prof. music, 1983—, dean emerita, prof. music, 1991—; artist-in-residence, head vocal studies Tanglewood Music Ctr., Tanglewood, Lenox, Mass., 1965—. Named Amb. for the Arts; tchr. master classes U.S., Can., Beijing, Moscow. Recital debut Town Hall, NYC, 1950, opera debut, NYC Opera in U.S. premiere of The Trial, 1953, recitals throughout, U.S. and fgn. countries; soprano soloist leading symphony orchestras; performer, tchr., Aspen Mus. Festival, 1953-57, appeared as Cressida in, Walton's Troilus and Cressida in, NY premiere, 1955; title role in Floyd's: Susannah, world premiere, Tallahassee, 1955; title role in: Darius Milhaud's Medea, U.S. premiere, Brandeis U., 1955; world premiere Floyd's opera Wuthering Heights, 1958, Floyd's Passion of Jonathan Wade, 1959, Flower and Hawk, 1971; U.S. Premier Peter Grimes, 1946; leading soprano: Vienna Staatsoper, 1960, 61; debut as Fiordiligi in Cosi Fan Tutte, Met. Opera Co., 1961, La Scala Opera, Milan, 1962; U.S. premiere Benjamin Britten's War Requiem, with Boston Symphony, 1963; world premiere of Darius Milhaud's opera La Mére Coupable, Geneva, 1966; U.S. premiere Dimitri Shostakovitch's Symphony No. 14, with, Phila. Orch., 1971. Recipient Alumnae Achievement award, Wellesley Coll., Nadia Boulanger Achievement award, Longy Sch. Music, Letter of Distinction for Svc. to Am. Music, Am. Music Ctr., Lifetime Achievement award, Nat. Opera Assn., 2005, Disting. Faculty award, Boston U., 2007. Home: 9 Seekonk Rd Great Barrington MA 01230-1558 Personal E-mail: curtinphyllis@msn.com.

CURTIN, THOMAS LEE, ophthalmologist; b. Columbus, Ohio, Sept. 9, 1932; s. Leo Anthony and Mary Elizabeth (Burns) C.; m. Constance L. Sallman; children: Michael, Gregory, Thomas, Christopher, Kenton. BS, Loyola U., LA, 1954; MD, U. So. Calif., 1957; cert. navy flight surgeon, US Naval Sch. Aerospace Med., 1959. Diplomate Am. Bd. Ophthalmology. Intern Ohio State U. Hosp., 1957-58; resident in ophthalmology U.S. Naval Hosp, San Diego, 1961-64; pvt. practice medicine specializing in ophthalmology Oceanside, Calif., 1967—. Mem. staff Tri City, Scripps Meml. hosps.; sci. adv. bd. So. Calif. Soc. Prevention Blindness, 1973-76; bd. dirs. North Coast Surgery Ctr., Oceanside, 1987-96; cons. in field. Trustee Carlsbad Unified Sch. Dist., 1975—83, pres., 1979, 1982, 1983; trustee Carlsbad Libr., 1990—99, pres., 1993, 1998; bd. dirs. Mission San Luis Rey, Oceanside, Calif., 2006—. Officer MC USN, 1958—67. Mem. AMA, Calif. Med. Assn., San Diego County Med. Soc., Am. Acad. Ophthalmology, Aerospace Med. Assn., San Diego Acad. Ophthalmology (pres. 1979), Calif. Assn. Ophthalmology (bd. dirs.), Carlsbad Rotary, El Camino Country Club. Repubican. Roman Catholic. Office: 3231 Waring Ct Ste S Oceanside CA 92056-4510

CURTIN, TIMOTHY JOHN, lawyer; b. Detroit, Sept. 21, 1942; s. James J. and Irma Alice (Sirotti) C.; m. B. Colleen Lindsey, July 11, 1964; children: Kathleen, Mary. BA, U. Mich., 1964, JD, 1967. Bar: Ohio 1968, Mich. 1970, U.S. Dist. Ct. (so. dist.) Ohio 1968, U.S. Dist. Ct. (we. dist.) Mich. 1970, U.S. Dist. Ct. (ea. dist.) Mich. 1980, U.S. Dist. Ct. Del. 1996, U.S. Dist. Ct. (no. dist.) Ill. 1999, U.S. Ct. Appeals (6th cir.) 1968. Assoc. Taft, Stettinius & Hollister, Cin., 1967-70, McCobb, Heaney & Van't Hof, Grand Rapids, Mich., 1970-72; ptnr. Schmidt, Howlett, Van't Hof, Snell & Vana, Grand Rapids, 1972-83, Varnum, Riddering, Schmidt & Howlett, Grand Rapids, 1983—2005, counsel, 2005—. Contbr. articles to legal publs. Treas. Kent County Dem. Com., 1976-78, chmn. 3rd Dist. Dem. Com., 1993—. Mem. ABA, Mich. Bar Assn., Grand Rapids Bar Assn., Fed. Bar Assn., Am. Bankruptcy Inst., Egypt Valley C.C. Democrat. Roman Catholic. Avocations: travel, fishing. Office: Varnum Riddering Schmidt & Howlett Box 352 333 Bridge St SW Grand Rapids MI 49501-0352 Office Phone: 616-336-6440. Business E-Mail: tjcurtin@varnumlaw.com.

CURTIS, ANTHONY R., communications educator; b. Marietta, Ohio, Oct. 31, 1940; s. Edwin Wyatt and Charlotte Suder Curtis; m. Judith Genevicz Curtis, Feb. 11, 1977. BA in journalism, Pa. State U., 1967, MA in polit. sci., 1970; PhD in mass comm., Union Inst. & U., 1997. Asst. prof. Pa. State U., University Park, 1971—77; v.p. TAB Books, Blue Ridge Summit, Pa., 1978—81; asst. prof. Hood Coll., Frederick, Md., 1981—84; pres. ARC Soft Pubs., Woodsboro, Md., 1981—92; instr. Salisbury State U., Md., 1992—97; assoc. dean Union Inst. & U., Cin., 1997—2002; prof. U. N.C., Pembroke, 2002—. Author: Space Almanac, 1989; editor: (online mag.) Space Today Online, 1994—; author: (cd rom book) Space: A Visual History of Manned Spaceflight, 1998. Mem. Raleigh Tavern Soc., Colonial Williamsburg Found., Williamsburg, Va., 1981—89. Recipient Apple Dist. Educator, Apple Computer, 2000—, Ednl. Adv., Am. Radio Relay League, 2000—, NASA Solar Sys. Ambassador, NASA Jet Propulsion Lab, 2002—. Mem.: Hist. of Sci. Soc., Friends of U. N.C. Pembroke Libr. (bd. pres. 2005—), Radio Amateur Satellite Corp., Highland Soc., Scotland Meml. Hosp. Found., W.A.R. Goodwin Soc., Colonial Williamsburg Found. Avocations: stamp collecting/philately, model railroading, amateur radio, photography. Home: 8000 Carnostie Dr Laurinburg NC 28352 Office: U NC PO Box 1510 Pembroke NC 28372 Office Phone: 910-521-6616. Office Fax: 910-522-5795. E-mail: acurtis@uncp.edu.

CURTIS, ARNOLD BENNETT, retired lumber company executive; b. Astoria, Oreg., May 5, 1940; s. Arnold Bennett and Irja Virginia (Thompson) C.; m. Erica Katherine Mitchell, Dec. 23, 1985; children: Braden Thomas, Bryce Bennett. BS, Oreg. State U., 1962. Brewing chemist Gen. Brewing, San Francisco, 1962-67; v.p. N.W. Hardwoods, Inc., Portland, Oreg., 1967-71, pres., 1971-80, also bd. dirs.; pres. N.W. Hardwoods divsn. Weyerhauser Co., Federal Way, Wash., 1980-97, v.p. Hardwood Bus. Group, 1990-98; ret., 1998. Bd. dirs. Puyallup Internat. Inc., Weyerhaeuser New Zealand Ltd., Pine Solutions Australia; chmn. bd. dirs. Columbia Forest Products, 2001. Mem. adv. bd. Ctr. Retail and Bus. Market Strategy. Mem. Hardwood Mfrs. Assn. (dir., exec. com. 1985-95, pres. 1993). *When you commit yourself to an answer it's best to always tell the truth - then you never have to worry about remembering what you said.*

CURTIS, BEN CLIFFORD, professional golfer; b. Columbus, Ohio, May 26, 1977; m. Candace Curtis. Student, Kent State U., Ohio. Profl. golfer, 2000—. Achievements include winning PGA Tour events including the British Open, 2003, Booz Allen Classic, 2006; winner, amateur events including the Ohio Amateur, 1999, 2000, Players' Amateur, 2000. Mailing: PGA TOUR 112 PGA TOUR Blvd Ponte Vedra Beach FL 32082

CURTIS, CAROLE ORTALE, executive recruiter, consultant; b. Inglewood, Calif., Aug. 15, 1944; d. Albert Thomas and Ann Irene Ortale; m. John Joseph Curtis, Oct. 19, 1968; children: Mark Gregory, Michelle Ann. BA in English and Edn., Cal State U., Long Beach, 1967, Grad. Cert. in Career Counseling, 1982. Career mgmt. cons. Image Plus, Rancho Palos Verdes, Calif., 1996—. Pers. mgr. Savage Info. Svcs., Torrance, 1989—91; career counselor Ednl. and Tutorial Svcs., Palos Verdes Peninsula, Calif., 1994—96; guidance counselor So. Calif. Regional Ctr., Torrance, 1997—98; dir. career ctr., career counselor Career Planning Ctr., Marina Del Rey, Calif., 2000—02; career adv. Casa De Los Angilitos, 2005—; cons. in field. Author: (poetry) A Time of Strife, 2003, The Tribute, 2004, A New Decade, 2004, Eyes of the Moon, 2006, To Die and Be Forgotten, 2006; photographer Artistic Visions; contbr. poetry to anthologies. Advocate Alzheimers Orgn., Rancho Palos Verdes, 2001—06; legislative chair Soleado Sch., Rancho Palos Verdes, Calif., 1980—81; assoc. Nat. Career Devel. Assn., 1997—2004; membership chair Las Ayudas, Rancho Palos Verdes, 1998—2000; minister St. John Fisher, Rancho Palos Verdes, Calif., 1995—99, co-chair women's group, 2006—, co-chmn. guild, 2006—07; bd. dirs. Casa de L.A., 2006. Nominee Most Disting. Alumni, El Camino Coll., 1998, Poet of Yr., 2006. Mem.: Internat. Soc. Poets, Calif. Assn. Career Counselors (assoc.), Beta Sigma Phi (v.p., treas. 1987—93). Avocations: writing poetry, photography, travel, dance. Home: 27510 Halescorner Rd Rancho Palos Verdes CA 90275 Home Phone: 310-541-6315. Business E-Mail: cccounselor@juno.com.

CURTIS, CAROLYN ANN, musician, educator; b. Akron, Ohio, May 1, 1943; d. Basil Lee and Mary Elinor Curtis. BS in Music Edn., U. Akron, Ohio, 1966; M in Music Performance, U. Mich., Ann Arbor, 1969. HS band dir. Detroit Bd. Edn., 1965—91; organist, choir dir. Charity Luth. Ch., Detroit, 1968—83, Our Saviour Luth. Ch., Detroit, 1983—85; min. music St. James Luth. Ch., Grosse Pointe, Mich., 1985—91; choir dir., organist Grace Luth. Ch., Akron, Ohio, 1993—2003; organist Bethany United Ch. of Christ, Cuyahoga Falls, Ohio, 2003—. Trumpeter Detroit Concert Band, 1970—73; solo cornetist, trustee, treas. Freedom Brass Band, Akron, 2003—; 1st trumpet Detroit Women's Symphony, 1965—75, Grosse Pointe Symphony, 1965—73. Mem.: Am. Fedn. Musicians, Am. Guild Organists, Internat. Trumpet Guild, Akron Symphony Guild, Friends of Music. Home: 332 Franklin Ave Cuyahoga Falls OH 44221

CURTIS, CHARLES B., former federal agency administrator; b. Upper Darby, Penn., 1940; m. Rochelle Elaine Curtis; 1 child. BA, BS, U. Mass.; JD, Boston U. Founding ptnr. Van Ness Feldman, P.C.; chmn. Fed. Energy Regulatory Commn., 1977—81; under sec. US Dept. Energy, Washington, 1994—95, dep. sec., 1995—97; ptnr., dir. energy group Hogan & Hartson LLP, 1997—99; exec. v.p., COO UN Found., 1999—2001; pres., COO Nuclear Threat Initiative, Inc., 2001—. Mem. Coun. Fgn. Rels.; bd. dirs. Edison Internat., 2006—. Served in USAR, 1965—71. Office: Nuclear Threat Initiative 1747 Pennsylvania Ave NW 7th Fl Washington DC 20006

CURTIS, CHARLES EDWARD, Canadian government official; b. Winnipeg, Man., Can., July 28, 1931; s. Samuel and May (Goodison) C.; m. Hilda Marion Simpson, Oct. 30, 1954; 1 dau., Nancy Maude. C.A., U. Manitoba, 1955. Chartered acct. Dunwoody & Co., Winnipeg, 1949-54; chief assessor nat. revenue, income tax bd. Province of N.B., Can., 1954-67; asst. dep. min. budget fin. and adminstrn. Province of Man., Winnipeg, 1967-75, dep. min., 1976-96. Past CEO Man. Energy Authority; acting CEO MTX subs. Man. Telephone Sys.; mem. investment coms. Superannuation Bd., WPG Found., Manitoba Mus. Man & Nature, Law Soc. Manitoba; exec.-in-residence faculty of mgmt. U. Man. Fellow Can. Inst. Chartered Accts. (past chmn. pub. sector acctg. and audit standards com.); mem. Man. Inst. Chartered Accts. (pres. 1975-76), Law Soc. of Man. (lay bencher), Order of Man., Rotary (hon. treas. 1974-2000), Man. Club. Home: 596 South Dr Winnipeg MB Canada R3T 0B1 Office: Provincial Govt Province MN 109-450 Broadway Ave Winnipeg MB Canada R3C 0V8 Office Phone: 204-475-0725.

CURTIS, CHARLES G., JR., lawyer; BA in History magna cum laude, Harvard U., 1978; JD, U. Chgo., 1982. Bar: Wis., Am. Bar Assoc., U.S. Supreme Ct., U.S. Ct. appeals, 7th cir., U.S. Dist. Ct., Nr. N.Y. Law Clerk Senior Judge David L. Bazelon, U.S. Ct. of Appeals, 1982—83, Justice William J. Brennan, Jr., U.S. Supreme Ct., 1984; ptnr. Foley & Lardner; atty., Co-Chair Appeals and Strategy Heller, Ehrman, White, & McAuliffe LLP, 2001—. Named one of The Best Lawyers in Am., 2003—04. Office: Heller Ehrman 1 Main St Ste 201 Madison WI 53703 Office Phone: 608-663-7480. Fax: 608-663-7499. E-mail: ccurtis@hewm.com.

CURTIS, D. JAY, lawyer; b. Stillwater, Okla., Dec. 9, 1942; s. Dale R. and Muriel (Morris) Curtis; m. Kathryn Hoops, Aug. 6, 1965; children: Dale, Jonathan, Tyler, Bryan, Andrew. BS in Acctg., U. Utah, 1968, JD, 1971. Bar: Utah 1971, US Dist. Ct. (dist. Utah) 1971, US Tax Ct. 1984. Ptnr. Kesler, Gordon & Curtis, Salt Lake City, 1971—76, Nielsen & Sr. and predecessor, Salt Lake City, 1977—89; shareholder Ray, Quinney & Nebeker, P.C., Salt Lake City. Served USAR, 1961—68. Named one of Top 100 Attys., Worth mag., 2006, Best Lawyers in Am., 2007. Mem.: Estate Planning Coun. Salt Lake City, Salt Lake County Bar Assn., Utah Bar State Assn. (chmn. lawyer benefits com. 1980—83), ABA, Mountain State Pension Conf. (mem. 1974, pres. 1979), Holy Cross Found. (planned giving com. 1985), Primary Children's Med. Ctr. (deferred gifts com. 1980—81). Republican. Mem. Lds Ch. Office: Ray Quinney & Nebeker PO Box 45385 36 S State St Ste 1400 Salt Lake City UT 84111-0385 Office Phone: 801-323-3314. E-mail: jcurtis@rqn.com.

CURTIS, DEANA A., electronics executive, small business owner; b. Rochester, NY, July 31, 1953; d. Dean A. and Patricia A. Prevost; m. Michael J Curtis, July 4, 2004. AS in Fashion and Interior Decorating, John Robert Powers, 1972. With advt. divsn. Dem. & Chronicle, Rochester, 1971—73; leasing adminstr., property tax mgmt. Xerox Corp., Webster, NY, 1976—; prin., owner Impressions Dating Svc., Rochester, 1996—98, Shadows of the Past, Rochester, 1996—; prin., co-owner Niagara Elec. Sales, Rochester, 1987—94. Vol. Holy Cross Ch., Rochester, 1980—96. Recipient Recognition award, Astoria, 1993. Republican. Roman Cath. Home: 4625 Kear Rd Canandaigua NY 14424 Office: Xerox Corp 800 Salt Rd Bldg 843 Webster NY 14580 Office Phone: 585-393-1975.

CURTIS, DOUGLAS HOMER, small business owner; b. Jackson, Mich., July 19, 1934; s. Homer K. and Luella D. (Hall) C.; m. Jean A. Breaux; children: Rebecca, Linda, Colleen, Robert. BA, Park Coll., Parkville, Mo., 1956. With Gen. Electric Co., 1958-69, mgr. Boston region Gen. Electric Supply Co. div., 1967-69; v.p. fin. and adminstrn. internat. Data Corp., Boston, 1969; v.p. fin. Franklin Electric Co. Inc., Bluffton, Ind., 1969-80; pres. Curtis Assocs., Inc., Bluffton, 1980-82; pres., COO Satelco, Inc., San Antonio, 1983-84; v.p. adminstrn. Lyall Electric Co., Kendallville, Ind., 1984-86; pres., owner Flexible Personnel Group of Cos., Inc., Ft. Wayne, Ind., 1987-97, Nat. On-Site Pers., 1991-2001, HR America, 1992—, On-Site Med. Staffing, 2000—. Bd. dirs. Wabash Valley Mfg., Inc., Silver Lake, Ind., Sentry Points; pres. Wells County (Ind.) Hosp. Authority, 1974-75 Served to capt. USMCR, 1956-58. Mem. Nat. Assn. Securities Dealers (vicechmn. fin. 1980, chmn. fin. com. 1980), Fin. Execs. Inst. (chpt. dir. 1975) Office: 1833 Magnavox Way Fort Wayne IN 46804-1539 Office Phone: 260-436-3878. Business E-Mail: dcurtis@hramerica.net.

CURTIS, EDWARD JOSEPH, JR., gas industry executive, management consultant; b. Boston, May 26, 1942; s. Edward Joseph and Violet Ella (Upton) C.; m. Virginia Carolyn Fye, May 9, 1976; children: Jane Mercedes, Sherri Jean, Virginia Amy. BSChemE, Worcester Polytech., 1964, MSChemE, 1966. Engr. Cabot Corp., Boston, 1966-68; mgr. corp. devel. Distrigas Corp., Boston, 1968-72; pres. E.J. Curtis Assocs., Inc., York Harbor, Maine, 1972—. Pres. Pine Hill Assocs., Inc., Hollis, N.H., 1976-80; ptnr. ABC Mgmt. Systems, Bellingham, Wash., 1977-82; mng. ptnr. Essex Cons. Svcs., Boston, 1981-82. Pres. York Harbor Neighborhood Assn., 1989-92. Mem. AIChE, Am. Gas Assn., New Eng. Gas Assn. (bd. dirs. 1988-91, 95-2001), Soc. Gas Lighting, Assn. Energy Engrs., Internat. Assn. Energy Economists, , Guild Gas Mgrs., York Golf and Tennis Club, Rosedale Golf and Country Club, Agamenticus Yacht Club, York Harbor Reading Rm., Theta Chi. Republican. Mem. Congl. Ch. Avocations: sailing, skiing, golf, computer science, music.

CURTIS, FRANK R., lawyer; b. Valley Stream, NY, Sept. 27, 1946; s. Frank and Rosalind (Vreeland) Curtis; m. Cynthia Mary Knapik, May 14, 1977; children: Lauren Josephine, Frank Edward, Michael Bennett. AB magna cum laude, Harvard Coll., 1968; JD, Yale U., 1971. Bar: N.Y. 1972, U.S. Dist. Cts. (so. and ea. dists.): N.Y. 1973, U.S. Ct. Appeals (2d cir.): 1975. Assoc. Hellerstein Rosier & Rembar, NYC, 1971—73; ptnr. Rembar Wolf & Curtis, NY, 1974—77, Rembar & Curtis, NYC, 1978—. Lectr. PLI, NYC, 1980, NYC, 88. Trustee North Salem Free Libr., NY, 1983—91. Mem.: N.Y. State Bar Assn., Copyright Soc. of the U.S.A., Assn. of Bar of City of N.Y. (sec. com. on copyright 1979—80), Harvard Club, Phi Beta Kappa. Home: PO Box 908 2 Juengstville Rd Croton Falls NY 10519-0908 Office: Rembar & Curtis 2 Juengstville Rd PO Box 908 Croton Falls NY 10519 Office Phone: 914-276-2920.

CURTIS, GEORGE WARREN, lawyer; b. Merrill, Wis., Sept. 24, 1936; s. George Gregory and Rose E. (Zimmerman) C.; m. Judith Olson, 1956 (div. 1966); m. Mary Pelman, 1967 (dec. 1973); children: George, Catherine Schmidt, Eric, Greg, Paul, David; m. Mary Ruth Kersztyn, Dec. 27, 1973 (div. 1999); children: Emily, Benjamin; m. Suzette Bigler Whyte, July 10, 1999; stepchildren: Erika, Evan. BA, U. Minn., 1959; JD, U. Wis., 1962. Bar: Wis. 1962, Fla. 1968. Assoc. Russell & Curtis, Merrill, 1962-68; ptnr. Nolan, Engler, Yakes & Curtis, Oshkosh, Wis., 1968-74, Curtis, MacKenzie, Haase & Brown, Oshkosh, 1974-83, Curtis, Wilde & Neal, Oshkosh, 1984-96, Curtis & Neal, Oshkosh, 1997-98; with Curtis Law Offices, 1999. Host (TV show) It's Your Law. Named Super Lawyer, Milw. Mag., 2005, 2006. Fellow: Wis. Bar Found.; mem.: ATLA (bd. govs.), Internat. Soc. Barristers, Wis. Acad. Trial Lawyers (bd. dirs. 1978—83, treas. 1984, sec. 1985, v.p. 1986, pres. 1987), Am. Bd. Trial Advocates (pres. Wis. chpt.), Am. Coll. Trial Lawyers. Democrat. Avocations: conservationist, dog trainer. Home: 7361 Canary Rd Pickett WI 54964-9724 Office: Curtis Law Offices 2905 Universal St Oshkosh WI 54904-6341 Office Phone: 920-233-1010. Business E-Mail: curtislw@execpc.com.

CURTIS, J. VAUGHAN, lawyer; b. Lexington, Ky., June 2, 1951; Student, Centre Coll.; BA, U. Ky., 1973, MA, 1975, JD with distinction, 1978. Bar: Ga. 1978, Ky. 1980. Atty. The White House, Ford Adminstrn.; joined Alston & Bird LLP, Atlanta, 1978—, ptnr., healthcare, corp. group Atlanta & NYC. Lead articles editor Ky. Law Jour., 1977-78. Mem. State Bar Ga., Ky. Bar Assn., Atlanta Bar Assn., Order of Coif., Phi Delta Phi. Office: Alston & Bird LLP One Atlantic Ctr 1201 W Peachtree St NW Atlanta GA 30309-3424 Office Phone: 404-881-7397. Office Fax: 404-881-7777. Business E-Mail: vaughan.curtis@alston.com.

CURTIS, JAMES THEODORE, lawyer; b. Lowell, Mass., July 8, 1923; s. Theodore D. and Maria (Souliotis) Koutras; m. Kleanthe D. Dusopol, June 25, 1950; children: Madelon Mary, Theodore James, Stephanie Diane, Gregory Theodosius, James Theodore Jr. BA, U. Mich., 1948; JD, Harvard U., 1951; ScD (hon.), U. Mass., 1972. Bar: Mass. 1951. Assoc. Adams & Blinn, Boston, 1951-52; legal asst., asst. atty. gen. Mass., 1952-53; pvt. practice law Lowell, 1953-57; sr. ptnr. firm Goldman & Curtis, and predecessors, Lowell and Boston, 1957—. Elected mem. Lowell Charter Commn., 1969—71; del. Dem. Party State Convs., 1956—60; chmn. Greater Lowell Heart Fund, 1967—68; mem. adv. bd. Salvation Army, sec., 1956—58; mem. bd. Higher Edn. Msss., 1967—72; bd. dirs. U. Mass. Rsch. Found., Lowell, 1965—72, Merrimack Valley Health Planning Coun., 1969—72; trustee U. Mass., Lowell, 1963—72, chmn. bd., 1968—72. With 10th mt. divsn. US Army, 1943—45, spl. agent counter intelligence corps. US Army, 1945—46. Decorated Knight Order Orthodox Crusade Holy Sepulcher. Mem.: ATLA, ABA, U. Mich. Alumni Assn., Harvard Law Sch. Alumni Assn., Am. Judicature Soc., Mass. Acad. Trial Lawyers, Middlesex Conty Bar Assn., Mass. Bar Assn., DAV, Lowell Hist. Soc., Harvard Club (Lowell, pres. 1969—71, bd. dirs.), Masons, Delta Epsilon Pi. Home: 111 Rivercliff Rd Lowell MA 01852-1471 Office: Goldman & Curtis PC 144 Merrimack St Ste 444 Lowell MA 01852-1789 Office Phone: 978-454-8804. Business E-Mail: law@goldman-curtis.com, jcurtis@goldman-curtis.com.

CURTIS, JAMIE LEE, actress; b. LA, Nov. 22, 1958; d. Tony Curtis and Janet Leigh (dec. 2004); m. Christopher Guest, Dec. 18, 1984; children: Annie, Thomas. Student, U. Pacific, Stockton, Calif., 1976. Actress: (films) Halloween, 1978, The Fog, 1980, Prom Night, 1980, Terror Train, 1980, Halloween II, 1981, Road Games, 1981, Trading Places, 1983, Love Letters, 1984 Grandview USA, 1984, The Adventures of Buckaroo Banzai: Across the 8th Dimension, 1984, Perfect, 1985, Welcome Home, 1986, A Man in Love, 1987, Amazing Grace and Chuck, 1987, Dominick and Eugene, 1988, A Fish Called Wanda, 1988, Blue Steel, 1990, Queens Logic, 1991, My Girl, 1991, Forever Young, 1992, My Girl 2, 1994, Mother's Boys, 1994 True Lies, 1994 (Golden Globe award Best Actress - Musical or Comedy), House Arrest, 1996, Ellen's Energy Adventure, 1996, Fierce Creatures, 1997, Homegrown, 1998, Halloween H2O, 1998, Virus, 1999, Drowning Mona, 2000, The Tailor of Panama, 2001, Daddy and Them, 2001, Rudolf the Red-Nosed Reindeer and the Island of Misfit Toys (voice), 2001, Halloween: Resurrection, 2002, Freaky Friday, 2003, Christmas with the Kranks, 2004, The Kid and I, 2005; (TV movies) Colombo: Bye-Bye Sky-High I.Q. Murder Case, 1977, Death of a Centerfold: The Dorothy Stratten Story, 1981, Money on the Side, 1982, As Summers Die, 1986, The Heidi Chronicles, 1995, Nicolas' Gift, 1998; (TV series) Operation Petticoat, 1977-78, She's in the Army Now, 1981, Anything but Love, 1990-93, Pigs Next Door, 2000; (TV appearances) Quincy, 1977, Hardy Boys/Nancy Drew Mysteries, 1977, Charlie's Angels, 1978, The Love Boat, 1978, Buck Rogers in the 25th Century, 1979, The Drew Carey Show, 1996; dir.: Anything But Love, 1990; author (children's books): When I Was Little: A Four-Year-Old's Memoir of Her Youth, 1993, Today I Feel Silly, 1998, Where Do Balloons Go? An Uplifting Mystery, 2000, I'm Gonna Like Me: Letting Off a Little Self-Esteem, 2002, It's Hard to Be Five, 2004, Is There Really a Human Race?, 2006. Office: Creative Artists Agy c/o Rick Kurtzman 9830 Wilshire Blvd Beverly Hills CA 90212-1804

CURTIS, JOHN J., medical educator; b. Rochester, NY, Jan. 16, 1944; s. John Joseph and Mabel (Leatherman) C.; m. Vicky Burleson, Oct. 2, 1987. BS, U. Scranton, 1966; MD, Georgetown U., 1970. Diplomate Am. Bd. Internal Medicine, Am. Bd. Nephrology. Asst. prof. medicine U. Ky. Med. Ctr., Lexington, Ky., 1974-79; assoc. prof. medicine U. Ala., Birmingham, 1979-85, prof. medicine, 1985—, prof. surgery, 1991—, Endowed prof. transplant surgery, 1991—, dir. The Transplant Ctr., 1999—. Program dir. Gen. Clin. Rsch. Ctr., Birmingham, 1988-98; mem. med. adv. bd. Ala. Kidney Found., Birmingham, 1989—. Asst. editor Am. Jour. Kidney Diseases, 1987-92; transplantion editor (book) Yearbook of Nephrology, 1992-96. 1st lt. USAR, 1970-72. Mem. Am. Soc. Nephrology, Internat. Soc. Nephrology, The Transplantation Soc., Am. Soc. Transplant Physicians, European Dialysis & Transplant Assn. Office: U Ala Birmingham Divsn Nephrology THT 643 1530 3rd Ave S Birmingham AL 35294-0006 Office Phone: 205-934-3217. E-mail: jjcurtis@uab.edu.*

CURTIS, JOHN JOSEPH, lawyer, writer; b. Fairmont, W.Va., Nov. 23, 1942; s. John Joseph and Marie Francis (Christopher) C.; m. Shirley Ann Slater, Oct. 15, 1971 (div. June 1993); children: Christopher, Kevin. AB, U. W.Va., 1964, JD, 1967. Bar: W.Va. 1967, Ill. 1972, Calif. 1979. Pvt. practice law, South Charleston, W.Va., 1967-68; chief counsel, asst. dir. W.Va. Tax Dept., Charleston, 1968-71; tax atty. Sears, Roebuck & Co., Chgo., 1971-73; chief tax counsel, dir. taxes Pacific Lighting, LA, 1973-87; ptnr. Baker & Hostetler, LA, 1987-93, Law Offices of John Curtis, LA, 1994—. Author: The Code, 2004. Com. mem. Pasadena Tournament Roses, 1978-93. Lt. comdr. USNR, 1968-80. Mem. ABA, L.A. County Bar

Assn. (chmn. com. 1989), Calif. Bar Assn., Inst. Property Tax, So. Calif.Tax Found. (pres. 1990-96), L.A. Taxpayers Assn. (pres. 1990-95), Calif. Taxpayers Assn. (pres. 1987-88). Avocations: skiing, scuba, fishing. Office: 2 Arado Rancho Santa Margarita CA 92688-2749 Home Phone: 949-888-9157; Office Phone: 949-888-9157. Business E-Mail: jcurtis595@aol.com.

CURTIS, JUDITH GENEVICZ, communications educator; b. Wilmington, Del., Mar. 21, 1953; d. Francis Stanley and Murryal Mannering Genevicz; m. Anthony R. Curtis, Feb. 11, 1977. BA in Journalism, Pa. State U., U. Pk., Pa., 1974; MA in Polit. Sci., Hood Coll., Frederick, Md., 1991; PhD in Mass Comm., Union Inst. and U., Cin., Ohio, 2000. Mng. editor TAB Books, Blue Ridge Summit, Pa., 1978—81; v.p. ARCsoft Pub., Woodsboro, Md., 1980—93; adj. faculty Salisbury State U., Md., 1994—97, Union Inst. and U., Cin., 1997—2002; asst. prof. U. N.C., Pembroke, NC, 2002—. Author: Favorite Recipes from America's 50 States, 1986, Handbook of Online Teaching, 2001; mng. editor: Space Today Mag., 1986—94; contbr. articles to profl. jours. Recipient Excellence in Tchg. award, Southwestern Ohio Coun. Higher Edn., 2001. Mem.: Assn. Edn. Journalism and Mass Comm., Mass Comm. Soc., Am. Radio Relay League (life), Friends Libr. U. N.C., Highland Soc., Goodwin Soc., Phi Kappa Phi. Avocations: photography, gardening, interior decorating, amateur radio. Home: 8000 Carnostie Dr Laurinburg NC 28352 Office: Univ North Carolina PO Box 1510 Pembroke NC 28372 Business E-Mail: jcurtis@uncp.edu.

CURTIS, KAREN HAYNES, lawyer; b. Laurel, Miss., Sept. 15, 1951; d. John Travis Haynes Jr. and Jeannine Burkett Tanner; children: Laurel Elizabeth Cornell, Jaime Rodriguez Cornell. BS in Biology, Tulane U., 1973; JD summa cum laude, Nova Law Ctr., 1978. Bar: Fla. 1978, US Ct Appeals (5th cir.) Fla. 1980, US Ct. Appeals (11th cir.) Fla. 1981, US Dist Ct. (so. dist.) Fla. 1986, US Dist Ct. (mid. dist.) Fla., 1986, US Supreme Ct. 1994; cert. in appellate practice Fla. Bar Bd. Legal Specialization and Edn., 1996. Law clk. Steel, Hector & Davis, Miami, Fla., 1978; law clk. to Judge William M. Hoeveler US Dist. Ct., Miami, Fla., 1978-80; assoc. Shutts & Bowen, Miami, Fla., 1980-84, ptnr., 1985-95; founding ptnr., pres. Gallwey Gillman Curtis & Vento, P.A., Miami, Fla., 1995—2004; ptnr. Clarke Silverglate & Campbell, P.A., Miami, 2004—. Dir. Ch. by the Sea, 1994—, treas., 2000-05. Listed in Leading Fla. Attys. civil appellate law, Fla. Super Lawyers appellate practice, 2006, Top 50 Female Lawyers in Fla., Fla. Trend's 2007, Fla. Legal Elite. Mem.: FBA, ABA, Am. Judicature Soc., Supreme Ct. Hist. Soc., Fla. Bar (grievance com. 1988—91, appellate ct. rules com. 1993—2002), Dade County Bar Assn. (ins. law com. 1990—91, appellate ct. com. 1991—, banking and corp. litig. com. 1992—93), Fla. Assn. Women Lawyers. United Ch. of Christ. Avocations: reading, piano, computer. Home: 18720 SW 33rd Court Miramar FL 33029 Office: Clarke Silverglate & Campbell PA 799 Brickell Plaza Ste 900 Miami FL 33131 Office Phone: 305-377-0700. Business E-Mail: kcurtis@csclawfirm.com.

CURTIS, MARK T., financial planner; B, Stanford Univ.; MBA, UCLA. Joined Smith Barney, 1981, mng. dir. wealth mgmt., corp. client group dir. Palo Alto, Calif. Past. pres. Assn. Profl. Investment Consultants. Named Top Fin. Advisor in Am., Barron's Mag., 2006—07; recipient Harry B. Irvine award, Consulting Group, 1996. Office: Smith Barney Ste 101 Bldg 4 1001 Pagemill Rd Palo Alto CA 94304*

CURTIS, MARY E. (MARY HOROWITZ), publishing executive; d. Lloyd E. and Jean Curtis; m. Irving Louis Horowitz, Oct. 30, 1979 AB cum laude, Washington U., St. Louis, 1968. Editl. dir. Transaction Pubs., New Brunswick, NJ, 1968-74, exec. v.p., 1987-97, pres., 1997—, chmn. bd. dirs., 1994-97; editor in chief Praeger Pubs. subs. CBS Ednl. Pub., NYC, 1974-79; v.p., pub. periodicals John Wiley and Sons, NYC, 1979-87; v.p. Scripta Techica subs. John Wiley and Sons, Washington, 1984-87; mem. mgmt. bd. MIT Press, 1998—; vice chair, trustee Horowitz Found. for Social Policy, 1998—. Chair adv. com. Serials Industry Systems, 1985-88; dir. Transaction Pubs. (U.K.) Ltd.; lectr. in field. Contbr. articles to profl. jours. Mem. Soc. Scholarly Pubs. (bd. dirs. 1984-88), Assn. Am. Pubs. (Freedom to Read com.). Jewish. Office Phone: 732-445-2280. Business E-Mail: mcurtis@transactionpub.com.

CURTIS, MICHAEL, lawyer; b. Albuquerque, Aug. 11, 1949; BA, Columbia U., 1971; JD, Willamette U., 1977. Bar: Oreg. 1977, U.S. Dist. Ct. Oreg. 1977. Ptnr. Curis & Correll, Portland, Oreg. Mem.: ABA, Am. Acad. Forensic Scis., Nat. Legal Aid and Defender Assn., Oreg. Criminal Def. Lawyers Assn. (life), Nat. Assn. Criminal Def. Lawyers (life). Office: Curtis & Correll 4300 NE Fremont St Ste 230 Portland OR 97213 Office Phone: 503-284-0763. E-mail: curtismichael@qwest.net.

CURTIS, PAUL JAMES, performance artist, director; b. Boston, Aug. 29, 1927; s. Lawrence D. and Madeleine Maria (Schwager) C. Studied directing with Erwin Piscator, New Sch. for Social Rsch., 1947-49. Dir. Deal Conservatory Theatre, 1948; founder, dir., performer Am. Mime Theatre, NYC, 1952—; founder Am. Mime, Inc., NYC, 1970—, Internat. Mimes & Pantomimists, 1972-74; chmn. mime dept. Am. Acad. Dramatic Arts, NYC, 1956-71; lectr. emeritas Cornell U., Ithaca, NY, 1969-89. Instr. mime Bennington Coll., Vt., Jacob's Pillow Dance Festival, Mass., Ohio U., Austin Coll., Goodman Sch. Drama, Chgo., Pace U., NYC, Hunter Coll., NYC, Met. Opera Ballet Sch., NYC, New Sch. Social Rsch., NYC, Gene Frankel Theatre Workshop, NYC, Guggenheim Mus., NYC, Johns Hopkins U., Balt., Am. Conservatory Theatre, San Francisco, Circle in Sq. Theatre Sch., NYC, Sarah Lawrence Coll., NY, D'Youville Coll., NY, Lincoln Sch., Calif., Fairleigh Dickinson U., NJ, Stockton State Coll. NJ, Rutgers U., New Brunswick, NJ, Clarke Ctr., NYC, Guggenheim Mus., NYC, The Family, NYC, Johns Hopkins, Balt., RI Sch. Drama, Am. Conservatory Theatre Arts Guild, NJ, Brown U., RI, Seven Arts Ctr., NYC, Rye H.S., NY, Footlight Ranch, Pa., Ohio U., Austin Coll., Tex., Internat. Dance Sch., NYC, Mamaroneck Sch. Performing Arts, NY, The Leonardo's, Paris; Am. mime course established at Salle Pleyel, Paris, 1998, 59 Rivoli Chez Robert, Electron Libre, Paris workshops, 2000. TV appearances NBC Exploring the Performing Arts, 1963, NBC Profile on the Arts, 1966, Nippon TV Japan, 1970, NBC To Tell The Truth, 1973, NY Live Cable TV, 1974, NBC Today Show, 1975, WNYC-TV, 1975, 1978, ABC Kids Are People Too, 1978, WNEW Broadway Extra, 1978, ABC The Last Word, 1983, TV appearance Documentary Film on the American Mime Theatre, 2003, film documentary Paul J. Curtis American Mime; author: American Mime, the Medium, 1952, (plays) The Pinball Machine, 1953, Fate, 1953, The Tell Tale Heart, 1953, Escapade, 1953, The Demon Lover, 1953, Of Identity, 1953, Once Upon An Island, 1954, Monolotry, 1954, The Triple Goddess, 1954, The Western, 1954, Improvisation, 1955, Presentation, 1955, Eden, 1956, Abstraction, 1956, Commedia, 1956, Dreams I, 1958, The Scarecrow, 1962, Dreams II, 1962, The Godstuff, 1962, The Lovers, 1963, Birds, 1965, Female, 1967, Light, 1968, Hurly-Burly, 1969, Evolution, 1973, Sludge, 1974, Six, 1975, Work in Progress, 1976, Abstraction, 1977, The Unitaur, 1982, Peepshow, 1988, Pageant, 1989, Music Box, 1991, Couplings, 1999. With USN, 1944—46. Mem. AEA, AFTRA, Nat. Movement Theatre Assn. Office: Am Mime Theatre 61 4th Ave Fl 2 New York NY 10003-5204 Home Phone: 212-677-9276; Office Phone: 212-777-1710. Personal E-mail: ammime@aol.com. Business E-Mail: Mime@Americanmime.org.

CURTIS, PAULA ANNETTE, elementary and secondary education educator; b. Natrona Heights, Pa., Apr. 16, 1953; d. Stephen John and Josephine Kathleen (Killian) C. BS in Edn., Geneva Coll., 1974; postgrad., U. Vt., 1975, Pa. State U., New Kensington, 1978. Cert. religious edn. tchr., Pitts. Diocese. Tchr. Transfiguration Sch., Russellton, Pa., 1979—, dir. religious edn., 1995-98; tchr. continuing edn. C.C. of Allegheny County, Pitts., 1992—, Pa. State U., New Kensington, 1988—; tchr. O'Mara Driving Sch., Lower Burrell, Pa., 1976—, Lenape Votech., 1990—; CCD tchr. Transfiguration Sch., Russellton, 1995-97, head tchr., head fine arts dept., 1995-97, head Spanish dept. K-8, 1979—. Chmn. vision and values in Pitts. Diocese, Transfiguration Sch., 1980-97; CCD tchr. St. Clement Parish, Tarentum, Pa., 1986-92, dir. religious edn., 1987-92; dir. religious edn. St. Joseph Parish, Natrona, Pa., 1992-93; product tester Nat. Family Opinion Poll, 1987—; model Van Enterprises, Cranberry, Pa., 1989-92; tchr. driver edn. Plum (Pa.) Sr. H.S., 1996-98; Act 48 presenter for Penn Hills Sch. Dist. and Pitts. Diocesan Schs., 2002—; freelance model, Fashion Bug, 1998—. Vol. Help Beautify the Cmty. with Art, Russellton. Mem. Nat. Cath. Educators Assn., Nat. English Tchrs. Assn. Democrat. Roman Catholic. Avocations: craft designs, needle work, collecting reptiles, collecting and breeding tropical birds, breeding shih-tzus. Home: 211 W 9th Ave Tarentum PA 15084-1241 Office: Transfiguration Sch CCD Office 100 Mckrell Rd Russellton PA 15076-1100 Office Phone: 724-265-3350.

CURTIS, PHILIP KERRY, executive recruiter, lawyer; b. Mineola, NY, Nov. 6, 1945; s. William Kerry and Cherry (Smith) C.; m. Janet (McDowell), Sept. 9, 1970; 1 child, Kerry Bowen. BA, Dartmouth Coll., 1967; JD, Harvard Law Sch., 1971; MBA, Harvard U., 1974. Bar: N.Y., 1971; Ga., 1976. Assoc. White and Case, NYC, 1971-72, Hansell and Post, Atlanta, 1975-76; counsel, asst. to pres. Wiggins and Assoc., Atlanta, 1976-82; exec. v.p. Coers, Steinemann, and Co., Atlanta, 1982-84; exec. v.p., ptnr. Western Devel. SE, Atlanta, 1984-87; ptnr., sr. v.p. Charter Properties, Inc., Atlanta, 1987-93; exec. v.p. JDN Realty Corp., Atlanta, 1994-96; pres. Habersham Ptnr., Atlanta, 1996—2002; ptnr. Matteson Ptnr., Atlanta, 2002—. Vis. lectr. real estate, Kennesaw Coll., Grad. Bus. Sch., 1992-93. Elder Peachtree Presbyn. Ch., Atlanta, 1983-86; dir. Met. Arts Found., Atlanta, 1983-87; 1st lt., USAR, 1970-78. Mem.: SAR (pres. Atlanta chpt. 2005—06), St. George Soc. (pres. Atlanta chpt. 2007—), Soc. War of 1812, Soc. Colonial Wars, Mil. Order World Wars (jr. vice comdr. Atlanta chpt. 2007—), Gen. Soc. SR, Old Guard (lt. col., chief of staff), Mil. Order Stars and Bars, Civil War Roundtable, Venerable Order St. John, Nat. Meml. Day Assn. Ga. (pres. 2006—), Burge Plantation Club, Buckhead Fifty Club (v.p. 2007), Sigma Chi Club Atlanta (bd. dirs. 1985—86), Ravinia Club Ga., Army and Navy Club, Atlanta Forum, Harvard Bus. Sch. Club of Atlanta (pres. 1982—83), Dartmouth Club of Ga. (pres. 1982—84), Buckhead Rotary Club (bd. dirs. 2006—), Cherokee Town and Country Club, Harvard Club of Ga., German Club (pres. 1986). Republican. Home: 3111 Arden Rd NW Atlanta GA 30305-1916 Office: Two Ravinia Dr Ste 310 Atlanta GA 30346

CURTIS, RICHARD, author, screenwriter; b. Wellington, New Zealand, Nov. 8, 1956; s. Anthony and Glynness Curtis; children: Scarlett Kate Freud Curtis, Jake Daniel Anthony Freud Curtis. Student, Harrow, Oxford U. Screenwriter: (films) The Tall Guy, 1989; screenwriter, co-exec. producer Four Weddings and a Funeral, 1994; screenwriter Bean, 1997; screenwriter, exec. producer Notting Hill, 1999; screenwriter Bridget Jones' Diary, 2001; screenwriter, director, exec. producer Love Actually, 2003; screenwriter Bridget Jones: The Edge of Reason, 2004; (TV films) Blackadder's Christmas Carol, 1988; screenwriter, exec. producer The Girl in the Cafe, 2005 (Emmy award for Best Writing for a Miniseries Movie or Dramatic Special, 2006); screenwriter: (TV series) Not The Nine O'clock News, 1979—82; Blackadder, Blackadder II, Blackadder the Third, Blackadder Goes Forth, 1983—89; The Lenny Henry Show, 1984; Spitting Image, 1984—96; Mr. Bean, 1989—2002; Bernard and the Genie, 1991; The Vicar of Dibley, 1994—2000; Blackadder Back and Forth, 2000. Office: c/o Peteus Fraser & Dunlop 34-43 Russell St London WC2B 5HA England

CURTIS, ROBERT ALLEN, lawyer; b. Sun Valley, Calif., Aug. 31, 1974; s. Ronald Cleo and Darlene Victoria Curtis; m. Amy Nichole Los, Apr. 7, 2002; children: Kaylee Nichole, Madeleine Taylor. BA in Econ., UCLA, 1996; JD, Pepperdine U., Malibu, Calif., 1999. Bar: Calif., US Dist. Ct. (ctrl. and no. dist.) Calif., US Dist. Ct. (we. dist.) Mich., US Ct. Appeals (9th cir.). Law clk. Foley, Bezek & Komoroske, Burbank, Calif., 1998—99; assoc. atty. Foley & Bezek, LLP, Santa Barbara, Calif., 1999—2003, ptnr., 2003—05, Foley, Bezek, Bhile & Curtis, LLP, Santa Barbara, 2005—. Bd. dirs. alumni adv. bd. Ctr. Entrepreneur and Tech., Pepperdine U., 2004—. Contbr. articles to profl. jours. Mem.: William L. Gordon Inns of Ct., Santa Barbara County Bar Assn., John Wooden Athletic Fund. Avocations: travel, basketball.

CURTIS, ROBERT O., mechanical engineer; b. Pontiac, Mich., Jan. 11, 1948; s. Robert F. and Mary M. Curtis; m. Maria I. Asis, June 23, 1983; children: Christian J., Sheila A. BA, Kalamazoo Coll., Mich., 1966—70; BS, Lawrence Inst. Tech., Southfield, Mich., 1974—78; MS, Oakland U., Rochester, Mich., 1978—83. Cert. profl. engr., Mich., 1981. Ils support & svc. engr. Detroit Diesel Corp., 1977—. Master: Math Counts (assoc.; Mich. dir. 1983—2006); mem.: Mich. Soc Prof Engr. (assoc.; pres. 1988—89, dir. engrs. in industry 2004—06, Mich. Outstanding Engr. in Industry award 2004). Achievements include research in combustion & emissions testing. Office: Detroit Diesel 13400 Outer Dr W Detroit MI 48239 Home Phone: 248-661-6628. Office Fax: 313-592-5802. Business E-Mail: bob.curtis@detroitdiesel.com.

CURTIS, RUSSELL GLENN, social studies educator; s. Russell and June Chapman Curtis; life ptnr. Tina Sapp Baker; children: Mary Jo Baker, Maggie Baker. B in Gen. Studies, Ohio U., Athens, 1985; M in Social Sci., Ohio U., 1998; BA, Morehead State U., Ky., 1990. Cert. tchr. social studies to adolescents and young adults Nat. Bd. Profl. Tchg. Stds., permanent cert. tchr. history, govt., econs., psycholgy and social studies Ohio Dept. Edn. Substitute tchr. Mason County Schs., Maysville, Ky., 1990—91; social studies tchr. Ripley-Union-Lewis-Huntington HS, Ohio, 1991—. Academic team sponsor Ripley-Union-Lewis-Huntington HS, 1992—, mock trial advisor, 1992—2006, Ohio stock market game advisor, 1993—2005, coord. field experiences in Washington, 1997—2000, student vol. program coord., 2000—05, field day coord., 2003—05, kids' philosophy slam coord., 2003—06; mid. sch. mock trial advisor Ripley-Union-Lewis-Huntington Mid. Sch., 2001—06. Dir.: Maysville Players Theatre Group. Sr. citizen prom coord. Ripley-Union-Lewis-Huntington HS, 1998—, sr. yr. cmty. svc. coord., 2001—, The Dictionary Project sponsor, 2002—; trivia challenge cons., participant Ledger Ind./WFTM, Maysville, 2001—05; trustee John P. Parker Hist. Soc., Ripley, 2001—05. Named Golden Apple Achiever, Ashland Oil, 1994, 1996, Staff Mem. of Yr., Ripley-Union-Lewis-Huntington Jr./Sr. HS Student Coun., 1995—96, Tchr. of Yr., Ripley-Union-Lewis-Huntington Sch. Dist., 1997—98; recipient Leadership in Ednl. Excellence award, Brown County Ednl. Svc. Ctr., 1998, Gov.'s Ednl. Leadership award, State of Ohio, 2003, Master Tchr. award, Martha Holden Jennings Found., 2005, Ohio Best Svc.-Learning Project award, Learn and Serve Ohio, 2005. Mem.: Ohio Ctr. for Law-Related Edn. (Eiler Mock Trial award for excellence in coaching 2002), Nat. Social Studies Suprs. Assn., Ohio Coun. Social Studies, Nat. Coun. Social Studies, Econs. Ctr. for Edn. and Rsch. (assoc.), Ctr. for Civic Edn. (assoc.). Office: Ripley-Union-Lewis-Huntington HS 1317 S 2d St Ripley OH 45167 Home Phone: 606-301-1691; Office Phone: 937-392-4384. Business E-Mail: curtisr@ripley.k12.oh.us.

CURTIS, SUSAN GRACE, lawyer; b. NYC, Apr. 24, 1950; d. Henry G. and Helen Curtis; m. Robert Y. Pelgrift Jr., June 8, 1974; children: Robert III, Henry, Victoria. AB, Yale Coll., 1971; JD, Columbia U., 1974. Bar: NY 1975, US Ct. Appeals (2d cir.) 1975. With Lord, Day & Lord, NYC, 1974-79, Shearman & Sterling, NYC, 1979-84, Proskauer, Rose, 1984-87, 93-98; ptnr. Epstein, Becker & Green, NYC, 1987-93; of counsel White & Case, NYC, 1998—; adj. asst. prof. law NYU, 1995-98; mem. faculty Practising Law Inst., 1990—. Contbg. editor: Jour. Pension Planning and Compliance, 1991—; mem. editl. adv. bd. BNA Pension Reporter, 1993—, tax mgmt. adv. bd., 1993—; contbr. articles to profl. jours. Mem. ABA (com. employee benefits), NY State Bar Assn. (com. employee benefits), Assn. Bar City NY (sec. com. employee benefits 1987-90).

CURTIS, SUSAN M., lawyer; b. Nashville, 1956; BA summa cum laude, U. Tenn., Knoxville; JD, Vanderbilt Univ., 1981. Bar: NY 1982. Ptnr., structured fin. Skadden, Arps, Slate, Meagher & Flom, NYC. Mem.: Phi Beta Kappa. Office: Skadden Arps Slate Meagher & Flom 4 Times Sq New York NY 10036 Office Phone: 212-735-2119. Office Fax: 917-777-2119. Business E-Mail: scurtis@skadden.com.

CURTIS, THOMAS PELHAM, II, artist, educator, small business owner; s. Thomas James and Elizabeth Delafield Curtis; m. Denise Dietrich Willman, Nov. 18, 1972; children: Elizabeth Longfellow, Thomas James II, Marguerite Willman, Anna Christina, Andrew Warren. AB in Arch., Harvard Coll., 1960; degree, US Army Commd. and Gen. Staff Coll., 1979; student in art, Corcoran Sch. Art, 1966. Commd. lt. U.S. Army, 1960, advanced through grades to lt. col., 1979, with corps. engrs., 1960—87; ret. USAR, 1987; freelance artist Washington, 1966—69; editl. cartoonist Milw. (Wis.) Sentinel, 1969—84; pvt. practice Curtis Studio, Milw., 1985—. Author (cartoonist): The Turn of A Decade, 1970, Curtis In Profile, 1983. Decorated Commendation medal US Army, Meritorious Svc. medal with oak leaf cluster, Knight Grand Cross Sovereign Mil. Order Temple of Jerusalem, Knight Grand Cross Imperial Ethiopian Order St. Mary of Zion, Knight comdr. Order St. Gregory The Great; recipient Disting. Svc. award, Sovereign Mil. Order Temple of Jerusalem, 2001. Mem.: Am. Soc. Portrait Artists, N.Y. State Soc. Cin. (pres. 2005—), Philadelphia Soc., Copley Soc. Boston. Episcopalian. Avocations: genealogy, history, bagpipes. Personal E-mail: thebruce@execpc.com.

CURTIS-FRANCIS, KELLEY ANN, pharmacist; b. Dorchester, Mass., Dec. 25, 1969; adopted d. Linda Emily and Merton Elden Curtis; m. Jerry Edward Francis, Sept. 11, 2004; 1 child, Sophia Grace Francis. BS in Pharmacy, Mass. Coll. Pharmacy, Boston, 1993; MBA in Health Adminstrn., Suffolk U., Boston, 1998; PharmD, St. John's U., Jamaica, NY, 2002. Registered pharmacist Mass., 1993, NY, 1999, Registered Pharmacist Ohio, 2002. Dir. drug info. Brigham and Women's Hosp., Boston, 1995—99; dir. drug info. svcs. VA Med. Ctr., NYC, 1999—2002; drug policy mgr. Premier Health Ptnrs., Dayton, Ohio, 2002—04; corp. dir. utilization and contracting clin. svcs. Cath. Healthcare Ptnrs., Cin., 2004—. Asst. prof. U. Cin., 2006—, LI U. Arnold and Marie Schwartz Coll. Pharmacy, Bklyn., 2000—02. Contbr. articles to profl. publs. Mem.: Am. Coll. Clin. Pharmacy, Am. Soc. Health Sys. Pharmacists. Independent. Roman Catholic. Office: Cath Healthcare Ptnrs 615 Elsinore Pl Cincinnati OH 45202 Home Phone: 513-755-2398; Office Phone: 513-639-0134. Personal E-mail: kelleypharm@aol.com.

CURTISS, CHARLES FRANCIS, retired chemist, educator; b. Chgo., Apr. 4, 1921; s. Ralph Charles and Camille (Guthormsen) C.; m. Lois Pauline Hruska, Mar. 23, 1946; children: Larry A., Glenn D., Ned S. BS, U. Wis., 1942, PhD, 1948. Faculty U. Wis., 1949—, prof. chemistry, 1960-89, emeritus, 1989—. Author: (with others) Molecular Theory of Gases and Liquids, 1954, Dynamics of Polymeric Liquids, 1977, 2d edit., 1987; contbr. articles to profl. jours. Fellow Am. Phys. Soc., AAAS; mem. Am. Chem. Soc. Home: 6317 Keelson Dr Madison WI 53705-4368 Personal E-mail: curtiss@chem.wisc.edu.

CURTISS, ELDEN FRANCIS, archbishop; b. Baker, Oreg., June 16, 1932; s. Elden F. and Mary (Neiger) C. BA, St. Edward Sem., Seattle, MDiv, 1958; MA in Ednl. Adminstrn, U. Portland, 1965; postgrad., Fordham U., U. Notre Dame. Priest Roman Cath. Ch., 1958. Campus chaplain, 1959—68; supt. schs. Diocese of Baker, Oreg., 1962—70; pastor, 1968—70; mem. ecumenical ministries State of Oreg., 1972; pres., ector Mt. Angel Sem., Benedict, Oreg., 1972—76, mem. bd. regents, 1976—93; mem. pastoral svcs. Oreg. State Hosp., Salem, 1975—76; bishop Diocese of Helena, Mont., 1976—93; archbishop Archdiocese of Omaha, 1993—. Chmn. bd. Boys Town USA, Cath. Mut. Relief Soc. Am.; mem. Pontifical Coun. for Family, Rome; Episcopal advisor Serra Internat. Mem.: Nat. Cath. Ednl. Assn. (bishops and pres's com. coll. dept., Outstanding Educator 1972). Office: Archdiocese of Omaha 100 N 62nd St Omaha NE 68132-2702

CURTISS, HOWARD CROSBY, JR., mechanical engineer, educator; b. Chgo., Mar. 17, 1930; s. Howard Crosby and Susan (Stephenson) Curtiss; m. Betty Ruth Cloke, Mar. 24, 1956 (dec. June 1985); children: Lisa Crosby, Jonathan Cloke; m. Elizabeth M. Fenton, May 22, 1988. B in Aero. Engring., Rensselaer Poly. Inst., Troy, NY, 1952; MS in Aero. Engring., Princeton U., NJ, 1957, PhD in Aero. Engring., 1965. Mem. rsch. staff dept. aerospace and mech. scis. Princeton U., 1956-65, mem. faculty, 1965—, prof., 1970-98, prof. emeritus, 1998—. Mem. Army Sci. Adv. Panel, 1972-77, Naval Rsch. Adv. Com., 1978-80, Army Sci. Bd., 1978-82; hon. prof. Nanjing Aero. Inst., China, 1985—. Author: (with others) A Modern Course in Aeroelasticity, 1978; editor: Jour. Am. Helicopter Soc., 1972-74; contbr. articles to sci. jours. Served with USN, 1952-54. Fellow Am. Helicopter Soc. (dir. 1978-79), AIAA; mem. Sigma Xi, Tau Beta Pi, Metedeconk River Yacht Club, Princeton Club NY. Home: 24 Chestnut St Princeton NJ 08542-3806 Office: Dept Mech and Aerospace Engring Princeton U Princeton NJ 08544-0001 Office Phone: 609-258-5149. Business E-Mail: b1002@princeton.edu.

CURTISS, JEFF, consumer products company executive, lawyer; BSBA, U. Nebr., 1970, JD, 1971; LLM in Taxation, Washington U., St. Louis, 1975. Bar: Nebr., Colo., Ill., Mo.; CPA, Colo. Various devel. positions to v.p. fin. G.D. Searle & Co., 9 yrs; CFO, Coleman Co.; exec. v.p., CFO, bd. dirs. Heritage Media, Dallas; CFO, sr. v.p. Browning-Ferris Industries, Inc., Houston, 1992-99; Svc. Corp. Internat., Houston, 2000—. Office: Svc Corp Internat PO Box 130548 1929 Allen Pkwy Houston TX 77219-0548 Mailing: PO Box 3151 Houston TX 77253-3151

CURTISS, RICHARD HOLDEN, magazine editor, writer; b. Grand Rapids, Mich., June 13, 1927; s. Fred Adelbert and Alma Clement (Holden) C.; m. Donna Jean Bourne, June 18, 1950; children: Diana Ruth Sreebny, Delinda Louise Hanley, Andrew Bourne, Raymond Holden. BA in Journalism, U. So. Calif., LA, 1949. Reporter OMGUS Observer, Berlin, Germany, 1946-47; editor/reporter Whittier (Calif.) Star Reporter, 1949-50; newsman UP, LA, 1950-51; pubs. officer U.S. Embassy, Djakarta, Indonesia, 1951-53, press attache Ankara, Turkey, 1957-59, Baghdad, 1963-66, pub. affairs officer Damascus, Syria, 1966-67, counselor for pub. affairs Beirut, 1973-76; info. officer Am. Consulate Gen., Stuttgart, Germany, 1954-56; newswriter USIA, Washington, 1959-62, program coord. Near East, South Asia, 1967-69, dep. asst. dir. Near East, North Africa, 1976-78, chief insp., 1979-80; dir. Voice of Am. Program Ctr., Rhodes, Greece, 1970-73; exec. dir. Am. Edn. Trust, Washington, 1981—. Exec. editor Washington Report on Mid. East Affairs, 1983—; founding dir. Mid.-East Policy Coun., Washington, 1981-82, Coun. for Nat. Interest, Washington, 1985-86. Author: A Changing Image: American Perceptions of the Arab-Israel Dispute, 1982, 2d edit., 1986, Stealth Pacs: Lobbying Congress for Control of U.S.-Mid. East Policy, 1990, 4th edit., 1996; co-editor: Seeing the Light: Personal Encounters with the Middle East and Islam, 1997; contbr. numerous articles to profl. jours. Recipient Edward R. Murrow award for excellence in pub. diplomacy Fletcher Sch. for Law and Diplomacy, 1976, Superior Honor award USIA, 1976, Lifetime Achievement award Am.-Arab Anti-Discrimination Com., 1992, Achievement award Ptnrs. for Peace, 1993, Dedicated Svc. award Islamic Assn. for Palestine in N.Am., 1994, Lifelong Dedication award United Muslims of Am., 1994, Cert. of Appreciation The Jerusalem Fund for Edn. and Cmty. Devel. and Ctr. for Policy Analysis on Palestine, 1995, They Dared to Speak Out award Coun. for Nat. Interest, 1995, Voice of Conscience of Am. Journalism award Am. Muslim Alliance, 1998, Cmty. award for journalism Coun. on Am. Islamic Rels., 1999, Constn. to World Awareness award Solidarity for Palestinian Human Rights Orgns. of McGill and Concordia Univs., Montreal, Liberty and Justice award Am. Muslim Coun., Muslim Am. Soc., and United Assn. for Studies and Rsch., 1999. Mem. Nat. Press Club. Avocations: archaeology, paleontology, environmental protection, human rights. Office: American Educational Trust 1902 18th St NW Washington DC 20009-1707 E-mail: wrmea@aol.com.

CURTISS, ROY, III, life sciences professor; b. May 27, 1934; m. Josephine Clark, Dec. 28, 1976; children: Brian, Wayne, Roy IV, Lynn, Gregory Clark, Eric Garth, Megan Kimberly. BS in Agr., Cornell U., 1956; PhD in Microbiology, U. Chgo., 1962; DSc (hon.), So. Ill. U., Edwardsville, 2003. Instr., rsch. asst. Cornell U., 1955-56; jr. tech. specialist Brookhaven Nat. Lab., 1956-58; fellow microbiology U. Chgo., 1958-60, USPHS fellow, 1960-62; biologist Oak Ridge Nat. Lab., 1963-72; lectr. microbiology U. Tenn., Knoxville, 1965-72, lectr. Grad. Sch. Biomed. Scis. Oak Ridge, 1967-69, prof., 1969-72, assoc. dir., 1970-71, interim dir., 1971-72; Charles H. McCauley prof. microbiology U. Ala., Birmingham, 1972-83; sr. scientist Inst. Dental Rsch., 1972-83, Comprehensive Cancer Ctr., 1972-83, dir. molecular cell biology grad. program, 1973-82; dir., sr. scientist Cystic Fibrosis Rsch. Ctr., 1981-83; prof. cellular and molecular biology Sch. Dental Medicine Washington U., St. Louis, 1983-91, George William and Irene Koechig Freiberg prof. biology, 1984—2005, chmn. dept. biology, 1983-93, dir. Ctr. Plant Sci. and Biotech., 1991-94, George William and Irene Koechig Freiburg prof. emeritus, 2005—; prof. life scis. Ariz. State U., Tempe, 2004—, co-dir. Ctr. Infectious Diseases and Vaccinology, Biodesign Inst., 2004—06, dir. Ctr. Infectious Diseases and Vaccinology, Biodesign Inst., 2007—, directorate mem. Biodesign Inst., 2007—. Mem. Ctr. Infectious Disease, Washington U., St. Louis; vis. prof. Inst. Venezolana de Investigaciones Científicas, 1969, U. P.R., 1972, U. Católica de Chile, 1973, U. Okla., 1982; recombinant DNA molecule program adv. com. NIH, 1974-77, genetic basis disease rev. com., 1979-83, chmn., 1981-83, vaccine study panel, 2001-04, chmn. bacterial biodefence rev. com., 2003-2004; genetic biology com. NSF, 1975-78; mem. diseases rsch. adv. bd. Midwest Regional Ctr. Excellence in Biodefense and Emerging Infections, 2003-05; mem. exec. com. Sch. Life Sci. Ariz. State U., 2005—. Editor: Jour. Bacteriology, 1970-76, Infection and Immunity, 1985-92, Escherichia coli and Salmonella: Cellular and Molecular Biology, 1993-96, 2006- , exec. editor-in-chief, 2000-05, exec. editor, 2006—. Active Oak Ridge City Coun., 1969-72, Cystic Fibrosis Found., rsch. devel. program rev. com. 1984-89, Conf. Rsch. Workers on Animal Diseases, Heiser Found. Sci. Adv. Bd., 1996-2004; bd. dirs. Am. Type Culture Collection, 1989-99, presdl. adv., 2003—; bd. dirs. Whitfield Sch., 1997-2005, exec. com., 2002-2005; founder, dir. and sci. adv. MEGAN Health, Inc., 1992-2000, v.p. rsch., 1998-99; bd. govs. Ariz. Arts Sci. Tech. Acad., 2006-; mem. Mo. Seed Capital Investment Bd., 2000-03. Recipient Sardinia Sci. award, 2003; named Mo. Inventor of Yr., 1997, Am. Biosci. Rschr. of Yr., 2007. Fellow: AAAS, Acad. Sci. St. Louis, Am. Acad. Microbiology; mem.: NAS, Ariz. Arts, Sci. and Tech. Acad., Internat. Soc. Vaccines, World Health Orgn. (steering com. immunology of TB 1982—85), Coun. Advancement Sci. Writing (dir. 1976—82, v.p. 1978—82), N.Y. Acad. Scis., Am. Soc. Microbiology (parliamentarian 1970—75, dir. 1977—80, editl. bd. ASM News 1987—99, dir. 1989—94, 1999—2004), Soc. Gen. Microbiology, Internat. Soc. Mucosal Immunology, Am. Assn. Avian Pathologists, Genetics Soc. Am. (chmn. genetics stock ctrs. com. 1987—89), Gateway Strikers Soccer Club (pres. 1995—2001, chmn. bd. dirs. 2001—05, founder), Sigma Xi. Home: 6732 N Joshua Tree Ln Paradise Valley AZ 85253-3245 Office: CIDV The Biodesign Inst Ariz State U Tempe AZ 85287-5401

CURTISS, THOMAS, JR., lawyer; b. Buffalo, Nov. 4, 1941; s. Thomas and Hope (Middleton Plumb) C. BA, Yale U., 1963; JD, Harvard U., 1970. Bar: Calif. 1971. Assoc. Musick, Peeler & Garrett, L.A., 1970-72, Macdonald, Halsted & Laybourne, L.A., 1972-76, ptnr., 1976-88, Baker & McKenzie, L.A., 1988—92, Kindel & Anderson, L.A., 1992-96, McKenna & Cuneo, L.L.P., L.A., 1996—2002; prin. Rodi, Pollock, Pettker, Galbraith & Cahill, L.A., 2000—. Adj. prof. Loyola U., L.A. Law Sch., 1982-93, 99. Mem. editl. bd. L.A. Lawyer, 1992-93; contbr. articles to profl. jours. Mem. vestry Trinity Episc. Ch., L.A., sr. warden, 1982, 84-86, canon of the diocese; mem. Commn. on Ordained Ministry, Diocese of L.A., 1983-88; legal com. Music Ctr. Found., 1988-94, dir. Cath. Ctr. St. Paul, 1989-94, treas., 1989-95; mem. AIDS Interfaith Coun. So. Calif., Inc., 1989-91; Class of 1959 agt. Phillips Exeter Acad., 1994-98; dir. Mental Health Assn., L.A. County, 1996-97. Maj., USMCR, 1963-78. Fellow Am. Coll. Trust and Estate Counsel; mem. ABA (mem. sect. real property, probate and trust law), L.A. County Bar Assn. (chmn. exec. com., probate and trust law sect. 1991-92), The Calif. Club, State Bar of Calif. (bd. of legal specialization, cert. specialist, estate planning, trust and probate law). Republican. Home: 2250 Micheltorena St Los Angeles CA 90039-3021 Home Phone: 323-660-8335; Office Phone: 213-438-5207. E-mail: tcurtissjr@sbcglobal.net.

CURTIS-TWEED, PHYLLIS MARIE, humanities educator; d. Cecil Morris and Alice Marie Curtis; m. Nicholas Genevieve-Tweed, May 30, 1992; 1 child, Lauren Genevieve-Tweed. BA, U. Md., College Park, 1978, MEd, 1985; PhD, Emory U., 1993. Rsch. assoc., instr. psychology dept. psychiatry Harvard Med. Sch., Judge Baker Children's Ctr., Boston, 1995—2001; assoc. prof., dir., freshman yr. program Medgar Evers Coll. CUNY, Bklyn., 2001—05; asst. prof. Medgar Evers Coll. CUNY, 2005—. Contbr. entry, articles to profl. publs. Leader Reach Out and Touch/Macedonia AME Ch., Flushing, NY, 2002. Recipient postdoctoral fellowship in psychology dept. psychiatry, Harvard U., 1993—95, Rsch. award, Childrens Studies at Harvard U., 1998—99, U.S. Achievement Acad. Nat. award, 1994; grantee, NIMH, 1995—2001. Mem.: Assn. for Moral Edn. (exec. bd. mem. 2005—). African Methodist Episcopal Church. Avocations: reading, writing, travel. Office: Medgar Evers Coll 1650 Bedford Ave Brooklyn NY 11225 Home Phone: 718-657-4799; Office Phone: 718-270-4960. E-mail: ptweed@mec.cuny.edu.

CURTS, HAROLD LAYNE, construction executive; b. Dallas, Oct. 30, 1957; s. Harold Franklin and Betty Ann (Moulton) C.; m. Trina Elizabeth Roach, Aug. 16, 1980; children: Steven Robert, Valerie Layne. AA in Design and Drafting, Mountain View Coll., 1978; AA in Civil Constrn., Tarrant County Coll., 1985; BS, Letourneau U., 1994. Project engr. Broyles & Broyles, Inc., Ft. Worth, 1978-80; project mgr. Precision Concrete and Constrn., Inc., Dallas, 1980-81; constrn. mgr. Methodist Hosps. of Dallas, 1981-83; v.p. constrn. Medco Constrn., Baylor Health Care System, Dallas, 1983-85; v.p. design and constrn. The Centra Group, Ft. Worth, 1985-91; pres. Tech. Interiors, Ft. Worth, 1991—. Mem. ASCE, Tex. Assn. Hosp. Engrs., Nat. Eagle Scout Assn. Republican. Baptist. Avocations: travel, fishing. Office: Technical Interiors PO Box 14824 Fort Worth TX 76117-0824 Home Phone: 817-589-7711; Office Phone: 817-589-7985. E-mail: hcurts@sbcglobal.net.

CURWEN, RANDALL WILLIAM, journalist, editor; b. Hazel Green, Wis., Apr. 18, 1946; s. Charles William and Theda (Hillary) C. BS, U. Wis., 1968. Reporter Rockford (Ill.) Morning Star, 1968-69, copy editor/asst. city editor, 1969-72; copy editor Chgo. Today, 1972-74; copy editor/asst. sect. editor Chgo. Tribune, 1974-80, assoc. features editor, 1980-91, co-editor evening edit., 1992, travel editor, 1992—. Recipient 1st place headline writing award Ill. UPI, 1977, Johnrae Earl award Chgo. Tribune, 1979, 96, Soc. Am. Travel Writers Ctrl. States award for best travel sect., 1994, 99, 2001, 02. Mem. Soc. Am. Travel Writers (Lowell Thomas award for best travel sect. 1995, 97), Nat. Lesbian and Gay Journalists Assn., Soc. Am. Travel Writers (v.p. 2005-06). Avocations: travel, baseball, films. Home: 930 W Roscoe Rear Coachhouse Chicago IL 60657 Office: Chgo Tribune Co 435 N Michigan Ave PO Box 25340 Chicago IL 60625-0340

CURWOOD, STEVE, television producer, host; m. Jennifer Curwood; 2 children. Reporter Boston Globe, CBS News, WBUR-FM/Boston and WGBH-TV/Boston, NPR. Lectr. environ. sci. and pub. policy Harvard Univ. Reporter (radio programs) Weekend All Things Considered, NPR, 1979, creator, host Living on Earth, NPR, 1990—. Co-recipient Pulitzer Prize for Public Svc., 1975, AAAS Sci. Journalism award for radio reporting, 2006; recipient New England Environ. Leadership award, Tufts Univ., 1992, Global Green award for Media Design, 2003, David A. Brower award for excellence in environ. reporting, Sierra Club, 2003. Mem.: World Media Found., Inc. (pres.). Office: Living on Earth 20 Holland Street Ste 408 Somerville MA 02144-2749 Office Phone: 617-629-3632. Business E-Mail: stevecurwood@loe.org.

CURY, BRUCE PAUL, lawyer, judge, educator; b. Englewood, NJ, Mar. 19, 1942; s. Beddy Galib and Violet (Maloof) C.; m. Orahdella Elizabeth Green, Oct. 14, 1972; 1 child, Lauren Elaine. BS, U. Ky., 1965; JD, U. Louisville, 1972. Bar: Fla. 1972, U.S. Dist. Ct. (mid. dist.) Fla. 1974, U.S. Ct. Appeals (5th cir.) 1980, U.S. Ct. Appeals (11th cir.) 1982, U.S. Supreme Ct. 1976. Assoc. George McDowell P.A., Tampa, Fla., 1972-73; sole practice Tampa, 1973-76; adj. prof. bus. law U. Tampa, 1977-85; adj. prof. criminal law U. South Fla., 1984-85, lectr., 1981-87; chief asst. pub. defender Office of Pub. Defender, Tampa, 1974-85; sole practice Tampa, 1985-90; gen. counsel Fla. Dept. Transportation, Bartow, 1990—. Magistrate traffic ct. Jud. 13 cir., Tampa, 1993—; chmn. Hills County Zoning Bd. Tampa, 1989-97; pres., dir. Bay Area Legal Svcs., Inc., Tampa, 1980-92; chmn. Hills County Land Use Appeals Bd. Tampa, 1997-1999. Legal counsel Big Bros./Big Sisters Greater Tampa, Inc., 1983-95; pres, bd. dirs. Rape Crisis Ctr., Tampa, 1982-84; bd. dirs. Hillsborough Edn. Found., Tampa, 1999—; chmn. Hillsborough County City-County Planning Commn., Tampa, 1999-2003, 2005-. 1st lt. US Army, 1966—69. Recipient Indigent Accused award Fla. Pub. Defender, 1985, Dirs. award Sexual Abuse Treatment Ctr. Tampa, 1986, Pres. and Dirs. award Bay Area Legal Svcs. Tampa, 1992, Sec. of Transp. Leadership award Fla. Dept. Transp., 2000, Outstanding contbn. svc, Hillsborough Cty., 2003, Bd of County Commn. award Outstanding Contribution and Svcs. to Hillsborough County. Mem. Criminal Def. Lawyers Assn. Hillsborough County, Fla. Bar Assn. (mem. several sects., chmn. 13th Jud. Circuit grievance com.), Hillsborough County Bar Assn. (mem. several coms., exec. counsel trial lawyers sect.), Fla. Leadership 2000, Am. Inn of Cts. (master). Republican. Methodist. Home: 1301 Bayshore Blvd Tampa FL 33606 Office: Fla Dept Transportation 801 N Broadway Ave Bartow FL 33830-3809 Office Phone: 800-292-3368. Business E-Mail: bruce.cury@dot.state.fl.us.

CURZAN, MYRON PAUL, lawyer; b. NYC, May 13, 1940; s. Lee and Hannah Rose (Tannenbaum) C.; m. Mary Hannah Curzan; children: Elisabeth, Anne, Katherine. BA, Columbia U., 1961, LLB, 1965; MA, Yale U., 1962. Bar: Calif. 1966, D.C. 1969. Clk. to chief justice Calif. Supreme Ct., 1965-66; legis. asst. to Senator Robert F. Kennedy Washington, 1966-67; ptnr. Arnold & Porter, Washington, 1967-91; CEO APCO Assocs., The Arnold & Porter Cons. Group, 1984-88; pres., CEO MPC & Assocs., Inc., 1984-91, chmn. bd., 1991-96; chmn. bd., CEO UniDev, LLC, 1996—; CEO Nat. Captioning Inst., 1996-98. Vice-chmn. bd. Conn. Mut. Life Ins. Co., 1991-93; counsel Arnold & Porter, 1993-98; trustee George Washington U.; bd. dirs. Rocky Mountain Inst., E Source Inc., Internat. Inst. for Energy Conservation. Contbr. articles to profl. jours. Address: 6404 Garnett Dr Chevy Chase MD 20815-6616 Home Phone: 301-656-9256; Office Phone: 301-656-7764. Personal E-mail: mcurzan@unidevllc.com.

CURZON, SUSAN CAROL, academic administrator; b. Poole, Eng., Dec. 11, 1947; came to U.S., 1952. d. Kenneth Nigel and Terry Marguerite (Morris) C. AB, U. Calif., Riverside, 1970; MLS, U. Wash., 1972; PhD, U. So. Calif., 1983. Spl. libr. Kennecott Exploration, San Diego, 1972-73; various positions LA County Pub. Libr., 1973-89; dir. libr. Glendale Pub. Libr., Calif., 1989-92; dean libr. Calif. State U., Northridge, 1992—. Cons. Grantsmanship Ctr., L.A., 1981-83; vis. lectr. Grad. Sch. Libr. and Info. Sci. UCLA, 1986-92. Author: Managing Change, Managing the Interview. Libr. of Year Libr. Jour., 1993. Mem. ALA, Calif. Libr. Assn. Democrat. Avocation: history. Office: Calif State U Libr Office of the Dean 18111 Nordhoff St Northridge CA 91330-8326 Office Phone: 818-677-2271.

CUSACK, JOAN, actress; b. NYC, Oct. 11, 1962; d. Richard and Nancy C.; m. Richard Burke 1993; 2 children. BA, U. Wis., 1985. Stage appearances include Road, 1988, Brilliant Traces, 1989, Cymbeline, 1989; TV appearances include Saturday Night Live (regular 1985-86 season), The Mother, 1994, What About Joan, 2001-02, A Very Merry Muppet Christmas, 2002; film appearances include Cutting Loose, 1980, My Bodyguard, 1980, Class, 1983, Grandview USA, 1984, Sixteen Candles, 1984, The Allnighter, 1987, Broadcast News, 1987, Stars and Bars (aka An Englishman in New York), 1988, Married to the Mob, 1988, Working Girl, 1988 (Acad. award nominee best supporting actress 1989), Say Anything, 1989, Men Don't Leave, 1989, My Blue Heaven, 1990, The Cabinet of Dr. Ramirez, 1991, Hero, 1992, Toys, 1992 (also musician), Addams Family Values, 1993, Corrina, Corrina, 1994, Nine Months, 1995, Two Much, 1996, Mr. Wrong, 1996, A Smile Like Yours, 1997, In and Out, 1997, Grosse Pointe Blank, 1997, Arlington Road, 1999, Runaway Bride, 1999, (voice) Toy Story 2, 1999, Arlington Road, 1999, Cradle Will Rock, 1999, High Fidelity, 2000, Where the Heart Is, 2000, School of Rock, 2003, Looney Toons-Back in Action, 2003, Raising Helen, 2004, The Last Shot, 2004, Ice Princess, 2005, (voice) Chicken Little, 2005, Friends With Money, 2006. Office: United Talent Agy Inc 9560 Wilshire Blvd Fl 5 Beverly Hills CA 90212

CUSACK, JOHN, actor; b. Evanston, Ill., June 28, 1966; s. Richard and Nancy Cusack Co-owner New Crime Productions. Actor: (films) Class, 1983, Sixteen Candles, 1984, Grandview USA, 1984, The Sure Thing, 1985, Journey of Natty Gann, 1985, Better Off Dead, 1985, Stand By Me, 1986, One Crazy Summer, 1986, Broadcast News, 1987, Hot Pursuit, 1987, Eight Men Out, 1988, Tapeheads, 1988, Say Anything, 1989, Fatman and Little Boy, 1989, The Grifters, 1990, True Colors, 1991, Shadows and Fog, 1992, Roadside Prophets, 1992, The Player, 1992, Map of the Human Heart, 1992, Bob Roberts, 1992, Money for Nothing, 1993, Bullets Over Broadway, 1994, The Road to Wellville, 1994, Floundering, 1994, City Hall, 1995, (voice) Anastasia, 1997, Con Air, 1997, Hellcab, 1997, Midnight in the Garden of Good and Evil, 1997, This is My Father, 1998, The Thin Red Line, 1998, Pushing Tin, 1998, Being John Malkovich, 1999, Live of the Party, 2000, Ango, 2000, America's Sweethearts, 2001, Serendipity, 2001, Identity, 2003, Runaway Jury, 2003, Must Love Dogs, 2005, The Ice Harvest, 2005, The Ice Harvest: Alternate Endings, 2006, Martian Child, 2007, 1408, 2007; actor, dir., writer Grosse Pointe Blank, 1997; prodr., actor Arigo, 1998, Max, 2002; actor, writer High Fidelity, 2000, The Cradle Will Rock, 1999; prodr. Cosmic Banditos, 2002, 2.2, 2002. Office: William Morris Agy 151 El Camino Dr Beverly Hills CA 90212*

CUSACK, JOHN T., lawyer; b. Sept. 10, 1958; BS magna cum laude, Drew Univ., 1980; JD, George Washington Univ., 1983. Bar: NY 1984, Ill. 1986. Ptnr., chair fin. group DLA Piper Rudnick Gray Cary, Chgo. and NYC. Mem.: ABA, Chgo. Bar Assn., Ill. State Bar Assn. Office: DLA Piper Rudnick Gray Cary 1251 Ave of the Americas New York NY 10020-1104 also: DLA Piper Rudnick Gray Cary Ste1900 203 N LaSalle St Chicago IL 60601-1293 Office Phone: 212-835-6049, 312-368-4049. Office Fax: 312-236-7516. Business E-Mail: john.cusack@piperrudnick.com.

CUSACK, JOHN THOMAS, lawyer; b. Oak Park, Ill., June 22, 1935; s. Thomas Jr. and Clare (Hock) C.; m. Mary Louise Coughlin, Nov. 1, 1969; children: John, James, Mary Helen, Cathleen. AB cum laude, U. Notre Dame, 1957; JD, U. Mich., 1960; postgrad., Harvard U., 1961-62. Bar: Ill. 1960, U.S. Dist. Ct. (no. dist.) Ill. 1961, U.S. Dist. Ct. (no. dist.) Ind. 1983, U.S. Tax Ct. 1984, U.S. Ct. Appeals (7th cir.) 1973, U.S. Ct. Appeals (5th and 9th cirs.) 1975, U.S. Ct. Appeals (3d cir.) 1986, U.S. Ct. Appeals (10th cir.) 1987, U.S. Ct. Appeals (11th cir.) 1988, U.S. Supreme Ct. 1966. Trial atty. antitrust div. U.S. Dept. Justice, 1962-70; assoc. Gardner, Carton & Douglas, Chgo., 1970-74, ptnr., 1974—, chmn. litigation dept., 1978-86, chmn. antitrust practice group, 1986—. Contbr. articles to legal jours. Trustee Fenwick H.S. 1st lt. JAGC, USAR, 1963-67. Mem. ABA (antitrust and litigation sect., health law com. 1960—), Chgo. Bar Assn., Law Club City Chgo. Roman Catholic. Home: 1030 Franklin Ave River Forest IL 60305-1340 Office: Gardner Carton & Douglas 191 N Wacker Dr Ste 3700 Chicago IL 60606-1698 E-mail: jcusack@gcd.com.

CUSACK, THOMAS JOSEPH, retired banker; b. NYC, Aug. 12, 1938; s. Thomas Joseph and Josephine (Mingalone) C.; m. Elizabeth Mary McAuliffe, June 4, 1960; children: Thomas, Elizabeth, Bridget. BBA, St. Francis Coll., 1968; grad., Stonier Grad. Sch. Banking, New Brunswick, NJ. Asst. v.p. Irving Trust Co., NYC, 1959-79; v.p., sr. ops. mgr. Mellon Bank Internat., NYC, 1979-83, gen. mgr., 1983-85; v.p., sr. ops. mgr. Creditanstalt, Greenwich, Conn., 1985-90, v.p. planning and devel., 1990-93, v.p., COO, 1993-94, sr. v.p., COO, 1995-98; ret., 1998. U.S. rep. Swift Documentary Credit Working Group, Brussels, Belgium, 1983-85; mem. Payments and Settlement Systems Com., Bankers Assn. Fgn. Trade, 1983-85. Chmn. fin. com. St. Vincent DePaul Roman Cath. Ch., Elmont, NY, 2006—. Mem. KC (4th degree), US Coun. on Internat. Banking (chmn. 1987-88). Avocations: camping, touring. Home: 10 John Ave Elmont NY 11003-1916 Personal E-mail: tjccat@verizon.net. *If we all would realize that the only lasting thing we leave in this world is our reputation, what a better world this would be.*

CUSH, JOHN PATRICK, priest, theology studies educator; b. Bklyn., Jan. 20, 1972; s. Edward Joseph Cush and Catherine Mary Flynn. BA in Philosophy and English, St. John's U., Jamaica, NY, 1994; STB in Theology, Gregorian U., Rome, 1997, STL in Theology, 1999. Parochial vicar Good Shepherd Roman Cath. Ch., Bklyn., 1998, St. Helen Roman Cath. Ch., Howard Beach, NY, 1999—2004; chaplain St. Edmund's H.S., Bkln., 1999—2000; instr. deacon program Diocese of Bklyn., 1999—2000, 2005—, mem. Cath.-Luth. bilaterals, 2000—, censor of books, 2001—; faculty Cathedral Prep. Sem., Elmhurst, NY, 2004—. Theology instr. Diocesan Pastoral Inst. for Formation of Lay Ecclesial Ministers, 2001—; presenter ministry workshops Diocesan Liturgical Commn., 2002—; spiritual dir. permanent diaconate, Diocese Bklyn., 2002—. Contbr. articles to Bklyn. Tablet; presenter Radio Maria USA, 2005—. Mem. Cath.-Episcopalian Bilaterals, 2005—. Mem.: Am. Cath. Philos. Assn., Cath. Biblical Assn. Am. Office: Cathedral Prep Sem 56-25 92nd St Elmhurst NY 11373

CUSHING, CHARLES R., architectural firm executive; BS, US Merchant Marine Acad., MIT; MS, SUNY; PhD, U. Wales. With Sea-Land Svc., Inc., 1961—68; founder, pres. C.R. Cushing & Co., Inc, NYC, 1968—. Bd. dirs. Transp. Rsch. Bd., Marine Bd.; bd. trustees Webb Inst. Mem.: NAE. Office: CR Cushing & Co, Inc 7th Fl 30 Vesey St New York NY 10007 Office Phone: 212-964-1180. Office Fax: 212-285-1334.

CUSHING, MARK L., lawyer; BA with honors, Stanford U., 1975; JD, Willamette U., 1981. Spl. asst. to Gov. Oreg.; ptnr. & litig. Tonkon, Torp, Galen, Marmaduke and Booth, LLP, Portland, Oreg., Ball, Janik and Novak, LLP, Portland, Oreg.; sr. v.p. Video Lottery Technologies Inc., 1993—94; pres. Automated Wagering Internat. Inc., 1994; asst. to chmn. Lynch Corp., Greenwich, Conn., 1996; pres. St. George Crystal, Jeanette, Pa., 1999; of counsel Winstead Sechrest & Minick PC, Austin, Tex., 2001—02, ptnr. Washington, 2002—04, chair govt rels. and pub. policy sect.; mem. Winstead Consulting Group LLC; ptnr., pub. law & policy strategies group Sonnenschein Nath & Rosenthal LLP, Washington, 2004—.

CUSHING, MICHAEL, federal agency administrator; b. Bangor, Maine, Sept. 9, 1947; BA, Harvard U., 1969, JD, 1974. Pvt. practice; with pvt. asset mgmt. co.; mng. dir. Nat. Transp. Safety Bd.; chief of staff, dir. Ctr. for Labor-Mgmt. Rels. U.S. Office Pers. Mgmt.; mng. dir. mgmt. svcs. Overseas Pvt. Investment Corp., Wash., 1997—; sr. v.p (resource mgmt.) Export-Import Bank, Wash., DC. Office: Export-Import Bank 811 Vermont Ave NW Washington DC 20571 Office Phone: 202-565-3946.

CUSHING, STEVEN, linguist, educator, writer, researcher, consultant; b. Brookline, Mass., June 25, 1948; s. Alfred Edward and Evelyn Cushing. SB, MIT, 1970; MA, UCLA, 1972, PhD, 1976. Rsch. asst. MIT, 1967-70, UCLA, 1973-74; instr. U. Mass., Boston, 1974-75, Roxbury C.C., Boston, 1975-77; rsch. staff Higher Order Software Inc., Cambridge, Mass., 1976-82; rsch. assoc. Rockefeller U., NYC, 1979; from master lectr. to assoc. prof. Boston U., 1986-94; rsch. fellow NASA-Ames Rsch. Ctr., Mountain View, Calif., 1987-88, Stanford U., Palo Alto, Calif., 1987-88, NASA-Langley Rsch. Ctr., Hampton, Va., 1989; asst. prof. St. Anselm Coll., Manchester, N.H., 1983-85, Stonehill Coll., North Easton, Mass., 1985-89; adj. prof. Union Inst. Grad. Sch., Cin., 1994—; lectr. Boston U., 2002—, Northeastern U., Boston, 2003; instr. Mass. Sch. Law, 2002; tchr. Hingham H.S., Mass., 2003—05, Belmont Hill Sch., Mass., 2004—, Advanced Math. and Sci. Acad., Marlborough, Mass., 2005—, dept. head, 2006—. Mem. bd. editl. commentators The Behavioral and Brain Scis., 1978—; chmn. software design Internat. Conf. Sys. Scis., Honolulu, 1978; mem. 1st fgn. del. USSR Acad. of Scis., 1989; session chmn. session on internat. comm. Internat. Pragmatics Conf., Kobe, Japan, 1993; invited spkr. Internat. Conf. on Maritime Edn. and Tng., Rijeka, Croatia, 1999. Author: Quantifier Meanings: A Study in the Dimensions of Semantic Competence, 1982, Fatal Words: Communication Clashes and Aircraft Crashes, 1994, Japanese edit., 2001; assoc. editor Language, 1998-2000; contbr. articles to profl. jours. and mags. Mem. nat. exec. coun. Nat. Ethical Youth Orgn., 1965—66; fiddler Strathspey and Reel Soc. N.H. Recipient New Eng. Regional award Future Scientists of Am., 1965, 1st pl. award U.S. Nat. Scottish Fiddle Composition Competition, 1996; NSF grantee, 1965, 70-71, NIMH grantee, 1970-71, NDEA grantee, 1970-73; Woodrow Wilson Found. fellow, 1970-71, NASA Summer Faculty fellow, 1987-89; rsch. affiliate MIT, 1978-79, Boston U., 1986-88. Mem. Linguistic Soc. Am., Nat. Ctr. for Sci. Edn., Internat. Pragmatics Assn., Computer Sci. Tchrs. Assn. Home: 20 Parks Dr Sherborn MA 01770 Personal E-mail: stevencushing@alum.mit.edu.

CUSHMAN, ELLEN, counselor; b. Worcester, Mass., Sept. 22, 1951; d. Roland George Lalone and Margaret Theresa Noonan; m. David Peyton Cushman, June 6, 1987; children: Heather Elizabeth, Lucas David. BFA in Art History and Art Edn., Mass. Coll. Art, Boston, 1975; MBA, Babson Coll., Wellesley, Mass., 1985. With MRC, Inc., 1977—85; fin. planning cons. Bank of New Eng., 1985—88; sr. fin. planning cons. Harvard U.,

1994—98; sr. retirement counselor MIT, Cambridge, Mass. Sloan Network Informing Orgnl. Reponse advisor Ctr. on Aging and Work, Boston Coll. Recipient MIT Excellence award, 2005. Office: MIT 77 Massachusetts Ave Cambridge MA 02139

CUSHMAN, HELEN MERLE BAKER, retired management consultant; b. Perth Amboy, NJ; d. Ivan F. and Lucile (Atkinson) Baker; m. Robert Arnold Cushman, June 2, 1945; children— Lucinda Ann, Robert Rorem. AB in History, Barnard Coll., 1942; postgrad., NYU, 1944. Route analyst intelligence divsn. Air Transport Command, Washington, 1943-44; personnel asst. Gen. Cable Corp., NYC, 1944-45; sr. staff asst. to chmn. bd. Trans World Airlines, NYC, 1945-50; pres. H.M. Baker Assocs., Westfield, N.J., 1958-93; ret., 1993. Past archivist-historian N.J. chpt. Am. Records Mgmt. Assn. Author: ARMA-New Jersey, The Founding Years, 1972, A History of Shreve, Crump and Low, 1974, Butterick and the Story of Sewing, 1975, The Anniversary Manual, 1976, Gears, Machines, Systems, 1978, Mountainside Chapel: Yesterday, Today, Tomorrow, 1981, Serving Westerly Since 1800, 1985, The Mill on the Third River, 1992, From Seed to Harvest, 1993, The Church at the Crossroads, 1999, Walter's World: Memoirs of W.E. Atkinson 1856-1944, 2004; editor, pub. Ministry Press, The Bus. History Letter; contbr. to Am. Archivist. Recipient Lit. award Am. Records Mgmt. Assn., 1972. Mem.: PEO Sisterhood (pres. chpt. AE, Princeton N.J.), various hist. socs., Newcomen Soc., Barnard Coll. Club North Ctrl. NJ (past pres.). Address: 321 Sharon Way Monroe Township NJ 08831-1561

CUSHMAN, JOHN C., III, real estate company executive; Grad., Colgate U., 1963; grad. advanced mgmt. program, Harvard U. Co-founder Cushman Realty Corp., 1963—78, Cushman Winery Corp., 1972, dir., CEO; chmn. Cushman & Wakefield, Inc., LA, 2001—, also bd. dirs. Bd. mem. Culinary Holdings Inc., D.A. Cushman Realty Corp., Inglewood Pk. Cemetery, La Quinta Corp., La Quinta Properties, Inc., Callaway Golf Co.; dir. and chmn. Cushman Winery Corp. Mem. Calif. Commn. on Jobs and Econ. Growth, 2004. Mem.: L.A. Turf Club (bd. mem.). Office: Cushman Wakfield Inc 601 S Figueroa St Los Angeles CA 90017*

CUSHMAN, KAREN LIPSKI, writer; b. Chgo. married; 1 child, Leah. BA in English/Greek, Stanford U., 1963; MA in Human Behavior, USIU, 1977; MA in Mus. Studies, JFK U., 1987. Faculty mus. studies dept. John F. Kennedy U., San Francisco. Author: Catherine, Called Birdy, 1994, The Midwife's Apprentice, 1995 (John Newberry award 1996), The Ballad of Lucy Whipple, 1996, Matilda Bone, 2000, Rodzina, 2003. Office: 17804 Thorsen Road Sw Vashon WA 98070

CUSHMAN, KEITH, English professor; b. Jefferson City, Mo., Dec. 23, 1942; s. Jerome and Hanna Cushman; m. Deborah Bell, Jan. 3, 1992; m. Judith Rabinowitz, June 22, 1969 (div.); 1 child, Phoebe; 1 child, Cameron Brett Berkman. AB, Harvard U., Cambridge, Mass., 1964; PhD, Princeton U., NJ, 1969. Asst. prof. U. Chgo., 1969—76; prof. dept. English U. NC, Greensboro, 1976—. Editor: (edition of letters) The Letters of D. H. Lawrence & Amy Lowell, (edition of literary work) D. H. Lawrence: Memoir of Maurice Magnus. Recipient Rsch. Excellence award, U. NC, Greensboro, 1991, Harry T. Moore award, D H Lawrence Soc. N.Am., 1998; fellow, Fulbright Found., 1964—65, 2001; grantee, Korea Found., 1992. Avocations: travel, reading, book collecting. Home: 1303 Clarendon Dr Greensboro NC 27410 Office: U NC Greensboro Greensboro NC 27412 Office Phone: 336-334-5660. Business E-Mail: keith_cushman@uncg.edu.

CUSHMAN, MARGARET JANE, herbalist, nurse; b. Pahokee, Fla., Nov. 17, 1948; d. Edmund Francis and Mary Margaret (Adams) C. Diploma in nursing, Johns Hopkins Hosp., 1969; BSN, U. Pa., 1972; MSN, Yale U., 1976; MS in Herbal Medicine, TAI Sophia Inst., 2004; postgrad., U. Mass., 2004—. Asst. dir. nursing St. Joseph's Hosp., Phila., 1972-74; asst. dir. Regional Vis. Nurse Agy., North Haven, Conn., 1976-78; exec. dir. Waterbury (Conn.) Vis. Nurse Assn., 1978-82; exec. v.p. VNA Health Care, Inc., Plainville, Conn., 1982-86; pres. Vis. Nurse And Home Care, Inc. (name changed to VNA Health Care, Inc.), Plainville, Conn., 1986-98; CEO Home Care U. Nat. Assn. for Home Care, Washington, 1998—2002, v.p., 1999—2002; exec. dir. Home Healthcare Nurses Assn., Nat. Assn. for Home Care, 1999—2002; editor-in-chief Caring Mag., Nat. Assn. for Home Care, 1999—2002; editl. cons. Caring Mag., 2003; clin. herbalist and cons. Herbs and Health LLC, Freeport, Maine, 2004—; rsch. asst. U. Mass., Boston, 2004—. Asst. clin. prof. Yale U. Sch. Nursing, New Haven, 1978-99, assoc. clin. prof., 1999—; asst. clin. prof. U. Tex. Sch. Nursing, San Antonio, 1990-97; cons. U. SC Sch. Nursing, 1987-89, U. Tex. Sch. Nursing, San Antonio, 1989-90; corporator Am. Savs. Bank, 1993-98, Hartford Hosp., 1993-2006, Hosp. for Special Care, 1994-98; adj. asst. prof. pharmacy practice, master applied natural products program, Mass. Coll. Pharm. and Health Sci., Boston. Contbg. author: Home Health Adminstration, 1988; mem. editl. bd. Home Healthcare Nurse, 1988-95; co-editor Certification for Home Care/Hospice Execs. Study Guide; contbr. articles to profl. jours. Mem. Conn. Gov.'s Blue Ribbon Com. to Investigate Nursing Home Industry in Conn., Hartford, 1975-77; mem. nat. adv. com. Ctr. for Health Policy Rsch., Denver, 1989-94; mem. Conn. Award for Excellence Health Adv. Task Force, 1993-94; sec. Found. for Hospice and Home Care, 1989-95; joint adv. coun. and pub. health adv. coun. Conn. Dept. Pub. Health and Addiction Svcs., 1994-95; bd. dirs. St. Mary's Hosp., Waterbury, Conn., 1996-98, Health Tech, 1997-98. Robert Wood Johnson/Nat. League for nursing fellow, 1975, fellow Found. for Hospice and Home Care, 1992; recipient Andrew Veckerelli prize Yale U. Sch. Nursing, 1976, Disting. Alumni award, 1986, Creative Thinking Assn. Tribute, 1990, Leadership award Conn. Assn. for Home Care, 1995, Student Leadership award, U. Mass., Boston, 2007. Fellow Am. Acad. Nursing; mem. ANA, Acad. Health, Ea. Nursing Rsch. Soc., Am. Herbalists Guild, Inst. of Noetic Scis., Nat. League for Nursing (nat. adv. coun. home health outcome study 1989-93), Nat. Assn. Home Care (chmn. 1986-88, sec. 1984-86, 91-94, vice chair 1995-98, Mem. of Yr. award 1984, 97, Virginia Henderson award for excellence in nursing 1997), Conn. Assn. Home Care (sec. 1981-85), Greater Hartford C. of C. (women execs. com. 1990-98), Coastal Ctr. for Entrepreneurship, Alumni Assn. Leadership Greater Hartford, Sigma Theta (mem. Tau Theta Alpha chpt. Doctoral Dissertation award 2007). Avocation: gardening. Home: 75 Shore Dr Freeport ME 04032 Personal E-mail: mcushman@herbsandhealth.com, mcushman@jhu.edu.

CUSHWA, WILLIAM, biology professor; b. Radford, Va. s. Charles and Nancy Cushwa; m. Susan Cushwa; children: Brooke, Matthew. BS, Va. Tech, Blacksburg, 1986; MS, U. Calif., Davis, 1990, PhD, 1995. Tchr. sci. John Handley H.S., Winchester, Va., 1988—90; prof. biology Clark Coll., Vancouver, Wash., 1995—. Contbr. articles to profl. jours. Men's group leader New Heights Ch., Vancouver, Wash., 1998—2007. Recipient Exceptional Faculty award, Clark Coll., 1999. Mem.: NEA (assoc.). Avocations: exercise, home remodeling projects. Office: Clark Coll 1933 Ft Vancouver Way Vancouver WA 98663 Office Phone: 360-992-2386. E-mail: wcushwa@clark.edu.

CUSICK, PATRICIA A., information technology executive; b. Scranton, Pa., Nov. 5, 1948; BS in Math., Marywood Coll., Scranton, 1970. Plant mgr., sys. supplies IBM, dir., info. sys. and logistics for comm. product group; dir., computer integrated mfg., mktg. & devel. IBM U.S.; dir., acct. technical programs IBM at Fort Motor Co.; mgr., info. tech. Digital Equipment Corp., Maynard, Mass.; joined Xerox Corp., 1991, v.p., info. mgmt., bus. group ops., v.p. & chief info. officer Webster, NY, 1999—. Named Woman of Yr. in Bus. and Industry, Raritan Valley C. of C., 1984. Office: VP & CIO Xerox Corp M/S 102-12A 800 Phillips Rd Webster NY 14580

CUSICK, ROBERT IRWIN, federal official, lawyer; b. Nashville, Jan. 31, 1944; BA, U. Louisville, 1965, JD, 1968. Bar: Ky. 1968. Ptnr. Wyatt, Tarrant & Combs, LLP, Louisville; dir. Office Govt. Ethics, Washington, 2006—. Mem. bar govs. 4th Supreme Ct. Dist., 1985-92; vice chmn. Fed. Jud. Selection Commn. of Ky., 1985-87, Ky. Bd. Bar Examiners, 1987-96. Editor-in-Chief Jour. of Family Law, 1966-67. Served in US Naval Reserves. Recipient Disting. Svc. award, Louisville Bar Assn., 1991. Fellow Am. Bar Found.; mem. ABA, Am. Judicature Soc., Fed. Bar Assn., Ky. Bar Assn. (bd. govs. 1992), ABA ctr. for Profl. Responsibility, Greater Louisville Inc., Navy League US. Office: Office Govt Ethics 1201 New York Ave NW Ste 500 Washington DC 20005

CUSSLER, CLIVE ERIC, author; b. Aurora, Ill., July 15, 1931; s. Eric E. and Amy (Hunnewell) C.; m. Barbara Knight, Aug. 28, 1955; children: Teri, Dirk, Dayna. Student, Pasadena City Coll., 1949-51; PhD in Maritime History, N.Y. State Maritime Coll., 1997. Owner Bestgen & Cussler Advt., Newport Beach, Calif., 1961-65; creative dir. Darcy Advt., Hollywood, Calif., 1965-67; chmn. Nat. Underwater and Marine Agy. Author: (novels) The Mediterranean Caper, 1973, Iceberg, 1975, Raise the Titanic!, 1976, Vixen 03, 1978, Night Probe, 1981, Pacific Vortex, 1982, Deep Six, 1984, Cyclops, 1986, Treasure, 1988, Dragon, 1990, Sahara, 1992, Inca Gold, 1994, Shock Wave, 1995, Sea Hunters, 1996, Flood Tide, 1997, Clive Cussler & Dirk Pitt Revealed, 1998, Atlantis Found, 1999, Valhalla Rising, 2001, Serpent, 1999, Blue Gold, 2000, Fire Ice, 2002, Sea Hunters II, 2002, White Death, 2003, Golden Buddha, 2003, Trojan Odyssey, 2003, Sacred Stone, 2004, (with Dirk Cussler) Black Wind, 2004; (with Paul Kemprecos) Lost City, 2004, Polar Shift, 2005; (with Jack DuBrul) Dark Watch, 2005, (with Paul Kemprecos) The Navigator, 2007, (with Jack Dubrul) Skeleton Coast, 2006; (children's books) The Adventures of Vin Fiz, 2006, The Chase, 2007. Served in USAF, 1950-54. Recipient Disting. Svc. award, Nat. Maritime Hist. Soc., Navy Meml. Heritage award, Nat. Trust for Hist. Preservation award, numerous advt. awards, Thriller Master Lifetime Achievement award, Internat. Thriller Writers. Fellow Nat. Soc. Oceanographers, N.Y. Explorers Club (Lowell Thomas Underwater Explorers award), Royal Geog. Soc. London, Classic Car Club Am. Achievements include discovery of over 60 historic shipwrecks.

CUSSLER, EDWARD LANSING, JR., chemical engineer, educator; s. Edward Lansing and Eleanor Christine (Lloyd-Jones) C.; m. Elizabeth Campbell Beidler. BS in Chem. Engring., Yale U., 1961; MS in Chem. Engring., U. Wis., 1963, PhD, 1965; DSc (hon.), U. Lund, 2002. Rsch. asst. U. Wis., Madison, 1961—65, postdoctoral fellow, 1961—65, U. Adelaide, Australia, 1965-66, Yale U., 1966-67; asst. prof. Carnegie-Mellon U., 1967-70, assoc. prof., 1970-73, prof., 1973-80, U. Minn., Mpls., 1980—. Mem. editl. bd. Jour. Membrane Sci., 1975—. Recipient William H. Frances S. Ryan award Carnegie-Mellon U., 1975, George Taylor Tchg. award U. Minn., 1987, Separations Sci. award ACS, 2002. Mem. NAE (Separations Sci. award 2002), AIChE (bd. dirs. 1989-92, v.p. 1993, pres. 1994, editl. bd. 1996—, Alan P. Colburn award 1975, W.K. Lewis award 2001), Am. Assn. Engrs. Soc. (chair 1996). Office: U Minn Chem Engring Dept 421 Washington Ave SE Minneapolis MN 55455-0373 Office Phone: 612-625-1596. Business E-Mail: cussl001@umn.edu.

CUSTEN, BARBARA S., library director; Dir. South State Coop. Libr. Sys., Calif., Santiago Libr. Sys., Met. Coop. Libr. Sys., Pasadena, Calif., Riverside Pub. Libr., Calif., 2006—. Bd. dirs. Califa. Office: Riverside Pub Libr 3581 Mission Inn Ave PO Box 468 Riverside CA 92502 Office Phone: 951-826-5213. Office Fax: 951-826-5407.

CUSTER, BETH, composer, musician; d. William Benjamin Custer and Jean Nancy Stewart. B in Musical Studies, SUNY, Potsdam, 1980; postgrad., Mich. State U., 1980; M in Clarinet Performance, San Francisco State U., 1985. Clarinet tchr., 1976—; tchr. Clarinet Monster annual clarinet ensemble workshops, Calif., 1990—; substitute prof. Mills Coll., Oakland, Calif., 1995—, adj. prof. composition, 2005—; prof. composition U. Calif., Berkeley, 2006. Musician: The Club Foot Orch., 1983—, Clarinet Thing, 1990, Trance Mission, 1992—98, Eighty Mile Beach, 1994, Dona Luz 30 Besos, 1998—2001, The Beth Custer Ensemble, 2001—, numerous recs. Mem.: Am. Music Ctr., Musicians Union, Am. Composers Forum, Dolphin Swim Club. Office Phone: 415-305-3242.

CUSTER, CHARLES FRANCIS, lawyer; b. Hays, Kans., Aug. 19, 1928; s. Raymond Earl and Eva Marie (Walker) C.; m. Irene Louise Macarow, Jan. 2, 1950; children: Shannon Elaine, Charles Francis, Murray Maxwell, Kelly Sue. AB, U. Chgo., 1948, JD, 1958. Bar: Ill. 1958, U.S. Dist. Ct. (no dist.) Ill. 1971, U.S. Supreme Ct. 1991. Assoc. Meyers & Matthias, Chgo., 1958-72; pvt. practice Chgo., 1972-78; ptnr. Vedder, Price, Kaufman & Kammholz, Chgo., 1978-98, of counsel, 1998—. Arbitrator, mediator. Past dir. Family Care Svcs., Chgo. Mem. ABA (mem. fed. regulation of securities and devels. in investment svcs. coms., dispute resolution sect.), Chgo. Bar Assn. (mem. securities law com., mem. investment cos. subcom., alternative dispute resolution com.), Cliff Dwellers (past officer and dir.). Avocations: music, theater. Home: 5210 S Kenwood Ave Chicago IL 60615-4006 Office: Vedder Price Kaufman & Kammholz 222 N La Salle St Ste 2600 Chicago IL 60601-1100 Office Phone: 312-609-7545.

CUSTER, JOHN CHARLES, portfolio manager; b. Chgo., Aug. 30, 1934; s. John Howard and Irene Lillian (McGovern) C.; m. Barbara Ann Welcher, Sept. 5, 1959 (dec. Sept. 1996); 1 child, John Thomas. AB, Ind. U., 1956; MHA, U. Minn., 1966; grad., Harvard U., 1975. Asst. adminstr. Johns Hopkins Hosp., Balt., 1966-67; clin. adminstr. Kaiser Permanente Med. Care Program, Oakland, Calif., 1967-69, dir. materials, 1969-70, mgr. health plan Cleve., 1970-74, v.p., health plan mgr., 1974-79; v.p. Kaiser Permanente Adv. Svcs., Oakland, 1979-84; pres., CEO Keystone Health Plan, Camp Hill, Pa., 1984—87, Custer & Assocs., Hummelstown, Pa., 1987—92; investment broker Legg Mason Wood Walker, Inc., 1992—2006, Smith Barney, 2006; ptnr. Heritage Wealth Advisors, Lemoyne, Pa., 2006—. Lectr. U. Minn. Grad. Sch. of Pub. Health, Mpls., 1981-85, Harvard U. Grad. Sch. of Pub. Health, Boston, 1977-80. Chmn. Pa. Assn. HMO's, Harrisburg, 1984-86. 1st lt. U.S. Army, 1956-58, col. USAR. Mem. APHA, Am. Coll. Health Care Execs., Am. Hosp. Assn., Med. Group Mgmt. Assn., Internat. Fedn. of Employee Benefit Plans, Pa. State C. of C. (health care cost contain com.), Pa. State Dept. of Pub. Welfare (health care adv. subcom. 1984-85), Oakmont Homeowners Assn. (pres.), Hershey Golf Club (trustee 2004—), Cosmos Club (Washington), Army-Navy Club (Washington), Harvard Club (N.Y.C.), Elks, Delta Upsilon. Episcopalian. Home: 589 Lovell Ct Hummelstown PA 17036-9156 Office: 635 N 12th St Lemoyne PA 17043 Office Phone: 717-737-9260 x 201. Fax: (717) 737-0800. Personal E-mail: custerj2@nationwide.com.

CUSUMANO, JAMES ANTHONY, filmmaker, vocalist, retired pharmaceutical, hotel, and recording industry executive; b. Elizabeth, NJ, Apr. 14, 1942; s. Charles Anthony and Carmella Madeline (Catalano) Cusumano; m. Jane LaVerne Melvin, June 15, 1985 (dec. June 2001); children: Doreen Ann, Polly Jean; m. Inez Sipulova, July 9, 2003. BA, Rutgers U., 1964, PhD, 1967; grad. Exec. Mktg. Program, Stanford U., 1981, Harvard U., 1988. Dir. catalyst rsch. Exxon Rsch. and Engring. Co., Linden, NJ, 1967-74; pres., chief exec. officer, founder Catalytica Inc., Mountain View, Calif., 1974-85, chmn., 1985-2000, also bd. dirs.; pres., CEO, bd. dirs. Catalytica Fine Chems., Inc., Mountain View, Calif., 1993-97; chmn., CEO, bd. dirs. Catalytica Pharms., Inc., 1997-99, chmn., chief strategic officer, 1999-2000; pres., CEO, founder Chateau Wally Films LLC, Ojai, Calif., 2000—; exec. dir. Sch. Neo-Alchemy, 2002—; vice chmn. World Bus. Acad., 2004—; prin., owner Chateau Mcely, Czech Republic. Bd. dirs. Ojai Film Festival, CBA Bus. Sch., Croatia; advisor Fulbright scholar progam Inst. Internat. Edn.; mem. dean's adv. bd. Rutgers U., 1997—; mem. com. on catalysts and environ. NSF; exec. briefings with Pres. George Bush and Cabinet mems., 1990, 92; bd. dirs. Catalytica Advanced Techs., Inc.; spkr. in field; lectr. and plenary lectr. in field. Author: Catalysis in Coal Conversion, 1978, (with others) Critical Materials Problems in Energy Production, 1976, Advanced Materials in Catalysis, 1977, Liquid Fuels from Coal, 1977, Kirk-Othmer Encyclopedia of Chemical Technology, 1979, Chemistry for the 21st Century, Perspectives in Catalysis, 1992, Science and Technology in Catalysis 1994, 1995; contbr. articles to profl. jours., chpts. to books; founding editor Jour. of Applied Catalysis, 1980, Hydrogen and the New Energy Economy, 2005; exec. prodr. feature film: What Matters Most, 2001; exec. prodr. documentary film: One Tough Biscotti: A Woman, A Film and A Fight, 2001; rec. artist with Royal Teens and Dino Take Five for ABC Paramount, Capitol and Jubilee Records, 1957-67; single records include Short Shorts, Short Shorts Twist, My Way, Hey Jude, Rosemarie, Please Say You Want Me, Lovers Never Say Goodbye; albums include The Best of the Royal Teens, Newies But Oldies; cd's for Global Children's Charities, Oldies for Youngies, 2004; appeared in PBS TV prodn. on molecular engring., Little by Little, 1989. Recipient Surface Chemistry award Continental Oil Co., 1964; Henry Rutgers scholar, 1963, Lever Bros. fellow, 1965, Churchill Coll. fellow Cambridge Univ., 1992. Mem.: ASCAP, AIChE, World Future Soc., Smithsonian Assocs., Pres.'s Assn., Am. Mus. Natural History, Soc. Organic Chems. MFrs. (bd. dirs. 1996), N.Y. Acad. Scis., Am. Phys. Soc., Am. Chem. Soc. (plenary lectr. to chem. educators nat. meeting 1994), Phi Lambda Upsilon, Sigma Psi. Roman Catholic. Achievements include 20 patents in catalysis and surface science. Office: Chateau MCELY SRO Parizska 3 110 00 Prague Czech Republic Home: U Stare Scholy 2 110 00 Prague 1 Czech Republic Office Phone: +420-325-600-000. Business E-Mail: jim@chateaumcely.com.

CUSWORTH, CHRISTYL J., conservator, artist; b. Neptune, NJ, Mar. 14, 1963; d. Christopher and Dorothy Cusworth. BA, Coll. N.J., 1986; student, Am. Coll. Greece, Athens, 1984; sculpture student, U. New Orleans, 1994. Registered profl. assoc. Am. Inst. for Conservation of Hist. and Artistic Works. Artist, bronze caster Antietam, Trenton, NJ, 1987—91; paintings conservator, artist Christyl Cusworth Paintings Conservator, Lambertville, NJ, 1995—. Bronze caste, art installer Artist Julian Schnabel, NYC, 1989—90; apprentice, artist Salah Hudson Conservation Studio, New Orleans, 1991—95; art installer Artist/Photojournalist Melina Mara, Washington, 2003. Oil painting, Star night over Lambertville (Bob and Joyce Byers award, 2004). Office: Christyl Cusworth Paintings Conservator 28 N Union St Lambertville NJ 08530 Home Phone: 609-397-5441. Personal E-mail: cus@pil.net.

CUTCHINS, CLIFFORD ARMSTRONG, IV, lawyer; b. Norfolk, Va., May 13, 1948; s. Clifford Armstrong III and Ann (Woods) Cutchins; m. Jane McKenzie, Aug. 14, 1971; children: Sarah Helen, Ann Woods. BA, Princeton U., 1971; JD, MBA, U. Va., 1975. Bar: Va. 1975, US Dist. Ct. Ea. Dist. Va. 1975, US Ct. Appeals 4th Cir. 1975. Assoc. McGuire, Woods, Battle & Boothe (now McGuireWoods LLP), Richmond, Va., 1975—82, ptnr., 1982—90, 2001—; sr. v.p., gen. counsel, sec. James River Corp. Va., Richmond, 1990-97, Ft. James Corp., Deerfield, Ill., 1997-2000. Bd. dirs. Arts Coun. Richmond, 1980-86, Richmond Heart Assn., 1980-83, St. Catherine's Sch., Richmond, 1983-86, Richmond Ballet, 1986-88, Richmond Children's Mus., 1986-94, Richmond on the James, 1986-88, Hist. Richmond Found., 1990-94, Richmond Met. Blood Svc., 1995-97, Kohl Children's Mus., Wilmette, Ill., 1998-2000, Richmond First Tee, 2001-, The Nature Conservancy Va. Chpt., 2002-, Assn. for Corp. Growth, Richmond; bd. trustees Henrico Doctors' Hosp., 1986-, Va. Commonwealth U. Sch. Engring. Found., 1997-. chmn. Fort James Found., 1997-2000. Mem.: Va. Bar Assn., Commonwealth Club (bd. dirs. 1983—86, 1996—97), Kinloch Golf Club, Country Club Va. (bd. dirs. 1990—93, 2003—, v.p. 2004—06, pres. 2007—). Avocations: golf, travel, reading. Office: McGuireWoods LLP One James Ctr 901 E Cary St Richmond VA 23219-4030 Office Phone: 804-775-4720. Office Fax: 804-225-5344. Business E-Mail: ccutchins@mcguirewoods.com.

CUTHBERTSON, GILBERT MORRIS, political science professor; b. Warrensburg, Mo., Nov. 20, 1937; s. Gilbert and Marion Darlington (Morris) C. BA, U. Kans., 1959; PhD, Harvard U., 1963. Asst. prof. Rice U., Houston, 1963-68, assoc. prof., 1968-77, prof., 1977—. Resident assoc. Will Rice Coll., Houston, 1964—. Author: (book) Political Myth and Epic, 1975, (monographs) Political Power, 1968, Myth, Power, Value, 1982; co-author: Teacher Immortal, 1984. Mem. curator's bd. Mus. of Printing History, 1998-2005. Recipient George R. Brown lifetime award for excellence in tchg., 1993; Summerfield scholar U. Kans., 1955-59; Woodrow Wilson fellow Harvard U., 1959-63; Wilson C. Morris fellow. Mem. Am. Polit. Sci. Assn., Scottish Heritage Found. (bd. dirs. Great Scot award), River Oaks Rotary (bd. dirs., Paul Harris fellow), Knife and Fork Club, Phi Beta Kappa (past pres. chpt.), Pi Sigma Alpha, Sigma Tau Gamma, Delta Phi Alpha. Democrat. Presbyterian. Avocation: bridge. Office: Rice U Dept Polit Sci Houston TX 77251-1892 Office Phone: 713-348-3363. E-mail: poli@rice.edu.

CUTHRELL, CARL EDWARD, retired clergyman, lawyer, educator; b. Norfolk, Va., Aug. 13, 1934; s. Cecil Edward and Edna Catherine (Kirby) C.; m. Naomi Lorene Marshall, Dec. 23, 1960; children: Byron Eugene, Benjamin Dean. LLB, LaSalle U. Law Sch., Chgo., 1959; diploma Egyptian studies, Oriental Inst., U. Chgo., 1960; BD, Brantridge Forest Sch., Eng., 1970; MA in Med. History, Sussex Coll. Tech., Eng., 1972; MA in Classical Studies, Christ Ch. Coll., Oxford, Eng., 1973; diploma Germanic langs., Heidelberg U., Fed. Republic Germany), 1975; BA, Upper Iowa U., 1979; MA, Covington Theol. Sem., 1982; BRE, Cen. Bapt. Bicle Coll., 1989. Pvt. practice, Hampton, 1960—; ordained to ministry Evang. Friends Ch., 1972; pastor Rescue (Va.) Friends Ch., 1968-96. Faculty dept. theology, Norfolk extension Washington Bible Coll., Lanham, Md., dept. spl. programs/history Coll. William and Mary, Williamsburg, Va., dept. secular studies Cen. Bapt. Bible Coll., Hampton, Va. Author: Ancient Mummies, 1967, Paul's Voyage, 1971; Contbr.: lit. criticisms to Times Herald Newspaper; also numerous short stories. Bd. dirs. Nat. Philatelic Inst.; trustee Quincy Coll., 1970, Nat. Coll. Surgeons Hall of Fame, 1972. Served with M.C. AUS, 1950-57, Korea. Decorated Silver Star; recipient Scouter's award Boy Scouts Am., 1956, Silver Beaver award, 1976, Nat. Tchrs. medal Freedoms Found., 1973, Peace medal UN, 1973, Good Citizenship medal SAR, 1976 Mem. U.S. Capital, Nat. hist. socs., S.R., Sons Confederate Vets., Christian Educators Assn., Va. Herpetological Soc., Mil. Order Stars and Bars. Republican. Home: Abbeyfield Cottage 600 Copperfield Ln Lexington NC 27292

CUTLER, ALEXANDER MACDONALD, manufacturing executive; b. Milw., May 28, 1951; s. Richard Woolsey and Elizabeth (Fitzgerald) C.; m. Sarah Lynn Stark, Oct. 11, 1980; children: David Alexander, William MacDonald. BA, Yale U., 1973; MBA, Dartmouth Coll., 1975. Fin. analyst Cutler-Hammer, Milw., 1975-77, bus. group contr., 1977-79; contr. custom distbn. and control divsn. Eaton Corp., Atlanta, 1979-80, plant mgr. custom distbn. and control divsn., 1981-82, mgr. custom distbn. and control divsn., 1982-83, mgr. power distbn. divsn. Milw., 1984-85, gen. mgr. indsl. control and power distbn., 1985-86, pres. controls group Cleve., 1986-91, exec. v.p. ops., 1992-93, exec. v.p., COO controls, 1993-95, pres., COO, 1995-2000, chmn., pres., CEO, 2000—, bd. dirs. Bd. dirs. Axcelis Techs., 2000—06. Bd. dirs. United Way Svcs. Cleve., 2000-06, N.E. Ohio Coun. on Higher Edn., 1993-97, Greater Cleve. Growth Assn., 2001-04, Cleve. Tomorrow, 2000-04, Greater Cleve. Roundtable, 2000-04; class agt. alumni fund Loomis Chaffee Sch., Windsor, Conn., 1969—; bd. dirs. alumni fund Yale U., New Haven, 1974-89; trustee The Cleve. Play House, 1987-2002,

Gt. Lakes Mus., Inc., 1988-91, Mus. Natural History, Cleve., 1989-97; bd. overseers Amos Tuck Sch. Bus. Dartmouth Coll., 1996-2006; trustee Loomis Inst., 2003-2006; active Keycorp., 2000—, Bus. Roundtable, 2002—; chmn. Greater Cleve. Partnership, 2004-06. Mem.: Nat. Elec. Mfrs. Assn. (indsl. automation divsn. 1986—90; bd. govs. 1987—99, treas. 1993—95, bd. govs. 1996—99), Elec. Mfrs. Club (bd. dirs. 1995—), Yale U. Alumni Assn. (pres. Cleve. chpt. 1991—93, exec. com. of vis. com. Weatherhood Sch. Mgmt. 1993—2002, Yale devel. bd. 1998—), Musical Arts Assn., Chagrin Valley Hunt Club. Avocation: tennis. Office: Eaton Corp 1111 Superior Ave Eaton Ctr Cleveland OH 44114-2584 Office Phone: 216-523-5000.

CUTLER, BERNARD JOSEPH, editor-in-chief, writer; b. NYC, May 26, 1924; s. Joseph Louis and Sophie (Appel) C.; m. Carol Ann Rataic, Mar. 6, 1948. BSME, Pa. State Coll., 1945. Reporter Pitts. Press, 1945-51; reporter N.Y. Herald Tribune, 1951-56, Moscow corr., 1956-58, chief Paris bur., 1958-60, mng. editor European edition Paris, 1960, editor European edition, 1961-66; European corr. Scripps-Howard Newspapers, Paris, 1966-69, fgn. editl. writer Washington, 1969-72, chief editl. writer, 1972-80, editor-in-chief, 1980-89, fgn. affairs columnist, 1989-95. Author: Reactionary! Sgt. Lloyd W. Pate's Story, 1956. Recipient Disting. Alumni award Pa. State U., 1972. Mem.: Gridiron, National Press. Office: 2735 P St NW Washington DC 20007-3065

CUTLER, BRUCE, lawyer; b. Bklyn., Apr. 29, 1948; BA, Hamilton College, 1970; JD cum laude, Brooklyn Law School, 1974. Bar: NY 1975, U.S. Supreme Ct. 1979, U.S. Ct. Appeals (2nd cir.) 1982. Supervising sr. trial atty. Homicide Bureau, New York, 1974—81; deputy chief Court Bureau, Office of the Dist. Atty., Kings County, NY; attorney Slotnick & Baker, 1981—87; pvt. practice, 1987—. Author: Closing Argument: Defending (and Befriending) John Gotti, and Other Legal Battles I Have Waged, 2003. Recipient American Jurisprudence Award in Criminal Law. Office: 260 Madison Ave New York NY 10016*

CUTLER, DAVID M., finance educator; BA in Econ. summa cum laude, Harvard U., 1987; PhD in Econ., MIT, 1991. Asst. prof. economics Harvard U., Cambridge, Mass., 1991—95, John L. Loeb assoc. prof. social sciences, 1995—97, prof. economics, 1997—2005, assoc. dean, faculty of arts & sciences, 2002—, Otto Eckstein prof. applied economics, 2005—; sr. staff economist Coun. Econ. Advisers, 1993; dir. Nat. Econ. Coun., 1993; rsch. assoc. Nat. Bur. Econ. Rsch. Mem. govt. adv. panel NIH, Social Security Adminstrn., Health Care Fin. Adminstrn.; sci. adv. bd. Alliance for Aging Rsch.; bd. dirs. Nat. Acad. Social Ins. Editor: (jour.) Jour. Health Econ.; author: Your Money or Your Life: Strong Medicine for America's Health Care System, 2004. Recipient Outstanding Mentor award, Harvard U. Grad. Sch. Arts & Sciences, 1999, Griliches prize for best paper, Quarterly Jour. Economics, 1999, Kenneth Arrow award, 2000, Eugene Garfield award, Research!Am., 2003, John Eisenberg Mentoring award, Agy. Health Care Quality & Rsch., 2004, David Kershaw prize, Assn. Pub. Policy & Mgmt., 2004; fellow Ctr. Advanced Study in Behavioral Sciences, 2000—01. Fellow: Am. Acad. Arts & Scis., Employee Benefit Rsch. Inst.; mem.: NAS, Inst. Rsch. Poverty, Inst. Medicine, Phi Beta Kappa. Avocations: history, running, ultimate Frisbee, walking along the Charles River. Office: Harvard U Dept Economics Littauer Ctr 1875 Cambridge St Cambridge MA 02138

CUTLER, EVERETTE WAYNE, history professor; b. Beaumont, Tex., Nov. 29, 1938; s. Homer Everette and Mary Abbie (Osborne) C.; m. Leta Harriet Rush; 1 child, Lori Catherine. BA, Lamar U., Beaumont, Tex., 1959; BD, So. Meth. U., Dallas, 1964; MA, U. Tex., Austin, 1967, PhD, 1971. Rsch. assoc. U. Tex., Austin, 1965-67, U. Ky., Lexington, 1970-75; assoc. prof. history Vanderbilt U., Nashville, 1975-87; rsch. prof. history U. Tenn., Knoxville, 1987—. Dir. Polk Project, Vanderbilt U., Nashville, 1975-87, Polk Project, U. Tenn., 1987—. Asst. editor Southwestern Hist. Quar., 1965-67; asst. editor: Papers of Henry Clay, vols. 4 and 5, 1970-75; editor: Correspondence of James K. Polk, vols. 5-10, 1975—, North for Union, 1986. Pres. Nashville Symphony Chorus, 1982-83; vestry St. George's Episc. Ch., Nashville, 1984-87; dir. Tenn. Pres. Trust, 1991—2005; commodore Concord Yacht Club, 2000-02. Grantee NEH, 1984, 88-96, 2002-03, Nat. Hist. Publs. and Records Commn., 1975—, Tenn. Hist. Commn., 1975—. Mem. Am. Hist. Assn., Orgn. Am. Historians, So. Hist. Assn., Assn. for Documentary Editing, Interscholastic Sailing Assn. (dir. bd. 2003—), Phi Kappa Phi, Alpha Tau Omega. Democrat. Episcopalian. Avocations: choral music, sailing, fiction writing. Home: 7901 High Heath Knoxville TN 37919-4410 Office: U Tenn Hoskins Libr 216 Knoxville TN 37996-0001 Home Phone: 865-690-3515; Office Phone: 865-974-0662. Business E-Mail: wcutler@utk.edu.

CUTLER, JOHN EARL, landscape architect; b. Houston, Nov. 21, 1943; s. John Cecil and Dorothy Evelyn (Hewett) C.; m. Paula Helene Murdy, Dec. 27, 1969; children: Christian Hewett, Leigh Helene. BS in Landscape Architecture, Tex. A&M U., 1967. Registered landscape arch., Tex. Landscape arch. Caudill Rowlett Scott, Houston, 1968-69, Marmon Mok Green, Houston, 1969-70; campus landscape arch. U. Houston, 1970-74; ptnr., landscape arch. Office of George Porcher, Houston, 1974-79; prin., landscape arch. The SWA Group, Houston, 1979—. Bd. dirs. Trees for Houston, 1984—. Recipient Oustanding Alumni award, Tex. A&M U., 2004. Fellow Am. Soc. Landscape Archs. Avocation: sailing. Home: 2235 Bartlett St Houston TX 77098-5201 Office: The SWA Group 1245 W 18th St Houston TX 77008-3392 Office Phone: 713-868-1676. Business E-Mail: jcutler@swagroup.com.

CUTLER, KARAN DAVIS, writer, columnist; b. Ill., Oct. 1, 1942; d. J. Cary and Ellen Esslinger Davis; m. Stephen J. Cutler, Apr. 25, 1968; children: Ellen M. Rock, Timothy S. BA, So. Ill. U., Carbondale, 1965; MA, MALS, U. Mich., Ann Arbor, 1968. Sr. editor Harrowsmith Country Life/Telemedia, Charlotte, Vt., 1989—94, mng. editor, 1994—96. Sch. libr., Vt., 1984—89; instr. C.C. Vt., Burlington, 1985—88; garden columnist Rutland Herald and Barre Times Argus, Barre, Vt., 1987—91. Author: (non-fiction) Pruning Trees, Shrubs and Vines, 2003, Herb Gardening for Dummies, 1995, Burpee-The Complete Vegetable and Herb Gardener, 1997 (Notable Book award Bklyn Botanic Garden, 1998), 2003, The New England Gardener's Book of Lists, 2000, Burpee - The Complete Flower Gardener, 2006; editor: (non-fiction) Vines, 1992, Salad Gardens: Gourmet Greens and Beyond, 1995, Essential Tools: Equipment and Supplies for Home Gardeners, 1995, Tantalizing Tomatoes: Smart Tips and Tasty Picks for Gardeners Everywhere, 1997, Starting From Seed: The Natural Gardener's Guide to Propagating Plants, 1998, Flowering Vines: Beautiful Climbers, 1999. Recipient Quill and Trowel award, Garden Writers Am., 1989, 1990, 1991, 1993, 1994, 1995. Home Phone: 802-899-4635. Personal E-mail: kdcutler@aol.com.

CUTLER, KENNETH B., JR., dermatologist, educator; b. Sept. 12, 1968; BA in Econ., Amherst Coll., Mass., 1990; MD cum laude, SUNY, Bklyn., 1994. Intern Columbia Presbyn. Med. Ctr., NYC, 1994—97; resident in dermatology NY Med. Coll., Valhalla, NY, 1997—2000; pvt. practice Stamford, Conn., 2000—01; pres., owner Stamford Dermatology Cons. PC, 2001—. Prof. dermatology NY Med. Coll., Valhalla, 2000—. Commr. pub. health City of Stamford, 2006—; active Nat. Rep. Congrl. Com., 2004—. Named Physician of Yr., Nat. Rep. Congl. Com., 2005; named one of America's Top Physicians, Nat. Consumer Rsch. Assn., 2004; recipient Congl. Merit award, Nat. Rep. Congl. Com., 2006. Fellow: Am. Acad. Dermatology; mem.: AMA, Fairfield County Med. Assn., Conn. State Dermatology and Dermatologic Surgery Soc., Conn. State Med. Assn., Stamford C. of C., Nat. Eagle Scout Assn., Met. Club (NY), Alpha Omega Alpha. Home: 293 Rocky Rapids Rd Stamford CT 06903 Office: Stamford Dermatology Cons 125 Strawberry Hill AVe Ste 302 Stamford CT 06902-2536 Office Phone: 203-323-9033. Personal E-mail: cutlerk@aol.com.

CUTLER, KENNETH BURNETT, lawyer, investment company executive; b. Muskegon Heights, Mich., June 19, 1932; s. Stanley and Lucile (Miles) C.; m. Cecelia Bilsly, Mar. 9, 1967; children: Kenneth Burnett, Randall Miles, Cynthia Bilsly, Robert Appleby, Jeffrey Lamont Derrick. BBA, U. Mich., 1954, JD, 1957. Bar: Mich. 1957, NY 1960. Assoc. Dewey Ballantine, Bushby, Palmer & Wood, NYC, 1957-66; v.p., gen. counsel The Lord Abbett Managed Funds, NYC, 1966—97; ptnr., gen. counsel Lord, Abbett & Co., NYC, 1972-97. Mem.: NASD (arbitration bd. 1976—), Bronxville Field Club, Winged Foot Golf Club, Met. Club, Phi Delta Phi, Delta Tau Delta. Avocations: golf, tennis, skiing. Home: 10 Westway Bronxville NY 10708-4311

CUTLER, LAURENCE JEFFREY, lawyer; b. Bklyn., May 23, 1945; s. Charles and Ruth (Grossman) C.; children: Rebecca L., Mitchell A. BA, Am. U., Washington, 1967; JD, U. Ky., 1970. Bar: N.J. 1970, U.S. Dist. Ct. N.J. 1970, U.S. Supreme Ct. 1974, U.S. Ct. Appeals (3rd cir.) 1982, N.Y. 1986; cert. matrimonial arbitrator and mediator Am. Acad. Matrimonial Lawyers. Pvt. practice, Morristown, N.J., 1970—. Mem. coms. civil practice N.J. Supreme Ct., 1976-79, matrimonial litigation, 1980-82, family part practice, 1985-87, 98—; guest lectr. Seton Hall U. Sch. Law, 1988-90, adj. prof. law, 1992—; lectr. Am. Acad. Matrimonial Lawyers, 1985, 93, N.J. Family Part Judges' Retreat, 1989, N.J. Jud. Coll., 1990, Nat. Bus. Inst., Inc., 1992, Inst. Continuing Legal Edn. N.J., 1978—, Morris County Bar Assn., 1986, 91, N.J. State Bar Assn., 1992, Am. Trial Lawyers Assn., 1993-96, 99—. Co-author: N.J. Family Law Practice, 3 vols., 2001; contbr. articles to profl. jours. Mem. Morris Plains Juvenile Conf. Com., 1973-82; bd. trustees Morris Plains Libr. Assn., 1982-87. Recipient Tishler award, 1993, Bar Register of Pre-Eminent Lawyers, 1994—; named to Best Lawyers in Am., 1995—, Best Lawyers in N.J., 1997—. Mem. AMA (litigation sect. 1987-90), Internat. Acad. Matrimonial Lawyers (bd. govs. U.S. chpt. 1994-98), Am. Acad. Matrimonial Lawyers (bd. govs. 1989-90, 91-94, arbitration com. 1993—, chmn. mktg. com. 1991-92, membership com. 1992-93, budget and fin. com. 1990-91, editl. bd. Law Jour. 1993—, chmn. SCUBA Network 1992-93, bd. mgrs. N.J. chpt. 1981—, pres. N.J. chpt. 1985-87, chmn. nominating com. 1992-93, chmn. scholarship com. 1991-94, membership com. 1991-94), Am. Coll. Family Trial Lawyers (exec. com. 1994—), N.J. Assn. Matrimonial Arbitrators (v.p. 1993—), N.J. State Bar Assn. (exec. com. 1975-93, appellate practice com. 1993-95, curriculum com. Inst. Continuing Legal Edn. 1982-91), Morris County Bar Assn. (mem. family law com. 1973-75, 80—, chmn. 1987, chmn. matrimonial early settlement program 1976), Inn of Ct. (N.J. master family law 1993—), N.J. Bd. of Atty. (cert. matrimonial). Avocations: computers, horses. E-mail: LJC@Cutlaw.com.

CUTLER, LAURENCE STEPHAN, architect, museum administrator, writer, advertising executive, educator; b. New Haven, Conn., Aug. 27, 1940; s. Hermann Shepard and Doris Winifred Cutler; m. Sherrie Stephens, Jan. 24, 1967 (div. 1992); children: A. Maximilian S., Zachary Wolf S.; m. Judy Goffman, Feb. 7, 1995; stepchildren: Jennifer Paige Greenawalt, Andrew Douglas Goffman. BA, U. Pa., 1962; MArch, Harvard U., 1966, MArch in Urban Design, 1967. Nationally cert. architect. Founder, co-prin. ECODESIGN, Cambridge, 1966; with ECODESIGN subs. Combustion Engring., Inc., 1972—79; founder C-E Tec Internat., Inc., 1972-79, ECODESIGN/SPC Internat., 1979—82; with Architects Collaborative, Eero Saarinen & Assocs.; group dir. Lodigiani U.S.A. Ltd., 1985-87, also bd. dirs. Prof. MIT, 1967-72, Harvard U., 1965-73, R.I. Sch. Design, 1965-68; group dir. N.Am. Gold Greenless Trott (USA) Holdings, Inc., London, 1988-91; adv. dir. Emery Roth Architects, 1984-90. Prin. archtl. works include: Chase Manhattan Bank Hdqrs. for Caribbean, St. Thomas, Ballys Park Pl. Casino Hotel, Sugarloaf/USA Ski Area, Maine, fire and police complex, Westford Mass., Lockhart Gardens Shopping Ctr., U.S. Virgin Islands, Am. Embassy housing, Lagos, Nigeria; author: (with Albert G.H. Dietz) Industrialized Building Systems for Housing, 1971, (with Sherrie Stephens Cutler) Recycling Cities for People: The Urban Design Process, 1976, 3d edit., 1983, Handbook of Housing Systems for Designers and Developers, 1974, (with Judy Cutler) Parrish & Poetry, 1995, 99, Maxfield Parrish: A Retrospective, 1996, 99,(with Judy Cutler) Maxfield Parrish, 2000, 04., Maxfield Parrish and the American Imagists, 2004. Incorporator Cambridge Sch. Weston; founder, trustee The Woodbridge Found.; adv. dir. Am. Illustrators Gallery, N.Y.C., 1984—, founder, chair ARTShows and Products, Corp., 1993—, Maxfield Parrish Orgn.; officer Paul Cezanne Family Orgn., Inc.; founder, chair Nat. Mus. Am. Illustration, Newport, R.I., 1998—; chair Am. Civilization Found., 1998—. Recipient Alpha-Rho Chi Gold medal Harvard U., 1966, Engring. Excellence award Colo. Cons. Engrs. Coun., 1973, Design and Environment award, 1975, Design Arts Program award NEA, 1980; Milton Fund grantee, Harvard U., 1966, Fulbright-Hays grantee, India, 1968. Mem. AIA (Regional Honors award 1974, 75), Royal Inst. Brit. Architects, Am. Soc. Planning Ofcls., Nat. Coun. Archtl. Registration Bds., Harvard Club N.Y., Nat. Arts Club, Carnegie Club, Skibo Castle Scotland, Carnegie-Abbey (Portsmouth, R.I.). Address: 18 E 77th St Ste 4B New York NY 10021-1700 also: Vernon Ct 492 Bellevue Ave Newport RI 02840 Home Phone: 401-846-2578; Office Phone: 401-851-8949 ext. 10. Business E-Mail: lcutler@americanillustration.org.

CUTLER, RICHARD W., lawyer; b. New Rochelle, NY, Mar. 9, 1917; s. Charles Evelyn and Amelia (MacDonald) C.; m. Elizabeth Fitzgerald, Oct. 18, 1947; children: Marguerite Blackburn, Alexander MacDonald, Judith Elizabeth. BA, Yale U., 1938, LLB, 1941. Bar: Conn. 1941, N.Y. 1942, Wis. 1950, D.C. 1975, U.S. Supreme Ct. 1980. Practiced in, NYC, 1941—49, Milw., 1949—87; assoc. Donovan, Leisure, Newton & Lumbard, 1941—42; atty. Legal Aid Soc., 1946—47, RCA Comm., Inc., 1947—49; ptnr. Quarles & Brady, and predecessors, 1954—87; gen. ptnr. Sunset Investment Co., Milw. Author: Zoning Law and Practice in Wisconsin, 1967, Greater Milwaukee's Growing Pains, 1950-2000: An Insider's View, 2001, Counterspy: Memoir of a Counterintelligence Officer in World War II and the Cold War, 2004. Chmn. Milw. br. Fgn. Policy Assn., 1951-53; pres. Childrens Service Soc. Wis., 1961-63, Neighborhood House, 1971-74; sec. Southeastern Wis. Regional Planning Commn., 1960-84, Yale Devel. Bd., 1973-79; bd. dirs. Wis. Dept. Resource Devel., 1967-68; Met. Milw. Study Commn., 1957-61; bd. dirs. Milw. Innovation Ctr., 1985-89, pres., 1984-85, exec. v.p., 1985-89; bd. dirs. Greater Milw. Com., 1982-89. Capt. USAAF, 1943-46 and OSS, 1944-46. Recipient Disting. Leadership award Am. Planning Assn., 1992. Mem. ABA, Wis. Bar Assn., Milw. Club, Milw. Country Club, Town Club, Phi Beta Kappa. Presbyterian. Home: 938 W Shaker Cir Mequon WI 53092-6032 Office: 411 E Wisconsin Ave Milwaukee WI 53202-4461 Home Phone: 262-241-4305. E-mail: rwc@quarles.com.

CUTLER, STEPHEN JOEL, sociologist, educator; b. Lawrence, Mass., Jan. 1, 1943; s. Lewis J. and Minnie C.; m. Karan Elizabeth Davis, Apr. 25, 1968; children: Ellen Min, Timothy Spence. BA, Dartmouth Coll., 1964; MA, U. Mich., 1965, PhD, 1969. Faculty Oberlin Coll., Ohio, 1969—84, prof. sociology-anthropology, 1979—84, chmn. dept., 1979—82; prof. sociology, Bishop Robert F. Joyce Disting. Prof. gerontology U. Vt., Burlington, 1984—, dir. Ctr. Study of Aging, 1993—96. Sr. fellow Ctr. Study Aging and Human Devel., Duke U., 1975-76; adv. bd. nat. data program social scis. Nat. Opinion Rsch. Ctr., 1980-85; mem. human devel. and aging study sect. NIH, 1979-84, 88-92, chmn., 1990-92; vis. scholar Oreg. State U., 2002; Fulbright scholar, 2003—. Co-author: Middle Start: An Experiment in the Educational Enrichment of Young Adolescents, 1978; co-editor: Major Social Problems: A Multidisciplinary View, 1979, Promoting Successful and Productive Aging, 1995; assoc. editor Gerontol. Monographs, 1976-82; mem. editl. bd. Internat. Jour. Aging and Human Devel., 1980—, Jour. Gerontology, 1981-86, Rsch. on Aging, 1982—, Am. Jour. Alzheimer's Disease, 2002—, Handbook of Aging and the Social Scis., 2005, Jour. Applied Gerontology, 2005—; editor Jour. Gerontology: Social Scis., 1990-93 Grantee, NIMH, NSF, NIH, Alzheimer's Assn.; Woodrow Wilson fellow, 1965, Univ. scholar, 2000—01, Fulbright scholar, 2003—04. Fellow Gerontol. Soc. Am. (exec. com. behavioral and social scis. sect. 1979-81, chmn. 1987, coun. mem. 1986-88, pres.-elect 1997, pres. 1998); mem. Am. Sociol. Assn. (coun. sect. on aging 1982-84, chmn.-elect 1993-94, chmn. 1994-95), Assn. for Gerontology in Higher Edn. (bd. dirs., exec. com. 1985-87, 95-97, Clark Tibbitts award 2001). Home: 54 Sleepy Hollow Rd Essex Junction VT 05452-2722 Office: U Vt Dept Sociology Burlington VT 05405-0001 Business E-Mail: scutler@uvm.edu.

CUTLER, STEPHEN M., lawyer, former federal agency administrator; b. 1961; BA summa cum laude, Yale U., 1982; JD, Yale Law Sch., 1985. Law clk. to Hon. Dorothy W. Nelson US Ct. Appeals (9th cir.), 1985—86; assoc. Wilmer, Cutler & Pickering LLP, 1987—93, ptnr., 1993—98; dep. dir. enforcement SEC, Washington, 1999—2001, acting dir. enforcement, 2001, dir. enforcement, 2001—05; ptnr. Wilmer, Cutler, Pickering, Hale & Dorr LLP, Washington, 2005—07; exec. v.p., gen. counsel JP Morgan Chase & Co., NYC, 2007—. Vis. fellow Ctr. Law in Pub. Interest, 1986—87. Editor: Yale Law Jour. Recipient Chmn. award Excellence, 1999, 2000, 2003. Office: JP Morgan Chase & Co 270 Park Ave New York NY 10017-2070*

CUTLER, TIMOTHY SPENCE, music educator, composer; b. Oberlin, Ohio, Feb. 2, 1973; s. Stephen Joel and Karan (Davis) Cutler; m. Ann Christine Fisher, July 24, 2004. MusB, Oberlin Conservatory of Music, Ohio, 1995; PhD, Yale U., New Haven, 2000. Expert U.S. Chess Fedn. Grad. asst. Yale U., New Haven, 1997—2000; asst. prof. music Austin Coll., Sherman, Tex., 2000—05, assoc. prof. music, 2005—07; prof. music theory Cleve. Inst. Music, 2007—. Founder and editor Internet Music Theory Database, 2003—; prin. second violin Sherman Symphony Orch., Sherman, Tex., 2000—; grading com. Advanced Placement Music Theory Exam, Princeton, NJ, 2000—; composer-in-residence Denison Heritage Performing Artists, Denison, Tex., 2001—; music divsn. editl. bd. Learning Object Learning Activities Project, Wesleyan, Conn., 2004—; presenter to profl. confs. Composer: Four Songs for Tenor and Piano (Included in ERM Media's CD-series Masterworks of the New Era, 2004), Symphony (Oberlin Conservatory, First Prize, Symphonic Composition, 1995), The Last Performance (Oberlin Conservatory, First Prize, Chamber Composition, 1995); contbr. articles to profl. jours. Tech. grantee, Associated Colls. of the South, 2003, 2005, 2006. Mem.: Tex. Soc. Music Theory (program com. 2001, 2005), Coll. Music Soc., Soc. Music Theory, Orpheus Alliance, Pi Kappa Lambda. Avocation: chess. Office: Cleve Inst Music 11021 East Blvd Cleveland OH 44106 Home Phone: 216-751-6724.

CUTLER, VERNE CLIFTON, engineering educator, consultant; b. Brookings, SD, Jan. 2, 1926; s. Jesse C. and Mabel Cutler; m. Norma K. Cutler, Feb. 18, 1948 (dec. Apr. 14, 2003); children: Susan, Janice, Diane, Robert, David; m. Charlene Yaunke Cutler, Oct. 23, 2004. BS, Kans. State U., 1950, MS, 1951; PhD, U. Wis., 1960. Registered engr., Wis. Design engr. Boeing Airplane Co., Wichita, 1951; instr. U. Wis., Madison, 1951-60, asst. prof., 1960-63, assoc. prof., 1963—67, prof., 1967—, dept. chair, 1963-73, ret. emeritus prof., 2001—. Cons., expert witness, Milw., 1963—; cons. Allis-Chalmers, Milw., 1984. Author: Encyclopedia Britannica-Compton's, 1988. Asst. scout leader Boy Scouts Am., Milw., 1964. Recipient ATT Tchg. Excellence award, 1990; U. Wis.-Milw. Alumni Assn. Tchg. Excellence award, 1988. Mem. Am. Soc. Engring. Edn. (Outstanding Campus Rep. 1990, Centennial cert. 1993), Sigma Xi. Republican. Methodist. Avocations: woodworking, gardening, hunting, fishing, tennis. Home: 8630 N Spruce Rd Milwaukee WI 53217-2126 Office Phone: 414-352-1893. E-mail: vccutler@aol.com.

CUTLER, WALTER LEON, diplomat, foundation executive; b. Boston, Nov. 25, 1931; s. Walter Leon and Esther Dewey (Bradley) C.; m. Sarah G. Beeson, Mar. 16, 1957 (div. 1981); children: Allen Bradley, Thomas Gerard.; m. Isabel K. Brookfield, Nov. 28, 1981. BA, Wesleyan U., Middletown, Conn., 1953; MA, Fletcher Sch. of Law & Diplomacy, 1954. Joined U.S. Fgn. Service, 1956; vice consul Am. consulate Yaounde, Cameroon, 1957-59; fgn. affairs officer Dept. State, Washington, 1959-60, staff asst. to sec. of state, 1960-62; 2d sec. Am. Embassy Algiers, Algeria, 1962-65; prin. officer Am. Consulate Tabriz, Iran, 1965-67; polit. officer, 1st sec. Am. Embassy Seoul, Korea, 1967-69, Saigon, Vietnam, 1969-71; spl. asst. for Vietnam Peace Negotiations U.S. Dept. State, 1971-73; mem. Sr. Seminar in Fgn. Policy, 1973-74; dir. Office Ctrl. African Affairs, 1974-75; amb. to Zaire, 1975-79; amb.-designate to Iran, 1979; prin. dep. asst. sec. for congl. rels. Dept. State, Washington, 1979-81; amb. to Tunisia, 1982-84, Saudi Arabia, 1984-87, 1988-89; rsch. prof. diplomacy Georgetown U., Washington, 1987-88; pres. Meridian Internat. Ctr., Washington, 1989—; spl. emissary for sec. gen. UN, NYC, 1994. Served with U.S. Army, 1954-56. Recipient Disting. Alumnus award Wesleyan U., 1983, King Abdul Aziz award Saudi Arabia, 1986, Presdl. Performance award, 1986, 87, Wilbur J. Carr award U.S. Dept. State, 1989, Dir. Gen.'s Cup award, 1993; decorated Order of the Leopard, Zaire, 1979. Mem. Coun. Fgn. Rels., Am. Fgn. Svc. Assn., Am. Acad. Diplomacy, Washington Inst. Fgn. Affairs, Mid. East Inst., Am. Tunisian Assn. (hon. com. The Am. Coms. on Foreign Rels.), Nat. Coun. for Internat. Visitors (mem. adv. coun.), Met. Club. Office: Meridian Internat Ctr 1630 Crescent Pl NW Washington DC 20009-4004 Office Phone: 202-667-6800. Business E-Mail: wcutler@meridian.org.

CUTLIP, RANDALL BROWER, retired psychologist, university president emeritus; b. Clarksburg, W.Va., Oct. 1, 1916; s. M.N. and Mildred (Brower) C.; m. Virginia White, Apr. 21, 1951; children: Raymond Bennett, Catherine Baumgarten. AB, Bethany Coll., 1940; cert. indsl. pers. mgmt., So. Meth. U., 1944; MA, East Tex. U., 1949; EdD, U. Houston, 1953; LLD, Bethany Coll., 1965, Columbia Coll., 1980; LHD, Drury Coll., 1975; ScD, S.W. Bapt. U., 1978; LittD, William Woods U., 1981. Tchr. adminstr. Tex. pub. sch., 1947-50; dir. tchr. placement U. Houston, 1950-51, supr. counselling, 1951-53; dean students Atlantic Christian Coll., Wilson, NC, 1953-56, dean, 1956-58; dean personnel, dir. grad. divsn. Chapman U., Orange, Calif., 1958-60; pres. William Woods Coll., Fulton, Mo., 1960-81, pres. emeritus, 1981—; trustee William Woods U., Fulton, Mo., 1981-85, 92—. Chmn. bd. dirs. Mo. Colls. Fund, 1973-75; chmn. Mid-Mo. Assn. Coll., 1972-76; bd. dir. Marina del Sol, bd. pres., 1985-90, 92-95. Mem. visitors' bd. Mo. Mil. Acad., 1966-70, chmn., 1968-72; trustee Schreiner Coll., Kerrville, Tex., 1983-92, Amy Shelton McNutt Charitable Trust, 1983—, Permanent Endowment Fund, 1987-96, Scholarship Found. and Res. Fund of Christian Ch., 1992-96, Christian Found., 1990—; bd. dir. Univ. of the Americas, 1984-96, exec. v.p., 1985-96; bd. dirs. Tex. State Aquarium, 1994, exec. com., 1994—, pres. 1998; elder emeritus Christian Ch., bd. dir., exec. com. Recipient McCubbin award, 1968, Delta Beta Xi award, 1959 Mem. Am. Pers. and Guidance Assn., Alpha Sigma Phi, Phi Delta Kappa, Kappa Delta Pi, Alpha Chi. Address: 1400 Ocean Dr Corpus Christi TX 78404-2109

CUTNAW, MARY-FRANCES, retired communications educator, writer, editor; b. Dickinson, ND, June 15, 1931; d. Delbert A. and Edith (Calhoun-Pritchard) C. BS, U. Wis., 1953, MS, 1957, postgrad., 1959—60, postgrad., 1967—68. Life tchg. license in speech, English and French, Wis. Vol. tchr. Vocat. Sch. for World War II Displaced Persons, Stevens Point, Wis., 1951-52; speech tchr. Pulaski H.S., Milw., 1953-55; tchg. asst. dept.

speech U. Wis., Madison, 1956-57, spl. asst. Sch. Edn., summer 1957; instr. speech U. Wis.-Stout, Menomonie, 1957-58, dean of women, 1958-59, asst. prof. speech, 1959-64, assoc. prof. speech, 1964-74, prof. emeritus, 1974—. Comm. and pers. cons., St. Paul, 1974—; writer, editor, pub. New Legal Press, 1995—. Author: How to Settle a Living Trust, 1996, 4th edit., 2003. Organizer, past advisor Young Dems., Menomonie, 1959—; founder Edith and Kent Cutnaw Scholarship, U. Wis., Stevens Point, 1960—; bd. dirs. Blaisdell Place, Mpls., 1980-85. Hon. scholar U. Wis., Madison, 1959-60, 67-68. Mem. ACLU, NOW, Internat. Platform Assn., Nat. Women's History Mus., Wis. Acad. Arts and Scis., Wis. Women's Network, Progressive Roundtable (Mpls.), Calhoun Beach Club (Mpls.), Amnesty Internat., World Jewish Congress (charter), US Holacost Mus., Drs. Without Borders, U. Club St. Paul, Greenpeace, Dunn County Humane Soc., Sierra Club, Soc. for Prevention of Cruelty to Animals, Humane Soc. U.S., Gamma Phi Beta, Phi Beta, Sigma Tau Delta, Pi Lambda Theta. Roman Catholic. Office: New Legal Press PO Box 282 Menomonie WI 54751-0282 Business E-Mail: cutnawm@uwstout.edu.

CUTRELL, CHARLES C., III, lawyer; b. Great Falls, Mont., Aug. 23, 1954; BA in gov. & econ., Oberline College, 1976; JD, U. Va., 1981. Assoc. Gaston & Snow, Boston, 1981—86; v.p., counsel The Boston Co., 1986—94; with State Street Corp., Boston, 1994—, exec. v.p., sec., 2004—, gen. counsel, 2004—06. Mem.: Am. Bankers Assn., Boston Bar Assn., Securities Assn., Greater Boston Legal Svcs. Office: State Street Corp 1 Lincoln St Boston MA 02111 Home Phone: 617-536-6050; Office Phone: 617-786-3000. Office Fax: 617-664-4006.*

CUTRER, FRED MICHAEL, neurologist; b. Jackson, Miss., July 16, 1956; s. Hugh Lowery and Rose (Wilson) C.; m. Lucinda Jane Turley, May 28, 1994. BMus, Belhaven Coll., 1978; MMus, Am. Conservatory of Music, 1980; MD, U. Miss., 1988. Diplomate Am. Bd. Psychiatry and Neurology. Intern U. Miss. Med. Ctr., Jackson, 1988-89; resident in neurology UCLA, 1989-92; fellow in neurology-migraine mechanisms Mass. Gen. Hosp./Harvard Med. Sch., Boston, 1992-94; asst. in neurology Mass. Gen. Hosp., Boston, 1994—; instr. in neurology Harvard Med. Sch., 1994—. Cons. Glaxo Pharms., Raliegh-Durham, 1995—; vis. migraine faculty Annenberg Ctr.-Eisenhower, Rancho Mirage, Calif., 1995-2000, Dept. Neurology Mayo Clinic, Rochester, N.Y., 2001—. Assoc. editor Up to Date in Neurology, 1995; author: Massachusetts General Hospital Handbook of Pain Management, 1995, Headache, 1996; editl. bd. Contemporary Neurology, 1995. Missions com. Trinitarian Congrl. Ch., Concord, Mass., 1995—. Recipient Clin. Investigator Devel. award Nat. Inst. for Stroke and Neurologic Disease, 1995; Glaxo fellowship Glaxo Pharms., 1992-93. Mem. Am. Acad. Neurology, Am. Assn. for the Study of Headache (Harold Wolff award 1996), Internat. Headache Soc. Avocations: music, print collecting, weightlifting, gardening. Office: Mass Gen Hosp 149 13th St # 6403 Charlestown MA 02129-2020

CUTRI, ROC MICHAEL, research scientist; Dep. exec. dir., Infrared Processing and Analysis Ctr. (IPAC) Calif. Inst. Tech., Pasadena. Co-recipient James Craig Watson medal, NAS, 2007. Achievements include being one of the project scientists& task lead for the Two Micron All Sky Survey (2MASS) project. Office: Infrared Processing and Analysis Ctr Calif Inst Tech MS 100-22 770 S Wilson Ave Pasadena CA 91125 Office Phone: 626-395-1828. Office Fax: 626-397-7018. Business E-Mail: roc@ipac.caltech.edu.*

CUTRIGHT, PHILLIPS, sociologist, educator; b. Wooster, Ohio, Mar. 1, 1930; s. Clifford R. and Eva N. (Goddin) C.; m. Karen L. Bowles, Oct. 31, 1965; children: Anuschka, Jennifer. AB, Coll. Wooster, 1955; PhD, U. Chgo., 1960. Mem. faculty Wash. State U., Pullman, 1960-61, Dartmouth, 1961-62; with Social Security Adminstrn., 1962-65; mem. faculty Vanderbilt U., Nashville, 1965-67, Washington U., St. Louis, 1967-68, Harvard-MIT, 1968-70; prof. sociology Ind. U., Bloomington, 1970—94. Cons. in field, 1971— Contbr. articles to profl. jours. Served with USAF, 1951-53. Home: 400 Winfield Cove Rd Saluda NC 28773 E-mail: cutright@tds.net.

CUTSHALL-HAYES, DIANE MARION, elementary school educator; b. Pitts., Jan. 15, 1954; d. William Edward and Irma Delores (Marion) Snowden; m. John Steven Baran, Jan. 11, 1975 (div. 1982); 1 child, Allison Rae; m. Dean F. Cutshall, Dec. 17, 1989. BA, Eureka Coll., 1975; BS, Ind. U., Ft. Wayne, 1986. First grade tchr. Hoover Elem. Sch., Schaumburg, Ill., 1976-79, Indian Meadows Elem. Sch., Ft. Wayne, Ind., 1979-80, 82-86, Perry Hill Elem. Sch., Ft. Wayne, 1981-82; second grade tchr. Indian Meadows Elem. Sch., Ft. Wayne, 1986—. Tchr. rep. State Ill. Rsch. Adv. Coun., 1991; active ISTEP Blue Ribbon Commn., Ill., 1989, State Ill. Lang. Arts Adv. Commn., 1988, Project REAP Adv. Bd., 1988. Spl. events chair Greater Ft. Wayne (Ind.) Crime Stoppers, 1992-95; active YMCA Camp Potawotami, Ft. Wayne, 1993—, Eureka Coll. Alumni Assn., 1992—, pres., 1995—. Christa McAuliffe fellow State of Ind., 1987; recipient Excellence in Edn. award Inst. Copy Corp., 1988, Outstanding Young Alumna award Eureka Coll., 1990, Armstrong Tchr. Educator award, 1998; named Ind. State Elem. Tchr. of Yr., 1993. Mem. Nat. Coun. Tchrs. Math., Internat. Reading Assn., Tchrs. Applying Whole Langs. Lutheran. Avocations: rollerblading, racquetball, reading, walking. Home: 5809 Eagle Creek Dr Fort Wayne IN 46814-3207 Office: Indian Meadows School 11420 Ernst Rd Roanoke IN 46783-9660

CUTSHAW, KENNETH ANDREW, lawyer; b. Knoxville, Tenn., Sept. 2, 1953; s. Harvey Audley and Frankie Janelle (Temple) C.; m. Diane Dracos. BA, U. Tenn., 1975, JD, 1978; LLM, Am. U., 1987. Bar: Tenn. 1978, D.C. 1987, U.S. Dist. Ct. (mid. dist.) 1978, Tenn., (ea. dist.) 1978, Tenn. Supreme Ct. 1978, U.S. Supreme Ct. 1987, U.S. Fed. cir., 1991. Sr. atty. State of Tenn. Legis., Nashville, 1979-80, The 1982 World's Affair, Knoxville, 1980-83, cons., 1984; campaign mgr. for candidate U.S. Senate, 1983-84; asst. dep., asst. sec. import adminstrn. Dept. Commerce, Washington, 1985-87, chief of staff export adminstrn., 1987-89, dep. asst. sec. export enforcement, 1989-91; ptnr. Miller & Steuart, Washington, 1991-93; pres. Global Trading Ptnrs., Inc., Washington, 1991-93; of counsel Troutman Sanders, LLP, Atlanta, 1993-95, Smith Gambrell & Russell, LLP, 1995-99; ptnr. Holland & Knight, LLP, Atlanta, 1999—2006; exec. v.p., gen. coun. Cajun Open Co. dba Church's Chicken, Atlanta, 2006—. Mem. U.S. Govt. Industry Adv. Com. on Customs and Trade, 1994-96; adj. prof. Ga. State U., 1997—, Emory U., 2002—, Ga. Tech., 2005—; hon. counsul Govt. of India; bd. dir. India, China Am. Inst.; Georgia; ptnr. KBS India. Author: Tennessee Criminal Law Statutes, 1980; co-author: Doing Business in China, 1995, Doing Business in Russia, 1999, Doing Business in India, 2001; contbr. articles to profl. jours. Vice chmn., exec. com. Tenn. Rep. Party, 1982-85; internat. chmn. Boy Scouts Am., Atlanta; mem. Bretton Woods Com.; co-chmn. Awakening Weekend; dir. Ctr. Global Bus. Leadership, 2002-. Roddy Acad. scholar U. Tenn., 1971-72. Mem. ABA, Internat. Bar Assn., Ga. Bar Assn., Atlanta Bar Assn., Tenn. Bar Assn. (com. chmn. 1983-84), D.C. Bar Assn., Am. Coun. Young Polit. Leaders (bd. dirs., co-chmn.), Coun. on Fgn. Rels., Atlanta Round Table (chmn.), World Trade Ctr. (bd. dirs.), Elks, Sigma Chi. Baptist. Avocations: flying, skiing, hiking, cultural events, golf. Home: 5560 Whitner Dr Nw Atlanta GA 30327-4745 Office: 980 Hammond Dr Ste 1100 Atlanta GA 30328 Home Phone: 404-312-5544; Office Phone: 770-350-3800. Office Fax: 770-512-3966. Business E-Mail: kcutshaw@churchs.com

CUTTER, JEFFREY S., music educator; b. Royal Oak, Mich., July 20, 1956; s. George E. and Joy G. (Dolby) Cutter. MusB with distinction, Wayne State U., 1978, MEd, M in Ednl. Leadership/Administrn., 1994. Cert. tchr. Mich. Performing arts facilitator Warren Consol. Cmty. Edn., 1980—2006; curriculum cons. Warren Consol. Schs., 2000—06; band dir. Paul K. Cousino HS, Warren, 2006—. Chmn. Warren Coun. Commn., Warren Cultural Commn., Warren-Ctr.-Line Thanksgiving Parade Ctr. Inc.; pres. Friends of Music, Wayne State U.; v.p. fin. Wayne State Coll. Fine, Performing, Comm. Arts Alumni Assn. Mem.: Assn. Dist. XVI (treas., past pres.), Warren Symphony Soc., Warren Concert Band, Inc. (pres., treas., past pres.), Mich. Sch. Band and Orch. Assn., Am. Sch. Band Dirs. Assn. (nat. pres. 2005—06, immediate past pres.). Home: 32774 McConnell Ct Warren MI 48092-3111 Office: Paul K Cousino HS 30333 Hoover Rd Warren MI 48093 Home Phone: 586-264-0959; Office Phone: 586-698-4605. Personal E-mail: cutterjeff@hotmail.com. Business E-Mail: cutter@wcs.k12.mi.us.

CUTTING, HEYWARD, designer, planner; b. NYC, Dec. 3, 1921; s. Heyward and Constance (Roberson) C.; m. Jeremy Hohenstein, 1948 (div. 1978); children: Heyward, Francis Brockholst, William Bayard; m. Joan Faulkner Randell, Nov. 3, 1979; Stepson, Thomas William Randell. Grad., Eton, 1939; student, Harvard, 1939-41; B.Sc., Ill. Inst. Tech., 1953. Ptnr. Chermayeff & Cutting (architects and indsl. designers), 1954-56; pvt. practice architecture Cambridge, 1957; mem. Geometrics, Inc. (architects, engrs. and cons. specialized structures), Cambridge, 1958-68, 73-86; pvt. practice cons., 1986—. Asst. dir. adminstrn. Mus. Fine Arts, Boston, 1968-73, trustee, 1961-68, 73-78 Former trustee Mt. Auburn Hosp., Cambridge; past mem. vis. com. dept. archaeology, also dept. fine arts Harvard U. Served to maj. KRRC, 60th Rifles Brit. Army, 1941-45, Egypt, Italy. Mentioned in despatches. Mem.: Tavern (Boston).

CUTTING, SEAN EUGENE, aeronautical engineer; b. Frankfurt, Germany, Oct. 7, 1976; s. Glenn Eugene Cutting and Carla Jean Vutting. BS in Aeronautical Engring., Rensselaer Polytech. Inst., Troy, NY, 1998. Cost engr. GE Power Systems, Schenectady, NY, 1999—2001; project controls engr. Stone & Webster, Inc., Stoughton, Mass., 2001—03; design engr. GE Aviation, Lynn, Mass., 2003—. Mem.: Am. Mensa.

CUTTS, CHARLES EUGENE, retired engineering educator; b. Sioux Falls, SD, May 15, 1914; s. Charles Clifford and Ethel May (Gardner) C.; m. Jane Bebensee, Mar. 16, 1946; children: George Gardner, Elizabeth Anne. B.C.E., U. Minn., 1936, MS in Civil Engring, 1939, PhD, 1949. Registered profl. engr., Minn., Fla., Mich. Instrumentman Milw. R.R., 1936- 38; teaching asst. dept. civil engring. U. Minn., 1938-39, instr., asst. prof., 1946-50; engr. C.F. Haglin & Sons, summer 1939; asst. prof. dept. civil engring. Robert Coll., Istanbul, Turkey, 1939-42; engr. Braithwaite Co., Ltd., Iskenderun, Turkey, summer 1942, 43; assoc. prof., assoc. rsch. engr. U. Fla., 1950-53; engr. Engring. Scis. Program NSF, Washington, 1953-56; profl. lectr. civil engring. George Washington U., 1955-56; prof., chmn. dept. civil engring. Mich. State U., 1956-69, prof., 1969-84, prof. emeritus, 1984—; ret., 1984. Cons. U. Minn. Morocco Project, 1986. Author: Structural Design in Reinforced Concrete, 1954, other tech. pubs. Served to maj C.E. AUS, 1943-46; lt. col. Res. ret. Mem. Nat. Acad. Scis. (fellowship com. 1961-63), ASCE (chmn. com. on mech. properties of materials 1965, pres. Mich. sect. 1967, chmn. com. on engring. edn. 1969-70), Am. Concrete Inst., Am. Soc. Engring. Edn. (chmn. civil engr. div. 1965-66, v.p. 1970—, chmn. constn. and bylaws com. 1981-83), Engrs. Coun. Profl. Devel. (chmn. region 5 1972-73), Nat. Soc. Profl. Engrs., Tau Beta Pi, Chi Epsilon. Home: 4599 Ottawa Dr Okemos MI 48864-2028 Office: Civil Engring Mich State Univ East Lansing MI 48824 Office Phone: 517-349-9590.

CVENGROS, JOSEPH MICHAEL, manufacturing company executive; b. Pana, Ill., Oct. 8, 1931; s. Joseph John and Mary Bernice (Sturgeon) C.; m. Mary Elizabeth Ainsworth, Feb. 11, 1956; children: Joseph J., Mary E., Andrew T., Katherine A., J. Michael, Robert A., David L., Susan M. BABS, Washington U., St. Louis, 1955; MBA, Northwestern U., 1960. Pers. mgr. Continental Baking Co., Chgo., 1956-57; asst. to chmn. bd. dirs. Automatic Canteen Co. divsn. ITT, Chgo., 1957-65; cons. Spencer Stuart and Assoc., Chgo., 1965-68; investor High Tech., Inc., Chgo., 1968—; chmn. bd. dirs., CEO Anaconda Metal Hose divsn. Anamet, Inc., Glen Ellyn, Ill., 1984—. Fellow Econ. Club Chgo. Office: Anamet Inc 739 Roosevelt Rd Ste 204 Glen Ellyn IL 60137-5873 Home Phone: 630-469-1826.

CVETANOVICH, DAN L., lawyer; b. Wheeling, W.Va., Oct. 2, 1952; s. Louis J. and Nila J. (Hall) Cvetanovich; m. Sharon M. Smith, Sept. 8, 1979; children: Gregory L., Steven W. BA, West Liberty State Coll., 1974; JD, Harvard U., 1977. Bar: Ohio 1977, US Dist. Ct. (so. dist.) Ohio 1978, US Ct. Appeals (6th cir.) 1980, US Dist. Ct. (no. dist.) Ohio 1984, W.Va. 1985, US Dist. Ct. (so. dist.) W.Va. 1985, US Ct. Appeals (4th cir.) 1986, US Dist. Ct. (we. dist.) Tex. 1998, US Dist. Ct. (no. dist.) W.Va. 2001. Assoc. Bricker & Eckler, Columbus, Ohio, 1977-82, ptnr., 1983-87, Arter & Hadden LLP, Columbus, 1987—2003; mem. Bailey Cavalieri LLC, Columbus, 2003—. Mem.: ABA, Columbus Bar Assn., W.Va. State Bar, Ohio State Bar Assn. Republican. Avocations: hunting, fishing, golf. Office: Bailey Cavalieri LLC One Columbus 10 W Broad St 21st Fl Columbus OH 43215-3422 Office Phone: 614-229-3291. Business E-Mail: Dan.Cvetanovich@baileycavalieri.com.

CWIERTNIAK, ROBERT L., psychologist, educator, consultant; b. Chgo., Dec. 30, 1945; s. Louis Florian Cwiertniak and Lillian Rosaline Brzdenkiewicz; m. Linda Jay Mathes; children: Laura, Wil. BA in Sociology/Psychology, St. Joseph's Coll., Rensselaer, Ind., 1967; MS in Edn. Counseling, Chgo. State U., 1969; EdD in Counseling Psychology, U. No. Colo., 1973. Cert. grades 6-12 tchg. for math., psychology and sociology Ill., 1968, lic. psychologist Wisc., 1979, nat. cert. counselor Nat. Bd. for Cert. Counselors, 1987, cert. sch. psychologist Ill. State Bd. Edn., 1973, counselor Ill. State Bd. Edn., 1973, clin. profl. counselor Dept. Profl. Regulation, Ill., 1999. Tchr. math. Gordon Tech. H.S., Chgo., Ill., 1967, coach track, 1967—68; jr. H.S. math. & sci. tchr. Our Lady Gate of Heaven Sch., Chgo., 1968—70; head night libr. Chgo. State U., 1973—76; sch. psychologist/spl. edn. coord. H.S. Dist. #214, Mt. Prospect, Ill., 1973—76; univ. counselor U. Wis., Stevens Point, 1978—84; coll. counselor Triton Coll., River Grove, Ill., 1985—2002; sch. psychologist Aero Spl. Edn. Coop., Burbank, Ill., 1984—86; pvt. practice Stevens Point, Wis., 2002—. Founder Full Earth Book Coop., Ft. Collins, Colo., 1971—75, Blue Bead Trading Co., Stevens Point, Wis., 1997—; adv. bd. Metro. Chgo. Disability Programs, River Grove, Ill.; faculty adv. to sch. bd. Our Lady Gate of Heaven Sch.; lectr., numerous workshops/seminars in field; adj. faculty psychology dept. Dominican U., River Forest, Ill., 1995—2001. Editor: (book) Coursewise-Perspectives in Abnormal Psychology, 1999. Mem.: APA, Ill. Fedn. Tchrs., Am. Fedn. Tchrs. Avocations: biodynamic gardening & farming, travel, reading, researching spirituality. Home: 2837 N Reserve Dr PO Box 268 Stevens Point WI 54481 Office: Monolith Inc PO Box 268 2514 Dewey Dr Stevens Point WI 54481

CYFORD, JANET IRENE, Spiritualist medium, meditation consultant; b. Walthamstow, London, Eng., June 21, 1939; d. Leonard George and Irene Olive Chapman; m. Albert Howard Cyford, Feb. 14, 1987; m. Michael Ernest Morton, Sept. 23, 1961 (div. Feb. 9, 1977); children: Angela Morton, David Morton. Diploma in bus. adminstrn. (hon.), Ramsgate Coll., 1976. Window display artist various stores, London, 1959—61; self employed restuarant owner Broadstairs, Kent, England, 1965—77; office mgr. Baverstock Pollock Accts., Great Dunmow, England, 1977—80; legal cashier Wade & Davis Solicitors, Barristers, Great Dunmow, England, 1980—; spiritualist medium, lectr., tchr. self employed, Balt., 1987—2006; meditation cons. Dept. of Pub. Safety & Correction Detention Ctr. SAP, ACT, Balt., 2000—02; pvt. practice medium Balt., 2002—06. Asst. sec. Inst. of Spiritualist Mediums, London, 1965—85; bd. mem. Stepping up & Helping Out Recovering Drug Addicts, Balt., 2001—02; meditation cons. Families in Recovery Maintenance, Balt., 2000—02. Author: The Ring of Chairs A Medium's Story, 2000; featured in book: Witness to the Unsolved by Edward Olshaker. Recipient Cert. of Appreciation, SAP/ACT Dept of Pub. Safety & Correctional Svcs., 2001. Mem.: Co-Freemasonry (master mason 1982—2002). Home Phone: 410-235-9116; Office Phone: 410-235-9116. Personal E-mail: JCMedsp@aol.com.

CYGANOWSKI, MELANIE L., bankruptcy judge; b. Chgo., June 8, 1952; d. Daniel F. and Sophia A. C.; married, 1989. AB in anthropology, Grinnell Coll., 1974; postgrad. in urban devel., Cornell U., 1975; JD magna cum laude, SUNY, Buffalo, 1981. Bar: N.Y. 1982, U.S. Supreme Ct., U.S. Ct. Appeals (2d cir.), U.S. Dist. Ct. (so., ea. and we. dists.) N.Y. Coord. program planning, planner, cons. dept. community devel. and human resources City of Buffalo, N.Y., 1974-78; dir. individual referral program Broadway-Filmore Area Coun., Inc., Buffalo, 1978-79; summer assoc. Hodgson, Russ, Andrews, Wood & Goodyear, Buffalo, 1980; law clk. to Hon. Charles L. Brieant U.S. Dist. Ct. (so. dist.) N.Y., 1981-82; litigation assoc. Sullivan & Cromwell, NYC, 1982-89; sr. atty. Milbank, Tweed, Hadley & McCloy, 1989-93; judge U.S. Bankruptcy Ct. (ea. dist.) N.Y., Ctrl. Islip, 1993—, chief judge, 2005—. Adj. prof. law bankruptcy program St. John's U. Sch. Law. Contbr. articles to legal jours. Fellow Am. Bar Found, ABA; mem. , Nat. Conf. Bankruptcy Judges, N.Y. State Bar Assn. Roman Catholic. Avocations: bicycling, gardening, fishing. Office: US Bankruptcy Ct The Long Island Fed Ct 290 Federal Plz Central Islip NY 11722 Office Phone: 631-712-5682. Business E-Mail: mcyganowski@yahoo.com.

CYLKE, FRANK KURT, librarian; b. New Haven, Conn., Feb. 13, 1932; s. Frank Anton and Helen Mary (Callahan) C.; m. Mary Elizabeth Newhouse, Dec. 28, 1962; children: Frank Kurt, Mary Amanda, Virginia Ann. BA, U. Conn., 1954; MLS, Pratt Inst., 1957; postgrad., Fairfield U., Am. U., Georgetown U. Libr. Graham-Eckes Sch., Palm Beach, Fla., 1957-58; reference libr. Bridgeport Pub. Libr., Conn., 1958-62; head pub. svc. New Haven Pub. Libr., 1962-65; asst. libr. Providence Pub. Libr., 1965-68; chief libr. rsch. US Office Edn., 1968-69; exec. dir. fed. libr. com. Libr. of Congress, 1970-73, dir. nat. libr. svc. for blind, physically handicapped, 1973—. Instr. Grad. Libr. Sch. U. RI, 1967-68; instr. Grad. Libr. Sch. Cath. U. Am., 1974—, bd. visitors, 1980—; exec. sec. panel edn. & tng. Com. Sci. and Tech. Inst.; chmn. librs. tech. com. Met. Washington Coun. Govts., 1970-71; sec. US Book Exch., 1972-74; sec.-treas. Joint Venture Pub. Activity, 1970-74; mem. E. Greenwich Free Libr. Corp., RI, 1967—; adv. bd. Ednl. Resources Info. Ctr./Clearinghouse Libr. and Info. Sci., 1970-72; bd. visitors Grad. Sch. Libr./Info. Sci., Pratt Inst., 1980—. Editor: Captains Shelf, 1964-66, FLC Newsletter, 1970-73, Library Service for the Blind and Physically Handicapped: An International Approach, 1979, Recipient Va. Cultural Laureate, 1992, Dayton M. Forman Meml. award Can. Nat. Inst. for the Blind, 1996, Newel Perry award Nat. Fedn. of Blind, 2005; grantee U.S. Office Edn., 1972 Mem.: KC, ALA (Joseph W. Lippincott award 1992, F.J. Campbell medal 1975—76), Friends of Librs. for Blind in N.Am. (founder, ex-officio bd. dirs.), Internat. Fedn. Libr. Assns. (founder, chmn. sect. for blind), World Blind Union, Am. Soc. Info. Sci. (sec. 1874—1975), Spl. Librs. Assn. (chpt. pres. 1975—76), Dinghy Cruising Assn., Shenandoah Nat. Park Assn., Mystic Seaport (pilot), Crow's Nest (St. John's, Nfld.), Mansion House Yacht Club, Fed. City Club, Ancient Order of Hibernians, Knights of Columbus. Roman Catholic. Avocations: sailing, birding. Home: PO Box 192 Great Falls VA 22066-0192 Office: Libr of Congress Nat Libr Svc for the Blind 1291 Taylor St NW Washington DC 20542-0002 Office Phone: 202-707-5104. Personal E-mail: kurt.cylke@verizon.net. Business E-Mail: fcyl@loc.gov.

CYMBLER, MURRAY JOEL, corporate financial executive; b. Germany, July 20, 1948; U.S., 1949; s. Harry and Adele C.; m. Carol Horowitz, Nov. 23, 1972; children: Adam, Robyn. BA, Hunter Coll., 1970. Tchr. N.Y. Bd. Edn., Bronx, 1970-71; contract analyst The Equitable Life Assurance Soc., NYC, 1972-86; chmn., CEO Astro-Stream Corp., Levittown, N.Y., 1986-91; mgr. fin. Landmark Plaza Properties Corp., Sayville, N.Y., 1991-99; gen. mgr. Intown Theaters, Sayville, 1999—2000; fin. sales rep. Met Life, 2001, Nat. Life, 2002. Achievements include invention of Orbi Sport-ball, 1985. Office: Orbico Inc 133 Ronni Dr East Meadow NY 11554-1330

CYMROT, MARK ALAN, lawyer; b. Queens, NY, Oct. 8, 1947; s. Irwin Maurice and Anne (Kipnis) C.; m. Janinne Dall'Orto; children: Isaac, Erin, Isabella. BA, George Washington U., 1969; JD, Columbia U., 1972. Bar: D.C. 1973, N.Y. 2000. Trial lawyer civil divsn. U.S. Dept. of Justice, Washington, 1972-77; sr. litigator Consumers Union of U.S. Inc., Washington, 1977-79; spl. litigation counsel civil divsn. U.S. Dept. of Justice, Washington, 1979-83; ptnr. Cole Corette & Abrutyn, Washington, 1983-91, Baker & Hostetler LLP, Washington, 1991—. Bd. dirs. Writers Ctr., Bethesda, Md. Contbr. articles to profl. jours. Named one of Best Lawyers in Washington, Washingtonian Mag. Avocations: photography, writing, golf, tennis. Office: Baker & Hostetler LLP 1050 Connecticut Ave NW Washington DC 20036-5304 Home Phone: 301-656-8939; Office Phone: 202-861-1677. Business E-Mail: mcymrot@bakerlaw.com.

CYNADER, MAX SIGMUND, psychology and physiology professor, researcher; b. Berlin, Feb. 24, 1947; arrived in Can., 1951; s. Samuel and Maria (Kraushar) C.; m. Ann Lynn Langford, Sept. 26, 2004; children: Madeleine Maria, Rebecca Kay, Alexandra Josephine. BSc, Mc Gill U., Montreal, Que., Can., 1967; PhD, MIT, 1972. Fellow neuroanatomy Max-Planck Inst. Psychiatry, Munich, 1972-73; asst. prof. psychology Dalhousie U., 1973-77, assoc. prof., 1977-81, assoc. prof. physiology, 1979-84, prof. psychology, 1981-84, Killam rsch. prof., 1984-88, prof. physiology, 1984-88; prof. psychology U. B.C., 1988—, prof. physiology, 1988—, prof. dept. ophthalmology, 1988—, dir., 1988-99; dir. Brain Rsch. Ctr., U. B.C. and Vancouver Hosp. and Health Scis. Ctr., 1997. Mem. pres.'s workshop on five yr. plan strengthening sci. support in Can. Natural Scis. and Engring. Rsch. Coun. Can., 1984, workshop for Steacie fellows, 1988; mem. task force on curriculum devel. in Can. neurosci., 1984; mem. spl. adv. panel on rsch. preparedness USAF, 1985; rep. Internat. Human Frontiers Sci. program Med. Rsch. Coun. Can., 1988; mem. grants com. behavioural scis. Med. Rsch. Coun. Can., program grants com. 1989—; referee senate rev. grad. program in neurosci. U. Western Ont., 1989; mem. math., computational and theoretical spl. rev. com. NIMH, 1989—; external reviewer Med. Rsch. Coun. Can., Alta. Heritage Fund Med. Rsch., NIH, NSF, USAF Office Sci. Rsch., Multiple Sclerosis Soc. Can., Vancouver Found., March of Dimes, Fight for Sight; CRC chair in brain devel., 2001-06. Mem. editorial bd. jours. Behavioral Brain Rsch., Clin. Vision Scis., Concepts in Neurosci., Devel. Brain Rsch., Exptl. Brain Rsch., Neural Networks, Visual Neurosci.; mem. adv. bd. series Rsch. Notes in Neural Computing; contbr. articles to profl. jours. Recipient Killam Rsch. prize U. B.C., 1989—; E.W.R. Steacie fellow Natural Sci. and Engring. Rsch. Coun. Can., 1979, Can. Inst. Advanced Rsch. fellow, 1986—, Bank of Montreal fellow Can. Inst. for Advanced Rsch., 1998; grantee Med. Rsch. Coun. Can., 1973—, Natural Sci. and Engring. Rsch. Coun. Can., 1975—, NIH, 1978-81, Killam Rsch. Prof., 1984, B.C. Sci. & Tech. Champion, 2004. Fellow Can. Inst. Advanced Rsch., Royal Soc. Can.; mem. Soc. Neurosci. (Halifax chpt., pres. 1985, edn. com. 1986-89), Can. Assn. Neurosci. (pres. 1986), Assn. Rsch. Otolaryngology, Assn. Rsch. in Vision and Opthalmology, Can. Physiol. Soc., Internat. Brain Rsch. Orgn., Internat. Soc. Devel. Neurosci., Internat. Strabismol. Assn., World Fedn. Neuroscientists. Achievements include being named semifinalist Can. Astronaut program, 1983. Office: U BC Vancouver Hosp Brain Rsch Ctr 2211 Wesbrook Mall Vancouver BC Canada V6T 2B5 Home Phone: 604-921-2418. Business E-Mail: cynader@brain.ubc.ca.

CYNAMON, DAVID J., lawyer; b. Phila., Jan. 27, 1949; AB, Brown U., 1970; JD, Harvard U., 1973. Bar: DC 1973, US Dist. Ct. Md, US Court of Appeals (DC, 2nd, 3rd, 4th, 7th, 8th, & 11th, cirs.,) US Court Fed. Claims, US Supreme Ct. Ptnr. Shaw, Pittman, Potts & Trowbridge, Wash., Pillsbury Winthrop Shaw Pittman, Wash., DC. Contbr. Co-chair, dir.coun. Wash. Lawyers Com. Civil Rights and Urban Affairs; exec. com. Ct. Excellence; co-chair Ct. Improvements Com. Office: Pillsbury Winthrop Shaw Pittman 2300 N St NW Washington DC 20037-1122 Office Phone: 202-663-8492. Office Fax: 202-663-8007. Business E-Mail: david.cynamon@pillsburylaw.com.

CYPRUS, NICHOLAS STANLEY, automotive executive, accountant; b. NYC, May 1, 1953; s. Nick and Niki Cyprus; m. Barbara Ann Helmick, Sept. 26, 1981; 1 child, Nicky. BS in Acctg., Fairleigh Dickinson U., 1977; MBA, NYU, 1990. CPA. Staff mgr. acctg. policy AT&T, Murray Hill, NJ, 1982-84, staff mgr. fin. assurance, 1984-85; asst. contr. portfolio acctg. AT&T Capital Corp., Morristown, NJ, 1985-87, asst. corp. contr., 1987-89, v.p., contr., 1989-95; asst. corp. contr. external reporting AT&T Inc., Morristown, NJ, 1995-98, v.p., contr. Basking Ridge, NJ, 1999—2004; contr., chief acctg. officer Interpublic Group of Cos., 2004—06, GM Corp., Detroit, 2006—. Contbr. articles to profl. jours. Bd. dirs. Ctr. for Enabling Techs., Whippany, N.J., 1997—. Mem. AICPA, N.J. Soc. CPAs (Outstanding CPA Bus. Leader award 1998-2000, 1999; mem. conf. bd. contr.'s coun.). Avocations: sport fishing, boating. Office: GM PO Box 300 Detroit MI 48265-3000*

CYR, ARTHUR I., political science and economics professor; b. LA, Mar. 1, 1945; BA, UCLA, 1966, MA, 1967; AM, Harvard U., 1969, PhD, 1971. Tchg. fellow Harvard U., 1970—71; program officer Ford Found., 1971—74; prof., adminstr. UCLA, 1974—76; program dir. Chgo. Coun. Fgn. Rels., 1976—81, v.p., 1981—96; pres., CEO, World Trade Ctr. Assn., Chgo., 1996—98; Clausen disting. prof. Carthage Coll., Kenosha, Wis., 1998—; dir. Clausen Ctr. World Bus., 2000—. Author: Liberal Politics in Britain, 1977, rev. edit., 1988, British Foreign Policy and the Atlantic Area, 1979, U.S. Foreign Policy and European Security, 1987, After the Cold War—American Foreign Policy, Europe and Asia, 1997, rev. edit., 2000, Taiwan: The Commercial State, 2003, rev. edit., 2005; contbr. Scripps Howard, articles to profl. jours. With USAR, 1966—73. Fellow, Harvard Knox, 1969—70. Mem. Internat. Inst. Strategic Studies, Royal Inst. Internat. Affairs, Royal United Svc. Inst., Coun. Fgn. Rels., Century, Phi Beta Kappa. Office: Carthage Coll Clausen Ctr Kenosha WI 53140-1994 Business E-Mail: acyr@carthage.edu.

CYR, CONRAD KEEFE, federal judge; b. Limestone, Maine, Dec. 9, 1931; s. Louis Emery and Kathleen Mary (Keefe) Cyr; m. Judith Ann Pirie, June 23, 1962 (dec. Mar. 1985); children: Keefe Clark, Jeffrey Louis Frederick; m. Diana Kathleen Sanborn, Sept. 25, 1987. BS cum laude, Holy Cross Coll., 1953; JD, Yale U., 1956; LLD (hon.), Husson Coll., 1991. Bar: Maine 1956. Pvt. practice, Limestone, 1956—59; asst. US atty., Bangor, Maine, 1959—61; pvt. practice Winchell & Cyr, Bangor, Maine, 1961—62; judge US Bankruptcy Ct., Bangor, 1961—81, US Dist. Ct., Bangor, 1981—83, chief judge, 1983—89; judge US Fgn. Intelligence Surveillance Ct., 1987—89, US Ct. Appeals (1st cir.), Boston, 1989—97, sr. judge, 1997—. Standing spl. master US Dist. Ct., Maine, 1974—76; chief judge Bankruptcy Appellate Panel Dist., Mass., 1980—81; mem. Jud. Council (1st cir.), 1987—; com. on adminstrn. of bankruptcy sys. Jud. Conf. US, 1987—. Founder, editor-in-chief: Am. Bankruptcy Law Jour., 1970—81, contbg. author, editor: Collier on Bankruptcy, vol. 10. Steering com. US AID Project for Assisting Bankruptcy and Reorgn. Procedures in Ctr. and Ea. Europe; treas. Limestone Rep. Com., 1958; chmn. budget com. Town of Limestone, 1959. Named one of Outstanding Young Men of Maine, 1963; recipient cert. of appreciation, Kans. Bar Assn., 1979, U. Maine, 1983, Nat. Judge's Recognition award, Nat. Conf. Bankruptcy Judges, 1979, Key to Town Limestone, 1983. Fellow: Am. Coll. Bankruptcy, Maine Bar Found. (charter); mem.: ABA, John Ballou Am. Inn of Ct., Aroostook Bar Assn., Am. Judicature Soc., Nat. Bankruptcy Conf. (exec. bd. 1974—77), Nat. Conf. Bankruptcy Judges (pres. 1976—77), Penobscot Bar Assn., Maine Bar Assn., Limestone C. of C. (pres.). Roman Catholic.*

CYR, J. V. RAYMOND, telecommunications industry executive; b. Montreal, Que., Can., Feb. 11, 1934; s. Armand and Yvonne (Lagace) Cyr; m. Marie Bourdon, Sept. 1, 1956; children: Helene, Paul Andre. Student, Ecole Poly.; BSc, U. Montreal, 1958; postgrad., Bell Labs., NJ, Nat. Def. Coll., 1972—73; LLD (hon.), Concordia U., Montreal, 1988. With Bell Can., 1992-96, engr., 1958-65, staff engr. Montreal, 1965-70, from v.p. ops. staff region to v.p., 1973-75, pres., 1983-85, chmn., pres., CEO, 1985-87, chmn. bd. dirs., 1987-89, pres., 1983-85, chmn., pres., CEO, 1985-87, chmn. bd., 1987-89, chief engr. Quebec City, 1970-73, from exec. v.p. to v.p. adminstrn., 1975-83, chmn., 1992-96; with BCE, Inc. (formerly Bell Can. Enterprises), 1987-93, pres. Montreal, 1987-88, pres., CEO, 1988-89, also bd. dirs., chmn., pres., CEO, 1989-90, chmn., CEO, 1990-92, chmn., 1992-93, dir., sr. advisor to chmn.'s office, 1993-97; chmn. Montreal Trust, 1989-90. Bd. dirs. Can. Nat., ART Advanced Rsch. & Techs. Inc., Polyvalor Inc., G.T.C. Transcontinental Ltd., Fonds de Solidarite des Travailleurs du Que., Triton Electronik Inc., Transp. Can. Pipelines, chmn. bd., 1989—92. Past chmn. Jr. Achievement Can., Montreal Mus. Contemporary Art, Opera de Montreal; assoc. gov. U. Montreal. Decorated officer Order of Can.; named chair in mgmt. in his honor, Ecole Polytechnique, Laureate Personnalite, 125th Anniversaire de l'Ecole Polytechnique, 1998; recipient Gold Medal award, Can. Egnrs., 1987, Ordre du Mérite des Diplies, U. Montreal, 1988, Laureate of Prix des comm. du Que., 1990, Mgmt. Achievement award, McGill U., 1991, Gt. Montrealer award, 1991, Commemorative medal, 125th Ann. Confederation Can., 1992. Mem.: Can. Acad. Engring. (founding), Islemere Club, St. James Club, St. Denis Club. Roman Catholic. Avocations: golf, swimming. Office: 1050 Beaver Hall Hill 19th Montreal PQ Canada H2Z 1S4 Office Phone: 514-870-8799. Office Fax: 514-870-4136.

CYR, KAREN D., lawyer; b. 1948; BS, Iowa State U.; JD, Duke U. Bar: 1977. Gen. counsel Nuclear Regulatory Commn., Fockville, Md., 1994—. Office: Nuclear Regulatory Commn One White Flint N 11555 Rockville Pike Rockville MD 20852-2738

CYR, LISA WATSON, lawyer; BA summa cum laude, U. Minn., Duluth, 1995; JD magna cum laude, William Mitchell Coll. Law, 1998. Bar: Minn. 1998. Atty. McCullough, Smith, Williams & Cyr, P.A., St. Paul. Guest lectr. Family Law Inst. Named a Rising Star, Minn. Super Lawyers mag., 2006. Mem.: Ramsey County Bar Assn. (mem. family law sect., co-chair family law sect. 2001—02), Minn. State Bar Assn. (mem. family law sect.), Phi Kappa Phi. Office: McCullough Smith Williams & Cyr PA 905 Parkway Dr Saint Paul MN 55117 Office Phone: 651-772-3446. E-mail: lwatsoncyr@mcculloughlawyers.com.*

CYRS, MICHAEL THOMAS, lawyer; b. Wausau, Wis., 1969; BBA, U. Notre Dame, 1991; MBA, JD, Marquette U., 1994. Bar: Wis. 1994, Ill. 1994, CFP: 2000. Atty. Hinshaw & Culbertson, 1994—97; ptnr. WilliamsMcCarthy, LLP, Rockford, Ill., 2002—. Mem.: Wis. Bar Assn., No. Ill. Estate Planning Coun., ABA, Ill. State Bar Assn., Winnebago County Bar Assn. (treas., dir. 2001—02, chmn. tax sect. 2000). Office: WilliamsMcCarthy LLP PO Box 219 120 W State St 4th Fl Rockford IL 61105-0219 Office Phone: 815-987-8900. Office Fax: 815-968-0019. E-mail: mcyrs@wilmac.com.*

CYRUS, BILLY RAY, country music performer, actor; b. Flatwoods, Ky., Aug. 25, 1961; s. Ron and Ruth Ann (Adkins) C., Cletis Adkins (stepfather), and Joan Cyrus (stepmother); m. Cindy Cyrus, 1987 (div. 1991); m. Leticia Finley, Dec. 12, 1993; children: Christopher Cody, Miley Hope, Braison Chance, Noah Lindsey, Brandi, Trace. Student, Georgetown Coll. Band mem. Sly Dog; signed to Mercury Records, 1990. Singer: (songs) Achy Breaky Heart, 1992, (albums) Some Gave All, 1992, It Won't Be the Last, 1993, Storm in the Heartland, 1994, Trail of Tears, 1996, Shot Full of Love, 1998, Southern Rain, 2000, Time Flies, 2003, The Other Side, 2003, Wanna Be Your Joe, 2006, Home at Last, 2007; actor: (films) Radical Jack, 2000, Mulholland Dr., 2001, Wish You Were Dead, 2002, Death and Texas, 2004, Elvis Has Left the Building, 2004; (TV films) Doc, 2001; (TV series), 2001—04, Hannah Montana, 2006—; performer: Dancing With the Stars, 2007. Grammy nomination, Best Country Vocal Collaboration for Romeo with Dolly Parton, Tanya Tucker, Kathy Mattea, Pam Tillis, & Mary-Chapin Carpenter, 1994, winner 5 TNN/Music City News awards for male vocalist, album, video, song, and single, 1998. Office: c/p Mitchell Gossett CESD Talent Agy 10635 Santa Monica Blvd Los Angeles CA 90025*

CYRUS, CYNTHIA J., dean, music educator; b. Seattle, Sept. 2, 1963; d. John D. and Virginia J. Cyrus; m. Thomas B. Dowling; children: Amelia Berle, Nathaniel Berle, Nissa Berle. BA, Pomona Coll., 1984; MA, U. N.C., 1987, PhD, 1990. Vis. asst. prof. U. Rochester, NY, 1991—92, SUNY, Stony Brook, NY, 1992—94; asst. prof. Blair Sch. Music Vanderbilt U., Nashville, 1994—2001, assoc. prof., 2001—, assoc. dean Blair Sch. Music, 2004—. Session organizer Internat. Medieval Congress, Kalamazoo, 2001—04; mem. adv. bd. rsch. jour. Vanderbilt U., 2004—07; lectr. in field. Editor: Online Reference Book for Medieval Studies, 1997—2007, De tous biens plaine: 28 Settings of Hayne, 2000; contbr. articles to profl. jours.; editor: Musical Intruction and Musical Learning, 1470-1650. Organizer Bellevue Project-Oriented Unschoolers, Nashville, 2002—06. Recipient Friends of Libr. award, Pontifical Inst. Mediaeval Studies, Toronto, Can., 2000; fellow, The Ohio State U., 1990—91; grantee, Univ. Rsch. Coun., 1995—96, Vanderbilt U., 1996, NEH Summer Inst., 2003, NEH Collaborative, 2004—05; Joseph E. Pogue fellowship, U. N.C., 1984—88. Mem.: Internat. Machaut Soc. (webmaster 2002—03, bd. dirs. 2002—05), Coll. Music Soc. (campus rep. 2002—04), Am. Musicol. Soc. (chmn. program com. S.C. chpt. 1995—96, mem. com. moderated elec. discussion list 2002—06, bd. com. on comm. 2005—08), Medieval Acad. Am. Office: Blair School Music Vanderbilt Univ 2400 Blakemore Ave Nashville TN 37212 Office Phone: 615-322-7693.

CYRUS, JAMAL D., artist; b. Houston, 1973; BFA in Digital Media and Photography, U. Houston, 2004. Instr., art prog. Project Row Houses, Houston; instr. Shade Tree Project Fashion Club, Houston; mem. artist Otabenga Jones & Assoc. Exhibitions include U. Mus., Southern Tex. U., Station Mus. Contemporary Art, Lawndale Art Ctr., Houston, Arthouse, Austin, Whitney Biennial, 2006. Office: Project Row Houses 2500 Holman PO Box 1011 Houston TX 77251-1011

CYS, RICHARD L., lawyer; b. Boulder, Colo., Oct. 9, 1944; BSChemE with honors, U. Colo., Boulder, 1966; JD, Georgetown U., 1969. Bar: DC 1969. Law clk. to Hon. John Pratt DC, 1969-70; asst. US atty. DC, 1970-77; mem. Davis Wright Tremaine LLP, Washington, co-ptnr.-in-charge, 2007—. Mem. ABA, Bar Assn. DC Office: Davis Wright Tremaine LLP 1500 K St NW Ste 450 Washington DC 20005-1272 Office Phone: 202-508-6617.*

CYWAR, ADAM WALTER, engineering executive; b. Kearny, NJ, Mar. 14, 1937; s. Adam Benjamin and Sophie Julia (Kurak) C.; m. Gloria Ella Beresford, Mar. 29, 1956 (div. May 1973); children: Victoria Cywar, Douglas A., Sophia; m. Rose Barter Tubb, May 11, 1973. BSME, N.J. Inst. Tech., Newark, 1960, MSMgtE, 1965. Design engr. Colgate-Palmolive, Jersey City, 1956-60; indsl. engr. Lionel Corp., Hillside, NJ, 1960-63; sr. engr. IBM Corp., Boca Raton, Fla., 1963-93; pres. Adam Cywar Indsl. Engr., Austin, Tex., 1993—. V.p. info. sys. RPM Assocs., Georgetown, Tex., 1993-97; founder IBM Worldwide Activity Based Mgmt. Competency Ctr. Author: Handbook of Industrial Engineering, 1982 (IBM Achievement award 1983). Chmn. Town of Poughkeepsie Rep. Com. to Elect Jim Buckley, 1968. Mem. ASME (sr. mem.), Inst. Indsl. Engrs. (sr., treas. 1975-90, dir. honors and awards 1970-75, Disting. Svc. award 1977). Avocations: writing, industrial engineering research. Home and Office: Adam Cywar Indsl Engr 4307 Las Palmas Dr Austin TX 78759-5062 Personal E-mail: acywar@yahoo.com.

CZACH, GABRIELA BOZENA, personal care industry executive; b. Nidzica, Poland, Aug. 1, 1953; arrived in U.S., 1983; d. Jenryk and Janina Krystkiewicz; m. Witold Edmund Czach, Dec. 1, 1951; 1 child, Jaroslaw. Midwife Gen. Swierczewski Hosp., Gdansk, 1975—78; mgmt. specialist Techino Svc. Co., 1978—83; med. asst. Phila. Med. Coll., 1983—86; manicurist Jean Marlyn Salon, Kenkintown, 1986—87; esthetician Pierre and Carlo Spa, Phila., 1990—97; esthetician cons. Metropolis Spa, Princeton, NJ, 1998—2002; owner Amber Spa, Pennington, 2003—. Cosmetic cons. Pierre and Carlo Spa, Phila., 1991—98, asst. mgr., 1993—96. Ind. cons. Women Cmty., Pennington, 2002; leader Girl Scouts Poland, Nidzica, 1966—72; asst. troop leader Girls Scouts U.S.A., Bucks County, Pa., 1996—99. Mem.: Polish Am. Mothers Assn. (sec. 1989—99), Polish Am. Orgn. (sec. 1986—95), Internat. Spa Assn. Republican. Roman Catholic. Avocations: skiing, travel, bicycling, gardening, tennis. Home: 1139 Buttonwood Ave Bensalem PA 19020 Office: Amber Spa 16 S Main St Pennington NJ 08534

CZACHOR, BRUCE, lawyer, consultant; b. Bklyn., May 7, 1961; BA in Polit. sci., SUNY, Binghampton, 1983; JD magna cum laude, NY Law Sch., 1987. Bar: NY 1988, NJ 1988, DC 1989, Calif. 2004. Letter of credit analyst Chase Manhattan Bank, NYC, 1983-84; law clk. to Hon. George Gallagher US Ct. Appeals (DC cir.), Washington, 1987-88; law clk. to Hon. Judge John Reilly; ptnr. Shearman & Sterling LLP, NYC & Toronto, 1988—94, mng. ptnr. Menlo Park, Calif., co-mng. ptnr. San Francisco. Mem. ABA, NY Bar Assn., NJ Bar Assn. Republican. Office: Shearman & Sterling LLP 525 Market St San Francisco CA 94105 Office Phone: 650-838-3632. Office Fax: 650-743-6630. Business E-Mail: bczachor@shearman.com.

CZAJKA, JAMES VINCENT, architect; b. Lackawanna, NY, Dec. 6, 1950; s. Joseph Martin and Livia Maria (Jengo) C. BS in Art and Design, MIT, 1972, MArch, 1975. Registered architect, NY. Asst. prof. architecture SUNY, Buffalo, 1975-79; architect Ehrenkrantz Group Architects and Planners, NYC, 1979-84, Beyer, Blinder, Belle Architects and Planners, NYC, 1984-91, assoc., 1987-91, studio dir., 1988-91; pvt. practice NYC, 1991-92; prin. Allanbrook Benic Czajka Architects & Planners, NYC, 1993-2001, James Vincent Czajka Architects, NYC, 2001—. Cons. Art Ctr. Old Forge, 2006. Prin. works include Baird Point Amphitheater, SUNY, Buffalo, 1978, Social Security Adminstrn. Bldg., Queens, NY, 1982, Paul Klapper Hall, Queens Coll., 1986, N.Y. Hall Sci. Master Plan, Queens, 1992, Am. Acad. Arts and Letters Master Plan, 1994, St. Joseph Parish Master Plan, Queens, 1994, World Monuments Fund Hdqrs., Manhattan, 1995, Loyola Sch. Sci. Ctr. renovation, Manhattan, 1996, Rutgers Ch. renovation, Manhattan, 1997, Bklyn. Conservatory of Music renovation, 1998, Blue Heron Arts Ctr., Manhattan, 1999, Preissner House, East Hampton, N., 2000, Conard House, Manhattan, 2000, The Rockwell Mus. of Western Art, Corning, NY, 2001, NY Soc. Libr. Master Plan, 2002, Lefferts Homestead Children's Mus., Bklyn., 2002, Elephant House Renovation, Bronx Zoo, 2003, Myerson House, Amagansett, NY, 2004, Third St. Music Sch. Master Plan, NYC, 2005; program arch. Art Ctr. of Old Forge, 2006. Mem. AIA, Nat. Coun. Archtl. Registration Bds. (cert.). Avocation: piano. Home: 303 E 84th St Apt 2F New York NY 10028-4435 Office: 611 Broadway Rm 817 New York NY 10012-2608 Office Phone: 212-475-1112. Business E-Mail: jvc@jvcarchitects.com.

CZAJKOWSKI, GERARD ZYGFRYD, physicist, researcher; b. Neustadt, Germany, Oct. 11, 1944; 1 child, Marcin. MS, Nicolaus Copernicus U., Toruń, Poland, 1967, PhD, 1971, DSc, 1975. Sci. asst. Nicholas Copernicus U., 1967-75; asst. prof. U. Tech. and Agr., Bydgoszcz, Poland, 1976-87, head dept. theoretical physics, 1977—, assoc. prof., 1987-94, prof. physics, 1994—. Vis. prof. physics Scuola Normale Superiore, Pisa, Italy, 1987-88, 95-96, 99-2000, 04-05. Contbr. articles to profl. jours. Fellow Alexander von Humboldt Found., Inst. Theoretical Physics Tech. U., Aachen, Germany, 1980-81, 84-85, Consiglio Nat. delle Ricerche, Rome, 1996, NATO-CNR fellow, 1995. Mem. European Phys. Soc., NY Acad. Scis., Polish Phys. Soc., Italian Phys. Soc., Soc. Humboldtiana Polonorum. Avocations: history, history of art, foreign languages, travel. Office: Inst Math Physics S Kaliskiego 7 U Tech/Life Sci PL 85796 Bydgoszcz Poland Business E-Mail: czajk@utp.edu.pl.

CZÁRÁN, LÓRÁNT, geographer, consultant; b. Sighisoara, Romania, Jan. 4, 1969; s. István and Klára (Kiss) C.; m. Andrea Judith Szász, Aug. 4, 1990; 2 children: Ciktoria, Alexandra. MSc, U. Cluj, Romania, 1993. Geog. info. sys. coord. U. Cluj, 1992-93; environ. cons. Civitas Found., Cluj, 1993-94; rsch. fellow Collegium Budapest, 1994-95; from vis. rschr. to project mgr. UN Environ. Programme Grid, Arendal, Norway, 1996—2002; geographic info. sys. officer UN Hdqrs., 2002—07, mgr. map ctr., 2007—. Served with Romanian mil., 1987-88. Jr. Rsch. grant Collegium Budapest, 1994. Mem. Planetary Soc., Global Spatial Data Infrastructure Assn. Roman Catholic. Avocations: skiing, caving, computers, mountain climbing, tennis. Address: 630 First Ave #20K New York NY 10016 Office Phone: 917-367-2467. Business E-Mail: czaran@un.org.

CZARNECKI, ANTHONY J., correction administrator, educator; b. Mt. Vernon, NY, Aug. 28, 1948; s. Stanley and Lucy (Calabrese) C.; m. Lorraine Portman, Oct. 9, 1971; children: David, Pamela. BA, Iona Coll., 1970; MA, John Jay Coll., 1975; MPA, Pace U., 1990. Probation officer, sr. probation officer, tng. dir. Westchester County Probation Dept., White Plains, N.Y., 1970-83; chief of staff Westchester County Correction Dept., Valhalla, NY, 1983—. Adj. prof. criminal justice Westchester C.C., Valhalla, 1976—, Iona Coll., New Rochelle, N.Y., 1981—. Editor-in-chief Jour. Probation and Parole, 1980-82; contbr. articles to profl. jours. Recipient Disting. Alumnus award, John Jay Coll. Criminal Justice, 2003. Mem. Am. Correctional Assn. (chmn. com. profl. ethics 2004—), Am. Probation and Parole Assn. (Probation officer Yr. award 1981), Am. Soc. Pub. Adminstrn., Middle Atlantic States Correctional Assn. (pres. 1997-99, trustee 1979—, Achievement award 1989, Leadership award 1997, Founders award 2000), N.Y. State Probation Officers Assn. (pres. 1978-80). Roman Catholic. Office: Westchester County Correction Dept PO Box 389 Hdq Bldg Valhalla NY 10595-0389 Office Phone: 914-231-1102.

CZARNECKI, GERALD MILTON, investment banker, venture capitalist; b. Phila., Mar. 22, 1940; s. Casimir M. and Rose-Mary (Grajek) C.; m. Lois Rae DiJoseph, July 9, 1965; 1 dau., Robyn Alexandra. BS, Temple U., 1965; MA, Mich. State U., 1967; LHD (hon.), Nat. U., 1994. C.P.A., Ill., Tex. With Continental Bank, Chgo., 1968-79, v.p., operating gen. mgr. trust ops. and gen. mgr. corp. svcs., 1971-78; pres. Fla. Computing Svcs., 1979; exec. v.p. Houston Nat. Bank, 1979-82; sr. v.p. fin. Republic Bank Corp., 1982-83, exec. v.p., 1983-84; pres., CEO Altus Bank, 1984-87; chmn., chief exec. officer Bank of Am. Hawaii, Honolulu, 1987-93; sr. v.p. human resources and adminstrn. IBM Corp., Armonk, NY, 1993-94; pres. UNC Inc., Annapolis, Md., 1994-95; chmn., CEO Deltennium Group, Inc., Boca Raton, Fla., 1995—, Renaissance, Inc., 1999—2001, also bd. dirs. Mem. faculty DePaul U., Chgo., 1975-78, Bank Adminstrn. Inst., 1978-85, Grad. Sch. Banking, U. Wis., 1979-86, Inroads Inc., Chgo. 1977-79 (chmn. bd. dir.), Inroads Inc. Houston, 1981; vis. prof. Jones Sch. Bus., Rice U., 1980; adj. prof. econs. Houston Bapt. U., 1980-82, policy and strategy So. Meth. U., 1983-84; mem. adv. com. Banking Ctr., Tex. So. U., 1980-82; chmn. securities processing sub-com. Am. Nat. Standards Inst., 1974-79; mem. Tuskegee Inst. State Adv. Coun., 1984-87; mem. treas., mem. exec. com., bd. dirs. Nat. Coun. Savs. Instns., 1984-90; pres. thrift adv. coun. Fed. Res. Bd., 1986-90; chmn. bd. dir. Great Clips Mid-Atlantic, Inc., 1997-2004, Deltennium Corp., 1996-, Renaissance Inc., 1999-2004; bd. dirs. State Farm Ins. Cos., State Farm Banks, ATM Nat. Inc., 2003-06, Software Internat. Inc. (lead dir., chair governance com.); chmn. audit com., mgr. bd. dirs., Del Global Techs. Inc., 2001—. Contbr. articles to profl. publs. Bd. dirs., treas. Hawaii Theatre Ctr., 1988-93; bd. dirs. Honolulu Econ. Devel. Corp., 1988-93, Nature Conservancy Hawaii, 1988-93, U. Hawaii Pres.' Coun., 1988-93, Aloha United Way, 1988-93; mem. Bus. Roundtable of Hawaii, 1989-93; chmn. Mil. Affairs Coun., 1992-93; mem. exec. and policy coms. Bus. Coun. N.Y. State, 1993-94; mem. adv. bd. Corp. Leadership Coun., 1993-94; nat. bd. dirs. Jr. Achievement, 1993—; trustee, vice chmn. Nat. U., 1994—, chair Nat. Leadership Inst, 2005—, InPractice, Inc., 2004—; bd. dirs. Jr. Achievement Worldwide, 1994—. Capt. US Army, 1960—63. Mem. AICPA, Am. Bankers Assn. (chmn. securities processing com. 1974-77, trust ops. com. 1978, mem. exec. com. ops. and automation div. 1980-83, rsch. com.), Am. Econ. Assn., Nat. Assn. Corp. Dirs. (bd. dirs. D.C. chpt. 1999—), Tex. Soc. CPAs, Fin. Execs. Inst., Consumer Bankers Assn. (bd. dirs. 1986-89), N. Am. Soc. Corp. Planners (bd. dirs. Dallas Chpt. 1982-83), Assn. for Corp. Growth, Orgn. Resource Counselors, Inc., Hawaii C. of C. (bd. dirs. 1988-89, chmn. bd. 1990-92), Omicron Delta Epsilon, Alpha Delta Phi. Office Phone: 561-620-2356, 561-994-6466. Business E-Mail: gmc@deltennium.com.

CZARNECKI, KELLY, librarian; MEd in Ednl. Policy Studies, U. Ill., Urbana-Champaign, 2001, MSLIS, 2002. Teen librarian, ImaginOn Public Libr. Charlotte and Mecklenburg Co., NC. Co-leader Teen Second Life Eye4You Libr. Alliance; co-chair, teen gaming discussion group Young Adult Library Services Assn. Named one of the Movers & Shakers, Libr. Jour., 2007. Office: Public Library Charlotte and Mecklenburg County 310 N Tryon St Charlotte NC 28202

CZARNEZKI, MARY ELAINE, media specialist; b. Milw., June 3, 1952; d. Gerald J. and Eleanor H. (Lietz) C. BS, U. Wis., Milw., 1973; MA, U. Wis., Madison, 1975; postgrad., U. Pitts., 1982. Cert. instructional library media specialist. Librarian for kindergarten through 8th grade Columbus (Wis.) Pub. Schs., 1976-90; media specialist Edgerton Elem. Sch., Hales Corners, Wis., 1990—. Mem. ALA, Am. Assn. Sch. Librarians (mem. pub. awareness com.), Wis. Libr. Assn., Wis. Assn. Sch. Librs., Milw. Met. Sch. Libr. Assn., Columbia County Libr. Assn. (past pres.), Beta Phi Mu, Kappa Delta Pi. Home: 8119 W Oklahoma Ave Milwaukee WI 53219-3514

CZEPIEL, LORI ANNE, lawyer; b. Chgo., Aug. 23, 1963; BA in economics, Northwestern U., 1981—84; JD cum laude, Boston U. Sch. of Law, 1984—87. Counsel, assoc. Skadden, Arps, Slate, Meagher & Flom LLP, Los Angeles, 1987—97; ptnr. Sidley Austin LLP, New York, NY, 1997—. Dir. Northwestern Alumni Assn., Evanston, Ill., 1998—2006, v.p., 1998—2006; exec. bd. mem. and pac fundraising chair Young Executives of Am., Los Angeles, 1996—97; mem. Northwestern U. Coun. of 100, Evanston, Ill., 1998—2006. Mem.: Assn. of the Bar of the City of NY, ABA. Office: Sidley Austin LLP 787 Seventh Ave New York NY 10019 Business E-Mail: lczepiel@sidley.com.

CZESTOCHOWSKI, JOSEPH STEPHEN, administrator, publisher, investor; b. NYC, Aug. 6, 1950; s. Joseph Stephen and Julia (Skowron) C.; m. Debra J. Kindred Nicholson, Nov. 18, 1972; 1 child, J. F. Stefan Parker. Diploma, Jagiellonian U., Krakow, Poland, 1971; BA, U. Ill., Champaign-Urbana, 1971, MA, 1973. Curator of collections Brooks Mus. Art, Memphis, 1973; dir. Decker Gallery, Md. Inst., Balt., 1975—78, The Dixon Gallery and Gardens, Memphis, 1994—98, Parker Cop., 1993—; exec. dir. Cedar Rapids Mus. Art, Iowa, 1978—94. Dir. Internat. Arts The Torch Press, 1993—; sr. examiner Accreditation Commn. of the AAM; field reviewer Inst. Mus. Svcs.; govt. and art com. Assn. Art Mus. Dirs. Author: (monograph) The Published Prints of Charles Burchfield, 1976, The Pioneers, 1977, John S. Curry - A Portrait of a Rural America, 1977, Go West, 1978, Polish Posters, 1979, The Combined Works of Arthur B. Davies, 1980, Prints by Childe Hassam, 1980, John S. Curry and Grant Wood - A Portrait of Rural America, 1981, The American Landscape Tradition 1738-1965, 1982, Marvin D. Cone, An American Tradition, 1985, Marvin D. Cone and Grant Wood - An American Tradition, 1990, James Swann - In Quest of a Printmaker, 1990, Marvin D. Cone - Art as Self-Portrait, 1990; contbr. pubs. in field, articles to profl. jours. Mem. adv. bd. Krannert Art Mus., Bronze Cir., LAS Coll., U. Ill. Urbana; mem. pres. coun. U. Ill. Found., Urbana. Fellow Vatican Mus. and Smithsonian Inst., 1976, Smithsonian Instn., 1977-79; recipient first Nancy Hanks Meml. award for profl. excellence Am. Assn. Mus., 1985; rsch. grant Brazil Minister Fgn. Affairs, 1995-98, Portugal Ministry Culture, 1998, Spain Ministry Culture, 1998. Mem. Am. Assn. Mus. Dirs., Internat. Coun. Mus., The Kosciuszko Found. (trustee 1988-96), The Polish Inst. Arts and Scis. in Am., Inc. (trustee 1986-96), Ctr. for the Study of the Presidency (trustee), Coll. Liberal Arts and Scis. U. Ill. Alumni Assn. (trustee 1994-96), Rotary Internat. Office: Internat Arts 1550 N Lake Shore Dr Apt 28C Chicago IL 60610 Business E-Mail: jc@internationalarts.org, interarts@parkers.com.

CZINDER, THOMAS BRADLEY, musician, director; b. Grand Haven, Mich., June 28, 1980; s. Lonnie Gene and Nancee Jeanne Czinder; m. Andrea Lynn Ward, Nov. 8, 2003. BA in Church Music, Concordia U., Ann Arbor, Mich., 2002. Dir. ch. and sch. music St. Paul Luth. Ch. and Sch., Flint, Mich., 2002—; accompanist Flint Festival Youth Singers, Flint Inst. Music, 2005—. Mem.: Am. Guild Organists (registrar 2005—). Office: St Paul Luth Ch and Sch 402 S Ballenger Hwy Flint MI 48532 Home Phone: 810-513-8610; Office Phone: 810-239-6200. Office Fax: 810-239-5466.

CZINGER, KEVIN ROBERT, entrepreneur, venture capitalist; b. Cleve., Apr. 15, 1959; s. Kenneth Robert and Ethel Mac (Hudock) C.; m. Katrin Julia Blucher, Aug. 28, 1987; children: Antonia, Lukas. BA, Yale U., 1982, JD, 1987. Bar: N.Y. 1987. Asst. U.S. atty. Manhattan U.S. Atty's. Office, NYC, 1988-90; exec. dir. Goldman Sachs Internat., London, 1990-94; exec. v.p., COO BMG Entertainment, NYC, 1994-96; CEO, founder Volcano Entertainment, LLC, NYC, 1996-98; mng. dir. Merrill Lynch & Co., Inc., 1998-99; COO Webvan.com, Foster City, 1999-2000; venture capitalist, entrepreneur-in-residence Benchmark Capital, 2000; with Angel Investor, 2001; ptnr., co-founder San Shan. Founder, bd. mem. Amistad Acad., Achievement First Org.; trustee Yale Law Sch.; mem. Yale President's Coun. Internat. Activities.*

CZOP, ANDREW PAUL, electrical engineer; b. West Warwick, RI, Oct. 6, 1982; s. Gregory J. and Linda L. Czop. BSEE, Western New Eng. Coll., Springfield, Mass., 2004. Robotics elec. engr. L3 Titan Corp., Indian Head, Md., 2004—. Contbr. articles to profl. jours. Presdl. scholar, Western New Eng. Coll., 2000, 2001, 2002, 2003. Achievements include patents pending for RAMBOT (A Low Cost Disposable Explosive Ordnance Disposal Robot). Home Phone: 401-465-9652; Office Phone: 301-744-6858 305.

CZOPEK, VANESSA, library director; County libr. Stanislaus County Libr., Modesto, Calif. Contbr. articles to profl. publs. Office: Stanislaus County Libr 1500 I St Modesto CA 95354 Office Phone: 209-558-7801. Office Fax: 209-529-4779. E-mail: czopkv@mail.co.stanislaus.ca.us.

CZYRNY, JAMES JOSEPH, physiatrist; b. Buffalo, July 22, 1955; s. John and Erma Czyrny; m. Debra S. Wilson; children: Julie M., Steven J. BA in Biology, SUNY, Buffalo, 1977, MD, 1981. Resident Consortium hosp. U. Buffalo, Buffalo, 1981—84; prof. clin. rehab. medicine SUNY, Buffalo, 1985—; clin. dir. rehab. medicine Erie County Med. Ctr., Buffalo, 1985—. Fellow: Am. Acad. Phys. Medicine and Rehab. Avocation: flying. Office: Erie County Med Ctr 4Grider St Buffalo NY 14215 Office Phone: 716-898-3106.

DAAB-KRZYKOWSKI, ANDRE, pharmaceutical and nutritional manufacturing company administrator; b. Warsaw, May 16, 1949; came to U.S., 1973, naturalized, 1981; s. Aleksy Czeslaw Crest Polkozic and Zofia (Dyszkiewicz crest Kudrys) Krzykowski; 1 child, Cecylia. MSChemE, Tech. U., Warsaw, 1973; MBA, Memphis State U., 1979. Rsch. chemist Schering-Plough, Memphis, 1974-77; process control mgr. Ralston Purina Co., Memphis, 1977-80; dir. pharm. projects Bristol-Myers Squibb Co., Mayaguez, P.R., 1980-90; process devel. group mgr. R&D Ross Labs. divsn. Abbott Labs., 1990—. Patentee in field. Served to 2d lt. Polish Army Res. Mem. Am. Mgmt. Assn., Am. Chem. Soc., Toastmasters (pres. local chpt. 1986). Republican. Lutheran. Avocations: sailing, scuba diving, Karate. Office: Ross Labs 625 Cleveland Ave Columbus OH 43215-1724 Office Phone: 614-624-3966. Business E-Mail: andre.daab-krzykowski@abbott.com.

DAANE, JAMES DEWEY, banker; b. Grand Rapids, Mich., July 6, 1918; s. Gilbert L. and Mamie (Blocksma) D.; m. Blanche M. Tichenor, Apr. 28, 1941 (div. 1952); 1 dau., Elizabeth Marie Daane Mallek; m. Onnie B. Selby, Jan. 23, 1953 (dec. Dec. 1961); m. Barbara W. McMann, Feb. 16, 1963; children: Elizabeth Whitney, Olivia Quartel. AB magna cum laude, Duke U., 1939; MPA, Harvard U., 1946, D in Pub. Adminstrn. (Littauer fellow), 1949. With Fed. Res. Bank, Richmond, Va., 1939-60, asst. v.p., 1953-57, v.p., 1957-60, also cons. to pres. bank, adviser to pres. Mpls., 1960; asst. to sec. treasury, 1960-61; dep. undersec. treasury for monetary affairs, 1961-63; mem. bd. govs. Fed. Reserve System, Washington, 1963-74; vice chmn. bd. dirs. Commerce Union Bank, Sovran Bank/Cen. South, Nashville, 1974-78; chmn. internat. policy com. Commerce Union Corp., 1978-87; dir. Nat. Futures Assn., Ill., 1983—2002; chmn. internat. policy com Sovran Fin. Corp., Nashville, 1988; chmn. money market com. Commerce Union Bank, 1974-87; chmn. money market com. cen. S. Sovran Bank, 1988-90. Assoc. economist Fed. Open Market Com., 1955-56, 58-59; chief IMF Fiscal Mission to Paraquay, 1950-51; vice chmn. Tennessee Valley Bancorp. Inc., 1975-78; Frank K. Houston prof. banking and fin. Owen Grad. Sch. Mgmt., Vanderbilt U., 1974-85, Valere Blair Potter prof. banking and fin., 1985-89, Frank K. Houston prof. emeritus, 1989—, Alan R. Holmes prof. econs. Middlebury Coll., 1991-93; bd. dirs. Chgo. Bd. of Trade, 1979-82; prof. fin. Vanderbilt U. Editor: (with David C. Colander) The Art of Monetary Policy. Bd. advisers Patterson Sch. Diplomacy and Internat. Commerce, U. Ky. Mem. J.F. Kennedy Sch. Govt. Assn. of Harvard U., Am. Econ. Assn., Am. Finance Assn. Home: 102 Westhampton Pl Nashville TN 37205-3439 Office: Vanderbilt U Owen Grad Sch Mgmt 401 21st Ave N Nashville TN 37203 Office Phone: 615-322-3632. E-mail: dewey.daane@owen.vanderbilt.edu.

DAAR, ERIC STEVEN, medical educator; b. LA, Oct. 21, 1959; s. David and Thelma Daar; m. Judith Freedel Daar, Dec. 25, 1983; children: Evan, Jared, Adam, Ryan. BA, UCLA, 1981; MD, Georgetown U., Washington, 1985. Intern and resident Cedars-Sinai Med. Ctr., LA, 1985—88, fellow infectious diseases, 1988—91, dir. AIDS program, 1991—2001, chief infectious diseases, 1994—2000; prof. medicine David Geffen Sch. Medicine, UCLA, 2000—; chief divsn. HIV medicine Harbor-UCLA Med. Ctr., Torrance, Calif., 2001—. Contbr. numerous articles to profl. jours. Bd. dirs. LA Biomed. Rsch. Inst., 2001—, AIDS Project LA, 2002—. Grantee, NIH, State of Calif. Office: Harbor-UCLA Med Ctr 1124 W Carson St N24 Torrance CA 90502 Office Phone: 310-222-2467. Fax: 310-533-0447. Business E-Mail: edaar@labiomed.org.

DAARSTAD, ERIK, cinematographer; b. Fjotland, Norway, June 27, 1935; arrived in U.S., 1953; s. Even Olsen Daarstad and Margit Elida Johnsen; m. Louanne Jo Frye, July 6, 1963; children: Kari Ann, Heather Britt, Erik Even. BA, U. So. Calif., 1957. Pres. Stadmor Film Co., Inc., Manhattan Beach, Calif., 1966—76; dir. photography Nat. Geog. Soc., Metro-Goldwyn-Mayer, Walt Disney; dir. photograph PBS, Am. Film Found., Saul Bass & Assocs., others. Dir. photography: (documentaries) The Exiles, 1961 (Golden Ducat award); Why Man Creates, 1969 (Acad. award); The Great Whales, 1978 (Emmy award); Four Stones for Kanemitsu, 1974 (Acad. award nomination); The Incredible Machine, 1975 (Acad. award nomination); Notes on the Performing Arts, 1977 (Acad. award nomination); Never Give Up, 1995 (Acad. award nomination); Sing!, 2002 (Acad. award nomination); Mysteries of the Mind, 1980 (Emmy award); Superliners: Twilight of an Era, 1980 (Emmy award, Peabody award). Bd. dirs. Pend Oreille Arts Coun., 1999—2001, Bonner County Hist. Soc., 2001—03, Panida Theater, 2004—. With US Army, 1959—61. Named Citizen of Yr., Sandpoint (Idaho) C. of C., 2002; recipient Cert. Commendation, Am. Assn. State and Local History, 2003. Democrat. Avocations: skiing, photography. Home: 1504 Northshore Dr Sandpoint ID 83864 Fax: 208-263-5790. Personal E-mail: eriklou@bossig.com.

DABAH, EZRA, apparel executive; Bd. dir., exec. officer Gitano Group Inc., 1972—93; founder, pres. Eva Joia Inc. (subs. of Gitano Group Inc.), 1983; chmn. The Children's Place Retail Stores Inc., Secaucus, NJ, 1989—2007, CEO, 1991—. Office: The Children's Place 915 Secaucus Rd Secaucus NJ 07094*

DABBAGH, MAHMOUD, language educator, linguist, researcher; b. Damascus, Syria, Aug. 14, 1964; 3 children. BA in French Language, Civilization, and Culture, magna cum laude, U. Damascus, Syria, 1987; MA in Gen. and Applied Linguistics, with highest distinction, René Descartes, Sorbonne Paris V, France, 1988; PhD in Literary Traductology, with highest distinction, Sorbonne Nouvelle Paris III, 1997. Cert. translator/interpreter Arabic-French-English French Translation Assn., Am. Translators Assn. Middle sch., HS tchr. Omar Bin Abdel-Aziz HS, Damascus, Syria, 1986—87; accredited translator, interpreter Tenth Mediterranean Games, Damascus, 1987, Oger Liban Translator/Interpreter, Damascus, 1987; French for Bus. Instruction For Adults Lang. and Computer Sch., Paris, 1991; interpreter, sales rep. Orient-Export, Paris, 1988—98; translator Al-Farabi Pub. Ho., Paris, 1999; postdoctoral rschr. Sorbonne Ctr. Contemporary Near-Eastern Studies, U. Paris, Paris, 1997—99; Arabic linguist instr. Mil. Linguists-Joint Lang. Ctr., Augusta, Ga., 2002; adj. lectr. course bldg. French, Arabic SUNY, Brockport, 2002—, Nazareth Coll., Rochester, 2002—. Author (translator): The Non-Observance of the Four Doctrines: The Most Dangerous Heresy that Threatens Divine Law, 1999. Mem.: MLA, ACLU, UUP, SPLC, SFT, IAF, ATA, AFT, Am. Translators Assn., French Translators Assn., French Embassy Cultural Ctr., Alliance Francaise (Rochester), Alliance Française, Wall of Tolerance, Cercle Francais Nazareth Coll. Avocations: reading, computer science, literary theory, translation science. Office: SUNY Fgn Lang and Lit Dept 116 Tower 350 New Campus Dr Brockport NY 14420-2914 Home: 2025 E Henrietta Rd Apt 1 Rochester NY 14623 Office: Nazareth Coll Bldg G381 4245 E Ave Rochester NY 14618-3790 Personal E-mail: mdabbagh@rochester.rr.com. Business E-Mail: mdabbagh@brockport.edu, mdabbag6@naz.edu.

DABDOUB, PAUL OSCAR, academic administrator; b. La Lima, Honduras, July 7, 1946; came to U.S., 1955; s. Jacob Abraham and Helen (McNabb) D.; m. Lorrie Suzanne Shell, Aug. 9, 1993; children by previous marriage: Desiree, John Kelly, Paul Jacob. B of Bible, Open Bible Coll., 1983; student, Liberty U., 1979; M of Theology, Andersonville Bapt. Sem., 1996, D of Pastoral Theology, 1996. Fin. mgr. 3d Nat. Bank, Nashville, 1973-78; min. Mooring Bapt. Ch., Tiptonville, Tenn., 1978-79, Kinfolks Ridge Bapt. Ch., Caruthersville, Mo., 1979-80; min., founder Victory Bapt. Ch., Caruthersville, 1980-91; adminstr., founder, min. Victory Bapt. Acad., Caruthersville, 1984—91; min. Ridge Meml. Bapt. Ch., Slidell, La., 1991—; sci. instr. Northlake Christian Sch., Covington, La., 1991. Founder, pres., instr. Slidell Bapt. Sem., 1994—. Avocation: wild turkey hunting. Home: 106 Jane St Slidell LA 70461 Office Phone: 985-726-9600. Personal E-mail: bpdkjv1@aol.com.

DABERKO, DAVID A., bank executive; b. Hudson, Ohio, 1945; BA, Denison U., 1967; MBA, Case Western Res. U., 1970. Mgmt. trainee Nat. City Bank, Cleve., 1968-72, asst. v.p., 1972-73, v.p. bank investment divsn., dept. head met. lending divsn., 1973-80, sr. v.p. corp. banking, 1980-82, pres., 1987-93; exec. v.p. corp. banking Nat. City Corp., Nat. City Bank, Cleve., 1982-85; pres., bd. dirs. Nat. City Bank (formerly BancOhio Nat. Bank), Columbus, 1985-87; dep. chmn. Nat. City Corp., Cleve., 1987-93, pres., CEO, 1993-95, chmn., CEO, 1995—2007, chmn., 2007—. Dir. Fed. Res. Bank, Cleve. Trustee Cleve. Tomorrow, Greater Cleve. Growth Assn., Case Western Res. U., Hawken Sch., Neighborhood Progress, Univ. Cir. Inc., Univ. Hosp. Health Sys.; co-chair Harvest for Hunger Campaign, 1992, 93. Mem. Bankers Roundtable. Office: Nat City Corp National City Center 1900 E 9th St Cleveland OH 44114-3401*

DABIDEEN, DARRIN, research scientist; b. San Fernando, Trinidad and Tobago, Aug. 31, 1972; arrived in US, 1997; s. Knollis Dabideen and Vindra Seecharan. BS with 1st class honors, U. of W.I., Trinidad, 1994, MPhil, 2000; PhD, CUNY, NYC, 2002. Rsch. scientist Feinstein Inst. for Med. Rsch., Manhasset, NY, 2004—; postdoctoral rschr. U. Calif., Davis, 2003—04. Recipient postgrad. scholarship, U. of W.I., 1994—96. Mem.: Am. Assn. for Pharm. Scientist (assoc.), Am. Chem. Soc. (assoc.). Achievements include development of a new class of inhibitors for macrophage migration inhibitory factor (MIF); novel synthetic strategies to spiroketal and tetrahydrofuran subunits; a novel glycosylation protocol using glycosyliodides and highly strained oxa and thio cycloailane acceptors. Office: Feinstein Inst for Med Rsch 350 Community Dr Manhasset NY 11030 Home Phone: 917-804-6357; Office Phone: 516-562-3472. Office Fax: 516-562-1022. E-mail: ddabidee@nshs.edu.

DABINETT, DIANA FRANCES, artist; d. Leslie Frank and Ivy Annie May; m. Patrick Dabinett, Aug. 1969; children: Emily Thomas. BA in fine arts, U. Cape Town, 1963. HS art tchr., Zimbabwe, 1965—66; HS English tchr. England, 1967—69; asst. curator London Art Gallery, Ont., 1969—73. Can. artists rep., Labrador, Nfld., 1980—97; visual arts advisor, adv. panel Fed.-Prov. Cultural Agreement, Nfld., Canada, 1992—2000; artist in residence, Hopedale, Labrador, 1998—99, Gros Morne Park, Nfld., 2001, Terra Nova Park, 2005. Exhibitions include Pathways, 1997-99; exhibited in group shows at Discovery Travelling Maritimes, 1997; One-woman shows include St. John's, 1989-92, 2006, 07, Lunenberg, NS, 1992, Christina Parker Fine Art St. John's, 1994, 98, 2000, 02, 04, 05, 06, Can. Embassy Tokyo, 2001, Can. Embassy Washington, 2003, Argyle Fine Art Gallery, Halifax, 2003, Prince Edward Island, Can., 2004, Devel. House, St. John's, 2006; collection HRH Queen Elizabeth II.; prin. works at Birthing Ctr. and Cancer Ctr., Cmty. Hosp. of Monterey Peninsula, St. Lawrence Hosp. and Labrador Health Ctr., Newfoundland, NS Health and Welfare Dept. Halifax, Labrador Straits; illustrator: Iceburgs-Castles in the Sea, 2000. Mem.: Canadian Soc. Water Colour Painters. Avocations: reading, snow shoeing, hiking. Address: Box 1005 Torbay NL Canada A1K 1K9 Business E-Mail: dianadabinett@nl.rogers.com.

DABLE, CAROL M., primary school educator; b. New Ulm, Minn., Jan. 14, 1943; d. Edwin A. and Emma Clara Helen (Laeslin) Nolte; m. Paul D. Dable, July 22, 1967; children: Ami McClure, Kala McClellan, Marci Gorman, Jon. BS, Dr. Martin Luther Coll., Minn., 1965. 1st and 2d grade tchr. Trinity Luth. Sch., Waukesha, Wis., 1965—71; elem. and HS substitute tchr. Lake Mills, Wis., 1971—74; pre-K, grades 3-5 and kindergarten tchr. Christ Luth., West Salem, Wis., 1975—. Bd. mem. Hist. Soc., West Salem, Wis.; dir. handbell choir Christ Luth. Avocations: reading, crocheting, canvas craft-stitching. Personal E-mail: cdable@christstjohns.org.

DABNEY, H. SLAYTON, JR., lawyer; b. Charlottesville, Va., Sept. 14, 1949; s. Hovey S. and Patricia S (Schmidt) D.; m. Donna C. Warns, Jan. 14, 1983; children: Slayton, Kate, Andrew. BA, U. Va., 1971, JD, 1974. Bar: Va. 1974, N.Y. 2005, U.S. Dist. Ct. (ea. and we. dists.) Va., U.S. Dist. Ct. D.C., U.S. Dist. Ct. (so. dist.) N.Y., U.S. Bankruptcy Ct. (ea. and we. dists.) Va., U.S. Ct. Appeals (4th cir.). Ptnr. King & Spalding, LLP, NYC. Mem. ABA, Am. Bankruptcy Inst. Office: King & Spalding LLP 1185 Avenue of the Americas New York NY 10036-4003 Office Phone: 212-556-2287. Business E-Mail: sdabney@kslaw.com.

DABRISHUS, MICHAEL JOHN, librarian; s. Michael Jerome and Elizabeth Agnes Dabrishus; m. Nancy Elizabeth Hooper, Apr. 28, 1973; children: Mara Elizabeth, Anna Elise. BA, We. Mich. U., 1971; MS in Libr. Sci., Wayne State U., 1975. Archivist Tex. State Libr., Austin, 1976—83; asst. dir. libr. U. Ark., Fayetteville, 1984—2002, U. Pitts., 2002—. Co-author: (book) William Grant Still: A Bio-Bibliography; contbr. book. Fellow: Tex. State Geneal. Soc.; mem.: Pa. State Hist. Records Adv. Bd., Soc. S.W. Archivists (pres. 1996—97), Soc. Am. Archivists, ALA. Office: Univ Pitts 7500 Thomas Blvd Pittsburgh PA 15260 Home Phone: 412-318-4250; Office Phone: 412-244-7065. Office Fax: 412-244-7077. E-mail: michaeld@pitt.edu.

DABROWSKA, DOROTA MARIA, statistician, educator; b. Warsaw, Dec. 10, 1954; arrived in U.S., 1981, naturalized, 1992; d. Emma K. Juhasz-Dabrowska and Cyryl A. Dabrowski. MA in Math., Warsaw U., 1978; PhD in Stats., U. Calif., Berkeley, 1984. Rsch. assoc. Polish Acad. Sci., Warsaw, 1978—81; asst. prof. Carnegie-Mellon U., Pitts., 1984—88, UCLA, 1988—91, assoc. prof., 1991—96, prof., 1996—. Assoc. editor: Jour. Multivariate Analysis, 1999—, Lifetime Data Analysis, 2002—, Annals of Statistics, 2004—06, Statistics Survey, 2007—; contbr. articles to profl. jours. Recipient Evelyn Fix Meml. medal, U. Calif., 1984; grantee, NSF, 1989—2003, NIH, 1995—2003, 2007—; Earl C. Anthony fellow, U. Calif., 1981—82, Regents fellow, 1982—83, UC Presdl. fellow, 1986—88. Fellow: Inst. Math. Stats.; mem.: Bernoulli Soc., Am. Statis. Assn. Office: Univ Calif LA Sch Pub Health/Biostatistics Los Angeles CA 90095-1772 Business E-Mail: dorota@ucla.edu.

DABROWSKI, DORIS JANE, lawyer; b. Paterson, NJ, May 20, 1950; BA, Rutgers U., 1972, JD, 1975. Bar: Pa. 1975, U.S. Dist. Ct. (ea. dist.) Pa. 1976, U.S. Ct. Appeals (3d cir.) 1977, N.J. 1979, U.S. Dist. Ct. N.J. 1979, U.S. Ct. Appeals (fed. cir.) 1985. Staff atty. Del. County Legal Assistance, Chester, Pa., 1975-77; assoc. Tabas, Horwitz & Furlong (later Tabas, Furlong & Roser), Phila., 1977-83; pvt. practice Pa., 1983—, NJ, 1983—. Arbitrator Nat. Assn. Securities Dealers; participant Nat. Pension Assistance Project, Patient Advocate Network; adv. coun. 18th Police Dist., 1997-2004. Mem. editorial bd. Women's Rights Law Reporter, 1974-75. Dir. Well Woman, Phila., 1983-87, Pa. Pro Musica, Phila., 1983-84; adv. bd. Clara Bell Duvall Edn. Fund, Phila.; gov. bd. Health Systems Agy., S.E. Pa., 1980-86; organist Holy Innocents St. Paul Episc. Ch., 2004—. Recipient Cert. of Achievement Bus. Women's Network, Phila., 1984; named Pa. Super Lawyer, 2006, 07. Mem. Nat. Employment Lawyers' Assn. (pres. Ea. Pa. chpt. 1992-98), Nat. Assn. Women Lawyers (amicus com., bd. dirs. 1994-95), Phila. Bar Assn. (evidence code task force 1992-93, chair support subcom. of small firm and sole practice com. 1992, exec. com. pub. interest sect., co-chair women's rights com. 2000-01, co-chair sole and small firm practice com. 2007), Assn. for Union Democracy, Am. Guild Organists (exec. com. 2002-03). Office: 1500 Walnut St Ste 900 Philadelphia PA 19102 Office Phone: 215-790-1115. Personal E-mail: dabrowskidoris@hotmail.com. Business E-Mail: dabrowsk@eticomm.net.

DABROWSKI, EDWARD JOHN, television technical director; b. Chgo., Nov. 16, 1957; s. Edward J. and Justina J. (Grilc) D. BS in Elec. Engring., Ill. Inst. Tech., Chgo., 1979. Engr. Sta. WMAQ-TV, Chgo., 1976-83, tech. dir., 1983—; enrg.-in-charge The Jenny Jones Show, 1995. Tech. dir. (NBC afternoon spl.) The Sixth Street Kids, 1984, (WMAQ-TV docu-drama) Fast Break to Glory: Dusable Panthers, 1988, Chgo. Sisslin (Chgo. Emmy award 1989), Chgo. Bears Pre-Season football, 1993, Engring. Devel. Group, 1996—. Emmy nomination, Chgo. Chpt., 1998; recipient Emmy award, 2000, 03; 1999 Millennium Spl. Coverage award, Tech. award Chgo. Marathon 2002 Mem. IEEE, Soc. Broadcast Engrs., NATAS (Emmy nominations Chgo. chpt. 1986), Nat. Assn. Broadcast Employees and Technicians (steward Chgo. chpt. 1981-87, mobilization coord. Chgo. 1994-95), Natl. Assn. of Broadcast Employees and Technicians, Broadcasting and Cable Television Workers Sector of the Communications Workers of Amer., AFL-CIO Steward and Exec. Bd. Mem. Chgo. Local 41 1999—, Am. Radio Relay Lague (life), Chgo.-Suburban Radio Assn., Mus. Broadcast Comm. (charter), Am. Fraternal Union, Slovene Nat. Benefit Soc. (rec. sec. lodge 449, pres. Chgo. dist. 2003—) Democrat. Roman Catholic. Avocations: amateur radio, photography. Office: Sta WMAQ-TV NBC Tower 454 N Columbus Dr Chicago IL 60611-5514 Office Phone: 312-836-5522. E-mail: edward.dabrowski@nbc.com.

DABROWSKI, THADDEUS E., art educator, consultant, painter; b. Bronx, NY, July 17, 1945; s. Theodore J. and Wanda K. (Curylo) D.; m. Althea M. Smith, May 17, 1970; children: Veronika D. Bulkin, Sibyl T. Jayne. BBA, U. Mass., 1968, MFA, 1970, MEd, 1972. Tech. specialist U. Mass., Amherst, 1972-78, adminstrv. asst., 1978-95, textbook adminstr., 1995—2001, adj. lectr. art, 1981—; art edn. cons., 2001—. Pres., v.p., treas. Leverette (Mass.) Artists and Craftsmen, 1982—; mem. Pub. Arts Commn., Amherst, 1990-94; cons. Nat. Edn. Systems, Amherst, 2001—. Solo exhbns. include Campus Cinema, Hadley, Mass., 1968, U. Mass. Student Union Gallery, Amherst, 1970, Leverett (Mass.) Crafts and Art Ctr., 1990, Burnett Gallery, Jones Libr., Amherst, 1995; showcase artist New Eng. Arts Festival, U. Mass., 1983. Loaned exec., mem. cabinet United Way of Hampshire, Amherst, 1987-2002; mem. Commonwealth of Mass. Employees Charitable Campaign Com., 1987—, Region 4 Charity Application Rev. Com., 1987-2003; elected town meeting mem. Town of Amherst, 2001—. Recipient Milton Bradley award Springfield (Mass.) Art League, 1976. Mem. NEA, Nat. Art Edn. Assn., Mass. Tchrs. Assn., Mass. Assn. for Ednl. Tech. (charter), Univ. Staff Assn. (steward, chief steward 1995-02), Rotary (sec. Amherst 1989-91, v.p. 1991-92, pres. 1992-93, Paul Harris fellow 1984—). Avocations: classic automobile preservation, piano, computer systems. Home: 9 Squire Ln Amherst MA 01002-3232 Office: U Mass Dept Art Amherst MA 01003 Business E-Mail: thaddeus@art.umass.edu.

D'ABRUZZO, STEPHANIE, actress; Grad., Northwestern U. Actor: (off-broadway plays) Avenue Q, 2003 (Drama Desk nominee, 2003); (TV series) Sesame Street, 1993—, The Wubbulous World of Dr. Seuss,

1996—98, Oobi, 2003—04, Scrubs, 2007, (voice actor) Sheep in the Big City, 2000—01, The Book of Pooh, 2000—01, Proof of Life on Earth, 2005,; (films) The Adventures of Elmo in Grouchland, 1999, Sesame Street 4D, 2003; (Broadway plays) Carnival, 2002, Chess, 2003—, Avenue Q, 2003 (Tony nominee, 2004, Theatre World award, 2004, Outer Critics Circle Special Ensemble award); (plays) I Love You Because, 2006.*

D'ACCONE, FRANK ANTHONY, music educator; b. Somerville, Mass., June 13, 1931; s. Salvatore and Maria (DiChiappari) D'A. MusB, Boston U., 1952, MusM, 1953; AM, Harvard U., Cambridge, Mass., 1955, PhD, 1960. Asst. prof. music SUNY at Buffalo, 1960-63, assoc. prof., 1964-68; prof. music UCLA, 1968-94, chmn. dept., 1973-76; chmn. faculty UCLA Coll. Fine Arts, 1976-79; chmn. dept. musicology UCLA, 1989-93. Vis. prof. music Yale U., 1972-73 Author: The History of a Baroque Opera, 1985, The Civic Muse, 1997, Music in Renaissance Florence, 2006, Music and Musicians in 16th Century Florence, 2007; editor: Music of the Florentine Renaissance, vols. 1-12, 1967-94; gen. editor Corpus Mensurabilis Musicae, 1986-2001; co-editor Musica Disciplina, 1990-2001; contbr. articles to profl. jours. Fellow Am. Acad. Rome, 1963-64, Fulbright Found., 1963-64, NEH, 1975; recipient G.K. Delmas Venetian Studies award, 1977, J.S. Guggenheim Found. award, 1980, Internat. Galilei prize, Pisa, 1997. Fellow Am. Acad. of Arts and Scis.; mem. Am. Musicol. Soc. (hon., dir. 1973-74), Internat. Musicol. Soc. Home: 725 Fontana Way Laguna Beach CA 92651-4010 Office: U Calif Dept Music Los Angeles CA 90024 Personal E-mail: fondac@cox.net.

DACEY, PAUL, artist; b. Toledo, July 16, 1960; s. Eleanor Dacey. BFA in Painting, Cleve. Inst. Art, 1984; course, Artists Environ. Found., 1982, Lacoste Summer Arts Program, France, 1982. Commns., Nokia US Hdqrs., Dallas, 1999, Credit Suisse First Boston, London, 1999—2000, US Embassy, Ottawa, Can., 1999, Kampala, Uganda, 2000, prin. works include Maxwell Davidson Gallery, NYC, one-man shows include Reconfigured, Interchurch Ctr., 1996, Wash. Square Windows, NYU, 1998, St. Peter's Ch., 1999, Maxwell Davidson Gallery, NYC, 1999, Manifest Destiny, Maxwell Davidson Gallery, 2001, exhibited in group shows at Cleve. Ctr. for Contemporary Art, Cleary/Gottlieb, NYC, Art Initiatives, Artists Space, Washington Sq. East Gallery, NYU, Max Fish, NYC, Tomasulo Gallery, Union CC, Cranford, NJ, ADAA, Art of the 20th Century, NYC, San Francisco Art Expo, Art Chgo., Art Miami, Art Cologne, Maxwell Davidson Gallery, Nancy Hoffman Gallery, NYC, Qualita Fine Art, Las Vegas, Transamerica Pyramid Gallery, San Francisco, Kunstverein Neuenhaus, Germany, 101 Calif., San Francisco, Toledo Mus. Art, Art LA, AAFair, NYC, Morgan Lehman Gallery, Lakeville, Conn., Krasdale Gallery, White Plains, NY, Parrish Art Mus., Southampton, NY, Wooster Arts Space, NYC, Artgalerie Markus, Lingen, Germany, Beijing New Art Projects, China, Davidson Contemporary, NYC, Represented in permanent collections Cleary Gottlieb, Progressive Mayfield Village, OH, Dechert LLP, NYC, Novell, Provo, Utah, Toledo Mus. Art, White & Case, NYC, Dechert LLP, Phila.; featured (book authored by Fre Ilgen) ART? No Thing! (Analogies between Art, Science, Philosophy). Ellen Battell Stoeckel fellow, Yale U., 1983. Home and Office: Apt 23 35-21 80th St Jackson Heights NY 11372 Office Phone: 718-457-6637. Personal E-mail: pauldacey@earthlink.net.

DACEY, ROBERT FRANK, accountant; b. Dayton, Ohio, Aug. 8, 1954; s. Frank Robert and Florence Helen (Duckro) D.; m. Lauri Solita Castillo, May 20, 1989. BBA magna cum laude, U. Cin., 1977; JD, George Mason U., 1996. CPA, Ohio. Sr. acct. Deloitte Haskins & Sells, Cin., 1977-79; bus. mgr., contr. United Press Internat., Inc., London, 1979-81; sr. mgr. Deloitte & Touche, Washington, NYC, Cin., 1981-91; dir. GAO, Washington, 1991—. Editor GAO Financial Audit Manual, 1992. Instr. Junior Achievement, Cin., 1983-85; pres. Milford (Ohio) Area Jaycees, 1984. Recipient merit award Milford Rotary Club, 1985, Meritorious Svc. award GAO, 1994, Arthur S. Flemming award The George Washington U. and The Arthur S. Flemming Awards Commn., 1997 Mem. AICPA. (cert. info. systems auditor), Beta Gamma Sigma Avocations: bicycling, hiking, scuba diving. Office: GAO 441 G St NW Washington DC 20548-0001 Home: 7114 Matthew Mills Rd Mc Lean VA 22101-2642

DACH, LESLIE ALAN, public relations company executive; b. NYC, Apr. 17, 1954; s. Joseph and Edith (Lipsyzc) D.; m. Mary Ann Dickie, Nov. 19, 1983; children: Jonathan Alexander, Eliza May. BS in Biology, Yale U., 1975; MPA, Harvard U., 1981. Staff scientist Environ. Def. Fund., Washington, 1977-79; assoc. dir. Nat. Audubon Soc., Washington, 1981-84, legis. dir., 1984-87; dir. scheduling Mondale-Ferraro campaign, Washington, 1984; spl. asst. to chmn. U.S. Senate Agr. Com., Washington, 1987; dir. comm. Dukakis for Pres., Boston, 1987-88; sr. v.p. Edelman Pub. Rels., Washington, 1989-90, exec. v.p., 1990-96, vice chmn., 1996—. Office: Edelman Pub Rels 1875 Eye St NW Ste 900 Washington DC 20006-5422

DACHOWSKI, PETER RICHARD, manufacturing executive; b. Hillingdon, Middlesex, Eng., June 2, 1948; came to U.S., 1969; s. Teodor and Mary D.; m. Victoria Kaplan, 1977. MA in Econs. with first class honors, Queens' Coll., Cambridge, Eng., 1969; MBA, U. Chgo., 1971. Fin. analyst Exxon Corp., 1971-73; mgr. Boston Cons. Group, 1973-76; asst. treas. CertainTeed Corp., Valley Forge, Pa., 1976-78, asst. to CEO, 1979-80; v.p. planning and devel. CertainTeed Co., Valley Forge, Pa., 1980-81, v.p., treas., 1981-83, v.p., compt., 1983-85; v.p., pres. Roofing Products Group, 1985-90, Vinyl Bldg. Products Group, Valley Forge, 1987-90; sr. v.p., pres. Exterior Products Group, 1990-93, exec. v.p., 1994—96, chmn., pres. , CEO, 2004—. Mem. corp. devel. staff Saint Gobain, Paris, 1978—79; pres. Worldwide Insulation Saint-Gobain, 1996—2004; adv. coun. Joint Ctr. Housing Studies Harvard U., 1990—, U. Chgo. Grad. Sch. Bus., 2002—06, U. Chgo. Paris Ctr., 2006—; bd. dirs. Ball Hort. Co. Trustee Alliance Francaise Phila., 1994-98, Internat. House of Phila., 1994-96, 2004-; bd. dirs. Phila. Orch. Assn., 2002—, Nat. Bldg. Material Distbrs. Assn., 2005—. Recipient Wall St. Jour. award Dow Jones-Chgo., 1971. Mem.: Union League Phila., World Pres. Orgn., Beta Gamma Sigma. Avocations: travel, music, sailing, scuba diving, gardening. Home: 321 Woodmont Cir Berwyn PA 19312-1431 Office: CertainTeed Corp PO Box 860 Valley Forge PA 19482-0860 Office Phone: 610-341-7749.

DACHS, ALAN MARK, investment company executive; b. NYC, Dec. 7, 1947; s. Sidney and Martha (Selz) D.; m. Lauren B. Dachs, June 23, 1973. BA, Wesleyan U., Middletown, Conn., 1970; MBA, NYU, 1978. Account officer Chem. Bank, NYC, 1971-74; various positions Bechtel Group, Inc., San Francisco, 1974-81; v.p., CFO Dual Drilling Co., Wichita Falls, Tex., 1981-82; sr. v.p., mng. dir. Bechtel Investments, Inc., San Francisco, 1982-89; pres., dir., mem. exec. com. and CEO Fremont Group, LLC, San Francisco, 1989—. Bd. dirs. Bechtel Group, Bechtel Enterprises, Inc. Charter trustee, chair bd. trustees Wesleyan U.; trustee The Brooking Instn., The Conf. Bd. Fellow: Am. Acad. Arts & Scis. Office: Fremont Group LLC 199 Fremont St Ste 2500 San Francisco CA 94105-2261*

DACIER, PAUL T., lawyer, information technology executive; b. Boston, Dec. 21, 1957; m. Kim Dacier; children: Jessica, Brittany, John. BA, Marquette U., 1980, JD, 1983. Bar: Wis. 1983, Mass. 1995. Assoc. counsel Apollo Computer, Inc., 1984-85, counsel, 1985-87, sr. counsel, 1987-89; corp. counsel EMC Corp., 1990—92, gen. counsel, 1993—, v.p., 1993—2000, sr. v.p., 2000—06, exec. v.p., 2006—. Mem. Mass. Bar Assn., State Bar Wis. (v.p., gen. counsel). Office: EMC Corp 176 South St Hopkinton MA 01748*

DACKAWICH, S. JOHN, sociology educator, academic administrator; b. Loch Gelley, W.Va., Jan. 31, 1926; s. Samuel and Estelle (Jablonski) D.; m. Shirley Jean McVay, May 20, 1950; children: Robert John, Nancy Joan. BA, U. Md., 1955; PhD, U. Colo., 1958. Instr. U. Colo., 1955-57, Colo. State U., 1957-59; prof., chmn. sociology Calif. State U., Long Beach, 1959-70, prof. sociology Fresno, 1970-94, chmn. dept., 1970-75, prof. sociology emeritus, 1994—. Pvt. practice survey rsch., 1962-. Author: Sociology, 1970, The Fiery Furnace Effect, 2000; contbr. articles and rsch. papers to profl. publs. Mem. Calif. Dem. Ctrl. Com., 1960-62; co-dir. Long Beach Ctrl. Area Study, 1962-64, Citizen Participation Study, Fresno. With USMCR, 1943-46, U.S. Army, 1950-53. Mem. Am. Sociol. Assn., Pacific Sociol. Assn. Home: 5841 W Judy Ct Visalia CA 93277-8601 Office: Calif State U Dept Sociology 5340 N Campus Dr Fresno CA 93740-8019 Personal E-mail: sjdack@peoplepc.com.

DACOSTA, CAROLINE LEE, small business owner; b. Slippery Rock, Pa., Dec. 13, 1941; d. John Edward and Eleanor Rose Allen; children: Yvonne Rene Shawgo, Tamara Kay Hufnagel, Andrea Lee Doods. Student Elem. Edn., Slippery Rock State Tchrs. Coll., 1960. Cert. Fingerprint Analyzation, Criminal Divsn. FBI, Wash., D.C., 1961. Asst. to pathologist and lab technician Grove City Hosp., Pa., 1962—64; book keeper Rice Clin. Lab, Santa Ana, Calif., 1964—65; exec. asst. to prin. Slippery Rock Area Sch. Dist., 1966—74; account exec. WMGW/WZPR AM/FM Radio, Meadville, Pa., 1975—76; account exec., office mgr. Butler Eagle Newspaper, Pa., 1975—81; account exec. UNSCO Linens, Youngstown, Ohio, 1981—83; owner, mgr. DaCosta Properties, Mercer, Pa., 1985—, Casa DaCosta Bed & Breakfast, Mercer, 2004—. Pub. spkr., presenter, specialist Mercer County Vocat., Tech. Sch., 1987—91. Author: (cookbook) My Kitchen Also Has a Stove. Make up artist Theater in Park, Grove City, 1975—76; asst. chairperson Heart Assn. Fund, Grove City, 1976—77; pub. spkr., adv. for elderly to obtain affordable prescription drugs Citizens for Consumer Justice, Phila., 2001—05. Mem.: Mercer County C. of C., Mercer County Conv. and Visitors Bur., Pa. Soc. Bed and Breakfast (co-founder, asst. dir.), Zelienople Lions Club (assoc.). Presbyterian. Achievements include One of the first women to be initiated as a full fledged Lion in Pennsylvania. Avocations: painting, hist. preservation and restoration of homes, travel, reading. Home: 116 West Market St Mercer PA 16137 Office: DaCosta Properties Casa DaCosta B & B 116 West Market St Mercer PA 16137 Home Phone: 724-662-5681; Office Phone: 724-662-5681. Office Fax: 724-662-1617. Personal E-mail: casadacosta@zoominternet.net.

DA COSTA, NEWTON CARNEIRO AFFONSO, JR., engineering educator, researcher; b. Curitiba, Parana, Brazil, Dec. 31, 1956; s. Newton Carneiro Affonso and Neusa Feitosa Affonso da Costa; m. Nebel Arguello Affonso Lanza, Dec. 29, 1995; 1 child, Isabela Arguello Affonso. BS in Engring., U. Sao Paulo, Brazil, 1980; MS in Engring., Fed. U. Santa Catarina, Florianopolis, Brazil, 1985; PhD, Getulio Vargas Found., Sao Paulo, 1991. Asst. prof. Fed. U. Santa Catarina, Florianopolis, 1985—86, vis. prof., 1991—93, assoc. prof., 1997—; vis. rschr. Lancaster U., England, 1989—91; assoc. prof. Fed. U. Rio de Janeiro, 1994—97; vis. scholar Columbia U., NYC, 1999—2000. Assoc. editor Brazilian Jour. Fin., Rio de Janeiro, 2006—; contbr. scientific papers in field. Grantee Rsch. grant, NRC, 1995—; Fulbright scholarship, Fulbright Found., 1999—2000. Mem.: Brazilian Fin. Assn. (assoc.; found. mem. 2001, fiscal bd. mem. 2005—), Brazilian Bus. Assn. (assoc.). Home: 2245 Bocaiuva St #302 Santa Catarina Florianopolis 88015-530 Brazil Personal E-mail: ncacjr@gmail.com. Business E-Mail: newton@cse.ufsc.br.

DACUNHA, JEFFREY J., oil industry executive, researcher; BS in Math. and Computer Sci., Baylor U., Waco, Tex., 2000, MS in Math., 2001, PhD in Math., 2004. Davies postdoctoral rsch. fellow US Mil. Acad., West Point, NY, 2004—05; rschr. Lufkin Automation, Houston, 2006—. Contbr. articles to profl. jours. Named Grad. Student of Yr., Baylor U., 2004; scholar, 2000—04; Davies Postdoctoral Rsch. fellow, NAS, 2004—05. Mem.: Soc. Petroleum Engrs., Pi Mu Epsilon (life). Avocations: flying, running. Office: Lufkin Automation 11375 W Sam Houston Pkwy S Ste 800 Houston TX 77031 Office Phone: 281-495-1100.

DACUS, DERON R., lawyer; b. Tyler, Tex., Aug. 21, 1967; BBA cum laude, Tex. A&M U., 1989; JD cum laude, Baylor U., 1994. CPA Tex., 1992; bar: Tex. 1994, US Dist. Ct. (ea. and no. dists. Tex.), US Ct. Appeals (5th cir.). Sr. level acct. Pricewaterhouse; atty. Ramey & Flock, P.C., Tyler, Tex. Named a Rising Star, Tex. Super Lawyers mag., 2006. Mem.: Nat. Homebuilders Assn., Tyler Area Builders Assn., Smith County Bar Assn., Def. Rsch. Inst., Tex. Assn. Def. Counsel (mem. bus. litig. sect.). Office: Ramey & Flock PC 100 E Ferguson Ste 500 Tyler TX 75702 Office Phone: 903-597-3301. E-mail: derond@rameyflock.com.*

DADAKIS, JOHN D., lawyer; b. NYC, Oct. 9, 1951; s. George and Lois (McKenzie) D.; m. Patty J. Palmieri, June 12, 1982. BA, Johns Hopkins U., 1973; JD, Fordham U., 1976. Bar: NY 1977, Fla. 1977, Calif. 1994. Assoc. Curtis, Mallet-Prevost, Colt & Mosle, NYC, 1976-80, Reavis & McGrath, NYC, 1980-84, ptnr., 1985-88, Fulbright & Jaworski, NYC, 1989, Rogers & Wells, NYC, 1989—99, Clifford Chance, 2000—03, Morrison & Foerster, 2003—05, Schiff Hardin LLP, NYC. Bd. trustees Merrill Lynch Trust Co., 2005—. Dir. Attys. Family-Held Enterprises; bd. dirs. Starlight Found., NY, 1988-93, Believe in Me Found., NY, 1993-03. Named one of Top 100 Attys., Worth mag., 2005. Mem. ABA (chair real property probate and trust sects., spl. problems bus. owners com. 1993-98), Fla. Bar Assn. Office: Schiff Hardin LLP 623 Fifth Ave 28th Fl New York NY 10022 Office Phone: 212-745-0860. Office Fax: 212-753-5044. E-mail: jdadakis@schiffhardin.com.

D'ADDARIO, ALICE MARIE, retired school system administrator; b. NYC, Feb. 9, 1942; d. Ralph and Rose Marie (Ventigmiglia) DeMartino; m. Joseph L. D'Addario, June 27, 1964; children: Joseph R., Paul T. BS in Social Studies, St. John's U., 1962, MS in Secondary Edn., 1963; MA in Liberal Studies, NYU, 1981. Cert. sch. adminstr., secondary educator of English and Social Studies, N.Y. Tchr. social studies So. Huntington Schs., Huntington Station, NY, 1963-83; dept. chair Walt Whitman H.S., Huntington Station, 1983—2005. Adj. prof. Adelphi U., Garden City, N.Y., 1989-02, inservice instr. S. Hungington Tchr. Ctr., 2002-2005; tchg. adv. panelist, program reviewer America, Pathways to the Present, Prentice Hall, 1998, program reviewer, tchr. adv. panel World History, Connections to Today, 1999; counselor Ind. Coll., 1988—; mem. dept. leadership adv. bd. Malloy Coll., 2004—; lead staff developer fed. grant improving the tchg. of Am. history Region 4 NYC Queens Coll.; lead staff developer grant CUNY Rsch. Ctr., Queens Coll.; lead staff developer grant C.W. Post U.; presenter in field. Author: Writing Across the Curriculum, 1988, Participationin Government-A Guide for Teachers I, 1989, II, 1991, Asian Studies Elective Curriculum. PTA pres. P.S. 144 Queens, 1981-83, Russell Sage Jr. High Sch. 190, Queens, 1983-85, Parents Assn. Hillcrest H.S., Queens, 1986-88, Queen's Confederation of Parents, 1987-88; mem. evaluation panel dept. leadership award Molloy Coll., 2004. Recipient Parent Svc. award Hillcrest H.S., Queens, 1986-88, Profl. Recognition award Bd. Edn. South Huntington Schs., 1983, Tchr. of Yr. award Walt Whitman H.S. Parent Assn., 1984, Spl. Tchrs. Are Recognized award Cornell U., 1992, Dartmouth Coll. Freshman Tchr. Recognition award, 1994, Outstanding Social Studies Supr. award L.I. Coun. for the Social Studies, 1997, Disting. Dept. Leader award Molloy Coll., 2004. Mem. L.I. Council for the Social Studies, Assn. Sch. Adminstrs., So. Huntington Chairperson Assn. (v.p. 1985-87, pres. 1987-2005). Democrat. Roman Catholic. Avocations: reading, theater, art museums, bicycling, jogging. Home: 68-47 Harrow St Forest Hills NY 11375-5157 Personal E-mail: aljog29@aol.com.

DADDY YANKEE, (RAYMOND AYALA), musician; b. Río Piedras, PR, Feb. 3, 1977; m. Mirredys Gonzalez, 1994; 3 children. Founder, lead prodr. Los Cangri's Inc., El Cartel Records. Musician: (albums) El Cartel, 2000, El Cartel II, 2001, El Cangri.com, 2002, Los Homerun-es, 2003, Barrio Fino, 2004 (Billboard Latin Music Awards, Reggaeton Album of Yr., 2005, Billboard Music Award, Latin Album of Yr., 2005, Reggaeton Album of Yr., Billboard Latin Music Awards, 2006), The King of New York, 2004, Ahora Le Toca al Cangri Live, 2005, Barrio Fino en Directo, 2005, Tormenta Tropical, Vol. 1, 2006, El Cartel: The Big Boss, 2007, (songs) Mayor Que Yo, 2005 (Reggaeton Song of Yr., Billboard Latin Music Awards, 2006); actor: (films) Vampiros, 2004; actor, exec. prodr. (films) Talento de barrio, 2007. Named Latin Album Artist of Yr., Billboard Music Awards, 2005, Outstanding Male Musical Performer, Nat. Coun. La Raza ALMA award (Am. Latin Media Arts), 2006; named one of 100 Most Influential People, Time Mag., 2006; recipient Albums Artist of Yr. award, Billboard Latin Music Awards, 2006. Office: c/o C+C Artistic Mgmt Calle Yaboa Real #874 Country Club San Juan PR 00924 Office Phone: 787-726-2027, 787-661-5050. Office Fax: 787-276-4132. E-mail: elcartel@gmail.com.

DADISMAN, JOSEPH CARROL, retired newspaper executive; b. Statesboro, Ga., May 24, 1934; s. Howard Dean and Mary Lou (Moore) D.; m. Mildred Jean Sparks, Aug. 19, 1956; children: David Carrol, Ellen Clarice. AB, U. Ga., 1956. Reporter, editorial writer, mng. editor Augusta (Ga.) Chronicle, 1956-66; editor Marietta (Ga.) Daily Jour., 1966-72; mng. editor Macon (Ga.) News, 1972-74; exec. editor, v.p. Columbus (Ga.) Ledger-Enquirer, 1974-80; gen. mgr. Tallahassee Dem., 1980-81, pub., pres., 1981-97; Knight Internat. Press fellow to Russia, 1998. Pres. adv. bd. U. Ga. Sch. Journalism, 1979-81, Fla. A&M U. Sch. Journalism, 1988-90; pres. Jr. Achievement of Columbus-Phenix City, 1977-78, United Way of Leon County, 1985-86, Ga. AP Assn., 1976-77; pres. Cmty. Found. of North Fla., 1997-2001. Served with AUS, 1957-59. Recipient Pub. Svc. award Cobb County C. of C., 1968, Fearless Editl. award Ga. Press Assn., 1963, Outstanding Alumnus award U. Ga. Sch. Journalism, 1994, Disting. Leader award Tallahassee Area C. of C., 1995, meritorious achievement award Fla. A&M U., 1996, Knight-Ridder excellence award in cmty. svc., 1997; named Young Man of Yr., Augusta Jaycees, 1962. Mem. Am. Soc. Newspaper Editors, Fla. Press Assn. (bd. dirs. 1984-86, v.p. 1986-87, pres. 1987-88), So. Newspaper Pubs. Assn. (bd. dirs. 1989-92), Econ. Club Fla. (pres. 1993-94, chmn. 1995-97), Govs. Club (bd. dirs. 2000-02, pres. 2002), Killearn Country Club, Capital Tiger Bay Club, Rotary. Methodist. Home: 1235 Live Oak Plantation Rd Tallahassee FL 32312-2509 E-mail: jcdadisman@aol.com.

DADLEZ, ANNA ROMANA, language educator; arrived in US, 1955; d. Roman Gasowski and Anna Gasowska; m. Tomasz Michal Dadlez, Feb. 11, 1956; children: Eva Maria Zofia, Alexandra Romana. BA, U. Durham, Newcastle on Tyne, England, 1955; MSLS, Syracuse U., NY, 1964, PhD in Polit. Sci., 1973. Cataloger fgn. publs. Syracuse U., Syracuse, NY, 1965—67, instr. Polish lang., 1976; instr. history and polit. sci. Onondaga CC, Syracuse, 1973—76; dir. Inst. Polish Studies, Saginaw Valley State Coll., University Center, Mich., 1976—82; prof. Polish lang., history, polit. sci. Saginaw Valley State U., University Center, Mich., 1976—. Author: (scholarly work) Political and Social Issues in Poland, 1946-85, 1989, (scholaly work, autobiogroplay) Journey from Innocence, 1998, (hist. novel) In Time Of War, 2006. Grantee, Saginaw Valley State U., 2000. Mem.: Mich. Acad. Sci., Arts and Letters (life), Polish Am. Congress. Roman Catholic. Home: 1453 Vermont St Saginaw MI 48602 Office: Saginaw Valley State U 7400 Bay Rd University Center MI 48710 Home Phone: 989-793-1079; Office Phone: 989-964-4315. Business E-Mail: adadlez@svsu.edu.

DADO, DIANE VALENTINA, plastic and reconstructive surgeon; b. Chgo., Feb. 14, 1952; d. Ralph N. and Violet M. Dado; 1 child, Joseph. BA, St. Xavier Coll., Chgo., 1973; MD, Loyola U., Maywood, Ill., 1976. Cert. Am. Bd. Plastic and Reconstructive Surgeery. Intern in surgery Loyola U. Med. Ctr., Maywood, Ill., 1976-77, resident in surgery, 1977-79, resident plastic surgery, 1979-82; fellow plastic surgery Children's Meml. Hosp., Chgo., 1982-83; instr. surgery Stritch Sch. Medicine Loyola U., Maywood, 1983, asst. prof. surgery 1983-89, prof. surgery, pediatrics, 1989—. Mem. plastic surgery rsch. coun. Loyola U. Cleft Palate/Craniofacial Team, 1983—; attending physician Loyola U. Med. Ctr. div. Plastic Surgery, 1983—. children's Meml. Hosp. div. plastic surgery, 1983—. Contbr. articles to profl. jours. Mem. Am. Soc. Plastic and Reconstructive Surgeons, Am. Acad. Pediatrics, ACS, Am. Cleft Palate Assn., Ill. Assn. Craniofacial Teams, Chgo. Soc. Plastic Surgery, Can. Soc. Plastic Surgeons, Desmond A. Kernahan Soc. (founding). Avocations: martial arts, scuba diving, sailing, skiing. Office: Loyola U Med Ctr 2160 S 1st Ave Maywood IL 60153-3304

DADRIAN, VAHAKN NORAIR, retired sociology educator; b. Istanbul, Turkey, May 26, 1926; came to U.S., 1947, naturalized, 1961; s. Hagop and Mayreni (Der Garabedian) D. Student (Alexander von Humboldt fellow), U. Berlin, Germany, U. Vienna, Austria; student (scholar), U. Zurich, Switzerland; MA, Wayne State U., 1950; PhD (Reynolds fellow), U. Chgo., 1954. Asst. prof. sociology Washington Coll., Chestertown, Md., 1955-56, Boston U., 1957-59; rsch. fellow Harvard Ctr. for Middle Eastern Studies, 1961-62; sr. analyst dept. strategic studies div. missiles and space Raytheon, 1962-63; lectr. Boston Coll., 1963-65; asso. prof. Wis. State U., Superior, 1965-67, Fla. Atlantic U., 1967-68, prof., 1968-70, SUNY, Geneseo, 1970-91; dir. genocide study project H.F. Guggenheim Found., Conesus, N.Y., 1991—. Vis. scholar Mass. Inst. Tech. Ctr. Internat. Studies, 1960-61; guest rschr. Inst. for Rsch. on Soviet Union, Munich, Germany, summer 1962; participant, Am. Sociol. Assn. grantee 6th World Congress of Sociology, Evian, France, fall 1966; vis. prof. Duke, summer 1971; dir. genocide study project NSF, 1977—; lectr. at univs., confs. and on TV in, U.S., Europe, Soviet Union, S.Am. Contbg. author: World Book Ency., 1972—, Encyclopedia of Genocide, 1999, Encylopedia Mondiale des génocides, 2001, Encylopedia of Genocide and Crimes Against Humanity, 2005; Cons. editor: Internat. Jour. Contemporary Soc; translator, editor: United and Independent Turania (Zarevand), 1971; Contbr. articles to profl. jours., newspapers. Recipient Wis. U. Bd. Regents award, 1966, St. Vardan medal for scholarship in field of Soviet nationalities Cardinal Aghadjanian, Rome, 1968, Ellis Island medal of honor, 2005, Lifetime Achievement award Internat. Assn. Genocide Scholars, 2005, Lifetime Achievement award Scholars Conf. on the Holocaust and the Churches, 2005, Fridjof Nanson Gold medal Humanitarian Svcs. award, 2006Hrant Dink Freedom award ABA, 2007; grantee Harvard Lab. Social Rels., 1959, Am. Philos. Soc., 1961, Am. Com. Travel, 1962, Wenner-Gren Found., 1963, 65, Am. Coun. Learned Socs., summer 1966, NSF, 1968, 73, 76, SUNY, 1974, H.F. Guggenheim Found., 1990-91. Mem. Delta Tau Kappa (hon.) Home: PO Box 99 Conesus NY 14435-0099 Office: Genocide Rsch Zoryan Inst PO Box 99 Conesus NY 14435-0099

DADY, ROBERT EDWARD, lawyer; b. NYC, Nov. 11, 1936; s. Edward Joseph and Florence (Scheidt) D.; m. Mollie D. Richman; children: Michael, Andrew, Rachel. BA, Queens Coll., 1958; LLB, Fordham U., 1961. Bar: N.Y. 1962, Fla. 1974. Asst. gen. counsel The Equity Corp., NYC, 1962-66; gen. atty. ITT_Levitt and Sons, Inc., Washington, Lake Success, NY, 1966-70; sr. v.p.-legal First Realty Investment Corp., Miami Beach, Fla., 1970-71; v.p.-legal, sec. Cavanagh Cmtys. Corp., Miami, Fla., 1971-75; ptnr. Mann & Dady, P.A., Miami, 1975-80, Mann, Dady, Corrigan & Zelman, P.A., Miami, 1980-83, Dady, Siegfried & Kipnis, P.A., Miami, 1984-85; pvt. practice Miami, 1985-87; ptnr. Kimbrell and Hamann, P.A., 1987-89; shareholder Popham, Haik, Schnobrich & Kaufman, Ltd., 1990-96; of counsel Fieldstone, Lester, Shear & Denberg, Coral Gables, Fla.,

1996—. Past adj. prof. law U. Miami Sch. Law.; bd. dirs. Spectrum Programs, Inc., pres., 1984-86, Spectrum Found., Inc., pres. 1988—. Author: Land Acquistion and Development, 1975. Bd. dirs., exec. comm. Miami Coalition for a Safe and Drug Free Cmty., 1992-99; vice-chmn. Childrens Home Soc. Found. Miami, 1993-96, bd. dirs., 1993-2004; appointed to (by gov.) Fla. Jud. Nom. Com., 1995-98; bd. dirs. Wellness Cmty., Greater Miami, 2001-06. Mem. Nat. Land Coun. (pres. 1974-81, vice chmn. bd. dirs. 1973—), Builders Assn. So. Fla. (life dir., gen. counsel 1982-2001), ABA (environ. law com., timesharing and recreation law com., vice chmn. 2004), Fla. Bar Assn. Democrat. Home: 8440 SW 143rd St Village of Palmetto Bay FL 33158-1457 Office: Fieldstone Lester Shear & Denberg Sun Trust Plaza 201 Alhambra Cir Ste 601 Coral Gables FL 33134-5107 Office Phone: 305-357-1001. Business E-Mail: bd@flsdlaw.com.

DAEHLER, MARVIN WILLIAM, psychology professor; s. Vernon C. and Rosy F. Daehler; m. June Kelsen, Aug. 28, 1965; children: Curtis C., Joshua E., Renee E. AB, U. Ill., Champaign Urbana, 1964; PhD, U. Minn., Mpls., 1968. Asst. prof. U. Mass., Amherst, 1968—74, assoc. prof., 1974—83, prof., 1983—. Fellow: APA; mem.: Soc. Rsch. in Child Devel. Achievements include research in cognitive development. Office: U Mass Dept Psychology Box 37710 Amherst MA 01003-7710 Home Phone: 413-253-3268; Office Phone: 413-545-2429.

DAEHN, GLENN STEVEN, materials scientist; b. Chgo., July 4, 1961; s. Ralph Charles and Beverly S. (Shanske) D.; m. Margaret A. Burkhart, Oct. 25, 1987; children: Andrew Joseph, Katrin Ellen, Matthew Charles. BS, Northwestern U., Evanston, Ill., 1983; MS, Stanford U., Calif., 1985, PhD, 1988. Rsch. asst. Stanford U., Palo Alto, Calif., 1983-87; asst. prof. dept. materials sci. and engring. Ohio State U., Columbus, 1987-92, assoc. prof. dept. materials sci. and engring., 1992-96, Fontana prof. dept. materials sci. and engring., 1996—. Co-founder, v.p. technology Excera Materials Group, 1992-2007. Co-editor: Modeling the Deformation of Crystalline Solids, 1991. Named Nat. Young Investigator, NSF, 1992; recipient Young Investigator award Army Rsch. Office, 1992, R.L. Hardy Gold medal TMS, 1992, Marcus Grossman award ASM Internat., 1990. Mem. ASM Internat., Am. Ceramic Soc., Materials Rsch. Soc., Minerals, Metals and Materials Soc. Achievements include description and practical applications of how temperature changes accelerate the deformation of composite materials; co-development of new class of ceramic-metal composites; development of hyperplasticity --practical application of extended metal ductility observed at high velocity. Home: 2076 Fairfax Rd Upper Arlington OH 43221-4319 Office: Ohio State U Materials Sci Dept 2041 N College Rd Columbus OH 43210-1124 Office Phone: 614-292-6779. Business E-Mail: Daehn.1@osu.edu.

DAEMMRICH, HORST SIGMUND, German language and literature educator; b. Pausa, Germany, Jan. 5, 1930; s. Arthur M. and Gertrud A. (Orlamunde) D.; m. Ingrid H. Guenther, June 10, 1962; children: JoAnn, Arthur. AB, Wayne State U., Detroit, 1958, MA, 1959; PhD, U. Chgo., 1964. Instr. U. Chgo., 1961-62; asst. prof. Germanic langs. and lits. Wayne State U., Detroit, 1962-66, assoc. prof., 1967-70, prof., 1971-80; prof., chair U. Pa., 1981-98. Resident dir. Jr. Year Inst. at U. Freiburg, Germany, 1972-73 Author: The Shattered Self, 1973, Literaturkritik in Theorie und Praxis, 1974 (with Ingrid Daemmrich) Wiederholte Spiegelungen, Themen und Motive in der Literatur, 1978, Karl Krolow, 1980, Wilhelm Raabe, 1981, Themes and Motifs in Western Literature: A Handbook, 1987, Themen und Motive in der Literatur, 1987, 2d edit, 1995, Spirals and Circles: A Key to Thematic Patternsn in Classicism and Realism, 2 vols., 1994, Themen and Motive in der Literatur, Handbuch, 1995; editor: The Challenge of German Literature, 1971, Studies on Themes and Motifs in Literature, 1990; gen. editor: Studies on Themes and Motifs in Literature, 1991-2005, 76 vols.; contbr. articles to profl. jours. Mem. Am. Soc. Aesthetics, Acad. Lit. Studies, Am. Lessing Soc., Am. Assn. Tchrs. German (mem. commn. on higher edn. 1974—), Am. Comparative Lit. Assn., MLA (sec. and chmn. 19th century lit. 1972-73), Midwest MLA (sec., chmn. modern Germanic lit. 1966-67), Phi Beta Kappa. Home: 307 Suffolk Rd Flourtown PA 19031-2119 Office: U Pa Dept Germanic Langs Philadelphia PA 19104-6305 Business E-Mail: hdaemmri@sas.upenn.edu.

DAENZER, BERNARD JOHN, insurance company executive, consultant; b. NYC, Jan. 15, 1916; s. Bernard Cornelius and Amelia Catherine (Heinze) D.; m. Valerie Antoinette Lee, June 8, 1941 (dec. Feb. 29, 2004); children: Peter, Jean Daenzer Aiken, John, Richard (dec.). AB, Fordham Coll., 1937, JD, 1942; LLD, Coll. Ins. NYC, 1981. Spl. agt. Loyalty Group, Westchester, NY, 1937-43; with Security-Conn. Group, 1943-57, exec. v.p., 1955-57; pres. Wohlreich & Anderson Ltd., Cranford, NJ, 1957-81. Dir. Alexander Howden Group Ltd., London, 1968-81; underwriter Lloyds of London, 1968-04; dir. emeritus RLI Corp., Peoria, Ill., 1972-07. Columnist: Weekly Underwriter, 1964-86; author 11 books, also other publs. and mystery stories. Trustee Loman Found., Malvern, Pa. Served with USNR, 1944-46. Mem.: Soc. Chartered Property and Casualty Underwriters, Coll. Ins. N.Y.C., Racquet Club, Card Sound Country Club, Ocean Reef Club. Republican. Roman Catholic. Office: Ocean Reef 29 Angelfish Cay Dr Key Largo FL 33037-5271 Office Fax: 305-367-3354. Personal E-mail: bjdlondon@aol.com.

DAFERMOS, CONSTANTINE MICHAEL, applied mathematics professor; b. Athens, Greece, May 26, 1941; came to U.S., 1964; s. Michael Constantine and Sophia (Raptarchis) D.; m. Stella Theodoracopoulos, Sept. 6, 1964; children: Thalia, Michael. Diploma, Athens Nat. Tech. U., 1964; PhD, Johns Hopkins U., 1967. Fellow Johns Hopkins U., 1967-68; asst. prof. Cornell U., 1968-71; assoc. prof. Brown U., 1971-76, prof. applied math., 1976—, Univ. prof., 1988—, dir. Lefschetz Ctr. for Dynamical Systems, 1988-94. Author: Hyperbolic Conservation Laws in Continuum Physics, 2000; mem. editl. bd. Archive for Rational Mechanics and Analysis, 1972—, Jour. of Thermal Stresses, 1978-2000, Quar. Applied Math., 1985—, Math. Modeling and Numerical Analysis, 1986-96, Proc. Royal Soc. Edinburgh, 1987—, Advances Math. Applied Sci., 1989—, Math. Models and Methods, 1990-97, Comm. on Applied Nonlinear Analysis, 1995—, , Ricerche di Matematica, 1997—, Jour. Am. Math. Soc., 1999—, Revista Matematica Complutense, 2000, Jour. Dynamics and Differential Equations, 2002--; contbr. articles to profl. jours. NSF grantee, 1970—, Office Naval Rsch. grantee, 1972-80, 92—, USAF grantee, 1972-73, U.S. Army grantee, 1973-96. Mem. Soc. Natural Philosophy (treas. 1975-76, chmn. 1977-78), Am. Math. Soc., Acad. of Athens, Am. Acad. Arts and Scis. Office: Brown U Lefschetz Ctr Dynamical Sys 182 George St Providence RI 02912-9056 E-mail: dafermos@dam.brown.edu.

DAFFORN, GEOFFREY ALAN, biochemist; b. Cunningham, Kans., Feb. 4, 1944; s. Francis Elston and Anna Elizabeth Dafforn; m. Gail McLaughlin, July 14, 1973; 1 child, Christine Elizabeth. BA cum laude, Harvard U., 1966; PhD, U. Calif., Berkeley, 1970. Postdoctoral fellow U. Calif., Berkeley, 1973; asst. prof. U. Tex., Austin, 1974; from asst. prof. to assoc. prof. Bowling Green (Ohio) State U., 1974-81; sr. chemist Syva Co., Palo Alto, Calif., 1982-87, rsch. fellow, 1987—, group mgr., 1999—2000; prin. scientist Nugen Techs., San Carlos, Calif., 2001—04; lectr. dept. chemistry Santa Clara U., Calif., 2005—. Author articles and abstracts; patentee in field. Grantee Army Rsch. Office, 1979-82, Am. Chem. Soc., 1975-80. Mem. AAAS, Am. Chem. Soc., Sierra Club. Office: Santa Clara U Dept Chemistry 500 El Camino Real Santa Clara CA 95053 E-mail: gdafforn@scu.edu.

DAFFRON, MARYELLEN, retired librarian; b. Richmond, Va., Nov. 12, 1946; d. William Charles and Ellen (Ahern) D.; m. Newton J. Frank. BA, Coll. Mt. St. Joseph on Ohio, Cin., 1968; MLS, Drexel U., 1970. Libr. Richmond Pub. Libr., 1969-73, FMC, Washington, 1973—93; with U.S. Immigration and Naturalization Svc. Office of Gen. Counsel, Washington, 1993—2003; law libr. Office of Prin. Legal Advisor, U.S. Immigration and Customs Enforcement, Washington, 2003—05, ret., 2005. Vol. No. Va. Hotline, Arlington, 1974-79. City of Richmond fellow, 1968. Mem.: Beta Phi Mu. Roman Catholic.

DAFOE, WILLEM, actor; b. Appleton, Wis., July 22, 1955; s. William Dafoe; 1 child. Student, U. Wis. Mem. Theatre X theatrical co., 1975, co-founder, The Wooster Group theatrical co., N.Y.C., 1977—. Actor (feature films) The Loveless, 1983, The Hunger, 1983, New York Nights, 1984, Roadhouse 66, 1984, Streets of Fire, 1984, To Live and Die in L.A., 1985, Platoon, 1986 (Acad. award nomination 1987), The Last Temptation of Christ, 1988, Off Limits, 1988, Mississippi Burning, 1988, Triumph of the Spirit, 1989, Born on the Fourth of July, 1989, Cry-Baby, Flight of the Intruder, Wild at Heart, 1990, White Sands, 1992, Light Sleeper, 1992, Body of Evidence, 1992, Far Away So Close!, 1993, The Night and the Moment, 1994, Clear and Present Danger, 1994, Tom and Viv, 1995, Victory, 1995, The English Patient, 1996, Basquiat, 1996, Speed 2: Cruise Control, 1997, Affliction, 1997, New Rose Hotel (also co-prod.), 1998, Lulu on the Bridge, 1998, eXisten Z, 1998, American Psycho, 1999, The Boondock Saints, 1999, Bullfighter, 2000, The Animal Factory, 2000, Shadow of the Vampire, 2000 (Oscar Nomination for Best Actor in a Supporting Role, 2000), The Gangs of New York, 2000, Pavillion of Women, 2001, Edges of the Lord, 2001, Spider-Man, 2002, Auto-Focus, 2002, Finding Nemo (voice only), 2003, Once Upon A Time in Mexico, 2003, Camel Cricket City (voice only), 2003, The Reckoning, 2004, The Clearing, 2004, Spider-Man 2, 2004, The Life Aquatic with Steve Zissou, 2004, The Aviator, 2004, Ripley Under Ground, 2005, Control, 2005, xXx: State of the Union, 2005, Inside Man, 2006, Am. Dreamz, 2006; TV appearances: The Hitchhiker, 1985, The Simpsons (voice only), 1997. Recipient Donostia prize, San Sebastian Film Fstival, 2005 Only actor to ever be nominated for an Oscar for playing a vampire.

DAGENAIS, SIMON, chiropractor, epidemiologist; b. Hull, Que., Can., Apr. 1, 1975; s. Jean-Pierre and Suzanne Dagenais. DC, PhD, LA Coll. Chiropractic/U. Calif., Irvine, 2005. Rsch. dir. CAM Rsch. Inst., Irvine, 2000—; scientist CHEO Rsch. Inst., Ottawa, Ont., Canada, 2005—. Editor: Principles and Practice of Chiropractic, 3rd edit., 2004. Mem.: N.Am. Spine Soc. Home Phone: 613-321-0736. Personal E-mail: simon@camresearch.com.

DAGIT, CHARLES EDWARD, JR., architect, educator; b. Phila., July 1, 1943; s. Charles E. and Janet (Donnelly) D.; m. Alice M. Murdoch, June 3, 1967; children: Charles Edward, J. Murdoch. BA, U. Pa., 1965, B.Arch., 1967, M.Arch., 1968. Registered architect, Pa., N.Y., N.J., Conn., Va., Md., Vt. Designer Henry D. Dagit & Sons, Phila., 1965-68, Mitchell, Giurgola Assocs., Phila., 1968-69; project designer Henry D. Dagit & Sons, Phila., 1969-70; ptnr. Dagit Saylor Architects, Phila., 1970—. Adj. asst. prof. Sch. Arch. and Engring., Temple U., 1973-80; adj. prof. dept. arch. Phila. Coll. Art, 1979-80; vis. prof. U. Pa., 1980; prof. dept. arch. Drexel U. Prin. works include Peale House of Pa. Acad. Fine Arts (Design award Phila. chpt. AIA 1983, Merit award Pa. Mus. and Hist. Com.), Agrl. Arena at Pa. State U. (Silver medal Pa. State U. 1985, Design award Phila. chpt. AIA 1985), Spring Garden Health Ctr. (runner-up for Rudi Brunner award), Phoenix City Ctr. for Arts (NEA grant), 1983, Cumberland Union Bldg. Shippensburg U. (Phila. chpt. AIA Design award 1992, Design award PSA 1992), Bartram's Garden (Pa. Mus. and Hist. Commn. Preservation award 1993), Campus Ctr. Bldg. Haverford Coll. (Phila. chpt. AIA Design award 1994, Design award PSA 1994, F.W. Olin Bldg. (Phila. chpt. AIA Design award 1992, Design award PSA 1992), Pa. Ballet (Design award PSA 1989), Gwynedd Mercy Coll. Lourdes Libr. Addition (Phila. chpt. AIA Design award 1986), Magee Rehab. Hosp. (Phila. chpt. Design award 1984), Logan Mus. Anthropology, Beloit Coll. (Phila. chpt. AIA Design award 1995, Internat. Illumination Design award, Preservation award WI Preservation Trust 1995), Grove Hall, Coll. Bus. Bldg., Shippensburg U. (Design award Phila. chpt. AIA 1999, Silver award Commonwealth Design Awards 10,000 Friends Pa. 2004, Honor award Phila. chpt. AIA 2005). Pres. Gladwyne Civic Assn., 1981-82; pres. Friends of St. Christopher's Hosp., Phila., 1977-78; trustee Bryn Mawr. (Pa.) Country Day Sch., 1975-79; bd. dirs. Phila. Zool. Soc., 1979-87; pres. bd. trustees Gladwyne Libr. Bd., 1990-91; trustee Acad. Cmty. Music, 1997—. Recipient Design award Progressive Architecture, 1974, 40 Under 40 award A&U Mag., Japan, 1977, View of World Contemporary Architecture award Japan Architect, 1977; winner nat. design competition Cultural Arts Pavillion, Newport News, Va., 1985. Fellow: AIA (pres.-elect Phila. chpt. 1989, pres. Phila. chpt. 1990, chair Nat. Design Conf. commn. on architecture for arts and recreation 1976, chair Nat. Design Conf. commn. on design Louis I. Kahn & Phila. Sch. 1991, chmn. designate commn. on design 1992, vice chmn. commn. design 1993, chmn. commn. design 1994, AIA PA chmn. leadership forum 2003—04, Silver medal Phila. chpt. 1976, Gold medal 1978, Silver medal 1985); mem.: AIA PA PAC (vice chmn. 2003—04, vice chair 2005, chmn. 2006), Facilities Planning Acad., Soc. Coll. and Univ. Planners, The Carpenters Co., U. Pa. Spinx Sr. Soc. (bd. dirs. 1973—76), Mask and Wig Club, Merion Golf Club (Ardmore, Pa.), Downtown Club Phila. (bd. dirs. 1986—89). Republican. Roman Catholic. Home: 381 Williamson Rd Gladwyne PA 19035-1618 Office: Dagit Saylor Architects 100 S Broad St Ste 1100 Philadelphia PA 19110-1003 Business E-Mail: cdagit@dagitsaylor.com.

DAGLIS, LISA GENINE, deputy attorney general; b. Northridge, Calif., Feb. 28, 1969; d. Abraham and Rosalynd Rohrberger; m. John P. Daglis, Apr. 21, 1988; 1 child, Brett John. AA pre law, Atlantic C.C., Mays Landing, NJ, 1985; BA Govt. and Politics, Widener U., Chester, Pa., 1997; JD, Widener U. Law Sch., Wilmington, Del., 2003. Bar: N.J. 2003. Staff South Jersey Legal Svcs., Atlantic City, 2004; law clk. Superior Ct. N.J., Mays Landing, 2004—; dep. atty. gen. State of NJ, 2006—. Legal aid vol. South Jersey Legal Svcs., 2004; campaign vol. Rep. Club, Atlantic County, Hamilton Twp., NJ. Recipient Zelda K. Hermann award, Widener Sch. of Law, 2003. Mem.: ABA, U. S.Holocaust Meml. Mus. Soc., So. Poverty Law Ctr., Phi Kappa Phi. Avocations: sailing, interior decorating, painting. Office Phone: 609-633-2038.

DAGNON, JAMES BERNARD, human resources executive; b. St. Paul, Jan. 31, 1940; s. James Lavern and Margaret Elizabeth D.; m. Sandra Ann McGinley, June 4, 1960; children: Sheri T. Dagnon Tice, Terry J., Laurie M. Zinn, Diana L. Felner. BS in Bus. with distinction, U. Minn., St. Paul, 1979, cert. in Indsl. Rels., 1978. Various clerical positions No. Pacific Ry. Co., St. Paul, 1957-70; supr., then mgr. pers. rsch. and stats. Burlington No. R.R. Co., St. Paul, 1970, mgr. manpower planning, 1970-78, dir. compensation and orgnl. planning, 1978-81; asst. v.p. compensation and benefits Burlington No. Inc., Seattle, 1981-84, from v.p. labor rels. to exec. v.p. employee rels. Ft. Worth, 1984-95; sr. v.p. employee rels. Burlington No. Santa Fe Rlwy. Co., Ft. Worth, 1995-97; sr. v.p. people The Boeing Co., Seattle, 1997—2002; pres. Christian Living Inst., 2004. Bd. dirs. Inroads Inc., Seattle Inroads Inc.; chmn. Corp. Champions, Ft. Worth, 1994—96; trustee Cook-Ft. Worth Children's Med. Ctr., 1995—97; bd. dirs. United Way Met. Tarrant County, 1995—97, Wash. State Gov.'s Commn. on Higher Edn. in 2020; trustee Bellevue C.C., 1999—2006; bd. dirs., trustee Wash. Early Learning Found., 1999—2003; pres. Cath. Evang. Outreach, Seattle, 1981—84, Christian Living Inst., 2004—; bd. dirs. Western Wash. Cath. Charismatic Renewal, 2004—. Capt. USAR, 1957—70. Fellow Nat. Acad. Human Resources; mem. Beta Gamma Sigma. Republican. Avocations: scuba diving, photography. Home: PO Box 605 Medina WA 98039-0605

D'AGOSTINO, JAMES SAMUEL, JR., corporate financial executive; b. Balt., July 4, 1946; s. James Samuel and Betty Ann (List) D'A.; m. Diane Martin Greener, Sept. 25, 1971; children: James Martin, Ann Diestel. BS in Econs., Villanova U., 1968; JD, Seton Hall Sch. Law, Newark, 1974; postgrad., Harvard U., 1993. Bar: N.J. 1974, Tex. 1979. Trust officer Fidelity Union Trust Co., Newark, 1968-73; asst. treas. The Chase Manhattan Bank, N.A., NYC, 1973-76; v.p. Citibank/Citicorp, Houston, 1976-86; v.p., treas. Am. Gen. Corp., Houston, 1986-90, sr. v.p. investor rels., 1990-91, sr. v.p. adminstrn., 1991-93, exec. v.p. adminstrn., 1993; pres., CEO Am. Gen. Life and Accident Ins. Co., Nashville, 1993-95, chmn., CEO, 1995-97; pres. Am. Gen. Corp., Houston, 1997-98; vice-chmn., group exec. Consumer Fin. Am. Gen. Corp., Houston, 1998-99; chmn., pres., CEO Encore Bank, 1999—. Republican. Presbyterian. Office: Encore Bank 9 Greenway Plaza Ste 1000 Houston TX 77046 Office Phone: 713-787-3103. E-mail: jdagostino@encorebank.com.

D'AGOSTINO, RALPH BENEDICT, mathematician, statistician, educator, consultant; b. Somerville, Mass., Aug. 16, 1940; s. Bennedetto and Carmela (Piemonte) D'A.; m. Lei Lanie Carta, Aug. 28, 1965; children: Ralph Benedict, Lei Lanie Maria. AB, Boston U., 1962, MA, 1964; PhD, Harvard U., 1968. Lectr. math. Boston U., 1964-68, asst. prof., 1968-71, assoc. prof., 1971-76, lectr. law, 1975-91, assoc. dean Grad. Sch., 1976-78, prof. math. and stats., 1976—, prof. pub. health, 1982—, dir. data analysis and stats. Framingham Heart Study, 1985—, chmn. dept. math., 1986-91, 2006—, dir. stats. cons. unit, 1986—, dir. Biostats MA/PhD Program, 1988—, prof. law, 1991—2004; adj. prof. Tufts U., 2004—. Mem. clin. care rsch. Tufts U., 1990—; exec. dir. data mgmt. and biostats. Harvard Clin. Rsch. Inst., 2002—; vis. lectr. Am. Statis. Assn., 1975-86, 88-92; vis. prof. biostats. clin. epidiology unit Univ. Hosp., Geneva, 1993; Rankin vis. prof. U. Wis., 1995; spl. lectr. clin. trials symposium U. Fla., 1995; vis. scientist NHLBI, 1993; Lowell Reed lectr. APHA, 1996; Remington lectr. AHA CV-EPI, 2006; spl. scientist Boston City Hosp., 1981-95, Boston Med. Ctr., 1996—, New Eng. Med. Ctr., 1990—; mem. Health Inst. New Eng. Med. Ctr., 1990—; cons. stats. United Brands, 1968-76, Diabetes and Arthritis Control Unit, Boston, 1971-75, City of Somerville, Mass., 1972, ednl. Harvard U. Dental Sch., 1969, Lahey Clinic Found., 1973-85, Walden Rsch., 1974-79, FDA Biometrics Divsn. and Over-the-Counter Divsn., 1975—, Cardio and Renal Divsn. FDA, 1987—, Gastrointestinal Drug Divsn., FDA, 1994-96, Medical Devise Divsn. 1999—, Oncology Drugs Divsn., 2002—, Arnold & Porter, 1980, Bedford Rsch. Assn., 1976-81, Corneal Scis., 1976, Biotek, 1979-88, GCA, 1979-87, Lever Bros., 1982-87, Conrail, 1981, FBI, 1984, Ctr. Psychiat. Rehab., Boston U., 1985-2004, NIMH, 1985, Dade Clin. Assays, 1986-90, Millipore, 1983-92, VLI Corp., 1985-90, New Eng. Coll. Optometry, 1985-93, Dupont Corp., 1985, Bristol Myers, 1986, 93, Cheeseborough Ponds, 1987-96, med. decision making divsn. and health svcs. rsch. unit Tufts New Eng. Med. Ctr., 1986—, Am. Inst. Rsch. in Social Scis., 1983-88, New Eng. Rsch. Insts., 1987-92, Thompson Med., 1987-96, Merck, Sharpe and Dohme, 1988-94, Carter Ctr., Emory U., 1969-75, Unilever, 1991-96, 99-, Miles, 1991-95, Ultra Fem., 1991-93, Health Effects Inst., 1992-2001, Forsyth Dental Clinic, 1992-93, 95—, Bard Vascular, 1990-95, Ultra Slim Fast, 1990-95, Block Med., 1993-95, Bayer Pharm., 1993-98, 2004-, Astra Pharm., 1993-97, Cytyc, 1993-97, Regua, 1994-96, SmithKline Beechman, 1994-95, Proctor and Gamble, 1994-96, 2000—, Sandoz, 1994-96, R W Johnson Pharms., 1997, Mass. Med. Assistance, 1995-97, Cambridge Heart, 1996—2000, Merck/ Johnson & Johnson, 1999—2007, Aventis, 2000—, Ajinomoto, 2000, Discovery Lab, 2000— Pfizer, 2000-, Vertex, 2005-, Gention, 2005-; mem. various FDA coms. including fertility and maternal health drugs adv. com, 1978-81, life support subcom., 1979-81, drug abuse adv. com., 1987-90, gastrointestinal drugs adv. com., 1990-94, nonprescriptive drug adv. com., 1995-99, 2007-, chair, 1996-98; cons. various FDA coms., Cardio-Renal com., 1995-98, arthritis com., 1997-, ob-gyn. devices, 2002-, oncological drugs com., 2004-; mem. task force on design and analysis of dental and oral rsch., 1979-2003, Harvard U. health tech. com., 1986-90; mem. Honolulu Heart Study Adv. Com., NIH, 1989-96, Balt. Longitudinal Study of Aging Adv. Com., 1990, NIH Consensus Panel on Liver Transplantation, 1983, Consensus Panel on Fresh Frozen Plasma, 1984, Consensus Panel on Geriatric Assessment Methods for Clin. Decision Making, 1987; mem. task force Office Tech. Assessment, 1980; mem. consensus panel on intraoral techniques ADA, 1990; mem. study sect. Agy. for Health Care Policy and Rsch., 1990-94; mem. Bethesda Conf. on Matching Intensity of Risk Factor Mgmt. With the Hazard for Coronary Disease Events, 1996; prin., co-prin. investigator or sr. statistician on grants Nat. Ctr. Health Svcs. Rsch., 1976-82, NHLBI, 1982—, USAF, 1980-85, Nat. Cancer Inst., 1985—, Nat. Inst. Criminal Justice, 1982-85, Nat. Ctr. Child Abuse and Neglect, 1982-85, Robert Wood Johnson Found., 1981-85, Social Security Adminstrn., 1982-86, 90-93, Motor Vehicles Mem. Assn., 1987, NIOSH, 1985, Nat. Insts. Aging, 1986—, Agency for Health Care Policy and Rsch., 1989—; grant and contract reviewer NAS, 1979—, Nat. Ctr. Health Svcs. Rsch., 1976, 89, NIH, 1983—, NSF, 1987-95, AHCPR, 1990; co-prin. investigator Framingham Heart Study, 1993-; chair spl. emphasis panel reviewing small bus. grant proposal Nat. Inst. Dental Rsch., 1996. Author: (with E.E. Cureton) Factor Analysis, An Applied Approach, 1983, (with Shuman and Wolf) Mathematical Modeling, Applications in Emergency Health Services, 1984, (with Stephens) Goodness of Fit Techniques, 1986, (with D. Schiff) Practical Engineering Statistics, 1996, (with Sullivan and Beiser) Introductory Applied Biostatistics, 2004, Tutorials in Biostatistics, 2005; assoc. editor Am. Statistician, 1972-76, Jour. Am. Statis. Assn., 1993-96; editor Emergency Health Svc. Rev., 1981-88, Stats. in Medicine (biostat. tutorials), 1993—, Stats. in Medicine, 1997—; mem. editl. bd. Biostatistica, 1990-99, Jour. Hypertension, 2004—; cons. Jour. New Eng. Medicine; editor Encyclopedia of CLinical Trials; book reviewer Houghton-Mifflin, Holden, Day, Duxbury Press, Prentice Hall, 1969; contbr. over 500 articles to profl. jours.; co-developer instrument for predicting acute ischemic health disease, stroke health risk appraisal function and coronary heart disease risk assessment function, global cardiovacular disease risk function. Recipient Spl. citation FDA Commr., 1981, 95, Metcalf awrd for excellence in teaching Boston U., 1985; Am. Heart Assn. fellow, 1991; pre-doctoral fellow NIH, 1962-68. Fellow Am. Statis. Assn. (pres. Boston chpt. 1972, v.p. 1971, mem. nat. coun. 1973-75, vis. lectr. 1976-78, 80—, Statistician of Yr. Boston chpt. 1993, chmn. sect. Health Policy Stats. 1996, chmn. sect. Epidemiology 2003); mem. APHA (Lowell Reed lectr. 1996, chmn. sect. emergency health svcs. 1982-83, governing coun. 1983-85), Am. Heart Assn. (Remington lectr., mem. cardiovasc. epidemiology coun. 2006), Inst. Math. Stats., Am. Soc. Quality Control, Biometrics Soc. (mem. regional adv. com. 1989-94), Phi Beta Kappa, Sigma Xi. Roman Catholic. Home: 5 Everett Ave Winchester MA 01890-3523 Office: Boston U Statistics & Cons Unit 111 Cummington St Boston MA 02215-2411 Office Phone: 617-353-2767. Business E-Mail: ralph@bu.edu.

D'AGOSTINO, THOMAS PAUL, federal agency administrator; m. Beth Ann Alemany; 2 children. BS, U.S. Naval Acad., 1980; MS, Johns Hopkins U., 1992, Naval War Coll., 1997. Various assignments US Dept. Energy, 1989—, program mgr. SEAWOLF submarine propulsion sys. naval sea sys. command, dep. dir. nuc. weapons rsch. and devel program., asst. dep. adminstr. program integration, dep. adminstr. for def. programs, Nat. Nuclear Security Adminstrn., 2006—07, dir. stockpile stewardship program, 2006—07, adminstr. Nat. Nuclear Security Adminstrn., 2007—, under sec. for nuclear security, 2007—. Capt. USNR. Decorated Navy Commendation Medal with Gold Stars, Navy Achievement Medal, Navy Expeditionary Medal, Meritorious Unit Commendation, Nat. Def. Svc. Medal, Predl. Rank Meritorious Exec. award, numerous others. Office: US Dept Energy Nat Nuclear Security Adminstrn 1000 Independence Ave SW Rm 7A-199 Washington DC 20585 E-mail: thomas.dagostino@nnsa.doe.gov.*

DAGUM, ALEXANDER B., plastic surgeon; MD, U. Ottawa, 1987. Diplomate in plastic surgery and surgery of the hand Am. Bd. Plastic Surgery. Resident in plastic surgery U. Toronto, fellow in microsurgery, hand and microsurgery; fellow hand and microsurgery SUNY, Stony Brook, assoc. prof., 2000—. Lectr. U. Toronto, 1995—2000; pres. Ont. Soc. Plastic Surgeons, 1999—2000; sect. chair plastic surgery Ont. Med. Assn., 1999—2000. Named one of Medical Marvels, NY Mag., 2006. Fellow: ACS, Royal Coll. Physicians and Surgeons (Can.) (cert. in plastic surgery). Office: Stony Brook Univ T-18 Health Sciences Ctr Stony Brook NY 11794-8181 also: 37 Research Way East Setauket NY 11733-3465 Office Phone: 631-444-8210. Office Fax: 631-444-8894. E-mail: alexander.dagum@stonybrook.edu.*

DAHAN, ANDRE, telecommunications industry executive; b. Mar. 16, 1949; B in Computer Sci., Jerusalem Inst. Tech. Pres. Dun & Bradstreet U.S., 1997—99; pres. N. Am. & global accounts The Dun & Bradstreet Corp., 1999—2000, sr. v.p. electronic commerce, 2000—01; pres. eccelerate.com, Inc., 1999—2001; pres. mobile multimedia svcs. AT&T Wireless Svcs., Inc., Redmond, Wash., 2001—04; pres., CEO Comverse Tech., Inc., Woodbury, NY, 2007—. Bd. dirs. PalmSource, Inc., 2005—, Red Bend Software, 2006—, Comverse Tech., Inc., 2007—. Office: Comverse Tech Inc 909 Third Ave New York NY 10022

DAHAN, RENE, retired oil industry executive; b. Aug. 26, 1941; Diploma in nautical sci., Sch. Hydrogeography, Bordeaux, France. Process technician Esso, Rotterdam, The Netherlands, 1963-73, mgr., 1973-74, mgr. refining dept., 1974-77; head corp. planning divsn. Esso Europe, London, 1977-78, mgr. natural gas dept., 1978-81; dep. mgr. petroleum products dept. Exxon Corp., 1981-83; exec. v.p. Esso B.V., Breda, The Netherlands, 1983-85, pres. CEO, 1985-91; exec. v.p. ECI, 1991-92; corp. v.p., pres. ECI Exxon Corp., 1992-95, sr. v.p., 1995-98, Exxon Mobil Corp., 1999—2001, exec. v.p., 2001—05. Mem. internat. adv. bd. Inst. Empresa.; supervisory bd. VNU NV, TPG NV, Aegon NV; internat. advisory bd. CVC Capital Ptnr.; bd. dir. Jr. Achievement Internat.; bd. trustees US Coun. Internat. Bus.; chmn. supervisory bd. Royal Ahold NV, 2004—. Office: Royal Ahold NV Piet Heikade 167-173 1019 Amsterdam Netherlands*

DAHAR, ELEANOR WILLIAM, lawyer; b. Manchester, NH, Dec. 2, 1961; d. Victor William and Eleanor Dahar. BA magna cuma laude, Wheaton Coll., 1984; JD, Boston Coll., 1987. Bar: NH 1988, Mass. 1989, US Dist. Ct. (Dist. NH) 1989, US Dist. Ct. (Dist. Mass.) 1989, US Supreme Ct. 1994, US Dist. Ct. (Dist. Mass.), US Dist. Ct. (Dist. NH). Assoc. Victor W. Dahar, P.A., Manchester, 1987—. Bd. dirs. Manchester Boys & Girls Club, 1992-2000, Federated Arts Coun., 1994-99, Optima Health, 1994, Mancester Economic Development Coun. 1996-97; v.p. and delegate Boston Coll. Alumni Coun., 2002. Mem. ABA (young lawyers div. 1989), NH Bar Assn. (pres.-elect 2006-07), Boston Bar Assn., Manchester Bar Assn. (v.p. 1996-97, social sec. 1995-96, exec. bd. 1991), Mass. Bar Assn., Assn. Trial Lawyers Am., NH Trial Lawyers Assn.; Manchester Rotary (pres. 1998-99, bd. mem. 1992-). Avocations: tennis, skiing, travel, opera. Office: Victor W Dahar PA 20 Merrimack St Ste 300 Manchester NH 03101-2207 Office Phone: 603-622-6595. E-mail: vdaharpa@worldnett.att.net.

DAHDAL, WAFA Y., pharmacologist, educator; b. Damascus, Syria, Dec. 22, 1968; d. Yousef Mousa and Soumaya Ibrahim Dahdal. AA with high honors, Loop Coll., 1989; PharmD with high honors, U. Ill., Chgo., 1993. Cert. pharmacotherapy specialist Bd. Pharm. Specialists, 1995. Pharmacy residency St. Louis Hosp., Coll. Pharmacy, St. Louis, 1994; asst. prof. St. Louis Coll. Pharmacy, 1994—2001; pres. Gateway Coll. Clin. Pharmacy, 1999—2000; assoc. prof. Midwestern U., Downers Grove, Ill., 2001—. Vice-chair, dept. pharmay practice Midwestern U., 2007—. Contbr. chapters to books, articles to profl. jours. Exec. bd. mem. Internat. Pharm. Fedn., Netherlands, 2004—07. Grantee Rsch. grant, Pharmacia & Upjohn, 1999, St. Louis Coll. Pharmacy, 1999, Pfizer, 2004, Scios, Inc., 2004. Mem.: Nat. Arab Am. Med. Assn. (pres.-elect 2007—), Heart Failure Soc. Am., Am. Heart Assn., Nat. Assn. Bds. Pharmacy (mem. continuing profl. devel. com. 2004—05), Am. Assn. Colls. Pharmacy (pharmacy practice ednl. outcomes & objectives task force 2006), Am. Coll. Clin. Pharmacy (mem. publ. com. 1998—99, mem. internat. affairs com. 1997—99), Internat. Pharm. Fedn (mem. steering com. 2002—07). Home: 7902 Stewart Dr Darien IL 60561 Office: Midwestern Univ 555 31st St Downers Grove IL 60515 Office Fax: 630-515-6958. Personal E-mail: wdahdal@hotmial.com. Business E-Mail: wdahda@midwestern.edu.

DAHER, EDOUARD, cardiologist; b. Kobayat, Akkar, Lebanon, Sept. 11, 1965; arrived in US, 1990; s. Raymond and Marie Daher. BS, Am. U., Beirut, 1986; MD, St. Joseph U., Beirut, 1990. Cert. Am. Bd. Internal Medicine, 1994, in Cardiovasc. Medicine Am. Bd. Cardiovasc. Disease, 1998, Am. Soc. Nuc. Cardiology, 1997, in Endovascular Medicine Am. Bd. Vascular Medicine, 2005. Resident Yale U. Sch. Medicine, New Haven, 1991—94, cardiovasc. fellow, 1994—98; asst. prof. medicine Wayne State U., Detroit, 1999—2004; attending cardiologist John D. Dingell VA Med. Ctr., 1999—2005; interventional peripheral fellow St. Elizabeth Med. Ctr., Boston, 2005; interventional cardiology fellow New Eng. Med. Ctr., 2005—. Dir. nuc. cardiology John D. Dingell VA Med. Ctr., Detroit, 1999—2004, chief sect. cardiology, 2001—04, dir. clin. rsch. ctr., 2002—04; staff physician Children's Hosp. Mich. PET Ctr., Detroit, 2001—04; dir. nuc. cardiology Harper U. Hosp., 2002—03. Contbr. chapters to books, scientific papers, articles to profl. jours. Recipient Process Improvement award, Vets. Integrated Svc. Network II, 2003, Rsch. Protected Time award, Wayne State U. Dept. Internal Medicine, 2000; Seed Money grant, 2000. Fellow: Am. Coll. Cardiology; mem.: Am. Heart Assn., Am. Soc. Nuc. Cardiology (dir. Mich. working group 2001—04, Young Investigator award 1997).

DAHIYA, RAJBIR SINGH, mathematics professor, researcher; b. Rattangarh, Haryana, India, Dec. 3, 1940; arrived in U.S., 1968; s. Ram S. and Kesar (Devi) D.; m. Krishna Tavathia, Dec. 11, 1966; children: Madhu, Ranjan. PhD, Birla Inst. Sci. and Tech., Pilani, India, 1967. Lectr. Birla Inst. Sci. and Tech., 1967-68; asst. prof. math. Iowa State U., Ames, 1968-72, assoc. prof., 1972-78, prof., 1978—. Reviewer math. revs. Zentrallblat; referee applied math. jours. Contbr. over 150 rsch. papers on delay and advanced differential equations, transform theory and spl. functions to U.S., European and Australian profl. jours. Mem. Am. Math. Soc. Democrat. Hindu. Home: 3144 Sycamore Rd Ames IA 50014-4510 Office: Iowa State U Dept Math Ames IA 50011-0001

DAHL, ARLENE, actress, writer, designer, cosmetics executive; b. Mpls., Aug. 11, 1928; d. Rudolph and Idelle (Swan) D.; m. Marc A. Rosen; children: Lorenzo Lamas, Carole Christine Holmes, Stephen Andreas Schaum. Student, U. Minn., 1943-44, Mpls. Inst. Art, 1945, Minn. Coll. Music, 1944, Minn. Bus. Coll., 1944. Pres. Arlene Dahl Enterprises, 1952-67; v.p. Kenyon & Eckhart, 1967-72; pres. Woman's World divsn. Kenyon & Eckhart Advt. Agy., 1967-72; nat. beauty and health advisor Sears Roebuck Co., 1970-75; internat. dir. Sales and Mktg. Execs. Internat., 1972-75; fashion dir. O.M.A., 1975-78; pres. Dahlia Parfums, Inc., 1975-80, Dahlia Prodns., Inc., 1978-81, Dahlmark Prodns., 1981—; pres., CEO Scandia Cosmetics, Ltd., 1978-80; pres., chmn. Lasting Beauty Ltd., 1986—. Author: Always Ask a Man, 1965, 12 Beautyscope books, 1968, rev. edit., 1978, Arlene Dahl's Secrets of Hair Care, 1969, Arlene Dahl's Secrets of Skin Care, 1972, Beyond Beauty, 1980, Arlene Dahl's Lovescopes, 1983, Arlene Dahl's Weekly Astro Forecast, yearly from 1991-2005, The Enquirer, 1991-2005, Celebrity Living mag. Weekly Forecast, 2005-, Arlene Dahl's Hollywood Horoscope internat. mag. weekly column, 1990-2005; actress: (Broadway plays) including Mr. Strauss Goes to Boston, Questionable Ladies, Cyrano de Bergerac, Applause (Tony award musical), (films) including (debut) My Wild Irish Rose, The Bride Goes Wild, Reign of Terror, A Southern Yankee, Ambush, The Outriders, Three Little Words, Watch the Birdie, Scene of the Crime, Inside Straight, No Questions Asked, Desert Legion, Slightly Scarlet, Sangaree, Caribbean Gold, Jamaica Run, Diamond Queen, Here Come the Girls, Bengal Brigade, Kisses for My President, Woman's World, Journey to the Center of the Earth, Wicked as They Come, She Played with Fire, Les Poneyettes, Du Blé Enliases, The Land Raiders, The Way to Kathmandu, Fortune Is a Woman, The Big Bank Roll, Who Killed Maxwell Thorn?, Midnight Warrior, 1991, (TV shows) Lux Video Theatre, 1952-53, guest starring appearances on The Love Boat, Fantasy Island, Love American Style, One Life to Live, 1981-84, Night of 100 Stars, 1983, Happy Birthday Hollywood, 1987, All My Children, 1995, Renegade, 1995, 96, 97, Air America, 1999; hostess (TV series): Pepsi-Cola Theatre, 1954, Opening Night, 1958, Arlene Dahl's Beauty Spot, 1966, Arlene Dahl's Starscope, 1979-80, Arlene Dahl's Lovescope, 1980-82; played throughout U.S. in One Touch of Venus, The Camel Bell, Blithe Spirit, Liliom, The King and I, Roman Candle, I Married an Angel, Bell, Book and Candle, Applause, Marriage Go Round, Pal Joey, A Little Night Music, Forty Carats, Life with Father, Murder Among Friends, Dear Liar; nightclub acts Flamingo Hotel, Las Vegas, Latin Quarter, N.Y.C., musical stage appearances: Carnegie Hall, 1997, London Paladium, 1992, 1998, Salute to MGM Musicals; internat. syndicated beauty columnist Chgo. Tribune/ N.Y. News Syndicate, 1950-70, Arlene Dahl's Lucky Stars Column, Globe Communications, 1988-90, Arlene Dahl's Starscope Weekly Column, 1991, 92, 93, 94, 95, 96, 97, 98, 99, 00, 01, 02, 03, 04, 05, Horoscope Yearly Forecast 1991-02; designer sleepwear for A.N. Saab & Co., 1952-57, In Vogue with Arlene Dahl (Vogue Patterns), 1980-85, Arlene Dahl Pvt. Collection Jewelry, 1989-94, Arlene Dahl's Jewels of Fortune Home Shopping Network, 1996. Hon. life mem. Father Flannagan's Boys Town; internat. amb. Pearl Buck Found.; founder, pres. Broadway Walk of Stars Found., Inc., 1999—; bd. dirs. Hollywood Mus. Recipient 10 Box Office Laurel awards, Hollywood Walk of Fame Star, 1961, Coup de Chapeau Deaville Film Festival award, 1982, 92; named Best Coiffed, Heads of Fame awards, 1967-72, 80; named Woman of the Yr., Advt. Club of N.Y.C., 1969, Mother of the Yr., 1982, Lifetime Achievement award WorldFest, 1994, Leadership in the Arts, 1997; named to Scandinavian Hall of Fame, 1997. Fellow: Vesterheim Norwegian/Am. Found. (life); mem.: UNIFEM, NATAS (trustee), Film Soc., Edward Grieg Soc., Authors Guild, Acad. Motion Picture Arts and Scis. (vice chair N.Y. spl. events), Acad. TV Arts and Scis. (bd. govs., v.p.), Smithsonian Assocs., Nat. Trust for Hist. Preservation, Commanderie de Bordeaux (N.Y.), Commanderie de Bontemps du Medoc et Graves, France. Office: Dahlmark Prodns PO Box 116 Sparkill NY 10976-0116 Office Fax: 212-628-0478.

DAHL, JONATHAN, magazine editor-in-chief; BA in Journalism, Columbia Univ., 1981. Reporter Houston Chronicle; reporter, Dallas Bur. Wall St. Jour., reporter, Chgo. Bur., weekend editor; exec. editor SmartMoney, NYC, 2004—06, editor-in-chief, 2006—. Office: Editor-in-Chief SmartMoney 2nd Fl 1755 Broadway New York NY 10019 Office Phone: 211-283-9200.

DAHL, LAWRENCE FREDERICK, chemistry professor; b. Evanston, Ill., June 2, 1929; s. Lawrence Gustave and Anne (Stuessy) D.; m. June Lomnes, Sept. 1, 1956; children: Larry, Eric, Christopher (dec.). BS in Chemistry, U. Louisville, 1951; PhD, Iowa State U., 1956; DSc (hon.), U. Louisville, 1991. Postdoctoral fellow Ames (Iowa State U.) Lab. AEC, 1957; from instr. to assoc. prof. chemistry U. Wis., Madison, 1957-64, prof., 1964—, R. E. Rundlechair, 1978—, Hilldale chair and prof., 1991—. Brotherton rsch. prof. U. Leeds, 1983 Recipient Inorganic Chemistry award Am. Chem. Soc., 1974, Disting. Alumnus award U. Louisville Coll. Letters and Sci., 1990, Sr. U.S. Scientist Humboldt award Alexander von Humboldt Stiftung, 1985, R.S. Nyholm medal Royal Soc. Chemistry, 1985, P. Chini medal Italian Soc. Chemistry, 1989, J.C. Bailar Jr. medal U. Ill., 1990, F. Basolo medal Northwestern U., 1995, Hilldale award in phys. scis. U. Wis., 1994, Willard Gibbs medal, Chgo. sect. Am. Chem. Soc., 1999, Pioneer award, Am. Inst. Chemists, 2000; named to Hon. Order Ky. Cols., 1982; Alfred P. Sloan fellow, 1963-65, U. Louisvlle Coll. Letters and Sci. fellow, 1990. Fellow AAAS, N.Y. Acad. Sci., Am. Acad. Arts and Scis.; mem. NAS. Home: 4817 Woodburn Dr Madison WI 53711-1345 Office: Univ of Wis Madison Dept of Chemistry 1101 University Ave Madison WI 53706-1322 Fax: 608-262-6143. E-mail: dahl@chem.wisc.edu.

DAHL, MARK VICTOR, dermatologist, educator; b. Mpls., Aug. 24, 1942; s. Victor E. and Edith M. D.; m. Arlene C., July 1, 1966; children: Kristian Mark, Jonathan Mark. BA, Wesleyan U., 1964; MD, U. Minn., 1968. Diplomate in dermatology, immunodermatology and dermatopathology Am. Bd. Dermatology. Intern U. Ore. Med. Sci. Ctr., Portland, 1968-69; fellow in dermatology U. Copenhagen, 1969-70; rsch. assoc. Walter Reed Army Med. Ctr., Washington, 1970-72; resident dermatology U. Calif., San Francisco, 1972—74; from asst. prof. to prof. dermatology U. Minn. Med. Sch., Mpls., 1974—2000, chmn. dept. dermatology, 1995—2000, prof. emeritus, 2000—; prof. dermatology Mayo Clinic Ariz., Scottsdale, 2000—07. Pres. Mark Dahl & Assocs., Inc., 1994-2002. Author: Clinical Immunodermatology, 1981, 3d edit., 1996, Common Office Dermatology, 1983, Clinical Dermatology, 1990, 4th edit., 2007, Dermatology, 1991; mem. editl. bd. jours. in field; contbr. articles to profl. jours. Founder Camp Discovery for children with severe skin diseases. Maj. M.C., U.S. Army, 1970-72. Mem. Am. Soc. Allergy and Immunology (pres. 1981-82), Am. Acad. Dermatology (hon., pres. 1993-94, Henry Stelwagen award 1972, Gold Triangle award 1998, Gold medal 2002, Master Dermatologist 2006), Am. Dermatologocal Assn., Assn. Profs. Dermatology, Internat. Soc. Dermatology, Soc. Investigative Dermatology (v.p. 1994-95), Br. Dermatol. Assn. (hon.), Mex. Acad. Dermatology (hon.), Can. Dermatol. Assn. (hon.), Minn. Dermatol. Soc., Phoenix Dermatol. Soc., South Africa Dermatology Soc. (hon.), Pacific Dermatology Assn. (hon.). Office: Mayo Clinic Scottsdale 13400 Shea Blvd Scottsdale AZ 85259 Business E-Mail: dahl.markv@mayo.edu.

DAHL, PETER STEFFEN, geologist, educator; b. Port-of-Spain, Trinidad and Tobago, Nov. 17, 1948; s. Ole Steffen and Diana Eleanor Dahl; m. Susan Marie Petroski, Jan. 14, 1984; 1 child, Elena Katherine. BA in Chemistry, Ind. U., Bloomington, 1969, MA in Geology, 1970, PhD in Geology, 1977. Lic. 1st class radiotelephone and television, FCC, 1972. Analytical chemist OA Labs., Inc., Inpls., 1970—71; chem. engr. (electroplating) GM (Delco Electronics divsn.), Kokomo, Ind., 1973—74; prof. geochemistry Kent State U., Ohio, 1977—. Exploration cons. (gold) Homestake Mining Co., Lead/Deadwood, SD, 1993—97; dir., geology summer field camp Kent State U., Spearfish, SD, 1985, 89, 91, 93, 96, 2005; prof. field geology Ind. U., Cardwell, Mont., 1987; vis. rsch. sci. Bern, Copenhagen, Stockholm, 2007—. Assoc. editor: American Mineralogist; contbr. scientific papers to profl. jours. Chair fin. com., past pres., mem. coun. Trinity Luth. Ch., Kent, Ohio, 1997—. With USNR, 1971—73. Decorated Nat. Def. medal USN, US Congl. Antarctic Svc. medal NSF and US Congress; finalist Alumni Disting. Tchg. award, Kent State U., 1980; recipient Glenn W. Frank Disting. Tchg. award, Dept. Geology, Kent State U., 1986; fellow, Ind. U., 1969—70, Texaco, 1976—77; grantee, Cottrell Rsch. Corp., 1978, Homestake Mining Co., 1993—97; Rsch. grant, NSF, 1981—83, 1993—94, 1997—2004. Mem.: No. Ohio Geol. Soc., Am. Geophys. Union, Geol. Soc. Am. (rep. Kent State U. 1980—85), Mineral. Soc. Am. (chair disting. lectr. com. 2003—05), Sigma Xi. Achievements include formulated the empirical quantitative relationship between mineral composition/structure and sequences of cooling ages observed for the same minerals; documented the high accuracy of a new, total-Pb technique for dating the mineral monazite and its microtextures in metamorphic rocks; contributed to unravelling ancient plate-tectonic history of the Wyoming microcontinent from 2600 to 1600 million years ago; determined the accuracy/precision of published mineral-pair geothermometers and calibrated two others; design of two electroplating processes for plating key electronic components of the first electronic ignitions, and scaled up these processes to production levels. Avocations: piano, golf, travel, reading. Home: 1430 River Edge Dr Kent OH 44240 Office: Kent State Univ Dept Geology Lincoln at Summit Sts Kent OH 44242 Office Phone: 330-672-2218. Office Fax: 330-672-7949. Personal E-mail: pdahl@neo.rr.com. Business E-Mail: pdahl@kent.edu.

DAHL, ROBERT ALAN, political science professor; b. Inwood, Iowa, Dec. 17, 1915; s. Peter Ivor and Vera (Lewis) D.; m. Mary Louise Bartlett, 1940 (dec. 1970); children: Ellen Kirsten, Peter Bartlett (dec.), Eric Lewis, Christopher Robert; m. Ann Goodridge Sale, 1973. AB, U. Wash., 1936; PhD, Yale U., 1940; LLD (hon.), U. Mich., 1985, U. Alaska, 1987; D of Philosophy (hon.), U. Oslo, 1994; LLD (hon.), Law Sch. for Social Rsch., 1996, Harvard U., 1998; D honoris causa, U. Madrid Complutense, 2001; LLD, Grinnell Coll., 2001; LittD, Columbia U., 2005. Mgmt. analyst USDA, 1940; economist Office Prodn. Mgmt., Office Price Adminstrn. and Civilian Supply, War Prodn. Bd., 1940-42; faculty Yale U., 1946—, Eugene M3yer prof. polit. sci., 1955-64, Sterling prof. polit sci., from 1964, Ford Rsch. prof., 1957-58, chmn. dept. polit. sci., 1957-62. Lectr. polit. sci., Flacso, Santiago, Chile, 1967; pres. Am. Polit. Sci. Assn., 1967. Author: Congress and Foreign Policy, 1950, (with E. Browne) Domestic Control of Atomic Energy, 1951, (with C.E. Lindblom) Politics, Economics and Welfare, 1952, A Preface to Democratic Theory, 1956, (with Haire and Lazarsfeld) Social Science Research on Business, 1959, Who Governs?, 1961, Modern Political Analysis, 1963, Political Oppositions in Western Democracies, 1966, After the Revolution?, 1970, Polyarchy: Participation and Opposition, 1971, Regimes and Oppositions, 1972, Democracy in the United States, 1972, (with E.R. Tufte) Size and Democracy, 1973, Dilemmas of Pluralist Democracy, 1982, A Preface to Economic Democracy, 1985, Controlling Nuclear Weapons, 1985, Democracy, Liberty and Equality, 1986, Democracy and the Critics, 1989, The New American Political (Dis) Order, 1994, Toward Democracy: A Journey Reflections: 1940-1997, 1997, On Democracy, 1999, Politica e virtu, 2001, How Democratic Is the American Constitution?, 2002, Intervista sul Pluralismo, 2002, On Political Equality, 2006. With U.S. Army, 1943-45. Decorated Bronze Star with cluster; Cavaliere of Republic of Italy, 1988; recipient Woodrow Wilson prize, 1963, 90, Talcott Parsons prize, 1977, Wilbur Lucius Cross medal, 1986, Elaine and David Spitz award, 1991; Guggenheim fellow, 1950, 78, fellow Ctr. for Advanced Study in Behavioral Scis., 1955-56, 67. Fellow Am. Acad. Arts and Scis. (Talcott Parsons prize 1977); mem. NAS, Am. Philos. Soc., Am. Polit. Sci. Assn. (pres. 1966-67, Woodrow Wilson prize 1963, James Madison prize 1978, Gladys Kammerer award 1983, Benjamin Lippincott award 1989, Johan Skytte prize 1995), New Eng. Polit. Assn. (pres. 1951), ACLU, Brit. Acad., Phi Beta Kappa. Home: 200 Leeder Hill Dr Hamden CT 06517-2750 Office Phone: 203-432-5283. E-mail: robert.dahl@yale.edu.

DAHLBEN, SALIN ABRAHAM, neuropsychiatrist; b. Rio de Janeiro, Nov. 2, 1945; came to U.S., 1973; s. Abraham and Emilia D.; m. Sonia Sapolnik, July 8, 1971 (div. 1975); m. Jean Annette Leupold, Nov. 7, 1982 (div. 1996); children: Deborah, Rachael Emily, Lindsay Johanna, Joshua Robert, Brian Andre. BS, Hebrew Coll., Rio de Janeiro, 1963; MD, Fed. U., Rio de Janeiro, 1969. Cert. Bd. Med. Quality Assurance, Calif.; diplomate Am. Bd. Psychiatry and Neurology in gen. psychiatry and with added cert. in geriatric psychiatry. Mem. med. staff Naval Hosp., Rio de Janeiro, 1970-71; intern Mt. Sinai Hosp. Svcs., NYC, 1973-74; resident Boston City Hosp., 1974-75; fellow in neurosurgery Lahey Clinic, Boston, 1975-76; resident in neurosurgery U. Iowa Hosps., Iowa City, 1976-78, VA Hosp., Iowa City, 1978; resident in psychiatry U. Iowa Hosps., Iowa City, 1979-80; chief resident Mt. Sinai Hosp. Med. Ctr., Chgo., 1981; med. unit dir. Bridgewater State Hosp., 1983-85; med. dir. Dorchester Mental Health Ctr., Mass., 1985-87; asst. psychiatrist McLean Hosp., Belmont, Mass., 1983—; asst. clin. prof. Tufts U. Sch. Medicine, Boston, 2005—. Clin. instr. psychiatry Harvard Med. Sch., Boston, 1983—; clin. assoc. Mass. Gen. Hosp., 1988—98, Mass. Mental Health Ctr., 1999—; assoc. Cambridge Hosp., 1990—; unit med. dir. psychiatry Metro Boston Lemuel Shattuck Hosp., Boston, 2001—; asst. clin. prof. Tufts U. Sch. of Medicine, 2005—. 1st lt. M.D. Brazilian Navy, 1970-71. Recipient prize Assn. Med. Students, Rio de Janeiro, 1968, 69, Abbey Norman Prince award Mt. Sinai Hosp. Med. Ctr., Chgo., 1981; named one of Am.'s Top Psychiatrists in Neuropsychiatry, Consumers Rsch. Coun. Am., 2003; scholar Nat. Coun. for Rsch., 1969-70. Mem. Mass. Med. Soc., NY Acad. Scis., Am. Mensa, Harvard Faculty Club, Harvard Club NY, Sigma Xi (MIT chpt.), Harvard Club NY. Office: 25 Mount Alvernia Rd Chestnut Hill MA 02467-1057 Business E-Mail: sdahlben@hms.harvard.edu.

DAHLBERG, ALBERT EDWARD, biochemistry professor; b. Chgo., Sept. 19, 1938; s. Albert Archer and Thelma Elizabeth (Ham) D.; m. Pamela Kathy Voth, June 29, 1963; children: Albert Andrew, Krista Katherine, Paul Eric BS, Haverford Coll., Pa., 1960; MD, U. Chgo., 1965, PhD in Biochemistry, 1968. Rsch. assoc. Nat. Cancer Inst.-NIH, Bethesda, Md., 1967-70; European Molecular Biology Orgn. fellow Molecular Biol. Inst., U. Aarhus, Denmark, 1970-72; prof. biochemistry Brown U., Providence, 1972—, chmn. dept. biochemistry, 1985, 87. Vis. prof. U. Wis., Madison, 1978-79; v.p. rsch. Mora Pharms., Inc., Miami, Fla., 1983—; founder, bd. dirs. Milkhaus Lab. Inc., Delanson, NY, 1993—; mem. bd. sci. counselors divsn. cancer biology diagnosis and ctrs. Nat. Cancer Inst., 1992-95; mem. Corp. of Haverford Coll., 1995—. Contbr. articles to profl. jours., chpts. to books NIH grantee, 1972—; recipient USPHS Rsch. Career Devel. award NIH, 1975-80 Fellow AAAS, Am. Soc. Microbiology; mem. Am. Soc. Biochemistry and Molecular Biology (sec. 2001—04), The Monroe Inst. Mem. Society Of Friends. Home: 554 Wayland Ave Providence RI 02906-4723 Office: Brown U Dept Molecular and Cell Biology and Biochemistry Box G- L254 Providence RI 02912 Home Phone: 401-421-9688. Business E-Mail: AE_Dahlberg@Brown.edu.

DAHLBERG, CARL FREDRICK, JR., entrepreneur; b. New Orleans, Aug. 20, 1936; s. Carl Fredrick and Nancey Erwin (Jones) D.; m. Constance Weston, Dec. 30, 1961; children: Kirsten Erwin Dahlberg Turner, Catherine Morgan Dahlberg Stokes BSCE, Tulane U., 1958; MBA, Harvard U., 1964. Regional mgr. bond dept. E.F. Hutton & Co., Inc., New Orleans, 1965—67; chmn. exec. com. Dahlberg, Kelly & Wisdom, Inc., New Orleans, 1967—71; pres. St. Mary Galvanizing Co., Inc., New Orleans, 1971—2000, chmn., 2000—; pres. The South Coast Co., LLC, 2004—. Co-organizer, dir. Charter Med. Corp., 1969-72; adv. dir. Rathborne Cos., 1985-91; with Internat. Trade Mart, 1974-89, exec. com., 1981-84, treas., 1983-84; consul gen. of Monaco, New Orleans, 1981-98; treas. Consul Corps of New Orleans, 1990-94 Co-author: Hydrochloric Acid Pickling, 1979 Trustee Metairie Park Country Day Sch., New Orleans, 1976-85, treas., 1980-82, chmn., 1982-84; trustee Eye, Ear, Nose and Throat Hosp., New Orleans, 1980-96, exec. com., 1980-83; trustee Eye, Ear, Nose and Throat Found., 1980-83, U. South, Sewanee, Tenn., 1984-90; bd. dirs. New Orleans Tech. Coun., 1993-98, Mus. Arts Soc. New Orleans, 2000-06, Metro. Crime Comm. New Orleans, 2006—; vis. com. Monroe libr. Loyola U., New Orleans, 2002-06; vestryman Christ Ch. Cathedral, New Orleans, 1981-85. With U.S. Army, 1958-59 Mem. ASCE, Nat. Assn. Mfrs. (bd. dirs. 1997-2003), Venerable Order Hosp. of St. John of Jerusalem, Mil. and Hospitaller Order St. Lazarus, Order of Merit of Italian Republic, Order of Grimaldi (Monaco), New Orleans Country Club, Pickwick Club, Army and Navy Club Washington, The Brook Club NYC

Republican. Episcopalian. Home: 199 Audubon Blvd New Orleans LA 70118-5538 Office: 201 Saint Charles Ave Ste 2531 New Orleans LA 70170-1000 Office Phone: 504-599-5960. E-mail: fritzdahl@aol.com.

DAHLBERG, ERIC ROSS, music educator; b. Mpls., Nov. 7, 1962; s. Jerome E. and Marilyn D. Dahlberg; m. Suzanne Marie Parenteau, May 22, 1993; children: Madeline Rae, Heather Marie. MusB, U. Minn., 1985, MEd, 1999; MAEd, Hamline U., 2006. Lic. tchr. State Minn., cert. environ. edn. Hamline U., 2002. Pvt. instrumental music instr., Minn., 1985—; instr. longterm band, strings, classroom music Hopkins Pub. Schools #270, Golden Valley, Minn., 1985—86; dir. orch. Oskaloosa (Iowa) Cmty. Schs., 1987—90; tchr. instrumental music St. Paul Pub. Schools #625, St. Paul, 1993—. Mem. cello sect. Bloomington Symphony Orch., Minn., 1990—2000; condr. Rondo Cmty. Orch. (formerly 'Capitol Hill Symphony'), St. Paul, 1995—2000, Woodbury Youth Orch., 2001—05. Writer (article) Gopher Music Notes, photographer (photograph/color print) Voyage Through Time, Lasting Illusions. Recipient Reserve Champion ribbon, Washington County Fair, 2003, Champion ribbon, Ramsey County Fair, 2004, 2005. Mem.: Minn. Music Educators Assn. (Minn. All State Orch. award 1979—81), Minn. Band Dirs. Assn., Music Educators Nat. Conf. (no. state coord. - student chpt. 1984—85). Achievements include Have held the position of 'Principal Cello' for the following orchestras:Armstrong Sr. H. School; University of Minnesota, Duluth, Symphony Orchestra & Chamber Orchestra; Oskaloosa Community Orchestra; Currently hold a 'Brown Belt' in karate. Have won 1st, 2nd, and/or 3rd place trophies at 'Green, Blue and Red' belt levels at local karate tournaments. Avocations: photography, Karate, fishing, alpine skiing, travel. Office: Linwood A+ Elem School 1023 Osceola Ave Saint Paul MN 55105

DAHLBERG, KENNETH C., engineering executive; b. Camden, NJ, Oct. 19, 1944; BSEE, Drexel U., 1967; MSEE, U. So. Calif., 1969; student, UCLA bus. sch.for advanced edn. for execs. Various engring., program mgmt., leadership positions Hughes Electronics Corp., 1967, corp. v.p.; sr. v.p. Hughes Aircraft Co.; pres., COO Raytheon Sys. Raytheon Co., Washington, 1997—2000, exec. v.p. bus. devel., 2000—03; exec. v.p. Gen. Dynamics; pres., CEO Sci. Applications Internat. Corp., San Diego, 2003—, chmn., 2004—. Mem. IEEE, Am. Soc. Naval Engrs., Nat. Def. Indsl. Assn. (bd. dirs.), Surface Navy Assn., U.S. Navy League (life), Assn. U.S. Army. Office: Sci Applications Internat Corp 10260 Campus Point Dr San Diego CA 92121*

DAHLBURG, JOHN-THOR THEODORE, news correspondent; b. Orange, NJ, Apr. 30, 1953; s. Donald Russell and Madeline (Blackadore) D.; m. Yvonne Michelle Bastien, Nov. 18, 1980; children: Cecile, Charlotte. BA summa cum laude, Wash. and Lee U., Lexington, Va., 1975; LLD with highest honors, U. Toulouse, France, 1980. Reporter, pub. affairs dir. Sta. WLUR-FM, Lexington, Va., 1971-75; stringer Lynchburg News, Va., 1974-75; news clk., intern Time Mag., Paris, 1974; reporter, editor Boca Raton News, Fla., 1980-81; newsman AP, Miami, Paris, 1981-83, editor, fgn. desk NYC, 1984-86, corr. Moscow, 1986-90, LA Times, Moscow, 1990—93, bur. chief New Delhi, 1993—96, Paris, 1996—2001, Miami, 2001—06; state editor South Fla. Sun-Sentinel, 2006—. Journalistes en Europe fellow, 1983-84; recipient George Polk award L.I. U., 1993, Excellence citation Overseas Press Club Am., 1993, Hal Boyle award, 1996, Cert. of Merit AP News Execs. Coun., 1993, Robert F. Kennedy Journalism award, 1996, Soc. Profl. Journalists award for internat. reporting, 1997; named finalist Pulitzer Prize in internat. reporting, 1992, 93. Mem.: Soc. Profl. Journalists (bd. dirs. South Fla. chpt.). Avocations: Model T Ford restoration, rowing, Salsa dancing.

DAHLE, CAROL JO, secondary school educator, director; b. St. Cloud, Minn., Dec. 29, 1951; d. Calvin John and Kathleen Florence Repulski; m. Thomas Alan Dahle, June 30, 1953; 1 child, Stephen Thomas. BMus in Applied Music, NW State U., Natchitoches, La., 1974; BS in Music Edn., St. Cloud State U., 1976; postgrad., U. Wis., River Falls, 1977. Band, choir dir. Allen HS, Robeline, La., 1975—76; mid. sch./jr. high choir dir., tchr. Hudson (Wis.) Sch. Dist., 1976—. Active Phipps Ctr. for the Arts, Hudson, 1985—, music dir. for musicals, 1980, past pres.; choir dir. Trinity Luth. Ch., Hudson, 1984—. Recipient Star Excellence award, Hudson Edn. Found., 1998. Mem.: St. Croix Valley Mus. Edn. Assn. (pres. 1976—, treas., sec.), Wis. Sch. Music Assn., Wis. Choral Dirs. Assn. (guest dir. Singing in Wis. music festival 1996, rep. N.W. dist. 2001—05, guest dir. Singing in Wis. music festival 2006, 5 Star award 2003, 2004, 2005, 2006, Outstanding Mid. Level Choir Dir. 2004). Democrat. Lutheran. Avocations: reading, gardening, travel. Office: Hudson Mid Sch 1300 Carmichael Rd Hudson WI 54016

DAHLE, JOHANNES UPTON, retired academic administrator; b. Ada, Minn., Nov. 28, 1933; s. Upton Emmanuel and Marte (Goli) D.; m. Arlene Isabel Powell, Dec. 27, 1956; children: Randall Douglas, Lisa Johanna. BS, U. Minn., 1956, MA, 1966. Choral dir. U. Minn., Mpls., 1960-62-63-66; dir. choirs Macalester Coll., St. Paul, 1962-63; dir. student activities and univ. programs U. Wis., Eau Claire, 1966-71, dir. univ. ctrs., 1971-84, dir. devel., 1984-95, ret., 1995. Pres., dir. Eau Claire Conv. Tourism Bur., 1979-84; v.p., dir. Eau Claire Regional Arts Coun., 1982-84; bd. dirs. United Way of Eau Claire; mem. Plymouth Congrl. Ch., Mpls. Capt. USAF, 1956-60. Mem. Internat. Assn. Coll. Unions, Coun. for Advancement and Support Edn., Kiwanis (pres. Eau Claire chpt. 1975-76), Phi Kappa Phi (sec. 1982-84), Omicron Delta Kappa (sec. 1981-84), Phi Mu Alpha Sinfonia. Home: 1929 Hunter Hill Rd Hudson WI 54016-5818

DAHLGREN, CARL HERMAN PER, performing company executive, educator; b. NYC, July 2, 1929; s. Harry W.A. and Ester Florence (Carlson) D.; m. Ella Kate Bowes, Oct. 8, 1960; children: Robert C., John L., Per M., Eva B. MusB, Westminster Choir Coll., Princeton, NJ, 1954. Project dir. Benson & Benson, Princeton, 1954-55; asst. head spl. research and analysis Gallup & Robinson, Princeton, 1956-57; v.p., artist mgr. Columbia Artists Mgmt., Inc., NYC, 1958-68, dir., 1962-68; v.p. Hurok Concerts, Inc., NYC, 1968-70, assoc., 1970-74; pres. Dahlgren Arts Mgmt., Inc., Denver, 1970-78; sr. ptnr. Dahlgren, Schiffmann & Assocs., NYC, 1978-80; assoc. prof. arts adminstrn. U. Cin., 1978—, acting head broadcasting divsn., 1979-80. Dir. masters program in arts adminstrn. Coll. Conservatory of Music, 1978—, prof., 1989—, prof. emeritus, 1992; prin. Dahlgren & Yaffe, Arts Cons., 1992; acting exec. dir. Assn. for Advancement of Arts Edn., Cin., 1995-96; mem. faculty senate U. Cin., 1988-90. Co-founder, exec. dir. Westminster Choir Coll. Alumni Fund Assn., 1954-59; mgr. Princeton Symphony Orch., 1957-59; gen. mgr., dir. Central City (Colo.) Opera House, 1970-72; bd. dirs. Gilpin County Arts Assn., 1970-76; bd. dirs., sec. Colo. Celebration of Arts, 1974-76; pres. Classic Choral, 1975-78, Cin. Chamber Orch., 1982-91; trustee Westminster Choir Coll., 1967-74. With AUS, 1947-49. Decorated knight 1st Class Order of Lion, Finland; recipient Merit award Westminster Choir Coll. Mem. AAUP (v.p. U. Cin. chpt. 1990-92), Assn. Arts Adminstrn. Educators (trustee 1988, pres. 1990), Am. Assn. Mus., Faculty Club U. Cin. Episcopalian. Personal E-mail: chpdahl@theriver.com.

DAHLGREN, DOROTHY, museum director; b. Coeur d'Alene, Idaho; BS in Museology and History, U. Idaho, 1982; M in Orgnl. Leadership, Gonzaga U., 1998. Dir. Mus. North Idaho, Coeur d'Alene, 1982—. Mem. Kootenai County Hist. Preservation Commn. Author: (with Simone Carbonneau Kincaid) In All the West No Place Like This: A Pictorial History of the Coeur d'Alene Region, 1996. Mem. no. region com. Idaho Heritage Trust. Office: Mus N Idaho PO Box 812 Coeur D' Alene ID 83816 Office Phone: 208-664-3448. E-mail: dd@museumni.org.

DAHLING, GERALD VERNON, lawyer, director; b. Red Wing, Minn., Jan. 11, 1947; s. Vernon and Lucille Alfrieda (Reuter) D.; m. Edell Marie Villella, July 26, 1969; children: David (dec.), Christopher, Elizabeth, Mary. BS, Winona State Coll., Minn., 1968; MS, U. Minn., 1970; PhD, Harvard U., 1974; JD, William Mitchell Coll. of Law, 1980. Bar: U.S. Patent Office 1979, Minn. 1980, Ind. 1980, Pa. 1997, U.S. Dist. Ct. (so. dist.) Ind. 1980. Patent atty. Eli Lilly and Co., Indpls., 1980-84, mgr. biotech. patents, 1984-86, asst. patent counsel biotech., 1986-89, asst. patent counsel biotech. and fermentation products, 1990, asst. gen. patent counsel, 1991-95; dir. intellectual property Pasteur Mérieux Connaught, Lyon, France and Swiftwater, Pa., 1995-97, corp. v.p., dir. intellectual property, 1997-98, sr. v.p. intellectual property Lyon, France, 1998-99, Rhone Poulenc Rorer, Collegeville, Pa., 1998—99; sr. v.p. global patents Aventis Pharms., Bridgewater, NJ, 2000—05; v.p., gen. counsel, global patent litig. and life cycle mgmt. Sanofi-Aventis, 2005, v.p. global group patent counsel, 2005—. Mem. ABA, Ind. Bar Assn., Pa. Bar Assn., Am. Intellectual Property Law Assn., Intellectual Property Owners Assn. (bd. dirs.), INTERPAT. Democrat. Roman Catholic. Office: Sanofi-Aventis 20 Avenue Raymond Aron 92105 Antony France Home: 15 Rue Montorgueil 75001 Paris France

DAHLINGER, MARTHA LOUISE, elementary school educator; b. Tampa, Fla., Mar. 28, 1936; d. Carl Bowman and Etta Louise Burkhalter; m. Russell Allen Dahlinger, 1958 (div. 1968); children: Jeffrey, Deborah, Daniel, Maria. BA in Edn., Mich. State U., 1965; MA in Edn., Western Mich. U., 1988. Classroom tchr. Vicksburg (Mich.) Pub. Schs., 1958—60, Kalamazoo (Mich.) Pub. Schs., 1969—94, Numazu (Japan) Bd. Edn., 1994—95, Kalamazoo (Mich.) Pub. Schs., 1995—98. Co-chair program and events Kalamazoo County Juvenile Home, 1963—65; troop leader Girl Scouts Am., 1965; tchr. rep. ARC, 1971—91; host family exchange students Western Mich. U., 1971—80; chair pub. affairs Kalamazoo Edn. Assn., 1972; appt. by state rep. to Friend of Ct. rev. com. Mich. Women's Commn., 1979—80; pub. affairs com. Planned Parenthood, 1977—79, state del., 1978—85; bd. dirs. Western Mich. U. Partners in Dance, 2001—05, v.p., 2003, pres., 2004, co-chair programs and events, 2003—05; vol. Portage Pub. Libr., 2002—06, 2002—05; mem. exec. com. Dem. Party Kalamazoo County, 1972—86, county and state convs. del., 1972—86, mem. state platform com., 1978, candidate county commn., 1987, mem. state ctrl. com., 1979—84, campaign mgr. 6th congl. dist., 1986; bd. dirs. South Ctrl. Mich. ACLU, 1983—93, pres., 1988—90, bd. dirs. Mich. affiliate, 1986—93, mem. exec. bd., 1987—93, nat. del., 1989—91, chair Mich. delegation, 1989; bd. dirs. Planned Parenthood/Reproductive Health South Ctrl. Mich., Inc., 1972—85; mem. polit. action com. Mich. Edn. Assn., 1975—89, mem. governing bd., 1976—78, chair 3d congl. com., 1976, 1978, 46th dist. house com. chair, 1976, 1978. Named Outstanding Vol., Planned Parenthood South Ctrl. Mich., 2005; recipient award, Kalamazoo Pub. Schs. Hispanic Program, 1983, award for participation in Classrooms of Tomorrow Computer Program, Gov.of Mich., 1990. Mem.: Western Mich. Univ. Ptnrs. in Dance (bd. dirs. 2001—05, v.p 2003, program and events co-chair 2003—05, pres. 2004), Kalamazoo/Numazu Sister City Com. (life; host family com. chair 2003, exch. tchr. com. chair 2003, 2004). Democrat. Unitarian Universalist. Avocations: reading, music, dance, water related activities, gardening. Home: 2612 Chopin Kalamazoo MI 49024-6634

DAHLK, THOMAS HARLAN, lawyer; b. Madison, Wis., Aug. 22, 1952; s. Harlan Edward and Ardys (Hanson) D.; m. Janice Kay Larson, Dec. 21, 1973; children: Lesley Anne, Thomas Larson. BA with distinction, U. Wis., 1974; JD magna cum laude, Creighton U., 1977. Bar: Nebr. 1977, Nebr. Supreme Ct. 1977, U.S. Dist. Ct. (Nebr., Okla., Iowa, Minn., Ariz., Ga., Fla., Kans., wc. dist. Mo., so. dist. NY), U.S. Ct. Appeals (8th, 10th, 11th cir.), U.S. Supreme Ct. 1992. Assoc. Fitzgerald and Brown, Omaha, 1977-83, ptnr., 1983—88; ptnr. Lieben Dahlk Whitted Houghton Slowiaczek & Jahn, 1988-98; ptnr., bus. & comml. litig. Blackwell Sanders Peper Martin LLP, 1998-, Omaha office mng. ptnr. 2003-. Adj. faculty Creighton Law Sch., Omaha, 1981—. Trustee Brownell-Talbot Sch., Omaha; gov. mem. Omaha Symphony. Contbr. articles to legal publs., lead articles editor Creighton Law Rev. Fellow Nebr. bar Found.; mem. ABA (com. fed. securities regulation 1982—), Nebr. Bar Assn. (chmn. mentoring com. 2001-03), Nebr. Assn. Trial Attys., Omaha Bar Assn. Lutheran. Office: Blackwell Sanders Peper Martin LLP Ste 2100 1620 Dodge St Omaha NE 68102 Office Phone: 402-964-5031. Office Fax: 402-964-5050. Business E-Mail: tdahlk@blackwellsanders.com.

DAHLMAN, SIMON JACQUES, journalist, educator; b. Ft. Lauderdale, Fla., Nov. 22, 1958; s. Louis Jacques and Amanda Bess (Geesink) D.; m. Melissa Ann Roy, May 18, 1980; children: Sarah Elizabeth, Emily Rachael. BA cum laude, Milligan Coll., 1980; MA, U. Cin., 1998. Ordained to ministry Christian Ch., 1979. Youth min. First Christian Ch., Erwin, Tenn., 1979-81; min. Platt Bridge Ch. of Christ, Wigan, Eng., 1982-87; editor Christian Fellowship Mag., Birmingham, Eng., 1984-87; assoc. editor The Lookout Std. Pub., Cin., 1987-90, editor The Lookout, 1990-96; editor Pastor's Family, Colorado Springs, Colo., 1996—99; assoc. prof. comm. Milligan Coll., 1999—. Instr. Cin. Bible Coll., 1994-95; editl. dir. Std. Pub., Cin., 1992-96. Contbr. articles to mags. and jours. Mem. Evang. Press Assn., Religious Newsletter Assn. Avocation: soccer.

DAHLSTROM, BECKY JOANNE, journalist; b. Olympia, Wash., Sept. 24, 1957; d. Timothy Craddick and Shirleen (Stout) Roan; m. Kenneth W. Dahlstrom, Mar. 17, 1978 (div. Aug. 1984); children: Levi, Olivia; m. Robert Salley, Sr., Feb. 21, 1986 (div. Sept. 1994); 1 child, Robert, Jr. Student, Am. Coll., 1985-86. Writer Hospital, 1988-89; admitting clerk County Ventura (Calif.) Healthcare Agy., 1989—. Writer, editor West Fork (Ark.) Elem. Sch., 1970-73. Author: (poem) My Authority, 1980 (Hon. mention 1980). Mem. Future Bus. Leaders Am. Republican. Baptist. Avocations: drawing, writing, horseback riding, ceramics.

DAHMS, BRUCE JOHN, secondary school educator; b. Manchester, Conn., Aug. 10, 1946; s. Francis Arthur Dahms and Doris Margaret Porterfield. BS in Edn., U. Maine, 1969. Tchr. Southeastern NH Christian Academy, Somersworth, 1973—. Mem. organizing com. New England Christian Sports League, 1981—82. With US Army, 1969—71, Vietnam. Decorated Bronze Star; recipient Golden Apple, New England Assn. Christian Schs., 2000. Republican. Baptist. Avocation: painting. Home: 18 Noble St Somersworth NH 03878 Office: Southeastern NH Christian Academy 12 Rocky Hill Rd Somersworth NH 03878

DAHN, CONNEY COLLEY, special education educator; m. Larry Dahn; 3 children. BA, Univ. Ala. Spl. edn. tchr., 1974—, South Fork H.S., 1990—93, Martin County H.S., 1993—2004, Jensen Beach (Fla.) H.S., 2004—. Founder Friends Chorus for mentally and physically challenged students, 1989; coach Spl. Olympics. Named Christa McAuliffe Ambassador for Edn., Fla. Dept. Edn., Fla. Tchr. of Yr., 2007, Sch. Tchr. of Yr., Martin County Sch. Dist. (twice). Mem.: Kappa Delta. Avocation: running. Office: Jensen Beach High Sch 2876 NW Goldenrod Rd Jensen Beach FL 34957 E-mail: cdahn@adelphia.net.*

DAHN, JEFF RAYMOND, physics professor; b. Bridgeport, Conn., Jan. 9, 1957; arrived in Can., 1970; s. Raymond Charles and Margery (Halsted) D.; m. Katherine Mary Lillian Macdonald, July 1, 1987 (div.); children: Hannah, Tara, Jackson. BSc in Physics with honors, Dalhousie U., Halifax, NS, Can., 1978; MSc in Physics, U. B.C., Vancouver, Can., 1980, PhD in Physics, 1982. Rsch. assoc. Nat. Rsch. Coun. Can., Ottawa, Ont., 1982-83, mem. continuing staff, 1983-85; project leader materials sci. Moli Energy Ltd., Vancouver, 1985-87, rsch. dir., 1987-90; assoc. prof. physics Simon Fraser U., Burnaby, B.C., 1990-94, prof. physics, 1994-96; prof. physics and chemistry Dalhousie U., Halifax, N.S., 1996—, Can. rsch. chair, 2003—. Cons. Moli Energy (1990) Ltd., 1990-96, 3M Co., 1996—. Contbr. more than 315 sci. papers to profl. jours.; patentee in field. Recipient Medal for Innovation in Physics from Can. Assn. Physicists, 1987, Herzberg medal Can. Assn. Physicists, 1996, Gold medal B.C. Sci. Coun., 1996. Fellow Royal Soc. Can.; mem. Am. Phys. Soc., Electrochem. Soc. (Lash Miller award Can. sect. 1993, Battery divsn. Rsch. award 1996), Internat. Battery Materials Assn. (Rsch. award 1995). Avocations: woodworking, basketball, hiking in mountains. Office: Dalhousie U Dept Physics Halifax NS Canada B3H 3J5 Office Phone: 902-494-2991. E-mail: jeff.dahn@dal.ca.

DAHRENDORF, LORD RALF GUSTAV, sociologist, educator; b. Hamburg, Germany, May 1, 1929; s. Gustav and Lina (Witt) D.; m. Christiane Klebs, April, 2004. PhD, U. Hamburg, 1952, London Sch. Econs., 1954; 26 hon. degrees from various univs. Privatdozent sociology U. Saar, Fed. Republic Germany, 1957; fellow Ctr. for Advanced Studies in Behavioral Scis., Palo Alto, Calif., 1957-58; prof. sociology U. Hamburg, 1958-60, U. Tubingen, 1960-66; prof. U. Constance, 1966-69, dean faculty social scis., 1966-67; mem. Fed. Parliament Govt. of Fed. Republic Germany, 1969-70; parliamentary sec. of state in German Fgn. Office, 1969-70; mem. Commn. of the European Cmtys., 1970-74; dir. London Sch. Econs., 1974-84; warden St. Antony's Coll., Oxford, 1987-97; mem. House of Lords, London, 1993—, chmn. delegated powers select com., 2002—06; rsch. prof. Social Sci. Ctr., Berlin, 2005—. Trustee Ford Found., 1976-87; mem. Coun. of Brit. Acad., 1980-83, House of Lords, 1993—; chmn. bd. Friedrich-Naumann Stiftung, 1982-87, Delegated Powers Select com., 2002-06. Author: Marx in Perspective, 1953, Industrie-und Betriebssoziologie, 1956, Class and Class Conflict, 1959, Die angewandte Aufklä rung, 1963, Gesellschaft und Demokratie in Deutschland, 1965, Pfade aus Utopia, 1967, Essays in Theory of Society, 1968, Konflikt und Freiheit, 1972, Plä doyer für die Europä ische Union, 1973, The New Liberty, 1975, Life Chances, 1980, On Britain, 1982, Die Chancen der Krise, 1983, The Modern Social Conflict, 1988 (all transl. into many langs.), Reflections on the Revolution in Europe, 1991, LSE: A History of the London School of Economics 1895-1995, 1995, Morals, Revolution and Civil Society, 1997, After 1989, 1997, Liberal und unabhängig, Gerd Bucerius und seine Zeit, 2000, Universities after Communism, 2000, Über Grenzen, 2002, Auf der Suche nach einer neuen Ordnung, 2003, Der Wiederbeginn der Geschichte, 2004, Versuchungen der Unfreiheit, 2006. Mem. Hansard Soc. of Electoral Reform, 1975-76; mem. Royal Commn. on Legal Svcs., 1976-79; mem. Com. to Rev. the Functioning of Fin. Instns., 1977-80; mem. German PEN Ctr., 1971—. Decorated knight comdr. Order Brit. Empire, also by decorated by govts. of Senegal, Luxembourg, Fed. Republic Germany, Austria, Belgium, Italy. Fellow Anglo German Soc. (presidium), British Acad., Royal Soc. Arts, Royal Coll. Surgeons (hon.); mem. AAAS (hon.), NAS (fgn. assoc.), Am. Philos. Soc., Royal Irish Acad. (hon.), others. Office: House of Lords London SW1A 0PW England

DAHSE, KENNETH WILLIAM, photographer, writer, educator; b. Teaneck, NJ, May 3, 1949; s. William Charles Dahse and Dorothy Rose Devine; m. Carol Salminen (div.); 1 child, Lisa; m. Linda Jewell, Feb. 23, 1974; 1 child, Shannon. BA, Montclair State U., 1972, MA, 1977. Secondary educator Bogota (N.J.) Pub. Schs., 1977—; adj. instr. Bergen C.C., Paramus, N.J., 1991—. Author: RVing America's Backroads, 1989, The Hell Riders, 2005; contbr. articles to jours. including Am. Legion, Trailer Life, Motorcycle Tour & Cruiser, Motor/Home, Rider, Roadbike, Family Motor Coaching. Environ. activist C.L.E.A.N., Inc., Ringwood, N.J. Mem. NJ Edn. Assn., Bogota Edn. Assn. (pres. 1995-2004), Sierra Club, Appalachian Mt. Club. Avocations: motorcycle riding, backpacking, hiking, kayaking. Personal E-mail: kennethdahse@yahoo.com.

DAI, GUANG-MING GEORGE, optics scientist; b. Nanan, Fujian, China, July 16, 1965; adopted s. Shiqin Dai and Lizhen Chen; m. Wendy Wenqun Liu; children: Percy, Perry. BS, Xiamen U., Xiamen, China, 1986; PhD, Lund U., Lund, Sweden, 1995. Prin. scientist Advanced Med. Optics, Santa Clara, Calif., 2001—. Author: Wavefront Optics for Vision Correction; contbr. scientific papers, chapters to books. Head coach Forest Pk. Sch. Sci. Olympiad Teams, Fremont, Calif., 2005—07. Post-doctoral fellowship, Swedish Natural Sci. Rsch. Coun., 1995. Fellow: Am. Acad. Optometry; mem.: Assn. for Rsch. in Vision and Ophthalmology (corr.), Internat. Soc. for Optical Engrs. (corr.), Optical Soc. Am. (corr.). Achievements include patent for Iterative Fourier reconstruction for laser surgery and other optical applications; patents pending for; invention of Sys. and methods for prediction of objective visual acuity based on wavefront measurements; Compound modulation transfer function for laser surgery and other optical applications; Database sys. for centralized clin. and rsch. applications with data from wavefront aberrometers; Systems and methods for correcting high order aberrations in laser refractive surgery; Volumetric point spread function for eye diagnosis and treatment; Transformation methods of wavefront maps from one vertex distance to another; Residual accommodation threshold for correction of presbyopia and other presbyopia correction using patient data. Office: Advanced Med Optics 3400 Ctrl Expressway Santa Clara CA 95051 Office Phone: 408-773-7188. E-mail: george.dai@amo-inc.com.

DAI, WEILI, information technology executive; b. China; m. Sehat Sutardja; 2 children. BS in Computer Sci., U. Calif., Berkeley. Positions in software devel. and project mgmt. Canon Rsch. Ctr. Am., Inc.; co-founder Marvell Tech. Grp. Ltd., 1995, v.p., corp. sec., bd. dirs., 1995, exec. v.p. and gen. mgr. comm. and consumer bus. grp., 1999—, COO, 2006—. Named one of 400 Richest Ams., Forbes mag., 2006. Office: Marvell Semiconductor Inc 5488 Marvell Ln Santa Clara CA 95054

DAI, YUAN-SHUN, education educator; b. Shanghai, Apr. 3, 1978; s. Li-Gen Dai and Lai-Di Yang; m. Jia-Feng Liu, July 3, 2000. B in Engring., Tsinghua U., China, 2000; PhD, Nat. U. Singapore, 2004. Asst. prof. Ind. U.-Purdue U., Indpls., 2004—. Reviewer European Jour. Operational Rsch., 2002, Internat. Jour. Reliability, Quality and Safety Engring., 2003; author: (book) Computing Systems Reliability, 2004; contbr. articles to profl. jours. Scholarship, Tsinghua U., 1997, 1998, Presdl. Grad. Fellowship, Nat. Univ. Singapore, 2002—03. Mem.: Reliable Grid Alliance, IEEE. Avocations: classical music, reading, golf, swimming, skating. Office: Ind Univ Purdue Univ Computer Sci Dept 723 W Michigan St SL 280 Indianapolis IN 46202 Home: 805 Lockefield St Apt A Indianapolis IN 46202 Office Fax: 317-274-9742. Personal E-mail: ydai@cs.iupui.edu.

DAIDONE, LEWIS EUGENE, finance company executive; b. Perth Amboy, NJ, Aug. 6, 1957; s. Eugene John and Gertrude Rose (Sawyer) D.; m. Kathleen Eleanor Ward, May 11, 1985; children: Eugene Joseph, Brittany Nicole, Lewis Peter. BA, Rutgers U., 1979, MBA, 1980. CPA, NY, NJ. Sr. acct. Ernst & Young, NYC, 1980-82; asst. controller Reserve Group, NYC, 1982-84; mgr. commodity acctg. Dean Witter Reynolds, NYC, 1984; v.p., treas., sec. Cortland Distbrs., Inc., Hackensack, NJ, 1984-89; sr. v.p., CFO Cortland Fin. Group, Inc., Hackensack, NJ, 1984—89; mng. dir., CFO mutual funds Salomon Smith Barney, Inc., NYC, 1990—2004; sr. v.p., dir. Smith Barney Fund Mgmt. LLC, NYC, 1990—2004; sr. v.p., treas. Smith Barney Funds., Inc., NYC, 1990—2004, Smith Barney Money Funds, Inc., NYC, 1990—2004, Smith Barney Muni Funds, NYC, 1990—2004, Smith Barney Tax-Free Money Fund, NYC, 1990—2004, Smith Barney Intermediate Mcpl. Fund, NYC, 1992—2004, Smith Barney Mcpl. Fund, Inc., NYC, 1992—2004, Smith Barney High Income Opportunity Fund, Inc., NYC, 1993—2004; chmn. Global Horizon Investment Series, Brit. West Indies, 1992—2000, Smith Barney Internat. Funds, Luxembourg, 1993-97; and CFO/Chief Adminstrv. Officer 150 other investment cos. with Salomon Smith Barney. Head funds adminstrn.

Citigroup Asset Mgmt., 1998-2004; CFO LOG-NET, Inc., 2005—; COO, 2006-; v.p., treas. Cortland Trust, Inc., Hackensack, 1984-89; cons. in field, 1981-82. Trustee Wyndmoor Condominium Assn., Woodbridge, NJ Named one of Outstanding Young Men Am., U.S. Jaycees, 1979. Fellow N.J. State Soc. CPAs; mem. AICPA, N.Y. State Soc. CPAs, Beta Gamma Sigma. Avocations: golf, racquetball. Office: LOG-NET Inc 230 Half Mile Rd Red Bank NJ 07701

DAIGLE, BARBARA DIANNE, elementary school educator; b. East Liverpool, Ohio, Feb. 2, 1960; d. Jack Earl and Barbara Ann Talbott; m. Kenneth Alan Daigle, July 24, 1982; children: Kellie Elise, Emily Kate. BA in Polit. Sci., Youngstown State U., 1982; MEd, Marygrove Coll., 1999. Cert. tchr. in elem. edn. (K-8) Ohio, 1988, reading validation (K-12) 1987. Reading, math. tchr. E.J. Blott Elem. Sch., Youngstown, Ohio, 1988—90; elem. tchr. Roosevelt Elem. Sch., McDonald, Ohio, 1992—, mem. textbook selection com.; mem. sch. improvement com. Bldg. rep. teaming to impact student achievement Trumbull County, 2005; mem. textbook com. Roosevelt Elem. Sch., McDonald, Ohio, 2003—04, mem. sch. improvement com., 2004—05. Co-author (editor): (plays) The Rainforest, 2000; contbr. columns in newspapers. Participant Hands Across Am., Salem, Ohio, Relay for Life, Youngstown, 2005, com. mem., 2005; missions com. mem. United Meth. Ch., Girard, Ohio, 2004, 2005. Mem.: NEA, Trumbull Area Reading Coun., OH Edn. Assn., McDonald Edn. Assn., Nat. Sci. Tchrs. Assn. Democrat. Methodist. Avocations: reading, exercise, photography, travel, theater. Office: Roosevelt Elem Sch 410 W 7th St Mc Donald OH 44437 Home Phone: 330-530-4500. Personal E-mail: iluvrus43@yahoo.com.

DAIL, JOSEPH GARNER, JR., retired judge; b. Elloree, SC, June 15, 1932; s. Joseph Garner and Esther Vernette (Harbort) D.; m. Martha E. MacReynolds; children: Edward Benjamin, Mary Holyoke. BS, U. N.C., 1953, JD with honors, 1955. Bar: N.C. 1955, Va. 1976. Pvt. practice, Washington, 1959-76; ptnr. Croft, Dail & Vance (and predecessor), 1966-76; sole practitioner McLean, Va., 1976—83; counsel Gabeler, Ward & Griggs, 1983-87; judge U.S. adminstrv. law Fresno, Calif., 1987-94, San Francisco, 1994-97, Tampa, 1997-99; sr. U.S. adminstrv. law judge, 1999—2005; ret., 2005. Assoc. editor: N.C. Law Rev, 1954-55. Lt. USNR, 1955-59; capt. Res. (ret.). Mem. N.C. Bar Assn., Va. Bar Assn., Transp. Lawyers Assn. (Disting. Svc. award 1976), Order of Coif, Phi Beta Kappa. Republican. Home: 103 Masters Ln Safety Harbor FL 34695-3722 Personal E-mail: macdail@aol.com.

DAILEY, COLEEN HALL, magistrate; b. East Liverpool, Ohio, Aug. 10, 1955; d. David Lawrence and Deloris Mae (Rosensteel) Hall; m. Donald W. Dailey Jr., Aug. 16, 1980 (div. May 2001); children: Erin Elizabeth, Daniel Lester. Student, Wittenberg U., 1973-75; BA, Youngstown State U., 1977; JD, U. Cin., 1980. Bar: Ohio 1981, U.S. Dist. Ct. (no. dist.) Ohio 1981. Sr. libr. assoc. Marx Law Libr., Cin., 1979-80; law clk. Kapp Law Office, East Liverpool, 1979, 1980-81, assoc., 1981-85; pvt. practice East Liverpool, 1985-95; magistrate Columbiana County, Ohio, 1995—. Spl. counsel Atty. Gen., Ohio, 1985—92. Pres. Columbiana County Young Dems., 1985-87; bd. dirs. Big Bros./Big Sisters Columbiana County, Inc., Lisbon, Ohio, 1984-87, Planned Parenthood Mahoning Valley, Inc., 1993-97; trustee Ohio Women Inc., 1991-95; mem. Columbiana County Progress Coun., Inc. Mem.: ABA, Ohio Women's Bar Assn. (trustee 1997—99), Columbiana County Bar Assn., Ohio Assn. Magistrates (chmn. domestic rels. sect. 1998—2000, 2002—07), Ohio Bar Assn. (Ohio Supreme Ct. Joint Task Force on Gender Fairness, family law specialization bd.). Democrat. Lutheran. Office: Columbiana County Common Pleas Court 105 S Market St Lisbon OH 44432-1255 Office Phone: 330-424-7777 ext 1102. Business E-Mail: cdailey@ccclerk.org.

DAILEY, DANIEL OWEN, artist, educator, product designer; b. Phila., Feb. 4, 1947; s. David Bireley and Barbara Tarleton (Tricebock) D.; m. Linda MacNeil, Aug. 19, 1977; children: Allison MacNeil, Owen MacNeil. B.F.A., Phila. Coll. Art, 1969; M.F.A., R.I. Sch. Design, Providence, 1972. Tchr., fellow MIT Ctr. for Advanced Visual Studies, Cambridge, 1975-80; founder, prof. glass program Mass. Coll. Art, Boston, 1973-89; mem. faculty Pilchuck Glass Sch., Stanwood, Wash., 1974—; designer, artist Cristallerie Daum, Paris and Nancy, France, 1975—; designer Steuben Glass, Corning, NY, 1982—. Tchr. glass R.I. Sch. Design, 1970-72, Haystack Mountain Sch. Crafts, Deer Isle, Maine, 1976—; owner Dan Dailey Inc., Kensington, N.H., 1977—; mem. faculty Mass. Coll. Art, 1989—; bd. govs. Mus. Arts and Design, N.Y.C., 2000—. One-man and group shows throughout U.S. and Europe, 1970—; represented in permanent collections Renwick Gallery, Smithsonian Inst., Washington, Toledo Mus. Art, J.B. Speed Mus., Louisville, Creative Glass Ctr. Am., Millville, NJ, Morris Mus., Morristown, NJ, Royal Ont. (Can.) Mus., Met. Mus. Art, NYC, Smithsonian Inst., Washington, Corning (NY) Mus. Glass, Huntington (W.Va.) Mus., New Indian Mus., Flagstaff, Ariz., Les Archives Daum, Nancy, France, U. Ill. Art Gallery, Normal, Brockton (Mass.) Art Mus., Nat. Gallery Victoria, Melbourne, Australia, Nat. Mus. Modern Art, Kyoto, Japan, St. Louis Mus. Art, High Mus. Art, Atlanta, Phila. Mus. Art, Kestner Mus., Hannover, Fed. Republic Germany, Mus. Art, Darmstatt, Fed. Republic Germany, Indpls. Mus. Art, Mus. Arts & Design, NYC, LA County Mus. Art, Mus. des Arts Decoratifs, Paris, Boston Mus. Fine Arts, Detroit Inst. Art, Yokohama Mus. Art, Japan, Mus. Design et Dárts Appliques Contemporairs, Lausanne, Switzerland, Wheaton Mus., Millville, NJ, Milw. Mus. Art, Boca Raton (Fla.) Mus. Art, Carnagie Mus. Art, Pitts., Racine Art Mus., Wis., Currier Gallery of Art, Manchester, NH, Darmstatt Mus., Germany, Dayton Art Inst., Ohio, Greatest Bar on Earth, Windows on the World Corp., One World Trade Ctr. Towers, NYC, Hunter Mus. Am. Art, Chattanooga, Tenn., Pilchuck Glass Collection at City Centre and U.S. Bank Centre, Seattle, WA, Pacific First Ctr., Seattle, Rockefeller Ctr. Corp., NYC, Chase Manhattan Bank Collection, NYC, Town of Vail, Colo., Toyama Inst. Glass, Toyama City, Japan, Visions, NYC, Mus. Art Royal Ontario Mus., Toronto, Can., Renwick Gallery, Smithsonian Inst., Washington; exhibitions include Renwick Gallery, 1987, Smithsonian Inst., 1987, Mus. Am. Art, 1987, Habatat Galleries, Boca Raton, 1987-2005, Leo Kaplan Modern, NYC, 1990-2005; commns. include Jasper's Restaurant, Boston, Dreyfus Corp. Hdgrs., Met Life Bldg., NYC, Children's Hosp., Boston, No. Essex County Courthouse, Newburyport, Mass., Rockefeller Ctr., Rainbow Room, NYC, Commonwealth Energy Svcs. Corp. Hdqrs., Cambridge, Mass., Town of Vail, Colo., 1992-2005, LA County Mus., 1993, pvt. residence, Zurich, Switzerland, NYC, Boca Raton (Fla.) Mus. Art, Windows on the World, NY, 1996, 92d St. Y, NYC, 1998, Mayo Clinic, Rochester, 2001, Restaurant Daniel, NYC, 2002, Providence Performing Arts Ctr., 2004; represented in pvt. collections. Trustee Haystack Mountain Sch., Deer Isle, Maine, 1983-92, Urban Glass; nat. adv. bd. U. Arts, Phila., 1989—, Renwick Gallery, Smithsonian Instn., Washington; bd. govs. Mus. Arts and Design, NYC, 2000— Fulbright Hayes fellow Venice, Italy, 1972-73; Glass fellow NEA, 1979, Masters fellow Creative Glass Ctr. Am., 1989, Mass. Coun. for Arts, 1980, 85-87, MIT Ctr. Advanced Visual Studies fellow, 1975-79, Grad. Tchg. fellow RISD, 1970-72, fellow award Am. Craft Coun., 1998; recipient Libensky award Chateau St. Michelle Vineyards and Winery, 2000, Masters of the Medium award Renwick Smithsonian, 2001, Pres. Disting. Artist award U. of the Arts, Phila., 2001, Art of Liberty award Nat. Liberty Mus Fellow Am. Craft Coun.; mem. Glass Art Soc. (pres., chmn. bd. dirs. 1980-82, hon. life). E-mail: studio@idandailey.com.

DAILEY, DELL LEE, federal agency administrator, military officer; b. 1949; BA, US Mil. Acad., 1971; MA, Shippensburg U. Comdr. 160th Aviation Spl. Ops. Group Airborne, Ft. Campbell; coord. for counterterrorism US Dept. State, Washington, 2007—. Office: US Dept State Office Coord for Counterterrorism Harry S Truman Bldg 2201 C St NW Rm 2509 Washington DC 20520 Office Phone: 202-647-9892.*

DAILEY, DIANNE K., lawyer; b. Great Falls, Mont., Oct. 10, 1950; d. Gilmore and Patricia Marie (Linnane) Halverson. BS, Portland State U., 1977; JD, Lewis & Clark Coll., 1982. Assoc. Bullivant, Houser, Bailey PC, Portland, Oreg., 1982-88, ptnr., 1988—, pres., 2002—06. Contbr. articles to profl. jours. Fellow: Am. Bar Found.; mem.: ABA (chair task force on involvement of women 1990—93, governing coun. 1992—99, liaison to commn. on women 1993—97, vice chair tort and ins. practice sect. 1995—96, chair-elect tort and ins. practice sect. 1996—97, standing com. environ. law 1996—99, chair tort and ins. practice sect. 1997—98, chair sect. officers conf. 1998—2001, governing coun. 2003, del. 2003, ins. coverage litigation com., chair task force CERCLA reauthorization, law practice mgmt. sect., comm. com.), Fedn. Ins. and Corp. Counsel, Def. Rsch. Inst., Multnomah Bar Assn. (bd. dirs. 1994—95), Oreg. State Bar, Wash. Bar Assn. Office: Bullivant Houser Bailey PC 300 Pioneer Tower 888 SW 5th Ave Ste 300 Portland OR 97204-2089 Office Phone: 503-499-4430. Business E-Mail: dianne.dailey@bullivant.com.

DAILEY, FRANKLYN EDWARD, JR., electronic image technology company executive, analyst, consultant; b. Rochester, NY, Feb. 5, 1921; s. Franklyn Edward and Isabel Louise (Lasher) D.; m. Marguerite Virginia Parker, Apr. 1, 1944; children: Franklyn III, Michael, Philip, Elizabeth, John, Paul, Thomas, Vincent. BS, U.S. Naval Acad., 1942; BSEE, U.S. Naval Postgrad. Sch., 1950; MS in Applied Physics, UCLA, 1951. Commd. ensign USN, 1942, advanced through ranks to capt.; mgr. planning and engrng. ops. Stromberg-Carlson Co., Rochester, NY, and San Diego, 1956-61; treas. Stati-Systems Inc., Springfield, Mass., 1962-65; dir. mfg. Tecnifax Corp., Holyoke, Mass., 1965-66; asst. dir. rsch. The Plastic Coating Corp., South Hadley, Mass., 1966-67; asst. v.p. mktg. Scott Graphics Inc., South Hadley, 1967-68, v.p. new bus. devel., 1968-70, v.p. rsch., 1970-76; cons. Image Tech. & Application, Wilbraham, Mass., 1977—; prin. Dailey Internat. Pub., 1996—. Pres. Photon Chroma Inc., Westfield, Mass., 1982, 84; image cons. McGraw-Hill, N.Y.C., 1978, Isomet Corp., Springfield, Va., 1980; v.p. mfg. Coulter System Corp., Bedford, Mass., 1981; chmn. Electronic Imaging Conf., Boston, Anaheim, 1985-90; speaker in field. Author: Joining the War at Sea, 1939-45, 1998, 3d edit., 2006, My Times with the Sisters and Other Events, 2000, 3d reprinting, 2005, The Triumph of Instrument Flight: A Retrospective in the Century of U.S. Aviation, 2004. Pres. Pioneer Valley chpt. Am. Diabetes Assn., 1986-88. Roman Catholic. Avocations: tennis, biking. Office Phone: 413-596-3752. Personal E-mail: franklyn@daileyint.com.

DAILEY, GARRETT CLARK, publisher, lawyer; b. Bethesda, Md., Mar. 22, 1947; s. Garrett Hobart Valentine and Margaret (Clark) Dailey; m. Carolynn Farrar, June 21, 1969; children: Patrick, Steven. AB, UCLA, 1969; MA, Ariz. State U., 1974; JD, U. Calif., Davis, 1977. Bar: Calif. 1977, U.S. Dist. Ct. (no. dist.) Calif. 1969. Assoc. Stark, Stewart, Simon & Sparrowe, Oakland, Calif., 1977-80; ptnr. Davies & Dailey, Oakland, 1980-85, owner, 1986-90; ptnr. Blum, Davies & Dailey, Oakland, 1985-86; pres., pub. Attys. Briefcase, Inc., Oakland, 1989—, pres., CEO, 1989—. Lectr. U. Calif. Davis Sch. Law, 1988-90, Golden Gate U. Grad. Sch. Taxation, San Francisco, 1986—95. Author: SupporTax, 2001—, Dissomaster, 2004; contbg. author Attorney's Briefcase, Calif. Family Law, 1990—, Calif. Evidence, 1993—, Children and the Law, 1992—, Calif. Lawgic Marital Termination Agreements, 1996—, Calif. Divorce Guide, 1997—, Lawgic Premarital Agreements, 1997— Bd. dirs. Amigos de las Americas, San Ramon Valley, Calif., 1980-85, Rotary 517 Found., Oakland, 1985, Kid's Turn, 1993. Recipient Hall of Fame award Calif. Assn. Cert. Family Law Specialists, 1995, Spencer Brandeis award LA County Bar Assn., 2003. Fellow Am. Acad. Matrimonial Lawyers (named Family Law Person of Yr., 2006); mem. Assn. Cert. Family Law Specialists (Hall of Fame award 1995). Democrat. Congregationalist. Home: 1651 W Livorna Rd Alamo CA 94507-1018 Office: Attys Briefcase Inc 2915 McClure St Oakland CA 94609 Office Phone: 510-465-3920. E-mail: briefcase@aol.com.

DAILEY, JANET, writer; b. Storm Lake, Iowa, May 21, 1944; d. Boyd and Louise Haradon; m. William Dailey; 2 stepchildren. Student pub. schs., Independence, Iowa. Sec., Nebr., Iowa, 1963-74. Author: No Quarter Asked, 1976, After the Storm, 1976, Boss Man From Ogallala, 1976, Savage Land, 1976, Land of Enchantment, 1976, Fire and Ice, 1976, The Homeplace, 1976, Dangerous Masquerade, 1977, Night of the Cotillion, 1977, Valley of the Vapors, 1977, Fiesta San Antonio, 1977, Show Me, 1977, Bluegrass King, 1977, A Lyon's Share, 1977, The Widow and the Wastrel, 1977, Giant of Mesabi, 1978, The Ivory Cane, 1978, The Indy Man, 1978, Darling Jenny, 1978, Reilly's Woman, 1978, To Tell the Truth, 1978, Sonora Sundown, 1978, Big Sky Country, 1978, Something Extra, 1978, Master Fiddler, 1978, Beware of the Stranger, 1978, The Matchmakers, 1978, For Bitter or Worse, 1979, Green Mountain Man, 1979, Six White Horses, 1979, Summer Mahogany, 1979, Touch the Wind, 1979, Strange Bedfellow, 1979, Low Country Liars, 1979, Sweet Promise, 1979, For Mike's Sake, 1979, Sentimental Journey, 1979, A Land Called Deseret, 1979, The Bride of the Delta Queen, 1979, Tidewater Lover, 1979, Lord of the High Lonesome, 1980, Kona Winds, 1980, The Boston Man, 1980, The Rogue, 1980, Bed of Grass, 1980, The Thawing of Mara, 1980, The Mating Season, 1980, Southern Nights, 1980, Ride the Thunder, 1980, Enemy in Camp, 1980, Difficult Decision, 1980, Heart of Stone, 1980, One of the Boys, 1980, Wild and Wonderful, 1981, A Tradition of Pride, 1981, The Traveling Kind, 1981, The Hostage Bride, 1981, Dakota Dreamin', 1981, For the Love of God, 1981, Night Way, 1981, This Calder Sky, 1981, Lancaster Men, 1981, Terms of Surrender, 1982, With a Little Luck, 1982, Wildcatter's Woman, 1982, Northern Magic, 1982, That Carolina Summer, 1982, This Calder Range, 1982, Foxfire Light, 1982, The Second Time, 1982, Mistletoe and Holly, 1982, Stands a Calder Man, 1983, Separate Cabins, 1983, Western Man, 1983, Calder Born, Calder Bred, 1983, Best Way to Lose, 1983, Leftover Love, 1984, Silver Wings, Santiago Blue, 1984, The Pride of Hannah Wade, 1985, The Glory Game, 1985, The Great Alone, 1986, Heiress, 1987, Rivals, 1989, Masquerade, 1990, Aspen Gold, 1991, Tangled Vines, 1992, Riding High, 1994, The Proud and The Free, 1994, Touch the Wind, 1994, Summer Mahogany, 1995, Legacies, 1996, Homecoming, 1997, Illusions: A Novel, 1997, The Prodigal Daughter, 1998, This Calder Sky, 1999, Calder Pride, 1999, A Capital Holiday, 2001, Green Calder Grass, 2002, Calder Promise, 2004, Lone Calder Star, 2005. Recipient Golden Heart award Romance Writers Am., 1981, Romantic Times Contemporary award, 1983.

DAILEY, JIM, former mayor; b. Little Rock, July 31, 1942; m. Patti Murphy, 1965; 4 children. BSBA, U. Ark. Mayor City of Little Rock, 1995—2006. Exec. com., past v.p. Ark. Mcpl. League; active participant Domestic Violence Commn., Youth Task Force, Workforce Investment Bd., Advt. and Promotion Commn., Little Rock; bd. dirs. Gtr. Little Rock Regional C. of C., Metroplan, Little Rock, Cmtys. in Schs., Little Rock, Sister Cities Commn., Little Rock, New Futures, Little Rock.

DAILY, DEIRDRE LYNN, systems analyst; b. Santa Monica, Calif., Sept. 28, 1976; d. Karen Lynn Daily. AA, Moorpark Coll., 1997; BS, Calif. State U., Northridge, 1999, postgrad., 2006—. Intern managed care West Hills Hosp., Calif.; provider rels. rep. Family Healthcare Med. Group, Simi Valley, Seaview IPA, Oxnard, 2002; regional sales rep. CIMS- a Wellpoint subsidiary; lead user applications analyst Wellpoint, Inc., Newbury Park, 2005—06; contract compliance advisor Compliance WellPoint, Inc., 2006. Vol. ONE Adult Day Care, Northridge. Avocations: photography, art, music, hiking, camping. Personal E-mail: deirddaily@aol.com.

DAILY, FRANK J(EROME), lawyer; b. Chgo., Mar. 22, 1942; s. Francis Jerome and Eileen Veronica (O'Toole) D.; m. Julianna Ebert, June 23, 1996; children: Catherine, Eileen, Frank, William, Michael. BA in Journalism, Marquette U., 1964, JD, 1968. Bar: Wis. 1968, U.S. Dist. Ct. (ea. dist.) Wis. 1968, U.S. Dist. Ct. (we. dist.) Wis. 1971, U.S. Dist. Ct. (ctrl. dist.) Ill. 1990, U.S. Dist. Ct. (ea. dist.) Mich. 1994, U.S. Ct. Appeals (7th cir.) 1977, U.S. Ct. Appeals (3d and 5th cirs.) 1985, U.S. Ct. Appeals (4th, 6th, 8th, 9th, 10th, 11th cirs.) 1990, U.S. Supreme Ct. 1998, U.S. Dist. Ct. (no. dist.) Ill. 1999. Assoc. Quarles & Brady, Milw., 1968-75, ptnr., 1975—. Lectr. in product liability law and trial techniques Marquette U. Law Sch., U. Wis., Harvard U.; lectr. seminars sponsored by ABA, State Bar Wis., State Bar S.D., State Bar S.C., Product Liability Adv. Coun., Chem. Mfrs. Assn., Wis. Acad. Trial Lawyers, Trial Attys. Am., Marquette U., Southeastern Corp. Law Inst., Risk Ins. Mgmt. Soc., Inc.; life mem. pres.'s coun. Wake Forest U., U. Dayton, Boston Coll. Author: Your Product's Life Is in the Balance: Litigation Survival-Increasing the Odds for Success, 1986, Product Liability Litigation in the 80s: A Trial Lawyer's View from the Trenches, 1986, Discovery Available to the Litigator and Its Effective Use, 1986, The Future of Tort Litigation: The Continuing Validity of Jury Trials, 1991, How to Make an Impact in Opening Statements for the Defense in Automobile Product Liability Cases, 1992, How Much Reform Does Civil Jury System Need, 1992, Do Protective Orders Compromise Public's Right to Know, 1993, Developments in Chemical Exposure Cases: Challenging Expert Testimony, 1993, The Spoliation Doctrine: The Sword, The Shield and The Shadow, 1997, Trial Tested Techniques for Winning Opening Statements, 1997, Litigation in the Next Millennium -- A Trial Lawyer's Crystal Ball Report, 1998, What's Hot and What's Not in Non-Daubert Products Liability In the Seventh Circuit, 1998. Commr. for chief judge Milwaukee County, Wis., 2001; bd. visitors Wake Forest U. Law Sch.; bd. trustees U. Ala. Law Sch. Named Marquette U. Law Alumnus of Yr., 2000. Fellow Internat. Acad. Trial Lawyers; mem. ABA (past co-chair discovery com. litigation sect., vice chmn. products, gen. liability and consumer law com. of sect. tort and ins. practice, litigation sect. and mfrs. liability subcom.), ATLA, AAAS, Trial Atty. of Am., Wis. Bar Assn., Milw. Bar Assn., 7th Cir. Bar Assn., Am. Judicature Soc., Def. Rsch. Inst., Supreme Ct. Hist. Soc., Indsl. Truck Assn. (lawyers com.), Am. Law Inst., Product Liability Adv. Coun., Am. Agrl. Law Assn., Wis. Acad. Trial Lawyers, Assn. for Advancement of Automotive Medicine (life), Nat. I-Club U. Iowa, U. Ala. Nat. Alumni Assn., Circle of Champions. Roman Catholic. Office: Quarles & Brady 411 E Wisconsin Ave Ste 2040 Milwaukee WI 53202-4497 Office Phone: 414-277-5381. E-mail: fjd@quarles.com.

DAILY, GRETCHEN CARA, ecologist, environmental services administrator; b. Wash., Oct. 19, 1964; d. Charles Dennis and Suzanne Rachel (Schubert) D. BS, Stanford U., 1986, MS, 1987, PhD, 1992. Ctr. for Conservation Biology/Nature Conservancy fellow Stanford (Calif.) U., 1988-92; Winslow/Heinz postdoctoral fellow U. Calif., Berkeley, 1992—; assoc. prof. biology Stanford (Calif.) U., dir., Tropical Rsch. Program, Ctr. for Conservation. Sci. advisor IPAT Prodns. (film), Stanford, 1995. Author (with PR Ehrlich & AH Ehrlich) The Stork and the Plow: The Equity Solution to the Human Dilemma, 1995, Nature's Services: Societal Dependence on Natural Ecosystems, 1997, (with Katherine Ellison) The New Economy of Nature: The Quest to Make Conservatoin Profitable, 2002; Contbr. over 150 articles to profl. jours. Recipient Frances Lou Kallman award Stanford U., 1992, 21st Century Scientist award, 2000; Named Pew scholar in conservation and environ., Pew Found., 1994, Fellow, Aldo Leopard Leadership Program, 1999, Smith Sr. Scholar, The Nature Conservancy, 2003. Mem. Rocky Mtn. Biol. Lab; Fellow, Am. Acad. Arts & Sciences, NAS. Office: Stanford U Ctr Conservation Biology 385 Serra Mall Stanford CA 94305 Office Phone: 650-723-9452. Office Fax: 650-725-1992. E-mail: gdaily@stanford.edu.

DAILY, THOMAS A., lawyer; b. Ft. Smith, Ark., Jan. 8, 1946; BA, U. of the South, 1967; JD with honors, U. Ark., 1970. Bar: Ark. 1970. Ptnr. Daily & Woods PLLC, Ft. Smith, Ark. Mem.: ABA, Ark. Bar Assn. (pres.-elect 2002, pres. 2003).

DAIM, TUGRUL UNSAL, technology management specialist, educator; b. Istanbul, May 22, 1967; s. Turhan Hasan and Tulay Ayse D.; m. Yonca Tarman. BS, Bogazici U., Istanbul, 1989; MSc, PhD, Portland State U., 1998. Program mgr. Intel Corp., Hillsboro, Oreg., 1995—2005; assoc. prof. Portland State U., Oreg., 2005—. Adj. prof. Portland State U., 1997—, Oreg. Grad. Inst. Sci. and Tech., Beaverton, 1999—; cons. KOC Corp., Istanbul, 1992-93, Turkpetrol Corp., Istanbul, 1993-96. Contbr. articles to profl. jours., chpts. to books. Pres. Turkish Am. Students Cultural Assn., Portland, 1993-95, Suadiye LEO Club, Istanbul, 1989. Mem. IEEE, Am. Soc. Engring. Mgmt., Nat. Geographic Soc., Internat. Assn. Mgmt. Tech., Product Devel. Mgmt. Assn., Inst. Ops. Rsch. and Mgmt. Sci., Portland Downtown Lions Club (dir. 1995-96), Omega Rho (pres. chpt. 1995-97), Sigma Xi, Tau Beta Pi. Avocations: european comics, soccer, tennis, gourmet cooking. Home: 16125 SW Kessler Tigard OR 97224 Office: Portland State Univ ETM 1900 SW 4th Ave Portland OR 97201 Office Phone: 503-806-2791. Fax: 503-725-4667. Business E-Mail: tugrul@emp.pdx.edu.

DAINES, N. GEORGE, lawyer; b. 1949; m. Mindy Daines; 6 children. BA, Utah State U.; JD, Yale U. Bar: Utah 1976. Chief judge U.S. Ct. Appeals (10th Cir.); ptnr. Barrett & Daines, Logan, Utah, Daines, Wyatt & Allen, LLP, Cache County, 2003—. Tchr. bus. and real estate law Utah State U.; founder, prin. owner Cache Valley Bank; bd. dirs. Utah Prosecution Coun. Mem. bd. editors: Yale Law Jour. Active in the historical renovation of prime historic sites in Cache Valley. Mem.: Utah State Bar (mem. exec. com., jud. evaluation com., pres.-elect 2003—04, pres. 2004—). Office: Daines Wyatt & Allen LLP 101 N Main Logan UT 84321 Office Phone: 435-716-8361. Office Fax: 435-716-8381. E-mail: george@legal.state.ut.us.*

DAINES, RICHARD F., state health commissioner, former health services executive; b. Preston, ID, Feb. 17, 1951; m. Linda Daines; 3 children. BA in History, Utah St. U., 1974; MD, Cornell U., 1978. Cert. Am. Bd. Internal Medicine, Am. Bd. Internal Medicine, Critical Care. Missionary Church of Jesus Christ of Latter-day Saints, Bolivia, 1970—72; intern NY Hosp., 1978—79, resident, 1979—81; med. dir. St. Barnabas Med. Ctr., Bronx, NY, 1987—99, sr. v.p. for profl. affairs, 1994—2000; med. dir., sr. v.p. med. affairs St. Luke's-Roosevelt Hosp. Ctr., NYC, 2000—02, pres., CEO, 2002—07; commr. of health State of NY, Albany, 2007—. Avocation: skiing. Office: NY Dept of Health Corning Tower Empire State Plz Albany NY 12237*

DAITZ, RONALD FREDERICK, lawyer; b. NYC, Sept. 1, 1940; s. Abraham and Anne (Birnbaum) D.; m. Linda Fay Rosenberg, Aug. 2, 1964; children: Paul Bennett, Charles Spencer. AB, Amherst Coll., 1961; LLB, Harvard U., 1964. Bar: N.Y. 1966, Colo. 1964, U.S. Dist. Ct. Colo. 1964, U.S. Ct. Appeals (10th cir.) 1964, U.S. Dist. Ct. (so. dist.) N.Y. 1979. Assoc. Henry & Adams, Denver, 1964-65; from assoc. to ptnr. Weil, Gotshal & Manges LLP, NYC, 1965—. Mem. ABA (fed. regulation of securities com., bus. law sect. 1979—), Am. Coll. Comml. Fin. Lawers, N.Y. State Bar Assn. (mem. com. securities regulation, bus. law sect. 1984—, chmn. 1990-93, sec. bus. law sect. 1994-95, 2d vice-chair and fiscal officer 1995-96, mem. exec. com. 1991-2001, 1st vice chair 1996-97, chair 1997-98), Assn. Bar City N.Y. (com. corp. law 1975-77, 87-88, 95-97). Office: Weil Gotshal & Manges LLP 767 5th Ave Fl Concl New York NY 10153-0119 Office Phone: +44 207 903-1404.

DAJANI, VIRGINIA, art association administrator; Exec. dir. Am. Acad. Arts and Letters, NYC, 1990—. Office: Am Acad Arts and Letters 633 W 155th St New York NY 10032-7501 Office Phone: 212-368-5900. E-mail: academy@artsandletters.org.

DAJNOWICZ, JAN, software and hardware designer, researcher; arrived in US, 1998; BSc in Electronics and Telecomm., Silesian Tech. U., Gliwice, Poland, 1995. Engr. Welding Inst., Gliwice, 1982—92, group leader, 1992—95, head computer sci. dept., 1995—98; programmer JLA, Park Ridge, NJ, 1998—2001; I/T specialist IBM Corp., Armonk, NY, 1998—2004, Southbury, Conn., 2005; tech. specialist UPS, Morristown, NJ, 2005—. Con./programmer AVREX, Gilwice, 1990—93, Technologia, Gilwice, 1993—95, Gambit, Gilwice, 1995—98. Contbr. chapters to books, articles to profl. jours. Recipient Silver medal, Eureka, Brussels, 1995—97, award of gt. invention competition, Ministry Environ. Protection Natural and Forest, Warsaw, 1997. Mem.: N.Y. Acad. Scis., Am. Assn. Artificial Intelligence. Achievements include inventions in field. Avocations: Karate, Japanese and Chinese cultures. Business E-Mail: jdajnowi@sdf.lonestar.org.

DAKE, MARCIA ALLENE, retired nursing educator, dean; b. Bemus Point, NY, May 22, 1923; d. Earl B. and Bernice DeLeo (Haskin) D. Diploma, Crouse Irving Hosp., 1944; BS, Syracuse U., 1951; MA, Columbia U., 1955, EdD, 1958. RN. Tchr., sch. nurse various locations, 1946—48; chmn. health dept. SUNY, Oneonta, 1952—56; dean coll. nursing U. Ky., Lexington, 1958—72; dir. dept. nursing edn. ANA, Kansas City, 1972—74; project dir. program devel. nursing ARC, Washington, 1975—79; dir. nursing edn. James Madison U. Coll. Nursing, 1979—81; prof. dean Coll. Nursing, 1981—88; ret., 1988. Editor, resident photographer: Greenspring Village Photo Directories, 2000—; programmer, host Closed Circuit TV Studio, 2000. Mem. Ky. Bd. Nursing Edn. Nurse Registration, 1969-72, pres., 1970-72; pres. Va. Coun. Deans of Baccalaureate Nursing Programs, 1981-84; nurse officer Civil Def. Otsego County, N.Y., 1953-56; mem. Def. Adv. Com. on Women in Svcs., 1963-65; mem. Ky. Comprehensive Health Planning Coun., 1968-71; pres. Ky. League for Nursing, 1961-65; bd. dir. Cmty. Ch. Coll., Sun City Ctr., Fla., 1989-92, Sun City Ctr. Guardianship Found., 1990-98; trustee United Cmty. Ch., Sun City Ctr., 1993-96, chmn. pers. com., 1994-96, fin. com., 1994-95, vice chmn. bd. trustees, 1995-96, stewardship com., 1996-98, mem. pastoral rels. com., 1996-98, mem. long range planning com., 1996-97, chmn. pastoral rels. com., 1998—; sec. Caloosa Women's Golf Assn., Sun City Ctr., 1991-92; treas. Greater Sun City Ctr. Disaster Coun., 1992-94; mem., vice chmn. resident adv. com. Greenspring Village, Springfield, Va., 1999-2000, corr. sec. resident adv. com., 2001; prodr., host Channel 6 T.V Greenspring Village, 2001; prodr., pub. resident/staff photo directories, 2000-. 1st lt. U.S. Army Nurse Corps., 1945—46. Fellow Nat. League Nursing; mem. ANA, Va. Nurses Assn. (pres. dist. 9 1983-85), Va. Soc. Profl. Nurses (treas. 1983-88), Va. Assn. Colls. Nursing (sec. 1980-82, pres. 1982-85), Alliance Nursing Orgns. (chmn. Va. 1985-88), LWV, Delta Kappa Gamma, Kappa Delta Pi, Pu Lambda Theta. Address: 222 7442 Spring Village Dr Springfield VA 22150-4444

DAKIN, CHRISTINE WHITNEY, dancer, educator; b. New Haven, Aug. 25, 1949; d. James Irving, Jr. and Jean Evelyn (Coulter) Crump; m. Robert Ford Dakin, June 21, 1969 (div. Sept. 1982); m. Stephen J. Mauer, Aug. 1, 1985. Student, U. Mich., 1967-71; D of Arts (hon.), Shenandoah U., 1996. Performer, teacher Ann Arbor Dance Theater, Mich., 1965-71; tchr. Ann Arbor Pub. Schs., 1967-70, Lincoln Ctr. Inst., NYC, 1978, Guanajuato U., Mex., 1982; vis. artist USIA Vladivastock, Vladivastock, Russia, 1992; ArtsLink grantee, vis. artist Vladivastock, 1996; tchr., faculty advisor, choreographer Ballet Nacional de Mex., 1993—, U. Colima, Mexico, 2000—; vis. artist USIA Ballet Contemporaneo, Buenos Aires, 1993; prin. dancer Martha Graham Dance Co., NYC, 1976—. Dancer, rehearsal dir. Pearl Lang. Dance Co., 1972-76, Kazuko Hirabayashi Dance Co., 1974-76; faculty Martha Graham Sch., 1972—, Juilliard Sch., 1992—, Alvin Alley Am. Dance Ctr., 1989-93. Appeared in: It's Hard to Be a Jew, 1972, The Dybuk, 1975; appeared (with Martha Graham Dance Co.) Covent Garden, London, 1976, Met. Opera, 1980, Bklyn. Acad. Music, 1994, Sta. WNET Dance in Am. Series, 1979; Young Artist in Performance at The White House, Sta. WNET, 1982, (with Rudolph Nureyev) Paris Opera, Berlin Opera, 1984, N.Y. State Theater, 1985; NHK Film, Japan, 1990, Paris Opera Film, 1991, (documentary film) Les Printemps du Sacre, 1993; assoc. founder Buglisi/Foreman Dance, 1994, (with Buglisi/Foreman Dance) Runes of the Heart, Kennedy Ctr., 1997; assoc. artistic dir. Martha Graham Dance Co., 1997, artistic dir., 2001. Am. Dance Festival scholar, 1969, Garcia-Robles Sr. scholar Fulbright Found., 1999; recipient award Dance Mag., 1994, U. Mich. Alumni award, 2000, Bessie award, 2004; grantee Rockefeller U.S.-Mex. Fund for Culture, 1997-98, 2001. Mem. Am. Guild Mus. Artists (life, bd. govs.)

DALE, ADRIANNE MARIE, information technology executive, consultant; d. Almore Marcus and Marie Antoinette (Howard) Dale. BS, Howard U., Washington, 1961. Cert. med. technologist Am. Soc. for Clin. Pathology, 1967. Med. technologist Providence Hosp., Washington, 1967—71; med. tech. instr. D.C. Gen. Hosp., 1971—72; assoc. prof., med. tech. Prince Georges C.C., Largo, Md., 1972—87; cons. D.C. Commn. Women, Washington, 1987—87; adminstrv. asst. Episcopal Ch. Women Diocese of Washington, 1989—90; program officer Episcopal Diocese of Washington, 1990—99; founder and CEO Mouse Calls, LLC, 2000—. Editor: (anthology) People of the Promise; author: (biography) Earl Neil: Black Civil Rights Reformer. Vol. D.C. Crisis Hotline, Washington, 1995, Arena Stage, 2003—; diocesan/parish cons. Episcopal Diocese Washington, 1985—99; lay leader Trinity Episc. Ch., Washington, 1987—2003; mem. All Souls Unitarian Choir, 2003—; sec. Episcopal Sr. Ministries, 1993—99; mem. ByteBack Cmty. Computer Ctr., 2005, Oracle Set Found., 1999—. Recipient Vol. of the Yr. cert., ByteBack Cmty. Computer Ctr., 2005. Episcopalian. Avocations: yoga, crossword puzzles, reading, jazz piano, travel. Office: Mouse Calls LLC Washington DC 20017-2621 Home Phone: 202-529-8497; Office Phone: 202-529-8934. Personal E-mail: info@mousecalls-llc.com.

DALE, DAVID C., physician, educator; b. Knoxville, Tenn., Sept. 19, 1940; s. John Irvin and Cecil (Chandler) D.; m. Rose Marie Wilson, June 22, 1963 BS magna cum laude, Carson-Newman Coll., 1962; MD cum laude, Harvard U., 1966. Intern and resident Mass. Gen. Hosp., 1966-68; resident U. Wash. Hosp., Seattle, 1971-72; clin. assoc. NIH, 1968-71; prof., assoc. chmn. dept. medicine U. Wash., Seattle, 1976-82, dean Sch. of Medicine, 1982-86. Contbr. numerous articles to profl. jours. Served to comdr. USPHS, 1968-70, 72-74 Mem. Am. Soc. Hematology, Assn. Am. Physicians, Am. Soc. for Clin. Investigation, ACP Avocations: woodworking, gardening, backpacking, sports. Office: U Wash Sch Medicine PO Box 356422 Seattle WA 98195-6422 Business E-Mail: dcdale@u.washington.edu.

DALE, DEBORAH, foundation executive; b. 1967; Chief devel. officer Primavera Found., Tucson. Involved with Voices for Edn., Ariz. Women's Conf., Southern Ariz. Ctr. Against Sexual Assault; Taste of Nation founding com. mem. Share Our Strength; com. mem. Mayor's Costume Ball for Arts; former bd. mem. Cmty. Shares; former bd. chair Mus. Contemporary Art; co-chair Tucson Suffragettes Virgin Voter Ball. Named one of 40 Under 40, Tucson Bus. Edge, 2006. Mem.: Assn. Fundraising Professionals (govt. rels. chair). Office: Primavera Foundation 702 S 6th Ave Tucson AZ 85701 Office Phone: 520-623-5111. Office Fax: 520-623-6434.

DALE, ERWIN RANDOLPH, retired lawyer, writer; b. Herrin, Ill., July 30, 1915; s. Henry and Lena Bell (Campbell) D.; m. Charline Vincent, Aug. 27, 1955; children: Allyson Ann (Mrs. Earl A. Samson III), Kristan Charline (Mrs. Victor L. Zimmermann). BA, U. Tex., El Paso, 1937; JD, U. Tex., 1943. Bar: Tex. 1943, D.C. 1953, Mich. 1956, N.Y. 1960. Atty. IRS, 1943-56, chief reorgn. and dividend br., 1954-56; legal staff Gen. Motors Corp., 1956-57; ptnr. Chapman, Walsh & O'Connell, NYC and Washington, 1957-59, Hawkins, Delafield & Wood, NYC, 1959-84; of counsel Hutchison, Price, Boyle & Brooks, Dallas, 1985-86, Jenkens, Hutchison & Gilchrist, Dallas, 1986, Hutchison, Boyle, Brooks & Dransfield, Dallas, 1986—87, ret., 1987—. Lectr. tax matters; dir. Md. Electronics Mfg. Corp., 1948-58; dir., treas. The Renaissance Corp., 1968-72; dir., asst. treas. Shancom Reconstrn. Corp., 1968-72, Newhaven Corp., 1968-72 Author numerous articles on fed. tax matters; bd. editors: Tex. Law Rev., 1941-42, 42-43. Mem. ABA (chmn. com. consol. returns sect. taxation 1959-60), Tex. Bar Assn., Mich. Bar Assn., N.Y. State Bar Assn. (chmn. corp. tax com. tax sect. 1967-68, mem. exec. com. 1968-70), Tax Inst. Am. (bd. dirs. 1967-69, treas. 1966), Assn. of Bar of City of N.Y., Nat. Tax Assn., Nat. Assn. Bond Lawyers, Am. Coll. Tax Counsel, Ex-Students Assn. U. Tex., Ex-Students Assn. U. Tex., El Paso, Bronxville Field Club (N.Y.), Masons. Home: 10 Holly Ln Darien CT 06820-3303 Home Fax: 203-662-9386. Personal E-mail: erdale@aol.com.

DALE, JOHN SORENSEN, investment company executive, portfolio manager; b. Mpls., Sept. 30, 1945; s. John Sorensen and Ruth Elaine (Bergstrom) D.; m. Cheryl Lee Woolley, June 19, 1965; children: John, Christopher. BA in Mktg. and Humanities, U. Minn., 1968. CFA. Securities analyst, portfolio mgr. Norwest Corp., Mpls., 1968-78, v.p., sr. trust investment strategist, 1978-84, sr. v.p., mgr. equity advisors, 1984-87; sr. v.p., sr. portfolio mgr. Peregrine Capital Mgmt., Mpls., 1987—. Fellow Inst. Chartered Fin. Analysts; mem. Assn. Investment Mgmt. and Rsch., Twin Cities Soc., Security Analysts, Internat. Soc. Fin. Analysts. Avocations: travel, fishing, hunting. Office: Peregrine Capital Mgmt LaSalle Plz Ste 1850 8th and LaSalle Minneapolis MN 55402-2018

DALE, JUDY RIES, religious organization administrator, consultant; b. Memphis, Dec. 13, 1944; d. James Lorigan and Julia Marie (Schwinn) Ries; m. Eddie Melvin Ashmore, July 12, 1969 (div. Dec. 1983). BA, Rhodes Coll., 1966; M in Religious Edn., So. Bapt. Theol. Sem., 1969, grad. specialist in religious edn., 1969. Cert. tchr. educable mentally handicapped, secondary English, adminstrn. and supervision spl. edn. EMH tchr., curriculum writer, tchr. trainer Jefferson County Bd. Edn., Louisville, 1969-88, ednl. cons., 1988-90; dist. coord. Gt. Lakes dist. Universal Fellowship Met. Cmty. Chs., Louisville, 1990—2002, spl. asst. comm. and lay resources, 2006—. Lectr. U. Louisville, 1976—77, 1987—90, Jefferson CC, Louisville, 1987—93; mem. program adv. com. Internat. Conf. Spl. Edn., Beijing, 1987—88; mem. faculty Samaritan Inst. Religious Studies, 1992—98. Editor, writer: A Manual of Instructional Strategies, 1985, Handbook for Begining Teachers, 1989. Bd. sec. Com. Ten, Inc., Louisville, 1987—91; v.p. GLUE, 1988—92, pres., 1992—94; mem. steering com. Ky. Fairness Alliance, 2005—06, treas., 2005—06; mem. membership com. Cmty. Health Trust, 1991—94; chair acad. affairs com. Samaritan Inst. Religious Studies, 1996—97, trustee, 1992—98; mem. programs and budget divsn. Universal Fellowship Met. Cmty. Chs., 1990—97, mem. gen. coun., 1990—2002, active women's secretariat steering com., 1991—95, mem. core team, 1993—2000, chair, 1997—2000, fin. team, 1997—2005, bd. adminstrn., 2003—05, chmn. risk mgmt. team, 2003—05, sec., 2004—05, chair, 2005. Named Outstanding Elem. Tchr. Am., 1975; recipient Hon. Order of Ky. Cols., 1976, MCC Disting. Lay Leadership award, 1999. Mem.: ACLU, NOW, AAUW, Ky. Coun. Exceptional Children (bd. dirs. 1978—90, Mem. of the Yr. 1987), Coun. Exceptional Children (keynote spkr., mem. exec. com. 1984—88, internat. pres. 1986—87, bd. govs. 1981—88), Women's Alliance, Parents, Family and Friends Lesbians and Gays, Nat. Gay & Lesbian Task Force, Nat. Ctr. Lesbian Rights, Internat. Platform Assn., Gay and Lesbian Assn. Anti-Defamation, Lambda Legal Def. and Edn. Fund, Phi Kappa Phi. Democrat. Avocations: reading, handwork. Home and Office: 1300 Ambridge Dr Louisville KY 40207-2410 Personal E-mail: judydale13@aol.com.

DALE, KAREN MCCALL, music educator; b. Charlotte, NC, May 6, 1959; m. B. Edwin Dale III; children: Melody, Caroline, Benjamin. A of Fine Arts, Brevard Coll., NC, 1979; BA, Winthrop Coll., Rockhill, SC, 1982; MusM, East Carolina U., Greenville, NC, 1984. Tchr. music Southeast Elem. Sch., Kinston, NC, 1985—86; min. music Spilman Meml. Bapt. Ch., 1985—90; dir. choral South Lenoir H.S., 1986—91; tchr. music Banks ELem. Sch., 1991—94; tchr. music, drama Arendell Panott Acad., 1994—96; assoc. prof. comm., fine arts Jackson State C.C., Tenn., 1999—. Vis. prof. music Union U., Jackson, 1997—2000. Performer: (soprano) Memphis Vocal Arts, 1999—; prodr.: (soprano) West Jackson Choir, 2003—; performer: (flute) West Jackson Orch., 2003. Recipient Outstanding Young Educator, Lenoir County Jaycees, Tchr. Yr., South Lenoir. Mem.: West Tenn. Vocal Music Educators Assn., Music Educators Nat. Conf., Am. Choral Dirs. Assn., NAt. Assn. Tchrs. Singing. Home: 10 Buckthorn Cove Jackson TN 38305 Office: JAckson State C C 2046 N Parkway Jackson TN 38301 Personal E-mail: kmdsing@yahoo.com.

DALE, ROBERT GORDON, investment company executive; b. Toronto, Ont., Can., Nov. 1, 1920; s. Gordon McIntyre and Helen Marjorie (Cartwright) D.; m. Mary Austin Babcock, Apr. 3, 1948; children: Robert Austin, John Gordon. Student, U. Toronto Schs., 1930-39, Trinity Coll., U. Toronto, 1939-40. Cert. in bus. adminstrn., 1946. With Maple Leaf Mills, Ltd., Toronto, 1947—, plant mgr., 1957-61, gen. product mgr., 1961-65, asst. to pres., 1965-67, exec. v.p., 1967-68, chmn., pres., chief exec. officer, 1968-86, dir.; chmn. Upper Lakes Group Inc., Toronto, 1993—95; dep. chmn. Upper Lakes Group, Inc., Toronto, 1996—; pres. Pinedale Investments Inc., Toronto, 1994—. Hon. pres. Air Cadet League Can.; past chmn. Ont. Provincial Com.; trustee United Comty. Fund Greater Toronto; past chmn. bd. govs. Can. Corps Commissionaires, Canadian Exec. Svc. Orgn.; bd. dirs. Sunnybrook Med. Ctr.; past pres. Branch 165 Royal Can. Legion. With RCAF, 1940-45. Decorated D.F.C., Can. Forces Decoration, Disting. Service Order. Mem. Phi Kappa Pi. Clubs: Rosedale Golf, Nat, Royal Can. Mil. Inst., Empire. Conservative. Anglican. Office: Upper Lakes Group Inc 49 Jackes Ave Toronto ON Canada M4T 1E2 Personal E-mail: daleroberg@hotmail.com.

DALE, SHANA L., federal agency administrator; b. 1964; BS, U. Tulsa; JD, Calif. Western Sch. Law. Bar: Calif. 1991, DC 1991. Asst. vice-chancellor fed. rels. U. Tex.; Rep. counsel sci., space com. US House Com. Sci., Space, Tech., 1991—95, staff dir. subcommittee Space, Aeronautics, 1995—2000; chief of staff, gen. counsel Office of Sci., Tech. Exec. Office Pres., 2005, dep. dir. Homeland & Nat. Security; dep. adminstr. NASA, 2005—. Spkr. in field. Mem.: Women in Aerospace (Outstanding Alumnus award 2000). Achievements include becoming highest ranking female official in histroy of NASA, 2005. Office: NASA HQ Suite 1M32 Washington DC 20546-0001

DALE, T.D., architectural firm executive; CEO, pres. Dale & Assocs., P.A., Jackson, Miss. With Sch. Architecture Adv. Coun. Mem.: Miss. State Bd. Architecture (sec., treas. 1986, pres. 1992), Am. Inst. Architects Miss. (bd. dir. 1996, chmn. 1996, sec. treas. 1997, chmn. state conv. 1999).

DALEN, JAMES EUGENE, cardiologist, educator; b. Seattle, Apr. 1, 1932; s. Charles A. and Muriel E. (Joanise) Robinson. BS, Wash. State U., 1955; MA, U. Mich., 1956; MD, U. Wash., 1961; MPH, Harvard U., 1972. Intern and asst. med. resident Boston City Hosp., 1961—63; sr. resident New Eng. Med. Ctr., Boston, 1963—64; rsch. fellow in cardiology Harvard Med. Sch., Peter Bent Brigham Hosp., Boston, 1964—67, assoc. dir. cardiovasc. lab., 1967—75; instr., asst. prof., assoc. prof. medicine Harvard Med. Sch., 1967—75; chmn. dept. cardiovasc. medicine U. Mass. Med. Sch., 1975—77, prof., chmn. dept. medicine, 1977—88; physician-in-chief U. Mass. Hosp., 1977—88; acting chancellor U. Mass., Worcester, 1986—87; editor Archives Internal Medicine, 1987—2004; dean, vice provost med. affairs U. Ariz. Coll. Medicine, Tucson, 1988—95, dean, v.p. health scis., 1995—2001. Mem. editl. bd. Jour. AMA, 1987—2004; contbr. articles to profl. jours. With USN, 1951—53. Mem.: ACP, Am. Coll. Chest Physicians (pres. 1985—86), Am. Coll. Cardiology, Assn. Univ. Cardiologists. Home: 5305 N Via Velazquez Tucson AZ 85750-5989 Office: 1840 E River Rd Ste 120 Tucson AZ 85718 Personal E-mail: jamesdalen@yahoo.com.

DALES, SAMUEL, microbiologist, virologist, educator; b. Warsaw, Aug. 31, 1927; emigrated to Can., 1948, naturalized, 1953; s. James and Helen (Ochs) D.; m. Laura L.R.J. Fischer, Dec. 28, 1952 (dec.); children: Adam Charles, Pamela Ann. BA with honors, U. B.C., 1951, MA, 1953; PhD, U. Toronto, 1956. Postdoctoral fellow Nat. Cancer Inst. Can., 1957-60; rsch. assoc., asst. prof. Rockefeller U., NYC, 1960-66; assoc. prof., mem., chief cytobiology Pub. Health Rsch. Inst. City of N.Y., Inc., 1966-76; prof. U. Western Ont., Can., London, Can., 1975-93, prof. emeritus, 1993—, chmn. microbiology and immunology, 1975-80. Research prof. NYU Med. Sch., 1969-75; mem. adv. bd. spl. virus cancer program Nat. Cancer Inst., NIH, 1969-73; mem. virology study sect. NIH, 1971-75, ad hoc, 1977, 79; mem. sci. adv. bd. Banting Rsch. Found., 1978-80; mem. rev. panels virology and cancer USPHS, Med. Rsch. Coun. Can.; adj. prof. Rockefeller U., 1996—. Author: Biology of Poxviruses, 1981; mem. editl. bd. Virology, 1963—, Jour. Cell Biology, 1973-76, Intervirology, 1973-91, Virus Rsch., 1983-92, Microbial Pathogenesis, 1985—, Jour. Virology, 1989-97, Ency. Virology, 1990-95; contbr. sci. articles and revs. to profl. publs. Fellow Royal Soc. Can.; Macy Found. scholar, 1981-82; rsch. grantee USPHS; rsch. grantee Med. Rsch. Coun. Can.; rsch. grantee Multiple Sclerosis Soc. Fellow AAAS; mem. Fedn. Am. Socs. for Exptl. Biology, Harvey Soc., Am. Soc. Cell Biology, N.Y. Soc. Electron Microscopy (coun. 1968-70), Amyotrophic Lateral Sclerosis Soc. An. (sci. adv. bd.) Home: 262 Central Park W Apt 4C New York NY 10024-3512 Home Phone: 217-787-7139. Personal E-mail: drssdfr@aol.com.

D'ALESANDRO, PHILIP ANTHONY, parasitologist, immunologist, retired medical educator; b. Bound Brook, NJ, Apr. 2, 1927; s. Philip and Antoinette Ann (Vaccaro) D'A.; m. Rosemary Natale Falzarine, Nov. 25, 1961. BSc, Rutgers U., 1952, MSc, 1954; PhD, U. Chgo., 1958. Rsch. assoc. U. Chgo., 1958-59; assoc. prof. Rockefeller U., NYC, 1959-75; assoc. prof., acting head divsn. tropical medicine Columbia U., NYC, 1975-92, emeritus prof., 1992—. Chmn. tropical medicine and parasitology study sect. NIH, Bethesda, Md., 1976-80. Author: (with others) Immunity to Parasitic Animals, 1970, Pathogenicity of Trypanosomes, 1979, Parasitic Protoza, Vol. 1, 1991; editor Jour. Protozoology, 1980-88; contbr. articles to profl. jours. Sgt. U.S. Army Air Corps, 1945-46. Grantee NIH, 1972-90, 79-82. Fellow AAAS; mem. Phi Beta Kappa. Avocations: antique cars, model railroading, photography. E-mail: pdalesand@aol.com.

D'ALESSANDRI, ROBERT M., academic administrator, retired dean; b. NYC, June 26, 1945; m. Elaine D'Alessandri; 2 children. BA, Fordham U., 1967; MD, N.Y. Med. Coll., 1971. Diplomate Am. Bd. Internal Medicine, Am. Bd. Infectious Diseases. Intern dept. medicine Met. Hosp., NYC, 1971—72; fellowship divsn. infectious diseases U. Fla., Gainesville, 1974—76, resident dept. medicine, 1976—77; instr., chief resident dept. medicine W.Va. U. Sch. Medicine, 1977—78, asst. prof. dept. medicine, 1978—81, assoc. prof. dept. medicine, 1981—84, prof. dept. medicine, 1985—, chief sect. of comprehensive medicine dept. medicine, 1979—87, assoc. dean ambulatory svcs. dept. medicine, 1987—90, dean Sch. of Medicine dept. medicine, 1989—2004; v.p. for health scis. W.Va. U., 1992—; pres. Blanchette Rockefeller Neurosciences Inst. Bd. dirs. Nat. Bank of W.Va., Morgantown, MountainView Regional Rehab. Hosp., W.Va. U. Rsch. Corp., Chestnut Ridge Psychiat. Hosp., W.Va. U. Hosps., W.Va. U. Med. Corp., Morgantown HealthRight Clinic, Morgantown Hospice; commentator Sta. WNPB, W.Va. Pub. Radio; host weekly Doctors on Call; weekly med. corr. Sta. WCHS-TV, Charleston, Sta. WDTV, Clarksbur, Sta. WTRF, Wheeling; elected shc. medicine rep. Univ. Faculty Senate, 1980-84; chair credentials com. W.Va. Hosps., 1984-85, med. exec. bd. chair 1985-86, chair infection control com., 1985-86, exec. com. chair 1986-87, mem. 1983-87, chair hosp. med. records com., 1986-87, chair hosps. patient care rev. com., 1986-87, chair ambulatory care bldg. com., 1987-89, chair dean's com. VA Med. Ctr., Martinsburg, 1991—, Clarksburg, 1989—; chair sch. of medicine ednl. adv. coun. W.Va. U. Health Scis. Ctr., 1989—, chair sch. of medicine exec. faculty, 1989—, chair health scis. ctr. exec. com., 1992—; coord. intro. clin. medicine dental studies, 1979-84, coord. intro. to clin. medicine, phys. diagnosis course, 1979-84; spl. lectr. Guiyang (China) Med. Coll., 1988, Hangzhou (China) Red Cross Hosp., 1988. Contbr. numerous articles to profl. jours. Bd. dirs. Monongalia Arts Ctr., Morgantown, 1989—. Mem. AMA, Am. Coll. of Physicians, Infectious Diseases Soc., Soc. for Gen. Internal Medicine, Nat. Rural Health Assn., W.Va. State Med. Assn., Monongalia County Med. Soc. Office: RC Byrd Health Scis Ctr 1150 Health Scis N PO Box 9000 Morgantown WV 26506-9000 Office Phone: 304-293-4511. Office Fax: 304-293-4973. Business E-Mail: rdalessandri@hsc.wvu.edu.

D'ALESSANDRO, DANIEL, lawyer, educator, coach; b. Jersey City, Oct. 10, 1949; s. Donato Marino D'Alessandro and Rose Teresa (Casamassimo) Drennan; m. Beth Anne Lill, Sept. 2, 1978; children: Daniel Patrick, Eric Charles. BA, St. Peter's Coll., 1971; JD, Seton Hall U., South Orange, NJ, 1974; LLM in Criminal Justice, NYU, 1981. Bar: NJ 1975, NY 1982, US Dist. Ct. NJ 1975, US Dist. Ct. (so. dist.) NY 1989, US Supreme Ct. 1985; cert. ct. approved family law mediator, civil law mediator. Law clk. to presiding judge Juvenile and Domestic Relations Ct., Hudson County, NJ, 1974-75; pub. defender City of Jersey City, 1975-76; prosecutor Town of Secaucus, NJ, 1976-77; prin. D'Alessandro & Assocs., Jersey City, 1977-82; ptnr. D' Alessandro & Tutak, Jersey City, 1982-90; pres. D'Alessandro, Tutak & Aschoff, PC, Jersey City, 1990-92; ptnr. D'Alessandro & Aschoff, PC, Jersey City, 1992—93; pvt. practice Jersey City, 1994—2003; ptnr. D'Alessandro & Cieckiewicz, P.C., Jersey City, 2003—. Adj. prof. Middlesex County Coll., Edison, NJ, 1981—83, St. Peter's Prep., 1981—83; arbitrator automobile arbitration program NJ Supreme Ct., mem. ethics com. dist. VI, vice-chair fee arbitration com.; counsel Employees Retirement Sys. Jersey City, 1985—89; lectr. in field. Vol. probation officer Hudson County Probation Dept., 1977; pro bono counsel Anthony R. Cucci Civic Assn., Jersey City, 1981—89, Battered Women's Shelter, Jersey City, 1982, Mayor's Task force for Handicapped, Jersey City, 1985—89; v.p. Jersey City Boys Club, 1991, pres., 1993—98, also trustee; baseball coach Jersey Shore Thunderbirds, NJ AAU, 1993—2001, Monmouth Monarchs Atlantic Baseball Coll. League, 2003, Mater Dei HS, 2000—02, 2004—, football coach, 2006—. Named Prof. of Yr., Secaucus Patrolmen's Benevolent Assn., 1980, Super Lawyer in Gen. Practice, NJ Monthly mag., 2005, Super Lawyer in Family Law, 2006, 2007; recipient Disting. Svc. award, Jersey City Police Dept., 1988, Cert. of Merit, NJ Supreme Ct., Meritorious Pub. Svc. award, 1990, Outstanding Bd. Mem. award, NJ Boys and Girls Clubs Hudson County, 1998, Cmty. Svc. award, Boys & Girls Clubs, 2003. Mem.: ABA, Hudson County Bar Assn. (treas. 1991, sec. 1992, v.p. 1994, 1995, pres.-elect 1996, pres. 1997—98, past chmn., mem. various coms., trustee, Outstanding Bd. Mem. award 1998, Cmty. Svc. award 2001—02, Family Lawyer of Yr. 2007), NJ State Bar Assn. Democrat. Roman Catholic. Avocations: renovating old homes, sports, renovating scholastic athletic fields. Office: 3279 John F Kennedy Blvd Jersey City NJ 07306-3418 Office Phone: 201-653-4340. Business E-Mail: dad@dadlc.com.

D'ALESSANDRO, DAVID FRANCIS, insurance company executive; b. Utica, NY, Jan. 6, 1951; s. Dominick Vincent and Rosemary (Pallaria) D'A.; children: Michael, Andrew. BA, Utica Coll. of Syracuse U., 1972. Account supr. Daniel J. Edelman Inc. Pub. Rels., 1972-74; info. programs mgr. svc. bur. Control Data Corp., 1974-77, comm. mgr. data svcs., 1977-79, gen. mgr. comml. credit, 1980-84; asst. v.p. Citibank Comm. Svcs., 1979-80; v.p. John Hancock Fin. Svcs., Boston, 1984-85, sr. v.p., 1985-88, pres. corp. sector, mem. mgt. com., 1988-91, sr. exec. v.p. retail sector, 1991, pres., CEO, 1996—2004. Author: Brand Warfare: 10 Rules for Building the Killer Brand, 2001, Career Warfare: 10 Rules for Building a Successful Personal Brand and Fighting to Keep It, 2003. Trustee, mem. exec. com. Wang Ctr. for Performing Arts, Boston, 1989—; chmn. Harvard U. Kennedy Sch. Govt., 1990—; bd. trustees Syracuse U., 1990—, Utica (N.Y.) Coll., 1988—.

D'ALESSANDRO, DIANNE MARIE, public defender; b. NYC, Apr. 20, 1952; d. Frank and Marie A. D'A.; m. John P. Foley, July 24, 1977; children: Maria, James. BA in Psychology, Upsala Coll., East Orange, NJ, 1974; JD, NY Law Sch., 1981. Bar: NJ 1981, US Dist. Ct. NJ 1981. Staff atty. Bergen City Legal Svc., Hackensack, N.J., 1981-83; sr. trial atty. Office Pub. Defender, Hackensack, 1983—. Dist. II B ethics com., Office of Atty. Ethics of the Supreme Ct. of NJ, 1992-95; bd. dir. Bergen County Legal Svc. Recipient citation from Susan Reisner, Pub. Advocate, for work done on State vs. Harris, also Co-Worker Recognition award State of N.J., 2004. Mem.: Women Lawyers in Bergen County, Friends of Ringwood Manor, Nat. Trust for Hist. Preservation, Nat. Assoc. Criminal Def. Lawyers. Avocations: reading, hiking, historic preservation. Office: Office of Pub Advocate/Pub Defender 60 State St Hackensack NJ 07601-5451 Office Phone: 201-996-8030 2410. Business E-Mail: dalessandro_d@opd.state.nj.us.

DALESSIO, DONALD JOHN, internist, neurologist, educator; b. Jersey City, Mar. 2, 1931; s. John Andrea and Susan Dorothy (Minotta) Dalessio; m. Jane Catherine Schneider, Sept. 4, 1954 (dec. Mar. 1998); children: Catherine Leah, James John, Susan Jane. BA, Wesleyan U., 1952; MD, Yale U., 1956. Diplomate Am. Bd. Internal Medicine. Intern N.Y.C. Hosp., 1956—57, asst. resident in medicine and neurology, 1959—61; resident in medicine Yale Med. Ctr., 1961—62; pres. med. staff Scripps Clinic, La Jolla, Calif., 1974—78; chmn. dept. medicine Scripps Clin., La Jolla, 1974—89, chmn. emeritus, 1989—, cons., 1982—, pres. med. group, 1980—81; clin. prof. neurology U. Calif., San Diego, 1973—. Physician in chief Green Hosp., La Jolla, 1974—89; pres. Am. Assn. Study Headache, Chgo., 1974—76; chmn. Fedn. We. Soc. Neurology, Santa Barbara, Calif., 1976—77; Musser-Burch lectr. Tulane U., 1979; Kash lectr. U. Ky., 1979. Author: (book) Wolff's Headache, 7th edit., 2001, Approach to Headache, 1973, Approach to Headache, 6th edit., 1999; editor: Headache jour., 1965—75, 1979—84, Scripps Clinic Personal Health Letter; mem. editl. bd. Jour. AMA, 1977—87; columnist: San Diego Tribune. Pres. Nat. Migraine Found., Chgo., 1977—79. Capt. US Army, 1957—59. Recipient Disting. Alumnus award, Wesleyan U., 1982. Fellow: ACP; mem.: World Fedn. Neurology (Am. sec. 1980—90, rsch. group migraine), Am. Acad. Neurology (assoc.), La Jolla Beach/Tennis Club, La Jolla Country Club. Avocations: tennis, squash, piano. Home: 8891 Nottingham Pl La Jolla CA 92037-2131 Office: Scripps Clinic & Rsch Found 10666 N Torrey Pines Rd La Jolla CA 92037-1092

D'ALESSIO, FREDERICK D., telecommunications company executive; b. NJ; BSEE, N.J. Inst. Tech., MS in Engring.; MBA, Rutgers U. With N.J. Bell, from 1971; v.p. ops. and engring. Bell Atlantic Corp., 1990-91; pres., CEO, Bell Atlantic-Md., Inc., 1991-95; pres. Bell Atlantic-Consumer Svcs., Arlington, Va., 1995—, group pres. NYC; pres. advanced svcs. Verizon Comms., Inc., NYC. Non-exec. dir. Spirent PLC, 2004—, Network Equipment Technologies, Inc., 2005—. Bd. govs. Nat. Aquarium, Balt.; bd. dirs. Balt. Symphony Orch., Greater Balt. Com., Inc., Kennedy Krieger Inst.; trustee Goucher Coll. Office: Verizon Comms Inc 1095 Avenue Of The Americas New York NY 10036-6704

D'ALESSIO, VALAIDA CORRINE, artist, consultant; b. Dwight, Ill., Jan. 7, 1938; d. Roy Selmer and Agnes Irene (Seversen) Christiansen; m. Terald Ramon Stevens, July 5, 1958 (div. Dec. 1974); children: Christian Stevens, Curt Stevens, Kirsten Stevens, Karlin Stevens; m. Paul D'Alessio, July 16, 1976 (dec. Apr. 2000). Student, Joliet Jr. Coll., Ill., 1957, Aurora U., 1964, Am. Acad. Art, Chgo., 1969. Experienced-based master ednl. resources Joliet Twp. High Schs. Adult art educator Joliet Jr. Coll., 1980-88; art workshop leader various art leagues, Chgo. area, 1980-96, State of Ill. Gallery, Lockport, 1994. Art cons. Lockport St. Gallery, Plainfield, Ill., 1994—96, Prairie View Gallery, Lockport, 1999—2000; represented by Village Galleries Contemporary, Lahaina, Maui, Hawaii, 2001—. Contbr. (paintings and mixed media collages) Watercolor and Collage Workshop, 1988, (books) Layering: An Art of Time and Space, 1992, Creative Collage Techniques, 1994, Best of Watercolor 2, 1997, Best of Watercolor 2 Painting Texture, 1997, Bridging Time and Space, Essays on Layered Art, 1998, Art and Healing (Barbara Ganin), 1999, The Art of Layering Making Connections, 2004. Vol. Crisis Line Will County, 1990—96. Mem.: North Coast Collage Soc., Soc. Exptl. Artists, Soc. Layerists Multi-Media. E-mail: valaida@aol.com.

DALEY, ARTHUR JAMES, retired magazine publisher; b. St. Paul, Aug. 15, 1916; s. John and Mary (Mayer) D.; m. Lorayne Mary Mongan, June 7, 1941; children: Michael, Kay. Student pub. schs., Fond du Lac, Wis. Advt. salesman Fond du Lac Commonwealth Reporter, 1936, sports editor, 1937-40; sports writer Green Bay (Wis.) Press-Gazette, 1941-43, sports editor, 1946-68, telegraph, picture editor, 1968-78; pub. Green Bay Packer Yearbook, 1960-83, assoc. pub., 1984-88, ret., 1988. Columnist: Green Bay Packer Report, 1974—, Green Bay Packer Scrapbook, 2002. Mem. Wis. Hall of Fame Com. With AUS, 1943-46, ETO. Named to Green Bay Packer Hall of Fame, 1993. Mem. Pro Football Writers Am., Nat. Football League Alumni Assn., Oneida Golf and Country Club. Home: 1146 Highview Ln Green Bay WI 54304-2222

DALEY, CLAYTON CARL, JR., consumer products company executive; b. Canton, Ohio, Nov. 6, 1951; s. Clayton and Jane Daley; m. Meredythe Lee Gray, Mar. 10, 1979; children: Clayton III, Graeme. AB in Econs., Davidson Coll., 1973; MBA, Ohio State U., 1974. Mgr. cost dept. Procter & Gamble Co., Green Bay, Wis., 1974-76, acctg. and office mgr. Cape Girardeau, 1976-78, forecaster paper divsn., 1978-79, fin. analysis supr. tissue brands, 1979-80, mgr. fin. analysis dept. paper divsn., 1980-82, mgr. soap cost acctg. dept. PS&D divsn., 1982-84, dir. fin. info. systems project, comptr.'s divsn., 1984-86, dir. corp. planning, 1986-88, divsn. comptr. PS&D divsn., 1988-89, divsn. comptr. PS&D divsn., BS&HCP divsn., 1989-90, comptr. soap products, 1990-91; comptr. US ops. Procter & Gamble USA, 1991-92; v.p., comptr. Procter & Gamble Internat., 1992-93, team leader, v.p., compt., 1993-94; v.p., treas. Procter & Gamble Co., 1994-98, CFO, 1999—2007, vice-chmn., CFO, 2007—. Trustee Fin. Execs. Inst., 1994, Fin. Execs. Rsch. Found., 1994. Bd. dirs. Boy Scouts Am., Dan Beard Coun., 1997, Am. Cancer Soc., Hamilton County Unit, Cancer Family Care, Inc. Mem. Cin. Rotary. Office: Procter & Gamble Co 1 Procter And Gamble Plz Cincinnati OH 45202-3393*

DALEY, GEORGE QUENTIN, hematologist, biomedical research scientist; b. Catskill, NY, Nov. 13, 1960; s. Frank Leonard and Natalie Alcine (Evans) Daley; m. Amy Claire Edmondson, 1995. AB, Harvard U., 1982; PhD in Biology, MIT, 1989; MD summa cum laude, Harvard U., 1991. Diplomate Am. Bd. Internal Medicine. Chief resident in internal medicine Mass. Gen. Hosp., Boston, 1994-95; fellow Whitehead Inst. for Biomedical Rsch., MIT, Cambridge, Mass., 1995; clin. rsch. fellow hematology/oncology Children's, Brigham, Women's and Dana Farber Cancer Ctr. Inst.; assoc. prof., biol. chemistry and molecular pharmacology Harvard Med. Sch., 2002—; with divsn. hematology/oncology Children's Hosp., Boston, 2003—, assoc. dir. stem cell/devel. biology rsch., assoc. prof., pediatrics. Chmn. pre-med. adv. com. Quincy House, Harvard U., Cambridge, 1987-95. Contbr. articles to sci. jours. Recipient rsch. award for Clin. Trainees NIH, 1992, Burroughs-Wellcome Fund Career award, Scholar award, Leukemia and Lymphoma Soc. Am., Pioneer award, NIH, 2004; nat. scholar Harvard U., 1978-91. Mem. AAAS, Am. Soc. Clin. Investigation. Achievements include creation of mouse model for chronic myelogenous leukemia; research in stem cells of the blood to define the molecular basis for human leukemia; self-renewal and differentiation of human ES cells, target directed chemotherapy for chronic myelogenous leukemia (CML); first creation of functional sperm cells from embryonic stem cells (cited a "Top Ten" breakthrough for 2003 by Science magazine). Office: Childrens Hosp Boston 300 Longwood Ave Karp-7 Boston MA 02115 Office Phone: 617-919-2013. Office Fax: 617-730-0222.*

DALEY, HENRY J., lawyer; b. Boston; BS, Worcester Polytechnic Inst., 1978; PhD in Physics, U. Arizona, 1984; JD, Northeastern U., 1996. Bar: Mass. 1997, DC 1999, US Patent and Trademark Office. Former rsch. scientist Daresbury Lab., England, MIT, Lincoln Lab.; former assoc. Pillsbury Winthrop, Va., ptnr. Washington, 2002—05; ptnr., intellectual property group Venable LLP, Washington, 2005—. Former visiting scholar Yale U., Kernfysisch Versneller Inst., Netherlands. Office: Venable LLP 575 7th St NW Washington DC 20004 Office Phone: 202-344-4362. Office Fax: 202-344-8300. Business E-Mail: hjdaley@venable.com.

DALEY, JENNIFER, internist, educator; b. Springfield, Mass., Sept. 10, 1949; d. Edward Murray and Elizabeth (Bloom) D.; children: John, Benjamin, Sarah, Beth, Liane. BA magna cum laude, Brown U., 1972; MD, Tufts U., 1976. Diplomate Am. Bd. Internal Medicine. Resident in internal medicine New Eng. Med. Ctr., Boston, 1976-79; fellow in gen. medicine Harvard Med. Sch., Boston, 1985-87; asst. prof. Tufts U. Sch. Medicine, Boston, 1979-87; staff physician Beth Israel Hosp., Boston, 1987-99; asst. prof. medicine Harvard Med. Sch., Boston, 1991-98, assoc. prof., 1998—2002; dir. Ctr. for Health Sys. Design, Mass. Gen. Hosp., Boston, 1999—2002; chief medical officer Tenet Healthcare Corp., Dallas, 2002—. Health svcs. rschr. VA, West Roxbury, Mass., 1990; v.p. health care quality Beth Israel Deaconess Med. Ctr., Boston, 1996-99; health care cons. Author: Using Hospital Mortality Data, 1991; editor: Through the Patient's Eyes, 1994; contbr. over 140 articles to med. jours. Grantee VA, 1990. Fellow ACP, Am. Assn. Health Svcs. Rsch.; mem. AMA, Soc. Gen. Internal Medicine. Mailing: Tenet Healthcare PO Box 809088 Dallas TX 75380-9088 Office: Tenet Healthcare 13737 Noel Rd Dallas TX 75240*

DALEY, MICHAEL JOSEPH, lawyer; b. Phila., Aug. 9, 1955; s. Robert Charles and Agnes Theresa (Brophy) D. BA with honors, U. Denver, 1977; JD, Loyola U., Chgo., 1980; MLA, U. Chgo., 2006. Bar: Ill. 1980, U.S. Dist. Ct. (no. dist.) Ill. 1980, Trial Bar (no. dist.) Ill. 1983, U.S. Ct. Appeals (7th cir.) 1985, U.S. Supreme Ct. 1985, U.S. Dist. Ct. (no. dist.) Ind. 1994, U.S. Tax Ct. 1994. Asst. state's atty. Cook County State Atty.'s Office, Chgo., 1981-83; assoc. Nisen & Elliott, Chgo., 1983-86, ptnr., 1986—. Instr. trial advocacy Loyola U. of Chgo., 1986—, Nat. Inst. Trial Advocacy, 2000-. Recipient Lewis Powell Medal for Advocacy, Am. Coll. Trial Lawyers, 1980, Robert Bellarmine award Loyola U. Chgo., 1995. Mem. Bar Assn. 7th Fed. Cir., Assn. of Transp. Practitioners, Nat. Assn. R.R. Trial Counsel, Union League Club Chgo. Avocations: skiing, bicycling, golf. Office: Nisen & Elliott 200 W Adams St Ste 2500 Chicago IL 60606-5283 E-mail: mdaley@nisen.com.

DALEY, PAMELA, diversified services, technology and manufacturing company executive; b. Springfield, Mass., Oct. 1, 1952; d. Edward Murray and Elizabeth Bloom Daley; m. Randall Lee Phelps, Aug. 26, 1995. AB summa cum laude in Romance Langs. and Lit., Princeton U., 1974; JD magna cum laude, U. Pa., 1979. Bar: Pa. 1979, N.Y. 1991. Lectr. partnership taxation law U. Pa., Phila., 1982-89; assoc. tax sect. Morgan, Lewis & Bockius, Phila., 1979-86, ptnr., 1986-89; tax counsel GE, Fairfield, Conn., 1989-91, v.p., sr. counsel for transactions, 1991—2004, sr. v.p. bus. devel., 2004—. Bd. outside advisor Va. Tax Review assn., 1982-92. Editor-in-chief U. Pa. Law Review; contbr. articles to profl. jours. Trustee MacDuffie Sch., Springfield, 1986-92; bd. govs. Pa. Economy League, 1986-89; mem. bd. overseers Law Sch. U. Pa., 1999—; bd. dirs. G.E. Found., 1999—, Genworth Fin., Inc.; bd. dirs. World Wildlife Fund, 1999—. Teaching fellow Salzburg Seminar on Am. Law and Legal Instns., 1986; named to Acad. Women Achievers YWCA, 1992. Mem. Order of Coif, Phi Beta Kappa. Office: GE 3135 Easton Tpke # E3 Fairfield CT 06828

DALEY, PAUL PATRICK, lawyer; b. Boston, July 10, 1941; s. Patrick Joseph and Catherine Josephine (Ford) D.; m. Barbara Sabin, May 24, 1980; 1 child, Patrick. AB, Boston Coll., 1963; MBA, JD, Harvard U., Cambridge, Mass., 1973; grad., US Army Airborne Sch., Ft. Benning, Ga. Bar: Mass. 1973, U.S. Ct. Appeals (1st cir.) 1974, U.S. Dist. Ct. (Mass.) 1974, U.S. Ct. Appeals (5th cir.) 1980, U.S. Supreme Ct. 1980, N.Y. 1983, U.S. Ct. Appeals (2d cir.) 1998. Assoc. Hale and Dorr LLP, Boston, 1973-78; jr. ptnr. Hale and Dorr, Boston, 1978-82; sr. ptnr. Wilmer Cutler Pickering Hale and Dorr LLP, Boston, 1982—. Lectr. CLE programs. Assoc. editor Mass. Law Rev., 1998—; contbr. articles to profl. jours. Trustee Mass. Sch. Profl. Psychology, Boston, 1985-03, chair, 1994-03; trustee St. Sebastians Sch., Needham, Mass. 1981-1982, Naval War Coll. Found., 1996—, pres., 2000-02, chmn., 2002-04; bd. dir. Am. Sail Train Assn., Newport, RI, 1982-86; dir. Brain Aneurism Rsch. Trust, 2006-. Capt. USNR, 1963—94. Decorated Disting. Flying Cross, Air Medals (16), Navy Commendation medal with Combat V, Vietnamese Air Gallantry Cross, Meritorious Svc. medal. Fellow Am. Coll. Bankruptcy; mem. ABA, Mass. Bar Assn. (past chmn. bus. bank com., bus. law sect., fee arbitation bd.), Boston Bar Assn. (coun.), Am. Bankruptcy Inst., Nat. Def. U. Found., U.S. Naval Inst., Naval Res. Assn., Assn. Naval Aviation, Tailhook Assn., Comml. Law League, Navy League, Windsor Club (Waban, Mass.), Brae Burn Country Club, Miacomet Golf Club, Wardroom Club (treas. and dir. 2006-). Democrat. Roman Catholic. Avocations: flying, golf, bicycling, reading, theater. Home: 9 Crofton Rd Waban MA 02468-1931 Office: Wilmer Cutler Pickering Hale and Dorr LLP 60 State St Boston MA 02109-1816 Office Phone: 617-526-6720. Office Fax: 617-526-5000. Business E-Mail: paul.daley@wilmerhale.com.

DALEY, RICHARD MICHAEL, mayor; b. Chgo., Apr. 24, 1942; s. Richard J. and Eleanor (Guilfoyle) D.; m. Margaret Corbett, Mar. 25, 1972; children: Nora, Patrick, Elizabeth. BA, DePaul U., Chgo., 1964, JD, 1968. Bar: Ill. 1969. Ptnr. Simon and Daley, Chgo., 1970-72, Daley, Riley & Daley, Chgo., 1972-80; mem. Ill. State Senate, 1973-80, chmn. Judiciary I Com., 1975, 77; state's atty. Cook County, Ill., 1980-89; mayor Chgo., 1989—; pres. U.S. Conf. Mayors , 1996. Headed the US Conf. Mayors, 1996. Bd. dirs. Little City Home; mem. Citizens Bd. U. Chgo.; mem. adv. bd. Mercy Hosp., Chgo.; bd. mgrs. Valentine Boys Club; active Nativity of Our Lord Parish, Chgo. Named Outstanding Leader, Ill. Assn. Social Workers, 1978, Outstanding Legislator of Yr., Lt. Gov. Sr. Legis. Forum, 1979, Outstanding Leader in Revision of Ill. Mental Health Code, Ill. Assn. Retarded Citizens, 1979, Municipal Leader of Yr., American City and County mag., 1997, Pub. Official of Yr., Governing mag., 1997, Politician of Yr., Library Jour., 1997, Official of Yr., Alliance for Great Lakes, 2006; named one of One of the Five Best Big-city Mayors, Time mag., 2005; recipient Golden Rule plaque, Chgo. Boys Club Am., Education Excellence award, Nat. Conf. for Cmty. and Justice, 1999, Pub. Svc. Leadership award, Nat. Coun. for Urban Econ. Develop., 1999, J. Sterling Morton award, Nat. Arbor Day Found., 1999, Keystone award, Am. Architectural Found., 1999, Martin Luther King/Robert F. Kennedy award, Coalition to Stop Gun Violence/Education Fund To End Handgun Violence, 1999, Openlands Project Conservation Leadership award, 2000, National Trust's Trustee's award for Outstanding Achievement in Pub. Policy, 2000, National Trust for Historic Preservation National Preservation award, 2000, 2002, Ill. Coalition Against Domestic Violence (ICADV) Human Dignity award, 2001, Chgo. Innovation award, Sun-Times, 2002, Extreme City 'Digie' (Digital Innovation) award, 2002, Waste Management, Inc. Top honors in City Livability award, US Conf. of Mayors, 2002, Lifetime Achievement award, Am. for Arts & U.S. Conf. Mayors, 2005, Kevin Lynch award, MIT, 2005. Mem. Chgo. Bar Assn., Ill. State Bar Assn., ABA, Cath. Lawyers Guild. Democrat. Roman Catholic. Office: Office of the Mayor City Hall Rm 507 121 N La Salle Chicago IL 60602-1202*

DALEY, ROBERT EMMETT, retired foundation executive; b. Cleve., Mar. 13, 1933; s. Emmett Wilfred and Anne Gertrude (O'Donnell) D.; m. Mary Berneta Fredericks, June 7, 1958; children: Marianne Fredericks, John Gerard. BA in English, U. Dayton, 1955; MA in Polit. Sci., Ohio State U., 1968, MA in Pub. Adminstrn., 1976. Local govt. reporter, Washington corr., fin. editor Jour. Herald, Dayton, Ohio, 1957-65, pub. affairs reporter, 1967; staff writer Congressional Quar., Inc., Washington, 1966; pub. affairs reporter Dayton Daily News, Dayton, 1969; dir. pub. affairs & comm. Charles F. Kettering Found., Dayton, 1977-94, ret., now assoc., 1994—. Part-time copy boy, sports reporter Jour. Herald, Dayton, 1953-55. Past pres., bd. trustees St. Joseph Home for Children; former mem. adv. bd. Ctr. for Religious Telecomms., U. Dayton; traveling press sec. sen. candidate John J. Gilligan, 1968, for gubernatorial candidate, 1970-71, asst. to Gov. Gilligan, 1971-75; media rels. dir. Nat. League of Cities, Washington, 1976-77; Soc.; past mem. Ind. Sector Pub. Info. & Edn. Com. With U.S. Army, 1955-57. Mem. Soc. Profl. Journalists, Nat. Press Club, KC, Ancient Order Hibernians. Roman Catholic. Home: 888 Cranbrook Ct Dayton OH 45459-1525 Office: Charles F Kettering Found 200 Commons Rd Dayton OH 45459-2788 Business E-Mail: daley@kettering.org.

DALEY, RON(ALD EUGENE), playwright, poet, theater director, theater producer; b. Washington, Sept. 24, 1945; s. Russell Eugene and Dorothy Sybil (Krouse) D.; m. Virginia Ann Bean, Nov. 7, 1986; children: Jackson Phillip Wesley, Bryan Augustin, Geoffrey Eugene. BA in Philosophy, North Park Coll., 1967; MA in English with honors, Roosevelt U., 1968; MA in Drama, Syracuse U., 1975. founder ACT-Argyle, 1999—. Instr. English/Philosophy Malcolm X C.C., Chgo., 1968-70, Orange County C.C., Middletown, N.Y., 1970-73; English N.Y.C. C.C., Bklyn., 1975-78; dir., designer various theatre companies, 1978-80; producer Jerron Prodns., NYC, 1980-81; assoc. artistic dir. New World Theatre, NYC, 1981-82; artistic dir. Nat. Shakespeare Co., NYC, 1982-85; resident dir., producer Riverside Shakespeare Co., NYC, 1986; exec. dir. RED Prodns., Argyle, Wis., 1985—; writer No Evil Prodns., 2003—07. Guest dir. Broom St. Theatre, Madison, 1987-94, Classic Theatre, N.Y.C., 1979-84, AMDA Studio One, N.Y.C., 1977-78, Camden (Maine) Shakespeare Festival, 1979; co-founder Mercury Players, Madison, 1994—. Author of plays off Broadway including Beyond the Veil, Damphools and Wowsers, Argyle Wisconsin 53504, In the Matter of John David Hutchins, It's Gotta Be the Shoes, Nobody Dies, 5:45, Badger Orpheus, The Third Blackhawk War, Journeys with Nanabozo, The Abrazo, The Knight of the Burning Pestle, The Red Palace; editor Amphibious Maneuvers. Prodr. Free Shakespeare in the Parks, N.Y.C., 1986. Mem Soc. of Stage Dirs. and Choreographers, Dramatists Guild, U.S. Holocaust Meml. Mus., ACLU. Avocations: fishing, gardening, carpentry. Home: PO Box 196 Argyle WI 53504-0196

DALEY, RUTH MARGARET, advertising agency administrator; b. Buffalo, Apr. 12, 1950; d. Russell Short and Emma Pleasant (Wear) Garrick; m. Jeffrey George Vanghel (dec. 1988); m. Patrick L. Daley. Student, Villa Maria Coll., Buffalo. Sec. McKesson & Robbins Drug Co., Cheektowaga, NY, 1972-78; sales rep. Nasco Inc., Springfield, Tenn., 1978-80; telemktg. sales rep. L.M. Berry & Co., Amherst, NY, 1980-81, mgr. telemktg. sales unit, 1981-83, mgr. telemktg. sales dept., 1984-90; mgmt. cons. Ameritech, Troy, Mich., 1990-92; mgr. tng. White Directory Pub. (The Talking Phone Book), Buffalo, 1992—2002, telephone sales mgr., 2002—. Grad. asst. Dale Carnegie Inst., Buffalo, 1985. Avocations: dance, reading, travel. Home: 66 Parktrail Ln Buffalo NY 14227-2545 Office: The Talking Phone Book 1945 Sheridan Dr Buffalo NY 14223-1203 Home Phone: 716-656-0240; Office Phone: 716-875-9100 x80142. Business E-Mail: rdaley@talkingphonebook.com.

DALEY, SANDRA, retired artist, filmmaker, photographer; b. Fargo, ND, Feb. 28, 1940; d. Cecil Raymond and Margaret (Anderson) D. AB cum laude, Oberlin Coll., Ohio, 1961; MFA with high distinction, Calif. Coll. Arts and Crafts, Oakland, 1965. Co-editor (Geoffrey C. Ward): Contemporary Photographer Magazine, 1960; show (with Andy Warhol and Roy Lichtenstein), Dwan Gallery, LA, 1964, show (with Nicholas Quennell), 1965, Experiments in Art and Tech., Osaka Pavilion, World's Fair, 1970; prodr., dir.: (film (with Sally Potter) London Mysteries, 1964; (film (with Robert Mapplethorpe and Patti Smith) Robert Having His Nipple Pierced, 1970; (film (Patti Smith, Sam Shepard and Vali) Patti Having Her Knee Tattooed, 1971; prodr., dir. (live mixed media performance (with Alan Lanier and Patti Smith) Cine Probe, The Mus. of Modern Art, N.Y.C., 1971. Avocations: writing, drawing.

DALEY, SUSAN JEAN, lawyer; b. New Britain, Conn., May 27, 1959; d. George Joseph and Norma (Woods) Daley. BA, U. Conn., 1978; JD, Harvard U., 1981. Bar: Ill. 1981. Assoc. Altheimer & Gray, Chgo., 1981-86, ptnr., 1986—2003, Perkins Coie LLP, Chgo., 2003—. Mem.: ABA (real property, probate and trust law sect. 1983—, employee benefits com. taxation sect. 1984—, chmn. welfare plans com. real property, probate and trust law sect. 1989—95, chmn. employee benefits, securities law com. taxation sect. 2001—), Chgo. Coun. Fgn. Rels., Chgo. Bar Assn. (chmn. employee benefits divsn. fed. taxation com. 1985—86, chmn. employee benefits com. 1990—91, chmn. fed. taxation com. 1992—93), Ill. Bar Assn. (chmn. employee benefits divsn. fed. taxation sect. 1984—86, chmn. employee benefits sect. 1995—96), Nat. Assn. Stock Plan Profls. (pres. Chgo. chpt. 1995—). Avocation: marathons. Home: 1636 N Wells St Apt 415 Chicago IL 60614-6009 Office: 131 S Dearborn St STE 1700 Chicago IL 60603-5559 Home Phone: 312-399-3348; Office Phone: 312-324-8645. Business E-Mail: SDaley@perkinscoie.com.

DALEY, SUZANNE, editor; Grad., Hampshire Coll., 1978. Joined NY Times, 1978, reporter met. desk, 1982, dep. met. editor, 1994—95, South Africa bur. chief, 1995—99, Paris bur. chief, 1999—2002, edn. editor, 2002—05, contbr. Thursday Styles sect., 2004, nat. editor, 2005—. Office: NY Times 229 W 43rd St New York NY 10036 Office Phone: 212-556-4119. Office Fax: 212-556-3758. E-mail: daley@nytimes.com.

DALEY, VINCENT RAYMOND, JR., real estate company executive, consultant; b. Evanston, Ill., June 21, 1940; s. Vincent R. and Carole V. Daley; m. Viola (Vi) Elizabeth Bursiek, May 6, 1967; children: Kathleen Marie, Colleen Patricia. AA, Lincoln Coll., Ill., 1961; BS, Loyola U., Chgo., 1963; student in real estate, Roosevelt U., Chgo., 1964. From salesman to store mgr. Sears Roebuck & Co., Chgo., 1962—73; v.p., cons. Kencoe Corp., Des Plaines, Ill., 1973—74; pres. Daley & Assocs., Chgo., 1974—; chmn. Wacker Real Estate Svcs., Chgo., 1997—. Chmn. Wacker Mgmt. Corp., Chgo. State legis. asst. 8th Legis. Dist., Chgo., 1985—93; mem. econ. devel. com. State of Ill., Springfield, 1985—88; bd. trustees Lincoln Col. Chartered Lincoln U., 2001—. Plt. sgt. Ill. Nat. Guard, 1961—67. Recipient Pres. award, Realtors Land Inst., 1989, Good Neighbor award, Chgo. Assn. Realtors, 1998. Mem. Chgo. Bd. Realtors (life; bd. dirs.), Nat. Assn. Realtors (bd. regents), Ill. Assn. Realtors (bd. dirs.), Realtors Land Inst. (bd. govs.), Cert. Comml. Investment Mems. Inst., Internat. Real Estate Fed. (sr. cert. valuer, registered internat. mem., cert. investment financier). Democrat. Roman Catholic. Avocation: travel. Home: 1807 N Orleans St Chicago IL 60614-5325 Office: Wacker Real Estate Svcs 400 N Michigan Ave Ste 600 Chicago IL 60611-4129 Office Phone: 312-787-7554. Personal E-mail: vincevidaley@aol.com.

DALEY, WILLIAM M., bank executive, former federal government official; b. Aug. 8, 1948; m. Loretta Daley; 3 children. BA, Loyola U., 1970; LLB, John Marshall Law Sch., Chgo., LLD (hon.), 1975. Bar: Ill. 1975. With Daley and George, Chgo.; ptnr. Mayer, Brown & Platt; vice chmn. Amalgamated Bank, Chgo., 1989, pres., COO, 1990-93; atty., advisor to Mayor Richard M. Daley, Chicago, 1993—97; sec. Dept. Commerce, Washington, 1997-2000; chmn., v.p. Al Gore's presidential campaign, 2000; vice chmn. Evercore Capital Partners L.P., 2000—01; pres. SBC Communications, 2001—04; chmn. Midwest region J.P. Morgan Chase & Co., 2004—. Bd. dirs. Merck & Co., Boston Properties, Coun. Foreign Rels., John F. Kennedy Ctr. Performing Arts, Com. US-China Foreign Relations; spl. counsel to Pres. for NAFTA. Served in Army Nat. Guard & Air Nat. Guard, 1970—76. Recipient St. Ignatius award fro Excellence in the Practice of Law, 2995, World Trade award World Trade Ctr., Chgo., 1994, World Standards Day 2002 Hon. Chair & Ron Bown award, Alliance for Telecomm. Industry Solutions. Office: SBC Comm 175 E Houston San Antonio TX 78205*

D'ALFONSO, MARIO JOSEPH, lawyer; b. Phila., Nov. 3, 1951; s. Albert Carmine and Yolanda (Zanfrisco) D'A.; m. Rita F. Borrelli, Apr. 26, 1975; 1 child, Mario C. BA, Villanova U., 1973; JD, Widener U., 1979. Bar: Pa. 1979, N.J. 1979, U.S. Dist. Ct. (ea. dist.) Pa. 1979, U.S. Dist. Ct. N.J. 1979, U.S. Ct. Appeals (3d cir.) 1980, U.S. Supreme Ct. 1983, U.S. Ct. Appeals (5th cir.) 1989. Assoc. Avena, Hendren & Friedman, Camden, N.J., 1979-81; ptnr. Avena, Hendren, Friedman & D'Alfonso, 1981-84, D'Alfonso & Camacho, P.A., Haddon Heights, N.J., 1984—. Cons. Marbert Construction, Haddon Heights, N.J., 1982—. Mem. Am. Arbitration Assn. (Svc. award 1984), Assn. Criminal Def. Lawyers, Camden County Bar Assn., N.J. Trial Lawyers Assn., Phi Delta Phi (pres. 1978), Phi Kappa Phi. Roman Catholic. Home: 64 Lady Diana Cir Marlton NJ 08053-3705 Office: 1814 Rt 70 E Ste 350 Cherry Hill NJ 08003 Office Phone: 856-779-7777.

D'ALFONZO, SAMUEL DONALD, real estate company executive; b. Catonsville, Md., Oct. 1, 1924; s. Samuel Joseph and Blanche Margaret D'Alfonzo; m. Mary Marguerite Oles, May 11, 1993; m. Shirley Mae Mitchell (dec.); children: Donald Wayne, Stephen Michael. BA, U. Md., College Park, 1949. Pres. D&D Properties Inc., Balt., 1964—84, owner, 1984—. Pres. Am. Metaseal Corp., Balt., 1953—2005, Moldform Plastics, Inc., Balt., 1967—85; ptnr. SEI, Balt., 1984—. Contbr. articles to profl. jours. Sgt. US Army, 1942—45, Pacific. Mem.: Am. Soc. Metals (life), Soc. Plastic Engrs. (sr.), 517th Field Artillery Assn. (sec.), Am. Foundry Men's Soc., Exch. Club Catonsville (past treas., past sec., past pres., Outstanding Treas. 1991—92). Avocations: sport cars, travel. Office: D&D Properties 1801 Old Sulphur Spring Baltimore MD 21227

DALGARNO, ALEXANDER, astronomy educator; b. London, Jan. 5, 1928; s. William and Margaret (Murray) D.; m. Barbara W.F. Kane, Oct. 31, 1957 (div.); children: Penelope, Rebecca, Piers, Fergus; m. Emily K. Izsak, June 23, 1972 (div.). BSc, U. London, 1947, PhD, 1951; MA (hon.), Harvard U., Cambridge, Mass., 1967; DSc (hon.), Queen's U. Belfast, 1980, York U., Can., 2000. Lectr. Queen's U., Belfast, Northern Ireland, 1951-56, reader, 1956-61, prof. math. physics, 1961-67, dir. computation lab., 1961-66; prof. astronomy Harvard U., Cambridge, Mass., 1967—, Phillips prof., 1977—, chmn. dept., 1971-76; dir. Inst. for Theoretical Atomic and Molecular Physics, 1989-93. Assoc. dir. Ctr. for Astrophysics Harvard U., 1973-80; acting dir. Harvard Coll. Obs., 1971-73; rsch. scientist Smithsonian Astrophys. Obs., Cambridge, Mass., 1967—; Vikram A. Sarabhai prof. Phys. Rsch. Lab., Ahmedebad, 2002; Jan Hendrik Oort prof. U. Leiden, 2003; Charles M. and Martha Hitchcock prof. U. Calif., Berkeley, 2003; vis. scholar Sackler Inst. Adv. Studies Tel Aviv U., 1995-96. Editor: Astrophys. Jour. Letters, 1973—2002; contbr. articles to profl. jours. Recipient Hodgkins medal Smithsonian Instn., 1977, Spiers Medal, Royal Soc. Chemistry, 1992; fellow UMIST, 1992, Univ. Coll. London, 1976. Fellow: Internat. Acad. Quantum Molecular Sci. (ann. prize 1967), Internat. Acad. Astronautics, Royal Astron. Soc. (Gold medal 1986), Am. Acad. Arts and Scis., Am. Geophys. Union (Fleming medal 1995), Optical Soc. Am. (Meggers award 1986), Am. Phys. Soc. (Davisson-Germer award 1980), Inst. Phys. (U.K.), Royal Soc. (Hughes medal 2002), Royal Irish Acad. (hon.); mem.: NAS. Home: 27 Robinson St Cambridge MA 02138-1403 Office: Harvard-Smithsonian Ctr Astrophysics 60 Garden St Cambridge MA 02138 Home Phone: 617-354-8660; Office Phone: 617-495-4403. Business E-Mail: adalgarno@cfa.harvard.edu.

DALGLEISH, STUART MCNAUGHT, retired manufacturing executive; b. Manchester, Eng., Mar. 21, 1933; permanent resident, US, 2006; s. John McNaught and Ethel Florence (Harris) Dalgleish; m. Rosemary Janet Ford, Sept. 3, 1960; children: Paul McNaught, Grant Louis. BSc with honors, Queen's U., Belfast, Northern Ireland, 1955. Ind. dir. 3ls, Manchester, 1991—2006; chmn. McConomy Co., Ltd., Liverpool, England, James Briggs Ltd., Oldham, England; non-exec. dir. Mita (UK) Ltd., Wales; chmn., mng. dir. Comfalux Mfg. Ltd., Southport, England, 1961—2006; vice-chmn. Daryl Industries Ltd., Wirral, England, 2001—05; ret. Vol. prison visitor, chaplain Wymott Prison, Lanes, England, 1985—2006; vol. prison chaplain Hardee Correctional Inst., Fla., 2007. Fellow: Inst. Bus. Advisors, Assn. Internat. Accts. Home: 3411 Winding Oaks Dr Longboat Key FL 34228 Personal E-mail: dalgleish1@verizon.net.

DALIANIS, LINDA STEWART, state supreme court justice; BA cum laude, Northeastern U., 1970; JD, Suffolk U., 1974, JD (hon.), 2001. Bar: N.H. 1974, U.S. Dist. Ct. N.H. 1974, U.S. Supreme Ct. 1974. Pvt. law practice, Nashua, NH, 1974-79; marital master NH Superior Ct., 1979-80, assoc. justice, 1980—2000, chief justice, 2000; assoc. justice NH Supreme Ct., Concord, 2000—. Chair Interbranch Criminal and Juvenile Justice Com.; mem. Edn. Coms. N.H. Supreme and Superior Cts., Northern New Eng. Jud. Edn. Com.; mem. Jud. Adv. Com. N.H. Dept. Corrections; mem. Marital Masters Com., Alternative Dispute Resolution Com. N.H. Supreme Ct. First woman to hold seat on N.H. Supreme Ct. Office: Supreme Ct Bldg One Noble Dr Concord NH 03301-6160*

DALINKA, MURRAY KENNETH, radiologist, educator; b. Bklyn., May 13, 1938; s. Joseph and Gertrude (Cohen) D.; m. Janice L. Kolber, Feb. 28, 1982; 1 son, Bradford Gordon; children by previous marriage: Ilene, Ian Scott. BS, U. Mich., 1960, MD, 1964. Diplomate Am. Bd. Radiology. Intern Pa. Hosp., Phila., 1964-65; resident in radiology Montefiore Hosp., NYC, 1965-68; instr. radiology Harvard Med. Sch., 1970-71; from asst. prof. to assoc. prof. radiology Thomas Jefferson U. Hosp., Phila., 1971-76, prof., 1976—; chief orthop. radiology Hosp. U. Pa., 1976—. Chief diagnostic radiology Thomas Jefferson U. Hosp., Phila., 1974-76;. cons.hila. Naval Hosp., 1974-79, Walson Hosp., Ft. Dix Army Base, 1972-77. Author: Arthography, 1980, Symposium on Orthopedic Radiology, 1983; mem. editorial bd. Bone Syllabus IV, 1982—, Skeletal Radiology, 1982—, Conversations in Radiology, 1977-79; guest editor Emergency Medicine Clinics of North America, Vol. 3, 1985; editor: (with J.J. Kaye) Radiology in Emergency Medicine Clinics in Emergency, Vol. 3, 1984, (with J. Edeiken and D. Karasick) Edeiken's Roentgen Diagnosis of Diseases of Bone, 4th edit. Served to capt. USAF, 1968-70. James Picker research fellow, 1972-73; recipient Honor Orator award, Phila. Roentgen Ray Soc., 2005. Mem. Internat. Skeletal Soc. (past pres.), Radiol. Soc. N.Am. (Outstanding Educator award 2003), Am. Coll. Radiology (chmn. panel on musculoskeletal imaging, mem. task force on appropriateness criteria/diagnostic patient care guidelines), Phila. Roentgen Ray Soc. (past pres.). Home: 318 S 21st St Philadelphia PA 19103-6531 Office: U Pa Hosp Dept Radiology 3400 Spruce St Philadelphia PA 19104-4206 E-mail: dalinka@oasis.rad.upenn.edu.

DALIO, RAYMOND T., investment company executive; MBA in Fin., Harvard U., 1973. Head Instl. Futures Dept. Shearson Hayden Stone; dir. commodities Dominick and Dominick; founder, pres. Bridgewater Associates, Westport, Conn., 1975—, chief investment officer. Office: Bridgewater Associates One Glendinning Pl Westport CT 06880 Office Phone: 203-226-3030. Office Fax: 203-291-7300.

DALIS, IRENE, mezzo soprano, performing arts association administrator; b. San Jose, Calif., Oct. 8, 1925; d. Peter Nicholas and Mamie Rose (Boitano) D.; m. George Loinaz, July 16, 1957; 1 child, Alida Mercedes. AB, San Jose State Coll., 1946; MA in Teaching, Columbia U., 1947; MMus (hon.), San Jose State U., 1957; studied voice with, Edyth Walker, NYC, 1947-50, Paul Althouse, 1950-51, Dr. Otto Mueller, Milan, Italy, 1952-72; MusD (hon.), Santa Clara U., 1987; DFA (hon.), Calif. State U., 1999. Prin. artist Berlin Opera, 1955-65, Met. Opera, NYC, 1957-77, San Francisco Opera, 1958-73, Hamburg (Fed. Republic Germany) Staatsoper, 1966-71; prof. music San Jose State U., Calif., 1977—2004; founder, gen. dir. Opera San Jose, 1984—. Dir. Met. Opera Nat. Auditions, San Jose dist., 1980-88. Operatic debut as dramatic mezzo-soprano Oldenburgisches Staatstheater, 1953, Berlin Staedtische Opera, 1955; debut Met. Opera, N.Y.C., 1957, 1st Am.-born singer, Kundry Bayreuth Festival, 1961, opened, Bayreuth Festival, Parsifal, 1963; commemorative Wagner 150th Birth Anniversary; opened 1963 Met. Opera Season in Aida; premiered: Dello Joio's Blood Moon, 1961, Henderson's Medea, 1972; rec. artist Parsifal, 1964 (Grand Prix du Disque award); contbg. editor Opera Quar., 1983. Recipient Fulbright award for study in Italy, 1951, Woman of Achievement award Commn. on Status of Women, 1983, Pres.'s award Nat. Italian Am. Found., 1985, award of merit People of San Francisco, 1985, San Jose Renaissance award for sustained and outstanding artistic contbn., 1987, Medal of Achievement Acad. Vocal Arts, 1988; named Honored Citizen City of San Jose, 1986; inducted into Calif. Pub. Edn. Hall of Fame, 1985, others. Mem. Beethoven Soc. (mem. adv. bd. 1985—), San Jose Arts Round Table, San Jose Opera Guild, Am. Soc. Univ. Women, Arts Edn. Week Consortium, Phi Kappa Phi, Mu Phi Epsilon. Office: Opera San Jose 2149 Paragon Dr San Jose CA 95131 Office Phone: 408-437-4450. Business E-Mail: dalis@operasj.org.

DALKE, CARL D., school system administrator, consultant; b. Inman, Kans, Nov. 10, 1924; s. Peter and Helena C. (Heidebrecht) Dalke; m. Jeanette Harper (div.); children: Terry J., Patricia L., Deborah J. Campbell. AA, Hutchinson Jr. Coll., Kans., 1947; BS, MS, Kans. State U., Manhatten, 1950; postgrad., U. Chgo., 1950—53. From v.p. to pres., CEO BBB, Chgo., 1953—66; exec. v.p., CEO Ill. Consumer Fin. Assn., Chgo., 1967—84; v.p. client svcs. Sanford Orgn., Inc., 1980; self-employed orgnl. cons. CD Orgn. Mgmt., Park Forest, Ill., 1981—. Spkr. in field. With 101st airborne divsn. US Army, 1943—46, ETO. Mem.: Chgo. Soc. Assn. Execs., Am. Soc. Assn. Execs., Ill. Clergy Econ. Workships, Ill Coun. Econ. Edn., Nat. Inst. Consumer Credt Mgmt. (chmn. bd. 1976—79, bd. govs.), Rotary Club Chgo., Chgo. Press Club. Avocations: golf, Scrabble, bicycling, skydiving. Office: CD Orgn Mgmt Svcs 376 Dogwood St Park Forest IL 60466

DALLAS, H. JAMES, medical products executive; b. Lithonia, Ga., Aug. 1, 1958; BS in Acctg., U. SC, Aiken, 1983; MBA, Emory U., 1994. Equipment cleaner Pepperidge Farms, Aiken, SC, 1981—83; br. auditor C & S Nat. Bank, 1983—84; cost acct. Gypsum divsn. Ga.-Pacific Corp., 1984—85, programmer corp. info. tech., 1985—87, analyst corp. info. tech., 1987—89, mgr. info. sys.-transp. divsn., 1989—92, gen. mgr. transp. divsn., 1992—94, dir. strategy and planning corp. info. tech., 1994—96, group dir. bldg. products mfg. info. tech., 1996—98, group dir. bldg. products mfg. and distbn. info. tech., 1998—2000, v.p. bldg. products distbn. sales and logistics Mid-Atlantic and S.E. regions, 2000—01, pres. lumber, 2001—02, v.p., CIO info. tech., 2002—06; sr. v.p., chief info. officer Medtronic, Inc., Mpls., 2006—. Mem. adv. bd. Habitat for Humanity, Atlanta; mem. exec. com. Nat. Eagle Leadership Instn.; mem. resource devel. com. Cool Girls; mem. CIS adv. bd. Kennesaw State U.; former mem. assoc. com. Interdenominational Theol. Ctr. Office: Medtronic Inc 710 Medtronic Pkwy Minneapolis MN 55432-5604

DALLAS, SANDRA, writer; b. Wash., June 11, 1939; d. Forrest Everett and Harriett (Mavity) Dallas; m. Robert Thomas Atchison, Apr. 20, 1963; children: Dana Dallas, Povy Kendal Dallas. BA, U. Denver, 1960. Asst. editor U. Denver Mag., 1965-66; editl. asst. Bus. Week, Denver, 1961-63, 67-69, bur. chief, 1969-85, 90-91, sr. corr., 1985-90; freelance editor, 1990—2001. Book reviewer Denver Post, 1961—, regional book columnist, 1980—. Author: Gaslights and Gingerbread, 1965, rev. edit., 1984, Gold and Gothic, 1967, No More Than 5 in a Bed, 1967, Vail, 1969, Cherry Creek Gothic, 1971, Yesterday's Denver, 1974, Sacred Paint, 1980, Colorado Ghost Towns and Mining Camps, 1985, Colorado Homes, 1986, Buster Midnight's Cafe, 1990, reissued, 1998, The Persian Pickle Club, 1995, The Diary of Mattie Spenser, 1997, Alice's Tulips, 2000, The Chili Queen, 2002, The Quilt that Walked to Golden, 2004, New Mercies, 2005, Tallgrass, 2007; editor: The Colorado Book, 1993; contbr. articles to popular mags. Bd. dirs. Vis. Nurse Assn., Denver, 1983—85, Hist. Denver, Inc., 1979—82, 1984—87, Rocky Mountain Quilt Mus., 2001—04, Historic Georgetown, Inc., 2002—05. Recipient Wrangler award Nat. Cowboy Hall of Fame, 1980, Lifetime Achievement award Denver Posse of Westerners, 1996, disting. svc. award U. Colo., 1997; named Colo. Exceptional Chronicler of Western History by Women's Library Assn. and Denver Pub. Library Friends Found., 1986; finalist Spur award We. Writers of Am., 1998, Women Writing the West Willa award, 2001, 03, 05, recipient, 2003, Benjamin Franklin award Ind. Book Pub. Assn., 2005 Mem. Women's Forum Colo., Denver Woman's Press Club, Western Writers Am. (Spur award 2003), Women Writing the West. Democrat. Presbyterian. Home and Office: 750 Marion St Denver CO 80218-3434

DALLAS, SATERIOS (SAM DALLAS), aerospace engineer, researcher, consultant; b. Detroit, May 9, 1938; s. Peter and Pauline (Alex) D.; m. Athena Ethel Spartos, July 12, 1964; children: Gregory Dean, Paula Marie. BS in Aero. Engrng., U. Mich., 1959, BS in Engrng. Math., 1960; MS in Astrodynamics, UCLA, 1963, PhD in Engrng., 1968. Rsch. engr. astrodynamics dept. Jet Propulsion Lab., Pasadena, Calif., 1965-78, supr. tech. group mission design, 1978-82, flight engrng. office mgr. Voyager Project, 1982-84, sci. and mission design mgr. Magellan Project, 1984-89, tech. mgr. spacecraft analysis, 1989-90, mission mgr. Mars Observer Project, 1990-93, mission mgr. Mars Global Surveyor Project, 1994-97, mission mgr. space interferometry mission, 1997-99, flight project mentor, 2002—04, cons., 2004—. Instr. Pepperdine U., Malibu, Calif., 1973-75; lectr. on space missions Kennedy Space Ctr., Cape Canaveral, Fla., 1988, Australian Dept. Industry, Tech. and Commerce, Canberra, 1988, USAF-CAP-PLR Ctr. Aerospace Edn., Las Vegas, Neb., 1991. Author: Progress in Astronautics and Aeronautics, 1964, Natural and Artificial Satellite Motion, 1979; contbr. articles to sci. jours. Coach Glendale (Calif.) Little League, 1979-82; com. mem. troop 125 Boy Scouts Am., Glendale, 1980. Recipient Apollo achievement award NASA, 1969, cert. of recognition, 1974, Laurels award Aviation Week, 1989, 94, Exceptional Achievement award NASA, 1998. Mem. AIAA, Am. Astron. Soc. (astrodynamics tech. com. 1970-80). Republican. Greek Orthodox. Avocations: skiing, hiking, woodworking, tennis, computer applications development. Home: 3860 Karen Lynn Dr Glendale CA 91206-1218 E-mail: ssd1938@hotmail.com.

DALLAS, WILLIAM MOFFIT, JR., lawyer; b. Cedar Rapids, Iowa, May 7, 1949; s. William Moffit and Winifred Mae (Lillie) D.; m. Lynne Louise Russo, July 30, 1977 (div. July 1984); m. Janet Neustaetter, Apr. 19, 1985; children: Sarah Anne, Steven Kurt. AB, Oberlin Coll., 1971; JD, Harvard U., 1974. Bar: N.Y. 1975, U.S. Dist. Ct. (so. and ea. dists.) N.Y. 1975, U.S. Ct. Appeals (2d cir.) 1976, U.S. Ct. Appeals (3d cir.) 1983, U.S. Ct. Appeals (8th cir.) 1984. Assoc. Sullivan & Cromwell, NYC, 1974-82, ptnr., 1982—. Fed. mediator U.S. Dist. Ct., 1995—. Contbr. articles on antitrust issues to law revs., 1978—, chpt. to book. Served to lt. USN, 1971-77. Mem. ABA, Assn. of Bar of City of N.Y. (chmn. com. on judicial admin., 1999—, sec. judiciary com. 1977-80, chmn. com. jud. adminstrn. 1999-2002), N.Y. County Lawyers' Assn. (chmn. com. on trade regulation 1978-81), India House Club (N.Y.C.). Office: Sullivan & Cromwell 125 Broad St New York NY 10004-2489 Office Fax: 212-558-3588. Business E-Mail: dallasw@sullcrom.com.

DALLEK, ROBERT, historian, professor, writer; b. Bklyn., May 16, 1934; s. Rubin and Esther (Fisher) Dallek; m. Ilse F. Shatzkin, Nov. 20, 1959 (dec. Oct. 1962); m. Geraldine R. Kronmal, Aug. 22, 1965; children: Matthew J., Rebecca R. BA, U. Ill., 1955; MA, Columbia U., 1957, PhD, 1964. Lectr. history CCNY, 1959-60; instr. history Columbia U., NYC, 1960-64; from asst. prof. to prof. UCLA, 1964—94, prof., 1994, vice-chmn. dept. history, 1972-74; prof. history Boston U., 1996—2002; vis. prof. Dartmouth Coll., 2004—05. Rsch. assoc. So. Calif. Psychoanalytic Inst., LA, 1981—85; Commonwealth Fund lectr. Univ. Coll., London, 1984; Thompson lectr. U. Wyo., Laramie, 1986; Charles Griffin lectr. Vassar Coll., Poughkeepsie, NY, 1987; George W. Littlefield lectr. U. Tex., Austin, 1990; vis. Harmsworth prof. Oxford U., England, 1994—95; cons. ABC, NYC, 1981—82, Ednl. Film Ctr., Annandale, Va., 1988, Sta. KCET-TV, LA, 1988, KERA-TV, Dallas, 1989—91. Author: Democrat and Diplomat: the Life of William E. Dodd, 1968, Franklin D. Roosevelt and American Foreign Policy, 1932-1945, 1979, The American Style of Foreign Policy: Cultural Politics and Foreign Affairs, 1983, Ronald Reagan: The Politics of Symbolism, 1984, Lone Star Rising: Lyndon Johnson and His Times, 1908-1960, 1991, Hail to the Chief: The Making and Unmaking of American Presidents, 1996, Flawed Giant: Lyndon Johnson and His Times 1961-1973, 1998, An Unfinished Life: John F. Kennedy, 1917-1963, 2003, Lyndon B. Johnson: Portrait of a President, 2003, Let Every Nation Know: John F. Kennedy in His Words, 2006, Nixon and Kissinger: Partners in Power, 2007; editor: 3 books; contbr. article to profl. jours. Mem. adv. com. on diplomatic documents Dept. State, Washington, 1985—88; mem. adv. com. Mayor Tom Bradley, LA, 1986; mem. adv. com. on ethics L.A. City Coun., 1989—90; bd. dirs. FDR and Eleanor Roosevelt Inst., 2003—, Nat. Portrait Gallery, 2003—04. John Simon Guggenheim fellow, 1973—74, sr. fellow, NEH, 1976—77, Humanities fellow, Rockefeller Found., 1981—82, Am. Coun. Learned Socs. fellow, 1984—85, Rsch. grant, Eleanor Roosevelt Inst., 1976—77, Lyndon B. Johnson Found., 1984—85, 1988—89, Montgomery fellow, Dartmouth Coll., 2004, 2005. Fellow: Am. Acad. Arts and Scis., Soc. Am. Historians (pres. 2004—05); mem.: Com. on History Second World War, Soc. for Historians of Am. Fgn. Rels. Office Phone: 202-588-8963.

DALLEN, RUSSELL MORRIS, JR., investment company and publishing company executive, lawyer; b. Biloxi, Miss., Jan. 20, 1963; s. Russell Morris and Faye Annette (Werner) D.; m. Claire Lucia (Hodgson), May 27, 1995; children: Allegra Julia Faye, Arabella Sarah Emma. BA in econ. and polit. sci., U. Miss., 1985; M in internat. affairs, Columbia U., 1987; diploma in internat. law, Nottingham U., Eng., 1988; BA in jurisprudence, Oxford U., Eng., 1990, MA in law, 1994. Fgn. corr. Newsweek, London, 1990-91; sr. fellow, dir. UN Assn., USA, NYC, 1991-93; assoc. Morgan Stanley and Co., Inc., NYC, 1994-96; ptnr. Stires, O'Donnell and Co., Inc., 1996-99, Brisbane, Mendez de Leon and Co., Fahnestock and Co.,Inc., Oppenheimer and Co., Inc., 2000—; pres., editor in chief The Daily Jour., NAL Jour., 2003—06. Co-author: Revitalizing The United Nations, 1993; Issues Before the United Nations, 1989, A Global Agenda, 1992; contbr. articles to profl. jour. Bd. dirs. Venezuelan-Am. Amistad Assn., 2005—; bd. govs. Harold W. Rosenthal Fellowship, Washington, 1985—; exec. com. Manhattan coun. Boy Scouts Am., N.Y.C., 1992—; vol. Big Bros. and Big Sisters, N.Y.C., 1992—. Recipient Ner Tamid Leadership Award; Nat. Jewish Com. on Scouting, 1979; Kluwer Internat. Law Award, 1990; Article of Yr. Award Common Market Law Rev.; named Century III Leader, 1981; Harry S. Truman scholar, 1983; U.K. Fgn. and Commonwealth Office scholar, 1987; Harold Rosenthal Fellow, 1985; Am. Fellow European Communities, 1986; Ctr. Fellow Ctr. for Study of Presdy., 1985. Mem. N.Y. State Bar Assn.; N.Y. County Lawyers Assn. (chmn. sub-com. 1992—); Oxford and Cambridge Club; Squadron A Club; Cornell Club; Landsdowne Club. Avocations: sailing, flying, riding. Home: M365 PO Box 3340 New York NY 10185-3340 Home Phone: 212-227-1492. E-mail: rmdallen@aol.com.

DALLEY, GEORGE ALBERT, lawyer, consultant; b. Havana, Cuba, Aug. 25, 1941; s. Cleveland Ernest and Constance Joyce (Powell) D.; m. Pearl Elizabeth Love, Aug. 1, 1970; children: Jason Christopher, Benjamin Christian. AB, Columbia U., 1963, JD, MBA, Columbia U., 1966. Bar: NY 1966, DC 1971, US Supreme Ct. 1972. Asst. to pres. Met. Applied Rsch. Ctr., NYC, 1967-69; counsel The Children's Found., Washington, 1970-71; assoc. counsel Stroock and Stroock and Lavan, Washington, 1970-71, Com. on Judiciary, US Ho. of Reps., Washington, 1971-72; adminstrv. asst. to Rep. Charles B. Rangel, NYC, Washington, 1973-77, counsel, staff dir., 1985-89; dep. asst. sec. for human rights and social affairs Bur. Internat. Orgns. Affairs Dept. State, Washington, 1977-80; mem. CAB, 1980-82; dep. dir. Mondale for Pres. Com., Washington, 1983-84; counsel, staff dir. Congressman Charles B. Rangel, US Ho. of Reps., Washington, 1985-89; sr. v.p. Neill and Co., Washington, 1989-93; ptnr. Neill, Dalley, Carroll, Nealer and Assevero, Washington, 1992-93; sr. ptnr. Holland and Knight, Washington, 1993—2001; counsel, and staff dir. to Congressman Charles Rangel, Washington, 2001—. Adj. prof. Am. U. Sch. Law. Mem. legal adv. com. Dem. Nat. Com., 1975-76; bd. dirs. Africare, TransAfrica; Joint Ctr. for Polit. and Econ. Studies Internat. Inst., Jamaica Nats. Devel. Found. Mem. ABA, Nat. Bar Assn., Coun. Fgn. Rels. Home: 1328 Vermont Ave NW Washington DC 20005-3607 Office: Rm 2354 US House Rep Washington DC 20515 Office Phone: 202-225-4365. Personal E-mail: gdalley@aol.com. Business E-Mail: george.dalley@mail.house.gov.

DALLMANN, DANIEL F., artist, educator; b. St. Paul, Mar. 21, 1942; BS, Minn. State U., 1965; MA, U. Iowa, 1968, M.F.A., 1969. Prof. Tyler Sch. Art, Phila., 1969—. One-man shows include Schoelkopf Gallery, N.Y.C., 1980, 84, 87, J. Rosenthal Fine Arts, Ltd., Chgo., 1989, Tatischeff Gallery, N.Y.C., 1993, Davidson Gallery, Seattle, 1994, Payne Gallery of Moravian Coll., Bethlehem, Pa., Kendall Gallery of Miami-Dade Coll., Miami, Fla., 1997, Dartmouth Coll. Hanover N.H., Lied Art Gallery, Creighton U., Omaha, 1998, Charles More Gallery, Phila., 2000-02; exhibited in group shows, including Allan Frumkin, N.Y.C., 1982, Berkshire Mus., Pittsfield, Mass., 1983, Hudson River Mus., Yonkers, N.Y., 1984, 86, San Francisco Mus. Modern Art, 1985, Orlando (Fla.) Mus. Art at Loch Haven, 1986, NAD, N.Y.C., 1988, NAS, Washington, 1989, Md. Inst., Balt., 1990, So. Alleghenies Mus. Art, Loretto, Pa., 1992, 93, Forum Gallery, N.Y.C., 1994, Smith Coll., Northampton, Mass., 1996, Hackett-Freedman Gallery, San Francisco, 1998, Art Inst. Chgo., 1999, Emporia (Kans.) State U., 2000, Frye Mus. of Art, Seattle, 02; represented in permanent collections Woodmere Art Mus., Phila., J.B. Speed Mus.,

Louisville, Nat. Mus. Am. Art, Washington, Art Inst. Chgo., Amity Art Found., Woodbridge, Conn., also corp. collections. Office Phone: 267-261-3152. E-mail: dallmann@temple.edu.

DALLMANN, WILLIAM CHARLES, speech educator, writer; b. Detroit, Nov. 16, 1929; s. Bertram and Lillian Dallmann; m. Constance Joan Covington; children: Shane, Alan, Lara. AB in Speech and Drama, San Francisco State U., 1957, MA in Drama, 1963; PhD in Speech Pathology, Purdue U., 1973. Cert. Am. Speech Hearing and Lang. Assn. Prof. communicative disorders Valparaiso (Ind.) U., 1964—84; Ju-Jutsu sensei Pacific Acad. Life Arts, Monterey, Calif., 1984—89; freelance writer Monterey, 2001—. Pvt. investigator Wittlinger Agy., Indpls., 1982—84; speech pathologist, clin. hypnotist Counseling Assocs., Valparaiso, 1976—81, exec. dir., 1976—81; dir. Speech Lang. Clinic, Valparaiso, 1964—84. Author: The Children of Prometheus, 1999, 2 Kill or Not to Kill, 2001. With USN, 1948—49, 1st lt. US Army, 1951—53, Korea. Mem.: ACLU, Inst. Gen. Semantics, Vets. for Peace, Amnesty Internat., 25th Infantry Divsn. Assn. (life). Lutheran. Avocations: reading, languages, quantum physics, theology, semantics. Home: 4080 Los Altos Drive Pebble Beach CA 93953 Personal E-mail: raven@redshift.com.

DALLOS, PETER JOHN, neurobiologist, educator; b. Budapest, Hungary, Nov. 26, 1934; arrived in US, 1956, naturalized, 1962; s. Ernest and Maria Dallos; m. Joan Usis, Aug. 18, 1977; 1 child by previous marriage, Christopher. Student, Tech. U. Budapest, 1953-56; BS, Ill. Inst. Tech., 1958; MS, Northwestern U., 1959, PhD, 1962. Rsch. engr. Am. Machine and Foundry Co., 1959; cons. engr., 1959-60; mem. faculty Northwestern U., 1962—, prof. audiology and elec. engring., 1969—, prof. neurobiology and physiology, 1981—, chmn., 1981-84, 86-87, assoc. dean Coll. Arts and Scis., 1984-85, John Evans prof. neurosci., 1986—, Hugh Knowles prof. audiology, 1994—2003, acting v.p. for rsch., 2003—. Vis. scientist Karolinska Inst., Stockholm, 1977-78; chmn. behavioral and neurosci. rev. panel No. 5 Nat. Inst. Neurol., Communicative Disorders and Stroke, NIH, 1982-85, mem. nat. adv. council, 1984-87 Author: The Auditory Periphery: Biophysics and Physiology, 1973; editor: The Cochlea, 1996; contbr. articles to profl. jours. Recipient 12th ann. award Beltone Inst. Hearing Rsch., 1977, Internat. prize Amplifon Rsch. and Study Ctr., 1984, Senator Jacob Javits Neurosci. Investigator award, 1984, Honors of Assn. award Am. Speech-Lang.-Hearing Assn., 1994, Bekesy medal of Acoustical Soc. Am., 1995, Sigma Xi Disting. Nat. lectr., 1997-98, Acta Otolaryngologica Internat. prize, 1997, Kresge-Mirmelstein prize La. State U., 2000; Guggenheim fellow, 1977-78; McKnight sr. fellow, 1997-2000, Guyot prize, 2004, Hugh Knowles prize, 2005. Fellow IEEE (life), AAAS, Acoustical Soc. Am., Am. Acad. Arts and Scis.; mem. Soc. for Neurosci., Assn. for Rsch. in Otolaryngology (pres. 1992-93, award of merit 1994), Am. Physiological Soc., Collegium Otolaryngologicum Amicitae Sacrum, Hungarian Acad. Scis., Sigma Xi, Tau Beta Pi, Eta Kappa Nu. Office: Northwestern U 2240 Campus Dr Evanston IL 60208-0837 Business E-Mail: p-dallos@northwestern.edu.

DALLURA, SAL ANTHONY, physician; b. Flushing, NY, Nov. 7, 1960; s. Russ and Mayann (Taranto) D.; m. Donna Ann Baldassare, Aug. 6, 1983 (div. Mar. 1993); children: Christopher Anthony, Corinne Elizabeth; m. Stacy Elizabeth Carberry, July 1, 1995 (div. Jan. 1999); 1 child, Matthew Anthony; m. Tammy L. Chance, Dec. 27, 1999. BS in Pre-Profl. Studies cum laude, U. Notre Dame, South Bend, Ind., 1982; MD with honors, NY Coll. Osteo. Medicine, Old Westbury, 1986. Diplomate Am. Acad. Family Physicians, 1990, 1996, 2002. Mng. ptnr. Flashner Med. Ptnrship., Babylon, NY, 1989-91; assoc. physician Moriches Med. Care, Center Moriches, NY, 1989-91, Digiovanna, Massepequa Park, NY, 1991-92, Tippecanoe Family Physicians, Tipp City, Ohio, 1992-98, Milton Union Med. Ctr., West Milton, Ohio, 1998-2000; physician mng. ptnr. After Hours Family Care, Tipp City, 1994-98; physician Upper Valley Profl. Corp., 1994-2000, Kenbrook Med. Ctr., 2000—02, St. Marys Family Practice, Ohio, 2002—05, Holzer Clinic, Jackson, Ohio, 2005—. Expert witness malpractice def., case revs., depositions, testimony for family practice. Recipient Excellence in Gastroenterology award, 1986. Fellow Am. Acad. Family Practice; mem. Am. Osteo. Assn., Am. Acad. Urgent Care Medicine, Ohio Osteo. Assn., Alpha Epsilon Delta. Republican. Roman Catholic. Avocations: model railroading, coin and stamp collecting, reading, audio and video entertainment, computer research. Office: 280 Pattonsville Rd Jackson OH 45640 Home Phone: 419-629-3029; Office Phone: 740-395-8889. Business E-Mail: sdallura@nktelco.net.

DALLY, JAMES WILLIAM, mechanical engineering educator, consultant; b. Sardis, OH, Aug. 2, 1929; s. William Hiram and Martha (Siebert) D.; m. Anne Evangeline Tziritas, Dec. 22, 1955; children: Lisa, William, Michelle. BSME, Carnegie Mellon U., 1951, MSME, 1953; PhD, Ill. Inst. Tech., 1958. Registered profl. engr., Md. Asst. dir. rsch. Armour Research Found., Chgo., 1961-64; prof. Ill. Inst. Tech., Chgo., 1964-71; prof., chmn. dept. U. Md., College Park, 1971-79; dean Coll. Engring. U. R.I., Kingston, 1979-82; mgr. mech. devel. IBM, Manassas, Va., 1982-84; prof. mech. engring. U. Md., College Park, 1984-97. Disting. vis. prof. USAF Acad., 1995-96; mem. tech. assessment bd. Army Rsch. Lab., 1997-2000; pres. College House Enterprises, LLC, 1998—. Author: Photoelastic Coatings, 1977, Engineering Measurements, 1984, 2nd edit., 1993, Packaging Electronic Systems, 1990, Product Engineering and Manufacturing, 1998, Design Analysis of Structural Elements, 3rd edit., 2003, 4th edit., 2004, Experimental Stress Analysis, 2005, Introduction to Engineering Design, Book 9, 2006, 2nd edit., 2007; contbr. articles. Recipient Boeing Outstanding Educator award, 1996. Fellow ASME, Am. Acad. Mechanics (bd. dirs. 1984-88, pres. 1990-91, Disting. Svc. award 2004), Soc. Exptl. Mechanics (hon., pres. 1970-71, Murray lectureship 1979, Past Pres. award 1971, M.M. Frocht award 1976, Hetenyi award 1995, F.G. Tatnall award 2001, Charles E. Taylor award 2002); mem. Nat. Acad. Engring., U.S. Nat. Com. Theoretical and Applied Mechanics (chmn. 1982-84, vice-chmn., 1984-86). Achievements include patents in field. Office Phone: 865-558-6111. Personal E-mail: jdally0829@comcast.net.

DALLY, WILLIAM J., computer science educator; Past prof., dept. Elec. Engring. and Computer Sci. MIT; Willard R. and Inez Kerr Bell Prof. Computer Sci. Stanford Univ., chmn. Dept. Computer Sci. Key role in the founding of Avici Sys., 1997—, Stream Processors Inc., 2004—; chief tech. officer Velio Comm., 1999—2003; worked with Cray, 1989—; spkr. in field. Contbr. articles to numerous profl. jours. Fellow: Am. Acad. Arts & Scis., Assn. Computing Machinery (Maurice Wilkes award 2000), IEEE (Seymour Cray award 2004). Office: Computer Sci Dept Stanford Univ 353 Serra Mall Gates Rm 301 Stanford CA 94305-9025 Office Phone: 650-723-2273 ext. 5-8945. Business E-Mail: bill.dally@cs.stanford.edu.*

DALMAU, MICHELLE, library and information scientist; b. Miami, Fla. d. Fernando Victorino Dalmau and Carmen Maria Poll. BA in English and Art History, magna cum laude, Fla. Internat. U., 1997; M in Info. Sci., Ind. U., 2004, MLS, 2004. Membership and pub. info. coord. Mus. Contemporary Art, North Miami, Fla., 1998; web developer, Departmental Info. Services Univ. Info. Tech. Services, 2000—01, web developer, Oncourse, 2001—02; interface & usability specialist Ind. U. Digital Libr. Prog., 2002—06, digital projects & usability librarian, 2006—. Usability cons. teiPublisher, 2004—; XTM/topic map encoding and usability cons. Top Map for Charles Algernon Swinburne, 2005; designer and technical support Digital Humanities Quarterly, 2005; co-dir. Your Art Here, 2005—. Mem. Spl. Interest Group on Computer-Human Interaction. Named one of the Movers & Shakers, Libr. Jour., 2007. Mem.: Assn. for Computing Machinery, Assn. for Computers and the Humanities, Am. Soc. Info. Sci. & Tech., ALA, Beta Phi Mu. Office: Indiana Univ Digital Library Program Rm E170 1320 E 10th St Bloomington IN 47405 Office Phone: 812-855-1261. E-mail: mdalmau@indiana.edu.

D'ALOIA, G(IAMBATTISTA) PETER, manufacturing executive; b. Sao Paulo, Brazil, Jan. 10, 1945; s. John and Rosali (Picarelli) D'Aloia; m. Marguerite Ann Fuccello, Aug. 3, 1946; children: Jonelle, Tara. BS in Acctg., NYU, 1966, LLM in Taxation, 1976; JD, St. John's U., 1969. Bar: NY 1969. Tax atty. Arthur Young and Co., NYC, 1969-72, Allied Chem. Co., Morristown, NJ, 1972-79; chief tax counsel Allied Corp., Morristown, NJ, 1979-81, dir. taxes, 1981-83; v.p. taxes Allied-Signal Inc., Morristown, NJ, 1983-88, v.p., treas., 1988-92, v.p., contr., 1992-95, v.p. devel., CFO, 1995-2000; sr. v.p., CFO Am. Standard Companies, Inc., Piscataway, NJ, 2000—. Mem. Bd. Edn., Mendham, NJ, 1977—80. Mem.: NY State Bar Assn., Assn. of Bar City of NY, ABA. Roman Catholic. Avocations: jogging, sailing, gardening. Office: Amer Standard Cos One Centennial Ave PO Box 6820 Piscataway NJ 08855-6820*

DALOIA, RACHEL ROSEMARY, music educator; b. New Hyde Park, NY, Nov. 2, 1976; d. Gregory Francis and Rose Mary Spano; m. Michael Nicholas Daloia, Oct. 18, 2003; children: Gianna Lahela, Anthony Michael. B Voice Performance, B Music Edn., U. Del., 1999; M Music Edn., Five Towns Coll., 2004. Cert. K-12 music tchr. NY. 5th-6th grade choir dir. Island Trees Mid. Sch., Levittown, NY, 1999—2000; jr. high choir dir. North Country Rd. Mid. Sch., Miller Place, NY, 2000—00; jr./sr. high choir dir. Sewanhaka HS, Floral Park, NY, 2000—. Varsity and jr. high gymnastics coach Roslyn (NY) HS/Mid. Sch., Roslyn, NY, 2002—03. Mem.: Nassau Music Educator's Assn., Music Educator's Nat. Conf. Republican. Roman Catholic. Avocations: gymnastics, camping, crafts, musical theater. Home: 1602 Broadway New Hyde Park NY 11040 Office: Sewanhaka HS 500 Tulip Ave Floral Park NY 11001 Home Phone: 516-775-2793; Office Phone: 516-488-9627. Personal E-mail: musicdaloia@yahoo.com.

DAL PAN, GERALD J., federal agency administrator; Dir. clin. rsch. Guilford Pharma., HHI, LLC, Clin. Rsch. and Statistical Services; med. reviewer, divsn. of anesthetic critical care and addiction drug products FDA, Rockville, Md., 2000—03, dir., divsn. of surveillance, rsch., and communication support, office of drug safety in CDER, 2003—05, dir. drug safety, 2005—. Faculty John Hopkins U. Sch. Medicine, part-time asst. prof., dept. neurology. Office: FDA 5600 Fishers Lane Rockville MD 20857

DALPINO, IDA JANE, retired secondary school educator; b. Newhall, Calif., Oct. 20, 1936; d. Bernhardt Arthur and Wahneta May (Blyler) Melby; m. Gilbert Augustus, June 14, 1963 (div. 1976); 1 child, Nicolette Jane. BA, Calif. State U., Chico, 1960; postgrad., Sacramento State, 1961—65, Sonoma State, 1970—71; MA, U. San Francisco, 1978. Cert. cmty. counselor, learning handicapped, c.c. instr., exceptional children, pupil pers. specialist, secondary tchr., resource specialist. Tchr. Chico High Sch., 1959-60; counselor Mira Loma High Sch., Sacramento, 1960-66; tchr. ESL Phoenix Ind. High Sch., 1968-69; resource specialist Yuba City (Calif.) High Sch., 1971-2000; ret., 2000. English tchr. Rough Rock Demonstration Sch., summers, 1975, 76. Office sec. Job's Daus., North Bend, Oreg., 1953—; active Environ. Def. Fund, Centerville Hist. Assn., Chico, 1991—. Mem. NEA, Calif. Tchrs. Assn., Chico State Alumni Assn., Sierra Club, Nature Conservancy, Audubon, Greenpeace, Sigma Kappa Alumni. Democrat. Mem. Science of the Mind Church. Avocations: reading, ecology, genealogy. Home: 6 Navajo Ln Corte Madera CA 94925 Personal E-mail: idajane@comcast.net.

DAL PORTO, MARK DANIEL, music educator; b. Sacramento, July 29, 1955; s. Dante and Shirley Louise Dal Porto. BA, Calif. State U., Sacramento, 1978, MA, 1981; DMA, U. Tex., 1985. Vis. asst. prof. music Tex. State U., San Marcos, 1987—89; from asst. prof. to assoc. prof. music No. State U., Aberdeen, SD, 1989—94, Tex. Woman's U., Denton, 1994—2001; assoc. prof. music Ea. N.Mex U., Portales, 2001—. Presenter at confs. and meetings. Author: (music composition) Galactica for Symphonic Wind Ensemble, Spring, the Sweet Spring for Choir with Piano Accompaniment (winner Denton Cmty. Chorus Composition Contest, 2001), Domestic Suite: Scenes and Memories from Childhood for Piano Solo, 2001, When Your Song Rang Out to Me, 2003, Song of the Night for Oboe, Voice, and Piano, 2004, Midnight Song for Oboe, Mixed Choir and Piano, 2005, Peace Resounds for Mixed Choir and Piano, 2006, At MIdnight for Brass Quintet, Percussion and Mixed Choir, 2006, Song of Eternity for Orchestra, 2006. Mem.: ASCAP (Royalties 1986 - present), Soc. Composers, Inc., Coll. Music Soc., Am. Music Ctr., Am. Composer's Forum. Home: 1116 Gemini Drive Portales NM 88130-6134 Office: Eastern New Mexico University Department of Music Station 16 Portales NM 88130 Office Phone: 505-562-2271. Business E-Mail: mark.dalporto@enmu.edu.

DALRYMPLE, CHRISTOPHER GUY, chiropractor; b. Beaumont, Tex., Sept. 2, 1958; s. Guy H. and Betty Jane (Williams) D.; m. Angela Hackley, Dec. 15, 1979; children: Sarah E., William C., Clayton G. Student, Baylor U., 1976-78; D in Chiropractic Medicine, Tex. Chiropractic Coll., 1982. Diplomate Nat. Bd. Chiropractic Examiners, Tex. Bd. Chiropractic Examiners; ordained Baptist Deacon, 1988. Chiropractor Brassard Chiropractic Clinic, Beaumont, 1982-85; chiropractic physician, adminstr. Brenham (Tex.) Chiropractic Clinic, 1985—. Host Back Talk, 1987-88; chair Tex. Chiropractic PAC; cons., lectr. in field. Author: Brenham & Masonry 150 Years Together, 1995; contbr. articles to profl. jours. Team chiropractor track team Blinn Coll., Brenham, 1987-94, Tex. track and field participants Olympics, 1992; Sunday sch. dir. First Bapt., 1986-87, 90-93, Sunday sch. tchr., 1987-89, bd. trustees Calvary Bapt. Ch., Brenham, 1992-94, Sunday sch. tchr. youth, 1993-94, actor, playwright ch. pageants, 1993-94, 96, 98, 99, 03, deacon. chmn., 1994-98, chmn. pers. com., 1995-98, chmn. long range planning com., 1995-98, adult Sunday sch. tchr., 1995-99; treas. Brenham Ind. Sch. Devel.-PAC, 1994; participant Health Occupation Students of Am. Program, Brenham H.S. Recipient State Sweepstakes Winner "Jake", Tex. Jaycees, 1984, Outstanding Officer, 1984. Fellow: Internat. Coll. Chiropractors; mem.: Tex. Chiropractic Assn. (labor rels. 1983, dist. 9 sec. 1983—84, chmn. publ. com. 1987—99, editor-in-chief 1987—99, membership com. 1994—95, dist. 8 state dir. 1996—99, state sec. 1999, pres.-elect 2000, pres. 2001, internal affairs coord. 2002—06, state com., Young Chiropractor award 1997, Pres.'s award 1999, 2004, 2006), Am. Chiropractic Assn., Masons (Knight Comdr., Knight Templar), Gideons Internat. (Bible chmn. 1994—2005), Tex. Chiropractic Coll. Alumni Assn., Baylor Alumni Assn. (life), K.T., Masons, Graham Masonic Lodge (various offices), Delta Sigma Chi (sec. 1981, bd. dirs. 1982). Republican. Baptist. Avocation: kendo. Office: Brenham Chiropractic Clinic PO Box 2350 Brenham TX 77834-2350 Office Phone: 979-836-4610. Business E-Mail: cdal@fixback.com.

DALRYMPLE, GARY BRENT, research geologist; b. Alhambra, Calif., May 9, 1937; s. Donald Inlow and Wynona Edith (Pierce) D.; m. Sharon Ann Tramel, June 28, 1959; children: Stacie Ann, Robynne Ann Sisco, Melinda Ann Dalrymple McGurer. AB in Geology, Occidental Coll., 1959; PhD in Geology, U. Calif., Berkeley, 1963; DSc (hon.), Occidental Coll., Los Angeles, 1993. Rsch. geologist U.S. Geol. Survey, Menlo Park, Calif., 1963-81, 84-94, asst. chief geologist we. region, 1981-84; dean, prof. Coll. Oceanic and Atmospheric Sci., Oreg. State U., Corvallis, 1994-2001, dean and prof. emeritus, 2001—. Vis. prof. sch. earth scis. Stanford U., 1969-72, cons. prof., 1983-85, 90-94; disting. alumni centennial spkr. Occidental Coll., 1986-87. Author: Potassium-Argon Dating, 1969, Age of Earth, 1991, Ancient Earth, Ancient Skies, 2004; contbr. chpts. to books and articles to profl. jours. Fellow NSF, 1961-63; recipient Meritorius Svc. award U.S. Dept. Interior, 1984, Public Svc. award Geological Soc. Am., 2001, Nat. medal Sci., 2003. Fellow Am. Geophys. Union (pres.-elect 1988-90, pres. 1990-92), Am. Acad. Arts and Scis.; mem. NAS (chair geology sect. 1997-2000), Am. Inst. Physics (bd. govs. 1991-97), Consortium for Oceanographic Rsch. and Edn. (bd. govs. 1994-2001), Joint Oceanographic Inst. (bd. govs. 1994-2001, chair 1996-98). Achievements include discovery that the earth's magnetic field reverses polarity and determination of time scale of these reversals for the past 3.5 million years; development of ultra-fast high-sensitivity thermoluminescence analyzer for studying lunar surface processes; development and refinement of K-Ar and 40 Ar/39 Ar dating methods and instrumentation, continuous laser probe for determining ages of microgram-sized mineral samples; research on volcanoes in the Hawaiian-Emperor volcanic chain, chronology of lunar basin formation, development and improvement of isotopic dating techniques and instrumentation, geomagnetic field behavior, plate tectonics of the Pacific Ocean basin, evolution of volcanoes, various aspects of Pleistocene history of the western U.S. Home: 1847 NW Hillcrest Dr Corvallis OR 97330-1859 Personal E-mail: brentandsharon@comcast.net.

DALRYMPLE, JACK, lieutenant governor, former state legislator; b. Mpls., Oct. 16, 1948; m. Betsy Wood Dalrymple; 4 children. BA in Am. Studies, Yale U., 1970. Farmer, 1970—; mem. N.D. Ho. of Reps from 22 Dist., 1985—2001, chmn. appropriations com.; lt. gov. State of N.D., Bismarck, 2001—. Bd. dirs. Prairie Pub. TV, N.D. State U. Devel. Found., Golden Growers Coop.; mem. Edn. Broadcasting Coun.; co-founder Share House Inc. Recipient Outstanding Young Farmer award, 1983. Mem. Cass County Rural Water Users Assn. (past bd. dirs.), Casselton Econ. Devel. Found., Univ. Pres. Agr. Club (pres.), Durum Growers Assn. (bd. dirs.), Jaycees. Republican. Address: PO Box 220 Casselton ND 58012-0220 Office: Office Lt Governor Dept 101 600 E Boulevard Ave Bismarck ND 58505 Office Phone: 701-328-4222. Office Fax: 701-328-2205.*

DALRYMPLE, ROBERT ANTHONY, III, civil engineering educator; b. Camp Rucker, Ala., May 30, 1945; s. Robert Anthony and Helen Nancy (Wright) D.; m. Candice VuHaggie, June 22, 1968; 1 child, Melissa Jane. AB, Dartmouth Coll., 1967; MS, U. Hawaii, 1968; PhD, U. Fla., 1973. Registered profl. engineer, Del. Asst. in engring. U. Fla., Gainesville, 1968-71, grad. rsch. assoc., 1971-73; asst. prof. civil engring. and marine studies U. Del., Newark, 1973-77, assoc. prof., 1977-84, prof., 1984—2004, prof. emeritus, 2004—; Willard & Lillian Hackerman prof. civil engring. Johns Hopkins U., 2002—, chmn. Dept. Civil Engring., 2002—04. Asst. dean Coll. Engring. U. Del., 1980-82; dir. Ctr. for Applied Coastal Rsch. U. Del., 1989—; civilian mem. Coastal Engring. Rsch. BD. U.S. Army Corps of Engrs., Vicksburg, Miss., 1989—. Fellow ASCE; mem. NAE, Am. Geophys. Union, Internat. Assn. for Hydraulic Rsch., Soc. for Indsl. and Applied Math., Am. Acad. Mechanics, Am. Shore and Beach Preservation Assn., Del. Assn. Profl. Engrs. (coun. mem. 1990—). Office: Dept Civil Engring Johns Hopkins U 210 Latrobe Hall Baltimore MD 21218 Office Phone: 410-516-7923. Office Fax: 410-516-7473. E-mail: rad@jhu.edu.

DALRYMPLE, RONALD GERALD, psychologist; b. Denver, Nov. 24, 1949; s. Claeton Gerald and Norma Ethel (Shafer) D. BS, U. Md., 1971, MA, 1982, PhD, 1984. Lic. psychologist, Md. Pvt. practice Kent Island Psychol. Svcs., Inc., Chester, Md., 1986—. Author: Increase Your Power of Creative Thinking in Eight Days, 1985, The Inner Manager, 1989, The Feeding, 1995. Mem. Mensa, Phi Beta Kappa. Home: PO Box 414 216 Dominion Rd Chester MD 21619-2634 Office: Quantum Psychology Press PO Box 414 216 Dominion Rd Chester MD 21619-2634

DALRYMPLE, THOMAS LAWRENCE, retired lawyer; b. Wellsburg, W. Va., May 20, 1921; s. Lawrence Chester and Ethel May (Taylor) D.; m. Marjorie May Keeler; children: Bruce Lawrence, Dale Brian. AB, U. Mich., 1943, JD, 1947. Bar: Ohio 1947, U.S. Supreme Ct. Practiced in, Toledo, 1947-96; assoc. Williams, Eversman & Morgan and successor firms, 1947-50, Welles, Kelsey, Fuller, Harrington & Seney and successor firms, 1950-52; ptnr. Fuller & Henry and predecessor firms, 1953-96. Mem. Trout Unltd., Toledo Mus. Art. Served to capt. inf. AUS, 1943-46. Decorated Combat Inf. badge, Silver Star medal, Purple Heart. Fellow Am. Coll. Trial Lawyers, Am. Bar Found., Ohio Bar Found.; mem. Order of Coif, Phi Beta Kappa. Home: 4307 Stannard Dr Toledo OH 43613-3636

DAL SANTO, DIANE, retired judge, writer, arbitrator, mediator; b. East Chicago, Ind., Sept. 20, 1949; d. John Quentin and Helen (Koval) D.; m. Fred O'Cheskey, June 29, 1985. BA, U. N.Mex., 1971; cert., Inst. Internat. and Comparative Law, Guadalajara, Mex., 1978; JD, U. San Diego, 1980. Bar: N.Mex. 1980, U.S. Dist. Ct. N.Mex. 1980. Ct. planner Met. Criminal Justice Coordinating Coun., Albuquerque, 1973-75; planning coord. Dist Atty.'s Office, Albuquerque, 1975-76, exec. asst. to dist. atty., 1976-77, asst. dir. atty. for violent crimes, 1980-82; chief dep. city atty. City of Albuquerque, 1983; assoc. firm T.B. Keleher & Assocs., 1983-84; judge Met. Ct., 1985-89, chief judge, 1988-89; judge Dist. Ct., 1989-2000. Faculty Nat. Jud. Coll., 1990-95, 97-2000, trustee, 1995-96; adj. faculty Internat. Law Enforcement Acad., Roswell, N.Mex., 2002-06. Columnist Albuquerque Jour., 1996-98. Mem. Mayor's Task Force on Alcoholism and Crime, 1987—88, N.Mex. Coun. Crime and Delinquency, 1987—97, Task Force Domestic Violence, 1987—94, Metro Criminal Justice Coordinating Coun., 1998—2000; bd. dirs. Nat. Coun. Alcoholism, 1984, S.W. Ballet Co., Albuquerque, 1982—83, Youth Devel., Inc., 2004—; founder Pennies for the Homeless, 1993, vp. bd. dirs., 2002—06; bd. dirs. N.Mex. Coun. Crime and Delinquency, 1992—94, bench, bar, media com., 1987—, pres., 1992; rules evidence com. Supreme Ct., 1993—96, chair com. access to pub. records, 1988; steering com. N.Mex. Buddy Awards, 1995—97. U. San Diego scholar, 1978-79; recipient Women on the Move award YWCA, 1989, Disting. Woman award U. N.Mex. Alumni Assn., 1994, Outstanding Alumnus Dept. Sociology U. N.Mex., 1995; named Woman of Yr. award Duke City Bus. and Profl. Women, 1985. Mem. ABA (Jud. Excellence award Nat. Conf. State Trial Judges 1996), LWV, AAUW, Am. Judicature Soc., N.Mex. Women's Found., N.Mex. State Bar Assn. (silver gavel award 1997), N.Mex. Women's Bar Assn. (bd. dirs. 1991-92, Power and Caring award 2000), Albuquerque Bar Assn., Nat. Assn. Women Judges (bd. dist. dirs. 1999-00), Greater Albuquerque C. of C. (steering com. 1989), N.Mex. Magistrate Judges Assn. (v.p. 1985-89), Dist. Judges Assn. (pres. 1994-95). Home Phone: 505-266-0663. Personal E-mail: dianedalsanto@aol.com.

DALSING, MICHAEL CLETUS, surgeon, educator; s. Vincent John and Nellie Mary Dalsing; m. Rosa Marie Olejniczak, May 20, 1978; children: Jessica Rose, Rachael Augusta, Heather Matilda. BA in Biology, St. Mary's Coll., Winona, Minn., 1974; MD, The Med. Coll. Wis., Milw., 1978. Cert. in vascular surgery Am. Bd. Surgery, 1986, in gen. surgery Am. Bd. Surgery, 1984, in surg. critical care Am. Bd. Surgery, 1992. Internship in surg. Sch. Medicine, Indiana U., Indpls., 1978—79, residency in surg., 1979—82, chief residency in surg., 1982—83; fellowship in vascular surgery Northwestern U., Chgo., 1983—84; from asst. prof. to prof. surgery Sch. Medicine Ind. U., Indpls., 1984—2004, E. Dale and Susan E. Habegger prof. surgery Sch. Medicine, 2004—, dir. vascular surg. residency program Sch. Medicine, 2001—. Pres. med. staff Clarian Health Care Sys., Indpls., 2005—. Contbr. chapters to books, over 100 articles to profl. jours. Named alumnus mem., Alpha Omega Alpha, 1988; Conrad Jobst fellow, Northwestern U., 1983. Fellow: ACS (gov. from ind. 2004—); mem.: Assn. Program Dirs. Vascular Surg., Midwestern Vascular Surg. Soc. (pres. 2005—06), Am. Venous Forum (pres. 2006—), Ctrl. Surg. Assn., Soc. Clin. Vascular Surg., Soc. Vascular Surg., Am. Surg. Soc. Roman Cath. Achievements include research in vascular surgery esp regarding venous valves, carotid artery surgery, collateral blood vessel development and other unusual vascular disorders. Avocations: travel, tennis, football. Office: Indiana University School of Medicine 1801 North Senate Blvd MPC-2 S-3500 Indianapolis IN 46202 Office Phone: 317-962-0280. Office Fax: 317-962-0289. Business E-Mail: mdalsing@iupui.edu.

DALTAS, ARTHUR JOHN, management consultant, software services manager; b. Mpls., Aug. 5, 1945; s. John Howard Locken and Adella Marie (DeChaney) D.; stepfather, John Paul Daltas; m. Ellen Causey Peckham, Feb. 23, 2001; children: Alexander, Andrew, Elizabeth; stepchildren: Samuel Peckham, Anne Peckham. BA, Coll. St. Thomas, Forth Worth, Tex., 1968; MBA with high honors, Boston U., 1973. Tchr. U.S. Dept. Def., Frankfurt, Germany, 1970-71; treas., mgr. Cambridge Comm. Group, Inc., Mass., 1973-78; v.p. The MAC Group/Gemini Inc., Cambridge, 1978-84; founder, pres. The Mgrs. Group, Concord, Mass., 1984-87; prin., chmn. Concord Cons. Group, 1987-2000. Pres. Exec. Advisors Corp., 1997, Progress Software Corp., 2000; mgr. Open Edge Product Programs. Contbg. author: Implementing Strategy, 1982, Marketing Management, 1991; contbr. articles to various publs. Bd. dirs. Make a Wish Boston, 1991-96; asst. scoutmaster Boy Scouts Am., 1999-2002; deacon, standing com. Hancock Ch., 2000—. With U.S. Army, 1968-70. Mem. Nat. Alumni Coun. Boston U., SMG Alumni Bd. Dirs. Boston U., Beta Gamma Sigma. Avocations: skiing, hiking, golf. Office: Progress Software Corp 14 Oak Park Bedford MA 01730

DALTON, ALLAN D., real estate company executive; Sr. exec. Cendent Corp., 1997; sr. v.p. NRT Inc., 1998—2002; exec. v.p. Coldwell Banker Hunneman, Coldwell Banker New England Metro, 2002; pres., CEO Realtor.com, 2002—06; pres. Real Estate Services Divsn. Move, Inc., 2006—07, divisional pres., 2007—. Named one of Real Estate's 25 Most Influential Thought Leaders, Realtor Mag., 2006. Office: Move Inc 30700 Russell Ranch Rd Westlake Village CA 91362 Office Phone: 805-557-2300. Office Fax: 805-557-2680.*

DALTON, ANNE, lawyer; b. Pitts., Dec. 6, 1951; d. Thomas John and Mary Olive (Paul) D.; m. Oliver E. Martin, Dec. 26, 1987. BA in Polit. Sci., NYU, 1973; JD, Fordham U., 1977. Bar: NY 1978, US Dist. Ct. (so. and ea. dists.) NY 1979, Pa. 1987, Fla. 1990. Assoc. Mendes & Mount, NYC, 1979-80; atty. news divsn. ABC, NYC, 1980-85; TV news prodr. ABC Network, NYC, 1985-86; sr. atty. Radio City Music Hall Prodns., Inc., NYC, 1986-87; pvt. practice Stroudsburg, Pa., 1987-91; asst. county att., asst. port authority atty. Lee County, Ft. Myers, Fla., 1991-94; pvt. practice Ft. Myers, 1994—. Spl. hearing master 20th Jud. Cir., Fla., 1991—, ct. Commr., gen. magistrate family civil and probate divsn., 1995—; adj. prof. Edison CC, Ft. Myers, Barry U., Ft. Myers; Fla. family, cir. civil, dependency, county, fed. mediator, 1995; arbitrator, state ct., 1998. Recipient Clio award, Internat. Clio Award Com., 1978. Mem. Pa. Bar Assn., Fla. Bar Assn., NY Bar Assn., Lee County Bar Assn. Roman Catholic. Avocations: reading, gardening. Office: 2044 Bayside Pkwy Fort Myers FL 33901-3102 Office Phone: 239-337-7900.

DALTON, CHERYL RENEE, entrepreneur; b. Jersey City, May 16, 1960; d. Ronald McGowan and Marie Funchess; m. Allen Brett Dalton, Sept. 3, 1995; children: Sha-nia Nell Smith, Ebony Elisa Casley 1 stepchild, Ebony Johnsen. Student, Barnwell Vocat. Sch., 1992. Cert. nursing asst., S.C. Pvt. nurse Atty. George Crawford, Orangeburg, SC, 1992—95; nursing asst. Dehec Home Health, 1992—; owner, dir. Dalton's CMC Residential Care Facility, Orangeburg, 2007—; CEO Dalton & Dalton Enterprise, 2007—. Founder, dir. Edisto Fork Family Info. Referral, Orangeburg, 2003—. Author: A Path From Destruction (Then & Now), 2001; writer poetry for gospel songs:. Mem.: NAACP, Order Ea. Star. Methodist. Achievements include patents for adhesive weave and fast track. Avocation: softball. Home and Office: 356 Cimmaron St Orangeburg SC 29115 Office: Daltons CMC Residential Care Facility 1231 Eutaw St Orangeburg SC 29115 Home Phone: 803-533-5599; Office Phone: 803-533-5599. E-mail: crdalton_29115@hotmail.com, orangeburgrenee@aol.com.

DALTON, DAN R., finance educator, former dean; BA, Calif. State U., 1970, MS, 1975; PhD, U. Calif., Irvine, 1979. Owner retail bus. Middle Earth, 1971—73; owner D&H Industries, 1971—73; mem. staff GE; faculty mem. UCLA, Santa Ana Coll., Calif. State U. Long Beach, Kelley Sch. Bus. Ind. U., Bloomington, Ind., 1979—, assoc. dean for acad. affairs, Samuel and Pauline Glaubinger Prof. Mgmt., 1995—98, dean, 1997—2004, Harold A. Poling Chair in Strategic Management, 1998—, dean emeitus, 2004—; dir., Inst. for Corp. Governance, 2004—. Contbr. numerous articles to profl. jours. Recipient numerous awards and citations for excellence in tchg. Office: Indiana Univ Kelley School Business 1309 E 10th St Bloomington IN 47405-1701

DALTON, DAVID ROBERT, chemistry professor; b. Chgo., Nov. 16, 1936; s. William Edward and Ethel (Shaykin) D.; m. Cecile Kaplan, Aug. 31, 1958; children: Nathaniel, Rachel, Aaron. BA, Northwestern U., 1957; PhD, UCLA, 1962. Chemist G. D. Searle & Co., Skokie, Ill., 1958-63, Monsanto Rsch. Corp., Dayton, Ohio, 1963-64; postdoctoral instr. Ohio State U., Columbus, 1964-65; asst. prof. chemistry Temple U., Phila., 1965-68, assoc. prof. chemistry, 1968-73, prof. chemistry, 1973—, assoc. dean rsch. and grad. studies, 1993-95, chmn. dept. chemistry, 2000—03, Honors prof., 2005. Cons. Noramco, Wilmington, Del., 1987—, Auxillium Pharm. Co., 99—, McNeil Pahrm. Co., 99—, Inkine Pharm. Co., 99—. Author: The Alkaloids, 1979, Organic Chemistry in the Lab, 1979. Recipient Scroll award Am. Inst. Chemists, 1982, Section award undergrad. edn. Am. Chem. Soc., 2003; named Hons. Prof. 2005, Temple U., 2005 Mem.: AAAS, Am. Chem. Soc. (Undergrad. Edn. award 2003, Temple U. Hon. Prof. of Year 2005). Home: 143 Gulph Hills Rd Radnor PA 19087-4615 Office: Temple U 13th And Norris St Philadelphia PA 19122 Office Phone: 215-204-7138. Business E-Mail: david.dalton@temple.edu.

DALTON, DENNIS GILMORE, political science professor; b. Morristown, NJ, Mar. 12, 1938; s. Andrew John and Emily Snow (Smith) D.; m. Sharron Louise Scheline, May 22, 1961; children: Kevin Andrew, Shaun Michael. BA, Rutgers U., 1960; MA, U. Chgo., 1962; PhD, U. London, 1965. Lectr. politics U. London, 1965-69; Ann Whitney Olin prof. polit. sci. Barnard Coll., Columbia U., NYC, 1969—. Condr. series of e-seminars Nonviolent Power, M.K. Gandhi, M.L. King, Jr. and Nonviolent Resistance Around the World, Columbia U. Digital Knowledge, 2002. Author: Indian Idea of Freedom, 1982, Mahatma Gandhi: Nonviolent Power in Action, 1993; editor: States of South Asia, 1983, Mahatma Gandhi: Selected Political Writings, 1996. Mem. War Resisters League, N.Y.C., 1969—. Recipient Emily Gregory Disting. Teaching award, 1978; Am. Coun. Learned Socs. grantee, 1975, Am. Philos. Soc. grantee, 1975; Am. Inst. Indian Studies fellow, 1974; Fulbright scholar to Nepal, 1994-95. Home: 390 Riverside Dr Apt 3e-1 New York NY 10025-1867 Office: Columbia Univ Barnard Coll 606 W 120th St New York NY 10027-5706 Office Phone: 212-854-5006. Business E-Mail: ddalton@barnard.edu. *My research for the last four decades on the life and thought of Mahatma Gandhi has convinced me that his example carries universal implications for the study of conflict resolution. The theory and practice of nonviolence offer us today a system of values and a hope for the future that should serve to inspire humanity.*

DALTON, HARRY JIROU, JR., (JERRY DALTON), public relations executive; b. San Antonio, Feb. 7, 1927; s. Harry Jirou and Dorothy Bess (Black) D.; m. Marion Packard Hume Dalton, Aug. 21, 1954; children: Cynthia Kay, Robert Hume, Steven Jirou. BBA in Advt., U. Tex., 1949, postgrad., 1949-50, Boston U., 1958, U. Nebr., Omaha, 1958-60. Commd. 2d lt. USAF, 1950, advanced through grades to brig. gen., 1975; from assoc. to dir. corp. com. EDS Corp., Dallas, 1980-84; mgr. corp. comm. The LTV Corp., Dallas, 1984-92, Vought Aircraft Co., Dallas, 1992-93; pvt. practice as pub. rels. counsel Dallas, 1994—. Named Outstanding Govt. Pub. Info. Officer Aviation/Space Writers Assn., Washington, 1974. Fellow Pub. Rels Soc. Am. (pres. 1990); mem. Tex. Pub. Rels. Assn. (Outstanding Pub. Rels. Practitioner in Tex. award 1989, Silver Spur award 1991). Presbyterian. Home and Office: 6411 Laurel Valley Rd Dallas TX 75248-3904 Home Phone: 972-960-0145; Office Phone: 972-960-0145. Personal E-mail: jerrydalton@sbcglobal.net.

DALTON, JAMES EDGAR, JR., health facility administrator; b. Gretna, Va., Sept. 17, 1942; married. Bachelors degree, Randolph-Macon Coll., 1964; Masters degree, Va. Commonwealth U., 1966. Adminstrv. resident Lynchburg (Va.) Gen. Hosp., 1965-66, adminstrv. asst., 1966-69, asst. adminstr., 1969-70; adminstr. Princeton (W.Va.) Cmty. Hosp., 1970-72; regional adminstr. Humana Inc., Dallas, 1972-73, regional v.p. Tampa, Fla., 1973-76; dir. hosp. svcs. Am. Medicorp Inc., Atlanta, 1976-77, Dallas, 1977-78; v.p. Hosp. Corp. Am., Nashville, 1978-79, Arlington, Tex., 1979-87, HealthTrust, Inc., Arlington, 1987-89, Nashville, 1989-90; pres., CEO Quorum Health Group, Inc., Brentwood, Tenn., 1990-2001; pres. Edinburgh Assocs., Inc., 2001—. Chmn. Signature Hosp. Corp., 2006—, Hosp. Corp., 2006—. Home and Office: 6505 Edinburgh Dr Nashville TN 37221-3707 Personal E-mail: jdalton561@aol.com.

DALTON, JOHN JOSEPH, lawyer; b. NYC, Feb. 7, 1943; s. John Henry and Anna Veronica D.; m. Martha Warren Egan, Feb. 24, 1968; children: Martha G., J. Michael, W. Brian. BBA, Fairfield U., 1964; JD, Northwestern U., 1967. Bar: Ill. 1967, Ga. 1970, US Dist. Ct. (no. and mid. dists.) Ga., US Dist. Ct. (no. dist.) Ill., US Ct. Appeals (2d, 4th, 5th, 7th, 10th and 11th cirs.), US Tax Ct., US Supreme Ct. Atty. Clausen, Miller, Gorman, Caffrey & Witous, Chgo., 1967-69; ptnr. Troutman Sanders (formerly Troutman, Sanders, Lockerman & Ashmore), Atlanta, 1970—. Chmn. adv. bd. Atlanta Vol. Lawyers Found., 1993. With US Army, 1968—69. Fellow: Am. Bar Found., Am. Coll. Trial Lawyers (regent 2001—05, sec. 2005—06, treas. 2006—07, pres. elect 2007—); mem.: Atlanta Bar Assn. (chmn. bd. Ga. Justice Project 2003—04, bd. dirs.), Highlands Country Club, Peachtree Golf Club, Piedmont Driving Club. Office: Troutman Sanders 600 Peachtree St NE Ste 5200 Atlanta GA 30308-2216 Office Phone: 404-885-3120. Office Fax: 404-962-6539. Business E-Mail: john.dalton@troutmansanders.com.

DALTON, MARTHA GOMER, music educator; d. Roy Paul and Gladys Gomer; m. Ronnie Thomas Dalton, Oct. 15, 1977; children: John, James, Stephen. MusB, Trevecca Nazarene U., 1976; MusM in Vocal Performance, Miami U., 1994; MusM in Vocal Pedagogy, Roosevelt U., 2004. Grad. tchg. asst. Miami U., Oxford, Ohio, 1991—92; prof. music Olivet Nazarene U., Bourbonnais, Ill., 1996—. Mem.: Nat. Assn. Tchrs. Singing, Am. Choral Dirs. Assn. Office: Olivet Nazarene U One University Ave Bourbonnais IL 60914 Home Phone: 815-933-4537. Business E-Mail: mdalton@olivet.edu.

DALTON, ROBERT EDGAR, retired mathematician, computer scientist; b. Boston, May 2, 1938; s. Robert Evelyn and Mildred Louise (Zoellick) D.; m. Sally (Turner), Sept. 12, 1961 (div. 1977); children: Stephen Howard, Alena Lynn BS in Math., U. Chgo., 1959; MS in Applied Math., N.C. State U., 1961, PhD in Applied Math., 1964; MS in Computer Sci., Fla. State U., 1982. Systems analyst RCA Svc. Co., Cocoa Beach, Fla., 1964—65; mem. tech. staff TRW Systems Group, Cocoa Beach, Fla., 1965—71; ops. rsch. analyst Naval Underwater Systems Ctr., West Palm Beach, Fla., 1971—79; grad. tchg. asst. Fla. State U., Tallahassee, 1980—81; asst. prof. Am. U., Washington, 1981—83; mem. tech. staff Mitre Corp., Greenbelt, Md., 1983—85; prin. investigator Vitro Corp., Silver Spring, Md., 1985—93; sr. software devel. engr. Raytheon Co., Bedford, Mass., 1995—2003. Adj. prof. Fla. Inst. Tech., 1964-68, Fla. Atlantic Univ., 1979. Contbr. chapters to books, articles to journals. Chmn. U. Chgo. Alumni Fund, Palm Beach County, Fla., 1975-79 Recipient Spl. Achievement award Naval Underwater Sys. Ctr., 1974, 76; named Jaycee of Yr., Boynton Beach, Fla., 1974 Mem.: Carolina Mountain Club. Achievements include rsch. in underwater acoustics, knowledge acquisition and learning, computer games, pattern recognition, knowledge based sys. devel., and decision support with fuzzy logic. Home: 100 Park Lane S Black Mountain NC 28711 Personal E-mail: bobdalton@charter.net.

DALTON, WILLIAM STEVEN, oncologist, educator; b. Ft. Worth, 1949; BA in Chemistry/Philosophy, U. N.Mex., 1971; MD, Ind. U., 1980, PhD in Toxicology/Med. Life Scis., 1976. Diplomate Am. Bd. Internal Medicine, Am. Bd. Oncology. Intern Ind. U., Indpls., 1980-81; resident in internal medicine U. Ariz., Tucson, 1981-83, fellow in oncology, 1983—; assoc. dir. clin. investigations H. Lee Moffitt Cancer Ctr., Tampa, Fla., 1997—99, dep. dir., 1999—2001, CEO, exec. dir., 2002—. Faculty medicine, pharmacology U. Ariz. Coll. Medicine, 1985—96, prof., 1993—96, dean, 2001—02; prof. oncology, medicine, and biochemistry U. South Fla., 1997—99, prof., chmn. Dept. Interdisciplinary Oncology, 1999—2001. Mem. ACP, Am. Osteo. Assn., Sigma Xi. Office: H Lee Moffitt Cancer Ctr 12902 Magnolia Dr Tampa FL 33612-9416 E-mail: dalton@moffitt.usf.edu.

DALTREY, ROGER HARRY, singer; b. London, Mar. 1, 1944; s. Harry and Irene D.; m. Jacqueline Jan. 29, 1964 (div. 1968); children: Simon; m. Heather Taylor (July 19, 1971); children: Rosie Lea, Willow Amber, Jaimie. Lead singer The Who, 1965—. (albums with The Who) The Who Sings My Generation, 1965, Happy Jack, 1966, The Who Sell Out, 1967, The Magic Bus: The Who on Tour, 1968, Tommy, 1969, Live At Leeds, 1970, Meaty Beaty Big & Bouncy, 1971, Who's Next, 1971, Quadrophenia, 1973, Odds & Sods, 1974, The Who By Numbers, 1975, Who Are You, 1978, Face Dances, 1981, Hooligans, 1981, It's Hard, 1982, Who's Greatest Hits, 1983, Who's Last, 1983, Who's Missing, 1985, Two's Missing, 1987, Who's Better, Who's Best, 1988, Join Together, 1990, Thirty Years of Maximum R&B, 1994, Live at the Isle of Wight Festival 1970, 1996, My Generation: The Very Best of The Who, 1996, The BBC Sessions, 1999, The Blues to the Bush, 1999, The Ultimate Colllection, 2002, Live at the Royal Albert Hall, 2003, The Who: Then & Now, 2004, Live from Toronto, 2006, Endless Wire, 2006; (soundtracks) The Kids Are Alright, 1979, Quadrophenia, 1979; (solo albums) Daltrey, 1973, Ride A Rock Horse, 1975, One of the Boys, 1977, McVicar, 1980, Parting Should Be Painless, 1984, Under a Raging Moon, 1985, Can't Wait to See the Movie, 1987, Rocks in the Head, 1992, Martyrs & Madmen: The Best of Roger Daltrey, 1997; performer (films) Monterrey Pop, 1968, Woodstock, 1970, The Kids Are Alright, 1979, The Who Rocks America, 1982; actor (films) Tommy, 1975, Lisztomania, 1975, The Legacy, 1979, Bitter Cherry, 1983, Pop Pirates, 1984, Murder: Ultimate Grounds for Divorce, 1984, The Hunting of the Snark, 1987, The Little Match Girl, 1987, Gentry, 1987, Three Penny Opera, 1988, Cold Justice, 1989, Mack the Knife, 1989, Buddy's Song, 1990, If Looks Could Kill, 1991, Lightning Jack, 1994, Bad English I: Tales of a Son of a Brit, 1995, 1996, Like It Is, 1998, Best, 2000, Chasing Destiny, 2001, .com for Murder, 2002, Johnny Was, 2006; (TV movies) The Beggar's Opera, 1983, The Comedy of Errors, 1983, Forgotten Prisoners: The Amnesty Files, 1990, (voice only) The Real Story of Happy Birthday to You, 1992, The Wizard of Oz in Concert: Dreams Come True, 1995, The Magical Legend of the Leprechauns, 1999, Dark Prince: The True Story of Dracula, 2000, Strange Frequency 2, 2001, Chasing Destiny, 2001, Trafalgar's Battle Surgeon, 2005; (TV mini-series) Pirate Tales, 1997; (TV appearances) One of the Boys, 1977, Buddy, 1986, Crossbow, 1987, How to Be Cool, 1988, Midnight Caller, 1991, Tales from the Crypt, 1993, Lois & Clark: The New Adventures of Superman, 1996, Sliders, 1997, Fitzcairn, 1997-98, Highlander, 1998, The Bill, 1999, Rude Awakening, 1999-2000, That 70's Show, 2002, Witchblade, 2001-02, Once Upon a Time on the Westway, 2006, CSI: Crime Scene Investigation 2006; actor, prodr. (films) McVicar, 1980; exec. prodr. (films) Quadrophenia, 1979 Named to The Rock & Roll Hall of Fame (as mem. of The Who), 1990; recipient Ivor Novello award for Contribution to British Music, 1982, BRIT award for Outstanding Contribution to British Music, 1988, honorary Knight Comdr. of the Most Excellent Order of the British Empire, 2005. Office: WEA/Atlantic 75 Rockefeller Plz New York NY 10019-6908*

DA'LUZ VIEIRA-JONES, LORRAINE CHRISTINE C., acupuncturist, researcher; b. London, Apr. 30, 1955; arrived in US, 1999; d. Archibald Carlyle and Christine Heather Da Luz Vieira; m. Schuyler M. Jones, Dec. 23, 1998; children: Jesse Christopher, Cassandra Laurie. Licentiate in Acupuncture, C.T.C.M., Leamington Spa, Eng., 1983, B in Acupuncture, 1986, M in Acupuncture, 1989; M in Anthropology, Oxford U., Eng., 1994, MPh in Med. Anthropology, 1995, DPhil, 1999; DOM (hon.), Chelsea U., Eng., 2004; diploma in Acupuncture (hon.), 2002. Lectr. Coll. Traditional Chinese Medicine, England, 1985-96; cons. Drug and Alcohol Rehab. Centre, London, 1994-97; pvt. practice acupuncturist Oxford, 1982—99, Wichita, Kans., 2000—. Cons. to various clinics, Canada, United States, Europe, 1983—, England, 1987—; lectr. hosps., England, 1984—, Acad. 5 Element Acupuncture, Miami, Fla., 2002—; lectr., cons. 10 hosps., China, 1993; adj. prof. WSU, Kans. Bd. dirs. O.A.C.M., Oxford, England, 1981, W.I.S.E., Netherlands, Denmark, 1979—82. Grantee, Oxford U., 1997. Fellow: Am. Assn. Integrative Medicine, Am. Integrative Medicine Assn.; mem.: Traditional Acupuncture Soc., Brit. Acupuncture Coun., Am. Assn. Oriental Medicine. Avocations: travel, reading, cooking, tapestry, music. Mailing: 1570 N Ridgewood Dr Wichita KS 67208 Office Phone: 316-841-4745. Personal E-mail: drlorijones@cs.com.

DALY, ANN MICHELLE, broadcast executive; BA in Economics, U. Calif., LA. Pres. N.Am. Buena Vista Home Video; head feature animation DreamWorks SKG, 1997—2004; COO DreamWorks Animations SKG, 2004—. Named one of 100 Most Powerful Women in Entertainment, Hollywood Reporter, 2006. Mailing: Dreamworks Animations Inc 1000 Flower St Glendale CA 91201*

DALY, BENEDICT DUDLEY THOMAS, JR., cardiothoracic surgeon; b. Boston, Nov. 28, 1939; s. Benedict Dudley Thomas and Alice Margaret (Groden) D.; m. Joan Marie Behenna, Sept. 25, 1971; children: Jennifer, Benedict, Matthew. AB, Georgetown U., 1961; MD, Boston U., 1965. Intern, Boston City Hosp., 1965-66, resident, 1966-72; assoc. surgeon Tex. Heart Inst., Houston, 1972-75; dir. cardiothoracic surgery St. Elizabeth Hosp., Brighton, Mass., 1976-78; surgeon New Eng. Med. Ctr., Boston, 1978-87, sr. surgeon, 1987—; chief cardiothoracic surgery VA Med. Ctr., Boston, 1987-2002, Newton Wellesley Hosp., 1986-93; clin. dir. gen. thoracic surgery Boston Med. Ctr., 2002-, dir. Ctr. Thoracic Oncology, 2003-; assoc. prof. Tufts U., Boston, 1976-84, prof. cardiothoracic surgery, 1984-02, prof. cardiothoracic surgery Boston U. Sch. Medicine, 2003. Contbr. articles to profl. jours. NIH-NHLBI grantee, 1978-84; Am. Heart Assn. grantee, 1973-74. Fellow ACS, Coll. Chest Physicians, Am. Coll. Cardiology; mem. Soc. Thoracic Surgeons, Am. Assn. Thoracic Surgery. Home: 12 Wildwood Cir Wellesley MA 02482-6465 Office: Boston Med Ctr Ctr Thoracic Oncology Robinson B405 88 E Newton St Boston MA 02118 Office Phone: 617-638-5600. Business E-Mail: benedict.daly@bmc.org.

DALY, CARSON JONES, television personality; b. Santa Monica, Calif., June 22, 1973; s. J. D. Daly and Pattie Day Caruso, Richard Caruso (Stepfather). Student, Loyola Marymount U., LA. With Sta. KOME; VJ MTV Networks, NYC, host Total Request Live, 1998—2003; host Last Call with Carson Daly, NBC, 2002—, "Carson Daly's Most Requested", New Year's Eve with Carson Daly, 2004—; founder 456 Entertainment, LLC, New York, 2003—; exec. prodr. Carson Daly Productions. Voice Is It Fall Yet?, 2000, guest appearance Sabrina, The Teenage Witch, 2002, Mad TV, 2002, The Apprentice, 2004, The Ashlee Simpson Show, 2005, My Name is Earl, 2005. Scholar Golf, Loyola Marymount U.

DALY, CHARLES ULICK, foundation executive; b. Dublin, May 29, 1927; came to U.S., 1934, naturalized, 1940; s. Ulick deBurgh and Violet (Sealy-King) D.; m. Mary Larmonth, June 11, 1949 (dec.); children: Michael, Douglas; m. Christine Sullivan, Nov. 5, 1988; children: Charles, Kevin. BA in Internat. Rels., Yale U., 1949; MS in Journalism, Columbia U., 1959. Mgr. then v.p. Mexican subs. Pacific Molasses Co., San Francisco, 1949-50, 52-58; congl. fellow Am. Polit. Sci. Assn., 1959-60; editor Stanford U., Calif., 1961; staff asst. Pres. Kennedy and Pres. Johnson, 1962-64; v.p. U. Chgo., 1964-71; v.p. govt. and cmty. affairs Harvard U., Cambridge, Mass., 1971-76; editor Media and the Cities, The Quality of Inequality, Urban Violence; pres. Joyce Found., Chgo., 1978-86; dir. John F. Kennedy Found., Boston, 1988-2001, dir. emeritus, 2001—. Mem. Lloyd's of London, 1976—; freelance writer, 1958—. Mem. Commn. on Adminstrv. Rev., U.S. Ho. of Reps.; chmn. Donor's Forum, Chgo., 1980; bd. dirs. Am. Ireland Fund, Joyce Fedn., Ind. News and Media, Ireland; adv. on HIV/AIDS. With USNR, 1945-46; USMCR, 1950-52. Decorated Silver Star, Purple Heart. Mem. Bantry Sailing Club (Ireland), Boca Grande Club (Fla.), Wightman Tennis Club. Home: 32 Forest Ridge Rd Weston MA 02493 E-mail: daly4charlesu@aol.com.

DALY, CHERYL, communications and broadcast executive; b. Providence, Apr. 20, 1947; d. Francis Patrick and Mary Ann (Wallis) D.; m. Arthur James Generas, July 18, 1970; 1 child, Caroline. BA, Rutgers U., 1969; postgrad., New Sch. for Social Rsch., 1975-78. Account exec. Phil Dean Assocs., NYC, 1969—72; dir. pub. rels. Kirkland Coll., Clinton, 1972—75; mgr. press svcs. CBS Radio, NYC, 1976—80; assoc. dir. internal comm. CBS, Inc., 1980—81, dir. corp. info., 1981—83; v.p. pub. rels. Group W Satellite Comm., 1984—95, sr. v.p. pub. rels., 1995—97, CBS Cable, 1997—2000; sr. v.p. comm. TNN, MTV Networks, 2000—01; v.p. media relations MSNBC, 2002; pub. rels. cons. NYC, 2002—05; dir. comms. NATAS, 2005—. Examiner Westinghouse Quality Awards, Pitts., 1990. Recipient Best Co. Comm. award Cable TV Bus., 1986, Mktg. award Westinghouse Broadcasting Co., 1991. Mem. Cable TV Pub. Affairs Assn. (bd. dirs. 1985-87), Media Mommies (co-founder 1987). Democrat. Roman Catholic. Home: 1 W 67th St New York NY 10023-6200 Office: NATAS 111 W 57th St Ste 600 New York NY 10019 Office Phone: 212-484-9446. E-mail: dcheryl311@aol.com, cdaly@emmyonline.tv.

DALY, DONALD F., retired engineering company executive; b. Morristown, NJ, Jan. 10, 1933; s. John F. and Sophie E. (Podeski) D.; m. Bennie L. London, Nov. 2, 1963; children: Stephen, David, Eric. ME, Stevens Inst. Tech., 1955. Equipment engr. Corning (N.Y.) Glass Works, 1955-56; sales engr. Mundet Cork, 1958-60; process engr. Thiokol Chem. Corp., 1961-65; dir. engring. Syntex Corp., 1966-78; v.p., project mgr. Indsl. Design Corp., 1978-2000; dir. Tech. Design & Constrn. Co., Portland, Oreg., 1992-94; ret., 2000. Republican. Avocations: golf, skiing.

DALY, FRANK, anatomist; BS in Biology, Stonehill Coll., North Easton, Mass., 1991; PhD in Anatomy and Neurobiology, Boston U., 1997. Rsch. assoc. Howard Hughes med. inst. Mass. Gen. Hosp., Boston, 1997—99; asst. prof. anatomy U. New Eng., Biddeford, Maine, 1999—2005, assoc. prof. anatomy, 2005—. Contbr. articles to profl. jours. Recipient Russek Grad. Student Achievement award, Boston U. Sch. Medicine, 1997, Disting. Academic Svc. award, U. New Eng. Phys. Therapy, 2002, Summers Meml. Tchg. award, U. New Eng. Coll. Arts and Sci., 2003.

Mem.: Assn. Rsch. in Vision and Ophthalmology, Am. Assn. Anatomists, Am. Assn. Clin. Anatomists, Alpha Epsilon Lambda. Office: Univ New England 11 Hills Beach Rd Biddeford ME 04005 Office Phone: 207-602-2415. Business E-Mail: fdaly@une.edu.

DALY, GAIL M., law librarian, educator, dean; b. Detroit; BA in Edn., U. Mich., 1968, MA in Libr. Sci., 1969; JD, U. Minn., 1989. Former assoc. dir. U. Minn. Law Sch. Libr.; assoc. dean for libr. and tech., assoc. prof. law So. Meth. U. Dedman Sch. Law, Dallas. Former mng. editor Minn. Law Rev.; vis. assoc. law Rsch. Librs. Group Stanford U., Mountain View, Calif.; mem. Nat. Mus. and Libr. Svcs. Bd., Washington, 2004—. Mem.: ABA, Am. Assn. Law Librs., Assn. Am. Law Schs. Office: So Meth Univ Underwood Law Libr 6550 Hillcrest Ave Dallas TX 75275 Office Phone: 214-768-1873. Business E-Mail: gdaly@mail.smu.edu.*

DALY, GEORGE GARMAN, dean; b. Painesville, Ohio, Oct. 5, 1940; s. George Ferdinand and Helen May (Garman) D.; m. Barbara Leigh Anthony, Mar. 13, 1977. AB in Economics, Miami U., Oxford, Ohio, 1962; MA in Economics, Northwestern U., 1965, PhD, 1967. Asst. to assoc. prof. Miami U., Oxford, 1965-69; asst. prof. U. Tex., Austin, 1969-70; chief economist Office of Energy Rsch. and Devel., 1974; asst. dir. Inst. Def. Analysis, 1977—79; asst. prof. to prof. U. Houston, 1971-77, dean Coll. Social Sci., 1979-83; dean U. Iowa Tippie Coll. Bus., Iowa City, 1983-93, NYU Stern Sch. Bus., NYC, 1993—2002, Albert Fingerhut prof. bus. adminstrn.; dean McDonough Sch. Bus., Georgetown U., Washington, 2005—. Office: McDonough Sch Business Georgetown Univ 206 Old North Washington DC 20057 Office Phone: 202-687-3883. E-mail: dalyg@georgetown.edu.*

DALY, HEATHER EILEEN, toxicologist; b. Rochester, NY, Sept. 21, 1969; d. Cornelius Joseph and Gladys Lonie Daly. BA in Biomath., Rutgers U., New Brunswick, NJ, 1991; PhD in Toxicology, U. Rochester, NY, 1997; M Spiritual Psychology, U. Santa Monica, Calif., 2001. Predoctoral fellow U. Rochester, 1992—97; cons. toxicologist Gradient Corp., Cambridge, Mass., 1997—99; toxicologist Clorox Co., Pleasanton, Calif., 1999—2003; founding Ctr. Health and Well-Being, Rochester, 2004—. Sr. instr. Slo Kwon-do Martial Arts, Rochester, 2004—; coord. numerous health events; presenter seminars in field. Editor: Let's Not Call It Meditation, 2006; presenter: (CD) Introduction to Basic Meditation Techniques, 2005; contbr. articles to profl. publs. Foodlink vol. Rochester Single Vols. Mem.: Gates Continuing Edn., Soc. Women in Math. and Sci., Soc. Risk Analysis, Soc. Toxicology, Inst. Noetic Scis. Avocations: dance, martial arts, music. Home: 1706 S Carmelina Ave Los Angeles CA 90025

DALY, JIM, medical products executive; BS in Pharmacy, SUNY, Buffalo, 1984, MBA, 1985. Hosp. pharmacist, Buffalo; various positions including v.p., gen. mgr. respiratory and anti-infectives bus. divsn. Glaxo Wellcome/GlaxoSmithKline; v.p., gen. mgr. US Oncology bus. unit Amgen, Inc., Thousand Oaks, Calif., 2002—05, sr. v.p. N.Am. comml. ops., 2005—. Office: Amgen Inc One Amgen Center Dr Thousand Oaks CA 91320-1799 Office Phone: 805-447-1000. Office Fax: 805-447-1010.*

DALY, JOHN M., surgeon, educator; b. Phila., Dec. 10, 1947; m. Mary F. Bonner, Aug. 1971; children: John M. Jr., William L., Brian P., Timothy J., Patrick T., Maureen P. BA cum laude, LaSalle Coll., 1969; MD, Temple U., 1973. Diplomate Am. Bd. Surgery. Intern Hermann Hosp. U. Tex. Med. Sch., Houston, 1973-74; resident in gen. surgery U. Tex. Med. Sch., Houston, 1974-78, chief resident in gen. surgery, 1977-78, instr. surgery, 1978; faculty assoc. in surgery M.D. Anderson Hosp., Houston, 1978-79; asst. prof. surgery U. Tex. Med. Sch., Houston, 1978-80, M.D. Anderson Hosp. and Tumor Inst., Houston, 1979-80; assoc. attending surgeon Meml. Sloan-Kettering Cancer Ctr., NYC, 1980-85; prof. surgery, chief div. surgical oncology U. Pa., Phila., 1986—93; asst. prof. surgery Weill Med. Coll. of Cornell U., NYC, 1980-81, Lewis Atterbury Stimson prof., 1993—2002, prog. dir., gen. surgery residency prog., 1993—2002, chair, surgery dept., 1993—2002; surgeon-in-chief NY Presbyterian Hosp., 1993—2002; dean Temple U. Med. Sch., 2002—. Vis. assoc. physician Rockefeller U. Hosp., N.Y.C., 1980; asst. mem. Sloan-Kettering Inst., 1981-84, assoc. mem., 1984-85; assoc. attending physician N.Y. Hosp., 1983; Jonathan E. Rhoads prof. surgery U. Pa. Sch. Medicine, Phila., 1986; cons. in surgery Meml. Sloan-Kettering Cancer Ctr., N.Y.C., 1986. Contbr. numerous articles in sci. and profl. jours. Rsch. grantee Smith Kline and French, 1967; named one of Outstanding Young Men of Am., 1972; recipient Rsch. award So. Med. Soc., 1974, Resident Rsch. award, 1977-78, George Waldren award for Outstanding Chief Resident in Surgery, U. Tex. Med. Sch., 1978, Sam E. Roberts Nutrition Found. medal U. Kans. Sch. Medicine, 1981. Mem. AMA (Joseph B. Goldberger Rsch. award 1970-72), Am. Cancer Soc. (bd. dirs. Phila. divsn., nominating com., profl. edn. com., pub. edn. com., Clin. Rsch. award 1977-78, jr. faculty clin. fellowship 1979-82), ACS (Schering Rsch. award 1977-78), AAAS, Am. Assn. Cancer Rsch., Am. Gastroent. Soc., Am. Soc. for Parenteral and Enteral Nutrition (program chmn. 4th clin. congress, chmn. edn. com. 1980-81, treas. and exec. com. 1981-83, pres. 1985-86), Am. Soc. Clin. Oncology, Am. Soc. Clin. Nutrition, Am. Surg. Assn., Assn. Acad. Surgery (program com. 1979-80, 80-81, com. on issues 1980-82, nominating com. 1983-84, councilman 1984-86), Collegium Internationale Chirurgiae Digestivae, Fedn. Am. Socs. Exptl. Biology and Medicine, Am. Inst. Nutrition, Internat. Soc. Surgery, Internat. Soc. Parenteral Nutrition, N.Y. Cancer Soc., N.Y. Surg. Soc., Phila. Acad. Surgery, Phila. Coll. Physicians, Soc. Surgery of Alimentary Tract, Soc. Clin. Surgery, Soc. Surg. Oncology (pres. 2002-03), Soc. Univ. Surgeons. Clubs: Surg. Biology III. Office: Temple U Sch Medicine 3400 N Broad St Philadelphia PA 19140 Office Phone: 215-707-8773.

DALY, JOHN PATRICK, professional golfer; b. Carmichael, Calif., Apr. 28, 1966; m. Sherrie Daly; 3 children. Student, U. Ark. Profl. golfer PGA Tour, 1991—. Author: (biography) My Life in and Out of the Rough, 2006. Winner golf tournaments including PGA Championship, 1991, B.C. Open, 1992, Bell South Classic, 1994, Brit. Open, 1995, Buick Invitational, 2004; mem. Dunhill Cup, 1993, 98, 2000. Address: care PGA Am 100 Avenue Of Champions Palm Beach Gardens FL 33418-3653

DALY, JOHN T, research scientist; s. John Paul and Lillian Jean Daly; m. Catherine Marie Sheil, Jan. 8, 1994; children: Nathan Christopher, Sarah Elizabeth, Hannah Catherine. MSE, Princeton U., NJ, 1995. Application analyst Raytheon Intelligence and Info. Sys., Garland, Tex., 1995—2004; tech. staff memory Los Alamos Nat. Lab., N.Mex., 2004—. Achievements include research in reliability, resilience, and modeling for high performance computing. Office: Los Alamos Nat Lab M/S T080 Los Alamos CA 87545 Home Phone: 505-661-7043; Office Phone: 505 667-7665. Office Fax: 505 667-9644. Business E-Mail: jtd@lanl.gov.

DALY, JOSEPH LEO, law educator; b. Phila., July 31, 1942; s. Leo Vincent and Genevieve Delores (McGinnis) D.; m. Kathleen Ann Dolan, July 24, 1965; children: Michael, Colleen. BA, U. Minn., 1964; JD, William Mitchell Coll. Law, 1969. Bar: Minn. 1969, U.S. Dist. Ct. Minn. 1970, U.S. Supreme Ct. 1972, U.S. Ct. Appeals (8th cir.) 1973, U.S. Ct. Appeals (D.C. cir.) 1974; cert. mediator and arbitrator alternative dispute rev. bd. Minn. Supreme Ct. Ptnr. Franke & Daly, Mpls., 1969-74; prof. law Hamline U. Sch. Law, St. Paul, 1974—. Arbitrator Am. Arbitration Assn., N.Y.C., 1980—, U.S. Fed. Mediation and Conciliation Svc., Washington, 1988—, for the states of Minn., Hawaii, Idaho, Ind., Mass., Mich., N.D., Pa., Oreg., Wisc., V.I and City of L.A.; arbitrator Bur. Mediation Svcs., St. Paul, 1978—; vis. scholar Ctr. for Dispute Resolution, Willamette U., Salem, Oreg., 1985; facilitator Minn. Internat. Health Vols., Kenya, 1985; observer Philippine Constl. Conv., Manila, 1986; participant European Arab Arbitration Congress, Bahrain, 1987; human rights investigator in the Philippines, 1989; vis. scholar U. Oslo, 1990, 91, 92, 96, 97; lectr. on trial skills for human rights lawyers, The Philippines, 1989; lectr. to leaders at Site 2 Cambodian Refugee Camp, Thai/Cambodian border, 1989; lectr. U. Cluj-NAPACA, Romania, 1991; vis. lectr. for developing countries Internat. Bar Assn., 1991-92; lectr. U. Tirana, Albania, 1992, London, 1993, Nat. Econs. U., Hanoi, Vietnam, 1993, 94, Danang (Vietnam) Poly. U., 1993, Ho Chi Minh Econs. U., Saigon, Vietnam, 1993, U. Hanoi Law Sch., 1994, U. Modena, Italy, 1994, Hanoi, Danang and Saigon, 1995, Phnom Penh, Cambodia, 1995, Hong Kong, 1996, Shenzhen, China, 1996, Oslo, Norway, 1996, Karolinska Inst., Stockholm, 1997; vis. prof. So. Cross U., Lismore, Australia, 1998, 99, U. Bergen, Norway, 1999, Tongji U., Shanghai, China, 1999, U. Saigon, Vietnam, 1999, 2000; cons. Chua U., Tokyo, 2001; team leader UN Devel. Programme mid-term evaluation of UN project, Vietnam, Hanoi, 2001; vis. prof. U. Queensland, Brisbane, Australia, 2001, 02, 2003, 2004; Fulbright scholar U. Montevideo, Uruguay, 2002, 2003, 2004; lectr., Rome, 2007. Co-author: The Law, the Student and the Catholic School, 1981; co-author, editor: The Student Lawyer: A High School Handbook of Minnesota Law, 1981, rev. edit., 1986, Strategies and Exercises in Law Related Education, 1981, International Law, 1993, The American Trial System, 1994, International Commercial Negotiation and Arbitration, 2001, Leading American Attorneys in ADR, 2003, Arbitration: The Basics, 2006; contbr. more than 50 articles to profl. jours. Mem. Minn. Legislature Task Force on Sexual Exploitation by Counselors and Therapists, St. Paul, 1984-85, Nat. Adv. Com. on Citizen Edn. in Law, 1982-85; bd. dirs. Scenic Am., Washington, 1989-92. Recipient Spurgeon award Mayor and Citizens of St. Paul and Indianhead Scouting, 1983; named a Leading Am. Atty. in Alternative Dispute Resolution: Employment Law; fellow U. Miss. Law Sch.; Fulbright sr. specialist, 2005, 06, 07. Mem. ABA (contbg. editor Preview of U.S. Supreme Ct. Cases mag. 1984—), Internat. Bar Assn. (London, vis. lectr. for devel. countries 1991—), Minn. State Bar Assn., Minn. Lawyers Internat. (human rights com., rep. to Philippine Constl. Conv. 1986), St. Paul Athletic Club, Phi Alpha Delta. Avocations: jogging, sailing. Office: Hamline U Sch Law 1536 Hewitt Ave Saint Paul MN 55104-1205 Office Phone: 651-523-2121. Business E-Mail: jdaly@hamline.edu.

DALY, KENNETH, business association executive; BS in Acctg., U. Del., 1967; attended, U. Pa. Wharton Sch., KPMG's Ptnr. Devel. Prog., KPMG's Internat. Ptnr. Prog., Burgenstock, Switzerland. Ptnr. KPMG, 1978—2005; dir. KPMG Audit Comm. Inst., 2006; pres., CEO Nat. Assn. Corp. Directors, 2007—. Trustee Upper Main Line YMCA, Lutheran Seminary at Germantown Found. Bd. Mem.: Am. Inst. of Cert. Public Accountants, Pa. Inst. Certified Public Accountants. Office: Nat Assn Corp Directors 1133 21 St NW Ste 700 Washington DC 20036*

DALY, MARY, college administrator; b. Erie, Pa., Dec. 29, 1943; d. Damian John and Letitia (Lawson) D. BS, Mercyhurst Coll., 1966; MA, Fairfield U., 1987; student, Pitts. Inst. Mortuary Sci., 2003. Cert. funeral assocs., funeral celebrant, grief counselor. From dir. found. rsch. to dir. spl. events and presdl. functions Mercyhurst Coll., Erie, Pa., 1966—80, dir. spl. events and presdl. functions, 1980—, asst. dir. devel., 1972-80, asst. to the pres. for external affairs, 1980-89, sr. asst. to the pres., 1989-91, v.p. pub. rels., 1991—, website developer, content resource mgr., 1997-98, sr. asst. to pres. bd. trustees, 2002—06, liaison to bd. trustees, 2006—. Comm. cons. Sisters of Mercy of Erie County, Erie, 1970—; polit. cons. Rep. Joseph Giles, Erie, 1980-90, Mayor Joyce Savocchio, Erie, 1986, 89, 93, 97. Creative dir. for publs. Bd. dirs. Gannondale, Erie, 1990-92, Internat. Inst., Erie, 1988-90, Zonta club Erie, 1980-83, March of Dimes, Erie, 1981-82, Muscular Dystrophy, Erie, 1981-82, Florence Crittendon Home, Erie, 1983-87, Millcreek Hall of Fame, 1995—, Multiple Sclerosis Soc., 2000-, Cath. Daughters Am., 2002-; mem. pub. rels. com. Libr. 21-Erie County Libr.; mem. merchandising, pub. rels. and mktg. com. Greater Erie Bicentennial; mem. pub. rels. com. Warner Theatre Restoration. Fulbright scholar for summer study in Egypt, 1977. Mem. Coun. for Advancement and Support of Edn. (Silver Medal Recognition awards 1986). Democrat. Roman Catholic. Avocations: piano, reading, travel, web-site developer. Office: Mercyhurst Coll Glenwood Hills 501 E 38th St Erie PA 16546-0002 Home: 501 E 38th St Erie PA 16546-0002 Office Phone: 814-824-2285.

DALY, MARY C., dean, law educator; BA, Thomas More Coll., 1969; JD cum laude, Fordham U. Sch. Law, 1972; LLM in Comparative Law, NYU Sch. Law, 1975—78. Assoc. Rogers & Wells, 1973—75; asst. U.S. Atty. Civil Div., 1975—80; chief of civil div. U.S. Atty. Office, So. Dist. N.Y., 1981—83; prof. Fordham Law Sch., 1983—2004, co-dir. Louis Stein Ctr. for Law and Ethics, dir. Grad. Prog., James H. Quinn Prof. Legal Ethics; dean, John V. Brennan Chair Law and Ethics St. John's U. Sch. Law, 2004—. Grantee Zichkla Fellow, Université de Paris, Faculté de Droit, 1973. Mem.: ABA (reporter Commn. Multidisciplinary Practice 1998—2000, mem. Out-of-the Box Com.), Fed. Bar Coun. (trustee 1997—2004), Assn. Bar N.Y.C. (chair Com. Profl. and Judicial Ethics 1996—99, mem. Delegation to Chile, Rwanda and Brazil 2002—03). Office: St Johns U Sch Law 8000 Utopia Parkway Jamaica NY 11439 E-mail: dalym@stjohns.edu.

DALY, MIRIAM SHAMER, retired family physician; b. Balt., Jan. 26, 1925; d. Maurice Emory and Bertha (Tapman) Shamer; m. Harold L. Daly, Jr., June 28, 1948 (dec. July 2, 1989); children: John, Martha, Thomas, David. AB, Goucher Coll., 1946; MD, U. Md., 1950. Diplomate Am. Bd. Family Practice. Intern Luth. Hosp. of Md., Balt., 1950-51, resident, 1951-52; clinic physician Balt. City Health Dept., Md. State Health Dept., 1952-55; practicing physician Balt., 1952-55; physician pvt. practice Albion, Mich., 1955-93; ret., 1993. Leader, camp counsellor Girl Scouts, South Ctrl. Mich., 1955—, pres. Irish Hills Coun., 1993-97, coord. Albion ARC blood drives, 1994—, mem. Sweet Adelines, 2003-05; bd. dir., 1990-97, Albion Ambulance Svc., 1989-95, ARC Calhoun County chpt., 1993—, Great Lakes Region Blood Svcs., ARC, 1994-95; bd. dirs. Albion-Homer United Way, 1999-2005, pres., 2001, 02; mem. allocation com. Calhoun County Sr. Village, 2000—. Recipient Girl Scouts Thanks Badge, Irish Hills Girls Scouts Coun., 1977, 1993, Cmty. Recognition award, Albion Coll., 1996, Athena award, Greater Albion C. of C., 2000. Mem. AMA, AAUW, NAACP (exec. bd. 2005—, bd. dirs. Albion br.), Mich. State Med. Soc. (Frederick and Besse Moulton Plessner Meml. award 1996), Calhoun County Med. Soc., Am. Acad. Family Practice, Mich. Acad. Family Practice, Rotary. Avocations: piano, photography, gardening. Personal E-mail: msdaly@hotmail.com.

DALY, PATRICK F., real estate executive, architect; b. Chgo., Jan. 25, 1949; s. John F. and Margaret M. (Gleason) D.; m. Shirley J. Kumis, June 25, 1971; children: Sean P., James P. BArch with honors and distinction, U. Ill., Chgo., 1972, BA in Archtl. History with honors and distinction, 1972. Cert. architect. Chmn. bd. Dalan Realty Corp., Chgo., 1980—, Dalan Devel. Corp., Chgo., 1986—2005; pres. Dalan/ Jupiter, Inc., Chgo., 1987—; mng. ptnr. Rising Sun Riverboat Casino and Resort, LLC, Chgo., 1995—; chmn. The Daly Group LLC, 1995—. Bd. dirs. Private Bancorp Inc., Private Bank & Trust Co., Chgo., Affiliated Network Svc., Inc.; vice chmn. bd. mgrs. U. Ill. Rsch. Parks, LLC, 2003—. Contbr. articles to profl. jours. Chmn. Ill. Ambs., Chgo., 1990-98; vice chmn. Met. Pier & Expn. Authority, Chgo., 1985-2002; commr. Nat. Adv. Commn. U.S. Dept. Labor, Washington, 1991-93; trustee Fund Am. Studies, 1993—, Univ. Ill. Found., 1993-99, dir. emeritus 1999; trustee Inst. Cmty. Empowerment, 1991-98, Chgo. Acad. Scis., 2001—, chmn., 2002-05; trustee Chgo. Hist. Soc., 2006—; chmn. Chancellor's Corp. adv. com. U. Ill., Chgo., 1995-2004; adv. bd. mem. Ind. Univ. Ctr. Real Estate Studies, 1994—, Roosevelt U. Sch. Real Estate, 2000—; dir. U.S. Com. for UNICEF/Chgo., 1996-2005, U.S.O., Chgo., 1998—; chmn. U. Ill. Alumni Assn., 1997-99; mem. leadership com. United Way, 1998; mem. coun. Brookings Instn.; co-chmn. Chgo. Am. Heartwalk, Am. Heart Assn., 2002. Recipient Alumni Achievement award U. Ill., 1993, City Ptnr. award, 2004; inducted into Chgo. Area Entrepreneurship Hall of Fame, 2002. Mem. Alpha Rho Chi. Office: The Daly Group 20 N Wacker Dr Ste 1500 Chicago IL 60606-2903 Business E-Mail: pdaly@thedalygroup.com.

DALY, PAUL SYLVESTER, former mayor, retired academic administrator, management consultant; b. Belmont, Mass., Jan. 8, 1934; s. Matthew Joseph and Alice Mary (Hall) D.; m. Maureen Teresa Kenny, May 25, 1957; children: Judith Mary, Paul S. Jr., Susan Marie, John Joseph, Maureen Hall. BS in Engring. Sci., Naval Postgrad. Sch., 1968; MBA, U. W. Fla., 1971. Commd. ensign USN, 1955; advanced through grades to capt., 1979; coll. dean Embry-Riddle Aero. U., Daytona Beach, Fla., 1979—81, chancellor Ariz., 1981—95; mayor City of Prescott, Ariz., 1996—99; mgmt. cons., 1999—; legis. affairs cons. Lectr. seminars, 1979-85; cons. British Aerospace, 1979-84, McDonnell Douglas, 1979-84, IBM, 1983-84; sr. faculty U. Phoenix, 1983-86. Bd. dirs. Yavapai Regional Med. Ctr., Prescott, Ariz., 1983-86, Prescott C. of C., 1982-84; chmn. Ariz. State Bd. Pvt. Postsecondary Edn.; pres. Ind. Coll. and Univs. of Ariz., Phoenix, 1982—; pres., founder West Yavapai County Am. Heart Assn. Chpt., chmn. affiliate of Am. Heart Assn./Ariz. Decorated Legion of Merit. Mem. Ret. Officers Assn. Republican. Roman Catholic. Avocation: sports. Personal E-mail: daly@myway.com.

DALY, RADLEY HUTCHINSON, retired academic administrator; b. Stamford, Conn., Aug. 6, 1925; s. Gerald Hutchinson and Marguerite (Radley) D.; m. Patricia Skinner, Apr. 26, 1952; children: Peter Hutchinson Daly, Susan Farwell Daly. BS, Yale U., 1949. Asst. Can. mktg. mgr. Vick Chem. Co., NYC, 1949-51; dir. product devel. Pepperidge Farm Inc., Norwalk, Conn., 1951-68; assoc. libr. Yale U., New Haven, Conn., 1968-75, assoc. provost, 1975-78, dir. adminstrv. svcs., 1978-87, assoc. sec. of the U., 1987-90, dep. sec. and marshal, 1990-96. Pres. Pequot Libr., Southport, Conn., 1986-87; treas. Kingsley Trust Assn., New Haven, 1974-94; mng. trustee M.C. Scholarship Found., New Haven, 1980—; pres. Mory's Assn., 2003-05. Mem. Conn. Acad. Arts and Scis., Elizabethan Club, Pequot Yacht Club (commodore 1977-79), Sigma Xi, Tau Beta Pi. Republican. Avocation: book restauration. Home: 26 Mill Hill Rd Southport CT 06890-1252 Office: Yale U 149 Elm St New Haven CT 06511-6608 Home Phone: 203-259-6090; Office Phone: 203-432-1092. Personal E-mail: rdaly1925@aol.com.

DALY, ROBERT ANTHONY, international relief organization, former professional sports team and film company executive; b. Bklyn., Dec. 8, 1936; s. James and Eleanor Daly; m. Carole Bayer; 1 stepchild, Cristopher Bacharach; children: Linda Marie, Robert Anthony, Brian James. Student, Bklyn. Coll.; PhD in Fine Arts (hon.), Am. Film Inst.; DHL (hon.), Trinity Coll. From dir. bus. affairs to v.p. bus. affairs, to exec. v.p. CBS TV Network, 1955—80; pres. CBS Entertainment Co., 1977—80; chmn., CEO Warner Bros., Burbank, Calif., 1982—94; chmn., co-CEO Warner Music Group, 1995—99; chmn., CEO, mng. ptnr. L.A. Dodgers, 1999—2004; chmn. Save the Children Fedn., Inc., Westport, 2005—. Bd. dirs. Am. Film Inst. Trustee Am. Film Inst. Mem.: NATAS, Hollywood Radio and TV Soc., Motion Picture Pioneers, Acad. Motion Picture Arts and Scis. Roman Catholic. Office: 10877 Wilshire Blvd #610 Los Angeles CA 90024 also: Save the Children 2000 M St NW Ste 500 Washington DC 20036

DALY, SEAN G., bank executive; With KPMG, Providence; various fin. mgmt. positions FleetBoston Corp., Citizens Fin. Group, Putnam Investments, Melville Corp.; COO QGO, LLC, RI; dir. bus. devel. QC2, LLC, RI; v.p., CFO Camden Nat. Corp., Camden, Maine, 2005—. Office: Camden Nat Corp 2 Elm St Camden ME 04843 Office Phone: 207-236-8821. Office Fax: 207-236-6256.*

DALY, STEPHEN JEFFREY, artist, educator; b. Governor's Island, NY, July 4, 1942; s. Doris (Leanord) Daly; m. Sharon Jane Able, Aug. 24, 1964; 1 child, Sabina. BA in Art, San Jose State U., 1964; MFA in Sculpture, Cranbrook Acad. Art, 1967. Instr. U. Minn., Mpls., 1967-69; asst. prof. Humboldt State U., Arcata, Calif., 1969-73, assoc. prof., 1975-79; asst. prof. U. Tex., San Antonio, 1979-81, Austin, 1981-86, assoc. prof., 1986-91, prof. art, 1992—. Vis. artist, U. Hawaii, Manoa, Honolulu, 1983, U. Ohio Sch. Art, Athens, 1984, So. Ill. U., Carbondale, 1985, U. Wash., Seattle, 1988, U. Okla. Sch. Art, Norman, 1992, etc.; art and architecture panel Tex. Commn. on Arts, 1980-82; curator Patrick Gallery, 4th Tex. Sculpture Symposium, Austin, 1983, San Antonio Art Inst., 1985. One-man shows include Am. Acad., Rome, 1975, Triton Mus., Santa Clara, Calif., 1977, Graham Gallery, Houston, 1983, William Campbell Contemporary Art, Ft. Worth, 1986, 87, 89, 93, 2000, Polytech. U., Valencia, Spain, 2002, others; exhibited in group shows at Hooks-Epstein Gallery, Houston, 1991, Ramapo Coll., Mahwah, NJ, 1994, Foothills Art Ctr., Golden, Colo., 1995, Old Navy Pier, Chgo., 1997, Grounds for Sculpture (I.S.C.), Hamilton, NJ, 2001, Hooks-Epstein Gallery, Tex., 1993, Blue-Star Art Space, Tex., 2002, 04-05, Galleria via Larga, Florence, Italy, William Havu Gallery, Colo., 2002, 05, 07; represented in pub. collections Oakland Art Mus., Calif., Bank San Antonio, Codema, Cuba, 2000, Polytech. U. Spain, 2006, others. Recipient Rome prize in sculpture Am. Acad. Rome, 1973-75, Louis Comfort Tiffany award in sculpture Tiffany Found., 1977-78, Summer Rsch. award U. Rsch. Inst., U. Tex., Austin, 1984, Outstanding Prof. award U. Tex., Austin, 2006; Reinhart fellow in sculpture Am. Acad. Rome, Md. Inst. Art, 1974-75, Grace Milam Centennial fellow in fine arts Coll. Fine Arts, U. Tex., 1984-85, 1990-91, Foxworth Centennial fellow, 1988-89; Rsch. grantee U. Rsch. Inst., U. Tex., 1984, 88, 01, 06, Resident fellow Hungarian Multicultural Ctr., Budapest. Democrat. Home: 31350 Ranch Rd 12 Ste C Dripping Springs TX 78620 Business E-Mail: stevesculpt@mail.utexas.edu.

DALY, TYNE, actress; b. Madison, Wis., Feb. 21, 1946; d. James Daly and Hope Newell; m. Georg Stanford Brown (div.); children: Alyxandra, Kathryne, Alisabeth. Student, Brandeis U., Am. Music and Dramatic Acad. Performed at Am. Shakespeare Festival, Stratford, Conn.; appeared on Broadway in Gypsy, 1990, 91 revivals, The Seagull, 1992, Rabbit Hole, 2006; films include Angel Unchained, 1970, The Enforcer, 1976, The Entertainer, 1976, Speed Trap, 1977, Telefon, 1977, Zoot Suit, 1982, The Aviator, 1985, Movers and Shakers, 1985; made TV debut in series The Virginian; guest appearances in various TV series including Veronica's Closet, 1996, appearances in TV series include Cagney & Lacey, 1982-88 (Emmy awards 1983, 84, 85, 88), Christy, 1994, (Emmy award 1996), Judging Amy, 1999-, (Emmy award best sup. actress, 2003); TV films include In Search of America, 1971, A Howling in the Woods, 1971, Heat of Anger, 1972, The Man Who Could Talk to Kids, 1973, Larry, 1974, Intimate Strangers, 1977, Better Late Than Never, 1979, The Women's Room, 1980, A Matter of Life and Death, 1981, The Great Gilly Hopkins, 1981, Your Place or Mine, 1983, Kids Like These, 1987, Stuck With Each Other, 1989, The Last to Go, 1990, Face of a Stranger, 1991, On the Town, 1993, Scattered Dreams, 1994, Colombo: Bird in the Hand, 1994, Bye Bye Birdie, 1994, Columbo: Undercover, 1994, The Forget-Me-Not Murders, 1994, Cagney and Lacey: The Return, 1994, Cagney and Lacey: Together Again, 1995, A Perfect Mother, 1996, Autumn Heart, The Simian Line, Shades of Gray, Three Secrets, Tricks, 1997, The Perfect Mother, 1997, Vig, 1998, Execution of Justice, 1999, The Wedding Dress, 2001; appearance one-woman show Mystery School. Recipient Tony award for Mama Rose role in Gypsy, 1990; nominated 2nd Antoinette Perry (Tony) award role in Rabbit Hole, 2006. Address: 272 S Lasky Dr Unit 402 Beverly Hills CA 90212-3671

DALY, WALTER JOSEPH, medical educator; b. Michigan City, Ind., Jan. 12, 1930; m. Joan Brown, June 12, 1953; children: Lois Kay, Alice Louise. AB, Ind. U., 1951, MD, 1955, ScD, 1998. Diplomate Am. Bd. Internal Medicine. Intern Ind. U., 1955-56, resident, 1956-57, 59-62, instr. medicine, 1962-63, asst. prof., 1963-65, assoc. prof., 1965-68, prof., 1968-77, John B. Hickam prof., 1977-80, J.O. Ritchey prof., 1980-95, J.O. Ritchey prof. emeritus, 1995—; chmn. dept. medicine, 1970-83; dean Sch. Medicine, 1983-95; dean emeritus Ind. U., 1995—. Dir. Regenstrief Inst. Health Rsch., 1976-83. Capt. M.C., U.S. Army, 1957-59. Master ACP (gov. 1980-84), Am. Physiol. Soc., Ctr. Soc. Clin. Rsch. (pres. 1980-81), Am. Soc. Clin. Investigation, Am. Clin. and Climatol. Assn. (v.p. 2004-05), Assn. Am. Physicians. Office: Ind U Sch Medicine 1120 South Dr Indianapolis IN 46202-5135 Office Phone: 317-274-7109.

DALY, WILLIAM JOSEPH, lawyer; b. Bklyn., Mar. 19, 1928; s. William Bernard and Charlotte Marie (Saunders) D.; m. Barbara A. Longenecker, Nov. 19, 1955; children: Sharon, Nancy, Carol. BA, St. John's U., 1951, JD, 1953. Bar: N.Y. 1954, U.S. Dist. Ct. (so. and ea. dists.) N.Y. 1958, U.S. Ct. Mil. Appeals 1969, U.S. Ct. Claims 1969, U.S. Tax Ct. 1969, U.S. Supreme Ct. 1973. Assoc. Garvey & Conway, Esquires, NYC, 1954-55, Wing & Wing, Esquires, NYC, 1955-58; ptnr. Daly Lavery & Hall, Esquires and predecessors, Ossining, NY, 1958—. Adj. prof. law Mercy Coll., Dobbs Ferry, N.Y. V.p. Legal Aid Soc., Westchester County, N.Y., 1983—; mem. 9th Jud. Dist. Grievance Com., 1981-89, chmn. 1988-89; spl. referee in disciplinary procs.; trustee Supreme Ct. Libr. at White Plains, 1985—. With U.S. Army, 1946-48; ret. col. JA-AUS, 1978; mem. Hall of Fame U.S. Army Officer Cand. Sch., Ft. Benning, Ga. Fellow Am. Bar Found., N.Y. Bar Found.; mem. ABA, N.Y. State Bar Assn. (ho. of dels. 1977-89, 90-96, exec. com. 1983-89, 90-96, v.p. 1985-89, 90-96), Westchester County Bar Assn. (pres. 1979-81, dirs. coun. 1981—), Westchester County Bar Inst. (bd. dirs. 1982-98), Ossinging Bar Assn. (pres. 1966-67), ATLA, N.Y. State Trial Lawyers Assn., Res. Officers Assn. U.S., Skull and Circle, Phi Delta Phi. Roman Catholic. Home: 232 Hunter Ave Sleepy Hollow NY 10591-1317 Home Phone: 914-631-3816; Office Phone: 914-941-7000.

DALZELL, RICK, information technology executive; BS in Engring., US Mil. Acad. Bus. devel. mgr. E-Sys., Inc., 1987—90; with info. sys. divsn. Wal-Mart Stores, Inc., 1990—94, v.p. info. sys., 1994—97; v.p., chief info. officer Amazon.com, Seattle, 1997—2000, sr. v.p., chief info. officer, 2000—01, sr. v.p. worldwide arch. and platform software, chief info. officer, 2001—. With US Army, 1983—90. Office: Amazon.com 1200 12th Ave S Seattle WA 98144*

DALZELL, ROBERT FENTON, JR., historian, educator; b. Cleve., Apr. 28, 1937; s. Robert Fenton and Lucile (Cain) D.; m. Lee Baldwin, June 18, 1960; children: Frederick, Jeffery, Victoria, Alex. BA, Amherst Coll., 1959; MA, Yale U., 1962, PhD, 1966. Instr. history Yale U., New Haven, 1962-66, asst. prof., 1966-70; assoc. prof. history Williams Coll., Williamstown, Mass., 1970-75, prof., 1975-77, Ephraim Williams prof. Am. history, 1977—2003, Willmott Family Third Century prof., 2003—07, Frederick Rudolph prof. Am. culture, 2007—, chmn. Am. civilization program, 1981—91, dep. coll. marshal, 1984—87, coll. marshal, 1987—95. Vis. prof. U. Va., 1985-86; mem. Mmass. Found. Humantities and Pub. Policy, 1982-89, v.p. 1987-88; trustee Hist. Deerfield, 1983-2003, Bennington Mus., 2000-02. Author: American Participation in the Great Exhibition of 1851, 1960, Daniel Webster and the Trial of American Nationalism, 1973, Enterprising Elite: The Boston Associates and the World They Made, 1987, (with Lee B. Dalzell) George Washington's Mount Vernon: At Home in Revolutionary America, 1998. Morse fellow, 1968-69, Guggenheim fellow, 1973-74, Charles Warren fellow, 1973-74, Williams Coll. Ctr. for Humanities and Social Scis. fellow, 1990; Mass. Soc. of the Cin. George Washington Disting. Prof., 1998-2003. Fellow Mass. Hist. Soc.; mem. Orgn. Am. Historians, Colonial Soc. Mass., Am. Studies Assn., Berkshire County Hist. Soc. Office: Williams Coll Stetson Hall Williamstown MA 01267 Office Phone: 413-597-2316. E-mail: rdalzell@williams.edu.

DAM, KENNETH W., law educator, former federal agency administrator; b. Marysville, Kans., Aug. 10, 1932; s. Oliver W. and Ida L. (Huepelsheuser) D.; m. Marcia Wachs, June 9, 1962; children: Eliot, Charlotte. BS, U. Kans., 1954; JD, U. Chgo., 1957; LLD (hon.), New Sch. Social Rsch., 1983. Bar: NY State 1959. Law clk. to justice U.S. Supreme Ct., 1957-58; assoc. Cravath, Swaine & Moore, NYC, 1958-60; faculty U. Chgo. Law Sch., 1960-82, prof., 1964-71, 74-82, Harold J. and Marion F. Green prof., 1976-82, provost, 1980-82, Max Pam prof. Am. and fgn. law, 1992—2001, 2003—04, sr. lectr., 2004—; dep. sec. U.S. Dept. State, 1982-85; v.p. law and external rels. IBM Corp., 1985-92; pres., CEO United Way Am., 1992; dep. sec. U.S. Dept. Treasury, Washington, 2001—03, acting sec., 2002—03; sr. fellow Brookings Instn., 2003—. Vis. prof. U. Freiburg, Germany, 1964; asst. dir. nat. security and internat. affairs Office Mgmt. and Budget, 1971-73; exec. dir. Coun. Econ. Policy, 1973; dir. Alcoa, 1987-2001, Xyleco, Inc., 2007-; adv. bd. BMW of N.Am., 1990-95. Author: The GATT: Law and International Economic Organization, 1970, Oil Resources: Who Gets What How?, 1976, The Rules of the Game: Reform and Evolution in the International Monetary System, 1982, The Rules of the Global Game: A New Look at U.S. International Economic Policymaking, 2001, Law-Growth Nexus: The Rule of Law and Economic Development, 2006; co-author: Federal Tax Treatment of Foreign Income, 1964, Economic Policy Beyond the Headlines, 1977, 2d edit., 1998; co-editor: Cryptography's Role in Securing the Information Society, 1996; chair bd. advisors Fgn. Affairs jour., 1997-2001. Bd. dirs. Am. Coun. on Germany, 1986-95, Am.-China Soc., 1989-99, Atlantic Coun., 1985-92, 2004—, Coun. on Fgn. Rels., 1992-2001, Chgo. Coun. on Fgn. Rels., 1992-2001; trustee Brookings Inst., 1989-2001, 03-; co-chmn. Aspen Strategy Group, 1991-2001. Recipient Raimar Lust award, Thyssen and Humboldt Found., Germany, 2007. Mem. Am. Acad. Arts and Scis., Am. Acad. Diplomacy, Am. Law Inst., Nat. Acad. (sci., tech. and law panel, 2003-), Shadow Fin. Regulatory Com., Munich Intellectual Property Law Ctr. (trustee, 2004-), Fin. Svcs. Vol. Corps (bd. dirs. 2005—), Com. Econ. Devel. (trustee) 2006-), Met. Club (Washington), Quadrangle Club. Office: U Chgo Law Sch 1111 E 60th St Chicago IL 60637 Business E-Mail: kdam@law.uchicago.edu.

DAMADIAN, RAYMOND VAHAN, biophysicist; b. Forest Hills, NY, Mar. 16, 1936; s. Vahan and Odette (Yazedjian) Damadian; m. Elizabeth Donna Terry, June 4, 1960; children: Timothy, Jevan, Kiera. Attended studied violin, Juilliard Sch. Music, 1944—52; BS in Math., U. Wis., 1956; MD, Albert Einstein Coll. Medicine, 1960. Univ. rsch. fellow in biophysics Harvard U., Cambridge, Mass., 1963—65; sr. investigator Sch. Aerospace Medicine, USAF, 1965—67; asst. prof. SUNY, Bklyn., 1967—71, assoc. prof., 1971—80; founder, pres., chmn. Fonar Corp., Melville, NY, 1978—. Career investigator Health Rsch. Coun., NYC, 1967—72. Capt. USAF, 1963—65. Named to National Inventors Hall of Fame, 1989; recipient Lawrence Sperry award, 1984, Nat. medal of Tech., 1988, Lemelson-MIT Lifetime Achievement award, 2001, Benjamin Franklin medal and Bower award for Bus. Leadership, Franklin Inst., 2004, Nat. Inventor of Yr. award, Intellectual Property Owners Edn. Found., 2007; Ford Found. Scholar, U. Wis., 1944—52. Mem.: AAAS, Soc. for Med. Innovation and Tech., Internat. Soc. for Magnetic Resonance in Medicine, Biophys. Soc., Am. Chem. Soc., Sigma Xi. Achievements include development of MRI (detecting cancer in tissue) in 1980; Upright Multi-Position (tradmarked) Magnetic Resonance Imaging (MRI) technology; holds over 45 patents for improvements to MRI scanner. Office: Fonar Corp 110 Marcus Dr Melville NY 11747-4292*

DAMAN, ERNEST LUDWIG, mechanical engineer; b. Hannover, Germany, Mar. 14, 1923; came to U.S., 1940, naturalized, 1944; s. Fritz and Ruth Edith (Meyer) Dammann; m. Jan. 20, 1945 (div.); children: Diane Cathrine, Cynthia Ruth, Bruce Hershey; m. Dorothy Russo, June 21, 1980; stepchildren: Christopher Walsweer, Jonathan Walsweer. BS in Mech. Engring, Poly. Inst. Bklyn., 1943. With Foster Wheeler Corp., Livingston, NJ, 1947—; dir. rsch. Foster Wheeler Energy Corp., Livingston, NJ, 1960-73, v.p., 1973-81, sr. v.p., 1981-88; chmn. Foster Wheeler Devel. Corp., Livingston, NJ, 1977-88, chmn. emeritus, 1988—; chmn., chief exec. officer HDS Fibers Inc., 1986-89; tech. exec. Exec. Office of Pres., The White House, Washington, 1995-97. Chmn. Nat. Materials Property Data Network, Inc., 1986-94; mem. sci. and tech. info. bd. NRC, 1989-91; lectr. in field. Patentee in field. Chmn. Westfield (N.J.) Democratic Com., 1956-60, Westfield Area Com. for Human Rights, 1962-68; mem. Westfield Charter Study Commn., 1964. Served with U.S. Army, 1944-46. Decorated Bronze Star. Fellow: ASME (pres.-elect 1987, pres. 1988—89), AAAS; mem.: NAE, United Engring. Trustees (bd. dirs. 1989—92, trustee 1989—2000, chmn. 1993), Am. Assn. Engring. Socs. (chmn. engring. roundtable 1993, bd. dirs.), Welding Rsch. Coun. (chmn. 1985), Westfield Tennis Club, Pi Tau Sigma. Achievements include development of advanced naval propulsion machinery, fluidized bed combustion, fast breeder reactor steam generators and intermediate heat exchangers; patents for energy conversion processes and heat system. Home: PO Box 1944 Edgartown MA 02539-1944 Office: Foster Wheeler Corp 12 Peach Tree Hill Rd Livingston NJ 07039-5701 Office Phone: 508-627-8323. Personal E-mail: damande@verizon.net. *As a naturalized citizen my life has been influenced by my strong admiration for American Democracy and all that it implies.*

DAMARLA, THYAGARAJU, electronics engineer; b. Mangalagiri, India, Aug. 2, 1948; s. Ramakantha Rao and Ramulamma Damarla; m. Komala Bai Sriperambuduru, Oct. 20, 2001; m. Rohini Velagapudi, Dec. 9, 1973 (div. May 17, 2001); children: Chanakya Chakravarthy, Mahendra. BSc with honors, Indian Inst. of Tech., 1965—68, BS in Tech. with honors, 1968—71, MS in Tech., 1971—73; PhD, Boston U., 1983—87. Sr. engr. Indian Space Rsch. Orgn., Sriharikota, India, 1973—79; sr. rsch. engr. Indian Inst. of Tech., 1979—82; rsch. asst. ECE Dept., Boston U., 1983—87; asst. prof. EE Dept., U. of Ky., 1987—94; rsch. assoc. NRC, Washington, D.C., DC, 1994—96; electronics engr. U.S. Army Rsch. Lab., Adelphi, Md. Nrc advisor U.S. Army Rsch. Lab., Adelphi, Md., 1996—. Contbr. articles to profl. jours. Tutor High Point H.S., Beltsville, Md., 2001—05. Recipient Governor's Vol. Svc. Cert., Govt. of Md., 2004. Mem.: IEEE. Hindu. Achievements include patents for; invention of methods and computer programs for minimizing logic circuit design using identity cell; implementation of signature analysis for analog and mixed signal circuits; a built-in self test method for identification of faulty chips in multi chip modules. Avocations: gardening, tennis, golf, skiing. Home: 9812 Robinson Blvd Laurel MD 20723 Home Phone: 301-498-9393; Office Phone: 301-394-1266. Personal E-mail: tdamarla@hotmail.com.

D'AMATO, ALFONSE M., lawyer, senator; b. Bklyn., Aug. 1, 1937; m. Penelope Ann Collenburg, 1960 (div. 1995); children: Lisa, Lorraine, Daniel, Christopher. BS, Syracuse U., 1959, JD, 1961. Bar: N.Y. 1962. Adminstr., Nassau County, N.Y., 1965-68; receiver of taxes Town of Hempstead, LI, N.Y., 1971-77, presiding supr., vice chmn. county bd. suprs., 1977-80; U.S. senator from N.Y., 1981-98; lawyer, comm. Fox News, 1999—; mng. dir. Park Strategies LLC, 1999—. Chmn. banking, housing and urban affairs com., mem. fin. com., caucus on internat. narcotics control; co-chmn. U.S. Commn. on Security and Coperation in Europe. Author: Power, Pasta, and Politics, 1996. Mem. Island Park Vol. Fire Dept. Mem. Lions, Sons of Italy, KC. Roman Catholic. Avocations: reading, piano. Office: Park Strategies LLC 101 Park Ave, Ste 2506 New York NY 10178

D'AMATO, ANTHONY, law educator; b. NYC, Jan. 10, 1937; s. Anthony A. and Mary (DiNicholas) D'A.; m. Barbara W. Steketee, Sept. 4, 1958; children: Brian, Paul. BA, Cornell U., 1958; JD, Harvard U., 1961; PhD, Columbia U., 1968. Bar: NY 1963, US Supreme Ct. 1963, US Tax Ct. 1987. Instr. Wellesley Coll., 1963-66; of counsel S.W. Africa Cases, NYC, 1965-66; Woodrow Wilson fellow U. Mich., Ann Arbor, 1966-67; Leighton prof. law Northwestern U. Law Sch., Chgo., 1968—. Author: The Concept of Custom in International Law, 1971, (with O'Neil) The Judiciary and Vietnam, 1972, (with Hargrove) Environment and the Law of the Sea, 1976 (with Wasby and Metrailer) Desegregation from Brown to Alexander, 1977, (with Weston and Falk) International Law and World Order, 1980, 2d edit., 1990, Jurisprudence: A Descriptive and Normative Analysis of Law, 1984, International Law: Process and Prospect, 1987, 2d edit., 1995, How to Understand the Law, 1989, (with Jacobson) Justice and the Legal System, 1992, International Law Anthology, 1994, International Law Coursebook, 1994, International Environmental Law Anthology, 1995, International Law and Political Reality, 1995, Analytic Jurisprudence Anthology, 1995, International Intellectual Property Anthology, 1996, Introduction to Law and Legal Thinking, 1996, International Law Studies, 1996, International Law Studies, 1997, International Intellectual Property Law, 1997, European Union Law Anthology, 1998, The Alien Tort Claims Act: An Analytical Anthology, 1999, International Intellectual Property Coursebook, 2000, International Law Sources: Collected Papers, Vol. 3, 2004; bd. editors Am. Jour. Internat. Law, 1981-95. Recipient Annual Book award Am. Soc. Internat. Law., 1981, Carl L. Fulda award for Outstanding Contbn. to Internat. Law, 1988. Mem. Internat. Law Assn., Am. Soc. Legal and Polit. Philosophy (chair inter-bar study group on ind. of lawyers and judges), ABA (coun. internat. law and practice), Am. Soc. Internat. Law (chair human rights interest group). Home: 5807 Lakeshore Dr N Holland MI 49424-1019 Office: Northwestern U Sch Law 357 E Chicago Ave Chicago IL 60611-3059 E-mail: a-damato@law.northwestern.edu. *All goals in life pale in comparison to the one issue of transcendant planetary importance: preventing nuclear war. We must establish mutually stable deterrence systems to prevent the temptation to initiate a nuclear attack. As a student of international and constitutional law, I pledge to use whatever I have learned in order to promote the recourse to law and justice that may help to establish conditions of international stability and trust.*

D'AMATO, SANDY, chef; m. Angela D'Amato. Grad., Culinary Inst. Am., 1974. Chef John Byron's Restaurant, Milw., 1980; co-owner, exec. chef Sanford Restaurant, Milw., 1989—, Coquette Cafe, 1999—, Harlequin Bakery, 2005—. Columnist (newspaper) Kitchen Technician, Milw. Jour. Sentinel, weekly guest chef (TV series) Always in Good Taste, CBS, appearance include Dining Around, TV Food Network, Great Chefs/Great Cities, PBS Julia Child Spl., America's Rising Star Chefs. Finalist Am. Culinary Gold Cup, Bocuse D'or, 1988; named Perrier Jouet Best Chef: Midwest, James Beard Found., 1996; named one of Top 25 Hot New Chefs, Food and Wine mag., 1985; recipient gold medal, Am. Seafood Challenge, 1989, Fine Dining Hall of Fame award (for Sanford Restaurant), Nation's Restaurant News, 1994, Disting. Restaurants of N. Am. award (for Sanford Restaurant), 1994, Ivy award (for Sanford Restaurant), Restaurants and Institutions Mag., 1995. Achievements include being one of 12 chefs selected to cook for Julia Child's 80th birthday, 1992; being one of 45 chefs selected nationally to cook for 2002 Salt Lake City Olympics, US Art of the Table. Office: Sanford Restaurant 1547 N Jackson St Milwaukee WI 53202 Office Phone: 414-276-9608.*

DAMAZ, PAUL F., architect; b. Portugal, Nov. 8, 1917; came to U.S., 1947, naturalized, 1953; s. Pierre L. and Maria A. (Leite) D.; m. Solange Guillon, Dec. 26, 1981. BA in Architecture, Ecole Speciale d'Architecture, 1941; M. Town Planning, U. Paris, Sorbonne, 1946. Archtl. designer UN Hdqrs., NYC, 1948-51, Harrison & Abramowitz, NYC, 1951-53; chief designer Cajetan Baumann, NYC, 1953-61; ptnr. Damaz & Weigel, NYC, 1962-76; pres. Adasco Tech Internat., NYC, 1976-81; prin. Paul Damaz Assos., East Hampton, NY, 1981—. Design critic Columbia, 1953; writer, critic, lectr. maj. univs. and TV. Dir. N.Y. Fine Arts Fedn.; Mem. nat. panel arbitrators Am. Arbitration Assn. Author: Art in European Architecture, 1956, Art in Latin American Architecture, 1962. Capt. French Army, 1939—45, POW in Germany. Fellow AIA; mem. French Ordre des Architectes, Archtl. League N.Y. (past v.p., Arnold W. Brunner award 1958), Mcpl. Arts Soc., French-Am. Soc., Am. Inst. Planners. Office: 218 Old Stone Hwy East Hampton NY 11937-1621 E-mail: psdamaz@yahoo.com.

D'AMBOISE, JACQUES JOSEPH, former dancer, choreographer, educator, director; b. Dedham, Mass., July 28, 1934; s. Andrew Ahearn and Georgette d'Amboise; m. Carolyn George, Jan. 1, 1956; children: George Jacques, Christopher R., Charlotte Lorraine, Catherine Liza. DHL, DFA, Coll. New Rochelle, 1976, Bates Coll., 1978; DHL (hon.), St. Peters Coll., 1978; DFA (hon.), Monmouth U., 1984; DHL, DFA, Conn. Coll., 1991, The Juilliard Sch., 2000; DHL (hon.), Franklin Pierce Coll., 2000; DFA (hon.), U. of the South, 2001; DHL (hon.), St. Joseph Coll., 2003. With N.Y.C. Ballet Co., 1949-84; prin. Dancer, 1953-84; instr. Sch. Am. Ballet; prof., dean SUNY Sch. Dance, Purchase, 1977-80. Founder Nat. Dance Inst., NYC, 1976—; dancer (films) Seven Brides for Seven Brothers, 1954, The Best Things in Life Are Free, 1956, Carousel, 1956, Off Beat, 1986, He Makes Me Feel Like Dancin', 1983; co-author: Teaching the Magic of Dance, 1983; choreographer Scherzo Opus 42, Valse-Scherzo Concert Fantasy, Celebration, The Chase, Tschaikovsky Suite No. 2, Sarabande and Danse II, Quatouor, Prologue and Saltarelli. Recipient Paul Robeson award, 1988, Capezio award, 1990, Disting. Svc. to Arts award, Am. Acad. Arts and Letters, 1993, Kennedy Ctr. Honors, 1995, St. Elizabeth Ann Seton award, NCEA, 1996, Nat. Medal of Arts award, U.S. Pres., 1998, Dance Mag. award, 1999, Arison award, Nat. Assn. for Advancement of Arts, 2002, James Keller award, The Christophers, 2002, Town Hall Friend of Arts award, 2000, Heinz award for Arts and Humanities, 2001, others; MacArthur fellow, 1990. Fellow: Am. Acad. Arts & Scis. Office: Nat Dance Inst Inc 594 Broadway Rm 805 New York NY 10012-3257*

D'AMBROSIO, JODY (GIGI) LYNN, art educator; b. Spartanburg, SC, Oct. 4, 1961; d. George Franklin and Jody Thomas Henderson; m. Francis Xavier D'Ambrosio, Dec. 31, 1989; children: Alexis Helena, Georgia Lynn. BA in Studio Art, Converse Coll., Spartanburg, SC, M in Art Edn. Elem. art tchr. Inman Elem. Sch., SC, 1984—. Pub. rels. chmn. Inman First Bapt. Ch., SC, 2001—05, mem. decorating com., 2001—06. SC. Tchr. Incentive grant, Teachers in SC., 1991, 1994, 2002, 2005. Mem.: Nat. Art Edn. Assn. Bapt. Avocations: travel, swimming. Home: 190 Johnny's Rd Inman SC 29349 Office: Inman Elem Sch 25 Oakland Ave Inman SC 29349 Office Phone: 864-472-8403. Personal E-mail: gigid_ambrosio@charter.net.

D'AMBROSIO, LOUIS J., telecommunications industry executive; BS summa cum laude, Pa. State Univ., 1986; MBA, Harvard Univ., 1992. Mgmt. position AT&T; mgmt. positions IBM, 1987—2002, gen. mgr. Asia Pacific Tokyo, v.p. mktg. develop. & execution, v.p. worldwide sales & mktg. software; group v.p. global services Avaya Inc., Basking Ridge, NJ, 2002—04, group v.p. global sales channels & mktg., 2004—05, sr. v.p., pres. global sales & mktg., 2005—06, pres., CEO, 2006—. Office: Avaya Inc 211 Mount Airy Rd Basking Ridge NJ 07920*

D'AMBROSIO, RALPH G., communications systems company executive; BBA summa cum laude, Iona Coll., New Rochelle, NY, 1989; MBA with honors, NYU, 1997. CPA. Sr. mgr. acctg. and auditing dept. Coopers & Lybrand LLP; various fin. mgmt. positions L-3 Comm. Holdings, Inc., NYC, 1997—2000, contr., 2000—01, v.p., contr., 2001—05, v.p. fin., prin. acctg. officer, 2005—07, v.p., CFO, 2007—. Office: L-3 Comm Holdings Inc 600 Third Ave New York NY 10016 Office Phone: 212-697-1111. Office Fax: 212-805-5477.*

DAME, CATHERINE ELAINE, acupuncturist; b. Holyoke, Mass., Oct. 1, 1951; d. Josaphat Charles and Lillian Geneva (Archer) Boulanger; m. William Henry Dame, Jan. 9, 1970 (div. May 1999); 1 child, Cristinna Lian. Acupuncture Diplomate, N.E. Sch. Acupuncture, Watertown, Mass., 1992; student, Ind. U., 1988-93; MEd, Cambridge Coll., 1994. Lic. acupuncturist, Mass.; nat. bd. diploma in acupuncture. Dept. mgr. Zayre Dept. Store, Chicopee, Mass., 1969; retail sales clk. Woodward & Lothrop Store, Alexandria, Va., 1971-72; dept. mgr. Steiger Dept. Store, Enfield, Conn., 1972-73; retail sales clk. Point Dept. Store, Ft. Walton Beach, Fla., 1973-74; assembly, repair mfg. Texas Instruments, Ft. Walton Beach, 1974-75; tller Third Nat. Bank, Springfield, Mass., 1975-81, customer svc. rep., 1981-82; teller Bank of N.E./Fleet Bank, Springfield, 1990-93; owner, mgr. Acupuncture Svcs., Chicopee, 1994—. Cons. Cambridge Coll., Springfield, Mass., 1994-95; bus. office liaison Cambridge Coll., 1995-98; Traditional Chinese Med. tour, China, 2001. Mem. People to People Internat. Mem.: Acupuncture Soc. Mass., Nat. Commn. Cert. of Acupuncturists Directory, Am. Assn. Oriental Medicine, Assn. Profl. Genealogists, New Eng. Hist. Geneal. Soc., Chicopee C. of C., Kings Bridge Equine Rescue, Inc., Granby Regional Horse Coun. Office: Acupuncture Svcs Chicopee 665 Prospect St Chicopee MA 01020-3064 Home Phone: 413-374-4332; Office Phone: 413-536-4534.

DAME, RICHARD FRANKLIN, marine biology educator; b. Charleston, SC, Nov. 16, 1941; s. Richard F. and Laurie M. (Heisser) D.; m. Amanda M. Roberts, Apr. 29, 1967; children: Caroline, Elizabeth. BS, Coll. of Charleston, 1964; MA, U. N.C., 1967; PhD, U. S.C., 1971. Tchr. St. Andrews High Sch., Charleston, 1966-68; prof. Coastal Carolina Coll. U. S.C., Conway, 1971-90, Palmetto prof., 1990—; dir. ecosystems program NSF, Washington, 1992-93, ecology cluster leader, 1993-94. Cons. Smithsonian Instn., Washington, 1985, U. Md., Solomons Island, 1991, Va. Commonwealth U., 2006, Va. Tech. U., 2006; panel mem. NSF, Washington, 1986, 89, 90, 2005, EPA, 2006; keynote spkr. European Marine Biology Symposium, 1991. Author, editor: Marsh Estuarine Systems Simulation, 1979, Ecology of Marine Bivalves: A Ecosystem Approach; author newspaper/TV course Oceans and Man, 1980, The Role of Bivalve Filter Feeders in Estuarine and Coastal Ecosystem Processes, 1993, Comparative Roles of Estuarine Feeders and Ecosystems, 2005; gen. editor Marine Ecology Progress Series; contbr. articles to profl. jours. Vestry Trinity Episcopal Ch., Myrtle Beach, S.C., 1979-81; bd. dirs. Litchfield Beaches Homeowners Assn., Pawleys Island, S.C., 1974-76, mem. Baruch Found. Property Mgmt. Bd., 1999-2002. Named one of Outstanding Young Men Am., 1975, Disting. Alumnus Coll. Charleston, 1989; fellow Belle Baruch Found., 1970-71. Mem. AAAS, Am. Soc. Limnology and Oceanography, Estuarine Rsch. Fedn., Southeastern Estuarine Rsch. Soc. (pres.-elect 1994-95, pres. 1996-98), Sigma Xi. Achievements include being first to measure oyster metabolism and growth; research in the importance of oyster reefs to estuarine water quality, Outwelling hypothesis, influence of oyster reefs on water chemistry, estuarine continuum theory; oyster reefs as complex systems. Office Phone: 843-722-8102.

DAME, WILLIAM PAGE, III, bank executive, educational administrator; b. Balt., July 6, 1940; s. William Page Dame Jr. and Hally Carrington (Brent); m. Laura Jacqueline Cordier, June 28, 1968 (div. 1975); children: William Page IV, Laura Alexandra; m. Beverly Ann Reece, July 4, 1998 BA, U. Va., 1963. Ofcl. asst., asst. treas. Bankers Trust Co., NYC, 1963-68, dep. rep. Tokyo, 1968-70, asst. treas. NYC, 1970-71; asst. v.p. Franklin Nat. Bank, NYC, 1971-72, regional rep. Singapore, 1972—74; v.p. Riggs Nat. Bank, Washington, 1974-76, Security Pacific Nat. Bank, LA, 1976-77,

San Francisco, 1977-79, Sydney, Australia, 1979-80, J. Henry Schroder Bank and Trust Co., NYC, 1981-82; sr. v.p. Palmer Nat. Bank, Washington, 1982-84; v.p. Sovran Bank, Arlington, Va., 1985-86; chief fin. officer DITT, Inc. subs. Electricité de France, Washington, 1986-88; v.p. Am. Security Bank, Washington, 1988-91; internat. fin. cons. Washington, 1991-93; adminstr. Grace Episc. Day Sch., Silver Spring, Md., 1993-95, Evergreen Sch., Kensington, Md., 1995-98, Alexandria Country Day Sch., Alexandria, Va., 1998—2002; asst. headmaster Lyndon Inst., Lyndon Ctr., Vt., 2002—. Corporator Passumpsic Savs. Bank, St. Johnsbury, Vt., 2004—. Sr. warden St. Paul's Episc. Ch., Washington, 1995-96; dir. Woodley Ensemble, Washington, 1997-2002, Piggery Theater, N. Hatley, Que., 2003—04, N. Hatley Club, 2003-, Assoc. Property Owners Lake Massawippi N. Hatley, Quebec. Mem. Soc. Colonial Wars, Am. Bus. Coun.-Singapore (founding mem.), Old Asian Hands Soc., BT Alumni Assn., Soc. of the Cin., North Hatley Club, Tanglin Club, Singapore Cricket Club, U. Club Montreal Democrat. Episcopalian. Home: 235 Skyline Dr Lyndonville VT 05851 Office: College Rd Box 127 Lyndon Center VT 05850 Office Fax: 802-626-6129. Personal E-mail: chantman@charter.net. Business E-Mail: page.dame@lyndoninstitute.org.

DAMELIN, HAROLD D., lawyer, former federal agency administrator; b. 1946; m. Harriet Damelin; 2 children. BA magna cum laude (hon.), Boston Coll., 1969; JD magna cum laude, Boston Coll. Law Sch., 1972. Fed. prosecutor, fraud & pub. integrity section, criminal divsn. US Dept. Justice, Wash., DC, 1974—86, asst. US atty. DC, 1974—86; ptnr. Powers, Pyles, Sutter & Verville, Wash., DC, 1986—95; staff dir. US Senate Permanent Subcomm. on Invest., Wash., DC, 1995—97; sr. counsel US Senate Comm. on Govtl. Affairs, Wash., DC, 1997—98; atty. Pyles, Sutter & Verville, Wash., DC, 1999—2003; insp. gen. US Small Bus. Admin., Wash., DC, 2003—05, US Dept. Treasury, Wash., 2005—07; ptnr. Blank Rome LLP, Phila., 2007—. Office: Blank Rome LLP Watergate 600 New Hampshire Ave NW Washington DC 20037 E-mail: Damelin@BlankRome.com.

D'AMELIO, FRANK ANTHONY, pharmaceutical executive, former telecommunications industry executive; b. Jersey City, Dec. 9, 1957; s. Joseph and Rose (Giordano) D'A.; m. Carmel Rachel Zampaglione, Mar. 31, 1984. BS, St. Peter's Coll., 1979; MBA, St. John's U., 1983. Asst. fin. analyst AT&T Bell Labs., Short Hills, NJ, 1979-80, sr. asst. fin. analyst, 1980-81, supr. payroll dept., 1981-82, fin. analyst, 1982-83, supr. fin. services, 1983-84, property mgr., 1984, mgr., services and personnel div., 1984-85, mgr. engring., adminstrn., 1985-86, mgr. facility ops. Murray Hill, NJ, 1986-88, mgr. govt. systems fin. and corp. customer relations Short Hills, NJ, 1988—94; controller AT&T Network Systems, 1994—96, CFO, 1996—98; exec. v.p., CFO Lucent Technologies, Murray Hill, NJ, 2001—06, COO, 2006, chief technology officer; sr. v.p. integration, chief adminstrv. officer Alcatel Lucent, 2006—07; sr. v.p., CFO Pfizer Inc., NYC, 2007—. Mem. Bldg. Owner's Mgmt. Assn. Republican. Roman Catholic. Avocations: weightlifting, football, basketball, real estate, water sports. Office: Pfizer Inc 235 E 42d St New York NY 10017-5755*

DAMERIS, THAD THANO, lawyer; b. Houston, Feb. 27, 1960; BBA, So. Methodist Univ., 1982; JD with honors, Univ. Tex., 1986. Bar: Tex. 1986, US Dist. Ct. (no., so., ea., we. dist. Tex., Ariz., so., no. dist. Calif., DC, so., ea. dist. NY, we. dist. Ark.), US Ct. Appeals (5th, 8th, 9th cir.), US Supreme Ct. Ptnr., co-leader Aviation Aerospace & Transp. industry team Pillsbury Winthrop Shaw Pittman, Houston. Contbr. articles to profl. jours. Fellow: Tex. Bar Found., Houston Bar Found.; mem.: ABA (chmn. Aviation & Space Law com., vice chmn. Aviation Litigation com., co-chmn. mfg. div. Forum on Air & Space Law), Am. Bd. Trial Advocates, Internat. Bar Assn., Am. Soc. Internat. Law, NTSB Bar Assn., Def. Rsch. Inst., Lawyer Pilot Bar Assn., Tex. Assn. Def. Counsel, State Bar Tex. Office: Hogan & Hartson LLP 711 Louisiana St Ste 2100 Houston TX 77002 Office Phone: 713-425-7322. Office Fax: 713-425-7373. Business E-Mail: thad.dameris@pillsburylaw.com.

DAMES, VIVIAN LOYOLA, social sciences educator; b. Philippines; d. Angeles Acero and Bernice Shirley Dames; married. Student, Seattle U., Colegio Victoria, Guadalajara, Mex., 1969; BA in Psych., U. Wash., Seattle, 1972; MSW, Wayne State U., Detroit, 1974; PhD in Social Work and Polit. Sci., U. Mich., Ann Arbor, 2000. Coord. rehab. Mich. Cancer Found.; instr. to assoc. prof. social work/women & gender studies U. Guam, 1977—. Vis. prof. U. South Pacific, Fiji, 1986, U. Papua New Guinea, Port Moresby; social sci. analyst US Dept. Census, 1994. Contbr. chapters to books. Recipient US Prof. of Yr. award, Carnegie Found. for Advancement of Tchg. and Coun. for Advancement and Support of Edn., 2006. Mem.: Nat. Assn. Social Workers, Guam chpt., Guam Assn. Social Workers. Avocations: reading, travel, yoga. Office: Sch Nursing Social Work & Health Scis Coll Profl Studies U Guam UOG Station Mangilao GU 96923 Office Phone: 671-735-2871. Office Fax: 671-734-1203. E-mail: vdames@uog9.uog.edu.*

DAMIANO, RALPH JAMES, JR., cardiovascular and thoracic surgeon; b. White Plains, NY, Nov. 3, 1954; BS in Biology (summa cum laude), Dartmouth Coll., 1976; MD, Duke U., 1980. Cert. Thoracic Surgery, Surgery. Resident, gen. surgery Duke U. Med. Ctr., Durham, NC, 1980—88, rsch. fellow, 1984, sr. residency, surgery, 1988—89; faculty mem., hosp. appointment Med. Coll. Va., Richmond, Va., 1989—96, asst. prof. surgery, 1989—96, dir., surgical electrophysiology, Cardiothoracic Surgery Rsch. Lab.; chief cardiac surgery Barnes Jewish Hosp. Washington U. Sch. Medicine, St. Louis, 1996; prof. surgery, chief divsn. cardiothoracic surgery Pa. State U., Milton S. Hershey Med. Ctr., 1996—2000; John M. Shoenberg Prof. Surgery, chief cardiac surgery Washington U. Sch. Medicine, St. Louis, 2000—. Invited lectr. in field. Contbr. articles to profl. jours.; assoc. editor Journal of Thoracic and Cardiovascualr Surgery, mem. editl. bd. Jour. Cardiovascular Surgery, Jour. Thoracic and Cardiovascular Surgery, Jour. Laparoendoscopic and Advanced Surgical Techniques, editl. review group chair Cardiothoracic Surgery, Doody Publishing. Named one of America's Top Doctors, 2006, Best Doctors in Am., Best Doctors, Inc., 2006; recipient Nat. Rsch. Svc. award, NIH, ComputerWorld Smithsonian award, Am. Coll. Surgeons Faculty Fellowship award, Clin. Tchr. Yr. award, 2006. Mem.: Alpha Omega Alpha. Achievements include the development of robotically-assisted cardiac surgery; performed the first robotically-assisted coronary artery bypass graft procedure in North America in 1998; internationally recognized for innovative research in surgical robotics and minimally invasive heart surgery. Office: Ctr for Advanced Medicine Heart and Vascular Ctr 4921 Parkview Pl Ste A Fl 8 Saint Louis MO 63110 Address: Barnes Jewish Hosp Queeny Tower Ste 3108 One Barnes-Jewish Hospital Plz Saint Louis MO 63110 Office Phone: 314-362-7327, 314-362-7327. Office Fax: 314-747-0917.*

DAMIANOS, SYLVESTER, architect, sculptor; b. McKeesport, Pa., Dec. 31, 1933; s. Tsambikos and Melanie (Barboteau) D.; m. Eva Lu Spears, Dec. 28, 1957; children: Lynne Lucille, Laurie Elizabeth, Leigh Ann. BArch, Carnegie Inst. Tech., Pitts., 1956; postgrad., Tech. Inst. Delft, Netherlands, 1957. Registered arch., Pa. Assoc. ptnr. Celli-Flynn, McKeesport, Pa., 1960-67; prin. Damianos & Pedone, Pitts., 1967-79; pres. Damianos & Assocs., Pitts., 1979-89; chmn. Damianos Brown Andrews Inc., Pitts., 1989-95; pres. Damianos + Anthony, Pitts., 1995—, Damianos-group, 2001—. Pres. Pitts. Plan for Art, 1960-82; bd. dirs. Action-Housing, Inc. Arch. bldg. renovation, 601 Grant St. Office Bldg. (Design 1993); exhibited works of sculpture, Mus. Art Carnegie Inst., 1975, Westmoreland County Mus. Art, 1966, N.Y.C., London. Chmn. planning com. Borough of Edgewood, Pa., 1976-77, mem. coun., 1977-81; bd. dirs. Met. Pitts. Pub. Broadcasting, Am. Wind Symphony, Pitts., 1975-76; sec. Pitts. Art Commn., 1970-78; chmn. bd. regents Am. Archtl. Found., 1991-94; chair pub. art adv. com. Pitts. Cultural Trust, 1994—, co-chair dist. design com., 2004— Fulbright grantee USIS, Netherlands, 1956 Fellow AIA (regional dir. 1985-87, v.p. 1988, 1st v.p. 1989, nat. pres. 1990, pres. Pitts. chpt. 1980, vice chancellor Coll. of Fellows 2002, chancellor elect 2001, chancellor 2002-03, Kemper award 1996, Medal of Distinction, Pa. chpt. 1997), Fedn. Archs. Republic Mex. (hon.), Royal Can. Inst. Archs. (hon.), Japan Inst. Archs. (hon.); mem. Pa. Soc. Archs. (bd. dirs., v.p. svcs.), Pitts. Archtl. Club (pres. 1963-64), Soc. Sculptors (dir. 1977-79), Assoc. Artists Pitts. (pres., dir. 1963-65, 93—), Edgewood Club (pres., dir. 1969-75). Greek Orthodox. Home: 328 Locust St Pittsburgh PA 15218-1457 Office: Damianos Group 328 Locust St Pittsburgh PA 15218 Home Phone: 412-242-6919; Office Phone: 412-398-6974. Personal E-mail: syld@comcast.net. Business E-Mail: syl@damianosgroup.com.

DAMICH, EDWARD JOHN, federal judge; b. Pitts., June 19, 1948; s. John James and Josephine Mary (Lovrencic) D. BA, St. Stephen's Coll., Dover, Mass., 1970; JD, Cath. U. Am., 1976; LLM, Columbia U., 1983, JSD, 1991. Bar: DC 1976, Pa. 1984. Asst. prof. law Widener U. Del. Law Sch., Wilmington, 1976-80, assoc. prof., 1980-84, George Mason U. Law Sch., Arlington, Va., 1985-89, prof., 1990; commr. Copyright Royalty Tribunal, 1992—93; chief intellectual property counsel Judiciary Com. US Senate, 1995—98; judge US Ct. Fed. Claims, Washington, 1998—, chief judge, 2002—. Witness subcommittee on intellectual property US Ho. Reps., Washington, 1993; commr. Copyright Royal Tribunal, 1992-93. Author: Actions and Remedies: Wills and Trusts, 1986, Federal, State and Common Law Protection of the Moral Rights of Authors, 1991; contbr. articles to legal jours. Fellow Columbia U., 1982. Mem. ABA, Pa. Bar Assn., DC Bar Assn., Assn. litteraire et artistique internationale. Office: US Ct Fed Claims 717 Madison Pl NW Washington DC 20005*

D'AMICO, ANDREW J., lawyer; b. Phila., Feb. 18, 1953; s. Joseph J. and Alice H. (Falotica) D'A.; m. Georgiana R. Etheridge, Feb. 25, 1978; children: Andrew J. Jr., Joseph W., Jennifer T., Theresa J. BA, St. Joseph's U., Phila., 1975; JD, Villanova U., 1978. Bar: Pa. Supreme Ct. 1978, U.S. Dist. Ct. (ea. dist.) Pa. 1979, U.S Ct. Appeals (3d Cir.) 1981. U.S Supreme Ct. 1982. Sole practitioner Law Offices Andrew J. D'Amico, Media, Pa., 1979—. Coach Llanerch Hills Little League, Drexel Hill, Pa., 1986-96, St. Bernadette CYO Basketball, 1996-2000. Mem.: ATLA, Assn. Conflict Resolution (Delaware Valley chpt. bd. dirs. 2004—06), Guy G. deFuria Am. Inn of Ct., Delaware County Bar Assn. (bd. dirs. 1991—92, chmn. ADR com. 1996—, bd. dirs. 1997—98, chmn. civil trial practice com. 2001), Pa. Trial Lawyers Assn., Alpha Sigma Nu. Roman Catholic. Avocations: music, coaching sports, reading. Office: PO Box 605 115 N Monroe St Media PA 19063-3037 Office Phone: 610-565-6700. Business E-Mail: damicolaw@verizon.net.

D'AMICO, ANTHONY VICTOR, radiation oncologist; b. NYC, June 9, 1961; BS in Physics, MIT, BS in Nuclear Engring., MS in Nuclear Engring., MIT, 1984, PhD in Radiation Physics, 1986; MD, U. Pa., 1990. Diplomate Am. Bd. Radiology. Intern Pa. Hosp., Phila., 1990-91; resident in radiation oncology Hosp. of U. Pa., Phila., 1991-94; asst. prof. radiation oncology Harvard U. Med. Sch., Boston, 1994—, assoc. prof. radiation oncology; chief genitourinary radiation oncology Dana-Farber Cancer Inst. Mem. AMA, Am. Radium Soc., Am. Soc. Clin. Oncology, Am. Soc. for Therapeutic Radiology and Oncology, Am. Urol. Assn., Mass. Med. Soc., Alpha Omega Alpha. Office: Dana Farber Cancer Inst Brigham and Womens Hosp 44 Binney St Tower L2 Boston MA 02115 Office Phone: 617-732-7936. Business E-Mail: adamico@partners.org.

DAMICO, DAVID A., lawyer; b. Pitts., Apr. 15, 1959; BS magna cum laude, Wash. and Jefferson Coll., 1981; JD, U. Pitts. Sch. Law, 1984. Bar: Pa. 1984, Ohio 1991, US Supreme Ct., US Ct. Appeals, Third and Sixth Circuits. Founding ptnr. Burns, White & Hickton LLC, 1987—. Past v.p. Nat. Assn. Railroad Trial Counsel (NARTC). Named to Pa. Super Lawyers, Phila. Mag., 2004. Mem.: ABA, Ohio Bar Assn., Pa. Bar Assn., Allegheny County Bar Assn. Office: Four Northshore Ctr 106 Isabella St Pittsburgh PA 15202 Home Phone: 412-967-1980; Office Phone: 412-394-2508, 412-995-3208. Business E-Mail: dadamico@bwhllc.com.

DAMICO, JACK SAMUAL, speech educator; b. Alexandria, La., Jan. 20, 1952; s. Anthony James and Hula Louise Damico; m. Holly Lynette Woolsey, Apr. 14, 1996; 1 child, Tommy Eugene. BA, Northwestern State U., Natchitoches, La., 1974; MS, U. Okla., Okla. City, 1976; PhD, U. N.Mex., Albuquerque, 1985. Cert. clin. competence Am. Speech-Lang.-Hearing Assn., 1977. Speech-language pathologist Albuquerque Pub. Schs., 1976—81; asst. prof. La. State U., Baton Rouge, 1985—89, assoc. prof., 1989—91; Doris B. Hawthorne eminent scholar and prof. U. La., Lafayette, 1991—. Cons. in field. Author: (book) Limiting Bias in the Assessment of Bilingual Students, Childhood Language Disorders, Clinical Aphasiology: Future Directions, Special Education Considerations for the English Language Learner, Whole Language for the Exceptional Child; editor: Professional discourse in Clinical and Educational Contexts; author: Multicultural Language Intervention; contbr. over 100 articles to profl. jours. Cons. Points Light Found., Washington, 1991—96, Nat. Student Speech-Lang.-Hearing Assn., Rockville, Md., 1989—94. Fellow: Am. Speech-Lang.-Hearing Assn. (Rsch. Higher Edn. Mentoring award, Jour. Editor's award, New Investigator's award); mem.: Linguistics Soc. Am., Internat. Pragmatics Assn., Internat. Clin. Linguistics and Phonetics Assn. Democrat. Avocations: travel, baseball, reading. Home: 130 Chantilly Cir Lafayette LA 70508 Office: The Univ La Lafayette PO Box 43170 Lafayette LA 70504-3170 Home Phone: 337-234-3941; Office Phone: 337-482-6551. Business E-Mail: jsdamico@louisiana.edu.

D'AMICO, MICHAEL, architect, urban planner; b. Bklyn., Sept. 11, 1936; s. Michael and Rosalie (Vinciguerra) D'Amico; m. Joan Hand, Nov. 26, 1955; children: Michael III, Dion Charles. BArch, U. Okla., 1961; postgrad., So. Meth. U. Sch. Law, 1962—63, Coll. Marin, 1988—89, San Francisco Law Sch., 1994—. Supr. advanced planning sect. Dallas Dept. City Planning, 1961—63; designer, planner in charge Leo A. Daly Co., San Francisco, 1963—66; project planner Whisler, Patri Assocs., San Francisco, 1966—67; arch., urban planner D'Amico & Assocs., San Francisco, NY, Guam, 1967—73; pres. D'Amico & Assocs., Inc., Mill Valley and San Francisco, Calif., and Guam, 1973—, Jericho Alpha Inc., 1979—82, Alpha Internet Sys., Inc., 1996—; chief ops. officer Patri Merker, 2006—. Cons. arch., planner City of Seaside, Calif., 1967—72, 1979—81, 1989—; cons. urban devel., Eureka, Calif., 1967—82; cons. planner, Lakewood, Calif.; redevel. cons., Daly City, Calif., 1975—77; redevel. advisor Tamalpais Valley Bus. Assn., 1975—77; archtl. and hist. analyst Calif. Dept. Transp., 1975—77; agt. Eureka, Calif., Coastal Commn., 1977—79; devel. cons. City of Scotts Valley, 1977—95, City of Suisun, 1988—89, City of Union City, 1989—91. Mem. steering com. San Francisco Joint Com. Urban Design, 1967—72. Recipient 1st prize, Port Aransas (Tex.) Master Plan Competition, 1964, Design award, Karachi Mcpl. Authority, 1987, Merit award, St. Vincent's/Silveira. Mem.: AIA (inactive, Cmty. Design award 1970), Solar Energy Soc. Am., World Future Soc., Calif. Assn. Planning Cons. (sec.-treas. 1970—72), Am. Planning Assn., Am. Inst. Cons. Planners. Office: 525 Midvale Way Mill Valley CA 94941-3705 Business E-Mail: alphais@alphais.com.

DAMICO, NICHOLAS PETER, lawyer; b. Chester, Pa., June 29, 1937; s. Ralph A. and Mary C. (Ametrane) D.; m. Patricia Ann Swatek, Aug. 26, 1967; children: Christine, Gregory. BS in Acctg., St. Joseph's U., 1960; LLB, U. Pa., 1963; LLM, Georgetown U., 1967. Bar: Pa. 1963, D.C. 1967, Md. 1986. Tax law specialist IRS, Washington, 1963-66; assoc. Silverstein & Mullens, Washington, 1966-72, ptnr., 1972-76; prin. Damico & Assocs., Washington, 1976—2003; sole practice Bethesda, Md., 2003—. Adj. prof. Georgetown U. Law Ctr., Washington, 1973-75. Mem. ABA. Office: 7272 Wis Ave Ste 300 Bethesda MD 20814

D'AMICO, SANDRA HATHAWAY, art educator; b. Torrington, Wyo., Dec. 3, 1954; d. Stanley Knapp and Roberta Harley Hathaway; m. John Chris D'Amico, May 24, 1980; children: Andrew, Christine. BFA, U. Denver, 1977; M of Humanities, U. Colo., Denver, 1998. Tchr. art Aurora (Colo.) Pub. Schs., 1977—81; artist-in-residence Wilder Elementary Sch., Littleton, 1988—90; art tchr. on spl. assignment Littleton Pub. Schs., 1989—90; tchr. art Creekside Elem. Sch., Aurora, 1990—92, Laredo Mid. Sch., 1992—98, Smoky Hill H.S., 1998—. Visual arts coord. Smoky Hill H.S., Aurora, Colo., 2000—. Mem.: ArtSource Colo. (adv. coun., chair staff devel. 2003—), Colo. Art Edn. Assn. (Outstanding H.S. Art Educator 2003). Office: Smoky Hill HS 16100 E Smoky Hill Rd Aurora CO 80015

DAMJANOV, IVAN, pathologist, educator; b. Subotica, Yugoslavia, Mar. 31, 1941; came to U.S., 1967; s. Milenko and Ana (Pavkovic) D.; m. Andrea Zivanovic, Jan. 18, 1964; children: Nevena, Ivana, Milena. MD, Zagreb U., Croatia, 1964, PhD, 1971. Lic. physician, Croatia, Pa., Kans.; diplomate Am. Bd. Pathology. Intern Gen. Hosp., Zagreb, 1964-65; resident in pathology U. Zagreb, 1966-67; intern in pathology Cleve. Met. Gen. Hosp., 1967-68; resident in pathology Mt. Sinai Hosp., NYC, 1968-69; asst. in pathology U. Zagreb, 1969-71; postdoctoral fellow Fels Rsch. Inst., Temple U., Phila., 1971-72; asst. prof. pathology U. Zagreb, 1972-73; from asst. prof. to assoc. prof. U. Conn., Farmington, 1973-77; from assoc. prof. to prof. Hahnemann Med. Coll. and Hosp., Phila., 1977-86; prof. pathology Jefferson Med. Coll. of Thomas Jefferson U., Phila., 1986-94; prof. pathology, chmn. U. Kans. Sch. Med., Kansas City, 1994-98, prof. pathology, 1998—. Cons. pathologist VA Hosp., Newington, Conn., 1975-77, Cancer Info. Dissemination and Analysis Ctr. for Virology, Immunology and Cancer-Related Biology, Franklin Inst., Phila., 1977-82, VAMC, Kansas City, Mo., 1995—, Pathology Stedman's Med. Dictionary, Phila., Pa., 2001-06; group for rsch. in pathology edn. U. Iowa, 1977-82; ad hoc reviewer, site vis. teams and study sects. NIH, Bethesda, Md., 1978—94; basic sci. merit award bd. VA, 1989-92; mem. Croatian Acad. Arts and Scis., 1992; mem. coun. U.S.-Can. Acad. Pathology, 1996-99; vis. prof. U. Novi Sad, Serbia, 2007—. Mem. editl. bd. Ultrastructural Pathology, 1985-96, Virchows Archiv, 1986-2003, In Vivo, 1988—, Modern Pathology, 1989—, Hosp. Physician, 1990-96, Human Pathology, 1991—, Croatian Med. Jour., 1992-2006, Lab. Investigation, 1994—, Pathology Rsch. Practice, 1998-2002, Jour. Urologic Pathology, 1991-2000, editor-in-chief, 2000-02, Internat. Jour. Devel. Biology, 2005-, Ann. Clin. Lab. Sci., 2005-; mem. editl. bd. Am. Registry of Pathology, Washington, 2000—; assoc. editor Lab. Investigation, 1982-94; regional editor N.Am. Differentiation, 1985-96; co-editor Anderson's Pathology, 10th edit., 1996; mem. editl. rev. group chair for pathology/surg. pathology Doody's Health Sciences Book Rev. Jour., 1998—. Recipient Christian R. and Mary F. Lindback award Jefferson Med. Coll., Phila., 1988, Tom Kent award Group for Rsch. in Pathology Edn., 2007. Mem. Am. Soc. Investigative Pathology, Internat. Acad. Pathology, European Soc. Pathology. Office: U Kansas Sch Med Dept Pathol & Lab Med 3901 Rainbow Blvd Kansas City KS 66160-0001 Personal E-mail: idamjanov@kc.rr.com. Business E-Mail: idamjano@kumc.edu.

DAMJANOVICH, CHASLAV M. (CASEY DIAMOND), filmmaker, television producer, writer; b. Ohrid, Yogoslavia, Sept. 25, 1932; arrived in U.S., 1973; s. Milan S. Damjanovich and Darinka Dj. Kosanovic; m. Ljiljana Jankovic (div.); m. Lana Grant (div.); 1 child, Srdjan C. Diploma in English Lit. and Lang., U. of Philosophy, Belgrade, Yugoslavia, 1955, diploma in Comparative World Lit., 1960. WW2 UFA news rsch. Cinematique, Belgrade, Serbia and Montenegro, 1954—55, mgr., 1956—58; filmmaker Avala Film, 1959—72; sr. broadcasting prodr. Broadcast Bd. of Gov. (formerly Voice of Am.), Washington, 1984—. Cons. on Yogoslav history U.S. Congress, Washington, 1984—87; writer newspaper Liberty, Serbia and Montenegro, 1985—91. Prodr.: (films) The Gangsters, 1959—73; dir.: Operation Cross Eagles, 1969; writer-dir.: Bomb at 10:10, 1968 (Golden Globe nominee, 1969); The Last Train to Berlin, 1970; (TV series) The Frontier Remote, 1982, dir.: (TV commls.); co-dir.: (films) Guestarbeiter, 1959—73, Window to the World, 1959—73; writer-translator: Majestic, 1991. Capt. Yugoslavian Army, 1959—60. Named Best VOA Prodr. European divsn., 1987. Republican. Avocations: Sumerian mythology, development of religious propaganda, development of mythology. Office: VOA 333 Constitution Ave SW Washington DC 20024

DAMMERMAN, DENNIS DEAN, diversified technology and services company executive; b. Fairfield, Iowa, Nov. 4, 1945; s. Morris Melvin and Mary Louise (Watson) D.; m. Patricia Anne Bryk, July 9, 1967; children: Dwight David, Heather Lynne. BS, U. Dubuque, 1967. Fin. mgmt. trainee GE, 1967-69, corp. auditor, 1969-74, mgr. acquisitions analysis, lighting bus. group, 1974-76, mgr. ops. analysis, consumer products and services sector, 1976-78; v.p., comptr. Gen. Electric Credit Corp., Stamford, Conn., 1978-81; v.p. Comml. Fin. Svcs., 1981, Real Estate Fin. Svcs. div., 1981-84; sr. v.p. fin., CFO GE, 1984—98, vice chmn., 1998—; chmn., CEO, Capital Svcs., Stamford, 1998—; chmn., CEO Kidder, Peabody Group, Inc., 1994—95. Mem. bd. dirs. GE, 1994—. Trustee Fairfield U., Fin. Acctg. Found.; bd. dirs. U. Dubuque. Mem. Coun. Fin. Execs., Fin. Execs. Inst., Officers Conf. Group. Republican. Office: GE Capital Svcs 260 Long Ridge Rd Stamford CT 06927

DAMON, EDMUND HOLCOMBE, retired plastics company executive; b. St. Louis, Aug. 5, 1929; s. Ralph Shepard Damon and Harriet (Dudley) Holcombe; m. Florence Elizabeth Drake, Apr. 14, 1956; children: Elizabeth, Leslie. BA, Amherst Coll., 1951; MA, U. Bridgeport, 1991. Contr., treas. Strategic Materials Corp., NYC, 1955-63; ops. analyst Norton Co., Troy, NY, 1964-65; v.p. corp. devel. Singer Co., Stamford, Conn., 1965-82; pres., chief exec. officer Pantasote Inc., Greenwich, Conn., 1983-89. Elder First Presbyn. Ch., Greenwich, 1970-88; bd. dirs. Child Guidance Ctr., Stamford, 1983-84, Fairfield County Cmty. Found., exec. com., 1991-97; pres. Greenwich United Way, 1986-92, Greenwich Cmty. Fund, 1992-97; bd. dirs., vice chmn. Greenwich chpt. ARC, 1989-92; mem. ARC N.E. regional commn., 1992-93; chmn. adminstrv. coun. First Ch. of Round Hill, Greenwich, 1989-97; bd. dirs. United Way, York County, Maine, 1998—2004, Brick Store Mus., Kennebunk, Maine, 1998-2000; adminstrv. coun. Ch. on Cape, Cape Porpoise, Maine, 1997-98; pres. Edn. Found. of Kennebunks, 2006-. Mem. Webhannet Golf Club (Kennebunk, Maine). Home: 5 Annies Way Kennebunk ME 04043-7533

DAMON, JOHNNY, professional baseball player; b. Ft. Riley, Kans., Nov. 5, 1973; m. Michelle Mangan, Dec. 30, 2004. Baseball player Kansas City Royals, 1995—2000, Oakland A's, 2001, Boston Red Sox, 2002—05, New York Yankees, 2005—. Co-author (with Peter Golenbock): Idiot: Beating the Curse and Enjoying the Game of Life, 2005. Named to MLB All-Star game, 2002, MLB All-Star Game, 2005. Achievements include led the American League in runs (136), stolen bases (46), 2000; being a member of World Series Champion Boston Red Sox, 2004. Office: c/o New York Yankees Yankee Stadium E 161st St and River Ave Bronx NY 10452

DAMON, MATT (MATTHEW PAIGE DAMON), actor; b. Cambridge, Mass., Oct. 8, 1970; m. Luciana Barroso, Dec. 9, 2005; 1 child, Isabella 1 stepchild, Alexa. Actor: (films) Mystic Pizza, 1988, School Ties, 1992, Geronimo: An American Legend, 1993, Courage Under Fire, 1996, Glory Daze, 1996, Chasing Amy, 1997, The Rainmaker, 1997 (nominee Blockbuster Entertainment award Favorite Actor-Drama), Rounders, 1998, Saving Private Ryan, 1998 (nominee SAG award Outstanding Performance by a Cast), The Talented Mr. Ripley, 1999 (nominee Best Performance by Actor in Motion Picture Drama Golden Globe award, 2000), Dogma, 1999,

All the Pretty Horses, 1999, Titan A.E. (voice), 2000, The Legend of Bagger Vance, 2000, Jay and Silent Bob Strike Back, 2001, The Majestic (voice), 2001, Oceans Eleven, 2001, Gerry, 2002, The Bourne Identity, 2002, Spirit: Stallion of the Cimarron (voice), 2002, Confessions of a Dangerous Mind, 2002, Stuck on You, 2003, Eurotrip, 2004, The Bourne Supremacy, 2004, Ocean's Twelve, 2004, The Brothers Grimm, 2005, Syriana, 2005, The Departed, 2006, The Good Shepherd, 2006, Ocean's Thirteen, 2007, The Bourne Ultimatum, 2007; actor, writer (film) Good Will Hunting, 1997 (nominee SAG award Outstanding Performance by a Male Actor in a Leading Role, MTV Movie awards Best Kiss, Best Male Performance, Best On-Screen Duo, ALFS award London Critics Cir. Actor of Yr., Screenwriter of Yr., Writers Guild Am. Screen award Best Screenplay written directly for screen, Golden Satellite award Best Action in Motion Picture, Golden Globe award Best Performance by an Actor in a Motion Picture-Drama, 3d pl. Boston Soc. Film Critics award Best Screenplay, Blockbuster Entertainment award Favorite Actor-Video, Oscar award Best Actor, Golden Satellite award Best Motion Picture Screenplay, Golden Globe award Best Screenplay-Motion Picture, Fla. Film Critics Cir. award Newcomer of Yr., Chgo. Film Critics Assn. award Most Promising Actor, BFCA award Breakthrough Artist, Berlin Internat. Film Festival Silver Berlin Bear award Outstanding Single Achievement, Oscar award Best Writing, Screenplay Written Directly for Screen), actor, exec. prodr. The Third Wheel, 2002; exec. prodr.: (films) Speakeasy, 2002, The Battle of Shaker Heights, 2003, Feast, 2005; prodr.: Stolen Summer, 2002; (TV series) Project Greenlight, 2001—05, Push, Nevada, 2002. Named one of 50 Most Powerful People in Hollywood, Premiere mag., 2005—06, 100 Most Powerful Celebrities, Forbes.com, 2007; recipient Star on the Hollywood Walk of Fame, 2007.*

DAMON, STEVEN WILLIAM, music educator; b. Greenfield, Mass., Nov. 12, 1969; s. William Herbert and Martha Janice Damon; m. Joyana Jill Dean, July 14, 2002; 1 child, Isaac William. MusM, U. Conn., 1997; MusB, U. Mass. Lowell, 1992; Fine Arts Dir. Cert., Fitchburg State Coll., 1999. Tchr. music Greenfield Pub. Schs., 1997—2003, Athol (Mass.)/Royalston Regional Sch. Dist., 1994—97, Belchertown (Mass.) Pub. Schs., 1993—94; oboe studio dir. Northfield Mt. Herman Sch., 2002—; tchr. music Holyoke Pub. Schs., 2004—. Fine arts organizer Learning Ctr. at Oak Courts, Greenfield, 1999—2005; editl. bd. mem. Mass. Music News, Falmouth, Mass., 2001—. Composer: Jupiter's Joy -a wedding march, 2002. Big brother Big Bros./Big Sisters of Franklin County, Greenfield, 2002; bd. dirs. Shelburne Falls Art Bank, Gill Cultural Coun., 2006—; condr. Shelburne Falls Mil. Band, 2000; founder, coord. TubaChristmas, Shelburne Falls, 1996; guest condr. Brattleboro Summer Pk. Band, Brattleboro, Vt., 2001, Conn. Valley Music Festival, Hartford, Vt., 2006. Grantee Grants, various Mass. Arts Couns., 1998—2006. Mem.: Music Educators Nat. Conf., Nat. Assn. Music Edn., Mass. Music Educators Assn. (mgr. All-State Jazz Ensemble 2001—02, K-9 rep. 2001—03, instrumental coord. western dist. 2001—03, chair western dist. 2003—05), Internat. Assn. for Jazz Edn. (vol. bugler-bugles across Am. 2005—). Baptist. Avocation: maple sugaring, dairy farming, red sox fan. Home: 475 Main Rd Gill MA 01354 Office: Sulivan Sch 400 Jarvis Ave Holyoke MA 01040 Office Phone: 413-534-2060. Personal E-mail: steve_damon@nmhschool.org.

DAMON, WILLIAM VAN BUREN, developmental psychologist, educator, writer; b. Brockton, Mass., Nov. 10, 1944; s. Philip Arthur and Helen (Meyers) D.; m. Wendy Obernauer (div. 1982); children: Jesse Louis, Maria; m. Anne Colby, Sept. 24, 1983, 1 child, Caroline. BA, Harvard U., 1967; PhD, U. Calif., Berkeley, 1973. Social worker N.Y.C. Dept. Social Svcs., 1968-70; prof. psychology Clark U., Worcester, Mass., 1973-89, dean Grad Sch., 1983-87, chmn. dept. edn., 1988-89; Disting. vis. prof. U. P.R., 1988; prof., chair edn. dept. Brown U., Providence, 1989-92, prof., Mittlemann Family dir. Ctr. for Study of Human Devel., 1993-98, univ. prof., 1997-98; fellow Ctr. for Advanced Study in the Behavioral Scis., 1994-95; prof., dir. Ctr. on Adolescence Stanford (Calif.) U., 1997—. Sr. fellow Hoover Instn., 1999—; mem. study sect. NIMH, Bethesda, Md., 1981-84; cons. State of Mass., 1976, State of Calif., 1978, Allegheny County, Pa., 1979, Pinellas County, Fla., 1990, Com. of Va., 1993, Hawaii, 1995, Children's TV Workshop, 1991-09, Annenberg Adv. Coun. on Excellence in Children's TV, 1996-99, Project for Excellence in Journalism, 2000-; mem. nat. adv. bd. Fox Family TV Network, 1998-2001. Author: Social World of the Child, 1977, Social and Personality Development, 1983, Self-Understanding in Childhood and Adolescence, 1988, The Moral Child, 1988, Child Development Today and Tomorrow, 1989, Some Do Care, 1992, Greater Expectations, 1995 (Parent's Choice Book award, 1995), The Youth Charter, 1997, Handbook of Child Psychology, 2006;; Good Work, 2001, Bringing in a New Era in Character Education, 2002, Noble Purpose, 2003, The Moral Advantage, 2004, Taking Philanthropy Seriously, 2006; editor: New Directions for Child Devel., 1978—2005. Trustee Bancroft Sch., Worcester, Mass., 1982-84; mem. adv. bd. Ednl. Alliance, 1991—; mem. bd. advisors John Templeto Found., 2005—. Grantee Carnegie Corp., N.Y.C., 1975-79, 97—, Spencer Found., 1980, 92-96, 98-2001, N.Y. comty. Trust, 1984-88, Inst. Noetic Scis., 1988-90, MacArthur Found., 1990-95, Pew Charitable Trusts, 1990-95, 98-2000, Ross Inst., 1996—, Hewlett Found., 1997—, The Templeton Found., 1998—, Atlantic Philanthropies, 2003-. Mem. APA, Jean Piaget Soc. (bd. dirs. 1983-87), Am. Ednl. Rsch. Assn., Soc. for Rsch. in Child Devel., Nat. Acad. Edn., Harvard Clubs of N.Y. and Boston. Republican. Episcopalian. Office: Stanford U Ctr on Adolescence Cypress Bldg C Stanford CA 94305-4145 Office Phone: 650-725-8205. Business E-Mail: wdamon@stanford.edu. *Learn to thrive on the risks and challenges themselves rather than merely on the prospects of winning; expect that every right and privilege must be vigorously defended; and through it all never give up the principle of common decency.*

DAMOS, CRAIG, construction executive; B in Bus., U. Iowa. CPA. Sr. v.p. econ. units RSM McGladrey, Inc., bd. dirs., ptnr.-in-charge Des Moines and Mason City offices, 1997—2000; strategic CFO Weitz Co., Des Moines, 2000, sr. v.p., pres., CEO, 2006—. Chair bd. dirs. Anawim Housing. Mem.: AICPA, Iowa Soc. CPAs. Office: Weitz Co 5901 Thornton Ave Des Moines IA 50321 Office Phone: 515-246-4700. Office Fax: 515-246-4799.*

DAMPF, BETH ANN, music educator; b. Marshfield, Mo., June 2, 1964; d. Joe Perry and Mary Edith Atterberry; m. Douglas Alan Dampf, Aug. 17, 2001; children: Grace Ann, Peter Garrett. MusB Edn., Southwest Bapt. U., Bolivar, Mo., 1986. Tchr. music Moniteau County R-I Schs., California, Mo., 1986—. Athletic dir. Moniteau County R-I Schs., 2003—05; dir. chancel choir United Ch. Christ, California, 2002—05. Chairperson Mo. FFA, Jefferson City, 1991—2006; mem. California Performing Arts Ctr., 2003—06. Named Educator of Yr., Moniteau County R-I Schs., Outstanding Young Woman Am., Outstanding Am. Tchr., Nat. Honor Roll, Outstanding Tchr., U. Mo. Coll. Agr.; named to Who's Who Among Am. Tchrs. Mem.: Nat. Found. HS Actvities-Music, Music Educators Nat. Conf., Mo. Choir Dirs. Assn., Delta Kappa Gamma. Avocations: sports, reading, photography, singing, gardening.

DAMRON, JAYNE, librarian; BA, Wayne State U., 2002, MLIS, 2004. Libr. aide Southfield Pub. Libr., Mich., 2001—03; children's program asst. Milford Pub. Libr., Mich., 2003—04; children's preprofessional Farmington Cmty. Libr., Mich., 2004, children's libr. Mich., 2005, children's outreach libr. Mich., 2005—. Reviewer Sch. Libr. Jour. Named one of the Movers & Shakers, Libr. Jour., 2007. Mem.: Mich. Libr. Assn. (judge Thumbs Up! Award for Teen Literature), Phi Beta Kappa. Office: Farmington Cmty Libr 32737 W 12 Mile Rd Farmington Hills MI 48334-3302 Office Phone: 248-553-0300. Office Fax: 248-553-3228.

DAMROSCH, LEOPOLD, JR., English educator; b. Manila, Sept. 14, 1941; s. Leopold and Elizabeth (Hammond) D.; m. Sheila Raymond (div.); children: John, Christopher; m. Joyce Van Dyke; children: Luke, Nicholas. BA, Yale U., 1963; MA, Cambridge U., 1966; PhD, Princeton U., 1968. From asst. prof. to prof. U. Va., 1968-83; prof. English U. Md., 1983-89; Ernest Bernbaum prof. English Harvard U., Cambridge, Mass., 1989—. Author: Samuel Johnson and the Tragic Sense, 1972, The Uses of Johnson's Criticism, 1976, Symbol and Truth in Blake's Myth, 1980, God's Plot and Man's Stories, 1985, The Imaginative World of Alexander Pope, 1987, Fictions of Reality in the Age of Hume and Johnson, 1989, The Sorrows of the Quaker Jesus, 1996, Jean-Jacques Rousseau: Restless Genius, 2005. Fellow: Am. Acad. Arts & Scis. Office: Harvard Univ Dept English 12 Quincy St Cambridge MA 02138*

DAMSBO, ANN MARIE, psychologist; b. Cortland, NY, July 7, 1931; d. Jorgen Einer and Agatha Irene (Schenck) D. BS, San Diego State Coll., 1952; MA, U.S. Internat. U., 1974, PhD, 1975. Diplomate Am. Acad. Pain Mgmt., Am. Coll. Forensic Examiners, Am. Bd. Psychol. Spltys. Commd. 2d lt. U.S. Army, 1952, advanced through grades to capt., 1957; staff therapist Letterman Army Hosp., San Francisco, 1953—54, 1956—58, 1961—62, Ft. Devers, Mass., 1955—56, Walter Reed Army Hosp., Washington, 1958—59, Tripler Army Hosp., Hawaii, 1959—61, Ft. Benning, Ga., 1962—64; chief therapist U.S. Army Hosp., Ft. McPherson, Ga., 1964—67; ret. U.S. Army, 1967; med. missionary So. Presbyn. Ch., Taiwan, 1968—70; psychology intern So. Naval Hosp., San Diego, 1975; pre-doctoral intern Naval Regional Med. Ctr., San Diego, 1975—76, postdoctoral intern, 1975—76, chief, founder pain clinic, 1977—86. Adj. tchr. U. Calif. Med. Sch., San Diego; lectr., U.S., Can., Eng., France, Australia; cons. forensic hypnosis to law enforcement agys.; approved cons. in hypnosis. Contbr. articles to profl. jours., chapters to books. Tchr. Sunday Sch. United Meth. Ch., 1945—; Rep. Nat. Candidate Trust Presdl. adv. com., platform planning commn. at-large-del.; ARC psychology vol. Naval Hosp., San Diego; vol. VA Hosp., LaJolla, Calif. Fellow Am. Soc. Clin. Hypnosis (psychology mem.-at-large, exec. bd. 1989-90), San Diego Soc. Clin. Hypnosis (pres. 1980); mem. AAUW, Am. Phys. Therapy Assn., Calif. Soc. Clin. Hypnosis (bd. govs.), Am. Soc. Clin. Hypnosis Edn. Rsch. Found. (trustee 1992-94), Internat. Platform Assn., Mil. Officers Am. (past pres. local chpt.), Ret. Officers Assn. (bd. dirs. Hidden Valley chpt., rep. presdl. task force, pres. adv. com.), Toastmasters (local pres.), Job's Daus. Republican. Home and Office: 1062 W Fifth Ave Escondido CA 92025-3802 Home Phone: 760-745-6640; Office Phone: 760-745-6640. *A purpose in life is essential to happiness. Success is a matter of making the most of the talents we are given, not receiving greater talents. Time is the most important gift. We can ill afford to waste it or wish it away. All accomplishment is meaningless unless one walks in harmony and fellowship with her maker and her fellow human beings. I am grateful to my parents and teachers for their examples and for providing me the opportunity for self-actualization.*

DAMSEL, CHARLES H., JR., lawyer; b. Apr. 30, 1929; s. Charles H. and Dorothy Mae (Carter) Damsel; m. Margaret W. Damsel, Aug. 25, 1951 (dec.); children: Charles H. III, Cherie Damsel Boone. BSBA, U. Fla., 1950, JD, 1956. Bar: Fla. 1956, U.S. Dist. Ct. Fla. 1956, U.S. Ct. Appeals (5th cir.) 1958, U.S. Supreme Ct. 1969, U.S. Ct. Appeals (11th cir.) 1981, cert.: Fla. (civil trial lawyer), adv.: Nat. Bd. Trial Advocacy, diplomate: Nat. Bd. Trial Advocacy, civil mediator: Fla. Supreme Ct., diplomate: Am. Bd. Trial Advocates. Assoc. Gurney, McDonald & Handly, Orlando, Fla., 1956—58; mem. Jones & Foster, P.A., West Palm Beach, Fla., 1958—86, Damsel & Gelston, P.A., 1987—98; sole practitioner, 1999—. Contbr. articles to profl. jours. With US Army, 1951—53. Mem.: ATLA, Am. Arbitration Assn., Def. Rsch. Inst. (area chmn.), Fedn. Ins. Counsel (v.p. 1978—79), Fla. Bar (bd. of legal specialization, exec. coun. trial lawyers sect.), Fed. Bar Assn. (pres. local chpt. 1977), Fla. Def. Lawyers Assn. (pres. 1976—77), Palm Beach County Trial Lawyers Assn., Palm Beach County Bar Assn. (pres. 1971), Fla. Blue Key (pres. 1954), Masons, Kappa Sigma, Pi Epsilon Delta, Alpha Phi Omega, Alpha Kappa Psi, Phi Delta Phi. Republican. Presbyterian. Office: 1803 S Australian Ave Ste A West Palm Beach FL 33409 Office Phone: 561-296-9390. Office Fax: 561-296-9396. Personal E-mail: cdamsel@aol.com.

DAMSGAARD, KELL MARSH, lawyer; b. Darby, Pa., May 16, 1949; s. Kjeld and Dorothy (Fanck) D.; m. Katherine Elizabeth Stark, June 17, 1972; children: Peter Kjeld, Christopher William, David Zentner. BA cum laude, Yale U., 1971; JD, U. Pa., 1974. Bar: Pa. 1974, U.S. Dist. Ct. (ea. dist.) Pa. 1975, U.S. Ct. Appeals (3d cir.) 1984, U.S. Ct. Appeals (D.C. cir.) 1989, U.S. Ct. Appeals (8th cir.) 1990, U.S. Ct. Appeals (10th cir.) 1991, U.S. Ct. Appeals (9th cir.) 2003, U.S. Supreme Ct. 1991. Law clk. to judge Superior Ct. of Pa., Phila., 1974-75; assoc. Morgan, Lewis & Bockius LLP, Phila., 1975-81, ptnr., 1981—, firm adminstrv. ptnr., 1996—2006. Fellow Am. Coll. Trial Lawyers; mem. ABA, Phila. Bar Assn. Avocations: skiing, jogging, tennis, antiques. Office: Morgan Lewis & Bockius LLP 1701 Market St Philadelphia PA 19103-2903 Home Phone: 610-827-7372; Office Phone: 215-963-5592. Office Fax: 215-963-5001. Business E-Mail: kdamsgaard@morganlewis.com.

DAMSGAARD, PATRICIA RAE, artist, educator; b. Chgo., Ill., Dec. 29, 1931; d. Harold John Carlson and Rachel Marie Berti; m. Conrad Damsgaard; children: Susan Rae, Kristine Anita, Elizabeth Lynn. BA, Ill. Coll., Jacksonville, 1953, DHL (hon.), 2004. Cert. tchr. Mo. Legal sec. Gilbert & Polance, Chgo., 1954—56; alumni sec. Ill. Coll., Jacksonville, 1956—57; legal sec. Irwin, Deneke & Penner, Chgo., 1957—59; tchr. art Parkway Continuing Edn., St. Louis, 1979—81; tchr. art, program coord. St. Louis Artist Guild, 1986—89; tchr. art Spring Branch Continuing Edn., Houston, 1992—2000, Houston, 2000—04. Paintings, Casa Tavanoti-Watercolor USA, 2000. Trustee Ill. Coll., Jacksonville, 1996—2004; tutor Literacy Advance, Houston, 1992—94; moderator Ivy Chapel, St. Louis, 1984—86. Mem.: St. Louis Art Assn. (show chmn. 1976—77), St. Louis Watercolor Soc., Soc. Watercolor Artists, Houston Watercolor Soc. (mem. nominating com. 1999—2000, 2004—05), St. Louis Artist Guild (life). Democrat. United Church Of Christ.

DAMSON, BARRIE MORTON, oil and gas exploration company executive; b. NYC, Jan. 29, 1936; s. Harry and Ethel (Brody) Damson; m. Joan Selig, Feb. 29, 1972; children: Blair, Laura, Bethany. AB, Harvard U., 1956; LLB, NYU, 1959. Bar: N.Y. 1959. Pres. Damson Petroleum Corp., NYC, 1963-69, Bronco Oil Corp., Midland, Tex., 1965-69, Delta Minerals Inc., Lake Charles, La., 1967-69; pres., chmn. bd. Damson Oil Corp., NYC, 1969-91. Pres., chmn. bd. First Crescent Corp.; chmn. Crescent Natural Resources, Inc.; bd. dirs., chmn., nominating com. Am. Stock Exch., 1981—91, bd. govs., chmn. audit com.; chmn. Damson Natural Resources, Inc., 1991, Damson Investment Group, Inc., European Am. Oil Co., Inc., 1991—94, Stagebill, 1993; bd. dirs. United Gas Holding Corp., 1993—97. Chmn. bd. mem. N.Y.C. Econ. Devel. Corp., 1992—96; dir. Robert Steel Found. for Pediat. Cancer Rsch., 1995; bd. trustees Hosp. Spl. Surgery, 2002; mem. Am. Bus. Conf., 1980—94; mem. Dean's Coun. Harvard Sch. Pub. Health. Mem.: Bar. Assn. N.Y., Harvard Club. Address: 1095 Pequot Ave Southport CT 06890-1421

DAN, BERNARD W., former commodities exchange executive; b. Chgo., Dec. 17, 1960; BS in Acctg., St. John's U., Collegeville, Minn., 1982. With Nat. Futures Assn., 1983—85; adminstrv. mgr. oper. activities Cargill Investor Svcs., Ltd., London, 1986—89, adminstrv. mgr. NYC, 1989—91, asst. v.p., 1991—93, v.p., 1993—94; dir. Cargill Investors Svcs. (Singapore) Pty. Ltd., 1994—97; v.p., Global Head of Execution Cargill Investors Svcs., Chgo., 1997—98; pres., CEO Cargill Investor Svcs., Chgo., 1998—2001; exec. v.p. Chgo. Bd. Trade, Chgo., 2001—02, pres., CEO, 2002—07; spl. adv. CME Group Inc., Chgo., 2007—. Gov. Bd. of Trade Clearing Corp., mem. bd. govs., 1st vice chmn. Mem.: The Comml. Club of Chgo., One Chgo., The Executives Club of Chgo., Nat. Futures Assn., Operation Hope Incorporated, Regional Bd. of Dir. Office: CME Group Inc 20 S Wacker Dr Chicago IL 60606*

DAN, MICHAEL T., security firm executive; Exec. v.p. Brink's Inc., 1985—92, pres. No. Am. ops., 1992—93, CEO, 1993—, pres., 2002—04; pres., CEO Brink's Holding Co., 1995—; chmn. BAX Global Inc., 1998—2006; pres., CEO The Brink's Co. (formerly Pittston Co.), Richmond, Va., 1998—, chmn., 1999—. Office: Brink's Co 1801 Bayberry Ct PO Box 18100 Richmond VA 23226-8100*

DANA, EDWARD RUNKLE, retired physician; b. Columbus, Ohio, May 20, 1919; s. Lowell Brockway and Helen (Runkle) D.; m. Lorraine Kirschner, Aug. 2, 1945; children— Edward R., H. Richard. AB, Wesleyan U., 1941; MD, Johns Hopkins U., 1944. Diplomate: Am. Bd. Radiology. Intern Univ. Hosps., Cleve., 1944-45; resident radiology Johns Hopkins Hosp., 1947-50; dir. radiology Mercy Hosp., Balt., 1950-64; asst. prof. radiology Johns Hopkins Med. Sch., 1960-68, asso. prof., 1968-69; chief diagnostic radiology Orange (Calif.) County Med. Ctr., 1969—2005; asso. prof. radiology U. Calif. Med. Sch., Irvine, 1969-79, prof., 1979—2005, joint prof. gastroenterology, 1969—2005, chief gastrointestinal radiology, 1976-77, co-chief, 1977—2005; co-dir. swallowing ctr. U. Calif. Med. Ctr., Coll. Medicine, Irvine; ret., 2005. Cons. gastroent. radiology Long Beach (Calif.) VA Hosp., 1974— Contbr. articles to profl. jours. Served to capt. M.C. U.S. Army, 1945-47. Named Tchr. of Yr. U. Calif. Irvine Coll. Med., 1996. Mem. Soc. Gastrointestinal Radiologists, Mensa, Sigma Chi, Phi Chi. Clubs: Md.

DANA, F(RANK) MITCHELL, theatrical lighting designer; b. Washington, Nov. 14, 1942; s. John Daskum Mitchell and Elizabeth Francis (Woods) D.; m. Wendy Karen Bensinger, Dec. 31, 1967; children: Scott Cameron, Ian Michael. BFA, Utah State U., 1964; MFA, Yale Drama Sch., 1967. Asst. to Jo Mielziner, NYC, 1968—69; tech. dir. Yale Drama Sch., New Haven, 1970-71; assoc. lighting dir. Ferd Manning, NYC, 1978-88. Guest lectr. U. Wash., So. Meth. U., San Francisco State U.; lectr. Mason Gross Sch. Arts, Rutgers U., 1982-97, asst. prof., 1997-99, assoc. prof., 2000-06, prof., 2006—. Prodn. mgr.: Stratford Festival, Pitts. Civic Light Opera; prodn. supr. Yale Repertory Theatre; lighting designer: Broadway Plays include The Freedom of the City, 1974, Once in a Lifetime, 1978, Inspector General, 1978, Man and Superman, 1978, The Suicide, 1980 (Drama Logue award), Mass Appeal, 1981, Monday After the Miracle, 1982, The Babe, 1984, Oh Coward, 1986; off-Broadway Plays include Three Acts of Recognition, 1982, A Coupla White Chicks, 1980, Mass Appeal, 1980, Oh Coward, 1981, Calling in Crazy, 1969, Songs My Mother Never Sang Me, 1982, Husbandry, 1984, A Hell of a Town, 1984, The Ninth Step, 1984, Daughters, 1986, Cold Sweat, 1988, Other People's Money, 1989, King Fish, 1991, Lust 1995, PaPa 1996, Pete 'n' Keely, 2000, Rounding Third, 2003; operas World Premier of Harriet: The Woman Called Moses, Orphee, Patria II, Tempest 94, Turandot, Royal Opera, Covent Garden, 1984, Olympic Arts Festival, 1984, L.A. Rondine, N.Y.C. Opera, 1984, Magic Flute, 1985, Merry Widow, 1986, Cleve. Symphony, Un Ballo in Maschera Va. Opera, 1985, Opera Festival of N.J., 1989-2001 Turandot, Royal Opera/Covent Garden at Wembly Arena, 1991, Carmen for L.A. Opera and Seville Expo92, La Traviata for Barcelona's Gran Licieu, 1992; Makropolous Case, Traviata, Midsummer Night's Dream, 1992, Elgato Montez, Madama Butterfly, Faust, Electra, Don Giovanni, L.A. Opera, 1994, Ky. Opera, 1999—, other opera cos.; also Pitts. Civic Light Opera, 1973-74, 79, 84-87; tours Hello Dolly, 1981, Mass Appeal, 1982, Guys and Dolls, 1984, George M., Jesus Christ Superstar, 1985, Stop the World, 1986, Other People's Money, Okla., 1990; regional theaters Am. Conservatory Theatre, 1972-80, BAM Theatre Co., 1977, 78, 80, 81, Goodman Theatre, 1973-82, McCarter Theatre, 1969-71, 82, 86-90, Nat. Arts Ctr., Ottawa, 1982-84, others including Mark Taper Forum, Paper Mill Playhouse, Phila. Drama Guild, Va. Mus. Theatre, Crossroads Theatre Co., Geva Theater, Folger Theater, Hartford Stage Co., Interact Theatre, Olney Theatre Ctr., Ala. Shakespeare Co., Cin. Playhouse, St. Louis MUNY, Repertory Theatre St. Louis, Syracuse Stage, Seattle Repertory, Stratford Shakespeare Festival, Studio Arena Theatre, Stratford Festival Theatre, Roundabout Theatre, 1987, 88, George Street Playhouse, Interact Theatre Co., Derby Playhouse (U.K.). Mem. Internat. Alliance Theatrical Stage Employees, United Scenic Artists USA 829 (lighting trustee 1970-72, 96-2003, nat. v.p. 2002--). Republican. Office: 221 W 82d St New York NY 10024-5406 Office Phone: 212-873-1229. E-mail: fmdld@earthlink.net.

DANA, HOWARD H., JR., lawyer, retired state supreme court justice; b. 1940; m. Susan B. Dana. AB, Bowdoin Coll., 1962; LLB, MA, Cornell, 1966; LLM, U. Va., 1998. Law clk. to Hon. E.T. Gignoux US Dist. Ct., Maine, 1966—67; atty. Verill Dana LLP, Portland, Maine, 1967—93, counsel, 2007—; assoc. justice Maine Supreme Ct., Portland, Maine, 1993—2007. Bd. dirs. Legal Svcs. Corp., 1982, 1990—93; vice chmn. Just. Action Group; chmn. Ct. Alternative Dispute Resolution Conf.; co-chmn. JAG Self Representation Task Force; liaison Maine Sup. Jud. Ct. to Lawyers Fund for Client Protection. Recipient Pro Bono Publico award, ABA, 1985, Pub. Svc. award, Maine State Bar Assn., 1986, Arthur Von Briessen award, Nat. Legal Aid & Defender Assn., 1993, Gordon S. Hargraves Freedom prize, Bowdoin Coll., 1997. Mem.: Am. Law Inst., Cumberland Bar Assn., Maine State Bar Assn., ABA (bd. gov. 2002—05). Office: Verrill Dana LLP One Portland Sq Portland ME 04112 E-mail: hdana@verrilldana.com.*

DANA, WILL, editor; m. Ellen Tien; 1 child. BA, Middlebury Coll., 1985. Intern Harper's Mag., 1985; asst. editor Interview Mag., Seven Days Mag.; editor Worth Mag., Outside Mag., Details Mag.; mng. editor Rolling Stone Mag. Recipient Interactive Feature award, Nat. Mag. Awards, Am. Soc. Mag. Editors, 2007. Office: Wenner Media LLC 2nd Fl 1290 Avenue of the Americas New York NY 10104-0298*

DANAHER, JOHN ANTHONY, III, prosecutor; b. New Haven, Aug. 22, 1950; s. John Anthony Jr. and Grace Elizabeth (Burkett) D.; m. Anne Elizabeth Morrison, May 11, 1985; children: Ceara Morrison Danaher, Brendan Ahearn, Austin Spellman, Mary Kate Shea. Awd, Fairfield U., 1972; MA, U. Hartford, 1977; JD, U. Conn., 1980. Bar: Conn. 1980; U.S. Dist. Ct. Conn. 1980; U.S. Ct. Appeals (2d cir.) 1982; U.S. Supreme Ct. 1987. Law clk. to hon. judge T. Emmet Clarie U.S. Dist. Ct. Conn., Hartford, Conn., 1980-81; trial atty. Day, Berry & Howard, Hartford, Conn., 1981-86; with NH US Atty.'s Office US Dept. Justice, Hartford, Conn., 1986—, US atty. Dist. NH, 2001—02. Editor Conn. Law Rev. 1978-80. Mem. Red Cross blood svcs. com., Hartford, 1981-85; active Conn. Rivers Coun., Boy Scouts Am., 1994—. Recipient Disting. Svc. award Atty. Gen. of U.S., Washington, 1990; 14 Superior Achievement awards Dept. of Justice, Hartford, 1988, 90-2000. Mem. Fed. Bar Assn. (pres. Hartford County chpt. 1985-86). Office: US Attys Office Ct Fin Ctr 157 Church St PO Box 1824 New Haven CT 06508

DANAHER, MALLORY MILLETT (MALLORY JONES), actress, photographer, film and theater producer; b. St. Paul, 1939; d. James Albert and Helen Rose (Feely) Millett; m. Thomas C. Danaher, Mar. 1985; 1 child from previous marriage, Kristen Vigard. BA, U. Minn. CFO Sheets & Co., NYC, Happy Camper Inc., NYC, Everwarm, Inc., Mallory Inc., Happyhometex, LLC. Actress: original cos. of Annie, The Best Little Whorehouse in Texas; stage roles: Dodsworth, Berkshire Theatre Festival; House of Blue Leaves; Hedda Gabler; Kennedy's Children; Edward Albee's Everything in the Garden (dir. Shelley Winters); Lincoln Ctr. Libr. Theatre; Stella; Cocteau's one-character play The Human Voice at Deutsches-Haus,

NYU; Full Moon and High Tide; (off-Broadway prodn.) Loose Connections, Judith Anderson Theatre; actor: (TV series) Love of Life, Another World, Hunter, Thirtysomething, Superior Court, Divorce Court, The Judge, Eischied: Only the Pretty Girls Die (NBC Movie of the Week); (films) Tootsie, Hell Hath No Fury with Barbara Eden, Alone in the Dark; exhibitions include Third Eye Gallery, NYC, Modernage Discovery Gallery, Gallery of St. Clement's; author: Fatherless Child, numerous poems; co-prodr.: (films) Three Lives; exec. prodr., lead actress: Deleting Spam; prodr.: (Broadway plays) Epic Proportions. Active NY Theatre; bd. dirs. David Horowitz Freedom Ctr., mem. governance com. Mem.: Women in Theatre, Legatus, The Actors Studio (chmn. auditions 2002—06), The Friars Club.

DANAS, ANDREW MICHAEL, lawyer; b. Redwood City, Calif., Apr. 25, 1955; s. Michael George and Marjorie Jean (Bailey) D.; m. Barbara C. Matthews. BA in Polit. Sci. and History, U. Conn., 1977; JD, George Washington U., 1982. Bar: DC 1982, US Dist. Ct. (DC cir.) 1983, US Dist. Ct. Md. 1987, US Ct. Appeals (Fed. cir.) 1984, US Ct. Appeals (11th cir.) 1987, US Ct. Appeals (3d and 4th cirs.) 1988, US Ct. Appeals (6th cir.) 1990, US Ct. Appeals (2d cir.) 1998, US Ct. of Claims 1984, US Supreme Ct. 1994, US Ct. of Internat. Trade 2003. Atty. Assn. Am. R.R., Washington, 1983-84; assoc. Grove Jaskiewicz & Cobert, Washington, 1984-90, Ptnr., 1991—. Contbg. author: Freewheeling; author legal column Intermodal Reporter, 1986-94; contbr. articles to profl. jour. Exec. com. Friends Assisting the Nat. Symphony, Washington, 1996-97. Mem.: ABA, Transp. Lawyers Assn. (chmn. legis. com. 1995—98, co-chmn. 1999—2001, co-chmn. antitrust com. 2003—, Disting. Svc. award 1996), Transp. Law Inst. (chair 1993—94), Euro-Am. Lawyers Group (mgmt. com. 2000—, sec. 2002—), Internat. Bar Assn., Mensa, Univ. Club (Washington) (mem. internat. com.), Phi Alpha Theta. Avocations: skiing, music, travel. Office: Grove Jaskiewicz and Cobert 1730 M St NW Ste 400 Washington DC 20036-4579 Office Phone: 202-296-2900 x219. Business E-Mail: adanas@gjcobert.com.

DANBERG, CARL CHRISTIAN, state agency administrator, former state attorney general; b. Aug. 29, 1964; m. Barbara Snapp; 2 children. JD, Widener U. Dep. atty. gen. State of Del., chief dep. atty. gen. Wilmington, 2004—05, atty. gen., 2005—07; dep. prin. asst. to commr. Del. Dept. Corrections, commr. of correction, 2007—. Adj. prof. U. Del. Mem. bd. Mt. Aviat Acad., St. Patrick's Day Soc. Mem.: Knights of Columbus. Office: Del Dept Corrections 245 Mckee Rd Dover DE 19904*

D'ANCA, JOHN ARTHUR, psychotherapist, educator; b. Chgo., Apr. 19, 1950; s. John Joseph and Josephine Rose (Bartolotta) D.; m. Carol Amendola; 1 son, Matthew John; stepdaughters, Ingrid, Heidi. BA, DePaul U., 1972; MA, Governors State U., 1975; CAS, No. Ill. U., 1978, EdD, 1982; PsyD, Chgo. Sch. Profl. Psychology, 1996; studied, Harvard U., 1994-95. Cert. eye movement desensitization and reprocessing; lic. clinician, Ill. Mem. counseling faculty Fenwick H.S., Oak Park, Ill., 1973-75; instr. psychology, counselor Triton Coll., River Grove, Ill., 1975-78; assoc. dir. Ball Found., Glen Ellyn, Ill., 1978-79; prof. student devel. Oakton Coll., Des Plaines, Ill., 1979—; pvt. practice psychology Park Ridge, Ill., 1975—. Extern John J. Madden Mental Health Ctr., Dept. of Psychiatry Chgo. Osteo. Hosp.; intern in psychology svc. Edward Hines Jr. VA Hosp., Hines, Ill., 1990—; mem. staff Bayside Clinic, Kenosha, Wis., 1993-97, mem. staff, psychiat. svcs., 1998—; cons. Molex Internat., 1986; lectr. in field; cons. Ill. Dept. Edn., Am. Med. Technologists, Goodwill Industries Internat.; cons., expert witness Ill. Dept. Profl. Regulation; mem. bd. Healthy Cmtys. Program Mental Health; mem. crisis response team psychol. trauma and mental health Des Plaines, Park Ridge, Ill. Contbr. articles to profl. jours. Bd. dirs. Chgo. Bd. of Mental Health, Northwest, 1974-75; mem. Oakton Coll. Crusade of Mercy Appeal, 1982; mem. Regional Med. Reserve Corps, 2006; eucharistic min. Roman Cath. Ch.; lector Roman Cath. Ch. Sears grantee, 1986—; recipient NISOD award for Coll. Tchg. Excellence, U. Tex., Austin, 2003, Silent Benefactor award Shrine of Our Lady of Pompeii, Chgo., 2006. Mem. NEA, APA, Internat. Soc. Traumatic Stress Studies (presenter 1996), Ill. Edn. Assn., Am. Soc. Clin. Hypnosis, Soc. Clin. and Exptl. Hypnosis, Joint Civic Commn. Italian Americans, Midwest Psychol. Assn., N.Am. Assn. Adlerian Psychology, Ill. Guidance and Pers. Assn., Ill. Coll. Pers. Assn., Phi Delta Kappa. Home: 935 Evergreen Way Highland Park IL 60035-3739 Office: 1600 E Golf Rd Des Plaines IL 60016-1234 Office Phone: 847-635-1966. E-mail: johnd@oakton.edu.

DANCE, FRANCIS ESBURN XAVIER, communication educator; b. Bklyn., Nov. 9, 1929; s. Clifton Louis and Catherine (Tester) D.; m. Nora Alice Rush, May 1, 1954 (div. 1974); children: Clifton Louis III, Charles Daniel, Alison Catherine, Andrea Frances, Frances Sue, Brendan Rush; m. Carol Camille Zak, July 4, 1974; children: Zachary Esburn, Gabriel Joseph, Caleb Michael, Catherine Emily BS, Fordham U., 1951; MS, Northwestern U., 1953, PhD, 1959. Instr. speech Bklyn. Adult Labor Schs., 1951; instr. humanities, coord. radio and TV U. Ill. at Chgo., 1953—54; instr. Univ. Coll. U. Chgo., 1958; asst. prof. St. Joseph's (Ind.) Coll., Ind., 1958—60; asst. prof., then assoc. prof. U. Kans., 1960—63; mem. faculty U. Wis., Milw., 1963—71, prof. comm., 1965—71, dir. Speech Comm. Ctr., 1963—70; prof. U. Denver, 1971—, John Evans prof., 1995—; prof. homiletics St. John Vianney Theol. Sem., 2002—05, John Evans prof. emeritus, 2006—. Content expert and mem. faculty adv. bd. to Internat. U. on Knowledge Channel, 1993-95; cons. in field. Author: The Citizen Speaks, 1962, (with Harold P. Zelko) Business and Professional Speech Communication, 1965, 2d edit., 1978, Human Communication Theory, 1967, (with Carl E. Larson) Perspectives on Communication, 1970, Speech Communication: Concepts and Behavior, 1972, The Functions of Speech Communication: A Theoretical Approach, 1976, Human Communication Theory, 1982, (with Carol C. Zak-Dance) Public Speaking, 1986, Speaking Your Mind, 1994, 2d edit., 1996; editor Jour. Comm., 1962-64, Speech Tchr., 1970-72; adv. bd. Jour. Black Studies; editl. bd. Jour. Psycholinguistic Rsch; contbr. articles to profl. jours. Bd. dirs. Milw. Mental Health Assn., 1966-67. 2d lt. AUS, 1954-56. Knapp Univ. scholar in comm., 1967-68; recipient Outstanding Prof. award Std. Oil Found., 1967; Master Tchr. award U. Denver, 1985, Univ. Lectr. award U. Denver, 1986. Fellow Internat. Comm. Assn. (pres. 1967); mem. Nat. Comm. Assn. (pres. 1982), Psi Upsilon. Office: U Denver Dept Human Comm Studies Denver CO 80208-0001 *Life should include a personal commitment to excellence with a corresponding humane tolerance for failure in self or in others. A belief in the progressive acquisition of autonomy can help guide both personal and professional decisions.*

DANCE, GLORIA FENDERSON, dance studio executive, ballet administrator; b. Portsmouth, Va., Mar. 10, 1932; d. Charles Bourrell and Ottillia Lavinia (Korn) Fenderson; m. Walter Forrest Dance III, June 4, 1951; children: Walter Forrest IV, Jon Marlon, Gloria Cherie. Student pub. schs., Petersburg. Cert. promotional dir., modeling/finishing and charm sch., cosmotologist. Assoc. tchr. Boyer/Traylor Dance Acad., Richmond, Va., 1952-60; founder, owner, dir. Gloria F. Dance Sch. Dancing, Petersburg, 1960—; artistic dir. Petersburg Ballet, Inc., 1984—. Block leader Ind. Voters, Walnut Hill, 1955—; chairwoman Jr. Woman's Club, Petersburg; Va. chairwoman Petersburg Dance Festival, White House Performance, Aug. 1984; chairwoman 1985 July 4 Festival, Petersburg. Recipient hon. award Optimist Club, Colonial Heights, Va., 1950-63, Va. Hon. award Va. Nat. Dance Week, 1984, Petersburg Pub. Service award Alumni Gloria F. Dance Sch., 1980, award Best Actress-Actress/Dancer, Liot, South Pacific, Mosque, Richmond, 1950; named Miss Virginia in Miss Am. Pageant, Atlantic City, Sept., 1950; prin. judge Miss America Preliminaries, Va., Md., N.C., Tenn., 1950's-80's; Dance Library Dedication (Gloria F. Dance Collection), Petersburg Pub. Library. Mem. Dance Educators Am. (life), Profl. Dance Tchrs., Miss America Sorority (life). Clubs: Petersburg Country Club; Ft. Lee Country Club (Va.); Battlefield Park and Racquet, Duck Woods Country Club (Nags Head N.C.). Presbyterian. Avocations: boating, swimming, skiing, dance. Home: 1806 Brandon Ave Petersburg VA 23805-1612 also: 413 E Albatross St Nags Head NC 27959 Office: Petersburg Ballet Inc 44 Goodrich Ave Petersburg VA 23805-2120 Office Phone: 804-733-9998. Personal E-mail: gloriadance@50470.com.

DANCEWICZ, JOHN EDWARD, investment banker; b. Boston, Feb. 12, 1949; s. John Felix and Teresa Sophia (Lewandowski) D.; m. Barbaragail Jarrett, Jan. 23, 1971; children: John Lawrence, Jill Elizabeth, Jenna Gail. BA in Econs., Yale U., 1971; MBA, Harvard U., 1973. Project adminstr. fin., cons. Nat. Shawmut Bank Boston, 1972-73; v.p., founder, mgr. U.S. investment banking Continental Ill. Nat. Bank Chgo., 1973-82; sr. mng. dir., mgr. corp. fin. Bear Stearns & Co. Inc., Chgo., 1982-96; founder, mng. ptnr. DN Ptnrs. LLP, DN Ptnrs. LP and DN Ptnrs. LP II, 1996—. Chmn. bd. dirs. Ctrl. Can Co., Inc., FCL Graphics, Inc., M & M Pump & Supply, Inc., Aztec Outdoor Advt. Co., dir. Country Pine Foods, Inc. Contbr. articles to profl. jours. Active schs. com., Yale U., campaign com., spl. gifts com., chmn. 25th reunion fundraising, sec. class 1971; sec. Harvard Bus. Sch. sect.; mem. spl. gifts com. Harvard Bus. Sch. Found. Recipient Pres.'s award, Yale Alumni Assn. Mem. Scholarship and Guidance Assn. (bd. dirs., v.p. 1982—), Lake Forest H.S. Ice Hockey Assn. (pres.), Harvard Bus. Sch. Club Chgo., Econ. Club, Univ. Club, East Bank Club, Mid-Am. Club. Home: 969 Spring Ln Lake Forest IL 60045-2302 Office: 77 W Wacker Dr Ste 4550 Chicago IL 60601 Office Phone: 312-332-7960. Business E-Mail: info@dupartners.com.

DANCEY, CHARLES LOHMAN, retired newspaper executive; b. Pekin, Ill., Nov. 28, 1916; s. Albert Duane and Bertha (Lohman) D.; m. Nina Evelyn Manker, Dec. 10, 1944; children: Richard, Burt Lee, Clinton Dancey. BS, U. Ill., 1938. Reporter Peoria (Ill.) Star, 1938-40, Peoria Jour., 1946-50; editor Peoria Jour. Star, 1958-80, asst. pub., 1980-87, cons., 1987-96, dir., 1993-96; dir., exec. bd. Dirksen Congrl. Rsch. Ctr., 1994-99, ret., 1999. Owner rep., mgmt. bd. WTVH-TV, Peoria, 1956-58 Ill. state comdt. Marine Corps League, 1947; City councilman, commr. fire and plice, Pekin, 1946-50. Col. USMCR, 1941-46, 50-51. Recipient Peoria chpt. B'nai B'rith Citizenship award, 1964 Mem. Inter-Am. Press Assn. (dir., exec. bd.), Am. Soc. Newspaper Editors. Clubs: Mason. Home: 419 Haines Ave Pekin IL 61554-4229 E-mail: china@dpc.net.

DANCHI, WILLIAM C., astrophysicist; BS with honors in Physics, Calif. Inst. Tech., Pasadena, 1978; AM in Physics, Harvard U., Cambridge, Mass., 1979, PhD in Physics, 1983. Postgraduate rsch. physicist U. Calif. Berkeley Space Scis. Lab., 1983—86, asst. rsch. physicist, 1987—92, sr. fellow, 1992—98, assoc. rsch. physicist, 1993—2000, sr. space fellow, 1998—99; astrophysicist NASA Goddard Space Flight Ctr. Infrared Astrophysics Br., 1999—2001, acting head, 2001—02, head, supervisory physicist, 2002—04; sr. astrophysicist, sr. scientist interferometry NASA Goddard Space Flight Ctr. Lectr. physics dept. U. Calif., Berkeley, 1994; vis. astronomer Obs. de la Cote d'Azur, Nice, France, 2000. Contbr. articles to sci. jours. Office: Exploration of the Universe Divsn NASA Goddard Space Flight Ctr Code 667 Exoplanets and Stellar Astrophy Greenbelt MD 20771 E-mail: william.c.danchi@nasa.gov.

DANCO, LÉON ANTOINE, management consultant, educator; b. NYC, May 30, 1923; s. Léon A. and Alvira T. (Gomez) D.; m. Katharine Elizabeth Leck, Aug. 25, 1951; children: Suzanne, Walter Ten Eyck. AB, Harvard, 1943, MBA, 1947; PhD, Case Western Res. U., 1963. Asst. to divsn. pres. Interchem. Corp., NYC, 1947-50; sales promotion mgr. Risdon Mfg. Co., Waterbury, Conn., 1950-55; mgmt. cons. Cheshire, Conn., 1955-57; prof., assoc. dir. mgmt. program Case Inst. Tech., Cleve., 1957-58, lectr., 1959—; mgmt. cons. L.A. Danco & Co., 1957—; lectr. John Carroll U., Cleve., 1959-66, prof., dir. mgmt. confs., 1966—. Vis. prof. econs. Cleve. Inst. Art, 1966-69, Kent State U., 1966-67; exec. dir. Univ. Svcs. Inst., Cleve., 1967-69, pres., 1969—, chmn., 1989—2007; pub. The Family in Business (newsletter), 1978—; pres. Center for Family Bus., 1978—, chmn. Ctr.for Family Bus., 1991-2007. Author: Beyond Survival-A Business Owners Guide for Success, 1975, Inside the Successful Family Business, 1979, Outside Directors in the Family Owned Business, 1981, Someday It'll All Be.Whose?, 1990; (in French) L'Entreprise Familiale, 1998; (in Spanish) La Empresa Familiare, 1998; syndicated columnist: It's Your Business, 1973—. Lt. (j.g.) USCG, 1942-46, PTO. Mem. Am. Econ. Assn. Home: 32000 Fairmount Blvd Pepper Pike Cleveland OH 44124 Personal E-mail: grummi@aol.com. *Whatever success we may achieve in this life will come from the purpose to which we put God's priceless gift of time.*

DANCYGER, RUTH, art historian; b. Cleve., Nov. 11, 1918; d. Henry and Nellie (Friedman) Steuer; married, Dec. 21, 1939; widowed, July 1968; children: Polly Sherard, Emily Edelstein. Student, Goucher Coll., 1936-38; BA, Case Western Res. U., 1942; MA, John Carroll U., 1966. Art historian John Carroll U., Cleve., 1987-93, Cleve. Artists Found., 1986—, also bd. dirs.; art historian Cleve. Artists Now, 1993-95; archivist, historian Temple Tifereth Israel, Cleve., 1998—. Lectr. Midwest Art History Found., 1995-96; catalogue rsch. asst. Cleve. Mus. Art and Ohio Univ. Press, 1996. Author (book) The Temple Tifereth Israel 1850-2000, 1999, Kubinyi and Hall: Cleveland Partners in Art, 1988, Edris Eckhardt, Cleveland Sculptor, 1990, Samuel Bookatz, Cleveland Artist in the Nation's Capital, 1993, Phyllis Seltzer Cleveland Printmaker, 1996. Bd. dirs. Temple Mus., 1984—; mem. mayor's com. Adopt-A-Sculpture, 1993; women's coun. Cleve. Mus. Art, 1994-2004, Cleve. Ctr. for Contemporary Art, 1985—, docent coun. of Mus. of Contemporary Art Ctr., 1989-2000; mem. Cleve. Artists' Found., 1987—, recording sec., 1990-93. Ohio Bell Telephone Co. grantee, 1987. Mem. Cleve. Soc. for Contemporary Art (program and travel planner 1989-96), Print Club of Cleve. (recording sec., 2000-04), Dirs. Cir. Cleve. Mus. Art. Home: 2632 S Green Rd Cleveland OH 44122-1536

DANDO, WILLIAM ARTHUR, academic administrator, geography and geology educator; b. Newell, Pa., June 13, 1934; s. Carl Frederick and Myrtle Jane (Foster) D.; m. Caroline Zaporowsky, July 19, 1958; children: Christina Elizabeth, Lara Margaret, William Arthur II. BS, Calif. U. Pa., 1959; MA, U. Minn., 1962, PhD, 1969. Vis. instr. U. Manitoba, Winnepeg, Can., 1961; instr. U. Md., College Park, 1965-66, lectr., 1967-69, asst. prof., 1970-75; assoc. prof. U. N.D., Grand Forks, 1975-80, prof., 1980-89, chair geography, 1977-82; prof. Ind. State U., Terre Haute, 1989—2002, chair geography, geology and anthropology, 1989—2002, dir. Sr. Scholar Acad., 2002—. Prin. investigator NSF Meteorology-Climatology Project, 1985—92, NIH Multiple Sclerosis Project, 1988—91, NSF Phys. Geography Inst., 1992—96, Dept. Edn. Project GEO, 1992—97, Geo-Technology-GIS Project, 1995—2000, Nat. Coun. Geographic Edn. Climatic Change Project, 2006—. Author: Introduction to Maryland, 1970, The Geography of Famine, 1980, Food and Famine, A Reference, 1991, Russia and the Independent Nations of the Former USSR: Geofacts and Maps, 1995; editor: Innovations in Land Use Management, 1977, World Hunger and Famine, 1995, Russia, 2003, The Geography of the Holy Land: Perspectives, 2005, Climatic Change and Variation: A Primer for Teachers, vol. I and vol. II, 2007; contbr. articles to profl. jours. Pres. Univ. Luth. Ch., Grand Forks, 1979, Christus Rex Luth. Campus Ministry, 1979-87, ND Luth. Campus Ministry Com. 1986-88; chmn. fin. com. Trinity Luth. Ch., Terre Haute, 1992-97, v.p., 1996-97. Recipient Disting. Tchg. Achievement award Nat. Coun. for Geographic Edn., 1986, 98, Burlington Northern Found. Faculty Achievement award, 1988, Illustrious Alumni Calif. State U. award, 1976, Ind. State U. Pres. award, 1997, Ind. State U. Disting. Prof. award, 2000. Mem. Assn. Am. Geography (chair Mid. Atlantic divsn. 1973-74, chair Great Plains-Rocky Mt. divsn. 1978-80, chair West Lakes divsn. 1994-95, regional councillor 1997-2000, West Lakes Divsn. Disting. Svc. award 2002, Am. Geographic Richard W. Pill Miller Svc. award 2002), Nat. Coun. for Geog. Edn. (annual meeting chair 1998), Assn. N.D. Geographers (pres. 1976-80), Geography Educators Network Ind. (dir. devel. 1991-2000), Sigma Xi (U. N.D. chpt. pres. 1986-87, Ind. State U. chpt. v.p. 1991-92, pres. 1992-93, Individual Excellence in Scientific Rsch. award 1983). Lutheran. Avocations: fishing, hiking, auto restoration. Home: 7785 S Carlisle Rd Terre Haute IN 47802-9343 Office: Ind State U Sr Scholar Acad Terre Haute IN 47809-0001 Office Phone: 812-237-7874. Business E-Mail: wdando@isugw.indstate.edu.

DANDONOLI, PATRICIA A., not-for-profit fundraiser; b. 1954; V.p. devel. & exec. dir. planning Am. Mus. Nat. Hist., NYC; dir. strategic initiatives Sundance Inst., Beverly Hills, Calif.; dir. resource devel. Office of Her Majesty Queen of Jordan Rania al-Abdullah, NYC; pres., CEO WaterAid Am., NYC, 2006—. Office: Wateraid America Inc 232 Madison Ave Rm 1201 New York NY 10016-2901 Office Phone: 646-344-7201.

D'ANDREA, DANA M., medical/surgical nurse, lawyer; b. Evergreen Park, Ill., Oct. 21, 1962; d. Anthony Emil and Adrienne Lynn D'Andrea. BS, Ill. State U., 1984; JD, U. Tulsa, 1988; assoc. deg. nursing, Gateway Tech. Coll., 2000. Bar: Ill. 1992; RN. Sr. coord. bids and contracts Fujisawa Healthcare, Inc., Northbrook, Ill., 1993—97; asst. pub. defender Lake County Pub. Defender Office, Waukegan, Ill., 1994—98; nurse St. Luke's Episcopal Hosp. Sys., Houston, 2002—; clinic adminstr. dept. internal medicine Northwestern Outpatient. Mem.: ABA, Lake County Bar Assn., Assn. Women Attys., Ill. State Bar Assn. Home: PO Box 58 Ingleside IL 60041 E-mail: lglnurse2@aol.com.

D'ANDREA, PATRICIA CARLISLE, marketing professional, communications executive; d. James Donald and Stella Fleck Carlisle; m. Steven F. D'Andrea, July 24, 1999; children: Stephen, Lindsay. BS in Tech. Writing, Carnegie-Mellon U., Pitts., 1984; MBA, CUNY, NYC, 1999. Publs. specialist AT&T Bell Labs Publs. Ctr., North Andover, Mass., 1984—87; documentation stds. mgr. AT&T Bell Labs Architecture Area, Holmdel, NJ, 1987—89; sr. publs. cons. AT&T Bell Labs Quality Orgn. (QUEST), Holmdel, 1989—94; comm. mgr. AT&T Transmission Systems, Holmdel, 1994—96; bus. mgr. Lucent Network Systems, Holmdel, 1996—98; market devel. sr. mgr. Lucent Optical Networking, Holmdel, 1998—2002; dir. bus. devel. Intertech Assocs., Inc., Freehold, NJ, 2003—. Adj. prof. Brookdale C.C., Lincroft, NJ, 2002—. Author: AT&T Quality Library: Quality Manager's Handbook, 1990, AT&T Quality Library: Reengineering Handbook, 1991; editor: AT&T Quality Library: Quality Improvement Team Helper, 1990, History of Otisco Lake, NY, 1996. Coun. mem. Redeemer Luth. Ch., Neptune, NJ, 2005—07, dir. music, 1989—2007; fin. devel. chairperson Monmouth Civic Chorus, Red Bank, NJ, 2006—07, singer, accompanist, 1987—2007. Mem.: Soc. Mktg. Profl. Svcs., Assn. Luth. Ch. Musicians (assoc.), Am. Guild Organists (assoc.), Carnegie-Mellon U. Princeton Alumni Orgn., Delta Delta Delta Alumni. Liberal. Lutheran. Avocations: singing, travel, pets, piano, organ. Office: Intertech Associates Inc 77-55 Schanck Rd Ste A-14 Freehold NJ 07728 Office Phone: 732-431-4336. Personal E-mail: carldand@aol.com. Business E-Mail: pdandrea@intertechassociates.com.

DANDRIDGE, LENOR, paralegal; d. LeRoy and Lucille Dandridge; 1 child, LaMont Warren. Student, Malcolm X Coll., 1976—79, Roosevelt U., 1979—83, Harold Washington Coll., 2002—. Owner Dandridge Tutoring and Mentoring, Chgo., 1998—. Author: (children's coloring book) Color N History, 1992, poetry. Cons., vol. Home-Along-With Home, Chgo., 1987—; tutor, mentor YMCA, Chgo., 1998, Hull House, Chgo., 2002; vol., asst. Play and Learn Daycare, Burham, Ill., 1999—; respite worker Ada S. McKinley, Chgo., 2002; vol. Lincoln Park Zoo, Chgo., 2003. Avocations: writing, bowling, modern jazz dancing, exercising. Home: PO Box A3203 Chicago IL 60690-3203

DANE, ERIC, actor; b. San Francisco, Nov. 9, 1972; m. Rebecca Gayheart, Oct. 29, 2004. Actor: (TV films) Serving in Silence: The Margarethe Cammermeyer Story, 1995, Seduced by Madness: The Diane Borchardt Story, 1996, Ball & Chain, 2001, Helter Skelter, 2004, Painkiller Jane, 2005, Wedding Wars, 2006; (films) The Basket, 1999, Sol Goode, 2001, Feast, 2005, X-Men: The Last Stand, 2006, Open Water 2: Adrift, 2006; (TV series) Gideon's Crossing, 2000—01, The American Embassy, 2002, Charmed, 2003—04, Las Vegas, 2004, Grey's Anatomy, 2006—(Outstanding Performance by an Ensemble in a Drama Series, SAG, 2007), (voice): (video game) X-Men: The Official Game, 2006. Office: c/o Grey's Anatomy Los Feliz Tower 4th Fl 4151 Prospect Ave Los Angeles CA 90027*

DANE, STEPHEN MARK, lawyer; b. Chillicothe, Ohio, Mar. 27, 1956; s. Clyde and Rita M. (Murray) D.; m. Kim P. Piatt, July 7, 1979; children: Tara, Adam, Shannon, Alexandra, Courtney. BS with honors, U. Notre Dame, 1978; JD magna cum laude, U. Toledo, 1981. Bar: Ohio 1981, U.S. Ct. Appeals (6th and 10th cirs.) 1982, U.S. Dist. Ct. (no. dist.) Ohio 1983, U.S. Dist. Ct. (no. dist.) Tex. 1983, U.S. Ct. Appeals (5th cir.) 1984, U.S. Supreme Ct. 1985, U.S. Ct. Appeals (7th cir.) 1993. Law clk. US Ct. Appeals (6th cir.), Cin., 1981-82; ptnr. Cooper & Walinski, Toledo, 1986—2004; atty. Relman & Dane, Washington, 2005—. Judge pro tempore Perrysburg Mcpl. Ct., 1990—. Recipient Fair Housing award HUD, 1996, Spirit of Wood County award, 1988, Pub. Interest Law award Equal Access to Justice Com., 2000, Fair Housing award Oho Civil Rights Commn. 2001; named Lawyer of Yr. Lawyers Weekly, 1998; named to St. John's Jesuit H.S. Hall of Fame, 1991. Mem. ABA, Ohio State Bar Assn., Toledo Bar Assn. (chmn. fed. ct. com. 1987-89, trustee 2001--), Wood County Bar Assn. Roman Catholic. Home: 501 Hickory St Perrysburg OH 43551-2206 Office: Relman & Dane 1225 19th St NW Washington DC 20036-2456 Office Phone: 202-728-1888. Business E-Mail: sdane@relmanlaw.com.

DANEHY, ROBERT JOSEPH, aquatic biologist; b. Boston, Sept. 27, 1953; s. Paul Eugene and Mary Theresa Danehy; m. Maryellen Danehy; children: Clare, Ava. BS, Westfield State Coll., Mass., 1975; MS in Fishery Biology, SUNY, Syracuse, 1985, PhD in Aquatic Ecology, 1994. Cert. Certified Fisheries Scientist Am. Fisheries Soc., 1992. Soils rschr. Peace Corps, El Progresso, Honduras, 1976—78; biology tchr. Timberlane Regional HS, Plaistow, NH, 1978—81; staff scientist Lockheed, Las Vegas, Nev., 1985—86, Internat. Sci. and Tech., Reston, Va., 1987—88; restoration ecologist Biohabitats, Towson, Md., 1988—90; aquatic biologist Boise Cascade, Idaho, 1995—2001, Weyerhaeuser Co., Springfield, Oreg., 2001—. Chmn. watershed com. Nat. Coun. Air and Stream Improvement, Corvallis, Oreg., 2003—05; co-chmn. headwaters rsch. coop. Headwaters Rsch. Coop. Com., Corvallis. Editor: (spl. issue) Sci. and Mgmt. Forest Headwater Streams, 2007; contbr. articles to profl. jours. Fellow, Sea Grant, 1981—83. Mem.: Am. Inst. Fishery Rsch. Biologists, N.Am. Benthological Soc., Am. Fisheries Soc. (cert. fisheries scientist). Home Phone: 541-741-5219; Office Phone: 541-741-5219.

DANELO, DAVID JOSEPH, writer, editor; b. Tallahassee, May 7, 1976; s. Danny Michael and Kathleen Thompson Danelo; m. Mary Georgia Reggie, June 15, 2002. BS in Gen. Engring., US Naval Acad., Annapolis, Md., 1998. Commd. USMC, 1998, advanced through grades to capt., 2002; freelance writer Kingston, Pa., 2004—; editor online mil. jour. US Cav. ON Point, Radcliff, Ky., 2006—. Corr. US Naval Inst., Annapolis, 2005—. Author: (nonfiction book) Blood Stripes: The Grunt's View of the War in Iraq, 2006. Decorated Purple Heart, Navy Achievement medal with Combat V; recipient Disting. Author award, US Naval Inst., 2006. Mem.:

VFW, Mil. Writers Soc. Am. (Silver medal 2006), Marine Corps Assn., USMC Combat Correspondents Assn., US Naval Inst. Home Phone: 570-709-6090. Personal E-mail: danelo@dynamisventures.com.

DANES, CLAIRE, actress; b. NYC, Apr. 12, 1979; d. Chris and Carla Danes. Attended, Lee Strasberg Theater Inst., Yale U., 1998—2002. TV role as Angela Chase in series My So-Called Life, ABC, 1994-95 (nominee Emmy award for Best Lead in Drama Series 1995, Golden Globe award for Best Actress in a Drama 1995); appeared in HBO spl. More Than Friends: The Coming Out of Heidi Leiter, 1994; guest appearances on TV series Law and Order, 1990; film appearances include: Dreams of Love, 1992, 30, 1993, Little Women, 1994, Dead Man's Jack, 1994, How to Make an American Quilt, 1995, Home for the Holidays, 1995, The Pesky Suitor, 1995, I Love You, I love You Not 1996, To Gillian on Her 37th Birthday, 1996, as Juliet in William Shakespeare's Romeo and Juliet, 1996, Mononoke-hime (voice only), 1997, U-Turn, 1997, The Rainmaker, 1997, Les Misérables, 1998, Polish Wedding, 1998, The Mod Squad, 1998, Brokedown Palace, 1999, Hercules (voice only), 1998, Igby Goes Down, 2002, The Hours, 2002, It's All About Love, 2003, Terminator 3: Rise of the Machines, 2003, The Rage in Placid Lake, 2003, Stage Beauty, 2004, Shopgirl, 2005, The Family Stone, 2005, Evening, 2007, Stardust, 2007; NYC Theatre appearences include Christina Olson: American Model, 2005, Edith & Jenny, 2007. Named one of 50 most beautiful people in the world, People mag., 1997.*

DANFORTH, ARTHUR EDWARDS, finance executive; b. Cleve., Jan. 23, 1925; s. Arthur Edwards and Jane (Hillyard) D.; m. Elizabeth Wagley, Mar. 17, 1956; children: Hillyard Raible, Nicholas Edwards (dec.), Jonathan Ingersoll, Elizabeth Wagley, Michael Stowe. BA, Yale U., 1948. With Hayden Miller Co., Cleve., 1949-54, First Nat. City Bank (predecessor to Citibank N.A.), NYC, 1954-63, asst. mgr. Buenos Aires office, 1959-61; treas. Bunge Corp., NYC, 1963-65; sr. v.p., treas. Colonial Bank & Trust Co., Waterbury, Conn., 1965-70; chmn., CEO Farmers Bank of Del., Wilmington, 1970-76; prin. Danforthgroup, New Canaan, Conn., 1976-98; ret., 1998. Past bd. dirs. United Way of Del., Boys Club of Wilmington, Grand Opera House Inc. of Del., NCCJ, Audubon Soc. Conn., Greater Wilmington Devel. Coun. Ensign USNR, 1943-46. Mem.: Quail Valley Rivers Club (Vero Beach, Fla.), Yale Club (N.Y.C.), Nantucket Yacht Club, Sankaty Head Golf Club.

DANFORTH, BRYAN NICHOLAS, entomologist, educator; BS in Zoology, Duke U., Durham, NC, 1983; MS in Entomology, U. Kans., Lawrence, 1987, PhD in Entomology, 1991. Asst. prof. Cornell U., Ithaca, NY, 1995—2001, assoc. prof., 2001—. Contbr. articles to sci. jours., chapters to books; co-author: Bee Genera of North and C.Am. (Hymenoptera: Apoidea), 1994. Office: Dept Entomology 3124 Comstock Hall Cornell U Ithaca NY 14853-2601 E-mail: bnd1@cornell.edu.*

DANFORTH, DAVID NEWTON, JR., surgeon, oncologist; b. NYC, June 25, 1942; s. David Newton and Gladys Margaret (Blaine) D.; m. Anne Walker Nickson, Apr. 13, 1985; 1 child, Laura. BA, Northwestern U., Evanston, Ill., 1965; MD, Northwestern U., Chgo., 1971; MS, U. N.Mex., Albuquerque, 1967. Diplomate Am. Bd. Surgery. Intern, then resident Cornell Med. Ctr., NYC, 1971-74, 77-79; clin. assoc. NIH, Bethesda, Md., 1974-77; surg. fellow M.D. Anderson Hosp., Houston, 1979-80; sr. staff fellow NIH, Bethesda, 1980-82; sr. investigator Nat. Cancer Inst., NIH, Bethesda, 1982—. Editor: Diagnosis and Management of Breast Cancer, 1988; contbr. articles to profl. jours. Served to lt. comdr. USPHS, 1974-76. Fellow Am. Cancer Soc., 1979-80. Fellow ACS, Soc. Surg. Oncology, Am. Soc. Clin. Oncology, Am. Assn. Cancer Rsch., Endocrine Soc. Republican. Episcopalian. Avocations: travel, sports, reading. Home: 7301 Meadow Ln Chevy Chase MD 20815-5009 Office: Nat Cancer Inst Surgery Br Bldg 10 Rm 2B38 Bethesda MD 20892 Home Phone: 301-657-4020. Business E-Mail: David_Danforth@nih.gov.

DANFORTH, ELLIOT, JR., medical educator; b. Bainbridge, NY, Oct. 21, 1933; s. Elliot and Ellen (Roberts) D.; m. Joan C. Garrett, Dec. 26, 1959; children: Kimberly H., Noel, Peter E. AB, Dartmouth Coll., 1956; MS, Ohio State U., 1958; MD, Albany Med. Coll., NY, 1962. Resident Dartmouth Affliated Hosps., Hanover, NH, 1962-65; instr. Dartmouth Med. Sch., Hanover, 1965-66; rsch. internist Walter Reed Army Inst. Rsch., Washington, 1966-70; asst. prof. U. Vt. Coll. Medicine, Burlington, 1970-74, assoc. prof., 1974-79, prof., 1979-94, prof. emeritus, 1993—, dir. clin. rsch. ctr., 1980-93, chief divsn. endocrinology, metabolism and nutrition, 1990-93; dir. Sims Obesity/Nutrition Rsch. Ctr., 1992-93; exec. dir. cardiovasc. metabolic rsch. Lederle Labs., Am. Cyanamid Co., 1993-95; med. cons. to pharm. industry, 1996—; pres., CEO Beartown Pharma, Underhill, Vt., 1998—. Cons. Walter Reed Gen. Hosp. Mem. editl. bd. J. Clin. Endocrinology and Metabolism, Jour. Gerontology, Obesity Rsch., Jour. Gerontology: Biol. Scis.; contbr. articles to profl. jours. Served to cpt. U.S. Army, 1966-68. NIH grantee, Washington, 1970-94. Mem. AAAS, Endocrine Soc., Am. Diabetes Assn., Am. Thyroid Assn., Am. Fedn. Clin. Rsch., Soc. Exptl. Biology and Medicine (mem. editl. bd. procs., coun. mem.), Internat. Assn. for Study of Obesity, N.Y. Acad. Scis., N.Am. Assn. Study Obesity. Avocations: travel, farming, fishing. Home and Office: 84 Beartown Rd Underhill VT 05489-9365 Office Phone: 802-899-2349. Personal E-mail: edanforth@adelphia.net.

DANFORTH, JOHN CLAGGETT, lawyer, former ambassador, senator; b. St. Louis, Sept. 5, 1936; s. Donald and Dorothy (Claggett) D.; m. Sally B. Dobson, Sept. 7, 1957; children: Eleanor, Mary, Dorothy, Johanna, Thomas. BA (hon.), Princeton U., 1958; BD, LLB, Yale U., 1963, MA (hon.); LHD (hon.), Lindenwood Coll., 1970, Ind. Central U.; LLD (hon.), Drury Coll., 1970, Maryville Coll., Rockhurst Coll., Westminster Coll., Culver-Stockton Coll., St. Louis U.; DD (hon.), Lewis Clark Coll.; HHD (hon.), William Jewell Coll.; STD (hon.), Southwest Bapt. Coll.; degree (hon.), Va. Theol. Sem., 1990, Holy Cross Coll., 1992, Harris Stowe Coll., 1992, Wash. U., 1995, U. Mo., 1995. Bar: NY 1963, Mo. 1966, DC 1994. With firm Davis Polk Wardwell Sunderland & Kiendl, NYC, 1964-66; ptnr. Bryan, Cave, McPheeters and McRoberts (now Bryan Cave LLP), St. Louis, 1966—68, 1995—2004, 2005—; atty. gen. State of Mo., 1969-76; US senator from Mo., 1976-94; spl. presidential envoy to Sudan The White House, Khartoum, 2001—02; permanent U.S. rep. to UN US Dept. State, NYC, 2004—05; ordained deacon Episc. Ch., 1963, priest, 1964; asst. rector NYC, 1963-66; assoc. rector Clayton, Mo., 1966-68, Grace Ch., Jefferson City, 1969; hon. assoc. St. Alban's Ch., Washington, 1977-94. Chmn. Mo. Law Enforcement Assistance Council, 1973-74; asst. chaplain Meml. Sloan-Kettering Cancer Ctr. of N.Y.C.; asst. rector Ch. of Epiphany in N.Y.C., Ch. of St. Michael and St. George, Clayton, Mo.; hon. canon Christ Ch. Cathedral, St. Louis. Author: Faith and Politics: How the Moral Values Debate Divides America and How to Move Forward Together, 2006. Republican nominee US Senate, 1970; assoc. rector Ch. of the Holy Communion, Univ. City, Mo., 1995—. Recipient Disting. Svc. award St. Louis Jr. C. of C., 1969, Disting. Missourian and Brotherhood awards NCCJ, Presdl. World Without Hunger award, 1985, Disting. Lectr. award Avila Coll., Chancellors medal UMKC, 1995; named Outstanding Young Man Mo. Jr. C. of C., 1968, St. Louis Man of Yr., 1994; Alumni fellow Yale U., 1973-79 Mem. Mo. Acad. Squires, Alpha Sigma Nu (hon.), bd. dirs., Dow Chemical Co., 1996-, Met. Life Insurance Co., 2000-. Republican. Office: Bryan Cave LLP One Met Sq 211 N Broadway Ste 3600 Saint Louis MO 63102-2750 E-mail: johncdanforth@bryancave.com.

DANFORTH, WILLIAM HENRY, retired academic administrator, physician; b. St. Louis, Apr. 10, 1926; s. Donald and Dorothy (Claggett) D.; m. Elizabeth Anne Gray, Sept. 1, 1950; children: Cynthia Danforth Prather, David Gray, Maebelle Reed, Elizabeth D. Sankey. AB, Princeton U., 1947; MD, Harvard U., 1951. Intern Barnes Hosp., St. Louis, 1951—52, resident, 1954—57; now mem. staff; asst. prof. medicine Washington U., St. Louis, 1960—65, assoc. prof., 1965—67, prof., 1967—, vice chancellor for med. affairs, 1965—71, chancellor, 1971—95, chmn., bd. trustees St. Louis, 1995—99, vice-chmn. bd. trustees, chancellor emeritus, 1999—. Pres. Washington U. Med. Sch. and Assoc. Hosps., 1965-71; program coord. Bi-State Regional Med. Program, 1967-68. Trustee Danforth Found., Am. Youth Found., 1963—, Princeton U., 1970-74, St. Louis Christmas Carols Assn., 1958-74, chmn., 1975—; co-chmn. Barnes/Jewish Hosp., 1996-2002; chmn. bd. trustees Donald Danforth Plant Sci. Ctr. Named Man of Yr., St. Louis Gloe-Democrat, 1978. Fellow: AAAS, Am. Acad. Arts and Scis.; mem.: Inst. Medicine. Home: 10 Glenview Rd Saint Louis MO 63124-1308 Office: Washington U West Campus Campus Box 1044 7425 Forsyth Blvd Ste 262 Saint Louis MO 63105-2161

DANG, CHI VAN, hematology and oncology educator; b. Saigon, Vietnam, Nov. 2, 1954; came to U.S., 1967; s. Chieu Van and Nga Ngoc (Nguyen) D.; m. Mary Doreen Seeley, May 18, 1985; children: Eric Van, Vanessa Marie. BS in Chemistry, U. Mich., 1975; PhD in Chemistry, Georgetown U., 1978; MD, Johns Hopkins U., 1982. Diplomate Am. Bd. Internal Medicine, Am. Bd. Med. Oncology. Resident in internal medicine Johns Hopkins Hosp., Balt., 1982-85; fellow in hematology and oncology U. Calif., San Francisco, 1985-87; asst. prof. medicine Johns Hopkins U., 1987-91, assoc. prof., 1991-97, assoc. prof. oncol., pathology, molecular biology & genetics, 1995-97, dir. hematology, 1993—2003, prof. medicine, oncology, and pathology, 1997—, prof. cell biology, 2001—, dep. dir. basic rsch., dept. medicine, 1996-99, co-dir. immunology and hematopoiesis, oncology, 1998-2000; vice dean rsch. Johns Hopkins Sch. Medicine, 2000—; Johns Hopkins Family prof. oncology rsch., 2004—. Mem. oncological scis. path B NIH, Bethesda, Md., 1993-97; cons. Abbott Lab., 2002, Novartis, East Hanover, NJ, 1993-98, Genentech, South San Francisco, Calif., 1995; sci. adv. bd. Lion Pharm. Corp., Balt.; bd. scientific counselors Nat. Cancer Inst. Contbr. articles to profl. jours. including Nature, Molecular and Cellular Biology, Genes and Devel. Sci.; mem. editl. bd. Jour. Clin. Invest., 1998—, Neoplasia, 1999—, Jour. Molecular Medicine, 2005—, Molecular Cell Biology, 2006-, Cancer Rsch., 2000—, sr. editor, 2003— Scholar Leukemia Soc. Am., 1992-97, Stohlman scholar award Leukemia Soc. Am., 1996, Merit award NIH/NCI, 1999. Mem. Assn. Am. Physicians, Am. Soc. for Clin. Investigation (pres. 2002-03), Inst. Medicine NAS, Phi Beta Kappa, Alpha Omega Alpha, Phi Lambda Upsilon. Avocations: india ink sketching, poetry. Home: 217 Upnor Rd Baltimore MD 21212-3425 Office: Johns Hopkins Univ Sch Med Ross 1032 720 Rutland Ave Baltimore MD 21205-2109 Business E-Mail: cvdang@jhmi.edu.

DANG, CHINH, information scientist; BA in Biology, U. Denver; MS in Info. Sys., U. Colo. Dir., tech., Allen Brain Atlas project Allen Inst. for Brain Sci., Seattle. Co-recipient Rave award-Science, WIRED Mag., 2007. Office: Allen Inst for Brain Sci 551 N 34th St Seattle WA 98103

DANG, KIMBERLY ALLEN, energy executive; B in Acctg., Tex. A&M U., College Station; MBA, Northwestern U. With venture capital firm, Austin, Tex.; legis. asst. US Congressman Jack Fields, Washington; with real estate investment area Goldman Sachs; dir. investor rels. Kinder Morgan, Houston, 2001—02, v.p. investor rels., 2002—, treas., 2004, CFO. Office: Kinder Morgan 500 Dallas St Ste 1000 Houston TX 77002 Office Phone: 713-369-9000.*

DANG, MARVIN S.C., lawyer; b. Honolulu, 1954; s. Brian K.T. and Flora Dang. BA with distinction, U. Hawaii, 1974; JD, George Washington U., 1978. Bar: Hawaii 1978, U.S. Dist. Ct. Hawaii 1978, U.S. Ct. Appeals (9th cir.) 1979. Atty. Gerson, Steiner & Anderson and predecessor firms, Honolulu, 1978-81; pvt. practice Honolulu, 1981—. Sr. v.p., bd. dirs. Rainbow Fin. Corp., Honolulu, 1984-95; bd. dirs. Foster Equipment Co. Ltd., Honolulu, 1986-, Hawaii Cmty. Reinvestment Corp., 1994-96; vice chmn. Hawaii Fin. Svcs. Assn. Polit. Action Com., 1988-95, sec./treas., 1999—; hearings officer (per diem) Adminstrv. Drivers License Revocation Office, Honolulu, 1991-95. State rep., asst. minority floor leader Hawaii State Legislature, Honolulu, 1982-84, mem. Hawaii identity theft task force, 2005-, vice-chmn., 2006-; chmn., vice chmn., mem. Manoa Neighborhood Bd., Honolulu, 1979-82, 84-87; pres., v.p., mem. Hawaii Coun. on Legal Edn. for Youth, Honolulu, 1979-86; mem. Hawaii Bicentennial Commn. of U.S. Constn., Honolulu, 1986-88. Recipient Cert. of Appreciation award Hawaii Speech-Lang.-Hearing Assn., Honolulu, 1984; named one of Ten Outstanding Young Persons of Hawaii, Hawaii State Jaycees, 1983. Mem. ABA (spl. com. youth edn. for citizenship 1979-85, 89-92, Hawaii membership chmn. 1981-93, standing com. law and electoral process 1985-89, exec. coun. young lawyers divsn. 1986-88, coun. fund for justice and edn. 1993-99, standing com. group and prepaid legal svcs. 2000-03, standing com. delivery of legal svcs. 2003-06, coalition for justice 2006—), Hawaii State Bar Assn. (bd. dirs. young laywers divsn. 1990, bd. dirs. collection law sect. 1999—, chair collection law sect. 1999-2005), Am. Prepaid Legal Svcs. Inst. (bd. dirs. 2000-2003), Hawaii Fin. Svcs. Assn. (sec. 1991, 2002-03, treas. 1992, 2003—, v.p. 1993, pres. 1994, lobbyist 1996—). Avocations: law, politics. Office: PO Box 4109 Honolulu HI 96812-4109 Office Phone: 808-521-8521. Business E-Mail: dangm@aloha.net.

D'ANGELO, CHRISTOPHER SCOTT, lawyer; b. Phila., Aug. 30, 1953; s. George Anthony and Antonia Scott (Billett) D'A.; m. Betsy Hart Josephs, May 22, 1982; children: John Robert, Christopher Hart, Caroline Colt, Jennifer Scott. BA with honors and distinction, U. Va., 1975, JD, 1978. Bar: Pa. 1978, U.S. Dist. Ct. (ea. dist.) Pa. 1978, (mid. dist.) Pa. 1992, U.S. Ct. Appeals (3d cir.) 1978, U.S. Supreme Ct. 1981. From assoc. to ptnr. Montgomery, McCracken, Walker & Rhoads, LLP, Phila., 1978—, chmn. product liability, mass tort sect., 1996—, vice chmn. sports, entertainment, amusements practice group, 2006—. Sustaining mem. Products Liability Adv. Coun., 1985—, case selection com. 1988-91, experts com., 1991—, restatement project com., 1993-2000, bd. dir., 1998-2002, aggregation claims project com., 1998-2005, chmn. bylaws com.; mem. Am. Law. Inst., 1996—, mem. consultative group-products liability, mem. consultative group-Aggregation Claims, mem. consultative group-torts, 1996—; lectr. in field. Co-founder The Declaration (U. Va. newsweekly), 1973-75; Editor: Counsel Table, 1990-94; contbr. articles to profl. jours. Mem. Internat. Vis. Ctr., Phila., 1982—, bd. dir., 1987-90, chmn. long range fin. com., 1987-89, counsel for COMPASS (young profl. and spl. events div. of ctr.), 1982-89, exec. com., 1982-89; selection com. Jefferson Scholars U. Va., Phila., 1980-84, chmn., 1981-82; fundraiser U.S. Ski Team, Phila., 1979-90, chmn., 1982-83, 87; fundraiser Acad. Natural Scis., Phila, 1979-88; trustee Episcopal Acad., Merion, Pa., 1988-2006, emeritus trustee, 2006—, fin. com., 1988-97, 2000-06, property com., 1998-2006, exec. com., 1999-2006; chmn. ann. giving campaigns Episcopal Acad., 1983-88; bd. mgrs. Episc. Acad. Alumni Soc., Merion, Pa., 1983-92, treas., 1984-85, v.p. 1985-88, pres. 1988-91; treas., exec. com., bd. dirs. Phila. Art Alliance, 1980-86; bd. dir. English Speaking Union U.S., 1979-82, chmn. young mem. group, 1980-83; bd. dirs. English Speaking Union Phila., 1980-88, chmn. fin. com., 1985-88; counsel honor com. and judiciary com. U. Va., 1976-78; nominating com. St. Christopher's Ch., Gladwyne, Pa., 1989-91; fundraiser Friends Sch., Haverford, Pa., 1987-89; lay reader, min. Ch. of the Redeemer, Bryn Mawr, Pa., 1992—, mem. capital campaign, 1993-1995, head usher, 1993-2001, chmn. Stewardship Com., 1997-98, vestry, 1997-2000; trophy com. Devon (Pa.) Horse Show, 1978—; mem. com. Benjamin Franklin Inst. Nat. Meml. Awards, 1995-98, bd. dir. Haverford Civic Assn., 2004-. Mem. ABA (mem. sect. litigation, products liability com., sect. internat. law, corp. counsel com. sect. intellectual property), Pa. Bar Assn. (exec. com. young lawyers divsn. 1979-85), Phila. Bar Assn., Products Liability Adv. Coun. (mem. Am. Law Inst. com., 1993-2000, case selection com., 1988-91, mem. experts com. 1991—, bd. dir. 1998-2002, chmn. bylaws com. 1998—), Def. Rsch. Inst. (products liability com., bus. litigation com., drug and med. device com., co-chmn European Corporate Outreach Com. 2002, vice chmn. internat. law com. 2001-03, chmn. 2003-05), Fedn. Def. and Corp. Counsel, Internat. Assn. Def. Counsel (chmn. bylaws com. 2003—, bd. dir. 2004-, mem. mgmt. task force 2006—, mem. fin. com. 2006—, mem. products liability com., bus. litigation com., chmn. 2001-03, drug and med. device com., complex class action com., internat. com., vice chmn. 2003-05, corp. counsel com.), Acad. Natural Scis., Anthenaeum, Phila. Mus. Art, Phila. Zoo, Merion Cricket Club (Haverford), Penn Club, IV St. Club, The Assemblies, Phila. Club. Republican. Avocations: sailing, photography, travel, squash. Office: Montgomery McCracken Walker & Rhoads LLP 123 S Broad St Fl 28 Philadelphia PA 19109-1099 Office Phone: 215-772-7397. E-mail: cdangelo@mmwr.com.

DANGELO, EUGENE MICHAEL, elementary school educator; b. Greensburg, Pa., Oct. 6, 1955; s. Louis Anthony and Dolores Joan (Sylvester) D. BS in Music Edn., Duquesne U., 1977, MusM in Composition, 1979; PhD in Tchr. Devel., U. Pitts., 1985. Cert. music edn. grades K-12, elem. sch. prin. grades K-8, Pa. Educator music, dir. choral & orch. Winchester-Thurston Sch., Pitts., 1985—88; educator music, dir. choral Mt. Pleasant Area Sch. Dist., Pa., 1988—99, dir. elem. band, 1999—. Mus. dir., prin. condr. Greensburg (Pa.) Mus. Soc. Philharm. Winds, 1990-95; adj. asst. prof. grad. edn. Seton Hill U., Greensburg, 1995—; adj. grad. outreach edn. faculty Gannon U., 2005—; edn. adv. bd. Tim Murphy U.S. Congress, Pa., 2005— Composer: All That I Might Be, 1987, Centennial Suite, 1987, The B. Cool Jingle, 1992, Millenium Fanfare and March, 2000, With Fire of Love, 2004, Psalm 27, 2005, Blue Rhumba, 2005. Westmoreland County Labor Conf. rep. Am. Fedn. Musicians Local 339, Greensburg, 1992; adv. bd. exemplary tchr. database US Dept. Edn., 1998—; oranist, cantor St. Paul Ch., 1982—92, voting mem. parish coun., 1986—87, dir. liturgical music, 1989—92; dir. music and liturgy St. Bede Ch., Bovard, Pa., 1993—96; dir. music St. Pius X Ch., Mt. Pleasant, 1998—2002; voting mem. St. Paul Elem. Sch. Bd. Edn., Greensburg, 1991—95; devel. adv. bd. Holy Cross Elem. Sch., Youngwood, Pa., 1998; mem. adv. coun. Greensburg Ctrl. Cath. HS, 2005—; dir., supr. liturgy and music Mt. Pleasant Cath. Chs., 2000—02; dir. music St. Mary Czestochowa Cath. Ch., 2005—06, St. Bede Ch., Bovard, Pa., 2006—, St. Mary Ch., Forbes Road, Pa., 2006—. Mem. ASCD, Nat. Assn. Pastoral Musicians, Am. Choral Dirs. Assn., U. Pitts. Doctoral Assn. Educators (life), Pa. Music Educators Assn., Music Educators Nat. Conf. (nat. registered music educator, 1991—), Mt. Pleasant Choral Soc. (founder, mus. dir. 2003-05), Pa. State Edn. Assn. Westmoreland Edn. Coun., Pi Lambda Theta Democrat. Roman Catholic. Avocations: genealogy, coin collecting/numismatics, stamp collecting/philately, radio communications, astronomy, auto restoration. Home: 271 Iowa St Greensburg PA 15601-3905 Office: Mt Pleasant Area Sch Dist RR 4 Mount Pleasant PA 15666-9804 Office Phone: 724-547-4100 3003. Personal E-mail: dremdangelo@verizon.net. Business E-Mail: Edangelo@mpasd.net, dangelo@setonhill.edu.

D'ANGELO, FRANK JOSEPH, literature and language professor; b. New Orleans, Nov. 29, 1928; s. Francesco and Mariana D'Angelo; m. Sylvia Snoddy D'Angelo; children: Frank, Susan, Marc, Stephen, Lori Ann. BS cum laude, Loyola U., New Orleans, 1960; MA, Tulane U., New Orleans, 1963; PhD, U. Nebr., Lincoln, 1970. Prof. English Ariz. State U., Tempe, 1970—95, dir. composition, 1971—79, prof. emeritus, 1995—. Spkr. in field. Author: A Conceptual Theory of Rhetoric, 1975, Process & Thought in Composition, 1985, Composition in the Classical Tradition, 2000; advisory editor: Rhetoric Rev., 1982—95, Jour. Advanced Composition, 1986—95, Encyc. Rhetoric & Composition, 1995—96; contbr. articles to books and jours. Staff sgt. US Army, 1961—63. Recipient Richard Braddock award, Conf. Coll. Composition, Urbana, Ill., 1977, Edward Corbett award, Focuses Jour., 1992. Mem.: Rhetoric Soc. Am. (bd.d irs. 1982—86), Nat. Coun. Tchrs. English (mem. exec. com. 1980), Modern Lang. Assn. (chair writing divsn. 1985). Democrat. Roman Catholic. Avocations: reading, music. Home: 2482 E Nathan Way Chandler AZ 85225

D'ANGELO, JOSEPH FRANCIS, publishing executive; b. Astoria, NY, July 4, 1930; s. Frank and Matilda (Oliveri) D'A.; m. Marcia Elaine Mackie, Mar. 4, 1965; children: Elena, Joseph Francis. BBA, St. John's U., 1952; PhD (hon.), St. John's U., William Penn Coll. Mem. Haskins & Sells CPAs, NYC, 1952-61; treas., contr. internat. ops. Borden Co., Panama and P.R., 1961-65; from v.p. to pres. King Features Syndicate divsn. Hearst Corp., NYC, 1973-96, chmn., 1997—; resident contr., 1965-73; bus. mgr., 1968-73; gen. mgr., 1973-75; pres., dir. King Features Syndicate, Inc., 1973-97. Pres., bd. dirs. Cowles Syndicate Inc., 1986-97, NAS, Inc., 1987-97; chmn. King Features Syndicate, Inc., Cowles, Inc., NAS, Inc., 1997—. Mem. Com. of 300 Archdiocese of N.Y.; bd. dirs. Alcoholism Coun. Greater N.Y.; trustee Emerson Coll., Boston, North Shore Univ. Hosp., pres. Mus. Cartoon Art and Hall of Fame, Boca Raton, Fla., Bd. of Trade. Mem. Artists and Writers Assn., Nat. Cartoonists Soc., Newspaper Features Coun., N.Y. Newspaper Pubs. Assn., N.Y. State Soc. Newspaper Editors, So. Newspaper Pubs. Assn., Sigma Delta Chi, Dutch Treat Club, Friars Club, N.Y. Athletic Club, Overseas Press Club, Wheatley Hills Golf Club, Knights of Malta. Republican. Roman Catholic. Office: King Features Syndicate Inc 300 West 57th St New York NY 10019 Business E-Mail: jdangelo@hearst.com.

D'ANGELO, ROBERT WILLIAM, lawyer; b. Buffalo, Nov. 10, 1932; s. Samuel and Margaret Theresa Guercio D'A.; m. Ellen Frances Neary, Sept. 17, 1959; children: Christopher Robert, Gregory Andrew. BBA, Loyola U., LA, 1954; JD, UCLA, 1960. Bar: Calif. 1960; cert. specialist taxation law. Practiced in, LA, 1960-89; mem. firm. Myers & D'Angelo, Pasadena, Calif., 1967—. Adj. prof. law, taxation Whittier Coll. Sch. of Law., 1981. Served to capt. USAF, 1954—57. Mem. ABA, AICPA, State Bar Calif., L.A. County Bar Assn., Wilshire Bar Assn., Pasadena Bar Assn., Calif. Soc. CPAs, Am. Assn. Atty. CPAs, Calif. Assn. Atty. CPAs (pres. 1980), Phi Delta Phi, Alpha Sigma Nu. Home: 1706 Highland Ave Glendale CA 91202-1265 Office: 301 N Lake Ave Ste 800 Pasadena CA 91101-4108 Office Phone: 626-792-0007. Personal E-mail: m-dlaw@pacbell.net.

D'ANGELO, VINCENT A., diversified financial services company executive, consultant; b. Lanciano, Chieti, Italy, Apr. 2, 1944; arrived in US, 1957; s. Rocco and Antonietta D'Angelo; m. Marie Lopez, Sept. 20, 1969; children: Claudine Marie, Adam Rocco. BBA in Acctg., St. Francis Coll., Bklyn., 1965. CPA NY, NJ, Conn. Ptnr. Coopers & Lybrand LLP, NYC, 1968—98, Pricewaterhouse Cooper LLP, NYC, 1998—2005; cons. Kinnelon, NJ, 1995—96; sr. v.p. fin. L-1 Identity Solutions, Stamford, Conn., 1996—. Mem. Columbus Citizens found., 1991. Sgt. US Army, 1965—67, Vietnam. Decorated Bronze Star with V. Mem.: AICPA. Avocations: skiing, reading.

D'ANGELO MELBY, DONNA MARIE, lawyer; BA, U. Calif., 1972; JD, Calif. Western Sch. Law, 1978. Bar: Calif. 1979. Ptnr. Sonnenschein, Nath & Rosenthal LLP, LA. Apptd. Jud. Sect. Adv. Panel; spkr. in field. Contbr. articles to profl. jours. Bd. dirs. Wellness Cmty. Foothills. Named one of Top 30 Women Litigators, L.A. and San Francisco Daily Jour., 2002, 2003, 2004, 100 Most Influential Attys. in Calif., L.A. Daily Jour., San Francisco Recorder, 2004, Top 5% So. Calif. Super Lawyers, Los Angeles Mag. & Law and Politics, 2004, 2005. Fellow: Internat. Soc. Barristers, Am. Coll. Trial Lawyers; mem.: ABA (mem. litigation sect., labor sect., employment sect), Fedn. Def. and Corp. Counsel, Internat. Assn. Def. Counsel, Def. Rsch. Inst., State Bar Calif. (trustee legal svcs. trust fund commn. 1985—86, 1997), L.A. Bar Assn. (mem. labor and employment law sect.), Fed. Bar Assn., Women Lawyers Assn. L.A., Calif. Women Lawyers, Am. Bd. Trial Advocates (exec. com. L.A. chpt. 1995—, mem. pres.'s coun. 1997, co-chair civil justice and nat. office com. 2001, nat. bd. dirs., nat. pres. 2005, pres. L.A. chpt. 2004). Office: Sonnenschein Nath & Rosenthal LLP 601 S Figueroa St Ste 1500 Los Angeles CA 90017 Office Phone: 213-892-5027. Business E-Mail: dmelby@sonnenschein.com.

DANGERFIELD, JOSEPH ALLEN, composer, educator; b. Beckley, W.Va., Feb. 12, 1977; s. C. Allen and Jo Ellen Dangerfield; m. Ami Leigh Dean, Sept. 29, 2001; children: Conner Allen, Piper Elyana. MusM, Bowling Green State U., Ohio, 2002; PhD, U. Iowa, Iowa City, 2005. Asst. prof. McNeese State U., Lake Charles, La., 2005—06, Coe Coll., Cedar Rapids, Iowa, 2006—. Composer: (songs) A Parable of Shadows, 2002 (Young and Emerging Composers award, 2002), Stone Memories, 2005 (Excellence in Composition Pelzer prize, 2005), The Waves Roll on, Thundering and Shimmering, 2006, Dreams of Fin, 2007. Home: 2096 Vista CIR NW Cedar Rapids IA 52405 Office: Coe Coll Music Dept 1220 1st Ave NE Cedar Rapids IA 52402 Home Phone: 319-550-5120; Office Phone: 319-399-8638. Business E-Mail: jdangerf@coe.edu.

D'ANGIO, CARL T., pediatrician, educator; b. Boston, Mar. 27, 1957; s. Giulio John and Jean Terhune D'Angio; m. Donna D. D'Angio, Aug. 22, 1981; children: Sara Jean, Rachel Anne. AB, Princeton U., NJ, 1979; MD, Johns Hopkins U., Balt., 1983. Diplomate Am. Bd. Pediat., 1989. Chief pediat. Ft. Defiance Indian Hosp., Ariz., 1989—91, staff pediatrician, 1998—99; asst. prof. pediat. U. Rochester, NY, 1995—2001, assoc. prof. pediat., 2001—. Contbr. chapters to books. Lt. comdr. USPHS, 1988—91. Recipient Nat. Rsch. Svc. award, Nat. Heart, Lung and Blood Inst., 1995; grantee Mentored Clin. Scientist Devel. award, 1997—2002, Indian Health Svc., 1989—90, Am. Heart Assn., 1997—99, Nat. Inst. Allergy and Infectious Diseases, 1998—2007, Nat. Inst. Child Health and Human Devel., 2001—06, Thrasher Rsch. Fund, 2007—. Fellow: Am. Acad. Pediat.; mem.: Perinatal Rsch. Soc., Soc. Pediatric Rsch. Office: Golisano Children's Hospital at Strong 601 Elmwood Avenue Box 651 Rochester NY 14534 Office Phone: 585-275-2972.

D'ANGIO, GIULIO JOHN, radiologist, educator; b. NYC, May 2, 1922; s. Carlo and Rosa (Calderazzo) D'A.; m. Jean Chittenden Terhune, Aug. 27, 1955 (dec. Nov. 2004); children: Carl, Peter; m. Audrey Evans, Feb. 1, 2005. AB, Columbia U., 1943; MD, Harvard U., 1945; D. Medicine and Surgery (hon.), U. Bologna, 1983. Diplomate: Am. Bd. Radiology, Am. Bd. Therapeutic Radiology. Surg. intern Children's Hosp., Boston, 1945-46. tng. in pathology, 1948-49; resident in radiology Boston City Hosp., 1949-53; also mem. staff; radiation therapist Children's Hosp., Boston, 1956-62; researcher Donner Lab., also Lawrence Radiation Lab., U. Calif., Berkeley, 1962-63; dir. divsn. radiation therapy U. Minn. Med. Sch., 1964-68; chmn. dept. radiation therapy Meml. Hosp., NYC, 1968-76; dir. children's cancer rsch. ctr. Children's Hosp., Phila., 1976-89; prof. radiation oncology Hosp. of U. Pa., Phila., 1976-92, vice chmn., clin. dir. dept. radiation oncology, 1989-92, prof. emeritus, 1992—; prof. pediatric oncology U. Pa. Med. Sch., Phila., 1976-92. Chmn. Nat. Wilms Tumor Study Com., 1968-91; past chmn. cancer clin. investigation rev. com. Nat. Cancer Inst. Editor-in-chief Med. and Pediat. Oncology, 1996-2003; contbr. numerous articles to med. jours. Capt. M.C. AUS, 1946-48. Decorated Commendation medal; recipient ann. award Am. Cancer Soc., 1978, Heath Meml. award M.D. Anderson Tumor and Cancer Inst., 1979. Am. Soc. Therapeutic Radiation Oncologists Gold medal, 1999, U., Prague Gold medal, 2003, cert. merit Pres. Italian Republic, 2003. Fellow Royal Coll. Radiology, Am. Acad. Pediatrics; mem. Am. Acad. Pediat. (past chmn. sect. oncology-hematology), AAAS, Am. Assn. Cancer Rsch., Am. Coll. Radiology, Am. Soc. Therapeutic Radiologists, Mass. Med. Soc., Pa. Med. Soc., Royal Soc. Medicine, Internat. Soc. Pediat. Oncology (pres. 1987), Radiol. Soc. N.Am., Am. Radium Soc., Soc. Pediat. Radiology (Gold medal, 2000), Phi Beta Kappa. Episcopalian. Home: 201 S 18th St # 1818 Philadelphia PA 19103 Office: U Pa Hosp Dept Radiation Oncology 3400 Spruce St Philadelphia PA 19104-4206

DANGL, JEFFERY L., biology professor; b. NAR; BS, Stanford U., 1981, MS, PhD, 1986. Prof. John N. Couch Disting. Prof., UNC- Chapel Hill, 1995—; assoc. dir. Carolina Ctr. for Genome Sci. Contbr. articles to profl. jour. Recipient John Lassiter Sanders Teaching Award, UNC, 1998. Mem.: NAS, Bd. on Life Sci. Office: U of NC at Chapel Hill Dangl Lab CB# 3280 Coker Hall Chapel Hill NC 27599 Office Phone: 919-962-5838, 919-962-5624. E-mail: dangl@email.unc.edu.*

DANGOOR, DAVID EZRA RAMSI, consumer goods company executive; b. Teheran, Iran, Aug. 3, 1949; arrived in Sweden, 1950, came to U.S., 1987; s. Selim Eliaho and Ruth (Lehr) D.; m. Ida (Ide) Weitzen, May 24, 1992; children: Rebecca Frances, Diana Katherine, Louisa Faye, Selim Edward. Civilekonom (MBA), Stockholm Sch. Econs., Sweden, 1973 Asst. dir. Scandinavian Supplies AB, Stockholm, 1970-74; asst. corp. treas. AGA Group AB, Stockholm, 1974-76; asst. to v.p. Philip Morris Europe, Middle East & Africa, Lausanne, Switzerland, 1976; dept. mktg. dir. Philip Morris Co. Germany, Munich, Fed. Republic Germany, 1977-80; area dir. No. Europe Seven Up Internat., London, 1980-84; pres. Benson & Hedges Can. Inc., Philip Morris Internat., Montreal, Que., Canada, 1984-86; sr. v.p. mktg. Philip Morris USA, NYC, 1987-92; exec. v.p. Philip Morris Internat., Rye Brook, NY, 1992—. Bd. dirs. Rothmans, Benson & Hedges, Inc., Toronto, 1987—; mem. bd. dirs. and exec. com. Swedish Am. C. of C., N.Y., 1996-2001, chmn., 1998-2001; bd. dirs. Fgn. Policy Assn. N.Y., 1997—. Exec. v.p. Student Assn. Palmgrenska Samskolan, Stockholm, 1966-68; bd. dirs. Student Assn. Stockholm Sch. Bus. Adminstrn. and Econs., 1969-72, Am. Scandinavian Found., 1999—; officer Royal Swedish Coast Art; exec. bd. dirs. Raoul Wallenberg Com. of U.S., 1990-93; trustee Arthur F. Burns Fellowships, 1997—; mem. internat. devel. com. Internat. Fedn. Multiple Sclerosis Socs., 1993-95. Fellow Amaranten, Sweden, 1971. Mem. Swedish Am. C. of C. (bd. dirs. exec. com. 1996—), Sallskapet Club (Stockholm), Hurlingham Club (London), Hillside Tennis Club (Montreal), Southampton (N.Y.) Bath and Tennis Club, The Tuxedo Park (N.Y.) Club. Avocations: squash, tennis, sailing, bridge.

DANGREMOND, DAVID W., art history educator; b. Norristown, Pa., June 8, 1952; s. James L. and Joan O. (Kross) D.; m. Mary Plant Spivy, Oct. 18, 1980; children: Saumel Plant Chapin, Augustus Welles Ewing. BA cum laude, Amherst Coll., 1974; MA, U. Del., 1976, Yale U., 1987, MPhil, 1990. Dir. Webb-Deane-Stevens Mus., Wethersfield, Conn., 1976-80, Bennington Mus., Vt., 1980-96; adj. prof. art history Trinity Coll., Hartford, Conn., 1996—. Adj. prof. art history U. Hartford, Conn., 1977-80; tutor Historic Deerfield, Mass., 1975; trustee Williamstown Regional Art Conservation Lab., Mass., 1981-86, 2001—, Florence Griswold Mus., Old Lyme, Conn., 1987—, v.p., 1992—; trustee Conn. Humanities Coun., 1997—, Essex Savings Bank, 2001—; mem. adv. bd. Gunston Hall Plantation, Lorton, Va., 1985—, Nat. Trust Hist. Preservation; dir. Attingham Summer Sch., Shropshire, Eng., 1980—; profl. adv. bd. Victoria Mus., Portland, Maine, 1985—; bd. overseers Strawberry Banke Mus., Portsmouth, NH, 1987—, v.p., 1988-90; mem. exec. com. Yale U. Art Gallery Assocs., 1987-93; mus. cons. various mus., 1995-; chmn. Newport Symposium, 2002—. Foreword author: Heritage Houses: the American Tradition in Connecticut 1660-1900, 1979; contbr. articles to jours. Bd. dirs. Hartford Architecture Conservancy, 1978-80; mem. adv. bd. Deacon John Grave Found.; mem. art and antiques coun. Conn. Pub. TV, Hartford, 1977-80; mem. concert com. Vt. Symphony Orch., 1980-86; trustee Musical Masterworks, 1992—, v.p. 1998—, pres. 2003—; div. head United Way Bennington County, 1982-84; del. Gov.'s Conf. on Future of Vt.'s Heritage, Montpelier, 1982; sr. warden St. Peter's Episcopal Ch., 1985—; bd. govs. Hill-Stead Mus., Farmington, 1990—; trustee Wadsworth Atheneum, Hartford, 1991—, exec. com., 1995—, chmn. curatorial com., 1995—, chmn. ethics com. 1996—, v.p. 1998—; trustee Conn. Hist. Soc., 1989—, v.p. 2003—. Fellow Historic Deerfield, 1973; Winterthur fellow H.F. duPont Winterthur Mus., 1974-76; Sir George Trevelyan scholar Attingham summer sch., Shropshire, Eng., 1976; recipient: Disting. Advocate for the Arts award, Conn. Commn. on the Arts, 1999, Thomas Hooker awards, 2006. Mem. Am. Assn. for State and Local History (state awards chmn.), New Eng. Mus. Assn. (exec. com. 1985-86), Am. Assn. Mus. (accreditation vis. com., mus. assessment program cons.), Am. Antiquarian Soc., Vt. Mus. and Gallery Alliance (pres. 1983-86), Greater Hartford Assn. of Historic Houses (bd. dirs.), Decorative Arts Soc., Am. Ceramics Circle, Coll. Art Assn., Soc. Archtl. Historians, Century Assn. (NYC), Knickerbocker Club (NYC), Grolier Club (NYC), Hartford Club, Old Lyme Country, Yale Club NYC, Lawn Club (New Haven), Dauntless Club (Essex), Newport Reading Rm. Episcopalian.

DANI, sculptor, painter; b. LA, Mar. 11, 1933; d. Gordon Hale and Gladys Christine Daniels; m. Lowell James Leyrer, Nov. 13, 1954; children: Jacque Sue Fait, Lori Kay Leyrer. Student, Pasadena City Coll., Calif., 1948—51, Laguna Beach Sch. Art, 1980, Orange Coast Coll., Costa Mesa, Calif., 1987—90, Calif. State U., Long Beach, 1990. Art instr. Pks. and Recreation, Costa Mesa, Calif.; tchrs. aide spl. edn. Newport/Mesa Unified Schs., 1968—73; corp. coord. Aminco Internat., Irvine, 1992—98; prin., owner Studio Dani, Ramona, 1972—. Exhibitions include Calif Art Club, 1966, San Bernardino Mus. Art, Calif., 1976—79, U. Miss. Nat. Show, 1977, Nat. Acad. Design, N.Y., 1978, Hudson Valley Art Assoc., 1978, Sothby's, 1996, 1998, Salmagundo Club, 2000, CLWAC Show, 2007. Pres. PTA Assn., Costa Mesa, 1965—66; co-chair Orange County Showcase, 2000; bd. dirs. Costa Mesa Sr. Ctr., 1999. Recipient Mrs. John Newington award, Hudson Valley Art Assn., N.Y., 1981, 1st Pl. Sculpture, Catharine Lorillard Wolfe Show, N.Y., 1995, Sculptor's award, Hillcrest Invitational, 1970, 1982, Art Fest award, Am. Artists Profl. League, 1998, H.A. Fadhi Sculpture award, 2002, Leila Gardin Sawyer Meml. award, 2002. Mem.: Acad. Fine Arts Found. (Rembrandt mem. 2002—), San Vicente Valley Club (pres. 2005—06). Republican. Methodist. Avocations: tennis, golf, swimming, walking. Office Phone: 760-787-9813. Business E-Mail: dani1001@aol.com.

DANIEL, ARLIE V., speech education educator; b. Spencer, Iowa, May 15, 1943; s. Arlie Verl and Eleanor Marie (Grover) D. AA, Iowa Lakes C.C., 1963; BA, Morningside Coll., 1965; MA, U. Iowa, 1978; PhD, U. Nebr., 1981. High sch. tchr. Missouri Valley (Iowa) Pub. Schs., 1965-68, Clinton (Iowa) Pub. Schs., 1971-78; dir. speech edn. East Ctrl. U., Ada, Okla., 1981—. Linscheid disting. prof., 2006—. Co-author: Project Text for Public Speaking, 6th edit., 1991; co-author chpt. in Basic Communication Course Annual, 1994; editor: Activities Integrating Oral Communication Skills for Students in Grades K-8, 1992; contbr. chpt. to Teaching and Directing the Basic Communication Course, 1993; contbg. author Creating Competent Communicators: Activities for Teaching, Speaking, Listening and Media Literacy in the K-12 Classroom, 2003. 1st lt. U.S. Army, 1968-71. Recipient Tchg. Excellence award, East Ctrl. U., 1995, Linscheid Disting. Tchg. Prof., 2006. Mem. AAUP, Assn. Tchr. Educators, Internat. Comm. Assn., Okla. Speech Theatre Comm. Assn. (pres. 1986-87, exec. sec. 1989-92, Outstanding Comm. Educator award 1985, Josh Lee Svc. award 1992, Spl. award for contbns. to profession 1994), Ctrl. States Comm. Assn. (life, exec. dir. 1994-97, v.p., 1997-98, pres. elect, 1998-99, pres. 1999-2000, past pres. 2000-2001, Outstanding Young Speech Tchr. award 1985), Nat. Comm. Assn. (life), Rotary Internat. (chair youth com. Ada chpt. 1994-2003, pres. elect 2002-03, pres. Ada 2003-04, v.p. 2004-2005, dist. 5770 Interact chair 1995-2003, Rotaract chair, 2003—), Pi Kappa Delta. Democrat. Methodist. Avocations: golf, bowling, wine making. Home: 1206 Tower Rd Ada OK 74820-6106 Office: East Cen U Communication Dept Ada OK 74820-6899 Office Phone: 580-559-5214. E-mail: adaniel@csca.ecok.edu.

DANIEL, CHARLES DWELLE, JR., retired military officer; b. San Antonio, Oct. 30, 1925; s. Charles Dwelle and Jean Elizabeth (Stormont) D.; m. Ann Meredith Carter, June 7, 1946; children: Charles Dwelle III, Peter C. BS, U.S. Mil. Acad., 1946; MS, Tulane U., 1961, PhD, 1968; BA in Studio Art, Am. U., 1987. Joined U.S. Army; advanced through grades to maj. gen.; F.A. battery comdr. U.S. Army (3d inf. divsn.), Republic of Korea, 1950—52; adviser Ky. N.G., Louisville, 1953-55; F.A. missile officer 7th U.S. Army Europe, 1956-59; physicist Def. Atomic Support Agy., Washington, 1963-66; F.A. bn. and divsn. artillery comdr. 1st inf. divsn. Viet Nam, 1966-67; divsn. chief, dir. Office of Chief of U.S. Army R & D, 1968-71; commdg. gen. I Corps, Arty., Republic of Korea, 1971; dep. commdg. gen. Korean Support Command, 1971-72; dir. army rsch. Dept. Army, Washington, 1972-74, dir. combat support systems. 1974; dep. comdt. Nat. War Coll., Ft. McNair, Wash., 1974-75; spl. asst. to commdg. gen. U.S. Army Material Command, Alexandria, Va., 1975-77; commdg. gen. U.S. Army Electronics R & D Command, Adelphi, Md., 1977-79; ret., 1979. Dir. target acquisition BDM Corp., McLean, Va., 1979-80; cons. Burdeshaw Assocs., 1981—. Decorated D.S.M., Silver Star, Legion of Merit with oak leaf cluster, D.F.C., Bronze Star with 4 oak leaf clusters, Air medal with 16 oak leaf clusters, Joint Svc. Commendation medal, Army Commendation medal U.S., Vietnamese Cross of Gallantry with silver star; named Hon. Col. 33d Regiment, U.S. Field Artillery, 2003. Mem. SAR, Assn. U.S. Army, Assn. Grads. U.S. Mil. Acad., Jamestown Soc. Magna Carta Barons. Home: 4904 Baltan Rd Bethesda MD 20816-2404 Office: Burdeshaw Assocs Ltd 4701 Sangamore Rd Bethesda MD 20816-2508

DANIEL, CHARLES TIMOTHY, transportation engineer, consultant; b. NYC, Aug. 3, 1958; s. John Carl and Eleanor Daniel; m. Melissa J. Sanft, Mar. 4, 1995. BA in Engring., Lafayette Coll., 1980; MS in Transp., MIT, 1982; MBA, NYU, 1991. Staff engr. George Beetle Co., Phila., 1983-84; project engr. Transamerica Leasing, Purchase, NY, 1984-87. mgr. tech. svcs. White Plains, 1987-89, engring. cons., 1989—. Treas. Midtown Daniel Corp., 1990—, pres., 1995—; mem. domestic freight container stds. subcom. Internat. Standardization Orgn. Tech. Com. Freight Containers, 1986—88. Mem. alumni bd. Rutgers Preparatory Sch., Somerset, NJ, 1985—; bd. advisors Princeton Com. on Fgn. Rels.; county committeeman Middlesex County Dem. Orgn., NJ, 1992—. Mem.: ASCE, Sigma Xi, Beta Gamma Sigma. Lutheran. Achievements include development of code structure for electronic data interchange of freight container chassis repair data. Home: 33 North Dr East Brunswick NJ 08816-1124 Office: Midtown Daniel Corp 34 North Dr East Brunswick NJ 08816-1122

DANIEL, COLDWELL, III, economist, educator, entrepreneur; b. New Orleans; s. Coldwell Jr. and Josephine Agnes (Weick) D.; children: Anne Alexis, Coldwell IV. BBA, Tulane U., 1949; MBA, Ind. U., 1950; PhD, U. Va., 1959; postdoctoral, U. Chgo., 1964-65. Instr. stats. U. Va., 1955-56; instr. econs. Pomona Coll., 1956-57; prof. econs., dept. chmn. U. So. Miss., 1958-65; prof. econs. U. Houston, 1965-70, U. Memphis, 1970—2004, prof. emeritus econs., 2004—. Rsch. coord. So. Calif. Rsch. Coun., 1956-57; vis. prof. La. State U., 1959; sr. Fulbright prof. econs. Dacca U., Bangladesh, 1961-62; Disting. Fulbright lectr. Shanghai Jiao Tong U., 2001; project dir. Miss. Test Facility Econ. Impact Study NASA, 1963; prin. The Anwell Co., Memphis, 1974—; Fulbright lectr. Shanghai Jiao Tong U., 2001; Fulbright sr. specialist U. Sofia, 2006; pres. Coastal Castles, Inc., 2004—06. Author: Mathematical Models in Microeconomics, 1970; reader Jour. Econ. and Bus., 1991-2004, Social Sci. Jour., 1988-2004, Am. Jour. Econs. and Sociology, 1990-2004, Jour. Econ. Edn., 1997-2004, Internat. Econ. Jour., 1999-2004, Am. Econ. Rev., 2000; founder, chmn. bd. editors, The So. Quar., 1962-64; co-founder and manuscript rev. editor Jour. Econs. and Fin., 1977-91; mem. editl. bd. Jour. Econs. and Fin., 1991-94, Jour. Econs. and Fin. Edn., 2002-2004; assoc. editor for econs. Social Sci. Quar., 1968-70, mem. editl. bd., 1972-84; contbr. articles to profl. jours. Trustee Christ United Meth. Ch. With USAF, 1945-46; 1st lt. US Army, 1951-53. Decorated Bronze Star; NSF Sci. Faculty fellow, 1964-66. Fellow Acad. Econs. and Fin.; mem. Am. Econ. Assn., Pakistan Econ. Assn. (life), Southwestern Econs. Assn., Acad. Econs. and Fin. (co-founder, pres. 1977-78, area coord. Indsl. Orgn. and pub. Policy, 1990-94, Disting. Svc. award 1979, Cert. Appreciation 1981), Mo. Valley Econs. Assn. (pres. 1984-85, Meritorious Svc. award 1986), So. Econ. Assn., Atlantic Econ. Soc. (exec. com. 1991-94, area coord. Indsl. Orgn. and Pub. Policy 1989-94), The Raven Soc., Sigma Xi, Beta Gamma Sigma, Omicron Delta Kappa, Pi Kappa Pi, Omicron Delta Epsilon, Pi Gamma Mu, Delta Tau Kappa, Phi Beta Delta, Pi Sigma Epsilon, Delta Sigma Pi. Home Phone: 901-650-5834. Business E-Mail: cdaniel1@memphis.edu.

DANIEL, DAVID EDWIN, academic administrator, civil engineer; b. Newport News, Va., Dec. 20, 1949; s. David Edwin and Betty Ruth (Aschenback) D.; m. Frances Louise Locker, June 12, 1971 (div.); children: Katherine Ruth, William Monroe; m. Susan Nielsen Brady, May 12, 1989; 1 child, Alexander David. BS, U. Tex., 1972, MS, 1974, PhD, 1980. Staff engr. Woodward-Clyde, San Francisco, 1974-77; asst. prof. U. Tex., Austin, 1981-85, assoc. prof., 1985-91, prof., 1991-96; prof., head dept. civil engring. U. Ill., Urbana, 1996-2001, dean, Coll. Engring., Gutgsell prof. civil engring., 2001—05; pres. U. Tex., Dallas, 2005—. Mem. ASCE (Norman medal 1975, Cross medal 1984, 2000, Middlebrooks award 1995, Richard R. Torrens award 1995), NAE Office: Univ Texas Dallas Office of Pres PO Box 830688 Richardson TX 75083-0688 Business E-Mail: dedaniel@utdallas.edu.

DANIEL, DAVID RONALD, management consultant; b. Hartford, Conn., Feb. 26, 1930; s. David Richard and Marion (Ingalls) D.; m. Lise C. Scott; children: David, Peter, Stephen. AB, Wesleyan U., Middletown, Conn., 1952; MBA, Harvard U., 1954; LHD (hon.), Wesleyan U.; DL (hon.), Harvard U. Assoc. McKinsey & Co. Inc., NYC, 1957-63, prin., 1963-68, dir., 1968—, mng. dir. NY office, 1970-76, mng. dir. firm, 1976-88. Contbr. articles to profl. jours. Chmn. emeritus Wesleyan U.; trustee Brandeis U., Thirteen/WNET, NY; chmn. Libr. of Am.; trustee emeritus Rockefeller U., Brookings Instn. Mem. Coun. on Fgn. Rels. Home: 580 Park Ave New York NY 10021-7313 Office: McKinsey & Co Inc 55 E 52nd St Fl 21 New York NY 10055-0183

DANIEL, DECKLER, engineering educator; b. Tiffin, Ohio, Aug. 23, 1963; s. Carl and Sandra Deckler; m. Jan Rowles. PhD, U. Akron, Ohio, 2002. Registered profl. engr., Ohio. Devel. engr. Loral Def. Systems, Akron, 1986—91; prof. engring. Wayne Coll., U. Akron, Orrville, Ohio, 1991—. Author: Six-Minute Solutions for Mechanical PE Exam Thermal and Fluids Systems Problems. Mem.: IEEE, ASME (assoc.), Am. Soc. Engring. Edn. (assoc.). Office: U Akron Wayne Coll 1901 Smucker Rd Orrville OH 44667 Home Phone: 330-497-7684; Office Phone: 330-684-8761. Office Fax: 330-684-8989. Business E-Mail: dcd@uakron.edu.

DANIEL, DONALD CLIFTON, academic administrator, aerospace engineer; b. Mar. 21, 1942; s. Ben Melton and Jimmie Elizabeth (Dobbs) D.; m. Donna Maria Brown, June 13, 1976; 1 child, Jennifer Sim. BS in Aerospace Engring., U. Fla., 1964, MS in Aerospace Engring., 1965, PhD in Aerospace Engring., 1973. Chartered engr., UK. Rsch. engr. The Boeing Co., Huntsville, Ala., 1965-68; rsch. assoc. U. Fla., Gainesville, 1971-72; aerospace engr. Air Force Armament Lab., Eglin AFB, Fla., 1973-88; chief scientist Arnold Engring. Devel. Ctr., Arnold AFB, Tenn., 1988-94; dep. dir. sci. and tech., chief scientist Hdqs. Air Force Material Command, Wright-Patterson AFB, Ohio, 1994-97, acting dep. asst. sec., 1995; exec. dir. Air Force Rsch. Lab., Wright Patterson AFB, Ohio, 1997—99; prin. rsch. engr. Ga. Tech. Rsch. Inst., Atlanta; disting. rsch. prof. Nat. Def. U. Ctr. Tech. & Nat. Security Policy; chmn. NATO Rsch. & Tech. Orgn.; assoc. v.p. U. Tenn., 2006—; COO U. Tenn. Space Inst., Tullahoma, 2006—. Bd. dirs. U. Tenn. Space Inst. Nat. Adv. Bd., Tullahoma, 1984—, Von Karman Inst., Brussels, Belgium, 1991-97; mem. editorial adv. bd. AIAA Jour. of Spacecraft and Rockets, Washington, 1988—. Contbr. articles to profl. jours. Mem. Tullahoma Rotary Club, 1988-94. Recipient Civilian Career Svc. award, USAF, 2002. Fellow AIAA, Royal Aero. Soc. Office: U Tenn Ms01 Frank G Clement Bldg 411 B H Goethert Pkwy Tullahoma TN 37388 Office Phone: 931-393-7213. E-mail: ddaniel@utsi.edu.

DANIEL, ELNORA D., academic administrator; d. Stephen and Cecelia Bell; m. Herman Daniel, Mar. 25, 1961; 1 child, Michael. BS, N.C. Agrl. and Tech. U., Greensboro, 1964; MEd, Columbia U., NYC, 1968; EdD, Columbia U., 1978. RN N.C., 1964. V.p. for acad. affairs Hampton U., Va., 1991—93, v.p. for health, 1994—95, exec. v.p. and provost, 1995—98; pres. Chgo. State U., 1998—. Bd. dirs. LaRabida Children's Hosp., Am. Assn. State Colls. and Univs. (AASCU), Am. Coun. Edn. (ACE), Commn. Adult Edn., Nat. Assn. Equal Opportunity Higher Edn. (NAFEO), Beverly Bank & Trust Co., Little Co. Mary Hosp., Seaway Nat. Bank; nat. adv. bd. Millennium Leadership Initiative Am. Assn. State Colls. and Univs. (AASCU). Contbr. articles to profl. jours., chpts. to books. Mem. LWV Chgo., 1999, Ill. Commn. 50th Anniversary Brown vs. Bd. Edn.; mem. advisory bd. Cmty Violence Prevention Program Ctrl State. U.; prin. mem. Chgo. United; mem. Econ. Club Chgo., Women's Network Chgo., Chgo. Consortium Higher Edn., Comml. Club Chgo., Univ. Club Chgo.; mem. women's bd. Field Mus. Ret. col. Nurses Corp. US Army, 1991. Named to Hall of Fame, Today's Chgo. Woman, 2002; recipient Dir.'s Oustanding Achievement award, Ill., 2002. Fellow: Am. Acad. Nursing; mem.: Jr. Achievement Chgo. Independent. Office: Chicago State Univ 9501 S King Dr ADM/313 Chicago IL 60628 Office Phone: 773-995-2400. Business E-Mail: ed-daniel2@csu.edu.

DANIEL, GEORGE K., cardiologist; b. Cairo, Sept. 2, 1963; s. Kamel E. and Victoria F. Daniel; m. Mariam N. Azer, Aug. 30, 2004. MD, Tanta U., Egypt, 1981. Diplomate in internal medicine Am. Bd. Internal Medicine, 1997, in cardiology Am. Bd. Internal Medicine, 2000, in interventional cardiology Am. Bd. Internal Medicine, 2001, in endovascular medicine Am. Bd. Vascular Medicine, 2005, in vascular medicine Am. Bd. Vascular Medicine, 2005. Resident internal medicine U. Ark., Little Rock, 1994—97; fellow cardiology Ind. U., Indpls., 1997—2000, fellow interventional cardiology, 2000—01, chief cardiology fellow, 2000—01; fellow vascular and endovascular Wash. Hosp. Ctr., 2001—02; dir. vascular inst. Heart Ctr. Ind., Indpls., 2002—06; dir. endovascular medicine cardiovascular lab. John F Kennedy Med. Ctr., Atlantis, Fla., 2006—. Recipient William Nasser Cardiovasc. Fellowship award, Ind. U., 1999, Ann. Fellow Cardiovasc. Rsch. award, Pfizer, 2000. Fellow: Soc. Cardiovasc. Angiography and Interventions, Am. Coll. Cardiology; mem.: ACP (Merit cert. 1995). Achievements include research in trials for novel devices and therapies for minimally invasive treatment of vascular and heart disease; first to use Carotid stents in Indianapolis; use Stent graft for treatment of aortic aneurysm in Indianapolis. Office: Palm Beach Heart Assocs 5503 South Congress Ave Ste 206 Atlantis FL 33462 Home Phone: 561-876-9955; Office Phone: 561-434-0353. Personal E-mail: gkdaniel@pol.net.

DANIEL, J. CHRISTOPHER, health facility executive, family medicine physician, military officer; b. Phila., Apr. 15, 1958; s. Frank V. and Regina Luff Daniel; m. Lorraine Yetsuko Higa, June 19, 1993; children: Penelope Nicole Michiko, Nicholas Wayne. AB cum laude, Princeton U., 1980; MD, Jefferson Med. Coll., Phila., 1984; MBA, Yale U., 2007. Diplomate Am. Bd. Family Medicine (added qualification in adolescent medicine). Spl. asst. for health care matters Office of Sec. of Navy, Washington, 1981—82; basic surgery intern Naval Hosp., San Diego, 1984—85; flight surgeon U.S

Naval Hosp., Subic Bay, Zambales, Philippines, 1986—89, Fleet Composite Squadron FIVE, Naval Air Station Cubi Point, Zambales, 1989—90; family practice resident Naval Hosp., Camp Pendleton, Calif., 1991—93; family physician U.S. Naval Hosp., Naval Air Station Sigonella, Catania, Italy, 1993—96; adolescent medicine fellow Naval Med. Ctr., San Diego, 1996—98; chief med. staff, family and adolescent medicine physician Naval Med. Clinic, Annapolis, Md., 1998—2002; exec. officer U.S. Naval Med. Rsch. Unit Two, Jakarta, Indonesia, 2002—04; commdg. officer Naval Submarine Med. Rsch. Lab., Groton, Conn., 2004—06, Naval Med. Rsch. Ctr., Silver Spring, Md., 2006—. Sr. med. officer, dir. Br. Med. Clinic, NAS Cubi Point, 1987—90; AHA ACLS affiliate faculty, program dir. U.S. Naval Hosp., Naval Air Station Sigonella, 1994—96; founder, dir. Travel Medicine Clinic, U.S. Naval Hosp., Naval Air Station Sigonella, 1994—96; co-founder, dir. San Diego H.S. Football Head Injury Project, 1997—98; clin. instr., dept. family and preventive medicine U. Calif., San Diego, 1997—98; assoc. prof. dept family medicine Uniformed Svcs. U. of Health Scis., Bethesda, Md., 1997—2002; mem. editl. adv. bd. Am. Family Physician, Leawood, Kans., 2002—. Capt. USN, 1980—. Named one of America's Top Family Drs., Consumer's Rsch. Coun. Am., 2002—07; recipient Outstanding Scholar Athlete award, Phila. Evening and Sunday Bull., 1976, 1st prize staff rsch. project, Naval Med. Ctr., San Diego, 1999. Fellow: Am. Acad. Family Physicians; mem.: Naval Submarine League, World Orgn. Family Drs., Am. Coll. Physician Execs. (life), Aerospace Med. Assn. (life), Uniformed Svcs. Acad. Family Physicians, Soc. for Adolescent Medicine (chair internat. adolescent health profls. in tng. 1996—98). Roman Catholic. Avocations: sports, travel. Office: Naval Med Rsch Ctr 503 Robert Grant Ave Silver Spring MD 20910

DANIEL, JAMES RICHARD, accountant, corporate financial executive; b. Chgo., June 26, 1947; s. Elmer Alexander and June B. (Bush) D.; m. Marsha Ruth Stone, Nov. 8, 1969; children: Jennifer Rae, Michael James. BS in Acctg., U. Ill., 1970; MBA, Loyola U., 1974. CPA, Ill., La. Dir. fin. Baxter Travenol Labs., Chgo., 1974-79; corp. contr. Bio-Rad Labs. Inc., Richmond, Calif., 1979-81; v.p., treas., contr. Lykes Bros. Steamship Co. Inc., New Orleans, 1981-84; CFO SCI Systems Inc., Huntsville, Ala., 1984-91; sr. v.p., CFO Dell Computer Corp., Austin, Tex., 1991-93; exec. v.p., CFO, pres. hdqrs. support, treas. MicroAge, Inc., Tempe, 1993-2000; cons., 2000-01; sr. v.p., CFO PetsMart Inc., Phoenix, 2001. Mem. issuer affairs com. NASDAQ, 1995-2001. With U.S. Army, 1970-73. Recipient Outstanding Alumnus award Loyola U. Grad. Sch. Bus., 1995. Mem. AICPA. Republican. Home: 1695 Cherokee Ln Wickenburg AZ 85390 Office Phone: 928-684-6189. E-mail: jdanieletal@aol.com.

DANIEL, JONATHAN ALEXANDER, chiropractor, educator; b. NYC, June 16, 1947; s. Lewis C. Daniel and Hildreth Leona Alexander. BA, U. Calif., Berkeley, 1966—69; DC, We. States Chiropractic Coll., Portland, Oreg., 1974—77; MSCM, Am. Coll. Traditional Chinese Medicine, San Francisco, 1989—92. Lic. chiropractor Oreg., 1977, Calif., 1977, Pa., 1977, NY, 1978, acupuncturist NY, 1992, Calif., 1993, NJ, 1996, Conn., 2003. Prof. Pacific Coll. Oriental Medicine, NYC, 1993—. Commr. Nat. Commn. Certification Acupuncture & Oriental Medicine, Alexandria, Va., 2006. Fellow: Brit. Inst. Homeopathy. Home Phone: 212-206-8368. Personal E-mail: jdaniel1@nyc.rr.com.

DANIEL, KATHRYN HUTCHINS, musician, educator; b. Houston, June 4, 1953; d. Melvin Goodrich and Robbie Edwards Hutchins; m. Robert Norvell Daniel, May 27, 1977; 1 child, Leslie Alison. MusB in Edn. with honors, Tex. Tech U., Lubbock, 1971—75; MusM in Flute Performance, Cath. U. Am., DC, 1978—81. Cert. music & math. tchr. Tex., 1975, Orff Schulwerk, level 1 U. St. Thomas, Minn., 1994, Kodaly Calif. State U., 2003, Kodaly, level 2 Calif. State U., 2004. Prin. flutist USN Band, DC, 1978—87; freelance flutist Kennedy Ctr. Opera Ho. Orch., US Air Force Band, Mid-Atlantic Chamber Orch., Washington, 1987—93; music tchr. Holy Trinity Episcopal Day Sch., Bowie, Md., 1993—96; asst. prof. music Sch. Music, Sam Houston State U., Huntsville, Tex., 1999—. Coord. flute festival Houston Flute Club, 2006—07; pvt. flute tchr., Houston, 1996—99; presenter in field. Children's choir dir. First United Meth. Ch., Conroe, Tex., 1998—2001. Chief petty officer USN, 1978—87, DC. Mem.: Tex. Flute Soc., Nat. Flute Assn., Houston Flute Club (flute fest coord. 2006—07), Alpha Lambda Delta, Pi Kappa Lambda. Achievements include being the first woman to be an instrumental tour soloist with the US Navy Band in DC. Avocations: travel, reading, history. Home: 10926 Kaleo Way Conroe TX 77304 Office: Sam Houston State Univ PO Box 2208 Huntsville TX 77341-2208 Home Phone: 936-441-1914. Personal E-mail: rkldan@consolidated.net. Business E-Mail: kdaniel@shsu.edu.

DANIEL, MARILYN S., lawyer; b. Tulsa, Okla., July 30, 1940; d. Basil M. and Kathryne (Shannon) Stewart; m. John A. Daniel, June 15, 1962; 1 child, John S. BA, Rhodes Coll., 1962; JD, U. Ky. Coll. of Law, 1976. Bar: Ky. Sec. math. tchr., Ky, NJ, 1962—71; legal clerk U.S. Dist. Judge, Lexington, Ky., 1977; asst. U.S. atty. U.S. Dept. Justice, Lexington, 1978—81; gen. counsel Mason & Hanger Corp., Lexington, 1982—, v.p. adminstrn., 1992—96, sr. v.p., 1996—99. Dir. The Mason Co., Lexington, 1990—99, Ky. Bar Assn. for Women, 1991—93; vol. dir. Maxwell St. Legal Clinic, 1999—. Mem. Fayette County Bd. Edn., 1985—88; trustee Transylvania Presbytery, 1985—98; elder Maxwell St. Presbyn. Ch., 1993—. Recipient Women of Achievement award YWCA, 1993. Mem. ABA, KBA (CLE chair ann. conv. 1992), Fayette County Bar Assn. (Henry T. Duncan award 1994. Avocations: gardening, cooking, hiking, quilting, handwork.

DANIEL, PATRICK D., energy executive; m. Dora Daniel; 2 children. BS chem. engring., Univ. Alta.; MS chem. engring., Univ. BC. Pres. IPL Energy U.S.; CEO Interprovincial Pipe Line Inc.; exec. v.p., COO energy transp. svc. Enbridge Energy, pres., COO, pres., CEO, 2001—. Office: Enbridge Energy 3000 Fifth Ave Pl 425 First St SW Calgary AB T2P 3L8 Canada*

DANIEL, ROBERT MICHAEL, lawyer; b. Rocky Mount, NC, Aug. 21, 1947; s. Harvey Derby and Edna Lois (McCullen) D.; m. Kaye Ruth Coates, Aug. 31, 1968; children: Robert M. Jr., John Matthew. AB in Econs., U. N.C., 1968, JD, 1971. Bar: N.C. 1971, Pa. 1976; U.S. Dist. Ct. (we. dist.) Pa. 1976; U.S. Tax Ct. 1979. Judge adv. U.S. Marine Corps., 1971-74; ptnr. Smith & Daniel, Pittsboro, NC, 1974-75; trust officer Mellon Bank, N.A., Pitts., 1975-78; assoc. Buchanan Ingersoll, Pitts., 1978-82, ptnr., 1982—2001; dir. Cohen & Grigsby PC, Pitts., 2002—. Bd. dirs. Cohen & Grigsby, Pitts., 2002; mem. Nat. Adv. Coun., 2005—. Pres. Greater Pitts. coun. Boy Scouts Am., 1996-99, bd. dirs. N.E. region. Col. USMCR, 1966-98, ret. Fellow Am. Coll. Trust and Estate Counsel; mem. Pa. Bar Assn. (past chmn. real property, probate and trust law sect. 1998-99), Duquesne Club. Presbyterian. Avocations: travel, reading. Home: 1491 Redfern Dr Pittsburgh PA 15241-2956 Office: Cohen & Grigsby PC 11 Stanwix St 15th Fl Pittsburgh PA 15222-1319 Office Phone: 412-297-4989.

DANIEL, ROYAL THOMAS, III, lawyer, mechanical engineer, accountant; b. Portsmouth, Va., July 30, 1956; s. Royal Thomas Daniel, Jr. and Lillian Martha (Ellis) Daniel; m. Holly Ann Walsh, Oct. 30, 1993; children: Andrew Joseph, Royal Thomas IV, James David, John Walsh. BS in Nuclear Engring., N.C. State U., 1978, MS in Indsl. Mgmt., 1980; MS in Acctg., Bentley Coll., 1985, MS in Computer Info. Systems, 1986; JD, Suffolk U., 1990; degree in advanced mgmt. program, U. Pa., 2005. Bar: NC 1991, Mass. 1991, DC 1992, NY 2003, NJ 2003, US Tax Ct. 1993, NY 2003, NJ, 2003; registered profl. mech. and indsl. engr., Mass., NC; CPA, Md., NC; cogeneration profl. Assn. Energy Engrs. Sr. proposal engr. Combustion Engring. Power Sys., Inc., Windsor, Conn., 1979—80; coordinating specialist Boston Edison Co., 1980—85, power supply coord., 1985—92; prin. Daniel Law Offices, P.A., Raleigh, NC, 1992—94; v.p. PSEG Asia, Ltd., Hong Kong, 1994—2000; bd. dirs., v.p. Meiya Power Co. Ltd., Hong Kong, 1995—98, 2002—04; pres., bd. dirs. Energy Infrastructure Devel., Bangkok, 1998—2000; vice chmn. ops. and fin. Sri U-Thong, Bangkok, 1998—2000; corp. devel. PSEG Global LLC, NJ, 2000—01, US bus. mgr., 2001—07; dir. mergers and acquisitions PSEG Svcs. Corp., NJ, 2007—. Contbr. chapters to books. Exec. dir. Patriot's Path Coun. Boy Scouts Am., NJ. Mem. NSPE, ABA, Am. Inst. Certification of Computer Profls., Am. Arbitration Assn. (panel arbitrators), Nat. Assn. Accts. (cert. Inst. Cert. Mgmt. Accts.), NC Assn. CPA, NC Bar Assn., DC Bar Assn., Inst. Cert. Computer Profls. (cert. data processor, sys. profl.), Rotary, Order St. Patrick, Phi Delta Phi, Tau Beta Pi. Baptist. Home: 333 Boulevard Mountain Lakes NJ 07046-1517 Office Phone: 973-430-7286. Personal E-mail: royal_daniel@hotmail.com.

DANIEL, SAMUEL J., hospital administrator, medical educator; b. Leeward Islands, Sept. 13, 1950; BA in Chemistry, CUNY, 1974; MD, Columbia U., 1978. Diplomate Am. Bd. Internal Medicine, Am. Bd. Gastroenterology. Intern Roosevelt Hosp., NYC, 1978—79, resident in internal medicine, 1979—80, St. Lukes-Roosevelt Hosp., NYC, 1980—81, resident in gastroenterology, 1981—83; dir. medicine N. Gen. Hosp., NYC, 1995—2001, CEO, 2001—. Asst. clin. prof. Columbia U.; assoc. clin. prof. Mt. Sinai Sch. Medicine, 2001—. Office: 1789 Madison Ave New York NY 10035 Address: 1879 Madison Ave New York NY 10035-3832 Office Phone: 212-360-5090. Business E-Mail: samuel.daniel@ngsc.org.

DANIEL, SUSAN QUALLS, secondary school educator; b. Gary, Ind., Apr. 11, 1958; d. Raymond Dee Qualls; 1 child, Jordan Taylor. BA, Nat. U., San Diego, 1986, MA, lifetime CC credential, Nat. U., San Diego, 1988. Tchr. Oceanside Unified Sch. Dist., Calif., 1990—, night sch. adult edn. tchr., 1997—2001; ESL instr. Mira Costa C.C., Oceanside, 1986—90. Gifted and talented class tchr. Murrieta Sch. Dist., Calif., 1988—90. Author: (anti-graffiti video) California Youth Against Graffiti Video (Outstanding Educator Appreciation award City of Oceanside, 1995). Recipient Marvin T. Levin scholarship. Mem.: Oceanside Tchrs. Assn. (corr.; site rep. 2000—02), Calif. Tchrs. Assn. (life). Avocations: writing, reading, oil painting. Home: 31130 El Torito Ct Temecula CA 92592 Office: Ocean Shores Continuation High School 3131 Oceanside Blvd Oceanside CA 92056 Home Phone: 951-764-5040; Office Phone: 760-439-3142. Office Fax: 760-439-5588. Personal E-mail: susieqintemecula@aol.com.

DANIEL, T., mime performer, theater director, choreographer; b. Chgo., Aug. 23, 1945; s. Theodore Charles and Thelma L. (Soderlind) Heagstedt; m. Laurie Willets, July 14, 1976. BS, Ill. State U., 1967, postgrad., 1969. Cert. Ecole Internat. de Mime. Performer, creator, artistic dir. T. Daniel Productions (Movement & Movement Theatre), Chgo., 1971—. Choreographer (film) Poltergeist III, 1988; choreographer, performer (video) Sweets for the Sweet, 1984; performer, creator (plays) Fantasmia, 1984, Merlin & The Color of Magic, 1986, Structures on Silence, 1988, The Magic of Mime, 1973, A World of Mime, 1971, ImVentionS, musical mims quartet, 2000 Home and Office: 6619 N Campbell Chicago IL 60645

DANIEL, THOMAS L., zoology educator; b. NYC, Aug. 21, 1954; BS in Anthropology and Engring., U. Wis., 1976, MS in Zoology and Engring., 1978; PhD in Zoology, Duke U., 1982; postgrad., Calif. Inst. Tech. Myron A. Bantrell postdoctoral fellow in sci. and engring. Calif. Inst. Tech., 1982-84; asst. prof. dept. zoology U. Wash., Seattle, 1984-88, assoc. prof. dept. zoology, 1988-92, prof. dept. zoology, 1992—, Joan and Richard Komen Chair of Biol. External grad. faculty Oreg. State U., 1987—; mem. various coms. at U. Wash. including chair grad. admissions dept. zoology, 1989-91, chair grad. program dept. zoology, 1991-94, dir. math. biology tng. program, 1993—; panel mem. physiol. processes NSF, 1991—; presenter in field. Mem. editl. bd. Jour. Exptl. Biology, Cambridge U., 1988-90, 93—; contbr. articles to profl. jours. Grantee NSF, 1984-87, 88-91, 91-93, 93, U. Wash., 1987-88, J. Fluke Co., 1988, Reticon, Inc., 1988, Am. Soc. Zoologists Symposium on Efficiency in Organisms, 1988-89, Whitaker Found. for Biomed. Rsch., 1988-91, Howard Hughes Found., 1989-94, M.J. Murdock Meml. Trust, 1989-94, Apple Computer, 1991; MacArthur fellow, 1996. Office: U Wash Dept Biology 106 Kincaid Hall PO Box 351800 Seattle WA 98195-1800

DANIEL, WILLIAM WALTER, JR., retired radiologist; b. Kenosha, Wis., Sept. 30, 1938; s. William Walter and Virginia Mae Daniel; m. Elisabeth Jacqueline Bonomo, Apr. 7, 1960 (div. Mar. 16, 1972); 1 child, Jacqueline Elise. BS, Northwestern U., Evanston, Ill., 1961, MD, 1965. Diplomate Am. Bd. Radiology. Resident Mayo Grad. Sch Medicine, Rochester, Minn., 1968—71; asst. prof. U. Sherbrooke Sch. Medicine, Que., Canada, 1971—73, U. Ala., Birmingham, 1973—77, assoc. prof., 1977—81, prof., 1981—92, U. Iowa Sch. Medicine, Iowa City, 1994—97; with Mayo Clinic, Scottsdale, Ariz., 2000—06; ret., 2006. Pres. Soc. Skeletal Radiology, Schaumburg, Ill., 1984—86; assoc. editor jour. Arthritis and Rheumatism, Birmingham, 1985—90. Contbr. articles to profl. publs. Dir., pres. The Cottonwood Found., Scottsdale, 1997—2006. Capt. USAF, 1966—68. Decorated commendation medal for meritorious svc. USAF. Fellow: Am. Coll. of Radiology (life), Northwestern U. Med. Sch. Alumni Assn. (disting.); mem.: Internat. Skeletal Soc., Soc. of Skeletal Radiology, Radiol. Soc. of N.Am., Alpha Omega Alpha. Avocations: jogging, scuba diving, skiing, travel, history.

DANIEL-DREYFUS, SUSAN B. RUSSE, information technology executive; b. St. Louis, May 30, 1940; d. Frederick William and Suzanne (Mackay) Russe; m. Don B. Faerber, Nov. 27, 1962 (div. Nov. 1968); 1 child, Suzanne Mackay; m. Marc Andre Daniel-Dreyfus, Aug. 9, 1969; 1 child, Cable Dunster. Student, Smith Coll., 1958-60, Corcoran Sch. Fine Arts, 1960-61, Washington U., St. Louis, 1961-62; MEd, Cambridge Coll., 1991. Mng. ptnr. Comm., Inc., 1980-82; asst. dir. Harvard Bus. Sch. Fund, Cambridge, 1982-86; pres. SCR Assocs. Corp., Cambridge, 1986—. Mem. bd. advisors Odysseum, Inc.; bd. dirs. Future Mgmt. Systems. Mem. St. Louis-St. Louis County White House Conf. on Edn., 1966-68; mem. Mo. 1st Gov.'s Conf. on Edn., 1966, 2d Conf., 1968; bd. dirs. Tunbridge Sch., 1973-78, St. Louis Smith Coll.; hon. bd. dirs. New Music Circle; mem. woman's bd. dirs. Washington U., New Music Circle, 1963-67; mem. woman's bd. Mo. Hist. Soc.; bd. dirs. Non-Partisan Ct. Plan for Mo., Young Audiences Inc., 1967-69; bd. dirs. Childrens Art Bazaar, 1968-70; founder St. Louis Opera Theater; chmn. Art. Mus. Bond Issue election St. Louis, 1966; jr. bd. dirs. St. Louis Symphony, 1966-68, Opportunities Indsl. Center, Boston; legis. chmn. bd. dirs. Boston LWV, 1969-72; mem. coun., bd. dirs. Jr. League Boston, 1970-72, 74-76, v.p. Bd. of Family Counseling Services-Region West, Boston, 1979—; pres. Family Counseling Bd., Brookline, Mass.; trustee Chestnut Hill Sch., Boston, Brookline Friendly Soc.; mem. steering com. ann. fund Boston Children's Hosp. Med. Center, 1980-84; v.p. Nat. Friends Bd., Joslin Diabetes Found., 1980-83; mem. corp. bd. Joslin Diabetes Ctr.; v.p. bd. dirs. Boston Ctr. Internat. Visitors, 1979-82; Boston bd. dirs. Mass. Soc. Prevention of Cruelty to Children, 1980-84; exec. v.p. Ctr. for Middle East Bus., 1978-82; pres. bd. Brookline Community Fund, 1984—; overseer Old Sturbridge Village, 1987—. Mem. Colonial Dames, Soc. Art Historians. Clubs: Women's City (dir., Boston); Vincent (dir.). Home: PO Box 638 Altona 3018 Australia

DANIELE, GRACIELA, choreographer; b. Buenos Aires, Dec. 8, 1939; arrived in US, 1963; d. Raul and Rosa (Almoina) Daniele; m. Jules Fisher. Grad., Theater Colon, Ballas Artes, Buenos Aires. Choreographer (Broadway plays) The Most Happy Fella, 1979, The Pirates of Penzance, 1981, Zorba, 1983, The Rink, 1984, The Mystery of Edwin Drood, 1985, Dangerous Games, 1989, Once on This Island, 1990, Chronicle of a Death Foretold, 1995, A New Brain, 1998, Annie Get Your Gun, 1999, Marie Christine, 1999, Little Fish, A Song Cycle, Chita Rivera: The Dancer's Life, 2005; choreographer and dir. (plays) Bernarda Alba, 2006, The Glorious Ones, 2007, musical staging (Broadway plays) A History of American Film, 1978, The Goodbye Girl, 1993, Ragtime, 1998; performer: (Broadway plays) What Makes Sammy Run?, 1964, Here's Where I Belong, 1968, Promises, Promises, 1968, Coco, 1969, Follies, 1971, Chicago, 1975; choreographer (films) Mighty Aphrodite, Everyone Says I Love You, Pirates. Named to Theater Hall of Fame, 2005; recipient Mr. Abbott award for outstanding achievement by a dir./choreographer, 1998. Mem.: Soc. Dirs. and Choreographers (exec. bd. 1985). Avocation: gardening.

DANIELL, HERMAN BURCH, pharmacologist; b. Cadwell, Ga., May 25, 1929; s. Walter and Ruby Florence (Burch) Daniell; m. Mickey Marucheau, May 24, 1952 (dec.); m. Lorraine Smith, June 30, 1957 (dec.); children: Kimberley Ann, Anthony Burch, Walter Herman. BS in Pharmacy, U. Ga., 1951, MS in Pharmacology, 1964; PhD in Pharmacology, Med. U. S.C., 1966. Owner-operator retail pharmacies, Savannah, Ga., 1953-62; instr. U. Ga., 1962-64; USPHS trainee Med. Coll. S.C., Charleston, 1964—66; mem. faculty Med. U. S.C., 1966-92, prof. pharmacology, 1978-92, prof. emeritus, 1992—. Contbr. articles to profl. jours. Served to capt. M.S.C. US Army, 1951—53. Grantee, USPHS, 1966—85, S.C. Heart Assn., 1966—73. Mem.: Am. Soc. Pharmacology and Exptl. Therapeutics, Sigma Xi, Kappa Sigma, Rho Chi. Episcopalian. Home: 1549 Burningtree Rd Charleston SC 29412-2630

DANIELL, JERE ROGERS, II, retired historian; b. Millinocket, Maine, Nov. 28, 1932; s. Warren Fisher and Mary (Holway) D.; m. Sally Ann Wellborn, Dec. 1955 (div. 1969); children: Douglas, Alexander, Matthew; m. 2d Elena Lillie, July 19, 1969; stepchildren: Breena Daniell, Clifford Brodsky. AB, Dartmouth Coll., 1955; MA, Harvard U., 1962, PhD, 1964. Asst. prof. history Dartmouth Coll., 1964-69, assoc. prof., 1969-74, prof., 1974—2003, chmn. dept., 1979-83; class of 1925 prof., 1984—; head tutor Heritage Found., Old Deerfield, Mass., 1960-64; ret., 2003. Author: Experiment in Republicanism: N.H. Politics and the American Revolution, 1970, Colonial N.H.: A History, 1981; bd. editors: Univ. Press of New England, 1978-86. Served to lt (j.g.) USN, 1955-58. Mem. Colonial Soc. Mass., N.H. Hist. Soc. (bd. trustee 1979-86, 1999—), Vt. Hist. Soc., Maine Hist. Soc., Mass. Hist. Soc. Home: 11 Barrymore Rd Hanover NH 03755-2401 Office: Dartmouth Coll Dept History Hanover NH 03755 E-mail: jere.r.daniell@dartmouth.edu.

DANIELLI-GAROFALO, DONATELLA, mathematics professor; arrived in US, 1992; d. Giorgio Danielli and Carmen Festi; m. Nicola Garofalo, Jan. 4, 1992; children: Andrea Garofalo, Francesco Garofalo, Fabio Garofalo, Alessandro Garofalo. Degree cum laude, U. Bologna, 1989; PhD, Purdue U., West Lafayette, Ind, 1999. Asst. prof. Johns Hopkins U., Balt., 1999—2001; assoc. prof. Purdue U., West Lafayette, Ind., 2001—. Vis. asst. prof. Mittag-Leffler Inst., Djursholm, Sweden, 2000. Recipient Tchg. for Tomorrow award, Purdue U., 2004—05; grantee Career award, NSF, 2003—. Mem.: Assn. Women in Math., Am. Math. Soc. Office: Purdue U 150 N University St West Lafayette IN 47907 Office Phone: 765-494-1920. Office Fax: 765-494-0548. Business E-Mail: danielli@math.purdue.edu.

D'ANIELLO, DANIEL A., investment company executive; b. Pitts., Sept. 14, 1946; s. Beatrice V. (Laconi) D'A.; m. Gayle V. Yanicky, Oct. 9, 1976; children: Dana F., Bethany A. BS, Syracuse U., 1968; MBA, Harvard U., 1974. Sr. fin. analyst Trans World Airlines, NYC, 1974-76; dir. planning Pepsico, Purchase, N.Y., 1976-80; v.p. corp. fin. planning Marriott Corp., Washington, 1980-86; CFO, v.p. devel. Marriott Inflite, Washington, 1986-87; co-founder, mng. dir. The Carlyle Group, Washington, 1987—. Bd. dirs. CB Comml., Elgar Electronics Corp., GTS Duratek, Internat. Tech., Inc., Pharm. Rsch. Assocs., Inc., Baker & Taylor Inc., vice chmn. Author: A Model for Airline Route Analysis, 1973, (case study) Braniff International, 1974. Bd. dirs. Fight for Children, Inc., 1992—; vice chmn. events U.S. Holocaust Meml. Found., Washington, 1992; selection com. Pres.' Commn. White Ho. Fellow, Washington, 1993. Lt. (j.g.) USN, 1968-71. Fellow Teagle Found., 1973; named Disting. Grad. Butler (Pa.) Area H.S., 1993. Mem. City Club Washington. Avocations: golf, reading, opera. Office: The Carlyle Group 1001 Pennsylvania Ave NW Washington DC 20004-2505*

DANIELOVITCH, ISSUR See DOUGLAS, KIRK

DANIELS, CAROLINE, publishing executive; b. San Francisco, Dec. 11, 1948; d. William L. and Gladys Daniels; m. Jack Wernick, Nov. 30, 1985 (div.); children: Martin Wernick, Katherine Wernick. Student, U. Dijon, France, 1965; BA in Psychology, U. Colo., 1970; postgrad., Harvard U., 1983-85. Export agt. Air Oceanic Shippers, San Francisco, 1972-73; library supr. Aircraft Tech. Pubs., San Francisco, 1973-75, ops. mgr., 1975-80, v.p., 1980-82, exec. v.p. Brisbane, Calif., 1982-84, pres., 1984—86, CEO, chmn. bd. dirs., 1984—. Pres. adv. bd. Embry Riddle Aero. U.; bd. dirs. Acad. Art U., San Francisco; past bd. dirs. Jr. Achievement of Bay Area. Mem.: Gen. Aviation Mfg. Assn. (bd. dirs., former exec. com., former chmn. pub. affairs com., chmn. safety affairs com.), San Francisco Opera Guild (bd. dirs.). Office: Aircraft Tech Pubs 101 S Hill Dr Brisbane CA 94005-1251 Office Phone: 415-330-9500.

DANIELS, CHARLIE, musician, lyricist; b. Wilmington, NC, Oct. 28, 1936; Founder Charlie Daniels Memorabilia Mus., Nashville, 2001—. Mem. (band) Jaguar band, 1958—67, session man (in Nashville with Flatt and Scruggs) Marty Robbins, Claude King, Pete Seeger, Bob Dylan, others, founder, mem. (band) Charlie Daniels Band, 1971—, recorded for (record cos.) Kama Sutra and Sony/Epic Records, —, records include (albums) Te John, Charlie Daniels, 1971, Grease and the Wolfman, 1972, Uneasy Rider, 1973, Whiskey, 1974, Fire on the Mountain, 1974, Nightrider, 1975, Saddle Tramp, 1976, Volunteer Jam Capricorn, 1976, Volunteer Jam III and IV, 1978, Volunteer Jam VI, 1980, Volunteer Jam VII, 1981, High Lonesome, 1976, Whiskey, 1977, Midnight Wind, 1977 (Grammy award best single of yr. Devil Went Down to Georgia), Million Mile Reflections, 1979, Full Moon, 1980, Windows, 1982, Decade of Hits, 1983, Me and the Boys, 1985, Powder Keg, 1987, Homesick Heroes, 1988, Simple Man, 1989, Christmas Time Down South, 1990, Renegade, 1991, America, I Believe in You, 1993, All Time Greatest Hits, 1993, The Door, 1994, Same Ole Me, 1995, CDB Live, How Sweet the Sound, 2002, Redneck Fiddle Man, 2002, A Merry Christmas to All, 2002, Freedom and Justice For All, 2003, 1st Christian Album The Door, 1994, Super Hits, 1994, 2d Christian album Steel Witness, 1996, SONY Legacy releases 1st CDB box set, The Roots Remain, 1996, By the Light of the Moon, 1997, Road Dogs, 2000, founder (record label) Blue Hat debut for label, 1998, Fiddle Fire, 1998, Tailgate Party, 1999; songwriter:, songs recorded by (songs) Elvis Presley, Gary Stewart, Tammy Wynette, others; actor(appeared in): (TV films) PBS TV film The Lone Star Kid, 1986; also composed score; author: (short stories) The Devil Went Down to Georgia; songs This Ain't No Rag It's a Flag, 2001 (Biggest Single for CDB in 10 yrs.); Gospel album (albums) How Sweet The Sound: 25 Favorite Hymns and Gospel Greats; author: (handbook) Aint No Rag, 2003. Recipient 3 Country Music Assn. awards, 1979, Grammy award for best performance by a country group, 1980, Toys for Tots Man of Yr. award, 1992, Humanitarian award Country Radio Broadcasters Seminar, 1992; named Instrumentalist of Yr., Instrumental Group of Yr., Winner Acad. Country Music's Pioneer award, 1998, Winner TNN Music City News Living Legend award, 1999; named to Wilmington, NC, Walk of Fame, 2002.

Office: The Charlie Daniels Band CDB Inc 17060 Central Pike Lebanon TN 37090-8019 Fax: 615-443-3140. E-mail: paulacdb@aol.com.

DANIELS, CHARLIE L., state official; b. Parker's Chapel, Ark., Dec. 7, 1939; m. Patricia Burleson (dec.); children: Marsha, Chuck. Student, So. Ark. U., U. Ark., Little Rock; LHD (hon.), Shorter Coll. Dir. Ark. Dept. Labor, 1974—80; dir. govt. affairs Ark. Electric Cooperatives, 1980—84; commr. state lands State of Ark., Little Rock, 1984—2002, sec. state, 2003—. Mem. Parker's Chapel Sch. Bd., 1972—74. Served in USAF, served in USAFR. Mem.: Nat. Assn. Secs. State, Ea. Land Resources Coun., Western States Land Commrs. Assn., Ark. Natural and Cultural Resources Coun., Natural Resources Com., State Bd. Apportionment, Info. Network Ark. Bd. Baptist. Office: Office Sec State 256 State Capitol Bldg Little Rock AR 72201 Office Phone: 501-682-1010. Office Fax: 501-682-3510. Business E-Mail: cdaniels@sosmail.state.ar.us.*

DANIELS, CHERYL LYNN, pediatrics nurse; b. Paterson, NJ, June 15, 1951; d. Nathan and Frances Avonna (Bradshaw) D. RN, Martland Hosp. Sch. Nursing, Newark, 1971; AAS in Health and Community Svc., NYU, 1984, BA in Journalism, 1987. Evening charge nurse Martland Hosp. Unit, Newark, 1971-73; staff nurse Heal Econs. Advancement League, Paterson, NJ, 1972-74; neonatal intensive care nurse St. Joseph's Hosp. & Med. Ctr., Paterson, NJ, 1973-77, charge nurse neonatal intensive care, 1977—79, pediat. neonatal ICU, 1979-89, intensive care nurse, pediatric HIV outpatient nurse, 1989-90; rsch. outpatient HIV/SJH case mgmt. nurse Aids Clin. Trial Group, 1990-2001; case mgr. outpatient pediat. HIV Clinic, 1989—; pediat. sedation nurse for CT scan procedures, 2001—02. Mentor Career Beginning Program, Paterson, 1988-90. Recipient Gobetz award, NYU, 1984. Mem. ARC, AACN (cert. pediat. nursing), Alpha Sigma Lambda. Baptist. Avocations: clarinet, swimming, reading, writing, painting. Office: Saint Joseph Hosp 703 Main St Paterson NJ 07503-2691 Office Phone: 973-754-4703. Personal E-mail: danielscheryl@msn.com. Business E-Mail: danielsc@sjhmc.org.

DANIELS, CHRISTOPHER, mechanical engineer, educator; BS in Mech. Engring., U. Akron, Ohio, 1994, MS in Mech. Engring., 1996, PhD in Mech. Engring., 2000. Sr. rsch. assoc. Ohio Aerospace Inst., Clev., 2000—03; rsch. asst. prof. U. Akron, 2003—. Advanced Seal Devel. grant, NASA, 2000—03, Emerging Sealing Tech. grant, 2003—04, Advanced Sealing Tech, Devel. grant, 2004—07. Mem.: AIAA, ASME. Achievements include patents pending for seal with integrated shroud for androgynous docking and berthing in space environments. Office: Univ Akron 302 Buchtel Common Akron OH 44325-3901 Office Phone: 216-433-6714.

DANIELS, DANIEL BAKER, information technology manager, small business owner; b. Jersey City, Oct. 9, 1980; s. Daniel Baker Daniels, Jr. and Debra Jean Higgins. BBA in Info. Tech., Oakwood Coll., Huntsville, Ala., 2006. Info. tech. assoc. Office for Regional Conf. Ministry, Huntsville, 2005—; owner/founder Daniels Media, Huntsville. Fellow: Assn. for African-Am. Collegians, Oakwood Coll. Computer Club; mem.: Phi Beta Lambda, Zeta Alpha Gamma Psi Frat. Inc. Home Phone: 256-658-5838. Home Fax: 530-658-5836. Personal E-mail: daniels_media@yahoo.com.

DANIELS, DANIEL LLOYD, lawyer; b. New Milford, Conn., Nov. 17, 1962; s. C. Ross Jr. and Fayne M. (McGrath) D.; m. Jennifer A. Matteis, Aug. 27, 1988; children: Benjamin T., Elizabeth S. AB summa cum laude, Dartmouth Coll., Hanover, NH, 1984; JD cum laude, Harvard U., Cambridge, Mass., 1987. Bar: NY 1988, Conn. 1991. Law clk. Mass. Supreme Ct., Boston, 1987-88; assoc. Sullivan & Cromwell, NYC, 1988-89; prin. Settle Agy., Inc., Danbury, Conn., 1989-91; assoc. Cummings & Lockwood, Stamford, Conn., 1991-96, ptnr., 1997—2004, chmn. pvt. clients grp., 2005—. Contbg. author: The 401(K) Plan Handbook, 1997; columnist Trusts & Estates Mag., 2005-. Mem. Danbury Econ. Devel. Commn., 1991; bd. dirs. Cmty. Ctrs., Inc., Greenwich, Conn., 1994-96, Cmty. Answers at Greenwich Libr., 1996-98, Fairfield County Com. Fedn., 2005-. Named one of Top 100 Attys., Worth mag., 2005—06. Fellow Am Coll. Trust and Estate Counsel; mem. ABA, Conn. Bar Assn. (presenter 1996, mem. estates and probate exec. com. 1999—), NY State Bar Assn., Stamford-Norwalk Regional Bar Assn., Harvard Law Sch. Assn. Conn. (trustee Stamford 1995—). Avocations: a capella singing, gilbert and sullivan, musical theater. Office: Cummings & Lockwood 6 Landmark Sq Stamford CT 06901 Office Phone: 203-351-4203. E-mail: ddaniels@cl-law.com.

DANIELS, DEBORAH JEAN, lawyer, former federal agency administrator; BA, De Pauw U., 1973; JD, Ind. U. Bar: Ind. 1977, admitted to practice: US Dist. Ct. (So. Dist.) Ind. 1977, US Ct. Appeals (7th Cir.) 1977, US Supreme Ct. 1987. Chief counsel, Marion County, Ind.; ptnr. Kreig DeVault, LLP, Indpls., 1991—96, 2005—; US atty. U.S. Dist. Ct. (So. Dist.) Ind., 1988—93; first dir. exec. office Weed and Seed US Dept. Justice, 1992—93, asst. atty. gen. justice programs Washington, 2001—05. Exec. dir. Greater Indpls. Progress Com., Inc., 1994—96. Office: Krieg DeVault LLP One Indiana Sq Ste 2800 Indianapolis IN 46204 Office Phone: 317-238-6253. Office Fax: 317-636-1507. E-mail: ddaniels@kdlegal.com.

DANIELS, DIANA M., lawyer, retired publishing executive; b. Dillon, Mont. children: Dana, Daphne. BA, Cornell U., 1971; JD, Harvard U., 1974; M of City Planning, MIT, 1974; diploma, U. Edinburgh, 1976. Bar: N.Y. 1975, U.S. Dist. Ct. (ea. and so. dists.) N.Y. 1975, U.S. Ct. Appeals (2d cir.) 1975, D.C. 1978, U.S. Supreme Ct. 1988. Assoc. Cravath, Swaine & Moore LLP, NYC, 1975—78; asst. counsel The Wash. Post Co., 1978—79, gen. counsel, 1988—89, v.p., gen. counsel, 1989—91, v.p., gen. counsel, sec., 1991—2007; v.p., counsel Newsweek, NYC, 1979—85, v.p., gen. counsel, 1985—88. Trustee Cornell U., 1995—, vice chmn., 2004—06, chmn. exec. com., 2006—; trustee ABA Mus. Law, 1997—2004, Appleseed Found., 1998—2004, Ctr. Study of Presidency, 1997—2001, Am. Law Inst., 2003—, Goldman Sachs Trust, 2007—; mem. legal adv. com. NY Stock Exch., 2003—06. Office Phone: 202-362-4104.

DANIELS, EDGAR ROTH, educator; b. Flushing, NY, Apr. 16, 1948; s. Edgar Roth and Patricia Jean Daniels; m. Jessica Radcliffe, Nov. 11, 1972; children: Jonathan Edgar, Megan Marie. B, Widener U., Pa., 1970; M, LI U., 1976, Stony Brook U., NY, 1985. Cert. Nat. Bd. for Profl. Tchg. Stds., 1997. Tchr. Smithtown Ctrl. Sch. Dist., 1973—2003; lectr. Stony Brook U., 1990—; asst. prof. St. Joseph's Coll., Patchogue, NY, 2006—. Exec. dir. Daniels' Ednl. Svcs., Levittown, NY. Author: (ednl. material) The Cooperative Companion, The PACT Co-Teaching Inclusion Model. Bd. mem. Levittown (N.Y.) Pub. Libr., 1983—88, Levittown (N.Y.) Sch. Bd., 1985—87. Recipient Pioneer award, Nat. Bd. for Profl. Tchg. Stds., 1994, Golden Apple award, March of Dimes, 1998, All Star Tchr., SCOPE, 2000. Home Phone: 516-735-5932.

DANIELS, ELIZABETH ADAMS, English language educator; b. Westport, Conn., May 8, 1920; d. Thomas Davies and Minnie Mae (Sherwood) Adams; m. John L. Daniels, Mar. 21, 1942; children: John L., Eleanor B. (dec.), Sherwood A., Ann S. AB, Vassar Coll., 1941; A.M., U. Mich., 1942; PhD, N.Y. U., 1954. From instr. to prof. English Vassar Coll., Poughkeepsie, NY, 1948-85, dean freshmen, 1955-58, dean studies, 1965-73, chmn. dept. English, 1974-76, 81-84, acting dean faculty, 1976-78, chmn. self-study, 1978-80, Vassar historian, 1985—. Author: Jessie White Mario, Risorgimento Revolutionary, 1972, Main to Mudd, Bridges to the World, 1994, Main to Mudd, and More, 1996; co-author: (with Clyde Griffen) Full Steam Ahead in Poughkeepsie, The Story of Coeducation at Vassar 1966-74, 2000, (with Maryann Bruno) Vassar College 1861-2000, 2000, (with Ron Patkus, Kari Strickland and Marian Thomas) Administrative History of Vassar College, 2004; contbr. articles to publs. Bd. dirs. Alzheimer's Assn. Mid-Hudson Valley, World Affairs Coun. Hudson Valley. Recipient Grad. award Alumnae Assn. N.Y. U., 1954, Spirit of Vassar Alumnae award, 2006; Vassar fellow, 1941; Nat. Endowment Humanities summer stipend, 1981. Mem. MLA, AAUP, Poughkeepsie Tennis Club, Phi Beta Kappa. Democrat. Home: 56 Muirfield Ct Poughkeepsie NY 12603 Office: Vassar Coll PO Box 74 Poughkeepsie NY 12602-0074 *Growing up with intellectual ambitions, I was able to work out a very satisfactory career combining teaching, college administration, scholarship, family life, and a good marriage slightly forerunning the feminist movement of the late nineteen-sixties. I owe much of this to Vassar College, the first endowed woman's college in the U.S.*

DANIELS, FRANK EMMETT, mathematician, educator; b. Miami, Fla., Sept. 28, 1963; s. Dan and Jewell Rae (Morgan) D. BS, U. Fla., Gainesville, 1985, MS, 1987, PhD, 1994. Grad. teaching asst. math. dept. U. Fla., Gainesville, 1985-92; teaching asst. math. dept. Santa Fe Community Coll., 1992-94; prof. sys. adminstr. Great Basin Coll., Ely, Nev., dept. chair, 1999—2003. Co-designer 2dary Edn. program, 2003—04; faculty senate chmn. Great Basin Coll., 2003—04, chair bachelor of arts program in integrative and profl. studies, 2004—. Mem. Campus Advance (pres. 1988-91), Campus Christian Fellowship (pres. 1991-92), Phi Beta Kappa. Republican. Avocations: comic book collecting, collecting Beatles items, Bibl. studies, role-playing games. Office: Great Basin Coll 2115 Bobcat Dr Ely NV 89301-3107 Office Phone: 775-289-3589. Business E-Mail: fdaniels@gbcnv.edu.

DANIELS, GEORGE BENJAMIN, federal judge; b. Allendale, SC, May 13, 1953; s. Rufus Jacob and Florence (Morten) D. Student, Suffield Acad., 1967-71; BA, Yale U., 1975; JD, U. Calif., Berkeley, 1978. Bar: D.C. 1978, N.Y. 1979, Calif. 1981, N.J. 1983, U.S. Supreme Ct. 1982; notary public, N.Y. Trial atty. criminal def. div. Legal Aid Soc. N.Y., NYC, 1978-80; law clk. to presiding justice Calif. Supreme Ct., San Francisco, 1980-81; litigation atty. Skadden, Arps, Slate, Meagher & Flom, NYC, 1981-83; asst. U.S. atty. U.S. Atty.'s Office, Bklyn., 1983-89; judge Criminal Ct. City N.Y., 1989-90; counsel to mayor City of N.Y., 1990-93; judge Criminal Ct., NYC, 1993-95; justice Supreme Ct. N.Y., 1995-2000; judge U.S. Dist. Ct. (so. dist.) N.Y., 2000—. Adj. prof. Bklyn. Law Sch., 1988-91. Bd. trustees Suffield (Conn.) Acad., 1986—; bd. dirs. Andrew Glover Youth Program, N.Y.C., 1982—. Mem. ABA. Office: US Courthouse 40 Foley Sq New York NY 10007

DANIELS, GREGORY MARTIN, screenwriter; b. NYC, June 13, 1963; m. Susan Daniels, Sept. 1991. BA, Harvard U., 1985. Staff writer cable TV show Not Necessarily the News, Hollywood, Calif., 1985-87; staff writer TV show The Wilton-North Report, Hollywood, 1987; freelance co-writer TV pilots The Rich Hall Show, Goodnight America, 1987; staff writer TV show Saturday Night Live, NYC, 1988—90; co-exec. prodr. The Simpsons; exec. prodr. King of The Hill, 1997—; prodr., writer, dir. The Office, 2005—. Recipient Emmy award for Outstanding Animated Series, 1999, Danny Thomas Prodr. of Yr. award in Episodic TV - Comedy, Producers Guild of Am., 2007. Mem. Writers Guild Am. West, AFTRA, ASCAP. Address: 846 1/4 N Formosa Ave Los Angeles CA 90046-7648*

DANIELS, JAMES DOUGLAS, retired academic administrator; b. Harmony, NC, Nov. 14, 1935; m. Marie Brown, Oct. 6, 1957; children: Christopher James, Gregory John, Susan Marie. AB, Davidson Coll., 1957; MA, U. N.C., 1962, PhD, 1968. Exec. tng. program Deering-Milliken Textile Corp., Gainesville, Ga., 1957-58; history instr. Hargrave Military Acad., Chatham, Va., 1961-62, chmn., divsn. social sci., 1962-65, dean students, summer sch., 1964-65; asst. prof. history Valdosta (Ga.) State Coll., 1968-71, assoc. prof. history, 1971-78, history prof., 1978, dean, sch. arts, sci., 1970-80; pres., prof. history Coker Coll., Hartsville, SC, 1981—2002; ret., 2002. Bd. dirs. Byerly Hosp., 1981-85; Sunday sch. tchr. First Presbyn. Ch. Hartsville, 1981—. Com. on ministry Pee Dee Presbytery of S.C., 1985—, moderator, 1985; adv. bd. Bank of Am., 1988—, Pee Dee Heritage, 1982—, Darlington County Mental Health Citizens, 1987—. With US Army, 1958—60. NDEA fellow, U. N.C., 1966-68; recipient Man and Boy award Valdosta Boys' Club Bd. Dirs., 1970. Mem. Greater Hartsville C. of C. (bd. dirs. 1982-88, v.p. 1986, pres. 1987, chmn. bd. 1988), Hartsville H.S. Acad. Boosters Club and Band Boosters, Rotary (bd. dirs. 1982-99, Citizen of Yr. award 1989), Order of Palmetto, Omicron Delta Kappa. Presbyterian. Avocations: reading, fishing. Home: 206 Persimmon Fork Rd Blythewood SC 29016

DANIELS, JAMES MAURICE, retired physicist; b. Leeds, Eng., Aug. 26, 1924; emigrated to Can., 1953, naturalized, 1971; came to U.S., 1984, naturalized, 1992. s. Bernard and Mary Mahala (Proctor) D.; married; children: Ian Nicolas James, Maurice Edward Bruce. BA, Oxford U., Eng., 1945, MA, 1949, DPhil, 1952. Exptl. asst. Radar R & D Establishment, Malvern, England, 1944-46; tech. officer explosives div. Imperial Chem. Industries, Ardeer, Scotland, 1946-47; rsch. fellow Clarendon Lab., Oxford (Eng.) U., 1952-53; asst. prof. physics U. B.C., Vancouver, Canada, 1953-56, assoc. prof., 1956-60; UNESCO expert U. Buenos Aires, Argentina, 1958-59; prof. U. Toronto, 1961-87, prof. emeritus, 1987—, chmn. dept. physics, 1968-73, chmn. dept. stats., 1983-84. Vis. prof. Instituto de Fisica, S.C. de Bariloche Argentina, 1960-61, Helsinki U. Tech., 1974, Columbia U., 1978-79, Princeton U., 1984-85, Ecole Normale Superieure Paris, 1985-86, Nat. Tsing Hua U., Hsinchu, Republic of China, 1990, 91-92; vis. disting. prof. Oakland U., Rochester, Mich., 1994-95; pres. U. Toronto Faculty Assn., 1976-77; v.p. Can. Assn. Univ. Tchrs., Ottawa, 1979-80; sec., treas. Can. Inst. Particle Physics, Ottawa, 1970-73. Author: Oriented Nuclei, Polarized Targets and Beams, 1965; contbr. numerous articles to profl. jours. Alfred P. Sloan fellow, 1962-65, Guggenheim fellow, 1978-79 Fellow London Phys. Soc., London Inst. Physics (chartered physicist), London Royal Soc. Arts, Royal Soc. Can.; mem. Can. Assn. Physicists, Am. Phys. Soc., N.Y. Acad. Scis., Can. Inst. Particle Physics (sec-treas. 1971-73). Achievements include patents for Doppler radar; instrument for measure the polarization of 3 He; first to achieve successful production of spatially oriented atomic nuclei; compressed spin-polarized 3 He; application of the Mossbauer effect for determining spin arrangements in magnetic materials. Personal E-mail: jmdaniels314@hotmail.com.

DANIELS, JAMES WALTER, lawyer; b. Chgo., Oct. 13, 1945; s. Ben George and Delores L. (Wolanin) D.; m. Gail Anne Rihacek, June 14, 1969; children: Morgan, Abigail, Rachel. AB, Brown U., 1967; JD, U. Chgo., 1970. Bar: Calif. 1970, U.S. Dist. Ct. (ctrl. dist.) Calif. 1970, U.S. Tax Ct., 1972, U.S. Supreme Ct. 1979. Assoc. firm Latham & Watkins, L.A. and Newport Beach, Calif., 1970-77, ptnr., 1977—2005. Arbitrator Orange County Superior Ct., Santa Ana, Calif., 1978—88, judge pro tem, 1979—87. Fin. dir. St. Elizabeth Ann Seton Parish, Irvine, Calif., 1975-82; sec. Turtlerock Tennis Com., Irvine, 1981-83, 86—, pres., 1985-86; bd. dirs. Turtlerock Terr. Homeowners Assn., 1983-85, 87-89. Mem. Irvine Racquet Club, Palm Valley Country Club, Indian Ridge Country Club. Democrat. Roman Catholic. Home: 19241 Beckwith Ter Irvine CA 92603 Office: 3315 Fairview Rd Costa Mesa CA 92626

DANIELS, JEFF, actor, playwright; b. Athens, Ga., Feb. 19, 1955; m. Kathleen Treado, July 13, 1979; 3 children. Student, Cen. Mich. U. Apprentice Circle Repertory Co., NYC; founder Purple Rose Theatre Co., Chelsea, Mich. Actor: (stage prodns.) The Farm, 1976, My Life, 1977, Brontosaurus, 1977, Feedlot, 1977, Lulu, 1978, Slugger, 1978, The Fifth of July, 1978, 79, 80-81, Johnny Got His Gun, 1982 (Obie award), Three Sisters, 1982-83, The Golden Age, 1984, Short-Changed Review, Redwood Curtain, 1993, Blackbird, 2007; (films) Ragtime, 1981, Terms of Endearment, 1983, The Purple Rose of Cairo, 1985, Marie, 1985, Heartburn, 1986, Something Wild, 1986, Radio Days, 1987, The House on Carroll Street, 1988, Sweet Hearts Dance, 1988, Grand Tour, 1989, Checking Out, 1989, Arachnophobia, 1990, Welcome Home, Roxy Carmichael, 1990, Love Hurts, 1990, The Butcher's Wife, 1992, Gettysburg, 1993, Speed, 1994, Dumb and Dumber, 1994, Fly Away Home, 1996, 2 Days in the Valley, 1996, 101 Dalmations, 1996, Trial and Error, 1997, Pleasantville, 1998, My Favorite Martian, 1999, All the Rage, 1999, Chasing Sleep, 2000, Blood Work, 2002, The Hours, 2002, Gods and Generals, 2003, I Witness, 2003, Imaginary Heroes, 2004, Because of Winn-Dixie, 2005, The Squid and the Whale, 2005, Good Night, and Good Luck, 2005, RV, 2006, Infamous, 2006, The Lookout, 2007; (TV films) A Rumor of War, 1980, An Invasion of Privacy, 1983, The Caine Mutiny Court Marshall, 1988, No Place Like Home, 1989, Disaster in Time, 1992, Redwood Curtain, 1995, The Crossing, 2000, Cheaters, 2000, The Goodbye Girl, 2004, The Five People You Meet in Heaven, 2004; actor, dir., writer (films)Escanaba in da Moonlight, 2001, Super Sucker, 2001 (Best Comedy award, US Comedy Film Festival, Aspen, Colo. 2001); playwright: Shoeman, 1991, The Tropical Pickle, 1992, The Vast Difference, 1993, Thy Kingdom's Coming, 1994, Escanaba in da Moonlight, 1995, Across the Way, 2002, Recipient Michigan Filmmaker award, Traverse City Film Festival, 2006. Office: Internat Creative Mgmt Inc 8942 Wilshire Blvd Beverly Hills CA 90211*

DANIELS, JENNIFER M., lawyer; b. 1963; BA, U. Penn., 1985; JD, Harvard Law Sch., 1988. Bar: NY 1989. Joined IBM Inc., 1990; v.p., gen. counsel IBM Americas; v.p., asst. gen. counsel, chief trust and compliance officer IBM Internat.; v.p., gen. counsel, sec. Barnes & Noble, Inc., 2007—. Office: Barnes & Noble Inc 122 Fifth Ave 2nd Fl New York NY 10011 Office Phone: 212-633-4062.*

DANIELS, JOHN DRAPER, lawyer; b. Bklyn., Feb. 11, 1939; s. Draper L. and Louise Parker-Lux (Cort) D.; m. Sara Josephine Sears, Dec. 27, 1962; children: Stephen Draper, Elizabeth Marie, Rebecca Cort. AB, Princeton U., 1961; JD, U. Chgo., 1964. Bar: Ill. 1964, U.S. Dist. Ct. (no. dist.) Ill. 1967. Assoc. Jacobs & McKenna, Chgo., 1964-70, Law Offices Dale L. Schlafer, Chgo., 1970-73; assoc. then ptnr. Jacobs, Williams & Montgomery, Chgo., 1973-87; ptnr. Sanchez & Daniels, Chgo., 1987—2004; of counsel Sanchez Daniels & Hoffman, LLP, Chgo., 2005—. Arbitrator Cir. Ct. of Cook County. Mem. admissions screening panel Princeton Alumni Coun. Capt. U.S. Army, 1964-66. Mem. ABA, Ill. Bar Assn. (chmn. ins. sect. coun. 1985), Chgo. Bar Assn., Am. Arbitration Assn. (arbitrator 1977—), Internat. Assn. Def. Counsel, Soc. Trial Lawyers (bd. dirs. 1990, '92), Am. Bd. Trial Advs., Ill. Assn. Defense Trial Counsel, Trial Lawyers Club of Chgo., Tower of Chgo. Club (bd. trustees. 1985-87), East Bank Club. Roman Catholic. Avocations: guitar, musical composition, tennis, fishing, golf. Home: 1611 Wilmette Ave Wilmette IL 60091-2424 Office: Sanchez Daniels & Hoffman LLP 333 W Wacker Dr Chicago IL 60606-1220 Office Phone: 312-641-1555. Business E-Mail: jdaniels@sanchezdh.com.

DANIELS, JOHN HANCOCK, agricultural products company executive; b. St. Paul, Oct. 28, 1921; s. Thomas L. and Frances (Hancock) D.; m. Martha H. Williams, Dec. 23, 1942; children: Martha M., John Hancock, Jane P. Daniels Moffett, Christopher W. Student, St. Paul Acad., 1932-37; grad., Phillips Exeter Acad., 1939; BA, Yale, 1943; grad., Advanced Mgmt. Program, Harvard, 1957. With Archer-Daniels-Midland Co., Mpls., 1946-96, successively mem. staff linseed oil div., prodn. mgr. alfalfa divsn., mgr. feed divsn., v.p., dir., 1946-53, pres., dir., 1958-67, chmn., 1967-72, dir., mem. exec. com., 1972-96. With Mulberry Resources Inc. Author: Nothing Could Be Finer, 1996, Affectionately H, 1999, In The Boat, 2004. With Bus. Coun.; trustee Com. Econ. Devel.; chmn. 1972 Decatur United Way Campaign. Served from 2d lt. to capt. F.A., AUS, 1943-46. Decorated Bronze Star medal. Mem. Elizabethan Club, Links Club (N.Y.C.), Mpls. Club, Woodhill (Minn.) Club, Sprindale Hall Club (Camden, S.C.), Grolier Club, Lafayette Club. Episcopalian. Home: Mulberry Plantation PO Box 1349 Camden SC 29020-1349 Personal E-mail: CDE322@aol.com.

DANIELS, JOHN PETER, lawyer; b. NYC, Feb. 5, 1937; s. Jack Brainard and Isabelle (McConachie) D.; m. Lynn Eldridge, Aug. 28, 1978 (div. Jan. 1980); m. Susan Gurley, Apr. 1, 1983. AB, Dartmouth Coll., 1959; JD, U. So. Calif., 1963. Bar: Calif. 1964; diplomate Am. Bd. Trial Advocates. Assoc. Bolton, Groff and Dunne, LA, 1964-67, Jones and Daniels, LA, 1967-70, Acret and Perrochet, LA, 1971-81; ptnr. Daniels, Baratta and Fine, LA, 1982-99, Daniels, Fine, Israel & Schonbuch, LA, 1999—. Mem. Assn. So. Calif. Def. Counsel (bd. dirs. 1975-80), Fedn. Ins and Corp. Counsel. Clubs: Wilshire Country (Los Angeles). Avocations: scuba diving, golf, hunting. Office: Daniels Fine Israel & Schonbuch 1801 Century Park E Fl 9 Los Angeles CA 90067-2302 Office Phone: 310-556-7900. Business E-Mail: daniels@dfis-law.com.

DANIELS, JOHN R., oncologist, educator; b. Detroit, May 9, 1938; BA, Stanford U., 1959, MD, 1964. Diplomate Am. Bd. Internal Medicine. Postdoctoral fellow dept. cell biology Albert Einstein Coll. Medicine, 1964; intern in medicine Stanford U. Sch. Medicine, 1964-65; rsch. assoc. Nat. Inst. Dental Rsch., NIH, 1966-69; sr. resident in medicine Stanford U. Sch. Medicine, 1969-70, instr. div. oncology, 1970-71, asst. prof. div. oncology, 1971-78, clin. assoc. prof. div. oncology, 1978-79; v.p. for sci. and tech. affairs Collagen Corp., 1978-79; CEO, dir. Target Therapeutics, 1985-89; assoc. prof. medicine div. oncology U. So. Calif. Sch. Medicine, LA, 1979—, assoc. prof. radiology, 1990—. Bd. dirs. Collagen Corp. Contbr. over 85 articles to profl. jours.; 9 patents in field. Mem. Am. Assn. for Cancer Rsch., Am. Soc. Clin. Oncology. Home: 842 N Las Casas Ave Pacific Palisades CA 90272-2340

DANIELS, JOHN W., JR., lawyer; b. Birmingham, Ala., June 11, 1948; BA, North Ctrl. Coll., 1969; MS, U. Wis., 1972; JD, Harvard U., 1974. Bar: Wis. 1974. Ptnr. Quarles & Brady, Milw. Dir. V&J Foods, Inc., Met. Milw. Assn. Commerce, Diemakers, Inc.; dir. & sec. Med. Coll. Wis., 1995—; chair North Milw. State Bank; bd. Ganton Technologies. Dir. Greater Milw. Com., Med. Coll. Wis., Met. Milw. Assn. Commerce, Ralph Evinrude Found., Boys & Girls Clubs Milw., Holy Redeemer Christian Acad., Milw. Symphony Orch. (past dir.), Milw. Neighborhood House (past dir.). Recipient Best Lawyers in Am., Chambers USA, 1993; grantee Ford Found. fellow, Nat. Sci. Found. fellow. Mem. ABA (nat. v.p. LSD 1973-74, nat. vice chmn. YLD corporation, banking and bus. law 1974-75, mem. nat. coun. real property, probate and trust law sect. 1981-84, 90—), Am. Coll. Real Estate Attys., State Bar Wis., Milw. Young Lawyers Assnn. (pres. 1981-82), Milw. Bar Assn., Am. Coll. Real Estate Lawyers (nat. v.p.) 1997-98. Office: Quarles & Brady 411 E Wisconsin Ave Ste 2040 Milwaukee WI 53202-4497 Office Phone: 414-277-5103. Office Fax: 414-978-8903. Business E-Mail: jwd@quarles.com.

DANIELS, JOSEPH, neuropsychiatrist; b. Linden, NJ, Mar. 18, 1931; s. Bennie and Dora (Chese) D.; m. Shirley Perkins, July 20, 1996; children: Joan Marie, Jean Dorene. BA cum laude, Lincoln U., 1953; MD, Howard U., 1957. Rotating intern Med. Ctr. Jersey City, 1957—58; resident internal medicine Worcester City Hosp., Worcester, Mass., 1958—59; resident psychiatry Ancora Hosp., NJ, 1962—65; dir. outpatient clinic Christian Health Care Ctr., Wyckoff, NJ, 1966—70; dir. outpatient dept. Cmty. Mental Health Ctr., N.J. Coll. Medicine, Newark, 1970—79; med. dir., pres. Ctr. for Growth and Reconciliation, East Orange, NJ, 1979—87; sr. staff psychiatrist Pine Rest Christian Hosp., Grand Rapids, Mich., 1987—96; cons. Kent County Cmty. Mental Health Ctr., Grand Rapids, 1996—. Mem. Healthy Kent 2000 Health Com., 1993-94; cons. psychiatrist Newark Bd. Edn., 1976-84, East Orange Bd. Edn., Victory House,

Newark, 1976-82, Project Rehab, Grand Rapids, 1990-91. Author: The Urban Mission, 1974. Founder, pres., chmn. bd. Ministry Reconciliation Fellowship, 1980-87; bd. dirs. Grand Rapids Reach Inc., pres., 1991-93; selected mem. Leadership Grand Rapids, 1993-94. Capt. M.C., U.S. Army, 1959-62. Fulbright Sr. scholar U. Zimbabwe Sch. Medicine, 1998-99; decorated Am. Medal of Honor, 2001 Mem.: Beta Kappa Chi. Baptist. Avocations: sports, writing, reading. Office: 901 Eastern Ave NE Grand Rapids MI 49503-1201 Personal E-mail: drsdsapd@juno.com. E-mail: jdaniels1054@sbcglobal.net.

DANIELS, JOSEPH CARL, foundation administrator; b. July 6, 1972; s. Lawrence Stephen and Susan Daniels; m. Naomi Metzger, July 15, 2000; children: Caleb, Maerose. BA in Hist., Washington U., St. Louis; JD, U. Pa. Law Sch. Assoc. Cravath, Swaine & Moore, NYC; cons. McKinsey & Co., NYC; chief, External Initiatives Robin Hood Found., NYC; gen. counsel World Trade Ctr. Meml. Found., NYC, 2005—06, acting pres., 2006, pres., CEO, 2006—. Chair, Strategic Planning Com. The Hope Prog., NYC, 2002—. Office: World Trade Ctr Meml Found One Liberty Plz 29th Fl New York NY 10006 Office Phone: 212-227-7722. Office Fax: 212-227-7931.*

DANIELS, KATHLEEN ANGELA, educational association administrator; b. Detroit, Jan. 21, 1945; d. Leondro Cardinez and Lillian Mary (Murray) Castro; m. Donald W. Daniels, Jan. 30, 1971 (div. May 1983); 1 child, Donald. BA in Environ. Design, Wayne State U., 1967; student, U. Calif., LA, 1969. Photographic artist Jana Taylor & Co., Venice, Calif., 1985-88; rep., founder Am. Child Found., Venice, 1986-88; exec. dir. Cmty. Assns. Inst., LA, 1989—2000; interior plantscaper, owner Ms. Green Thumb, 2003—; owner Let's Get Organized, 2003—. Mem. NOW, NAFE, Nat. Woman's Polit. Caucus, Am. Soc. Assn. Execs., Sierra Club, Nat. Dem. Club. Avocations: gardening, ceramic animal collector, reading, walking. Home and Office: Ms Green Thumb 1903 W 9th St San Pedro CA 90732-3303 Office Phone: 310-339-0898. E-mail: msgreenthumb8@yahoo.com.

DANIELS, KURT R., speech and language pathologist; b. Chgo., Oct. 22, 1954; s. Donald R. and Phyllis D. (Lenz) D.; m. Renee Perry, July 5, 1980. BS, Ea. Ill. U., 1976, MS, 1977. Cert. clin. competence speech/lang. pathology; lic. speech/lang. pathologist, nursing home adminstr; tchr's. cert. spl. K-12th grades. Hearing and speech specialist Shapiro Devel. Ctr., Kankakee, Ill., 1977-80; dysphagia specialist lead profl. W.A. Howe Ctr., Tinley Pk., Ill., 1980—. Adv. bd. program in comm. disorders Govs. State U., clin. adj. prof.; cons., presenter in field Recipient Editor's Choice award Nat. Libr. Poetry, 1994, 95. Mem. Am. Speech, Lang. and Hearing Assn., Ill. Speech, Lang. and Hearing Assn., Internat. Soc. Poets. Achievements include research in dysphagia and developmental disabilities. Office: 7600 W 183d St Tinley Park IL 60477 Home Phone: 815-469-7091; Office Phone: 708-614-4355.

DANIELS, LEE ALBERT, state legislator; b. Lansing, Mich., Apr. 15, 1942; s. Albert Lee and Evelyn (Bousfield) D.; m. Pamela Mesha; children: Laurie Lynn, Rachael Lee, Julie, Thomas, Christina. BA, U. Iowa, 1965; JD, John Marshall Law Sch., 1967. Rep. precinct committeeman, 1965-74; mem. bd. auditors York Twp., Ill., 1966-73; vice chmn. York Twp. Rep. Comty. Orgn., 1973-74; former minority spokesman judiciary com. Ill. Ho. of Reps.; spl. asst. atty. gen., 1973-75; Ill. state rep. 46th Dist., 1975—, majority whip, 1981-82, minority leader, 1983-94, spkr. Ho., 1995—97. Full ptnr. Katten, Muchin & Zavis, 1984-91; ptnr. Bell, Boyd & Lloyd, Chgo., 1992— Trustee Elmhurst Hosp.; chmn. Ill. Rep. Party, 2001-2002. Recipient Everett McKinley Dirksen award, 1995; named one of Outstanding Legislators in Country, Nat. Rep. Legis. Assn., 1991, Legislator of Yr., Ill. Hosp. Assn., 1986, DuPage Mayors and Mgrs. Conf., 1995. Mem. ABA, Ill. Bar Assn., DuPage County Bar Assn., Shriners, Masons, Moose. Republican. Home: 105 S York Rd Ste 550 Elmhurst IL 60126 Office: 200 5N Stratton Springfield IL 62706-0001

DANIELS, LYDIA M., health care administrator; b. Louisville, Dec. 21, 1932; d. Effort and Gladys T. (Turner) Williams; children by previous marriage: Danny Winston, Jeffrey Bruce, Anthony Wayne. Cert., Samuel Merritt Hosp. Sch. Med. Record Adminstrs., Calif., 1959; student, Ctrl. State Coll., Wilberforce, Ohio, 1950—52; Calif. State U., Hayward, 1967, student, 1969—72; BA, Golden Gate U., 1992, MS, 1993; postgrad., So. Calif. U., 2007. Sec. chemistry dept. Ctrl. State Coll., Wilberforce, 1950-52; co-dir. Indian Workcamp Pala Indian Reservation, Calif., 1956-58; clk.-typist Camarillo State Hosp., Calif., 1956-58; student med. record adminstr. Samuel Merritt Hosp., Oakland, Calif., 1958-59, asst. med. record adminstr., 1962-63, asst. chief med. record adminstr., 1965, chief med. record adminstr., 1965-72; med. record adminstr. Albany Hosp., Calif., 1964-65; asst. med. record adminstr. Children's Hosp., San Francisco, 1960; co-dir. interns in cmty. svc. Am. Friends Svc. Com., San Francisco, 1960-61; med. record adminstrs. Pacific Hosp., Oakland, 1963-64; med. record cons. Tahoe Forest Hosp., Truckee, Calif., 1969-73; chief med. record adminstr. Highland Gen. Hosp., Oakland, 1972-74; dir. med. record svcs. U. Calif. San Francisco Hosps. and Clinics, 1975-82; mgr. patient appointments, reception/registration Kaiser-Permanente Med. Ctr., 1982-88, dir. ambulatory adminstrv. svcs., 1988-94, asst. dir. human resources, 1994-96; dir. human resources Brookside Hosp., San Pablo, Calif., 1996-97; cons. human resources Daniels Consultation Svcs., San Pablo, 1996-98; dir. human resources Alameda County Med. Ctr., San Leandro, Calif., 1998—2002; adj. prof. human resources mgmt. Dominican U. Calif., San Rafael, 2002—. Adj. prof. human resources mgmt., labor mgmt. rels. Golden Gate U., 1978—; pres. Daniels Consultation Svcs., Berkeley, 1988—, mgmt. tng. human resources cons., 1997—. Author: Health Record Documentation: A Look at Cost, 1981; Inservice Training as a Tool in Managing the Changing Environment in the Medical Record Department, 1983; The Budget as a Management Tool, 1983; issues editor: Topics in Health Record Management, Parts I and II, 1983. Leader Girl Scouts Am. Oakland area coun., 1960-62; Sunday Sch. tchr. Soc. of Friends, Berkeley, Calif., 1961-63, mem. edn. com., 1965-68; mem. policy and adv. bd. Far West Lab Demonstration Sch., Oakland, 1973-75; bd. dirs. The Californians, Oakland, 1993-97, Patrons of the Arts and Humanities, Oakland, 1994-97, YWCA, Berkeley, 1995-2001, Operation Dignity, Inc., 2002-2004. Recipient Mgmt. Fellowship award U. Calif., San Francisco, 1979-80. Mem. Am. Med. Record Assn., Calif. Med. Record Assn. (editl. bd. 1976-77, pres. 1974-75), East Bay Med. Record Assn. (chmn. edn. com. 1971-72, pres. 1969-70), Assn. Systems Mgmt., Am. Mgmt. Assn., San Francisco Med. Records Assn. (pres.-elect 1982-83, pres. 1983-84), Am. Assn. Tng. and Devel. (Golden Gate chpt., v.p. prof. devel. 1994-96). Office Phone: 510-525-0848. Personal E-mail: ldancon@aol.com.

DANIELS, MARY P., academic administrator, technologist; b. P.G. County, Md., Feb. 16, 1961; d. William Clarence Proctor and Eva Rostta Bricsoe; children: Zanisha, Bobby Jr., Nathaniel, Jeremiah. BBA, BRE, Mgmt. Wash. Sat. Coll., DC, 1993; MRE, DD, Breakthrough Bible Coll., Suithand, Md., 2003; DHL, Breakthrough Bible Coll., Md., 2005. Commn. technologist WMATA, Washington, 1981—2000; v.p. fin./bus. Breakthrough Bible Coll., Suitland, Md., 2000—; commn. technologist Met. Area Transit Authority, Washington, 2000—. Bd. dirs., CEO Wells of Water Ministries, Inc., Washington, 1989—; bd. dirs. Britt Quinn Enterprise, Md., 2003—; exec. bd. dirs. Breakthrough Bible Coll., 2000. Author: Establishing Your Church, Church Law, 2004. Democrat. Avocations: walking, travel, cooking, reading. Office Phone: 202-546-8228. E-mail: drmarypdaniels@aol.com.

DANIELS, MICHAEL E., information technology executive; Mgmt. positions in sales, mktg. & services IBM, 1976—94, gen. mgr. positions, 1994—99; global services head IBM Asia Pacific, 1999—2002; gen. mgr. sales & distbn. Americas IBM, 2002—05, sr. v.p. global tech. services, 2005—. Office: IBM 1 New Orchard Rd Armonk NY 10504-1722*

DANIELS, MICHAEL PAUL, lawyer; b. Maplewood, NJ, Apr. 22, 1930; s. Samuel and Lena E. (Oxman) D.; m. Lora Lee, June 23, 1949 (div. Aug. 1964); children: Lisa J., Rachel L., Aaron N.; m. Elaine Makris, Sept. 1, 1964; children: Anthony P., Maria, Alexander P. BA, U. Chgo., 1949, JD, 1952; student, U. Tokyo Sch. Law, 1958-59. Bar: U.S. Ct. Appeals (D.C. cir.) 1955, U.S. Supreme Ct., U.S. Ct. Internat. Trade; U.S. Ct. Appeals (fed. cir.). Atty. U.S. Congl. Reference Service, Washington, 1955-56; assoc. Becker & Maguire, Washington, 1956-57, Stitt & Hemendinger, Washington, 1958-63; ptnr. Stitt, Hemindinger & Daniels, Washington, 1963-67, Daniels, Houlihan & Palmeter, Washington, 1968-84; ptnr., internat. dept. head Mudge, Rose, Guthrie, Alexander & Ferdon, Washington, 1984-95; ptnr. Graham & James, Washington, 1995-97, Powell Goldstein Frazer & Murphy, Washington, 1997—2000; of counsel Sidley Austin Brown & Wood LLP, 2001—02; ptnr., chmn. internat. trade group Loeffler Group LLP, 2003—. Cons. Fasturn Inc., 2000—03. Served with U.S. Army, 1952-54, Korea. Decorated Meritorious Bronze Star; fellow Fulbright fellow. Mem. ABA, D.C. Bar Assn. Home: 5615 Bent Branch Rd Bethesda MD 20816-1049 Office Phone: 202-775-4427. Personal E-mail: MikeElaineDaniels@comcast.net. Business E-Mail: mdaniels@loefflerllp.com.

DANIELS, MITCHELL ELIAS, JR., governor, former federal official; b. Monongahela, Pa., Apr. 7, 1949; s. Mitchell Elias and Dorothy Mae (Wilkes) D.; m. Cheri Lynn Herman, May 20, 1978; children— Meagan, Melissa, Meredith, Margaret. AB, Princeton U., 1971; JD, Georgetown U., 1979. Bar: Ind. 1979. Exec. v.p. Campaign Communicators, Inc., Indpls., 1971-74; dep. to mayor City of Indpls., 1974-75; campaign mgr. Lugar for U.S. Senate, Indpls., 1976; adminstrv. asst. to U.S. Senator Dick Lugar U.S. Senate, Washington, 1977-83; exec. dir. Nat. Rep. Sen. Com., Washington, 1983-85; asst. to the Pres. The White House, Washington, 1985—87; CEO Hudson Inst., 1987—90; pres. N. Am. pharmaceutical ops. Eli Lilly and Co., 1993—97, sr. v.p. corp. strategy, policy, 1997—2001; dir. Office Mgmt. & Budget Exec. Office of the Pres., Washington, 2001—03; gov. State of Ind., Indianapolis, 2005—. Vice pres., trustee Am. Council Young Polit. Leaders, Washington, 1983—; mem. adv. com. Responsible Govt. for Am. Found., Washington, 1983—; bd. dirs. Fund for Hoosier Excellence, 1984—, Ind. Nat. Bank, Ind. Power & Light, Angie's List. Recipient Graham award Ind. Am. Legion, 1966, "Hero of the Taxpayer" award, American for Tax Reform, 2002, Chauncey Rose award, Rose-Hulman Inst. Tech., 2003; Presdl. scholar, 1967 Mem. Ind. Bar Assn. Clubs: Columbia (Indpls.). Republican. Presbyterian. Office: Office of Governor 206 State House Indianapolis IN 46204 Office Phone: 317-232-4567. Office Fax: 317-232-3443.*

DANIELS, NORMAN, philosopher, educator; b. NYC, June 30, 1942; s. Manus and Evelyn (Auerbach) D.; m. Anne L. Hooker; 1 child, Noah. AB summa cum laude, Wesleyan U., 1964; BA, MA, Balliol Coll., Oxford, Eng., 1966; PhD, Harvard U., 1970. Asst. prof. philosophy Tufts U., Medford, Mass., 1970-76, assoc. prof. philosophy, 1976-81, prof. philosophy, 1981—2002, chmn. philosophy dept., 1983—2002; prof., sch. of public health Harvard U., Boston, 2002—. Faculty Harvard extension, Cambridge, Mass., 1976—; vis. assoc. prof. bioethics Brown U., Providence, 1979; reviewer NEH, NSF, 1982-85; panel mem. NSF-NEH Ethics and Values in Sci. and Tech., 1982. Author: (book) Thomas Reid's Inquiry: The Geometry of Visibles and the Case for Realism, 1974, Reading Rawls: Critical Studies of John Rawls' A Theory of Justice, 1975, In Search of Equity: Health Needs and the Health Care System, 1983, Just Health Care, 1985, Am I My Parent's Keeper? An Essay on Justice Between the Young and the Old, 1988; editorial bd. Australasian Jour. Philosophy, Ethics, Jour. Medicine and Philosophy; editor (with Keith Lehrer) series of philosophy textbooks; referee Isis, Nous, Philos. Forum, Philos. Studies, Social Theory and Practice, Jour. Medicine and Philosophy, Bus. and Profl. Ethics Jour., Milbank Meml. Fund Quar., Philosophy and Econs., Philosophy and Phenomenology Research; reviewer Wadsworth Pub. Co., Dickenson, Prentice-Hall, Oxford, Princeton, Garland Pub. Co., Cornell U. Press, Rowman and Littlefield, Cambridge U. Press. Recipient George Plimpton Adams prize, 1970, Woodrow Wilson Career Devel. award, 1980, Mass. Found. Humanities and Pub. Policy and Matchette Found. award, 1980; Harvard Grad. Nat. fellow, 1966-69, NEH Individual fellow, 1977-78; grantee Marsden Found., 1966, Nat. Ctr. Health Svcs. rsch. grantee, 1978-79, 79-80, 80-81, 81-82, NEH, 1983-85, 89—, Retirement Rsch. Found., 1983-86, NSF, 1987, USPHS, 1989—. Mem.: Nat. Institute of Health, 1999-, AAAS, AAUP, Am. Philos. Assn., Philosophy of Sci. Assn., Phi Beta Kappa. Office: Harvard Sch Pub Health 665 Huntington Ave Rm 1104C Boston MA 02115

DANIELS, PATSY JEAN, literature professor; b. Columbia, Tenn., Mar. 19, 1944; d. Johnnie D. Daniels and Retha Lorene Stanfill; m. Jerry Lee Ballard, Nov. 13, 1959 (div. 1975); children: Jerry Lee Ballard Jr., Robert Daniel Ballard; m. Jerry Leon Jackson, Feb. 17, 1990; 1 child, Danielle Marie Jackson. BA in Liberal Studies, U. Nebr., Omaha, 1975, MA in English, 1978; PhD in Lit. and Criticism, Ind. U. Pa., 1998. Adminstrv. asst. gerontology program U. Nebr., Omaha, 1977—80; dir. publs. Ctr. Health Svcs. Rsch. U. Colo. Health Svcs. Ctr., Denver, 1980—81, instr., rsch. asst. dept. preventive medicine Sch. Nursing, 1980—81; instr. dept. langs. and lit. Austin Peay State U., Clarksville, Tenn., 1988—93; instr. dept. langs., lit. and philosophy Tenn. State U., Nashville, 1994—98; asst. prof. English, coord. English Ln. Coll., Jackson, Tenn., 1998—99, asst. prof., coord. English, chmn. divsn. liberal studies and edn., 1999—2001, assoc. prof., coord. English, chair divsn. liberal arts and edn., 2001—04; acad. scholar Chinese Acad. Social Scis., Beijing, 2001; assoc. prof. dept. English and modern fgn. langs. Jackson State U., Miss., 2004—. Mentor Mellon-Mays Undergraduate Rsch. Fellowships, Jackson, Tenn., Ronald McNair Undergraduate Rsch. Fellow, Jackson State U., Jackson, Miss. Author: (book) The Voice of the Oppressed in the Language of the Oppressor, 2001. Cub scout den mother Boy Scouts of Am., Cedar Rapids, Iowa, 1968—69; asst. troop leader Girls Scouts US, Clarksburg, 1999—2004; vol. reader spl. edn. classes Clarksburg Sch., 1999—2004; vol. Habitat for Humanity, Jackson, 2002, 2005; program coord. Shambhala Tng., Boulder, Colo., 1987—88. Named Faculty Mem. of Yr., Ln. Coll., 2000—01; fellow, East-West Ctr., U. Hawaii, Honolulu, 2005, Nat. Endowment for Humanities, U. Okla., Norman, 2007; grantee, Ln. Coll., 2000, Ctr. U. Scholars, Jackson State U., 2005—07; scholar, Nebr. Bd. Regents, 1972—75. Mem.: MLA, Internat. Assn. for Asian Studies, South Ctrl. MLA, Nat. Assn. Native Am. Studies, Nat. Assn. Hispanic and Latino/a Studies, Soc. Ethnic Literatures of US, Nat. Assn. African Am. Studies (area coord. 1999—2000, bd. mem. 2000—01), Nat. Coun. Tchrs. English, Sigma Tau Delta (print and electronics publications com. mem. 2004—). Buddhist. Avocation: travel. Office: Jackson State U 1400 John R Lynch St Jackson MS 39217 Home Phone: 601-845-4623; Office Phone: 601-979-1480. Office Fax: 601-979-3732. Business E-Mail: patsy.j.daniels@jsums.edu.

DANIELS, RANDY A., investment company executive, former state official; b. Chgo., Nov. 30, 1951; m. Jacqueline Daniels; children: Asha, Toure. BA in Govt. and Journalism, So. Ill. U., 1972. Prof. adj. journalism CCNY, Columbia U.'s Grad. Sch. Journalism; reporter WVON Radio, Chgo., 1970—72; corr. CBS News, Chgo., 1972—77, fgn. corr. Nairobi, Kenya, 1977—80, nat. corr. NYC, 1980—82; mng. editor Jacaranda Nigeria Ltd., 1982—84; dir. Comm. N.Y.C. Coun. Pres.'s Office, 1986—88; Press Sec. Prime Min. of Bahamas, 1988—92; v.p. Hirshfeld realty, NYC, 1993—95; sr. v.p., dep. commr. econ. revitalization Empire State Corp. (ESDC), 1995—99; sr. v.p. Canyon Johnson Urban Fund, L.L.P., 1999—2001; sec. state State of NY, Albany, 2001—05; vice chmn. Gilford Securities Inc., NYC, 2007—. Mem.: Exec. and Fin. Coms., SUNY (vice chmn.bd. trustees, chmn. invetsment com., co-chmn. coms. on gen. edn. and charter schs.). Office: Gilford Securities Inc 777 Third Ave New York NY 10017*

DANIELS, ROBERT VINCENT, history professor, former state senator; b. Boston, Jan. 4, 1926; s. Robert Whiting and Helen Underwood (Hoyt) D.; m. Alice May Wendell, July 2, 1945; children: Robert H., Helen L. Turcotte, Irene L., Thomas L. AB, Harvard U., 1945, MA, 1947, PhD, 1951; LLD (hon.), U. Vt., 1994. Rsch. assoc. MIT, Cambridge, 1951-52; social sci. faculty Bennington (Vt.) Coll., 1952-53, 57-58; asst. prof. Slavic studies Ind. U., 1953-55; rsch. assoc. Columbia U., 1955-56; from asst. prof. history to prof. U. Vt., Burlington, 1956-88, prof. emeritus, 1988—, chmn. dept., 1964-69, dir. exptl. program, 1969-71; mem. Vt. Senate, 1973-82, asst. minority leader, 1977-80, minority leader, 1981-82. Chmn. Vt. Gov.'s Commn. Med. Care, 1974-75; mem. Vt. Health Policy Corp., 1977-80; mem. adv. com. on East Europe and USSR, Coun. on Internat. Exch. of Scholars, 1983-85; adv. coun. Ctr. for Internat. Polit. Studies, Rome, 1989—; mem. sister state com. Vt.-Karelia, 1991—, co-dir. self-govt. tng. program, 1993-94; dir. U. Vt. Petrozavodsk U. partnership program, 1994-95; mem. supervisory bd. Internat. Coop. Ctr. Karelian br. St. Petersburg Acad. Pub. Adminstrn. Author: The Conscience of the Revolution, 1960, Documentary History of Communism, 1960, rev. edit., 1993, The Nature of Communism, 1962, Studying History, 1966, Red October, 1967, The Russian Revolution, 1972, Fodor's Europe Talking, 1975, Russia-The Roots of Confrontation, 1985, Is Russia Reformable?, 1988, Year of the Heroic Guerrilla, 1989, Trotsky, Stalin and Socialism, 1992, The End of the Communist Revolution, 1993, Soviet Communism from Reform to Collapse, 1994, Russia's Transformation, 1997, The Fourth Revolution, 2005, The Rise and Fall of Communism in Russia, 2007; editor: The University of Vermont: The First Two Hundred Years, 1991. Mem. Chittenden County (Vt.) Dem. Com., 1959—; mem. Burlington City Dem. Com., 1965—; chmn. policy and planning platform com. Vt. Dem. Party, 1962-66, 69-73, 76-80, mem. exec. com., 1981-85; alt. Dem. Nat. Conv., 1968; mem. Dem. Platform Com., 1980; bd. visitors USAF Acad., 1965-67. Ensign USNR, 1944-46. U.S.-Soviet Cultural Exch. scholar U. Moscow, 1966, USSR Acad. Scis. scholar, 1976, 84, 88; NEH fellow, 1971-72, Guggenheim fellow, 1980-81, Kennan Inst. fellow, 1985. Fellow Vt. Acad. Arts and Scis.; mem. Am. Hist. Assn. (pres. conf. Slavic and East European history 1976-77), Am. Assn. Advancement Slavic Studies (bd. dirs. 1968-71, v.p. 1991, pres. 1992, chmn. com. on govt. affairs 1993-94, Disting. Contbns. award 2001), Can. Assn. Slavists, Authors' Guild, Vt. Hist. Soc. (trustee 1968-71), Vt. Coun. World Affairs, Norwich Ctr./Bridges for Peace (bd. dirs. 1988-94), Harvard Club Vt. (pres. 1974-75). Democrat. Home: 195 S Prospect St Burlington VT 05401-3519 Office: University of Vermont Dept Of History Burlington VT 05405-0001 Home Phone: 802-864-7645; Office Phone: 802-656-3180. Business E-Mail: rdaniels@zoo.uvm.edu.

DANIELS, RONALD DALE, conductor; b. San Mateo, Calif., Aug. 19, 1943; s. Worth W. and Margurite Pearl (Chandler) D.; 1 child, Ryan Stark. BMus, San Francisco Conservatory, 1968. Condr., music dir. Musical Arts of Contra Costa (Calif.) County, 1968-75, U. Calif., Berkeley, 1973-75, Contra Costa Symphony, 1976-79, Reno (Nev.) Philharm., 1979-98, conductor Laureate, 1998—. Guest conductor various orchs.; grants rev. cons. in field. With USMC, 1966. Recipient Lucien Wulsin award Baldwin Piano Co., Tanglewood Festival, 1968, Gov.'s Art award State of Nev., 1981. Avocations: ice skating, skiing, sailing, hiking, astronomy. Office: Reno Philharm Assn Ste 3 925 Riverside Dr Reno NV 89503 Home: 19430 SE 30th St Camas WA 98607-9437

DANIELS, RONALD GEORGE, theater director; b. Niteroi, Rio de Janiero, Brazil, Oct. 15, 1942; arrived in U.S., 1991; s. Percy and Nellie (Chalmers) D.; m. Anjula Harman; children: Alexis, Eliena. Student, Fundacão Brasileira de Teatro, Rio de Janiero. Assoc. artistic dir. Am. Reperatory Theatre, Cambridge, Mass., 1991—96; head acting and directing programs Inst. for Advanced Theatre Tng. Harvard U., 1991—96. Hon. assoc. dir. Royal Shakespeare Co., Stratford-upon-Avon, London; lectr. Shakespeare Inst., U. Birmingham, Friends Royal Shakespeare Co., NYU, others. Dir.: (stage) Coriolanus, Major Barbara, Who's Afraid of Virginia Wolf, Sweeney Todd, Ghosts, Hamlet, Drums in the Night, The Samaritan, Time Travelers, The Long and Short and the Tall, The Word, Measure for Measure, Fear and Miseries of the Third Reich, The Insect Play, Twelfth Night, A Midsummer Night's Dream, Pillars of the Community, Man is Man, The Children's Crusade, Female Transport, Sgt. Musgrave's Dance, Into the Mouth of Crabs, By Common Consent, The Motor Show, Made in Britain, Bang, Afore Night Come, Bingo, Puntila and His Servant Matti, Ivanov, Destiny, T'is Pity She's a Whore, The Lorenzaccio Story, The Sons of Light, Pericles, The Suicide, Timon of Athens, Hippolytus, Camille, Hansel and Gretel, Peer Gynt, Romeo and Juliet, Ashes, The Beastly Beatitudes of Balthazar B, Across from the Garden of Allah, Playing with Trains, The Tempest, Julius Cesar, Maydays, Breaking the Silence, The Danton Affair, The Women Pirates, Real Dreams, They Shoot Horses, Much Ado About Nothing, The Plain Dealer, The Clockwork Orange, Earwig, Richard II, The Seagull, As You Like It, The Dream of The Red Spider, Silence, Cunning, Exile, Cakewalk, Henry IV parts I and II, The Cherry Orchard, Henry V, The Threepenny Opera, The Tempest, Slaughter City, Long Day's Journey into Night, Blinded by the Sun, Anthony and Cleopatra, The Shepherd King, One Flea Spare, Madama Butterfly, Henry V and Richard II, Richard III, Macbeth, Remember This, King Lear, Carmen, Hedda Gabler, The Feast of Snails, The Turn of the Screw, Sana que Sana, Havana is Waiting, Tosca, Cosi Fan Tutti, La Forza del Destino, Points of Departure The Suitcase Triology, The Front Page; exec. prodr. Lawn Dogs. Mem. Soc. Stage Dirs. and Choreographers, Dirs. Guild Gt. Britain, Am. Guild Musical Artists, Nat. Assn. Latino Ind. Prodrs. E-mail: rondaniels000@aol.com.

DANIELS, RUSSELL, information technology executive; BS, Ohio Univ. Developer-related positions Apple Computer; gen. mgr., application devel. ops. Hewlett-Packard Co., chief tech. officer, software global bus. unit, v.p., chief tech. officer, Software and Adaptive Enterprise, Software Bus. Unit, Tech. Solutions Palo Alto, Calif. Named one of Top 25 Chief Tech. Officers, InfoWorld mag., 2006. Office: Hewlett Packard 3000 Hanover St Palo Alto CA 94304 Office Phone: 650-857-1501.*

DANIELS, STEPHEN M., government official; b. Boston, Mar. 28, 1947; s. Everett Jerome and Helen Dorothy (Ettinger) Daniels; m. Maygene Louise Frost, June 25, 1972; children: Edward Frost, Leah Lillian. BA, Yale U., 1968, JD, 1972. Bar: Calif. 1972, DC 1973, U.S. Supreme Ct. 1980. Asst. to asst. sec. for legis. HEW, Washington, 1969-70; legis. analyst U.S. Office of Mgmt. and Budget, Washington, 1971; legis. asst. to Congressman U.S. Ho. Reps., Washington, 1972-73, with Com. on Govt. Ops., 1973-87, minority counsel Com. on Govt. Ops., 1980-87, minority staff dir. Com. on Govt. Ops., 1984-87; bd. contract appeals GSA, Washington, 1987—2007, chmn., 1992—2007, bd. US civilian contract appeals, 2007—, chmn. bd. US civilian contract appeals, 2007—. Treas. Capitol Hill Cmty. Found., Washington, 1999—. Commr. Congl. Softball League, Washington, 1977—81; pres. Capitol East Children's Ctr., Washington, 1982—83; trustee Capitol Hill Day Sch., Washington, 1988—92. Capt. USAR, 1970—71. Mem.: ABA, Calif. Bar Assn., D.C. Bar Assn., Fed. Bar Assn. Avocations: bicycling, baseball, home restoration, camping. Home: 816 Massachusetts Ave NE Washington DC 20002-6016 Office: 1800 F St NW Washington DC 20405-0001 Business E-Mail: stephen.daniels@gsa.gov.

DANIELS, SUSANNE, broadcast executive; m. Greg Daniels. Grad., Harvard U. Asst. mgr. devel. Broadway Video Entertainment, mgr. devel.; dir. variety, reality and specials ABC TV Network; dir. comedy devel. The Fox Broadcasting Co.; pres. entertainment, lifetime svcs. entertainment The WB Network, Burbank, Calif., 2005; pres. entertainment Lifetime Entertainment Services, 2005—. Spkr. in field; developer (for Lorne Michaels) Saturday Night Live, Kids in the Hall, Am. Detective, America's Funniest People, Living Single, Martin, Buffy the Vampire Slayer, Dawson's Creek, Felicity, Roswell, Angel, Gilmore Girls, 7th Heaven; responsible for overseeing (ABCs spls.) Academy Awards, Muhammad Ali's 50th Birthday Spl., Am. Comedy Awards. Bd. dirs. The Nat. Campaign to Prevent Teenage Pregnancy. Named in the Power Issue Entertainment Weekly, 1997; named one of 100 Most Powerful Women in Entertainment, Hollywood Reporter, 1998, 1999, 2000, 2005, 2006; recipient Gemini award, Am. Women in Radio & Television, 2001. Mem.: Acad. TV Arts and Sci. Office: Lifetime Entertainment Services World Wide Plz 309 West 49th St New York NY 10019 Office Phone: 212-424-7000. Office Fax: 212-957-4447.*

DANIELS, SYDNEY ROBERT, theater director, educator; b. Sept. 16, 1941; s. James Monroe and Marie P. Daniels. BS in Edn., Ill. State U., Normal, 1963, MS in Edn., 1967. Art tchr. Wendell Phillips H.S., Chgo., 1965—67; instr. Harold Washington Coll., Chgo., 1967—70, asst. prof., 1971—89, assoc. prof., 1989—92, prof., 1992—. Tech. dir. theatre Harold Washington Coll., 1968—69, assoc. dir. theatre, 1969—74, dir. theatre, 1974—. Mem. Joseph Jefferson Theatre Awards Com., Chgo., 1970—. Recipient Excellence award, Nat. Inst. for Staff Devel., 1996, Alumni Achievement award, Ill State U. Alumni Assn., 1998, 25 Yr. Svc. award, Joseph Jefferson Theatre Awards Com., 2005. Roman Catholic. Avocations: painting, theater, gardening, singing.

DANIELS, WILLIAM BURTON, retired physicist, educator; b. Buffalo, Dec. 21, 1930; s. William C. and Sophia (Penner) D.; m. Adriana A. Braakman, Sept. 2, 1958; children: Charlotte Mary, William Fredrik, Donald Christopher. BS in Physics, U. Buffalo, 1952; MS, Case Inst. Tech., 1955, PhD, 1957. Instr. to asst. prof. Case Inst. Tech., 1957-59; rsch. scientist Union Carbide Corp., 1959-61; mem. faculty Princeton U., 1961-72, prof. solid state scis., 1967-72; Unidel prof. physics U. Del., Newark, 1972-2000, Unidel prof. emeritus, 2001—. Rsch. collaborator Brookhaven nat. Lab.; cons. U.S. Army Rsch. Lb.; guest scientist rsch. facility, Denmark, 1976; invité Coll. France, 1977; exch. prof. U. Paris, 1977; guest scientist IBM Zurich Lab., 1977; guest scientist Max Planck Inst. for Festkoerperforschung; vis. faculty Geophys. Lab., Carnegie Inst. of Washington, 2000. Recipient Alexander von Humboldt Sr. Scientist award, 1981, 92; John S. Guggenheim Meml. fellow, 1976-77. Fellow Am. Phys. Soc. Achievements include research in properties materials at high pressure, equation of state of solids, experimentation on solidified permanent gases, electronic structure of compressed solids, instrumentation high pressure research, non-linear optics. E-mail: Family_Daniels@yahoo.com.

DANIELS, WILLIAM DAVID (BILL DANIELS), actor; b. Bklyn., Mar. 31, 1927; s. David and Irene D.; m. Bonnie Bartlett, June 30, 1951; children: Michael, Robert. Grad., Northwestern U. Broadway debut in Life With Father, 1939; appeared in plays Richard II, N.Y.C., 1951; Seagulls Over Sorento, 1952; The Man Who Corrupted Hadleyburg, 1953; The Man Who Had All The Luck, also Ladies in Retirement, 1954; Cat on a Hot Tin Roof, 1957; Look Back in Anger, 1958; The Iceman Cometh, 1956; The Legend of Lizzie, 1959; The Zoo Story, 1960; S. Am. tour, 1961; A Thousand Clowns, 1962; Dear Me The Sky is Falling, 1963; One Flew Over the Cuckoo's Nest, 1963; On a Clear Day You Can See Forever, 1965; Daphne in Cottage D, 1967; 1776, 1969; A Little Night Music, 1973; films include Ladybug Ladybug, 1963, A Thousand Clowns, 1965, Two for the Road, 1967, The Graduate, 1967, 1776, 1972, The Parallax View, 1974, Black Sunday, 1977, Oh, God!, 1977, The One and Only, 1978, The Blue Lagoon, 1980, All Night Long, 1981, Blind Date, 1987, Her Alibi, 1989, Magic Kid II, 1994, Blades of Glory, 2007; TV appearances: Somerset Maugham Theater, ABC, 1952, Profiles in Courage, NBC, 1965; television films include Murdock's Gang, 1973, The Fabulous Dr. Fable, 1973, A Case of Rape, 1974, Sarah T., Portrait of a Teenage Alcoholic, 1975, One of Our Own, 1975, Francis Gary Powers, 1976, Instant Family, 1977, Killer on Board, 1977, The Court Martial of George Armstrong Custer (Hallmark Hall of Fame), 1977, Big Bob Johnson and His Fantastic Speed Circus, 1978, Sergeant Matlovich vs. the U.S. Air Force, 1978, City in Fear, 1980, The Million Dollar Face, 1981, The Wonderful World of Philip Malley, 1981, Nuts and Bolts, 1981, Rehearsal for Murder, 1982, Rooster, 1982, Drop Out Father, 1982, The Little Match Girl, 1987, Howard Beach: Making a Case for Murder, 1989, On Thin Ice: The Tai Babilonia Story, 1990, Clara, 1991, Back to the Streets of San Francisco, 1992, The Lottery, 1996, Crazy Love, 2003; appeared in television series Captain Nice, 1966-67, mini-series The Adams Chronicles, 1976, The Nancy Walker Show, 1976, mini-series Blind Ambition, 1979, Freebie and the Bean, 1980, Knight Rider (voice), 1982-87, St. Elsewhere, 1982-88. Served to staff sgt. U.S. Army, 1945-47; ETO. Recipient Clarence Derwent award, Village Voice Off-Broadway award for The Zoo Story, 1960; Argentina Drama Critics award, The Zoo Story, 1962. Recipient 1986 Emmy Award as best actor in a drama series for Saint Elsewhere. Office: c/o Artists Agy 10000 Santa Monica Blvd Ste 305 Los Angeles CA 90067-7007

DANIELSEN, ALBERT LEROY, economics professor, energy and utilities consultant; b. Council Bluffs, Iowa, May 26, 1934; s. Moroni Lloyd and Geneva Gale (Williford) Danielsen; m. Eleanor Jean Gibson, June 7, 1958; children: Bartley Roland, Lea Anne, Albert William. BS, Clemson U., 1960; PhD, Duke U., 1966. From asst. prof. to prof. econs. U. Ga., Athens, 1963—97, prof. emeritus, 1997—; dir. Office Internat. Market Analysis, U.S. Dept. Energy, Washington, 1976—78, James C. Bonbright Utilities Ctr., U. Ga., 1991—; pres. Nat. Bus. and Econ. Edn. Assocs. Inc., 1988—, UBM Am., 2005—. Econ. cons. on pvt. contracts, regulation, elec. restructuring and privitization Czech Republic, Egypt, India, Malasia, Panama and U.S.; testified before numerous regulatory agys.; dir. nat. utility confs., 1980—. Author: Evolution of OPEC, 1982, Principles of Public Utility Rates, 1988, OPEC, Encyclopedia Britannica, 2002; contbr. articles to profl. jours.; author: documents in field. Grantee, Social Sci. Rsch. Coun., 1982. Mem.: Am. Econs. Assn., Internat. Assn. Energy Economists. Baptist. Avocations: swimming, golf. Office Phone: 706-202-2534. Personal E-mail: danielsen@bellsouth.net. Business E-Mail: bonbright@terry.uga.edu.

DANIELSON, ELENA SCHAFER, retired archivist; d. Louis and Hilda Schafer; m. Ronald Danielson; 1 child, Erik. AB, U. of Calif., Berkeley, 1969, MLS, 1979; PhD, Stanford U., 1975. Archivist Hoover Instn., Stanford, Calif., 1997—2002, assoc. dir., 2002—05, dir. of libr. and archives, 2002—05, ret., 2005. Author and archival cons. Contbr. articles to profl. jours. Recipient Ernst Posner award, Soc. of Am. Archivists, 2005, Nat. Order of Merit award, Romania, 2004, Laurel award, Prime Min. of Poland, 2001. Office: Hoover Instn Archives 434 Galvez Mall Stanford CA 94305-6010 Office Phone: 650-723-3563.

DANIELSON, GARY R., lawyer; b. Detroit, June 8, 1953; s. Ronald Gregory and Catherine (Gibson) D. BA in Psychology, Oakland U., Rochester, Mich., 1976; JD cum laude, Wayne State U., 1983. Bar: Mich. 1983, U.S. Dist. Ct. (ea. dist.) Mich., 1985, U.S. Supreme Ct. 1987. Sr. job placement counselor Ferndale (Mich.) Sch. Dist., 1976-79; employment and tng. adminstr. Oakland County Govt., Pontiac, Mich., 1979-82; sr. corp. labor rels. rep. Harper-Grace Hosps., Detroit, 1982-83; corp. labor rels. mgr. Vis. Nurse Assn., Detroit, 1983-85; atty., v.p., cons. Indsl. Rels., Inc., Detroit, 1985-90; pres. The Danielson Group, P.C., Chesterfield, Mich., 1988—. Mem. ABA, Mich. Bar Assn., Indsl. Rels. Rsch. Assn. Republican. Avocation: sailing. Office: Danielson Group PC 55921 Gratiot Chesterfield MI 48051 Office Phone: 586-749-6400. Business E-Mail: gdanielson@dgrouppc.com.

DANIELSON, GILBERT LAWRENCE, consumer products company executive; b. Monmouth, Ill., Aug. 22, 1946; BS, Drake U., 1968. With Arthur Andersen & Co., Chgo.; various sr. fin. positions; v.p. fin., CFO Aaron Rents, Inc., Atlanta, 1990-98, exec. v.p., CFO, 1998, also bd. dirs. Bd. dirs. Abrams Industries, Inc. 1st lt. U.S. Army, Vietnam. Office: Aaron Rents Inc 309 E Paces Ferry Rd NE Atlanta GA 30305-2377 Business E-Mail: Gil.Danielson@aaronrents.com.

DANIELSON, GORDON KENNETH, JR., cardiovascular surgeon, educator; b. Burlington, Iowa, Dec. 5, 1931; s. Gordon Kenneth and Helen H. (Hill) Danielson; m. Sondra Jean Bolich, Jan. 21, 1961; children: Gordon Kenneth III, Laura, Karen, Keith, Bruce, Susan, Jennifer. BA in Chemistry, U. Pa., Phila., 1953, MD, 1956, postgrad., 1960. Diplomate Am. Bd. Surgery, Am. Bd. Thoracic Surgery. Intern U. Mich. Hosp., Ann Arbor, 1956-57; asst. resident in surgery Hosp. of U. Pa., 1957-61, chief resident in surgery, 1961-62, gen. and thoracic surgeon, 1962-65, asst. chief surg. div. I, 1962-65; vis. fellow in thoracic surgery Thorax Kliniken, Stockholm, 1963-64; practice medicine specializing in thoracic and cardiovascular surgery Phila., 1963-65, Lexington, Ky., 1965-67, Rochester, Minn., 1967—2003. Assoc. prof. surgery U. Ky. Med. Sch.; chief cardiac surgery Univ. Hosp., 1965-67; faculty Mayo Grad. Sch. Medicine, Rochester, Minn., 1967-2003, prof. surgery, 1975—, Joe M. and Ruth Roberts prof. surgery, 1987-2004; past chmn. divsn. thoracic and cardiovascular surgery, cons. cardiovascular and thoracic surgery Mayo Clinic/Mayo Found., 1967-2003, St. Mary's Hosp., Meth. Hosp., Rochester, 1967-2003; Am. Heart Assn. vis. tchr., Singapore, 1975, Amman, Jordan, 1981, W.W.L. Glenn lectr., 1999. Editor: Cardiovascular Surgery, 1972—78; contbr. numerous articles to profl. jours. Recipient Albert Einstein award, 1956, Roche award, 1956, Spencer Morris prize, 1956; Markle Acad. Medicine scholar, 1962—67, Congenital Heart Disease Fellow, US USSR Health Exch. Program, 1973, Pfizer, Senatorial, Clark scholar, 1956. Fellow ACS, Am. Coll. Cardiology; mem. Am. Assn. Thoracic Surgery, Am. Surg. Assn., Am. Heart Assn. (fellow coun. cardiovascular surgery), Soc. Thoracic Surgeons (a founder), Soc. Univ. Surgeons, Soc. Vascular Surgery, Mexican Soc. Cardiology (hon.), Assn. Thoracic and Cardiovascular Surgeons of Asia (hon.), India (hon.), Chile Soc. Cardiology and Cardiovascular Surgery (hon.), Colombian Soc. of Cardiology (hon.), Congenital Heart Surgeons Soc., Peruvian Soc. of Cardiology (hon.), Phi Beta Kappa, Alpha Omega Alpha. Home: 6000 16th Ave NW Rochester MN 55901-2107 Office: Mayo Med Ctr Plummer N-10 Rochester MN 55905-0001 Office Phone: 507-284-2691. Business E-Mail: danielson.gordon@mayo.edu.

DANIELSON, JAMES WALTER, retired research microbiologist; b. Miller, SD, June 6, 1940; s. Walter Henry and Florence Marie (Manning) Danielson. BS, S.D. State U., 1968. Microbiologist FDA, Mpls., 1969—80, rsch. microbiologist, 1980—2000; ret., 2000. Germicide testing project officer FDA, 1990—92. Contbr. articles to profl. jour. Recipient Pub. Health Svc. Spl. Recognition award, Washington, 1988. Mem.: Am. Soc. for Microbiology, Assn. Ofcl. Analytical Chemists. Democrat. Roman Catholic. Achievements include development of methods for detecting ethylene oxide residuals in plastics and other materials; determination of effects of disinfectants on dialyzer membranes; determining leached compounds from rubber and plastic in parenteral solutions; sporicidal testing of germicides and determination of glutaraldehyde and phenol in germicides. Avocations: dance, tennis, volleyball. Home: 5925 Halifax Ave N Minneapolis MN 55429-2424 Personal E-mail: jwdan2@netzero.net.

DANIELSON, JOHN M., educational consultant, former federal agency administrator; b. Houston; Grad., U. Tex., Austin. Spl. asst. to sec. US Dept. Edn., Washington, 1991—93; nat. comty dir. AMERICA 2000, 1993—94; founder, prin. Comty. Edn. Ptnrs., 1994—2002; chief of staff to sec. US Dept. Edn., Washington, 2002—03; pres., CEO Chartwell Edn. Group LLC, NYC, 2005—. Office: Chartwell Education Group LLC Empire State Bldg Ste 7506 New York NY 10118 E-mail: danielson@chartwelleducation.com.

DANIELSON, PAUL E., state supreme court justice; m. Elizabeth "Betsy" Danielson; 1 child, Erik. BA, Fla. State U., Tallahassee; JD with honors, U. Ark., Fayetteville, 1975. Bar: Ark. 1975. Law clk. to Assoc. Justice Frank Holt Ark. Supreme Ct., assoc. justice position 5, 2007—; pvt. practice atty.; dep. pros. atty. 6th and 15th jud. dists. State of Ark.; city atty. City of Booneville, Ark.; cir. judge 15th jud. cir. Ark. Cir. Ct., 1994—2007. Instr. U. Ark. Sch. Law. Named Outstanding Trial Judge of Yr., Ark. Trial Lawyer Assn., 2003. Fellow: Ark. Bar Found.; mem.: Ark. Jud. Coun., Ark. Bar Assn. Office: Ark Supreme Ct Justice Bldg 625 Marshall St Little Rock AR 72201*

DANIELS-ROGERS, LATAUSHA, social sciences educator, entrepreneur; d. David D. and Lenora Daniels; m. Marcus Diego Rogers, Nov. 3, 2001 (div. Oct. 14, 2003); 1 child, Marcus Diego Rogers Jr. BS in Secondary Social Sci. Edn., Judson Coll., Marion, Ala., 2001; MA in Tech. Edn., Lesley U., Cambridge, Mass., 2007. Cert. tchr. Ala., highly qualified tchr. Ala. Dept. of Edn. and No Child Left Behind. Social studies tchr. permanent supply Birmingham City Schs., 2002—03; social studies tchr. Holy Family Cath. HS, Birmingham, 2003—04, Birmingham City Schs. Whatley K-8, 2004—07; Midfield bd. edn. Rutledge Mid. Sch., 2007—. Cheer coach Ala. HS Athletic Assn., Birmingham, 2003—; tchr. cons. and presenter Nat. Urban Alliance, Birmingham, 2005—; tchr. rep. Whatley Cmty. Forum, Birmingham, 2004—05; tchg. Am history grant tech. asst., 2006; founder Rebirth Soc. Women, 2006. Grantee Generation Next: Promoting Change, Cmty. and Voting Literacy, Columbia U. Tchrs. Coll., 2005, Photojournalism award Tchg. of Am. History, 2007. Mem.: AAUW, NEA, Birmingham Edn. Assn., Nat. Coun. Social Studies. Avocations: poetry, dance. Home: 160 20th St Hueytown AL 35023 Office: Midfield Bd Edn Rutledge Mid Sch 1221 8th St Midfield AL 35228 Home Phone: 205-497-9731; Office Phone: 205-780-8647.

DANIEN, ELIN C., archaeologist, researcher; b. NYC, July 17, 1929; m. Wilton R. Danien, Mar. 26, 1964. BA, U. Pa., 1982, MA, 1989, PhD, 1998. Pub. programs coord. U. Pa., Mus. Archaeology and Anthropology, Phila., 1981—97, rsch. assoc., 1998—. Initiator, organizer Annual Maya Weekend (Dir.'s award for Outstanding Contributions to Pub. Edn. in Archaeology, 1997); editor: Maya Folktales from the Alta Verapaz; author: Guide to the Mesoamerican Gallery; editor: New Theories on the Ancient Maya; exhibitions include Painted Metaphors: Pottery and Politics of the Ancient Maya; author: (biography) Mary Louise Baker: Painter of Maya Painted Pottery. Recipient Alice Paul award, U. Pa. Assn. Women Faculty and Adminstrs., 1991, Disting. Svc. award, U. Pa. Coll. Gen. Studies, 2001, award of distinction, 2007, Alumni award, U. Pa. Mem.: Am. Anthrop. Assn., Soc. Am. Archaeology (chair pub. rels. com. 1995—98), Phi Beta Kappa. Achievements include created Bread Upon the Waters, unique scholarship for women part-time students at U Pa. Office: U Pa Mus Archaeology 3260 South St Philadelphia PA 19104 Office Phone: 215-898-4000. Business E-Mail: edanien@sas.upenn.edu.

DANIKAS, DIMITRIOS, plastic surgeon; MD, U. Patras Med. Sch., Patras-Rion, Greece, 1991. Resident dept. gen. surgery St. Andrews' Gen. Regional Hosp., Patras, Achaia, Greece, 1992—94; intern N.Y. Hosp. Med. Ctr. Queens, Flushing, 1994—95; resident dept. surgery Monmouth Med. Ctr., Long Branch, NJ, 1995—2001; rschr. dept. plastic surgery So. Ill. U., Springfield, 2001—02; plastic surgeon dept. plastic surgery SUNY, Bklyn., 2002—03; plastic surgeon divsn. plastic surgery N.Y. Presbyn. Hosp., 2003—05, Plastic and Cosmetic Surgery Ctr., Eatontown, NJ, 2005—. Chief resident gen. surgery Beth Israel Med. Ctr., Newark, 2000—01, Monmouth Med. Ctr., Long Branch, NJ, 2000—01. Contbr. articles, chapters to books, presentations. Mem.: Am. Acad. of Anti-Aging Medicine, Mediterranean Council for Burns and Fire Disasters, Plastic Surgery Rsch. Council, Northeastern Soc. Plastic Surgeons, Hellenic Med. Soc. N.Y., Am. Soc. Gen. Surgeons, Soc.Laparoendoscopic Surgeons (hon. Outstanding Laparoendoscopy award 2000), Soc. Am. Coll. Surgeons (assoc.; candidate). Avocations: history, philosophy. Office: Plastic and Cosmetic Surgery Ctr 32 Corbett Way Eatontown NJ 07724 Home: 1 Channel Dr Unit 1105 Monmouth Beach NJ 07750-1340 Office Phone: 732-460-9555. Office Fax: 732-460-0699. Personal E-mail: ddanikas@yahoo.com.

DANILOV, VICTOR JOSEPH, museum administrator, educator, writer; b. Farrell, Pa., Dec. 30, 1924; s. Joseph M. and Ella (Tominovich) D.; m. Toni Dewey, Sept. 6, 1980; children: Thomas J., Duane P., Denise S. BA in Journalism, Pa. State U., 1945; MS in Journalism, Northwestern U., 1946; EdD in Higher Edn., U. Colo., 1964. With Sharon Herald, Pa., 1942, Youngstown (Ohio) Vindicator, 1945, Pitts. Sun-Telegraph, 1946-47, Chgo. Daily News, 1947-50; instr. journalism U. Colo., 1950-51; asst. prof. journalism U. Kans., 1951-53; with Kansas City Star, 1953; mgr. pub. rels. Ill. Inst. Tech. and IIT Rsch. Inst., 1953-57; dir. univ. rels. and pub. info. U. Colo., 1957-60; pres. Profile Co., Boulder, Colo., 1960-62; exec. editor, exec. v.p. Indsl. Rsch. Inc., Beverly Shores, Ind., 1962-69, pub., exec. v.p., 1969-71; dir., v.p. Mus. Sci. and Industry, Chgo., 1971-77, pres., dir., 1978-87, pres. emeritus, 1987—. Dir. mus. mgmt. program U. Colo., 1987-2004, adj. prof., 1987-2004; rural industrialization adv. group Dept. Agr., 1967; mem. panel internat. transfer tech. Dept. Commerce, 1968; sci. info. coun. NSF, 1969-72; chmn. Conf. on Implications Metric Change, 1972, Nat. Conf. Indsl. Rsch., 1966-70; chmn. observance Nat. Indsl. Rsch. Week, 1967-70; chmn. Midwest White House Conf. on Indsl. World Ahead, 1972, Internat. Conf. Sci. and Tech. Museums, 1976, 82; task force on fin. acctg. and reporting by non bus. orgns., others. Author: Public Affairs Reporting, 1955, Starting a Science Center, 1977, Science and Technology Centers, 1982, Science Center Planning Guide, 1985, Chicago's Museums, 1987, rev. edit., 1991, America's Science Museums, 1990, Corporate Museums, Galleries, and Visitor Centers: A Directory, 1991, A Planning Guide for Corporate Museums, Galleries, and Visitors Centers, 1992, Museum Careers and Training: A Professional Guide, 1994, University and College Museums, Galleries, and Related Facilities, 1996, Hall of Fame Museums: A Reference Guide, 1997, Colorado Museums and Historical Sites, 2000, Museums and Historic Sites of the American West, 2002, Sports Mus. and Halls of Fame Worldwide, 2005, Women and Museums: A Comprehensive Guide, 2005; editor: Crucial Issues in Public Relations, 1960, Corporate Research and Profitability, 1966, Innovation and Profitability, 1967, Research Decision-Making in New Product Development, 1968, New Products--and Profits, 1969, Applying Emerging Technologies, 1970, Nuclear Power in the South, 1970, The Future of Science and Technology, 1975, Museum Accounting Guidelines, 1976, Traveling Exhibitions, 1978, Towards the Year 2000, 1981; editor profl. procs.; contr. various profl. articles Trustee Women of the West Mus., 1991-99, v.p., 1991-99; trustee La Rabida Children's Hosp. and Rsch. Ctr., 1973-83; mem. U. Chgo. Citizens Bd., 1978-87. Mem. Am. Assn. Mus. (exec. com. 1976-77, bd. dirs. 1985-88, chmn. mus. studies task force 1988-89), AAAS, Assn. Sci.-Tech. Ctrs. (bd. dirs. 1973-84, sec.-treas. 1973-74, pres. 1975-76), Internat. Coun. Mus. (com. on sci. and tech. mus. 1972—, vice chmn. 1977-87, chmn. 1982-83, bd. dirs. 1985-88), Chgo. Coun. on Fine Arts (chmn. 1976-84), Ill. Arts Alliance (bd. dirs. 1983-86), Sci. Mus. Exhibit Collaborative (pres. 1983-86), Mus. Film Network (pres. 1984-86). Home and Office: 1426 Chicago Ave Evanston IL 60201 Office Phone: 847-328-5256.

DANILOVICH, JOHN J., federal official, former ambassador; b. Calif., June 25, 1950; m. Irene Forte, Mar. 19, 1977; children: John Charles, Alice, Alexander. Grad., The Choate Sch., 1968; BA in Polit. Sci., Stanford U., 1972; MA in Internat. Rels., U. So. Calif., London, 1980. Ptnr., cons. The Eisenhower Inst., Washington, 1987—90; US amb. to Costa Rica US Dept. State, San Jose, 2001—04, US amb. to Brazil, Brasilia, 2004—05; CEO Millenium Challenge Corp., Washington, 2005—. Bd. dirs. numerous shipping and property cos. Bd. dirs., chmn. transition com. Panama Canal Commn., 1991—96; former trustee Am. Mus. in Britain; former chmn. Republicans Abroad; former bd. dirs. Stanford U. Trust, U.S.-U.K. Fulbright Commn. Recipient Orden Nacional Juan Mora Fernandez award, Govt. Costa Rica. Mem.: Coun. on Fgn. Rels., White's (London), Pacific Union Club (San Francisco), Knights of Malta. Office: Millennium Challenge Corp 875 Fifteenth St NW Washington DC 20005 Business E-Mail: ketchemaj@mcc.gov.*

DANILOW, GREG A., lawyer; b. NYC, Feb. 23, 1949; BA cum laude, Lehigh U., 1970; JD, Fordham U., 1974. Law clerk to Judge John M. Cannella US Dist. Ct., So. Dist. NY, 1974—76; ptnr., co-head bus. and securities litigation dept. Weil, Gotshal & Manges LLP, NYC. Lectr. in field. Writing and rsch. editor Fordham Law Review, 1973—74. Office: Weil Gotshal & Manges LLP 767 Fifth Ave New York NY 10153 Office Phone: 212-310-8182. Office Fax: 212-310-8007. Business E-Mail: greg.danilow@weil.com.

DANISHEFSKY, SAMUEL J., chemistry professor; b. Bayonne, NJ, Mar. 10, 1936; BS, Yeshiva U., 1956; PhD in Chemistry, Harvard U., 1962. Fellow chemistry Columbia U., NYC, 1961-63, prof. chemistry, 1993—; asst. to prof. chemistry U. Pitts., 1963-79; prof. chemistry Yale U., New Haven, 1979-93, chmn. dept. chemistry, 1981-88; dir. Lab. for Bioorganic Chemistry Meml. Sloan-Kettering Inst., NYC, 1991—, Eugene W. Kettering chair, 1993—. Cons. Merck Sharp & Dohme, 1973—, GE Co., 1977—, vis. prof. Iowa State U., 1974, U. Calif., 1977, Rice U., 1977, Tex. A&M, 1986; vis. lectr. Tex., 1979; scientific adv. bd. Conforma Therapeutics. Recipient Wolf award in chemistry, Wolf Found., Israel, 1995, Claude S. Hudson award in Carbohydrate Chemistry, 1997, Tetrahedron prize, 1996, Bristol-Myers Squibb Lifetime Achievement award, Benjamin Franklin medal in Chemistry, Franklin Inst., 2006, Bristol-Myers Squibb Disting. Achievement award in Organic Synthesis, 2006. Fellow AAAS, Am. Acad. Arts and Sci.; mem. NAS (award in Chemical Sciences, 2006), Am. Chem. Soc. (Ernest Guenther award in the Chemistry of Natural Products, 1981, Aldrich award for Creative Work in Synthetic Organic Chemistry, 1986, Arthur C. Cope award 1998, Claude S. Hudson Award in Carbohydrate Chemistry, 1997, Nichols medal 1999, F.A. Cotton award for Excellence in Chemical Rsch., Tex. A&M U. sect., 2001, Roger Adams award in Organic Chemistry, 2007), Swiss Chem. Soc., Japanese Chem. Soc. Office: Sloan Kettering Inst 1275 York Ave New York NY 10021-6094 also: Dept Chemistry Columbia U 3000 Broadway mail code 3106 New York NY 10027 Office Phone: 212-639-5502, 212-854-6195. Office Fax: 212-854-7142, 212-772-8691. Business E-Mail: dshefsky@chem.columbia.edu, s-danishefsky@ski.mskcc.org.*

DANITZ, MARILYNN PATRICIA, choreographer, video specialist; b. Buffalo; BS in Chemistry, Le Moyne Coll.; MS in Chem. Engring., Columbia U. Artistic dir. High Frequency Wavelengths/Danitz Dances, 1976—. Assoc. prof. Tainan Cheng Chuan Coll., Taiwan, 1984; profl. dancer Ballet Mcpl. Strasbourg, France, Ballet Mcpl. Geneva, Switzerland; choreography commns. performances include The 11th Internat. Ballet Comp. Varna, Bulgaria, 1983, Tbilisi Ballet co., USSR, Nat. Ballet of Colombia, Nat. Inst. Arts, Taiwan, Nanatsudera Theatre, Nagoya, Japan, Shanghai Ballet and Shanghai Jiao Tung U., People's Republic of China,

Nat. Cheng Kung Dance Group, Taiwan, Jacob's Pillow Dance Festival, Mass., 6th Internat. Dance Theatre Festival, Poland, 5th Anniversary Celebration Kannon Ctr., St. Petersburg, Russia, 15th Internat. Festival of Modern Choreography, Belarus, Opening Ceremony World Congress UNESCO, Larnaka, Cyprus, 2005, others; master choreography workshops include Ctrl. Ballet, Beijing, Chinese Cultural U., Taipei, Taiwan, Okuda Studio, Nagoya, Ballet Philippines, Manila, NSW Coll. Dance, Sydney, The Ballet Sch., Bogota, Colombia, Lublin, Lodz, Poznan and Bytom, Poland, Vitebsk, Belarus, UNESCO 19th World Congress on Dance Rsch., Cyprus, others; video prodn. Reel Art Ways Nat. Residency, funded by NEA, 1990; video art collaboration with Allen Ginsberg. Presentations include Internat. Conf. on Dance and Tech., 1993, Naropa Inst. 20th Anniversary Celebration, 1994, Lincoln Ctr., N.Y.C., 1995, Hanyang U., Seoul, Korea, 1997, others; video work in permanent collection Lincoln Ctr. Dance Collection; TV prodns. of works include Nat. Broadcasting, Venezuela, Colombia, Bulgaria, Poland, Russia, Belarus, Cyprus, Pub. Broadcasting, Albany, N.Y.C., Mpls.; works performed by Nat. Ballet with the Nat. Philharm. Orch. of Colombia Gala Performance, 1984; co. tours include China, Japan, Taiwan, Europe, Hawaii, Philippines, Can, Europe, S.Am., Russia and Belarus, Cyprus; co-editor Branching Out, Oral Histories of the Founders of Six National Dance Orgns.; juror competitions. Recipient Outstanding Dance-Theater Work of 1986 award Dance Brew-ATV Cable Manhattan, award for disting. choreography Nat. Assn. Regional Ballet, 1982; Bessie Schoenberg Lab. for Experienced Choreographers Dance Theater Workshop; NIH fellow; Gold Medal scholar Conservatoire Geneve, N.Y. State Regents scholar, Le Moyne Coll. Chemistry scholar, others. Mem. UNESCO Internat. Dance Coun., Dance Theater Workshop, Am. Dance Guild (pres., editor Am. Dance, bd. dirs., nat. conf. planning com.), Soc. Dance History Scholars, Dance Films Assn., Congress on Rsch. in Dance Address: 560 Riverside Dr Apt 16E New York NY 10027-3208 also: PO Box 216 Sand Lake NY 12153-0216 Address: 2242 Beech St Virginia Beach VA 23451 Personal E-mail: HFW2000@aol.com.

DANK, LEONARD DEWEY, medical illustrator, audio-visual consultant; b. Birmingham, Ala., Dec. 21, 1929; s. George and Ellen (Balsam) D.; B.A. in Zoology, Cornell U., 1952; grad. Sch. Med. Illustration, Mass. Gen. Hosp., 1955; m. Beryl Eileen Jealous, Sept. 30, 1961; 1 dau., Amelia Theresa. Staff med. artist, plastic surgery clinic Manhattan Eye, Ear & Throat Hosp., 1955-57, Eye Bank for Sight Restoration, 1957-59; owner Leonard D. Dank Med. Illustration Studio, 1959-79; pres. Med. Illustrations Co., 1979— (all N.Y.C.); cons. med. illustrator St. Luke's Hosp., 1961-83, trans-vision div. Milprint, Inc., 1965— , Woman's Hosp., 1963-83, H.S. Struttman, Inc., 1964— , Home Library Press, 1960-70 (all N.Y.C.), Synapse Communications, Inc. (Conn.), 1973-75, Contemporary Orthopaedics and Contemporary Surgery, 1981-85, P.W. Communications, Inc., 1982-89, Esquire Mags. Health and Fitness Clinic, 1985-88, Whittle Communications, 1988—. Recipient 1st prize certificate merit A.M.A., 1959, 1st prize citation of merit in motion picture program A.C.S., 1959, 62; Better Teller award Assn. Indsl. Advertisers, 1973, Outstanding Sci. Book award for Children Nat. Sci. Tchrs. Assn., 1982, Cert. of Merit Soc. of Illustrators, 1986. Mem. Assn. Med. Illustrators, Guild Natural Sci. Illustrators. Roman Catholic. Co-author: Gynecologic Operations, 1978; med. illustrator for numerous med. books, jours., elementary textbooks, juvenile books, encys. Fax: 631-734-5496. Home and Office: PO Box 944 Cutchogue NY 11935-0944 Office Phone: 631-734-6199.

DANKANYIN, ROBERT JOHN, management consultant; b. Sharon, Pa., Sept. 4, 1934; s. John and Anna (Kolesar) D.; m. Dorothy Jean Kuchel, Aug. 9, 1958 (div. June 1975); children: Douglas John, David Jay, Dana Jean; m. Georgia C. Oleson, Apr. 2, 1988 (dec. Sept. 1990); m. Charlene Marcella Bassett, May 16, 1998 BSCE, Pa. State U., 1956; MBA, U. So. Calif., 1961; MSEE, UCLA, 1963; DBA, Belford U., 2006. Cert. level 2 Profl. Ski Instrs. Am. From mgr. mobile ICBM systems engrng. dept. to mgr. space system lab. Hughes Aircraft Co., Culver City, Calif., 1956-68; program mgr. Litton Industries, Beverly Hills, Calif., 1968-70; v.p. program mgmt. Litton Ship Systems, Culver City, 1970-71, Litton Ship Sys., Pascagoula, Miss., 1971-73; asst. mgr. for U.S. Roland program, Canoga Pk., Calif. Hughes Aircraft Co., Culver City, Calif., 1975-77, asst. divsn. mgr. missile devel. div. Canoga Pk., Calif., 1977-84, mgr. land combat systems divsn. Culver City, Calif., 1984-86, group v.p. missile systems group, 1986-87; v.p., asst. group exec. missle systems group Canoga Park, Calif., 1987-88; v.p., asst. group exec. space and communication group, El Segundo, Calif. Hughes Aircraft Co., Culver City, Calif., 1988-89, corp. sr. v.p. diversification LA, 1989-92, sr. v.p. bus. devel., 1992-93; sr. v.p., pres. Hughes Indsl. Electronics Co., LA, 1993-95; group exec. Whittaker Corp., Westwood Village, Calif., 1973-75; pres., chmn. bd. Whittaker Cmty. Devel. Corp., Englewood, Colo., Knoxville, Tenn., Westwood Village, San Juan, P.R., 1973-75; internat. bus. and mgmt. cons., pres., CEO ITI, Malibu, Calif., 1995—. Chmn. Hughes Program Mgr. Devel. Course, L.A., 1976-88; chmn., bd. dirs. Light Valve Products, Inc., 1988-92, Hughes/Japan Victor Tech. Inc., 1992-95, Hughes Micro Electronics Ltd., Glenrothes, Scotland, Hughes Europa Ltd., Brussels, Belgium, 1993-95; bd. dirs. Hughes Environ. Sys., Inc., Long Beach, Calif.; Hughes España, Madrid, Spain, Aero Sys., Inc., Paris; mem. adv. bd. Pulse Link Inc., San Diego, 2002-05; dir. several wholly owned subs. including Direct TV, Spectrolab, Hughes Network Sys., RF Identification Sys.; lectr., guest spkr., author on tech. mgmt.; bus. ventures, fgn. mktg., def. conversion, diversification and entrepreneurship. Editor Inter Fraternity/Sorority Newsletter Pa. State U., 1955-56. Chmn. indsl. and profl. adv. coun. Coll. Engrng. Pa. State U.; ski instr. Bear Mountain Ski Resort, Big Bear Lake, Calif., 1990-2005; chmn. several indsl. task forces reporting to U.S. congl. coms. Voted Ordo Honorium by Kappa Delta Rho Fraternity, 1991, outstanding Engr. of the Yr. by Pa. State U., 1991; honored as outstanding engineering alumnus, 1992. Mem. Am. Def. Preparedness Assn. (bd. dirs. 1986-94, chmn. fin. com. 1990-94), Hughes Mgmt. Club, Aero Club So. Calif., Marina City Club, Riviera Country Club (bd. govs. 1999—2004), Calif. Yacht Club. Republican. Roman Catholic. Avocations: skiing, scuba diving, sailing, hiking, fishing, golf. Home: 20700 Rockpoint Rd Malibu CA 90265 Office Phone: 310-508-6863. Personal E-mail: IamBobbyD@aol.com.

DANKE, VIRGINIA, educational administrator, travel consultant; b. Spokane, Wash., Mar. 9, 1925; d. William Ernest and Daisy May (Norton) Danke. BS, Wash. State U., 1947; MEd, Whitworth Coll., 1950; postgrad., LaSalle U., 1973. Cert. tchr. Counselor Clarkston (Wash.) Sch. Dist., 1947—48; head phys. edn. dept. Lewis & Clark H.S., Spokane Sch. Dist., 1948—77; travel cons. Viking Travel, Spokane, 1982—, Empire Tours, Spokane, 1982—. Co-author (editor): Marching Together, 1955. Treas. Fedn. Western Outdoor Clubs, 1980—92; com. mem. Future Spokane, 1981—, bd. dirs., Pacific Crest Trail Conf., Santa Ana, Calif., 1984; mem. Am. Red Cross Disaster Unit; vol. Meals on Wheels, 2004—. Named to Wash. State Officials Hall of Fame, 2003, Inland Empire Softball Hall of Fame, 2004; recipient Scroll of Honor-Hall of Fame, Spokane C. of C., 1983, Greater Spokane Sports Assn., 1973, Wash. Interscholastic Activites Assn., 1990, State Officiating, 1992, Red Cross award, 2006, spl. award, ARC, 2006. Mem.: Spokane Ret. Tchrs. Assn. (pres. 1981—82), Wash. State Ofcls. Assn. (Meritorious Svc. award 2002, named to Hall of Fame 2003), Wash. State Ret. Tchrs. Assn. (bd. dirs. 1987—), Nat. Ret. Tchrs. Assn., Wash. Edn. Assn., Spokane Edn. Assn. (com. chmn. 1960—70, pres. 1981—82), Friends Centennial Trail (bd. dirs. 1994—96), Soroptimist (pres. 1970), Hangman Golf Club (Spokane pres. 1997), Hobnailers Club (pres. 1966—67, 1986—87). Home: 1103 E 14th Ave Spokane WA 99202-2541

DANKNER, JAY WARREN, lawyer; b. Bklyn., June 15, 1949; s. Morris and Frances Dankner; m. Iris Rose Terens, May 15, 1983; children: Danielle Renee, Nicole Beth. BA cum laude, Bklyn. Coll., 1970, JD cum laude, 1973. Bar: N.Y. 1974, Fla. 1974, U.S. Dist. Ct. (ea. and so. dists.) N.Y. 1974, U.S. Ct. Appeals (2d cir.) 1974, U.S. Supreme Ct. 1977, U.S. Dist. Ct. (no. dist.) N.Y. 1986. From assoc. to ptnr. Sullivan & Liapakis P.C., NYC, 1974-94; ptnr. Dankner & Milstein, P.C., NYC, 1994—. Lectr. Practicing Law Inst., N.Y.C., 1983-87, N.Y. State Trial Lawyers Inst., 1985—, continuing legal edn. program Bklyn. Law Sch., 1986—, N.Y. State Bar Assn. CLE Programs, Nassau County Bar Assn., Queens Bar Assn.; mem. Bklyn. Law Rev., 1972-73; bd. dirs. Atty's Info. Exchange Group, Inc., 1981—. Author: Products Liability Practice Guide, 1988, Masters of Trial Practice, 1988, Deposing Corporate Defendants in Products Liability Actions, 1988, Trial Strategy - Plaintiffs View, 1988; contbr. articles to profl. jours. Named a NY Super Lawyers, 2006; named one of Best Lawyers in Am., Town & Country, 1985, 2007, NY Area's Best Lawyers, 2006—07, Best Lawyers in Am., 2007, Leading Plaintiffs' Lawyers in Am., Lawdragon, 2007; named to NY Super Lawyers, 2006—07, Million Dollar Advs. Forum, 1994—. Mem. ABA, NY State Bar Assn. (spl. com. for jud. discipline 1987-89), Assn. of Bar of City of NY (mem. products liability com. 1993-97, 2005-07), Fla. Bar Assn., Assn. Trial Lawyers Am., NY State Trial Lawyers Assn. (chair products liability com. 1991, 93-94, mem. products liability com. 1992-93), NY County Lawyers Assn. (mem. products liability com. 1992-93). Home: 524 E 72nd St New York NY 10021-9801 Office: Dankner & Milstein PC 41 E 57th St New York NY 10022-1908 Office Phone: 212-751-8000. Business E-Mail: jwd@danknermilstein.com.

DANKO, GARY J., chef; b. Massena, NY, Dec. 31, 1956; s. Frank J. and Opal (Self) D. Assoc. Occupational Studies, Culinary Inst. Am., 1977. Head chef White Pillars Inn, Norwood, NY, 1977-78, Vanity Fair, Bookstore and Bistro, San Francisco, 1978-80; chef, cons. Anthony's Classic Cuisine, Plattsburgh, NY, 1980-81; head chef, kitchen mgr. Powder Hound Inn, Warren, Vt., 1981-82; head chef Tucker Hill Country Inn/Restaurant, Waitsfield, Vt., 1982-84; exec. chef Beringer Vineyards, St. Helena, Calif., 1985-86; chef de cuisine Calif. Festival, Palace Hotel, Tokyo, 1987-88; exec. chef Chateau Souverain Winery and Restaurant, Geyserville, Calif., 1986-90; chef The Restaurant The Ritz-Carlton, San Francisco, 1991-92, exec. chef The Dining Room, 1992—. Guest chef Holidome, Ann Arbor, Mich., 1986; chef de cuisine Calif. Festival, Palace Hotel, Tokyo, 1987, 88; faculty mem. Sch. for Am. Chefs at Beringer Vineyards, 1989-90; guest chef Cunard Sea Goddess, 1991, Draegers Culinary Ctr., Menlo Park, Calif., 1993, 94, 95; cons. Stouffer Corp., Culinary Round Table, Solon, Ohio, 1992, Ketchum Pub. Rels., Sun Dried Tomato Promotion, 1992; restaurant cons. Ed Moose and Assocs., 1992—; cons. chef The Newport Rm., The Hotel Arts, Barcelona, Spain, 1993—. Recipes pub. in LA Times, San Francisco Chronicle, San Francisco Examiner, Times Tribune, Wine Country, Susan Costner's Great Sandwiches, Good Friends, Great Dinners, New California Cuisine, California Wine Country Cooking, Madeleine Cooks, Cuisine of the Wine Country; chef Madeleine Cooks, Md. Pub. TV, Breger Video. Recipient James Beard award Best Chef Calif., 1995, Outstanding Service award, 2006, Best 10 New Chef in Am. Domaine Mumm Food & Wine Mag., 1989. Home: 5 Russian Hill Pl San Francisco CA 94133-3605*

DANKO, GEORGE, engineering educator; b. Budapest, Hungary, Apr. 3, 1944; came to U.S., 1986; s. Gyorgy and Ilona (Mihaly) D.; m. Eva Arvay, Dec. 14, 1976; 1 child, Reka. BSME, Tech. U. Budapest, 1968, PhD, 1976; MS in Applied Math., Eotvos U. of Scis., Budapest, 1975; PhD, Hungarian Acad. Scis., Budapest, 1985. Cert. Profl. Ski Instrs. Am. Assn. Asst. prof. Tech. U. Budapest, 1968-75, assoc. prof., 1979-86; fellow Hungarian Acad. Scis., Budapest, 1975-79; rsch. assoc. U. Nev., Reno, 1986-90, assoc. prof., 1990-95, prof. mining engring., 1995—. Cons. Sierra Sci., Reno, 1990—; chmn. High-Level Radioactive Waste Mgmt. Conf., 1991, 92; portrait artist, Reno, 1987-92. Co-author: Methods for the Calculation of Pipeline Transients, 1976, Warming-up and Cooling of Electrical Machinery, 1982; contbr. articles to profl. jours. Com. rep. Truckee River Steering Com., Reno, 1993-94. Grantee U.S. Bur. Mines, 1986-97, U.S. Dept. Energy, 1991—, Clarkson Co., 1992-98. Mem. ASME, ISES (internat. organizing com. 1993-94), IFAC (internat. program com. 1995—), Soc. Mining Engrs., Am. Nuclear Soc. Achievements include patents for methods and apparatus for the determination of the heat transfer coefficient, process and apparatus for the determination of thermophysical properties, underground cooling enhancement for nuclear waste repository, method and apparatus for underground nuclear waste repository, others. Office: U Nev Reno Mining Engrng Dept 173 Reno NV 89557-0001

DANN, EMILY, mathematics educator; b. Albany, Ga., July 26, 1932; d. Jesse Lyman and Evelyn (Calhoun) Dann; m. Christian A. Hansen, June 7, 1977; children: Leslie Montgomery Przybyzewski, Ann Christiansen, Robin Hansen, Randall Hansen, Rhonda Hansen McAleaivey, Rheta Hansen. BA, Huntingdon Coll., 1954; MS in Math., U. Houston, 1966; MS in Computer Sci., Monmouth U., W. Long Branch, NJ, 1993; EdD, Rutgers U., 1976. Instr. Lee Coll., Baytown, Tex., 1965-67; prof. Middlesex County Coll., Edison, N.J., 1967-81; dir. human resources Hanlin Group (formerly LCP Chem. & Plastics Co.), Edison, N.J., 1981-84, systems analyst, 1986-89; v.p. Assoc. Svcs., Edison, N.J., 1989-91; sr. math. edn. assoc. Rutgers U. Sch. Edn., New Brunswick, N.J., 1991-95, 99—, sr. math. edn. specialist, 1995-99; asst. prof. edn. CCNY, NYC, 1995-99; sr. math. edn. specialist Rutgers U. Grad. Sch. Edn., 1999—. Vis. assoc. prof. math. Drew U., 1984-86; cons. Title I math. program Bedminster (N.J.) Pub. Sch., 1976-77; mem. co-adj. faculty Grad. Sch. Edn., Rutgers U., 1976-81, Kean Coll., 1980-81. Contbr. articles to profl. jours. Mem. ASTD, Acad. Mgmt., Orgn. Devel. Network, Am. Math. Assn., Jean Piaget Soc. Home: 1 Scenic Dr Highlands NJ 07732-1329 Personal E-mail: edann75@comcast.net.

DANN, MARC, state attorney general, former state senator; b. Evanston, Ill., Mar. 12, 1962; m. Alyssa Lenhoff; 3 children. BA in Hist., U. Mich., 1984; JD, Case Western Res. U., 1987. Ptnr. Betraz and Dann, 1991—99, Dann and Falgiani, Youngstown, Ohio, 1999—2007; mem. Ohio State Senate from Dist. 32, Columbus, 2003—07, ranking minority mem., mem. agr., highways and transp., judiciary civil justice, judiciary criminal justice, ways and means, and econ. devel. coms.; atty. gen. State of Ohio, Columbus, 2007—. Mem. regional bd. Anti-Defamation League; mem. bd. edn. Liberty Twp., Ohio, 2001—02. Named Legislator of Yr., Ohio Farmers Union, 2005, Amvets, 2005; recipient Pro Bono award, N.E. Ohio Legal Svcs. Mem.: Mahoning and Trumbull County Bar Assns., Tobacco-Free Youth, Youngstown-Warren Regional C. of C., Jewish Cmty. Ctr. Democrat. Office: Office of Atty Gen State Office Tower 30 E Broad St 17th Fl Columbus OH 43266-0410*

DANN, OLIVER TOWNSEND, psychoanalyst, psychiatrist, educator; b. Mansfield, Ohio, Aug. 10, 1935; s. Edward William and Mary Virginia (Townsend) D.; m. Linda Marie Schweers, July 15, 1961; children: Sara Katharine, Jonathan William Jenner, Luke Nathan Townsend, Jesse Charles. AB, Columbia U., 1958; MD, Yale U., 1962. Diplomate Am. Bd. Psychiatry and Neurology. Resident in psychiatry Sch. Medicine Yale U., New Haven, 1963-67, asst., assoc. prof. psychiatry Sch. Medicine, 1967-79; clin. prof. psychiatry Miller Sch. Medicine U. Miami, Fla., 1980—; dir. Fla. Psychoanalytic Inst., 1997—2001, chair edn. com., 2003—05. Pvt. practice, Miami, 1979—. Contbr. articles to profl. jours. Fellow APA (disting. life), Ctr. for Advanced Psychoanalytic Studies; mem. SAR, Am. Psychoanalytic Assn., Internat. Psychoanalytic Assn., Western New England Inst. Soc. Psychoanalysis, Balt.-Washington Inst. Soc. Psychoanalysis, Fla. Psychanalytic Inst. Soc. Found., Mayflower Soc., Jamestowne Soc., Huguenot Soc., Explorers Club, Phi Beta Kappa. Avocations: sailing, canoeing, hiking. Home and Office: 4550 SW 74th St Miami FL 33143-6271 Office Phone: 305-665-5677.

DANNEMILLER, JOHN C., transportation company executive; b. Cleve., May 17, 1938; s. John Charles and Jean I. (Bage) D.; m. Jean Marie Sheridan, Sept. 22, 1962; children— David, Peter BS, Case Western Res. U., 1960, MBA, 1964; postgrad., Stanford U., 1975, Columbia U., 1974, Tuck Exec. program Dartmouth Coll., 1976. Vice pres. foods div. Diamond Shamrock, 1978-81, dir. planning, 1981-83; v.p. SDS Biotech Corp., Cleve., 1984-85; group v.p. leasing group Leaseway Transp., Cleve., 1984-85, pres., chief operating officer, 1985-88, exec. v.p., chief oper. officer, 1988—; exec. v.p. Bearings Inc., Cleve., 1988—, now chmn., ceo, b d. dirs. Bd. dirs. Lamson & Sessions, Cleve., Star Bank, Cleve. Bd. dirs., advisor Jr. Achievement, Cleve., 1962-64; bd. dirs. Luth. Med. Found.; fund raiser United Way, Cleve. and St. Louis Mem. Bearing Speciality Assn., Cleve. Athletic Club, Lakewood Country Club, Union Club, Univ. Club, Beta Gamma Sigma. Republican. Presbyterian. Avocations: tennis, water-skiing, boating, skiing, golf. Office: Bearings Inc PO Box 6925 3600 Euclid Ave Cleveland OH 44115-2515

DANNENBERG, ARTHUR MILTON, JR., experimental pathologist, immunologist, educator; b. Phila., Oct. 17, 1923; s. Arthur Mansbach and Marion (Loeb) D.; m. Aileen Rose Hart, Mar. 30, 1948; children: Arlene Dannenberg Bowes, Andrew Loeb, Audrey Ann. AB, Swarthmore Coll., 1944; MD, Harvard U., 1947; MA, U. Pa., 1951, PhD, 1952. Diplomate: Nat. Bd. Med. Examiners. Intern Albert Einstein Med. Ctr., Phila., 1947-48; rsch. resident Children's Hosp., Phila., 1948-49; fellow Henry Phipps Inst. U. Pa., Phila., 1950-52, asst. prof., 1956-64; fellow U. Utah, 1952-54; assoc. prof. environ. health scis. Johns Hopkins U. Bloomberg Sch. Pub. Health, Balt., 1964-73, prof., 1973—, prof. joint faculty sch. medicine dept. pathology, 1976—. Mem. editl. bd. Am. Rev. Respiratory Diseases, 1973-75, 79-84, Infection and Immunity jour., 1976-78; contbr. articles to profl. jours. and chpts. to books. Lt. comdr. Med. Rsch. Unit 1, USN, 1954-56. Mem. Am. Soc. Investigative Pathology, Histochem. Soc., Am. Soc. Microbiology, Soc. for Leukocyte Biology (sec. 1975-76), Am. Assn. Immunologists, Am. Thoracic Soc., Soc. Investigative Dermatology. Home: 12 Lake Manor Ct Baltimore MD 21210-1017 Office Phone: 410-955-3062. Office Fax: 410-955-0105. Business E-Mail: artdann@jhsph.edu.

DANNENBERG, KONRAD K., aeronautical engineer; b. Weissenfels, Germany, Aug. 5, 1912; came to U.S. 1945. s. Hermann and Klara (Kittler) D.; m. Ingeborg M. Kamke, Apr. 8, 1944 (dec.); 1 child, Klaus Dieter; m. Jacquelyn E. Staiger, Mar. 31, 1990. MS Engring., Techn. U., Hannover, Ger., 1938. Asst. Tech. U., Hannover, 1938, engr. Frankfurt, Germany, 1939; rschr. HAP-Peenemuende, Germany, 1940-45; mgr. U.S. Army Ordnance, Ft. Bliss, Tex., 1945-50, ABMA, Huntsville, Ala., 1950-60, NASA/MSFC, Huntsville, 1960-73; assoc. prof. UTSI-U. Tenn., Tullahoma, 1973-78; cons. The Space & Rocket Ctr., Huntsville, 1978—. Author: In Memory of H. Oberth, 1990, Vahrenwald to Dresden, 1990; (with E. Stuhlinger) Rocket Center Peenemünde, 1993, Albert Püllenberg and the Gesellschaft für Raketenforschung, 1995, (with Donald Tarter) Mitchell R. Sharpe-Aerospace Historian, 1997. Lt. German Army, 1939—40. Recipient Meritorious Svc. award U.S. Army, 1960, Exceptional Svc. award NASA, 1969, Konrad K. Dannenberg scholarship, 1992, Gov. of Ala. Commendation, 2002, Genesis award Ala. Info. Tech. Assn., 2004. Fellow AIAA (chpt. chmn. 1967, Durand lectr. pub. svc. 1990), Holger N. Toftoy award, Hermann Oberth award 1996); mem. Hermann Oberth Soc. (hon., Golden Hermann Oberth medal 1994), Nat. Space Soc. (charter), Am. Rocket Soc. (chmn. 1962). Lutheran. Achievements include patents in rocket engine design. Home and Office: 233 Cheswick Dr Madison AL 35757-8712 Personal E-mail: konrad2@aol.com.

DANNER, BLYTHE, actress; b. Phila., Feb. 3, 1943; d. Harry Earl and Katharine D.; m. Bruce W. Paltrow, Dec. 14, 1969 (dec. Oct. 3, 2002); children: Gwyneth Kate, Jake, Laura. BA in Drama, Bard Coll., 1965, DFA (hon.), 1981; LHD (hon.), Hobart-Smith Coll., 1981. Appeared as Laura in Glass Menagerie, 1965; repertory at Theatre Co. Boston, The Knack, and 7 new Am. Plays, 1965-66; appeared as Helena in repertory Midsummer Night's Dream, Trinity Sq. Playhouse, R.I.; appeared as Irena in repertory Three Sisters, Trinity Sq. Playhouse, R.I., 1967; with Lincoln Ctr. Repertory Co. in Summertree, 1968, Cyrano de Bergerac, 1968, Elise in the Miser, 1969 (Theatre World award); appeared on Broadway as Jill Tanner in Butterflies Are Free (Tony award 1971); also appeared in Major Barbara, 1971, Twelfth Night, 1972, The Seagull, 1974, Ring Around The Moon, 1975, Betrayal, 1980 (Tony award nominee), Blithe Spirit, 1987, A Streetcar Named Desire, 1988, Sylvia, 1995, Moonlight, 1995, Suddenly Last Summer, 2006; actor (films) 1776, 1972, To Kill a Clown, 1972, Lovin' Molly, 1974, Hearts of the West, 1975, The Seagull, 1975, Futureworld, 1976, The Great Santini, 1980, Too Far to Go, 1982, Man, Woman, And Child, 1983, Brighton Beach Memoirs, 1986, Another Woman, 1988, Mr. and Mrs. Bridge, 1990, Alice, 1990, The Prince of Tides, 1991, Husbands and Wives, 1992, To Wong Foo, Thanks for Everything, Julie Newmar, 1995, The Myth of Fingerprints, 1997, The X Files, 1998, The Farmhouse, 1998, Forces of Nature, 1999, The Love Letter, Meet the Parents, 2000, The Invisible Circus, 2001, 3 Days of Rain, 2002, The Quality of Life, 2003, Sylvia, 2003, Meet the Fockers, 2004, (voice) Howl's Moving Castle, 2004, The Last Kiss, 2006; (TV movies) To Confuse the Angel, 1970, Dr Cook's Garden, 1971, George M!, 1972, The Scarecrow, 1972, F. Scott Fitzgerald and "The Last of the Belles", 1974, Sidekicks, 1974, Eccentricities of a Nightingale, 1976, The Court-Martial of George Armstrong Custer, 1977, A Love Affair: Eleanor and Lou Gehrig, 1978, Are You in the House Alone?, 1978, Roots: The Next Generations, 1979, Too Far to Go, 1979, You Can't Take It With You, 1979, Inside the Third Reich, 1982, In Defense of Kids, 1983, Helen Keller-The Miracle Continues, 1984, Guilty Conscience, 1985, A Streetcar Named Desire, 1988; Tattinger's, 1988, Judgment, 1990, Never Forget, 1991, Cruel Doubt, 1992, Getting Up and Going Home, 1992, Homage, 1995, Saint Maybe, 1998, We Were the Mulvaneys, 2002, Back When We Were Grownups, 2004; (TV series) Adam's Rib, 1973, Healthcare Crisis, 2000, Presidio Med, 2002-03, Huff, 2004- (Emmy award for outstanding supporting actor in a miniseries or a movie, 2005, Emmy award for outstanding supporting actress in a drama series, 2006). Recipient Theatre World award, 1969; Best Actress award Vevey Film Festival, Switzerland, 1982*

DANNER, BRYANT CRAIG, lawyer; b. Boston, Nov. 18, 1937; s. Nevin Earle and Marjorie (Harms) D.; m. Judith I. Baker, Aug. 23, 1958; 1 child Debra Irene. BA, Harvard U., 1960, LLB, 1963. Bar: Calif. 1963, U.S. Dist. Ct. (cen. dist.) Calif. 1963. Assoc. Latham & Watkins, LA, 1963-70, ptnr., 1970-92; sr. v.p., gen. counsel So. Calif. Edison Co., Rosemead, Calif., 1992-95, exec. v.p., gen. counsel, 1995—2005, Edison Internat., Rosemead, 2000—05. Mem. L.A. County Bar Assn. (chmn. environ. sect. 1988-89). Avocations: fly fishing, astronomy.*

DANNER, KATHLEEN FRANCES STEELE, federal official; b. Kansas City, Mo., Oct. 28, 1960; m. Steve Danner, Jan. 18, 1996. Admissions counselor N.E. Mo. State U., Kirksville, 1980-83, assoc. dir. admissions, 1983-86, programming coord. dept. pub. svcs., 1986-87; Iowa, N.H. dir. Gephardt for Pres., St. Louis, 1987-88; mem. Mo. Ho. of Reps., Jefferson City, 1988-94; state dir. Clinton for Pres., 1991-92; regional dir. U.S. Dept. HHS, Kansas City, Mo., 1994—, acting dir. intergovtl. affairs Washington, 1998—. Pres. Greater Kansas City Fed. Exec. Bd. Pres. Greater Mo. Found.; exec. com. Heart of Am. United Way; mem. White House Outreach Task Force on CHIP. Recipient Hammer award V.P. Gore, 1999, award for disting. svc. Sec. Shalala, 1998. Mem. Ctrl. Exch., Nat. Women's Polit. Caucus. Roman Catholic. Avocations: sports, dance, reading, politics. Office: US Dept Health and Human Svcs 601 E 12th St Ste 210 Kansas City MO 64106-2826 Home: 306 Earnhardt Dr Branson MO 65616

DANNER, PATSY ANN, former congresswoman; b. Louisville, Ky., Jan. 13, 1934; d. Henry J. and Catherine M. (Shaheen) Berrer; children: Stephen, Stephanie, Shane, Shavonne.; m. C.M. Meyer, Dec. 30, 1982. Student, Hannibal-LaGrange Coll., 1952; BA in Polit. Sci. cum laude, N.E. Mo. State U., 1972. Dist. asst. to Congressman Jerry Litton, Kansas City, Mo., 1973-76; fed. co-chmn. Ozarks Regional Commn., Washington, 1977-81; mem. Mo. State Senate, 1983-1992, 103rd-106th Congress from 6th Mo. dist., 1993-2001. Mem. internat. rels. com., transp. and infrastructure com. Mem.: LWV (bd. mem., health chairwoman Columbia-Boone County, Mo.). Democrat. Roman Catholic.

DANNER, RICHARD ALLEN, dean, law educator; b. Marshfield, Wis., Aug. 26, 1947; s. Reuben Mathias and Evelyn (Fischer) D.; m. Cheryl Clark Sanford, Jan. 27, 1973; children— Zachary Allen, Katherine Elizabeth BA, U. Wis., 1969, MS, 1975, JD, 1979; postgrad., MIT, 1973. Bar: Wis. 1979. Environ. law libr. U. Wis. Law Libr., Madison, 1975-79; assoc. law libr. Duke U. Sch. Law, Durham, NC, 1979-80, acting law libr., instr., 1980-81, dir. law libr., 1981-93, asst. prof. law, 1981-82, assoc. prof., 1982-85, prof., 1985—, assoc. dean, 1993-98, sr. assoc. dean info. svcs., 1998—. Dir. Triangle Rsch. Librs. Network, 1984-97. Author: Legal Research in Wisconsin, 1980, Strategic Planning: A Law Library Management Tool, 1991, 2d edit., 1996, Toward a Renaissance in Law Librarianship, 1997; editor Law Library Management Tool, 1991, Law Libr. Jour., 1984-94; co-editor: Introduction to Foreign Legal Systems, 1994; contbr. articles to profl. jours. With U.S. Army, 1969-71 Decorated Bronze Star Mem. ABA, Am. Assn. Law Librs. (pres. 1989-90), ALA, State Bar Wis. Home: 2419 Tryon Rd Durham NC 27705-5511 Office: Duke U Sch Law Libr PO Box 90361 Durham NC 27708-0361 Office Phone: 919-613-7115. E-mail: danner@law.duke.edu.

DANNEY, MARK MAXWELL, pediatrician; b. Buffalo, Oct. 23, 1946; s. Ervin Arnold and Elizabeth Gertrude Danney; m. Shaun Allison Hartford, Feb. 14, 1992; children: Melissa Marie, Christopher Marc, Angela Michelle, Nicholas Matthew. BS, USAF Acad., 1968; MD, Johns Hopkins U., 1972. Diplomate Am. Bd. Pediat., 1977, Am. Bd. Pediatric Endocrinology, 1978. Pediatric resident Wilford Hall USAF Med. Ctr., San Antonio, 1972—74, pediatric endocrinologist, 1976—84, chmn. pediat. residency, 1985—88, ret., col., 1988; pediatric fellow in pediatric endocrinology U. Iowa, Iowa City, 1974—76; asst. chmn. pediat. David Grant USAF Med. Ctr., Travis AFB, Calif.; assoc. prof. pediat. U. Tex. Health Sci. Ctr., San Antonio, 1988—94, prof. pediat., 1994—2002; pediatric endocrinologist Diabetes and Glandular Disease Clinic, San Antonio, 2002—. Contbr. articles to profl. jours. Co-founder and camp dir. Camp Independence of San Antonio, 1987—2006. Col. USAF, 1972—88. Decorated Legion of Merit USAF; recipient Champion of Diabetes Award, Alamo Area Chpt. Am. Diabetes Assn., 1996, Outstanding Cadet in Life Scis., USAF Acad., 1968, Alpha Omega Alpha Honor Soc., Johns Hopkins U. Sch. of Medicine, 1972, Pediatric Tchg. Award, Wilford Hall USAF Med. Ctr., 1981, 1983, David Grant USAF Med. Ctr., 1985, Patient Edn. Award, Tex. Affiliate Am. Diabetes Assn., 1990, Vol. of the Yr., 1992, Pediatric Tchg. Award, U. of Tex. Health Sci. Ctr. at San Antonio, 1991, Youth Services Award, Tex. Affiliate Am. Diabetes Assn., 1994. Fellow: Am. Acad. Pediat. (chpt. chmn. 1984—87); mem.: Lawson Wilkins Pediatric Endocrinology Soc. Lutheran. Avocations: coaching youth baseball, photography, orienteering. Office: Diabetes and Glandular Disease Clinic 5107 Medical Dr San Antonio TX 78229 Home Phone: 830-981-8297. Office Fax: 210-615-1666. Business E-Mail: mdanney@dgdclinic.com.

DANNHAUSER, STEPHEN J., lawyer; b. NYC, May 23, 1950; s. Frank A. and Irene (Tinney) Dannhauser; m. Mary Elizabeth Robinson, July 1, 1973; children: Benjamin, Todd, Jess. BA with honors, SUNY, Stonybrook, 1972; JD with honors, Bklyn. Law Sch., 1975. Bar: NY 1976. Atty. Weil Gotshal & Manges LLP, NYC, 1975—, exec. ptnr., 1989—2001, chmn., 2002—. Mem. NYC Bar Assn. Com. to Enhance Diversity; mem., Internat. Policy Com. US C. of C. Mem., decisions editor: Bklyn. Law Rev., 1974—75. Pres. NY Police and Fire Widows' and Children's Benefit Fund, NYC, 1985—; chair, mem. various coms. Nat. Minority Bus. Coun., Assn. for the Help of Retarded Children, Catholic Charities, Covenant House, Legal Aid Soc., United Way, Ronald McDonald House, NY Blood Ctr., Boy Scouts Am., Police Athletic League and other orgns., NYC, 1993; chmn., bd. dirs. Boys and Girls Harbor, Inc., East Harlem, NY; hon. mem. Honor Legion of the Police Dept. City NY. Named Hon. Asst. Chief, Fire Dept. City NY, New Yorker for N.Y., Citizens for N.Y.C.; recipient award, Fed. Bar Coun. and its Pub. Svc. Com., NYC Police Dept. Bomb Squad, Ellis Island Medal of Honor, Founder's Medal, Boy's & Girl's Harbor, Inc., Chairman's award, Nat. Minority Bus. Coun., Michael Bolton Charities Lifetime Achievement award. Fellow: Am. Bar Found.; mem.: ABA (ABA Law Firm Pro Bono Project Adv. Com.). Avocations: running, golf. Office: Weil Gotshal & Manges LLP c/o Grace F Lopez 767 5th Ave 10th Flr New York NY 10153-0119 Office Phone: 212-310-8326. Office Fax: 212-310-8007. E-mail: stephen.dannhauser@weil.com.

DANNI, F. ROBERT, town official; b. Pitts., Oct. 26, 1939; s. Anthony Joseph and Lucille Marie (Kromer) D.; m. Patricia Arlene Maslona, Aug. 14, 1965 (div. Dec. 1980); children: Mark, Traci, Scott, Todd; m. Kathleen Anne Zimpfer, Jan. 13, 1990; 1 child, Adam. BS, U.S. Mcht. Marine Acad., 1961. Lic. chief stationary engr., City of Buffalo; lic. profl. engr., N.Y.; lic. officer U.S. Merchant Marine. Third asst. engr. Am. Export Lines, Hoboken, N.J., 1961-63; project engr. GM, Tonawanda, N.Y., 1964-69; asst. commr. of bldg. Town of Amherst, N.Y., 1969—. Chmn. Western Region Bd. Rev., 1984—. Instr. Baker Victory Rifle Drill Team, Lackawanna, N.Y., 1969-75; gen. chmn. Armed Forces Week Western N.Y., Buffalo, 1988, 93, 98, 2003; asst. scoutmaster Troop 440, Boy Scouts Am., Williamsville, N.Y. Capt. USNR, 1961-91; rear admiral N.Y. Naval Militia, 1991—, Region III comdr., 1984-98. Mem. N.Y. State Soc. Profl. Engrs. (pres. Erie-Niagara chpt. 1990-91, Basinski-Wohler distinguished svc. award 2000), N.Y. State Bldg. Ofcls. Conf. (tech. chmn. 1985-91), Naval Res. Assn. (life), Mil. Officers Assn. (life), Rotary Club Williamsville N.Y. (youth chmn. 1982-97, Rotarian of Yr. award 1997). Avocations: music, health club. Office Phone: 716-631-7080. Personal E-mail: frobertd@adelphia.net. Business E-Mail: frdanni@amherst.ny.us.

D'ANNIBALLE, PRISCILLA LUCILLE, contracting company executive; b. Martins Ferry, Ohio, Oct. 28, 1950; d. James Louis and Smyrna Isabell (Prieto) D'A. BE, U. Toledo, 1973. Credit mgr. Kabat Distbg. Co., Toledo, 1973-80; comml. ops. officer Ohio Citizens Bank, Toledo, 1980-81, credit officer, 1981-82, mktg. officer, 1982-83, mortgage banking officer, 1983-85; owner, pres. D'Ann Enterprises, Inc. dba Paul Davis Restoration, Holland, Ohio, 1985—; pres. dist. V Paul Davis Systems, Toledo, 1992-95, mem. nat. exec. com., 1992-95, treas. nat. exec. com., 1994-95. Chmn. arbitration com. Paul Davis Systems, 1991; dist. 3 acting pres. Paul Davis Restoration, 2002, dist. 3 v.p., 2001—06. Mem. fund drive United Way, Toledo, 1982, Jr. Achievement, Toledo, 1983; bd. dirs. Voluntary Action Ctr., Toledo, 1981-82, Better Bus. Bur., 2002-, bd. mem., 2002-. Mem. Nat. Assn. Credit Mgmt. (bd. dirs. 1981-87, bd. dirs. Ednl. Forum 1976-82, pres. 1980, Credit Person of Yr. award 1982, Credit Exec. of Yr. award 1987), Holland-Springfield C. of C. (exec. bd. dirs. 1990-95, v.p. 1991-92, pres. 1993), Paul Davis Restoration Franchisee Assn. (pres. 1991). Roman Catholic. Avocations: golf, swimming, gardening, antiques, travel. Home: 704 Oak Park Dr Toledo OH 43617-2024 Office: D'Ann Enterprises Inc 1035 S Mccord Rd Holland OH 43528-9596

DANO, LINDA, actress; b. LA, May 12, 1943; m. Frank Attardi, 1977. BA in Design, Calif. State U., Long Beach. Writer, model, fashion designer; owner Strictly Personal. Actress (TV series) As the World Turns, 1981-82, One Life to Live, 1978-80, 1999-2004, Another World, 1982-99, All My Children, 1999-2000, Port Charles, 2000, Gen. Hospital, 2000-01, 2003, Guiding Light, 2005; (pilots) The Montefuscos, 1975, The Fess Parker Show, 1978, (TV films) The Last Survivors, 1975, The Nurse Killer, 1975, The Night That Panicked America, 1975, Rage of Angels: The Story Continues, 1986, Perry Mason: The Case of the Killer Kiss, 1993, When the Vows Break, 1995, See Jane Date, 2003; (guest appearances) Police Story, 1973, Ironside, 1974, Police Women, 1974, Harry O, 1975, Rockford Files, 1976, 1977, Starsky & Hutch, 1977, Charles Angels, 1977, Barney Miller, 1978, CHiPs, 1978, The Six Million Dollar Man, 1978, Homicide: Life on the Street, 1997, Desperate Housewives, 2005, What I Like About You, 2006; (spls.) 14th, 17, 18, 21st and 22d Ann. Daytime Emmy Awards, 1987-95, 50 Years of soaps: An All-Star Celebration, 1994, 11th Ann. Soap Opera awards, 1995, others; narrator Legends in Love, 1991, Diana: The Making of a Princess, 1989; film appearances include Wishbone Cutter, 1978; casting dir. Somewhere in the City, 1998; host Attitudes, 1987, The Another World Reunion, 2003; replacement host Soap Talk, 2006; co-author: Looking Great.It Doesn't Have to Hurt, 1997, (as Felicia Gallant) Dreamweaver, 1984 Trustee HeartShare Human Svcs. of N.Y. Mem. Alzheimer's Assn. (hon. chair 1997). Office: Care Another World 30 Rockefeller Plz Rm 1204 New York NY 10112-0002

DANO, PAUL FRANKLIN, actor; b. Wilton, Conn., June 19, 1983; BA in English, NYU. Lead guitar and vocals Cherry Revision. Actor: (films) The Newcomers, 2000, L.I.E., 2001 (Best Debut Performance, Independent Spirit Awards, 2002), The Emperor's Club, 2002, Light and the Sufferer, 2004, The Girl Next Door, 2004, Taking Lives, 2004, The Ballad of Jack and Rose, 2005, The King, 2005, Weapons, 2006, Fast Food Nation, 2006, Little Miss Sunshine, 2006 (Critics Choice award, Broadcast Film Critics Assn., 2007, Outstanding Performance by a Cast in a Motion Picture, SAG, 2007), There Will Be Blood, 2007; (TV films) Too Young to Be a Dad, 2002; appeared on (TV series) The Sopranos, 2002, 2004.*

DANOFF, DUDLEY SETH, surgeon, urologist; b. NYC, June 10, 1937; s. Alfred and Ruth (Kauffman) D.; m. Hevda Amrani, July 1, 1971; children: Aurele, Doran. BA summa cum laude, Princeton U., 1959; MD, Yale U., 1963. Diplomate Am. Bd. Urology. Surg. intern Columbia-Presbyn. Med. Ctr., NYC, 1963-64; resident in surgery Yale New Haven Med. Ctr., 1964-65; resident in urologic surgery Squier Urologic Clinic, Columbia-Presbyn. Med. Ctr., 1965-69; NIH trainee Francis Delafield Hosp., NYC, 1969; asst. in urology Columbia U.Columbia-Presbyn. Hosp., NYC, 1969; cons., surgeon New Orleans VA Hosp., 1970; asst. surgeon Tulane U., New Orleans, 1970; pvt. practice urologic surgery LA, 1971—. Attending urologic surgeon Cedars-Sinai Med. Ctr., L.A., VA Hosp., L.A.; attending urologic surgeon, clin. faculty UCLA Author: Superpotency, 1998, Impotence, It's Reversible, 1999; contbr. articles to profl. jours. Bd. dirs. Tel-Hashomer Hosp., Israel, Christian Children's Fund, Beverly Hills Edn. Found.; trustee Anti-Defamation League; mem. prof. adv. bd. The Wellness Comty.; mem. nat. exec. bd. Gesher Found.; mem. adv. com., past pres. Med. divsn. L.A. Jewish Fedn. Coun.; mem. nat. leadership cabinet United Jewish Appeal; chmn. Am. Friends of Assaf Harofeh Med. Ctr., Israel; pres. western states region and internat. bd. govs. Am. Friends Hebrew U. Jerusalem; pres. western region Am. Commn. for Shaare Zedek Med. Ctr. Jerusalem. Recipient Excellence in Medicine award, Israel Cancer Rsch. Found., 1998. Fellow ACS; mem. AMA, Internat. Coll. Surgeons, Israeli Med. Assn., Am. Fertility Soc., Soc. Air Force Clin. Surgeons, Am. Urologic Assn., Societe International d'Urologie, Transplant Soc. So. Calif., Los Angeles County Med. Assn., Soc. for Laparoendoscopic Surgeons, Am. Technion Soc., Profl. Men's Club of L.A. (past pres.), Princeton Club So. Calif., Yale Club So. Calif., Hillcrest Country Club, Phi Beta Kappa, Sigma Xi, Alpha Omega Alpha, Phi Delta Epsilon (past pres., exec. com.). Achievements include research in laparoscopic urologic procedures. Avocations: golf, swimming, reading, writing. Office: Cedars-Sinai Med Ctr 8635 W 3d St #1W Los Angeles CA 90048-5912 Office Phone: 310-854-9898. Office Fax: 310-854-0267.

DANOFF, ERIC MICHAEL, lawyer; b. Waukegan, Ill., June 30, 1949; m. Barbara Madsen, May 27, 1979; children: Nicholas Madsen Danoff, Alexander Madsen Danoff. AB, Dartmouth Coll., 1971; JD, U. Calif., Berkeley, 1974. Bar: Calif. 1974, U.S. Dist. Ct. (no., cen., ea. and so. dists.) Calif., U.S. Ct. Appeals (9th cir.), U.S. Supreme Ct. Assoc. Graham & James, San Francisco, 1974-80, ptnr., 1981-97, Kaye, Rose & Ptnrs., San Francisco, 1998-2001, Emard Danoff PortTamulski & Paetzold LLP, San Francisco, 2001—. Contbr. articles to profl. publs. Mem. Maritime Law Assn. Office: Emard Danoff Port Tamulski & Paetzold LLP Ste 400 49 Stevenson St San Francisco CA 94105 Office Phone: 415-227-9455. E-mail: edanoff@edptlaw.com.

DANOS, HARRY JOHN, architect, educator, artist; b. Enfield, Conn., May 5, 1924; s. John Christopher and Alice (Panagiota) D.; m. Catherine Magiopoulos, Sept. 5, 1948; 1 child, Michael (dec.). Apprentice program, GE Co., 1943; USAF tng., Amherst Coll., Mass., 1943—44, Yale U., New Haven, Conn., 1943—44; student, Springfield Jr. Coll., Mass., 1946-47; BArch, Syracuse U., NYC, 1952; MArch, Rice U., Houston, 1953; studied watercolors with, Carlton Plummer, Barbara Nechis, Irving Shapiro and others. Registered arch., Conn., Vt., R.I., Mass. Arch., designer C.P. Kantianis, AIA, Springfield, Mass., 1952-55, Robert Carroll May (apprentice Frank Lloyd Wright), Hartford, 1955-57, Moore and Salsbury, U. Hartford, 1957-62, Charles DuBose Constn. Plz., 1952-55; prin., archtl. firm Harry Danos, AIA, Avon, 1955-80, Danos and Assocs., Archs., Hartford, 1962-80; staff arch., constrn. mgr. Associated Constrn. Co., Hartford, 1980-82; asst. dir. Bur. Pub. Works State of Conn., Hartford, 1982-84; profl. arch., devel. cons., 1984—. Instr. art and arch. Syracuse U., Rice U., U. Hartford, Boston Archtl. Ctr., Guilford Handcrafts and Art Ctr, 1984—, Mystic Art Assn., Conn., Von Leibig Art Ctr., Naples, Fla. Exhbns. include Peel Gallery, Danby, Vt., Leverett Gallery, Amherst, Mass., Hartford Nat. Bank, Waterford, Conn., E. Lyme Cmty. Ctr. Libr., Nat. Greek Am. Artists, Springfield, Mass.; represented in pvt. collections. Past chmn. E. Lyme Art League; exec. mem. E. Lyme Arts Coun.; mem. zoning and planning commn. Town of Avon, Conn., 1959-65; rep. Capitol Region Planning Agy., Avon, 1962-65. Commd. officer SAC, USAF, 1944-46, WWII, PTO. Recipient Archtl. Award of Merit, Am. Assn. Sch. Adminstrs., 1965, Carl E. Shawyer award of merit Archtl. Precast Assn., 1975, Facilities Excellence award World Wide Volkswagen Corp.-Porsche-Audi Ea. Div., 1981, various achievement awards; named Winner, Chgo. Tribune Better Rooms Competition, 1950; fellowship grantee Rice U., 1952-53. Mem. AIA (corp., Medal 1952), Am. Arbitration Assn. (arbitrator), Conn. Watercolor Soc., Mystic Art Assn., Salmagundi Club, Avon Lions Club (past treas.). Avocation: watercolorist teacher. Home and Office: 148 Old Black Point Rd Niantic CT 06357-3303

DANOS, PAUL, dean, accounting educator; m. Mary Ellen Danos; children: Amanda, Melissa. BS in acctg., U. New Orleans, 1964, MBA in acctg., 1968; PhD in acctg., U. Tex., Austin, 1974. CPA La. Acct. in charge chem. divsn. Freeport Minerals Co., 1964—70; instr. U. New Orleans, 1970—71; tchg. asst. U. Tex., 1971—74; asst. prof. Sch. Bus. Adminstrn., U. Mich., 1974—78, assoc. prof., 1978—83, prof., 1983—95, chmn. acctg., 1984—91, Arthur Andersen & Co. prof. actg., 1985-95, dir. Paton Acctg. Ctr., 1988-91, assoc. dean, 1991—93, sr. assoc. dean, 1993—95; dean Tuck Sch. Bus., Dartmouth Coll., Hanover, NH, 1995—, Laurence F. Whittemore prof. bus. adminstrn., 1995—. Adv. bd. Assn. Advance Collegiate Schools of Bus., Grad. Mgmt. Admissions Coun., Ledyard Nat. Bank, Nat. Taiwan U., The Rassias Found. Bd. Overseers, LEAD Coun. of Deans, Accentus, U. Notre Dame Coll. Bus. Adminstrn.; bd. dirs. Grad. Mgmt. Admissions Coun., BJ's Wholesale Club, Inc., General Mills, Inc., 2004—. Author two text books; contbr. articles to profl. jours. Mem.: Assn. to Advance Collegiate Schools of Bus. Office: Office of Dean Tuck School of Business 100 Tuck Hall Hanover NH 03755-9027 Office Phone: 603-646-2460. Business E-Mail: paul.danos@dartmouth.edu.*

DANOS, ROBERT MCCLURE, retired oil company executive; b. New Orleans, Dec. 9, 1929; s. Joseph A. and Muriel R. (McClure) D.; m. Barbara Umbach, Apr. 30, 1955; children: Robert M., Sally C., Susan M., Julie A., Richard F., Renee R. BS in Geology, Tulane U., 1950; MS, La. State U., 1952. Geologist Texaco, Inc., New Orleans, 1955-67, staff geologist Houston, 1967, divsn. geologist Tulsa, 1968-70, exploration mgr. Denver, 1970-80; sr. v.p. K N Energy, Inc., Lakewood, Colo., 1980-83; pres., CEO Midlands Energy Co., Lakewood, 1983-84; pres. McMoRan-Midlands Oil Co., New Orleans, 1984-86; pres., chief ops. officer McMoRan Oil & Gas Co., New Orleans, 1986-89; pres. Plains Petroleum Oper. Co., Lakewood, Colo., 1989-95; dir. Am. Exploration Co., Houston, 1996-97. 1st lt. U.S. Army, 1954. Mem. Am. Assn. Petroleum Geologists (del.), New Orleans Geolog. Soc. (v.p. 1965-67), Rocky Mountain Geolog. Assn., Bienville Club, Cherry Hills Country Club, Pickwick Club, Arlberg Club. Home: 124 High St Denver CO 80218-4018 E-mail: rmdanos@msn.com.

DANS, MICHAEL JAY, dermatologist, educator; b. Calif. MD with hons., PhD with hons., NYU. Diplomate Am. Bd. Dermatology, 2005, lic. physician Calif., 2004. Clin. instr. sch. medicine U. Calif., San Francisco, 2005—; staff physician Kaiser Permanente, San Rafael, Calif., 2005—. Author: Guidebook to the Extracellular Matrix, Anchor, and Adhesion Proteins, 2d edit., 1999, Cancer of the Skin, 2004; contbr. articles to profl. jours. Fellow, NIH, 1993—2001; scholar, Regents U. Calif., 1989—93, U. Calif., Davis, 1989—93. Fellow: Am. Acad. Dermatology; mem.: AMA, Calif. Pacific Med. Assn., Am. Soc. Dermatologic Surgery. Avocations: jogging, skiing, piano, hiking. Office: 490 Post St Ste 320 San Francisco CA 94102 Office Phone: 415-781-1932. Office Fax: 415-781-1947.

DANSBY, JOHN WALTER, retired oil industry executive; b. Logan, W.Va., Dec. 29, 1944; s. Charles Eugene and Lillian (Maggard) Dansby; m. Karen Navarin, June 20, 1970; children: Andrew, David. BS in Econs, U. Pa., 1966; MBA, Emory U., 1967; PhD in Econs, U. Ky., 1976. Fin. analyst Ashland (Ky.) Oil, Inc., 1970-71, staff economist, 1975-77, mgr. fed. energy programs, 1977-81, exec. asst., 1981, v.p. strategic planning, 1981-84, v.p. planning, 1984-92, adminstrv. v.p. and treas., 1992-98; ret., 1998. Part-time instr. No. Ariz. U., 2000—. Treas. Verde Valley Sinfonietta, 2005—; bd. dirs. Verde Valley Sanctuary. Mem.: The Sedona 30. Home: 75 Rim Shadows Cir Sedona AZ 86336-2196

DANSE, ILENE HOMNICK RAISFELD, physician, educator, toxicologist, sculptor; b. NYC; d. Jack and Henrietta Homnick; m. James Atherton Danse, Aug. 10, 1982; children: Arthur Raisfeld, Robin Raisfeld. BS, CUNY, 1960; MD, NYU, 1964; student, Pratt Inst., Art Students League, Bklyn. Mus. Art Sch. Diplomate Nat. Bd. Med. Examiners, Am. Bd. Internal Medicine, Am. Bd. Toxicology. Assoc. prof. internal medicine SUNY, Stony Brook, 1975-83, assoc. prof. pharmacology, 1977-83, dir. clin. pharmacology and toxicology Sch. Medicine, 1978-83; acting chairperson clin. pharmacology Northport VA Hosp., LI, N.Y., 1978-83; sr. advisor Chevron Environ. Health Ctr., San Pablo, Calif., 1982-84; prin. ENVIROMED Health Svcs., Inc., Novato, Calif., 1984-99; ind. med. examiner toxicology and internal medicine Dept. Indsl. Rels., State of Calif., 1985—; assoc. clin. prof. dept. medicine div. occupl. and environ. medicine U. Calif., San Francisco, 1986—2006, assoc. clin. prof. dept. epidemiol. and preventive medicine Davis, 1991—. Cons. in fields of toxicology, pharmacology, environ., occupl. and internal medicine, 1984-2000; mem. bd. sci. advisors Am. Coun. Sci. and Health; mem. sci. rev. panel Hazardous Substances Data Base, Nat. Libr. Medicine. Author: Common Sense Toxics in the Workplace, 1991; contbr. articles to sci. publs.; exhibitions include Sonoma Mus. Visual Art, Santa Rosa, Calif., Bolinas Mus., Calif., Ohr-O'Keefe Mus. Art, Biloxi, Miss., Kellogg Gallery, Pomona, Calif., John Toki Gallery, Richmond, Calif., Calif. Clay Competition, Davis. Mem. sci. rev. panel Hazardous Substances Data Base, Nat. Libr. of Medicine; Mem. past bd. sci. advisors Am. Coun. on Sci. and Health Recipient various art awards. Fellow ACP, Am. Coll. Clin. Pharmacology; mem. AAAS, Am. Acad. Clin. Toxicology, Am. Chem. Soc. (environ. health and safety sect.), Am. Coll. Occupl. Medicine, Am. Indsl. Hygiene Assn. (occupational medicine sect.), Am. Coll. Toxicology, Am. Soc. Pharmacology and Therapeutics, Soc. Toxicology, Western Occupational Med. Assn. Achievements include patent for epithelial cell growth-regulating composition containing polyamines, and method of its use.

DANSKY, IRA M., lawyer; b. NYC; BS, U. R.I., 1967; JD, Vanderbilt U., 1970; LLM in Taxation, NYU, 1973. Bar: NY 1971, Conn. 1989. Gen counsel Jones Apparel Group, Inc., NYC, 1996—, sec., 2001—, exec. v.p., 2002—. Mem.: ABA, Conn. Bar Assn., N.Y. State Bar Assn. Office: Jones Apparel Group Legal Dept 1411 Broadway New York NY 10018 Office Phone: 212-642-3860, 212-536-9526. Office Fax: 212-785-1228. Business E-Mail: jdansky@jny.com.*

DANSON, TED (EDWARD BRIDGE DANSON III), actor; b. San Diego, Dec. 29, 1947; s. Edward B. and Jessica (McMaster) D.; m. Randall Lee Gosch, Aug. 1970 (div. 1975); m. Cassandra Coates, July 30, 1977 (div. 1993); children: Kate, Alexis; m. Mary Steenburgen, Oct. 7, 1995. Student, The Kent Sch., Conn., 1961-66, Stanford U., 1966-68, Carnegie-Mellon U., 1968-72. Tchr. The Actors' Inst., L.A., 1978. Off Broadway plays include: The Real Inspector Hound, 1972, Comedy of Errors, Comedians; actor (daytime dramas) The Doctors (TV films) The Women's Room, 1980, Once Upon a Spy, 1980, Dear Teacher, 1981, Our Family Business, 1981, Allison Sydney Harrison, 1983, Cowboy, 1983, Something About Amelia, 1984, Gulliver's Travels, 1996, Thanks of a Grateful Nation, 1998, Living with the Dead, 2004, It Must Be Love, 2004, Our Fathers, 2005, Knights of the South Bronx, 2005; actor, exec. producer: (TV films) When The Bough Breaks, 1986, We Are The Children, 1987; (films) The Onion Field, 1979, Body Heat, 1981, Creepshow, 1983, A Little Treasure, 1985, A Fine Mess, 1986, Just Between Friends, 1986, Three Men and a Baby, 1987, Cousins, 1989, Dad, 1989, Three Men and A Little Lady, 1990, Made in America, 1993, Getting Even With Dad, 1994, Pontiac Moon, 1994(also exec. prodr.), Loch Ness, 1996, Jerry & Tom, 1998, Homegrown, 1998, Saving Private Ryan, 1998, Mumford, 1999, Fronterz, 2004, The Moguls, 2005, Bye Bye Benjamin (also exec. prodr.), 2006, Nobel Son, 2007; (TV series) Somerset 1975-76, Cheers, 1982-1993 (Emmy award Best Comedy Actor, 1990, 1993, Golden Globe award 1990, 91), Ink, 1996 (also exec. prodr.), Becker, 1998-2004, Help Me Help You, 2006-; co-prodr. (TV series) Down Home, 1990; guest appearances B.J. and the Bear, 1979, Laverne & Shirley, 1980, Family, 1980, Tucker's Witch, 1982, Benson, 1981, Magnum P.I., 1981, Taxi, 1982, Frasier, 1995, Diagnosis Murder, 1999, Veronica's Closet, 1998, Curb Your Enthusiasm, 2002, 2004, 2005, Heist, 2006, Help Me Help You, 2006, Damages, 2007; (voice) The Simpsons, 1994, Grosse Pointe, 2000, Gary the Rat, 2003, The Magic 7, 2006 Recipient Presdl. End Hunger award AID, 1989, Am. Comedy Award, 1991, The Peoples Choice Award for Favorite Male TV Performer, 1992, Emmy for Best Actor in Comedy Series, 1990, 93,

Golden Globe awards, 1985, 90, 91, Star on Walk of Fame, 1999, TV Land award, 2006, 2007. Office: care Creative Artists Agy c/o Josh Liberman 9830 Wilshire Blvd Beverly Hills CA 90212-1804*

DANTO, ARTHUR COLEMAN, writer, philosopher, critic; b. Ann Arbor, Mich., Jan. 1, 1924; s. Samuel Budd and Sylvia (Gittleman) D.; m. Shirley Rovetch, Aug. 9, 1946 (dec. July 1978); children: Elizabeth, Jane; m. Barbara Westman, Feb. 15, 1980. BA, Wayne State U., 1948; MA, Columbia U., 1949, PhD, 1952; postgrad., U. Paris, 1949-50; D (hon.), Parsons Sch. Design, 1990, Sch. Visual Arts, 1995, Pa. Acad. Fine Arts, 1996, Conn. Coll., 1997, Wayne State U., 1999, Coll. Art & Design, Detroit, 2001, Mass. Coll. Art; DLitt, Columbia U., 2004. Instr. U. Colo., Colo., 1950-51; mem. faculty Columbia U., 1952—, Johnsonian prof. philosophy, 1975-92, chmn. dept., 1979-87, co-dir. Ctr. for Study of Human Rights, 1978-92; prof. emeritus, 1992. Andrew W. Mellon Fine Arts lectr., 1995; Albertus Magnum prof. U. Cologne, 2005. Author: Analytical Philosophy of Knowledge, 1968, What Philosophy Is, 1968, Analytical Philosophy of Hist., 1965, Nietzsche as Philosopher, 1965, Analytical Philosophy of Action, 1973, Mysticism and Morality, 1972, Jean-Paul Sartre, 1975, The Transfiguration of the Commonplace, 1981 (Lionel Trilling Book prize 1982), Narration and Knowledge, 1985, The Philosophical Disenfranchisement of Art, 1986, The State of the Art, 1987, Connections to the World, 1989, Encounters and Reflections: Art in the Hist. Present, 1990 (Nat. Book Critics Circle Prize for Criticism, 1990), Beyond the Brillo Box: Art in the Post Hist. Period, 1992, Mark Tansey: Visions and Revisions, 1992, Robert Mapplethorpe, 1992, Embodied Meanings: Critical Essays and Aesthetic Meditations, 1994, Playing with the Edge: The Photographic Achievement of Robert Mapplethorpe, After the End of Art: Contemporary Art and the Pale of Hist., 1997 (Eugene Kayden prize 1997), The Body/Body Problem, 1999, Philosophizing Art, 1999, The Madonna of the Future, 2000, The Abuse of Beauty: Aesthetics and the Concept of Art, 2003, Unnatural Wonders: Essays in the Gap Between Art and Life, 2004; editor Jour. Philosophy, 1965—, pres., 1987—; art critic The Nation, 1984—; contbg. editor ARTFORUM; cons. editor for various other publs. Bd. dirs. Amnesty Internat., 1970-75, gen. sec., 1973. Served with AUS, 1942-45. With US Army, 1942—45, N. Africa, Italy. Recipient prize for disting. criticism Mfr.-Hanover/Art World, 1985, George S. Polk award for criticism, 1985, Nat. Book Critics Circle prize for criticism, 1990, ICP Infinity prize for writing in photography, 1993, Prix Philosophie, 2003, Icelandic Lit. prize, 2005; fellow Fulbright Found., 1949, Guggenheim Found., 1969, 82, Am. Coun. Learned Socs., 1961, 70; Fulbright disting. prof. Yugoslavia, 1976; Phi Beta Kappa prof. Arts and Scis. Fellow AAAS; mem. Am. Philos. Assn. (v.p. 1969, pres. 1983), Am. Soc. Aesthetics (v.p. 1987, pres. 1989), Coll. Art Assn. (Frank Jewett Mather prize for criticism). Office: 420 Riverside Dr New York NY 10025-7773 Office Phone: 212-666-3588. Business E-Mail: acd1@columbia.edu.

D'ANTONI, MIKE (MICHAEL ANDREW D'ANTONI), Professional basketball coach and sports team executive, former player; b. Mullens, W.Va., May 8, 1951; m. Laurel D'Antoni; 1 child, Michael. Student, Marshall U. Draft pick Kans. City-Omaha Kings (now Sacramento Kings), 1973, player, 1973—75, Am. Basketball Assn. Spirits of St. Louis, 1975—76, San Antonio Spurs, 1976, scout, 1999—2000; player Italian League Philips Milan, 1976—89, head coach, 1990—94, Italian League Benetton Treviso, 1994—97, 2001—02; dir. player pers. Denver Nuggets, 1997-98, head coach, 1998-99; asst. coach Portland Trail Blazers, 2000—01, Phoenix Suns, 2002—03, head coach, 2003—, exec. v.p. basketball ops., 2006—, gen. mgr., 2006—07. Head coach NBA Western Conf. All-Star Team, 2007. Co-author (with Dan Peterson): Playmaker; co-author: (with Tullio Lauro) Vivendo Giacando. Named Top Point Guard of All Time, Italian League, 1990, NBA Coach of Yr., 2005; named to All-NBA Rookie Second Team, 1974, Marshall U. Hall of Fame, 1997. Achievements include winning 5 Italian League Championships, 2 Cups of Europe, 2 Cups of Italy, 1 Korac Cup and 1 Intercontinental Cup as a member of Philips Milan; won the Korac Cup as head coach of Philips Milan, 1993; won the Cup of Europe, 1995, Cup of Italy, 1995, and Italian League Championship, 2002, as head coach of Benetton Treviso. Office: Phoenix Suns 201 E Jefferson St Phoenix AZ 85004*

D'ANTONI, PHILIP, television producer; b. Bronx, NY, Feb. 19, 1929; s. Peter and Josephine (Elici) D'Antoni; m. Ruth Ann Wiederecht, Sept. 12, 1953; children: Christopher, Jeanne, Carol, James, Robert. Student, Fordham U., 1948-50. Prodn. asst., asso. producer CBS-TV, 1949-53; v.p., dir. Mut. Broadcasting Sys., 1955-61; pres. D'Antoni/Weitz TV Prodns. Prodr.: (TV series) Movin' On, 1961—73; (films) Bullitt, 1968, The French Connection, 1971 (Acad. award, 1971), (spls.) Elizabeth Taylor in London, 1964, Sophia Loren in Rome, 1965, Melina Mercouri in Greece, 1966, (dir): (films) The Seven Ups, 1974; (TV films) Strike Force, The Connection, Cabo, Inside-Outside, In Tandem, Rubber Gun Squad, 1974—77. With US Army, 1946—48. Mem.: Motion Picture Acad., Screenwriters Guild, Dirs. Guild Am. Home: care of St Andrews G C 10 Old Jackson Ave Hastings On Hudson NY 10706

D'ANTONIO, JAMES JOSEPH, lawyer; b. Tucson, Jan. 13, 1959; s. Lawrence Patrick and Rosemary Catherine (Kane) D'A. Student, Tufts U., 1978-79; BA, U. Ariz., 1981, JD, 1984. Bar: Ariz. 1984, U.S. Dist. Ct. Ariz. 1984, U.S. Ct. Appeals (9th cir.) 1993. Assoc. Law Office of D'Antonio and D'Antonio, Tucson, 1984-93; pvt. practice law Law Offices of James J. D'Antonio, Tucson, 1993—. Chmn. bd. govs. U. Ariz. Coll. Law, 1983-84; mem. Pima County Teen Ct. Adv. Bd; mem. Health South Rehab. Inst., Tucson Cmty. Adv. Bd.; bd. dirs. Coyote Task Force. Named Outstanding Pro Bono Lawyer Pima County Vol. Lawyers Program, 1993. Fellow Ariz. Bar Found.; mem. ABA, Assn. Trial Lawyers Am., Ariz. Bar Assn., Ariz. Trial Lawyers Assn., Pima County Bar Assn. Office: 751 N Country Club Rd Tucson AZ 85716

DANZA, TONY, actor; b. Bklyn., Apr. 21, 1951; m. Rhonda Yeoman (div.); 1 child, Marc Anthony; m. Tracy Robinson 1986; children: Katherine Anne, Emily Lyn. Grad., U. Dubuque. Began career as profl. boxer; appeared in films Hollywood Knights, 1980, Going Ape, 1981, Cannonball Run II, 1984, She's Out of Control, 1989, Angels in the Outfield, 1994, Dear God, 1996, Illtown, 1996, A Brookln State of Mind, 1997, Meet Wally Sparks, 1997, Glam, 1997, The Girl Gets Moe, 1997, A Brooklyn State of Mind, 1997, Glam, 2001, Crash, 2004, The Whisper, 2004; TV series include Taxi, ABC, 1978-83, Who's the Boss?, ABC, 1984-92 (also dir.), Baby Talk, 1992, Hudson Street, 1995, The Tony Danza Show, 1997, Homewood P.I., 2000, Family Law, 2000-02; TV films include Doing Life, Wall of Tyranny, Single Bar, Single Women, Freedom Fighters (also exec. prodr.), Bob Hope: Laughing With the Presidents, 1996, 12 Angry Men, 1997, North Shore Fish, 1997, The Garbage Picking Field Goal Kicking Philadelphia Phenomenon, 1998, Noah, 1998, Stealing Christmas, 2003; co-exec. prodr. (TV films) Doing Life, 1986; exec. prodr. (TV films) The Whereabouts of Jenny, 1991, Bermuda Triangle, 1996, Sudden Terror: The Hijacking of School Bus #17, 1996, Crowned and Dangerous, 1997, (TV series) George, 1993, Hudson Street, 1995, (films) The Jerky Boys, 1995; host, co-exec. prodr. (TV series) The Tony Danza Show, 2004-; stage appearance Wrong Turn at Lungfish, 1993, A View from the Bridge, 1998, I Remember You, 2006, The Producers, 2006. Avocations: softball, running. Office: c/o ABC TV 57 W 66th St New York NY 10023-6298*

DANZBERGER, ALEXANDER HARRIS, retired chemical engineer, consultant; b. NYC, Mar. 23, 1932; s. George Harris and Ruth P. (Alexander) D.; m. Jacqueline P. Pilcher, Mar. 12, 1954; children: Alison, Alexander, Diana, Robert; m. Anne Griggs Pierson, Apr. 23, 1977; stepchildren: Jennifer Pierson, Priscilla Pierson, Stephanie Pierson BSChemE, MIT, 1953. Registered profl. engr., Mass., Colo. Mem. staff Arthur D. Little Inc., Cambridge, Mass., 1953-60; engring. mgr. Linde div. Union Carbide Corp., Tonawanda, N.Y., N.Y.C., 1961-70; chief engr. Booz, Allen & Hamilton, Florham Park, NJ, 1971—72, Marcom Cons., NYC, 1973-75; v.p. Hydrotechnic Corp., NYC, 1976-81; mgr. pollution control group Dames & Moore, Golden, Colo., 1982-83; pres. Danzberger and Assocs., Inc., Lakewood, Colo., 1983—2004; ret. Adj. prof. dept. arts and scis. Johnson and Wales U., Providence, 2001—03. Served to 1st lt. U.S. Army, 1956-58. Recipient Kenneth B. Allen award N.Y. Water Pollution Control Assn., 1983. Fellow: AIChE; mem.: ASME (life), Masons. Republican. Presbyterian. Home and Office: 273 N Farm Dr Bristol RI 02809-1560 Home Phone: 401-254-9712. E-mail: aharrisd@fullchannel.net.

DANZER, GERALD ARLIN, history professor; b. Oak Park, Ill., Nov. 9, 1938; s. Harold Elmer Danzer and Gertrude Alma Soidtke Danzer; m. Magdalene A.M. Insel, June 11, 1960; children: Nadine, Gerald D., Timothy. BS in Edn., Concordia Tchrs. Coll., River Forest, Ill., 1959; MA in History, Northwestern U., Evanston, Ill., 1961, PhD in History, 1967. From asst. prof. to prof. history U. Ill., Chgo., 1967—2000, history prof. emeritus, 2000—. Coord. City in History Conf., Chgo., 1970—93; dir. Chgo. Neighborhood History Project, 1980—85, Cartographic Traditions Project, Chgo., 1991—99. Author: Public Places, 1987, Discovering World History Through Maps, 1991, Word History: An Atlas, 1998; contbr. more than 100 articles to profl. jours., chpts. to books. Organizer historic preservation Old Walnut St., Itasca, Ill., 1970—. Recipient Superior Achievement award, Ill. State Hist. Soc., 1986. Mem.: Assn. Am. Geographers, Orgn. Am. Historians, Am. Hist. Assn. (James Harvey Robinson prize 1987, 1990). Avocations: historic preservation, collecting books and maps. Home: 200 S Walnut St Itasca IL 60143 Office: U Ill Chgo Dept History 198 601 S Morgan St Chicago IL 60607

DANZIG, FREDERICK PAUL, newspaper editor; b. Springfield, Mass., Sept. 17, 1925; s. Phillip and Sylvia (Levin) D.; m. Edith Goret, Mar. 16, 1952; children: Steven, Ellen Kay. BA, Washington Sq. Coll., NYU, 1949. Copy boy AP, NYC, 1943; reporter Herkimer (N.Y.) Evening Telegram, 1949, Port Chester (N.Y.) Daily Item, 1950-51; reporter, columnist UPI, NYC, 1951-62; sr. editor Advt. Age, NYC, 1962-68, exec. editor, 1969-84, editor, 1984-94; contbg. editor, 1995—. Advt. newscaster Sta. WQXR, 1979-81, Sta. WMCA, 1982-86; adj. instr. New Sch. Social Rsch., N.Y.C.; pub. radio commentator, 1989-90; media cons. Comprehensive Cmty. Revitalization Program, N.Y.C, 1994-98; mem. adv. bd. Youth Law Ctr., Washington. Author: (with Ted Klein) How to be Heard, 1974, Publicity, 1985. Served with inf. AUS, 1943-46. Decorated Bronze Star, Purple Heart; recipient Alumni Achievement award NYU, 1983. Mem. 29th Inf. Divsn. Assn., Amagansett Hist. Assn., The Battle of Normandy Found., U.S. Holocaust Meml. Mus., Internat. Mus. Cartoon Art (adv. bd.). E-mail: fredpep@aol.com.

DANZIG, VOLEEN H., marketing professional, educator; b. Adrian, Mich., Apr. 7, 1978; d. Peter Daniel and Helen Marie (Blacksmith) Wilkes; m. James Patrick Danzig, Feb. 14, 2001; children: James Patrick Jr., Rachel Helen, Benjamin Todd. BA in Bus., U. Pitts., 2000; MBA, U. Mich., Ann Arbor, 2002. Mktg. rep. McMahon Comm., Ann Arbor, 2000—02, Meriks Creative Group, Southfield, Mich., 2002—05, dir. mktg., 2005—. Adj. lectr. mktg. Ctrl. Mich. U., Southfield, 2006—. Mem.: Am. Acad. Advt., Am. Mktg. Assn., Omicron Delta Kappa, Delta Zeta (life). Democrat. Roman Catholic. Avocations: travel, tennis, exercise.

DANZIGER, BRUCE EDWARD, structural engineer; b. NYC, Feb. 14, 1964; s. Frederick Benjamin Danziger and Elise Lee (Saranow) Gold. BS in Archtl. Engring., Calif. Poly. U., 1988. Lic. structural engr. Calif. Assoc. Ove Arup & Ptnrs., London, 1988-90, Sevilla, Spain, 1990-92, LA, 1992-93, 2002—, NYC, 1993-97, San Francisco, 1997—2002, project engr., 2002—. Mem. faculty So. Calif. Inst. Architecture; Bedford vis. prof. RPI, 2006—. Recipient 1st prize MakMax Membrane Design Competition, 1993, Hon. Mention award, 1995, 96, Bamboo Bridge Honor award Am. Inst. Architects, 2006. Office: ARUP 12777 W Jefferson Blvd Ste 200 Los Angeles CA 90066 Office Phone: 310-578-4182. Business E-Mail: bruce.danziger@arup.com.

DANZIGER, GLENN NORMAN, retired chemicals executive; b. NYC, Apr. 7, 1930; s. Victor and Freda (Lazar) Danziger; m. Florence Spielvogel, June 7, 1953; children: Jill Marla Hetson, Amy L. Tenenbaum, Beth J. Keyes(dec.). AB, Columbia U., 1952, BSChE, 1953. Chemist Breinig Bros., Hoboken, NJ, 1955-61; v.p., tech. dir. Flood and Conklin, Newark, 1961-65; tech. sales rep. Seaboard Chem. Corp., Lodi, NJ, 1965-75; pres. Seaboard Sales Corp., Paterson, NJ, 1975—2002; ret., 2002. Author: Formulation of Organic Coatings, 1967. Lt. (j.g.) USNR, 1953—55. Jewish. Avocations: travel, golf, skiing, reading.

DANZIGER, JAMES NORRIS, political science professor; b. LA, May 28, 1945; s. Edward and Beverly Jane Danziger; m. Lesley Robson, June 12, 1971; children: Nicholas James, Vanessa Margaret. BA, Occidental Coll., LA, 1966; MA, Sussex U., Brighton, Eng., 1968; MA, PhD, Stanford U., 1974. Prof. polit. sci. U. Calif., Irvine, 1972—, chmn. dept. polit. sci., 1974-76, 81-83, 88-92, assoc. dean Sch. Social Scis., 1978-81, chmn. acad. senate, 1994-95, dean of undergrad. edn., 1995-99; rsch. assoc. Ctr. Rsch. Info. Tech. and Orgns., Irvine, 1974—, dir., 2000-01, assoc. dir., 2001—; scholar-in-residence LaVerne (Calif.) U., 1983-84. Vis. prof. U. Pitts., 1996, Aarhus (Denmark) U., 1985. Author: Making Budgets, 1978, Understanding the Political World, 1991, 8th edit., 2007; co-author: Computers and Politics, 1982, People and Computers, 1986; mem. editl. bd. Local Govt. Studies, 1981—2003; assoc. editor Social Sci. Computer Rev.; mem. editl. bd. Internat. Jour. Electronic Govt. Rsch. Bd. dirs. South Laguna Civic Assn., 1983-86, chair South Laguna Annexation Task Force, 1986, bd. dirs. Irvine Campus Housing Authority, 1996-2004. Recipient Disting. Teaching award U. Calif., 1979, Daniel Aldrich disting. svc. award, 1997; Marshall scholar Govt. of U.K., 1966-68; named Disting. Faculty Lectr. U. Calif. Acad. Senate, 1987, IBM Faculty fellow, 2003—; NSF grantee, 1973-79, 80-83, 1996-98, 99—. Mem. Am. Polit. Sci. Assn. (Leonard White award 1974), ASPA (Marshall Dimock award 1977), Phi Beta Kappa (pres. local chpt. 1988-89, sec.-treas. local chpt. 1996-99, Pi Sigma Alpha (pres. local chpt. 1987—). Avocations: travel, basketball, literature. Office: U Calif Sch Social Scis Irvine CA 92697-5100 Office Phone: 949-824-5533. E-mail: danziger@uci.edu.

DANZIGER, LUCY, editor; married; 2 children. Grad., Harvard U. Reporter Star-Ledger, Newark, 1982—86; mag. assoc. editor, 1986—88; founding mng. editor 7 Days, 1988—90; exec. editor Manhattan, Inc., NYC, 1990—92; freelance writer, 1992—95; freelance editor Allure; editor style and news dept. NY Times, NYC, 1994—95; founding editor Women's Sports & Fitness, 1997—2001; editor-in-chief SELF mag., NYC, 2001—. Mem.: Am. Soc. Mag. Editors (bd. dirs. 2007—). Office: Salf Mag 4 Times Sq New York NY 10036

DANZIGER, RAPHAEL, political scientist, researcher; b. Haifa, Israel, June 26, 1944; came to U.S., 1968; s. Norbert and Hanna Danziger; m. Carla Danziger, June 12, 1970; children: Elon, Tamar. BA in Polit. Sci. and History Islamic Countries, Hebrew U., Jerusalem, 1965; MA in Near Ea. Studies, U. Wash., 1970; MA in European and Near Ea. History, Princeton U., 1972, PhD in Near Ea. Studies, 1974. Rschr. Shiloah Ctr. for Mid. Ea. Studies Tel Aviv (Israel) U., 1975-76; dep. dir. Inst. Mid. Ea. Studies U. Haifa (Israel), 1976-77; policy analyst commn. on internat. affairs Am. Jewish Congress, NYC, 1981-86, asst. dir. commn. on internat. affairs, 1986-90; dir. rsch. and info. Am. Israel Pub. Affairs Com., Washington, 1990—. Cons. Hudson Inst., Croton-on-Hudson, N.Y., 1974-75; vis. rsch. fellow dept. history U. Bergen, Norway, 1980; vis. fellow dept. Near Ea. studies Princeton (N.J.) U., 1981; lectr. dept. Mid. East history U. Haifa, 1975-81; vis. asst. prof. dept. history U. Wash., Seattle, 1980-81; lectr. in field. Author: Abd al-Qadir and the Algerians: Resistance to the French and Internal Consolidation, 1977; editor Near East Report, 1992—; contbr. articles to profl. jours. Lt. Israeli Army, 1965-68. Mem. Mid. East Studies Assn., Mid. East Inst. Office: Am Israel Pub Affairs Com 440 1st St NW Ste 600 Washington DC 20001-2017 Office Phone: 202-639-5268. Business E-Mail: rdanziger@aipac.org.

DANZL, DANIEL FRANK, emergency physician; b. Cin., Apr. 2, 1950; s. Frank Bernard and Mary Ellen (Doerger) D.; m. Joanna Colosimo Danzl, Nov. 25, 1978; children: Maggie, Julia. BS magna cum laude, U. Cin., 1972; MD, Ohio State U., 1976. Diplomate Am. Bd. Emergency Medicine. Intern St. Francis Med. Ctr., Peoria, Ill., 1976-77; resident in emergency medicine U. Louisville, 1977-79, asst. prof. emergency medicine, 1979-83, assoc. prof. emergency medicine, 1983-89, prof. emergency medicine, 1989-91, prof., chair, 1991—. Bd. dirs., councilman-at-large Univ. Assn. for Emergency Medicine, 1988-89, indsl./govtl. rels. com., 1984-85, nominating com., 1987-88; bd. dirs. Soc. for Acad. Emergency Medicine, 1989, mem. annals of emergency meidcine task force, 1989; bd. dirs. Am. Bd. Emergency Medicine, sec.-treas., 1995-96, pres.-elect, 1996-97, pres. 1997—, mem. ad hoc com., oral examiner, 1982—; mem. Com. to Advise the Nat. ARC, 1984-87; reviewer for various med. jours. Author book chpts., monographs and textbooks including Airway Management in the Trauma Patient in the Clinical Practice of Emergency Medicine, 1991; editl. bd. Jour. Emergency Medicine, 1983—, Poisindex-Emergindex, 1982—, Jour. Wilderness Medicine, 1991—; contbr. more than 70 articles to Jour. Wilderness Medicine, Jpur. Emergency Medicine, Annals of Emergency Medicine, Am. Jour. Emergency Medicine, others. Mem. Water Safety Com. Nat. Safety Coun.-Pub. Safety Div., 1981-84; alternate med. dir. Jefferson Vocat. Edn.-Louisville EMS Paramedic Tng. Program, 1989-90, 90-91. Recipient Silver Tongue Orator award Soc. Tchrs. of Emergency Medicine, 1986, 88; grantee Office of Naval Resources, 1983-85, Key Pharmaceuticals, 1985, Hoffman-LaRoche, Inc., 1988, 89. Fellow Am. Coll. Emergency Physicians (nat. coun. mem. 1981-93, reference com. mem. 1981, 85, 89, rsch. com. mem. 1982-83, 83-84); mem. AMA (Physician's Recognition awards), NAS, Am. Soc. Circumpolar Health, Soc. for Acad. Emergency Medicine (bd. dirs. 1989, task force 1989), Nat. Rsch. Coun., Undersea and Hyperbaric Oxygen Med. Soc., Ky. Chpt. Am. Coll. Emergency Physicians (councillor 1981-93, sec.-treas. 1983-84, pres.-elect 1984-85, pres. 1985-86), Wilderness Med. Soc., Phi Beta Kappa, Beta Theta Pi, Alpha Omega Alpha, Phi Eta Sigma. Roman Catholic. Achievements include research on hypothermia. Home: 4804 Smith Rd Floyds Knobs IN 47119-9238 Office: U Louisville Dept Emergency Med 530 S Jackson St Louisville KY 40202-1675 Office Phone: 502-588-5689.

DAO, KATHRYN H., rheumatologist; arrived in US, 1995; BS in Microbiology suma cum laude, U. Tex., Arlington, 1995; MD, U. Tex., Dallas, 1999. Diplomate in rheumatology Am. Bd. Internal Medicine, 2004. Intern, resident Washington U. Med. Ctr., Barnes Jewish Hosp., St. Louis, 1999—2002; fellow rheumatology U. Tex. S.W. Med. Ctr., 2002—04; staff rheumatologist Presbyn. Hosp., Dallas, 2004—. Rschr. Presbyn. Hosp., Dallas, 2004—. Editor: (book) Washington Manual of Rheumatology; contbr. articles to profl. jours. Scholar, Pfizer, 2004. Mem.: ACP, Tex. Med. Assn., Am. Coll. Rheumatology. Roman Catholic. Avocations: cooking, photography, travel. Office: Arthritis Consultation Ctr 9301 N Ctrl Expressway Ste 675 Dallas TX 75231 Office Phone: 214-345-8200. Office Fax: 214-345-7999.

DAO, THUY DINH, personal care industry executive; b. Bac Ninh, Vietnam, Apr. 12, 1942; arrived in U.S., 1991, naturalized, 1997; s. Tan Dinh Dao, Thu Thi Pham, Hoi Thi Nguyen (Stepmother); m. Dung Ngoc Tran, Mar. 30, 1968; children: Thuy-Van, Khai, Tri. B with honors, Tri-Duc Cath. Sch., Da-Lat, Vietnam, 1961; cert. Radio/TV Technician, Can-Tho U., Vietnam, 1987; cert. Computer/Elec. Cable Tech., Amtek Inst., Arlington, Va., 1992; student, Lycee Yersin, Da-Lat. A+ cert. Nova C.C., Alexandria, Va., 2001, cert. nail tech. Falls Ch., Va. Interpreter, transplator U.S. Adv. Teams, Chau Doc,Hong Ngu,Kien Giang, Vietnam, 1965—70; tinsmith Can-Tho, Vietnam, 1976—81; owner coffee shop Ho-Chi-Minh City, Vietnam, 1983—88; with The Ritz Carlton Pentagon City, Arlington, Va., 1991—96; owner Elegant Nails, New Castle, Del., 1999—2000, mgr. Alexandria, 2001—02, Belle Beauté and Hollywood Image Inc., Wilmington, Del., 2003—, Bella Nails, Wilmington, 2003—04; asst. T&D Home Improvement, Inc., Falls Church, Va., 2004—. Trader Fgn. Currency Agy., (IMEX Can Tho) Can Tho, Vietnam, 1981—82; owner thuydaogift.com. Author: The Siren, 1980, numerous poems; contbr. articles to profl. jours. With Army South Vietnam, 1970—75. Mem.: Internat. Biog. Assn. Avocations: music, movies, travel, reading, sports. Office: T&D Home Improvement Inc 3059 Sleepy Hollow Rd Falls Church VA 22042 Personal E-mail: thuy_dao_1999@yahoo.com, thuy_dao@att.net.

DAOUD, GEORGE JAMIL, hotel and motel consultant; b. Beirut, Oct. 20, 1948; came to U.S., 1958, naturalized, 1970; s. Jamil G. and Shafika E. Daoud; divorced; 5 children. BS, NYU, 1967; MPS, Cornell U., 1969; PhD in Bus. Adminstrn., U. Palmer Green, 1986. Gen. mgr. Holiday Inn, New London and Groton, Conn., 1974-75, Gentle Winds Beach Resort, St. Croix, V.I., 1975-78; pres., cons. Motor Inn Mgmt., Inc., Dayton, Ohio, 1973—. Pres. Cen. Svcs. Group, Inc., First Group, Inc., Host Mgmt., Inc., Inn Group, Inc., 1981—, Metro Markets, Inc., Dayton, Triac Ventures, Inc., 1980-86. Mem Am. Hotel and Motel Assn. (cert. hotel adminstr., mem. Ednl. Inst.), Ohio Hotel and Motel Assn., Nat. Assn. Rev. Appraisers, Cert. Real Estate Rev. Appraisers, Masons. Republican. Roman Catholic. Office: Hotelvest Inc 864 N Main St Dayton OH 45405-4630

DAOUK, HAZEM, finance educator; Diploma in accounting and finance, Inst. Comml. Superieur, Paris, France, 1993; MBA, U. Md., College Park, 1995; PhD in Finance, Ind. U., Bloomington, 2001. Fin. analyst Compagnie Fiduciaire pour le Commerce et l'Industrie, Paris, 1992—93; fin. prof. U. Mich., Ann Arbor, 2001—02, Cornell U., Ithaca, NY, 2002—. Author: (article) Jour. of Fin. Econs. (Best Acad. Paper award Internat. Investment Forum, U. Chgo., 1998), Jour. Fin. (Nomination for Best Paper in Jour. of Fin., 2002, 2002), Accounting Review (Best Paper award Conf. on the Theories and Practices of Securities and Fin. Markets, Taiwan, 2002), Jour. of Corp. Fin.; referee: over 20 jours., reviewer: NSF, 2003. Achievements include research featured in Barron's, Business Week, Boston Globe, Chicago Tribune, Economic Intuition, Money Magazine, Reuters News, The Economist, Financial Times and the Washington Post; ranked 227 out of 77,000 total authors in the world on the Social Sciences Research Network (ssrn.com) in terms of total number of downloaded copies of papers (over 12,000). Avocation: intraday trading of stocks and futures. Office: Cornell Univ Warren Hall Rm 446 Ithaca NY 14853 Office Phone: 607-255-6459. Office Fax: 607-255-9984. E-mail: hd35@cornell.edu.

DAOUST, DONALD ROGER, pharmaceutical executive, microbiologist, cosmetics executive; b. Worcester, Mass., Aug. 13, 1935; s. G. Arthur and Alice Anne (Lavalee) D.; m. Johanna K. Kalinoski, May 30, 1959 (div. 2003); children: Donna Jean, Stephen Michael, Sandra Marie; m. Barbara Neubert, 2005. BA, U. Conn., 1957; MS, U. Mass., 1959, PhD, 1962. Sr. rsch. microbiologist Merck Sharp & Dohme, Rahway, NJ, 1962-70, rsch. fellow, 1970-72, mgr. biol. quality control West Point, Pa., 1972-75; dir. quality control Armour Pharm. Co., Kankakee, Ill., 1975-76, v.p. quality assurance and regulatory compliance Phoenix, 1976-78; v.p., quality control Carter-Wallace, Inc., Cranbury, NJ, 1978—2001. Contbr. articles o profl. jours., chapters to books. Mem. Borough Coun., South Plainfield, N.J., 1970-72; treas. George Washington coun. Boy Scouts Am., 1981-84, pres., 1984-87, area v.p., bd.dirs. NE region U.S., 1987—2004. Recipient Disting. Svc. award South Plainfield Jaycees, 1969, silver Beaver award Boy Scouts Am., 1988, Silver Antelope award N.E. region, 1992; named Outstanding Young Man, N.J. Jaycees, 1970. Mem.: AAAS, Pharm. Mfrs. Assn. (quality control adminstrn. 1979—82, adv. bd. 1982—94, vice chmn 1988—90, chmn. 1990—92), Am. Soc. for Quality Control, Am. Soc. Microbiology, Laurel Oak Country Club (Sarasota, Fla.). Achievements include patents in field. Avocations: golf, jogging, reading, gardening. Home: 3254 Chas MacDonald Dr Sarasota FL 34240 Personal E-mail: dondaoust@comcast.net.

DA PENA, EILEEN, psychologist; b. Carmel, Calif., Sept. 11, 1972; d. Ramon Da Pena and Eileen Schmidt. BA in Psychology, U. Calif., Santa Barbara, 1994; MA in Psychology, Calif. Sch. Profl. Psychology, 1997, D of Clin. Psychology, 2002, MS in Clin. Psychopharmacology, 2004; cert. in advanced grad. gerontology, U. South Fla., 1998. Lic. psychologist Calif. Bd. Psychology. Asst. psychologist, La Jolla, Calif., 2002—04; postdoctoral fellow U. Calif., San Diego, 2002—04; postdoctoral fellow clin. neuropsychology Fielding Grad. Inst., Santa Barbara, 2005—. Psychologist Sharp Healthcare, San Diego, 2005—; clin. psychologist, San Diego, 2005—; adj. instr. Alliant Internat. U., San Diego, 2005—. Vol. Alzheimer's Assn., San Diego, 1998—. Recipient Recognition award, Operation Promote Liberty Panama, 1990, Diversity award, Calif. Sch. Profl. Psychology, 1995—2000; scholar, U. South Fla., 1997—98, USA Scholarship Group Found., 2000—02. Mem.: APA, Internat. Neuropsychol. Soc., Nat. Acad. Neuropsychology. Democrat. Avocations: travel, reading, movies, learning new languages.

DAPKUS, PAUL D., engineering educator; BS, U. Ill. at Urbana-Champaign, 1966, MS, 1967, PhD, 1970. Joined Viterbi Sch. Engring., U. So. Calif., LA, 1982, William M. Keck chair. Contbr. articles to profl. jours. Recipient Nick Holonyak Jr. Award, Optical Soc. Am., 2005. Fellow: AAAS, IEEE (Engring. Achievement Award 1995, David Sarnoff Tech. Field Award in Electronics 2001), Am. Physical Soc.; mem.: NAE. Office: U So Calif Viterbi Sch Engring Mailcode 0243 Los Angeles CA 90089 Office Phone: 213-740-4414. Office Fax: 213-740-6022. E-mail: dapkus@usc.edu.

DAPRON, ELMER JOSEPH, JR., communications executive; b. Clayton, Mo., Jan. 14, 1925; s. Elmer Joseph and Susanna (Kruse) D.; m. Sharon Kay Neuling, Feb. 22, 1977 (dec. Apr. 1987). Employed in constrn., Fairbanks, Alaska, 1947-48; tech. writer-editor McDonnell-Douglas Corp., St. Louis, 1948-57; freelance writer Paris, 1957; with Gardner Advt. Co., St. Louis, 1960-78, v.p., 1969-78; sr. v.p. Kenrick Advt. Inc., 1978-83; pres. Cornucopia Communications, Inc., 1979—. Producer syndicated radio and TV show Elmer Dapron's Grocery List; advt. and mktg. cons. to govt. and industry; commentator The Grocery List Armed Forces Radio Network (worldwide); contbr. articles to publs. Mem. Nat. Dem. Com., candidate for Gov. of Mo., 1992; nat. pres. Iwo Jima Task Force Two, 1994—; nat. chmn. Korea Task Force 2000, 1997—. With USMCR, 1943-45, PTO, 50-51, Korea. Recipient advt. awards including New Filming Techniques award Internat.-Film Festival; hon. fellow Harry Truman Libr. Inst. Mem. Nat. Agrl. Mktg. Assn., Miss. Valley Farm Mktg. (Man of Yr. 1974), Assn. R.R. Advt. and Mktg. (nat. membership chmn.), Marine Corps League (nat. vice comdt. 1967-69, nat. press officer 4th Marine Div. Assn. 1989—, publicity chmn.), Media Club, St. Louis Track Club. Democrat. Office: 21440 Lakeview Estates Dr Warrenton MO 63383-5258 Home Phone: 636-456-7122; Office Phone: 636-456-0154.

D'AQUINO, THOMAS, lawyer, educator, entrepreneur; b. Trail, BC, Can., Nov. 3, 1940; m. Susan Marion Peterson, 1965. BA, U. B.C., 1962, LLB, 1965; LLB, LLM, U. London, 1967; LLD (hon.), Queen's U., 1996, Wilfred Laurier U. Adj. prof. law U. Ottawa, Ont., Canada; chmn. Intercounsel Ltd.; pres., chief exec. Can. Coun. Chief Execs. (CCCE), Ottawa, 1981—. Former exec. asst. to Fed. Min., spl. asst. to Prime Min., Can., 1969-72; internat. cons. firm in London and Paris, 1972-75; frequent guest lectr.; bd. dirs. Manulife Fin Corp., CGI, Inc.; mem. Chmn's Internat. Adv. Coun. of the Am.'s Soc.; founding mem. Pacific Coun. on Internat. Policy; adv. bd. Lazard Can.; chmn. Nat. Gallery of Can. Found., N.Am. security and prosperity initiative, Can. Coun. Chief Execs., co-chmn. task force on environ. leadership. Co-author: Northern Edge: How Canadians Can Triumph in the Global Economy, 2001; contbr. articles to profl. jours. Mem. World Econ. Forum Geneva, Inst. for Strategic Studies, London. Mem. Can. Bar Assn., Internat. Bar Assn., B.C. Law Soc. Office: Can Coun Chief Execs 99 Bank St Ste 1001 Ottawa ON Canada K1P 6B9

DARAM, SUMANTH REDDY, medical educator; m. Hima Reddy, Jan. 10, 2006. MD, St. Louis U., 2004. Diplomate Am. Bd. Internal Medicine, 2005. Clin. asst. prof. medicine Med. Coll. Wis., Milw., 2004—; academic hospitalist St. Joseph Regional Med. Ctr., Milw., 2004—. Scholar, Nat. Coun. for Ednl. Rsch. and Tng., 1990—92. Mem.: ACP, Soc. Hosp. Medicine. Achievements include research in nephrology and hematology. Office Phone: 414-874-4763.

D'ARBANVILLE, PATTI, actress; b. NYC, May 25, 1951; m. Roger Mirmont, 1976 (div. 1977); m. Steve Curry, 1980 (div. 1981); m. Terry Quinn, June 15, 1993 (div. 2000); children: Emmelyn, Alexandra, Liam, Jesse. Appeared in films Flesh, 1968, Bilitis, 1976, Big Wednesday, 1978, Time After Time, 1979, The Fifth Floor, 1980, Modern Problems, 1981, THe Boys Next Door, 1985, Call Me, 1988, Fresh Horses, 1988, Crossing the Mob, 1988, Wired, 1989, Snow Kill, 1990, The Fan, 1996, Father's Day, 1997, I Know What You Did Last Summer, 1997, Archibald the Rainbow Painter, 1998, Bad to the Bone, 1997, Celebrity, 1998, Personal Velocity: Three Portraits, 2002, A Tale of Two Pizzas, 2003, World Trade Center, 2006, Perfect Stranger, 2007, (TV series) Another World, 1992-93, New York Undercover, 1994-97, The Guiding Light, 1998-2000, (TV episodes) Eddie Capra Mysteries, 1978, Barnaby Jones, 1980, Charlies Angels, 1980, Darkroom, 1982, Murder, She Wrote, 1984, Miami Vice, 1985, Crime Story, 1986, Midnight Caller, 1988, The Hitchhiker, 1989, Wiseguy, 1989, Law & Order, 1992, South Beach, 1993, L.A. Law, 1994, Nip/Tuck, 2003, The Sopranos, 2004, Third Watch, 2004-05, Rescue Me, 2006.*

DARBEE, PETER A., utilities executive; b. 1954; BA in Econ., MBA, Darmouth Coll.; Nuclear Reactor Technology Program, MIT. Mgmt. Salomon Brothers, AT&T; investment banker, v.p. Goldman Sachs; v.p., CFO, controller Pacific Bell; v.p., CFO Advance Fibre Commns., Inc.; sr. v.p., CFO, treas. PG&E Corp., 1999—2005, pres., CEO, 2005, chmn., CEO, 2006—. Mem. San Francisco Com. on Jobs. Office: PG&E 1 Market Spear Tower San Francisco CA 94105*

DARBELNET, ROBERT LOUIS, automobile association executive; b. Portland, Maine, Dec. 14, 1951; s. Jean Louis and Elizabeth (Matheson) D.; m. Mary Ann McCaughey, Aug. 27, 1977; children: John Kevin, Mary Jennifer. LLB, Laval U., Quebec City, 1978. Dir. consumer protection dept. Que. (Can.) Automobile Club, Quebec City, 1973-76, dir. road and tech. svcs., 1976-78, dir. gen. ins. dept., 1978-79, asst. gen. mgr., 1980-83, dir. gen., 1983-90, pres., 1990-94. Tchr. bus. Coll. Sainte Foy (Que.), 1978—84, v.p., 1981—82, pres., 1982—86; bd. dirs. Ont. Corp., Muncie, Ind., ITS Am., vice chair, 2002; mem. Nat. Petroleum Coun.; pres. Alliance Internat. Tourisme, 2001—, chair mgmt. com., 2001—; chair world bd. Alliance Internat. Tourisme/Fedn. Internat. de'lAutomobile, 2002; mem. Fedn. Internat. del'Automobile Senate, 1997—. Mem. Fedn. Internat. de l'Automobile, Paris, 1990—, dep. pres., 2001—; bd. dirs. Corp. de la Salle Albert Rousseau, 1990—94, Enfant Jesus Hosp., 1993—94, Union Canadienne Ins., 1993—94; bd. govs. Coll. Sainte-Foy, 1980—88, bd. govs. alumni fund, 1980—88, v.p., 1982—88; trustee AAA Found. for Traffic Safety, 1990—, sec., 1993—94; v.p. Internat. Tourism Commn., 1995—, world tng. coun., 1995—, mem. mgmt. com., 1995—. Mem.: Am. Automobile Assn. (pres., CEO 1994—). Office: 1000 Aaa Dr Heathrow FL 32746-5063

D'ARBELOFF, ALEXANDER V., electronics executive; Co-founder Teradyne Corp., Boston, 1960—99, pres., 1971—96, CEO, 1971—97, chmn. bd. dirs., 1977—; hon. chair. MIT, Cambridge. Chmn. bd. trustees MIT, Cambridge, 1997—2003. Office: 77 Massachusetts Ave E52-586 Cambridge MA 02139-4307 Office Phone: 617-253-4034.

DARBY, EDWIN WHEELER, retired columnist; b. Oakland, Md., Jan. 7, 1922; s. John Dade and Nell (Bosley) D.; children— Ann Wheeler, John Dade; m. Susan E. Kroening, Mar. 14, 1970; 1 son, George Kroening. BS in Journalism, Ohio U. White House corr. Time mag., 1948-55; midwest corr. Time and Fortune mags., 1956-58; financial editor, columnist Chgo. Sun-Times, 1958-95; ret., 1995. Author: The Fortune Builders, 1987. Recipient Marshall Field award, 1974, Loeb award, 1975 Mem. Tavern Club. Home: 2703 W Logan Blvd Chicago IL 60647-1831

DARBY, G(EORGE) HARRISON, lawyer; b. NYC, Jan. 24, 1942; s. Stephen John and Madge B. (Leh) D. BA, Muhlenberg Coll., 1963; LLB, Bklyn. Law Sch., 1967. Bar: N.Y. 1967. Of counsel Jackson Lewis LLP, L.A. and other offices, 1967—. Mem. child adv. group Internat. Inst. of L.A., 1989-96. Office: Jackson Lewis LLP 725 South Figueroa St Los Angeles CA 90017-5408

DARBY, JOSEPH M., reservist; s. Dale (Stepfather) and Margaret; m. Bernadette Darby, 1998. First to report prisoner abuse at Abu Ghraib prison in Iraq. Reservist 372nd Mil. Police Co. US Army, Iraq. Recipient Spl. Profile in Courage, John F. Kennedy Libr. Found., 2005.

DARBY, KAREN SUE, law educator; b. Columbus, Ohio, Sept. 15, 1947; d. Emerson Curtis and Kathryn Elizabeth (Bowers) Dum; m. R. Russell Darby, Dec. 21, 1974; children: David Randolph, Michael Emerson. BA magna cum laude, Capital U., Columbus, 1969; JD, Ohio State U., 1980. Bar: Ohio 1980, Pa. 1998, U.S. Dist. Ct. (so. dist.) Ohio 1981. High sch. English tchr. Columbus Pub. Schs., 1969-72; employee rels. specialist GE, Circleville, Ohio, 1972-74, mgr. EEO and manpower programs chem. met. div. Worthington, Ohio, 1974-77; atty. Ohio Legal Rights Svc., Columbus, 1980-81; pvt. practice Columbus, 1981-90; assoc. dir. Ohio Continuing Legal Edn. Inst., Columbus, 1989-95; dir. Phila. Bar Edn. Ctr., 1995-97; assoc. dir. Pa. Bar Inst., Phila., 1997—2002; exec. dir. Ill. Inst. for Continuing Legal Edn., 2002—. Mem. rules adv. com. Supreme Ct. Ohio, Columbus, 1989-94. Author, editor: Civil Commitment in Ohio - A Manual for Respondents' Attorneys, 1980. Mem. divorce mediation panel Ohio State U. Commn. on Interprofl. Edn., Columbus, 1988-91; vol. Boy Scouts Am., Columbus, 1988-92, Columbus Pub. Schs., 1984-95. Fellow: Ill. State Bar Found.; mem.: ABA, Govt. Bar Assn., Chgo. Bar Assn., Assn. Continuing Legal Edn. (dir.-at-large), Ill. State Bar Assn., Univ. Club of Chgo. Democrat. Lutheran. Avocations: organ, piano, gardening. Office: IICLE 2395 W Jefferson St Springfield IL 62702 Home Phone: 217-787-9255; Office Phone: 217-787-2080. Business E-Mail: kdarby@iicle.com.

DARBY, MICHAEL RUCKER, economist, educator; b. Dallas, Nov. 24, 1945; s. Joseph Jasper and Frances Adah (Rucker) D.; children: Margaret Loutrel, David Michael; Lynne Ann Zucker-Darby, 1992; stepchildren: Joshua R. Zucker, Danielle T. Zucker. AB summa cum laude, Dartmouth Coll., 1967; MA, U. Chgo., 1968, PhD, 1970. Asst. prof. econ. Ohio State U., 1970-73; vis. asst. prof. econ. UCLA, 1972-73, assoc. prof., 1973-78, prof., 1978-87, 96—, prof. Anderson Grad. Sch. Mgmt., 1987-94, Warren C. Cordner prof. money and fin. mkts., 1995—, vice-chmn., 1992-93; dir. John M. Olin Ctr. for Policy, 1993—; assoc. dir. orgnl. rsch. program UCLA Inst. for Social Sci. Rsch., 1995—2000; assoc. dir. Ctr. Internat. Sci., Tech., Cultural Policy Sch. Pub. Affairs, UCLA, 1996—; rsch. assoc. Nat. Bur. Econ. Rsch., 1976-86, 92—; asst. sec. for econ. policy U.S. Dept. Treasury, Washington, 1986-89; mem. Nat. Commn. on Superconductivity, 1988-89; under sec. for econ. affairs U.S. Dept. Commerce, Washington, 1989-92; adminstr. Econs. and Stats. Adminstrn., 1990-92. V.p., dir. Paragon Industries, Inc., Dallas, 1964—83; mem. exec. com. Western Econ. Assn., 1987—90, v.p., 1998—99, pres.-elect, 1999—2000, pres., 2000—01; chmn. The Dumbarton Group, 1992—; adj. scholar Am. Ent. Inst. for Pub. Policy Rsch., 1992—; economist stats. income divsn. IRS, 1992—94; mem. regulatory coord. adv. com. Commodity Futures Trading Commn., 1992—96. Author: Macroeconomics, 1976, Have Controls Ever Worked: The Post-War Record, 1976, Intermediate Macroeconomics, 1979, 2d edit., 1986, The Effects of Social Security on Income and the Capital Stock, 1979, The International Transmission of Inflation, 1981, Labor Force, Employment, and Productivity in Historical Perspective, 1984, Reducing Poverty in America: Views and Approaches, 1996; editor Jour. Internat. Money and Fin., 1981-86, mem. editl. bd., 1986—; mem. editl. bd. Am. Econ. Rev., 1983-86, Contemporary Policy Issues, 1990-93, Contemporary Econ. Policy, 1994—, Internat. Reports, 1992—. Bd. dirs. The Opera Assoc., 1992—; mem. acad. adv. bd. Ctr. Regulation and Econ. Growth of the Alexis de Tocqueville Instn., 1993-96. Recipient Alexander Hamilton award U.S. Treasury Dept., 1989; sr. fellow Dartmouth Coll., 1966-67, Woodrow Wilson fellow, 1967-68, NSF grad. fellow, 1967-69, FDIC grad. fellow, 1969-70, Harry Scherman rsch. fellow Nat. Bur. Econ. Rsch., 1974-75, vis. fellow Hoover Instn., Stanford U., 1977-78. Mem. AAAS, Am. Econ. Assn., Am. Fin. Assn., Am. Statis. Assn., Am. Law & Econs. Assn., Nat. Assn. Bus. Economists, Royal Econ. Soc., So. Econ. Assn., Western Econ. Assn., N.Y. Acad. Scis., Capitol Hill Club (D.C.), Nat. Econ. Club. Episcopalian. Home: 18108 Meandering Way Dallas TX 75252-2763 Office: UCLA Anderson Grad Sch Mgmt Los Angeles CA 90095-0001

D'ARCHE, DOUGLAS D., lawyer; b. San Diego, Feb. 7, 1968; BS in Bus. Econs., Willamette U., 1990; JD cum laude, U. Houston Law Ctr., 1995. Bar: Tex. 1995, US Dist. Ct. (we. and so. dists. Tex.) 1996, US Ct. Appeals Fifth Cir. 1996, US Dist. Ct. (no. and ea. dists. Tex.) 1997. Ptnr. Baker Hostetler, Houston. Contbr. articles to profl. publs. Named a Rising Star, Tex. Super Lawyers mag., 2006. Mem.: Houston Bar Assn., Tex. Young Lawyers Assn. (Outstanding Dir. award 2005, Pres.'s Award of Merit 1997). Office: Baker Hostetler 1000 Louisiana Ste 2000 Houston TX 77002-5009 Office Phone: 713-646-1379. Office Fax: 713-751-1717. E-mail: ddarche@bakerlaw.com.

DARCHUN, LINO AUKSUTIS, real estate professional; b. Chgo., Mar. 4, 1942; s. Joseph and Ursula (Shimkus) D.; m. Mary Lynn Burchette, Nov. 11, 1983; 1 child, Matthew. Student, So. Ill. U., 1960-62, 65, U. Ill., Chgo., 1966; grad., Realtor Inst., 1991. Cert. residential specialist, residential broker, internat. property specialist. Agt. Ea. Airlines, Chgo., 1967-68; sta. mgr. World Airways, Oakland, Calif., 1968-71; mgr. The Bulls Restaurant-Nightclub, Chgo., 1971-73, pres., 1977-88; v.p. Leber-Darchun, Inc., Chgo., 1973-74; adminstr. dept. aviation City of Chgo., 1974-77; assoc. realtor Palormo Realty, Chgo., 1987-88, realtor, 1988-93, v.p., 1990-93; realtor Rubloff, Inc., Chgo., 1988-90; asst. br. mgr. Coldwell Banker Residential Lincoln Park, Chgo., 1993-95, br. mgr., 1995-97; broker assoc. Coldwell Banker Residential Real Estate, Chgo., 1997—. Bd. dirs. Northwewstern U. Cognitive Neurology and Alzheimers Disease Ctr. Chmn. com. Old Wicker Park, Chgo., 1972-73; vol. Grant Hosp., Chgo.; v.p. Lincoln Park Inter-Agy. Coun., 1988; mem. adv. bd., bd. dirs. Friends of Lincoln Park/Lakeview Schs.; mem. Chgo.-Vilnius (Lithuania) Sister City Com.; mem. adv. bd. Acapulco (Mex.) Children's Home. Sgt. U.S. Army, 1962-65. Fellow Internat. Real Estate Fedn.; mem. Nat. Assn. Realtors, Chgo. Assn. Realtors (chmn. 2004, mem. multiple listing svcs. com.), Grievance Com., Internat. Real Estate Fedn., Internat. Cmty. Affairs, Lincoln Park C. of C. (v.p. 1991—, chmn. human svcs. com. 1987—, bd. dirs.), Lincoln Park Zool. Soc., Lincoln Park Conservation Assn. (1st v.p. 1988, bd. dirs., v.p. 1998-2000), Chgo. Pub. Schs. Alumni Assn. Democrat. Unitarian Universalist. Avocations: travel, music, epicure, arts. Home: 2731 N Wilton Ave Chicago IL 60614-1423 Office: Coldwell Banker Residential Lincoln Park 1840 N Clark St Chicago IL 60614-5881 Office Phone: 312-397-3082. Business E-Mail: lino@linodarchun.com.

D'ARCY, GERALD PAUL, engineering executive, consultant; b. Jackson, Mich., June 6, 1933; s. Merlin Wellington and Jessie Elizabeth (Sober) D.; m. Dorothy Lee Cordell, Nov. 27, 1953; children: Sherry, Janet, Nancy, Deborah, Helen. BSMechE, U. Tex., 1956; MSMechE, U. Colo., 1962; PhD, U. Tex., 1973. Registered profl. engr., Tex. Commd. 2d lt. USAF, 1956, advanced through grades to col., ret., 1986; asst. chief soil and rock mechanics group Air Force Weapons Lab., Kirtland AFB, N.Mex., 1962-67; rsch. assoc. Lawrence Radiation Lab., Livermore, Calif., 1967-70; chief phys. & engring. scis. divsn. Air Force Systems Command, Andrews AFB, Md., 1973-74; chief guns, rockets & explosives divsn. Air Force Armament Lab., Eglin AFB, Fla., 1975-79; vice comdr., later comdr. Air Force Geophysics, Hanscom AFB, Mass., 1979-84; comdr., dir. Air Force Office of Sci. Rsch., Bolling AFB, 1984-86; v.p. Applied Rsch. Assocs. Inc., Albuquerque, 1986-94; ret., 1994. Mech. engring. vis. com. U. Tex., Austin, 1976-79. Inventor soil stress gage; author more than 20 articles. Decorated Legion of Merit; recipient Meritorious Svc. award for nuclear weapons devel. U. Calif., Livermore, 1970; named Disting. Engring. Grad. U. Tex., Austin, 1985. Mem.: U. Tex. Mech. Engring. Acad. Dist. Alumni, Phi Kappa Phi. Democrat. Methodist. Avocation: woodworking. Home: 808 Plantation Way Panama City FL 32404-8603 E-mail: utdeg@aol.com.

DARCY, KEITH THOMAS, finance company executive, educator, not-for-profit developer; b. NYC, June 18, 1948; s. Donald and Geraldine (Kindermann) Darcy; m. Lynne Alison Cumming, June 17, 1972; children: Erin Lyn, Timothy James. BS in Econs., Fordham U., 1970; MBA, Iona Coll., New Rochelle, NY, 1974; postgrad., NY Theol. Sem., 1988-89. With Bankers Trust Co., NYC, 1970—77; v.p. Marine Midland Bank N.A., NYC, 1977—82; CEO, IGM divsn. Gen. Reins. Corp., Stamford, Conn., 1982—83; dir. human resource divsn. Marine Midland Bank, NYC, 1984—89; pres., CEO, The Leadership Group, Inc., NYC, 1989—94; v.p., assoc. ethics officer Prudential Securities Inc., NYC, 1994—96, sr. ethics advisor, 1996—97; assoc. dean, disting. prof. bus. Georgetown U., Washington, 1995—96; exec. v.p. office of the pres. IBJ Whitehall Bank and Trust Co., NYC, 1997—2002; chmn. Darcy Ptnrs. Inc., Pound Ridge, NY, 2003—; exec. dir. Ethics & Compliance Officer Assn. (formerly Ethics Officer Assn.), Waltham, Mass., 2005—; pres. Ethics & Compliance Officer Assn. Found., Waltham, Mass., 2006—. Adj. faculty Marymount Coll., 1978-96, Mercy Coll., 1975-96; faculty advanced exec. edn. Wharton, U. Pa., 1994—; faculty grad. mgmt. program Antioch U., Seattle, 1989-96; exec.-in-residence U. Md. U. Coll., 2004—; exec.-in-residence Manhattanville Coll., Purchase, NY, corp. adv. bd., 1989—; exec. fellow Ctr. for Bus. Ethics, Bentley Coll., Waltham, Mass., 1993—, exec. com.; tchg. fellow Smith Sch. Bus., U. Md., College Park, 2002—, fellow, Ethics Resource Ctr., Washington, 2006; bd. dirs. Barat House, Purchase, NY; dir. emeritus Ethics Officer Assn.; steering com. Caux (Switzerland) Round Table, 1996-99; nat. adv. bd. Worktalk, 1999-2006; vice chmn. Ctr. for Values-Based Leadership, 1999-2004, chmn., bd. trustees BBB Found., 2001—; bd. dirs. E*Trade Bank, E*Trade Savings Bank, ETB Holdings Inc., bd. United Med. Savings, 2007—; com. on effects of mktg. on obesity in children and youth Inst. Medicine, Washington; faculty Insead, France and Singapore, 2004-05 Co-author: Change Management, 1993, The Ethics Companion, 1999, The Crisis in Corporate Governance-HR's Role, 2003, Food Marketing to Children and Youth, 2005; mem. editl. bd., contbr.: At Work: Stories of Tomorrow's Workplace, 1992-2006; featured in The Ethical Edge, The Portable Executive, Merchants of Vision, Career Crossroads, Winning the People Wars, Survival Skills in the Fin. Svcs. Industry. Treas. Westchester County Rep. Com., White Plains, NY, 1979-89; asst. treas. NY State Friends for Jim Buckley, 1976; dir. NCCJ, 1977-85; trustee Bedford Presbyn. Ch., NY, 1982-87, Better Bus. Bur. Found., NY, 2001—; mem. Westchester Blue Ribbon Commn. to Formulate County Housing Policy, 1979; trustee March of Dimes, Westchester, 1978-84, chmn. Exec. Walkathon, 1978-81. Mem. Ethics Officers Assn. (dir. emeritus, exec. dir.), Caux (Switzerland) Round Table (affil.), Soc. Friendly Sons of St. Patrick (pres. 1985), Ethics Resource Ctr. (fellow). Office: 27 Horseshoe Hill W Pound Ridge NY 10576 Home Phone: 914-764-0403; Office Phone: 781-647-9333. E-mail: keith.darcy@ethicsinleadership.com.

D'ARCY, MARGARET JEANETTE, volunteer; b. Chgo., Apr. 18, 1927; d. Harry Bernard and Margaret Ruth O'Donnell; m. John Walsh D'Arcy, Aug. 20, 1949; children: Margaret, John, Kevin, Terry, Patrick, Candy, Michael, Thomas. BA, U. St. Francis, Joliet, Ill., 1949. Cert. tchr. Ill. Past pres., mem. Visitation and Aid Soc., Joliet, 1950—, Women of Rotary, Joliet, 1975—; past pres., charter mem. Provena St. Joseph Med. Ctr. Women's Aux., Joliet, 1955—, Joliet Area Cmty. Hospice Guild, 1980—; past mem. lay adv. bd. Provena St. Joseph Med. Ctr., Joliet, 1980—88, mem. found. bd., 2005—; mem. women's coun. Brain Rsch. Found., U. Chgo., 1995—; bd. dirs. Chgo. Drama League, 1994—. Named Jean Placher Disting. Alumna, U. St. Francis, 1994, Joliet Cath. Acad. Alumna of Yr., 2004; recipient Franciscan Heritage award, St. Joseph Med. Ctr., 1995, De La Salle award for cmty. svc., Lewis U., Romeoville, Ill., 1997, Signum Fidelis award, 2005, Rabbi Herschman Cmty. Svc. award, C. of C., Joliet, 1999. Home: 1580 Naperville Rd Plainfield IL 60544

DARCY, ROBERT EMMETT, political science and statistics professor; b. Elizabeth, NJ, Feb. 25, 1942; s. John William and Jane (Alton) D.; m. Lynne C. Murnane, Aug. 30, 1975; children: Mary Frances, Catherine Rose. BA, U. Wis., Madison, 1965; MA, U. Ky., Lexington, 1970, PhD, 1971. Asst. prof. George Washington U., Washington, 1971—77, Okla. State U., Stillwater, 1977—80, assoc. prof. polit. sci. and stats., 1980—85, prof., 1985—90, Regents prof., 1991—. Expert witness on racial disparities, ballot and election procedures Atty. Gen., State of Okla., Oklahoma City, 1984-86, 91-95, 98, 2002, Ohio, 1991, NH, 1995, 2004-05, NC, 1998, NY, 1999, Fed. Dist. Ct., 2002, 03, 04, 05; vis. prof. U. Conn., 1984, U. New Orleans, 1985, Queen's U., Belfast, 1987, Nat. U. Ireland, Galway, 1988, Australian Def. Force Acad., 1991, U. NSW, 1991, Trinity Coll., Dublin, 1993, U. Tel Aviv, 2007; mem. Okla. Commn. on Status Women, 1997—, co-chmn. summit 1997, 99; mem. Okla. Jud. Evaluation Commn., 1997-2001, Legis. Task Force on Jud. Selection, 1999-2000; vice chmn. gen. faculty Okla. State U., 2004-05, faculty coun., 2004-05, chair gen. faculty, 2005-06, faculty coun., 2005-06; lectr. in field. Author: Women, Elections and Representation, 1987, 90, 94, Guide to Quantitative History, 1995, Okla. Women's Almanac, 2005; co-editor Jour. Okla. Politics, 1991-99, 2005, Social Sci. Jour., 1983-85, Korean Jour. Pub. Policy, 2005-; contbr. articles to profl. jours. Recipient Liberty Bell award Okla. Bar Assn., 1999, Commendation, Okla. Ho. of Reps., 2000; Bruce fellow Keele U., Eng., 1998; vis. rsch. scholar Acad. Korean Studies, Seoul, 1983. Mem. AAUP (chpt. pres. 1984, 88), Polit. Studies Assn. Ireland, Am. Polit. Sci. Assn., Am. Assn. Pub. Opinion Rsch., Western Social Sci. Assn., Okla. Polit. Sci. Assn. (pres. 1992, Outstanding Okla. Polit. Scientist award

1993), So. Polit. Sci. Assn., Midwestern Polit. Sci. Assn., Rotary, Sigma Xi Republican. Home: 2215 W 5th Ave Stillwater OK 74074-2818 Office: Okla State U Dept Polit Sci Stillwater OK 74078-0001 Office Phone: 405-744-5641. Business E-Mail: bob.darcy@okstate.edu.

DARDAI, SHAHID MOINUDDIN, computer science educator; b. India, May 11, 1940; Prof. computer sci. dept. Richard J. Daley Coll., Chgo., 1993—, data processing coord. Chairperson computer sci. dept. Richard J. Daley Coll., 1993—; adj. faculty math. and computer sci. dept. Chgo. State U., 1993—. Recipient Disting. Prof. award, City Coll. Chgo., 2000—01. Mem. Data Processing Mgmt. Assn., Phi Theta Kappa. Office: Richard J Daley Coll 7500 S Pulaski Rd Chicago IL 60652-1242 Fax: (312) 838-7524. E-mail: sdardai@hotmail.com, sdardai@ccc.edu.

DARDEN, CHRISTOPHER ALLEN, lawyer, actor, writer; b. Martinez, Calif., Apr. 7, 1956; m. Marcia Carter, Aug. 31, 1997. BA in Criminal Justice, Calif. State U., San Jose; JD, U. Calif., San Francisco, 1980. Bar: Calif. 1980. Former atty. Nat. Labor Rels. Bd.; former asst. head dep. in spl. investigations divsn. L.A. County Dist. Attys. Office, former dep. dist. atty. in maj. crimes divsn.; actor, writer, 1996—; faculty Calif. State Univ., Los Angeles, 1995; assoc. prof. law Sch. Law Southwestern U., LA, 1996—99; atty. Darden & Assoc., Los Angeles, 1999—. Former legal commentator NBC, CNBC and CNN. Author: (with Jess Walter) In Contempt, 1996; author (with Dick Lochte) The Trials of Nikki Hill, 1999, L.A. Justice, 2000, The Last Defense, 2002, Lawless, 2004. Recipient Crystal Heart award, Loved Ones of Homicide Victims, 1998, Humanitarian of the Year, Eli Home, 2000. Mem.: Am. Trial Lawyers Assn., Nat. Bar Assn. (life). Office: Darden & Associates 5757 W Century Blvd Los Angeles CA 90045 Office Phone: 310-568-1804. Business E-Mail: dardenatty@aol.com.

DARDEN, CLAIBOURNE HENRY, JR., marketing research professional; b. Greensboro, NC, June 26, 1943; s. Claibourne Henry and Gerry (Bonkemeyer); m. Anita McMurry; children: Claibourne III, Prentiss. BS, Washington & Lee U., 1966; MBA, Emory U., 1968. Pres. Darden Rsch. Corp., Atlanta, 1968—. TV commentator, spkr. in field. Bd. dirs. Nat. Wild Turkey Fedn., Edgefield, SC, 1985—2000, Quality Deer Mgmt. Assn., Bogart, Ga., 2001—06, Ga. Conservancy, 1985—91, Washington & Lee Alumni Assn., Atlanta, 1986—87. Mem. Am. Mktg. Assn. (bd. dirs. Atlanta chpt. 1970-75, Mktg. Profl. of Yr. 1976), N.Y. Yacht Club, Druid Hills Golf Club. Presbyterian. Avocations: hunting, sailing, fishing. Office: Darden Rsch Corporation 1534 N Decatur Rd NE Atlanta GA 30307-1022

DARDEN, DERRICK CAROLYLE, civilian military employee, educator; b. Newark, Nov. 6, 1959; s. Mozell and Beatrice G. Darden; m. Anita Darden; children: Derrick Jr., Briana, Kamal. BSBA, Liberty U., Lynchburg, Va., 1992; MS in Human Rels., U. Okla., Norman, 1998. Supply systems technician US Army, 1987—2000; supply systems technician/sr. project leader Comm. Electronics Command, NJ, 1997—2000; supply systems technician Dept. Army, Ft. Irwin, Calif., 2000—04, logistics mgmt. specialist, 2004—07, govt. contract specialist, 2007—. Served with US Army, 1987—2004. Mem.: Warrant Officer Assn., Barstow Rotary Club (leaders facilitator 2004—05, Paul Harris fellow 2005). Avocations: travel, indoor sports. Office Phone: 760-380-6513.

DARDEN, EDWIN SPEIGHT, SR., architect; b. Stantonsburg, NC, Oct. 14, 1920; s. Edwin Speight and Sallie (Jordan) D.; m. s. Pauline K. Bartlett, Feb. 26, 1944; children: Edwin Speight III, Judith Ann, Diane Russell. BS in Archtl. Engring., Kans. State U., 1947. Registered architect, Calif. Assoc., Fred L. Swartz and William G. Hyberg, Fresno, Calif., 1949-59; ptnr. Nargis and Darden (Architects), Fresno, 1959-69; pres. Edwin S. Darden Assocs., Inc., Fresno, 1969-85, cons., 1985—2005. Bd. dirs. Murphy Bank; mem. state adv. bd. Office of Architecture and Constrn., 1970-78; cons. ednl. facilities, 1975—. Prin. works include Clovis (Calif.) High Sch., 1969, Clovis W. High Sch., 1976, Ahwahnee Jr. High Sch., Fresno, 1966, Tehipite Jr. High Sch., Fresno, 1973, Fresno County Dept. Health, 1978, Floyd B. Buchanan Edn. Ctr., Clovis, 1990. Served to 1st lt. C.E., AUS, 1942-46. Fellow AIA; mem. Sigma Phi Epsilon, Alpha Kappa Psi. Clubs: Fresno Rotary. Presbyterian. Office: Edwin S Darden Associates Inc 6790 N West Ave #104 Fresno CA 93711-1393 E-mail: esda@pacbell.net.

DARDEN, GEORGE WASHINGTON, III, (BUDDY DARDEN), former congressman, lawyer; b. Sparta, Ga., Nov. 22, 1943; s. George and Frances Darden; m. Lillian Budd; c. Christy & George. Student, North Ga. Coll., 1961-62, George Washington U., 1962-63; BA, U. Ga., 1965, JD, 1967. Bar: Ga. 1967. Asst. dist. atty. Cobb County, Marietta, Ga., 1968-72, dist. atty., 1973—76; sole practice law Marietta, 1977-78; assoc. Awtrey & Parker, Marietta, 1979-83; mem. Ga. Ho. of Reps., 1980—83; mem. from 7th Dist. Ga. US Ho. of Reps, 1983—95, mem. appropriations com., mem. standards and official conduct com., mem. armed svc. com., mem. interior and insular affairs com.; ptnr. McKenna Long & Aldridge LLP, Atlanta. Intern to US Senator Richard Russell, Washington, 1962, to Congressman Carl Vinson, Washington, 1963 Bd. dirs. Atlanta Area council Boy Scouts Am., Cobb County Emergency Aid, Marietta; mem. bd. trustees LaGrange Coll., Ga., 2002- Mem. Nat. Assn. Dist. Attys., ABA, Ga. Bar Assn., Cobb County Bar Assn. Lodges: Kiwanis (past pres. Marietta). Democrat. Office: McKenna Long & Aldridge LLP Ste 5300 303 Peachtree St NE Atlanta GA 30308 Office Phone: 404-527-4130. Office Fax: 404-527-4198. E-mail: bdarden@mckennalong.com.

DARDEN, JOSEPH SAMUEL, JR., health educator; b. Pleasantville, NJ, July 25, 1925; s. Joseph Samuel and Blanche Catherine (Paige) D.; m. Barbara Cassandra Sellers, Dec. 30, 1955 (div. July 1979); 1 child, Michele Irene; m. Barbara L. Simpson, Oct. 21, 1987. AB, Lincoln U., 1948; MA, NYU, 1952, EdD (Danforth Found. fellow), 1963. Instr. biol. scis. Clark Coll., Atlanta, 1952-55; asst. prof. Albany (Ga.) State Coll., 1955-58, prof., 1959-64; asst. prof. Kean U. of N.J., Union, 1964-67, prof. health edn., 1970—2002, coord. health, 1977-79, chmn. dept. health and recreation, 1979-84, coord. health, 1984—2002, dir. minority enrollment, 1988-94, prof. emeritus, 2002—. Adj. prof. health Wagner Coll., S.I., N.Y., 1965-88; cons. N.J. Dept. Edn., 1968-73, 76-88. Author: (with others) Growth Pattern and Sex Education, 1967, Updated Supplement to Growth Pattern and Sex Education, 1972, Toward a Healthier Sexuality: A Book of Readings, 1997; editor, co-author: Critical Health Issues Reader, 2002. Bd. advisors Marylawn of Oranges, 1971-73; bd. dirs. N.J. Coun. Family Relations, 1981-83; trustee Planned Parenthood of Essex County, N.J., 1985—; trustee Planned Parenthood of Met. N.J, 1985-2003. With AUS, 1944-46. Recipient Alumni Achievement award, Lincoln U., 1993, Presdl. Excellence award, Kean U., 2002. Fellow Am. Assn. Health Edn. (charter), Am. Sch. Health Assn. (governing coun. 1970-73, Disting. Svc. award 1971); mem. AAHPERD (Eastern dist. v.p. for health edn. 1971-72, dist. pres. 1974-75, Eastern dist. rep. 1979-82, honor award Eastern dist. 1976, nat. honor award 1985, Outstanding Tchr. award Eastern dist. 1983, Charles D. Henry award 1988, Edwin B. Henderson award 1991), Assn. Advancement Health Edn. (dir. 1975-78, Profl. Svc. award 1990, presdl. citation 1996), N.J. Health Edn. Coun. (founder 1967, honor award 1975), N.J. Assn. Health, Phys. Edn. and Recreation (v.p. health edn. 1967-68, Honor fellow award 1972, Disting. Leadership award 1975), Alpha Phi Alpha. Home: 1519 Silo Hill Ln Breinigsville PA 18031

DARDEN, LAURETTA, elementary school educator; b. Kinston, NC, Dec. 1, 1956; d. Robert Lee and Sallie Lorraine Brown; m. Gregory Maurice Darden, July 2, 1988; 1 child, Loreal Sallie Lorraine. BA, Fayetteville State U., NC, 1978. Elementary Education NJ., 1979, Nursery NJ. Elem. tchr. Paterson Bd. of Edn., Paterson, NJ, 1979—. Recipient Governor's Tchr. Recognition, Paterson Bd. of Edn., 2001, Mayor's Award (outstanding civic contbn.), Mayor Barnes Paterson, N.J., 2001, Golden Apple Award, The NJ. Herald News, 2002. Mem.: NJ. Edn. Assn. (assoc.), Paterson Edn. Assn. (assoc.), Alpha Kappa Alpha Sorority Inc. (life). Avocations: reading, sewing, drawing, travel. Home Phone: 973-942-0870. Personal E-mail: hunnybrown2@yahoo.com.

DARDEN, WILLIAM HOWARD, JR., biology professor; b. Tuscaloosa, Ala., Apr. 25, 1937; s. William Howard and Jannie Belle (Herring) D.; m. Caroline Jackson, July 15, 1959; children: Leanne Carol, Michael Howard. BS, U. Ala., Tuscaloosa, 1959, MS, 1961; PhD, Ind. U., 1965. Asst. prof. biology U. Ala., Tuscaloosa, 1965-68, assoc. prof., 1969-73, prof., assoc. chmn. dept. biology, 1973-74, prof., chmn. dept. biology, 1974-96; prof. emeritus, 1996—. Contbr. articles to sci. jours. Bd. dirs. Springhill Lake Assn., 1980-85, So. Grass Tennis Club, 1979-81, Ala. Credit Union, 1987—. Predoctoral fellow NIH, 1963-65; grantee NSF, 1972, U. Ala., Tuscaloosa, 1965-71 Mem. Sigma Xi, Beta Beta Beta, Omicron Delta Kappa, Phi Kappa Phi. Am. Baptist. Home: 3628 Rainbow Dr Tuscaloosa AL 35405-5331 Office: U Ala PO Box 870344 Tuscaloosa AL 35487-0001 E-mail: dardoc@aol.com.

DARDENNE, JAY (JOHN LEIGH DARDENNE JR.), state official, former state legislator, lawyer; b. Baton Rouge, Feb. 6, 1954; s. John Leigh Sr. and Janet Lucille (Abramson) Dardenne; m. Catherine Eloise McDonald, Aug. 20, 1983; children: John Leigh III, Matthew Michael. BA in Journalism, La. State U., 1976; JD, La. State U. Law Ctr., 1979. Bar: La. 1979. Law clk. to Hon. Frank J. Polozala US Dist. Ct. La., Baton Rouge, 1979-81; ptnr. Kennon, Odom & Dardenne, L.L.C., Baton Rouge, 1981—; mem. Baton Rouge Met. Coun., 1989—91, La. State Senate from 16th dist., Baton Rouge, 1992—2006, mem. edn. com., mem. joint legis. com. on budget, mem. judiciary B com., mem. retirement com., mem. senate and govtl. affairs com.; sec. state State of La., Baton Rouge, 2006—. Author: (book) Milk and Donuts Forever, 1977. Chmn. Leadership Greater Baton Rouge Alumni, Inc., 1986-87, Baton Rouge Sports Commn., 1989-92; pres. River City Festivals Assn., Baton Rouge, 1986-87, Muscular Dystrophy Assn., Baton Rouge, 1981-84, mem. nat. bd., 1993—; pres. Cerebral Palsy Assn., Baton Rouge, 1985-86, La. State U. Alumni Fedn., 1984-85. Recipient Disting. Leader award Nat. Assn. Cmty. Leadership Orgns., 1986; named Outstanding Young Person in La., La. Jaycees, 1987, Outstanding Young Person in Baton Rouge, Baton Rouge Jaycees, 1977, 86. Fellow Brit.-Am. Project; mem. ABA, La. State Bar Assn. (Outstanding Young Lawyer in La. 1986), Baton Rouge Bar Assn., Sigma Chi. Clubs: Baton Rouge Touchdown (bd. dirs. 1984—), Sigmachi (Baton Rouge) (pres. 1979-81). Lodges: Rotary. Republican. Jewish. Office: Office Sec State PO Box 94125 Baton Rouge LA 70804*

DARDIK, HERBERT, vascular surgeon, general surgeon; b. Long Branch, NJ, May 17, 1935; s. Morris and Sarah D.; m. Janet E. Goldstein, June 23, 1958; children: Alan, Michael, Sharon. BA magna cum laude, NYU, 1956, MD, 1960. Diplomate Am. Bd. Med. Examiners, Am. Bd. Surgery, cert. spl. competency in vascular surgery; lic. physician NJ, NY. Intern Montefiore Hosp. and Med. Ctr., NYC, 1960-61, asst. surg. resident to chief surg. resident, 1961-65; instr. surgery Albert Einstein Coll. Medicine, NYC, 1964-65, asst. prof. surgery, 1967-77; clin. assoc. prof. surgery N.J. Coll. Medicine, Newark, 1981-91; clin. prof. in surgery Sch. Medicine U. Pa., Phila., 1991—2002, clin. prof. surgery Sch. Medicine, 2003—; clin. prof. surgery Mt. Sinai Sch. Medicine, NYC, 1991—; staff surgeon USAF Hosp. Andrews AFB, Washington, 1965-67; assoc. dir. surgery to dir. surgery Montefiore-Morrisania Affiliate, NYC, 1967-71, cons. in surgery, 1971-76; assoc. attending surgeon Montefiore Hosp. and Med. Ctr., NYC, 1970-77; cons. surgery North Ctrl. Bronx Hosp., NY, 1976; assoc. attending surgeon Englewood (NJ) Hosp., 1973-79, active attending surgeon and chief vascular surg. svc., 1979—, chief dept. surgery, 1984, 1995, 2000—. Sr. rsch. scientist Lab. for Exptl. Medicine and Surgery in Primates, NYU Med. Ctr., 1973-78; numerous visiting professorships, 1976-95, at Good Samaritan Hosp., Cin., U. Munich, U. Laval, Que., Can., Rigshospitalet, Copenhagen, Karolinska Inst., Stockholm, Semmelweis Med. U., Budapest, First Internat. Course on Vascular Traumatology, Mexico City, Inst. of Vascular Surgery of U. Milan, Groote Schuur Hosp., Cape Town, South Africa, U. Orange Free State, Bloemfontein, South Africa, Johannesburg Hosp. of U. of Witwatersrand, South Africa, Allegheny Gen. Hosp., Pitts., Wilmington (Del.) Med. Ctr., Mercy Hosp., Pitts., U. Cologne, Germany, Jewish Gen. Hosp., Montreal (Harry C. Vallon Vis. Prof.), U. Md., Balt., Maritime Vascular Soc., North Sydney Hosp., N.S., Can., Pa. Hosp., Phila., U. Colo. Health Sci. Ctr. and Affiliated Hosps., Denver, Mary Imogene Basset Hosp., Cooperstown, N.Y., Cooper Hosp./Univ. Med. Ctr., Camden, N.J., Gulf Coast Vascular Soc., Tulane U., La. State U. Ochsner Med. Clinic, New Orleans, St. Vincent's Med. Ctr., N.Y.C., U. Trondheim, Norway, Broadgreen Hosp., Liverpool, Eng., U. Colo. Rose Med. Ctr. (guest lectr.), Queen Elizabeth Hosp., Montreal, Wright State U., Dayton, Ohio, Cleve. Vascular Soc., N.Y. Meth. Hosp., Bklyn.; surgeon by invitation Mass. Gen. Hosp., Bosotn, 1979, Milan, 1981, Sydney, N.S., 1985, Colo. Health Sci. Ctr., 1985, U. Trondheim, 1992, Paul Brousse Hosp., Paris, 1995, Utrecht, The Netherlands, 1997; internat. adv. com. Internat. Vascular Symposium, London, 1981, Internat. Coll. Angiology, Athens, 1985, 14th World Congress Internat. Union Angiology, Munich, 1986. Contbr. over 300 articles and abstracts to profl. jours., chpts. to books; presenter in field; creator exhibits in field; dir. numerous symposia in field; patentee in field; editor SCVS Newsletter, 1987—; editl. bd. Jour. Englewood Hosp., 1989—, Fitness Swimmer, 1992-95, Vascular Forum, 1993-95, guest editor 1994, Vascular Surgery, 1995—; Creativity editor Jour. Am. Coll. Physician Inventors, 1992-95; invited reviewer Jour. Vascular Surgery, European Jour. Vascular Surgery, Am. Jour. Surgery. Capt. USAF Med. Corps, 1965-67. Recipient George Schwartz prize in biology, 1954, Wortis Biol. prize, 1956, Herbert Dardik awards, Ann. Vascular Fellows Abstract Presentation, Humanitarian award, Retired Sr. Vol. Program, 2001. Mem. ACS (bd. govs. 1991-94, adv. coun. vascular surg. 1995—), ACP, AMA (Hektoen Gold medal 1976), Assn. Acad. Surgery, Soc. Vascular Surgery, Internat. Soc. Cardiovasc. Surgery, Soc. Internat. de Chirurgia, Soc. Clin. Vascular Surgery (hon., various offices and coms., pres. 1984-85, exec. com. 1982—, Lifetime Achievement award 2001), Soc. Surgery of the Alimentary Tract, Am. Coll. Gastroenterology, Collegium Internat. Chirurgia Digestive, Am. Coll. Physician Inventors (founding mem., sec. 1992—), Eastern Vascular Soc. (adv. coun. 1991—, exec. com. 1996-95, pres. 1990-91), NJ Vascular Soc. (pres.-elect 1983-84, pres. 1984-85, dir. exec. com. 1982-83, postgrad. surg. edn. award 1983), NY Soc. Cardiovasc. Surgery, NY Surg. Soc., Bergen County Med. Soc., Maine Vascular Soc. (hon.), Mex. Soc. Angiology (hon.), Israel Soc. Vascular Surgery (hon.), Rocky Mountain Vascular Soc. (hon.), Cleve. Vascular Soc. (hon.), Phi Beta Kappa. Office: Englewood Hosp & Med Ctr Dept Surgery 350 Engle St Englewood NJ 07631-1823 E-mail: hdardik@ehmc.com.

DAREHSHORI, NADER FARHANG, publishing sales executive; b. Shiraz, Iran, Dec. 15, 1936; came to U.S., 1961, naturalized, 1972; s. Zaki F. and Rokhsar (Farsimadan) D.; m. Anne C. Wagnild, Dec. 14, 1969 (dec.); m. Cynthia McGuffey, Aug. 3, 1991. BA in Econs., U. Wis., 1966, postgrad., 1966. Supt. village schs., Shiraz, 1959-61; from salesman to midwest sales mgr. Houghton Mifflin Co., Geneva, Ill., 1966-84, from v.p., gen. mgr. coll. divsn. midwest to chmn., CEO, 1984-91; chmn., pres., CEO Houghton Mifflin Co. (sold to Vivendi), Boston, 1991—2002; now co-founder, CEO, chmn. Cambium Learning, Natick, Mass. Named to Assn. Ednl. Pub. Hall of Fame, 2002; recipient Charles E. Rogerson award for cmty. svc., Rogerson Communities, 2003, Medal of Hope, Orgn. for a New Equality (O-N-E), 2004. Democrat. Office: Cambium Learning 313 Speen St Natick MA 01760 Office Phone: 508-647-1340. Office Fax: 508-647-1346.

DAREN, SYLVIA, poet; b. NYC, Apr. 2, 1920; d. Louis Millman and Rose Beresnoger; m. Joseph Daren, Dec. 24, 1939; children: Edythe Hepner, Marsha. Student, grad. H.S., 1937. Lectr. Singles Group, NYC; poet laureat Temple Emeth; bd. mem. & by-law co-chair Temple Emeth Sisterhood; Instalation Chmn. Gold Coast Cancer Rsch. of Palm Greens, Women's Club of Palm Green; fund raising chair Delray B'nai B'rith; Poet and Mistress of Ceremonies Palm Greens Entertainers; actor, poet, story teller Yiddish Club of Palm Greens. Author (childrens poetry): Moses, The Hebrew Giant; author: (poetry book) How I Earned My Bachelor of Life Degree --You Can COunt Your Credits Too !!!; author: (plays and poetry) various including Temple Emeth of Delray Beach (Poet Laureat); co-dir.: Oakland Sr. Citizens -Oakland Jewish Ctr., 1962—80; editor (newspaper): Palms West O.R.T.; actor(co-author): (plays) My Unfair Lady. Leader Girl Scouts of Am., Queens, NY, 1953—54; vol. Creedmore Hosp., Queens; v.p. and trustee, adv. girls, fund raising, cmty. svc., jewish edn., Aid to Israel for Queens, vol. B'nai B'rith, Bayside, NY, 1953—2003, various Fla., 1953—2003; founder Marsha Daren Fund Long Island Jewish Med. Ctr., Long Island, 1975—89. Recipient Honorary Mem. of Am. Legion, Am. Legion, 1933, Honoree- This is Your Life, Oakland B'nai B'rith, 1959, Honoree, Org. of people Undaunted by Stroke, 1976, United Jewish Appeal & Federation of Jewish Philanthropies, 1976, Jewish Nat. Fund Temple Emeth, 0955—2003, Mem. award, B'nai B'rith Dist. 5, Woman of Achievement award, Women's League of Conservative Judaism, 2005. Mem.: Bowling League, B'nai B'rith. Jewish. Avocations: poetry, acting, bowling, golf, volunteering.

DARGAN, PAMELA ANN, systems engineer, consultant; b. Norfolk, Va. d. Thomas J. and Stana E. (Verich) Piazza; m. W. Scott Dargan, Dec., 1990. BS in Math., Va. Poly. and State U., 1979; MS in Computer Sci., George Mason U., 1993. Programmer Control Data Corp., Rockville, Md., 1979—80; tech. staff BDM Corp., McLean, Va., 1980—81, TRW Fed. Sys. Group, McLean, 1981—87; dep. program mgr. Mystech, Inc., Alexandria, Va., 1987—89; lead engr. MITRE Corp., McLean, 1989—98, prin., 2001—02, Litton Tasc, Inc., Chantilly, Va., 1998—2001; sr. cons. Scitor Corp., Chantilly, 2002—03; prin. sys. engr. SAIC, Reston, Va., 2003—. Program chair East Coast Artificial Intelligence Work Sta. Users Group, 1984-85; author on open sys. for internat. confs. and publs. Author: Open Systems and Standards for Software Product Development, 2005; contbr. chpts. to books, articles to profl. jours. Mem. IEEE, Assn. Computing Machinery, Internat. Coun. on Sys. Engring. Home Phone: 703-591-4070. Personal E-mail: pdargan@erols.com. Business E-Mail: pamela.a.dargan@saic.com.

DARGEL, COREY, composer, singer; b. McAllen, Tex., Oct. 19, 1977; s. Russell Vernon Dargel, Jr. and Connie Lynne Dargel; life ptnr. Yvan Greenberg. MusB in Composition, Oberlin Coll., Ohio, 2001. Composer: (albums) Less Famous Than You, 2006, Other People's Love Songs, 2007, (songs) All the Notes and Rhythms I've Ever Loved, 2006, (plays) Removable Parts, 2006—07, (songs) Gay Cowboys, 2006; contbr. articles to mags. Named one of Composers on the Edge, New Yorker Mag., 2006. E-mail: corey@automaticheartbreak.com.

DARGEL, JAN KAY, college administrator, institute president, lawyer; b. Peoria, Ill., Oct. 11, 1953; d. Merle William and Adeline Marie Dargel; m. Ivor G. Hughes, Mar. 17, 1984. BA, Am. Coll. Switzerland, 1973; MA, U. Chgo., 1974; postgrad., Oxford U., 1980; JD, Ill. Inst. Tech., Chgo., 1982. Project liaison officer NACRO, London, 1974-77; ct. liaison Cts. Alternative Project, San Francisco, 1978; asst. pub. defender Office of Pub. Defender, Tampa, Chgo., 1983-85, 85-86; prof. polit. sci. U. Tampa, 1986-95, dean arts and scis., 1995-98; pres. The Eiger Inst., San Francisco, 1998—; dean arts and scis. Coll. of Marin, Kentfield, Calif., 1998—2002, v.p. acad. affairs, 2002—. Mem. Tampa Bay com. on fgn. rels. Contbg. editor Encyclopedia of Human Rights, 2d edit., 1997; author: (with others) Censorship. Grad. Leadership Tampa, 1997; bd. dirs., chair Inst. for Cmty. Rsch., Tampa, 1995-98. Mem. Am. Polit. Sci. Assn. Office: Coll of Marin 835 College Ave Kentfield CA 94904-2529

DARGIS, MANOHLA, film critic; b. NYC; M in Cinema Studies, NYU. With Village Voice, NYC, 1987—94; film editor LA Weekly, Calif., 1994—2002; film critic LA Times, Calif., 2002—04; co-chief film critic NY Times, NY, 2004—. Adj. prof., critical studies dept. Univ. So. Calif., 2001. Contbr. Harper's Bazaar, Sight and Sound, Film Comment; author: LA Confidential, 2003. Mem. selection com. NY Film Festival; mem. nominating com. Someone to Watch Award. Mem.: Nat. Soc. Film Critics, LA Film Critics Assn. (former pres.), Slate's Annual Movie Club. Office: NY Times 229 W 43rd St New York NY 10036 Office Phone: 212-556-7411. Office Fax: 212-556-1516. Business E-Mail: dargis@nytimes.com.

DARIEN, STEVEN MARTIN, management consulting company executive; b. NYC, Oct. 29, 1942; s. Leo and Laura Darien; m. Susan Ruth Kinsley, Nov. 29, 1942; children: Jodi Ellen, Andrew Todd. AB, Rutgers U., 1963; MBA, Columbia U., 1966. Claims settler Equitable Life, NYC, 1963-64; mgmt. trainee Merck & Co., Inc., Rahway, N.J., 1966-69, mgr. coll. rels., 1969-74, exec. dir. pers. resources, 1974-79, exec. dir. U.S. Pers., 1979-85, v.p. employee rels., 1985-89, v.p. worldwide pres., 1989-90, v.p. human resources, 1990-96; pres. Darien Assocs., 1996-98; chmn., CEO The Cabot Adv. Group, Washington, 1998—. Bd. dirs. Somerset Hosp. Chmn. Olin Inst. for Employment Practice and Policy; chmn. Olin Found. for Employment Policy and Practice. Mem. Columbia U. Bus. Sch. Alumni Assn. (v.p.). Office Phone: 908-704-1888. E-mail: steve@sdarien.com.

DARIOTIS, TERRENCE THEODORE, lawyer; b. Chgo., Feb. 28, 1946; s. Theodore S. and Dorothy Mizzen D.; m. Jeanne Elizabeth Gibbons, Oct. 24, 1970; children: Sara, Kristin, Jennifer. BA in Philosophy, St. Joseph's Coll., Rensselaer, Ind., 1969; JD, Loyola U., Chgo., 1973; LL M. in Taxation, U. Fla., 2003. Bar: Ill. 1973, Fla. 1975, US Tax Ct. 1993, US Supreme Ct., 1978; bd. cert. in wills, trust and estates law Fla. Bar, 2001. Law clk. to presiding justice Appellate Ct. of Ill. (2d dist.), Waukegan, 1973-74; assoc. Keith Kinderman, Tallahassee, 1975-76; sole practitioner Tallahassee, 1976—82, 2000—; ptnr. Kahn and Dariotis, P.A., Tallahassee, 1982-96, Warfel, Goldberg, Dariotis, Waldoch & Olive, P.A., Tallahassee, 1996-00. Adj. prof. Fla. State U. Coll. Bus., 1987-93. Office: 1695 Metropolitan Cir Ste 6 Tallahassee FL 32308-3731 Office Phone: 850-523-9300. E-mail: tdariotis@nettally.com.

DARKO, DENIS F., research scientist, educator, physician; b. Indpls., July 13, 1947; s. Charles O. and Agnes Mary (Lauck) Darko; m. Ann Marie Barker, Oct. 15, 1983; children: Emily Marie, Roseann Michelle. BS in Physics, U. Notre Dame, 1969; MD, Ind. U., 1975. Diplomate Am. Bd. Psychiatry and Neurology. Staff rsch. assoc. biols. divsn. Eli Lilly Co., Indpls., 1970, U. Co. Sch. Medicine, 1971; resident physician family practice Maricopa County Hosp., 1975, Scottsdale (Ariz.) Meml. Hosp., 1975—76; resident physician psychiatry Good Samaritan Med. Ctr., Phoenix, 1977—80, chief resident in psychiatry, 1979—80; pvt. practice psychiatry Scottsdale, 1980—83; cons. psychiatrist Phoenix Indian Med. Ctr., 1980—81; supr. psychiatry residency program Maricopa County Med. Ctr., 1980—83; instr. family practice residency program Scottsdale Meml. Hosp., 1980—83; fellow in consultation/liaison psychiatry U. Calif.-San Diego Med. Ctr., 1983—84, fellow in psychopharmacology and psychobiology Clin. Rsch. Ctr., 1984—85; asst. prof. psychiatry U. Calif., San

Diego Sch. Medicine, 1985—92, assoc. adj. prof., 1992—2004, assoc. clin. prof., 2004—07, chmn. diagnostic com. NIMH mental health clin. rsch. ctr., 1984—89, rsch. fellow in immunology and allergy divsn. immunology and allergy Dept. Pediats., 1985—87, chmn. resident rsch. com. dept. psychiatry, 1989—92; attending physician Univ. Hosp., 1985—94; ward chief San Diego VA Med. Ctr., 1985—87, staff psychiatrist, 1985—93, med. dir. mental health clinic, 1987—92, chief psychiat. emergency svc., 1988—92; dir. Mood Disorders Rsch. Clinic U. Calif. San Diego Sch. Medicine and San Diego VA Med. Ctr., 1987—90; med. dir. NIMH Mental Health Clin. Rsch. Ctr., 1987—88; vis. scientist Scripps Clinic and Rsch. Found. Dept. Neuropharmacology, 1990; assoc. adj. prof. Scripps Rsch. Inst. Dept. Neuropharmacology, 1991—92, assoc. prof., 1993—2002; attending physician Scripps Clin. Dept. Medicine, Divsn. Psychiatry, 1991—2002, head divsn. psychiatry and behavioral medicine, 1997—2002; head neuroimmunology lab., dept. neuropharmacology Scripps Rsch. Inst., 1993—2002; med. dir., v.p. Calif. Clin. Trials, LLC, 2002—03; dir. clin. rsch., neurosci. AstraZeneca PLC, Wilmington, 2003—06, exec. dir. global neurosci. licensing, 2006—. Chmn. grant application rev. com., dept. acad. affairs Scripps Clinic Found., 1995—2002; cons. Hybritech, 1991—94. Recipient review article award, Am. Coll. Allergists, 1986; fellow, USPHS, 1972. Fellow: ACP, Am. Psychiat. Assn. Office: AstraZeneca PO Box 15437 Wilmington DE 19850-5437 Home Phone: 610-558-2111.

DARLING, ALBERTA HELEN, state legislator, art gallery director, marketing professional; b. Hammond, Ind., Apr. 28, 1944; d. Albert William and Helen Anne (Vaicunas) Statkus; m. William Anthony Darling, Aug. 12, 1967; children— Elizabeth Suzanne, William Anthony. BS, U. Wis., 1967. English tchr. Nathan Hale High Sch., West Allis, Wis., 1967—69, Castle Rock High Sch., Castle Rock, Colo., 1969—71; mem. Wis. State Assembly, 0990—1992, Wis. Senate from 8th dist., Madison, 1992—. Cons. orgn. devel., Milw., 1982—; dir. mktg. and communications Milw. Art Mus., 1981-88; exec. dir. mktg. architectural firm, 1988-90; State Rep. Wis., 1990—, mem. urban edn. com., children and human svcs. com., tourism com., homelessness com., teeenage pregnancy com., vice chmn. gov.'s housing policy commn., assembly coms. Pres. Community Action Seminar for Women, 1979-80; a founder Goals for Greater Milw. 2000, 1980-84; co-chair Action 2000, 1984-86; co-chmn. Icebreaker Am. Winterfestival; chmn. Community Action Seminar for Women, 1988; bd. dirs., exec. com. United Way, Milw., 1982-1992, chair project 1985, 1984-85, chmn. policy com. 1988; founder Today's Girls/Tomorrow's Women, Milw., pres. Jr. League Milw., 1980-82, Planned Parenthood Milw., 1982-84, Future Milw., 1983-85; vice chmn. State of Wis. Strategic Planning Council, 1988—, chmn. small bus./entrpreneur com.; mem. Greater Milw. Com.'s Mktg. Task Force, 1987-88; chmn. United Way Policy Com., 1987-88; participant Bus. Ptnrs. White House Conf., 1987; mem. summerfest adv. com. on Winter Festivals, 1989; founder Women's Fund of Milw. Found; actuve Juvenile Justice Leadership Com. Recipient Vol. Action award Milw. Civic Alliance, 1984, Community Service award United Way, 1984, Leader of Future award Milw. Mag., 1988, Nat. Assn. Community Leadership Orgn. award, 1986, Today's Girls/Tomorrow's Women Leadership award, 1987, Future Milw. Community Leadership award, 1988, Friend of Edn. Leadership award Head Start, 1994, William Steiger Humanitarian award, 1994. Mem. Greater Milw. Com., TEMPO Profl. Women, Am. Mktg. Assn. (Marketer of Yr. 1984), Pub. Relations Soc. Am., Ctr. for Pub. Representation (state bd. 1988), ARC (bd. dirs., exec. fin. coms. 1987—), Women's Fund (steering com. 1988), Internat. Assn. Bus. Communicators, Greater Milw. Com. Republican. Avocations: travel, art history, contemporary american literature, golf, tennis. Home: 1325 W Dean Rd Milwaukee WI 53217-2537 Office: State Capitol PO Box 7882 Madison WI 53707-7882 Office Phone: 608-266-5830. Business E-Mail: sen.darling@legis.wisconsin.gov.

DARLING, GEORGE CURTIS, minister, administrator; b. Xenia, Ohio, Nov. 23, 1928; s. Russell M. and Mary Elizabeth (Young) D.; m. Edna Pearlen Phillips, May 1, 1960; (div. Apr. 1973) 1 child, Curtis; m. Mary Elizabeth Miller, Oct. 24, 1952 (div. Aug. 1956), 1 child, Kirk; m. Evelyn Cornelia Woodfork, Apr. 10, 1976 (dec. Nov. 1998; m. Anna Jean Parks, Aug. 30, 2002. Adrloma in Theology, Am. Bapt. Theol. Sem., Dayton, Ohio, 1970. Ordained to ministry Bapt. Ch., 1963. Pastor 2nd Bapt. Ch., Del., Ohio, 1966-71; supply pastor Tabernacle Bapt. Ch., Columbus, Ohio, 1974; pastor Flintridge Bapt. Ch., Columbus, 1980-91; asst. pastor Peace Bapt. Ch., Columbus, 1993—. V.p. Springfield (Ohio) Dist. Sunday Sch. and Bapt. Tng. Union. Author: How to Find God, 1969. Bd. dirs., pres. Liberty Ctr., Delaware, Ohio, 1968-70; mem. Delaware County Community Action Orgn., 1967; vol. motivational spkr. to stroke patients, 1996—. With U.S. Army, 1950-52, Korea.; ret. USAF, 1988. Recipient Hon. Sci. award, Bausch & Lomb, 1946. Mem. Eastern Union Missionary Bapt. Assn. (statis. clk. Ohio 1981-85, 3d vice moderator 1985-87, 2d vice moderator, 1987-91), Columbus Bapt. Ministers and Laity Bible League (instr. 1987-96, parliamentarian 1999—). Home: 884 E Weber Rd Columbus OH 43211-1174 *On cloudy days when the sun is hidden from view, flying above the clouds enables one to see the brightness of the sun. When things go wrong in my life, I take a spiritual trip beyond the darkness of the moment into the sunlight of hope.*

DARLING, JOHN ROTHBURN, business educator; b. Holton, Kans., Mar. 30, 1937; s. John Rothburn and Beatrice Noel (Deaver) D.; m. Melva Jean Fears, Aug. 20, 1958; children: Stephen, Cynthia, Gregory. BS, U. Ala., 1959, MS, 1960; PhD, U. Ill., 1967; PhD (hon.), Chung Yuan Christian U., Taiwan, 1998; D in Econs. (hon.), Helsinki Sch. Econs., 2001. Divisional mgr. J.C. Penney Co., 1960-63; grad. teaching asst. U. Ill., Urbana, 1965-66; asst. prof. mktg. U. Ala., Tuscaloosa, 1966-68; assoc. prof. mktg. U. Mo., Columbia, 1968-71; prof. adminstrn., coord. mktg. Wichita State U., 1971-76; dean, prof. mktg. Coll. Bus. Adminstrn. So. Ill. U., Carbondale, 1976-81; v.p. acad. affairs and rsch., prof. internat. bus. Tex. Tech U., Lubbock, 1981-86; provost, v.p. acad. affairs, prof. mktg. and internat. bus. Miss. State U., Mississippi State, 1986-90; chancellor, disting. prof. internat. bus. La. State U., Shreveport, 1990-95; pres. Pittsburg State U., Kans., 1995-99, prof. mktg. and internat. bus., 1995-2000; vis. disting. prof. mktg. Rockhurst U., 2000—03; disting. prof. mgmt. Tex. State U., San Marcos, 2003—07; disting. sr. lectr. U. Tex., San Antonio, 2007—. Mktg. rsch. cons. Southwestern Bell, 1970; sr. v.p. Boothe Advt. Wichita, 1972; pres. Bus. Rsch. Assocs., 1972-76; cons. Bus. Rsch. Assocs., 1976-82; spl. cons. FTC, Washington, 1972-75, U.S. Dept. Justice, 1973-74, Atty. Gen., State of Kans., 1972-76, Dist. Atty. 18th Jud. Dist., Wichita, 1972-76, Maya Internat. Inc., Houston, 1995—2000, Morrison and Assocs., Inc., Shreveport, 1995-97; vis. disting. prof. internat. mktg. Helsinki Sch. Econs. and Bus. Adminstrn., 1993—. Author: (with Harry A. Lipson) Marketing Fundamentals, Text and Cases, 1980, (with Raimo Nurmi) International Management Leadership: The Primary Competitive Advantage, 1997; mem. bd. cons. editors Jour. Advt., 1984—97; mem. editl. rev. bd. Jour. Internat. Bus. Studies, 1991—96, Jour. Entrepreneurship, 1997—; contbr. articles to profl. jours. Bd. dirs. Outreach Found., 1973-79, v.p., 1975-77; trustee Graceland Coll., Lamoni, Iowa, 1976-82; mem. mgmt. com. Park Coll., Kansas City, 1976-79. With USAR, 1954—62. Decorated Comdr. Order of the Lion of Finland Republic of Finland; recipient Disting. Eagle Scout award, Boy Scouts Am., 1997. Mem. Internat. Coun. Small Bus., Am. Mktg. Assn., Am. Mgmt. Assn., Acad. Internat. Bus., Am. Econs. Assn., Am. Arbitration Assn., (mem. nat. panel arbitrators and mediators 1993-99), Nat. Assn. Intercollegiate Athletics (mem. governing bd. 1994-95), So. Bus. Adminstrn. Assn., So. Mktg. Assn., So. Econs. Assn., So. Assn. Colls. and Schs. (chair reaccreditation com. 1982-95, chair faculty qualifications criteria com. 1989-90, com. to rev. criteria for accreditation 1990-92, commr. 1992-95), Nat. Assn. State Univs. and Land-Grant Colls. (chair regional accreditation rev. com. 1989-90), Sales and Mktg. Execs. Internat., Beta Gamma Sigma, Phi Kappa Phi, Omicorn Delta Kappa, Phi Delta Kappa, Kappa Delta Phi, Mu Kappa Tau, Pi Sigma Epsilon, Alpha Kappa Psi, Chi Alpha Phi, Alpha Phi Omega, Phi Eta Sigma, Delta Mu Delta, Alpha Mu Gamma. Avocations: golf, tennis. Home: 29622 Terra Bella Fair Oaks Ranch TX 78015 Office: U Tex Ctr Profl Excellence One UTSA Cir San Antonio TX 78249 Office Phone: 210-458-4778. Personal E-mail: jrd@gvtc.com.

DARLING, ROBERT EDWARD, theater director, designer; b. Oakland, Calif., Oct. 1, 1937; s. Irving Jackson and Helen Ellen (Hebel) D.; m. Ann Farris, Aug. 22, 1970. BA, San Francisco State U., 1959; M.F.A., Yale U. Sch. Drama, 1963; student, Bayreuth Festspiel Meisterclasse, 1965, Columbia U., NYC, 1978. Creative problem solving, idea design/graphic facilatation and transition mgr. MG Taylor Corp., 1984—; with Robert Darling & Assoc., Darling Assoc. Garden Design, 1991—. Former mem. opera-musical theatre policy panel Nat. Endowment for Arts; panelist Nat. Opera Inst., Nat. Inst. for Music Theater, OPERA Am., 1977-97. Designer, dir. numerous opera, theatre and ballet prodns. throughout U.S. and Can., 1960—; N.Y.C. debut with Another Evening with Harry Stoones, 1962; San Francisco Opera debut with L'Elisir d'Amore, 1967; Santa Fe Opera debut with Anna Bolena, 1970, Chgo. Lyric Opera debut with Don Carlo, 1972; N.Y.C. Opera debut with Der Fliegende Hollander, 1976, Hidden Valley Opera Don Giovanni, 1975, Seattle Opera Tannhaüser, 1984; dir. and designer world premiers of Medea, 1972, Colonel Johnathan the Saint, 1972, The Infanta, 1975, The Last of the Mohicans, 1976, The Face on the Barroom Floor, 1978, Soyazhe, 1979, Freddy the Leaf, 1987, 90-91, Recollections RLS, 1993, Williamstown Theatre Festival debut season J.B., 1963, Williamstown Theatre Festival: Marat/Sade, 1990, Speed The Plow, 1991, Miami City Ballet, Pan Nuit Suite, Jewels, 1993, debut Utah Festival Opera (Pagliacci, Gianni Schicchi), 1998; dramaturg-Coyote Tales Score, Kansas City Lyric Opera, 1998, Hidden Valley Opera La Boheme, 2002; artistic coord. Spring Opera Theatre, San Francisco, 1972, artistic adv. Kans. City (Mo.) Lyric Theatre, 1973; co-founder, prin. dir. Hidden Valley Opera Ensemble, Carmel, Calif., 1974-77; artistic dir. Central City Opera House Assn., Denver, 1977-82, Hidden Valley Opera, 1985-89, 2002—; illustrations, E.C. Schirmer, 2000; artistic prodr. Acorn Theatre, Washington, 1988-98; site coord., founding mem. Alliance for New Music-Theater, 1994-2007, v.p. 2005-07; founding mem. Internat. Forum and Visual Practioneers, 2003—; designs represented in collection Am. design Smithsomian Mus., Mus. of the City of N.Y., Prague Quadrennial Scenographic Design, 1987; contbr. articles to profl. jours. Mem. United Scenic Artists, Am. Guild Mus. Artists, Actors Equity-Can., OPERA Am., Logan Circle Assn., Washington Daffodil Soc. (past pres.). Democrat. Lutheran. Office Phone: 202-483-2126. Personal E-mail: darlingr@aol.com.

DARLING, ROBERT HOWARD, lawyer; b. Detroit, Oct. 29, 1947; s. George Beatson and Jeanne May (Mainville) D.; m. Cathy Lee Trygstad, Apr. 30, 1970; children: Bradley Howard, Brian Lee, Kara Kristine, Blake Robert. BS in Mech. Engring., U. Mich., 1969, MS in Mech. Engring., 1971; JD, Wayne State U., 1975. Bar: Mich. 1975, U.S. Dist. Ct. (ea. dist.) Mich. 1975, U.S. Ct. Appeals (6th cir.) 1975. Engr. Bendix Corp., Ann Arbor, Mich., 1970, Ford Motor Co., Dearborn, Mich., 1972-73; ptnr. Philo, Atkinson, Darling, Steinberg, Harper & Edwards, Detroit, 1975-81; sr. ptnr. Sommers, Schwartz, Silver & Schwartz, Southfield, Mich., 1981—. Assoc. editor Wayne State U. Law Review. Mem. ABA, Assn. Trial Lawyers Am., Mich. Trial Lawyers Assn. (exec. bd. 1981—, publs. chmn. 1981-85, products liability chmn. 1986—), Met. Detroit Trial Lawyers Assn., Oakland County Trial Lawyers Assn., State Bar Mich., Detroit Bar Assn., Plymouth Hist. Soc., Pi Tau Sigma. Avocation: golf. Office: Sommers Schwartz Silver Schwartz 2000 Town Ctr Ste 900 Southfield MI 48075-1100 Address: 8785 Warren Rd Plymouth MI 48170-5119 E-mail: rdarling@s4online.com.

DARLING, SCOTT EDWARD, lawyer; b. LA, Dec. 31, 1949; s. Dick R. and Marjorie Helen (Otto) D.; m. Cynthia Diane Harrah, June 1970 (div.); 1 child, Smokie; m. Deborah Lee Cochran, Aug. 22, 1981; children: Ryan, Jacob, Guinevere. BA, U. Redlands, 1972; JD, U.S.C., 1975. Bar: Calif. 1976, U.S. Dist. Ct. (cen. dist.) Calif. 1976. Assoc. atty. Elver, Falsetti, Boone & Crafts, Riverside, 1976-78; ptnr. Falsetti, Crafts, Pritchard & Darling, Riverside, 1978-84; pres. Scott Edward Darling, A Profl. Corp., Riverside, 1984—. Grant reviewer HHS, Washington, 1982-88; judge pro tem Riverside County Mcpl. Ct., 1980, Riverside County Superior Ct., 1987-88; bd. dirs. Tel Law Nat. Legal Pub. Info. System, Riverside, 1978-80. Author, editor: Small Law Office Computer Legal System, 1984. Bd. dirs. Youth Adv. Com. to Selective Svc., 1968-70, Am. Heart Assn. Riverside County, 1978-82, Survival Ministries, 1986-89; atty. panel Calif. Assn. Realtors, L.A., 1980—; pres. Calif. Young Reps., 1978-80; mem. GI Forum, Riverside, 1970-88; presdl. del. Nat. Rep. Party, 1980-84; asst. treas. Calif. Rep. Party, 1981-83; Rep. Congl. candidate, Riverside, 1982; treas. Riverside Sickle Cell Found., 1980-82, recipient Eddie D. Smith award; pres. Calif. Rep. Youth Caucus, 1980-82; v.p. Riverside County Red Cross, 1982-84; mem. Citizen's Univ. Com., Riverside, 1978-84, World Affairs Council, 1978-82, Urban League, Riverside, 1980-82. Calif. Scholarship Fedn. (life). Named one of Outstanding Young Men in Am., U.S. Jaycees, 1979-86. Mem. ABA, Riverside County Bar Assn., Speaker's Bur. Riverside County Bar Assn., Riverside Jaycees, Riverside C. of C. Lodges: Native Sons of Golden West. Avocations: skiing, swimming, reading. Office: 3697 Arlington Ave Riverside CA 92506-3938 Office Phone: 951-788-2889. Business E-Mail: info@darlinglawoffices.com.

DARLINGTON, DAVID WILLIAM, management consultant; b. Boston, Oct. 3, 1945; s. Horace and Maude Beatrice (Pfalzgraf) D.; m. Stacey A. Mitchell, May 24, 1986; children: Elizabeth Joy, Christine Rebecca. BS, Babson Coll., 1974; MBA, 1976; postgrad., Northeastern U., 1977-80. Planning engr. Stone & Webster Engring. Corp., Boston, 1974-75; project adminstr. Northrop Corp., Norwood, Mass., 1975-80; mgr. program adminstrn. internat. sys. divsn., bus. mgr. Sanders Assocs., Inc., Nashua, NH, 1980-82; cons., program mgr., contr. Arthur D. Little, Cambridge, Mass., 1982—2002; fin. dir. ICF Cons., Inc., 2002—03; acctg. mgr. M/A-com Tyco Electronics, 2003—05; acctg. mgr. iRobot Corp., 2005—. Cons., program mgr., contr. Arthur D. Little, Cambridge, Mass., 1982-2002; fin. dir. ICF Cons., Inc., 2002-03; acctg. mgr. M/A-com Tyco Electronics, 2003—. With USN, 1964—71. Mem. Am. Prodn. and Inventory Control Soc. (cert.), Nat. Contract Mgmt. Assn. (cert.), Inst. Cost Analysis (cert.), Inst. Mgmt. Accts., Appalachian Mountain Club, Betta Gamma. Home: 378 Charles Bancroft Hwy Litchfield NH 03052-8033

DARLINGTON, HENRY, JR., retired investment broker; b. NYC, Jan. 8, 1925; s. Henry and Dorothy (Stone-Smith) D.; m. Frances Elizabeth Richardson, June 5, 1948 (div. Feb. 1965); children: Henry Darlington III, Elizabeth Aldrich, Victoria Wilde Darlington Yoder; m. Dorothea Fiske Page, July 1965 (div. Dec. 1973); m. Carla P. Barratt-Brown, June 1990. BA, Columbia U., 1949; LHD (hon.), St. Paul's Coll., Lawrenceville, Va., 1987. Salesman IBM, 1949-52; security salesman Cosgrave, Miller & Whitehead, 1952-55; gen. ptnr. Hill, Darlington & Co., 1955-62; v.p. B.J. Van Ingen & Co., Inc., 1956-59; registered rep. Cruttenden, Podesta and Miller, 1962; with syndicate dept. Loeb, Rhoades & Co., 1962-64, br. office adminstr., 1964-67, v.p., 1967-71, registered rep., 1972-79; investment exec. Shearson Loeb Rhoades, Inc. (now Salomon, Smith Barney), 1979-92; ret. Trustee Hoosac Sch., Hoosick, NY, 1968-75, Ch. Heavenly Rest Day Sch., NYC, 1968-74, Search and Care, NYC, 1972-87, vestryman Ch. Heavenly Rest, 1969-75; bd. dirs. Fedn. Protestant Welfare Agys., 1962-89, asst. treas., 1971-79; bd. dirs. Episcopal Mission Soc., 1979-89, St. Paul's Ch., Rome, 1975-99, St. James' Ch., Florence, Italy; trustee Bd. Fgn. Parishes, 1975-97; warden Eglise Francaise du Saint Esprit, 1984-88. With USNR, 1943-46, lt. Res., 1946-65. Named to Order Ky. Cols. Mem. SAR, St. Nicholas Soc. (pres. 1976-78), St. Andrews Soc., St. George's Soc., The Soc. of the Cin., The Huguenot Soc. (pres. 1986-89), Soc. Colonial Wars in the State of NY, Fla. and Vt. (gov. 1991-93), Mil. Order of World Wars (NY chpt.), NY Soc. Mil. and Naval Officers World War, Navy League U.S. (past sec., treas. We. Conn. Coun.), Naval Order, Pilgrim Soc., St. Andrew's Soc., Most Venerable Order of Hosp. of St. John of Jerusalem, Army and Navy Club, Union Club, Univ. Club, Everglades Club, Piping Rock Club, Palm Beach Yacht Club, The Lansdowne Club, Delta Psi (trustee Alpha chpt. 1953-58). Home: 30 E 62d St New York NY 10006

DARLINGTON, RICHARD BENJAMIN, retired psychologist, educator, researcher; b. Woodbury, NJ, Nov. 16, 1937; s. Charles Joseph and Eleanor (Collins) D.; m. Elizabeth Day, June 13, 1959; children: Jean Susan, Lois Heather. BA, Swarthmore Coll., 1959; PhD, U. Minn., 1963. Asst. prof. psychology Cornell U., Ithaca, NY, 1963—68, assoc. prof., 1968—80, prof., 1980—2005; prof. emeritus, 2005—; rschr. neurosci. Cornell U., 2005—. Author: Radicals and Squares, 1975, (with others) Lasting Effects of Early Education, 1982, (with Patricia M. Carlson) Behavioral Statistics: Logic and Methods, 1987, Regression and Linear Models, 1990; contbr. articles to profl. jours.; contbr. chpts. to books. Project dir. Am. Friends Svc. Com., 1960, 61. Fellow NSF, 1959-60, Woodrow Wilson Found., 1959-60; grantee HEW, 1977-81, Office of Edn., 1966-67, 70-71, Dept. of Labor, 1980-81 Fellow AAAS; mem. Phi Beta Kappa Mem. Soc. Of Friends. Avocation: folk dancing. Home: 204 Fairmount Ave Ithaca NY 14850-4804 Business E-Mail: rbd1@cornell.edu.

DARLOW, GEORGE ANTHONY GRATTON, investor; b. Rochester, NY, June 16, 1938; s. Alfred Miltenberger and Lillian (Gratton) D.; m. Helen Julia Donovan, Mar. 2, 1971 (div.); 1 child, Gillian Darlow Jones; m. Christiana Sewall Alden (div.). BA, Yale U., 1961; JD, Columbia U., 1971; LLD, Yale U., 1979, Columbia U., 1979, U. Rochester, 1979, Sweet Briar Coll., 1979. Trustee Am. Indian Archeol. Inst., Washington, Conn., 1973-93; chmn., trustee Inst. Am. Indian Studies, Washington, Conn., 1993—. With USN, 1961-64; lic. capt. USCG. Mem. Colony Found. (trustee 1995—), Ancient Free Accepted Masons (32nd Degree), Rotary Internat., Berzelius Soc., Beta Theta Pi, Lions Club, Yale Club (N.Y.C.), Royal Palm Yacht Club, Mory's (New Haven). Republican. Episcopalian. Home: 18925 S River Rd Alva FL 33920

DARLOW, JULIA DONOVAN, lawyer; b. Detroit, Sept. 18, 1941; d. Frank William Donovan and Helen Adele Turner; m. George Anthony Gratton Darlow (div.); 1 child, Gillian; m. John Corbett O'Meara. AB, Vassar Coll., 1963; postgrad., Columbia U. Law Sch., 1964-65; JD cum laude, Wayne State U., 1971. Bar: Mich. 1971, U.S. Dist. Ct. (ea. dist.) Mich. 1971. Assoc. Dickinson, Wright, McKean, Cudlip & Moon, Detroit, 1971-78; ptnr. Dickinson, Wright, Moon, Van Dusen & Freeman and predecessor, Detroit, 1978—2001; sr. v.p. Detroit Med. Ctr., 2001—01; cons. mem. Dickinson, Wright PLLC, Detroit, 2002—04; counsel Varnum, Riddering, Schmidt & Howlett, LLP, 2005—06; bd. regents U. Mich., 2007—. Chair corp. governance com. Internet Corp., 2004-05; adj. prof. Wayne State U. Law Sch., 1974-75, 96; commr. State Bar Mich., 1977-87, exec. com., 1979-83, 84-87, sec. 1980-81, v.p., 1984-85, pres.-elect 1985-86, pres. 1986-87, coun. corp. fin. and bus. law sect. 1980-86, coun. computer law sect. 1985-88; mem. State Officers Compensation Commn., 1994-96; chair Mich. Supreme Ct. Task Force on Gender Issues in the Cts., 1987-89 Bd. dirs. Hutzel Hosp., 1984—2003, chair, 2002—03; bd. dirs. Mich. Opera Theatre, 1985—, mem. exec. com., 1992—; bd. dirs. Mich. Women's Found., 1986—91, Detroit Med. Ctr., 1990—2003, Marygrove Coll., 1996—2006, sec., 2003—06; trustee Internat. Inst. Met. Detroit, 1986—92; trustee Mich. Met. coun. Girl Scouts USA, 1988—91; trustee Detroit coun. Boy Scouts Am., 1988—98; mem. exec. com. Mich. Coun. Humnanities, 1988—92; mem. Blue Cross-Blue Shield Prospective Reimbursement Com., Detroit, 1979—81; v.p., mem. exec. com. United Found., 1988—95; mem. Mich. Gov.'s Bilateral Trade Team for Germany, 1992—98. Fellow Am. Bar Found. (Mich. State chair 1990-96); mem. Detroit Bar Assn. Found. (treas. 1984-85, trustee 1982-85), Mich. Bar Found. (trustee 1987-94), Am. Judicature Soc. (bd. dirs. 1985-88), Internat. Women's Forum (global affairs com. 1994-03), Women Lawyers Assn. (pres. 1977-78), Mich. Women's Campaign Fund (charter). Democrat. Office: Ste 400 200 E Liberty St Ann Arbor MI 48104 Office Phone: 313-690-3054.

DARMAN, RICHARD, investor, former federal official; b. Charlotte, NC, May 10, 1943; m. Kathleen Emmet, Sept. 1, 1967; children: William Temple Emmet, Jonathan Warren Emmet, Christopher Temple Emmet BA cum laude, Harvard U., 1964, MBA, 1967, DSc (hon.); DLaw (hon.). Dep. asst. sec. US Dept. Health, Edn. & Welfare, Washington, 1971-72; asst. to sec. US Dept. Def., Washington, 1973; spl. asst. to atty. gen. US Dept. Justice, Washington, 1973; fellow Woodrow Wilson Internat. Center for Scholars, Washington, 1974; prin., dir. ICF, Inc., Washington, 1975, 77-80; asst. sec. US Dept. Commerce, Washington, 1976-77; lectr. public policy and mgmt. Harvard U., 1977-80; asst. to Pres. The White House, Washington, 1981-85; dep. sec. US Dept. Treasury, Washington, 1985-87; mng. dir. Shearson Lehman Hutton Inc., NYC, 1987-88; dir. Office Mgmt. & Budget Exec. Office of the Pres., Washington, 1989-93; prof. JFK Sch. Govt. Harvard U., 1998—2002; ptnr. The Carlyle Group, 1993—; chmn. bd. dir. AES Corp., Arlington, Va., 2003—. Bd. dirs. Frontier Ventures Corp., 1993—. Editor: Harvard Ednl. Rev, 1970; contbg. editor U.S. News & World Report, 1987-88; author: Who's in Control?, 1996; contbr. articles to profl. jours. Trustee Bennington Coll., 1974—75, The Brookings Inst., 1987—88, Howard Hughes Med. Inst., 2005—; bd. dirs. Smithsonian Nat. Mus. Am. History, 2000—, vice chmn. bd., 2003—05, chmn. bd., 2005—; trustee NATIXIS Funds, 1996—, Loomis Sayles Funds, 2003—; mem. overseers com. to visit Kennedy Sch. Govt. Harvard U., 1988—98, 2003—, Harvard Med. Sch., 1994—99; dir. Matha's Vineyard Mus., 2007—. Office: The Carlyle Group 1001 Pennsylvania Ave NW Washington DC 20004-2505

D'ARMAND, JOHN BERGER, music educator; b. Knoxville, Tenn., Nov. 15, 1935; s. Roscoe Carlisle and Virginia Luck Berger D'Armand; m. Susanne Buchinger, Dec. 24, 1987; children: Cynthia Luck Sullivan, Jeannette Noël, Maureen. BS, U. of Tenn., 1954—58; MusB, Baldwin-Wallace Coll., 1960—63; MusM, U. of Ill., 1963—65; D of musical arts, U. of Cin., 1967—80; Kodály Diploma, U. of Calgary, 1982—84; Med, U. of Alaska, 1990—2004. Type A Teaching Certificate State of Alaska, 1999. Chorister Robert Shaw Chorale, NYC; artist in residence Concordia Coll., Moorhead, Minn., 1964—67; assoc. prof. of music U. of Mass., 1968—80; lectr. in music Wesleyan U., Middletown, Conn., 1970—72; music dir. WFCR, Amherst, Mass., 1973—75; prof. of music U. of Alaska, 1980—. Founder and exec. dir. Paul Ulanowsky Found. for Chamber Musicians, Deerfield, Mass., 1969—; voice coach Oren Brown Voice Seminar, Amherst, Mass., 1980; pres. of the faculty senate U. of Alaska, 1997—98. Singer: (rca victor choral recording) Bach: Mass in B minor (Grammy winner for best sacred choral rec., 1960). Recipient Independent Students Association Man of the Yr., U. Tenn., 1958, Baldwin-Wallace College Alumni Achievement award, 1984; scholarship, Berkshire Music Ctr. at Tanglewood, 1960, Oglebay Pk. Opera Workshop, Wheeling, W.Va., 1960, Performing Assistantship in opera performance, U. of Ill., 1963—64, scholarship, Yale Summer Sch. of Music and Art, 1967, Grad. Assistantship in opera and conducting, U. of Cin., 1967—68. Mem.: Pi Kappa Lambda, Delta Phi Alpha. Home: P O Box 210623 Auke Bay AK 99821-0623 Home Phone: 907-789-4956. Home Fax: 907-789-3981. Personal E-mail: jbd@gci.net.

DARMENTO, RALPH JOSEPH, religious organization administrator, educator, school system administrator; b. Bklyn., Mar. 4, 1952; s. Ralph R. and Elvira M. Darmento. BS, Manhattan Coll., 1973; MA, Columbia U., 1976, U. San Francisco, 1980; postgrad., Fordham U., 1997. Cert. math. tchr. NY, adminstr. NY. Math. tchr. Bishop Loughlin Meml. HS, Bklyn., 1973—76; chmn. math. dept. La Salle Acad., NYC, 1993—96, 1987—88, Providence, 1976—79, math tchr., vice prin., 1980—84; chmn. math. dept. Sacred Heart HS, Yonkers, NY, 1979—80; prin. St John's Coll., Washington, 1984—87; chmn. math. dept., counselor La Salle Mil. Acad., Oakdale, NY, 1988—89; prin. Archbishop Carroll HS, Washington, 1989—92, St Raphael Acad., Pawtucket, RI, 1992—93; assoc. supt. Archdiocese of Newark, Newark, 1996—2000, dep. supt., 2000—. Commr. Commn. on Secondary Schools, Phila., 2003—; reviewer William H. Sadlier, NYC, 2005—. Recipient St Philip Neri award, Oratory Prep. Sch., 2003, Pro Ecclesia et Pontifice, Pope John Paul II, 1991. Mem.: ASCD (assoc.), Nat. Coun. Tchrs. Math. (assoc.), Nat. Cath. Edn. Assn. (assoc.), Chief Adminstrs. Cath. Edn. (assoc.). Roman Catholic. Office: Archdiocese of Newark 171 Clifton Ave Newark NJ 07104 Home: 1216 Beverley Rd Brooklyn NY 11218 Home Phone: 718-857-4311; Office Phone: 973-497-4260. Office Fax: 973-497-4249. Personal E-mail: rjdfsc@gmail.com.

DARMSTANDLER, HARRY MAX, retired military officer; b. Indpls., Aug. 9, 1922; s. Max M. and Nonna (Holden) D.; m. Donna L. Bender, Mar. 10, 1957; children: Paul William, Thomas Alan. BS, U. Omaha, 1964; MS, George Washington U., 1965; grad., Nat. War Coll., 1965. Commd. 2d lt. USAAF, 1943; advanced through grades to maj. gen. USAF, 1973; served with 15th Air Force, 1943, 5th Air Force, Republic of Korea, 1952; comdr.-in-chief Pacific, 1960—63; served with joint chiefs of staff, 1965—68; supreme comdr. Allied Powers Europe, 1969—71; comdr. 12th Air Divsn. SAC, 1972, dep. chief of staff for plans, 1973; spl. asst. to chief of staff USAF, 1974—75; chmn. bd., CEO Rancho Bernardo Savs. Bank, San Diego, 1983—90; ptnr. Allied Assocs., Colorado Springs, Colo., 1968—, D & H Inc., Woodland Park, Colo., 1979—; founding ptnr. Assocs. Group, San Diego, 1995—2005. Cons. Mid East matters and bd. dirs. Palomar Pomerado Health Found, San Diego; bd. dirs. Clean Found., San Diego. Author numerous articles on nat. def. requirements. Elder, Rancho Bernardo Community Presbyn. Ch., San Diego. Decorated D.S.M. with oak leaf cluster, Legion of Merit with oak leaf cluster, D.F.C., Air medal with 3 oak leaf clusters; research fellow UCLA, 1969. Mem. AIAA, Order Daedalians, Soc. Strategic Air Command, Eagle Scout Alumni Assn., Bernardo Heights Country Club (San Diego, past pres.), Phi Tau Alpha. Home: La Jolla Village Towers 8515 Costa Verde Blvd #1707 San Diego CA 92122 Personal E-mail: dhank32@sbcglobal.net.

DARNALL, ROBERTA MORROW, educational association administrator; b. Kemmerer, Wyo., May 18, 1949; d. C. Dale and Eugenia Stayner (Christmas) Morrow; m. Leslie A. Darnall, Sept. 3, 1977; children: Kimberly Gene, Leslie Nicole. BS, U. Wyo., Laramie, 1972. Tariff sec., ins. adminstr. Wyo Trucking Assn., Casper, 1973-75; asst. clerical supr. Wyo. Legislature, Cheyenne, 1972-77, congrl. campaign press aide, 1974; pub. rels. dir. Casper, Wyo., Wyo. Rep. Ctr. Com., 1976-77; asst. dir. alumni rels. U. Wyo., 1977-81; exec. dir. Alumni Assn., 1981—. Bd. dirs. recognition, planned giving, and golf coms. Ivison Meml. Hosp. Found.; mem. Altar Guild, lector, usher, vestry, former acolyte, coord. St. Matthew's Ch. Mem. Coun. for Advancement and Support of Edn., Higher Edn. Assn. Rockies, Am. Soc. Assn. Execs., Laramie C. of C. (past edn.com.), U. Wyo. Alumni Assn., Cowboy Joe Club, PEO (former courtesy com., officer). Republican. Episcopalian. Home: 15 Snowy View Ct Laramie WY 82070-5358 Office: 214 S 14th St Laramie WY 82070 Home Phone: 307-742-5889; Office Phone: 307-766-4166. E-mail: robbie@uwyo.edu.

DARNELL, JAMES EDWIN, JR., molecular biologist, educator; b. Columbus, Miss., Sept. 9, 1930; s. James Edwin and Helen (Hopkins) D.; m. Jane Roller, 1957; children: Christopher, Robert, Jonathan; m. Kristin Holby, 2002. BS, U. Miss., 1951; MD, Washington U., 1955, DSc, 1996. Intern Barnes Hosp., 1955-56; asst. to sr. surgeon USPHS, Bethesda, Md., 1957-60; asst. and assoc. prof. MIT, Cambridge, 1961-64; prof. Albert Einstein Coll. Medicine, NYC, 1967, Columbia U., 1968-74, chmn. dept. biol. scis., 1971-74; Vincent Astor prof. Rockefeller U., NYC, 1974—, v.p. acad. affairs, 1990-91. Co-author: (textbooks) General Virology, 1967, 77, Molecular Cell Biology, 1986, rev. edits., 1990, 1995, 2000, 03. Recipient H.T. Rickets award U. Chgo., 1979, Internat. award Gairdner Found., Toronto, Ont., Can., 1986, Paul Janssen prize in Advanced Biotech. and Medicine, 1994, Bertner award in cancer rsch., 1996, Passano award, 1997, Milstein award, 1997, City of Medicine, 1998, E.B. Wilson award, 1998, Lynen medal, 1999, Dickson Prize in Medicine, 1999, William B. Coley award, 1999, Gerald D. Aurbach lecture award The Endocrine Soc., 1999, Novartis/Drew award in biomed. rsch., 2000, N.Y. Acad. Medicine medal for disting. contbns. in biomed. sci., 2002, Albert Lasker award for Spl. Achievement in Med. Sci., 2002, Nat. Medal of Science award, 2002. Mem. NAS, Am. Acad. Arts and Scis. (award 1973), Royal Soc. (fgn.), Japanese Biochem. Soc. (hon.), Royal Swedish Acad. Aci. (fgn.), European Acad. Scis. Office: Rockefeller U Molecular Cell Biology 1230 York Ave New York NY 10021-6399

DARNELL, RILEY CARLISLE, state official, lawyer; b. Clarksville, Tenn., May 13, 1940; s. Elliott Sinclair and Mary Anita (Whitefield) D.; m. Mary Penelope Crockarell, June 2, 1963; children: Neil Whitefield, Duncan Edward, Mary Eve, Penelope Joy, Dawson Riley. BS, Austin Peay State U., 1962; JD, Vanderbilt U., 1965. Bar: Tenn. 1965. Gen. practice, Clarksville, 1965-66, 69—; mem. Tenn. Ho. Reps. from 67th dist., 1971—80, treas. ho.-senate caucus, 1971—86, sec. ho. com. ways & means, chmn. joint ho. -senatefiscal rev. com., 1975—80; men. Tenn. State Senate, 1980—92, chmn. transp. com., 1982—86, chmn. joint com. children & youth, 1987—89, majority leader, 1988—92; sec. state State of Tenn., Nashville, 1993—. Served to Capt. JAGC, USAF, 1966-69. Fellow Tenn. Bar Found.; mem. ABA, Montgomery County Bar Assn., Tenn. Trial Lawyers, Tenn. Bar Assn., Nat. Conf. State Legislators (jud. task force), So. Lesig. Conf. (mem. fiscal affairs com.) Democrat. Mem. Ch. Of Christ. Office: Office Sec State State Capitol First Floor 600 Charlotte Ave Nashville TN 37243 Office Phone: 615-741-2819. Business E-Mail: riley.darnell@state.tn.us.*

DARNEY, PHILIP DEMPSEY, gynecologist, educator; b. Granite, Okla., Feb. 27, 1943; s. Walter Preston and Corene (Barton) D.; m. Virginia Grant (div. 1981); children: Blair, Barton; m. Uta Landy, Oct. 13, 1984; 1 child, Andrew. AB, U. Calif., Berkeley, 1964; MD, U. Calif., San Francisco, 1968; MSc, London Sch. Hygiene, 1972. Diplomate Am. Bd. Preventive Medicine, Am. Bd. Ob-Gyn. Intern USPHS Hosp., San Francisco, 1968-69; resident in ob-gyn Brigham and Women's Hosp., Boston, 1973-76; dep. dir. div. reproductive health Ctrs. Disease Control, Atlanta, 1971-73; asst. prof. ob-gyn Harvard Med. Sch., Boston, 1976-78; assoc. prof. ob-gyn Oreg. Health Scis. U., Portland, 1978-80; prof. ob-gyn U. Calif. Sch. Medicine, San Francisco, 1981--. Cons. AID, Washington, 1971-74, Pathfinder Internat., Boston, 1973-83, The Population Coun., Family Health Internat., Internat. Projects Assistance Svc., Family Planning Internat. Assistance, Johns Hopkins U., 30 countries;lectr., writer in field. Author: Protocols for Office Gynecologic Surgery, 1996, Clinical Guide for Contraception, 1992, 4th edit., 2005; contbr. chpts. to books; reviewer 20 med. jours.; contbr. over 200 articles to profl. jours Bd. dirs. Engender Health, Planned Parenthood Fedn. Am., Alan Guttmacher Inst. Named Outstanding Young Profl. Am. Pub. Health Assn., 1984, recipeint Schultz award 2004 Fellow Am. Coll. Obstetricians and Gynecologists, Am. Coll. Preventive Medicine, Am. Gyn. and Obstetric Soc., Inst. Medicine. Democrat. Avocations: surfing, sailing, sculling. Office: San Francisco Gen Hosp Dept Ob-Gyn San Francisco CA 94110 Business E-Mail: darneyp@obgyn.ucsf.edu.

DARNIS, GERAUD, manufacturing executive; Grad, Inst. Superieur du Commerce, Paris. Mgmt. positions United Technologies Corp., 1983—, v.p. fin. Carrier Europe, 1992—93, mng. dir. Carrier France, 1993—96, pres. Carrier European transcontinental ops., 1996—99, pres. Carrier Asia Pacific ops., 1999—2001, pres. UTC Power, 2001, pres. Carrier bus. unit, 2001—. Office: United Technologies Corp United technologies Bldg Hartford CT 06101*

DARNTON, ROBERT CHOATE, library director, historian, educator; b. NYC, May 10, 1939; s. Byron and Eleanor (Choate) D.; m. Susan Lee Glover, June 29, 1963; children: Nicholas Campbell, Catherine Choate, Margaret Townsend. BA, Harvard U., 1960; BPhil, Oxford U., Eng., 1962, DPhil, 1964. Reporter NY Times, NYC, 1964; jr. fellow Harvard U., 1964-68; asst. prof. history Princeton U., NJ, 1968-71, assoc. prof. NJ, 1971-72, prof. NJ, 1972—2007, Shelby Cullom Davis prof. European history; Carl H. Pforzheimer univ. prof. Harvard U., 2007—; dir. Harvard U. Libr., 2007—. Author: Mesmerism and the End of the Enlightenment in France, 1968, The Business of Enlightenment: A Publishing History of the Encyclopédie, 1775-1800, 1979 (Am. Hist. Assn. Leo Gershoy prize 1979), The Literary Underground of the Old Regime, 1982, The Great Cat Massacre and Other Episodes in French Cultural History, 1984 (LA Times book prize), The Kiss of Lamourette: Reflections in Cultural History, 1989, Edition et Sédition, L'univers de la littérature clandestine au XVIII e siècle, 1991 (Prix Chateaubriand), Berlin Journal, 1989-90, 1991, Gens de lettres, gens du livre, 1992, The Forbidden Best-Sellers of Pre-Revolutionary France, 1995 (Nat. Book Critics Circle award 1996), The Corpus of Clandestine Literature in France, 1995, Jacques-Pierre Brissot, His Career and Correspondence, 1779-1787, 2001, George Washington's False Teeth. An Unconventional Guide to the Eighteenth Century, 2003. Decorated officer Ordre des Arts et des Lettres, chevalier Légion d'Honneur, 1999; recipient Koren prize Soc. French Hist. Studies, 1973, MacArthur Found. prize, 1982, Gutenberg prize Internat. Gutenberg Soc. and City of Mainz, Germany, 2004. Fellow Am. Acad. Arts and Scis., Am. Philos. Soc., Brit. Acad. (corr. 2001); mem. Am. Hist. Assn. (pres.-elect 1998, pres. 1999-00), Am. Soc. 18th-Century Studies (Clifford prize 1971, 73), Internat. Soc. 18th-Century Studies (pres. 1987-1992), Academia Europaea, Belgian Royal Acad. French Lang. and Lit. Office: Office of Dir Wadsworth House 1341 Massachusetts Ave Cambridge MA 02138*

DAROFF, ROBERT BARRY, neurologist, educator; b. NYC, Aug. 3, 1936; s. Charles and May (Wolin) D.; m. Jane L. Abrahams, Dec. 4, 1959; children: Charles II, Robert Barry, Jr., William Clayton BA, U. Pa., 1957, MD, 1961. Cert. in Neurology Am. Bd. Psychiatry and Neurology, 1969. Intern Phila. Gen. Hosp., 1961-62; resident in neurology Yale-New Haven Med. Ctr., 1962-65; fellow in neuro-ophthalmology U. Calif. Med. Ctr., San Francisco, 1967-68; prof. neurology, assoc. prof. ophthalmology U. Miami Med. Sch.; dir. ocular motor neurophysiology lab. Miami Va. Med. Ctr., 1968-80; Gilbert W. Humphrey prof., chmn. dept. neurology Case Western Res. U. Med. Sch.; dir. dept. neurology Univ. Hosps., Cleve., 1980-93; prof. neurology Case Western U., 1980—, assoc. dean, 1994—2003, interim vice dean edn. and acad. affairs, 2004—06, interim chair, 2006—; staff neurologist Cleve. Va. Med. Ctr., 1980-93; chief of staff, sr. v.p. acad. affairs U. Hosp., Cleve., 1994—2003; chief med. officer St. Vincents Charity, St. Johns West Shore Hosps., 2004—05. Med. sci. adv. bd., chmn. sci. program com. Myasthenia Gravis Found., 1984—87, exec. com., 1992—2003, sec., 1995—96, vice chair, 1997—99, chair, 1999—2001, chair nominating com., 2002—03; adv. bd. Nat. Multiple Sclerosis Found., 1988—90, Soc. Progressive Supranuclear Palsy, 1991—94; nat. adv. eye coun. sensory and motor disorders vision panel NIH, 1980—83; steering com. neurological disorders in comml. drivers US Dept. Transp., chmn. task force, 1987; lectr. T.S. Srinivasan Endowment, Madras, India, 1994; Cumings lectr. Migraine Trust, London, 1994; lectr. Am. Coun. Headache Edn., 1996, vice chair, 2000—02; Soriano lectr., 2001; prof. (hon.) Astana-State Med. Acad., Kazakhstan, 1999; bd. advisors Capnia, Inc., 2000—; lectr. 7th Ann. Vijjajiva, Mahidol U., Bangkok, 2006. Book rev. editor: Neuro-ophthalmology, 1981-86, mem. editl. bd., 1987-2003; assoc. editor Jour. Biomed. Sys., 1970-72; editor Neurol. Progress, Anns. Neurology, 1981-84; editor-in-chief Neurology, 1987-96, sci. integrity adv., 2004-; co-editor World Neurology, 1991-98, editl. adv. bd. 1998—2003; mem. editl. bd. Archives of Neurology, 1976, Annals of Neurology, 1977-86, Neurology and Neurosurgery Update Series, 1978-93, Headache, 1980-86, sr. edit. advisor, 2004-; Contemporary Neurology Series, 1989-93, Neurosci., Saudi Arabia, 2003-06, conculting sr. editor, 2007—, Practical Neurology, 2003—; mem. editl. adv. bd. Jour. Neuro-ophthalmology, 2001—; mem. editl. coun. Neurologia Croatica, 1991-2004; mem. editl. commn. Valeology, Kazakhstan, 2002-05, The Scientific World Neurology Jour., 2006-; contbr. articles to profl. jours. Chmn. Young Tae Kwon Do Acad., North Miami, 1977-80; bd. dirs. Benign Essential Blepharospasm Rsch. Found., 1983-; trustee Fairhill Ctr. for Aging, 1988—, The Learning Corp., 1992-00, Edison Bio Tech. Ctr., 1994-01, Great Lakes Sci. Ctr., 1994-01, Myasthenia Gravis Found. Am., 1999-01; mem. tech. adv. coun. BIOMEC, Inc., 1999-2007; bd. trustees Greater Cleve. chpt. ARC, 1999-05, mem. exec. com., 2000-03; mem. cmty. bd. St. Vincent Charity Hosp., 2003-05, St. John West Shore Hosp., 2003-05. With USAR, 1965—67. Recipient Ernst Jung-Medaille Fur Medizin in Gold, 1993, Silver Jubilee Oration award Med. Coll. Trivandrum, India, 1994, John H. Budd Disting. Mem. award Cleve. Acad. Med., 2002, Disting. Grad. award U. Pa., 2003, Lifetime Achievement award, Neurosciences India Group, 2005; named hon. dir. life Fairhill Ctr., 2006. Fellow: Am. Headache Soc. (pres. 2002—04, bd. dirs., sec., John R. Graham Svc. Clin. Forum award 2005); mem.: AMA, World Neurology Found. (bd. dirs. 2006—), Internat. Neurology Forum (chair internat. organizing com. 2004—07), Eastern Mediterranean Association of Med. Editors, World Assn. Med. Editors, Internat. Headache Soc., Neuromuscular Disease Assn. Romania (internat. sci. com. 1991—93), Acad. Med. Scis. Kazakhstan, Alliance Brain Initiatives (founding mem.), Dana Found., Am. Neurol. Assn. (hon.; program adv. com. 1977—78, chmn. 1978, councillor 1980—82, membership adv. com. 1980—83, chmn. 1981—83, nominating com. 1984, chmn. Annals of Neurology oversight com. 1984—86, sec. 1985—89, pres.-elect 1989—90, pres. 1990—91, past pres. 1991—92, history com. 2004—06), Am. Acad. Neurology (hon.; chmn. sci. program com. 1973—75, exec. bd. 1987—96, Netter lectr. 1989, pub. com. 1993—2001), Assn. Colombiana Neurologia (hon.), Coun. Sci. Editors, World Fedn. Neurology (fin. com. 1985—, exec. com. Rsch. group on Neuro-Ophthalmology 1987—95, publs. com. 1987—, chmn. 1990—2001), Clin. Eye Movement Soc. (founder), Barany Soc., Internat. Neuro-Ophthalmology Soc. (organizing com. 1986), N.Am. Neuro-Ophthalmology Soc. (bd. dirs. 1986—94, chair cert. and accreditation com. 1997—98, publs. com. 1999—2001), Rocky Mountain Neuro-Ophthalmology Soc. (bd. dirs. 1980—86), Vietnam Vets. Inst. (bd. scholars 1998—, Ea. Med. Assn. Med. Editors, ethics and sci. misconduct com. 2005—, united coun. of neurolgic subspecialists, alternate dir. 2005—, com. on publ. ethics 2005—), Alpha Omega Alpha. Office: Univ Hosp Rm HAN 503 11100 Euclid Ave Cleveland OH 44106 Office Phone: 216-844-3193. Business E-Mail: robert.daroff@case.edu.

DARR, ALAN PHIPPS, curator, historian; b. Kankakee, Ill., Sept. 30, 1948; s. Milton Freeman, Jr. and Margaret (Phipps) D.; m. Mollie Hayden Fletcher, June 28, 1980; children: Owen, Alexander. BA, Northwestern U., 1970; MA, Inst. Fine Arts, NYU, 1975, PhD in Art History, 1980; Cert., Mus. Tng., Met. Mus. Art, 1976, Mus. Mgmt. Inst., U. Calif. Berkeley, 1980. Grad. intern Met. Mus. Art, NYC, 1976; instr. NYU, 1976; asst. curator Detroit Inst. Arts, 1978-80, assoc. curator, 1980-81, curator in charge European sculpture and decorative arts, 1981—, Walter B. Ford II Family curator European sculpture and decorative arts, 1997—; postdoctoral fellow Harvard U. Ctr. for Italian Renaissance Studies at Villa I Tatti, Florence, 1988-89; adj. prof. Wayne State U., Detroit, 1982—; Paul Mellon vis. sr. scholar Ctr. Advanced Study in Visual Arts, Nat. Gallery, Washington, 1994. Co-editor/co-author: Italian Renaissance Sculpture in the Time of Donatello, 1985-86, Donatello Studien, 1989, Verrocchio and Late Quattrocentro Italian Sculpture, 1992, The Dodge Collection of Eighteenth Century French and English Art in the Detroit Institute of Arts, 1996, Woven Splendor: Five Centuries of European Tapestry in the Detroit Institute of Arts, 1996, Catalogue of Italian Sculpture in the Detroit Inst. of Arts, 2 vols., 2002, The Medici, Michelangelo and the Art of Late Renaissance Florence, 2002, Large Bronzes in the Renaissance, Studies in the History of Art, vol. 64, Nat. Gallery of Art, 2003, others; contbr. articles to profl. jours. Nat. Endowment Arts Mus. Profls. Fellow, 1983; John J. McCloy fellow, 1980-81, Ford Found. fellow, 1975-78, Met. Mus. Art fellow, 1975. Office: Detroit Inst Arts 5200 Woodward Ave Detroit MI 48202-4094

DARR, WALTER ROBERT, financial analyst; b. Phila., June 19, 1956; s. John Fluke, Sr. and Lois Marilyn (Fry) Darr. BS in Commerce, Rider U., Lawrenceville, NJ, 1978, MBA, 1991. Mgmt. cert., Zenger-Miller Front Line Leadership Mercer County CC, NJ, 1996, mgmt. cert., Total Quality Mgmt. Mercer County CC, NJ, 1997. Collateral analyst First Nat. Bank & Trust Co., Beverly, NJ, 1978-84, First Peoples Bank NJ, Westmont, 1984-88, loan rev. analyst, 1988-92; loan acctg. tech. NJ Nat. Bank, Trenton, 1992-93; sr. credit analyst Carnegie Bank, N.A., Princeton, NJ, 1993-94, asst. cashier, sr. credit analyst, 1994-97; credit officer, credit dept. supr. Broad Nat./Independence Cmty. Bank, Newark, 1997-99; asst. sec., bus. banking divsn. Ind. Cmty. Bank, Newark, 1999-2000, asst. v.p. SBA lending, 2001—06; sr. underwriter, bus. banking div. Summit Bank, Dayton, NJ, 2000-2001; asst. v.p., branch bus. banking, SBA Sovereign Bank, Villanova, Pa., 2006—. Treas. Cinnaminson Bapt. Ch., NJ, 1983—87, deacon, 1988—89, 1993—94, Princeton Presbyn. Ch., 2005—; chmn.-treas. Mercer County chpt. Child Evangelism Fellowship NJ, 1996—99; mem. Lewis Shearer Chorale/Garden State Chorale, NJ, 1982—94. Recipient Sch. award, Am. Legion Post, Medford, NJ, 1974. Mem.: Rider U. Alumni Assn. (bd. dirs. 2002—, sec. 2003—05), Gideons (camp pres. 2002—05, Mercer West Camp, NJ 2002—, camp sec. 2005—06). Republican. Presbyterian. Avocations: classic cars, bicycling, classical music, Victorian architecture. Home: 107 Manlove Ave Apt E-B Hightstown NJ 08520-3234 Home Phone: 609-448-2190; Office Phone: 610-526-6215. Personal E-mail: wdarr56@aol.com. Business E-Mail: wdarr1@sovereignbank.com.

DARRELL, NORRIS, JR., lawyer; b. Berlin, May 10, 1929; s. Norris and Doris Clare (Williams) D. (parents Am. citizens); m. Henriette Maria Haid, July 31, 1962; 1 child, Andrew. AB, Harvard U., 1951, LL.B. cum laude, 1954. Bar: NY 1955, US Supreme Ct. 1965. Assoc. Sullivan & Cromwell, NYC, 1956-65, ptnr., 1965-92, sr. ptnr. European office Paris, 1968-71, sr. counsel, 1993—. Trustee Cold Spring Harbor Lab., Inc., NY, 1974-81, United Student Aid Funds, Inc., Fishers, Ind., 1974-94, USA Group Inc., Fishers, Ind., 1993-2000, East Woods Sch., Oyster Bay, NY, 1974-79; hon. trustee Heckscher Mus., Huntington, NY; bd. dirs. Lumina Found. for Edn., Inc., Indpls., Ind. With US Army, 1954—56. Harvard Club NY, Pilgrims Soc., River Club NY (bd. govs. 1978-98), Cold Spring Harbor Beach Club, Edgartown Yacht Club. Home: 44 Walnut Tree Ln Cold Spring Harbor New York NY 11724 Personal E-mail: norrisd482@aol.com.

DARRETTA, ROBERT J., pharmaceutical executive; BS in Econs., Villanova U.; postgrad., Stanford U. Fin. mgmt. trainee to chief fin. officer Ethicon Johnson & Johnson, New Brunswick, NJ, 1968-78, mng. dir. Ethicon S.P.A. Italy, 1984-88, pres. Iolab, 1988-97, treas., corp. officer New Brunswick, NJ, 1995-97, v.p. fin., CFO, 1997—2002, exec. v.p., CFO, 2002—04, vice chmn., CFO, 2004—. Bd. dirs. Oper. Smile; bd. trustees Healthcare Leadership Coun. Office: Johnson & Johnson 1 Johnson & Johnson Plz New Brunswick NJ 08933-0001*

D'ARRIGO, STEPHEN, JR., agricultural company executive; b. Stockton, Calif., Mar. 8, 1922; s. Stephen and Constance (Picciotto) D;A.; m. Rosemary Anne Murphy, Aug. 20, 1949 (dec. Sept. 2006); children: Stephen III, Kathleen Anne, Joanne Marie, Michael Anderw, Dennis Patrick, Patrick Shane. BS, U. Santa Clara, 1947. Sec.-treas. D'Arrigo Bros. Co. Calif., San Jose, 1946-62, Salinas, 1962-83; ret., 1983; sec.-treas. Santa Cruz Farms (co. merged with D'Arrigo Bros. 1970), Eloy, Ariz., 1947-52, pres., gen. mgr., 1952-70, bd. dirs., 1947-70. Mem. Nat. Def. Exec. Res. 2d lt. US Army, 1943—46. Decorated Bronze Star, Belgian Fouragere; recipient Disting. Svc. award, Santa Clara Heart Assn. Mem. NRA (life), Springfield Armory Mus. (life), Smithsonian Assocs. (nat. chrter), Mil. Order World Wars, Assn. U.S. Army, Co. Mil. Historians, Am. Soc. Arms Collectors, Tex. Gun Collectors Assn. Home: 2241 Dry Creek Rd San Jose CA 95124-1216

DARROW, EMILY M., public relations executive, writer; b. Kingston, NY, Sept. 21, 1964; d. H. Van Wyck and Marianne Darrow; m. Brendon Paul McCrane, Oct. 5, 2002. Student, Vassar Coll., 1983—84; BA, Hunter Coll., 1989; postgrad., Inst. of FIne Arts, NYU, 1992. Mus. mgr., edn. mgr. Hist. Hudson Valley-Montgomery Pl., Annandale-on-Hudson, NY, 1995; dir. pub. rels. and promotions Mohonk Mountain Ho., New Paltz, NY, 1997—98; pub. rels. assoc. Bard Coll., Annandale-on-Hudson, 1998—; asst. to exec. dir. Inst. Advanced Theology Bard Coll., Annandale-on-Hudson, 2001—. Rschr. Salander O'Reilly Gallery-Stuart Davis Catalogue Raisonne Project, NYC, 1989—90; writer, rschr. Art Commn. City of N.Y., 1989—90; internship in pub. rels. Opera Garnier de Paris-Paris Opera Ballet, Paris, 1990—91, N.Y.C. Ballet, 1982—84; cons., writer Vikarmasila Found., NYC, 1999—; mem. Woodstock Arts Bd., 2004—. Mem. Woodstock (N.Y.) Arts Bd., 2004—. Recipient Zabar grad. scholarship, Hunter Coll., 1989; fellow Leon Levy and Shelby White, Inst. of Fine Arts/NYU, 1990. Mem.: Coll. Art Assn. and Pub. Rels. Soc. Am., Jr. League Kingston (rec. sec. 1991—96, pub. rels. dir. 1991—96). Home: 250 Morton Rd Rhinebeck NY 12572 Office: Bard Coll Annandale Hotel Annandale On Hudson NY 12504 Personal E-mail: EMDarrow87@alum.vassar.edu.

DARROW, JILL E(LLEN), lawyer; b. NYC, Jan. 6, 1954; d. Milton and Elaine (Sklarin) D.; m. Michael V.P. Marks, May 14, 1987. AB in English, Barnard Coll., 1975; JD, U. Pa., 1978; LLM in Tax Law, NYU, 1983. Bar: Pa. 1978, NY 1979, US Tax Ct. 1982. Assoc. Shearman & Sterling, NYC, 1978-79, Rosenman & Colin, NYC, 1979-86, ptnr., 1987—2002, Katten Muchin Rosenman LLP, NYC, 2002—. Mem. ABA, NY State Bar Assn., Pa. Bar Assn., Phi Beta Kappa. Home: 300 Central Park W New York NY 10024 Office: Katten Muchin Rosenman LLP 575 Madison Ave Fl 12 New York NY 10022-2511 Office Phone: 212-940-7113. Business E-Mail: jill.darrow@kattenlaw.com.

DARROW, KURT L., manufacturing executive; b. 1954; m. Renee M. Darrow. BA, Adrian U., 1977. V.p. sales La-Z-Boy Inc., 1987—99, sr. v.p., sales & mktg., 1999—2001, pres., residential divsn., 2001—03, pres., CEO, 2003—. Office: La Z Boy Inc 1248 N Telegraph Rd Monroe MI 48162*

DARROW, WILLIAM RICHARD, retired pharmaceutical company executive, consultant; b. Middletown, Ohio, 1939; s. Richard William and Nelda D.; m. Janet Elizabeth Swan, 1964; children: James William, Susan Elizabeth, Margaret Ellen. BA, Ohio Wesleyan U., 1960; MD, Western Res. U., 1964; PhD in Pharmacology, Case-Western Res. U., 1969. Intern Univ. Hosps., Cleve., 1964; sr. clin. rsch. assoc. CIBA Pharm. Co., 1969, asst. dir. clin. pharmacology, 1969—70; dir. clin. pharmacology CIBA-GEIGY Corp., 1970—75, exec. dir. clin. rsch., 1975—76; sr. v.p. rsch., med. dir. Wallace Labs. divsn. Carter Wallace, Inc., Cranbury, NJ, 1976—80; med. dir. Schering Labs. divsn. Schering-Plough Corp., Kenilworth, NJ, 1980; v.p. med. and regulatory affairs Schering-Plough Rsch., Kenilworth, 1981—82; sr. v.p. med. ops. Schering-Plough Corp., Kenilworth, 1982—94, sr. med. advisor, 1994—2003; ret., 2003. Bd. dirs. AltaRex Corp., 2001-02; chmn. rsch. com. N.J. Health Scis. Group, 1973-76, mem. exec. com., 1973-74, 76-86, treas., 1977-80, v.p., 1980-86; mem. Bernards Twp. Bd. Health, 1979-93, v.p., 1980, pres., 1981-85, 86-93; chmn. Bernards Twp. Deer Study Task Force, Deer Mgmt. Adv. Com., 1999—; bd. dirs. N.J. chpt. Arthritis Found., 1990-2004, exec. com., 1991-2004, vice chmn., 1995-97, chmn. bd. dirs., 1997-2001, past chmn., 2001-04; bd. dirs. Pharm. Ednl. and Rsch. Inst., 1993-2000, chmn. curriculum com., 1993-95; bd. dirs. Junior Achievement No. N.J., 1996; mem. sci. adv. bd. Clin. Rsch. Ctr. Robert Wood Johnson Med. Ctr., 1990-2000; mem. U.S. del. Internat. Conf. on Harmonization, 1991-99; mem. N.J. State Adv. Coun. on Arthritis, 2000-05; mem.Somerset County (NJ) Med. Res. Corps, 2005—. Recipient Roche award, 1962, Humanitarian of Yr. award Arthritis Found. N.J., 1994; USPHS postdoctoral fellow, 1965-69. Fellow: Royal Soc. Medicine, Am. Acad. Pharm. Physicians (life); mem.: AMA, Pharm. Rsch. Mfrs. Am. Found. (sci. adv. bd. 1990—, chmn. 1994—, chief sci. advisor 1997—), Pharm. Rsch. Mfrs. Am. (steering com. med. sect. 1984—96, program chmn. 1988—89, vice-chmn. 1989—90, chmn. 1990—92, past chmn. 1992—96), Drug Info. Assn., Lakeside Country Club (Penn Yan, N.Y.), Basking Ridge (N.J.) Country Club, Pi Delta Epsilon, Omicron Delta Kappa, Phi Rho Sigma, Phi Gamma Delta. Republican. Presbyterian.

DARSEY, JEROME ANTHONY (JERRY DARSEY), chemistry professor, consultant; b. Houma, La., Aug. 26, 1946; s. Elmer Joseph and Arline (Houghton) D.; m. Patricia Ann Bukowski, June 10, 1989; children: Brittany Angéle, Joseph Anthony, Mary Catherine. BS in Physics, La. State U., 1970, PhD in Chemistry, 1982. Asst. prof. chemistry and physics Gordon Coll. U. Ga. System, Barnsville, 1983-84; asst. prof. Tarleton State U./Tex. A&M U., Stephenville, Tex., 1984-88, assoc. prof., 1988-90; asst. prof. U. Ark., Little Rock, 1990-93, assoc. prof., 1993-96, prof., 1996—. Univ. scholar natural scis. Tarleton State U., Tex. A&M U., 1989-90; cons. Oak Ridge (Tenn.) Nat. Lab., 1990-95; co-chmn. 1st workshop neural network applications to material scis. Dept. Energy, 1994; chmn. 1st APS Symposium on Applications of Artificial Neural Networks to Chemical Systems; invited lectr. 21st Australian Polymer Symposium, 1996. Contbr. scientific papers to profl. jours. Named Outstanding Univ. Rschr., U. Ark., Little Rock, 1995, Outstanding Rschr. Coll. Sci. and Math., 1995, 2000; grantee Am. Chem. Soc., 1986, 90, NSF, 1992, 96, NASA, 1994-2001. Fellow AAAS; mem. Am. Chem. Soc. (chmn. Ark. sect. 1993), Am. Phys. Soc., Ark. Acad. Sci., S.W. Theoretical Chemistry Conf. (chmn. 1986-87), Tex. Acad. Sci. (vice chmn. chemistry divsn. 1986-87, chmn. 1987-88). Achievements include patents in field. Home: 1514 Alberta Dr Little Rock AR 72227-5803 Office: U Ark Dept Chemistry 2801 S University Ave Dept Little Rock AR 72204-1099 Office Phone: 501-569-8828. E-mail: jadarsey@ualr.edu.

DARSIE, RICHARD FLOYD, JR., medical entomologist; s. Richard Floyd and Helen Colvin Darsie; m. Hilda Asturius Darsie; 1 child, Helen. BA, Bethany Coll., W.Va., 1937; MS, U. Pitts., 1941; PhD, Cornell U., 1949. Assoc. prof. U. Del., Newark, 1950—62; instr. Franklin & Marshall Coll., Lancaster, Pa., 1949—50; malaria specialist AID, Katmandu, Nepal, 1963—67; tng. officer Malaria Tng. Ctr., Manila, 1967—71; chief vector-borne disease tng. CDC, Atlanta, 1971—76, rsch. entomologist divsn. vector-borne and viral diseases Ft. Collins, Colo., 1982—85; rsch. entomologist Ctrl. Am. Rsch. Sta., San Salvador, El Salvador, 1976—79, Med. Entomology Rsch. and Tng. Unit, Guatemala City, Guatemala, 1979—82, U. SC, Georgetown, 1985—96, U. Fla., Vero Beach, 1996—. Author: Identification and Geographical Distribution of the Mosquitoes of North America, 2005. 1st lt. USAF, 1941—45. Mem.: Am. Mosquito Control Assn. (Meritorious Svc. award 1983), Entomol. Soc. Washington, Entomol. Soc. Am. Avocations: music, sports.

DARST, DAVID MARTIN, investment banker, writer, educator; b. Knoxville; s. Guy Bewley and Susan Mary (McGinnis) Darst; m. Diane Wassman; children: Elizabeth Mathews, David Martin. BA, Yale U., 1969; MBA, Harvard U., 1971. CFA. Assoc. Goldman, Sachs & Co., NYC, 1971-75, v.p., mgr., 1981—, v.p., resident mgr. Zurich, Switzerland, 1975-81, CFO global equities divsn., 1991—96; mng. dir. Morgan Stanley, NYC, 1996—; founding pres. Morgan Stanley Investment Group, 1998—; chief investment strategist global wealth mgmt. divsn., dir. Morgan Stanley Trust Co., NYC, 2001—. Vis. lectr. Coll. and Sch. Mgmt., Yale U., New Haven, 1981—, Bus. Sch., Harvard U., Boston, 1987—; mem. investment com. NY Acad. Scis., Phi Beta Kappa Found. Author: The Complete Bond Book, 1975, The Handbook of the Bond and Money Markets, 1981, The Art of Asset Allocation, 2003, Mastering the Art of Asset Allocation, 2007; contbr. articles to profl. jours. Bd. dirs. Deer Park Assn., 1985—, pres., 1989—; bd. dirs. Can.-U.S. Found. Ednl. Exch., 1996—, Student Sponsor Partnership, 2002—; bd. profl. adv. N.Y.C. Ballet, 1997—; corp. adv. bd. Sch. Am. Ballet, NYC, 2002—. William H. Donaldson Disting. Faculty fellow, Sch. Mgmt. Yale U., 1986—87. Mem.: CFA Inst., NY Soc. Security Analysts, Assn. Internat. Bond Dealers (mem. edn. com.), Yale Alumni Assn. Greenwich (bd. dirs. 1996—), Phelps Assn. (v.p., gov. 1974—), Yale Club N.Y.C. (coun. 1987—, chmn. fin. com. 1987—), Money Marketeers. Office: Morgan Stanley 12th Fl 522 5th Ave New York NY 10036-7601

DART, JOHN SEWARD, journalist, editor; b. Peekskill, NY, Aug. 1, 1936; s. Seward Homer and Vella Marion (Haverstock) D.; m. Gloria Joan Walker, Aug. 31, 1957; children— Kim, John W., Randall, Christopher. BA, U. Colo., 1958. Staff writer UPI, Indpls. and L.A., 1961-65; sci. writer Calif. Inst. Tech., Pasadena, 1966-67; religion writer L.A. Times, 1967-98; news editor Christian Century mag., 2000—. Author: The Laughing Savior, 1976, The Jesus of Heresy and History, rev., expanded edit., 1988, Decoding Mark, 2003; co-author: Unearthing the Lost Words of Jesus, 1998; contbr. reports for Freedom Forum First Amendment Ctr., Vanderbilt U. Served with U.S. Army, 1958-61 Recipient Supple Meml. award Religion Newswriters Assn., 1980, Merrell Meml. award Jim Merrell Religion Liberty Found., 1980, William F. Leidt award Episcopal Ch., 1980, Angel award Religion in Media, 1985, News Reporting award Am. Acad. Religion, 2004; NEH fellow Stanford U., 1973-74, First Amendment Ctr. fellow Vanderbilt U., 1992-93. Mem. Religion Newswriters Assn. (pres. 1990-92), Soc. Bibl. Lit. (mem.-at-large exec. com. Pacific Coast region 1990-95, nat. website editl. bd. 2004—). Avocation: table tennis (nationally ranked player). Home and Office: 12122 Bowmore Ave Northridge CA 91326-1002

DARTER, ROBERT WELLS, surgeon, physician; b. Berkeley, Calif., Aug. 26, 1933; s. Robert James and Lizbeth Amy (Wells) Darter; m. Jan Marie Darter, Mar. 13, 1996; children: Robert, Michael, James, John, Kimberly. BS in Pub. Health, U. Calif., Berkeley, 1954; MS in Microbiology, Northwestern U., Chgo., 1957, MD, 1958. Lab. asst. Calif. State Dept. Pub. Health, Berkeley, 1949—54; med. lab. tech. Augustana Hosp., Chgo., 1955—58; intern Alameda County. Hosp., Oakland, Calif., 1958—59; epidemic intelligence officer USPHS, Atlanta, 1959—61; physician, surgeon St. Helena, Calif., 1961—. Clin. instr. family practice U. Calif., San Francisco, 1965—86. Med. advisor Napa County Head Start Program, 1968—70; mem. Calif. Sch. Health Alliance, 1976—88, treas., 1978—88; co-founder, chmn. bd. Vintage Savs. and Loan, 1976—82; mem. nat ski patrol aux. Boreal Ridge Resort, 1987—96. Named Citizen of Yr., Am. Legion, 1971; recipient Lifetime Achievement award, St. Helena C. of C., 2006. Mem.: Kiwanis Club (St. Helena chpt. pres. 1969, St. Helena chpt. treas. 1971—78, St. Helena chpt. sec. 1978—92, 1997—, divsn. gov. 8 1970—71, chmn. vocat. guidance com. 1971—72, chmn. agrl. & conservation com. 1973—74, chmn. adminstrn. zone 1 1974—75, chmn. major emphasis com. 1975—76, chmn. learning disabilities 1976—77, chmn. anatomical gift act com. 1982—83, 1983—84). Office: Napa Valley Family Med Group 1222 Pine St Saint Helena CA 94574-9554

DARTER, THOMAS EUGENE, JR., composer, musician, writer; b. Livermore, Calif., Feb. 13, 1949; s. Thomas Eugene and Vivian Lorene Darter; m. Sibyl Heishman, Dec. 3, 1977 (div. Feb. 1992); children: Erika Borges, Lisa, Allana; m. Karen Lucille Hogan, Sept. 21, 1996. BA summa cum laude, Cornell U., 1969, MFA, 1972, D in Musical Arts, 1979. Instr. music theory and composition Roosevelt U., Chgo., 1972-75; editor Keyboard Mag., Cupertino, Calif., 1975-85, mng. editor, 1991-94, editor San Mateo, Calif., 1994-97, pub., 1997-98; editor AfterTouch Mag., Buena Park, Calif., 1986-89; engring. publs. mgr. Coactive Networks, Sausalito, Calif., 2000-01; freelance musician, writer, 1998—. Dir. contemporary music ensemble Roosevelt U., Chgo., 1972-75; lectr. music/film dept. U. So. Calif., LA, 1984-88; cons. editor Keyboard Mag., Cupertino, 1990-91. Composer, pianist Scatter: Manring Kassin Darter Live in San Francisco, 2002; arranger Monk Suite (Kronos Quartet), 1985, Music of Bill Evans (Kronos Quartet), 1986. 1st prize Nat. Fedn. Music Clubs, 1969, 71. Mem. Am. Fedn. Musicians, Phi Beta Kappa, Phi Kappa Phi. Home: 750 South L St Livermore CA 94550 Personal E-mail: tdarter@sbcglobal.net.

DARVAROVA, ELMIRA, musician, concertmaster; b. Bulgaria; came to U.S., 1986; MusB, State Conservatory, Sofia, Bulgaria, 1977, MusM, 1979; certificate, Guildhall Sch. Music, London, 1982; artist's diploma, Ind. U., 1987. Concertmaster Plovdiv (Bulgaria) Philharm. Orch., 1979-86, Owensboro (Ky.) Symphony Orch., 1986-88, Evansville (Ind.) Philharm., 1987-88; artistic dir., concertmaster Evansville Chamber Orch., 1987-88; assoc. instr. violin Ind. U. Sch. Music, Bloomington, 1986-88; acting concertmaster Rochester (N.Y.) Philharm., 1988. Vis. lectr. Ind. U. Sch. Mus., 1988; guest concertmaster Columbus Symphony Orch., Columbus, Ohio, 1988; concertmaster Met. Opera Orch., NYC, 1989-2002, Chgo. Grant Park Symphony, 1990-2003; founding mem. New World Trio, 1991; performer at various recitals and concerts throughout the world. Recipient 1st medal internat. competition, Barcelona, Spain, 1979, hon. diploma, prize Tchaikovsky competition, Moscow, 1982, silver medal Viotti internat. competition, Vercelli, Italy, 1984, 3d prize internat. competition, Sion, Switzerland, 1985. Achievements include first woman concertmaster in Metropolitan Opera history. Avocations: reading, languages.

DARVILL, ALAN G., biochemist, botanist, educator; b. Redditch, Worchester, Eng., Jan. 27, 1952; came to U.S., 1976; s. Bryan Richard and Pamela Mary Darvill; m. Janet Elizabeth Jones, July 12, 1975; 1 child, Sarah Jayne. BS in Plant Biology, Wolverhampton Poly., UK, 1973; PhD in Plant Physiology, Univ. Coll. Wales, Aberystwyth, 1976. Postdoctoral assoc. U. Colo., Boulder, 1976—78, sr. rsch. assoc., 1978—83, asst. prof. dept. molecular, cellular and devel. biology, 1983—84, assoc. prof., 1984—85; assoc. prof. dept. biochemistry and plant biology U. Ga., Athens, 1985—87, prof., 1988—2003, Regents prof., 2003—, assoc. dir. Complex Carbohydrate Rsch. Ctr., 1985—87, dir., 1987—, co-dir. Ctr. for Plant & Microbial Complex Carbohydrates, 1987—. Adminstrv. dir. NIH Nat. Ctr. Rsch. Resources Integrated Glycotech, 1999—; adminstrv. dir. NIH/NCRR integrated tech. Biomed. Glycomics, 2004—. Contbr. more than 199 articles to profl. jours. Mem. AAAS, Am. Chem. Soc. (exec. com. divsn. carbohydrate chemistry 1993—, chmn. divsn. carbohydrate chemistry 1994-95), Soc. for Complex Carbohydrates. Office: U Ga Complex Carbohydrate Rsch Ctr 315 Riverbend Rd Athens GA 30602-4712

DARVISH, DANIEL K., research and development company executive, director; s. Shan and Shoku Darvish; m. Sheila H. Alviar, Apr. 12, 2003. MD, George Washington U., DC, 1993. Diplomate Am. Bd. Internal Medicine, 1996. Bd. mem. Advancement Rsch. Myopatheis, Encino, Calif., 1999—2002; clin. dir., cons. HIBM Rsch. Group, Encino, 2003—. Grantee, Advancement of Rsch. for Myopathies, 2003—. Mem.: Am. Soc. Gene Therapy. Achievements include development of non-profit clinical laboratory model; accelerated the development of a treatment for a rare muscle disease known as Hereditary Inclusion Body Myopathy (HIBM) or Distal Myopathy with Rimmed Vacuoles (DMRV). Office: HIBM Rsch Group 16661 Ventura Blvd #311 Encino CA 91436 Home Phone: 818-621-2395; Office Phone: 818-789-1044. Home Fax: 818-337-7250. Personal E-mail: ddarvish@hibm.org.

DARWIN, DAVID, engineering educator, consultant; b. NYC, Apr. 17, 1946; s. Samuel David and Earle D.; m. Diane Marie Mayer, June 29, 1968; children: Samuel David, Lorraine Marie. BS in Civil Engring., Cornell U., 1967, MS in Structural Engring., 1968; PhD in Civil Engring., U. Ill., 1974. Lic. profl. engr., Kans. Asst. prof. civil engring. U. Kans., Lawrence, 1974-77, assoc. prof., 1977-82, prof., 1982—, Deane E. Ackers disting. prof. civil engring., 1990—, dir. Structural Engring. and Materials Lab., 1982—; dir. Infrastructure Rsch. Inst., 1998-2001, 2003—. Cons. David Darwin, Lawrence, 1976—. Author: Steel and Composite Beams with Web Openings, 1990; co-author: Concrete, 2d edit., 2003, Design of Concrete Structures, 13th edit., 2004; contbr. articles to profl. jours. Mem. Uniform Bldg. Code Bd. Appeals, Lawrence, 1978-84. Capt. U.S. Army, 1967-72, Vietnam. Decorated Bronze Star with oak leaf cluster; recipient Miller award, U. Kans., 1986, Irvin Youngberg Rsch. Achievement award, 1992, Civil and Environ. Engring. Alumni Assn. Disting. Alumnus award, U. Ill., 2003; grantee, NSF, 1976—2003, Kans. Dept. Transp., 1980—82, 1990—, Air Force Office Sci. Rsch., 1985—92, Civil Engring. Rsch. Found., 1991—95, Fed. Hwy. Adminstrn., 1994—98, 2001—, SD Dept. Transp., 2001—, Nat. Coop. Hwy. Rsch. Program, 1994—95; Bellows scholar, 2001, Miller scholar, 2004. Fellow ASCE (editor Jour. Structural Engring. 1994-00, bd. govs. Structural Engring. Inst. 2000-04, treas. 2003-04, Kans. sect. v.p., pres.-elect 2001-02, pres. 2002-03, Huber Rsch. prize 1985, Moisseiff award 1991, state-of-the-art of civil engring. award 1996, 2000, Richard R. Torrens award 1997), Am. Concrete Inst. (pres. Kans. chpt. 1975, bd. dirs. 1988-91, 2005—, v.p. 2005-07, exec. com. 2005—, pres. 2007—, Bloem Disting. Svc. award 1986, Arthur R. Anderson award 1992, Structural Rsch. award 1996, Joe W. Kelly award 2005); mem. AAAS, ASTM (award of appreciation 2003), Am. Soc. Engring. Edn., Am. Inst. Steel Constrn., Prestressed Concrete Inst., Post-Tensioning Inst., Concrete Rsch. Coun. (chmn. 1990-96), Structural Engring. Inst. (bd. govs. 2000-04, treas. 2003-04), Wire Reinforcement Inst. (hon.), Phi Kappa Phi (pres. U. Kans. chpt. 1976-78). Democrat. Unitarian Universalist. Achievements include development of standard method of design for structural steel and composite beams with web openings. Avocations: swimming, walking. Office: U Kans Civil Environ and Archtl Engring Dept 2142 Learned Hall 1530 W 15th St Lawrence KS 66045-7609 Home Phone: 785-841-2888; Office Phone: 785-864-3827. E-mail: daved@ku.edu.

DARWOOD, JOHN JOSEPH, physician; b. Van Wert, Ohio, Feb. 6, 1956; s. Arthur Joseph and Marilyn Ruth Darwood; m. Maria Lynne Darwood; children: Elizabeth Ruth, Rachel Ann. BS, Toledo U., Ohio, 1978; MD, Wright State U., 1983, MS, 1989. Diplomate Am. Bd. Family Practice, Am. Bd. Preventive Medicine, Am. Bd. Occupl. Medicine, Am. Bd. Aerospace Medicine. Resident in family practice Good Samaritan Hosp., Dayton, Ohio, 1983-86; occupl. medicine physician Indsl. Med. Ctr., Dayton, 1986-90; physician Comprehensive Health Svcs. Kennedy Space Ctr. NASA, Fla., 1990—. Fellow Am. Acad. Family Physicians, Am. Coll. Occupl. and Environ. Medicine; mem. Nat. Mgmt. Assn. (chpt. pres. 1995-96, 2000-01, chpt. chmn. bd. dirs. 1997-99). Office: Chs 005 Kennedy Space Center FL 32899-0001

DAS, ASHOKE KUMAR, internist, consultant; b. Calcutta, W. Bengal, India, Nov. 1, 1934; came to U.S., 1974; s. Srikrishna and Durgeshnandini (Bose) D.; m. Geeta Mukhopadhyay, Aug. 15, 1961 (dec. 1993); 1 child, Arnab. MBBS, Calcutta U., 1957, MD, 1962, PhD, 1971. Diplomate Royal Coll. Physicians London, Am. Bd. Internal Medicine. Rotating intern NRS Med. Coll. Hosp., Calcutta, 1956, resident, 1957-58; chief resident Stafford Gen. Infirmary UK, 1970; chief resident internal medicine and cardiology Rush Green Hosp. UK, 1971-74; attending physician Our Lady Mercy Med. Ctr., Bronx, 1976—; chief sect. internal medicine Morrisania Clin., Bronx, 1980-83; pvt. practice Bronx, 1983—; attending physician St. Barnabas Hosp., Bronx, 1983—, Bronx Lebanon Hosp. Ctr., 1983—. Clin. asst. prof. medicine NY Med. Coll.; cons. in field. Indian Coun. Med. Rsch. grantee, 1958-59. Fellow ACP, Royal Coll. Physicians. (Eng.), Royal Soc. London; mem. AMA, NY State Med. Soc., Bronx Med. Soc., U. Calcutta Med. Assn. Am., Assn. Physicians India (US), Lions Club (mem. fundraising campaign 1995—, v.p. 1999, pres. 2001, dir. 2005-). Avocations: walking, travel. Office: 2940 Grand Course Apt SA Bronx NY 10458 Office Phone: 718-933-6655.

DAS, BISWAJIT, electrical engineer, educator; BS with honors, Indian Inst. Tech., Kharagpur, India, 1980; PhD, Purdue U., West Lafayette, 1989. Asst. prof. U. Notre Dame, Ind., 1990—94; assoc. prof. W.Va. U., Morgantown, 1994—2002; prof. U. Nev., Las Vegas, 2003—; dir. Nev. Nanotechnology Ctr., Las Vegas, 2006—. Cons. in field; lectr. in field. Recipient Outstanding Tchg. award, U. Notre Dame, 1991, W.Va. U., 1996, 1997, Barrick Disting. Scholar award, U. Nev., 2007; grantee, NSF, 1991—2007, Dept. Energy, 1991—2007, Dept. Def., 1991—2007. Mem.: AAAS, Electrochem. Soc. (assoc.), Am. Chem. Soc. (assoc.), Optical Assn. Am. (assoc.). Achievements include invention of Datta-Das transistor; research in the field of Spintronics; nonlithographic nanoparticles; discovery of lifting of spin degeneracy in two dimensonal systems; development of nonlithographic nanomanufacturing system; patents pending in field. Office: Univ Nevada 4505 Maryland Pkwy Las Vegas NV 89154 Office Phone: 702-895-2530. Office Fax: 702-254-9928. Personal E-mail: eeprofessor@hotmail.com.

DAS, JAGABANDHU, chemist, researcher; b. Gadi Bero, West Bengal, India, June 14, 1950; s. Gopal Krishna and Siddeswari Das; m. Chandra Datta, Dec. 31, 1985. BS with honors, Calcutta U., 1971; MS, Patna U., India, 1973; PhD, U. NB, Fredericton, 1978. Rsch. fellow Harvard U., Cambridge, Mass., 1978—82, Bristol-Myers Squibb Co., Princeton, NJ, 1982—. Contbr. articles to profl. jours. Recipient Patna U. Gold medal, Patna U., India, 1973; Nat. scholar, Govt. of India, 1967—70, N. L. scholar, 1971—73. Mem.: NY Acad. Sci., Am. Chem. Soc. Achievements include patents in field; invention of anti-cancer drug dasatinib, trade name SPRYCEL. Office: Bristol-Myers Squibb Co Rt 206 & Provinceline Rd PO Box 4000 Princeton NJ 08543-4000 Office Phone: 609-252-5068. Office Fax: 609-252-6804.

DAS, KALYAN, lawyer; b. Calcutta, India, June 23, 1956; s. Amulyaratan and Chaitaly (Mitra) D.; m. Pia Mukherjee, Feb. 18, 1986; children: Sabrina, Rahul. Barrister-at-Law, The Lincoln's Inn, London, 1979; diploma, Assoc. of the Chartered Inst. of Arbitrators, London, 1980; LLM, NYU, 1989. Bar: Eng. 1979, Wales 1979, N.Y. 1983; advocate Supreme Ct. India, 1981; barrister and solicitor Melbourne, Australia, 1984. Barrister-at-law Fountain Ct. Temple, London, 1980-81; assoc. Malcolm A. Hoffmann, NYC, 1981-82, White & Case, LLP, NYC, 1983-88, Milbank, Tweed, Hadley & McCloy, LLP, NYC, 1988-90, Seward & Kissel LLP, NYC, 1990-93, ptnr., head global banking and instl. fin. restructuring/workout group, 1993—. Editor: Company Law, 1980. Internat. life v.p. Internat. Students' Trust, London, 1987—. Fellow Am. Coll. Investment Counsel (co-chair ann. meeting 1998, trustee 2004—); mem. ABA, N.Y. State Bar Assn., Assn. Bar City of N.Y., Am. Arbitration Assn. (panel mem.), Hon. Soc. Lincoln's Inn, Wine Soc. London, Met. Club (N.Y.C.). Avocation: travel. Home: 107 W 89th St Penthouse A and B New York NY 10024-1944 Office: Seward & Kissel LLP 1 Battery Park Plz Fl 23 New York NY 10004-1485 also: Seward & Kissel LLP No 1 Poultry London EC2R 8JR England Office Phone: 011-49-207-405-4048, 212-574-1391. Business E-Mail: das@sewkis.com.

DAS, KOUSHIK K., industrial researcher; arrived in US, 1998; s. Bishnu Pada and Gita Das; m. Neepa Biswas, Jan. 5, 2003. B in Tech. with honors, Indian Inst. Tech., Kharagpur, India, 1998; MS in Engring., U. Mich., Ann Arbor, 2000, PhD, 2003. Grad. student rsch. asst. U. Mich., Ann Arbor, 1998—2003; rsch. staff mem. IBM TJ Watson Rsch. Ctr., Yorktown Heights, NY, 2003—. Mem. conf. organizing com. IBM TJ Watson Rsch. Ctr., Yorktown Heights, NY, 2005—06, mem. tech. program com., 2005—06; presenter in field. Contbr. chapters to books, articles to profl. jours. Joint sec. Lipilekha, West Chester, NY, 2006—07, exec. com. mem., 2006—07. Recipient Pres. India Gold medal, Indian Inst. Tech., 1998, First Plateau Invention Achievement award, IBM; fellow, Princeton U., 1998, Cornell U., 1998. Mem.: IEEE (tech. conf. program com. 2004—06, conf. tech. program com. 2005, track chair, session chair), Assn. Computing Machinery (symposium tech. program com. 2005—06, session chair), Delta Epsilon Iota (life). Achievements include patents for a method of reducing leakage current in Sub-1 V SOI Circuits; low-leakage integrated circuits and dynamic logic ckts; patents pending in field. Home: 6 Laurie Rd Cortlandt Manor NY 10567 Office: IBM TJ Watson Research Center PO Box 218 Yorktown Heights NY 10598 Business E-Mail: kkdas@us.ibm.com.

DAS, SUMAN KUMAR, plastic surgeon, researcher; b. Calcutta, India, May 6, 1944; came to U.S., 1980; s. Bisweswar and Devi Rani (Ghosh) D.; m. Carole Ellen Simmons, July 10, 1976 (div. Apr. 1984); children: Louise Angelique, Natalie Krishna; m. Rosyln Tanner, Mar. 22, 1991. B of Medicine and Surgery, Calcutta U., India, 1967; MD, Ednl. Commn. Fgn. Med. Grad., 1981. Diplomate Am. Bd. Plastic Surgery. Intern R.G. Kar Med. Coll. and Hosp., Calcatta, 1966-67, resident in gen. surgery, house officer, 1967-68; sr. house officer in accident and emergency, orthopaedics Royal Infirmary, Bolton, Lancs, Eng., 1968-69, house surgeon in gen. surgery, 1969-70; sr. house officer in gen. surgery Royal United Hosp., St. Martin's Hosp., Bath, Eng., 1970-72; house officer in medicine Whiston Hosp., Prescot, Liverpool, Eng., 1970; registrar in gen. surgery Frenchay Hosp., Bristol, Eng., 1972-73, sr. house officer in plastic surgery, 1973-74; registrar in plastic surgery Frenchay Hosp., Bristol, Eng., 1974, Royal Victoria Infirmary, Fleming Meml. Children's Hosp., Newcastle-Upon-Tyne, Eng., 1974-77; fellow in plastic and reconstructive surgery Hosp. for Sick Children, Toronto, Ont., Can., 1978; fellow in micro and hand surgery St. Vincent's Hosp., Melbourne, Australia, 1979-80, asst. plastic surgeon, 1979-80; rsch. assoc. in plastic surgery UCLA Med. Ctr., 1980-82; co-dir. microsurgery tng. program Harbor/UCLA Med. Ctr., 1980-82; dir. plastic surgery rsch. VA Wadsworth Med. Ctr., LA, 1980-82; resident in plastic surgery U. Miss. Med. Ctr., Jackson, 1982-83, sr. and chief resident in plastic surgery, 1983-84; pvt. practice Jackson, 1984-86; chief and asst. prof. div. plastic surgery U. Miss. Med. Ctr., Jackson, 1986-87, chief and assoc. prof. div. plastic surgery, 1987-90, prof. plastic surgery, chief div. plastic surgery, chief, 1990-95, clin. prof. plastic surgery, 1995—. Cons. plastic surgery Miss. Bapt. Med. Ctr., River Oaks Hosp.; attending Meth. Rehab. Ctr., U. Miss. Med. Ctr., River Oaks East Hosp., St. Dominiso

Hosp.; vis. prof. dept. surgery divsn. plastic surgery U. Calif., San Francisco, 1981, U. Ala., 1992; mem. patient care com. U. Miss., Jackson, 1990—92; pres. internet co. Nxmed.com. Inc., 1999—2003; dir. St. Dominic Ambulatory Surgery Ctr., 1999—2004; med. dir. St. Dominic's Ambulatory Surgery Ctr., 1999—2004, pres., 2003—04; dir. outreach program St. Dominic Hosp.; presenter and exhibitor in field at numerous profl. meetings. Author: (with others) Manual of Operative Plastic and Reconstructive Surgery, 1980, Textbook of Surgery, 2nd edit., 1988, Ency. of Flaps, 1990; mem. editorial bd. So. Med. Jour., 1993-1999; contbr. articles to Brit. Jour. Surgery, Brit. Jour. Plastic Surgery, Indian Jour. Dermatology, Hand, Plastic Surgery Forum, Jour. Singapore Acad. Sci., Jour. Oral Surgery, Plastic Reconstrn. Surgery, Acta Anatomica, Jour. Clin. Pathology, others; inventor turmeric on wound healing. Pres. NxMed.com Internet Distant Edn., 2000—. Recipient prize North Eng. Surg. Soc., 1977, Plastic Surgery Ednl. Found. Rsch. grant 1983-84, other grants Eli Lilly 1989, Tyra, 1989, Collagen Corp. 1989, 90-91, NIH, 1989, Am. Soc. Aesthetic Plastic Surgery, 1990, 91. Fellow ACS, Royal Coll. Surgeons London, Royal Coll. Surgeons Edinburgh (traveling scholarship 1976); mem. AMA, AAAS, Am. Fedn. for Clin. Rsch., Am. Assn. Hand Surgery (rsch. grant com. 1990-91, chmn. rsch. grant com. 1992), Am. Assn. Acad. Plastic Surgeons (fellowship com. 1990), Am. Soc. Plastic and Reconstructive Surgeons, Am. Assn. Plastic Surgeons, Internat. Soc. Burn Injuries, Internat. Soc. Reconstructive Microsurgery, Internat. Soc. Surgery, Internat. Soc. Emergency Medicine and Critical Care (charter), Brit. Assn. Plastic Surgeons (best prize and cert. 1967), Brit. Soc. Surgery of Hands (European traveling scholarship 1977), Soc. N.Am. Skull Base Surgery (founding), Miss. State Med. Assn., Plastic Surgery Rsch. Coun., N.Y. Acad. Sci., S.E. Soc. Plastic and Reconstructive Surgeons (program com. 1990—, trustee 1997-2000, historian 2000-01, chmn. CME com. 1999—, asst. sec. 2001—, v.p. 2005-06, pres. elect 2006-07, pres. 2007—), Miss. Acad. Scis. (chmn. 1992), Acad. Surg. Rsch., Assn. for Acad. Surgery, Southeastern Surg. Congress, Internat. Fedn. Surg. Colls., So. Med. Assn. (chmn. 1992), Miss. Children's Mus. (ptnrs. advisory bd. mem.) 2007, Cmty. Found. of Greater Jackson (trustee 2007-), Lions Club (Flora), Sigma Xi. Achievements include discovery that silicone does not elicit any change in T cell population; that capsular contracture with silicone implant is not an immunological effect; rsch. on best treatment for finger tip amputation in children, size and lengthening of human omentum, muscle transplantation by microvascular technique fatigue like normal muscle. Home: 242 Highland Hills Ln Flora MS 39071-9613 Office: 2629 Ct House Cir Flowood MS 39232 Office Phone: 601-362-0611. Office Fax: 601-362-0192. Personal E-mail: Sushrata@aol.com.

DAS, SUNIL R., computer scientist, educator; s. Tarak N. and Kshiroda S. Das; m. Sipra Roy, July 23, 1967; 1 child, Polly Mukherjee. Intermediate in sci., U. Calcutta, India, 1954, BSc in Physics with honors, 1956, MSc in Tech., 1960, PhD in Radiophysics, 1965. Lectr. U. Calcutta, Inst. Radiophysics & Electronics, 1965—67, pool officer, reader, 1972—77; postdoctoral fellow, vis. prof. Elec. Engring. Dept. U. Ottawa, 1967—72, from assoc. prof. to full prof. Elec. & Computer Engring. Dept., 1982—2002, prof. emeritus sch. info. tech. engring., 2002—; prof. CIS Dept. Troy U., Montgomery, Ala., 2003—. Vis. rsch. prof. Inst. Computer Engring. Nat. Chiao Tung U., Hsinchu, Taiwan, 1977—82; vis. prof. ctr. reliable computing Stanford U., Calif., 1991; vis. scientist Computer Sci. Divsn. U. Calif., Berkeley, 1997. Author: (book) Distributed Mutual Exclusion Algorithms, 1992; contbr. articles to profl. jours. Recipient Good People, Good Deeds award, ROC, 1981, Best Paper award, Rudolph Christian Karl Diesel, 2000, C.V. Ramamoorthy Disting. Scholar award, Soc. Design & Process Sci., 2007; fellow, 1998, Can. Acad. Engring., 2002; grantee Rsch. fellow, Engring. Inst. Can., 2005. Fellow: IEEE (life; editor 1991—, Tech. Achievement award 1996, Meritorious Svc. award 1997, Golden Core award 1998, Certificate of Appreciation award 1998, Donald G. Fink Prize Paper award 2003, Certificates of Appreciation award 1999); mem.: Soc. Design and Process Sci., Internat. Assn. Sci. and Tech. for Devel., Assn. Computing Machinery. Hinduism. Achievements include research in switching circuit theory and computer design; built-in self-test in very large-scale integration and data compression; microarchitecture and microprogram optimization; system-on-chip design and test; graph theory and combinatorics. Avocation: travel. Office: Troy Univ Computer and Info Sci Dept Maxwell-Gunter AFB 100 Turner Blvd Montgomery AL 36103 Office Phone: 613-562-5800 ext. 6216. Personal E-mail: das@site.uottawa.ca. Business E-Mail: sdas@troy.edu.

DASARI, GANESWARA R., oil industry executive; s. Venkat R and Seeta R Dasari; m. Usha S Chava, Dec. 22, 1996; children: Shobha, Shourav. B Engring., Andhra U., 1988; M Tech., Indian Inst. Tech. Kharagpur, 1991; PhD, Cambridge U., 1996. Offshore engr. Fugro Ltd, London, 1996—97; rsch. assoc. Cambridge U., England, 1997—2000; asst. prof. Nat. U. Singapore, 2000—03; sr. rsch. engr. ExxonMobil Upstream Rsch. Co., Houston. Cons. Drb Hicom, Kaulalumpur, Malaysia, 2000—. Mem.: ASCE (assoc.), Soc. Petroleum Engrs. (assoc.), Cambridge Commonwealth Trust (life), Cambridge Philos. Soc. (life). Achievements include research in role of geomechanics in reservoir engineering; development of methodology to predict mine burial for Office of Naval Research. Office: ExxonMobil Upstream Research Company 3120 Buffalo Speedway URC-N344 Houston TX 77252-2189 Home Phone: 281-412-9300; Office Phone: 713-431-4844. Business E-Mail: ganeswara.r.dasari@exxonmobil.com.

DASBURG, JOHN HAROLD, restaurant executive; b. NYC, Jan. 7, 1943; s. Jean Henry and Alice Etta Dasburg; m. Mary Lois Diaz, July 6, 1968; children: John Peter, Kathryn. AA, U. Miami, 1963; BS in Indsl. Engring., U. Fla., 1966, MBA, 1971, JD, 1973. Bar: Fla. 1974; CPA, Fla., Md. Staff Peat Marwick Mitchell & Co., Jacksonville, Fla., 1973-78, tax ptnr. in charge, 1978-80; v.p. tax Marriott Corp., Washington, 1980-82, v.p. fin., 1982-84, sr. v.p., 1984-85, exec. v.p., CFO, chief real estate officer, 1985-88, pres. lodging group, 1988-89; pres., CEO Northwest Airlines, 1990-2001; chmn. Burger King Corp., Miami, Fla., 2001—03, pres., CEO, 2001—02; chmn., CEO, pres. Astar Air Cargo, Inc., Miami, 2003—. Bd. dirs. St. Paul Travelers Cos., WCI Cmtys., Inc., Winn Dixie Stores, Inc. Contbr. articles to profl. jours. Lt. (j.g.) USN, 1966-69, Vietnam. Republican. Roman Catholic. Office: Astar Air Cargo Inc 2 S Biscayne Blvd Ste 3663 Miami FL 33131 Office Phone: 305-982-0500.

DASCHER, PAUL EDWARD, dean, accounting educator; b. Oct. 1, 1942; s. Albert Jacob abd Ruth (Mountney) D.; m. Nancy Patricia Byrne; children: Mitchell Paul, Heidi Beth. BS, Pa. State U., 1964, MS, 1966, PhD, 1969. Instr. acctg. Pa. State U., 1968-69; asst. prof. acctg. Va. Poly. Inst., Blacksburg, 1969-71, assoc. prof. acctg., 1971-73; prof. acctg. Drexel U., Phila., 1973-93, dept. head, 1974-77, dean Coll. of Bus. and Adminstrn., 1977-93; dean Sch. Bus. Adminstrn. Stetson U., Deland, Fla., 1993—2004, prof. acctg., 1993—, M.E. Rinker, Sr. dist. prof., 2002—. Vis. prof. Northeastern U., Boston, 1976; cons. Price Waterhouse and Co., N.Y.C., 1974-75; lectr. in field. Co-author: Financial Accounting, 1980, 4th edit., 1995, Accounting Readings, 1982, Managerial Accounting, 1985, 11th edit., 2002; contbr. numerous articles to profl. jours. Fellow Price Waterhouse & Co., Armstrong Cork Co.; recipient Socio-Econ. Disting. Svc. award Nat. Assn. Accts., 1973, 75, 81, Faculty Appreciation award Drexel U., 1977, Commendation medal Phila. chpt. Pa. Inst CPAs, 1977, Meritorious Svc. award Cmty. Accts., 1981; named one of Outstanding Young Men of Am., 1979 Mem. Am. Acctg. Assn., Fin. Execs. Inst., Inst. Mgmt. Accts. (nat. v.p. 1989-90), Accts. for Pub. Interest (pres. 1986-89), Alpha Kappa Psi, Beta Alpha Psi, Beta Gamma Sigma. Republican. Lutheran. Avocations: tennis, reading. Office: Stetson U Sch Bus Adm Deland FL 32723 Office Phone: 386-822-7404. Business E-Mail: pdascher@stetson.edu.

DASCHLE, THOMAS ANDREW, former senator; b. Aberdeen, SC, Dec. 9, 1947; m. Linda Hall Daschle; children: Kelly, Nathan, Lindsay. BA, S.D. State U., 1969. Fin. investment rep.; chief legis. aide, field coordinator Sen. James Abourzek, 1973-77; mem. 96th-97th Congresses from 1st S.D. Dist., U.S. Ho. of Reps., 1979—87, 98th-99th Congresses at large, 1983-87; U.S. senator from S.D., 1987—2005; minority leader U.S Senate, 1996—2001, 2003—04, majority leader, 2001—03; spl. policy advisor Alston & Bird LLP, Washington, 2005—. Mem. agrl. nutrition and forestry com., mem. fin. com., rules com., co-chmn. Sen. Dem. steering and coord. com., co-chair Sen. Dem. tech. and comm. com., chmn. Sen. Dem. conf. com., co-chmn. Sen. Dem. policy com.; leader bipartisan effort; author, enforcer Agent Orange Act, 1991; authored, reformulated gasoline provisions of Clean Air Act Amendment 1990; bd. dir. Mascoma Corp., 2007-. Founder Am. Grown Found., 1987. Served to 1st lt. USAF, 1969-72. Recipient Nat. Commdr.'s award Disabled Am. Vets., 1980, Disting. Alumni award S.D. State U., 1997, VFW Congl. award VFW, 1997, Legislator of Yr. award Vietnam Vets. Am., 1997, Cert. Appreciation, Nat. Assn. Federally Impacted Sch., 1997, Congl. Leadership award Cmty. Anti-Drug Coalitions Am., 1997, Golden Triangle award Nat. Farmer's Union, 1997-98, Outstanding Vets. Adv. of Yr. award Disabled Am. Vets. Dept. S.D., 1998, Pres. Recognition award Nat. Indian Impacted Schs. Assn., 1998, Cert. Appreciation, Nat. Assn. Alcoholism and Drug Abuse Counselors, 1998, Diplomat award Rapid City C. of C., 1998, Disting. Svc. award Nat. Rural Electric Coop. Assn., 2000; named Outstanding Young Man of Yr., U.S. Jaycees, 1981, Friend of Edn., S.D. Edn. Assn., 1997, Person of the Yr., Nat. Assn. Concerned Vets., 1997, Legislator of Yr., Renewable Fuels Assn., 1998, Maj. Gen. Williamson's S.D. Nat. Guard Militia Man of 1998, S.D. Nat. Guard. Democrat. Roman Catholic. Office Phone: 202-756-3156. Business E-Mail: tom.daschle@alston.com.

DASENBROCK, REED WAY, state official, former academic administrator, literature educator; b. Sept. 18, 1953; Degree, McGill U., Oxford U.; PhD, Johns Hopkins U., 1982. Asst. prof. N.Mex. State U., Las Cruces, 1982—86, assoc. prof., 1986—91, prof. Eng., 1991—2001, dept. head, 1994; prof. English & dean Coll. Arts & Sci. U. N. Mex., Albuquerque, 2001—05, interim provost & v.p. acad. affairs, 2005—06, provost & v.p. acad. affairs, 2006—07; cabinet sec. higher end. N.Mex. Higher Edn. Dept., Santa Fe, 2007—. Jerome S. Cardin vis. chair humanities Loyola Coll., Md., 1992—93. Author (or editor): of 8 books & over 100 scholarly papers. Office: NMex Higher Edn Dept NMex Sch for Deaf campus 1068 Cerrillos Rd Santa Fe NM 87505-1650 Office Phone: 505-476-6500. Office Fax: 505-476-6511.*

DASGUPTA, ANIRBAN, statistician, researcher; b. Calcutta, India, Dec. 8, 1957; s. Pabitra Kumar and Mukti Dasgupta. BSc, Indian Statis. Inst., 1977, MSc, 1978, PhD, 1983. Assoc. prof. Purdue U., West Lafayette, Ind., 1989—93, prof., 1994—. Assoc. editor Jour. Am. Statistics Assn., 1996—99, Sankhya, 1998—2005, Annals of Statistics, 1998—2006;, author 75 jour. articles, over 100 publs. Fellow: Inst. of Math. Statistics (mem. broad editl. activities 1998—); mem.: Am. Math. Soc., Inst. Of Math. Stats. (jour. editorships 1998—2006). Achievements include research in Theory and Applications of Statistics and Probability. Office: Purdue Univ 150 N University St West Lafayette IN 47907 Home Phone: 765-463-1482; Office Phone: 765-494-6033. Office Fax: 765-494-0558; Home Fax: 765-494-0558. Business E-Mail: dasgupta@stat.purdue.edu.

DASGUPTA, ARIJIT (BAPI), agricultural products executive; b. Calcutta, India, Aug. 30, 1957; s. Mihir and Mira Dasgupta; m. Anna M. Dasgupta, Oct. 13, 1984; children: Ariana, Gianna. BSc, U. Bombay, 1979; MS, U. Akron, Ohio, 1981, PhD, 1985; MBA, Washington U., St. Louis, 2001. Comml. devel. mgr. Monsanto, St. Louis, 1995—96, corp. growth dir., 1996—97; country dir. Solutia, Bombay, 1997—98, bus. dir., aviation prodn. St. Louis, 1998—2000, bus. dir., nylon fibers Atlanta, 2000—03; dir. product mgmt. and innovation Johns Manivlle, Denver, 2003—05, dir., bldg. sci. platform Littleton, Colo., 2005—. R&d specialist Monsanto, Springfield, Mass., 1985—91, r&d mgr., 1993—95, r&d mgr, Brussels, 1991—95. Contbr. articles to profl. jours. Mem.: ASHRAE, Am. Soc. Healthcare Engrs., Am. Chem. Soc., Energy Efficient Bldg. Assn., Industry Rsch. Inst. Achievements include 7 patents in field. Avocations: guitar, trivia, native American history. Office: Hhns Manville 10100 Westute Ave Littleton CO 80127

DASGUPTA, INDRANIL, physician, educator; b. Barielly, India, May 24, 1960; arrived in US, 1961; s. Sunil Pryia and Krishna Dasgupta. BA in Philosophy, Duke U., 1982; MPH in Internat. Health, Loma Linda U., 1987; cert. epidemiology, Johns Hopkins U., 1987; MBA in Fin., George Washington U., 1989; MD, St. George U., Grenada, 1994. Diplomate Am. Bd. Internal Medicine, 1999, Am. Bd. Cardiovasc. Disease, 2005. Congl. intern US Ho. of Reps., Washington, 1983; rsch. asst. Harvard Med. Sch., Boston, 1983-84, Dartmouth U. Med. Sch., Hanover, NH, 1985-86; rsch. assoc. Loma Linda Sch. Pub. Health, Calif., 1986-87; congl. intern US Senator Ed Kennedy, Washington, 1988-89; med. resident Med. Coll. Pa.-Hahnemann U. Hosps., Phila., 1995-98, rsch. assoc., 1998-99, geriatric fellow Phila., 1998-99; cardiology fellow Robert Wood Johnson Med. Sch. U. Medicine and Dentistry NJ, Camden, 1999—2002, rsch. assoc., 1999—2002; clin. asst. prof. divsn. cardiology Jefferson Med. Coll., Phila., 2002—; attending cardiologist Thomas Jefferson U. Hosp., Phila., 2002—. Contbr. articles to profl. jours. Vol. Muscular Dystrophy Assn., Winston-Salem, NC, 1981, US Spl. Olympics, Wilmington, Del., 1985, Dem. Fund Raising, Washington, 1988; rsch. intern Select Com. Aging US House of Reps., 1983. Fellow: Am. Coll. Physicians, Soc. Geriatric Cardiology, Am. Coll. Cardiology; mem.: ACP, Am. Soc. Nuclear Cardiology, Internat. Soc. Heart and Lung Transplantation, NY Acad. Scis., NJ Acad. Sci., Nat. Assn. Advancement Sci., Am. Heart Assn., Delta Omega, Sigma Alpha Epsilon. Democrat. Avocations: travel, sailing, snorkling, soccer. Home: 2528 Tigani Dr Wilmington DE 19808 Office: Thomas Jefferson U Hosp Jefferson Heart Inst 925 Chestnut St Mezzanine Level Philadelphia PA 19107 Personal E-mail: indranildasgupta@aol.com.

DASGUPTA, PURNENDU KUMAR, chemist, educator, department chairman; b. Calcutta, India, Dec. 5, 1949; came to U.S., 1973; s. Nirmal Kumar and Mina (Sen) D.; m. Kajori Dasgupta; children: Michael Akash, Rivu Nalok. MSc, U. Burdwan, India, 1970; PhD, La. State U., 1977. Grad. asst., then instr. La. State U., Baton Rouge, 1973-78; asst. rsch. chemist U. Calif., Davis, 1979-81; asst. prof., then assoc. prof. Tex. Tech. U., Lubbock, 1981-88, prof. chemistry, 1988-92, Paul Whitfield Horn prof., 1992—; prof., chair U. Tex. at Arlington, 2007—. Chmn. sulfur subcom. Intersoc. on Analysis, Phila., 1986—. Assoc. editor Atmospheric Environ., 1990—; editl. bd. Talanta, 1990—, Analytica Chimica Acta, 1992—, Process Control and Quality, 1995—; co-author: Ion Chromatography, 1987, Measurement Challenges in Atmospheric Chemistry, 1993; contbr. over 300 articles to peer-reviewed jours. Recipient Frank Blood award Soc. Toxicology and Pharmacology, 1981, Traylor Creativity award Dow Analytical Scis., 1989, A.A. Benedetti-Pichler award, Am. Microchemical Soc., 1998, Scientistof the Yr. award ARCS, 2005, Outstanding Achievement award in ion chromatography, 2005. Mem. Am. Chem. Soc., Sigma Xi. Achievements include 17 U.S. patents. Office: U Tex Arlington Dept Chemistry Arlington TX 76019 Office Phone: 817-272-3171. Business E-Mail: dasgupta@uta.edu.

DAS GUPTA, SUBAL, physics professor, researcher; b. Calcutta, India, Aug. 11, 1939; emigrated to Can., 1960; s. Subodh Chandra and Pritilata (Sen) Das G.; m. Sanjukta Sen Gupta, Aug. 12, 1965; children: Monidipa, Nandini. MSc, Calcutta U., 1959; PhD, McMaster U., 1963. Nat. Scis. and Engring. Rsch. Coun. Can. post-doctoral fellow AECL, Chalk River, Ont., Can., 1963-64; rsch. sci. Tata Inst. for Fundamental Rsch., Bombay, 1964-65; postdoctoral fellow in physics McGill U., Montreal, Que., Can., 1965-66, asst. prof. physics, 1967-71, assoc. prof., 1972-77, prof., 1978—, chair dept. physics, 1993-97, prof. physics, 1997—2004, prof. emeritus, 2005—. Contbr. articles to profl. jours. Oper. grantee Nat. Sci. and Engring. Rsch. Coun., 1966—. Office: McGill U Dept Physics ERP 319 3600 University St Montreal PQ Canada H3A 2T8 Business E-Mail: dasgupta@physics.mcgill.ca.

DASGUPTA, SUMANTRA, education educator, researcher; b. Kalyani, India, Dec. 31, 1976; s. Saktibrata and Maitreyi Dasgupta. BE, Birla Inst. of Tech., India, 2000; MS, Tex. A&M U., College Station, 2003. Rsch. asst. Tex. A&M U., College Station, 2000—05, tchg. asst., rsch. assoc., advisor, 2006—. Recipient Tech Brief award, Johnson Space Ctr. NASA, 2004; scholar, Elec. Engring. Dept., Tex. A&M U., 2000; Rsch. Grant, Tex. Higher Edn. Coordination Bd., Advanced Tech. Program, 2000—02, Johnson Space Ctr. NASA, 2002—05. Mem.: Informs-Student Chpt., TAMU. Avocation: music. Home: 601 Cross St Apt #52 College Station TX 77840 Office: Texas A&M Univ University Dr College Station TX 77840 Home Phone: 979-229-1390; Office Phone: 979-229-1390. Personal E-mail: dsumantrad@gmail.com. Business E-Mail: sumantra-dasgupta@neo.tamu.edu.

DASH, LEON DECOSTA, JR., journalist; b. New Bedford, Mass., Mar. 16, 1944; s. Leon DeCosta and Ruth Elizabeth (Kydd). BA, Howard U., 1968; DHD, Lincoln U., 1996. Reporter Washington Post, 1966—68, 1971—79, African bur. chief, 1979—83, with investigations desk, 1984—98; prof. journalism U. Ill., Champaign, 1998—99, Swanlund chair prof. journalism, 2000—01, Swanlund prof. journalism, 2001—; prof. journalism Ctr. Advanced Study, 2003—. Vis. prof. U. Calif.-San Diego, 1978. Author (with Ben H. Bagdikian): (book) The Shame of the Prisons, 1972; author: When Children Want Children: The Urban Crisis of Teenage Childbearing, 1989, Rosa Lee: A Mother and Her Family in Urban America, 1996 (Polit. Book award Washington Monthly Mag., 1997, 1st prize Harry Chapin Best Book award World Hunger Yr. Orgn., 1997). Vol. Peace Corps, Kenya, 1969—70. Co-recipient Editl. award for news series, Chesapeake AP, 1987, Editl. award, 1989; named one of Best 100 Works in 20th Century Am. Journalism for 8-part series Rosa Lee's Story for Washington Post, 1999; recipient George Polk Meml. award, Overseas Press Club, 1974, award for internat. news reporting, Washington-Balt. Newspaper Guild, 1974, hon. mention, 1975, Internat. Reporting award, Africare, 1984, Capitol Press Club, 1984, 1st Place Journalism award for gen. news, Nat. Assn. Black Journalists, 1986, Investigative Reporters and Editors award, 1987, 1st Prize award, Washington-Balt. Newspaper Guild, 1987, Pres.'s award, Washington Ind. Writers Assn., 1989, Martha Albrand Spl. Citation for Nonfiction, PEN, 1990, Pulitzer Prize for explanatory journalism, 1995, 1st Prize Robert F. Kennedy award for print journalism, 1995, Emmy award for pub. affairs, NATAS, 1996, Polit. Book award, The Washington Monthly mag., 1997, Prevention for a Safer Soc. award, Nat. Coun. on Crime and Delinquency for Rosa Lee book, 1997; Henry J. Kaiser Family Found. fellow, 1995—96. Mem.: Kappa Tau Alpha. Office: U Ill Dept Journalism 119 Gregory Hall 810 S Wright St Urbana IL 61801-3644 Home Phone: 217-344-5169; Office Phone: 217-265-5055. Business E-Mail: leondash@uiuc.edu.

DASH, SANFORD MARK, aerospace scientist; b. NYC, May 26, 1943; s. Jack and Rachael (Calamar) D.; m. Barbara Gaile Held; children: David, Kenneth, Jonathan, Naomi. BSME, CCNY, 1964; MS in Aeronautics and Astronautics, NYU, 1966, PhD in Aeronautics and Astronautics, 1969. Rsch. scientist Gen. Applied Sci. Labs., Westbury, N.Y., 1969-77; cons. Aero. Rsch. Assocs. Princeton, N.J., 1977-80; v.p., mgr. propulsive scis. divsn. Sci. Applications Internat. Corp., Princeton, N.J., 1980-94; pres., chief scientist Combustion Rsch. and Flow Tech., Inc., Pipersville, Pa., 1994—. Cons. in field. Contbr. over 250 articles to profl. pubs., chpts. to books. Recipient Cert. of Recognition, NASA, 1975, USAF, 1985. Fellow: AIAA (assoc.; chmn. aero-acoustics tech. com. 1997—99, Aerospace Profl. of Yr. 2002); mem.: NATO and Joint Army, Navy, NASA, Air Force Coms. Achievements include development of U.S. standard plume flowfield models for aircraft and missiles; rsch. on Nat. Aerospace Plane Program; formulation of jet noise reduction concepts for military aircraft; research on scramjet technology for next generation missile system. Business E-Mail: dash@craft-tech.com.

DA SILVA, ERCIO MARIO, physician; b. Catajuczes, Minas, Brazil; s. Mario and Rosa (Pinto) da S.; m. Doris Hale da Silva, Aug. 22, 1953; children: Robert, Suzanne. MD, U. Mines, Brazil, 1949. Diplomate Am. Bd. Colon Rectal Surgery. Physician U.S. Mil. Base, Columbia, SC, 1988—. Mem. Am. Soc. Colon Rectal Surgery, Columbia Med. Soc. Home: 413 Brookshire Dr Columbia SC 29210-4203

DASILVA, LYNN JUDITH, special education educator; d. John and Sonia Luz DaSilva; children: Christian Daniel, Samantha Lillian. M in profl. studies, Adelphi U., Garden City, 1985. Cert. advanced studies Coll. St. Rose, N.Y., 2005, administrative supr. Coll. St. Rose, N.Y., 2005, dist. adminstr. Coll. St. Rose, N.Y., 2005, physical edn. tchr. K-12 1985. Pre-school hearing and speech impairments tchr. North Shore Hosp. Affiliate, Westbury, NY, 1984; physical edn. tchr. grades 1-8 Rockville Ctr. Union Free Sch. Dist., NY, 1985—; in-state head coach Nassau County Spl. Olympics, NY, 2000—02, area coord. NY, 2000—02. Roundtable spkr. N.Y. Health Dept., NY, 2005. Author: (book) Theatre of the Mind, 2005. Recipient Jenkins award, Spl. Edn. PTA, 1997, Jennie E. Hewitt PTA, 2002, Master Educator award, RVC Dist. Tchrs., 2003, Cert. of Achievement, N.Y. Health Dept., 2003, 2004, 2005, 2006. Mem.: Assn. for Athletics, Physical Edn., Recreation and Dance, N.Y. Assn. for Health, Physical Edn., Recreation and Dance. Avocations: writing, painting, bicycling, hiking, running. Home: 437 Little East Neck Rd S Babylon NY 11702 Personal E-mail: ldasilva21@optonline.net.

DASKIN, MARK STEPHEN, engineering educator; b. Balt., Dec. 3, 1952; s. Walter and Betty Jane (Fax) D.; m. Babette Reva Levy, July 2, 1978; children: Tamar, Keren. BSCE, MIT, 1974, PhD in Civil Engring., 1978; postgrad. study in Engring., Cambridge, England, 1975. Tchg. asst. trans. sys. divsn. civil engring. MIT, Cambridge, 1976-77; asst. prof. civil engring. U. Tex., Austin, 1978-79, Northwestern U., Evanston, Ill., 1980-83, assoc. prof. civil engring., 1983-89, prof., 1989—2006, chair dept. indsl. engring. and mgmt. scis., 1995—2001, Bette and Neison Harris prof. of tchg. excellence, 2006—. Author: Network and Discrete Location: Models, Algorithms and Applications, 1995; editor-in-chief Transp. Sci., 1991-94; assoc. editor Location Sci., 1991-2000; contbr. articles to profl. jours. Bd. dirs. North Suburban Synagogue Beth El, Highland Park, Ill., 1991-94. U. Tex. Bur. Engring. Rsch. grantee, 1978-79, Northwestern U. Transp. Ctr. grantee, 1980, 81, NSF grantee, 1980-82, 84-90, 93-96, 95-98, 96-99, 1998-2002, 02-04, 05—, Urban Mass Transp. Adminstr. grantee, 1982-84, 84-85, United Parcel Svc. grantee, 1983-86, 91-92, Thermo-King Corp. grantee, 1990-91, 92-94, Heartland Blood Ctr. grantee, 1992, 96, grantee Office Naval Rsch., 2005, other grants; recipient Fulbright Rsch. award, 1989-90, Burlington No. Found. Faculty Achievement award, 1985, NSF Presdl. Young Investigator award, 1984, Scott Paper Leadership award, 1973-75, IIE Tech. Innovation award in indsl. engring., Fred C. Crane disting. svc. award; INFORMS fellow, 2004 Fellow Inst. Indsl. Engrs. (editor-in-chief IEE Transactions 2001—04, Fred C. Crane award for disting. svc. 2005); mem. INFORMS (v.p. publs. 1996-99, pres.-elect 2005, pres. 2006, past pres. 2007), Ops. Rsch. Soc. Am. (jour. editor 1991-94), Inst. Mgmt. Sci., Sigma Xi, Tau Beta Pi, Chi Epsilon. Avocations: swimming, photography. Office: Northwestern U Dept Indsl Engring Mgmt Sci Evanston IL 60208-0001 Office Phone: 847-491-8796. Business E-Mail: m-daskin@northwestern.edu.

DASSANOWSKY, ROBERT VON, language and film professor, writer, producer; b. NYC, Jan. 28, 1960; s. Elfi von Dassanowsky. Grad., Am. Acad. Dramatic Arts, Pasadena; BA with honors, UCLA, 1985, MA, 1988, PhD, 1992. Actor, 1975—; asst. prof. German, UCLA, 1992-93; asst. prof. German U. Colo., Colorado Springs, 1993-99, assoc. prof. German and film, 1999—2006, head German studies, 1999—2006, dir. film studies, 1999—, interim chair dept. visual and performing arts, 2000-01, chair dept. langs. and cultures, 2001—, prof. German and film, 2006—. Vis. prof. German UCLA, 2007—. Author: (plays) The Birthday of Margot Beck, 1980, Briefly Noted, 1981, Vespers, 1982 (Beverly Hills Theatre Guild award 1984), Tristan in Winter, 1986, Songs of a Wayfarer, 1986, Coda, 1991, (criticism) Phantom Empires: The Novels of A. Lernet-Holenia and the Question of Postimperial Austrian Identity, 1996, Verses of a Marriage, Translation of Poetry Collection by Hans Raimund, 1996, Telegrams from the Metropole: Selected Poetry, 1999, Gale Encyclopedia of Multicultural America, 2nd edit., 2000; contbg. editl. advisor: International Dictionary of Films and Filmmakers, 4th edit., 2001, Mars in Aries, trans. of novel by A. Lernet-Holenia, 2003, Austrian Cinema: A History, 2005; co-editor New Austrian Film, 2008; founding editor Rohwedder: Internat. Jour. Lit. and Art, 1986-93; editor Pen Center mag., 1992-98; contbg. editor Osiris, Rampike, Poetry Salzburg Rev.; mem. editl. bd. Modern Austrian Lit., 1997-01; exec. prodr. The Nightmare Stumbles Past, 2002, Semmelweis, 2001, Wilson Chance, 2005; co-prodr. Epicure, 2002, Believe, 2003; assoc. prodr. The Archduke and Herbert Hinkel, 2007; columnist Celluloid Mag., Austria; mem. editl. bd. Modern Austrian Literature, 1997-2001; editl. adv. bd. Ariadne Press, 1999—; editor Press. of South, 2004-. Mem. bd. dirs. The Internt. Exptl. Cinema Exposition, Denver Brit. Film Festival. Recipient Order of the Vitez (Hungary), Decoration of Honor in Silver, Austria, 2005; Cultural grantee City of L.A., 1990, 91, 92; Pres.'s Fund for Humanities grantee U. Colo., 1996, 2001; named Colo. Prof. of Yr., Carnegie Found./Coun. for Advancement and Support of Edn., 2004; recipient Residency award Karolyi Found., France, 1979, Letters, Arts and Scis. Rsch. and Creative Work award U. Colo., 2002. Mem. MLA, PEN (West bd. dirs. L.A. 1992-99, founder and pres. Colo. chpt. 1994-99 2002-03), PEN Austria, Internat. Lernet-Holenia Soc. (v.p. 1998-2006), Austrian Am. Film Assn. (v.p. 1997—), Austria Mundi (US rep. 2002—), Soc. Cinema and Media Studies, Poets and Writers, Modern Austrian Lit. and Culture Assn. (mem. exec. coun. 2006—), L.A. Poetry Festival, SAG, Concordia Assn. Journalists and Writers (Austria), Am. Coll. Heraldry (bd. govs. 2000—), European Acad. Arts and Scis., U.S. Fencing Assn., Constantinian Order St. George, Mensa. Office: U Colo Dept Langs and Cultures Colorado Springs CO 80933-7150 Office Phone: 719-262-3562. E-mail: belvederefilm@yahoo.com.

DASSEL-STUKE, DONNA JANE, psychologist, educator; b. Evansville, Ind., Feb. 29, 1956; d. Forrest James Dassel and Doris Eileen (Edmonson) Vowels; m. Michael Charles Stuke, July 7, 1985; 1 child, James Conrad. Student, Harlaxton Coll., England, 1976; BS cum laude, U. Evansville, 1977, MS, 1981; postgrad., Kans. State U., Fort Hays State U., Emporia State U., Peru State Coll., Pitts. State U. Cert. sch. psychologist (nat.), 1988, endorsement early childhood 1992. Work adjustment supr. So. Ind. Rehab. Ctr., Boonville, 1978, work adjustment specialist, 1978—79; grad. asst. U. Evansville, 1979; vocat. evaluator Rehab. Ctr., Evansville, 1979—81; intern Evansville Vanderburgh Sch. Corp. & Rehab. Ctr., 1981; sch. psychologist Twin Lakes Co-op., Clay Center, Kans., 1981—83, Marshall-Nemaha Co. Edn. Svc. Co-op., Seneca, 1983—99; substitute tchr. Holton, 1999—2005, Sabetha, 1999—2005, Wetmore, Kans., 1999—2005, Hiawatha, Kans., 1999—2005, Fall City, Nebr., 1999—2005; prof. Highland C.C., Kans., 2000—. Mem.: Kans. Assn. Sch. Psychologists, Nat. Assn. Sch. Psychologists, Delta Kappa Gamma, Alpha Lambda Delta. Democrat. Presbyterian. Avocations: piano, swimming, fishing, baseball, basketball. Home: 311 S Mathews St Bern KS 66408-0151

DASTIN, BARRY L., lawyer; BA magna cum laude, Yale U., 1975; JD cum laude, Harvard U., 1978. Bar: NY 1979, Calif. 1985. Ptnr. corp. and fin. dept. Kaye Scholer LLP, LA. Office: Kaye Scholer LLP Ste 1700 1999 Ave of the Stars Los Angeles CA 90067 Office Phone: 310-788-1070. E-mail: bdastin@kayescholer.com.

DASTRUP-HAMILL, FAYE MYERS, city official; b. Sanford, Colo., Dec. 15; d. Earl Dixon and Kady Florence (Cornum) Faucett; m. Sherly K. Myers (dec.); children: Carla Pearce, Susan Kitley (dec.), Mary Jane James, Elizabeth Ireland; m. Merrill E. Dastrup, Sept. 22, 1972 (dec. July 1987); m. Wayne A. Hamill, Mar. 23, 1991. Student, L.D.S. Bus. Coll., 1934-35; grad., Dale Carnegie Inst., 1953; degree in mcpl. works adminstrn., Mt. San Antonio Coll., 1960; student, Syracuse U. Inst., 1968; degree in tech. reporting, Chaffey Coll., 1970. Legal sec. W. W. Platt, City Atty., Alamosa, Colo., 1935-40; sec. pub. works dept. City of Ontario, Calif., 1957-60, dep. city clk., dep. city treas. Calif., 1960-64, city clk. Calif., 1964-73, city coun. mem., mayor and mayor pro tem Calif., 1974-92; mem. part 150 implementation com. Ontario Airport, Calif., 1993—, chmn. noise adv. com., dept. trans. State of Calif., 1994—. Sec. pers. dept. L.A. Housing Authority, 1948; mem. legis. subcom. So. Calif. Assn. Govts., chmn. hist. preservation and cultural arts com.; mem. revenue and taxation com. League of Calif. Cities, vice-chmn., chmn. Clks. Inst., gen. resolutions com., com. on environ. quality Inland Empire divsn.; chmn. San Bernardino County Planning Com., Criminal Justice; prese. So. Calif. City Clks. Assn., chmn. legis. com.; mem. exec. com. Valley Assn. of Cities; city coun. rep. Ontario Libr. Bd. Trustees. Escort sch. classes through City Hall; judge sci. fairs and sch. and comty. events; life mem. Friends of Ontario Libr.; mem., donor Friends of Mus. of History and Art, Ontario; pres., treas., trustee Ontario (Calif.) City Libr., 1993—; choir dir., life mem. Ch. of Jesus. Recipient plaque with gold gavel So. Calif. City Clks. Assn., 1972, Women Helping Women award Soroptimist Internat. of Ontario, 1981, 1990 Woman of Yr. award State Legislature, State of Calif., 1990, Woman of Achievement award 90s Women's Conf., 1990, 1994 YWCA Woman of Achievement award West End YWCA, 1994, Elizabeth S. Genee Lifetime Achievement award, West End YWCA, 1994, Bryce Denton award Mus. of History and Art, 1996, Outstanding Effort with Calif. Water plaque San Bernardino County Waterworks Dist. #8, 1986, Outstanding Svc. plaque Ontario Air N.G., 1990, Leadership plaque San Bernardino County Sheriff's Dept., 1993, Founding, Support and Encouragement of Crime Stoppers Spl. Recognition plaque Ontario Police Dept., 1993, Outstanding Comty. Svc. plaque U.S. Congressman Jay Kim, 1994, Plaque and Spl. Cert. congratulating receipt of Elizabeth Genee Lifetime Achievement award, 1994, Pub. Svc. Award trophy Adrian Meewis, 1972, plaque for dedicated and meritorious svc. to Ontario, as mayor City Coun. and City Clk., 1986, Lifetime Achievement plaque San Bernardino County Supr. Larry Walker, 1994, Svc. plaque South Coast Air Quality Mgmt. Dist., 1987, decorated plaque Salvation Army, 1992, others. Mem. Calif. Assn. Libr. Trustees and Commrs., Comty. Concert Assn. Pomona Valley (donor), Ontario C. of C. (life, Svc. Award plaque 1992), Musicians Club of Pomona Valley. Mem. Ch. of Jesus Christ of LDS. Avocation: vocal soloist. Home: 761 W Hawthorne St Ontario CA 91762-1510

DATA, ART J., information technology executive; B in Mech. Engring., Marquette Univ., 1972; MBA, DePaul Univ., 1985. With Danly Machine Tool Corp., 1968—75; joined Internat. Truck & Engine Corp. (operating co. of Navistar Internat. Corp.), Warrenville, Ill., 1975, various positions, including process engr. chief engr. computer tech., sr. project engr. for CAD engring., dir. bus. and tech. sys for engine group, 1975—93, v.p. info. tech., 1993—. Mem.: Tech. Executives Club, AITP, SIM, Soc. of Mfg. Engineers, Soc. of Automotive Engineers. Office: Internat Truck & Engine Corp 4201 Winfield Rd PO Box 1488 Warrenville IL 60555 Office Phone: 630-753-5528. Office Fax: 630-753-3982.

DATARS, WILLIAM ROSS, physicist, researcher; b. Desboro, Ont., Can., June 14, 1932; s. Albert John and Leona Alberta (Fries) D.; m. Eleanor Wismer, 1959 (dec. Oct. 2002); children: Timothy, Andrew, David. B.Sc., McMaster U., Hamilton, Ont., 1955; M.Sc., 1956; PhD, U. Wis., 1959. Physicist Def. Research Bd., 1959-62; mem. faculty McMaster U., 1962—, prof. physics, 1969-96, prof. emeritus, 1996—. E.W.R. Steacie fellow, 1968-70 Fellow Royal Soc. Can., Am. Phys. Soc.; mem. Can. Assn. Physics Lutheran. Home: RR 2 Lynden ON Canada L0R 1T0 Office: McMaster U Dept Physics & Astronomy Hamilton ON Canada L8S 4M1 Business E-Mail: datars@mcmaster.ca.

DATCU, IOANA, artist; b. Bucharest, Romania, Apr. 22, 1944; d. Marin and Niculina Datcu; m. Vasile Porcisanu, Aug. 5, 1967 (div. 1983); 1 child, Isabelle Ioana. BA, Pedagogical Inst., Bucharest, 1967; BFA summa cum laude, U. Minn., 1987, MFA, 1991. Tchr. biology high sch., Argova, Preasna, Romania, 1967—74; photography asst. U. Minn., St. Paul, 1985—86; photographer civil rights dept. City Hall, St. Paul, 1986—87; darkroom supervisor Film in the Cities, St. Paul, 1987—88; gallery asst., curator Paul Whitney Gallery, St. Paul, 1987—91; art instr. Minn. Mus. Am. Art, St. Paul, 1993—94; instr. drawing & painting U. Minn., Mpls., 1996—97. One-woman shows include Flanders Contemporary Art, Mpls., 1994, Winona (Minn.) State U, 1995, Mont. State U., Billings, 1996, Ea. Wash. U., Cheney, 1996, Indpls. Art Ctr., 1996, Kansas City (Mo.) Artists Coalition, 1997, Grants Pass (Oreg.) Mus. Art, 1997, Trinity Presbyn. Ch., Denton, Tex., 1998, South Bend (Ind.) Mus. Art, 1998, U. Dayton, Ohio, 2000, Concordia U., Seward, Nebr., 2004, exhibited in group shows at North Park Coll., Chgo., 1991, Hist. Trinity, Detroit, 1993, 1995—96, Barrett House Galleries, Poughkeepsie, N.Y., 1994, 1996, Katherine E. Nash Gallery, Mpls., 1992, 1995—96, Minot (ND) State U., 1995, Coll. St. Catherine, St. Paul, 1995, St. John's U., NY, 1995, Focal Point Gallery, NYC, 1996, SoHo Photo Gallery, 1997, Greater Lafayette Mus. Art, 1997, Truman State U., Mo., 1998, McNeese State U., La., 1998, Attelboro (Mass.) Mus. Art, 1998—99, New World Art Ctr., NYC, 1999, Ctrl. Mo. State U., 1999, Am. Bible Soc. Gallery, NYC, 2000, Internat. Print Triennial, Cracow, Poland, 2000, 2006, Krakow Nürnberg, Messezentrum Mus., Germany, 2000, Jewish Cmty. Ctr. Greater New Haven, Woodbridge, Conn., 2001, New American Pairings, Open Studio Press, 1995, Images of the Spirit Traveling Exhibit, 1995—97, CIVA CODEX III traveling exhibit, 1997—2001, Korean Cultural Ctr., LA, 2001, Grand Forks Art Gallery, Can., 2004, represented in, CD-Rom collections of Art Comms. Internat., 1995, Artmax Internat., 1995, Ency. Internat. Women Artists, Alliance Women Artists, 1997, New Art Internat., Book Art Press, 1997, Christianity and the Arts Jour., Internat. Print Triennial, 1999, Bridge to the Future, Nurnberg, 2000, The Missing Mary (by Charlene Spretnak), 2004, Faith and Vision: Twenty Five Years of Christians in the Visual Arts, 2005. Grantee Pollock-Krasner Found., 1992, Minn. State Arts Bd., 1994; Jerome Found. Residency fellow, 1994; McKnight Photography fellow, 1992, fellow Arts Midwest NEA, 1994-95, Clowes Fund regional residency fellow, Indpls., 1997; Vt. Studio Ctr. Residency award, Johnson, Vt., 1997. Mem. Christians in the Visual Arts, Nat. Assn. Women Artists, Inc. Mem. Eastern Orthodox Ch. Avocations: classical music, movies, yoga, literature. Home: 507 W 5th St Vermont IL 61484 Personal E-mail: ioanadatcu@yahoo.com.

DATE, ELAINE SATOMI, physiatrist, educator; b. San Jose, Calif., Feb. 19, 1957; BS, Stanford U., 1978; MD, Med. Coll. Pa., 1982. Diplomate of Nat. Bd. Med. Examiners. Diplomate Am. Bd. Phys. Medicine and Rehab. Dir. phys. medicine and rehab. Stanford (Calif.) U. Sch. Medicine, 1985—, rehab. medicine sect. chief, 1988-90, head phys. medicine and rehab. div., 1990—, assoc. prof. dept. functional rehab., 1995—; rehab. medicine chief Palo Alto (Calif.) VA Med. Ctr., 1988—. Fellow Am. Acad. Phys. Medicine and Rehab., Am. Assn. Electromyography and Electrodiagnosis. Avocations: reading, jogging.

DATILES, MANUEL BERNALDES, III, ophthalmologist, researcher; b. Manila, Feb. 26, 1951; arrived in U.S., 1979; s. Roberto Aguiling and Loretta (Bernaldes) Datiles; m. Jacqueline Romero, Mar. 13, 1976; children: Michelle, Joyce, Margaret, Jennifer, Manuel IV, Michael. BS cum laude, U. Santo Tomas, 1970, MD cum laude, 1974. Intern Jose Reyes Meml. Hosp. (North Gen. Hosp.); rsch. fellow Philippine Eye Rsch. Inst. U. Philippines, Manila, 1975—76; resident in ophthalmology U. Philippines-Philippine Gen. Hosp., Manila, 1976—79; rsch. scholar, vis. scientist Lab. Vision Rsch. Nat. Eye Inst.-NIH, Bethesda, Md., 1979—82; clin. fellow corneal and cataract surgery Wilmer Eye Inst.-Johns Hopkins U. Hosp., Balt., 1982—83; sr. staff ophthalmologist Nat. Eye Inst.-NIH, Bethesda, 1983—88, acting chief cornea and cataract sect., clin. svc. br., 1989—92, chief cornea and cataract sect., clin. svcs. br., 1992—2006; chmn. surg. adminstrv. com. NIH Clin. Ctr. Hosp., 1994—95; clin. staff Wilmer Eye Inst., Johns Hopkins U., Balt., 2007—; med. officer, sr. clin. investigator Nat. Eye Inst., NIH, 2007—. Vis. lectr. Wilmer Eye Inst.-Johns Hopkins U., Balt., 1984, Osaka U., Japan, 1986, U. Munich, 1988, Harkness Eye Inst., Columbia U., NYC, 1994—97, Washington Hosp. Ctr., 2006, Wilmer Eye Inst., Johns Hopkins U., Balt., 2007—; cons. on eye/cataract rsch. NASA, VA, pharm. cos.; presenter in field. Editor: cataract sect. Duane's Clinical Ophthalmology Textbook series, 1989—; guest editor: Jour. Investigative Ophthalmology and Visual Sci., 1999, 2000; contbr. chapters to books, articles to profl. jours.; reviewer jours. in field:. Recipient Most Outstanding Silver Jubilarian in Med. Rsch. award, U. Santo Tomas Alumni Assn. Am., 1999, Cert. Appreciation For Work With Indigents, James Cardinal Hickey and Archidiocese of Washington, Ophthalmology Rsch. award, Assn. Philippine Ophthalmologists in Am., 2001. Mem.: Philippine Am. Acad. Sci. and Engring., Contact Lens Assn. Ophthalmologists, Wilmer Eye Inst. Residents' Assn., Md. Soc. Eye Physicians and Surgeons, Washington Acad. Ophthalmology, Internat. Assn. Ocular Surgeons, Johns Hopkins Med. Surg. Assn., Castroviego Soc. Corneal Surgeons, Am. Acad. Ophthalmology, Assn. Rsch. in Vision and Ophthalmology, Johns Hopkins Alumni Assn. Roman Catholic. Achievements include research in medical nonsurgical treatment cataracts and early detection and documentation of cataracts; causes of cataracts. Avocations: sketching, soap carving, target shooting, guitar, chess. Office: NIH Nat Eye Inst Rm 10n226 Bethesda MD 20892-1860 Home Phone: 301-424-4008. Business E-Mail: datilesm@nei.nih.gov.

DATIRI, BENJAMIN CHUMANG, soil and environmental scientist; b. Sho, Plateau, Nigeria, May 1, 1953; came to U.S., 1983; s. Chumang Dangyang and Antele (Pam) D.; m. Roseline Chundung Gwott, Apr. 5, 1980; children: Simidarwei, Teyeidarwei, Ninratdarwei, Yeipyeng, Noro. BSc, Ahmadu Bello U., Zaria, Nigeria, 1978, MSc, 1982; PhD, U. Wis., 1989. Ordained and installed pastor Mt. Traveler Bapt. Ch., 2004; registered lab. animal technologist AALAS, 2004. Mem. Nigerian Youth Svc. Program, Onicha-Olona, 1978-79; agrl. officer II Plateau State Ministry of Agr., Lafia, Nigeria, 1979; grad. asst. Ahmadu Bello U., 1979-80, asst. lectr., 1980-82; rsch. asst. U. Wis., Madison, 1983-84; rsch. assoc. Tuskegee (Ala.) U., 1990-93, rsch. technician, 1993-95; assoc. rsch. prof., rsch. coord. Selma (Ala.) U., 1996-98; rsch. assoc. prof. biomed. dept. Tuskegee U., 1998—, asst. dir. animal care Comparative Medicine Resource Ctr., 2003—. Contbr. articles to profl. publs. Recipient Ch. Recreation League Leadership award Macon County of Ala., 1992, Basketball Coaches award Tuskegee-Macon County YMCA, 1994; Plateau State grad. scholar Govt. of Nigeria, 1983-86. Mem. Am. Soc. Agronomy, Soil Sci. Soc. Am., Sigma Xi (Tuskegee U. chpt. Outstanding leadership 1992, Dedicated Svc. award 1992). Achievements include discovery that chisel and no-till tillage systems do reduce surface runoff and increase infiltration, that wetting front migrations were found to be much deeper in soil profile than in conventional moldboard planting; hence, although surface water pollution may be reduced by conservation tillage, it could present a potential for groundwater pollution. Office: Tuskegee Univ Comparative Medicine Resource Ctr Tuskegee Institute AL 36088

DATSYUK, PAVEL, professional hockey player; b. Sverdlovsk, Russia, July 20, 1978; married; 1 child. Center Detroit Red Wings, 2001—, Dynamo Moscow (Russian Elite League), 2004—05. Player NHL Young-Stars Game, 2002, NHL All-Star Game, 2004. Recipient Lady Byng Trophy, 2006, 2007. Achievements include being a member of bronze medal winning Russian Hockey Team, Salt Lake City Olympics, 2002; being a member of Stanley Cup Champion Detroit Red Wings, 2002. Office: Detroit Red Wings Joe Louis Arena 600 Civic Ctr Detroit MI 48226*

DATTA, RAJIV V., oncologist, surgeon, department chairman; s. Virendra N. and Usha Datta; m. Arti R. Shetty, Aug. 15, 1990; children: Tanya, Saumya. Lic. physician Bombay, India, 1984. Clin. asst. prof. surgery Downstate Med. Sch., Bklyn., 2001; dir, divsn. surg. oncology South Nassau Hosp., Valley Stream, NY, 2001—, chmn. dept surgery, 2007—. Liason South Nassau Cancer Ctr., Valley Stream, 2003—07. Contbr. articles to profl. jours. Recipient Solomon Ciprut Outstanding Chief Resident award, Maimonides Med. Ctr., Bklyn., 1998; fellow, Tata Meml. Cancer Ctr., Mumbai, India, 1990, Meml. Sloan-Kettering Cancer Ctr., NY, 1996, Roswell Pk. Cancer Ctr., Buffalo, NY, 1999, 2000; scholar, Am. Assn. Cancer Rsch., 1999; Abrahman Mandelberg Traveling fellowship, Maimonides Med. Ctr., Bklyn., 1997. Fellow: Internat. Coll. Surgeons, Royal Coll. Surgeons, Am. Head and Neck Soc., Soc. Surg. Oncology, Nassau Surg. Soc. (assoc.; sec. 2007, treas. 2007); mem.: ACS (bd. dirs. Bklyn. LI chpt. 2006—07, rep. young surgeons 2005). Office: South Nassau Hosp 1 S Ctrl Ave Valley Stream NY 11580 Office Phone: 516-632-3350. Office Fax: 516-632-3355. Business E-Mail: rdatta@snch.org.

DATTA, RUPALI, geochemist, educator; d. Hemendra Kumar and Gayatri Datta. BS, Osmania U., 1987; MS, U. Hyderabad, 1989, MPhil, 1992, PhD, 1997. Postdoctoral rschr. Niigata (Japan) U., Japan, 1997—98, U. Fla., Gainesville, Fla., 1998—2002; from postdoctoral assoc. to asst. profl. U. Tex., San Antonio, 2002—04, asst. prof., 2004—, assoc. dir. Environ. Geochemistry Lab., 2002—. Mem. lead task force, San Antonio, 2004. Fellow, 16th Internat. Union of Biochemistry and Plant Molecular Biology Congress, 1994, Japanese Soc. Promotion of Sci., 1997—99; grantee, US EPA-Sci. to Achieve Results, 2002, HUD, 2004, NIH, 2004. Mem.: Geol. Soc. Am., Am. Soc. Plant Biologists, Crop Sci. Soc. Am., Am. Soc. Agronomy, Soil Sci. Soc. Am. Achievements include research in genetic characterization of phytochelatin biosynthetic pathways in arsenic hyper-accumulators; arsenic stress responses in plants; chemical and phytoremediation of arsenical pesticide contaminated soils; chemical and phytoremediation of lead contaminated soils. Office: Univ Tex San Antonio Earth and Environ Sci One UTSA Cir San Antonio TX 78249 Office Phone: 210-458-5168. Office Fax: 210-458-4469. Business E-Mail: rupali.datta@utsa.edu.

DATTA, SUDIP, finance educator; b. Kanpur, India, Feb. 2, 1962; s. Provash Chandra and Maya (Sinha) Dutta; m. Mai Elias Iskandar Datta, Mar. 26, 1993; children: Arun Basel, Anita Leela. BS in Econs., Presidency Coll., 1984; MA, SUNY Binghamton, 1987, PhD, 1989. Instr. SUNY, Binghamton, 1987-89; asst. prof. Bentley Coll., Waltham, Mass., 1989-95, assoc. prof., 1995-97, Robert and Julia Dorn prof. fin., 1997—2004; T. Norris Hitchman endowed chairholder, prof. fin. Sch. Bus. Adminstrn., Wayne State U., Detroit, 2004—. Contbr. articles to profl. jours. Fellow Am. Fin. Assn., Fin. Mgmt. Assn. (program com.), So. Fin. Assn. (program com.), We. Fin. Assn. Avocations: investing, travel, cooking, soccer, chess. Office: Wayne State Univ 5201 Cass Ave Prentis 216 Detroit MI 48202 Office Phone: 313-577-0408. Business E-Mail: sdatta@wayne.edu.

DATTILO, THOMAS A., retired manufacturing executive; b. June 12, 1951; BA, OH State U.; JD, U. Toledo; graduate of Advanced Mgmt. Program, Harvard Bus. Sch. Mem., corporate legal staff Dana Corp., 1977-82, with ins. operations dvsn., 1982-85, v.p. then gen. mgr., Precision Control Divsn., and other sr. mgmt. positions Laurinburg, NC, 1985—98; pres., CEO Hayes-Dana Inc., St. Cahtarines, Ont., Canada; pres. Victor Reinz Products, N. Am., Lisle, Ill.; pres., sealing products group Dana Corp., Toledo, 1997—99; pres., COO Cooper Tire and Rubber Co., Findlay, Ohio, 1999—2000, chmn., pres., CEO, 2000—06. Mem.: Mfr. Alliance (vice chmn.), Rubber Mfr. Assn. (chmn.), Automotive Parts Manufacturer's Assn., Young President's Orgn.

DATZ, ISRAEL MORTIMER, information systems specialist; b. NYC, Feb. 11, 1928; s. A. Mark and Lillian (Barkin) D.; m. Gerd Elin Alme-Torkildsen, Apr. 30, 1956. BS, CCNY, 1950; postgrad., U. Bergen, Norway, 1951-55. Chief programming group Internat. Inst. Meteorology, Stockholm, 1958-59; head support svcs. sect. NASA Goddard Space Flight Ctr., Greenbelt, Md., 1959-61; mathematician Army Strategy and Tactics Analysis Group, Bethesda, Md., 1961-63; acting chief div. ops. analysis Dept. Commerce Maritime Adminstrn., Washington, 1963-64; head computer div. marine engring. lab. Annapolis (Md.) div. Naval Ship R & D Ctr., 1964-68, rsch. coord. math., 1968-72, tech. adv. ops. rsch., 1972-79; pvt. practice, 1979-84, 92—; chief studies and analysis U.S. Army Engr. Sch., Ft. Leonard Wood, Mo., 1984—92. Author: Planning Tools for Ocean Transportation, 1971, Power Transmission and Automation for Ships and Submersibles, 1975, Planning in a Military Context: An Army Perspective, 1998, Military Operations Under Special Conditions of Terrain and Weather, 2004; contbr. articles to profl. jours. Recipient summer stipend, Woods Hole Oceanographic Instn., 1949, rsch. stipend, The Geophysics Inst., Bergen, Norway, 1953. Fellow AAAS; mem. N.Y. Acad. Scis., Inst. Ops. Rsch. and Mgmt. Sci., Assn. Computing Machinery, Nat. Def. Indsl. Assn., Am. Soc. Naval Engrs., Marine Tech. Soc., Soc. Naval Architects and Marine Engrs., U.S. Naval Inst., Navy League U.S. Home and Office: 1343 California Dr Rolla MO 65401-4529 Office Phone: 573-341-3870. Personal E-mail: mortdatz@prodigy.net.

DAUB, HAL (HAROLD JOHN DAUB JR.), lawyer; b. Fayetteville, NC, Apr. 23, 1941; s. Harold John and Eleanor M. (Hickman) D.; m. Mary Mernin; children: Natalie Ann, John Clifford, Tammy Rene. BSBA, Washington U., St. Louis, 1963; JD, U. Nebr., Lincoln, 1966. Bar: Nebr. 1966, US Ct. Appeals (8th cir.), US Ct. Customs and Patent Appeals, US Supreme Ct. Staff intern US Sen. Roman Hruska, Nebr., 1966; assoc. Fitzgerald, Brown, Leahy, McGill & Strom, 1966—70; v.p., gen. counsel Standard Chem. Mfg. Co., 1971-80; mem. 97th-100th Congresses from 2nd Nebr. dist., 1981-1989, mem. ways and means com., subcoms. on health and social security, pub. works & transportation, govt. ops. & small bus. com., 1981—89; prin., nat. dir. fed. govt. affairs Deloitte & Touche Acctg. and Cons. Firm, 1989—94; mayor City of Omaha, 1995—2001; ptnr. Blackwell & Sanders, LLP, 2001—; pres., CEO Am. Health Care Assn. and Nat. Ctr. for Assisted Living, Washington, 2004—05. Presdl. appointee Nat. Adv. Coun. on Pub. Svc., 1992—94; prin. Coun. for Excellence in Govt.; pres. Rep. Mayors and Local Elected Ofcls. Assn., 1995—2000; adv. bd. US Conf. Mayors, 1999—2001; chmn. Nat. League of Cities Pub. Safety and Crime Prevention Com., 1997, bd. dir., 1997—99; mem. Bush-Cheney Transition Team, Agr. Policy, 2000—01; presdl. appointee chmn. Social Security Adv. Bd., 2002—06; del. & keynote spkr. White House Conf. Aging, 2005. Jr. pres. Nebr. Founders' Day, 1971, sr. pres., 2001; exec. com., bd. dirs. Combined Health Agys. Drive, 1976; treas. Douglas County Rep. Party, Nebr., 1971-74, chmn., 1974-77; mem. Nebr. State Rep. Ctrl. Com., 1974-77; mem. Congl. Regulatory Reform Task Force, 1981-83, Congl. Rep. Agrl. Task Force, 1981-88; co-founder

Liability Ins. and Tort Reform Task Force, 1986; exec. com. Rep. Nat. Congl. Com., 1981-88; co-founder, co-chmn. Budget Reform Task Force, 1981-84; bd. dirs. Metro Arts Coun., 1989-93; nat. bd. dirs. Cmty. Health Agys. of Am., 2003-, chmn., 2006-; pres. Douglas-Sarpy unit Nebr. Heart Assn.; elder Presbyn. Ch.; nat. committeeman Rep. Party, 2005—; del. conf. aging. White Ho., 2005; chmn.-elect bd. dirs. Cmty. Heatlh Charities, 2005-, chmn., 2006-; active Children's Mus., Durham Western Heritage Mus., Joslyn Mus., Henry Doorly Zoo, Humane Soc. & Friends Forever, Salvation Army, United Way/CHAD Divsn. Chmn.; bd. dir. Freedoms Found. Capt. US Army, 1963—68. Decorated Army Commendation medal with oak leaf cluster, Expeditionary medal; named Outstanding Young Nebraskan, 1964, Outstanding Young Omahan, Jaycees, 1975, Outstanding Vol. of Yr. award Douglas-Sarpy unit Nebr. Heart Assn., 1976, Disting. Eagle Scout, 2000, Citizen of the Yr. Mid. Am. Boy Scout Coun., 2003; recipient Svc. award SAC, 1976, Leadership awards (4) Coalition for Peace Through Strength award, 1981-1989, Guardian of Small Bus. awards (4), 1981-89, Omaha C. of C. award, Watchdog of Treasury awards (5), 1981-89, Nebr. Reserve Officers, Minutemen of the Year, 1985, Humanitarian award, Grand Masonic Lodges of Nebr., 2004, Silver Beaver award, 2004, Communications & Leadership award, Toastmasters Int., 2005, Disting. Nebraskan award Nebr. Soc. Wash., DC, 2005, others; named to Omaha C. of C. Bus. Hall of Fame, 2004. Mem. Omaha Bar Assn., Nebr. Bar Assn., Nat. Assn. Credit Mgmt. (1st v.p. 1977), Res. Officers Assn., Urban League Nebr., Optimists Internat., Masons (33 degree), Shriners, Optimists Internat., Am. Judiature Soc., Air Force Assn., Am. Heart Assn. (Nebr. affiliate), Assn. Govt. Accountants, Fontenelle Forrest Assn., Multiple Sclerosis Soc., Nebr. Diplomats, Nebr. U. & Washington U. Alumni Assn., Am. Legion, Red Cross Gallon Club, Sisters Cities Assn., VFW, SAR, Kappa Sigma, Alpha Kappa Psi, Omicron Delta Kappa, Delta Theta Phi (Outstanding Law Fraternity Student in the Nation, 1965); fellow Nebr. State Bar Found. Republican. Office: Blackwell Sanders LLP 1620 Dodge St Ste 2100 Omaha NE 68102 Office Phone: 402-964-5019. Business E-Mail: hdaub@blackwellsanders.com.

DAUB, PEGGY ELLEN, library administrator; b. Bluffton, Ohio, Oct. 15, 1949; d. Perry J. and Olive L. (Hoover) D.; m. Jeffrey H. Cooper, Dec. 13, 1975; 1 child, William P. Cooper-Daub. MusB summa cum laude, Miami U., 1972; MA, Cornell U., 1975; MSLS, U. Ill., 1980; PhD, Cornell U., 1985. Acting asst. music libr. Yale U., 1980-81, head of music tech. svcs., rare books libr. Music Libr., 1981-82; head Music Libr. U. Mich., Ann Arbor, 1982-89, head Spl. Collections & Arts Librs., 1989-99, head Spl. Collections Libr., 2000—. Presenter Rare Books and Manuscript Sect. Pre-Conf., New Orleans, 1993, Bloomington, 1995 and others. Contbr. articles to profl. jours. Co-clk. Ann Arbor Friends Meeting, 1997-2001. Travel grantee Ctr. for Internat. Studies, Cornell U., 1977. Mem. ALA (Assn. Coll. and Rsch. Librs. rare books and manuscripts sect., mem. task force on interlibr. loan 1991-93, mem. preconf. program planning com. 1992-94), Music Libr. Assn. (bd. dirs. 1985-87, mem. resource sharing and collection devel. com. 1982-91), Rsch. Librs. Group (chairperson music program com. 1985-87, mem. steering com. 1982-87), Am. Musicol. Soc. (mem. coun. 1988-91, mem. coun. com. on minorities/diversity 1988-91), Phi Beta Kappa. Mem. Soc. Of Friends. Office: U of Mich Spl Collections Libr 711 Graduate Libr Ann Arbor MI 48109-1205 Office Phone: 734-764-9377. E-mail: pdaub@umich.edu.

DAUBE, JONATHAN MAHRAM, academic administrator; b. Cambridge, Eng., Nov. 23, 1937; arrived in U.S., 1963; s. David Daube and Herta Babette Simon; m. Linda Lindquist Daube, Aug. 29, 1964; children: Andrew Carl, Katharine Paula, Matthew Jeremy. MA with honors, U. Aberdeen, Scotland, 1957; Postgrad. Cert. with distinction, U. London, 1958, Acad. diploma, 1960; EdD, Harvard U., 1968. Tchr. English, math. Watford Grammar Sch., England, 1958—60; tchr. English, Manchester Grammar Sch., England, 1960—63, Newton H.S., Mass., 1963—65; asst. to supt. Newton Pub. Schs., Mass., 1967—68; sr. lectr. U. Malawi, Limbe, 1968—70; supt. schs. Martha's Vineyard Pub. Schs., Mass., 1970—75; dir. Union Grad. Sch., Yellow Springs, Ohio, 1975—78; pres. Berkshire C.C., Pittsfield, Mass., 1978—87, Manchester C.C., Conn., 1987—. Chair governing bd. Great Path Acad., Manchester, Conn., 2000—; founding mem., pres. bd. dirs. U. Aberdeen Devel. Trust; adj. prof. U. Mass., Amherst. Corporator Ea. Conn. Health Network, Manchester. Democrat. Office: Manchester CC Great Path Manchester CT 06045 Office Phone: 860-512-3100. Office Fax: 860-512-3101. Business E-Mail: jdaube@mcc.commnet.edu.

DAUBERT, ERIK JOSEPH, organization administrator, consultant; b. Goshen, NY, June 21, 1966; s. Robert Louis and Madeline J.; m. Andrea Miele, Oct. 4, 1997. BA, U. N.C., Chapel Hill, 1989; postgrad. in non-profit mgmt., Duke U., 1992; MBA, Campbell U., 2002; postgrad., Stanford U., 2005. Cert. fund raising exec. Exec. dir. Eco-Logical, Durham, NC, 1991-95; v.p. devel. YMCA Triangle Area, Raleigh, NC, 1996—2006; cons. ptnr. We Improve It, 2006—. Cons. Research Triangle Park, NC, 1995—2006; mem. coun. N.Am. YMCA Devel. Officers, 2005-06; fin. devel. cons. YMCA of USA, 2006-. cons. in field. Vice chair Sierra Club, Durham, 1991-93; pres. bd. dirs. Child Advocacy Commn., Durham, 1995-97; bd. dirs. Eno River Assn., 2003-, chair. resource devel. com., 2004-06; bd. advisors Nourish Internat., 2006-. Named Outstanding Vol., N.C. Pub. Allies, 1994, Cmty. Hero-Torchbearer, 1996 Olympic Games, 1996; recipient cert. merit The Nat. Arbor Day Found., 1993, 94; Stanford U. Grad. Sch Bus. Ctr. for Social Innovation fellow, 2005, 40 Under 40 Leadership Recognition award, Triangle Bus. Jour., 2005. Mem.: Assn. Fundraising Profls., Boardsource. Avocations: canoeing, camping, bicycling, reading, people. Home: 2917 Beech Grove Dr Durham NC 27705 Office: YMCA of the USA 2917 Beech Grove Dr Durham NC 27705 Home Fax: 919-383-3092. Business E-Mail: erik.daubert@ymca.net.

DAUBS, JAMES DANIEL, educational assessment specialist; b. Mt. Carmel, Ill., Nov. 18, 1958; s. Hubert Doyle and Iona Doty Daubs. BA, Butler U., Indpls., 1980; MA, U. Ill., Urbana-Champaign, 1983, PhD, 1988. Assessment specialist, group leader Ednl. Testing Svc., Princeton, NJ, 1991—2004; sr. content specialist The Coll. Bd., NYC, 2004—. Mem.: TESOL, Conf. on Coll. Composition and Comm., Nat. Coun. Tchrs. English, Stonewall Dems., Kappa Sigma. Episcopalian. Avocations: writing poetry, theater, reading, travel. Office: The College Bd 45 Columbus Ave New York NY 10023 Office Phone: 212-649-8403.

DAUCH, RICHARD E., automotive executive; b. 1942; BS, Purdue U., 1964. With Gen. Motors Corp., Detroit, 1964-75; group v.p. mfg. Volkswagen of Am., Detroit, 1976-80; v.p. Chrysler Corp., Detroit, 1980, exec. v.p. diversified ops., 1980-81, exec. v.p. stamping assembly diversified ops., 1981-84, exec. v.p. mfg., 1984-1994; co-founder, CEO Am. Axle and Mfg., Detroit, 1994—, pres., 1994—2001, chmn., 2001—. Recipient Eli Whitney Meml. Award Soc. Mfg. Engr., 1987, Ellis Island Medal of Honor, 1997; named Industry Leader of the Yr., Automotive Hall of Fame, 1997; Mfr. of the Yr., Mich. Mfg. Assn., 1997; Newsmaker of the Yr., Crain's Detroit Bus., 1998, World Trader of the Yr., Detroit Regional Chamber, 2002, Mich. Exec. of the Yr., Wayne State U. Coll. Bus. Adminstrn., 2002. Mem.: Nat. Assn. Mfr. (chairman 2003). Office: American Axle and Mfg 1840 Holbrook St Detroit MI 48212-3442*

DAUCHER, DONALD ALFRED, lawyer; b. Buffalo, Apr. 2, 1945; BS, U. Rochester, 1967; JD, Duke U., 1971. Bar: Calif. 1972. Mng. ptnr. Paul, Hastings, Janofsky & Walker, San Diego, 1971—. Mem. Order Coif, Beta Gamma Sigma. Office: Paul Hastings Janofsky & Walker LLP 695 Town Ctr Dr Costa Mesa CA 92626 Office Phone: 714-668-6257. Office Fax: 714-668-6357. Business E-Mail: dondaucher@paulhastings.com.

DAUER, DONALD DEAN, investment company executive; b. Fresno, Calif., June 1, 1936; s. Andrew and Erma Mae (Zigenman) D.; m. LaVerne DiBuduo, Jan. 23, 1971; children: Gina, Sarah. BS in Bus. Adminstrn., Calif. State U. Fresno; postgrad., U. Wash., 1964. Loan officer First Savs. and Loan, Fresno, 1961-66, v.p., 1966-71, sr. v.p., 1971-81, exec. v.p., 1978-81; pres. Uniservice Corp., Fresno, 1976-81, Don Dauer Investments, Fresno, 1981—; pres., chief oper. officer Riverbend Internat. Corp., Sanger, Calif., 1985-89. Chmn. bd. dirs. Univ. Savs. and Loan, 1991-92, acting pres., CEO, 1992; loan officer Norwest Mortgage, 1993-95; mgr. CMB Fin., 1995-96. Chmn. bd. dirs. City of Fresno Gen. Svcs. Retirement Bd., 1973-83, West Fresno Econ. and Bus. Devel. Program Bd., 1980-83; pres. bd. dirs. Cen. Calif. United Cerebral Palsy Assn., 1979-82; bd. dirs. Valley Children's Hosp. Found., Fresno, 1984-93; trustee, chmn. Valley Children's Hosp., 1987-93; bd. dirs. Youth for Christ USA, 1988-94, Twilight Haven Inc., 2000—; vice chmn. Riverbend Internat., 1975-91. Mem. Soc. Real Estate Appraisers (past pres.). Office: 2733 W Palo Alto Ave Fresno CA 93711-1110 Office Phone: 559-431-2764. E-mail: dddauer@yahoo.com.

DAUER, EDWARD ARNOLD, law educator; b. Providence, Sept. 28, 1944; s. Marshall and Shirley (Moverman) Dauer; m. Carol Jean Egglestone, June 16, 1966; children: E. Craig, Rachel P. AB, Brown U., 1966; LLB cum laude, Yale U., 1969; MPH, Harvard U., 2001. Bar: Conn. 1978, Colo. 1986. Asst. prof. law sch. U. Toledo, 1969-72; assoc. prof. law U. So. Calif., LA, 1972-74; assoc. prof. Yale U., New Haven, 1975-85, assoc. dean, 1978-83, dep. dean Law Sch., 1983-85; dean, prof. U. Denver, 1985-90, dean emeritus, prof., 1991—2007. Of counsel Popham, Haik, Schnobrich and Kaufman, 1990—97; vis. scholar Harvard U. Sch. Pub. Health, 1996—2004; pres. CAEJAD Aviation Corp.; assoc. Health Care Negotiations Assocs., Inc. Author: (book) Materials on a Nonadversarial Legal Process, 1978, Conflict Resolution Strategies in Health Care, 1993, Manual of Dispute Resolution: ADR Law and Practice, 1994 (CPR Book award, 1994), Health Care Dispute Resolution, 2000; contbr. articles to profl. jours. Founder, pres. Nat. Ctr. Preventive Law; bd. dirs. New Haven Cmty. Action Agy., 1978—81; mem. Colo. Commn. Higher Edn., 1987—91; bd. dirs. Cerebral Palsy Found., Denver, 1989—, pres., 1992—95; commr. Colo. Advanced Tech. Inst., 1989—91; pres. Legacy Found. Cerebral Palsy, 2007—, Common Good Colo., 2007—; treas. Colo. Coalition Patient Safety, 2007—. Recipient W. Quinn Jordan award, Nat. Blood Found., 1994, Paelia award, Harvard Sch. Pub. Health, 1996, Sanbar award, Am. Coll. Legal Medicine, 1999. Mem.: Am. Law Inst. (life), Univ. Club, Cherry Creek Athletic Club, Order of Coif. Republican. Home: 127 S Garfield St Denver CO 80209 Office: U Denver Coll Law 2255 E Evans Ave Denver CO 90208 Office Phone: 303-871-6278. Business E-Mail: edauer@law.du.edu.

DAUGAARD, DENNIS M., lieutenant governor, former state senator; b. Garretson, SD, June 11, 1953; m. Linda Kay Schmidt; children: Laura, Sara, Christopher BS, U. SD, 1975; JD, Northwestern U., 1978. Bar: SD. Atty. Supena & Nyman, 1978-79, Shand Morahan & Co., 1979-81; bank trust officer 1st Bank SD, 1981-90; devel. dir. Children's Home Soc., 1990—; mem. SD State Senate from 9th dist., Pierre, 1997—2003; lt. gov. State of SD, Pierre, 2003—. Mem. Nat. Soc. Fund Raising Execs., SD Bar Assn., SD Planned Giving Coun., Siox Falls (SD) Estate Planning Coun., Rotary. Republican. Lutheran. Office: Office Lt Governor State Capitol Bldg 500 E Capitol Ave Pierre SD 57501-5070 Office Phone: 605-773-3821. Office Fax: 605-773-4711.

DAUGHDRILL, JAMES HAROLD, JR., academic administrator; b. LaGrange, Ga., Apr. 25, 1934; s. James Harold and Louisa Coffee (Dozier) D.; m. Elizabeth Anne Gay, June 26, 1954; children: James Harold III, Louisa Rish Daughdrill Hoover, Elizabeth Gay Daughdrill Boyd. Student, Davidson Coll., 1952-54, DD, 1974; AB, Emory U., 1956; BD, Columbia Theol. Sem., 1967, M.Div., 1969. Ordained to ministry Presbyn. Ch., 1967. Pres. Kingston Mills, Inc., Cartersville, Ga., 1956-64; minister St. Andrews Presbyn. Ch., Little Rock, 1967-70; sec. of stewardship Presbyn. Ch. in U.S., Atlanta, 1970-73; pres. Rhodes Coll., 1973-99. Past chmn. Nat. Adv. Com. on Instl. Quality and Interity, Dept. Edn.; past chair Assn. Am. Colls.; past dir. Am. Coun. on Edn.; mem. Blue Ribbon adv. com. Memphis Pub. Schs.; dir. So. Univ. Conf., pres., 1998—; bd. dirs. Bulab Holdings, Inc., Union Planters Nat. Bank, Buckman Labs. Author: Man Talk, 1972; co-author: New Directions for Higher Education Source Book. Past chmn. Tenn. Coun. Pvt. Colls.; past pres. Coll. Athletic Conf.; past chmn. bd. So. Coll. Univ. Union; past trustee Memphis-Brooks Art Gallery, Hutchinson Sch.; past bd. dirs. Tenn. Ind. Colls., Liberty Bowl, Chickasaw coun. Boy Scouts Am., Memphis U. Sch., Memphis Ptnrs.; mem. exec. bd. Dixon Gallery and Gardens; trustee The Frank E. Seidman Award in Polit. Economy; mem. blue ribbon adv. com. to the supt. Memphis Pub. Schs. Named Educator of Yr. Greater Memphis State, Memphis Planner of Yr., Pillar of Memphis Jewish Nat. Fund; recipient Spirit of Life award City of Hope, Svc. award Rotary Club Memphis Community, 1987, McCallie Sch. Alumnus of Yr. award 1978, Disting. Nat. Eagle Scout award, 1991; honored by Tenn. Legislature for disting. svc. to higher edn. and to State of Tenn., 1998. Mem. NCJJ (nat. trustee), Assn. Presbyn. Colls. and Univs. (bd. dirs.), World Bus. Coun. (young pres.' orgn., Young Man of Yr. 1961), Chief Execs. Orgn. (past), Memphis C. of C. (past bd. dir.), Univ. Club (N.Y.C.), Phi Delta Theta, Omicron Delta Kappa, Kappa Delta Epsilon (nat. hon.). Home: 4035 Dumaine Way Memphis TN 38117-2909 Office: Rhodes Coll 2000 N Parkway Office Pres Memphis TN 38112-1690

DAUGHENBAUGH, RANDALL JAY, retired chemical company executive, consultant; b. Rapid City, SD, Feb. 10, 1948; s. Horace Allan and Helen Imogene (Reder) Daughenbaugh; m. Mary R. Wynja, Aug. 25, 1973; children: Jason Allan, Jill Christen. BS, S.D. Tech., 1970; PhD, U. Colo., 1975. Rsch. chemist Air Prod. and Chem., Allentown, Pa., 1975-80; rsch. dir. Chem. Exch. Industries, Boulder, Colo., 1980-83; pres. Hauser Chem. Rsch., Inc., Boulder, 1983-93, chief tech. officer, exec. v.p., 1993-99; ret. Contbr. articles to profl. jours. Named Engrepreneur of the Yr., Inc. Mag., 1992; recipient IR-100 award, R&D Mag., 1993. Mem.: Am. Chem. Soc. Achievements include patents in field. Home: 10755 Sheridan Lake Rd Rapid City SD 57702-6506 Office Phone: 605-343-1126. Personal E-mail: rjdaugh@rapidnet.com.

DAUGHENBAUGH, TERRY L., metal products executive; b. Latrobe, Pa., July 20, 1939; m. Cristine Zubaty, May 1, 1999; children: Thomas, Todd, Tracey stepchildren: Leslie, Neil. BS, U. Pitts., 1968; postgrad., Columbia U., 1985. With Kennemetal Corp., Latrobe, Pa., 1957-58, Latrobe (Pa.) Steel Co., 1958-92, project engr., 1968-70, melt shop supt., 1970-73, mgr. primary ops., 1973-85, gen. mgr. mfg., 1985-88, gen. mgr. primary ops. and engring., 1988-92; pres. Innovative Water Tech., Inc. divsn. Innovative Group, Latrobe, 1992; pres., owner Spl. D Co., Latrobe, 1992-96; pres., chmn. bd. dirs. Baker Pyromet, Inc., Greenville, Pa., 1994-2000; gen. mgr. LWB Refractories, Greenville, 2000—05. Cons. steel industry, 2005—. Chmn. bd. Ea. Westmoreland Devel. Corp., Latrobe, 1995—96, chmn. transp. com., 1989—99; mem. home rule com. Borough of Latrobe, 1994—98; coach, mgr., commr. Latrobe-Derry Area Teener League, 1974—84; mem. citizens adv. bd. Laurel Valley Transp. Improvement Project, 2004—; chmn. citizens adv. panel Southwestern Planning Commn., 2005—; bd. dirs. Latrobe Area C. of C., 1995—98, Valley Players of Ligonier, 1997, Laurel Ballet, 1990—94, Westmoreland Blind Assn., 1987—89, Econ. Growth Connection, 1998—, Western Pa. chpt. Juvenile Diabetes Rsch. Found., 2004—. Mem.: Ingot Metallurgy Forum, Alumni Elec. Metal Makers Guild, Latrobe Area Devel. Coun., Loyalhanna Watershed Assn., Ligonier Country Club. Republican. Lutheran. Avocations: skiing, golf, hunting. Home: 1129 Lauralynn Dr Latrobe PA 15650-4718

DAUGHERTY, F(RANCIS) MARK, music educator, conductor, theater director; b. Reading, Pa., May 28, 1951; s. Francis Rodman Daugherty and Lucy Eddinger. MusB, Eastman Sch. Music, 1973; MusM, Temple U, 1997; JD, Temple U., 1978. Bar: Pa. 1978. Editor Musicdata, Inc., Phila., 1984—99; tchg. asst. Temple U., 1995—97; tchr. Chestnut Hill Acad., 1997—. Artistic dir. Ambler Choral Soc., Pa., 1985—; accompanist Orpheus Club Phila., 1986—; dir. music Unitarian Soc. Germantown, 1983—; musical dir. Old York Rd. Temple Beth Am, Abington, 1984—; music dir. Camp Tecumseh, Center Harbor, NH, 1991—; condr. musical performance tour, Normandy, France, 2004. Editor: (bibliographic reference) Sacred Choral Music In Print, 2nd Ed., Secular Choral Music In Print, 2nd Ed., Sacred Choral Music In Print, '92 & '95 Supps., Secular Choral Music In Print, '91 & '93 Supps, Organ Music In Print: '90 Supplement, Classical Vocal Music In Print, 1985 Supplement. Recipient Elaine Brown Tribute award, Boyer Coll. of Music, Temple U, 1996; fellow, Chorus Am., 1996; scholar, Boyer Coll. Music, Temple U., 1995—96, 1996—97. Mem.: Unitarian Universalist Musicians Network, Guild Temple Musicians, Am. Guild Organists, Am. Choral Dirs. Assn., The Musical Fund Soc., Pi Kappa Lambda. Avocations: travel, fitness, environmental conservation, world music. Home: 21 Leamy House 115 Roumfort Rd Philadelphia PA 19119 Office: Chestnut Hill Acad 500 West Willow Grove Ave Philadelphia PA 19118 Home Phone: 215-242-0697; Office Phone: 215-247-4700. Personal E-mail: fmdleamy@aol.com. Business E-Mail: mdaugherty@chestnuthillacademy.org.

DAUGHERTY, JAMES ALBERT, retired aeronautical engineer; s. James Calloway and Effie Alberta Daugherty; m. Edith June Shofner (dec. 1975); 1 child, James Michael; m. Frances Mae Vaughan, Mar. 6, 1976. Grad. H.S., Ottawa, Kans. Lic. airplane and power plant mechanic, Civil Aeronautics Adminstrn.; ordained deacon Bapt. Ch., 1984. Assembly line worker Cessna Aircraft Co., Wichita, Kans., 1941—42, crew chief Hutchinson, Kans., 1942—43; from mechanic to sr. project engr. Trans World Airline, Kansas City, Mo., 1945—83. Pres., chmn. bd. Vets. Quindaro Homes, Inc., Kansas City, Kans., 1953—55; pres. TWA 1,100 Mem. Mgmt. Club, Kansas City, Mo., 1977—78; mem. adv. coun. McWherter Sr. Ctr., Memphis; active Ran for Polit. Office Charter Rev. Commn., Memphis, 2006. Cpl. USAF, 1943—45. Mem.: Am. Mensa. Avocations: writing, golf, bridge, line dancing, photography. Home: 5354 Fontana Ave Memphis TN 38115 Home Phone: 901-362-1340. Personal E-mail: jadshome@att.net.

DAUGHERTY, KENNETH EARL, research company executive, educator; b. Pitts., Dec. 27, 1938; s. Thomas Hill and Laura Elizabeth (Schuda) D.; m. Joan Kay Ogrosky, Dec. 22, 1961; children: Brian Earl, Kirsten Kay. BS in Chemistry, Carnegie-Mellon U., 1960; PhD in Analytical Chemistry, U. Wash., 1964; M in Bus. Econs., Claremont Grad. Sch., 1971. Chemist Marbon Chem.-Borg Warner, Washington, W.Va., 1960; rsch. chemist Rohm and Haas Corp., Bristol, Pa., 1964; group leader, sr. staff Amcord, Riverside, Calif., 1966-71; assoc. prof. chemistry U. Pitts., 1971-73; dir. research and devel. Gen. Portland Inc., Dallas, 1973-77; dir. energy and materials sci. Inst. Applied Scis. North Tex. State U., Denton, 1977-79, prof. chemistry, 1979—2000, chmn. analytical divsn., 1980—95; owner TRAC Labs., Denton, 1981—. Pres., CEO, KEDS Inc., KD Cons., 1977—; adj. prof. chemistry U. Pitts., 1973-2000, North Tex. State U., Denton, 1974-2000; adj. faculty Army Command and Gen. Staff Coll., 1983—; cons. in field. Author numerous publs. in field; patentee in field. Col. US Army, 1964—66, col. USAR, 1966—95. Decorated Army Commendation medal, Army Achievement medal, Army Meritorious Svc. medal; fellow DuPont, Shell Oil, Std. Oil, NSF, 1964. Fellow Am. Inst. Chemists; mem. Research Soc. Am., ASTM, Rilem, Nat. (transp. research bd.), NY Acad. Scis., Am. Ceramic Soc. (program chmn. 1986), Am. Chem. Soc. (chpt. pres. 1960, chmn. Dallas-Ft. Worth 1986, Argonne Nat. Lab. Achievement award 1987), Applied Spectroscopy Soc., Soc. Petroleum Engrs., Soc. Plastics Engrs., Sr. Army Comdrs. Assn., Sigma Xi, Pi Kappa Alpha, Omicron Delta Epsilon, Phi Lambda Upsilon, Alpha Chi Sigma, Masons (32d degree), Shriners, Rotary. Republican. Methodist. Home and Office: 1912 Hunskor Rd Oak Harbor WA 98277-8666 Personal E-mail: kedsinc@whidbey.net.

DAUGHERTY, LINDA HAGAMAN, real estate company executive; b. Denver, Jan. 25, 1940; d. Charles B. and Agnes May (Wall) Hagaman; m. Thomas Daniel Daugherty, Nov. 20, 1965; children: Patrick, Christina Marie. BS in Bus., U. Colo., 1961; postgrad., Tulane U., 1963-64, U. St. Thomas, 1990-91. Sr. systems analyst Lockheed Electronics NASA, Houston, 1966-73; sr. systems cons. TRW Systems Internat., Caracas, Venezuela, 1973-74; sy. systems cons. TRW Systems, LA, 1974-75; mng. ptnr. TDD-LHD Investments, LP, Katy, Tex., 1976—; pres. Nottingham Country Day Sch., Katy, 1977—2006; sr. systems analyst Intercomp, Houston, 1979-80; pres. Daugherty Fin. Svcs., Inc., Katy, 1979—91, Williamsburg Country Day Sch., Katy, 1983—2006. Mem. Epiphany Ch. Social Works Commn., San Antonio World Affair Coun.; pres. Mason Creek Women Reps. Club, Katy, 1980; treas. Nottingham Country Civic Club, Katy, 1979; mem. adv. bd. Nottingham Country Club, 1982—85; co-founder Friends of Archaeology U. St. Thomas, pres., 1991—93; pres., treas. Friends of Boerne Pub. Libr., 1997—99; asst. curator Archaeology Gallery, U. St. Thomas. Mem. Houston Archeology Soc., Tex. Archeology Soc., Archaeology Inst. of Am., Boerne Women's Club. Roman Catholic. Avocations: archaeology, bridge. Office: Motivated Child Learning Ctr PO Box 489 Boerne TX 78006-0489

DAUGHERTY, PATRICIA ANN, retired elementary school educator; b. Rockford, Ill., May 19, 1949; d. Bjarne John and Mary Rita (Ryan) Jacobsen; m. Greg A. Kramer, June 23, 1973 (div. Apr. 1988); 1 child, Josie Kramer. BS, No. Ill. U., 1971, MS, 1978. cert. elem. tchr., Ill., spl. edn. tchr., Ill. Tchr. Aurora East Sch. Dist., Ill., 1971—2004, ret., 2004; adj. faculty dept. edn. Aurora U., 2004—06. Mem. choir Our Lady of Mercy Cath. Ch. Mem. AAUW (2d v.p. membership 2005-07, gift honoree 1996), Am. Fedn. Tchrs. (bldg. rep. 1995-2004), Ill. Ret. Tchrs. Assn. Avocations: reading, gardening, skiing, golf. Home: 340 Inverness Dr Aurora IL 60504-6925

DAUGHTREY, MARTHA CRAIG, federal judge; b. Covington, Ky., July 21, 1942; d. Spence E. Kerkow and Martha E. (Craig) Piatt; m. Larry G. Daughtrey, Dec. 28, 1962; 1 child, Carran. BA cum laude, Vanderbilt U., 1964, JD, 1968. Bar: Tenn. 1968. Pvt. practice, Nashville, 1968; asst. US atty., 1968—69; asst. dist. atty., 1969—72; asst. prof. law Vanderbilt U., Nashville, 1972—75; judge Tenn. Ct. Appeals, Nashville, 1975—90; assoc. justice Tenn. Supreme Ct., Nashville, 1990—93; circuit judge US Ct. Appeals (6th cir.), Nashville, 1993—. Lectr. law Vanderbilt Law Sch., Nashville, 1975—82, adj. prof., 1988—90; mem. faculty NYU Appellate Judges Seminar, NYC, 1977—90, NYC, 1994—. Contbr. articles to profl. jours. Pres. Women Judges Fund for Justice, 1984—85, 1986—87; active various civic orgns. Named Woman of the Yr., Women Prof. Internat., 1976; recipient Athena award, Nat. Athena Program, 1991. Mem.: ABA (chmn. appellate judges conf. 1985—86, ho. of dels. 1988—91, chmn. jud. divsn. 1989—90, standing com. on continuing edn. of bar 1992—94, commn. on women in the profession 1994—97, bd. editors ABA Jour. 1995—2001, Margaret Brent award 2003), past mem., bd. visitors, Memphis State Sch. of Law, past mem., ed. bd., Judge's Journal, Lawyers Assn. for Women (pres. Nashville 1986—87), Nat. Assn. Women Judges (pres. 1985—86), Am. Judicature Soc. (bd. dirs. 1988—92), Nashville Bar Assn. (bd. dirs. 1988—90), Tenn. Bar Assn. Office: US Ct Appeals 300 Customs House 701 Broadway Nashville TN 37203-3944*

DAUGHTRY, CHRISTOPHER ADAM, singer; b. Roanoke Rapids, NC, Dec. 26, 1979; s. Pete and Sandra Daughtry; m. Deanna Daughtry, Nov. 2000; children: Hannah, Griffin. Former lead singer Absent Element;

signed to 19 Entertainment/RCA, 2006—; band founder & lead singer Daughtry, 2006—. Contestant (TV series) American Idol, 2006 (Top 12 contestant, 4th place winner); singer: (albums) Daughtry, 2006. Office: c/o 19 Entertainment Ltd 33 Ransomes Dock 35-37 Parkgate Rd London SW11 4NP England*

D'AUGUSTINE, ROBERT, academic administrator, lawyer; b. Tacoma, Wash., Apr. 22, 1947; s. Anthony Patrick and Marie Colette; m. Marcia Morgan, June 6, 1970; children: Matthew, Allie. BA, U. Pa., 1968, MA, 1971; MBA, Rutgers U., 1982, JD, 1996. Exec. asst. to dean U. Medicine and Dentistry N.J., Newark, 1977-83, asst. v.p. acad. affairs, 1983-87, assoc. v.p. acad. adminstrn., 1987-98, assoc. v.p. faculty adminstrn. New Brunswick, 1998-2000; exec. dir. budget and planning Rowan U., Glassboro, N.J., 2000—. Contbr. articles to scholarly and profl. jours. Co-founder, pres. Citizens for Quality Edn., Metuchen, NJ, 1988—93; pres. bd. trustees Vis. Nurse and Homemaker Svcs., Inc., Hainesport, NJ. With US Army, 1968—70. Mem. Beta Gamma Sigma. Home: 110 Woodlane Ct Glassboro NJ 08028 Office Phone: 856-256-4194. Business E-Mail: daugustine@rowan.edu.

DAUM, DAVID ERNEST, machinery manufacturing company executive; b. Pitts., July 31, 1939; s. Edward Charles and Esther (Horn) D.; children—Anjeanette R., Matthew C. BSE, Princeton U., 1960; MBA, U. Calif., Long Beach, 1972. Sales engr. Joy Mfg. Co., Seattle and San Francisco, 1960-68, dist. mgr. Mpls., 1968-70; pres. Sullair of So. Calif., Long Beach, 1970-75; v.p. Sullair Corp., Michigan City, Ind., 1975-85, Safway Steel Products, Milw., 1986-92; pres., owner Daum & Assocs., 1992—. Trustee, pres. Scaffolding, Shoring and Forming Inst. Am.; bd. dirs. Montessori Sch., Michigan City, 1970. Mem. Beta Gamma Sigma. Republican. Lutheran. Address: PO Box 1277 Friday Harbor WA 98250-1277 Office Phone: 360-542-4060. Personal E-mail: daumicilio@gmail.com. E-mail: daumicilio@prodigy.net.mx.

DAUM, JOHN F., lawyer; b. Washington, May 9, 1943; BA summa cum laude, Harvard U., 1965; LLB, Yale U., 1969. Bar: D.C. 1971, Calif. 1972. Ptnr. O'Melveny & Myers LLP, LA, mem. policy com. Lectr., fed. cts. and fed. jurisdiction U So. Calif. Law Sch. Mem. Yale Law Jour., 1967—69. Mem. ABA, LA County Bar Assn.(mem. com. of fed. procedure), Order of the Coif, Phi Beta Kappa. Office: O'Melveny & Myers LLP 400 S Hope St Los Angeles CA 90071-2899 Office Phone: 213-430-6111. Office Fax: 213-430-6407. Business E-Mail: jdaum@omm.com.

DAUM, JOHN LAVERN, retired band director, educator; b. Centralia, Ill., July 3, 1929; s. John Albert and Miriam Daum; m. Emma Elizabeth Kent, Oct. 17, 1954; children: John Thomas, Susan Lucille Daum-Bartling, Nancy Jane Daum-Durham, Brian Lee. AA in Edn., Centralia Jr. Coll., 1952; BA in Music Edn., So. Ill. U., Carbondale, 1954, MA in Music Edn., 1962. Band dir., tchr. Sch. Dist. 1, Vienna, Ill., 1954—58, Reorganized Dist. 1, Matthews, Mo., 1958—62, Cmty. Unit 1, Charleston, Ill., 1962—88; ret., 1988; band dir., originator Charleston Cmty. Band, 1977—. Commr. Park & Recreation Adv., Charleston, 1990—2005; music adjudicator Ill. HS Assn., 1968—2005, Ill. Elem. Sch. Assn., 1968—2005. Leader Boy Scouts Am., staff Nat. Jamboree, 1977, 1981, 1985, 1989, 1993, 1997, 2001, 2005. Recipient Vigil Honor, Boy Scouts Am., 1980, Woodbadge, 1982, Silver Beaver award, 1985, Jefferson award, Am. Inst. Pub. Svc., 2004. Mem.: Nat. Fedn. HS Music Assn., Nat. Band Assn. Methodist. Home: 1600 C St Charleston IL 61920

DAUMAN, PHILIPPE P., multi media company executive; b. Mar. 1, 1954; BA, Yale U., 1974; JD, Columbia U. Law Sch., 1978. Ptnr. Shearman & Sterling, NYC, 1978—93; sr. v.p. Viacom, Inc., NYC, 1993—96, gen. counsel, sec., 1993—98, exec. v.p., 1994—2000, dep. chmn., 1996—2000, pres., CEO, 2006—; co-chmn., CEO DND Capital Partners, LLC, 2000—. Bd. dirs. Viacom, Inc., 1996—98, 2006—; bd.dirs. Nat. Amusements, Inc., Lafarge Corp., Blockbuster, Inc., Genuity Inc. Bd. trustees Mus. City of NY; bd. visitors Columbia U. Law Sch. Office: Viacom Inc 1515 Broadway New York NY 10036-8901*

DAUPHINEE, JO ANNE LOUISE, retired nurse; b. Nov. 20, 1950; Student, U. Maine, Orono. Nurse asst. Bangor Mental Health Inst., Maine, 1974—2004. Recipient Women's award, Maine Progressive Newspaper, 1991, Women's Health Achievement award, Mabel Wadsworth Women's Health Ctr., 1999. Mem.: Peace and Justice Ctr. Ea. Maine (past bd. mem.), Nat. Assn. to Advance Fat Acceptance, Maine Women's Lobby (leadership pro-choice group 1971—), Maine Nat. Orgn. for Women (legis. coord. 1970, bd. activist 1971—, polit. action founder, treas. 1978, state coord. 1978—80, 1984, asst. state coord. 2001—06). Home: 87 Sunset Strip Brewer ME 04412

D'AURIOL, BRIAN J., engineering educator, researcher; PhD, U. New Brunswick, Fredericton, Canada, 1995. Vis. asst. prof. Wright State U., Dayton, Ohio, 1994—96; asst. prof. U. Man., Winnipeg, Manitoba, Canada, 1996—97; vis. asst. prof. U. Akron, Ohio, 1997—2000; asst. prof. U. Tex., El Paso, 2000—05; sr. sys. developer, engr. Ohio Supercomputer Ctr., Columbus, 2005—06; rsch. prof. Kyung Hee U., Yongin, Gyeonggi, Republic of Korea, 2006—. Contbr. articles to prof. jours. Mem.: IEEE, Assn. Computing Machinery. Office: Kyung Hee Univ Dept Computer Engring Sochen-dong Giheung-ku Gyeonggi Yongin 446-701 Republic of Korea Business E-Mail: dauriol@oslab.khu.ac.kr.

DAUS, ARTHUR STEVEN, neurological surgeon; b. Louisville, Feb. 6, 1957; s. Arthur Theodore Daus Jr. and Marilyn Ann (McCord) Hanish; m. Victoria Lynn Schilla, July 10, 1982; children: Arthur S. Jr., Haley N. BS in Physics magna cum laude, Vanderbilt U., 1977; MD, St. Louis U., 1981. Diplomate Nat. Bd. Med. Examiners, Am. Bd. Neurol. Surgery, Fedn. State Licensing Examiners; lic. physician, Ky., N.Mex., Ariz., Mo., Calif. Rotating intern in surgery U. Ky. Med. Ctr., Lexington, 1981-82, resident neurosurgeon, 1982-88; pvt. practice Midwest Neurosurgery Ctr., Joplin, Mo., 1988—. Instr. cervical spine instrumentation A.M.E. Med. Co., Kansas City, Mo., 1992. Mem. Nat. Coalition of Physicians Against Family Violence, Chgo., 1994—. Recipient Ky. State Residents award ACS com. on trauma, 1985; named Ky. Col. State of Ky., 1985—. Mem. AMA (Physician's Recognition award 1990-94, 2003-05, 06-, Physician's Recognition award with spl. commendation 1993-2003), So. Med. Assn., Jasper-Newton County Med. Soc., So. Neurosurg. Soc., Congress Neurol. Surgeons, Am. Assn. Neurol. Surgeons (Continuing Edn. award 1990-2004), Nat. Audubon Soc., Phi Beta Kappa, Phi Eta Sigma. Republican. Roman Catholic. Avocations: chess, swimming, archery, riflery, horseback riding. Home: 5 Teal Dr Joplin MO 64804-5816 Office: Midwest Neurosurgery Ctr 1111 McIntosh Cir Ste 305 Joplin MO 64804-3693

DAUSSMAN, GROVER FREDERICK, electrical engineer, consultant; b. Warrick County, Ind., May 6, 1919; s. Grover Cleveland and Madeline (Springer) D.; m. Elli Margrite Kilian, Dec. 27. 1941; children: Cynthia Louise Daussman Quinn, Judith Ann, Margaret Elizabeth Daussman Davidson Cooper. Student, U. Cin., 1936-38, Carnegie Inst. Tech., 1944-45, George Washington U., Washington, DC, 1948-56; BSEE, U. Ala., 1963, postgrad., 1963-64, 77, Indsl. Coll. Armed Forces, 1955-63; PhD (hon.), Hamilton State U., 1973. Registered profl. engr. , Ala., Va., DC; cert. fallout shelter analyst. Coop. engr. Sunbeam Elec. Mfg. Co., Evansville, Ind., 1936-38; engr., draftsman Phila. Navy Yard, 1941-42; resident engr., supr. shipbldg. USN, Neville Island, Pa., 1942-45; engr. Pearl Harbor Navy Yard, 1945-48; sect. head Bur. Ships USN, Washington, 1948-56; head guidance and control tech. liaison Army Ballistic Missile Agy., Huntsville, Ala., 1956-58, chief program coordination Guidance and Control Lab., 1958-60; chief program coordination Astrionics Lab., Marshall Space Flight Ctr., Huntsville, 1960-63, dir's staff asst. for advanced rsch. and tech., 1963-70, engring. cons., 1970—. Project dir. fallout shelter surveys Mil Dept. Tenn., 1971-73; head drafting dept. Alverson-Draughon Coll., Huntsville, 1974-77; instr. Ala. Christian Coll., 1977-79; engring. draftsman Reisz Engring., 1979; chief engr. Sheraton Motor Inn, 1979; sr. engr. Sperry Support Services, 1980; assoc. Techni-Core Profls., Huntsville, 1980-81; elec. engr. Reisz Engring., Huntsville, 1981-86; tutor in mathematics, scis. and engring. North Ala. Ctr. for Ednl. Excellence, Huntsville, 1986-2000, and U.S. Dept. Vet. Affairs, 2000-. Chmn. cmty. spl. gifts com. Madison County Heart Assn., 1965; active mem. Population Action Coun., Huntsville Track Club, Mended Hearts, Inc., Prayer Power Club, Nat. Assn. Sr. Friends, Sierra Club; treas. Huntsville United Ch. of Christ, Ala., 1959-61; mem. ch. council St. John's United Ch. of Christ, Cullman, Ala., 1964-66; sec. ch. council, program com. chmn. ch. council 1965-66; vice moderator Ala.-Tenn. Assn. 1965-68; bd. dirs. Southeast conf. 1965-66, mem. budget and finance com. 1965-66. Recipient Appreciation cert. North Ala. Ednl. Opportunity Ctr., Inc., 1987, 88, 89, 90, 91. Fellow: Explorers Club; mem.: ACLU, AARP, AIAA, NSPE (state dir. 1962—65, chpt. pres. 1966—67, state dir. 1968—71, 1985—91), AAAS, IEEE (life; sr. mem. sect. chmn. No. Ala. sect. 1961—62, founder, chmn. engring. mgmt. chpt. 1964—65, mem. inst. rsch. com. 1965—67, mem. adminstrv. com. engring. mgmt. soc. 1966—86, sec. soc. 1968—85, mem. Region 3 exec. com. 1969—79, mem. inst. bd. dirs., regional del. dir. S.E. region 1972—73, appreciation certs. Huntsville sect. 1960—62, Disting. Svcs. award 1964, Engr. of Yr. award 1969, Inst. Centennial medal 1984, Centennial Hon.Role of Outstanding Vols 1986, Ednl. Activities award 1987), Huntsville Jr. Engring. Tech. Soc. (organizer local high sch. chpts.), US Naval Inst., Am. Soc. Naval Engrs., Huntsville Assn. Tech. Socs. (sec. 1969—70, v.p. 1970—71, founder), Nat. Assn. Retarded Children, Internat. Platform Assn., Am. Def. Preparedness Assn. (post dir. Tenn. Valley 1963—66), Am. Inst. Urban and Regional Affairs, Ala. Soc. Profl. Engrs. (state dir. 1962—65, chpt. pres. 1966—67, state dir. 1968—71, regional Math Counts coord. 1981—91, state dir. 1985—91, state math. counts coord. 1988—89, Chpt. Engr. of Yr. 1968, 1982, Cert. of Appreciation 1982, Chpt. Engr. of Yr. 1989, Pres. award 1989), Planetary Soc. (charter), Hellenic Profl. Assn. Am. (hon.), MSFC Retirees Assn. (v.p. 1973—74, pres. 1974—75), Nat. Assn. Ret. Fed. Employees, Assn. US Army, Missile, Space and Range Pioneers (life), Cousteau Soc., U. Ala. Alumni Assn., Redstone Arsenal Officers Club. Democrat. United Ch. Of Christ. Office: 200 Westside Sq Ste 205 Huntsville AL 35801 Personal E-mail: gdauss@yahoo.com.

DAUSTER, WILLIAM GARY, lawyer, economist; b. Sacramento, Nov. 25, 1957; s. William Joe and Marianne Dauster; m. Ellen Lisa Weintraub, May 10, 1986; children: Matthew Isaac, Natanya Miriam, Emma Sophia. BA in Econs., Polit. Sci. and Internat. Rels., U. So. Calif., 1978, MA in Econs., 1981; JD, Columbia U., 1984. Bar: N.Y. 1985, U.S. Dist. Ct. (so. and ea. dists.) N.Y. 1985, D.C. 1986, U.S. Supreme Ct. 1997. Assoc. Cravath, Swaine & Moore, NYC, 1984-86; chief counsel com. on budget U.S. Senate, Washington, 1986-94, acting staff dir., chief coun., 1994, Dem. chief of staff, chief coun., 1995-97, Dem. dep. staff dir., gen. coun. com. labor & human resources, 1997, Dem. chief of staff, chief coun., 1997-98; counselor Wellstone Pres. Exploratory Com., Washington, 1998-99; dep. asst. to the Pres. for econ. policy, dep. dir. Nat. Econ. Coun., The White House, Washington, 1999-2000; sr. counselor to Senator Russ Feingold U.S. Senate, Washington, 2000—01, legis. dir., 2001—03. Dem. gen. coun. com. on fin. U.S. Senate, 2003, Dem. dep. staff dir., gen. coun., 2003—. Author: Congressional Budget Act Annotated, 1990, Budget Process Law Annotated, 1991, 1993, Trade Promotion Authority Annotated, 2007; editor-in-chief Columbia Jour. Law and Social Problems, 1983—84; contbr. articles to profl. jours. Bd. visitors Columbia Law Sch., 1992—2000. Recipient Order of Palm, 1978, trustee scholarship, U. So. Calif., 1974, Harlan Fiske Stone scholar, 1982—84. Mem.: N.Y. Bar Assn., D.C. Bar Assn. Democrat. Jewish. Home: 9713 Connecticut Ave Kensington MD 20895-3528 Business E-Mail: bill_dauster@finance-dem.senate.gov.

DAUTARTAS, MINODAUGAS (MINO) FERNAND, physical chemist; b. Cleve., Oct. 5, 1952; s. Zigmas and Madeleine Dautartas; m. Barbara Ann Renner, June 26, 1976; children: Angela Madeleine, Jennifer Ileine. BS in Chemistry, Ohio State U., 1977; PhD in Analytical Chemistry, U. Minn., 1982. Fellow U. Minn., Mpls., 1977—82; prin. investigator Bell Labs., Breinigsville, Pa., 1982—2000; chief tech. officer Haleos, Blacksburg, Va., 2000—02, Luna Innovations, Blacksburg, 2002; prin., owner LightVortex, Blacksburg, 2002—. Cons. MFD Consulting, Blacksburg, 2004—. Mem. City Coun., Alburtis, Pa., 1993—94. Mem.: IEEE (chmn. optoelectronics com. 1998—2000, Outstanding Paper award 1993). Achievements include patents for 74 U.S. patents in fiberoptics & integrated optics; invention of low cost miniture laser package; development of laser package, provided 1/3 World Market and brought in $2Billion in Revenue to Lucent; first to invent organometalic solar cell without a semiconductor. Home and Office: LightVortex Inc MFD Consulting 2006 Sycamore Trail Blacksburg VA 24060 Home Phone: 540-953-2160; Office Phone: 540-953-2160. Office Fax: 540-953-2164. Personal E-mail: mino.dautartas@verizon.net.

DAUTEL, CHARLES SHREVE, retired mining company executive; b. Cleve., Apr. 5, 1923; s. Robert Poe and Frances (Shreve) D.; m. Isabell Francis Brown, June 11, 1947; children: Charles Warren, Louis Craig. BSc, Ohio U., 1948; JD, U. Cin., 1952. Bar: Ohio 1952. With Nichols, Wood, Marx & Ginter, Cin., 1952-55, Eagle-Picher Industries, Inc., Cin., 1955-88, asst. sec., asst. gen. counsel, 1958-70, sec., 1970-87, v.p., 1980-87. With AUS, 1942-46. Mem. Phi Delta Theta, Phi Delta Phi. Clubs: Hidden Valley Lake Country. Home: 1448 Brookridge Circle Dr Lawrenceburg IN 47025-9332

DAUTEN, DALE ALAN, newspaper columnist; b. Fairfield, Iowa, Sept. 30, 1950; s. Joel John and Jeri (Muck) D.; m. Sandy Kelley; children: Hilary, Trevor, Joel. BS, Ariz. State U., 1971, MS, 1972; postgrad., Stanford U., 1972-73. Rsch. analyst AMERCO, Phoenix, 1972-74; rsch. mgr. Armour-Dial Corp., Phoenix, 1974-75; v.p. Hollander Assn., Atlanta, 1975-80; owner, founder Rsch. Resources, Atlanta and L.A., 1980-88; columnist King Features, NYC, 1992—; owner/founder The Innovators' Lab, 2002—. Cons., Tempe, Ariz., 1988—; syndicated columnist The Corporate Curmudgeon, 1992—, Kate & Dale Talk Jobs, 1996—. Author: Quitting, 1980, Taking Chances, 1986, The Max Strategy, 1996, The Gifted Boss, 1999, The Laughing Warriors, 2003, Better Than Perfect, 2006, Great Employees Only, 2006. Mediator State Atty. Gen., Phoenix, 1992-98; commr. Tempe Planning and Zoning commn., 1993-98; v.p., bd. dirs. Tactile Mus. for the Blind, Tempe, 1995-2000, Tempe Dream Commn., 1999-2000; vol. instr. East Valley Men's Ctr., 2002—. Office: c/o King Features 235 E 45th St New York NY 10017-3305 Office Phone: 480-839-8999. E-mail: dale@dauten.com.

DAUTH, FRANCES KUTCHER, journalist, editor; b. St. Louis, Aug. 20, 1941; d. David Jacob Kutcher and Dorothy Marie (Baugh) Hedges; m. Jerry Donald Dauth, July 5, 1964 (div. Dec. 1980). BA, U. Colo., 1963; cert. mgmt. program, Smith Coll., 1989. Staff writer Alameda (Calif.) Times Star, 1966—67, Contra Costa Times, Walnut Creek, Calif., 1968—69, Oakland (Calif.) Tribune, 1969—77; project editor San Francisco Examiner, 1977—82; asst. city editor Phila. Inquirer, 1982, dep. N.J. editor, 1983, suburban editor, 1984—85, city editor, 1985—89, nat. editor, 1989—91, fgn. editor, 1991—94, assoc. mng. editor, 1994—96; mng. editor Star Ledger, Newark, 1996—2004, editor editl. pages, 2004—. Office: Star Ledger Newark NJ 07102 Office Phone: 973-392-1536. Business E-Mail: fdauth@starledger.com.

DAVATZES, NICKOLAS, retired broadcast executive; 2 children. BA, M, St. John's U. Various exec. positions Xerox Corp., 1965—75, v.p. sales and mktg., 1975—77; pres. Intext Comm. Sys., 1978—80; pres., CEO A&E TV Networks, NYC, 1983—2005, CEO emeritus, 2005—. Mem. adv. bd. Colls. Bus. Adminstrn. St. John's U.; bd. govs. Banff TV Festival. Founder Conn. Found. Childhood Leukemia; trustee St. John's U. Formerly with USMC. Co-recipient Salute to Freedom award, USS Intrepid Found., 1995; named to Broadcasting and Cable Hall of Fame, 1999; recipient Hist. Found. Heritage award, USMC, Chevalier des Arts et Lettres, French Govt., 1989, Pres.'s award, Cable TV Pub. Affairs Assn., 1996, Vanguard award, Nat. Cable TV Assn., 1994, Hellenic Heritage Achievement award, Am. Hellenic Inst., 2000, Nat. Humanities Medal, NEH, 2006. Mem.: NATAS (dir. internat. coun.), Brit. Acad. Film and TV Arts (east coast, trustee).*

DAVE, TUSHAR A., Indo-US venture capital company executive; BS in Physics and Math., Bombay U.; MS in Computer Engring., Syracuse U., 1981. Design engr., advanced processor develop. group Intel Corp.; strategic mktg. mng., mem. corp. strategic team VLSI Technology, Inc., San Jose, Calif.; co-founder, chmn., pres., CEO Arcus Technology, Inc. (acquired by Cypress Semiconductor); founder, chmn., pres., CEO Armedia, Inc. (acquired by Broadcom Corp.), 1997; v.p., bus. develop. Broadcom Corp.; co-founder, mng. ptnr. NewPath Ventures, LLC, Santa Clara, Calif., 2002—. Created Vengines, Inc.; bd. dir. Nevis Networks, Inc., HelloSoft, Inc.; chmn. Emuzed. Achievements include being a pioneer in building Indo-US start-ups. Office: NewPath Ventures LLC 3945 Freedom Cir Ste 1050 Santa Clara CA 95054 Address: NewPath Ventures LLC 26 Cunningham Rd Bangalore 560 052 India Office Phone: 408-919-9900. Business E-Mail: tushar@newpathventures.com.

D'AVELLA, BERNARD JOHNSON, JR., publishing executive, lawyer; b. Orange, NJ, Jan. 6, 1945; s. Bernard Johnson and Aida Santa (Magliacane) D'A.; m. Elaine Anne Benucci, Aug. 11, 1973; children: Bernard J. III, Anthony N. Student, Princeton U., 1962-66; AB, Rutgers U., 1970; JD, U. Penn., 1973. Bar: N.J. 1973, U.S. Dist. Ct. N.J. 1973. Assoc. atty. Hannoch Weisman, Newark, 1973-78, ptnr., dir. Newark, Roseland, Trenton, NJ, 1978-98, mng. ptnr., dir., 1980-91; pres., COO Prudent Pub. Co. and The Gallery Collection, Ridgefield Park, NJ, 1998—. Former class pres. Princeton U., mem. exec. com., 25th, 30th, 35th and 40th reunion coms., former chmn. Maclean fellow sel. com.; former treas., trustee The Joint Connection; former chmn. ethics commn. Borough of Roseland, N.J.; chmn. Juvenile Conf. Com. Twp. of Essex Fells, N.J.; chmn. bd. govs. N.J. State Opera. Sgt. U.S. Army, 1967-69. Decorated Bronze Star, Bronze Star with oak leaf cluster, Air medal, Army Commendation medal. Mem. ABA, N.J. State Bar Assn., Assn. Fed. Bar, Essex County Bar Assn., Princeton Alumni Assn. Essex County (exec. com., alumni schs. com., past pres.), Essex Fells Country Club, Fellsbrook Paddle and Tennis Club, Mantoloking Yacht Club (sec., bd. govs.). Avocations: opera, house restoration and design, antiques and classic automobiles, tennis, golf. Office: Prudent Pub Co Inc 65 Challenger Rd 1st Fl Ridgefield Park NJ 07660-2111

DAVENPORT, AARON CHRISTOPHER, military officer; adopted s. Carlton Phillips and Lois Crocker Davenport; m. Kendra Mary Ennis, Sept. 23, 1989; children: Tatum Katherine, Payton Grace, Aelish Claire. BS in Marine Sci., US Coast Guard Acad., New London, Conn., 1984; MS in Environ. Health Sci., U. Calif., LA, 1995; grad. in Minor Hazardous Materials, UCLA, 1995. Cert. govtl. office World Safety Orgn., 1997, govt. safety officer World Safety Orgn., 1997, merchant marine master US Coast Guard, Dept. Homeland Security, 2004, safety exec. World Safety Orgn., 2007. Asst. chief, safety and health US Coast Guard, Norfolk, Va., 1995—98; ops., safety and command security officer US Coast Guard Cutter Hamilton, San Pedro, Calif., 1998—99; exec., safety officer US Coast Guard Cutter Tahoma, New Bedford, Mass., 1999—2001; exec. officer, counterdrug ops. US So. Command, Miami, Fla., 2001—03; sec., counterterrorism joint interagency coord. group US Hdqs., So. Command, Miami, 2001—03; commdg. officer US Coast Guard Cutter Valiant, Miami Beach, 2003—05; dep. chief, office counterterrorism and spl. missions US Coast Guard Hdqs., Washington, 2005—06; nat. security fellow Rand Corp., Nat. Def. Rsch. Inst., Arlington, Va., 2006—07; spl. advisor, homeland security affairs Exec. Office of V.P. USA, Washington, 2007—. Contbr. articles to profl. jours. Capt. master sail tng. vessel argus US Boyscouts Am., Newport Beach, Calif., 1993—99. Decorated Spl. Ops. award US Coast Guard, Commendation medal, Spl. Ops. award, Commendation medal, Def. Meritorious Svc. medal Dept. Def., Global War On Terrorism Svc. medal US So. Command, Dept. Def., Mil. Outstanding Vol. Svc. award, Armed Forces Expeditionary medal US So. Command, Meritorious Svc. medal US Coast Guard Atlantic Area Comdr., Presdl. Unit citation Pres. of USA. Mem.: Air Waste Mgmt. Assn. (internat. jour. peer reviewer 2000—). Achievements include research in co and nox exposure during car carrier off-loading operations. Avocations: equine sports, scuba diving, yachting. Office: Exec Office VP Homeland Security Affairs Purcellville VA 20132 Home Phone: 540-338-5360.

DAVENPORT, ALAN GARNETT, civil engineer, educator; b. Madras, India, Sept. 19, 1932; naturalized, Can. s. Tom and May Davenport; m. Sheila Rand Smith, Apr. 13, 1957; children: Thomas Sidney, Anna Margaret, Andrew Hope, Clare Rand. BA, Cambridge U., Eng., 1954, MA, 1958; MASc, U. Toronto, Ont., Can., 1957, DEng (hon.), 1989; PhD, U. Bristol, Eng., 1960; D. in Applied Sci. (hon.), U. Louvain, Belgium, 1979; D. in Tech. (hon.), Tech. U. Denmark, 1982; DSc (hon.), McGill U., Montreal, Que., Can., 1983, U. Toronto, Ont., 1989; DEng (hon.), Waterloo U., Ont., Can., 1986; DSc (hon.), U. Guelph, Ont., 1993, U. La Plata, Argentina, 1993; DEng, Carlton U., 1996, U. Bristol, 1998; DSc (hon.), U. Western Ontario, London, Canada, 2002. Lectr. U. Toronto, Ont., Canada, 1955-57; research officer Nat. Research Council, Ottawa, Ont., Canada, 1957-58; asst. prof., then prof. U. Western Ont., London, Canada, 1960—, founding dir. boundary layer wind tunnel lab., 1965—, rsch. dir. Inst. for Catastrophic Loss Reduction, 1999; dir. Ctr. for Studies in Constrn., 1990—. Cons. World Trade Ctr., NYC, CN Tower, Toronto, Sears Bldg., Chgo., Sunshine Skyway Bridge, Fla., Hong Kong and Shanghai Bank Bldg., Bank China Bldg., Hong Kong, Gt. Belt Bridge, Denmark, Normandy Bridge, France, Millau Viaduct, France, others. Editor: Can. Jour. Civil Engring., 1974—79; mem. editl. bd. Can. Jour. Civil Engring., 1979—81. Chmn. Can. nat. com. UN-Internat. Decade Natural Disaster Reduction, 1993—. Decorated Order of Can.; named to Engring. Hall of Distinction, U. Toronto, 1999; recipient Nobel prize, 1963, Cancam medal, Cancam 83, Saskatoon, Can., 1983, Queen Elizabeth medal, 1952—77, Gold medal, Inst. Structural Engrs., 1987, Oleg A. Kerensky medal, 1988, Ernest C. Manning award of distinction, Can. Confedn. medal, 1967—92, Killam prize, 1993, Can. Gold medal for sci. and engring., Natural Sci. and Engring. Rsch. Coun. Can., 1994, Gold ribbon d'Or award, French Autoroute Authority, Hellmuth prize for rsch., U. Western Ont., Otto H.G Flaschbart medal, Wind Engring. Soc. Germany, Austria and Switzerland, 2000, John F. Kennedy medal, Engring. Inst. Can., 2000, Albert Caquot prize, French Assn. Civil Engrs., 2001, Spl. Achievement award, Am. Inst. Steel Constrn., 2005, Lynn S. Beedle award, Coun. Tall Bldgs and Urban Habitat, 2005. Fellow: Royal Soc. Can. (Rutherford lectr. 1988), Engring. Inst. Can. (Duggan medal 1960, Gzowski medal 1963, 1978, Julian C. Smith medal), Can. Soc. Civil Engring. (A. B. Sanderson award 1985); mem.: ASCE (State of Art Civil Engring. award 1973, Can.-Am. Civil Engring. award 1977, Jack Cermak medal 2003), Coun. Tall Bldgs. and Urban Habitat (Lynn S. Beedle Achievement award), Am. Inst. Steel

Constrn. (Spl. Achievement award 2005), Royal Acad. Engring. (fgn. mem.), Can. Acad. Engring. (pres.), Nat. Acad. Engring. (assoc.), Internat. Assn. Shell Structures (Tsubai prize 1997), Internat. Assn. Bridge and Structural Engring. (award of Merit), Assn. Profl. Engrs. Ont. (Silver medal 1977, Bell Can. Forum award 1992), Can. Meteorol. Soc. (prize in Applied Meteorology 1965), Am. Meteorol. Soc. Avocations: sailing, squash, tennis. Home: 412 Lawson Rd London ON Canada N6G 1X8 Office: U Western Ont Boundary Layer Wind Tunnel Lab Engring Sci London ON Canada N6A 5B9 E-mail: agd@blwtl.uwo.ca.

DAVENPORT, ANN ADELE MAYFIELD, retired home care agency administrator; b. New Orleans, Nov. 12, 1941; d. Henry Louis and Myrtie Iola (Cason) Mayfield; m. John Wayne Davenport, June 18, 1966; children: Steven Lyle, Daniel Ryan, Eline Adele. BA, Southeasten La. Coll., 1963; MA in Edn., George Peabody Coll., 1965; MA in Sociology, Tex. Tech. U., 1971. Tchr. various schs., 1963—70; instr. of sociology Tex. Tech. U., Lubbock, 1970—74, James Madison U., Harrisonburg, Va., 1981—82, Ga. So. Coll., Statesboro, 1982—84; 5th grade tchr. Bulloch County Schs., Statesboro, Ga., 1985—87; gerontology project coord. Dept. of Nursing Ga. So. Coll., 1987—89; project dir. Sr. Companion Program Ctr. for Rural Health and Rsch., Ga. So. U., Statesboro, 1988—93; instr. dept. health sci. edn. Ga. So. Coll., Statesboro, 1993—95; exec. dir. Ogeechee Home Health Agy., Statesboro, 1995—96, Homebound Svcs., Statesboro, 1996—2002; ret., 2002. Editor various newsletters, 1987-2002. Bd. dirs. Citizens Against Violence, Statesboro, 1987-88, Habitat for Humanity, 1990-2002; pres. Coun. on Children and Parents, Statesboro, 1988-89, 93-94; mem. steering com. Bulloch County Commn. on Human Svcs., 1989-2002; adminstrv. bd. dirs., coun. on ministries, nominating com. Pittman Park United Meth. Ch.; pres. Ogeechee Wellness Coun., 1992-2002; bd. dirs. Ogeechee Home Health Agy., 1989-93. Mem. Ga. Rural Health Assn. (sec. 1988-89, editor state newsletter 1989-96), So. Sociol. Soc., Ga. Gerontol. Assn., Ga. Sociol. Assn., AAUW (newsletter editor Statesboro 1987-89), Am. Soc. on Aging, Nat. Coun. on the Aging, Am. Rural Health Assn. Avocations: tennis, reading.

DAVENPORT, ANNE MARILYN, dietitian; b. Queens Village, NY, Nov. 29, 1947; d. Alfred Francis Morel and Charlotte Adelaide Ward; m. John Howard Pearson, June 27, 1981 (div. July 1989); m. Terry Del Davenport, Sept. 10, 1995. AA in Liberal Arts, So. Seminary Jr. Coll., Buena Vista, Va., 1967; BS in Math. & Secondary Edn., U. Mass., Amherst, 1969, MS in Nutrition & Computers in Nutrition, 1975. Math. tchr. Highland Falls H.S., NY, 1969—71; clin. dietitian Aspen Valley Hosp., Colo., 1974—75; head clin. dietitian Cabell Huntington Hosp., W.Va., 1977—78, St. Mary's Hosp. & Med. Ctr., Grand Junction, Colo., 1978—82; nursing home cons. Powell County Nursing Home, Deerlodge, Mont., 1989—94; adminstrv. cons., bookkeeper Nat. Housebuilders Constrn. Co., Victor, Mont., 1995—. Author: (sci. fiction) Earthero, 2000. Mem.: New World Order Ministry for Universal Peace, Mont. Dietetic Assn., Am. Dietetic Assn. Avocations: jogging, walking. Home: 260 Indian Prairie Loop Victor MT 59875 Office Phone: 406-642-6863.

DAVENPORT, DAVID, lawyer, educator, academic administrator; b. Sheboygan, Wis., Oct. 24, 1950; s. E. Guy and Beverly J. (Snoddy) D.; m. Sally Nelson, Aug. 13, 1977; children— Katherine, Charles, Scott. BA, Stanford U., 1972; JD, U. Kans., 1977. Bar: Calif. 1977, U.S. Dist. Ct. (so. dist.) Calif., 1977. Assoc. Gray, Cary, Ames & Frye, San Diego, 1977—78; min. Ch. of Christ, San Diego, 1979; law prof. Pepperdine U., Malibu, Calif., 1980—99, gen. counsel, 1981—83, exec. v.p., 1983—86, pres., 1985—2000, dist. prof. pub. policy, 2003—. Rsch. fellow Hoover Instn., 2001—. Co-author: Shepherd Leadership; contbr. Fed. Antitrust Law, 1985, articles to profl. jourls. Mem. Adminstrv. Conf. of U.S., Washington, 1984-86; bd. overseers Hoover Inst., Stanford U.; bd. dirs. Am. Internat., Salem Cmty., Forest Lawn Meml. Parks Assn.; bd. dirs. Common Sense Calif., co-chair. Mem. Order of Coif. Republican. Office: Pepperdine U 24255 Pacific Coast Hwy Malibu CA 90263-0002 Business E-Mail: david.davenport@pepperdine.edu.

DAVENPORT, KIRK ADDISON, lawyer; b. Sept. 20, 1959; s. William and Gertrude (Perkins) D.; children: Lydia, Addison. BA, Brown U., 1981; JD, U. Mich., 1984. Bar: N.Y. 1984. Ptnr. Latham & Watkins, NYC, 1985—. Office: Latham & Watkins 885 3rd Ave Ste 1000 New York NY 10022-4834

DAVENPORT, LAWRENCE FRANKLIN, academic administrator; b. Lansing, Mich., Oct. 13, 1944; s. Theodore and Bernice (Alexander) D.; m. Cecelia Jackson, Sept. 24, 1966; children— Laurence, Anita, Anthony BA, Mich. State U., 1966, MA, 1968; Ed.D., Fairleigh Dickinson U., 1975; MS, Leicester Univ., Eng., 2002. V.p. devel. Tuskegee Inst., Ala., 1972-74; pres. ednl. complex San Diego C.C., 1974-79, provost, 1979-81; assoc. dir. ACTION, Washington, 1981-82; asst. sec. U.S. Dept. Edn., Washington, 1982-87; asst. sec. mgmt. and adminstrn. U.S. Dept. Energy, Washington, 1987-89; assoc. vice chancellor U. Calif., San Francisco, 1989-92; pres. Lawrence Davenport & Assocs., Mercer Island, Wash., 1989—2003; CFO, Seattle Pub. Schs., 1992-94; v.p. fin. and ops., CFO Milton Hershey (Pa.) Sch., 1994-2000; sr. v.p. Antin Neher Assocs., Hershey, 2000—01; dep. chief adminstrv. officer U.S. Ho. of Reps., 2001—02; exec. dir. Hale House Ctr. Inc., NYC, 2002—04; exec. v.p. Fla. Atlantic U., Boca Raton, 2004—06, exec. v.p. univ. advancement, 2006—07; interim pres. Paragon Found., West Palm Beach, Fla., 2007—. Co-author (with Petty): Career Education and Minorities, 1973. Presbyterian. Personal E-mail: lfdavenport@adelphia.net.

DAVENPORT, LEE LOSEE, physicist; b. Schenectady, NY, Dec. 31, 1915; m. Anne S. Davenport, 1944; children: Jeanne Treder, Carol Davenport. BS, Union Coll., 1937; MS, U. Pitts., 1940, PhD in Physics, 1946. Rsch. assoc. radar MIT, Cambridge, Mass., 1941-46; rsch. fellow constrn. cyclotron Harvard U., Cambridge, Mass., 1946-50; exec. v.p. Perkin-Elmer Corp., Norwalk, Conn., 1950-57; pres. Sylvania Corning Nuclear Corp., Bayside LI, NY, 1957-60; v.p. planning Sylvania Elec. Prodn., Inc., NYC, 1960-62; pres. GTE Labs, Inc., Stamford, Conn., 1962-77; v.p., chief scientist GTE, 1977-80, cons. telecomm., 1980—. Asst. dir. Electronics Rsch. Lab., U. Pitts, 1946, corp. dir., 1980-92. Fellow IEEE, Am. Phys. Soc.; mem. Nat. Acad. Engring. (life), Sci. Rsch. Soc. Am. Home: 61 Winding Ln Greenwich CT 06831-3704 E-mail: lld@sanglier.net.

DAVENPORT, LINDSAY, professional tennis player; b. Palos Verdes, Calif., June 8, 1976; d. Wink and Ann Lindsay; m. Jon Leach, 2003. Profl. tennis player, 1993—. Mem. U.S. Women's Olympic Tennis Team, Atlanta, 1996, Sydney, 2000, U.S. Fed Cup Team, 1993—2000, 2002. Named Rookie of the Yr., TENNIS Magazine, 1993, World Team Tennis, 1993, MVP, 1997, Player of the Year, TENNIS Magazine, 1998, Tour Player of the Year, WTA, 1998, 1999. Achievements include winning a gold medal in US Women's singles, Atlanta Olympic Games, 1996; singles champion, US Open, 1998, Wimbledon, 1999, Australian Open, 2000; doubles champion, Roland Garros (with Mary Jo Fernanadez), 1996, U.S. Open (with Jana Novotna), 1997, Wimbledon (with Corina Morariu), 1999; being WTA Tour Champion, 1999; winner of 48 career singles titles, 35 doubles titles, WTA Tour. Office: US Tennis Assn 70 W Red Oak Ln White Plains NY 10604-3602*

DAVENPORT, PAUL, economics professor; BA in Econs. with gt. distinction/honors, Stanford U., 1969; MA, U. Toronto, 1970, PhD, 1976, LLD (hon.), 2000, U. Alta., 1994; PhD (hon.), Internat. U. Moscow, 2002. Prof. econs. McGill U., Montreal, Que., Canada, 1972-89, assoc. dean grad. studies, 1982-86, vice prin. planning and computer svcs., 1986-89; pres., vice chancellor U. Alta., Edmonton, Alta., Canada, 1989-94, U. Western Ont., London, Canada, 1994—. Chair Assn. Univs. and Colls. Can., 1997-99, Coun. Ont. Univs., 1999-2001. Editor: (with Richard H. Leach) Reshaping Confederation: The 1982 Reform of the Canadian Constitution, 1984; contbg. author Renovating the Ivory Tower, 2002. Chair United Way Campaign, London and Middlesex, 2005. Decorated Chevalier Legion of Honor (France); Officer Order of Can. Mem.: Am. Econ. Assn., Can. Assn. Economists, Phi Beta Kappa. Office: U Western Ont Office of Pres Stevenson-Lawson Bldg London ON Canada N6A 5B8 Office Fax: 519-661-3676. Business E-Mail: pdavenpo@uwo.ca.

DAVENPORT, SANDRA, cultural organization administrator; d. Charles Adams and Katy Ann Davenport; 1 child, Suerain S. BA in Classics, St. John's Coll., Annapolis, Md., 1975; MSW, Ariz. State U., 1986. Lic. master social worker Ariz. Bd. Behavioral Health Examiners. Dir. Home Based Montessori Pre-Sch., Tucson, 1980—82; counselor, program coord. Family Counseling Agy., Tucson, 1986—89; therapist Tri Cmty. Counseling, Oracle, 1989—92; med. social worker Carondelet St. Mary's Hosp., Tucson, 1993—2001; exec. dir. Pima County/Tucson Women's Commn., Tucson, 2003—. Presenter, trainer Ariz. Child Abuse Prevention Conf., Phoenix, 1999; mem. steering com. Ariz. Women's Conf., Tucson, 2003—04; mem. hon. com. Micro Bus. Advancement Ctr. Luncheon, Tucson, 2004—05; founding mem., facilitator Pay Equity Initiative Cmty. Collaboration. Active Mayor's Task Force on Domestic Violence, Tucson, 1995; coord. Cmty. Collaboration on Domestic Violence Intervention in Healthcare, 1998—2001; mem. site visit team Ariz. Perinatal Trust, Phoenix, 2000; bd. mem., com. chair Am. Friends Svc. Com., Tucson, 2002—04. Recipient Mayor's cert. of recognition for role in Elder Shelter Program Devel. Team, Excellence award, Mayor George Miller, Tucson, 1998, Cmty. Collaboration award, Carondelet Cmty. Trust, 1999, Spl. Recognition Cert. award, Office Gov. Janet Napolitano, 2007, Cert. Honor award, Pima County Bd. Suprs. Chmn. Richard Elias, 2007, Appreciation and Recognition award, Office Mayor Robert Walkup, City Tucson, 2007. Mem.: NASW (Ariz. br. steering com., Social Worker of Yr. 2000), Black Women's Task Force, Ariz. Women's Polit. Caucus. Achievements include developed and implemented area protocol for domestic violence screening in hospitals. Avocations: painting, hiking, dance. Home: 3242 N El Tovar Tucson AZ 85705

DAVENPORT, THOMAS HERBERT, small business owner; b. Sandusky, Ohio, Mar. 15, 1933; s. Orme and Elva Mae (Bragg) D.; m. Annetta Henman, June 22, 1963; children: Deborah Ann, Mark Thomas, Brenda Kay. Grad., Coyne Electronic Sch., 1954-55. Lic. FCC gen. radio telephone. Clk. Nickel Plate R.R., Bellevue, Ohio, 1951, 1954; electronic technician various firms, Sandusky, 1955-56; prin. Bellevue Radio and TV, 1955—. Numerous inventions in field. Cpl. U.S. Army, 1952-53, 2d. lt USAF Aux., 1980-84. Mem. Am. Legion. Republican. Avocations: inventing, cartooning, gardening, poetry, reflexology. Home: 111 Seneca Dr Bellevue OH 44811-1635 Office: Bellevue Radio & TV 109 W Center St Bellevue OH 44811-1351

DAVERNE, STEVEN RICHARD, advertising director, artist, illustrator, behavior analyst, marketing professional, consultant; b. Patuxant, Md., July 10, 1955; s. Ronald Richard and Joan Beverly DaVerne. BA, U. South Fla., Sarasota, 1980; AS, Tampa Tech. Inst., 1990. Cert. Supervision and Employee Management Fla. Mental Health Inst., 1985, U. So. Fla., 1985. Therapist, behavior analyst Tampa Heights Hosp., 1980—84; behavior analyst, rschr. Fla. Mental Health Inst., Tampa, 1984—88; graphic designer, art dir. and illustrator numerous advt. and mktg. cos., 1988—98; creative dir. US West Comms., Denver, 1998—2000; owner, operator DaVerne Creative Group, Denver, 2000—; v.p. creative svcs. G.A. Wright Mktg., Inc., Denver, 2002—; founder, prin. Interact Tutorial Svcs., LLC, 2006—. Cons. Young Authors Conf., Tampa, Fla., 1991, Communique Group Advt., Denver, 2000—01; judge, creative cons. Henry Wurst Press Inc., Denver, 2000—01. Exhibitions include American 76th Nat. Exhbn., Nat. Arts Club, Patrons Internat. Exhbn., others, Represented in permanent collections Carter Presdl. Ctr., Atlanta. Nat. children's cancer soc. nat., 1988—2002; presenter behavioral tng. seminars Fla. Mental Health Inst., Tampa, Fla., 1984—88. Recipient Am. Graphic Design award, Bus. Mktg. Awards, 1999, Internat. Summit Creative award, Summit Awards, 1999, 2000. Mem.: Assn. Behavior Analysis, Art Dirs. Club. Achievements include supr. in the establishment of the first pilot research program for mainstreaming severely emotionally disturbed (SED) children in the Florida education system; development of paintings called the Learning Series which intrepreted and documented the social rsch. experience of (SED) children. Avocations: composing and performing music, skiing, water-skiing, sailing. Office Phone: 303-861-0539. Personal E-mail: steven@makup.net.

DAVES, DON MICHAEL, minister; b. Wichita Falls, Tex., Mar. 4, 1938; s. Floyd Lee and Johnnie Majorie (Dunn) D.; m. Patricia N. McLean, Aug. 29, 1958; children: Paul Lee, Donna Michelle. BA, Midwestern U., 1959; ThM, So. Meth. U., 1963; D. Humanities (hon.), Southwestern Coll., 1971. Ordained to ministry Meth. Ch., 1963. Pastor 1st Meth. Ch., Holliday, Tex., 1963-66, Prairie Heights Meth. Ch., Grand Prairie, Tex., 1966-72; minister to soc. North Tex. Conf. United Meth. Ch., 1972-77; pastor Meml. United Meth. Ch., Dallas, 1977-78; assoc. pastor Preston Hollow United Meth. Ch., Dallas, 1978-81, 1st United Meth. Ch., Duncanville, Tex., 1981-85, pastor Cedar Hill, Tex., 1985-91; assoc. pastor Walnut Hill United Meth. Ch., Dallas, 1992-95; pastor First United Meth. Ch., VanAlstyne, Tex., 1995-99; ret., 1999. Ret. mem. North Tex. Conf.; trustee Charlton Meth. Hosp., Dallas, 1986-95; mentor pastor Perkins Sch. Theology Intern Program, 1996-97; registrar Sherman-McKinney Bd. Ministry, 1996-99. Author: Devotional Talks for Children, 1961, Famous Hymns & Their Writers, 1962, Sermon Outlines on Romans, 1962, Meditations on Early Christian Symbols, 1963, Come with Faith, 1964, Young Readers Book of Christian Symbolism, 1967 (Best Children's Book by Tex. Author, Tex. Inst. Letters 1968), Advent: A Calendar of Devotions, 1971, Joy is Now, 1988. Active United Meth. Ch. Mem. Am. Assn. Pastoral Counselors, Dallas Hall Soc. So. Meth. U., Order of St. Luke, Disciplined Order Christ, Perkins Cir. Home: 5200 Keller Springs Rd Ste 231 Dallas TX 75248-2739

DAVES, GLENN DOYLE, JR., science educator, chemist, researcher; b. Clayton, N.Mex., Feb. 12, 1936; s. Glenn Doyle and Billye (Parker) D.; m. Pamela Gannarelli, Sept. 5, 1959; children: Laura Lee Daves Schantz, Anne Kathryn Crothers, Glenn Graham BS, Ariz. State U., 1959; PhD, MIT, 1964; PharmD (hon.), U. Uppsala, Sweden, 1987. Rsch. chemist Midwest Rsch. Inst., Kansas City, Mo., 1959-61, Stanford Rsch. Inst., Palo Alto, Calif., 1964-67; asst. prof. chemistry Oreg. Grad. Ctr., Beaverton, 1967-72, assoc. prof., 1972-74, prof., 1974-81, chmn. dept., 1972-79; prof., chmn. dept. chemistry Lehigh U., Bethlehem, Pa., 1981-88; dean provost Rensselaer Poly. Inst., Troy, 1989—2000, dean Project Kaleidoscope, Summer Insts., 2000—, dean provost, 2002—03. Vis. scientist NIH, Bethesda, Md., 1988. Co-editor: Advances in Polyamine Research, Vols. 1-2, 1978, Biologically Active Principals of Natural Products, 1984; contbr. numerous articles to profl. jours. Recipient numerous grants NIH, Am. Cancer Soc., U.S. Forest Svc., 1971—. Mem. Am. Chem. Soc., Internat. Soc. Heterocyclic Chemistry, Coun. for Chem. Rsch. (governing bd. 1985-86, chair manpower and resource com. 1984-87, mem. membership com. 1991). Democrat. Personal E-mail: davesgd@yahoo.com.

DAVES, SANDRA LYNN, poet, lyricist; b. Sacramento, Mar. 14, 1950; d. Willard Glen and Rachel Lucille Humbert; m. Tommy Wilburn Daves, Nov. 16, 1971 (dec. 2006); children: Todd Eric, Brice Aaron. Student, Internat. Libr. Poetry, 2003, Inst. Childrens Lit., 2006. Sec. McClellan AFB, Sacramento, 1969, Fish and Game Dept., Sacramento, 1970—71; poet, 1994—. Lyricist: songs Songs of Praise, Star of Bethlehem, America At War!, Gospel Millennium Celebration, Home For Christmas, Your Very Special Place, Kingdom of Angels (Four Star award for song Pray Without Ceasing, 2004), Celebrating Christmas with Jesus, The Joy and Splendor of Christmas, America, Producer's Showcase, Land That I Love, Hurricane, Songs of Love and Romance, 2006, Christmas By Candle Light, 2006; author: Diverse Verse, 2007; contbr. poetry to lit. publs. Recipient Poet of Merit, Fla., 2005. Mem.: ASCAP, Internat. Libr. Poetry, Am. Soc. Poets (founding laureate mem., founding laureate), Internat. Soc. Poets (Editor's Choice award Poet of Merit, Md. chpt. 2000—05, Poet of Merit Hollywood chpt. 2002, Poet of Merit Fla. chpt. 2003, Poet of Yr. Fla. chpt. 2003, Poet Laureate 2003, Poet of Merit DC chpt. 2003, Poet of Merit Fla. chpt. 2004, 2005, named Poet of Merit Las Vegas chpt. 2006, Poet of Merit Washington chpt., Poet of Merit Las Vegas chpt. 2007), Am. Biog. Inst. (life), Internat. Biog. Assn. (life). Avocations: reading, writing, walking, crossword puzzles. Home: 6825 Susanna Ct Citrus Heights CA 95621 Personal E-mail: sandilovespoetry-lyrics@comcast.net.

DAVEY, ADAM, gerontologist, researcher; BSc, U. Toronto, 1987—91; MSc, U. Guelph, 1992—94; PhD, Pa. State U., 1994—97. Assoc. prof. U. Ga., Athens, 1997—2004; sr. rsch. scientist Polisher Rsch. Inst., North Wales, Pa., 2004—3006; assoc. prof. Coll. Health Professions, Temple U., Phila., 2006—. Contbr. papers to profl. jours. and pubs. Bd. mem. Athens-Clarke County Coun. on Aging, 2001—03. Fellow: Gerontol. Soc. Am. (student awards com. 1995—97); mem.: APA (chair, divsn. 20 student awards com. 2003—05), Psychometric Soc., Am. Sociol. Assn. Office: Temple U Coll Health Professions 1700 N Broad St Ste 313 Philadelphia PA 19122 Office Phone: 215-204-7881. Office Fax: 215-204-1386. Business E-Mail: adavey@temple.edu.

DAVEY, CHARLES BINGHAM, soil scientist, educator; b. Bklyn., Apr. 7, 1928; s. Francis Joseph and Mary Elizabeth (Bingham) Davey; m. Elizabeth Anne Thompson, July 11, 1952; children: Douglas Alan, Barbara Lynn, Andrew Martin. BS, Syracuse U., 1950; MS, U. Wis., 1952, PhD, 1955. Soil scientist Rsch. Svc. Dept. Agr., Beltsville, Md., 1957-62; assoc. prof. N.C. State U., Raleigh, 1962-65, prof., 1965—, Carl Alwin Schenck Disting. prof., 1978—, Alumni Disting. prof., 1989, head dept., 1970-78. Editor: Tree Growth and Forest Soils, 1970; assoc. editor: Soil Sci. Soc. Am. proc., 1967—72; contbr. articles to profl. jours. With US Army, 1955—57. Fellow: AAAS, Soc. Am. Foresters (Barrington Moore Rsch. award), Soil Sci. Soc. Am. (pres. 1975—76, Disting. Svc. award), Am. Soc. Agronomy; mem.: Internat. Soc. Tropical Foresters, Sigma Xi (Rsch. award), Xi Sigma Pi, Gamma Sigma Delta, Phi Kappa Phi. Achievements include patents in field. Home: 5219 Melbourne Rd Raleigh NC 27606-1619 Office: Forestry Dept 3113 Faucette Dr Raleigh NC 27695-8008 Personal E-mail: char1168@bellsouth.net. Business E-Mail: cdavey@unity.ncsu.edu.

DAVEY, CLARK WILLIAM, newspaper publisher; b. Chatham, Ont., Can., Mar. 3, 1928; s. William and Marguerite (Clark) D.; m. Joyce Gordon, Sept. 13, 1952; children: Richard Gordon, Kevin William, Clark Michael. BA in Journalism, U. Western Ont., 1948, LLD (hon.), 1986. With Chatham Daily News, 1948-51; mng. editor No. Daily News, Kirkland Lake, Canada, 1951; hydro. seaway corr. Globe and Mail., 1951-55; mem. Parliamentary Press Gallery, Ottawa, 1956-60; fgn. editor Globe and Mail, 1960-63, mng. editor, 1963-78; pub. Vancouver (B.C., Can.) Sun, 1978-83, Montreal Gazette, 1983-89; pres., chmn. The Canadian Press, 1981-83; pub. Ottawa Citizen, 1989-92; v.p. Southam Inc., 1983-92; dir. Am. Press Inst., 1988-94; commr. Ottawa Hydro, 1999-2000. Pres. Michener Awards Found., 1993-98. Named to Can. News Hall of Fame, 1992. Office: 29 Madawaska Dr Ottawa ON Canada K1S 3G5 E-mail: waldosplace@rogers.com.

DAVEY, DIANE DAVIS, pathologist, educator; b. Sioux Falls, SD, June 23, 1956; d. Donald L. and Cara Lee Davis; children: James, Steven. BS with honors, Cornell U., Ithaca, NY, 1978; MD, Washington U., St. Louis, 1981. Diplomate Am. Bd. Pathology, Hematology, Cytopathology, Anatomic and Clin. Pathology. Resident in pathology Ind. U., Indpls., 1981—84; resident U. Iowa, Iowa City, 1984—85, fellow, 1985—86, assoc. pathology, 1986—88; asst. prof. pathology U. Ky., Lexington, 1988—94, assoc. prof. pathology, 1994—2000, prof. pathology, 2000—, dir. Cytopathology Lab., 1988—, vice chair, 2004—. Mem. panel, cons. FDA, Rockville, Md., 1995—; moderator Bethesda 2001 Workshop Nat. Cancer Inst., 2000—04; mem. adv. bd. Nat. Cancer Inst., 2004—; trustee Am. Bd. Pathology, Tampa, 2004—; assembly and task force mem. Am. Bd. Med. Specialists, 2005—. Co-author: The Bethesda System for Reporting Cervical Cytology, 2005; contbr. articles to profl. jours.; mem. editl. bd.: Diagnostic Cytopathology, 1996—, Cancer Cytopathology, 1996—; mem. editl. bd. Archives of Pathology and Laboratory Medicine, 2005—. Fellow, Acad. Medicine, 2006—07. Mem.: Papanicolaou Soc. Cytopathology (com. chair 1993, 2004), Coll. Am. Pathologists (com. chair 1998—2001, William Kuehn Outstanding Communicator award 2001), Am. Soc. Cytopathology (exec. bd. dirs. 1995—2003, v.p. 1999—2000, pres.-elect 2000—01, pres. 2001—02, Papanicolaou award 2007). Office: U Ky Med Ctr MS 117 Pathology 800 Rose St Lexington KY 40536 Office Phone: 859-257-9547. Business E-Mail: diane.davey@uky.edu.

DAVEY, KENNETH GEORGE, biologist, educator, academic administrator; b. Chatham, Ont., Can., Apr. 20, 1932; s. William and Marguerite (Clark) D.; m. Jeannette Isabel Evans, Nov. 28, 1959 (separated); children: Christopher Graham, Megan Jeannette, Katherine Alison. BSc, U. We. Ont., 1954, MSc, 1955, DSc (hon.), 2002; PhD, Cambridge U., 1958. NRC Can. fellow U. Toronto, Ont., 1958—59; Drosier fellow Gonville and Caius Coll., Cambridge U., 1959—63; assoc. prof. parasitology McGill U., Montreal, Que., Canada, 1963—67, prof. parasitology and biology, 1967—74, dir. Inst. Parasitology, 1964—74; prof., chmn. dept. biology York U., Downsview, Ont., 1974—81, dean of sci., 1982—85, disting. rsch. prof., 1984—2000, disting. rsch. prof. emeritus, 2001—, v.p. acad. affairs, 1986—91. Past pres. Huntsman Marine Lab.; pres. Biol. Coun. Can., 1979-81; mem. animal biology grant selection com. Natural Scis. and Engring. Rsch. Coun. Can., 1980-83, group chmn. life scis., 1983-86, mem. com. grants and scholarships, 1983-86; mem. panel on tropical health NIH, 1978-82; pres. World Exec. Coun., Inst. de la Vie, 1987-2003; coun. Royal Can. Inst., 1996—, v.p., 1998-2000, pres. 2000-02; mem. Nat. Coun. on Ethics in Human Rsch., 1998—2005, pres., 2002—04. Author: Reproduction in the Insects, 1965; editor Internat. Jour. Invertebrate Reprodn., 1978-86; mem. editl. bd. Internat. Jour. Parasitology, 1973-80, Exptl. Parasilology, 1970-76, Can. Jour. Zoology, 1966-76, editor, 1994—2004; assoc. editor Ency. Reprodn.; contbr. articles to profl. jours. Decorated officer Order of Can.; recipient Queen's Jubilee medal Govt. Can., 1977, 2002, Hitschfeld award Can. Assn. Rsch. Adminstrs., 1997, Wigglesworth medal Royal Entomol. Soc. London. Fellow Royal Soc. Can. (sec. Acad. Sci. 1979-85), Royal Entomol. Soc. Can. (Gold medal 1985), Royal Entomol. Soc. (hon. fellow); mem. Soc. Exptl. Biology, Internat. Union Biol. Scis. (Can. nat. com. 1977-82), Can. Soc. Zoologists (pres. 1981-82, Fry medal 1987), Can. Com. Univ. Biology Chmn. (chmn. 1975-77, Disting. Biologist medal 1992), Biol. Coun. Can. (Gold medal 1987). Office: York Univ Dept Biology North York ON Canada M3J 1P3 Office Phone: 416-736-2100 33804. Personal E-mail: davey@yorku.ca.

DAVEY, LYCURGUS MICHAEL, neurosurgeon; b. NYC, Feb. 20, 1918; s. Michael Marco and Elizabeth (Delaveris) D.; m. Artemis Diana Pappas, June 7, 1942 (dec. Aug. 2003); children: Michael Dean, Elaine Anne, Elizabeth. BA, Yale U., 1939, MD, 1943. Diplomate Am. Bd. Neurol. Surgery, 1954. Surg. intern New Haven Hosp., 1943-44, asst.

resident in surgery, 1946-50, William Harvey Cushing fellow, 1947-48, resident neurosurgeon, 1951-52; asst. resident in neurosurgery Hartford Hosp., 1950-51; clin. clk. Nat. Hosp., London, summer 1954; clin. instr. neurosurgery Yale U., 1952-60, asst. clin. prof., 1960-68, asso. clin. prof., 1968-77, clin. prof., 1977—. Assoc. fellow Trumbull Coll. Yale U., 1959—; cons. practice in neurosurgery New Haven, 1952-2002; emeritus staff Mid State Med. Ctr. (formerly Vets Meml. Med. Ctr.); emeritus Hosp. St. Raphael; hon. staff mem. Yale-New Haven Med. Ctr., 1952-01, pres. med. staff, 1971-72, assoc. sect. chief, 1954-91, emeritus, 1991-2001, hon. staff mem., 2002-; bd. dirs. Tex. Citrus Found. Editl. bd. historian Neurosurgery. Class sec. Yale U. Class of 1939, 1999—. Served to comdr. USNR, 1942-46, 52-54; capt. Res. ret. 1973. Fellow ACS, Internat. Coll. Surgeons; mem. AMA, Naval War Coll. Found., Inc. (life), U.S. Naval Inst. (life), Naval Res. Assn. (life), Navy League of U.S. (life), Conn. Med. Soc. (chmn. sect. on neurosurgery 1971-72), Conn. Soc. Neurol. Surgeons (hon. spkr. 2000), New Haven County Med. Soc. (pres. 1987), New Haven Med. Assn. (pres. 1972), Am. Assn. Neurol. Surgeons, New Eng. Neurosurg. Soc., Congress Neurol. Surgeons (mem. editl. bd., historian Neurosurgery 2001—, Disting. Svc. award 1966), Assn. Rsch. in Nervous and Mental Diseases, Soc. Med. Cons. to Armed Forces, Assn. Yale Alumni in Medicine (pres. 1995-97, Disting. Alumni Svc. award 1997, Peter Parker, M.D. Dean's medal 2003). Home (Summer): 1010 Hartford Tpke North Haven CT 06473-3038 Office: 2 Church St S Ste 304 New Haven CT 06519-1717 Office Phone: 203-781-0278. Personal E-mail: lmdavey@hotmail.com. *My life has been enriched by treating tasks as a challenge to my resourcefulness, knowledge, originality, inventiveness and faith. The task becomes a game rather than a chore.*

DAVID, CHRISTOPHER MARK, lawyer; b. Buffalo, Nov. 19, 1965; s. Thomas Leonard and Anne (Nickodemus) D.; m. Elizabeth Martina Wilson, Aug. 31, 1991; 1 child, Taylor Dawn. AA, Miami Dade C.C., 1989; BA, U. Fla., 1990; JD, U. Miami, 1993. Bar: Fla. 1993, U.S. Dist. Ct. (so. dist.) Fla. 1995. Atty. Hall, David and Joseph, P.A., Miami, Fla., 1993—2005, David and Joseph, PL, 2006—. Sgt. US Army, 1983—87. Mem.: ATLA, ABA, Dade County Bar Assn. Office: David and Joseph PL 1001 Brickell Bay Dr Ste 2002 Miami FL 33131 Home Phone: 305-251-0751; Office Phone: 305-374-5030, 786-364-7990. Business E-Mail: cdavid@davidjosephlaw.com.

DAVID, CLIVE, events executive; b. Manchester, Eng., June 6, 1934; came to U.S., 1957, naturalized, 1962; s. Marcus Wiener and Claire Rose (Levy) Wiener Kattenburg. Student, Blackpool Tech. Coll., 1951-52, Royal Coll. Art, 1955-57. Designer Chippendale's, London, 1955-57; asst. to pres. pub. relations Maybruck Assocs., NYC, 1959; Ea. regional dir. City of Hope, Phila., 1960-62; pres. Clive David Assocs., NYC, Clive David Enterprises div. Party Enterprises Ltd., Beverly Hills, Calif., Party Enterprises, Ltd., Beverly Hills, 1962—. Lectr. Party Planning par excellence, 1966—. Arranger major parties including Miss Universe Coronation Ball, Miami Beach, 1965, State visit of Queen Elizabeth and Prince Philip, Duke of Edinburgh, Bahamas, 1966, An Evening at the Ritz-Carlton, Boston, 1967, 69, Un Ballo in Maschera, Venice, 1967, An Evening over Boston, 1968, M.G.M. Cavalcade of Style, L.A., 1970, Symposium on Fund Raising through Parties, L.A., 1970, Great Midwest Limestone Cave Party, Kansas City, 1972, Une Soiree de Gala, Phila., 1972, 11th Anniv. of the Mike Douglas Show, Phila., 1972, The Mayor's Salue to Volunteers, Los Angeles, 1972, Twenty Fifth Anniv. Salute to Israel, Jerusalem, 1973, The Bicentenary, 1976, The World Affairs Council Silver Ball, Boston, 1977, The Ohio Theatre Jubilee, Columbus, 1978, Mayor's Salute to Vols., 1978, Dedication and Gala Performance, Northwestern U. Performing Arts Ctr., 1980, Metromedia Gala, Los Angeles Bicentennial, 1981, The Albemarle Weekend, Charlottesville, 1985, The La Costa Weekend, Carlsbad, 1987, The Embassy Ball, N.Y.C., 1987, The Lagoon Cycle Premiere, Los Angeles, 1987, State Visit Gala for Her Majesty Queen Elizabeth, Miami, 1991, The Grand Brazilian Clambake, Southampton, 1995, The Democratic Senatorial Campaign Committee Gala, Charlottesville, 1996, DSCC reception for Hillary Rodham Clinton, 1996, Rep. Nat. Conv. Team 100 Reception, San Diego, 1996; mem. Pres.' Summit for Am.'s Future Leadership Roundtable, Phila., 1997, Rep. Govs. Conf. Opening Banquet, 1999; contbr. articles to profl. jours. Served with Royal Arty. Brit. Army, 1953-55. Recipient Freedom Found. award Valley Forge, Pa., 1961, City of Hope award Phila., 1962, Mayor's medal for vol. services Los Angeles, 1972, Shalom award State of Israel, 1974, Mayor's medal City of Columbus; named hon. citizen City of Columbus. Mem. AFTRA Jewish. *I consider myself so fortunate to participate in events that bring joy, employment and funds to diversified causes, and maybe leave a miniscule contribution to history.*

DAVID, EDWARD EMIL, JR., electrical engineer, executive, management consultant; b. Wilmington, NC, Jan. 25, 1925; s. Edward Emil and Beatrice (Liebman) D.; m. Ann Hirshberg, Dec. 23, 1950; 1 dau., Nancy. BS, Ga. Inst. Tech., 1945; MS, MIT, 1947, ScD, 1950; DEng (hon.), Stevens Inst. Tech., 1971, Poly. Inst. Bklyn., 1971, U. Mich., 1971, Carnegie-Mellon, 1972, Lehigh U., 1973, U. Ill.-Chgo., 1973, Rose-Hulman Inst. Tech., 1978, U. Fla., 1982, Rensselaer Poly. Inst., 1982, Rutgers U., 1984, N.J. Inst. Tech., 1985, U. Pa., 1985. Exec. dir. research Bell Telephone Labs., Murray Hill, NJ, 1950-70; sci. adviser to Pres. Nixon; dir. Office Sci. and Tech., Washington, 1970-73; exec. v.p. Gould, Inc., 1973-77; ind. cons., 1977, 86—; v.p. Exxon Corp., NYC, 1978-80; pres. Exxon Research and Engring. Co., Florham Park, NJ, 1977-86, EED, Inc., Bedminster, NJ, 1986—; affiliate Washington Adv. Group, 1997—2004, 2004—; founder Bio Avrion, Tecumseh, Mich. Bd. dirs. Spacehab, Inc., Houston, Medjet Inc., Edison, NJ, Newire, Nashville, BioAvrion, Tecumseh, Mich., Ronson Corp., Somerset, NJ; cons. NSC, 1974—77; mem. def. sci. bd. U.S. Dept. Def., 1974—75; mem. tech. adv. bd. Chrysler Corp., 1985—93; chmn. Nat. Task Force on Tech. and Soc.; U.S. rep. to NATO Sci. Com., 1979—95; mem. adv. bd. AMP, Inc., Harrisburg, Pa., Bellcore, Livingston, NJ, Electric Power Rsch. Inst., Palo Alto, Calif., Inst. Def. Analyses, Alexandria, Va., 1993—95, Poly Ventures, Farmingdale, NY, Rowan Coll. N.J., Glassboro; active White House Sci. Coun., 1980—88, N.J. Commn. on Sci. and Tech.; chair sci. adv. com. NASA. Patentee in field. Mem. Bicentennial adv. com. Chgo. Mus. Sci. and Industry, 1974-75; mem. adv. bd. Office of Phys. Scis., NRC, 1976-81; mem. Pres.'s Commn. on Nat. Medal of Sci., 1975-78; mem. vis. com. to div. phys. scis. U. Chgo., 1976—; mem. adv. coun. Humanities Inst., 1976—; trustee Aerospace Corp., 1974-81, chmn. bd. trustees, 1975-81; life mem. corp. MIT, 1974—, also mem. exec. com., energy adv. bd.; bd. dirs. Summit (N.J.) Speech Sch., 1967-70; mem. Marshall Scholarships Adv. Coun.; mem. adv. and resource coun. Princeton U.; mem. cons. sci. com. Chateaubriand Scholarships; trustee Carnegie Instn. of Washington, 20th Century Fund, John Simon Guggenheim Meml. Found. Served with USNR, 1943-46. Recipient Outstanding Young Engr. award Eta Kappa Nu, 1954, George W. McCarty award Ga. Inst. Tech., 1958, award Summit Jr. C. of C., 1959, award of merit ASME, 1971, Harold Pender award Moore Sch., U. Pa., 1972, N.C. award, 1972, award for disting. contbn. Soc. Rsch. Adminstrs., 1980, N.J. Sci. and Tech. medal, 1982, medal Indsl. Rsch. Inst., 1983, Scientist of Yr. award R & D mag., 1984, Fahrney medal Franklin Inst., 1985, Pub. Svc. award Conf. Bd. Math. Scis., 1985, Silver Stein award MIT, 1991; named to Hall of Fame, Ga. Inst. Tech., 1994. Fellow IEEE, AAAS (bd. dirs. 1974-75, 77-82, pres. 1977-78, chmn. bd. dirs. 1979-80), Acoustical Soc. Am., Am. Acad. Arts and Scis., Audio Engring. Soc.; mem. NAS (coun. 1995), NAE (Bueche award 1984), Am. Philos. Soc., Assn. Computing Machinery, Am. Soc. for Engring. Edn. (Hall of Fame 1993), Engring. Soc. Detroit, Nat. Acad. Pub. Adminstrn. Office: EED Inc PO Box 435 Bedminster NJ 07921-0435

DAVID, GEORGE, psychiatrist, economic theory lecturer; b. NYC, Feb. 19, 1940; s. Norman and Jennie (Danziger) D. BA, Yale U., 1961; MD, NYU, 1965. Intern Children's Hosp., San Francisco, 1965; resident in psychiatry Colo. Psychiat. Hosp., Denver, 1965-66; practice medicine specializing in psychiatry San Francisco; staff Calif. Pacific Med. Ctr., San Francisco, 1966-67, San Mateo County (Calif.) Mental Health Svcs., 1968-71; lectr. on application of econ. theory to personal decision making. Mem. San Francisco Clin. Hypnosis (v.p. 1973-74). Libertarian. Office: 399 Laurel St San Francisco CA 94118-1951 Personal E-mail: davgeo@msn.com.

DAVID, GEORGE ALFRED LAWRENCE, manufacturing executive; b. Bryn Mawr, Pa., Apr. 7, 1942; s. Charles Wendell and Margaret (Simpson) David; m. Barbara Osborn, Sept. 4, 1965; children: Eliza Pell, Hannah Lawrence, Henry Gibb. BA, Harvard U., 1965; MBA, U. Va., 1967. Asst. prof. fin. and acctg. U. Va., Charlottesville, 1967—68; v.p. The Boston Cons. Group, 1968—75; sr. v.p. corp. planning and devel. Otis Elevator Co., NYC, 1975—77, sr. v.p., gen. mgr. Latin Am. ops. West Palm Beach, Fla., 1977—81, pres. N.Am. ops. Farmington, Conn., 1981—85, pres., CEO, 1985—89, chmn., 1989—97; sr. v.p. (parent co.) United Techs. Corp., 1988—89, exec. v.p., pres. comml./indsl., 1989—92, COO, 1992—94, pres., 1992—99, 2002—, CEO, 1994—, chmn., 1997—. Chmn. Greater Hartford chpt. ARC, 1985—87; former chmn. US-ASEAN Coun. Bus. and Tech., Nat. Minority Supplier Devel. Coun.; trustee Wadsworth Atheneum, Hartford, 1984—; bd. dirs. Inst. Internat. Econs., Washington. Republican. Episcopalian. also: Otis Elevator Co 10 Farm Springs Rd Farmington CT 06032-2526 Office: United Technologies United Technologies Bldg Hartford CT 06101*

DAVID, HAL, lyricist; m. Eunice Forester, Sept. 2, 1988; children: Jim, Craig. MusD (hon.), Lincoln Coll., 1991; DHL (hon.), Claremont Grad. U., 2000. Books: What the World Needs Now and Other Love Lyrics, Bacharach and David Songbook; Songs include Raindrops Keep Fallin' On My Head (Acad. award), The Look of Love (Acad. award nomination), What's New Pussycat? (Acad. award nomination), Alfie (Acad. award nomination), Wives and Lovers, Casino Royale, It Was Almost Like a Song (all Grammy award nomination), What the World Needs Now is Love, To Love a Child (written for Foster Grandparents' Program), To All the Girls I've Loved Before (recorded by Julio Iglesias and Willie Nelson), America Is (official song of Liberty Centennial campaign for restoration of Statue of Liberty and Ellis Island); chief collaborator: Burt Bacharach; other collaborators include Henry Mancini, Joe Raposo; Broadway show Promises, Promises (Grammy award, Tony award nomination); films include April Fools; record producer for Dionne Warwick. Elected Songwriters Hall Fame, Nashville Songwriters Hall Fame Internat.; recipient Presdl. award National Association Recording Merchandisers, Creative Achievement award B'nai B'rith, Entertainer of Yr. award Cue Mag. Mem. ASCAP (pres. 1980—), Songwriters Guild Am., Lyricists Guild Am., Dramatist Guild, Authors League. Address: 15 W 53rd St New York NY 10019-5401 *How do you create a hit? I don't know. When I sit down to work, I write what I feel. What happens afterwards is out of my hands. The only thing I'm sure of is you can't write a hit if you don't write a song. Of course, the act of creation, itself, is only one part of being a professional songwriter. To succeed and sustain, you have to have a knowledge of the other parts of the music business. You have to recognize that you are in business for yourself, and as president of your own company, you must be on top of all its aspects.*

DAVID, HERBERT ARON, retired statistician, educator; b. Berlin, Dec. 19, 1925; arrived in U.S., 1957, naturalized, 1964; s. Max and Betty (Goldmann) David; m. Vera Reiss, May 13, 1950 (dec.); 1 child, Alexander John; m. Ruth Finch, Dec. 1, 1992. BSc, Sydney U., Australia, 1947; PhD, London U., 1953. Rsch. officer Commonwealth Sci. and Indsl. Rsch. Orgn., Sydney, 1953-55; sr. lectr. dept. stats. U. Melbourne, Melbourne, Australia, 1955-57; prof. stats. Va. Poly. Inst., 1957-64; prof. U. N.C., Chapel Hill, 1964-72, Iowa State U., Ames, 1972-96, Disting. prof. liberal arts and scis., 1980-96, disting. prof. emeritus, 1996—, dir. stat. lab., head dept. stats., 1972-84; ret., 1996. Author: (book) The Method of Paired Comparisons, 1963, 2d edit., 1988, Order Statistics, 1970; co-author: 3d edit., 2003, Annotated Readings in the History of Statistics, 2001; co-editor: Advances in Biometry, 1996. Recipient J. Shelton Horsley award, Va. Acad. Scis., 1963, Wilks award, Army Rsch., 1983. Fellow: AAAS, Inst. Math. Stats., Am. Statis. Assn.; mem.: Internat. Statis. Inst., Biometric Soc. (editor Biometrics 1967—72, pres. 1982—83). Jewish. Home: 2334 Hamilton Dr Ames IA 50014-8201 Office Phone: 515-294-7749. Business E-Mail: hadavid@iastate.edu.

DAVID, LARRY, television scriptwriter and producer, actor; b. Bklyn., July 2, 1947; m. Laurie Lennard, Mar. 31, 1993 (separated 2007); 2 children. BA in History, U. Md., College Park. Staff writer: Fridays, 1980-82, Saturday Night Live, 1984-85; creator, writer: Norman's Corner, 1989; exec. prodr., co-creator TV series The Seinfeld Chronicles, 1989, Seinfeld, 1990-98 (Emmy award outstanding comedy series 1993, Emmy award outstanding writing comedy series 1993); writer/dir. Sour Grapes, 1998; exec. prodr., writer, actor HBO comedy special Larry David: Curb Your Enthusiasm, HBO series Curb Your Enthusiasm, 2000- (AFI award best comedy series, 2001, Emmy nomination best lead actor & best comedy series, 2002, 2003); film appearances include Second Thoughts, 1983, Can She Bank a Cherry Pie?, 1983, Radio Days, 1987, New York Stories, 1989.*

DAVID, MARTIN HEIDENHAIN, economics professor; b. Heemstede, The Netherlands, Jan. 21, 1935; s. Hans Theodor and Frances (Heidenhain) D.; m. Elizabeth Jane Likert, Sept. 7, 1957; children— Peter Rensis, Margaret Meigs, Andrew John. AB with honors, Swarthmore Coll., 1955; MA, U. Mich., 1957, PhD, 1960. Study dir. Inst. Social Research, Ann Arbor, Mich., 1959-61; asst. prof. econs. U. Wis., Madison, 1961-63, assoc. prof., 1964-66, prof., 1967—2001; fiscal economist U.S. Treasury, 1961-62; chmn. Social Sci. Reseach Inst., U. Wis., Madison, 1970-71; vis. prof., program dir. Inst. Social Research, U. Mich., 1971-72; vis. prof., sr. fellow Inst. Devel. Studies, U. Nairobi, 1974-76. Mem. Social Sci Rsch. Coun. Com. on Social Indicators, Washington, 1980-83; mem. exec. com. Conf. on Income and Wealth, Nat. Bur. Econ. Research, Cambridge, Mass., 1980-83; mem. com. on stats. on family assistance NRC, Washington, 1980-82, com. on nat. stats., 1988-94; chmn. Social Sci. Rsch. Coun. Com. on Survey of Income and Program Participation, 1982-88; vis. prof. Wirtschafts U. Vienna, 1993; rsch. prof. U. Md., JPSM, 2001-03; assoc. scholar Urban Inst., Washington, 2003-06; mem. adv. com. German Socio-econ. Panel, 1990-96. Author: Family Composition and Consumption, 1962, Income and Welfare in the U.S., 1962, Alternative Approaches to Capital Gains Taxation, 1968, Linkage and Retrieval of Micro-Economic Data, 1974; author, editor: Technical, Conceptual and Administrative Lessons of the Income Survey Development Program, 1982, Buying a Better Environment: Cost-Effective Regulation Through Permit Trading, 1983, Horizontal, Equity, Uncertainty, and Economic Well-Being, 1985; contbr. articles to profl. jours. Mem. Tax Reform Commn., State of Wis., 1978-79 Recipient Fred M. Taylor award, 1958; open scholar, 1951-55; doctoral dissertation fellow Ford Found., 1958-59; sr. post-doctoral fellow NSF, 1967-68 Fellow Am. Statis. Assn. (fellowship 1982-83); mem. Am. Econ. Assn. (census adv. com. 1979-84), Internat. Assn. Pub. Fin., Econometric Soc. Unitarian Universalist. Office Phone: 608-238-2181.

DAVID, MILES, marketing executive; b. Newark, Mar. 29, 1926; s. Samuel Harry and Estelle Rachel (Sklower) Ginsberg; m. Florence Cotton, Dec. 7, 1952; children: Steven, Amelia, Heidi. BA, NYU, 1946; postgrad., Columbia U., 1946. Assoc. editor Sci. Illustrated mag. McGraw-Hill Co., NYC, 1946-48; editor Sponsor mag., NYC, 1948-58; with Radio Advt. Bur., NYC, 1958-86, formerly v.p. and dir. promotion, exec. v.p., pres., vice chmn., chief exec. officer, bd. dir., adv. bd. dir.; pres. Am. Values: The Community Action Network; pres. nat. mktg. strategy nat. advertisers Mkt. Soundings subs. TradeOne Mktg. Inc., NYC, 1986—88; vice chmn. TradeOne Mktg. Inc., 1988—99; pres. Miles David Assocs., Inc., 1999—2004; solutions officer Campbell-Ewald Ad Agy., 2004—. Lectr. Tobe-Coburn Sch. Fashion Careers; speaker in field to nat., internat. groups.; bd. dir. Advt. Coun. Editor: Sponsor mag. (George W. Polk award). Former chmn. Scarsdale Adv. Coun. on Cable TV; mem. nominating com. Scarsdale Village Trustees; mem. procedure com. Non-Partisan Elections, Scarsdale; pres. Am. Values Cmty. Action Network. With AUS, 1943-45, ETO. Recipient Morris Meister award; named Outstanding Alumnus Bronx High Sch., Sci. Man of Yr. Radio Trade Assn., 1975, 76; named to Hall of Fame of Co-op Advt., 1997. Mem. Internat. Radio, TV Soc., Broadcast Pioneers, Perstare et Praestare, Trade Promotion Mgmt. Assn. (bd. dirs. 1998—), Scarsdale Club (N.Y.), Town Club (com. pub. rels. 1970-74). Jewish. Achievements include adminstr. Higbee Study, use of radio for dept. stores, and All-Radio Methodology Study, how to measure radio. Home and Office: 167 E 61st St 11A New York NY 10021 E-mail: mdavid.campbellewald@gmail.com.

DAVID, PAUL ALLAN, economist, economic historian; b. NYC, May 24, 1935; s. Henry and Evelyn D.; m. Janet M. Williamson, May 24, 1958 (div.); m. Sheila Ryan Johansson, Sept. 19, 1982; children: Rachel, Matthew; step-children: Kenneth, Elizabeth. AB summa cum laude in Econs, Harvard U., 1956, PhD, 1973; postgrad., Pembroke Coll., Cambridge U., Eng., 1956-58; MA, Oxford U., Eng., 1994; D hon. causa, U. Turin, 2003. Asst. prof. econs. Stanford U., 1961-66, assoc. prof., 1966-68, prof., 1969—2004, prof. history (by courtesy), 1976—2004, William Robertson Coe prof. Am. econ. history, 1978-94, chmn. dept., 1979-83, prof. emeritus, 2004—; sr. rsch. fellow All Souls Coll., Oxford, 1994—2002, emeritus fellow, 2002—; prof. econ. and econ. history U. Oxford, 1997—2002. Sr. fellow Oxford Internet Inst., Stanford Inst. Econ. Policy Research, Stanford U.; Pitt prof. Am. history and instns., vis. prof. Harvard U., 1972-73; vis. professorial fellow Churchill Coll., Cambridge U., 1977-78; vis. fellow All Souls Coll., Oxford (Eng.) U., 1967-68, 93-94; fellow Center for Advanced Study in Behavioral Scis., 1978-79; vis. prof. U. Paris-Dauphine, U. Maastricht, U. Ancona; mem. coun. Royal Econ. Soc., 1996-2001; mem. editl. bd. Jour. Network Industries, 1998-, Jour. Econ. Methodology, 1998-, Jour. Telecom. Policy, 1999-, Mind and Soc., 2005-; mem. adv. bd. OSSWatch, Eng., Sci. Commons, US, École Economie de Paris, Atta Scuola Politechnico, Milan, Turin, Italy, Erasmus Inst. Philosophy and Econ., Ctr. Econ. History and Theory Moscow State U.; cons. in field. Author: Nations and Households in Economic Growth: Essays in Honor of Moses Abramovitz, 1974, Technical Choice, Innovation and Economic Growth: Essays on American and British Experience in the Nineteenth Century, 1975, Reckoning with Slavery: A Critical Study in the Quantitative History of American Negro Slavery, 1976, The Economic Future in Historical Perspective, 2003; founding editor Jour. Econ. of Innovations and New Tech.; contbr. numerous articles to profl. jours. Bd. dirs. La Compagnie de Saint Gobain. Fulbright scholar, 1956-58; Guggenheim fellow, 1975-76. Fellow: Am. Philos. Soc., Brit. Acad., Internat. Econometric Soc., Am. Acad. Arts and Scis.; mem.: Econ. History Assn. (v.p., pres. 1988—89), Compagnie de Saint Gobain (bd. dir.). Office: Stanford U Dept Econs Stanford CA 94305-6072 also: Oxford Internat Inst 1 St Giles' Oxford OX1 3JS England Business E-Mail: pad@stanford.edu. E-mail: paul.david@economics.ox.ac.uk.

DAVID, REUBEN, lawyer; b. Baghdad, Iraq, June 12, 1928; arrived in U.S., 1951; s. Isaac Solomon David and Tefaha (Nisan) Solomon D.; m. Nesta Paley David; 1 child, Aram. License in Law, Iraqi Law Coll., Baghdad, 1951; BA, NYU, 1958; JD, N. Y. Law Sch., 1962. Bar: Iraq 1951, N.Y. 1969. Asst. corp. counsel City of N.Y., 1970-76, chief legal unit dept. personnel, 1976-78; dep. dir. for legal affairs N.Y.C. Employees' Retirement System, 1978—2002; pvt. practice law, 2002—. Mem. ABA, N.Y. State Bar Assn. Home: 30 Fifth Ave Apt 12E New York NY 10011-8812 Office Phone: 212-260-4956.

DAVID, ROBERT JEFFERSON, lawyer; b. New Roads, La., Aug. 10, 1943; s. Joseph Jefferson and Doris Marie (Olinde) D.; m. Stella Marie Scott, Jan. 21, 1967; children: Robert J. Jr., Richard M. BA, Southeastern La. U., 1966; JD, Loyola U., New Orleans, 1969. Bar: U.S. Dist. Ct. (ea. dist.) La. 1969, U.S. Dist. Ct. (mid. dist.) La. 1969, U.S. Dist. Ct. (we. dist.) La. 1975. Assoc. Gainsburgh, Benjamin, Fallon, David, New Orleans, 1969-74; ptnr. Gainsburgh, Benjamin, David, New Orleans, 1974—. Adj. faculty mem. Tulane U. Sch. Law, New Orleans, 1982-84, law sch. Loyola U., New Orleans, 1996; mem. hearing com. La. Atty. Disciplinary Bd.; Staff mem. Loyola U. Law Rev., 1967-69; bd. dir Loyola Law Sch. Alumni Assn., 2001-02, vis. com. Loyola Law Sch., 2002—, nominatimg com., 2007—; mem. Gov.'s Commn. on Med. Profl. Liability; lectr., spkr. continuing legal edn. seminars. Reader, recorder for La. Blind and Handicapped, 1986-91; charter mem. Lawyers for Alliance for Nuclear Arms Control, New Orleans, 1986-1990; pres. Arden Hill Acad. Parent Tchr. League, 1979-80. Fellow: Am. Coll. Trial Lawyers, Am. Bar Endowment (life); mem.: ATLA, ABA, New Orleans Bar Assn. (chair, med. jurisprudence com. 1994—96, mem. profls. commn. 2005—), La. Trial Lawyers Assn. (contbg. editor Civil Trial Tactics manual 1981, bd. govs. 1981—83, chmn. sect. med. malpractice 1992—94, bd. govs. 1995—96, exec. com. 1996—97, coun. of dirs. 1997—, legis. com.), La. Bar Found., La. State Bar Assn. (spl. inst. commn. 1974—82, asst. examiner commn. on bar admissions 1974—93, med. legal interprofl. com. 1987—, contbr. La. Bar Assn. Jour. column on Profl. Liability 1989—, co-chmn. 1991—94, disciplinary com.), Am. Bd. Profl. Liability Attys., Nat. Bd. Trial Advocacy, Phi Alpha Delta, Kappa Sigma. Avocation: sports. Home: 21 Cypress Point Ln New Orleans LA 70131-3351 Office: Gainsburgh Benjamin David 2800 Energy Ctr New Orleans LA 70163 Office Phone: 504-522-2304.

DAVID, RUTH A., public-service research institute executive; BSEE, Wichita State U., 1975; MSEE, Stanford U., 1976, PhD in Elec. Engring., 1981. With Sandia Nat. Lab., 1975—94, dir., develop. testing ctr. to dir. advanced info. technologies, 1991—94; dep. dir. for Sci. and Tech. CIA, 1995—98; pres., CEO Analytic Services, Inc., 1998—. Adj. prof. U. N.Mex.; mem. Dept. Homeland Security Adv. Coun., vice-chair, sr. adv. com. academia and policy rsch.; former pres. President's Homeland Security Adv. Coun.; mem. Corp. for the Charles Stark Draper Lab. Inc.; chair, com. on tech. insight-gauge, evaluate and review NRC, mem. com. on scientific communication and nat. secutiry, mem. com. on info. for terrorism prevention, mem. naval studies bd.; mem. adv. bd. Nat. Security Agy.; mem. adv. bd., tech. divsn. Jet Propulsion Lab.; mem. external adv. com Purdue U. Homeland Security Inst.; mem. Def. Sci. Bd., Dept. Energy Nonproliferation and Nat. Security Adv. Com., Senate Select Com. on Intelligence Tech. Adv. Group, Securities and Exchange Commn. Tech. Adv. Group; frequently provided speeches, interviews, lectures, briefings and articles on many aspects of homeland security. Co-author of three books on signal processing algorithms; contbr. scientific papers. Mem. mat. adv. com. Wichita State U. Found. Fellow: AIAA (assoc.); mem.: AAAS (mem. com. on scientific freedom & responsibility), Armed Forces Communications and Electronics Assn. (mem. internat. bd. dir.), NAE (councillor 2007—, com. on engring. edn.), Eta Kappa Nu, Tau Beta Pi. Office: Analytic Services Inc 2900 South Quincy St Ste 800 Arlington VA 22206 Office Phone: 703-416-2000.*

DAVID, SUSAN HOLCOMBE, child and family therapist; b. Plainfield, NJ, Aug. 29, 1949; d. Paul Thorne Holcombe and Marilyn Jean Lennon; children: Mark Christian, Jason Esser, Michael John, Karen Marie. BA in

Edn., Clemson U., SC, 1971; MA in Cmty. counseling, U. Phoenix, 2002. Lic. profl. counselor, nat. bd. cert. counselor. Tchr. Cath. Elem. Sch., Tampa, Fla., 1971; therapist Jewish Family & Childrens Svc., Phoenix, 2002—; therapist, educator E. Valley Family Resource Ctr., Mesa, Ariz., 2002—; therapist Child Crisis Ctr., Mesa, Ariz., 2003—04. Co-chmn., co-founder Morton Plant Hosp. Cruisin' the 60s Ann. Fund-raiser; co-founder Kimberly Home, Kimberly-Brian David Birthing Ctr., Jr. League Clearwater Dunedin, 1986—90. Mem.: Chi Sigma Iota (treas. 2002), Chi Omega. Roman Catholic. Avocations: art, sewing, scrapbooks, theater. Office: Jewish Family & Childrens Svc 1930 S Alma Sch Rd Ste A-104 Mesa AZ 85210 Office Phone: 480-820-0825 ext 11087. Personal E-mail: powerperson@cox.net.

DAVID, THEOHARIS LAMBROS, architect, educator; b. Farmingdale, NY, June 9, 1938; s. Lambros L. and Thalia (Joaniddes) D.; m. Margarita T. Leptos, July 29, 1967; children: Melissa T., Alexis L. BArch, Pratt Inst., 1961; MArch, Yale U., 1964; studied with Serge Chermayeff and Paul Rudolph. Registered arch., N.Y., N.J., Republic of Cyprus; cert. Nat. Coun. Archtl. Registration Bd. Designer Whittlesy & Conklin Archs./Planners, NYC, 1964-65, William F. Pedersen Assocs., NYC, 1965-66, K. Vafeades, Arch., Nicosia, Cyprus, 1965-66; asst. arch. J & A Philippou, Archs., Nicosia, 1966-67, 72; sr. designer Max O. Urbahn Assocs., NYC, 1968-72; ptnr. David & Dikaios Assocs., Architecture/Planning, Nicosia, NYC, Bahrain, 1973-87; prin. Theo David & Assocs., NYC, 1987—, Theo David Cons. Arch./Planner, Nicosia, 1992—. Founding dir. CAEC Architecture/Engring. Cons., Ltd., Cyprus, 1975; mem. faculty Pratt Inst., Bklyn., 1968-69, asst. prof. arch., 1969-79, assoc. prof., 1979-83, prof. arch., 1983—; nominator Aga Khan Award for Arch., 1984—; disting. juror 1st Presdl. Arch. Awards, Cyprus, 1992; guest lectr. U. Thessaloniki, Greece, 1972, Hellenic Conf. on Tall Bldgs., Athens, Greece, 1975, U. So. Calif., L.A., Archtl. Assn., London, 1982, Cyprus Archs. Assn. and Am. Ctr., Nicosia, 1982, 92, Tex. A&M U., 1984, Cyprus Popular Bank Cultural Ctr., Nicosia, 1987, 91, Hellenic Bank Cultural Ctr., Limassol, Cyprus, 1993, many others; guest critic CCNY, N.Y.C., Archtl. Assn., London, Temple U., Phila., Columbia U., N.Y.C., Yale U., New Haven, U. So. Calif., L.A., others. Author: Housing of a Culture/Cyprus, 1982; exhbns. include Pratt Manhattan Ctr., N.Y.C., 1971, 83, Pratt Inst. Gallery, Bklyn., 1978, Urban Ctr., N.Y.C., 1981, Cyprus House, N.Y.C., 1984, 92, Shafler Gallery Pratt Inst., Bklyn., 1987, Mcpl. Arts Soc., N.Y.C., 1987, Disting. Drawing Gallery, N.Y.C./AIA, 1988, Parson Sch. Design, N.Y.C., 1991, Higgins Hall Gallery, Pratt Inst., 1994, Famagusta Gate Nicosia, Cyprus Cooper Union Gallery, N.Y.C., 2004; contbr. articles to profl. jours. Mem. design adv. com. Pub. Devel. Corp., N.Y.C., 1986; 1st v.p. Am. Cyprus Congress, N.Y.C., 1990-94; appointed mem. adv. com. for New Cultural Ctr., Cyprus Govt., 1992. Served U.S. Army, 1962-63. Grantee N.Y. State Coun. on Arts, 1982, Pratt Rsch. Coun., 1983; recipient Design award Nat. Inst. Archtl. Edn., 1961, Bard Honor award City Club, N.Y., 1992, 1st prize G.S.P. Stadium Competition, Cyprus, 1993. Fellow AIA (N.Y. chpt., mem. overseas practice com. 1980-82, chmn. design awards program 1989-90, honors com. N.Y.C. chpt. 2003, Interior Design award AIA Jour. 1988, Design Excellence citation 1993, Design citation 1993, Archs. Designers & Planners for Social Responsibility Project award 1994, Cyprus State Architecture award 2001), Am. Planning Assn. (chmn. com. on N.Y. Waterfront 1984-86), Inst. Urban Design, Congress Internat. Modern Archs. (pres. 2004). Greek Orthodox. also: PO Box 20319 Nicosia Cyprus also: Pratt Inst Sch Arch Brooklyn NY 11205 Office: Theo David Architects 306 W 37th St New York NY 10018 Office Phone: 212-226-0788. Personal E-mail: tdanyc@aol.com.

DAVID, TODD R., lawyer; b. NYC, Dec. 3, 1956; BA, Queens Coll., 1982; JD, Northeastern Univ., 1985. Bar: Ga. 1986. Law clk., Hon. Marvin H. Shoob US Dist. Judge (no. dist.), Ga.; ptnr., co-coord. litig. practice Alston & Bird LLP, Atlanta. Contbr. articles to profl. journals. Bd. dir. ALS Soc. Ga., Synchronicity Performance Group. Office: Alston & Bird LLP One Atlantic Ctr 1201 W Peachtree St NW Atlanta GA 30309-3424 Office Phone: 404-881-7357. Office Fax: 404-253-8242. Business E-Mail: tdavid@alston.com.

DAVID, VALENTINA S., physics professor; d. Samuel and Mercy Yohan; m. Sunil Kumar David, June 4, 1971. BS in Edn., U. Indore, India, 1970; BSc in Biology, U. Poona, Pune, India, 1972; MSc in Botany, U. Poona, 1974, PhD in Physics, 1983. Cert. tchr. U. Indore, 1970. Instr. biology Vidya Bhavan Jr. Coll., Pune, Maharastra, India, 1981—91; biology lab. mgr. Bethune-Cookman Coll., Daytona Beach, Fla., 1992—93, instr., 1994—96, asst. prof., 1996—2003, assoc. prof., 2003—. Lead tchr. VISION, Daytona Beach, 1999—2002; lead tchr. MASTT project Bethune-Cookman Coll., Daytona Beach, 2003—04, project mgr. MASTT project, 2004—, project dir. UNCF-FAPT project, 2002—; lectr. in fiel; condr. workshops in field. Author: online course in phys. sci.; contbr. articles to profl. jours. Recipient Faculty Honors award, Bethune-Cookman Coll., 1999, Provost's award for Outstanding Svc., 1999, award Divsn. Sci. and Math., 2003, Pres.'s award for Faculty Mem. of the Yr., 2003, Best Paper award, CIBER/TLC Conf., Las Vegas, 2004, ABR/TLC Conf., Orlando, 2005, cert. of achievement for completing GLOBE Land Cover, Hydrology, and Soil Protocol, NASA Stennis Space Ctr., 2005; fellow, So. Edn. Found., 2003—04; grantee, NASA, 2004—05. Mem.: Assn. for Advancement of Computing in Edn. (corr.). Office: Bethune-Cookman Coll 621 Dr Mary McLeod Bethune Blvd Daytona Beach FL 32114 Home Phone: 386-761-2088; Office Phone: 386-481-2667.

DAVIDO, SCOTT, retail executive; b. 1961; BS in Acctg. and Econs., Case Western Reserve U., JD. Ptnr. Jones, Ray, Reavis & Pogue, Pittsburgh; sr. v.p., gen. counsel/sec. Elder-Beerman, Dayton, Ohio, 1997-99, exec. v.p., CFO, treas., 1999—2002; sr. v.p., gen. counsel, sec. NRG Energy, 2002—04, exec. v.p., pres. Northeast region, 2004—06; CFO Calpine Corp., San Jose, Calif., 2006—. Bd. dirs. Stages Stores, Inc., Special Metals Corp. Contbr. articles to profl. jours. Office: Calpine Corp 50 W San Fernando St San Jose CA 95113 Office Phone: 408-995-5115. Office Fax: 408-995-0505.

DAVIDOFF, JOANNE MALATESTA, multi-media specialist; d. John Ruben and Erma Carpinelli Malatesta; children: Cynthia Louise Bernstiel, Michael John. BA, Chestnut Hill Coll., Phila, 1954; MEd., Temple U., 1959. Cert. tchr. visually and multihandicapped Cath. U. Am., Washington, D.C., 1952, tchr. Commonwealth Pa., 1963. Dir. Upsal Day Sch. for Blind Children, Phila., 1955—69; coord. Nat. Exhibits for Blind Artists, Phila., 1981—82; coord. first GED for disabled persons Phila. Free Libr., Phila., 1981—83; classroom tchr. K-12 Overbrook Sch. for Blind, Phila., 1985—2000; educator for ind. living skills Del. County Assn. for Blind, Chester, Pa., 1996—2004; braille specialist, lang. arts Overbrook Sch. for the Blind, Phila., 2000—. Bd. mem. Associated Svcs. for the Blind, Phila., 1982—, pres., 1984—87, Overbrook Sch. for Blind Alumni, Phila., 1985—90, Liberty Bell Chpt. Pa. Assn. for Blind, Phila., 1990—; bd. mem. Nat. Exhibits for Blind Artists, Phila., 1990—, Montgomery County Assn. for Blind, North Wales, Pa., 1995—2004, Pa. Council of the Blind, Harrisburg, 1997—2001. Coord. Cath. Christian Doctrine Classes, Seven Dolors, Wyndmoor, Pa. Named Most Beautiful Blonde Girl in Am., NY Assn. Mem.: Cath. League of Persons with Disabilities (pres. 2001—04), Phila. Reg. Chpt. Pa. Council of Blind, Nevilaires (pres. 2000—), Oreland Lions Club. Roman Catholic. Avocations: music, reading, tandem cycling. Home: 7808 Pine Rd Wyndmoor PA 19038 Office: Overbrook Sch for the Blind 6333 Malvern Ave Philadelphia PA 19151

DAVIDOV, LUDMILA G., psychiatrist; arrived in U.S., 1993; d. Grigoriy Solomonovitch Davidov and Alexandra Yakovlevna Davidova; m. Alex P. Levy, July 4, 1974; children: Elena Levy, Alla Levy. MD, Med. SCh., Tajikistan, 1975. Cert. Bd. Cert. Psychiatry NY, 2003. Fellowship Citi Hosp., Tajikistan, 1975—77; internist City Hosp., Tajikistan, 1975—84, chief of dept., 1984—93; interperter 113 Hillside Divsn., Great Neck, NY, 1996—97, mental health worker, 1997—98; residency Nassau Univ. Med. Ctr., NY, 1998—2002; MD Comprehensive Counseling Ctr., Rego Pk., NY, 2003—; staff psychiatrist HIP Mental Health Clin., NY, 2002—; pvt. practice Rego Pk., 2006—. Contbr. articles to profl. jour. Recipient Best Physician of Year, Tajikistan, 1979. Mem.: Am. Psychiatric Assn. Avocations: piano, travel, reading, music. Office: 64-33 99th St Rego Park NY 11374 Office Phone: 718-459-1225.

DAVIDOVICH, LUIZ, physics professor; b. Rio de Janeiro, June 25, 1946; married; 4 children. BSc, Pontifical Cath. U., Rio de Janeiro, 1969; PhD, U. Rochester, NY, 1975. Rsch. asst. U. Rochester, NY, 1969—75; asst. prof. Inst. Theoretical Physics, Swiss Fed. Inst. Tech. Zurich, 1976—77, Pontifical Cath. U., Rio de Janeiro, 1977—82, assoc. prof., 1982—93, prof., 1993—94, Fed. U. Rio de Janeiro, 1994—. Vis. prof. Kastler-Brossel Lab. l'École Normale Sup'erieure, Paris, 1986—87, 1991, 94, 95, 97, 2001, 2001—02; mem. physics com. Brazilian Nat. Sci. Found., 1988—89, 1998—2000; vis. prof. Max-Planck Inst. Quantum Optics, Garching, Germany, 1989, U. N.Mex Ctr. Advanced Studies, Albuquerque, 1989, 1991—92, 1998, U. Paris VI, 2001, 05; vis. rschr. Atomic Physics Svc. Ctr. Atomic Energy, Saclay, France, 1991; vis. scientist Inst. Theoretical Physics U. Calif., Santa Barbara, 1996, 2001; vis. rschr. Isaac Newton Inst. U. Cambridge, England, 1999; head Brazilian Millennium Inst. Quantum Info., 2001—; mem. deliberative coun. Brazilian Nat. Rsch. Found., 2005—; vis. rschr. Tex. A&M U., Coll. Sta., 2006; mem. sci. coun. Internat. Ctr. Condensed Matter Physics, Brasilia, Brazil, 2006—. Contbr. articles to sci. jours., chapters to books; mem. adv. editl. bd.: Optics Comm., 1994—2000, Jour. Optics B: Quantum and Semiclassical Optics, 1998—2001, assoc. editor: Jour. Brazilian Assn. Advancement of Sci., 1995—2000, mem. editl. bd.: UNICAMP Pub. Ho., 2002—04, Annals of Brazilian Acad. Scis., 2003—, Phys. Rev. A, 2005—. Recipient Grand-Cross of Nat. Order of Sci. Merit, Pres. of Brazil, 2000. Mem.: Brazilian Assn. Advancement of Sci. (councillor 1993—95), Brazilian Phys. Soc. (sec. gen. 1981—83, councillor 1997—2001, 2002—06), Brazilian Acad. Scis. (dir. 2004—), Third World Acad. Scis. (Physics prize 2001), NAS (fgn. assoc.). Office: Inst Física Fed Univ Rio de Janerio Caixa Postal 68528 21941-972 Rio de Janeiro Brazil E-mail: ldavid@if.ufrj.br.

DAVIDOVSKY, MARIO, retired composer; b. Medanos, Buenos Aires, Argentina, Mar. 4, 1934; came to U.S., 1960; s. Natalio and Perla (Bulanska) D.; m. Elaine Blaustein, Nov. 19, 1961; children: Matias Gabriel, Adriana. Dir. Electronic Music Center, Princeton and Columbia univs., 1964-94; vis. lectr. Sch. Music, U. Mich., 1964; guest prof. Inst. di Tella, Buenos Aires, 1965; prof. music CCNY, 1968-80, Columbia U., 1981-94; prof. emeritus Harvard U., 1994—2004. Dir. Composer's Conf. Wellesley (Mass.) Coll. Composer chamber music, orchestral works, also works for electronic music.; recs. on, Columbia, Sonnova, C.I.R. Nonesuch, Turnabout, New World, Wergo, Bridge records. Bd. dirs. The Koussevitsky Music Found. in Libr. Congress; founder, bd. dirs. Robert Miller Fund for Music. Recipient award Koussevitzky Found., 1964, award Libr. of Congress, 1964, Nat. Inst. Arts and Letters, 1965, Creative Arts award Brandeis U., 1965, Aaron Copeland award Tanglewood, 1966, Naumburg award, 1971, Pulitzer prize in music, 1971, Seamus Nat. award, 1994, Cristoph & Stephan Kaske music prize, Munich, 1997; Guggenheim fellow, 1961-62, 62-63; Rockefeller fellow, 1964, 65. Mem. Am. Acad. Arts and Letters, Am. Acad. Arts and Scis. Home: 490 West End Ave New York NY 10024 Personal E-mail: mario.davidovsky@verizon.net.

DAVIDOW, CHARLES E., lawyer; b. June 25, 1954; BA magna cum laude, Amherst Coll., 1976; JD magna cum laude, Harvard Univ., 1979. Bar: DC 1980, NY 2000. Law clk. Judge Walter R. Mansfield, US Ct. Appeals (2d cir.), 1979—80; ptnr., co-chmn. Securities Enforcement Litigation group Wilmer Cutler Pickering Hale & Dorr, Washington. Adj. prof. Georgetown Univ. Law Ctr., 1991. Editor (& treas.): Harvard Law Rev. Office: Wilmer Cutler Pickering Hale & Dorr 2445 M St NW Washington DC 20037 Office Phone: 202-663-6241. Office Fax: 202-663-6363. Business E-Mail: charles.davidow@wilmerhale.com.

DAVIDS, JODY R., information technology executive; BBA, MBA, San Jose State U. Computer programmer Apple Computer, Inc., Cupertino, Calif., 1982, various positions, including Asia Pacific divsn., dir. supply chain reengring.; dir. tech. svcs. Nike, Inc., Beaverton, Oreg., 1997—2000; sr v.p. IT pharm. distbn. bus. unit Cardinal Health, Inc., Dublin, Ohio, 2000—03, exec. v.p., chief info. officer, 2003—. Office: Cardinal Health Inc 7000 Cardinal Pl Dublin OH 43017 Office Phone: 614-757-5000.*

DAVIDS, NORMAN, engineering educator, researcher; b. NYC, Mar. 17, 1918; s. Max and Sarah (Flint) Davidowitz; m. Frances White, Mar. 17, 1945; children: Gerald, Laura, Stuart. BS, CCNY, 1937; MS, NYU, 1938, PhD, 1940. Instr. CCNY, 1941; physicist C.E., Cin., 1942; mathematician Carnegie Inst. Tech., Washington, 1943-45; instr. Johns Hopkins U., Balt., 1945-47; assoc. prof. engring. mechanics Pa. State U., University Park, 1947-53, prof., 1953-78, prof. emeritus, 1978—. Mem. Inst. Advanced Study, Princeton, NY, 1941-42; project dir. NIH, Bethesda, Md., 1968-78, Ballistics Rsch. Labs., Aberdeen, Md., 1961-66; sr. sci. adviser Army Rsch. Office, Durham, NC, 1961 Editor: International Symposium on Stress Waves, 1960; contbr. articles to profl. jours. Recipient Naval Ordnance Devel. award Carnegie Inst., 1945; Fulbright scholar Israel Inst. Tech., 1959 Fellow Am. Acad. Mechanics (past treas., dir.); mem. ASME, Soc. Engring. Sci., Phi Beta Kappa, Sigma Xi Democrat. Jewish. Office: Pa State U Engring Sci and Mechs Dept University Park PA 16802 Home: 500 E Marylyn Ave G104 State College PA 16801-6103 Office Phone: 814-865-4523. Business E-Mail: nxd2@psu.edu.

DAVIDS, ROBERT NORMAN, retired petroleum exploration geologist; b. Elizabeth, NJ, Apr. 27, 1938; s. William Scheible and Anna Elizabeth (Backhaus) D.; m. Carol Ann Landauer, Apr. 20, 1957; 1 child: Robert Norman. AB in Geology, U. Va., 1960; MS, Rutgers U., 1963, PhD, 1966. With Exxon Co. USA, 1966—, micropaleontologist New Orleans, 1965-71, uranium geologist Denver, 1971-72, Albuquerque, 1972-78, supervisory geologist Tex. area exploration Corpus Christi, 1978-80, N.W. area supr., 1981, dist. geologist so. dist. New Orleans, 1981-84, divsn. exploration tng. coord., spl. trades unit geologist, 1984-86, geol. tng. advisor Houston, 1986-89; rsch. geologist Exxon Prodn. Rsch. Co., 1989-92; exploration geologist Exxon Exploration Co., 1992—2000. Contbr. articles to profl. jours. Formerly active local Little League Baseball, Jr. Achievement. NSF grad. fellow, 1964-65. Mem. Soc. Econ. Paleontologists and Mineralogists (treas. Gulf Coast sect. 1971), Am. Assn. Petroleum Geologists, Explorers Club, Krewe of Endymion, Sigma Xi, Beta Theta Pi.

DAVIDSON, ABRAHAM ABA, art historian, educator, photographer; b. Dorchester, Mass., June 27, 1935; s. Isaac and Ruth (Feinsilver) D. AB in Archtl. Scis. cum laude, Harvard U., Cambridge, Mass., 1957; postgrad., Hebrew U., Jerusalem, 1957—58; AM in Art History, Boston U., 1960; B in Jewish Edn., Hebrew Tchrs. Coll., Boston, 1960; PhD in Art History, Columbia U., NYC, 1965. Vis. lectr. art history U. Iowa, 1963-64; instr. Wayne State U., Detroit, 1964-65; asst. prof. Oakland U., Rochester, Mich., 1965-68; mem. faculty Tyler Sch. Art, Temple U., Phila., 1968—, prof. art history, 1975—. Vis. asst. prof. U. Mass., Amherst, summers 1965-67, U. Colo., summer 1968; Thomas P. Johnson disting. vis. scholar Rollins Coll., Winter Park, Fla., 1997; cons. Burlington County C.C., Pemberton, NJ, 1976-77. Author: The Story of American Painting, 1974, 79, Japanese transl., 1976, The Eccentrics and Other American Visionary Painters, 1978, Early American Modernist Painting, 1910-1935, 1981, 3d edit., 1990, Ben Solowey, 1988, Ralph Albert Blakelock, 1996, The Paintings of E.M. Saniga, 2001, Abraham A. Davidson, Photographs, 1964-2004, 2005, also articles; one-man exhbns. of photographs Temple U., 1972, 82, Painted Bride Gallery, Phila., 1974, Burlington County C.C., 1978, Gloucester County Coll., NJ, 1979, 92, Villanova U., 1982, Pavilion Galleries Burlington County Hosp., Mt. Holly, NJ, 1987, 1521 Café Gallery, 1997, Phila. C.C., 2001, Northampton County Libr., Richboro, Pa., 2004, 05; represented in permanent collections Bank Leumi, Cigna Corp., Lehigh U., Sch. Pharmacy, Temple U., Villanova U., Sheldon Meml. Art Gallery, U. Nebr., Free Libr. Phila., Newark Pub. Libr., Hudson-United Bank, Jefferson divsn.; numerous TV appearances. Recipient Group 17 prize photography Detroit Inst. Arts, 1969, NEH grantee, 1985 Office: Tyler Sch Art Temple Univ Beech and Penrose Aves Elkins Park PA 19126 Office Phone: 215-204-6933. Business E-Mail: adavidso@temple.edu.

DAVIDSON, ANN D., lawyer, aerospace transportation executive; b. Upper Montclair, NJ, 1952; BA, Ohio U.; JD, U. Dayton, 1979; attended, Georgetown U. Sch. of Foreign Service. Bar: 1979. Assoc. Coolidge, Wall, Womsley & Lombard, Dayton, Ohio, 1979—80; atty. US Navy, 1980—83; various positions including assoc. gen. counsel Honeywell, 1983—90; dep. gen. counsel Alliant Techsystems, 1990—93; v.p., gen. counsel, corp. sec. Power Control Technologies, Inc., Kalamazoo, 1993—98; assoc. gen. counsel, asst. sec. Parker Hannifin Corp., Cleveland, 1998—2001; v.p., gen. counsel Alliant Techsystems, 2001—03, v.p., gen. counsel, corp. sec., 2003—04, sr. v.p., gen. counsel, corp. sec., 2004—. Office: Alliant Techsystems Inc 5050 Lincoln Dr Edina MN 55436

DAVIDSON, ANTHONY R., education educator, consultant; b. Southport, Eng., July 31, 1958; s. Benjamin and Janet Davidson; m. Linda B. Steinmetz, Mar. 21, 1988; children: Nechama R., Leah, Binyamin, Yehuda Y. BBA, CUNY, 1982, MBA, 1985; PhD, City U. London, 1998. Electronic Document Profl. Xplor Internat. Cert. Commn., Calif., 2002. Instr. Bernard M. Baruch Coll. CUNY, 1985—90; asst. prof. Adelphi U., Garden City, NY, 1990—2000; prof., dean divsn. programs bus. NYU, NYC, 2000—. Pres. Perfect Impressions Cons., NYC, 1988—. Author: (article) TQM Mag. (Literati Club award for Excellence: Outstanding Paper of Yr., 2002), Telecomm. Sys. Jour., 2003, IEEE Computer, 2004, (book) Interdisciplinary Research, 2004; rev., contbr. (book) Managing Customer Relationships; contbr. chapters to books. Bd. dirs., exec. adv. bd. of e-learn AACE, Norfolk, Va., 2000; advisor RCCS Cancer Soc., Bklyn., 2002; bd. dirs., bd. trustees Med-Smart, Ann Arbor, Mich., 2002; regional chmn. Child Life Soc. Cystic Fibrosis, 2003; mem. steering com. IPSI, Belgrade, Serbia, 2004; advisor JCSE Ctr. for Spl. Edn., Bklyn., 1993—2004; chmn. QTL Free Lending Libr., Queens, 1990—97. Cecilia S. Cohen scholar, CUNY, 1982. Mem.: Beta Gamma Sigma, Sigma Iota Epsilon (chpt. pres. 1983—84). Avocations: skiing, soccer, football, chess. Office: NYU 11 W 42nd St - Ste 429 New York NY 10036 Office Phone: 212-992-3330. Business E-Mail: anthony.davidson@nyu.edu.

DAVIDSON, BARRY A., plastic surgeon; b. Newark, 1939; MD, Columbia U. Coll. Physicians and Surgeons, 1964. Cert. Am. Bd. Plastic Surgery, Am. Bd. Surgery. Intern, gen. surgery Tufts New England Med. Ctr., Boston, 1964—65; resident, plastic surgery New England Med. Ctr and Boston City Hosp., Boston, 1966—69, Inst. Reconstructive Plastic Surgery, NYU Med. Ctr., NYC, 1969—71, fellow; chief, divsn. plastic surgery Deaconess Waltham Hosp., Mass., 1971—96; clin. instr. Harvard U., 1971—; private practice Plastic & Cosmetic Surgery, Inc., Newton, Mass., 1971—. Chmn., surgical technique and operating com. Newton-Wellesley Hosp. Fellow: ACS; mem.: Mass. Med. Soc., Plastic Surgery Ednl. Found., Lipoplasty Soc. N.Am., Am. Soc. Laser Surgery, Northeastern Soc. Plastic & Reconstructive Surgery, Mass. Soc. Plastic & Reconstructive Surgery, New England Soc. Plastic & Reconstructive Surgeons, Am. Soc. Plastic Surgeons, Am. Soc. for Aesthetic Plastic Surgery (Certificate of Advanced Tng. in Cosmetic Surgery). Office: Plastic and Cosmetic Surgery Inc 2000 Washington St Ste 545 Newton MA 02462 Office Phone: 617-964-2000. Office Fax: 617-964-6235.*

DAVIDSON, BARRY SHELDON, academic administrator, comparative and adult education educator; b. Bklyn., Sept. 18, 1949; s. Jack and Iva Irene Davidson. BS, Pittsburg State U., Kans., 1971, MS, 1973; EdS, Vanderbilt U., 1974; EdD, U. Ark., 1977. Cert. permanent 7-12 tchr. NY. Vis. prof. East Carolina U., Greenville, NC, 1977—80; assoc. dir. admissions U. Nevada-Reno, Reno, 1980—90; dir. admissions Pittsburg (Kans.) State U., 1990—91; acad. historian Am. Cmty. Sch., Athens, Greece, 1991—2000; asst. prof. edn. Lander U., Greenwood, SC, 2000—01, McNeese State U., Lake Charles, La., 2001—02, Troy U., Ala., 2002—. Guest scholar Adam Mickiewicz U., Poznan, Poland, 1989, European Humanities U., Minsk, Belarus, 1998, Internat. Solomon U., Kiev, Ukraine, 1999, Ind. U. Tbilisi, Georgia, 1999; presenter Oxford U. Roundtable, 2005. Assoc. editor: Nat. Forum Jour., 2004—; contbr. articles to profl. jours. Chmn. No. Nev. Soccer League Disciplinary Com., Reno, 1980—84; vol. Probation and Parole, Reno, 1987—90; campaign vol. United Way, Pittsburg, Kans., 1990—91; cross country and track coach ACS Varsity Boys and Girls, Greece, 1991—96. Recipient Outstanding Young Alumnus award, Pittsburg State U., 1987. Mem.: AAUP. Avocations: travel, gardening, coin and stamp collecting. Home: 1122 S Brundidge Boulevard Troy AL 36081-3112 Office: Troy U 232 Gen Academic Bldg Troy AL 36082 Personal E-mail: vandy49@hotmail.com.

DAVIDSON, BONNIE JEAN, gymnastics educator, sports management consultant; b. Rockford, Ill., Nov. 19, 1941; d. Edward V. and Pauline Mae (Dubbs) Welliver; m. Glenn Duane Davidson, June 4, 1960 (dec. Oct. 1993); children: Lori Davidson Aamodt, Wendy Davidson Seerup; m. James A. Johnson, Sept. 15, 2001. Student, Rockford Coll., Ill., 1965, Rock Valley Coll., Rockford, Ill., 1969—77. Founder, owner, dir. Gymnastic Acad. Rockford, 1977-95; pres., dir., owner Springbrook, Ltd., swim and tennis club, Rockford, 1986-95. Rep. trampoline and tumbling com. AAU, 1989-99; coach nat. and world champion athletes; mgr., judge, head del. U.S.A. gymnastics teams, 1980—2004; speaker, lectr., clinician in field.; mem. organizing coms. world championships, also others, 1982-99. Contbr. World Book Ency. Bd. dirs. U.S. Olympic Com., 1995-2005, U.S.A. Gymnastics, 1991-2005; instr. ARC. Named one of Most Interesting People, Rockford mag., 1987; named to USA Gymnastics Hall of Fame, 2003; recipient YWCA Janet Lynn Sports award, 1996. Mem. Internat. Fedn. Trampoline and Tumbling (internat. judge, mem. tech. com. 1986-99—, del. to congress 1976-86, hon. lifetime mem. 1998), Internat. Fedn. Sport Acrobats (internat. judge), U.S.A. Trampoline and Tumbling Assn. (hon. life; nat. tumbling chairperson 1980-88, advisor 1988-99—, Coach of Yr. award 1980, Outsanding Contbn. to the Sport award 1987, 96, Master of Sport award 1989), U.S. Sports Acrobatics Fedn. (hon. life; v.p. 1984-95), Nat. Judges Assn. (exec. dir.). Republican. Avocations: skiing, boating, bicycling, birdwatching, flying. E-mail: johnsonbj11@insightbb.com.

DAVIDSON, BROOK A., lawyer; b. Gainesville, Ga., Nov. 21, 1979; d. Thomas Bayton Atkinson and Rebecca Racioppi, Susan Lamancusa Atkinson (Stepmother) and Stephen Gerard Racioppi (Stepfather); m. Timothy Allen Davidson, May 3, 2002; children: Timothy Allen, Nicholas Calhoun. BA, Brenau U., Gainesville, Ga., 2002; JD, Ga. State U., Coll. Law, Atlanta, 2005. Law clk. Andrew, Merritt, Reilly & Smith, LLP, Lawrenceville, Ga., 2004—05, assoc. atty., 2005—. Mediator Ga. Office Dispute Resolution, 2003—. Mem. Planning and Zoning Bd., 2004—05, chmn., 2005—07. Denise Marchesseau scholar, Brenau U., 2001. Mem.: Delta Delta Delta (alumni advisor 2004—05, lifetime mem. advisor 2005—), State Bar Ga. (sec. fiduciary law sect. younger lawyers divsn. 2007, younger lawyers elder law section sect. 2007—). Libertarian. Roman

Catholic. Avocations: reading, travel, tennis. Office: Andrew Merritt Reilly & Smith LLP 7 Lumpkin St Lawrenceville GA 30045 Office Phone: 770-513-1200. Office Fax: 770-513-1201. Business E-Mail: bdavidson@amrslaw.com.

DAVIDSON, CHANDLER, sociologist, educator; b. May 13, 1936; m. Sharon Lavon Plummer, Nov. 1, 1986. BA, U. Tex., 1961; PhD, Princeton U., 1969. Rsch. prof. sociology Rice U., Houston, 1966—, prof. polit. sci., 1997—2003, prof. emeritus, 2003—, Radoslav Tsanoff prof. pub. affairs, 2000—03, chair dept. sociology, 1979-83, 86-89, 1995—2003. Co-prin. investigator NSF, 1988-92, Rockefeller Found., 1990. Author: Biracial Politics, 1972, Race and Class in Texas Politics, 1990, Protecting Minority Voters, 2006; editor: Minority Vote Dilution, 1984, (with Bernard Grofman) Controversies in Minority Voting, 1992, (with Grofman) Quiet Revolution in the South, 1994. Mem. Nat. Commn. on the Voting Rights Act, 2005. With USN, 1962. Fulbright scholar, 1961-62; Woodrow Wilson fellow, 1963-64, rsch. fellow Nat. Endowment for Humanities, 1976-77; recipient Gustavus Myers Ctr. Human Rights award for outstanding book on human rights, 1993, Ally award Ctr. for the Healing of Racism, 1996, Brown award for superior tchg., Rice U., 1997, 99, 2000, 2002, Brown award for excellence in tchg. Rice U., 1998. Mem. Am. Polit. Sci. Assn. (Fenno prize 1995), Phi Beta Kappa. Office: Rice U Dept Sociology 6100 S Main St Houston TX 77251-1892 Business E-Mail: fcd@rice.edu.

DAVIDSON, CHARLES D., energy executive; m. Nancy Davidson. BSChE, Purdue Univ., 1972; MS, Univ. Tex., Dallas, 1980. With ARCO Oil & Gas, 1972—93, sr. vice-pres., Eastern District, 1992—93; sr. v.p. Vastar Resources, Inc., 1993—97, pres., CEO, 1997—2000, Noble Energy Inc., 2000—01, chmn., pres., CEO, 2001—. Chmn. offshore com. Independent Petroleum Ass. Am. Mem. adv. bd. Univ. Tex., Dallas. Mem.: Am. Inst. Chem. Engineers, Soc. Petroleum Engineers. Office: Noble Energy Ste 100 100 Glenborough Houston TX 77067 Office Phone: 281-872-3100. Office Fax: 281-872-3111.*

DAVIDSON, CHARLES THOMAS, lawyer; b. Jacksonville, Fla., Feb. 26, 1943; s. John Boyce and Dorothy (Rogers) D.; m. Joyce Ann Fernandez, June 21, 1975; 1 child, Johnathan Boyce. BS, U. Tenn., 1965; JD, U. Fla., 1972. Bar: Fla. 1973; cert. ct. mediator, Fla. Asst. state atty., 13th Jud. Cir. State Attys. Office, Tampa, Fla., 1973-83; lawyer, pres., shareholder McWhirter Reeves & Davidson, P.A., Tampa, 1983—. Mem. Greater Tampa (Fla.) C. of C., 1985— Capt. US Army, 1966—70. Mem.: ABA (forum com. on the constrn. industry 1985), FBA, Fla. Bar Assn. (trial lawyers sect., exec. coun. trial lawyers sect. 1987—88), Hillsborough County Bar Assn., Am. Arbitration Assn. (Nat. Panel of Arbitrators), Kiwanis Club Tampa. Office: McWhirter Reeves & Davidson PA 400 N Tampa St Ste 2450 Tampa FL 33602-5842 Office Phone: 813-224-0866. E-mail: tdavidson@mac-law.com.

DAVIDSON, COLIN HENRY, architect, educator; b. Exeter, Eng., Mar. 4, 1928; emigrated to Can., 1968, naturalized, 1975. s. Douglas Nangle and Dulcie Rose (Winter) D.; m. Lucienne Fiant, Jan. 18, 1956; children: Dominique, Philip. Diploma architecture, Brussels Royal Acad., 1951; M.Arch., M.I.T., 1955. Archtl. asst. Luccichenti/Monaco, Rome, 1951-54; asst. architect Architects' Collaborative, Cambridge, Mass., 1954-55, London County Council, 1956-60; pres. C.H. Davidson Cons., London, 1960-68; prof. architecture U. Montreal, 1968—; dean Faculty Environ. Design, 1976-85. Founder Indsl. Forum Rsch. Group, 1969; founder, pres. IF Rsch. Corp.; exec. dir. Cibat-Montreal Internat. Bldg. Ctr. Prin. works include Cosmos and SB2 industrialized bldg. sys.; author numerous works in field of info. sci. in bldg. including 4 thesauri in bldg. sci. and tech., bldg. procurement, tech. transfer, and post-disaster reconstruction. Counselor Galaxie Jeunesse. Named Bldg. Communicator of Yr., Internat. Union of Bldg. Ctrs., 1991, Domus Personality of Yr., Provincial Assn. of Home Builders, Quebec, 1991; recipient Disting. Prof. award, Assn. Collegiate Sch. Architecture, 1987, Program Com. commendation, Internat. Coun. for Rsch. and Innovation in Bldg. Construction, 2006. Mem. Internat. Coun. Rsch. and Innovation in Bldg. and Constrn.-CIB, Order of Archs. Que. Achievements include development of web-based question-and answer system for the construction sector. Office: U Montreal PO Box 6128 Montreal PQ Canada H3C 3J7 Office Phone: 514-343-7420. Personal E-mail: colinhdavidson@sympatico.ca. *I have constantly been torn by the dilemma of the Architect: man-of-the-arts or man-of-science. Having opted for the latter (perhaps out of fear of the former), I find I must work in a scientific near-vacuum. For this reason, I dedicate my life to problems of research and its application, to the transfer of information in the building process.*

DAVIDSON, DAN EUGENE, educational association administrator, director, language educator; b. Wichita, Kans., Sept. 18, 1944; s. Clerin D. and Fay E. (Scott) D.; m. Maria D. Lekic, Apr. 20, 1976; children: Michael Scott, Paul Eugene. BA, U. Kans., 1966; MA, Harvard U., 1971, PhD, 1972; DSc (hon.), Russian Acad. Scis., 1995, Almaty State U., Kazakhstan, 1996, U. World Langs., Uzbekistan, 1997. Asst. prof., then assoc. prof. Amherst (Mass.) Coll., 1971-76; from assoc. prof. to prof. Russian Bryn Mawr (Pa.) Coll., 1976—; exec. dir. Am. Coun. Tchrs. of Russian, Washington, 1980—; pres. Am. Couns. for Internat. Edn. ACTR/ACCELS, 1998—. Adj. faculty U. Pa., Columbia U., Harvard U., 1975; cons. UN, N.Y.C., 1987, 88, 91, U.S. Dept. Edn., NEH, Washington; co-chair Internat. Task Force on Ednl. Reform in Russia, Ukraine, Belarus, Kyrgyzstan, Kazakhstan, 1992-94 (Soros Founds.); chmn. Alliance for Internat. Ednl. and Cultural Exch., 1997-99. Series editor: Soviet-American Textbook Series of Russian, 1974—; author, co-author, editor univ. and high sch.-level textbooks on English and Russian; editor, co-editor scholarly collections, jours.; contbr. articles to scholarly publs. Bd. dirs. numerous non-profit ednl. orgns.; mem. leadership com. co-chmn. ann. fund and major gifts, Barrie Sch., 1995-96, trustee, 1997-2000; mem. Fair Share Campaign Sidwell Friends Sch., 1992-97. Recipient Pushkin medal, 1982, Order Internat. Friendship, USSR, 1990; inducted into Russian Acad. Edn., 1995; recipient Disting. Svc. to Profession award, Am. Assn. Tchrs. Slavic Langs., 1995, Disting. Svc. award Assn. Depts. Fgn. Langs./MLA, 1997; hon. fellow Woodrow Wilson Found., 1966. Mem. MLA, Am. Assn. Advancement Slavic Studies, Am. Coun. Tchrs. of Russian (pres. 1975-79), Internat. Assn. Tchrs. Russian Lang. and Lit. (v.p. 1975-80, 91—), Harvard Club, Phi Beta Kappa, Delta Phi Alpha. Democrat. Episcopalian. Avocations: travel, music, swimming. Office: Am Couns Ste 700 1776 Massachusetts Ave NW Washington DC 20036-1904 Office Phone: 202-833-7522. Personal E-mail: ddavidson@rcn.net. Business E-Mail: ceo@americancouncils.org.

DAVIDSON, DANIEL IRA, lawyer; b. Bklyn., Sept. 19, 1936; s. Mitchell and Minnie (Needleman) D.; m. Susan Bettina Thomas, Mar. 13, 1966; 1 child, Jill. AB, Columbia Coll., 1957; JD, Columbia U., 1959. Bar: N.Y. 1959, U.S. Ct.Appeals (2d cir.), 1960, U.S. Ct. Appeals (D.C. cir.), 1970, D.C., 1972, U.S. Ct. Appeals (9th cir.), 1975, U.S. Ct. Appeals (5th cir.), 1980, U.S. Ct. Appeals (10th and 11th cirs.), 1981, U.S. Supreme Ct., 1982. Editor Columbia Law Rev., 1958-59; law clk. to Judges Harold R. Medina and Learned Hand U.S. Ct. Appeals 2d Cir., 1960; assoc. Cravath, Swaine & Moore, NYC, 1961-65; spl. asst. to asst. sec. state East Asia and Pacific Affairs, Washington, 1965-67; spl. asst. to ambassador U.S. Dept. State, Washington, 1967-68; U.S. del. to Paris Peace Talks on Vietnam Paris, 1968-69; mem. staff Nat. Security Coun., Washington, 1969; assoc. Wilmer, Cutler & Pickering, Washington, 1969-70; exec. asst. to W. Averell Harriman Washington, 1971-72; assoc. Prather, Levenberg, Seeger, Doolittle, Farmer & Ewing, Washington, 1972-73, Spiegel & McDiarmid, Washington, 1973-74, ptnr., 1974—. Mem. Com. on Internat. Affairs Dem. Policy Coun., Washington, 1971-72; cons. U.S. Dept. State, Washington, 1978-79, pub. mem. fgn. svc. selection bd., 1995; mem. Coun. on Fgn. Rels.; lectr. in polit. sci. CUNY, 1960. Editor: Columbia Law Review; contbr. articles and book revs. to The Economist, NY Times, LA Times, Wash. Post, London Times, Fin. Times, The Atlantic, others; featured in: (documentary) The Trials of Henry Kissinger, Wiretapped by Richard Nixon. 1st lt. USAR, 1960-66. Fellow Salzburg Seminar in Am. Studies, 1959. Mem. Cosmos Club, Phi Beta Kappa. Jewish. Home: 2900 Brandywine St NW Washington DC 20008-2138 Office: Spiegel & McDiarmid 1333 New Hampshire Ave NW Washington DC 20036 Office Phone: 202-879-4000. Personal E-mail: did11@starpower.net.

DAVIDSON, DANIEL MORTON, lawyer; b. Lynbrook, NY, July 9, 1950; BA summa cum laude, Williams Coll., 1972; JD magna cum laude, Harvard U., 1975. Bar: D.C. 1975, Calif. 1977, U.S. Tax Ct. 1979, U.S. Supreme Ct. 1992. Law clk. Mass. Supreme Ct., 1975-76; ptnr. Sidley & Austin, Washington, 1985-98, Hogan & Hartson, L.L.P., Washington, 1998—. Contbr. articles to profl. jours. Mem. ABA, D.C. Bar Assn., State Bar Calif., Phi Beta Kappa. Office: Hogan & Hartson LLP 555 13th St NW Ste 900W Washington DC 20004-1109 Office Phone: 202-637-5865. Business E-Mail: dmdavidson@hhlaw.com.

DAVIDSON, DAVID SCOTT, retired architect; b. Great Falls, Mont., Dec. 17, 1925; s. David Adams and Florence Mae (Scott) D.; m. Marjorie Luella Huffman, Sept. 10, 1949; children: Carol M., Marilyn S., Scott L., Bruce F., Craig S. Student, U. Utah, 1943, Pasadena City Coll., 1944; BS in Architecture, Mont. State U., 1950. Registered architect, Mont. Architect in tng. Shanley & Shanley Architects, Great Falls, 1950-52; architect van Teylingen, Knight, van Teylingen, Great Falls, 1952-54; prin. David S. Davidson, Architect, Great Falls, 1954-56; ptnr. Davidson & Kuhr Architects, Great Falls, 1956-75; pres. Davidson & Kuhr Architects, P.C., Great Falls, 1975—2002. Dir., pres. Great Falls Arts Assn., 1980-83; dir., pres. Mont. Inst. Arts, 1981—; mem. state constrn. adv. coun. State of Mont., 1983-84; dir., v.p. Paris Gibson Square, Great Falls, 1982—88. Mem. Great Falls Zoning Bd., 1972-75; mem. rehab. com. Great Falls Housing Task Force, 1975-78; chmn. architecture div. United Way, 1975-78; dir. Great Falls Symphony Assn., 1992-93. Served with U.S. Army, 1943-46. Recipient 1st honor Mont. chpt. AIA, 1973, 75; recipient honor award in architecture Mont. chpt. AIA, 1973, 74, 78, 83, merit in architecture Mont. chpt. AIA, 1965, 2 awards U.S. Dept. Energy, 1986, Interior Design award Arch. Record, 1976, Internat. Union Bricklayers and Allied Crafts award, 1986, 87, 92. Fellow AIA (chpt. pres. 1965-66, dir. 1962-66), Great Falls Soc. Architects (pres. 1958-59), Jr. C. of C. (dir. 1956-60) Home: 1212 Buena Dr Great Falls MT 59404-3750

DAVIDSON, DIANE (MARIE DAVIDSON), publisher; b. LA, Mar. 6, 1924; d. Charles Casper and Stella Ruth (Bateman) Winnia; divorced, 1953; children: David William, Ronald Mark. AB, U. Calif., Berkeley, 1943; MA, Calif. State U., Sacramento, 1959. cert. secondary tchr., 1944. Tchr. Campbell (Calif.) High Sch., 1944-45; actress Pasadena (Calif.) Playhouse, 1945, U.S.O. Camp Shows, NYC, 1946-47; tchr. El Camino H.S., Sacramento, 1954-85. Illustrator, pub. and editor Swan Books, Fair Oaks, Calif., 1979—99. Author: Feversham, 1969, (with Josephine Van Essi) Pablo's Gold, 2007; editor: 18 Easy-to-Read Shakespeare Plays Without Changing the Words, History of Trinity Episcopal Church, Folsom, California, 1996. Mem. NEA, PEN, Authors Guild, Calif. Writers Club, Calif. Tchrs. Assn., Phi Beta Kappa, Pi Lambda Theta. Democrat. Episcopalian. Avocations: gardening, writing.

DAVIDSON, DONALD WILLIAM, advertising executive; b. Toronto, May 18, 1938; s. John Harvie and Harriet Gertrude Davidson; m. Olive Margaret Somerville, July 28, 1962; children: Scott, Susan. Degree, U. Toronto, York U. Account exec. E.L. Ruddy, Toronto, 1957-68, Foster & Kleiser, Detroit, 1968-70; v.p. Outdoor Advt. Sales, 1971-72, Montreal, 1972-73, v.p. mktg. group, 1973-75; v.p. nat. sales Claude Neon Ltd., Toronto, 1975-77, exec. v.p., 1977-79; pres. Mediacom Inc., Toronto, 1979-80, chmn., pres., 1980-84; exec. v.p., COO Gannett Outdoor, NYC, 1984-86, pres., CEO, 1986-96, Trading Bay LLC, NYC, 2005—; pres. Trading Bay Media, 1996—; ptnr., pres. DCR Media Inc. Past vice chmn. Traffic Audit Bur. Mem. The Advt. Coun. (bd. dirs.), Lambton Golf and Country Club, Bigwin Golf Club. Home: 40 Las Brisas Way Naples FL 34108 Office: Trading Bay LLC 230 Park Ave Ste 1000 New York NY 10169-0005

DAVIDSON, DONETTA LEA, federal official, former state official; b. Liberal, Kans., Aug. 14, 1943; d. Edwin Donald Owens and Loretta May (Conrad). County clk. and recorder Bent County, Las Animas, Colo., 1978-86; dir. of elections State of Colo., Denver, 1986-94; county clerk & recorder Arapahoe County, Littleton, Colo., 1995—99; sec. state State of Colo., Denver, 1999—2005; commr. US Election Assistance Commn., 2005—. Accreditation bd. Nat. Assn. State Election Directors Voting Sys./Ind. Test Authority, 1998—; bd. dirs. Election Ctr., 1998—. Henry Toll Fellowship of Coun. of State Govts., 1993. Mem.: Nat. Assn. Secretaries of State (treas. 2003—04, pres. elect 2004—05, pres. 2005), Postal Svc. Task Force (chairperson, joint elections officials liaison cmty. 1997—), Fed. Election Commn. Adv. Panel (mem. 1995—), Internat. Assn. Clks., Recorders, Election Officials, and Treasurers (mem. 1995—), Nat. Assn. State Election Dir. (pres. 1994), Colo. State Assn. of County Clk. and Recorders (pres. 1983—84). Republican. Office: US Election Assistance Commn 1225 NY Ave NE Ste 1100 Washington DC 20005 Office Phone: 303-894-2200. Business E-Mail: sos.admin1@sos.state.co.us.

DAVIDSON, DOUGLAS E., lawyer; b. NYC, 1946; BS, Georgetown U., 1968; JD summa cum laude, George Washington U., 1971. Bar: NY 1972. Ptnr. Thelen Reid & Priest LLP, NYC, vice chmn., bus. dept., co-chmn., Latin Am. & Global Fin. & Securities Practice Group, co-chmn., Energy Utilities & Infrastructure Practice Group. Editor-in-chief George Washington Law Rev., 1970—71. Mem.: Assn. Bar City NY (chmn. nuclear tech. & law com. 1982—85), NY State Bar Assn., Fed. Energy Bar Assn., ABA, Order of Coif. Office: Thelen Reid & Priest LLP 875 Third Ave New York NY 10022-6225 Office Phone: 212-603-8977. Office Fax: 212-603-2001. Business E-Mail: ddavidson@thelenreid.com.

DAVIDSON, ERIC HARRIS, molecular and developmental biologist, educator; b. NYC, Apr. 13, 1937; s. Morris and Anne D. Davidson. BA, U. Pa., 1958; PhD, Rockefeller U., 1963. Research asso. Rockefeller U., 1963-65, asst. prof., 1965-71; asso. prof. devel. molecular biology Calif. Inst. Tech., Pasadena, Calif., 1971-74, prof., 1974—, Norman Chandler prof. cell biology, 1981—. Author: Gene Activity in Early Development, 3d edit., 1986, Genomic Regulatory Systems, 2001, Regulatory Genome, 2006; contbr. scientific papers. Grantee, NIH, 1965—, NSF, 1972—. Mem.: NAS. Achievements include research in DNA sequence organization; gene expression during embryonic development; gene regulation; evolutionary mechanisms; gene networks. Office: Calif Inst Tech Div Biology Mail Code 156 29 Pasadena CA 91125-0001 Office Phone: 626-395-4937. Business E-Mail: davidson@caltech.edu.

DAVIDSON, ERNEST ROY, chemist, educator; b. Terre Haute, Ind., Oct. 12, 1936; s. Roy Emmette and Opal Ruth (Hugunin) D.; m. Reba Faye Minnich, Jan. 27, 1956; children: Michael Collins, John Philip, Mark Ernest, Martha Ruth. BSc, Rose-Hulman Inst. Tech., 1958, DEng (hon.), 1998; PhD, Ind. U., 1961; PhD (hon.), Uppsala U., 2000. NSF Postdoctoral fellow U. Wis.-Madison, 1961-62; asst. prof. chemistry U. Wash., 1962-65, assoc. prof., 1965-68, prof., 1968-84, Ind. U., Bloomington, 1984-86, disting. prof., 1986—2002, chmn. dept. chemistry, 1999—2002; prof. U. Wash., Seattle, 2002—. Disting. vis. prof. Ohio State U., 1974-75; vis. prof. IMS, Japan, 1984, Technion, Israel, 1985; vis. scholar U. N.C., 2002—; Boys-Rahman lectr. Royal Soc. Chemistry, 2002; adj. prof. U. N.C., Chapel Hill, 2005—. Editor: Jour. Computational Physics, 1975-98, Internat. Jour. Quantum Chemistry, 1975—, Jour. Chem. Physics, 1976-78, 98—, Chem. Physics Letters, 1977-84, Jour. Am. Chem. Soc., 1978-83, Jour. Phys. Chemistry, 1982-90, Accounts of Chem. Rsch., 1984-92, Theoretica Chimica Acta, 1985-98, Chem. Revs., 1986—; contbr. numerous articles on density matrices and quantum theory of molecular structure to profl. jours. Union Carbide fellow Rose-Hulman Inst. Tech., 1958; NSF fellow Ind. U., 1961; recipient Hirschfelder prize in theoretical chemistry, 1997-98, Schrodinger medal, 2001, Nat. medal of sci., 2002; Sloan fellow, 1967-68; Guggenheim fellow, 1974-75; laureate l'Academie Internationale des Sciences Moleculaires Quantiques, 1971. Fellow Am. Phys. Soc., Sigma Xi; mem. NAS, Am. Chem. Soc. (Computers in Chemistry award 1992, Theoretical Chemistry award 2000), Am. Acad. Arts and Scis., Ind. Acad. Sci. (Chemist of Yr. award 1999), Phi Lambda Upsilon, Tau Beta Pi. Office: U Wash Dept Chemistry Bagley 303A Seattle WA 98195-1700

DAVIDSON, EUGENE ABRAHAM, biochemist, educator, academic administrator; b. NYC, May 27, 1930; s. Jack and Sophie Miriam (Deutsch) D. BS, UCLA, 1950; PhD, Columbia U., 1955. Postdoctoral fellow, instr. U. Mich., 1955-58; asst. prof. biochemistry Duke U., 1958-62, assoc. prof., 1962-65, prof., 1965-67; prof., chmn. dept. biol. chemistry M.S. Hershey Med. Center, Pa. State U., 1967-87, assoc. dean for edn., 1975-87; chmn. dept. biochemistry and molecular biology Georgetown U., Washington, 1988—2002, prof., 2003—. Mem. Nat. Bd. Med. Examiners, Part I; cons. in field. Author: Carbohydrate Chemistry, 1967; contbr. numerous articles to profl. publs.; Editorial reviewer for numerous jours. Guggenheim fellow, 1965-66; NIH grantee, 1958— Mem. AAAS, Am. Soc. Biol. Chemists, Assn. Med. Sch. Depts. Biochemistry, Biochem. Soc., Am. Assn. Cancer Research, Soc. Complex Carbohydrates, Glycoconjugate Soc. (pres. 1985-87), Sigma Xi. Office: Georgetown U Dept Biochem/Molecular Biology Washington DC 20057 Office Phone: 202-687-1100. Business E-Mail: davidson@georgetown.edu.

DAVIDSON, EZRA C., JR., obstetrician, gynecologist, academic administrator, educator; b. Water Valley, Miss., Oct. 21, 1933; s. Ezra Cap and Theresa Hattie (Woods) Davidson; children: Pamela, Gwendolyn, Marc, Ezra K. BS cum laude, Morehouse Coll., 1954; MD, Meharry Med. Coll., 1958. Diplomate Am. Bd. Ob-Gyn. (examiner 1973-). Intern San Diego County Gen. Hosp., 1958—59; resident in ob-gyn. Harlem Hosp., NYC, 1963—66, asst. attending ob-gyn, obstet. coordinator maternal and infant care clinics, 1967—68; dir. departmental research, assoc. attending, acting chmn. ob-gyn, co-dir. coagulation research lab. Roosevelt Hosp., NYC, 1968—70; fellow blood coagulation, asst. ob-gyn Columbia U. Coll. Physicians and Surgeons, NYC, 1966—67, instr. dept. ob-gyn, 1967—69, asst. clin. prof., 1970; cons. ob-gyn Office Health Affairs, OEO, Washington, 1970—72; prof. Charles R. Drew U. of Medicine and Sci., LA, 1971—, acad. v.p., 1982—87, chmn. dept. ob.-gyn., 1971—96, assoc. dean primary care, 1997—; prof. U. So. Calif., Los Angeles, 1971—80, UCLA, 1980—. Chief svc. dept. ob-gyn. King/Drew Med. Ctr., LA, 1971—96; attending physician dept. ob-gyn. L.A. County-U. So. Calif. Med. Ctr., 1971—80; mem. nat. med. adv. com. nat. found. March of Dimes, 1972—76; bd. cons. Internat. Childbirth Edn. Assn., 1973—81; mem. sec.'s adv. com. population affairs HEW, 1974—77, chmn. svcs. task force, 1975—77; chmn. bd. dirs. L.A. Regional Family Planning Coun., 1975—77; bd. dirs. Nat. Alliance Sch. Age Parents, 1975—79; mem. corp. bd. Blue Shield, Calif., 1989—; chair DHHS Sec.'s Adv. Com. on Infant Mortality, 1990—93; active FDA, 1990—96, chmn. fertility and maternal health drugs adv. com., 1992—96; mem. adv. com. to the dir. NIH, 1995—98, mem. dirs. adv. panel on clin. rsch., 1995—98; mem. roundtable on health care quality Inst. on Medicine, 1995—98; mem. coun. grad. med. edn. HHS, 1997—2000; bd. dirs., chair med. policy com. Blue Shield of Calif., 1998—2002. Bd. dirs. The Calif. Wellness Found., 1995—, chmn., 1996—98; bd. dirs. Children's Bur. So. Calif., 1999—, v.p., 1995—99, pres., 1999—2002; bd. dirs. Jacobs Inst. of Womens Health, 1999—; chmn. bd. trustees Blue Shield Calif. Found., 2004—. With USAF, 1959—63. Fellow Johnson Found. Health Policy, Inst. Medicine, NAS, 1979—80. Fellow: ACS, L.A. Ob-Gyn. Soc. (pres. 1982—83), Royal Coll. Ob-Gyn., Am. Coll. Ob-Gyn. (nat. sec. 1983—89, pres.-elect 1989—90, pres. 1990—91); mem.: Calif. Tech. Assessment Forum (chair 2002—), Assn. of Acad. Minority Physicians (pres. 2002—03), Golden State Med. Assn. (pres. 1989—90), Assn. Profs. Ob-Gyn. (pres. 1989—90), Nat. Med. Assn. (chmn. nat. sect. ob-gyn. 1975—77, mem. sci. coun. 1979—88, bd. trustee 1989—95, chmn. bd. trustees 1992—95), Ob-Gyn. Assembly So. Calif. (chmn. 1989—90), Pacific Coast Ob-Gyn. Soc., N.Am. Soc. Pediatric and Adolescent Gynecology (pres.-elect 1993—94, pres. 1994—95), Am. Ob-Gyn. Soc. Office: 12021 Wilmington Ave Los Angeles CA 90059-3019

DAVIDSON, FRANK PAUL, retired macroengineer, lawyer; b. NYC, May 20, 1918; s. Maurice Philip and Blanche (Reinheimer) D.; m. Izaline Marguerite Doll, May 19, 1951; children: Roger Conrad, Nicholas Henry, Charles Geoffrey. BS, Harvard U., 1939, JD, 1948; DHL (hon.), Hawthorne Coll., 1987; D in Engring. and Diplomacy (hon.), Roger Williams U., 2003. Bar: NY 1953, US Dist. Ct. (so. dist.) NY 1953. Dir. mil. affairs, gen. counsel Houston C. of C., 1948—50; contract analyst Am. Embassy, Paris, 1950-53; assoc. Carb, Luria, Glassner & Cook, NYC, 1953-54; pvt. practice law NYC, 1955-70; founding pres., counsel, bd. dirs. The Inst. for the Future, 1967-70; rsch. assoc. MIT, Cambridge, Mass., 1970-96, also chmn. system dynamics steering com. Sloan Sch. Mgmt., coord. macro-engring. Sch. Engring. Pres., gen. counsel Tech. Studies Inc., NYC, 1957—96; vice chmn. Inst. for Ednl. Svcs., Bedford, Mass., 1980—84; co-founder Channel Tunnel Study Group, London and Paris, 1957, governing bd., 1957—85; NAS del. Renewable Resources Workshop, Katmandu, Nepal, 1981; mem. adv. bd. Tech. in Soc., Elmont, NY, 1981—, project appraisal, 1986—98; mem. editl. bd. Interdisciplinary Sci. Revs., 1985—; apptd. to exploration task force NASA, Washington, 1989; spl. lectr. Société des Ingénieurs et Scientifiques de France, 1991; mem. internat. sci. and tech. com. Ocean Cities Symposium, Monaco, 1995. Author: Macro: A Clear Vision of How Sci. and Tech. Will Shape Our Future, 1983, Macro: Big is Beautiful, 1986; co-author: Building the World: An Encyclopaedia of the Great Engineering Projects in History, 2006; editor: series of AAAS books on macroengring., Tunneling and Underground Transport, 1987; co-editor: Solar Power Satellites, 1978, 2d edit., 1998. Bd. dirs. Internat. Mountain Soc., Boulder, Colo., 1981-2000, Assn. Prospective 2100, Paris, 1997; trustee Norwich (Vt.) Ctr., 1980-83, mem. steering com. Am. Trails Network, 1986-88, bd. dirs. Am. Trails Washington, 1988-90. RCAC, 1941-46, ETO; Troop Leader 10th Cdn., Armoured Rgt. (Fort Garry Horse), Intelligence Officer and Squadron Leader; GSO III (Intelligence) Second Armoured Brigade Group, maj. Tex. State Guard; apptd. to Senate Ft. Garry Horse, 1995, bd. overseers Roger Williams U., 2004. Decorated Bronze Star medal, 1945-46; Chevalier Legion of Honor (France), 1999; named hon. major Fort Garry Horse, 2004; recipient Key to City Osaka, Japan, 1987, Twice the Citizen award Royal Mil. Inst., Man., Can., 1999, William James award Rensselaerville Inst., 2001; elected Mem. Honoraire, Pres. d'Honneur Assn. Louis Armand, Paris, 1996-99; Lewis Mumford fellow Rensselaerville Inst., 1982. Mem. ABA, Internat. Assn. Macro-Engring. Socs. (bd. dirs. 1987—, hon. chmn. 1997-2000), Am. Soc. Macro-Engring. (bd. dirs. 1982—, vice chancellor 1983-97, pres. 1997-98, chmn. 1998), Assn. Bar City N.Y. (internat. law com. 1959-62), Major Projects Assn. (mem. overseas adv. com. U.K. 1995—), Knickerbocker Club, St. Botolph Club, MIT Quarter Century Club. Home: 151 Main St Concord MA 01742-2436

DAVIDSON, GEORGE ALLAN, lawyer; b. NYC, Apr. 6, 1942; s. George Roger and Jean Allan (McKaig) D.; m. Annette L. Richter, Sept. 4, 1965; children: Emily, Charlotte. AB, Brown U., 1964; LLB, Columbia U., 1967. Bar: N.Y. 1967, U.S. Dist. Ct. (so. and ea. dists.) N.Y. 1969, U.S. Ct. Appeals (2d cir.) 1970, U.S. Supreme Ct. 1974, U.S. Tax Ct. 1974, U.S. Ct. Appeals (D.C. cir.) 1976, U.S. Dist. Ct. (no. dist.) Calif. 1980, U.S. Ct. Appeals (9th cir.) 1981, U.S. Ct. Appeals (5th cir.) 1982, U.S. Dist. Ct. (no. dist.) N.Y. 1982, U.S. Ct. Appeals (11th cir.) 1983, U.S. Ct. Appeals (1st cir.) 1986, U.S. Ct. Appeals (7th cir.) 1992, U.S. Ct. Appeals (fed. cir.) 2005. Law clk., 1967-68; assoc. Hughes Hubbard & Reed, NYC, 1968-74, ptnr., 1974—; dir. P.R. Legal Def. and Edn. Fund, Inc., 1980-84. Dir. Legal Aid Soc., 1979-92, pres. 1987-89, N.Y. Lawyers for Pub. Interest, Inc., 1984-86, Columbia Law Sch. Alumni Assn., 1987-91, Practicing Attys. for Law Students, 1989-2006, VIP Cmty. Svcs., 1994—, Greenwich House, Inc., 2002—, chmn., 2004—; chmn. Fed. Defenders N.Y., Inc., 2005—. Contbr. articles to profl. jours. Fellow Am. Coll. Trial Lawyers; mem. ABA, Internat. Bar Assn., Fed. Bar Coun., Am. Law Inst., N.Y. State Bar Assn., Assn. Bar City N.Y., Nat. Assn. Coll. and Univ. Attys., Union Internationale des Avocats, Century Assn. Office: Hughes Hubbard & Reed LLP 1 Battery Park Plz Fl 12 New York NY 10004-1482 Office Phone: 212-837-6585. E-mail: davidson@hugheshubbard.com.

DAVIDSON, GILBERT, city manager; b. 1975; Dep. town mgr., Marana, Ariz. Adv. coun., Student Affairs U. Ariz.; undergraduate adv. bd. Eller Coll. Mgmt. Bd. mem. Ariz. Town Hall. Named one of 40 Under 40, Tucson Bus. Edge, 2006. Mem.: Rotary Club, Elks Lodge, Masonic Lodge. Avocation: U. Ariz. sporting events. Office: Town Manager 11555 W Civic Ctr Dr Marana AZ 85653 Office Phone: 520-382-1999.

DAVIDSON, GLEN HARRIS, federal judge; b. Pontotoc, Miss., Nov. 20, 1941; s. M. Glen and Lora (Harris) D.; m. Bonnie Payne, Apr. 25, 1973; children: Glen III, Gregory P. BA, U. Miss, 1962, JD, 1965. Bar: Miss. 1965, admitted to practice: US Ct. Appeals (5th Cir.) 1965, US Supreme Ct. 1971. Asst. dist. atty. First Jud. Dist., Tupelo, Miss., 1969-74, dist. atty., 1975; US atty. US Dist. Ct. (No. Dist.) Miss., Oxford, 1981-85, US dist. judge Aberdeen, Miss., 1985—2000, chief judge, 2000—, Jud. Conf. U.S., 2004. Atty. Lee County Sch. Bd., Miss., 1974—81. Bd. dirs. Cmty. Devel. Found., Tupelo, 1976-81; exec. bd. Yocona Coun. Boy Scouts Am., 1972—. Maj. USAF, 1966-69. Mem.: Kiwanis (pres. Tupelo 1978), Miss. Prosecutors Assn., ATLA, Lee County Bar Assn. (pres. 1974), Miss. Bar Found., Fed. Bar Assn. (v.p. 1984). Presbyterian. Office: US Dist Courthouse 301 W Commerce St Ste 342 PO Box 767 Aberdeen MS 39730-0767 Office Phone: 662-369-6486. Office Fax: 662-369-8339. Business E-Mail: Glen_Davidson@msnd.uscourts.gov.

DAVIDSON, GORDON, theater producer and director; b. Bklyn., May 7, 1933; s. Joseph H. and Alice (Gordon) D.; m. Judith Swiller, Sept. 21, 1958; children: Adam, Rachel. BA, Cornell U.; MA, Case Western Res. U.; LHD (hon.), Bklyn. Coll.; D. Performing Arts (hon.), Calif. Inst. Arts; DFA (hon.), Claremont U. Ctr. Stage mgr. Phoenix Theatre Co., 1958-60, Am. Shakespeare Festival Theatre, 1958-60, Dallas Civic Opera, 1960-61, Martha Graham Dance Co., 1962; mng. dir. Theatre Group at UCLA, 1965-67; founding dir./prodr. Center Theatre Group Mark Taper Forum, Ahmanson Theatre, Kirk Douglas Theatre, 1967—2005; co-founder New Theatre For Now, Mark Taper Forum, 1970. Past mem. theatre panel Nat. Endowment for Arts; past pres. Theatre Communications Group; mem. adv. council Internat. Theatre Inst.; mem. adv. com. Cornell Ctr. for Performing Arts; cons. Denver Center for the Performing Arts; bd. dirs. several arts orgns. including Am. Arts Alliance. Producer, dir. over 150 major theatrical prodns. including The Deputy, 1965, Candide, 1966, The Devils, 1967, Who's Happy Now, 1967, In the Matter of J. Robert Oppenheimer, 1968 (N.Y. Drama Desk award), Murderous Angels, 1970, Rosebloom, 1970, The Trial of the Catonsville Nine, 1971 (Obie award, Tony award nomination), Henry IV, Part I, 1972, Mass, 1973, Hamlet, 1974, Savages, 1974 (Obie award), Too Much Johnson, 1975, The Shadow Box, 1975 (Tony award, Outer Critics Circle Best Dir. award), And Where She Stops Nobody Knows, 1976, Getting Out, 1977, Black Angel, 1978, Terra Nova, 1979, Children of a Lesser God, 1979, The Lady and the Clarinet, 1980, Chekhov in Yalta, 1981, Tales from Hollywood, 1982, The American Clock, 1984, The Hands of Its Enemy, 1984, Traveler in the Dark, 1985, The Real Thing, 1986, Ghetto, 1986, A Lie of the Mind, 1988; dir. operas including Cosi Fan Tutte, Otello, Beatrice and Benedick, Carmen, La Boheme, Il Trovatore, Harriet, A Woman Called Moses, A Midsummer Night's Dream, 1988; TV film The Trial of the Catonsville Nine, 1971; exec. producer Zoot Suit, 1981; producer for TV It's the Willingness, PBS Visions Series, 1979, Who's Happy Now?, NET Theatre in Am. Series; dir. A Little Night Music, 1990. Trustee Ctr. for Music, Drama and Art; past pres. League Resident Theatres; past v.p. Am. Nat. Theatre Acad; advisor Fund for New Am. Plays; mem. adv. bd. Nat. Found. for Jewish Culture. Recipient N.Y. Drama Desk award for direction, 1969; recipient Los Angeles Drama Critics Circle awards for direction, 1971, 74, 75, Margo Jones award New Theatre for Now, 1970, 76, Obie award, 1971, 77, Outer Critics Circle award, 1977, Tony award for direction, 1977, award John Harvard, award Nat. Acad. TV Arts and Scis., award Nosotros Golden Eagle, award N.Y. League for Hard of Hearing, award N.Y. Speech and Hearing Assn., award Am. Theatre Assn., award Los Angeles Human Relations Commn.; Guggenheim fellow, 1983, Pulitzer Prize in Drama for the Kentucky Cycle and Angels in America (Part One- Millennium Approaches). Mem. League Resident Theatres (past pres.), ANTA (v.p. 1975), Nat. Endowment for the Arts. Office: Mabery Road Prods INC 4211 Jackson Ave Culver City CA 90232 Office Phone: 213-972-7353, 310-842-8886.

DAVIDSON, GORDON BYRON, lawyer; b. Louisville, June 24, 1926; s. Paul Byron and Elizabeth (Franz) D.; m. Geraldine B. Geiger, Dec. 21, 1948; children: Sally Burgess, Stuart Gordon. AB, Centre Coll., Danville, Ky., 1949; JD, U. Louisville, 1951; LLM, Yale U., New Haven, Conn., 1952. Law clk. Supreme Ct. U.S., 1954; of counsel Wyatt, Tarrant & Combs, Louisville, 1955-92, mng. ptnr., 1978-92. Chair emeritus Norton Healthcare, Inc., Warben, Inc. Pres. Louisville Ctrl. Area, Inc., 1971-73; chmn. River City Mall Com., 1973-74, Louisville Devel. Com.; trustee Louisville Area C. of C., 1986; bd. dirs. The Ky. Ctr.; bd. dirs., chmn. Norton Childrens Hosps., 1973-75, Louisville Fund for Arts, 1987-93; trustee emeritus Centre Coll. Recipient Louisville Citizen of Yr. award, 1973-74, Mayor's Fleur de Lis award, 1974, Louisville Man of Yr. award, 1981, Outstanding Lawyer of Ky. award, 1984, Disting. Alumnus award U. Louisville Law Sch., 1982, Disting. Citizen award City of Louisville, 1987, Man of Vision award, 1991, Ky. Commonwealth award, 1995, Caritas Found. award, 1998, U. Louisville Alumni Fellows award, 2005; Alumni fellow Brandeis Sch. Law, U. Louisville, 2005; named to Louisville Male HS Hall of Fame, 1989, Jr. Achievement Bus. Hall Fame, 2007. Mem. Jefferson Club, Louisville Country Club, Dennbarr Club, Lawyers Club, River Valley Club, Gulf Stream Bath and Tennis Club, Gulf Stream Golf Club Democrat. Presbyterian. Home: 435 Lightfoot Rd Louisville KY 40207-1853 also: 1102 Vista Del Mar Dr N Delray Beach FL 33483-7146 Office: Wyatt Tarrant & Combs PNC Plz Louisville KY 40202-2823

DAVIDSON, GORDON KIRBY, lawyer; b. Port Chester, NY, July 30, 1948; BSEE with great distinction, Stanford U., 1970, MS in Elec. Engring. and Computer Systems, 1971, JD, 1974. Bar: Calif. 1974. Law clk. to Judge Ben C. Duniway U.S. Ct. Appeals (9th cir.), 1974-75; ptnr. Fenwick & West LLP, Mountain View, Calif., 1980—, chmn., 1995—. Named a Nathan Abbott scholar, Stanford U. Law Sch., 1974; named one of 100 Most Influential Lawyers, Nat. Law Jour., 2000, 2006, 50 Most Powerful Venture Capital Dealmakers, Forbes Mag., 2001, 100 People Who Changed Our World, Upside Mag., 2001, ten best corp. lawyers in Calif., Calif. Lawyer Mag., 2004, ten best lawyers in Northern Calif., San Francisco Mag., 2004, top 100 venture capital deal makers, Forbes Mag.'s Midas List, 2004, 2005. Mem. ABA, State Bar Calif., Order Coif, Phi Beta Kappa. Office: Fenwick & West LLP Silicon Valley Center 801 California St Mountain View CA 94041*

DAVIDSON, HERBERT M., JR., (TIPPEN), newspaper owner; b. Chgo., Aug. 10, 1925; s. Herbert Marc and Liliane (Refregier) D.; m. Josephine Field, Dec. 27, 1947 (dec. July 1995); children: Marc, Julia. Student, Juilliard Sch., 1942-43, 45-46; Mus.D. (hon.), Stetson U., 1975. Reporter Chgo. Daily News, 1949-50; city editor Daytona Beach (Fla.) News-Jour., 1951-53, mng. editor, 1953-56, gen. mgr., 1957-85, pub., 1985-98, co-editor, 1985—, pres., CEO, 1998—. Pres. Ctrl. Fla. Cultural Endeavors, Inc., Daytona Beach, 1963—; chmn. Fine Arts Coun. of Fla., 1970-75, 81-82; mem. Fla. Alliance for Arts, 1998—; mem. Fla. Arts Coun., 1998-2000; prodr., artistic dir. Seaside Music Theater, Daytona Beach, 1976—. Cpl. U.S. Army, 1942-44, PTO. Named Ambassador of the Arts, State of Fla., Tallahassee, 1982, Hon. mem. London Symphony Orch., 1989, honoree Daytona Beach Community Coll.'s Tippen and Josephine Field Davidson Endowment for the Arts, 1992; hon. officer Civil divsn. Order of the Brit. Empire, 1998. Mem. Am. Soc. Newspaper Editors Avocations: music, theater, handicraft, stamp collecting/philately. Home: 1608 N Oleander Ave Daytona Beach FL 32118-3415 Office: Daytona Beach News-Jour 901 6th St Daytona Beach FL 32117-3352 Home Phone: 386-252-0524; Office Phone: 386-252-1511. Business E-Mail: tippen@news-jrnl.com.

DAVIDSON, HUGH MACCULLOUGH, French language and literature educator; b. West Point, Ga., Jan. 21, 1918; s. Robert Calvin Davidson Sr. and Anne Della Stripling; m. Loretta Jane Miller, June 15, 1951; 1 child, Anne Stripling Davidson. AB in Romance Langs., U. Chgo., 1938, PhD in Romance Langs., 1946; MA (hon.), Yale U., 1967. Instr. French U. Chgo., 1946-48, asst. prof. French, 1948-53, asst. dean coll., 1951-53; asst. prof. romance langs. Dartmouth Coll., 1953-56, prof. romance langs., 1956-62, chmn. dept. romance langs., 1957-59; prof. romance langs. Ohio State U., 1962-67, 68-73; prof. French lit. U. Va., 1973-78, commonwealth prof. French lit., 1978, 1978-90, commonwealth prof. French lit. emeritus, 1990—. Vis. prof. French U. Mich., 1967; univ. examiner French and gen. linguistics, humanities U. Chgo., 1946-48; chmn. Coll. French staff U. Chgo., 1948-53; Thomas Jefferson fellow Downing Coll., Cambridge U., Eng., 1979-80; vis. prof. U. Paris Sorbonne, 1982-83; vis. com. humanities and arts Case We. Res. U., 1967; cons. div. edn. programs NEH, 1977; conducts seminars in field. Author: Audience, Words, and Art, 1965, The Origins of Certainty: Means and Meanings in Pascal's Pensées, 1979, Blaise Pascal, 1983, Pascal and the Arts of the Mind, 1993; co-author: A Concordance to the Pensées of Pascal, 1975, A Concordance to Pascal's Les Provinciales, 1980; asst. editor: The Idea and Practice of General Education, 1948; mem. editl. bd. Continuum: Problems in French Literature from the Late Renaissance to the Early Enlightenment, EMF: Studies in Early Modern France; contbr. articles to profl. jours. Capt. USAF, 1942—46. Gen. Edn. fellow Carnegie Found., 1948-49; Fulbright Sr. fellow for rsch. in France, 1959-60; Sr. Rsch. fellow Nat. Found. Arts and Humanities, 1967-68. Mem. MLA (editl. com. publs. 1968-73), Am. Assn. Tchrs. French, Am. Soc. Eighteenth-Century Studies, N. Am. Soc. Seventeenth-Century French Lit., Assn. internat. des études françaises, Soc. Internat. d'étude du XVIIe siècle, Soc. internat. d'étude du XVIIIe siècle, Soc. des amis de Inst. Lit. Française U. Paris Sorbonne, Soc. des amis de Port-Royal, Phi Beta Kappa (nat. Senate 1982-88). Episcopalian. Avocations: sculpture, architecture, music, history, philosophy. Address: 250 Pantops Mountain Rd Apt 319 Charlottesville VA 22911 Office: U Va Dept French Lit 302 Cabell Hl Charlottesville VA 22908-0001

DAVIDSON, JACK LEROY, academic administrator; b. Indpls., July 14, 1927; s. Lawrence L. and Emma (Jones) D.; m. Ina Stanfill, June 20, 1948; children: William (dec.), Nancy, Evan. BA, Franklin Coll., 1949; MA, Ind. U., 1955, Ed. Adminstrn., 1961, PhD, 1967. Tchr., guidance counselor, coach Mitchell (Ind.) Pub. Schs., 1949-57; elem. prin., supervising prin. Vincennes (Ind.) Pub. Schs., 1957-59; supt. Worthington (Ind.) Pub. Schs., 1959-61, Salem (Ind.) Pub. Schs., 1961-65, Oak Ridge (Tenn.) Pub. Schs., 1965-68, Manatee County (Fla.) Pub. Schs., 1968-70, Austin (Tex.) Pub. Schs., 1970-80, Tyler (Tex.) Public Schs., 1980-91; spl. asst. to pres. U. Tex., Tyler, 1991-96. Vis. prof. U. Tex.; chmn. Tex. Adv. Com. on Ednl. Improvement. Schs.; cons. Tex. Edn. Agy. Author: Effective School Board Meetings, 1970, The Superintendency & Leadership for Effective Schools, 1987; Contbr. articles to ednl. jours. Bd. dirs., pres. Southwest Ednl. Devel. Lab.; charter mem. Tex. Commn. on Inter-Govtl. Rels.; bd. dirs. Austin Jr. Achievement; pres. bd. dirs. Salvation Army, pres. adv. bd., 2005-07. With USNR, 1945-47. Recipient Super Supt. award Tex. PTA, 1982, award of honor Nat. Sch. Pub. Rels. Assn., 1990, Disting. Svc. award AASA, 1992, Founders award Tyler Ind. Sch. Dist. Found., 2005; named one of 100 Top Exec. Educators Exec. Educator mag., 1984, 89; Dr. Jack L. Davidson Conf. Ctr. named in his honor, 2004. Mem. Am. Assn. Suprs. Curriculum Devel., Am. Assn. Sch. Adminstrs., Tex. Assn. Sch. Adminstrs., Rotary (pres. Tyler club), Phi Delta Kappa (outstanding educator award 1992). Methodist (deacon, dir.). Home: 1807 Picadilly Pl Tyler TX 75703-2409 Office Phone: 903-561-7154. Personal E-mail: davidsonji@suddenlink.net. *The only real profit in life comes from the satisfaction gained in service to others.*

DAVIDSON, JAMES JOSEPH, III, lawyer; b. Lafayette, La., July 27, 1940; s. James Joseph and Virginia Lee (Dunham) Davidson; m. Kay Cecile Holloway, Aug. 7, 1962; children: Kimberly Kay, James Joseph IV, Lynda Leigh, Virginia Holland. BA, U. SW La., 1963; JD, Tulane U., 1964. Bar: La. 1964, US Dist. Ct. (we. dist.) La. 1965, US Ct. Appeals (5th cir.) 1972, US Supreme Ct. 1975, US Dist. Ct. (ea. dist.) La. 1979, US Ct. Appeals (11th cir.) 1981, US Dist. Ct. (mid. dist.) La. 1986. Ptnr. Davidson, Meaux, Sonnier & McElligott, Lafayette, La., 1964—. Mem. exec. bd. Evangeline area coun. Boy Scouts Am., 1969—80; trustee U. La. Lafayette Found., 1980—, pres., 1988—91. Fellow: Am. Bar Found. (life); mem.: ABA (ho. dels. 2002—04, 2006—), Assn. Transp. Practitioners, Assn. Def. Trial Attys., Internat. Assn. Def. Counsel, Am. Counsel Assn., Am. Bd. Trial Advs. (adv. bd.), Nat. Assn. RR Trial Counsel, La. Assn. Def. Counsel (dir. 1975—77), La. State Law Inst. (coun. 2002—), La. Bar Found., La. State Bar Assn. (bd. gov. 2007—, del. 1970—96). Republican. Baptist. Home: 539 Girard Park Dr Lafayette LA 70503-2601 Office: PO Box 2908 Lafayette LA 70502-2908 Office Phone: 337-237-1660.

DAVIDSON, JEANNIE, costume designer; b. San Francisco, Mar. 21, 1938; d. Willis H. and Dorothy J. (Starks) Rich; children from previous marriage: David L. Schultz (dec. Jan. 1996), Mark P. Schultz, Seana Davidson, Michael Davidson; m. Bryan N. St. Germain, June 14, 1980. BA, Stanford U., Calif., 1961, postgrad., 1965-68. Resident costume designer Oreg. Shakespearean Festival, Ashland, 1969-91; owner, designer Ravenna Fabric Studio, Inc., Medford, Oreg., 1994—. Mfr. custom ch. vestments and hand-dyed wearable art. Designer over 150 prodns. including all 37 of Shakespeare's plays. Recipient numerous awards for excellence in costume design. Mem. U.S. Inst. for Theatre Tech., Phi Beta Kappa. Avocations: fabric design, painting, writing, quilting. E-mail: jsaintg@earthlink.net.

DAVIDSON, JO ANN, political organization executive, retired state legislator; children: Julie, Jenifer. Mem. Ohio Ho. of Reps., Columbus, 1981—2001, minority leader, speaker, 1995—2001; interim dir. Ohio Dept. Jobs and Family Services, 2001; owner JAD & Assoc. Government Cons. Firm, 2001; campaign chmn. Ohio Valley Bush-Cheney '04, 2004; co-chmn. Rep. Nat. Com., Washington, 2005—. Chmn. Ohio Ho. Rep. Campaign Com., 1986-2000. Mem. Reynoldsburg (Ohio) City Coun., 1968-77; former vice chmn. Ohio Turnpike Commn.; trustee Franklin U., U. Findlay, Ohio, Ohio State U. Named Legislator of Yr., Nat. Rep. Legislators Assn., 1991; named to Ohio Women's Hall of Fame, 1991. Republican. Office: Rep Nat Com 310 First St SE Washington DC 20003

DAVIDSON, JOHN, professional sports team executive, former hockey analyst; b. Ottawa, Ont., Feb. 27, 1953; m. Diana Davidson; children: Lindsay, Ashley. Goaltender St. Louis Blues, 1973—75, NY Rangers, 1975—83; hockey analyst MSG Network, NYC, 1983—84, 1986—2006, Hockey Night in Can., Can. Broadcasting Corp. (CBC), 1984—86; pres. St. Louis Blues, 2006—. Lead analyst hockey coverage Olympic Games on NBC, Albertville, France, 1992, Lillehammer, Norway, 94, Nagano, Japan, 98, Salt Lake City, 2002; analyst FOX, 1995—99; studio and game analyst ABC Sports, 1999—2004; analyst lead broadcast team NHL on NBC, 2006; host In the Crease, NHL.com, JD on Ice, MSG Net work, 2003—04; co-host Inside the NHL; panalist After 40 Minutes, CBC; contbr. Satellite Hotstove, CBC. Mem. selection com. Hokcey Hall of Fame. Co-recipient Lester Patrick Award, 2004; recipient NY Emmy award for Outstanding On-Camera Achievement, 1995, 2001. Office: St Louis Blues Hockey Club Savvis Ctr 1401 Clark Ave Saint Louis MO 63103

DAVIDSON, JOHN HUNTER, agriculturist; b. Wilmette, Ill., May 16, 1914; s. Joseph and Ruth Louise (Moody) D.; m. Elizabeth Marie Boynton, June 16, 1943 (dec. Feb. 2005); children: Joanne Davidson Hildebrand, Kathryn Davidson Bouwens, Patricia. BS in Horticulture, Mich. State U., 1937, MS in Plant Biochemistry, 1940. Field rschr. agrl. chems. Dow Chem. Co., Midland, Mich., 1936-42, with R&D dept. agrl. products, 1946-72, tech. adviser R&D agrl. products, 1972-80, tech. adviser govt. rels., 1980—86, cons., 1984—. Contbr. articles on plant pathology, horticulture and weed control to profl. jours. Lt. USNR, 1945. Mem. Am. Chem. Soc., Am. Soc. Hort. Sci., Weed Sci. Soc., Am. Pathol. Soc., Exch. Club of Midland, Phi Kappa Phi, Alpha Zeta. Republican. Home: 2325 Rockwell Dr Apt 264 Midland MI 48642-9327

DAVIDSON, JOHN KENNETH, SR., sociologist, educator, researcher, writer, consultant; b. Augusta, Ga., Oct. 25, 1939; s. Larcie Charles and Betty (Corley) D.; m. Josephine Frazier, Apr. 11, 1964; children: John Kenneth Jr., Stephen Wood. Student, Augusta Coll., 1956-58; BS in Edn., U. Ga., 1961, MA, 1963; PhD, U. Fla., 1974. Asst. prof. dept. psychology and sociology Armstrong State Coll., Savannah, Ga., 1963-67; asst. prof. sociology Augusta Coll., 1967-74; acting chmn., asst. prof. dept. sociology Ind. U., South Bend, 1974-76; assoc. prof. sociology U. Wis., Eau Claire, Wis., 1976-78, prof., 1978—2004, prof. emeritus, 2004—, chmn. dept. sociology, 1976-80, asst. spl. projects to dean grad. studies and univ. rsch., 1987-91, coord. family studies, 1990—2004, acting chmn., dept. sociology (summer), 2003—05. Cons. family life edn.; rsch. cons. dept. ob-gyn. Med. Coll. Ga., Augusta, 1969-74, pediatrics, 1972-73, assoc. dir. health care project, 1971-73, rsch. instr., 1971, rsch. assoc., 1972-73, rsch. cons. dept. community dentistry, 1974-79; program coord. Community Devel. in Process Phase II and III, Title I Higher Edn. Act of, 1965, 1970; sociology and anthropology com. Univ. System Ga., 1970-74, chmn. curriculum sub-com., 1970-72; dir. Sex Edn., The Pub. Schs. and You project Ind. Com. on Humanities, 1975; summer asst. spl. projects U. Wis., Eau Claire, 2003, 2004, 2005. Co-author: Marriage and Family, 1992, Marriage and Family: Change and Continuity, 1996; co-editor: Speaking of Sexuality: Interdisciplinary Readings, 2001, 2005, Cultural Diversity and Families, 1992; editor (assoc.): Jour. Marriage and the Family, 1975—85, Sociol. Inquiry, 1986—92, Sociol. Imagination, 1993—2004; editor: (cons.) Jour. Sex Rsch., 1991—95; editor: (cons) Sociol. Inquiry, 2001—05; reviewer: Jour. Deviant Behavior, 1979—90, Sociol. Spectrum, 1985—2005, Jour. Family Issues, 1995—2004, Jour. Sex Rsch., 1996—2005; contbr. articles to profl. jours. Past state chmn. pub. affairs Ind. Assn. Planned Parenthood Affiliates, 1975-76; past bd. dirs. Planned Parenthood North Cen. Ind., chmn. pub. affairs com., 1975-76; past bd. dirs., 1st v.p., resources allocation com. Wis. Family Planning Coordinating Council; past bd. dirs., exec., info., internat. and edn. coms., chmn. social sci. rsch. com. Assn. for Vol. Sterilization; past pres. citizens adv. bd. Eau Claire and Chippewa Falls Planned Parenthood Clinics; past mem. dirs. Planned Parenthood of Wis., Inc.; past mem. Eau Claire Coord. Coun., Eau Claire County Adv. Health Forum, Eau Claire County Task Force on Family Planning, Eau Claire Task Force on Teen Pregnancy. Mem Nat. Coun. Family Rels. (past chmn. com. stds. and criteria for cert., former mem. devel. com. and cert. com., Ernest G. Osborne award 2003, 2004), Am. Sociol. Assn., Wis. Sociol. Assn., So. Sociol. Soc., Mid-South Sociol. Assn. (pres.-elect 1998-99, pres. 1999-2000, past pres. 2000-01, hotel negotiator, 2003-06), Midwest Sociol. Soc., Groves Conf., Wis. Coun. Family Rels. (bd. dirs., exec. com., past pres.), Soc. Sci. Study Sex., Tex. Coun. Family Rels., Augusta Coll. Alumni Soc., U. Fla. Alumni Soc., U. Ga. Alumni Soc., Pres. Club. U. Wis.-Eau Claire, Kappa Delta Pi, Phi Kappa Phi (chpt. pres. 1991-92, Nat. Forum editl. com. 1992-99), Phi Theta Kappa, Alpha Kappa Delta (editor nat. newsletter 1979-83, nat. v.p. 1992-94, nat. pres.-elect 1994-96, nat. pres. 1996-98, nat. past pres. 1998-2000, exec. coun. 1992-2000) Episcopalian. Personal E-mail: davidsj@ulwec.edu.

DAVIDSON, JOHN ROBERT, retired dentist; b. Peru, Ind., Apr. 28, 1947; s. John Howard and Kathryn (Loughran) Davidson; m. Jean-Marie Dobler, Jan. 23, 1965 (div. Oct. 1972); children: James Michael, Jennifer Renee; m. Linda Mary Seasock, Oct. 22, 1977 (dec. Aug. 1997); children: Kathryn Cherise, John Richard. BS, Purdue U., 1969; DDS, UCLA, 1972. Diplomate Am. Bd. Forensic Dentistry, Am. Bd. Forensic Examiners. Gen. practice dentistry, Granada Hills, Calif., 1972—74; prof. clin. and cmty. dentistry, dir. of clinics Ferris State Coll., Big Rapids, Mich., 1974—75; pvt. practice dentistry specializing in oral implantology Peru, Ind., 1975—2004; ret., 2003. Chief dental staff Dukes Meml. Hosp., Peru, 1975—96; dep. coroner Miami County, 1987—2003. Recipient Citizen of the Yr. award, Peru, 1978, Pride award, Grissom AFB Cmty. Coun., Peru, 1980. Fellow: Internat. Congress of Oral Implantologists, Am. Coll. Oral Implantaologists (assoc.); mem.: ADA, Ind. Soc. Forensic Odontology (charter), Peru Area C. of C. (bd. dirs. 1976—83, Oustanding Svc. award 1979), Wabash Valley Dental Soc., Ind. Dental Assn., Am. Coll. Forensic Examiners, Mensa, Scottish Rite, Rotary (chmn. scholarship com. Peru 1975—95), Elks, Masons. Home: 200 Rainbow Dr #10042 Livingston TX 77399-2000 Office Phone: 765-473-4421.

DAVIDSON, JOHN ROBERT (JAY), bank executive; b. LA, Mar. 30, 1950; s. John Robert Davidson and Carolyn Rose Monson; m. Kristina Maria Jonsson, Dec. 29, 1978; children: Joshua Kingseley, Michelle Maria. BSME, U. ND, 1972; postgrad., AMP Corp. Leadership Coll., 1990. Engr. Dow Chem. Co., Pauls Valley, Okla., 1972-74; real estate investor Mpls., 1974-77; account exec. AMP Inc., Boulder, Colo., 1977-83, mkt. mgr. Harrisburg, Pa., 1983-86, dist. mgr. Denver, 1986-90, nat. mgr., 1990—95; founder 1st Am. State Bank of Colo., 1995, chmn. bd., CEO, pres., 1995—; dir. funds mgmt. com. Am. State Bank, Williston, ND, 1994—2005, dir. exec. com., 1996—2005; founder, CEO, chmn. bd. dirs. First Am. State Bank, Denver, 1995—; CEO, chmn. bd. First Am. Bancorp, 1998—. Chmn. bd. dirs. Colo. Housing and Fin. Authority, 1999—2007; bd. dirs. Step 13, Kenneth King Found.; co-chair FASB Fitness Festival. Supporter Denver Ctr. Performing Arts, F.A.C.E.S., Boy Scouts Am, Children's Hosp., Arthritis Found., Cherry Creek Sch. Found. and Cmty. Asset Program; event co-chmn. Western Fantasy Gala Vols. of Am., 2005; bd. dirs. Kempe Children's Found., 1997—2005, treas., exec. com., chmn. fin. com., chair allocations com., 1998—2002; past bd. dirs., sec., chmn. devel. bd. Am. Heart Assn.; past. bd. dirs. Easter Seals Colo., event co-chmn.; co-chmn. Denver Ctr. Performing Arts New Years Gala, 2000; co-chair First Am. State Bank Fitness Festival, 2001—, Saturday Night Alive Gala;

bd. dirs., sec. Denver Metro Area, 2000—. Named Pillar of the Cmty., Arapahoe House, 2000; named Villager of Yr., 2005; recipient Presdl. Legion of Merit. Mem.: NRA (life), Glenmoore Country Club, Met. Club, Masons. Avocations: skiing, mountain biking, photography, computers, music. Home: 5780 S Goldsmith Pl Greenwood Village CO 80111-3522 Office: 1st Am State Bank 8390 E Crescent Pkwy Greenwood Village CO 80111-2811 Office Phone: 303-694-6464. Personal E-mail: fasb32@earthlink.net. Business E-Mail: jdavidson@fasbank.com.

DAVIDSON, JOY ELAINE, retired mezzo soprano; b. Ft. Collins, Colo., Aug. 18, 1940; d. Clarence Wayne and Jessie Ellen (Bogue) Ferguson; m. Robert Scott Davidson, Aug. 9, 1959; children: Lisa Beth, Robert Scott II, Jeremy Fergus, Bonnie Kathleen, Jordan Christian. BA, Occidental Coll., Los Angeles, 1959; postgrad., Fla. State U., 1961-64. Dir. vocal/opera dept. New World Sch. Arts Coll./Conservatory Divsn., Miami, Fla., 1992—2002; ret., 2001. Robert A. Carrie Mastronardi endowed prof., 1995—. Debut 1965 with Miami Opera; has performed with Met. Opera, opera cos. throughout U.S. and Can., La Scala, Vienna State Opera, Bayerische State Opera, Lyons (France) Opera, Welsh Opera, Florence (Italy) Opera, Torino (Italy) Opera. (recipient Gold medal Internat. Competition Young Opera Singers, Sofia, Bulgaria 1969), Rio de Janeiro; performed with numerous orchs. including N.Y. Philharm., Los Angeles Philharm., Boston Orch., Pitts. Orch., Columbus (Ohio) Orch.; rec. artist. Named Outstanding Miami Artist at Orange Bowl; recipient Mastronardi endowed chair, 1995, NISOD award for tchg. excellence, 1996, Roberta Rymer Balfe award Fla. Grand Opera. Mem. PEO, United Meth. Women, Sigma Alpha Iota, Zeta Tau Zeta. Methodist. Avocations: swimming, camping, bicycling, church activities. Home: 413 Walnut St #5032 Green Cove Springs FL 32043 Office Phone: 305-510-5131. E-mail: davidsons123@hotmail.com. *Success awaits those who dare to dream big enough. The success achiever is the possibility thinker.*

DAVIDSON, JUSTIN, music critic; b. Rome; m. Ariella Budick; 1 child, Milo. BMus, Harvard U.; D of Music, Columbia U. Dir. editl. Sony Classical, NYC, 1995—96; music critic Newsday, Melville, NY, 1996—. Adj. prof. music Columbia U. Contbr. articles to profl. jours. and newspapers. Recipient Pulitzer prize, 1999, award, Press Club of L.I., Deems Taylor award, ASCAP. Office: Newsday 235 Pinelawn Rd Melville NY 11747-4250

DAVIDSON, KEAY, newswriter; Sci. writer Sentinel Star, Orlando, Fla., 1979—81, L.A. Times San Diego Bur., 1981—85, San Francisco Examiner, 1986—2000, San Francisco Chronicle, 2000—. Author (with George Smoot): Wrinkles in Time, 1993; author: Twister: The Science of Tornadoes and the Making of a Natural Disaster Movie, 1996, Carl Sagan: A Life, 1999; contbg. writer: Scientific American, New Scientist, National Geographic, Sky and Telescope, NY Times, Washington Post, Best Am. Sci. Writing, 2004. Recipient Westinghouse Sci. Journalism award, 1986, Sci. in Soc. award, Nat. Assn. Sci. Writers. Office: San Francisco Chronicle 901 Mission St San Francisco CA 94103-2988 Office Fax: 415-896-1107. Business E-Mail: kdavidson@sfchronicle.com.

DAVIDSON, MARGARET A., federal agency administrator, lawyer; JD, La. State U.; MS in Marine Policy and Resource Econ., U. RI. Spl. counsel & asst. atty. gen. State of La.; exec. dir. SC Sea Grant Consortium, 1983—95; dir. Coastal Services Ctr. Nat. Oceanic & Atmospheric Adminstrn., Charleston, SC, 1996—, acting asst. adminstr. Services and Coastal Zone Mgmt., 2000—02. Former fulbright scholar Prince of Songkhla U., Thailand, 1992—93; prof. U. Charleston; adjunct prof. Clemson U., U. SC. Office: NOAA Coastal Services Ctr 2234 So Hobson Ave North Charleston SC 29405*

DAVIDSON, MARILYN COPELAND, writer, musician, educator; b. New Castle, Ind., Sept. 2, 1934; d. Clyde Harrison and Hazel Copeland; m. Douglass Albert Davidson, Dec. 28, 1961; children: Jennifer Juntwait, Diana Valencia. BS, Ball State U., 1955; diploma in piano, Juilliard Sch., 1956. Music tchr. Dallas Public Schs., 1956—57, Shortridge H.S., Indpls., 1957—62, Port Washington (NY) Pub. Schs., 1962—66, Troy State U., Troy, Ala., 1966—70, South Lyon (Mich.) Middle Sch., 1970—72, Fairleigh Dickinson U., Teaneck, NJ, 1979—83, Bergenfield (NJ) Pub. Schs., 1972—84, Our Redeemer Luth. Ch., Dumont, NJ, 1973—78, Evangelical Luth. Ch., Hasbrouck Heights, NJ, 1980—82, Pequannock (NJ) Pub. Schs., 1986—90, 1992—95; coord. author MacMillan/McGraw Hill, Inc., NYC, 1984—. Presenter Internat. Reading Assn., NJ, 1995, N.J. Music Supervisors Assn., 1985, Bruno Walter Hall, Lincoln Ctr., NYC, 1994, Carnegie Hall, NYC, 2000, Technology Symposium, Fla. State U., Tallahassee, 2000, Suffolk County Music Educators, 2001, workshops, throughout US;; presenter in field. Author: (textbook series) Music and You, 1988, 1991, Spotlight on Music, 2005; author: (with Bob McGrath) Music for Fun, 2000; author: (textbook series) Share the Music, 1992, 1995; composer: (orchestrations) Tops in Pops, 1995, An Acoustic Jam, 1996, Folk Songs From A World Apart, 2004; contbr. articles to profl. newsletters, teacher's guides and other publs.; author (with Bob McGrath): (profl. training video) Music and the Curriculum; author: Using Music to Help Children Learn, 2004, It's Elementary, 2005; co-author (with Bob McGrath): Curriculum Connections: Using Music to Help Children Learn; pianist: solo performances Muncie, Ind., Symphony, Hawthorne, NJ, Symphony, North Jersey Symphony, Rockland, NY, Symphony. Coun. mem., soloist and accompanist for recitals Bergenfield Coun. for the Arts, 1974—80; accompanist Carley Singers Chamber Choir, Indpls., 1957—61; educational cons. New Jersey Symphony, 1987—92; education com. mem., clinician, tnr. N.J. Symphony Master Tchr. Project; lectr. N.Y. Philharm. Children's Series, 1995; lectr., performer Bergenfield Pub. Libr., 1996; piano soloist Hawthorne Chamber Symphony, 1996, 1997, 1998, North Jersey Symphony, Tenafly, 1996, 2001, Rockland NY Symphony, 2003. Named Outstanding Alumnus, Ball State U. Sch. Music, 1993; recipient Young Artists award, Muncie Symphony, 1953, Gov.'s Tchr.'s Recognition award, NJ, 1995. Mem.: NEA, N.J. Edn. Assn., Music Educators Nat. Conf. (music selection com. 1993, nat. assembly, writer for teacher's guides), N.J. Music Educators Assn. (writer "It's Elementary" 1988—96), Northern N.J. Orff Schulwerk Assn. (co-founder, treas., sec., pres., mem-at-large), Am. Orff-Schulwerk Assn. (hon.; life mem., regional rep., chairperson higher edn., nat. v.p., nat. pres., higher edn. post-level III adv. com., AOSA celebrity advocacy panel selection com.), Orgn. Am. Kodaly Educators, Delta Kappa Gamma, Pi Kappa Lambda, Sigma Alpha Iota. Home and Office: 31 Martin St Bergenfield NJ 07621 Home Phone: 201-385-4723; Office Phone: 201-385-8521.

DAVIDSON, MAYER B., endocrinologist, educator, researcher; b. Balt., Apr. 11, 1935; s. David and Esther (Crockin) D.; m. Naomi Berger, Nov. 25, 1961 (div. 1977); children: Elke W., Seth J.; m. Roseann Herman, Aug. 31, 1980. AB, Swarthmore Coll., 1957; MD, Harvard U., 1961. Diplomate Am. Bd. Internal Medicine, Am. Bd. Endocrinology and Metabolism. Intern Bellevue Hosp., NYC, 1961-62, jr. asst. resident, 1962-63; sr. asst. resident U. Wash. Affiliated Hosps., Seattle, 1963-64; rsch. fellow dept. endocrinology and metabolism King County Hosp., U. Wash., Seattle, 1964-66; asst. prof. medicine UCLA Sch. Medicine, 1969-74, acting chief div. endocrinology and metabolism, 1973-74, from assoc. prof. to prof., 1974-95, clin. prof., 1996—2006; with Drew U., 2006—. Dir. diabetes program Cedars-Sinai Med. Ctr., L.A., 1979-95; assoc. dir. clin. diabetes City of Hope Nat. Med. Ctr., 1995-98; dir. clin. trials unit Charles R. Drew U.; nat. advisor Diabetes Ctr. Humana Hosp., Phoenix, 1985-91; attending physician diabetic clinic Boston City Hosp., 1966-68; clin. asst. Harvard Med. Sch., 1968-69; cons. AMA Dept. Drugs. Author: Diabetus Mellitus: Diagnosis and Treatment, 4th edit., 1998, The Complete Idiot's Guide to Type 2 Diabetes, 2005; founding editor: Current Diabetes Reports, 2000—02, editor-in-chief: Diabetes Care, 2002—06; contbr. chapters to books. Co-founder, bd. dirs. free med. facility Venice (Calif.) Family Clinic, 1970. Maj. Med. Svc. Corps U.S. Army, 1966-69. USPHS rsch. fellow Nat. Inst. Arthritis and Metabolic Diseases, 1965-66; recipient Upjohn award for Outstanding Diabetes Educator, 1990, Robert H. Williams/Rachmiel Levine award for sci. contbns. and humanism in tng. young rschrs., 1995, Banting medal for Disting. Svc., 1998; named to Best Doctors in Am., 1992-93, 95-96, 96-97. Fellow ACP; mem. AAAS, Am. Diabetes Assn. (rsch. prizes 1965, 66, R&D award 1974-75, rsch. 1978-81, bd. dirs. 1986-89, 93-99, v.p. 1995-96, pres.-elect 1996-97, pres. 1997-98), Am. Fedn. Clin. Rsch., Western Soc. Clin. Rsch., Endocrine Soc., Am. Soc. Clin. Investigation, Western Assn. Physicians, Am. Assn. Diabetes Educators (editl. bd. jour. 1980-83), Boylston Med. Soc., Am. Diabetes Assn. (pres. 1997-98), Sigma Xi. Democrat. Jewish. Business E-Mail: mayerdavidson@cdrewu.edu.

DAVIDSON, MEDORA LEA, dance educator; b. Merriam, Kans., July 2, 1930; d. John Archibald and Mabel Adelaide Davidson; m. Daniel Howe Hoge, Jr., Feb. 6, 1971 (div. June 14, 1984); m. Harry Lee Lydick, June 21, 1953 (div. Nov. 5, 1965); children: Harry Lee Lydick, Jr., Robin Louis Lydick. Instr. ballet, tap, jazz, gymnastics, ballroom dance, low-impact aerobics Davidson Dance Studio, Prairie Village, Kans., 1950—89; dance instr. N.A.D.A.A. city chpts., St. Paul, St. Louis, Omaha, Tulsa, Dallas, 1957—59; jazz dance instr. nat. faculty Nat. Assn. Dance and Affiliated Artists, Inc., L.A., Dallas, Chgo., 1957—59; choreographer outdoor mus. shows Johnson County (Kans.) Pks. and Recreation, 1971—73; choreographer Kansas City (Mo.) Royals Banquet shows, 1972—74; tchr. ballet, tap, gymnastics Visitation Parochial Sch., Kansas City, Mo., 1989—91; former owner, instr. ballet, tap, jazz, gymnastics, low-impact aerobics Davidson Dance Studio, Ottawa, Kans., 1991—99; tchr. low-impact aerobics Albuquerque Sr. Ctrs., 1999—2000; tchr. modern dance and children's drama Carnegie Cultural Ctr., Ottawa, 2000—02, tchr. piano, 2002—06; instr. Kindermusik Internat., Ottawa, 2002—04, tchr. yoga, 2002—07. Dance therapist activity dept. Psychiat. Receiving Ctr., Western Mo. Mental Health Ctr., Kansas City, 1969—; taped 65 half-hour ballet class lessons for children Medora and Me, 1970—71; taped 65 half-hour interviews for women The Feminine Touch, 1970—71; dir. Picnic A.C.T. Ottawa!, Ottawa Cmty. Theatre, 1997; writer, dir. 3 plays Fine Arts Singles, Johnson County, Kans., 1990—91; dir. Show Boat Baldwin Cmty. Theater, Baldwin City, Kans., 1999; formed Crackerjack Children's Theatre, Ottawa, 2001; writer, dir. Coventown A.C.T. Ottawa!, Ottawa, 2001, dir. An Old Time Radio Show, 02, dir. Playboy of the Western World, 02; dir. Crackerjack Children's Theatre Christmas Reader's Theatre, 2001, Nunsense 2003, Baldwin City Cmty. Theatre, 2003, Another Old Time Radio Show, Ottawa Cmty. Theatre, 2003, Bye, Bye, Bye Birdie, Baldwin City Cmty. Theatre, 2003, One Magical Christmas Eve, Ottawa Cmty. Theatre, 2003, Quilters, Ottawa Cmty. Theatre, 2004, Murder at the Goon Show, Crackerjack Children's Theatre, 2005, Crackerjack Children's Theatre Prodn., 2006. Actor: (plays) Gypsy, 1973, Lady Audley's Secret, 1976, The Farsighted Dragon and the Nearsighted Knight, 1985, Night of January 16th, 1994, Greater Tuna, 1996, The Tempest, 1998, Nunsense, 1999, 2003, Diamonds to Die For, 2000, Cabaret, A Black Tie Affair, 2001, Cabaret, For Ladies Only, 2003, Cabaret, Back & Better, 2004, Driving Miss Daisy, 2005, Cabaret 8 to the Bar, 2005, Cabaret, Our Way, 2005, Cabaret Goes Country, 2006, Driving Miss Daisy, 2006, Best of Cabaret II, 2006, Steel Magnolias, 2006, The Curious Savage, 2007; dir.: Anchors Aweigh, 2006, Pride & Prejudice, 2007; sculpture works include, Wrought Iron Restoration Winder Bldg, Washington, 1978, Bas Relief of Watts Mill, Mo., Kans. State Line Bridge, 1976. Vol. dance therapist Johnson County Mental Health Ctr., Overland Park, Kans., 1967—69. Avocations: gardening, painting, sewing, reading. Home: 1103 S Main St Ottawa KS 66067-3523 E-mail: medorad@sbcglobal.net.

DAVIDSON, MICHAEL H., cardiologist, researcher; b. Dayton, Ohio, Nov. 22, 1956; MD, Ohio State U., 1981. Med. dir. Chgo. Ctr. for Clin. Rsch., 1986—96; prof. medicine Rush U. Med. Ctr., Chgo., 1986—; pres., CEO Protocare Trials Chgo. Ctr. for Clin. Rsch., 1996—2003, exec. med. dir., 1998—2003; dir. preventive cardiology Rush U. Med. Ctr., Chgo., 2001—; exec. med. dir. Radiant Rsch., Chgo., 2003—. Office: Radiant Research 515 N State St Ste 2700 Chicago IL 60610 Office Fax: 312-494-2217. Business E-Mail: michaeldavidson@radiantresearch.com.

DAVIDSON, NANCY BRACHMAN, artist, educator; b. Chgo., Nov. 3, 1943; d. Philip and Jane (Blanch) Brachman; m. Donald Davidson, July 15, 1961 (div. 1977); 1 child, Lance A.; m. Greg Drasler, June 15, 1985. BEd, Northeastern Ill. U., 1965; BA, U. Ill., Chgo., 1972; MFA, Sch. Art Inst., Chgo., 1975. Vis. asst. prof. U. Ill., Champaign, 1977-79, Williams Coll., Williamstown, Mass., 1980-84; vis. artist, assoc. prof. SUNY, Purchase, 1984—. One-woman shows include Berkshire Mus., Pittsfield, Mass., 1982, Marianne Deson Gallery, Chgo., 1978, 1981, 1983, 1988, Richard Anderson Gallery, N.Y.C., 1991, 1993, 1995, Shoshana Wayne Gallery, Santa Monica, Calif., 1997, Nova Sin Gallery, Prague, Czech Republic, 1998, Neuberger Mus., Purchase, N.Y., 1998, Dorsky Gallery, N.Y.C., Inst. Contemporary Art, U. Pa., Phila., 1999, Vedanta Gallery, Chgo., 2000, The Contemporary Arts Ctr., Cin., 2001, Robert Miller Gallery, N.Y.C., 2001, Regina Gouger Miller Gallery, Carnegie Mellon U., Pitts., 2002, exhibited in group shows at Albright-Knox Gallery, Buffalo, 1980, Mus. Contemporary Art Chgo., 1984, Art Inst. Chgo., 1974, 1978, 1979, Bad Girls West-UCLA, 1994, Corcoran Biennial, 2002. Fellow NEA, 1978, Mass. Coun. Arts, 1981, Ford Found., 1978; Mass. Coun. Arts grantee, 1984, Anonymous Was a Woman grantee, 1997, Pollock-Krasner grantee, 2001, Creative Capital Artist grantee, 2005. Home: 137 Duane St Apt 4W New York NY 10013-3892

DAVIDSON, RICHARD J., retired medical association administrator; b. Phila., 1936; m. Janet Davidson. BA in secondary edn., West Chester U., Pa.; EdM in edn., Temple U.; PhD in edn., George Washington U. Former tchr., principal, Del.; dir. edn. Md.-DC-Del. Hosp. Assn.; pres. Md. Hosp. Assn., 1969—91, Am. Hosp. Assn., Chgo & Washington, 1991—2007. Bd. dir. Health Rsch. & Ednl. Trust, Internat. Hosp. Fedn. Founding. dir. Inst. for Diversity. Co-recipient Nat. Healthcare Leadership award, Nat. Ctr. for Healthcare Leadership, 2006; recipient Bd. Dirs. award, Healthcare Fin. Mgmt. Assoc., 2000.*

DAVIDSON, RICHARD J., psychology and psychiatry professor, researcher; PhD in Psychology, Harvard U., 1976. With U. Wis.-Madison, 1984—, William James and Vilas Rsch. prof. psychology and psychiatry, dir., Lab. for Affective Neuroscience, dir., Waisman Lab. for Brain Imaging & Behavior. Spkr. in field; dir. NIMH funded Wis. Ctr. for Affective Sci., Ctr. for Mind-Body Interaction, NIMH Tng. Program on Emotion Rsch.; core mem. MacArthur Found. Rsch. Network in Mind-Body Interaction, MacArthur Found. Mind-Brain-Body and Health Intiative; mem. bd. scientific counselors NIMH; mem. NAS Panel to Evaluate the Validity of the Polygraph, 2001—02. Contbr. articles to profl. jours., chapters to books;, author. Named one of Most Influential People, Time Mag., 2006; recipient Nat. Inst. Mental Health Rsch. Scientist award, Merit award, NIMH, Established Investigator award, Nat. Alliance for Rsch. in Schizophrenia and Affective Disorders (NARSAD), Disting. Investigator award. Fellow: Am. Psychological Soc. (Disting. Scientific Lectr. 1997, co-editor, Emotion, Disting. Scientific Contribution 2000, William James Fellow award), APA, AAAS, Am. Acad. Arts & Sciences; mem.: Soc. for Psychophysiological Rsch. (past pres.), Soc. for Rsch. in Psychopathology (past pres.), Sigma Xi. Office: Waisman Lab for Brain Imaging and Behavior U Wis-Madison Waisman Ctr Office T-225 1500 Highland Ave Madison WI 53705 also: U Wis-Madison 538 Psychology Bldg W J Brogden 1202 W Johnson St Madison WI 53706 Office Phone: 608-265-8189. Office Fax: 608-262-8972. Business E-Mail: rjdavids@wisc.edu.

DAVIDSON, RICHARD LAURENCE, geneticist, educator; b. Cleve., Feb. 22, 1941; BA, Case Western Res. U., 1963, PhD, 1967. Asst. prof. Harvard Med. Sch., Boston, 1970-73, assoc. prof. microbiology and molecular genetics, 1973-81; research assoc. human genetics Children's Hosp. Med. Ctr., Boston, 1970-81; head dept. molecular genetics U. Ill. Med. Ctr., Chgo., 1981—, Benjamin Goldberg prof. genetics, 1981—. Co-dir. Cell Cult Ctr., MIT, Boston, 1975-81; mem. mammalian genetics study sect. NIH, 1975-81; mem. human cell biology adv. panel NSF, 1973-75. Editor-in-chief: Somatic Cell Genetics. U.S. Air Force Office Research-NRC fellow, 1967-68, Ctr. Molecular Genetics, Paris, 1967-70. Mem. AAAS, Tissue Culture Assn., Cell Biology Assn. Office: U Ill at Chicago Head Dept Mol Gen (M/7 669) 900 S Ashland Ave Ste 669 Chicago IL 60607-4046

DAVIDSON, RICK, employment services executive; BSEE, Ariz. State U. V.p. global info. svcs. Haworth, Inc.; sr. v.p., chief info. officer CNH Global N.V.; acting global chief info. officer for Manpower Feld Group; sr. v.p., global chief info. officer Manpower, Inc., Milw., 2003—. Office: Manpower Inc 5301 N Ironwood Rd Milwaukee WI 53217 Office Phone: 414-961-1000. Office Fax: 414-961-6500.*

DAVIDSON, ROBERT A., trucking executive; BSIE, MBA, U. Ark. Mem. econ. analysis dept. ABF Freight Sys., Inc., Ft. Smith, Ark., 1972—83, v.p. pricing, 1983—97, v.p. mktg., 1997—2003, pres., CEO, 2003—05; pres., COO Arkansas Best Corp., Ft. Smith, Ark., 2005—06, pres., CEO, 2006—. Chmn. Nat. Motor Freight Traffic Assn.; dir. Motor Freight Carriers Assn. Past chmn. Nat. Classification Com.; mem. U. Ark. Engring. Adv. Coun. Capt. transp. corps USAR. Office: Arkansas Best Corp 3801 Old Greenwood Rd Fort Smith AR 72903 Mailing: Arkansas Best Corp PO Box 10048 Fort Smith AR 72917-0048*

DAVIDSON, ROBERT BRUCE, retired lawyer; b. NYC, May 6, 1945; BS in Econs. cum laude, U. Pa., Phila., 1967; JD, Columbia U., NYC, 1972. Bar: NY 1973, US Dist Ct (so and ea dists) NY 1973, US Ct Appeals (2d cir) 1975, US Ct Appeals (DC cir) 1981, US Supreme Ct 1979, US Tax Ct 1984, US Ct Appeals (fed cir) 1989, US Ct Appeals (3d cir) 1990. Assoc. Baker & McKenzie, NYC, 1972—79, ptnr., 1979—2003; ret., 2003. Exec. dir. JAMS Arbitration Practice, NYC, 2003—; prof. arbitrator and mediator JAMS Panel; panel of arbitrators Hong Kong Internat. Arbitration Ctr., NASD, ICC; mem. internat. and ins. panels Ctr. Pub. Resources. Contbr. articles to profl jours, chapters to books. Vol US Peace Corps, The Philippines, 1968—70. Fellow: Am. Bar Found., Coll. Comml. Arbitrators (bd. mem.); mem.: ABA (dispute resolution and internat. law sects.), Am. Fgn. Law Assn., Assn. Bar City NY (chair com. arbitration 1982—85, com. internat. law 1986—89, chmn. com. arbitration 2003—06, com. internat. law 2007—). Office: JAMS 280 Park Ave West Bldg 28th Flr New York NY 10017 Home Phone: 914-921-5240; Office Phone: 212-607-2752. Business E-Mail: rdavidson@jamsadr.com.

DAVIDSON, ROBERT WILLIAM, not-for-profit executive; b. Colfax, Wash., Sept. 18, 1949; s. William Martin and Lena (Soli) D.; m. Molly Evoy, Apr. 16, 1977; children: Ford Patrick, Matthew Harpur, Marshall Andrew. AB, Harvard U., 1971; MBA, U. Wash., 2000. Exec. dir. Sabre Found., Cambridge, Mass., 1971-72; adminstrv. asst. Congressman Joel Pritchard, Washington, 1973-79; asst. sec. state State of Wash., Olympia, 1979-80; pres. Frayn Fin. Printing, Seattle, 1982-87, Frayn Printing Co., Seattle, 1985-87; exec. dir. Woodland Park Zool. Soc., Seattle, 1987—94, pres., 1986—87; prin. Alistar Capital Group, Bellevue, Wash., 1994—2001; CEO Seattle Aquarium Soc., Seattle, 2002—. Chmn. pub. funding com. Mayor's Zoo Commn., Seattle, 1984-85; bd. dirs. Discovery Inst., 1992-2004, Internat. Snow Leopard Trust, 1994-96; sch. bd. Cath. Archdiocese Seattle, 1995-98; active King County Bond Oversight Com., 1986-93 Mem. N.W. Devel. Officers Assn. (pres. 1994), Downtown Rotary Club (v.p. found. 1997-98, bd. dirs. 2005-), Wash. Athletic Club. Republican. Roman Catholic. Avocation: photography. Office: 1415 Western Ave # 505 Seattle WA 98101 Home Phone: 425-455-5760; Office Phone: 206-838-3910. Business E-Mail: bob@aquariumsociety.org.

DAVIDSON, ROGER H(ARRY), political science professor; b. Washington, July 31, 1936; s. Ross Wallace and Mildred (Younger) D.; m. Nancy Elizabeth Dixon, Sept. 29, 1961; children: Douglas Ross, Christopher Reed. AB magna cum laude, U. Colo., 1958; PhD, Columbia U., 1963. Asst. prof. govt. Dartmouth Coll., Hanover, NH, 1962-68; assoc. prof. polit. sci. U. Calif., Santa Barbara, 1968-71, prof., 1971-83, assoc. dean letters and sci., 1978-80, vis. prof., 1994, 1999—; sr. specialist Congl. Rsch. Svc., Washington, 1980-88; prof. govt., politics U. Md., College Pk., 1981-99. Profl. staff mem. U.S. Ho. of Reps., Washington, 1973—74; rsch. dir. U.S. Senate, Washington, 1976—77; cons. White House, 1970—71, U.S. Com. on Violence, Washington, 1968—69, Ctr. for Civic Edn., 2002—; Leon Sachs vis. scholar Johns Hopkins U., Balt., 1997; John Marshall Disting. Fulbright prof. Debrecen U., Hungary, 2002. Author: The Role of the Congressman, 1969; co-author: A More Perfect Union, 4th edit., 1989, Congress and Its Members, 11th edit., 2007; editor: The Postreform Congress, 1992; co-editor: Masters of the House, 1998, Workways of Governance, 2004, Understanding the Presidency, 4th edit., 2006; contbr. articles to profl. jours. Co-chmn. Upper Valley Human Rights Coun., Hanover, N.H., 1966-68; chmn. Goleta Valley Citizens Planning Group, Santa Barbara, 1974-76; rsch. com. of legis. specialists Internat. Polit. Sci. Assn.; adv. commn. on records of Congress Nat. Archives and Records Adminstrn., 1995-99; bd. dirs. Governance Inst., 1986—, Archtl. Found. of Santa Barbara, 2003—, U. Calif. Santa Barbara Affiliates, 2006—. Woodrow Wilson Nat. Found. fellow, 1958, Gilder fellow Columbia U., 1960, Faculty fellow Dartmouth Coll., 1965-66, Disting. Polit. Scientist Santa Barbara City Coll., 2005-06. Fellow Nat. Acad. Pub. Adminstrn.; mem. Nat. Capital Area Polit. Sci. Assn. (pres. 1985-86), Legis. Studies Group (charter, nat. chmn. 1980-81), Am. Polit. Sci. Assn. (joint com. project 87-Am. Hist. Assn./Am. Polit. Sci. Assn., chmn. congl. fellowship com. 1990, 93, endowed programs com. 1994-95, chmn. 1995-96, co-chmn. exec. com. centennial campaign 1997-2003, bd. dirs. centennial ctr. 2006—), Western Polit. Sci. Assn. (bd. editors 1977-78). Baptist. Avocations: music, history. Home: Villa L 400 E Pedregosa St Santa Barbara CA 93103-1970 Office: Dept Polit Sci U Calif Santa Barbara CA 93106 Personal E-mail: publius10@cox.net.

DAVIDSON, RONALD CROSBY, physicist, researcher; b. Norwich, Ont., Can., July 3, 1941; s. William Crosby and Annie Beatrice (Caley) D.; m. Jean Farncombe, May 18, 1963; children: Cynthia Christine, Ronald Crosby Jr. BSc, McMaster U., 1963; PhD, Princeton U., 1966. Faculty dept. physics U. Md., 1968-78; prof. physics MIT, 1978-91; prof. astrophys. scis. Princeton U., 1991—. Vis. scientist Los Alamos Sci. Lab., 1974-75; asst. dir. for applied plasma physics Office of Fusion Energy Dept. Energy, Washington, 1976-78; dir. Plasma Fusion Center MIT, Cambridge, Mass., 1978-88; chmn. magnetic fusion adv. com., 1982-86; dir. Princeton Plasma Physics Lab., 1991-96. Author: Methods in Nonlinear Plasma Theory, 1972, Theory of Nonneutral Plasmas, 1974, 2d edit., 89, Physics of Nonneutral Plasmas, 1990. Recipient Disting. Assoc. award Dept. Energy, 1986, Leadership award Fusion Power Assocs., 1986, Kaul Found. Excellence award, 1993, Particle Accelerator Sci. and Tech. award, 2005; Ford Found. fellow, 1963-64, Imperial Oil fellow, 1963-66, Sloan Rsch. Found. fellow, 1970-72. Fellow AAAS, Am. Phys. Soc. (chmn. div. plasma physics, 1983-84). Office: Princeton U Plasma Physics Lab PO Box 451 Princeton NJ 08543-0451 Business E-Mail: rdavidson@princeton.edu.

DAVIDSON, SHEILA KEARNEY, lawyer, insurance company executive; b. Paterson, NJ, Dec. 16, 1961; d. John James and Rita Barbara (Burke) Kearney; m. Anthony H. Davidson, Oct. 5, 1996; children: Andrew John, Patrick Kearney. BA cum laude, Fairfield U., 1983; JD, George Washington U., 1986. Bar: N.Y. 1987, U.S. Dist. Ct. (so. dist.) N.Y. 1987, D.C. 1989. Assoc. Shearson Lehman Bros., Inc., NYC, 1986-87; staff atty. Nat. Assn. Securities Dealers, NYC, 1987-89, regional atty., 1989-90, sr. regional atty., 1990-91; regional counsel NY Life Ins. Co., NYC, 1991-93, assoc. counsel, 1993-94, asst. gen. counsel, 1994-95, v.p., assoc. gen. counsel, 1995-97, sr. v.p. in charge of corp. compliance dept., 1998-00, sr. v.p., gen. counsel, 2000—05, exec. v.p. law and corp. adminstrn., 2005—. Trustee Fairfield U., 2003—, Madison Sq. Park Conservancy, 2004—. Mem.: D.C. Bar Assn., Phi Delta Phi. Republican. Roman Catholic. Office: NY Life Ins Co 51 Madison Ave New York NY 10010-1603

DAVIDSON, THOMAS FERGUSON, retired chemical engineer; b. NYC, Jan. 5, 1930; s. Lorimer Arthur and Elizabeth (Valentine) D.; m. Nancy Lee Selecman, Nov. 10, 1951; children: Thomas Ferguson, Richard Alan, Gwyn Ann. BS in Engring., U. Md., College Park, 1951; HHD (hon.), Weber State U., Ogden, Utah, 1998. Sr. project engr. Wright Air Devel. Ctr., Dayton, Ohio, 1951-58; dep. dir. Solid Sys. Divsn., Edwards, Calif., 1959-60; mgr. govt. ops. Thiokol Chem. Corp., Ogden, Utah, 1960-64, dir. aerospace mktg. Bristol, Pa., 1965-67, dir. tech. mgmt. Ogden, 1968-82; v.p. tech. Morton Thiokol Inc., Chgo., 1983-88, Thiokol Corp., Ogden, 1989-90; cons. Ogden, 1990-99. Subcom. lubrications and wear NACA, Washington, 1955-57; chmn. Joint Army, Navy, NASA, Air Force exec. com., 1959-60. Editor: National Rocket Strategic Plan, 1990; contbr. articles to profl. jours. Trustee Family Counseling Svc., Ogden, 1991—98, Weber State U. Found., 1999—, Weber State U., 1999—2007, chair trustees, 2005—07; trustee Ogden Dinosaur Park, 2000—03; mem. Utah State Bd. Edn., 1992—94; mem. allocations com. United Way; bd. dirs. Habitat for Humanity Internat., 1991—93; chmn. bd. dirs. Wesley Acad., Ogden, 1994—98; bd. dirs. Utah Musical Theatre, 1997—2005, ARC No. Utah, 1999—2001, Ogden Weber Applied Tech. Coll. Found., 2001—03; mem. athletic bd. Weber State U., 1999—2005. Fellow AIAA (assoc., sect. chmn. 1979-80, chmn. rocket propulsion com. 1987-90, mem. aerospace tech. com. 1987-90, Wyld Propulsion award 1991, WSU Crystal Crest award 2001); mem. Am. Newcomen Soc., Smithsonian Instn., Exch. Club (Book of Golden Deeds award 2001), Ogden Golf and Country Club, Weber State Wildcat Club (bd. dirs. 1996-2000). Republican. Methodist. Home: 4755 Banbury Ln Ogden UT 84403-4484

DAVIDSON, THOMAS MAXWELL, oil industry executive; b. NYC, Dec. 14, 1937; s. Alfred Edward and Claire Helen (Dreyfus) D.; m. Ruth Elizabeth Bovenkerk, Dec. 8, 1962; children: Douglas Edward, Anne Elizabeth. BA, Vanderbilt U., 1959; MBA, Columbia U., 1961. Mgr. Ford Motor Co., Dearborn, Mich., 1963-72; dir. credit ops. White Motor Corp., Eastlake, Ohio, 1972-73, v.p., treas., 1976-77; sr. v.p., COO White Motor Credit Corp., Cleve., 1973-75, pres., CEO, 1975-77, also bd. dirs.; sr. v.p. fin., CFO, dir. Tex. Gas Transmission Corp., Owensboro, Ky., 1977-81; exec. v.p., CFO Arrow Electronics, Inc., NYC, 1981-87, exec. v.p. Greenwich, Conn., 1987-89, also bd. dirs., 1981-94; pres., CEO Global TeleSystems Group, 1989-93, also bd. dirs., 1990-93; pres., CEO Internat. Techs., Inc., Greenwich, 1993—. Med. Info. Internat., 1995-98. Bd. dirs. SOVAM Teleport Russia, Sovintel, Russia, Baltic Comms., Ltd., Russia; bd. dirs., chair CEO XXI Century Hotel Network Ltd., 1998—2000; co-founder, sr. v.p. Vytek Wireless, Inc., 2000—01; mng. dir. Southporter Mgmt. Group, 2002—; dir. Seguas Corp., 2005; mng. dir. Digital Entertainment Svcs. LLC, 2006. Served with U.S. Army, 1959. Mem.: N.Y. Athletic Club. Home: 131 Doubling Rd Greenwich CT 06830-4040 Office: Internat Techs Inc 35 Mason St Greenwich CT 06830-5433 Office Phone: 203-661-4875.

DAVIDSON, THOMAS NOEL, metal products executive; b. Evansville, Ind., Oct. 4, 1939; s. Harry R. and Helen E. Davidson; m. Sally Anne Fries, 1958; children: Thomas N. Jr., John C., James R., Jennifer J. BSc with honors, Mich. State U., 1961. Chmn. bd. dirs. Quarry Hill Group, Nutech Precision Metals Inc., Azure Dynamics Inc. Past prin. owner Am. Brass Co., Ansonia Brass, Atco Controls, Inc., Buffalo Brass Co., Carborundum Abrasives, Inc., Cramco, Inc., Hanson Inc., Jensen Fitting Mfg., Ltd., Jensen Fittings Corp., PCL Industries Ltd., Sandbright & Co., Sklar-Peppler Furniture Inc., Stephenson's Rent-all Inc., Union Drawn Steel Ltd., Volstatic, Inc.; chmn. bd. Azure Dynamics, LP; bd. dirs. TLC Laser Eye Ctrs., MDC Corp., Occulogix Inc., Nutech Precision Metals, TLC Eye Ctr.; bd. dirs. Nat. Marine Sanctuary, Clemmer Industries; past chmn. Gen. Trust Corp., Henson Chem. Past chmn. Ocean Reef Hist. Soc., Ocean Reef Found., Hugh MacMillan Children's Found.; past chmn. Can. CPGA Golf Championship, Metro Toronto Conv. Ctr.; past bd. dirs. Con. Smythe Rsch. Found., Westhem Corp., USF&G, Can., Nat. Club, Can. Club, Silcorp Ltd., others; bd. dirs., past chmn. Ocean Reef Cmty. Found.; chmn. Ocean Reef Cultural Ctr.; founding chmn. Ocean Reef Club, Inc. Recipient Fin. Post Can. award 1979; named Entrepreneur of Yr. by Fin. Post. Mem. Soc. Plastics Engrs. (past dir.), Soc. Plastics Industry (past chmn., Man of Yr. award 1985), Variety Ability Systems Inc. (past dir.), Variety Village (past dir.). Young Pres. Orgn. (internat. pres. 1988-89), World Pres. Orgn. (bd. dirs., internat. pres. 1997), Can. Club (past bd. dirs., N.Y. and Toronto), Nat. Club Toronto (past bd. dirs.), Rosedale Golf Club (Toronto), Card Sound Golf Club (bd. dirs.), English Turn Golf and Country Club (New Orleans), Griffith Island Club (Wiarton, Ont., past chmn.), Ocean Reef Club (past chmn.), Bonefish and Tarpon Unltd. (founding chmn.), The Caledon Mountain Trout Club (Inglewood, Ont.), Tau Beta Pi, Pi Tau Sigma. Home: 7 Sunrise Cay Rd Key Largo FL 33037-5301 Office: Quarry Hill Group 24 Dockside Ln PO Box 83 Key Largo FL 33037-0083

DAVIDSON, TOM WILLIAM, lawyer; b. Madison, Wis., Oct. 10, 1952; s. Alvin William and Louise Elizabeth (Zeratsky) D.; m. Linda Mary Greiber, July 27, 1974; children: Jessica, Heather, Thomas. BA, U. Wis., 1977, JD, 1974. Bar: Wis. 1977, U.S. Dist. Ct. (we. dist.) Wis. 1977, U.S. Ct. Appeals (D.C. cir.) 1986, U.S. Supreme Ct. 1986, Va. 2001. Gen. atty. FCC, Washington, 1977-79, trial atty., 1979; assoc. Sidley & Austin, Washington, 1980-84, ptnr., 1985-91, Akin, Gump, Struass, Hauer & Feld, LLP, Washington, 1992—, and chair. comm. practice group. Active Burke (Va.) Ctr. Cmty. Assn., 1977-79; chmn. Bass Pond Cluster Bd., 1977-78. Mem. ABA, FBA, Fed. Comm. Bar Assn., Lowe's Island Club, Tournament Players Club at Avenal, Phi Beta Kappa, Phi Eta Sigma, Phi Kappa Phi. Avocations: golf, softball, soccer, basketball, racquetball. Office: Akin Gump Strauss Hauer & Feld Ste 400 1333 New Hampshire Ave NW Washington DC 20036-1564 Office Phone: 202-887-4011. Business E-Mail: tdavidson@akingump.com.

DAVIDSON, WILLIAM M., manufacturing executive, professional sports team owner; b. Dec. 5, 1922; m. Karen Davidson; children from previous marriage: Ethan, Maria. BBA, U. Mich., 1947; JD, Wayne State U., 1949; LHD (hon.), Jewish Theol. Sem. Am., 1996, U. Mich., 2001. Pres., CEO Guardian Glass Co., Northville, Mich., 1957-68; pres., CEO, dir. Guardian Industries Corp., 1968—; mng. ptnr., part owner NBA Detroit Pistons, 1974—; owner Women's NBA Detroit Shock, 1998—, NHL Tampa Bay Lightning, 1999—; majority owner Palace Sports and Entertainment; former owner Arena Football League Detroit Fury. Donated to the establishment of William Davidson Inst., U. Mich. Sch. Bus. Adminstrn., 1992, William Davidson Grad. Sch. of Jewish Edn. at Jewish Theological Seminary of Am., NY, Davidson Inst. of Science Edn. at Weizmann Inst. of Sci., Rehovot, Israel, 1999; founder Pistons/Palace Found. Served in USN. Named one of Am.'s most generous donors, New York Times, 1997, Forbes' Richest Ams., 1999—, World's Richest People, Forbes mag., 2001—; recipient honors for lifelong philanthropy, Coun. of Mich. Foundations, 1997. Office: Guardian Industries Corp 2300 Harmon Rd Auburn Hills MI 48326 also: Detroit Pistons 5 Championship Dr Auburn Hills MI 48326*

DAVIDSON-SHEPARD, GAY, secondary school educator; b. Long Beach, Calif., Dec. 15, 1951; d. Leyton Paul and Ruth Leona (Gritzmaker) Davidson; m. Daniel A. Shepard, June 24, 1983. BA, U. Calif., Irvine, 1972; MA, Columbia Pacific U., 1986. Cert. elem. and secondary edn. tchr. Tchr. mid. sch. Ocean View Sch. Dist., Huntington Beach, Calif., 1973—; team mem. Calif. learning assessment system State Dept. of Edn., Sacramento, 1987—; chief reader Orange County pentathlon and decathlon Orange County Dept. Edn., Costa Mesa, Calif., 1980—; sr. reader new standards State Dept. Edn., Sacramento, 1995—. Lang. arts cons. various sch. dists., Calif., 1976—; chief reader Calif. Learning Assessment System, Sacramento, 1993—; sr. reader New Stds., 1995—; chief reader, asst. chief reader, table reader Golden State Exams, 1997—; item writer Calif. H.S. Exit Exam, 2000—. Author/cons.: Teacher's Guide for Direct Assessment Writing, 1990; test writer Acad. Pentathlon Test, 1984—, Dist. Lang. Art Proficiency Test, 1980—. Mem. NEA, AAUS, AAUW, Nat. Assn. Tchrs. of English, Calif. Reading Assn., Mensa, Calif. Tchrs. Assn., Ocean View Tchrs. Assn. Democrat. Avocations: reading, camping, travel, cooking. Home: 6782 Rook Dr Huntington Beach CA 92647-5641 Office: Mesa View Sch 17601 Avilla Ln Huntington Beach CA 92647-6612 Office Phone: 714-842-6608. Personal E-mail: davshep1@verizon.net.

DAVID-WEILL, MICHEL ALEXANDRE, retired investment banker; b. France, Nov. 23, 1932; came to US, 1977; s. Pierre Sylvain and Berthe Marie (Haardt) David-W.; m. Hélène Lehideux, July 20, 1956; children: Beatrice David-Weill Stern, Cecile David-Weill, Natalie Merveilleux du Vignaux, Agathe David-Weill Mordacq. Student, Inst. Scis. Politiques, 1953. Ptnr. Lazard Freres & Co., 1961-65; ptnr. Lazard Freres & Cie, 1965—, sr. ptnr., 1975—2005, Lazard Freres & Co., NYC, 1977-95, chmn., 1995—2005; ret., 2005. Bd. dirs. Eurazeo, 1972—, pres., 2003; vice chmn. Groupe Danone, 1970; bd. dirs. Publicis Groupe S.A., 1990. Bd. gov. Soc. of NY Hosp.; trustee Met. Mus. Art, 1985—. Named one of Top 200 Collectors, ARTnews Mag., 2004. Mem. Academie des Beaux-Arts (mem. inst.). Clubs: Brook (NYC), Knickerbocker (NYC). Avocation: collector of 17th to 19th century French paintings. Office: 820 Fifth Ave New York NY 10065

DAVIE, JILL, chef; Grad., U. Calif., Santa Cruz, Culinary Inst. Am. Externship LuLu, San Francisco; chef de cuisine Hans Rockenwagner, Rock; vis. chef Tru, Blackbird, Trotters; chef Josie Restaurant, Santa Monica, 2000—03, chef de cuisine, 2003—. Featured in Art Culinaire mag., Food Arts mag., Gourmet mag., appearances on Recipe TV, Ultimate Restaurants, Date Plate, Food Network. Named Top Ten Student of Yr., Culinary Inst. Am.; named one of LA's Rising Stars, StarChefs.com, 2006; recipient Food and Wine Baby Chef award, Julia Child, 1996. Office: Josie 2424 Pico Blvd Santa Monica CA 90405 Office Phone: 310-581-9888.*

DAVIES, ANGELA, oncologist, educator; BS, Wilfrid Laurier U., Waterloo, Ont., 1993; MD, McMaster U., Hamilton, Ont., 1996. Cert. Am. Bd. Internal Medicine, Am. Med. Internal Medicine, Med. Oncology. Resident internal medicine U. Toronto, 1996—99; fellowship, med. oncology McMaster U., Hamilton, Ont., 1999—2001; asst. prof. hematology/oncology U. Calif. Davis Lung Cancer Clinic and Develop. Therapeutics Clinic, 2001—, physician, 2001—. Contbr. articles to profl. jours. Named one of Top Doctors, Sacramento Mag. Mem.: Southwest Oncology Group, Royal Coll. Physicians (Can.), Assn. Northern Calif. Oncologists, Am. Soc. for Clin. Oncology. Office: U Calif Davis Cancer Ctr 4501 X St Ste 3016 Sacramento CA 95817 Office Phone: 916-734-3700.*

DAVIES, CHARLES R., retired lawyer; BS, Duquesne U., 1964; JD, Georgetown U., 1967. Bar: D.C. 1968. Joined Geico Corp., Washington, 1968, asst. v.p., asst. gen. counsel, 1978, v.p., 1987—98, dep. general counsel, 1987—92, gen. counsel, 1992—2006, group v.p., 1998—2000, sr. v.p., 2000—06, ret., 2006. Office: Geico Corp Geico Plz Washington DC 20076-0001

DAVIES, COLLEEN T., lawyer; b. Sacramento, Oct. 22, 1958; married; children: Katie, Patrick. BA with honors in English lit., U. Calif., Davis, 1980; JD, Santa Clara U., 1983. Bar: Calif. 1983. With Crosby, Heafey, Roach & May (combined with Reed Smith LLP, 2003), 1983—2003; ptnr., mem. exec. com. Reed Smith LLP, Oakland, Calif., 2003—. Comments editor Santa Clara Law Rev., 1982—83; mem. Product Liability Adv. Coun. Mem.: ABA, Def. Rsch. Inst. (pharm. & med. device sect.), Alameda County Bar Assn., Calif. State Bar, Phi Beta Kappa. Office: Reed Smith LLP 1999 Harrison St Ste 2400 Oakland CA 94612 Office Phone: 510-763-2000. Office Fax: 510-273-8832. Business E-Mail: cdavies@reedsmith.com.

DAVIES, DAVID B., communications executive; b. 1969; BS, MS, Mass. Inst. Tech.; MBA, Harvard U. Grad. Sch. Bus. Sr. assoc. Booz, Allen & Hamilton Inc.; v.p., Strategy and Product Mktg. for Subscriber Networks Sci. Atlanta, Inc., Ga. Named one of 40 Executives Under 40, Multichannel News, 2006. Mem.: Soc. for Cable Telecom. Engineers, Cable & Telecom. Assn. for Mktg. Office: Scientific Atlanta 5030 Sugarloaf Pkwy Lawrenceville GA 30044 Office Phone: 770-236-5000. Office Fax: 770-236-4775.

DAVIES, DAVID GEORGE, lawyer, educator; b. Waukesha, Wis., July 19, 1928; s. David Evan and Ella Hilda (Degler) D.; m. Elaine Kowalchik, May 12, 1962; children: Thea Kay, Bryn Ann, Degler Evan. BS, U. Wis., 1950, JD, 1953. Bar: Wis. 1953, Ariz. 1959. Trust rep. First Nat. Bank of Ariz., Phoenix, 1957-58, asst. trust officer, 1958-62, trust officer, head bus devel. in trust dept., 1962-66, v.p., trust officer, 1966; practice in Phoenix, 1967—; assoc. Wales & Collins, 1967-68; ptnr. Wales, Collins & Davies, 1968-75, Collins, Davies & Cronkhite, Ltd., 1975-85, David G. Davies, Ltd., 1986—. Instr. bus. law local chpt. C.L.U.s, 1965; instr. estate and gift taxation, 1973—; instr. estate planning Phoenix Coll., 1968—; past instr. Maricopa County Jr. Coll. Pres. Central Ariz. Estate Planning Council; pres., bd. dirs. Vis. Nurse Service, United Fund Agy.; chmn. bd. Beatitudes Campus of Care; bd. dirs. Phoenix chpt. Nat. Hemophilia Found.; bd. dirs., treas. trusteeship St. Luke's Hosp. Med. Ctr., Phoenix, 1982—; mem. adv. bd. planned giving com. Salvation Army, 1997—. Served to capt. JAGC, AUS, 1953-57. Mem. Central Assn. Life Underwriters (asso.), ABA, Wis. Bar Assn., State Bar Ariz., Am. Assn. Homes for Aged (legal affairs com., future com.) Congregationalist (chmn. bd. trustees, moderator). Office: 5110 N 40th St Ste 236 Phoenix AZ 85018-2151 Office Phone: 602-956-1521.

DAVIES, DAVID HUW, electronics executive, engineering company executive; b. Tredegar, Monmouthshire, Wales, Oct. 29, 1942; arrived in US, 1967; s. Vivian Jones and May Nance Davies; m. Josephine Lockwood, July 28, 1966; children: Susan Elaine Sheely, Sarah Beth. BSc, U. Coll. London, 1964, PhD, 1967; MBA, U. Pitts., 1974. Sr. scientist Westinghouse Electric, Pitts., 1967—77; v.p. Kylex Inc, Mountain View, Calif., 1977—81, Ampex Corp, Redwood City, Calif., 1992—97; optical rec. gen. mgr. 3M Co, St. Paul, 1981—92; sr. v.p. SIROS Corp, Mountain View, 1997—99; chief tech. officer DPHI Inc., Boulder, Colo., 1999—. Cons. SBR Assocs., Boulder, Colo., 1999—; adv. bd. Optical Data Storage Conf., 2005—. Editor: Storage & Retrieval Systems, 1990; contbr. articles to profl. jours. Recipient Consumer Product of Yr. award, Consumer Electronics Soc., 2001. Fellow: Soc. Optical Engring. (chpt. chair 1987—97); mem.: IEEE. Achievements include 16 patents in field; development of optical storage technology; novel miniature optical disc drives; creation of CD ROM standard. Avocations: sailing, skiing, genealogy. Home: 151 Boulder View Ln Boulder CO 80304 Office: DPHI Inc dba DataPlay 2580 55th St Boulder CO 80301 Home Phone: 303-938-0522; Office Phone: 303-952-2464. Office Fax: 303-444-5120. Personal E-mail: davedavies@qwest.net.

DAVIES, GRACE LUCILLE, real estate educator; b. Providence, Apr. 6, 1926; d. Leonard Cerulle and Eleanor De Prete; m. David John Davies, Feb. 8, 1948; children: Mary Ellen, David L., Pamela, Amy. AA, Long Beach City Coll., 1946; BA, U. Calif., Berkeley, 1948; MA, Calif. State U., Long Beach, 1965. Gen. elem. credential Calif., life elem. credential Calif., elem. sch. adminstr. credential Calif., life elem. sch. adminstr. Calif. Elem. educator ABC Unified Sch. Dist., Artesia, Calif., 1956—85, MGM coord., 1960—70, bilingual coord., 1960—70, asst. prin., 1970—80; real estate, bus., investment D. Davies & Assoc., Long Beach, Calif., 1985—. Clk. Long Beach (Calif.) Election Bd., 1990—; mem., vol. Long Beach City Campaign, 1998. Mem.: Calif. Ret. Tchrs. Assn. (legis. chair 1985—, pres. 2000—04, area membership chair 2004—), Apt. Mgmt. Assn., Delta Kappa Gamma (v.p., pres., Golden Rose award 1996), Pi Lambda Theta (treas., v.p., pres., Outstanding Contbn. Edn. award 1996). Avocations: travel, reading, theater, camping, music. Home: 6215 Parima St Long Beach CA 90803

DAVIES, HUGH MARLAIS, museum director; b. Grahamstown, South Africa, Feb. 12, 1948; came to U.S., 1956; s. Horton Marlais and Brenda M. (Deakin) D.; children: Alexandra, Dorian; m. Lynda Forsha; 1 stepdaughter, Mackenzie Forsha Fuller. AB summa cum laude, Princeton U., 1970, MFA, 1972, PhD, 1976. Dir. Univ. Gallery, U. Mass., Amherst, 1975-83; David C. Copley dir. Mus. Contemporary Art (formerly La Jolla Mus. Contemporary Art), San Diego, 1983—. Vis. prof. fine arts Amherst Coll., 1980-83; mem. adv. coun. dept. art and archeology Princeton U., 1989—, panel mem. fed. adv. com. internat. exhbns., 1990-94; co-curator Whitney Mus. Am. Art Biennial, 2000. Author: (book) Francis Bacon: The Papal Portraits of 1953, 2001, Francis Bacon: The Early and Middle Years, 1928-1958; co-author: Sacred Art in a Secular Century: 20th Century Religious Art, 1978, Francis Bacon (Abbeville), 1986. Nat. Endowment Arts fellow, 1982, 95. Mem. Am. Assn. Mus., Coll. Art Assn., Assn. Art Mus. Dirs. (trustee 1994-2001, pres. 1997-98). Office: Mus Contemporary Art San Diego 700 Prospect St La Jolla CA 92037-4228 Office Phone: 858-454-3541.

DAVIES, J. CLARENCE (TERRY DAVIES), public information officer, consultant; b. NYC, Nov. 16, 1937; BA cum laude, Dartmouth Coll., 1959; PhD in Am. Govt., Columbia U., 1965. Instr. govt., dir. Bur. Rsch. in Mcpl. Govt. Bowdoin Coll., Brunswick, Maine, 1963-65; chief examiner environ. and consumer protection Bur. of Budget Exec. Office of Pres., Washington, 1965-67, sr. staff mem. Coun. Environ. Quality, 1970-73; asst. prof. politics and pub. affairs Princeton (N.J.) U., 1967-70; fellow, asst. dir. instns. and pub. decisions divsn. Resources for Future, Inc., Washington, 1973-76; exec. v.p. Conservation Found., Washington, 1976-89; asst. adminstr. policy, planning and evaluation U.S. EPA, Washington, 1989-91; exec. dir. Nat. Commn. on Environment, Washington, 1991-92; dir. Ctr. for Risk Mgmt. Resources for Future, Washington, 1992-2000, sr. fellow, 2000—; sr. adv. Woodrow Wilson Internat. Ctr. for Scholars, 2005—. Cons. U.S. Bur. of Budget, 1967-68, U.S. Dept. Health, Edn. and Welfare, 1968-69, Pres.'s Adv. Coun. on Exec. Orgn., 1969-70, NSF, 1976-79; mem.-at-large exec. com. sci. adv. bd. EPA, 1976-81, chmn. adminstr.'s adv. com. toxic substances, 1977-78, co-chmn. com. on econs. sci. adv. bd., 1979-80, mem. subcom. environ. statis. Nat. Adv. Coun. for Environ. Policy and Tech., 1991-95; mem. sr. steering com. Ctr. Tech. and Adminstrn., Am. U., 1976-79; mem. sci. adv. bd. Internat. Joint Commn. U.S.-Can., 1984-87; mem. adv. bd. Ctr. for Chem. Process Safety, 1985-89; mem. bd. govs. Environ. Health and Safety Inst., Nat. Safety Coun., 1986-89; mem. adv. panel on systems at risk from climate change U.S. Office Tech. Assessment, 1991-92; bd. dirs. Inst. Coop. Environ. Mgmt., 1991-93; chmn. bd. dirs. Resolve, Inc., 1993-2001. Author: Neighborhood Groups and Urban Renewal, 1966, The Politics of Pollution, 2d edit., 1975, Pollution Control in the United States, 1998; co-author: Training for Environmental Groups, 1984, Determining Unreasonable Risk, 1979, Significant New Use Rules for Existing Chemicals, 1983, Controlling Cross-Media Pollutants, 1984; author: (with others) Growing Against Ourselves: The Energy-Environment Tangle, 1974, Federal Environmental Law, 1974, Environmental Management in the Colorado River Basin, 1974, The Governance of Common Property Resources, 1974, Social Research and Public Policies, 1975, Air Pollution and Administrative Control, 1977, Mechanisms of Toxicity and Hazard Evaluation, 1980, Strategies for Public Health, 1981, TSCA's Impact on Society and the Chemical Industry, 1983, Environmental Policy in the 1980s, 1984, Pollutants in a Multimedia Environment, 1986, Integrated Pollution Control in Europe and North America, 1990, Keeping Pace with Science and Engineering: Case Studies in Environmental Regulation, 1993, Encyclopedia of the Environment, 1994, Reforming Permitting, 2001, Managing the Effects of Nanotechnology, 2006, EPA and Nanotechnology, 2007; co-editor: Business and Environment: Toward Common Ground, 1977, Risk Communication, 1987; mem. editl. bd. Toxic Substances Jour., 1979-89. Mem. bd. dirs. Wildlife Habitat Enhancement Coun., 1987-89. Ford Found. Met. Region fellow. Fellow AAAS; mem. NAS (com. environ. indices 1973-74, com. on environ. decision making 1975-77, com. on prevention significant deterioration under Clean Air Act 1979-81, com. on instl. means for assessment risks to pub. health 1982-83, environ. studies bd. 1983-85, com. on multimedia pollutants 1986-88, chmn. com. on prins. decision making for regulating chemicals in environment 1974-75, com. social and behavioral sci. rsch. priorities for environ. decision making 2003-05, climate change sci. program com., 2006-07), Nat. Inst. for Chem. Studies (nat. adv. bd. 1986-89), NAE (steering com. symposium on environ. regulation 1992-93), Nat. Acad. Pub. Adminstrn. (panel on econ. incentives 1992-93, panel on EPA priorities 1993-95), Phi Beta Kappa. Office: 1616 P St NW Washington DC 20036-1434 Home Phone: 301-469-6271; Office Phone: 202-328-5080. Personal E-mail: jcd3@verizon.net. E-mail: davies@rff.org.

DAVIES, JOHN ARTHUR, retired physics professor, engineering educator, research scientist; b. Prestatyn, North Wales, Mar. 28, 1927; emigrated to Can., 1940; s. Francis James and Doris Annie (Edkins) D.; m. Florence Smithson, July 29, 1950; children: Susan, Chris, Cathy, Paul, Jim, Anne. BA with honors in Chemistry, St. Michael's Coll., Toronto, 1947; MA in Phys. Chemistry, U. Toronto, 1948, PhD in Phys. Chemistry, 1950; DSc (hon.), Royal Roads Mil. Coll., 1984, Salford U., Eng., 1993. With Atomic Energy of Canada, Chalk River, Ont., 1950-85; prof. engring. and physics McMaster U., Hamilton, 1969-92, prof. emeritus, 1992—. Vis. prof. physics U. Aarhus, Denmark, 1964-65, 69-70; vis. physicist Nobel Inst. Physics, Stockholm, Sweden, 1962, Calif. Inst. Tech., 1969, Osaka U., Japan, 1972. Author: (with J.W. Mayer, L. Eriksson) Ion Implantation, 1970; contbr. over 200 articles to prof. jours. Can. Ramsay Mem. fellow, 1954-56; recipient Noranda medal Chem. Inst. Can., 1965, Callinan award Am. Electrochem. Soc., 1968, W.B. Lewis medal Can. Nuc. Soc., 1998. Fellow Royal Soc. Can., Bohmische Phys. Soc.; mem. Chem. Inst. Can., Can. Assn. Physics, Danish Royal Soc. Roman Catholic. Home and Office: Box 224 7 Wolfe Ave Deep River ON Canada K0J 1P0

DAVIES, KATHERINE STEFANIE, environmental scientist, educator; b. London, Eng., Nov. 17, 1956; d. Stefan Frankel and Audrey Lloyd; m. George Manter DuWors, Feb. 2, 2007; 1 child, Jonathan Richard Cromwell. BSc in Biochemistry with honors, Sheffield U., Eng., 1978; MA in Cultural Anthropology and Social Transformation, Calif. Inst. Integral Studies, San Francisco, 2002; DPhil, Oxford U., Eng., 1981. Mgr., environ. protection office City Toronto, 1985—90; prin. Ecosystems Consulting, Ottawa, Ontario, Canada, 1990—2002; core faculty, ctr. creative change Antioch U., Seattle, 2003—. Bd. dirs. Can. Environ. Law Assn., Toronto; steering com. Collaborative Health and Environ., Freeland, Wash.; mem. Ont. Pesticides Adv. Com., Toronto, 1986—88; mem. & chair health com. Can. Environ. Assessment Rsch. Coun., Ottawa, 1987—91; mem. sci. adv. bd., co-chair health com. Internat. Joint Commn., Ottawa, 1988—90, Washington, 1988—90; mem. Ont. Environ. Assessment Bd., Toronto, 1990—94; bd. dirs. Wash. Citizens for Resource Conservation, Seattle, 2004—; vice chair, adv. bd. dirs. Inst. Children's Environ. Health, Freeland, Wash., 2005—. Contbr. articles to profl. jours. Recipient Svc. Above Self award, Rotary Club Seattle, 2004; grantee, Seattle Biotech Legacy Found., 2005, 2006, 2007. Mem.: APHA, Wash. State Pub. Health Assn. Office: Antioch Univ 2326 Sixth Ave Seattle WA 98121 Office Phone: 206-268-4811. Business E-Mail: kdavies@antiochsea.edu.

DAVIES, LAURA, professional golfer; b. Coventry, Eng., Oct. 5, 1963; Profl. golfer LPGA, 1987—. Mem. European Solheim Cup Team, 1990, 92, 94, 96, 98. 15 career victories, including Circle K LPGA Tucson Open, 1988, Jamie Farr Toledo Classic, 1988, Lady Keystone Open, 1989, Inamori Classic, 1991, McDonald's Championship, 1993, Standard Register Ping, 1994, 95, 96, 97, Sara Lee Classic, 1994, Chick-fil-a Charity Championship, 1995, Star Bank LPGA Classic, 1996, LPGA Tour Championship, 1996, L.A. Womeen's Championship, 2000, The Philips Invitational, 2000; recipient Rolex Player of Yr. award, 1996; named Mem. Brit. Empire, Queen Elizabeth II, 1988. Office: care LPGA 100 International Golf Dr Daytona Beach FL 32124-1082

DAVIES, PAUL LEWIS, JR., retired lawyer; b. San Jose, Calif., July 21, 1930; s. Paul Lewis and Faith (Crummey) D.; m. Barbara Bechtel, Dec. 22, 1955 (dec. June 2001); children: Laura (Mrs. Segundo Mateo), Paul Lewis III. AB, Stanford U., 1952; JD, Harvard U., 1957. Bar: Calif. 1957. Assoc. Pillsbury, Madison & Sutro, San Francisco, 1957—63, ptnr., 1963—89; gen. counsel Chevron Corp., 1984—89. Hon. trustee Calif. Acad. Scis., trustee, 1970-83, chmn., 1973-80; pres. Herbert Hoover Found.; bd. overseers Hoover Instn., chmn., 1976-82, 91-93; hon. regent U. of Pacific, regent, 1959-90. Lt. U.S. Army, 1952-54. Mem. Bohemian Club, Pacific-Union Club, Villa Taverna, Claremont Country Club, Cypress Point Club, Sainte Claire Club, Collectors Club, Explorers Club, Links Club, Met. Club, St. Francis Yacht Club, Palo Alto (Calif.) Club, Phi Beta Kappa, Pi Sigma Alpha Republican. Office: 3697 Mt Diablo Blvd Ste 205 Lafayette CA 94549 Office Phone: 925-284-8180. E-mail: pauldaviesjr@yahoo.com.

DAVIES, PAUL LEWIS, III, venture capitalist; b. Oakland, Calif., June 29, 1961; s. Paul Lewis Jr. and Barbara Bechtel Davies; m. Pilar Hanigan, Feb. 14, 1963; children: Robert H., Natalie L., Tyler S. BS in Indsl. Engring., Stanford U., 1983, MBA, 1987. With Bechtel Group, Inc., San Francisco, 1987-93; prin. Brentwood Assocs., Menlo Park, Calif., 1993-94, Fremont Group, San Francisco, 1995; mng. prin. Cambria Group, Menlo Park, 1996—. Bd. dirs. Crossbow Tech., Inc., San Jose, Calif., Lakeside Corp., Lafayette, Calif.; chmn. bd. dirs. DSA/Phototech, Inc., L.A. Bd. overseers Hoover Instn., Stanford, Calif.; pres., bd. dirs. Llagas Found., Lafayette; bd. dirs. Lakeside Found., Lafayette, Hoover Found., Ohio; vice chmn. bd. trustees Menlo Sch., Atherton, Calif. Mem. Inst. Indsl. Engrs., Bohemian Club, Pacific Union Club, Parairo Club, Menlo Circus Club, Stanford Golf Club. Republican. Office: The Cambria Group 1600 El Camino Real Ste 155 Menlo Park CA 94025 Office Phone: 650-329-8600. Office Fax: 650-329-8601. Business E-Mail: davies@cambriagroup.com.

DAVIES, PERCY (PETE) CHARLES, mechanical engineer; b. Pontrilas, Sask., Can., Sept. 18, 1920; s. George Davies, Alice Fanny Wall; m. Nancy Naidee Clark, June 28, 1941 (div. Feb. 1959); children: Denise Diane, Leslie Ann, Joyce Natalie; m. Betty Jean Martin; 1 child, Michael Lane. BSME, U. Wash., 1953. Cert. comml. balloon pilot FAA. Machinist inspector Continental Can Corp., Seattle, 1949—53; gen. mgr. Cert. Mfg., Seattle, 1953—58, Smith-Williston Co., Seattle, 1958—59, Dependable Bldg. Maint., Seattle, 1960—65; owner, gen. mgr. Dictamatic Corp., Portland, 1965—77; owner, chief pilot Rainbow Balloon Flights, Sun City, Ariz., 1983—87; owner Adna Press, Sun City, 1987—. Chmn. bd. Dictamatic Corp., Portland, 1965—77. Author: The Spartan Rebel, 2003, Big Man on Campus, 2003, Kidnapping Susan, 2003, TASER, 2005. With US Merchant Marines, 1945. Mem.: Nat. Assn. Bldg. Svc. Contrs. (nat. bd. dirs. 1965), Tau Beta Pi. Republican. Church Of The Nazarene. Avocations: writing, woodworking, travel, photography, portrait painting. Home and Office: 9206 W Glen Oaks Cir N Sun City AZ 85351 Personal E-mail: iampcd1@aol.com.

DAVIES, PETER JOHN, plant physiology educator, researcher; b. Sudbury, Middlesex, Eng., Mar. 7, 1940; came to U.S., 1966; s. William Bertram and Ivy Doreen (Parmentier) D.; m. Linda Kay DeNoyer, Aug. 2, 1976; children: Kenneth DeNoyer, Caryn Parmentier. BSc with honors, U. Reading, Eng., 1962; MS, U. Calif., Davis, 1964; PhD, U. Reading, 1966. Instr. Yale U., New Haven, 1966-69; asst. prof. plant physiology Cornell U., Ithaca, NY, 1969-75, assoc. prof., 1975-83, prof., 1983—, chmn. sect. plant biology, 1992-96. Vis. prof. Cambridge (Eng.) U., 1976-77, Univ. Coll. of Wales, Aberystwyth, 1983-84, U. Minn., 1984, U. Tasmania, Australia, 1996-97, 2006, U. Bologna, Italy, 2006. Author: (with others) The Life of the Green Plant, 1980, Control Mechanisms in Plant Development, 1970; editor: Plant Hormones and Their Role in Plant Growth and Redevelopment, 1987, Plant Hormones: Physiology, Biochemistry and Molecular Biology, 1995, Plant Hormones: Biosynthesis Signal Transduction, Action!, 2004; editor-in-chief Plant Growth Regulation, 1987-92. Mem. Am. Soc. Plant Physiology, Internat. Plant Growth Substance Assn. (coun. 1991-98). Office: Cornell U Plant Biology Ithaca NY 14853 Office Phone: 607-255-8237. Business E-Mail: pjd2@cornell.edu.

DAVIES, RICHARD WARREN, lawyer; b. 1946; BA, Salem State Coll., 1967; MA, Purdue U., 1968; JD, Boston U., 1971. Bar: Mass. 1971, Conn. 1972. Law clk. Conn. Supreme Ct., 1971—72; assoc. Hirschberg, Pettengill, Strong & Nagle, 1972—74; asst. gen. counsel Hubbell, Inc., Orange, Conn., 1974—87, asst. sec., 1980—82, sec., 1982—, gen. counsel, 1987—, v.p., 1996—. Mem.: Am. Soc. Corp. Secretaries. Office: Hubbell Inc 584 Derby Milford Rd Orange CT 06477-4024 Office Phone: 203-799-4230. Office Fax: 203-799-4333.*

DAVIES, ROBERT ABEL, III, consumer products company executive; b. Englewood, NJ, Sept. 10, 1935; s. Robert Abel Jr. and Lillian Louise (Vila) D.; m. Marilyn Jean Doering, June 16, 1957 (div.); children: Bruce Gregory, Mark Richard, Eric Doering, Nancy Louise; m. Diane M. Church, Sept. 2, 1995, children; Alexander Church, Sophia Catherine. AB, Colgate U., 1957; MBA, Columbia U., 1963. Salesman Proctor & Gamble Co., Cin., 1960-61; product mgr. Colgate Palmolive Co., NYC, 1963-66; group product mgr. Boyle-Midway div. Am. Home Products, NYC, 1966-69; v.p., mktg. Church & Dwight Co., Inc., Princeton, NJ, 1969-76, v.p., gen. mgr., 1976-81, pres., chief oper. officer, 1981-84, bd. dir., 1981-84; pres., chief exec. officer Calif. Home Brands Inc., Terminal Island, Calif., 1985-89; prin. Gold Coast Calamari Inc., Oxnard, Calif., 1990-94; pres. Church & Dwight Co., Inc., Princeton, NJ, 1995-2001, CEO, 1990—2004, chmn., 2001—04, bd. dir., 1995—, non-exec. chmn., 2004—07. Served to lt. (j.g.) USNR, 1957-60. Office: Church & Dwight Co Inc 469 N Harrison St Princeton NJ 08543-5297

DAVIES, THOMAS MOCKETT, JR., history professor; b. Lincoln, Nebr., May 25, 1940; s. Thomas Mockett and Faith Elizabeth (Arnold) D.; m. Eloisa Carmela Monzón Abate, June 10, 1968 (dec. Jan. 1994); 1 dau., Jennifer Elena; m. Rosemarie Adele Lindsay, Jan. 7, 1995. BA, U. Nebr., 1962, MA, 1964; student, Universidad Nacional Autonóma de México, 1961; PhD, U. N.Mex., 1970; postdoctoral fellow, U. Tex., Austin, 1969-70. Lectr. U. N.Mex. Peace Corps Tng. Center, 1964-66; asst. prof. Latin Am. history San Diego State U., 1968-72, asso. prof., 1972-75, prof. Latin Am. history, 1975—2001, dir. Ctr. for Latin Am. Studies, 1979—2001, chmn. Latin Am. studies, 1979—2001, prof. dir. emeritus ctr. Latin Am. studies. Author: (with others) Historia, problema y promesa. Homenaje a Jorge Basadre, 1978, Research Guide to Andean History: Bolivia, Chile, Ecuador and Peru, 1981, The Spanish Civil War: American Hemisphere Perspectives, 1982, EL APRA de la Ideología a la Praxis, 1989, Latin American Military History: An Annotated Bibliography, 1992; author: Indian Integration in Peru: A Half Century of Experience, 1900-48, 1974 (co-winner Herbert Herring Meml. award Pacific Coast Coun. on Latin Am. Studies 1973), (with Victor Villaneuva) 300 Documentos Para la Historia del APRA; Conspiraciones Apristas de 1935 a 1939, 1979, Secretos Electorales del APRA: Correspondencia y Documentos de 1939, 1982; (with Brian Loveman) The Politics of Anti-Politics: The Military in Latin America, 1978, 3d rev. edit., 1997, Che Guevara: Guerrilla Warfare, 1985 (Hubert Herring Meml. award 1985, 3d rev. edit., 1997); mem. editorial bd. Hispanic Am. Hist. Rev., 1985-1990; Contbr. (with Brian Loveman) articles to profl. jours. Recipient Outstanding Faculty award San Diego State U. Alumni Assn., 1981, 97, 1st ann. Internat. Scholar award Phi Beta Delta, 1992, Wiley W. Manuel award Calif. State Bar Assn., 1995, 98; grantee Dept. Edn. for Nat. Resource Ctr. for L.Am. Studies, 1979-2001, San Diego State U. Found., 1971-73, 75, 76, 79, 80, San Diego State U., 1988, 89, 90, William and Flora Hewlett Found., 1997-2001; fellow Henry L. and Grace Doherty Charitable Found., 1966-68 Mem. Latin Am. Studies Assn., Conf. Latin Am. History (exec. sec. 1979-84), Pacific Coast Council Latin Am. (bd. govs. 1989-91, pres. 1996-97), Rocky Mountain Council on Latin Am. Studies (exec. com. 1980—2001, pres. 1996-97), Am. Hist. Assn., Consortium L.Am. Studies Programs (exec. sec.-treas. 1994-2001). Home: 7524 Maplewood Dr NW Albuquerque NM 87120-3923

DAVIES-VENN, CHRISTIAN, environmental engineer; b. Freetown, Sierra Leone, Apr. 24, 1952; came to U.S., 1982; s. Reynold Jonathan and Mary Arabella (Davies) Venn; m. Rebecca Princess Thomas, Apr. 26, 1980; children: Esther, Cynthia. B in Engring., U. Sierra Leone, 1976; MS, U. Cin., 1984; PhD, U. Ark., 1989. Registered profl. engr., Va., Md., DC, Mich.; bd. cert. Am. Acad. Environ. Engrs. Project engr. Techsult & Co. Engrs., Freetown, 1976-78, office mgr., 1978-82; rsch. assoc. U. Cin., 1984-87, U. Ark., Fayetteville, 1987-90; mgr. process devel. Parsons Engring. Sci., Inc., Fairfax, Va., 1990-94; sr. project mgr., process engring. program mgr., dir. water and wastewater svcs., v.p. PEER Cons., P.C., Rockville, Md., 1994—. Ptnr. Techsult & Co., Freetown, 1978-83; mem. nutrient removal com. Parsons Engring.-Sci., Inc., Pasadena, Calif., 1992-94; bd. dirs. Water and Wastewater Svcs. Contbr. articles to profl. jours. Chmn. stewardship com. Oakton (Va.) United Meth. Ch., 1992-94; mem. Gideons Internat.; chmn., bd. trustees Fairhaven United Meth. Ch.; active Gideons Internat. Nat. scholar Govt. Sierra Leone, 1972, merit scholar, Govt. Republic of Germany, 1972; African grad. fellow African-Am. Inst., N.Y.C., 1982-89; recipient 1st pl. student presentation Ark. Water Works & Poll Control, 1988. Mem.: NSPE, ASCE, Coun. Engring. Splty. Bds. (award and admission com., com. profl. engring. splty. cert.), Internat. Assn. Water Quality, Am. Acad. Environ. Engrs. (treas.), Am. Water Resources Assn., Am. Water Works Assn., Chesapeake Water Environment Assn., Fed. Water Quality Assn., Water Environment Fedn., Gideons Internat., Phi Kappa Phi, Chi Epsilon. Avocations: creative writing, classical music, computer programming, volleyball, soccer. Office: PEER Consultants PC 12300 Twinbrook Pkwy Ste 410 Rockville MD 20852-1650 Home Phone: 301-515-1475; Office Phone: 202-787-2759. Personal E-mail: daviesvennc@att.net. Business E-Mail: daviesc@peercpc.com.

D'AVIGNON, ROY JOSEPH, lawyer; b. Dallas, July 20, 1942; s. Roy J. and Ann (Ham) D'Avignon; m. Tania M. Mychajlyshyn, Nov. 29, 1969; children: Larissa A., Markian W. BSS, Loyola U., New Orleans, 1964; LLB, Harvard U., 1967. Bar: Tex. 1967, Mass. 1969. Assoc. Hutchins & Wheeler, Boston, 1969-77; counsel Raytheon Co., Lexington, Mass., 1977-86, div. counsel, 1986-90, asst. gen. counsel, 1990-99; v.p., sect. and gen. counsel Simplex Time Recorder Co., Gardner, Mass., 1999—2001; sole practitioner, 2001—. Capt. M.I. US Army, 1967—69. Mem.: Boston Bar Assn., Tex. Bar Assn., Mass. Bar Assn., APA.

DAVILA, ROBERT R., academic administrator; b. July 1932; m. Donna Davila; 2 children. BA, Gallaudet U., 1953; M in Spl. Edn., Hunter Coll., 1963; PhD in Ednl. Tech., Syracuse U., 1972. Faculty mem. Dept. Edn. Gallaudet U., Washington, dir. Kendall Sch., dean Model Secondary Sch. for Deaf, v.p. Pre-College Programs, pres., 2007—; asst. sec. Office of Spl. Edn. and Rehabilitative Svcs. US Dept. Edn., Washington, 1989—93; headmaster NY Sch. for Deaf, White Plains, 1993—96, chmn. bd. dirs., 2001; v.p. National Tech. Inst. for Deaf, Rochester Inst. of Tech., 1996—2004; chair Studies in Tech. and the Adult Learner Nat. U., La Jolla, Calif. Former pres. Coun. on Edn. of Deaf; mem. Nat. Coun. on Disability. Mem.: Convention of Am. Instructors of Deaf (former pres.). Office: Office of Pres Gallaudet U 800 Florida Ave, NE Washington DC 20002 Office Phone: 202-651-5005.*

DAVIS, AARON W., lawyer; b. Waterloo, Iowa, Oct. 10, 1973; BA, Minn. State U., 1997; JD, William Mitchell Coll. Law, 2001. Bar: Minn. 2002, US Dist. Ct. (dist. Minn.) 2002, US Dist. Ct. (we. dist. Wis.) 2002, US Dist. Ct. (dist. Colo.) 2002, US Ct. Appeals (Fed. cir.), US Ct. Appeals (5th, 7th and 8th cirs.). Assoc. Patterson, Thuente, Skaar & Christensen, P.A., Mpls. Named a Rising Star, Minn. Super Lawyers mag., 2006. Mem.: Minn. Intellectual Property Law Assn., Am. Intellectual Property Law Assn., ABA (mem. forum on the entertainment and sports industries, mem. intellectual property law sect.), Minn. State Bar Assn. (chair entertainment & sports sect.), Hennepin County Bar Assn., Minn. Music Acad. (treas.). Office: Patterson Thuente Skaar & Christensen PA 4800 IDS Ctr 80 S 8th St Minneapolis MN 55402 Office Phone: 612-349-5754. E-mail: davis@ptslaw.com.*

DAVIS, ADDIE L., mathematics educator; d. Joe Smith and Margieree Crosby; m. Clarence L. Davis, June 27, 1970; children: Raymond DeJoe Smith, Maurice Lamar. BSBA, Roosvelt U., Chgo., 1975; MA, Chgo. State U., 1979; ABD, Capella U., 2003. Assoc. prof. Olive-Harvey Coll., Chgo., 1983—. Sr. faculty advisor Phi Theta Kappa Olive-Harvey Coll., 2002—. Women's dept. chair Little Mountain Hope, Chgo., 2005—. Recipient Woman of Yr., Assn. Women in Cmty. Colleges-Local, 2003—04, Dist. Prof., Olive-Harvey Coll., 2003—04, Dist. Adv. Paragon award, Phi Theta Kappa, 2005. Mem.: Am. Assn. Math. (assoc.). Democrat-Npl. Avocations: reading, travel, swimming, singing. Office: Olive-Harvey Coll 10001 S Woodlawn Ave Chicago IL 60628 Home Phone: 773-846-2698; Office Phone: 773-291-6428. Office Fax: 773-291-6304. Business E-Mail: addavis@ccc.edu.

DAVIS, ALAN JAY, lawyer; b. Phila., Feb. 4, 1937; s. Rudolph Alan and Adele (Saver) Davis; m. Roslyn Kutcher; children: Jennifer C., Michael R. BA, U. Pa., 1957; JSD, Harvard U., 1960. Bar: Pa. 1961, US Dist. Ct. (ea. dist.) Pa. 1961, US Ct. Appeals (3d cir.) 1961, US Supreme Ct. 1979. Law clk. to chief judge US Ct. Appeals (3d cir.), Phila., 1960-61; assoc. Wolf, Block, Schorr & Solis-Cohen, Phila., 1961-66, ptnr., 1968-91, chmn. litig. dept., 1987-91; chief asst. dist. atty. Office Dist. Atty., Phila., 1966-68; sr. litig. ptnr. Ballard Spahr Andrews & Ingersoll, Phila., from 1991. Spl. master to investigate prison sys. and sheriff's dept. Ct. Common Pleas, Phila., 1968—70; lectr. law U. Pa. Sch. Law, Phila., 1973—77; city solicitor City of Phila., 1980—82, chief labor negotiator, 1991—93, Southeastern Pa. Transp. Authority, Phila., 1982, Sch. Dist. Phila., 1984, 96. Chmn. met. adv. bd. Anti-Defamation League B'nai B'rith, Phila., 1986—88; mem. sch. com. Germantown Friends Sch., Phila., 1986—88; trustee Free Libr. Phila., 1995—98; mem. bd. trustees The Pew Charitable Trusts, 2004—07; chmn. Third Cir. Lawyers Adv. Com., 2007; pres. U. Pa. Law Sch. Am. Inns of Ct., 1998—2000. Fellow: Internat. Acad. Trial Lawyers, Am. Coll. Trial Lawyers; mem.: ABA, Am. Law Inst., Phila. Bar Assn., Pa. Bar Assn., Jr. Legal Club, Legal Club. Home: Philadelphia, Pa. Died May 9, 2007.

DAVIS, ALLEN, professional football team executive; b. Brockton, Mass., July 4, 1929; s. Louis and Rose Davis; m. Carol Segall, July 11, 1954; 1 child, Mark. Student, Wittenberg Coll., 1947; AB, Syracuse U., 1950. Asst. football coach Adelphi Coll., 1950—51; head football coach Ft. Belvoir, Va., 1952—53; player-personnel scout Baltimore Colts, 1954; line coach The Citadel, 1955—56, U. So. Calif., 1957—59; asst. coach San Diego Chargers, 1960—62; gen. mgr., head coach Oakland Raiders, 1963—66, owner, mng. gen. ptnr., 1966—82, LA Raiders, 1982—95; now pres., gen. ptnr. Oakland Raiders, 1995—. Former mem. mgmt. council and competition com. NFL. With AUS, 1952—53. Named Profl. Coach of Year, AP, UPI, Sporting News, Pro-Football Illustrated, 1963, Young Man of Yr., Oakland, 1963, only individual in history to be an asst. coach, head coach, gen. mgr., league commr. and owner; named to Pro Football Hall of Fame, 1992. Mem.: Am. Football Coaches Assn. Office: Oakland Raiders 1220 Harbor Bay Pkwy Alameda CA 94502-6570

DAVIS, ALLEN FREEMAN, history professor, writer; b. Hardwick, Vt., Jan. 9, 1931; s. Harold Freeman and Bernice Susan (Allen) D.; m. Roberta Hazel Green, June 16, 1956 (div.); children: Gregory Freeman, Paul Studley. AB, Dartmouth Coll., 1953; MA, U. Rochester, 1954; PhD, U. Wis., 1959. Instr. history Wayne State U., Detroit, 1959—60; asst. prof. history U. Mo., Columbia, 1960—63, assoc. prof., 1963—68; prof. Temple U., Phila., 1968—99, prof. emeritus, 1999—. Vis. prof. U. Tex., Austin, 1983, U. Amsterdam, 1986-87, John Adams chair. Co-author: March of American Democracy, Vol. V, 1966, Spearheads for Reform, 1967, 84, American Heroine, 1973, 2000, Postcards From Vermont, 2002; (with others) The American People, 1986, 7th edit., 2006; (with Jim Watts) Generations, 1974, 3d edit., 1983; (with Fredric Miller and Morris Vogel) Still Philadelphia, 1983, Philadelphia Stories, 1988; editor: (with Harold D. Woodman) Conflict and Consensus in American History, 1966, 9th edit., 1997; (with Mary Lynn McCree) Eighty Years at Hull House, 1969; (with Mark Haller) The Peoples of Philadelphia, 1973, 2d edit., 1998, Jane Addams on Peace, War and International Understanding, 1974, For Better or Worse, 1980; (with Mary Lynn Bryan) 100 Years at Hull House, 1990, Series in American Civilization, 1978-2000; contbr. articles to profl. jours. Served with AUS, 1954-56. Recipient Friends of Lit. award, 1970, Christopher award, 1974; Danforth Grad. fellow, 1953-59, Am. Council Learned Socs. sr. fellow, 1971-72, NEH fellow, 1975-76, Fulbright fellow, 1986-87; Am. Philos. Soc. grantee, 1962, 65. Mem. Am. Hist. Assn., Orgn. Am. Historians, Am. Studies Assn. (treas. 1971-72, exec. sec. 1972-77, pres. 1989-90, Bode-Pearson award 1996), Soc. Am. Historians. Home: 2032 Waverly St Philadelphia PA 19146-1343 E-mail: davisafd@aol.com.

DAVIS, ANDREW NEIL, lawyer, educator; b. Boston, Nov. 7, 1959; s. Gerald Stanley and Sarah Lee D.; m. Suzanne Frances DiBenedetto, Oct. 11, 1992; children: David R. Bray, Hannah M., Zachary G. BS in Biology, Trinity Coll., 1981; MS in Botany, U. Mass., 1983, PhD in Botany, 1987; JD, George Washington U., 1990. Bar: Conn. 1990, U.S. Dist. Ct. Conn. 1991, Mass. 1998. Atty. Pepe & Hazard, Hartford, Conn., 1990-93, Brown, Rudnick, Freed & Gesmer, Hartford, 1993-94; ptnr. LeBoeuf, Lamb, Greene & MacRae LLP, Hartford, 1994—. Adj. prof. environ. studies Conn. Coll., 1994—. Sr. author/co-author: The Home Environmental Sourcebook, 1996, ISO 14001: Meeting Business Goals Through An Effective Environmental Management System, 1998; contbr. articles to profl. jours. Mem. Leadership Greater Hartford, 1997; chmn. lake adv. commn. Town Marlborough, 1992-2006, zoning commn., 1993-95. Recipient Hon. Sci. award Bausch & Lomb, 1977; Albert L. Deslisle Botany fellow, 1982. Mem. Am. Arbitration Assn. (environ. adv. com. 1993-95), Conn. Bar Assn. (exec. com. environ. law sect. 1996-2000), Conn. Bus. and Industry Assn. (environ. policies coun. 1991-). Avocations: photography, sailing, scuba diving, travel, reading. Office: LeBoeuf Lamb Greene & MacRae LLP 225 Asylum St Fl 13 Hartford CT 06103-1529 Office Phone: 860-293-3514. E-mail: adavis@llgm.com.

DAVIS, ANGELA YVONNE, political activist, educator, writer; b. Birmingham, Ala., Jan. 26, 1944; D.B. Frank and Sally E. Davis. Studied under Theodor Adorno, Frankfurt Sch., 1960-62; student, U. Paris, 1963-64; BA magna cum laude, Brandeis U., 1965; MA, U. Calif., San Diego, 1968. Mem. faculty San Francisco State U.; tchr. U. Calif., San Diego, 1968; asst. prof. philosophy UCLA, 1969; prof. history of consciousness dept. U. Calif., Santa Cruz, 1991—, presdl. chair in African American and feminist studies, 1995-97. Adv. bd. Prison Activist Resource Ctr., spkr. in field. Removed from teaching position in philosophy dept., UCLA, 1969. On FBI's 10 Most Wanted List, 1970. Captured, tried and acquitted, 1972. Gov. Ronald Reagan vowed she would never teach in Univ. Calif. sys. Candidate for US v.p., Communist Party ticket, 1980. Author: If They Come in the Morning: Voices of Resistance, 1971, Angela Davis: An Autobiography, Women, Race, and Class, 1981, Women, Culture, and Politics, 1989, Violence Against Women and the Ongoing Challenge to Racism, 1992, Resisting State Violence: Radicalism, Gender, and Race in US Culture, 1996, The Angela Y. Davis Reader, 1998, The House That Race Built, 1998, Blues Legacies and Black Feminism: Gertrude "Ma" Rainey, Bessie Smith, and Billie Holiday, 1998, Are Prisons Obsolete?, 2003. Mem. Black Panthers. Mem. Communist Party. Office: History of Consciousness Dept UC Santa Cruz 1156 High St Santa Cruz CA 95064 Office Phone: 831-459-0111.

DAVIS, ANNA JANE RIPLEY, elementary school educator; b. Uhrichsville, Ohio, Sept. 7, 1931; d. Emmet Frank and Lillie Hazel (Kinsey) Ripley; m. H. Joe Davis, Mar. 16, 1951; children: Alan Joe, Kendal Jay. A, Asbury Coll., 1953; BS with honors, Kent State U., 1962, MEd with honors, 1978, postgrad., 1980—96; student, Richmond Coll., London U., St. Andrews U., Dundee U., Cambridge U., U. Paris, U. Rome, U. Amsterdam, Ohio U. Cert. elem. tchr., Ohio. Tchr. Kenston Schs., Chagrin Falls, Ohio, 1953-55, 58-62, Firestone Rubber Plantation, Harbel, Liberia, West Africa, 1962-64, Newbury (Ohio) Schs., 1964-65, Orange Schs., Pepper Pike, Ohio, 1965-99. Chaperone, counselor Am. Inst. for Fgn. Study, British Isles and Europe, summers 1968-81. Author children's books. Active Kenston PTA, Chagrin Falls and Pepper Pike PTA, Am. Field Svc., Chagrin Falls, Geauga County Personal Growth Com. for workshops; bd. dirs. Friends Geauga County Pub. Libr.; bookmobile project vol. traveling libr. Geauga County Pub. Libr. for Amish Schs., traveling libr., 1994—; elem. sch. tutor, 1998—; vol. ARC, 1955—. Food Pantry and Clothing for Needy, Kiwanis, bookmobile projects Geauga County Pub. Lib. Friends; mem. edn. com., libr., home care, Care Bears com., Prayer Chain, Sunday sch. com., Sunday Sch., membership com., libr. com. Pepper Pike Garfield Meml. United Meth. Ch. Mem. NEA (life), ASCD, Ohio Edn. Assn., N.E. Ohio Tchrs. Assn., Orange Tchrs. Assn. Avocations: travel, bicycling, hiking, reading, writing.

DAVIS, ANTONIO LEE, professional basketball player; b. Oct. 31, 1968; m. Kendra Davis; 2 children. Degree in computer sci., U. Tex., El Paso. Profl. basketball player Ind. Pacers, 1993—99, Toronto Baptors, 1999—2003, Chgo. Bulls, 2003—05, NY Knicks, 2005—06, Toronto Raptors, 2006—. Players pres. NBA Players Union, 2005—; basketball player Team USA World Basketball Championship, 2002. Contbr. to various charities. Mem.: Oakland Area Profl. Athletes. Office: Air Canada Ctr 40 Bay St Toronto ON M5J 2X2 Canada

DAVIS, AQUILLA, diversified financial services company executive; d. Mallie Harmon Woodberry and Rosa Lee Davis; children: Meshelliah Davis Hayward, Genonyus Damorris, Jawanda Lecress. BSc, Benedict Coll., 1973—77; MA, Webster U., 2001—05. Data entry operator Champus BC/BS, Florence, SC, 1989—92; asst. mgr. J.L. Income Tax & Gen. Acctg. Svc, Georgetown, SC, 1993—2005. County office clk. Farmers Home Adminstrn., Kingstree, SC, 1979—86; owner Davis Tax & Poetry Svc, Johnsonville, SC, 2002—05. Author: (poem writer) Inspire Poems of Love, Joy and Peace (Editors award, 2003). Asst. vp dir. Young People Dept., Johnsonville, SC, 1997—2005. Scholar, Minority Access, Inc, 2005. Ame. Avocations: reading, singing, travel. Home: 718 Poston Rd Johnsonville SC 29555 Home Phone: 843-386-3973; Office Phone: 843-386-3973. Personal E-mail: aquilladavis2003@yahoo.com.

DAVIS, ARTUR, congressman, lawyer; b. Montgomery, Ala., Apr. 9, 1967; BA in Govt. cum laude, Harvard U., 1990, JD cum laude, 1993. Intern So. Poverty Law Ctr.; law clk. U.S. Dist. Ct. Judge, 1993—94; asst. U.S. atty. Mid. Dist., Ala., 1994—98; pvt. practice Birmingham, Ala., 1998—2002; mem. U.S. Congress from 7th Dist., Ala., 2003—. Mem. budget com. fin. svc. com. U.S. Congress 7th Dist. Ala. Recipient Most Influential Black Americans, Ebony mag., 2006; scholar, Harvard U. Democrat. Office: US Ho Reps 208 Cannon Ho Office Bldg Washington DC 20515-0107 also: Dist Office 2 20th St N Ste 1130 Birmingham AL 35203 Office Phone: 202-225-2665. Office Fax: 202-226-9567.*

DAVIS, BARBARA SNELL, education educator; b. Painesville, Ohio, Feb. 21, 1929; d. Roy Addison and Mabelle Irene (Denning) Snell; children: Beth Ann Davis Schnorf, James Lee, Polly Denning Davis Spaeth. BS, Kent State U., 1951; MA, Lake Erie Coll., 1981; postgrad., Cleve. State U., 1982-83. Cert. reading specialist, elem. prin., Ohio. Dir. publicity Lake Erie Coll., Painesville, 1954-59; tchr. Mentor (Ohio) Exempted Village Sch. Dist., 1972-86, prin., 1986-97; prof., supr. Lake Erie Coll., 1997—. Author: Who Says You Can't Change the World?, 2005; contbr. articles to profl. jours. Former trustee Mentor United Meth. Ch. Mem. Delta Kappa Gamma (pres. 1982-84), Phi Delta Kappa (pres. 1992-93), Theta Sigma Phi (charter). Home: 7293 Beechwood Dr Mentor OH 44060-6305 Office: 326 College Hall Lake Erie Coll Painesville OH 44077

DAVIS, BARON, professional basketball player; b. Apr. 13, 1979; Attended, UCLA. Basketball player Charlotte Hornets (later New Orleans Hornets), 1999—2005, Golden State Warriors, 2005—. Named to NBA All-Star Team, 2004; recipient Skills-challenge award, NBA, 2004. Achievements include holding rookie franchise record for assists in a season, Charlotte Hornets (now New Orleans Hornets). Office: Golden State Warriors 1011 Broadway Oakland CA 94607

DAVIS, BARRY E., energy executive; BA finance, Texas Christian U. V.p., marketing & development Endevco, Inc.; founder Ventana Natural Gas Company (now Crosstex Engergy), 1992; pres., CEO Comstock Natural Gas, Inc., Crosstex Energy, 1996—. Office: c/o Crosstex 2501 Cedar Springs Rd Dallas TX 75201*

DAVIS, BENJAMIN ALANDO, lawyer; s. Carolyn Davis; m. Aysha Khan, July 13, 2004; 1 child, Benjamin Sikander. AS, U. Md., 1991; BS, Columbus U., 1993; JD, U. Ga., 1996. Bar: Ga. 1996. Assoc. Scott, Quarterman and Wells, Athens, Ga., 1995—96; prin. Davis Law Firm, P.C., Atlanta, 1997—. Law clk. to Hon. Steve Jones, Athens, 1994—96. Judge Nat. H.S. Mock Trial, Atlanta, 1996—2004. Cpl. US Army, 1987—91. Scholar, U. Ga. Sch. Law, 1991. Mem.: Ga. Assn. Criminal Def. Lawyers (assoc.). Office: Davis Law Firm PC Ste 200 1201 Peachtree St Atlanta GA 30361 Office Phone: 404-233-0120. Business E-Mail: davislawfirm@msn.com.

DAVIS, BENJAMIN GEORGE, theologian, educator; b. Honesdale, Pa., July 6, 1941; s. Benjamin George and Laura Teneyck (Swingle) D.; m. Janet Marie Gorden, June 21, 1980; children: Leslie Anne, John Nathan. AB, U. Mich., 1967, AM, 1969; MTh, U. Nottingham, England, 1982; DMin, St. Mary's Sem. and Univ., Balt., 1985; MBA, North Ctrl. U., 2004, PhD, 2005; MS, Am. Milt. U., 2007. Draftsman, designer Munson Mill Machinery Co., Utica, N.Y., 1961-62; design engr. Gen. Motors Corp., Warren, Mich., 1963-66; devel. coord. City of Ann Arbor, Mich., 1967; research economist Exec. Office of the Pres., Washington, 1970; sr. assoc. RMC Research Corp., Bethesda, Md., 1971-75; dir. Research Svcs., Inc., Clinton, Md., 1975-80; regional dir. World Relief, Landover, Md., 1981-86; dir. Evangelicals for Social Action, Washington, 1987-89; pastor St. John United Ch., Columbia, Md., 1989-90; prof. St. Mary's Sem. and U., Balt., 1986—; assoc. dean Balt. Internat. Coll., 1988-95. Exec. dir. The Religious Coalition, Frederick, Md., 1995-98; dean, campus dir. Potomac Coll., Washington, 1998-03; dir. acad. affairs U. Phoenix, Columbia, Md., 2003-06; provost Stratford U., Falls Ch., Va., 2006; pres. U. Coll. of U. Northern Va., 2007-. Author: A Modern Interpretation of Revelation, 1982, Understanding World Cultures: The United States and Canada, 1990, 2d edit., 2000, Economics: An Integrated Approach, 1997; editor: The Dictionary of Essential English, 1987. Pres. Fgn.-born Info. and Referral Network, Columbia, 1986-92; chmn. Coalition for Refugee Resettlement, Washington, 1985-86; chairperson Md. Refugee Adv. Coun., Balt., 1985-86. Recipient Gov.'s Citation State of Md., 1985, 86; NDEA fellow in economics U. Md., 1969-71, Rickard's fellow in theology U. Nottingham, 1980-81. Mem. Assn. for Psychol. Type, Assn. Overseas Educators, Mensa, Omicron Delta Epsilon. Avocations: jazz, photography, motorcycling. Home: 6580 Madrigal Ter Columbia MD 21045-4628 Office Phone: 703-392-0771. Business E-Mail: bdavis.admin@unva.edu. *The search for certainty in life leads only up blind alleys. Accept the ambiguity and moving forward in faith is all.*

DAVIS, BETTY BOURBONIA, real estate company executive; b. Ft. Bayard, N.Mex., Mar. 12, 1931; d. John Alexander and Ora M. (Caudill) Bourbonia; children: Janice Cox Anderson, Elizabeth Ora Cox. BS in Elem. Edn., U. N.Mex., 1954. Gen. ptnr. BJD Realty Co., Albuquerque, 1977—. Mem. Friends of Little Theatre, 1973—85, Friends of Art, 1978—85, Mus. N.Mex Found.; bd. dirs. Albuquerque Opera Build, 1977—79, 1981—83, 1985—87, membership co-chair, 1977—78; mem. Hodgin Hall preservation com. U. N.Mex. Recipient Matrix award for Journalism, Jr. League. Mem.: N.Mex Hist. Soc., Albuquerque Guild Santa Fe Opera, Mt. Vernon Ladies Assn., Alumni Assn. N.Mex, Internat. Platform Assn., Order Rainbow Girls (mem. state exec. com. N.Mex Order 1986—2002, chair pub. rels. com., co-chair gen. arrangemtns com. 1990—97, mem. grand exec. com., past grand worthy advisor N.Mex, past mother advisor Friendship Assembly 50), Jr. League Albuquerque (sustainer), Albuquerque Mus. Assn., N.Mex Symphony Guild, Las Amapolis Club, Tanoan Country Club, Albuquerque Knife and Fork Club, Order Eastern Star, Alpha Chi Omega (chpt. advisor bdlg. corp. 1962—77). Republican. Methodist. Home: 9505 Augusta Ave NE Albuquerque NM 87111-5820

DAVIS, BETTYE JEAN, school system administrator, state legislator; b. Homer, La., May 17, 1938; d. Dan and Rosylind (Daniel) Ivory; m. Troy J. Davis, Jan. 21, 1959; children: Anthony Benard, Sonja Davis Wade. Cert. nursing, St. Anthony's, 1961; BSW, Grambling State U., 1971; postgrad., U. Alaska, 1972. Psychiat. nurse Alaska Psychiat. Inst., 1967-70; asst. dir. San Bernardino (Calif.) YWCA, 1971-72; child care specialist DFYS Anchorage, 1975-80, soc. worker, 1980-82, foster care coordinator, 1982-87; dir. Alaska Black Leadership Edn. Program, 1979-82; exec. dir. Anchorage Sch. Bd., 1982-89; mem. Alaska Legislature, 1990—2000, Alaska Senate, 2000—. Chair Children's Caucus Alaska Legis., 1992—. Pres. Anchorage Sch. Bd., 1986-87; bd. dirs. Blacks in Govt., 1980-82, March of Dimes, 1983-85, Anchorage chpt. YWCA, 1989-90, Winning with Stronger Edn. Com., 1991, Alaska 2000, Anchorage Ctr. for Families, 1992—, active Anchorage chpt. NAACP, bd. dirs., 1978-82; mem. State Bd. Edn., 1997-2000. Toll fellow Henry Toll Fellowship Program, 1992; named Woman of Yr., Alaska Colored Women's Club, 1981, Child Care Worker of Yr., Alaska Foster Parent Assn., 1983, Social Worker of Yr., Nat. Foster Parents Assn., 1983, Outstanding Bd. Mem, Assn. Alaska Sch. Bds., 1990,; recipient Outstanding Achievement in Edn. award Alaska Colored Women's Club, 1985, Outstanding Women in Edn. award Zeta Phi Beta, 1985, Boardsmanship award Assn. Alaska Sch. Bds., 1989, Woman of Achievement award YWCA, 1991, Outstanding Leadership award Calif. Assembly, 1992. Mem. LWV, Nat. Sch. Bd. Assn., Nat. Caucus of Black Sch. Bd. Mems. (bd. dirs. 1986-87), Alaska Black Caucus (chair 1984—), Alaska Women's Polit. Caucus, Alaska Black Leadership Conf. (pres. 1976-80), Alaska Women Lobby (treas.), Nat. Caucus of Black State Legis. (chair region 12, 1994—), Women Legislators Lobby, Women's Action for New Directions, North to Future Bus. and Prof. Women (pres. 1978-79, 83), Delta Sigma Theta (Alaska chpt. pres. 1978-80). Clubs: North to Future Bus. and Profl. Women (past pres.). Democrat. Baptist. Avocations: cooking, Scrabble, stamp collecting/philately, coin collecting/numismatics, reading. Home: 2240 Foxhall Dr Anchorage AK 99504-3350 E-mail: bdavis@ak.net.

DAVIS, BEVERLY WATTS, federal agency administrator; b. Cincinnati; BS in economics, polit. sci., and social sciences, Trinity U., San Antonio; postgrad. in mgmt. and human resources, Webster U., Jeffersonville, Ind. Statewide coord. Texans' War on Drugs, 1988; cons., then dir. cmty. health Travis County Tex. Health Dept.; exec. dir. San Antonio Fighting Back Anti-Drug Cmty. Coalition; sr. v.p. United Way of San Antonio and Bexar County; dir. Ctr. for Substance Abuse Prevention, Substance Abuse and Mental Health Svcs. Adminstrn., Rockville, Md., 2003—. Mem. Minority-and Women-Owned Bus. Commn. Named Vol. of the Yr., U.S. Atty. Gen., 1997, Advocate of the Yr., Palmer Drug Abuse Program, Yellow Rose of Tex., Gov. of Tex., Outstanding Minority Bus. Owner, Greater Austin C. of C., 1985; named to San Antonio Women's Hall of Fame, 1998; recipient Dir.'s Award for Cmty. Leadership, FBI, Commendation Award, US Dept. Justice, Comdr.'s Award for Outstanding Leadership, Dept. Def., Vol. Award, Gov. Tex., Award for Neighborhood Action, Tex. Atty. Gen.'s Office, Outstanding Citizen Advocate Award, Nat. Crime Prevention Coun. Office: Substance Abuse and Mental Health Svc Adminstrn Rm 4-1057 1 Choke Cherry Rd Rockville MD 20857 Office Phone: 240-276-2420.

DAVIS, BILLIE JOHNSTON, school counselor; b. Charleston, W.Va., Sept. 24, 1933; d. William Andrew Jr. and Garnet Macil (Johnston) D. BS, Morris Harvey Coll., 1954; MA, W.Va. U., 1959. Nat. bd. cert. counselor; W.Va. lic. profl. counselor. Tchr. math. Kanawha County Schs., Charleston, 1954-59, counselor, 1959-98. Pub. edn. study commn. W.Va. Legislature, 1980. Mem. W.Va. Commn. on Juvenile Law, 1982-97; bd. dirs. W.Va. Com. for Prevention Child Abuse, W.Va. Sch. Health Adv. Com.; apptd. W.Va. rep. at Tchr.'s Inaugural Experience for Inauguration of Pres. George Bush by Gov. of W.Va., 1989; mem. subcom. W.Va. Health Care Task Force, 1992; trustee W.Va. Youth Advocate Program, 1993-95, Nat. Youth Adv. Program, 1994-95; oversite com. W.Va. Juvenile Predisposition Plan, 1993-97; adv. bd. James H. Morton Juvenile Ctr., 2005— Mem. adv. bd. W.Va. Divsn. Juvenile Svcs., 2001—, James H. Tiger Morton Juvenile Detention Ctr., 2005— Recipient Anne Maynard award W.Va. Sch. Counselor Assn., 1986; named Am. mid./jr. high Sch. Counselor of Yr. Am. Sch. Counselors Assn., 1987, Citizen of Yr., Dunbar Lions Club, 1987. Mem. Am. Assn. Counseling and Devel. (Spl. Recognition award 1991), W.Va. Assn. Counseling and Devel. (pres. 1964-66, legis. chmn. 1974-98, spl. award legis. svcs. 1981), W.Va. Edn. Assn. (past legis. chmn.), Kanawha County Sch. Counselors Assn. (pres., legis. chmn. 1974-98), W.Va. Sch. Counselors Assn. (chmn. gov. rels., parliamentarian), Alpha Delta Kappa (past chpt. pres.), Phi Delta Kappa. Democrat. Baptist. Home: Charleston, W.Va. Died June 2007.

DAVIS, BLONDELL GILLIAM, business manager, evangelist, artist, author, poet; b. Ft. Pierce, Fla., Dec. 21, 1942; d. Fred Douglas and Mary Louise Gilliam; m. Levoid Davis, July 15, 1962; 1 child, Sherry Yvonne AA, Lincoln Jr. Coll., 1962. Ordained to ministry Apostolic (Holiness) House of Prayer. State evangelist House of Prayer, Tampa, Fla., 1980—, mgr. bakery, 1987—, gen. evangelist, 2006—07, promotions, gen. mother, 2007—. Author: Miracles on the Mind, 1993, Miracles Never Cease; editor Ho. of Prayer Gospel Press. Avocations: writing, cooking, drawing, painting, sewing. Home: 3210 E Lambright St Tampa FL 33610-3609 Office: The House of Prayer 3006 E Ellicott St Tampa FL 33610-2136 Office Phone: 813-238-5221.

DAVIS, BONNIE CHRISTELL, judge; b. Petersburg, Va., July 13, 1949; d. Robert Madison and Margaret Elizabeth (Collier) Davis. BA, Longwood Coll., Farmville, Va., 1971; JD, U. Richmond, 1980. Bar: Va. 1980, US Dist. Ct. (ea. dist.) Va. 1980, US Ct. Appeals (4th cir.) 1982. Tchr. Chesterfield County Schs., Chesterfield, Va., 1971-77; pvt. practice Chesterfield, 1980-83; asst. commonwealth atty. Chesterfield County, 1983-93; judge Juvenile and Domestic Rels. Ct. for 12th Jud. Dist. Va., 1993—. Adviser Youth Svcs. Commn., Chesterfield, 1983-93; cons. Task Force on Child Abuse, 1983-93, Met. Richmond Multi-Discipline Team on Spouse Abuse, 1983-93, Va. Dept. of Children for handbook Step by Step Through the Juvenile Justice System in Virginia, 1988; nat. adv. com. for prodn. on missing and runaway children Theatre IV; adv. group to set stds. and tng. for Guardians Ad Litem, Supreme Ct. Va., 1994; chmn. jud. adminstrn. com. Jud. Conf. Va. for Dist. Cts., 1995-97, 2001-03; state adv. com. for CASA and children's Justice Act, 1998-2002. Co-author: Juvenile Law and Practice in Virginia, 1994. Task force on core values Chesterfield County Pub. Schs., 1999. Mem.: Chesterfield-Colonial Heights Bar Assn., Met. Richmond Women's Bar Assn., Va. Trial Lawyers Assn., Va. Bar Assn., Va. State Bar (bd. govs. family law sect. 1997—2001, bd. govs. sr. lawyers conf. 2005—, bd. govs. gen. practice sect. 2005—), State-Fed. Jud. Coun. Va. Home: 415 Lyons Ave Colonial Heights VA 23834-3154 Office: Chesterfield Juvenile and Domestic Rels Dist Ct 7000 Lucy Corr Blvd Chesterfield VA 23832-6717 Office Phone: 804-751-4115.

DAVIS, BRANTLEY PIERCE, physician, researcher; b. June 29, 1925; s. Frank Pierce Cleveland and Mary Hamilton Keen Davis; m. Frances Marie Stirrett, June 26, 1954; children: Paula Leigh Misner, Loren Brantley, Natalie Ann Jones. AA, Lower Columbia Coll., Longview, Wash., 1947; BS, U. Wash., Seattle, 1949, MD (hon.), 1953. Pvt. practice, Bellingham, Wash., 1955—77; plant physician Arco Refinery, Ferndale, Wash., 1976—82. County jail physician Whatcom County, Bellingham, 1957—67; plant physician Intalco Aluminum Co., Ferndale, 1967—86; staff physician We. Wash. U., Bellingham, 1968—69; v.p., med. dir. Whatcom Physicians Svc., Bellingham, 1971—93; chief of staff St. Luke's Hosp., Bellingham, 1966. Sgt. US Army, 1943—46, ETO. Mem.: AMA, Am. Coll. Occup. and Environ. Medicine, Am. Acad. Family Physicians, Wash. State Med. Assn., Whatcom County Med. Soc. (pres. 1969), Phi Theta Kappa, Phi Chi, Pi Kappa Alpha (v.p. 1949). Protestant. Home: 501 Park Ridge Rd Bellingham WA 98225-7914

DAVIS, BRIAN KEITH, biophysicist, researcher; b. Sydney, Australia, May 15, 1937; arrived in US, 1962, naturalized, 1981; s. Ruby Constance Davis; m. Nelida Villanueva, Aug. 3, 1963; 1 child, Simon. BSc, U. NSW, Sydney, 1957, PhD, 1961, DSc, 1982. Tchg. fellow U. NSW, 1958—61; Ford Found. fellow Worcester Found. for Exptl. Biology, Shrewsbury, Mass., 1962—63; rsch. fellow Harvard U., Cambridge, Mass., 1963—65, McGill U., Montreal, Que., 1966—68; sci. officer Med. Rsch. Coun. Lab. Molecular Biology, Cambridge, England, 1965—66; scientist Worcester Found. Exptl. Biology, Shrewsbury, Mass., 1970—78; rsch. prof. SUNY, Stony Brook, 1978—82; exec. dir. Rsch. Found. So. Calif., La Jolla, 1983—. Warden Basser Coll., Sydney, 1961; chmn. Gregory Pincus Meml. Com., Shrewsbury, Mass., 1976; acting divsn. dir. LI Rsch. Inst., Stony Brook, NY, 1979—81. Contbr. over 100 papers to profl. jours. and pubs. Vol. sci. tchr. Primary schools, Shrewsbury, Mass., 1974—77; mem. Rsch. Found. for Mental Hygiene, NY, 1979—81. With Australian Army, 1954—57. Recipient Publ. Fund award, U. NSW, 1961; fellow Reproductive Physiology, Ford Found., 1962; grantee, NIH, 1973—83, U.S. State Dept., AID, 1974. Mem.: AAAS, NY Acad. Sci., Am. Chem. Soc. Achievements include initiating the use of hydrogel implants for administration of insulin and other substances; demonstration of Fisher's fundamental theorem on how natural selection applies to competitive RNA replication during exponential growth; relating Curie's principle to complexity transmission; research in devised ribosome-triplet tRNA binding assay to establish codon assignments; proposed generalized entropy measure of physical complexity; devised immunochemical procedure to isolate specific messenger RNA from polysomes; formulated rapid-reading principle in template directed polymerization; identified membrane vesicle inhibitor (decapacitation factor) of mammalian spermatozoa fertilizing capacity; proposed membrane-cholesterol depletion as mechanism of mammalian spermatozoa capacitation; theory depicting molecular evolution as a damping response to scalar forces capable of generating Non-Darwinian attractors; proposed model of genetic code evolution equating temporal order of amino acid entry into code with synthesis path length. Avocations: tennis, reading philosophy and biographies. Office: Rsch Found So Calif PO Box 13595 La Jolla CA 92039 Business E-Mail: davis@resfdnsca.org.

DAVIS, BRITTON ANTHONY, retired lawyer; b. Highland Park, Ill., Jan. 2, 1936; s. James Archie and Anita (Blanke) D.; m. Lynn Marriott Wegner, 1958 (dec. 1975); children: Hilary, Shepard; m. Peggy M. Swint, 1986; children: Stephen Swint, Thomas Swint. Student, Denison U., 1954-57; BS in Law, Northwestern U., 1959, LLB, 1960. Bar: Ill. 1960. Assoc. Haight & Hofeldt, Chgo., 1959-89; pvt. practice Winnetka, Ill., 1989—96; ret., 1996. Vol. Children's Spl. Edn. Programs, Winnetka. Mem.: ABA, Patent Law Assn. Chgo., Bar Assn. 7th Fed. Cir., Chgo. Curling Club, Indian Hill Club (Winnetka). Home: 4616 Forest Edge Ln Long Grove IL 60047

DAVIS, BUTCH (PAUL HILTON DAVIS), college football coach; b. Tahlequah, OK, Nov. 17, 1951; m. Tammy Davis; 1 child, Andrew. BS in Biology & Life Sci., U. Ark., 1974. Head coach Rodgers HS, Tulsa, 1978; asst. Okla. State U. Cowboys, 1979—83; defensive line coach U. Miami Hurricanes, 1984—88, Dallas Cowboys, 1989—93, defensive coord., 1993—94; head coach U. Miami Hurricanes, 1995—2001, Cleve. Browns, 2001—04, U. N.C. Tar Heels, Chapel Hill, 2006—. Office: U NC Tar Heels Keenan Field House 8500 Chapel Hill NC 27599*

DAVIS, C. VANLEER, III, lawyer; b. Camden, NJ, 1942; AB summa cum laude, Princeton U., 1964; LLB magna cum laude, Harvard U., 1967. Bar: Pa. 1969. Law clk. to Hon. Abraham L. Freedman U.S. Ct. Appeals (3d cir.), 1967-68; ptnr. Dechert LLP, Phila. Lectr. Pa. State U. Tax Conf., 1980, mem. planning com., 1986—, chair, 1991-92; lectr. grad. tax program Temple U., 1988-89. Author: (with Jay Zagoren) Pennsylvania Limited Liability Company Forms and Practice Manual, 1996; co-editor (with Patrick Dolan) Securitization Handbook, 2000-05. Mem. Phi Beta Kappa. Office Phone: 215-994-2528. E-mail: van.davis@dechert.com.

DAVIS, CALVIN DE ARMOND, historian, educator; b. Westport, Ind., Dec. 3, 1927; s. Harry Russell and Abbie Jane (Moncrief) Davis. AB, Franklin Coll., Ind., 1949; MA, Ind. U., 1956, PhD, 1961. Tchr. Wilson Sch., Columbus, Ind., 1949-51, 53-54; asst. prof. history Ind. Central Coll., Indpls., 1956-57; teaching assoc. Ind. U., 1958-59; asst. prof. history U. Denver, 1959-62, Duke U., Durham, NC, 1962-64, assoc. prof., 1964-76, prof., 1976-96, prof. emeritus, 1996—. Cons. NEH, 1974. Contbr. articles to profl. jours.; author: (essays) Ency. U.S. Fgn. Rels., 1997, Oxford Companion to American Military History, 1999, Scribner's Ency. Am. Fgn. Policy, 2002, The United States and the First Hague Peace Conference, 1962 (Albert J. Beveridge award, 1961), The United States and the Second Hague Peace Conference, 1976; contbg. author: American Statesmen Secretaries of State from John Jay to Colin Powell, 2004. With US Army, 1951—53. Mem.: Soc. Historians Am. Fgn. Rels., Orgn. Am. Historians, Am. Hist. Assn. Home: 511 E Nightingale Dr Greensburg IN 47240-8589 Office: Duke U Dept History Durham NC 27708

DAVIS, CATHERINE LUCY, psychologist, diabetes researcher; b. Stamford, Conn., Oct. 28, 1968; d. Flavius Eugene Davis IV and Constance Anne Russell; m. Francisco Ignacio Robles, Nov. 9, 2002. AB in Psychology magna cum laude, Dartmouth Coll., 1990; MS in Clin. Health Psychology, U. Miami, 1995, PhD in Clin. Health Psychology, 1997. Lic. psychologist. Psychology resident Geisinger Med. Ctr., Danville, Pa., 1996—97; postdoctoral fellow U. Miami, Coral Gables, Fla., 1997—2000; asst. prof. pediat. Med. Coll. Ga., Augusta, 2000—. Mem. acad. coun. Med. Coll. Ga., Augusta, 2002—05; investigator Ga. Ctr. for Prevention of Obesity and Related Disorders, Athens/Augusta, 2001—04; ad hoc reviewer Jour. Pediat. Psychology, 2001—, Obesity Rsch., 2001—, Internat. Jour. Obesity, 2002—, Am. Jour. Pub. Health, 2004—, Hosp. Physician Cardiology Bd. Rev. Manual, 2005—, Health Psychology, 2005—, Biol. Psychology, 2005—, Ethnicity & Disease, 2005—; grant reviewer NIH, Am. Diabetes Assn., 2004—, Dutch Diabetes Rsch. Found., 2005—. Contbr. articles to profl. jours. Mem., vol. Cat Network, Miami, 1998—2000; treas. Ch. of Augusta, 2005—. Grantee, NIH NIDDK, 2003—; Rufus Choate scholar, Dartmouth Coll., 1990, Benjamin J. Benner '69 Rsch. Support fellow, 1989, Summer Diabetes Student Rsch. Program fellow, Juvenile Diabetes Found., 1992, Maytag fellow, U. Miami, 1992—95, T32 Rsch. fellow, NHLBI/NIH, 1997—2000, Diabetes rsch. grantee, Fraternal Order of Eagles in Augusta, 1999, Summer Inst. on Behavioral Medicine Interventions grantee, NIH, 2001, Summer Inst. on Behavioral Randomized Clin. Trials grantee, NIH, Office Behavioral and Social Sci. Rsch., 2002. Mem.: APA (divsn. 38 health psychology, divsn. 54 Soc. Pediat. Psychology), Soc. Pediat. Rsch., NAASO The Obesity Soc., Soc. Behavioral Medicine, Am. Heart Assn., Am. Diabetes Assn. (chair profl. sect. coun. on behavioral medicine and psychology 2003—05), Vol. Assn. Cultural Hispanoamericana, Phi Beta Kappa, Alpha Theta (pres. 1988—89). Liberal. Unitarian Universalist. Avocation: music. Office: Ga Prevention Inst Med Coll Ga 1499 Walton Way HS 1640 Augusta GA 30912

DAVIS, CHARLES MEMATH, SR., non-commissioned officer; b. Olula; s. Edward Daniel, Sr. and Alice Thelma (Coperand) Davis. AA, Phillips Bus. Coll., Augusta, Ga., 1982. Enlisted US Army, non-commd. officer Oreuxairbise, France, Ft. Carson, Colo., sr. non-commd. officer Nanau, Germany, Ilovf, Vietnam, Grailshan, Germany. Mem.: DAV, VFW, Am. Legion. Democrat. Methodist.

DAVIS, CHARLES RAYMOND, political scientist, educator; b. Hampton, Va., Jan. 16, 1945; s. Cecil Raymond and Fronda Gail (Bradshaw) D.; m. Terry Lorraine Barr, Oct. 1, 1963 (div. July 1979); children: Kimberly Dawn Ingram, Charles Robert; m. Raymonda Carolyn Mays, Feb. 12, 1982. BA in Polit. Sci., U. Louisville, 1974; MA in Polit. Sci., U. Ky., 1975, PhD of Polit. Sci., 1985. Instr. Jefferson Community Coll., Louisville, 1976; claims rep. Aetna Casualty, Madisonville, Ky., 1977-78; rsch. asst. U. Louisville, 1979-80; rsch. analyst Ky. Health Svcs., Frankfort, 1981-85; asst. prof., masters degree program coord. U. So. Miss., Long Beach, 1986-89, asst. prof. Hattiesburg, 1989, assoc. prof., 1991-99, prof., 1999—. Policy analyst Ky. Gov's. Coalition on Health Costs, Frankfort, 1982; acting dir. grad. studies, U. So. Miss., Hattiesburg, 1990. Author: Organization Theories and Public Administration, 1996; editl. bd. Internat. Jour. Orgn. Theory & Behavior, 1997; contbr. numerous articles to profl. jours. Mem. AAUP, ASPA, Am. Polit. Sci. Assn., So. Polit. Sci. Assn., Miss. Polit. Sci. Assn., Miss. chpt. ASPA. Mem. Ch. of Christ. Avocations: photography, travel, reading, music, history of old west. Home: 417 Browns Bridge Rd Hattiesburg MS 39401-8703 Office: U So Miss Dept Polit Sci Southern Sta # 5108 Hattiesburg MS 39406 Business E-Mail: raymond@usm.edu.

DAVIS, CHRISTOPHER JAMES, television producer; b. Port Jefferson, NY, Apr. 19, 1974; s. James Athur and Deborah Carol Davis. BFA in Film & Animation, Rochester Inst. Tech., NY, 1996—2000. Freelance dir. photography Nickelodeon, The Daily Show & Alan Weiss Prodns., NYC, 2002—06; freelance editor Nickelodeon, Spike & MTV, NYC, 2004—06; supervising prodr. Nickelodeon, 2006—. Dir., dir. photography, editor (Converse commls.) Eat and Run (Directing, Editing & Low Budget Tellys, 2004), F=ma (Directing, Cinematography & Low Budget Tellys, 2004); editor: (48 hour film fest) Valuable Things (Audience Choice award, 2006); dir.: Project Greenlight II Good Cinema (Finalist Project Greenlight Top 10 Dirs., 2003), Nickelodeon promo Interpretive Angelica (Bronze award Promax, 2007). Mem. WNYC, 2004—06. Mem.: Greater NY Mensa. Independent. Avocations: skiing, hiking, swimming, photography, music. Office: Nickelodeon 1515 Broadway New York NY 10036 Home Phone: 646-823-8176.

DAVIS, CHRISTOPHER KEVIN, SR., sales executive; b. Ogden, Utah, Apr. 8, 1959; s. James LaVerne and Margaret Mary (Brewer) D.; m. Christine Marie Davis, Oct. 27, 1984; children: Jennifer Lee, Christopher Kevin, Kelly Anne. A in Liberal Arts, Meremac Coll., St. Louis, 1979; B of Gen. Studies, U. Mo., St. Louis, 1988. Lic. health, variable annuities and life ins. sales; real estate sales. Prodn. supr. Survival Tech., St. Louis, 1982-84; salesman Cardinal Properties Real Estate Co., St. Louis, 1981-84; packaging supr. Sigma Aldrich Chem., St. Louis, 1984-85; sales mgr. Gen. Turf and Grounds Equipment Co., St. Louis, 1985-86, TNT Golf Car & Equipment Co., St. Peters, Mo., 1986-91, gen. mgr., 1991-93; pres., CEO Gateway Power Equipment, St. Louis, 1993-2001; pres. Eco-Green Techs., Inc., St. Louis, 1996-2000; pres., CEO Gateway Power Comm., Inc., St. Louis, St. Charles, Springfield, 1999—2002, pres. Lake Ozark, Mo., 2000—02; v.p. Magic Melt, LLC, Silex, Mo., 2000-01; PLC divsn. mgr. Outdoor Equipment Co., 2001—02; boat sales Bass Pro Shops, Sportsman Warehouse, 2002—03; sales staff Precision Office Installers, St. Louis, 2002—03, Premier Wireless Sales, Destin, Fla., 2003—04; health and life ins. sr. sales agt. UGA (United Group Assoc.) Assn. Field Svcs., 2003—; pres. Affordable Health and Dental Ins., 2004—. Mem.: Miracle Strip Bassmasters, Twin Cities Bass Club. Roman Catholic. Avocations: hunting, fishing, golf. Office: AFS Assn Svcs 290 Tequesta Dr Destin FL 32541 Office Phone: 850-259-7108. Personal E-mail: cdavisnow@aol.com.

DAVIS, CHRISTOPHER LEE, lawyer; b. Washington, Dec. 1, 1950; s. Martin Thomas and Margaret (Babcock) D.; married; children: Finn Christian, Ian Dunmore. BA with honors, Middlebury Coll., 1972; JD cum laude, Union U., 1975. Bar: Vt. 1975, U.S. Dist. Ct. Vt. 1975, U.S. Ct. Appeals (2d cir.) 1975. Assoc. Gear & Kittell, Burlington, Vt., 1975-78; ptnr. Gear, Kittell & Davis, Burlington, 1979-81, Gear & Davis, Inc., Burlington, 1981-90, Gear, Davis & Kehoe, Inc., 1991-92, Langrock, Sperry & Wool, Burlington, 1992—; bd. dirs. Vt. Legal Aid, Burlington, 1983-88; mem. Vt. Profl. Conduct Bd., 1984-93; mem. adv. com. Vt. Civil Rules, 1985-96; mem. Vt. Jud. Conduct Bd., 1998—, chair, 2001-06; bd. dirs. Tree Farm Mgmt. Group. Chief notes editor Albany Law Rev. Bd. dirs. Children's Legal Services, Burlington, 1981-83. Mem. ABA, Vt. Bar Assn. (bd. mgrs. 1980-84), Chittenden County Bar Assn., Burlington Rugby Football Club (pres. 1978-83, 86-88). Office: Langrock Sperry & Wool 210 College St #400 Burlington VT 05401-8376 Home Phone: 802-863-3862; Office Phone: 802-864-0217. E-mail: cdavis@langrock.com.

DAVIS, CLARENCE CLINTON, JR., lawyer; b. Alexandria, La., Sept. 24, 1956; s. Clarence Clinton Sr. and Julia Isabel (Pace) D.; m. Lisa Cheryl Russell, Aug. 6, 1977 (div. Aug. 1978). BS with hons., Northwestern State U., 1977; JD cum laude, So. Meth. U., 1980. Bar: Fla. 1980, U.S. Tax Ct. 1981, U.S. Ct. Appeals (5th cir.) 1981, Tex. 1982; cert. tax law Tex. Bd. Legal Specialization; CPA, Tex. Assoc. Trenam, Simmons, Kemker, Scharf, Barkin, Frye & O'Neill, Tampa, Fla., 1980-81, Moore & Peterson, Dallas, 1981-85, mem., 1986-89; ptnr. Krage & Jarvey, LLP, Dallas, 1989—. Author: Partnership Taxation in Theory and Practice, 1991-95, Advanced Problems in Partnership Taxation, 1992—, Fundamentals of LLC and Partnership Taxation, 1996—, Understanding LLC and Partnership Allocations and Basis, 1996—, Real Estate and Tax Deferred Exchanges, 1996-99, Tax Advice for Real Estate and Small Business, 2004—. Mem. ABA (taxation sect.), Tex. Bar Assn. (tax exempt orgn. subcom. taxation sect. 1986-87), Fla. Bar Assn., Dallas Bar Assn., Coll. State Bar Tex., Tex. Soc. CPAs, Order of Coif, Phi Kappa Phi. Republican. Episcopalian. Home Phone: 972-991-6314; Office Phone: 214-969-7500. Business E-Mail: ccdavis@kjllp.com.

DAVIS, CLARICE MCDONALD, lawyer; b. New Orleans, Jan. 20, 1941; d. James A. and Helen J. (Ross) McDonald. BA cum laude, U. Tex., 1962, MA, 1964; JD magna cum laude, So. Meth. U., 1968. Bar: Tex. 1969, U.S. Dist. Ct. (no. dist.) Tex. 1970, U.S. Ct. Appeals (5th cir.) 1971, U.S. Supreme Ct. 1973. Law clk. to presiding justice U.S. Ct. Appeals (5th cir.), Dallas, 1969-71; ptnr. Akin, Gump, Strauss, Hauer & Feld LLP, Dallas, 1971—, gen. counsel. Comments editor Southwestern Law Jour., 1967-68; instr. Southern Methodist Univ. Sch. of Law, 1968-69. Bd. visitors So. Meth. U., Dallas, 1979-82, v.p. Law Sch. Alumni Adv. Coun., 1992, pres. 1993-94, mem. bd. govs., 1995-98. Avocations: photography, swimming, running, golf. Office: Akin Gump Strauss Hauer & Feld LLP 1700 Pacific Ave Ste 4100 Dallas TX 75201-4675 Office Phone: 214-969-2711. Office Fax: 214-969-4343. Business E-Mail: cdavis@akingump.com.

DAVIS, CLAUDE-LEONARD, lawyer, academic administrator; m. Margaret Crowley; 1 child, Margaret Michelle. BA in Journalism, U. Ga., 1966, JD, 1974. Bar: Ga. 1974. Broadcaster Sta. WKLE Radio, Washington, Ga., 1958-62; realtor Assocs. Realty, Athens, Ga., 1963-66; bus. cons. Palm Beach, Fla., 1970-71; asst. to dir. Ga. Coop. Extension Svc., Athens, 1974-81; atty. Office of Pres. U. Ga., Athens, 1981—; mem. faculty, regent Ga. Athletics Inst., 1988-98; broadcaster Leonard's Losers.com, Athens, Ga., 2000—. Cons. numerous agrl. chem. industry groups nationwide, 1977-86, Congl. Office Tech. Assessment, Washington, 1978-79, USDA, Washington, 1979-80; del. Kellogg Nat. Leadership Conf., Pullman, Wash., 1980. Summer editor and contbr. Ga. Jour. of Internat. and Comparative Law, 1972-74; contbr. articles on agr. and fin. planning to profl. jours.; author and editor: DAWGFOOD: The Bulldog Cookbook, 1981, Touchdown Tailgates, 1986. Del. So. Leader Forum, Rock Eagle Ctr., Ga., 1976-99; trainer Ga. 4-H Vol. Leader Assn., 1979—99; coord. U. Ga. Equestrian Team, Athens, 1985-87; mem. Clarke County Sheriff's Posse, 1985-2000. Capt. U.S. Army, 1966-70. Chi Psi Scholar, 1965; Recipient Outstanding Alumnus award Chi Psi, 1972, Service to World Community award Chi Psi, 1975. Mem. Nat. Assn. Coll. and Univ. Attys., DAV, Poets Soc., Am. Legion, Rotary, The Pres.'s Club, Gridiron Secret Soc., UGA Charter Club, UGA Ptnrs., Chi Psi (advisor 1974). Baptist. Avocations: martial arts, creative writing, music, gardening. Office: U Ga Peabody Hall Ste 3 Athens GA 30602

DAVIS, CLAYTON, writer, pilot, photographer; b. Portersville, Ala., Feb. 27, 1931; s. Horace Milton Davis and Agnes Zama Meadows; m. Irene Alice Brink, Apr. 8, 1952; children: Lynne, Keith Harold. AA in Math. and History, San Antonio Coll., 1966; BA in Russian and Russian Studies, Syracuse U., 1967; postgrad., U. Md., 1971-75. Cert. comml. pilot and airline transport pilot, Md. Enlisted USAF, 1947, advanced through grades to master sgt., 1966, ret., 1970; math. tchr. Anne Arundel County Schs., Annapolis, Md., 1970-77; pilot Met. Air Charter, Balt., 1977-89, dir. ops., 1981-87. Flight instr., Md. Author: Flying Secrets, 1992, Flying Stories, 1992, So, You Want to Be a Pilot, 1999, Kindness: A Little Drop of Water Cures Everything, 2002, Where Pheasants Sing: Life in South Dakota 1900-2000, 2002, Medical Miracle in Maryland, 2004, Amelia, Jet Pilot, 2005; contbg. editor Pvt. Pilot Mag.; contbr. to Redfield (SD) Press, Golden Times, SD, Severna Park Voice, Md., aviation mags., others. Founding mem. Md. Aviation Hist. Task Force. Recipient St. Ignatius Gold medal, Azov Acad., Russia, 2003. Mem. Nat. Writers Assn. (founder, pres. Balt.-Washington chpt. 1993). Republican. Lutheran. Avocations: photography, flying, gardening. Home: 2 Brenda Ct Severna Park MD 21146-3604 Office Phone: 410-647-6148. Personal E-mail: cd19@verizon.net.

DAVIS, CLIVE JAY, record company executive; b. Bklyn., Apr. 4, 1933; s. Herman and Florence (Brooks) Davis; children: Fred, Lauren, Mitchell, Douglas. BA magna cum laude, NYU, 1953; LLB cum laude, Harvard U., Cambridge, Mass., 1956. Bar: NY 1957. Assoc. firm Rosenman Colin Freund Lewis & Cohen, NYC, 1958—60; gen. atty. Columbia Records, 1960—65, pres., 1966—73, Arista Records, Inc., NYC, 1974—2000, pres., CEO, 1974—2000; co-founder J Records, 2000—02; chmn., CEO RCA Records, NY, 2002—04, BMG N.Am., 2004—. Author: Clive: Inside the Record Business, 1975. Named Man of Yr., Am. Parkinson Disease, 1972, Record Co. Exec. of Yr., Nat. Assn. TV and Radio Announcers, 1973, Nat. Pop Music Survey, 1974, 1978, 1980, 1984, 1987, 1990—93, Pres. of Yr., Man of Yr., City of Hope, 1978, Man of Yr., Martell Found. for Cancer, Leukemia and AIDS Rsch., 1980, 1985, Humanitarian of Yr., Am. Cancer Soc., 1985; named to, Rock and Roll Hall of Fame, 2000; recipient Humantarian award, Anti-Defamation League, 1970, Martin Luther King Humanitarian of Yr. award, Congress Racial Equality, 1991, Man of Yr. award, Friars Club Orgn., 1992, Amfar, 1998, Grammy Lifetime Achievement award, 2000, Hitmaker award, Nat. Acad. Songwriters Hall of Fame, 2003, Brass Ring award, Children's Diabetes Found., 2006, Music Visionary of Yr. award, UJA Fedn., 2007. Mem.: Record Industry Assn. Am. (pres., chmn. bd. 1972—73, now dir.). Office: BMG Label Group 745 Fifth Ave New York NY 10151 *Experience has taught me to speak out again and again and, with right on one's side, the voice is eventually heard. Cheers for the reasoned vigilantes in society who prevent those in power from overwhelming the rights of the individual who otherwise cannot surface.*

DAVIS, CRAIG ANDERSON, school system administrator, educator; b. St. Augustine, Fla., July 15, 1969; s. Terrell Gene and Cornelia Rosalie Davis; m. Ellen Michelle Burke, Aug. 10, 1996; children: Autumn Leigh, Anderson Phillip. AA, St. John's River Cmty. Coll., 1994; BA in English, U. North Fla., 1997, MEd in Ednl. Leadership, 2002; PhD in Ednl. Leadership, U. Fla., 2007. Dep. sheriff St. John's County Sheriff's Office, St. Augustine, 1989—90, 1991—93; police officer St. Augustine Police Dept., 1990—91; acct. Davis & Davis, St. Augustine, 1998—99; tchr. English and humanities Palatka H.S., Fla., 1999—2003; adminstr. Duval County Pub. Schs., Fla., 2006—07, St. Johns County Sch. Dist., 2007—. Alumni fellow, U. Fla., 2003. Mem.: Nat. Assn. Secondary Sch. Prins., Assn. Supervision and Curriculum Devel., Am. Ednl. Rsch. Assn., Phi Delta Kappa. Republican. Avocations: reading, exercise. Home: 7422 Crill Ave Palatka FL 32177-8934 Office: St Johns County Sch Dist Bartram Trail HS 2050 Roberts Rd Jacksonville FL 32259

DAVIS, CRESWELL DEAN, lawyer, consultant; b. Abilene, Tex., Sept. 12, 1932; s. Emmett Dean and Marye (Creswell) D.; m. Mollie Villeret, Aug. 9, 1958; children: Addison Dean Davis, Kevin Tucker Davis. BA with honors, U. North Tex., 1953; JD, U. Tex., 1958. Bar: Tex. 1958. Asst. atty. gen. State of Tex., Austin, 1958-61; sr., mng. ptnr. Davis & Davis, P.C., Austin, 1961—. Dir. Tex. Jr. Bar Conf., 1964-65. Author: Texas Legal and Consent Manual for Texas Hospitals, 1967-90; contbr. articles to profl. jours. Mem. U. North Tex. bd. regents, 1967-88, chmn., 1988; mem. U. North Tex. Health Sci. Ctr. and Tex. Coll. Osteopathic Medicine, 1967-88, chmn. 1988; adj. prof. hosp. law, Trinity U., San Antonio, 1967-90; adj. prof. pharmacy jurisprudence, U. Tex., 1969—. Recipient Disting. Svc. award Tex. Pharm. Assn., 1973, Outstanding Achievement award Tex. Assn. Life Underwriters, 1986, Outstanding Svc. award Tex. Assn. Child Care Facilities, 1984, Disting. Alumnus award U. North Tex., 1990. Mem. Rotary, Masons, Phi Alpha Delta. Episcopalian. Avocations: ranching, horses, education. Office: Davis & Davis PC 9442 N Capital Of Texas Hwy Austin TX 78759-7262

DAVIS, CRISPIN, publishing company executive; b. Mar. 19, 1949; Asst. brand mgr. Procter & Gamble, 1970—78, mktg. dir. U.K. ops., v.p. U.S. food ops., 1978—90; mng. dir. European ops. United Distillers, 1990—92, group mng. dir., bd. mem. Guinness (parent co.) Edinburgh (Scotland), London, 1992—94; CEO Aegis Group plc, London, 1994—99; exec. chmn. Reed Elsevier NV, Amsterdam, 1999—2000; co-chmn. Reed Elsevier plc, London, 1999—2000; CEO Reed Elsevier plc, Reed Elsevier NV, 1999—. Office: Reed Elsevier NV 25 Victoria St London SW1H 0EX England E-mail: crispin.davis@reedelsevier.co.uk.

DAVIS, D. LAVELDA, dean, academic administrator; d. Howard and Alice Mae Davis; 1 child, Shawnelle Tatianna White. BA in Polit. Sci., Syracuse U., NY, 1980; MDiv, All Faiths Sem. Internat., NYC, 2003; PhD in Divinity, Commonwealth Open U., NY, 2004, Dr. of the Univ. (hon.), 2006. Lic. interfaith min. New Light Temple, NY, 2002, cert. theol. youth leader NY Theol. Sem., 1996, ordained deaconess Bapt. Ch., 1996; cert. notary signing agent. Human resouce generalist GreenPoint Bank, Lake Success, NY, 1998—2001, mem. staff NYC, 2001—05; assoc. dean All Faiths Sem. Internat., NYC, 2004—05, dean, 2005—; engring. adminstr. Hofstra U., Hempstead, NY, 2006—; sr. pastor New Light Temple, 2005—. Owner, CEO Davida Enterprises, Bklyn., 2003—; founder Counseling for Clerics, Bklyn., 2005—; spiritual advisor All Faiths Sem., NYC, 2002—03; founding mem. Tribeca Spiritual Ctr., NYC, 2001—03, celebration chmn., 2001—03, chmn. bd. trustees, 2001—03. Contbr.: audio book New Light Temple Internat. New Light Temple International, 2004. Contbr. United Spinal Assn., Milford, NH, 1997—2006. Mem.: Assn. Interfaith Ministers, Nat. Notary Assn., So. Poverty Law Ctr. (assoc.; named to Wall of Tolerance 2005—06), Thirteen NY, Build the Dream (assoc.; founding sponsor 2006), Wildlife Conservation (assoc.), Schomberg Soc. (assoc.). Dfl. Avocations: sports, travel, reading, crafts, crocheting. Office: All Faiths Sem Internat 7 West 96th St Ste 19B New York NY 10025 Home: 72-11 Austin St Ste 359 Forest Hills NY 11375 Office Phone: 718-261-0583. Personal E-mail: revdavida@verizon.net. E-mail: veldi84@mgn.com.

DAVIS, D. SCOTT, delivery service executive; b. Oreg. BS in Fin., Portland State U.; advanced mgmt. program, Wharton Sch. Bus., U. Pa. CPA. CFO, then CEO II Morrow, 1986—91; mgmt. positions UPS, 1986—98; CEO Overseas Ptnrs., Ltd., Bermuda, 1998—2000; v.p. fin. UPS, Atlanta, 2000—01, sr. v.p., CFO, treas., 2001—, vice-chmn., bd. dir., 2006—. Bd. dir. Honeywell Internat., 2005—; dep. chmn. Fed. Res. Bank of Atlanta. Mem. fin. coun. Ga. Coun. Econ. Edn. Office: UPS Corp Hdqrs 55 Glenlake Pkwy NE Atlanta GA 30328*

DAVIS, DANIEL M., curator, librarian; b. Ft. Dix, NJ, Jan. 31, 1971; s. John Wayne and Celia Anne Davis; m. Ashlee Timothy. BA in History, U. Wyo., Laramie, MA in History, 1995. Photog. archivist U. Wyo., Laramie, 1996—2000; photog. curator Utah State U., Logan, 2000—. Pres. Cache Valley Hist. Soc., Logan, 2006—07. Mem.: Soc. Am. Archivists. Democrat. Office: Utah State U 3000 Old Main Hill Logan UT 84322-3000 Office Phone: 435-797-0890.

DAVIS, DANNY K., congressman; b. Parkdale, Ark., Sept. 6, 1941; m. Vera Davis; children: Jonathon, Stacey BA, Ark. A. M. & N. Coll., 1961; MA, Chgo. State U., 1968; PhD, Union Inst., 1977. Mem. U.S. Congress from 7th Ill. dist., 1997—; mem. com. on govt. reform and oversight, com. on small bus.; mem. subcom. of census; mem. com. on edn. & workforce. Chgo. alderman, 1979-90; commr. Cook. County, 1990-96; candidate Chgo. mayor, 1991; founder, pres. Westside Assn. for Community Action; pres. Nat. Assn. Community Health Ctrs.; co-chmn. Clinton/Gore/Moseley-Braun Ill. campaigns, 1992; bd. dirs. Nat. Housing Partnership. Recipient Most Influential Black Americans, Ebony mag., 2006. Democrat. Office: 1526 Longworth House Office Bldg Washington DC 20515-1307 also: 2301 Roosevelt Rd Broadview IL 60155 Home Phone: 773-261-3164; Office Phone: 202-225-5006, 708-345-6857.*

DAVIS, DARRELL L., retired automotive executive; b. Sharon, Pa., Aug. 8, 1939; s. Paul Darrell and Dorothy Jane (Snyder) D.; m. Jacqueline Donna Pain, July 18, 1986; children: Paul Darrell II, Robert Tod. BS, Youngstown State U., 1963; cert. Stanford Exec. Program, Stanford U., 1987; cert. Global Leadership Program, U. Mich., 1993. Svc. rep., warranty mgr., dist. mgr., asst. zone mgr. Chrysler Motors Corp., Orlando, Fla., 1966-77, zone mgr. Omaha, 1977-78, Troy, Mich., 1978-79, nat. distbn. mgr., regional mgr., gen. mgr. import export ops., gen. sales mgr. Detroit, 1979-88; pres., chief exec. officer Alfa Romeo Distbrs. N. Am., Orlando, 1988-91; gen. sales mgr. Chrysler Corp., Orange, Calif., 1991-93; v.p. Chrysler Internat. Corp., Detroit, 1993-95; gen. mgr. Europe Chrysler Corp., Detroit, 1993-95; pres., COO Chrysler Fin. Corp., Southfield, Mich., 1995-97, chmn., CEO, 1997-98; v.p. Chrysler Corp., 1997—98; sr. v.p. Daimler Chrysler Corp., 1998—2001; bd. mgmt. Daimler Chrysler Svcs. AG, 1999—2000; CEO Daimler Chrysler Fin. Svcs. N.Am., LLC, 1999-2000; sr. v.p., gen. mgr. global svc. and parts divsn. Daimler Chrysler Corp., 2000—01, ret., 2001—. Author automotive profl. materials. Hon. judge Pebble Beach Concours d'Elegance, 1999—; bd. dirs. Boys and Girls Clubs of S.E. Mich., 1998—2001, Walter P. Chrysler Mus., 2001—; bd. advisors Beeghly Coll. of Edn., Youngstown State U., Ohio, 2004—. Lt. US Army, 1963—65. Mem.: Classic Car Club Am. (treas. Fla. region 2001—06), Antique Auto Club Am. (pres. Fla. region 2007). Republican. Avocations: auto collecting, American history. Office Phone: 407-330-9100. Personal E-mail: ddavis8839@aol.com.

DAVIS, DAVID BRION, historian, educator; b. Denver, Feb. 16, 1927; s. Clyde Brion and Martha (Wirt) Davis; m. Toni Lisa Hahn, Sept. 9, 1971; children: Adam Jeffrey, Noah Benjamin;children from previous marriage: Jeremiah Jonathan, Martha Elizabeth, Sarah Brion. AB summa cum laude, Dartmouth Coll., 1950, LittD, 1977; AM, Harvard, 1953, PhD, 1956; MA, Oxford U., 1969; LHD, U. New Haven, 1986; LittD, Columbia U., 1999. Scheduler Cessna Aircraft Co., Wichita, Kans., 1950-51; instr. history Dartmouth U., 1953-54; mem. faculty Cornell U., 1955-69, prof., 1963-69, Ernest I. White prof. history, 1964-69; prof. Yale U., 1969—2001, Farnam prof. history, 1972-78, Sterling prof. history, 1978—2001, Sterling prof. emeritus, 2001—, assoc. dir. Nat. Humanities Inst., 1975, dir. Gilder Lehrman Ctr. Study Slavery Resistance Abolition, 1998—2004, dir. emeritus, 2004—. Tchr. summer course Gilder-Lehrman Inst., 1994-2000; John Hope Franklin lectr. Adelphi Coll., 1995; Paley lectr. Hebrew U., Jerusalem, 1995, Taft lectr. U. Cin., 1996, Byrn lectr. Vanderbilt U., 1996, Keynote lectr. U. Chgo., 1997, Wachova lectr. Coll. of Charleston, 1997, Keynote lectr. Rutgers U., 1997, Maisel lectr. Cornell U., 1998, Popkin lectr. UCLA, 1999, Jefferson lectr. U. Cal., Berkeley, 2004; Confs. with Disting. Historians U. Houston, 2000, 01; lectr. Black History Month Coll. Charleston, Commentator on Muslim-Christian mutual enslavement, Am. Hist. Assn., 2001, Tercentennial Symposium Yale U., 2001, Hart lectr. Pomona Coll., 2001, Nathan I. Huggins lectr. Harvard U., 2002, After dinner lectr., Libr. Congress Civil War Sypusium, 2002; keynote lectr. conf. on global slavery Emory U., 2003, N.Y. Pub. Libr., 2003, N.Y. Hist. Assn., 2004, Nantucket Hist. Assn., 2004, others; Jefferson lectr. U. Calif., Berkeley, 2004; Tanner lectr. in human values Stanford U., 2006; keynote lectr. McGill U., Montreal, 2007, Westminster, London, 2007. Author: Homicide in American Fiction 1790-1860, A Study in Social Values, 1957, The Problem of Slavery in Western Culture, 1966, 1988, 2001, The Slave Power Conspiracy and the Paranoid Style, 1969, The Problem of Slavery in the Age of Revolution, 1770-1823, 1975, 1999, Slavery and Human Progress, 1984, From Homicide to Slavery: Studies in American Culture, 1986, Revolutions: Reflections on American Equality and Foreign Liberations, 1990, In the Image of God: Religion, Moral Values, and Our Heritage of Slavery, 2001, Challenging the Boundaries of Slavery, 2003, Inhuman Bondage: The Rise and Fall of Slavery in the New World, 2006; co-author: The Great Republic, 1977, 1992, The Antislavery Debate, 1992; editor: Ante-Bellum Reform, 1967, The Fear of Conspiracy, 1971, Ante-Bellum American Culture: An Interpretive Anthology, 1979, 1997; contbg. author: The Stature of Theodore Dreiser, 1955, The Province of Pose, 1956, Why Man Takes Chances, 1968, Surveillance and Espionage in a Free Society, 1972, Perspectives and Irony in America Slavery, 1976, The Amerian Family: Dying or Developing, 1979, Slavery and Freedom in the Age of the American Revolution, 1983, British Capitalism and Caribbean Slavery, 1987, Lincoln, the War President, 1992; co-editor: The Boisterous Sea of Liberty: A Documentary History of America From Discovery Through the Civil War, 1998; contbg. author: Essays in Slavery, Secession, and Southern History, 2000, American Places: Encounters with History: America's Leading Historians Talk about the Sites Where the Past Comes Alive for Them, 2000; contbr. N.Y. Review of Books; Free at Last: A History of the Abolition of Slavery in America. Mem. subcom. internal security Dem. Nat. Policy Coun., Pulitzer Prize Com., 1968, Bancroft Prize Com., 1989; co-chair adv. bd. Gilder-Lehrman Inst. Am. History, 1995—. With AUS, 1945-46. Recipient Anisfield Wolf award in race relations, 1967, Pulitzer prize for nonfiction, 1967, Mass Media award NCCJ, 1967, Bancroft prize, 1976, Nat. Book award for history and biography, 1976, Presdl. medal Dartmouth Coll., 1991, Kidger award Improving Tchg. History in New Eng., 2004; Guggenheim fellow, 1958-59; Fulbright grantee, 1980; NEH fellow, 1983-84, Gilder-Lehrman Inaugural fellow, 1996-97. Fellow Am. Acad. Arts and Scis., Brit. Acad. (corr.); mem. Am. Philos. Soc. (adminstrv. bd. Benjamin Franklin papers), Mass. Hist Soc., Am. Hist. Soc. (Albert J. Beveridge award 1975, award for scholarly achievement 2007), Inst. Early Am. History and Culture (coun. 1976-79), Am. Antiquarian Soc., Soc. Am. Historians (Bruce Catton prize for lifetime achievement 2004), Orgn. Am. Historians (pres. 1988-89, chair Frederick Jackson Turner award com. 1989, Lincoln prize com. 1992), Am. Histor. Assn. (Scholarly Achievement award 2007), Assn. Am. Pubs. (Best Book in History award 2006), Milan Group in Early U.S. Hist. Jewish. Home: 733 Lambert Rd Orange CT 06477-1806 Business E-Mail: david.b.davis@yale.edu.

DAVIS, DAVID LEE, congressman; b. Anderson, Ind., Nov. 6, 1959; m. Joyce Engle; children: Matthew, Rachel. AAS in Respiratory Therapy, Calif. Coll., 1983; BS in Orgnl. Mgmt., Milligan Coll., 1991. Cert. Respiratory Therapist East Tenn. State U., 1979, Hyperbaric Technologist. Pres. Shared Health Services, Inc.; clin. adj. faculty mem. Respiratory Care Dept., East Tenn. State U.; mem. Tenn. Ho. Reps from Dist. 9, 1998—2006, US Congress from 1st Tenn. dist., 2007—. Mem. Sportsman Legis. Caucus, Northeast Caucus, Tourism Caucus, Farm Bur., Coalition for Kids, Communities in Schools, Leadership Johnson City, Leadership Kingsport, President's Coun. Milligan Coll., Johnson City Chamber of Commerce; bd. mem. Crumley House Head Injury Rehab Ctr., Sci. Hill High Sch.-Alternative Learning Ctr.; chmn. Unicoi County Rep. Party, 1995—96; mem. Washington County Rep. Party, Conservative Round Table. Named Respiratory Care Practioner of Yr., 1994, Home Med. Equipment Supplier of Yr., Legislator of Yr., Tenn. Podiatric Assn., 2005; recipient Health Care Hero award, 2004. Mem.: Nat. Fedn. Ind. Bus. (mem., Leadership Coun.), Tenn. Assn. Home Care (chmn., Medicare Part B, John W. Hines award), Johnson City Rotary Club. Republican. Baptist. Office: 514 Cannon Ho Office Bldg Washington DC 20515 also: 320 W Center St PO Box 769 Kingsport TN 37660 Office Phone: 423-773-8861, 202-225-6356. Office Fax: 202-225-5714.*

DAVIS, DAVID M., air transportation executive; BS in Aerospace Engring., U. Minn., MBA in Fin. Dir. fin. customer svc. divsn. Delta Air Lines; v.p. fin. planning and analysis Budget Group Inc., 2000—02, US Airways Group Inc., 2002—04, exec. v.p. fin., CFO, 2004; CFO KRATON Polymers, LLC, Houston; with NW Airlines Corp., 2005—, sr. v.p. fin., contr., exec. v.p., CFO, 2007—. Bd. dirs. Compass Airlines, Inc., Mesaba Aviation, Inc.; bd. dirs., chmn. audit com. ARINC, Inc. Bd. dirs. Minn. Zoo Found. Office: NW Airlines Corp 2700 Lone Oak Pky Eagan MN 55121 Office Phone: 612-726-2111.*

DAVIS, DAVID OLIVER, radiologist, educator; b. Danville, Ill., June 25, 1933; s. Oliver and Anna Marie (Collignon) D.; m. Agnes Layden, Dec. 26, 1955; children: Karen, Kathy, Diane, Janet, Nancy. BS, U. Ill., 1954; MD, St. Louis U., 1958. Diplomate Am. Bd. Radiology. Intern Starkloff Meml. Hosp., St. Louis, 1958-59; resident USPHS Hosp., SI, NY, 1959-61, Columbia Presbyn. Med. Ctr., NYC, 1962-63; asst. prof. radiology Washington U., St. Louis, 1966-68, assoc. prof., 1968-70; prof. U. Utah, 1970-72, George Washington U., 1972—, prof. neurology, 1977—, chmn. dept. radiology, 1978-82, 91-96, prof. neurosurgery, 1985—. Vis. prof. U. Calif., San Francisco, 1985; cons. UCLA, 1995-96, UNS; sec.-gen. 12th Internat. Symposium on Neuroradiology. Editor: Principles of Diagnostic Radiology, 1971, Reconstruction Tomography in Diagnostic Radiology and Nuclear Medicine, 1977; mem. editl. bd. Jour. Computer Assisted Tomography, 1977-88, Am. Jour. Neuroradiology, 1979-90, Neuroradiology, 1971-80; mem. editl. exec com. Jour. Investigative Radiology, 1971-80. With USPHS, 1959-64. Recipient Golden Apple award George Washington U., 2000; NIH spl. fellow, 1964-66. Fellow Am. Coll. Radiology (mem. coun. steering com. 1992-94, mem. bd. chancellors 1994-99), Am. Heart Assn. (stroke coun.); mem. AMA, Am. Soc. Neuroradiology (sec. 1971-74, pres. 1979-80, chmn. publs. com. 1988-92, counselor 1992-94, Gold medal 2002), D.C. Med. Soc., D.C. Radiol. Soc. (pres. 1983-84, counselor 1985-91), Assn. Univ. Radiologists, 1973-1990, Soc. Chmn. Acad. Radiology Depts. (sec.-treas. 1981-83), Acad. Radiology Rsch. (bd. dirs. 1994-99), Internat. Microcirculation Soc., Blue Grass Radiology Soc. (hon.), Radiol. Soc. N.Am., Am. Roentgen Ray Soc. (mem. exec. coun. 1992-95, alt. del. to AMA 1995-99, del. 1999-2000), North Pacific Soc. Neurology and Psychiatry (hon.), Am. Head and Neck Radiology, Phila. Roentgen Soc. (hon.), Western Neuroradiology Soc., Am. Soc. Spine Radiology Splty. and Svcs. Soc., Alpha Omega Alpha. Office: George Washington U Med Ctr Dept Radiology 900 23rd St NW Washington DC 20037 Office Phone: 202-715-5192. E-mail: daveandagnes@yahoo.com.

DAVIS, DAVID SCOTT, academic administrator, chemistry professor; b. Danville, Va., July 26, 1963; s. Jerry O'Neil and Patricia Ann Davis; m. Cathy Louise Daniel, July 18, 1998; children: Ryan Matthew Glisson, Miller Ann, Layne Elizabeth. BS, Erskine Coll., SC, 1985; PhD, Emory U., Atlanta, 1990. Asst. prof. Mercer U., Macon, Ga., 1991—96, assoc. prof., 1996—2004, prof., 2004—, vice provost, 2004—07, sr. vice provost for rsch., 2007—, dean grad. studies, 2007—. Author numerous scientific articles in scientific jours. Pres. Huguenin Heights Neighborhood Assn., Macon, Ga., 1998—99; mem. nominating com. Ga. Sports Hall of Fame; adminstrv. bd. Mulberry St. United Meth. Ch., Macon, Ga., 2003—06; bd. mem. Flying Fleet Club of Erskine Coll., Due West, SC, 2002—05, Intown Macon (Ga.), 1997—2000. Recipient ILI Program award, NSF, 1997—99, CCLI Program, 2002—04; Fellowship, Coun. on Undergraduate Rsch., 1994, Athletic scholarship, Erskine Coll., 1981—85. Mem.: Am. Conf. of Academic Deans, Am. Assn. of Higher Edn., Coun. of Colls. of Arts and Scis., Coun. on Undergraduate Rsch., Ga. Acad. of Sci., The Am. Chem. Soc., Sigma Xi, Phi Kappa Phi, Pi Alpha. Methodist. Avocations: golf, reading, woodworking. Home: 624 Bellgrove Pointe Macon GA 31220 Office: Mercer Univ 1400 Coleman Ave Macon GA 31207 Home Phone: 478-461-5971; Office Phone: 478-301-2024. Office Fax: 478-301-5576; Home Fax: 478-301-5576. Business E-Mail: davis_ds@mercer.edu.

DAVIS, DEBORAH LYNN, lawyer, art dealer; b. NYC, Apr. 23, 1948; d. Melvin Jerome and Beatrice (Greenapple) D. BS, Case Western Res. U., Cleve., 1970, JD, 1973. Bar: NY 1974, US Dist. Ct. (ea. and so. dists.) NY 1974. Staff atty., dir. litigation Community Action for Legal Svcs., Inc., Bklyn., 1974-77, 78-81; atty. BLS Legal Svcs., NYC, 1977-78; assoc. Gallet & Dreyer, NYC, 1981-86; ptnr. Wagner, Davis & Gold, P.C., NYC, 1986-99, of counsel, 1999—; ptnr. El-Baz Gallery NY Ltd., NYC, 1999-2000; pres., owner Deborah Davis Fine Art Inc., Hudson, NY, 2000—. Contbg. author chpts. in book. Incorporator, officer, bd. dirs. NY Svc. Program for Older People, Inc., 1978-91; mem. Family Ct. Panel Screening and Oversight com. 1st Jud. Dept., 1985-88, vice-chair screening applicants, 1985-87. Mem. NY State Bar Assn., NY County Lawyers Assn., NY Women's Bar Assn., Fourthdown Block Assn. (treas. 2003-06), Hudson Bus. Alliance (treas. 2002—). Office: 510 Warren St Hudson NY 12534 Home: PO Box 332 Hudson NY 12534 Office Phone: 518-822-1890. Personal E-mail: deborahdavisfineart@earthlink.net.

DAVIS, DON H., JR., multi-industry high-technology company executive; Engring. sales trainee Allen-Bradley (aquired by Rockwell 1985), 1963-66, dist. mgr. Birmingham, Ala., 1966-79, gen. mgr. programmable contr. divsn., 1979-80, v.p. programmable contr. divsn., 1980-82, v.p., gen. mgr. indsl. control divsn., 1982-85, sr. v.p., 1985-86, head indsl. control group, 1986-87, sr. v.p., gen. mgr. indsl. computer and comm. group, 1987-89, pres., 1989-93, corp. sr. v.p., pres. automation, 1993-95, pres., COO, 1995-97, pres., CEO, 1997-98; chmn., CEO Rockwell Automation, Inc., 1998—2004, chmn., 2004—. Bd. dirs. Sybron Internat., Ingram Micro, Inc. Nat. trustee Boys and Girls Clubs Am.; chmn. bd. L.A. Mfg. Learning Ctr.; regent Milw. Sch. Engring. Mem. Internat. Soc. for Measurement and Control (hon. chmn.), Nat. Elec. Mfrs. Assn. (past chmn. bd. govs.), Bus. Roundtable, The Conf. Bd. (sr.). Office: Rockwell Internat Corp 777 E Wisconsin Ave Ste 1400 Milwaukee WI 53202-5302

DAVIS, DON P., retail executive; Fin. analyst and various positions including sr. v.p. info. systems PayLess Drug Stores, Wilsonville, Oreg., 1982—94; sr. v.p. info. systems Thrifty PayLess, 1994; v.p. application delivery Lowe's Cos., Inc., North Wilkesboro, NC; sr. v.p., chief info. officer Rite Aid Corp., 2000—. Office: Rite Aid Corp 30 Hunter Lane Camp Hill PA 17011 Office Phone: 717-761-2633.*

DAVIS, DONALD ALAN, news correspondent, writer, lecturer; b. Savannah, Ga., Oct. 5, 1939; s. Oden Harry and Irma Artice (Gay) Davis; m. Robin Murphy, Mar. 17, 1983 (dec. May 11, 2005); children from previous marriage: Russell Glenn, Randall Scott. BA in Journalism, U. Ga., 1962. Reporter Athens (Ga.) Banner-Herald, 1961-62, Savannah Morning News, 1962; with UPI, 1963-65, 1967-83, Vietnam corr., 1971-73, New Eng. editor, 1977-80, White House corr., 1981-83; reporter, editor St. Petersburg (Fla.) Times, 1965-66; polit. reporter, columnist San Diego Union, 1983-91; pub. Pacific Rim Report newsletter, 1985-88. Instr. journalism Boston U., 1979; instr. writing U. Colo., 1998-99; lectr. U.S. Naval War Coll., 1983, Queen Elizabeth 2, 1991. Author: The Milwaukee Murders, 1991, The Nanny Murder Trial, 1992, Bad Blood, 1994, Death of an Angel, 1994, Fallen Hero, 1994, Appointment with the Squire, 1995, Death Cruise, 1996, A Father's Rage, 1996, The Gris-Gris Man, 1997, Hush, Little Babies, 1997, The Last Man on the Moon, 1999, JonBenet, 2000, Dark Waters, 2002, Lightning Strike, 2005, Shooter, 2005. Fellow Keizai Koho Ctr., Tokyo, 1985, Overseas Press Club, 2000. Unitarian. E-mail: tedsalad@mesanetworks.net.

DAVIS, DONALD GLENN, lawyer; b. San Gabriel, Calif., Sept. 15, 1958; BS in Acctg., Calif. State U., Pomona; JD, U. So. Calif. Assoc. O'Melveny & Meyers, LA; prof. of law Southwestern U. Law Sch., LA, 1972-80; gen. counsel Republic Corp., LA, 1973; ptnr. Danielson, St. Clair & Davis, LA, 1974-77; mng. ptnr. Davis & Assocs., LA, 1980—, DGD Enterprises P.V., LA, 1980—, DGD Investment Banking, LA, 1980—. Exec. editor Law Rev. jour., U. So. Calif., 1968-69. Vice-pres. student body, Calif. State U., Pomona, 1964-65; candidate 42nd Congl. Dist., Calif., 1988. Mem. ABA, L.A. Bar Assn. (chmn. securities cooperative seminar 1988, chmn. bus. lawyers sect. 1986-87), Order of Coif, Calif. Club, Balboa Bay Club. Office Phone: 310-823-8300.

DAVIS, DONALD RAY, entomologist; b. Oklahoma City, Mar. 28, 1934; s. Esker Arnold and Mildred Louise (Fortson) D.; m. Mignon Marie Bush, Sept. 29, 1972; children: Marisa Marie, Steven Ray. BA, U. Kans., 1956; PhD, Cornell U., 1962. With Smithsonian Instn., Washington, 1961—, assoc. curator, then curator entomology, 1961-76, chmn. dept., 1976-81, curator entomology, 1981—. Contbr. articles to profl. jours. Recipient Smithsonian Instn. Rsch. Found. award, 1966-67, 73-74, Scholarly Studies grantee, 1990-2003, Am. Philos. Soc. grantee, 1963; Rsch. Opportunity awardee, various yrs. Mem. Biol. Soc. Washington (pres. 1984-85), Lepidopterists Soc. (Jordan medal 1977, pres. 1985), Assn. Tropical Biology, Entomol. Soc. Am., Hennig Soc., Nat. Speleological Soc., Soc. Systematic Zoology, Entomol. Soc. Washington (pres. 1979), Washington Biologists Field Club. Office: Smithsonian Instn Entomology NHB 127 PO Box 37012 Washington DC 20013-7012 E-mail: davis.don@nmnh.si.edu. *I believe that life's major goal should be to contribute something of lasting value to earth's diverse heritage. Perhaps the most permanent heritage anyone can bequeath lies in the discovery of new knowledge. By thus enriching our common heritage, I feel that I can partially repay, in my own humble way, for the enormous privilege of having once lived on this fascinating planet.*

DAVIS, DONALD ROBERT, nutritionist, researcher, consultant; b. La Jara, Colo., Mar. 19, 1941; s. Robert Cristopher and Ida Mary (Blissard) D.; m. Vera Elaine Wilson, June 27, 1980 (div. Aug. 15, 1989). Student, Calif. Inst. Tech., 1962; PhD, UCLA, 1965. Postdoctoral fellow, instr. Calif. Inst. Tech., Pasadena, 1965-67; asst. prof. U. Calif., Irvine, 1967-74; rsch. scientist assoc. U. Tex., Austin, 1974-86, rsch. assoc., 1986—. Trustee Internat. Acad. Nutrition and Preventive Medicine, 1983-85, The Wacker Found., 1987—; dir. Roger J. Williams Nutrition Inst., 1987-90; sr. rsch. cons. Ctr. for Improvement of Human Functioning, Wichita, Kans., 1989—. Editor-in-chief Jour. Applied Nutrition, 1986-91; mem. editl. bds. Jour. Applied Nutrition, 1978—, Jour. Internat. Acad. Preventive Medicine, 1983-85, Jour. Advancement in Medicine, 1997—; contbr. more than 50 articles to profl. jours; co-developer nutrient content software, NutriCircles, 1985—. Instr. Lifetime Learning, Austin, 1978—. Rsch. fellows NSF, Washington, 1965-67; grantee Found. for Nutritional Advancement, Washington, 1986. Mem.: AAAS, Am. Coll. Nutrition. Office: Univ Tex Biochem Inst Austin TX 78712 E-mail: d.r.davis@mail.utexas.edu.

DAVIS, DOROTHY SALISBURY, writer; b. Chgo., Apr. 26, 1916; d. Alfred Joseph and Margaret Jane (Greer) Salisbury; m. Harry Davis, Apr. 25, 1946 (dec.). AB, Barat Coll., Lake Forest, Ill., 1938. Mystery and hist. novelist, short story writer. Author: A Gentle Murderer, 1951, A Town of Masks, 1952, Men of No Property, 1956, Death of an Old Sinner, 1957, A Gentleman Called, 1958, The Evening of the Good Samaritan, 1961, Black Sheep, White Lamb, 1963, The Pale Betrayer, 1965, Enemy and Brother, 1967, God Speed The Night, 1968, Where the Dark Streets Go, 1969, Shock Wave, 1972, The Little Brothers, 1973, A Death in the Life, 1976, Scarlet Night, 1980, A Lullaby of Murder, 1984, Tales for a Stormy Night, 1985, The Habit of Fear, 1987, In the Still of the Night, 2000. Recipient Life Achievement award Bouchereon, 1989. Mem. Authors Guild, Mystery Writers of Am. (former pres., recipient Grand Master award 1985), Adams Roundtable. Home: PO Box 595 Palisades NY 10964-0595

DAVIS, DWIGHT, cardiologist, educator; b. Winston-Salem, NC, Apr. 11, 1948; s. James C. Davis; m. Lorna Jean Enck, July 30, 1988; 1 child, Nathan James. BS, N.C. A&T State U., 1970; MD, U. Rochester, 1975. Rsch. asst. U. Rochester, NY, 1970-71; intern in medicine Boston U. Hosp., 1975-76, resident in medicine, 1976-78; cardiology fellow Duke U. Med. Ctr., Durham, NC, 1978-81; asst. prof. medicine, cardiology divsn. Pa. State U., Hershey, 1981-87, assoc. prof., 1987-92, disting. lectr., 1986, prof. medicine, 1992—, cardiology dir. heart transplantation, artificial organs and preclinical tchg. program, dir. cardiology preclinical tng. program, 1984—, dir., cardiology fellow tng. program, 1984-87, dir. cardiac catheterization lab., 1987—, med. dir. cardiac rehab. program, 1988—, dir. clin. cardiology program, 1991—, asst. dean for admissions, 1994-99, assoc. dean admissions and student affairs, 1999—. Vice chmn. faculty affairs faculty senate Pa. State U., University Park, 1988—; mem. med. alumni coun. U. Rochester Sch. Medicine and Dentistry, 1992—; various disting. lectureships. Contbr. numerous articles to profl. jours.; editorial reviewer Annals Internal Medicine, 1983—; editorial adv. bd. Primary Cardiology, 1985—. Mem. Pa. Coun. on Aging, Harrisburg, 1989—. Recipient Outstanding Physician award Pa. State U. Sch. Medicine, 1984, Disting. Tchg. awards, 1988-89, Tchr. of Yr. award, 1991, Disting. Prof. award for tchg., 1991, Outstanding Tchr. of Yr. award med. sch. class of 1995, 93, Outstanding Tchr. of Yr. award med. sch. class of 1997, 1995, Alumni Excellence award N.C. A&T State U., 1986, Disting. Alumni award Nat. Assn. Equal Opportunity in Higher Edn., 1987; Joy McCann scholar, 2005. Fellow Am. Coll. Cardiology, Am. Coll. Angiology; mem. AAAS, Am. Heart Assn. (fellow coun. on clin. cardiology, rsch. com. Pa. affiliate 1992—, pres. elect Pa. affiliate 1997, pres. elect Pa./Del affiliate 1998, Disting. Svc. award Pa. Del. affiliate 2000), Am. Fedn. Clin. Rsch., Am. Assn. Med. Colls. (pres. elect North East group on student affairs 1998), Am. Assn. Cardiovasc. and Pulmonary Rehab. (expert panel cardiac rehab. guidelines project 1992—, chair cardiac rehab. criteria devel. panel 1995—), N.Y. Acad. Scis., Alpha Omega Alpha. Mem. United Ch. of Christ. Achievements include discovery that abnormalities of the sympathetic nervous system in patients with heart failure is due to an increase in norepinephrine spillover and a decrease in norepinephrine clearance from the circulation. Office: Pa State U Coll Medicine Divsn Cardiology PO Box 850 Hershey PA 17033-0850

DAVIS, EARL JAMES, chemical engineering professor emeritus; b. St. Paul, July 22, 1934; s. Leo Ernest and Mary (Steiner) D.; children: Molly Kathleen, David Leo. BS cum laude, Gonzaga U., 1956; PhD, U. Wash., 1960. Design engr. Union Carbide Chems. Co., South Charleston, W.Va., 1956; from asst. prof. chem. engring. to assoc. prof. Gonzaga U., Spokane, Wash., 1960-68, dir. computing ctr., 1967-68; rsch. fellow Imperial Coll., London U., 1964-65; assoc. prof. chem. engring. Clarkson U., 1968-73, head socio-environ. program, 1972-74, prof., 1973-78, chmn. chem. engring. dept., 1973-74, assoc. dir. Inst. Colloid and Surface Sci., 1974-78; prof., chmn. chem. and nuclear engring. dept. U. N.Mex., 1978-80; dir. engring. divsn., prof. Inst. Paper Chemistry, Appleton, Wis., 1980-83; rsch. fellow in chem. engring. U. Wash., Seattle, 1957-60, prof. chem. engring., 1983—, assoc. vice provost for rsch., 2001—03. Guest prof. Tech. U. of Vienna, Austria, 2000; sr. scientist, cons. Unilever Rsch. Lab., Port Sunlight, Eng., 1974-75; vis. scholar NAS/Chinese Acad. Scis., China, 1989; adj. prof. Sichuan U., Chengdu, China, 2001—. Assoc. editor Aerosol Sci. and Tech., 1993-97; mem. editl. bd. Jour. Colloid and Interface Sci., 1984-86; mem. editl. bd. Jour. Aerosol Sci., 1992-98, editor-in-chief, 1999—; mem. adv. bd. Surface and Colloid Sci., 2000—; regional editor (N.Am. and S.Am.) Colloid and Polymer Sci., 1994-99; contbr. articles to sci. publs. NSF fellow, 1964-65, grantee, 1963-89, 92—2003; recipient Burlington No. award for rsch., 1988; Leeds and Northrup fellow U. Wash., 1960. Fellow AAAS, mem. AIChE (adminstr. Design Inst. Multiphase Processing 1979-87), Am. Chem. Soc., Am. Assn. Aerosol Rsch. (treas. 1990-92, David Sinclair award 1991, v.p. 1996-97, pres. 1997-98), Soc. Applied Spectroscopy, Gesellschaft für Aerosolforschung, Sigma Xi. Achievements include research in air pollution control, aerosol physics and chemistry and colloid science. Office: U Wash Dept Chem Engring PO Box 351750 Seattle WA 98195-1750 Business E-Mail: davis@cheme.washington.edu.

DAVIS, EDDIE JOE, academic and foundation administrator; b. Wichita Falls, Tex., Jan. 20, 1945; s. Dennis Drapper and Ruby Mae (Callaway) D.; m. Jo Ann Meuse, June 8, 1968; children: Phillip Michael, Jennifer Ann. BS in Journalism, Tex. A&M U., 1967, MEd in Adminstrn., 1974, PhD in Higher Edn., 1980; student, Harvard Grad Sch. Bus., 1971. Dir. mgmt. svcs. Tex. A&M U., College Station, 1972-78, assoc. v.p. bus., 1978-80, v.p. fiscal affairs, 1983-87, prof. ednl. adminstrn., dep. chancellor fin. and adminstrn., 1987-91, dep. chancellor, 1991-93, interim pres., 2006—; pres. Tex. A&M Found., College Station, 1993—; v.p. fiscal affairs, treas. North Tex. State U., Denton, 1980-83. Bd. dirs. Coun. Govtl. Rels., Washington, chmn. costing policies com., 1992-93. Pres., Brazos County A&M Club, 1978; bd. dirs. Brazos County United Way, Tex., 1980; mem. formula adv. com. State Coord. Bd., 1981—, chair formula study com., 1992-93. Col. AUS, 1967-90, Vietnam. Mem. Tex. Assn. State Sr. Coll. and Univ. Bus. Officers (pres. 1985-86), Southern Assn. Coll. and Univ. Bus. Officers (chmn. 1984-85), Endowed Diamond Century Club, 12th Man Found. Adv. Bd., A&M Legacy Soc. Roman Catholic. Home: 6004 Augusta Cir College Station TX 77845-8984 Office: Tex A&M Found 401 George Bush Dr College Station TX 77840-2811 Office Phone: 409-845-8161. E-mail: edavis@tamu.edu.*

DAVIS, EDGAR GLENN, healthcare executive, educator; b. Indpls., May 12, 1931; s. Thomas Carroll and Florence Isabelle (Watson) Davis; m. Margaret Louise Alandt, June 20, 1953; children: Anne-Elizabeth, Amy Alandt, Edgar Glenn Davis Jr. AB, Kenyon Coll., 1953; MBA, Harvard U., 1955. With Eli Lilly & Co., Indpls., 1958—63, mgr. budgeting and profit planning, 1963—66, mgr. econ. studies, 1966—67, mgr. Atlanta sales dist., 1967—68, dir. market rsch. and sales manpower planning, 1968—69, dir. mktg. plans, 1969—74, exec. dir. pharm. mktg. planning, 1974—75, exec. dir. corp. affairs, 1975—76, v.p. corp. affairs, 1976—90, v.p. health care policy, 1990; pres., chmn. bd. dirs. Centre for Health Sci. Info., Boston, 1990—; fellow Ctr. for Bus. and Govt. Kennedy Sch. of Govt. Harvard U., 1991—95; adj. prof. Butler U., Indpls., 1995—. Exec. in residence Butler U. Coll. Bus.; mem. Inst. Ednl. Mgmt., Harvard U. Grad. Sch. Edn., 1987; chmn. staff Bus. Roundtable Task Force on Health, 1981—85; U.S. rep. UN Indsl. Devel. Orgn. Conf., Lisbon, 1980, Casablanca, 81, Budapest, 83, Madrid, 87; participant meeting of experts on pharms UNIDO , 1981; rep. to UN Commn. on Narcotic Drugs, Vienna, 1981, UN Econ. and Social Coun., NYC, 1981, UN Indsl. Devel. Orgn. Conf.; Ctr. for Bus. and Govt. fellow Kennedy Sch. Govt., Harvard U.; co-chmn. Harvard Conf. on Govt. Role in Civilian Tech., 1992, Harvard Conf. Pharmaceutical Rsch., Innovation and Pub. Policy, 1993, Harvard Biotech. Roundtable, 1991—; vis. scholar, advisor Health and Welfare Unit, Inst. for Econ. Affairs, London; vis. scholar Green Coll. Oxford (Eng.) U., 1994—; chmn. Nat. Fund for Med. Edn., 1994—; dir. English Speaking Union, Indpls.; gov. Soc. Indiana Pioneers; lectr. in field. Contbr. articles to profl. jours. Pres. Eli Lilly and Co. Found., 1976—88; pres., chmn. bd. Indpls. Health Inst., 1988—91; trustee Kenyon Coll., Gambier, Ohio, Ind. Hist. Soc.; pres. bd. trustees Boston Biomed. Rsch. Inst., 1991—95, trustee emeritus; chmn. Nat. Fund for Med. Edn., 1996—; bd. dirs. Carnegie Coun. on Ethics and Internat. Affairs, 1985—92; accredited nongovtl. observer rep. to UN Goodwill Fund. Ind. Inc., 1987—95; bd. dirs. Sta. WFYI Pub. TV, Indpls., 1983—91, Am. Symphony Orch. League, 1987—92, mem. dirs. coun., 1987—; bd. dirs. Nat. Health Coun., 1984—91, Pub. Affairs Coun., Washington, 1984—92, Nat. Fund for Med. Edn.; bd. advisors Christian Theol. Sem., Bishops Sch., LaJolla, Calif.; chmn. bd. dirs. Ind. Repertory Theatre, 1979—85; vice chmn., exec. com., bd. dirs. Indpls. Symphony Orch. and Ind. State Symphony Soc., 1977—91; chmn. task force on fine arts Commn. for Future of Butler U.; chmn. exec. com. Pan Am. Econ. Leadership Conf. 10th Pan Am. Games, Indpls.; mem. Chgo. Coun. on Fgn. Rels.; bd. govs. Soc. Ind. Pioneers. Mem.: NAM (vice-chmn. health policy com. 1987—91, bd. dirs.), Am. Symphony Orch. League N.Y. (mem. dir. coun.), Inst. Medicine NAS, Ind. Soc. Pioneers (bd. govs.), Dramatic Club of Indpls., Univ. Club (Indpls.) (bd. dirs.), Literary Club Indpls., Reform Club London, N.Y. Yacht Club, Edgartown Golf Club, Chappaquiddick Beach Club, Contemporary Club, Woodstock Club, Naples Yacht Club, Edgartown Yacht Club , Naples (Fla.), Met. Club (Washington). Office: Butler U Coll Bus Adminstrn 4600 Sunset Ave Indianapolis IN 46208-3487 Office Fax: 317-940-9455.

DAVIS, EDMOND RAY, lawyer; b. Glendale, Calif., Sept. 4, 1928; s. Archie Allen and Eve Mae (Hoover) D.; m. Ruby Evelyn Davis, Oct. 17, 1954; children: Phillip A., Sandra A. Student, Pepperdine Coll.; JD, U. Calif., San Francisco, 1952. Bar: Calif. 1952, U.S. Dist. Ct. (cen. dist.) Calif. 1952. Assoc. Bailie, Turner & Sprague, 1955-60; trust counsel Security Pacific Nat. Bank, 1960-67; ptnr. Overton, Lyman & Prince, LA, 1967-87, Brobeck, Phleger & Harrison, LA, 1987-99, Davis & Whalen, North Hollywood, Calif., 1999—. Chmn., pub. adminstr. Pub. Guardian Adv. Commns., Los County Bd. Suprs., 1974-76; bd. dirs. Braille Inst. Am., Inc., Children's Bur. So. Calif., Children's Bur. Found., Fifield Manors, Inc.; pres. LA Jaycees, 1962; mem. legal com. Music Ctr. Found., Performing Arts Council, LA county, 1980-85. With U.S. Army, 1952-54. Recipient Alumni award Pepperdine Coll., 1962. Fellow Am. Coll. Trust and Estate Counsel (chmn. Calif. chpt. 1981-86); mem. Internat. Acad. Estate and Trust Law (academician), State Bar of Calif. (chmn. estate planning, trust and probate law sect. 1977-78), L.A. County Bar Assn. (exec. com., probate and trust law sect. 1986-89, Arthur K. Marshall award Probate and Trust Law sect. 1991), Order of Coif, Calif. Club, Chancery Club. Office: 5200 Lankershim Blvd Ste 380 North Hollywood CA 91601-3155 Home Phone: 626-799-7234; Office Phone: 818-752-2880. Office Fax: 818-752-2990. Business E-Mail: edavis@daviswhalen.com.

DAVIS, EDWARD BERTRAND, retired federal judge, lawyer; b. W. Palm Beach, Fla., Feb. 10, 1933; s. Edward Bertrand and Mattie Mae (Walker) D.; m. Patricia Lee Klein, Apr. 5, 1958; children: Diana Lee

Davis, Traci Russell, Edward Bertrand, III. JD, U. Fla., 1960; LLM in Taxation, N.Y. U., 1961. Bar: Fla. 1960. Pvt. practice, Miami, 1961-79; counsel High, Stack, Lazenby & Bender, 1978-79; U.S. dist. judge So. Dist. Fla., 1979-2000; shareholder Ackerman Senterfitt, Miami, 2000, chair state wide litig. practice. Served with AUS, 1953-55. Mem.: Fla. Bar Assn., Dade County Bar Assn. Office: Akerman Senterfitt Suntrust Internat Ctr One SE 3d Ave 28th Fl Miami FL 33131 Office Phone: 305-755-5850. Fax: 305-374-5095. E-mail: edavis@akerman.com.

DAVIS, EDWARD WILSON, business administration educator; b. Thomaston, Ga., Aug. 4, 1935; s. James Royland, Jr. and Hazel (Bass) D.; m. Patricia Gail Forrest, Oct. 20, 1962; children: Matthew Wilson, Edward Royland. BS in Mech. Engring, Ga. Inst. Tech., 1957, MS in Indsl. Engring, 1959; postgrad., Swiss Fed. Inst. Tech., 1957-58; MPhil, Yale U., 1967, PhD, 1968. Project leader Ops. Research, Inc., Washington, 1960-64; asst. prof. Harvard Bus. Sch., Cambridge, Mass., 1968-73; vis. asso. prof. Sloan Sch. Mgmt., M.I.T., Cambridge, 1973-74; assoc. prof., then prof. U. N.C., Chapel Hill, 1974-78; prof. Grad. Sch. Bus. Adminstrn., U. Va., Charlottesville, 1978—, Oliver Wight prof. bus. adminstrn., 1984—, Isidore Horween rsch. prof., 1991-96. Cons. various pvt. and public cos., U.S. and Europe. Author: Case Studies in Material Requirements Planning, 1978; co-author: Project Management with PERT & CPM, 3d edit., 1983, The Extended Enterprise, 2003; editor: Project Management, 1974, 2d edit., 1982. Council mem. Pilgrim Congregation Ch., 1972-74; cub scout and boy scout leader Occoneechee council Boy Scouts Am., 1974-77. IBM faculty fellow in internat. bus., 1976 Mem.: Prodn. Ops. Mgmt. Soc. (v.p. edn. 2003—05), Inst. Mgmt. Scis., Am. Inst. Indsl. Engrs., Project Mgmt. Inst., Am. Inst. Decision Scis., Am. Prodn. and Inventory Control Soc. (dir. Ednl. and Research Found., presdl. award 1974, 1989), U. Va. Raven Soc., Westminister Canterbury of the Blue Ridge (bd. dirs. 2000—04). Presbyterian. Office: PO Box 6550 Charlottesville VA 22906-6550 Office Phone: 434-924-4819. Business E-Mail: ewd@virginia.edu.

DAVIS, EGBERT LAWRENCE, III, lawyer; b. Winston-Salem, NC, Dec. 30, 1937; s. Egbert Lawrence Jr. and Eleanor (Layfield) D.; m. Alexandra Holderness, Aug. 25, 1962; children: Alexandra Davis Hipps, Egbert L. IV, Lucinda Davis, Pamela Davis. AB, Princeton U., 1960; LLB, Duke U., 1963; MBA, George Washington U., 1966. Bar: NC 1963. Assoc. Womble, Carlyle, Sandridge & Rice, Winston-Salem, NC, 1965-70, ptnr., 1970-82, Raleigh, NC, 1982-97, of counsel, 1997—. Sec. Wachovia Realty Investments, Winston-Salem, 1969—82. Mem. editl. bd. Duke U. Law Jour., 1963. Chmn. N.W. Environ. Preservation Com., Inc., Winston-Salem, 1980; chmn. bd. trustees N.C. Bapt. Hosp., Winston-Salem, 1981—82; chmn. N.C. Family Bus. Forum, 1993—94; co-chmn. Raleigh Wake Leadership Found., 2002—04; mem. state coun. N.C. Prison Fellowship, 1994—97; bd. dirs. NC Found. for Econ. Edn., 1996—2006; exec. com. Ea. Ctr. for Regional Devel., 1996—97; rep. N.C. Ho. of Reps., Raleigh, 1970—74; senator N.C. Senate, Raleigh, 1974—78; chmn. N.C. Dem. Party, 1989—91; bd. dirs. Ctr. for Citizenship, Enterprise and Govt., 2003—05. Capt. US Army, 1963—65. Named Citizen of Yr. Winston-Salem Mayor's Com. on Employment of the Handicapped, 1971, Young Man. of Yr. Winston-Salem Jaycees, 1972; recipient Freedom Guard award N.C. Jaycees, 1973, U.S. Jaycees, 1973. Mem. N.C. Bar Assn. (bd. govs. 1979-82), Duke Law Alumni Assn. (bd. dirs. 2006—), Coastal Conservation Assn. (bd. dirs. 1997-2006), Raleigh Rotary Club (pres. 1986-87), Duke U. Law Sch. Alumni Assn. (bd. dirs. 2006—). Republican. Presbyterian. Avocations: reading, writing, tennis, biking, fishing. Office: Womble Carlyle Sandridge PO Box 831 Raleigh NC 27602-0831 Office Phone: 919-755-2103. Personal E-mail: eldiii@aol.com. Business E-Mail: ldavis@wcsr.com.

DAVIS, ELIZABETH EILEEN, education educator; b. West Point, NY, Nov. 3, 1967; d. Buster Keaton and Rita Ann Davis. AA in Info. Sys., Anne Arundel Cmty. Coll., 1990; BS in Info. Systems, U. Balt., 1992, BS in Bus. Mgmt., 1992; advanced tchg. cert., Coll. Notre Dame, 1996, MEd, 2000. Computer operator Nat. Security Agy., Ft. Meade, Md., 1985—86; mktg. rep. Spl. Programs Inc., Glen Burnie, Md., 1990—96; elem. sch. tchr. Balt. City Sch. Sys., 1996—, spl. edn. tchr., 2003—04. Coord. Balt. symphony orch. Balt. Pub. Sch., 1996—98. Sunday sch. tchr. Glen Burnie Evangelical Presbyn., 1987. Mem.: ASCD.

DAVIS, ELLEN MARIE, business educator; b. Boston, June 9, 1958; d. Charles F. and Ellen (Fahy) Sargent; m. Jack C. Davis, Oct. 13, 1982; children: Elaine, Melissa. BS in Bus. Edn., Salem Coll., Mass., 1981; postgrad., Cameron U., Lawton, Okla., 1988—89; postgrad, Cameron U., Lawton Okla., 1991, Cameron U., Lawton, Okla., 2001—05. Cert. K-12 tchr., Okla., Mass. Instr. Big Bend C.C., Friedberg, Germany, 1983-88, Fischer Ednl. Svcs., Lawton, 1989-91; tchr. bus. Am. Coll., Lawton, 1992-93; owner Checker Wrecker and Auto Salvage and E&M Car Ctr., Lawton, 1993—; instr. Douglass Learning Ctr., Lawton Pub. Schs., 2004—. Pres. Howell Elem. Sch. PTA, 1994-95. Named Tchr. of Month (2), Am. Coll., 1992. Mem. Okla. Alliance for Geog. Edn., Smithsonian Assocs., Internat. Reading Assn. Avocations: reading, crafts. Home: PO Box 3738 Lawton OK 73502-3738 Office: 520 S Sheridan Lawton OK 73501 E-mail: okdragonlady@yahoo.com.

DAVIS, ERROLL BROWN, JR., academic administrator, former utilities executive; b. Pitts., Aug. 5, 1944; s. Erroll Brown and Eleanor Margaret (Boykin) D.; m. Elaine E. Casey, July 13, 1968; children: Christopher, Whitney BS in elec. engring., Carnegie-Mellon U., 1965; MBA in Fin., U. Chgo., 1967. Corp. fin. staff Ford Motor Co., Detroit, 1969-73, Xerox Corp., Rochester, 1973-78; v.p. fin. Wis. Power and Light Co., Madison, 1978-82, v.p. fin and pub. affairs, 1982-84, exec. v.p., 1984-87, pres., 1987—98, pres., CEO, 1988-98; pres. WPL Holdings, Inc., 1990—98, Alliant Energy Corp., Madison, 1998—2003, CEO, 1990—2005, chmn., 2000—06; CEO Alliant Energy Resources, Inc.; chmn. Edison Electric Inst., 2000—03; chmn., CEO Interstate Power and Light Co., 2000—05; chancellor U. Sys. Ga., Atlanta, 2006—. Bd. dirs. BP plc, Union Pacific Corp., GM Corp., 2007—. Mem. bd. regents U. Wis., 1987-94; bd. dirs. United Way Dane County, 1984-89, chmn. bd. dirs., 1987; life trustee Carnegie Mellon U., chmn. bd. trustees, 2000-03; mem. bd. trustees U. Chgo., 2005—. Recipient Black Engineer of Yr. Award, 1998, Ellis Island Medal of Honor, 2001, Dr. Martin Luther King Jr. Award, City of Madison, 2001. Mem. Am. Soc. Corp. Execs., Electric Power Rsch. Inst. (bd. dirs. 1990-2006), Assn. Edison Illuminating Cos. (bd. dirs. 1993-2006), Edison Electric Inst. (bd. dirs. 1995-2006, chmn. 2002-03), US Olympic Com. (bd. dirs.). Avocations: biking, golf. Office: U Sys of Ga Bd Regents 270 Washington St SW Atlanta GA 30334-1450

DAVIS, EVAN ANDERSON, lawyer; b. NYC, Jan. 18, 1944; s. Richard T. and Charlotte (Upham) Davis; m. Mary Carroll Rothwell; children: Sara Mei-Ping, Charlotte Zhong Xue, Phoebe Ming Ming. BA, Harvard U., 1966; JD, Columbia U., 1969. Bar: N.Y. 1970, U.S. Dist. Ct. (so. dist.) N.Y. 1973, U.S. Ct. Appeals (2d cir.) 1973, U.S. Dist. Ct. (ea. dist.) N.Y. 1978, U.S. Supreme Ct. 1979. Law clk. to judge U.S. Ct. Appeals (D.C. cir.), 1969-70; law clk. to Justice Potter Stewart U.S. Supreme Ct., 1970-71; gen. counsel N.Y.C. Budget Bur., 1971-72; chief consumer protection div. N.Y.C. Law Dept., 1972-74; task force leader, impeachment inquiry staff U.S. Ho. of Reps., 1974; assoc. Cleary, Gottlieb, Steen & Hamilton LLP, NYC, 1975-78, ptnr., 1979—86, 1991—; counsel to gov. of N.Y., 1985-90. Vice chmn. Fund N.Y.C., 1982—85; trustee Columbia U., 1993—2005, mem. exec. com., 1994—, chair bd. fin. com., 1999—2005, vice chair bd., 2001—05. Editor-in-chief: Columbia Law Rev., 1968—69. Treas. Sch. Field Studies, 1991—95; bd. dirs. Franklin and Eleanor Roosevelt Inst., 1993—98, mem. exec. com., 1994—2002; bd. dirs. Mus. Hudson Highlands, 1997—98, Storm King Sch., 1991—98, Adirondack Coun.; bd. visitors Helen Hayes Hosp., 1992—98; trustee Spence Sch., 2005—; rep. Ctr. for Family; chairperson N.Y. Fair Elections Project, 1998—; mem. Coun. Fgn. Rels. Recipient Hopkins medal, St. David's Soc., N.Y., 1988, Bruckner medal, Fed. Bar Coun., 1990, Aquarium Environ. award, Wildlife Conservation Soc., 1995, Milton Gould award for Outstanding Advocacy, Office Appellate Defender, 1998, award, Brennan Ctr., 1999, Law and Soc. award, N.Y. Lawyers Pub. Interest, 2000, 1844 award, N.Y. Correctional Assn., 2001, award, Bklyn. Legal Svcs., 2004. Mem.: ABA (ho. of dels. 1983—85, 1991—93, 2000—02, chmn. spl. com. youth edn. citizenship 1986—88, chmn. standing com. pub. edn.), N.Y. State Bar Assn. (mem. com. stds. atty. conduct 1992—, mem. commn. mid. income access legal svc. 1995—2002, chief judge's commn. jud. election 2003—), Am. Law Inst., Legal Aid Soc. (v.p. 1983—85, 1983—84, mem. exec. com. 1992—2000), Assn. Bar City of N.Y. (chmn. exec. com. 1982—83, v.p. 1983—84, pres. 2000—02). Office: Cleary Gottlieb Steen & Hamilton LLP 1 Liberty Plz New York NY 10006-1470 Office Phone: 212-225-2850. Business E-Mail: edavis@cgsh.com.

DAVIS, FERD LEARY, JR., law educator, consultant; b. Zebulon, NC, Dec. 4, 1941; s. Ferd L. and Selma Ann (Harris) D.; m. Joy Baker Davis, Jan. 25, 1963; children: Ferd Leary III, James Benjamin, Elizabeth Joy. BA, Wake Forest U., 1964, JD, 1967; LLM, Columbia U., 1984. Bar: N.C. 1967. Editor Zebulon (N.C.) Record, 1958; tchr. Davidson County Schs., Wallburg, NC, 1966; ptnr. Davis & Davis and related law firms, Zebulon and Raleigh, NC, 1967—76; asst. pros. Wake County Dist. Ct., Raleigh, 1968—69; town atty. Town of Zebulon, 1969—76; founding dean Campbell U. Sch. Law, Buies Creek, NC, 1975—86, prof. law, 1975—2005; founding dean, prof. law Elon U. Sch. Law, Greensboro, NC, 2005—. Dir. Inst. to Study Practice of Law and Socioecon. Devel., 1985-2005; chmn. The Davis Cons. Group, Inc., Greensboro, 1987-2005; pres. LAWLEAD/NIELLP, 1998—; cons. U. Charleston, W.Va., 1979; vis. scholar Ctr. for Creative Leadership, 1993. Assoc. editor Wake Forest U. Law Rev. Trustee Wake County Pub. Librs., 1971-75, Olivia Raney Trust, 1969-71; mem. N.C. State Dem. Exec. Com., 1970-72, N.C. Gen. Statutes Commn., 1977-79, Commn. on the Future of N.C., 1980-83; dir., Howard Meml. Christian Edn. Fund, N.C. BarCares. 1st Lt. USAR, 1959-66. Babcock scholar Wake Forest U., 1963-67; Dayton Hudson fellow Columbia U., 1982-83. Fellow Coll. Law Practice Mgmt.; mem. ABA, N.C. Bar Assn., N.C. State Bar, Am. Judicature Soc. (nat. adv. com. 2005—), Rotary, Phi Delta Phi, Delta Theta Phi, Omicron Delta Kappa. Democrat. Office: Elon U Sch Law 201 N Greene St Greensboro NC 27401 Office Phone: 336-278-9201. E-mail: davislaw@elon.edu.

DAVIS, FLORENCE ANN, lawyer; b. Pitts., Feb. 22, 1955; d. Richard Davis and Charlotte (Saul) McGhee; m. Kevin J. O'Brien, May 28, 1978; children: Rebecca Davis, Sarah Davis. AB, Wellesley U., 1976; JD, NYU, 1979. Bar: N.Y. 1980, U.S. Dist. Ct. (ea. and so. dists.) N.Y., N.Y. Ct. Appeals (2d cir.), U.S. Tax Ct., U.S. Supreme Ct. Assoc. atty. Sullivan & Cromwell, NYC, 1979-86; litigation counsel Morgan Stanley & Co., NYC, 1986-88, v.p., 1988-90, dir. compliance, 1989-90, prin., 1990-95; v.p., gen. counsel Am. Internat. Group, NYC, 1995—. Pres. Starr Found. Root-Tilden scholar NYU Law Sch., 1976-79. Mem. Securities Industry Assn. (v.p. edn. Compliance and Legal div. 1992, exec. com. Compliance and Legal div. 1990-92). Office: American International Group Inc 70 Pine St New York NY 10270-0094

DAVIS, FRANK TRADEWELL, JR., lawyer; b. Atlanta, Feb. 2, 1938; s. Frank T. and Sue (Burnett) D.; m. Winifred Storey, June 23, 1961; children: Frank, Frederick, Gordon. AB, Princeton U., 1960; JD, George Washington U., 1963; LLM, Harvard U., 1964. Bar: Ga. 1963, U.S. Ct. Appeals (5th cir.) 1963, D.C. 1966, U.S. Supreme Ct. 1968, U.S. Ct. Appeals (11th cir.) 1982, U.S. Ct. Appeals (10th cir.) 2003. Assoc. Hansell, Post Brandon & Dorsey, Atlanta, 1964-67; ptnr. Hansell & Post, Atlanta, 1968-77, 79-86, Long, Aldridge & Norman, Atlanta, 1986—2002, McKenna, Long & Aldridge, Atlanta, 2002—. Ptnr., gen. counsel Pres.'s Reorgn. Project Office of Pres., 1977-79; vis. instr. U. Ga. Law Sch., 1964-66, Ga. State U. Law Sch., 1988-90; vis. prof. Emory U. Law Sch., 1992—; dir. Red and Black Newspaper U. Ga., 2005-. Author: Business Acquisitions, 1977, (2d edit.), 1982; contbr. articles to legal jours. Bd. dirs. Nat. Inst. Justice, 1980—81, Westminster Schs., 1969—, chmn. bd. dirs., 1984—89; bd. dirs. Va. Sem., 1980—94, exec. com., 1985—89; mem. Atlanta Charter Commn.; chmn. Atlanta Crime Commn., 1977; mem. bd. councilors Carter Presdl. Ctr., 1988—; chmn. Regional Ednl. Found. Atlanta; commr. Atlanta Regional Commn., 1999—; bd. dirs, Ga. First Amendment Found., 1996—; sr. warden All Saints' Episcopal Ch., 1982, 2002, vestry, 2000—03. Lt. USNR, 1960—62. Fellow Am. Bar Found. (life); mem. Am. Law Inst. (life), Atlanta C. of C. (bd. dirs. 1975-77), Piedmont Driving Club (Atlanta), Capital City Club (Atlanta), Cedar Creek Racquet Club (Cashiers, N.C.), The Army and Navy Club (Washington), Rotary (pres. Atlanta chpt. 1990-91, bd. dirs., sec. 1988-89, chmn. bd., 1991-92, chmn. Ednl. Found. 1997—). Home: 2525 Peachtree Rd 11 Atlanta GA 30305 Office: 303 Peachtree St NE Ste 5300 Atlanta GA 30308-3264 Home Phone: 404-233-4020; Office Phone: 404-527-4080. Personal E-mail: ftd@mckennalong.com.

DAVIS, FRANK WAYNE, lawyer; b. Ada, Okla., Aug. 24, 1936; s. Roscoe Gladstone and Neva Dell (Peck) Davis; m. Kay Diane Higginbotham, Aug. 12, 1961; children: David, Paul. Student, U. Ill., Urbana, 1956-57; BA, East Cen. U., 1958; LLB, U. Okla., Norman, 1959. Bar: Okla. 1959, U.S. Dist. Ct. (we. dist.) Okla. 1965, U.S. Ct. Appeals (10th cir.) 1976. Acting postmaster U.S. Postal Service, Ada, 1959-61; assoc. Denny W. Falkenburg, Medford, Okla., 1961; county atty. Logan County, Guthrie, Okla., 1961-65; sole practice Guthrie, 1965—85, 1988—; ptnr. Davis and Hudson, Guthrie, 1985-88. Mcpl. judge City of Guthrie, 1974—78; rep. State of Okla., Oklahoma City, 1978—2004; vice chmn. judiciary com. Okla. Ho. of Reps., 1981—82, 1989, 1991—2004, minority fl. leader, 1982—86, asst. minority fl. leader, 1986—90. Scoutmaster Troop # 850 Boy Scouts Am., Guthrie, 1961—2000; del. Rep. Nat. Convs., 1984, 1996, alt. del., 2000; chmn. Logan County Reps., Guthrie, 1964—69; del. gen. conf. United Meth. Ch., Portland, Oreg., 1976; trustee Okla. United Meth. Found. Recipient Silver Beaver award, Boy Scouts Am., 1978. Mem.: Logan County Bar Assn. (pres. 1972—73), Okla. Bar Assn., Am. Legion, Masons, Lions (v.p. 2004—05, pres. 2005—06, zone chmn. 2007—), Gideons. Methodist. Avocations: fishing, stamp collecting/philately, farming, oil and gas production. Office: 115 N Division St Guthrie OK 73044-3240 Home: 2121 N Walnut Guthrie OK 73044 Home Phone: 405-282-1478; Office Phone: 405-282-1420. Personal E-mail: repfwdavis@wmconnect.com.

DAVIS, FRED, journalist, educator; b. Columbia, SC, Feb. 14, 1947; s. Nathaniel Lewis Sr. and Arneatha Pearl (Robinson) D.; m. Joan Sineta Walker, Jan. 14, 1967; children: Alex LaMar, Kevin Alexander. BS in English Edn., N.C. A&T State U., 1969; MBA in Gen. and Exec. Mgmt., Fla. Metro. U., 2005; ME In Integrated Learning Techs., Jacksonville U., Fla., 2007. City/coun. reporter WFMY-TV/CBS, Greensboro, NC, 1969-70; govtl. reporter WJRT-TV/ABC, 1970-74, dir. documentaries and pub. affairs, 1974-75; anchor-reporter WMAL-TV (WJLA-TV/ABC), Washington, 1975; various positions in field to reporter, news editor WRC-TV/NBC News, Washington, 1975; gen. assignment, news program svc. reporter KNBC-TV/NBC News, Burbank, Calif., 1976; writer/reporter KHJ-TV/Ind., Hollywood, Calif., 1976-78; anchor/editor WIS-TV/NBC, Columbia, SC, 1978-80; asst. news dir., sr. producer WJXT-TV/CBS, Jacksonville, Fla., 1980-81; staff writer Jacksonville Jour./Fla. Pub. Co., 1981; news dir. ABC Direction Radio Network/ABC News, NYC, 1981-88; weekly commentator CBS-owned radio stas., 1992; self-syndicated columnist S.C. newspapers, 1992—; Disting. prof. mass media mgmt. Wash. State U., Pullman, 1995-97; columnist The Seattle Times, The Spokesman-Rev., 1996—98. Adj. prof. Edward R. Murrow Sch. of Comm., Wash. State U., Pullman, 1997—2000; cons./host Sta. KWSU-TV (PBS), 1997—; owner media svcs./broadcast news consultancy, 1989—; vis. lectr. Benedict Coll., Columbia, 1979—80, Columbia, 1990, Coll. Journalism U. S.C., 1987, Coll. Journalism & Mass Comm., U. Nebr., Lincoln, 1997—99; mem. Journalism and Mass Comm. del. to China, Citizens Ambassador Program, 1996, Journalism and Mass Comm. del. to Italy, Switzerland, Austria, Citizens Ambassador Program, 1997, Journalism and Mass Comm. del. to S. Africa, Citizens Ambassador Program, 1999; expert media witness Libel Def. Resource Ctr., San Diego, 1997; del. People to People Internat., Russia, 1998, Finland, 98; cons., host KWSU-TV, KUON-TV, 1997; cons., writer The Gallup Org., Lincoln, Nebr., 1999—; del. News World conf., Barcelona, 1999; lectr. Coll. Journalism & Mass. Comm., U. Nebr., Lincoln, 1997—99, U. Nebr., Lincoln, 1999—; adj. instr. U. Fla. Coll. Journalism and Comm., 2001—; journalism instr. James Weldon Johnson Coll. Prep. Mid. Sch., Jacksonville, 2005—; cons. Vista Rsch. (Std. and Poors), NYC, 2006—. Contbr. articles USA Today; provider (news commentaries) CBS-owned radio stas., N.Y., L.A., Chgo., Phila., San Francisco, Detroit, Mpls., columnist (newspaper) The Seattle Times, 1996—97, The Royal Gazette, Bermuda, 1996—97, The Spokesman-Rev., 1996—97, prodr./cons. (global bus. report) Bermuda Broadcasting Co., 2000—01, writer (jour.) Jacksonville Bus. Jour., 2001, prodr./moderator ("Socratic" Roundtables TV series) WJCT-TV (PBS), Jacksonville, Fla., 2001. Bd. visitors, N.C. A&T State U., Greensboro, 1988—; del. Russia and Finland People to People Internat., 1998. Recipient award, Leadership Flint (Mich.), 1973, Internat. Radio Festival of N.Y., 1983—88, Ohio State award, ABC Radio, 1986, award, Nat. Press Club, 1984, 1985, Comm. Excellence to Black Audiences award of distinction, ABC Dir./Radio Network, 1987, b'nai b'rith Edward R. Murrow Brotherhood award, 1986, Disting. Alumni award, Nat. Assn. for Equal Opportunity in Higher Edn., 1988, Disting. Acheivement award, Mass Media Mngmt. Studies, Coll. Liberal Arts, Wash. State U., 1996. Mem.: U.S. Tennis Assn. (USTA), Broadcast Edn. Assn., Assn. for Edn. in Journalism and Mass Comm., S.C. Press Assn., Nat. Assn. Black Journalists, Acad. TV Arts and Scis., Am. Fedn. TV and Radio Artists, Radio-TV News Dirs. Assn., Internat. Platform Assn., PGA Ptnrs., Broadcast Edn. Assn., Assn. for Edn. in Journalism and Mass Comm., Nat. Geog. Soc., Soc. Profl. Journalists, Nat. Assn. Black Journalists, Acad. TV Arts and Scis., Am. Fedn. TV and Radio Artists, Radio-TV News Dirs. Assn., Internat. Platform Assn., PGA Ptnrs. (charter mem., charter), U.S. Tennis Assn., U.S. Golf Assn., The Folio Soc., Planetary Soc., Nat. Geog. Soc., The Folio Soc., S.C. Press Assn., U.S. Golf Assn., Planetary Soc., Alpha Phi Alpha, Alpha Phi Alpha. Baptist. Avocations: gourmet cooking, racquetball, golf, tennis, barbecue judging. Office: Davis Media Svcs & Syndication LLC/ U Fla Coll Journalism & Comm PO Box 56741 Jacksonville FL 32241-6741

DAVIS, FREDERICK BENJAMIN, retired law educator; b. Bklyn., Aug. 21, 1926; s. Clifford Howard and Anne Frances (Forbes) D.; m. Mary Ellen Saecker, Apr. 21, 1956; children: Judith, Robert, James, Mary. AB, Yale U., 1948; JD, Cornell U., 1953; LLM with honors, Victoria U. of Wellington, New Zealand, 1955. Bar: N.Y. 1953, Mo. 1970, Ohio 1981. Assoc. Engel Judge & Miller, NYC, 1953-54; instr. U. Pa. Law Sch., 1955-56; asst. prof. NYU, 1956-57, U. S.D., 1957-60, assoc. prof., 1960-62, Emory U., 1962-63, prof., 1963-66, U. Mo.-Columbia, 1966-70, Edward W. Hinton prof. law, 1970-81, Edward W. Hinton prof. emeritus, 1981—; dean, prof. law U. Dayton Sch. Law, 1981-86; dean, prof. Memphis State U., 1987-92, prof., 1992-98, prof., dean emeritus, 1998—. Cons. adminstrv. procedure Mo. Senate, 1974-77; vis. prof. Wake Forest U. Sch. Law, 1980, 86-87, U. Wis., 1960, George Washington U., 1965, Tulane U., 1966, U. Mo.-Kansas City, 1973, U. Ky., 1977. Contbr. numerous articles, comments, revs., notes to profl. jours. Served with USNR, 1944-46. Mem. ABA (coun. sect. adminstrv. law 1969-75), Am. Law Inst., Rotary Club (Memphis Ctrl. chpt.), Crescent Club. Republican. Episcopalian. Personal E-mail: freddyandmary@gmail.com.

DAVIS, GEENA (VIRGINIA DAVIS), actress; b. Wareham, Mass., Jan. 21, 1957; m. Richard Emmolo, March 25, 1982 (div. Feb. 26, 1983); m. Jeff Goldblum, Nov. 1, 1987 (div. Oct. 17, 1990); m. Renny Harlin, Sept. 18, 1993 (div. June 21, 1998); m. Reza Jarrahy, Sept. 1, 2001; children Alizeh Keshvar Davis Jarrahy, Kian William, Kaiis Steven. BFA, Boston U., 1979; attended, New England Coll., Henniker, NH. Founder Genial Pictures; mem. My. Washington (N.H.) Repertory Theatre Co. Actor: (films) Tootsie, 1982, Fletch, 1985, Transylvania 6-5000, 1985, The Fly, 1986, Beetlejuice, 1988, The Accidental Tourist, 1988 (Academy award Best Supporting Actress, 1989), Earth Girls Are Easy, 1989, Quick Change, 1990, Thelma and Louise, 1991 (Acad. award nominee Best Actress 1991, British Acad Film and TV Arts award Best Actress in leading role 1991, Golden Globe award nominee Best Actress 1991), A League of Their Own, 1992, Hero, 1992, Princess Scargo and the Birthday Pumpkin (voice), 1993, Angie, 1994, Speechless, 1994 (also prodr.), Cutthroat Island, 1995, The Long Kiss Goodnight, 1996, Stuart Little, 1999, Stuart Little 2, 2002; TV series: Buffalo Bill, 1983-84 (also wrote), Sara, 1985, The Geena Davis Show, 2000 (also co-exec. prodr.), Commander-in-Chief, 2005-06(Best Performance by an Actress in a TV Series-Drama, Hollywood Fgn. Press Assn (Golden Globe award), 2006; appeared in TV film Secret Weapons, 1985; exec. prodr. Mistrial, 1996; TV appearances include Knight Rider, 1983, Fantasy Island, 1984, Family Ties 1984, Remington Steele, 1985, Will & Grace, 2004. Recipient Matrix award for arts & entertainment, NY Women in Comm. Inc., 2006. Avocation: archery. Office: Creative Artists Agy 9830 Wilshire Blvd Beverly Hills CA 90212

DAVIS, GENE, public relations executive, state legislator; b. Salt Lake City, July 2, 1945; s. John Albert and Glenna Rachel (Cameron) D.; m. Penny Lou Hansen, Mar. 9, 1971; children: James, Pamela. Cert. in electronic engring., Radio Operational Engring., Burbank, Calif., 1963; LLB, LaSalle Ext. U., Chgo., 1974. Announcer Radio Sta. KNAK, Salt Lake City, 1965-75; prodn. continuity dir. Radio Sta. KALL AM/FM, Salt Lake City, 1976-86; owner G. Davis Advt., Pub. Rels., Salt Lake City, 1986-91; pub. rels. profl. Valley Mental Health, Salt Lake City, 1990—; mem. Utah Senate, Dist. 3, Minority Whip, Salt Lake City, 1998—. Treas. Comm. Fed. Credit Union, Salt Lake City, 1981-86. Vice-chair East County Recreation Bd., Salt Lake City, 1991—2000; rep. Utah State House of Reps., Salt Lake City, 1986—98; mem. bus. & labor com., retirement com., exec. appropriations com., coun. of state govt.-health capacity task force Utah State Senate, Salt Lake City. Mem. Sugar House Rotary Club (pres. 2003-04), Sugar House Cmty. Coun. (chmn. 1984-85). Democrat. Mem. Lds Ch. Avocations: golf, gardening, politics. Home: 865 Parkway Ave Salt Lake City UT 84106-1704 Office: Valley Mental Health 4460 S Highland Dr Ste 450 Salt Lake City UT 84124 Office Phone: 801-273-6394. Business E-Mail: gened@vmh.com. E-mail: gdavis@utahsenate.org.

DAVIS, GENE, retired civil engineer; b. Lower Peach Tree, Ala., Apr. 21, 1935; s. Edgar Thomas and Una (Smith) D.; m. Betty Marie Davidson; children: Jean Marie Davis, Jenifer Davis Cerny, Joanna Davis Palladino, James Andrew Davis. BSCE, U. Ala., 1958; MS in Mgmt., Naval Postgrad. Sch., 1969; cert., Armed Forces Staff Coll., 1974. Commd. ensign USN, 1958, advanced through grades to Capt., 1980; resident engr. Navy Project Office, Cape Canaveral, Fla., 1960-63, Dir. of Constrn. in South East Asia, Bangkok, Thailand, 1963-65; program mgr. Pacific divsn., Naval Civil Engring., Honolulu, 1965-68; exec. officer Naval Constrn. Bat. 121, Gulfport, Miss., 1968-70; dir. constrn. planning Hdqrs., Naval Civil Engring., Washington, 1974-76; comdg. officer Naval Constrn. Bat. 133, Gulfport, 1976-78; chief of staff Naval Constrn. Regiment, Port Hueneme, Calif., 1978-81; comdr. officer Pub. Works Ctr., Great Lake, Ill., 1981-83; vice comdr. Pacific divsn., 1983-86; dir. constrn. Diego Garcia, 1986-87;

retired USN, 1987; sr. group engr. Martin Marietta, Orlando, 1987-92; ops. mgr. Brown & Root Inc., Houston, 1992-2001; civil engr. cons., 1997-98; v.p. RSI, Inc., 1997-98; ret., 2001. Author: Analysis of the Imperial Iranian Navy Construction Program, 1974. Mem. Soc. Am. Mil. Engrs. (pres. Diego Garcia post 1992), USN Inst. Republican. Roman Catholic. Home: PO Box 535 Thomasville AL 36784-0535

DAVIS, GEOFF, congressman; b. Montreal, Que., Can., Oct. 26, 1958; m. Pat Davis; 6 children. BS, US Mil. Acad., West Point, 1981. Pres. Capstone Inc., 1992—2004; mem. US Congress from 4th Ky. dist., 2005—. Mem. bd. adv. No. Ky. C. of C.; bd. mem. Regional Ct. Appointed Spl. Advocate Assn. Served Rangers, 82d Airborne div. US Army, 1976—87. Mem.: West Pont Assn. Graduates, US Army Ranger Assn., 82d Airborne Assn., NRA (life). Republican. Christian. Office: US Ho Reps 1541 Longworth Ho Office Bldg Washington DC 20515-1704 Office Phone: 202-225-3465. Office Fax: 202-225-0003.*

DAVIS, GEORGE DONALD, executive land use policy consultant; b. Oneida, NY, Nov. 19, 1942; s. Pearl Floyd and Kathrine Virginia (Connolly) D.; m. Anita Face Riner, June 26, 1976; children: Maria Lisa, Brett Hollis, Sarah Bessie, Lara Emily; stepchildren: Andrea G. Riner, Joel S. Riner. BS in Forestry, SUNY, 1964; postgrad., Cornell U., 1971. Forester, pub. land adminstr. U.S. Forest Svc. Dept. Agr., Colo., 1964-68; ecologist Gov. Rockefeller's N.Y. State Temp. Study Commn. on Future of Adirondacks, 1969—71; pvt. land use and natural resources cons. Ithaca, NY, 1971; dir. planning Adirondack Park Agy., Ray Brook, NY, 1971-76; exec. dir. Wilderness Soc., Washington, 1976-77; spl. asst. U.S. Forest Svc., Washington, 1977-79; dep. forest supr. Idaho Panhandle Nat. Forests, Coeur d'Alene, 1979-82; land use, natural resource cons. Wadhams, NY, 1982-94; program dir. Adirondack Coun., 1983-88; exec. dir. Adirondack Land Trust, 1984-88; prin. Davis Assocs., 1988—. Pres. Ecol. Sustainable Devel., Inc., 1994—97; coord. Global Assocs. in Sustainable Devel., 1997—2002; project dir. Land Use Policy and Allocation Program for Lake Baikal Watershed in Russia, 1991—93, Lake Hovsgol/Selenge River Wateshed in Mongolia, 1992—94, Ussuri River Watershed in Russian Far East and China, 1993—97, Altai Rep., Russia, 1994—97; exec. dir. Gov. Cuomo's Commn. on Adirondacks in the 21st Century, 1989—90; mem. environ. task force Rockefeller Bros. Fund; mem. Hudson Basin project task force Rockefeller Found. Co-author: The Unfinished Agenda, 1977, Developing a Land Conservation Strategy, 1987; author: Ecosystem Representative as a Criterion for World Wilderness Designation, 1987, 2020 Vision: Fulfilling the Promise of the Adirondack Park, 1988, Completing the Adirondack Wilderness System, 1990, The Lake Baikal Region in the Twenty-First Century: A Model of Sustainable Development or Continued Degradation?, 1993, A Comprehensive National Program of Sustainable Land Use Policies for the Lake Hovsgol-Selenge River Watershed, 1994, A Sustainable Land Use and Allocation Program for the Ussuri/Wusuli River Watershed and Adjacent Territories, 1996; contbr. to profl. publs. Active Gov. N.Y. State Forest Industry Task Force, 1987-89, N.Y.-New Eng. Gov. Task Force on No. Forest Lands, 1988-90. MacArthur fellow, 1989—. Roman Catholic. Home and Office: 2482 N 32d St Springfield OR 97477-7900 E-mail: davisassoc1@aol.com. *The basic goal of my life has been to promote land and natural resource stewardship, through direct action and example, to help insure that our planet's resources are more equitably distributed among members of the present generation and are sufficient for future generations.*

DAVIS, GEORGE EDWARD, industrial designer; b. Hugo, Okla., July 3, 1928; s. Silas William and Florence Elva (White) D.; m. Betty Sue Walker, July 21, 1951; children: Susan Elizabeth, Laura Ellen. Student, U. Tex., 1946—49; BA, Art Ctr. Coll. Design, LA, 1956. Registered interior designer, Tex. Staff designer Friedrich Refrigeration Co., San Antonio, 1957; design dir. comml. divsn. Woodarts Co., Houston, 1958-59; staff designer Brede, Inc., Houston, 1960-61; designer, co-founder Concept Planners and Designers, Houston, 1962-64; mgr. archtl. dept. Lockheed-Calif. Co., NASA Manned Spacecraft Ctr., Clear Lake, Tex., 1965-66; staff designer office products divsn. Litton Industries, Austin and San Antonio, 1967-68; staff designer Clegg Design Group, San Antonio, 1969-76; ind. design cons. San Antonio, 1977—. Interior designer for USAA, San Antonio, 1991-2001; dir. Systemics, Inc., San Antonio, Christian Bookmark, Inc., San Antonio, 1972-88. Trustee, San Antonio Christian Sch., 1973-82, chmn. bd., 1979-80; bd. elders Christ Presbyn. Ch., San Antonio, 1982-85; mem. Zoning Commn., City of Castle Hills, 1983-93, mem. City Coun., 1993-94, mem. Archtl. Rev. Com., 1995-2001. Served with USAF, 1950-54. Decorated DFC, Air medal with 3 oak leaf clusters. Mem. AIA (profl. affiliate), Tex. Soc. Architects (profl. affiliate, award of merit 1968). Home: 205 Wisteria Dr Castle Hills TX 78213-2109 Office: PO Box 13385 San Antonio TX 78213-0385 Personal E-mail: gdavis22@satx.rr.com.

DAVIS, GEORGE LINN, banker; b. Des Moines, July 9, 1934; s. James Cox and Elizabeth (Linn) D.; m. Anne Roberts, May 1955 (div. Jan. 1967); children: James, Elliott, George Linn; m. Mary Elizabeth Graham, Apr. 27, 1968; children: Stephen, Thomas. BA, Yale U., 1956; MBA, Harvard U., 1958. Sr. v.p. Citibank NA, NYC, 1958-81; exec. v.p. First Chgo. Corp., Chgo., 1981-87; Citicorp/Citibank group exec. N.Am. Fin. Group, NYC, 1987-90; chmn. Scarborough Ptnrs., Inc., NYC, 1990—; pres., CEO, bd. dirs. 1st Am. Bankshares Inc., Washington, 1990-91. Bd. dirs. Sealy Inc.; CEO Banco de Venezuela Internat., Syscon Inc.; chmn. Emex, Inc. Trustee Central Park Conservancy; chmn. Nat. Stroke Assn. Mem. Robert Morris Assocs., Assn. Equipment Lessors (bd. dirs. 1974-76), Chgo. Club, Glenview Club, Sleepy Hollow Country Club, Univ. Club. Republican. Office: Scarborough Partners Inc 450 Park Ave Fl 6 New York NY 10022-2605 Office Phone: 212-634-1180. E-mail: GD@JFLPartners.com.

DAVIS, GEORGE S., manufacturing executive; Grad. in Econs. and Polit. Sci., Claremont McKenna Coll., Calif.; MBA, UCLA. Sr. pres. fin. Europe, Mid. East and Africa Atlantic Richfield Co.; corp. treas. Applied Materials, Inc., 1999—2005, head corp. bus. devel. group, 2005—06, sr. v.p., CFO, 2006—. Chmn. North Am. adv. bd. Semiconductor Equipment and Materials Internat. Bd. trustees San Jose Repertory Theatre. Office: Applied Materials Inc PO Box 58039 Santa Clara CA 95052-8039 Office Phone: 408-727-5555.*

DAVIS, GLEN ANTHONY, pediatrician; b. Kalamazoo, Mar. 18, 1972; s. Charles Alexander and Clementine Johnson Davis; m. Tamera Raeann Davis, Aug. 19, 2005. BS in Biomedical Scis., U. Mich., Ann Arbor, 1998, MD, 1998. Resident Children's Hosp. Mich., Detroit, 1998—2001; pediatrician Elkhart Gen. Hosp., Ind., 2001—04, South Bend Clinic, 2005—. Mag. columnist Ask the Pediatrician Gt. Lakes Family Mag., 2004—05; mem. children's hosp. steering com. Meml. Hosp., South Bend, Ind., 2005—; TV host Ask Dr. D, WSBT-TV, 2005—. Recipient Charles Gibson award, U. Mich. Med. Sch., 1998. Fellow: Am. Acad. Pediat.; mem.: AMA. Avocations: running, reading. Office: South Bend Clinic 211 N Eddy St South Bend IN 46617 Office Phone: 574-233-7337. Personal E-mail: gdavismd98@msn.com.

DAVIS, GLENN CRAIG, psychiatrist; b. Columbia, Mo., Apr. 26, 1946; s. Morris S. and Dorothy (Hall) Davis; children: Jason Michael, Galen Brent. BA, Reed Coll., 1968; MD, Duke U., 1972. Diplomate Am. Bd. Psychiatry and Neurology. Intern, then resident Duke U. Med. Ctr., Durham, NC, 1972-75; clin. assoc. NIMH, Bethesda, Md., 1975-77, chief of drug abuse unit, biological psychiatry br., 1977-79; assoc. prof. U. Tenn. Ctr. Health Scis., Memphis, 1979-81; assoc. prof. then prof. Sch. of Medicine Case Western Reserve U., Cleve., 1981-87; dir. psychiat. rsch. to chief of staff Cleve. VA Med. Ctr., 1981-87; chair psychiatry Henry Ford Med. Ctr., Detroit, 1987-92; v.p. behavioral svcs. Henry Ford Health System, Detroit, 1991-94, v.p. acad. affairs, 1992—2001, chief med. officer suburban regions, 1996-98, assoc. dean Case Western Reserve U., 1993—2001; prof. psychiatry Case Western Reserve U., Cleve., 1994—2001; pres. Am. Bd. Psychiatry & Neurology, Deerfield, Ill.; dean coll. of human medicine Mich. State U., East Lansing, Mich., 2001—05; sr. client ptnr. Korn Ferry Internat., Phila., 2005—. Clin. prof. U. Mich. Sch. Medicine, Ann Arbor, 1988—2001. Author numerous sci. rsch. papers and book chpts.; contbr. articles to profl. jours. Lt. comdr. USPHS US Army, 1975—79. Fellow: Am. Psychopathological Assn., Am. Psychiat. Assn.; mem.: AMA, AAAS, Am. Bd. Med. Specialties, Am. Bd. Psychiatry and Neurology (dir. 1996—2003, pres. 2000), Alpha Omega Alpha, Sigma Xi. Office: Korn Ferry Internat 1835 Market St Philadelphia PA 19103 Office Phone: 215-656-5356. Business E-Mail: gdavis@kornferry.com.

DAVIS, GLORIA WHITTIE, educational association administrator; d. Jim Daniel Whittie and Sadie Whittie Smith; m. Clarence Earl Davis, June 10, 1995; 1 child, Eric Wayne Whittie. BA in Criminal Justice, Lamar U., 1991; MA in Counseling, Prairie View A&M U., 1998, MA in Vocat. Edn., 2005. Dir. Tobacco Prevention Program, Beaumont, 2000; program coord. Family Literacy Program, Beaumont, 2001—. Employment supr. Tex. Work Force, Beaumont, 1973—99. Singer, writer, actor (performance) Gospel Music Work Shop of America (Excellence award, 2005). Registrar Tex. Mass Choir, Beaumont, 1993; bd. mem. Even Start, Beaumont, 2000, com. mem. Austin, Tex., 2004; instr. Texas Honors Leadership Program; choir pres. City Wide Musical; vol. Cmty. Outreach Program; deaconess Word of God Christian Ch., Beaumont, 1999. Recipient Beaumont Leadership award, 1984, Tex. Honors Leadership award, Tex., 2001-2004, Black Gospel Music award, Beaumont, 2004, Leadership Coun. Wall of Tolerance, So. Poverty Law Ctr., 2004. Mem.: Am. Counselling Assn., Nat. Ctr. Family Literacy, Internat. Assn. Pers. Employment Sys., Ea. Star. Home: 13350 Moss Hill Dr Beaumont TX 77713 Office: Lamar U PO Box 10034 Beaumont TX 77710 Home Phone: 409-753-2757. Office Fax: 409-880-1880; Home Fax: 409-753-2261. Personal E-mail: gdavis@aol.com. E-mail: gdavis7646@aol.com.

DAVIS, GORDON J., lawyer; b. Chgo., Aug. 7, 1941; AB, Williams Coll., 1963; JD, Harvard U., 1967; LLM (hon.), Williams Coll., Bard Coll. Bar: Ill. 1968, N.Y. 1973, U.S. Dist. Ct. (so. and ea. dists.) N.Y. 1973. Commr. NYC Dept. Parks and Recreation, 1978-83; ptnr. LeBoeuf Lamb Green & MacRae, LLP. Screening panel fed. magistrates U.S. Dist. Ct. (so. dist.) N.Y., 1983-90; co-founder Ctrl. Partk Conservancy. Mem. N.Y. City Planning Commn., 1973-78; bd. dirs. Harlem Studio Mus., 1981, Lincoln Ctr. Performing Arts, 1983, Mcpl. Art Soc., 1983, Dance Theatre of Harlem, 1984, N.Y. Public Libr., 1993; chmn. Jazz at Lincoln Ctr., 1996; v.p., bd. dirs. N.Y. Shakespeare Festival. Named one of Am.'s Top Black Lawyers, Black Enterprise mag., 2003; recipient Karel Shook Founders Award, Dance Theatre of Harlem, Harlem Sch. Arts Founders Medal, Frederick Law Olmsted Medal, Ctrl. Park Conservancy, Judicial Friends Award for Leadership, Assn. African-Am. Fed. , State and City Judges. Mem.: Assn. of Bar of City of N.Y. (com. to enhance profl. opportunities for minorities 1990), N.Y. Chap., Am. Inst. Architects (hon.). Office: LeBoeuf Lamb Green & MacRae 125 W 55th St New York NY 10019-5369 Office Phone: 212-424-8366. E-mail: gdavis@llgm.com.

DAVIS, GORDON RICHARD FUERST, retired biologist, translator; b. Prince Albert, Sask., Can., Apr. 5, 1925; s. Louis James Davis and Nora Sylvia Fuerst; m. Marie Bérengère Pauline Bérubé, May 25, 1949 (sep. 2003); children: Joseph Richard Kevin (dec.), Elyse Bruce, Marie Raymonde Joceline, Marie-Thérèse Danielle. B.Sc. in Zoology with honors, McGill U., 1948, M.Sc., 1949, PhD, 1952. Agrl. scientist biol. control unit Can. Dept. Agr., Que., 1948-52, research officer research br. Saskatoon, Sask., 1952-65, research scientist research br., 1965-85; translator Co-Operators Fin. Svcs. Ltd., Regina, Sask., Can., 1987-90; pres., mng. dir. Triple-D Translation Svcs., Regina, Sask., 1990-95. Mem. Div. III sci. curriculum com. Sask. Dept. Edn., 1974-80 Contbr. articles to profl. jours. Bd. trustees Saskatoon Catholic Bd. Edn., 1974-77; mem. Sask German Council, Inc., rep to Concordia German Language Sch., 1986-87, v.p., 1986-87. Served with Royal Can. Navy Vol. Res., 1944-45. Carpenter Teaching fellow, 1950-51 Mem. Nutrition Soc. Can. (sec. 1973-77, v.p. 1979-80, pres. 1980-81), Can. Fedn. Biol. Socs. (dir. 1973-77, 80-81, hon. sec.-treas. 1980-84), Sask. Geneal. Soc., Can.'s Nat. History Soc. Roman Catholic. *A knowledge of as many areas of learning as possible and a general understanding of related and unrelated fields helps to push back the limitations of our horizons; a dedication to one goal at a time; a desire to improve the environment for the general good and acknowledgement by future inquirers of the value of the contributions that one has made: all provide their own opportunities in a hostile world.*

DAVIS, GRAY (JOSEPH GRAHAM DAVIS), lawyer, former governor; b. NYC, Dec. 26, 1942; m. Sharon Ryer, Feb. 20, 1983. BA cum laude, Stanford U., 1964; JD, Columbia U., 1967. Chief of staff to Gov. Jerry Brown State of Calif., Sacramento, 1975—81, mem. Calif. State Assembly, 1983—87, state contr., 1987—95, lt. gov., 1995-99, gov., 1999—2003; of counsel Loeb & Loeb, LA, 2004—. Chmn. Housing and Community Devel. Com., Calif. Coun. on Criminal Justice, Franchise Tax Bd., State Lands Commn.; mem. Bd. Equalization, State Tchrs. Retirement System, Pub. Employees Retirement System, Nat. Coun. Institutional Investors; U. Calif. Regent, Calif. State U. trustee; mem. intergovtl. policy adv. com. on trade Office of U.S. Trade Rep. Founder Calif. Found. for the Protection of Children. Capt. US Army. Democrat. Office: Loeb & Loeb 1010 Santa Monica Blvd Ste 2200 Los Angeles CA 90067

DAVIS, GUY DONALD, research scientist; b. Newport News, Va., June 15, 1952; s. Donald Arthur and Elinor Wilson (Ware) Davis; m. Norma May Hensler, June 30, 1990; children: Christiana Ashley May, Hensler. BS in Physics cum laude, Rensselaer Poly. Inst., 1974; MS in Physics, U. Wis., 1975, MS in Materials Sci., 1979, PhD in Materials Sci., 1982. Scientist Martin Marietta Labs., Balt., 1980—85, sr. scientist, 1985—88, staff scientist, group leader, 1988—93, tech. mgr., 1993—95; prin. scientist DACCO SCI., Inc., Columbia, Md., 1995—. Mem. sci. coun. Md. Acad. Sci., 1987—92. Editl. bd. Surface and Interface Analysis, 1987—96, Surface Sci. Spectra, 1991—, Jour. Adhesion Sci. and Tech., 1993—; contbr. articles tech. journals, chpts. to books. Named Disting. Young Scientist, Md. Acad. Scis., 1987; recipient Gov.'s Citation, State of Md., 1987, Citizen's Citation, City of Balt., 1987. Fellow: Electrochemical Soc. (chmn. Nat. Capital sect. 2001—02, William Blum award 1998), Am. Vacuum Soc. (chmn. applied surface sci. divsn. 1993—94), ASM Internat.; mem.: ASTM (2d vice-chmn. E-42 com. 1988—93), Fed. Materials Soc. (trustee 2005—), Soc. Adhesion and Adhesives, Adhesion Soc. (treas. 1988—95, v.p. 1995—96, pres. 1996—98, Robert L. Patrick fellow), NACE Internat., Soc. Advancement Material and Process Engrng., Internat. Stds. Orgn. (chmn. TC201 SC2 1993—95). Democrat. Lutheran. Office: DACCO SCI INC 1 S Beechwood Ave Baltimore MD 21228 Business E-Mail: davis@daccosci.com.

DAVIS, HARLEY CLEO, retired military officer; b. Van Buren, Ark., May 7, 1941; s. Aleta (Johnson) Davis; m. Patricia Ann White, Mar. 9, 1985. BS, Ark. Tech. U., 1963; MA, Ea. Ky. U., 1972; exec. devel. program, U. N.H., 1987. Commd. 2d lt. U.S. Army, 1963, advanced through grades to maj. gen., 1993; platoon leader 1st Bn., 50th inf., 2d Armored Div., 1963; various assignments, 1963-80; comdr. 3d Bn., 5th Spl. Forces Group, Ft. Bragg, NC, 1980-82; chief leadership br. Hdqrs. Dept. of the Army, Washington, 1982-84; chief of staff JFK Spl. Warfare Ctr. and Sch., Ft. Bragg, 1985-86; comdr. 5th Spl. Forces Group, Ft. Campbell, Ky., 1987-89; asst. comdt. JFK Spl. Warfare Ctr. and Sch., Ft. Bragg, 1989-91; dep. comdg. gen. U.S. Army Sp. Ops. Command, Ft. Bragg, 1991-92; comdg. gen. U.S. Army Spl. Forces Command (Airborne), Ft. Bragg, 1992-95; dep. comdg. gen. Fifth U.S. Army (west), Ft. Lewis, Wash., 1995-97. Sr. mentor Jt. Spl. Ops. U., 2007—. Decorated DSM with oak leaf cluster, Legion of Merit, Soldier's medal, Bronze Star with two oak leaf clusters, Air medal with oak leaf cluster. Home Phone: 301-570-6253.

DAVIS, HARRY REX, political science professor; b. Ozona, Tex., Nov. 9, 1921; s. Rex Otis and Mima (Gowin) D.; m. Ruth Elizabeth Greenlee, Sept. 6, 1947; children: Peter Gowin, Scott Andrew, Martha Greenlee. BA summa cum laude, Tex. Christian U., 1942; AM, U. Chgo., 1949, PhD, 1951; postdoctorate, Union Theol. Sem., 1952-53. Teaching fellow Tex. Christian U., 1945-46; mem. faculty dept. govt. Beloit (Wis.) Coll., 1948-90, assoc. prof., 1956-59, prof., 1959-90, chmn. dept., 1959-84, prof. emeritus, 1990—. Cons. ch. and soc. dept. World Council Chs., 1969. Author: (with others) Small City Government, 1962, Colleges and Commitments, 1971; Editor: (with others) Reinhold Niebuhr on Politics, 1960, 2d edit., 2007. Active Beloit City Coun., 1959-60, Beloit Bd. Ethics, 1975-81, Wis. Gov.'s Coun. on Jud. Selection, 1983-86, Beloit Bd. Health, 1996-2002, chmn., 1996-98; chmn. Beloit Dem. Com., 1956, 61-63; local mgr. campaigns congl. candidates. With USAAF, 1942-45. Ford faculty fellow, 1952-53; grantee Social Sci. Rsch. Coun., Rockefeller Found. Mem. Midwest Polit. Sci. Assn. (sec.-treas. 1959-65, mem. exec. coun. 1966-68), Am. Polit. Sci. Assn. (chmn. Burdette award com. 1979), Am. Soc. Polit. and Legal Philosophy, Soc. Christian Ethics. Democrat. Presbyterian (elder, coun. on ch. and society 1965-72, Gen. Assembly commr. 1991). Office: Beloit Coll Dept Government Beloit WI 53511 Home: 2423 Stonehedge Ln Beloit WI 53511-6727

DAVIS, HELEN GORDON, retired state senator; b. NYC, 1926; m. Gene Davis; children: Stephanie, Karen, Gordon. BA, Bklyn. Coll.; postgrad., U. South Fla., 1967—70. Tchr. High Sch. Commerce, NYC, Hillsborough High Sch., Tampa, Fla.; grad. asst. U. South Fla., 1968; mem. Fla. Ho. of Reps. (1st woman to be elected in 1974 from Hills Co., 1st woman to chair the legis. del.), 1974-88; state senator Fla., 1988-92; mem. Fla. Supreme Ct. Commn. on Gender Bias in the Cts., 1988-90, Fla. Supreme Ct. Commn. on Mediation and Arbitration, 1987—. Chmn. senate appropriations subcom. human svcs., mem. rules com., internat. trade and econ. devel. com., health and rehab. svcs. com. Jud. chmn. Local Govt. Study Commn. Hillsborough County (Fla.), 1964; mem. Tampa Commn. on Juvenile Delinquency, 1966-69, Mayor's Citizens Adv. Com., 1966-69, Quality Edn. Commn., 1966-68, Gov.'s Citizen Com. for Ct. Reform, 1972, Hillsborough County Planning commn., 1973-74; mem. Gov.'s Commn. on Jud. Reform, 1976; mem. employment com. Commn. Cmty. Rels., 1966-69; by-laws chmn. Arts Coun. Tampa, 1971-74; 1st v.p. Tampa Symphony Guild, 1974; bd. dirs. U. South Fla. Found., 1968-74, Stop Rape, 1973-74; past pres. PTA; active adv. commn. Nat. Child Care Action Campaign, Nat. Ctr. for Crime and Delinquency; chair Hillsborough Dem. Exec. Com., also pres.; active Fla. Com. on the Status of Women, 2001. Recipient U. South Fla. Young Dems. Humanitarian award, 1974, Diana award NOW, 1975, Woman of Achievement in Arts award Tampa, 1975, Tampa Human Rels. award, 1976, Hannah G. Solomon Citizen of Yr., 1980, St. Petersburg Times/Fla. Civil Liberties award, 1980, Friend of Edn. award, 1981, Fla. Alliance for Responsible Parenting award, 1981, Humanitarian award Judeo-Christian Clinic, 1984, Fla. Network of Runaway Youth award, 1985, Ctr. for Women Leader-adv. Friend award, 1985, Nat. Assn. Juvenile Ct. Judges Appreciation award, 1987, AAUW Leadership award, 1987, Hillsborough County Halfway House appreciation award, 1988, Martin Luther King award City of Tampa, 1988, Appreciation award Nat. Fedn. Dem. Women, 1989, Dept. Legal Affairs appreciation, 1990, Superwoman award Mus. Sci. and Industry, 1990, Nat. Childcare Merit award NASP, 1992, Am. Judicature award Am. Judicature Assn., 1993, Woman of Courage award City of Tampa, 2000, Liberty Bell award, Hillsborough Bar Assn., 2005; named Fla. Motion Picture and TV Outstanding Legislator, 1990; named to Fla. Women's Hall Fame, 1999. Mem. LWV (pres. Hillsborough County 1966-69, Fla. adminstrn. of justice chmn. 1969-74, First Leadership Achievement award 2004, Highest Achievement award 2006), Am. Arbitration Assn., Hills County Bar Assn. (Liberty Bell award 2005), Hills County Expy. Authority, Fla. Supreme Ct. Commn. Arbitration. Democrat. Home: 45 Adalia Ave Tampa FL 33606-3301 Home Fax: 813-253-0393.

DAVIS, HENRY BARNARD, JR., lawyer; b. East Grand Rapids, Mich., June 3, 1923; s. Henry Barnard and Ethel Margaret (Turnbull) Davis; m. Margaret Lees Wilson, Aug. 27, 1946; children: Caroline Dellenbusch, Laura Davis, George B. BA, Yale U., 1945; JD, U. Mich., 1950; LLD, Olivet Coll., 1983. Bar: Mich. 1951, U.S. Dist. Ct. (we. dist.) Mich. 1956, U.S. Ct. Appeals (6th cir.) 1971, U.S. Supreme Ct. 1978. Assoc. Allaben, Wiarda, Hayes & Hewitt, 1951-52; ptnr. Hayes, Davis & Dellenbusch PLC, Grand Rapids, Mich., 1952—2002, Davis & Davis Law Office PLC, Grand Rapids, 2002—. Mem. Kent County Bd. Commrs., 1968-72; mem. Cmty. Mental Health Bd., 1970-94, past chmn.; trustee, sec. bd. Olivet Coll., 1965-91, trustee emeritus, 1991—; bd. dirs. Jr. Achievement Grand Rapids, 1960-65; chair Grand Rapids Historic Preservation Com., 1977-79; trustee East Congregational Ch., 1979-81. Served with USAAF, 1943-46, Philippines. Mem. ABA, Mich. Bar Assn., Grand Rapids Round Table (pres. 1969), Masons. Republican. Home: 30 Mayfair Dr NE Grand Rapids MI 49503-3831 Office: 535 Fountain St NE Grand Rapids MI 49503-3421 Office Fax: 616-458-8638. Personal E-mail: hbdavis@mac.com.

DAVIS, HERBERT OWEN, lawyer; b. Washington, June 11, 1935; s. Owen Stier and Claudie Lea (Pointer) D.; children: Herbert O. Jr., Ann P., Paul B. BA, U. N.C., 1957; JD, Duke U., 1960. Bar: N.C. 1960, U.S. Dist. Ct. (mid. dist.) N.C. 1960. Assoc. Smith Moore Smith Schell & Hunter, Greensboro, NC, 1960—66, ptnr., 1966—86, Smith Helms Mulliss & Moore, Greensboro, 1986—2002, Smith Moore LLP, Greensboro, 2002—05, of counsel, 2006—. Editor in chief Duke Law Jour., 1959—60. Mem. ABA, NC Bar Assn., Greensboro Country Club, Carolina Club, Phi Beta Kappa Home: 2303 Danbury Rd Greensboro NC 27408-5123 Office: Smith Moore LLP 300 N Greene St Ste 1400 Greensboro NC 27401-2171 Business E-Mail: bert.davis@smithmoorelaw.com.

DAVIS, HIRAM JOE, public school administrator; b. Spartanburg, SC, Feb. 13, 1930; s. Flake Revere and Dolorus Jane (Haigler) D.; m. Anna Jane Ripley, Mar. 16, 1951; children: Alan Joe, Kendal Jay. AB, Asbury Coll., 1951; MEd, Kent State U., 1957. Cert. supt., prin., supervisor, tchr. Elem. sch. tchr., Antrim, Ohio, 1951-52; tchr. Auburn Elem. Sch., Chagrin Falls, Ohio, 1952-57; prin. Kenston Elem. Schs., Chagrin Falls, Ohio, 1957-62; prin., dir. of 16 schs. Firestone Rubber Plantation, Harbel, Liberia, West Africa, 1962-64; asst. high sch. prin. Orange Schs., Pepper Pike, Ohio, 1964-66, prin. Brady Mid. Sch., 1966-84; interim prin. Kenston Schs., Chagrin Falls, Ohio, 1984-98. Past bd. mem. Am. Inst. Fgn. Study, Greenwich, Conn., 1968-84, prin. summer sch. groups to Europe, 1968-82; attendee White House Conf. on Edn.; owner JD Mailboxes. Chmn. trustees Garfield Meml. United Meth. Ch., Pepper Pike, mem. p.p.r. com., mission com.; vol. traveling libr. for Geauga County Pub. Libr. to Amish schs.; scoutmaster troop 1 Liberian Boy Scouts and Boy Scouts Am., Harbel, Liberia, 1962-64; summer session missionary svc. Liberia, 1985, Kenya, 1987; founder Chagrin Valley Jr. Athletic Conf. Mid. Schs. Recipient Dedicated Svc. award Chagrin Valley Jr. Athletic Conf., Garfield Meml. award for dedicated svc. in all areas of churchmanship, Harry Denman Evangelism award for lay leader United Meth. Ch. Conf., Cmty. Svc. award Fedn. Orange Cmties. Mem. NEA (life dept. Nat. Elem. Sch. Prin.), Kiwanis (pres. Lander Cir. chpt. 1969-70, 2004—05, George F. Hixon award 2001). Avocation: raising registered belgians. Office Phone: 440-543-4206. Personal E-mail: farmerhj@webtv.net.

DAVIS, HOWARD TED, engineering educator; b. Hendersonville, NC, Aug. 2, 1937; s. William Howard and Gladys Isabel (Rhodes) D.; m. Eugenia Asimakopoulos, Sept. 15, 1960 (dec. July 1996); children: William Howard II, Maria Katherine; m. Catherine Asimkopoulos, Mar. 9, 2000. BS in Chemistry, Furman U., 1959; PhD in Chem. Physics, U. Chgo., 1962. Postdoctoral fellow Free U. of Brussels, 1962-63; asst. prof. U. Minn., Mpls., 1963-66, assoc. prof., 1966-69, prof., 1969-80, prof., head chem. engring. and materials sci., 1980-95, dean Inst. Tech., 1995—2004, Regent's prof., 1997—; Humboldt rschr. Cologne U., Germany, 2005. Editor: Springs of Creativity, 1981; author: Statistical Mechanics of Phases, Interfaces and Thin Films, 1995, (with K. Thomson) Linear Algebra and Linear Operators in Engineering, 2000; contbr. over 500 articles to sci. and engring. jours. Fellow Sloan Found., 1967-69, Guggenheim Found., 1969-70. Mem. AAAS, AIChE (Walker award for excellence in publs. 1990), NAE, Am. Chem. Soc., Soc. Petroleum Engrs., Minn. Fedn. Engring. Socs. (Disting. Engr. 1998). Democrat. Avocations: tennis, golf, reading, movies. Office: U Minn 421 Washington Ave SE Minneapolis MN 55455-0373 Home: 4330 Tyrol Crest Golden Valley MN 55416 Office Phone: 612-625-4088. Personal E-mail: htdavismn@yahoo.com. Business E-Mail: davis@cems.umn.edu.

DAVIS, IRVIN, advertising, public relations and broadcast executive; b. St. Louis, Dec. 18, 1926; s. Julius and Anna (Rosen) D.; m. Adrienne Bronstein, Apr. 25, 1968; 1 child, Jennifer Alison. BSBA, Washington U., 1950; postgrad., St. Louis U., 1952; DHum (hon.), Nat. Coll., 1981, Logan Coll., 2004. Pres. Clayton-Davis & Assoc., Inc., St. Louis, 1953—, Admiral Broadcasting Corp., St. Louis, 1983—. C.p., bd. dirs. Nat. Acad. TV Arts and Scis., 1982—; bd. dirs. Truman Bank; pres. Galtex Broadcasting; pres. Celebrities Prodns. Author: Room for Three, Comprehensive Tng. in Advt. and Pub. Relations; producer (film) Family Album, 1974, Use It in Good Health, Charlie, 1975. Pres. Child Assistance Program, 1986—92; v.p. Boys and Girls Town Mo., St. James, 1976—99, Make Today Count, 1985—86; bd. dirs. Jackie Joyner Kersee Found., 1997—2001, Crusade Against Crime, St. Louis, 1984—; pres. St. Louis Artists Guild. Sgt. USAF, 1945—47, PTO. Recipient Freedom Found. award, 1975, Internat. Film and TV Festival award, 1973-75, Internat. Broadcasting award Hollywood Advt. Club, 1965, 77, 82, 83, Cinegolden Eagle award Coun. on Internat. Non-Theatrical Events, 1975, Nat. Emmy award, 1991; inductee Nat. TV Acad. Silver Cir., 2004. Mem.: AFTRA, Am. Med. Writers Assn., Pub. Rels. Soc. Am. (accredited), St. Louis Club, Press Club, Advt. Club. Office: Clayton Davis and Assoc Inc 230 S Bemiston Ave Ste 1400 Saint Louis MO 63105

DAVIS, J. ALAN, writer, film and television producer; Student, Marlborough Coll., Eng., 1979; BA with distinction, So. Meth. U., 1983; JD with honors, U. Tex., 1987. Bar: Calif. 1988. Assoc. O'Melveny & Myers, LA, 1987-89, Rosenfeld, Meyer & Susman, Beverly Hills, Calif., 1989-90; pvt. practice LA, 1990-94; ptnr. Davis & Benjamin, LA, 1995-98, Garvin, Davis & Benjamin, LLP, LA, 1998-99; head legal and bus. affairs Warner Bros. Internat. TV Prodn., Burbank, Calif., 2000—02; pres. Periscope Ltd., LA, 2002—. Mem. Calif. Bar Assn., Beverly Hills Bar Assn., Brit. Acad. Film and TV Arts, L.A. (mng. dir. 1998, bd. dirs., chmn. Britannia awards 2004). Avocations: skiing, scuba diving, tennis.

DAVIS, J. MORTON, investment company executive, venture capitalist, economist; b. NYC, Jan. 7, 1929; s. Morris and Sylvia (Mandel) Davidowitz; m. Rosalind Selengut, Sept. 24, 1949; children: Esti Davis Stahler, Ruki Davis Renov, Rivka Davis Rosenwald, Laya Davis Perlysky. AB in Econs. magna cum laude, Bklyn. Coll., 1957; MBA with distinction, Harvard U., 1959. Account exec. Shields & Co., NYC, 1959-62; sr. pres. D.H. Blair & Co., Inc., 1962-75, pres., chmn., chief exec. officer, 1975-92, D.H. Blair Investment Banking Corp., 1992—. Pres., chmn. bd. Engex, Inc., 1968—; lectr. econs. CUNY; allied mem. N.Y. Stock Exchange; past chmn. Am. Pub. Priorities Inst. Author: Making America Work Again, 1983, From Hard Knocks to Hot Stocks: How I Made a Fortune from Smart Investing and How You Can Too, 1998. Bd. dirs. N.Y.'s Finest Found., Inc.; trustee Yeshiva U., CUNY Grad. Sch.; dir. Am-Israel Friendship League. Mem. Harvard Club, Inwood Tennis Club, Phi Beta Kappa. Office: D H Blair Investment Banking Corp 44 Wall St New York NY 10005-2401 *I believe if you work very hard, it's easy to succeed! The corollary to that is that if you work easy, it's virtually impossible to succeed. If you contribute fully of your time, energy, knowledge, resources, etc., you ultimately get the rewards, at least commensurate with that contribution, and more, for you also have the joy of achieving and giving as much of what you are to this world. The harder you work, the luckier you get! You not only are ultimately well paid but you make your mark. You achieve success with recognition and the gratifying feeling that you really earned it.*

DAVIS, JACK WAYNE, JR., retired publishing executive; b. Toledo, May 21, 1947; s. Jack Wayne and Virginia (Moore) D.; m. Amélie Claiborne Matthews, June 24, 1977; 1 child, Claiborne Levering. Grad., Harvard Coll., 1969. Mng. editor Figaro, New Orleans, 1972-73; reporter, columnist, asst. city editor, city editor The States-Item, New Orleans, 1973—80; metro editor The Times - Picayune, New Orleans, 1980-83; assoc. metro editor, night metro editor, metro editor The Chgo. Tribune, 1983-87; editor, v.p. Daily Press, Newport News, Va., 1987-94, pres., pub., CEO, 1994-98; pres. Tribune Interactive Inc., 1998—99, v.p. planning Tribune Pub., 1999—2000; pres., pub. CEO The Hartford Courant, Hartford, Conn., 2000—07. Frank Knox fellow U. Rajasthan, India, 1971, Profl. Journalism fellow Stanford U., 1977-78. Mem. Wadsworth Atheneum Mus. of Art (bd. dirs.), MetroHartford Alliance, The Antiquarian and Landmarks Soc., The Pirate's Alley Faulkner Soc., Hartford Courant Found., Hartford's Camp Courant. Avocations: sculling, reading, squash.

DAVIS, JACQUELINE ZURAT, library director, arts administrator; b. Bradford, Pa., Oct. 30, 1946; d. Frank Joseph and Rosemary (Fedele) Zurat; m. Michael James Davis; m. Michael James Davis, Dec. 13, 1969; children: Adam, Ashley. BA, Dunbarton Coll. of Holy Cross, 1969; MA, U. Kans., 1973; Degre Superieur, L'Institut Catholique, Paris, 1973. Staff asst. US Sen. Edward Kennedy office, Washington, 1967-71; dir. concert, chamber music and new directions series U. Kans., Lawrence, Kans., 1980—93, dir. to exec. dir. Lied Ctr., 1993—2000; Barbara G. and Lawrence A. Fleischman exec. dir. NY Pub. Libr. for the Performing Arts, NYC, 2000—. Bd. mem. Chamber Music Am., Dance USA, Am. Arts Alliance; co-chairperson Midwest Regional Booking Conf., Mpls., 1987; founder Swarthout Soc., 1980; founder, pres. Lyric Opera Guild, 1974-80; co-commr. multi-media Festival 2000: SenseUs, 1990, dance David Gordon's "United States", 1989; site visitor/panelist Nat. Endowment for the Arts, 1985. Trustee Leadership Lawrence, 1982, bd. dirs., 1987. Recipient Kans. Governor's Arts award, 1994; named Outstanding Citizen of Yr. Lawrence Sch. Dist., 2000; named one of 11 Outstanding Presenters Pew Charitable Trusts, 1999, 10 Most Influential U. Presenters in US. Internat. Arts Mgr., 1999; named to Univ. Kans. Women's Hall of Fame, 2000; Grantee NEA, 1981; Fellow Nat. Endowment for Arts, 1987. Mem. Assn. Performing Arts Presenters (nat. pres. 1990-92, nat. v.p. 1988-90, nat. conf. chair 1986), Lawrence C. of C. (cultural affairs com.). Democrat. Roman Catholic. Avocations: tennis, reading, travel, eating in great restaurants. Office: NYPL for Performing Arts 40 Lincoln Ctr Plz New York NY 10023-7498

DAVIS, JAMES ALLAN, gerontologist, educator; b. Portland, Oreg., May 20, 1953; m. Louis Carol Lindsay. BS, U. Oreg., 1975, MS, 1976, EdD, 1980. State mental health gerontologist Oreg. Mental Health Div., Salem, 1978-80; project dir. Oreg. Long Term Care Tng. Project, Salem, 1979-80; tng. specialist Nat. Assn. Area Agys. on Aging., Washington, 1981; asst. dir. for internships and vol. svc. exptl. learning programs U. Md., 1981-86, mem. rsch. and instructional faculty, 1982-86; com. adminstr. Oreg. State Human Resources Com., Salem, 1987; exec. dir., legis. dir. Oreg. State Coun. Sr. Citizens, Salem, 1987—2002; program coord. for sr. mental health care Oreg. Sr. and Disabled Svc. Div., Salem, 1989—2001; pres. James A. Davis and Assocs. Inc., Portland, 1991—; state project dir. Oreg. Assn. RSVPs, 1995—; assoc. prof. dept. human scis. Marylhurst U., Oreg., 2005—. Vis. asst. prof. Ctr. for Gerontology, U. Oreg., 1990-92; co-chair Audio-Visual Program, Internat. Congress Gerontology, 1985; nat. gerontology acad. adv. panel, Nat. Hosp. Satellite Network, 1983-85; lobbyist United Srs. Oreg., Oreg. State Coun. Sr. Citizens, Oreg. State Denturist Assn., Oreg. State Pharmacist Assn., Oreg. Soc. Physician Assts., Oreg. Legal Techs. Assn., Oreg. Dental Lab. Assn., Wash. Denturist Assn., Nat. Denturist Assn.; adj. asst. prof. Urban Studies Inst. on Aging, Portland State U., 2003—; assoc. prof. human scis. dept. Marylhurst U., 2001—, co-chair diversity com.; presenter in field Co-author: TV's Image of the Elderly, 1985; contbg. editor Retirement Life News, 1988-92; sr. issues editor Sr. News, 1989-96; contbr. articles to profl. jours.; producer, host approximately 400 TV and radio programs. Founding pres. Oreg. Alliance for Progressive Policy, 1988-89; co-chair mental health com., vice chair legis. com., Gov.'s Commn. on Sr. Svcs., 1988-89; exec. coun., media chair Human Svcs. Coalition Oreg., 1988-89; bd. dirs. Oreg. Health Action Campaign, 1988-92; 2d v.p., bd. dirs. Oreg. State Coun. for Sr. Citizens, 1977-80, 90-92, Oreg. Medicaid Com., 1996—2002; co-chair Oreg. Medicare/Medicaid Coalition, 1995—2001, Oreg. Long Term Care Campaign, 1996-98; mem. Gov's. Task Force for Volunteerism, State of Md., 1983-84, State Legis. Income Tax Task Force, 1990; vice chair Oreg. State Bd. Denture Technology, 1991-96; mem. com. for assessment on needs for volunteerism, Gov.'s Vol. Coun., State of Md., 1984-86; project dir. Oreg. Assn. Ret. and Sr. Vol. Programs, 1995—; mem. exec. bd. dirs. Oreg. Advocacy Coalition of Srs. and People with Disabilities, 1997—; chmn., bd. dirs. Oreg. Campaign for Patient Rights, 1997—2003. Recipient Disting. Svc. award City of Salem, 1980, Spl. Human Rights award, 1981, Svc. award U. Md., 1984, Hometown U.S.A. award Community Cable TV Producers, 1988, Disting. Svc. award Oreg. State Coun. Sr. Citizens, 1991. Mem.: Oreg. State Coun. of Sr. Citizens (Disting. Svc. of Sr. award 2000), Alzheimers Assn. of Oreg. (Pub. Policy award 2000), Nat. Denturist Assn. (exec. dir. 1982—89), Gerontol. Soc. Am. (mental health task force 1982—84, co-chmn. 1983—84), Nat. Assn. State Mental Health Dir. (nat. exec. com. 1978—80, vice chmn. 1979—80, spl. cons.81 1981—82, mem. aging div., co-chmn. nat. program com. 1984—87, nat. media chair 1985—92), Nat. Gray Panthers (nat. exec. com. 1984—87, nat. bd. dirs. 1984—92, program co-chmn. nat. biennial conv. 1986, nat. health task force 1981—, co-chmn. 1983—84, chmn. mental health subcom. 1981—86, editor Health Watch 1982—84, state program developer Oreg. chpt. 1979—80, 1989, lobbyist 1987—, gov.'s patient protection work group 2000—01). Democrat. E-mail: davisjasr@aol.com.

DAVIS, JAMES HENRY, retired psychology educator; b. Effingham, Ill., Aug. 6, 1932; s. Kenneth E. and Forest (Naylor) D.; m. Elisabeth Bachman, June 27, 1954; children— Stephen J., Kristin E., Leah E. BS, U. Ill., 1954; MA, Mich. State U., 1958, PhD, 1961. Asst. instr. psychology Mich. State U., East Lansing, 1959-60; instr. psychology Miami U., Oxford, Ohio, 1960-61, asst. prof. psychology, 1961-65, assoc. prof. psychology, 1965-66; vis. assoc. prof. psychology Yale U., New Haven, 1966-67, U. Ill., Champaign, 1967-68, assoc. prof., 1968-70, prof. psychology, 1970-97, prof. emeritus psychology, 1997. Fellow Ctr. for Advanced Study in Behavioral Scis., 1987-88. Author: Group Performance, 1969; editor: (with W. Brandstatter and H.C. Schuler) Dynamics of Group Decisions, 1978, (with W. Brandstatter and G. Stocker-Kreichgauer) Group Decision Making, 1982, (with G.M. Stephenson) Progress in Applied Social Psychology, Vol. I, 1981, Vol. II, 1984, (with Erich Witte) Understanding Group Behavior, Vol. 1 and Vol. 2, 1996; contbr. articles to profl. jours. With US Army, 1954—56. Fellow AAAS, Am. Psychol. Soc.; mem. Psychonomic Soc., Midwestern Psychol. Assn., Soc. Exptl. Social Psychologists, Soc. for Judgment and Decision Making, Soc. Math. Psychology, Sigma Xi Home: 10 Lake Park Rd Champaign IL 61822-7101 Business E-Mail: j-davis@uiuc.edu.

DAVIS, JAMES LEE, lawyer; b. High Point, NC, May 2, 1940; AB with high honors, Guilford Coll., 1968; JD with honors, U. N.C., 1971. Bar: N.C. 1971. With Ward and Smith P.A., New Bern, NC. Charles A. Dana scholar. Mem. N.C. State Bar, N.C. Bar Assn. (chmn. real property sect. coun. 1981-82), Craven County Bar Assn. (pres. 1978-79), Order of Coif. Office: Ward and Smith PA PO Box 867 1001 College Ct New Bern NC 28562-4972 Home Phone: 252-633-3358; Office Phone: 252-672-5404. E-mail: jld@wardandsmith.com.

DAVIS, JAMES RICHARD, software engineer, consultant; b. Somerset, Ky., Oct. 9, 1970; s. James Ralph and Priscilla Carrender Davis; m. Melissa Joy Bertram, Aug. 1, 2004. B in Elec. Engring., Vanderbilt U., Nashville, 1993, MSEE, 1995, PhD in Elec. Engring., 2000. Rsch. scientist Vanderbilt U., 2000—04; sr. software engr. Kendro Lab. Automation, Nashville, 2004—05, Thermo Electron Corp., Nashville, 2005—06, Thermo Fisher Sci., Nashville, 2006—. Mem.: IEEE, Phi Eta Sigma, Tau Beta Pi, Eta Kappa Nu, Alpha Lambda Delta. Baptist. Avocations: softball, computers, offroading. Office: Thermo Fisher Sci 7109 Baker's Bridge Ave Brentwood TN 37027

DAVIS, JAMES ROBERT, cartoonist; b. Marion, Ind., July 28, 1945; s. James William and Anna Catherine (Carter) D.; m. Jill Carol Davis; 1 son, James Alexander. Artist, Groves & Assocs., advt., Muncie, 1968-69; asst. to cartoonist: Tumbleweeds comic strip, 1969-78; cartoonist: Garfield comic strip, 1978—; TV script Here Comes Garfield, 1982, Garfield on the Town, 1983 (Emmy award 1984), Garfield in the Rough, 1984 (Emmy award 1985), Garfield's Halloween Adventure, 1985 (Emmy award 1986), Garfield in Paradise, 1986, Garfield Goes Hollywood, 1987, The Garfield Christmas Special, 1987; author: Garfield at Large, 1980, Garfield Gains Weight, 1981, Garfield Bigger Than Life, 1981, Garfield Weighs In, 1982, Garfield Takes the Cake, 1982, Garfield Treasury, 1982, Here Comes Garfield, 1982, Garfield Sits Around the House, 1983, Garfield Second Treasury, 1983, Garfield Eats His Heart Out, 1983, Garfield Tips the Scale, 1984, Garfield Loses his Feet, 1984, Garfield: His Nine Lives, 1984, Garfield Makes It Big, 1985, Garfield Rolls On, 1985, Third Garfield Treasury, 1985, Garfield Out to Lunch, 1986, The Unabridged, Uncensored, Unbelieveable Garfield Book, 1986, Garfield Food for Thought, 1987, The 4th Garfield Treasury, 1987, The Garfield Cat Naming Book, 1988, Garfield Chews the Fat, 1989, The 5th Garfield Treasury, 1989, Happy Birthday, Garfield, 1989, Garfield, Tiens Bon La Rampe, 1989, Garfield's Longest Catnap, 1989, Garfield The Big Star, 1989, Garfield in the Park, 1989, Garfield and the Tiger, 1989, Mini-Mysteries featuring Garfield, 1990, Garfield: The Me Book: A Guide to Superiority, How to Get It, Use It, and Keep It, 1990, Garfield's Judgement Day, 1990, Garfield's Feline Fantasies, 1990, Garfield Stories, 1990, Garfield on the Farm, 1990, Garfield Hangs Out, 1990, Garfield Goes to Waist, 1990, The Sixth Garfield Trasury, 1991, Garfield: The Truth About Cats, 1991, Garfield: Seasons Greetings, 1991, Garfield Thanksgiving Special, 1991, Garfield Takes Up Space, 1991, Garfield Says a Mouthful, 1991, Garfield Gets a Life, 1991, Garfield's Ghost Stories, 1992, Garfield Vacation Greetings, 1992, Garfield Learns About Thoughtfulness: Don't Be Late!, 1992, Garfield Learns About Planning: Surprize Party, 1992, Garfield Learns About Money: Money Madness!, 1992, Garfield Learns About Fire Safety: Where's the Fire?, 1992, Garfield Learns About Cooking: Any Cat Can Cook, 1992, Garfield Learns about Conservation: Endangered Odie?, 1992, Garfield Keeps His Chin Up, 1992, Garfield By the Pound, 1992, Garfield Birthday Greetings, 1992, The Seventh Garfield Treasury, 1993, Garfield's Big Fat Hairy Joke Book, 1993, Garfield Takes His Licks, 1993, Garfield Hits the Big Time: His 25th Book, 1993, Garfield's Tales of Mystery, 1994, Garfield's Night Before Christmas, 1994, Garfield's Insults, 1994, Garfield's Haunted House: And Other Spooky Tales, 1994, Garfield's Furry Tales, 1994, Garfield's Big Fat Scary Joke Book, 1994, Garfield's Big Fat Holiday Joke Book, 1994, Garfield Insults, Put-Downs, 1994, Garfield Fat Cat, 1994, Garfield Discovers America, 1994, Garfield's Son of Big, Fat Hairy Jokes, 1994, Big Hairy Garfield, 1994, Garfield, The Easter Bunny?, 1995, Garfield's Stupid Cupid: And Other Silly Stories, 1995, Garfield Fat Cat 3 Pack, 1995, Garfield Dishes It Out, 1995, Mr. Potato Head, 2001, Garfield: The Movie, 2004, Garfield: A Tail of Two Kitties, 2006. With USMC, 1967. Named to Mktg. Hall of Fame award Am. Mktg. Assn., 1982; recipient Disting. Alumnus award Am. Assn. State Colls. Univs.; named Garfield comic strip as most widely distributed comic in the world Guiness Book of World Records, 2003 Mem. Nat. Cartoonists Soc. (Best Humor Strip of 1981, 86, Segar award 1985, Cartoonist of Yr. 1990), Newspaper Comics Council. Protestant. Republican. Office: Universal Press Syndicate 4520 Main St Ste 700 Kansas City MO 64111-7701

DAVIS, JAMES S., lawyer; b. 1945; BA, Harvard U., 1966, JD, 1969. Bar: Mass. 1969. Mem. Bingham, Dana & Gould, Boston; of counsel Bingham McCutchen, Boston. Mem.: ABA, Boston Bar Assn. Office: Bingham McCutchen 150 Federal St Fl 15 Boston MA 02110-1726 Office Phone: 617-951-8000. E-mail: james.davis@bingham.com.

DAVIS, JANE G., lawyer; b. Norwich, NY, May 3, 1949; BA in French, Elmira Coll., NY, 1971; MA in French, U. Pitts., 1973; JD, Duquesne U., 1978. Bar: Pa. 1978, US Dist. Ct. We. Dist. Pa. 1978. Assoc. gen. counsel Limbach Co., Pitts., 1978—81; atty. Joy Technologies Inc., Pitts., 1981—88, v.p., gen. counsel, sec., 1988-95, York Internat. Corp., York, Pa., 1995—. Mem. ABA, Pa. Bar Assn. Office: York Internat Corp 631 S Richland Ave York PA 17403

DAVIS, JANICE, school system administrator; BS, U. NC, Chapel Hill, MA in Tchg., PhD in Curriculum and Instruction. Asst. supt. Granville County, NC, supt. NC, 1994—2000; asst. supt. for curriculum and instruction Durham, NC, 2000—03; dep. state supt. NC Dept. Pub. Instrn., 2003—, interim supt., 2005. Office: NC Dept Pub Instrn 301 N Wilmington St Raleigh NC 27601 Office Phone: 918-807-3441. E-mail: jdavis@dpi.state.nc.us.

DAVIS, JEREMY MATTHEW, chemist; b. Bakersfield, Calif., Aug. 5, 1953; s. Joseph Hyman and Mary (Pavetto) D.; m. Bernadette Sobkiewicz, Aug. 28, 1976 (div.); children: Andrew Jeremy, Christopher Peter. BS in Biol. Scis., U. Calif., Irvine, 1974; M in Pub. Adminstrn., Calif. State U., Long Beach, 1983; cert. in Facilities Mgmt., U. Calif., Irvine, 2006. Chemist I, II, Orange County Water Dist., Fountain Valley, Calif., 1977—84, supervising chemist, 1984—. Papers in field; TV appearance contestant on Jeopardy, 2001. Named Lab. Person of Yr., Calif. Water Environment Assn., Santa Ana River Basin, 1984. Mem. MENSA, Intertel, Toastmasters Internat. (pres. Watermeisters club 1996, 99, 2003, gov. founder's dist. area C-5, 1999-2001, gov. divsn. C 2001-2002). Office: Orange County Water Dist PO Box 8300 Fountain Valley CA 92728-8300 Office Phone: 714-378-3244. Business E-Mail: jdavis@ocwd.com. E-mail: jermedavis@hotmail.com.

DAVIS, JESSICA G., geneticist; b. Bklyn., Apr. 3, 1934; d. Nathan S. and Sylvia (Teplitz) Grosof; m. Andrew R. Davis, June 17, 1956; children: Jennifer Davis Hall, David. BA, Wellesley Coll., 1955; MD, Columbia U., 1959. Diplomate Am. Bd. Med. Genetics. Intern pediatrics St. Luke's Hosp.-Columbia U.; fellow Albert Einstein Coll. Medicine Yeshiva U., NYC, 1961-68, instr. Albert Einstein Coll. Medicine, 1962, asst. prof. Albert Einstein Coll. Medicine, 1968-74; assoc. prof. clin. pediatric Well Coll. Medicine Cornell U., NYC, 1974—. Cons. March of Dimes, N.Y.C., 1974—, Hastings Inst., Garrison, N.Y., 1979—; mem. sickle cell adv. com. NIH. Contbr. articles to profl. jours. Recipient Antoine Marfan award Nat. Marfan Found., 2005, numerous grants. Fellow: Am. Coll. Med. Genetics (founding fellow, CME officer); mem.: N.Y. Acad. Medicine, Coun. Regional Genetics Network (pres. 1991—94), Am. Soc. Human Genetics. Office: Weill Med Coll Cornell U NY-Presbyn Hosp 525 E 68th St Rm Box 128 New York NY 10021-4870 Home Phone: 518-733-5829; Office Phone: 212-746-1496. Business E-Mail: jgdavis@med.cornell.edu.

DAVIS, JIM, lawyer, former congressman; b. Oct. 11, 1957; m. Peggy Bessent; children: Peter, William. BA, Washington and Lee U., 1979; JD, U. Fla., 1982. Atty. Carlton Fields, Tampa, Fla., 1982—87; ptnr. Bush, Ross, Gardner, Warren and Rudy, Tampa, Fla., 1988—96; mem. Fla. Ho. of Reps., 1988—96, majority leader; mem. U.S. Congress from 11th Fla. dist., 1997—2007, mem. budget com., house adminstrn. com., internat. rels. com., mem. energy and commerce com., 2003—07, co-chair, New Dem. Coalition; ptnr. Holland & Knight LLP, Tampa, 2007—. Mem. Tampa Bay Partnership Judeo Christian Health Clinic. Mem.: ABA, Hillsborough County Bar Assn., Fla. Bar Assn. Democrat. Office: Holland & Knight LLP 100 N Tampa St, Ste 4100 Tampa FL 33602-3644 Office Fax: 813-229-0134. E-mail: jim.davis@hklaw.com.

DAVIS, JIMMY FRANK, prosecutor; b. Lubbock, Tex., June 14, 1945; s. Jack and Fern Lisemby D.; M. Joyce Zelma Hart, Nov. 6, 1976; children: Jayme Leigh, Julee Ellen. BS in Edn., Tex. Tech. U., Lubbock, 1968; JD, U. Tex., Austin, 1972. Bar: Tex. 1972, U.S. Supreme Ct. 1975, U.S. Dist. (no dist.) Tex. 1976, U.S. Ct. Appeals (5th cir.) 1976, U.S. Ct. Appeals (11cir.) 1981. Asst. criminal dist. atty. Lubbock County, 1973—77, adminstrv. asst., 1976-77; county and dist. atty. Castro County, Tex., 1977-92; asst. atty. gen. State of Tex., 1993—; mem. forms com. Atty. Gen. Office, 1999—2001. Mem. State Bar of Tex. (com. admissions dist. 16 1974-78, dist. 13 1983-92, govt. lawyers sect., coun. mem. 1991-92), Tex. Dist. and County Attys. Assn., Lubbock County Jr. Bar Assn. (pres. 1977), Tex. Tech. Ex Students Assn. (dist. rep. 1981-84, bd. dirs. 1985-90), Coll. of State Bar of Tex. (continuing legal edn. 1984-93, 2007—), Kiwanis of Lubbock (pres. 1977), Kiwanis of Dimmitt (pres. 1981), Delta Theta Phi. Office Phone: 806-763-3981. Business E-Mail: jimmy.davis@cs.oag.state.tx.us.

DAVIS, JO, naturopathic physician; b. Pecos, Tex., Jan. 6, 1937; d. Johnnie Rex and Laura (Swann) D.; children: Cassandra Ann, Charles Rex. AA in Nursing, N.Mex. State U., 1992; BS in Nutrition, Clayton Coll. Naturahealth, 1995, MS in Nutrition, 1996; DD, Am. Inst. Theology, 1996; PhD in Nutrition, Clayton Coll. Naturahealth, 1997; PhD in Hypnotherapy, Am. Pacific U.; D Naturopathy, Clayton Coll. Natural Health, 1995. Diplomate Am. Psychotherapy Assn.; cert. hypnotherapist, advanced therapy Emotional Freedom Technique, 2004; RN, Kans., Mo., Tex., N.Mex. Asst. coord. Carlsbad Hospice, Inc., N.Mex., 1992—98; prin., owner Natural Health Tng. and Resource Ctr., Carlsbad, 1994—98; dir. New Directions, Inc., Oak Grove, Mo., 1999—. Cons. Westbrooke Chiropractic, Lee's Summit, Mo., 1999—, Chiropractic Physicians, Independence, Mo., 1999—; instr. Continuing Edn. RN, Tex.; cert. trainer Neuro-Linguistic Programming, Inst. for Time Line Therapy Tng. Contbr. articles to newspapers; newsletter editor, 1994-96. Mem. Internat. Good Neighbor Coun., Mex., U.S.A., 1994-96; pres. Wildlife Rescue, Inc., Carlsbad, 1992-96; ordained min. Reverend Universal Life Ch. Named N.Mex. Woman of Yr. State of N.Mex., 1992. Mem. AAUW, Am. Assn. Nurse Assessment Coords. (cert.), Internat. Guild Hypnotists, Am. Bd. Hypnotherapy, Am. Holistic Health Assn., Nat. Audobon Soc., The Nature

Conservancy, Order Ea. Star. Avocations: raising horses, shaman studies, native american culture. Home and Office: 8311 S Hillside School Rd Oak Grove MO 64075-8245 Office Phone: 816-215-4363. Personal E-mail: doctordavis@weblue.com.

DAVIS, JO, nurse, writer, professional speaker, small business owner, photographer; b. St. Louis, Feb. 9, 1947; d. Jesse Marshall Davis and JoAnn (Charlsie Mae) (Skaggs) McCants; children: Jo Alice Gallagher, Andrew W. Lingle, Jr., James M. Lingle, Daniel V. Lingle(dec.) , Elizabeth K. Nash. AS in Sci., Forest Park Coll., 1980, AS in Liberal Arts, 1982; studied, State Fair Coll., 1980—81, U. Mo., Columbia, 1980, Kirkwood Coll., 1993; grad., Pacific Inst. Aromatherapy, San Raphael, Calif., Internat. cert., 2000; postgrad., Sarasota Acad. Christian Counseling. Lic. practical nurse, Mo., 1981. Active field of nsg., 1982—89; owner Exterm Pest Control, 1986—93; over-the-road truck driver Salem, Ill., 1993—98; columnist Driving Force Mag./Pollard Pub., Ala., 1996—2001; nurse, 1997—; creator, tchr. safe driving course; census taker Census Bur. US Dept. Commerce. Spkr. in field. Author: Victims of Domestic Violence, 1982, (poetry collection) Wings, 1998, Motivational Seven Steps to Assuming Responsibility, 1999; author: (as J. Marshall Davis) The Write to Kill, 1999; author: Tribal Dancer (Hon. Mention), How to Escape Abuse; editor: The Scene Newspaper, Down Home Mag.; contbr. multiple mag. articles and short stories. Leader Girl Scouts Am., Overland, Mo., 1972—73, Boy Scouts Am., Sedalia, Mo., 1981—82; asst. Brownie leader, 1971; asst. dist. missions coord. membership nurture and outreach United Meth. Women; sec. Arcadia Valley United Meth. Women. Named Most Valued Leader, Boy Scouts Am., Sedalia, 1982; recipient Presenter's award for serving as a role model, 18th Nat. Women's Tng. Program, New Horizons, St. Louis, Safety Essay Grand award, T.T.C., Inc., Salem, Ill., Pres. award for literary excellence, Iliad Press, 1st, 2nd, 3d Pl. writing contest, State Fair Coll., Cert. of Achievement, Profl. Spkrs. Tng. Program, Wis., 1999. Mem.: Mo. Writers Guild, Truck Writers Nat. Assn., Internat. Women's Writers Guild, Nat. Writers Union, Mo. Women of Today, Mo. Nurses Assn., Nat. Geog. Soc., Phi Theta Kappa. Methodist. Achievements include research in the effects of essential oils on the human body. Avocations: horseback riding, ice skating, free hand climbing, photography, violin. Home: Rte 1 Box 171A Arcadia MO 63621 Office Phone: 573-546-2947. Personal E-mail: jdavisnow@aol.com.

DAVIS, JO ANN S., congresswoman; b. Rowan County, NC, June 29, 1950; m. Charles E. Davis II; children: Charlie, Chris. Student, Hampton Roads Bus. Coll., Va. Owner Davis Mgmt. Co., 1988, Jo Ann Davis Realty, 1990; mem. Va. State Gen. Assembly, 1997—2001, mem. gen. laws com., mem. health welfare & insts., mem. sci. & tech. com., mem. claims com., mem. Chesapeake and its tributaries com.; mem. US Congress from 1st Va. dist., 2001—, mem. armed svcs. com., mem. internat. rels. com., mem. permanent select com. on intelligence, chair terrorism, human intelligence, analysis and counter-intelligence subcommittee, mem. def. rev. threat panel. Republican. Mem. Assembly Of God Ch. Office: US Ho Reps 1123 Longworth Ho Office Bldg Washington DC 20515-4601 Office Phone: 202-225-4261.*

DAVIS, JOAN CARROLL, retired museum director; b. Sept. 20, 1931; d. Homer Leslie and Ruby Isabelle (Stone) G.; m. Frederic E. Davis, Aug. 22, 1953; children: Timothy, Terri, Tami, Traci, Todd, Tricia. Student, Bob Jones U., 1949-52. Supr. Day Care Ctr. Bob Jones U., Greenville, SC, 1953-63; docent Univ. Art Gallery, Greenville, 1964-73, dir., 1974—; ret., 1999. Republican. Baptist. Office: 217 Stadium View Dr Greenville SC 29609 Personal E-mail: fedjed@juno.com.

DAVIS, JOE A., lawyer; b. Alexandria, La., Apr. 1, 1960; married. BS, Univ. Tex., Dallas, 1982; JD, Baylor Univ. Law Sch., Waco, 1985. Ptnr. Hunton & Williams LLP, Dallas, 1985—2005; exec. v.p., gen. counsel Crosstex Energy LP, Dallas, 2005—. Mem.: Natural Gas & Electric Power Soc., N. Tex. (past pres.), N. Tex. Chapter, Gas Processors Assn., Texas State Bar. Office: Crosstex Energy LP 2501 Cedar Springs Ste 100 Dallas TX 75201 Home Phone: 214-520-6242; Office Phone: 214-721-9246. Business E-Mail: joe.davis@crosstexenergy.com.*

DAVIS, JOE DAUGHTRY, III, communications educator, writer; b. Greatfalls, Mont., Oct. 21, 1958; m. Genine Ann Underwood, Aug. 6, 1983; 1 child, Marie. MA, U. No. Mich., Marquette, 1998. Med. specialist U.S. Army, Fort Bragg, NC, 1977—80; emergency med. technition Bisak Ambulance, Greatfalls, Mont., 1980—82; nursing asst./unit clk. U. Iowa Hosp. and Clinc, Iowa City, 1983—96; writing instr. Rust Coll., Holly Springs, Miss., 1998—2000; writing and speech instr. NIACC, Mason City, 2000—. Learning communities dir. NIACC, Mason City, 2006—. Author: article, short story. Spec 4 US Army, 1977—80, Fort Bragg. Mem.: CCCC (assoc.). Democrat. Catholic. Home: 719 6th St Rudd IA 50471 Office: NIACC 500 College Dr Mason City IA 50401 Home Phone: 641-395-2632; Office Phone: 641-422-4121.

DAVIS, JOEL, publisher; b. Chgo., Apr. 5, 1934; s. Bernard George and Sylvia (Friedman) D.; m. Carol Sue Barnett, Aug. 3, 1958; children: Charles Michael, Andrew Barnett, Jonathan William. BA, Brown U., 1957; student, Columbia U., summer 1953. With Davis Publs., Inc., NYC, 1957-92, exec. v.p., 1959-68, pres., 1969-92, Sylvia Porter's Personal Fin. Mag. Co., 1982-89, Woodworker, Inc., Westport, Conn., 1993-95; ptnr. Davis/Herschbein & Assocs., L.L.C., Westport, 1996—2003; pres. Archtl. Designs, Inc., Wilton, Conn., 1996—. Bd. dirs. Mut. N.Y., Mony Series Fund Inc., 1971-2004. Nat. chmn. univ. fund Brown U., 1965—68; bd. dirs. Brit. Am. Ednl. Found., 1977—80; mem. exec. com. gen. devel. coun. Brown U., 1962—77, Young Pres. Orgn., 1971—83; vice chmn. Brown Devel. Coun., 1968—69; regional dir. Assoc. Alumni Brown U., 1965—67, trustee, mem. corp., 1968—73; mem adv. and exec. com. Brown U., 1971—73, chmn. budget and fin. com., 1971—73, chmn. nat. alumni schs. program, 1982—85; trustee Westport Pub. Libr., 1992—2001; chmn. Westport Libr. Adv. Coun., 2001—; trustee Brookfield Craft Ctr., 1992—94; pres. Westport Pub. Libr., 1997—99. Mem. Am. Arbitration Assn. (mem. nat. panel), Mag. Pubs. Am. (bd. dirs. 1969-94, sec. 1979-81, vice chmn. mktg. com. 1969-73, mem. exec. com. 1971-88, mem. fin. com. 1974-88, chmn. membership com. 1975-91), Brown Club (mem. N.Y.C. bd. govs. 1963-69). Home: 15 Crooked Mile Rd Westport CT 06880-1124 Office: Archtl Designs Inc 57 Danbury Rd Ste 203 Wilton CT 06897 E-mail: prez@architecturaldesigns.com.

DAVIS, JOHN A., film producer; b. Denver; Prodr. (films) Predator, 1987, Three O'Clock High, 1987, Taffin, 1988, License to Drive, 1988, Little Monsters, 1989, The Last of the Finest, 1990, Enid is Sleeping, 1990, Shattered, 1991, Storyville, 1992, The Firm, 1993, The Thing Called Love, 1993, Gunmen, 1994, Grumpy Old Men, 1994, Richie Rich, 1994, The Hunted, 1995, Waterworld, 1995, The Grass Harp, 1995, Grumpier Old Men, 1995, Courage Under Fire, 1996, The Chamber, 1996, Daylight, 1996, Out to Sea, 1997, Bad Manners, 1997, Digging to China, 1998, Doctor Dolittle, 1998, The Settlement, 1999, Dudley Do-Right, 1999, Rights of Passage, 1999, Labor Pains, 2000, Heartbreakers, 2001, Dr. Dolittle 2, 2001, Behind Enemy Lines, 2001, Life or Something Like It, 2002, 29 Palms, 2002, Happy Hour, 2003, Daddy Day Care, 2003, Devil's Pond, 2003, Paycheck, 2003, Garfield, 2004, I, Robot, 2004, First Daughter, 2004, Flight of the Phoenix, 2004, At Last, 2005, When a Stranger Calls, 2006, Garfield: A Tale of Two Kitties, 2006, Eragon, 2006, Norbit, 2007, (TV films) Silhouette, 1990, Voyage, 1993, This Can't Be Love, 1994, The Last Outlaw, 1994, One Christmas, 1994, Kidnapped, 1995, Asteroid, 1997, Volcano: Fire on the Mountain, 1997, Miracle at Midnight, 1998, The Jesse Ventura Story, 1999, Little Richard, 2000, Bobbie's Girl, 2002, Nadine in Date Land, 2005, Life is Ruff, 2005, Jump In!, 2007. Office: Davis Entertainment Ste 2900 2121 Avenue Of The Stars Los Angeles CA 90067-5057*

DAVIS, JOHN CHARLES, lawyer; b. Kansas City, Mo., Mar. 4, 1943; s. Ralph B. Jr. and Helen M. (Schneider) D.; m. C. Jane Reusser, June 18, 1966; children: Tracy A., Matthew S. BA, U. Kans., 1965; JD, U. Mich., 1968. Bar: Mo. 1968, Kans. 1983. Ptnr. Stinson Morrison Hecker LLP, Kansas City, 1968—. Chmn. Fed. Estate Tax Symposium, 1986-87 Chmn. Bacchus Found., Kansas City, 1974; bd. dirs. Crittenten, Kansas City, 1988-94, vice chmn., 1990-92; trustee Schutte Found., Kansas City, 1986—, UMKC, 1989—, treas., 1994-96, counsel, 1996—; trustee Village Presbyn. Ch. Found., chmn., 1991-93; elder Village Presbyn. Ch., 1994-97; bd. dirs. Gamma O Edn. Found., Heart of Am. coun. Boy Scouts Am., exec. com., 1996—; bd. dirs. John County C.C. Found Fellow Am. Coll. Trust and Estate Counsel (by-laws com. 1987-96, chmn. 1996-99, 2002-05, program com. 1993-96); mem. ABA, Mo. Bar Assn., Kans. Bar Assn., Estate Planning Soc. Kansas City (pres. 1990-91), Nelson-Atkins Mus. Soc. Fellows, Kansas City Club (v.p. 1989-90), Indian Hills Country Club (Mission Hills, Kans.), River Club (Kansas City, Mo.), Rotary, Gamma Omicron (pres., bd. dirs. 1979-85) Presbyterian. Avocations: squash, Hopi art, Marklin trains, travel, photography. Home: 6421 High Dr Mission Hills KS 66208-1935 Office: Stinson Morrison Hecker LLP 1201 Walnut St Ste 2900 Kansas City MO 64106 Office Phone: 816-691-3252. Business E-Mail: jcdavis@stinsonmoheck.com.

DAVIS, JOHN EDWARD, music educator, musician; b. Omaha, Nebr., July 7, 1954; s. William Edward and Dorothy Ann Davis; m. Susan Lynn Aronovici, June 10, 1990; children: Evan William, Andrew Russell. MusB magna cum laude, San Francisco State U., 1990, MusM, 1991; D in Musical Arts, U. Ariz., 1997. Ordained elder Presbyn. Ch. Saxophonist San Francisco Saxophone Quartet, 1980—87, Nuc. Whales Saxophone Orch., Santa Cruz, Calif., 1987—91; grad. tchg. asst. San Francisco State U., 1990—91, U. Ariz., Tucson, 1991—94, grad. rsch. asst., 1994—95; asst. prof. of music Berry Coll., Mt. Berry, Ga., 1995—2001; flutist Rome (Ga.) Symphony Orch., 1995—; assoc. prof. music Berry Coll., Mt. Berry, Ga., 2001—07, prof. music, 2007—. Arranger (musical arrangement) Brandenburg Concerto No. 3: For Flute Choir. J. S. Bach, 1998, String Quartet No. 4, K. 157: For Saxophone Quartet. W. A. Mozart, 1999, Three Madrigals: For Flute Quartet or Flute Choir Orlando di Lasso, 1999, Concerto Grosso, Op. 3, No. 8: For Flute Choir. Antonio Vivaldi, 1999, Quartet in C Minor, Op. 18, No. 4: For Saxophone Quartet L. van Beethoven, 1999, Quartet, No. 58, Op. 54, No. 2: For Saxophone Quartet Franz Josef Haydn, 1999, Divertimento, K. 138: For Flute Choir W. A. Mozart, 1999, Lady Radnor's Suite: For Flute Choir. C. Hubert H. Parry, 1999, Sheep May Safely Graze: For Saxophone Sextet, 2000, Intermezzo, Op. 118, No. 2: For Flute Choir Johannes Brahms, 2000, Souvenir de Porto Rico: For Flute Choir. Louis Moreau Gottschalk, 2000, Gloria, from Missa Tu Es Petrus: For Flute Choir. Palestrina, 2000, Trio in G Major, Op. 53, No. 1: For Flute Trio, 2000, Concerto Grosso, Op. 6, No. 3: For Flute Choir. G. F. Handel, 2000, What Wondrous Love: For Flute Choir, 2001, Finale, from Serenade, Op. 22: For Flute Choir Antonin Dvorak, 2001, Allegro, from Sinfonia Concertante: For Flute Choir. J. C. Bach, 2001, Tarentelle Styrienne: For Flute Choir, 2002, I Need Thee Every Hour. Robert Lowry, 2002; arranger: musical arrangement Enigma Variations: For Flute Choir, Edward Elgar, 2003; arranger (musical arrangement) Jig, from St. Paul's Suite: For Flute Choir, 2004, Madrigali di Monteverdi: For Flute Choir, 2004, Menuet, from Tombeau de Couperin: For Flute Choir, 2004, Danza Española: For Flute Choir, 2004, Allegro, from Flute Concerto No. 3 in C Major for Flute Choir, 2006, Veni, Sancto Spiritus, For Flute Choir, 2006, others, saxophonist (recording) Thar They Blow. Nuclear Whales Saxophone Orchestra. Whaleco Music, Whalin'. Nuclear Whales Saxophone Orchestra, Bach/Mozart. The San Francisco Saxophone Quartet, The San Francisco Saxophone Quartet; contbr. articles to profl. jours. Conducting Fellow, Conductors Inst. SC., 1998. Mem.: ASCAP (Std. award, annually 1999—2005), Music Educators Nat. Conf., Nat. Flute Assn., Nat. Assn. Coll. Wind and Percussion Instrs., Coll. Music Soc., Phi Kappa Phi, Pi Kappa Lambda, Phi Mu Alpha. Avocations: photography, bicycling, tennis. Office: Berry College 11 Berry College Mount Berry GA 30149 Home: 12 E Clinton Dr Rome GA 30165 Office Phone: 706-290-2176. Business E-Mail: jdavis@berry.edu.

DAVIS, JOHN JAMES, religion educator; b. Phila., Oct. 13, 1936; s. John James and Cathryn Ann (Nichols) D.; m. Carolyn Ann. BA, Trinity Coll., Dunedin, Fla., 1959, DD (hon.), 1968; MDiv, Grace Coll. & Grace Theol. Sem., Winona Lake, Ind., 1962, ThM, 1964, ThD, 1967. Instr. Grace Coll. & Grace Theol. Sem., 1963-65, prof. Old Testament, 1965—2004, exec. v.p., 1976-82, pres., 1986-93; exec. dean Near East Sch. Archaeology, Jerusalem, 1970-71. Area supr. Tekoa Archeol. Expdn., Jordan, 1968, 70, Raddana Expdn., Jordan, 1974, Heshbon Expdn., Jordan, 1976, Abila Archeol. Expdn., Jordan, 1982, 84, Khirbet el-Maqatir Expdn., Israel, 2000, Khirbet Nisya, Israel, 2003. Author: Paradise to Prison, 1975 (Book of Yr.), The Perfect Shepherd, 1979 (Book of Yr.), 16 other books. Chmn., bd. dirs. Kosciusko Comty. Hosp., 1994—. Recipient Gold award United Way, 1980, Conservation award Barbee Property Owners Assn., 1983; named Outdoor Writer of Yr., Ind. Dept. Natural Resources, 1986, to the Koscivsko County Rep. Hall of Fame, 1992. Mem. Am. Schs. of Oriental Research, Near East Archeol. Soc., Outdoor Writers Assn., Hoosier Outdoor Writers Assn. (pres. 1984-86). Avocations: fishing, hunting, photography, music. Home: PO Box 557 Winona Lake IN 46590-0557 Business E-Mail: johnjdavis@mchsi.com.

DAVIS, JOHN KERR, philosopher, educator, lawyer; b. Bremerton, Wash., June 26, 1956; s. Donald Dewitt and Judith Lee (Moxon) D. BA, Reed Coll., 1981; JD, NYU, 1985; PhD in Philosophy, U. Wash., 2001. Assoc. Elam, Burke & Boyd, Boise, Idaho, 1984-86, Weinstein, Fischer, Riley, Erickson & Wolfe, Seattle, 1988-95; pvt. practice Seattle, 1995-2001; asst. prof. med. humanities Brody Sch. Medicine, East Carolina U., Greenville, NC, 2001—04; asst. prof. philosophy U. Tenn., Knoxville, 2004—. Independent. Office: Univ Tenn Dept Philosophy 816 McClung Tower Knoxville TN 37996-0480 Business E-Mail: jdavis95@utk.edu.

DAVIS, JOHN MACDOUGALL, lawyer; b. Seattle, Feb. 20, 1914; s. David Lyle and Georgina (MacDougall) D.; m. Ruth Anne Van Arsdale, July 1, 1939; children: Jean, John, Bruce, Ann, Margaret, Elizabeth. BA, U. Wash., 1936, LLB, JD, 1940. Bar: Wash. 1940. Assoc. Poe, Falknor, Emory & Howe, Seattle, 1940-45; pvt. practice Seattle, 1945-46; ptnr. Davis & Riese, Seattle, 1946-48, Emory, Howe, Davis & Riese, Seattle, 1948-50, Howe, Davis & Riese, Seattle, 1951-53, Howe, Davis, Riese & Aiken, Seattle, 1953-58, Howe, Davis, Riese & Jones, Seattle, 1958-68, Davis, Wright, Todd, Riese & Jones, Seattle, 1969-85; of counsel Davis, Wright & Jones, Seattle, 1985-89, Davis Wright Tremaine, Seattle, 1990—. Lectr. U. Wash. Law Sch., 1947-52; pres. Seattle Bar Assn., 1960. Bd. dirs. Virginia Mason Hosp., Seattle, 1952-79, pres., 1970-72; bd. dirs. Pacific Sci. Ctr., 1971-90, dir. emeritus, 1990—, past pres., past chmn.; trustee Whitman Coll., 1971-86, chmn., 1983-86; bd. dirs. Blue Cross Wash. and Alaska, 1982-89, Diabetic Trust Fund, 1954—, Wash. Student Loan Guaranty Assn., 1978-83; mem. adv. bd. Chief Seattle council Boy Scouts Am.; mem. Mercer Island Sch. Bd., 1956-66. With USNG, 1931—34. Recipient Disting. Eagle Scout award, 1982 Mem. ABA, Wash. State Bar Assn. (merit award 1965), Seattle-King County Bar Assn. (pres. 1960-61), Order of Coif, Rainier Club (Seattle), The Mountaineers Club (Svc. award, 1974), Phi Delta Phi, Alpha Delta Phi. Clubs: Rainier (Seattle). Presbyterian. Avocation: mountain climbing. Home: 9104 Fortuna Dr #3305 Mercer Island WA 98040-3166 Office: Davis Wright Tremaine 2600 Century Sq 1501 4th Ave Ste 2600 Seattle WA 98101-1688

DAVIS, JOHN RIPOLL, manufacturing executive; BS, U. State of NY, 1991. V.p. Turbines & Pumps, Inc., Odessa, Tex., 1980—84; CEO Omnitek Internat., Inc., Odessa, 1984—89; ptnr. Jacqueline Co., Wyomissing, Pa., 1990—99; prin. Prototypes, Wilmington, Del., 1999—; owner Davis Oil and Gas Investments, Wilmington, 2006—. Mem.: ASM, Am. Soc. Quality, Soc. Mfg. Engrs., Faculty Club U. Pa., Penn Club. Achievements include design of improved nozzle ring performance, turbochargers; development of protocol for welding hot short cracking aluminum alloys in cryogenic service. Avocations: sociology, history of technology, music, literature, travel. Office: 2207 Concord Pike Ste 464 Wilmington DE 19801 Home Phone: 610-223-5833. Personal E-mail: jdavis@bluetruck.net.

DAVIS, JOHN ROWLAND, academic administrator; b. Mpls., Dec. 19, 1927; s. Roland Owen and Dorothy (Norman) D.; m. Lois Marie Falk, Sept. 4, 1947; children— Joel C., Jacque L., Michele M., Robin E. BS, U. Minn., 1949, MS, 1951; postgrad., Purdue U., 1955-57; PhD, Mich. State U., 1959. Hydraulic engr. U.S. Geol. Survey, Lincoln, Nebr., 1950-51; instr. Mich. State U., 1951-55; asst. prof. Purdue U., 1955-57; lectr. U. Calif., Davis, 1957-62; hydraulic engr. Stanford Rsch. Inst., South Pasadena, Calif., 1962-64; prof. U. Nebr., Lincoln, 1964-65, dean coll. engring. and architecture, 1965-71, faculty rep. intercollegiate athletics; prof., head dept. agrl. engring. Oreg. State U., Corvallis, 1971-75, instl. athletic rep., 1972-87, dir. Agrl. Expt. Sta., assoc. dean Sch. Agr., 1975-85, dir. spl. programs Office of Academic Affairs, assoc. dir. athletics, 1987-89, prof. emeritus, assoc. dir. athletics, 1989—. Governing bd. Water Resources Research Inst., 1975-85; dir. Western Rural Devel. Center, 1975-85, Agrl. Research Found., Jackman Inst.; cons. Stanford Research Inst., Dept. Agr., Consortium for Internat. Devel.; dir. Engrs. Council Profl. Devel., 1966-72; pres. Pacific-10 Conf., 1978-79. Contbr. articles to profl. jours. Mem. budget commn. City of Corvallis, 2003—. With USNR, 1945-46. Fellow Am. Soc. Agrl. Engrs. (dir. 1971-73, Agrl. Engr. Yr. award Pacific N.W. region 1974), NCAA (v.p. 1979-83, sec.-treas. 1983-85, pres. 1985-87), Heartland Humane Soc. (pres. bd. dirs. 2002). Home: 2940 NW Aspen St Corvallis OR 97330-3307 Office: Oreg State U Gill Coliseum Corvallis OR 97331 Personal E-mail: davisjrd@aol.com.

DAVIS, JOHN WARREN, real estate broker, consultant; b. York, Pa., Feb. 14, 1946; s. Frank Asbury Jr. and Lillian Margaret (Billings) D. BA in Polit. Sci., Drake U., Des Moines, 1968; AA in Real Estate, San Diego City Coll., 1976; MS in Acquisition and Contract Mgmt., West Coast U., LA, 1987; postgrad., Walden U., 1992—; grad., Kellogg Brown, 2005, Root Procurement Acad., 2005. Real estate sales staff, 1972-79; clk. GS 3 Naval Ocean Sys. Ctr., 1979-80; contract intern, contract adminstr. Office of Naval Rsch., 1980-84; contract specialist, warranted ordering officer Gen. Svc. 1102-11 Naval Weapons Sta., 1984-86; contract specialist Gen Svc. 1102-12 Navy Space Sys. Activity, 1986-88; procurement analyst Gen Svc. 102-12 COMNAVAIRPAC, 1988-98; def. contract mgr. Def. Contract Mgmt. Command, 1998—2000; sr. v.p. Azan Corp. Group, San Diego, 2001—03; subcontract adminstr. Kellogg, Brown & Root, Houston, 2005—06; contractor cons., 2006—. Del. San Diego State U. to the Nat. Acad. Conf. for Contract Mgmt. Educators, 1991, 92, 93; profl. cons. Computer Applications, Inc., 1992; mem. tech. program com., chairperson for electronic data interchange Soc. of Logistics Engrs., 1995; mem. Golden Hill planning com. City of San Diego; adj. prof. San Diego State U., chmn. curriculum rev. com. for acquisition. Author, Paperless Contracting, The EDI Revolution, 1995, contbr. articles to profl. publs. With U.S. Army, Vietnam, 1968-72. Fellow Nat. Contract Mgmt. Assn. (life; cert. profl. contract mgr.); mem. ABA (mem. sub-com. pub. law sector, sub-com. on intellectual property), SAR (nat., Calif. and San Diego chpts.), VFW (life), Am. Arbitration Assn. (nat. panel mem.), Soc. Govt. Meeting Planners (v.p. San Diego chpt.), Soc. Logistics Engrs., San Diego Athletic Club, San Diego Writers and Editors Guild, Author's Guild (past pres.). Episcopalian. Avocations: swimming, travel. Personal E-mail: jwdsandiego@yahoo.com.

DAVIS, JON L., logistics consultant; b. Louisiana, Mo., Mar. 1, 1934; s. Lloyd Israel Davis and Mary Isabelle (Cory) Stone; m. Rita Marie Pitts, July 21, 1957; children: Michael Louis, Catherine Faith, Laurie Marie BSBA magna cum laude, U. Albuquerque, 1977. Cert. profl. logistician. Enlisted USAF, 1956, advanced through grades to col., 1979, ret., 1985; col., dep. comdr. maintenance 479th Tactical Tng. Wing, Holloman AFB, N.Mex., 1979—81, 67 Tactical Reconnaissance Wing, Bergstrom AFB, Tex., 1981—83; col., dir. logistics USAF Operational Test & Evaluation Ctr., Kirtland AFB, N.Mex., 1983—85; asst. v.p. Los Alamos Tech. Assocs., Albuquerque, 1985—2000; logistics cons. Albuquerque, 2000—. Author Air Force manuals Mem. Austin-Bergstrom Cmty. Coun., Austin, Tex., 1981-83, Alamogordo Mil. Adv. Com., N.Mex., 1980-81 Decorated Legion of Merit, D.F.C., 12 Air medals Mem. Internat. Soc. Logistics (sr., chpt. chmn. 1991), USAF Logistics Officers Assn., Air Force Assn. (life), Red River Valley Assn. (life). Republican. Home and Office: 9706 Camino Del Sol NE Albuquerque NM 87111-1510 E-mail: jdavis502@comcast.net.

DAVIS, JONATHAN, JR., broadcast executive; b. Aug. 7, 1971; Intern NBC, NYC; writers' asst. Politically Incorrect ABC; asst. DreamWorks TV; dir. alternative programming and latenight devel. Fox Broadcasting Co., Beverly Hills, Calif., 2002—05, dir. comedy devel., 2005—06, v.p. comedy devel., 2006—. Achievements include overseeing development of the TV series Til Death and Happy Hour. Office: Fox Broadcasting Co PO Box 900 Beverly Hills CA 90213*

DAVIS, JORDAN S., venture capitalist; BA in econ., State U. NY, Binghamton; MBA, J.L. Kellogg Grad. Sch. Mgmt. Northwestern U. Co-founder Cambridge Heart, Inc., Voxware, Inc.; with Morgan Stanley & Co., Inc.; mng. dir. KBL Healthcare, Inc.; co-founder, v.p., dir. KBL Healthcare Acquisition Corp.; co-founder, mng. ptnr. Radius Ventures, LLC, 1997—. Bd. dirs. Health Language, Inc., ZettaCore, Inc., Implant, Inc., Am. Banknote, Holographics, Inc. Office: Radius Ventures LLC 400 Madison Ave 8th Fl New York NY 10017 Office Phone: 212-897-7778. Office Fax: 212-397-2656.

DAVIS, JOSEPH LLOYD, academic administrator, consultant; b. Crawfordsville, Iowa, May 4, 1927; s. Whitfield and Jane (Lloyd) D.; m. Margaret Florence Cooper, Dec. 28, 1949; children: Stephen Joseph, Thomas Whitfield, Jane Ellen. BSc, Ohio State U., 1949, MA, 1955, PhD, 1967. Reporter Ohio State Jour., 1943-49, 52-53; tchr. Morey Jr. H.S., Denver, 1949-52, Central H.S., Columbus, Ohio, 1953-54; asst. dir. adminstrv. rsch. Columbus Public Schs., 1954-56, dir. publs. and public info., 1956-60, exec. asst. to supt., 1960-64, asst. supt. spl. svcs., 1964-77, supt. of schs., 1977-82; exec. dir. Ohio Coun. Vocat. Edn., 1985-96. Past pres. Columbus Rotary; adj. prof. Ohio State U., 1983—; founder, dir. emeritus Ohio State U. Nat. Acad. for Supt.; cons. and author in field. Mem., bd. trustees Kids Voting/Ctrl. Ohio Region, 1999—2007; past pres. Friends Bd. WOSU AM, FM and TV, Ohio State U., Columbus, 1986—98, 2000—06; vice chmn. bd. trustees Union Cemetery Assn., Columbus, 2005—. With USN, 1945—46, with USN, 1950—51. Recipient award for civic leadership Columbus Area C. of C., 1980, Liberty Bell award Columbus Bar Assn., 1980; named to Pub. Schs. Hall of Fame, Columbus, Ohio, 1993. Mem. Am. Assn. Sch. Adminstrs. (disting. svc. award 1989). Nat. Sch. Pub. Rels. Assn. (pres.'s award 1980), Assn. for Career and Tech. Edn., Ohio Assn. for Career and Tech. Edn., Buckeye Assn. Sch. Adminstrs., Nat. Soc. Study Edn., Horace Mann League, Ohio State U. Alumni Assn. (leadership consortium 2003—), Ohio State Advocates, Rotary

(Rotarian of Yr. award 1994), Torch Club Columbus, Phi Delta Kappa, Epsilon Pi Tau (laureate 1994, Disting. Svc. award 2000), Kappa Delta Pi, Omicron Tau Theta. Presbyterian. Personal E-mail: jdavis59@columbus.rr.com.

DAVIS, JUDY, actress; b. Perth, Australia, Apr. 23, 1955; m. Colin Friels, 1984; children: Jack, Charlotte. Student, Nat. Inst. Dramatic Art, Sydney, Australia. Appearances include: (films) Clean Straw for Nothing, 1976, High Rolling, 1977, My Brilliant Career, 1979 (Best Actress Sammy award Australian Film and TV Awards 1979, Best Actress award Brit. Acad. Film and TV Arts 1981, Best Newcomer Brit. Acad. Film and TV Arts 1981), Hoodwink, 1981 (Best Supporting Actress Sammy award Australian Film and TV Awards 1981), Winter of Our Dreams, 1981 (Best Actress Sammy award Australia Film and TV Awards 1981), Heatwave, 1982, The Final Option, 1983, A Passage to India, 1984 (Acad. award nominee for best actress 1984), Kangaroo, 1986, High Tide, 1987, Georgia, 1988, Alice, 1990, Impromptu, 1991, Barton Fink, 1991, Naked Lunch, 1991 (Best Supporting Actress award N.Y. Critics Cir. 1991), Where Angels Fear to Tread, 1991, Husbands and Wives, 1992 (Acad. award nominee for best supporting actress 1992), The Ref, 1994, The New Age, 1994, Children of the Revolution, 1996, Absolute Power, 1996, Blood and Wine, 1996, Deconstructing Harry, 1996, Celebrity, 1997, The Echo of Thunder, 1998, Gaudi Afternoon, 2000, The Man Who Sued God, 2001, Swimming Upstream, 2003, Marie-Antoinette, 2006, The Break-Up, 2006; (TV movies) Water Under the Bridge, 1980 A Woman Called Golda, 1982 (Emmy award nominee 1982), The Merry Wives of Windsor, 1982, Rocket to the Moon, 1986, One Against the Wind, 1991, Serving in Silence: The Margarethe Cammermeyer Story, 1995 (Emmy award), Echo of Thunder (Emmy nomination), 1997, Dash & Lily, 1997 (Emmy nomination), A Cooler Climate, 1998, Life With Judy Garland: Me and My Shadows, 2000 (Golden Globe award, Am. Screen Actors award, Golden Satellite award, Broadcast Critics Choice award, Am. Film Inst. award, Emmy award), The Reagans, 2003, Coast to Coast, 2004, A Little Thing Called Murder, 2006. Office: care Shanahan Mgmt PO Box1509 Darlinghurst NSW 1300 Australia

DAVIS, JULIA A., lawyer, retail executive; BA in Economics, John Carroll U., 1982; JD with honors, Ohio State U. Sch. of Law, 1985. Assoc. then prtnr. Vorys, Sater, Seymour and Pease, Columbus, Ohio, 1987—2003; exec. v.p., gen. counsel Retail Ventures (Value City Dept. Stores), Columbus, Ohio, 2003—. Nat. bd. mem. ACLU, nat. bd. mem. exec. com., 1999—, nat. affirmative action officer, 2000—. Mem.: Columbus Bar Assn. (ethics com.). Office: Retail Ventures Inc 3241 Westerville Rd Columbus OH 43224

DAVIS, JUNE FIKSDAL, medical facility owner, floral designer; b. Alexnadria, Minn., June 18, 1944; d. Mads and Gladys Lillian Katherine (Engstrom) Fiksdal; m. Merrill Nathaniel Davis III, June 20, 1971; adopted sons: Kim Geoffrey, Marc Lee. Cert. with highest honor, Am. Sch. Floral Arts, Chgo., 1965. Floral designer Fiksdal Flowers, Rochester, Minn., 1960-70; prin. floral designer, nat. design tchr. Retail Florists, Kansas City, Mo., Houston, 1970-81; pres. owner, founder The Gables Found., Inc., Rochester, 1982—; floral designer, 1981—. Author: Floral Design, 1973 (Am. Inst. Floral Design award 1974). Cellist Rochester Symphony Orch., 1960-69; bd. dirs., fin. planner United Way, 1974; real estate placement Riverplace Devel., 1980; bd. dirs. Rochester Ballet, 1975; chair Symphony Ball, Rochester Symphony, 1975; coord. music program, new pipe organ, harpischord Unitarian Ch., 1975-81 (Outstanding Svc. award 1977), project pres. Walden Hill Bach Soc., 1975-82; vol. Mayo Clinic Visitors Bur. Mem. Am. Inst. Floral Design, Bus. and Profl. Women. Avocations: gourmet cooking, water sports, winter sports, skiing, European travel.

DAVIS, KAREN, insurance company executive, educator; b. Blackwell, Okla., Nov. 14, 1942; d. Walter Dwight and Thelma Louise (Kohler) Padgett; 1 child, Kelly Denise Collins. BA, Rice U., 1965, PhD, 1969. Asst. prof. econs. Rice U., 1969—70; econ. policy fellow Social Security Adminstrn. Brookings Instn., Washington, 1970—71, rsch. assoc., 1971—74, sr. fellow, 1974—77; dep. asst. sec. for planning and evaluation, health HEW, Washington, 1977—80; adminstr, health resources adminstrn. USPHS, Washington, 1980—81; prof. Johns Hopkins U., Balt., 1981—92, chmn., 1983—92; exec. v.p. Commonwealth Fund, NYC, 1992—94, pres., 1995—. Mem. Physican Payment Rev. Commn., 1986-94; dir. Commonwealth Fund Commn. on Elderly People Living Alone, 1985-91; vis. lectr. Harvard U., 1974-75; nat. adv. com. Agy. for Health Care Rsch. and Quality, 1999-2003; bd. dirs. Geisinger Health Sys. Author: National Health Insurance: Benefits, Costs and Consequences, 1975, Health and the War on Poverty, 1978, Medicare Policy: New Directions for Health and Long-Term Care, 1986, Health Care Cost Containment, 1990. Mem.: Inst. Medicine, Phi Beta Kappa. Democrat. Methodist. Home: 1365 York Ave 27K New York NY 10021 Office: The Commonwealth Fund The Harkness House 1 E 75th St New York NY 10021-2692 Office Phone: 212-606-3825. Business E-Mail: kd@cmwf.org.

DAVIS, KELLI ANSLEY, social studies educator; b. Houston, Oct. 29, 1976; BA in History, Stephen F. Austin State U., Nacogdoches, Tex., 2000. Cert. tchr. Tex., 2005. Social studies educator Dayton H.S., Tex., 2002—. Mem.: ASCD, Nat. Coun. Social Studies, Assn. Tex. Profl. Educators. Office: Dayton High Sch 3200 Cleveland Dayton TX 77535 Home Phone: 281-812-6150; Office Phone: 936-258-2510.

DAVIS, KELVISHA LASHAE, forensic specialist; b. Oct. 19, 1980; BA, Fisk U., Nashville, 2002; MS, Tenn. State U., Nashville, 2004. Rsch. lab. asst. Tenn. State U., Nashville, 2002—04; forensic lab. technician Orchid Cellmark, Nashville, 2004—06. Home: 3251 Vailview Dr Nashville TN 37207

DAVIS, KENNETH BOONE, JR., dean, law educator; b. Louisville, Sept. 1, 1947; s. Kenneth Boone and Doris Edna (Gordon) D. m. Arrietta Evoline Hastings, June 2, 1984; children: Peter Hastings, Mary Elizabeth, Kenneth Boone III. AB, U. Mich., 1969; JD, Case Western Res. U., 1974. Bar: D.C. 1975, Ohio 1974. Law clk. to chief judge U.S. Ct. Appeals (9th cir.), San Francisco, 1974-75; assoc. Covington & Burling, Washington, 1975-78; prof. law U. Wis., Madison, 1978—, assoc. dean for academic affairs, 1996, James E. and Ruth B. Doyle-Bascom prof. law, 1997—, dean law sch., 1997—. Visiting prof. U. Calif. L.A., U. Pa., Case Western Reserve. Contbr. articles to profl. jours. Recipient President's Award of Excellence, State Bar Wis., 1990. Mem. ABA, Am. Fin. Assn., Am. Law Inst., Wis. Bar Assn. (reporter, corp. and bus. law com.). Office: U Wis Law Sch 975 Bascom Mall Madison WI 53706-1399 Office Phone: 608-262-0962. E-mail: kbdavis@wisc.edu.

DAVIS, KENNETH LEON, psychiatrist, pharmacologist, medical educator; b. NYC, Sept. 10, 1947; married, 1972; 2 children. BA, Yale U., 1969; MD, Mt. Sinai Med. Sch., 1973. Diplomate Am. Bd. Psychiatry and Neurology. Intern Stanford U., 1973-74, resident, 1973-76, life sci. rsch. assoc., 1975-76; rsch. assoc. Stanford Psych. Clin., 1974-79; asst. dir. Stanford Psych. Clin. Rsch. Ctr., VA Med. Ctr., 1975-79; clin. psychiat. cons. Santa Clara Valley Med. Ctr., 1976-79; chief dept. psychiat. VA Med. Ctr., 1979-87; assoc. prof. psychiatry and pharmacology Mt. Sinai Sch. Medicine, 1979-84; dir. schizophrenia biol. rsch. ctr., 1981-91; prof. Mt. Sinai Sch. Medicine, 1984—, chair dept. psychiatry, 1987—, Esther and Joseph Klingenstein prof., 1994—2003, dean, 2003—; pres., CEO Mt. Sinai Med. Ctr., 2003—. Editor Alzheimer's Disease and Associated Disorders, Biol. Psychiatry, Clin. Neuropharmacology, Harvard Review of Psychiatry, Internat. Jour. Geriatric Psychiatry, Internat. Jour. Geriatric Psychopharmacology, Jour. Geriatric Psychiatry & Neurology, Jour. Psychiatric Rsch., Jour. Am. Geriatrics Soc., Schizophrenia Rsch., Neuropsychopharmacology, Jour. Exptl. Cognitive and Behavioral Neurosci., Molecular Psychiatry, Sociedade de Psiquiatria Do Rio Grande Do Sul; author, co-author over 500 sci. articles. Recipient A. E. Bennett Clin. Sci. Rsch. award, 1977, Saul Horowitz Jr. Meml. award, 1977-78, Solomon Silver award, 1981, Joel Elkes Internat. award ACNP, 1986, Daniel H. Efron Excellence in Rsch. award, 1990, Rita Hayworth award Alzheimer's Assn., 1991, Lifetime Sci. award Inst. Advanced Sci. in Immunology and Aging, 1992. Mem. NAS, Am. Coll. Neuropsychopharmacology (pres.-elect 2004-05, pres. 05-06), Am. Psychiat. Assn. (APA/KEMPF award 1999), Soc. Biol. Psychiatry (Gold medal award 1999, APA award Rsch. in Psychiatry 2001), Inst. Medicine of NAS. Achievements include research in the biological basis of senile dementia of the Alzheimers' type, and schizophrenia. Office: Mount Sinai Med Ctr - Mount Sinai Sch Medicine Presidents Office One Gustave L Levy Pl Box 1220 New York NY 10029-6574 Business E-Mail: kenneth.davis@mssm.edu.

DAVIS, KENNETH WAYNE, language educator, business communication consultant; b. Chariton, Iowa, June 22, 1945; s. Wayne Pitman and Jeanne Frances (West) Davis; m. Bette Hargrove, Nov. 28, 1970; children: Cassandra Alice, Evan Thomas. BA, Drake U., 1967; MA, Columbia U., 1968; PhD, U. Mich., 1975. From asst. prof. English to assoc. prof. U. Ky., Lexington, 1975-88; assoc. prof. to prof. Ind. U.-Purdue U., Indpls., 1988—, dept. chair, 1998-2001; edn. dir. Am. Cabaret Theatre, 2001—05. Bus. cons., Lexington, 1977-88; pres. Komei, Inc., 1994—. Author: Better Business Writing, 1983, (with others) Business Communication for the Information Age, 1988, Rehearsing the Audience, 1988, (with others) Writing: Process, Product, and Power, 1993, The McGraw-Hill 36-Hour Course in Business Writing and Communication, 2005, Mandarin translation, 2006; prodr.: 2001: Lessons in Leadership videoconf., 1991; numerous other books and articles. Bd. dir. Shepherd's House, Inc., Lexington, 1986-88, Waycross Camp and Conf. Ctr., 1995-2000, World Trade Club Ind., 1998-2001. Sgt. US Army, 1968-71. Woodrow Wilson fellow, 1967; recipient Faculty Service award Nat. Univ. Continuing Edn. Assn., 1987. Mem.: ASTD, Assn. Profl. Comm. Cons. (pres. 2006—), Assn. Bus. Comm. (bd. dirs. 2003—), Toastmasters Internat., Hon. Order Ky. Col., Freemasons. Episcopalian. Avocations: theater, travel. Office: Ind U-Purdue U Dept English 425 University Blvd Indianapolis IN 46202-5148 Office Phone: 317-274-0084. Business E-Mail: kdavis@iupui.edu.

DAVIS, KEVIN E., law educator; b. 1970; BA in Econ., McGill U., Montreal, 1990; LLB, U. Toronto, 1993; LLM, Columbia U., 1996. Law clk. to Justice John Sopinka Supreme Ct. of Can.; assoc. corp. dept. Torys LLP, Canada; asst. prof. to prof. law U. Toronto; vis. prof. law NYU Sch. Law, 2003, prof., 2004—. Vis. prof. & John M. Olin rsch. fellow U. So. Calif. Law Sch.; vis. fellow Clare Hall, Cambridge U.; vis. lectr. U. West Indies, Barbados. Office: NYU Sch Law Vanderbilt Hall Rm 335 40 Washington Sq S New York NY 10012-1099 Office Phone: 212-992-8843. E-mail: davisk@juris.law.nyu.edu.

DAVIS, LANITA IRENE, secondary school educator; d. George Michael and Beulah Elizabeth Soffa; m. James Edward Davis, May 6, 2000; children: Brittany Sue, Adam James. BS in Secondary Math., U. Colo., Denver, 1993, MA in Curriculum and Instrn., 1997. Cert. tchr. Colo. Mid. sch. math. tchr. Douglas County Sch. Dist., Highlands Ranch, Colo., 1996—, sports coach, 1998—. Eucharistic min. St Francis Cath. Ch., Castle Rock, Colo., 2000—. Mem.: Nat. Coun. Tchrs. Math. Office Phone: 303-387-3300.

DAVIS, LANT B., lawyer; b. Birmingham, Ala., Mar. 6, 1954; BA summa cum laude, Duke U., 1976; JD, Yale U., 1979. Bar: Ala. 1979. Atty. Bradley, Arant, Rose & White, Birmingham, Ala.; pvt. practice Terre Haute, Ind. Mem. ABA, Am. Acad. Hosp. Attys., Nat. Health Lawyers Assn., Ala. State Bar (chmn. health law sect. 1992-93, vice chmn. 1990-92), Birmingham Bar Assn., Healthcare Fin. Mgmt. Assn. Mem. editorial bd.: Yale Law Jour., 1978-79. Office: 2100 Ohio Blvd Terre Haute IN 47803 Office Phone: 812-235-7026. Office Fax: 812-232-5040. Business E-Mail: cpcpastor1@verizon.net.

DAVIS, LARRY E., academic administrator; b. Saginaw, Mich., May 11, 1946; m. Shirley Salmon; children: Amani, Naeem, Keanu. BS in Psychology, Mich. State U., 1968; MSW, U. Mich., 1973, MA in Psychology, 1975, PhD in Social Work and Psychology, 1977. Asst. prof. Washington U., St. Louis, 1983—96, prof. social work and psychology, 1998, E. Desmond Lee prof. racial and ethnic diversity, 1998—2001; dir. Ctr. on Race and Social Problems U. Pitts., Pitts., 2001—, dean and Donald M. Henderson prof., 2001—. Author: Black and Single: Finding and Choosing a Partner Who's Right for You, 1993, 3d edit., 2003, Working with African American Males: A Guide to Practice, 1999. Mem. Gov.'s Adv. Com. on African Am. Affairs, Harrisburg, Pa., 2002—; bd. dirs. United Way of SW Pa., Pitts., 2003—, Pa. Cancer Control Consortium, Pitts., 2003—, Pitts. Zoo and PPG Aquarium, 2005—. Mem.: NASW, Coun. on Social Work Edn., Nat. Assn. Black Social Workers. Home: 944 N Sheridan ave Pittsburgh PA 15206 Office: U Pitts Sch Social Work 2117 Cathedral of Learning Pittsburgh PA 15260 E-mail: LEDavis@pitt.edu.

DAVIS, LAURA ARLENE, retired foundation administrator; b. Battle Creek, Mich., Apr. 14, 1935; d. Paul Bennett and Daisy E. (Coston) Borgard; m. John R. Davis, Aug. 7, 1955; children: Scott Judson, Cynthia Ann Davis Welker. BS, Ctrl. Mich. U., 1986. Sec. Mich. Loan Co., Battle Creek, 1952-56; legal sec. Ryan, Sullivan & Hamilton, Battle Creek, 1957-64; exec. sec. W.K. Kellogg Found., Battle Creek, 1965-76, adminstrn./program asst., 1976, fellowship dir., 1977, asst. v.p. adminstrn., asst. corp. sec., 1978-84, v.p. corp. affairs, corp. sec., 1984-95, spl. asst. to pres., CEO, 1996-97. Cons. Mich. State U., 1998-2000. Pres. bd. dirs. Charitable Union, Battle Creek, 1983-85; mem. allocations panel United Way of Battle Creek, 1983, v.p. cmty. rels., 1990-91, 1st v.p., 1994, pres. of bd., 1995-97; bd. dirs. Battle Creek Gas Co., 1988—2004, Riding for the Handicapped Cheff Ctr., 1991-96, sec., 1992; trustee Binder Park Zoo; mem. adv. coun. Argubright Bus. Coll., 1989-90; mem. Visionquest 5000, 1989; mem. selection com. Cmty. Leadership Acad.; bd. dirs. Coun. Mich. Founds., 1994-97; mem. membership com. Recipient Athena award C. of C., Cmty. Svc. award J.C. Penney. Mem. Adminstrv. Mgmt. Soc. (pres. chpt. 1982-83), Am. Mgmt. Assn., Nat. Touring Network (bd. mem. 1997-99, sec. 1998-99), Battle Creek C. of C. Home: 101 Brighton Park Battle Creek MI 49015-9615

DAVIS, LAWRENCE WILLIAM, radiation oncologist; b. N. Braddock, Pa., Sept 5, 1935; s. William Paul Davis and Julia Helen Zukas; children: James G., Karen E. BS, Juniata Coll., Huntington, Pa., 1957; MA, U. Pa., 1969; MBA, Temple U., 1984; MD, Georgetown U., 1961. Diplomate Am. Bd. Radiology (trustee 1981-95, asst. exec. dir. radiation oncology 1994-04, assoc. exec. dir. 2004—), lic. physician Pa., Md., l, NY, Ga. Asst. instr. radiology U. Pa., Phila., 1962-66, instr. radiology, 1966, 68-69, asst. prof. radiology, 1969-72, assoc. prof. radiology, 1972-75; prof. radiation therapy Thomas Jefferson Sch. Medicine, 1975-84; prof. and chmn. radiation oncology Albert Einstein Coll. Medicine, Bronx, 1984-91, Emory U., Atlanta, 1991—. Cons. Armed Forces Radiobiology Rsch. Inst., Bethesda, 1968-70; exec. com. of med. staff Montefiore Med. Ctr., 1984-87, 1990-91, div. coun., 1988-89; prof. svc. com. Phila. div. Am. Cancer Soc., 1970-75; trustee 1981-95, asst. exec. dir. radiation oncology 1994-03, assoc. exec. dir. radiation oncology, Am. Bd. Radiology, 2003-. Assoc. editor Internat. Jour. Radiation Oncology, 1986—, mem. editl. bd. Neuro Oncology, 1989—99, assoc. editor, 1991—2003, mem. editl. bd. Am. Jour. Clin. Oncology, 1991—2003; contbr. numerous articles to profl. jours. Capt. USAF, 1966—68. Fellow Am. Cancer Soc., Phila., 1963-64, NIH, 1964-66, Am. Cancer Soc. traineeship, 1968-71 Fellow Am. Coll. Radiology; mem. AAAS, Am. Assn. Cancer Rsch., Am. Coll. Radiology (commn. on radiation oncology 1981-90, bd. chancellors 1993-99), Am. Soc. Therapeutic Radiology and Oncology (chmn. bd. 1988-89, pres. 1987-88), Am. Coll. Hosp. Adminstrs., Am. Mgmt. Assn., Am. Radium Soc. (pres. 1992-93), Am. Soc. Clin. Oncology, NY Acad. Scis., Radiation Rsch. Soc., Radiol. Soc. N.Am., Alpha Omega Alpha. Office: Emory Clinic 1365 Clifton Rd NE Atlanta GA 30322-1013 Home Phone: 678-289-0687; Office Phone: 404-778-5323. Business E-Mail: davis@radonc.emory.org.

DAVIS, LEON, oil industry executive; b. Arkansas City, Kans., Nov. 15, 1918; s. Miriam Kahan; m. Elene Meyer Davis, July 29, 1952; children: Lynn, Lance, Ross, Evan. BA, U. Okla., 1940. Co-owner Davis Bros., Tulsa, Houston, 1945—. Chmn. bd. dirs. Alliance S.B.I. Co., Tulsa. Pres. Urban League, Tulsa, 1964; chmn. Okla. Civil Rights Commn., 1966; co-founder, chmn. Interferon Found., Houston, 1979—90; bd. dirs. M. D. Anderson Hosp. Col. USAAF, 1940—48. Mem.: Kiwanis (pres. 1965). Avocation: tennis. Home: 502 Thamer Ln Houston TX 77024-6920 Office: Davis Bros 1221 Mckinney St Ste 3100 Houston TX 77010-2009 Office Phone: 713-659-3131. Business E-Mail: leondavis@davisbros.com.

DAVIS, LEWIS BERKLEY, mechanical engineer; b. Owensboro, Ky., Mar. 3, 1944; s. Lewis Berkley and Elizabeth (Miller) D.; m. Gloria Jean Whitaker, Dec. 15, 1966 (div. 1982); m. Katharine Frances Herrick, Sept. 20, 1986. BSME, U. Ky., 1966, MSME, 1970, PhD, 1972. With Gas Turbine div. GE, Schenectady, NY, 1972—, mgr. advanced combustion design, 1979-81, 82-85, mgr. low emissions devel., 1988, mgr. combustion engring., 1992—96, chief engr., 1996—. Patentee, gas turbine combustors; contbr. sci. papers to various profl. publs. Named to, Ky. Engring. Hall of Distinction, 2007; recipient Steinmetz award, GE, 1991; NASA fellow, 1967—70. Fellow ASME (visitor for accreditation bd. for engring. and technology 1980-88); mem. NAE. Achievements include 20 patents in field. Office: GE Energy Bldg 40-355 1 River Rd Schenectady NY 12345

DAVIS, LEWIS U., JR., lawyer; b. Pitts., Mar. 25, 1950; s. Lewis Uber and Myrtle Elizabeth (Otte) D.; children: Shannon Lynn, Christin Lynn; m. Laraine Frazzini, May 22, 1993; 1 child, Laura Fitzgerald. BS in Engring. summa cum laude, Lehigh U., 1972; JD summa cum laude, Cornell U., 1975. Bar: Pa. 1975, U.S. Dist Ct. (we. dist.) Pa. 1975, U.S. Ct. Appeals (3d cir.) 1978. Assoc. Buchanan Ingersoll, Pitts., 1975-82, ptnr., shareholder, 1982—, v.p. tech., chief technology officer, 1994—. Contbr. articles to profl. jours. Mem. ABA, Am. Bankruptcy Inst., Pa. Bar Assn. Avocations: computers, tennis, golf. Office: Buchanan Ingersoll & Rooney PC One Oxford Centre 301 Grant St Fl 20 Pittsburgh PA 15219-1410 Office Phone: 412-562-8953. Business E-Mail: lewis.davis@bipc.com.

DAVIS, LINCOLN, congressman; b. Pall Mall, Tenn., Sept. 13, 1943; m. Lynda Compton; 3 children. BS in Agronomy, Tenn. Technol. U., 1966. Soil scientist USDA, 1966; mem. Tenn. State Ho. Reps, 1980—84; operator Diversified Constrn., Tenn.; mem. Tenn. State Senate, 1996—2002, Dem. majority whip, vice chmn. transp. com., mem. environment com., 1996—2002, mem. conservation com., 1996—2002, mem. tourism com., 1996—2002; mem. US Congress from 4th Tenn. dist., 2003—, mem. transp. and infrastructure com., mem. sci. com., mem. agr. com., mem. Blue Dog Coalition. Mayor, Town of Byrdstown, 1978-82; former mem. Upper Cumberland Devel. Dist., Upper Cumberland Human Resource Agy., LBJ&C Devel. Corpn. Named Legislator of Yr., Tenn. Nurses Assn., 1997, Tenn. County Ofcls. Assn., 1998, Tenn. Devel. Dist., 1999, Tenn. Human Resource Agy., 2000, Tenn. Primary Care Coun., 2001, Citizen of Yr., Domestic Violence Coun., 1999; recipient Legislator of Yr., Tenn. Realtor's Assn., 1997. Mem.: Tenn. Jaycees (past state pres.). Democrat. Baptist. Office: US Ho Reps 410 Cannon Ho Office Bldg Washington DC 20515 Office Phone: 202-225-6831.*

DAVIS, LINDA LENNON MCCONNELL, critical care nurse; b. Kingstree, SC, Mar. 1, 1943; d. Murdoch and Vandetta (Vandergrift) Lennon; m. Robert John McConnell, Apr. 20, 1963 (div. 1971); children: Susan McConnell Kennedy, Amber Virginia Smith; m. S.E. Felkel, 1974 (div. 1984); m. Hal Davis, 1998. Grad. with honors, Mercy Sch. Nursing, 1968; student, U. NC, 1972; BS in History with honors, Charleston So. U., 1990. Cert. BLS; RN SC, NC, Fla. Head nurse neurosurgery intensive care Med. U. Hosp., Charleston, SC, 1968—70; head nurse respiratory intensive care Duke U. Med. Ctr., 1971—73. Author: Charleston's Historical Churches and Chapels of Ease, 1998; co-author: Angel Oak Story, 1981. Hist. guide City of Charleston, 1983; active Gibbes Mus. Art Women's Coun., 1978—; vol. Hospice, Jacksonville, Fla., 2001; women's council Gibbes Mus. Art; women's coun. membership chair Unitarian Ch., Charleston, SC, 1979, religious edn. tchr., 1980. Recipient Svc. award, Gibbes Mus. Art Women's Coun., 1997. Mem.: AAUW. Home and Office: The Grand Reserve #926 13810 Sutton Park Dr N Jacksonville FL 32224 Office Phone: 904-821-9479. Business E-Mail: revolution1779@aol.com. E-mail: revolution1779@comcast.net.

DAVIS, LISA E., lawyer; b. Flushing, NY, Feb. 6, 1960; BA, Harvard U., 1981; JD, NYU Sch. Law, 1985. Bar: NY 1986. Law clk. to Honorable Constance Baker Motley, US Dist. Ct., So. Dist. NY, 1985—86; assoc. Kramer Levin Naftalis & Frankel LLP; ptnr., entertainment, publ., media Frankfurt Kurnit Klein & Selz, PC, NYC. Contbr. articles to law jour. Named one of Top 50 Black Power Brokers in Entertainment, Black Enterprise Mag., 2002, Am. Top Black Lawyers, 2003; recipient Jacob K. Javits Achievement award, Bedford Stuyvesant Restoration Corp., 2003. Mem.: Black Entertainment and Sports Lawyers Assn., Nat. Bar Assn. (Intellectual Property Sect.), Assn. Bar City of NY. Office: Frankfurt Kurnit Klein & Selz PC 488 Madison Ave New York NY 10022 E-mail: ldavis@fkks.com.

DAVIS, LOURIE IRENE BELL, retired computer education and information systems specialist; b. Las Vegas, N.Mex., Apr. 8, 1930; d. Currie Oscar and Minnie I. (Rodgers) Bell; m. Robert Eugene Davis, Aug. 21, 1950; children: Judith Anne, Robert Patrick, (adopted) Jaime Alleyn, (adopted) Flint Christopher. Student, Ea. N.Mex. U., 1947—49; BS, West Tex. U., 1959; postgrad., U. Tulsa, 1980—81. Cert. tchr. Tex., Okla. Programmer/analyst Nat. Bank Tulsa, 1968—71, Blue Cross/Blue Shield Okla., Tulsa, 1972—75, mgr. sys., 1977—81, dir. info. sys., 1981—82, mgr. project control, 1983, mgr. info. ctr., 1984—85, mgr. profl. cons. and tng., 1985—87; faculty devel. coord. CAID Okla. State U., Okmulgee, 1987—90; dir. Region 8 Intertel, Inc., Tulsa, 1987—91, adminstrv. officer, 1991-95, pres., CEO, 1995-2000, treas., CFO, 2001—05; publ. Integra, the jour. of Intertel, Inc., 1991—2006; ret., 2006. Sys. curriculum coord., computer sci. instr. Tulsa Jr. Coll., 1975-76, mem. computer sci. adv. bd., 1976-83, adj. instr., 1977-83, 93-94; computer bus. and edn. cons. Davis Cons., 1991-2002; mem. steering com. US Senate bus. adv. bd., 1981-88; ind. cons., Tulsa, 1987; lectr. computer assisted instr. Success League of Innovation Conf., St. Louis, 1989, Music Users Group Conf., U. Tenn., Chattanooga, 1989, Pres.'s Day Des Moines Area C.C., 1990. Mem. budget panel United Way Tulsa, 1981-87, Allocations Exec. Com. Appreciation award, 1987; mem. US Rep. Presdl. Task Force, 1982-93, Rep. Nat. com., 1983-91; mem. Holy Family Sch. Bd., 1991-95, nominating com. chair, 1993, sec., 1993-95. Recipient Internat. Merit award, Assn. Sys. Mgmt., 1980, 1984, winner, Leage of Innovation for C.C.S. Competition, IBM, 1989. Mem.: NEA, AAUW, NAFE, Okla. Edn. Assn., Tulsa Classroom Tchrs. Assn., Higher Edn. Acad. Coun. of Okla., Tulsa Area Sys. Edn. Assn. (recorder 1980—81), Intertel (nat. acceptance com. chair 1978, dir. region VIII 1987—91, membership officer 1991—95, pub. Integra, Jour. of Intertel 1992—2005, pres.and chmn. bd. 1995—2000, treas. 2001—05, lifetime mem. and appreciation award 1997, Continuous Outstanding Svc. award 2004, spl. appreciation award 2005, 2006), Habitat for Humanity, Arbor Day Found., Sierra Club, Mensa, Alpha Chi. Republican. Mem. Unity Ch. of Christianity. Home and Office: 2403 W Oklahoma St Tulsa OK 74127-3027 Office Phone: 918-906-6089. Personal E-mail: LourieD@aol.com.

DAVIS, LOYD EVAN, defense industry marketing professional; b. Newark, Ohio, Apr. 10, 1939; s. Paul Edwin and Eleanor Amanda (Loyd) D.; m. Delores Madeline Wells, Nov. 10, 1959 (div. 1975); children: Mark Evan, Geoffrey Scott; m. Judith Ann Lambert, Sept. 15, 1977; 1 child, James Richard. BSEE, Okla. State U., 1963, MSEE, 1968. Commd. 2d lt. USAF, 1964, advanced through grades to maj., 1974; served in various locations, then ret. U.S. Air Force, 1979; mem. sr. profl. staff Dynatrend, Inc., Arlington, Va., 1979—82; mktg. mgr. govt. systems sector Harris Corp., Alexandria, Va., 1982—87; mktg. mgr. E-Systems Melpar Divsn., Falls Church, Va., 1987—90; mem. sr. profl. staff Adroit Systems, Inc., Alexandria, 1990—95; dir. mktg. comm. L3 Comm. Corp., Salt Lake City, 1996—. Mem.: Armed Forces Comm. Electronics Assn., Air Force Assn., Nat. Def. Indsl. Assn., Assn. U.S. Army, Mt. Vernon Amateur Radio Club (pres. 1987—88), Davis County Amateur Radio Club (v.p. 1997), Woodbridge Wireless Club (pres. 1972—73, 1988—89), Masons (worshipful master 2002, sec. 2003—, grand chaplain 2004, grand orator 2005, jr. grand warden 2006, sr. grand warden 2007). Republican. Methodist. Avocation: amateur radio. Home: 1476 Madera Hills Dr Bountiful UT 84010-1523 Office: L3 Comms Corp Comm Systems West 640 North 2200 West Salt Lake City UT 84116-0850 Home Phone: 801-296-8546; Office Phone: 801-594-2297. Personal E-mail: k8ei@arrl.net.

DAVIS, LUTHER, writer, theater producer, motion picture producer; b. NYC, Aug. 29, 1921; s. Charles Thomas and Henriette (Roesler) D.; m. Dorothy deMilhau, Nov. 3, 1943 (div. 1961); children: Noelle, Laura Duval; m. Joan Bassie. BA, Yale U., New Haven, Conn., 1938. Author: (play) Kiss Them for Me, 1945, (libretto with Charles Lederer) Kismet (Tony award 1953); prodr. Timbuktu, 1978 (Tony nomination 1979), (libretto) Grand Hotel, 1989 (Tony nomination 1990, Olivier award London, England, 2005), 15 solo screenplays including The Hucksters, 1946, A Lion Is in the Street, 1950, Across 110th Street, 1972; author, prodr. Lady in a Cage, 1964; numerous TV series, pilots and episodes. Served to maj. USAAF, 1942-45, CBI, ETO. Mem. Dramatists Guild Am., Writers Guild Am.-West, League Am. Theaters and Prodrs., Acad. Motion Picture Arts and Scis., PEN. Personal E-mail: ludavis212@aol.com.

DAVIS, LYNN ETHERIDGE, political scientist, educator; b. Miami, Fla., Sept. 6, 1943; d. Earl DeWitt and Louise (Featherston) Etheridge. BA, Duke U., 1965; MA, Columbia U., 1967, PhD, 1971; DHL (hon.), Va. Theol. Sem., 2000. Lectr. Miles Coll., Birmingham, Ala., 1966-67; asst. prof. polit. sci. Barnard Coll., Columbia U., NYC, 1970-74; rsch. assoc. Internat. Inst. for Strategic Studies, London, 1973; program analysis staff Nat. Security Council, 1974; asst. prof., lectr. dept. polit. sci. Columbia U., 1974-76; prof., staff mem. Senate Select Com. on Intelligence, 1975-76; dep. asst. sec. of def. for policy plans and nat. security affairs Office of the Under Sec. for Policy, Dept. Def., Washington, 1977-79, asst. dep. under sec. for policy planning, 1979-81; rsch. Internat. Inst. Strategic Studies, London, 1981-82; prof. national security affairs National War Coll., Washington, 1982-85; dir. studies Internat. Inst. Strategic Studies, London, 1985-87; hon. sr. rsch. fellow, dept. war studies Kings Coll., London, 1988-90; rsch. fellow John Hopkins Fgn. Policy Inst, Paul H. Nitze Sch. Advanced Internat. Studies, 1988-91; v.p. army rsch. divsn., dir. Arroyo Ctr. RAND, Santa Monica, Calif, 1991-93, sr. fellow Washington, 1997—2001, sr. polit. scientist, 2001—06, dir., 2006—; under sec. for arms control and internat. security affairs Dept. State, Washington, 1993-97. Author: The Cold War Begins, Soviet American Conflict Over Eastern Europe, 1974. Woodrow Wilson fellow, 1965-66, 69-70, 81-82; Columbia U. fellow, 1965-66, 68-69; recipient David D. Lloyd prize Harry S. Truman Library, 1976 Mem.: Coun. on Fgn. Rels., Phi Beta Kappa. Home: 827 S Lee St Alexandria VA 22314-4333 Office: RAND 1200 S Hayes St Arlington VA 22202-5050 Office Phone: 703-413-1100 x5399. E-mail: Lynn_Davis@rand.org.

DAVIS, MAMIE (DENISE DAVIS), writer; b. Florence, SC, July 28, 1943; divorced; 1 child, Jacqueline J. Maslin. Cert. IBM data entry, NYC, 1981. From clk grade 2 to prin. admin. assoc. NYC Civil Svc., 1962—86; freelance writer, composer NYC and, SC, 1986—. Tchg. coord., cons. NYC-DSS/HRA, 1980—86; stock actor Pilgrim Dramatic Playhouse. Author: (plays) So Many Drops of Rain (showcased at NATAS), Sam Blood's Secret, Sibling of Evil, Agency Procedures: Lust and Corruption, 2002, (novel and screenplay) Jessie's Folly, 2000, over 30 short stories; actor: numerous feature films, (Off-Broadway plays) Medea, Damn That Miss Anne, The Nurse, Civil Rights Worker. Mem.: ASCAP. Avocations: fashion design, dressmaking, book cover design. Personal E-mail: maymee7000@bellsouth.net.

DAVIS, MARGARET BRYAN, paleoecology researcher, educator; b. Boston, Oct. 23, 1931; AB, Radcliffe Coll., 1953; PhD in Biology, Harvard U., 1957; DSc (hon.), U. Minn., 2002. NSF fellow dept. biology Harvard U., Cambridge, Mass., 1957-58; dept. geosci. Calif. Inst. Tech., Pasadena, 1959-60; rsch. fellow dept. zoology Yale U., New Haven, 1960-61, prof. biology, 1973-76; rsch. asoc. dept. botany U. Mich., Ann Arbor, 1961-64, assoc. rsch. biologist Gt. Lakes Rsch. divsn., 1964-70, rsch. biologist, assoc. prof. dept. zoology, 1966-70, rsch. biologist, prof. zoology, 1970-73; head dept. ecology and behavioral biology U. Minn., Mpls., 1976-81, prof. dept. ecology, evolution and behavior, 1976-82, Regents prof. ecology, 1983—2000. Vis. prof. Quaternary Rsch. Ctr., U. Wash., 1973; vis. investigator environ. studies program U. Calif., Santa Barbara, 1981-82; adv. panel ecology NSF, 1976-79; sci. adv. com. biology, behavior and social scis., 1989-91; adv. panel geol. record of global change, NRC, 1991-92, planetary biology com., 1981-82, global change com; 1987-90, mem. screening com. in plant scis., internat. exch. of persons com., 1972-75, sci. and tech. edn. com., 1984-86, vis. rsch. scientist scholarly exch. com. NAS/NRC, People's Republic China, mem. grand challenges in environ. sci. com., 1999-2000; U.S. nat. com. internat. Union Quaternary Rsch., 1966-74; bd. trustees Inst. for Ecosys. Studies, 2000—. Mem. editl. bd. Quaternary Rsch., 1969-82, Trends in Ecology and Evolution, 1986-92, Ecosystems, 2000-03. Bd. dir. Ricon Inst., 2005—. Recipient Sci. Achievement award Sci. Mus. Minn., 1988, alumnae Recognition award Radcliffe Coll., 1988, Nevada medal, 1993, Merit award Bot. Soc. Am., 1998, award for Contbn. Grad. Edn., U. Minn., 1999, Centennial award Bot. Soc. Am., 2006. Fellow: AAAS, Geol. Soc. Am., Am. Acad Arts and Scis.; mem.: NAS, Am. Quaternary Assn. (councillor 1969—70, 1972—76, pres. 1978—80, Dist. Career award 2001), Brit. Ecol. Soc. (hon.), Am. Soc. Naturalists (hon.), Ecol. Soc. Am. (pres. 1987—88, Eminent Ecologist award 1993), Nature Conservancy (bd. dirs. Minn. chpt. 1979—85), Internat. Assn. Gt. Lakes Rsch. (bd. dirs. 1970—73), Sigma Xi, Phi Beta Kappa. Office: U Minn Dept Ecology Evolution & Behavior 100 Ecology Bldg 1987 Upper Buford Cir Saint Paul MN 55108-1051 Business E-Mail: mbdavis@ecology.umn.edu.

DAVIS, MARGARET THACKER, retired critical care, medical and surgical nurse; b. Greensboro, NC, June 7, 1925; d. Tiller Foltz and Lucy Wright (Spencer) Thacker; m. Joe Southard Davis, Feb. 4, 1961; 1 child, Dana Lee. Diploma in nursing, Baylor U., Dallas, 1947; student, Ea. N.Mex. U., Roswell, 1978. RN, N.Mex., Tex., Fla. Office nurse Drs. Britt & Cafaro, St. Augustine, Fla., 1947-50, Dr. Robert J. Rowe, Dallas, 1950-61, Dr. F.A. English, Roswell, 1964-74; charge nurse post anesthesia care unit Ea. N.Mex. Med. Ctr., Roswell, 1990-91, ret., 1991. Named Employee of Month, Ea. N.Mex. Med. Ctr., 1985; recipient N.Mex. Nursing Legends award, 2005. Mem. ANA, Am. Soc. Post Anesthesia Nurses (charter), Post Anesthesia Nurses Assn. N.Mex. (bd. dirs. 1980-86, sec. 1986-87, legis. com. 1989-90), N.Mex. Nurses Assn. (dist. 5 sec. 1983-85, 91-93, pres. 1986-88, bd. dirs. 1988-90, 92-94, 96-98, membership chmn. 1988-90, chmn. nominating com. 1990, Nurse of Yr. award 1989, search for excellence award 1990, dist. 5 honored nurse 1995,N.Mex. Nursing Legends award 2005), Baylor U. Sch. Nursing Alumni Assn. Personal E-mail: maggied53@aol.com.

DAVIS, MARGUERITE HERR, judge; b. Washington, Nov. 12, 1947; d. Norman Phillip and Margaretha Joanna Herr; m. James Riley Davis, June 20, 1970; children: Amy Marguerite, Christine Riley. AA with honors, St. Petersburg J. Coll., Clearwater, Fla., 1966; BA with honors, U. of South Fla., 1968; JD with honors, Fla. State U., 1971. Bar: Fla. 1971, U.S. Dist. Ct. (no. dist.) Fla. 1971, U.S. Dist. Ct. (mid. dist.) Md. 1985, U.S. Ct. Appeals (11th cir.) 1985, U.S. Supreme Ct. 1986. Atty. workers compensation div. U.S. Dept. Labor, Tallahassee, 1971; sr. legal aide Fla. Supreme Ct., Tallahassee, 1971-85, exec. asst. to Hon. Chief Justice Alderman, 1982-84; ptnr. Swann & Haddock, Tallahassee, 1985-87, Katz, Kutter, Haigler, Alderman, Davis & Marks, Tallahassee, 1987-93; judge Dist. Ct. of Appeal (1st dist.) Fla., Tallahassee, 1993—. Mem. editl. bd. Trial Advocate Quar., 1991-93; contbr. chpts. to books. Mem. ABA, Fla. Bar Assn. (appellate ct. rules com. Tallahassee chpt. 1995-2002, appellate ct. rules com. chair, 1995-97, grievance com., disciplinary rev. com., chmn. supreme ct. local rules adv. com., jud. cir. grievance com., rules of jud. adminstrn. 1995-2006, chair 1997-98, chair jud. evaluation com. 1999-2000, chair 2001-03, exec. coun. appellate advocacy sect.), Fla. State Fed. Jud. Coun. (exec. dir. 1985—), Tallahassee Women Lawyers, Fla. Def. Lawyers Assn. (amicus curiae com.), Fla. Supreme Ct. Hist. Soc., Am. Arbitration Assn. (ad hoc com. stds. for appellate practice cert.), Altrusa Club of Tallahassee (treas. 1971-76), Fla. State U. Alumni Assn. (bd. dirs. 1975-76), Jud. Mgmt. Coun. (appellate ct. workload and jurisdiction com. 1996—, chair appellate rules liaison com., appellate practice and advocacy sect. 1996-98), Univ. So. Fla. (bd. dirs. Alumni Assn. 1999), Phi Theta Kappa. Methodist. Avocations: quilting, sewing, knitting, running, reading.

DAVIS, MARICA NANCI ELLA RIGGIN, retired artist; b. Phila., Apr. 13, 1934; d. Dale Thomas and Anna (Kudla) Purtle; m. Donald Allen Riggin, Sept. 11, 1954 (dec. Nov. 10, 1970); children: Ralph Allen Riggin, Ronald Dale Riggin, David Wayne Riggin; m. Leonard Nettleton Davis, July 3, 1976; 3 stepchildren. Student, Montgomery Coll., Rockville, Md., 1975—78, student, 1983, student, 1988, student, 1993. Electro-mech. drafter Philco, Phila., 1952—55, Vitro Labs. Automated Industries, Aspen Hill, Md., 1971—73; designer, printer Sears Roebuck, Bethesda, Md., 1970; drafer, illustrator Watkins-Johnson Co. divsn. CEI, Gaithersburg, Md., 1973—86, IDEAS/SAIC, Columbia, Md., 1987—98. Instr. adult edn. craft class Montgomery County, Md.; jury Damascus County Fair Art Show. Juried and award winning shows, Sugar & Frichtle, Kensington, Md., Town Ctr., Ten Oaks, Md., Gurmukh Galleries, Md., Gaithersburg Coun. Arts, Woodlawn Mansion, Md., Kentland Mansion, McCrillus Gardens, Audubon Soc., Unitarian Universalitic Ch., Pyramid Atlantic, Sandy Spring Mus., Visual Sys. Art Ctr., Strathmore Hall, Rockville Arts Pl., Delapaine Visual Arts Ctr., Md., Café Monet, Kensington, Kent Island Federation Art, Md., Sumner Mus., Washington, Saxon Swan Gallery, Del., Dietricks Gallery, Sta. Gallery, Dover (Del.) Art League, one-woman shows include Open Studio Gallery, 2000, 2001, 2002, 2004, Kent Island Fedn. Art, Md., 2003, 2004. Pres. Episcopal Ch. Women, Beathany Beach, Del., 2003. Mem.: Ga. Miniature Art Soc., Miniature Art Soc. Fla. Inc., Cider Painters Am., Printmakers Plus, Olney Art Assn. (pres. 1995, 1996), S. Ea. Del. Artists Studio Tour, Miniature Painters Sculptors and Gravers Soc. (receiver 1989—98), Nat. League Am. Pen Women (membership chair Holly chpt.), Md. Printmakers (assoc.; folio chair 1996), Phi Theta Kappa. Home: 306 Steamboat Ln Dagsboro DE 19939-9226 Personal E-mail: ezdavis306@aol.com.

DAVIS, MARK E., chemical engineering educator; b. Ellwood City, Pa. m. Mary P. Davis; 3 children. BS, U. Ky., Lexington, 1977; MS, U. Ky., 1978, PhD in chem. engring., 1981. Asst. prof., assoc. prof., to chaired prof. chem. engring. Va. Poly. Inst. and State U., Blacksburg, 1981—91; prof. dept. chemistry Calif. Inst. Tech., Pasadena, prof. chem. engring., 1991—93, Warren and Katharine Schlinger Prof. Chem. Engring., 1993—. Sci. adv. bd. Alnylam, NovoDynamics, Symyx; founder Insert Therapeutics, Pasadena, chief sci. adv., bd. dirs.; founding scientist Calando Pharms., Duarte, Calif.; mem. Exptl. Therapeutics Prog. City of Hope Comprehensive Cancer Ctr., Duarte; lectr. Co-editor Fundamentals Chem. Reaction Engring.; founding editor: CaTTech, assoc. editor: Chemistry of Materials, AIChE Jour.; contbr. articles sci. jours. Recipient Dow Outstanding Young Faculty award, Am. Soc. Engring. Edn., 1985, Presdl. Young Investigator award, 1985, Donald Breck award, Internat. Zeolite Assn., 1989, Alan T. Waterman award, NSF, 1990, Paul H. Emmett award, North Am. Catalysis Soc., 1995. Mem.: Materials Rsch. Soc., Am. Inst. Chem. Engrs. (Allan P. Colburn award 1989, Profl. Progress award 1999), Am. Chem. Soc. (Ipatieff prize 1992), NAS, NAE, Tau Beta Pi, Omega Chi Epsilon, Phi Eta Sigma. Achievements include pioneering work in the synthesis of new catalytic materials. Office: Calif Inst Tech Dept Chemistry 210-41 1200 E California Blvd Pasadena CA 91125-0001

DAVIS, MARK M., microbiologist, educator; b. Paris, Nov. 27, 1952; BA in Molecular Biology, Johns Hopkins U., 1974; PhD in Molecular Biology, Calif. Inst. Tech., 1981. Fellow lab. of immunology NIH, Bethesda, Md., 1980-82, staff fellow lab. of immunology, 1982-83; asst. prof. med. microbiology Stanford (Calif.) U. Sch. Medicine, 1983-86, assoc. prof. microbiology and immunology, 1986-91, prof. microbiology and immunology, 1991—, Burt & Marion Avery prof. immunology, dir. predoctoral program in immunology, 1994—, chair microbiology & immunology, 2002—04, dir. Stanford Inst. Immunity, Transplantation, & Infection, 2004—; assoc. investigator Howard Hughes Med. Inst., Stanford U., 1987-91, faculty coord., 1989—, investigator, 1991—. Instr. Cold Spring Harbor (N.Y.) Lab., 1983; mem. sci. adv. bd. Damon Runyon-Walter Cancer Found., 1985-88; co-organizer UCLA Symposium, 1987; mem. allergy and immunology study sect. divsn. rsch. grants NIH, 1988-92. Recipient Intra-Sci. Rsch. Found. award 1980, Youth Scientist award Passano Found., 1985, Eli Lilly award 1986, Kayden award N.Y. Acad. Scis., 1986, Howard Taylor Ricketts award U. Chgo., 1988, Gairdner Found. award, 1989, King Faisal Internat. prize 1995, Sloan prize Gen. Motors Rsch. Found., 1996; scholar PEW Found. 1985-89. Mem. Nat. Acad. Scis., Inst. Medicine (2004). Office: Howard Hughes Med Inst Beckman Ctr B221 279 Campus Dr Stanford CA 94305-5323

DAVIS, (ALICE) MARLECE, secondary school educator, director; d. Rex S. and E. Lucille Treadwell; children: Lindsey, Cody. BA in Elem. Edn. and English, Houston Bapt. U., Tex., 1970; MEd, Stephen F. Austin U., Nacogdoches, Tex., 1981, degree in Mid-Mgmt., 1981. Cert. tchr. Tex., 1970. Tchr. elem., mid. schs. Humble Ind. Sch. Dist., Tex., 1974—81, administrator, 1981—2004; tchr. mid. sch. Holy Trinity Episc. Sch., Houston, 2004—, dir. devel., 2005—07. Adj. prof. Kingwood Coll., Tex., 2000—; sponsor sch. newspaper Holy Trinity Sch., 2003—06, pvt. sch. inter-scholastic assn. coach, 2003—07, yell leader sponsor; student sponsor svc. learning Rosemont Assisted Living, Atascocita, Tex., 2002—06, Jesse Jones State Pk., Houston, 2005—06. Author: Creative Writing for Teachers, 1985. Bd. dirs. Kingwood Christian Ch., 1991—93, dir. edn., 2001—03, dir. small group, 2003—05. Named Tchr. of Yr., Humble Walmart, Tex., 2006; recipient Take Pride in Am. award, US Dept. Interior, 2006—07; grantee, Houston Endowment, 2005—06, 2006—07, Astro-CocaCola-Minute Maid, 2006. Mem.: PTA (life). Democrat. Home: 1303 St Andrews Kingwood TX 77339 Office: Holy Trinity Episc Sch 11810 Lockwood Houston TX 77044

DAVIS, MARTHA FRANCES, lawyer; b. Wichita, Kans., Apr. 4, 1957; d. Robert Louis and Marian (Larson) D. AB in Anthropology, Harvard U., 1979; BA, Trinity Coll., Oxford, Eng., 1981, MA in Jurisprudence, 1987; JD, U. Chgo., 1983. Bar: Ill. 1983, N.Y. 1985, U.S. Supreme Ct. 1988. Law clk. to judge U.S. Dist. Ct. (no. dist.) Ind., Hammond, 1983-85; assoc. Cleary, Gottlieb, Steen & Hamilton, NYC, 1986-90; staff atty. NOW Legal Def. and Edn. Fund, 1990—. Bd. dirs. Ctr. for Immigrants Rights; Kate Stoneman vis. prof. Albany Law Sch., 2000; adj. prof. NYU Sch. Law. Author: Brutal Need: Lawyers and the Welfare Rights Movement, 1960-73. Bunting Inst. fellow, Radcliffe Coll., 1988-89; Wasserstein fellow, Harvard Law Sch., 1998. Mem. N.Y.C. Bar Assn. (chair adminstrv. law com.). Mem. Soc. Of Friends. Avocations: music, writing.

DAVIS, MARVIN ARNOLD, manufacturing executive; b. St. Louis, Nov. 16, 1937; s. Sam and Pauline (Neuman) D.; m. Trudy Brenda Rein, Aug. 11, 1968; children: Julie, Jeffrey. BS in Chem. Engring., Washington U., St. Louis, 1959; MBA in Fin.and Mktg., Washington U., 1966. Lead engr. Standard Oil Calif., San Francisco, 1962-64; product mgr. Shell Chem. Co., NYC, 1966-69; group controller Pfizer, Inc., NYC, 1969-75; exec. v.p. Good Hope Industries, New Orleans, 1975-77; pres., chief exec. officer Reed Industries, Inc., Stone Mountain, Ga., 1978-79; pres. Sentrex Ltd., Atlanta, 1977-82; v.p. Sentry Ins., 1982-84; chmn., CEO Petrowax PA Inc., 1991-93, Datamax Corp., 1996—2002; cons., pres. Grisanti Galef Goldress, 1984-97, mng. ptnr., 2001—. Chmn., CEO Petrowax PA, Inc., 1992-94, Signal Apparel Corp., 1993-94; chmn. Folger Adams Corp., Simplicity Pattern Co., Pandick Press; instr. Farleigh Dickinson U., 1968-71; lectr. Washington U., 1966, 77; cons. in field; bd. dirs. Wherehouse Enterntainment Corp., Fairlanes Bowling Corp., Celluland Corp., Northwest Pipe and Casing Co., Z Axis Corp., Crown Crafts Corp., Turn Around Mgmt. Assn., Cherokee Corp.; pres. AMA Fund, Inc. Author: The Profit Prescription, 1985, Turnaround, 1987, The Turnaround Formula, 2002, Take No Prisoners, 2007. Served to lt. USNR, 1959-62. Scholar Washington U., 1959, fellow, 1968. Mem. DeKalb C. of C., Citrus Club, Beta Gamma Sigma, Alpha Chi Sigma. Jewish. Office: Grisanti Galef and Goldress 333 Sandy Springs Cir Ste 106 Atlanta GA 30328 Home Phone: 770-396-7557; Office Phone: 404-441-3970. Personal E-mail: mdavis2866@aol.com. Business E-Mail: mdavis@gggcrisismanager.com.

DAVIS, MARY BYRD, conservationist, researcher; b. Cardiff, Wales; came to U.S., 1947; d. John Dymond and Joanna Inger (Falconer) Byrd; m. Robert Minard Davis; children: Carol, John. BA, Agnes Scott Coll., 1958; MA, U. Wis., 1968, PhD, 1972; MLS, Simmons Coll., 1974. Acquisitions libr. No. Mich. U., Marquette, 1974—75; asst. libr. Georgetown (Ky.) Coll., 1975—78; libr. U. Ky., Lexington, 1978—83; freelance writer and editor Georgetown, 1983-90, 93—; staff writer, office mgr. Earth First Jour., Canton, NY, 1990; co-founder and pub. Wild Earth, Canton, NY, 1991—92, assoc. editor Richmond, Vt., 1993—98; dir. Yggdrasil Inst., Georgetown, Ky., 1994—. Author: The Military Civilian Nuclear Link, 1988, Guide de L'Industrie Nucleaire Francaise, 1988, The Green Guide to France, 1990, Going Off the Beaten Path: An Untraditional Travel Guide to the U.S., 1991, Old Growth in the East: A Survey, 1993, rev. edit., 2003, La France nucléaire: matières et sites, 1997, 2002, The U.S. Enrichment Establishment 1999, 1999; co-author: Les Déchets nucléaires militaires Français, 1994, Weapons of Mass Destruction, 2006; editor: Eastern Old-Growth Forests: Prospects for Rediscovery and Recovery, 1996, Eastern Old-Growth Notes, 1997-2000. Bd. dirs. Centre de Documentation et de Recherche sur la Paix et les Conflits, Lyon, France, 1989—, Wildlands Ctr. for Preventing Roads, Missoula, Mont., 1996-99. Mem. Nat. Writers Union, Sierra Club (editor energy report 1986-87, exec. com. Cumberland chpt. 1982-84), Phi Beta Kappa.

DAVIS, MARY ELIZABETH, speech pathologist, educator, counselor; b. Larned, Kans., July 1, 1930; d. LeRoy D. and Katheryn (Herndon) Harris; m. W.G. Davis, Apr. 3, 1969; children: Pamela Koch, Michelle Dalton; 1 stepchild, Wendy Garton. BA, Calif. State U., Fresno, 1959, MA, 1982. Cert. resource specialist, speech pathologist tchr., deaf tchr., counselor, Calif. Dir. recreation and occupl. therapy Wyo. State Hosp., Evanston, 1956-58; tchr. Fresno Unified Sch. Dist., 1960-80, Barton County C.C., Great Bend, Kans., 1990-98. Bd. dirs. Larned Historical Soc., Santa Fe Trail Ctr., Larned, Kans., 2001—04. Mem. Am. Counseling Assn., Nat. Bd. Cert. Counselors. Home: 3100 Nutmeg LN #D Hutchinson KS 67502-2968

DAVIS, MARY ELLEN K., educational association administrator; MLS, U. Ill.; MA, Ctrl. Mich. U. Sr. assoc. exec. dir. Assn. Coll. and Rsch. Librs., 1993—2001, exec. dir., 2001—, dir. comm. and systems, publs. program officer; ref. libr., bibliographer Ctrl. Mich. U. Recipient Girl Scouts Outstanding Vol. award. Mem.: ALA, U. Ill. Grad. Sch. Libr. and Info. Sci. Alumni Assn. (bd. dirs., pres.), Am. Soc. Assn. Execs., Soc. Scholarly Publishing, Phi Kappa Phi, Beta Phi Mu. Office: 50 East Huron St Chicago IL 60611 Office Phone: 800-545-2433. E-mail: acrl@ala.org.

DAVIS, MARY HELEN, psychiatrist, educator; b. Kingsville, Tex., Dec. 2, 1949; d. Garnett Stant and Emogene (Campbell) D. BA, U. Tex., 1970; MD, U. Tex., Galveston, 1975; grad. in adult and child psychoanalysis, Inst. for Psychoanalysis, Chgo., 1982-92. Cert. Nat. Bd. Med. Examiners, Am. Bd. Psychiatry and Neurology, Child and Adolescent Psychiatry. Intern, then resident in psychiatry SUNY, Buffalo, 1975-78; fellow in child psychiatry U. Cin., 1978-80; asst. prof. Med. Coll. Wis., Milw., 1980-89, clin. assoc. prof., 1989-93; med. dir. adolescent treatment unit Milw. Psychiat. Hosp., 1981-86, Schroeder Child Ctr., 1986-89; pvt. practice, 1989-93; med. dir. Devereux-Victoria (Tex.) Psych. Residential Treatment Ctr., 1993-94; pvt. practice Lancaster, Pa., 1995—. Cons. Milw. Mental Health Cons., 1980-93, Children's Svc. Soc., Milw., 1982-93, Cath. charities, Harrisburg, Pa., 1996—, Sch. Dist. Lancaster, 1998—. Bd. dirs. Next Generation Theatre, Milw., 1988-90, Next Act Theatre, Milw., 1990-92, Lancaster Guidance Ctr., 2002-06. Mem. Am. Med. Women's Assn., Assn. for Child Psychoanalysis, Am. Psychoanalytic Assn., Am. Acad. Child and Adolescent Psychiatry. Baptist. Avocations: science fiction, music, computers, crochet. Office Phone: 717-392-7062. E-mail: mdsquare@juno.com.

DAVIS, MARY MARTHA (MARTY DAVIS), small business owner, consultant; b. Canton, Ohio, May 6, 1939; d. John Newton Reed and Mary Maria Schrengost; m. Richard Paul Davis, Dec. 23, 1961; children: John Newton, Scott Reed. BA, Grove City Coll., Pa., 1961; post grad., Pa. State U., State Coll., 1961—. Cert. YMCA PE Springfield, Mass., 1985, grad. Sheffield Sch. Design, N.Y.C., 1995. Tchr. Spanish Penn Hills H.S., Pitts., 1962; tchr. English Corning & Elmira Sch. Dists., NY, 1963, 1964; mgr. and buyer Smith's Dept. Store, 1973—76; assoc. exec. dir., instr. and program mgr. YMCA, 1980—93; owner Marty R. Davis Interior Design, Corning, Chautauqua and Hilton Head, NY, 1995—. Cons. and workshop presenter Coop Ext. Ctr., Ithaca, NY, 1972—75, Hosp. Aux. N.Y. State, 1975—89; pres., dir. and advisor Women's Ctr., Corning, 1980—89. Campaign dir Easter Seals, St. Lawrence County, NY, 1974; dir. and legis. liaison 7 Lakes Coun. Girl Scouts U.S.A., 1982—96; spkr. hosp. assn. and aux. convs., 1981—89; pres. Kiwanis, Corning, 1994; trustee, elder 1st Presbyn. Ch., Corning, NY, 1980—99; trustee Corning Philharmonic Soc., Corning and Elmira, NY, 1984—94; bd. trustees Hosp. Assn. N.Y. State, Albany, 1981—83, chair Com. on Hosp. Aux., 1981—83; trustee Presbyn. Ho. Assn., chair auqua bldg. and grounds com., 2000—; trustee Hist. Assn., Canton, NY, 1973—79, Corning, NY, 1985—90. Master: Am. Contract

Bridge League (life; cert. dir.); mem.: Investment Club (sec. Hilton Head chpt. 2000—04), Palmetto Rowing Club (treas. 2003—06, instr.), Northshore at Chautauqua (trustee 2004—). Republican. Avocations: golf, reading, bridge, rowing. Home: 5 Yard Arm Palmetto Dunes Hilton Head Island SC 29928-5247 Address: Chautauqua Institution 20 Elm Lane C1 Chautauqua NY 14722 E-mail: martyrdid@yahoo.com.

DAVIS, MATTHEW SCOTT, curator, history professor; s. Edward J. Davis, Jr. and Kathrywn W. Davis; m. Lisa Ann Pepple, June 19, 2004. BS summa cum laude in History, Ga. Coll. and State U., 2002, MA in History, 2004. Asst. curator edn. The Old Gov.'s Mansion, Milledgeville, Ga., 2004—. Adj. prof. history Ga. Mil. Coll., Milledgeville, 2003—. Mem.: Am. Assn. State and Local History, Am. Assn. Mus., Ga. Assn. Mus. and Galleries, Ga. Trust Historic Preservation, Ga. Hist. Soc., Am. Hist. Assn., Phi Kappa Phi, Phi Alpha Theta, Gamma Beta Phi, Omicron Delta Kappa. Republican. Bapt. Avocations: saxophone, hiking, reading, travel. Home: 239 Autumn Ridge Ct Gray GA 31032 Office: The Old Govs Mansion 120 S Clarke St Milledgeville GA 31061

DAVIS, MELLAR PILGRIM, oncologist; b. Columbus, Ohio, Dec. 22, 1951; s. Mellar and Lola (Zimmerman) D.; m. Deborah Doan, Aug. 21, 1976; children: Luke, Amanda, Meghan, Jessamyn. BA, Otterbein Coll., 1974; MD, Ohio State U., 1977. Diplomate Am. Bd. Internal Medicine. Intern, then resident Riverside Meth. Hosp., Columbus, 1977-80; fellow in oncology/hematology Mayo Clinic, Rochester, Minn., 1980-83; pvt. practice Toledo Clinic, 1983-84, Millhon Clinic, Columbus, 1984-87, Columbus Oncology Assocs., 1987—2006; dir. rsch. Harry R. Horvitz Ctr. for Palliative Medicine, Cleve. Clinic Found., 2006—. Instr. medicine Mayo Med. Sch., 1982; mem. community adv. bd. James Comprehensive Cancer Ctr., Ohio State U., Columbus; mem. rsch. com. Riverside Regional Cancer Inst., Columbus; mem. residence evaluation com. Riverside Meth. Hosp.; mem. Taussig Cancer Ctr., Cleve. Clinic.; mem. dept. bioethics Cleve. Clinic. Contbr. articles to profl. jours. Fellow Am. Coll. Chest Physicians; mem. Am. Soc. Hematology, Am. Soc. Clin. Oncology Business E-Mail: davismb@ccf.org.*

DAVIS, MICHAEL, medical educator; b. Bronxville, NY, Nov. 14, 1942; s. Pearce and Lucia D.; children: Nathaniel, Alexander. BA, Northwestern U., 1965; PhD, Yale U., 1969. Rsch. assoc. Yale U. Sch. Medicine, New Haven, 1969-70, asst. prof., 1970-75, assoc. prof., 1975-84, prof., 1984-98, 1998—; Robert W. Woodruff prof. psychiatry Emory U. Sch. Medicine, Atlanta, 1998—. Contbr. more than 225 articles to profl. jours.;, author 85 book chpts. Named one of Highly Cited Scientists, Inst. Scientific Info.; recipient USPHS Rsch. Scientist award, NIMH, 1975—79, 1980—99, Merit award, 1991—, Matthew Wayner-Noke Pharmaceuticals award, Internat. Behavioral Neuroscience Soc., 2005, Pavlovian Rsch. award, Pavlovian Soc., 2006; Woodrow Wilson fellow, 1965, NSF fellow, 1966—69, Sterling fellow, Yale U., 1969. Fellow Am. Psychol. Assn. (Disting. Scientific Contbrn. award 2006), Am. Psychol. Soc., Am. Coll. Neuropsychopharmacology, AAAS; mem. Soc. for Neurosci., Soc. for Psychophysiology, Phi Beta Kappa. Office: Emory U Sch Medicine Psychiatry Yerkes Primate Ctr 954 Gatewood Dr Rm 5200 Atlanta GA 30329 Business E-Mail: mdavis4@emory.edu.

DAVIS, MICHAEL J., judge; b. 1947; BA, Macalester Coll., 1969; JD, U. Minn., 1972; LLD (hon.), Macalester Coll., 2001. Law clk. Legal Rights Ctr., 1971-73; with Office Gen. Counsel Dept. Health, Edn. and Welfare, Social Security Adminstrn., Balt., 1973; criminal def. atty. Neighborhood Justice Ctr., 1974, Legal Rights Ctr., 1975—78; pub. defender Hennepin County, 1978-83; judge Hennepin County Mcpl. Ct., 1983-84, Hennepin County Dist. Ct. (4th jud. dist.), 1984-94; atty., commr. Mpls. Civil Rights Commn., 1977-82; judge U.S. Dist. Ct. Minn., St. Paul, 1994—. Constnl. law instr. Antioch Mpls. C.C., 1974; criminal def. trial practice instr. Nat. Lawyer's Guild, 1977; trial practice instr. William Mitchell Coll. Law, 1977-81, Bemidji Trial Advocacy Course, 1992, 93; adj. prof. U. Minn. Law Sch., 1982—, Hubert H. Humphrey Sch. Pub. Affairs, 1990; instr. Minn. Inst. Legal Edn., Civil Trial Practice Inst., 1991-92; lectr. FBI Acad., 1991, 92. Mem. Minn. Superior Ct. Racial Bias Task Force, 1990—93, U.S. Dist. Ct.; chmn. Pretrial Release & Bail Evaluation Com., 1997—. Recipient Outstanding Alumni award Macalester Coll., 1989, Good Neighbor award WCCO Radio, 1989, Disting Svc. award William Mitchell Coll. of Law, 2000. Mem. ABA, Nat. Bar Assn., Minn. Minority Lawyers Assn., Am. Inns. of Ct., Fed. Bar Assn., Fed. Judges Assn., Hennepin County Bar Assn., Minn. State Bar Assn., Minn. Lawyers Internat. Human Rights Com. (past mem. bd. dirs.), Internat. Acad. Trial Judges, Nat. Assn. for Pub. Interest Law (bd. dirs.), 8th Cir. Jury Instruction Com., U.S. Assn. Constitutional Law. Office: US Dist Ct Minn 300 S 4th St Ste 14E Minneapolis MN 55415-2251 Office Phone: 612-664-5070. Business E-Mail: mjdavis@mnd.uscourts.gov.

DAVIS, MICHAEL STEVEN, lawyer; b. Brookline, Mass., Aug. 1, 1947; s. Ralph and Beatrice (Levy) D.; m. Madelyn O. Davis, Aug. 16, 1970; children: Gregory, Adam, Bethany. AB, U. Rochester, NYC, 1969; JD cum laude, Boston U., 1972. Bar: N.Y. 1973, U.S. Dist. Ct. (so. and ea. dists.) N.Y. 1974, U.S. Ct. Appeals (2d cir.) 1974, U.S. Supreme Ct. 1979, U.S. Ct. Claims, 1980. Assoc. Chadbourne & Parke, NYC, 1972-82; sr. counsel corp. litigation Am. Internat. Group, NYC, 1982-88; ptnr. Zalkin, Rodin & Goodman, LLP, NYC, 1988-99, Zeichner, Ellman & Krause, LLP, NYC, 1999—. Asst. adj. prof. C.W. Post Ctr., L.I. U., Glen Cove, NY, 1975—79. Editor: Boston U. Law Rev., 1970—72. Mem. Citizens Ctr. for Children of NY, Inc., 1978—87; trustee The Harvey Sch., Katona, NY, 1994—97; pres. Pelham (NY) Jewish Ctr., 1986—88; v.p. Sinai Free Synagogue, 2003—04. Mem. ABA, Assn. Bar City of N.Y., Am. Arbitration Assn., ARIAS-US AIDA Reinsurance and Ins. Arbitration Soc. (cert. arbitrator), Huguenot Bridge Club. Democrat. Office: Zeichner Ellman & Krause LLP 575 Lexington Ave New York NY 10022-6102 Business E-Mail: mdavis@zeklaw.com.

DAVIS, MICHAEL W., lawyer; b. NYC, Nov. 12, 1950; BA magna cum laude, SUNY, Binghamton, 1972; JD cum laude, Northwestern U., 1975. Bar: Ill. 1975, Supreme Ct. Ill. 1975, US Dist. Ct. no. dist. Ill., ea. divsn. 1975, no. dist. Calif. 1981, ctrl. dist. Ill. 2002, US Supreme Ct. 1981, US Ct. of Appeals 2nd cir. 1980, 4th cir. 1986, 6th cir. 1986, 7th cir. 1988. Ptnr. Sidley & Austin, Chgo., and head, product liability and mass tort group, sec. exec. com. Prof. products liability law Chgo. Kent Coll. Law, 1984-88. Mem. drug and med. device steering com. Def. Rsch. Inst. Mem. Internat. Assn. Defense Coun., Legal Club Chgo. Office: Sidley & Austin Bank One Plz 10 S Dearborn Chicago IL 60603 Office Fax: 312-853-7036. Business E-Mail: mdavis@sidley.com.

DAVIS, MICHELE A., federal agency administrator, former mortgage company executive; b. Louisville, Ky. BS in Fgn. Svc., Georgetown U., Washington, 1988; M in Econs., Am. U. Economist Citizens for Sound Economy; economist minority leader staff Joint Econ. Com. US Congress, Washington, chief spokesperson majority leader's office, adv. house Rep. leadership, comms. dir. house majority leader Dick Armey, 1997—2001; asst. sec. for pub. affairs US Dept. Treasury, Washington, 2001—02, 2006—; sr. v.p. regulatory policy Fannie Mae, Washington, 2003—05; dep. asst. to Pres. & dep. nat. security adv. for strategic comm. & global outreach NSC, Washington, 2005—06. Republican. Office: US Dept Treasury Pub Affairs 1500 Pennsylvania Ave NW Rm 3438 Washington DC 20220*

DAVIS, MINNIE P., minister; d. George Andrew Prince and Dorothy Prince Blakely, Rosevelt Blakely (Stepfather); m. Fred Davis, July 3, 1971; children: Gregory David Prince, Tammy LaVette, Dontrece, Denita La'Chele, Nicolette Robertson. Attended, Reading Area CC, 1977—79, Pace Bus. Inst., 1980—81, Urskin Theol. Seminary, 1989—90. Pastor Sandy Grove AME Ch., Warrenton, Ga., 1988—91, Mt. Taber AME Ch., Keysville, Ga., 1991—95, Liberty Hill AME Ch., Thomson, Ga., 1995—98, St. James AME Ch., Tennile, Ga., 1998—2000, Wesley Chapel AME Ch., Milledgeville, Ga., 2000—01, Ward Chapel AME Ch., Augusta, Ga., 2001—02, Spring Bethel AME Ch., Louisville, Ga., 2004—. Chaplain U. Hosp., Augusta, 1989—92, mem. bd. ethics, 1990—92; adv. bd. mem. Ga. Health Decisions, Atlanta, 1995—99; tchr. African Meth. Bd. Examiners, Augusta, 1997—; bd. trustees AME Ch., Augusta, 2001—; spkr. Predatory Lending Practices US Senate. Founder Citizens Addressing Pub. Svcs. Trustee AME Ch., Atlanta, 1997. Recipient Unsung Heroine, Top Ladies of Distinction, 1995, Citizen of Yr., Kappa Chpt. TAU Gamma Delta Sorority, 1995, Cmty. Svc. award, Augusta Lincoln League, 1995. Mem.: Women in Ministries AME Ch. (assoc.). Home: 3534 Prince Rd Augusta GA 30906 Home Phone: 706-796-1571; Office Phone: 706-589-1316.

DAVIS, MORRIS, lawyer; BA, Rice U.; JD, U. Tex. Mng. ptnr. McGinnis, Lochridge & Kilgore, Austin, Tex.; gen. counsel Temple-Inland Inc., Austin, Tex., 2006—. Office: Temple-Inland Inc 1300 Mopac Expressway S Austin TX 78746 Office Phone: 512-434-5800. Office Fax: 512-434-8001.*

DAVIS, MORRIS D., military officer, lawyer; b. Shelby, NC, July 31, 1958; BS, Appalachian State U., NC, 1980; JD, NC Ctrl. U. Sch. Law, 1983; LLM, Army JAG Sch., 1992, George Washington U. Nat. Law Ctr., 1992. Bar: US Supreme Ct., Ct. Appeals Armed Forces, Air Force Ct. Criminal Appeals, DC, NC. Chief mil. justice Eastern Space & Missile Ctr., Patrick, Fla., 1983—85; area def. counsel, 1985—88; cir. trial counsel, ea. cir. Bolling, DC, 1988—89; appellate govt. counsel, 1989—91; civil law divsn. instr. Air Force JAG Sch., Maxwell, Ariz., 1992—95, dep. comdt., 2000—03; staff judge adv. 14th Flying Training Wing, Columbus, Miss., 1995—97, 7th Bomb Wing, Dyess, Tex., 1997—2000; dir. Air Force Legal Info. Svcs. Air Force Legal Svcs. Agy., Maxwell, Ariz., 2003—05; staff judge adv. 20th Air Force, F.E. Warren, Wyo., 2005; chief prosecutor US Dept. Defense Office Mil. Commns., Washington, 2005—. 1st lt. USAF, 1983—84, cpt., 1984—91, maj., 1991—96, lt. col., 1996—2001, col., 2001—. Decorated Air Force meritorious Svc. medal with 4 oak leaf clusters, Air Force commendation medal with 2 oak leaf clusters, Air Force achievement medal with 1 oak leaf cluster, SW Asia svc. medal. Office: Office Mil Commns The Pentagon Washington DC 20301*

DAVIS, MORRIS SCHUYLER, astronomer; b. Bklyn., Dec. 14, 1919; s. Nathan Samuel and Helen (Gross) D.; m. Dorothy Irene Hall, May 26, 1945; children: Glenn Craig, Elizabeth Davis Nyblade, Cynthia Louise Davis, Deborah Susan Davis, Katherine Davis Stalberg, Martha Davis Werlen. BA, Bklyn. Coll., 1946; MA, U. Mo., 1947; PhD, Yale U., 1950. Dir. Computer Ctr., Yale U., New Haven, 1956-66, also research assoc. astronomy; pres. dir. Triangle Univs. Computation Ctr., Research Triangle Park, N.C., 1966-70; Morehead prof. astronomy U. N.C., Chapel Hill, 1970-85, Morehead prof. astronomy emeritus, 1985—. Fellow AAAS; mem. Univ. Research Assn. (trustee 1977-83, exec. editor Celestial Mechanics 1985-89), Am. Astronom. Soc., Internat. Astron. Union. Unitarian Universalist. Office: U N C CB#3255 Dept Physics and Astronomy Phillips Hall 039A Chapel Hill NC 27599-3255 Home: 700 Emory Dr Chapel Hill NC 27517-3008 E-mail: morrisdavis@mindspring.com.

DAVIS, MULLER, lawyer; b. Chgo., Apr. 23, 1935; s. Benjamin B. and Janice (Muller) D.; m. Jane Lynn Strauss, Dec. 28, 1963 (div. July 1998); children: Melissa Davis Muller, Muller Jr., Joseph Jeffrey; m. Lynn Straus, Jan. 23, 1999. BA magna cum laude, Yale U., 1957; JD, Harvard U., 1960. Bar: Ill. 1960, US Dist. Ct. (no. dist.) Ill. 1961. Practice law, Chgo., 1960—; assoc. Jenner & Block, 1960-67; ptnr. Davis, Friedman, 1967—. Lectr. continuing legal edn., matrimonial law and litig.; legal adviser Michael Reese Med. Rsch. Inst. Coun., 1967-82; co-chair com. to study and recommend a comprehensive rules design for the domestic rels. divsn. Circuit Ct. of Cook County, Ill., 2003—. Author: (with Sherman C. Feinstein) The Parental Couple in a Successful Divorce, 1984; Illinois Practice of Family Law, 1995, (with Jody Meyer Yazici), 7th edit., 2007; contbg. author Marriage, Health and the Professions, 2002; mem. editl. bd. Equitable Distbn. Jour., 1984—; contbr. articles to law jour. Bd. dirs. Infant Welfare Soc., 1975-96, hon. bd. dirs., 1996—, pres., 1978-82; co-chmn. gen. gifts 40th and 45th reunions Phillips Exeter Acad., chair class capital giving, 1994-98, 50th reunion gift com. Yale Class Coun. 2002—. Capt. US Army, Ill. N.G., 1960-67. Fellow Am. Acad. Matrimonial Lawyers (bd. mgrs. Ill. chpt. 1996-99), Am. Bar Found.; mem. ABA, FBA, Ill. Bar Assn., Chgo. Bar Assn. (matrimonial com. 1968-83, sec. civil practice com. 1979-80, vice chmn. 1980-81, chmn. 1981-82), Am. Soc. Writers on Legal Subjects, Chgo. Estate Planning Coun., Legal Aid Soc. (vice chmn. matrimonial bar 1991-95, vice chmn. 1995-97, chmn. 1997-99), Lawyers Club Chgo., Tavern Club, Lake Shore Country Club, Chgo. Club. Republican. Jewish. Home: 161 E Chicago Ave Apt 34 E Chicago IL 60611-2601 Office: Davis Friedman 135 S LaSalle St 36th Fl Chicago IL 60603 Office Phone: 312-782-2220. Business E-Mail: mdavis@davisfriedman.com.

DAVIS, NATHANIEL, humanities educator; b. Boston, Apr. 12, 1925; s. Harvey Nathaniel and Alice Marion (Rohde) Davis; m. Elizabeth Kirkbride Creese, Nov. 24, 1956; children: Margaret Morton Davis Mainardi, James Creese, Thomas Rohde, Helen Miller Davis Presley. Grad., Phillips Exeter Acad., 1942; AB, Brown U., 1944, LLD, 1970; MA, Fletcher Sch. Law and Diplomacy, 1947, PhD, 1960; postgrad., Columbia, Cornell U., Middlebury Coll., 1953—54, U. Central de Venezuela, 1961—62, Norwich U., 1989. Asst. history Tufts Coll., 1947; joined U.S. Fgn. Service, 1947; 3d sec. Prague, Czechoslovakia, 1947-49; vice consul Florence, Italy, 1949-52; 2d sec. Rome, 1952-53, Moscow, USSR, 1954-56; Soviet desk officer State Dept., 1956-60; 1st sec. Caracas, Venezuela, 1960-62; acting Peace Corps dir., Chile, 1962; spl. asst. to dir. Peace Corps, 1962-63, dept. assoc. dir., 1963-65; U.S. minister to Bulgaria, 1965-66; sr. staff Nat. Security Coun. (White House), 1966-68; U.S. amb. Guatemala, 1968-71, Chile, 1971-73; dir. gen. Fgn. Service, 1973-75, asst. sec. of state for African affairs, 1975; U.S. amb. Switzerland, 1975-77; State Dept advisor and Chester Nimitz prof. Naval War Coll., 1977-83; Alexander and Adelaide Hixon prof. humanities Harvey Mudd Coll., Claremont, Calif., 1983—2002, faculty exec. com., 1986-89, acting dean of faculty, 1990, emeritus prof., 2002—. Lectr. in field. Author: The Last Two Years of Salvador Allende, 1985, Equality and Equal Security in Soviet Foreign Policy, 1986, A Long Walk to Church: A Contemporary History of Russian Orthodoxy, 1995, 2d edit., 2003. Mem. ctrl. com. Calif. Dem. Party, 1987—90, 1991—, mem. exec. bd., 1993—, mem. bus. and profl. caucus, 1992—; mem. L.A. County Dem. Ctrl. Com., 1988—90, 1992—, regional vice chmn., 1994—96; del. Dem. Nat. Conv., 1988, 1992, 1996, 2000; del. So. Calif. conf. United Ch. of Christ, 1986—87. Lt. (j.g.) USNR, 1944—46. Recipient Cinco Aguilas Blancas Alpinism award, Venezuelan Andean Club, 1962, Disting. pub. Svc. award, USN, 1983, Elvira Roberti award for outstanding leadership, Los Angeles County Dem. Com., 1995, spl. merit award (as author), So. Calif. Motion Picture Coun., 1998, Prism award for nat., state, county and local svcs., Jerry Voorhis Claremont Dem. Club, 1999; Fulbright scholar, Moscow, 1996—97. Mem.: AAUP (pres. Claremont Coll. chpt. 1992—96, 1998), Am. Acad. Diplomacy, Coun. on Fgn. Rels., Am. Fgn. Svc. Assn. (bd. dirs., vice chmn. 1964), Cosmos Club, Phi Beta Kappa. Home: 1783 Longwood Ave Claremont CA 91711-3129 Office: Harvey Mudd Coll 301 E 12th St Claremont CA 91711-5901 Office Phone: 909-624-8022.

DAVIS, NATHANIEL (NATE) A., broadcast executive; BE, Stevens Inst. Tech., NJ, 1976; Masters in Engring. Computer Sci., Moore Sch. at Pa.; MBA, Wharton Sch., U. Pa., 1982. Sr. v.p., network ops., COO, sr. v.p., fin. & v.p. sys. develop. MCImetro; various sr. engring. and fin. roles MCI Comm., 1986—98; CFO MCI Telecommunications, 1996—98; exec. v.p., network and technical services Nextel Comm., 1998—99; pres., COO XO Comm. (formerly Nextlink Comm. Inc.), 2000—03; exec. in residence Columbia Capitol, 2003—06; pres., COO XM Satellite Holdings, Inc., Washington, 2006—07, interim CEO, 2007—, also bd. dir., 1999—. Mng. dir., owner RANND Advisory Group, Oakton, Va., 2003—06; bd. dir. Mutual of Am. Capitol Mgmt. Corp., Charter Comm., 2005—, XO Comm. (formerly Nextlink Comm. Inc.), 2000—03. Office: XM Satellite Radio Holdings Inc 1500 Eckington Pl NE Washington DC 20002-2194*

DAVIS, NICHOLAS HOMANS CLARK, finance company executive; b. NYC, Dec. 1, 1938; s. Feltz Cleveland and Loraine Vanderpool (Homans) D.; children from previous marriage: Loraine, Helen, Alexandra, Eleanor; m. Brenda Jean Molen, Dec. 18, 1982; children: Nicholas, Elizabeth. BA in Geology with honors, Princeton U., 1961; MBA in Fin., Stanford U., 1963. Chartered fin. analyst. Research analyst Fahnestock & Co., NYC, 1963-67; mgr. research Andresen & Co., NYC, 1967-71; dir. research Boettcher & Co., Denver, 1971-75; v.p. corp. fin. White Weld & Co., Denver, 1975-78; v.p. asset mgmt. Paine Webber Co., Denver, 1978-92; pres. Mont. Investment Advisors, Inc., Bozeman, 1991—. Trustee, investment officer Thenen Found., Montclair, N.J., 1966—. Bd. dirs., treas Predator Conservation Alliance; bd. dirs. Eagle Mount Rehab. Ctr. Mem. Riverside Country Club, Rotary (pres. Bozeman Noon). Avocations: skiing, fly fishing, deepwater voyaging, writing, backpacking. Home: 85 Limestone Meadows Ln Bozeman MT 59715 Office: Mont Investment Advisors Inc 104 E Main St # 416 PO Box 7090 Bozeman MT 59771-7090 Office Phone: 406-586-7711. Personal E-mail: mintnd@aol.com.

DAVIS, NIGHTA J., photographer, artist; d. Betty J. Stephens Spratling and Elmer R. Spratling; m. Reuben G. Davis, Sept. 12, 1992; 1 child, Vanessa Alana Flanders-Freuen. AA, GTC, Ga., 1985. Pres./chairwoman Ltd. Signature Edit., Hiawassee, Ga., 1999—. Prin. works include ltd. signature edit. photographic art. Mem. apptd. by the gov. Children and Youth Coordinating Coun. of Ga., Statewide, Ga., 2004—. Mem.: Blue Ridge Art Assn., Ga. Mountain Cultural Alliance, Ga. Assembly Cmty. Arts, Ga. Born Artists Group (founder), North Ga. Arts Guild, Soc. of Children's Book Writers and Illustrators (assoc.), Mountain Arts Assn. (assoc.). Achievements include Her work hangs in the Atlanta Capitol Building in Atlanta, Ga., the Congressional and US Senate Building in Washington, D.C.as well as many prestigous institutions and homes throughout the world; Some of her finest works hang in the homes and offices of U.S. Senators, Governors and State Senators. Avocations: travel, collecting various items of interest, classical music, writing, hiking. Office: Ltd Signature Edit 794 Ramey Mountain Rd Hiawassee GA 30546 Home Phone: 706-896-9021; Office Phone: 706-896-9021. Personal E-mail: nider77777@alltel.net.

DAVIS, OSCEOLA A., opera singer; d. Percy and Ever Davis; m. Alfred B. Smith, Nov. 26, 2004. MusB, U. Arts, Phila., 1970, B in Music Edn., 1970; diploma in opera, Curtis Inst., 1972. Soloist: Met. Opera, 1981—89; Finnish Nat. Opera, 1983—94; singer: as Rosina in Barbiere di Seville, as Blondchen in Die Entfuhrung aus dem Serail, as Papagena in Die Zauberflote, as Queen of the Night in Die Zauberflote, as Zerbinetta in Ariadne auf Naxos, as Gilda in Rigoletto. Soloist 1st Ch. of Christ Scientist, Boston, 1989—97. Named Woman of Yr., Nat. Assn. Negro Bus. and Profl. Women; recipient Commendation award, Pres. City Coun., 2001, Mayor of Camden, 2001. Mem.: Am. Guild Music Artists (bd. govs.), Rotary (pres. 2004, 2006). Personal E-mail: oa4d@earthlink.net.

DAVIS, OWEN KIDDER, physician, endocrinologist; b. NYC, Aug. 16, 1956; s. Stephen Edward and Joyce Baldwin (Kidder) D.; m. Marianne Alida Gawain, Nov. 19, 1983; children: Zoe Catherine, Alida Ashby. BA, Swarthmore Coll., 1978; MD, Bowman Gray Sch. Medicine, 1982. Diplomate Am. Bd. Ob-gyn., Am. Bd. Reproductive Endocrinology. Intern, resident N.Y. Hosp., Cornell Med. Ctr.; fellow Brigham and Women's Hosp., Boston; instr. Harvard U., Boston, 1986-88; assoc. prof. Cornell U. Med. Coll., NYC, 1988—; assoc. ob-gyn. Brigham & Women's Hosp., Boston, 1986-88; assoc. attending ob-gyn. N.Y. Presbyn. Hosp., 1988—. Acting chief gynecology Cornell Med. Ctr., assoc. dir. In Vitro Fertilization. Contbr. articles to profl. jours. Med. dir. Am. Fertility Assn.; chair instl. rev. bd. N.Y. Presbyn. Hosp.; chief of gynecology Cornell Med. Ctr. John Lockwood Meml. fellow Swarthmore Coll., 1978. Fellow: N.Y. Acad. Medicine (sec. sect. ob-gyn. 1991—92), Am. Coll. Ob-Gyn.; mem.: AMA, Soc. for Reproductive Endocrinologists, Soc. Assisted Reproductive Tech. (pres., exec. coun., past chair membership and practice com.), Am. Soc. for Reproductive Medicine (legis. monitor, practice com., govt. rels. com. 1987—, bd. dirs., mem. editl. bd. of fertility and sterility, editl. bd. on fertility and sterility), Alpha Omega Alpha. Avocations: music, travel, tennis. Office: Weill Med Coll of Cornell U 505 E 70th St New York NY 10021-4872 Home: 165 E 72d St Apt 16A New York NY 10021 Office Phone: 212-746-1765. E-mail: okdavis@med.cornell.edu.

DAVIS, PAIGE (MINDY PAIGE DAVIS), television personality and host; b. Phila., Oct. 15, 1969; m. Patrick Page, 2001. Grad., Meadows Sch. Arts, So. Meth. U., Dallas. Dancer Beach Boys tour; performer: (plays) Company, Pippin, Hello, Dolly, A Chorus Line, (nat. tour) Chicago, Beauty and the Beast, 1995—98, (Off-Broadway plays) The Vagina Monologues, 2003; performer: (lead) (Broadway plays) Chicago: The Musical, 2004; performer: Sweet Charity, 2007; host: (TV series) Trading Spaces, 2001—; author: Paige by Paige: A Year of Trading Spaces, 2003. Office: Trading Spaces Banyan Prodns 530 Walnut St Ste 276 Philadelphia PA 19106*

DAVIS, PAMELA BOWES, pediatric pulmonologist; b. Jamaica, NY, July 20, 1949; d. Elmer George and Florence (Welsch) Bowes; m. Glenn C. Davis, June 28, 1970 (div. Mar. 1987); children: Jason, Galen. AB, Smith Coll., 1968; PhD, Duke U., 1973, MD, 1974. Cert. Am. Bd. Internal Medicine, 1977, in Pulmonary Diseases 1980, Am. Bd. Pediat., 1996, in Pediatric Pulmonology 2000. Internal medicine intern Duke Hosp., 1973-74, resident in internal medicine, 1974-75; sr. investigator NIAMD/NIH, Bethesda, Md., 1977-79; asst. prof. U. Tenn. Coll. Medicine, Memphis, 1979-81, Case Western Res. U. Sch. Medicine, Cleve., 1981-85, assoc. prof., 1985-89, prof., 2002, Arline H. and Curtis F. Garvin Rsch. prof., 2005—, chief pediatric pulmonary divsn., 1985—, vice chmn. rsch. dept., 1994—96, vice dean rsch., 2005—, interim dean, v.p. med. affairs, 2006—. Pres. Am. Fedn. for Clin. Rsch., Thorofare, NJ, 1989—90; trustee Rsch. Am, Arlington, Va., 1989—90; mem. adv. coun. Nat. Inst. Diabetes, Digestive and Kidney Diseases, 1992—96; mem. bd. sci. counselors NHLBI, 2001—06, chmn., 2004—06; founding scientist Copernicus Therapeutics, Inc., Cleve. Contbr. articles to profl. jours. Chmn. med. adv. coun. Cystic Fibrosis Found., Bethesda, 1988-90. With USPHS, 1975—79. Named Rainmaker of Yr., Edn. Rsch. Northeast Ohio Live Mag., 2002; named to, Clevel. Med. Hall of Fame, 2001; recipient Samuel Rosenthal award in acad. pediat., 1996, Maurice Saltzman award, Mt. Sinai Health Care Found., 1998, Smith Coll. medal, 2001, Paul di Sant'Agnese award, Cystic Fibrosis Found., 2006. Fellow ACP; mem. Am. Pediatric Soc., Am. Acad. Pediatrics, Am. Physiol. Soc., Am. Thoracic Soc., Am. Soc. Gene Therapy, Biophys. Soc., Soc. for Pediatric Rsch., Assn. Am. Physicians,

Phi Beta Kappa, Sigma Xi, Alpha Omega Alpha. Achievements include 7 patents in field. Office: Rainbow Babies/Child Hosp 2101 Adelbert Rd Cleveland OH 44106-2624 Business E-Mail: pbd@case.edu.

DAVIS, PATRICIA MARGARET ALICE, psychology and religion educator; b. LA, Mar. 2, 1955; d. Robert Joseph and Sallianne Nissen Davis; m. Daniel Sperling, June 28, 1981; 1 child, Rhiannon Elizabeth Davis Sperling. BA, U. Calif. San Diego, 1978; MBA, U. Calif. Berkeley, 1982; MA in theol. studies, San Francisco Theol. Sem., 2004. Rsch. analyst Calif. Pub. Utilities Commn., San Francisco, 1978—80, So. Pacific RR, San Francisco, 1982—83, asst. mgr., 1984; supr., planning and analysis Am. Pres. Lines, Oakland, Calif., 1985—86, mgr., planning and control, 1987—88; instr., psychology and religion Grad. Theol. Union Summer Session, Berkeley, Calif., 2005. Instr. summer session Pacific Sch. Religion, 2006. Co-author: Future Drive: Electric Vehicles and Sustainable Transportation; contbr. chapters to books. Vice-chair San Francisco Shakespeare Festival, 2003—, bd. dirs., 2003—. Recipient Newhall Tchg. award, Grad. Theol. Union, 2006. Mem.: Soc. for the Sci. Study of Religion, Am. Acad. of Religion, APA, Internat. Assn. for the Study of Dreams, Met. Club (mem. com. 2003—05). Office: San Francisco Shakespeare Festival PO Box 460937 San Francisco CA 94146-0937 Home Phone: 510-524-0341.

DAVIS, PATTI, writer; b. LA, Oct. 22, 1952; d. Ronald Reagan (former U.S. pres., dec. June 2004) and Nancy Davis Reagan; m. Paul Grilley, 1984 (div. 1990). Attended, Northwestern U., U. So. Calif. Hostess, singer Gt. Am. Food and Beverage Co., Santa Monica, Calif. Conducted seminars on dysfunctional families. Appeared in Vega$, Nero Wolfe, Trapper John, M.D.; author: Home Front, 1986, Deadfall, 1989, A House of Secrets, 1992, The Way I See It, 1993, Bondage, 1994, The Long Goodbye, 2004; featured in Playboy Mag., June 1994. Office: Simon & Schuster Ste 383 1230 Avenue Of The Americas Fl Concl New York NY 10020-1586

DAVIS, PAUL B., retired mechanical and civil engineer; b. NYC, Jan. 20, 1909; s. Samuel and Esther (Schwartz) D.; m. Sally Vogel (dec.), Nov. 24, 1932; children: Gerald Joseph, Audrey Thea Coll; m. Beatrice Fibus, Aug. 17, 1999. Student, Poly. U. N.Y., 1928. Engring. draftsman Mcpl. Pub. Works, NYC, 1929-41; asst. engr. Bd. Water Supply, NYC, 1941-42; sr. designer to asst. supt. design hydro/nuc./fossil fuel electric generating stas. Ebasco Svcs., Inc., NYC, 1942—66; mgr. Spanish projects Ebasco Overseas Corp., Madrid, 1966-72; project engring. mgr. Burns & Roe, Hempstead, N.Y., 1973-76; ednl. coord. Argonne Nat. Lab., Argonne, Ill., 1977. Dir. Poinciana Condominium Assn., Lake Worth, Fla., 1979-86. Mem. NSPE (life), N.Y. State Soc. Profl. Engrs., Nat. Wildlife Fedn., The Nature Conservancy, Sierra Club, Zionist Orgn. Am., World Jewish Congress, B'nai B'rith. Avocations: spanish culture, painting, bridge, swimming. Home: 3520 Whitehall Dr Apt 303 West Palm Beach FL 33401-1072 E-mail: bababe@bellsouth.net.

DAVIS, PAUL JOSEPH, endocrinologist; b. Chgo., Oct. 28, 1937; s. Paul Albert and Maxine Lydia (Mason) D.; m. Faith Ainsworth Baker, Dec. 8, 1962; children: Matthew, John, Sarah. BA magna cum laude, Westminster Coll., 1959; MD cum laude, Harvard U., 1963. Intern Bronx Mcpl. Hosp. Ctr., 1963-64, resident in medicine, 1964-67; clin. assoc. NIH, Bethesda, Md., 1967-69, sr. staff assoc., 1969-70; head endocrinology div. Balt. City Hosps., 1970-75; prof. medicine, head endocrinology div. SUNY, Buffalo Med. Sch., 1975-90, also vice chmn. dept. medicine; prof., chmn. dept. medicine Albany Med. Coll., Albany Med. Ctr., NY, 1990-99, sr. assoc. dean for clin. rsch., 1998—; chief med. svc. VA Med. Ctr., Buffalo, 1980-90. Mem. merit rev. bd. endocrinology, oncology VA; bd. dirs. Am. Bd. Internal Medicine; mem. nat. adv. coun. W.Va. U. Health Sci. Ctr.; dir. Ordway Rsch. Inst., Albany, N.Y., 1999—. Editor-in-chief Immunology, Endocrine and Metabolic Agents in Medicinal Chemistry, 2007—. Trustee Westminster Coll., Fulton, Mo., 2000—; sci. dir. Charitable Leadership Found. Master ACP (gov. Upstate N.Y. region, pres. N.Y. chpt.), Gerontol. Soc.; mem. Am. Fedn. Med. Rsch., Am. Soc. Biochemistry and Molecular Biology, Am. Thyroid Assn. (bd. dirs., pres. 1997-98, Disting. Svc. award 2003), Endocrine Soc., Bd. Sci. Counselors, Nat. Inst. Aging. Achievements include research and publs. on mechanisms of action of thyroid hormone, effects of aging on endocrine function. Home: 35 Old South Rd West Sand Lake NY 12196-2104 Office: Ordway Research Inst Inc 150 New Scotland Ave Albany NY 12208 Home Phone: 518-674-3383; Office Phone: 518-641-6410. Business E-Mail: pdavis@ordwayresearch.org.

DAVIS, PETER FRANK, filmmaker, writer; b. Santa Monica, Calif., Jan. 2, 1937; s. Frank and Tess (Slesinger) D.; m. Johanna Mankiewicz, Sept. 13, 1959 (dec. July 1974); children: Timothy, Nicholas; m. Karen Zehring, June 10, 1979 (div. Dec., 1995); children: Jesse, Antonia; m. Alicia Anstead, July 4, 2003; stepchild: Kristen Anstead. AB magna cum laude, Harvard U., 1957. Editl. asst. N.Y. Times, 1958-59; writer, interviewer Sextant Film Prodns., NYC, 1961-64; writer, assoc. prodr. NBC News, NYC, 1964; writer, prodr. CBS News, NYC, 1965-72; freelance filmmaker NYC, 1972-82; freelance writer, 1976—; artist-in-residence The New Sch., NYC, 2006—07. Vis. lectr. various univs., 1974-75. Documentary cons. Pumping Iron, 1978, Gilda Live, 1980; writer, prodr.: (TV documentaries) The Heritage of Slavery, 1968, The Battle of East St. Louis, 1969, The Selling of the Pentagon, 1971 (Emmy award 1971, Peabody award 1971, Writers Guild Am. award 1971, George Polk award 1971); prodr. The Best Hotel on Skid Row, 1990; writer Age 7 in America, 1991; prodr., writer JACK, 1993; assoc. prodr., writer (documentary) Hunger in America, 1968 (Writers Guild Am. award 1968); dir., prodr.: (films) Hearts and Minds, 1974 (Oscar award 1975), Middletown, 1982; co-writer (TV film) Haywire, 1980; contbg. editor Esquire Mag., 1985-92; author: Hometown, 1982, Where is Nicaragua?, 1987, If You Came This Way, 1995; Iraq correspondent The Nation, 2003; contbr. articles to mags. Served with AUS, 1959-60. Recipient Saturday Rev. award, 1970, 71, Peace and Friendship among Nations medal, 2003; Poynter fellow Yale U., 1971, assoc. fellow, 1972—. Mem. Writers Guild Am., Authors Guild Am., Acad. of Motion Picture Arts and Sci. Democrat. Home and Office: PO Box 357 Castine ME 04421-0357

DAVIS, R. STEVEN, lawyer, telecommunications industry executive; m. Kim Davis; 2 children. BS, JD, U. Kans., Lawrence. Bar: Kans. 1978, Mo. 1981, Tex. 1986. Pvt. practice atty., Kans., 1978—81; v.p. law and state govt. affairs AT&T, Basking Ridge, NJ, 1981—2000; sr. v.p., asst. gen. counsel policy and law Qwest Comm. Internat., Inc., Denver, 2000, sr. v.p. policy and law, dep. gen. counsel. Office: Qwest Comm Internat Inc 1801 California St Denver CO 80202 Office Phone: 303-896-4200. Office Fax: 303-896-8515. E-mail: steve.davis@qwest.com.*

DAVIS, RANDY LEE, soil scientist; b. LA, Nov. 23, 1950; s. Willie Vernon and Joyce Christine (Manes) D. AA, Yuba Community Coll., 1972; BS in Soils and Plant Nutrition, U. Calif., Berkeley, 1976. Vol. soil scientist U.S. Peace Corps, Maseru, Lesotho, 1976-79; soil scientist Hiawatha Nat. Forest, Sault Saint Marie, Mich., 1979-86; project soil scientist Bridger-Teton Nat. Forest, Jackson, Wyo., 1986-91, forest soil scientist, 1991-97, soil and water program leader, 1997-2001; nat. soils program leader USDA Forest Svc., Washington, 2001—. Detailed soil scientist Boise (Idaho) Nat. Forest, 1989, 92, Mendocino (Calif.) Nat. Forest, 1996, San Bernardino (Calif.) Nat. Forest, 1999; detail assignment Brookings Inst. legis fellow, 2004; Nat. Burned Area Emergency Rehab. program leader, Washington, 2000, 2002-03; acting nat. program leader Wetland and Riparian Program, USDA Forest Svc., 2002—03. Author (poems) My Diary, 1977; editor Soil Classifiers newsletter; contbr. articles to profl. jours. Pres. Sault Community Theater, Sault Saint Marie, 1984-86. Named to Yuba Coll. Athletic Hall of Fame, 1971—72, Basketball team, Marysville, Calif., 2006. Mem. Soil Sci. Soc. Am., Soil and Water Conservation Soc. (bd. dirs. 1991-92, chpt. pres. 1993-97), Internat. Soc. Soil Sci., Am. Assn. for Advancement of Sci. Methodist. Avocations: gardening, photography, history. Home: 208 12th SE Washington DC 20003 Office: USDA Forest Svc 1400 Independence SW Washington DC 20250-0003 Home Phone: 202-547-3163; Office Phone: 202-205-1082. Personal E-mail: randyd83001@yahoo.com. Business E-Mail: rdavis03@fs.fed.us.

DAVIS, RAYMOND P., bank executive; b. 1950; Former pres. US Banking Alliance, Atlanta; dir. Umpqua Bank, Portland, Oreg., 1994—, pres., CEO, 1994—2000, CEO, 2002—03, pres., CEO, 2003—, Umpqua Holdings Corp., 1999—. Named Ernst & Young Entrepreneur of the Yr., 2004. Office: Umpqua Holdings Corp Ste 1200 One SW Columbia St Portland OR 97258

DAVIS, REBECCA C., insurance company executive; Student, Auburn U., Ala.; BBA, Columbus State U., Ga. With AFLAC, 1973—, asst. v.p. policyholder svc. dept., 1978, v.p. mktg. adminstrn. and ops., 1984, v.p. client svcs. and adminstrn., 1987, sr. v.p., asst. dir. mktg., 1992, sr. v.p., chief adminstrv. officer, 1999, exec. v.p., chief adminstrv. officer, 2004—. Office: AFLAC 1932 Wynnton Rd Columbus GA 31999 Office Phone: 706-323-3431.*

DAVIS, RENDELL ASHTON, retired minister, social worker; b. Hackensack, NJ, Nov. 6, 1922; s. Myrtus Ashton and Elizabeth (Chapman) Davis; m. Elaine McMurtrie (div.); children: Rendell Jr., Roxanne, Pierce; m. Florence Van Volkenburgh. BA, Wesleyan U., Middleton, Vt., 1944; ThM, McCormich Theol. Sem., 1950. Ordained minister Presbyterian Ch., 1950, United Ch. of Christ, 2003. Fraternal worker Presbyn. Ch., Japan, 1950—61; pvt. practice acctg. Eldora, Ohio, 1961—68; pastor 1st Presbyn. Ch., Whiteland, Ind., 1968—69, Ocean City, Md., 1984—86; exec. dir. Pub. Action in Correctional Export, Indpls., 1969—72, Pa. Prison Soc., Phila., 1972—84; ret., 1986. Youth comm. fraternal dir. United Ch. of Christ in Japan, Tokyo, 1955—61. Chmn. legis. dist. Dem. Party, Tucson, 1948—2001; bd. dirs. SW Conf., United Ch. of Christ, Phoenix, 2003—05, Am. Correctional Assn., Balt., 1986. Home: 3700 N Campbell Ave #1026 Tucson AZ 85719-1914

DAVIS, REX DARWIN, business consultant; b. Skiatook, Okla., June 11, 1924; s. Ivan Francis and Ruth Mae (Nabors) D.; m. Amelia Roberts Fry, Apr. 14, 1979; children by previous marriage: Deborah Ruth, Kathleen Marie. LLB, U. Okla., 1949; postgrad., Princeton U., 1966. Exec. asst. to asst. regional commr. Bur. Alcohol Tobacco and Firearms, Cin., 1962-66, asst. regional commr., 1966-70; dir. alcohol tobacco and firearms Dept. of the Treasury, Washington, 1972—78; pres. Nat. Assn. Beverage Importers, Inc., Washington, 1978-85, Delta Cons., Inc., Washington, 1985—2001; pres., chief exec. officer New Europe Wines, Inc., 1991-95; exec. dir. Pres.'s Forum of Beverage Alcohol Industry, 1990—2001. Chmn. Lic. Beverage Info. Coun., exec. dir. Pres.'s Forum of Beverage Alcohol Industry, Washington, 1981—85, Internat. Fedn. Wine & Spirits, Paris, 1982—85; advisor to dir. on history of the bur. Bur. Alcohol, Tobacco, Firearms and Explosives, Dept. Justice, 2004—05. Author: Federal Searches and Seizures, 1964 Vice chmn. Sky Ranch Found., Washington, 1983—85; pres. Treas. Hist. Assn., 1978—79, 2006—; mem. leadership coun. Brady Ctr. to Prevent Gun Violence. 1st lt. USAAF, 1943—45. Decorated Purple Heart, Air medal with 2 oak leaf clusters; recipient Chevalier de Merite Agricole French Gov., 1983, award for exceptional svc. Dept. Treasury, 1978, Meritorious Svc. award 1977, Lifetime Achievement award Bur. Alcohol, Tobacco, Firearms, 2001; named Fed. Employee of Yr. Cin. chpt. Fed. Bus. Assn., 1965; Meritorious award William A. Jump Found., 1959, Cert. of Appreciation Nat. Law Enforcement Officers Meml. Fund, 2005. Mem. Am. Soc. Assn. Execs., Okla. Bar Assn., Am. Legion, Pi Kappa Alpha, Internat. Club, Princeton Club. Avocations: golf, tennis, snorkeling, stamp collecting/philately. Home: 311 10th St SE Washington DC 20003 Home Phone: 202-547-1058.

DAVIS, REX LLOYD, insurance company executive; b. Des Moines, Dec. 29, 1929; s. Leon Mack and Mercedes Johanna (Lamar) D.; m. Sally JoAnne Richard, Apr. 14, 1952; children: Kristine Lynn, Craig Thomas JD, Drake U., 1952. Bar: Iowa, US Dist. Ct. Iowa, US Supreme Ct.; CPCU, CLU. With Employers Mut. Casualty Co., Des Moines, 1954—66, regional v.p. Phila., 1966—72; exec. v.p. Ranger Ins. Co., Houston, 1972—75, pres., 1975—84; pres., COO Ranger Ins. Mgrs., Ranger Internat. Ins. Ltd., Ranger County Mut.; atty.-in-fact Ranger Lloyds, Houston, 1975—84; pres., COO Rex L. Davis & Assocs., Inc., 1984—2007; chmn. United Republic Reins. Co., 1986—92, also bd. dirs. Major USAR, major Nat. Guard. Mem. Houston Bar Assn., Soc. CPCU, Soc. CLU, Lakeside Country Club (Houston), Petroleum Club (Houston), Delta Theta Phi Avocations: golf, exercise, dance. Business E-Mail: rexldavis@sbcglobal.net.

DAVIS, RICHARD BRADLEY, pathologist, educator, internist; b. Iowa City, Iowa, Nov. 6, 1926; s. Bradley Nelson and Gladys Mae (Fairbanks) D.; m. Jean Nixeen Anderson, June 22, 1957; children— Janet, Stephen, Catharine. BS, Yale U., 1949; MD, State U. Iowa, 1953; PhD, U. Minn., 1964. Intern Mary Fletcher Hosp., Burlington, Vt., 1953-54, resident, 1954-56; instr. U. Minn., Mpls., 1959-64, asst. prof. medicine, 1964-69; vis. investigator Sir William Dunn Sch. Pathology, Oxford, England, 1964-65, MRC Blood Coagulation Research Unit, Churchill Hosp., Oxford, 1965; asso. prof. medicine U. Nebr., Omaha, 1969-73, prof. medicine, 1973-94, acting dir. div. hematology, 1974-76, prof. pathology, 1976-94, dir. hematology div., 1976-79, emeritus prof. internal medicine, 1994—. Contbr. articles to sci. publs. Served with U.S. Army, 1945-46. Borden Undergrad. Med. Research grantee, 1953; USPHS career devel. awardee, 1961-69 Fellow A.C.P., Central Soc. Clin. Research, Am. Fedn. Clin. Research, Am. Soc. Exptl. Pathology, N.Y. Acad. Scis., Am. Assn. History of Medicine Soc. Exptl. Biology and Medicine, Am. Soc. Hematology, Royal Micros. Soc., Internat. Soc. Haemostasis and Thrombosis, Omaha Mid-West Clin. Soc., Sigma Xi, Alpha Omega Alpha, Phi Beta Pi, Theta Kappa Psi. Home: 103 Woodhall Spa Williamsburg VA 23188-9138 Personal E-mail: rbd7@verizon.net.

DAVIS, RICHARD EARL, lawyer; b. Jackson, Mich., Aug. 13, 1951; s. Richard Allen and Velva Elizabeth (England) Davis; m. Paula Hurst, Dec. 9, 1972; children: Richard Seth, Tessa Rebecca. BA, U. So. Fla., 1973, MA, 1975; JD cum laude, Stetson U., 1977. Bar: Fla. 1978, US Ct. Appeals (11th cir.), US Dist. Ct. (mid. dist.) Fla., bd. cert. city, county and local govt. law: Fla., cert.: (cir. civil mediator), bar: U.S. Supreme Ct. Asst. county atty. Hillsborough County, Fla., 1978-85; assoc. Holland & Knight, Tampa, Fla., 1985-88, ptnr., 1988-96, Richard E. Davis, P.A., Tampa, 1997—. Lectr. in field. Mem.: ABA, Stetson Lawyers Assn., Fla. Bar Assn., Hillsborough County Bar Assn., Tampa Downtown Partnership, Phi Sigma Alpha, Phi Kappa Phi. Office: 220 E Madison St Ste 512 Tampa FL 33602-4826 E-mail: tpaland@earthlink.net.

DAVIS, RICHARD FRANCIS, city government official; b. Providence, Aug. 18, 1936; s. Walter Francis and Mary Elizabeth (Gearin) D.; m. Virginia Catherine Oates, Aug. 27, 1960; children: Walter Douglas, John Richard, Theresa Catherine. BS, U. Ark., Little Rock, 1964; student city and regional planning, MIT, summer, 1964; postgrad., Carnegie Mellon U., 1973. Planner Met. Area Planning Commn., Little Rock, 1964-66; mem. Met. Planning Commn. Kansas City, Mo., 1966-67, dir. econs., 1967-69, dir. ops., 1969-71; exec. dir. Mid-Am. Regional Council, Kansas City, 1972-77; gen. mgr. Kansas City Area Transp. Authority, 1977-2000; instr. city planning U. Mo., Kansas City, 1973-74; Planning commr. City of Gladstone, Mo., 1967—69, 1981—90, 2003—04, city councilman Mo., 1969-71, mayor Mo., 1971-72, chmn. park bd. Mo., 1972-76, mem. bd. zoning adjustment, 1993—2004; bus. devel. Olsson Assocs., 2002—. Mem. Gladstone Econ. Betterment Coun., 2003-04, chmn., 2004; mem. Clay County (Mo.) Indsl. Devel. Commn., 1972-77, Coun. on Edn., Kansas City, 1974-82, treas., chmn. interdist. rels. com. Coun. adv. Major League Baseball Players Trust for Children, 2000-2003; v.p. Brooktree Homeowners Assn., 1979-80; total transp. adv. com. MidAmerica Regional Coun., 1977-2000, chmn. transit adv. com., 1997-2000; bd. dirs. Mo. Pub. Transit Assn., 1979-2000, pres., 1987-89, 1999-2000; bd. dirs. Kans. Pub. Transit Assn., 1979-2000; trustee Black Econ. Union, 1984-88; bd. dirs., treas. Heart of Am. United Way Vol. Ctr., 1985-87; mem. Kansas City Port Authoriry, 2006—; With USAF, 1955-59. Recipient Transp. Svc. award Kansas City chpt. Conf. of Minority Transit Officials, 1987. Mem. Am. Soc. Pub. Adminstrn. (pres. Kansas City chpt. 1980, Pub. Adminstr. of Yr. award 1973, L.P. Cookingham award 1991), Am. Planning Assn., Am. Pub. Transit Assn. (bd. dirs. 1980-93, 94-2000, govtl. affairs and legis. steering com., v.p. mgmt. and fin. com. 1984-86, v.p. govt. affairs com. 1991-93, Outstanding Pub. Transp. Mgr. award 2000), Kansas City Royal Lancers (bd. dirs. 2001-04, v.p. 2001-02, pres. 2002-03), Northland Regional C. of C., Brookhill Home Assn. (bd. dirs., 2005—, pres., 2006), Kansas City Port Auth. Bd. Commrs. Home and Office: 5826 N Kensington Ave Kansas City MO 64119

DAVIS, RICHARD HUNT, JR., historian; b. Highland Park, Mich., Sept. 30, 1939; s. Richard Hunt and Helen Grace Davis; m. Jeanne Elizabeth Gruber, May 28, 1939; children: Richard Francis, Jonathan Edward. BA, Grinnell Coll., 1961; MA, U. Wis., 1965, PhD, 1969. Prof. history, now prof. emeritus U. Fla., Gainesville, 1967—, dir. Ctr. for African Studies, 1979—88, dir. internat. studies and programs, 1993—94. Author: Encyclopedia of African History and Culture, Volumes 4&5, 2005, (monograph) Bantu Edn. and the Edn. of Africans in South Africa, 1972; editor: Mandela, Tambo, and the African Nat. Congress, 1991, Apartheid Unravels, 1991. Sec. U. Pk. Neighborhood Assn., Gainesville, 2001—03; troop leader Boy Scouts Am., Gainesville, 1978—88; com. mem. So. Africa Fulbright Rev. Com., Coun. for Internat. Exch. of Scholars, Washington, 2001—03. Sr. Fulbright scholar, Coun. for Internat. Exch. Scholars, 1999, Woodrow Wilson fellow, Woodrow Wilson Found., 1961—62, NDEA Title VI Fgn. Lang. fellow, U.S. Dept. Edn., 1964—66, Younger Humanist fellow, Nat. Endowment for the Humanities, 1973—74. Mem.: United Faculty Fla. (treas., v.p. 1972—78), African Studies Assn. (editor African Studies Rev. 1980—88), World History Assn. Presbyterian. Avocations: travel, reading, politics. Home: 1812 NW 6th Ave Gainesville FL 32603 Office: Univ Florida History Dept PO Box 117320 Gainesville FL 32611-7320 Business E-Mail: hdavis@cns.ufl.edu.

DAVIS, RICHARD JOEL, former government official, lawyer; b. NYC, Mar. 27, 1946; s. Herbert H. and Sylvia (Ginesin) D.; m. Nancy R. Davis. BA in History, U. Rochester, 1966; JD magna cum laude, Columbia U., 1969. Bar: NY 1970, US Dist. Ct (So. Dist. NY) 1973, DC 1974. Law clk. to Judge Jack B. Weinstein, US Dist. Ct. for Ea. Dist. NY, 1969-70; mem. criminal divsn., asst. chief appellate atty. corruption unit US Atty. Office, So. Dist. NY, 1970-73; task force leader Watergate Spl. Prosecution Force, Washington, 1973-75; asst. sec. of the treasury for enforcement and ops. Dept. Treasury, Washington, 1977-81; assoc. Weil, Gotshal and Manges LLP, NYC, 1976-77, ptnr., gen. counsel adminstrn., litigation, white collar crime, complex settlement negotiations, internal regulatory, and government investigations, 1981—; instr. in trial advocacy Harvard U.; instr. Nat. Inst. Trial Advocacy. Notes and comments editor Columbia U. Law Review, 1968-69; Co-author: American Hostages in Iran, 1988. Mem. Task Force on Ops. of Phila. Police Force, 1986, Citizens Task Force on Use and Security of Central Park (v.p. for development 1987-91), mem. Mayor's Commn. on Police Corruption, 1995—, chmn. 1996—, mem. Mayor's Task Force on Police-Cmty. Rels., Pro Bono Spl. Master for Investment Policy for the Agent Orange Settlement Fund; chmn. Randall's Island Sports Found.; mem., chmn. Citizen's Union, 1994-. Recipient Curtis J. Berger award, The Bridge, Inc., 1999, Whitney North Seymour award, Fed. Bar Coun., 2000, Ari Halberstam award, Jewish Children's Mus., 2000. Mem. ABA, Legal Aid Soc. NYC (v.p. 1987-91, bd. dirs. 1987-92), Citizens Union (bd. dirs. 1991-97, vice chmn. 1993-97), Boys Harbor (bd. dirs. 1993—, co-chmn. lawyers com. on violence 1994-98, bd. dirs. parks coun. 1994—), Assn. Bar City NY, City Bar Assn. (co-chmn. criminal justice coun.). Responsible for overseeing the freeze on Iranian assets and other sanctions imposed as a result of the seizure of hostages during the Carter Adminstration and participated in the development of the US-Iran Hostage Release Agreements in January, 1981. Office: Weil Gotshal & Manges LLP 767 5th Ave New York NY 10153 Office Phone: 212-310-8860. Office Fax: 212-310-8007. Business E-Mail: richard.davis@weil.com.

DAVIS, RICHARD K., bank executive; b. 1958; married; 3 children. B in econ., Calif. State U. Various consumer banking positions Security Pacific Nat. Bank, 1978—92, exec. v.p., 1992—93, Star Banc Corp., 1993—98; vice chmn. consumer banking Firstar Corp., Mpls., 1998—2001, U.S. Bancorp, Mpls., 2001—03, vice chmn., comml. & consumer banking, 2003—04, pres., COO, 2004—06, pres., CEO, 2006—. Bd. dir. Xcel Energy Inc.; bd. mem. Visa Internat., Visa USA. Bd. mem. Nat. Underground Railroad Freedom Ctr., Mpls. YMCA, Mpls. Orch., Guthrie Theatre. Mem.: Am. Bankers Assn. (bd. mem.). Office: US Bancorp 800 Nicollet Mall Minneapolis MN 55402 E-mail: richard.davis@usbank.com.*

DAVIS, RICHARD RALPH, lawyer; b. Houston, July 28, 1936; s. William Ralph and Virginia (Allison) D.; m. Christina R. Zelkoff, June 1, 1974; 1 child, Virginia Lee Allison. BA, Yale U., 1962, LLB, 1965; MBA, Columbia U., 1965. Bar: N.Y. 1966. Law clk. FAA, Washington, 1964; assoc. Chadbourne & Parke, NYC, 1965-73, ptnr., 1974-83; sr. v.p., gen. counsel Inspiration Resources Corp., NYC, 1983-91; sr. v.p., sec., gen. counsel Bessemer Securities Corp./Bessemer Trust Co., NA, NYC, 1991—2006, cons., 2007—. With U.S. Army, 1956-59. Mem. ABA. Home: 1185 Park Ave Apt 6-g New York NY 10128-1309 E-mail: davis@bessemer.com.

DAVIS, RICHARD WATERS, lawyer; b. Rocky Mount, Va., July 9, 1931; s. Beverly Andrew and Julia (Waters) D.; m. Mary Alice Woods; children: Debra, Julie, Richard Jr., Bob, Bev. B, Hampden-Sydney Coll., 1952; LLB, U. Richmond, 1959. Bar: Va. 1959. Pvt. practice, Radford, Va., 1959—. Dist. judge City of Radford, 1962-80; mem. Pub. Defenders Commn. Va., 1993-2004, chmn. 2002-04; mem. Va. State Bar Coun., 1989-95; assoc. prof. bus. law Radford U.; lectr. Va. Trial Lawyers Assn. Fellow Am. Coll. Trial Lawyers, Am. Bar Found., Va. Law Found. (fellows coun. 1992-98); mem. ABA. Va. Bar Assn. Home: 101 5th St Radford VA 24141 Office: PO Box 3448 Radford VA 24143-3448 Office Phone: 540-639-9081. Business E-Mail: dickdavis@davisattys.com.

DAVIS, ROBERT, JR., art educator, artist; b. Allendale, S.C., Sept. 11, 1920; s. Robert and Lula Fuller Davis; married, Apr. 26, 1942; children: Constance D. Lindsay, Iris Davis Huff, Sheila. BA, Temple U., Phila., 1964. Drafting tchr. Spencers H.S., Phila., 1942—65; draftsman Spencer Studios, Phila., 1943; tchr. Strawberry Mansion H.S., Phila., 1965—83, dept. head, 1980—. Capt. Civil Air Patrol, Mt. Gomery, Conn., 1970—. Democrat. Baptist. Home: 7915 Green Ln Wyncote PA 19095

DAVIS, ROBERT EDWARD, retired communications educator; b. Wichita, Kans., Apr. 2, 1931; s. Edward Lorenzo and Dorrinda Belle (Packer) D.; m. Jacqueline Peggy Baas, Aug. 22, 1955 (div. 1979);

children: Robert J., Sarah J., James E.; m. Martha Toni Merrill, Jan. 8, 1983. BA, U. No. Iowa, 1953; MA, U. Iowa, 1956, PhD, 1965. Instr. Grundy Ctr. (Iowa) High Sch., 1953-54; asst. to dir. radio and TV U. No. Iowa, Cedar Falls, 1954-58; lectr., instr. dept. speech and theatre Hunter Coll., NYC, 1961-63, 65-66; asst. prof. dept. speech U. Mich., Ann Arbor, 1966-69; from assoc. prof. to prof. and chmn. dept. cinema and photography So. Ill. U., Carbondale, 1969-74; prof. and chmn. Dept. Radio-TV-Film, U. Tex., Austin, 1974-87, John T. Jones Jr. Centennial prof. in communication, 1987-89, now emeritus, 1989—. Author: Response to Innovation, 1976; co-producer, dir. (film) Maple Sugar Farmer, 1973 (7 nat. and internat. awards); writer, performer, dir., producer over 1000 ednl. radio and tv programs; contbr. articles to profl. jours. Mem. Pacific Grove City Coun., 1990—98; mayor pro tem Pacific Grove, 1994—98; mem. Pacific Grove Planning Commn., 1999—, chair, 2005—07; bd. dirs. Heritage Soc. Pacific Grove, 2001—. Mem.: Pacific Grove Citizens Police Acad. Alumni Assn. (bd. dirs. 2000—, chmn. 2005—07). Republican. Methodist. Avocations: travel, photography. Home: 1212 Del Monte Blvd Pacific Grove CA 93950-2029 Personal E-mail: rtdavis@aol.com.

DAVIS, ROBERT EDWARD, plant pathologist; b. Bklyn., Jan. 27, 1939; s. Robert Samuel and Cecilia Bernadette (Hall) D.; m. Maryann Starr, June 23, 1962; children: Peter James, Michael Robert. BSc in Botany, U. R.I., 1961; PhD in Plant Pathology, Cornell U., 1967. Lab. asst. botany dept. U. R.I., Kingston, 1958, jr. asst. in rsch. dept. plant pathology, 1959-60; rsch. asst. dept. plant pathology Cornell U., Ithaca, N.Y., 1961-66; lectr. dept. plant pathology and physiology U. Minn., St. Paul, 1965; postdoctoral rsch. assoc. Plant Virology Lab., Agrl. Rsch. Svc., USDA, Beltsville, Md., 1966-67, rsch. plant pathologist, 1967-85, rsch. leader, 1985-93, leader Molecular Plant Pathology Lab., 1994—. Adj. prof. Cornell U., 1984—, Dimock Meml. lectr., 1983; Lockwood lectr. Conn. Agrl. Exptl. Sta., New Haven, 1984; mem. sci. com. Jour. Rivista di Patologia Vegetale; disting. lectr. USDA, Beltsville, 2005. Assoc. editor Jour. Phytopathology, 1972-75, 89-91; contbr. articles to Virology, Sci., Phytopathology, DNA & Cell Biology, Can. Jour. Microbiology. Judge sci. fairs, Md., 1969-79; chmn. citizens adv. com. Crofton (Md.) Woods Sch., 1976. Decorated Order of Knight's Cross Republic of Lithuania; named a Disting. Sr. Profl., 2004; recipient Silver Plow award, USDA, 1998, Presdl. Rank award. Fellow AAAS, Am. Phytopathol. Soc. (chmn. bacteriology com. 1987-88, Ruth Allen award), Washington Acad. Sci. (Biol. Scis. award 1983); mem. Pacific Sci. Assn., NAS, Sigma Xi. Achievements include patent in liquid density gradient zone electrophoresis apparatus, discovery and characterization of spiroplasmas, research in field of spiroplasmas and mycoplasmalike organisms (phytoplasmas) that infect plants. Home: 1793 Rochester St Crofton MD 21114-2611 Office: ARS-USDA BARC West Molecular-Plant Path Lab Beltsville MD 20705 Office Phone: 301-504-6290. E-mail: davisr@ba.ars.usda.gov.

DAVIS, ROBERT EDWARD, state supreme court justice; b. Topeka, Aug. 28, 1939; s. Thomas Homer and Emma Claire (Hund) D.; m. Jana Jones; children: Edward, Rachel, Patrick, Carolyn, Brian. BA in Polit. Sci., Creighton U., 1961; JD, Georgetown U., 1964. Bar: Kans. 1964, U.S. Dist. Ct. Kans. 1964, U.S. Tax Ct. 1974, U.S. Ct. Mil. Appeals 1965, U.S. Ct. Mil. Review, 1970, U.S. Ct. Appeals (10th cir.) 1974, U.S. Supreme Ct. 1982. Pvt. practice, Leavenworth, Kans., 1967-84; magistrate judge Leavenworth County, 1969-76, county atty., 1980-84, judge dist. ct., 1984-86; judge Kans. Ct. Appeals Jud. Br. Govt., Topeka, 1986-93; justice Kans. Supreme Ct., Topeka, 1993—. Lectr. U. Kans. Law Sch., Lawrence, 1986-95. Capt. JAGC, U.S. Army, 1964-67, Korea. Mem. Am. Judges Assn., Kans. Bar Assn., Leavenworth County Bar Assn. (pres. 1977), Judge Hugh Means Am. Inn of Ct. Charter Orgn. Roman Catholic. Office: Kansas Supreme Ct 301 W 10th Ave Topeka KS 66612

DAVIS, ROBERT EDWIN, lawyer; b. New Orleans, July 2, 1934; BA, JD, So. Meth. U., Dallas, 1958. Bar: Tex. 1958. Ptnr. Hughes & Luce, LLP, Dallas. Mem. adv. com. Tex. Supreme Ct. Named a Tex. Super Lawyer, Tex. Monthly, 2003—06; named one of Best Lawyers in Dallas, D Mag., 2005. Mem.: Am. Coll. Tax Counsel, Dallas Bar Assn. (chair Sect. Taxation 1977, chair 1977, pres. 1980), ABA, Tex. Bar Found., State Bar Tex. (chair Sect. Taxation 1976—77, dir. 1981—82). Office: Hughes & Luce LLP 1717 Main St Ste 2800 Dallas TX 75201 Office Phone: 214-939-5447. Office Fax: 214-939-5849. E-mail: bob.davis@hughesluce.com.*

DAVIS, ROBERT G., insurance company executive; degree, MBA, U. Tex. Acct. exec. E.F. Hutton & Co., LA; chmn., CEO MBank, Brownville, Tex., MCorp. (acquired by Banc One), San Antonio, 1985-89; chief credit officer Bank One Tex.; pres., CEO Bank One Columbus, 1991-95, Banc One Credit Corp., 1995-96, USAA (United Svcs. Automobile Assn.), San Antonio, 1996—, chmn., 2002—. Served in US Army. Decorated Silver Star, DFC, Air Medals, Bronze Star, Vietnam Cross of Gallantry, Purple Heart. Office: USAA 9800 Fredericksburg Rd San Antonio TX 78288 Office Phone: 210-498-2211.*

DAVIS, ROBERT HEATER, chemical engineering educator; b. Paris, Mar. 26, 1957; arrived in US, 1957; s. Richard Malcolm and Helen (Heater) D.; m. Shirley Lynn Giles, Dec. 28, 1982. BS in chem. engring., U. Calif., Davis, 1978; MS in chem. engring., Stanford U., 1979, PhD in chem. engring., 1982. Postdoctoral fellow dept. applied math. and theoretical physics Cambridge U., England, 1982-83; asst. prof. chem. engring. U. Colo., Boulder, 1983-88, assoc. prof., 1988—92, prof., 1992—, chair chem. engring., 1992—2002, Patten Prof., Dept. Chem. Engring., 1997—, dean Coll. Engring. and Applied Sci., 2002—. Vis. prof. MIT, 1990—91, U. Calif., Santa Barbara, 1997—98. Contbr. articles to profl. jours. Bd. dirs. univ. program First. Presbyn. Ch., Boulder, 1985—. Recipient Presdl. Young Investigator Award, NSF, 1985, Jr. Faculty Devel. Award, U. Colo., 1985, Outstanding Undergrad. Tchg. in Chem. Engring. Award, Omega Chi Epsilon, 1989, Outstanding Rsch. Award, U. Colo. Coll. Engring. and Applied Sci., 1993, Outstanding Svc. Award, 1999, Outstanding Tchg. Award, 2000, Outstanding Grad. Tchg. Award, Dept. Chem. Engring., U. Colo., 1996, 2002, Outstanding Rsch. Award, U. Colo. Boulder Faculty Assembly, 2000, Svc. Award, 2003; NATO Postdoctoral Fellowship in Sci., 1982, Guggenheim Fellowship, 1990, U. Colo. Faculty Fellowship, 1997. Mem.: Soc. Indsl. Microbiology, Am. Soc. Engring. Edn. (Rocky Mountain Sec. Dow Outstanding Young Faculty Award 1990), Am. Chem. Soc., Am. Phys. Soc., AIChE (Outstanding Paper Award 1995). Republican. Avocations: hiking, bicycling. Office: Coll Engring and Applied Sci U Colo 422 UCB Boulder CO 80309-0422

DAVIS, ROBERT J., internet company executive; BSc summa cum laude, Northeastern U.; MBA with high distinction, Babson Coll.; D in Comml. Sci. (hon.), Bentley Coll., 1999; D (hon.), Northeastern U., 2000. From mem. staff to pres., CEO Lycos Inc. (merged with Terra Networks), Waltham, Mass., 1995—2000; former CEO Terra Lycos, former vice chmn.; now venture ptnr. Highland Capital, Lexington, Mass. Bd. dirs. Boston Coll. H.S., The Greater Boston C. of C., Mass. Interactive Media Coun., The Man. com. Office: Highland Capital 92 Hayden Ave Lexington MA 02421 Office Phone: 781-861-5500. Business E-Mail: bdavis@hcp.com.

DAVIS, ROBERT LARRY, lawyer; b. Lubbock, Tex., June 6, 1942; s. R. H. and Bernice (Pray) Davis; m. Peggy Saunders, Jan. 23, 1965; children: Lee Michael, Melissa Lynn. BA, Rice U., 1964; LLB (with honors), U. Tex., 1967. Bar: Tex. 1967, U.S. Dist. Ct. (we. dist.) Tex. 1969, U.S. Dist. Ct. (so. dist.) Tex. 1989. Assoc. Royston Rayzor & Cook, Houston, 1967-68; from assoc. to ptnr. Brown McCarroll, Austin, Tex., 1968—. Bus. sect. coord., mem. mgmt. com. Parliamentarian, mem. exec. com. Downtown Revitalization Task Force, Austin, 1978—80; mem., past pres. Boys Club, Austin, Travis County, 1981—; trustee Eanes Ind. Sch. Dist., Austin, 1986—93, pres., 1990—93. Methodist. Avocations: sports, music, reading. Home: 3607-3 Pinnacle Rd Austin TX 78746 Office: Brown McCarroll 1400 One Congress Plz III Congress Austin TX 78701 Home Phone: 574-327-1806; Office Phone: 512-479-9706. E-mail: rdavis@mailbmc.com.

DAVIS, ROBERT LAWRENCE, lawyer; b. Cin., Apr. 5, 1928; s. Bryan and Henrietta Elizabeth (Weber) D.; m. Mary Lee Schulte, June 14, 1952; children: Gregory, Randy, Jenny, Bradley. BA, U. Cin., 1952; JD with honors, Salmon P. Chase Coll. Law, 1958. Bar: Ohio 1958, U.S. Supreme Ct. 1966. Assoc. Trabert & Gay, Cin., 1958—62; ptnr. Trabert, Gay & Davis, Cin., 1962—68, Gay, Davis & Kelly, Cin., 1969—71; pvt. practice Cin., 1972—. Lectr. Mt. St. Joseph Coll, 1972-82; arbitrator Am. Arbitration Assn.; assoc. adj. prof. Salmon P. Chase Coll. Sch. Law, 1969-80; lectr. Good Samaritan Hosp. Sch. Nursing, 1960-71; mentor Ohio Supreme Ct. Mentoring Program. Pres. bd. trustees Cmty. Ltd. Care Dialysis Ctr., 1978—86; asst. sec. Hamilton County Ohio Hosp. Commn., 1986, Kidney Found. Greater Cin., 1989, 1992; mentor Ohio Supreme Ct. Mentor Program. Served to capt. US Army, 1946—48, 1952—53. Decorated Bronze Star medal, Army Commendation medal. Fellow: Am. Coll. Trial Lawyers (state chmn. 1994—95); mem.: KC, Am. Bd. Trial Advocates (adv., pres. Cin. chpt. 1996), Cin. Bar Assn. (John P. Kiely Professionalism award 2002), Ohio Bar Assn., Order of Curia, Lawyers Club (pres. 1962—63), Omicron Delta Kappa, Sigma Sigma, Phi Alpha Delta, Phi Delta Theta. Home: 9969 Voyager Way Cincinnati OH 45252-1962 Office: 3600 Carew Tower Cincinnati OH 45202 Home Phone: 513-741-4630; Office Phone: 513-241-3500. Personal E-mail: rdavis@choice.net.

DAVIS, ROBERT LEACH, retired federal official; b. Torrington, Conn., July 20, 1924; s. Clarence Adelbert and Ruth Mabel (Leach) D.; m. Lorraine Lillian Szabla, Sept. 16, 1950; children: Russell, Cynthia, Vicki, Scott, Gregg. BA in Psychology, U. Mich., 1949. Claims examiner Social Security Adminstrn., Chgo., 1950-52; investigator and personnel specialist U.S. CSC, Chgo., 1952-67; personnel dir. U.S. Post Office Region, Chgo., 1967-71; div. chief, asst. bur. dir. U.S. CSC, Washington, 1971-78; dep. asst. sec. for adminstrn. and mgmt. Dept. Labor, Washington, 1978-82. Served with AUS, 1943-46. Decorated Purple Heart. Democrat. Unitarian-Universalist. Home: 275 Briarcrest Dr #186 Ann Arbor MI 48104 Office Phone: 734-395-1717. E-mail: rdavis3330@aol.com.

DAVIS, ROBERT LEIGH, language educator; b. Princeton, NJ, Apr. 1, 1956; s. Robert Newman and Fran Helen Davis; m. Laurie King Brubaker, Mar. 22, 1980; children: Emily Sarah, Hannah Lynn. BA in English, Stanford U., Calif., 1976—78, MA, 1980—81; PhD in English, U. Calif., Berkeley, 1985—92. Tchr. English, Serra HS, San Mateo, Calif., 1980—85; prof. English, Wittenberg U., Springfield, Ohio, 1992—, dir. first-yr. seminars, 2003—06. Author: (literary criticism) Whitman and the Romance of Medicine. Homeless adv. Interfaith Hospitality Network, Springfield, 1997—2006. Recipient Excellence in Tchg. award, Wittenberg U., 1996, Edith B. and Frank C. Matthies award for faculty rsch., 1998, Alumni Assn. award for disting. tchg., 2005, Excellence in Tchg. award, SW Ohio Coun. Higher Edn., 2006; NEH fellow. Democrat. Achievements include research in American literature, literature and medicine, college teaching. Avocation: bicycling. Home: 3388 Petre Rd Springfield OH 45502 Office: Dept English Wittenberg U Springfield OH 45501 Business E-Mail: rdavis@wittenberg.edu.

DAVIS, ROBERT M., medical products executive; B in fin., Miami Univ.; MBA, JD, Northwestern Univ. Fin. mgmt. positions through dir. corp. fin. planning Eli Lilly & Co., 1990—2004; treas. Baxter Internat. Inc., Deerfield, Ill., 2004—06, corp. v.p., treas., CFO, 2006—. Office: Baxter Internat 1 Baxter Pkwy Deerfield IL 60015-4625*

DAVIS, ROBERT NOLAN, federal judge, educator; b. Kewanee, Ill., Sept. 20, 1953; s. Ezekiel Robert and Rose Marie (Hodge) D. BA, U. Hartford, 1975; JD, Georgetown U., 1978. Bar: Iowa 1980, Va. 1993. Law clk. U.S. Senate, Washington, 1976-78; legal asst. FTC, Washington, 1976; fin. atty. U.S. Commodity Futures Trading Com., Washington, 1978-80, trial atty., 1980-83; gen. atty. U.S. Dept. Edn., Washington, 1983-87; spl. asst. U.S. Atty. U.S. Dept. Justice, Washington, 1987; assoc. prof. law U. Miss., Oxford, Miss., 1987—94, prof. law, 1994—2002, Stetson U., Gulfport, Fla., 2002—; judge US Ct. Appeals Vets. Claims, Washington, 2004—. Adj. prof. Am. U., Washington, 1986-87; instr. mil. law Naval Aviation Schs. Command, Pensacola, Fla., summer, 1989; vis. prof. law, Washington and Lee U., Lexington, Va., 1989-90, Stetson U. Coll. Law, 2001-02; arbitrator D.C. Bar, Washington, 1982-87; comml. arbitrator and mediator Am. Arbitration Assn., N.Y.C., 1985—; commr. Nat. Conf. of Commrs. on Uniform State Laws, 1993. Founder Jour. Nat. Security Law, 1995. Expert sports witness Miss. State Senate, Jackson; mem. law sch. admissions com. U. Miss., mem. dean search com., mem. athletic com., mem. student recruitment com.; dir. basic res. intelligence tng. program, region eight USNR, 1993—. Mem. ABA, Fed. Bar Calif., Iowa State Bar Assn., Va. State Bar Assn., Federalist Soc. (vice chair internat. law). Avocation: sports. Office: US Ct Appeals Vets Claims 625 Indiana Ave NW Ste 900 Washington DC 20004 Office Phone: 202-501-5863. Business E-Mail: rdavis@vetapp.gov.

DAVIS, ROBERT W., computer company executive; BS in Commerce and Acctg., U. Va.; MBA, Columbia U. Bus. Sch. CPA. Staff acct. Price Waterhouse, sr. mgr., SEC Svcs. Dept.; asst. corp. controller MCI Comm. Corp.; v.p. worldwide fin. and planning, Enterprise Systems Group Dell, Inc., 1996—99, v.p. worldwide corp. planning, 1999—2001, v.p., corp. fin., 2001, chief acctg. officer, 2002; exec. v.p., CFO Computer Assocs. Internat., Inc., Islandia, NY, 2005—06. Mem. bus. adv. bd. U. Vir. McIntire Sch. Commerce. Mem.: Fin. Exec. Internat. (mem. com. on corp. reporting, mem. corp. exec. bd. strategy and fin. sects.).

DAVIS, ROBIN JEAN, state supreme court chief justice; b. Boone County, W.Va., Apr. 6, 1956; m. Scott Segal; 1 child, Oliver. BS, W.Va. Wesleyan Coll., 1978; MA in Indsl. Rels., W.Va. U., 1982, JD, 1982. With Segal & Davis L.C., 1982-96; justice W.Va. Supreme Ct. of Appeals, 1996—, chief justice, 1998—2002, 2006—. Mem. W.Va. U. Law Inst., W.Va. Bd. of Law Examiners, 1991-96. Contbr. articles to W.Va. Law Rev.; co-author Litigation Handbook on West Virginia Rules of Civil Procedure. Recipient Dist. West Virginian award, 2000. Mem. ABA, Assn. of Trial Lawyers of Am., Kanawha County Bar Assn., Am. Acad. Matrimonial Lawyers. Office: Supreme Ct of Appeals Bldg 1 Rm E 301 State Capitol Charleston WV 25305 Office Phone: 304-558-4811. Business E-Mail: robindavis@courtswv.org.*

DAVIS, ROGER EDWIN, lawyer, retired retail executive; b. Lakewood, Ohio, Dec. 29, 1928; s. Russell G. and Irma (Aboline) D.; m. Eva Grace Keeler, July 25, 1953 (div. Feb. 1980); children: Susan Lee, Lisa Ann, Steven Russell; m. Yvonne L. Berich, June 1, 1980 (dec. Aug. 2005); m. Collene Erb, Aug. 14, 2006. AB, Harvard U., 1950; LLB, U. Mich., 1953. Bar: Mich. 1953. Pvt. practice, Detroit, 1955-60; assoc. Langs, Molyneaux & Armstrong, 1955-60; counsel Avis Enterprises, 1961-62; with legal dept. S.S. Kresge Co. (now Kmart Corp.), 1963-70, v.p., gen. counsel, sec., 1970-85, sr. v.p., gen. counsel, sec., 1985-91, ret., 1991. Served with AUS, 1953-55. Mem. State Bar Mich., Fla. Bar, Bonita Bay Club. Personal E-mail: roger1498@embarqmail.com.

DAVIS, ROGER LEWIS, lawyer; b. New Orleans, Jan. 27, 1946; s. Leon and Anada A. Davis; m. Annette Vucinich; 1 child, Alexandra. BA, Tulane U., 1967; MA, UCLA, 1969, PhD, 1971; JD, Harvard U., 1974. Bar: Calif. 1974. Assoc. Orrick, Herrington & Sutcliffe, L.L.P., San Francisco, 1974—79, ptnr., 1980—, chmn. pub. fin. dept., 1981—, mem. exec. com. Mem. mcpl. fiscal adv. com. Mayor of San Francisco; tech. adv. com. Calif. Debt & Investment Adv. Commn. Named a Dealmaker of the Yr., Am. Lawyer mag., 2006. Fellow: Am. Coll. Bond Counsel (bd. dirs.); mem.: Calif. Pub. Securities Assn. (bd. dirs., infrastructure subcom. of State Strategic Com. on Terrorism), Nat. Assn. Bond Lawyers. Office: Orrick Herrington & Sutcliffe LLP The Orrick Building 405 Howard St San Francisco CA 94105 Business E-Mail: rogerdavis@orrick.com.

DAVIS, RONALD WAYNE, genetics researcher, biochemistry educator; b. Moroa, Ill., July 17, 1941; s. Lester and Gerzella Mary (Brown) D.; m. Janet L. Dafoe, May 2, 1949; children: Whitney Allen, Ashley Halcyon. BS, Ea. Ill. U., 1964; PhD, Calif. Inst. Tech., 1970. Postdoctoral fellow Harvard U., Cambridge, Mass., 1970-71; asst. prof. biochemistry Stanford (Calif.) U., 1972-77, assoc. prof., 1977-80, prof., 1980—. Mem. sci. adv. bd. Collaborative Rsch., Bedford, Mass., 1978—. Author: Manual for Genetic Engineering, 1980. Recipient Eli Lilly award in microbiology, 1976, U.S. Steel award in molecular biology, 1981, Louis S. Rosenstiel award Brandeis U., 1992. Mem. NAS. Avocation: backpacking. Office: Stanford U Dept Biochemistry 855 California Ave Stanford CA 94305

DAVIS, ROY WALTON, JR., lawyer; b. Marion, NC, Jan. 15, 1930; s. Roy Walton and Mildred Gertrude (Wilson) D.; m. Madeline Burch Combs, Sept. 10, 1955; children: R. Walton III, Madeline Trent, Rebekah Wilson, Sally Fielding. BS, Davidson Coll., 1952; JD with honors, U. N.C., 1955. Bar: N.C. 1955, U.S. Dist. Ct. (we. dist.) N.C. 1960, U.S. Ct. Appeals (4th cir.) 1963. Ptnr. Davis & Davis, Marion, 1959-60; from assoc. to ptnr. and pres. Van Winkle, Buck, Wall, Starnes & Davis, Asheville, N.C., 1960—. Lectr. in field. Contbr. articles to profl. publs. Chancellor Episc. Diocese of Western N.C., 1980—. With U.S. Army, 1956-59. Fellow: Internat. Soc. Barristers, Am. Coll. Trial Lawyers (state chair 1994—96), Am. Bar Found.; mem.: ABA (Ho. of Dels. 1989—92, ins. practice and litig. sects.), N.C. Assn. Def. Attys., N.C. State Bar (pres. 1985—86, trustee IOLTA 1987—93, bd. law examiners 2002—), N.C. Bar Assn. (chmn. young lawyers divsn. 1965—66, chair adminstrn. of justice task force 1999—2002, v.p. 2004—06, Gen. Practice Hall of Fame), Order of the Coif. Democrat. Home: 359 Country Club Rd Asheville NC 28804-2639 Office: Van Winkle Buck Wall Starnes & Davis 11 N Market St Asheville NC 28801-2932 Home Phone: 828-253-5983; Office Phone: 828-258-2991. Business E-Mail: rdavis@vwlawfirm.com.

DAVIS, RUBY DEE See DEE, RUBY

DAVIS, RUSSELL HADEN, psychotherapist, consultant; b. Washington, Nov. 26, 1940; s. Walter Haden Davis and Virginia (Russell) Edge; m. Iva Lee Crocker, 1964; children: Brandon Denise, Haden Arnold. BA, U. Va., 1962; MDiv, Union Theol. Sem., NYC, 1965, STM, 1978, PhD, 1986; ThM, So. Bapt. Theol. Sem., Louisville, 1966. Ordained to ministry So. Bapt. Ch., 1961, endorsed to chaplaincy Alliance of Baptists in the USA, 2000. Clin. chaplain Ky. State Reformatory, LaGrange, 1966-71, Ctrl. State Hosp., Milledgeville, Ga., 1971-77; assoc. min. The Riverside Ch., NYC, 1977-86; pvt. practice pastoral psychotherapy, 1974-98; asst. prof. psychiatry and religion Union Theol. Sem., NYC, 1986-91; mem. faculty Blanton-Peale Grad. Inst. Pastoral Psychotherapy, NYC, 1989-91; dir. Psy-Law, NYC, 1989-91; asst. prof. U. Va., 1994, assoc. prof., 1994-95; exec. dir. Assn. for Clin. Pastoral Edn., Inc., Decatur, Ga., 1995-98; pres. Legacy Group Internat., 1998—; founder sch. clin. pastoral edn. Sentara Norfolk (Va.) Gen. Hosp., 2001—. Adj. prof. Va. Commonwealth U., 2001—06, John Leland Ctr. Theol. Studies, 2004—06. Author: Freud's Concept of Passivity, 1993; also articles. Founder Sch. of Clin. Pastoral Edn., Sentara Hosps., Norfolk, 2001; bd. dirs. Tidewater Pastoral Counseling Svcs., Norfolk, 2001—05, Inst. for Relationship Therapy, NY, 1981—88, Counseling Ctr., Riverside Ch., NY, 1978—82. Named Ky. Col., State of Ky., 1970; fellow Union Theol. Sem., 1979-81, rsch. grantee, 1987-90; fellow Oaklawn Found., 1980. Mem.: Assn. Profl. Chaplains (bd. cert. chaplain 1974—99), Assn. for Clin. Pastoral Edn. (cert. supr., v.p. racial, ethnic, multicultural network 2006—07). Office: Sch Clin Pastoral Edn Sentara Norfolk Gen Hosp 600 Gresham Dr Norfolk VA 23507 Business E-Mail: rhdavis@sentara.com.

DAVIS, RUTH MARGARET, information technology executive; b. Sharpsville, Pa., Oct. 19, 1928; d. W. George and Mary Anna (Ackermann) D.; m. Benjamin F. Lohr, Apr. 29, 1961. BA, Am. U., 1950; MA, U. Md., 1952, PhD, 1955; PhD (hon.), CMU, 1978, U. Md., 2000. Statistician FAO, UN, Washington, 1946-49; mathematician Nat. Bur. Standards, 1950-51; head ops. rsch. div. David Taylor Model Basin, 1955-61; staff asst. Office Dir. Def. Rsch. and Engring. Dept. Def., 1961-67; asso. dir. rsch. and devel. Nat. Libr. Medicine, 1967-68; dir. Lister Hill Nat. Center for Biomed. Communications, 1968-70; dir. Inst. for Computer Scis. and Tech. Nat. Bur. Standards, 1970-77; dep. undersec. def. for rsch. and engring., 1977-79; asst. sec. resource applications U.S. Dept. Energy, 1979-81; chmn., pres., CEO Pymatuning Group Inc. FMR, 1981-2000. Chmn. Aerospace Corp., 1994—2001; lectr. U. Md., 1955—57, Am. U., 1957—58; vis. prof. computer sci. U. Pa., 1969—72; adj. prof. U. Pitts.; mem. Md. Gov.'s Sci. Adv. Coun., 1971—77; chmn. nat. adv. coun. Elec. Power Rsch. Inst., 1975—76. Contbr. articles to profl. jours. Recipient Rockefeller Tech. Mgmt. award, 1973, Fed. Woman of the Yr. award, 1973, Systems Profl. of Yr. award, 1979, DSM, U.S. Dept. Def., 1979, U.S. Dept. Energy, 1981, Gold medal, 1981, Ada A. Lovelace award, 1984, Disting. Alumnus award, U. Md., 1993, Disting. Alumna award, 1995, Alumna of Yr. in Math. and Sci. award, 2003; inducted into Computer News Hall of Fame, 1988. Fellow AIAA, Soc. for Info. Display; mem. AAAS, Am. Math. Soc., Math. Assn. Am., Nat. Acad. Engring. (counselor), Nat. Acad. Pub. Adminstrn., Nat. Acad. Arts and Scis., Washington Philos. Soc., Sigma Pi Sigma, Tau Beta Pi. Office Phone: 703-671-3500. Personal E-mail: rmdavis5@aol.com. *The rapid rate of change in our lives due principally to technology and changing personal values makes adaptability and flexibility key ingredients to success. The one essential invariant of success is integrity, accompanied by compassion.*

DAVIS, SAMUEL, hospital administrator, educator, consultant; b. NYC, Sept. 30, 1931; s. Morris and Ethel (Levowitz) D.; m. Ellen Darce Kalker, June 16, 1957; children: Joseph Evan, Thomas Adam, Jonathan Edward, Jessica Ann. BA, CCNY, 1952; MS, Columbia U., 1957. Acct. Roosevelt Hosp., NYC, 1954-55; relief adminstr. Meml. Center Cancer and Allied Diseases, NYC, 1955-56; adminstrv. resident, then adminstrv. asst. to dir. and dir. ambulatory care services Roosevelt Hosp., 1956-59; mem. adminstrv. staff Hillside Hosp., Glen Oaks, NY, 1959-72, exec. v.p., 1970-72; exec. cons. L.I. Jewish-Hillside Med. Center, New Hyde Park, NY, 1972; exec. pres. Mt. Sinai Hosp., Mpls., 1972-75, dir. NYC, 1975-81, pres., 1981-85; sr. v.p. Mt. Sinai Med. Center, NYC, 1975-77, exec. v.p., 1978-84; pres. EcuMed, NYC, 1984-85; prin. Sam Davis & Assocs., Rye, NY, 1986—; sr. dir. Delta Cons. Group, NYC, 1990-98; assoc. prof. adminstrv. medicine Mt. Sinai Med. Sch., 1975-79, acting chmn., 1977-79, Edmond A. Guggenheim prof. health care mgmt., chmn. health care mgmt., 1979-84, disting. service prof. health care mgmt., 1984—; adj. prof. health care adminstrn. Baruch Coll., CUNY, 1978-87; prof. mgmt., clin. prof. Sch. Pub. Health Columbia U., 1988—; cons. health care strategy and orgnl. change, 1976—; pres. Sam Davis & Assoc., 1999—. Dir. health care research, The Ctr. for Mgmt., CUNY; vice chmn. bd. dirs. Hennepin County (Minn.) Health Coalition, 1973-75; mem. health adv. com. Minn. Met. Health Bd., 1974-75; mem. Hennepin County Health and Social

Services Adv. Bd., 1974-75. Author: Decision Analysis in Hospital Administration, 1974; contbr. articles to profl. jours. Trustee Mpls. Fedn. Jewish Service, 1973-75; chmn. health and welfare div. N.Y.C. Fedn. Jewish Philanthropies, 1975-76; trustee, mem. exec. com. Montefiore Med. Ctr., Bronx, N.Y., 1985—. Served with AUS, 1952-54. Recipient Humanitarian award NCCJ, 1984; fellow social studies and humanities CCNY, 1952; WHO fellow, 1970; sr. fellow Wharton Sch. U. Pa., 1986—. Fellow Am. Coll. Hosp. Adminstrs., Am. Pub. Health Assn.; mem. Am. Assn. Hosp. Planning, Am., Am. Acad. Dramatic Arts (bd. dirs., exec. com.), N.Y. State hosp. assns., Am. Mgmt. Assn., Herman Biggs Soc. Home Phone: 914-698-5549.

DAVIS, SAMUEL MARION, dean, law educator, researcher; b. Pascagoula, Miss., Nov. 24, 1944; s. Marion Fuller and Ida Belle (Butler) D.; m. Carolyn Mary Peele, aug. 23, 1964; children: Samantha Carrie, Sarah Ellen. BA, U. So. Miss., 1966; JD, U. Miss., 1969; LLM, U. Va., 1970. Bar: Miss. 1969, U.S. Dist. Ct. (no. dist.) Miss. 1969, U.S. Supreme Ct. 1978, U.S. Ct. Appeals (11th cir.) 1982, U.S. Ct. Appeals (5th cir.) 1992. From asst. prof. to assoc. prof. U. Ga. Law Sch., Athens, 1970-78, asst. dean, 1973-75, prof., 1978-97, assoc. dean, 1986-92, assoc. v.p. for acad., 1994-97; dean U. Miss. Law Sch., Oxford, 1997—, Jamie L. Whitten chair law & govt., 1998—. Vis. assoc. prof. Washington and Lee U. Law Sch., Lexington, Va., 1975-76. Author: Rights of Juveniles, 1974; co-author: Children in the Legal System, 1983, 3d edit., 2004, Children's Rights and the Law, 1987. Fellow: Miss. Bar Found.; mem.: ABA, Miss. Bar, Am. Law Inst. Democrat. Methodist. Avocations: sailing, reading, travel. Office: Office of the Dean Univ Miss Law Sch PO Box 1848 University MS 38677 Home Phone: 662-234-4118; Office Phone: 662-915-6900. Business E-Mail: smdavis@olemiss.edu, smdavis2003@bellsouth.net.

DAVIS, SARAH FRANCES, management consultant, bishop; b. Beaumont, Tex., Feb. 4, 1948; d. Cornelius N. and Thelma (Levy) Taylor; m. Claytie Davis Jr., June 20, 1970; children: Claytie III, Corey Carrington. BA, North Tex. U., 1970; MS, Pace U., 1979; doctorate ministry, So. Methodist Univ. Dist. mgr. Southwestern Bell, Houston, 1970-83; pres. Strategic Mgmt. & Cons. Co., Houston, 1983—. Active awareness program Boy Scouts Am., Houston, 1987—; bd. dirs. south Houston dist. Bible Readers Outreach, 1987—. Mem. Internat. Assn. Fin. Planners (bd. dirs. 1987-88). Methodist. Achievements include third woman in history of African Methodist Episcopal Church elected Bishop. Avocation: bible study. Office: AME Church PO Box 223 nMesaru 100 Lesotho South Africa

DAVIS, SARAH IRWIN, retired language educator; b. Louisburg, NC, Nov. 17, 1923; d. M. Stuart and May Amanda (Holmes) Davis; m. Charles B. Goodrich, Nov. 18, 1948 (div. 1953). AB, U. N.C., 1944, AM, 1945; PhD, NYU, 1953. Tchg. asst. English dept. NYU, 1948-51; tchr. English Elizabeth Irwin HS, NYC, 1951-53; editor coll. texts Henry Holt, NYC, 1953-55; editor coll. texts, encylopedias McGraw-Hill, NYC, Rome, 1955—60; asst. prof. English Louisburg Coll., NC, 1960-63, Randolph-Macon Woman's Coll., Lynchburg, Va., 1963-70, assoc. prof. English, 1970-75, chairperson Am. studies, 1971-87, prof. English and Am. studies, 1975-87, ret., 1987. Contbr. articles to profl. jours. Mem. MLA, Am. Studies Assn., NC-Va. Coll. English Assn. (various coms.), Franklin County Hist. Soc. (pres. 1989-94). Home: Carol Woods 139 750 Weaver Dairy Rd Chapel Hill NC 27514

DAVIS, SCOTT CHARLES, music educator, political activist; b. Abington, Pa., Oct. 6, 1955; s. Rothmeyer and Diane Davis. BA in History, West Chester U., 1978. Cert. Secondary Sch. Tchr. Pa., 1984. Music tchr., Pa., Md., Va., NJ, NY, Del., 1968—; piano technician Pa., Md., Va., DC, Del., NJ, NY, Conn., 1978—. Polit. cons., Pa., Md., Va., DC, Del., NH, NY, 1982—; real estate investor, Phila., 1991—; broadcaster WGCB-FM, Red Lion, Pa., 1995. Songwriter, performer: US, Europe, Can., 1960—2005; songwriter Hope, 2004, Yes, 2004; editor: New English Revised Sacred Annotated Scriptures, 2004—05. Observer Town Watch, Phila., 1980—; chmn. Solvency Party. Am., 1994—2001; chmn. nat. exec. com. Sovereignty Party Am., 2001—04, Party Am. Revolution, 2004—; founder Christian Assn. Reconciliation, 2004. Reconciliationist. Achievements include worked successfully with Congress and the White House to limit the scope of the Lebanese War; formulated cease-fire proposal used by Lebanese government. Avocations: languages, geography, history. Office: Party American Revolution PO Box 877 Edgemont PA 19028-0877 Office Phone: 215-233-5369.

DAVIS, SCOTT JONATHAN, lawyer; b. Chgo., Jan. 8, 1952; s. Oscar and Doris (Koller) D.; m. Anne Megan, Jan. 4, 1981; children: William, James, Peter. BA, Yale U., New Haven, Conn., 1972; JD, Harvard U., Cambridge, Mass., 1976. Bar: Ill. 1976, U.S. Dist. Ct. (no. dist.) Ill. 1976, U.S. Ct. Appeals (7th cir.) 1977, US Ct. Appeals (8th cir.) 1986. Law clk. to judge US Ct. Appeals (7th cir.), Chgo., 1976—77; assoc. Mayer Brown LLP, Chgo., 1977—82, ptnr., 1983—. Law lectr. U. Chgo. Law Sch., 2007—. Bd. editors: Harvard Law Rev., 1974—76; contbr. articles to profl. jours. V.p. Chgo. Police Bd. Home: 838 W Belden Ave Chicago IL 60614-3236 Office: Mayer Brown LLP 71 S Wacker Dr Chicago IL 60606 Office Phone: 312-701-7311. Business E-Mail: sdavis@mayerbrown.com.

DAVIS, SHANI, Olympic athlete; b. Chgo., Ill., Aug. 13, 1982; Achievements include winning Jr. Age Group Nat. Championships, 1995, 1997, 1999, 2000; first place 1500 meter, Jr. Country Match 2002, Jr. World Championships, 2002; first African-American to qualify for Olympic Short Track Team, 2002; World Champion, 1500 meter, World Single Distance Championships, 2004; U.S. Allround Speedskating Champion, 2003-2005; winner, Allround World Longtrack Championships, 2005; Gold Medal in 1000 meter Speed Skating, Torino Olympics, Italy, 2006; first black athlete to win gold medal in an individual event in Winter Olympics history, 2006. Office: Team Shani Davis 815 Dempster St Evanston IL 60201

DAVIS, SHELBY MOORE CULLOM, investment company executive, consultant; b. Phila., Mar. 20, 1937; s. Shelby Cullom and Kathryn (Wasserman) D.; m. Wendy Ann Adams, June 20, 1959 (div. 1975); children: Andrew, Christopher, Victoria; m. Gale Abbie Lansing, Apr. 17, 1976; children: Lansing, Alida, Edith. AB with honors, Princeton U., 1958. V.p. in charge equity rsch. Bank of N.Y., NYC, 1958-66; founding ptnr. Davis, Palmer & Biggs, NYC, 1966-78; sr. v.p. Fiduciary Trust Co., NYC, 1978-83, cons., 1983-98; pres. various mut. funds Davis Selected Advisers, Santa Fe, 1983-98, also dir. all mut. funds, 1969-78, 83-98. Contbr. articles to Fin. Analysts Jour. Bd. dirs., trustee Beekman Downtown Hosp., N.Y.C., early 1960s; bd. dirs. Am. Cancer Soc., N.Y.C., early 1970s; trustee United World Coll., 1988—, Teton Sci. Sch., 2001-06, Princeton U., 2006—; mem. adv. bd. Coll. of the Atlantic, 1999—; founder Davis United World Coll. Scholars Program, 1998—. Mem. N.Y. Soc. Security Analysts (bd. dirs. 1965), Univ. Club, River Club (N.Y.C.), Harbor Club (Seal Harbor, Maine), Tuxedo Club (Tuxedo Park, N.Y.), Jupiter Island Club, Jackson Hole Golf and Tennis Club. Republican. Avocations: skiing, hiking, travel, swimming, tennis. Home: PMB 25185 PO Box 20000 Jackson WY 83001-7000 Office: PO Box 362 Tuxedo Park NY 10987

DAVIS, SMITH WORMLEY, lawyer; b. West Chester, Pa., Mar. 7, 1948; s. John Aubrey and Mavis Elizabeth (Wormley) D.; m. Wendy Ann Butler, July 14, 1975 (div.). BA magna cum laude, Yale U., 1970, JD, 1974. Bar: D.C. 1978. Assoc. Milbank, Tweed, Hadley & McCloy, NYC, 1974-76; law clk. to presiding justice U.S. Dist. Ct. D.C., 1976-77; counsel judiciary com. Ho. of Reps., Washington, 1978-79; assoc. Akin, Gump, Strauss, Hauer & Feld, Washington, 1979-84, ptnr., 1985—. Gen. counsel Womens Senate Rep. Victory com., 1990; spl. counsel Nat. Rep. Senatorial com., 1991—94; sr. adv. Phil Gramm for Pres. com., 1995—96; mem. adv team Bush-Cheney HUD Transition, 2000. Mem.: DC Bar Assn. Republican. Presbyterian. Home: 5923 Woodfield Estate Dr Alexandria VA 22310-1895 Office: Akin Gump Strauss et al Ste 400 1333 New Hampshire Ave NW Washington DC 20036-1532 Office Phone: 202-887-4098. Office Fax: 202-955-7720. Business E-Mail: sdavis@akingump.com.

DAVIS, STACEY ANN, lawyer; b. Long Beach, Calif., Nov. 15, 1976; d. Daniel Jack and Sharon Diane Davis; m. Nichalaus Alexander Sims, Sept. 4, 2005. BA, Mich. State U., E.Lansing, 1998; MBA, JD, U. Conn., Hartford, 2002. Bar: Ala. 2002. Atty. Berkowitz, Lefkovits, Isom & Kushner, Birmingham, Ala., 2002—03, Baker, Donelson, Bearman, Caldwell & Berkowitz, PC, Brimingham, 2003—. Chair entertainment & sports law task force Ala. State Bar, Birmingham, 2006. Editor-in-chief (journal) Conn. Jour. Internat. Law, technology editor. Com. head Sidewalk Moving Picture Festival, Birmingham, 2003, Birmingham SHOUT Festival, 2006; dir., sec. Ala. Moving Image Assn., Inc., Birmingham, 2004. Recipient Best of Bar-Entertainment Law award, Birmingham Bus. Jour., 2006. Mem.: ABA (entertainment & sports law sect.), Ala. State Bar, Birmingham Bar Assn. Office: Baker Donelson et al 420 20th St N Ste 1600 Birmingham AL 35203 Business E-Mail: sdavis@bakerdonelson.com.

DAVIS, STACY NICOLE, religious studies educator; b. Waukegan, Ill., Oct. 6, 1973; d. John Michael and Melissa Ann Davis. BA, U. Tulsa, 1996; M. in Theol. Studies, Phillips Theol. Sem., 1998; PhD, U. Notre Dame, 2003. Instr. theology U. Notre Dame, 2002; asst. prof. religious studies St. Mary's Coll., Notre Dame, Ind., 2003—. Mem. African Am. bibl. hermeneutics steering com. Soc. Bibl. Lit., 2004—. Contbr. articles to profl. jours. Mem. Amnesty Internat., 1992; advisor Sex Offense Svcs., South Bend, Ind., 2004. Grantee Ctr. for Academic Innovation faculty tchg. grant, St. Mary's Coll., 2005. Mem.: Soc. Bibl. Lit., Phi Beta Kappa. Avocations: reading, listening to music, traveling. Office: Saint Mary's Coll Box 38 161 Madeleva Hall Notre Dame IN 46556 Home Phone: 574-258-9004; Office Phone: 574-284-4700. Business E-Mail: dsn1973@aol.com.

DAVIS, STANLEY NELSON, hydrologist, educator; b. Rio de Janeiro, Aug. 6, 1924; s. Nelson Caryl and Mary Faye (Caulkins) D.; m. Barbara Jean Wickham, Apr. 14, 1949 (div.); children: Gerald Nelson, Ruth Ann, Darlene Grace, Randall Wayne, Betty Jean, Nancy Faye.; m. Augusta G. Felty, Feb. 12, 1982; children— Tara Devi, Locana Kamala BS in Geology, U. Nev., 1949; MS, U. Kans., 1951; PhD, Yale, 1955. Geologist U.S. Bur. Reclamation, 1949, Mo. Geol. Survey, 1952, 53, 55; instr. U. Rochester, 1953-54; mem. faculty Stanford, 1954-67, prof. geology, 1965-67, U. Mo., 1967-73, chmn. dept., 1969-72; asso. dean Coll. Arts and Scis., 1972-73; prof. geology Ind. U., Bloomington, 1973-75; prof. hydrology U. Ariz., Tucson, 1975—, head dept. hydrology and water resources, 1975-79. Vis. prof. U. Chile, Santiago, 1960-61; tchr. Bowling Green U., summer 1963, Princeton, summer 1965, U. Hawaii, fall 1966; instr. U. Oriente in Venezuela, summer 1967-68, 72; lectr. Am. Geol. Inst.; mem. East Greenland Expdn., Arctic Inst. N. Am., summer 1959; cons. to govt. and industry, 1955— Author: Hidrogeología, 1961, (with R.M. DeWiest) Hydrogeology, 1966, (with P. Reitan and R. Pestrong) Geology, Our Physical Environment, 1976, (with D.J. Campbell, H.W. Bentley, T.J. Flynn) Ground Water Tracers, 1984, Hydrogeology in the United States, 1780-1950, 2005; also articles. Served with AUS, 1943-46, PTO. Fellow AAAS, Geol. Soc. Am. (O.E. Meinzer award 1989), Am. Geophys. Union; mem. Assn. Ground Water Scientists and Engrs., Soc. Econ. Paleontologists and Mineralogists, Sigma Xi. Home: 6540 W Box Canyon Dr Tucson AZ 85745-9681 Office: U Ariz Dept Hydrology & Water Resou Tucson AZ 85721-0001 Business E-Mail: sndavis@u.arizona.edu.

DAVIS, STEPHEN, professional football player; b. Mar. 1, 1974; m. Virginia Davis; children: Dentia, Sherrell, Stephen Davis Jr., Stephanie. Degree in vocat. edn., Auburn. Profl. football player Washington Redskins, 1996—2003, Carolina Panthers, Charlotte, 2003—. Founder Rushing for Remembrance. Named to NFC Pro-Bowl Team, 1999, 2003. Achievements include led NFL in rushing touchdowns (17), 1999. Office: Carolina Panthers 800 S Mint St Charlotte NC 28202

DAVIS, STEPHEN EDWARD FOLWELL, banker; b. Auckland, N.Z., July 12, 1964; s. George Folwell and Elizabeth Ann (Strother) D. BA, Harvard Coll., 1987. Rsch. intern The Brookings Instn., Washington, 1984; sales intern Lotus Devel. Corp., Cambridge, Mass., 1986-87; fin. analyst Salomon Bros. Inc., NYC, 1987-89; interest rate swap trader Kidder Peabody & Co., NYC, 1989-90; derivatives trader Deutsche Bank AG, NYC, 1990-95; proprietary trader Dai-Ichi Kangyo Bank, Ltd., 1995-96; head derivatives trading Hypo Bank AG, NYC, 1996-97; pres. Nuuanu Real Estate Investors, Honolulu, 1997—. Researcher book: The Ultimate Insiders, 1989. Homesteading coord., dir. Crimson Impact Inc., N.Y.C., 1991-95; treas. The Quadrille Soc., N.Y.C., 1991—; vol. Habitat for Humanity, 2002. JFK Sch. Govt. grantee, 1984; Lindsay Exeter Meml. scholar, 1983. Mem. Fgn. Policy Assn., Harvard Club of N.Y. Avocations: foreign policy, golf, running. Home: 757 Ocean Ave Unit 203 Santa Monica CA 90402 E-mail: sdavis@post.harvard.edu.

DAVIS, STEPHEN HOWARD, applied mathematics professor; b. NYC, Sept. 7, 1939; s. Harry Carl and Eva Leah (Axelrod) D.; m. Suellen Lewis, Jan. 15, 1966. BEE, Rensselaer Poly. Inst., 1960, MS in Math, 1962, PhD in Math., 1964; BSc honoris causa, U. Western Ont., 2001. Research mathematician Rand Corp., Santa Monica, Calif., 1964-66; lectr. in math. Imperial Coll., London U., 1966-68; asst. prof. mechanics and materials sci. Johns Hopkins U., 1968-70, assoc. prof., 1970-75, prof., 1975-78; prof. engring. sci. and applied math. Northwestern U., 1979—, Walter P. Murphy prof., 1987—, McCormick Sch. prof., 2000—. Dir. Ctr. for Multiphase Fluid Flow and Transport, 1986-88; cons. in field; vis. prof. math. Monash U., Australia, 1973; vis. prof. chem. engring. U. Ariz., 1977; vis. prof. aerospace and mech. engring., 1981; vis. scientist Institut für Aerodynamik-ETH, Zurich, Switzerland, 1971; vis. scientist Dept. Math. Ecole Polytechnique Federale, Lausanne, Switzerland, 1984, 85, vis. prof. 1987, 88, 91; mem. U.S. Nat. Com. for Theoretical and Applied Mechanics, 1978-87. Asst. editor Jour. Fluid Mechanics, 1969-75, assoc. editor, 1975-89, editor-in-chief, 2000—; contbr. articles to profl. jours. Recipient Alexander von Humboldt award, 1994, Fluid Dynamics prize Am. Phys. Soc., 1994, G.I. Taylor medal Soc. for Engring. Sci., 2001. Fellow Am. Phys. Soc. (chmn. divsn. fluid dynamics 1978-79, 87-88, councillor divsn. fluid dynamics 1980-82); mem. NAS, NAE, Am. Acad. Arts and Scis., Soc. Indsl. and Applied Math. (coun. 1983-87), Sigma Xi, Pi Mu Epsilon. Home: 1199 Edgewood Rd Lake Forest IL 60045-1308 Office: Northwestern U McCormick Sch Engring/Applied Scis Sheridan Rd Evanston IL 60208-0001 Business E-Mail: sdavis@northwestern.edu.

DAVIS, STEPHEN N., endocrinologist; m. Frances Louise Hunt, Sept. 17, 1982; children: Ian, Stuart, Hugh. MBBS, London U., 1979; MD, Vanderbilt U., Nashville, 1993. Cert. endocrinology, diabetes and metabolism Royal Coll. Physicians and Surgeons Eng., 1982. Qualified Royal Free Hosp., Sch. Medicine, London, 1979; ho. physician acad. depts. diabetes and nephrology Royal Free Hosp., London, 1979—80; ho. surgeon acad. depts. surgery and gynecology Royal Free Hosp., London U., 1980, sr. ho. officer accident, emergency and ICU, 1980—81, sr. ho. officer acad. depts. diabetes, medicine, rheumatology and respiratory medicine, 1981—83; med. registrar acad. depts. gen. medicine, diabetes, endocrinology, geriatric medicine and cardiology Newcastle Gen. and Freeman Hosps., U. Newcastle upon Tyne, England, 1983—84; Eli Lilly rsch. fellow dept. medicine Royal Victoria Infirmary, U. Newcastle upon Tyne, 1984—85, med. rsch. coun. dept. medicine, 1985—87, hon. sr. registrar dept. medicine, 1985—87; sr. registrar infirmary Freeman Hosps., U. Newcastle upon Tyne, 1987—88; Med. Rsch. Coun. traveling fellow dept. molecular physiology and biophysics Vanderbilt U. Sch. Medicine, Nashville, 1988—89, Juvenile Diabetes Found. fellow depts. molecular physiology, biophysics and medicine, 1989—91, asst. prof. dept. medicine Diabetes Rsch. and Tng. Ctr., 1991—94, assoc. prof. dept. medicine Diabetes Rsch. and Tng. Ctr., 1994—99, assoc. prof. dept. molecular physiology and biophysics, 1994—99, chief divsn. diabetes, endocrinology and metabolism, 2000—, prof. dept. molecular physiology and biophysics, 2000—, Rudolph Kampmeier prof. dept. medicine, 2000—; assoc. dir. Diabetes Rsch. and Tng. Ctr. Vanderbilt U., Nashville, 1999—, assoc. dir. Gen. Clin. Rsch. Ctr., 1999—; dir. Nashville VA/Juvenile Diabetes Found. Internat. Diabetes Rsch. Ctr., Nashville, 1997—2002. Mem. med. bd. Vanderbilt U., Nashville, mem. dept. medicine awards com., mem. physicians scientist awards com., mem. masters clin. investigation entry and rev. com., mem. clin. rsch. scientist entrance and rev. com.; mem. exec. com. Vanderbilt U. Sch. Medicine, Nashville; mem. nat. organizing com. Veterans Affairs Coop. Study #565; chair hypoglycemia and clin. complications Annual Am. Diabetes Assn. Meeting, 2005. Contbr. articles to profl. jours. Recipient Peel Med. Rsch. award, 1986, award, Mason Med. Rsch. Found., 1987, Newcastle Rsch. and Sci. Com. Rsch. award, 1988, So. Sect. AFCR Young Faculty award, 1993, Novartis award for Diabetes Rsch., Am. Soc. Clin. Investigation, 2000, Mary Jane Kugel award, Juvenile Diabetes Rsch. Found. Internat., 2002, Grant W. Liddle award for clin. rsch., Vanderbilt U., 2005; grantee, NIH/Nat. Inst. Diabetes and Digestive and Kidney Diseases, 1997—, 2004—, 2004—, Dept. Veterans Affairs, 2000—, NIH/Nat. Heart, Lung and Blood Inst., 2002—, NIH/ Nat. Heart, Lung and Blood Inst., 2005—, 2006—, NIH/Nat. Ctr. for Rsch. Resources, 2002—, NIH, 2005—. Fellow: Royal Coll. Physicians; mem.: Am. Assn. Clin. Endocrinologists, Am. Physiology Soc., Endocrine Soc., Am. Soc. Clin. Investigation, So. Soc. Clin. Investigation, Juvenile Diabetes Found. Internat., Brit. Med. Assn., Am. Fedn. Clin. Rsch., Brit. Diabetes Assn., Am. Diabetes Assn. (chair hypoglycemia and clin. complications annual meeting 2005, chair hypoglycemia and complications annual meeting 1997). Office: Vanderbilt University 715 PRB 2220 Pierce Ave Nashville TN 37232-6303 Office Phone: 615-936-1649. Office Fax: 615-936-1250. Business E-Mail: steve.davis@vanderbilt.edu.

DAVIS, STEVEN A., restaurant company executive; m. Lynnda Davis; children: Brittany, Stephanie, Cassaundra. BS, Univ. Wis., Milw.; MBA, Univ. Chgo. Mgmt. positions through dir. mktg. Kraft Gen. Foods, 1984—93; mgmt. positions through sr. v.p. Pizza Hut Yum! Brands Inc., 1993—2002, pres. Long John Silver's & A&W All-Am. Food Restaurants, 2002—06; chmn., CEO Bob Evans Farms Inc., Columbus, Ohio, 2006—. Chmn. Summerbridge Louisville, 2003—; bd. mem. Turner 12, Dallas, 2000—03. Named one of 75 Most Powerful Black Men in Am. Bus., Black Enterprise mag., 2005. Office: Bob Evans Farms Inc 3776 S High St Columbus OH 43207*

DAVIS, SUANNA JEANETTE, mezzo-soprano, retired music educator; b. Conway, Ark., Jan. 22, 1938; d. Anthony William and Dolly Dimple (Evans) Flake; m. John M. Burnau (dec.); 1 child, Jennifer Suanna Burnau; m. Franklin L. Davis, June 25, 1979; 1 stepchild, Lisa Hill. BS in Music Edn. and Voice, U. Ark., 1960, MEd in Music Edn. and Voice, 1970. Cert. tchr. music K-12, elem. edn. Ark. Mezzo-soprano Ark. State Opera Co., Little Rock, 1960—62; mezzo-soprano soloist Trinity Episc. Cathedral, 1960, Temple B'nai Israel, Little Rock, 1960—62, Kansas City Lyric Theatre, 1962, Temple B'nai Israel, 1965—68, St. Mark Episc. Ch., 1960—62, Little Rock Philharmonic Orch., 1961, Kansas City Starlight Theatre, 1962—63, Unity Temple Mother Ch., Kans. City, 1962—63; mezzo-sporano soloist 1st Am. Baptist Ch., Kans. City, 1963—64; mezzo-soprano soloist Christ Episc. Ch., Little Rock, 1965—70, Springhill Ave. Temple, Mobile, Ala., 1970—72; music tchr., elem. classroom tchr. Little Rock Sch. Dist., 1967—69, 1971—97, ret., 1997; music dir., soloist, 1979—80; soloist various trips to UK and other European countries, 1980—95; soprano soloist First Presbyn. Ch., 1994—, mezzo-soprano soloist, 1994—, mem. worship com., mem. congressional care com. Condr. student nurses glee club St. Vincent's Infirmary Sch. Nursing, 1960—62; vis. instr. voice U. Ctrl. Ark., 1965—72. Soloist numerous oratorios, cantatas, recitals and motets; singer: numerous operatic roles. Corr. sec. Presbyn. Women. Grantee, Little Rock Sch. Dist., 1990; Chatham Opera scholar, Am. Fedn. Music Clubs. Mem.: AARP, Actor's Equity, Am. Guild Musical Artists, Nat. Assn. Tchrs. Singing (continuing emeritus mem.), Nat. Ret. Tchrs. Assn., Altruistic Tchrs. Soc. (historian, v.p., pres.), Alpha Delta Kappa (past pres.). Presbyterian. Avocations: gemology, etymology, travel, writing poetry. Home: 7007 Gingerbread Ln Little Rock AR 72204 Office Phone: 501-372-1804.

DAVIS, SUSAN A., congresswoman; b. Cambridge, Mass., Apr. 13, 1944; m. Steve, 1970; children: Jeffrey, Benjamin. BA in Sociology, U. Calif., Berkeley, 1965; MA in Social Work, U. N.C. Social worker; exec. dir. Aaron Price Fellowship Program, 1990-93; served Calif. State Assembly, 1994-2000; mem. U.S. Congress from 53rd Calif. dist., 2000—, Ho. Com. on Veteran Affairs. Mem. Congressional com. House Armed Svcs., Edn. and Workforce; chaired Women's Caucus for Senate and Assembly, Consumer Protection, Govt. Efficiency, Econ. Devel. com.; created and co-chaired Select com. on Adolescence. Mem. San Diego City Sch. Bd., 1983-1992, pres. and v.p.; pres. League of Women Voters San Diego., Democrat. Office: US Ho Reps 1224 Longworth House Office Bldb Washington DC 20515-0553*

DAVIS, SUSAN F., human resources specialist; BS, MS, Beloit Coll.; MBA, U. Mich. From strategic planner to corp. mgr. tng. and devel. Hoover Universal Corp., 1983-85; various positions including v.p. orgnl. devel. automotive group Johnson Controls, Inc., Milw., 1983—94, v.p. human resources, 1994—2006, exec. v.p. human resources, 2006—. Bd. dirs. Quanex Corp., Butler Mfg. Co. Mem.: HR Policy Assn. (vice chair). Office: Johnson Controls Inc 5757 N Green Bay Ave Milwaukee WI 53209-4408 Office Phone: 414-228-1200. Office Fax: 414-524-2077.*

DAVIS, SUSAN LYNN, musician, educator; b. Arcadia, Calif., May 4, 1963; d. David Russell Aronovici and Merlyn Sue Smith, Herb Moreno (Stepfather) and Kathryne DeLorme (Stepmother); m. John Edward Davis, June 10, 1990; children: Evan William, Andrew Russell. AA, Cabrillo Coll., 1983; MusB, San Francisco State U., 1986, MusM, 1990; Tchg. Certification in Music, U. Ariz., 1995. Cert. tchr. support specialist Ga. Profl. Standards Commn., 2004, music in edn. Yamaha Nat. Tchg. Inst., Mich., 1999, Orff-Schulwerk: Levels 1 & 2 U. Ariz., 1994. Music specialist Rome City Schs., Rome, Ga., 1995—; flute and saxophone instr. ABC Music Store, San Bruno, Calif.; flute instr. Rome Music Acad., 1996—2000; kindermusik instr. Berry Coll., Mt. Berry, Ga., 1996—99; flute instr. Shorter Coll. Prep. Dept., Rome, 1996—99, Tanque Verde Sch. Dist., Tucson, 1992—95; music technician Red Rock Elem. Sch., Red Rock, Ariz., 1991—94. Flutist Specifically Winds Woodwind Quintet, San Francisco, 1985—91, City Winds Woodwind Trio, San Francisco, 1985—91; prin. flutist Palo Alto Chamber Orch., 1987—91, San Francisco City Coll. Summer Opera Orch., 1987—91; flutist Twentieth-Century Forum, San Francisco, 1988—91; saxophonist San Francisco City Coll. Cmty. Jazz Band, 1988—90; prin. flutist Redwood Symphony, Redwood City, 1989—91; flutist and saxophonist So. Ariz. Light Opera Co., Tucson, 1994—95; prin. flutist Chamber Players of the South, Rome, 1996—; flutist Dogwood Chamber Ensemble, Rome, 1998—; prin. flutist Catalina Chamber Orch., Tucson, 1991—95; flutist Davis/Harding Flute and Guitar Duo, Tucson, 1991—95; prin. flutist Master's Sinfonia Orch., Belmont, Calif., 1991; flutist Davis/Huckabee Flute and Guitar Duo, Rome, 1996—99; saxophonist Clocktower Jazz Ensemble, Rome, 1996—; prin.

flutist Rome Symphony Orch., Rome, 1999—. Musician: (flutist) Nat. Flute Assn. Conv. Profl.l Flute Choir, (flute soloist) Miss Calif. State Pageant Contestant (First Pl. Talent award, 1982), (saxophonist) Aptos HS Jazz Band (European Jazz Festival Concert Tour, 1981), (flutist) Santa Cruz County Symphony Talent Bank (First Pl. Flute and Chamber Ensemble Winner, 1983). Flutist/chorus dir. Floyd Med. Ctr. Arts Program, Rome, 2003—; vol. (music & charities) Westminster Presbyn. Ch., Rome, 1997—2005; bd. dir. Rome/Floyd (Ga.) Humane Soc., 2000—; sch. improvement com. West Ctrl. Elem. Sch., Rome, 1997—2005; profl. devel. steering com. mem. Berry Coll./West Ctrl. Elem., Rome, 2002—05; tchr. mentor Berry Coll. Sch. of Edn., Ga., 2002—05. Recipient Tchr. of Year, West Ctrl. Elem., 2004—05. Mem.: Nat. Flute Assn. (assoc.), Ga. Music Educator's Assn. (assoc.), Music Educator's Nat. Conf. (assoc.), PA of Ga. Educators (assoc.). Democrat. Presbyterian. Avocations: travel, tennis, reading, movies, animals. Home: 121 E Clinton Dr Rome GA 30165 Office: West Central Elem Sch 409 Lavender Dr Rome GA 30165 Home Phone: 706-234-4605. Office Fax: 706-234-5854. Business E-Mail: susdavis@rcs.rome.ga.us.

DAVIS, SUSAN RAE, lawyer; b. Salem, Oreg., July 15, 1948; d. William Ray and Pearl E. (Lundin) Catlin; m. Donald K. Davis, June 13, 1970. BA, U. Wash., 1969, JD, 1977. Bar: Wash. 1977, U.S. Dist. Ct. (we. dist.) Wash. 1977, U.S. Ct. Appeals (9th cir.) 1977, U.S. Dist. Ct. (ea. dist.) Wash. 1989. Writer, editor AP, Seattle, 1969—70; news dir. Sta. KUUU, Seattle, 1970-71; reporter, photographer Sta. KXLY-TV, Spokane, Wash., 1971-73, Sta. KHQ-TV, Spokane, 1973-74; ptnr. Burns, Schneiderman, Davis & Finkle P.S., Seattle, 1977-86, The Davis Firm, Seattle, 1987—2005, mediator, arbitrator, 2005—; writer, editor Wash. Law & Politics Super Lawyer, 2001—03. Instr. journalism Eastern Wash. State Coll., Spokane, 1973-74. Mem. tribunal Wash. State Human Rights Commn., Seattle, 1974-79; arbitrator King County Mandatory Arbitration Panel, Seattle, 1985-2005; bd. visitors U. Puget Sound, 1986-87. Mem. ATLA, Settlement Now (mediator 1988-97), Am. Bd. Trial Advs., Trial Lawyers for Pub. Justice, Wash. State Bar Assn., Wash. State Trial Lawyers Assn. (leadership award 1984, bd. dirs. 1980-82, treas. 1982-83, v.p. west 1983-84, v.p. pub. affairs 1984-85, pres. elect 1985-86, pres. 1986-87). Democrat. Avocation: photography. Home: PO Box 31239 Seattle WA 98103-1239 Office Phone: 206-789-1056. Personal E-mail: susandavis@seanet.com.

DAVIS, TERRY HUNTER, JR., lawyer; b. Charlottesville, Va., Mar. 19, 1931; s. Terry Hunter and Mattie May (Parsons) D.; m. Mary Jane Irwin, Sept. 3, 1960 (dec. Nov. 2004); 1 child, Terry Hunter III; m. Betty Rachel Logon Cloud, Oct. 29, 2005. BA, Va. Mil. Inst., 1953; LLB, U. Va., 1958. Bar: Va. 1958, NY 1959, NC 1999. Assoc. Thacher, Proffitt, Prizer, NYC, 1958-60; law clk. Chief U.S. Dist. Judge, Norfolk, Va., 1960-61; assoc., ptnr. Taylor, Gustin, Harris, Norfolk, 1961—64; ptnr. Harris, Fears, Davis, Lynch & McDaniel, Norfolk, 1964—2006; pvt. practice Norfolk, 2006—. Instr. ins. law. Contbg. author Virginia Lawyer's Basic Practice Handbook, 1964, Federal Special Master, 1964. Chmn. Norfolk Electoral Bd., 1971-72; candidate Va. State Ho. Reps., 1967, 69, 82. 1st lt. U.S. Army, 1953-55. Mem. ABA, Va. Bar Assn., Va. State Bar (com. mem. 1972-73), Norfolk/Portsmouth Bar (com. chmn. 1962-63), SAR (treas. 1962-64), Jamestown Soc., Kiwanis. Republican. Episcopalian. Avocations: jogging, tennis. Home: 7451 North Shore Rd Norfolk VA 23505-1770 Office: 215 East City Hall Ave Norfolk VA 23510 Office Phone: 757-477-3191. Personal E-mail: Tdavis5735@aol.com.

DAVIS, THOMAS M., III, congressman; b. Minot, ND, Jan. 5, 1949; m. Peggy Davis; 3 children. BA in Polit. Sci., Amherst Coll., 1971; JD, U. Va., 1975. Legis. asst. Va. State Ho. Dels., 1964-67; lawyer pvt. practice, 1975-79; v.p., gen. counsel Advanced Techs., 1979-90; mem. bd. suprs. Mason Dist., Fairfax, Va., 1980—94, chair bd. suprs. Fairfax County, Va., 1992—94; v.p., gen. counsel then corp. counsel and chair PRC, Inc., McLean, Va., 1990-94; mem. US Congress from 11th Va. dist., 1995—, chmn. govt. reform com., mem. homeland security com., chmn. Nat. Rep. Congl. Com., 1998—2002. Mem. adv. bd. Afghanistan-Am. Found.; bd. dirs. Boys and Girls Club, Partnership for Pub. Svc.; mem. adv. bd. Women in Govt. Rels. Leader; chair adv. bd. Va. Legal Svcs.; mem. Fairfax County, Va. Tenant-Landlord Assn., Nat. Capitol Planning Commn., No. Va. Transp. Commn., Va. Assn. Cities, Gen. Govt. Steering Com.; chair Effective Govtl. Policy Com. Va. Mcpl. League; pres. Washington Met. Coun. Govts. Served in US Army, 1971, 1st lt. USAR, served in Va. N.G. Named to Am. Electronics Assn. High Tech Hall of Fame, 2000; recipient Congl. Tech. Policy award, Electronic Industry Alliance, 1999, Friend of the Shareholder award, Am. Shareholders Assn., 2002, Guardian of Small Bus. award, Nat. Fedn. of Ind. Bus., 2002, Hero of Taxpayer award, Ams. for Tax Reform, 2002, Jefferson award, Citizens for a Sound Economy, 2002, RSA Conf. award for Pub. Policy, RSA Security, 2002, Sr. Guardian Medal of Honor, Seniors Coalition, 2002, Tech. Champion award, Nat. Assn. State Chief Info. Officers, 2003, Azimuth award, Chief Info. Officers Coun., 2004. Mem.: Baileys Crossroads Rotary Club (charter mem., past pres.). Republican. Office: US Ho Reps 2348 Rayburn Ho Office Bldg Washington DC 20515-4611 Office Phone: 202-225-1492.*

DAVIS, TOM, biology professor; b. Grand Island, Nebr., Feb. 8, 1947; s. Elvin Charles and Lillian Mae Davis. BSEE, U. Minn., Mpls., 1969; MS, U. Minn., Duluth, 1979. Biomedical rsch. engr. Medtronic, Inc., Mpls., 1969—73; rsch. fellow U. Minn., Duluth, 1976—79; wildlife biologist US Fish and Wildlife, Patuxent, Md., 1986—88; adj. prof. Santa Fe C.C., 1991—97, asst. prof., 2002—; mgr. Outback Tours, Santa Fe, 1997—2001. Avocations: volleyball, singing, photography. Office: Santa Fe CC 6401 Richards Ave Santa Fe NM 87508 Office Phone: 505-428-1757. Business E-Mail: tdavis@sfccnm.edu.

DAVIS, TRAYTON M., lawyer; b. Milwaukee, Wis., 1955; BA, Haverford Coll., 1977; JD, NYU, 1980. Bar: N.Y. 1981. Ptnr. & co-chmn. Global Fin. Group Milbank Tweed Hadley & McCloy, NYC, 1993—. Mem.: ABA (Bus. & Internat. Law sect.), Am. Coll. Investment Counsel. Office: Milbank Tweed Hadley & McCloy 1 Chase Manhattan Plz New York NY 10005-1413 Office Phone: 212-530-5349. Office Fax: 212-530-5219. Business E-Mail: tdavis@milbank.com.

DAVIS, VERNON THOMAS, military officer, researcher; b. Bremerton, Wash., Jan. 19, 1960; married. BS, US Mil. Acad., West Point, NY, 1981; MS in Physics, MIT, Cambridge, 1991; PhD in Physics, Am. U., Washington, 2002; MS in Strategic Studies, U.S. Army War Coll., Carlisle, Pa., 2005. Ops. and tng. officer Multi-National Forces, Haiti, Port-au-Prince, Haiti, 1994—95; arty. bn. ops. officer 25th Inf. Divsn. (Light), Schofield Barracks, Hawaii, 1995—96, arty. bn. exec. officer, 1996—97; instr., asst. prof. physics U.S. Mil. Acad., West Point, NY, 1991—94, dir., photonics rsch. ctr., 2003—05; ops. and tng. officer Office of Mil. Cooperation-Afghanistan, Kabul, Afghanistan, 2004—05; chief, test divsn. detachment 2 Def. Threat Reduction Agy., Dugway, Utah, 2005—. Col. US Army, 1977—2006. Decorated Meritorious Svc. medal US Army, Humanitarian Svc. medal, Armed Forces Expeditionary medal, Global War on Terror Expeditionary medal. Mem.: US Army Field Artillery Assn. (life), Phi Kappa Phi, Sigma Pi Sigma. Home: 25 Officer's Cir Tooele UT 84074 Office: DTRA Test Divsn Detachment 2 Bldg R0423B 3rd St Ditto Area Dugway UT 84022-5000 Home Phone: 435-843-0120; Office Phone: 435-831-7255. Office Fax: 435-831-7252. Business E-Mail: davisv@dpg.army.mil.

DAVIS, W. JEREMY, retired lawyer, dean; b. Pitts., Apr. 13, 1942; s. Winthrop Neuffer and Eleanor (Power) D.; m. Jacqueline Dvoracek, June 11, 1966; children: Jeremy Michael, Sarah Elizabeth. BSBA, U. Denver, 1964, JD, 1970; LLM, Yale U., 1980. Bar: Colo. 1970, N.D. 1973. Pvt. practice law, Denver, 1970-71; asst. prof. U. N.D., Grand Forks, 1971-74, assoc. prof., 1975-82, dean, prof. law, 1983—2002, gen. counsel, 1993-2000, dir. legal affairs, 2000—02; dean, Sutin prof. law Appalachian Sch. Law, 2003—05, v.p., 2005—06; ret., 2006. With U.S. Army, 1965-68. Fellow Bush Found., 1979-80. Mem. State Bar Assn. N.D. (bd. govs. 1982-2002), N.D. Trial Lawyers Assn. (bd. govs. 1986-2002), Va. State Bar Assn. (assoc.). Home: 1622 Earl Cir Grand Forks ND 58201 Home Phone: 701-775-8807. Personal E-mail: wjeremy.davis@gmail.com.

DAVIS, WAYNE ALTON, computer science educator; b. Ft. Macleod, Alta., Can., Nov. 16, 1931; s. Frederick and Anna Mary (Barr) D.; m. Audrey M. Zorolow, July 17, 1959 (div. 1989); children: Fredrick M., Peter W., Timothy M.; m. Patricia Ruth Syme, Mar. 24, 1990. BSE, George Washington U., 1960; MSc, U. Ottawa, 1963, PhD, 1967. Sci. officer Def. Resch. Bd., Ottawa, Ont., 1960-68; research scientist Dept. Comms., Ottawa, 1968-69; vis. scientist NRC, Ottawa, 1975-76; assoc. prof. U. Alta., Edmonton, 1969-77, prof. computing sci., 1977-91, prof. emeritus, 1991—, acting chmn. computing sci., 1982-83; acting dir. Alta. Centre for Machine Intelligence and Robotics, 1988-89. Lectr. U. Ottawa, 1965-69; sessional lectr. Carleton U., 1967; cons. Editor: The Barrs of Ardenville, 1978; editor Procs. Graphics Interface, 1994, 95, 96, 97, 98. Grantee NRC, 1970-78; rsch. grantee Natural Scis. and Engring. Rsch. Coun., 1978-92; strategic grantee Natural Scis. and Engring. Rsch. Coun., 1981-83; grantee Def. Rsch. Bd., 1974-76; hon. prof. Harbin Shipbldg. Engring. Inst., China, 1985. Mem. Can. Info. Processing Soc. (pres. 1978-79), Can. Human Computer Comms. Soc. (pres. 1981-96), Can. Soc. Computational Study of Intelligence (treas. 1976-86), Faculty Club. Anglican. Home: Box 817 605-21st St Fort Macleod AB Canada T0L 0Z0 Office: U Alta Dept Computing Sci Edmonton AB Canada T6G 2E8 E-mail: davis@cs.ualberta.ca.

DAVIS, WAYNE PITMAN, public relations executive; b. Phillipsburg, Mo., Sept. 9, 1920; s. William Riley and Alice (Pitman) D.; m. Jeanne Frances West, May 28, 1944 (dec. June 1975); children: Kenneth Wayne, Polly Jeanne Davis Montgomery (dec.); m. Ferne Gater Bonomi, Apr. 20, 1991. BA, The Principia Coll., 1939; B of Journalism, U. Mo., 1941; MS, Iowa State U., 1988. Publisher The Moravia (Iowa) Union, 1942-45; mgr. The Mille Lacs Messenger, Isle, Minn., 1946-47; publisher The Seymour (Iowa) Herald, 1947-77; dir. mktg., pub. rels. and sales Iowa State Ctr., Ames, 1977-87; instr. Iowa State U., Ames, 1988-98. Chmn. Bd. Mcpl. Utilities, Seymour, 1969-75; pres. Genoa & Seymour Farmers Mutual Telephone Co., 1954-61; dir., v.p. Ctrl. Iowa Symphony Bd., Ames, 1989-99. 2d lt. U.S. Army, 1945-46, col. USAR, 46-76. Decorated Meritorious Svc. medal; recipient James W. Schwartz Dist. Svc. to Journalism award Greenlee Sch. Journalism and Comm., Iowa State U., 2005. Mem. Pub. Rels Soc. Am. (accredited, sec. ctrl. Iowa chpt. 1980-8, bd. dirs. 1982-85, newsletter editor 1980-82, 1999-2005), Iowa Newspaper Assn. (Iowa master editor-pub. 1971, Disting. Svc. award 2007), Iowa Newspaper Found. (bd. dirs. 1989-93, pres. 1992), Res. Officers Assn., Soc. Profl. Journalists, Am. Legion, Lions (Seymour 1954-77). Avocation: travel. Home: 1003 Kennedy St Ames IA 50010-4247 Business E-Mail: wdavis@iastate.edu.

DAVIS, WENDELL, JR., lawyer; b. NYC, June 22, 1933; m. Penelope Case, May 17, 1969; children: Jennifer C., Virginia W. Hartung, Peter T. AB cum laude, Harvard U., 1954, LL.B. cum laude, 1961. Bar: Conn. 1961, NY 1963, US Dist. Ct. (so. and ea. dist.) NY 1964, US Dist. Ct. Conn. 1966, US Ct. Appeals (2d cir.) 1966, US Ct. Appeals (5th cir.) 1972, US Supreme Ct. 1973. Law sec. to Justice Charles D. Breitel, NYC, 1964-65; ptnr. Scheuermann & Davis and predecessor firms, NYC, 1975-78, 92-00, Emmet, Marvin & Martin, NYC, 1978-91. Pres. Carnegie Hill-90th St. Inc., 1977-80 Bd. dirs. United Way Larchmont, 1984-91. Lt. USNR, 1957. Mem. Am. Law Inst., Harvard Club, Sawgrass Country Club. Home: 35 Village Walk Dr Ponte Vedra Beach FL 32082

DAVIS, WILLIAM ALBERT, parks director; b. New Haven, Sept. 10, 1946; s. Arthur Wilson Davis and Dorothy May (Hellyer) Jordan; m. Rebecca Marsden Haile, Apr. 8, 1965; children: William Albert Jr., Anna Catherine. BA in Profl. Arts, Brooks Inst. Photography, 1971; BSBA, San Diego State U., 1980. Photographer, owner Davis-Hixon Photography, Santa Ana, Calif., 1971-73; photographer Sea World, Inc., San Diego, 1973, sales rep., 1974-76, sales mgr., 1976-78, mktg. mgr. fast food subs., 1978-80, corp. planning assoc., 1980-81; dir. mktg. Sea World Ohio, Aurora, 1981-85, v.p. mktg., 1985-86, pres., 1986-88, Sea World Fla., Orlando, 1988-97; exec. v.p., gen. mgr. Sea World of Calif., 1997-2001; corp. v.p. guest svcs. Busch Entertainment Corp., St. Louis, 2001—03; mng. dir. Universal Mediterranea, Tarragona, Spain, 2003—04; v.p., gen. mgr. Six Flags Marine World, Vallejo, Calif., 2005—; pres., COO, Universal Orlando Resort, 2006—. Bd. dirs. Hubbs-Sea World Rsch. Inst., San Diego, Marine Rsch. Ctr., Sea World, Orlando, Calif. Travel and Tourism Commn. Bd. dirs., exec. com. Conv. and Visitors Bur. Orange County, Orlando, 1988-97, pres.-elect, 1990, pres., 1991, chmn., 1992-93; mem. bd. Efficient Transp. for Community Orlando, 1988-97; mem. adv. coun. Dick Pope Sr. Inst. Tourism Studies, Orlando, 1989-97; commr. Fla. Tourism Commn., 1991—; trustee United Arts of Ctrl. Fla., 1992—; mem. U. Ctrl. Fla. Found., 1994-97; mem. White House Com. on Tourism, 1995, mem. exec. com. San Diego Conv. and Visitors Bur., 1997—, Super Bowl XXXII Host com. Staff sgt. USAF, 1965-69, Vietnam. Fellow Am. Assn. Zool. Parks and Aquariums; mem. San Diego C. of C. Roundtable, Brooks Inst. Alumni Assn., Kiwanis (bd. dirs. Aurora club 1985-87, 1st v.p. 1987—) Avocations: golf, photography. Home: 210 Acadia Terr Celebration FL 34747-5004 Office: Six Flags Marine World 2001 Marine World Vallejo CA 94589 Office Phone: 407-224-6944. Business E-Mail: badavis@sftp.com. E-mail: bill.davis@universalorlando.com.

DAVIS, WILLIAM ALLISON, II, retired lawyer; b. High Point, NC, May 2, 1942; s. Robert Dorsey and Frances Elizabeth (Taylor) D.; m. Elizabeth Gray Heefner, June 18, 1966; children: Sarah Scott, Elizabeth Taylor. AB in Econs., U. N.C., 1964; LLB, Duke U., 1967; LLM in Taxation, NYU, 1968; student, NC State U. Sch. Design, 2004—. Bar: N.C. 1967. Assoc. Womble Carlyle Sandridge & Rice, Winston-Salem, NC, 1968-72, ptnr., 1972—2005. Trustee NC Sch. Arts, Winston-Salem, vice chmn., 1990, chmn., 1992—96, NC Film Coun., 1994—96, Winston-Salem Piedmont Triad Film Commn., 1993—96; trustee The Penland (NC) Sch., 1998—2005, vice chmn., 2000, chmn., 2001—02; trustee Winston Sch. State Univ. Found., 2001—04, NC Audubon, 2003—. Democrat. Avocations: hiking, skiing, travel, fishing.

DAVIS, WILLIAM C., JR., judge; b. Knoxville, Tenn., Jan. 27, 1948; s. William C. and Burla A. (Monger) D.; m. Elaine Elizabeth Quinn, Sept. 18, 1971; children: Jeff, Tim, Ruth, Mike. BS in Chemistry, U. Ill., 1970, JD, 1974. Atty. pvt. practice, Lewistown, Ill., 1975—2006; judge 9th Jud. Cir. Ill., Lewiston, 2006. Dir., Lewistown High Sch. Acad. Found., 1990—. Mem. Toastmasters.

DAVIS, WILLIAM E., lawyer; b. Northampton County, NC, Mar. 3, 1943; AB, Univ. N.C., 1965; JD, William and Mary, 1968. Bar: US Dist. Ct. (Dist. DC) 1971, DC Ct. Appeals 1974, Md. Ct. Appeals 1984, US Supreme Ct. 1974. Mem. Ross, Marsh & Foster, Washington. Adj. prof., trust and estates George Washington Law Sch., Washington; dir. Coun. for Ct. Excellence. Mem.: DC Bar Assn., Md. State Bar Assn., Am. Bar Assn., NC State Bar, George Washington Am. Inn of Ct. (membership chair), DC Superior Ct. Adv. Com. on Probate and Fiduciary Rules, Bar Assn. DC (pres. 2004, sec.), Phi Delta Phi. Office: Ross Marsh & Foster Ste 400 2001 L St NW Washington DC 20036 Office Phone: 202-822-8888. Office Fax: 202-775-9330. Business E-Mail: wdavis@rossmarshfoster.com.*

DAVIS, WILLIAM EUGENE, federal judge; b. Winfield, Ala., Aug. 18, 1936; s. A. L. and Addie Lee (Lenahan) Davis; m. Celia Chalaron, Oct. 3, 1963. JD, Tulane U., 1960; BS, Samford U., 2006. Bar: La. 1960. Assoc. Phelps Dunbar Marks Claverie & Sims, New Orleans, 1960—64; ptnr. Caffery Duhe & Davis, New Iberia, La., 1964—76; judge US Dist. Ct., Lafayette, La., 1976—83, US Ct. Appeals (5th cir.), Lafayette, 1983—. Recipient Order of the Coif. Mem.: ABA, Maritime Assn. US, La. Bar Assn. Republican. Office: US Ct Appeals 800 Lafayette St Ste 5100 Lafayette LA 70501-6883 Office Phone: 337-593-5280.*

DAVIS, WILLIAM HOWARD, lawyer; b. Monmouth, Ill., May 24, 1951; s. Orville Francis and Alice Gertrude (Hennenfent) D.; m. Susan Claire Parris, April 11, 1981; children: Benjamin Patrick, Jackson Mitchell, Claire Marie. BA with honors, U. South Fla., 1974; JD with high honors, Fla. State U., 1977. Bar: Fla. 1977, U.S. Dist. Ct. (no. dist.) Fla. 1977, U.S. Dist. Ct. (mid. dist.) Fla. 1986, U.S. Ct. Appeals (11th cir.) 1986, U.S. Supreme Ct. 1996. Assoc. Thompson, Wadsworth, Messer & Rhodes, Tallahassee, 1977-80; ptnr. Wadsworth & Davis, P.A., Tallahassee, 1980—2002; of counsel Messer, Caparello and Davis PA, Tallahassee, 2003—05; ptnr. Dobson, Davis & Smith, 2006—. Instr. legal writing Fla. State U., 1976-77; emeritus mem., ex officio Fla. Supreme Ct. Commn. Professionalism, 2002—; trustee Fla. Supreme Ct. Hist. Soc., 2006-. Editor: (notes and comments) Fla. State U. Law Rev., 1976-77. Bd. dirs. Legal Aid Found., Inc., 1980-81, Fla. Legal Svcs., Inc., 1988-96, pres., 1993; pres. student govt., chmn., state coun. student body pres. State U. Sys. Fla., 1973-74. Mem. ABA, Acad. Fla. Trial Lawyers, Nat. Assn. Criminal Def. Lawyers, Fla. Bar (2d cir. judge nominations commn. 1986-90, chmn. 2d cir. jud. grievance com. 1988-90), Fla. Bar Found. (bd. dirs. 1993-94, 97—, sec.-treas. 2002-04, pres 2005-06, chmn., trustee endowment trust 2006—, chmn. legal assistance to poor grant com. 1993-04, exec. com. 2000-06), Tallahassee Bar Assn. (bd. dirs. 1982-88, 2006-07, pres. 1986-87), Fla. Supreme Ct. Hist. Soc. (trustee 2006—), Fla. Assn. Criminal Def. Lawyers, Am. Inns of Ct. (master of bench emeritus, exec. com. Tallahassee 1994-96), Coalition for Juvenile Justice, Am. Judicature Soc., Cath. Charities (bd. dirs. Tallahassee region 1995-2002, pres. 1999-2001), Leadership Tallahassee, Gulf Winds Track Club, Capital Tiger Bay Club, Omicron Delta Kappa, Phi Sigma Alpha. Office: 610 N Duval St Tallahassee FL 32301 Home: PO Box 38309 Tallahassee FL 32315-8309 Business E-Mail: billdavislaw@gmail.com.

DAVIS, WILLIAM MAXIE, JR., lawyer; b. Elizabethtown, NC, June 7, 1932; s. Willie Maxie and Lucy Victoria (Dowless) D.; m. Shirley Jane Smith, Mar. 24, 1987. B. in Gen. Edn., U. Nebr., 1965; MA, U. So. Calif., 1970; JD, NC Ctrl. U., 1986. Bar: NC 1986, US Dist. Ct. (we., ea. and mid. dists.) NC, US Ct. Appeals (4th cir.), US Supreme Ct. 1989; cert. criminal trial advocacy Nat. Bd. Trial Advocacy, 1993. Enlisted USAF, 1950, commd. 2d lt., 1958, chief systems implementations br. (OIC ICBM telemetry program) Hdqrs. SAC, 1971-73, chief career devel. and assignments specialized officers, 1973-75, advanced through grades to lt. col, 1974, ret., 1975; chief sys. analysis br. DCA, Vietnam, 1966—67; dir. plans, programs UK Comm. Region, Eng., 1967-71; asst. county mgr., personnel officer, dir. of planning, dir. of emergency mgmt. Bladen County, Elizabethtown, 1977—83; asst. pub. defender NC 26th Jud. Dist., Charlotte, 1986—2006. Pres. Help Every Loving Parent, 1988-2006; county dir. Boy Scouts Am., Bladen County, NC, 1976-80; pres. bd. dirs. Vistana SPA Condo Homeowners Assn., 1992—2005. Recipient Spl. award NC Dist. Atty. & Pub. Defender, Order of Long Leaf Pine (with rank of amb. extraodinaire) Gov. NC, 2006; profiled in Champion mag., Nat. Assn. Criminal Def. Lawyers, 1992, Testimony mag., Internat. Fellowship Christian Businessmen, 1993, Charlotte Observer. Mem. NC Bar, NC Acad. Trial Lawyers, Elizabethtown-White Lake C. of C. (bd. dirs. 1975-77), Nat. Bd. Trial Advocacy, Am. Legion (life), VFW (life), DAV (life). Home and Office: PO Box 1085 Clinton NC 28329 Office Phone: 910-592-4549. Office Fax: 910-592-4549. Business E-Mail: billdavislaw@aol.com.

DAVIS, WYNNDI P., elementary school educator; d. William Prince and Wardie Jones; m. Patrick Davis, May 4, 1992. Ed.S Specialist's in Ednl. - Adminstrn., The U. of So. Miss., Gulfport, MS, 2004; EdS in Elem. Edn., William Carey Coll., Hattiesburg, Miss., 2005; MBA, William Carey Coll., Gulfport, Miss., 2005, MEd in Elem. Edn., 2005, B in Gen. Studies, 2005. Lic. profl. educator Miss., 2001. Tchr. Twenty-Eighth St. Elem. Sch., Gulfport, 2001—06; curriculum specialist Ctrl. Elem., Gulfport, 2006—. Mem.: Miss. Profl. Educators (assoc.). Office: Gulfport Sch Dist Ctrl Elem 1043 Pass Rd Gulfport MS 39501 Home Phone: 228-214-0167; Office Phone: 228-865-4642. Office Fax: 228-865-0281. Business E-Mail: wynndi.davis@gulfportschools.org.

DAVIS-FERNANDES, TINA DENISE, secondary school educator, coach; b. LA, Dec. 10, 1967; d. Lenious Samuel Davis and Martha Lee Callegari-Davis; m. Sean Anthony Fernandes, June 29, 1991; children: Anthony Fernandes, Denise Fernandes. MEd, Argosy U., Orange, 2005. Coach girls head track & field Compton Unified Sch. Dist., Calif., 1991—95; tchr. spl. ecdn. ECKO-Multi-Center, 1992—95; tchr. Lynwood Unified Sch. Dist., 1995—; coach track & field U. So. Calif., LA, 1999—. Recipient West Regional Asst. Coach Yr. Sprints/Hurdles, NCAA, 2005. Mem.: Women's Track & Field, AAHPERD (none), USA Track & Field (none). Achievements include Coached over 20 All-American Titles for USC; Assisted USC Track & Field Team to the First National Title in 2001. Office: USC / Lynwood Unified School District 3501 Watt Way Los Angeles CA 90089 Home Phone: 213-725-3534; Office Phone: 213-821-2170. Office Fax: 213-740-7289; Home Fax: 213-740-7289. Personal E-mail: davisfer@usc.edu.

DAVIS-JEROME, EILEEN GEORGE, educational consultant, principal; b. NYC, Nov. 10, 1946; d. Rennie and Flora May (Compton) George; m. Bruce Davis, Aug. 8, 1970 (div. 1978); m. Frantz Jerome, Sept. 7, 1982; 1 child, Thais Davis BFA, Pratt Inst., Bklyn., 1968; MA, CUNY, 1971, PD, 1990; EdD, Nova Southeastern U., Ft. Lauderdale, Fla., 1998. Lic. ednl. adminstr., prin., instrn. specialist, N.Y. Tchr. fine arts Herbert Lehman H.S., Bronx, NY, 1971—75; tchr. English, fine arts Jr. H.S. 131, Bronx, 1975—76; tchr. English Jr. H.S. 22, Bronx, 1976—79; admissions counselor Fashion Inst. Tech., SUNY, 1983—85; tchr. fine arts Andrew Jackson H.S., Cambria Heights, NY, 1979—83, coord. art dept., 1986—92; project dir. Andrew Jackson Magnet H.S., Cambria Heights, 1993—, prin. Humanities and Arts, 1994—2003, project dir. Humanities and Arts, 1994—; coord. Queensborough Coll. Project Prize, Bayside, NY, 1991—92; ednl. adminstr. Queens H.S. Office, N.Y.C. Pub. H.S., Corona, NY, 1993—94. Coord. internat. studies Friends Jackson H.S., Cambria Heights, 1986-93, equal opportunity coord., 1989-92; exam asst. N.Y.C. Bd. Edn., Bd. Examiners, Bklyn., 1983-87; curriculum/career cons. Fashion Inst., SUNY, Detroit, Washington, Phila., 1983-86 Curriculum writer N.Y. State Project Implement Career Edn., 1975, N.Y. State Futuring, 1984; proposal writer Magnet Sch. Funding, 1993; author: Resource Book, 1989 Mem., spkr. Cambria Heights Civic Assn., 1983; mem. N.Y. Urban League, N.Y.C.; vol. Mayor's Vol. Action/Alpha Sr. Cr., Cambria Heights, 1984; vol. Black Spectrum Theatre Co., 1983-86; mem. coord. coun. h.s. divsn. N.Y.C. Bd. Edn., 1997—; v.p. for edn. Madam C.J. Walker Found., 2001— Named Educator of Yr., NAACP/ACT-S0, N.Y.C., 1992; recipient Recognition award, Black Spectrum Theatre Co., 1983, Spkrs. award, N.Y.C. Bd. Edn. Open Doors, 1983—84, Black Exec. Exch. Program Nat. Urban League, N.Y.C., 1984, Developer Grant award, Impact II Grant, N.Y.C., 1989, Laurelton Club Prol. award, 1996, Disting. Educator award, L.I. br. Nat. Assn. U. Women, 2001, Life Membership award, NAACP, N.Y.C., 2001, Excellence in Edn. award, Omega Psi Phi, 2002, Disting. Educator award, Newsday, 2003, Outstanding Citizen citation, N.Y.C. Coun., 2003, Performace award, N.Y.C. Dept. Edn., N.Y.C. Coun. Suprs. and Adminstrs, 2002—03. Mem. ASCD, UN Assn., N.Y. State Art Tchrs. Assn., N.Y.C. Art Tchrs. Assn. (v.p., sec. 1983-85, cert. 1983-86), Cultural Heritage Alliance (assoc., Recognition award 1986), Greater Queens Chpt. The Links, Inc., Delta Sigma Theta (chair arts and letters 1991-97, Golden Life award 1991), Phi Delta Kappa (Disting. cert. 1994) Democrat. Episcopalian. Avocations: painting, travel, dance, writing, theater. Office: Magnet HS Humanities and the Arts 20701 116th Ave Jamaica NY 11411-1038

DAVIS-LEWIS, BETTYE, nursing educator; b. Egypt, Tex., Sept. 19, 1939; d. Henry Sr. and Eliza (Baylock) Davis; divorced; children: Kim Michelle, Roderick Trevor. BS, Prarie View A&M U., 1959; BA in Psychology, U. Houston, 1972; MEd, Tex. Southern U., 1974, EdD, 1982. Dir. edn. Houston Internat. Hosp., 1987—; dir. nurses Mental Health & Mental Retardation Auth. Harris County, Houston, 1982-87, Riverside Gen. Hosp., Houston; CEO, owner Diversified Health Care Systems, Inc., Houston, 1985—; asst. clin. prof. psychiat. nursing U. Tex., 1987-88; asst. prof. allied health sci. Tex. So. U., Houton, 1989—. Adj. prof. Coll. Nursing, Prairie View A&M U., 1986—; lectr. in field; leadership extern. Mem. Harris County Coun. Orgns., 1987—; mem. polit. action com. Coalition 100 Black Women, 1988—; founder, mem. Hattie White Aux. br. NAACP, 1988; mem. grievance com. State Bar Tex., 1988—; chmn. S.W. Regional Nat. Black Leadership Initiative on Cancer, 1988—; grad. Leadership Tex.; bd. dirs. Theatre Under the Stars. Recipient Disting. Rsch. award Internat. Soc. Hypertension, Disting. Crystal award, Impact award Wheeler Ave. Bapt. Ch.; fellow Internat. Leadership Forum, Am. Leadership Forum; named one of Most Influential Black Americans, Ebony mag., 2005, 06. Fellow Internat. Soc. Hypertension in Blacks; mem. ANA, Nat. Black Nurses Assn. (past mem. bd. dirs., pres.), Sigma Theta Tau, Chi Eta Phi. Office: Diversified Health Care Sys Inc #2 4811 Jackson Houston TX 77004 also: Nat Black Nurses Assn 8630 Fenton St, Ste 330 Silver Spring MD 20910-3803

DAVISON, BRUCE, actor; b. Phila., June 28, 1946; s. Marian E. and Clair W. D.; m. Jess Walton, May 20, 1972 (annulled); m. Lisa Pelikan, 1986 (div.); 1 child; m. Michele Correy, Apr. 30, 2006; 1 child. BFA, Pa. State U., NYU. Stage appearances include Oh Dad, Poor Dad, Mama's Locked You in the Closet and I'm Feelin' So Bad, 1966; Broadway debut Tiger at the Gate, 1967, King Lear, 1968, A Home Away From Home, 1969, Streamers, L.A., 1978, A Life in the Theatre, 1980, The Elephant Man, 1980, Sorrows of Stephen, 1981, The Front Page, 1982, Richard III, 1984, The Glass Menagerie, 1984, Caine Mutiny Court Martial, 1984, The Normal Heart, 1986, The Cocktail Hour, 1989-90; TV appearances (series) Hunter, 1984-86, Harry and the Hendersons, 1991-92, Close to Home, 2005-; (TV films) Deadman's Curve, 1978, Summer of My German Soldier, 1979, The Lathe of Heaven, 1980, Mind Over Murder, 1980, Tomorrows Child, 1982, The Gathering, 1982, Incident at Crestridge, 1982, Ghost Dancing, 1983, Poor Little Rich Girl: The Barbara Hutton Story, 1987, Lady in a Corner, 1989, Stolen: One Husband, 1990, Live! From Death Row, 1992, Down Out and Dangerous, 1995, Hidden in America, 1996, After Jimmy, 1996, Color of Justice, 1997, Little Girl Fly Away, 1998, A Memory in my Heart, 1999, Locked in Silence, 1999; film appearances Last Summer, 1969, Strawberry Statement, 1970, Willard, 1971, Jerusalem File, 1972, Peege, 1972, Ulzana's Raid, 1973, Mame, 1974, Mother, Jugs and Speed, 1975, Short Eyes, 1978, Brass Target, 1978, High Risk, 1981, A Texas Legend, 1982, Lies, 1983, Crimes of Passion, 1984, Spies Like Us, 1985, The Ladies Club, 1986, Misfit Brigade, 1988, Longtime Companion, 1990, Steel and Lace, 1990, Short Cuts, 1993, 6 Degrees of Separation, 1993, Homage, 1994, Farm From Home: The Adventures of Yellow Dog, 1995, The Skateboard Kid II, 1995, The Cure, 1995, the Baby-Sitters Club, 1995, Grace of My Heart, 1996, The Crucible, 1996, Lovelife, 1997, Apt pupil, 1998, Paulie, 1998, Vendetta, 1999, Summer Catch, 2000, The King is Alive, 2000, X-Men, 2000, Crazy/Beautiful, 2001, Summer Catch, 2001, High Crimes, 2002, Dahmer, 2002, Manfest, 2002, X2, 2003, Runaway Jury, 2003, Rules of the Game, 2003, Evergreen, 2004, On the Couch, 2004, Hate, Crime, 2005, Confession, 2005, Going Shopping, 2005, Touched, 2005, The Dead Girl, 2006, Breach, 2007. Office: William Morris Agy care Brian Dubin 1325 Avenue Of The Americas New York NY 10019-6026*

DAVISON, CALVIN, retired lawyer; b. Norwood, Ohio, Jan. 9, 1932; s. Emberson and Hazel Hildreth (Jenz) D.; m. Carole Ann Sawyer, Apr. 3, 1971; 1 child, Douglas Sawyer. AB cum laude, Miami U., Oxford, Ohio, 1953; JD cum laude, Harvard U., 1959. Bar: D.C. 1959, U.S. Dist. Ct. D.C. 1959, U.S. Ct. Appeals (D.C. cir.) 1959, U.S. Ct. Appeals (6th cir.) 1973, U.S. Ct. Appeals (2d cir.) 1979, U.S. Ct. Appeals (4th cir.) 1991, U.S. Supreme Ct. 1964. Assoc. Pogue & Neal, Washington, 1959-65, ptnr., 1965-67, Jones, Day, Reavis & Pogue, Washington, 1967-79, Crowell & Moring, Washington, 1979-97. Contbr. articles to profl. jours. Lt. j.g. USN, 1953-56 Mem. ABA, D.C. Bar Assn., Univ. Club. Avocations: swimming, tennis. Home: 4950 Quebec St NW Washington DC 20016-3231

DAVISON, EDWARD JOSEPH, electrical engineering educator; b. Toronto, Ont., Can., Sept. 12, 1938; s. Maurice and Agnes (Quinlan) D. Assoc., Royal Conservatory of Music, Toronto, 1957; BA, U. Toronto, 1960, MA, 1961; PhD, Cambridge U., 1964, ScD, 1977. Asst. prof. dept. elec. engring. U. Toronto, 1964-66, assoc. prof., 1968-74, prof. dept. elec. engring. and computers, 1974-2000, univ. prof., 2001—04, univ. prof. emeritus, 2004—. Asst. prof. dept. elec. engring. and computer scis. U. Calif., Berkeley, 1966-67; dir. Elec. Engring. Consociates Ltd., Toronto, 1977—; elected Hon. prof. of Beijing Inst. of Aeronautics and Astronautics, 1986; pres. Elec. Engring. Consociates, Ltd., Toronto, 1997-99. Assoc. editor: Jour. Automatica, 1974-87, Jour. Large Scale Systems: Theory and Applications, 1979-90, Jour. Optimal Control and Methods, 1983—; cons. editor IEEE Transactions on Automatic Control, 1985. Contbr. numerous articles infield to profl. jours. Athlone fellow, 1961-63; E.W.R. Steacie Meml. fellow, 1974-77; Killam Rsch. fellow, 1979-80, 81-83; named to U. Toronto Engring. Alumni Hall of Distinction, 2003; recipient Killam Engring. prize Can. Coun., 2003. Fellow Royal Soc. Can., IEEE (v.p. Control Systems Soc. 1979-80, mem. adminstrv. com. 1977-83, dir. Soc. mag. 1980-82, assoc. editor jour. Trans. on Automatic Control 1974-76, editl. adv. bd. IEEE Procs. 1980-81, Centennial medal 1984, elected disting. mem. 1984), Can. Acad. Engring. 2005, Internat. Fedn. Automatic Control (vice chmn. theory com. 1978-87, chmn. 87-90, Quazza medal 1993, vice chmn. tech. bd. 1990-93, coun. mem. 1990-96, vice chmn. IFAC policy com. 1996-99, IFAC adminstrv. and fin. com. 1999-2005, IFAC Outstanding Mem. Svc. award 1996, elected fellow of Internat. FEDN Automatic Control, 2005); mem. IEEE Control Systems Soc. (pres.-elect 1982-83, pres. 1983-84, Hendrik W. Bode Lectr. prize 1997), Profl. Engrs. Ont. (cons. engr. 1979—), Russian Acad. Nonlinear Scis. Office: U Toronto Dept Elec Engring-Computers Toronto ON Canada M5S 1A4 Home Phone: 416-444-9381. Business E-Mail: ted@control.utoronto.ca.

DAVISON, HELEN IRENE, secondary school educator, counseling administrator; b. Oskaloosa, Iowa, Dec. 19, 1926; d. Grover C. and Beulah (Williams) Hawk; m. Walter Francis Davison, June 20, 1953 (div.); 1 child, Linda Ellen. BS in Zoology, Iowa State U., 1948; MS in Biol. Sci., U. Chgo., 1951; MA in Ednl. Psychology and Counseling, Calif. State U., Northridge, 1985. Med. rsch. technician U. Chgo. Med. Sch., 1951-53; tchr. sci. Lane High Sch., Charlottesville, Va., 1953-55; med. rsch. asst. U. Va. Med. Sch., Charlottesville, 1955-56, U. Mich., Ann Arbor, 1956-60; tchr. sci. Monroe High Sch., North Hills, Calif., 1966-98, chmn. sci. dept., 1990-91, sch. site coun., 1993-94, ret., 1998. Rsch. technician Los Alamos Sci. Labs., 1954; counselor psychotherapy Forte Found., Encino, Calif., 1987-92, Tarzana, Calif., 1993-2000, Northridge, Calif., 2000-04. V.p. San Fernando Valley chpt. Am. Field Svc., 1980-81; vol. counselor Planned Parenthood Am., L.A., 1982-88. Fellow, NSF, 1985—86. Mem. Calif. Tchrs. Assn., Calif. Assn. Marriage and Family Therapists, Iowa Acad. Sci. (assoc.), AAUW. Avocations: travel, history, cooking.

DAVISON, RICHARD, internist, educator; b. Buenos Aires, Nov. 7, 1937; came to U.S., 1966; s. Charles Edward and Matilde (Muller) D.; m. Lisette Glusberg, July 1, 1965; 1 child, Sebastian. MD, U. Buenos Aires, 1963. Diplomate Am. Bd. Internal Medicine, Am. Bd. Cardiovascular Diseases, Am. Bd. Critical Care Medicine. Intern Inst. Med. Rsch., Buenos Aires, 1964; resident Passavant Meml. Hosp., Chgo., 1966-68, chief resident, 1968-69; cardiology fellowship VA Hosp., Chgo., 1969-71; asst. prof. Northwestern U. Sch. Medicine, Chgo., 1973-81, assoc. prof., 1981—, chief sect. critical care medicine, 1982—2003, chief sect. cardiology, 1988-92; dir. med. intensive care area Northwestern Meml. Hosp., Chgo., 1973—2003. Contbr. articles to profl. jours. Recipient Thrombolysis in Myocardial Infarction award NIH. Fellow Am. Coll. Cardiology, Am. Coll. Physicians, Council of Clin. Cardiology (Am. Heart. Assn.), Soc. Critical Care Medicine; mem. Am. Heart Assn., Alpha Omega Alpha. Office: Northwestern Meml Hosp Divsn Critical Care 201 E Huron St Galter 10-240 Chicago IL 60611-2908 Office Phone: 312-695-2745.

DAVIS-WEXLER, GINIA, singer, director; b. Phila., Mar. 10, 1918; d. Meyer and Hilda (Emery) D.; m. Morris M. Wexler, Oct. 1968 Student drama, Carnegie Inst. Tech., 1939—41; vocal pupil, Frances Lewando, Doris Monteux, 1939—50; coached with, Povla Frijsh, Pierre Monteux, Queena Mario, Pablo Casals, Madeleine Grey. Voice tchr. Mich. State U., East Lansing, 1962; dir. Hancock County Chamber Music Soc. (now Hancock County Friends of Arts), East Sullivan, Maine, 1962—; dir. free programs for children Farmstead Barn, Sullivan, Maine, 1970—. Performed as Polly Peachum in The Beggar's Opera, 1941, Bar Harbor (Maine) Stock Co., Chautauqua, NY Bucks County Playhouse; leading roles New Moon, Toledo Light Opera Co., 1945; appeared on Broadway in Susan and God, 1942, Call Me Mister, 1946; made operatic debut as Gretel in Hansel and Gretel with Pitts. Opera Soc., 1943; ann. recital NYC, 1948-65; toured U.S.A. with unique recital program, Portraits in Song, 1947-67, Europe, 1949, 50; appeared at Holland Festival, 1950; in 1st U.S. performances of Flaminio of Pergolesi, 1953; performances at Royal Opera of Brussels, 1955, broadcasts, US, Europe; appeared with symphony orch., US, Europe, Mid.-East, 1955-67; made six months world tour, Africa, Asia, 1966, guitar concerts, 1965; dir. performing arts for children series, Hancock Grand County Auditorium, 1976-89, h.s. touring program, 1980-89, recs. songs Music Libr. Records, Inc., folk music divsn., Libr. Congress; mem. Surry, Maine Opera Co., 1984-90; dir. Sullivan Bicentennial Chorus, 1989; lead role in play All Thru the Night, 1989; appearances Am. Folksong Festival; adviser folk music, Nat Arts Found.; authority on folksongs; collector, transcriber, interpreter: (with Jean Thomas) folklore Ky. mountains (the Traipsin' Woman), 1950-55, also other locations; entertainer Armed Forces, US, Europe. (Recipient grand prize Internat. contest interpretation French song 1958) Chmn. Sullivan Conservation Commn., 1973-83; pres. Pierre Monteux Sch. for Condrs., Hancock, Maine, 2005-07. Home: The Farmstead 2816 US Hwy 1 Sullivan ME 04664-3522 Home Phone: 207-422-3615, 954-561-1943. Personal E-mail: gdwexler@msn.com.

DAVOREN, PETER J., construction executive; b. 1956; married. Grad. in Constrn. Mgmt., Pratt Inst., NY, 1978. Field engr. Turner Constrn. Co., Boston, 1978—80, with NYC, 1980, ops. mgr. interiors divsn., 1990—95, v.p. interiors divsn., 1995—96, gen. mgr. NY office, 1996—2000, sr. v.p. NY, NJ, Phila. and Pitts. offices, 2000—03, pres., 2003—; COO The Turner Corp., 2003—07, chmn., CEO, 2007—. Bd. dirs. ACE Mentor Program. Office: Turner Constrn Co 375 Hudson St New York NY 10014 Office Phone: 212-229-6000. Office Fax: 212-229-6390.*

DAVOREN, STEVEN MICHAEL, marketing professional, psychologist; b. NYC, Nov. 29, 1968; s. Michael Thomas and Helen Adele Davoren. BS in Mktg., Seton Hall U., 1992, MA in Psychol. Studies, 1996; PhD in Natural Health, Clayton Coll., 2004. Cert. crisis counselor Contact We Care, Inc. Asst. project dir. Statis. Rsch., Inc., Westfield, NJ, 1985—93; market rsch. cons. Fortune 500 Corps., NYC, 1993—95; project dir. FRC Rsch. Corp., NYC, 1996—97; primary rsch. mgr. Blue Cross Blue Shield, Newark, 1998—2000; rsch. cons. Blue Cross Blue Shield and JP Morgan, NYC, 2000—. Soup kitchen server St. Joseph's Social Svc. Ctr., Elizabeth, NJ, 1994—95; grant proposal writer Westfield Cmty. Ctr., NJ, 1995—96. Mem.: APA (assoc.), Nat. Campaign for Tolerance (founding mem. 2005), Am. Mktg. Assn. Roman Catholic. Avocations: running, music, comparative religion, animals, nature walks. Home: 641 Maye St Westfield NJ 07090

DAVY, LUCILLE E., school system administrator; m. James M. Davy; children: James, Andrew. BA in Math, Seton Hall U., 1978; JD, U. Notre Dame Law Sch. Bar: NJ 1980, Fed. Dist. Ct. 1980; cert. Math Tchr. Practiced law; edn. policy advisor State Dem. Com., NJ, 2000—01; spl. counsel to Gov. on Edn. Policy, NJ, 2002—05; acting commr. edn. State of NJ Dept. Edn., NJ, 2005—06, commr. edn. NJ, 2006—. Rep. State Bd. Edn., NJ, Comm. on Higher Edn., NJ Tech. Bd. Trustees; chairwomen NJ State Bd Examiners; adj. prof. math. St. Mary's Coll., Ind., Mercer County Cmty. Coll., NJ. Tchr. Confraternity of Christian Doctrine St. James Ch., Pennington, NJ; mem. Westfield Sch. Parent Teacher Coun., NJ, 1996—2000. Office: Office of Commr 100 River View Plaza PO Box 500 Trenton NJ 08625-0500 Office Phone: 609-292-4450, 609-292-4469. Office Fax: 609-777-4099.*

DAVY, MICHAEL FRANCIS, civil engineer, consultant; b. Springfield, Mo., Mar. 24, 1946; s. Philip Sheridan and Caecilia Magdelen (Thiemann) D.; m. Joyce Kay Young, Aug. 17, 1968; children: Mark Sheridan, Katherine Ann, Jennifer Mary. BS, U. Wis., 1969. Diplomate Am. Acad. Environ. Engrs. Project engr. Davy Engring. Co., La Crosse, Wis., 1969-74, v.p., 1975-88; mgr. Davy Labs., La Crosse, 1975—; pres. Davy Engring. Co., La Crosse, 1989—. Dir. St. Francis Med. Ctr., 1993-95, Wis. Mfrs. and Commerce, 1995-98, Wells Fargo Bank-LaCrosse, 1998—. Mem. Gov.'s Clean Water Task Force, 1988—89; bd. dirs. Gateway Area coun. Boy Scouts Am., La Crosse, 1973—, pres. exec. bd., 1989—91; bd. dirs. La Crosse Family YMCA, 2000—03. Recipient Silver Beaver award Gateway Area Coun. Boys Scouts Am., 1987. Mem. NSPE (nat. bd. dirs. 1987-93), ASCE (Young Engr. Yr. 1980), Wis. Soc. Profl. Engrs. (Engr. Yr. 1987,pres. 1984-85, sec. 1980-82, Young Engr. Yr. 1976), Am. Coun. Engring. Cos. Wis. (bd. dirs. 1987-90), Profl. Engrs. in Pvt. Practice (vice chmn. 1981-83, Merit award 1990), LaCrosse Country Club (dir. 1993-99, pres. 1997-99). Roman Catholic. Avocations: swimming, boating. Home: 615 23rd St N La Crosse WI 54601-3853 Office: Davy Engring Co 115 6th St S La Crosse WI 54601-4153

DAW, AMY W., music educator; b. Salisbury, NC, June 18, 1956; d. John Caldwell Ridenhour and Helen Gold Owen; m. Edward A. Daw, Oct. 5, 1990; children: Richard Creed Wood, Dorthy Gail Wood, Jennifer Lynn, Christopher Edward. MusB Edn. in Edn., U. N.C., 1978. Lic. music edn. K-12 N.C. Dept. Edn., 1988, cert. Nat. Bd. Profl. Tchg. Standards, 2005. Music educator No. H.S., Durham, NC, 1989—. Organist Mt. Bethel Presbyn. Ch., Durham, NC, 1995, children's music, 1996—, deacon, 2001—02. Grantee, Durham Edn. Network, 2001—03. Mem.: Am. Choral Dirs. Assn. (show choir repertoire and standards chair 2004—, women's all state coord. 2003—), N.C. Music Educators Assn. (dist. pres. 1999—2003, coalition chair 2003—), Alta Delta Kappa (assoc.), Nat. Educators Assn. (assoc.). Avocation: travel. Home: 6 Dalton Ct Durham NC 27705 Office: Northern High Sch 117 Tom Wilkinson Rd Durham NC 27712 Home Phone: 919-382-0023; Office Phone: 919-560-3956. Office Fax: 919-479-3001. Personal E-mail: amygail@nc.rr.com. E-mail: amy.daw@dpsnc.net.

DAW, HAROLD JOHN, lawyer, director; b. NYC, July 6, 1926; s. Joseph and Dorothy (Dannenberg) D.; m. Meryl Kann, Sept. 25, 1960. AB, Union Coll., 1950; LL.B., Columbia U., 1954. Bar: N.Y. 1955. Assoc. Shearman & Sterling, NYC, 1954-62, ptnr., 1962-89. Served with USN, 1944-46, ETO. Mem. ABA, N.Y. State Bar Assn., Bar Assn. City N.Y., Phi Beta Kappa Clubs: University. Home: 15 Buena Vista Dr Westport CT 06880-6602

DAWDY, DORIS OSTRANDER, writer; d. Archie and Lydia (Matz) Ostrander; m. David R. Dawdy, Feb. 21, 1951; 1 child, Barbara Dahl. Student music, MacPhail Sch. Music, Mpls. Cons. in field. Composer: I Keep Telling Myself, 1947; author: Artists of the American West, vols. I, 1974, vol. II, 1981, vol. III, 1985, 2d edit., 1987, Congress in its Wisdom: The Bureau of Reclamation and the Public Interest, 1989, George Montague Wheeler: The Man and the Myth, 1993; editor: A Voice in Her Tribe, 1980, 3d edit. 1984, The Wyant Diary/An Artist with the Wheeler Survey, 1980, others. Named David Russell Dawdy and Doris Ostrander Dawdy Geoscis. Libr. Rsch. Fund in her honor, San Francisco State U., 2006. Mem. Mus. Soc. San Francisco., San Francisco Mus. and Hist. Soc., Nat. Mus. Women in Arts Office Phone: 415-681-0957.

DAWDY, SHANNON LEE, archaeologist, historical anthropologist; BA in Anthropology, Reed Coll., Portland, Oreg., 1988; MA in Anthropology, Coll. William and Mary, Williamsburg, Va., 1994; MA in History, U. Mich., Ann Arbor, 2000, PhD in Anthropology and History, 2003. Docent coun. adminstr. Fine Arts Mus. San Francisco, 1989—92; archaeologist Colonial Williamsburg Found./Coll. William and Mary, Va., 1992—93; consulting ethnohistorian Meherrin Indian Tribe, Winton, NC, 1994—95; project mgr. Earth Science, Inc., New Orleans, 1994—95; rsch. assoc., dir. greater New Orleans archaeology program U. New Orleans, 1995—98, vis. scholar, Coll. Urban and Pub. Affairs, 2004—; grad. student instructor, dept. anthropology and history U. Mich., Ann Arbor, 1999—2001; adj. instructor, dept. history Triton Coll., River Grove, 2003; lectr., dept. social sciences Harold Washington Coll., Chgo., 2003; asst. prof. anthropology and social sciences in the coll. U. Chgo., 2004—. Fieldwork experience in Oreg., So. New England, Va., NC, Cuba, New Orleans, La., 1987—; reading group coord., doctoral program in anthropology and history, 1998—99; dept. rep. Grad. Employee Orgn., 1999—2000; grant writer for team project Social Sci. Rsch. Coun., Cuba Program, 2001—02; spkr. in field. Contbr. articles to prof. jours., chapters to books; manuscript reviewer Jour. of Social History, Louisiana History, bd. dir., newletter editor La. Archaeological Conservancy, 1996—98, guest editor Historical Archaeology, Vol. 34, 1999—2000. Rackham Regents Fellowship, 1998—2001, Inst. for Humanities Fellow, 2001—02, Am. Soc. for Eighteenth Century Studies Fellow, Newberry Libr., 2002. Mem.: La. Archaeological Soc., Soc. for Am. Archaeology (session organizer, chair, Cuban Archaeology for conf. 2002), French Colonial Hist. Soc., La. History Assn., Soc. for Hist. Archaeology (session organizer, chair, Creolization for conf. 1998), Am. Anthropology Assn. Office: Dept Anthropology Haskell 202 U Chgo 1126 E 59th St Chicago IL 60637 Office Phone: 773-834-0829. Business E-Mail: sdawdy@uchicago.edu.

DAWE, JAMES ROBERT, lawyer; b. Bristol, Conn., Aug. 12, 1945; s. John Grosvenor and Madeline Rose Dawe; m. Mary Gardner, July 5, 1970; children: Emily, Jeremy, Sarah. BA, Lehigh U., 1967; M City Planning, San Diego State U., 1974; JD, U. San Diego, 1976. Bar: Calif. 1976, U.S. Dist. Ct. (so. dist.) Calif. 1976. Atty. Seltzer Caplan McMahon Vitek, San Diego, 1976—. Chair Urban Librs. Coun., Evanston, Ill., 1993-94, San Diego Pub. Libr. Commn., 1986-94; past chair Libr. Calif. Bd., Sacramento, Downtown San Diego Partnership, San Diego City Mgr. Ballot Com.; chair San Diego Pub. Libr. Found.; vice chair, steering com. Downtown San Diego Ctr. City Cmty. Plan Update. Mem. ABA (real property sect.), Urban Land Inst., Calif. Bldg. Industry Assn. (legal action com.). Office: Seltzer Caplan McMahon Vitek 750 B St Ste 2100 San Diego CA 92101-8177

DAWES, DOMINIQUE, Olympic athlete; b. Silver Spring, Md., Nov. 20, 1976; BS, U. Md., 1999. Mem. U.S. Olympic Team, Barcelona, 1992, Atlanta, 1996. Actor: (TV series) The Jersey; (Broadway plays) Grease. Named U.S.A. Gymnastics Athlete of Yr., 1993, Sportsperson of Yr., USA Gymnastics, 1994, 3d pl. team, Olympic Games, Barcelona, Spain, 1992, 2d pl. all around and floor exercise, 1st in vault and balance beam, 3d uneven bars, Coca Cola Nat. Championships, Salt Lake City, 1993, 2d in uneven bars and balance beam, World Gymnastics Championships, Birmingham, Eng., 1993, 1st pl. in all around, vault, balanve beam and floor exercise, McDonald's Am. Cup, Orlando, Fla., 1994, 1st pl. in all around, vault, uneven bars, balance beam and floor exercise, Cola Cola Nat. Championships, Nashville, 1994, 1st pl. in all around, NationsBank World Team Trials, Richmond, Va., 1994, 2d pl. team, World Championships, Dortmund, Germany, 1994, 1st pl. in uneven bars and floor exercise, 3d pl. in balance beam, Coca Cola Nat. Championships, New Orleans, 1995; recipient Arch McDonald award, Touchdown Club Washington, 1995, McDonald's Balancing It All award, 1995, Harry P. Iba Citizen Athlete award, 1995, Gold medal Team Competition, Olympic Games, Atlanta, 1996. Avocations: reading, dance, acting. Office: care USA Gymnastics Pan Am Plz 201 S Capitol Ave Ste 300 Indianapolis IN 46225-1058

DAWES, ROBERT LEO, mathematician, consultant; b. Big Spring, Tex., Mar. 5, 1945; s. William Robert and Josephine Melloo (Duflot) D.; m. Rosemary Mae Nelson, Oct. 10, 1970; children: Sara Michelle, Karen Melissa. BS in Math., Tex. Tech U., 1966, MS in Math., 1968; PhD in Math., U. Tex., 1977. Mem. tech. staff Tex. Instruments, Inc., Dallas, 1975-81; sr. specialist E-Systems, Inc., Garland, Tex., 1981-85; pres. Martingale Rsch. Corp., Allen, Tex., 1985-94; asst. prof. math. Hampton (Va.) U., 2002—04; pres. QED Corp., Bedford, Tex., 1995—2006; co-founder, chief scientist Advanced Receiver Techs. LLC, Dallas, 2006—. Founder, chair Metroplex Inst. Neural Dynamics, Dallas, 1986-90. Mem. city coun. City of Parker (Tex.), 1987-99. Lt. USNR, 1968-71. Mem. (sr.) IEEE (chmn. Dallas chpt. Acoustics, Speech and Signal Processing Soc. 1988), Internat. Neural Network Soc. (chair math. and theory spl. interest group 1990-92). Avocation: quantum mechanics. Home: 2217 Bedford Cir Bedford TX 76021

DAWES, ROBYN MASON, psychology professor; b. Pitts., July 23, 1936; s. Norman H. and Zita (Hill) D.; children by previous marriage: Jennifer, Molly. BA in Philosophy, Harvard U., 1958; MA in Clin. Psychology, U. Mich., 1960, PhD in Math. Psychology, 1963; PhD (hon.), U. Goteborg, Sweden, 1999. Rschr. Ann Arbor (Mich.) VA Hosp., 1962-67; lectr. U. Mich., Ann Arbor, 1963-66, asst. prof., 1966-67; assoc. prof. psychology U. Oreg., Eugene, 1967-71, prof., 1971-85, co-head dept. psychology, 1972-73, acting head, 1979-80, head, 1981-85; prof. psychology Carnegie Mellon U., 1985—, head dept. social and decision scis., 1985-90, 95-96, univ. prof., 1992—, Charles J. Queenan Jr. univ. prof., 1997—. Rsch. scientist Oreg. Rsch. Inst., Eugene, 1967-76, v.p., 1973-74; NATO lectr., The Hague, The Netherlands, 1968; vis. prof. U. Calif., Santa Barbara, 1975-75; cons. numerous insts. and orgns.; Olof Palme vis. prof. U. Stockholm and U. Goteborg, 1999. Author: Fundamentals of Attitude Measurement, 1972, Rational Choice in an Uncertain World, 1988 (William James book award div. gen. psychology Am. Psychol. Assn.), House of Cards: Psychology and Psychotherapy Built on Myth, 1994, paperback edit., 1996, Irrationality in Everyday Life, How Pseudo-Scientists, Lunatics and the Rest of Us Systematically Fail to Think Rationally, 2001, paperback edit., 2003; co-author: (with C.H. Coombs and A. Tversky) Mathematical Psychology: An Elementary Introduction, 1970, (with R. Hastie) Rational Choice in an Uncertain World, (2d edition), 2001; contbr. articles to profl. jours; mem. editl. bds., cons numerous profl. jours. and publs. Rackham Summer fellow, 1961, James McKean Cattell Sabbatical fellow, 1978-79; del. NAS, USA-USSR Acad. Scis. Seminar Decision Making, Moscow-Tblisi, USSR, 1979; fellow Ctr. Advanced Study in Behavioral Scis., 1980-81, Ctr. for Rationality and Interactive Decision Making The Hebrew U. of Jerusalem, 1994. Fellow AAAS, Am. Acad. Arts and Scis., Am. Psychol. Soc., Am. Assn. Applied and Preventive Psychology (exec. bd. 1991—), Am. Statis. Assn.; mem. Oreg. Psychol. Assn. (pres. 1984-85), Pub. Choice Soc., Psychometric Soc., Judgement and Decision Making Rsch. Soc. (chmn. 1986, exec. bd. 1988, exec. bd. 1994-95), Soc. Advancement of Socio-Econs. (exec. bd. 1991-98), Sigma Xi, Phi Kappa Phi (sr.). Office: Carnegie Mellon U Dept Social & Decision Scis Pittsburgh PA 15213 Office Phone: 412-268-2055. Office Fax: 412-268-6938. Business E-Mail: rd1b@andrew.cmu.edu. *It took a while to understand the wisdom of Herodotus to "take good counsel with (ourselves); for even if the event turns out contrary to one's hopes, still one's decision was right"--always drawing support from the knowledge that the future is uncertain.*

DAWES, TREVOR A., school librarian; b. Jamaica, WI; arrived in US, 1980; AB in Sociology, Columbia U., 1990, MA in Ednl. Adminstrn., 1994; MLS, Rutgers U., 2001; MA in Edn., Columbia U., 2002. Technical services supr. Thomas J. Watson Libr. Bus. and Economics Columbia U. Libraries, NYC, 1988—89, head serials unit Sch. of Law Libr., 1989—90, access services supr. Sci. and Engring. Libraries, 1990—92, head Libr. Info. and Privileges Office, 1992—99, acting head Butler Circulation Dept., 1995, head Circulation and Support Services Dept., 1999—2004; adj. instr. Coll. Info. Sci. and Tech. Drexel U., Phila., 2006—; dir. Circulation Services Divsn. Princeton U. Library, NJ, 2004—. Mem. Am. Soc. for Info. Sci. and Tech., 1999—2002, Assn. Libr. collections and Tech., 1993—98, 2003—05; mem. programming com. Black Librarians Network of NJ, 2005—06. Founding mem., sec. GABLES Columbia U., 1993. Named one of the Movers & Shakers, Libr. Jour., 2007; Gilbert H. Kelly Fellowship, Rutgers U. Sch. Comm., Inf. and Libr. Studies, 1999—2001. Mem.: ALA (chmn. HW Wilson Staff devel. award jury 2006—07), Assn. Coll. and Rsch. Libraries (vice chmn. excellence in acad. libraries award nominating com. 2003—05, chmn. profl. devel. coord. com 2006—08), Black Caucus of Am. Libr. Assn. (mem. exec. bd. 2005—07), Libr. Adminstrn. and Mgmt. Assn., NJ Libr. Assn. (mem. profl. devel. com. 2005—07, co-chmn. mentoring com. 2006—07, sec. coll. and univ. sect. 2007—08). Avocations: travel, reading, movies. Office: Princeton Univ Library One Washington Rd Princeton NJ 08544 E-mail: trevor@trevordawes.com.

DAWISHA, ADEED, political science professor; b. Baghdad, Nov. 2, 1944; m. Karen Hurst, Jan. 1, 1972; children: Nadia, Emile. PhD, London Sch. Econs., 1974. Lectr. Lancaster U., England, 1974—76, Keele U., Stoke-on-Trent, England, 1977—78; sr. rsch. assoc. Internat. Inst. Strategic Studies, London, 1978—79; dep. dir. studies Royal Inst. Internat. Affairs, London, 1979—85; prof. George Mason U., Fairfax, Va., 1985—2000, Miami U., 2000—. Cons. Dept. of State, Wash., CIA. Author: (book) Arab Nationalism in the Twentieth Century, The Arab Radicals, Syria and the Lebanese Crisis, Egypt in the Arab World; editor: The Making of Foreign Policy in Russia and the New States of Eurasia, Beyond Coercion: The Durability of the Arab State, Islam in Foreign Policy, The Soviet Union in the Middle East. Recipient Fulbright fellow, 1990—91; Fellow, Social Sci. Rsch. Coun., Eng., 1981, Consulting fellow, Coun. Fgn. Rels., 1984—85, fellow, Woodrow Wison Internat. Ctr. Scholars, 1985—86, scholar, Carnegie, 2004—05. Mem.: Internat. Studies Assn., Mid. East Studies Assn., Mid. East Inst., Am. Hist. Assn., Am. Polit. Sci. Assn. Home: 478 White Oak Dr Oxford OH 45056 Office: Polit Sci Miami U High St Oxford OH 45056 Home Phone: 513-524-1305; Office Phone: 513-529-2332. Personal E-mail: dawisha@muohio.edu.

DAWKINS, RICHARD (CLINTON RICHARD DAWKINS), ethologist, evolutionary biologist, educator, writer; b. Nairobi, Kenya, Mar. 26, 1941; arrived in came to Eng., 1949; s. Clinton John and Jean Mary Vyvyan (Ladner) Dawkins; m. Marian Ellina Stamp, Aug. 19, 1967 (div. 1984); m. Eve Barham, June 1, 1984 (div.); 1 child, Juliet Emma; m. Lalla Ward, 1992. BA, Oxford U., 1961, MA, DPhil, Oxford U., 1966, DSc, 1989; LittD (hon.), St. Andrews U., 1995, Australian Nat. U., Canberra, 1996; DSc (hon.), U. Westminster, 1997, U. Hull, 2001; D Univ. (hon.), Open U., 2003. Rsch. asst. to prof. N. Tinbergen FRS, 1965—67; asst. prof. zoology U. Calif., Berkeley, 1967—69; rsch. student Oxford U., 1962—66, univ. lectr., zoology England, 1970—90, Ad hominem reader, zoology, 1990—95, Charles Simonyi Prof. of the Pub. Understanding of Sci. England, 1995—; fellow New Coll., 1970—90, Professorial fellow, 1995—. Humanist laureate Internat. Acad. Humanism; com. fellow Scientific Investigation of Claims of the Paranormal, Skeptical Inquirer; hon. assoc. New Humanist; coun. mem. Assn. for the Study Animal Behavior, 1972—79; mem. sci. consultative com. British Broadcasting Corp., 1986—91; hon. chmn., sci. engring. tech. com. Oxford U., 1996; hon. assoc. Nat. Secular Soc. Ltd., London, 1996; mem. Internat. Centre for Life Scientific Adv. Group, Newcastle upon Tyne, 1997; cons. Independent Schools Parents' Orgn., 1999; chmn. Michael Faraday award Selection Com., 2003; judge, selection com. Grierson Awards Sci. Sect., 2003, BAFTA TV Awards, 2003; pub. engagement com. Natural History Mus., London, 2003, mem. David Attenborough Studi Com., 05; patron Sunday Times Oxford Lit. Festival, 2003; mem. selection com. for Dawkins Prize Balliol Coll., Oxford, 2004; invited lectr. in field. Author: The Selfish Gene, 1976, 1989, The Extended Phenotype, 1982, The Blind Watchmaker, 1986 (Royal Soc. Lit. award, 1987, LA Times Literary prize, 1987), River Out of Eden: A Darwinian View of Life, 1995 (Number One Bestseller, Sunday Times List), Climbing Mount Improbable, 1996 (Number One Bestseller, Observer List), Unweaving the Rainbow: Science, Delusion and the Appetite for Wonder, 1997, A Devil's Chaplain, 2003, The Ancestor's Tale: A Pilgrimage to the Dawn of Evolution, 2004, The God Delusion, 2006 (Publsihers Weekly Bestseller); columnist, sr. editor Free Inquiry, Council for Secular Humanism, advisor British Acad. TV Awards, edited with M. Dawkins and T.R. Halliday The Tinbergen Legacy, 1991, editl. advisor to several jours., european editor Animal Behavior Monographs, 1972—73, Animal Behaviour, 1974—78, exec. editor Oxford Surveys in Evolutionary Biology, 1983—86, founding editor Episteme Jour., 2002; editor: Best American Science and Nature Writing, 2003; bd. advisor TIME Future of Life Summit, 2003, mem. adv. bd. Encyclopedia of Evolution, Oxford U. Publishing, Artificial Life, mem. editl. adv. bd. Websters Encarta Encyclopedia, Journal of Memetics, mem. editl. bd. Biology and Philosophy, mem. external adv. bd. Oxford Today, cons. Young Encyclopedia of Science, Oxford U. Publishing, televised lecture on the Evolution of Human Purpose, 1982, presenter BBC Horizon Programme: Nice Guys Finish First, 1985, BBC Horizon Programme: The Blind Watchmaker, 1986 (Sci. Tech prize for Best TV Documentary Sci. Programme of the Yr., 1987), BBC Discussion Programme: Thinking Aloud, 1986, presenter, author Break the Science Barrier with Richard Dawkins, Channel 4, Equinox, 1996, and other TV interviews, discussions, and presentations, edited in several jours.; contbr. articles to profl. jours.; invited forwards in books; writer, presenter: Documentary The Root of All Evil?, 2006. Founder, bd. trustee Richard Dawkins Found. for Reason and Sci., 2006—; advisor The Vega Sci. Trust, U. Sussex, 1999; mem. British Mus. Develop. Trust Coun., 2001, Oxford Trust Centre for Sci. Comm. in Oxfordshire, 2002. Named one of Top 100 Pub. British Intellectuals, Prospect Mag., 2004, The World's Most Influential People, TIME Mag., 2007; recipient Zoological Soc. London Silver medal, 1989, Michael Faraday award, Royal Soc. London, 1990, Nakayama prize for Achievement in Human Sci., 1994, Humanist of the Yr. award, 1996, Internat. Cosmos prize, Osaka, Japan, 1997, Kistler prize, U.S.A., 2001, Medal of Presidency of the Italian Republic, Rimini, Italy, 2001, Bicentennial Kelvin medal, Royal Philos. Soc. Glasgow, 2002, Shakespeare prize for contribution to British Culture, Alfred Toepfer Found., Hamburg, Germany, 2005, Golden Plate award, Acad. Achievement, 2006; Hon. Fellowship, Regent's Coll., London, 1988, Hon. Fellow, Balliol Coll., Oxford U., 2004. Fellow: Royal Soc., Royal Soc. Lit.; mem.: British Humanist Assn. (v.p. 1996), British Assn. for the Advancement of Sci. (pres., biol. sciences sect. 1997), Trinity Coll. Univ. Philos. Soc. (hon. patron 2004). Avocation: computer programming. Office: New Coll U Oxford Oxford OX1 3BN England also: RichardDawkinsnet PO Box 13604 Savannah GA 31416*

DAWSON, CARON, medical and legal consultant; b. London, Sept. 21, 1956; d. Douglas and Patsy Dawson. Diploma, NW Surrey Dist. Sch. Nursing, Chertsey, England, 1978; BA in Polit. Sci. (hon.), Old Dominion U., Norfolk, Va., 1987; JD, U. Miami, 1990, LLM in Internat. Law, 1991. Bar: Fla. 1991; RN Fla., 1978, Ill., 2001. Med.-legal cons. pvt. practice, Chgo., 1991—. Recipient Outstanding Polit. Sci. award, Old Dominion U., 1986—87. Mem.: ATLA, Phi Kappa Phi. Home: 47 W Division St Ste 1 Chicago IL 60610-2220 Home Phone: 773-477-8610. Personal E-mail: carondawson@cdrnjd.com.

DAWSON, CARROLL, professional sports team executive; Student, Paris Jr. Coll.; grad., Baylor U., Waco, Tex. Asst. coach Baylor U., head coach, 1973—77; asst. coach Houston Rockets, 1980—96, gen. mgr., 1996—; exec. v.p. basketball Houston Comets. Named to Paris Jr. Coll. Hall of Fame, Baylor U. Hall of Fame, Tex. Assn. Basketball Coaches Hall of Fame, Tex. Sports Hall of Fame, 2003. Office: Houston Rockets Toyota Ctr 1510 Polk St Houston TX 77002*

DAWSON, CHANDLER ROBERT, ophthalmologist, educator; b. Denver, Aug. 24, 1930; married; 3 children. AB, Princeton U., 1952; MD, Yale U., 1956. USPHS epidemiologist Communicable Disease Ctr., 1957-60; resident dept. ophthalmology Sch. Medicine U. Calif., San Francisco, 1960-63; asst. clin. prof. U. Calif., San Francisco, 1963-66, asst. prof. in residence, 1966-69, assoc. prof. opthalmology, 1969-75, prof. ophthalmology, 1975-97, prof. emeritus, assoc. dir. Francis I. Proctor Found., 1970-84, dir., 1984-95. Fellow Middlesex Hosp. Med. Sch., London, 1963-64; co-dir. WHO Collaborating Ctr. for Reference and Rsch. on Trachoma and other Chlamydial Infections, 1970-79, dir. Collaborating Ctr. for Prevention of Blindness and Trachoma, 1979—97. Recipient Knapp award AMA, 1967, 69, Medaille Trachome, 1978. Mem. Am. Soc. Microbiology, Am. Acad. Ophthalmology, Assn. Rsch. Vision & Ophthalmology. Achievements include rsch. in epidemiology of infectious eye diseases and cataracts; prevention of blindness; pathogenesis of virus diseases of the eyes; electron microscopy of eye diseases; clinical trials of treatment for trachoma and for herpes simplex eye infections. Office: U Calif San Francisco Francis I Proctor Found Rsch Ophthalmology San Francisco CA 94143-0412

DAWSON, DENNIS RAY, lawyer, manufacturing executive; b. Alma, Mich., June 19, 1948; s. Maurice L. and Virginia (Baker) D.; m. Marilynn S. Gordon, Nov. 26, 1971; children: Emily Lynn, Brett Thomas. AA, Gulf Coast Coll., 1968; AB, Duke U., 1970; JD, Wayne State U., 1973. Bar: Mich. 1973, U.S. Dist. Ct. (ea. dist.) Mich. 1973, U.S. Dist. Ct. (we. dist.) Mich. 1975. Assoc. Watson, Wunsch & Keidan, Detroit, 1973-75; mem. Coupe, Ophoff & Dawson, Holland, Mich., 1975-77; staff atty. Amway Corp., Ada, Mich., 1977-79; corp. counsel Meijer, Inc., Grand Rapids, Mich., 1979-82; sec., corp. counsel Tecumseh Products Co., 1982-92; corp. counsel, asst. sec. Holnam Inc., Dundee, Mich., 1992-93; v.p., gen. counsel, sec. Denso Internat. Am. Inc., Southfield, Mich., 1993-2000, sr. v.p., gen. counsel, sec., 2000—. Exec. com. Bank of Lenawee, Adrian, Mich., 1984-93, also bd. dirs.; adj. prof. Aquinas Coll., Grand Rapids, 1978-82; govt. regulation and litigation com. Outdoor Power Equipment Inst. Inc., Washington, 1982-92. Trustee Herrick Meml. Hosp., 1988-91, Tecumseh Civic Auditorium, 1986-89; mem. adv. coun. Montessori Children's House and Acad., Adrian, 1987-93; mem. adv. bd. Eastern Mich. U. Coll. Bus., 2004. Mem. ABA, Mich. State Bar Assn., Am. Corp. Counsel Assn., Mich. Mfrs. Assn. (lawyers com. 1987-92), Lenawee C. of C. (bd. dirs. 1988-92). Office: Denso Internat America Inc PO Box 5133 24777 Denso Dr Southfield MI 48034-5244

DAWSON, EARL BLISS, medical educator; b. Perry, Fla., Feb. 1, 1930; s. Bliss and Linnie (Calliham) Dawson; m. Winnie Ruth Isbell, Apr. 10, 1951; children: Barbara Gail, Patricia Ann, Robert Earl, Diana Lynn. BA, U. Kans., 1955; postgrad., Bowman Gray Sch. Medicine, 1957—59; MA, U. Mo., 1960; PhD, Tex. A&M U., 1964. Rsch. instr. dept. ob-gyn. U. Tex. Med. Br., Galveston, 1963—65, rsch. asst. prof., 1965—68, rsch. assoc. prof., 1968—89, assoc. prof., 1989—. Cons. Interdeptl. Com. Nutrtion Nat. Def., 1965—68, Nat. Nutrition Survey, 1968—69. Author: Effect of Water Borne Nitrites on the Environment of Man; contbr. articles to profl. jours., chapters to books. Scoutmaster Boy Scouts Am., 1969—. With USNR, 1947—52. Scholar, NSF, 1961—62; Nutrition Rsch. fellow, 1960—61, Rsch. fellow, NIH, 1962—63. Mem.: NY Acad. Scis., Tex. Acad. Scis., Soc. Environ. Geochemistry and Health, Soc. Exptl. Biology and Medicine, Am. Fertility Soc., Am. Coll. Nutrition, Am. Soc. Clin. Nutrition, Am. Inst. Nutrition, Mic-O-Say Club (Kansas City, Mo.), Sigma Xi, Phi Rho Sigma. Baptist. Achievements include research in prenatal nutrition, male fertility, epidemiology of lithium in Texas, biochemical changes associated with pre-menstrual syndrome. Home: Apt 8 3431 S Peach Hollow Cir D Pearland TX 77584-8006 Office: U Tex Med Br Dept Ob-Gyn Galveston TX 77550 Personal E-mail: winniearl@cs.com.

DAWSON, EDWARD JOSEPH, merger and acquisition executive; b. Rochester, Pa., Apr. 1, 1944; s. Ralph Edward and Evelyn May (Riggle) D.; m. Lynda Sue Weir, 1975; 5 children. BS in Indsl. Mgmt., Carnegie Mellon U., 1966; MBA in Fin., U. Chgo., 1968. Lic. security broker/dealer, real estate broker. Computer systems analyst, corp. fin. analyst Tex. Instruments Corp., Dallas, 1968-70, product planning mgr. digital systems divsn., 1970-72, mgr. comml. equipment bus. objective, 1972-74, mgr. mktg. electronic watch divsn., 1975-76, mgr. mktg. home video systems, 1976-77; sr. v.p. ops. and mktg. Capital Alliance Corp., Dallas, 1977-80, exec. v.p. merger ops., 1980-81, chmn. bd., CEO, pres., 1981—. Sec. M&A Internat., 1988, v.p., 89, 96, pres., 90, 97; mem. faculty Bus. Leadership Ctr. So. Meth. U., 1999—; mem. entrepreneurship adv. coun. Carnegie Mellon U., 1998—. Author 4 books. Pres. Marina del Rey Homeowners Assn., 1982-84. Mem. Omicron Delta Kappa, Beta Theta Pi. Mem. Ch. of Christ. Home: 818 Stratford Dr Southlake TX 76092-7109 Office: Capital Alliance Corp 2777 N Stemmons Fwy Ste 1220 Dallas TX 75207-2293 Office Phone: 214-638-8280. Business E-Mail: ed.dawson@cadallas.com.

DAWSON, GERALDINE, medical educator, social worker; b. Huntington, Pa., Oct. 2, 1945; d. Donn and Evelyn Koontz; m. Nathan Maniam. BA, Pa. State U., 1967; MSW, Smith Coll., 1969; MD, Albert Einstein Coll. Medicine, 1988. Fellow Harvard Med. Sch.-Mass. Gen. Hosp., Boston, 1980—82, All India Inst. Med. Sci., New Delhi, 1987—88; med. resident Lenox Hill Hosp., NYC, 1988—89; cons. Dept. of Def., Washington, 1990—92; assoc. prof. Marywood U., Scranton, Pa., 1993—. Contbr. articles to profl. jours. Mem. adv. coun. Regional Health Edn. Ctr. N.E. Pa., Scranton, 2001—; mem. Pa. Health Edn. Interdisciplinary Task Force, Hershey, 2002—. Named N.E. Woman, Scranton Times, 2000, Excellence in Their Field, Johnstown Tribune Democrat, 2000. Mem.: Pa. Nat. Alliance Mentally Ill, Pa. Nat. Assn. Social Workers (chairperson profl. stds. com. 1997—2003), Am. Psychotherapy Assn. (diplomate). Office Phone: 570-348-6282 ext 2390. Business E-Mail: dawson@marywood.edu.

DAWSON, HOWARD ATHALONE, JR., federal judge; b. Okolona, Ark., Oct. 23, 1922; m. Marianne Atherholt, Feb. 2, 1946; children: Amy, Suzanne. BS in Commerce, U. NC, 1946; JD, George Washington U., 1949. Bar: DC 1949, Ga. 1958. Pvt. practice, Washington, 1949-50; atty. civil divsn. Office Chief Counsel, IRS, 1950-53, asst. regional counsel Atlanta region, 1953-56, regional counsel, 1957, asst. chief counsel adminstrn. Washington, 1958-62; judge US Tax Ct., Washington, 1962—73, 1977—83, chief judge, 1973-77, 83-85, sr. judge, 1990—; prof. law, dir. grad. tax prog. U. Balt., 1986-89. David Brennan Disting. prof. law U. Akron Sch. Law, spring 1986; Disting. adj. prof. law U. San Diego Sch. Law, spring 1991. Served with AUS, 1943-45, ETO; capt. Res. Mem. ABA, DC Bar Assn., Fed. Bar Assn., Chi Psi, Delta Theta Phi. Office: US Tax Court 400 2nd St NW Washington DC 20217-0002*

DAWSON, JAMES CLIFFORD, environmental science educator, geologist; b. Toronto, Ont., Can., Apr. 19, 1941; arrived in US, 1961; s. Clifford and Winifred Mary (Tadman) D.; m. Caroline Weiss, June 12, 1971. AA, Mt. San Antonio Coll., 1963; BA, UCLA, 1965, MS, 1967; PhD, U. Wis., Madison, 1970. Asst. prof. geology SUNY, Plattsburgh, 1970—74, assoc. prof., 1974—80, prof. environ sci., 1980—91, Disting. Svc. prof., 1991—. Pres. Nat. Assn. State Bds. Edn., 1998. Chmn. Adirondack Land Trust, Inc., Elizabethtown, N.Y., 1984-89; bd. dirs. Adirondack Coun., Elizabethtown, 1982-2000; pres. Assn. for Protection of Adirondack, Schenectady, N.Y., 1982-83; mem. exec. coun. Lake Champlain Com., Inc., Burlington, Vt., 1976-98, bd. regents N.Y. State, 1993—. Mem.: AAAS, Am. Assn. Petroleum Geologists, Am. Geophys. Union, Geol. Soc. Am., Sigma Xi. Home: 2 Birchwood Dr Peru NY 12972-2600 Office Phone: 518-564-4035. Business E-Mail: james.dawson@plattsburgh.edu.

DAWSON, JOHN JOSEPH, lawyer; b. Binghamton, NY, Mar. 9, 1947; s. Joseph John and Cecilia (O'Neill) D. BA, Siena Coll., 1968; JD, U. Notre Dame, 1971. Bar: Ariz. 1971, Nev. 1991, Calif. 1993, D.C. 1994, N.Y. 1996. Nat. practice group chair, bankruptcy and creditors rights practice group Quarles & Brady LLP, Phoenix. Reporter local rules ct. U.S. Bankruptcy Ct. for Dist. Ariz.; atty. rep. U.S. Ct. Appeals (9th cir.), 1992-95 Co-author: Advanced Chapter 11 Bankruptcy, 1991. Fellow Ariz. Bar Found.; mem. State Bar Ariz. (chmn. bankruptcy sect. 1976-77, 80-81), Am. Bankruptcy Inst. Republican. Roman Catholic. Avocations: sports, reading, movies, travel, writing. Office: Quarles & Brady LLP Renaissance One Two North Central Ave Phoenix AZ 85004-2391 Home Phone: 602-266-2769; Office Phone: 602-229-5414. Business E-Mail: jdawson@quarles.com.

DAWSON, MARY RUTH, curator, educator; b. Highland Park, Mich., Feb. 27, 1931; d. John Elson and Olga Josephine (Down) D. BS, Mich. State Coll., 1952; postgrad., U. Edinburgh, 1952-53; PhD, U. Kans., 1957; D of Humanities (hon.), Chatham Coll., 1983; DSc (hon.), Mich. State U., 2005. Instr. zoology Smith Coll., 1958-61; asst. program dir. NSF, Washington, 1961-62; mem. staff Carnegie Mus., Pitts., 1962—, curator, 1971—, chmn. earth sci. div., 1973-97, acting dir., 1982-83, curator emeritus, 2003. Adj. prof. earth scis. U. Pitts., 1971—. Contbr. articles to profl. jours. Named Disting. Dau. Pa., 1987, Honoree, Women and Girls Found., 2006; recipient Arnold Guyot award, Nat. Geog. Soc., 1981, Woman in Sci. award, Chatham Coll., 1983, Disting. Alumni award, Mich. State U., 2003, Romer-Simpson medal, Soc. Vertebrate Paleontology; fellow, AAUW, 1958—59; Fulbright scholar, 1952—53, Rsch. grant, NSF, 1961—62, 1965—. Fellow Geol. Soc. Am., Arctic Inst. N.Am., Paleontol. Soc.; mem. Soc. Vertebrate Paleontology (hon.; v.p. 1972-73, pres. 1973-74), Paläontologische Gesellschaft, Bernese Mountain Dog Club Am., Am. Soc. Mammalogists, Phi Beta Kappa. Achievements include research on Tertiary Lagomorpha, early Tertiary Holarctic rodents, Arctic paleontology. Office: Carnegie Mus 4400 Forbes Ave Pittsburgh PA 15213-4080 Business E-Mail: dawsonm@carnegiemnh.org.

DAWSON, MICHAEL C., political science professor; m. Alice Furumato-Dawson. BA, U. Calif. Berkeley, 1982; PhD, Havard U., 1986. Assoc. prof. U. Chgo., 1992—2001, William R. Kenan Jr. prof., dept. polit. sci. and the coll., 2001—02, chair, polit. sci. dept., John D. MacArthur Disting. Svc. prof., dept. polit. sci. and the coll., 2005—; faculty mem. Harvard U., 2002—05. Founder, faculty mem. Ctr. for the Study of Race, Politics and Culture U. Chgo.; co-principal investigator 1988 Nat. Black Election Study; prin. investigator with Ronald Brown 1993-1994 Nat. Black Politics Study; prin. investigator Black Civil Soc. Study; with Lawrence Bobo conducted six pub. opinion studies on racial divide in the US, 2000—04. Author: Black Visions: The Roots of Contemporary African-Am. Political Ideologies, 2001, Behind the Mule: Race and Class in African -Am. Politics, 1994; co-editor (with Lawrence BoBo): Du Bois Review; contbr. numerous articles on African-Am. polit. behavior and race and Am. politics. Fellow: Am. Acad. Arts & Sciences. Address: Ctr for the Study of Race Politics and Culture U Chgo 5733 S University Ave Chicago IL 60637 Office Phone: 773-702-8932. Office Fax: 773-702-1689. Business E-Mail: medawson@uchicago.edu.

DAWSON, MIMI WEYFORTH, public policy consultant; b. St. Louis, Aug. 31, 1944; d. Francis Griffin and Jeanne (Gething) Weyforth; m. Rhett Brewer Dawson, Jan. 15, 1976; 2 children: Elizabeth Stuart, Andrew Brewer. AB, Washington U., St. Louis, 1966. Press sec., legis. asst. to Rep. James Symington, Mo. Dist., 1973; pres. sec., chief staff Sen. Bob Packwood, Oreg., 1973-81; commr. FCC, Washington, 1981-87; dep. Sec. U.S. Dept. Transp., Washington, 1987-89; sr. pub. policy cons. Wiley Rein and Fielding LLP, Washington, 1989—. Apptd. U.S. Holocaust Meml. Coun., 1992-98; adj. fellow Ctr. for Strategic and Internat. Studies. Mem. Atlantic Coun. U.S. (bd. dirs. 1995—). Republican. Roman Catholic. Office: Wiley Rein and Fielding LLP 1776 K St NW Washington DC 20006-2304 Office Phone: 202-719-7034. Business E-Mail: mdawson@wrf.com.

DAWSON, PATRICIA LUCILLE, surgeon; b. Kingston, Jamaica, W.I., Sept. 30, 1949; arrived in U.S., 1950; d. Percival Gordon and Edna Claire (Overton) D.; children: Alexandria Zoe Hiserman, Wesley Gordon Hiserman BA in Sociology, Allegheny Coll., 1971; MD, N.J. Med. Sch., Newark, 1977; MA in Human and Orgn. Devel., The Fielding Inst., 1996, PhD in Human and Orgnl. Sys., 1998. Membership dir. N.J. ACLU, Newark, 1972; resident in surgery U. Medicine and Dentistry N.J. N.J. Med Sch., 1977-79; resident in surgery Virginia Mason Med. Ctr., Seattle, 1979-82; pvt. practice specializing in surgery Arlington, Wash., 1982-83; dir. med. staff diversity Group Health Coop., Seattle, 1993-98, staff surgeon, 1983-98; pvt. practice Seattle, 1998—2003; breast surgeon Swedish Cancer Inst., 2004—. Author: Forged by the Knife—The Experience of Surgical Residency from the Perspective of a Woman of Color, 1999 Fellow ACS, Seattle Surg. Soc.; mem. Physicians for Social Responsibility, Assn. Women Surgeons, Wash. Black Profls. in Health Care, NOW. Avocations: fiction, walking, cooking. Office: Providence Comp Breast Ctr Jefferson Twr 1600 E Jefferson St Ste 300 Seattle WA 98122-5645 Home Phone: 206-725-1223; Office Phone: 206-320-4880.

DAWSON, PETER A., corporate financial executive; Exec. v.p. telecom. and indsl. bus. unit Bechtel Corp., sr. v.p., CFO, 2002—. Office: Bechtel Group 50 Beale St San Francisco CA 94105 also: PO Box 193965 San Francisco CA 94119 Office Phone: 415-768-1234. Office Fax: 415-768-9038.*

DAWSON, ROBERT G., telecommunications industry executive; b. 1946; B, Ga. Inst. Tech.; MBA, Ga. State U. Registered profl. engr., Ala., Fla., Ga., Miss. Coop. edn. student Southern Co. Svcs. Southern Co., 1964, various exec. and mgmt. positions in generation, power delivery and fuel svcs., v.p. fuel svcs., v.p. power generation and delivery Miss. Power, 1992—94, v.p. L.Am. and Caribbean assets Southern Energy (now Mirant Corp.), pres., CEO SouthernLINC Wireless and Southern Telecom, 1995—. Bd. dirs. Am. Mobile Telecom. Assn., CTIA. Office: Southern-LINC Wireless 30 Ivan Allen Jr Blvd NW Atlanta GA 30308 Office Phone: 404-506-5000. Office Fax: 404-506-0455.*

DAWSON, ROSARIO, actress, singer; b. NYC, May 9, 1979; Actor: (films) Kids, 1995, Girls Night Out, 1995, He Got Game, 1998, Side Streets, 1998, Light It Up, 1999, Down to You, 2000, Josie and the Pussycats, 2001, Sidewalks of New York, 2001, Trigger Happy, 2001, Chelsea Walls, 2001, King of the Jungle, 2001, Love in the Time of Money, 2002, Ash Wednesday, 2002, The First $20 Million Is Always the Hardest, 2002, Men in Black II, 2002, The Adventures of Pluto Nash, 2002, 25th Hour, 2002, This Girl's Life, 2003, Shattered Glass, 2003, The Rundown, 2003, Alexander, 2004, This Revolution, 2005, Sin City, 2005, Little Black Dress, 2005, Rent, 2005, A Guide to Recognizing Your Saints, 2006, Clerks II, 2006, Descent, 2006, Grindhouse (Death Proof segment), 2007.*

DAWSON, ROSE DOROTHY, retired elementary school educator; b. Waukesha, Wis., Feb. 16, 1931; d. Frank Peter and Rose M. (Cisler) Zaic; m. Keith W. Dawson, June 13, 1953 (dec. May 1987); children: Kenneth, Richard, Michael, Gail, Allen. BS, U. Wis., Whitewater, 1970; postgrad., U. Wis., Parkside, 1983-85. Cert. elem. tchr., Wis. Tchr. Magee Sch., Genesee Depot, Wis., 1951-53, Union Grove Middle Sch., 1986-91, Union Grove Grade Sch., Wis., 1953-54, 65-86, Wis., 1991-94, ret. Wis., 1995. Mem. NEA, Wis. Edn. Assn., Union Grove Area Edn. Assn., Am. Rose Soc. Lutheran. Avocations: gardening, crocheting, knitting, stamp collecting/philately, hummel collection. Home: 18906 58th Rd Union Grove WI 53182-9611 Office: 1745 Milldrum St Union Grove WI 53182

DAWSON, STEPHEN EVERETTE, lawyer; b. Detroit, May 14, 1946; s. Everette Ivan and Irene (Dresser) D.; m. Consiglia J. Bellisario, Sept. 20, 1974; children: Stephen Everette Jr., Gina C., Joseph J. BA, Mich. State U., 1968; MA, U. Mich., 1969, JD, 1972. Bar: Mich. 1972, U.S. Dist. Ct. (ea. dist.) Mich. 1972, U.S. Supreme Ct. 1978, U.S. Ct. Appeals (6th cir.) 1980. Assoc. Dickinson, Wright, Moon, Van Dusen & Freeman, Detroit, 1972-79; ptnr. Dickinson, Wright, PLLC, Bloomfield Hills, Mich., 1979—. Adj. prof. law U. Detroit, 1986-88. Mem. ABA, Am. Coll. Real Estate Lawyers, Mich. State Bar Assn. (mem. coun. real property law sect. 1986-93, chair 1992-93, land title stds. com. 1999—), Mich. State Bar Found., Phi Beta Kappa. Avocation: reading. Office: Dickinson Wright PLLC 38525 Woodward Ave Ste 2000 Bloomfield Hills MI 48304-5092 Office Phone: 248-433-7200. E-mail: sdawson@dickinsonwright.com.

DAWSON, SUZANNE STOCKUS, lawyer; b. Chgo., Dec. 29, 1941; d. John Charles and Josephine (Zolpe) Stockus; m. Daniel P. Dawson Sr., Sept. 1, 1962; children: Daniel P. Jr., John Charles, Michael Sean. BA, Marquette U., 1963; JD cum laude, Loyola U., Chgo., 1965. Bar: Ill. 1965, U.S. dist. Ct. (no. dist.) Ill. 1965. Assoc. Kirkland & Ellis, Chgo., 1965-71, ptnr., 1971-82, Arnstein & Lehr, Chgo., 1982-89, Foley & Lardner, Chgo., 1989-94; spl. counsel publicly held corps., 1995-97; corp. counsel Baxter Healthcare Corp., Deerfield, Ill., 1997-98, sr. counsel, 1998—2004, asst. gen. counsel, chief transactions counsel, 2004—06; comml. arbitrator Am. Arbitration Assn., 2006—. Mem. various coms. United Way Chgo.; corp. adv. bd. Sec. State of Ill., 1973; past mem. bd. advisors Loyola of Chgo. Law Sch.; trustee Lawrence Hall Youth Svcs., Chgo., 1983-98, pres., 1991-93, chair 1993-96; mem. adv. bd. Cath. Charities Chgo., 1985—, bd. dirs., 2002—, chair north suburban regional adv. bd., 2002—; mem. exec. com., bd. governance Notre Dame High Sch., Niles, Ill., 1990-97. Recipient Founder's Day award Loyola U., 1980, St. Thomas More award Loyola of Chgo. Law Sch., 1983. Mem. ABA, Am. Arbitration Assn. (appointed mem. nat. panel comml. arbitrators 1996—, comml. arbitrator 2006—), Ill. Bar Assn. Roman Catholic. Avocations: piano, choir singing, gardening, skiing, gourmet cooking. E-mail: suzannedawson@auditrecovery.net.

DAWSON, VALINA L., science educator; BS in Environ. Toxicology, U. Calif., Davis, 1983; PhD in Pharmacology, U. Utah, 1989. Fellow dept. neurology Hosp. of U. Pa., Phila., 1989—90; fellow Addiction Rsch. Ctr. Nat. Inst. Drug Abuse, Balt., 1990—93; dir. neurobiology of disease program dept. neurology Johns Hopkins U. Sch. Medicine, Balt.; assoc. prof. neurology, neurosci., and physiology Johns Hopkins Hosp., 1994—2001, prof., vice chmn. neurology, prof. neurosci. and physiology, 2001—. Contbr. articles to profl. jours. Named Internat. Soc. for Neurochemistry Young Investigator, 1999, Staglin Music Festival Investigator, 1998; recipient Mary Lou McIlhany scholarship, 1999, Am. Heart Assn. Grant-in-Aid award, 1996, award, Muscular Dystrophy Assn., 1995, Alzheimer's Assn. Scholar award, 1994, Am. Heart Assn. Grant-in-Aid award, 1994, AmFar Scholar award, 1994, ADAMHA Intramural Rsch. Tng. award, 1992, Nat. Inst. Drug Abuse Staff Fellow award, 1992, Winter Conf. on Brain Rsch. fellowship, 1991, NIH PRAT fellowship, 1990. Achievements include research in molecular mechanisms of neurodegeneration and regeneration; experimental models of stroke; gene discovery of novel cell survival pathways; cell based therapies for the treatment of neurologic disorders. Office: Inst for Cell Engring Dept Neurology 733 N Broadway St Ste 711 Baltimore MD 21205 E-mail: vdawson@jhmi.edu.

DAWSON, VIRGINIA SUE, retired editor; b. Concordia, Kans., June 6, 1940; d. John Edward and Wilma Aileen (Thompson) Morgan; m. Neil S. Dawson, Nov. 28, 1964; children: Shelley Diane Dawson Sedwick, Lori Ann Dawson Hughes, Christy Lynn. BS in Home Econs. and Journalism, Kans. State U., 1962. Asst. publs. editor Ohio State U. Coop. Ext. Svc., Columbus, 1962-64; home editor Ohio Farmer mag., Columbus, 1964-78; food editor Columbus Dispatch, 1978—2000, ret. Recipient Commn. award Ohio Poultry Assn., 1980. Mem. Assn. Food Journalists. Avocations: biking, reading, cooking, hiking. Personal E-mail: ndawson1@cox.net.

DAWSON, WILLIAM B., lawyer; b. Amarillo, Tex., Aug. 24, 1949; BBA, Tex. Tech U., 1972, JD with highest honors, 1975. Bar: Tex. 1975. Atty. Carrington, Coleman, Sloman & Blumenthal LLP, Dallas; ptnr., co-head Litig. Sect. Vinson & Elkins LLP, Dallas. Bd. editors: Tex. Tech Law Rev., 1974-75. Fellow Am. Coll. Trial Lawyers; mem. ABA, Order of Coif, Phi Kappa Phi, Delta Theta Phi. Office: Vinson & Elkins LLP Trammell Crow Ctr 2001 Ross Ave, Ste 3700 Dallas TX 75201 Office Phone: 214-220-7926. E-mail: bdawson@velaw.com.

DAWSON, WILLIAM RYAN, zoology educator; b. LA, Aug. 24, 1927; s. William Eldon and Mary (Ryan) D.; m. Virginia Louise Berwick, Sept. 9, 1950; children: Deborah, Denise, William. Student, Stanford, 1945-46; BA, UCLA, 1949, MA, 1950, PhD, 1953; DSc, U. Western Australia, 1971. Faculty zoology U. Mich., Ann Arbor, 1953-94, prof., 1962-94, D.E.S. Brown prof. biol. scis., 1981-94, chmn. div. biol. scis., 1974-82, dir. Mus. Zoology, 1982-93, D.E.S. Brown prof. emeritus, 1994—. Lectr. Summer Inst. Desert Biology, Ariz. State U., 1960-71, Maytag prof., 1982; rschr. Australian-Am. Edn. Found., U. Western Australia, 1969-70; Carpenter lectr. San Diego State U., 1996; mem. Speakers Bur., Am. Inst. Biol. Sci., 1960-62; mem. adv. panel NSF environ. biology program, 1967-69; mem. adv. com. for rsch. NSF, 1973-77; adv. panel NSF regulatory biology program, 1979-82; mem. R/V Alpha Helix New Guinea Expdn., 1969; chief scientist R/V Dolphin Gulf of Calif. Expdn., 1976; mem. R/V Alpha Helix Galapagos Expdn., 1978. Editorial bd.: Condor, 1960-63, Auk, 1964-68, Ecology, 1968-70, Ann. Rev. Physiology, 1973-79, Physiol. Zoology, 1976-86; co-editor: Springer-Verlag Zoophysiology and Ecology series, 1968-72; assoc. editor: Biology of the Reptilia, 1972, Birds of N.Am., 1997-2004. Served with USNR, 1945-46. USPHS postdoc. rsch.fellow, 1953; Guggenheim fellow, 1962-63; recipient Russell award U. Mich., 1959, Disting. Faculty Achievement award, 1976; Wheeler lectr. U. N.D., 1986. Fellow Am. Ornithol. Union (Brewster medal 1979); mem. Soc. Integrative Comparative Biology (pres. 1985), Am. Physiol. Soc., Ecol. Soc. Am., Cooper Ornithol. Soc. (hon., Painton award 1963, Miller Rsch. award 1996), Phi Beta Kappa, Kappa Sigma. Home: 1376 Bird Rd Ann Arbor MI 48103-2351 Office Phone: 734-615-6903. Business E-Mail: wrdawson@umich.edu.

DAY, ANNETTE J., music educator; d. Edward Leroy and Ada June Shives; m. Mark Stephen Day, June 9, 1984; 1 child, Erin Taylor. BA in Music Edn., Shepherd U., 1981. Tchr. music Music Tchrs. Nat. Assn., 2004, Prin., owner Day Music Studio, Berkeley Springs, W.Va., 1976—, piano pedagogy instr. Peachtree City, Ga., 1974—. Dir. girl's choir, 2004—. Co-founder Peachtree City Piano Camp; music coord. 1st United Meth. Ch., Berkley Springs, 1974—77, Francis Asbury United Meth. Ch., Berkley Springs, 1977—81; dir. adult and youth choir Christ Our Shepherd Luth. Ch., Peachtree City, 2000—02, girl's choir dir., 2004—. McMurran scholar, Shepherd Coll., 1980. Mem.: Nat. Fedn. Music Clubs, Nat. Guild Piano Tchrs., Music Tchrs. Nat. Assn. (pres.-elect. south metro Atlanta 2000—02, v.p. Cowetta-Fayette 2002—04, pres. 2004—, nat. cert. music tchr. 2004). Office: Day Music Studio 214 Columns Ln Peachtree City GA 30269 Business E-Mail: daystudio@earthlink.net.

DAY, BARBARA D., education educator, association administrator; BS, East Carolina U., 1959; MEd, U. NC, Chapel Hill, 1962, PhD, 1968; MDiv, Duke U., 2002. Tchr., prin. and asst. supt. schs.; dir. tchg. fellows prog. U. NC, Chapel Hill, 1989—99, coord. early childhood edn., elem. edn. and tchg. & learning progs., prof., coord. curriculum and instrn. doctoral prog. Chair Early Childhood Consortium Assn. Supervision and Curriculum Devel., 1987—92; mem. Early Childhood Edn. Task Force Nat. Assn. State Bds. of Edn. Editor: Education in the 21st Century. Key Issues: Leadership, Literacy, Legislation and Learning, 1985, Teaching and Learning in the New Millennium, 2002; author: Early Childhood Education: Developmental/Experiential Teaching & Learning, 4th ed., Good Schools for Young Children, 5th ed. Recipient CINE Golden Eagle award for Media Publ., 1987, Nat. Leadership award, Nat. Assn. Internat. Honor Societies, 2000. Mem.: Phi Delta Kappa, Kappa Delta Pi (pres. 1998—2000), Delta Kappa Gamma Soc. Internat. (pres. 2006—). Office: Sch Edn U NC CB 3500 Peabody Hall Chapel Hill NC 27599-3500 Office Phone: 919-962-7739. Office Fax: 919-962-1533. E-mail: bday1@email.unc.edu.*

DAY, BURNIS C., artist, educator; b. Hepzibah, W.Va. s. Jeff Monroe and Willie Etta (Porter) Day. Student, Ctr. for Creative Studies Coll. of Art and Design, Detroit, 1964—66, Famous Artists Sch., Westport, Conn., 1965—67; AAS, Oakland C.C., Farmington Hills, Mich., 1969. Keyliner and photostat operator Freuhauf Corp., Detroit, 1970-71; art dir. Urban Screen Process, Detroit, 1971-73; instr. art Pittman's Galleries, Inc., Detroit, 1973-74; art assoc. Cal Summers' House of Art, Detroit, 1971-77; with 21st Century Video, Detroit; free-lance advt. and painting, Detroit, 1977—. Comml. commissions Chrysler Corp., J.L. Hudson Co.; instr. art Wayne County C.C., 1985—98, St. Scholastica Summer Day Camp, Detroit, 1995—98; juror Mich. State Fair, Detroit, 1992, Arts for Parks, Jackson Hole, Wyo., 1994; field videographer Inst. for Survey Rsch., Temple U., Phila., 1992—93; instr. painting on TV satellite UAW-Chrysler Nat. Tng. Ctr., Detroit, 1995—99; panelist Mich. Arts and Humanities Touring Dir., 2000—03; art slide registry collections Nat. Mus. of Am. Art, Washington, Nat. Portrait Gallery, Smithsonian Inst., Art Inst. Chgo., Indpls. Mus. of Art, Nigerian Nat. Coun. Arts and Culture. Prin. works include Friendship, a collector's item, one-man shows include Pittman Galleries, Detroit, 1981, Gov. James J. Blanchard's Showplace Display, Lansing, Mich., 1985, exhibited in group shows at The Gallery Tanner, L.A., 1984, The Laramie Art Guild, Wyo., 1979, The N.Mex. Art League, 1979, Nat. Theatre, Lagos, Nigeria, 1977, Represented in permanent collections Detroit Inst. Arts, Detroit Main Libr., Denver Pub. Libr., City of N.Y., U. Utah Mus. Fine Arts, Mus. No. Ariz., Mus. Art, Ponce, P.R., Las Vegas Art Mus., Kauai Regional Libr., Lihue, Hawaii, Former Pres. Bill Clinton's Pvt. Collection from the White House, U. Mo. Mus. Art and Archaeology, Washington County Mus. Fine Arts Md., U. Mont. Mus. Fine Arts, N.Mex. Highlands U., Ft. Smith (Ark.) Art Ctr., Fisk U. Art Galleries, Tenn., Hofstra U. Mus., N.Y., Mus. City N.Y., Oprah Winfrey's pvt. collection, Chgo., Mus. of Art and Archaeology, Univ. Mo.-Columbia, Univ. S.D. Art Galleries, Charles B. Goddard Ctr. for the Visual and Performing Arts, Ardmore, Okla., The Carsey-Werner Co., Astoria, N.Y., Sally Jesse Raphael, Phil Donahue, many others; author: Burnis Calvin Day's Neogeometric Paintings (His Travels, Insight on Art and Artists), 2003, translator. Vol. svc. camera operator pub. access program Comcast Cable TV, 1988. Recipient awards for art, 1st pl. award for mural, People's Art and Detroit Recreation Dept., 1976, 2d pl., 1977, cert. of recognition, US Zone Com., Lagos, Nigeria, 1977. Avocations: nature, outdoors, Go. Office: PO Box 0255 Detroit MI 48231-0255 Personal E-mail: burnisday@yahoo.com.

DAY, CECIL LEROY, agricultural engineering educator; b. Dexter, Mo., Oct. 4, 1922; s. Cecil Lawrence and Katherine (Kleffer) D.; m. Peggy Eunice Thrower, Aug. 29, 1948; children: Stanley K., Thomas L. BS in Agrl. Engring., U. Mo., 1945, MS, 1948; PhD, Iowa State U., 1957. Mem. faculty U. Mo. at Columbia, 1945-85, prof. agrl. engring., 1962-85; prof. emeritus, 1985—; chmn. dept., 1969-82. Vis. prof. U. Thessaloniki, Greece, 1972; pres. Penreico, Inc., 1968-79. Author articles, bulls. Chmn. elec. appeals bd., Columbia, 1966-76; elder Ch. of Christ, 1993-98; alumni bd. dirs. U. Mo. Coll. Engring., 1992-2004. Fellow Am. Soc. Agrl. Engrs. (outstanding individual of yr. Mo. sect. 1982); mem. Agrl. Engrs. of Mo. Inc. (pres. 1987-2000), Lakeshore Villa Homes Assn. Inc. (treas. 1985-99, pres. 1996-98), Columbia Golden K Kiwanis Club (pres. 1995-96). Home: 104 Clinkscales Rd Apt 702 Columbia MO 65203 *"And we know that all things work together for good to them that love God."*

DAY, CHARLES WILLIAMSON, commentator; b. Chgo., Apr. 30, 1931; s. Lewis Andrew and Isabel Gillette (Williamson) Day; m. Carla Louise Dean, Nov. 30, 1963; children: Charles Williamson Jr., Allison Parker, Spencer Dean. BA, Yale U., 1954; MS, Columbia U., 1957; MA, U. Chgo., 1958. Accreditation Pub. Rels. Soc. Am., 1981. Speech writer Ford Motor Co., Washington, 1960—62, ednl. affairs, 1962—63, mgr. non-product legis., 1963—79, dir. King Ct. project, 1979—80, mgr. Lincoln Mercury pub. rels., 1980—87, mgr. spl. events, 1988—90, mgr. Washington pub. affairs, 1990—94, dir. Washington pub. affairs, 1994—97; classical music host WGMS-FM, 1998—2007. Chmn. Rd. Gang Washington, 1970—71; pres. Capitol Hill Club Toastmasters Internat., 1973—74, pres. U.S.Senate Club, 1974—75; guest lectr. journalism sch. George Washington U., 1978—79. Author: (column) Roll Call Newspaper, The Toastmaster Magazine; contbr. articles to profl. jours. Advisor Mich. Metro Girl Scouts Coun., Detroit, 1981—87. Capt. USAF, 1954—56. Recipient Sackett prize Libel Law, Columbia U. Grad. Sch. Journalism, 1957, Thoth award Best Radio Promotion, Pub. Rels. Soc. Am., Washington Chpt., 1998, Radio award Best Fill-in Talent, 1999; scholar, C. J. LaRoche, 1957—58. Mem.: Book and Snake Soc., Lowes Island Club, Cosmos Club (life), Beta Theta Pi. Episcopalian. Achievements include first to hold transatlantic auto industry TV news conference; created GreenWire service of Political Hotline, division of National Journal; invention of in-car cell phone (Ford production option); raised funds to complete Martin Luther King, Jr. Center, Atlanta. Avocations: running, art, travel, fine scale modeling. Home: 101 Sinegar Pl Potomac Falls VA 20165 Office: WGMS-FM 3400 Idaho Ave NW Washington DC 20016 Home Phone: 703-406-4112. Personal E-mail: bday2@earthlink.net.

DAY, DELBERT EDWIN, ceramic engineering educator; b. Avon, Ill., Aug. 16, 1936; s. Edwin Raymond and Doris Jennings (Main) D.; m. Shirley Ann Foraker, June 2, 1956; children: Lynne Denise, Thomas Edwin. BS in Ceramic Engring., Mo. Sch. Mines and Metallurgy, 1958; MS in Ceramic Tech., Pa. State U., 1960, PhD in Ceramic Tech., 1961; DSc (hon.), U Mo.-Rolla, 2004. Registered profl. engr., Mo. With U. Mo., Rolla, 1961—, dir. Indsl. Rsch. Ctr., 1965-72, dir. Grad. Ctr. Materials Rsch., 1983-92, Curators' prof. ceramic engring., 1981—; founder, chmn., CEO Mo-Sci Corp., Rolla, Mo., 1985—; dir. State of Mo. Tech. Corp., 1999—2004. Vis. prof. chemistry Miss. Coll., 1963, Eindhoven Tech. U., The Netherlands, 1971; mem. tech. staff Sandia Nat. Labs., Albuquerque, 1981, 91; sr. vis. faculty scientist Battelle Pacific N.W. Labs., Richland, Wash., 1990; asst. dean grad. studies Mo. Sch. Mines and Metallurgy, 1979-81; chmn. acad. coun. U. Mo., Rolla, 1978-79, active numerous other coms.; cons. Los Alamos Nat. Labs., 1983-95, NASA, 1974-88, numerous other glass and refractories cos., 1958—; vice-chmn. Gordon Rsch. Conf. on Glass, 1990-92, chmn., 1992-94; tech. program dir. confs. on glass including Baden-Baden, Germany, 1973, Rolla, 1975, XII Internat. Glass Congress, Albuquerque, 1980, Internat. and 7th U. Conf. Glass Sci., Clausthal-Zellerfeld, Germany, 1983; founder, CEO MO-Sci. Corp., Rolla. Editor: 3 books; contbr. articles to profl. jours. Chmn. bd. Wesley Found.; chmn. United Ministries Higher Edn. Bd. Dirs., 1969; adv. Explorer Scout Post 82, 1964-69; bd. dirs. Rolla Cmty. United Fund, 1975-81, Mo. Incutech Found., 1984-87; mem. bd. adjustment City of Rolla, 1973-79; fin. chmn. United Meth. Ch., 1978-80; pres., bd. dirs. Rolla Cmty. Devel. Corp., 1967-71, 82-90. 1st lt. C.E., U.S. Army, 1958-64. Recipient Outstanding Young Man award Clinton (Miss.) Jaycees, 1963, Rolla (Mo.) Jaycees, 1968, Cmty. Builder award Fraternal Order of Eagles, 1971, Pres.'s award for rsch. and creativity U. Mo., 1996, Chancellor medal U. Mo.-Rolla, 2003, Hosler Alumni Scholar medal Pa. State U., 2003. Fellow Am. Ceramic Soc. (life, v.p. rsch. 1990-91, trustee 1986-98, trustee glass divsn. 1986-89, chmn. glass divsn. 1982-83, fellows com. 1987-92, publs. com. 1980-82, 90-95, v.p. Publs. 1992-93, treas. 1993-94, pres.-elect 1994-95, pres. 1995-96, others, Outstanding Educator award 1991, G.W. Morey Rsch. award 2001, Samuel Geijsbeek award 2001, Harry E. Ebright award 2002, W.D. Kingery award 2004), Am. Nat. Inst. Ceramic Engrs., Soc. Glass Tech. (Great Britain); mem. NAE, Am. Soc. Engring. Edn. (chmn. mineral engring. div. 1968-69, program chmn. mineral engring. div. 1967-68), Nat. Inst. Ceramic Engrs. (Profl. Achievement in Ceramic Engring. award 1971, Greaves Walker award 2001), Materials Rsch. Soc., Mo. Acad. Sci. (corp. mem. com. 1989-90), Keramos, Blue Key, Tau Beta Pi, Phi Kappa Phi, Sigma Gamma Epsilon, Sigma Xi (treas. U. Mo.-Rolla chpt. 1966-67, sec. 1967-68, v.p. 1968-69, pres. 1969-70). Achievements include 44 U.S. and foreign patents (with others) for Alumina Zircon Bond for Refractory Grains, Chemically Durable Nitrogen Containing Phosphate Glasses Useful for Sealing to Metals; first to include Radioactive Biologically Compatible Glass Microspheres, Radioactive Glass Microspheres, iron phosphate glasses for vitrifying hazardous wastes, others; co-invention of TheraSphere used for treatment of liver cancer. Home: PO Box 357 Rolla MO 65402-0357 Office: U Mo-Rolla Grad Ctr Material Rsch 109 Straumanis Hl Rolla MO 65409-1170 Office Phone: 573-341-4354. Business E-Mail: day@umr.edu.

DAY, DONALD LEE, retired engineering educator; b. Leedey, Okla., Aug. 14, 1931; m. Sarah F. Day; children: Cheryl, Keith, Dennis. BS in Agrl. Engring., Okla. State U., 1954, PhD in Agrl. Engring., 1962; MS in Agrl. Engring., U. Mo., 1958. Registered profl. engr., Ill. Engr. Allis Chalmers Mfg. Co., Milw., 1954; instr. Tex. Tech U., Lubbock, 1957-58; asst. prof. U. Ill., Urbana, 1962-67, assoc. prof., 1967-71, prof., 1971-97; ret., 1994. Adviser UN/WHO, Romania, 1972—75, US Food Grain Coun., Russia, Poland, Czech Republic, 1975; cons. Internat. Exec. Svc. Corps., Mexico, 1978; leader structures and environ. divsn. agrl. engring. dept. U. Ill., 1989—94. Author: Livestock Manure Management, 1983; contbr. articles to profl. jours. Active Twin City Bible Ch., Urbana, Ill. Pilot USAF, 1954—57. Grantee, various orgns.; fellow, Japan Soc. Promotion Sci., 1992, USDA Office Internat. Coop. and Devel. Fellow: Am. Soc. Agrl. Engrs. (Rsch. Paper award 1966); mem.: Ill. Pilots Assn., Coun. Agrl. Sci. and Tech., Agrl. Honor Orgns., Aircraft Owners and Pilots Assn. Achievements include invention of electrical conversion of organic matter. Business E-Mail: dl-day@uiuc.edu.

DAY, DONALD SHELDON, lawyer; b. Boston, Nov. 3, 1924; s. Israel and Frances (Goldberg) D.; m. Edythe Greenberg, July 8, 1945; children: Clifford L., Richard J., Halee Beth. BA, Bates Coll., 1946; LLB, Cornell U., 1948. Bar: N.Y. 1948. Past chmn. bd. Saperston and Day P.C., Buffalo, 1979-96; pres. World Union for Progressive Judaism, 1988-95. Bd. dirs. various corps. Gen. chmn. United Jewish Fund Campaign, Buffalo, 1971-73, 75; past co-chmn. Western N.Y. chpt. NCCJ; past pres. United Jewish Fedn. Buffalo; past chmn. bd. Childrens Hosp. Buffalo, Union Am. Hebrew Congregations; trustee Forest Lawn Cemetery and Crematory, Hebrew-Union Coll. With AUS, 1942-45. Mem. Am., N.Y. State, Erie County bar assns., Order of Coif, Phi Kappa Phi. Jewish (past pres. temple). Office: Hiscock & Barclay 3 Fountain Plz Buffalo NY 14203-1486 Business E-Mail: dday@hiscockbarclay.com.

DAY, DORIS (DORIS VON KAPPELHOFF), singer, actress; b. Cin., Apr. 3, 1924; d. Frederick Wilhelm and Alma Sophia von Kappelhoff; m. Al Jorden, Mar. 1941 (div. 1943); 1 son, Terry; m. George Weilder, 1946 (div. 1949); m. Marty Melcher, Apr. 3, 1951 (dec. 1968); m. Barry Comden, Apr. 1976 (div.) Student pub. schs., Cin. Made profl. dancing appearance with Doherty & Kappelhoff, Glendale, Calif.; singer Karlin's Karnival, Sta. WCPO-Radio, with bands Barney Rapp, Bob Crosby, Fred Waring, Les Brown; singer, leading lady, Bob Hope NBC radio show, 1948-50, Doris Day CBS show, 1952-53; singer Columbia Records, 1950—, Hooray for Hollywood col.1, 1988, A Day At The Movies, 1989, The Essence of Doris Day, 1993, Duet with The Andre Previn Trio, 1996; star Warner Bros. Studio; motion pictures include Romance on the High Seas, 1948, My Dream is Yours, 1949, Young Man With a Horn, 1950, Tea For Two, 1950, West Point Story, 1950, Lullaby of Broadway, 1951, On Moonlight Bay, 1951, I'll See You in My Dreams, 1951, April in Paris, 1952, By the Light of the Silvery Moon, 1953, Lucky Me, Yankee Doodle Girl, 1954, Love Me or Leave Me, 1955 (selected as 1 of 10 best films by N.Y. Herald Tribune), Pajama Game, 1957, Teacher's Pet, 1958, Tunnel of Love, 1958, It Happened to Jane, 1959, Pillow Talk, 1959, Midnight Lace, 1960, Jumbo, 1962, That Touch of Mink, 1962, The Thrill of It All, 1963, Please Don't Eat the Daisies, 1960, Lover Come Back, 1962, Send Me No Flowers, 1964, Do Not Disturb, 1965, The Glass Bottom Boat, 1966, Caprice, 1967, The Ballad of Josie, 1968, Where Were You When The Lights Went Out, 1968, With Six You Get Eggrolls, 1968, Sleeping Dogs, Hearts and Souls, 1993, That's Entertainment III, 1994; TV series The Doris Day Show, 1970-73, Doris Day & Friends, 1985-86, Doris Day's Best, 1985-86; appeared on TV spl. The Pet Set, 1972; guest appearance Six Feet Under, 2005. Founder Doris Day Animal League, Washington, 1987. Winner 1st prize (with Jerry Doherty) as best dance team in Cin.; recipient Laurel award as leading new female persoanlity in motion picture industry, 1950; named top audience attractor, 1962; recipient Am. Comedy Lifetime Achievement award, 1991. Christian Scientist. Office: care Doris Day Animal League Ste 100 227 Massachusetts Ave NE Washington DC 20002-4963 also: Columbia Records 550 Madison Ave New York NY 10022-3211

DAY, EDWARD FRANCIS, JR., lawyer; b. Portland, Maine, Nov. 4, 1946; s. Edward Francis and Anne (Rague) Day; m. Claire Ann Nicholson, June 27, 1970; children: Kelley Ann, John Edward. BA, St. Anselm Coll., 1968; JD cum laude, U. Maine, 1973; LLM in Taxation, NYU, 1976. Bar: NJ 1973, US Dist. Ct. NJ 1973, US Tax Ct. 1974, NY 1981. Assoc. Hannoch, Weisman, Stern & Besser, Newark, 1973-74, Carpenter, Bennett & Morrissey, Newark, 1974-78, ptnr., 1979-93, sr. ptnr., 1994-98, of counsel, 1999—2004, McElroy, Deutsch, Mulvaney & Carpenter, LLP, Morristown, NJ, 2004—. Instr. employee benefits and comml. law The Am. Coll., Valley Forge, Pa., 1981-82; exec. v.p., gen. counsel Main Steel Polishing Co., Inc., Tinton Falls, NJ, 1999—. Editor Maine Law Rev., 1972-73. Mem., vice-chmn. Allenhurst Bd. Adjustment, NJ, 1983-85; mem., vice-chmn. Allenhurst Planning Bd., 1985-87; mem. Nat. Ski Patrol, Denver, 1985—; scoutmaster Monmouth coun. Boy Scouts Am., Ocean Twp., 1987-90; mem. 10th Mountain Divsn. Assn., Aspen, Colo., 1996—. With mil. police corps, US Army, 1968-70. Named One of Outstanding Young Men of Am., 1979; Ford Found. scholar, 1966-68. Mem.: ABA, Appalachian Mountain Club (Boston), Estate Planning Coun. No. NJ, Essex County Bar Assn., NJ Bar Assn., 10th Mountain Divsn. Assn. (Aspen, Colo.), TPC Sawgrass (Ponte Vedra Beach, Fla.), Jumping Brook Country Club (Neptune, NJ), Jersey Coast Club of Red Bank (v.p. 1976—77), Deal (NJ) Golf and Country Club (bd. dirs. 1985—92, sec. 1991—92), Am. Legion. Roman Catholic. Avocations: golf, skiing, piano. Home: 225 Spier Ave Allenhurst NJ 07711-1120 Office: McElroy Deutsch Mulvaney & Carpenter LLP 3 Gateway Ctr Newark NJ 07102-4079 also: Main Steel Polishing Company Inc 2 Hance Ave Eatontown NJ 07724-2726 Office Phone: 973-565-2020, 732-450-0110. Office Fax: 732-450-0511. Personal E-mail: edward.day@verizon.net.

DAY, EMERSON, physician; b. Hanover, NH, May 2, 1913; s. Edmund Ezra and Emily Sophia (Emerson) D.; m. Ruth Fairfield, Aug. 7, 1937 (dec. Oct. 1994); children: Edmund Perry, Robert Fairfield, Nancy, Bonnie, Sheryl; m. Germaine Scherman, Sept. 24, 1999. BA, Dartmouth Coll., 1934; MD, Harvard U., 1938. Intern Presbyn. Hosp., NYC, 1938- 40; fellow in cardiology Johns Hopkins U., 1940-42; asst. resident medicine N.Y. Hosp., 1942; med. dir. internat. divsn. Trans World Airline, NYC, 1945-47; asst. prof. preventive medicine and pub. health Cornell U. Med. Coll., 1947-50, assoc. prof. clin. preventive medicine and pub. health, 1950-54, prof. preventive medicine Sloan Kettering divsn., 1954-64; chmn. dept. preventive medicine Meml. Hosp., NYC, 1954-63; dir. Strang Cancer Prevention Clinic, 1950-63; mem., chief divsn. preventive medicine Sloan-Kettering Inst., NYC, 1954-64; cons. in geriat. Cold Spring Inst., Cold Spring-on-Hudson, NY, 1952-57; dir. N.Y.C. Dept. Health Cancer Detection Ctr., 1947-50, Strang Clinic/Meml. Sloan Kettering Cancer Ctr., 1950-63, PMI-Strang Clinic, 1963-69; pres. Preventive Medicine Inst., Strang Cancer Prevention Ctr., 1969—; hon. pres., mem. bd. trustees Preventive Medicine Inst., 1969—; v.p., med. dir. Medequip Corp., 1969-76, sr. med. cons., 1976-82; med. v.p. Health Mgmt. Internat., Inc., 1982-84; med. dir. Physicians for Med. Cost Containment, Inc., 1984-94; prof. medicine Northwestern U. Med. Sch., 1976-81, prof. emeritus, 1981—; assoc. dir. Northwestern U. Cancer Ctr., 1976-81; med. dir. Portes Cancer Prevention Ctr., 1978-79; attending physician Northwestern Meml. Hosp., 1976-81, vis. physician, 1981-99. Lectr. Cook County Grad. Sch. Med., 1977-90; mem. Northwestern U. Med. Assocs., 1980-81; med. dir., chmn. dept. internal medicine Chgo. Splty. Hosp. and Med. Ctr., 1981-84; hon. staff physician Evanston, Glenbrook hosps., 1976-99; attending physician, mem. med. bd. James Ewing Hosp., Meml. Hosp., N.Y.C., 1950-64; founder, sr. mem. PMX Med. Group, N.Y.C., 1956— 70; adj. prof. biology N.Y. U., 1965-70; mem. cancer detection com. Internat. Union Against Cancer, 1954-70; pres. N.Y.C. div. Am. Cancer Soc., 1963-64; med. cons. Medidata Health Svcs., Inc., 1985-90; mem. Dean's Coun. for Future of Dartmouth Med. Sch. Contbr. numerous articles to profl. jours. Dir. Am. Found. for Children and Youth. Served as flight surgeon ATC USAAF, 1942-45. Recipient Bronze medal Am. Cancer Soc., 1956, professorship in early detection Ill. divsn., 1976-79, Lifetime Achievement award Strang Cancer Prevention Ctr., 2003. Fellow ACP, N.Y. Acad. Medicine, N.Y. Acad. Scis. (pres. 1965), APHA, Am. Occupl. Med. Assn., Am. Geriat. Soc., Internat. Acad. Cytology (hon.); mem. AMA, Am. Soc. Cytopathology (founder, pres. 1958, hon., Papanicolaou award 1978), Am. Soc. Preventive Oncology, Internat. Health Evaluation Assn., Soc. for Advanced Med. Sys. (founding dir. 1969-81), Am. Assn. Med. Sys. and Informatics (founding dir. 1981-84), Harvey Soc., Chgo. Clin. Ethics Program (charter), Century Assn., Ill. Med. Soc., Chgo. Med. Soc., Med. Cons. Svcs. Assn., Dartmouth Club (mem. dean's coun., award 1955), Phi Beta Kappa, Alpha Omega Alpha, Zeta Psi. Home and Office: 1420 Sheridan Rd Apt 4A Wilmette IL 60091

DAY, HOWARD WILMAN, geology educator; b. Burlington, Vt., Nov. 17, 1942; s. Wilman Forrest and Virginia Louise (Morton) D.; children: Kristina, Sarah, Susan; m. Judy Lynn Blevins. AB, Dartmouth Coll., 1964; MS, Brown U., 1968, PhD, 1971. Prof. geology U. Okla., Norman, 1970—76, U. Calif., Davis, 1976—, chmn. dept., 1990-96. Co-editor Jour. Metamorphic Geology, 1985-92; contbr. articles to profl. jours. Fulbright fellow, Norway, 1964, Alexander von Humboldt fellow, Fed. Republic Germany, 1977. Fellow Geol. Soc. Am., Mineral Soc. Am.; mem. Am. Geophys. Union. Office: U Calif Dept Geology Davis CA 95616 Business E-Mail: hwday@ucdavis.edu.

DAY, JAMES, television executive; b. Alameda, Calif., Dec. 22, 1918; s. James Magee and June (Reeve) D.; m. Beverley Anne Hare, Apr. 12, 1943; children: Meredith Johnson, Douglas Craig, Alan Kent, James Ross. BA, U. Calif., Berkeley, 1941; postgrad., Stanford U., 1951; LHD (hon.), Newark State Coll., Newark, NJ, 1972. Dir. pub. svc. NBC, San Francisco, 1946-49; radio specialist Civil Info. & Edn. Sect./Supreme Commdr. Allies/Pacific, Tokyo, 1949-51; dep. dir. Radio Free Asia, San Francisco, 1951-53; pres., gen. mgr. KQED (TV-FM), San Francisco, 1953-69; pres. Nat. Ednl. TV, NYC, 1969-71, WNET-TV, NYC, 1971-73; prof. radio, TV Bklyn. Coll., CUNY, NYC, 1976-89, prof. emeritus, 1989—; pres. Publivision, Inc., NYC, 1973—. Pres. Timely Prodns. for TV, N.Y.C., 1989—; founding dir. Children's TV Workshop, Pub. Broadcasting Svc., Internat. Pub. TV Screening Conf., Comm. Improvement, Inc.; chmn. adv. bd. City Univ. TV. Author: The Vanishing Vision: The Inside Story of Public Television, 1995, interviewer: (TV) Kaleidoscope, 1954-69, Day at Night, 1973-74, Conversations with Eric Hoffer, 1967, Conversations with Arnold Toynbee, 1968; sr. prodr. Black Writers in America. Capt. U.S. Army, 1941-46. Recipient Robert C. Kirkwood award, San Francisco Found., 1966, Golden Plate award, Am. Acad. Achievement, Dallas, 1968, 50th Anniversary Dirs. award, Ohio State U., Columbus, 1986; resident scholar Rockefeller Study Ctr., Bellagio, Italy, 1978. Mem. Internat. Inst. Comm., Soc. Profl. Journalists. Avocations: photography, swimming. Home: 115 E 86th St New York NY 10028-1057 Office: Publivision Inc One Lincoln Pla New York NY 10023 Office Phone: 212-875-6150. Personal E-mail: jdayny@cuny.tv.

DAY, JAMES MCADAM, JR., lawyer; b. Detroit, Aug. 18, 1948; s. James McAdam and Mary Elizabeth (McGibbon); children: Cara McAdam, Brenna Marie, Michael James; m. Kathleen C. Henderson. AB, UCLA, 1970; JD magna cum laude, U. Pacific, Sacramento, 1973. Bar: Calif. 1973, US Dist. Ct. (no. dist.) Calif. 1973, US Ct. Appeals (9th cir.) 1975. Assoc. Downey, Brand, Seymour & Rohwer, Sacramento, 1973-78, ptnr., 1978—, chmn. natural resources dept., 1985—90; mng. ptnr. Downey, Brand, Seymour & Rohmer, Sacramento, 1990—94, chmn. nat. resources dept., 2002—03, mng. ptnr., 1997—2001; ptnr. Day Carter & Murphy LLP, Sacramento, 2006—. Contbr. articles to profl. jours. Pres., bd. dirs. Sacramento Soc. for Prevention of Cruelty to Animals, 1976-79, Children's Home Soc. of Calif., Sacramento, 1979-85; bd. dirs. Sta. KXPR/KXJZ, Inc. Pub. Radio, Sacramento, 1984-94, chmn., 1990-93; bd. dirs. Calif. State Libr. Found., 1995-2000, chmn., 1995-2000. Mem. ABA (natural resources sect. 1998), Calif. Bar Assn. (exec. com. 1985-89, chmn. real property law sect. 1988), Rocky Mountain Mineral Law Found., Sacramento Petroleum Assn., Calif. Mining Assn., U. Pacific McGeorge Law Sch. Alumni Assn. (bd. dirs. 1980-83). Avocations: yachting, fishing. Office: Day Carter & Murphy LLP 3620 Am River Dr Ste 205 Sacramento CA 95864 Home: 411 Burbank Way Sacramento CA 95864

DAY, JOHN ANTHONY, JR., pulmonologist; b. Washington, Sept. 7, 1949; s. John Anthony and Marcia (O'Brien) Day; m. Jane Marie Doyle, July 9, 1983; children: Margaret Eugenie, Nicholas Paul, Helen Elizabeth. AB, Harvard Coll., 1973; MD, Cornell U., 1981. Diplomate Am. Bd. Critical Care Medicine, Am. Bd. Internal Medicine. Intern, resident in internal medicine Vanderbilt U. Hosp., Nashville, 1981-84; instr. medicine Brown U., Providence, 1984-85, fellow in pulmonary medicine, 1985-87; attending physician Carney Hosp., Boston, 1987-93; asst. prof. medicine U. Mass. Med. Sch., Worcester, 1993—. Attending physician Day Kimball Hosp., Putnam, Conn. Fellow: Am. Coll. Chest Physicians; mem.: Am. Thoracic Soc. Home: 270 Old Turnpike Rd Woodstock CT 06282 Office: 346 Pomfret St Putnam CT 06260 Office Phone: 860-928-4344.

DAY, JOHN DENTON, small business owner, animal breeder; b. Salt Lake City, Jan. 20, 1942; s. George W. and Grace (Denton) Jenkins; m. Susan Hansen, June 20, 1971; children: Tammy Denton Wadsworth (dec.), Jeanett B. Barber. Student, U. Utah, Salt Lake City, 1964-65; BA in Econs. and Bus. Adminstrn. with high honors, Westminster Coll., Salt Lake City, 1971. Riding instr., wrangler Uinta wilderness area U-Ranch, Neola, Utah, 1955-58; wrangler, riding instr. YMCA Camp Rodger, Kamas, Utah, 1957; stock handler, driver, ruffstock rider Earl Hutchinson Rodeo Contractor, Idaho, 1959; with Mil. Data Cons., Inc., LA, 1961-62, Carlseon Credit Corp., Salt Lake City, 1962-65; sales mgr. sporting goods Western Enterprises, Salt Lake City, 1965-69; founder Rockin d Ranch, Millcreek, Utah, 1969; ski instr. Brighton Ski Sch., Utah, 1969-71; Western rep. PBR Co., Cleve., 1969-71; owner, founder, pres. John D. Day, mfrs. reps., 1972—; dist. sales rep. Crown Zellerbach Corp., Seattle and LA, 1971-73; dist. sales mgr. Surfonics Engrs., Inc., Woods Cross, Utah, 1976-78, Garland Co., Cleve., 1978-81; pres., founder Dapco paper, chem., instl. food and janitorial supplies, Salt Lake City, 1973-79; rancher Heber, Utah, 1976-90, horse tng. facility, horsemanship sch. and ranch, Temecula, Calif., 1984-90, St. George, Utah, 1989-99; pres., founder John D Day Greeting Cards and Award Winning Art Works, 1990—; horse training Horsemanship Sch., Quarter Horse Breeding Facility, Yerington, Nev., 1999—2004; owner Quarter Horse Breeding Facility, Art Studio, Dammeron Valley, Utah, 2004—. Sec. bd. Acquadyne, 1974, 75. Actor, dir., prodr. (movies) The Big Sky, 1952, Rebel Without a Cause, 1955, Devils Brigade, 1967, Biography of the Horse Expensive Hobby, 1985, Coyote Summer, 1995, (music videos) Someday Soon, 1993, A Tour of Snows Canyon, 1993, All For the Love of Horse, 1982-83, Biography of the Horse Expensive Hobby, 1985, Stallion Management, 1985, Advanced Training for Horses and Horse Lovers, 2006, others; tv spls. and commls., Chev., Palmer, The Osmonds, others; standup comic; contbr. articles to jours., including Western Artist. Group chmn. Tele-Dex fund raising project Westminster Coll.; founder, supr. vol. group Day's Rangers, 1990-99, 2004—; vol. Dixie Nat. Forest, 1989-94, 2004—, USDA Forest Svc.; 1st U.S. wilderness ranger USDA, US Forest Svc., Dixie Nat. Forest, Pine Valley Ranger Dist., Pine Valley Mountain Wilderness, So. Utah, 1993-99; vol. State of Nev. Ft. Churchill State Hist. Pk. & Pony Express Tr., 1999-2004; vol. Dixie Nat. Forest, 2004—. With AUS, 1963-64. Recipient grand nat. award Internat. Custom Car Show, San Diego, 1962, Award of Excellence Winternationals Nat. Hot Rod Assn., others, 1962-63, Key to City, Louisville, Ky., 1964, Champion Bareback Riding award, 1957, Vol. award USDA Forest Svc., 1991, 92, 93, 97, 2005, 06, Safety award Dixie Nat. Forest, P.V.R.D., 1992-99, Outstanding Performance award USDA, 1995, 98, Cert. Appreciation, 1997, Outstanding Svc. award DNF, 1997, Pine Valley Mountain Wilderness award Nev. State Parks, Appreciation cert. Fort Churchill State Historic Park, 1999-2004, Nat. Vol. award US, 2006; Dally team roping heading and heeling champion, 1982; nominated US Vol. award 1994. Mem. Internat. Show Car Assn. (co-chmn. 1978-79), Am. Quarter Horse Assn. (life, Horseback Riding Program 5000 Hour award 2002, 10 Yr. Breeder award, 20 Yr. Breeder award), Profl. Horseman Assn. (high point reining champion 1981, awarded Nat. Reining Horse Assn. Bronze, qualified for world championship, Dodge, Toyota Fall Futurite Circuit Champion Working Cowhorse 1994-95, World Championship Show qualifier and participant Oklahoma City Sr. Cutting 1994, regional championships, region 7, ring steward, 4A horse-testride, 2005), Intermountain Quarter Horse Assn. (sr. reining champion 1981, champion AMAT reining 1979-81), Utah Quarter Horse Assn. (state champion AMAT reining 1979, 80, AMAT barrel racing 1980, working cowhorse champion 1982, trained working cowhorse and rider champion 1992, 98, 2003, trained amateur reining horse and rider champion 1996, 2003, open cutting res. champion 1993-95, 97, open cutting champion 1994, Menlove Dodge Toyota Fall Futurity circuit champion working cowhorse, 1994-95, open working cowhorse champion & broadmare halter champion 1995, Rose cir. working cowhorse champion 1995, 98, Rose Cir. Open working cowhorse champion, showed cir. champion Brodmare at Halter Rose cir. open cutting champion 1996, 97, bd. dirs. 1992-94, trained amateur barrel racing and amateur pole bending horse and rider 1998, State Reserve Champion amateur cutting horse and rider, trained state champion team roping champion roper, heading and heeling, 2003, 06, team roping heeling champion 2004, 05), Profl. Cowhorseman's Assn., Nat. Cutting Horse Assn. (affiliate), Profl. Cowhorseman's Assn. (world champion team roping, heeling 1986, 88, high point rider 1985, world champion stock horse rider 1985-86, 88, world champion working cowhorse 1985, PCA finals open cutting champion, 1985-88, PCA finals 1500 novice champion 1987, PCA finals all-around champion 1985-88, inducted into Hall of Fame 1988, first on record registered Tex. longhorn cutting contest, open champion, PCA founder, editor newsletter 1985-89, pres. 1984-88), World Rodeo Assn. Profls. (v.p. Western territory 1989-98, judge nat. high sch. rodeo, cutting horse and rodeo queen contest, 1990—, hon. life v.p. Western Terr. US 1998—, Calif. Sports Person of Yr., 1986-87, Calif. Athlete of Yr., 1988), Future Farmers Am. (horse judge 2003—), Nevada Quarter Horse Assn. (mem. com., Am. Quarter Horse Assn., Ride 2000, "Let Freedom Ride", Fall Circuit 2000 Open Cutting Champion), Nev. Quarter Horse Assn. (Summer Circuit Champion), 2002, Utah Qt. Horse Assn. (mem. com.)

DAY, JOHN SIDNEY, management sciences educator; b. Newton, Mass., Oct. 13, 1917; s. Franklin Everett and Marion (Guild) D.; m. Barbara Jane Felch, Nov. 20, 1940; children: John Sidney, Stephen L. Student, Tufts U., 1935-37, Oxford Sch. Bus. Adminstrn., 1939; MBA with distinction, Harvard U., 1950, DCS, 1956; D in Mgmt. (hon.), Purdue U., 1993. Asst. to pres. C. Carlson Co., Boston, 1939-40, 45-46; instr. Oxford Sch. Bus. Adminstrn., Cambridge, Mass., 1946-48; rsch. asst. Harvard Grad. Sch. Bus. Adminstrn., Cambridge, Mass., 1950-51, rsch. assoc., 1951-53, asst. prof., 1953-56; assoc. prof. Purdue U., Lafayette, Ind., 1956-59, prof. indsl. mgmt., 1959-83, dean Krannert Grad. Sch. Mgmt., 1969-78, v.p. for devel., 1978-83, Krannert prof. mgmt., 1983-86, v.p. emeritus, 1986—. Author: (with L. Bollinger) Management of New Enterprises, 1952, Subcontracting Policy in the Airframe Industry, 1956, (with P. Donham) New Enterprise and Small Business Management, 1960. Bd. dirs. Purdue Rsch. Found., 1980-83; mem. Tippecanoe County (Ind.) chpt. ARC, 1968-74, chmn., 1974; treas. Tippecanoe County Easter Seal Soc., 1972-78; mem. West Lafayette Econ. Devel. Commn., chmn., 1975-83; mem. nat. adv. coun. SBA; trustee Joint Coun. on Econ. Edn., 1976-78; pres. Oak Point Cmty. Assn., Inc., 1980-86; bd. dirs. Home Hosp., 1972-78, pres., 1977; bd. dirs. Am. Assemblies Collegiate Schs. Bus., 1974-78, pres., 1977-78. Served to col. USMCR. Decorated Bronze Star with combat V (2); Baker scholar; Ford Found. fellow, 1959-60; named Hon. Sec. of State Ind.; recipient Sagamore of the Wabash. Mem. 1st Marine Divsn. Assn., Masons. Home and Office: 25 River Mead Rd Peterborough NH 03458 Personal E-mail: josidday@comcast.net.

DAY, JOHN T., academic administrator, dean; b. Poughkeepsie, NY, Mar. 1, 1948; s. John T. and Catherine M. Day; m. Sharon R. MacFarland, July 4, 1970; children: Caitlin A., Laura E., Nathaniel A. BA summa cum laude, Coll. of the Holy Cross, 1970; MA, Harvard U., 1971, PhD, 1977. Allston Burr sr. tutor Harvard U., Cambridge, Mass., 1976—79; from asst. to full prof. English St. Olaf Coll., Northfield, Minn., 1979—2002, assoc. dean for interdisciplinary studies, 1999—2002, asst. v.p. for acad. affairs, 2000—02; English prof. Roanoke Coll., Salem, Va., 2002, v.p. acad. affairs, dean, 2002—. Trustee Roanoke Higher Edn. Authority, 2002—. Editor: (collection of essays) Word, Church, and State: Tyndale Quincentenary Essays; book reviewer: Sixteenth Century Jour., author essays. Office: Roanoke College 221 College Ln Salem VA 24153 Home Phone: 540-375-2185; Office Phone: 540-375-2203.

DAY, JONATHAN S., lawyer; b. Houston, 1940; AB, Princeton U., 1962; JD, U Tex., 1965. Bar: Tex. 1965. City atty. City of Houston, 1974—76; ptnr., Pub. Law Andrews Kurth LLP, Houston, mem. mgmt. com. Mem.: ABA, State Bar Tex., Houston Bar Assn., Phi Delta Phi. Office: Andrews Kurth LLP 600 Travis St Ste 4200 Houston TX 77002-3090 Office Phone: 713-220-4715. Office Fax: 713-238-7365. Business E-Mail: jonathanday@andrewskurth.com.

DAY, JULIAN C., retail executive; b. Scarborough, England, May 14, 1952; s. Stephen Bradshaw and Gwendolyn Adams; m. Kathleen Lynn Healy; 2 children. BA, Oxford U., 1974, MA, 1979; MBA, London Bus. Sch., 1979. Sr. engagement mgr. McKinsey & Co., 1980-85; v.p., European devel. mgr. Chase Manhattan Bank, 1985-87; exec. mgmt. cons. Kohlberg, Kravis, and Roberts & Co., 1987-93; exec. v.p., CFO Safeway, Inc., 1993-98, Sears, Roebuck & Co., Hoffman Estate, Ill., 1999—2002; pres, COO Kmart Holding Corp., Troy, Mich., 2002—03, pres, CEO, 2003—04; chmn., CEO RadioShack Corp., Ft. Worth, 2006—. Bd. dirs. Petco Animal Supplies, Inc., KMart Holding Corp. Office: RadioShack Corp 300 Radioshack Cir Fort Worth TX 76102*

DAY, KAHLIL AMYN, mediator, lawyer; b. Mpls., Aug. 16, 1958; s. Stacey B. Day and Noorbibi K. Day-Good; m. Atiya B. Day, Dec. 8, 1988; 1 child, Zara Noor. BA, Cornell U., Ithaca, NY, 1980; MSL, Vt. Law Sch., South Royalton, 1990; JD and certs. in environ., ocean and coastal laws, U. Oreg., Eugene, 1985; MBA, Orlando Coll., Fla., 1991. Bar: Fla. 1986, US Dist. Ct. (mid. dist.) Fla. 1986, US Ct. Appeals (11th cir.) 2002, US Supreme Ct. 1990, Fla. Supreme Ct. (cir. and county ct. mediator) 1992, Fla. Supreme Ct. (family mediator) 2000, Mid. Dist. Fla. (fed. mediator) 1997. Law clk., atty. and mediator, 1982—; asst. pub. defender Orange County Pub. Defender's Office, Orlando, 1993—2002; state mediator Divsn. Adminstrv. Hearings, Jacksonville, Fla., 2002—. Mem. Mediation Qualification Bd., 1996—2006; grievance mediator Fla. Bar, 2000—. Author: Mediation, A Citizen's Handbook, 2004, Fifty Clues to Conflict Resolution, 2004, Keys to a Successful Pro Se Workers' Compensation Mediation, 2006. Recipient Outstanding Adv. (mock trial winner) award, U. Oreg., 1985; NY Regents scholar, 1976. Mem.: ABA, Fla. Bar (grievance com. 18A mem., vice chair 1993—96, chair-elect 9th cir. UPL com. 2002—03, sec. 2007—), Cornell Club of Greater Jacksonville, Delta Kappa Epsilon (bd. dir. Delta Chi chpt. 1996—97), Phi Delta Phi (life). Independent. Avocations: travel, East Indian coins. Personal E-mail: teamday@aol.com.

DAY, KEVIN THOMAS, retired business executive, investment banker, foundation administrator; b. London, Aug. 24, 1937; came to U.S., 1957; s. William Stanley and Mary Ann (Hook) Day; m. Mary Violet Scheuber, Aug. 1960. BA, Brisbane Tech. Coll., Queensland, Australia, 1957. Pres. Americana Investments, San Francisco, 1960-63; stockbroker Sutro and Co., San Francisco, 1963-66; regional v.p. Am. Express Investment Co., San Francisco, 1966-70; dir. mktg. ITT Fin. Svcs., NYC, 1970-78; pres. Exec. Assocs., Reno, 1978-83, First Interstate Bank Found., Reno, 1983-1991; exec. dir. Cath. Community Svcs., Reno, 1991—2004; ret. Cath. Community Svcs., Reno, 2004. Chmn. Nev. Fgn. Trade Zone, Reno, 1986-91, Desert Rsch. Inst., Reno. Pres. Econ. Devel. Authority, Reno, 1985, Nev. Mus. Art, 1989-91; mem. exec. com. Western Indsl. Nev., Reno, 1985-90; commr. Nev. Commn. on Econ. Devel., Carson City, 1987-90. Named Man of Yr., Reno mag., 1988; recipient Torch of Liberty award Nat. Conf. Comty. and Justice, 1989, Nev. Order of Silver Spur, 1990. Republican. Roman Catholic. Avocations: archaeology, travel, art. Home: 3600 Worthington Way Plano TX 75023 Personal E-mail: kevaday@msn.com.

DAY, LINCOLN HUBERT, demographer, educator; b. Ames, Iowa, Jan. 7, 1928; s. John Armstrong and Vera (Hills) Day; m. Alice Taylor, Nov. 26, 1952; children: Thomas Hills, Caroline Day Santesteban. BA, Yale U., 1949; MA, Columbia U., 1951, PhD, 1957. Instr., asst. prof. sociology Mt. Holyoke Coll., South Hadley, Mass., 1955—58; asst. prof. sociology Princeton (NJ) U., 1958—59; rsch. assoc. Bur. Applied Social Rsch. Columbia U., NYC, 1959—62; vis. fellow in demography Australian Nat. U., Canberra, 1962—64, sr. fellow in demography, 1973—94; rsch. assoc. Sch. Pub. Health Harvard U., Boston, 1964—65; assoc. prof. pub. health and sociology Yale U., New Haven, 1965—70; chief demographic and social stats. br. UN, NYC, 1970—73; Hofstee fellow Netherlands Interdisciplinary Demographic Inst., Den Haag, 1994. Vis. prof. sociology Columbia U., 1976. Co-author (with Alice Taylor Day): Too Many Americans, 1964; co-author: (with A.J. Jaffe) Disabled Workers in the Labor Market, 1964; author: Analysing Population Trends, 1983, The Future of Low-Birthrate Populations, 1992; co-editor (with D.T. Rowland): How Many More Australians?, 1988; co-editor: (with Ma Xia) Migration and Urbanization in China, 1994; contbr. numerous articles to profl. jours. Mem. adv. bd. Environ. Film Festival, Washington; bd. dirs. Ctr. for Arms Control and Non-Proliferation, Washington. Cpl. US Army, 1953—55. Fellow, Fulbright Found., 1968; scholar-in-residence, Bellagio (Italy) Study and Conf. Ctr., 1990. Mem.: Am. Sociol. Assn., Sustainable Population Australia, Nature and Soc. Forum, Internat. Union for Sci. Study of Population, Population Assn. Am., Amnesty Internat., Coun. for a Livable World, ACLU, Cosmos Club. Democrat. Avocations: travel, politics, gardening. Home: 2124 Newport Pl NW Washington DC 20037-3001 Personal E-mail: at-lhday@verizon.net.

DAY, LUCILLE LANG, museum administrator, educator, writer; b. Oakland, Calif., Dec. 5, 1947; d. Richard Allen and Evelyn Marietta (Hazard) Lang; m. Frank Lawrence Day, Nov. 6, 1965 (div. 1970); 1 child, Liana Sherrine; m. Theodore Herman Fleischman, June 23, 1974 (div. 1985); 1 child, Tamarind Channah Fleischman; m. Richard Michael Levine, Aug. 25, 2002. AB, U. Calif., Berkeley, 1971, MA, 1973, PhD, 1979; MA, San Francisco State U., 1999, MFA, 2004. Tchg. asst. U. Calif., Berkeley, 1971-72, 75-76, rsch. asst., 1975, 77-78; tchr. sci. Magic Mountain Sch., Berkeley, 1977; specialist math. and sci. Novato (Calif.) Unified Sch. Dist., 1979-81; instr. sci. Project Bridge Laney Coll., Oakland,

1984-86; sci. writer and mgr. precoll. edn. programs Lawrence Berkeley Nat. Lab., 1986-90, life scis. staff coord., 1990-92, mgr. Hall of Health, Children's Hosp. & Rsch. Ctr. at Oakland, 1992—2004, dir. Hall of Health, 2004—. Lectr. St. Mary's Coll. Calif., Moraga, 1997—2000. Author: numerous poems, articles and book reviews; author: (with Joan Skolnick and Carol Langbort) How to Encourage Girls in Math and Science: Strategies for Parents and Educators, 1982; author: Self-Portrait with Hand Microscope, 1982, Fire in the Garden, 1997, Wild One, 2000, Lucille Lang Day, Greatest Hits, 1975-2000, 2001, Infinities, 2002, Chain Letter, 2005, The Book of Answers, 2006, God of the Jellyfish, 2007. Recipient Joseph Henry Jackson award in lit., San Francisco Found., 1982; Grad. fellow, NSF, 1972—75. Mem.: Soc. Pub. Health Edn. (No. Calif. chpt.), Math./Sci. Network, Nat. Assn. Sci. Writers, No. Calif. Sci. Writers Assn., Phi Beta Kappa, Iota Sigma Pi. Home: 1057 Walker Ave Oakland CA 94610-1511 Office: Hall of Health 2230 Shattuck Ave Berkeley CA 94704-1416 Office Phone: 510-549-1564. Business E-Mail: lucyday@hallofhealth.org.

DAY, MARK RONALD, history educator, reenactor; b. Rhinebeck, NY, May 28, 1952; s. Ronald Augustus and Henrietta Martha Day; m. Barbara Jean Day, June 3, 1978; children: Matthew Mark, Carolyn Anne. BS in Sociology, SUNY, Excelsior Coll., Albany, 1993. Ops. specialist USN, 1971—95, ret., 1995; tchr. history Liberty H.S., Bedford, Va., 1995—2001, tchr. history, chmn. social studies dept., 2002—. Va. ch. conf. del. Heritage United Meth. Ch., Lynchburg, 2005—06; mem. NJ Light Inf. Revolutionary War Re-enactment Unit, Hiawasee, Ga., 1998—2006, 105th Pa. Civil War Re-enactment Unit, 2005—06. Decorated Navy Commendation medals (2), Navy Achievement medals (2), Armed Forces Expeditionary medal, Kuwait Liberation medal, Combat Action ribbon. Mem.: Nat. Coun. Social Studies, Nat. Model RR Assn., Lynchburg N-scale Model Club, Sons Union Veterans Civil War (patriotic instr. 2005—06, mem. dept. del. to nat. conv. 2006, jr. vice comdr. Taylor Wilson Comp 10 2007), VFW (life). Independent. Methodist. Avocations: model trains, reading. Office: Liberty High School 100 Liberty Minutemen Drive Bedford VA 24523 Home Phone: 434-385-7283; Office Phone: 540-586-2541. Business E-Mail: mday@bedford.k12.va.us.

DAY, MARLENE E., elementary school educator; b. Biddeford, Maine, July 16, 1955; d. Vincent Louis and Marguerita Marcella Noella Angelosante; widowed; children: Shauna, Chaz; m. Charles E. Day Jr., Oct. 1, 2003. BS, U. Maine, 1977; MS in Reading, U. So. Maine, 1982. Tchr. Old Orchard Beach (Maine) Elem. Sch., 1977—80, Lorange Mid. Sch., Old Orchard Beach, 1980—. Mem. Commn. for Children with Spl. Needs., Augusta, Maine, 1983—84, Gov.'s Commn. Excellence in Edn., Augusta, 1983—85; religious edn. tchr., lectr. St. Margaret Cath. Ch., Old Orchard Beach. Named Maine State Tchr. of Yr., 1983; recipient Project Seed award, 1994. Mem.: Maine Tchrs. Assn., Phi Delta Kappa (past sec.). Roman Catholic. Avocations: reading, gardening, travel. Home: 1 Smith Ave Old Orchard Beach ME 04064 Office: Old Orchard Beach Sch Dept Loranger Mid Sch 148 Saco Ave Old Orchard Beach ME 04064 Business E-Mail: mday@oobschools.org.

DAY, MARY ANN, medical/surgical nurse; b. Covington, Tenn., Apr. 9, 1944; m. George Day, Jan. 17, 1980; children: Maurice, Michele, Shawn, Corey. AAS, Joliet Jr. Coll., Ill., 1989; BSN, Lewis U., 1995; student, U. St. Francis, 1998—. RN, Ill.; cert. emergency nurse pediat. course. Staff nurse Michael Reese Hosp., Chgo., 1989-91, MacNeal Hosp., Berwyn, Ill., 1991-99, Westlake Hosp., Melrose Park, Ill., 1999—; adj. faculty/LPN program Triton Coll., River Grove, Ill., 1996—, instr. RN continuing edn. course, 1998—; asst. patient care mgr. St. Joseph Hosp., Joliet, Ill., 1999—; IV therapist Ctrl. Dupage Hosp., Winfield, Ill., 1999—; nursing supr. St. Anthony's Hosp., Chgo., 2001—. Mem. diversity task force com., Westlake Hosp., 1999; instr. in nursing assistance Waubonsee Coll., 2002; weekend supr. VNA Home Health; adj. faculty nurse asst. program, Moraine Valley CC, 2005. Nominee Black Profl. Female scholarship, Minority Student of Yr., 1989. Avocations: classical music, classical pianist. Home: 6 Puffin Cir Bolingbrook IL 60440-1236

DAY, MELVIN SHERMAN, information and telecommunications company executive; b. Lewiston, Maine, Jan. 22, 1923; s. Israel and Frances (Goldberg) D.; m. Louisa Walker; children: Cynthia Day Solganick, Wendy Day Young, Robert Marshall, Guy Carlton. BS, Bates Coll., 1943; postgrad., U. Tenn., 1953—54. Chemist Metal Hydrides Inc., Beverly, Mass., 1943-44, Tenn. Eastman Corp., Oak Ridge, 1944-46; sci. analyst AEC, Oak Ridge, 1946-48, asst. chief tech. info. svc. ext., 1950-56, chief, 1956-58, dir. tech. info. divsn. Washington, 1958-60; dep. dir. Tech. Info. and Edml. Programs Office, NASA, Washington, 1960-61, dir. Sci. and Tech. Info. divsn., 1961-67, dep. asst. adminstr. tech. utilization, 1967-70; head Office Sci. Info. NSF, Washington, 1970-72; dep. dir. Nat. Libr. Medicine, HEW, Bethesda, Md., 1972-78; dir. Nat. Tech. Info. Svc. Dept. Commerce, 1978-82; v.p. Info. Tech. Group, 1982-84, Rsch. Publs., 1984-86; sr. v.p. Herner & Co., 1986-88; pres. M. Day Cons. Internat., Inc., Arlington, Va., 1988—; exec. v.p. BIIS Corp., Herndon, 1991-94; v.p. GlobeNet Holding Corp., 1994-97. Cons. IAEA, 1960; adviser OECD, 1970, 75; U.S. mem. OECD info. policy group; U.S. mem. NATO Tech. Info. Panel, 1960-70, 79-82, chmn., 1970; chmn. com. on sci. and tech. info. Fed. Coun., 1970-72, chmn. com. on intergovtl. sci. rels., 1969-70, chmn. sci. info. exch. adv. bd., 1963-69, mem. chem. abstracts adv. bd., 1964-68; mem. Fed. Libr. Com., 1968-78, chmn. exec. bd., 1973-75; trustee Found. Ctr. 1972-78, trustee emeritus, 1991—; U.S. mem. adv. com. on librs., documentation and archives UNESCO; pres. abstracting bd. Internat. Coun. Sci. Unions, 1977-83; bd. dirs. Internat. Coun. for Sci. and Tech. Info., 1983—, Inst. for Internat. Info. Programs, 1985-88; trustee Engrng. Info., Inc., 1981-84, bd. dirs., 1993-98; del. numerous panels; cons., adviser and lectr. in field; mem. adv. com. HHS Health Svcs. Rsch. Dissemination and User Liaison, 1990-92, also mem. dissemination com. Mem. editl. bd. Health Comm. and Informatics, 1977-80, Infomediary, 1990-93, Yearbook of the Database Info. Industry, 1990-91. Bd. visitors U. Pitts. Grad. Sch. Info. Sci., 1977-83. With U.S. Army, 1944-46. Recipient Exceptional Svc. medal NASA, 1971, Superior Svc. award USPHS, 1976. Fellow AAAS, Nat. Fedn. Abstracting and Info. Svcs. (hon. fellow); mem. Am. Soc. Info. Sci. (chmn. internat. rels. com. 1972-75, pres. 1975-76, coun. 1975-77, editl. bd. bull. 1977-80), Am. Chem. Soc., Spl. Libr. Assn., Am. Soc. Cybernetics (bd. dirs. 1975-79), Venezuelan Acad. Scis. (hon. corr.), Internat. Coun. Sci. and Tech. Info. (hon., Disting. Svc. award 1997), Cosmos Club. Home: 4309 Chesapeake St NW Washington DC 20016-4509 Personal E-mail: louisaday@verizon.net.

DAY, MICHAEL GORDON, information technology executive, educator; b. Madison, Wis., July 30, 1951; s. Lee Monroe and Joan (Meredith) D.; m. Donna Kay Corl, May 26, 1979 (div. Apr. 1986); children: Thomas Lee, Anne Elizabeth; m. Carol Ann Stefanko, Apr. 12, 1997. BA, Pa. State U., 1973; JD, George Washington U., 1976. Bar: Pa. 1976. Assoc. Alan Ellis, Esq., State College, Pa., 1976-77; pvt. practice State College, Pa., 1977-85; with Profl. Planning Cons., State College, Pa., 1985-86, Century Fin. Svcs., State College, Pa., 1986-96; solutions expert Netscape, 1996-99; dir. Info. Tech. Inst./Shepherd Coll., Shepherdstown, W.Va., 1999—. Instr. bus. law Pa. State U., University Park, 1978-79, instr. continuing legal edn., 2002; counsel Boccardo Law Firm, San Jose, Calif., 1983, Rees Law Firm, Washington, 1983; sr. v.p. Century Mortage Corp., 1991-96. Chmn. Com. to Elect Mel Hodes Senator, Pa., 1982, Dem. Com., State College, 1982-84; active Exec. Com. Centre County, 1982-84, United Pennsylvanians, 1982-83; gen. counsel CLEAN, 1982-85; v.p. Mt. Nittany Conservancy, 2000-02; candidate for Pa. Ho. Reps., 1980; candidate for dist. justice 49th Dist. Pa., 1977, chmn. Potomac Alliance for Kerry, 2004; owner www.4kerry.com, 2004; mem. Md. for Kerry Steering Com.; coord. Washington County Md. for Kerry; founder Free State, 2005—; founder Free State Polit. Action Com., 2005. Mem. Lions Paw Alumni Assn. (pres. 1999-2001), Parmi Nous, Omicron Delta Kappa, Delta Sigma Rho. United Ch. Of Christ. Office: 400 W Stephen St Martinsburg WV 25401 Business E-Mail: michael@michaelday.org.

DAY, NATALIE MARIE, music educator, director; b. Dubuque, Iowa, July 30, 1981; d. Steven Ralph and Tammi Marie Day. B in Music Edn., U. Wis., Madison, 2004; M in Music Edn., U. Wis., Milw., 2006—. Lic. Tchr's. Wis., 2004. Elem. gen. music tchr. Hillcrest Elem. Sch., Waukesha, 2004—05; choral dir. Waukesha West HS, 2004—06, Waukesha South HS, 2005—; mid. sch. choral dir. Ctrl. Mid. Sch., 2006—. Adjudicator Wis. Sch. Music Assn., Waukesha, 2004—. Swim lesson coord. Waukesha Parks, Recreation and Forestry, 1998—2006. Mem.: MENC, The Voice-Care Network, Am. Choral Dirs. Assn., Wis. Choral Dirs. Assn. Avocations: camping, bicycling, swimming, reading. Home: 1018 River Pl Blvd #8 Waukesha WI 53189 Office: Ctrl Mid Sch 400 N Grand Ave Waukesha WI 53186 Home Phone: 262-424-4490; Office Phone: 262-970-3246. Personal E-mail: nmday30@hotmail.com.

DAY, PETER RODNEY, geneticist, educator; b. Chingford, Essex, Eng., Dec. 27, 1928; came to U.S., 1963; m. Lois Elizabeth Rhodes, May 26, 1951; children: Susan Catherine, Rupert Peter, William Rodney. BS in Botany, Birkbeck Coll., Eng., 1950; PhD, U. London, 1954. Sr. scientific officer John Innes Inst., Hertford, Eng., 1957-63; assoc. prof. Ohio State U., Columbus, 1963-64; chief, genetics dept. Conn. Agrl. Expt. Sta., New Haven, 1964-79; dir. Plant Breeding Inst., Cambridge, Eng., 1979-87; prof. genetics, dir. Rutgers U., New Brunswick, NJ, 1987—2002, prof. emeritus, 2002—. Sec. Internat. Genetics Fedn., 1984-93; trustee Internat. Ctr. for Maize and Wheat Improvement, Mexico City, 1986-92; chmn. Mng. Global Genetic Resources Bd. on Agrl., NAS, Washington, 1986-93. Author: Genetics of Host-Parasite Interaction, 1974; co-author: (with J.R.S. Fincham) Fungal Genetics, 1963, (with H.H. Prefl) Plant-Fungal Pathogen Interaction, 2001. Commonwealth Fund fellow U. Wis., 1954-56; Guggenheim Meml. fellow U. Queensland, 1972. Home: 8200 Tarsier Ave New Port Richey FL 34653 E-mail: p1rd@verizon.net.

DAY, RENEE NOELLE, secondary school, special education educator, special education educator; m. Robert Stuart Day, Oct. 19, 1991. BA in Polit. Sci., U. Calif., Riverside, 1989, credential in Secondary Social Sci., 1998, credential in Specialist Spl. Edn., 1998. Lic. profl. clear single subject specialist Calif. Commn. on Tchr. Credential, 1998. From spl. edn. social studies tchr. to coord. Ramona HS, Riverside, Calif., 2000—01, coord. achievement testing Dept. Spl. Edn., 2001—, chmn. Dept. Spl. Edn., 2004—. Facilitator academic impact team Ramona H.S., 2000—02, mem. leadership team, 2005—06, coord. history day, 2003—05, adviser model UN club, 2003—. Contbg. author Chicken Soup for the Working Woman's Soul: A Mother's Choice, 1998—99. Vol. Multicultural Youth Festival, Riverside, 2004—, Hidden Springs Elem. Sch., Moreno Valley, Calif., 1999—2000, mem. site coun., 1999—2000; organizer walk UN World Food Program, Riverside, 2005—; organizer food and clothing bank Ramona HS, 2005—06. Named Outstanding Educator, Inland Empire Coun. Social Studies, 2002, Everyday Hero, YWCA Riverside County, 2006; recipient Making a Difference Spl. Edn. award, Cmty. Adv. Com., 2002. Mem.: NEA, Calif. Tchrs. Assn., Nat. Coun. Social Studies, Am. Polit. Sci. Assn., UN Assn. (adv. student alliance 2005—), Phi Delta Kappa, Am. Polit. Sci. Acad. Office: Ramona HS 7675 Magnolia Ave Riverside CA 92504 Home Phone: 951-924-8757; Office Phone: 951-352-8429. Business E-Mail: rnday@rusd.k12.ca.us.

DAY, RICHARD ALLEN, retired chemistry professor; b. Kellogg, Iowa, Apr. 4, 1931; s. Clarence Hodson and Della (Mendenhall) Day; m. Lyn Tibbits, Aug. 19, 1956; children: Eric, Sylvia. Student, William Penn Coll., 1949-50; BS, Iowa State U., 1953; Phd, MIT, 1958. Rsch. assoc. MIT, Cambridge, 1957-59; asst. prof. chemistry U. Cin., 1959-63, assoc. prof. chemistry, 1963-68, prof. chemistry, 1968—, prof. biol. chemistry Coll. of Medicine, 1972—. Faculty rep. to U. Cin. Bd. Trustees, 1990-93; exec. com. Ohio Valley Chromatography Symposium; bd. dirs. DataChem, Inc., Indpls., BioCin Inc., Cin. Patentee in field. Recipient numerous grants. Fellow AAAS; mem. Am. Chem. Soc. (chmn. Cin. sect. 1982-83), Am. Soc. Mass Spectrometry, Am. Soc. Microbiology, Am. Soc. Biochem. & Molecular Biology, Protein Soc.

DAY, RICHARD EARL, lawyer, educator; b. St. Joseph, Mo., Nov. 2, 1929; s. William E. and Geneva C. (Miller) D.; m. Melissa W. Blair, Feb. 2, 1951; children: William E., Thomas E. BS, U. Pa., 1951; JD with distinction, U. Mich., 1957. Bar: Ill. 1957, D.C. 1959, S.C. 1980. Assoc. Kirkland & Ellis, Chgo., 1957-58, Howrey Simon Baker & Murchison, Washington, 1958-61; asst. prof. law U. N.C., Chapel Hill, 1961-64; assoc. prof. Ohio State U., Columbus, 1964-66, prof., 1966-75, U. S.C., Columbia, 1975-76, 80-86, dean, 1977-80, John William Thurmond chair disting. prof. law, 1986-99, disting. prof. law emeritus, 1999—. Cons. U.S. Office Edn., 1964-66; course dir. Ohio Legal Ctr. Inst. Columbus, 1970-75; vis. prof. law U. Southampton (Eng.), fall 1988. Author: The Intensified Course in Antitrust Law, 1972, rev. edit., 1974; book rev. editor Antitrust Bull., 1968-71, adv. bd., 1971—; adv. bd. Antitrust and Trade Regulation Report, 1973-76, Jour. Reprints for Antitrust Law and Econs., 1974—. Ohio commr. Nat. Conf. on Uniform State Laws, 1967-75, S.C. commr., 1977-80; mem. Ohio Gov.'s Adv. Coun. Internat. Trade, 1972-74, S.C. Jud. Coun., 1977-80; chmn. S.C. Appellate Def. Coun., 1977-80, S.C. Com. Intellectual Property and Unfair Trade Practices Law, 1981-87. Lt. USNR, 1952-55. Named John William Thurmond Disting. Prof. Law. Mem. ABA, S.C. Bar Assn. (bd. govs. 1977-80), Am. Law Inst. Methodist. Home: 204 Saint James St Columbia SC 29205-3074 Office: U SC Law Ctr Main And Green Sts Columbia SC 29208-0001 Personal E-mail: rdaycolumbia@aol.com.

DAY, RICHARD M., computer educator; m. Mary Pagliero. BA in Philosophy, U. S.Ala., Mobile, 1984—89; MS in Computer & Info. Sci., Troy U., Montgomery, Ala., 2001—04. Mgr. of area computing services U. Ala., Tuscaloosa, 1993—96; mgr. area computer svcs. U. W.Ala., Livingston, Ala., 1996—98, asst. prof. computer & info. sys., 2004—; IT project mgr. Ala. Dept. Pub. Safety, Montgomery, 1998—2002, IT sr. systems specialist, 2002—04. Specialist 5, e5 US Army, 1978—82. Decorated Nat. Def. Svc. medal US Army, Army Achievement medal, Good Conduct medal. Mem.: IEEE, IEEE Computer Soc., Brit. Computer Soc. (MBCS, CITP), Assn. Computing Machinery, Phi Kappa Phi. Office: Univ W Ala UWA Station 21 Livingston AL 35470 Home Phone: 205-652-3645. Business E-Mail: richard.day@acm.org.

DAY, RICHARD PUTNAM, marketing professional, arbitrator, employee benefits consultant; b. Hartford, Conn., Feb. 13, 1930; s. Godfrey Malbone and Sheila (Wilson) D.; m. Patricia Ann Brady, Jan. 26, 1957; children: Richard Jr., Stephen, Thomas (dec.), Gregory, Katharine, Martha, Ward, Emily. Student, The Choate Sch., 1948; AB, Middlebury Coll., 1952. With group field sales Conn. Gen. Life Ins. Co., Hartford, Detroit, Toledo, Phoenix, 1952-61; dir. sales group Bankers Life Nebr. (name changed to Ameritas Life Ins. Corp.), Lincoln, 1961-73, v.p. group, 1973-87, exec. v.p. group, 1987-91, exec. v.p. bus. devel., 1991-93; prin. R.P. Day Consulting, Paradise Valley, Ariz., 1993—. Dir. Nat. Health Care Svcs., Jacksonville, Fla., 1985—95. Trustee, pres. bd. Madonna Profl. Care Ctr., Lincoln, 1970-80, trustee Lincoln Gen. Hosp., 1980. Lt. USN, 1952-56. Mem. VFW, Internat. Soc. Cert. Employee Benefit Specialists (bd. dirs. pres. governing coun., chmn. bd. 1986), Am. Soc. CLUs, Internat. Found. Employee Benefit Plans, Profl. Ins. Mass-Mktg. Assn., Mass-Mktg. Ins. Inst., Nat. Assn. Dental Plans, Am. Legion, Mil. Officers Assn., Country Club of Lincoln, Scottsdale Country Club, Blue Key Honor Soc., Phi Kappa Tau. Republican. Episcopalian. Avocation: golf. Home: 6530 N 61st St Paradise Valley AZ 85253 Office Phone: 480-368-0916. Personal E-mail: daypvaz@aol.com.

DAY, ROBERT ADDISON, JR., investment management company executive; b. LA, Calif., 1943; married; 3 children. BS in Economics, Claremont McKenna Coll., 1965. With White, Weld and Co., NY; founder Trust Co. of the West, NY, 1971, chmn., CEO NY; chmn., pres., CEO W.M. Keck Found., trustee, 1998—. Dir. Freeport-McMoRan Copper & Gold, Inc., 1995—, Syntroleum Corp., Société Générale, McMoRan Exploration Co. Former trustee Claremont McKenna Coll.; trustee Brookings Institution, 1998—; mem. adv. bd. Fgn. Intelligence. Named one of Forbes' Richest Americans, 2003, 2006. Mem.: Coun. on Fgn. Relations, Bus. Coun., Ctr. for Strategic & Internat. Studies, Alfalfa Club. Address: W M Keck Found 550 South Hope St Ste 2500 Los Angeles CA 90071

DAY, ROBERT ANDROUS, literature and language professor, retired library director, editor, publisher; b. Belvidere, Ill., Jan. 18, 1924; s. Floyd Androus and Mabel May (Dorn) D.; m. Betty Lucy Johnson, Aug. 27, 1949; children— Nancy, Barton, Robin BA, U. Ill., 1949; MS, Columbia U., 1951. Librarian, Sci. and Tech. div. Newark Pub. Library, 1951-53; librarian, editor Inst. Microbiology Rutgers U., 1953-60, dir. Coll. of South Jersey Library, 1960-61; mng. editor Am. Soc. Microbiology, Washington, 1961-80; dir. ISI Press, Phila., 1980-86; v.p. Inst. for Sci. Info., Phila., 1984-86; prof. English, U. Del., Newark, 1986-2000, prof. emeritus, 2000—. Tchr. sci. writing; pub. cons. NSF, NIH, others Author: How to Write and Publish a Scientific Paper, 1979, 6th edit., 2006, Scientific English: A Guide for Scientists and Other Professionals, 1992, 2d edit., 1995. With USAAF, 1943-46. Mem. AAAS, Coun. Science Editors (chmn. 1977-78), Soc. Scholarly Pub. (pres. 1982-84), Am. Med. Writers Assn., Soc. Tech. Comm., European Assn. Sci. Editors, Assn. Tchrs. Tech. Writing. Home: 77 Ritter Ln Newark DE 19711-5174 Business E-Mail: bday@udel.edu.

DAY, ROBERT DWAIN, JR., foundation administrator, lawyer; b. Stockton, Calif., Dec. 14, 1950; s. Robert Dwain and June Rita Day; m. Carol Robin Tyler; children: Leslie Carroll, Ryan Tyler. BS, Va. Tech., 1974; JD, U. S.C., 1977. Bar: S.C. 1977, D.C. 1978. Forester USDA Forest Svc., Washington and Columbia, SC, 1973-77; dir. resource policy Soc. Am. Foresters, Bethesda, Md., 1977-81; resident fellow Resources for the Future, Washington, 1981-82; exec. dir. Renewable Natural Resources Found., Bethesda, 1982—; corp. sec. RNRF Title Holding Corp., 1997—. Cons. Office of Tech. Assessment U.S. Congress, Washington, 1981-82; nat. task force Soc. Am. Foresters, Bethesda, 1982-83; advisor Conservation Found., Washington, 1978-79; adv. coun. Coll. Natural Resources, Utah State U., 1992-96, Va. Tech., 1999—; nat. adv. coun. Environ. Careers Orgn., 2004-; nat. awards coun. for environ. sustainability Renew Am. Inc., 1997-98; non-govtl. orgn. rep. Global Environment Facility, 2000—; del. Afghanistan-Am. Summit on Recovery and Reconstn., Washington, 2002; del. White House Conf. on Global Climate Change, Washington, 1997, White House Conf. on Coop. Conservation, St. Louis, 2005. Columnist: Jour. Forestry, 1977-81; editor: Renewable Resources Jour., 1982—. Appt. by county exec. to 9/11 Econ. Impact Panel Montgomery County , 2001. Mem. AAAS, D.C. Bar Assn., Soc. Am. Foresters, Soil and Water Conservation Soc., Environ. Law Inst., Coun. Engrng. and Sci. Soc. Execs., Montgomery County Soc. for Assns. (exec. com. 1992-94, 98-05, vice chmn. 1999-00, chmn. 2000). Home: 2191 Canterbury Way Potomac MD 20854-6105 Office: Renewable Natural Resources 5430 Grosvenor Ln Ste 220 Bethesda MD 20814-2142 Office Phone: 301-493-9101. Business E-Mail: day@rnrf.org.

DAY, ROBERT WINSOR, preventive medicine physician, researcher; b. Framingham, Mass., Oct. 22, 1930; s. Raymond Albert and Mildred (Doty) Day; m. Jane Alice Boynton, Sept. 6, 1957 (div. Sept. 1977); m. Cynthia Taylor, Dec. 16, 1977; children: Christopher, Nathalia, Natalya, Julia. Student, Harvard U., 1949—51; MD, U. Chgo., 1956; MPH, U. Calif., Berkeley, 1958, PhD, 1962. With USPHS, 1956—57; resident U. Calif., Berkeley, 1958—60; research specialist Calif. Dept. Mental Hygiene, 1960—64; asst. prof. Sch. Pub. Health and Sch. Medicine UCLA, 1962—64; dep. dir. Calif. Dept. Pub. Health, Berkeley, 1965—67; prof., chmn. dept. health services Sch. Pub. Health and Community Medicine, U. Wash., Seattle, 1968—72, dean, 1972—82, prof., 1982—2005, emeritus prof. and dean, 2005—; pres., dir. Fred Hutchinson Cancer Rsch. Ctr., Seattle, 1981—97, pres., dir. emeritus, 1997—, mem. pub. health scis., 1997—. Mem. Nat. Cancer Adv. Bd., 1992—98, Nat. Cancer Policy Bd., 1996—2000; chief med. officer Epigenomics, Inc.; sci. dir. Internat. Consortium Rsch. Health Effects Radiation, 2001—04; founder, chmn. Targeted Growth, Inc., 1998—; chmn. Sci. and Mgmt. of Addictions, 2005—; mgr. Sci. Group, DLC, Investment Co.; cons. in field. Fellow: APHA, AAAS, Am. Coll. Preventive Medicine; mem.: AMA, Am. Soc. Addiction Medicine, King County Med. Soc., Wash. State Med. Assn., Am. Assn. Cancer Insts. (bd. dirs. 1983—87, v.p. 1984—85, pres., chmn. bd. dirs.), Assn. Schs. Pub. Health (pres. 1981—82), Am. Assn. Cancer Rsch., Am. Soc. Preventive Oncology, Am. Soc. Clin. Oncology. Office: 1872 E Hamlin St Seattle WA 98112 Office Phone: 206-954-9922. Personal E-mail: dlcllc@comcast.net.

DAY, ROLAND BERNARD, retired judge; b. Oshkosh, Wis., June 11, 1919; s. Peter Oliver and Joanna King (Wescott) D.; m. Mary Jane Purcell, Dec. 18, 1948; 1 dau., Sarah Jane. BA, U. Wis., 1942, JD, 1947. Bar: Wis. 1947. Trainee Office Wis. Atty. Gen., 1947; assoc. mem. firm Maloney & Wheeler, Madison, Wis., 1947-49; 1st asst. dist. atty. Dane County, Wis., 1949-52; prnt. firm Day, Goodman, Madison, 1953-57; firm Wheeler, Van Sickle, Day & Anderson, Madison, 1959-74; legal counsel mem. staff Sen. William Proxmire, Washington, 1957-58; justice Wis. Supreme Ct., Madison, 1974-95, chief justice, 1995-96. Mem. Madison Housing Authority, 1960-64, chmn., 1961-63; regent U. Wis. System, 1972-74. Served with AUS, 1943-46. Mem. ABA, ATLA, State Bar Wis., Ygdrasil Lit. Soc. (pres. 1968), Madison Torske Klubben, Masons (33rd degree). Mem. United Ch. of Christ. Clubs: Madison, Madison Lit.

DAY, RONALD RICHARD, retired financial executive; b. York, Pa., Nov. 14, 1934; s. Russell Aldinger and Rosa Ellenora (Reever) D.; m. Patricia Glee Duncan, Nov. 24, 1956. BS in Econs., Lebanon Valley Coll., Annville, Pa., 1956; postgrad., U.S. Army Fin. Sch., Indpls., 1957, Lehigh U., Bethlehem, Pa., 1961. Mgr. cost control and sys. Mack Trucks, Inc., Allentown, Pa., 1963—67; mgr. cost acctg. Am. Chain divsn. Acco Babcock Co., York, 1967—70, divsn. contr., 1970—82, v.p. fin. and acctg. Chain and Forged Products Group, 1982—89; pres., sr. v.p., contr., chief fin. officer AAA So. Pa., 1990—; ret., 2001. Committeeman York County Rep. Party, 1972-74; bus. chmn. York County chpt. Am. Heart Assn., 1987-89. Served to 1st lt. U.S. Army, 1957-59. Mem. York Area C. of C., Internat. Platform Assn., Lafayette Club, Jeffersonian Club, Outdoor Country Club, Masons, Shriners, Order of DeMolay (adv. bd. 1975-89), Rotary (sec. West York club 1988-92, pres. 1993-94)/ Lutheran. Avocations: golf, hunting, fishing, boating, travel. Home: 2430 Ramblewood Rd York PA 17404-3941 Home Phone: 717-764-9974.

DAY, RUSSELL CLOVER, state agency administrator; b. Concord, NH, June 29, 1943; s. Alan C. and Lois M. (Huntington) D.; m. Carol Ann Tasker, July 9, 1965; children: Jennifer Marie, Jeffrey Russell. BA, New England Coll., 1965; postgrad., Fairfield U., 1965, U. N.H., 1965-67; M in Human Svcs. Adminstrn., Antioch U., Keene, NH, 1978. Examiner State of N.H. Soc. Security Disability Determination Svc., Concord, 1969-73, supr., 1973-81, dep. dir., 1981-85, adminstr., 1985—2005; exec. dir. NH Psychol. Assn., 2005—06. Trustee New England Coll., 1987-89; supervisory com.

NH Fed. Credit Union, chair, 1995-2007, bd. dirs., 1997—; mem. NH House of Reps., 2007—; vice chair Goffstown Rep. Town Com.; mem. solid waste commn. Goffstown. Recipient Vol. Achievement award N.H. Credit Union League, Edward Filene award, Social Security Commrs. citation, 2000, 05, Assoc. Commrs. citation, 2000, Excellence in Govt. award Greater Boston Fed. Exec. Bd., 2002, Social Security Commrs.'s citation, 2005. Mem. Nat. Coun. Disability Determination Dirs. (exec. com. 1991-94), Masons, Lions Club (pres. 1983-84, chmn. region I, dist. chmn. 1995-96, bd. dirs. 1984—, zone chmn. 1982-83, 94-95, Melvin Jones fellow 2000, trustee Goffstown Lions scholarship 2006—), New Eng. Coll. Alumni Assn. (chmn. 1987-89). Republican. Congregationalist. Avocations: fishing, boating, photography, golf. Home: 73 Wallace Rd Goffstown NH 03045 Office Phone: 603-271-3065. Personal E-mail: rcday2@verizon.net. Business E-Mail: russell.day@leg.state.nh.us.

DAY, SARAH JANE, actor; b. Madison, Wis., Oct. 30, 1958; d. Roland Bernard and Mary Jane (Purcell) Day. BA, U. Wis., 1980. Mem. Core Co. Am. Players Theatre, Spring Green, Wis., 1986—; actor Milw. Repertory Theater, Milw. Chamber Theater, First Stage Milw., Next Act Theatre, Milw., Madison Repertory Theatre, Madison. Guest artist Univ. Theatre, Madison. Bd. mem. Spring Green Literary Festival, Wis., Friends of the Spring Green Library; founding bd. mem. Spring Green Area Arts Coalition. Democrat. Home: E3516 US Hwy 14 & 60 Spring Green WI 53588

DAY, STACEY BISWAS, physician, educator; b. London, Dec. 31, 1927; came to U.S. 1955, naturalized 1977. s. Satis B. and Emma L. (Camp) D.; m. Ivana Podvalova, Oct. 18, 1973; children Kahil Amyn, Selim. MD, Royal Coll. Surgeons, Dublin, Ireland, 1955; PhD, McGill U., 1964; DSc, Cin. U., 1971. Intern King's County Hosp., SUNY Downstate Ctr., 1955-56; resident fellow in surgery U. Minn. Hosp., 1956-60; hon. registrar St. George's Hosp., London, 1960-61; lectr. exptl. surgery McGill U., Montreal, Que., Canada, 1964; asst. prof. exptl. surgery U. Cin. Med. Sch., 1968-70; assoc. dir. basic med. rsch. Shriner's Burn Inst., Cin., 1969-71; from asst. to assoc. prof. pathology, head Bell Mus. Pathobiology U. Minn., Mpls., 1970-74; dir. biomed. comm. and med. edn. Sloan-Kettering Inst., NYC, 1974-80; mem. Sloan-Kettering Inst. for Cancer Rsch., 1974-80; mem. adminstrv. coun., field coordinator, 1974-75; prof. biology Sloan Kettering divsn. Grad. Sch. Med. Sci. Cornell U., 1974-80; clin. prof. medicine divsn. behavioral medicine NY Med. Coll., 1980-92; prof. biopsychosocial medicine, chmn. dept. cmty. health U. Calabar Sch. Medicine, Nigeria, 1982-85; prof. internat. health, dir. Internat. Ctr. for Health Scis. Meharry Med. Coll., Nashville, 1985-89, dir. WHO Collaborating Ctr. ICHS, 1987-89; founding dir. WHO Collaborating Ctr., Nashville, 1987-89, emeritus dir., 1989; adj. prof. family and cmty. medicine U. Ariz. Coll. Med. Scis., Tucson, 1985-89; univ. prof. internat. health U. Calabar, Nigeria, 1989—; permanent vis. prof. med. edn. Oita Med. U., Japan, 1992-99. Arris and Gale lectr. Royal Coll. Surgeons, England, 1972; vis. lectr., Ireland, 72; vis. prof. U. Bologna, 1977, Kyushu, Japan, 90, U. Mauritius, 1991, Bratislava U., 1991, U. Tokyo, Japan, 1992—93, U. Nagasaki, Japan, 1992—93, Beijing, 1993; vis. prof. health comm. U. Santiago, Chile, 1979—80, Colombo, Sri Lanka, 1996; vis. prof. Oncologic Rsch. Inst., Tallinn, Estonia, 1976, All India Insts. Health, 1976, U. Maidugari, 1982, Vellore U., India, 1996, De Quito, Ecuador, 1996; vis. acad. Oxford (Eng.) U., 1993—95; moderator med. cartography and computer health Harvard U., 1978, Acad. Scis., Czech Republic, 1987, Australia, 88; Fulbright prof. Charles U., Czech Republic, 1989; prof. (hon.) Coll. Health Scis. U. San Francisco de Quito (Ecuador), 1996; cons. Pan Am. Health Assn., 1974—90, US-USSR Agreement for Health Cooperation, 1976, WHO Collaborating Ctr. Meharry Med. Coll., Nashville, 1985, NAFEO/USAID, 1986—89; mem. expert com. for health, manpower devel. WHO, 1986—90, cons. divsn. strengthening health care resources, 1987—90, UN-FSSTD, 1987, AID/Joint Memorandum of Understanding Africa, Kenya, 1987—89, West Africa, 1987—89, Sudan, 1985—89; cons. to dean med. coll. faculty med. and health scis. ABHA, Asir, Saudi Arabia, 1981; cons. to dir. High Tatras symposia Post Grad. Med. Inst., Bratislava, 1990—; cons. to rector U. Autónoma Agraria Antonio Narro, Saltillo, Mexico, 1987—89; pres., chmn. Pub. Cultural and Ednl. Prodns., Montreal, Canada, 1966—85; bd. dirs., v.p. Am. Sci. Activities Mario Negri Found., 1975—80; bd. dirs. Internat. Health, African Health Consultancy Svc., Nigeria, Ekologia & Zivot, Slovakia; founding chmn. (hon.), bd. dirs. Lambo Found. U.S.; v.p., trustee Cancer Relief Found., Calabar; pres., exec. dir. Internat. Found. Biosocial Devel. and Human Health, 1978—86, chmn., 1986—; mem. Medzinárodny Poradny Vybor Nadácie Ekológia Zivot, Slovakia, 1995—; cons. Inst. Health, Lyfford Cay, Bahamas, 1981, Govt. Cross River State, Nigeria, Itreto State and H.H. Obong of Calabar, Nat. Bd. Advisors, Am. Biog. Inst., 1982—; cons. cmty. health and health comms. Navaho Nation, Sage Meml. Hosp., Ganado, Ariz., 1984; founder, cons. Primary Self-Health Clinics, Oban, Ikot Oku Okono and Ikot Imo, Nigeria, 1982—84; cons. High Tatras Internat. Health Symposia, Slovakia, 1990—; apptd. ab. Gov. State of Tenn., 1986—; adj. clin. prof. medicine NY Med. Coll.; prof. (hon.) Colegio Ciencias Salud U. San Francisco, Quito, 1965—. Author: (verse) Collected Lines, 1966, (plays) By the Waters of Babylon, 1966, (verse) American Lines, 1967, (plays) The Music Box, 1967, Three Folk Songs Set to Music, 1967, Poems and Etudes, 1968, (novels) Rosalita, 1968, The Idle Thoughts of a Surgical Fellow, 1968, Edward Stevens-Gastric Physiologist, Physician and American Statesman, 1969, Letters to Ivana from Calabar, 2001, (novella) Bellechasse, 1970, A Leaf of the Chaatim, 1970, Ten Poems and a Letter from America for Mr. Sinha, 1971, Curling's Ulcer: An Experiment of Nature, 1972, Tuluak and Amaulik: Dialogues on Death and Mourning with the Innuit Eskimo of Point Barrow and Wainwright, Alaska, 1974, East of the Navel and Afterbirth: Reflections from Rapa Nui, 1976, Health Communications, 1979, The Biopsychosocial Imperative, 1981, What Is Survival: The Physician's Way and the Biologos, 1981, Developing Health in the West African Bush, 1995; author: (in Czech) Moudrost Samuraju, 1998; author: Selected Poems and Embers of a Medical Life, 1999, In the Shadow of the Bush - Letters from Calabar, 2000, Vitaesophia of Integral Humanism, 2001, The Klacelka in a Slavic Woodland, 2003, The Wisdom of Hagakure, 1996; editor: Death and Attitudes Toward Death, 1972, Membranes, Viruses and Immune Mechanisms in Experimental and Clinical Disease, 1972, Ethics in Medicine in a Changing Society, 1973, Communication of Scientific Information, 1975, Trauma: Clinical and Biological Aspects, 1975, Molecular Pathology, 1975; editor: (with Robert A. Good) (series) Comprehensive Immunology, 9 vols., 1976—80; editor: Cancer Invasion and Metastasis-Biologic Mechanisms and Therapy, 1977, Some Systems of Biological Communication, 1977, Image of Science and Society, 1977, What Is A Scientist?, 1978, Sloan Kettering Inst. Cancer Series, 1974—80; editor: (with K. Inokouchi) Selections from the Chronicle of the Hagakure as Wisdom Literature: The Way of The Samurai of Saga Domain, 1993; editor-in-chief, mem. editl. bd. Health Communications and Informatics, 1974—80, editor in chief The American Biomedical Network: Health Care System in America Present and Past, 1978, A Companion to the Life Sciences, Vol. 1, 1979, A Companion to the Life Sciences, Vol. 2, Integrated Medicine, 1980, A Companion to the Life Sciences, Vol. 3, Life Stress, 1981, Advance to Biopsychosocial Health, 1984, editor in chief, mem. editorial bd. Health Communications and Biopsychosocial Health; editor (with others): Cancer, Stress and Death, 1979, 2nd edit., 1986; editor: Computers for Medical Office and Patient Management, 1981, Readings in Oncology, 1980, Biopsychosocial Health, 1981, Primary Health Care Guidelines: A Training Manual for Community Health, 2nd edit., 1986; editor: (with T.A. Lambo) Contemporary Issues in International Health, 1989; sr. editor, with Salat and others Health and Quality of Life in Changing Europe in the Year 2000, 1992, sr. editor, with H. Koga Hagakure-Spirit of Bushido, 1993, sr. editor, with K. Inokuchi Selections from the Chronicles of the Hagakure as Wisdom Literature: The Way of the Samurai of Saga Domain, 1993, sr. editor, with Salát Health Management, Organization, and Planning in Changing Eastern Europe, 1993, sr. editor, with M. Kobayashi and K. Inokuchi, in Japanese The Medical Student and the Mission of Medicine in the Twenty First Century, 1995, sr. editor Developing Health in the West African Bush, 2 parts, 1995, Letters of Owen Wagensteen to a Surgical Fellow: with a memoir, 1996, Man and Mu: The Cradle of Becoming and Unbecoming, 1997, Czech Caesura: Golden Prague and the Black Years (Notes from Diaries 1970-1990), 1998, Moudrost Samuraju Trigon (in Czech), 1998, Poems and Embers of a Medical Life, 1998, The Surgical Treatment of Ischaemic Heart Disease with An Account of the Coronary and Intercoronary Circulation in Man and Animals, 1999, Introduction-Comprehensive Medicine (Oriental-Occidental Overview), 2000, Letters to Ivana from Calabar, 2001, Purkynje Address and Other Health Care Lectures Czechoslovakia 1989-1999, 2002, Pliskova's Butterflies-When God Says Enough, 2003, mem. editl. bd. Annual Reviews on Stress, Jour. Stress, cons. editl. bd. Comprehensive Medicine (Japan), Wilhelm Von Humboldt Über Die Unter Dem Namen Bhagavad Gita with commentary, 2001, Purkyne Address and Other Healthcare Lectures, 1989-1999; co-editor: various publs.; contbr. articles; prodr.: TV and health edn. programs, 1982—85, (TV film) Onchocerciasis-River Blindness in Africa, 1988; co-author: A Season of Flowers in Death Valley and the California Deserts, 2005; co-author: (with Ivana P. Day) In Search of the Desert Five Spot, 2006. Served with Brit. Army, 1946-49. Recipient Moynihan medal Assn. Surgeons Gt. Britain and Ireland, 1960, Reuben Harvey triennial prize Royal Coll. Physicians, Ireland, 1957, Arris and Gale award Royal Coll. Surgeons, Eng., 1972, disting. scholar award Internat. Communication Assn., 1980, Sama Found. medal, 1982, disting. citation Hagakure Soc., 1992, Nat. Svc. medal Royal Brit. Legion, 1993; named to Hon. Order Ky. Cols., 1968; named Chieftan Ntufam Ajan of Oban Ejagham People, Cross River State, Nigeria, 1983; hon. prof. Del Colegio De Ciencas De La Salud De La Universidad San Francisco De Quito, 1996; recipient Chieftan Obong Nsong Idem Ibibio Nigeria, 1983, Mgbe (Ekpe) honor Nigeria, commendation WHO address Fed. Govt. Nigeria, Calabar, 1983, Leadership in Internat. Med. Health citation Pres. US, 1987, WHO medal, 1987, Agromedicine citation Commr. of Agr., State of Tenn., 1987, Assembly citation State of N.Y., 1987, Citation Congl. Record., 1987; Maestro Honorifo, U. Autonoma Agraria, Coahuila, Mex., 1987; presented Key to the City of Nashville, 1987; recipient Vice-Chancellor's Citation and Presentation for Primary Health Care Teaching in Nigeria, U. Calabar, 1988; Pamétni medal Postgrad. Med. Coll., Prague, 1991, Gold medal U. of Bratislava, 1991, Disting. Citation Hagakure Rsch. Soc., Japan, 1992, Nat. Svc. medal Royal Brit. Legion, 1993, Citation Commendation from Pres. Kyoto Prefectural U. Medicine, Japan, 1993, Citation Commendation on Contbn. to Med. Edn. from Pres. Oita Med. U., Japan, 1997; addresses presented by people of Ikot Imo, Nsit Anyang, Oban, 1982-84, Commendation from King of Calabar, 1984; Ciba fellow Can., 1965; Stacey Day Ward named in his honor by Fed. Min. and Gov. of Cross River State, Calabar Med. Ctr., Nigeria, 1986; charter mem. U.S. Normandy Com., 1988; 1st fgn. hon. mem. Hagakure Res. Soc. (Samurai), Kyushu, Japan, 1991. Fellow: African Acad. Med. Scis. (founder), African Acad. Sci., World Acad. Arts and Scis., Japanese Found. for Biopsychosocial Health (internat. hon. fellow and most disting. mem.), Zool. Soc. London Royal Micros. Soc., Royal Soc. Health; mem.: APHA, AMA, AAS, Adelaide Hosp. Soc. (Ireland), Soc. Med. Geographers USSR, Am. Rural Health Assn. (v.p. internat. sci. affairs, bd. dirs.), Am. Anthrop. Assn., Am. Inst. Stress (bd. dirs.), Am. Assn. History Medicine, NY Acad. Scis., Can. Authors Assn., Internat. Burn Assn., Am. Burn Assn. Home: 6 Lomond Ave Chestnut Ridge NY 10977 Home (Summer): Ruzinovska 1228 14200 Prague Czech Republic E-mail: camp27day@yahoo.com. *I have tried to assimilate all that is good in many cultures and to bring about a synthesis of these expressions in my own life and writings. It is as if I must find a third eye that can see what is best in all men, to integrate them newly into a changing world, and to be as much a releasing force as to be an absorbing force. This direction, I believe, commits one to an unceasing philosophy to unlearn and to relearn.*

DAY, STOCKWELL BURT, government official; b. Barrie, Ont., Can., Aug. 16, 1950; s. Stockwell and Gwendolyn (Gilbert) D.; m. Valorie Martin Day, Oct. 2, 1971; children: Logan, Luke, Ben. Auctioneer, Alta., Canada, 1972-74; dir. Teen Challenge Outreach Ministries, Edmonton, Alta., Canada, 1974-75; contractor Comml. Interiors, Alta., Canada, 1976-78; sch. adminstr./asst. pastor Bentley (Alta) Christian Centre, 1978-85; mem. Legis. Assembly Alta. Legis., Edmonton, 1986—, govt. caucus whip, 1989-92, govt. house leader, 1994-97, min. of labor, 1992-96, min. of family and social svcs., 1996-97, provincial treas., acting premier, 1997-2000; leader The Can. Alliance, Calgary, 2000—01, sr. critic fgn. affairs, 2002—05; min. pub. safety Ho. Commons, Ohawa, Canada, 2006—. Chmn. Alta. Tourism Edn. Coun., Edmonton, 1987-89, Premier's Coun. on Family, Edmonton, 1990-92. Mem. Rotary Club. Avocations: tennis, roller blading, backpacking, reading. Office: Minister Pub Safety 517S Center Block House Commons Ohawa ON KIA OA6 Canada Office Phone: 613-995-1702. Business E-Mail: days@parl.gc.ca.

DAY, SUSAN MARIE, music educator, composer; b. Kingston, NY, June 12, 1949; d. Joseph and Esther Besdesky Hartman; children: Andrew, Casey. BSc in Music Edn., Ithaca Coll., 1971; MA in Music Edn., Columbia U., 1972. String tchr. Cherry Creek Schs., Englewood, Colo., 1972—80, Douglas County Schs., 1988—. Violinist Arapahoe Philharm., Englewood, Colo., 1984—; guest condr. youth symphonies, Colo., 1994—; contest adjudicator in field, Colo., 1994—. Composer: SMHD Music, 1994—, ASCAP, 2005, Reverie, 2004, over 25 other compositions in field; author: Teaching Orchestra on a Year Round Calendar, 1996. Recipient Winner String Orch. Composition Contest, Tex. Orch. Dirs. Assn., 2006. Mem.: Nat. Sch. Orch. Assn., Am. String Tchrs. Assn. (mem. string industry coun., named Outstanding String Tchr. 2000), Music Educators Nat. Conf., Colo. Music Educators' Assn. Avocations: hiking, bicycling, Scrabble, reading, movies. Home and Office: 8091 S Albion St Littleton CO 80122 Office Phone: 303-773-3185. Personal E-mail: sday@ecentral.com.

DAY, TWILA M., food service executive; b. Champaign, Ill. m. Bill Day; 5 children. B in Bus. Mgmt., Our Lady of the Lake, San Antonio, Tex., 1989. Various position in the banking and oil industry, 1983—92; sr. programmer analyst, information tech. dept. Sysco Corp., Houston, 1992—93, team leader, Sysco Uniform Systems, 1993—95, project mgr., 1995—96, sr. mgr., application develop., 1996—97, sr. dir., operating comp. support team, 1997—99, sr. dir., application develop., 1999—2000, asst. v.p., tech. and applications, 2000—05, v.p., information tech., 2005, v.p., CIO, 2005—. Office: Sysco Corp 1390 Enclave Pkwy Houston TX 77077-2099

DAYAL, VIJAY SHANKER, physician, educator; b. Ranchi, Bihar, India, Sept. 20, 1936; came to U.S., 1986; s. Ram Shanker Dayal and Vindhyachal (Devi) Devi; m. Susheela Sadhu, Oct. 10, 1961; children: Aneeta, Anjali, Amit. MBBS, Patna Med. Coll., India, 1959; MSc, McGill U., Montreal, Can., 1966. Resident in otolaryngology McGill U., Montreal, 1960-61, 62-64, resident in surgery, 1961-62; clin. tchr. U. Toronto (Can.), 1967-68, asst. prof., 1968-75, assoc. prof., 1975-81, prof., 1981-86, U. Chgo., 1986—. Mem. editl. bd. Am. Jour. Otolaryngology, 1989—, Otolaryngology Head and Neck Surgery, 1990; author: Clinical Otolaryngology, 1981; contbr. over 70 articles to profl. jours. V.p. Am. Neurotology Soc., 1983-84. Fellow Am. Acad. Otolaryngology, Am. Otological Soc., Am. Trilogical Soc., Barany Soc. Achievements include patent (with others) for Artificial Replacement for Larynx. Office: U Chgo Dept Surgery 5841 S Maryland Ave # 412 Chicago IL 60637-1463

DAYHOFF, DIANE, retail executive; B in Polit. Sci., Northwestern U., MBA. CFO Birraporitti's Restaurant; staff v.p. fin. Continental Airlines; v.p. investor rels. Home Depot, 2003—. Office: Home Depot 2455 Paces Ferry Rd Atlanta GA 30339 E-mail: diane_dayhoff@homedepot.com.

DAY-LEWIS, DANIEL MICHAEL BLAKE, actor; b. London, Apr. 29, 1957; s. Cecil and Jill (Balcon) D.-L; m. Rebecca Miller Nov. 11, 1996; children: Gabriel Kane, Ronan Cal, Cashel Blake. Student, Bedales and Bristol Old Vic Theatre Sch. Appeared in plays Class Enemy, Funny Peculiar, Bristol, Eng., Look Back in Anger, Dracula, Bristol and London, Another Country, London, Futurists, Romeo, Thisbe, R.S.C., Hamlet, 1989; appeared in TV show Insurance Man; films include: Sunday Bloody Sunday, 1971, Ghandi, 1982, The Bounty, 1984, A Room with a View, 1986, My Beautiful Laundrette, 1986, Nanou, 1986, The Unbearable Lightness of Being, 1988, Stars and Bars, 1988, Eversmile, New Jersey, 1989, My Left Foot, 1989 (Academy Award best actor 1989), The Last of the Mohicans, 1992, The Age of Innocence, 1993, In the Name of the Father, 1993 (Academy Award nomination best actor 1993), The Crucible, 1996, The Boxer, 1997, Gangs of New York, 2002 (Best Actor in Leading Role, British Acad. Film Award (BAFTA) 2003), The Ballad of Jack and Rose, 2005. Office: Julian Belfrage Assoc 46 Albemarle St London W1S 4DF England also: Parseghian/Planco Mgmt 23 E 22nd St Ste 3 New York NY 10010

DAYNARD, RICHARD ALAN, law educator; b. NYC, July 19, 1943; s. David M. and Sarah (Weidenbaum) D.; m. Carol S. Iskols, Aug. 9, 1975; children: David J., Gabriela C. BA, Columbia U., 1964, MA in Sociology, 1970; JD, Harvard U., 1967; PhD in Urban Studies and Planning, MIT, 1980. Bar: N.Y. 1967, U.S. Ct. Appeals (6th cir.) 1986, U.S. Supreme Ct. 1986, U.S. Ct. Appeals (11th cir.) 1987, U.S. Ct. Appeals (5th cir.) 1996. Law clk. 2d cir. US Ct. Appeals, NYC, 1967-68; tchg. fellow Columbia U., NYC, 1968-69; asst. prof. law Northeastern U., Boston, 1969-71, assoc. prof. law, 1971-73, prof. law, 1973—, assoc. dean acad. affairs, 2004—06; William Cahan disting. prof. Flight Attendants Med. Rsch. Inst., Miami, Fla., 2005—. Chmn. law and obesity project Pub. Health Advocacy Inst., 2002—; lectr., cons. in field. Editor-in-chief Tobacco Products Litigation Reporter, 1985-2006; assoc. editor: Tobacco Control: An Internat. Jour., 1998—; contbr. articles to profl. jours. Chmn. Tobacco Products Liability Project, Boston, 1984—; pres. Group Against Smoking Pollution of Mass., Boston, 1983-, Clean Indoor Air Ednl. Found., Boston, 1983-92, Tobacco Control Resource Ctr., Inc., Boston, 1993-2006, Pub. Health Advocacy Inst., 2006—; pres. Stop Teenage Addiction to Tobacco, 1996-98; chair lay adv. bd. Flight Attendants Med. Rsch. Inst., 2003-05; bd. mem. Framework Conv. Alliance, 2006—, exec. com., 2007—. Mem. ABA, Am. Pub. Health Assn., Law and Soc. Assn., Phi Beta Kappa. Home: 90 Commonwealth Ave Boston MA 02116-3040 Office: Northeastern U Sch Law 400 Huntington Ave Boston MA 02115-5005 Office Phone: 617-373-2026. E-mail: r.daynard@neu.edu.

DAYS, DREW S., III, lawyer, educator; b. 1941; m. Ann Ramsay Langdon, 1966; children: Alison, Elizabeth. Degree in Eng. Lit. with honors, Hamilton Coll., 1963; LLB, Yale U., 1966. Bar: Ill. 1966, NY 1970. Assoc. Cotton, Watt, Jones & King, Chgo., 1966-67; vol. Peace Corps., Honduras, 1967-69; assoc. counsel NAACP Legal Def. Fund, NYC, 1969-73, 75-77; assoc. prof. Temple U., 1973-75; asst. atty. gen. Dept. of Justice, Washington, 1977—80; assoc. prof. Yale U., New Haven, 1981-86, prof., 1986-93, Alfred M. Rankin chair Law Sch., 1992—; solicitor gen. Dept. Justice, Washington, 1993-96; of counsel Morrison & Foerster LLP, 1997—. Founding dir. Orville H. Schell, Jr. Ctr. for Internat. Human Rights Yale U. Law Sch., 1988-93. Bd. dirs. John D. and Catherine T. MacArthur Found., Petra Found., Hamilton Coll. Mem. Am. Law Inst., Am. Bar Found., Am. Acad. Arts and Scis., Am. Acad. Appellate Lawyers, Coun. on Fgn. Rels., Inter-Am. Dialogue. Office: Yale Law Sch PO Box 208215 New Haven CT 06520-8215 Home Phone: 203-787-7452; Office Phone: 203-432-4948. Business E-Mail: drew.days@yale.edu.

DAYS, MICHAEL, editor; b. Phila., 1953; m. Angela Dodson; 4 children. BA, Coll. of Holy Cross, 1975; MA, U. Mo., 1976. With Wall St. Jour.; joined as reporter Phila. Daily News, 1986, dep. mng. editor, 1998—2004, mng. editor, 2004—05, editor, exec. v.p., 2005—. Mem.: Nat. Assn. Black Journalists. Office: Phila Daily News 400 N Broad St PO Box 7788 Philadelphia PA 19130 Home Phone: 609-394-7632; Office Phone: 215-854-5984. Business E-Mail: daysm@phillynews.com.

DAY-SALVATORE, DEBRA LYNN, medical geneticist; b. Hoboken, NJ, Oct. 23, 1953; m. Francis P. Salvatore, Sr., Dec. 24, 1988. BA in Biology, Harvard U., 1975; MS in Pharmacology, NYU, 1979, PhD in Pharmacology, 1982; MD, Case Western Res. U., 1986. Diplomate Am. Bd. Med. Genetics, Am. Bd. Pediats. Grad. fellow dept. pharmacology NYU Med. Ctr., 1978-79; sr. rsch. asst. dept. medicine Case Western Res. U., Cleve., 1979-82, rsch. assoc. dept. molecular biology and microbiology, 1982-84; pediatric and adolescent medicine resident Cleve. Clinic Found., 1986-89; med. genetics fellow Robert Wood Johnson Med. Sch., New Brunswick, NJ, 1990-91, asst. prof. pediatrics, 1990—, coord. perinatal genetics dept. ob-gyn., 1991-92, dir. divsn. reproductive and perinatal genetics dept. ob-gyn., 1992—, asst. prof. ob-gyn. and reproductive scis. and pediatrics, 1992—, acting chief divsn. clin. genetics, dept. ob-gyn. and reproductive scis., 1993—; physician Robert Wood Johnson Univ. Hosp., New Brunswick, 1990—, St. Peter's Med. Ctr., 1992—, chief divsn. clin. genetics, 1996—. Mem. genetic adv. bd. N.J. State Dept. Health's Parental and Child Adv. Com.; mem. med. adv. bd. Cryo-Cell Internat. Genetics editor Jour. of Perinatology, 1993—; contbr. articles, abstracts to profl. jours. Cons. N.J. Interagency Adoption Coun. Mem. AAAS, AMA, Am. Acad. Pediatrics (mem. N.J. chpt.), Am. Soc. Cell Biology, Am. Soc. Human Genetics, Human Genetics Assn. N.J. (mem. legis. com.), N.Y. Acad. Sci. Office: Saint Peter's Univ Hosp 254 Easton Ave # 4410 New Brunswick NJ 08901-1766 Home Phone: 732-274-1192. E-mail: Day-Salva@comcast.net.

DAYTON, MARK BRANDT, former senator; b. Mpls., Jan. 26, 1947; children: Eric, Andrew. BA cum laude in Psychology, Yale U., 1969. Tchr. gen. sci. N.Y.C. Pub. Sch., 1969-71; counselor, adminstr. Social Svc. agency, Boston, 1972-76; legis. asst. to Senator Walter Mondale US Senate; staff mem. for Gov. Rudy Perpich State of Minn., 1977, commr. econ. devel., 1978, commr. energy and econ. devel., 1983—86, state auditor, 1991—95; US Senator from Minn., 2001—07. Mem. Senator Paul Wellstone's re-election campaign, 1995-96; agr., armed svcs., rules, gov. affairs com., state of Minn. Recipient President's award, NAACP Minn. chpt., 1995, Disting. Citizen award, Minn. Veterans Fgn. Wars, 1995, Golden Triangle, Minn. Nat. Farmers Union, 2002, 2003, Legis. of Yr., Am. Ambulance Assn., 2003, Public Svc. award, Minn. State Fedn. Cons. for Exceptional Children, 2003. Democrat.*

DAYTON, SKY, telecommunications company executive; b. NYC, Aug. 8, 1971; m. Arwen Elys; 3 children. Grad., Delphian Sch., 1988. Mgr. computer graphics dept. Mednick & Assocs., 1988-90; founder Cafe Mocha, LA, 1990-92; co-founder Dayton Walker Design, 1992-94; founder Earthlink Inc., Pasadena, Calif., 1994, chmn., 1994—2005; co-founder ECompanies, 1999—; founder, non-exec. chmn. Boingo Wireless, 2001—; CEO HELIO LLC (formerly SK-EarthLink), Westwood, Calif., 2005—. Bd. dirs. Earthlink, Inc., Business.com, NeoPets; mem. adv. bd. Ctr. Pub. Leadership, John F. Kennedy Sch. Govt. Mem. Assn. Online Profls. (bd. dirs.), Internet Access Coalition. Avocations: surfing, snowboarding. Office: HELIO LLC 10960 Wilshire Blvd Ste 600 Los Angeles CA 90024

DAYWALT, LEE ERIC, minister, museum administrator; b. Chambersburg, Pa., Dec. 31, 1970; s. Colin Roy and Dixie Lee Daywalt. Associate, Pa. State U., Mont Alto, 1991; B in History, Shippensburg U., Pa., 1993; Master, Winebrenner Theo. Sem., Findlay, Ohio, 1996. Adminstr. Preserving Our Heritage Archives and Mus., South Mountain, Pa., 2001—; pastor New Balt. Ch. of God, South Mountain, 2001—. Author: (books) In the Beginning, 2003, The world that then was, 2005, Gleanings 1853-1875, 2006. Mem. Vision 2015, Waynesboro, Pa., 2006—, Quincy Twp. Planning Commn., Quincy, Pa., 2006—; dir. Waynesboro Area Sch. Bd., 2007—. Fellow Centennial Fellowship award, Pa. State U., Mont Alto Campus, 2003. Mem.: Pa. Forest Fire Mus. (historian 2001—06). Conservative. Achievements include founder of local history archives and museum. Home: 5050 Spruce Rd Fayetteville PA 17222 Office: New Baltimore Ch God 4947 Spruce Rd Fayetteville PA 17222 Home Phone: 717-749-3826; Office Phone: 717-762-2367. E-mail: new_baltimore_church_of_god@hotmail.com.

DCAMP, CHARLES BARTON, music educator; b. Feb. 16, 1932; s. Glenn Franklin and Nina Clarice (Larson) Dc.; m. Ruth Joyce MacDonald, June 27, 1953; children: James Charles, Douglas Kevin, David Michael, Richard Manley, Paul Frederick, Jon Barton. BS, U. Ill., Champaign-Urbana, 1956, MS, 1957; PhD, U. Iowa, Iowa City, 1980. Tchr. Watervliet Pub. Sch., Mich., 1958-61; tchr. music United Twp. HS, East Moline, Ill., 1961-63; band dir. Pleasant Valley Schs., Iowa, 1963-74; prof. music St. Ambrose U., Davenport, Iowa, 1974-97, prof. emeritus, 1997—, dir. bands, chmn. divsn. fine arts, chmn. dept. music. Guest dir., adjudicator festivals, music contests, Iowa, Ill., Minn.; prodr. Quad-City Music Guild, 1973-77, music dir., 1967—; chmn. Iowa All-State Band, 1971-74; instr. woodwinds Bemidji State U. Band Camp, 1967-92. Pub. arrangements for concert band; contbr. articles to profl. jours. Active Riverdale Vol. Fire Co., 1966-75, pres., 1971-73; active Red Cross Constantine; founder, 1st condr. Quad-City Wind Ensemble, 1987—; choirmaster Bettendorf Presbyn. Ch. Choir, 1982-94. With AUS, 1952-55. Recipient Karl King Disting. Svc. award Iowa Bandmasters, 1987, Disting. Svc. to Music Edn. award Iowa Music Educators Assn., 1995; named to Quad City Music Guild Hall of Fame, 1997. Mem. Iowa Bandmasters Assn. (past pres., Karl King Disting. Svc. award 1987), Coll. Band Dirs. Nat. Assn., Music Educators Nat. Conf., Iowa Music Educators (pres., past pres., editor Iowa Music Educator mag., 1978-80, Disting. Svc. award 1995), Am. Fedn. Musicians, Am. Philatelic Soc., Nat. Band Assn. (Iowa state chmn.), Quad City Stamp Club (editor newsletter 1993-98), Masons (master 2007; sec. Brubaker Lodge 2000-03, Grand Musician Grand Lodge Iowa 2000-01, 04-05), Hi-12 (Davenport chpt., sec. 1999-2005, pres. 2005—06), Shriners (Kaaba shrine), Scottish Rite (32 degree, Master of Kadosh 2006, personal rep. 2007-), York Rite, Phi Mu Alpha Sinfonia, Phi Delta Kappa, Tau Kappa Epsilon. Republican. Methodist. Home: 803 W Rusholme St Davenport IA 52804-1927 Office: Saint Ambrose U Music Dept Davenport IA 52803 Business E-Mail: dcampcharlesb@sau.edu.

DCAMP, KATHRYN ACKER, human resources executive; b. Hartford, Conn., Jan. 12, 1956; d. Donald Jalmer and Virginia Ruth (Wainman) Acker; m. Glenn William DCamp, July 17, 1978; 1 child, Kristen Louise. AA, Ball State U., 1976, BS magna cum laude, 1978. Cert. compensation profl., sr. profl. in human resources. Actuarial/analyst pensions Aetna Life & Casualty, Hartford, Conn., 1980-81, compensation analyst, 1981-82, compensation cons., 1982-84, compensation adminstr., 1984-85, exec. compensation cons., 1985-86, sr. adminstr./exec. programs, 1986-88; compensation cons. The Assoc. Group, Indpls., 1988, compensation mgr., 1989-90, dir. exec. compensation benefits, 1990-93, dir. compensation, mgmt. edn. and exec. benefits, 1993-94; compensation leader GE Capital Corp., Stamford, Conn., 1994-2000; v.p., global compensation leader Cisco Sys., Inc., San Jose, Calif., 2000—01, sr. v.p. human resources, 2001—06, sr. exec. advisor, 2006—. Ind. cons., 1986-93, Motivation by Design, 1993-99; spkr. compensation topics; faculty advisor Univ. Evansville, Ind., 1990—; bd. dirs. Technology Solutions Co., 2007-; area rep. Ind. and Ky. World at Work, mem. nat. adv. bd. on exec. compensation, 1998-2000; columnist Talent Mgnt. Mag., 2006-. Co-author: Spot Gainsharing Personnel Journal, 1989. Mem.: Internat. Bar Assn., World at Work, Soc. Human Resources Mgmt. Lutheran. Office: Cisco Systems Inc 170 W Tasman Bldg 10 San Jose CA 95134-1619 Office Phone: 408-219-5391. E-mail: kdcamp@cisco.com.

DEA, DAVID YOUNG FONG, electrical engineer, consultant; b. Hong Kong, Mar. 6, 1924; came to U.S., 1937; s. Chun Fong and Teung Heung (Chow) D.; m. Mary Gin, Dec. 17, 1955; 1 child, George Hong. BSEE, U. Calif., Berkeley, 1950; postgrad., U. So. Calif., 1951-54. Mem. tech. staff Hughes Aircraft Co., Culver City, Calif., 1950; sect. mgr. Firestone Missile Div., Southgate, Calif., 1956-57; pres. Dea Electronics Co., LA, 1957-59; dept. mgr. on missiles Hughes Aircraft Co., Culver City, 1959-63; project mgr. avionics Teledyne Corp., LA, 1963-65; regional mgr. Bunker Ramo Corp., Canoga Park, Calif., 1965-66; project engr. LTV Corp., Dallas, 1966-73, Lear Siegler Corp., Grand Rapids, Mich., 1973-80; dir. engring. advanced battle tank devel. Nat. Water Lift Corp., Kalamazoo, 1980-82; cons. engr. McDonnell Douglas Corp., St. Louis, 1982-86; project mgr. Simmons Precision Corp., Vergennes, Vt., 1986-87; cons. engr. Control Data Corp., St. Paul, 1987-89; cons. M1 Tank Program Gen. Dynamics Corp., Sterling Heights, Mich., 1990-98; cons. weapon tech. United Defense LP, Mpls., 1998-2000; cons. General Dynamics Corp., Tallahassee, 2001—. Contbr. articles to profl. jours. Violinist Inglewood (Calif.) Symphony. With USAF, 1943-46, Philippines, Japan. Mem. IEEE (sr.), Computer Soc. of IEEE. Republican. Achievements include patents in field. Office: General Dynamics Corp 2930 Commonwealth Rd Tallahassee FL 32303 Home: 29 Santa Bella Rd Rolling Hills Estates CA 90274 E-mail: daviddea@gdls.com.

DEA, FAY SUEY, counselor, educator; d. William and Jean Dea. AB in History magna cum laude, UCLA, 1972, MA in History, 1973, MA in Edn., 1981. Counselor Coll. of Letters UCLA, 1975—79; staff aide to dean adminstrn. svcs. L.A. City Coll., 1979—81; dir. outreach cmty. svcs. L.A. Valley Coll., 1981—82, counselor, instr., 1988—; staff asst. to dir. student svcs. L.A. C.C. Dist., 1982—84, budget analyst, 1984—87; dir. C.C. rels. Calif. State U., Long Beach, 1987—88. Mem. acad. senate L.A. Valley Coll., 1996—. Mem.: Faculty Assn. Calif. C.C.'s, Am. Fedn. Tchrs., Pi Gamma Mu, Phi Lambda Theta, Phi Beta Kappa. Avocations: collecting literary first editions, photography, travel, opera. Office: LA Valley Coll 5800 Fulton Ave Van Nuys CA 91401

DEA, PETER ALLEN, gas industry executive, geologist; b. Worcester, Mass., Aug. 28, 1953; s. Allen Pearson and Beverly Jane (Brown) D. B.A. in Geology, Western State Coll., Gunnison, Colo., 1976; M.S. in Geology, U. Mont., 1981. Geologist Novanda Exploration, Missoula, Mont., 1977, WGM, Inc., Anchorage, 1976-77, Converse Cons., Lakewood, Colo., 1980-81; prof. geology Western State Coll., Gunnison, 1980-82; sr. geologist Exxon Co., U.S.A., Corpus Christi, Tex., 1982; positions through exec. v.p. exploration, Barrett Resources Corp., vice-chmn., CEO, 1994-2000, chmn., CEO, 2000-2001; pres., CEO Western Gas Resources , Inc., 2001-. Bd. dirs. EchoStar Comm. Corp. Contbr. articles to profl. jours. Mem. Am. Assn. Petroleum Geologists, Corpus Christi Geol. Soc. Avocations: skiing; sailing; mountain climbing; kayaking; writing.

DE ABREU, SUE, elementary school educator; b. Honolulu, Dec. 29, 1947; d. Lawrence and Mary (Jones-Howard) de Abreu-Morris; 1 child, Steven. AA, Gulf Coast Coll., Panama, 1967; BA, Fla. State U., 1971; BS, Harvard U., 1968; MS, Ga. So. Coll., 1984; MA, U. West Fla., 1985. Cert. art edn. tchr. K-12th, elem. tchr., sci. specialist 5th-6th grades, Fla. Reading specialist Craig Elem. Sch., Vail, Colo., 1980; tchr. sci. 7th-8th grade Ludowic County Schs., Jesup, Ga., 1981-84; tchr. sci. 5th-6th grade Gulf County Pub. Schs., Port St. Joe, Fla., 1985-98. State judge Fla. State Sci. and Engring. U. Fla, instr.; spl. news cons. Time Mag., 2001. Inventor Learning Through Creative Designs series, 2000. Chmn. Gulf County-N.W. Fla. chpt. Nat. Dem. Senatorial Com., 2001; pres. DeAbreu Plantation Nurseries; landscape designer, pres. Abreu Landscaping Design Svcs. Recipient Outstanding Fla. Artist award, Fedn. Fla. Women's Clubs Am., 2000-01. Mem. NEA, ASCD, Nat. Art Edn. Assn., Nat. Middle Sch. Assn., Nat. Wildlife Fedn. (Gulf County dir.), Wewahitchka Fedn. Women's Club (v.p. 1994-96). Home: 211 Abreu Rd Wewahitchka FL 32465-7719

DEACH, JANA AUNE, lawyer; b. Fergus Falls, Minn. BA magna cum laude, U. ND, 1993; JD with distinction, U. ND, Grand Forks, 1999. Bar: Minn. 1999, US Dist. Ct. (dist. Minn.) 1999. Assoc. Moss & Barnett, P.A., Mpls. Contbr. articles to profl. publs.; symposium editor: U. ND Law Rev. Named a Rising Star, Minn. Super Lawyers mag., 2006. Mem.: ABA, Minn. State Bar Assn., Hennepin County Bar Assn., Phi Alpha Theta. Office: Moss & Barnett PA 4800 Wells Fargo Ctr 90 S 7th St Minneapolis MN 55402 Office Phone: 612-877-5305. E-mail: deachj@moss-barnett.com.*

DEACON, DAVID EMMERSON, advertising executive; b. Toronto, Ont., Can., July 22, 1949; s. Donald Mac Kay and Florence (Campbell) D.; m. Kathryn Robinson (divorced); m. Mary Cecilia Eberle, July 23, 1982 (divorced). Student, Brock U., St. Catherines, Ont., 1968-70, Casa Sch. Fine Arts, Paris, 1970-71. Chmn. election orgn. Liberal Party Ont., Toronto, 1973-75; chmn., editor polit. alerts F.H. Deacon, Hodgson Inc., Toronto, 1975-79, v.p. retail sales, 1979-84; gen. mgr. Porsche div. VW Can., Toronto, 1984-87; pres. Deacon Day Advt., Toronto, 1988-94; chmn. Lowe SMS, Toronto, 1994-96; mng. dir., COO, CFO Padulo Integrated, Toronto, 1996-2000; ptnr. Investment Profile, Inc., Toronto, 2000—; pres. Azure Dynamics Corp., Toronto, 2001—05, dep. chmn., exec. v.p. bus. devel., 2005—, 2005—; chmn. group DKG, 2006—. Illustrator: (poetry) Sun Street, 1970; records include Over the Line, 1994, The Iron Clock, 1996, Stranger in the Morning, 1999; narrator Discovery Channel prodn. Frontiers of Construction, 2001, 02, 03. Chmn. campaign tng. Fed. Liberty Party, 1977-79; pres. Ont. Liberal Party, 1983-85; chmn. Ont. campaign John Turner Leadership, 1984. Winner Can. Endurance Racing championship Can. Automobile Sport Club, 1980. Mem.: Toronto Club. Avocations: skiing, tennis, sailing. Home Phone: 416-928-2708. Personal E-mail: ddeacon@azuredynamics.com.

DEACON, JOHN C., lawyer; b. Newport, Ark., Sept. 26, 1920; BA, U. Ark., 1941, JD, 1948. Bar: Ark. 1948. Ptnr. Barrett & Deacon, Jonesboro, Ark. Commr. from Ark. to Nat. Conf. Commrs. on Uniform State Laws, 1966—, chmn. exec. com., 1977-79, pres. 1979-81. Recipient Ark. Outstanding Lawyer-Citizen award, 1973. Fellow Am. Coll. Trial Lawyers, Internat. Acad. Trial Lawyers (bd. dir. 1978-84), Southwestern Legal Found. (trustee 1975-95, chmn. Research Fellows 1983-85); mem. ABA (chmn. sect. bar activities 1967-68, Ark. del. 1967-79, bd. govs. 1980-83, 92-93, chair sr. lawyers divsn. 1994-95), Craighead County Bar Assn. (pres. 1968-69), N.E. Ark. Bar Assn. (pres. 1966-68), Ark. Bar Assn. (pres. 1970-71, Legacy award 2006), Am. Counsel Assn. (pres. 1974-75), Am. Bar Found. (pres. 1994-96), Internat. Assn. Def. Counsel, Nat. Assn. R.R. Trial Lawyers, Delta Theta Phi. Office: PO Box 1700 Jonesboro AR 72403-1700 also: Barrett & Deacon PA 300 S Church St Jonesboro AR 72401-2911 Office Phone: 870-931-1700. E-mail: jdeacon@barrettdeacon.com.

DEACY, THOMAS EDWARD, JR., lawyer; b. Kansas City, Mo., Oct. 14, 1918; s. Thomas Edward and Grace (Scales) D.; m. Jean Freeman, July 10, 1943 (div. 1988); children: Bennette Kay Deacy Kramer, Carolyn G., Margaret Deacy Vickrey, Thomas, Ann Deacy Krause; m. Jean Holmes McDonald, 1988. JD, U. Mo., 1940; MBA, U. Chgo., 1949. Bar: Mo. 1940, Ill. 1946. Practice law, Kansas City, 1940-42; ptnr. Taylor, Miller, Busch & Magner, Chgo., 1946-55, Deacy & Deacy, Kansas City, 1955—. Lectr. Northwestern U., 1949-55, U. Chgo., 1950-55; dir., mem. exec. com. St. L.-S.F. Ry., 1962-80; dir. Burlington No. Inc., 1980-86; mem. U.S. team Anglo-Am. Legal Exchange, 1973, 77. Mem. Juv. Protective Assn. Chgo., 1947-55, pres., bd. dirs., 1950-53; mem. exec. bd. Chgo. coun. Boy Scouts Am., 1952-55; pres. Kansas City Philharmonic Orch., 1961-63, chmn. bd. trustees, 1963-65; trustee Sunset Hill Sch., 1963-73; trustee, mem. exec. com. u. Kansas City, 1963—; trustee Mo. Law Sch. Found., pres., 1973-77, Kans. chpt. The Nature Conservancy, 1994-99. Capt. AUS, 1942-45. Fellow Am. Coll. Trial Lawyers (regent 1968— , treas. 1973-74, pres. 1975-76), Am. Bar Found; mem. Am. Law Inst., Jud. Conf. U.S. (implementation com. on admission of attys. to fed. practice 1979-86), ABA (commn. standards jud. adminstrn. 1972-74, standing com. fed. judiciary 1974-80), Ill. Bar Assn., Chgo. Bar Assn., Mo. Bar, Kansas City Bar Assn., Lawyers Assn. Kansas City, Chgo. Club, La Jolla (Calif.) Country Club, La Jolla Beach and Tennis Club, Kansas City Club, Kansas City Country Club, River Club, Q.E.B.H. Sr. Hon. Soc. of Mo. Univ., Beta Gamma Sigma, Sigma Chi. Home: 2724 Verona Cir Shawnee Mission KS 66208-1265 Office: 920 Main St Ste 1900 Kansas City MO 64105-2010 Business E-Mail: ted@deacylaw.com.

DEAKTOR, DARRYL BARNETT, lawyer; b. Pitts., Feb. 2, 1942; s. Harry and Edith (Barnett) D.; children: Rachael Alexandra, Hallie Sarah. BA, Brandeis U., 1963; LLB, U. Pa., 1966; MBA, Columbia U., 1968. Bar: Pa. 1966, Fla. 1980, N.Y. 1980, Calif. 2003. Assoc. firm Goodis, Greenfield & Mann, Phila., 1968-70, ptnr., 1971; gen. counsel Life of Pa. Fin. Corp., Phila., 1972; asst. prof. U. Fla. Coll. Law, Gainesville, 1972-74, assoc. prof., 1974-80; with Mershon, Sawyer, Johnston, Dunwody & Cole, Miami, Fla., 1980-81, ptnr., 1981-84, Walker Ellis Gragg & Deaktor, Miami, 1984-86, White & Case LLP, Miami, 1987-95, Johannesburg, 1995-2000, Palo Alto, Calif., 2000—01, ret. ptnr., 2002—07, ptnr. of counsel Miami, 2007—. Mem. Dist. III (Fla.) Human Rights Advocacy Com. for Mentally Retarded Citizens, 1974-78, chmn., 1978-80; mem. adv. bd. Childbirth Edn. Assn. Alachua County, Fla., 1974-80; mem. resource devel. bd. Mailman Ctr. for Child Devel., 1981-88. Mem. Fla. Bar, NY Bar, Calif. Bar. Mailing: 1330 Mariposa Ave Boulder CO 80302-7842 Office Phone: 305-371-2700. E-mail: dbd@ionsky.com.

DEAKYNE, WILLIAM JOHN, library director, musician; b. Harrisburg, Pa., June 25, 1936; s. William John and Hazel (Brown) D. MusB, U. Hartford, 1961; MLS, Villanova U., 1962; Diploma in French, Berlitz Sch., Phila., 1967, Berlitz Sch., Stamford, Conn., 1969. Cert. libr., NJ, Mass., NY, Wash. Dir. Meuser Meml. Libr., Easton, Pa., 1962-64, Coyle Free Libr., Chambersburg, Pa., 1964-65, Free Libr. Springfield Twp., Phila., 1965-68, Darien (Conn.) Libr., 1968-78, East Lyme (Conn.) Libr., 1979—, East Lyme Libr. Found., 1991—. Founding mem. Librs.-on-Line, Inc., 1983. Organist, pianist, composer Jeu de Clochette, 1964; contbr. articles to profl. jours. V.p. East Lyme C. of C., Niantic, Conn.; mem. Am. Cathedral of the Holy Trinity, Paris, 1998—; charter mem. Founders Planned Giving Soc., U. Hartford, 1996—. Mem. ALA (del. to Internat. Fedn. Libr. Assn. meetings Chgo., Copenhagen 1969), Les Amis de Vielles Maisons. Democrat. Avocations: restoration of pipe organs in France, promotion of English organs in U.S. Home: Westchester Dr East Lyme CT 06333 Office: East Lyme Pub Libr 39 Society Rd Niantic CT 06357-1100 Office Phone: 860-739-6926.

DEAL, JILL B., lawyer; b. Stockton, Calif., Sept. 3, 1942; d. Ronald Emerson and Otilia (MacDonald) Brady; m. Timothy E. Deal, Sept. 5, 1964; children: Christopher, Bartholomew. BA, U. Calif., Berkeley, 1964; JD, Cath. U., 1979. Bar: D.C. 1979. Rsch. asst. FTC, Washington, 1974-78, policy analyst, 1978-79; atty. Arnold & Porter, Washington, 1979-81; Am. legal advisor Gen. Electric Co., p.l.c., London, 1981-85; atty. Rogers & Wells, Paris, 1985-88, of counsel Washington, 1988—96; principal, regulatory group Fish & Richardson, 1996—2000; ptnr., FDA, bioscience and pharmaceuticals Venable LLP, Washington, 2000—. Speaker FDLI Conference on Generic Biologics, 2003, CBI Annual Forum on Generic Drugs, 2003, Biopharmaceutical Comparability Conference, 2004; presenter in field. Co-author Biotechnology: Patents, Licensing and FDA Practice, 2001, Liability for Generic Drug Products: Issues to Consider, 2003, (with Matthew Bender) Reilly, Homeland Security Deskbook; contbr. articles to profl. jours. Mem. ABA (sec. on antitrust), DC Bar. Office: Venable LLP 575 7th St NW Washington DC 20004 Office Phone: 202-344-4713. Office Fax: 202-344-8300. Business E-Mail: jdeal@venable.com.

DEAL, KEVIN PAUL, furniture designer; b. Chgo., Oct. 3, 1956; s. Paul Sydney Deal and Bernice Lorraine Chowning-Deal; m. Nancy Kaye Ream, Oct. 1, 1988 (div. Jan. 1993); 1 child, Veronica Victoria. AS in fire sci., Crafton Hills Coll., 1997, AS in emergency med. svc., 1998. Owner Wood Dr., San Diego, 1984—90; owner, furniture repair Wood Magic, Riverside, 1990—2003; firefighter, EMT Riverside County Fire Dept., Calif., 1994—99; owner Kevin Deal Fine Woodworking, 2003—. Scholarship chmn. San Diego Fine Woodworkers, 1987—90. Author: (paper) UR, Home of the Ziggurat, 1997. Mem.: Smithsonian Inst., Nat. Geographic Soc., Exptl. Aircraft Assn., Archeol. Inst. of Am., Valley Coll. Fencing Club, Alpha Gamma Sigma (life). Roman Catholic. Avocations: archaeology, history, archery, sailing, swordsmith. Office: Kevin Deal P O Box 701 Riverside CA 92502 Office Phone: 951-684-6084. Business E-Mail: kdeal1956@sbcglobal.net.

DEAL, NATHAN J., congressman, lawyer; b. Millen, Ga., Aug. 25, 1942; m. Sandra Dunagan; children: Jason, Mary Emily, Carrie, Katie. BA, Mercer U., 1964, JD, 1966. Atty. priv. practice, 1979—82; asst. dist. atty. N.E. cir. Hall County, Ga., 1970—71, judge, juvenile court Ga., 1971-72, atty., 1977—79; mem. Ga. State Senate, 1981—93, pres. pro tempore, 1991—93; mem. U.S. Congress from 9th Ga. Dist., 1993—2003, 2005—, chmn. energy and commerce com.; mem. U.S. Congress from 10th Ga. Dist., 2003—05. Mem. Congressional Boating Caucus, Congressional Caucus on Unfunded Mandates, Congressional Travel and Tourism Caucus, Congressional Vietnam-Era Veterans Caucus, Rural Health Care Coalition, Speaker's Immigration Task Force. Capt. JAGC, U.S. Army, 1966-68. Republican. Office: US Ho Reps 2133 Rayburn Ho Office Bldg Washington DC 20515-1009

DEAL, TIMOTHY, association executive, former diplomat; b. St. Louis, Sept. 17, 1940; s. Edward F. and Loretta (Fuemuller) D.; m. Jill Brady, Sept. 5, 1964; children; Christopher, Bart. BA, U. Calif., Berkeley, 1962; postgrad., San Francisco State Coll., 1964-65, Am. U., 1972-73. With Am. Embassy, Tegucigalpa, Honduras, 1966-68, Warsaw, Poland, 1969-72, econ. counselor London, 1981-85; various fgn. svcs. assignments Dept. State, Washington, 1972-76; sr. staff mem. NSC, The White House, Washington, 1976-81; dep. U.S. rep. to U.S. Mission to OECD, Paris, 1985-88; dir. office Ea. European/Yugoslav affairs Dept. State, 1988-89; spl. asst. to pres. for nat. security affairs NSC, The White House, 1989-92; minister, dept. chief of mission Am. Embassy, London, 1992-96; ret., 1996; sr. v.p. U.S. Coun. for Internat. Bus., Washington, 1996—. Bd. dirs. Banner Life Ins. Co., William Penn Life Ins. Co., Legal and Gen. Am. Capt. U.S. Army, 1963-65. Avocations: theater, cinema, sports. Home: 5721 Macarthur Blvd NW Washington DC 20016-5304 Office: 1400 K St NW Ste 905 Washington DC 20005 Home Phone: 202-244-3177; Office Phone: 202-371-1316. E-mail: tdeal@uscib-dc.org.

DEAL, WILLIAM BROWN, medical school dean, physician, educator; b. Durham, NC, Oct. 4, 1936; s. Harold Albert and Louise (Brown) D.; m. April Autrey, May 2, 1998; children: Kimberly Deal Wolpert, Kathleen Louise. AA, Mars Hill Coll., 1956; AB, U. N.C., 1958, MD, 1963. Intern in medicine U. Fla. Hosp., Gainesville, 1963-64, asst. resident, 1966-68, fellow in infectious diseases Gainsville, 1968—69, chief resident, instr. dept. medicine Gainesville, 1969-70; asst. prof. dept. medicine U. Fla., 1970-73, assoc. dean Coll. of Medicine, 1973-77, assoc. prof. dept. cmty. health and family medicine, 1973-75, assoc. prof. dept. medicine, 1973-75, prof., 1975-88, acting dean Coll. of Medicine, 1977-78, dean Coll. of Medicine, v.p. clin. affairs, 1978-88, clin. prof. medicine, 1988—; assoc. dean, prof. medicine U. Ala. Sch. of Medicine, 1991-96, sr. assoc. dean, prof. medicine, 1996-97, dean, 1997—2004, prof. medicine Birmingham; interim CEO UAB Health Sys., 1998-99; v.p. medicine U. Ala., Birmingham, 2000—, sr. v.p., dean emeritus, 2004—. Pres. Maine Med. Ctr. Found., Portland, Maine, 1988—90; asst. to sr. v.p. AMA, 1980; lectr. Northwestern U., 1980; vis. clin. tutor City Hosp. U. Edinburgh, Scotland, 1967; chair nat. adv. com. Summer Med. Dental Edn. Program. Contbr. articles to numerous profl. jours. Fellow: ACP, Royal Soc. Medicine; mem.: AMA (liaison com. on med. edn. 1982—87, chmn. governing coun. sect. on med. schs. 1986—87, exec. com. AAMC 1986—88, disting. svc. mem. AAMC 2005—), Med. Assn. State of Ala., Jefferson County Med. Soc., Zool. Soc. of Ala., Noble Order of the Flea, Alpha Omega Alpha (bd. dirs. 1986—95, pres. 1993—95), Beta Theta Pi, Phi Chi. Office: Sch of Medicine FOT 856 UAB Birmingham AL 35294-0001 Office Phone: 205-934-9401. Business E-Mail: wdeal@uab.edu.

DEAL, WILLIAM THOMAS, retired school psychologist; b. Dec. 18, 1949; s. Richard Lee and Rheta Lucille (Gerber) Deal; m. Paula Nespeca, Aug. 5, 1972. BS, Bowling Green State U., 1972; MA, John Carroll U., 1977; postgrad., Kent State U., 1979—. Sci. tchr. Westlake Schs., 1972-76; intern sch. psychologist Garfield Heights Schs., 1976-77; pvt. practice Parma Heights, Ohio, 1982—84; sch. psychologist, 1977—2007; ret., 2007. Named Psychologist of the Yr., Cleve. Sch., 1990; recipient cert. of Recognition, Garfield Heights Bd. Edn., 1980, Outstanding Achievement award, Cleve. Assn. Children with Learning Disabilities, Inc., 1980. Mem.: Cleve. Assn. Sch. Psychologists, Ohio Sch. Psychology Assn., United Tchg. Profession, Nat. Assn. Sch. Psychologists, Phi Delta Kappa. Democrat. Methodist. Home: 5290 Kings Hwy Cleveland OH 44126-3059

DE ALESSI, ROSS ALAN, lighting designer; b. San Francisco, Apr. 16, 1955; s. August Eugene De Alessi and Angela Maria (Caredio) Leonard; m. Susan Tracey Stearns, Aug. 11, 1990; 1 child, Chase Arthur. BFA, Stephens Coll., 1978. In-house lighting designer GUMP'S, San Francisco, 1981-84; prin. Ross De Alessi & Assoc., San Francisco, 1984-87, Luminae Lighting Design, San Francisco, 1987-93; prin., co-founder Ross De Alessi Lighting Design, Seattle, 1993—. Works include GUMP'S Christmas Windows, San Francisco (award of Distinction Gen. Electric, 1986, Spl. Citation 1989, Edwin F. Guth award Illuminating Engring. Soc. 1989, 90), TAB Products Showroom, L.A. (award of Distinction Gen. Electric 1987), St. Augustine's Ch., Pleasanton, Calif. (Sect. award Illuminating Engring. Soc. 1988), L.A. Quinta (Calif.) Resort Plz. Fountains (award of Excellence Gen. Electric 1988, Paul Waterbury award Illuminating Engring. Soc. 1989), McKesson Bldg. Lobby, San Francisco (award of excellence Gen. Electric 1988, Edwin F. Guth award Illuminating Engring. Soc. 1989), Brown & Bain, Phoenix (Merit award Gen. Electric 1989), Saxe Gallery, San Francisco (Edwin F. Guth award Illuminating Engring. Soc. 1989), Plz. Pk., San Jose, Calif. (Paul Waterbury Spl. Citation Illuminating Engring. Soc. 1990), The Palace Fine Arts, San Francisco (Edison Award Gen. Electric 1990, Paul Waterbury award Illuminating Engring. Soc. 1991, award of Excellence Internat. Assn. Lighting Designers 1991), Le Touessrok, Island of Mauritius (Merit award Gen. Electric 1993, Sect. Award Illuminating Engring. Soc. 1994, Paul Waterbury award 1994), St. Patrick's Sem., Menlo Park, Calif. (Edison award Gen. Electric 1993, Edwin F. Guth award Illuminating Engring. Soc. 1994, Citation Internat. Assn. Lighting Designers 1994), Palace of the Lost City, Republic of Boputhatswana (Award of Merit Gen.

Electric 1992, Paul Waterbury award Internat. Assn. Lighting Designers 1993), Wells Fargo Bank-Flagship Bank, San Francisco (award of excellence Gen. Electric 1992, Merit award Illuminating Engring. Soc. 1993, citation Internat. Assn. Lighting Designers 1993), Santa Barbara County Courthouse, Santa Barbara (Paul Waterbury award Illuminating Engring. Soc. 1995, award of excellence Internat. Assn. Lighting Designers 1995), City of Bridges, Cleve. (Edison award 1995, Paul Waterbry award Illuminating Engring. Soc. 1997), MGM Grand Gateway of Entertainment, Las Vegas (award of excellence Gen. Elec. 1998, Edwin F. Guth award Illuminating Engring. Soc. 1999, Merit award Internat. Assn. Lighting Designers 1999), Helsinki Master Plan-Esplanade (Edison award 1999, Award of Distinction, Illuminating Engring. Soc. 2000, Merit award Internat. Assn. Lighting Designers), Space Needle (award of excellence Gen. Electric 2000, Illuminating Engring. Soc. 2001, Merit award Internat. Assn. Lighting Designers 2001), Forth Bridge (award of excellence Internat. Assn. Lighting Designers 2002), Montecasino (Merit award Gen. Electric 2001, Sect. award Internat. Assn. Design awards 2002). Mem. Internat. Assn. Lighting Designers (lighting cert.), Nat. Coun. on the Certification Lighting Profls., Illuminating Engring. Soc., Washington Athletic Club. Avocations: scuba diving, travel. Office: Ross De Alessi Lighting Design 2330 Magnolia Blvd W Seattle WA 98199-3813

DEALEY, LYNN TOWNSEND, artist; b. Smithfield, NC, July 16, 1954; d. John Sims and Rebecca Barnes Townsend; m. Russell Edward Dealey, May 4, 1985. AS in Advt. Design, Art Inst. Ft. Lauderdale, 1977; BS in Health Edn., U. N.C. Greensboro, 1976. Mem. adv. bd. Artreach, Dallas, 1991—92; spkr. in field. Illustrator: A Coon Creek Chronicle, 1992; featured, Texans and Their Pets, 2006, cover, Philanthropy in Tex., 2002, featured, Texas Women: Trailblazers, Shining Stars and Cowgirls, 2003, Enchanted Galleries, 2004—, mural, Dallas Zoo, 1998; co-author: Splenda: Is It Safe?, 2005. Mem.: Dallas Country Club, Dallas Social Dir. Avocations: science, biology, cartooning, travel, cooking. Office: PO Box 191406 Dallas TX 75219 Office Phone: 214-890-8123.

DEALY, JOHN MICHAEL, chemical engineer, educator; b. Waterloo, Iowa, Mar. 23, 1937; s. Milton David and Ruth Marion (Dorton) D.; m. Jacqueline Dery, Aug. 22, 1964; 1 child, Pamela. BS, U. Kans., 1958; MS, U. Mich., 1959, PhD, 1963; postdoctoral fellow, 1964. Asst. prof. chem. engring. McGill U., Montreal, Que., Canada, 1964-67, assoc. prof., 1967-72, prof., 1972—2004, prof. emeritus, 2004, chmn. dept., 1993-94, dean engring., 1994-99. Cons. indsl. rheology and polymer processing Author: 4 books on melt rheology and plastics processing; contbr. articles. Fellow: Can. Acad. Engring., Royal Soc. Can., Soc. Plastics Engrs.; mem.: Soc. Rheology (pres. 1987—89), Sigma Xi, Theta Tau, Tau Beta Pi. Home: 315 Roslyn Ave Montreal PQ Canada H3Z 2L7 Office: McGill U Chem Engring Dept 3610 University St Montreal PQ Canada H3A 2B2 Home Phone: 514-937-5037; Office Phone: 514-398-4264. E-mail: john.dealy@mcgill.ca.

DEAMANT, CATHERINE D., internist; b. 1960; MD, Rush Med. Coll., 1987. Resident Michael Reese Hosp.; founder Connections' Health Svc., Chgo., 1990—; internist, dir., palliative care program Cook Co. Bur. Health Svcs., Chgo., 2001—. Named one of Chgo.'s 100 Most Influential Women, Crain's Chicago Business, 2004. Office: Cook County Bur Health Svcs 1835 W Harrison St Chicago IL 60612

DEAMER, BARTLEY C., lawyer; b. San Francisco, Jan. 16, 1945; BA, Stanford U., 1966; student, Free Univ. Berlin, Germany, 1966—67; JD cum laude, Harvard U., 1970. Bar: Calif. 1972. Law clk. to Hon. Irving R. Kaufman U.S. Ct. Appeals (2nd cir.) N.Y., 1970-71; atty. McCutchen, Doyle, Brown & Enersen, San Francisco; ptnr. Bingham McCutchen LLP. Note editor Harvard Law Rev., 1969-70, active, 1968-70. Recipient Silicon Valley's Top Attorneys, San Jose mag., 2005, No. Calif. Super Lawyer, Law & Politics and San Francisco mag., 2004—06, Best Lawyers in Am., 2007. Fellow Am. Coll. Investment Counsel, ABA. Office: Bingham McCutchen LLP 3 Embarcadero Center San Francisco CA 94111 Office Phone: 650-849-4868. Business E-Mail: bart.deamer@bingham.com.

DE AMICIS, DON S., lawyer; AB, Harvard Coll., 1976; JD, Harvard Univ., 1979. Bar: Mass. 1980, DC 1980. Ptnr., bankruptcy, bus. restructuring Ropes & Gray LLP, Boston. Mem.: Mass. Bar Assn. (Internat. Law Com.), Boston Bar Assn. (Internat. Law Sect. Steering Com.), Internat. Bar Assn., Am. Bankruptcy Inst., ABA (bd. govs. 2005—). Office: Ropes & Gray LLP One International Pl Boston MA 02110 Office Phone: 617-951-7732. Office Fax: 617-235-0019. Business E-Mail: don.deamicis@ropesgray.com.

DEAN, ALAN, lawyer; b. NYC, Dec. 31, 1951; AB, Harvard U., 1973; MA, U. Calif., Berkeley, 1974; JD, Harvard U., 1978. Bar: NY 1979, US Dist. Ct. (so. & ea. dist.) NY 1979. Assoc. Davis Polk & Wardwell, NYC, 1978-85, ptnr., 1986—. Office: Davis Polk & Wardwell 450 Lexington Ave New York NY 10017 Office Phone: 212-450-4126. Office Fax: 212-450-3126. Business E-Mail: alan.dean@dpw.com.

DEAN, BEALE, lawyer; b. Ft. Worth, Feb. 26, 1922; s. Ben J. and Helen (Beale) Dean; m. Margaret Ann Webster, Sept. 3, 1948; children: Webster Beale, Giselle Liseanne. BA, U. Tex., Austin, 1943, LLB, 1947. Bar: Tex. 1946, U.S. Dist. Ct. (no., we. and ea. dists.) Tex., U.S. Cir. Ct. (5th and 11th cirs.) 1952, U.S. Supreme Ct. 1954. Asst. dist. atty., Dallas, 1947-48; assoc. Martin, Moore & Brewster, Ft. Worth, 1948-50; mem. Martin, Moore, Brewster & Dean, 1950-51, Pannell, Dean, Pannell & Kerry (and predecessor firms), 1951-65; ptnr. Brown, Herman, Scott, Young & Dean, Ft. Worth, 1965-71, Brown, Herman, Scott, Dean & Miles, Ft. Worth, 1971-98, Brown, Herman, Dean, Wiseman, Liser & Hart, LLP, Ft. Worth, 1998—2003; sr. counsel Brown, Dean, Wiseman, Liser, Proctor & Hart, LLP, Ft. Worth, 2003—06, Brown, Dean, Wiseman, Proctor, Hart & Howell, LLP, Ft. Worth, 2007—. Spl. asst. Atty. Gen., Tex., 1959—61. Regent Nat. Coll. Dist. Attys., 1985—2003. With USAAF, 1942—45, ETO. Named Tex. Super Lawyer, Law and Polit., Tex. Monthly, 2003—04, 2003—06. Mem.: ABA, Nat. Coll. Dist. Attys. (regent 1985—2005), Tex. Bar Found. (charter mem.), Am. Bar Found., State Bar Tex. (bd. dirs. 1973—75), Am. Coll. Trial Lawyers, Ft. Worth-Tarrant County Bar Assn. (past pres. 1971—72, Blackstone award 1991), Bar Assn. Fifth Fed. Cir., Ft. Worth Club, Ridglea Country Club, Ft. Worth Boat Club. Presbyterian. Office: 200 Fort Worth Club Bldg 306 W 7th St Fort Worth TX 76102-4905

DEAN, BILL VERLIN, JR., lawyer; b. Oklahoma City, Jan. 11, 1957; s. Bill V. and Mary Lou (Dorman) D.; m. Christine Potter; children: Bill V. III, Mary Megan. BS, Ctrl. State U., 1978; JD, Oklahoma City U., 1991. Bar: Okla. 1982, U.S. Dist. Ct. (we. dist.) Okla. 1983, (no. dist.) Okla. 1986, (ea. dist.) Okla. 1987, Tex. 1990, N.Y. 1992, U.S. Ct. Appeals (10th cir.) 1986; U.S. Supreme Ct., 2002; lic. real estate broker and ins. agt. Second dep. assessor Okla. County Assessor, Oklahoma City, 1978—80; atty. Struthers Oil and Gas Corp., Oklahoma City, 1980—82; cons. Bill Dean & Co., Jones, Okla., 1979—; ptnr. Dean & Assocs. P.C., Jones, 1982—; pres. Dean Ins. Agy. Ltd., 1986—, Casualty Corp. Am., Inc., 1999—; pres., CEO Madewell Holding Corp., 2004—. Bd. dirs. Union Mut. Ins. Co., Madewell & Madewell, Inc., Madewell Holding Corp., 2004—; CEO Casualty Corp. of Am., Inc., 1999—. Mem. Okla. County Bar Assn., Okla. Bar Assn., Tex. Bar Assn., N.Y. Bar Assn., Shriners. Methodist. Home: 200 Cherokee St Jones OK 73049-7709 Office: Dean & Assocs P C PO Box 1060 110 W Main St Jones OK 73049-1060 Home Phone: 405-399-2324; Office Phone: 405-399-9111. Business E-Mail: bdean@deannet.com.

DEAN, BRUCE LINTON, radiologist; b. Richmond, Ind., May 7, 1951; s. Calvin Curtis and Geneva Dean; m. Gail Lynn Chaney, June 3, 1989; children: Troy, Ryan. BS in Chemistry, Purdue U., West Lafayette, Ind.; MD, Ind. U., Indpls. Neuroradiologist Barrow Neurol. Inst., Phoenix, 1987—. Vol. Phoenix Resuce Mission, Food for Hungry, Phoenix. Grantee, NIH, NSF. Home: 6045 E Monticeto Ave Scottsdale AZ 85251

DEAN, CAROLE LEE, film company executive; b. Dallas, Mar. 23, 1939; d. Roy Webster and Dorothy Lee Dean; children: Richard Dean, Carole Joyce. Student, UCLA. Pres. Studio Film and Tape, LA, 1969-2000, NYC, 1970-2000, Chgo., 1994—2000, From the Heart Prodn., LA, 1992—. Spkr. in field. Prodr., host Health Styles, 1994-97; author: Heal Thyself, 1999, The Art of Funding Your Film: Alternative Financing Concepts, 2003, The Art of Manifesting: Create Your Future, 2005. Established Roy W. Dean film, video and writing grants, 1992. Mem. Nat. Arts Club. Republican. Avocations: skiing, equesterian. Personal E-mail: caroleedean@att.net.

DEAN, E. JOSEPH, lawyer; b. Astoria, Oreg., May 20, 1949; s. Charles Herbert Dean and Sarah (Barnard) Leino; m. Judith A. Buszko, Sept. 2, 1972; children: Rebecca Ann, William Thomas, Margaret Ruth. BA in Econs., U. Oreg., 1971, BA in Math., 1971; JD cum laude, Harvard U., 1974. Bar: Oreg. 1974, US Ct. of Appeals (1st cir.) 1975, US Dist. Ct. Oreg. 1975, US Ct. of Appeals (9th cir.) 1980, US Tax Ct. 1984, US Ct. of Appeals (8th cir.) 1989, US Ct. of Appeals (fed. cir.) 1990, US Supreme Ct. 1991, Oreg. Supreme Ct., Dist. of Colo. Law clk. to Edward M. McEntee US Ct. Appeals (1st cir.), Providence, 1974-75; assoc. Davies, Biggs, Strayer, Stoel & Boley, Portland, Oreg., 1975-81; ptnr. Stoel, Rives, Boley, Jones & Grey (now Stoel Rives LLP), Portland, Oreg., 1981-95, Stoel Rives LLP, Portland, 1996—. Contbr. Mem. Multnomah County Local Profl. Responsibility Com., Portland, 1981-84, State Profl. Responsibility Bd., Portland, 1984-87; bd. dirs. Morrison Ctr. Youth and Family, Portland, 1985-91, v.p., 1988-89, pres., 1989-91. Recipient Best Lawyers in Am., 2005—06. Mem. Multnomah Bar Assn. ACLU, sec. Oreg. State Bar (uniform state laws com.) 1983-84, mem. State Profl. Responsibility Bd. 1984-87, spl. counsel Oreg. Jud. Fitness Commn. Avocation: farming. Office: Stoel Rives LLP 900 SW 5th Ave Ste 2600 Portland OR 97204-1268 Office Fax: 503-220-2480. Business E-Mail: ejdean@stoel.com.

DEAN, EDWIN BECTON, entrepreneur; b. Danville, Va., Feb. 7, 1940; s. Edwin Becton and Lois (Campbell) D.; m. Deirdre Anne Jacovides, Aug. 16, 1964; children: Jennifer E., Kristin R., Brian N. BS in Physics, Va. Poly. Inst. and State U., 1963, MS in Math., 1965; postgrad., George Washington U., 1974-77; cert. profl. study engring. mgmt., Old Dominion U., 1998. Technician, assoc. engr. Johns Hopkins U. Applied Physics Lab., Laurel, Md., 1959-64; physicist, mathematician, electronic engr., and ops. rsch. analyst Naval Surface Warfare Ctr., Silver Spring, Md., 1964-79; owner, mgr. Gen. Bus. Svcs. and Beta Systems, Virginia Beach, Va., 1979-84, Virginia Beach Communique Inc., Virginia Beach, Va., 1980-81; registered rep. First Investors Corp., Arlington, Va., 1971-85; dir. Tips Club of Virginia Beach, Inc., 1980-82; computer specialist Naval Supply Systems Command, Norfolk, Va., 1982-83; head cost estimating office NASA Langley Rsch. Ctr., Hampton, Va., 1983-90, tech. resource mgr. Space Exploration Initiative Office, 1990-94, sr. rsch. engr. multidisciplinary optimization br., 1994-98; owner The DFV Group, Virginia Beach, Va., 1996-98; pres. The DFV Group, Inc., Virginia Beach, 1999—2002. Presenter in field; distbr. Shaklee, 1999—. Contbr. articles to profl. jours. NASA fellow, 1963-65. Mem. IEEE, Assn. for Computing Machinery, Internat. Soc. Parametric Analysts (past chmn. bd. dirs.), Am. Soc. for Quality Control, Am. Assn. Cost Engrs., Internat. Neural Network Soc., Sigma Pi Sigma, Pi Mu Epsilon, Phi Kappa Phi.

DEAN, EDWIN ROBINSON, economist, educator, consultant; b. South Bend, Ind., July 25, 1933; s. William Stover and Eleanor (Hatcher) D.; m. Emily Rebecca Finlay, Feb. 2, 1963; children: Gabrielle N., Natalie R. BA in Philosophy magna cum laude, Yale U., 1955; postgrad., Gokhale Inst. Politics-Econs., Poona, India, 1955—56; PhD in Econs., Columbia U., 1963. Instr., then asst. prof. econs. Columbia U., NYC, 1960-68; assoc. prof. Queens Coll., CUNY, 1968-72; program dir. Am. Friends Svc. Com., NYC, 1970-73; supervisory equal opportunity specialist in econs. U.S. Commn. on Civil Rights, 1973-80; sr. assoc. Nat. Inst. Edn., Washington, 1980-83, acting asst. dir., 1983; supervisory economist Bur. Labor Stats., Washington, 1983-85, chief divsn. productivity rsch., 1985-89, assoc. commr. Office Productivity and Tech., 1989-99, ret., 1999; adj. prof. econs. George Wash. U., Washington, 2000—03. Cons. to World Bank, 2001-03; mem. exec. com. Conf. Rsch. Income and Wealth, 1994-2000; chair working party industry stats. OECD, 1998-2000. Author: The Supply Responses of African Farmers: Theory and Measurement in Malawi, 1966, Plan Implementation in Nigeria, 1962-66, 1972; contbg. author: The Challenge Ahead: Equal Opportunity in Referral Unions, 1976, Nonreferral Unions and Equal Employment Opportunity, 1982; editor: The Controversy over the Quantity Theory of Money, 1965, Education and Economic Productivity, 1984; contbr. articles to profl. jours. Recipient Julius Shiskin award, Nat. Assn. Bus. Econs., 2000; fellow, NSF, 1961—62; grantee rsch., Columbia U. Coun. for Rsch. in Social Scis., 1964, Rockefeller Found., Ibadan, Nigeria, 1965—67; scholar, Yale U., 1951—55; Howland travel fellow, 1955, Seager fellow in econs., 1956, 1957, William Bayard Cutting travel fellow, Columbia U., 1958. Mem.: Am. Econ. Assn.

DEAN, GEOFFREY, book publisher; b. Newcastle-upon-Tyne, Eng., Sept. 18, 1940; s. Thomas Craig and Mildred Catherine (Hoggard) D.; m. Philma Marina Patterson, Aug. 10, 1963; children: Andrea Samantha, Christopher Michael. BA, U. Toronto, 1961. With McGraw-Hill Co. Can. Ltd., 1961-66, coll. editor Scarborough, Ont., 1962-66; sales mgr. Methuen Publs., Toronto, 1966-70; v.p. mktg. Van Nostrand Reinhold Ltd., Toronto, 1970-76; pres., dir. John Wiley & Sons. Can. Ltd., Toronto, 1976-86; cons. Geoffrey Dean Enterprises, 1986—; pres. Tech. Instrnl. Products Inc., 1987-88, Scriptographic Communications Ltd., Toronto, 1989-91. Dir. Youth Employment Svc., Toronto, 1995-2000; mem. adv. bd. on sci. pub. Nat. Rsch. Coun. Can., 1982-84; chmn. Book and Periodical Coun., 1988-89; mem. project assessment com. Book Pub. Industry Devel. Program, Govt. Can., 1987-91; internat. cons. Dept. of Edn., Rep. of Philippines, 1996-97. Bd. dirs. Can. Diabetes Assn., 1987-89. Mem. Can. Book Pubs. Coun. (pres. 1983), Ont. Bus. Edn. Assn. (hon. pres. 1982-84), Rotary (Paul Harris fellow 2006). Home and Office: 33 Deepglade Crescent Toronto ON Canada M2J 1B3 Home Phone: 416-497-0104; Office Phone: 416-805-1210. E-mail: geoffdean01@hotmail.com.

DEAN, H. CLARK, retired civil engineer, genealogist; b. Evanston, Ill., Jan. 22, 1931; s. Herbert Franklin and E(lla) Frances (Clark) D.; m. Mary Margaret McHugh, Aug. 20, 1960; children: Merrick Stephen McHugh, Nancy Lauck Dean Cacioppo. BSCE, Swarthmore Coll., 1953; MBA, U. Chgo., 1964. Registered profl. engr., Pa.; registered structural engr., Ill.; cert. genealogist Bd. for Cert. Genealogists. Engr. Pratt & Whitney, East Hartford, Conn., 1954; jr. engr. Modjeski & Masters, Harrisburg, Pa., 1954, engr., 1956-61, Harza Engring. Co., Chgo., 1961-67, asst. to v.p., 1967-72, asst. project mgr., 1972-74, project mgr., 1974-76, asst. dept. head, 1976-80, dept. head, 1980-97; ret., 1997. Contbr. articles to profl. jours. including Am. Genealogist., Nat. Geneal. Soc. Quar., New Eng. Hist. and Geneal. Register, NY Geneal. and Biog. Record, Mayflower Quar. With C.E., U.S. Army, 1955-56. Mem. ASCE (life), New Eng. Hist. and Geneal. Soc., Nat. Geneal. Soc., Soc. Mayflower Descs. in Ill. (treas. 1967-70, bd. assts., 1990-98, gov. 1998-2001), Order Founders and Patriots Am., Ill. Soc. War of 1812, Assn. Profl. Genealogists, North Suburban Geneal. Soc. (pres. 1976) Home: 422 Kelling Ln Glencoe IL 60022-1113 Personal E-mail: hclarkdean@juno.com.

DEAN, HOWARD BRUSH, III, political organization administrator, former governor; b. NYC, Nov. 17, 1948; s. Howard Brush and Andrea (Maitland) D.; m. Judith Steinberg, 1981; children: Anne, Paul. BA, Yale U., 1971; MD, Albert Einstein Coll. Medicine, 1978. Intern, then resident in internal medicine Med. Ctr. Hosp. Vt., 1978-82; practice medicine specializing in internal medicine Shelburne, Vt.; mem., house edn. com., mcpl. corps. and elections com., rules com. Vt. House of Reps., Montpelier, 1983-86, asst. minority leader, 1985-86; lt. gov. State of Vt., Montpelier, 1986-91, gov., 1991—2003; chmn. Dem. Nat. Com., 2005—. Asst. clin. prof. medicine U. Vt. Coll. Medicine; ran for Democratic nomination in Presdl. election., 2004; established political action com. Democracy for America, 2004; guest host CNBC's Topic A with Tina Brown, 2004. Bd. dirs. Vt. Developmental Capabilities Council, U. Vt. Council, Vt. Adv. Commn. Intergovtl. Affairs, Vt. State Bd. Nat. Forests; founder Vt. Youth Conservation Corps; sponsor Long Trail Preservation Fund. Democrat. Office: Dem Nat Com 430 S Capitol St SE Washington DC 20003

DEAN, J. THOMAS, lawyer; b. Cleve., Feb. 22, 1933; s. John Ladd and Margaret Caroline (Blakely) Dean; m. Patricia Jean Whitmore, Aug. 6, 1960; children: Thomas W., Carol M., Joan G. BA, Ohio Weslyan U., 1956; JD, Western Res. U., 1959. Bar: Ohio 1959. Asst. pros. atty. Lake County, Ohio, 1960; assoc. Blakely, Rand, Painesville, Ohio, 1961—67; ptnr. Blakely & Dean, 1967—76, Blakely, Dean, Wilson & Klingenberg, Painesville, 1975—90, Blakely, Dean & Klingenberg, 1990—92, Blakely, Dean & Wagner, 1992—97. Law dir. North Perry Village, Ohio, 1970—90. Mem. Painesville Bd. Zoning Appeals, 1971—76, Planning Commn., 1967—79, chmn., 1970—77; pres. Painesville Sr. Citizens, 1982—84; clk. Painesville Twp. Park, 1962—; mem. Lake County Planning Commn., 1997—2000; mem Lake County Bd. Elections, 1964—84, 1988—90; chmn. Lake County Rep. Com., 1970—74, 1982—84; mem. Ohio Rep. Cen. Com., 1980—88; bd. trustees Lake County Vis. Bur., 1996—; mem. Lake County Found. Bd., 1978—2000, sec., 1978—90. Mem.: Lake County Bar Assn. (pres. 1979—80), Ohio State Bar Assn., Kiwanis (pres. 1980—81). Republican. Methodist. Avocation: swimming. Office: Blakely & Dean PO Box 526 Painesville OH 44077-0526 Office Phone: 440-354-5636. E-mail: jtdean222@aol.com.

DEAN, JAMES BENWELL, lawyer; b. Dodge City, Kans., May 23, 1941; s. James Harvey and Bess (Benwell) D.; m. Sharon Ann Carver, Sept. 1, 1962 (div. 1991); m. Patricia A. Bostick, Aug. 23, 1993 (div. 1999); children: Cynthia G. Dean Vosburgh, James M.; m. Gail M. Cohen, Sept. 21, 2002. Student, Southwestern Coll., 1959-60, U. Colo., 1961; BA, Kans. State U., 1962; JD, Harvard U., 1965. Bar: Colo. 1965, U.S. Dist. Ct. Colo. 1965, U.S. Tax Ct. 1966, Nebr. 1971, U.S. Ct. Appeals (10th cir.) 1971. From assoc. to ptnr. Tweedy & Mosley, Denver, 1965-71, Kutak Rock Cohen Campbell Garfinkle & Woodward, Omaha, 1971-73; ptnr. Mosley, Wells & Dean, Denver, 1973-77, Kutak Rock & Huie, Denver, 1977-81, James B. Dean, P.C., Denver, 1981-91, Dean, McClure, Eggleston & Husney, Denver, 1991-95, James B. Dean, PC, Denver, 1995-2000, Dean & Stern, LLC, Denver, 2001—05, Dean, Dunn & Phillips LLC, Denver, 2005—. Lectr. U. Ark. Law Sch., Fayetteville, 1982—86, C.C. Aurora, Colo., 1996—97; spl. asst. atty. gen. State of Colo., Denver, 1989—; assoc. reporter, drafting com. on uniform ltd. coop. assns. act Nat. Conf. Commrs. on Uniform State Laws. Co-editor Agricultural Law Jour., 1979-84; contbr. articles to profl. jours. Recipient Erwyn E. Witte Colo. Cooperator award, Colo. Coop. Coun., 1996. Mem.: ABA (advisor bd. forum com. on rural lawyers and agrl. bus. 1983—89), Am. Agrl. Law Assn. (bd. dirs. 1981—83, pres.-elect 1985—86, pres. 1986—87, strategic planning com. 2000—01, Disting. Svc. award 1989), Denver Bar Assn., Colo. Bar Assn. (bd. dirs. 1989—2001, sec. agrl. law sect. 1991—94, chair, Colo. coop. statute revision com. 1995—), Nebr. Bar Assn. Avocations: photography, woodworking, hiking, piano. Office: 4155 E Jewell Ave Ste 703 Denver CO 80222-4511 Home Phone: 303-756-8689; Office Phone: 303-756-6744. Business E-Mail: jim@lawatddp.com.

DEAN, JAMES EDWARD, retired state official; b. Atlanta, Mar. 14, 1944; s. Steve and Dorothy (Cox) D.; m. Vyvyan Ardena Coleman, June 11, 1966; children: Sonya Velika, Monica Alexis. BA in Sociology, Clark U., 1966; MSW, Atlanta U., 1968; postgrad., Fisk U., 1967, Emory U., 1975-76. Cert. instr. interaction mgmt. system. Rep. Atlanta Daily World, 1960-70, Atlanta Inquirer, 1962-68; asst. manpower dir. Econ. Opportunity Atlanta, Inc., Atlanta, 1965-66; human resources rep. Butler St. YMCA, Atlanta, 1968-85; project dir. Atlanta Urban League, Inc., 1969-71; dir. alumni affairs Clark Coll., Atlanta, 1971-78; asst. dir. so. region Nat. Urban League, Atlanta, 1978-82; EEO officer Ga. Dept. Transp., Chamblee, 1982-88, EEO review officer, 1988—2006; ret., 2006. V.p. Cmty. Svcs., Inc., Atlanta, 1982—. Mem. Ga. Ho. of Reps., 1968-75; pres. In-Betweeners Club, Friendship Bapt. Ch., Atlanta, 1982; mem. Atlanta chpt. Frontiers Internat. Named One of 5 Outstanding Young Men, Atlanta Jaycees, 1973; recipient Presdl. citation Clark Coll., 1974, spl. achievement award Ga. Dept. Transp., 1988; named hon. lt. col. a.d.c. Staff of Gov., State of Ga., 1979, hon. adm. Ga. Navy, 1971; Nat. Urban League fellow, 1966, Leadership Ga. fellow, Coun. Religion and Internat. Affairs feellow; Atlanta U. scholar. Fellow Internat. Biog. Assn.; mem. NASW, Internat. Platform Assn., Nat. Tech. Assn., Ctr. for Study of Presidency, Am. Fedn. Police, So. Ctr. Internat. Studies, Black-Jewish Coalition, Nat. tchrs. Assn., Frontiers Internat., Clark Coll. Alumni Assn. (Alumni Dir. award 1978), Men Clark Coll. (sec. governing bd. 1989), 2nd Tuesday Black Stamp Collectors Club, Joyner Club (sec. Atlanta chpt.), Frontier Internat., Inc., Acad. of Cert. Social Workers, Alpha Phi Alpha (lt. col., staff of gov. 1991). Democrat. Home: 87 Burbank Dr NW Atlanta GA 30314-2941 Office: Ga Dept Transp 5025 New Peachtree Rd Atlanta GA 30341-3124 Office Phone: 404-788-1109.

DEAN, JOHN F., federal judge; b. Washington, 1946; BS, Mich. State U., 1970; JD, Catholic U. Am., 1975; M of Law in Taxation, Georgetown U., 1985. Bar: DC 1975, admitted to: US Supreme Ct., Fed. Dist. Ct., No. Dist. Tex., Dist. Md., US Tax Ct. With Office of Chief Counsel, IRS, Dallas Dist. Counsel, 1975—78, Balt. Dist. Counsel, 1978—86, Office of Assoc. Chief Counsel Internat., 1986—94; spl. trial judge US Tax Ct., 1994—. Adj. prof. law Howard U., 1999—. Mem.: Wash. Bar Assn. (vice chair jud. counsel 2002—03). Office: US Tax Ct 400 2nd St NW Washington DC 20217

DEAN, JOHN GUNTHER, diplomat; b. Germany, Feb. 24, 1926; came to U.S., 1939, naturalized, 1944; s. Joseph and Lucy (Askenaczy) D.; m. Martine Duphenieux, Dec. 26, 1952; children: Catherine Dean Curtis, Paul, Joseph. BS magna cum laude, Harvard U., 1947, MA, 1950; Doctorate, U. Paris, 1949. With ECA, Am. embassy, Paris, 1950-51, Am. embassy, Brussels, 1951-53, asst. econ. commr. Saigon, 1953-56; polit. officer Am. Embassy, Laos, 1956—58; consul Am. consulate, Togo, 1959-60; chargé d'affaires Am. Embassy, Mali, 1960-61; with Dept. State, Washington, 1961-65; polit. officer Am. Embassy, Paris, 1965—69; regional dir. CORDS in Central Vietnam, 1970-72; dep. chief mission Am. Embassy, Laos, 1972—74, amb. to Cambodia, 1974—75, Denmark, 1975—78, Lebanon, 1978—81, Thailand, 1981—85, India, 1985—88. Adv. U.S. delegation to UN, 1963; now mem. adv. bds. several nat. and internat. cos. and instns. Served to 2d lt. AUS, 1944-46. Fellow Center for Internat. Affairs Harvard, 1969-70 Mem.: Harvard (N.Y.C.); Kenwood Golf and Country (Washington). Office: 29 Blvd Jules Sandeau 75116 Paris France Home: Chalet Crettaz BP 1318 1936 Verbier Valais Switzerland Office Phone: 0033-1-45-04-71-84. Personal E-mail: johnmartinedean@aol.com.

DEAN, JOHN WESLEY, III, investment banker, former federal official; b. Akron, OH, Oct. 14, 1938; m. Maureen (Mo) Dean, 1972; 1 child from previous marriage. Student, Colgate U.; BA, Coll. of Wooster, 1961; JD, Georgetown Univ., 1965. Law clk. Hollabaugh & Jacobs, 1964; jr. assoc. Welch & Morgan, Washington, 1965—66; chief minority counsel for Judiciary Com. US Ho. Reps., Washington, 1966—67; assoc. dep. atty. gen., Office Criminal Justice US Dept. Justice, Washington, 1969—70; counsel to Pres. The White House, Washington, 1970—73; private investment banker; writer; lectr.; columnist FindLaw. Assoc. dir. Nat. Commn. on Reform of Fed. Criminal Laws, Washington, 1967—68. Author: Blind Ambition, 1976, Lost Honor, 1982, The Rehnquist Choice: The Untold Story of the Nixon Appointment that Redefined the Supreme Court, 2001, Unmasking Deep Throat, 2002, Warren G. Harding (American Presidents Series), 2004; co-author (with Robertson Dean): Worse than Watergate: The Secret Presidency of George W. Bush, 2004. Key figure in Watergate scandal; convicted of obstruction of justice, served four months in prison.

DEAN, KASEEM, music producer; b. Bronx, NY, 1979; Prodr. Full Surface Records, 2001—. Contbr. numerous film soundtracks; prodr.: (albums with artists such as Jay Z, Eve, and DMX). Named one of 40 Under 40, Crain's NY Bus. Mag., 2006; recipient New York award, New York Mag., 1999.*

DEAN, LESLIE ALAN (CAP DEAN), international economic, social and political development consultant, interagency and defense analyst; b. Indpls., June 18, 1940; s. Henry Lloyd and Margaret Ann (Pfafman) Dean; m. Jeanne Louise Lambert, Apr. 14, 1962; children: David Richard, Laura Elizabeth. BA, U. Ill., 1963, MA, 1966; postgrad., U. Pitts., 1968-69. Internat. loan analyst Bank Calif., San Francisco, 1970; joined Fgn. Svc., 1970; devel. officer US AID, Washington, 1970, 77-79, Vientiane, Laos, 1971-75, Kathmandu, Nepal, 1975-77, Islamabad, Pakistan, 1979-83, Dar Es Salaam, Tanzania, 1983-85, asst. mission dir. Lusaka, Zambia, 1985-87, mission dir. sr. fgn. svc., 1988-90, office dir. Washington, 1990-92, mission dir. Pretoria, South Africa, 1992-96, dep. asst. adminstr. Africa Bur. Washington, 1996-98; dir. integrated devel. programs sub-Saharan Africa Internat. Found. Edn. and Self Help, Phoenix, 1999—2003, v.p. ops., 2003; regional coord. for Baghdad Coalition Provisional Authority, Baghdad, Iraq, 2004; interim mayor Baghdad, 2004; interim gov. Baghdad Province, 2004; internat. econ. and social devel. cons., 2004—05; sr. lead specialist, def. and interagency analyst Gen. Dynamics and US Joint Forces Command, 2005—. Elder Pinnacle Presbyn. Ch., 2002—, chair mission com., 2002—03, mem. mission com., 2004—; trustee Pinnacle Presbyn. Found., 2006—. Capt. USAF, 1964—68. Mem.: Fgn. Policy Assn., Am. Fgn. Svc. Assn., Phi Eta Sigma. Avocations: swimming, reading, travel. Personal E-mail: cdean@deanaz.com.

DEAN, MICHAEL M., lawyer; b. Phila., Jan. 7, 1933; BA, Antioch Coll., 1954; JD cum laude, U. Pa., 1957. Bar: Pa. 1957. Fulbright fellow U. London, 1962-63; ptnr. Wolf, Block, Schorr & Solis-Cohen, Phila., 1966-2000, of counsel, 2000—. Dir. Univ. City. Sci. Ctr., Phila., 1993—2004, chmn., 2000—02. Bd. dirs. emeritus Ctrl. Phila. Devel. Corp., 1996—, pres., 1987—90, chmn., 1990—95; counsel, bd. dirs., exec. com., chmn. endowment trust Diagnostic and Rehab. Ctr., Phila., 1980—2003; exec. com., bd. dirs., sec. Ctr. City Dist., 1990, solicitor, 1991—. E-mail: mdean@wolf.block.com.

DEAN, NANCY, literature educator, retired playwright; d. Archie Leigh Dean and Ella Cecille Lang; life ptnr. Beatrice Eva Eastman, Sept. 2, 1963. BA with honors, Vassar Coll., 1952; MA in Tchg., Radcliffe Coll., 1953; PhD, NYU, 1963. Tchr. The Madeira Sch., Greenway, Va., 1953—55, Wakefield H.S., Arlington, Va., 1955—56; instr. Robert Coll., Istanbul, Turkey, 1956—59; from instr. to full prof. Hunter Coll., CUNY, NYC, 1963—90; ret. Author: (plays) Ophelia's Laughter, 1988, Blood and Water, 1988, Burning Bridges, 1991, Upstairs? In the Afternoon?, 1995, That Ilk, 2000, Criseyde, 2003, Libretto, Criseyde, 2005; author: (as Elizabeth Lang) (novels) Anna's Country, 1981; author: (screenplay) Ophelia's Rainbow, 2005; co-editor: (short stories) In the Looking Glass, 1977, (plays) Intimate Acts, 1997; translator: Molière's Misanthrope, 1991. Founder The Astraea Found., NYC, 1977—85; co-founder with Beatrice Eva Eastman Open Meadows Found., NYC, 1986. Recipient Significant Achievement As Playwright & Supporter of Other Lesbian Playwrights, Sisters On Stage, 1995; Ford fellow, Vassar Coll., 1953, Louise Hart Van Loon fellow, 1959—60, Woodrow Wilson fellow, NYU, 1962—63, Penfield scholar, 1961, Jay F. Krakauer Meml. grantee, NYU Grad. Sch. Alumni, 1962—63. Mem.: AAUW, Pen and Brush (chair playwrights 2002—04), Washington Sq. Playwrights, Times Sq. Playwrights, Dramatists Guild (assoc.). Democrat. Buddhist. Office: Grimalkyn Ltd 620 King Ave Bronx NY 10464 Personal E-mail: enndean@mindspring.com.

DEAN, PATRICEA LOUISE, lawyer, educator, small business owner; b. Kansas City, Mo., Sept. 25, 1928; d. Merville Francis Davies and Marie Margaret (Dorsch Davies) Damron; m. Richard Wallace Dean, Mar. 14, 1948 (dec. July 20, 1987); children: Phyllis Carol(dec.) , Katherine Ann, Carol Anne. AA, Met. Jr. Coll., Kansas City, 1947; BA, Pepperdine U., 1968, JD, 1971. Bar: Calif. 73, U.S. Supreme Ct. 87, U.S. Tax Ct. 92. Pvt. practice, Anaheim and Sacramento, Calif., 1973—2001; instr. various colls. and law schs., Calif., 1975—2001; continuing edn. instr. N.W. Coll., Powell, Wyo., 2001—04; founder, pres. Office@Home, Inc., 1998—. Legis. coord. Western Manufactured Housing Inst., 1977—83; atty., lobbyist, presenter seminars Golden State Manufactured Home Owners League, 1984—89; dir., pres. telecomms., software and internet businesses, 1990—. Author: Guide to Manufactured Housing, 1980; contbr. articles to profl. publs. Pres. Friends of Cody Libr., 2002—04; precinct worker Dem. Party, Mo. and Calif., 1949—53; campaign mgr. Dist. Atty. race, Iron County, Utah, 1962—63; precinct committeewoman Rep. Party, Park County, Wyo., 2002—03. Achievements include helped draft federal and state laws on building, siting, zoning and taxation of manufactured homes.

DEAN, PAUL JOHN, magazine editor; b. Pitts., May 11, 1941; s. John Aloysius and Perle Elizabeth (Thompson) D.; m. Jo-ann Tillman, Aug. 19, 1972 (div. Mar. 1981); children: Jennifer Ann, Michael Paul. Student engring., Pa. State U., 1959-60. Gen. mgr. Civic Ctr. Honda Co., Pitts., 1965-68, Washington-Pitts. Cycle Co., Canonsburg, Pa., 1968-70; nat. svc. mgr. Yankee Motor Co., Schenectady, 1970-73. Competition congressman Am. Motorcyclist Assn., 1971, 72, trustee, sec. bd., 1988-91, chmn., 1991-97; bd. dirs. AMA ProRacing, 1997-2006; adv. bd., guest speaker L.A. Trade Tech. Coll., 1974-90; trustee Am. Motorcyclist Heritage Found., 1990-91. Engring. editor Cycle Guide mag., Compton, Calif., 1973-74, editor-in-chief, 1974-80, editorial dir., 1980-84; editor-in-chief Cycle World mag., Newport Beach, Calif., 1984-88, editorial dir. Cycle and Cycle World mags., 1988-92; v.p., editorial dir. Cycle World Mag. Group, 1992-2005, v.p., sr. editor, 2005—; author manuals. Served with AUS, 1964-65. Named to, Nat. Motorcycle Mus. and Hall of Fame, 2002. Home: 5915 Arabella St Lakewood CA 90713-1203 Office: Hachette Filipacchi Media US 1499 Monrovia Ave Newport Beach CA 92663-2752 Office Phone: 949-720-5386. E-mail: CW1Dean@aol.com.

DEAN, PAUL REGIS, retired law educator; b. Leetonia, Ohio, July 12, 1918; s. Edward Joseph and Catherine (Sheets) D.; m. Delores M. Fitch, July 14, 1945 (dec. 1987); children— Mary E., Lawrence E. (dec.), Patricia (dec.), John, Paul, William, Delores, Teresa, Brian, Student, DeSales Coll., Toledo, 1936-38; BA, Youngstown State U., 1940; LLB, Georgetown U., 1946, LLM, 1952, LLD, 1969. Bar: D.C. 1946, Va. 1954. Law clk. to presiding judge D.C. Ct. of Appeals, 1946-47; prof. law Georgetown U., 1947-54, 69-88; dean U. Law Ctr., Georgetown U., 1954-69, dean emeritus and prof. emeritus, 1988—. Legal adviser to Pres.'s Com. Govt. Contract Compliance, 1952-53; neutral trustee United Mine Workers Am. Health and Retirment Funds, 1971-94; mem. Pres.'s Commn. Pension Policy, 1979-81, D.C. adv. com. U.S. Civil Rights Commn., 1961-63; trustee, v.p. Loyola Found. Inc., 1957—. Served to lt. USNR, 1942-46. Fellow Am. Coll. Trust and Estate Counsel; mem. Am. Arbitration Assn., Va. Bar Assn., Bar Assn. D.C. (Lawyer of Yr. award 1971), Delta Theta Phi. Office: 600 New Jersey Ave NW Washington DC 20001-2022

DEAN, RICHARD ANTHONY, mechanical engineering executive; b. Bklyn., Dec. 22, 1935; s. Anthony David and Anne Mylod Dean; m. Sheila Elizabeth Grady, Oct. 5, 1957; children: Carolyn Anne, Julie Marie, Richard Drews. BSME, Ga. Inst. Tech., 1957; MSME, U. Pitts., 1963, PhDME, 1970. Registered profl. engr., Calif. From jr. engr. to mgr. thermal and hydraulic engring. Westinghouse Nuclear Energy Sys., 1959-70; v.p., tech. dir. water reactor fuels General Atomics, San Diego, 1970-74, v.p. uranium and light water reactor fuel, 1974-80, sr. v.p., 1980-92; pres. Leading Edge Engring., San Diego, 1993—; pres., CEO Cutting Edge Products, Inc., San Diego, 1997—. Cons. U.S. Congress Office Tech. Assessment. 1st lt. U.S. Army, 1957-59. Mem. AAAS, ASME (former chmn. nuclear fuels tech. com.), Am. Nuclear Soc. (gen. chmn. annual meeting 1993), Global Found. (bd. advisors), Internat. Thermonuclear Experimental Reactor (adv. bd.). Achievements include the develpoment of commercial nuclear power stations; advanced the understanding of boiling heat transfer phenomena; invention of advanced nuclear fuel assembly. Home: 6699 Via Estrada La Jolla CA 92037-6432 Office: Leading Edge Engring # 313 13240 Evening Creek Dr San Diego CA 92128 Office Phone: 858-513-1203. Business E-Mail: dean@leeinc.us.

DEAN, RICHARD N., lawyer; b. Providence, Mar. 5, 1955; BA, Vanderbilt Univ., 1977; MA, JD, Univ. Va., 1980. Bar: NY 1981, DC 1995. Atty. Coudert Bros., NYC, 1980—85, Sydney, Australia, 1985—87, Moscow, 1988—91, ptnr., head Russia, Ukraine & Ctrl. Asia practice Washington, 1991—. Lectr. Univ. Va. Sch. Law, 1993—. Editor (sr.): Va. Jour. Internat. Law; contbr. chapters to books.

DEAN, ROBERT BRUCE, architect; b. Brockton, Mass., Jan. 15, 1949; s. Robert George and Marjorie Gertrude (O'Donnell) D.; m. Mary Hood Hoskinson, June 18, 1977; children: Robert Maxwell, Anne, Claire. BA, U. Pa., Phila., 1971; MArch, Columbia U., NYC, 1976. Registered architect, NY, Conn. Staff architect Skidmore, Owings & Merrill, Architects, NYC, 1976-77; job capt. Stephen Jacobs & Assn., NYC, 1977-78; staff architect Johnson-Burgee Architects, NYC, 1978-79; pvt. practice architecture NYC and Syracuse, 1979-85; project architect Robert A.M. Stern Architects, NYC, 1985-86; pres. Dean Design, Inc., New Canaan, Conn., 1986—. Adj. assoc. prof. Columbia U., NYC, 1978-83; asst. prof. Syracuse U., 1980-84. Contbr. articles to profl. jours. Planning Commn. Town of Redding, Dem. Town com. Grantee Syracuse U., 1982, grantee Nat. Endowment Arts, 1983-84; William Kinne Fellow, 1976. Mem. AIA, Conn. Soc. Architects. Democrat. Congregationalist. Avocation: history. Office: Dean Design Inc 111 Cherry St New Canaan CT 06840-5530 Office Phone: 203-966-8333. Business E-Mail: rdean@deandesign.net.

DEAN, ROBERT FRANKLIN, insurance company executive; b. Houston, Nov. 1, 1942; s. Claude Nathan and Nellie Gladis (Davis) D.; m. Kathy Copeland, Aug. 16, 1963 (div. Jan. 1970); 1 child, Robert Franklin Jr.; m. Betsy Ellen Kniehl, Sept. 20, 1975 (dec. Jan. 1994); children: James, Kyle, Courtney Elizabeth. BBA in Bus. Mgmt., U. Houston, 1968. Cert. safety profl. Safety engr. Gulf Ins. Group, Houston, 1968-69, Indsl. Indemnity Ins., Houston, 1969-75; loss control mgr. Crum & Forester Ins. Group, Houston, 1975-78; sr. mktg. cons. Aetna Ins. Co., Houston, 1978-80; v.p. mktg. div. Stanley Ins., Houston, 1980-81; pres., chief exec. officer Dean & Draper Ins. Agy. Inc., Houston, 1981—. Mem. Mut. Tier One Agt., Travelers' Personal Lines Agts. Counsel, 1998—2006, United Fire Agt. Coun., 2006; agt. Hartford Platinum, 2003—06. Head football coach Alief Youth Assn., Houston, 1975-81; mem. steering com. Rep. Party, Houston, 1988; bd. trustees Harris County Impact Polit. Action Com., 1991-96; mem. Hartford Prodr. Coun., 2002-03, Tex. Mut. Prodr. Coun., 2001-04. Recipient Cert. of Appreciation, Spring Br. Sch. Dist., 1985, Outstanding Svc. award Tex. Automotive Assn., 1985, Am.'s First Pres. award, 2004-05; named Agt. of Yr. Travelers Ins. Co., 1999-06, Travelers Elite Agt. in personal and comml. ins., 1999-06, United Fire Ins. Diamond Agt., 2002-03, United Fire Agt. of Yr., 2004, 05. Mem. Am. Soc. Safety Engrs. (cert. com. on edn. Houston chpt. 1975-76), Houston Gemini Automation Group (bd. dirs. Houston chpt. 1989-90, pres. 1990-92), Ind. Ins. Agts. of Am. (bd. dirs. Houston chpt. 1991-96, 05-06), Houston Assn. of Ins. Agts. (legis. com. 1993-94, 06, recreation com., charitable events bd. liaison, bd. dirs. charitable found.), Ind. Agts. of Tex. Wind Storm Taskforce Com., Gemini User of Am. Republican. Episcopalian. Avocations: golf, health, motorcycling, choir, swimming. Office: Dean & Draper Ins Agy 3131 W Alabama 4th Fl Houston TX 77098 E-mail: bdean@deandraper.com.

DEAN, ROSEMARIE DENISE, medical transcription supervisor; d. William Perry and Helga Elsa Dean. Degree in Secretarial Svcs., Rochester C.C., Minn., 1985. Cert. med. transcriptionist Calif., 2004. Coord. med. transcription ops. Orlando Regional Healthcare Sys., Orlando, Fla., 1987—. Personal asst. Willie B. Newman, M.D., J.D., Longwood, Fla., 1994—95; spkr. in field. Editor: Stedman's Medical Books; contbr. articles to profl. jours. Group organizer Youth For Christ, Longwood, Namibia, 2000; group leader Youth for Christ, Namibia, 2000; tchr. English Lang. Inst. China, LA, China, 1997; vol. CCSM, Raleigh, NC, China, 1998—98; with social svcs. Presbyn. Ch., Longwood, Brazil, 2006—06. Fellow: Am. Assn. Med. Transcription (assoc.); mem.: Ctrl. Fla. Chpt. Med. Transcription (assoc.). Home Phone: 407-314-6757; Office Phone: 321-841-5285.

DEAN, SCOTT P., music educator, director; b. Santa Ana, Calif. s. Frank and Barbara Dean; m. Cynthia Limb; children: Nathan P., Elizabeth L. BA in Music Edn., Calif. State U., 1979, MusM in Conducting, 1986. Dir. music St. Paul's Luth. Ch., Sunny Hills, Calif., 1978—79, Good Shepherd Luth. Ch., Buena Park, Calif., 1979—80, Red Hill Luth. Ch., Tustin, Calif., 1982—89; artisitic dir. and founder South Coast Chamber Singers, Newport Beach, Calif., 1982—89; dir. music First Presbyn. Ch. of Bellevue, Wash., 1989—. Master class participant, chorus mem. Oreg. Bach Festival, Eugene, Oreg., 1976—91; lectr., adjudicator, clinician Various organizations, We. US, 1985—; mentor for MDiv candidates music and worship Seattle Area Theol. Ext. (Fuller), Seattle, 1995—99; guest condr. Cappella Nymphenburg, Maria Ward Choir, Munich, 2000. Conductor (recordings) Blessings, Fount of Every Blessing, Songs of the Spirit. Recipient Outstanding Contbn. to the Choral-Vocal Area, Calif. State U. of Fullerton, Music Dept., 1977—78, Outstanding Svc. to the Dept. of Music, Calif. State U., Fullerton, 1978—79. Mem.: Presbyn. Assn. of Musicians, Am. Guild of English Handbell Ringers, Choristers Guild, Am. Choral Dirs. Assn. (assoc.; chair we. Wash. 1991—93, chair NW divsn. music and worship 1992—2001, nat. chair music in worship 2001—), Phi Mu Alpha Sinfonia (life). Achievements include first to The Company of Heaven-Benjamin Britten (Northwest premiere); Benedicite-Andrew Carter (We. U.S. premiere); Requiem-Mozart, completed by Robert Levin (Wash. state premiere); Requiem-Brahms, translated Robert Bullock (We. U.S. premiere); International Music Ministry Abroad performances in Austria, Czech Republic, Germany, Hungary, Italy, Poland, Slovakia, Slovenia, Switzerland; research in The British Library (London); Biblioteque Nationale (Paris); Various libraries (Rome). Avocations: travel, photography, music. Office: First Presbyn Ch of Bellevue 1717 Bellevue Way NE Bellevue WA 98004 Office Phone: 425-454-3082.

DEAN, THOMPSON, diversified financial services company executive, investment banker; b. Taipei, Taiwan, Apr. 2, 1958; s. David and Mary Alice (Larson) D. BA in Fgn. Affairs, U. Va., 1979; MBA with high distinction, Harvard U., 1984. Asst. treas. Irving Trust Co., NYC, 1979-82; v.p. spl. fin. group (leveraged transactions) Goldman, Sachs & Co., NYC; v.p. merchant banking group DLJ Merchant Banking Ptnrs. (merged with Credit Suisse First Boston in 2000), 1988, mng. dir., 1991, mng. ptnr., 1995, co-chmn. investment com. and mng. ptnr. MBP I, MBP II, and MBP III Funds; mng. dir., head of Leveraged Corp. Private Equity Credit Suisse First Boston, 2001—05. Former chmn. bd. Arcade Holding Corp., DeCrane Aircraft Holdings, Inc., Von Hoffmann Press, Inc., Fiberite Holdings, Inc., Katz Media Group, Inc., IVAC Holdings, Inc.; dir. Charles River Lab., Inc., Formica Corp., Insilco Holding Co., Mfr. Svc. Ltd., Mueller Holdings (N.A.), Inc., Nycomed Holdings, Inc., 2005—; mng. ptnr., CEO Avista Capital Partners. Dir. Lenox Hill Neighborhood Assn.; mem. various com. Soc. Meml. Sloan Kettering, Mus. City NY, Boys Club, NY, U. Va. Echols scholar U. Va., 1975, Baker scholar Harvard U., 1984. Republican. Avocations: golf, basketball, squash, sailing, tennis, skiing.

DEAN, WILLIAM EVANS, aerospace engineer, engineering company executive, consultant; b. Greenville, Miss., July 6, 1930; s. George Thomas Dean and Martha Myrtle (Evans) Carlton; m. Dorothy Sue Hamilton, Oct. 14, 1953; children: Janet Lea, Jody Anne, Justin H. B in Aero. Engring., Ga. Inst. Tech., 1952; MBA, Pepperdine U., 1970; grad., USAF Air Command and Staff Coll., 1970. FAA cert. airplane and instrument flight instr. Commd. officer USAF, 1952, advanced through grades to maj., 1962; divsn. mgr., dir. Rockwell Internat. Corp., LA, 1962-67, v.p., divsn. gen. mgr., 1967-80; exec. v.p. Acurex Corp., Mountain View, Calif., 1981-82, pres., COO, 1982-83, pres., CEO, 1983-90, vice chmn., 1990-91; assoc. dir. Ames Rsch. Ctr. NASA, Moffett Field, Calif., 1991-93, dep. ctr. dir., 1994-97; v.p., dir. Univs. Space Rsch. Assn., Columbia, Md., 1997—2002; founder, mng. dir. The Dean Group, LLC, Santa Ana, Calif., 2002—. Lectr. Calif. State U., Chico, 1988, Santa Clara U., 1993-98, USAF Acad., 1961, 75. Contbr. articles on gen. mgmt. and aero. engring. to profl. jours. Bd. dirs. NCCJ, San Jose, Calif., 1984-97, co-chmn., 1988-91; bd. dirs. Santa Clara County Mfg. Group, San Jose, 1984-91, vice-chmn., 1988-91; bd. dirs. Saddleback Community Coll., Mission Viejo, Calif., 1976-77, United Fund, Orange County, Calif., 1971; United Way, Santa Clara County, San Jose, 1985-91; vice-chmn., bd. advisors Leavey Sch. Bus., Santa Clara U., 1987-97, vice chmn., 1989-91; tech. com. Orange County Bus. Coun., 1998-2000. Decorated Air Force Commendation medal with oak leaf cluster; recipient Spl. Svc. award United Way, 1986, NASA Astronaut Personal Achievement award, 1972, 84, Outstanding Contbn. to Manned Exploration of the Moon award, 1972, Medal for Outstanding Leadership, 1995, Group Achievement awards, 1995, Disting. Svc. medal, 1997; Silver Knight of Mgmt. award Nat. Mgmt. Assn., 1978, Commendation Cert. Calif. State Assembly, 1986, Pres. award Santa Clara U., 1993, Disting. Alumnus award Woodward Acad., 1999, Acad. Disting. Engring. Alumni award Ga. Inst. Tech., 1995; inducted to Engring. Hall of Fame, Ga. Inst. Tech., 1997. Fellow AIAA (bd. dirs. 1979-86, 91-95, fin. com. 1995—, Space Shuttle award 1984), Internat. Acad. Astronautics (Paris), Am. Astron. Soc., Nat. Space Soc.; mem. Am. Electronics Assn. (edn. found. 1982-88), Aircraft Owners and Pilots Assn. (command pilot), Air Force Assn. Republican. Baptist. Office: The Dean Group 13422 Laurinda Way Santa Ana CA 92705-1926 Office Phone: 714-544-5020. Business E-Mail: wedean@thedeangroup.com.

DEANDRADE, KRISTY A., elementary school educator; d. Alan and Joyce Kirkland; m. Richard Floyd; children: Katee, Elizabeth; m. William DeAndrade (dec.). B of Edn., U. Md., College Park, 1998; postgrad., U. Md., Balt., 2004—. Advanced Profl. Cert. Md., cert. group cycling instr. Tchr. Ctr. Marine Biotech., Balt., 1998; tchr. 6th grade sci. and math. Meade Mid. H.S., Ft. Meade, 1998—; counselor, tchr. Md. Sci. Ctr., Balt., 2000—. Faculty coun. chair, regional rep. Meade Mid. Sch., Ft. Meade, 1999—2005, team leader, 2004—; mem. materials of instrn. selection bd. Anne Arundel County Pub. Schs., Annapolis, Md., 1999—2003. Youth fitness instr., 2003—; liaison, staff mem. Young Marines, Laurel, Md., 1997—2001; liaison svc. learning Meade Mid. Sch., Ft. Meade, 2004—. Cpl. USMC, 1992—94. Nominee Disney Tchr. of Yr., 2001, 2002, 2005; recipient U.S. Achievement Acad. scholarship, 1996, 1997, Chancellor's award, U. NC, Wilmington, 1996. Mem.: Am. Fitness and Aerobics Assn. (cert. group fitness instr.), Phi Theta Kappa, Lambda Delta. Avocations: fitness, bicycling, bowling, music, reading.

DEANE, DEBBE, psychologist, journalist, editor, consultant; b. Coatesville, Pa., July 30, 1950; d. George Edward and Dorothea Alice (Martin) Mays; widowed; children: Theo, Vonisha, Lorise, Voniece. AA in Psychology, Mesa Coll., 1989; BA Psychology, San Diego State U., 1993; MA in Psychology, Nat. U., 1995; D of Psychology, Calif. Sch. Profl. Psychology, 2005. Announcer Sta. KBPI, Denver, 1969-70, Sta. WKXI, Jackson, Miss., 1970-72; news anchor Sta. WNGE-TV, Nashville, 1973-76; news dir. Sta. KLDR, Denver, 1976-78; host, reporter Sta. KMGH-TV, Denver, 1978-81; news anchor, editor Sta. KHOW, Denver, 1978-79; news & pub. affairs dir. Sta. KLZ, Denver, 1979-80, Sta. KCBQ, San Diego, 1980-82; news anchor Sta. KOGO, San Diego, 1983-84; news anchor, reporter Sta. KCST-TV, San Diego, 1984-87; dir. comm. Omni Corp., San Diego, 1987—; news anchor Sta. KFI, LA, 1990-91; sr. psychiat. therapist Behavioral Health Group, San Diego, 1993—. Media liaison United Negro Coll. Fund, San Diego, 1990-92; dir. comm. United Chs. of Christ, San Diego, 1989-92; cons. San Diego Assn. Black Journalists, 1985-92, San Diego Coalition Black Journalists, 1985-92; cons. in field. Campaign fin. analyst San Diego County Registrar of Voters, San Diego, 1990; cons. San Diego County Office Disaster Preparedness, 1990-91, Nu Way Youth Ctr. & Neighborhood House, Inc., San Diego, 1991-92; counselor Project STARRT, San Diego, 1991-92; cons. United Way Home Start, Inc. Family Self-Sufficiency Program, 1996—; cons. and program coord. San Diego Healthy Start, Inc., 1997—. Samuel L. Gompers Secondary Inst. Math., Sci. & computer Tech., 1997—; coord. Clin. program rsch. treatment, TeleCare, Inc., 1999-. Recipient San Diego Black Achievement award Urban League, 1989, Best News Show & Spot News award San Diego Press Club, 1985, Golden Mike award So. Calif. Broadcast Assn., L.A., 1986; named one of Top 25 Businesswomen Essence Mag., 1978, Outstanding Humanitarian Worldvision, 1993, Outstanding Humanities Alumna Mesa Coll., 1993, Woman of the Year, Outstanding Humanitarian, Habitat for Humanity, Outstanding Humanitarian, Feed-the-Children, Outstanding Humanitarian, Teach Tolerance Project. Mem. AFTRA, APA, Am. Women in Radio & TV, Women in Comm., Black Students Sci. Orgn. (sec. 1989-91), Africana Psychol. Soc. (media coord. 1990-92), San Diego Assn. Black Psychologists (media coord. 2003-06), Psi Chi. Democrat. Achievements: first African-Am. in U.S. lic. to teach radio & TV broadcast prodn. Home: 3545 Valley Rd No 1 Bonita CA 91902-4164 Personal E-mail: debbedeane@msn.com.

DEANE, JAMES GARNER, editor, conservationist; b. Hartford, Conn., Apr. 5, 1923; s. Julian Lowrie and Miriam (Grover) D. BA, Swarthmore Coll., 1943. Mem. editorial staff Washington Star, 1944-60, edn. editor, 1952-57, classical recs. critic, 1952-60; ind. researcher, vol. in conservation activity, 1961-68; assoc. editor Nat. Parks Mag., 1968-69, editor, 1969; asst. editor The Living Wilderness, Washington, 1969-71, exec. editor, 1971-75, editor, 1975-81; editor Defenders mag., Washington, 1981-2001, editor emeritus, 2001; v.p. Defenders of Wildlife, Washington, 1997-2001. Washington corr. Mus. Courier, 1945-55; contbg. editor High Fidelity mag., 1953-55; mem. com. transp. environ. rev. process Transp. Research Bd. NRC, 1974-77; Am. co-chmn. Can. U.S. Environ. Coun., 1975-81. Bd. dirs. Arctic Internat. Wildlife Range Soc., 1979—; trustee Com. of 100 on Federal City, 1967-90, 1st vice chmn., 1967-69; chmn. Potomac Valley Conservation and Recreation Council, 1967. Served with AUS, 1946-47. Recipient award, Edn. Writers Assn., 1956, Public Svc. award, Washington

Newspaper Guild, 1956, Charles Carroll Glover award, Nat. Park Svc., 1967. Home: 111 Audubon Rd PO Box 104 Leeds MA 01053 Business E-Mail: jdeane111@comcast.net. *Protection of as many as possible of the remaining wild places and, with them, of the marvelous diversity of living species on our crowding planet is one of the imperatives of our time. This need can be met only by developing worldwide understanding of its crucial importance. That is the challenging task of the nature-conservation movement. I find it exhilarating to be making some contribution, however modest, to the accomplishment of that task through the techniques of journalism.*

DEANE, LELAND MARC, plastic surgeon, director; b. NYC, June 18, 1952; s. Maurice Allen and Barbara Elaine (Ushkow) D.; m. Danielle Anne Sheft, Nov. 21, 1993; children: Ashby Bennett, Galen Ames. BS, Union Coll., 1974; MD, SUNY, Bklyn., 1978. Diplomate Am. Bd. Surgery, 1984, Am. Bd. Plastic Surgery. Intern, then resident in surgery New Eng. Med. Ctr., 1978-83; resident in plastic surgery Ea. Va. Grad. Sch. Medicine, 1983-85; fellow in hand surgery Jefferson Med. Coll., 1986; pvt. practice LI Plastic Surg. Group P.C., Garden City, NY, 1986—; chief divsn. plastic surgery North Shore/LI Jewish Southside Hosp., Bayshore, NY, 2006—. Mem. surg. rev. com. Winthrop U. Hosp., Mineola, N.Y., 1986-98, mem. resident edn. com., 1992-98; instr. surgery Cornell Med. Coll., 1989—. Contbr. articles to profl. jours. Advisor Mothers of Super Twins, L.I., 1995—. Grantee So. Med. Assn., 1984. Fellow ACS; mem. Am. Soc. Plastic and Reconstructive Surgeons, Northea. Soc. Plastic Surgeons, N.Y. Regional Soc. Plastic and Reconstructive Surgery, Seawanhaka Corinthian Yacht Club, N.Y. Yacht Club. Office: LI Plastic Surg Group PC 999 Franklin Ave Garden City NY 11530-2913 Office Phone: 516-742-3404.

DEANE, RICHARD HUNTER, JR., former federal judge, lawyer; b. Oct. 18, 1952; BA, U. Ga., 1974, JD, 1977; LLM, U. Mich., 1979. Bar: Ga. 1977. Asst. U.S. atty. No. Dist. Ga., 1980-88; chief gen. crimes sect. U.S. Attys. Office, 1988-91, chief criminal divsn., 1991-94; magistrate judge U.S. Dist. Ct. (no. dist.) Ga., Atlanta, 1994-98; U.S. atty. No. Dist. Ga., Atlanta, 1998—2002; with Jones Day, Atlanta, 2002—. Office: Jones Day 1420 Peachtree St NE Ste 800 Atlanta GA 30309-3053 Office Phone: 404-581-8502. Business E-Mail: rhdeane@jonesday.com.

DEANGELIS, CATHERINE D., pediatrics educator; b. Scranton, Pa., Jan. 2, 1940; m. James C. Harris. BA, Wilkes Coll., 1965; MD, U. Pitts., 1969; MPH, Harvard U., 1973. Diplomate Nat. Bd. Med. Examiners, Am. Bd. Pediat.; RN Pa., N.Y. Intern in pediat. Children's Hosp., Pitts., 1969—70; resident in pediat. Johns Hopkins Hosp., Balt., 1970—72, teaching fellow pediat. dept. internat. health Sch. Pub. Health, 1972; pediatrician Roxbury Comprehensive Health Clinic, Boston, 1972—73; asst. prof. pediat. Coll. Physicians and Surgeons, asst. prof. health svc. adminstrn. Sch. Pub. Health Columbia U., 1973—75; mem. staff divsn. pediatric ambulatory care, dir. med. edn. Child Care Project Columbia Presbyn. Med. Ctr., 1973—75; asst. prof. pediat. Sch. Medicine U. Wis., 1975—77, assoc. prof. pediat. Sch. Medicine, 1977—78; dir. ambulatory pediatric svcs. U. Wis. Hosps., 1975—78; assoc. prof. pediat. Johns Hopkins Sch. Medicine, 1978—85; dir. pediatric primary care and adolescent medicine Johns Hopkins Hosp., 1978—84, co-dir. adolescent pregnancy program, 1979—82; with dept. health svcs. adminstrn. and dept. internat. health Johns Hopkins Sch. Hygiene and Pub. Health, 1980—90; dir. residency tng. dept. pediat. Johns Hopkins Hosp., 1983—90, dir. divsn. gen. pediat. and adolescent medicine, 1984—90; deputy chmn. dept. pediat. Johns Hopkins Sch. Medicine, 1983—90, prof. pediat., 1986—90, assoc. dean acad. affairs, 1990—93, sr. assoc. dean acad. affairs and faculty, 1993—94, vice dean acad. affairs and faculty, 1994; editor Jour. AMA, 2000—. Mem. Gov.'s Task Force to Evaluate Health Care in Wis. State Prisons, 1975—78; chmn. ambulatory care com. U. Wis. Hosp., 1976—78; mem. med. sch. admissions com. U. Wis. Sch. Medicine, 1976—78, chmn., 1977—78; mem. exec. coun. dept. pediat. and Children's Ctr. Johns Hopkins U. Sch. Medicine, 1982—90, chmn. fin. com. dept. pediat., 1984—85, chmn. assoc. prof.'s promotion com., 1985—88, chmn. com. developing Women's Health Ctr. at Johns Hopkins Med. Instns., 1993; mem. Md. Gov.'s Task Force on Women's Health, 1993—, chair, 1994; mem. search com. U. Wis., 1976, Johns Hopkins Sch. Medicine, 1984, 88, 92, 93; mem. nat. rev. com. for accreditation of nurse practitioners Am. Nurses' Assn., 1975—79, co-chmn., 1977; mem. peer rev. com. nurse practitioner programs divsn. nursing Health Resources Agy., Dept. HEW, 1979—81. Author: Basic Pediatrics for the Primary Care, 1984; editor: An Introduction to Clinical Research, 1990; editor: (with others) Principles and Practice of Pediatrics, 1990, 1994; assoc. editor Pediatric Annals, 1990, editor Archives of Pediatrics and Adolescent Medicine, 1993—. Cons. Robert Wood Johnson Found., 1973—; mem. adv. group on improving outcomes for children Pew Charitable Trusts, 1991—92; mem. adv. panel medicine Pew Health Profn.'s Commn.; mem. nat. adv. com. Robert Wood Johnson Clin. Scholars Program, 1992—; mem. steering com. Rural Health Planning, Wis. Recipient George Armstrong award, Ambulatory Pediatric Assn., scholarship, Acad. Adminstrn. and Health Policy, Assn. Health Ctrs., 1993; fellow NIH, 1973. Fellow: APHA, Am. Acad. Pediat. (govt. affairs com. 1984—88, chpt. III youth com. N.Y. chpt. 1974—75, chmn. adolescent com. Md. chpt. 1981—84); mem.: Inst. Medicine Coun., Soc. Adolescent Medicine, Am. Bd. Pediat. (examiner 1986—, long-range planning com. 1990—91, chmn. long-range planning com. 1992—, bd. dirs. 1990—, fin. com. 1991—, sec., treas. 1993—95, chair-elect 1995—96, chair 1996, search com. 1990), Am. Pediatric Soc. (sec., treas. 1989—), Alpha Omega Alpha. Address: JAMA 515 N State St Chicago IL 60610-4325 Office: Johns Hopkins Sch Medicine 720 Rutland Ave Ste 106 Baltimore MD 21205-2109

DE ANGELIS, FLAVIO, electrical engineer, researcher; b. Rome, May 16, 1972; arrived in US, 2001; s. Bruno De Angelis and Franca De Mico; life ptnr. Noemi Perez-Paz. Degree summa cum laude in Telecom. Engring., U. Rome Tor Vergata, Italy, 1999; MPhil in Elec. Engring., CUNY, N.Y.C., 2002, PhD in Elec. Engring., 2005. Engr. network sys. Comverse Network Sys., Rome, 2000—01; rschr. CUNY, 2001—06; sr. sys. engr. Qualcomm, Inc., San Diego, 2006—. Adj. instr. Borough Manhattan C.C., NYC, 2002—04, La Guardia C.C., NYC, 2002, CCNY, NYC, 2002—05; assoc. cons. Marinuzzi & Assocs., Rome, 2005—. Contbr. articles to profl. jours. Carabiniere Carabinieri Army, 1998—99, Italy. Fellow, CCNY, 2001—03, 2002—03, The Grad. Ctr., CUNY, 2004—05. Mem.: IEEE. Office: AS-730W 5775 Morehouse Dr San Diego CA 92121 Home Phone: 858-455-9161; Office Phone: 858-658-3165. Personal E-mail: flaviodeangelis@hotmail.com.

DE ANGELIS, JUDY, anchorwoman; b. Passaic, NJ, Oct. 1, 1949; d. Fredrick and Patricia (Zollo) De An.; m. Barry Sheffield, Aug. 28, 1977; children: Alexader, Katelin, Corrine. Student, Hartt Sch. Music, Hartford, Conn., 1968-69; BA in Speech and Drama, U Hartford, 1971; MA in Edn., Montclair State U., 1973. Lic. 3d class operator FCC. Anchor Sta. WALK-AM-FM, Patchogue, NY, 1978-79, Sta. WGBB-FM, Freeport, NY, 1979-80, Sta. WKJY-FM, Hempstead, NY, 1980, Sta. WHLI, Hempstead, 1980, Sta. WCBS-FM, NYC, 1980-81; reporter, anchor Sta. WNBC, NYC, 1981-88; morning anchor Sta. WINS, NYC, 1988—; morning drive anchor WNEW-FM, NYC, 2004—; co-owner Sheffield Studios, Mahwah, NJ. Freelance anchor The Source, 1982-88; freelance anchor NBC Radio Network, 1982-888, host talk-net, 1989-90; news anchor HBO Entertainment, 1988; indsl. voice-over Odyssey Prodns., N.Y.C., 1981-88; comml. voice-over DWJ, Ridgewood, N.J., 1994—, Gourvitz Comm., N.Y.C., 1995—; cons. Media Placement Svcs., Glen Rock, N.J., 1994—. Author: (documentary) Child Abuse: The Darker Side of Growing Up, 1982 (Olive awrd N.Y.C. Coun. of Chs., 1983; appeared on Broadway in Rockabye Hamlet, 1976. Lectr. on broadcasting all ednl. levels, 1985—; dir. religious edn. Christ Episcopal Ch., Ridgewood, 1995—; troop leader Girl Scouts U.S.A., 1994—. Recipient award for pub. svc. N.Y. Deadline Club, 1982, spl. citation Office N.Y.C. Comptr., 1983; name Best Radio Newscaster, N.Y. AIR, 2000, 01. Mem. AFTRA, Actors Equity, Ramapo-Bergen Animal Refuge. Democrat. Avocations: carpentry, gardening, crossword puzzles, sailing, swimming. Office: 1010 WINS Radio 888 7th Ave New York NY 10106-0001

DE ANGELIS, ROSEMARY ELEANOR, actress; b. Bklyn., Apr. 26, 1933; d. Francis and Antoinette (Donofrio) De A.; m. Kenneth Richard Bridges, Sept. 12, 1965 (div. 1983); 1 child, Laurel Ann. BA, Empire State Coll., 1998. Tchr. HB Studio, NYC, 2004—, Uta Hagen Herbert Berghof Studio. Tchr. Practice of Acting HB Studios, NYC. Appeared in plays Spinning into Butter, Over The River and Through the Woods, Queen and the Rebels, High Time, Six Characters in Search of an Author, Mrs. Klein (Barrymore award 1993), The Paradise Kid, In the Summer House, The Transfiguration of Benno Blimpie (Drama Desk award-Best Actress), N.Y. Sharespeare Fest. (with Joseph Papp dir.), numerous others; appeared in movies Frequency, Hit and Runway, Two Family House, The Wanderers, Enormous Changes at the Last Minute, Nothing Lasts Forever, Out of Darkness, Household Saints, Mamma Mia, Angie, Two Bits, The Juror; appeared in TV shows 100 Centre St., Guiding Light, As The World Turns, Monkey, Monkey, The Death of Ivan Ilyich, P.B.S. Theatre in Am., Baker's Dozen, The Equalizer, Law and Order; co-writer (screenplay) Burning Intentions, 1992-99; dir.: Shadow Boxers, 1998; author: The Nightingales; author numerous poems. Recipient residency award, Edna St. Vincent Millay writer's colony, N.Y.C. Mem. AFTRA, SAG, Actors Equity Assn. Avocations: painting, photography. Personal E-mail: redtoes100@aol.com.

DEANGELO, JOSEPH J., consumer products company executive; B in Acctg. and Econs., SUNY, Albany. Fin. and operating positions CL Marvin, PLC; fin. and operating position Ga. Pacific; with aerospace GE, with power generation, with plastics, with elec. distbn. and control, appliances COO, pres., CEO capital transport internat. pool and modular space; exec. v.p. Stanley Works, 2003—04; sr. v.p. PRO Bus. and Tool Rental Home Depot, Atlanta, 2004—05, sr. v.p. Home Depot Supply and PRO Bus. and Tool Rental, 2005, exec. v.p. Home Depot Supply, 2005—, COO, 2007—. Office: Home Depot 2455 Paces Ferry Rd Atlanta GA 30339*

DEANGELO, LEANNA MARIE, research health psychologist, writer; b. Independence, Mo., Aug. 18, 1962; d. Peter Anthony and Carolyn Frances (Dunn) DeA.; m. David Webb Stockburger, May 23, 1999. MA, Pepperdine U., 1987; PhD, Saybrook Inst., San Francisco, 1998. Author: Germs on Our Mind: The Psychology of Contagion, 2005; contbr. articles to profl. jours. Office Phone: 303-818-9488.

DEANO, EDWARD JOSEPH, JR., lawyer, retired state legislator; b. New Orleans, Jan. 17, 1952; s. Edward Joseph and Alice Evelyn (Lanusse) D.; m. Susan Kathleen Bailey, Mar. 17, 1990. BS, U. Southwestern La., 1973; JD, La. State U., 1976. Atty. City of Mandeville, La., 1980—83; former prosecutor Mandeville Misdemeanor Ct.; ptnr. Deano & Deano, Mandeville; state rep. La. Ho. of Reps., Baton Rouge, 1984—96; town atty. Town of Abita Springs, 1996—. Mem. civil law com., 1984-88, mcpl. and parochial affairs com., 1984-88, commerce com., 1988-92, ways and means com., 1992—, ins. com., 1992-96; chmn. house sub-com. on recreation, 1984-88, subcom. econ. devel., 1988-92; bd. dir. Area Health Edn. Coun., Mandeville Trail Head. Past pres. St. Tammany Humane Soc., St. Tammany Taxpayer's Assn., Mandeville Horizons; charter mem. Habitat for Humanity; past mem. Mandeville Vol. Fire Dept.; past coord. asst. St. Tammany dist. Boy Scouts Am.; mem. Mandeville City Charter Commn.; founder Krewe of the Emerald Trapazoid. Named Conservationist of Yr. St. Tammany Sportsmen's League, 1985, La. Wildlife Fedn., 1995, Legislator of Yr. La. Preservation Alliance, 1988, Alliance for Good Govt., 1988, 89, La. Alliance for Mentally Ill, 1989, La. Assn. Justices of the Peace and Constables, 1989, 94; named to 25 Mem. Cmty. Hall Fame of Century, St. Tammany News Banner, 1999; recipient Gov.'s award. Mem. US Supreme Ct. Bar Assn., La. Bar Assn., Covington Bar Assn., Krewe of the Emerald Trapazoid. Democrat. Roman Catholic. Avocations: outdoors, historical research, travel, crabbing. Office: Deano & Deano 895 Park Ave Mandeville LA 70448-4920 Office Phone: 985-626-1001. Personal E-mail: deanoanddeano@bellsouth.net.

DEANS, PATRICIA HERRMANN, investment banker; b. Monmouth Beach, NJ, Oct. 28, 1956; d. Joseph Charles and Caroline (Hauck) Herrmann; m. Jamie Robertson Deans, Feb. 29, 1981 (div. Mar. 1992). BA, U. Mass., Boston, 1980; M Internat Fin, Rutgers U., 1984. Account mgr., media & telecomm. Bank Montreal, NYC, 1984-86; v.p. Media corp. fin. Chase Securities, Inc., NYC, 1986—, mng. dir., sr. ptnr. in global syndicated fin., 1996—; head telecomm. media and tech. Syndicated Leveraget Fin., J./P. Morgan, 2002—. Mem. Lawrence Beach Club, Norfolk Country Club, Phi Beta Kappa. Roman Catholic. Avocations: skiing, running, travel, violin. Office: Chase Securities Inc 5th Fl 270 Park Ave Fl 5 New York NY 10017-2014 Address: 771 W End Ave Apt 4D New York NY 10025-5537 also: 26 Windom Rd Norfolk CT 06058-1126 Office Phone: 212-270-4872.

DE ANTONI, EDWARD PAUL, lab administrator; b. San Francisco, Mar. 7, 1941; s. Attilio Mario and Zita Elizabeth (Lolich) DeA.; m. Karen Dolores Thode, Jan. 22, 1966; children: Marc Edward, Christopher Earl. AB, U. San Francisco, 1962; PhD, Cornell U., 1971. Vol. Peace Corps, Turkey, 1964-66; sr. analyst Planning Bur. State of S.D., Pierre, 1973-76; dir. health planning Dept. Health, 1976-81; asst. dir. Assoc. Sch. Bds. S.D., 1981-84; dir. cancer control program Colo. Dept. Health, 1986-90; rsch. dir. Cancer Ctr., Porter Meml. Hosp., Denver, 1991-92; chair genitourinary cancer control Southwest Oncology Group, 1991-97; rsch. dir. Prostate Cancer Edn. Coun., 1991-97; asst. prof. urology Health Sci. Ctr., U. Colo., Denver, 1992-99, sr. instr., 2000—, sr. instr pathology/urology, 2001—. Woodrow Wilson fellow, 1962-63; ESEA fellow, 1966-69 Business E-Mail: ed.deantoni@uchsc.edu. *The life of the mind, inspired by a classic liberal education and by a faith in truth, has been a major force in my life. I realize, however, that such learning enriches most when it is embedded in a life of practical affairs, when it enlivens my relationships with others, and when it is used to seek a good beyond myself.*

DEAR, RONALD BRUCE, retired social work educator; b. Phila., Sept. 23, 1933; s. John David and Margaret (McDade) D.; 1 child, Bruce. BA, Bucknell U., 1955; honors cert., U. Aberdeen, Scotland, 1955; MSW, U. Pitts., 1957; PhD in Social Work, Columbia U., 1972. Cert. social worker, N.Y., Wash. Chief social worker Mental Hygiene Cons. Svc., Aberdeen Proving Ground, Md., 1958-60; chief Neuropsychiat. Clinic, 7th Inf. Divsn., Korea, 1960-61; residence dir. Horizon House, Inc., Phila., 1961-64; prof. U. Wash., Seattle, 1970—2003, prof. emeritus, 2003—. Vis. prof. U. Bergen, Norway, 1984, U. Trondheim, Norway, 1996; faculty lobbyist U. Wash., 1983-85, 88-91, faculty pres., 1993-95; master tchr. Coun. on Social Work Edn., 1991, 93, 94, 97; mem. adv. bd. Internat. Population and Family Assocs. Author: Social Welfare Policy: Trends and Issues, 6th edit., 2001, Teaching Social Policy in Social Work Education: Model Syllabus, 2003; editor: Poverty in Perspective, 1973; mem. The Social Policy Jour., 2002—; contbr. articles to profl. jours. and encys. Apptd. by gov. to income assistance adv. com., 1987-93, to adv. com. for Dept. Social and Health Svcs., 1980-83, Human Svcs. Policy Ctr., 1996—, adv. com. Wash. State Econ. Svcs., 1996-2004; mem. nat. adv. bd. Influencing State Policy, 1997—; appeared in centennial program of Columbia U. Sch. Social Work, 1998; pres. U. Wash. Ret. Assn., 2007—. 1st lt. U.S. Army, 1957-61. Mem. NASW (Social Worker of Yr. Wash. chpt. 1981, mem. staff legis. N.Y.C. chpt. 1968-69), Acad. Cert. Social Workers. Avocations: travel in over 50 countries, photography, hiking. Home: 7328 16th Ave NE Seattle WA 98115-5737 Business E-Mail: rdear@u.washington.edu.

DEARANI, JOSEPH ALBERT, medical educator; BA in Biology, Fordham U., 1982; MD, Georgetown U., Washington, 1986. Cons. Mayo Clinic, Rochester, Minn., 1996—, assoc. prof. surgery, 2002—. Contbr. articles to profl. jours. Mem.: Congenital Heart Surgeons Soc., Soc. Thoracic Surgeons, Am. Assn. Thoracic Surgery, Alpha Omega Alpha. Office: Mayo Clinic 200 1st St SW Rochester MN 55905

DE ARAÚJO, ALOISIO PESSOA, mathematics professor; PhD in Stats., U. Calif., Berkeley, 1974. Prof. Inst. Pure and Applied Math., Rio de Janeiro. Contbr. articles to profl. jours. Fellow: Third World Acad. Scis., NAS (fgn. assoc.); mem.: Am. Acad. Arts & Scis. (hon. fgn. mem.). Office: Inst Pure and Applied Math Praia de Botafogo 190 Sala 1100 22250900 Rio de Janeiro Brazil E-mail: aloisioa@fgv.br.

DEARBORN, MAUREEN MARKT, speech and language clinician; b. Brockton, Mass., Jan. 19, 1948; d. Francis Joseph and Marjorie Agnes (White) M.; m. James Clement Bovin, Nov. 6, 1970 (div. June 1973); m. David C. Dearborn, Jan. 14, 1989. BA in Speech Pathology and Audiology, U. Mass., 1970; MA in Ednl. Psychology, Am. Internat. Coll., Springfield, Mass. Speech and lang. clinician Holyoke (Mass.) Pub. Schs., 1970—. Chmn. Holyoke Cancer Crusade, 1985; voter registration chmn. Holyoke Dem. Com., 1987; chmn. deaconesses 2d Congl. Ch. Holyoke. Mem.: DAR (historian Eunice Day 1984—), Mass. Tchrs. Assn., Mass. Speech, Hearing and Lang. Assn., Am. Speech, Hearing and Lang. Assn. (continuing edn. adv. bd. 1988—91, congl. action contact 1988—90), Holyoke Tchrs. Assn., Hampden County Tchrs. Assn. (pres. 1981, 1987, sec. 1982, v.p. 1984—86, treas. 1988—), Dorchester Hist. Soc., Wrentham Hist. Soc., Assn. for Gravestone Studies, Friends of the Libr. Coun. (treas. 1992—2000), Mass. Geneal. Soc., New Eng. Hist. and Geneal. Soc. Avocations: bicycling, antiques, genealogy, aerobics. Home: 257 W Franklin St Holyoke MA 01040-2210 Office: Holyoke Pub Schs 57 Suffolk St Holyoke MA 01040-5015 Home Phone: 413-532-3692; Office Phone: 413-534-2067. E-mail: dearborn@massed.net.

DEARING, REINHARD JOSEF, curator, retired city official; b. Bamberg, Fed. Republic of Germany, May 1, 1947; m. Michele Jack, Feb. 14, 1967 (div. Oct. 1980); 1 child, Lauren; m. Patricia Lee Pollack, Jan. 2, 1982; 1 child, Bradford. AA, La. State U., Baton Rouge, 1968, BA, 1975, MA, 1977, postgrad., 1979; PhD, Northwestern U., 2003. CPM, Tulane U., 1989. Adminstrv. officer La. Nat. Bank, Baton Rouge, 1972-75; tchg. asst. La. State U., 1975-79; adj. asst. prof. U. So. Miss., Natchez, 1977-79; chief of staff, chief adminstrv. officer City of Slidell, La., 1979—2007; ret., 2007; curator City of Slidell, 2007—. Cons. La. Mcpl. Assn., Baton Rouge, 1985-87. Author: The Waffen-SS: A Representative Study, 1977, General James Dearing and the Cause of the Confederacy, 2001, SS General Karl Wolff and his Italian Odyssey, 2003; contbr. articles to profl. jours. Mem. Gov.'s Mcpl. Policy Task Force, PJPHS sch. bd. Officer U.S. Army, 1968-72. Col. La. State Guard, 1984—96, col., 2003—07, ret., 2007. Decorated Silver Star; named Hon. State Senator, La. Mem. La. Mcpl. Assn., Nat. League Cities, St. Tammany Mcpl. Assn., Am. Pub. Works Assn., La. State U. Alumni Assn. (dir. 1985-87), Assn. US Army, Am. Legion, VFW, Internat. City Mgrs. Assn., Mil. Order of Stars and Bars, Order of So. Cross, SCV. Independent. Avocations: historic research, fencing, racquetball, jogging. Office: City of Slidell PO Box 828 Slidell LA 70459-0828 Personal E-mail: rdearing@charter.net.

DEARING, TERESA ALLISON, librarian; b. Westfield, NY, July 8, 1950; d. Claude Wilbur Dearing and Beulah Berenice Hess; m. Robert James Canuti, Aug. 21, 1971 (div. Apr. 30, 1991); 1 child, Timothy Robert Canuti. BA, SUNY, Geneseo, 1972, MLS, 1975; AS, Genesee C.C., 1994. Pub. libr. profl. cert. NY. Libr. dir. Mt. Morris (NY) Libr., 1973—76, Dansville (NY) Pub. Libr., 1976—. Sec. Dansville Econ. Devel. Corp., 1988—2006. Mem.: NY Libr. Assn., Dansville Rotary Club (sec. 1995—, Paul Harris fellow 1998). Methodist. Office: Dansville Pub Libr 200 Main St Dansville NY 14437-1316 Home Phone: 585-335-3466; Office Phone: 585-335-6720. Business E-Mail: director@dansville.lib.ny.us.

DEARMAN, ANDREW J., III, utilities executive; b. 1953; Jr. engr. Ala. Power Southern Co., 1975, various exec. positions in power generation and delivery, divsn. v.p. Ala. Power, sr. v.p., chief tech. officer Southern Energy (now Mirant Corp.), exec. v.p., chief transmission officer, 2001—. Office: Southern Co 30 Ivan Allen Jr Blvd NW Atlanta GA 30308 Office Phone: 404-506-5000.*

DE ARMAS, FREDERICK ALFRED, foreign language educator; b. Havana, Cuba, Feb. 9, 1945; came to U.S., 1959, naturalized, 1968; s. Alfredo and Ana Maria (Galdos) De A. BA magna cum laude, Stetson U., DeLand, Fla., 1965; PhD (Carnegie fellow 1965-68), U. N.C., 1968. Mem. faculty La. State U., Baton Rouge, 1968-88, prof. Spanish, 1978-88, acting chmn. dept., 1979-80, dir. grad. studies, 1980-85; prof. Spanish and comparative lit. Pa. State U., 1988-91, Disting. prof. Spanish and comparative lit., 1991-98, Edwin Erle Sparks prof. Spanish and Comparative Lit., 1998-2000, fellow Inst. for Arts and Humanities, 1989-2000; prof. Spanish U. Chgo., 2000-01, Andrew W. Mellon prof. humanities, 2001—, chmn. dept. romance langs. and lit., 2005—. Vis. assoc. prof. U. Mo., Columbia, 1977, vis. prof., 1986; vis. prof. Duke U., 1994 Author: The Four Interpolated Stories in the Roman Comique, 1971, Paul Scarron, 1972, The Invisible Mistress, 1976, The Return of Astraea, 1986, The Prince in the Tower, 1993, Heavenly Bodies, 1996, A Star-Crossed Golden Age, 1998, Cervantes, Raphael and the Classics, 1998, Writing for the Eyes in the Spanish Golden Age, 2004, Ekphrasis in the Age of Cervantes, 2005, Quixotic Frescoes: Cervantes and Italian Renaissance Art, 2006; editor: Pa. State U. Studies in Romance Literatures, 1991-2001; co-editor: European Literary Careers, 2002; mem. editl. bd. Bull. Comediantes, 1981—, Hispanófila, 1981-88, 2001—, PMLA, 1985-89, South Central Rev., 1987-89, Comparative Literature Studies, 1989-2001, Hispania, 1993-95, Jour. Interdisciplinary Lit. Studies, 1993-2000, South Atlantic Rev., 2003—, Revista Didascalia, 2004—, Revue Romane, 2004—;, Modern Philology, 2006—; contbr. articles to profl. jours. NEH grantee, 1979; NEH fellow, 1985, 95, summer inst., 1989, dir. summer inst., 1994, dir. summer seminar, 2003. Mem. MLA, Comparative Lit. Assn., Renaissance Soc. Am., Am. Assn. Tchrs. Spanish and Portuguese, Assn. Internat. Hispanistas, Hispanic Soc. Am. (corr.), Cervantes Soc. Am. (v.p. 2003-07, pres. 2007—). Office: U Chgo Dept Romance Lang 1115 E 58th St Chicago IL 60637 Office Phone: 773-702-8481. Business E-Mail: fdearmas@uchicago.edu.

DEARMIN, CHRISTOPHER CARL, medical technician; b. Long Beach, Calif., Dec. 13, 1966; s. Robert Edward Dearmin and Verna Opal Daermin. Cert. respiration therapy, Calif. Paramedical and Tech. Coll., Long Beach, 1988, Mt. San Antonio Coll., Walnut, Calif., 1995. Cert. neonatal and pediat. respiratory care specialist Nat. Bd. fRespiratory Care, 2003, registered respiratory therapist Nat. Bd. Respiratory Care, 1995. Lead respiratory therapist Humana Hosp., Westminster, Calif., 1988—91; respiratory care supr. Vencor Hosp. Orange County, Westminster, 1992—95, Sunrise Hosp. and Med. Ctr., Sunrise Children's Hosp., Las Vegas, Nev., 1995—98; respiratory care mgr. Vencor Hospital-Las Vegas East, Las Vegas, Nev., 1998—98; respiratory care practitioner iii Hoag Meml. Hosp. Presbyn., Newport Beach, Calif., 1998—2006; respiratory therapist Torrance Meml. Med. Ctr., Calif., 2002—06, Children's Hosp. and Healthcare Ctr., San Diego, 2006; respiratory care practitioner Children's Hosp. Austin, Tex., 2006—06, St David's Round Rock Med. Ctr., Tex., 2006—, Smithville Regional Hosp., 2006—. Recipient Amb. Courtesy award, Las Vegas C. of C., 1998, Vencor Touch award, Vencor Hosp., 1992—95, Svc. Excellence Advisor award, Hoag Meml. Hosp. Presbyn., 2000, Magic award, Children's Hosp. San Diego, 2005. Mem.: Tex. Soc. Respiratory Care (assoc.), Am. Assn. Respiratory Care (assoc.), Am. Coll. Chest Physicians (assoc.; allied health mem. 2006—07). Home: 14409 Little Eagle Ct Elgin TX 78621 Office: Smithville Regional Hosp 800 East Hwy 71 Smithville TX 78957 Home Phone: 512-285-6180; Office Phone: 512-237-3214. Home Fax: 512-687-5375. Personal E-mail: cdearmin@austin.rr.com. Business E-Mail: cdearmin@srhnet.org.

DEASON, DARWIN, information technology executive; b. Ark. With MTech Corp., Dallas, 1968—88, CEO, dir., 1978—88; founder Affiliated Computer Services, Inc., Dallas, 1988, CEO, 1988—99, chmn., 1988—. Office: ACS Inc 2828 North Haskell Dallas TX 75204*

DEASON, ELLEN MURIEL See WELLS, KITTY

DEASON, HEROLD MCCLURE, lawyer; b. Alton, Ill., July 24, 1942; s. Ernest Wilburn and Mildred Mary (McClure) D.; m. Wilma Lee Kaemmerle, June 18, 1966; children: Sean, Ian, Whitney. BA, Albion Coll., 1964; JD, Northwestern U., 1967. Bar: Mich. 1968. Assoc. Bodman LLP, Detroit, 1967-74, ptnr., 1975—. City atty. Grosse Pointe Pk., Mich., 1978—. Vice chmn. Detroit, Windsor Freedom Festival, 1978-92; bd. dirs. Spirit of Detroit Assn., 1980-2003. Recipient Spirit of Detroit award, Detroit City Coun., 1986. Mem. ABA, Mich. Assn. Mcpl. Attys. (pres. 1995-97), Detroit Bar Assn., Can.-U.S. Bus. Assn. (pres. 2005), Grosse Pointe Yacht Club (commodore 1992-93), Detroit Racquet Club, Windsor Club. Home: 1044 Kensington Ave Grosse Pointe Park MI 48230-1437 Office: Bodman LLP 6th Fl at Ford Field 1901 St Antoine St Detroit MI 48226 Home Phone: 313-885-5507; Office Phone: 313-393-7556. Business E-Mail: hdeason@bodmanllp.com.

DEASON, JONATHAN PIERCE, environmental engineer, federal agency administrator; b. Charleston, SC, Feb. 8, 1948; married; 3 children. BS in Civil Engring., U.S. Mil. Acad., 1970; MBA in Mgmt., Golden Gate U., 1975; MS in Environ. Engring., Johns Hopkins U., 1978; PhD in Environ. Systems, U. Va., 1984. Registered profl. engr., Va. Commd. U.S. Army, 1970, advanced through grades to capt.; engr. officer U.S. Army Corps of Engrs., 1970-75, civil engr. North Atlantic Divsn., 1975-78; chief water resources program U.S. Bur. Indian Affairs, 1978-82; sr. policy advisor office of water policy U.S. Dept. Interior, 1982-83; spl. asst. Office Asst. Sec. of Army, 1983-86; mgr. Nat. Irrigation Water Quality Program U.S. Dept. of Interior, Washington, 1986-89, dir. Office of Environ. Policy and Compliance, 1989-94; v.p. environ. affairs Am. Rd. and Transp. Builders Assn., Washington, 1994-96; prof. environ. and energy mgmt. program George Washington U., Washington, 1994—. Adj. prof. environ. and energy mgmt. George Wash. U., 1984-94; chmn. fed. liaison group Bd. Environ. Studies and Toxicology Nat. Rsch. Coun./NAS, 1990-91; mem. nat. panel of experts U.S. Com. Irrigation and Drainage, 1987; chmn. Pres.'s Task Force Indian Water Resources Devel., 1978-80. Author: (with others) Risk Based Decision Making in Water Resources, 1989; contbr. over 50 articles to profl. jours. Col. USAR. Recipient Engring. Achievement award Va. Engring. Found., 1993, Founder's medal and Fed. Engr. of Yr. award Nat. Soc. Profl. Engrs., 1992, Arthur S. Flemming award Jr. C. of C., 1984. Mem. Am. Soc. Civil Engrs. (bd. trustees scholarship trust 1992-93, pres. nat. capital sect. 1990-91, Meritorious Svc. award 1988), Am. Water Resources Assn. (dir. Chesapeake region 1989-91). Office: Policy and Compliance Environ Policy and Compliance George Washington U Washington DC 20052-0001 Home: 1331 14th St N Arlington VA 22209-3705

DEASON, STEPHEN EARL, computer company executive; b. Laredo, Tex., Jan. 19, 1972; s. Dale and Ruth Holt Deason; m. Maggie Neuton Deason, Aug. 6, 2006. BS in Mechanics and Chemistry, U. Ala., Birmingham, 1992; MS, So. Meth. U., Dallas, 1999. Co-founder Applied Media Resources, Dallas, 1994; gen. mgr. Consolidated Svcs. Group, Dallas, 1994—95; sr. tech. support mgr. Affiliated Computer Svcs., Dallas, 1995—96; sr. mktg. cons. Lawson Software, Dallas, 1996—97; sr. mktg. mgr. J.D. Edwards Dracle Corp., Atlanta, 1997—98; prin. architect Servicesoft/Kana, Atlanta, 1999—2001; ptnr. Affiliated Computer Svcs., Atlanta, 2001—. Bd. dirs. We Are At Your Svc., Inc., Atlanta. Co-author: Medicaid & Managed Care, 2006. Cons. Habitat for Humanity, Alphanetta, Ga., 2004—, HAnds on Atlanta, 2002—05; dir. Healthcare for Alantans, Atlanta. Mem.: Project Mgmt. Inst., Toastmasters, Tau Kappa Epsilon. Avocations: golf, rock climbing, running, billiards, fishing. Home: 1102 Thornborough Dr Alpharetta GA 30004 Office: Affiliated Computer Svcs 3 Ravinia Dr Ste P750 Atlanta GA 30346 Office Phone: 770-350-5371. Business E-Mail: stephen.deason@waays.com.

DEASY, CORNELIUS MICHAEL, retired architect; b. Mineral Wells, Tex., July 19, 1918; s. Cornelius and Monetta (Palmo) D.; m. Lucille Laney, Sept. 14, 1941; children: Diana, Carol, Ann. BArch, U. So. Calif., 1941. Practice architecture, LA, 1946—76; ptnr. Robert D. Bolling, 1960—76, ret., 1976. Prin. works include prin. offices student union, Calif. State U., LA; author: Design for Human Affairs, 1974, Designing Places for People, 1985, Gifts From America, 2003. V.p. LA Beautiful; dir. Regional Plan Assn.; commr., LA Bd. Zoning Appeals, 1973-. Recipient numerous design awards, Nat. Endowment Arts award, 1983. Fellow AIA (past pres., dir. So. Calif. chpt., chmn. com. rsch.). Home and Office: Davenport Creek Farm 4979 Davenport Creek Rd San Luis Obispo CA 93401-8109 Personal E-mail: c_deasy@sbcglobal.net.

DEASY, IRENE M., retired protective services official; d. Earnest August Markley and Clara Matilda Larson; m. Howard Gale Ledgerwood (dec.); m. William H. Deasy (dec.). Grad., Sarachon-Hooley Secretarial Sch., Kansas City, Mo., 1942; RN, BSN, Hunter Coll., 1973. Stenographer clk. US Naval Air Sta., Olathe, Kans., 1942—43, stenographer, disc jockey Jacksonville, Fla., 1943—45; stenographer, sec. US Dept. Immigration, NYC, 1945—49; policewoman NYC Police Dept., 1949—73. Co-author: In That Very Day, 1995, The Civil War, 1996, The Holy Spirit, Your Divine Companion, 1996, Money Is Power, 1997. Vol. Marantha Internat., Sacramento; mem. Internat. Effort for Am. Armed Forces; v.p., treas. Consolidated Mgmt. Corp.; nominee v.p. U.S.A. Ind. Prty, 2004. Scholar, Bellevue Hosp., Hunter Coll.; Four scholarships NYC policewoman. Mem.: AAUW. Avocations: reading, political activities. Home: 217 W Evans Ave Pueblo CO 81004

DEATHERAGE, WILLIAM VERNON, lawyer; b. Drumright, Okla., Apr. 17, 1927; s. William Johnson and Pearl Mae (Watson) D.; m. Priscilla Ann Campbell, Sept. 16, 1932; children: Thomas William, Andrea Susan. BS, U. Oreg., 1952, LLB with honors, 1954. Bar: Oreg. 1954, U.S. Dist. Ct. Oreg. 1956. Ptnr. Frohnmayer, Deatherage, Pratt, Jamieson & Moore, Medford, Oreg., 1954—. Bd. dirs. Oreg. Law Inst., U. Oreg. Found. With USN, 1945-48. Mem. Am. Coll. Trial Lawyers, Internat. Acad. Trial Lawyers, Delta Theta Phi, Rogue Valley Country Club (pres. 1988), Rogue River Valley Univ. Club. Democrat. Episcopalian. Address: 2592 E Barnett Rd Medford OR 97504-8345 Home Phone: 541-773-4498; Office Phone: 541-779-2333. E-mail: deatherage@fdfirm.com.

DEATON, BRADY J., academic administrator; m. Anne Deaton; children: Tony, Brady Jr., Christina, David. BS in Agrl. Econs., U. Ky., 1966, MA in Diplomacy and Internat. Commerce, 1968; PhD in Agrl. Econs., U. Wis., 1972. Assoc. prof. U. Tenn., 1972—78; dir. Va. Poly. Inst. and State U., 1978—89; prof., Agricultural Econ, dept. chair & social sci. unit leader U. Mo., Columbia, Mo., 1989—98, chief staff, dep. chancellor, provost, 1998—2004, interim chancellor, 2004, chancellor, 2004—. Chair Nat. Assn. State Univs. and Land Grant Colls. Contbr. articles to profl. jours. Office: Office of the Chancellor 105 Jesse Hall Univ Mo Columbia MO 65211 Office Phone: 573-882-3387. Office Fax: 573-882-9907. Business E-Mail: chancellor_office@missouri.edu.

DEATON, CHAD C., oil and gas industry executive; married; 3 children. BS in Geology, U. Wyo. With Schlumberger Oilfield Svcs., 1976—99, exec. v.p., 1998—99, sr. adv., 1999—2001; pres., CEO Hanover Compressor Co., 2002—04; chmn., CEO Baker Hughes Inc., Houston, 2004—. Bd. dirs. Baker Hughes Inc., 2004—, Carbo Ceramics, Ariel Corp. Mem.: Petroleum Equip. Suppliers Assn. Office: Baker Hughes Inc 3900 Essex Lane Houston TX 77027 Mailing: Baker Hughes Inc PO Box 4740 Houston TX 77210-4740*

DEATS, SUZANNE, writer, editor, artist; b. Abilene, Tex., Nov. 14, 1937; d. Otto and Susan Reynolds Deats; m. Ben Bedford, Aug. 27, 1960 (dec. Jan. 19, 1978); children: Aaron Bedford, John Bedford. BA in Fine Arts, U. N.Mex., 1981. Juror Santa Fe Art Festival, Main St. Show, Ft. Worth, Mus. S.W., Midland, Tex. Author: Evelyne Boren, 1998, Michael Dunbar, 2006; co-author: Santa Fe Design w. Elmo Baca, 1990, Abstract Art w. Stuart Ashman, 2004, Western Traditions w. Michael Duty, 2005, New Mex. Landscape w. Suzan Campbell, 2006; exhibitions include Hill's Gallery, Santa Fe, Art du Monde, Japan; exhbn. (catalog) Kevin Red Star, Yellowstone Art Mus., Billings, Mont.; contbr. articles to periodicals. Mem.: Mensa. Avocations: fiction, design, cooking, travel. Office Phone: 817-999-6894. Personal E-mail: suzdeats@aol.com.

DEAVER, JAMES T.H., lawyer; b. Santa Monica, Calif., Feb. 2, 1961; BS, Wharton Sch. Bus. U. Pa., 1985; JD cum laude, Temple U., 1991; LLM, NYU, 1992. Bar: NY 1993. Ptnr. Wilson, Elser, Moskowitz, Edelman & Dicker LLP, NYC. Mem.: ABA, Assn. of the Bar of the City of NY. Office: Wilson Elser Moskowitz Edelman & Dicker LLP 23rd Fl 150 E 42nd St New York NY 10017-5639 Office Phone: 212-490-3000 ext. 2775. Office Fax: 212-490-3038. Business E-Mail: deaverj@wemed.com.

DEAVER, PHILLIP LESTER, lawyer; b. Long Beach, Calif., July 21, 1952; s. Albert Lester and Eva Lucille (Welton) D. Student, USCG Acad., 1970-72; BA, UCLA, 1974; JD, U. So. Calif., 1977. Bar: Hawaii 1977, U.S. Dist. Ct. Hawaii 1977, U.S. Ct. Appeals (9th cir.) 1978, U.S. Supreme Ct. 1981. Assoc. Carlsmith, Wichman, Case, Mukai & Ichiki, Honolulu, 1977-83, ptnr., 1983-86, Bays, Deaver, Lung, Rose & Holma, Honolulu, 1986, mng. ptnr., 1986—95. Contbr. articles to profl. jours. Bd. dirs. Parents and Children Together, 1993-2006, v.p. 2000-2002, chmn. bd., 2003-05. Mem. ABA (forum com. on the Constrn. Industry), AIA (affiliate Hawaii chpt.), Am. Arbitration Assn. (arbitrator). Home: 2471 Pacific Heights Rd Honolulu HI 96813-1029 Office: Bays Deaver Lung Rose and Holma PO Box 1760 Honolulu HI 96806-1760 Office Phone: 808-523-9000. E-mail: pdeaver@legalhawaii.com.

DEAVERS, JAMES FREDERICK, optometrist, clinical nutritionist; b. Saint Augustine, Florida, Apr. 23, 1947; s. James Lonnie and Gwen Eula (Fields) D.; m. Janet (Allen), Jan. 1, 1995; children: Samuel, Chris, Marie, Robin, Shea, Christy. BS, So. Coll. of Optometry, Memphis, 1979, OD, 1978. Optometrist Berkeley Eye Care, 1980—95, Cmty. Eye Care Specialists, Moncks Corner, SC, 1995—99, Eyeplus, Lexington, SC, 1997—99, America's Best, North Charleston, SC, 1999—2003, Eyeplus, Summerville, SC, 2004—. Staff sgt. USAF, 1965—69. Republican. Avocations: travel, running. Office: Eyeplus Summerville SC 29483 Personal E-mail: james.deavers@gmail.com.

DEB, ARUN KUMAR, environmental engineer; b. Calcutta, Bengal, India, May 1, 1936; came to US, 1974; s. Hemanta Kumar and Chapala (Sen) D.; m. Dhriti Raha, June 8, 1962; 1 child, Bhaskar. BSCE, U. Calcutta, 1957; MSCE, U. Wis., 1961; PhDCE, U. Calcutta, 1968. Registered profl. engr., Pa., NY, DC; diplomate Acad. Environ. Engrs. Asst. prof. U. Calcutta, 1961-71; sr. rsch. fellow Univ. Coll., London, 1971-73; vis. prof. U. Notre Dame, Ind., 1974; v.p. Roy F. Weston, Inc., West Chester, Pa., 1974, ret. Contbr. tech. papers to profl. jours. Co-recipient Grainger Challenge Silver award, 2007; recipient Engrs. Gold Medal award Inst. Engrs., India, 1972, Lifetime Achievement award, Pa. Am. Water Works Assn., 1999, Ken Miller Founder award Water for People, 2002; NSF grantee. Fellow ASCE (chmn. publs. com. 1982-84, session progs. com. 1987-88, editor jour. 1982-84, chmn. awards com. 1994-95, Stephen D. Bechtel award 2003); mem. Water Environ. Fedn., Am. Waterworks Assn. Home: 100 Trowbridge Ln Downingtown PA 19335-4413 Personal E-mail: arundeb@msn.com.

DEBACKER, MICHAEL LEE, automotive executive, lawyer; b. 1947; JD, Washburn U. Bar: Kans. 1972, Okla. 1975. Asst. gen. counsel Dana Corp., Toledo, 1986—2001, v.p., 1994—, gen. counsel, sec., 2001—07. Office: Dana Corp PO Box 1000 Toledo OH 43697-1000 Business E-Mail: mike.debacker@dana.com.

DEBAKEY, MICHAEL ELLIS, surgeon, educator; b. Lake Charles, La., Sept. 7, 1908; s. Shaker Morris and Raheeja (Zorba) DeBakey; m. Diana Cooper, Oct. 15, 1936; children: Michael Maurice, Ernest Ochsner(dec.) , Barry Edward, Denis Alton; m. Katrin Fehlhaber, July 1975; 1 child, Olga Katarina. BS, Tulane U., 1930, MD, 1932, MS, 1935; degrees (hon.). Diplomate Nat. Bd. Med. Examiners, Am. Bd. Surgery, Am. Bd. Thoracic Surgery. Intern Charity Hosp., New Orleans, 1932—33, asst. surgery, 1933—35, U. Strasbourg, France, 1935—36, U. Heidelberg, Germany, 1936; instr. surgery Tulane U., New Orleans, 1937—40, asst. prof., 1940—46, assoc. prof., 1946—48; prof., chmn. dept. surgery Baylor Coll. Medicine, 1948—93, Disting. svc. prof., 1968—, v.p. med. affairs, 1968—69, CEO, 1968—69, pres., 1969—79, Olga Keith Wiess prof. of surgery, 1981—, chancellor, 1978—96, chancellor emeritus, 1996—; pres. The DeBakey Med. Found., 1961—; dir. Nat. Heart Blood Vessel Rsch. Demonstration Ctr., Baylor Coll. Medicine, 1974—84; dir. DeBakey Heart Ctr., Baylor Coll. Medicine, 1985—. Surgeon-in-chief Ben Taub Gen. Hosp., 1963—93; sr. attending surgeon Meth. Hosp.; clin. prof. surgery U. Tex. Dental Br.; cons. surgery VA Hosp., U. Tex. M.D. Anderson Cancer Ctr., St. Luke's Hosp., Tex. Children's Hosp., Tex. Inst. Rehab. and Rsch., Houston, Brooke Gen. Hosp., Brooke Army Med. Ctr., Ft. Sam Houston, Tex., Walter Reed Army Hosp., Washington, D.C.; mem. med. adv. com. Office Sec. Def., 1948—50; mem. task force med. svcs. Hoover Commn., 1949; founding bd. dirs. Friends of Nat. Libr. of Medicine, 1985—; mem. bd. regents Nat. Libr. of Medicine, 1956—60, 1994—98, chmn., 1959, 98; past mem. nat. adv. heart coun. NIH; mem. Nat. Adv. Health Coun., 1961—65, Nat. Adv. Coun. Regional Med. Programs, 1965—, Nat. Adv. Gen. Med. Scis. Coun., 1965, Program Planning Com., Com. Tng., Nat. Heart Inst., 1961—; mem. civilian health and med. adv. coun. Office Asst. Sec. Def.; chmn. Pres.'s Commn. Heart Disease, Cancer and Stroke, 1964; mem. adv. coun. Nat. Heart Lung and Blood Inst., 1982—87; chmn. Found. Biomedical Rsch., 1988; trustee, v.p. Baylor Med. Found.; adv. Dag Hammarskjöld Med. Sci. Prize Com.; trustee Baylor Coll. Medicine, 1996; fgn. adj. prof. Karolinska Inst., 1997. Author (with Robert A. Kilduffe): Blood Transfusion, 1942; author: (with Gilbert W. Beebe) Battle Casualties, 1952; author: (with Alton Ochsner) Textbook of Minor Surgery, 1955; author: (with T. Whayne) Cold Injury, Ground Type, 1958; author: A Surgeon's Visit to China, 1974, The Living Heart, 1977, The Living Heart Diet, 1985, The Living Heart Brand Name Shopper's Guide, 1992, The Living Heart Guide to Eating Out, 1993, The New Living Heart Diet, 1996, The New Living Heart, 1997; editor: Yearbook of surgery, 1958—70; chmn. adv. editl. bd.: Medical History of World War II, founding editor: Jour. Vascular Surgery, 1984—88; contbr. over 1600 articles to med. jours. Disting. mem. U.S. Army Med. Dept. Rgt., 1989; cons. to Surgeon Gen., 1946—. Col. Office Surgeon Gen. US Army, 1942—46, now Col. Res. US Army. Decorated Legion of Merit, 1945; named in his honor Michael E. DeBakey Dept. Surgery, Baylor Coll. Medicine, 1999, in his honor Michael E. Debakey Heart Inst. Kan., Hays Med. Ctr., 1999, in his honor Michael E. DeBakey Internat. Surgery Chair, Uniformed Svc. Univ. Health Sci., 2000, in his honor Michael E. DeBakey Inst. Comparative Cardiovascular Sci. and Biomedical Devices, Tex. A&M Univ., 2000, innumerable honors and awards including Leader in Medicine, AMA, 1997, charter mem., Tex. Sci. Hall Fame, 2001, in his honor Michael E. DeBakey Vet. Affairs Med. Ctr., 2004; named an inductee Space Tech. Hall Fame, 1999; named one of 200 Most Influential People in Telemedicine, Ctr. Pub. Svc. Comm., 1996, Top Ten Heroes, Millenium Soc., 1996; named to Health Care Hall of Fame, Modern Healthcare, 1996, Houston Hall Fame, 1999, Sci. in Tex. Hall Fame, 2000; recipient Rudolph Matas award, 1954, Disting. Svc. award, Internat. Soc. Surgery, 1958, Modern Medicine award, 1957, Leriche award, Internat. Soc. Surgery, 1959, Great medallion, U. Ghent, 1961, Grand Cross, Order Leopold, Belgium, 1962, Albert Lasker award for clin. rsch., 1963, Order of Merit Chile, 1964, St. Vincent prize med. scis., U. Turin, 1965, Centennial medal, Albert Einstein Med. Ctr., 1966, Gold Scalpel award, Internat. Cardiology Found., 1966, Eleanor Roosevelt Humanities award, 1969, Meritorious Civilian Svc. medal, Office Sec. Def., 1970, Medal of Freedom with Distinction Presdl. award, 1969, Inst. Med. Nat. Acad. Sci., 1981, Theodore E. Cummings award, 1987, Nat. Med. of Sci. award, 1987, First Issue Michael DeBakey medal, ASME, 1989, Inaugural award, Scripps Clinic and Rsch. Found., 1989, DeBakey-Bard Chair in Surgery, Baylor Coll. of Medicine, 1990, Disting. Svc. award, Am. Legion, 1990, Lifetime Achievement award, Found. for Biomed. Rsch., 1991, Maxwell Finland award, Nat. Found. for Infectious Diseases, 1992, Acad. of Athens award, 1992, Pres. Disting. Svc. award, Baylor Coll. Medicine, 1992, Gibbon award, Am. Soc. Extracorporeal Tech., 1993, named in his honor Michael E. DeBakey Libr. Svc. Outreach award, Friends of the Nat. Libr. Medicine, 1993, Alton Ochsner award relating smoking to health, 1993, Thomas Jefferson award, AIA, 1993, Lifetime Achievement award, Am. Heart Assn., 1994, prize for basic biomed. rsch., Giovanni Lorenzini Med. Fedn., 1994, Disting. Svc. award, Tex. Soc. Biomed. Rsch., 1994, Heart Saver award, Save A Heart Found., Cedars-Sinai Med. Ctr., 1994, Honor award, United Meth. Assn. Health & Welfare Ministries, 1995, Michael E. DeBakey chair in Pharm., Baylor Coll. Medicine, 1995, Nat. Order of Medicine Vasco Nunez de Balboa, Panama, 1995, Pub. Svc. award, AIAA, 1997, Boris Petrovsky Internat. Surgeons award, 1997, Premio Giuseppe Corradi award, Bevagna, Italy, 1997, Rotary Nat. award, 1997, Sesquicentennial medal, Tulane Coll., 1997, Fire of Genius award, So. Utah U., 1997, Commonwealth Trust award for invention and sci., 1997, Michael E. DeBakey Heart Inst. Wis. named in his honor, Kenosha Hosp. and Med. Ctr., 1992, Michael E. DeBakey, M.D. award for Excellence in Visual Edn. named in his honor, 1993, DeBakey Scholar in Cardiovasc. Scis. MD-PhD Program named in his honor, Baylor Coll. Medicine, 1994, Michael E. DeBakey, MD Excellence in Rsch. award named in his honor, 1994, dedication of Northwestern U. Med. Sch. book, 1995, Michael E. DeBakey H.S. Health Professions named in his honor, 1996, Med. Ctr. of LA Found. Inaugural Spirit of Charity award, 1998, Leader in Medicine honor, AMA, 1997, John P. McGovern Lecture award, Cosmos Club Found., 1998, Lifetime Achivement award, Rsch. Am., 1998, Michael E. DeBakey Presdl. Excellence award named in his honor, 1998, Mus. Health and Med. Sci. Lifetime Membership award, 1999, Disting. Svc. award, Soc. Vascular Surgery, 1999, Sci. Achievement award, Am. Assn. Thoracic Surgery, 1999, inaugural Michael E. DeBakey award contbns. to Am.'s Health, AIA, 1999, Bicentennial Living Legends award, Libr. Congress, 2000, Lifetime Achievement Outstanding Alumnus award, Tulane Med. Alumni Assn., 2000, Tall Texan award, Muscular Dystrophy Assn., 2001, Invention Yr., DeBakey Ventricular Assist Device, NASA, 2001, Mendal Medal award, Villanova U., Pa., 2001, Living Legend award, World Artificial-Organ, Immunology, Transplant Soc., Ottawa, Can., 2001, Inspired Leadership award, Am. Bible Soc., 2001, Wall of Honor tribute for lifetime contributions, 2002, Lifetime Achievement award, Internat. Health and Med. Film Festival, 2002, Lindbergh-Carreell Prize, 2002, Michael E. DeBakey Med. Student Poetry award, 2003, Michael E. DeBakey Dept. of Surgery award for excellence in acad. surgery, 2003, award of excellence for tireless work in the field of heart failure, Cleve. Clinic Found. Kaufman Ctr., 2003, Ben Taub Humanitarian award, Harris County Hosp. Dist., 2003, Hon. Alumnus award, Ochsner Clinic Found. Fellows' Alumni Assn., 2003, Millennium Doctor award, People Caring for the Cmty., Inc., 2003, Olaf Acrel Medallion, Swedish Surgical Soc., 2003, Lomonosov Gold medal, Russian Acad. Scis., 2004, David E. Rogers award, Assn. Am. Med. Colls. and Robert Wood Johnson Found., 2004, Lifetime Achievement award, Nat. Arab Am. Med. Assn., 2004, Cert. Congl. Recognition, U.S. Ho. Reps., 2004. Fellow: Internat. Acad. Cardiovascular Scis. (hon.), Am. Coll. Cardiology (hon.), Royal Coll. Physicians and Surgeons of U.S. (hon. disting. fellow 1992), Inst. of Medicine Chgo. (hon.); mem.: AMA (Hektoen Gold medal 1954, Disting. Svc. award 1959, Hektoen Gold medal 1970), AAAS, Uniformed Svc. Alumni Assn. (life hon.), Internat. Soc. Surgery, Soc. Univ. Surgeons, Assn. Internat. Vascular Surgeons (pres. 1983), Internat. Cardiovascular Soc. (pres. 1958, pres. N.Am. chpt. 1964), Am. Assn. Thoracic Surgery (pres. 1959), So. Surg. Assn. (pres. 1989—90, chmn. coun. 1995—), Am. Surg. Assn. (pres. 1989, Disting. Svc. award 1981), Soc. Vascular Surgery Lifeline Found. (pres. 1989), Soc. Vascular Surgery (pres. 1954), Am. Heart Assn. (Nat. Chpt. Lifetime Achievement award 2004), Royal Soc. Medicine, Assn. Française de Chirurgie (hon.), Med. Libr. Assn. (hon.), Hellenic Surg. Soc. (hon.), Mex. Acad. Surgery (hon.), Telemedicine 200 Ctr. for Pub. Svcs., Acad. of Athens, University Club (Washington), Houston Club (hon.), Alpha Omega Alpha, Sigma Xi (William Procter prize for sci. achievement 1995). Episcopalian. Achievements include development of roller pump universally used in heart-lung machine; Dacron artificial arteries and Dacron-velour arteries as surgical replacement of diseased arteries; first successful patch-graft angioplasty; fundamental concept of therapy in arterial disease; left ventricular bypass pump for cardiac assistance and first successful clinical application; first successful resection and graft replacement of fusiform aneurysm; establishment of Meth. DeBakey Heart Ctr., Meth. Hosp., Houston, 2001; establishment of DeBakey USU Brigade, 2001; establishment of Michael E. DeBakey award for Long-life Well-lived in Svc. to Mankind, Huffington Ctr. on Aging, 2001; establishment of Michael E. DeBakey Scholarship in Grad. Sch. Biomedical Sci., Baylor Coll. Medicine, 2001; establishment of Michael E. DeBakey Journalism award, Found. Biomedical Rsch., 2002.

DEBAKEY, SELMA, communications educator, writer, editor; b. Lake Charles, La. BA, postgrad., Newcomb Coll., Tulane U., New Orleans. Dir. dept. med. communication Ochsner Clinic and Alton Ochsner Med. Found., New Orleans, 1942-68; prof. sci. communication Baylor Coll. Medicine, Houston, 1968—; editor Cardiovascular Research Ctr. Bull., 1970-84. Mem. panel judges Internat. Health and Med. Film Festival, 1992. Author: (with A. Segaloff and K. Meyer) Current Concepts in Breast Cancer, 1967; past editor Ochsner Clinic Reports, Selected Writings from the Ochsner Clinic; contbr. numerous articles to sci. jours., chpts. to books. Named to Tex. Hall of Fame. Mem. AAAS, Soc. Tech. Communication, Assn. Tchrs. Tech. Writing, Am. Med. Writers Assn. (past bd. dirs.; publ., nominating, fellowship, constn., bylaws, awards, and edn. coms.), Council Biol. Editors (past mem. trn. in sci. writing com.), Soc. Health and Human Values, Modern Med. Monograph Awards Com., Nat. Assn. Standard Med. Vocabulary (former cons.).

DE BARBIERI, MARY ANN, not-for-profit management consultant; b. Winston-Salem, NC, May 1, 1945; d. Robert Carroll and Annie Louise (Neal) Hutcherson; m. Alfredo Emanuelle De B.; children: Maria Luisa, Riccardo Roberto. BA in Theatre Arts, Mary Washington Coll., 1967; student, Herbert Berghof Studio, 1967—69. With J. Walter Thompson, NYC, 1967-68; asst. to prodr. Norman Twain Prodns., NYC, 1968-69, Contemporary Theatre Co., NYC, 1971-74; co. mgr. Folger Theatre Group, Washington, 1974-77, bus. mgr., 1977-80; mng. dir. Shakespeare Theatre at the Folger, Washington, 1980-90; performing arts cons. Alexandria, Va., 1990-92; dir. The Found. Ctr., Washington, 1992-94; pres. De Barbieri and Assocs., 1994—. Adj. prof. arts mgmt. grad. program Am. U., 1994-99; treas. League of Washington Theatres, 1983-86; chair selection com. The Washington Post/Washington Coun. Agys. Award for Excellence in Non-profit Mgmt., 1997, 98, 99, mem. selection com. 1996-99, The Washington Post Grants in the Arts, 1997—; curriculum design cons., core faculty Choral Mgmt. Inst. of Chorus Am., 2002—; presenter in field. Bd. dirs. Washington Area Lawyers for Arts, 1984-94; bd. dirs. Cultural Alliance Greater Washington, 1986-96, v.p., 1990-96; bd. dirs. Nat. Soc. Fundraising Execs., 1993-96, v.p. edn., 1995, treas., 1996; bd. dirs. Ctr. for Nonprofit Advancement, 2000-06, pres., 2004, 05; chair Performing Arts Coun., Alexandria, Va., 1981-84; founder, first chair Alexandria Commn. for Arts, 1984-88, theater commr., 1984-94; contbr. to study of downtown stages for new theater in Washington, 1985; mem. panel Va. Commn. for the Arts, 1990-96, 2005—. Recipient Outstanding Svc. to Theatre Cmty. award League of Washington Theatres, 1990. Office: 525 Beauregard Dr SE Leesburg VA 20175 Home Phone: 703-777-5052; Office Phone: 703-777-3585. Business E-Mail: debarasso@aol.com.

DEBARTOLO, EDWARD JOHN, JR., real estate developer, former professional football team owner; b. Youngstown, Ohio, Nov. 6, 1946; s. Edward J. and Marie Patricia DeBartolo; m. Cynthia Ruth Papalia, Sept. 27, 1968; children: Lisa Marie, Tiffanye Lynne, Nicole Anne. Student, U. Notre Dame, 1964—68. With Edward J. DeBartolo Corp., Youngstown, Ohio, 1960—, v.p., 1972—76, exec. v.p., 1976—79, chief adminstrv. officer, 1979—94, pres., CEO, 1995—; owner San Francisco 49ers, 1977—97; chmn. bd. DeBartolo Realty Corp., 1994—; chmn., CEO DeBartolo Entertainment, Inc. Mem. Nat. Cambodia Crisis Com., 1980—; adv. coun. Nat. Assn. People with AIDS, 1992; trustee Youngstown State U., 1974—77; nat. adv. coun. St. Jude Children's Rsch. Hosp., 1978—, local chmn., 1979—80; chmn. local fund drive Am. Cancer Soc., 1975—; chmn. 19th Ann. Victor Warner award, 1985, City of Hope's Spirit of Life Banquet, 1986; apptd. adv. coun. Coll. Bus. Adminstrn. U. Notre Dame, 1988; bd. dirs. Cleve. Clinic Found., 1991; lifetime mem. Italian Scholarship League. With US Army, 1969. Named one of Forbes' Richest Americans, 2006; recipient Man of Yr. award, St. Jude Children's Hosp., 1979, Boy's Town of Italy in San Francisco, 1985, Sportsman of Yr. award, Nat. Italian Am. Sports Hall of Fame, 1991, Cert. of Merit, Salvation Army, 1982, Warner award, 1986, Silver Cable Car award, San Francisco Conv. and Visitors Bur., 1988, NFL Man of Yr. award, Football News, 1989, Svc. to Youth award, Cath. Youth Orgn., 1990, Hall of Fame award, Cardinal Mooney High Sch., 1993. Mem.: Internat. Coun. Shopping Ctrs., Dapper Dan Club (bd. dirs. 1980—), Fonderlac Country Club, Tippecanoe Country Club. Office: Debartolo Corp 7620 Market St Youngstown OH 44512-6076 also: De Bartolo Holdings 100 Debartolo Pl # 300 Youngstown OH 44512 *Personal philosophy: Success in business and sporting competition relies on the same basic ingredients--hire the best qualified people and then provide them with the leadership and best resources to accomplish the task.*

DEBARTOLO, HANSEL MARION, JR., otolaryngologist, plastic surgeon; b. Aurora, Ill., May 13, 1947; s. Hansel Marion and Rosemary (Boetto) Debartolo; m. Susan Elizabeth Debartolo, June 26, 1977; children: Doré, Hansel III, Merrit, Janae, Raquel. BA cum laude, U. Minn., 1969; MD, Loyola U., Chgo., 1972; JD, William Howard Taft U. Diplomate Am. Bd. Otolaryngology, Nat. Bd. Med. Examiners, Am. Acad. Anti-Aging (bd. examiner). Intern, resident Mayo Clinic and Mayo Found., Rochester, Minn.; fellow in surgery Mayo Clinic, Rochester; fellow in otorhinolaryngology Geisinger Clinic, Danville, Pa.; former chief staff AmSurg, Joliet, Ill. Ptnr. Chgo. White Sox, H.M.D., Racing Stables, Chgo. Metro TV, Sportsvision, CETUS Internat., Granada Cosmisky Parks Assocs., Hard Master Recording; CEO H.M.D. Devel.; attending surgeon Mendota (Ill.) Hosp. Contbr. articles to profl. jours. Bd. dirs. Debartolo Rsch. Found. Fellow: Drs. Mayo Soc. Life, Priestly Surg. Soc., Am. Rhinologic Soc., Chgo. Larynigol. and Otological Soc., Am. Acad. Anti-Aging Medicine, Am. Acad. Otorhinolaryngology (legis. key physician Ill., mem. bd. govs.), Deafness Rsch. Assn. (life); mem.: AAAS, Am. Soc. Cosmetic Dermatology, Pa. Acad. Ophthalmology and Otolaryngology, Ill. Soc. Opthalmology and Otolaryngology (mem. exec. coun., sec.-treas., chief editor proceedings), Am. Acad. Advancement Medicine, Hunter Boat Owners Assn., Sailboat Harbor Prairie Harbor Yacht Club, Aurora Country Club. Roman Catholic. Avocations: tennis, skiing, golf, bicycling, amateur radio. Home: 20 Dorchester Ct Aurora IL 60506-9139 Office: Debartolo Clinic 11 Debartolo Dr Sugar Grove IL 60554-9584 Home Phone: 630-466-4140; Office Phone: 630-859-1818. Office Fax: 630-859-1830. Personal E-mail: debartolohansel@sbcglobal.net.

DEBEAR, RICHARD STEPHEN, library planning consultant; b. NYC, Jan. 18, 1933; s. Arthur A. and Sarah (Morrison) deB.; m. Estelle Carmel Grandon, Apr. 27, 1951; children: Richard, Jr., Diana deBear Fortson, Patricia deBear Talkington, Robert, Christopher, Nancy deBear Naski. BS, Queens Coll., CUNY, 1953. Sales rep. Sperry Rand Corp., Blue Bell, Pa., 1954-76; pres. Libr. Design Assocs., Plymouth, Mich., 1976-97, Am. Libr. Ctr., Plymouth, 1981—. Bldg. cons. to numerous librs., 1965—; mem. interior design program profl. adv. com. Wayne State U. Mem. ALA, Mich. Libr. Assn. (oversight com. Leadership Acad. 1990—). Home Phone: 734-453-0912; Office Phone: 734-254-8080. Business E-Mail: ddebear@americanlibrary.com.

DEBELLEVUE, LUCKY, sculptor; b. Lafayette, La., 1957; BFA, U. Soutwestern La., 1983; MFA, U. New Orleans, 1987. One-man shows include Feature Gallery, 1997, Realismus Studio, Berlin, 1997, Mus. Contemporary Art, Chgo., 1999, Whitney Mus. Am. Art, Altna, NY, 2002, Ingalls & Assocs., Miami, Fla., 2004, exhibited in group shows at Contemporary Arts Ctr., New Orleans, 1986, Four Walls, Bklyn., 1992, Artists Space, NYC, 1992, The Drawing Ctr., 1993, U. Buenos Aires, 1995, Bklyn. Mus. Art, 1997, Dalarnas Mus., Falun, Sweden, 1997, D'Amelio Terras Gallery, NYC, 1998, Galerie Emmanuel Perrotin, Paris, 1998, Stephen Friedman Gallery, London, 1999, Grand Arts, Kansas City, 1999, Netherland Gallery Art, Rotterdam, 1999, Mus. D'hondt-Dhaenens, Deurl, Belgium, 2000, PS 1 Contemporary Art Ctr., LI City, NY, 2000, Delfina Project Space, London, 2000, Galeria d'Arte Moderna, Bologna, Italy, 2002, Wexner Galleries, Columbus, Ohio, 2004, Ludwig Mus., Köln, Germany, 2006. Joseph H. Hazen Rome Prize Fellowship in Visual Arts, Am. Acad. in Rome, 2004—05. Office: Feature Inc 530 W 25th St New York NY 10001 Office Phone: 212-675-7772.

DEBENEDET, RACHEL, actress; Actor: (Broadway plays) Nine, 2003, Dirty Rotten Scoundrels, 2005—06, (off-broadway plays) The King and I, 1995, Love and War, Adrift in Macao, 2007 (Barrymore award Outstanding Leading Actress in a Musical, 2006). Office: Phila Theatre Co 1714 Delancey St Philadelphia PA 19103*

DEBENEDETTI, PABLO GASTON, chemical engineering professor; b. Buenos Aires, Mar. 30, 1953; came to the U.S., 1980; U.S. citizen; s. Sergio Isaias and Francine Fanny (Lehmann) D.; m. Silvia Irene Strauss, July 11, 1987; children: Gabriel Alejandro, Dina Sonia. BS in Chem. Engring., Buenos Aires U., 1978; MS, MIT, 1981, PhD, 1985. Rsch. engr. O de Nora Impianti Elettrochimici, Milan, 1978-80; asst. prof. dept. chem. engring. Princeton (N.J.) U., 1985-90, assoc. prof., 1990-94, prof. chem. engring., 1994—, dept. chair, 1996—2004, Class of 1950 prof., 1998—. Vaughan lectr. Calif. Inst. Tech., 1992; Katz meml. lectr. CUNY, 1997; Wohl meml. lectr. U. Del., 1997; Cary lectr. Ga. Inst. Tech., 1998; Berkeley lectr. in chem. engring. U. Calif., Berkeley, 2003, Smith disting. lectr., Davis, 07; Collaboratus disting. lectr. Rutgers U., 2003; Katz lectr. chm. engring. U. Mich., 2005; Patten disting. lectr. U. Colo., Boulder, 2006; Rilley lectr. U. Notre Dame, 2007; Abbott lectr. Rensselaer Polytechnic Inst., 2007. Author: Matastable Liquids Concepts and Principles, 1996; mem. editl. bd.: Jour. Supercritical Fluids, 1988—, Revs. in Chem. Engring., 1999—, Chem. Engring. Edn., 2000—, Indsl. and Engring. Chem. Rsch., 2001—04, Physica A, 2001—, Jour. Chem. Physics, 2006—; contbr. articles to profl. jours. including Journ. Chem. Physics, Jour. Phys. Chemistry, Nature, Phys. Rev. Letters, Molecular Physics, Am. Inst. Chem. Engr. Jour., others. Named NSF Presdl. Young Investigator, 1987; European Econ. Cmty. fellow, 1978, Camille and Henry Dreyfus Tchr. scholar, 1989, Guggenheim fellow, 1991, elected to Nat. Acad. Engring. 2000, Prausnitz award 2001. Mem.: NAE, AAAS, Am. Phys. Soc., Am. Chem. Soc., Am. Inst. Chem. Engrs. (assoc. editor AIChE jour. 2006—, Profl. Progress award 1997), Sigma Xi. Achievements include protein processing and separations with supercritical fluids; theory of supercritical fluids and mixtures; thermodynamics of confined supercooled and glassy water; thermodynamics and statistical mechanics of metastable systems; thermodynamics of polyamorphic phase transitions; structure, dynamics, and thermodynamics of glasses. Office: Princeton U Dept Chem Engring Princeton NJ 08544-0001

DEBERRY, DONNA, retail executive; b. 1955; Attended, Calif. State U. Worked with NFL, U.S. Olympic Com., The Oprah Winfrey Show; exec. v.p. global diversity and corp. affairs Wyndham Internat. Inc.; CEO, founder DRP Internat.; v.p. diversity Nike, Inc., 2006—. Bd. dirs. Nat. Hispanic Corp. Coun., U.S. Hispanic C. of C., Nat. Coalition of Black Meeting Planners, Nat. Assn. Black Hotel Owners, Operators and Developers; mem. adv. coun. eWomen Network Found.

DEBERTIN, JAY D., energy and food products executive; B in Econs., U. ND, Grand Forks, 1982; MBA, U. Wis., Madison, 1984. With petroleum divsn. CHS Inc., 1984, v.p. crude oil supply Denver, 1998—2001, sr. v.p. energy ops. St. Paul, 2001, exec. v.p., COO processing Inver Grove Heights, Minn., 2005—. Bd. dirs. Nat. Coop. Refinery Assn., Horizon Milling, Ventura Foods, LLC, US BioEnergy, 2006—. Office: CHS Inc PO Box 64089 Saint Paul MN 55164-0089 Office Phone: 651-355-6000.*

DEBEVOISE, CHARLES HENRY, lawyer; b. Providence, May 17, 1958; s. Charles Conklin DeBevoise and Dolores Annette (Anderson) Brunt; m. Janet Shensa; children: Robert Raymond, Edward Raymond. BA in Polit. Sci., Providence Coll., 1980; JD, Am. U., 1983. Bar: R.I. 1983, Mass. 1984, D.C. 1985, U.S. Dist. Ct. R.I. 1984. Law clk. Supreme Ct. R.I., Providence, 1983—84; assoc. Edwards & Angell, Providence, 1987—92, ptnr. Providence, Boston, 1992—95, Bowditch & Dewey, Framingham, Mass., 1999—2004; shareholder Davis, Malm & D'Agostine, P.C., Boston, 2004—. Bd. dirs. Narragansett coun. Boy Scouts Am., Providence, 1987-95; sr. warden St. Dunstan's Episcopal Ch., Dover, Mass., 2000-2003. Mem. ABA, R.I. Bar Assn., Mass. Bar Assn., D.C. Bar Assn., Boston Bar Assn., Dedham Country and Polo Club (bd. govs. 2006—), Pi Sigma Alpha. Republican. Episcopalian. Avocations: reading, tennis, golf, gardening. Home: 10 Cedar Hill Rd Dover MA 02030-1624 Office: Davis Malm & D'Agostine PC One Boston Pl 37th Fl Boston MA 02108 Home Phone: 508-785-2037; Office Phone: 617-589-3846. E-mail: cdebevoise@davismalm.com.

DEBEVOISE, DICKINSON RICHARDS, federal judge; b. Orange, NJ, Apr. 23, 1924; s. Elliott and Josephine (Richards) D.; m. Katrina Stephenson Leeb, Feb. 24, 1951; children: Kate, Josephine Debevoise Davies, Mary Debevoise Rennie, Abigail D. Boozan. BA, Williams Coll., 1948; LLB, Columbia U., 1951. Bar: N.J. 1953, U.S. Supreme Ct. 1956. Law clk. to Hon. Phillip Forman, chief judge U.S. Dist. Ct. for Dist. N.J., 1952-53; assoc. firm Riker, Emery & Danzig, Newark, 1953-56; ptnr. firm Riker, Danzig, Scherer, Debevoise & Hyland, Newark, 1957-79; judge U.S. Dist. Ct. for N.J., 1979—. Pres. Newark Legal Svcs. Project, 1965-70; chmn. N.J. Gov.'s Workmen's Compensation Study Commn., 1972-73; mem. N.J. Supreme Ct. Adv. Com. on Jud. Conduct, 1974-78; chmn. N.J. Disciplinary Rev. Bd., 1978-79; mem. Lawyers Adv. Com. for 3d Cir., 1975-79, chmn., 1979; chmn. N.J. Legal Svcs. Adv. Coun., 1976-78. Assoc. editor: N.J. Law Jour, 1959-79. Trustee Ramapo Coll., NJ, 1969-73, chmn. bd., 1971-73; trustee Williams Coll., 1969-74, Fund for NJ, 1985—; trustee Hosp. Ctr. at Orange, NJ, v.p., 1975-79; trustee, v.p. NJ Inst. Social Justice, 2002-; pres. Dems. for Good Govt., 1956-60, active various presdl., senatorial, gubernatorial campaigns; active St. Stephens Episcopal Ch. Sgt. U.S. Army, WWII, 1st lt. Korean War. Decorated Bronze Star. Fellow Am. Bar Found.; mem. ABA, N.J. Bar Assn., Fed. Bar Assn. (v.p. 1976), Assn. Fed. Bar State N.J. (v.p. 1977-79), Essex County Bar Assn. (treas. 1960-64, trustee 1968-71), Am. Law Inst., Judicature Soc., Columbia Law Sch. Assn. (bd. dirs., pres. 1992-94). Office: US Dist Ct PO Box 999 Newark NJ 07101-0999 Home Phone: 908-273-7097; Office Phone: 973-645-6121.

DEBEVOISE, ELI WHITNEY, II, federal official, lawyer; b. Morristown, NJ, Feb. 8, 1953; BA summa cum laude, Yale Coll., 1974; JD, Harvard U., 1977. Bar: D.C. 1977. Law clk. to Hon. William J. Holloway Jr. US Ct. Appeals (10th cir.) Okla., Oklahoma City, 1978-79; ptnr., internat. practice group Arnold & Porter LLP, Washington, 1979—2007; US exec. dir. Internat. Bank Reconstruction & Devel. (The World Bank), Washington, 2007—. Mem. Council on Foreign Rels., ABA (coun. mem. sect. on internat. law), Am. Soc. Internat. Law (exec. coun.), Internat. Bar Assn. Office: US Exec Dir Internat Bank Reconstrn & Devel 1818 H St Mail Stop MSN-MC13-1307 Washington DC 20433

DE BEVOISE, LEE RAYMOND, editor, writer; b. Paterson, NJ, Aug. 24, 1948; m. Sharon De Bevoise; children: Suzanne, Richard (dec.). Student, Glassboro State Coll., 1968; ASN, Cumberland C.C., Vineland, NJ, 1974; student, Stockton State Coll., 1991; MS in Comm. summa cum laude, La Salle U., 1996. RN, N.J., Nebr. Editor The Artery Millville Hosp., NJ, 1970—73; staff instr. ARC, Phila., 1981—96; v.p. De Bevoise & Assocs., Friend, Nebr., 1993—. Adj. prof. La Salle U., 1996-2003; clin. info. sys. liaison Bryan Home Health Care Svc., Lincoln, 1998-2006; fin. analyst Nat. Student Loan Program, Lincoln, Nebr., 2006—07. Columnist Daily Jour., Millville, NJ, 1990-97; columnist The Sentinel, 2005; field editor Disabled Outdoors mag., 1994-97; editor South Jersey Angler Mag., 1996-97, The Sentinel Friend, 2007—. Asst. advisor Med. Explorer Post, Millville, 1971-72; trustee Millville Day Care Ctr., 1974-77; co-chmn. adv. com. State Assemblyman Salmon, Millville, 1986-89; trustee, deacon, treas. Open Bible Bapt. Ch., Millville, 1986-95; music dir., choir dir., elder, co-youth group leader Friend Berean Ch., Friend, Nebr., 2000—06; vol. rep. Dare 2 Share Ministries, 2003—; dir. pub. rels. Meadowwood Environ. Sanctuary, Millville, 1990-97, S.J. Sportsmen's Jamboree, Maurice River Twp., NJ, 1990-96; chmn., emcee Friend Talent Show, 1999-2000; co-founder Isaiah 6 Ministries, 2004-06, South East Nebr. Youth Rally, 2004—. With USN, 1969-70. Recipient 1st pl. award, Bi-cenntenial Photography, 1976, Nebr. State Svc. award, Nat. Assn. Home Care and Hospice, 2004. Mem. Boat Writers Internat., Boating Writers Internat., Kodak Profl. Network, Internat. Freelance Photographers Orgn., Internat. Webmasters Assn., IEEE Computer Soc., Mason-Dixon Outdoor Writers Assn. (Gatco Best Mag. column award, Pete Greer Meml. award 1st runner up for best black and white photography), HTML Writers Guild. Avocations: personal computers, fishing, shooting sports, environmental concerns, boating. Home: 607 S Pine St Friend NE 68359-1534 Office: De Bevoise & Assocs 607 S Pine St Friend NE 68359-1534 Home Phone: 402-947-9311. E-mail: lee@fishdreams.com.

DEBIEC, JACEK, psychiatrist, research scientist, educator; s. Henryk Debiec and Barbara (Malinowska) Malinowska-Debiec; m. Monika Isabella Tang. MD, Jagiellonian U., Cracow, Poland, 1994, PhD in Med. Sci., 2000; MA, Pontiff Acad. Theology, Cracow, 1997, PhD in Philosophy of Sci., 2000. Cert. psychiatrist Cracow. Attending psychiatrist, academic instr. dept. psychiatry Jagiellonian U. Coll. Medicine, Cracow, 1997—2002; rsch. scientist NYU Ctr. for Neural Sci., NYC, 2003—. Author: Possession: A Psychopathological Approach To The Problem, 2000, Mathematics And The Brain, 2002, The Self; From Soul to Brain, 2003. Recipient Neal E. Miller New Investigator award, Acad. Behavioral Medicine Rsch., 2007; Herder fellow, Alfred Toepfer Stiftung, Hamburg, Germany and Vienna U., Austria, 1998—99, Fulbright fellow, Polish-Am. Fulbright Commn., 2000—03. Mem.: NY Acad. Scis., Nearoethics Soc., Am. Psychiat. Assn., Soc. Neurosci. Achievements include research in neural basis of fear and fear learning, mechanisms of memory consolidation and reconsolidation. Office: Ctr for Neural Sci NYU 4 Washington Pl Rm 809 New York NY 10003 Office Fax: 212-995-4704. Business E-Mail: jacek@cns.nyu.edu.

DE BLASI, TONY (ANTHONY ARMANDO DE BLASI), artist; b. Alcamo, Italy, Jan. 1, 1933; came to U.S., 1938, naturalized, 1959; s. Frank and Josephine (Frisella) De B.; m. Eva Machauf; children from previous marriage: Keith, Eric. Student, Art Students League, NYC, 1957—59; BA, U. RI, 1961; MFA, Ind. U., 1963; studied with William Leete, Kingston, RI, 1959—61; studied with Jo Cain, 1959—61; studied with James McGarrell, Bloomington, Ind., 1961—63; studied with William Bailey and Dr. Albert Elsen, Bloomington, 1961—63, studied with Rudy Pozzatti, 1961—63. Chmn., instr. dept. art Washington and Jefferson Coll., Washington, Pa., 1963-66; prof. painting and drawing Mich. State U., East Lansing, 1966-86; instr. Sch. Visual Arts, NYC, 1988-90. One-man shows include Kresge Art Mus., Mich. State U., East Lansing, 1969, 72, 76, Spectrum Gallery, NYC, 1968, 69, 71, 73, Detroit Art Inst., 1972, Razor Gallery, NYC, 1975, 77, Western Mich. U., Kalamazoo, 1979, Wake Forest U., Winston-Salem, NC, 1980, Urban Inst. Contemporary Art, Grand Rapids, Mich., 1981, Andrews U., Berrien Springs, Mich., 1983, Louis K. Meisel Gallery, NYC, 1985, 87-89, 91, 93, 95, Hokin Kaufman Gallery, Chgo., 1988, Hokin Gallery, Bay Harbor Island, Fla., 1990, 92, SUNY Fine Arts Gallery, Oneonta, NY, 1998; exhibited in group shows at Mus. Modern Art, Penthouse Gallery, NYC, 1968, Henri Gallery, Washington, 1968, 70, Riverside Mus., NYC, 1970, Spectrum Gallery, 1970, 71, Eastern Mich. U., Ypsilanti, 1972, Corcoran Gallery, Washington, 1973, Razor Gallery, NYC, 1975, 77-79, Grand Rapids Art Mus., 1980, Neill Gallery, NYC, 1980, Detroit Inst. Arts, 1969-70, 82, Ball State U. Gallery, Muncie, Ind., 1983, Louis K. Meisel Gallery, NYC, 1984-90, NJ Ctr. Visual Arts, Summit, 1985, 69th Regement Armory, NYC, 1988, Islip Art Mus., NY, 1993, Jaffe Baker Blau Gallery, Boca Raton, Fla., 1995, Dorothy Blau Gallery, Bay Harbor Island, Fla., 1997, Heuser Art Ctr. Gallery, Bradley U., Peoria, Ill., 2001, Thorne-Sagendorph Gallery, Keene St. Coll., Keene, NH, 2007; represented in permanent collections Detroit Art Inst., Ind. U. Mus. Fine Arts, Bloomington, Golden Artist Colors, New Berlin, NY, Ulrich Mus. Art, Wichita, Kans., Rose Art Mus., Brandeis U., Waltham, Mass., City Nat. Bank, Detroit, Greenfield Energy Corp., LA, Best Products Co. Inc., Richmond, Kresge Art Mus., East Lansing, Mich., also numerous pvt. collections; represented by Louis K. Meisel Gallery, NYC, 1984-96, Dorothy Blau Gallery, Bay Harbor Island, Fla., 1997-2003. Served with USN, 1951-55. Recipient Albert Kahn Assoc. Archs. and Engrs. prize, 1969, Founders Purchase prize (1st prize), Detroit Art Inst., 1970, Mich. Fine Arts Competition award of excellence, Birmingham-Bloomfield Art Ctr., 1982; fellow, N.Y. Found. Arts, 2006; grantee, Tiffany Found., 1966, Individual Artist grantee, Mich. Coun. for Arts, 1983. Office Phone: 212-226-6475. E-mail: tonydeblasi@gmail.com.

DE BLASIS, JAMES MICHAEL, performing company executive, theater producer; b. NYC, Apr. 12, 1931; s. James and Sarah (de Felice) de B.; m. Ruth Hofreuter, Aug. 25, 1957; 1 child, Blythe. BFA, Carnegie Mellon U., 1959, MFA, 1960. Mem. drama faculty Carnegie Mellon U., 1960-62; head drama dept. Onondaga C.C., Syracuse, NY, 1963-72; head Opera Workshop, Syracuse, 1969-70; adv. of opera Corbett Found., Cin., 1971-76; gen. dir. Cin. Opera Assn., 1973-87, artistic dir., 1988-96. Internat. ind. stage dir. of opera, 1962—; pvt. coach, Dramatic Interpretation of Operatic Roles, 1995—. Artistic advisor, Pitts. Opera, Inc., 1979-83. With U.S. Army, 1951-53. Recipient award Omicron Delta Kappa, 1959, Alumni award Bellaire High Sch., 1974, award in arts adminstrn. Gov. Ohio, 1989, Post/Corbett award for performing artist Corbett Found./Cin. Post, 1989. Mem. Actors Equity, Am. Guild Mus. Artists, Drama Alumni Carnegie Mellon U., Beta Theta Pi, Omicron Delta Kappa. Republican. Episcopalian.

DEBLOOM II, JAMES ROBERT, surgeon; b. Rochester, NY, Aug. 7, 1973; BA, Harvard U., Cambridge, 1995; MS, Roswell Pk. Cancer Inst., Buffalo, 1997; MD, Jefferson Med. Coll., Phila., 2001. Intern internal medicine Rochester Gen. Hosp., NY, 2001—02; resident dermatology U. Iowa Hosps. and Clinics, Iowa City, 2002—05; fellow mohs surgery Shadyside Med. Ctr., U. Pitts., 2005—06; pres., med. dir. SC Skin Cancer Ctr., Greenville, 2006—. Resident rep. Am. Soc. Dermatol. Surgery, Chgo., 2004—05. Fellow: Am. Coll. Mohs Micrographic Surgery and Cutaneous Oncology, Am. Acad. Dermatology; mem.: Alpha Omega Alpha Med. Honor Soc. Office: SC Skin Cancer Ctr 300 Ashby Park Ln Greenville SC 29607 Home: 6 Cricken Tree Dr Simpsonville SC 29681 Office Phone: 864-288-1154.

DEBO, VINCENT JOSEPH, lawyer, director, manufacturing executive; b. Bklyn., Feb. 14, 1940; s. George and Letitia (Ruggiero) D.; m. Linda Mellucci, June 25, 1966; 1 child, Jennifer Lynn. BS, Fordham U., 1961, JD, 1964. Bar: N.Y. 1965, U.S. Dist. Ct. (so. and ea. dists.) N.Y. 1967, U.S. Tax Ct. 1969, U.S. Ct. Appeals (2d cir.) 1967, U.S. Supreme Ct. 1969. Assoc. various law firms, NYC, 1964-70; corp. counsel Bangor Punta Corp., Greenwich, Conn., 1970-73; from asst. gen. counsel, asst. sec. to v.p., gen. counsel Internat. Rheem Mfg. Co., NYC, 1973—. Dir., officer various corp. subs. and joint ventures. Mem. ABA (subcoms.). Home: 4 Greenlea Ct Westport CT 06883-3016 Office: Rheem Mfg Co 405 Lexington Ave Fl 22D New York NY 10174-0307 Office Phone: 212-916-8100. Business E-Mail: vince.debo@rheem.com.

DEBOCK, RONALD GENE, real estate company executive; b. Buckley, Wash., Sept. 12, 1928; m. Donna J. DeBock, Sept. 24, 1949; children: Beverly J. DeBock Satter, Gary, Janice. BA, N.W. Coll., Kirkland, Wash., 1953; MDiv., Western Evangelical Sem., Portland, Oreg., 1960; AA, Tacoma CC, Wash., 1979; PhD, Calif. Grad. Sch. Theology, Glendale, 1979. Ordained minister Assemblies of God Ch., 1953-96. Commd. ensign USNR, 1957, advanced through grades to lt. comdr., 1971, chaplain, 1958-71; founder, owner Rainier Rentals (now Rainier Rentals & Sales), Puyallup, Wash., 1975—, Fireball Publs., Puyallup, 1993—. Instr. Am. sign lang. Cmty. Ednl. Opportunity, Orting, Wash., 1995-96. Author: Practice What You Preached, 1993. Active Aloha Hotel Chapels Ministry, Honolulu, 1988-96; bd. dirs. Romanian Renewal Internat., 1993-96, v.p., 1995-96; del. Pierce County Rep. Conv.; charter mem. Rep. Presdl. Task Force; patriotic program presenter. Decorated Vietnam Cross of Gallantry with palm; recipient Delta Epsilon Chi award, 1975, Paul Harris award Rotary,

1992; named Alumnus of Yr. NW U., 1967. Mem. Wash. Assn Realtors, Inc., Puyallup C. of C., Mil. Chaplains Assn. USA, VFW, DAV. Avocations: Scrabble, languages, real estate investing. Personal E-mail: rainierron@aol.com.

DE BOER, PIETER CORNELIS TOBIAS, mechanical and aerospace engineering educator; b. Leiden, Netherlands, May 21, 1930; s. Pieter and Willemina (Zuydam) deB.; m. Joan Lieshout, June 7, 1956; children: Maarten P., Claire E., Yvette E. MechE degree, Delft U. Tech., 1955; PhD in Physics, U. Md., 1962. Rsch. asst., assoc. Tech. U. Delft, 1954-55; rsch. assoc. U. Md., 1957-62, rsch. asst. prof., 1962-64; asst. prof. Cornell U., 1964-68, assoc. prof., 1968-74; prof. Sibley Sch. Mech. and Aerospace Engring., Cornell U., 1974—2000, assoc. dir., 1982-91; prof. Sibley Sch. Mech. and Aerospace Engring., Cornell U. Grad. Sch., Ithaca, NY, 2000—. Tech. staff Aerospace Corp., 1963, 65, 67, 95, 97, 99, Ford Motor Co., 1971-73, gas turbine div. GE Co., 1978-78, Commissariat Atomic Energy, Grenoble, France, 2000-01; vis. prof. von Karman Inst. for Fluid Dynamics, Belgium, 1968, Cornell Aero. Lab., Buffalo, 1969, Tech. U. Delft, 1985-86; tech. staff; cons. Conelec, Elmira, NY, Allied Chem., Inc., Mt. Clemens, Mich., Inst. for Def. Analyses, Arlington, Va., others. Am. editor Applied Sci. Rsch., 1987-98; contbr. articles to profl. jours. With Dutch Army, 1955-57. NATO fellow, 1968. Fellow AIAA (assoc.); mem. ASME, AAUP, Am. Phys. Soc., Am. Soc. Engring. Edn., Royal Inst. Engrs. (The Netherlands), Royal Netherlands Acad. Scis. (corr.), Golden Key, Finger Lakes Cycling Club, Finger Lakes Runners Club, Cayuga Nordic Ski Club, Carcadilla Boat Club (treas.), Sigma Xi, Pi Tau Sigma, Sigma Pi Sigma. Office: Cornell U Sibley Sch Mech Aerospace Upson Hall Ithaca NY 14853 Office Phone: 607-255-3583. Business E-Mail: ptdl@cornell.edu.

DE BOER, SIDNEY B., automotive executive; Attended, Stanford U., U. Oregon. Chmn., CEO Lithia Motors Inc., Medford, Oreg., 1968—. Mem. Presidents Club NADA; mem. DaimlerChrysler Nat. Dealer Council. Bd. mem. So. Oreg. Univ. Found., Oreg. Cmty. Found., Oreg. Shakespeare Festival. Recipient All-Star Dealer award, Sports Illustrated mag., 1990, Quality Dealer award, Time Mag., 1997. Office: Lithia Motors Inc 360 E Jackson St Medford OR 97501*

DE BOLD, ADOLFO J., pathologist, educator, physiologist, researcher; b. Paraná, Argentina, Feb. 14, 1942; arrived in Can., 1968; s. Adolfo E.G. and Ana (Patriarca) deB.; m. Mercedes L. Kuroski; children: Adolfo A., Alejandro J., Cecilia I., Gustavo A., Pablo G. B.Sc. (hon.), Faculty Chem. Sci., Cordoba, Argentina, 1968; M.Sc. in Pathology, Queen's U., Kingston, Ont., 1971, PhD in Pathology, 1973. Cert. clin. chemist. Demonstrator in physics Nat. U. Cordoba, 1961-62, demonstrator normal and path. histology, 1964-67; resident, chief resident Nat. Hosp., Clinicas, Cordoba, 1966-68; asst. prof., lab. scientist Queen's U. and Hotel-Dieu Hosp., Kingston, 1974-82, assoc. prof., 1982-85, prof., 1985-86; prof. pathology and physiology U. Ottawa, Ont., Canada, 1986—. Bd. dirs. research U. Ottawa Heart Inst. at Ottawa Civic Hosp., 1986—. Discovered Atrial Natriuretic Hormone, 1981, patented, 1986; contbr. over 100 sci. articles and chpts. to books in field. Bd. dirs. Heart Inst., Ottawa, 1986-93. Decorated officer Order of Can.; recipient Queen Elizabeth II Golden Jubilee medal, Gairdner Internat. award Gairdner Found., Toronto, 1986, Manning Prin. award Manning Found., Alta., Can., 1986, Sci. Achievement award Am. Soc. Hypertension, 1986, rsch. achievement award Can. Cardiovasc. Soc., 1986, CIBA award Am. Heart Assn., 1994; Disting. Rsch. Prof. award Ont. Heart and Stroke Found. Fellow Royal Soc. Can.(McLaughin medal of excellence in rsch. 1988), Royal Coll. Physicians and Surgeons (Can.), AAAS; mem. Can. Hypertension Soc., Am. Soc. for Hypertension, Internat. Soc. Hypertension (Rsch. Achievement award), Internat. Soc. Heart Rsch., Am. Sect. Can. Fedn. Biol. Socs., Histochem. Soc., U.S. Acad. Pathology, Can. Acad. Pathology, Am. Soc. Cell Biology, Can. Soc. Cell Biology, Internat. Acad. Pathology, Am. Assn. Pathology, Fedn. Am. Soc. Exptl. Biology, Microscopial Soc. Can., Soc. Exptl. Biology and Medicine, Can. Soc. Anatomy, N.Y. Acad. Sci. Roman Catholic. Avocation: classical guitar. Office: U Ottawa Heart Inst 40 Ruskin St Ottawa ON Canada K1Y 4W7 Home Phone: 613-761-4326; Office Phone: 613-761-4265. E-mail: adebold@ottawaheart.ca.

DEBOLD, JOSEPH FRANCIS, psychologist, educator; b. Boston, Nov. 3, 1947; s. Joseph Francis and Patricia (Miltimore) DeB.; m. Carol Lynn Hook, Dec. 20, 1969. AB, UCLA, 1969; PhD, U. Calif., Irvine, 1976. Trainee U. Calif. NICHD Devel. & Reproductive Biology, Irvine, 1971-75; instr., rsch. assoc. Mich. State U., East Lansing, 1975-77; asst. prof. Carnegie-Mellon U., Pitts., 1977-79, Tufts U., Medford, Mass., 1979-83, assoc. prof., 1983-91, prof., 1991—, chmn. dept. psychology, 1990-93, 2002—05; vis. rsch. assoc. Children's Hosp. Med. Ctr., Boston, 1981-85. Advisor NSF, Washington, 1989-92. Mem. editl. bd. Hormones and Behavior, 1987-92; contbr. articles to profl. jours., chpts. to books. Grantee NSF, 1986-99, Nat. Inst. Alcoholism and Alcohol Abuse, 1980-2002, 03—, Biomed. Rsch. Support Program, 1990-91. Mem. AAAS, Soc. for Neurosci., Nat. Assn. Advisors for Health Professions, NY Acad. Scis., Rsch. Soc. on Alcholism, Sigma Xi, Psi Chi. Avocations: motorcycling, tennis, volleyball. Office: Tufts U Dept Psychology 490 Boston Ave Medford MA 02155 Office Phone: 617-627-5901.

DEBOLT, PAUL A., lawyer; b. Lorain, Ohio, Sept. 16, 1963; BA, John Carroll U., 1986; JD, Ohio State U., 1989. Bar: Ohio 1989, DC 1997, US Ct. of Military Appeals. Former assoc. Venable LLP, Washington, ptnr., govt. contracts, 2000—. Capt. US Army, 1990—95. Mem.: ABA (mem. public contract law section), Nat. Contract Mgmt. Assn., Bd. of Contract Appeals Bar Assn. Office: Venable LLP 575 7th St NW Washington DC 20004 Office Phone: 202-344-8384. Office Fax: 202-344-8300. Business E-Mail: padebolt@venable.com.

DE BOOR, CARL-WILHELM R., mathematician; b. Stolp, Germany, Dec. 3, 1937; m. Matilda C. Friedrich, Feb. 6, 1960 (div. Sept. 12, 1984); children: C. Thomas, Elisabeth, Peter, Adam; m. Helen L. Bee, Jan. 2, 1991. Student, Universitaet Hamburg, 1956-59, Harvard U., 1959-60; PhD, U. Mich., 1966; doctorate in Sci. (hon.), Purdue U., 1993, Technion, 2002. Rsch. mathematician Gen. Motors Research Labs., 1960-64; asst. prof. math., computer sci. Purdue U., 1966-68, assoc. prof., 1968-72; prof. math., computer sci. U. Wis.-Madison, 1972—2003, prof. emeritus, 2003—. Vis. staff mem. Los Alamos Sci. Labs., 1970-95, affiliated prof. U. Wash., 2004-. Author: (with S. Conte) Elementary Numerical Analysis, 1972, 1980, A Practical Guide to Splines, 1978, 2001, (with J.B. Rosser) Pocket Calculator Supplement for Calculus, 1979, Spline Toolbox for Matlab, 1990, (with K. Höllig and S. Riemenschneider) Box Splines, 1993. Named John Von Neumann lectr. Soc. Indsl. and Applied Math., 1996, recipient Nat. medal of Sci., 2003, 05. Fellow Am. Acad. Arts and Scis.; mem. Nat. Acad. Engring., Nat. Acad. Sci., Soc. Indsl. and Applied Math., Polish Acad. Sci., Leopoldina, Phi Beta Kappa Office: PO Box 1076 Eastsound WA 98245

DE BORCHGRAVE, ARNAUD, editor, writer, lecturer; b. Brussels, Oct. 26, 1926; s. Count Baudouin and Audrey (Townshend) de B.; m. Dorothy Solon, Apr. 1950; 1 child, Arnaud; m. Eileen Ritschel, Mar. 31, 1959; 1 child, Trisha; m. Alexandra D. Villard, May 10, 1969 Student, Maredsous, Belgium, 1936—39, King's Sch., Canterbury, Eng., 1940—42. Free-lance writer, Ea. Europe, 1946—47; staff United Press, We. Europe, 1947—51; mgr. Benelux Countries, 1949—51; European Corr. Newsweek, Paris, North Africa, Mid. East, Indo-China, 1951—54, fgn. editor, sr. editor, 1955—59, chief fgn. corr., 1959—62, mng. editor internat. edits., 1962—63, chief Newsweek Corr., 1964—80; columnist, TV host; sr. assoc. Ctr. for Strategic and Internat. Studies, 1981—85; editor in chief The Washington Times and Insight Mag., 1985—91; dir. Transnat. Threats Initiative, sr. advisor Ctr. for Strategic and Internat. Studies, Washington, 1991—; pres., CEO, UPI, Washington, 1999—2001. Editor-at-large, Washington Times and UPI, 2001— Served with Brit. Royal Navy, 1942-46 Decorated commandeur de l'Ordre de Leopold II, Medaille Maritime Belge; recipient Medal of Honor Def. Coun., 1980, Medal of Honor World Bus. Coun., 1981, Washington Dateline award Soc. Profl. Journalists, also numerous awards for fgn. reporting Mem. Am. Soc. Newspaper Editors, Internat. Press Inst., Inter-Am. Press Assn., Coun. Fgn. Rels., Racquet and Tennis Club, Met. Club, Econ. Club Washington, Nat. Press Club Home: 2801 New Mexico Ave NW Washington DC 20007-3921 Office: Ctr for Strategic and Internat Studies 1800 K St NW Washington DC 20006-2202 Home Phone: 202-333-5434; Office Phone: 202-775-3282.

DEBOW, JAY HOWARD CAMDEN, public relations executive; b. Flushing, NY, Sept. 21, 1932; s. Thomas Howard and Dorothea (Camden) DeB.; m. Audrey Ellison, May 4, 1957 (div. 1985); children: Stacy, Carolyn, Jennifer, Hollis; m. Suzanne Hayat, Nov. 12, 1986. AB, U. Ga., 1955. Reporter Athens (Ga.) Banner Herald, 1954; news writer UPI, NYC, 1955; v.p. pub. rels. Merrill Anderson Co., NYC, 1956—60; founder, pres. Jay DeBow & Ptnrs., Inc., NYC, 1960—89; pres. Jay DeBow & Ptnrs. Omnicom Pub. Rels. Network, NYC, 1990—92; founder, mng. prin. The Energy Team, 1993—; mng. ptnr. DeBow Mellow Palmer Group, LLC. Chair Jay DeBow & Ptnrs., Inc., 1992—; chmn. bd. advisors Salvation Army Manhattan. Recipient Ad Week Nat. Mktg. Program award, 1990, Cipra award Inside PR Mag., 1991. Mem. Nat. Investor Rels. Inst. (former chmn. govt. affairs com., ethics com., mem. steering com., sr. Investor Rels. Roundtable), Pub. Rels. Soc. Am. (Silver Anvil award 1991), Internat. Inst. Comms., Counselors Acad., Internat. Pub. Rels. Assn., N.Y. Soc. Security Analysts, Assn. Investment Mgrs., Soc. Profl. Journalists, Nat. Press Club (Washington), Met. Club (N.Y.C.; bd. govs., chmn., mem. com.). Home: 530 Park Ave Apt 6J New York NY 10021-8015 Address: 142 Barefoot Cove Hypoluxo FL 33462 Home Phone: 212-758-8117; Office Phone: 212-906-9192. E-mail: jaydegbow@aol.com.

DEBRASKI, SARAH CORNISH, librarian; m. Paul Debraski; 1 child, Clark. MLS, U. Pitts. Children's libr. Allen County Libr. Sys. Tecumseh Br., Ind.; libr. Vineyard Haven Pub. Libr., Martha's Vineyard, Mass.; young adult libr. Somerset County Libr. Sys. Warren Township Br., NJ, head Youth Services Dept. NJ. Mem.: NJ Libr. Assn., Young Adult Libr. Services Assn. (v.p./pres.-elect 2007—), ALA (chair prog. clearinghouse com., rep. to conf. planning coordinating team, bd. dirs. 2004—07). Avocations: reading historical romance novels, board games, word games, cooking, baking.

DEBRECZENY, PAUL, retired language educator, writer; b. Budapest, Hungary, Feb. 16, 1932; came to U.S., 1960; s. Zsigmond and Margit Ibolya (Csanady) D.; m. Gillian Marjorie Butterworth, Oct. 30, 1959; children: Louise, Martin. BA in Russian Studies, Eotvos U., Budapest, 1953, BA in Hungarian Studies, 1955; PhD in Russian Lit., U. London, 1960. Research assoc. Inst. Lit. Studies, Hungarian Acad. Scis., Budapest, 1955-56; trans. editor Pergamon Press, Oxford, Eng., 1959-60; from asst. to assoc. prof., dept. chmn. Tulane U., New Orleans, 1960-67; assoc. prof. U. N.C., Chapel Hill, 1967-74, prof., chmn., 1974-79, prof. Slavic langs., 1979-83, Alumni disting. prof. Russian and comparative lit., 1983-99, prof. emeritus, 1999—, chmn. humanities divsn., 1984-86; dir. Ctr. for Slavic, Eurasian and East European Studies U. N.C.-Duke U., Chapel Hill, 1991-94. Author: Nickolay Gogol and His Contemporary Critics, 1966, Temptations of the Past, 1982, The Other Pushkin, 1983, 2d rev. edit. in Russian, 1996, Social Functions of Literature: Alexander Pushkin and Russian Culture, 1997; translator: The Captain's Daughter and Other Stories by Alexander Pushkin, 1992; translator, editor: Literature and National Identity, 1970, Alexander Pushkin's Complete Prose Fiction, 1983; editor: Chekhov's Art of Writing: A Collection of Critical Essays, 1977, American Contributions to the Ninth International Congress of Slavists, Vol. 2: Literature, 1983; editor: Russian Visual and Narrative Art: Varieties of Seeing, 1994; mng. editor: The Pushkin Journal, 1993-96, the Pushkin rev., 1997-98. Awarded Golden Key City of New Orleans, 1967; named outstanding graduating sr. award in his name U. NC, Chapel Hill, 2000—, disting. prof. award in his name U. NC Coll. Arts and Scis., 2004—. Mem. AAUP, MLA, Am. Assn. Tchrs. Slavic and East European Langs. (v.p. 1978-79), Am. Assn. for Advancement of Slavic Studies, So. Conf. on Slavic Studies (v.p. 1979, pres. 1980, Sr. Scholar award 1987), N.Am. Pushkin Soc. (pres. 1993). Democrat. Home: 304 Hoot Owl Ln Chapel Hill NC 27514-2743 Office: U NC Dept Slavic Langs Chapel Hill NC 27599-3165 Business E-Mail: pdebrecz@email.unc.edu.

DE BREMAECKER, JEAN-CLAUDE, geophysics educator; b. Antwerp, Belgium, Sept. 2, 1923; came to U.S., 1948, naturalized, 1963; s. Paul J.C. and Berthe (Bouché) De B.; m. Arlene Ann Parker, Nov. 29, 1952 (dec.); m. Ruth F. Baer, July 6, 1998 (dec.); children— Christine, Suzanne. MS in Mining Engring, U. Louvain, Belgium, 1948; MS in Geology, La. State U., 1950; PhD in Geophysics, U. Cal. at Berkeley, 1952. Research scientist, sr. research scientist Inst. pour la Recherche Sci. en Afrique Centrale, Bukavu, Congo, 1952-58; Boese postdoctoral fellow Columbia, 1955-56; postdoctoral fellow Harvard, 1958-59; faculty Rice U., Houston, 1959—, prof. geophysics, 1965-94, prof. emeritus, 1994. Research asso. U. Calif., Berkeley, 1966; vis. mem. Tex. Inst. for Computational Mechanics, U. Tex., Austin, 1977; vis. prof. U. Paris, 1980-81 Author: Geophysics, the Earth's Interior, 1985. Chmn. Citizens for McCarthy, Houston, 1968. Served with Belgian Army, 1944-45. Mem. AAUP, Am. Geophys. Union, Fedn. Am. Scientists, Internat. Assn. Seismology and Physics of Earth's Interior (assoc. sec. gen. 1963-71, sec. gen. 1971-79). Home: 3115 Broadmead Dr Houston TX 77025-3819 Office: Rice U Dept Earth Sci Box 1892 Houston TX 77251 Office Phone: 713-348-4886. Business E-Mail: deb@rice.edu.

DE BRIER, DONALD PAUL, lawyer, oil industry executive; b. Atlantic City, Mar. 20, 1940; s. Daniel and Ethel de B.; m. Nancy Lee McElroy, Aug. 1, 1964; children: Lesley Anne, Rachel Wynne, Danielle Verne. BA in Hist., Princeton U., 1962; LLB with honors, U. Pa., 1967. Bar: NY 1967, Tex. 1977, Utah 1983, Ohio 1987. Assoc. firm Sullivan & Cromwell, NYC, 1967-70, Patterson, Belknap, Webb & Tyler, NYC, 1970-76; v.p., gen. counsel, dir. Gulf Resources & Chem. Corp., Houston, 1976-82; v.p. law Kennecott Corp. (former subs. BP America Inc.), Salt Lake City, 1983-89; assoc. gen. counsel BP America Inc., Cleve., 1987-89; gen. counsel BP Exploration Co. Ltd., London, 1989-93; exec. v.p., gen. counsel Occidental Petroleum Corp., LA, 1993—. Bd. dirs. LA Philharm., 1995—. Lt. USNR, 1962—64. Mem. Calif. Club, Riviera Tennis Club (chmn. adv. bd. govs. 2002-). Office: Occidental Petroleum Corp 10889 Wilshire Blvd Los Angeles CA 90024-4201

DE BRIGARD, EMILIE, anthropologist, consultant; b. NYC, Dec. 11, 1943; d. A. Lincoln and Ruth Emilie (Jaeger) Rahman; m. Raul de Brigard, June 11, 1966; 1 child, George. BA, Harvard Coll., 1963; MA, U. Calif., 1972. Guest curator dept. of film Mus. of Modern Art, NYC, 1972-73; asst. to dir. human studies film archives Smithsonian Instn., Washington, 1975-77; prin. programmer Margaret Mead Film Festival Am. Mus. Natural History, NYC, 1977-78; faculty Harvard Summer Sch., Cambridge, Mass., 1980-86; pres. Internat. Film Seminars, Inc., NYC, 1981-83; vis. lectr. dept. anthropology Yale U., New Haven, 1989-91; pres. Soc. for Visual Anthropology, Washington, 1995-97, FilmResearch, Higganum, Conn., 1970—. Author: The History of Ethnographic Film, 1971, Anthropological Cinema, 1973, Cine Antropológico, 1978; producer (film) Margaret Mead: A Portrait by a Friend, 1978. Trustee Wadsworth Atheneum, Hartford, Conn., 2000—; pres. Friends of the Ixchel Mus., Guatemala, 2005-07; adv. bd. Arden Inst., Shakespeare & Co. Fellow Am. Anthrop. Assn., Royal Anthrop. Inst.; mem. Soc. Woman Geographers, Harvard Club So. Conn. (v.p. 1995—). Avocation: costume and textiles. Home: 285 Riverside Dr Apt 7D New York NY 10025-5227 Office: FilmResearch 8 Christian Hill Rd Higganum CT 06441-4030 E-mail: debrigard@att.net.

DEBRINCAT, SUSAN JEANNE, nutritionist; b. Detroit, Oct. 7, 1943; d. Lloyd Brode and Florence Claire Greenleaf; m. Raymond Frank DeBrincat, June 19, 1965; children: David Lloyd, Mark Joseph. BS magna cum laude, Mich. State U., 1965. Cert. med. technologist, Am. Soc. Clin. Pathologists. Med. technologist Harper Hosp., Detroit, 1965-66, South Macomb Hosp., Warren, Mich., 1966; art tchr. YWCA, Berkley, Mich., 1969-80; master coord. Shaklee Corp., 1977—, sr. master coord., facilitator Pacific Inst., 1987—, lifetime master, 1990—, nutritional counselor, fashion, color, image and makeup counselor, mgmt. and leadership trainer, motivational spkr., 1977—2007. Interior designer. Painter oil, acrylic, watercolors. Mem. Rep. Nat. Com. Pres.'s Club, Found. Club, Phi Kappa Phi, Delta Zeta. Roman Catholic. Avocations: painting, art and antiques, reading, travel, boating. Office Phone: 770-538-9982. E-mail: healthychoices@charter.net.

DEBRUIN, DONALD J., church musician; b. Paterson, NJ, Apr. 10, 1957; s. Donald and Marion Campbell DeBruin. MusB, Syracuse U., NY, 1979; MusM, U. Colo., Boulder, 1981; MArch, NJ Inst. Tech., Newark, 1991. Dir. music, organist Ch. Radburn, Fair Lawn, NJ, 1982—86, Preakness Ref. Ch., Wayne, NJ, 1987—92; dir. music First Presbyn. Ch., Freehold, NJ, 1992—97; dir. music ministries First Congl. UCC, Madison, Wis., 1997—. Composer: (organ composition) Processional for Organ and Bells, Trio on a Tune of Harold Arlen, (handbell composition) Christmas Fanfare. Pres. Assn. Ch. Musicians, 2002—03, bd. member-at-large, 1998—2004. Mem.: Choristers Guild, Am. Guild English Handbell Ringers, Presbyn. Assn. Musicians, Am. Guild Organists, Assn. Ch. Musicians. Avocations: reading, antiques, home improvement. Office: First Congregational UCC 1609 University Ave Madison WI 53726 Home Phone: 608-824-9516; Office Phone: 608-233-9751. Business E-Mail: ddebruin@firstcongmadison.org.

DE BRUIN, JERRY MARK, retail executive; BSc in Pharmacy, U. Utah, 1982. Various positions including mgr. and dir. Managed Health Care Am. Drug Stores, 1982—94; COO, v.p. ops. RxAMERICA LLC, 1994—97, CEO, gen. mgr. Salt Lake City, 1997—99; v.p. managed care and pharmacy procurement Albertson's, Inc., 1999—2003; sr. v.p. pharmacy svcs. Rite Aid Corp., 2003—05, exec. v.p. pharmacy, 2005—. Office: Rite Aid Corp 30 Hunter Lane Camp Hill PA 17011 Office Phone: 717-761-2633.*

DEBRUIN SAMPLE, ANNE, human resources specialist; Formerly with Whirlpool Corp., Benton Harbor, Mich.; numerous human resources positions including mgr. human resources Pepsi-Cola N.Am. PepsiAmericas, Inc., Mpls., 1988—2001, sr. v.p. human resources, 2001—. Office: PepsiAmericas 4000 Dain Rauscher Plz 60 S Sixth St Minneapolis MN 55402 Office Phone: 612-661-4000. Office Fax: 612-661-3737.

DEBRUYN, MAXINE, performing arts educator; b. Mayville, Mich., May 8, 1937; d. Willard C. Harris and Madge L. Griswold; m. Maxine Mae Harris, June 17, 1961; 1 child, Margret Christine. BS, Mich. State U., East Lansing, 1959. Prof. dance Hope Coll., Holland, Mich., 1965—. Recipient Lifetime Achievement award in dance edn., Mich. Dance Council, Faculty Achievement award for outstanding tchg. & leadership, Hope College Ruth and John Reed, Honor award, Mich. Assn. Health, Physical Education, Recreation & Dance. Mem.: Nat. Dance Edn. Orgn. (pres. 2006—), Dance and Child Internat. (exec. com. mem.-at-large). Office: Hope Coll 168 E 13th St Holland MI 49423 Office Fax: 616-395-7090; Home Fax: 616-395-7090. Business E-Mail: debruyn@hope.edu.

DEBS, RICHARD A., investment banker; b. Providence, Oct. 7, 1930; s. Abraham George and Madge (Fatool) D.; m. Barbara Knowles, July 19, 1958; children: Elizabeth Anderson, Nicholas. BA summa cum laude, Colgate U., 1952; postgrad. (Fulbright scholar), Cairo U., 1952-53; MA, Princeton U., 1956, PhD, 1963; LLB, Harvard U., 1958, grad. Advanced Mgmt. Program, 1973. Bar: N.Y. 1960. Researcher joint project Harvard-Princeton, 1958-59; with Fed. Res. Bank of N.Y., NYC, 1960-76, legal dept., 1960-64, asst. counsel, 1964-69, sec. of bank, 1965-69, v.p. govt. bonds and securities, 1969-72, v.p. loans and credits, 1969-72, v.p. open market ops., 1972, sr. v.p., 1973, 1st v.p., chief adminstrv. officer, 1973-76; alt. mem. Fed. Open Market Com., 1973-76; mng. dir. Morgan Stanley & Co., Inc., 1976-87; pres. Morgan Stanley Internat. Inc., 1976-87; chmn. R.A. Debs & Co., 1987—; adv. dir. Morgan Stanley, 1987—; chmn. The Malaysia Fund Inc., 1987—. Bd. dir. Gulf Internat. Bank, London, Mizuho Corp. Bank, Mizuho Securities Co.; chmn. com. fiscal agy. ops. Fed. Res. System, 1969-76; mem. Fed. Res. Steering Com. on Payments Mechanism, 1973-76, Fed. Res. Steering Com. on Internat. Banking, 1973-76; allied mem. N.Y. Stock Exchange, chmn. adv. com. internat. capital markets; com. multinat. enterprises U.S. coun. Internat. Bus.; mem. internat. capital markets adv. com. Fed. Res. Bank of N.Y.; mem. Nat. Commn. on Pub. Svc. (The Volcker Commn.); mem. Overseas Devel. Coun.; mem. U.S. Office Pers. Mgmt. Task Force on Pay Reform; mem. World Bank Adv. Group on Pvt. Sector Devel.; bus. adv. coun. European Bank for Reconstrn. and Devel., Russian-Am. Banking Forum; mem. Carnegie Commn.; mem. Take Stock in Am. Com., 1973-76; mem. Egypt-U.S. Bus. Coun.; mem. adv. coun. Near Eastern program Princeton U., Mid. East Inst., Columbia U.; mem. N.Y. State Savs. Bond Com., 1973-76; adv. coun. Am. Inst. Banking, 1973-76; advisor Bank Julius Baer, 1987—, United Gulf Group (Kuwait), 1987—, Dai-Ichi Mut. Life, Tokyo, 1988—, Nissho Iwai Corp., Tokyo, 1990—; mem. adv. bd. Mid. East Inst. Columbia U. Contbr. articles to profl. jours. Chmn. emeritus, trustee Carnegie Hall; bd. dir. Fedn. Protestant Welfare Agys., Inst. Internat. Edn.; trustee Carnegie Endowment for Internat. Peace, Am. Univs. Field Staff; trustee Am. U., Beirut, vice chmn., 1981-94, chmn., 1994—; bd. dirs. Am. Council on Germany; mem. vis. com. Middle East Center Harvard U., 1976-82, mem. vis. com. Ctr. Internat. Affairs; mem. Group of 30, Reuters Carnegie Global Pub. Policy Group, 1999—; also mem. exec. com. Bretton Woods Com.; U.S. chmn. U.S.-Saudi Arabia Bus. Coun. Recipient Lifetime Achievement award, Fulbright Assn., Fedn. Protestant Welfare Agencies, Third St Music Sch. Settlement, Nat. Acad. Design, King Abdul Aziz medal, Govt. Saudi Arabia, Cedars of Lebanon medal, Govt. of Lebanon. Mem. ABA (com. Middle Eastern law), Assn. Bar City N.Y., Coun. Fgn. Rels., C. of C. U.S. (internat. policy com., chmn. subcom. on internat. econ. devel. 1979-87), Egyptian Am. C. of C. (chmn.), N.Y. C. of C. and Industry, Japan Soc., Asia Soc., Fgn. Policy Assn. (bd. govs.), Econs. Club, Century Assn. (N.Y.C.), Larchmont Yacht (N.Y.), River Club, Phi Beta Kappa Assocs. Office: Morgan Stanley & Co 1585 Broadway 31st Fl New York NY 10036-1001 E-mail: Richard.Debs@morganstanley.com.

DEBUNDA, SALVATORE MICHAEL, lawyer; b. Phila., June 17, 1943; s. Salvatore and Marie Ann (Carilli) DeB.; children: Lauren, David. BS in Econs., U. Pa., 1965, JD, 1968. Bar: Pa. 1968, U.S. Supreme Ct. 1977. Law clk. to justice Phila. Ct. of Common Pleas, 1968-69; asst. gen. counsel ARA Services, Inc., Phila., 1969-74; sr. assoc. Cohen, Verlin, Sherzer & Porter, Phila., 1974-75; v.p., sec., gen. counsel AEL Industries, Inc., Montgomeryville, Pa., 1975-80; v.p., gen. counsel Cooper Assocs., Inc., Marlton, NJ, 1980-81; v.p. cable TV devel. Greater Media, Inc., East Brunswick, NJ, 1981-85; ptnr., chmn. media/entertainment law group Fox, Rothschild, O'Brien & Frankel, Phila., 1985-91; shareholder, dir. Pelino &

Lentz, PC, Phila., 1991—. Mem. ABA, Pa. Bar Assn., Phila. Bar Assn., Fed. Comm. Bar Assn. Avocations: sports, owning thoroughbred horses. Office: Pelino & Lentz PC 1650 Market St One Liberty Pl 32d Fl Philadelphia PA 19103-7393

DE BURLO, COMEGYS RUSSELL, JR., investment company executive, educator, retired treasurer; b. Phila. s. Comegys Russell and Margaret (Whitehurst) de B.; m. Edith Power Thatcher; children: Jane Thatcher, Charles Russell, John Todd. BS, Swarthmore Coll.; MBA, U. Pa.; DBA, Harvard U. Past CFO Tufts U., v.p., prof., treas., hon. treas. V.p. Ednl. Testing Svc., Princeton, N.J.; dir. UST Corp., NIH, Nat. Cancer Inst., Cancer Program Adv. Com., Cancer Rsch. Ctrs. Rev. Com., Am. Coun. on Edn., Com. on Taxation; pres., prin. The de Burlo Group Inc., 1987—. Past adv. com. No. Calif. Cancer Program; past mem. sci. adv. com. U. N.Mex. Cancer Treatment Ctr., Ohio State U. Comprehensive Cancer Ctr., 1983-97; pres. Mass. Assn. Schs. and Colls.; trustee Cambridge Friends Sch., Belmont Hill Sch., Moses Brown Sch., Lincoln Sch., BB&N Sch.; bd. mgrs. New Eng. Yearly Meeting; trustee Obadiah Brown/Sarah Swift Fund; commr. pub. trust funds. With USNR. Mem. Assn. for Investment, Mgmt. and Rsch., Boston Security Analysts Soc., Internat. Assn. for Comparative Rsch. on Leukemia and Related Diseases (treas.), Am. Rhododendron Soc. (asst. treas. Mass. chpt.), Harvard Club, Green Mountain Club, Appalachian Mountain Club, Tau Beta Pi. Office: 50 Federal St Boston MA 02110-2500 Office Phone: 617-482-0275. E-mail: edith@bloomberg.net.

DEBUS, ALLEN GEORGE, historian, educator; b. Chgo., Aug. 16, 1926; s. George Walter William and Edna Pauline (Schwenneke) D.; m. Brunilda Lopez-Rodriguez, Aug. 25, 1951; children: Allen Anthony George, Richard William, Karl Edward. BS, Northwestern U., 1947; A.M., Ind. U., 1949; PhD, Harvard U., 1961; postgrad., U. Coll. London, 1959-60; D.Sc. h.c., Cath. U. Louvain, 1985. Research chemist Abbott Labs., North Chicago, Ill., 1951-56; asst. prof. U. Chgo., 1961-65, assoc. prof. history, 1965-68, prof., 1968-78, Morris Fishbein prof. history sci. and medicine, 1978-96, Morris Fishbein prof. emeritus, 1996—; dir. Morris Fishbein Ctr. for Study History Sci. and Medicine, 1971-77. Disting. vis. prof. Ariz. ctr. for medieval and renaissance studies Ariz. State U., 1984; vis. prof. Inst. Chemistry, U. São Paulo, Brazil, 1990; mem. internat. adv. com. Tel-Aviv U. The Cohn Inst. History and Philosophy of Sci. and Ideas, Ctr. for History and Philosophy of Sci. of Hebrew U. of Jerusalem; mem. internat. adv. bd. Annali dell'Istituto e Museo di Storia della Scienza di Firenze; cons. lit. and sci. curriculum Ga. Inst. Tech. Author: The English Paracelsians, 1965, 66, (with Robert P. Multhauf) Alchemy and Chemistry in the 17th Century, 1966, The Chemical Dream of the Renaissance, 1968, 2d edit., 1972, Science and Education in the 17th Century, 1970, (with Brian Rust) The Complete Entertainment Discography, 1973, 2d rev. edit., 1989, The Chemical Philosophy, 2 vols., 1977, 2d edit., 2002, Japanese transl., 1999, Man and Nature in the Renaissance, 1978, 15th rev. edit., 1995, Italian transl., 1982, Spanish transl., 1985, 86, 2d edit., 1995, Japanese transl., 1986, Chinese transl., 1988, 2000, Greek transl., 1997, Portuguese trans., 2002, Robert Fludd and His Philosophical Key, 1979; Science and History: A Chemist's Appraisal, 1984, Chinese tranl., 1999, Chemistry, Alchemy and the New Philosophy, 1550-1700, 1987, The French Paracelsians: The Chemical Challenge to Medical and Scientific Tradition in Early Modern France, 1991, 2002, Paracelso e la Tradizione Paracelsiana, 1996, Chemistry and Medical Debate: Van Helmont to Boerhaave, 2001, The Chemical Promise, 2006; editor: World Who's Who in Science from Antiquity to the Present, 1968, Science, Medicine and Society in the Renaissance, 2 vols, 1972, Medicine in Seventeenth-Century England, 1974; editor reprint: Theatrum Chemicum Britannicum (1652), 1967, John Dee's Mathematicall Praeface (1570), 1975; editor: (with Ingrid Merkel) Hermeticism and the Renaissance: Intellectual History and the Occult in Early Modern Europe, 1988, (with Michael T. Walton) Reading the Book of Nature: The Other Side of the Scientific Revolution, 1998, Alchemy and Early Modern Chemistry: Papers from Ambix, 2004; essayist: Festschrift: Experiencing Nature: Essays for Allen G. Debus (edited by Paul Theerman and Karen Parshall, 1997); mem. bd. adv. editors Physis Rivista internazionale de storia della scienza, Nuncius, The 16th Century Jour.; adv. editor: History of Science; hon. bd. editors Incognita; programmed 3 records released by Smithsonian Instn. Music of Victor Herbert, 1979; notes to CD releases by Archeophone-Bert Williams, Nora Bayes and Jack Norworth, 2003-04, Monarchs of Minstrelsy, 2006; contbr. articles to profl. jours.; patentee in field. Social Sci. Rsch. Coun. fellow, 1959-60; Fulbright fellow, 1959-60; Fels Found. fellow, 1960-61; Guggenheim fellow, 1966-67; overseas fellow Churchill Coll. Cambridge (Eng.) U., 1966-67, 69; mem. Inst. Advanced Study Princeton, N.J., 1972-73; NEH fellow Newberry Libr., Chgo., 1975-76; fellow Inst. for Rsch. in Humanities U. Wis., Madison, 1981-82, NEH, 1987, Folger Shakespeare Libr., Washington; rsch. grantee Am. Philos. Soc., 1961-62, Wellcome Trust, 1962, NIH, 1962-70, 74-75, 77-78, 92-97, NSF, 1961-63, 71-74, 80-83, Am. Coun. Learned Socs., 1966, 70, 71. Fellow AAAS (mem. electorate nominating com., sect. L 1974-77, chmn. com. 1974); mem. History of Sci. Soc. (council 1962-65, 87-90, program chmn. 1972, Pfizer award 1978, Sarton medal 1994, Disting. lectr. 1996), Soc. Study Alchemy and Early Chemistry (mem. council 1967—), Am. Assn. for History Medicine (program com. 1975), Brit. Soc. for History Sci., Internationale Paracelsus Gesellschaft, Am. Chem. Soc. (asso. mem. history of chemistry div., exec. com. 1969-72, Dexter award 1987), Soc. Med. History of Chgo. (sec.-treas. 1971-72, v.p. 1972-74, pres. 1974-76, mem. council), Académie Internat. d'Histoire de la Medecine, Société Internationale d'Histoire de la Medecine, Academie Internat. d'Histoire des Scis. (corr. 1971, membre effectif 1991), Am. Inst. History of Pharmacy (Edward Kremers award 1978, adv. panel hist. activity 1979-81, awards com. 1981—), Am. Soc. Reformation Research, Assn. Recorded Sound Collections., Midwest Junto for History of Sci. (pres. 1983-84), Academia das Ciencias de Lisboa. Office: U Chgo Dept History Chicago IL 60637 Office Phone: 773-702-8391. Personal E-mail: adebus@midway.uchicago.edu.

DEBUSK, CHARLES RICHARD, engineer, consultant; s. Charles Malcolm and Margaret DeBusk; m. Mary Elizabeth Roberts, Sept. 5, 1981; stepchildren: Amy Henderson, James Roberts 1 child, Margaret Amelia Monroe. B.S. in Indsl. Engring., Va. Poly. Inst. & State U., 1974—79; M.S. in Indsl. Engring., U. Tenn., 1981—87. Professional Engineer, Tenn., 1984; Certified Six Sigma Master Black Belt GE, 2001. Master black belt/sr. mgr. GE Healthcare, Milwaukee, 1991—; sr. mgr. RSM McGladrey, Minneapolis, 1985—91; corp. dir. of cost acctg. The Health Ctrl. Sys., Minneapolis, 1985—86; mgmt. systems cons. HCA, Nashville, 1983—85. Instr. St. Mary's U. of Minn., Minneapolis, Minn., 1986—92. Mem.: Inst. of Indsl. Engring., Am. Soc. for Quality, Alpha Pi Mu. Office: GE Healthcare PO Box 43280 Brooklyn Park MN 55443 Home Phone: 763-561-3654; Office Phone: 763-561-9230. E-mail: charles.debusk@med.ge.com.

DEBUSK, LORRAINE, elementary school educator; b. Bklyn., Oct. 1, 1941; d. John and Muriel Holley; m. Jeffrey Crawford (div.); children: Sean Crawford, Kimberly Crawford; m. Jack DeBusk, Feb. 5, 1987. AA, Clark County CC, 1984; BA, U. Nev., Las Vegas, 1989; degree in Tchg., Nat. U., Las Vegas, 1991; MS, Nova U., Las Vegas, 1994, postgrad. Cert. sch. adminstr. Nev. Pvt. practice, NYC; med. technician, nurse Sunrise Hosp., Las Vegas; GATE specialist Clark County Sch. Dist., Las Vegas, tchr., 1991—. Tchr. English to adults CCSD, Las Vegas, 2002. Mem.: Humane Soc. US, Planetary Soc., Greenpeace. Avocations: raising parrots, gardening. Office: Clark County Sch Dist Doris Reed Elem Sch Las Vegas NV 89108 Office Phone: 702-799-4777.

DE CAMILLI, PIETRO V., cell biologist; b. Cittiglio, Italy; BA, Lyceum Manzoni, Milan, 1966; MD magna cum laude, U. Milan, 1972. Assoc. prof. Yale U. Sch. Med., 1988—92, prof., 1992—, chmn. cell biology dept., 1997—2000, Eugene Higgins prof. cell biology, 2003—; investigator Harold Hughes Med. Inst., 1992—. Keith Porter Lectr. Am. Soc. Cell Biology, 1997; adv. bd. European Molecular Biology Org. Jour. Mem.: Am. Acad. Arts & Sciences, European Molecular Biology Org., Inst. Medicine, Nat. Acad. Sciences. Mailing: Dept Cell Biology Yale U Sch Medicine PO Box 208002 333 Cedar St New Haven CT 06520-8002 Office: BCMM 236 295 Congress Ave New Haven CT 06519-1418 Office Phone: 203-737-4461, 203-737-4457, 203-737-4469. Office Fax: 203-737-4436. E-mail: pietro.decamilli@yale.edu.

DECAMINADA, JOSEPH PIO, retired insurance company executive; b. Gebo, Wyo., Oct. 17, 1935; s. Pio and Ida (Franch) Decaminada; m. Genevieve Caputo, Aug. 30, 1958; 1 child, Joseph. BA magna cum laude, St. Francis Coll., 1956; JD, St. John's U., 1959; postgrad., Harvard U., 1978-79. CPCU, CLU, chartered fin. cons. From corp. sec. to sr. v.p., sec. Atlantic Mut. Ins. Co., Centennial Ins. Co., NYC, 1971-86, exec. v.p., sec., 1986-96. Past chmn. bd. dirs. CPCU-Harry J. Loman Found., Motor Vehicle Accident Indemnification Corp., N.Y. Property Ins. Underwriting Assn., Ind. Fedn. N.Y. Contbr. articles to profl. jours. Bd. dirs., chmn. bd. Coll. Mt. St. Vincent, Riverdale, NY. Decorated Knight of Malta; named named Ins. Man of Yr., Recovery Forum, 1978; recipient Brotherhood award, NCCJ, 1991; Anglo-Am. fellow, B.D. Cooke & Ptnrs., Ltd., London, 1966. Mem. Soc. CPCU (nat. pres. 1984-85, Disting. Svc. award 1989, Eugene A. Toale Meml. award N.Y. chpt. 1974), Soc. CLU. Home: 3 Ridgecrest N Scarsdale NY 10583-2013

DE CANI, JOHN STAPLEY, retired statistician, educator; b. Canton, Ohio, May 8, 1924; s. John Mustin and Ada Louise (Stapley) deC.; m. Jessie Montrose Farr, Dec. 17, 1955 (dec. Sept. 1969). BS, U. Wis., 1948; MBA, U. Pa., 1951, PhD, 1958. Mem. faculty U. Pa., Phila., 1948—, assoc. prof. stats., 1963-72, prof., 1972-95; prof. emeritus, 1995—; chmn. dept. stats. U. Pa., 1972-78. Cons. USN, 1957— , NAACP, 1967— , EEOC, 1976— Author: (with R. C. Clelland) Basic Statistics, 1973; contbr. articles to profl. jours. Served with USAAF, 1943-45. Recipient Disting. Tchg. award Lindbach Found., 1964; recipient Wharton disting. tchg. award, 1978, 95, 97; Fulbright grantee Norway, 1959-60 Fellow: Royal Statis. Soc., Am. Statis. Assn.; mem.: Biometric Soc., Inst. Math. Stats., Second Air Divsn. Assn. (exec. v.p. 2004—05, pres. 2005—06). Home: 226 W Rittenhouse Sq Apt 1715 Philadelphia PA 19103 Personal E-mail: j.decani@att.net.

DECARAVA, ROY R., photographer, educator; b. NYC, Dec. 9, 1919; s. Andrew DeCarava and Alfreda Ferguson; m. Sherry Forsythe, June 16, 1947; children: Susan, Wendy, Laura. Student, Cooper Union Art Sch., NYC, 1938-40; PhD (hon.), R.I. Sch. Design, 1985. Sign painter and display artist, N.Y., 1936-37; tech. draftsman, 1939-42; comml. artist and illustrator, 1944-58; freelance photographer for various advt. agys., rec. and TV cos., mags. including Scientific American, Fortune, McCall's, Look, Newsweek, Time, Life, 1959-68, 75—; contract photographer Sports Illustrated mag., NYC, 1968-75; prof. art Hunter Coll., 1978, disting. prof. art, 1989—. Founder, dir. A Photographers Gallery, N.Y.C., 1954-56, Kamolinge Workshop for Black Photographers, N.Y.C., 1963-66; adj. prof. photography Cooper Union Inst., 1969-72, assoc. prof., 1975-78; mem. curatorial council Studio Mus., Harlem, N.Y., 1976. One-man shows include 44th Street Gallery, N.Y.C., 1950; Countee Cullen Br. N.Y. Pub. Library, 1951; Little Gallery N.Y. Pub. Library, 1954; A Photographers Gallery, N.Y.C., 1955; Studio Mus., Harlem, N.Y., 1969; Sheldon Meml. Art Ctr. U. Nebr., Lincoln, 1970; U. Mass., Amherst, 1974; Mus. Fine Arts, Houston, 1975; Corcoran Gallery, Washington, 1976; Benin Gallery, N.Y.C., 1976; Witkin Gallery, N.Y.C., 1977; Light Work Gallery, Syracuse, N.Y., 1977; Port Washington Pub. Library, N.Y.C., 1978; Friends of Photography, Carmel, Calif., 1980; Akron Art Inst. (Ohio), 1980; group exhbns. include Mus. Modern Art, N.Y.C., 1953, 55, 78, Met. Mus. Art, N.Y.C., 1964, Nat. Gallery of Can., Ottowa (toured Can. and U.S.), 1967, Ctr. Creative Photography, U. Ariz., Tucson, 1980, Tampa (Fla.) Mus., 1983, Barbican Art Gallery, London (toured Eng.), 1985, Fotografiska Museet, Stockholm, 1986; represented in permanent collections Mus. Modern Art, N.Y.C., Met. Mus. Art, N.Y.C., Harlem Art Collections, N.Y. State Office Bldg., N.Y.C., Andover Art Gallery Phillips Acad. (Mass.), Corcoran Gallery; Atlanta U., Sheldon Meml. Art Gallery U. Nebr., Mus. Fine Arts, Houston, Ctr. for Creative Photography U. Ariz., Tucson; photographer books: The Sweet Flypaper of Life (text by Langston Hughes), 1955, 2d edit., 1984; Photographs/DeCarava, (text by Sherry Turner) 1981; The Sound I Saw, 1983 (exhibited throughout Japan and Near East 1986). Served with U.S. Army, 1943. Recipient Art Svc. award Mt. Morris United Presbyn. Ch., N.Y.C., 1969; Benin Creative Photography award, 1972; Artistic and Cultural Achievement award Cmty. Mus. of Bklyn., 1979; Nat. Medal Arts Nat. Endowment Arts, 2006; named hon. citizen of Houston, 1975; Guggenheim fellow. Mem. Am. Soc. Mag. Photographers. Office: Hunter College Dept Art 11019 HN 695 Park Ave New York NY 10021 Office Phone: 212-650-3750. E-mail: rdecarav@hunter.cuny.edu.*

DECARLO, JOHN T., lawyer; b. Phila., Nov. 6, 1950; BS, Villanova U., 1972; JD, U. San Fernando Valley, 1975. Bar: Calif. 1976, US Dist. Ct., Cent. Dist. Calif. 1978, DC 1995, US Dist. Ct., DC 1996. Ptnr. DeCarlo & Connor, P.C., LA; gen. coun. United Brotherhood Carpenters & Joiners of Am. Mem.: ABA, LA County Bar Assn. Office: DeCarlo & Connor 9th Fl 533 S Fremont Ave Los Angeles CA 90071-1706

DECARO, ANGELO ANTHONY, JR., data processing executive; b. Poughkeepsie, NY, June 24, 1951; s. Angelo A. and Carmela (Gasparro) D.; m. Beverly Ann Fulvio, June 25, 1983; children: Francesca, Julianne. BSME, Northeastern U., Boston, 1974; MBA, Pace U., White Plains, NY, 1987. Assoc. engr. IBM, Poughkeepsie, 1974-77, sr. assoc. engr., 1977-78, planning/m.e. mgr., 1978-83, sr. engr./mgr., 1983-84, mfg. mgr., 1984-85, mfg. engring. mgr., 1985-86, tech. asst. to v.p. corp. mfg. Armonk, N.Y., 1986-87, asst. plant mgr. Poughkeepsie, 1987-89, plant mgr. Austin, Tex., 1989-93; pres., COO Xetel Corp., Austin, Tex., 1993—. Bd. mem. Austin Quality Coun., dir. Tycom Corp. Active various charitable orgns. in past. Recipient IBM Div. award, 1980. Roman Catholic. Avocations: golf, racquetball. Office: Xetel 2525 Brockton Dr Austin TX 78758-4463

DECASTRO, CRISTINA L., secondary school educator; b. Westerly, RI, Jan. 23, 1973; d. David G. and Nelia L. deCastro. BS in Edn., U. Conn., Storrs, 1995; EdM, U. Hartford, West Hartford, Conn., 2001; M in Math., Quinnipiac U., Hamden, Conn., 2005. Cert. elem. edn. grades K-6 tchr. Conn., 2001, math. tchr. grades 4-8 Conn., 2004. Program dir. St. Paul's Luth. Day Sch., Savannah, Ga., 1997—98; after-sch. program coord. St. Andrew's Sch., Savannah, Ga., 1998—99; math. tchr. summer sch. Rockville H.S., Vernon, Conn., 1999—2002; substitute tchr. Salem Sch., Conn., 2000—02; grade 4 tchr. West Broad St. Sch., Stonington, Conn., 2001—02; grade 6 math./lang. arts tchr. Dr. Robert H. Brown Mid. Sch., Madison, Conn., 2002—03; grade 8 math. tchr. East Lyme Mid. Sch., Niantic, Conn., 2004—. Mem.: NEA, Nat. Coun. Tchrs. Math., Conn. Edn. Assn., Kappa Delta Pi (Pi Phi chpt.). Office Phone: 860-739-4491 3462.

DE CASTRO, HUGO DANIEL, lawyer; b. Panama City, Sept. 12, 1935; arrived in U.S., 1947; s. Mauricio Fidanque and Armida Rebecca (Salas) de C.; m. Isabel Shapiro, July 25, 1958; children: Susan M., Teresa A., Andrea L., Michele L. BSBA in Econs. cum laude, UCLA, 1957, JD summa cum laude, 1960. CPA Calif.; bar: Calif. (ret.) 1961. Prin. de Castro, West, Chodorow, Glickfeld & Nass Inc., LA, 1961—2005. Lectr. UCLA, 1962-67, 68, counsel to dean Law Sch., 1963—; commr. tax adv. com. State Bar Calif. Editor UCLA Law Rev., 1959-60, Taxation for Lawyers, 1971-88; contbr. articles to profl. jours. Former trustee Stephen S. Wise Temple, Jewish Fedn. Cmty. Found.; trustee, bd. dir., chmn. fin. com. UCLA Found.; bd. dirs. Western LA Found., Hebrew Union Coll., Law Found.; bd. govs. Trustee Endowment Trusts. Mem. ABA chmn. taxation subcom.), ACLU, LA C. of C. (former chmn., dir.), LA World Affairs coun., Am. Jewish Com., Del Rey Yacht Club (Calif., former dir., officer), Founders of Music Ctr., Las Hadas Country Club (Mex.), Pi Lambda Phi. Office: 10877 Wilshire Blvd Ste 300C Los Angeles CA 90024 E-mail: hugo4ucla@gmail.com.

DE CELLES, CHARLES EDOUARD, theologian, educator; b. Holyoke, Mass., May 17, 1942; s. Fernand Pierre and Stella Marie (Shooner) De C. BA, U. Windsor, Ont., Can., 1964; MA in Theology, Marquette U., Milw., 1966; PhD, Fordham U., 1970; MA in Religion, Temple U., Phila., 1979. m. Mildred Manzano Valdez, July 17, 1978; children: Christopher Emanuel, Mark Joshua, Salvador Isaiah. Mem. faculty Dunbarton Coll. of Holy Cross, Washington, 1969-70, Marywood Coll. (became Marywood U., 1997), Scranton, Pa., 1970—, prof. religious studies, 1980—. Mem. bd. examiners U. Calicut, Kerala, India, 1985—86; subject specialist Accrediting Commn. of Distance Edn. and Tng. Coun., 1995; moderator Students Organized to Uphold Life, Marywood Coll., 1982—, co-chmn. Task Force Social Justice and Environment, 1992—93, corrector off-campus degree program, 1977—, dept. scribe, 1995—. *Professor DeCelles has written theological essays at various levels. Besides a book and study guides, DeCelles has authored journal and professional articles in such publications as The American Benedictine Review, The American Ecclesiastical Review, Social Justice Review, Spirituality Today, and The Priest. He has authored popular articles in magazines such as Catholic Digest, Sign, Our Sunday Visitor, Our Family, Eucharist, Messenger of St. Anthony, Franciscan Message, and Way of St. Francis. He has written eight Liguori pamphlets and published numerous columns in Catholic newspapers including National Catholic Register and The Catholic Observer. He wrote for the opinion magazine America.* Author: Paths of Belief, Vol. 2, 1977, editor, prin. co-author rev. edit., 1987, 2007; The Unbound Spirit: God's Universal Sanctifying Work, 1985, Jesus: The Eternally Begotten of the Father as Human Being, 1993; editor Biographical Directory Cath. Acad. Scis. in U.S.A., 1994, Science and Religion in Dialogue, 1999; also pamphlets, articles, book revs., guest editorials, columns, letters, occasional columnist Nat. Cath. Register, 1983-87, The Dunmorean, 1996-97; regular columnist The Catholic Observer, 1996-2005; regular feature writer The Catholic Leader, 2005—; contbr. articles to profl. jours., mags. and newspapers. Mem. ProLife Prep. Commn. Scranton Diocese Synod, 1984—85; mem. Filipino-Am. Assn. NE Pa., 1984—91, pub. rels. officer, 1985—91, editor newsletter, 1988—91; mem. pack com. Boy Scouts, Scranton, 1990—95, Cath. religious emblems counselor, 1993—96; mem. Ecumenism and Inter-faith Commn. Diocese of Scranton, 1992—, theol. cons., 1990—2003; mem. Ecumenism and Inter-faith Commn. Ecumenical Leadership Com. (now Christian Cmtys. Gathering of Northea. Pa.), 1999—; leader Cath. Charismatic Prayer Group, Scranton, 1970—76; chmn. Prolife com. Immaculate Conception parish, 1994—; bd. dirs. Scranton UN Assn., 1974—75, chmn. UN Day, 1974; bd. dirs. Scranton chpt. Pennsylvanians for Human Life, 1983—, v.p., 1994—. Recipient cert. of appreciation, U.S. Cath. Conf., 1976, Disting. Svc. award, UN Assn. U.S., 1974, Svc. award, Filipino-Am. Assn. N.E. Pa., 1990, cert. appreciation, Boy Scouts Am., 1991, 1992, 1993, 1994, 1995, Defender of Life cert. of appreciation, Susan B. Anthony List, 2003, several athletic awards for rd. running yearly, 1987—96, multiple awards for speed walking, 1990—96, 2000—02, admitted to the Order Cor Mariae, Marywood Coll., 1990, invested knight, Equestrian Order of the Holy Sepulchre of Jerusalem, 1994, Ronald Reagan Rep. Gold Medal award, Congl. Com., 2004, Cert. Recognition for Commitment and Svc., Marywood U. Distance Learning Program, 2004; Fordham U. Presdl. scholar, 1966—68. Mem. Cath. Acad. Sci. U.S.A. (pub. com. 1991-2001, chmn. program com. 1993-96, chmn. pub. com. 1997-2001, v.p. 1997-2003), Coll. Theology Soc. Am., Men of the Sacred Heart (Scranton chpt.), Theta Alpha Kappa (chpt. moderator 1982—). Roman Catholic. Home: 923 E Drinker St Dunmore PA 18512-2644 Office: Marywood U Dept Religious Studies Scranton PA 18509-1598 Office Phone: 570-348-6211 2305. Business E-Mail: decelles@es.marywood.edu. *What the world needs is compassion. It needs me to climb out of the confines of my own little ego and embrace humankind: humanity created not in my image but God's - including the senile man, the habitual alcoholic, the AIDS victim, the starving Somalian, the abused woman, the child in the womb.*

DECESARE, DONALD E., broadcast executive; b. Jersey City, Mar. 6, 1947; s. Emilio D. and Anita T. DeCesare; m. Catherine M. Fahey, June 20, 1970; 1 child, Elizabeth Ann. BA, U. Pitts., 1967; MA, U. Conn., 1969. News dir. Sta. WGCH-AM, Greenwich, Conn., 1972—74; reporter Westinghouse Broadcasting Corp., NYC, 1974—76; writer CBS News divsn. CBS Inc., NYC, 1976—78, news editor, 1978—80, fgn. prodr., 1980—83, sr. fgn. prodr., 1983—85, mgr. N.Y./New Eng. bur., 1985—87, fgn. editor, 1987—89, v.p. news coverage, 1989—90, v.p. ops., 1990—96; v.p. CBS News, 1990—96; pres. Crossroads Comm. of Old SaybrookLLC, Norwalk, Conn., 1996—, Crossroads Comm. / Enterprises; owner/operator WMRD-AM, Middletown, Conn., 1996—, WLIS-AM, Old Saybrook, Conn., 1996—. Bd. dirs. Middlesex County United Way, Norwalk Symphony Soc. Recipient Columbia DuPont award Columbia U., 1989; Overseas Press Club award, 1990. Mem.: Conn. Pub. Access Network (bd. dirs., treas.), Conn. Broadcasters Assn. (chmn., 1st vice chmn.), Old Saybrook C. of C. (bd. dirs., pres. 2002—04). Avocations: latin american art, furniture making, computers. Office: Crossroads Comm LLC 157 N Seir Hill Rd Norwalk CT 06850-1333 also: PO Box 1150 777 River Rd Middletown CT 06457-3922 also: PO Box 1420 77 Springbrook Rd Old Saybrook CT 06475-1225 Office Phone: 860-347-9673. E-mail: don@wliswmrd.net.

DE CESPEDES, JORGE L., pharmaceutical executive; b. Cuba; arrived in US, 1961; m. Yvonne M. de Cespedes; 3 children. BA in bus. adminstrn., Fla. Internat. U. Sales positions with Smith Kline Laboratories, Miami; co-founder, pres., COO Pharmed Group Corp., Miami, 2005—; co-founder, mng. ptnr. The Astri Group. Minority owner Bobcats Basketball Holdings LLC, 2004—. Office: Pharmed Group Corp 3075 NW 107th Ave Miami FL 33172-2134 Office Phone: 305-592-2324. Office Fax: 305-591-9643.

DE CHAMPEAUX DE LABOULAYE, DENNIS, computer scientist; BS in Math., U. Amsterdam, The Netherlands; PhD in Math., U. Leiden, The Netherlands. Rschr. U. Amsterdam, 1970-82; assoc. prof. Tulane U., New Orleans, 1982-84; staff engr. ADAC Labs., San Jose, Calif., 1984-86; engr., scientist Hewlett-Packard, Palo Alto, Calif., 1986-93; sr. SW cons. Rational, Santa Clara, Calif., 1993-94; cons. Scopus, Emeryville, 1994, Libr. U. Calif., Berkeley, 1994, NET, Redwood City, Calif., 1994, McKesson, San Francisco, 1995, Nat. Semiconductor, Santa Clara, 1995-96, KLA, San Jose, 1996, AllTell, San Jose, 1996, Kaiser Permanent, Oakland, Calif., 1996, KLA, San Jose, 1997, Sabre Decision Systems, Ft. Worth, 1997—98, Fireman's Fund, Novato, Calif., 1998, Sprint, Dallas, 1999, Blue Cross and Blue Shield, Jacksonville, 1999; pres. New Channel, Redwood City, Calif., 2000, Onto00 Inc., 2001—. Mem. AAAI, Assn. Computing Machinery, Sigart.

DECHANT, VIRGIL C., retired fraternal organization administrator; b. Antonino, Kans., Sept. 24, 1930; s. Cornel J. and Ursula (Legleiter) D.; m. Ann Schafer, Aug. 20, 1951; children: Thomas, Daniel, Karen, Robert. Degree (hon.), Pontifical Coll. Josephinum, Columbus, Ohio, St. Anselm's Coll., Manchester, NH, St. Leo's Coll., Fla., Mt. St. Mary's Coll., Emmitsburg, Md., St. John's U., SI, NY, Providence Coll., Sacred Heart U., Bridgeport, Conn., Pontifical U. Santo Tomas, Manila, Assumption Coll., Worcester, Mass., Albertus Magnus Coll., New Haven, St. Thomas U., St.

Paul, Kans. Newman Coll., Wichita, Franciscan U., Steubenville, Ohio, Benedictine Coll., Atchison, Kans., St. Thomas U., Fredericton, NB, Can., Dallas U. With KC, 1948—63, dir., asst. supreme sec., supreme master 4th degree, 1963, supreme sec., 1967-77, supreme knight, CEO New Haven, 1977—2000. Appointee Pontifical Coun. for the Family, 1982—; consultor, Pontifical Coun. for Social Comm., 1990—; hon. councilor of state, Vatican City State, 2001, 05; mem. Coun. of Superindency, Inst. for Works of Religion (Vatican Bank), 1990—. Bd. dirs. Nat. Shrine Immaculate Conception, Washington, Pontifical Coll. Josephinum, Columbus; past trustee Cath. U. Am.; commr. Christopher Columbus Quincentenary Commn. for founding of Ams., 1992; apptd. auditor Snyod Am., 1997. Decorated Knight St. Gregory the Great promoted to comdr. with Star elevated to Knight Grand Cross, Knight Grand Cross Equestrian Order Holy Sepulchre, Holy Land Pilgrim Shell, Knight Grand Cross Order Pius IX, Knight Sovereign Mil. Order of Malta; named one of Gentleman of His Holiness, Pope John Paul II, 1987; appointed to Extraordinary Synod of Bishops in Vatican, 1985, Synod of Bishops on Laity, 1987, Synod of Bishops for Am., 1997; recipient Cross of Merit with Golden Star of Holy Sepulchre of Jerusalem, 1990.

DECHAR, PETER HENRY, artist; b. NYC, Apr. 19, 1942; s. Edouard and Diane D.; m. Natasha Gratcheva, Apr. 23, 1999; 1 child, Antonina. Prin. Peter Dechar Inc. Archtl. Furniture. One-man shows include Cordier & Ekstrom Gallery, NYC, 1967, 69, 75, Twentieth Century Art from the Rockefeller Collection, NYC, 1969, Mus. Modern Art, NYC, 1969; exhibited in group shows at Larry Aldrich Mus., Ridgefield, Conn., 1967, Krannert Art Mus., 1967, Whitney Mus. Art, NYC, 1967, 69; represented in permanent collections Mus. Modern Art, NYC, Whitney Mus. Art, NYC, Larry Aldrich Mus., Ridgefield, Conn., Walker Art Ctr., Fiberglass Tower Art Collection, Julien Levy Collection, Chase Manhatten Collection, Rockefeller Collection. Personal E-mail: pdechar@aol.com.

DE CHASTELAIN, A(LFRED) JOHN G(ARDYNE) D(RUMMOND), Canadian army officer, diplomat; b. Bucharest, Rumania, July 30, 1937; emigrated to Can., 1955, naturalized, 1962; s. Alfred George G. and Marion Elizabeth (Walsh) de C.; m. MaryAnn Laverty, Sept. 9, 1961; children: Duncan John, Amanda Jane. Student, Fettes Coll., Edinburgh, Scotland, 1950-55, Mt. Royal Coll. Calgary, Can., 1956; BA with honors in History, Royal Mil. Coll., Can., 1960; grad., Brit. Army Staff Coll., 1966; D in Mil. Sci. (hon.), Royal Mil. Coll. Can., 1996; LLD in Conflict Resolution (hon.), Royal Rds. U., 2001; EdD (hon.), Nipissing U., 2006; LLD (hon.), Carleton U., 2006, Queen's U., Kingston, 2007. Commd. 2d lt. Can. Army, 1960, advanced through grades to gen., 1989; comdg. officer 2d Bn. Princess Patricia's Can. Light Inf., 1970-72; comdr. Can. Forces Base, Montreal, Que., 1974-76; comdr. Can. Contingent UN Force in Cyprus, 1976-77; comdt. Royal Mil. Coll. Can., Kingston, Ont., 1977-80; comdr. 4th Can. Mechanized Brigade Group, Lahr, Fed. Republic Germany, 1980-82; dir. Gen. Land Doctrine Nat. Def. Hdqrs., Ottawa, 1982-83; dep. comdr. Mobile Command, St. Hubert, Que., 1983-86; asst. dep. min. pers. Nat. Def. Hdqrs., Ottawa, Ont., Canada, 1986-88, vice chief of Def. Staff, 1988-89, chief of Def. Staff, 1989-93; Can. amb. to U.S. Washington, 1993. Past v.p. Scouts Can.; chief Defence Staff, 1994-95; mem. Internat. Body on Decommissioning of Arms in No. Ireland, 1995-96; mem. ind. chmn. No. Ireland Peace Talks, 1996-98; chmn. Ind. Internat. Commn. on Decommissioning of Arms in No. Ireland, 1997—. Decorated comdr. Order Mil. Merit (Can.), officer Order of Can., comdr. Order St. John of Jerusalem, Legion of Merit (U.S.), Companion of Honour (U.K.); recipient Hellenic Commendation medal of Merit and Honor (Greece), Vimy award, Conf. Def. Assocs.; fellow, Lady Margaret Hall, Oxford, 2006. Mem. Dominion of Can. Rifle Assn. (past pres.), Royal Scottish Country Dance Soc., St. Andrew's Soc., Royal Mil. Coll. Club, Royal Can. Legion, Royal Can. Mil. Inst, Col. of the Regiment, PPCLI, 2000-2003 Home: 170 Acacia Ave Ottawa ON Canada K1M 0R3 Personal E-mail: ajgd.dec@sympatico.ca.

DECHENE, ARTHUR C., JR., philosopher, religious studies educator; b. Washington, Sept. 27, 1939; m. Joy Boenig, Jan. 1, 2001. BA, U. Notre Dame, South Bend, Ind., 1961; MA, Cath. U. Am., Washington, 1965, McMaster U., Hamilton, Ont., 1975; PhD, Columbia Pacific U., San Rafael, Calif., 1982. Lectr. Loyola Coll., Montreal, Quebec, Canada, 1963—66; adj. prof. Austin C.C., Tex., 2001—. Contbr. articles to profl. jours. With USMCR, 1957—63. Woodrow Wilson fellow, Woodrow Wilson Nat. Fellowship Found., 1961—62. Home Phone: 512-303-5853; Office Phone: 512-223-6201. Personal E-mail: acdechene@gmail.com.

DECHENE, JAMES CHARLES, lawyer; b. Petaluma, Calif., May 14, 1953; s. Harry George and Domenica Theresa Dechene; m. Teresa Marie Caserza, Aug. 2, 1975; children: Michelle, Mark, Sabrina, Diane. BS summa cum laude, Santa Clara U., 1975; JD magna cum laude, U. Mich., 1978, AM in Econs., 1978, PhD in Econs., 1980. Bar: Ill. 1979, U.S. Dist. Ct. (no. dist.) Ill. 1980, U.S. Ct. Appeals (7th cir.) 1993, U.S. Dist. Ct. (ea. dist.) Wis. 1996. Assoc. Sidley & Austin, Chgo., 1980-86; ptnr. Sidley Austin LLP, Chgo., 1986—. Adj. prof. Health Law Inst. DePaul U. Coll. of Law, 1987—; bd. dirs. Med. Sci. Labs., Wauwatosa, Wis., 1991-95. Author: Establishing a Physician Organization, 1993; author: (with others) Health Law Practice Guide, 1993-2004, Financing and Liability, 1994, Health Law Handbook, 1989, 90, 91, 93, Managed Care, 1996, Telemedicine and E-Health Law, 2004; contbr. articles to profl. jours. Mem. Ill. Bar Assn., Am. Health Lawyers Assn., Am. Econs. Assn. Roman Catholic. Office: Sidley Austin LLP One S Dearborn St Chicago IL 60603-2000 Home Phone: 630-852-8578; Office Phone: 312-853-7275. Business E-Mail: jdechene@sidley.com.

DECHERD, ROBERT WILLIAM, newspaper and broadcasting executive; b. Dallas, Apr. 9, 1951; s. Henry Benjamin Jr. and Isabelle Lee (Thomason) D.; m. Maureen Healy, Jan. 25, 1975; children: William Benjamin, Audrey Maureen. AB cum laude, Harvard U., 1973. Exec. v.p. Dallas Morning News, 1980-83, Belo Corp., Dallas, 1981-84, pres., chief operating officer, 1985-86, chmn., chief exec. officer, 1987-94, chmn., pres. and CEO, 1994—2007, chmn., CEO, 2007—. Dir. Kimberly-Clark Corp., 1996—. Pres. Dallas Symphony Assn., 1979-80, Dallas Symphony Found., 1984-86, St. Mark's Sch., Tex., 1988-91; chmn. Dallas Parks Found., 1985-87, Dallas Soc. Profl. Journalists, 1978; trustee Tomas Rivera Policy Inst., 1992—; incorporator, pres. Freedom. of Info. Found. Tex., 1978. Recipient Disting. Svc. award Dallas Jaycees, 1985, Am. Newspaper Exec. of Yr. award Adweek mag., 1985, citation of honor AIA, 1988, Seymour Preston award Nat. Assn. Ind. Schs. Coun. Advancement and Support Edn., 1989, James Madison award Freedom of Info. Found. Tex., 1989, Henry Cohn Humanitarian award Anti-Defamation League, 1992, Freedom of Speech award The Media Inst., 1998; named to the Tex. Bus. Hall of Fame, 1995; recipient St. Mark's Disting. Alumnus award, 1998. Mem. Tex. Soc. Architects (hon.), Newspaper Assn. Am. (mem. exec. bd. 1992-96). Office: Belo Corp PO Box 655237 Dallas TX 75265-5237*

DE CHERNEY, ALAN HERSH, obstetrics and gynecology educator; b. Phila., Feb. 13, 1942; s. William Aaron and Ruth (Hersh) De Cherney; m. Deanna Faith Saver, June 26, 1966; children: Peter, Alexander. BS in Natural Scis., Muhlenberg Coll., 1963; MD, Temple U., 1967; MA (hon.), Yale U., 1985. Diplomate Am. Bd. Ob-Gyn (examiner 1984-, bd. dirs. 1995-), Am. Bd. Reproductive Endocrinology (bd. dirs. 1988-94), Nat. Bd. Med. Examiners (examiner 1987-90). Intern in gen. medicine U. Pitts., 1967-68; resident in ob-gyn. U. Pa., Phila., 1968-72, instr. dept. ob-gyn, 1970-72; asst. prof. ob-gyn. Yale U. Sch. Medicine, New Haven, 1974-78, assoc. prof., 1979-84, prof., 1984-91, John Slade Ely prof. ob-gyn, 1987-92, dir. div. reproductive endocrinology, dept. ob-gyn, 1982-92, lectr. dept. biology, 1985-92; Louis E. Phaneuf prof., chmn. dept. ob-gyn. Tufts U. Sch. Medicine, 1992-96; prof. dept. ob-gyn. UCLA, 1996—2006; chief Reproductive Biology and Medicine Br. NIH, Bethesda, Md., 2006—. Editor-in-chief: Fertility and Sterility, 1996—. Maj. US Army, 1972—74. Recipient Disting. Alumni award, Temple U., 1989, 2002, Muhlenberg Coll., 1994. Fellow: IOM, ACOG, Soc. Gynecologic Investigation (pres. 1994—95), Soc. Study Reproduction, Soc. Gynecologic Surgeons, European Soc. Human Reproductions and Embryology, Endocrine Soc., Soc. Reproductive Surgeons (charter, pres. 1991), Soc. Reproductive Endocrinologists (pres. 1988), Soc. Assisted Reproductive Tech. (pres. 1987—88), Am. Assn. History Medicine, Am. Fertility Soc. (pres. 1994—95). Office: NIH Reproductive Biology and Medicine Br Nat Inst Child Health and Human Devel Bldg 10 CRC 1 E Rm 1-3140 10 Center Dr M Bethesda MD 20892-5800 Home Phone: 310-770-9667; Office Phone: 301-791-5800, 301-496-5800. Business E-Mail: decherney@mail.nih.gov, dcherney@mednet.ucla.edu.

DECHIARA, DOMINICK, lawyer; BSBA cum laude, Am. U.; JD cum laude, Fordham U. Bar: NJ, NY. Ptnr. & leveraged buyouts practice group leader Nixon Peabody LLP, NYC, 2006—. Mem.: Practicing Law Inst., Assn. of the Bar in the City of New York. Office: Nixon Peabody LLP 437 Madison Ave New York NY 10022 Office Phone: 212-940-3772. Office Fax: 866-402-0836. E-mail: ddechiara@nixonpeabody.com.

DECI, EDWARD LEWIS, psychologist, educator; b. Clifton Springs, NY, Oct. 14, 1942; s. Charles Henry and Janice Margaret (Upchurch) Deci. AB, Hamilton Coll., 1964; postgrad., London Sch. Econs., 1965; MBA, U. Pa., 1967; PhD, Carnegie-Mellon U., 1970. Postdoctoral fellow Stanford U., 1973-74; mem. faculty U. Rochester, NY, 1970—, prof. psychology, 1978—, chair dept. psychology, 1993—94, Helen F. and Fred H. Gowen prof. social scis., 2005—; pvt. practice psychotherapy, 1975—; pres. Inst. for Rsch. and Reform in Edn., 1995-97, chmn., 1997—. Lectr. in field; cons. in field. Author: (book) Intrinsic Motovation, 1975, The Psychology of Self-Determination, 1980; co-author: Industrial and Organizational Psychology, 1977, Intrinsic Motivation and Self-Determination in Human Behavior, 1985, Why We Do What We Do, 1995. Pres. Monhegan Mus. Assn., 1984—; trustee Monhegan (Maine) Conservation Assocs., 1982—89, 1992—95, Monhegan Artist Residency Corp., Maine, 1998—, Monhegan Island Sustainable Cmty. Assn., 2001—06. Grantee NIMH, 1977—78, 1989—94, NSF, 1981—83, Nat. Inst. Child Health and Human Devel., 1986—89, 1990—96, Bill and Melinda Gates Found., 2006—07, Inst. Edn. Scis., 2007—. Fellow: APA, Assn. Psychol. Sci. Office: U Rochester Psychology Dept Rochester NY 14627 Business E-Mail: deci@psych.rochester.edu.

DECIUTIIS, ALFRED CHARLES MARIA, oncologist, television producer; b. NYC, Oct. 16, 1945; s. Alfred Ralph and Theresa Elizabeth (Manko) deCiutiis; m. Catherine L. Gohn. *Family originated in Aquila. Key dates in family history include: 893, first ranked among the nobles of Italy; In 1140, at the assizes of Ariano, merged by Roger II with the Campaneschi; 1527, merger of Italian and Spanish branches; 1629, created "Princes of the Holy Roman Empire"; 1711, ancestor Giovanni Nocerino, discovered remains of Herculaneum; 1860, numbered among Garibaldi's 1000; 1901, Count Salvatore de Ciutiis, translated work leading to Concordate of 1929; 1920s, Count Vincenzo de Ciutiis appointed ambassador to Spain by Italy; Count Vincente de Ciutiis, Count of Madrid, assassinated in Spanish Civil War. The family has both Italian and Spanish branches. Paternal grandfather awarded the order of the Holy Spirit and buried in a church in Naples dedicated to the nobles of Spain. He was also responsible for the renovation of the Church of Santa Chiara in Naples, which was nearly destroyed in World War II. Around the turn if the century, the Marquesa of Salerno was also a de Ciutus. A paternal cousin, Msgr. Vincenzo de Ciutiis, would regularly preside at the famous festival of San Gennero in Naples. Family is related to the Patriazi clan where one member is considered "Blessed" by the Roman Catholic Church.* BS summa cum laude, Fordham U., 1967; MD, Columbia U., 1971. Diplomate Am. Bd. Internal Medicine, Am. Bd. Med. Oncology. Intern N.Y. Hosp.-Cornell Med. Ctr., NYC, 1971-72, resident, 1972-74; fellow in clin. immunology Meml. Hosp.-Sloan Kettering Cancer Ctr., NYC, 1974-75, fellow in clin. oncology, 1975-76, spl. fellow in immunology, 1974-76; guest investigator, asst. physician exptl. hematology Rockefeller U., NYC, 1975-76; pvt. practice specializing in med. oncology LA, 1977—. Mem. adult bone marrow transplant team Memorial Sloan-Kettering Cancer Ctr., 1974—76; chief oncology svc. Miseracordia Hosp. (now Mercy Hosp. Cornell Med. Ctr.), Bronx, NY, 1976; mem. med. adv. com. Olympics, 1984; co-founder Medtrina Med. Ctr., Torrance, Calif., physician asst. supr., 1994; mem. fgn. policy leadership project Ctr. Internat. Affairs, Harvard, Ill. *Dr. deCiutiis was first to note a clinical syndrome in 1976 while at Memorial Sloan-Kettering Cancer Center. Later it became known as Chronic Epstein Bar Virus and still later Chronic Fatigue Syndrome. As a third year medical student he had an article published in The Lancet on the delayed onset of renal failure from a hemolytic transfusion reaction secondary to minor blood group incompatibilities. He, while at R.U. was privileged to work with two professors who already had their Nobel prizes: Drs. George Pallade and René Dubois. Professionally, Dr. deCiutiis was privileged to participate in the care of numerous celebrities including Aristotle Onassis, Nobel Laureate Ralph Bunch, Madam Chang Kai Shek, Acadamy Award Winner Melvin Douglas, and Winthrop Rockefeller, among many other notables.* Host cable TV shows, 1981—, med. editor Cable Health Network, 1983—, Lifetime Network, 1984—; syndicated columnist: Coast Media News, 1980; prodr.: numerous med. TV shows; interviewed: numerous stars; author: (Landmark sci. paper) Defects in the Alternate Pathway of Complement Activation post Splenectomy; contbr. articles to profl. jours. Mem. gov. bd. med. coun. Italian-Am. Found.; mem. Italian-Am. Civic Com., LA, 1983, Cath. League Civil and Rel. Liberty, World Affairs Coun., LA, Boston Mus. Fine Arts, Met. Mus.; founder Italian-Am. Med. Assn., 1982; co-founder Italian-Am. Legal Alliance, LA, 1982—; mem. UCLA Chancellor's Assocs. Served to capt. M.C. US Army, 1972—74. Leukemia Soc. Am. fellow, 1974—76. Fellow: ACP, Internat. Coll. Physicians and Surgeons; mem.: AAAS, AMA (Physician's Recognition award 1978—80, 1982—85, 1986—89, 1989—91, 1991—94, 1994—96, 1996—99, 1999—2002, 2002—04), Am. Soc. Hematology (emeritus), Internat. Platform Assn., Drug Info. Assn., Chinese Med. Assn., Am. Geriat. Soc., Am. Pub. Health Assn., N.Y. Acad. Sci. (life), Internat. Health Soc., Am. Union Physicians and Dentists, Los Angeles County Med. Assn., Calif. Med. Assn., Am. Soc. Clin. Oncology, Mensa, Smithsonian Instn., Nat. Geog. Soc. (life), Fondazione Giovanni Agnelli, Nature Conservancy, Nat. Wildlife Fedn., Sigma Xi, Alpha Omega Alpha, Phi Beta Kappa. Achievements include participated on some of the first bone marrow transplants in the USA; 1st comprehensive clinical description of chronic fatigue syndrome as a neuro-immunologic acquired disorder. Office: PO Box 384 Agoura Hills CA 91376-0384

DECK, RICHARD ALLEN, political scientist, consultant, writer, volunteer; b. Concord, NH, May 6, 1953; s. Herbert Heller Jr. and Eleanor DuVall (Deyo) D.; m. Jo Ann Marie Passariello, Nov. 15, 1986. Student, Ripon Coll., 1972—73, Waseda U., Japan, 1974—75; BA in Polit. Sci. and East Asian Studies summa cum laude with honors, Macalester Coll., 1977; cert. in Urban and Regional Planning and Design, Harvard U., 1978; Grad. Cert. in Brit. Fgn. Policy, Oxford U., Eng., 1980; MA in Econs., Pub. Policy and Adminstrn., U. Manchester, Eng., 1982; M in City Planning, U. Calif., Berkeley, 1982; AM in Polit. Sci., Stanford U., 1985, PhD in Polit. Sci., 1997; MALS, Dartmouth Coll., 1994. Internat./intercultural rels. seminar leader Assn. Current English Keio U., Japan, 1975; mag. writer and interviewer English Jour., Japan, 1975; rschr., writer Dem. Farmer Labor Party, Mpls., 1976; survey rschr. and analyst Project on Volunteerism Adelphi U., LI, 1978; legis. analyst rschr. Assembly Edn. Com. NY State Assembly, Albany, 1979; co-chair external affairs Grad. Assembly U. Calif., Berkeley, 1981—82; fellow internat. peace and security studies Social Sci. Rsch. Coun. and John D. and Catherine T. MacArthur Found., SE Asia, 1986—88; vis. joint fellow nat. and internat. security U. So. Calif., UCLA, 1989; rsch. fellow and project coord. Asian Regionalization Asia/Pacific Rsch. Ctr., Stanford U. and The Asia Found. San Francisco, 1991—92; v.p. Catalyst Concepts, Berkeley, 1992—2000, pres., 2001—; founding dir. Asia/Pacific Reg. Policy Rsch. Inst., Berkeley and Emeryville, Calif., 1998—; prodr., dir. Asian Democracy and Human Rights Webcasting Sta. Alliance for Reform and Democracy in Asia, Berkeley and Emeryville, 2001—. Social sys. dir., bd. dirs. U. Calif. Space Working Group, U. Calif., Berkeley, 1979-82; grad. rep. from Berkeley campus for the student body pres. coun. U. Calif., 1981-82; tchg. asst. Stanford U., Calif., 1983, 86, grad. studies com., 1983-84, head tchg. asst., 1984, observer Project Peace and Coop. Asia-Pacific Region, 1984, internat. rels. sr. faculty search com., 1985-86, co-instr., 1991; seminar group discussion leader, M.A.L.S. Colloquium on Ctrl. Am., Darmouth Coll., 1984; participant Project Soviet Internat. Behavior, U. Calif., Berkeley and Stanford U., 1985-86; lectr. Inst. SE Asian Studies, 1988, Nat. U. Singapore, 1988, Asean Insts. Conf. on US-Asean Rels., Singapore, 1988; conf. participant and delegate 40th Anniv. Commemoration of the Signing of the United Nat. Charter in San Francisco, 1985; ofcl. observer US del. Pacific Econ. Cooperation Coun., PECC Gen. Meeting/Conf., San Francisco, 1992; global media dir. US-SE Asian Alliance for a Dem. Asia, Cambridge, Mass., 1998-2000; cons. Def. & Diplomacy, The Newshour with Jim Lehrer, PBS-TV, Washington and Arlington, Va., 2000; panelist God Governance and Dem. Reform in Asia-Ideals in Action, Press Conf. and Staff Briefing, Congl. Human Rights Caucus, Washington, 2001, Democracy and Human Rights in Asia, ARDA's Democracy Index, Mems. Briefing Congl. Human Rights Caucus, Capitol Hill, DC, 2006; mem. Nat. Bus. Adv. Coun., Washington, 2002-04; cons. Lawyer's Com. on Human Rights, NYC, 2003, Nat. Dem. Inst. Internat. Affairs, Washington, 2003-04, Sweden-Singapore Initiative for Democracy, Olaf Palme Inst., Swedish Internat. Liberal Ctr., Jarl Hjalmarsson Found., Stockholm, Singapore Dem. Party, 2003-06; liason to US Democratic Nat. Convention for Alliance for Reform and Democracy in Asia, Boston, Mass., 2004, ASEAN Sect. leader Burma Pro-Democracy Conf., San Francisco, 2004, organizer, exec. dirs. tour Alliance for Reform and Democracy in Asia, 2004; panel moderator Tibet Day The Presidio, San Francisco, 2005; panelist in field; spkr., lectr. and spkr. in field. Author: US official delegation Dialogue Partners session, First ASEAN Economic Congress, ASEAN Chambers of Commerce and Industry, and the Institute of Strategic and International Studies, 1987, Fourth ASEAN Institutes Conference on the Association of Southeast Asian Nations and the United States, 1988; (with others) Peace, Conflict, and Strategic Cultures in the Asia-Pacific Region, 1999; (with others) The Singapore Puzzle, 1999, Strategic Cultures in the Asia-Pacific Region, 1999 (paper edit.); co-author, co-editor Asia Democracy Index, Singapore, 2005; mem. editl. bd. and survey design team Asia Democracy Index, 2005-, (with others) Those Who Dare: Voices of Asia's Democrats, 2006; mem. editl. bd., edtl. writer, polit. corr., and polit. feature writer Stanford Daily, 1982-83; contbr. articles to profl. jours.; interview subject (TV) Friday Background, Current Affairs Unit, Singapore Broadcasting Corp., 1987, Berita (Evening news), RTM (Malaysian govt. network), 1987, Official Questionner of Malaysian Prime Minister Mahathir bin Mohamad, Iseas Singapore Lecture, Inst. Southeast Asian Studies, 1988, Bada's Draft the Lady Campaign for UN Sec. Gen. Daw Aung San Suu Kyi of Burma, Buddha by the Bay, Berkeley, 2006; (film) co-narrator and co-interviewer The Pennsylvania Underground: The Sanctuary Movement and Illegal Ctrl. Am. Refugees in Philadelphia, 1986; (newspaper) Internat. Herald Tribune, Republic of Singapore, 1987, (radio) The Michael Fay Caning Affair, The World Tonight with Phil Till Show, Radio Can., Vancouver, 1994; spl. contbr. Asiaweek newsmag., Hong Kong, 1998, mem. editl. bd. Asia Democracy Index, Alliance for Reform and Democracy in Asia, Taiwan, 2005-. Chmn. NH Govs.' Youth Hwy. Safety Adv. Com., 1972; del. 40th Anniversary Commemoration of the Signing of the UN Charter in San Francisco: Conf. Assessing the UN After 40 Yrs., UN Assn. San Francisco and World Affairs Coun. No. Calif., 1985; spl. fellowship coord. Open Soc. Inst., NYC, 1997—98, 2000; interim chairperson panel of experts and resource persons on Asian democratization Alliance for Reform and Democracy in Asia, Washington, 2000—01, co-dir. Asia Democracy Index Project Osaka, Japan, Berkeley/Emeryville, 2001—, steering com. Singapore, Washington and Kuala Lumpur, 2004—, liaison ofcl. to US Dem. Nat. Conv. Boston, 2004, West Coast organizer exec. dir.'s tour San Francisco, 2004, co-chair Assn. Scholars and Rschrs. for Asian Dem. Studies Berkeley, Emeryville, 2001—04, US western rep. Emeryville, Calif., 2006—; co-chair Assn. Scholars and Rschrs. for Asian Dem. Studies, Alliance for Reform and Democracy in Asia, 2004—06; bd. dirs., exec. bd. various cities Burmese Am. Dem. Alliance, Calif., 2004—; dir. various campaigns Daly City, Calif., 2006—; panelist on Asia Democracy Index and World Forum for Democratization in Asia Staff Briefing and Press Conf., Congl. Human Rights Caucus, Washington, 2005; del., panelist World Forum for Democratization in Asia, Taipei, 2005; founding mem. Supoort Free Burma, San Francisco, 2007—; Del. candidate NH Pres. preference primary Dem. Nat. Conv., Keene, 1972; Del. candidate Calif. Pres. Primary, Stanford, 1984, Berkeley, 1992; candidate NH Constl. Conv., Keene, 1974; city and campus chair Calif. Dem. Pres. Primary Campaign, Stanford U. and Palo Alto, 1984, 1992; staff intern Minn. Dem. Farmer Labor Party Hdqs., 1976; coord. "Draft the Lady" campaign Daw Aung San Suu Kyi for UN Sec.-Gen. Burmese Am. Dem. Alliance, San Francisco and Union City, 2006; co-coord. Burmese Am. Alliance's and Support Free Burma's Congresspersons, Senator's and Gov.'s Rescue Mission to Rangoon Campaign, San Francisco, Union City and Albany, 2007; dir. Burmese Am. Dem. Alliance's Asian Charter Human Rights Campaign, San Francisco, Union City and Albany, 2007; bd. dirs. U. Manchester Postgrad. Soc., England, 1980—81. Recipient World Affairs Coun. Staff award, 1985, Nat. Small-Bus. Legis. Leadership Achievement award Bus. Adv. Coun., Washington, 2002; Nat. Forensics League scholar Ripon Coll., 1972-73; Harry Sherman scholar Macalester Coll., 1976-77; John W. Searle Meml. scholar Macalester Coll., 1976-77, Outstanding Sr. award, Minn. Jaycees, Coll. Ct. of Honor, 1977; NY State Assembly Grad. Scholar fellow, 1979; Roothbert Fund fellow U. Calif., Berkeley, 1979-80, 81-82; Inst. Internat. Edn. scholar Oxford U., 1980; Rotary Internat. Grad. fellow U. Manchester, 1980-81; Lasker scholar U. Calif., Berkeley, 1981-82; Newhouse fellow U. Calif., Berkeley, 1981-82; Eisenhower Meml. Grad. scholar Stanford U., 1982-83; AMVETS scholar Stanford U., 1982-86; Stanford U. Grad. fellow 1982-86; MALS Grad. fellow Dartmouth Coll., 1984, 86; UN Assn. and World Affairs Coun. scholar, 1985; Fgn. Lang. and Area Studies grantee US Dept. Edn., 1985; SSRC/MacArthur found. fellow in Internat. Peace and Security, NYC and Chgo., 1986-88; USC-UCLA Vis. Joint fellowship in Nat. and Internat. Security, LA, 1989; rsch. fellow Asia/Pacific Rsch. Ctr. Stanford U. and the Asia Found., San Francisco, 1991-92; co-nominee (with Dr. Chee Soon Juan, Singapore) Nobel Peace Prize, 1999-07. Mem. Internat. Studies Assn. (presenter 1998), Assn. Asian Studies, Acad. Polit. Sci., Am. Polit. Sci. Assn., Pi Kappa Delta, Phi Alpha Theta, Pi Sigma Alpha, Phi Beta Kappa. United Ch. of Christ. Avocations: reading, movies. Office: Catalyst Concepts PO Box 8393 Berkeley CA 94707-8393 E-mail: radcatalyst@webtv.net, radcatalyst@gmail.com.

DECKARD, STEVE WAYNE, science educator, academic administrator; b. Lawrenceville, Ill., Apr. 9, 1953; m. Mary E. Chester, May 15, 1982; 1 child, Daniel. BA in Biology, McKendree Coll., 1975; MS, U. Ill., 1980; attended, No. Ill. U., 1981—85, OH U., 1976, Vincennes U., 1976, Parkland Coll., 1978, Beloit Coll., 1983, U. Mo., 1990; EdD in Curriculum and Evaluation, U. Sarasota, 1993. Cert. secondary biology tchr. Ill., 1975, life certs. in biol. scis., profl. edn., supervision, and chief academic officer Calif. CC, 1989, adminstrv. cert. Assn. Christian Schs. Internat., Calif.,

1990, lic. pastor Berean Coll., 1987, Harvest Fellowship, Calif., 2001, notary pub. Calif., 2002. Secondary biology tchr. Ill. Sch. Dists., 1975—83; instr. Kishwaukee Coll., 1984—87; jr. hs educator West Covina Christian Sch., 1988—89; dir. housing McKendree Coll., 1989—90; asst. prof. edn., and sci. The King's Coll., Briarcliff, NY, 1990—93; asst. prof. sci. edn. Inst. Creation Rsch., Santee, Calif., 1991—, cons. to COO and acad. dean, 2006, cons., adj. prof.; v.p. academic affairs Trinity Bible Coll., 1998—2000, Vision Internat. Coll. and U., Ramona, Calif., 2000—04; prof. doctoral studies in ednl. leadership Liberty U., Lynchburg, Va., 2004—, mem. undergraduate honors thesis coms., 2004; mem. dissertation coms. Adj. prof. Newport U., Newport Beach, Calif.; adj. faculty mem. Azusa Pacific U., 1988—98, Bethany Coll., 1994—96, Nat. U., 1996—98; bd. chair Creation Rsch. Resources, 1994—98; adv. bd. mem. Nehemiah Inst.; presenter in field; spkr. in field; cons. in field; program developer in field; workshop and seminar attendee in field. Author: Homes schooling laws all fifty states, 1986, 10th edit., 2002; (with S. DeKoven) Research writing made easy: A guide to writing college papers: The masters thesis, the doctoral dissertation and the doctoral project, 2002, (with D. DeWitt) Worldview studies book one: Developing a Creator-centered worldview, 2003; contbr. articles to profl. jours. Recipient Appreciation cert., Creation Edn. Resources Bd., 1994—98; grantee, Alexander Found., 2001. Mem.: Am. Ctr. Law and Justice. Office Phone: 434-582-2417. Business E-Mail: sdeckard@liberty.edu.

DECKELBAUM, NELSON, lawyer; b. Washington, Apr. 1, 1928; s. Fred and Rose (Egber) D.; m. Louann Jacobs, Oct. 19, 1952; children: David Alan, Todd Stuart. BS, Georgetown U., 1950, JD, 1952. Bar: D.C. 1952, Md. 1957, U.S. Supreme Ct. 1966. Practice law, Washington, 1952—; sr. ptnr. Deckelbaum Ogens & Raftery, Chartered, 1974—. Staff mem. Commn. on Govt. Security, 1956; dir. Independence Savs. Bank. Chmn. Democratic precinct, Montgomery County, Md., 1958. Served with USAF, 1952-54. Named in Best Lawyers in Am. Fellow Am. Coll. Bankruptcy; mem. ABA, Md. Bar Assn., D.C. Bar Assn., Am. Judicature Soc., Georgetown U. Alumni Assn., Woodmont Country Club, Univ. Club (pres. 1994-95). Home: 4200 Massachusetts Ave NW Apt 115 Washington DC 20016 Office: Deckelbaum Ogens & Raftery 3 Bethesda Metro Ctr Bethesda MD 20814-5330 Office Phone: 301-961-9200. E-mail: ndeckelbaum@deckelbaum.com.

DECKELMAN, WILLIAM L., JR., lawyer; b. Crossett, Ark., Aug. 19, 1957; s. William and Marion Deckelman; m. Lisa Deckelman. BA, Ark. State U., 1978, MBA, 1979; JD, U. Ark., 1981. Bar: Tex. 1982. Assoc. Winstead Sechrest & Minick, Dallas, 1981—85; with MTech Corp. (acquired by Electronic Data Systems Corp. in 1988), 1985—88; sr. v.p., gen. counsel, sec. Affiliated Computer Services Inc., Dallas, 1989—93, exec. v.p., gen. counsel, sec., 1993—95, 2000—, dir., 2000—03; atty. pvt. practice, 1995—2000; mng. shareholder Munsch Hardt Kopf & Harr PC, Austin, Tex., 1996—2000. Mem.: State Bar Tex. Office: Affiliated Computer Services Inc 2828 N Haskell Bldg 1 Dallas TX 75204 Office Phone: 214-841-6144. E-mail: bill.deckelman@acs-inc.com.*

DECKER, BRETT M., bank executive; b. Sandusky, Ohio, Nov. 5, 1970; s. John Erie and Sharon Rose Decker. BA, Albion Coll., Mich., 1989—93; MA, Johns Hopkins U., Balt., 1996—99, US Naval War Coll., Newport, RI, 2007. Tchg. asst. Gerald R. Ford Inst., Albion, Mich., 1991—92; litig. law clk. Office of Gen. Coun. Ford Motor Co., Dearborn, Mich., 1995; nat. polit. reporter Evans & Novak Inside Report, 1996—99; tv prodr., script writer, booker Insights with Robert Novak, 1996—99; Wash. polit. corr. Nat. Cath. Register, Hamden, Conn., 1998; speechwriter, editorialist Office of Majority Whip Tom Delay US Ho. Reps., 1999—2000; editl. page writer Wall St. Jour., Hong Kong, 2000—03; editor Asian culture & thought page Asian Wall St. Jour., Hong Kong, 2001—03; editl. writer Far Ea. Econ. Rev., Hong Kong, 2001—03; editl. bd. mem. Wash. Times, 2003—04; spokesman, speechwriter to bd. dirs. Export-Import Bank US, 2004—05, sr. v.p., 2005—. Author: (biography) The Global Filipino, 2006, (book manuscript) Terror in the Jungle: Al Qaeda's Threat to America from Southeast Asia; contbr. columns in newspapers. Founder, chmn. Decker Found. for Philippine Free Press, Alexandria, Va., 2004—. Recipient award for commentary writing on human rights in China, Amnesty Internat., 2002; grantee Journalism fellowship, Phillips Found., 2003. Mem.: Nat. Press Club, Overseas Press Club, Detroit Athletic Club, Fgn. Correspondents' Club Hong Kong (life; gov. 2002—03), Sigma Chi Frat. (life; pres. 1992—92). Republican. Roman Catholic. Avocations: military history, motoring, baseball, poetry, Latin liturgy. Office: Export-Import Bank US 811 Vermont Ave NW Washington DC 20571 Office Phone: 202-565-3200. E-mail: brett.decker@exim.gov.

DECKER, JOHN WILLIAM, metal products executive; b. Cleve., July 15, 1948; s. James William and Betty Erdmann (Smith) Decker; m. Elaine Marie Metz, Aug. 30, 1971; children: Amanda Elaine, Gregory John. BS, Lincoln Meml. U., 1966-70; MEd, Kent State U., Ohio, 1970-72. Cert. tchr., adminstr. Ohio. Elem. tchr. Parma (Ohio) City Schs., 1970-78; corp. sec., treas. Decker Steel & Supply, Inc. (formerly Decker Reichert Steel & Supply, Inc.), Cleve., 1978-83, v.p., 1983-85, pres., chmn., CEO, 1985—. Mem. Am. Theater Orgn. Soc., Plahouse Sq. Vol. Group; co-chmn. cmty. fin. com. Parma City Schs., 1994—97; apptd. Parma Bd. Edn., 1997, elected, 1998—2001, v.p., 1999—, pres., 2000—01; ruling elder Parma South Presbyn. Ch., Parma Heights, Ohio, 1979—81, 1983—92, 1996—, clk. of session, 1983—94, chmn. fin. com., 1995—96, 2004—06, chmn. properties coun., 1997—2000, properties chair, 2005—07, adminstrv. coun. chairperson, 2001. Mem.: Greater Cleve. Growth Assn., Masons. Republican. Avocations: choral group singing, pipe organ playing, repair and building, collecting antique telephones, collecting victorian lighting. Home: 9634 Greenbriar Dr Cleveland OH 44130-4756 Office: 4500 Train Ave Cleveland OH 44102-4515 Home Phone: 440-888-7192.

DECKER, MARK JONATHAN, radiologist; b. Suffern, NY, Oct. 3, 1966; s. Alan Barry and Shelley Decker; m. Dina Loren, June 12, 1993; children: Jake, Alexandra, Nicholas, Christopher. BS, Union Coll., Schnectady, NY, 1988; postgrad., NYU, NYC, 1988—89; MD, Mt. Sinai Sch. Medicine, NYC, 1993. Diplomate Am. Bd. Radiology. Radiology resident Mt. Sinai Hosp., Miami, Fla., 1993—97; musculoskeletal fellow Hosp. Spl. Surgery, NYC, 1997—98; dir. MRI Radiologic Health Sci., Smithtown, NY, Port Jefferson, NY, 1998—2001; dir. orthop. radiology Zwanger & Peseri, Plainview, NY, Massapequa, NY, 2001—04; dir. MRI & orthop. radiology Met. Diagnostic Imaging P.C., NYC, Forest Hills, Garden City, Bklyn., 2004—. Mem.: Radiologic Soc. N.Am., Am. Coll. Radiology, Soc. Skeletal Radiology. Avocations: hockey, soccer, lacrosse, baseball, drums.

DECKER, MICHAEL JOHN, neuroscientist; b. Chattereaux, France, Mar. 5, 1960; s. Ronald Malcolm and Barbara Janet Decker; m. Debra Dee Williams, Aug. 10, 1991; 1 child, Michael John. BN, Case Western Res. U., Cleve., 1994, PhD, 1999. Respiratory Therapist Ohio Respiratory Care Bd., 1990; RN Ohio Bd. of Nursing, 1994. Dir. clin. svcs. Fusion Sleep, Suwanee, Ga., 2005—; asst. prof. neurology Emory U. Sch. of Medicine, Atlanta, 2000—; adj. prof. Ga. State U., Atlanta; vis. scientist Centers for Disease Control, Atlanta. Medcial adv. bd. InVacare Corp., Elyria, Ohio, 2005—; cons. Medcare/Flaga, Reykjavik, Iceland, 2002—05; consulant Respironics, Murrysville, Pa., 1991—95; cons. Medtronics, Mpls., 1991—92. Recipient Rsch. Excellence Award, Am. Profl. Sleep Soc., 1999, Steward Award in Anatomy, Case Western Res., 1999; grantee High Altitude Studies in Tibet, Bolivia, Ethiopia, Nat. Geog., 1991-1995, Episodic Neonatal Hypoxia Impairs Sleep & Cognition, NIH, 2001-2005. Office: Fusion Sleep 4265 John s Creek Pkwy Suwanee GA 30024 Home Phone: 678-352-7790; Office Phone: 678-990-3962. Office Fax: 678-840-3777; Home Fax: 678-840-3777. Personal E-mail: mdecker@emory.edu. E-mail: mdecker@fusionsleep.com.

DECKER, MICHAEL LYNN, lawyer, judge; b. Oklahoma City, May 5, 1953; s. Leroy Melvin and Yvonne (Baird) D. BA, Oklahoma City U., 1975, JD, 1978; grad., Nat. Jud. Coll., U. Nev., Reno, 1990. Bar: Okla. 1978, U.S. Ct. Appeals (10th cir.) 1979, U.S. Dist. Ct. (we. dist.) Okla. 1985, U.S. Supreme Ct. 1994, U.S. Ct. Appeals (5th cir.) 2004. Assoc. Bay, Hamilton, Lees, Spears, and Verity, Oklahoma City, 1978-80; assoc. dir. devel. Oklahoma City U., 1980-81, asst. dean, Sch. of Law, 1981-82; sr. oil and gas adminstrv. law judge Okla. Corp. Commn., Oklahoma City, 1982-92, sr. asst. gen. counsel oil and gas conservation, 1992-95, deputy gen. counsel oil and gas conservation, 1995—2005, dir. office adminstrv. procs., 2005—. Campaign staff intern US Senator Henry Bellmon's Re-election Campaign, 1974; mem. Civil Arbitration Panel, US Dist. Ct. (we. dist.) Okla., 1985—; mem. dean's adv. com. Oklahoma City U. Law Sch., 1986; mem. sys. rev. bd. Okla. Corp. Commn., 1990-93, mem. process mgmt. rev. team, 1995-96; mem. legal and regulatory affairs com. Interstate Oil and Gas Compact Commn., 2000—, mem. coun. state oil and gas attys., 2001-, chair, 2004-05; mem. revision subcom. Model Oil and Gas Conservation Act, Interstate Oil and Gas Compact Commn., 2003; lectr., spkr. in field. Trustee Oklahoma City U., 1989—91, mem. alumni bd. dirs., 1986—2000; mem. com. of twenty Oklahoma City Art Mus., 1987—95, co-chair omelette party, 1990; vol. Contact Teleminister, Oklahoma City, 1986—91; mem. Class XI Leadership Oklahoma City, 1993; area rep. Okla. Mozart Festival, Bartlesville, 1988—; pres. alumni assn. Oklahoma City U., 1988—92; youth shelter vol. Okla. Lawyers for Children, 2006—; mem. FBI Citizens Acad., Okla., 2006; mem. adminstrv. bd. St. Luke's United Meth. Ch., 1988—92, chair missions com., 1993—94; mem. nat. alumni bd. dirs. Oklahoma City U., 2000—, mem. devel., long range planning, adminstrv. liaison, student rels., centennial alumni banquet and centennial coms.; bd. dirs. Eldercare Access Ctr., Inc., 2001—06, Contact Teleminister, Oklahoma City, 1987—90, March of Dimes Western Okla., 1990—93. Mem.: Oklahoma City Mineral Lawyers Soc., Okla. County Bar Assn. (exec. com. young lawyers sect. 1978—82, mem. law day com. 1979—88, chmn. law day luncheon spkr. com. 1979—88), Okla. Bar Assn. (chair environ. law sect. 2007, mem. mineral law sect.), Raymer Soc. for the Arts (bd. dirs., Lindsborg, Kans. 1999—2005, sec. 2002—05, long range planning com. 2006—), Lions, Lambda Chi Alpha (Outstanding Alumnus award 1983, treas. bldg. corp. 1984—89, pres. 1989—91), Phi Alpha Delta. Republican. Home: 2008 NW 44th St Oklahoma City OK 73118-1902 Office: Okla Corp Commn State Capitol Complex Jim Thorpe Bldg PO Box 52000 Oklahoma City OK 73152-2000 Office Phone: 405-521-2241. Personal E-mail: bloomin2@cox.net.

DECKER, RAYMOND FRANK, chemicals and metal products executive; b. Afton, NY, July 20, 1930; s. Bernett Hurd and Mildred (Bisbee) Decker; life ptnr. Mary Birdsall, Dec. 27, 1951; children: Susan, Elizabeth, Catherine, Laura. BS, U. Mich., Ann Arbor, 1952, MS, 1955, PhD, 1958. With Inco Ltd., 1958-82, v.p. corp. tech. and diversification ventures, 1978-82; v.p. rsch. and corp. rels. Mich. Technol. U., Houghton, 1982-86; pres., CEO Univ. Sci. Ptnrs., Inc., 1986-98; pres. ASM Internat., 1986-87; founding chmn., pres., CEO Thixomat, Inc., 1988—2004, chair, pres., CEO, 2004—05, also bd. dirs., CTO, 2005—; founding chmn. Wavemat, Inc., 1987-88. Bd. dirs. Lindberg Corp., 1989—2001, Spl. Metals Corp., 1990—2003; adj. prof. Poly. Inst. Bklyn., 1962—66, NYU, 1968, U. Mich., 1997—; cons. KMS Fusion, Inc., Howmet turbine Components, Alcoa, GE, GM, 1985—; Van Horn Disting. lectr. Case-Western Res. U., 1975; mem. materials adv. bd. NASA, 1969, Nat. Bur. Stds., 1973, NSF, 1985—86; mem. Nat. Materials Adv. Bd., 1982—88; mem. exec. com. Strategic Hwy. Rsch. Program, 1986—93; long-range planning com. Metall. Soc., 1985—87, State Rsch. Fund Panel Mich., 1983—86; chmn. rsch. & tech. coordinating com. Fed. Hwy. Adminstrn., 1995—98; trustee Foundry Ednl. Found., 1975—77, Welding Rsch. Coun., 1975—80; chmn. bd. trustees Mich. Energy and Resource Rsch. Assn., 1985—86; keynote spkr. on superalloys Seven Springs Conf., 1980, NAE, 1980—. Author: (book) Strengthening Mechanisms in Nickel-Base Superalloys; editor: Maraging Steels. Chmn. alumni com. dept. material sci. and engring. U. Mich., Ann Arbor, chmn. class of 1952 reunion; chmn. Ch. Coun., 2001—03. Recipient IR-100 award, 1964, Sesquicentennial award, U. Mich., 1967, Disting. Grad. award, 1994, Innovation award, Mobile Computing, 1999, Inc 500 award, 1999. Fellow: Am. Soc. Metals Internat. (chmn. materials sys. and design divsn. 1971—73, trustee 1976—79, chmn. diamond decade com. 1980—81, Campbell Meml. lectr. 1985, chmn. organizing com. World Materials Congress 1988, hon. mem. 1991, Alpha Sigma Mu lectr. 2001, Woodside lectr. 2003, Gold medal 1981); mem.: NAE, AAAS, AIME (lectr. Inst. Metals divsn. 1973, R. F. Mehl medal 1973), Afton Ctrl. Sch. Alumni Assn. (v.p. 2004—). Congregationalist. Achievements include co-inventing maraging steels, Thixomolding machine. Home: Apt 204 505 E Huron Ann Arbor MI 48104 Office Phone: 734-995-5550. Business E-Mail: rdecker@thixomat.com.

DECKER, RICHARD JEFFREY, lawyer; b. Manhasset, NY, Aug. 26, 1959; s. Alan B. and Shelley T. (Belkin) D.; m. Carrie Ann Gordon, Aug. 13, 1989. BA, Union Coll., Schenectady, NY, 1981; JD, Boston U., 1984. Bar: N.Y. 1985, Calif. 1985, Mass. 1985, U.S. Dist. Ct. (cen. dist.) Calif. 1985. Assoc. Turner, Gesterfeld, Wilk & Tigerman, Beverly Hills, Calif., 1985-86, Shapiro, Posell & Close, LA, 1986-90, Katten, Muchin, Zavis & Weitzman, LA, 1990-93; ptnr. Stephan, Oringher, Richman Theodora & Miller, LA, 1993—. Mem. Los Angeles County Bar Assn., Beverly Hills Bar Assn., Century City Bar Assn. Avocations: sports, guitar playing, travel, reading. Office: Stephen Oringher Richman Theodora & Miller 2029 Century Park E Ste 600 Los Angeles CA 90067-2907

DECKER, RICHARD KNORE, lawyer; b. Lincoln, Nebr., Sept. 15, 1913; s. Fred William and Georgia (Kilmer) Decker; m. Fern Iona Steinbaugh, June 12, 1938. AB, U. Nebr., 1935, JD, 1938. Bar: Nebr. 1938, U.S. Supreme Ct. 1941, D.C. 1948, Ill. 1952. Trial atty. antitrust div. Dept. Justice, 1938-52; ptnr. Lord, Bissell & Brook, Chgo., 1953-84, of counsel, 1984—2005. Trustee Village of Clarendon Hills (Ill.), 1960-64; chmn. bd. elders Community Presbyn. Ch., Clarendon Hills, 1963-66; mem. Union Ch. of Hinsdale; chmn. bd. Community House, Hinsdale, Ill., 1976, Robert Crown Ctr. for Health Edn., Hinsdale, Ill., 1981-83, also bd. dirs, 1976-2005. With USNR, 1942-45, lt. comdr. ret. Mem. ABA (chmn. antitrust sect. 1971-72), Ill. Bar Assn. (gov. 1969-73, chmn. antitrust sect. 1964-66), Chgo. Bar Assn. (chmn. antitrust law com. 1956-59), The Lawyers Club Chgo., Hinsdale Golf Club (pres. 1968). Republican. Home: 196 Pheasant Hollow Dr Burr Ridge IL 60527-5051

DECKER, ROBERT OWEN, history professor, clergyman; b. Lafayette, Ind., Nov. 6, 1927; s. Samuel Owen and Helen Dale (Noble) D.; m. Margaret Ann Harris, May 30, 1948 (dec. July 2005); 1 child, Terry Lynn Decker DeIulis; m. Jeannine Adams Pitkin, March 11, 2006. AB, Butler U., 1953; AM, Ind. U., 1958; PhD, U. Conn., 1970. Ordained to ministry Congregational Ch., 1990. Instr. City of LaPorte (Ind.) Schs., 1956—59, Ctrl. Conn. State U., New Britain, 1959-63, asst. prof., 1963-73, assoc. prof., 1973-77, prof. history, 1977-89, prof. emeritus, 1989—. Editor manuscripts Wesleyan U. Press, 1977-89; advisor NEH, 1977-89, Connecticut River Found. Author: Whaling Industry of New London, 1973, The Whaling City: A History of New London, 1976, A Student Guidebook to American History, 1983, Hartford Immigrants, 1987, The New London Merchants, 1986, Cromwell, Connecticut 1650-1990: The History of A River Port Town, 1991; contbr. articles and book revs. to profl. jours. Mem. Christian Activities Coun., Hartford, 1965—, pres., 1972-74, 76-78, historian, 1983—, life mem., 1996—; bd. dirs. Hartford Inner City Exch., 1971-81, chmn. bd., 1977-80; chmn. state legis. adv. com. Conn. Devel. Disabilities Coun., 1973-75; evaluator programs Conn. Humanities Coun.; historian Rocky Hill (Conn.) Congl. Ch., 1985-89, Conn. 350th Com., 1985-89; justice of peace, Rocky Hill, 1985-89, 2000—, constable, 1986-89, 2002-06, apptd. town historian, 1988—; mem. Assn. Conn. Mcpl. Historians, 1988—, membership sec., 1994—, pres., 1996-97; pastor Eagle Rock Congl. Ch., 1989-93, Bozrah Centre Congl. Ch., 1994-95, supply pastor, 1995-2001; mem. exec. bd. Conn. Congl. Christian Chs., 1995-2001; pastor Barkhamstead Ctr. Congl. Ch., 2001—; mem. UCC Hist. Com., 1989-92, Rep. Town Comm., Rocky Hill, 2000—; dir. Old Towne Tourism Dist. Conn., 1989-90; justice of peace, 1998—. Served with U.S. Army, 1946-52. Asian Studies grantee, 1959; Am. Studies grantee, 1959; Danforth grantee, 1962; Munson Maritime grantee, 1961; Smithsonian Inst. grantee, 1963; recipient Pierport Edwards award Grand Lodge Ct., 2003. Mem. AAUP, Orgn. Am. Historians, Am. Hist. Assn., New Eng. Hist. Assn., Conn. Hist. Assn., Assn. for Study of Conn. History, New London County Hist. Soc., Am. Waldensian Aid Soc. (pres. Hartford chpt. 1986-89), Masons (Master Stepney Lodge 1990, 92, Master's award 1992, Arthur E. Warner award 1996, Master Silas Dean Lodge 2001-02, 2003-2004, Grand Chaplain 1997-2003, High Priest Delta chpt. 1998-99, Knight Mason 1998—, master Philosophic Lodge Rsch., worshipful master 2000-01, Master's award 2001, 2002, eminent comdr. 2001—02, thrice illustrious master Walcott Coun. I 2000-01, high priest 2001—02, assoc. grand prelate, 2002-), Royal Arch Masons (Pierpont Edward Bronze medal 2003), Masonic Vet. Assn. Conn. (Venerable Master 2005-06), Phi Alpha Delta. Republican. Congregationalist (life deacon). Home: 2623 Main St Rocky Hill CT 06067-2507 Office: Barkhamsted Cong Ch 6 Olde Town Hall Rd Pleasant Valley CT 06063 Office Phone: 860-379-5864. E-mail: decker7900@sbcglobal.net.

DECKER, ROGER WALTER, biologist, researcher; b. Troy, NY, Aug. 9, 1971; BS in Biology, Mercy Coll., Dobbs Ferry, NY, 2000. Rsch. assoc. Genzyme Pharmaceuticals, Okla. City, 2000—04; scientist ii Wyeth, Sanford, NC, 2004—. Author: (book) Uproar (Best Writer Okla. City award, 2004). Mem.: ASME. Home: 2772 Mallard Cove Rd Sanford NC 27330 Office: Wyeth Pharmaceuticals 4300 Oak Pk Sanford NC 27330 Home Phone: 919-478-9307; Office Phone: 919-478-9307. Personal E-mail: roger3841@yahoo.com.

DECKER, SUE (SUSAN LYNNE DECKER), Internet company executive; b. Nov. 1962; married; 3 children. BS in Computer Sci. & Economics, Tufts U., 1984; MBA, Harvard U. Cert. Charterd Fin. Analyst. With Donaldson, Lufking & Jenrette (DLJ), 1986—2000, publ. and advtsg. rsch. anlayst, dir. global head rsch., 1998—2000; sr. v.p. fin. & adminstrn. Yahoo! Inc., Sunnyvale, Calif., 2000—02, CFO, 2000—07, exec. v.p. fin. & adminstrn., 2002—07, exec. v.p, head advt. & pub. group, 2007, pres., 2007—. Mem. Fin. Acctg. Standards Adv. Coun., 2000—04; bd. dir. Costco Wholesale, 2004—. Stanford Inst. of Econ. & Policy Rsch., 2005—, Intel Corp., 2006—, Berkshire Hathaway. Named one of 50 Women to Watch, Wall St. Jour., 2006, 50 Who Matter Now, Business 2.0, 2007. Office: Yahoo! 701 1st Av Sunnyvale CA 04089*

DECKER, WALTER JOHNS, toxicologist; b. Tannersville, NY, June 13, 1933; s. H. Russell and Leola May (Coons) D.; m. Barbara Allen Hart, Aug. 19, 1961; children: Karl Hart, Reid Johns, Sam Travis. BA, SUNY, Albany, 1954, MA, 1955; PhD, George Wash. U., Washington, DC, 1966. Commd. 2d lt. US Army, 1955, advanced through grades to lt. col., 1970, ret., 1975; assoc. prof. U. Tex. Med. Br., Galveston, 1976-83; pres. Toxicology Cons. Svcs., El Paso, Tex., 1984-97. Adj. clin. prof. Tex. Tech. U., El Paso, 1991—. Contbr. articles to jours. Clin. Toxicology, Vet. and Human Toxicology, Toxicology and Applied Pharmacology, others. Mem. sci. rev. panel Nat. Libr. Medicine's Hazardous Substance Data Bank, Bethesda, Md., 1985-2000; chair steering com. West Tex. Poison Ctr., El Paso, 1994-96. Recipient Aesculapius award, Tex. Med. Assn., 1977, Career Achievement award, Am. Acad. Clin. Toxicology, 2001. Fellow: Am. Acad. Clin. Toxicology (Career Achievement award 2001); mem.: Soc. Toxicology. Episcopalian. Achievements include research in toxicology. E-mail: bdecker173@centurytel.net.

DECKER, WAYNE LEROY, meteorologist, educator; b. Patterson, Iowa, Jan. 24, 1922; s. Albert Henry and Effie (Holmes) D.; m. Martha Jane Livingston, Dec. 29, 1943; 1 dau., Susan Jane. BS, Central Coll., Pella, Iowa, 1943; postgrad., UCLA, 1943-44; MS, Iowa State U., 1947, PhD, 1955. Meteorologist U.S. Weather Bur., Washington and Des Moines, 1947-49; mem. faculty U. Mo. at Columbia, 1949—, prof. atmospheric sci., 1958-67, prof., chmn. dept. atmospheric sci., 1967-91, prof. emeritus, 1992—, dir. coop. inst. applied meteorology, 1985-92; cons. climatologist, 1992—. Chmn. com. climatic fluctuations and agrl. prodn. NRC, 1975-76; bd. dirs. Council for Agrl. Sci. and Tech., 1978-85, mem. exec. com., 1981-85; chair organizing com. 16th Internat. Congress Biometeorology. Fellow Am. Meteorol. Soc.; mem. Internat. Soc. Biometeorology (treas. 1990-99, chair, 16th Internat. Congress Biometeorology), Am. Geophys. Union, Am. Agronomy Soc., Sigma Xi, Gamma Sigma Delta. Home: 23 Springer Dr Columbia MO 65201-5424 Office: Univ Mo 302A Anheuser-Busch Natural Resources Bl Columbia MO 65211-7040 Personal E-mail: janewaynedeck@centurytel.net.

DECKERS, PETER JOHN, dean; b. Boston, Feb. 13, 1941; married, 1964; 7 children. BA cum laude, Coll. of the Holy Cross, 1962; MD cum laude, Boston U., 1966. Diplomate Nat. Bd. Med. Examiners, Am. Bd. Surgery. Med. intern Boston City Hosp., 1966—67; jr. asst. resident gen. surgery Boston U. Med. Ctr., Univ. Hosp., 1967—68; clin. assoc. surgery br. Nat. Cancer Inst., NIH, Bethesda, 1968—70; resident gen. surgery Boston U. Med. Ctr., U. Hosp., 1971, UPSHS trainee in acad. surgyer, 1971—72, resident in gen. surgery, 1972—73, chief resident in gen. surgery, 1973—74; staff surgeon Boston City Hosp., 1974—84; asst. to assoc. prof. surgery Boston U. Sch. Medicine, 1974—78; dean U. Conn. Sch. of Medicine, 1995—2000, dean sch. of medicine and exec. v.p. health affairs, 2000—. Attending staff gen. surgery John Dempsey Hosp./U. Conn. Health Ctr., 1984—, VA Med. Ctr., 1984-89; sr. staff dept. surgery Hartford Hosp., 1984—; program dir. Hartford Hosp.-U. Conn. Integrated Surg. Residency Program, 1984-94; dir. divsn. of gen. surgery Hartford Hosp., 1984-87; sr. staff dept. surgery New Britain Gen. Hosp., 1989—, Dept. Surgery, Mt. Sinai Hosp., 1989—, St. Francis Hosp. and Med. Ctr., 1988—; chmn. dept. surgery Hartford Hosp., 1987-94, Murray-Heilig prof., chmn. dept. surgery U. Conn. Sch. of Medicine, 1987-95; surgeon-in-chief John Dempsey Hosp., 1990-94; program dir. U. of Conn. Integrated Gen. Surg. Residency Tng. Program, 1990-94; interim dean, 1992-94; exec. v.p. for clin. affairs U. Conn. Health System, 1994-95; exec. v.p. for physician practice orgn. U. Conn. Health System, 1995—. Editl. bd. Breast Surgery: Index and Reviews, 1993, Surg. Oncology, 1991; contbr. numerous articles to profl. jours. Recipient First Prize James Ewing Resident Rsch. award, 1971; recipient numerous grants. Mem. Transplantation Soc., Am. Assn. for Cancer Rsch., Eastern Coop. Oncology Group, Assn. for Acad. Surgery, Am. Assn. for Cancer Edn., Am. Fedn. for Clin. Rsch., Mass. Med. Soc., Am. Radium Soc. (exec. com. 1989-91), Am. Soc. of Clin. Oncology, Soc. of Surg. Oncology (mem. coms.), Soc. of Univ. Surgeons, New England Cancer Soc. (pres. 1993, pres.-elect 1992, exec. coun. 1991-94), Boston Surg. Soc., Societe Internationale de Chirurgie, Bay State Health Care, Soc. for the Surgery of the Alimentary Tract, New England Surg. Soc. (treas. 1996-98, pres. 1999), Assn. of Program Dirs. in Surgeons (pres.-elect 1990-91, pres. 1991-92), Conn. State Med. Soc. (mem. cancer coordinating com. 1990-91), Am. Cancer Soc. (Hartford chpt.), Connecticare, Hartford

County Med. Assn., Soc. of Surg. Chmn. Home: 44 Heritage Dr Avon CT 06001 Office: Univ Conn Health Ctr 263 Farmington Ave Farmington CT 06030-3800 E-mail: deckers@nso.uchc.edu.

DECKROSH, HAZEN DOUGLAS, retired state agency educator and administrator; b. Defiance, Ohio, Apr. 13, 1936; s. Lawrence L. and Martha L. Deckrosh; m. Carol Ann Everett, Nov. 25, 1970; children: Stephanie, Todd, Douglas, Nadia Nicole. BS, Ohio No. U., 1959; MEd, U. Toledo, 1980. Cert. tchr., Ohio. Phys. edn. and history tchr., coach Waynesfield (Ohio)-Goshen Jr. High Sch., 1959-61; coach, history, phys. edn. tchr. Coshocton (Ohio) Sacred Heart High Sch., 1961-63; health-phys. edn. tchr., coach West Holmes Jr. High Sch., Millersburg, Ohio, 1965-70; tchr. history and govt., coach Elida High Sch., 1970-73; occupational work experience tchr.-coord., coach Spencerville (Ohio) High Sch., 1973-77; occupational work edn. tchr., coord. Four County Vocat. Sch., Archbold, Ohio, 1977-82, 99—; vocat. supr. Jefferson County Vocat. Sch., Steubenville, Ohio, 1986-87; occupational work experience tchr., coord. Ohio Dept. of Youth Svcs., Columbus, 1987-94; ret., 1994. Pres. DYS Coordinators, Columbus, 1990-94; ski instr. Swiss Valley, Mich., 1995—; GED instr. Correction Ctr. Northwest Ohio. Editor: Threaded Fasteners, 1987; contbr. articles to profl. publs. Mem. Am. Youth Hostels, Lima, 1972—. Mem. NEA, Ohio Edn. Assn., Am. Vocat. Assn., Ohio Vocat. Assn., Occupl. Work Experience Coords. Assn. (state adv. coun., Lima rep. 1977-80, Columbus rep. 1991-94), Full Gospel Bus. Men's Fellowship Internat., Gideons Internat. (treas., then sec.), 5th Dist. Ofcls. Assn. (v.p., rules interpreter), Capitol West Umpires Assn. (rules interpreter 1991-93), Lima Umpires Assn. (sec.-treas. 1973-77), Ret. Tchrs. Assn. (pres.), Alpha Sigma Phi. Republican. Avocations: sports officiating, high school and college sports, teaching skiing. Home: 12265 County Road 150 Montpelier OH 43543-9613 Personal E-mail: blazinghazen@aol.com.

DECLERCQ, NICO FELICIEN, research scientist; b. Kortrijk, Belgium, Dec. 27, 1975; s. M. Declercq and N. Vangheluwe, adopted s. P. Vangheluwe and J. Verbrughe; m. Shirani O. de Silva, Feb. 25, 1978; children: Benjamin Jonathan Howard, Anna-Laura Florence Marion. BS, KULeuven Campus Kortrijk, Belgium, 1996; MS (hon.), KULeuven U., Belgium, 2000; PhD, Ghent U., Belgium, 2005; PhD (hon.), 2005. Doctoral rschr. Ghent U., Belgium, 2001—05, post-doctoral rschr., 2005—06; asst. prof. Ga. Inst. Tech., George W. Woodruff Sch. Mech. Engring., Atlanta, 2006—. Author 35 sci. papers, articles in sci. jours.; actor: (50 papers in conf. proceedings). Recipient Internat. Dennis Gabor award, Hungarian Parliament, 2006, Early Career award, Internat. Commn. Acoustics, 2007; grantee, NATO, NSF, Belgium. Mem.: IEEE, Am. Inst. Physics, Russian Acoustical Soc., French Acoustical Soc., Acoustical Soc. Am. Achievements include discovery of physical explanation of the Quetzal echo at the pyramid of Chichen Itza, Mexico and the acoustics of the famous Greek theater of Epidaurus; research in mystery of chirping pyramid decoded; explanation of extraordinary acoustics of Hellenistic amphitheatre of Epidaurus in Greece. Office: Ga Inst Tech George W Woodruff Sch Mech Engring 801 Ferst Dr Atlanta GA 30332-0405 Address: Georgia Tech Lorraine 2 rue Marconi 57070 Metz France Home Phone: 32 478 666719. Personal E-mail: declercq@ieee.org.

DE CONCINI, DENNIS, lawyer, retired senator, consultant; b. Tucson, May 8, 1937; s. Evo and Ora (Webster) DeC.; children: Denise, Christina, Patrick Evo. BA, U. Ariz., 1959, LLB, 1963. Bar: Ariz. 1963, D.C. 1963. Mem. firm Evo DeConcini; founder, ptnr. DeConcini & McDonald, Tucson, 1968-73; dep. Pima County atty. Sch. Dist. 1, 1971-72, county atty., 1972-76; U.S. Senator from Ariz., 1977-95; ptnr. De Concini, McDonald, Yetwin & Lacy, Tuscon, 1995—, Washington, 1995—, Parry, Romani, DeConcini & Symms, Washington, 1995—. Mem. appropriations com., U.S. Senate, chmn. subcom. on Treasury, Postal Svc. and Gen. Govt.; mem. subcom. on Def., subcom. on Energy and Water Devel., subcom. on Fgn. Ops., subcom. on Interior Related Agys.; mem. Jud. com.; chmn. subcom. on Patents, Copyrights and Trademarks; mem. subcom. on Antitrust, Monopolies and Bus. Rights, subcom. on the Constitution, com. on Rules and Adminstrn., com. on Vets. Affairs; chmn. select com. on Intelligence; chmn. Commn. on Security and Cooperation in Europe; select com. Indian Affairs; mem. Internat. Narcotics Control Caucus, West Coalition of Senators; former pres., bd. dirs. Shopping Ctrs., Inc.; bd. dirs. Fed. Home Mortgage Corp., Schuff Steel, Ariz. Bd. Regents, 2006-. Chmn. legis. com. Tucson Dem. Cmty. Coun., 1966-67; mem. major gifts com., devel. fund drive St. Joseph's Hosp., 1970, mem. devel. coun., 1971-73; chmn. bd. dirs. Nat. Ctr. Missing and Exploited Children, 2004-05; mem. major gifts com. Tucson Mus. and Art Ctr. Bldg. Fund, 1971; adminstr. Ariz. Drug Control Dist., 1975-76; precinct committeeman Ariz. Dem. Ctrl. Com., 1958—; mem. Pima County Dem. Ctrl. Com., 1958-67, Dem. State Exec. Com., 1958-68; state vice chmn. Ariz. Dem. Com., 1964-66, 70-72; vice chmn. Pima County Dem. Com., 1970-73. Served to 2d lt. JAG U.S. Army, 1959-60. Named Outstanding Ariz. County Atty., 1975 Mem. ABA, NAACP, Nat. Dist. Attys. Assn., Am. Judicature Soc., Ariz. Bar Assn., D.C. Bar Assn., Ariz. Sheriffs and County Attys. Assn., Ariz. Pioneer Hist. Soc., Pima County Bar Assn., U. Ariz. Alumni Assn., Pres.'s Club, Tucson Fraternal Order Police, Phi Delta Theta, Delta Sigma Rho, Phi Alpha Delta. Roman Catholic.: 2525 E Broadway 111 Tucson AZ 85716 Office Phone: 202-547-4000. Business E-Mail: ddeconcini@lobbycongress.com.*

DE CONINGH, LISE N., language educator; b. Milagro, Spain, June 13, 1957; arrived in US, 1981; d. Jean and Marie Navarro; m. Mathew de Coningh, Apr. 3, 1959; children: Isabelle, Matthew. BA, Paris U. X, Nanterre, France, 1984; EdM, John Carroll U., Cleve., 1998. Tchr. Les Violettes, Mantes la Jolie, France, 1976—77, Jean Macé, Les Mureaux, France, 1977—80, Denver Internat. Sch., 1980—86, Jules Ferry, St. Germain, France, 1986—87, Hathaway Brown Sch., Shaker Heights, Ohio, 1987—. Mem.: Am. Coun. Tchg. Fgn. Langs. Office: Hathaway Brown Sch 19600 N Park Blvd Shaker Heights OH 44122

DECOSTA, BENJAMIN R., airport executive; BA in Physics, Queens Col.; JD, NY Law Sch., 1975. With Port Authority NY, 1972—78; chief of staff, personnel and labor relations City of NY, 1978—83; gen. mgr. Newark Int. Airport, NJ, 1994—98; gen. mgr. aviation Hartsfield-Jackson Internat. Airport, Atlanta, 1998—. Office: Dept Aviation Hartsfield-Jackson Internat Airport 6000 N Terminal Pkwy, PO Box 20509 Atlanta GA 30320

DECOSTANZO, MARYBETH, language educator; b. Jersey City, Mar. 11, 1961; d. Ida DeCostanzo. B in Liberal Studies, Ind. U., Bloomington; MA in TESOL, Fairleigh Dickinson U., Madison, NJ; postgrad., Monmouth U. Events mktg. mgr. AT&T/Lucent Techs., Basking Ridge, NJ, 1984—2000; lang. specialist, ESL tchr. Perth Amboy, NJ, 2003—. Home: 36 Mountain Ct Bedminster NJ 07921

DE COU-LANDBERG, MICHELLE V., retired language educator; b. Chalon-Sur-Saône, France, Sept. 16, 1934; arrived in US, 1963, naturalized; d. Lucien-Louis and Suzanne (Fourneret) Vuillermet; m. James Herbert De Cou (div.); children: Claire De Cou-Rizzi, Michel-David De Cou, Jacques-Frédéric De Cou; m. Erik W. Landberg. Licence d'anglais, U. Dijon, France, 1957; postgrad., Claremont Grad. Sch., Calif., 1960—61; MA in English Lit., George Mason U., Fairfax, Va., 1976. Cert. English and French tchr. Va., 1967, elem. edn. Va., 1987. French asst. Diss Grammar Sch., Norfolk, England, 1956—57; English tchr. French govt., Chambéry Savoie, 1958—59, St. Jean de Maurienne, 1960—61, Luang-Prabang, Laos, 1961—62; French tchr. Arlington County Pub. Schs., Va., 1967—68, Fairfax County Pub. Schs., Fairfax, Va., 1972—73, ESL tchr., 1975—96; ret., 1996. Del. to Vietnam Citizen Ambs. Program, 1994. Author: The Global Classroom, vol. 1, 1994, vol. 2, 1995; contbr. articles to profl. jours. Pres. Common Ground Found., Reston, Va., 1977—79, Herndon-Reston F.I.S.H., Herndon, Va., 1982—85; chmn. coll. and career bound program Kids R First, Reston, 2000—. Named Reston Citizen of Yr., Reston Cmty. Assn., 1981; recipient Golden Eagle award, Fairfax County Pub. Schs., 1994; Fulbright travel scholar, 1960—67. Mem.: TESOL (chmn. elem. edn. sect. 1993). Democrat. Buddhist. Avocations: travel, hiking, genealogy, human rights issues. Personal E-mail: aillon@aol.com.

DE COURTEN-MYERS, GABRIELLE MARGUERITE, retired neuropathologist; b. Fribourg, Switzerland, Aug. 8, 1947; came to U.S., 1979; d. Maurice Edmond and Margrit (Wettstein) de Courten; m. Ronald Elwood Myers, Apr. 18, 1981; 1 child, Maximilian. BSBA, Akademikergemeinschaft, Zurich, Switzerland, 1967; MD, U. Zurich, 1974. Resident in psychiatry Hopital Psycho-Geriatrique, Gimel, Switzerland, 1974-75; resident in pediatrics U. Hosp. Zurich, 1977; resident in neuropathology U. Hosp. of Lausanne, Switzerland, 1976-78; rsch. assoc. NIH, Bethesda, Md., 1979-80; fellow in neuropathology Coll. of Medicine U. Cin., 1980-83, asst. prof. neuropathology Coll. of Medicine, 1983-88, assoc. prof. neuropathology Coll. of Medicine, 1988-89, tenured assoc. prof. Coll. of Medicine, 1989, full prof., 1999—2001; ret., 2007—. Cons. Vets. Affairs Med. Ctr., Cin., 1983—2006, Children's Hosp. Med. Ctr., Cin., 1984—2005, Good Samaritan Hosp., Cin., 1990—; adj. prof., U. Cin., 2001-07. Grantee VA, 1985—, NIH, 1986-90, 93—, Am. Heart Assn., 1991-94, Am. Diabetes Assn., 1995. Mem Am. Assn. Neuropathologists, Am. Acad. Neurology, Soc. Exptl. Neuropathology. Office: U Cin Coll of Medicine Dept Pathology PO Box 670529 231 Bethesda Ave Cincinnati OH 45267-0529 Home Phone: 513-625-6251; Office Phone: 513-558-0148.

DECRANE, ALFRED CHARLES, JR., petroleum company executive; b. Cleve., June 11, 1931; s. Alfred Charles and Verona (Marquard) DeCrane; m. Joan Elizabeth Hoffman, July 3, 1954; children: David, Lisa, Stacie, Stephanie, Sarah, Jennifer. BA, U. Notre Dame, 1953; JD, Georgetown U., 1959; LHD (hon.), Manhattanville Coll., 1990; DJD (hon.), U. Notre Dame, 2002. Cert. Va. Bar, 1959, D.C. Bar, 1959, Tex. Bar, 1961, N.Y. Bar, 1966. Legal dept. Texaco, Inc., Houston, 1959—65, NYC, 1964—66, asst. to vice chmn. bd., 1965—67, asst. to chmn. bd., 1967—68, gen. mgr. producing dept. Eastern hemisphere, 1968—70, v.p., 1970—76, sr. v.p., gen. counsel, 1976—77, sr. v.p., dir., 1977—78, exec. v.p., 1978—83, pres., 1983—86, chmn. bd. dirs., 1987—96, chmn., chief exec. officer, 1993—96. Life trustee U. Notre Dame. 1st lt. USMC, 1954—55. Mem.: ABA (sect. sec. 1964—67). Achievements include co-founder Natural Resources Law Jour. mineral law sect. Office: PO Box 1247 Greenwich CT 06836-1247

DECROSTA, SUSAN ELYSE, graphic designer; b. Cambridge, Mass., Aug. 28, 1956; d. Joseph Mario and Gertrude Ermelinda (Galligani) DeC. BFA, Mass. Coll. Art, Boston, 1980. certified art tchr., supr. Graphic artist Nixdorf Computer Corp., Burlington, Mass., 1981—86; artist, illustrator Rivers, Trainor, Doyle, Providence, 1987; lead artist, illustrator Raytheon Co., Andover, Mass., 1986—94; graphic designer Raytheon Svc. Co., Burlington, Mass., 1994—2004; art dir. Raytheon Tech. Svc., Burlington, 2004—. Freelance graphic artist, 1980—; guest spkr. to design and illustration students Northeastern U., 1992. Publ. Graphic Design U.S.A. Mag., 2000 (Am. Graphic Design award, 2000, 2003, 2005). Vol. AIDS Action Com., Boston; bd. dirs. Jeannette Neill Dance Scholarship Program, Boston, 1999-2006. Recipient Excellence award Soc. Tech. Comm. and Art Direction, 1986, In-House Am. Graphic Design awards Graphic Design USA Mag., 2005, 06, Graphic Design award Graphic Design USA, 2006, others. Mem.: Design Mgmt. Inst., Women's Initiative Network, Art Alumni Assn. Avocations: dance, painting. Office: Raytheon 880 Technology Dr Billerica MA 01821 Office Phone: 978-424-8541. Personal E-mail: sdecrosta1@verizon.net.

DECROW, KAREN, lawyer, educator, writer; b. Chgo., Dec. 18, 1937; d. Samuel Meyer and Juliette (Abt) Lipschultz; m. Alexander Allen Kolben, 1960 (div. 1965); m. Roger DeCrow, 1965 (div. 1972, dec. 1989). BS, Northwestern U., Evanston, Ill., 1959; JD, Syracuse U., NY, 1972; DHL (hon.), SUNY, Oswego, 1994. Bar: NY, US Dist. Ct. (no. dist.) NY. Resorts editor Golf Digest mag., Evanston, Ill., 1959-60; editor Am. Soc. Planning Ofcls., Chgo., 1960-61; writer Ctr. for Study Liberal Edn. for Adults., Chgo., 1961-64; editor Holt, Rinehart, Winston, Inc., NYC, 1965; textbook editor L.W. Singer, Syracuse, NY, 1965-66; writer Ea. Regional Inst. for Edn., Syracuse, 1967-69, Pub. Broadcasting System, 1977; tchr. women and law, 1972-74; nat. bd. mem. NOW, 1968-77, nat. pres., 1974-77, also nat. politics task force chair; cons. affirmative action; pvt. practice, Jamesville, NY, 1974—. Lectr. topics including law, gender, internat. feminism to corps., polit. groups, colls. and univs., US, Can., Mex., Finland, China, Greece, former USSR; nat. coord. Women's Strike for Equality, 1970; moot ct. judge, 1974--; NY State del. Internat. Women's Yr., 1977; originator Schs. for Candidates; participant DeCrow-Schlafly ERA Debates, from 1975; founder (with Robert Seidenberg, MD) World Woman Watch, 1988; gender issues advisor Nat. Congress for Men; mem. Task Force on Gender Bias. Author: (with Roger DeCrow) University Adult Education: A Selected Bibliography, 1967, American Council on Education, 1967, The Young Woman's Guide to Liberation, 1971, Sexist Justice, 1974, First Women's State of the Union Message, 1977, (with Robert Seidenberg) Women Who Marry Houses: Panic and Protest in Agoraphobia, 1983, Turkish edit., 1988, 2d Turkish edit., 1989, United States of America vs. Sex: How the Meese Commission Lied About Pornography, 1988, (with Jack Kammer) Good Will Toward Men: Women Talk Candidly About the Balance of Power Between the Sexes, 1994; editor: The Pregnant Teenager (Howard Osofsky), 1968, Corporate Wives, Corporate Casualties (Robert Seidenberg, MD), 1973; contbr. articles to USA Today, NY Times, NY Times Bus. Sect., LA Times, Chgo. Tribune, Nat. Law Jour., Women Boston Globe, Vogue, Mademoiselle, Ingenue, Newsday, Chgo. Sun Times, Penthouse, Washington Post, LA Times Mag., Policy Review, Miami Herald, Internat. Herald Tribune, Social Problems, Houston Chronicle, Pitts. Press, Nat. NOW Times, Syracuse U. Mag., San Francisco Chronicle, Civil Rights Quar., Women Lawyers Jour., other newspapers, mags.; regular columnist: Syracuse New Times, 1985—; columnist NY Times Spl. Features; recording: Opening Up Marriage, 1980. Hon. trustee Elizabeth Cady Stanton Found.; active Hon. Com. to Save Alice Paul's Birthplace; Liberal party candidate for Mayor of Syracuse, 1969. Recipient Profl. Recognition award for best newspaper column Syracuse Press Club, 1990, 94, 95, 96, 2000, Best Column award, 1994-95, 99, 2001, 02, Best Column award NY Press Assn., 1991-92, 95, award Barnard Coll., Vet. Feminists of Am. and the Barnard Ctr. for Rsch. on Women, Woman of Achievement/Distinction award Gov. George E. Pataki, 1998; Svc. to Soc. award Northwestern U. Alumni Assn., 2002, Achievement award The Post-Standard, Syracuse, 2003; named to Hall of Achievement Medill Sch. Journalism Northwestern U., 2007. Mem. NOW (pres. 1974-77, bd. dirs. 1968-74, v.p.), ACLU (Ralph E. Kharas Disting. Svc. in Civil Liberties award 1985), NY Women's Bar Assn. (ctrl. NY chpt. pres. 1989-90, jud. screening com., Joan L. Ellenbogen Founder's award 2003, Doris Hoffman medal 2005), Women's Bar Assn. State NY (founder, Ctrl. NY chapt., 1977, judicial screening com., ctrl. NY chapt. pres., 1989-90, nom. com., 1996, 2001, Doris Hoffman medal 2005), NY Bar Assn., Onondaga County Bar Assn. (profl. ethics com., fed. cts. com., grievance com., co-chair membership com. 2006, governance com. 2006, nominating com. 2006, bd. dirs. 2005—), Elizabeth Cady Stanton Found. (trustee), Feminists for Free Expression (adv. com.), Abortion Rights Mobilization (bd. dir.), Nat. Coalition Against Censorship, Working Women's Inst. (bd. advisors), Syracuse Friends Chamber Music, Atlantic States Legal Found., Yale Polit. Union (hon. life), Nat. Congress Men (gender issues advisor), Mariposa Edn. and Rsch. Found., Nat. Coun. Children's Rights (adv. panel), Wilderness Soc., Northwestern U. Alumni Assn., Women's Inst. Freedom Press, Art Inst. Chgo., Nat. Women's Polit. Caucus, Theta Sigma Phi. Address: 7599 Brown Gulf Rd Jamesville NY 13078-9636 Office Phone: 315-682-2563. *I feel especially lucky to be able to participate, as Holmes said, in the passion of our times. The movement to create equality between women and men is the most interesting and exciting during this period in history. My goal is a world where the gender of a baby will have little or no relevance to future pursuits or pleasures - personal, political, economic, social, or professional. It is exhilarating to watch society change in that direction.*

DECTER, EDWARD M., orthopedist, surgeon; b. 1948; BS, U. Md., 1970; MD, Creighton U., 1975. Diplomate Am. Bd. Orthopaedic Surgeons. Intern Temple U. Sch. Medicine, 1975—76; resident Hosp. Joint Diseases Orthopaedic Inst., NYC, 1976—80; attending orthopaedic surgeon St. Barnabas Med. Ctr., Livingston, NJ. Med. dir. West Orange Sports Medicine Ctr., 1980—86; team physician St. Benedicts Prep, NJ, 1993—, NJ Cosmos, 1995, NJ Dragons, 1996, NJ Riptide, 1996, NY Red Bulls (formerly NY/NJ MetroStars), 1999—, NJ Gladiators, 2002—03, NJ Storm, 2004; cons. Tahuichi Soccer Acad., Bolivia, 1999—. Contbr. articles to med. jours. Named one of Best Doctors in NY, NY Mag., 1999, Am.'s Top Surgeons, Consumer's Rsch. Coun. Am., 2002—03. Fellow: Am. Coll. Surgeons; mem.: Essex County Med. Soc., Am. Orthopaedic Soc. Sports Medicine, Am. Bd. Soc. for Sports Medicine, Knee Surgery and Sports Medicine, Internat. Soc. Arthroscopy, Arthroscopy Assn. N.Am., Am. Coll. Sports Medicine, Am. Med. Soccer Assn. Avocations: fishing, boating, golf, tennis, skiing. Office: Ctr Orthopaedics Ste 101 1500 Pleasant Valley Way West Orange NJ 07052 also: St Barnabas Ambulatory Care Ctr Sports Medicine Inst 200 S Orange Ave Livingston NJ 07039 Office Phone: 973-322-7330, 973-669-5600. Office Fax: 973-669-0269.*

DECTER, MIDGE, writer; b. St. Paul, July 25, 1927; d. Harry and Rose (Calmenson) Rosenthal; m. Norman Podhoretz, Oct. 21, 1956; children: Rachel, Naomi, Ruth, John. Student, U. Minn., 1945-46, Jewish Theol. Sem. Am., 1946-48. Asst. editor Midstream mag., 1956-58; mng. editor Commentary, 1961-62; editor Hudson Inst., 1965-66, CBS Legacy Books, 1966-68; exec. editor Harper's mag., 1969-71; book review editor Saturday Rev./World mag., 1972-74; sr. editor Basic Books, Inc., 1974-80; exec. dir. Com. for Free World, 1980-90; sr. fellow Inst. on Religion and Pub. Life, 1991—95. Author: The Liberated Woman and Other Americans, 1971, Liberal Parents, Radical Children, 1975, The New Chastity and Other Arguments Against Women's Liberation, 1997, An Old Wife's Tale: My Seven Decades in Love and War, 2001, Losing the First Battle, Winning the War, 2002, Rumsfeld: A Personal Portrait, 2003; mem. editl. bd.: First Things. Bd. dirs. Heritage Found., Ctr. for Security Policy, Phila. Soc.; founding mem. Coalition for Dem. Majority; former dir. Nicaraguan Freedom Fund. Recipient Nat. Humanities medal, 2003. Home: 120 E 81st St New York NY 10028-1428

DECUIR, BRYAN JUDE, automotive technician, computer engineer; b. New Rhodes, La., July 6, 1965; s. Eugene Noel DeCuir and Vera Mae Gossarand-DeCuir; m. Stephanie Ruth Baerga; children: Bryanna Joy, Ashley Rhae Grisby, Aralynne Nicole Baerga-Green, Elanni Arabella Baerga-Washington. Cert. master ASE technician ASE, Va., state inspector State of Va., Catepillar cert. Va., GM electronics cert. Va., Ford electronics Va., Bendix cert. Va. Sr. automotive technician II City of Hampton (Va.) Fleet Svcs., 1995—. Computer engr. Q's Autmotive, Newport News, Va., 1992—. Decorated S.W. Asian medal, Good Conduct medal. Mem.: Moose (life; legioneer 2005). Office: City of Hampton Fleet Svcs 413 N Armistead Ave Hampton VA 23669 Home Phone: 757-888-2788; Office Phone: 757-726-2958. Personal E-mail: bryandecuir@yahoo.com.

DEDE, MEHMET ISMET CAN, robotics researcher, educator; b. Bergama, Izmir, Turkey, June 19, 1977; s. Mustafa Ruhi and Nur Dede. BSc in Mech. Engring., Istanbul Tech. U., Turkey, 1995—99; MSc in Mech. Engring. with honors, Mid. E.Tech. U., Ankara, Turkey, 2000—03. Mechatronics design engr. Aselsan, Inc., Ankara, 2000—03; rsch. asst., instr. Fla. Internat. U., 2003—. Organizing com. chair Fla. Conf. Recent Advances in Robotics, Miami, 2006—06. Contbr. articles to profl. jours. Mem.: ASME, Turkish Student Assn., Fla. Internat. U. (pres. 2003—), Delta Epsilon Iota, Phi Beta Delta. Home: 2899 Collins Ave Apt 1403 Miami Beach FL 33140 Office: Fla Internat Univ 10555 W Flagler St Miami FL 33174 Home Phone: 305-498-4476. Business E-Mail: cdede002@fiu.edu.

DEDERICH-PEJOVICH, SUSAN RUSSELL, harpist; b. Rockville Center, NY, Oct. 4, 1951; d. Robert Marwood and Martha Annette (Geffs) D.; m. Svetozar Pejovich; 1 child, Mira Zorina. B. Performing Arts, Cleve. Inst. Music, 1973; student of, Alice Chalifoux. Prin. harpist Oklahoma City Symphony, 1973-74, New Orleans Symphony, 1974-77, Dallas Symphony, 1977—; adj. prof. harp So. Meth. U. Mem. contemporary music ensemble Voices of Change; founder Flute, Viola, Harp Trio Triptych; condr. So. Meth. U. Harp Ensemble; co-dir. Adriatric harp workshop, Krk, Yugoslavia, Summer Festival, Purgatory, Colo., Killington (Vt.) Music Festival; founder, mem. October Trio, 2002—. Musician: Dallas Mus., So. Meth. U., U. North Tex. Office: care Dallas Symphony Orch 2301 Flora St Ste 300 Dallas TX 75201-2404

DEDERICK, ROBERT GOGAN, economist; b. Keene, NH, Nov. 18, 1929; s. Frederic Van Dyck and Margaret (Gogan) D.; m. Margarida N. Magalhaes, Aug. 24, 1957; children: Frederic, Laura, Peter. AB, Harvard U., 1951, AM, 1953, PhD, 1958; postgrad., Cornell U., 1953-54. Econ. research mgr. New Eng. Mut. Life Ins. Co., Boston, 1957-64; assoc. economist No. Trust Co., Chgo., 1964, v.p., assoc. economist, 1965-69, v.p., economist, 1969-70, sr. v.p., chief economist, 1970-81, exec. v.p., chief economist, 1983-94, econ. cons., 1994—2003; mem. panel of econ. advisers Congl. Budget Office, 1991—2004; mem. econ. adv. bd. U.S. Commerce Dept., 1968-70, 75-76, 83-85, asst. sec. commerce for econ. affairs, 1981-82, under sec. commerce for econ. affairs, 1982-83; prin. RGD Econs., Hinsdale, 1994—. Fellow: Nat. Assn. Bus. Economists (pres. 1973—74, governing coun. 1969—75); mem.: Internat. Conf. Comml. Bank Economists, Am. Bankers Assn. (alumni coun.), Harvard Discussion Group Indsl. Economists, Conf. Bus. Economists (chmn. 1984—85), Dutch Settlers Soc. Albany, Capitol Hill Club, Hinsdale Golf Club, Harvard Club, Econ. Club. Home: 113 S County Line Rd Hinsdale IL 60521-4722 Office: RGD Economics 113 S County Line Rd Hinsdale IL 60521-4722 Office Phone: 630-325-7183. Personal E-mail: rdederick@aol.com.

DEDIO, ROBERT, otolaryngologist; BA, Colgate U., Hamilton, NY, 1981; MD, NYU, 1985. Intern Hosp. U. Pa., 1985—86, resident, 1986—90; asst. chief otolaryngology divsn. Leigh Valley Hosp., Allentown, Pa., 1991—. Fellow: ACS; mem.: Am. Acad. otolaryngology.

DEDMAN, BILL, journalist; b. Chattanooga, Oct. 14, 1960; s. Harold C. and Bobbye (Griswold) Dedman; m. Pamela J. Belluck, Sept. 5, 1993; children: Justin, Arielle, Jillian. Student, Wash. U., St. Louis, 1978—81. Reporter Warrensburg (Mo.) Star-Jour., 1981, Blue Springs (Mo.) Examiner, 1981—82, Chattanooga Free Press, 1983, Chattanooga Times, 1984—86, Knoxville News-Sentinel, 1986—87, Atlanta Journal-Constitution, 1987—89, Washington Post, 1989—91; fellow Freedom Forum Media Studies Ctr. Columbia U., NYC, 1992—93; contbg. writer Mother Jones Mag., 1993—94; dir. computer-assisted reporting AP, 1994—97; writer N.Y. Times, 1997—2001; corr. Boston Globe, 2001—05; mng. editor Telegraph, Nashua, NH, 2005—. Hearst vis. fellow U. Md.

Coll. Journalism, 1993—94; lectr. Northwestern U. Recipient Pulitzer Prize for investigative reporting, 1989, Robert F. Kennedy Journalism award grand prize, 1989, Worth Bingham prize, 1989, numerous others. Mem.: Investigative Reporters and Editors (bd. dirs. 1990—96, award 1989).

DEDRICK, JAMES R., prosecutor; Atty. US Dept. Justice, Knoxville, Tenn., 1983—; 1st atty. US Attys. Office, Ea. Dist. Tenn., 1989—, US Attys. Office, Ea. Dist. N.C., 1992-93; US atty. (ea. dist) Tenn. US Dept. Justice, 2005—. Office: US Attys Office 800 Market St Ste 211 Knoxville TN 37902-2342*

DE DUVE, CHRISTIAN RENÉ, chemist, educator; b. Thames-Ditton, Surrey, Eng., Oct. 2, 1917; s. Alphonse and Madeleine (Pungs) de Duve; m. Janine Herman de Duve, Sept. 30, 1943; children: Thierry, Anne, Françoise, Alain. MD, U. Louvain, Belgium, 1941, PhD, 1945; grad., Med. Nobel Inst., Stockholm, 1946—47; MSc, U. Louvain, Belgium, 1946; PhD (hon.), U. Turin, 1969, U. Leiden, 1970, U. Sherbrooke, 1970, U. Lille, 1973, Cath. U. Santiago, Chile, 1974, U. René Descartes, Paris, 1974, State U. Liege, 1975, State U. Ghent, 1975, Gustavus Adolphus Coll., St. Peter, Minn., 1975, U. Rosario, Argentina, 1975, U. Aix-Marseille II, 1979, U. Keele, 1982, Katholieke U. Leuven, 1984, Karolinska Inst., Stockholm, 1986, U. Montreal, 1992, Rockefeller U., 1997. Lectr. physiol. chemistry faculty medicine Cath. U. Louvain, 1947—51, prof., head dept. physiol. chemistry, 1951—85, emeritus prof., 1985—. Prof. biochem. cytology Rockefeller U., NYC, 1962—74, Andrew W. Mellon prof., 1974—88, prof. emeritus, 1988—; vis. prof. Albert Einstein Coll. Medicine, Bronx, NY, 1961—62, Chaire Francqui State U. Ghent, 1962—63, Free U., Brussels, 1963—64, State U., Liège, 1972—73, Facultés U. Notre-Dame de la Paix, Namur, 1990—91; Mayne guest prof. U. Queensland, Brisbane, Australia, 1972; pres. Internat. Inst. Cellular and Molecular Pathology, Brussels, 1974—91. Mem. editl. bd.: Subcellular Biochemistry, 1971—87, Preparative Biochemistry, 1971—80, Molecular and Cellular Biochemistry, 1973—80; author: A Guided Tour of the Living Cell, 1984, Blueprint for a Cell, 1991, Vital Dust, 1995. Conseil d'adminstrn. Fonds Nat. de la Rsch. Sci., 1958—61; conseil de gestion Fonds de la Rsch. Sci. Médicale, 1959—61, commn. sci., 1958—61; com. experts Conseil Nat. de la Politique Sci., 1958—61; adv. bd. Ciba Found., 1960—85; adult devel. and aging rsch. and tng. rev. com. Nat. Inst. Child Health and Devel., NIH, 1970—73; adv. com. for med. rsch. WHO, 1974—79; sci. adv. com. Max Planck-Inst. for Immunbiology, 1975—78, Ludwig Inst. Cancer Rsch., 1985—91, Mary Imogene Bassett Rsch. Inst., 1986—90, Clin. Rsch. Inst. Montreal, 1986—; biology adv. com. N.Y. Hall of Sci., 1986—; adv. sci. com. Basel Inst. for Immunology, 1989—93. Recipient Prix des Alumni, 1949, Prix Pfizer, 1957, Prix Francqui, 1960, Prix Quinquennal Belge des Scis. Médicales, Belgium, 1967, Merit award, Gairdner Found. Internat., Can., 1967, Dr. H.P. Heineken prize, The Netherlands, 1973, Nobel prize for physiology or medicine, 1974, Theobald Smith award, Albany Med. Coll., 1981, Jimenez Diaz award, 1985. Fellow: AAAS; mem.: NAS, Soc. Belge Physiology, N.Y. Acad. Scis., Internat. Soc. Cell Biology, European Cell Biology Orgn., European Molecular Biology Orgn., European Assn. Study Diabetes, Koninklyke Acad. voor Geneeskunde, German Acad. der Naturforscher Leopoldina, Soc. Belge Biochim. (pres. 1962—64), Soc. Chimie Biologique, Am. Soc. Cell Biology (coun. mem. 1966—69, E.B. Wilson award 1989), Pontifical Acad. Sci., Am. Soc. Biol. Chemists, Am. Philos. Soc., Biochem. Soc. (Harden award 1978), Am. Chem. Soc., Royal Acad. Belgium, Royal Acad. Medicine, German Assn. for Cell Biology (assoc.), Acad. Europaea (assoc.), Acad. Scis. d'Athénes (assoc.), Acad. Scis. Paris (assoc.), Royal Soc. Can. (assoc.), Royal Soc. London (assoc.), Am. Acad. Arts and Scis. (assoc.), Sigma Xi. Address: Rockefeller U 1230 York Ave New York NY 10021-6399 Mailing: ICP 75 Ave Hippocrate B-1200 Brussels Belgium

DEE, FRANCIS X., lawyer; b. NYC, July 13, 1944; BA, Manhattan Coll., 1966; JD, Cath. U. Am., 1969; LLM in Labor Law, NYU, 1975. Bar: N.Y. 1970, N.J. 1972, U.S. Supreme Ct. 1981. Atty. NLRB, 1969-72; labor counsel Litton Industries, 1972-76; sr. ptnr. Carpenter, Bennett & Morrissey, 1976—2004, McElroy, Deutsch, Mulvaney & Carpenter, LLP, Newark, 2004—. Fellow Am. Coll. Trial Lawyers (NJ state chmn. 1999-01, regent, 2005—), Internat. Acad. Trial Lawyers, Coll. Labor and Employment Lawyers, Am Bar Found.; mem. ABA (litigation sect., com. on devel. law under nat. labor rels. act labor and employment law sect. 1975—), NY State Bar Assn. (litig., labor and employment law sects.), NJ State Bar Assn. (litig. sect., del. to gen. coun. 1985-92, exec. bd. 1983-92, mgmt. co-chair com. on practice and procedure under nat. labor rels. act 1980-83, sec. labor employment law sect. 1987-89, vice chmn. 1989-91, chmn. 1991-92). Essex County Bar Assn., Trial Attys. NJ (Trial Bar award), Fed. Bar Assn. Office: McElroy Deutsch Mulvaney and Carpenter LLP Three Gateway Ctr 100 Mulberry St Fl 17 Newark NJ 07102-4004 Home Phone: 201-656-5350; Office Phone: 973-565-2018, 973-425-8708. Business E-Mail: fdee@mdmc-law.com.

DEE, IVAN RICHARD, book publisher; b. Chgo., Mar. 11, 1935; s. Jack Arthur and Jeanette Rose (Melcher) D.; m. Sandra Cohen, June 21, 1959 (div. 1973); m. Phyllis Kirz, Aug. 3, 1977 (div. 1981); m. Barbara Burgess, Apr. 15, 1989; children: Alexander, Sara, Jacob, Gabriel. BJ, U. Mo., 1956, MA, 1957. Pres. Ardivan Press, Macon, Ga., 1960-61; v.p., editor-in-chief Quadrangle Books, Chgo., 1961-72; assoc. editor Chgo. Tribune Book World, Chgo., 1972-73; exec. editor Pubs.-Hall Syndicate, Chgo., 1973-74; editor-in-chief Chicagoan Mag., Chgo., 1974-75; dir. pub. affairs Michael Reese Hosp. and Med. Ctr., Chgo., 1975-89; pres. Ivan R. Dee, Inc., Chgo., 1989—. V.p. South Side Planning Bd., Chgo., 1975-89; commr. Chgo. Baseball League, 1978-00; mem. adv. bd. Nat. Great Books Curriculum Acad. Cmty., 2005—. Lt. (j.g.) USN, 1957-60. Office: Ivan R Dee Inc 1332 N Halsted St Chicago IL 60622-2624 Business E-Mail: idee@ivanrdee.com.

DEE, RONDA, poet, photographer, small business owner, journalist; b. Bronx, NY, May 6, 1943; d. Maurice Dee and Rachel Hoffer. AA, Manhattan CC, NYC, 1974; BS, NYU, 1976. Cert. Isadora Duncan Dance Workshop, 1995, Trager massage Dallas. Sec. Book of Knowledge, NYC, 1962; pvt. tutor City Coll., 1963; tchr. head start Lennox Hill Neighborhood Assoc., NYC, 1970; tchr. k-3 NW Harlee Elem. Sch., Dallas, 1977; sec. City of Dallas, 1977; tchr., summer reading prog. Texas Dept. Human Resources, Dallas, 1978; pvt. practice childcare, 1980—83; adminstrv. asst. Contact Dallas Telephone Crisis Counseling, 1980; journalist Brookhaven Sch. News The Courier, Dallas, 1987; pvt. practice, 2004—; distbr., dealer Eco-Quest Internat. Co. Living Air Ozone Machines; journalist, photographer Decoy newspaper, Richland Coll., 2004—05, comedy writer, 2004—05, newspaper comedy writer, 2004—05; journalist Richland Chronicle, Dallas, 2003—; journalist, staff writer The Courier, Brookhaven Coll., 1987; news reporter Richland Coll. Web Radio, 2006. Pupeteer children's ward Mt. Sinai Hosp., 1968; adminstrv. asst. Contact Dallas, 1990; featured reader Barnes & Noble Booksellers, 2000—02; distbr. Cell Tech. Health Foods, 1991—95; radio reporter Richland Coll., 2005. Exhibitions include Brookhaven Coll., Dallas, 1988, Ward Nass Gallery, 1995, Mem. D'Art, Dallas, 1997, Wells Fargo Bldg. Plano, Tex., Richland Coll., 2002—03, 500 X Gallery, Dallas, 2003—04, Richland Coll., 2004—05, exhibited in group shows at Oak Lawn Pub. Libr., Dallas, 2006 (2d pl. digital prints); photographer Photograph: Walls of New York City, 2002, Touch of Tomorrow, 2004, Labour of Love, 2005, Timeless Voices, Internat. Libr. Poetry, 2006; author, photographer: Parallex, 2002—05; contbg. writer Rough Times, 1970; contbr. articles to profl. jours. and newspapers;, author numerous poems; actor: Hands Across the Sea; (documentaries) Homelessness, 1985; extra (films) Veritas, Prince of Truth, 2004. Intake sec. Big Brother and Big Sisters, Dallas, 1981; mem. Concerned Citizens Pesticide Control, Dallas, 2003—; social svc. worker Holy Trinity Ch., 1983—85. Named Digital Printshow winner, Richland Coll., 2005, 1st Pl Poetry winner; recipient Founders Day award, NYU, 1976, Juried Art Contest winner for charcoal design collage, Brookhaven Coll., 1986, League Innovation award, Richland Coll., 2002—04, 2006. Mem.: Tex. Visual Arts Assn., Internat. Soc. Photographers, Internat. Soc. Poets, Sierra Club, Phi Theta Kappa. Avocations: camping, theater, films, exercise, drums. Home: PO Box 823478 Dallas TX 75382-3478 Home Phone: 972-221-7511. Personal E-mail: rondadee2001@yahoo.com.

DEE, RUBY (RUBY DEE DAVIS), actress, writer, film director; b. Cleve., Oct. 27, 1924; d. Marshall Edward and Emma (Benson) Wallace; m. Ossie Davis, Dec. 9, 1948 (dec. Feb. 4, 2005); children: Nora, Guy, Hasna. BA, Hunter Coll., 1945; ArtsD (hon.), Fairfield U.; BA (hon. doctorate), Iona Coll., Va. State U.; apprentice, Am. Negro Theatre, 1941-44; LHD (hon.), SUNY, Old Westbury, 1990; DFA, Spelman Coll., 1991. Ind. actress, writer, dir., v.p. Emmslyn II Prodns., 1945—. Author: (poetry) Glowchild, 1972, (musical) Take It from the Top, (collected poetry, humor, short stories) My One Good Nerve, co-author (with Ossie Davis): With Ossie & Ruby: In This Life Together, 1998 (Grammy award for Best Spoken Word Album, 2007), Life Lit by Some Large Vision: Selected Speeches & Writings, 2006; adaptor: (African folk tales) Two Ways to Count to Ten, The Tower to Heaven, (play) Books With Legs, 1993; contbr. column NY Amsterdam News; co-writer (film) Uptight; dir., adaptor (stage prodn.) Zora is my Name!, 1983; stage appearances include Jeb, 1946, Raisin in the Sun, 1959, Purlie Victorious, 1961, The Imaginary Invalid, 1971, Wedding Band, 1972 (Drama Desk award 1972), Boesman and Lena, 1970 (Obie award 1971), Anna Lucasta, Taming of the Shrew, Checkmates, 1988, The Glass Menagerie, 1989, Flyin West, 1994, Two Hah-Hahs and a Homeboy, 1995; actress: (films) Gone are the Days, The Jackie Robinson Story, 1950, Take a Giant Step, St. Louis Blues, A Raisin in the Sun, Purlie Victorious, To Be Young, Gifted and Black, Buck and the Preacher, Countdown at Kusini, Cat People, 1982, Do the Right Thing, 1989 (NAACP Image award as best actress 1989), Jungle Fever, 1991, Cop & 1/2, 1993, Whitewash, 1994, Just Cause, 1995, Simple Wish, A, 1997, Baby Geniuses, 1999, Little Bill, 2001, Feast of All Saints, 2001, Unchained Memories, 2002, Baby of the Family, 2002, Dream Street, 2005, No. 2, 2006, The Way Back Home, 2006; narrator: Time to Dance: The Life and Work of Norma Canner, A, 1998, Unfinished Journey, 1999; numerous TV appearances including It's Good to be Alive, 1974, Today Is Ours, 1974, The Defenders, Police Woman, Peyton Place, (TV films) To Be Young, Gifted and Black, All God's Children, The Nurses, Roots: The Next Generation, I Know Why the Caged Bird Sings, Wedding Band, It's Good to be Alive, Decoration Day (Emmy award for Supporting Actress in a Miniseries or Special 1991), The Atlanta Child Murders, (TV spl. with Ossie Davis) Martin Luther King: The Dream and the Drum, The Winds of Change, Windmill of the Gods, TV miniseries Stephen King's The Stand, 1994, Tuesday Morning Ride, 1995, Mr. & Mrs. Loving, 1996, Captive Heart: The James Mink Story, 1996, Porgy and Bess: An American Voice, 1998, Passing Glory, 1999, Having Our Say: The Delany Sisters' First 100 Years, 1999, Finding Buck McHenry, 2000, A Storm in Summer, 2000, Taking Back Our Town, 2001, Their Eyes Were Watching God, 2005; co-producer: (TV spl.) Today is Ours, The Ernest Green Story, 1993, (radio show) Ossie Davis and Ruby Dee Story Hour, 1974-78, (TV series) With Ossie and Ruby, 1981, (home videotape) Hands Upon The Heart, 1991, Middle Ages, 1992, Hands Upon The Heart II, 1993; rec. artist poems and stories; host (with Ossie Davis) African Heritage Movie Network. Recipient Martin Luther King Jr. award Operation PUSH, 1972, Drama Desk award, 1974, (with Ossie Davis) Frederick Douglass award NY Urban League, 1970, (with Ossie Davis) NAACP Image award Hall of Fame, Master Innovator For Film award Sony, 1991, Nat. Medal of Arts, 1990; Kennedy Ctr. Honors (with Ossie Davis), 2004. Mem. NAACP, CORE, Student Non-Violent Coordinating Com., SCLC. Address: The Artists Agy 10000 Santa Monica Blvd Los Angeles CA 90067-7007

DEEB, LARRY CHARLES, pediatric endocrinologist, epidemiologist; b. Tallahassee, Fla., July 2, 1947; s. Charles Hobeica and Carol Anna (Goll) D.; m. Josephine Marie Sutter, Oct. 7, 1978; children: Michael Larry, Laura Elzabeth. BA in History, Emory U., 1969, MD, 1973. Diplomate Am. Bd. Pediatrics. Pediatric resident U. Minn., Mpls., 1973-75, pediatric endocrine fellow, 1975-77; epidemic intelligence svc. officer, diabetes control activity Ctrs. for Disease Control, Atlanta, 1977—79, head, epidemiology and statistics group, diabetes control activity, 1979—80; ckin. asst. prof., dept. pediatrics Coll. Medicine, U. Fla., 1981—88, assoc. clin. prof., dept. pediatrics, 1988—93, clin. prof., dept. pediatrics, 1993—; pediatric endocrinology Childrens Clinic, Tallahassee, 1980—; rsch. assoc. Ctr. for Study of Populations, Fla. State U., 1987—; assoc. in medicine Fla. State U., 1993—. Epidemiologist cons. State of Fla., Tallahassee, 1980-, Internat. Diabetes Fedn.; clin. prof. pediatrics U. Fla., Gainesville, 1980-; med. dir. Diabetes Ctr. at Tallahassee Meml. Hosp.; epidemiologist NIH, Bethesda, Md., 1988-93; bd. dirs. Fla. Camp for Children and Youth with Diabetes; assoc. in medicine Fla. State U. Coll. Medicine, 1993-, courtesy assoc. prof. behavioral and social medicine, 2004-, courtesy asst. prof., pediatrics, 2004-. Mem. editl. bd. practical Diabetes, 1987—. Clin. Diabetes, 1988-92, 96—, Meml. Rey Med. Ctr., 1992—, Diabetes Spectra, 1992; contbr. articles to profl. jours. Lt. comdr. USPHS, 1965-77. Recipient Frederick Clifton Moor award, Tallahassee Rotary Club, 2006. Fellow Am. Acad. Pediatrics, Lawson Wilkins Pediatric Endocrinology Soc., Internat. Soc. Pediatric and Adolescent Diabetes, Am. Assn. Clin. Endocrinologists; mem. Am. Diabetes Assn. (mem. programs com., 1984-85, chair, coun. on health care delivery and pub. health, 1986-87, chair, com. on affiliate edn. and program services, 1986-87, mem task force on epidemiology and statistics, 1988-, mem. publications com., 1989-91, bd. dir., 1990-93, chair, non-periodicals review panel, 1991-93, chair elect coun. on clin. endocrinology, 1992-94, mem. nominating com., 1993-95, chair coun. on clin. endocrinology and metabolism, 1994-96, chair coun. on diabetes in youth, 1996-97, publications policy com., 1996-97, chair publications policy com., 1997-97, mem. diabetes quality improvement com., 1998-2000, provider recognition com., 2000-2001, fin. com., 2002-2004, v.p., 2004-2005, pres.-elect, medicine and sci., 2005-2006, pres. medicine and sci., 2006-), Internat. Diabetes Fedn. (life), Rotary (Paul Harris fellow). Episcopalian. Home: 2307 Trescott Dr Tallahassee FL 32308-0929 Office: Children's Clinic 2416 E Plaza Dr Tallahassee FL 32308-5384 also: 1634 N Plaza Dr Tallahassee FL 32306 Address: Diabetes Ctr at Tallahassee Meml Hosp 1221 Hodges Dr Tallahassee FL 32308 Office Phone: 850-878-0184. Office Fax: 850-216-1537. E-mail: lcdeeb@attglobal.net, lcdeeb@deeb.org.

DEEB, MARY-JANE, editor, educator; b. Alexandria, Egypt, Aug. 27, 1946; arrived in U.S., 1973; d. Alix and Stephanie (Klanscek) Anhoury; m. Marius K. Deeb, Sept. 27, 1969; 1 child, Hadi K. BA in Sociology, Am. U., Cairo, 1967, MA in Sociology, 1972; PhD in Internat. Rels., Johns Hopkins U., 1987. Rsch. assoc. Ford Found., Beirut, 1972-73; cons. UN Econ. Commn. for Western Asia, Beirut, 1980, UNICEF, Beirut, 1980-81; project dir. U.S. AID, Beirut, 1982-83; asst. professorial lectr. George Washington U., Washington, 1988-89, 93, 97, Georgetown U., Washington, 1991, 94; asst. prof. Am. U., Washington, 1989-94, adj. assoc. prof., 1994—; editor Mid. East Jour., Washington, 1995-98; Arab world area specialist Libr. of Congress, Washington, 1998—2004, head Near East sect., 2004—05, chief African and Mid. Ea. divsn., 2005—. External reviewer for grant proposals U.S. Inst. Peace, Washington, 1991, 92, 97, Woodrow Wilson Ctr. for Scholars, 2003, NEH, 2005; testified on subcom. on Africa fgn. rels. com. U.S. Ho. of Reps., 1991, 92, 98; testified before the select com. on intelligence, U.S. Senate, 1996; testified on fgn. rels. com. U.S. Senate, 1997, UN Monitor of Algerian legislative elections, 1997; dir. Algeria program Corp. Coun. on Africa; leader Libr. of Congress Mission to Iraq, 2003; team mem. Libr. Congress Mission to Iran, 2004. Co-author (with Marius K. Deeb): Libya Since the Revolution, 1982; author: Libya's Foreign Policy, 1991; co-editor: Hasib Sabbagh from Palestinian Refugee to Citizen of the World, 1996, Cocktails and Murder on the Potomac, 2001, (novel) Murder on the Riviera, 2004, A Christmas Mystery in Provence, 2004; rev. editor Internat. Jour. Mid.-East Studies, 1989-94; contbr. articles, revs. to profl. jours. and encys., and chpts. to books; interviewed on numerous TV programs, including CBS Evening News, ABC News, NBC Nightly News, CNN Headline News, Fox Morning News, PBS, and in news publs., including N.Y. Times, Washington Post, Time mag., L.A. Times, The Christian Sci. Monitor, U.S.A. Today, Boston Globe, Tokyo Shimbum, Yomouri, others. Mem. UN Assn., Am. Polit. Sci. Assn., Internat. Studies Assn., Mid. East Studies Assn. N.Am., Women's Caucus for Polit. Sci., Am.-Tunisian Assn. (exec. bd. 1989—), Hannibal Club (founding mem. 1999), World Affairs Coun., Women in Fgn. Policy, Mystery Writers Am., Sisters in Crime, Cosmos Club. Roman Catholic. Office: Libr Congress African and Middle Ea Divsn Jefferson Bldg 101 Independence Ave SE Washington DC 20540-0002 Office Phone: 202-707-1221. Business E-Mail: mdee@loc.gov.

DEEGAN, JOHN, JR., academic administrator, educator, researcher; b. Elizabeth, NJ, Nov. 18, 1944; s. John and Margaret (Pignataro) D.; m. Anita Hope Rochelle, Dec. 19, 1964; children: Michael J., Matthew B. Student, Monmouth Coll., West Long Branch, NJ, 1962-64; BS, Evangel Coll., Springfield, Mo., 1967; MA, U. Mich., 1969, PhD, 1972. Asst. prof. Rice U., Houston, 1972-75, U. Rochester, NY, 1975-80, assoc. prof., 1980; spl. asst. to dep. adminstr. EPA, Washington, 1980; dir. Love Canal Project, 1980-82; assoc. dean Sch. Pub. Health U. Ill., Chgo., 1982-86, acting dean, 1983-85; prof. U. No. Iowa, Cedar Falls, 1986-89, dean Coll. Social and Behavioral Scis., 1986-89; provost, v.p. acad. affairs, prof. U. So. Maine, Portland, 1989-94; dean coll., v.p. acad. affairs, prof. Westminster Coll., New Wilmington, Pa., 1994—2002; pres., prof. St. Andrews Presbyn. Coll., Laurinburg, NC, 2002—. Cons. EPA, 1983-86; trustee Ill. Cancer Coun., 1983-86; bd. dirs. Leopold Ctr. for Sustainable Agr. State of Iowa, 1987-89. Contbr. articles to sci. jours. Recipient EPA Bronze medal award, 1982; U. Rochester fellow in preventive medicine, 1979, Acad. Adminstrn. fellow Am. Coun. on Edn., 1986-87. Mem. AAAS, APHA, Am. Chem. Soc., Sigma Xi, Delta Omega. Democrat. Presbyterian. Avocations: fishing, golf. Office: Office of the Pres St Andrews Presbyn Coll Laurinburg NC 28352 Business E-Mail: jdeegan@sapc.edu.

DEEGAN, MARY JO, sociologist; b. Chgo., Nov. 27, 1946; d. William James and Ida May (Scott) Deegan; life ptnr. Michael Ray Hill. AS, Lake Mich. Coll., 1966; BS, We. Mich. U., 1969, MA, 1973; PhD, U. Chgo., 1975. Asst. prof. U. Nebr., Lincoln, 1975—80, assoc. prof., 1980—89, prof., 1989—. Med. trainee U. Chgo. Ctr. for Health Adminstrn., 1972-75; grad. asst. Western Mich. U., 1969-71.; del. Conf. on Directions in Health Econs., New Orleans, 1972. Author: Jane Addams and Men of the Chicago School, 1892-1918, 1988 (Choice award, 1989), American Ritual Dramas, 1989, Race, Hull House, and the University of Chicago, 2002 (Outstanding Scholarly Book, history sociol. sect.ASA, 03, 2nd pl. Racial and Ethnic Oliver C. Cox award); editor: Women in Sociology, 1991, American Ritual Tapestry, 1998, Play, School and Society (by G.H. Mead), 1999, Essays on Social Psychology (by G.H. Mead), 2001, The New Woman of Color (by F.B. Williams), 2002, Women at the Hague, 2003; co-editor: Women and Disability, 1985, Women and Symbolic Interaction, 1987, Feminist Ethics in Social Research, 1989, With Her in Ourland (by C.P. Gilman), 1997, The Dress of Women (by C.P. Gilman), 2002, On Art, Labor, and Religion by E.G. Starr, 2003, Social Ethics (by C.P. Gilman), 2005; series editor Women & Sociological Theory, 2001; contbr. articles to profl. jours. Mem.: Harriet Martineau Sociol. Soc. (Ann. award 2007), Internat. Sociol. Assn., Am. Sociol. Assn. (mem. hist. soc. sect., Disting. Scholarly Career award in history of sociology 2002). Office: Dept Sociology 711 Oldfather Hall U Nebraska Lincoln NE 68588-0324

DEEL, FRANCES QUINN, retired librarian; b. Pottsville, Pa., Mar. 9, 1939; d. Charles Joseph and Carrie Miriam (Ketner) Q.; m. Ronald Eugene Deel, Feb. 5, 1983. BS, Millersville State Coll., 1960; M.L.S., Rutgers U., 1964; M.P.A., U. West Fla., 1981. Post librarian U.S. Army Armor (Desert Tng. Ctr.), Ft. Irwin, Calif., 1964-66; staff librarian Mil. Dist. of Washington, 1966-67; supervisory librarian 1st Logistical Command, APO San Francisco, 1967-68; tech. process specialist Naval Edn. and Tng. Supervisory Command, Washington, 1968-77, Pensacola, Fla., 1968-77; chief tech. library USAF Armament Lab., Eglin AFB, Fla., 1977-81; dir. command libraries Air Force Systems Command (Andrews AFB), Washington, 1981-92; mem. exec. adv. council Fed. Library and Info. Network, Washington, 1983-86; libr. Air Force Dist. of Washington (Bolling AFB), Washington, 1992-94; dir. Navy Dept. Libr., Washington, 1994; ret., 1994. Mem. ALA (dir.-at-large armed forces libraries sect. Chgo. 1983-86), Spl. Libraries Assn., D.C. Library Assn. Roman Catholic. Home: 99 Country Club Dr W Destin FL 32541-4433

DEELEY, C. CAREY, JR., lawyer; b. Balt., Sept. 30, 1951; BA, U. Va., 1973; JD, U. Balt., 1979. Bar: Md., 1979, US Dist. Ct., Md. Law clerk to Hon. Austin W. Brizendine Circuit Ct. for Balt. County, Md., 1978-79; ptnr. Venable LLP (formerly Venable, Baetjer & Howard), Towson, Md. Former chmn. Pretrial Release Project Advisory Com. Mem. bd. trustees St. Paul's School for Boys; legal advisor Alcoholic Beverage Med. Rsch. Found. Mem. ABA, Md. State Bar Assn. (bd. govs. 1985-86), Balt. County Bar Assn. (mem. exec. council 1987-98, pres. 1996-97), Balt. County Bar Found. (pres. 1997-98); fellow Md. Bar Found. Office: Venable LLP PO Box 5517 210 Allegheny Ave Baltimore MD 21204-4074 Office Phone: 410-494-6259. Office Fax: 410-821-0147. Business E-Mail: ccdeeley@venable.com.

DEEM, GEORGE, artist; b. Vincennes, Ind., Aug. 18, 1932; s. George C. and Laura (Bobe) D. Student, Vincennes U., 1951—52; BFA, Sch. Art Inst. Chgo., 1958. Instr. painting Sch. Visual Arts, NYC, 1965—66, Leicester Coll. Art and Design, England, 1966—67, U. Pa., 1968; artist in residence Mus. Arts and Sci., Evansville, Ind., 1979; vis. artist Ill. State U., Normal, 1982, Branson Sch., Ross, Calif., 1995. Sec. exec. com. MacDowell Colony Fellows, 1982-87. One-man shows include Allan Stone Gallery, NYC, 1963, 1964, 1965, 1966, 1968, 1969, 1975, 1977, Sneed Gallery, Rockford, Ill., 1968, 1969, 1972, 1976, 1980, Merida Gallery, Louisville, 1966, 1968, 1969, 1978, 1983, Indpls. Mus. Art, 1974, Witte Meml. Mus., San Antonio, 1975, Evansville Mus. Arts and Scis., 1979, 1993, 2001, Greenberg Gallery, St. Louis, 1979, On View Downtown Gallery, Indpls., 1986, Harn Mus. Art, U. Fla., Gainesville, 1993, Mitchell Mus. Art, Mt. Vernon, Ill., 1993, Polk Mus. Art, Lakeland, Fla., 1994, Ind. State Mus., Indpls., 1994, Eckert Fine Art Gallery, 1994, Capricorn Gallery, Bethesda, Md., 1994, Wichita Ctr. Arts, 1994, Nancy Hoffman Gallery, NYC, 2000, Las Vegas Art Mus., Nev., 2001, Pavel Zoubok Gallery, NYC, 2002, 2004, 2006, Yale U. Jonathan Edwards Coll. Master's Ho., New Haven, 2003, New Britain Mus. Am. Art, Conn., 2005, exhibited in group shows at Yale U. Art Gallery, 1964, Whitney Mus. Am. Art, NYC, 1978, Pa. Acad. Fine Arts, 1981, Allentown Art Mus., Pa., 1983, Ft. Wayne Mus. Art, Ind., 1984, Nancy Hoffman Gallery, 1985, 1986, 1987, 1988, 1989, 1990, 1991, 1994, 1996, Flint Inst. Arts, Mich., 1993, Nassau County Mus. Art, Roslyn Harbor, NY, 1984, 2000, Mus. Art U. Oreg., 1996, Pavel Zoubok/Mary Delahoyd Gallery, NYC, 1998, Allan Stone Gallery, 2000, Miami U. Art Mus., Oxford, Ohio, 2002, Herbert F. Johnson Mus. Art, Ithaca, NY, 2002, Musee Art Moderne Contemporain, Strasbourg, France, 2003, Represented in permanent collections Indpls. Mus. Art, Evansville Mus. Arts and Sci., Stiftung Ludwig, Aachen, Germany, Vassar Coll. Art Gallery, Mus. Fine Arts, Houston, Miami U. Art Mus., Oxford, Weatherspoon Art Mus. U. NC, Greensboro, JP Morgan Chase Bank, NYC, Cleary Gottlieb Steen &

Hamilton, NYC, Bank of Am., Fla. Internat. U., Frost Art Mus., Miami, Fla., Ariz. State U. Art Mus., Tempe, Hallmark Cards, Inc., Kansas City, Mo., State Russian Mus., St. Petersburg, Mus. Modern Art, San Francisco, Am. Gen. Fin., Inc., Evansville, Albrecht-Kemper Mus. Art, St. Joseph, Mo., Seven Bridges Found., Greenwich, Conn., Ogden Mus. So. Art U. New Orleans, Wellington Mgmt. Co., Boston, comms., Nutter, McClennen & Fish, Boston, 1988, Paul, Weiss, Rifkind, NY, 1989, Mirage Resorts, Las Vegas, 1998; author: Art School: Paintings by George Deem, 1993, 2005, Meister Klasse: Kunst Entdecken mit George Deem, 2005, How to Paint a Vermeer: A Painter's History of Art, 2004, Täuschend Echt: Die Kunst des Sehens, 2004; actor: (film) The Cold Eye, 1980. With US Army, 1953—55. Home and Office: 10 W 18th St New York NY 10011-4617 Business E-Mail: george.deem@verizon.net.

DEEMS, SHERRAN ELLEN (SHERRY), artist, educator, editor; b. Farmville, Va., Feb. 27, 1947; d. Donald and Laura Ellen (Stewart) D.; m. William Arthur Diamond; children: Jessica Lynn, Justin Stewart. BFA in Art History, Va. Commonwealth U., 1972, MFA in Painting and Printmaking, 1993. Dir. Life Drawing Studio, Roanoke, Va., 1977-78; mktg. rep. Nat. Retail Svcs., Georgetown, Conn., 1982-86; writer Commonwealth of Va. Parole Bd., Richmond, 1988; coord. Alumni Open Drawing Studio Va. Commonwealth U., Richmond, 1987-91, asst. to dir. Arts Libr., 1991, asst. dir. devel. Sch. Arts, 1993-94, grad. asst. painting and printmaking dept., 1991-93, adj. instr., 1991-93, 95—, editor VCU Arts alumni mag., 1994—; prof. Savannah Coll. Art and Design, Ga., 2001—, dir. Still Life Ctr., 2003—, faculty chair undergrad. studies coun., mem. leadership coun. Coord. art history program for elem. schs. Roanoke Fine Arts Mus., 1977-78; guest artist Richmond Pub. Schs., 1990, 91, 92, John Tyler C.C., Chester, Va., 1992, 95, Va. Union U., Richmond, 1992, Hanover County Pub. Schs., Hanover, Va., 1993, Richmond Montessori Sch., 1995; instr. drawing Petersburg (Va.) Area Art League, 1987-89, mem. adv. bd.; instr. printmaking Richmond Hand Workshop, 1995—; mem. reading programs curriculum rev. com.Petersburg Pub. Schs.; guest artist Richmond Pub. Schs., 1990-93, John Tyler C.C., 1992-95; presenter and juror in field One-woman shows Old Colony Gallery, Williamsburg, Va., 1978, John Tyler C.C., 1988, Va. Commonwealth U., 1990, Anderson Gallery, Richmond, 1993, Interior Dynamics, Inc., Richmond, 1993, Clark Pollard Gallery, Richmond, 1993, ArtSpace Gallery, Richmond, 1994, Arts in Hosp., Richmond, 1995, Richmond Montessori Sch., 1995, U. Richmond, 1995, Pinnacle Gallery, 2006; exhibited in group shows Petersburg Area Art League, 1988, 89, John Tyler C.C., 1988, Jewish Cmty. Ctr., Richmond, 1988, 90, 95, Gallery 24, Richmond, 1989, Va. Commonwealth U., 1989, 91, 92, 93, 95, Crestar Gallery, Richmond, 1990, Gallery 25, Richmond, 1990, Larrick Ctr., Richmond, 1990, James Ctr. Gallery, Richmond, 1991, 96, ArtSpace Gallery, Richmond, 1992, 96, Art in D.C., Washington, 1992, Rockville (Md.) Arts Place, 1992, Randolph-Macon Coll., Ashland, Va., 1993, Roanoke Coll., Salem, Va., 1993, Arts Coun. Richmond, 1994, Longwood Coll., Farmville, 1994, Galerie Corti, Brussels, 1995, U. Richmond, 1995, U.S. State Dept., 2000, SCAD Atlanta Gallery, 2003, Red Gallery Savannah (Ga.) Coll. Art and Design, 2003, Salt Works Gallery, Atlanta, 2004, Gallery GBK, Sydney, 2004, WARPhaus Gallery, 2005, also others; represented in permanent collections Va. Commonwealth U., Anderson Gallery, Va., Cabell Libr., Richmond, also pvt. and corp. collections; work reviewed in various publs.; author: (exhbn. catalog) Roger Baugh; contbr. articles to profl. publs. Mem. scholarship com. Richmond Women's Caucus for Art, also fundraising chmn., mem. adv. bd.; mem. Petersburg City Commn.-Day of Child; bd. dirs. Old Towne Mchts. Assn., Petersburg, Jr. Federated Women's Clubs, Va.; bd. dirs. Va. Commonwealth U. Alumni Assn., 1996-97. Recipient award of excellence, Sherwood Forest Competition, Larrick Ctr. Painting Show; Jessie Hibbs scholar, Va. Commonwealth U., Commonwealth of Va. fellow, Presdl. fellow, Savannah Coll. Art and Design, 2005. Mem. Richmond Artists Assn., Richmond Women's Caucus for Art. Office Phone: 912-525-6611. Business E-Mail: sdeems@scad.edu.

DEEN, PAULA H., television personality, restaurant owner, chef; b. Albany, Ga., Jan. 19, 1947; m. Michael Groover, Mar. 2004; 2 stepchildren;children from previous marriage: Bobby, Jamie. Owner catering bus. The Bag Lady; owner The Lady and Sons restaurant, Savannah, Ga., 1990—. Host (TV series) Paula's Home Cooking, Food Network, 2002—, Paula's Party; author: (cookbooks) The Lady and Sons Too, The Lady and Sons Just Desserts, 2002, The Lady and Sons Savannah Country Cookbook, 2005; co-author (with Martha Nesbit): Paula Deen & Friends: Living It Up, Southern Style, 2005; author: (mag.) Cooking with Paula Deen, 2006—; actor: (films) Elizabethtown, 2005. Provided sponsorships and donations of money, cookbooks and other services to cmty. groups and causes. Named Most Memorable Meal Yr. at The Lady and Sons restaurant, USA Today, 1999, Small Bus. Person Yr. in Ga., US Small Bus. Adminstrn., 2003; recipient Ga. Women Entrepreneurs (GWEN) award, Ga. Small Bus. Devel. Ctr., 2003. Office: Food Network Studios 604 W 52nd St New York NY 10019 also: Lady & Sons Restaurant 102 W Congress St Savannah GA 31401*

DEENY, RAYMOND M., lawyer; b. Oelwein, Iowa, Aug. 27, 1951; BA, Ariz. State U., 1974, JD, 1977. Bar: Ariz. 1977, Colo. 1978. Mem. Sherman & Howard, Colorado Springs, Colo. Contbg. editor Devel. Labor Law Jour., 1982. Mem. ABA (mgmt. mem. devel. law under nat. labor rels. act sect. labor rels. law 1980-81), Indsl. Rels. Rsch. Assn. (pres. Rocky Mountain chpt. 1983-85), State Bar Ariz. Office: Sherman & Howard 90 S Cascade Ave Ste 1500 Colorado Springs CO 80903-1699 Business E-Mail: rdeeny@sah.com.

DEEP THROAT, See FELT, MARK

DEER, (RICHARD) ALAN, lawyer; b. Apr. 15, 1963; m. Jill Verdeyen; 2 children. BS in Acctg., Auburn U., 1985; JD, U. Ala., 1988. Bar: 1988. Ptnr. Lange, Simpson, Robinson & Somerville, LLP, Birmingham, Ala., 1988—97; assoc. gen. counsel Regions Fin. Corp., Birmingham, Ala., 1997, chief legal officer, 2003—04, exec. v.p., gen. counsel, corp. sec., 2004—07. Chmn. banking law com. Ala. Bar Inst. for Continuing Legal Edn. Mem. Ind. Presbyn. Ch. Mem.: Ala. State Bar, Birmingham Bar Assn., ABA (consumer fin. svcs. com. of bus. law sect.).*

DEERE, JAMES DICKSON, singer, pianist, voice and music educator, writer; b. Johnson City, Tenn., Sept. 2, 1933; s. Hulon Ray and Omeria Winslow Deere; m. Celia Lynn Bryant (div.); 1 child, Celia Michelle. MusB, Baylor U., 1955; MBA, UCLA, 1977; PhD, U. NC, Greensboro, 2002. Lic. tchr. NC, SC. Opera, ch. and musical theater singer, 1959—73; exec. dir. arts mgmt. Nev. Coun. Arts, Lake George Opera, 1974—80; instr. Belmont U., Nashville, 1980—81; arts mgmt. exec. Opera Carolina, Charlotte, NC, 1981—82; instr. Greensboro (N.C.) Tech. C.C., Greensboro, 1995—96; pvt. voice and piano tchr. Greensboro, Reidsville, NC, 1998—, Mayodan, NC, 2006—. Author: No Diamonds Allowed!, 1971, Singing in the 20th Century, 2005. Vol. Dem. Party, Greensboro, 2004. Served with US Army, 1956—58. Mem.: Nat. Assn. Tchrs. Singing, Music Tchrs. Nat. Assn. Home: 3206-A Regents Park Ln Greensboro NC 27455 Home Fax: 336-286-9223. E-mail: jdeere@triad.rr.com.

DEERING, ALLAN BROOKS, retired soft drink company executive; b. Chappaqua, NY, Apr. 1, 1934; s. Clarence and Muriel Deering; m. Carol Ann Werle, Apr. 14, 1957; children: Peter Brooks, Andrew Werle. BA, Columbia U., 1956. Systems analyst IBM Corp., White Plains, NY, 1956-58; EDP mgr. R.H. Donnelly Corp., NYC, 1958-68; dir. systems and data processing W.R. Grace & Co., NYC, 1968-76, asst. v.p., 1975; dir. info. systems SCM Corp., NYC, 1976-81; dir. mgmt. info. svcs. Pepsi Co., NYC, 1981-86, v.p. mgmt. info. svcs., 1986—2000. Mem. Mayor's Industry Adv. Bd. for Data Processing, N.Y.C., 1978, adv. bd. Pace U. Sch. Computer Sci., Omicron. Mem. Data Processing Mgmt. Assn., Soc. Mgmt. Info. Systems (bd. dirs.), N.Y. Computer Execs. Roundtable, Grocery Mfrs. Am. (chmn. systems com.), Rocky Point Club, Old Greenwich Yacht Club, Milbrook Club. Home: 3 Perkley Ln Riverside CT 06878-2309 E-mail: abdeering@snet.net.

DEERING, ANTHONY WAYNE MARION, real estate developer; b. Washington, Jan. 28, 1945; s. George Aloysius and Maude Emma (Matheys) D.; m. Kathryn Evelyn Regan, May 31, 1969; children: Heather, Spencer, Maron. BS, Drexel U., Phila., 1968; MBA, Wharton Sch., U. Pa., 1970; postgrad., U. Exeter, Eng. Bus. planner Exxon Co., NYC, 1970-71; cons. Dunuck, Fulton Co., Phila., 1971—; pres., CEO, Rouse Co., Columbia, Md., 1971-98, chmn., CEO, 1998—. Dir. T. Rowe Price Prime Res., T. Rowe Price New Income, T. Rowe Price Mut. Funds, Kleinwort Benson Mcht. Bank, The Rouse Co. Trustee Friends Sch., Balt., Balt. Parks Found., Balt. Mus. Art. Home: 6011 Charlesmead Rd Baltimore MD 21212-2214 Office: The Rouse Company 10275 Little Patuxent Pkwy Columbia MD 21044-3455

DEERING, RONALD FRANKLIN, librarian, minister; b. Paxton, Ill., Oct. 6, 1929; s. Minor Franklin and Grace Gilmour (Perkins) D.; m. Geraldine Gibbons, June 27, 1953 (dec. Jan. 1965); m. Edith Ann Proctor, June 12, 1966; children: Mark David, Daniel Timothy. BA summa cum laude, Georgetown Coll., Ky., 1951; MDiv, So. Bapt. Theol. Sem., 1955, PhD, 1962; MLS, Columbia U., 1967. Ordained to ministry So. Bapt. Conv., 1950. Pastor 1st Hilltop Bapt. Ch., North College Hill, Ohio, 1949-50; instr. in Bible Georgeton (Ky.) Coll., 1950-51; pastor Blue River Bapt. Ch., Salem, Ind., 1954-59; instr. Greek, N.T. So. Bapt. Theol. Sem., Louisville, 1958-61, theol. libr., 1962-95, assoc. v.p. for acad. resources, 1995—. Chmn. So. Bapt. Hist. Commn., Nashville, 1987-90; interim pastor 31 chs. in Ind., Ky., 1961-90; del. Bapt. World Alliance, Miami, Fla., Toronto, Ont., Can., L.A., 1965, 80, 85. Contbr. articles to profl. jours. Eli Lilly Theol. Librarianship grantee, 1967. Mem. AAUP, ALA, Southeastern Libr. Assn., Am. Theol. Libr. Assn. (nat. pres. 1984-85), Ky. Libr. Assn., Phi Alpha Theta, Beta Phi Mu, Sigma Tau Delta. Democrat. Home: 3111 Dunlieth Ct Louisville KY 40241-2937 Office Phone: 502-897-4807. Personal E-mail: rondeering@bellsouth.net.

DEERING, SUZY, advertising executive; b. 1969; B, U. of Ga. Associated with Walt Disney Advt., Fitzgerald and Co. Advt. of Atlanta, AirTouch Cellular; head, mktg. comm. team, nine state so. region Verizon Wireless, 1999—2005, dir. brand mgmt. and integration, 2005—07, exec. dir.-brand, media, sponsorship and integration, 2007—. Named one of 40 under 40, Advt. Age, 2007. Office: Verizon Communications Inc 140 W St New York NY 10036 Office Phone: 212-395-2121.*

DEES, BOWEN CAUSEY, retired institute executive; b. Batesville, Miss., July 20, 1917; s. John Simeon and Ida Lea (Causey) D.; m. Sarah Edna Sanders, Aug. 25, 1937 (dec. 1999); 1 child, Sarah Edna; m. Dorothea Regina Simoneau, Sept. 24, 2001. AB, Miss. Coll., Clinton, 1937, DSc (hon.), 1963; PhD, NYU, NYC, 1942; LLD, Lehigh U., 1976, Phila. Coll. Textiles and Sci., 1979; DSc (hon.), Temple U., 1981. Prof. physics Miss. Coll., 1943-44; instr. elec comms. Radar Sch., MIT, 1944-45; asst. prof. physics Rensselaer Poly. Inst., 1945-47; physicist, then div. chief sci. and tech. div., gen. hdqrs. SCAP, Tokyo, 1947-51; program dir. fellowships NSF, 1951-56, dep. asst. dir. sci. personnel and edn., 1956-59, asst. dir., 1959-63, assoc. dir. for edn., 1963-64, assoc. dir. planning, 1963-66; v.p. U. Ariz., 1966-68, provost acad. affairs, 1968-70; pres. Franklin Inst., Phila., 1970-82, pres. emeritus, 1982—. Adv. com. U.S. Army Command and Gen. Staff Coll., 1967-69; sci. info. coun. NSF, 1970-74; mem. Sci. Manpower Commn., Washington, 1976-79; U.S. co-chmn. U.S.-Japan Com. on Sci. Cooperation, 1981-87. Author: Fundamentals of Physics, 1945, The Allied Occupation and Japan's Economic Miracle, 1997; contbr. articles to profl. jours. Mem. Cosmos (Washington). Home Phone: 760-749-3781. Personal E-mail: bcdees2@aol.com.

DEES, C. STANLEY, lawyer; b. Tulsa, June 24, 1938; AB, Princeton U., 1960; LLB, U. Va., 1963. Bar: Va. 1963, D.C. 1964. Ptnr. McKenna, Long & Aldridge LLP, Washington. Lectr. U. Va. Law Sch. Contbr. articles to profl. jours. Trustee Legal Aid Soc. D.C., 1970-83, pres., 1978-80; mem. Va. Dem. Ctrl. Com., 1971-74. Fellow Am. Bar Found.; mem. ABA (chmn. fed. cts. com. 1977-78, jud. remedies com. 1978-80, program com. 1980-81, coun. mem. 1981-84, sec. 1984-85, vice-chmn. pub. contract law sect. 1985-86, chmn. pub. contract law sect. 1987-88), U.S. Ct. Fed. Claims Bar, D.C. Bar (vice-chmn. 1974-75, chmn. 1975-77, steering com., govt. contracts and litigation divsn.), Va. State Bar, Coun. Def. and Space Indsl. Assns. (chmn. 1991-93), Nat. Security Indsl. Assn. (v.p. 1983-90, trustee 1990-96), D.C. Bar Found. (adv. com.), Order of Coif. Office: McKenna Long & Aldridge 1900 K St NW Washington DC 20006 Office Phone: 202-496-7628. Business E-Mail: sdees@mckennalong.com.

DEES, JULIAN WORTH, retired academic/research administrator; b. Henderson, NC, Feb. 20, 1933; s. Charles Andrew and Gertrude Elizabeth (Lancaster) D.; m. Bernita June Funk, Aug. 29, 1954; children: Sandra Eileen Dees Anthony, Mark Alan, Gregory Linn. BS in Radio Engring., Tri-State U., Angola, Ind., 1953, BS in Adminstrv. Engring., 1954; MSEE, U. Cin., 1955. Registered profl. engr., Ga. Microwave engr. IT&T Labs., Ft. Wayne, Ind., 1955-60; project mgr., sr. engr. Martin Marietta Corp., Orlando, Fla., 1960-71; dir. electromagnetic lab. Ga. Inst. Tech., Atlanta, 1971-80, assoc. v.p. rsch., dir. office contract adminstrn., prin. rsch. engr., 1980-98; ret., 1998. Asst. sec., asst. treas Ga. Tech. Rsch. Corp., Atlanta, 1980-98; bd. dir. Coun. on Rsch. & Tech., Washington. Contbr. articles to jours. in field; patentee in field. Named Author of Yr., Martin Marietta Corp., 1965. Fellow IEEE (Engr. of Yr. Orlando chpt. 1968); mem. Soc. Rsch. Adminstrs. (sr.), Coun. on Govtl. Rels., Nat. Coun. Univ. Rsch. Adminstrs. Avocations: woodworking, judging barbeque cook-offs. Home: 2128 Rosser Pl Stone Mountain GA 30087-1517

DEES, MORRIS SELIGMAN, JR., lawyer; b. Shorter, Ala., Dec. 16, 1936; s. Morris Seligman and Annie Ruth (Frazer) D.; m. Elizabeth Breen; children: Morris Seligman III, John Fuller, Ellie. BS, U. Ala., 1958, LLB, 1960. Bar: Ala. 1960. Chmn. bd. Fuller and Dees Pub., Inc. (merged with Times Mirror), 1960-69; ptnr. Levin and Dees, 1969-71; co-founder (with Joe Levin) and chief trial counsel So. Poverty Law Ctr., Montgomery, Ala., 1971—. Pres. Funding Group, 1983—; instr. criminal law Jones Law Sch., 1960-62; vis. fellow John F. Kennedy Sch. Govt., Harvard U.; elected fellow U. Pa. Law Sch., 1988. Co-author (with Steve Fiffer): A Season for Justice, 1991; author: Hate on Trial: The Case Against America's Most Dangerous Neo-Nazi, 1993, Gathering Storm: America's Militia Threat, 1996. Dir. nat. fund raising McGovern for Pres., 1972; nat. fin. chmn. Carter for Pres., 1976; nat. fin. dir. Kennedy for Pres., 1980; trustee Miles Coll. Named One of 10 Outstanding Young Men Am. U.S. Jaycees, 1967, 100 Top Lawyers, Nat. Law Jour., 2006; recipient Outstanding Svc. for Human Rights award Tuskegee Inst., 1976, Trial Lawyer of Yr. award Trial Lawyers for Pub. Justice, 1987, Pub. Svc. Achievement award Common Cause, 1988, Justice award So. Christian Leadership Conf., 1989, Martin Luther King Jr. Mem. Award, Nat. Edn. Assn., 1990, Humanitarian Award, U. Ala., 1993, Friend of Edn. Award, Nat. Edn. Assn, 2001. Mem. ABA (Young Lawyers Disting. Svc. award 1987), Ala. Bar Assn., Direct Mail Mktg. Assn. (bd. dirs., Showmanship award 1968), Beta Gamma Sigma. Unitarian (pres. ch. 1968). Home: Rolling Hills Rnch Mathews AL 36052 Office: So Poverty Law Ctr 400 Washington St Montgomery AL 36104-4344*

DEES, RICHARD LEE, lawyer; b. Harrisburg, Ill., Jan. 14, 1955; s. David Lee and Joann (Alvey) D.; children: Sarah Elizabeth, Elliott Richard, Spencer Barrett; m. Nora B. Flint, Apr. 21, 2001. AS, Southeastern Ill. Jr. Coll., 1975; BS, So. Ill. U., 1977; JD magna cum laude, U. Ill. Coll. Law, 1980. Bar: Ill. 1980, US Tax Ct. 1981. Ptnr. McDermott, Will & Emery, Chgo., 1980—. Invited witness Senate Fin. Com., 1989-90, House Ways and Means Com., 1990. Editor: Agrl. Law and Tax Report, 1984-89; topics editor U. Ill. Law Forum, 1979-80; contbr. articles to profl. jours. Named one of Top 100 Attys., Worth mag., 2005. Fellow Am. Coll. Trust and Estate Counsel; mem. Leading Ill. Attys., Order of Coif. Presbyterian. Office: McDermott Will & Emery 227 W Monroe St Ste 3100 Chicago IL 60606-5096 Office Phone: 312-984-7613. Office Fax: 312-984-7700. E-mail: rdees@mwe.com.*

DEES, SANDRA KAY MARTIN, psychologist, research scientist; b. Omaha, Apr. 18, 1944; d. Leslie B. and Ruth Lillian (May) Martin; m. Doyce B. Dees. BA magna cum laude, Tex. Christian U., 1965, MA, 1972, PhD, 1989. Cert. Montessori Soc., 1977. Adminstrv. asst., rsch. coord. Hosp. Improvement Project, Wichita Falls (Tex.) State Hosp., 1968-69; caseworker adoptions Edna Gladney Home, Ft. Worth, 1970-71; psychologist Mexia (Tex.) State Sch., 1971-72; sch. psychologist Ft. Worth Ind. Sch. Dist., 1971-78, program evaluator, 1978-86; pvt. counselor, 1986-88; rsch. scientist Tex. Christian U., Ft. Worth, 1989—2005, mem. adj. faculty, 1991-92, mem. grad. faculty, 1994—2005. Bd. dirs Because We Care, Ft. Worth, 1988-97, Hill Sch., 1994—. Contbr. articles to profl. jours. Dallas TCU Women's Club creative writing scholar, 1962-64, Virginia Alpha scholar, 1963; NASA rsch. asst., 1965-67; USPHS trainee, 1967-68. Mem. APA, Am. Ednl. Rsch. Assn., Mental Health Assn., Mortar Board, Mensa, Sigma Xi, Alpha Chi, Phi Alpha Theta, Psi Chi, Phi Delta Kappa. Home: 29 Bounty Rd W Fort Worth TX 76132-1003 Office: Tex Christian U Dept Psychology Fort Worth TX 76129-0001 E-mail: s.dees@tcu.edu.

DEES, STEPHEN PHILLIP, agricultural products executive, lawyer; b. Tulsa, Feb. 21, 1943; s. Jesse Raymond and Mary Adelia (Ledbetter) D.; m. Mary Louise Porter, June 26, 1966 (div. Oct. 1986); children: Emily Ann, Daniel Ledbetter, Matthew Louis; m. Kristine Ann Odenwald, Oct. 10, 1987 (div. Apr. 1992); 1 child, Charles Jesse; m. Linda Petsch, Sept. 3, 1995. BA, Washington U., 1965, JD, 1967. Bar: Mo. 1967. Assoc. Stinson, Mag, Thomson, McEvers & Fizzell, Kansas City, Mo., 1967-71; ptnr. Stinson, Mag & Fizzell, Kansas City, 1971-84; v.p., gen. counsel Farmland Industries Inc., Kansas City, 1984-87, sec., 1986-91, v.p. law and adminstrn., 1987-93, now exec. v.p. bus. development & internat. mktg., dir. gen., 1993-98; dir. gen. Farmland Industries, S.A. de C.V. of Mex., 1993-95; ptnr. Rochdale Prins., 1998—2000; of counsel Shook, Hardy & Bacon, Kansas City, Mo., 2000—. Officer, bd. dirs. Gt. Am. Basketball League, Shawnee Mission, Kans., 1979-86, commr., 1983-86; mem. Sister Cities Commn., Kansas City, 1982-90. Served with USAF, 1967, then with Res. Mem. ABA, Mo. Bar (vice chmn. labor law com. 1977-80, chmn. 1980-81), Lawyers Assn. Kansas City (bd. dirs. 1983-86, treas. 1989-91), Kansas City Met. Bar Assn., Order of Coif. Republican. Jewish. Avocations: stamp collecting/philately, racquetball, travel. Home: 4511 N Mulberry Dr Kansas City MO 64116-4652 Office: Shook Hardy Bacon 2555 Grand Blvd Kansas City MO 64108-2613 Office Phone: 816-559-2466.

DEESCH, VASTI F., museum registrar; d. José Ferreira da Silva and Creuza Ferreira de Souza; m. George P. DeEsch, Oct. 23, 1976; 1 child, George W. F. BA in English as a Second Lang., Portuguese, Fed. U. of Pernambuco, Brazil, 1970; MEd in Secondary Sch. Supervision, U. North Tex., Denton, 1974. Cert. mgmt. mus. collections Smithsonian Ctr. for Edn. and Mus. Studies, Washington, 2005. Portuguese, English tchr. Recife State H.S., Pernambuco, Brazil, 1969—71, Am. Bapt. H.S., 1969—71; Brazilian Portuguese instr. DeSales U., Center Valley, Pa., 1988—93; coop. advt. coord. H. Leh and Co., Allentown, Pa., 1986—89; allocator Phillips Van Heusen Corp., Reading, 1989—95; collections data mgr. Reading Pub. Mus., Pa., 1996—2002, asst. registrar, 2002—04, registrar, 2004—. Portuguese translator Am. Inst. Langs., Dallas, 1977—81; English, French & Spanish langs. lab asst. U. of North Tex., English and Fgn. Langs. Depts., Denton, 1974—76; interpreter in field. Translator articles, documents and books from English to Portuguese, of tech.translations for Tex. Instruments, of art articles from French to English. ESL vol., tchr. Faith Evang. Free Ch., Allentown, Pa., 2005. Mem.: Am. Assn. of Museums, Macungie Pa. Hist. Soc., Emmaus Hist. Soc., Linguistics Club, U. of North Tex. Achievements include South American countries representative, international students association of University of North Texas. Office: Reading Pub Mus 500 Museum Rd Reading PA 19611

DEESE, E(THEL) HELEN, retired literature and language professor; b. San Diego, Sept. 15, 1925; d. Clyde Thomas and Ethel (Findlay) Smith; m. Rupert Julian Deese, Mar. 4, 1951; children: Rupert Thomas, Mary Ann, Franklin William, Richard Samuel. BA, U. Calif., Riverside, 1968, MA, 1970, PhD, 1977. Lectr. U. Calif., Riverside, 1977—79, 1992—2005, Calif. State Poly. U., Pomona, 1979-81; assoc. prof. English Mt. St. Mary's Coll., Los Angeles, 1983-89; Fulbright lectr. Hungary, 1989-90, Macao, 1990-91. Critic So. Calif. drama, Shakespeare Bull., NYC, 1985—; author: Robert Lowell: A Reference Guide, 1982; editor: Robert Lowell: New Essays on the Poetry, 1986, Critical Essays on Wallace Stevens, 1988, Critical Essays on William Carlos William, 1995; contbr. Ency. Am. Poets and Poetry, 2005; contbr. N. Am. Players of Shakespeare, 2007. Mem. MLA, Internat. Fedn. Theatre Rsch., Assn. Lit. Scholars and Critics, Shakespeare Assn, N.Am. Players Shakespeare Democrat. Unitarian Universalist. Home and Office: 601 E Baseline Rd Claremont CA 91711-2237 Office Phone: 909-626-6135. Personal E-mail: hsdeese@msn.com.

DEESE, GEORGE E., food products company executive; With Flowers Foods, Inc., Thomasville, Ga., 1964; pres., COO Flowers Bakeries, 1983—2002, Flowers Foods, Inc., 2002—04, pres., CEO, 2004—06, chmn., pres., CEO, 2006—. Mem.: Quality Bakers Am. (mem. bd.), Grocery Manufacturers Am. (indus. affairs coun.), Am. Bakers Assn. (former chmn., board exec. com.). Office: Flowers Foods 1919 Flowers Cir Thomasville GA 31757*

DEESE, PAMELA MCCARTHY, lawyer; b. Abington, Pa., July 4, 1958; d. John Joseph McC. and Penny Ann (Wells) Knight; m. Charles Michael Deese, May 10, 1986; children: Spencer Michael, Charles Jameson, Kendall Ann. BS, The Am. U., 1980, JD, 1983. Bar: Pa. 1984, DC 1990, US Ct. Appeals (8th cir.) 1989 (4th cir.) 1992, US Supreme Ct. 1995, US Ct. Appeals (DC cir.) 1996. Asst. dir. GSP US Trade Rep., Washington, 1978-83; assoc. atty. Ablondi & Foster, Washington, 1983-86, Robins, Zelle, Larson & Kaplan, Washington, 1986-89; ptnr. Robins, Kaplan, Miller & Ciresi, Washington, 1990—99; ptnr., trademark licensing and advertising Dorsey & Whitney, LLP, 1999—2005; ptnr. intellectual property practice Arent Fox PLLC, Washington, 2005—. Vol. Offender Aid and Rep., Fairfax, Va., 1983-86; pres. Am. U. Alumni Assn., Washington, 1988-97; elder Lewinsville Presbyn. Ch., McLean, Va., 1989-92; trustee Am. U., 2002—; mem. Circles Bd. Kennedy Ctr., 2001—. Mem. ABA (vice chair sci. and tech. tech. stds. com. 2005—), Am. Intellectual Property Lawyers Assn., Licensing Industry Merchandising Assn. Democrat. Presbyterian. Avocations: skiing, reading, cooking, flower arranging, travel. Office: Arent Fox PLLC 1050 Connecticut Ave NW Washington DC 20036-5339 Office Phone: 202-828-3431. Office Fax: 202-857-6395. Business E-mail: deese.pamela@arentfox.com.

DEESE, WILLIE A., pharmaceutical executive; BA in Bus. Adminstrn., NC A&T State U., 1977; MBA, Western New England Coll., 1983. Buyer Digital Equipment Corp., 1977—79, sr. buyer, 1980—81, purchasing mgr., 1981—83, bus. materials mgr., 1983—85, site purchasing mgr., 1985—87, site materials mgr., 1987—89, disk operations mgr., 1989—90, site mgr., 1991—92; v.p. purchasing Kaiser Permanente, 1996—97; dir. purchasing SmithKline Beecham Clinical Laboratory Sector GlaxoSmithKline, 1992—95, v.p., dir. purchasing SmithKline Beecham Pharmaceuticals, 1995—96, sr. v.p., dir. purchasing Worldwide Supply Operations SmithKline Beecham Pharmaceuticals, 1997—2000, sr. v.p. global procurement and logistics, 2001—04; sr. v.p. global procurement Merck & Co., Inc., 2004—05, pres. Merck Mfg. Divsn., 2005—. Office: Merck PO Box 100 Whitehouse Station NJ 08889-0100*

DEETS, DWAIN AARON, retired aerospace technology executive; b. Bell, Calif., Apr. 16, 1939; s. Kenneth Robert and Mildred Evelyn (Bergman) D.; m. Catherine Elizabeth Meister, June 18, 1961; children: Dennis Allen, Danelle Alaine. AB, Occidental Coll., 1961; MS in Physics, San Diego State U., 1964; ME, UCLA, 1978. Rsch. engr. Dryden Flight Rsch. Ctr. NASA, Edwards, Calif., 62-78, 79-85, hdqrs. liaison engr. Washington, 1978-79, mgr. Edwards, 1979-85; dir. rsch. engring. Dryden Flight Rsch. Ctr., Edwards, 1990-96, dir. aerospace projects, 1996-97, dir. flight rsch. R&T, 1997-99; hdqrs. mgr. flight rsch. NASA, Washington, 1988-89; ret., 1999. Chmn. Reusable Launch Vehicles Non-Advocate Rev., 1995-96. Editor: (mag.) Secular Nat., 2006—, Atheist Alliance Internat.; contbr. articles to profl. jours. Recipient Exceptional Svc. medal NASA, 1988, Pres. Rank award SES, 1998, Founders award Atheists United, 2002 Fellow AIAA (assoc., Wright Bros. lectr. aeros. 1987); mem. Soc. Automotive Engrs. (chmn. aerospace control and guidance systems com. 1988-90), Toastmasters, Atheist Alliance Internat. (mem. bd. dirs.). Democrat. Home: 1770 Whitehall Rd Encinitas CA 92024-1036 Home Phone: 760-635-3719; Office Phone: 760-445-3242. E-mail: secularnation@cox.net.

DEETS, RICHARD M., secondary school educator, consultant; s. Richard M. Deets, Sr. and Mary E. Deets; m. Susan W. May; stepchildren: Kay May, Julie Daniels 1 child, Michelle R. BA, Calif. State U., LA, 1975; MA, Calif. State U., Northridge, 2000. Cert. resource specialist Calif., 1998, edn. adminstrn. Calif., 2000. Coord. coop. edn. L.A. Unified Sch. Dist., 1982—85, tchr., 1986—96, dean, 1996—2000, title I coord., 2000—01, resource specialist, 2001—. Mentor, tchr. LA Unified Sch. Dist., 2003—05. Author: (poetry) Poetic Divesities. Ednl. programs chair Sierra Madre (Calif.) Search and Rescue Team, 1989—2003; pres. Employment and Tng. Assn. Calif., LA, 1983—84. Named Coord. of the Yr., Vocat. Industry Clubs Am., 1982; recipient Poetry Grand prize, Internat. Soc. Poets, 2005. Mem.: Educare (assoc.), Phi Delta Kappa (assoc. 20 Yr. Svc. 2003). Republican. Episcopalian. Achievements include research in onsite Soviet Union space program. Avocations: mountain climbing, poetry, reading, mentor for high school students. Office: Los Angeles Unified School District 9229 Haskell Ave North Hills CA 91343 Personal E-mail: rdeets@socal.rr.com.

DE FABO, EDWARD CHARLES, photobiologist, research scientist, educator, photoimmunologist; b. Wilkes-Barre, Pa., June 10, 1937; s. Giovanni and Anna (Marconi) De F.; m. Athena Macris, Aug. 17, 1967 (dec. June 1985); m. Frances Patricia Noonan. BS, Kings Coll., 1958; PhD, George Washington U., 1974. Rsch. scientist USDA, Beltsville, Md., 1974-75, NCI-Frederick (Md.) Cancer Rsch. Ctr., 1978-81; scientist, adminstr. U.S. EPA, Washington, 1975-78; asst. rsch. prof. dept. dermatology George Washington U., Washington, 1981-86, assoc. rsch. prof. dept. dermatology, 1986-92, rsch. prof. dept. dermatology, 1992—. Chmn. project Sci. Com. on Problems of Environ. SCOPE ozone depletion and UV radiation, Paris, 1989-92; cons. U.S. EPA, 1984-85; chmn. project Internat. Arctic Sci. Com., Oslo, 1993—. Editor, organizer publ. Sci. Com. on Problems of Environment, 1992; contbr. articles to rsch. jours.; author: Immunology Today, 1992. Dir. congl. sci. fellowship program Am. Soc. Photobiology, Bethesda, 1981-85. Grantee Internat. Union Against Cancer, 1983, Am. Cancer Soc., 1987-89, U.S. EPA, 1987—, NIH, 1989—; fellow Smithsonian Inst., 1970-74, NSF, 1963-64; recipient Global Ozone award UN Environment Program, 1997, Elaine H. Snyder Cancer Rsch. award George Washington U., 1998. Mem. AAAS, Am. Soc. Photobiology (councilor 1980-83, dir. congl. sci. fellowship program 1981-85). Achievements include discovery (with F.P. Noonan)of a sunlight-activated immune-regulating photoreceptor on skin-urocanic acid; co-designer of unique UV monochromator for in vivo action spectrum studies.

DEFAZIO, LYNETTE STEVENS, dancer, choreographer, violinist, actress, educator; d. Honore and Mabel J. (Estavan) Stevens; children: J.H. Panganiban, Joanna Pang. Student, U. Calif., Berkeley, 1950—55, San Francisco State Coll., 1950—51; studied classical dance tchg. techniques and vocabulary with Gisella Caccialanza and Harold and Lew Christensen, San Francisco Ballet, 1952-56; D in Chiropractic, Life-West Chiropractic Coll., San Lorenzo, Calif., 1983; cert. techniques of tchg., U. Calif., 1985; BA in Humanities, New Coll. Calif., 1986. Lic. chiropracter, Mich.; diplomate Nat. Sci. Bd.; eminence in dance edn., Calif. C.C. dance specialist, std. svcs., childrens ctrs. credentials Calif. Dept. Edn., 1986. Contract child dancer Monogram Movie Studio, Hollywood, Calif., 1938-40; dance instr. San Francisco Ballet, 1953-65; performer San Francisco Opera Ring, 1960-67; performer, choreographer Oakland (Calif.) Civic Light Opera, 1963-70; dir. Ballet Arts Studio, Oakland, 1960; tchg. specialist Oakland Unified Sch. Dist., 1965-80; fgn. exch. dance dir. Academie de Danses-Salle Pleyel, Paris, 1966; instr. Peralta C.C. Dist., Oakland, 1971—, chmn. dance dept., 1985—. Cons., instr. ext. courses UCLA, Dirs. and Suprs. Assn., Pitts. Unified Sch. Dist., 1971-73, Tulare (Calif.) Sch. Dist., 1971-73; rschr. Ednl. Testing Svcs., HEW, Berkeley, 1974; resident choreographer San Francisco Childrens Opera, 1970—, Oakland Civic Theater; ballet mistress Dimensions Dance Theater, Oakland, 1977-80; cons. Gianchetta Sch. Dance, San Francisco, Robicheau Boston Ballet, TV series Patchwork Family, CBS, NYC; choreographer Ravel's Valses Nobles et Sentimentales, 1976. Author: Basic Music Outlines for Dance Classes, 1960, 1965, rev. edit., 1968, Teaching Techniques and Choreography for Advanced Dancers, 1965, Goals and Objectives in Improving Physical Capabilities, 1970, A Teacher's Guide for Ballet Techniques, 1970, Principle Procedures in Basic Curriculum, 1974, Objectives and Standards of Performance for Physical Development, 1975, Techniques of the Ballet School, 1970, rev. edit., 1974, The Opera Ballets: A Choreographic Manual Vols. I-V, 1986; assoc. music arranger: Le Ballet du Cirque, 1964, assoc. composer, lyricist: The Ballet of Mother Goose, 1968; choreographer Valses Nobles Et Sentimentales (Ravel), Transitions (Kashevaroff), 1991, The New Wizard of Oz, 1991, San Francisco Children's Opera (Gingold), Canon in D for Strings and Continuo (Pachelbel), 1979, Oakland Cmty. Orch. excerpts from Swan Lake, Faust, Sleeping Beauty, 1998, Rodeo, Alameda Coll. Cultural Affairs Program, 2000, The Gershwin Dances, 2004, solo dancer Three Stravinsky Etudes, Alameda Coll. Cultural Affairs Program, 1999, appeared in Flower Drum Song, 1993, Gigi, 1994, Fiddler on the Roof, 1996, The Music Man, 1996, Sayonara, 1997, Bye Bye Birdie, 2000, Barnum, the Circus Musical, 2001; musician (violinist): Oakland Cmty. Concert Orch., 1995—; condr.: Gil Gleason, coord.: Oakland Cmty. Orch., 2001—. Bd. dirs. Prodrs. Assocs., Inc., Oakland, 1999—; coord. Oakland (Calif.) Cmty. Orch., 2002—. Recipient Foremost Women of 20th Century, 1985, Merit award San Francisco Children's Opera, 1985, 90. Mem. Calif. State Tchrs. Assn., Bay Area Chiropractic Rsch. Soc., Profl. Dance Tchrs. Assn. Home and Office: 4923 Harbord Dr Oakland CA 94618-2506 Home Phone: 510-547-0477; Office Phone: 510-547-5477. Personal E-mail: LynetteDeFazio@comcast.net.

DEFAZIO, PETER ANTHONY, congressman; b. Needham, Mass., May 27, 1947; m. Myrnie Daut. BA in Econs. and Polit. Sci., Tufts U., Medford, Mass., 1969; postgraduate student, U. Oreg., Eugene, 1969-71, MS in Pub. Adminstrn./Gerontology, 1977. Sr. issues specialist, caseworker dist. field office Staff of US Rep. Jim Weaver of Oreg., 1977-78, legis. asst. Washington office, 1978-80, dir. constituent svcs., 1980-82; mem. Lane County Commn., Oreg., 1982-86, chmn.; mem. US Congress from 4th Oreg. dist., 1987—, dean Oreg. del., mem. transp. and infrastructure com., chmn. subcommittee on hwys. and transit, mem. homeland security com., mem. natural resources com. Mem. Lane County Econ. Devel. com., Intergovtl. Relations com.; bd. dirs. Eugene-Springfield Met. Partnership; Lane County Dem. precinct person, 1982. Served in USAFR. Mem. Assn. Oreg. Counties (legis. com.), Nat. Assn. Counties (tax and fin. com.). Democrat. Office: US House Reps 2134 Rayburn House Office Bldg Washington DC 20515-0001 Office Phone: 202-225-6416.*

DEFEIS, ELIZABETH FRANCES, lawyer, educator; b. NYC; d. Francis Paul and Lena (Amendola) D. BA, St. John's U., 1956, JD, 1958, JSD (hon.), 1984; LLM, NYU, 1971; postgrad., U. Milan, Italy, 1963-64, Inst. Internat. Human Rights, 1991. Bar: N.Y. 1959, U.S. Dist. Ct. (fed. dist.) 1960, U.S. Dist. Ct. (so. dist.) N.Y. 1961, U.S. Supreme Ct. 1965, U.S. Dist. Ct. (ea. dist.) N.Y. 1978, N.J. 1983. Asst. U. S. atty. So. Dist. N.Y., Dept. Justice, 1961-62; atty. RCA Corp., 1962-63; assoc. Carter, Ledyard & Milburn, NYC, 1963-69; atty. Bedford Stuyvesant Legal Svcs. Corp., 1969-70; prof. law Seton Hall U., Newark, 1971—, dean Sch. Law, 1983-88. Vis. prof. St. Louis U. Sch. Law, 1988, St. John's U. Sch. Law, 1990, 2001, U. Milan, Italy, 1996; Fulbright-Hays lectr., Iran, India, 1977-79; lectr. Orgn. Security and Cooperation in Europe, Russia, Turkmenistan, Tajikistan, Azerbaijan; vis. scholar Ctr. Study of Human Rights, Columbia U., 1989; project dir. TV series Women and Law, 1974-80; narrator TV series Alternatives to Violence, 1981; mem. com. women and cts. N.J. Supreme Ct., 1982-95; trustee Legal Svcs. N.J., 1983-88; mem. 3rd Cir. Task Force on Equality in the Cts., 1995-98; tech. cons. on Constitution of Armenia, 1992-95; project dir. T.V. series Pub. Internat. Law.; legal expert Armenia election OSCE, 1998; disting. chair fulbright program U. Naples, 2002. Chair Albert Einstein Inst., Boston, 1995—2001. Fulbright-Hays scholar Milan, Italy, 1963-64, Fulbright-Hays, Orgn. for Security and Cooperation in Europe scholar, Armenia, Russia, Italy, 1996; Ford Found. fellow, 1970-71. Mem. ABA, Columbian Lawyers Assn., Assn. of Bar of City of N.Y. (chmn. UN com.), N.J. Bar Assn., Nat. Italian Am. Found. Office: Seton Hall U Law Sch One Newark Ctr Newark NJ 07102 Business E-Mail: defeisel@shu.edu.

DEFELICE, EUGENE ANTHONY, internist, educator, magician; b. Beacon, NY, Dec. 24, 1927; s. Domenick and Louise (Grippo) DeF. BS, Columbia U., 1951; MD, Boston U., 1956. Ciba fellow, lectr. pharmacology Boston U. Sch. Medicine, 1954-57; intern Newton (Mass.) Wellesley Hosp., 1957; postgrad. tng. internal medicine/psychosomatic medicine Jackson Meml. Hosp., U. Miami Sch. Medicine, Miami, Fla., 1958—61; asst. dir. clin. rsch. Warner Lambert Rsch. Inst., Morris Plains, NJ, 1961-64; dir. clin. rsch. Bristol Labs. (now Bristol Meyers Squibb), Syracuse, NY, 1965-66, Sandoz Inc. (now Novartis Inc.), East Hanover, NJ, 1967-68, exec. dir. clin. research, 1969-70, dir. sci. affairs and comml. devel., 1970—73, v.p. corp. sci. devel., 1974-77, v.p. internat. med. rsch., med. advisor, 1977-83. Prof. biochemistry, microbiology and pub. health, dir. rsch. New Eng. Coll. Pharmacy, 1956-58; practice in medicine, cons. in medicine and med. rsch., Morristown, N.J., 1961-87, East Schodack and Albany, N.Y., 1988-2003, Niagara Falls, N.Y., 2004—; clin. assoc. prof. medicine Coll. Medicine and Dentistry N.J.-Rutgers Med. Sch., 1977-84; clin. prof. medicine UMD-Robert Wood Johnson Med. Sch., 1985—2003; clin. prof. anesthesiology UCLA, 1978-83. Co-author: Angiotensin Converting Enzyme Inhibitors, 1987, Prostaglandins, Platelets, Lipids: New Developemnts in Atherosclerosis, 1981, Health and Obesity, 1983, Beta Blockers in the Treatment of Cardiovascular Diseases, 1984, The Pharmacological Treatment of Cardiovascular Diseases, 1986; author: Web Health Info. Resource Guide, 2001, Breast Cancer, 2002, Overweight, Obesity and Health, 2002, Nutrition and Health, 2003, Web Health Information Resources, 2004, Prevention of Cardiovascular Disease, 2005, Stress and Health, 2006; mem. editl. bd. Triangle, Sandorama, 1977—81; contbr. articles to profl. jours. Served with U.S. Army, World War II. Named Hon. Citizen Italy; named to Notable Italian-Am. Hall of Fame; recipient Golden Merit award Med. Soc. NJ, 2006. Fellow Am. Geriat. Soc., Acad. Psychosomatic Medicine; mem. Soc. Am. Magicians, Internat. Brotherhood Magicians; emeritus mem. numerous profl. socs. Home and Office: 600 Spruce Ave Niagara Falls NY 14301 Office Phone: 716-285-2711. Personal E-mail: ead12209@yahoo.com. *Success in life comes from constancy of purpose, diligent work, living according to sound moral and religious principles, and having faith and hope in the future. Helping to make the world a better place to live in, autographing one's work in excellence, and doing good by others are the rewards which bring happiness.*

DE FELITTA, FRANK PAUL, film producer, writer; b. NYC; s. Pat and Genevieve (Sibilio) De F.; m. Dorothy Gilbert; children: Eileen Raymond. Student, U. N.C., New Sch. Social Research, 1948. Dir., writer: CBS, 1950-57; dir. programming: Nat. Telefilms Assocs., 1959-61; prodr., writer, dir.: NBC, from 1962; prodr., dir., writer: Universal Studios, 1968-69; film documentaries include Music of the South, 1955; sci. series Conquest, 1957; natural sci. series Adventure, 1953-55; hist. series Odyssey, 1958, The Chosen Child, 1962 (Writers Guild award), Emergency Ward, 1962 (Emmy award), Experiment in Excellence, 1963 (Sch. Bell award), Battle of the Bulge, 1964, The Stately Ghosts of England, 1964, The World of the Teenager, 1966 (Robert J. Flaherty award), Pearl Harbor, 1966 Golden Eagle award; dir., author: films Trapped, 1973, The Two Worlds of Jennie Logan, 1979 (Silver Halo award), Killer in the Mirror, 1986, Scissors, 1990; dir.: film Dark Night of the Scarecrow, 1981; (Brotherhood award of Nat. Conf. Christians and Jews for film Mississippi- A Self Portrait, George Washington Honor medal of Freedoms Found. for film The American Image.); author: films The First of January, 1970, The Savage Is Loose, 1971, Audrey Rose, 1977, The Entity, 1981; novels Oktoberfest, 1972, Audrey Rose, 1975, The Entity, 1978, Sea Trial, 1980, For Love of Audrey Rose, 1982, Golgotha Falls, 1984, Funeral March of the Marionettes, 1990, A Swift Death to Critics, 2000, Inch-A Dark Tale, 2006. Recipient Peabody award, 1954, 63, Thomas Alva Edison award, 1958, 5 Gold Eagle awards Coun. on Internat. Non-Theatrical Events. Mem. Writers Guild Am., Dirs. Guild Am.

DEFENDI, VITTORIO, medical association administrator, pathologist; b. Treviglio, Italy, Nov. 16, 1928; married, 1955; 3 children. MD, U. Pavia, 1951. Instr. pathology dept. U. Pavia, 1951-52; pathologist virus sect. Lederle Labs., NYC, 1956-58; assoc. pathologist Med. Sch., U. Pa., 1958-64, assoc. prof., 1964-68, Wistar prof., 1968-74; prof. pathology, chmn. dept. pathology Sch. NYU Sch. Medicine, NYC, 1974—2002. Brit. Coun. scholar Postgrad. Med. Sch., U. London, 1952-53; Fulbright fellow Med. Sch., U. Vt., 1953-54; rsch. fellow Detroit Inst. Cancer Rsch., 1954-56; assoc. mem. Wistar Inst., 1958-64, mem. staff, 1964-74; rsch. prof. Am. Cancer soc., 1973—. Leukemia Soc. scholar, 1962-66. Mem. Am. Soc. Cell Biology, Am. Soc. Exptl. Pathology, Histochem. Soc., Am. Assn. Immunology, Am. Assn. Cancer Rsch. Achievements include research in viral oncology; tumor biology; mechanism of immunological defense. Office: NYU Sch Medicine Dept Pathology 550 1st Ave New York NY 10016-6402 Business E-Mail: vittorio.defendi@med.nyu.edu.

DEFEO, CHARLES JOESPH, Internet company executive; b. Kansas City, Mo., Apr. 16, 1974; s. Charles Joesph DeFeo Jr. and Kelly DeFeo (Stepmother); m. Natasha Ann Graves, July 31, 1974. BA in Polit Sci., U. Mo., Kansas City, Mo., 1996. Tech. aide Office of U.S. Senator John Ashcroft, Washington, 1996—99; v.p. Campaign Solutions, Alexandria, Va., 1999; new media dir. Ashcroft for US Senate, St. Louis, 2000; dep. assoc. asst. atty. gen. US Dept. Justice, Washington, 2001—02; online comm. dir. Rep. Nat. Com., 2002—03; e-campaign mgr. Bush-Cheney '04, Arlington, Va., 2003—04; gen. mgr. Townhall.com, 2005—. Online dir. 55th Inaugural Com. for Pres. and v.p. US, Washington, 2004—05; asst. dir. internet alley 1996 Rep. Nat. Conv., San Diego, 1996. Online columnist (of polit. genre). Recipient Best Online Campaign award, George Wash. U. Golden Dot, 2004. Republican. Office: Townhall.com 1901 North Moore St Arlington VA 22209 Home Phone: 703-533-0373; Office Phone: 703-247-1222. Home Fax: 703-247-1259.

DEFEO, NEIL P., consumer products company executive; m. Sandra DeFeo; children: Julia, Lauren, Elizabeth. BCE, Manhattan Coll., 1968. With Procter & Gamble, 1968—93; group v.p. U.S. ops. Clorox Co., 1993—96; chmn., pres., CEO Remington Products Co., Bridgeport, Conn., 2001—03; pres., CEO Playtex Products Inc., Allendale, NJ, 2004—, chmn., 2006—. Bd. dir. Am. Woodmark Corp.; dir. Grocery Mfr. Assn., Cosmetic Toiletry & Fragrance Assn. Trustee Manhattan Coll. Office: Playtex Products Inc PO Box 701 Allendale NJ 07401-1600

DEFEO, PHILIP D., private equity firm executive; m. DeFeo H. Ann; 2 children. BA in Econ. and Internat. Fin., Iona Coll. Opers. mgr. Procter and Gamble; sr. v.p. internat. securities divsn. Bankers Trust Co., London; mng. dir. worldwide equities opers. Lehman Bros.; sr. v.p. and mem. oper. com. FMR Corp.; exec. v.p. & dir. mktg. and customer svc. Cedel Internat.; pres. and CEO Van Eck Assocs. Corp.; chmn. and CEO Pacific Exch. (now NYSE Arca), San Francisco, 1999—2005; co-founder mng. ptnr. Lithos Capital Partners LLC, Westport, Conn., 2006—. Non-exec. dir. Computershare Ltd., 2002—; chmn., trustee Market Vectors Trust, New York, 2006—; bd. dirs. Allied World Ins. Co., 2006—; ind. dir. Visa USA, Inc., 2006—. Mem.: Berea Coll. Bd. of Trustees. Office: Lithos Capital Ptnrs LLC Ste 215 1720 Post Road E Westport CT 06880 Office Phone: 203-259-7100. Office Fax: 203-259-5757. E-mail: info@lithoscapital.com.*

DEFEO, RONALD M., machinery manufacturing executive; B in Econs. and Philosophy, Iona Coll., 1974. Various positions Procter & Gamble, 1974-84; sr. v.p., mng. dir. JI case constrn. equipment Tenneco, Inc., 1984-92; pres. heavy equipment group TEREX Corp., 1992, pres., COO, 1993—95, pres., CEO, 1995—98, chmn., pres., CEO, 1998—2006, chmn., CEO, 2007—. Bd. dirs. United Rentals, Inc.; co-chmn. CONEXPO-CON/AGG. Mem. Constrn. Industry Mfrs. Assn. (mem. exec. com.), Young Pres. Orgn. Office: TEREX Corp Ste 320 500 Post Rd East Westport CT 06880*

DEFILIPPI, GEORGE, retired air force officer; b. Mobile, Ala., Sept. 6, 1947; s. George and Margaret Josephine (Lazzari) DeF.; m. Patricia Naismith McAdam, July 21, 1969; children: Jocelyn, Gwendolyn, Geoffrey, James. BS, USAF Acad., Colorado Springs, 1969; MS, Air Force Inst. Technology, Dayton, Ohio, 1977; cert. in bus. adminstrn., Georgetown Ctr. for Profl. Devel., 2005. Enlisted USAF, 1969, advanced through ranks to col., exec. sec., program mgr. Scientific Adv. Bd. HQ USAF, Washington, 1984-86, chief tng. divsn. 602d Tactical Air Control Wing Davis Mountain AFB, Ariz., 1986-88, cmdr. 22d Tactical Air Support Tng. Squadron, 1988-89, cmdr. 23d Tactical Air Support Squadron, 1989-90, cmdr. Air Liaison Office XVIII Airborne Corps Ft. Bragg, NC, 1991-93, cmdr. Air Liaison Office to 3d Rep. Korea Army Uijongbu, Korea, 1992-93, mil. staff specialist Undersec. Def. Acquisition & Tech. Washington, 1993-96, mil. asst. to dir. strategic tactical systems, 1996-99; ret., 1999; field dir. mil. requirements Carlton Life Support Systems, Inc., Arlington, Va., 1999—. Vol. Arlington Emergency Winter Shelter, 1993-99; active Arlington Com. of 100, 1994-2006; vestryman St. George's Episcopal Ch., 1996-99, Stephen min., leader, 1999—2005; abbot St. George's Urban Abbey, 2003-06; treas. St. George's Ch., 2005-. Mem. Assn. Unmanned Vehicle Sys. (bd. dirs. Capitol chpt. 1993-97), Air Force Assn. (Steele chpt. v.p. aerospace edn. 2006—, pres. 2004-06, v.p. ops. 2002-04, newsletter editor 1999—). Episcopal. Avocations: jogging, swimming. Office: Carlton Life Support Systems Inc 1215 S Clark St Ste 309 Arlington VA 22202 Office Phone: 703-414-5302. Business E-Mail: gdefilippi@carletonls.com.

DEFLEUR, LOIS B., academic administrator; b. Aurora, Ill., June 25, 1936; d. Ralph Edward and Isabel Anna (Cornils) Begitske; m. Melvin L. DeFleur (div.) AB, Blackburn Coll., 1958; MA, Ind. U., 1961; PhD in Sociology, U. Ill., 1965; HHD (hon.), U. Alaska, 1999. Asst. prof. sociology Transylvania Coll., Lexington, Ky., 1963-67; assoc. prof. Wash. State U., Pullman, 1967-74, prof., 1975-86, dean Coll. Liberal Arts, 1981-86; provost U. Mo., Columbia, 1986-90; pres. Binghamton U., SUNY, 1990—. Disting. vis. prof. USAF Acad., 1976-77; vis. prof. U. Chgo., 1980-81; bd. dirs. Energy East Corp., HealthNow, N.Y. Author: Delinquency in Argentina, 1965; (with others) Sociology: Human Society, 3d edit. 1981, 4th edit., 1984, The Integration of Women into All Male Air Force Units, 1982, The Edward R. Murrow Heritage: A Challenge for the Future, 1986; contbr. articles to profl. jours. Mem. Wash. State Bd. on Correctional Svcs. and Edn., 1974-77, State of N.Y. Edn. Dept. Curriculum and Assessment Coun., 1991-94, Trilateral Task for N.Am. Ednl. Collaboration, USIA, 1993-95. Recipient Disting. Alumni award Blackburn Coll., 1991, Chief Exec. Leadership awrd Coun. for Advancement and Support of Edn., 1999, Civic Leadership award Greater Binghamton C. of C., 2003, Woman of Distinction award Girl Scout Coun., 2002; grantee NIMH, 1969-79, NSF, 1972-75, Air Force Office, 1978-81. Mem. NCAA (pres. commn. 1996, exec. com. 1997-98), Am. Sociol. Assn. (publs. com. 1979-82, nominations com. 1984-86, coun. mem. 1987-90, com. on exec. office and budget), Pacific Sociol. Assn. (pres. 1980-82), Coun. Colls. of Arts and Scis. (bd. dirs. 1982-84, pres. 1985-87), Aircraft Owners and Pilots Assn., Internat. Comanche Soc., Nat. Assn. State U. and Land-grant Colls. (exec. com. 1990-93, chair coun. of pres. 1994-95, chmn. bd. dirs. 1996-97), Am. Coun. Edn. (bd. dirs. 1994-2000, v.p. chair-elect 1997-98, chair bd. dirs. 1998-99), Consortium Social Sci. Assns. (bd. dirs. 1993-96). Office: Binghamton U Office of Pres PO Box 6000 Binghamton NY 13902-6000 E-mail: ldefleur@binghamton.edu.*

DEFOOR, J. ALLISON, II, lawyer, priest; b. Coral Gables, Fla., Dec. 6, 1953; s. James Allison, Sr. and Marjorie (Keen) DeFoor; m. Terry Ann White, June 24, 1977; children: Melissa Anne, Mary Katherine, James Allison III. BA, U. So. Fla., 1976, MA, 1979; JD, Stetson U., 1979; STD, MDiv, Fla. Ctr. Theol. Studies, 1999, DMin, 2005. Bar: Fla. 1979, U.S. Dist. Ct. (so. dist.) Fla. 1980, U.S. Ct. Appeals (5th cir.) 1981, U.S. Ct. Appeals (11th cir.) 1982; ordained priest Episcopal Ch., 2007. Asst. pub. defender, 1979—80; asst. state's atty. 16th Cir., Key West, Fla., 1980—83, dir. narcotics task force, 1981—83; judge Monroe County, Plantation Key, Fla., 1983—87; assoc. Cunningham, Albritton, Lenzi, Warner, Bragg & Miller, Plantation Key, 1987—89; sheriff Monroe County, 1989—90; sr. v.p., CEO Wackenut Monitoring Sys. Inc., Coral Gables, 1991—92; gen. counsel, sec. HEM Pharm. Corp., Phila. and Key Largo, 1992—93; ptnr. Hershoff, Lupino, DeFoor & Gregg, Tavernier, Fla., 1993—99; Everglades policy coord. Office of Gov., State of Fla., Tallahassee, 1999—2000; gen. counsel Tidewater, Inc., Tallahassee, 2000—02; state coord. EarthBalance, Inc., Tallahassee and North Port, 2002—; dir. Beach Restoration, Inc., 2003—, Hydromentia, Inc., 2003—. Adj. faculty St. Leo Coll., Key West, 1980—81, U. So. Fla., Ft. Myers, Fla., 1981—82, Fla. Internat. U., Miami, 1985, U. Miami Law Sch., 1985—99, Fla. A&M U., 1999—2001; faculty Nat. Jud. Coll., Reno, 1985—86; lectr. Yale U., 2000, U. Pa. Law Sch., 2000. Editor: U. Miami Law Rev., 1985, St. Thomas Law Rev., 2000; author (with Schultz): Florida Civil Procedure Forms with Practice Commentary, 1989; author: Odet Philippe, Peninsular Pioneer, 1997. Trustee Fla. Dispute Resolution Consortium, Collins Ctr. for Pub. Policy, Fla. Chamber, 1000 Friends of Fla., Leroy Collins Inst.; bd. vis. Fla. State

U. Law Sch.; del. Rep. Nat. Conv., 1992, 2004; Rep. state committeeman Fla., 2004—; mem. Fla. Rep. Exec. Com., 1995—99, 2002—; Rep. nominee Lt. Gov. Fla., 1990; chmn. Wakulla County Rep. Exec. Com., 2001—04; vice chair Rep. Party Fla., 2003—07; bd. dirs. Associated Industries Fla., Fla. Taxwatch, 1000 Friends of Fla.; bd. govs. Fla. Chamber. Named one of Five Outstanding Young Men in Fla., Jaycees, 1984, Ten Outstanding Young Men in Am., 1985; recipient Merit award, Fla. Crime Prevention Commn., 1982, award, Leadership Fla. Class V, Chmn. award, Fla. Audubon, 1997. Mem.: Fla. Bar, Mensa, Key West Yacht Club, Islamorada Fishing Club, Gov.'s Club, Explorer's Club (N.Y.C.), Ocean Reef Club (Key Largo). Avocations: scuba diving, sailing, golf. Home: 359 River Plantation Rd Crawfordville FL 32327-1517 Office: Earth Balance 200 W College Ave Tallahassee FL 32301 Home Phone: 850-925-5693; Office Phone: 850-681-6465. Business E-Mail: adefoor@earthbalance.com.

DEFORD, FRANK, sportswriter, commentator, writer; b. Balt., Dec. 16, 1938; s. Benjamin F. Deford Jr. and Louise (McAdams) Deford; m. Carol Penner, Aug. 28, 1965; children: Christian McAdams, Scarlet Faith. BA, Princeton U., 1962. Writer Sports Illustrated mag., NYC, 1964-89, 98—; editor, pub. The Nat. Sports Daily, NYC, 1989-91; contbg. editor Newsweek, 1991-93, 96-98, Vanity Fair, 1993-96. Commentator Nat. Pub. Radio, Washington, 1980—, Cable News Network, NYC, 1980—86, NBC Sports, NYC, 1986—89, ESPN Radio, NYC, 1991—98, HBO, NYC, 1994—. Author: Five Strides on the Banked Track, 1971, There She Is, 1971, Cut 'n' Run, 1972, The Owner, 1976, Big Bill Tilden: The Triumphs and the Tragedy, 1976, Everybody's All-American, 1982, Alex: The Life of a Child, 1983, The Spy in the Deuce Court, 1986, The World's Tallest Midget, 1987, Casey on the Loose, 1989, Love and Infamy, 1993, The Best of Frank Deford, 2000, The Other Adonis, 2001, An American Summer, 2002, The Old Ball Game, 2005, The Entitled, 2007; author: (screenplays) Trading Hearts, 1988, Four Minutes, 2005. Trustee Cystic Fibrosis Found., Washington, 1973—, chmn., 1984—99, chmn. emeritus, 1999—. Named Sportswriter of Yr., Nat. Assn. Sportswriters and Sportscasters, 1982, 1984—88, Sportswriter Hall of Fame, 1998, Nat. Mag. Writer of Yr., Wash. Journalism Rev., 1987—88, Best U.S. Sportswriter, Am. Journalism Rev., 1992; recipient 1st Winner award for Excellence in Sport Journalism Ctr. for Study of Sport in Soc., Northeastern U., 1985, Disting. Svc. to Journalism award, U. Mo., 1987, Emmy award for TV Writing and Commentary, 1988, George Foster Peabody award for Documentary Writing, 1999, Nat. Mag. Award for Profiles, 1999. Democrat. Episcopalian. Home and Office: PO Box 1109 Greens Farms CT 06838-1109 Home Phone: 203-259-1784. Personal E-mail: frank6de@aol.com.

DEFORD, NANCY T., retired educational association and school system administrator; B in Art and Hist., Trinity U., Tex., M in Curriculum and Supervision; D in Comparative Edn., U. So. Calif., Heidelberg, Germany. Art tchr., San Antonio; tchr., adminstr., cons. England, France, Utah; positions including art edn. coord., dir. gifted progs., dir. gifted edn. and magnet schs., dir. ednl. planning and assessment, asst. prin., HS prin. Virginia Beach Pub. Schs.; supt. Pk. City Sch. Dist., Utah, 1996—2003; v.p. DeFord Ltd., Virginia Beach. Mem.: ACSD (pres., Va. bd. dirs. 1977, Va. rep. bd. dirs. 1992—94, at-large rep. to bd. 1996—98, Utah rep. 1998, 1999, 2001, mem. nominations com. 2000, pres. Utah chpt. 2002, at-large mem. bd. 2003—05). Office: DeFord Ltd 2712 Southern Blvd Ste 100 Virginia Beach VA 23452 E-mail: ndeford@cox.net.*

DE FOREST, SHERWOOD SEARLE, agricultural engineer, agricultural products executive; b. Ames, Iowa, Sept. 20, 1921; s. Frank Ray and Clara Maud (Searle) De F.; m. Virginia Mary Flynn, June 20, 1947; children: David, Debra, Denise, Kimberly. Student, U. Cin., 1939-40; BS, Iowa State U., 1943, MS, 1947. Instr. agrl. engring. Iowa State U., 1946-47, extension agrl. engr., 1947-52; engring. editor Successful Farming mag., Des Moines, 1952-59; with USX, Pitts., 1959-77, mgr. agrl. equipment mktg., 1964-70, indsl. rep., 1970-77; v.p., assoc. The Montgomery Group, Inc., Tallahassee, 1977-96; pollution prevention engr. Fla. Dept. Environ. Protection, Tallahassee, 1996-99; owner De Forest Agri-Svcs., Tallahassee, 1977-99. Pres. Ginande Corp., 1986-91; tech. transfer project leader No. Agrl. Energy Center, Sci. and Edn. Adminstrn., U.S. Dept. Agr., Peoria, Ill., 1980-81; cons. Pakistan, 1984, Portugal, 1985, 86; mem. indsl. and profl. adv. com. Coll. Engring. Pa. State U., 1966-71; mem. NE Regional Agrl. Research Planning Com., 1970-72; mem. Fla. Gov.'s Continuing Care Adv. Coun., 1996-2000. Author: The Vision That Cut Druggery From Farming Forever, 2007;contbg. author: Power to Produce, U.S. Dept. Agr. Yearbook, 1969, Steel in Agriculture, 1966; pub. TravelHost of Pitts. mag., 1982-83; tech. editor Soc. Automotive Engrs. Internat., 1987-89; editor: Memories of Dr. J. Brownlee Davidson, Father of Agricultural Engineering 2005; contbr. numerous articles to Successful Farming mag. Served to 1st lt. USAAF, 1942-46. Recipient Am. Soc. Agrl. Engrs.-Metal Bldg. Mfrs. Assn. award for disting. work in advancing knowledge and sci. of farm bldgs., 1964 Fellow: Am. Soc. Agrl. and Biol. Engrs. (pres. 1975—76); mem.: Fla. Life Care Residents Assn., Inc. (chpt. pres. 1999—2003, state bd. dirs. 2001—04, state treas. 2003—04). Presbyterian. Achievements include patents in field. Home and Office: 4173 Covenant Ln Tallahassee FL 32308-5766 Personal E-mail: ssdf@embarkmail.com.

DEFORGE, ANNA, professional basketball player; b. Apr. 14, 1976; d. Roger and Rosemary DeForge. Grad. in Bus. Adminstrn., U. Nebr., 1998. Guard Am. Basketball League San Jose Lasers, Calif., 1998, Nat. Women's Basketball League Springfield Spirit, Nat. Women's Basketball League Chgo. Blaze, WNBA Detroit Shock, 2000, WNBA Phoenix Mercury, 2003—05, WNBA Ind. Fever, 2006—; guard (off-season) Euro League Wisla Can-Pack, Poland, 2005—. Named MVP, Nat. Women's Basketball League, Polish League, 2006; named to Select All-Star Team, WNBA, 2004, Ea. Conf. All-Star Team, 2007. Achievements include winning Polish league titles as a member of Wisla Can-Pack, 2006, 07. Mailing: Ind Fever Conseco Fieldhouse One Conseco Court 125 S Pennsylvania St Indianapolis IN 46204 E-mail: anna@annadeforge.com.*

DE FRANCESCO, JOHN BLAZE, JR., public relations consultant, writer; b. Stamford, Conn., May 22, 1936; s. John Blaze and Mae (Matyscyk) DeF.; m. Louise C. Terlizzo, Nov. 1, 1958 (div. 1983); children: Daryl, Jay, Dana, Dorian; m. Diana Picchietti, Oct. 20, 1990. BS, U. Conn., 1958. Sr. v.p. Daniel J. Edelman, Inc., Chgo., 1967-77; exec. v.p. Ruder Finn & Rotman, Inc., Chgo., 1977-85; prin., CEO DeFrancesco/Goodfriend Pub. Relations, 1985-2001; exec. v.p. L.C. Williams & Assoc., Chgo., 2001—03; prin. DeFrancesco Artist and Writer, 2003—. Bd. dirs. Ill. Divsn. Vocat. Rehab., 1976-78; mem. pub. rels. adv. bd. Gov.'s State U., 1994-98. Comdr. USN, 1958-67; comdr. USNR; ret. 1979. Recipient 3 Silver Anvil awards Pub. Rels. Soc. Am., 6 Golden Trumpet awards Publicity Club, Chgo. Mem. Pub. Rels. Soc. Am., Navy League U.S., Mil. Officer Assn. Am. Roman Catholic. Home and Office: 18785 Saint Andrews Dr Monument CO 80132-8824

DEFRANCO, BONIFACE FERDINAND LEONARD (BUDDY DEFRANCO), clarinetist, bandleader; b. Camden, NJ, Feb. 17, 1923; m. Joyce O. Yount; 1 child, Charles Lee. Student, Mastbaum Music Sch., Phila. Alto saxophonist, solo clarinetist Johnny Scat Davis Band, on tour, 1939, Gene Krupa Orch., on tour, 1941-42, Charlie Barnett Orch., on tour, 1943; solo clarinet Tommy Dorsey Orch., on tour, 1944-48, Count Basie Septet, on tour, 1950; bandleader Buddy DeFranco Orch., 1951; featured clarinetist Jazz at the Philharm. All Star Tours, worldwide, 1952-54; condr. Glenn Miller Orch., 1966-74; leader, guest artist The Buddy DeFranco Group, Panama City, Fla., 1974—. Performer, clinician Yamaha Music Corp., Grand Rapids, Mich., 1973—; clinician, judge various univs., 1950—. Author: Buddy DeFranco Hand in Hand with Hanon, 1996, Buddy DeFranco on Jazz Improvisation, 1973, Mel Bay Presents Modern Jazz Compositions and Studies for the Clarinet, 1983; rec. artist numerous albums including Hark: Buddy DeFranco Meets the Oscar Peterson Quartet, 1994, Chip Off the Old Bop, 1994, You Must Believe in Swing, & Nobody Else But Me, with Metropole Orch., 1997, Flying Fingers of Art Tatum and Buddy DeFranco, Cross Country Suite with Nelson Riddle (Grammy award 1956), Mr. Lucky, Mood Indigo, Chicago Fire with Buddy DeFranco and Terry Gibbs, George Gershwin Songbook with Oscar Peterson, Buddy DeFranco/Dave McKenna: Do Nothing 'Till You Hear From Us, 1999, Buddy DeFranco: Cookin' the Books w/ John Pizzarelli Trio & Butch Miles, 2004 Named #1 Jazz Clarinetist over 45 times Downbeat mag., Metronome mag., Playboy Mag. All Stars-All Stars, Ency. Jazz Musicians poll; named 2006 Jazz Master, Nat. Endowment for Arts. Fellow Nat. Assn. Jazz Educators; mem. ClariNetowrk (bd. dirs. 1980—), ASCAP. Home (Summer): 978A Colorado Ave Whitefish MT 59937-3413 Address: 22525 Coral Ave Panama City FL 32413-3047 E-mail: harkii@hotmail.com.

DEFRANK, THOMAS MICHAEL, journalist; b. Houston, June 13, 1945; s. Pete and Lillian Margaret (McLaughlin) DeF.; m. Melanie Anne Cooper, May 6, 1990; children: Matthew Michael, Andrew Spencer. BA with high hons., Tex. A&M U., 1967; MA, U. Minn., 1968. Corr. Newsweek Mag., Washington, 1970-73, White House corr., 1974-85, sr. White House corr., dep. bur. chief, 1985-95; bur. chief NY Daily News, Washington, 1996—. Prin. reporter: (books) Quest for the Presidency 1984, 1985, 1988, 1989; co-author: Quest for the Presidency, 1992, 1994, The Politics of Diplomacy, 1995, Bare Knuckles and Backrooms, 1996, Write It When I'm Gone, 2007. 1st lt. US Army, 1968-70; US Army Res. 1970-92. Co-recipient Nat. Mag. award, Mag. Pubs. Assn. Am., NYC, 1993; recipient Gerald R. Ford prize for Disting. Reporting on the Presidency, 2006. Mem. White House Corrs. Assn. (pres. 1982-83, Aldo Beckman award 1993, Merriman Smith award 1983), Army & Navy Club, U. Club, Gridiron Club. Roman Catholic. Avocations: stamp collecting/philately, racquetball. Office: New York Daily News 1050 Thomas Jefferson St NW Washington DC 20007 Office Phone: 202-467-6670.

DEFRIES, RUTH S., earth system scientist, researcher; b. Washington, Oct. 20, 1956; d. Myron G. DeFries and Tamar D. Lieberman; m. Jitendra N. Bajpai, Nov. 23, 1980; children: Triveni, Avinash Bajpai. BA summa cum laude, Washington U., St. Louis, 1976; PhD, Johns Hopkins U., 1980. Hydrologist US Geol. Survey, Balt., 1979—80; rsch. assoc. Indian Inst. Tech., Bombay, 1981—83; sr. project officer environ. studies bd. NAS, Washington, 1983—87, sr. project officer global change com., 1987—91; assoc. rsch. scientist U. Md., College Park, 1991—99, assoc. prof., 1999—2005, prof., 2005—. Vis. scientist Carnegie Inst. Washington, Palo Alto, Calif., 1998; assoc. mem. MODLAND sci. team NASA, 1999—; mem. distributed active archive ctr. user working grp. Dept. Energy Oak Ridge Nat. Lab., 2000—; mem. global observations of forest cover Forest/Land Cover Implementation Team, 2001—04; sci. adv. bd. Nat. Ctr. Ecol. Analysis and Synthesis, Santa Barbara, Calif., 2001—04; mem. steering com. for workshop on direct and indirect human contbns. to terrestrial greenhouse gas fluxes NRC, 2003, mem. climate data records from operational satellies com., 2003—, mem. geog. scis. com., 2001—; mem. socioeconomic data and applications ctr. users' working grp. Internat. Earth Sci. Info. Network at Columbia U., 2004—. Contbr. articles sci. jours., chapters to books; co-editor: Global Change and Our Common Future: Papers from a Forum, 1989, Global and Regional Land Cover Characterization from Satellite Data, 2000, Ecosystems and Land Use Change, 2004; co-author: One Earth, One Future: Our Changing Global Environment, 1990; editl. bd. Regional Environ. Change, 2003—. Mem.: NAS, Ecol. Soc. Am. (Aldo Leopold leadership fellow 2001), Am. Geophys. Union (mem. spring meeting prog. com. 2001—02), Phi Beta Kappa. Office: U Md 2181 Lefrak Hall College Park MD 20742 Business E-Mail: rdefries@geog.umd.edu.

DE FRIESE, GORDON H., health services researcher; b. Trion, Ga., Apr. 25, 1942; BS, Middle Tenn. State U., 1963; MA, U. Ky., 1966, PhD, 1967. Instr. dept. behavioral sci. U. Ky. Med. Ctr., Lexington, 1966—67; asst. prof. sociology and social psychology Cornell U., Ithaca, NY, 1969—71; rsch. assoc. Cecil G. Sheps Ctr. for Health Svcs. Rsch. U. N.C., Chapel Hill, 1971—, asst. prof. sociology, 1971—77, asst. prof. family medicine Sch. Medicine, 1973—75, clin. assoc. prof. dept. epidemiology Sch. Pub. Health, 1978—82, assoc. prof. Sch. Medicine, 1976—82, prof. Sch. Medicine, 1982—, prof. Sch. Pub. Health, 1982—, prof. dept. dental ecology Sch. Dentistry, 1986—, co-dir. Robert Wood Johnson Found. Clin. Scholars Program, 1986—2000. Adj. asst. prof. Sloan Inst. Hosp. Adminstrn.; dir. U.S. Army Armor Sch. Electives Divsn., Fort Knox, Ky., 1967—69; co-dir. Comprehensive Health Planning Tng. Program of the Dept. of Sociology and City and Regional Planning and the Sloan Inst. Hosp. Adminstrn. Cornell U., Ithaca, NY, 1969—71; co-dir. grad. program in med. sociology Dept. Sociology U. N.C., Chapel Hill, 1971—76, dir. Cecil G. Sheps Ctr. for Health Svcs. Rsch., 1973—2000; pres., CEO N.C. Inst. Medicine; cons. and presenter in field; numerous other career related activities. Author (with B.D. Barker): Assessing Dental Manpower Requirements: Alternative Approaches for State and Local Planning, 1982; editor (with J.W. Bawden): Planning for Dental Care on a Statewide Basis: The North Carolina Dental Manpower Project, 1981; editor: (with T.C. Ricketts, J.S. Stein) Methodological Advances in Health Services Research, 1989; editor: Health Svcs. Rsch., 1983—96; co-editor (spl. issue): Jour. Family and Cmty. Health, 1982; assoc. editor: Social Forces, 1971—76, Drugs in Health Care, 1974—76, Jour. Health and Social Behavior, 1985—87, Am. Jour. Health Promotion, 1986—92, mem. editl. bd.: Health Care Mgmt. Rev., 1977—93, Med. Care, 1980—83, Internat. Jour. Health Scis., 1989—, Jour. Gerontology: Med. Scis., 1989—91, Comparative Health Policy: Nations, States, Cmtys., 1993—, book rev. editor: Health Svcs. Rsch., 1979—84; contbr. chapters to books, articles to profl. jours. Fellow: N.Y. Acad. Medicine; mem.: APHA (med. care sect.), Soc. for Gen. Internal Medicine, Found. for Health Svcs. Rsch. (bd. dirs. 1982—94, pres. 1986—87), Assn. for Health Svcs. Rsch. (bd. dirs. 1982—90, pres.-elect 1983—85, pres. 1985—86), Inst. Medicine, Sigma Xi. Office: Dept Social Medicine Med Sch Wing D U NC Campus Box 7240 Chapel Hill NC 27599-7240

DEGABRIELLE, DONALD J., JR., prosecutor; b. Lake Charles, La., 1953; s. Donald J. DeGabrielle and Jackie Rosenthal. BA, McNeese State U., 1975; JD, La State U., 1978. Spl. agent FBI, New Orleans and NYC, 1979—82; asst. dist. atty. to chief of trials Orleans Parish Dist. Atty.'s Office, New Orleans, 1982—85; assoc. atty. pvt. practice, 1985; asst. US atty. (so. dist.) Tex. US Dept. Justice, Houston, 1986—2002, first asst. US atty. (so. dist.) Tex., 2002—06, US atty. (so. dist.) Tex., 2006—. Resident legal advisor So. African Nat. Directorate of Pub. Prosecutors.*

DEGARMO, DENISE KAY, political scientist, educator; b. Syracuse, NY, Feb. 16, 1956; d. Arthur V. and Billie L. DeGarmo; children: Carroll Lamar, Casey Johnsen. AS, Monroe C.C., 1990; BS, SUNY, Buffalo, 1992; PhD, U. Mich., 2000. Fellow U. Mich., Ann Arbor, 1992, instr., 1992—2000; asst. prof. polit. sci. So. Ill. U., Edwardsville, 2000—. Facilitator fgn. policy's great decisions program So. Ill. U., Edwardsville, 2001—. Author: (book) The Disposal of Radioactive Wastes in the Metropolitan St. Louis Area: The Environmental and Health Legacy of Maluncerodt Chemical Works; contbr. articles to profl. jours. Active CAN-World Wildlife Fund, Washington, 2000—02; facilitator Fgn. Policy Assn.: Great Decisions Program, Edwardsville, 2001—02; commr. Ann Arbor City Market Commn., 1996—98; v.p. Ann Arbor Artisan Assn., 1996—98; active Slausen Middle Sch. PTO, Ann Arbor, 1992—99; hosts - helping one student to succeed Slausen Middle Sch., Ann Arbor, 1996; pres. Monroe C.C. Activities Club, Rochester, NY, 1989—90. Univ. Honors scholar, SUNY, 1990—92. Mem.: Internat. Studies Assn., Women in Internat. Security, Am. Polit. Sci. Assn., Phi Sigma Alpha, Phi Theta Kappa. Democrat. Office: So Ill Univ Box 1453 3233 Peck Hall Edwardsville IL 62026 Office Phone: 618-650-3375. Business E-Mail: ddegarm@siue.edu.

DEGENER, CAROL M., lawyer; d. John Michael and Marie-Laure Degener. BA magna cum laude with honors in Econ., Columbia U.; MA, Columbia U., N.Y.C.; JD, Harvard U., Cambridge, Mass. Bar: Mass. 1988, N.Y. 1990. Assoc. corp. fin. Goldman Sachs & Co., NYC, 1987—89; assoc. corp. dept. Donovan Leisure Newton & Irvine, NYC, 1989—95; counsel corp. fin. dept. Seward & Kissel LLP, NYC, 1996—. Mem.: Phi Beta Kappa. Office: Seward & Kissel LLP 1 Battery Park Plz Fl 20 New York NY 10004-1405 Business E-Mail: degener@sewkis.com.

DEGENERES, ELLEN, actress, comedienne, talk show host; b. Metairie, Jan. 26, 1958; d. Elliott and Betty DeGeneres. Began career as emcee local comedy club, New Orleans; performer various comedy clubs. Comedian (TV spls.) Young Comedians Reunion, HBO, Women of the Night, 1986, Command Performances: One Night Stand, 1989; author: My Point.And I Do Have One, 1995, The Funny Thing Is., 2003; actor: (films) Coneheads, 1993, Mr. Wrong, 1996, Goodbye Lover, 1998, (voice) Dr. Doolittle, 1998, EDtv, 1999, The Love Letter, 1999, Reaching Normal, 1999, (voice of Dory) Finding Nemo, 2003 (Annie award for Outstanding Voice Acting in Animated Feature Prodn., 2004); writer, dir., actor (films) My Short Film, 2004; actor: (TV films) On the Edge, 2001; (TV series) Open House, 1989, Laurie Hill, 1992; actor, exec. prodr. (TV films) If These Walls Could Talk 2, 2000, (TV series) The Ellen Show, 2001—02, actor, prodr., writer Ellen (originally named These Friends of Mine from 1993-94), 1993—98 (Emmy award for Outstanding Writing for Comedy Series, 1997, Peabody award, 1997), host, exec. prodr. The Ellen DeGeneres Show, 2003— (Best Talk Show, Daytime Emmy award, Nat. Acad. TV Arts and Sciences, 2005, Best Talk Show Host, Daytime Emmy award, Nat. Acad. TV Arts and Sciences, 2005, People's Choice awards, favorite daytime talk show host, 2006, Outstanding Talk Show, Daytime Emmy award, Nat. Acad. TV Arts and Sciences, 2006, Outstanding Talk Show Host, Daytime Emmy awards, Nat. Acad. TV Arts and Sciences, 2006, 2007), star, exec. prodr. (TV spls.) Ellen DeGeneres: The Beginning, 2000 (Am. Comedy award for Funniest Female Peformer in TV spl., 2001), Ellen DeGeneres: Here and Now, 2003, co-host 46th Annual Primetime Emmy Awards, 1994 (Am. Comedy award for Funniest Female Peformer in TV spl., 1995), host 53rd Annual Primetime Emmy Awards, 2001, 54th Annual Primetime Emmy Awards, 2002, 57th Annual Primetime Emmy Awards, 2005, 38th Annual Grammy Awards, 1996, 39th Annual Grammy Awards, 1997, VH1 Fashion Awards, 1998, VH1 Divas Las Vegas, 2002, 79th Annual Academy Awards, 2007, appeared as herself (documentaries) Wisecracks, 1991. Named Funny Female Star, People's Choice Awards, 2006, Favorite Talk Show Host & Funny Female Star, 2007; named one of 100 Most Influential People, Time Mag., 2006; recipient Funniest Person Am. for videotaped club performances in New Orleans, Showtime, 1982, Am. Comedy award for Funniest Female Stand-Up Comic, 1991, Golden Apple award as Female Discovery Yr., Hollywood Women's Press Club, 1994, Lucy award, 2000, Enduring Spirit award, Amnesty Internat., 2000, Best Television Series or Specialty (Variety), The Producers Guild of Am., 2006. Office: c/o Creative Artists Agy 9830 Wilshire Blvd Beverly Hills CA 90212*

DE GENNARO, EIDA MENDOZA, interpreter, real estate agent; b. Havana, Cuba, Sept. 21, 1944; arrived in US, 1961; d. Carlos and Aída Mendoza; m. Antimo G. De Gennaro, July 22, 1967; children: Aída Marie, Carl. BA, U. Nebr., 1967, MA, 1976. Fgn. lang. tchr., 1967—83; internat. lang. cons., 1983—; interpreter US Dept. State, Washington, 1983—; real estate agt. Dreamscape Realty, Inc., Aldie, Va., 1999—. Fundraising com. St. Jude Children's Hosp., Memphis, 1992—. Recipient award, US Dept. State, 2002. Mem.: Nat. Assn. Realtors, No. Va. Assn. Realtors. Republican. Roman Catholic. Avocations: reading, swimming. Home and Office: 6312 John Charles Landing Centreville VA 20121 Office Phone: 703-629-3851.

DE GENNARO, RICHARD, retired library director; b. New Haven, Mar. 2, 1926; s. Ralph and Acquilina (Pedicini) De G.; m. Birgit M. Erikson, June 12, 1953; children: Ralph, George, Christina. BA, Wesleyan U., 1951, MA, 1960; MS in LS, Columbia U., 1956; postgrad., Univs. Paris, Madrid and Perugia, 1951-55; grad. Advanced Mgmt. Program, Harvard U., 1971; DHL (hon.), Wabash Coll., 1991. Jr. acct. Atlas Constructors, Morocco, 1952-53; reference librarian N.Y. Pub. Libr., 1956-58, dir., 1987-90; successively reference librarian, asst. dir., assoc. univ. librarian systems devel., sr. assoc. univ. librarian Harvard U. Libr., 1958-70; dir. librs. U. Pa., 1970-86, adj. prof. English, 1979-86; libr. Harvard Coll., 1990-96. Vis. prof. Grad. Libr. Sch., U. So. Calif., 1968-69; cons. libr. bldgs., tech. and mgmt.; mem. overseers com. to visit libr., Harvard U.; cons. MIT, Johns Hopkins U.; mem. adv. bd. Chem. Abstracts Svc., 1967-70; mem. Palinet bd. Union Libr. Catalogue, 1970—; mem. com. internat. sci. and tech. info. programs NAS-NRC, 1977-79; mem. Mellon Found. JSTOR Bd., 1995—; sr. libr. advisor JSTOR; mem. governing bd. Rsch. Librs. Group, 1979-89, sr. vis. fellow, 1980-81, chmn., 1984-95; Bowker lectr., 1979; Lazerow lectr., 1984. Author: Shifting Gears, Information Technology and the Academic Library, 1984, Libraries, Technology, and the Information Marketplace, Selected Papers, 1987; contbr. articles to profl. jours. Bd. dirs. Ctr. for Rsch. Librs., 1977-81; trustee U. Pa. Press, 1978-82. With USN, 1942-46. Recipient Disting. Alumnus award Wesleyan U., 1991; Hugh Atkinson award, 1993; named Acad. Rsch. Libr. of Yr., 1991; Coun. Libr. Resources fellow, 1971; Rockefeller Found. Ctr. fellow, Bellagio, Italy, 1981; info. tech. fellow U. Edinburgh, 1984. Mem. Assn. Rsch. Librs. (pres. 1975, dir. 1973-76), ALA (pres. info. sci. and automation div. 1975), Am. Soc. Info. Soc. (Melvil Dewey medal 1986), Century Assn. Club, Grolier Club, Harvard Club. Home: Apt 1414 988 Blvd Of The Arts Sarasota FL 34236-4838

DEGENSHEIN, JAN, architect, planner; b. Bklyn., Sept. 15, 1946; s. Harry and Beverly (Oppenheimer) D.; m. Lynne Sheren, Sept. 1, 1968 (div. Mar. 1978); 1 child, Britta; m. Nadja Hoyer-Booth, June 1, 1980 (div. Mar. 2005); children: Oleg, Anya. BS Archtl. Scis., Washington U., 1967; BArch, MS in Planning, Pratt Inst., 1970; postgrad., CUNY, 1979-84. Registered architect, N.Y., N.J.; cert. Nat. Coun. Archtl. Registration Bds. 1975. Assoc. architect R.C. Weinberg & Assocs., NYC, 1968-70, Seiler Nakrosis Kerner, Liberty, NY, 1970-72; v.p. Degan Enterprises Inc., New City, NY, 1973-78; pres., prin. Jan Degenshein Architect-Planner, New City, 1975-83; pres. Degenshein Denker Assocs. P.C., Nyack, NY, 1983-88, Degenshein Denker Bodnar P.C., Nyack, 1988-91; prin., pres. Jan Degenshein Architects-Planners, Nyack, NY, 1991—. Guest critic Pratt Inst. Sch. Architecture, 1982, CCNY Sch. Architecture, 1990. Author: Atlantic-Schermehorn Corridor, 1970. Chmn., com. mem. Rockland County (N.Y.) Art in Pub. Places, 1987-1998; v.p., trustee Blue Rock Sch., West Nyack, 1989-95; mem. bd. advisors Martin Luther King Multi-Purpose Ctr., Spring Valley, N.Y., 1991—; vol., mem. bd. advisors, bd. dirs. Vol. Counseling Svcs., New City, 1994-02; mem. environ. adv. coun. U.S. Rep. Benjamin Gilman, 1993-96; mem. campaign cabinet Arts Fund for Rockland, Rockland County, 1990-92; mem. N.Y. State Bldg Ofcls. Conf., 1994—, Interfaith Forum on Religious Art and Architecture, 1983-01, Arts Coun. of Rockland, 1986—; adv. com. Rockland Ctr. Arts, 2004-, site plan com., 2005—; nominating com. Rockland County coun. Girl Scouts U.S., 1991-94; mem. Rockland Mcpl. Planning Fedn., 1990—, assoc. dir., 1997-2006; bd. dirs. Housing Action Coun., 1998-01, exec. bd., 1999-01, Internat. Codes Coun., 2004-; mem. retention and expansion com. Rockland Econ. Devel. Corp., 1996-01, cert. recognition, 1999; bd. dirs. Helen Hayes Hosp. Found., 1998-04, v.p., 2003-04, gala com., 1990-04, chmn., 2000-04; mem. citizens adv. bd. housing Town Clarkstown, 2002-04; mem. citizens adv. com. Rockland Psychiat. Ctr., Town of Orangetown 2000, 04-05; mem. nominating com. Keep Rockland Beautiful, 2005-06. Recipient archtl. excellence award Orange County Bd. Realtors, 1988, 89, Rockland County Execs. Arts award, 1995; winner Arts Coun. of Rockland poetry competition, 2002; named Bus. Man of Yr., Nat. Rep. Congl. Com., 2002, Bus. Leader of Yr., Rockland Jour. News, 2003, Rockland County Execs. Fair Housing award 2004, Poet of Year, Famous Poets Soc., 2005, Citizen of Yr. Child Care Resources Rockland, 2006. Mem. AIA (honor award for archtl. excellence Westchester/Mid-Hudson 1987, 88, 92, 94, 96, 2000; cmty.design awards; Rockland County Beautification award, 1992, 94, Rockland County Legislature Cert. of Recognition, 1999, Am. Inst. Cert. Planners, Am. Planning Assn., Rockland County Builders Assn. (Assoc. of Yr. 1978, Builder of Yr. 1980), Leadership Rockland (dir. 1994-2002, 2004—, pres. alumni assn. 1994-96, sec. 1999-2002, mem. selections com., fin. com., chmn. nominations com., recruitment com. coord. econ. devel. day 1995-2000, v.p., 2006—), Rockland Bus. Exch. (v.p., pres. membership com. 1993-97), Rockland Coalition for Democracy and Freedom (dir. 1995), Am. Forum for Global Edn. (advisor 1995-97) Hist. Soc. Rockland, Computer and Telecom. Initiative Rockland (chair nominating com. 1996, bd. dirs. 1997-2001, vice-chmn. 2006-), Rockland Bus. Assn. (mem. svcs. com. 1996, chair amb.'s com. 1996-98, comms. and advocacy com. 1997—, bd. dirs. 1997-2001, 2004—, chmn. affordable housing com. 2001-03, chmn. govt. affairs com. 2004-06, exec. bd. 2004—, chmn. econ. devel. com. 2007—, vice-chmn. 2007—), Nyacks C. of C. (v.p. 1988-89), Rotary Internat. Avocations: graphic arts, cooking, golf, writing. Office: 205 S Broadway Nyack NY 10960-4436 Office Phone: 845-358-8400. Business E-Mail: Jan@Degenshein.com.

DE GEORGE, LAWRENCE JOSEPH, diversified financial services company executive; b. NYC, May 6, 1916; s. Frank Phillip and Frances (Cavallo) DeG.; m. Florence A. Efel, Dec. 18, 1943; children: Lawrence F., Peter R. BSEE, Princeton U., 1936; MS, MIT, 1938; PhD in Advanced Math., Columbia U., 1939. Assoc. prof. elec. engring. Columbia U., 1938-39; field engr. Radio Engring. Lab., NYC, 1939-41; pres. Times Wire and Cable Co., Inc., div. Internat. Silver Co., Wallingford, Conn., 1946; also v.p., dir. Times Wire and Cable div., 1958-64, pres., 1964-68; v.p., dir. Insilco Corp., Meridan, Conn., 1968-72, exec. v.p., 1972-77, vice chmn., 1976-77; chmn., pres. Times Fiber Communications, Inc., Meriden, 1977-84, chmn., chief exec. officer, 1985-92, LPL Techs. Inc., Wallingford, Conn., 1985-97, Amphenol Corp., Wallingford, Conn., 1987-97; chmn., CEO DeG Capital Ptnrs. Ltd., Wallingford. Dir. Travelers Equities Fund, Inc., Hartford, Conn. Lt. comdr. USNR, 1941-46. Mem.: Club Collette, Admirals Cove Yacht Club, City Club, Palm Beach Yacht Club. Republican. Home: 176 Spyglass Ln Jupiter FL 33477-4037 Office: DeG Capital Ptnrs Ltd Ste 410 140 Intracoastal Pointe Dr Jupiter FL 33477-5094 Office Phone: 561-745-7000.

DE GETTE, DIANA LOUISE, congresswoman, lawyer; b. Tachikawa, Japan, July 29, 1957; came to U.S., 1957; d. Richard Louis and Patricia Anne (Rose) De G.; m. Lino Sigismondo Lipinsky de Orlov, Sept. 15, 1984; children: Raphaela Anne, Francesca Louise. BA magna cum laude, The Colo. Coll., 1979; JD, NYU, 1982. Bar: Colo. 1982, U.S. Dist. Ct. Colo. 1982, U.S. Ct. Appeals (10th cir.) 1984, U.S. Supreme Ct. 1989. Dep. state pub. defender Colo. State Pub. Defender, Denver, 1982-84; assoc. Coghill & Goodspeed, P.C., Denver, 1984-86; sole practice Denver, 1986-93; of counsel McDermott & Hansen, Denver, 1993-96; mem. Colo. Ho. of Reps., 1992-96, asst. minority leader, 1995-96; mem. U.S. Congress from 1st Colo. dist., 1997—; mem. commerce com. Editor: (mag.) Trial Talk, 1989-92. Mem. Mayor's Mgmt. Rev. Com., Denver, 1983-84; resolutions chair Denver Dem. Party, 1986; bd. dirs. Root-Tilden Program, NYU Sch. Law, N.Y.C., 1986-92; bd. trustees, alumni trustee Colo. Coll., Colorado Springs, 1988-94. Recipient Root-Tilden scholar NYU Sch. Law, NYC, 1979, Vanderbilt medal, 1982. Mem. Colo. Bar Assn. (bd. govs. 1989-91), Colo. Trial Lawyers Assn. (bd. dirs., exec. com. 1986-92), Colo. Women's Bar Assn., Denver Bar Assn., Phi Beta Kappa, Pi Gamma Mu. Democrat. Avocations: reading, backpacking, gardening.*

DEGEURIN, GEORGE MICHAEL, JR., (MIKE DEGEURIN), lawyer; b. Houston, 1971; BA, U. Colo., 1993; JD, St. Mary's U. Sch. Law, 1996. Bar: Tex. 1996, Ala. 1998, US Supreme Ct., US Dist. Ct. (so. and we. dists. Tex.). Briefing atty. Tex. Ct. Criminal Appeals, 1996—97; assoc. Joseph A. Turner LLC, Austin, Tex., 1997—99; asst. fed. pub. defender Houston, 1999—2002; assoc. Foreman, DeGeurin & Nugent, Houston, 2002—. Named a Rising Star, Tex. Super Lawyers mag., 2006. Mem.: Tex. Criminal Def. Lawyers Assn., Nat. Assn. Criminal Def. Lawyers, ABA, US Supreme Ct. Hist. Soc. Office: Foreman DeGeurin Nugent 300 Main St 3rd Fl Houston TX 77002 Office Phone: 713-655-9000.*

DEGEURIN, MIKE, lawyer; b. Austin, Tex., Jan. 9, 1945; s. Elias McDowell and Marguerite Effie (Smith) DeG.; m. Gayle Ross, Dec. 21, 1968; children: Michael, Katherine, Laura, Mack. BA, U. Tex., 1968; JD, Tex. Tech. Sch. Law, 1972. Bar: Tex., 1972, U.S. Supreme Ct. Tex., U.S. Dist. Ct. (all dists.) Tex., U.S. Ct. Appeals (5th, 10th, and 11th cirs.). Chief justice jud. counsel Tex. Tech. Sch. Law; law clk. John Wendell Odom Tex. Ct. Criminal Appeals, 1972-73; law clk. John Singleton So. Dist. Te., 1973-75; asst. fed. pub. defender Houston, 1975-77; ptnr. Forman, DeGeurin & Nugent (formerly Foreman, DeGeurin, Nugent & Gerger), Houston, 1977—. Named Outstanding Criminal Lawyer in Tex., Nat. Law Jour., 1989—90; named one of Top 50 Lawyers Under 50, 1989; recipient Justice Alliance award, Tex. Fellow Am. Bd. Trial Advocates, Tex. Bar Found.; mem. ABA, ATLA, Houston Bar Assn., State Bar Tex., Nat. Assn. Criminal Def. Lawyers, Harris County Criminal Lawyers Assn., Tex. Criminal Def. Lawyers Assn., Delta Theta Phi, Order of Barristers. Achieved international acclaim for his work in criminal defense. Office: Foreman DeGeurin & Nugent 300 Main St Houston TX 77002 Office Phone: 713-655-9000. Office Fax: 713-655-1812.*

DE GEUS, AART J., computer software company executive; MSEE, Swiss Fedn. Polytech Inst.; PhD Electrical Engring., So. Meth. U. Chmn., CEO Synopsys, Mountain View, Calif., 1986—. Vice chmn., edn. supporter Silicon Valley Mfrs. Group; vice chmn. Electronic Design Automation Consortium. Fellow: IEEE (Indsl. Pioneer award, Robert N. Noyce medal 2007). Office: Synopsys 700 E Middlefield Rd Mountain View CA 94043-4033*

DEGIOIA, JOHN J., academic administrator; b. Orange, Conn. m. Theresa Miller DeGioia; 1 child, John Thomas. BA in English, Georgetown U., 1979, PhD in Philosophy, 1995. Asst. to the pres. Georgetown U., Washington, 1982—85, dean of student affairs, 1985—92, assoc. v.p., chief adminstrv. officer, 1992—95, v.p., chief adminstrv. officer for main campus, 1995—98, prof. lectr., 1995—, sr. v.p., 1998—2001, pres., 2001—. Mem. exec. com. Fed. City Coun.; mem. Washington Bd. Trade; trustee Com. for Econ. Devel.; bd. dirs. MedStar Health. Named one of Young Leaders of the Acad., Change mag., 1998; recipient Chmn.'s award, Georgetown Alumni Admissions Program, 1997, Lifetime Achievement award for excellence in academia, Sons of Italy, 2004. Mem.: John Carroll Soc. (bd. govs.), Assn. Jesuit Colls. and Univs. (mem. exec. com., bd. dirs.), Bus.-Higher Edn. Forum, Coun. on Competativeness (mem. exec. com., regional innovation com. and global com.), Assn. Am. Colls. and Univs. (bd. dirs.), Consortium on Financing Higher Edn. (bd. dirs.), Am. Coun. on Edn. (bd. dirs., mem. com. on minorities in higher edn.). Office: Georgetown U Office of the Pres 204 Healy Hall Box 571789, 37th and O Streets, NW Washington DC 20057 Office Phone: 202-687-4134. Fax: 202-687-6660. Business E-Mail: president@georgetown.edu.*

DEGIORGIO, KENNETH D., lawyer, insurance company executive; BA with honors, Harvard U., Cambridge, Mass.; JD, MBA, UCLA. Atty. White & Case LLP, LA; regulatory and acquisition counsel First Am. Corp., Santa Ana, Calif., 1999—2001, v.p., assoc. gen. counsel, 2001—04, sr. v.p., gen. counsel, 2004—; exec. v.p. First Advantage Corp., 2003—. Bd. dirs. RP Data, 2006—. Office: First Am Corp 1 First American Way Santa Ana CA 92707 Office Phone: 714-250-3000.*

DEGIOVANNI-DONNELLY, ROSALIE FRANCES, biologist, educator; b. Bklyn., Nov. 22, 1926; d. Frank and Rose (Quartuccio) DeGiovanni; m. Edward Francis Donnelly, Sept. 23, 1961; children: Edward F. Jr., Francis M. BA, Bklyn. Coll., 1947, MA, 1953; PhD, Columbia U., 1961. Adj. prof. microbiology, genetics George Washington U., Washington, 1968—; rsch. biologist FDA, Washington, 1968-88. Contbr. articles to profl. jours. Recipient Merit award FDA, 1970. Mem. AAAS, AAUW, Italian Cultural Soc., Environ. Mutagen Soc., NY Acad. Scis., Am. Soc. Microbiology, McLean Indoor Club, Sigma Xi, Sigma Delta Epsilon. Democrat. Roman Catholic. Avocations: theater, swimming, tennis, travel, photography. Home: 1712 Strine Dr Mc Lean VA 22101-4744 Personal E-mail: edndol@earthlink.net.

DEGIULIO, LUCAS, artist; b. Dearborn, Mich., 1977; BFA in Mixed Media, Mpls. Coll. Art and Design, 2000. Exhibited in group shows at Midway Contemporary Art, Mpls., 2003, exhibitions include 6th Annual Monster Drawing Rally, Southern Exposure, San Francisco, 2006, Day for Night, Whitney Biennial, 2006, New Langton Arts, San Francisco, 2006.*

DEGN, DOUGLAS J., retired retail executive; b. Feb. 6, 1957; BS in Pharmacy, U. Kans., 1981. With Wal-Mart Stores USA, 1983—2007, pharmacy mgr., v.p. & divisional merchandise mgr., v.p. pharmacy merchandising & support, sr. v.p. & gen. merchandise mgr., exec. v.p. food & consumables merchandising, 2001—07. Recipient Sam M. Walton Entrepreneur of Yr. award, 1997.

DEGNAN, JOHN J., insurance company executive, lawyer; Grad. magna cum laude, St. Vincent Coll., 1966; JD, Harvard Law Sch., 1969; degree (hon.), Coll. St. Elizabeth, 1978, Seton Hall U., 1979. Law sec. to Justice John Francis NJ Supreme Ct.; atty. Clapp & Eisenberg, Newark; asst. counsel to Gov. Brendan T. Byrne State of NJ, 1974—77, chief counsel to Gov. Brendan T. Byrne, 1977—78, atty. gen., 1978—81; sr. ptnr. Shanley & Fisher; sr. v.p., gen. counsel Chubb & Son, 1990, pres., 1998, The Chubb Corp., Warren, NJ, 1996, vice chmn., chief adminstrv. officer, 2002—, chief ethics and compliance officer, 2005—. Bd. mem. Am. Inst. CPCUs, RAND Inst. Civil Justice; mem. disciplinary oversight com. Supreme Ct. NJ. Bd. mem. Sch. Risk Mgmt., Ins. and Actuarial Sci., St. John's U., St. Benedict's Prep. Sch., St. Barnabas Med. Ctr., NJ Performing Arts Ctr. Office: The Chubb Corp 15 Mountain View Rd Warren NJ 07059-6795 Office Phone: 908-903-2110.*

DEGNAN, JOHN JAMES, III, physicist; b. Phila., Dec. 10, 1945; s. John James Jr. and Ruth Dolores (Vece); m. Adele Susan Henry, June 27, 1969; children: Adam John, Andrew Paul. BS in Physics, Drexel U., Phila., 1968; MS in Physics, U. Md., College Park, 1970, PhD in Physics, 1979. Student trainee NASA Goddard Space Flight Ctr., Greenbelt, Md., 1964-67, physicist, 1968-72, sr. physicist, 1972-79, sect. head, 1979-89, dep. mgr. crustal dynamics project, 1989-93, head space geodesy and altimetry projects office, 1993-96, head geosci. tech. office, 1996—2003; chief scientist Sigma Space Corp., Lanham, Md., 2003—. Instr. Drexel U., Phila., 1967-68; assoc. mem. Adv. Group on Electron Devices, 1980-85, dep. mem. 1985-89; adj. prof. physics Am. U., Washington, 1988-93; chmn. CSTG SLR/LLR Subcommn., 1992-98, chmn. Internat. Laser Ranging Svc. Governing Bd., 1998-2002; tech. bd. Wegener, 1992-2000, chmn., 2000-03; mem. Am. Geophys. Union Steering Com. for Geodesy, 1998—. CSTG Exec. Bd. Contbr. articles to profl. jours; patentee, microaltimeter, 2002. Mem. Common Cause, Annapolis, Md., 1970—; v.p., treas. Pasadena Theatre Co., Md., 1982-84. Drexel Bd. Trustees scholar, 1963; recipient Marple-Newtown Sch. Dist. Hall of Fame award, Disting. Alumnus, 1989, Moe I. Schneebaum Meml. award for engring. NASA/GSFC, 1987, Tsiolkovsky medal, 2002, NASA Space Act award, 2003, Cir. of Distinction award Drexel U., 2005. Fellow Internat. Assn. Geodesy; mem. IEEE (sr.), ACLU, Optical Soc. Am., Am. Phys. Soc., Am. Geophys. Union (steering com. geodesy 1998—), Planetary Soc., Internat. Laser Comm. Soc. (charter), Common Cause Union Concerned Scientists, Nat. Space Club, Am. Volksmarch Assn., Sierra Club, Sigma Pi Sigma, Sigma Pi. Roman Catholic. Avocations: hiking, community theater. Home: 928 Barracuda Cove Ct Annapolis MD 21409-4719 Office: Sigma Space Corp 4801 Forbes Blvd Lanham MD 20706 Home Phone: 410-757-7899; Office Phone: 301-552-6300. Business E-Mail: john.degnan@sigmaspace.com.

DEGNAN, JOHN MICHAEL, lawyer; b. Mpls., Apr. 2, 1948; s. John F. and Lorraine A. Degnan; m. Barbara B. Degnan; children: Michael Gene Carland, John Patrick, Amy Marie, David Charles. BA, U. Minn., 1970; JD, William Mitchell Coll. Law, 1976. Bar: Minn. 1976, US Dist. Ct. Minn. 1976, US Ct. Appeals (8th cir.) Minn. 1976, US Supreme Ct. 1976. Ins. underwriter Marsh & McLennan, Mpls., 1973-76; lawyer Bassford, Lockhart, Truesdell & Briggs, P.A., Mpls., 1976—2003, Murnane, Conlin, White & Brandt, St. Paul, 2003—. Lectr. in field. Bd. dirs. Hennepin County Pub. Librs., 1980-84, Storefront Youth Action, 1981-83, Mediation Ctr., 1991—. 1st lt. US Army, 1971-72, Vietnam. Fellow: Am. Bd. Trial Advocates, Am. Coll. Trial Lawyers; mem.: ABA, Am. Soc. Law and Medicine, Def. Rsch. Inst., Minn. Def. Lawyers Assn. (bd. dirs. 1986—, pres. 1990—91), Am. Bd. Trial Advocates, Nat. Bd. Trial Advocacy (cert. civil trial specialist), Hennepin County Bar Assn. (professionalism com.), Minn. State Bar Assn. (ins. com., lectr. convs. 1984—85, civil trial cert. governing coun., cert. trial specialist), Richfield Jaycees (past pres.). Avocations: running, tennis, golf, sports. Office: Briggs and Morgan 2200 IDS Center 80 S 8th St Minneapolis MN 55402 Home Phone: 952-931-0514; Office Phone: 612-977-8660. Business E-Mail: jdegnan@briggs.com.

DE GOFF, VICTORIA JOAN, lawyer; b. San Francisco, Mar. 2, 1945; d. Sidney Francis and Jean Frances (Alexander) De G.; m. Peter D. Coppelman, May 2, 1971 (div. Dec. 1978); m. Richard Sherman, June 16, 1980. BA in Math. with great distinction, U. Calif., Berkeley, 1967, JD, 1972. Bar: Calif. 1972, U.S. Dist. Ct. (no. dist.) Calif. 1972, U.S. Ct. Appeals 1972, U.S. Supreme Ct. 1989; cert. appellate law specialist, 1996. Rsch. atty. Calif. Ct. Appeal, San Francisco, 1972-73; Reginald Heber Smith Found. fellow San Francisco Neighborhood Legal Assistance Found., 1973-74; assoc. Field, De Goff, Huppert & McGowan, San Francisco, 1974-77; pvt. practice Berkeley, Calif., 1977-80; ptnr. De Goff and Sherman, Berkeley, 1980—. Lectr. continuing edn. of bar, Calif., 1987, 90-92, U. Calif. Boalt Hall Sch. Law, Berkeley, 1981-85, dir. appellate advocacy, 1992; cons. Calif. Civil Practice Procedure, Bancroft Whitney, 1992; mem. Appellate Law Adv. Commn., 1995; apptd. applicant evaluation and nomination com. for State Bar Ct. by Calif. Supreme Ct., 1995, 2000; presented programs for Rutter Group Mastering Appellate Advocacy, 2004, Mastering the Stds. of Rev., 2005; apptd. by Chief Justice Calif. to Supreme Ct. Advisory Com. on publ. of ct. of appeals opinions, 2005-06; pvt. atty., clk. ct. com. Calif. Ct. Appeals, 1997-99; mem. com. on appellate practice ABA, 1997. Author: (with others) Matthew Bender's Treatise on California Torts, 1985. Apptd. to adv. com. Calif. Jud. Coun. on Implementing Proposition 32, 1984—85; mem. adv. bd. Hastings Coll. Trial and Appellate Adv., 1984—91; expert 20/20 vision project, commn. on future cts. Jud. Coun. Calif., 1993, apptd. to appellate standing adv. com., 1993—95; apptd. to Appellate Indigent Def. Oversight Adv. Com. State of Calif., 1995—; com. on appellate stds. of ABA Appellate Judges Conf., 1995—96; com. on appellate practice ABA, 1997; adv. bd. Witkin Legal Inst., Thompson Publishing Co., 1996—; officer Calif. Supreme Ct. Hist. Soc., 1999—; appointee 9th Jud. Cir. Hist. Soc. Hon. Cecil Poole Biography Project, 1998; chair Roger Traynor State Moot Ct. Com., 1999—; bd. dirs. Calif. Supreme Ct. Hist. Soc., State Bar Calif., 1996—2005; Appellate Law Cons. Group, 1994—95; bd. dirs. Ctr. for Youth Devel. Through Law, 2000—. Fellow Woodrow Wilson Found., 1967-68. Mem. Calif. Trial Lawyers Assn. (bd. govs. 1980-88, amicus-curiae com. 1981-87, editor-in-chief assn. mag. 1980-81, Presdl. award of merit 1980, 81), Calif. Acad. Appellate Lawyers (sec.-treas. 1989-90, 2d v.p. 1990-91, 1st v.p. 1991-92, pres. 1992-93), Am. Acad. Appellate Lawyers, Edward J. McFetridge Am. Inn of Cts. (counsellor 1990-91, edn. chmn. 1991-92, social chmn. 1992-93, v.p. 1993-94, pres. 1994-95), Boalt Hall Sch. Law U. Calif. Alumni Assn. (bd. dirs. 1989-91), Order of Coif. Jewish. Office: 1916 Los Angeles Ave Berkeley CA 94707-2419

DEGRAFFENREIDT, JAMES H., JR., gas company executive; BA, Yale Coll., 1974; MBA, JD, Columbia U., 1978. JD. Pres., COO Washington Gas Light Co., 1994—98, bd. dir., 1994—, pres., CEO, 1998, chmn., CEO, 1998—2000, chmn., pres., CEO, 2000—01, chmn., CEO, 2001—; bd. dir. WGL Holdings, 2000—, chmn., CEO, 2001—. Bd. dir. Harbor Bankshares Corp., Mass Mutual Fin. Group, Am. Gas Assn. Bd. dir. Alliance to Save Energy. Recipient Pioneers of the Profession award Minority Corp. Counsel Assn., 1997. Office: Washington Gas and Light Co 101 Constitution Ave NW Washington DC 20080-0002*

DE GRASSI, LEONARD, art historian, educator; b. East Orange, NJ, Mar. 2, 1928; s. Romulus-William and Anna Sophia (Sannicolo) DeG.; m. Dolores Marie Welgoss, June 24, 1961; children: Maria Christina, Paul. BA, U. So. Calif., 1950, BFA, 1951, MA, 1956; postgrad., Harvard U., 1953, Istituto Centrale del Restauro di Roma, 1959-60, U. Rome, 1959-60, UCLA, 1970-73. Tchr. art Redlands Jr. HS, Calif., 1951—53, Toll Jr. HS, Glendale, Calif., 1953—61, Wilson Jr. HS, Glendale, 1961; mem. faculty Glendale Coll., 1962—, prof. art history, 1974-92, chmn. dept., 1972, 89, prof. emeritus, 1992—. Tchr. Cite U., Paris, 1992, Istituto /Schuola Leonardo da Vinci, Florence, Italy, 1992. Prin. works include: (paintings) high altar at Ch. St. Mary, Cook, Minn., altar screen at Ch. St. Andrew, El Segundo, Calif., 1965-71, 14 Stas. of the Cross Ch. St. Mary, Cook, Minn., altar screen at Ch. of the Descent of the Holy Spirit, Glendale, 14 Stas. of the Cross at Ch. of St. Benedict, Duluth, Minn; research, artwork and dramatic work for Spaceship Earth exhbn. at Disney World, Orlando, Fla., 1980. Decorated Knight Grand Cross Holy Sepluchre, knight St. John of Jerusalem, 1976, knight Order of Merit of Republic of Italy, Cross of Merit; recipient J. Walter Smith Svc. award, 2001; named First Disting. Faculty, 1987, Outstanding Educator of Am., 1971. Mem. Art Educators Assn., Am. Rsch. Ct. Egypt, Tau Kappa Alpha, Kappa Pi, Delta Sigma Rho. Office: 1500 N Verdugo Rd Glendale CA 91208-2809 Office Phone: 818-240-1000 ext. 5742. Business E-Mail: degrassi@glendale.edu.

DEGRAVE, DOUGLAS MICHAEL, lawyer; b. Rochester, NY, May 23, 1954; s. Gorman Joseph and Elaine (Best) DeG.; m. Deborah Jean Horn, Jan. 11, 1975; children: Jacob Daniel, Jennifer Anne, Joshua Michael. AS in Adminstrn. Justice, U. HI., 1976; BA in Pol. Sci., Calif. State U., Long Beach, 1978; JD, Loyola U., 1981. Bar: Calif. 1981, U.S. Dist. Ct. (ctrl. dist.) Calif. 1982, U.S. Dist. Ct. (so. dist.) Calif. 1985, U.S. Ct. Appeals (9th cir.) 1986, U.S. Supreme Ct. 1987. Assoc. Stockdale, Peckham & Werner, Santa Ana, Calif., 1981-87; ptnr. Behrens, Recht, Finley & Hanley, Santa Ana, 1986-87; mng. ptnr. Parker.Stanbury, Santa Ana, 1987—2004, Poliquin & DeGrave LLP, Laguna Hills, Calif., 2004—. Adj. prof. Western State Univ. Coll. Law, 1998—. Contbr. articles to profl. jours.; speaker in field. Dir., v.p. Orange YMCA, 1986-89, YMCA Indian Guides/Princesses, 1983-96; v.p. Orange Jr. Soccer Club, 1986-87, pres. 1987-88, chmn. bd. 1989-90, coach 1982-90; mgr./coach South Sunrise Little Leage, Orange, 1992-2002. With US Army, 1973-76. Named one of Super Lawyers of Southern Calif., 2007. Mem. Assn. Southern Calif. Def. Counsel (amicus com. 1994), Am. Bd. Trial Adv. (pres.-elect Orange County Chpt.), Calif. Def. Counsel, Def. Rsch. Inst., Consumer Attys. Calif., Orange County Trial Lawyers, Orange County Bar Assn. Republican. Roman Catholic. Avocations: scuba diving, golf. Home: 18352 Serrano Ave Villa Park CA 92861-2711 Office: Poliquin & Degrave LLP 22972 Mill Creek Dr Laguna Hills CA 92653 Office Phone: 949-716-8230. Business E-Mail: ddegrave@pdattorneys.com.

DEGREGORIO, CARLO, social studies educator; b. Bronx, NY, Feb. 26, 1956; s. Vincent DeGregorio and Carmella Gaudio; divorced; 1 child, Andrew Anthony. BA, St. John's U., NYC, 1979; MA, Herbert H. Lehman Coll., NYC, 1993. Lic. Tchr. NY Dept. Edn., NYC. 4th grade tchr. St. Luke Sch., Bronx, 1979—80, Sacred Heart Sch., NYC, 1980—81; phys. therapist asst. Grand Manor Health Related Facilities, NYC, 1981—84; social studies tchr. St. John's Prep HS, Astoria, 1984—85, Alfred E. Smith Vocat. HS, Bronx, 1985—2000, New Sch. for Arts & Scis., Bronx, 2000—01; tchr., US history & govt. Met. Corp. Acad., Bklyn., 2001—02; tchr., 9th & 10th grade global studies New Sch. for Arts & Scis., 2002—04; mentor, 17 beginning HS tchrs. Region 10 HS, NYC, 2004—. Recipient Tchr. of Yr. award, Bronx Fedn. Parents Assn. Presidents, 1991. Mem.: ASCD, Nat. Coun. Social Studies. Avocations: coin collecting/numismatics, sci-fi movies. Home: 1631 Lurting Ave Bronx NY 10461 Office: NYC Dept Edn Region 10 New York NY Office Phone: 718-612-5967.

DEGROAT, WILLIAM CHESNEY, pharmacology educator; b. Trenton, NJ, May 18, 1938; s. William Chesney and Margaret (Welch) DeGroat; m. Dorothy Marion Albertson, June 13, 1959; children: Allyson L., Cynthia L., Jennifer L. BSc, Phila. Coll. Pharmacy and Sci., 1960, MSc, 1962; PhD, U. Pa., Phila., 1965, postgrad., 1965-66, Australian Nat. U., Canberra, 1966-67. Vis. research fellow John Curtin Sch. Med. Research, Canberra, 1967-68; asst. prof. U. Pitts. Med. Sch., 1968-72, assoc. prof., 1972-77, prof. pharmacology, 1977—, acting chmn. dept. pharmacology, 1978-80, adj. prof. pharmacy, 1978-88, prof. psychology, 1982-86, mem. ctr. of neurosci., 1984—, prof. dept. behavioral neurosci., 1986-94, prof. dept. neurosci., 1995-96. Vis. prof. U. Coll., London, 1998; mem. neurobiology study sect. NIH, 1983-88; vis. scientist NIAAA-NIH, 1989-90. Mem. editl. bd. Jour. Pharmacology and Exptl. Therapeutics, 1975—, Jour. Autonomic Nervous Sys., 1979—, assoc. editor, 1985-94, Neurourology and Urodynamics, 1982—, Am. Jour. Physiology, 1983-94, Life Scis., 1993—, Urology, 1996-98, Current Opinion in Central and Peripheral Nervous System Investigational Drugs, 1999-2006; editl. cons. profl. jours.; contbr. articles to profl. jours., chpts. in books. NSF fellow, 1962-63; pharmacology fellow Riker Pharm. Co., 1966-67; NSF fellow, 1966-67; recipient research Career Devel. award NIH, 1972-77, NIH Merit award, 2000. Fellow: AAAS; mem.: Dana Alliance for Brain Initiatives, Soc. for Urodynamics and Female Urology, Internat. Continence Soc., Internat. Soc. for Autonomic Neurosci. (exec. v.p.), Am. Autonomic Soc., Am. Motility Soc., Soc. for Basic Urologic Rsch., Internat. Med. Soc. of Paraplegia, Urodynamics Soc. (Lifetime Achievement award 1995), Am. Gastroent. Assn., Internat. Brain Rsch. Orgn., Soc. for Neurosci. (treas. 1994—95), Am. Soc. Pharmacology and Exptl. Therapeutics (award for exptl. therapeutics 2003), NY Acad. Scis., Am. Urol. Assn. (hon.), Japanese Urol. Assn. (hon.), Rho Chi. Sigma Xi. Republican. Methodist. Home:

6357 Burchfield Ave Pittsburgh PA 15217-2732 Office: U Pitts Med Sch W-1352 Biomed Sci Tower Terrace St Pittsburgh PA 15213 Office Phone: 412-648-9357. Business E-Mail: degroat@server.pharm.pitt.edu.

DEGROOT, LESLIE JACOB, medical educator; b. Ft. Edward, NY, Sept. 20, 1928; BS, Union Coll., 1948; MD, Columbia U., 1952. Intern, asst. resident in medicine Presbyn. Hosp., NYC, 1952-54; health physician Nat. Cancer Inst., 1954-55; physician U.S. Mission, Afghanistan, 1955-56; clin. and research fellow medicine Mass. Gen. Hosp., Boston, 1956, 58-60, resident, 1957-58, asst., 1960-64, asst. physician, 1964-66; assoc. prof. exptl. medicine MIT, 1966-68, assoc. dir. dept. nutrition and food sci. Clin. Research Ctr., 1966-68; prof. endocrinology Pritzker Sch. Medicine, U. Chgo., 1968—2005, chief thyroid study unit, 1968—2005, chief endocrinology sect., 1980—87; prof. medicine rsch. Brown U., Providence, 2005—. Nat. Cancer Inst. clin. fellow, 1954-55 Mem. Assn. Am. Physicians, Am. Thyroid Assn., Endocrine Soc., Am. Soc. Clin. Investigation, Am. Fedn. Clin. Research Office: Brown Univ Box G Rm E 308 70 Ship St Providence RI 02912 Home: Po Box P94 South Dartmouth MA 02748-0301 Office Phone: 401-863-6097. Business E-Mail: leslie_degroot@brown.edu.

DEGROOTE, MICHAEL G., management consulting company executive; Pres., CEO Laidlaw Inc., 1959-90, Republic Industries Inc., 1991-96, also chmn. bd. dirs.; pres. Century Bus. Svcs. Inc., Cleve., 1997-99, CEO, 1999—, also chmn. bd. dirs. Office: Century Bus Svcs Inc 6050 Oak Tree Blvd #500 Cleveland OH 44131-6951

DEGUERIN, DICK, lawyer; b. Austin, Tex., Feb. 16, 1941; s. E. Mack and Marguerite S. DeGuerin; m. Ann DeGuerin; children: Anna Michele, Ann Carlin; m. Janie Mitchell, Apr. 11, 1986. BA, U. Tex., 1963, LLB, 1965. Bar: Tex. 1965, US Dist. Ct. (so. dist. Tex.) 1968, US Ct. Appeals (5th cir.) 1971, US Supreme Ct. 1971, US Dist. Ct. (ea. dist. Tex.) 1973, US Ct. Appeals (8th cir.) 1974, US Dist. Ct. (no. dist. Tex.) 1979, US Ct. Appeals (11th cir.) 1981, US Dist. Ct. (ea. dist. Mich.) 1982, US Ct. Appeals (6th cir.) 1982, US Dist. Ct. (we. dist. Tex.) 1983, US Ct. Appeals (10th cir.) 1984, US Ct. Appeals (4th cir.) 1985; bd. cert. criminal law Tex. Bd. Legal Specialization. Asst. dist. atty. Harris County, Houston, 1965-68; assoc. Butler, Binion, Rice, Cook & Knapp, Houston, 1968-71; ptnr. Foreman & DeGuerin, Houston, 1971-82; sr. ptnr. DeGuerin, Dickson & Szekely, Houston, 1982-84, DeGuerin Dickson, & Hennessy (formerly DeGuerin & Dickson), Houston, 1984—. Spkr. in field. Contbr. articles to profl. jours. Named one of Top 10 Trial Lawyers in Am., Nat. Law Jour., 2004. Fellow Am. Coll. Trial Lawyers, Am. Bd. Criminal Lawyers, Am. Bd. Trial Advs., Internat. Soc. Barristers; mem. Tex. Bar Assn. (various coms.), Houston Bar Assn. (criminal law sect.), Houston Jr. Bar Assn. (coms. on law day, award, criminal law 1965-1976), Tex. Criminal Def. Lawyers Assn. (charter mem., dir. 1973-76), Harris County Criminal Lawyers Assn. (charter mem., dir. 1976-), Tex. Bd. Legal Specialization (cert.), Tex. Trial Lawyers Assn., Houston Trial Lawyers Assn., Nat. Assn. Criminal Def. Lawyers, Delta Theta Phi. Office: DeGuerin Dickson & Hennessy 7th Fl The Republic Bldg 1018 Preston Ave Houston TX 77002-1818 Office Phone: 713-223-5959. Office Fax: 713-223-9231. E-mail: ddeguerin@aol.com.*

DEGUILIO, JON E., lawyer; b. Hammond, Ind., June 15, 1955; s. Ernest Michael and Jeanne (Hochis) D.; m. Barbara Jo Wieser, Oct. 3, 1981; 1 child, Suzanne Jeanne. BA, U. Notre Dame, 1977; JD, Valparaiso U., 1981. Bar: Ind. 1981, U.S. Dist. Ct. (so. dist.) Ind. 1981, U.S. Dist. Ct. (no. dist.) Ind. 1981. Pub. defender Lake County Ct., Crown Point, Ind., 1984-87; dep. prosecutor Lake County Prosecutor's Office, Crown Point, 1981-84; 87-94; assoc. James Wieser Law Offices, Highland, Ind., 1981-93; U.S. atty. no. dist. Ind. Dept. Justice, Dyer, 1993-99. Atty. Highland Police Commn., Highland, Ind., 1987— and Highland Water Bd., 1987—; legal advisor, Lake County Sheriff, Crown Point, Ind., 1986-87; atty. Hammond and East Chgo. Fedn. of Tchrs., 1986—. Councilman Hammond City Council, 1984-87; mem. Lake County Med. Ctr. Devel. Agy., 1988—, Greater Hammond Community Services, 1987—; treas. Little Calumet River Basin Com., 1986. Mem. Lake County Bar Assn. (bd. dirs. 1988-90), Justinian Soc. Democrat. Avocations: basketball, bolf, reading. Home: 8944 Liable Rd Hammond IN 46322-2248 Office: US Attorneys Office 5400 Federal Plz #1500 Hammond IN 46320-1843

DEGUTIS, LINDA CHRISTINE, adult education educator, epidemiologist, researcher; b. Chgo., Dec. 16, 1953; d. William Joseph and Genevieve (Karons) D.; m. Robert F. Miller, Aug. 16, 1975 (div. Mar. 1983); m. Bruce Fenton Carmichael, Mar. 26, 1988. BS, DePaul U., 1975; MSN, Yale Sch. of Nursing, 1982; DrPH, Yale Sch. of Medicine, 1994. Cert. RN Conn., Ill. Staff nurse Rush-Presbyn. St. Luke's Med. Ctr., Chgo., 1975-78, Yale-New Haven Hosp., Conn., 1978-81; trauma program coord. Yale Sch. Medicine, New Haven, 1982-91, 92-95; lectr. in surgery Yale Sch. of Medicine, New Haven, 1984-95, asst. prof. sect. of emergency medicine, 1995—2003, assoc. prof. emergency medicine, pub. health, 2003—; trauma coord. Bridgeport (Conn.) Hosp., 1991-92; Robert Wood Johnson Health Policy fellow Office of Senator Paul Wellstone, Washington, 1996-97. Adv. mem. Conn. State com. on trauma; exec. com. mem. Conn. Adv. for Highway Safety, Hartford, Conn., 1995—. Contbr. articles to profl. jours. Founding mem. MADD-New Haven Chpt., 1983; vol. Conn. Spl. Olympic Games, New Haven, 1990-94, Internat. Spl. Olympic Games, New Haven, 1995; pres. Lake Point Condominium Assn. Bd., 1991. Mem. ACS, AAAS, Am. Pub. Health Assn. (exec. bd., chmn. injury control and emergency health svcs. sect.), Am. Trauma Soc., Nat. Assn. for Pub. Health Policy, Soc. Acad. Emergency Medicine. Office: Yale Sch Medicine 464 Congress Ave New Haven CT 06519-1361

DE GUZMAN, RICARDO D., retired physician; b. Gapan, Philippines, Feb. 22, 1930; s. Victorino De Guzman and Pascuala Domingo; m. Dolores I. De Guzman, Mar. 19, 1958; children: Robert, Raul. MD, U. Philippines, 1955. Staff physician VA Med. Ctr., Dayton, Ohio, 1967—2004. Home: 5017 James Hill Rd Kettering OH 45429

DE HAAN, HENRY JOHN, research psychologist; b. St. Clair County, Ill., Nov. 23, 1920; s. Henry J. and Fanny (Haislip) de H.; m. Mary J. Farrell, Oct. 22, 1943. AB, Washington U., St. Louis, 1942, AM, 1949; PhD, U. Pitts., 1960. Postdoctoral Coatesville VA Hosp., Pa., 1960—62; rsch. scientist George Washington U., Washington, 1962—64; rsch. psychologist Armed Forces Radiobiol. Rsch. Inst., Bethesda, Md., 1965—69, U.S. Army Rsch. Inst., Alexandria, Va., 1969—86; external rsch. prof. Krasnow Inst. for Advanced Study, George Mason U., Fairfax, Va., 2001—04. Mem. faculty USDA Grad. Sch., Washington, 1967-77. Author 10 U.S. govt. sci. and tech. reports, 1954-82; contbr. articles to Perception and Psychophysics, Jour. Comparative and Physiol. Psychology and other jours. With USN, 1944-46, PTO. Mem. AAAS (emeritus), APA (life), Am. Psychol. Soc., Ea. Psychol. Assn. (life), Soc. Neurosci. (emeritus), US Tennis Assn. (life), Internat. Primatol. Soc. (life), Psychonomic Soc. (life), Sigma Xi (emeritus). Achievements include research on perceptual and cognitive capacities of retarded children and adult psychotics, on effects of temperature on food intake and brain stimulation (in the rat), on effects of ionizing radiation on primate perceptual and cognitive capacities, and research on speech technology and speech compression, including a speech-rate intelligibility threshold. Home: 5403 Yorkshire St Springfield VA 22151-1203

DE HAAS, DAVID DANA, emergency physician; b. Hollywood, Calif., May 31, 1956; S. Martin and Norma (Deutsch) De H.; m. Mary Danuta Przybylowski, June 27, 1982; children: Lindsay Alexandra, Heather Brittany, Lance Austin. BS in Biochemistry, UCLA, Westwood, Calif., 1979; MD, Chgo. Med. Sch., 1983. Diplomate Am. Bd. Internal Medicine, Am. Bd. Emergency Medicine, Nat. Bd. Med. Examiners; cert. provider advanced trauma life support, ACLS, Pediatric Advanced Life Support, BCLS, Med. Disaster Response, instr. ACLS, Pediatric Advanced Life Support, Med. Disaster Response. Resident emergency medicine/internal medicine Kern Med. Ctr., Bakersfield, Calif., 1983-87; assoc. med. dir. Family Care Med. Assocs., Huntington Beach, Calif., 1987—; asst. clin. prof. medicine dept. internal medicine U. Calif.-Irvine Med. Ctr., Orange, 1989—; emergency physician St. Bernardine Med. Ctr., San Bernardino, Calif., 1991—; ptnr. Calif. Emergency Physicians Med. Group, San Bernardino, 1991—. Expert reviewer Med. Bd. Calif.; affiliate faculty ACLS, Pediatric Advanced Life Support, Am. Heart Assn.; vice chmn. dept. emergency medicine St. Bernardine Med. Ctr., ACLS dir., dir. quality assurance/continuous quality improvement dept. emergency medicine; mem. edn. com. Med. Disaster Response; ptnr.Calif. Emergency Physician Med. Group. Fellow ACP, Am. Coll. Emergency Physicians; mem. AMA, Calif. Med. Assn., Orange County Med. Soc., Soc. Orange County Emergency Physicians (bd. dirs.), Assn. Clin. Faculty U. Calif., Irvine Coll. Medicine. Avocations: gardening, pin collecting, reading. Home: 26882 Via La Mirada San Juan Capistrano CA 92675-4935 Office: St Bernardine Med Ctr 2101 N Waterman Ave San Bernardino CA 92404-4836

DEHAAS, JOHN NEFF, JR., retired architecture educator; b. Phila., July 4, 1926; s. John Neff and Sadie Lavinia (Hagel) DeH.; m. C. Bernice Wallace, Dec. 27, 1950; children: Kenneth Eric, Jocelyn Hilda. BArch, Tex. A&M U., 1948, MEd, 1950. Registered architect, Mont. Instr. Tex. A&M U., College Station, 1948-50, U. Tex., Austin, 1950-51; successively instr. to prof. Mont. State U., Bozeman, 1951-80. Supervisory architect Historic Am. Bldgs. Survey, summers San Francisco, 1962, Bozeman, 1963, 65, Milw., 1969; cons. Mont. Historic Preservation Office, Helena, 1977-78, mem. rev. bd., 1968-79. Author: Montana's Historic Structures, Vol. 1, 1864, Vol. 2, 1969, Historic Uptown Butte, 1977; editor quar. newsletter Mont. Ghost Town Preservation Soc., 1972— Bd. dirs. Mont. Assn. for Blind, Butte, 1984-95. Recipient Centennial Preservation award Mont. Historic Preservation Office, 1989, Dorothy Bridgman award for Outstanding Svc. to the Blind Montana Assn. for the Blind, 1990. Fellow AIA (com. on historic resources 1974—); mem. Mont. Hist. Soc. (trustee's award 1989). Republican. Methodist. Home: 2400 Durston Rd 50 Bozeman MT 59718

DEHART, JACOB, Internet company executive; Student, Purdue U., Ind. Co-founder, v.p. skinnyCorp, parent co. of Threadless.com (t-shirt site), NakedandAngry.com (wallpaper site), ExtraTasty.com (drink recipes site), others, Chgo., 2000—. Named one of Top 40 Under 40, Crain's Chgo. Bus., 2006. Office: skinnyCorp 5225 N Ravenswood Dr Ste 101 Chicago IL 60640*

DE HAVILLAND, OLIVIA MARY, actress; b. Tokyo, July 1, 1916; naturalized, 1941; d. Walter Augustus and Lilian Augusta (Ruse) de H. (parents British subjects); m. Marcus Goodrich, Aug. 26, 1946 (div.); 1 child, Benjamin Briggs Goodrich (dec.); m. Pierre Galante, Apr. 2, 1955 (div.); 1 child, Gisele. Student schs. and convent in, Calif.; DHL (hon.), Am. U., Paris, 1994. Made stage debut as Hermia in: Midsummer Night's Dream (Max Reinhardt prodn.), Hollywood Bowl, 1934; 1st motion picture in same role, 1935; actress: (films) including Captain Blood, Anthony Adverse, Robin Hood, Gone With the Wind (nominated for Acad. award 1939), Strawberry Blonde, Hold Back The Dawn (nominated for Acad. award 1941), Princess O'Rourke, To Each His Own (Acad. award for best actress 1946), Dark Mirror, The Snakepit (nominated for Acad. award 1948, N.Y. Critics Award 1948, Laurel Award for best performance 1948-53), The Heiress (Acad. award for best actress 1949, N.Y. critics award), My Cousin Rachel 1952, Not As A Stranger, 1954, Ambassador's Daughter, 1955 (Belgian Critics Prix Femina), Proud Rebel, 1957, Light in the Piazza, 1961, Lady in a Cage, 1963 (British films and filming award), Hush, Hush Sweet Charlotte, 1964, Airport '77, 1976, The Swarm, 1978, The Fifth Musketeer, 1979; TV appearances include Noon Wine, 1966, The Screaming Woman, 1972, Roots: The Next Generations, 1979, Murder is Easy, 1981, Charles and Diana: A Royal Romance, 1982, North and South, II, 1986, Anastasia: The Mystery of Anna, 1986 (Golden Globe award, Emmy nomination), The Woman He Loved, 1988; theatre includes (on Broadway) Romeo and Juliet, 1951, Candida, 1952, A Gift of Time, 1962, (summer stock) What Every Woman Knows, Westport, Conn., Easthampton, Long Island, 1946, Candida, same plus 9 other summer theatres, 1951; (legitimate) Transcontinental Tour Candida 1951-52, (245 Performances); lecture tours, U.S., 1971-80; toured Army and Navy hosps. in U.S., Alaska, Aleutians, South Pacific, 1943-44, Europe, 1957-61; pres. jury Cannes Film Festival, 1965; participant: narration of France's Bicentennial gift to U.S. Son et Lumiere, 1976, Bicentennial Service, Am. Cathedral in Paris, 1976; author: Every Frenchman Has One, 1962. Trustee Am. Coll. in Paris, 1970-71, Am. Libr. in Paris, 1974-81. Recipient Women's Nat. Press Club award for outstanding accomplishment in theater presented by Pres. Truman, 1950; Am. Legion Humanitarian award, 1967 Mem. Screen Actors Guild, Acad. of Motion Picture Arts and Scis. Democrat. Address: BP 156 75764 Paris Cedex 16 France

DEHAY, JERRY MARVIN, business educator, small business owner; b. Brownwood, Tex., Nov. 21, 1939; s. Marvin Edward and Willie Marie (Daniell) DeHay; m. Dana Lea Laxson, May 29, 1960 (div. June 30, 1973); children: David, Deanna; m. Marilyn Ann Lethco, July 28, 1973; children: Colin, Beva, Sue. BBA, A&M Coll. Tex., 1962; MBA, Tex. A&M U, 1966; PhD, North Tex. State U., 1978. Sales mgr. Procter and Gamble, Corpus Christi, Tex., 1962-65; instr. mktg. Tex. A&M U., College Station, 1966-69; asst. prof. bus. Howard Payne U., Brownwood, Tex., 1969-73; coord. food mktg. Tarrant County Jr. Coll. N.E., Hurst, Tex., 1973-75; instr. math. Brownwood State Sch., 1976-77; asst. prof. mktg. E. Tex. State U., Commerce, 1977-78, prof., 1979-83, dir. Small Bus. Inst., 1979—83; assoc. prof. bus. Hardin Simmons U., Abilene, Tex., 1978-79; dean Coll. Bus. Adminstrn. Tarleton State U., Stephenville, Tex., 1983-94, dir. Small Bus. Inst., 1983—87, dir. Small Bus. Devel. Ctr., 1987—89; CEO JMD Cons., Brownwood, Tex., 1994—; co-owner Recollections Antiques and Collectibles, Brownwood, Tex., 1996—; prof. bus. adminstrn. Howard Payne U., 2001—05, dir. continuing edn., 1971—73. Mem. adv. bd. Small Bus. Devel. Ctr. Co-author: Supervision, 1984; contbr. poems to anthologies; author, presenter (TV series) PBS Business File, 1985. Sec. bd. trustees Brownwood Ind. Sch. Dist., 1972; trustee Mullin (Tex.) Ind. Sch. Dist., 1979; chmn. regional adv. bd. SBA, Dallas; vice-chmn. Brownwood Bldg. Stds. Commn., 1997—2007; bd. dirs. Brown County Hist. Mus., pres., 1999, Tex. State Button Soc., 2007—, Brownwood City Coun., 2007—, mem., 2007—; bd. dirs. Brownwood Heritage Assn., 2006. Named Outstanding Educator of Am., 1973, 1974, 1975, Outstanding Am. of Bi-Centennial Era, 1976. Mem.: Sales and Mktg. Execs. Ft. Worth (educator mem.), Tex. Button Soc. (pres. 2007—), Pi Sigma Epsilon (educator v.p. 1984—85, adminstrv. v.p. 1985—86, nat. pres. 1987, Top Faculty Advisor award 1983), Mu Kappa Tau, Delta Sigma Pi. Baptist. Avocations: writing, singing, collecting buttons. Home and Office: 801 Quail Run Brownwood TX 76801-6314 Business E-Mail: dehay@bwoodtx.com. *Do all you can to help others to succeed in whatever endeavour they choose. If you are successful in this, there is no greater success.*

DEHAYES, DANIEL WESLEY, business educator; b. Columbus, Ohio, Sept. 23, 1941; s. Daniel Wesley and June Rosiland (Page) DeH.; children: Sarah Baxter, Benjamin Wesley. BA in Math. and Computer Sci., Ohio State U., 1963, MBA, 1964, PhD in Bus. Adminstrn., 1968. Asst. prof. systems analysis Naval Postgrad. Sch., Monterey, Calif., 1967-69; asst. prof. sch. bus. Ind. U., Bloomington, Ind., 1969-72, assoc. prof.sch. bus., 1972-79, prof. sch. bus., 1979—2005, prof. emeritus, 2005—, dean of acad. computing, 1981-86, asst. v.p. info. tech., 1987-88; dir. Ctr. For Entrepreneurship and Innovation, Ind. U., Bloomington, 1989-98. Exec. dir. Inst. Rsch. on the MIS, 1989-92; cons. in field. Textbook author; contbr. articles to profl. jours. Served to capt. U.S. Army, 1967-69 Recipient fellowships and grants Mem. Decision Scis. Inst. Republican. Methodist. Office: Indiana University Kelley School of Business Bloomington IN 47405 Office Phone: 317-342-1941. Business E-Mail: dehayes@indiana.edu.

DE HEER, WALTER A., physics professor; PhD, U. Calif., Berkeley, 1985. With Ecole Polytechnique, Lausanne, Switzerland, 1987—96; faculty mem. to prof. Sch. Physics Ga. Inst. Tech., Atlanta, 1996—. Contbr. articles to sci. jours. Named one of Sci. Am. 50, 2006. Achievements include refining techniques to grow graphene out of silicon carbide, potentially changing the way electronics are made in the future. Office: Sch Physics Ga Inst Tech 837 State St Atlanta GA 30332-0430 Office Phone: 404-894-7879. E-mail: deheer@electra.physics.gatech.edu.

DEHMELT, HANS GEORG, physicist, educator; b. Görlitz, Germany, Sept. 9, 1922; arrived in U.S., 1952, naturalized, 1962; s. Georg Karl and Asta Ella (Klemmt) Dehmelt; m. Diana Elaine Dundore, Nov. 18, 1989; 1 child from previous marriage, Gerd. Grad., Graues Kloster, Berlin, Abitur, 1940; D Rerum Naturalium, U. Goettingen, 1950; D Rerum Naturalium (hon.), Ruprecht Karl-Universitat, Heidelberg, 1986; DSc (hon.), U. Chgo., 1987. Postdoctoral fellow U. Goettingen, Germany, 1950—52, Duke U., Durham, NC, 1952—55; vis. asst. prof. U. Wash., Seattle, 1955, asst. prof. physics, 1956, assoc. prof., 1957—61, prof., rsch. physicist, 1961—. Cons. Varian Assocs., Palo Alto, Calif., 1956—76. Contbr. articles to profl. jours. Sr. pvt. German Army, 1940—45, (captured by US forces, POW to 1946). Recipient Humboldt prize, 1974, award in Basic Rsch., Internat. Soc. Magnetic Resonance, 1980, Rumford prize, Am. Acad. Arts and Scis., 1985, Nobel prize in Physics, 1989, Nat. medal of Sci., 1995; grantee NSF, 1958—. Fellow: Am. Phys. Soc. (Davisson-Germer prize 1970); mem.: NAS, Am. Optical Soc., Am. Acad. Arts and Scis., Sigma Xi. Office: Dept Physics U Wash FM-15 PO Box 351560 Seattle WA 98195-1560

DEHMER, GREGORY JOSEPH, cardiologist; b. Milw., Sept. 26, 1949; s. Joseph Anton and Bernadine Elizabeth (Bloom) D.; m. Sue Jane Vencil, Jan. 21, 1977; children: Jeffrey, Laura. BS, Carroll Coll., 1971; MD, U. Wis., 1975. Diplomate Am. Bd. Internal Medicine; cert in medicine, cardiology, and interventional cardiology. Dir. cardiac catheterization lab., asst. prof. medicine U. Tex. Health Sci. Ctr., Dallas, 1984-88; assoc. prof. medicine U. NC, 1988—2001; dir. cardiac catheterization lab U. NC Hosp., 1988—2001; prof. medicine, dir. cardiology divsn. Scott & White Clinic Tex. A&M U. Coll. Medicine, 2001—. Mem. editl. bd. Am. Jour. Cardiology, 1990—, Jour. Am. Coll. Cardiology, 1999-2003, Circulation, 1993-2004. Maj. USAF, 1981-83. Fellow ACP, Am. Coll. Cardiology, Am. Heart Assn. (pres.), Soc. Cardiovascular Angiography and Interventions; mem. AMA (panelist DATTA program 1991—). Mem. Ch. of Christ. Avocation: skiing. Office: 2401 South 31st St Temple TX 76508 Office Phone: 254-724-6782. Business E-Mail: gdehmer@swmail.sw.org.

DEHN, CATHLEEN PATTERSON, health facility administrator; b. Akron, Feb. 25, 1958; d. James Edward and Doris Elizabeth (Boyd) P.; m. James Keith Dehn, June 27, 1981; children: Benjamin Jameson and Alexander Hudson (twins). BSN, U. Akron, 1980; MSN, Case Western Res. U., 1988; MA Applied Psychology, NYU, 1995, postgrad., 1995—. RN, NY; cert. PNP, ANCC. Nurse technician Children's Med. Ctr. Akron, 1979-80, staff nurse, 1980-81; pediatric and advanced clin. nurse, asst. head nurse, clin. nurse specialist Rainbow Babies and Children's Hosp., Cleve., 1981-91, edn. coord., 1991-93; nurse, project coord. divsn. nursing NYU The Child Health Ctr., Bklyn., 1994-96; nurse dept. pediat. Inst. for Neurology and Neurosurgery Beth Israel Med. Ctr., NYC, 1996-2000; case mgr. dept. pediats. St. Vincent Hosp. and Med. Ctr., NYC, 2001—05, nurse mgr. NICU, pediat. divsn., 2005—07; nurse mgr. neonatal CCU and pediat. Lenox Hill Hosp., NYC, 2007—. Lectr., clin. instr. Frances Payne Bolton Sch. Nursing, Case Western Res. U., Cleve., 1990-93; mem. adj. faculty divsn. nursing NYU, 1994-96; project coord. Dance Cleve., 1989; nat. instr. Neonatal Resuscitation Program, 1990-91; regional instr. Neonatal Resuscitation Program, Am. Heart Assn., Am. Acad. Pediatrics. Exec. prodr. videos: Getting to Know the Unique Behavioral Capabilities of the Newborn, 1987, One Step at a Time: A Family's Guide to the Neonatal Intensive Care Unit, 1991. Co-founder Sick Kids Need Involved People, Cleve., 1987; team-walk capt. March of Dimes, Cleve., 1989-92 (Edn. grantee 1991); mem. Nat. Mus. Women in Arts. Recipient Samuel E. and Rebecca Elliott award for Cmty. Svc. Case Western Res. U., 1988; named One of Outstanding Young Women of Am., 1988; Fed. Profl. Nurse Trainee scholar, 1986-87. Mem. APA, Am. Ednl. Rsch. Assn., Kappa Delta Pi, Sigma Theta Tau, Pi Lambda Theta. Avocations: health outcomes research, teaching, educational evaluation. Home: 1 University Pl Apt 10L New York NY 10003-4518 Office Phone: 212-604-7875.

DEHN, JAMES KEITH, investment company executive; b. Buffalo, Jan. 29, 1957; s. Earl Sylvester and Kathryn Agnes (Pericak) D.; m. Cathleen Patterson, June 27, 1981; children: Benjamin Jameson and Alexander Hudson (twins) BA, Walsh U., North Canton, Ohio, 1979; MBA, SUNY, Buffalo, 1981; postgrad., NYU, 1996. Sales rep. Indsl. Metals, Inc., North Canton, Ohio, 1980-97; fin. advisor Prudential Securities, NYC, 1997-2000; fin. advisor pvt. client group UBS PaineWebber, NYC, 2000—04, Wachovia Securities, 2004—, v.p. investments, 2006—. Exec. prodr. (video) Getting to Know the Unique Behavioral Capabilities of the Newborn, 1987. Co-founder Friends of Footpath Footpath Dance Co., Cleve., 1988-90, bd. trustees, 1990-91; mem. capital campaign com. Ch. of the Ascension, NYC, 2006-. Recipient Heritage Home Renovation award Cleve. Heights Cmty. Congress, 1990. Mem. Washing Sq. Assn., Alumni Assn. SUNY Buffalo, Nat. Trust Historic Preservation. Avocations: tennis, sailing, culinary arts, historical preservation. Office: Wachovia Securities 1 Liberty Plz 46th Fl New York NY 10006 Office Phone: 212-978-1103.

DEHNER, JOSEPH JULNES, lawyer; b. Cin., Nov. 28, 1948; s. Walter Joseph and Bess (Humphries) Dehner; m. Noel Julnes, Nov. 19, 1983; children: Holly Julnes, Sara Julnes. AB, Princeton U., 1970; JD, Harvard U., 1973. Bar: Ohio 1973, U.S. Dist. Ct. (no. and so. dists.) Ohio 1975, Fla. 1986, U.S. Dist. Ct. (ea. dist.) Ky. 1988, U.S. Ct. Internat. Trade 1992. Law clk. to judge U.S. Ct. Appeals, Cleve., 1973-75; assoc. Kyte, Conlan, Wulsin & Vogeler, Cin., 1975-78, Frost Brown Todd LLC, Cin., 1978—; chmn. Universal Transactions Inc., 1991-95. Co-mgr. Ukraine Investments Ltd., 1995—99. Author: (book) Structured Settlements and Periodic Payment Judgments, 1986, A Guide to Soviet Businesspeople on American Business Law, 1991, Doing Business in Russia, 1992, Dispute Resolution in China, 1994, A Foreign Investors Guide to Ukraine, 1995; contbr. articles to profl. publs. Sec., v.p. Cin. Preservation Assn., 1978—86; mem. Cin. Planning Commn., 1984—85; pres. Charter Com. Greater Cin., 1982—86; chmn. Cin.-Kharkiv Sister City Project, 1988—91; Ohio commodore, 2003—; pres. French-Am. C. of C. of Greater Cin., 2004—06; chmn. So. Ohio Dist. Export Coun., 2003—, Fgn. Policy Leadership Coun. Greater Cin., 2005—; mem. exec. coun. MULTILAW, 1997—; chmn. Hamilton County/Cin. Pub. Libr. Found., 2006—; pres. European-Am. C. of C. of Greater Cin., 2007—; chancellor Episcopal Diocese So. Ohio, 1997—; trustee Princeton (N.J.) U., 1970—74, Ohio Hist. Soc., 1974—78. Mem.: ABA (vice chmn. internat. litig. com. 2002—04, mem. multilaw exec. coun.), 6th Cir. Jud. Conf., Cin. Bar Assn., Ohio Bar Assn. (chmn. internat. law com. 1989—91), Pub. Investors Arbitration Bar Assn.

Avocations: tennis, reading. Home: 822 Yale Ave Terrace Park OH 45174-1258 Office: Frost Brown Todd LLC 2200 PNC Ctr 201 E 5th St Ste 2200 Cincinnati OH 45202-4182 Office Phone: 513-651-6949. Business E-Mail: jdehner@fbtlaw.com.

DEHOFF, VALERIE S., music educator; d. Robert Ransome and Hazel Story Stone; m. George W. DeHoff, June 29, 1974; children: George W., Robert Stone, David Alan. BA, David Lipscomb Coll., 1974; MEd, Mid. Tenneessee State U., 1981. Lic. profl. tchr. Tenn., 1974. Pvt. piano tchr., Murfreesboro, Tenn., 1974—85; homebound tchr. Rutherford County Schools, Murfreesboro, 1978—79; English tchr. Thurman Francis Jr. H.S., Smyrna, Tenn., 1979—80; music tchr., choral dir. Mid. Tenn. Christian Sch., Murfreesboro, 1984—. Mem. Minerva Dr. Ch. of Christ, Murfreesboro, 1989—. Named Tchr. of Excellence, Tenn. Gov.'s Sch. for the Arts, 1999, 2003. Mem.: DAR, Am. Choral Dir. Assn. (assoc.), Mid. Tenn. Vocal Assn. (assoc.; exec. bd. 2000—, elem. honors chairperson 2000—05, pres. elect 2006—), Mid. Tenn. Choral Soc. (assoc.), Womans Club (assoc.). R-Conservative. Avocations: reading, genealogy. Home Phone: 615-890-5839; Office Phone: 615-893-0602.

DEHORATIUS, RAPHAEL JOSEPH, rheumatologist; b. Phila., Sept. 16, 1942; s. Pasquale P. and Edith R. DeH.; children: Nicole, Danielle. BS, St. Joseph's U., Phila., 1964; MD, Jefferson Med. Coll., 1968. Med. intern Jefferson Med. Coll., Phila., 1968-69, asst. prof. medicine, 1976-78, assoc. prof. medicine, 1978-82; med. resident U. N.Mex., Albuquerque, 1969-70, rheumatology fellow, 1972-74, asst. prof. medicine, 1974-76; prof. medicine Hahnemann U., Phila., 1982-92, Jefferson Med. Coll./Thomas Jefferson U., Phila., 1992—2006. Contbr. articles to profl. jours./publs. Maj. USAF, 1970-72. Recipient Lupus Rsch. grant Commonwealth of Pa., Arthritis Rsch. grant. Fellow: ACP, Am. Coll. Rheumatology (chmn. profl. meetings 1988—91, edn. coun. 1988—91, v.p. 2000—01, pres.-elect 2001—02, pres. 2002—03, chmn. nominations com. 2003—04); mem.: Assn. Am. Immunologists. Address: 800 Ridgeview Dr Horsham PA 19044 Home Phone: 856-467-6535. E-mail: rdehor@comcast.net.

DE HOYOS, DEBORA M., lawyer; b. Monticello, NY, Aug. 10, 1953; d. Luis and Marion (Kinney) de Hoyos; m. Walter C. Carlson, June 20, 1981; children: Amanda, Greta, Linnea. BA, Wellesley Coll., 1975; JD, Harvard U., 1978. Bar: Ill. 1978, U.S. Dist. Ct. (no. dist.) Ill. 1980. Assoc. Mayer, Brown & Platt, Chgo., 1978—84, ptnr., 1985—, mng. ptnr., 1991—. Bd. dirs. Evanston Northwestern Healthcare; bd. trustees Providence St. Mel. Sch. Contbr. chpt. to Securitization of Financial Assets, 1991. Trustee Chgo. Symphony Orch. Named one of the Ten Most Influential Women Lawyers in Ill., Am. Lawyer Media, 2000, Fifty Outstanding Women Graduates, Harvard Law Sch., 2003. Office: Mayer Brown Rowe Maw Llp 71L S Wacker Dr Chicago IL 60606-4637

DEICKEN, RAYMOND FRIEDRICH, neuropsychiatrist, neuroscientist; b. Honolulu, June 28, 1957; (parents Am. citizens); s. Raymond T. and Miriam (Ogata) D. AB, MS, Stanford U., 1980; MD, U. Calif., San Francisco, 1984. Diplomate Nat. Bd. Med. Examiners, Am. Bd. Psychiatry and Neurology; lic. physician Med. Bd. Calif. Resident physician U. Calif., San Francisco, 1984-88, rsch. fellow, 1988-91, asst. prof. psychiatry, 1991-97, assoc. prof., 1997—2003, prof., 2003—; staff physician VA Med. Ctr., San Francisco, 1991—, med. dir. Partial Hosp. Program, 2002. Lectr. in field; cons. Exodon Neurosci., 2001, Roche Biosci., 2001, Bristol-Myers Squibb, 2003. Reviewer manuscripts Biol. Psychiatry, 1987—, Psychiatry Rsch., 1992—; contbr. articles to profl. jours; mem. editl. bd. Jour. Integrative Neuroscis. Alumni mentor Stanford U. Student Alumni Mentor Program, 1993—. Recipient Young Investigator award Nat. Alliance for Rsch. on Schizophrenia and Depression, 1992, 94, Ind. Investigator award, 2000, 04, Stanley Found. rsch. award Nat. Alliance for Mentally Ill, 1997, 98, VA Physician Rsch. Assoc. Career Devel. award, 1991-95; Dista fellow Soc. Biol. Psychiatry, 1991. Fellow Collegium Internat. Neuropsychopharmacologicum, Royal Soc. Medicine (London), Internat. Soc. for Affective Disorders; mem. AMA, Soc. for Neuroscience, Soc. Biol. Psychiatry, Internat. Soc. Magnetic Resonance in Medicine, Am. Psychiat. Assn., Internat. Soc. Neuroimaging in Psychiatry, N.Y. Acad. Scis. Episcopalian. Office: Dept Veterans Affairs Med Ctr 4150 Clement St San Francisco CA 94121-1545 Office Phone: 415-221-4810. Business E-Mail: rfdeicken@gmail.com.

DEIGHTON, LEN, author; b. London, Feb. 18, 1929; Author: The Ipcress File, 1962 (motion picture U.S., 1963), Horse Under Water, 1963, U.S. edit. 1968, Funeral in Berlin, 1964 (motion picture U.S., 1965), Ou Est le Garlic/Basic French Cooking, 1965, 2d edit., 1979, U.S. edit., 1977, Action Cook Book, 1965, Cookstrip Cook Book, 1966, Billion Dollar Brain, 1966 (motion picture U.S., 1966), An Expensive Place to Die, 1967, Len Deighton's Dossier, 1967, Only When I Larf, 1968 (motion picture U.S., 1968), Bomber, 1970 (radio drama U.S., 1970), U.S. Edit. of Declarations of War, 1971, Close-Up, 1972, Spy Story, 1974 (motion picture U.S., 1974), Eleven Declarations of War, 1975, Yesterday's Spy, 1975, Twinkle, Twinkle, Little Spy, 1976, Catch a Falling Spy, 1976, Fighter, 1977, U.S. edit., 1978, SS-GB, 1978, U.S. edit., 1979, Blitzkrieg, 1979, U.S. edit., 1980, XPD, 1981, Goodbye Mickey Mouse, 1982, Berlin Game, 1983, Mexico Set, 1984, London Match, 1985, Winter: A Berlin Family 1899-1945, 1987, U.S. edit., 1988, Spy Hook, 1988, Spy Line, 1989, Spy Sinker, 1990, Basic French Cookery Course, 1990, ABC of French Food, 1989, U.S. edit., 1990, MAMista, 1991, City of Gold, 1992, Violent Ward, 1993, Blood, Tears & Folly, 1993, Faith, 1994, U.S. edit., 1995, Hope, 1995, U.S. edit., 1996, Charity, 1996; co-author: The Assassination of President Kennedy, 1967, Airshipwreck, 1978, U.S. edit., 1979, Battle of Britain, 1980, 2d edit., 1990, U.S. edit., 1980; (13-part TV series) Game, Set & Match, 1985. Office: care Jonathan Clowes Ltd 10 Iron Bridge House London NW1 8BD England E-mail: jonathanclowes@aol.com.

DEIHL, CHARLES L., former college president; b. Chgo., Dec. 12, 1937; s. Elmer Frank and Lois Olive (Waterman) D.; m. Peggy Ann Fleischman, May 1, 1938; children: Geoffrey Charles, Kristen Ann. BA, Ind. U., 1959; MA, Mich. State U., 1963, MFA, 1965. Asst. dir. publs. Ohio U., Athens, 1965-67, head graphic design, 1967-71, Bradley U., Peoria, Ill., 1971-74; head dept. fine arts U. Cin., 1974-79; dean arts and humanities SUNY, Buffalo, 1979-89; pres. Kendall Coll. Art and Design, Grand Rapids, Mich., 1989-95, Columbus Coll. of Art and Design, 1995—97. Mem. mgmt. devel. program Harvard U., Cambridge, Mass., 1986, seminar for new pres's., 1989; cons. graphic design and illustration in field. Artist to paintings and drawings in field. Sgt. USAF, 1962-63. Ind. U. merit scholar, 1955. Mem. Assn. Governing Bds. Univs. and Colls., Assn. Ind. Colls. and Univs. Mich., Assn. Ind. Colls. Art and Design, Univ. and Coll. Designers Assn. (pres. emeritus 1972—), Rotary Club Grand Rapids. Home: 7245 Sugar Bush Ln Chagrin Falls OH 44022-2667

DEIHL, MICHAEL ALLEN, federal agency administrator; b. Bluffton, Ind., Apr. 22, 1952; s. Robert W. and Betty J. (Miller) D.; m. Deborah Ann Crabb, June 16, 1973; 1 child, Samantha Lynn. BSEE, Colo. State U., 1974. East slope area mgr. ECPO Bur. Reclamation, Loveland, Colo., 1981-85, chief com. and control divsn., ECPO, 1985-87; chief maintenance divsn. Hoover Dam Bur. Reclamation, Boulder City, Nev., 1987-90; project mgr. Alaska Power Adminstrn., Dept. Energy, Juneau, 1990-92, dir. power divsn., 1992, adminstr., 1992-95; adminstr. Dept. Energy Southwestern Power Adminstrn., Tulsa, 1995—. Office: Southwestern Power Admin 1 W 3rd St Tulsa OK 74103-3502

DEIKE, KEITH LAWRENCE, lawyer; b. Owatonna, Minn., Aug. 9, 1952; s. Orvin Kenneth and Muriel Felicity Deike; m. Pamela Jean Schubbe, Apr. 8, 1988; children: Jacob Andrew, Maxwell James. BA magna cum laude, Mankato State U., 1979; JD, U. Minn., 1983. Bar: Minn. 1983, U.S. Dist. Ct. Minn. 1985. Sole practitioner Deike Law Offices, Waseca, Minn., 1983—94; assoc. Patton, Hoversten & Berg, P.A., Waseca, 1994—. Third dist. pub. defender State Bd. of Pub. Def., St. Paul, 1990—96; city prosecutor City of Waseca, 1991—94. Dir. Waseca Area C. of C., 1989—91, Waseca Area United Way, 1992—98; chair Sacred Heart Sch., Waseca, Minn., 1995—2001. Named Super Lawyer, Minn. Law & Politics Mag., 2000, Leading Personal Injury Atty., 2001. Mem.: Am. Assn. Justice, Minn. State Bar Assn. Home: 1200 4th St NE Waseca MN 56093 Office: Patton Hoversten & Berg PA 215 Elm Ave East Waseca MN 56093-0249 Home Phone: 507-835-5281; Office Phone: 507-835-5240. Office Fax: 507-835-1827. Business E-Mail: keith.deike@phblawoffice.com.

DEINES, KATRINA, architecture educator; BA in Art History, U. Minn., 1967, MA in Art History, 1974; MArch, U. Wash., 1979. Assoc. prof. dept. arch. U. Wash., Seattle, assoc. dean Coll. Arch. and Urban Planning, 1988—, co-dir. Rome Ctr., 1993—2000, dir. Rome Ctr., 2000—. Guest faculty mem. U. B.C., Sicily, Italy, 2000; mem. coll. exec. com. U. Wash., Seattle, 1988—, faculty senate, 1989—92, chair coll. awards com., 1996—, mem. campus art com., Bothell, 1998—, Wash. State Arts Commn., 1997—; internat. faculty coun., advisor to U. Wash. Pres. and Provost, 1998—. Mem. editl. bd.: Jour. Archtl. Edn., 1995—98, co-founder, mng. editor: N.W. Jour. for Arch. and Design, 1980—85. Soprano, treas., pres. bd. City Contabile Choir, 1986—92; active City of Seattle San Point Design Commn., 1998—99. Recipient Faculty Devel. Rsch. award, U. Wis. Coll. Arch. and Urban Planning, 1998. Office: U Wash Coll Arch and Urban Planning 208N Gould Hall Box 355720 Seattle WA 98195-5726

DEIRO, JUDITH ANNE, chemical dependency educator; d. Guido and Ruby Margaret Deiro. BA, Okla. State U., Stillwater, 1968; MA, U. Fla., 1970; PhD, U. Wash., 1994. Cert. alcohol studies Seattle U., developing capable young people Empowering People Inc., addiction sci. U. of Miami, chem. dependency counselor State of Wash. Vocat. rehab. counselor Dept. of Vocat. Rehab., Gainesville, Fla., 1970—72; rsch. assoc. State of Fla., Office of Drug Abuse, Tallahassee, 1972—73; clin. supr. Whatcom County Alcohol Ctr., Bellingham, Wash., 1974—77; mem. faculty Whatcom C.C., Bellingham, 1977—97; rsch. asst. U. of Wash., Seattle, 1991—94; mem. faculty Western Wash. U., Bellingham, 1997—. Cons. U.S. Office of Edn., Divsn. Addiction Scis., Miami, 1973; cons. to ednl. orgns., Seattle, 1977—; adj. faculty Western Wash. U., Bellingham, 1978—86, Seattle U., 1984—97; advisor Wash. State DSHS Adv. Bd., Olympia, 1980—84. Author: (book) Teachers DO Make a Difference, Teaching with Heart, Handbook for Portfolio Process -ERIC, Handbook for Learning Contracts; contbr. articles to profl. jours., chapters to books. Pres. N.W. Consortium of Chem. Dependency Educators, 1996; mem. Wash. State Adv. Bd. for Dept. Social and Health Svcs., 1980—84, Statewide Steering Com. for Presdl. Candidate, Seattle, 2002—04. Named Chem. Dependency Educator of Yr., State of Wash., N.W. Consortium of Chem. Dependency Educators, 1996; recipient Full-time Faculty Excellence award, Whatcom C.C., 1995, Excellence Among Women in Cmty. Colls. award, Assn. of Women in Cmty. and Jr. Colls., 1984; Rachel Royston scholar for Women Leaders in Edn., Rachel Royston Statewide Scholarship Com., 1992, 1993, 1994, James I. Doi Rsch. scholar, U. Wash., 1994, Fund for the Improvement of Postsecondary Edn. grantee, Post-secondary Consortium for Prevention, Prevention Program in Post-Secondary Sch. Mem.: NW Consortium of Chem. Dependency Educators (pres., (2 times) 1996—97). Democrat. Avocations: exercise, skiing, piano, beading, weightlifting. Home Phone: 425-774-1492.

DEISENHOFER, JOHANN, biochemistry professor, researcher; b. Zusamaltheim, Bavaria, Germany, Sept. 30, 1943; arrived in U.S., 1988, naturalized, 2001; s. Johann and Thekla (Magg) D.; m. Kirsten Fischer-Lindahl, June 19, 1989. Diploma in Physics, Technische U., Munich, 1971, PhD, 1974, Doctor habilis, 1987. Postdoctoral fellow Max-Planck Inst. Biochemie, Martinsried, Fed. Republic of Germany, 1974-76, staff scientist, 1976-88; investigator Howard Hughes Med. Inst., Dallas, 1988—; prof. biochemistry U. Tex., Dallas, 1988—. Contbr. mor than 100 sci. papers to profl. publs. Recipient Nobel prize for chemistry, 1988; co-recipient Biol. Physics prize Am. Phys. Soc., 1986, Otto Bayer prize, 1988; decorated Bavarian Order of Merit, knight comdr.'s cross (badge and star) Order of Merit of Germany, Roentgen-Plakette, 2004. Mem. AAAS, NAS, Am. Crystallographic Assn., German Biophys. Soc., Protein Soc., Biophys. Soc., Academia Europaea, German Acad. Natural Scientists Leopoldina. Office: Howard Hughes Med Inst U Tex Southwestern Med Ctr 6001 Forest Park Rd Dallas TX 75390-9050 Business E-Mail: Johann.Deisenhofer@UTSouthwestern.edu.

DEISLER, PAUL FREDERICK, JR., retired oil company executive; b. El Paso, Tex., Jan. 20, 1926; s. Paul Frederick and Jeanie Donnelly (Monroe) D.; m. Ellen Louise Bardwell, June 15, 1950; children: Jane Ellen, Paul Conrad, Julia Monroe. BS in Chem. Engring, Tex. A&M U., 1948; MS, Princeton U., 1949, PhD, 1952. With Shell Oil Co., 1952—86, v.p. transp. and supplies, 1969-71; dir. supply and refining Compañía Shell de Venezuela, 1971-73; v.p. Chem. Co., Houston, 1973-74; v.p. research and engring. products Shell Oil Co., Houston, 1974-76, v.p. health, safety and environment, 1976-86; dir. Chem. Industry Inst. Toxicology, 1975-86. Chmn. adv. coun. dept. chem. engring. Princeton U., 1978-81; vis. exec. prof. Sch. Bus., U. Houston, 1986-90, mem. curriculum adv. bd. Inst. Corp. Environ. Mgmt., 1992-93; exec. com. sci. adv. bd. EPA, 1986-94, cons., 1994-2000; environ. adv. coun. Rohm and Haas Co., 1989-93; adj. prof. environ. risk assessment U. Tex. Sch. Pub. Health, 1990-94; policy com. Ctr. for Global Studies, Houston Advanced Rsch. Ctr., The Woodlands, Tex., 1992-98; chair policy com. Houston Advanced Rsch. Ctr., The Woodlands, 1995-96; ret. 2003. Editor: Reducing the Carcinogenic Risk in Industry, 1984; area editor for health and environ. risk analysis Risk Analysis: An Internat. Jour., 1997, 98; author articles on environ. health risk assessment and mgmt. Bd. dirs. ARC, Houston, 1975-80; chmn. fin. com. Houston Sci. Fair, 1974-76; alumni councilor, trustee Tex. A&M Research Found., 1977-99, trustee; bd. dirs. Tex. Inst. for Advancement of Chem. Tech., 1988-2000; mem. governing coun. Inst. for Bus., Ethics and Pub. Issues, U. Houston, 1987-90. Served with USN, 1944-46, PTO. Fellow Soc. Risk Analysis (pres. 1986-87); mem. AAAS, AIChE, N.Y. Acad. Scis., U.S. Naval Inst., Assn. Princeton Grad. Alumni (bd. dirs. 1976-79), Am. Petroleum Inst. (chmn. health, environ. and safety gen. com. 1983-84), Am. Chem. Soc., Soc. for Regulatory Toxicology and Pharmacology, Sigma Xi, Tau Beta Pi, Phi Kappa Phi. Home: Apt 413 4409 Gaines Ranch Loop Austin TX 78735-6530 Home Phone: 512-721-3325. Personal E-mail: sinprisa@earthlink.net.

DEISSEROTH, KARL A., neuroscientist, educator; AB in Biochemical Scis., Harvard Coll., 1992; MD, Stanford U., Calif., 2000, PhD in Neuroscience, 2000. Asst. prof. bioengineering Stanford U., Calif., asst. prof. psychiatry and behavioral scis. Contbr. articles to profl. jours. Recipient Resident award, West Coast Coll. Biol. Psychiatry, 2003, Lilly Resident Rsch. award, Am. Psychiat. Assn., 2004, Culpepper Scholar award, Rockefeller Brothers Fund, 2004, Early Career Translational Rsch. award, Coulter Found., 2005, McKnight Technol. Innovations in Neuroscience award, 2005, NIH Dir.'s Pioneer award, 2005, Klingenstein Fellowship award, 2005, Whitehall Found. award, 2005, Young Faculty award, Am. Psychiat. Inst. Rsch. and Edn., 2005, Robert H. Ebert Clin. Scholar award, 2006, Presdl. Early Career award for Scientists and Engrs., Pres. George W. Bush, 2006—; grantee Rsch. Incentive grant, Office of Tech. Licensing, 2005. Office: Stanford U Clark Ctr W080 318 Campus Dr W Stanford CA 94305 Office Phone: 650-736-4325. E-mail: deissero@stanford.edu.*

DEISSLER, MARY ALICE, foundation executive; b. Oneonta, NY, Dec. 30, 1957; d. George W. and Carol (Zorda) Baker; m. James N. Deissler, Nov. 24, 1987; children: Benjamin, Eliza. BA, U. Mass., 1978; MBA, Babson Coll., 1982. Fin. analyst Digital Equipment Corporation, Maynard, Mass., 1978-82; devel. dir. Handel & Haydn Soc., Boston, 1984-89, gen. mgr., 1984-89, exec. dir., 1990—. Pres., bd. dirs. Studebaker Movement Theatre Co., Boston, 1986-88. Bd. dirs. Early Music Am., N.Y.C., 1989—, v.p., 1991—, pres., 1994; bd. dirs. Babson Coll., 1990-94, Chorus Am., 1991—, v.p., 1992, pres.-elect, 1996, pres., 1997, pres. bd. dirs., 1997; mem. bd. Arts/Boston, 1994—, pres. bd. dirs., 2003; bd. dirs. Am. Composers Fourm, 2000, chair, 2004—; bd. dirs. Berkshire Choral Soc., 2000—; treas. Handel House of Am. Found. Mem. Am. Symphony Orch. League. Office: Handel & Haydn Soc 300 Massachusetts Ave Boston MA 02115-4544 Business E-Mail: mdeissler@handelandhaydn.org.

DEISSLER, ROBERT GEORGE, fluid dynamics researcher; b. Greenville, Pa., Aug. 1, 1921; s. Victor Girard and Helen Stella (Fisher) D.; m. June Marie Gallagher, Oct. 7, 1950; children— Robert Joseph, Mary Beth, Ellen Ann, Anne Marie BS, Carnegie Inst. Tech., 1943; MS, Case Inst. Tech., 1948; PhD, Case Western Res. U., 1989. Researcher Goodyear Aircraft Corp., Akron, Ohio, 1943-44; aero. rsch. scientist NASA Lewis Rsch. Ctr., Cleve., 1947-52, chief fundamental heat transfer br., 1952-70, staff scientist, sci. cons. fluid physics, 1970-94, disting. rsch. assoc., 1994—. Fellow Lewis Rsch. Acad., 1983—; staff scientist sr. level emeritus, 1994. Author: Turbulent Fluid Motion, Taylor and Francis, 1998; contbr. articles to profl. jours.; areas of rsch. fluid turbulence, turbulent heat transfer, turbulent solutions of equations of fluid motion, nonlinear dynamics and chaos, meteorol. and astrophysical flows, radiative heat transfer in gases, heat transfer in powders. Served as lt. (j.g.) USNR, 1944-46 Recipient NACA/NASA Exceptional Svc. award, 1957, Outstanding Publ. award, 1978, Wisdom Soc. award, 2000; Lewis Rsch. Acad. fellow, 1983—. Fellow AIAA (Best Paper award 1975, Tech. Achievement award 1981), ASME (Heat Transfer Meml. award 1964, Max Jacob Meml. award 1975, Wisdom Hall of Fame 2000); mem. Am. Phys. Soc., Sigma Xi. Roman Catholic. Avocations: violin, reading, walking, natural theology. Home: 4540 W 213th St Fairview Park OH 44126-2106 Office: NASA Glenn Rsch Ctr 21000 Brookpark Rd Cleveland OH 44135-3191 *It is desirable that research be fundamentally based, even when it is undertaken with a view toward an application. Then the research will likely be worthwhile, regardless of whether or not the application materializes.*

DEITERS, SISTER JOAN ADELE, psychoanalyst, nun, chemistry professor; b. Cin., Apr. 28, 1934; d. Alfred Harry and Rose Catherine (Rusche) Deiters. BA, Coll. Mt. St. Joseph, Cin., 1963; PhD, U. Cin., 1967; M in Christian spirituality, Creighton U., Omaha, 1985. Joined Sisters of Charity, Roman Cath. Ch., 1952; cert. psychoanalyst, Westchester Inst. for Tng. in Psychoanalysis and Psychotherapy, 2000. Prof. chemistry Coll. Mt. St. Joseph, Cin., 1969-78; Matthew Vassar Jr. chair Vassar Coll., Poughkeepsie, NY, 1978-96. Contbr. articles to profl. jours. Mem. Am. Chem. Soc., Sisters of Charity, Sigma Xi; Nat. Assn. for Advancement of Psychoanalysis. Home: 10 Drouilhet Ln Apt 2 Poughkeepsie NY 12603 Office: 39 Collegeview Ave Poughkeepsie NY 12603-2415 Office Phone: 845-485-4920.

DEITRICK, WILLIAM EDGAR, lawyer; b. NYC, July 30, 1944; s. John English and Dorothy Alice (Geib) D.; m. Emily Jane Posey, June 22, 1968; children: William Jr., Elizabeth, Peter. BA, Johns Hopkins U., 1967; JD, Cornell U., 1971. Bar: Ill. 1972, U.S. Dist. Ct. (no. dist.) Ill. 1972, U.S. Ct. Appeals (7th cir.) 1976, D.C. 1981. Ptnr. Gardner, Carton and Douglas, Chgo., 1972—85; sr. v.p., dep. gen. counsel, mgr. litigation divsn. Continental Bank N.A., 1985—91; ptnr. Mayer, Brown, Rowe & Maw, Chgo., 1991—2003, sr. counsel, 2003—. Contbr. articles to profl. jours. Trustee North Shore Country Day Sch., 1992-97; gov. mem. Shedd Aquarium, 2000-04; With U.S. Army, 1968-70. Mem. ABA, Ill. Bar Assn., Chgo. Bar Assn., Johns Hopkins U. Alumni Assn. (class agt. 1967-95), Cornell Law Sch. Chgo. Alumni Assn. (chmn. 1985-87), Legal Club, Univ. Club Chgo. (bd. dirs. 2002-05), Indian Hill Club (bd. govs. Winnetka, Ill.). Home: 1360 N Lake Shore Dr # 1415 Chicago IL 60610 Office: Mayer Brown & Maw 71 S Wacker Dr Chicago IL 60606-4637

DEITZ, ROBERT L., lawyer; b. Phila., Feb. 7, 1946; BA cum laude, Middlebury Coll., 1968; MPA, Princeton U., 1972; JD magna cum laude, Harvard U., 1975. Bar: D.C. 1976. Law clerk to Hon. William O. Douglas, Hon. Potter Stewart, Hon. Byron R. White U.S. Supreme Ct., 1975-76; spl. asst. to dep. sec. state, 1979-81; mem. Perkins Cole, Washington; gen. coun. Nat. Security Agy., Fort Meade, Md. Editor Harvard Law Rev., 1973-74, supreme ct. note and note editor, 1974-75. Mem. Phi Beta Kappa. Office: Nat Security Agy 9800 Savage Rd Ste 6250 Fort George G Meade MD 20755 Office Phone: 301-548-3745. Office Fax: 301-688-4546.

DE JANOSI, PETER ENGEL, research manager; b. Pecs, Hungary, June 26, 1928; arrived in USA, 1947; s. Paul E. and Kitty De Janosi; m. Monica Reis, Nov. 30, 1963; children: Paul De Janosi, Nicholas De Janosi, Alexander De Janosi. BA, Conn. Wesleyan U., 1950; MA, U. Mich., 1951, PhD, 1956; PhD (hon.), Budapest U. Econs., 1997, Russian Acad. Scis., 2004. Economist Standard Oil Co. of NJ, NYC, 1956-62; program officer in charge Ford Found., 1962-80; v.p. Russell Sage Found., 1980-90; dir. Internat. Inst. Applied Systems Analysis, Laxenburg, Austria, 1990-96; sr. advisor Lead Internat., NYC, 1998—2004. Mem. adv. coun. Cornell U. coll. Human Ecology, Ithaca, NY, 1985—90; mem. gov. coun. Internat. Inst. Applied Systems Analysis, Laxenburg, Austria, 1987—90; mem. exec. com. The Internat. Fedn. Insts. Advanced Studies, 1993—96; governing bd. Inst. Internat. Global Environ. Strategies, Japan, 1997—2005, Grad. Faculty New Sch. U.; dir. Transforming Faces Worldwide. Recipient Cross of Honor first class, Republic of Austria, golden decoration, Province, City of Vienna. Mem.: Century Assn., Coun. Fgn Rels. Home: 5 Leroy Pl Chappaqua NY 10514-3207 E-mail: dejanosi@aol.com.

DEJARNATT, KITTY M., special education educator; b. Ogden, Utah, Mar. 3, 1947; d. Dean Ward Minson and Kitty Colleen Carr; m. Paul DeJarnatt, Nov. 28, 1964; children: Shalae Michelle, Stephenie Ann Dietz, Shawn Paul, Sheri Sue Giles, Stephen Ward, Sheryl Lynn, Shauna Leigh, Shannon Deane, Scott Thomas. BS in Spl. Edn., Utah State U., Logan, 1994, BS in Psychology, 1994. Special Education (Severe) Teacher Certification Utah State Bd. of Edn., 1994. Spl. edn. tchr. (severe) Davis H.S., Kaysville, Utah, 1994—99, Davis Sch. Dist. STEPS Program, Farmington, Utah, 1999—. Mandt trainer Davis Sch. Dist., Farmington, 1996—2003, autism team mem., 1998—, transition manual com. mem., 2002—04, spl. edn. graduation com., 2002—04, spl. edn. mentor, 2001—03, Utah spl. edn. program improvement planning sys. interview com., Farmington, 2004—05; best buddies advisor Davis H.S., 1996—99, U. of Utah, 2000—01; spl. edn. para-educator Box Elder Sch. Dist., Garland, 1988—94; presenter in field. Mem. LDS Ch. Mem.: NEA, Utah Edn. Assn., Davis Edn. Assn. (area rep. 2002—04, 2007—), Coun. for Exceptional Children (sec./treas. 1997—2000). Republican. Achievements include instrumental in development of transition program for students with severe disabilities from the ages of 18 to 22 years. Avocations: travel, crocheting, painting. Business E-Mail: kdejarnatt@dsdmail.net.

DEJARNETT, RODNEY, headmaster; married; 2 children. BS, Kutztown U.; MS in Natural Scis., Rensselaer Poly. Inst.; EdD, U. Pa., 2006. Math tchr., soccer coach Oley HS, Oley Valley Sch. Dist., Pa., 1977; math. scis. dept. chair Dennis-Yarmouth Regional HS, South Yarmouth, Mass.; math tchr. St. Paul's Sch., Concord, NH, 1996—2006, div. head, 1998—2001, academic dean, 2001—06; headmaster Dwight-Englewood Sch., Englewood, NJ, 2006—. Cons. U. Chgo. Sch. Math. Project, 1991—. Contbr. articles to profl. jours. Recipient Principals Award for Excellence in Teaching, Tandy Tech. Scholars Outstanding Tchg. Award, HS Educator of Yr. Mem.: Nat. Coun. of Tchrs. of Math. (past mem. Math Notes Com.). Office: Dwight-Englewood Sch 315 E Palisade Ave Englewood NJ 07631

DE JESUS, VERONICA, artist, educator; b. Cleve., Apr. 20, 1970; d. Agustin De Jesus and Elissa Cheng; life ptnr. Regina Clarkinia. MFA, U. Calif., Berkeley, 2003; BFA, San Francisco Art Inst., 1998. Art instr. Lighthouse For Blind, San Francisco, 1999—2002; vis. lectr. U. Calif., 2006—. Exhibitions include Dogkhat's Journey, 2004, Veronica De Jesus, Cue Art Found. Solo Show, 2005, publication piece for literary mag., Memorial Drawings, 2006, exhibitions include exhibit Personal Miracles, 2007. Recipient Kingsley Club Merit award, Sierra Coll., 1995, Gamblin Painting award, San Francisco Art Inst., 1997, Honors Studio award, 1997—98. Achievements include creating dialogue about personal stories. Personal E-mail: veronica@veronicadejesus.com.

DE JONG, DAVID SAMUEL, lawyer; b. Washington, Jan. 8, 1951; s. Samuel and Dorothy (Thomas) De J.; m. Tracy Ann Barger, Sept. 23, 1995; children: Jacob Samuel, Franklin Joseph. BA, U. Md., 1972; JD, Washington and Lee U., 1975; LLM in Taxation, Georgetown U., 1979. Bar: Md. 1975, US Dist. Ct. (dist. Md.) 1977, US Tax Ct. 1977, US Ct. Appeals (4th cir.) 1978, US Supreme Ct. 1979, DC 1980, US Dist. Ct. (dist. DC) 1983, US Ct. Claims, US Ct. Appeals (fed. cir.) 1983; CPA, Md. 1981; cert. valuation analyst 1998. Atty. Gen. Bus. Svcs., Inc., Rockville, Md., 1975-80; ptnr. Stein, Sperling, Bennett, De Jong, Driscoll & Greenfeig, P.C., Rockville, 1980—. Adj. prof. Southeastern U., Washington, 1979-85, Am. U., Washington, 1983-2000; instr. taxation U. Md., College Park, 1986-87, Montgomery Coll., Rockville, 1983; mem. character com. 7th Appeals Cir. Md. Ct. of Appeals. Co-author: (ann. book) J.K. Lasser's Year-Round Tax Strategies, 1989-2004; editor Notes and Comments, Washington and Lee U. Law Rev., 1974-75. V.p. Seneca Whetstone Homeowners Assn., Gaithersburg, Md., 1981-82, pres. 1982-83; treas. Met. Ctr. Visual Arts, 2005. Named one of Top 100 Attys. in US, Worth Mag., 2006. Mem. ABA, AICPA, Am. Assn. Atty.-CPAs (bd. dirs. 1998, sec. 1998-99, treas. 1999-2000, v.p. 2000-02, pres. elect 2002-03, pres. 2003-04), Md. Bar Assn. (mem. tax section coun. 2003), Montgomery County Bar Assn. (chmn. tax sect. 1991-92, treas. 1996-97), DC Bar Assn., Md. Assn. CPAs, DC Inst. CPA, Nat. Assn. Cert. Valuation Analysts v.p. Md. chpt. 2003-2007, pres., 2007—), Inst. Bus. Appraisers, Md. Soc. Accts., Estate Planning Coun. Suburban Md. (sec. 2004-05, v.p. 2005-06, pres. 2006—), Phi Alpha Delta. Office: Stein Sperling Bennett De Jong Driscoll & Greenfeig PC 25 W Middle Ln Rockville MD 20850-2214 Office Phone: 301-838-3204. Office Fax: 301-354-8104. E-mail: ddejong@steinsperling.com.

DE JONG, GORDON FREDERICK, demography professor, director; b. Berea, Ky., Aug. 6, 1935; s. Frederick Henry and Elizabeth (DeVries) De Jong; m. Caroline Jane Miller, July 1, 1961; children: Judith Kristen, Gregory Gordon, Graham Austin. BA, Ctrl. Coll., Pella, Iowa, 1957; MA, U. Ky., 1960, PhD, 1963. Instr. U. Ky., Lexington, 1961—63; from asst. prof. to prof. Pa. State U., University Park, 1963—91, disting. prof, dir. grad. program in demography, 1992—, dir. Population Rsch. Inst., 1974—76, 1982—88; sr. fellow East-West Ctr., Honolulu, 1978—79; vis. faculty Netherlands Grad. Sch. in Demography, 1994. Dir. Population Rsch. Inst., Pa. State Univ., 1974—76, 1982—88; rsch. cons. Govt. Thailand, Philippines, South Africa, 1983—. Editor: (acadmic book) Migration Decision Making, 1981, Social Demography, 1972, (journal) Demography, Population Assn. of Am., 1987—90; contbr. articles to profl. jour. Demographic advisor Exec. officers and Legislators Commonwealth of Pa., 1980—; Task Force on Aging, mem. Atty. Gen. Pa., 1993—2000; active Pa. 2020 Vision, 2006—. Mem.: Population Assn. Am. (chair), Am. Sociol. Assn. (chair). Achievements include research in 27 competitively awarded rsch. grants in demography issues internat; immigration and international migration; Founder and dir. of grad. program in demography, Pa. State Univ. Avocations: music, sports. Office: Population Rsch Inst 506 Oswald Tower University Park PA 16802

DE JONG, PIETER JOHANNES, finance educator, physical therapist; b. Zwijndrecht, Zuid Holland, Netherlands, Jan. 22, 1968; s. Pieter and Hendrieka de Jong; m. Leslie Jones, Aug. 11, 1966; children: Sophie Catherine, Nicolaas Pieter. BS in Physical Therapy, Hoge Sch., Rotterdam, Netherlands, 1990; MBA, U. Tex., Arlington, 2002, PhD in Fin., 2007. Physical therapist Dutch Royal Army, Netherlands, 1990—92, Harris Meth. Hosp., Fort Worth, Tex., 1992—96, Lockheed-Martin, Fort Worth, Tex., 1996—2002, Guardian Healthcare, Fort Worth, Tex., 2002—. Bus. fin. grad. tng. assoc. U. Tex., 2003—06. Contbr. articles to profl. jours. Sunday sch. tchr. United Meth. Ch., Arlington, Tex., 2000—. 1st lt. Dutch Royal Army, 1990—92, 't Harde, The Netherlands. Scholar Grad. Sch. scholar, U. Tex. at Arlington, 2002—06. Mem.: Beta Gamma Sigma (life). Methodist. Avocations: travel, running, soccer. Home: 6300 Woolwich Dr Arlington TX 76001 Home Phone: 817-465-6423; Office Phone: 817-272-7456.

DE JONGH, JOHN P., JR., governor, real estate company executive; b. VI, Nov. 13, 1957; s. John P. and Delores (Webb) de Jongh; m. Cecile Rene Galiber, 1986; 3 children. BA in Economics, Antioch Coll., 1981. With Tri-Island Econ. Devel. Coun; consumer mgr. Chase Manhattan Bank; commr. fin. US V.I., Charlotte Amalie, 1987—90, exec. asst. to commr. fin., 1990—92; sr. mng. cons. Pub. Fin. Mgmt., Inc., 1993—96; pres., CEO, dir. Lockhart Companies, Inc., Charlotte Amalie, 1996—; gov. US V.I., Charlotte Amalie, 2007—. Chmn. US V.I. Water and Power Authority, 1987—92; exec. dir. US V.I. Pub. Fin. Authority, 1988—90; chmn. US V.I. Tax Rev. Bd., 1987—90; sec. US V.I. Banking Bd., 1987—90; mem. US V.I. Small Bus. Devel. Agy., 1987—90; co-founder Chilmark Partners, LLC, 2003—. Pres. Karen Ingeborg Lockhart Found., Cmty. Found. US V.I., St. Thomas/St. John C. of C.; trustee Antilles Sch. Named Person of Yr., Rotary II, 2000. Democrat. Office: Office of Gov Govt House 21-22 Kongens Gade, Charlotte Amalie St Thomas VI 00802 Office Phone: 340-774-0001. Office Fax: 340-693-4374.*

DEJUD, CARLOS, psychologist; b. David, Panama, June 26, 1964; s. Luis Dejud and Abelina Dejud-Valenzuela; 1 child, Brian. BA, U. Ariz., Tucson, 1991, MA, 2000; EdS, PhD student, U. Ariz, Tucson, 2004—. Cert. sch. psychologist Ariz. Dept. Edn., spl. edn. tchr. k-12 Ariz. Dept. Edn. Counselor II La Frontera Ctr., Tucson, 1991—94, child family specialist, 1994—96, clinician III, 1996—98; grad. tchg. asst. U. Ariz., Tucson, 2000—04, rsch. asst., 2004—06; project coord U. Ariz, 2007—; asst. prof. U. Wis., Stout, 2007—. Cons. Tucson Urban League, 2006—; lectr., spkr. U. Med. Ctr., Tucson, 2003—. Contbr. articles to profl. jours. Bd. mem. Tucson Internat. Hariachi Conf., 1999—. Recipient Centennial Achievement award, U. Ariz., 1991, Advisor of Yr., Order of Omega, 2004. Mem.: APA, NASP, Omega Delta Phi (regional dir. 2007—), Omega Delta Phi Alumi Assn. (chmn. 2004—).

DEJUNEAS, PATRICIA ANN, lawyer; b. Elizabeth, NJ, Mar. 4, 1969; d. James Vincent and Patricia Mary Dejuneas. BS magna cum laude, Sacred Heart U., 1993; JD with high honors, U. Conn., 1996. Bar: Conn. 1996, Mass. 2001, US Dist. Ct. (Dist. Mass.) 2002, US Dist. Ct. (Dist. Conn.) 2002, US Ct. Appeals (1st Cir.) 2003. Law clk. to Hon. E. Eugene Spear Conn. Appellate Ct., 1996—97; law clk. to Hon. Donna F. Martinez US Dist. Ct. (Conn.), Hartford, 2000—02; assoc. Shipman & Goodwin, Hartford, Conn., Day, Berry & Howard LLP, Boston, Law Offices of Richard M. Egbert, PC, Boston. Mem.: Mass. Criminal Def. Lawyers Assn. Office: Law Offices of Richard M Egbert Ste 1800 99 Summer St Boston MA 02110-1251 Office Phone: 617-737-8222. Office Fax: 617-737-8223.

DE KANTER, ELLEN ANN, retired English and foreign language educator; b. Spokane, Wash., Mar. 10, 1926; d. George L. and Alison P. (Christy) Tharp; m. Scipio de Kanter, Feb. 2, 1949 (dec.); children: Scipio, Georgette, Robert, Adriana. BA, Mexico City Coll.-U. of Ams., 1947; MEd, U. Houston, 1972, MA in Spanish, 1974, EdD, 1979. Dir. bilingual edn. U. St. Thomas, Houston, 1979—2005; ret., 2005. Editor Tex. Assn. Bilingual Edn. Jour., 2004-05; Contbr. articles to profl. jours. 11 Tchr. Tng. grants undergrad. and grad. students, U. St. Thomas, 1986—2004. Mem. Nat. Assn. Bilingual Edn. (chmn. conf. 1989, program chmn. conf. 1993), Houston Area Assn. Bilingual Edn. (pres. 1987-88), Inst. Hispanic Culture (bd. dirs. 1989-90). Home: 3015 Meadowview Dr Missouri City TX 77459-3308 E-mail: dekanter@stthom.edu.

DEKASER, RICHARD J., bank executive; B in Econs., M in Econs., NYU. Staff economist US Dept. Commerce Bur. Econ. Analysis; sr. assoc. Data Resources, Inc. Std. and Poor's Corp.; sr. fin. economist Bank of Boston (now Bank of Am.); sr. v.p., chief economist Nat. City Corp. Chmn. fin. roundtable Nat. Assn. Bus. Econs. Mem. Gov.'s Coun. Econ. Advisors, Ohio. Named Top Economist, USA Today, 2006. Office: Nat City Corp Nat City Ctr 1900 E Ninth St Cleveland OH 44114-3484 Office Phone: 216-222-2000.*

DE KENESSEY, STEFANIA MARIA, composer; b. Budapest, Hungary, Oct. 6, 1956; came to U.S., 1967; d. Zoltan Elek and Stefania Ivanova Kenessey; m. Andrew Henry Chapman, June 20, 1976; children: Dora Rosalia, Jordan Spencer. BA, Yale U., 1976; MFA, Princeton U., 1978, PhD, 1984. Prof. music New Sch. U., NYC, 1980—2000, artist-in-residence, 2001—. Founder, artistic dir. The Derriere Guard, NYC, 1997—. Composer: (Operas) The Monster Bed, The Other Wise Man, (orchestra) Cutting Loose, Manned Flight, Wintersong, Summer Nights, Entrances and Departures, (chamber) Shades of Darkness, Beating Down, Magic Forest Dances, Sunburst, (songs) High Summer, In Memoriam, Autumn Elegy, The Muse Is Not Amused, The Daughters of Odessa, Girl in the Mirror, Jumping Jacks, Mothers and Daughters, Elizabethan Lyrics, (films) Art Under the Radar, The Last Angry Man, The Passing, (albums) Shades of Dark, Shades of Light, Two By three, Sunbursts, Sing for the Cure, An American Sampler, The Orchestra According to the Seven. Meet the Composer grantee, 1990—. Mem. ASCAP (Std. Music award 1990—), Nat. Assn. Composers (sec. East Coast chpt. 1985-92), Internat. Alliance for Women in Music (founding pres. 1993-94), Am. Women Composers (pres. 1990-93). Avocations: novels, poetry, theater, visual and fine arts. Home: 171 W 71st St Apt 2A New York NY 10023 Office: 65 W 11th St # 061 New York NY 10011 E-mail: dekeness@att.net.

DEKIEFFER, DONALD EULETTE, lawyer; b. Newport, RI, Nov. 8, 1945; s. Robert and Melissa (Hibberd) deKieffer; m. Nancy Kishida, June 27, 1970; 1 child, Nathan Hiroyuki. BA, U. Colo., 1968; JD, Georgetown U., 1971. Bar: U.S. Supreme Ct. 1982, U.S. Ct. Appeals (D.C. cir.) 1971, U.S. Dist. Ct. D.C. 1971, U.S. Ct. Claims 1971, U.S. Ct. Internat. Trade 1971. Mem. profl. staff Senate Rep. Policy Com., Washington, 1969—71; assoc. Collier, Shannon, Rill & Edwards, 1971—74; ptnr. Collier, Shannon, Rill, Edwards & Scott, 1974—80, deKieffer, Berg & Creskoff, 1980; gen. counsel U.S. Trade Rep., 1981—83; ptnr. Plaia, Schaumburg & deKieffer, 1983—84, Pillsbury, Madison & Sutro, 1984—92, deKieffer, Dibble & Horgan, 1992—. Mem. Presdl. Transition Team, 1980—81. Author: How to Lobby Congress, 1981, Doing Bus. with the USA, 1984, Doing Bus. with Romania, 1985, Doing Bus. in the U.S., 1985, Doing Bus. with the New Romania, 1991, Internat. Bus. Traveler's Companion, 1992, How Lawyers Screw Their Clients, 1996, The Citizen's Guide to Lobbying Congress, 1997. Mem.: ABA, Fed. Bar Assn., D.C. Bar Assn., Internat. Antitrust Soc., Am. Soc. Internat. Law. Office: deKieffer & Horgan 729 15th St NW Ste 800 Washington DC 20005-2105 Office Phone: 202-783-6900. E-mail: ddekieffer@dhlaw.com.

DEKKER, EUGENE EARL, biochemistry educator; b. Highland, Ind., July 23, 1927; s. Peter and Anne (Hendrikse) D.; m. Harriet Ella Holwerda, July 5, 1958; children: Gwen E., Paul D., Tom R. AB, Calvin Coll., 1949; MS, U. Ill., 1951, PhD, 1954. Instr. U. Louisville Med. Sch., 1954-56; instr. biol. chemistry U. Mich. Med. Sch., Ann Arbor, 1956-58, asst. prof., 1958-65, assoc. prof., 1965-70, prof., 1970-94, assoc. chmn. dept., 1975-88, emeritus prof., 1994—. With USN, 1945—46. Mem. AAAS, Am. Chem. Soc., Am. Soc. Biol. Chemists, Am. Soc. Plant Physiologists, Oxygen Soc., Protein Soc., Sigma Xi, Phi Lambda Upsilon. Mem. Christian Reformed Ch. Home: 4001 Glacier Hills Dr Apt 126 Ann Arbor MI 48105-3655 Office: U Mich Med Sch Dept Biol Chemistry Ann Arbor MI 48109-0606 Personal E-mail: eedekker@umich.edu.

DEKKER, GEORGE GILBERT, literature professor, writer, former academic administrator; b. Long Beach, Calif., Sept. 8, 1934; s. Gilbert J. and Laura (Barnes) D.; m. Linda Jo Bartholomew, Aug. 31, 1973; children by previous marriage: Anna Allegra, Clara Joy, Ruth Siobhan, Laura Daye. BA in English, U. Calif.-Santa Barbara, 1955; MA in English, 1958; M.Litt., Cambridge U., Eng., 1961; PhD in English, U. Essex, Eng., 1967. Lectr. U. Wales, Swansea, 1962-64; lectr. in lit. U. Essex, 1964-69, reader in lit., 1969-72, dean Sch. Comparative Studies, 1969-71; assoc. prof. English Stanford U., Calif., 1972-74, prof., 1974—2001, prof. emeritus, 2001—, chmn. dept., 1978-81, 84-85, Joseph S. Atha prof. humanities, 1988—, dir. program in Am. Studies, 1988-91, assoc. dean grad. policy, 1993—96, 2000—02. Author: Sailing After Knowledge, 1963, James Fenimore Cooper the Novelist, 1967, Coleridge and the Literature of Sensibility, 1978, The American Historical Romance, 1987, The Fictions of Romantic Tourism, 2005; editor: Donald Davie: The Responsibilities of Literature, 1983 Nat. Endowment Humanities fellow, 1977; Inst. Advanced Studies in Humanities fellow U. Edinburgh (Scotland), 1982; hon. fellow, Clare Hall Cambridge, 1997, Stanford Humanities Ctr., 1997. Mem. Am. Lit. Assn. Democrat. Office: Stanford Univ Dept English Stanford CA 94305 Office Phone: 650-723-2635. *Over the past forty years I have divided my personal and professional life between the U.S. and Britain; not England alone, but Ireland, Scotland and Wales, too. This experience has given the distinctive stamp to my work as a teacher and writer, making me as much at home with Scott as with Hawthorne, with a British as well as an American university.*

DEKKERS, MARIJN E., electronics executive; b. The Netherlands; B in Chem. Engring., Univ. Nijmegen, The Netherlands; MS in Chem. Engring., PhD in Chem. Engring., Univ. Eindhoven. Rsch. scientist R&D Ctr. GE, Schenectady, NY, various operating positions, 1985—95; positions through 1995—2000; COO Thermo Electron Corp., Waltham, Mass., 2000—02, pres., CEO, 2002—06, Thermo Fisher Scientific, Waltham, Mass., 2006—. Contbr. articles to profl. jours. Achievements include patents in field. Office: Thermo Fisher Scientific 81 Wyman St Waltham MA 02454*

DEKMEJIAN, RICHARD HRAIR, political science professor; b. Aleppo, Syria, Aug. 3, 1933; came to U.S., 1950, naturalized, 1955; s. Hrant H. and Vahede V. (Matossian) D.; m. Anoush Hagopian, Sept. 19, 1954; children: Gregory, Armen, Haig. BA, U. Conn., 1959; MA, Boston U., 1960; Middle East Inst. cert., Columbia U., 1964, PhD, 1966. Mem. faculty SUNY, Binghamton, 1964-86; prof., chmn. dept. polit. sci. U. So. Calif., Los Angeles, 1986-90, prof. internat. bus. Marshall Sch. Bus.; also master Hinman Coll., 1971-72. Lectr. Fgn. Svc. Inst., Dept. Def., Dep. State, 1976-87; vis. prof. Columbia U., U. Pa., 1977-78; cons. Dept. State, AID, USIA, UN, Dept. Def. Author: Egypt Under Nasir, 1971, Patterns of Political Leadership, 1975, Islam in Revolution, 1985, 2nd edit., 1995, Ethnic Lobbies in U.S. Foreign Policy, 1997, Troubled Waters: The Geopolitics of the Caspian Region, 2001, The Just Prince: A Manual of Leadership, 2003, Spectrum of Terror, 2007; contbr. articles to profl. jours. Pres. So. Tier Civic Ballet Co., 1973-76. Served with AUS, 1955-57. Mem. Am. Polit. Sci. Assn., Middle East Inst., Middle East Studies Assn., Internat. Inst. Strategic Studies, Skull and Dagger, Pi Sigma Alpha, Phi Alpha Theta. Office: U So Calif Dept Polit Sci Los Angeles CA 90089-0044 Office Phone: 213-740-3619. Business E-Mail: dekmejia@usc.edu.

DEKOK, DAVID, writer, reporter; b. Holland, Mich., July 17, 1953; s. Paul W. and Olga (Kilian) DeK.; m. Lisa W. Brittingham, Oct. 1, 1988; children: Elizabeth B., Lydia B. BA, Hope Coll., Holland, 1975. Reporter The News-Item, Shamokin, Pa., 1975-87, The Patriot-News, Harrisburg, Pa., 1987—, Blogger, By the River, 2006—. Cons. (TV film) Centralia Fire, PBS, 1982-83, The Town That Was, 2007; guest lectr. Bucknell U., Lewisburg, Pa., 1988-97. Author: Unseen Danger: A Tragedy of People, Government and Centralia Mine Fire, 1986, republished, 2000; appeared in documentary The Town That Was, 2007. Del. Mich. Dem. Conv., 1972; mem. St. Stephen's Episcopal Sch. Bd., 1999-2007, chmn. tech. com. Recipient Keystone Press award Pa. Newspaper Pubs. Assn., 1979, 86, 87, 90, 99, 2006, Pub. Svc. award Assoc. Press Mng. Editors of Pa., 1981, Gen. News Reporting award 2006, Janus award Mortgage Bankers Am., 1992. Mem. Investigative Reporters and Editors, Nat. Press Club (Freedom of the Press award 1995), Soc. Profl. Journalists (pres. ctrl. Pa. chpt. 1989-91, Spotlight award 1995), Newspaper Guild (pres. local 16 2004—06). Episcopalian. Home: 113 Conoy St Harrisburg PA 17104-1608 E-mail: ddekok@mac.com.

DEKOOL, L.M. (THEO DEKOOL), food products executive; With CPC Benelux, B.V., Buhrmann Tetterode; v.p. fin. Household and Pers. Care divsn. Sara Lee/DE, Netherlands, 1990—93, CFO, 1995—96, Blokker retail chain; v.p. Sara Lee Corp., Chgo., 1996—2001, sr. v.p., 2001, exec. v.p., CFO & chief adminstr. officer, 2002—. Office: Sara Lee Corp 3 First Natiolnal Plz Chicago IL 60602*

DEKOSKY, STEVEN TRENT, neurologist; b. Camden, NJ, Mar. 23, 1947; s. Aaron and Evelyn (Gorlen) DeK.; m. Beverly Nelson; children: Allison, Lauren. AB in Psychology, Bucknell U., 1968; MD, U. Fla., 1974. Diplomate in neurology Am. Bd. Psychiatry and Neurology. Postdoctoral fellow, instr. neurology U. Va. Sch. Medicine, Charlottesville, 1978-79; asst. prof. neurology, anatomy U. Ky. Coll. Medicine, Lexington, 1979-85, assoc. prof. anatomy and neurology, 1985-90, interim chmn. dept. neurology, 1985-87; grad. faculty U. Ky. Grad. Sch., Lexington, 1981-90; prof. psychiatry U. Pitts. Sch. Medicine, 1990—, prof. neurology, neurobiology, 1990—, grad. faculty, 1991—, interim chair dept. neurology, 2000—01, chair dept. neurology, 2002—. Vis. prof. psychology U. Calif., Irvine, 1983; co-dir. Alzheimer's disease rsch. ctr. U. Pitts. Med. Ctr., 1990-94, dir., 1994—, U. Ky. Med. Ctr., 1985-90; task force on Alzheimer's disease State of Ohio, Columbus, 1986-92; med. sci. adv. bd. Alzheimer's Assn., 1992—; dir. behavioral neurology of aging tng. program U. Pitts., 1990—. Mem. Am. Neurol. Assn. (Presd. award 1988), Am. Acad. Neurology, Am. Soc. Neurochemistry, Am. Heart Assn. (stroke coun.), N.Y. Acad. Scis., Soc. Neurosci., Soc. Exptl. Neuropathology (councillor 1990-92), Behavioral Neurology Soc., Am. Bd. of Psychiatry and Neurology. Office: U Pitts 3471 5th Ave Ste 811 Pittsburgh PA 15213-2593 Home Phone: 412-361-6116; Office Phone: 412-692-4622. Business E-Mail: dekoskyst@upmc.edu.

DEKU, AFRIKADZATA, African studies professor, writer; b. Kadjebi, Ghana, Dec. 13, 1949; m. Yayra Deku; children: Mawunyo, Nukunu Akusika, Mawulolo, Afrikamawuse, Afrikamawuedem, Afrikaworlanyo. BA with honors, U. Cape Coast, Ghana, 1977; MSc, U. Ife, Nigeria, 1981; diploma, Inst. Internat. D'Adminstrn. Pub., Paris, 1983; MPhil, U. Paris XI, Sorbonne, 1983, PhD, 1985; PhD in Internat. Mgmt. and Orgnl. Leadership (hon.), The Yorker Internat. U., Italy, 2006. Lic. mediator, arbitrator, negotiator. Ind. post-doctoral rsch. scholar U. Denver, 1986-87; founder, chief exec., prof. pan-Afrikan studies Afrikan Culture Inst., 1987—; vis. assoc. prof. Afrikan history Clark Atlanta U., 1990-91; vis. assoc. prof. Africana studies Morris Brown Coll., Atlanta, 1990; vis. assoc. prof. Afrikan culture, continuing edn. dept. Ga. State U., 1990; pub. The Afrikan Truth, 1994—; pub. internat. French, English Afrikan-Centric continental Afrikan scholar Continental Afrikan Pubs., 1990—. Vis. prof. French and Afrikan lit. Wofford Coll., Spartanburg, S.C., 1988-89, Converse Coll., Spartanburg, 1989; trainer, guest speaker Clemson U. 4-H Operation Pride, 1994—; ACT ESL placement test fairness reviewer and cons., 2000; participant ACT ESL Teleconf., 2000; resident guest artist Kennedy Middle Sch., Aiken, S.C., 1997, Jackson (S.C.) Mid. Sch., 1998, S.C. Writers Ann. Workshop Conf. Faculty, Manuscript Evaluator; poetry judge Pan-Afrikan Poetry Recitals, Myrtle Beach, 1998; founder, bd. chmn. Afrikamawu Miracle Mission made up of: Continental Afrikan Devel. Authority, KADA, Continental Afrikan Govt. Implementation Authority, KAGO, and Continental Afrikan Culture Promotions Authority, KAFO; guest artist Spartanburg Internat. Festival, 1999, Ea. Lit. Fellowship, Clinton, S.C., 1999, Greenville (S.C.) Internat. Festival Cultural Awareness summer jubilee, 2001, Greenville Summer Jubilee Festival for the Arts, 2001; guest author Lee County Young Authors Ann. Conf., Bishopville, S.C., 1999; lectr., spkr. and cons. in field. Author: (poetry) We Are All Continental Afrikans, 1991, Sacred Verses For My Afrikan Queens, 1992, Sacred Afrikan Spiritual Power From Within, 1993, Agbenoxevie Menye, Ablodesafui, Agbedefu (Ewe poetry), Courage, Mere Afrique, Cris de Tonnerre, Coups de Marteau, A Toi le Paradis de Ma Langue (Afrikan Poetry in French); (plays) No Where is Heaven, Breaking the Bloody Sword of Apartheid, (rsch. books) L'Union Continentale Africaine, vols. 1-3, 1986, Continental Afrikan Power Now, 1987, The Afrikan-Centric Perspective of the Afrikan World Crisis, 1988, Continental Afrikan Manifesto, 1999, Continental Afrikan Power in Figures, 1989, 2d edit., 2004, The Afrikan Gospel of Total Happiness Now and Always, 2006, The Power of Afrikan-Centricity, , 2006, AFRIKAMAWUNYA or the Holy Afrikan Bible, 2006, Continental Afrika: From Two Hundred Million Seasons to the Present, 2006, The Power and Benefits of Continental Afrikan Culture, 2007, How to Be a Continental Afrikan Again, 2007, Continental Afrikan Constitution of the Continental Afrikan Republic, 2007; Why the World Bank /IMF/UN etc. Are a Curse Rather Than a Blessing to Afrika, 2006, The Afrikan Origin of Humanity, 2005, Behold Your Continental Afrikan Savior Afrikadela Is Born, 2006, Passing Our ABC Test of our Afrikan-Centricity, 2007, spkr. in field. Founder Afrikan-Centricity Movement, Continental Afrikan Govt. Orgn., Continental Afrikan Found., Continental Afrikan Devel. Authority. Grantee S.C. Arts Commn., 1990-91; scholar Ghana Govt., 1970-72, 73-77, Commonwealth, 1975, 77, 78, French Govt., 1982-85; recipient OYO State Bursary award, 1980-81, Spartanburg, S.C. Arts Coun. award, 1989-90, S.C. Arts Commn. grant, 1990-91; named Mercedes-Benz of Expert Think Tank, Wall St. Jour., 2006. Mem. ABA, Am. Arbitration Assn., S.C. Coun. for Mediation and Alternative Dispute Resolution, Internat. Biog. Assn., Internat. Platform Assn., French PhD Holders Assn., African Studies Assn., African Heritage Studies Assn., Am. Polit. Sci. Assn. Home: 182 Stribling Cir Spartanburg SC 29301-1651 also: Box 209 Dansoman Accra Ghana Home Phone: 864-576-7992; Office Phone: 864-576-7992. Personal E-mail: afrikalion@aol.com, afrikafiaga@walla.com.

DE LAAT, GILBERT, automotive executive; b. Paterson, NJ, Apr. 2, 1957; s. Elmer Gilbert and Marjorie Lucille De Laat. BA, Columbia U., 1979; MPP, JD, Harvard U., 1984. Adminstr. legal and regulatory affairs Isuzu Motors Am., City of Industry, Calif., 1985-93; mgr. govt. affairs Nat. Hwy. Traffic Safety Adminstrn. Subaru Am., Inc., Cherry Hill, NJ, 1995—2001; mgr. GM govt. affairs Subaru R&D, Ann Arbor, Mich., 2001—. Congressional aid U.S. Congressman Andrew Maguire, Paramus, N.J., 1977-78. Mem. ABA, UN-USA, World Affairs Coun., Am. Trauma Soc., Am. Polit. Sci. Assn., Sonoma County Wine Growers Assn., N.Am. Riding Handicapped Assn. Republican. Roman Catholic. Avocations: sailing, martial arts, golf. Home: 385 Rolling Meadows Dr Ann Arbor MI 48103 Office: Subaru Rsch and Devel Inc 3995 Rearch Park Dr Ann Arbor MI 48108 E-mail: gdeLaat@subaru.com.

DELACATO, CARL HENRY, education educator; b. Pottstown, Pa., Sept. 10, 1923; s. Ercole S. and Julia (de Bartolomeo) D.; m. Janice E. Fernstrom, June 20, 1951; children— Elizabeth F., Carl Henry, David F. BS in Edn, West Chester State Coll., Pa., 1945; MS in Edn, U. Pa., Phila., 1948, EdD, 1952. Asst. headmaster Chestnut Hill Acad., Phila., 1945-64; founder, dir. Chestnut Hill Reading Clinic, 1948; prof. Avery Postgrad. Inst., Phila., 1963-73; prof., chmn. dept. devel. edn. U. Plano, Tex., 1965-70; asso. dir. inst. Para Le Orgn. Neurologica, Buenos Aires, 1967-70, Insts. Achievement Human Potential, Phila., 1953-73; dir. Inst. Rehab. of Brain Injured, Morton, Pa., 1974-89, Centrao de Rahabilitacao NS de Gloria, Sao Paulo, Brazil, 1976—. Pres. Delacato & Delacato Consultants in Learning, Plymouth Meeting, Pa., 1970—; cons. Asociacion Para Ayuda Lesionados Cerebales, Barcelona, Spain, 1970-89; hon. dir. of The Delacato Center, Holon, Israel, 1974—; dir. of Delacato project at Padagogische Hochschule Rheinland Abteilung fur Heilpadagoggik, Koln, W. Ger., 1975— , Delacato project TIKVA, Haifa, Israel, 1976—; bd. dirs. Delacato and Delacato, Naples, Italy, Delacato Consultation Ctr., Benelux; others. Author: The Treatment and Prevention of Reading Problems, 1959, Diagnosis and Treatment of Speech and Reading Problems, 1963, Elementary School of the Future, 1964, Neurological Organization and Reading, 1966, A New Start for the Child with Reading Problems, 1970, The Ultimate Stranger, The Autistic Child, 1974, contbr. numerous articles on rehab. and edn. to profl. jours.; editor: Am. Lectures in Edn. and Learning, 1969—. Vice pres. U.S. World Orgn. Human Potential, 1968-73; mem. Pa. Commn. Human Potential, 1969-70, Gov. Sergipe (Brazil) Commn. Human Potential, 1968-70; bd. dirs. Centre for Neurol. Rehab., Morton, Pa., 1974—. Recipient Disting. Alumnus award West Chester Coll., 1978, award Greater Long Beach (Calif.) Soc. for Autistic Children, 1977, Diploma Socio-Benmento Porto Allegra, Brazil, 1965, Diploma de Honra Ho Merito Piracioba, Brazil, 1965, Diploma de Reconheciemen, to Sao Paulo, 1965, Diploma e Medalha Comemorative de APAE Rio de Janeiro, 1965, Gold Medal Honor Brazil, 1960, Statuette with Pedestal award Internat. Rehab. Forum, 1966, 1st. Trailblazer award U. Plano, 1966 Mem. NSF. Home: Apt 1014 Lincoln Woods 9801 Germantown Pike Lafayette Hill PA 19444

DELACATO, CARL HENRY, lawyer; b. Aug. 18, 1955; BA, Haverford Coll., 1977; JD, Villanova Law Sch., 1980. Bar: Pa. 1980. Ptnr. Hecker Brown Sherry and Johnson, Phila., 1979—. Faculty Dickinson Law Sch. Trial Advocacy Seminar, 1991; fellow, faculty mem. Acad. Advocacy, Pa., 1992—. Mem. ABA (tort ins. practice sect.), Phila. Bar Assn. (chair ins. programs com., mem. civil litigation and real property sects., Chancellor's Spl. Recognition award 1994). Office: Hecker Brown Sherry Johnson 1700 Two Logan Sq 18th and Arch Sts Philadelphia PA 19103

DELACATO, JANICE ELAINE, special education educator, consultant; b. Bklyn., June 6, 1926; d. Frode Siegfried and Vilma Fernstrom; m. Carl Henry Delacato, June 20, 1951; children: Elizabeth Delacato Putnam, Carl Henry, David Fernstrom. AB, Bryn Mawr Coll., 1948. Tchr. Rydal Hall, Ogontz Sch., Pa., 1948-49, The Spence Sch., NYC, 1949-50, Chestnut Hill Acad., Phila., 1950-52; co-dir. The Chestnut Hill Reading Clinic, Phila., 1951-65, Delacato & Delacato Cons. in Learning, Phila., 1972-88; mgr. Morton (Pa.) Book Store, 1972-88; co-dir. The Delacato & Delacato Conf. Autism & Learning Disabilities, 1979-82. Editor newsletter Temple U. Med. Ctr. Women's Aux., Phila., 1953-65; class editor Bryn Mawr Coll. Alumnae Bull., 1966-79. Chmn. fund-raising com. Springside Sch., 1969-71; treas. Main St. Fair Antiques Booth, Chestnut Hill Hosp., 1965-77. Recipient Main St. Fair award Chestnut Hill Hosp., 1972. Mem. AAUW, Phila. Cricket Club. Republican. Unitarian Universalist. Home: Apt 1014 Lincoln Woods 9801 Germantown Pike Lafayette Hill PA 19444

DELACERDA, MELISSA GRINER, lawyer; b. St. Petersburg, Fla., Mar. 17, 1952; d. Joseph Henry and Dorothy Jean (Stephens) G.; m. Fred G. DeLacerda, June 17, 1972. BS, Memphis State U., 1973; JD, U. Tulsa, 1979. Bar: Okla. 1979. Tchr., elem. sch., Crowley, La., 1974-75; sports reporter Daily Advertiser, Lafayette, La., 1974-75; assoc. firm Bird & Hochderffer, Stillwater, Okla., 1979-80; sole practice law, Stillwater, 1980—. Bd. dirs. Alcoholism Council Area Okla., 1981-82, Stillwater Domestic Violence Svcs., 1979—. Mem. Okla. Bar Assn. (pres. elect, 2002-03, pres. 2003-04), Payne County Bar Assn. (sec. 1984), Am. Trial Lawyers Assn., Bus. and Profl. Women Stillwater (pres. 1985), Stillwater C. of C. (ambassador 1982-84). Office: Law Office of Melissa DeLacerda 301 S Duck St PO Box 1252 Stillwater OK 74076

DELA CRUZ, ACELIA CASTRO, elementary school educator; m. Ray Dela Cruz; children: Austing, Celestial Jewel. Tchr. Tanapag Elem. Sch., Saipan, No. Marianas. Named No. Mariana Islands Tchr. of Yr., 2007. Office: Tanapag Elem Sch PO Box 501370 Saipan MP 96950 E-mail: aceliacdelacruz@yahoo.com.*

DE LA CRUZ, CARLOS, wholesale distribution executive; b. Havana, Cuba; arrived in Miami, 1975; m. Rosa de la Cruz; 5 children. BS, U. Pa., 1962, MBA in fin., 1963; JD, U. Miami Sch. Law, Fla., 1972. Car dealership exec.; chmn. Eagle Brands, Coca-cola Bottlers, PR, Trinidad and Tobago. Co-founder Cuba Study Group; co-chmn. Mesa Redonda. Named one of top 200 art collectors, ARTnews Mag., 2004; recipient Silver Medallion Brotherhood Award, Nat. Conf. of Christians & Jews, Distinguished Svc. Award, Fla. Internat. U., Social Responsibility Award, Urban League, Alexis de Tocqueville Award for outstanding philanthropy, United Way, 1997, Simon Weisenthal Ctr. Nat. Cmty. Svc. Award, 1998. Achievements include becoming first hispanic chmn. United Way (1990) & U. Miami Bd. Trustees (1999). Avocation: collector of contemporary art, especially Latin Am. Mailing: 5 Harbor Pl Key Biscayne FL 33149-1715

DELA CRUZ, JOSE SANTOS, retired commonwealth supreme court justice; b. Saipan, Commonwealth No. Mariana Islands, July 18, 1948; s. Thomas Castro and Remedio Sablan (Santos) Dela C.; m. Rita Tenorio Sablan, Nov. 12, 1977; children: Roxanne, Renee, Rica Ann. BA, U. Guam, 1971; JD, U. Calif., Berkeley, 1974; cert., Nat. Jud. Coll., Reno, 1985. Bar: No. Mariana Islands, 1974, U.S. Dist. Ct. No. Mariana Islands 1978. Staff atty. Micro. Legal Svcs. Corp., Saipan, 1974-79; gen. counsel Marianas Pub. Land Corp., Saipan, 1979-81; liaison atty. CNMI Fed. Laws Commn., Saipan, 1981-83; ptnr. Borja & Dela Cruz, Saipan, 1983-85; assoc. judge Commonwealth Trial Ct., Saipan, 1985-89; commonwealth supreme ct. chief justice Supreme Ct. No. Mariana Islands, 1989—95; retired, 1995; gen. counsel No. Mariana Islands Port Authority, 1996—2003; sr. advisor Pacific Telecommunications, Inc., 2005—. Mem. Conf. of Chief Justices, 1989-95, Adv. Commn. on Judiciary, Saipan, 1980-82; chmn. Criminal Justice Planning Agy., Saipan, 1985-95. Mem. Coun. for Arts, Saipan, 1982-83; chmn. Bd. of Elections, Saipan, 1977-82; pres. Cath. Social Svcs., Saipan, 1982-85. Mem. No. Marianas Bar Assn. (pres. 1984-85). Roman Catholic. Avocations: golf, reading, walking. Personal E-mail: joedlc1@yahoo.com. *There is an inherent goodness in every person, no matter how bad that person may appear. Recognizing that goodness in each gives us hope that the future of mankind will not be destructive.*

DE LA CRUZ, ROSA, art collector; b. Havana, Cuba; m. Carlos de la Cruz; 5 children. Co-founder Moore Space, Fla., 2001. Curator (exhibitions) THAT PLACE, Moore Space, 2002. Named one of top 200 collectors, ARTnews Mag., 2004; recipient Alexis de Tocqueville Award for outstanding philanthropy, United Way, 1997, Simon Weisenthal Ctr. Nat. Cmty. Svc. Award, 1998. Mem.: Mus. Contemporary Art N. Miami, Miami Art Mus. (aquisition com.), Mus. Contemporary Art Chgo. (exhibitor com.). Avocation: collector of contemporary art, especially Latin Am. Mailing: 5 Harbor Pl Key Biscayne FL 33149-1715 E-mail: rdelacr@aol.com.

DE LA CRUZ-REYES, PILAR L., nursing administrator; b. Sanger, Calif., Nov. 6, 1946; d. Joe and Margaret Ybarra; m. Felix Reyes; m. Joe De La Cruz, Jr. (dec.); children: Stephen De La Cruz, Jeffrey De La Cruz. BSN, Calif. State U., Dominguez Hills, 1996, MSN, 2001. RN Calif. From nurse to exec. dir. Cmty. Med. Ctr., Fresno, Calif., 1969—2002, exec. dir., 2002—03; chief nurse exec. Fresno (Calif.) Heart Hosp., 2003—06. Sec. Nursing Leadership Coun., Fresno, 1984—85; chmn. bd. dirs. Am. Heart Assn., Fresno, 1981—82. Named RN of Yr., Nursing Leadership Coun., 1997; recipient Diversity award, Calif. Wellness Found., 2003. Mem.: Nat. Hispanic Nurses Assn., Assn. Calif. Nurse Leaders. Avocations: singing, antiques, bicycling, gardening, dance. Home: 3866 N Academy Ave Sanger CA 93657 Office: Hosp Coun No and Ctrl Calif Fresno CA 93720

DE LA FUENTE RAMIREZ, JUAN RAMON, academic administrator; b. Mexico City, Sept. 5, 1951; married; 3 children. MSc, U. Minn.; postgrad. psychiatry, Mayo Clinic. Prof. Nat. Nutrition Inst.; rschr. Mex. Inst. Psychiatry; dir. health rsch. program U.N.A.M., mem., 1980, dir. med. faculty, 1991—94, health sec., 1994; sec. health Govt. of Mex., Washington, 1995—99; served in Cabinet as rector U.N.A.M., 1999; rector Nat. Autonomous U. Mex. , 2002—; chief resident U. Minn. Vis. prof. several fgn. univs; v.p. Internat. Assn. Univs. Author books on health rsch. Vol. internat. health orgns.; investigator Nat. Inst. Nurtrition, Mex. Inst. Psychiatry, Mexico City. Recipient Eduardo Liceaga prize, Nat. Acad. Medicine. Office: Univ Nat Autonoma Mex DGSCA Circuito Exterior Ciudad U Delegacion Coyoacan Mexico City CP 04510 Mexico*

DE LA GARZA, LUIS ADOLFO, automotive executive, lawyer; b. Mission, Tex., Nov. 22, 1943; s. Adolfo and Carmen (Barrera) de la G.; m. Sherry Lynn Hatcher, Apr. 12, 1974; children: Miguel, Gabriel, Lucas. BBA, U. Tex., 1966; MBA, U. Hawaii, 1972; JD, U. Tex., 1975. Bar: Tex. 1975. Counsel El Paso Natural Gas Co., Tex., 1975-78; sr. counsel El Paso Co., Houston, 1978-81; sr. atty., asst. sec. Valero Energy Corp., San Antonio, 1981-87, v.p. corp. rels., 1987—97, PG&E Gas Transmission-Tex. Corp., 1997—2000; ptnr. Holland & Knight, LLP, 2001—03; v.p. adminstrn. Toyota Motor Mfg. Tex., Inc., 2005—. Co-founder, pres., CEO Texen Power Co., 2000. Chmn. March of Dimes San Antonio Walk Am., 1996, 97; bd. dirs., chmn. Latino leadership for the libr. campaign San Antonio Pub. Libr. Found.; bd. dirs. Tex. Equal Access to Justice Found., comms. com., 1994-2003; bd. dirs. Valero Polit. Action Com., San Antonio, 1984-97, chmn., 1987-97; bd. dirs. Valero Fed. Credit Union, 1987-88; bd. dirs. World Affairs Coun., San Antonio, 1987, exec. com., 1988-90; scout leader Boy Scouts Am., San Antonio, 1984-2005; mem. Witte Coun., Witte Com., San Antonio Mus. Assn., 1985-90; bd. dirs., chmn. United Way Tex., mem. pub. policy com., 2000-03; bd. dirs. Tex. Civil Justice League; mem. bus. adv. coun. U. Tex., San Antonio; commr. Tex. Equal Access Justice Commn., 2001-2003. Capt. USMC, 1966-72, Vietnam. Decorated Air medal with 15 oak leaf clusters; named One of the Hundred Most Influential Hispanics in Am. Hispanic Bus. Mag., 1990, One of the Corp. Elite in Am. Hispanic Mag., 1990-2000; recipient Breaking Barriers award Nat. Hispanic Employees Assn., 1993, Vol. of Yr. March of Dimes 1998. Fellow Tex. Bar Found.; mem. Tex. Bar Assn., San Antonio Bar Assn. (chmn. corp. counsel sect. 1986-88), Greater San Antonio C. of C. (govtl. affairs, edn. coun. steering com., bd. dirs. 1987-90), Southside C. of C. (bd. dirs. 1989-90, 05), San Antonio Hispanic C. of C. (bd. dirs. 1989-91). Methodist. Office: Toyota Motor Mfg Mail Code ADM-TX 1 Lone Star Pass San Antonio TX 78264-3463 Home Phone: 210-490-0582; Office Phone: 210-267-4110. E-mail: luis.delagarza@tema.toyota.com.

DELAGI, GREG, electronics executive; BSBA, Nichols Coll., Dudley, Mass., 1984. With Materials & Controls bus. Tex. Instruments, Inc., Attleboro, Mass., 1984, sales and mktg. position Semiconductor Group Austin, Tex. and Phoenix, mgr. sales ops. US Western region, with DSP ops., 1996, v.p., mgr. worldwide DSP Systems Bus. Unit, 2000, sr. v.p., gen. mgr. Wireless Terminals Bus. Unit, 2007—. Office: Tex Instruments Inc PO Box 660199 Dallas TX 75266-0199 Office Phone: 972-995-2011. Office Fax: 972-995-4360.*

DELAHANTY, REBECCA ANN, school system administrator; b. South Bend, Ind., Oct. 18, 1941; d. Raymond F. and Ann Marie (Batsleer) Paczesny; m. Edward Delahanty, June 22, 1963; children: David, Debbie. BA, Coll. of St. Catherine, Minn., 1977; MA, Coll. St. Thomas, Minn., 1983; PhD, Ga. State U., 1994. Cert. in adminstrn. and supervision Ga. Initiator, tchr. gifted kindergarten Dist. 284 Sch., Wayzata, Minn., 1977-83; gifted kindergarten coord. St. Barts Sch., Wayzata, 1983-85; prin. Dabbs Loomis Sch., Dunwoody, Ga., 1987-91; asst. to supt. Buford (Ga.) City Schs., 1993-98, supt., 1998-99; prof. Ga. State U., 1999-2000; ednl. cons., 2000—; adv. bd. U. Saint Thomas, Coll. Edu., 2001—. Staff devel. adv. coun. Ga. Contbr. Mem. adv. bd. Coll. Edn. U. St. Thomas , 2001—. Mem.: ASCD, Minn. Coun. Gifted and Talented, Minn. Assn. Gifted Children, Nat. Assn. Gifted Children, Am. Ednl. Rsch. Assn., Omicron Gamma, Phi Delta Kappa. E-mail: beckydelah@aol.com.

DELAHAY, JOHN N., orthopedist, surgeon; b. 1944; MD, Georgetown U., 1969. Cert. Orthopaedic Surgery, 1975. Intern Georgetown U. Med. Ctr., 1970, resident, 1974, prof., vice-chair edn. Dept. Orthopaedic Surgery. Named one of Top Doctors, Washingtonian.com. Mem.: Pediatric Orthopaedic Soc. N.Am. Office: Pasquerilla Healthcare Ctr Ground Fl Georgetown U Med Ctr Washington DC 20007 also: Georgetown Orthopaedics Chase Tower Bldg 4445 Willard Ave, Ste 202 Chevy Chase MD 20815 Office Phone: 202-444-1438, 240-235-2360.*

DE LA HOUSSAYE, BRETTE ANGELO-PEPE, electrical engineer, researcher, educator; b. LA, Aug. 20, 1960; s. Wilbert Joseph de la Houssaye and Paula Marie (Jones) Colby. BSEET, Devry Inst. Tech., 1989. Pvt. practice, Calif., 1990—; with Calcgate Software, 2003—; math tchr. LA Unified Sch. Dist., 2007—. Mem. IEEE, Am. Phys. Soc., Nat. Trust Historic Preservation, Am. Mus. Natural History. Achievements include discovery of alternate method for calculating work, using Newton's second Law of Motion and work energy theorem; programmed calcgate software which uses mathematical transform to calculate work, energy, and integral area. Home: 7719 Goodland Ave North Hollywood CA 91605-2041 Office Phone: 818-571-1960. Business E-Mail: brette@calcgate.com.

DE LA HOYA, OSCAR, boxer; b. LA, Feb. 4, 1973; s. Joel and Cecilia De La Hoya; m. Millie Corretjer, Oct. 5, 2001; 1 child, Oscar Gabriel; children: Jacob, Devon, Atiana Cecilia. Amateur boxer, 1984—92; profl. boxer, 1992—; founder, pres. Golden Boy Promotions, Inc., 2001—. Winner world title vs. Jimmi Bredahl by tech. knockout, jr. lightweight divsn. World Boxing Orgn., 1994, winner world title def. vs. Giorgio Campanella by tech. knockout, jr. lightweight divsn., 94, winner vacant world title vs. Jorge Paez by knockout, lightweight divsn., 94, winner world title def. vs. Carl Griffith by tech. knockout, lightweight divsn., 94, winner world title def. vs. John Avila by tech. knockout, lightweight divsn., 94, winner world title def. vs. John John Molina by unanimous decision, lightweight divsn., 95, winner world title def. vs. Rafael Ruelas by tech. knockout, lightweight divsn., 95, winner world title def. vs. Genaro Hernandez by tech. knockout, lightweight divsn., 95, winner world title def. vs. Jesse James Leija by tech. knockout, lightweight divsn., 95, winner world title vs. Felix Strum by unanimous decision, middleweight divsn., 2004; winner world title vs. Julio Cesar Chavez by tech. knockout, superlightweight divsn. World Boxing Coun., 1996, winner world title def. vs. Miguel Angel Gonzalez by unanimous decision, superlightweight divsn., 97, winner world title vs. Pernell Whitaker by unanimous decision, welterweight divsn., 97, winner world title def. vs. David Kamau by knockout, welterweight divsn., 97, winner world title def. vs. Hector Camcacho by unanimous decision, welterweight divsn., 97, winner world title def. vs. Wilfredo Rivera by tech. knockout, welterweight divsn., 97, winner world title def. vs. Patrick Charpentier by tech. knockout, welterweight divsn., 98, winner world title def. vs. Julio Cesar Chavez by tech. knockout, welterweight divsn., 98, winner world title def. vs. Ike Quartey by split decision, welterweight divsn., 99, winner world title def. vs. Oba Carr by knockout, welterweight divsn., 99, winner world title elimination vs. Derrell Coley by knockout, welterweight divsn., 2000, winner world title vs. Javier Castillejo by unanimous decision, superwelterweight divsn., 01, winner world title def. vs. Fernando Vargas by tech. knockout, superwelterweight divsn., 02, winner world title def. vs. Luis Ramon Campas by tech. knockout, superwelterweight divsn., 03, winner world title def. vs. Ricardo Mayorga by tech. knockout, superwelterweight divsn., 06. Musician: (album) Oscar De La Hoya, 2000 (Grammy nomination for single "Ven a Mi", 2001). Named Fighter of Yr., The Ring Mag., 1995, Pound for Pound Fighter, 1997, Best Boxer, ESPY awards, 2006; recipient Gold medal in lightweight divsn., US Olympics, Barcelona, 1992. Office: Golden Boy Promotions Ste 350 626 Wilshire Blvd Los Angeles CA 90017 Office Fax: 213-489-5631.*

DELAHUNT, WILLIAM D., congressman; b. Quincy, Mass., July 18, 1941; s. Bill Sr. and Ruth Delahunt; children: Kirstin, Kara. BA, Middlebury Coll., 1963; JD, Boston Coll., 1967. Asst. clk. Norfolk Superior Ct., 1968—70; legal counsel Quincy Police Dept., 1970; pvt. practice law, 1971-75; dist. atty. State of Mass., 1975—96; mem. US Congress from 10th Mass. dist., 1997—, mem. judiciary resources com., internat. relations com., co-chair Coast Guard caucus, Ho. Older Americans caucus. Mem. Quincy City Coun., 1971; mem. Mass. Ho. Reps., 1973-75, asst. majority leader. With USCGR, 1963-71. Democrat. Office: US Ho Reps 2454 Rayburn Ho Office Bldg Washington DC 20515-2110 Office Phone: 202-225-3111. Office Fax: 202-225-5658. E-mail: william.delahunt@mail.house.gov.*

DE LAMA, ALBERTO, artist; b. Havana, Cuba; s. Victorio and Carmen (Pena) de L.; m. June Rose Milazzo de Lama. AA, Am. Acad. Art, Chgo., 1965. Tchr. Am. Acad. Art, Chgo., 1969-75; pres. Graphic Direction, Tampa, Fla., 1982—. Works exhibited in various shows including Galeria Sans Souci, Caracas, Venezuela, Talisman Gallery, Bartlesville, Okla., LeBlanc's Wildlife Gallery, Minocqua, Wis., Univ. Club Tampa, Fla., Galeria Vanidades, Miami, Tampa Yacht Club, Fla.; represented in permanent collections Fla. Eye Ctr., Tampa, Pullman Bank, Chgo., Talman Home Fed. Savs., Chgo., Jim Walter Corp., Tampa, Delta Airlines, Atlanta, The Celotex Corp., Tampa, Galeria Vanidades, Miami. Recipient Diamond medal 1970-71, Gold medal, 1972-75 Palette and Chisel Acad.m Chgo. Home: 3005 W Horatio St Tampa FL 33609-4121

DELANEY, EUGENE A., electronics executive; BS, So. Ill. U.; MBA, DePaul U. Chmn. Motorola China Electronics Ltd. Motorola, Inc., 2002—, joined, 1978, fin. analyst comm. sector, 1978, contr. Motorola Credit Corp., 1986, ops. mgr. ctrl. region cellular bus., 1989—94, v.p., dir. ops. ctrl. and N.E. region Pan Am. wireless infrastructure group, 1994—95, v.p., gen. mgr. Japan cellular infrastructure divsn., 1995—97, corp. v.p. cellular infrastructure group, 1997—98, exec. v.p., pres. global rels. and resources orgn., 2002—05, sr. v.p. Europe, Middle East , Africa and Asia/Pacific Govt. Enterprise Mobility Solutions Schaumburg, Ill., 2005—. Office: Motorola Inc 1303 E Algonquin Rd Schaumburg IL 60196

DELANEY, JEFFREY J., lawyer; b. Queens, NY, Aug. 17, 1967; BA summa cum laude, Pace Univ., 1989, JD summa cum laude, 1992. Bar: Conn. 1992, NY 1993. Ptnr. corp. & securities practice, co-chmn. global energy industry team Pillsbury Winthrop Shaw Pittman, NYC. Contbr. articles to profl. jours. Editor (rsch. & writing): Pace Law Rev. Mem. and rsch. and writing editor Pace Law Rev. Office: Pillsbury Winthrop Shaw Pittman 1540 Broadway New York NY 10036 Office Phone: 212-858-1292. Office Fax: 212-858-1500. Business E-Mail: jeffrey.delaney@pillsburylaw.com.*

DELANEY, JOHN, protective services official; s. John Paul and Ellen Lee Delaney; m. Abigail Arellano Camargo, Oct. 10, 1978; children: Patricia, Kathleen, Stephanie, John Michael Jr. PhD in Bus. Adminstrn., Calif. Coast U., Santa Ana, 1998. Police officer, Blythe, Calif., 1986—90; pub. safety mgr. Cmty. Hosp. of San Bernardino, 1990—. Cons. Peace Offering Solutions, Colton, Calif., 1992—. Author: (novels) Lights Out, Gangz, Behind the Badge, The Green Shadow, The Zenith Resolution, The Ring Killer. Named Police Officer of Yr., City of Blythe, 1987; recipient City commendations, 1987, 1988. Democrat-Npl. Roman Catholic. Home Phone: 909-825-6461.

DELANEY, JOHN ADRIAN, academic administrator; b. Lansing, Mich., June 29, 1956; s. James Edward and Mary Ann (Langius) D.; m. Gena Barrett, Sept. 6, 1980; children: William Langius, Adrian Anne, Marye Margaret, James Barrett. BA in History, U. Fla., 1977, JD, 1981. Bar: Fla. 1981. With State Atty.'s Office, Jacksonville, Fla., 1981-91; chief asst. state atty. Jacksonville, Fla., 1986-91; gen. counsel City of Jacksonville, 1991-92, 94-95, chief of staff, mayor, 1992-94, mayor, 1995—2003; pres. U. North Fla., Jacksonville, 2003—. Mem. Leadership Jacksonville, 1986, Leadership Fla.-13; chmn. bd. St. Paul's Episcopal Sch. Mem. Inns of Ct., Fla. Blue Key (pres. 1980). Rotary, Delta Upsilon. Roman Catholic. Avocation: camping. Home: 110 Bowles St Jacksonville FL 32266-4917 Office: Office of the Pres U North Fla Jacksonville FL 32224-2648 Office Phone: 904-620-2500. Business E-Mail: jdelaney@unf.edu.

DELANEY, JOHN WHITE, lawyer; b. Springfield, Mass., Feb. 28, 1943; s. Frank T. and Emily (White) D.; m. Betsey Secor; children: Erin, Elizabeth. AB, Harvard U., 1964, JD, 1967. Bar: Mass. 1967, U.S. Dist. Ct. Mass. 1968. Staff asst. to U.S. senator Leverett Saltonstall, Washington, 1966; law clk. Mass. Superior Ct., Boston, 1967-68; asst. atty. gen. State of Mass., Boston, 1968-69; legis. asst. Gov. Commonwealth of Mass., Boston, 1969-73; asst. sec. consumer affairs and bus. regulation Commonwealth of Mass., 1973-76; exec. dir. Boston Mcpl. Rsch. Bur., 1976-80; dir. govt. and community affairs Bank of Boston, 1980-89; sr. ptnr. Hale and Dorr, Boston, 1989—2004; ptnr. Wilmer Cutler Pickering Hale and Dorr LLP, Boston, 2004—06; sr. counsel Wilmer Hale, Boston, 2007—. Dir. New England Legal Found., Boston, 1986—. Dir. Robert F. Kennedy Action Corps, Boston, 1973-92, mem. adv. coun., 2006—; sec. Harvard Class of 1964, 1979-, Coordinating Com., Boston, 1984-87; trustee, mem. exec. com. Mass. Taxpayers Found., Boston, 1986—; dist. rep. Dedham Town Meeting, Mass., 1986—; trustee Boston Mcpl. Rsch. Bur., 1991—. Brain Sci. Found., 2005—; mem. adv. coun. The Trustees of Reservations, 1993-99, 2000-06, bd. dirs., 2006-; dir. Greater Boston C. of C., 1992—; pres. Friends of RFK Children's Action Corps, Inc., 1996-03; mem. Mass.

IOLTA Com., 2004—. Fellow Mass. Hist. Soc.; mem. Boston Bar Assn. (mem. coun. 2003-06), Clover Club Boston (pres. 2006). Office: Wilmer Hale 60 State St Boston MA 02109-1800 Office Phone: 617-526-6939. Business E-Mail: john.delaney@wilmerhale.com.

DELANEY, KEVIN FRANCIS, retired military officer, consultant; b. Wolcott, Conn., Sept. 23, 1946; s. John and Mildred Delaney; m. Patricia Delaney, June 8, 1968; children: Kelly, Diana, Seana. BS in Engring., U.S. Naval Acad., Annapolis, Md., 1968; M in Bus., George Washington U., 1977; postgrad., MIT, 1984, Harvard U., 1993. Advanced through grades to rear admiral USN; comdg. officer Heli Anti-Sub Squadron 32, Norfolk, Va., 1980-82, 82-84; air boss USS Guadalcanal, 1984-86; commdg. officer HSL-31, wing comdr. Helo Sea Control Wing 3, Mayport, Fla., 1987—89; commdg. officer Naval Air Sta., Jacksonville, Fla., 1989-91; comdr. shore activities U.S. Atlantic Fleet, Norfolk, Va., 1993-94; dir. shore installation mgmt. Chief Naval Ops., Washington, 1994-95; comdr. Navy Region S.E. Jacksonville, 1995-98; ret. USN, 1998; exec. v.p. Coggin Automotive Group, Jacksonville, Fla., 1998-2000; exec. v.p., COO HealthScreen Am., Jacksonville, Fla., 2000—02; pres., CEO Delaney & Assocs. Consulting. Bd. mem. 12 Who Care, Jacksonville, 1995-, Vol. Jax, Inc., Jacksonville, 1995-98, Childrens' Haven, Orange Park, Fla., 1995-98; chmn. Navy/Marine Corp. Relief Soc., Jacksonville, 1995-98; bd. dirs. Salvation Army, United Way, USO, YMCA, Jr. Achievement, World Affairs Coun., Freedoms Found.; vice chmn. Toyota Gator Bowl; past chair United Way Campaign N.E. Fla.; pres. Ronald McDonald House; bd. govs., pres. Fla. C.C. Jacksonville Found; bd. trustees Jacksonville U., Fla. CC; bd. dirs. Jacksonville C. of C.; chmn. Jacksonville Beaches C. of C. Mem. Fla. C. of C., Rotary (pres. 2000), N.E. Fla. Safety Coun. (chmn.). Home: 4551 Swilcan Bridge Ln N Jacksonville FL 32224-5618 Office: Delaney and Assocs 8505 Baycenter Rd Ste 300 Jacksonville FL 32256 Office Phone: 904-733-7336 1453. E-mail: kdelaney@baywoodtech.com.

DELANEY, KIM, actress; b. Phila., Nov. 29, 1961; 1 child, Jack. Appeared in (TV series) All My Children, 1981-84, 94, Tour of Duty, 1987, The Fifth Corner, 1992, NYPD Blue, 1995-2001 (Emmy award 1997), Philly, 2001, CSI: Miami, 2002, 10.5: Apocalypse, 2005 (TV movies) First Affair, 1983, Perry Mason: The Case of the Sinister Spirit, 1987, Cracked Up, 1987, Christmas Comes to Willow Creek, 1987, All My Darling Daughters, Please Take My Daughters, 1988, Something Is Out There, 1988, The Broken Cord, 1992, Lady Boss, 1992, Closer and Closer, The Disappearance of Christina, 1993, Tall, Dark, and Deadly, 1995, Tall Dark and Deadly, 1995, All Lies End in Murder, 1997, The Devil's Child, 1997, Love and Treason, 2001, (films) That Was Then.This Is Now, 1985, The Delta Force, 1986, Hunter's Blood, 1987, Campus Man, 1987, The Drifter, 1988, Hangfire, 1991, Body Parts, 1991, The Force, 1994, Inferno, Darkman II: The Return of Durant, 1994, Dark Goddess, 1994, Serial Killer, 1995, Project: Metalbeast, 1995, Closer and Closer, 1995., Mission to Mars, 2000. Avocations: biking, swimming, working out, watching films. Office: care The Gersh Agy attn Bob Gersh 232 N Canon Dr Beverly Hills CA 90210-5302 also: care Melissa Prophet Mgmt 1041 N Formosa Ave Los Angeles CA 90046 also: CSI Miami Prodn Office El Segundo Studios 2265 E El Segundo Blvd El Segundo CA 90245

DELANEY, MATTHEW SYLVESTER, mathematics professor, academic administrator; b. Ireland, Nov. 26, 1927; arrived in U.S., 1947, naturalized, 1952; s. Joseph C. and Elizabeth M. (Bergin) Delaney. Student, St. John's Coll., 1947—51; BA, Immaculate Heart Coll., LA, 1958; MS, Notre Dame U., 1960; PhD, Ohio State U., 1971. Ordained priest Roman Cath. Ch., 1951. Assoc. pastor L.A. Cath. Diocese, 1951—55; instr. math., physics Pius X H.S., Downey, Calif., 1955—58, vice prin., 1960—62; instr. math. Immaculate Heart Coll., 1962—65, asst. prof., 1972—76, prof., 1976—, asst. acad. dean., 1973—78; dean acad. devel. Mt. St. Mary's Coll., LA, 1978—82, acad. dean, 1978—91, prof. math., 1991—96, prof. emeritus, 1996—. Contbr. articles to math. publs., profl. jours. Grantee, NSF, 1959—60, 1961. Mem.: NY Acad. Scis., Math. Assn. Am., Am. Math. Soc., Internat. Union Crystallography. Democrat. Achievements include Formal recognition of the eponyms, "Delaney Sets" and "The Delaney Symbol" in the disciplines of discrete geometry and math. crystallography. Home: Apt 32C 13700 El Dorado Dr Seal Beach CA 90740-3843 Office: Mount Saint Mary's Coll 12001 Chalon Rd Los Angeles CA 90049-1526 Personal E-mail: mdel2611@adelphia.net.

DELANEY, ROBERT FINLEY, retired columnist, political sociologist, lecturer; b. Fall River, Mass., Aug. 2, 1925; s. Joseph Patrick and Mary Gertrude (Finigen) Delaney; m. Mary Elizabeth Flynn, Jan. 21, 1950; children: Mary Ellen, Flynn, Nancy, Carrie, Deirdhre, Sarah; m. Patricia Ann Riley, Jan. 21, 1984. Student, Dartmouth Coll., 1943; BNS, Holy Cross Coll., 1946; postgrad., Harvard U., 1946, U. Vienna, 1956; MA, Boston U., 1948; BSLS, Cath. U. Am., 1955; DHL (hon.), U. Mass., 1981. Fgn. svc. info. officer Dept. of State, 1950—69; pub. affairs cons. Esso S.A., 1960—63; asst. dir. USIA, Washington, 1968-69; dir. Edward R. Murrow Center Public Diplomacy Fletcher Sch., Tufts U., Boston, 1969-70; pres. Thunderbird Grad. Sch. Internat. Mgmt., Phoenix, 1970-71; Milton Miles prof. internat. relations U.S. Naval War Coll., Newport, RI, 1971—81; adj. prof. internat. mgmt. Salve Regina U., Newport, 1972-78; pres. Michael W. Moynihan Public Affairs, Washington and NY, 1981—83; chmn. bd. dirs. RFD, Inc., Newport, 1983-91; pres. Global Scis., Ltd., 1985-89; sr. policy advisor US Space Sta., NASA, 1994-97; editor Newport This Week, 2003; ret., 2003. Author: Your Career in Foreign Service, 1957, Literature of Communism in America, 1958, The Psychology of Terror, 1980, Terror as a Tactic, 1988; editor: This is Communist Hungary, 1959, First Fifty Years of American Public Diplomacy, 1969, International Communications and the New Diplomacy, 1970, The Fourth Estate: The Impact of the Media on National Security Decision-Making, 2002. Incorporator Newport Hosp., 1979—82; mem. Rochambeau Bicentennial Commn., 1979—80; naval aide to Gov. of RI, 1976—81; RI press sec. Edward Kennedy primary campaign, 1980; bd. advisors Salvie Regina Coll., 1973—77. Served to capt. USNR, 1943—81, PTO, Vietnam. Decorated Air medal, medal of Merit Vietnam, Knight of St. Lazarus Mil. and Hospitalier Order of Jerusalem; recipient citation for, Inter-am. Cooperation Orgn. Am. States, 1965, Volker Found. award, 1954—55, Superior Svc. award, Dept. of State, 1962, Disting. Svc. award, 1965. Mem.: Met. Nat. Press Club (Washington), Am. Mgmt. Assn., Pres. Assn., Am. Fgn. Svc. Assn., Pub. Rels. Soc. Am., Inter Univ. Seminar Armed Forces, Naval War Coll. Found., Navy League, Dacor House Club, Reading Rm. Club (NewPort), NY Yacht Club (NYC), Alpha Sigma Nu, Delta Phi Epsilon. Roman Catholic. Home: 4265 Via del Villetti Venice FL 34293-7060

DELANEY, ROBERT VINCENT, former gas company executive, economic development consultant; b. NYC, Oct. 1, 1934; s. Charles Peter and Alice Mary (O'Rorke) D.; m. Marie Josephine Monaco, Oct. 13, 1956; children: Robert Vincent, Richard Clement, Charles John, Christopher Raymond, Elizabeth Marie. BS in Acctg., Fordham U., 1956; grad. advanced mgmt. program, Harvard U., 1979. Tax mgr. Bklyn. Union Gas Co., 1965-66, personnel mgr., 1966-71, asst. v.p. human resources, 1971-75, v.p. engring., 1975-81, sr. v.p. customer ops., 1981-88, group sr. v.p., chief adminstrv. officer, 1988-90; prin. CPS Cons., NYC, 1990—. Chmn. bd. Greater Jamaica Devel. Corp., N.Y.C.; bd. dirs. Queens Overall Econ. Devel. Corp., N.Y.C., Comprehensive Devel., Inc.; faculty advisor N.Y.C. Tech. Coll., 1968-92. Bd. dirs. Jr. Achievement N.Y., 1972-78, Coop. Edn. Commn. N.Y.C., 1977-82, N.Y. Hall Sci., N.Y.C., 1983-92, Queens Symphony Orch., 1981-91; pres. Harvard AMP Class of 1979, Cambridge; pub. mem. Bd. Cert. for Profl. Engrs. and Land Surveyors State of N.Y., Albany, 1977-87. Capt. arty., U.S. Army, 1957. Recipient Outstanding Svc. award Jr. Achievement, 1980, Disting. Citizen award Queens Symphony Orch., 1980, Bus. Friends of Arts award Borough of Queens, 1984, merit award Am. Legion, 1985, leadership award Greater Jamaica Devel. Corp., 1997, Disting. Svc. award Manhattan Comprehensive Night and Day H.S., 2001. Mem. Am. Gas Assn. (taxation com. 1962-64, customer acctg. com. 1965-67, chmn. pers. com. 1970-73, chmn. fin. and adminstrv. sect. 1982-83, award of merit 1979), Harvard Bus. Sch. Club of N.Y. (bd. dirs.), Harvard U. Club, Bklyn. Club, Beta Gamma Sigma. Republican. Roman Catholic. Avocations: tennis, stickball (three sewer hitter). Home and Office: 1025 Fifth Ave New York NY 10028-0134 E-mail: rvdny@aol.com.

DELANEY, TERENCE (TERRY) P., gas industry executive; b. Jan. 1956; Internal auditor Sunoco Inc., 1979, mgr. investor rels., 1995—2000, dir. investor rels. and strategic planning, 2000—03, v.p. investor rels. and planning Phila., 2003—. Office: Sunoco Inc Ten Penn Ctr 1801 Market St Philadelphia PA 19103-1699

DELANEY, WAYNE EDWARD, retired surgeon; b. Sherman, Tex., Sept. 5, 1933; s. Milton Loyd and Laura Alice Delaney; m. Mary Maxine Leslie Delaney, Aug. 15, 1953. BA, Tex. U., Austin, 1955; MD, U. Tex., 1959. Diplomate Am. Bd. Surgery, 1965. Intern Parkland Hosp., Dallas, 1959—60, gen. surgery resident, 1960—64. Bd. dirs. State Nat. Bank, Denison, Tex., 1975—, Smith Found., Denison, 1985—. Mem.: Chirugio Soc., Denison Country Club. Republican. Baptist. Avocations: tennis, golf.

DE LANGE, TITIA, research scientist, educator; BA, MS, U. Amsterdam, PhD in biochemistry; MS, Nat. Inst. Med. Rsch.; PhD in biochemistry, Netherlands Cancer Inst.; postdoctoral fellow, U. Calif., San Francisco, 1989; doctorate (hon.), U. Utrecht. Asst. prof. Rockefeller U., NYC, 1990—94, assoc. prof., 1994—97, prof., 1997—99, Leon Hess prof. and head lab. cell biology and genetics, 1999—. Recipient Rita Allen award, 1995, Burroughs Wellcome Fund Toxicology Scholar award, 1997, Cancer Rsch. award, NY Cmty. Trust, 1997, Sr. Scholar award, Ellison Med. Found., 2000, Paul Marks Prize, Meml. Sloan Kettering Cancer Ctr., 2001, AACR Women in Cancer Rsch. Charlotte Friend Meml. Lectureship, 2004, Dir.'s Pioneer Award, NIH, 2005. Fellow: Am. Acad. Arts & Scis.; mem.: Dutch Royal Acad. Scis., NAS (assoc.). Office: Rockefeller Univ 1230 York Ave New York NY 10021*

DELANO, VICTOR, retired naval officer; b. Washington, Dec. 20, 1919; s. Harvey and Marcia (Murdock) D.; m. Jacqueline Stinson (dec. 1990); children: Katherine Delano Jahnig, Harvey II. BSEE with distinction, US Naval Acad., 1941; MS in Physics, MIT, Lexington, Mass., 1949; postgrad., Indsl. Coll. Armed Forces, 1961-62. Ensign USN, 1941, advanced through grades to capt., 1959; staff comdr. 2d Fleet, 1956-58, Atlantic Fleet, 1963-65; chief of staff Atlantic Amphibious Force, 1966-67; with Office Chief of Naval Ops., 1967-69; ret., 1969; pres. Wichita Eagle-Beacon Pub., 1970-71. V.p., treas. Naval Hist. Found., Washington, 1980-99; trustee Naval Acad. Found.; trustee, bd. dirs. Avon Old Farms Sch., Conn., 1980-92, 95—; bd. dirs. Friends Nat. Zoo, Washington, 1971-80, Episc. Ctr. for Children, Washington, 1975-84, 88-94, Kingsbury Ctr., Washington, 1986-95. Decorated Legion of Merit (2), Bronze Star, Purple Heart. Mem. Naval Inst., Naval Acad. Alumni Assn., Mil. Order Carabao, Pearl Harbor Survivors Assn., Chevalier du Tastevin, Commanderie de Bordeaux (Naples), Chevy Chase Club, Metropolitan Club (Washington), Army-Navy Club, Grey Oaks Country Club (Naples, Fla.), Burning Tree Club. Avocation: golf. Home: 865 9th Ave South Naples FL 34102

DELANY, JIM (JAMES EDWARD DELANY), sports association administrator, lawyer; b. South Orange, NJ, Mar. 3, 1948; m. Catherine Fisher; children: Newman, James Chancellor. BA in Polit. Sci., U. N.C., 1970, JD, 1973. Counsel N.C. Senate Judiciary Com., 1973-74; staff atty. N.C. Justice Dept., 1974-75; enforcement rep. NCAA, 1975-79; commr. Ohio Valley Conf., 1979-89, Big Ten Conf., 1989—. Mem. spl. adv. com. to review recommendations regarding distribution of revenues NCAA, ad hoc com. to administer the conf. grant program, spl. com. to study factors affecting automatic qualification into divsn. I men's basketball championship, spl. basketball T.V. negotiating com.; NCAA rep. USA Basketball Coun. Active Spl. Olympics, YMCA. Named to Newark, NJ Hall of Fame, Ohio Valley Conf. Hall of Fame. Mem. N.C. Bar Assn., Black Coaches' Assn. (bd. advisors), Collegiate Commissioners Assn., Coll. Basketball Partnership, USA Basketball Exec. Com (v.p., 2000-) Office: Big Ten Conf 1500 Higgins Rd Park Ridge IL 60068-6300*

DELAP, TONY, artist; b. Oakland, Calif., Nov. 4, 1927; s. Truman Henry and Catherine (Yontz) D.; m. Kathleen Rose Campbell, Dec. 27, 1964; children— Kelly Rose, Jack Henry. AA, Menlo Jr. Coll., 1947; student, Claremont Grad. Sch., 1947-49. Prof. U. Calif. at Irvine, 1965-91. Exhibited group shows, San Francisco Mus., Oakland Mus., Whitney Mus., U. Ill., Mus. Modern Art N.Y., L.A. County Mus., Pasadena Mus., one man shows, Dilexi Gallery, San Francisco, 1963, 67, Robert Elkon Gallery, N.Y.C., Felix Landau Gallery, L.A., 1966, 68, U. Calif. at Irvine, Nicholas Wilder Gallery, L.A., 1972, 74, 76, Calif. Inst. Tech., 1974, Calif. State U., Long Beach, 1974, John Berggruen Gallery, San Francisco, 1972, 76, Jan Turner Gallery, L.A., 1987, 89, 91, Modernism Gallery, San Francisco, 1986, 89, 92, 96, Klein Gallery, Chgo., 1985, Beatrix Wilhelm Gallery, Stuttgart, Germany, 1992, Gudrun Spielvogel Gallery, Munich, 1993, Works Gallery, Santa Ana, Calif., 1992, Allene Lapides Gallery, Santa Fe, N.Mex., 1992, Mark Moore Gallery, Santa Monica, Calif., 1994-95, 98, Calif. State U., Fullerton, 1994, Peter Blake Gallery, Laguna Beach, 2000, 02, 04, 06, Charlotte Jackson Gallery, Santa Fe, N.Mex., 2002, 05, Patricia Faure Gallery, Santa Monica, Calif., 2004, 05, Tony DeLap Retrospective Ex. at OCMA, Newport Beach, 2000, San Jose Mus. Art, 2001; represented in permanent collections: Whitney Mus., Mus. Modern Art N.Y.C., Walker Art Inst., Tate Gallery, London, Long Beach Mus. Art, Los Angeles County Mus. Art, Santa Barbara (Calif.) Mus. Art, Newport Harbor Art Mus., Newport Beach, Calif., Guggenheim Mus., N.Y.C. Address: 225 Jasmine St Corona Del Mar CA 92625-3035

DELAPA, JUDITH ANNE, business owner; b. Bad Axe, Mich., Feb. 1, 1938; d. John Vincent and Ellen Agatha (Peters) McCormick; m. James Patrick DeLapa, Jan. 10, 1959; children: Joseph Anthony, James P. II, John M., Gina M. BS, Mich. State U., 1959, MA, 1985. Tchr. various schs., Mich., 1959-64; co-founder Saluto Foods Corp., Benton Harbor, Mich., 1963-76; founder Earthtone Interiors, St. Joseph, Mich., 1977-82, High Impact Coaching and Cons. Inc., Grand Rapids, Mich., 1987—. Mktg. rsch. and mgt. cons., writer various clients, nationwide. Author: High-Impact Business Strategies, 1993, The McCormick-DeLapa Family Cookbook, 1997, A Place Called Ireland, 2000, Was That Really Us God?, 2001. Past vice-chair exec. bd. Grand Rapids Symphony Orch.; bd. dirs., pres. Samaritan Found.; bd. dirs. Grand Rapids Art Mus.; trustee Mich. Colls. Found., Meijer Garden Found. Judith A. DeLapa Perennial Garden named in her honor Mich. State U. Avocations: reading, travel, theater. Office: High Impact Coaching & Cons Inc 2505 E Paris Ave SE Ste 195 Grand Rapids MI 49546 E-mail: jdelapa@high-impact.com.

DELAPP, TINA DAVIS, retired nursing educator; b. LA, Dec. 18, 1946; d. John George and Margaret Mary (Clark) Davis; m. John Robert DeLapp, May 31, 1969; children: Julia Ann, Sam, Scott Michael. Diploma, Good Samaritan Hosp., Phoenix, 1967; BSN, Ariz. State U., 1969; MS in Nursing, U. Colo., Denver, 1972; EdD in Post Secondary Edn., U. So. Calif., 1986. Health aide instr. Yukon-Kuskokwim Health Corp., Bethel, Alaska, 1970-71; asst. prof. nursing Bacone Coll., Muskogee, Okla., 1972-74; instr. nursing Alaska Meth. U., Anchorage, 1975-76; prof. nursing U. Alaska, Anchorage, 1976—84, assoc. dean nursing, 1984—92, dir. Sch. Nursing, 1996—2004, emeritus prof., 2004—. Mem. Alaska Bd. Nursing, 1989-92; cons. in field. Mem. editl. adv. bd. Jour. Nursing Edn., 2004—; contbr. articles to profl. jours. Treas. Alaska Nurses Found., 2004—. recipient Named Legend of Nursing, Alaska March of Dimes, 2004; recipient emeritus award, Am. Assn. Coll. Nursing, 2005. Fellow: We. Acad. Nursing; mem.: Alaska Nurses Found. (treas. 2004—), Am. Assn. Colls. Nursing (mem. nominating com. 2003, task force 2003—04, emeritus 2005), Nat. League for Nursing Accreditation Comn. (program evaluator 1986—, eval. review panel mem. 2000—05), We. Inst. Nursing (chair program com. 1994—95, sec.-treas. 1995—2005, gov.-at-large 2005—07, Jo Elinor Elliot Leadership award 2002, Anna Shannon Mentorship award 2006, Emeritus award 2007, Chancellor's award 1994), Sigma Theta Tau (pres. chpt. 1986—88, v.p. 1988—93, counselor 1995—2000). Avocations: knitting, reading, politics. Personal E-mail: tdelapp@ak.net.

DE LA RENTA, OSCAR, fashion designer; b. Santo Domingo, Dominican Republic, July 22, 1936; s. Oscar and Maria Antonia (deFiallo) de LaR.; m. Francoise de Langlade, Oct. 31, 1967 (dec. 1983); 1 adopted child, Moises; m. Anne France Engelhard, Dec. 26, 1989. Student, Santo Domingo U., Academia de San Fernando, Madrid. Launched signature fragrance Oscar de la Renta, 1977, fragrance for men, Pour Lui, 1980, Oscar for men, 1995, Intrusion, 2002. Mem. staff Balenciaga's AISA, Madrid; asst. to Antonio Castillo at Lanvin, Paris, 1961-63; chief designer Elizabeth Arden, NYC, 1963-65, Jane Derby, 1965-69 (became Oscar de la Renta Ltd.); chief designer, chmn. bd. dirs. Oscar de la Renta, Ltd., NYC, 1969—; designer Pierre Balmain, Paris, 1993—. Bd. dirs. La Casa del Nino Orphanage and Sch., Santo Domingo, Met. Opera, Carnegie Hall, Thirteen/WNET, Hispanic Designers, Spanish Inst., The Americas Soc., New Yorkers for Children, UNICEF. Decorated Order Juan Pablo Duarte, Order Cristobal Colon (Dominican Republic); recipient Coty awards, 1967, 68, Golden Tiberius award, 1968, Neiman-Marcus award, 1968, Perennial Success award, Fragrance Found. 1991, French Legion d'Honneur as Comdr., 1993, Living Legend award Am. Soc. Perfumers, 1995, Lifetime Achievement award Hispanic Heritage Soc., 1996, Gold Medal of Bellas Artes, King of Spain, 2000, Lifetime Achievement award, 1990; named to Coty Hall of Fame, 1973, Grand Marshall of NY Hispanic Day Parade, 2000. Mem.: Coun. Fashion Designers Am. (bd. dirs., pres. 1973—76, 1986—88, Lifetime Achievement award 1990, Womenswear Designer of Yr. award 2000, 2007). Achievements include helped build two schools incorporating orphanages and day-care centers in La Romana and Punta Cana, Dominican Republic. Office: Oscar de la Renta Ltd 550 7th Ave Fl 8 New York NY 10018-3207*

DE LARIOS, DORA, artist; b. LA, Oct. 13, 1933; d. Elpidio and Concha (Martinez) De L.; 1 child, Sabrina. BFA, U. So. Calif., 1957. Tchr. ceramics UCLA, 1979, U. So. Calif., L.A., 1959; curator 1st internat. ceramic exhbn., L.A., 1988. Ceramic artist, commd. work for site specific areas, including Montage Resort and Spa, Laguna Beach, Calif., 2003; over 40 major works located in Tahiti, Hawaii, Japan, N.J., Fla., pvt. residential projects. Democrat. Avocations: reading, collecting cook books, cooking, drawing edwin the rabbit. Studio: 8560 Venice Blvd Los Angeles CA 90034-2549 Office Phone: 310-839-8305. Personal E-mail: delarios@comcast.net.

DE LA RIVA, MYRIAM ANN, artist; b. Mexico City, Mex., Oct. 8, 1940; arrived in US, 1989; d. Adolfo De La Riva and Marianne Kayser; m. Conrado Gallegos, Feb. 26, 1961; children: Conrado Bernardo, Aileen, Eugenio Eduardo. Grad. Fine Arts, IberoAm. U.; student, Kent State U., U. Femenina Mex., Master Carlos Orozco Romero Studio, Master Gilberto Aceves Navarro Studio. V.p. World Coun. Visual Artists, Mexico City, 1994—96, bd. dirs., 2007—, Mus. Americas; coord. Artists Libr. European Cmty., 2003; coord. Mex. cultural month Latin Am. Art Mus., Miami, 2004; coord., creator World Trade Ctr., Veracruz, 2004. One-woman shows include over 46 internat. shows, 1988—2006, exhibited in group shows at including over 500 internat. shows, 1988—2007, prin. works include mural Today XX first Century. Vol. Tamayo Contemporary Art Mus., Mexico City, 2000—04, Nat. Mus. Art, San Carlos, 2000—02; mem. Miami Art Mus., 1991—2007, Nat. Mus. Women in Arts, 1991—2007, Global Culture Ctr., 1991—98. Named Hon. Mention Women in the Arts, Latin Am. Art Mus., Fla., 1994; recipient 1st prize, Sor Juana Found. Mex.-Lebanon Inst. Cultural, 1998, 3d prize, Francisco Goitia prize, 1994, Francisco Goitia prize, Ateneo del Anahuac, 1991, 1992. Mem.: World Coun. Visual Artists (bd. dirs. 2007—), Assn. Artac Aiap-Unesco, Soc. Mex. de Artistas Plasticos, Mex. Fine Artists Salon (bd. dirs. 2006—). Office: Delariva Bosque de Guayacanes #57 11700 Mexico City Mexico Home Phone: 011 52 555 5963623. Business E-Mail: delarivamyriam@hotmail.com.

DE LA ROCHA, CARLOS A., retired physician; b. Santo Domingo, Dominican Republican, Aug. 12, 1934; s. Carlos A. and Germania (Contin) de la R.; m. Penelope Lynn Lansing, May 20, 1961; children: C. Andrew, Maria L., Michael J., David L., Alicia M., Juan A. MD, Univ. de Santo Domingo, 1958. Diplomate Am. Bd. Surgery. Rotating intern City Hosp. at Elmhurst, Queens, NY, 1958-59; asst. resident surgery Albert Einstein Med. Ctr., Phila., 1959-60, Ellis Hosp., Schenectady, NY, 1960-62, chief resident surgery, 1962-63; tchg. fellow surgery St. Clares Hosp., Schenectady, 1963-65; asst. attending surgeon St. Clares and Ellis Hosp., 1965-69, attending surgeon, 1969-98; ret., 1998. Chmn. tissue unit Ellis Hosp., 1985-90; mem. Ellis Hosp. Found. Bd., 1988-94. Fellow Am. Coll. Surgeons; mem. AMA, Am. Soc. Gen. Surgeons, N.Y. State Soc. Surgeons, N.Y. State and County Med. Soc. Republican. Roman Catholic. Avocations: travel, classical music. Home: 44 Van Voast Ln Scotia NY 12302-9621 also: PO Box 1397 Schenectady NY 12301-1397 E-mail: delarochac@hotmail.com.

DE LA ROCHA, CASTULO, health services executive; b. Chihuahua, Mex., Dec. 1, 1948; s. Moises and Consuelo de la Roche; children: Marco Remi, Alexis, Milan. BA in Polit. Sci., U. Calif., Santa Barbara, 1972; JD, U. Calif., Berkeley, 1975. Cert. in Mgmt. Stanford U. Pres., CEO Alta Med. Health Svcs. Corp., LA, 1980—. Bd. dirs. Orthopaedic Hosp. of. So. Calif., Nat. Assn. Cmty. Health Ctrs.; mem. adv. bd. Edward R. Roybal Ctr. for Applied Gerontology, 1987, exec. com. mem. Latino Coalition for Healthy Calif. Bd. govs., treas. L.A. County Latino Coalition for Healthy Calif.; mem. bd. Latino Theater Co., The Theater Group. Recipient Nat. Project Health award US Commn. on Aging, 1986, Surgeon Gen.'s Gold medallion for pub. health, 1992, Chicano/Latino Med. Assn. award, 1991, Significant Achievement award Chicanos for Creative Medicine, 1995, Cmty. Svc. award Am. Diabetes Assn., 1995, Vantage award Vis. Nurses Found., 1996,; named Hispanic of Yr., Caminos, 1985, Program of Yr., United Way, 1982, #1 Nonprofit, Hispanic Bus. Mag.; named one of Top 10 Latinos in Healthcare LatinoLeaders mag., 2004 Office: Alta Med Health Svcs Corp 500 Citadel Dr Ste 490 Los Angeles CA 90040-1574

DE LA ROCHA, ZACK, singer, musician; b. Long Beach, Calif., Jan. 12, 1970; s. Beto de la Rocha. Band mem. Hardstance (name changed to Inside Out); lead singer Rage Against the Machine, 1991—2000. Played at Lollapalooza II, LA, 1992, Lollapalooza III, Phila., 1993, Lollapalooza, 1996, Latinpalooza, LA, 1994, Tibetan Freedom Concert, San Francisco, 1996, East Troy, Wis., 99, Woodstock 99, Coachella music festival, Indio, Calif., 1999, 2007. Musician: (albums) (with Inside Out) No Spiritual Surrender, 1990; singer (with Rage Against the Machine) Rage Against the Machine, 1992, Evil Empire, 1996, The Battle of Los Angeles, 1999, Renegades, 2000, Live at the Grand Olympic Auditorium, 2003, (songs) Tire Me, 1996 (Grammy award for Best Metal Performance, 1997), Guerilla Radio, 2000 (Grammy award for Best Hard Rock Performance, 2001).*

DE LASA, JOSÉ M., lawyer; b. Havana, Cuba, Nov. 28, 1941; came to U.S., 1961; s. Miguel and Conchita de Lasa; m. Maria Teresa Figueroa, Nov. 23, 1963; children: Maria Teresa, José, Andrés, Carlos. BA, Yale U., 1968, JD, 1971. Bar: N.Y. 1973. Assoc. Cleary, Gottlieb, Steen & Hamilton, NYC, 1971-76; legal dept. Bristol-Myers Squibb Co., NYC, 1976-94; exec. v.p., gen. counsel Abbott Labs., 1994—2005; of counsel Baker & McKenzie, Chgo., 2005—. Lectr. internat. law, various locations. Bd. dirs. Am. Arbitration Assn., The Resource Found., Coun. Fgn. Rels., NY, The Stovir Found. Mem. ABA, Assn. of Bar of City of N.Y., Assn. Gen. Counsel, North Shore Gen. Counsel Assn., Ill. State Bar Assn. Roman Catholic. Office: Baker & McKenzie 114 Avenue of the Americas New York NY 10036 Business E-Mail: jose.delasa@bakernet.com.

DE LA SABLIERE, JEAN-MARC, former international organization official; b. Athens, Greece, Nov. 8, 1946; married; 3 children. Student, Nat. Sch. Adminstrn., 1971—73. Appointed secrétaire des affaires etrangères French Ministry Foreign Affairs, 1973, with, 1973—75; private office French Min. of Foreign Affairs, 1975—77, tech. advisor in private office, 1977—78, dep. dir. of African and Malagasy Affairs, 1985—86, dep. dir., UN and Internat. Orgns. Directorate, 1986—89, dir. of African and Malagasy Affairs, 1992—96; chargé de mission in the private office of Prime Min., 1978—81; second counsellor Permanent Mission of France to the UN, NY, 1981—84; dep. permanent rep. for France UN, NY, 1989—92; French amb. Arab Republic of Egypt, 1996—2000; diplomatic advisor and sherpa Pres. of the French Republic, 2000—02; amb. extraordinary and plenipotentiary, permanent rep. of France to the Security Coun., head of French Mission to the UN, 2002—07.

DELATEUR, BARBARA JANE, medical educator; b. Hoquiam, Wash., Nov. 17, 1936; Student, Marylhurst Coll., Oreg., 1954-56; BS in Philosophy, St. Louis U., 1959; MD, U. Wash., 1963, MSc, 1968. Diplomate Am. Bd. Phys. Medicine and Rehab.; lic. physiatrist, Wash., Md. Rotating intern U. Hosp., U. Wash., 1963-64, resident dept. phys. medicine and rehab., 1964-67; instr. dept. phys. medicine and rehab. U. Wash. Sch. Medicine, 1967-68, asst. prof., 1968-71, assoc. prof., 1971-76, prof. dept. rehab. medicine, 1976-93; prof., dir. dept. phys. medicine and rehab. Johns Hopkins U. Sch. Medicine, Balt., 1993—2003, Lawrence Cardinal Shehan chair phys. medicine and rehab., 1993—2003, joint prof. health policy & mgmt. Sch. Hygiene & Pub. Health, 1994—; acting physiatrist-in-chief Rehab. Medicine Svc. Harborview Med. Ctr., Seattle, 1970-72, physiatrist-in-chief, 1972-93; dir. Muscular Dystrophy Clinic Meml. Hosp., Yakima, Wash., 1979-88; dir. dept. phys. medicine and rehab. Johns Hopkins Hosp., Balt., 1993—2003; med. dir. dept. rehab. medicine Good Samaritan Hosp., Balt., 1993—2003, disting. svc. prof. phys. medicine & rehab., 2006—, Lawrence Cardinal Shehan prof. emeritus phys. medicine & rehab., 2006—. Vis. prof. dept. rehab. medicine and dept. internal medicine SUNY, Syracuse, 1988; cons. physiatrist Johns Hopkins Geriatrics Ctr., Johns Hopkins Bayview Med. Ctr., Balt., 1994—; vis. lectr. dept. phys. medicine Coll. Medicine, Ohio State U., 1985; Arthur Grant lectr. U. Tex., San Antonio, 1992; Marquette lectr. Jefferson Med. Coll., Phila., 1993; spkr. various univs. and orgns.; pres. Phys.Medicine and Rehab./Edn. and Rsch. Found., 1990-94; mem. governing coun. sect. rehab. hosps. and programs Am. Hosp. Assn., 1993—; mem. adv. bd. Wash. State Divsn. Vocat. Rehab., 1979-84; vis. prof. U. Wash., 2005, Rehab. Inst. Chgo., 2005; spkr. in field. Contbr. articles to profl. jours.; mem. editl. bd. Archives Phys. Medicine and Rehab., 1978-84, Health After 50, Johns Hopkins Hosp., 1994—; reviewer Jour. Am. Geriatrics Soc., 1994—. Recipient Elizabeth and Sidney Licht award for sci. writing, 1990, Excellence in Tchg. award N.J. Med. Sch., 1992, Excellence in Rsch. Writing award Assn. Acad. Physiatrists and Am. Jour. Phys. Medicine and Rehab., 1992, Golden Goniometer award Phys. Medicine and Rehab. Residents, 1995, 2002, 04, 05, Labe Scheinberg award, Meeting of Consortium of MS Ctrs., Portland, Oreg., 1995. Fellow Am. Acad. Phys. Medicine; mem. AMA, Am. Acad. Phys. Medicine and Rehab. (bd. govs. 1983-90, v.p. 1986-887, pres-elect 1987-88, pres. 1988-89, Disting. Clinician award 1998, Frank M. Krusen award 2004), NAS, Am. Burn Assn., Am. Congress Rehab. Medicine, Assn. Acad. Physiatrists (Disting. Academician award 1998), Internat. Assn. for Study of Pain, King County Med. Assn., Northwest Assn. Phys. Medicine and Rehab. (pres. 1974-76), Gerontol. Soc. Am. (clin. medicine sect.), Wash. State Med. Assn. Office: Johns Hopkins Bayview Med Ctr PM&R AA Bldg Rm 1654 4940 Eastern Ave Baltimore MD 21224

DELATORRE, PHILLIP EUGENE, law educator; b. Chanute, Kans., July 6, 1953; s. Jose Crespin and Margaret (Alonzo) DeL.; m. Patrice Ann Kutz, Sept. 19, 1981; children: Edward Phillip, Daniel Patrick, Ryan Andrew. BA, U. Kans., 1975; JD, Harvard U., 1978. Bar: Mo. 1978, Kans. 1979. Assoc. Watson, Ess, Marshall & Enggas, Kansas City, Mo., 1978-80; prof. law U. Kans., Lawrence, 1980—. Commr. Kans. Human Rights Commn., 1991—. Contbr. articles to profl. jours. (recipient Best Article award 1985). Mem. ABA, Kans. Bar Assn., Mo. Bar Assn. Office Phone: 785-864-9240. Business E-Mail: ped@ku.edu.

DELATY, SIMONE, retired language educator; b. Valenciennes, France, Jan. 17, 1939; came to U.S., 1963; d. Georges and Hélène (Lagarde) D.; m. Joseph Szertics, Dec. 8, 1962 (div. 1978); 1 child, Claire Szertics. Lic. ès-Lettres, U. Grenoble, France, 1962; D in Comparative Lit., U. Bordeaux, 1970. Instr. French Bowling Green U., Bowling Green, Ohio, 1964-67, U. Iowa, Iowa City, 1968-69, asst. prof. French, 1969-76, assoc. prof. French, 1976-86, prof. French, 1986—96; ret., 1996; owner, operator of Simone's Plain and Simple-Artisan Bread and Farm Fresh Products, Wellman, Iowa, 1996—. Author: L'héritage espagnol de José-Maria de Heredia, 1975, Oeuvres poétiques complètes de J.M. de Heredia, 1984. Grantee Am. Philos. Soc., 1976, Am. Coun. Learned Socs., 1976. Mem.: MLA.

DELAUP, S. GUY, lawyer; b. New Orleans, Feb. 16, 1956; m. Mickey deLaup; 2 children. BS, La. State U., 1978, JD, 1981. Bar: La. 1981, US Dist. Ct. (Ea. Dist. La.) 1984, US Ct. Appeals (5th Cir.) 1984. Asst. dist. atty. Jefferson Parish, 1982—87; pvt. practice Metairie, La. Mem. La. Supreme Ct. Mandatory Continuing Legal Edn. Com., 1990—96, chmn., 1995—96. Pres. St. Catherine of Siena Sch. Bd.; pres. and treas. Beverly Knoll Civic Assn.; mem. bd. dirs. New Orleans Legal Aid Corp., 1984—88; mem. bd. dirs., past chmn. New Orleans Pro Bono Project, 1995—2002. Mem.: St. Thomas More Catholic Lawyers Assn., ABA, La. State Bar Assn. (pres.-elect 2006—07, Pro Bono Publico award 2002), Jefferson Bar Assn. (pres. 1989—90), John C. Boutall Am. Inn of Ct. Office: Atty at Law 2551 Metairie Rd Metairie LA 70001 Office Phone: 504-838-8777. Office Fax: 504-838-9903.

DE LAURENTIIS, DINO, motion picture producer; b. Torre Annunziata, Italy, Aug. 8, 1919; came to U.S., 1973; s. Rosario Aurelio and Giuseppina (Salvatore) De L.; m. Silvana Mangano, July 17, 1949 (dec. Dec. 16, 1989); children: Veronica, Raffaella, Frederico, Francesca; m. Martha Schumacher, Apr. 17, 1990; children: Carolyna, Dina. Student high sch. and comml. sch., Centro Sperimentale di Cinematografia, Rome. Prin. De Laurentiis Entertainment Group Studios, Wilmington, N.C., 1983-89; prin. De Laurentiis Entertainment Group, Inc., 1986-88, De Laurentiis Entertainment Ltd., Australia, 1986-88; founder, prin. Dino De Laurentiis Comm. (formerly FTC/Film and TV Co.), 1988—. Purchased Embassy Pictures, 1985; formed De Laurentiis Entertainment Ltd., Australia, 1986. Mem. actor's sch., Exptl. Film Center, Rome, 1937-39, organized first film prodn. co., 1941; productions include Bitter Rice, 1952, Ulysses, 1955, War and Peace, 1956, La Strada, 1956 (Acad. award), Nights of Cabiria, 1957 (Acad. award), This Angry Age, 1958, The Tempest, 1959, Under Ten Flags, 1960, The Best of Enemies, 1962, Barabbas, 1962, Three Faces of a Woman (Soraya), 1964, The Bible, 1966, Barbarella, 1967, Anzio, 1967, Waterloo, 1970, Valachi Papers, 1972, The Stone Killer, 1973, (moved to N.Y. 1973), Serpico, 1974, Death Wish, 1974, Mandingo, 1975, Three Days of the Condor, 1975, Lipstick, 1976, Face to Face, 1976, Buffalo Bill and the Indians, 1976, The Shootist, 1976, King Kong, 1976, Orca, 1977, The Serpent's Egg, 1977, The White Buffalo, 1977, King of the Gypsies, 1978, The Great Train Robbery, 1978, The Brink's Job, 1979, Hurricane, 1979, Flash Gordon, 1980, Ragtime, 1981, Striking Back, 1982, Conan The Barbarian, 1982, The Dead Zone, 1983, Firestarter, 1984, The Bounty, 1984, Conan The Destroyer, 1984, Dune, 1984, Cat's Eye, 1985, Red Sonja, 1985, Year of the Dragon, 1985, Marie, 1985, Silver Bullet, 1985, Raw Deal, 1986, Maximum Overdrive, 1986, Tai-Pan, 1986, Blue Velvet, 1986, King Kong Lives, 1986, Manhunter, 1986, Trick or Treat, 1986, Crimes of the Heart, 1986, Date With an Angel, 1987, The Bedroom Window, 1987, From the Hip, 1987, Million Dollar Mystery, 1987, Traxx, 1987, Weeds, 1987, Rampage, 1987, Collision Course, 1987, Dracula's Widow, 1987, Pumpkinhead, 1987, Adult Education, 1987, Desperate Hours, 1990, Kuffs, Once Upon a Crime, 1992, Body of Evidence, 1993, Army of Darkness, 1993, Assassins, 1995, Unforgettable, 1996, Breakdown, 1997, U-571, 2000, Hannibal, 2001, Red Dragon, 2002, Hannibal Rising, 2007.*

DE LAURENTIIS, GIADA, chef; b. Rome, Aug. 22, 1970; m. Todd Thompson. Degree in Social Anthropology, UCLA, 1996. Tng. Le Cordon Bleu, Paris; chef Ritz Carlton Fine Dining Room, Spago, Beverly Hills; food stylist Food & Wine Mag., 2001; founder GDL Foods. Spokesperson Barilla; judge Next Food Network Star. Host Everday Italian, Food Network, 2003—, Behind the Bash, 2005—, Giada's Weekend Getaways, 2007—, (TV special) An Italian Christmas with Mario and Giada, 2004, Giada in Paradise, 2007; author: Everyday Italian, 2005, Giada's Family Dinners, 2006, Everyday Pasta, 2007; contbg. corr. (TV series) Today Show, 2006—.*

DELAURO, ROSA L., congresswoman; b. New Haven, Conn., Mar. 2, 1943; m. Stanley Greenberg; 3 children. Student, London Sch. Econs. & Polit. Sci., 1962-63; BA in History and Polit Sci. cum laude, Marymount Coll., 1964; MA in Internat. Politics, Columbia U., 1966. Tng. assoc. Community Progress Inc., New Haven, 1967-69; instr. in internat. rels. Albertus Magnus Coll., 1967-68; adminstrv. asst. Nat. Urban Fellows, 1969-72, asst. dir., dir., 1972-75; city coord. Carter-Mondale Presdl. Campaign, New Haven, 1976; exec. asst. Mayor Frank Logue, New Haven, 1976-77, campaign mgr., 1977; exec. asst., devel. adminstr. City of New Haven, 1977-79; campaign mgr. Chris Dodd for U.S. Senate, 1979-80, 86; adminstrv. asst. U.S. Senator Christopher J. Dodd, Washington, 1981-87; state dir. Mondale-Ferraro Presdl. Campaign, NJ, 1986; ptnr. DeLauro-Geller, 1987-88; regional dir. Dukakis for Pres. Campaign, NY, NJ, Conn., 1988; exec. dir. EMILY's List, 1989; mem. U.S. Congress from 3rd Conn. dist., 1991—; mem. house appropriations com. and budget com. Del. to Dem. Nat. Conv., 1984; bd. dirs. Pax Ams. Past pres. New Haven Arts Coun. Assoc. fellow Timothy Dwight Coll., Yale U.; recipient Leadership award Am. Com. on Italian Migration. Mem. Nat. Italian-Am. Found., Dem. Women for Progress. Democrat. Roman Cath. Office: US House of Reps 2262 Rayburn Ho Office Bldg Washington DC 20515-0703 also: District Office 59 Elm Street New Haven CT 06510*

DE LAVALLADE, CARMEN, dancer, choreographer; b. Los Angeles, Mar. 6, 1931; m. Geoffrey Holder, June 26, 1955; 1 child, Leo. Dancer Lester Horton Dance Theater, 1949—50, lead dancer, 1950—54; prima ballerina Met. Opera, 1956; prin. John Butler Dance Co., 1956; guest artist Alvin Ailey Dance Co.; ptnr. De Lavallade-Ailey Dance Co.; guest artist Am. Ballet Theatre, 1965; choreographer & performer-in-residence Yale Sch. Drama, 1970, prof.; mem. Yale Repertory Theater. Dancer The Face of Violence, Lester Horton Dance Co., A Drum is a Woman, 1956, Roots of the Blues, Alvin Ailey Dance Co., 1958, Blues Suite, 1962, (Broadway plays) House of Flowers, 1954, (ballets) Flight, John Butler Dance Co., 1956, The Four Marys, Am. Ballet Theater, 1965, The Frail Quarry, 1965, (Operas) Amahl and the Night Visitors, 1957, Aida, Met. Opera, 1956, Sampson & Delilah, 1956, Carmina Burana, 1959, (films) Lydia Bailey, 1952, The Egyptian, 1954, Carmen Jones, 1954, (TV films) L'Enfance du Christ, 1964, choreographer Sweet Bitter Love, Alvin Ailey Am. Dance Theater, 2000, (Operas) Porgy & Bess, Met. Opera, 1990, Die Meistersinger, 1990, Rusalka, 1993; actor: (films) Odds Against Tomorrow, 1959, Lone Star, 1996, Big Daddy, 1999, The Other Brother, 2002, The Hours, 2002, Stone Mansion, 2004; (TV films) The Trial of Standing Bear, 1988, Blue Bayou, 1990; (plays) Othello, Death of a Salesman. Recipient Dance Mag. award, 1966, Clarence Bayfield award, Actors Equity, Capezio Dance award, 2007.*

DE LA VIÑA-SIERRA, DIANA MARIA, music educator; b. Holguin, Cuba, Apr. 22, 1956; arrived in U.S., 1962; d. Santos Rafael de la Viña and Ana Julia Viamonte-de la Viña; 1 child, Michael Arles. BA in Music Edn., Kean U., Union, NJ, 1980; cert., Villa Walsh Acad., 2005. Cert. piano tchr. Nat. Guild Piano Tchrs., 2003. Tchr. music Uruguay USA Sch., Elizabeth, NJ, 1983—86; tchr. voice, piano Newark Cmty. Sch. Arts, 1983—94, chmn. music dept., 1993—; head dept. music St. Hedwig's Sch., Elizabeth, NJ, 1997—2002; chmn. Spanish dept. Blessed Sacrament Sch., 2003—04; chmn. Dept. Music and Spanish St. Mary's Sch., 2004—. Author: (song) Danza Cubana. Head cultural affairs Pro Cuba Orgn., Elizabeth, 1990—94. Recipient Piano Competition First prize, Cath. Youth Orgn., 1969, Excellence in Tchg. award, Newark (N.J.) Cmty. Sch. Arts, 1993, Don Galaor award, La Tribuna newspaper; scholar, Villa Walsh Acad., 1971. Home: 151 Morristown Rd Elizabeth NJ 07208-1315

DELAWARE, RICHARD RAYMOND, mathematician, educator; b. Woonsocket, RI, Dec. 30, 1951; s. Raymond Rene and Lucille Hattie Delaware. BS cum laude, Santa Clara U., Calif., 1974; MA, U. Kans., Lawrence, 1977; PhD, U. Mo., Kans. City, 2000. Tchr. math. 9-12 Mo., 2002, tchr. gifted and talented tchr. K-12 Mo., 2003. Grad. asst. U. Kans., Lawrence, 1974—77; lectr. U. Mo., Kans. City, 1981—84, tchg. asst. Physics dept., 1983—84, math. coord. Math. and Physics Inst., 1984—2003, vis. instr., 1984—2003, assoc. clin. prof., 2004—. Assoc. dir., Math. and Physics Inst. U. Mo., Kans. City, 1998—2003; spkr. in field. Author: (videotape course) VSI Coll. Algebra, VSI Calculus I; contbg. editor: (newsletter) Math. and Physics Newsletter; contbr. scientific papers to profl. jours. Recipient Superior Tchg. Award, Sch. of Grad. Studies U. Mo. Kans. City, 1984, Ednl. Ptnrs. award, INROADS, Inc., 1989, Dean's award Outstanding Tchg., Sch. of Arts and Sciences U. Mo. Kans. City, 1995, Founding Faculty Mem. award, Math. and Physics Inst., 2003; U.G. Mitchell scholar, Dept. Math. U. Kans., 1975—77. Mem.: Gifted Assn. of Mo., Kans. City Area Tchrs. of Math., Mo. Coun. Tchrs. of Math., Nat. Coun. Tchrs. of Math., Math. Assn. of Am., Am. Math. Soc., Am.-French Geneal. Soc. (life), Alpha Sigma Nu SJ, Pi Mu Epsilon. Avocations: paleoanthropology, family genealogy, technical theatre. Office: U MO Kans City 5100 Rockhill Road Kansas City MO 64110 Business E-Mail: delawarer@umkc.edu.

DELAWIE, HOMER TORRENCE, retired architect; b. Santa Barbara, Calif., Sept. 24, 1927; s. Fred Ely and Gertrude (Torrence) D.; m. Billie Carol Sparlin (div. 1969); m. Ethel Ann Mallinger, Sept. 3, 1973; children: Gregory, Claire, Shandell, Tracy, Stephanie, Scott. BS in Archtl. Engring., Calif. Poly. State U., San Luis Obispo, 1951. Registered architect, Calif. Pvt. practice architecture, San Diego, 1958-61; founder, CEO Delawie Wilkes Rodrigues Barker & Bretton Assocs., San Diego, 1961—98, ret., 1998, ptnr. emeritus, 1998—. Mem. Planning Commn., City of San Diego, 1969-82; adv. bd. KPBS Pub. TV. Recipient Award of Merit Calif. chpt. Am. Inst. Planners, Lay Citizens award Phi Delta Kappa, 1975, award Calif chpt. Am. Planning Assn., 1982; named Disting. Alumnus, Calif. Poly. State U., 1972. Fellow AIA (over 60 design awards 1973—, Architects Svc. award Calif. coun. 1973, spl. award San Diego chpt. 1978, Pub. Svc. award Calif. coun. 1981, Outstanding Firm award San Diego chpt. 1986, Calif. Coun. Lifetime Achievement award 1998). Democrat. Home: 2749 Azalea Dr San Diego CA 92106-1132 Office: Delawie Wilkes Rodriques Barker & Bretton Assocs 2265 India St San Diego CA 92101-1725

DELAY, LARRY GENE, science educator, photographer; b. Springfield, Ill., Oct. 18, 1942; s. Charles A. and Frances V. DeLay; m. Cheryl Pyle, Apr. 2, 1966; 1 child, Brett Patrick. MAT in Ecology, Truman U., Kirksville, Mo., 1971. Cert. tchr. k-12 Ill. Tchr. biology Naperville Dist. 203, Ill., 1965—94; instr. anatomy and physiology Waubonsee CC, Sugar Grove, 1994—. Contbr. photo stories to automotive jours. Mem.: Human Anatomy and Physiology Soc., Nat. Assn. Biology Tchrs. Avocations: sports, automobiles, music, reading, German shepherds. Home: 22 Riverwood Ln Oswego IL 60543 Office: Waubonsee CC Waubonsee Dr Sugar Grove IL 60554

DELAY, TOM (THOMAS DALE DELAY), former congressman; b. Laredo, Tex., Apr. 8, 1947; s. Charles Ray and Maxine (Wimbish) DeL.; m. Christine Ann Furrh, Aug. 26, 1967; 1 child, Danielle BS, U. Houston, 1970. Gen mgr. Redwood Chem., Houston, 1970-73; owner, operator Albo Pest Control, Stafford, Tex., 1973-84, pres., 1984—; mem. Tex. State Ho. Reps., Austin, 1979-84, US Congress from 22d Tex. dist., 1985—2006, majority whip, 1995—2002, majority leader, 2002—05. Mem. Grace Caucus, Washington, US-Mexico Interparliamentary Del., Washington, 1985-86, Republican study com. Sci. and Tech. Task Force, 1985-86, mem. Rep. research com. Regulatory Reform Caucus, 1985-86. Co-author (with Stephen Mansfield): No Retreat, No Surrender: One American's Fight, 2007. Bd. dirs. Youth Opportunities Unltd., Houston; precinct chmn. Republican Party, Simonton, Tex., 1974-78; Gala chmn. Ft. Bend County "War on Drugs" Coalition, 1987; adv. bd. CloseUp Found.; active drug abuse and rehab. ctr. Odyssey House, Tex; adv. bd. Joint Ctr. for Urban Mobility Research, Houston; mem. Ft. Bend Arts Adv. Council. Recipient Legislator of Yr. award Tex. Assn. to Improve Distbn., 1983; ABC's Outstanding Legislator for the 67th Session Leadership award Young Conservatives of Tex., 1984; Nat. Security Leadership award Coalition Peace Through Strength, Washington, 1985-90; Freshman Class Rep., U.S. House GOP Com. on Coms., Washington, 1985-86; Golden Bulldog award Watchdog of the Treasury , 1985-90. Mem. Congl. Leaders for a Balanced Budget, Greater Houston Pest Control Assn. (former pres.), Tex. Pest Control Assn. (bd. dirs.), Southwest Energy Council, Am. Legis. Exchange Council, Nat. Conf. State Legislators, Fort Bend County Fair Assn. (life) Clubs: Sweetwater Country (Sugar Land, Tex.); Fort Bend 100. Lodges: Rotary. Republican. Baptist. Avocations: hunting, skiing, golf.

DELBANCO, NICHOLAS FRANKLIN, language educator, writer; b. London, Aug. 27, 1942; came to U.S., 1948; s. Kurt and Barbara Gabriele Delbanco; m. Elena Greenhouse, Sept. 12, 1970; children: Francesca Barbara, Andrea Katherine. AB, Harvard U., 1963; MA, Columbia U., 1966. Mem. faculty Bennington (Vt.) Coll., 1966-85; prof. English Williams Coll., Williamstown, Mass., 1983, Skidmore Coll., Saratoga Springs, NY, 1984; Robert Frost Collegiate prof. English U. Mich., Ann Arbor, 1985—2006, disting. prof., 2006—. Dir. MFA in writing program U. Mich., 1985—03; vis. prof. Iowa U. Writer's Workshop, Iowa City, 1980; vis. adj. prof. Columbia U., N.Y.C., 1981, 96-98; founding dir. Bennington Writing Workshops, 1978-85; chair fiction panel Nat. Book Awards, N.Y.C., 1997; vis. fellow Woodrow Wilson Nat. Found., Princeton, N.J., 1981—. Author: Group Portrait: Conrad, Crane, Ford, James & Wells, 1983, The Writer's Trade, 1990, Running in Place: Scenes from the South of France, 1991, In the Name of Mercy, 1995, Old Scores, 1997, What Remains, 2000, Sincerest Form, 2003, Vagabonds, 2004, Spring and Fall, 2006, others; editor: Stillness and Shadows, 1985, Speaking of Writing, 1990, Bernard Malamud on Life and Art, 1996, others. Mem. ant. adv. bd. Writers in Schs. PEN Faulkner, Washington, 2000—; mem. governing bd. Mich. Journalism Fellows Program, 1990—; mem. Arts Am. U.S. Info. Agy., Washington, 1992. Fellow Nat. Endowment for Arts, 1973, 82, J.S. Guggenheim Meml. Found., 1980; named Mich. Author of Yr., Mich. Assn. Librs., 2002. Fellow Internat. Am. Studies and Lang. Faculty Salzburg; mem. Authors Guild, Authors League, PEN, Century Assn., Signet Soc., Phi Beta Kappa. Office: U Mich Hopwood Rm Angell Hall Ann Arbor MI 48109 Office Phone: 734-764-6296. Business E-Mail: delbanco@umich.edu.

DELBENE, KURT, information technology executive; B in Indsl. Engring., U. Ariz.; MS, Stanford U.; MBA, U. Chgo. Software devel., systems engr. AT&T Bell Lab.; mgmt. cons. McKinsey & Co.; with Microsoft Corp., Redmond, Wash., 1992—, group mgr., systems divsn., group program mgr., Exchange client and schedule+, gen. mgr., Outlook, messaging and personal info. mgmt. application, v.p. authoring & collaboration svc. group, corp. v.p., office bus. platform group, 2006—. Office: Microsoft Corp One Microsoft Way Redmond WA 98052-7329

DEL BONO, IRENE LILLIAN (IRENE STONE GUILD DEL BONO), lawyer; b. Milford, Mass., May 27, 1949; d. Roy Prescott and Sara Lucretia (Snyer) Stone; children: Gregory Howe Jr., Daniel David. BS in Criminal Justice, Westfield State Coll., 1989; JD, Boston U., 1991, MA in Hist. Preservation, 1992. Bar: Mass. 1991, U.S. Supreme Ct. 1996, U.S. Dist. Ct. Mass. 2000. Asst. atty. gen. Office Atty. Gen., Boston, 1992-2001; atty. Irene Delbono, 2001—; chief environ. program State Mass. Dept. Conservation and Recreation, 2001—04, chief encroachment program, 2004—. Active Framingham Hist. Soc. Mem. Mass. Bar Assn. (property law sect.), Mass. Conveyancer's Assn., Nat. Trust Hist. Preservation, N.E. Legal Preservation Network. Avocations: writing, bicycling, hiking, internet. Home: 24 Nern St Natick MA 01760-3527 Office: State Mass Dept Conservation and Recreation Real Property Divsn 251 Causeway St Boston MA 02114 Office Phone: 508-655-8740. Personal E-mail: delbonolandlaw@hotmail.com.

DELBOURGO, JOËLLE LILY, publishing executive; b. Alexandria, Egypt, Sept. 10, 1953; arrived in US, 1960; d. Edward Daniel and J. Andrée (Domergue) D.; m. Lewis Foster Patton, May 16, 1976 (div. May 1996); children: Caroline Emily, Andrew David. Student, Vassar Coll., 1970-72; BA, Williams Coll., 1974; MA, Columbia U., 1975. Editorial asst. Bantam Books, NYC, 1975-76, asst. editor, 1976-78, assoc. editor, 1978-80; sr. editor Ballantine Del Rey Fawcett Books div. Random House Inc., NYC, 1980-81; exec. editor Ballantine Del Rey Fawcett Ivy Books div. Random House Inc., NYC, 1981-83, editor-in-chief, 1983-86, v.p., editor-in-chief trade books, 1986-89, editor-in-chief hard cover books and trade paperback, 1990-95; v.p., editl. dir. HarperCollins, NYC, 1996, sr. v.p., assoc. publ., editor-in-chief, 1997-99; CEO, pres. Joëlle Delbourgo Assocs. Inc. Lit. Mgmt., Pub. Cons., 1999—. Columbia faculty fellow, 1974—75. Mem.: Women's Media Group (bd. dirs., treas.), Phi Beta Kappa. Office: 516 Bloomfield Ave Ste 5 Montclair NJ 07042 Home Phone: 973-731-9729; Office Phone: 973-783-6800. Business E-Mail: info@delbourgo.com.

DEL CALVO, JORGE A., lawyer; b. Havana, Cuba, Oct. 13, 1955; BA with distinction, Stanford Univ., 1977; MA Latin Am. history, UCLA, 1978; MA pub. policy, Harvard Univ., 1981, JD cum laude, 1981; ND, Univ. Philippines, 1982. Bar: Calif. 1982. Assoc. Pillsbury Winthrop Shaw Pittman, Palo Alto, Calif., 1982—90, ptnr., 1990—. Bd. dirs. Berkeley Process Control; mem. adv. bd. Linklore LLC. Editor (coord.): Venture Capital & Pub. Offering Negotiation. Mem.: ABA, HispanicNet, Asian Multicultural Assn., Indus Entrepreneurs, Phi Beta Kappa. Office: Pillsbury

Winthrop Shaw Pittman 2475 Hanover St Palo Alto CA 94304-1114 Office Phone: 650-233-4537. Office Fax: 650-233-4545. Business E-Mail: jorge@pillsburylaw.com.

DEL CAMPO, MARTIN BERNARDELLI, architect; b. Guadalajara, Mex., Nov. 27, 1922; came to U.S., 1949; s. Salvador and Margarita (Bernardelli) Del C.; m. Laura Zaikowska, May 25, 1945; children: Felicia (dec.), Margarita, Mario. BA, Colegio Frances Morelos, Mexico City, 1941; archtl. degree, Univ. Nat. Autonoma de Mexico, Mexico City, 1948. Ptnr. Del Campo & Fruiht, architects, Santa Rosa, Calif., 1955-56, Del Campo & Clark, San Francisco, 1957-63; mgr. Hotel Victoria, Oaxaca, Mex., 1964-67; pres. Gulli-Del Campo, architects, San Francisco, 1968-70; ptnr. Del Campo Assocs., San Francisco, 1977-81. Lectr. archtl. design Coll. Environmental Design, U. Calif., Berkeley, 1973-74. Archtl. works include: Calif. Med. Facility South, Vacaville, Phillip Burton Fed. Bldg. remodeling, San Francisco, Hall of Justice, San Francisco, San Francisco Airport Internat. Terminal, Mex. Heritage Gardens, San Jose, Four Seasons Tower, San Francisco. Mem. AIA. Address: Del Campo & Maru Architects Inc 1504 Bryant St # 301 San Francisco CA 94103 Office: 1601 Shrader St San Francisco CA 94117-4253 Home Phone: 415-664-4379; Office Phone: 415-860-4379. Business E-Mail: martin@dcmsf.com.

DELCAMPO, ROBERT GREGORY, education educator; b. Ann Arbor, Mich., Aug. 6, 1977; s. Robert Louis and Diana Sammons DelCampo; m. Stephanie Guerra, May 27, 2001. Bachelors, U. N.Mex., 1999, MBA, 2000; PhD, Ariz. State U., 2004. Asst. prof. U. New Mex., Albuquerque, 2004—. Mem.: APA, Acad. Mgmt., Phi Beta Kappa. Office: Univ New Mex 1 University Albuquerque NM 87131-0001 Office Phone: 505-277-0018.

DEL CHIARO, MARIO ALDO, art historian, archaeologist, etruscologist, educator; b. San Francisco, Apr. 22, 1925; s. Casimiro and Elisa (Bianchi) A.; m. Christina Falkman, Sept. 13, 1958; children: Kari Louise, Marco Claudio, Paola Christina. AB, U. Calif.-Berkeley, 1950, MA, 1951, PhD, 1956. Teaching asst. art history U. Calif. at Berkeley, 1950-51, 55, Univ. fellow in art, 1951-52; John Wesley Britton traveling fellow in classics, 1952-53; Met. Mus. Art fellow NYC, 1953-54; grantee Am. Numismatic Soc. Seminar, 1954; faculty U. Calif., Santa Barbara, 1956—, prof. art history, 1966-94, prof. emeritus, 1994; chmn. dept. U. Calif.-Santa Barbara, 1969-72; Mem. archeol. staff for excavations in Turkey, Yugoslavia, Egypt, Sicily and Italy; dir. U. Calif.-Santa Barbara archeol. expdns. to, Tuscany, Italy. Author: The Genucilia Group: A Class of Etruscan Red-Figured Plates, 1957, Etruscan Red-Figured Vase-Painting at Caere, 1974, The Etruscan Funnel Group: A Tarquinian Red-Figured Fabric, 1974; exhbn. catalogues Greek Art in Private Collections of Southern California, 1963, Etruscan Art from West Coast Collections, 1967, Roman Art in West Collections, 1973, Etruscan Ghiaccio Forte, 1976, Re-exhumed Etruscan Bronzes, 1981; Classical Art, Sculpture in the Santa Barbara Mus. Art, 1984; editor: Corinthiaca, Studies in Honor of Darrell A. Amyx, 1986; contbr. book revs. and articles to profl. jours. Decorated Cavaliere Ufficiale Order of Merit (Italy); recipient Internat. award in archaeology, Tutto Maremma, Italy, 1990; grantee, Am. Philos. Soc., 1957, 1975, NEH, 1977; Prix de Rome fellow, Am. Acad. in Rome, 1958—60, Sr. Faculty fellow, Humanities Inst. U. Calif. at Berkeley, 1967—68. Mem. Archeol. Inst. Am., Explorers Club, Istituto Studi Etruschi ed Italici, Florence, Deutsches Archäologisches Inst., Istituto Archeologico Rome, European Acad. Scis. and Art, Salzburg, Phi Beta Kappa. Home: Hope Ranch 1376 Estrella Dr Santa Barbara CA 93110-2418

DELEHANT, JOSEPH HENRY, lawyer; b. New Haven, May 12, 1950; s. Raymond Francis and Lillian East (Tansey) D.; m. Marietta Barnes, Mar. 2, 1985; 1 child, Elisabeth Louise. AB magna cum laude, Harvard U., Cambridge, Mass., 1972; JD, U. Chgo., 1976. Bar: DC 1976, US Ct. Appeals (D.C. cir.) 1976, Mass. 1980, US Ct. Appeals (1st cir.) 1983. Dep. gen. counsel Gen. Dynamics Corp., Quincy, Mass., 1981-85; sr. counsel GTE Precision Materials, Danvers, Mass., 1986-93; gen. counsel Osram Sylvania Global Tungsten Products, Automotive Lighting, Danvers, Mass., 1993. Adj. prof. law So. Mass. Sch. of Law, Fall River, 1982-83. Contbr. articles to profl. jours. Mem.: Signet Soc., Harvard Club NY. Roman Catholic. Avocations: hiking, tennis, photography, films. Office Phone: 978-750-2479.

DELEHANTY, SUZANNE, museum director; b. Worcester, Mass., July 18, 1944; d. George B. and Catherine (Powers) D. BA with honors, Skidmore Coll., 1965; student, U. Pa., 1966-68. Curatorial asst. Inst. Contemporary Art, Phila., 1968-71, dir., 1971-78, Neuberger Mus., Purchase, NY, 1978-88, Contemporary Arts Mus., Houston, 1989—93; ind. curator and cons. NYC, 1994—95; dir. Miami Art Mus., 1995—. Mem. adv. coun. The Art Mus. at Princeton U., 1984—. Author: Agnes Martin, 1973, Cy Twombly and Video Art, 1975, George Segal/Environments, 1976, Fred Sandback/Sculpture, 1991. Mem. visual arts panel Tex. Commn. on Arts, 1990-91. Mem. Assn. Art Mus. Dirs., Urban League of Greater Miami. Office: Miami Art Mus 101 W Flagler St Miami FL 33130-1504 E-mail: sdeleha@miamidade.gov.

DE LEMOS, JAMES ANDREW, cardiologist, researcher; b. Riverside, Calif., Dec. 16, 1965; s. Robert and Anna de Lemos; m. Zena Perez, May 30, 1992; children: Nicholas, Mikaela, Benjamin. BA, U. Tex., Austin, 1987; MD, Harvard U., Boston, 1992. Diplomate in cardiology Am. Bd. Internal Medicine, 1999. Intern, resident, chief resident internal medicine U Tex. Southwestern Med. Ctr., Dallas, 1992—96, assoc. prof. medicine, 2000—; cardiology fellow Brigham & Women's Hosp., Boston, 1996—99. Dir. critical care unit Parkland Meml. Hosp., Dallas, 2000—; dir.,cardiology fellowship tng. program U. Tex. Southwestern Med. Ctr., 2005—. Contbr. more than 100 articles to med. pubs. Fellow: Am. Coll. Cardiology. Roman Catholic. Avocation: sports. Office: UT Southwestern Med Ctr 5909 Harry Hines Blvd HA 9133 Dallas TX 75390-9047 Office Phone: 214-645-7500.

DELEON, CHARLES, lawyer; married; 3 children. BA, George Mason U.; JD, George Washington U., 1995. Counsel, fed. contracts Electronic Data Systems Corp.; sr. counsel PSINet; gen. counsel CyBiz, Inc.; dep. gen. counsel GTSI Corp., Chantilly, Va., 2001—04, gen. counsel, corp. sec., 2005—. Former military intelligence officer US Army. Mem.: ABA, Va. State Bar. Office: GTSI Corp 3901 Stonecraft Blvd Chantilly VA 20151-1010 Office Phone: 703-502-2000.

DE LEON, LIDIA MARIA, magazine editor; b. Havana, Cuba, Sept. 10, 1957; d. Leon J. and Lydia (Diaz Cruz) de L. BA in Communications cum laude, U. Miami, Coral Gables, Fla., 1979. Staff writer Miami Herald, Fla., 1978-79; editorial asst. Halsey Pub. Co., Miami, 1980-81, assoc. editor, 1981, editor, 1981—, editor Delta Sky mag., 1983-95. Mem. Am. Soc. Mag. Editors, Am. Assn. Travel Editors, Golden Key, Sigma Delta Chi. Roman Catholic. Avocation: tennis. Office: 12550 Biscayne Blvd # 212 Miami FL 33181

DELEON, RUSS, Internet company founder; b. Sacramento, Calif., 1965; m. Ruth Parasol, 2003; 3 children. BA in Philosophy, Univ. Calif. Berkeley, 1987; JD, Harvard Law Sch., 1992. Exec. fell. Office of Governor George Deukmejian; assoc. atty., bus. dept. Morrison & Foerster, San Francisco; co-founder, cons. PartyGaming, 2001. Co-founder, gen. counsel San Francisco Multimedia Development Group; co-founder Evolve Software, 1995—2001, v.p. fin. Admin., gen. counsellor, treas., sec., 1995—. Named one of Forbes Richest Americans, 2006. Office: PartyGaming 711 Europort Gibraltar

DE LEON, SYLVIA A., lawyer; b. Corpus Christi, Tex., Mar. 2, 1950; m. Lynn R. Coleman; 3 children. BA, Briarcliff Coll., 1972; JD, U. Tex., 1976. Bar: Tex. 1976, DC 1977. Ptnr., founding mem. public law and policy practice group and mem. mgmt. com. Akin, Gump, Strauss, Hauer & Feld LLP, Washington. Adj. prof. law Georgetown U. Law Ctr., 1988-90; bd. dirs. (pres. apptd. senate confirmed) Amtrak, Nat. Railroad Passenger Corp., 1994—, vice chmn. 2003-, chair corp. strategy com. Bd. trustees U. Tex. Law Sch. Found. 2002-, U. Tex. Law Assn., 1985-89, 92-96, 2000-03, U. Tex. Devel. Bd., 1996—, bd. dirs. exec. com. Washington Ballet, 2001-; coord. issues transp. Clinton-Gore Presdl. Transition Team, 1992; presdl. appointee Nat. Commn. Ensure Strong Competitive Airline Industry, 1993, White House Conf. on Travel and Tourism. Mem. Bar Assn. DC, State Bar Tex. (chmn. fed. law and regulations com. 1984-87), Nat. Civil Aviation Rev. Commn. Office: Akin Gump Strauss Hauer & Feld Rm 1214 1333 New Hampshire Ave NW Washington DC 20036-1564 Business E-Mail: sdeleon@akingump.com.

DELFFS, DUDLEY J., writer, educator; b. Sewanee, Tenn., Nov. 27, 1964; s. Dudley Julian and Norma (Thompson) D.; m. Dorothy Kilpatrick Scruggs, May 14, 1989; children: Mary Elise, Annie Kilpatrick. BA in English, U. Tenn., 1987, MA in English, 1989; MA in Counseling, Colo. Christian U., 1992. Tech. writer, rschr. Energy, Environ. Resource Ctr., Knoxville, Tenn., 1990-91; instr. English U. Tenn., Knoxville, Tenn., 1988-91, Colo U., Lakewood, 1991-96; counseling intern Colo. Christian U., Morrison, 1993-94, asst. prof. English, 1996—; fiction editor Water-Brook Press (divsn. of Random House), Colorado Springs, Colo., v.p. and editor-in-chief, 2005—. Author: (novels) Forgiving August, 1993, The Martyr's Chapel, 1998, The Judas Tree, 1999; (non-fiction) Repentant Heart, 1995, Prayer Centered Life, 1997, Mastering Money: A Pilgrimage Small Group Guide, 1998, Seeking God's Will, 1998, Balm in Gilead: Healing for the Repentent Heart, 2002; contbr. poetry and short stories to lit. mags. Recipient Scholastic Press Poetry award Columbia U., 1986, award Fiction Editor, Mars Hill review. Mem. Nat. Coun. Tchrs. English, Am. Counseling Assn., Assembly on Lit. for Adolescents, Colo. Lang. Arts Soc., Colo. Authors' League. Avocations: mountain biking, hiking, fishing, movies and film, travel. Office Phone: 719-590-4999. Office Fax: 719-590-8977.

DELFINO, JOSEPH JOHN, environmental engineering sciences educator; b. Port Chester, NY, 1941; s. John J. and Frances C. Delfino; m. Dorothy Delfino; children: Janelle, Justin. BS in Chemistry, Holy Cross Coll., 1963; MS in Chemistry, U. Idaho, 1965; PhD in Civil and Environ. Engrng. & Water Chemistry, U. Wis., 1968. From instr. to assoc. prof. chemistry USAF Acad., Colorado Springs, Colo., 1968-72; sect. head, tech. mgr. IBT & Nalco Environ. Sci., Northbrook, Ill., 1972-74; sect. head environ. scis. Wis. State Lab. Hygiene, Madison, 1974-82; from asst. prof. to assoc. prof. U. Wis., Madison, 1974-80, assoc. dir. water resources ctr., 1977-78, prof. civil and environ. engring., 1980-82; prof. environ. engring. sci. U. Fla., Gainesville, 1982—, affiliate prof. chemistry, 1990—, chmn. dept. environ. engring. sci., 1990—99, interim chmn., 2002—03, affiliate prof. natural resources and environment, 1994—, interim dir. Ctr. for Wetlands and Water Resources, 1995. Writer, co-originator, chief tech. advisor documentary Fla. Water Story, Sta. WEDU-TV, Tampa, Fla.; assoc. editor Jour. Am. Water Resources Assn., 2004—; contbr. articles on water chemistry, environ. scis. and engring. to profl. publs. Mem. Citizens Environ. Quality Coun., Northbrook, Ill., 1972-74; mem. Mercury Tech. Adv. Com., State of Fla., 1991-93; mem. Alachua County Air Quality Commn., Fla., 1999; mem. T.M.D.L. tech. adv. com. Fla. Dept. Environ. Protection, 1999-00; mem. Water Mgmt. Com., Gainesville, 2006—. Capt. USAF, 1968-72. Recipient Pub. Svc. award Univs. Coun. on Water Resources, 1990. Fellow AAAS; mem. Am. Chem. Soc. (exec. com. environ. chem. divsn. 1973-76, editor Envirofacs environ. chem. divsn. 1973-76, student awards com. environ. chem. divsn. 1995-97, com. on environ. improvement 1998-01, Cert. of Merit environ. chem. divsn. 1991), Nat. Assn. State U. and Land Grant Colls. (ecology sect., exec. com. 1998-01), Assn. Environ. Engrs. and Sci. Profs., Am. Water Resources Assn., Fla. Acad. Scis. Office: U Fla Dept Environ Engring Scis PO Box 116450 Gainesville FL 32611-6450

DEL FORNO, ANTON, classical guitarist, recording artist, composer, educator; b. Dumont, NJ, Aug. 17, 1950; s. Vito and Mildred (Casio) Del F. MusB, Mannes Coll. Music, NYC, 1972. Musical debut Concrgebouw Hall, Holland, 1979; tchr. St. John's U., NYC, 1973-75; pvt. tchr. N.Y. and N.J., 1975—. Performer, lectr. numerous colls. and univs., 1973—. Debut Carnegie Recital Hall, N.Y., 1972, Concertgebouw Hall, Holland, 1979, Wigmore Hall, London, 1983, Alice Tully Hall, N.Y., 1983; composer mus. songs; sound recs. include Christmas Gifts, 1983, Anton Del Forno in Concert, Part I, 1985, Part II, 1988, Del Forno Plays Villa-Lobos, 1990, Del Forno Plays Del Forno, 2002; composer (guitar orchestra) The Flirtation Concerto, 2006. Mem. Broadcast Music, Inc. Roman Catholic. Avocation: vintage automobile collecting. Office: Legondary Artists Corner PO Box 362 New York NY 10113-0362 E-mail: antondelforno@att.net.

DELFS, ANDREAS, conductor, musical director; b. Flensburg, Germany; m. Amy Delfs; 4 children. Grad., Hamburg Conservatory, 1981; MA, Juilliard Sch., 1984. Staff conductor Lüneburg Stadttheater; music dir. Hamburg U. Orch.; musical asst. Hamburg State Opera; guest conductor Bremen State Theater, 1981; dir. Pitts. Youth Symphony; resident condr. Pitts. Symphony, 1986-90; music dir. Orch. Suisse Jeunes, 1984-95, Bern Opera, 1991-94; conductor N.Y. City Opera, 1995-96; music dir. Milw. Symphony Orch., 1997—; gen. music dir. Hannover State Opera and Orch., 1995—2000; music dir., artistic cons. St. Paul Chamber Orch., 2001—04. Guest condr. Phila. Orch. at Carnegie Hall, 1998, London Philharm., 1997, Dallas Symphony Orch., 1997, Houston Symphony, 1996—98, Junge Deutsche Philharmoni, Germany, 1995—98, Bern Symphony Orch., Minn. Orch., Detroit Symphony, Rochester Philharm. Bruno Walter scholar, Juilliard Sch., Steinburg fellow, Pitts. Symphony. Office: Milwaukee Symphony 700 N Water St #700 Milwaukee WI 53202-4239*

DELFYETT, PETER, engineering educator; PhD, Grad. Sch. & U. Ctr. CUNY, 1988. Mem. tech. staff Bell Comm. Rsch.; joined Sch. of Optics and Ctr. for Rsch. and Edn. in Optics and Lasers (CREOL), U. Ctrl. Fla., 1993—; trustee chair prof. optics, electrical and computer engring. and physics U. Ctrl. Fla. Editor-in-chief IEEE Jour. of Selected Topics in Quantum Electronics, assoc. editor IEEE Photonics Technology Letters; contbr. articles for profl. jours. and conf. proceedings. Recipient Bellcore Synergy award, Bellcore award for Appreciation, Presdl. Early Career award for Scientists and Engrs., Nat. Sci. Found., Researcher of Yr., U. Ctrl. Fla., 1999, Black Engr. of Yr. award, 2000, Nguzo Saba award, 2001, Disting. Rsch. Prof. award, 2002, Pegasus award, 2002, Tech. Innovation award, 2003, Outstanding Black Profl. in Sci. award, Sci. Spectrum, 2005, Trailblazer award, 2006. Fellow: IEEE/LEOS (fmr. mem. bd. gov.), Optical Soc. Am. Achievements include 12 US Patents. Office: Coll Optics & Photonics: CREOL & FPCE U Ctrl Fla PO Box 162700 Office CREOL 272 Orlando FL 32816-2700 Office Phone: 407-823-6812. Business E-Mail: delfyett@creol.ucf.edu.

DELGADILLO, ROCKARD J. (ROCKY DELGADILLO), lawyer; b. LA, July 15, 1960; m. Michelle Delgadillo; children: Christian, Preston. BA with honors, Harvard U.; JD, Columbia U. Tchr., coach L.A. Unified Sch. Dist.; sr. atty. O'Melveny and Myers, LA; dir. bus. devel. Rebuild L.A.; dep. mayor econ. devel. City of L.A., city atty., 2001—, re-elected city atty., 2005. City Atty., LA, 2001—. Bd. dirs. Arnold's All-Stars, Para Los Niños, Cath. Big Bros., 1st AME Ch. Renaissance Program, Franklin HS Scholarship Found., Friends Jordan HS, Workforce L.A.; leader L.A. ann. salute to Latino Heritage Month, 1993—. Named Disting. Young Alumnus, Columbia U., 1998, Alumnus of the Yr., 2002; named an All-Am. Football Player; recipient medal of excellence, Columbia U., John F. Kennedy Award, LA County Dem. Party, 2002. Office: 800 City Hall E 200 N Main St Los Angeles CA 90012-4131 Office Phone: 213-978-8100.

DELGADO, ARISTH See DJ CRAZE

DELGADO, CARLOS JUAN, professional baseball player; b. Aguadilla, Mayaguez, PR, June 25, 1972; Catcher St. Catharines/NY-Penn League, 1989-91; first baseman Toronto Blue Jays, 1993—2004, Fla. Marlins, 2005, NY Mets, 2006—. Named to Am. League All-Star Team, 2000, 2003; recipient Silver Slugger award, 1999—2000, 2003, Player of the Yr. award, Sporting News, 2000, Hank Aaron award, 2000, Roberto Clemente award, 2006. Achievements include led Am. League in RBI's (145), 2003. Office: NY Mets 123 01 Roosevelt Ave Flushing NY 11368*

DELGADO, JANE, health policy executive, writer, psychologist; b. Havana, Cuba, June 17, 1953; d. Juan Lorenzo Delgado Borges and Lucilla Aurora Navarro Delgado; m. Mark A. Steo, May 15, 1999; 1 child, Elizabeth A. Steo. BA, SUNY, New Paltz, 1973; MA, NYU, 1975; MS, W. Averell Harrimann Sch., 1981; PhD in Clin. Psychology, SUNY, Stony Brook, 1981. Children's talent coord. Children's TV Workshop, 1973-75; rsch. asst. SUNY, Stony Brook, 1975-79; social sci. analyst U.S. Dept. HHS, 1979-83, health policy advisor, 1983-85; pres., CEO Nat. Alliance for Hispanic Health, 1985—; pvt. practice in psychology, 1979—. Bd. dirs. Nat. Health Coun., 1986—97, Carter Ctr. Mental Health Taskforce, 1991—2000, Patient Safety Inst., 2001—; trustee The Kresge Found, 1997—, Found. Child Devel. , 1989—97. Author: Salud! A Latina's Guide to Total Health, 1997, 2d edit., 2002. Bd. dir. Kresge Found., 1997—, Lovelace Respiratory Rsch. Inst., 2002—, Health Found. Am., 2003—, Adams Respiratory Therapeutics, 2007—. Named SUNY Alumna of Yr., 1993; recipient Surgeon Gen.'s award, 1992, Florence Kelley award, 2002, Health and Sci. Latina Excellence award, 1995, FDA Commr.'s Citation award, 2005, Hispanic Heritage Found. award, 2005; W. K. Kellogg Found. Nat. fellow, 1988, NIMH fellow, 1975—79. Office: Nat Alliance for Hispanic Health 1501 16th St NW Washington DC 20036-1401 Office Phone: 202-797-4321. Business E-Mail: jdelgado@hispanichealth.org.

DELGADO, JOAO, emergency physician, toxicologist; b. Sao Felipe, Cape Verde; s. Jose Soares and Maria Celeste Delgado; m. Danica Bostock, July 31, 1994; 1 child, Annelie Grace. AB, Brown U., Providence, 1993; MD, Dartmouth U., Hanover, NH, 1997. Diplomate Am. Bd. Emergency Medicine, 2002, Am. Bd. Med. Toxicology, 2004. Fellow Rocky Mountain Drug & Poison Ctr., Denver, 2001—03; rsch. dir. Hartford Hosp. Divsn. Emergency Medicine, Conn., 2006—. Contbr. articles to profl. jours. Physician, team leader for internat. med. relief efforts Christian Med. Fellowship, Nigeria, 2005. Mem.: Am. Coll. Med. Toxicology, Soc. Academic Emergency Medicine, Am. Coll. Emergency Medicine. Office: Hartford Hosp 80 Seymour St Hartford CT 06102 Office Phone: 860-545-4547.

DELGADO, RAMON LOUIS, theater educator, author, director, playwright, lyricist; b. Dec. 16, 1937; s. Eloy Vincent and Hildegard E. (Chapman) D. BA, Stetson U., 1959; MA, Baylor U., 1960; MFA, YAle U., 1967; PhD, So. Ill. U., 1976. Tchr. Lyman HS, Longwood, Fla., 1960-62; mem. faculty Chipola Jr. Coll., Marianna, Fla., 1962-64, Ky. Wesleyan Coll., 1967-72, Hardin-Simmons U., 1972-74, So. Ill. U., 1974-76, St. Cloud State U., Minn., 1976-78; prof. speech and theater Montclair State U., Upper Montclair, NJ, 1978—2003, prof. emeritus, 2005. Evaluator N.J. Teen Arts Festival, 1980, 81; judge Am. Theatre Assn. Coll. Theater Festival, 1980, 82, 83, 84, 85, N.J. Teen Galaxy Competition, 1984. Playwright: Waiting for the Bus, 1968, Once Below a Lighthouse, 1972, The Jerusalem Thorn, 1979, A Little Holy Water, 1983, Stones, 1983, The Flight of the Dodo, 1990, Remembering Booth, 1997, The Iron Corset, 1999, Consider the Phoenix, 2000; editor: The Best Short Plays, 1981-89; author: Acting with Both Sides of Your Brain, 1986; contbr. articles to profl. jours. Sec. Forest St. Manor Condo Assn., 1997-99; bd. dirs. 12 Miles West Theatre, 2000-2002. Recipient Samuel French Play award, 1966, U. Mo. Play award, 1971, 75, playwriting awards Am. Coll. Theatre Festival, 1976, 77, 78, Grand prize Music City Song Festival contest, 1988, 7 hon. mentions, 1989; Midwest Profl. Playwrights fellow, 1978; Ford Found. grantee, 1961; playwright-in-residence INTAR, 1980 Mem. Dramatists Guild, Assn. for Theatre in Higher Edn., Nat. Theatre Conf., Theta Alpha Phi, Phi Kappa Phi. Democrat. Home: 16 Forest St Apt 107 Montclair NJ 07042-3519

DELGADO, ROGER RODRIGUEZ, surgeon, educator; b. El Paso, Jan. 11, 1946; s. Roger R. and Eva (West) D.; m. Linda Susan Ferguson, Dec. 27, 1968; children: Jessica Lorraine, Nathan Roger. BA, U. Tex. El Paso, 1966; MD, U. Tex. Galveston, 1970. Diplomate Am. Bd. Surgery. Intern R.E. Thomason Horst, El Paso, 1970-71; resident surgery Naval Regional Med. Ctr., Portsmouth, Va., 1971-75, staff surgeon lt. comndr. Camp Pendleton, Calif., 1975-78; pvt. practice surgeon Sebastopol, Santa Rosa, Calif., 1978—. Assoc. clin. prof. U. Cal. San Francisco, 1978—; chief staff Palm Dr. Hosp., Sebastopol, 1980-81, bd. trustees, 1980-83, 90-94, dir. surg. svcs., 1996—. Contbr. articles to profl. jours. Master: ACS; mem.: Southwest Surgical Congress and Am. Soc. of Breast Surgeons, Soc. Am. Gastrointestinal Endoscopic Surgeons, Soc. Clin. Vascular Surgery, Beta Beta Beta. Roman Catholic. Avocations: skiing, biking. Personal E-mail: rrdelgado@wildblue.net.

DELGADO-COLON, AIDA M., federal judge; b. 1955; BA cum laude, U. PR, 1977; JD cum laude, Pontifical Cath. U. PR, 1980. Bar: PR 1980. Dir. investigations PR Gov.'s Adv. Bd. on Labor Policy, 1980-82; asst. fed. pub. defender, 1982—93; 1st asst. fed. pub. defender San Juan, 1992—93; magistrate judge US Dist. Ct. PR, San Juan, 1994—2006, dist. judge, 2006—. Mem. Fed. Bar Exam. Com., 1986—; mem. local rules com. US Dist. Ct. PR 1991—; chmn. interpreters & ct. reports com., 1994-96, mem. criminal justice act com., 1994-96, EEO coord., 1995-99, EDR coord., 1999—; adj. prof. Pontifical Cath. U. PR Sch. Law, 2003-04. Mem. Fed. Magistrate Judges Assn., Women Judges Assn., PR Bar Assn., Cath. U. PR Law Sch. Alumni Assn., Nat. Hispanic Bar Assn. Office: Clemente Ruiz-Nazario US Courthouse Office 470 150 Carlos Chardon St San Juan PR 00918-1703 Office Phone: 787-772-3196.*

DELGADO GUAY, MARVIN OMAR, internist, geriatrician; b. Guatemala City, Guatemala, Sept. 14, 1974; s. Julio Anibal Delgado Chang and Ana Concepcion Guay Barahona. MD, Francisco Marroquin U., Guatemala, 1999. Cert. Am. Bd. Internal Medicine. Med. staff Nuestra Senora Pilar, Pvt. Hosp., Guatemala City, 1999—2001; med. staff. med. care patients with hiv/aids Clinica Familiar Luis Angel Garcia, 2001—02; resident Michael Reese Hosp., Chgo., 2002—05; geriatrics fellowship Beth Israel Deaconess Med. Ctr., Harvard U., Boston, 2005—06; palliative care and symptom control fellowship U. Tex., MD Anderson Cancer Ctr., Houston, 2006—. Leader Cath. juvenile groups Cristo Rey Ch., Franciscan Congregation, Guatemala City, 1990—96. Recipient Most Oustanding Intern award, Michael Reese Hosp., 2002—03; fellow, Beth Israel Deaconess Med. Ctr., Harvard Med. Sch., Boston, 2005—06. Mem.: AMA (assoc.), ACP (assoc.), Am. Geriat. Soc. (assoc.). Avocation: guitar. Home Phone: 713-741-4084.

DELGAUDIO, JULIAN JOSEPH, history professor; b. Hollywood, Calif., Jan. 3, 1950; s. Salvatore and Esther Mary DelGaudio; m. Rosalinda C. Dosta, Sept. 15, 2001; m. Virginia V. Valencia, Dec. 19, 1970 (div. July 10, 1998); children: Mercedes DelGaudio Carlos DelGaudio, Carlos M.,

Mercedes E., John C. Dosta, Elizabeth R. Dosta. PhD in History, U. Calif., Irvine, 1986. Staff historian Space and Missile Ctr., El Segundo, Calif., 1988—91; prof. history Long Beach City Coll., Calif., 1991—. Adj. instr. Calif. State U., Long Beach, 1983—90; staff historian Air Force Ballistic Missile Office, San Bernardino, Calif., 1985—87; chief historian U.S. Air Force Inspection and Safety Ctr., San Bernardo, Calif., 1987—88; adj. instr. Calif. State U., Northridge. Author (prodr.): Intercultural Sensitivity, Eunice: A Captivity Simulation, In Search of Freedom: Navigating a Slave's Narrative. Mem. Historians Against the War, 2005—07. Grantee, Calif. C.C., Chancellor's Office, 2002—03. Mem.: ACLU, Orgn. Am. Historians. D-Liberal. Office: Long Beach City Coll 4901 E Carson St Long Beach CA 90808 Home Phone: 562-429-0472; Office Phone: 562-938-4680. Business E-Mail: jdelgaudio@lbcc.edu.

DELGROSSO, DOUGLAS G., manufacturing executive; m. Kimberly DelGrosso; 1 child, Elle Marie. BS in Mech. Engring., Lawrence Technol. U.; MBA, Mich. State U. Design engr. Lear Corp., 1984, dir. product engring., 1991, v.p. ops. GM divsn., 1995, v.p./pres. Chrysler divsn., 1995, v.p./pres. GM divsn., 1997, sr. v.p. GM divsn., 1998, sr. v.p. interior sys. group and seat trim divsn., 1999, sr. v.p./pres. N.Am. and S.Am. ops., 1999, sr. v.p. product focus group, 2000, exec. v.p. internat. ops., 2001, pres., COO Europe, Asia and Africa Southfield, Mich., 2002—04, pres. COO Ams., 2004—05, pres., COO, 2005—. Bd. trustees Lawrence Technol. U., Southfield, Mich. Recipient Young Leadership and Excellence award, Automotive Hall of Fame, 1995, 40 Under 40 award, Crain's Detroit Bus., 1997. Office: Lear Corp 21557 Telegraph Rd PO Box 5008 Southfield MI 48086-5008 Office Phone: 248-447-1500.*

DEL GUERCIO, LOUIS RICHARD MAURICE, surgeon, educator; b. NYC, Jan. 15, 1929; s. Louis and Hortense (Ardengo) Del G.; m. Paula Marie Helene de Vautibault, May 18, 1957; children: Louis, Francsca, Paul, Catherine, Maria, Michelle, Christopher, Anthony. BS, Fordham U., 1949; MD, Yale U., 1953. Diplomate Am. Bd. Surgery, Am. Bd. Thoracic Surgery. Intern Columbia-Presbyn. Med. Ctr., NYC, 1953—54; resident St Vincent's Hosp., NYC, 1954—58, Cleve. City Hosp., 1958—60; practice medicine specializing in thoracic surgery, 1960—; assoc. prof. Albert Einstein Coll. Medicine, NYC, 1966—70, prof. surgery, 1970—71, dir. Clin. Rsch. Ctr.-Acute, 1967—71; clin. prof. surgery NJ Coll. Medicine, Newark, 1971—76; prof. surgery NY Med. Coll., NYC, 1976—, chmn. dept., 1976—2001, emeritus prof. surgery, 2001—; chief surgery Westchester County Med. Ctr., 1976—2001. Mem. surg. study sect. NIH, 1970-74; mem. com. on shock NRC-NAS, 1969-71; merit rev. bd. VA, 1971-74; mem. health care tech. study sect. Dept. HHS, 1980-84; cons. Nat. Ctr. Health Svcs. Rsch., 1980-84, NY State Office Profl. Med. Conduct, 2004—; chmn. bd. dirs. Daltex Med. Scis., Inc.; cons. in field. Author: (with B.G. Clarke) Urology, 1956, The Multilingual Manual for Medical History Taking, 1972, (with S.G. Hershey, R. McConn) Septic Shock in Man, 1971; editor-in-chief Critical Care Monitor, 1980-85, Complications in Surgery, 1990—; contbr. articles to med. jours.; patentee in field. Bd. trustees Maria Fareri Children's Hosp., Westchester Med. Ctr., 2006—. With Mcht. Marine, 1946-47; with AUS, 1949-51; col. med. dept. USAR, 1990—. Recipient award in medicine Fordham U. Alumni Assn., 1974, Gold award Am. Acad. Pediat., 1973, Humanitarian award Boys' Towns of Italy, 1994; grantee Health Rsch. Coun. NY, 1965-71, NIH, 1962-71. Fellow ACS, Coll. of Critical Care Medicine, Am. Thoracic Soc.; mem. Am. Trauma Soc. (founder), Soc. Critical Care Medicine (founder, pres. 1976), Am. Surg. Assn., Am. Physiol. Soc., Soc. Univ. Surgeons, French Nat. Acad. Surgery, Equestrian Order of Holy Sepulchre Jerusalem, Yale U. Sch. Medicine Alumni Assn. (exec. com. 2001—); hon. police surgeon City of N.Y. Home: 14 Pryer Ln Larchmont NY 10538-4021 Office: NY Med Coll Dept Surgery Valhalla NY 10595 Office Phone: 914-834-8265. Business E-Mail: lou@delguercio.com. *Adaptability and the determination of what is possible are the keys to personal success and contentment.*

DELHOMME, JAKE CHRISTOPHER, professional football player; b. Jan. 10, 1975; m. Keri Delhomme; 1 child. Grad., U. Louisiana-Lafayette. Quarterback Frankfurt Galaxy (NFL Europe), 1999, New Orleans Saints, 1999—2002, Carolina Panthers, 2003—. Named to NFC Pro Bowl Team, 2005. Achievements include being a member of World Bowl Champion Frankfurt Galaxy, 1999; led Carolina Panthers to their first Super Bowl appearance, Super Bowl XXXVIII, 2004. Office: c/o Carolina Panthers 800 South Mint Street Charlotte NC 28202

DELI, ANNE TYNION, retail executive; b. Milw., Apr. 18, 1956; m. Steven F. Deli; 2 children. BA in History and French, Georgetown U., 1978. Acct. exec. Dancer Fitzgerald Sample, NYC, 1978—80; acct. supr. Grey Advt., NYC, 1980—82; v.p. Wells Rich Greene, NYC, 1982—84; sr. v.p. Lawrence Charles Free, NYC, 1984—86; prin. Anspach Grossman Portugal, NYC, 1986—88; sr. v.p. Siegel & Gale, NYC, 1988—93; v.p., global mktg. Harley-Davidson, Inc., Milw., 1993—95; pres., founder North River Strategies, Milw./Chgo., 1995—2000; pres. Harley-Davidson Am. Rd. LLC/Orlando Harley-Davidson/Harley-Davidson Airport Stores, 2000—. Active Com. of 200; founder's coun. The Field Mus., Chgo.; bd. dirs. Milw. Zool. Soc., 1995—97, Chgo. Shakespeare Theatre, 2001—02, Orlando Mus. Art, 2002—05, Orlando and Orange County Conv. and Visitor's Bur. Named Bus. Woman of Yr., Orlando Bus. Jour., 2005. Mem.: Orlando Regional C. of C. (vice chmn. 2003—05). Republican. Avocations: world travel, tennis, theater, art. Office: H-D Am Rd LLC Ste 2144 875 N Michigan Ave Chicago IL 60611 Home Phone: 312-498-3622; Office Phone: 312-280-6001. Personal E-mail: annetdeli@aol.com.

D'ELIA, CHRISTOPHER FRANCIS, marine biologist, educator, academic administrator; s. Francis G. and Marian Frances (Wakeman) D'Elia; m. Jennifer Anne Hunnicutt, June 10, 1973; 1 child, Tallmadge Wakeman. AB, Middlebury Coll., 1968; PhD, U. Ga., 1974. Postdoctoral scholar UCLA, 1974; vis. asst. prof. U. So. Calif., LA, 1975; Noyes postdoctoral fellow Woods Hole (Mass.) Oceanog. Inst., 1975-77; from asst. prof. to assoc. prof. Chesapeake Biol. Lab. U. Md., Solomons, 1977—88, prof., 1988-99, SUNY, Albany, 1999—2004; dir. biol. oceanog. program NSF, Washington, 1987—89; dir. Md. Sea Grant Coll., 1989—98; v.p. rsch. SUNY, Albany, 1999—2002, prof. biology and pub. adminstrn. and policy, 2002—04; regional assoc. vice chancellor for rsch. and grad. studies, prof. environ. sci. and policy U. South Fla., St. Petersburg, 2004—, prof. marine science, dir. Center Sci. Pol. Applic. Coastal Environments, 2004—. Chair tech. adv. group Patuxent 208 Basin Plan, 1980—82; mem. adv. panel ocean scis. divsn. NSF, Washington, 1982—84, mem. fleet rev. com., 1999; chmn. Mid-Atlantic Regional Marine Rsch. Bd., 1991—96; mem. rsch. planning adv. group, priorities workgroup Chesapeake Bay Program, 1989—91, mem. sci. and tech. adv. com., 1993—98; cons. to govt. and industry, 1976—; regional rep. coastal resources adv. com., Md., 1982—83; mem. adv. com. Md. Sea Grant program, 1980—86; mem. sci. adv. bd. ecol. processes and effects com., marine monitoring com. EPA, 1991; mem. Leadership Md., 1997; mem. sea grant program assessment team NOAA, 2004, 06; mem. Nat. Ctr. for Environ. Rsch. panel, 2004, Leadership St. Petersburg, 2005, US Nat. Com. for Intergovtl. Oceanog. Commn., 2006—. Mem. editl. bd. Limnology and Oceanography, 1983—86; contbr. 65 articles in profl. jours. and books. Bd. dirs. Hudson River Found., 1998—; acad. adv. com. Indsl. Rsch. Inst., 2001—03; mem. exec. inst. Albany-Colonie C. of C., 2000; mem. Com. Water Leadership Program, 2004—, US Nat. Com. Intergovtl. Oceanographic Commn., 2006—; bd. dirs. Astrolabe, Inc., 1991—99, v.p., 1994—99; bd. dirs. Sci. Ctr. of Pinellas, 2004—, vice chair, 2005—06, chair, 2006—. Recipient Outstanding Service cert., Tri-County Coun., Meritorious Svc. award, Chesapeake Bay Program, Md., Gov.'s Salute to Excellence award, 1994; grantee, ERDA, 1976, EPA, 1978—82, Dept. Energy, 1979, NOAA, 1989—98, NSF, 1979—; Disting. Patrick scholar, Acad. Natural Scis., 1982—83. Fellow: AAAS (mem. exptl. program to stimulate competitive rsch. rev. teams 2005); mem.: Great Lakes Rsch. Consortium (bd. gov. 1999—2004), Indsl. Rsch. Inst. (mem. acad. advancment com. 2001—04), Coun. Soc. Pres. (sec. 1993—96, treas. 1997, chmn.-elect 1998, chmn. 1999, past chmn. 2000, chmn. emeritus 2001—), Coun. Sea Grant Dirs. (chmn.-elect, chmn. budget com. 1994), Sea Grant Assn. (pres. 1991—92, chmn. fed. rels. com. 1992—93, pres. 1999, President's award), N.Y. Acad. Sci., Nat. Assn. State Univs. and Land Grant Colls. (co-chmn. bd. dirs. 1994—95, coun. grad. rsch. and grad. edn. exec. com. 2000—01, bd. oceans and atmosphere, mem. exec. com., chmn. edn. com., chmn. spl. task force reorganization), Nat. Assn. Environ. Profs. (bd. dirs. Md. 1985—86), Internat. Soc. Reef Studies, Estuarine Rsch. Fedn. (v.p. 1989—91, pres. 1991—93, past pres. 1993—95), Ecol. Soc. Am. (chmn. pub. affairs com. 1989—91, vice chmn. 1991—92), Am. Soc. Limnology and Oceanography, Am. Chem. Soc., Oceanog. Soc. (life), Vinoy Club, Cosmos Club, Sigma Xi. Avocations: sailing, skiing, private pilot. Office: Office Academic Affairs U South Fla St Petersburg 140 7th Ave S Saint Petersburg FL 33701-5016 Office Phone: 727-873-4812. Business E-Mail: cdelia@spadmin.usf.edu.

D'ELIA, NICHOLAS, secondary school educator; b. NY, Sept. 22, 1959; s. Mario John and Angela Rose (Puma) D'Elia; m. Carolyne Gilroy, Aug. 24, 1984; children: Nicole, Michael, Philip. BA, CUNY, 1981; MS, Coll. S.I., 2004. V.p. prodn. Flying Tiger Comm., NYC, 1981-84; prodr., dir. Merrill Lynch Video Network, NYC, 1985-89; freelance dir. NYC, 1980-90; prodr., dir. Rainbow TV Prodns., Inc., NYC, 1990—94; tchr. Holy Name Sch., Bklyn., 1995—2001, New Utrecht HS, Bklyn., 2001—. Freelance dir. TV Generation, 1982 (U.S.A. Cable Video of the Week, 1983); freelance video engr. ABC Sports, 1981-85, ABC DayTime, N.Y.C. and remote locations, 1983-85, MacNeil-Lehrer News Hour, N.Y.C., 1983-85, CBS News, N.Y.C. and remote locations, 1983-84. Writer, producer (corp. mktg. tape) You Must Remember This., 1989 (AVCA Bronze award, 1989). Mem. NATAS, Internat. TV Assn. Roman Catholic. Avocations: performing and fine arts, scuba diving, auto racing. Office: New Utrecht HS 1601 80th St Brooklyn NY 11214

DELIGNE, PIERRE RENÉ, mathematician; b. Etterbeek, Belgium, Oct. 3, 1944; s. Albert and Renée (Bodart) D.; m. Elena Vladimirovna Alexeeva, Sept. 9, 1980; children: Natalia, Alexis. Licence en mathématiques, ULB (Université Libre de Bruxelles), Brussel, 1966, PhD in Mathematics, 1968. Jr. scientist Fond National de la Recherche Scientifique Belgium, Brussel, 1967-68; vis. mem. Institut des Hautes Etudes Scientifiques, Bures sur Yvette, France, 1968-70; permanent mem. Inst. des Hautes Etudes Scientifiques, Bures sur Yvette France, 1970-84; prof. Inst. for Advanced Study, Princeton, NJ, 1984—. Editor Pub. Math. Institut des Hautes Etudes Scientifiques, 1970; contbr. articles to profl. jours. Recipient Francois Deruyts prize, 1974, Henri Poincare Medal, Acad. Scis., Paris, 1974, Fields medal Internat. Math. Union, 1978, Crafoord prize, 1988, Balzan prize in Mathematics, 2004. Mem. Associé Etranger Academie des Sciences, AAAS (fgn. hon.), Royal Belgian Acad., Nat. Acad. Sciences (fgn. assoc.). Office: Inst for Advanced Study Sch Mathematics Einstein Dr Fuld Hall 210 Princeton NJ 08540 Business E-Mail: deligne@ias.edu.

DELIKAT, MICHAEL, lawyer; b. NYC, Apr. 3, 1952; s. Otto and Pearl (Soffer) D.; m. Alice Baron; children: Stacey, Jonathan. BS in Indsl. and Labor Rels., Cornell U., 1974; JD, Harvard U., 1977. Bar: N.Y. 1978, U.S. Dist. Ct. (so., ea. and we. dists.) N.Y. 1978, U.S Ct. Appeals (9th cir.) 1991, U.S. Supreme Ct. 1992. Ptnr. Baer Marks & Upham, NYC, 1977-91, Orrick Herrington & Sutcliffe LLP, NYC, 1991—, chair employment law practice group. Author: Summary Judgement Motion Practice, 1995, Legal Dangers in Diversity, 1995, Am. with Disabilities Act: New Fed. Rights for Disabled Employees, 1993, Protection Trade Secrets & Confidential Bus. Info.: Employer's Guide, 1993, Corporate Whistleblowing in the Sarbanes-Oxley Era, 2005. Fellow Coll. Labor Employment Lawyers; mem. ABA (equal employment opportunity com.), NY Univ. Ctr. Labor and Employment Law (bd. mem.), Cornell Club. Office: Orrick Herrington & Sutcliffe 666 5th Ave New York NY 10103-1798 Office Phone: 212-506-5230. Office Fax: 212-506-5151. Business E-Mail: mdelikat@orrick.com.

DELILLO, DON, author; b. NYC, Nov. 20, 1936; Student, Fordham U., 1954-58. Author: (plays) The Engineer of Moonlight, 1979, The Day Room, 1986; short stories in various collections, periodicals; (novels) Americana, 1971, End Zone, 1972, Great Jones Street, 1973, Ratner's Star, 1976, Players, 1977, Running Dog, 1978, The Names, 1982, White Noise, 1985 (Am. Book award 1985, Nat. Book Critics Circle award nominee 1985), Libra, 1988 (Internat. Fiction prize 1989), Mao II, 1991 (PEN-Faulkner award 1992), Underworld, 1997 (Runner Up, Best Fiction of the Past 25 Yrs., NY Times, 2006); Falling Man, 2007. Guggenheim fellow, 1979, Am. Acad. Inst. Arts and Letters Literature award, 1984.*

DE LISA, JOEL ALAN, rehabilitation physician, research executive; b. Seattle, Mar. 18, 1942; s. Joseph Phillip and Alice Georgia (Jensen) DeL.; m. Janet Hopper, July 25, 1971. BS in Zoology, Wash. State U., 1964; MD, U. Wash., 1968, MS, 1976. Diplomate Am. Bd. Phys. Medicine and Rehab. (chmn. 1993-98); diplomate spinal cord injury medicine. Intern St. Josephs Hosp., Phoenix, 1968-69; resident in phys. medicine and rehab. U. Wash., Seattle, 1972-75; med. dir., chief med. officer Kessler Inst. Rehab., West Orange, NJ, 1987-93; sr. v.p., chief med. officer Kessler Rehab. Corp., West Orange, 1994-2000; pres., CEO Kessler Med. Rehab. Rsch. and Edn. Corp., West Orange, 1998—. Prof., chmn. dept. phys. medicine and rehab. U. Medicine and Dentistry NJ, Newark, 1987—, interim dean, 2000; chmn. dept. phys. medicine and rehab. St. Barnabas Med. Ctr., Livingston, NJ, 1990-98, chair. ednl. commn. fgn. med. grad., 2005-06; vice chmn. Am. Bd. Med. Specialties, 2006-; chair elect coun. academic socs. Assn. Am. Med. Colls. Author: Principles and Practice of Physical Medicine and Rehabilitation, 2004, Manual of Nerve Conduction Study and Surface Anatomy and Needle Electromyography, 2004. Mem. AMA, Assn. Acad. Physiatrists, Am. Acad. Phys. Medicine and Rehab., Am. Congress Rehab. Medicine, Am. Paraplegic Soc. (hon., pres. Jackson Heights chpt. 1989-91, Excellence award 1995). Office: Kessler Med Rehab Rsch and Edn Corp 1199 Pleasant Valley Way West Orange NJ 07052-1424 Home Phone: 973-635-6200; Office Phone: 973-243-6806. Business E-Mail: delisaja@umdnj.edu.

DE LISI, NANCY, corporate financial executive; BA in Psych., U. Tex., Austin, MS in Profl. Acctg. Various exec. positions in multinational cos. and Citibank in internat. fin. and bus. devel., 1976—85; asst. treas. to v.p. fin. and treas. Altria Grp., Inc., NYC, 1985—2002, sr. v.p. mergers and acquisitions, 2002—. Bd. dirs. SABMiller, PLC. Office: Altria Group Inc 120 Park Ave New York NY 10017-5592*

DE LISIO, STEPHEN SCOTT, lawyer, director, pastor; b. San Diego, Dec. 30, 1937; s. Anthony J. and Emma Irving (Cheney) DeL.; m. Margaret Irene Winter, June 26, 1964; children: Anthony W., Stephen Scott, Heather E. Student, Am. U., 1958-59; BA, Emory U., 1959; LLB, Albany Law Sch., 1962; LLM, Georgetown U., 1963. Bar: N.Y. 1963, D.C. 1963, Alaska 1964. Practice law, Fairbanks, Alaska, 1963-71, Anchorage, 1972-96; asst. dist. atty. Fairbanks, 1963-65; assoc. McNealy & Merdes, 1965-66; lectr. U. Alaska, 1965-67; ptnr. Staley, DeLisio & Cook, 1966-93, DeLisio, Moran, Geraghty & Zobel, Inc., 1994—2003; pastor Anchorage Bible Fellowship. Bd. dirs. Woodstock Property Co., Inc., Pasit Inc., Challenger Films Inc.; vice chmn. Crosstown CBMC, 1986—87, chmn., 1987—88, 1990—91, area coord., 1987—92; city atty., Fairbanks, 1967—70, Barrow, 1969—72, Ft. Yukon and North Pole, 1970—72; past sec. U. Alaska Heating Corp., Inc.; past sec.-treas. Trans-Alaska Electronics, Inc., Baker Aviation, Inc.; former arbitrator, mem. Alaska regional coun. Am. Arbitration Assn. Author: (with others) Law and Tactics in Federal Criminal Cases, 1964. Past pres. Tanana Valley State Fair Assn.; past v.p. Fairbanks Mental Health Assn., Fairbanks United Good Neighbors Fund; bd. dirs. Anchorage Cmty. Chorus, 1975—77, Common Sense for Alaska, 1987—94, Alaska chpt. Lupus Found., 1989—96; chmn. bd. Alaska Voluntary Health Assn., 1993—96; former bd. dirs. Greater Fairbanks Cmty. Hosp. Found.; met. dir. Christian Businessmen's Outreach, 1993—94, bd. dirs. Anchorage, 1985—92; met. dir. Alaska Christian Businessmen's Com. U.S.A., 1994—2000; rep. precinct committeeman, 1970—76; chmn. Alaska Rep. Rules Com. Anchorage Rep. Com, 1973; v.p. We the People, 1977—79; vice chmn. Alaska Libertarian Party, 1983—84; mem. nat. com. Libertarian Party, 1982—85; deacon Anchorage Bible Fellowship, 1986—90, elder, pastor, 1990—; Alaska coord. Crown Ministries, 1991—93; bd. dirs. Projects Fe, Inc., 2001—07. Recipient Jaycee Disting. Service award, 1968 Mem. Am. Trial Lawyers Assn., Am. Judicature Soc., Alaska Bar Assn., DC Bar Assn., Anchorage Bar Assn., Spenard Bar Assn. (pres. 1975-77), U.S. Jaycees (past dir.), Alaska Jaycees (past pres.), Fairbanks Jaycees (past pres.), Chi Phi, Pi Sigma Phi, Woodstock Golf Inc. Club (pres. 1984-2007). Home: 5102 Shorecrest Dr Anchorage AK 99502-1329 Office: Anchorage Bible Fellowship 7348 Abbott Loop Rd Anchorage AK 99507 Home Phone: 907-243-5521. Personal E-mail: cbmcak@alaska.net. *A well-defined sense of values and the courage and determination to adhere to it is as essential to a life of purpose and fulfillment, as the rising of the sun is to life on this planet. The challenge is to develop values that are as relevant to the changes of tomorrow as to the reality of the now and the past. The "situation ethics" approach is as disastrous as a smashed rudder on a storm tossed vessel. The Way, the Truth and the Life is found only in Christ Jesus.*

DELK, CHARLOTTE TURLEY, elementary school educator; b. Ft. Benning Columbus, Ga., Sept. 27, 1964; d. Lester Albert Turley, Jr. and Charleen Whittle Turley; children: Joshua Turley Rusch, Whittle Harrison. BA, Valdosta State Coll., Ga., 1985; cert. T-4/Mid. Grades, Kennesaw State Coll., Ga., 1991. Staff writer Cherokee Tribune, Canton, Ga., 1986—89; tchr. M.A. Teasley Mid. Sch., Canton, Ga., 1991—94, Pelham City Mid. Sch., Pelham, Ga., 1994—97, Pearson Elem. Sch., Ga., 2003—. Baptist. Avocation: reading. Home: 505 North Chester Ave Douglas GA 31533 Office: Atkinson County Bd of Edn Pearson Elem Sch 563 N King St Pearson GA 31642 Office Phone: 912-422-3882. Business E-Mail: cdelk@atkinson.k12.ga.us.

DELL, CHARLENE ELIZABETH, music educator; d. Arthur Kenyon Dell and Gertrude May Poelma. MusB, SUNY, Potsdam, 1984; MS, We. Conn. State U., Danbury, 1989; PhD, U. SC, Columbia, 2003. Music educator Gouveneur Ctrl. Schs., NY, 1984—86, Arlington Ctrl. Schs., Poughkeepsie, NY, 1986—99; asst. prof. music edn. U. Okla., Norman, 2002—. Exec. adminstrv. dir. Sooner String Project, Norman, 2002—; asst. dir. for adminstrn. N.Y. State Summer Sch. of Arts, Saratoga Springs, 1983—96. Musician and soloist First Bapt. Ch., Norman, 2002—06. Tech. Grant, U. Okla. Sch. Music, 2004, Internat. Travel Grant, U. Okla., 2004. Mem.: Nat. Sch. Orch. Assn., Nat. Assn. Music Educators (assoc.), Am. String Teachers Assn. (assoc.; state pres. 2005—06). Home Phone: 405-573-2951; Office Phone: 405-325-0168.

DELL, MICHAEL SETH, computer company executive; b. Houston, Feb. 23, 1965; s. Alexander and Lorraine D.; m. Susan Lieberman, Oct. 23, 1989; 4 children. Student, U. Tex., 1983-84. Founder Dell Computer Corp. (formerly PC's Ltd.), Austin, 1984; chmn. Dell Inc. (formerly Dell Computer Corp.), Round Rock, Tex., 1984—, CEO, 1984—2004, 2007—. Bd. dirs. Dell Inc., 1984—; founder MSD Capital, LP., NYC, 1998—; IT Governor World Econ. Forum; mem. Internat. Bus. Coun., US Bus. Coun., President's Coun. of Advisors on Sci. & Tech.; mem. gov. bd. Indian Sch. of Bus., Hyderabad, India. Author: Direct From Dell: Strategies that Revolutionized an Industry, 1999. Founder, mem. bd. dirs. Michael & Susan Dell Found., Austin, 1999—. Recipient Entrepreneur of Yr. award Inc. Mag., 1990, Customer Satisfaction award JD Power, 1991, 93; named CEO of Yr. Fin. World Mag., 1993, Chief Exec. of Yr. Chief Exec. Mag., 2001; named one of Top 10 Most Powerful People in Bus. Fortune Mag., 2003, 04, Richest Americans Forbes Mag., 2005-2006, 50 Who Matter Now CNNMoney.com Bus. 2.0, 2006, World's Richest People Forbes Mag., 2007. Achievements include donated a collection of materials to the Smithsonian in 2007, including his employee badge, one of the company's newest computers and a PC Limited computer from 1985. Office: Dell Inc 1 Dell Way Round Rock TX 78682-0001*

DELL, RALPH BISHOP, retired pediatrician, researcher; b. Mt. Village, Alaska, July 31, 1935; s. Elwin B. and Elizabeth B. (Bishop) D.; m. Kathryn M. Bownass, June 17, 1957 (div. Dec. 1982); children: Laura, Kenneth; m. Karen K. Hein, Aug. 28, 1983; stepchildren: Ethan Hein, Molly Hein. BA, Pomona Coll., Claremont, Calif., 1957; MD, U. Pa., Phila., 1961. Diplomate Am. Bd. Pediat. Intern and resident Children's Hosp. Med. Ctr., Boston, 1961-63; NIH postdoctoral fellow Coll. Physicians and Surgeons, Columbia U., NYC, 1963-66, assoc., 1966-67, asst. prof. pediat., 1967-72, assoc. prof., 1972-78, prof., 1978-97; dir. Inst. for Lab. Animal Rsch. NRC, Washington, 1997-2000, ret., 2000. Author: 3 books, 100 rsch. papers; co-inventor amino acid solution. Program chair Windham World Affairs Coun., 2006—; trustee Whittingham Hist. Soc. Recipient Rsch. Career Devel. award NIH, 1966-71, Career Scientist award Health Rsch. Coun. N.Y., 1972-75; Fogarty Sr. Internat. fellow NIH, 1975-76. Mem. Am. Pediat. Soc., Am. Physiologic Soc., Am. Soc. Clin. Investigation, Soc. for Pediat. Rsch., Assn. for Computing Machinery, Am. Coll. Lab. Medicine (hon.), Am. Assn. Accreditation Lab. Animal Care (emeritus mem., coun. on accreditation), Lions Club. Democrat. Avocation: woodworking. Home: PO Box 607 Jacksonville VT 05342 Home Phone: 802-368-7568. Personal E-mail: rbdell@hughes.net.

DELL, ROBERT CHRISTOPHER, environmental engineer, educator, artist; b. Nyack, NY, Feb. 22, 1950; s. Edward John and Laurel Jean (McGrath) D.; children: Robert Carroll, Malcolm Vincent, Terrence Edward; m. Siena Gillan Porta, May 30, 1986. BS in Edn., SUNY, Oneonta, 1972; MFA in Sculpture, SUNY, New Paltz, 1975. Mem. Arch. and Cmty. Appearance bd. rev. Orangetown, NY, 1979-2001, vice-chmn., 1987-2001, mem. Planning Bd., 2001—; vis. artist Akureyri Sch. Visual Art, 1999, Am. Scandinavian Found. fellow, 1999-2000; adj. prof. Sch. Engring.2003-, Rsch. Fellow, 2004-, dir. Lab. for Energy Reclamation and Innovation, 2006-; dir., chief project engr. LED Traffic Light The Cooper Union, 2007—; spkr. in field; lectr. in field. One-man shows include Vorpal Gallery, Chgo., 1978, N.Y.C., 1981, 88, San Francisco, 1985, Blue Hill Cultural Ctr., Pearl River, N.Y., 1987, 98-99, Am. Embassy, Am. Cultural Ctr., Reykjavik, Iceland, 1988, geothermal sculpture installation, Country Park Reykjanesfolkvangur, Iceland, 1988, Perlan, Reykjavik (permanent geothermal sculpture installation) 1991,Castle and Old Faithful, Grotto Geyser Groups Yellowstone Nat. Park, Wyo., 1996, Kresge Oval MIT, 1997, Akureyri Art Mus., Iceland, 1999, The Great Geysir, Geysir Nature Conservation Area Haukadalur, Iceland, 1999, Akureyri Art Mus., Iceland, 1999, Reykjavik Mcpl. Art Mus. Harbour House, 2001, Albert Nerken Sch. Engring., Cooper Union, N.Y.C., 2004; The Lab Gallery, NYC, 2006 numerous group shows including most recently Noho Gallery N.Y.C., 2002, Hafnarborg Inst. Culture and Fine Art, Hafnarborg Museum, Hrafnarfurdor, Iceland, 2002, Museum House at Húsavík, Húsavík, Iceland, 2003, Regional Museum of Hornafjordur, Hofn, Iceland, 2003, McLevy Pk., Bridgeport, Conn., 2004-05; permanent collections include U.S. Embassy, Am. Cultural Ctr., Iceland, MIT, Fulbright Commn., Reykjavik, Syracuse U., Mus. Fine Art, Springfield, Mass., MacDowell Colony, Peterborough, N.H., SUNY, Town of Orangetown (N.Y.), Hafnarborg inst. Art and Cculture, Iceland; subject of video Hitavaetur MIT, Circumstantial Prodns., 1991, News Stories, Frettir, geothermal sculpture State TV Iceland, 1993-96; scenic artist motion pictures, TV shows; master scenic artist One Life to Live ABC, 1988-99 (Daytime Emmy honoree 1995); author: Hitavaettur and The Implications of Geothermal Sculpture, Leonardo, MIT Press 2000; several articles in field. Fellow MacDowell Colony, 1980, Am. Scandinavian Fdn., 1999-00, Fulbright Rsch. Fellow, 1988; Rsch. Fellow, 1993-95, Rsch. Assoc. 1995-7 MIT Ctr. for Advanced Visual Studies, Coun. Arts at MIT, 1997, N.Y. Found. for the Arts, 2001. Prin. Investigator, Charles A. and Ann Morrow Lindbergh Found. Waste Mgmt. and Minimization Grant, Anoka, Minn. 2006-7, Hon. Rsch. Assoc. NY Botanical Garden, Bronx, NY 2006-, prin. Investigator, Thermoelectric Power Generation, Phase I and II, 2004-6 Consolidated Edison, NYC Mem.: Am. Soc. Mechanical Engrs. Achievements include patents pending for. Home: 421 Washington St Tappan NY 10983-2703

DELL, ROBERT MICHAEL, lawyer; b. Chgo., Oct. 4, 1952; s. Michael A. and Bertha Dell; m. Ruth Celia Schiffman, May 29, 1976; children: David, Michael, Jessica. BGS, U. Mich., 1974; JD, U. Ill., 1977. Bar: U.S. Dist. Ct. (no. dist.) Ill. 1977, U.S. Ct. Appeals (7th cir.) 1977, U.S. Dist. Ct. (no. dist.) Calif. 1990. Law clk. to justice U.S. Ct. Appeals (7th cir.), Chgo., 1977—79; assoc. Latham & Watkins, Chgo., 1982—85, ptnr., 1985—, mng. ptnr. San Francisco office, 1990—94, firm chmn. and mng. ptnr., 1995—. Home: 19 Tamal Vista Ln Kentfield CA 94904-1005 Office: Latham & Watkins LLP 505 Montgomery St Ste 2000 San Francisco CA 94111-2552

DELL, SUSAN, foundation administrator, apparel designer; m. Micahel Dell; 4 children. BA in Fashion Merchandising & Design, Ariz. State U. Designer Susan Dell Collections, Austin, Tex., NYC; chmn. bd. Phi, NYC. Co-founder, chmn. bd. Michael & Susan Dell Found.; clothing designs featured in Am. Vogue, French Vogue, Harper's Bazaar, W Mag. Bd. mem. Austin Children's Hosp., Cooper Inst., St. Andrew's Episcopal Sch. Office: Cooper Inst 12330 Preston Rd Dallas TX 75203 also: Michael & Susan Dell Found One Dell Way Round Rock TX 78682

DELL, WARREN FRANK, II, management consultant; b. Louisville, Aug. 8, 1945; s. George Justus and Opal Lee (Roberts) D.; m. Theresa LoParco, July 11, 1970; child, Stacy Lee. BS, Northeastern U., 1968; MBA, Iona Coll., 1973. Cert. mgmt. cons. Systems analyst Am. Can Co., Greenwich, Conn., 1968-69; cons. Info. Techniques, Inc., Norwalk, Conn., 1969-70; systems analyst Colgate Palmolive, NYC, 1970-72, supr. mktg. stats., 1972-73, mgr. forecast and adminstrn., 1973-77; cons. Case and Co., Stamford, Conn., 1977-80, prin., 1980-83, sr. ptnr., dir., 1983-85; prin. Cresap, a Towers Perrin Co., NYC, 1985-86, v.p., 1986-90; pres. Dellmart & Co., Stamford, Conn., 1989—. Bd. dirs. JSL Perekriosrok. Contbr. articles to profl. jours. Mem. Coun. Logistics Mgmt., Warehouse Edn. Rsch. Coun., Food Distbn. Rsch. Soc., Am. Philatelic Soc., Inst. Mgmt. Cons. Avocations: stamp collecting/philately, golf, travel. Office: Dellmart & Co 125 Hardesty Rd Stamford CT 06903-4327 Office Phone: 203-968-8609. Personal E-mail: wfdell2@msn.com. Business E-Mail: Frank@Dellmart.com.

DELLA-GIUSTINA, JO-ANN, lawyer; b. Springfield, Mass., Sept. 6, 1951; d. Joseph Augustus and Jennie Delores (Subotin) Della-G. BA, Clark U., 1972; MA, Columbia Coll., Chgo., 1983; JD, Chgo.-Kent Coll. Law, 1987; PhD in Criminal Justice, CUNY, 2005. Bar: Ill. 1987, Mass. 1996, N.Y. 1998, U.S. Dist. Ct. (no. dist.) Ill. 1987, N.Y. 1998. Tchr. S.W. Ind. Sch. Dist., San Antonio, 1976-78, Malcolm X Coll., Chgo., 1978-80; dir. pub. rels. H&R Block, Chgo., 1983-85; asst. corp. counsel City of Chgo., 1987-89; sr. atty. Office of Cook County Pub. Defender, Chgo., 1989-90; judicial law clk. to Justice David Cerda Ill. Appellate Ct., Chgo., 1990-98; asst. prof. Bridgewater State Coll., Bridgewater, Mass., 2005—. Cons. Am. Planning Assn., Chgo., 1990—98; bd. dir. loan repayment and assistance program ITT Chgo., 1995—97, mem. exec. com. criminal justice PhD program, 2001—02; mem. curriculum com. criminal justice PhD program CUNY, 1999—2001, graduate tchg. fellow, 2001—04, mem. exec. com. PhD program, 2001—02; adj. asst. prof. John Jay Coll., 2001—05; presenter in field; mem. exec. com., PhD program CUNY, 2002—03; asst. prof. dept. criminal justice Bridgewater State Coll., Mass. Author: Blossom of the Flower, 1990; author (legal jour.) Land Use Law and Zoning Digest, 1990-98; contbr. articles to profl. jours. Pres. Greenwood Ct. Condominium Assn., Chgo., 1989-98. Mem. Justinian Soc. Lawyers, Nat. Assn. Women Lawyers (named Outstanding Law Grad. 1987), Women in Film (programs com. 1992-94), Acad. Criminal Justice Scis., Nat. Women's Studies Assn., Am. Soc. Criminology, Nat. Italian-Am. Bar Assn., Order of Coif, Homicide Rsch. Working Group, Justice Studies Assn. Avocations: travel, reading. Home and Office: 84 Fairway Dr Plymouth MA 02360 E-mail: jdgiustina@hotmail.com, jdellagiustina@bridgew.edu.

DELLAGLORIA, JOHN CASTLE, lawyer, educator; b. NYC, June 29, 1952; s. Arthur A. and Marianne Dellagloria; divorced; 1 child, Rebecca; m. Marilyn Castle Dellagloria, Sept. 25, 1988; 1 child, Caitlin. BA in English Lit., SUNY, Binghamton, 1976; JD, U. Miami, 1979. Bar: Fla. 1979, N.Y. 1986, U.S. Ct. Appeals (11th cir.) 1981, U.S. Dist. Ct. (so. dist.) Fla. 1980, U.S. Supreme Ct. Rsch. asst. 3rd Dist. Ct. Appeal, Miami, Fla., 1980-81; assoc. Cassel & Cassel PA, Miami, 1981-82; dep. city atty. City North Miami Beach, Fla., 1983-86; city atty. City South Miami, Fla., 1986-90; chief dep. city atty. City Miami Beach, Fla., 1990-96; city atty. City North Miami, Fla., 1995—2004; gen. counsel Miami Beach Housing Authority, 1997-2000, South Miami Cmty. Redevel. Agy., 1998—2002, City of Palm Bay Cmty. Redevel. Agy., Fla., 0200—. Lectr. Sch. Profl. Devel., U. Miami, 1982-88, dir. paralegal program, 1984-86, lectr. Sch. Bus., 1989—, lectr. real property program; lectr. govt. law sect. Fla. Bar; moderator Rachlin, Cohen & Holtz, Ann. Govt. Law Symposium, 1996—. Com. person Parrot Jungle Com., Pinecrest, Fla., 1998. Recipient Excellence in Tchg. award, U. Miami, 2004. Mem. Eugene P. Spellman Am. Inn of Ct. (alumnus). Democrat. Jewish. Avocation: long distance running. Home Phone: 305-255-4964; Office Phone: 305-392-4772. Personal E-mail: catdel@hotmail.com. E-mail: johndellagloria@dellaglorialaw.com.

DELLAPINA, MARIO JOHN, academic administrator; s. Joseph DellaPina and Emily Sidoli DellaPina; m. Mildred Murolo, June 30, 2006. BA, U. Miami, Fla., 1968. Cert. Fundraising Execs. Internat. , Va., 1998. Chmn. pres., CEO Evergreen Assocs., NYC, 1981—88; chief devel. officer Queens Coll. CUNY, Flushing, NY, 1988—, exec. dir. Queens Coll. Found., 1989—. Bd. mem. Louis Armstrong House and Archives, Flushing, NY, mem. adv. bd. Mem.: Explorers Club. Achievements include patents pending for theraputic whirlpool. Office: Queens Coll Found 65-30 Kissena Blvd Flushing NY 11367 Office Phone: 718-997-3920.

DELLA ROCCA, STEVEN, lawyer; BS cum laude, U. Pa., 1977; JD, NYU, 1980. Bar: Calif. 1980, NY 1998. Chmn., corp. dept. Latham & Watkins, NYC, 1991—2001, ptnr., 1988—, mem., exec. com., 2002—05. Mem.: ABA. Office: Latham & Watkins Ste 1000 885 Third Ave New York NY 10022-4834 Office Phone: 212-906-1200. Business E-Mail: steven.della.rocca@lw.com.

DELLA ROCCO, KENNETH ANTHONY, lawyer; b. Bridgeport, Conn., Sept. 5, 1952; BA, Sacred Heart U., Fairfield, Conn., 1974; JD, U. Bridgeport, 1982. Bar: Conn. 1983, U.S. Dist. Ct. Conn. 1985, N.Y. 1988, U.S. Supreme Ct. 1991. Assoc. Cummings & Lockwood, Stamford, Conn., 1982-88; from asst. gen. counsel to v.p. Melville Corp., Rye, NY, 1988—93, v.p. legal affairs, gen. counsel, 1993—95; counsel Cacace, Tusch & Santagata, Stamford, 1996—2002; ptnr. Martin, Lucas & Chioffi LLP, Stamford, 2003—. Mem. Conn. Bar Assn., Fairfield County Bar Assn. Office: Martin Lucas and Chioffi LLP 177 Broad St Stamford CT 06901 Office Phone: 203-973-5240.

DELLAS, ROBERT DENNIS, investment banker; b. Detroit, July 4, 1944; s. Eugene D. and Maxine (Rudell) D.; m. Shila L. Clement, Mar. 27, 1976; children: Emily Allison, Lindsay Michelle BA in Econs., U. Mich., Ann Arbor, 1966; MBA, Harvard U., Cambridge, 1970. Analyst Burroughs Corp., Detroit, 1966-67, Pasadena, Calif., 1967-68; mgr. U.S. Leasing, San Francisco, 1970-76; pres., dir. Energetics Mktg. & Mgmt. Assn., San Francisco, 1978-80; sr. v.p. E.F. Hutton & Co., San Francisco, 1981-85; prin. founder Capital Exchange Internat., San Francisco, 1976—. Gen. ptnr. Kanland Assocs., Tex., 1982, Claremont Assocs., Calif., 1983, Lakeland Assocs., Ga., 1983, Americal Assocs., Calif., 1983, Chatsworth Assocs., Calif., 1983, Walnut Grove Assocs., Calif., 1983, Somerset Assocs., N.J., 1983, One San Diego Assocs., Calif., 1984, Big Top Prodns., L.P., Calif., 1994. Bd. dirs. Found. San Francisco's Archtl. Heritage. Mem. U.S. Trotting Assn., Calif. Harness Horse Breeders Assn. (Breeders award for Filly of Yr. 1986, Aged Pacing Mare, 1987, 88, Colt of Yr. 1990), Calif. Golf Club San Francisco (bd. dirs.). Office: Capital Exch Internat 1911 Sacramento St San Francisco CA 94109-3419 Home Phone: 415-673-2195; Office Phone: 415-928-3062. Personal E-mail: bobdellas@earthlink.net.

DELLA TORRE, EDWARD, electrical engineer, educator; b. Milan, Italy, Mar. 31, 1934; came to U.S., 1940, naturalized, 1945; s. Rene and Anna (Rosner) Della Torre; m. Sonia Viola Peltz, Jan. 1, 1956; children—Neal, Marc, Cynthia. B.S.E.E., Bklyn. Poly. Inst., 1954; M.S.E.E., Princeton U., 1956; M.S. in Physics, Rutgers U., 1961; E.Sc.D., Columbia U., 1964. With elec. engring dept. Rutgers U., New Brunswick, N.J., 1956-67; with solid state physics lab. Bell Telephone Labs., 1967-68, with McMaster U., 1968-79, Wayne State U., 1979-82; George Washington U., Washington, 1982—. Author: Electromagnetic Field, 1969; Magnetic Bubbles, 1975; contbr. articles to profl. jours.; patentee in field. Recipient numerous grants, 1968—. Fellow IEEE (v.p. Magnetic Soc. 1997—, mem. bd. dirs. 2007-)Am. Phys. Soc.;Sigma Xi, Eta Kappa Nu, Tau Beta Pi. Office: George Washington U Elec Engring & Computer Sci Dept Washington DC 20052-0001

DELLAVECCHIA, MICHAEL ANTHONY, ophthalmologist, pathologist, educator; BA in Physics and Math., LaSalle Coll., Phila., 1970; MS in Biomed. Sci. and Engring., Drexel U., 1972, PhD in Biomed. Sci. and Engring., 1984; MD, Temple U., 1976. Diplomate Am. Bd. Med. Examiners, Am. Bd. Ophthalmology, lic. physician Pa., NJ. Resident in anatomical and clin. pathology Temple U. Hosp., Phila., 1977-80, chief resident, 1979-80, fellow in surg. pathology, 1980-81, resident in ophthalmology, 1981-84; fellow in ophthalmology Project Orbis, Inc., NYC, 1985; v.p., med. dir., co-founder Mega Med. Electronics, Hatfield, Pa., 1984-86; assoc. John Reichel MD, Ltd., Bryn Mawr, Pa., 1984-95; assoc. staff, clin. instr. Temple U. Hosp., Phila., 1986—; instr. Wills Eye Hosp., Phila., 1986—, Scheie Eye Inst., Phila., 1986-96; prof. dept. biomed. engring. Drexel U., Phila., 1991—; attending staff ophthalmology Grad. Health Sys. Phila. Coll. Osteo. Medicine, 1995—2002; assoc. surgeon Wills Eye Hosp., 2001—, attending surgeon, emergency rm., 2002—, dir. emergency dept., 2004—. Med. dir. Interstate Blood Bank, Inc., 1977—80; dir. med. info. Info. Mgmt. Corp., 1984—87; dir. med. rsch. Sonic Techs., Inc., 1984—86; med. dir., med. adv. bd. Lehigh Ultrasonics Group, 1985—87; pres., founder Dell Med. Inc., 1985—; pres., treas., co-founder Med. Design Assocs., 1985—86; co-founder, med. dir. Omega Nutrients, Inc., 1987—89; tech. advisor Project Orbis, Inc., 1986—; clin. instr. ophthalmology svc. Willis Eye Hosp., 1986—97, asst. prof., 1997—2000, assoc. prof., 2000—, dir. emergency dept., 2003—; clin. instr. ophthalmology svc. U. Pa., 1986—95, Temple U., 1984—; dir. labs. Am. Clin. Labs., 1985—94, Phila. Union Health Ctr., 1988—96; radiol. officer Emergency Mgmt. Assn., State of Pa., 1993—; co-founder Med. Surveillance Group, 1993—95; cons. Keystone Clin. Labs., 1994—95, NASA, 1992—; adj. prof. surgery dept. ophthalmology Phila. Coll. Osteo. Medicine, 1995—99; mem. editl. bd. laser medicine divsn. Emergency Care Rsch. Inst., 1995—2002; cons. Sensar divsn. Sarnoff Labs., 1993—2000, chmn. med. adv. bd., 1996—2000. Contbr. articles to profl. jours.; reviewer Physician's Info. and Ednl. Resources, 2005—, peer reviewer Jour. Biomed. Optics, 2006—; editor: Physicians Info. & Ednl. Resources ACP. Vol. counselor Boy Scouts Am.; chmn. instl. rev. bd. Phila. Retinal Endowment Fund, 2002—. Named one of Best Dr.'s in Am., 2003—; recipient numerous certs., Fed. Emergency Mgmt. Assn.; Presdl. Acad. scholar, LaSalle Coll., 1966—70, Pa. State Senatorial scholar, Temple U. Sch. Medicine, Rsch. fellow, Drexel U., 1976—77, Surg. Pathology fellow, Temple U. Hosp., 1980—81, numerous rsch. grantees. Fellow: ACS (bd. dirs. Phila. met. chpt. 2004—, treas. 2006—07, sec. 2007—, editl. cons. physicians info. and edn. resource 2006—), Phila. Coll. Physicians, Phila. Coll. Surgeons (bd. dirs. 2004—), Internat. Coll. Surgeons, Am. Acad. Ophthalmology (Lifetime Edn. in Ophthalmology award 1996—99); mem.: AMA (Physician Recognition award 1990—), IEEE, Lifelong Edn. Ophthalmology (with distinction 1999—), Chymian Soc., Newtonian Soc., Montgomery County Med. Soc., Pa. Med. Soc., Phila. County Med. Soc., Intercounty Opthal. Soc., Del. Vally Opthal. Soc., NY Acad. Scis., Am. Soc. Clin. Pathology, Engring. Medicine and Biology, Lase and Electro-Optics Soc., Internat. Biomedical Optics Soc. (inaugural), Internat. Soc. Photoinstrumentation Engrs., Internat. Bioelectrochem. Soc., Am. Soc. Laser Medicine and Surgery (mem. com. laser safety 2005—06, mem. com. constn. and by-laws 2006—07, mem. budget and fin. com. 2006—), Phila. Med. Club (bd. dirs. 2003—, chmn. membership com. 2004—), Brit. Officers Club (hon.), Lions, Sigma Xi, Alpha Epsilon Delta, Kappa Mu Epsilon. Achievements include patents for in engineering and medical devices; ophthalmic shield with removable compression device; medicament delivery systems and adaptive optics, and biometric identification. Office Phone: 215-928-3000. Business E-Mail: mdellavecchia@willseye.org.

DELLA-VOLPE, RALPH EUGENE, artist; b. Jersey City, May 10, 1923; s. Ralph and Caroline (Mischio) Della-V.; m. Helen Teresa Ray, 1948; children: Teresa Ray, Bronwyn Caroline, James Ralph. Student, Nat. Acad. Design, NYC, 1940-41, ARt Students League, 1945-48. Painter, Millbrook, N.Y., 1945—. Artist-in-residence Bennett Coll., Millbrook, 1949-78, chmn. art dept. One-man shows include Berkshire Mus., Pittsfield, Mass., Columbia Mus., S.C., Artists Gallery, N.Y.C., Babcock Gallery, N.Y.C.; exhibited in group shows at Grand Central Galleries, N.Y.C. Pfc. AUS, 1942-45. Recipient many prizes and awards in competition; MacDowell fellow, 1963. Independent. Presbyterian. Home: 241 South Rd Millbrook NY 12545-5540 E-mail: Della-Volpe@webtv.net.

DELLEUR, JACQUES WILLIAM, retired engineering educator; b. Paris, Dec. 30, 1924; came to U.S., 1952, naturalized, 1957; s. Georges Leon and Simone (Rossum) D.; m. DeLores Ann Horne, June 18, 1957; children: James Robert, Ann Marie. Civil and Mining Engr., Nat. U. Colombia, 1949; MS in Civil Engring., Rensselaer Poly. Inst., 1950; DEng Sci., Columbia U., 1955. Civil engr. R.J. Tipton and Assocs., 1950—52; from research asst. to instr. civil engring. and engring. mechanics Columbia U., 1952—55; mem. faculty Purdue U., 1955—95, prof. hydraulic engring. and hydrology, 1963—95, prof. emeritus hydraulic engring., 1995—, head hydromechanics and water resources area, 1965—76, head hydraulic and systems engring. area, 1981—90, 1991—92; assoc. dir. Purdue U. Water Resources Rsch. Ctr., 1971—89, acting dir., 1983. Rschr. fluid mechanics U. Grenoble, France, 1961-62, hydrology and environ. fluid mechanics French Nat. Hydraulics Lab., Chatou, France, 1968-69, 76-77, statis. hydrology U. Brussels, Belgium, 1991; NSF sr. exch. scientist U. Grenoble, France, 1983-84; vis. prof. U. Quebec, Canada, 1996—2005, Vrije U., Brussels, 1991—2005; mem. sci. coun. Revue des Sciences de L'eau/Water Scis. Sci. Interest Group/Nat. Inst. Sci. Rsch., Quebec, 1988—; vis. lectr. Ecole Polytechnique Federale de Lausanne, Switzerland, 1991, 93, 95, 97; coord. Consortium of U.S. and European Cmty. Univs. for Scholar and Multimedia Exchs. in Environ. and Water Resources Engring. and Scis., 1998-2003. Author and co-author 2 books on statis. hydrology; co-author book on urban hydorlogy; editor: Handbook of Groundwater Engineering, 1999, 2d edit., 2007; assoc. editor: Handbook of Civil Engineering, 1995, 2d edit., 2002; assoc. editor Jour. Hydraulic Engring., 2003—, also articles, reports in field. Recipient Ray K. Linsley award, Am. Inst. Hydrology, 2007. Fellow Ind. Acad. Sci.; mem. ASCE (Freeman fellow 1961-62, chmn. fluid dynamics com. 1964-66, task com. mechanics of turbulence 1964-69, task com. hydraulics of bridges 1963-68, task com. on urban drainage infrastructure 1988-90, co-chmn. task com. on urban drainage rehab. and techniques 1990-94, chmn. com. urban water resources 1994-95, chmn. com. sediment movement in urban drainage sys. 1998-2003, internat. bd. advisors Jour. Hydrologic Engring. 1996—, Svc. to the Profession award 2000, Ven Te Chow Hydrology award 2002, Type 2 award, Environ. and Water Resources Inst., 2003), Am. Geophys. Union (chmn. urban hydrology com. 1978-83), Am. Water Resources Assn., Am. Soc. Engring. Edn., Internat. Assn. Hydraulic Rsch. (U.S. del. joint com. on urban storm drainage with Internat. Assn. Water Quality 1987-93), Internat. Assn. Sci. Hydrology, Ind. Water Resources Assn. (Charles Harold Bechert award 1992), Wabash Area Lifetime Learning Assn. (pres. 2007—). Home: 124 Mohican Pl West Lafayette IN 47906-2159 Office: Purdue U Sch Civil Engring 550 Stadium Mall Dr West Lafayette IN 47907-2051

DELLI, BERTRUN H., art historian; b. Dresden, Germany, July 17, 1928; arrived in U.S., 1967; d. Johannes and Elfriede Tamme Delli. Degree in music, State Acad. Music and Theater, Dresden, 1949; PhD in Music and Art History, Free U., Berlin, 1957; diploma in lang. and culture, Ctr. de la Langue and Civila, Paris, 1967; MLS, Pratt Inst., 1978. Asst. prof. Concordia Coll., Seward, Nebr., 1972—73; asst. editor art index H.W. Wilson Co., NY, 1973—76, editor biography index NY, 1977—81, editor art index NY, 1981—94. Co-compiler: The Arts in America, a Bibliography, 1979-80, 1980. Named one of Cmty. Leaders and Noteworthy Ams., Am. Biog. Inst., 1978, Notable Ams., 1981; Clawson Mills Rsch. fellow, Met. Mus. Art, NYC, 1969—70. Mem.: ALA, Am. Musicology Soc.

DELLIBOVI, ALFRED A., bank executive, former federal agency administrator; b. Queens, NY, Feb. 1, 1946; m. Elizabeth Power; children: Robert, Christine. BA, Fordham Coll., 1967; MPA, Baruch Coll., 1973. High sch. tchr.; adminstrv. asst. to Assemblyman Alfred D. Lerner NY State Assembly, Albany, 1966—69, asst. to Spkr. Perry B Duryea, Jr, 1969, mem., 1971—78; adminstr. NY region Urban Mass Transp. Adminstrn., US Dept. Transp., NYC, 1981-84, dep. adminstr. Washington, 1984-87, adminstr., 1987-89; deputy sec. US Dept. Housing & Urban Devel., Washington, 1989-92; pres. Fed Home Loan Bank NY, 1992—. Roman Catholic. Office: Federal Home Loan Bank 101 Park Ave New York NY 10178-0500

DELLINGER, ROBERT J., corporate financial executive; BA in Econs., Ohio Wesleyan U., 1982. Pres., CEO Frankona Re GE, Munich, with fin. mgmt. program in consumer electronics bus. to corp. audit staff and exec. audit mgr., 1989, various mgr. positions, 1990—93, dir. fin. and bus. devel. plastics Singapore, 1993, mgr. fin. motor and indsl. sys., 1995, officer, exec. v.p., CFO, 1997; CFO, exec. v.p. Sprint Nextel Corp., Shawnee Mission, Kans., 2002—05; exec. v.p., CFO Delphi Corp., Troy, Mich., 2005—. Serve numerous bds. GE Plastics, GE Employers Reinsurance Corp. bds., Europe, Asia, US, Employers Reinsurance Corp., GE Frankona Re, GE Global Ins. Holdings, Employers Reinsurance Corp. Life, 2002—. Mem.: Fin. Execs. Inst. Office: Delphi Corp 5725 Delphi Dr Troy MI 48098-2815*

DELLINGER, WALTER ESTES, III, lawyer, educator; b. Charlotte, NC, May 15, 1941; s. Walter Estes and Grace Phelan (Lawing) D.; m. Anne Elizabeth Maxwell, June 12, 1965; children— Hampton, Andrew. AB with honors, U. N.C., at Chapel Hill, 1963; LLB, Yale U., 1966. Bar: N.C. 1970, DC, 1998. U.S. Supreme Ct. Assoc. prof. law U. Miss., 1966-68; law clk. to Justice Hugo L. Black, U.S. Supreme Ct., 1968-69; assoc. prof. law Duke U., 1969-72, Douglas B. Maggs prof., 1972-93, 98—; assoc. dean Duke U. Law Sch., 1974-76, acting dean, 1976-78; vis. prof. U. So. Calif. Law Ctr., 1973-74, U. Mich. Law Sch., 1977, Cath. U. Leuven, Belgium, 1985; prof. in residence U.S. Dept. Justice, Washington, 1980-81, advisor to the President, 1993; asst. atty. gen., head legal counsel U.S. Justice Dept., Washington, 1993-96; acting Solicitor Gen. U.S. Supreme Ct., 1996-97; chair, head appellate practice O'Melveny & Myers, Washington, ptnr. Cons., draftsman N.C. Criminal Code Commn., 1970-78; lectr. in the field. Mem. bd. editors Yale Law Jour., 1965-66, Am. Prospect; contbr. articles to profl. jours. Rockefeller Found. Humanities fellow, 1981-82; Nat. Humanities Ctr. Fellow, 1988-89. Mem. ABA, N.C. State Bar.; mem. exec. com. Yale Law Sch. Assn. Democrat. Home: 604 E Franklin St Chapel Hill NC 27514-3822 Office: Duke U Sch Law Box 90389 Science Dr & Towerview Rd Durham NC 27708

DELLO JOIO, NORMAN, composer; b. NYC, Jan. 24, 1913; s. Casimir and Antoinette (Garramone) Dello J.; m. Barbara Bolton, 1974; children: Victoria, Justin, Norman. Student, All Hallows Inst., 1926-30, Coll. City N.Y., 1932-34, Inst. Mus. Art, 1936, Juilliard Grad. Sch., 1939-41, Yale Sch. Music, 1941; MusD (hon.), Colby Coll., Lawrence Coll., U. Cin., 1967, St. Mary's Coll., 1969, Susquehanna U., 1980, U. So. Calif., 2006. Tchr. composition Sarah Lawrence Coll., 1945-50, Mannes Coll. Music, 1952—; commentator Met. Opera broadcasts; dean Sch. for the Arts, Boston U., 1972-78. Mem. rsch. adv. coun. US Office Edn.; adv. coun. State U. NY, Potsdam; chmn. policy com. contemporary music Ford Found. Composer: Ballet On Stage, 1944; piano and chorus Jubilant Song, 1945, Piano Sketchers, 2000, A Dream, 2000, Ricercari; for piano and orch., 1946, Variations- Chaccone-Finale, 1947, Diversion of Angels; dance, 1948, Concertante for Clarinet and Orch, 1949, New York Profiles; for orch., 1949, The Triumph of St. Joan; opera, 1950, Psalm of David; chorus and strings and brass orch., 1950, Song of Affirmation; soprano, chorus strings and brass , narrator, orch., 1950, Somebody's Coming; chorus and piano, The Tall Kentuckian; score for musical play, 1952, Song of the Open Road; chorus, 1952, (opera) The Ruby, 1953, The Lamentation of Saul, Baritone solo orch., 1954, The Trial at Rouen, 1955, Mediations on Ecclesiastes, 1956 (Pulitzer prize 1958), Air Power, symphonic suite, 1956, Ballad of the 7 Lively Arts, 1957, To St. Cecilia mixed chorus and brass, 1958, (opera) Blood Moon; also: Variations and Fantasy for Piano and Orchestra, 1961; (love songs) There is a Lady Sweet and Kind, Why So Wan, Pale Lover, Let Me Count the Ways, Meeting at Night; score Songs of Adieu, The Orch. Louvre, NBC TV, 1965 (Emmy award), Beyond Every Horizon; for Symphonic band Antiphonal Fantasy; organ, brass, strings, 1965, Songs of Walt Whitman for Orch. and Chorus, 1966, Capriccio; for piano, 1968, Fantasies on Theme of Haydn (orchestra), 1968, Time of Snow; ballet, 1968, Proud Music of the Storm; chorus, brass, organ, 1967, Days of the Modern; chorus, brass, percussion, 1968, Evocations; Variants on Medieval Tunel Band, 1965, chorus, orch., 1970, Psalm of Peace; chorus, organ, french horn, trumpet, 1971, Mass; chorus, organ, brass Concertante for Wind Instruments, 1972, Of Crows and Clusters; chorus and piano, 1972, Suite for Flute and Piano, 1973, Suite for Clarinet and Piano, 1973, Suite for Organ, 1973, Folio for Piano, 1973, Lyric Fantasies for Viola and Strings, 1973, The Poet's Song, 1973, Leisure, 1973, Songs of Abelard (band and voice) Mass to the Blessed Virgin; organ and chorus, 1974, Satiric Dances; band, 1974, Stage Parodies; piano 4 hands, 1974, Mass of the Eucharist in honour of Pope John XXIII; organ, brass, strings and chorus, 1975, Notes from Tom Paine; chorus and piano, 1975, Colonial

Variants; orch., 1976, Southern Echoes, 1976, Colonial Ballads; band, 1977, As of a Dream; orch., soloists, chorus, narrator and dancers, 1978, Sonata for Trumpet and Piano, 1978, Songs of Remembrance; voice solo and orch., 1978, Salute to Scarlatti; piano, 1978, The Psalmist's Meditation; chorus and piano, 1978, Variations; piano, 1980, Hymns Without Words; chorus and piano, 1979, Ballabili; dances for orch., 1981; chorus and piano Love Songs at Parting, 1982; string orch. East Hampton Sketches, 1983; piano and 4 hands Song at Springtide, 1984; concert band Aria and Roulade, 1983; chorus and concert band Let Us Sing a New Song, 1984, concert band Metaphrase, 1985, orch. Variants on a Bach Chorale, 1985, piano Introduction and Fantasies, 1985, Short Intervallic Etudes for Piano, 1986, Sing a Song Universal for chorus and piano, 1987, Nativity for chorus, soloists and orch., 1987, The Quest, 1990, mixed chorus and piano, A Memory: Men's Chorus and Piano, 1991, Songs of Memory, 1991, Variants on a Medieval Tune, 1993, Reflections on an Ancient Hymn for chamber orch., 1996, Salute to the Orch. Chamber Orch. Player, 1997, chamber orchestra Divertimento, 1997, Reflections on an Ancient Tune, 1997, piano 2 Songs Without Words, 1997, String Quartet, "Lyrical Interludes," 1998, concert band Fantasies, The Vigil for Mixed Chorus and Brass Instruments, band arrangement Jubilant Song, (music for TV series) Air Power, Directimento for Chamber Orch., 1997, mixed chorus and piano Passing Strangers, 2002; Lyrical Movement for string orch., 1995; Lyrical Interludes-string quartet Simple Sketches for piano, 2000, chorus and piano Dreamers, 2000, chorus and piano Passing Strangers, 2002, concert band City Scenes, 2003. Chmn. planning com. Ford Found.; Bd. dirs. Am. Music Center. Recipient Elizabeth Sprague Coolidge award, 1937; recipient Town Hall Composition award, 1941, N.Y. Music Critics Circle award, 1949, 58, Pulitzer prize for music, 1957, Emmy award for TV Score, Lifes Achievement award, Nat. Band Dirs. Assn., 2003; Grants and Scholarships in name of Norman Dello Joio awarded to Choral Soc. East Hampton students, 2003; Guggenheim fellow, 1943-44; Am. Acad. Arts and Letters grantee, 1945. Mem. Nat. Acad. Arts and Letters (coun.), Broadcast Music, Devon Yacht Club. Home: PO Box 154 East Hampton NY 11937-0154 *Whatever recognition I have received for my creative work, I owe for the most part, to an understanding mother and disciplinarian father. In this, my 70th year, I give thanks for a loving wife, a composer son whose music I feel will be an extension of myself into the future, and a son who is an Olympic equestrian of whom I am proud.*

DELLORUSSO, NEIL, astrochemist; b. Livingston, NJ, May 21, 1966; s. Neil B. and Roberta P. (Reichlen) D.; m. Kelly A. VanHouten, June 3, 1995. BA in Physics, Gettysburg Coll., Pa., 1988; PhD in Phys. Chemistry, U. Md., 1994. Tchg. asst. U. Md., College Pk., 1988-90, rsch. asst., 1990-94; Nat. Rsch. Coun. fellow Goddard Space Flight Ctr. (NASA), Greenbelt, Md., 1994-97; asst. rsch. prof. Catholic U./NASA Goddard Space Flight Ctr., Washington and Greenbelt, 1997—. Mem. Am. Astron. Soc. Achievements include laboratory study of nitriles inthe infrared for the purpose of identifying and quantifying nitriles in the atmosphere of Saturn's moon Titan, work on identifying and quantifying molecular species in comets. Office: Goddard Space Flight Ctr Code 693 Bldg 2 Greenbelt MD 20771-0001

DELL'OSSO, LOUIS FRANK, neuroscience educator; b. Bklyn., Mar. 16, 1941; s. Frank and Rose (Perrone) Dell'O.; m. Aquilina Marie Ferlo, May 22, 1965 (div. 1976); single ptnr. Charlene Hale Morse, Sept. 30, 1977. BEE, Bklyn. Poly. Inst., 1961, postgrad., 1961-63; PhD, U. Wyo., 1968. Co-dir. Ocular Motor Neurophysiology Lab. VA. Med. Ctr., Miami, Fla., 1972-80; asst. prof. biomed. engring. and surgery U. Miami, 1970-72, asst. prof. neurology, 1972-75, assoc. prof. neurology, 1975-79, prof. neurology, 1979-80; dir. Ocular Motor Neurophysiology Lab. VA Med. Ctr., Cleve., 1980—2004; prof. neurology and biomed. engring. Case Western Res. U., Cleve., 1980—, dir. Daroff-Dell'Osso Ocular Motility Lab., 2004—. Cons. Westinghouse Research Lab, Pitts, 1966-67, 70-71, Mt. Sinai Hosp., Miami, Fla., 1972-75. Bd. dirs. Vineland Galloway Civic Assn., Miami, 1973-76. Grantee NIH, 1971-77, VA Med. Ctr., 1972—, NSF, 1970. Fellow N.Am. NeuroOphthalmology Soc.; mem. IEEE, Engring. in Medicine and Biology Soc. (sr., chpt. chmn. 1977-78), Assn. Rsch. in Vision and Ophthalmology, Soc. Neurosci., NY Acad. Scis., Train Collectors Assn., CCCC Rod & Gun Club. Democrat. Home: 2356 Tudor Dr Cleveland OH 44106-3212 Office Phone: 216-421-3224. Business E-Mail: lfd@case.edu.

DELLO STRITTO, ELLEN M., retired social studies educator; b. Alliance, Nebr., Dec. 1, 1945; d. Howard John and Mary Margaret McCuin; m. Philip J. Dello Stritto, Nov. 28, 1970; children: Mary Ellen, Douglas, Katherine. BSc, SUNY Potsdam, 1967, MSc, 1970; postgrad., SUNY Oswego, 1992, Nat. Archives Wash. DC, 1992. Substitute tchr. then tchr. social studies Auburn City Sch. Dist., NY, 1967—2002; ret., 2002. Peer reviewer NY State Bd. Regents; mem. ethics com. Cayuga County Legis. Vol. Sacred Heart Ch., Auburn; bd. dirs. Cayuga Mus., 2007. Mem.: Ctrl. NY Ret. Tchrs. Orgn. (Region 7), NY State United Tchrs. Local Group, NY State Ret. Tchrs. Orgn. (life). Democrat. Roman Catholic. Avocations: reading, gardening. Home: 5599 W Lake Rd Auburn NY 13021

DELLUMS, RONALD VERNIE, mayor, retired congressman; b. Oakland, Calif., Nov. 24, 1935; m. Cynthia Lewis; 4 children. AA, Oakland City Coll., 1958; BA, San Francisco State Coll., 1960; MSW., U. Calif., 1962. Psychiatric social worker Calif. Dept. Mental Hygiene, 1962-64; program dir. Bayview Community Ctr., San Francisco, 1964-65; from assoc. dir. to dir. Hunters Point Youth Opportunity Ctr., 1965-66; planning cons. Bay Area Social Planning Coun., 1966-67; dir. concentrated employment program San Francisco Econ. Opportunity Coun., 1967-68; sr. cons. Social Dynamics, Inc., 1968-70; mem. US Congresses from 9th Calif. Dist., 1971-98; former chmn. house com. on D.C.; former mem. permanent select com. on intelligence; chmn. house armed svcs. com., 1993; pres. Healthcare Internat. Mgmt., Washington, 1998—2001; founder, sr. ptnr. Dellums & Assocs., LLC, Washington, 2001—; mayor City of Oakland, Calif., 2007—. Lectr. San Francisco State Coll., U. Calif., Berkeley; mem. U.S. del. North Atlantic Assembly, ranking minority mem. Nat. Security Com.; former chmn. Congl. Black Caucus, Calif. Dem. Congl. Del. Author: Defense Sense: The Search For a Rational Military Policy, 1983; co-author (with H. Lee Halterman): Lying Down with the Lions: A Public Life from the Streets of Oakland to the Halls of Power, 2000. Mem. Berkeley City Coun., 1967-71; served in USMC, 1954-56. Democrat. Office: City Hall One Frank H Ogawa Plz Oakland CA 94612*

DELMAR, EUGENE ANTHONY, architect; b. Gallitzin, Pa., June 8, 1928; s. Frank and Viola (Bocci) DiMaria; m. Bettie Hardin, Apr. 7, 1951; children: Diana, Daniel, David. B.Arch., Columbia U., 1954; M.Arch. in Urban Design, Catholic U. Am., 1971. Architect Ronald S. Senseman, FAIA, Washington, 1954-59; pres. Eugene A. Delmar, Silver Spring, Md., 1959-93, Delmar Architects, P.A., Olney, Md., 1993—. Mem. vis. com. Sch. Architecture U. Md., 1975. Important works include Electrophysics Lab., Columbia, Md., Montgomery County Jud. Ctr., Natatorium, Washington, Charlotte Hall Vets. Retirement Home, Denton Courthouse/Multi-Svc. Ctr., Brooke Grove Elem. Sch., F. Douglass HS, Springbrook HS, Rocky Hill Mid. Sch., Blake HS, Francis Scott Key Elem. Sch., Rockville Nursing Home, Treatment and Learning Ctr., G. James Gholson Midl Sch., Cora L. Rice Elem. Sch. Ednl. Complex, Huntingtown HS, Clarksburg HS. Mem. code enforcement bd. Dept. Econ. and Community Devel. Md., 1973-76; mem. Montgomery County Beautification Com., 1965, Montgomery County Sign Rev. Bd., 1968-71; bd. dirs. Rockville Nursing Home. Served to 2d lt. C.E., U.S. Army, 1946-48. Recipient Disting. Service award U.S. Jaycees, 1964, E.B. Morris Disting. Service award, 1976 Fellow AIA (First award design 1966, award of merit for design Potomac Valley chpt. 1966, bd. dirs. Potomac Valley chpt. 1992-97, pres. 1967-68); mem. Md. Soc. Architects (pres. 1972-73), Silver Spring Lions (pres. 1978-79), Columbia Univ., Sigma Chi. Office: Delmar Architects PA 3411 Olandwood Ct Ste 205 Olney MD 20832-1488 Office Phone: 301-774-9821. E-mail: genedelmar@aol.com.

DEL MEDICO, AMY, mathematics professor; MS in Math., No. Ill. U., DeKalb, 2000. Asst. prof. math. Waubonsee CC, Sugar Grove, Ill., 2001—. Faculty liaison, Ctr. for Tchg., Learning and Tech. Waubonsee CC, Sugar Grove, Ill., 2005—07, pres. faculty coun., 2007—. Treas. NOW Fox Valley Ill. Chpt., 2005—07. Mem.: Am. Math. Soc., USA Triathlon, Chgo. Area Runners Assn., Sigma Xi. Office: Waubonsee CC Rte 47 at Waubonsee Dr Sugar Grove IL 60554 Home Phone: 630-907-6124; Office Phone: 630-466-7900. Business E-Mail: adelmedico@waubonsee.edu.

DELMER, DEBORAH P., science educator; b. Indpls., Dec. 7, 1941; d. Thomas A. Pierson and Elizabeth Ellen Carpenter; m. Yoash Vaadia (dec. Dec. 1997); 1 child, Sarah Vaadia. BA, Ind. U., 1963; PhD, U. Calif., San Diego, 1968. Asst., then assoc. prof. Mich. State U., East Lansing, 1974-82; prin. scientist Arco Plant Cell Rsch. Inst., Dublin, Calif., 1983-86; prof. Hebrew U., Jerusalem, 1986-96; prof., chair U. Calif., Davis, 1997—2002, chair sect. plant biology; assoc. dir. food security Rockefeller Found., 2002—07, cons. internat. agr., 2007—. Contbr. articles to profl. jours. Grantee NSF, 1998—, U.S. Dept. Energy, 1997—, Cotton Inc., 1999—; recipient Anselme Payne award, ACS, 2003. Mem. NAS, Am. Soc. Plant Biologists(pres.), Internat. Soc. Plant Molecular Biology. Office: Apt 1A1 33 Riverside Dr New York NY 10023 Office Phone: 917-441-1264. Fax: (530) 752-5410. E-mail: dpdelmer@ucdavis.edu.

DEL MONTE, MONTE ANTHONY, medical educator; s. Anthony and Joyce Del Monte; m. Kristen De Pree, Oct. 16, 1976; children: Derek, Marcy. BA, Johns Hopkins U., 1971, MD, 1974. Diplomate Am. Bd. Ophthalmology, 1982. Skillman prof. pediatric ophthalmology U. Mich., Ann Arbor, 1985—. Pres. Am. Orthoptic Coun., Madison, Wis., 1992—96; dir. at large Am. Assn. for Pediatric Ophthalmology and Strabismus, San Francisco, 1994—97. Bd. dirs. Delta Gamma Med. Found., St Louis, 1982—87. Recipient Honor award, Am. Assn. Pediatric Ophthalmology and Strabismus, 1996, Sr. Achievement award, 2001. Achievements include patents pending for new treatment for Graves Eye Disease. Office: U Michigan 1000 Wall St Ann Arbor MI 48105 Office Phone: 734-764-4163. Business E-Mail: madm@umich.edu.

DEL NEGRO, JOHN THOMAS, lawyer; b. Springfield, Mass., Oct. 2, 1948; s. Angelo Antonio and Marguerite (Garofalo) Del N.; m. Linda Anne Mayberry, July 6, 1973. BA, George Washington U., 1970; JD, Cornell U., 1975. Bar: Conn. 1975, U.S. Dist. Ct. Conn. 1978, U.S. Tax Ct. 1981. Assoc. Murtha, Cullina, Richter & Pinney, Hartford, Conn., 1975-81, ptnr., 1982-95, Del Negro & Feldman, LLC, Hartford, 1995—2005, Del Negro & Del Negro, LLC, Hartford, 2005—. Author: (with Levenson) Depreciation and Investment Tax Credits, 1983. Bd. dirs. Conn. Opera Assn., 1990-2003, Watkinson Sch., 1992-2000. Mem. ABA, Conn. Bar Assn. (tax exec. com. 1992-2002). Office: Goodwin Sq 225 Asylum St Hartford CT 06103-1524 Business E-Mail: jdelnegro@delnegrolaw.com.

DELNIK, ALEXANDER, engineering executive, consultant; b. Zhitomir, Ukraine, Nov. 10, 1961; arrived in US, 1991; s. Yefim and Bera (Nevelskaya) Delnik. MS, Civil Engring. Inst., Kiev, Ukraine, 1983, PhD, 1987; MBA, UCLA, 1997. Registered profl. engr., Calif. Engr. Civil Engring. Inst., Kiev, 1987-88, sr. rschr., lectr., 1988-91; engr., lab. supr. Soil Tech, Inc., Temecula, Calif., 1991-93; project mgr. Dames & Moore, Inc., LA, 1993-98; mgr. strategic planning and new bus. devel. Edison Internat., Rosemead, Calif., 1998—; pres. PTP Group Americas Inc., Studio City, Calif., 2003—. Editor: English-Russian-Ukrainian Geotechnical Dictionary, 1992; contbr. articles to profl. jours.; editl. bd. Ukrainian Jour. of Found. Engring., 1990-92. Recipient Diploma of Sr. Rschr., Coun. Ministers of USSR, 1990; Ministry of Higher Edn. Lenin's scholar, 1982-83, grantee, 1989-91. Achievements include research and development of numerical techniques to simulate soil-structure interaction; major design and construction projects worldwide; risk management, strategic planning and development of major business opportunities for a leading energy company; development of technology-based businesses. Home: 12745 Sarah St Studio City CA 91604 Personal E-mail: alex.delnik@usa.net.

DELOACH, HARRIS E.(EUGENE), JR., manufacturing executive, lawyer; b. Aug. 7, 1944; s. Harris Eugene and Julia (Murdock) Del; m. Louise Hawes, June 12, 1969; children: Harris Eigene III, John Wilson Malloy, Jeanette Hawes. BBA, U.S.C., 1966; JD, 1969. Bar: S.C. 1969, U.S. Dist. Ct. S.C. 1969, U.S. Ct. Appeals (4th cir.) 1974. Ptnr. Wilmeth & DeLoach, Hartsville, S.C., 1972-85; v.p., gen. counsel Sonoco Products Co., Hartsville, S.C., 1986-90, exec. v.p., 1966-98, sr. exec. v.p., 2000, pres., CEO, 2002—05, chmn., pres., CEO, 2005—. V.p. HDFP, 1990-92; bd. dirsBank of Hartsville, Coker's Pedigreed Seed Co., Har tsville, Sonoco Products Co. Trustee Coker Coll., Hartsville, 1974-79, vice chmn., 1979; chmn. bd. trustees Byerly Hosp., Hartsville, 1976-79, chmn. 1997; chmn. bd. dirs. Thomas Hart Acad., Hartsville, 1984. Served to capt. USAF, 1969-72. Recipient Algernon Sydney Sullivan award Coker Coll., 1985, Disting. Alumnus award U. S.C., 1998. Mem. ABA, S.C. Bar Assn., 4th Jud. Cir. Assn., S.C. (v.p. 1974-78), Darlington County Bar Assn. (pres. 1984), Hartsville C. of C. (pres. 1977), Rotary (pres. Hartsville club 1977, Citizen of Yr. Hartsville club 1980). Presbyterian. Home: 620 W Home Ave Hartsville SC 29550-4430 Office: Sonoco Products Co North Second St Hartsville SC 29550-3305*

DELOATCH, CHERYL LEE, writer; b. Murfreesboro, NC, Dec. 30, 1963; d. Gilbert Lee and Susie Monger Deloatch. BA, U. N.C., 1988, MEd, 1993. Instr. Roanoke-Chowan C.C., Ahoskie, N.C., 1988-90; tchr. N.C. Pub. Schs., 1990-97; radio broadcaster Mortenson Broadcasting, Raleigh, 1998; tech. svc. specialist MCI World Comm., Cary, NC, 1998—2002; freelance writer. TV news asst. Sta. WRAL-TV 5, Raleigh, 1997-98; radio broadcaster Hertford Broadcasting, Ahoskie, N.C., 1988; writer, editor various cos., 1987—. Sec. Sunday sch. Mt. Sinai Bapt. Ch., Como, N.C., 1990-96; active Adopt-A-Student Program Weldon Elem. Sch., 1991-92; media vol. Spl. Olympics World Summer Games, 1999; grad. Avadon Profl. Devel. Program. Mem. Internat. Assn. of Bus. Communicators, N.C. Writers Network, Journalism Alumni and Friends Assn., Gen. Alumni Assn., N.C. Assn. of Govt. Info. Officers, N.C. Assn. of Educators. Avocations: reading, writing, music, movies and restaurants, theater.

DELONG, DONALD ALAN, lawyer; b. Detroit, Apr. 29, 1957; s. Dean Oliver and Marjorie Nell (Jones) DeL.; m. Leslie Carol Fleming, Oct. 18, 1981. BA with high honors, Mich. State U., 1979; student, U. Tex., 1979-80; JD cum laude, Wayne State U., 1985. Bar: Mich. 1985, U.S. Dist. Ct. (so. dist.) Mich. 1985. Assoc. Rockwell & Kotz, P.C., Detroit, 1985-90, Frank & Stefani, P.C., Troy, Mich., 1990-91; shareholder Kotz & Sangster, P.C., Detroit, 1991-94, Donald A. DeLong, P.C., Birmingham, Mich., 1994-96, Thompson, Morello, FeKaris, Radner & DeLong, P.C., Farmington Hills, Mich., 1996—98; sole practitioner Southfield, Mich., 1998—. Mem. ABA, State Bar Mich., Oakland County Bar Assn. Avocations: running, soccer, chess, reading. Office: Ste 380 25899 W 12 Mile Rd Southfield MI 48034-8315

DE LONG, JACOB EDWARD, real estate broker; b. Syracuse, NY, Oct. 5, 1939; s. Jacob Edward (dec.) and Eva Ann (Sposato) D. (dec.); children: Edward Andrew, Michael Anthony, Sean Michael (dec.). Grad. H.S., Fayetteville, NY. Sales rep. Ill. Shade Divsn., Slick Airways, Chgo., 1963-67; dir. mktg. Bean Bros. Inc., Walton, NY, 1967-71; real estate sales Longley Jones Assoc., Syracuse, 1971-73, Radclif Real Estate, Syracuse, 1973-76; comml. real estate sales J. Edward De Long Real Estate, Syracuse, 1976-80, Eagan Real Estate Inc., Syracuse, 1980—2005, Realist Real Estate Co., Liverpool, NY, 2005—. Pres. bd. dirs. The Andrew Nelson Self Help Ctr., Syracuse. Fund raiser, Friends of the Burnet Park Zoo, Syracuse, 1986. Sgt. USAF, 1957-62. Mem. NY State Bd. Realtors, Onandaga Bd. Realtors, Onondaga Ski Club, Syracuse Ski Hawks, Am. Legion, Rotary Club of Eastwood. Republican. Roman Catholic. Office: Realist Real Estate Inc 925 7th North St Liverpool NY 13088 Home Phone: 315-451-5419; Office Phone: 315-447-4408. Business E-Mail: edrealist@aol.com.

DELONG, MAHLON R., neurologist, educator; b. Des Moines, Iowa, Mar. 17, 1938; MD cum laude, Harvard U., 1966. Lic. Am. Bd. Psychiatry and Neurology, Nat. Bd. Med. Examiners. Asst. resident, intern Harvard Svc./Boston City Hosp., 1966—68; rsch. assoc. NIMH/Clin. Sci. Lab., Bethesda, Md., 1968—70, sr. staff fellow, 1970—71, NIMH/Neurophysiology Lab., Bethesda, Md., 1971—73; resident neurology Johns Hopkins U., Balt., 1973—76, asst. prof. neurology and physiology, 1975—80; chief neurology svc. Columbia (Md.) Med. Plan, 1976—80; dir. phys. diagnosis course Johns Hopkins Hosp., Balt., 1977—80; chief dept. neurology Baltimore City Hosps., 1980—85; assoc. prof. neurology and neurosci. Johns Hopkins Sch. Medicine, 1980—85, prof. neurology and neurosci., 1986—90; chmn. dept. neurology Emory U. Sch. Medicine, Atlanta, 2001—, prof. dept. neurology, 2001—, William Timmie Professor, dept. neurology; sect. chief dept. neurology Emory Clinic, Atlanta, 2001—. Mem. editl. bd.: Critical Revs. in Neurobiology, 1997—, Archives of Neurology, 1996—, mem. manuscript rev. com.: Sci., Jour. Neurophysiology, Annals of Neurology, others. Named William Patterson Timmie chair neurology, 1993—, Ga. Biomed. Rsch. scientist, 1995; named to Soc. Scholars, Johns Hopkins U., 1998; recipient Tchr.-Investigator award, Nat. Inst. Neurol. and Communicative Disorders and Stroke, 1974—79, Javitz Neuroscis. Investigator award, 1986, Fred Springer award, Am. Parkinson Disease Found., 1997, Disting. Leadership award, Huntington's Disease Soc. Am., 1998. Mem.: AAAS, Inst. Medicine, Assn. Univ. Profs. Neurology, Soc. for Neurosci., Am. Parkinson's Disease Assn. (sci. adv. bd. 1990—), Nat. Inst. Neurol. Disorders and Stroke (counselor 1993—99), Dystonia Med. Rsch. Found. (mem. grant rev. 1990—), Am. Neurol. Assn. (chmn. fin. com. 1995—96, 1994—96, councilor 1994—95, mem. fin. com. 1993—), Internat. Basal Ganglia Soc. (sec. 1995—98), Movement Disorder Soc. (mem. internat. exec. com. 1997—). Achievements include research in structure and focus of basal ganglia, motor functions of the basal ganglia; motor system physiology, movement disorders in man, pathophysiology of movement disorders, basal forebrain cholinergic system, and Alzheimer's Disease and related dementia. Office: Emory U Dept Neurology Ste 6000 1639 Pierce Dr Atlanta GA 30322

DELONG, RAY, editor; Copy editor Dayton Jour. Herald, Ohio, 1972-73; editor, reporter Chgo. Daily News, 1973-78; city editor Columbia Missourian, summer 1980; freelance writer, 1978—; editor Bus. Law Today ABA Pub., Chgo., 1986—. Asst. prof. journalism U. Ill., 1978-84; asst. prof. Medill Sch. Journalism, Northwestern U., 1984-86; lectr. Univ. Coll., Northwestern U., 1985-2001. Office: ABA Publishing 321 N Clark St Chicago IL 60610-4403*

DELONGE, THOMAS MATTHEW, JR., musician; b. Poway, Calif., Dec. 13, 1975; s. Connie and Thomas DeLonge; m. Jen Jenkins, May 26, 2001; children: Ava Elizabeth, Jonas Rocket. Co-founder, vocalist & guitarist Blink-182, 1992—2005; co-founder, lead vocalist, guitarist & bassist Box Car Racer, 2002—03; co-founder, lead vocalist & guitarist Angels & Airwaves, 2005—. Musician: (albums) (with Blink-182) Buddha, 1994, Cheshire Cat, 1994, Dude Ranch, 1997, Enema of the State, 1999, The Mark, Tom & Travis Show, 2000, Take Off Your Pants & Jacket, 2001, Blink-182, (with Boxcar Racer) Boxcar Racer, 2002, There Is, 2002, (with Angels & Airwaves) We Don't Need to Whisper, 2006, (songs) (with Blink-182) All the Small Things, 1999 (MVT Video Music award for Best Group Video, 2000), I Miss You, 2004 (Choice Love Song, Teen Choice Awards, 2004). Co-recipient Blockbuster Favorite Group-New Artist award, 2000, Choice Rock Group award, Teen Choice Awards, 2000—01, Choice Tour of Yr., 2004, Best New Act award, MTV Europe Awards, 2000, Best Rock Act award, 2001, Favorite Band award, Kid's Choice Awards, 2001, Woodie of Yr., mtvU Woodie Awards, 2006.*

DELORENZO, DAVID A., food products executive; b. 1947; BA, Colgate U.; MBA, U. Pa., 1970. With Dole Food Co., Inc., 1970—; pres. Dole Fresh Fruit Co., 1986—92, Dole Food Co., Inc., 1990—96, pres. internat. divsn., 1993—96, pres., COO, 1996—2001, vice chmn., 2001, cons., 2002—07, pres., CEO, 2007—. Bd. dirs. Dole Food Co., Inc. Office: Dole Food Co Inc 1 Dole Dr Westlake Village CA 91362-7300*

DE LORENZO, WILLIAM E., retired foreign language educator; BA in Spanish and Speech, Montclair State Coll., 1959, MA in Speech and Drama, 1964; PhD in Fgn. Lang. Edn. and Tchr. Edn., Ohio State U., 1971. Tchr. Spanish various locations, N.J.; asst. prof. Spanish, Montclair State Coll.; assoc. prof. emeritus, coord. fgn. lang. edn./2d lang. edn. U. Md., College Park; ret. Organizer, co-dir. symposium for fgn. lang. tchr. candidates. Recipient Florence Steiner award, 1992. Mem. Am. Coun. on Tchg. Fgn. Langs. (charter).

DELOREY, JOHN ALFRED, printing company executive; b. Malden, Mass., July 13, 1924; s. John Alfred and Alice Gertrude (Collins) D.; m. Ann M. Abbott, Dec. 27, 1952; children— Debra Ann, Michael John, David Abbott BS in Econs., Boston Coll., 1950; MBA, Harvard U., 1953. Plant mgr. Container Corp. Am., Renton, Wash., 1965-69, mgf. mgr. Carol Stream, Ill., 1969-73, gen. mgr. St. Louis, 1973-77, Carol Stream, 1977-81, v.p., divsn. gen. mgr. St. Louis, 1981-82; exec. v.p. W.F. Hall Printing Co., Chgo., 1982-87; v.p. Container Corp. Am., 1987-93; pres. DeLorey & Assocs., Oak Brook, Ill., 1993—. Dir. Container Corp. Am. Polit. Action Com., Chgo., 1981-86. Author: (with others) Consumer Packaging, 1953 Served to maj. USAF, 1942-53, ETO. Decorated DFC, Air medal with 3 oak leaf clusters, European Theater medal with 3 battle stars. Mem.: Paperboard Packaging Assn. (dir. midwest region 1977—81), Boston Coll. Club (Naples, Fla.), Kensington Country Club, Harvard Bus. Club, Butterfield Country Club. Avocations: golf, swimming, skiing, bridge, reading. Home and Office: DeLorey & Assocs 194 Briarwood Loop Oak Brook IL 60523-8714

DELOREY, JOHN FRANCIS, music educator; b. Weymouth, Mass., Aug. 24, 1959; s. John Francis and Janet Ireland Delorey. BA in Music History, Vassar Coll., NYC, 1981; MusM in Choral Conducting, The Boston Conservatory, 2003. Singer Scholar Cantorum of Boston, 1993—, Schola Discantus of San Francisco, 1993—, Boston Camarata, 1995—; dir. The Ethos Ensemble, 1996—, Choral Arts Soc., 1996—, Convivium, 1998—2000, 2004—; interim music dir. St. Mark's Sch., Southboro, Mass., 1998—99; prof., condr. Clark Univ., Worcester, Mass., 1999—2000, Worcester (Mass.) Polytechnic, 2001—; dir. Vox Futurae, 2001—; interim music dir. Holy Cross Coll., 2003—; choral condr. The Boston Conservatory, 2003—. Clinician Ethos Prodns., Shrewsbury, Mass., 1996—; adjudicator World Music Festivals, Mass., 2000—; bd. dirs. Arts Worcester, 2000—02; R&S chair Am. Choral Dirs. Assn., 2002—. Mem.: Am. Choral Dirs. Assn. (ex. divsn. tech. chair 2005—). Home: 496 Main St Shrewsbury MA 01545 Office: Worcester Polytechnic Inst 100 Inst Rd Worcester MA 01609 Office Phone: 508-831-5051. Business E-Mail: jfd@wpi.edu.

DELORIA, PHILIP S. (SAM), lawyer; m. Vivian BA, JD, Yale Univ. Dir. Am. Indian Law Ctr., Albuquerque, 1972—. Lectr. Univ. N. Mex. Sch. Law; past sec. gen. World Council Indigenous Peoples. Co-founder Commn. State-Tribal Rels., N.Mex.; mem. Nat. Inst. Rev. Bd., Indian Health Svc. Mem.: Standing Rock Sioux. Office: American Indian Law Center PO Box 4456 Station A Albuquerque NM 87196 Office Phone: 505-277-5462. Business E-Mail: deloria@law.unm.edu.

DELORME, MICHAEL, toxicologist, researcher; b. Detroit, Mich., Dec. 18, 1966; s. Lawrence and Carolyn DeLorme; m. Holly Hodgins, June 18, 1994; 1 child, Evan. BS, Wayne State U., 1985—89, MS, 1991—94, PhD, 1994—99. Registered Medical Technologist Am. Soc. for Clin. Pathology, Ill., 1989. Med. technologist Damon Clin. Laboratories at the Detroit Med. Ctr., 1989—90, Cottage Hosp., Grosse Point Farms, Mich., 1990—94; grad. rsch. asst. II Wayne State U., Detroit, 1994—99; postdoctoral fellow CIIT Centers for Health Rsch., Rsch. Triangle Pk., NC, 1999—2002; rsch. toxicologist - inhalation group DuPont Haskell Lab., Newark, Del., 2002—. Contbr. articles to profl. jours. AIHA Found. scholarship, Am. Indsl. Hygiene Assn., 1996. Mem.: Soc. of Toxicology, Am. Indsl. Hygiene Assn. Office: DuPont Haskell Lab PO Box 50 Newark DE 19714 E-mail: michael.p.delorme@usa.dupont.com.

DELORY, GREGORY TOWNSEND, aerospace scientist, consultant; b. San Francisco, July 27, 1968; s. Greg Delory and Candace Wheeler Jordan; m. Pamela Kim Washington, Aug. 7, 2005. PhD, U Calif., Berkeley, 1996. Lic. pvt. pilot FAA, cert. rsch. scuba diver U. Calif., Berkeley, black belt Okinawan Shorin-Ryu Karate Assn. Rsch. asst. Lawrence Berkeley Nat. Lab., Berkeley, 1985—89; engrng. aide dept. astronomy U. Calif., Berkeley, 1990—91, postdoctoral rschr. Space Scis. Lab., 1996—2000, rsch. physicist, 2001—03, sr. fellow, 2003—; project mgr. TelEvoke, Inc, San Francisco, 2000. Cons. Planetary Soc., Pasadena, Calif., 1997—; owner P & G Consulting, San Francisco, 2005—. Contbr. articles to profl. publs. Mars Atmosphere in the Optical and Radio grantee, NASA, 1999—2001, Mars Instrument Devel. Project grantee, 2002—06, Planetary Instrument Definition and Devel. grantee, 2002—04, Mars Data Analysis Program grantee, 2004—, Discovery Data Analysis Program grantee, 2006—. Mem.: AIAA, Aircraft Owners and Pilot's Assn., Am. Geophys. Union. Achievements include development of world's first microphone sensor for Mars; novel electromagnetic sounder to detect liquid water beneath the surface of Mars; world's first operational solar sail (first launch failed, next attempt in 2008-2010); research in electrodynamics of dust devils on Earth and Mars; first to physical mechanism responsible for Auroral Kilometric Radiation, an intense radio emission generated by the Earth into space; design of theory using atmospheric dust electrification to explain the toxicity of Martian soils as determined by the Viking landers. Avocations: weightlifting, cooking, running. Office: UC Berkeley Space Scis Lab 7 Gauss Way Berkeley CA 94720 Home Phone: 415-644-5720; Office Phone: 510-643-1991. Office Fax: 510-643-8302. Business E-Mail: cycles2059@mypacks.net.

D'ELOSUA, JENNIFER DAWN, music educator; b. Fort Sill, Okla., Aug. 19, 1977; d. Ralph Frederick and Kathy Taylor D'Elosua. BA in Music Edn., Shenandoah U., Winchester, Va., 1999. Performer Walt Disney World, Orlando, Fla., 1999—2002; music specialist Fairfax County Pub. Schs., Springfield, Va., 2002—. Tchr. rsch. leader Tchr. Rsch., Springfield, 2005—; dir., tchr. pvt. music studio, Springfield, 2002—; presenter in field; performer various sch. fundraising events. Dir., choreographer: (prodn.) King's Voices;, composer various songs for sch. programs. Mem.: Sigma Alpha Iota (corr.). Home: 8225 Crestmont Cir Springfield VA 22153 Office: Kings Park Elem Sch 5400 Harrow Way Springfield VA 22151 Home Phone: 703-493-9248; Office Phone: 703-426-7000. Personal E-mail: jdznygoof@aol.com.

DELOTTO, JEFFREY DANIEL, language educator, writer; b. Nassawadox, Va., Dec. 23, 1949; s. Mayo Andrew and Emalyn Crouch DeLotto. BA, U. Fla., Gainesville, 1973; MA, Fla. State U., Tallahassee, 1974, PhD, 1980. Vis. lectr. Tex. Wesleyan U., Lubbock, 1977—80; lectr. in English Yarmouk U., Irbid, Jordan, 1980—82; prof. English Tex. Wesleyan U., Ft. Worth, 1983—, interim dean, sci. and humanities, 1997—99; Fulbright lectr. in English U. Plovdiv, Bulgaria, 1992—93. Editor: AmarilloBay, 1995; author: Voices at the Door, 1995 (First pl. SW Poets Series, 1994), Days of a Chameleon Collected Poems, 2007. Fellow Fulbright Lectureship in Am. Lit., Coun. for Internat. Exch. of Scholars, 1992—93; NEH fellow, 1984, 1989. Mem.: Tex. Coll. English Assn. (pres. 2004—05), Conf. of Coll. Teachers of English (pres. 1999—2000, Best Paper award 1990, 2004, 2007), Coll. English Assn., Tex. Coun.Tchrs. English Lang. Arts (life; pres. 1990—91, Outstanding English Educator Post Secondary 1992), Ft. Worth Poetry Soc. Avocations: writing, poetry, sailing, painting. Home: 2415 Sandy Ln Fort Worth TX 76112 Office: Texas Wesleyan Univ 1201 Wesleyan St Fort Worth TX 76105 Home Phone: 817-531-4909; Office Phone: 817-531-4909. Business E-Mail: jdelotto@txwes.edu.

DELP, ROY EDWARD, music educator, singer; b. Newark, Oct. 14, 1943; s. Roy John and Jane Molenska Delp; m. Maryellen Butin, Apr. 16, 1966; children: George Edward, Roy Jonathan. MusB, Oberlin Coll. Conservatory Music, Ohio, 1965; MusM, New Eng. Conservatory, Boston, 1967. Asst. prof. music Augusta Coll., Ga., 1967—72; asst. prof. dept. music U. Wyo., Laramie, 1972—76; Walter S. James prof. voice coll. music Fla. State U., Tallahassee, 1976—, coord. voice and opera area faculty, 1976—. On-site reporter opera, musical theater program grant proposals NEA, Washington, 1991—93. Singer: Nat. Pub. Radio, (Operas) Lake George Opera Company, Orlando Opera Company, Orquesta Sinfonica de Chile; contbr. articles to profl. jours. Mem.: Music Tchrs. Nat. Assn., Nat. Assn. Tchrs. Singing (nat. pres. 1999—2004). Home: 1312 Lemond St Tallahassee FL 32308-0720 Office: Florida State Univ College Music Tallahassee FL 32306-1180 Home Phone: 850-386-6544; Office Phone: 850-644-4528.

DELP, WILBUR CHARLES, JR., lawyer; b. Cedar Rapids, Iowa, Oct. 26, 1934; s. Wilbur Charles and Irene Frances (Flynn) D.; m. Patricia Lynn Vesely, June 22, 1963; children: Marci Lynn, Melissa Kathryn, Derek Charles. BA, Coe Coll., 1956; LLB, NYU, 1959. Bar: Ill. 1960, U.S. Supreme Ct. 1962. Assoc. Sidley Austin, Chgo., 1959—68, ptnr., 1968—2000, sr. counsel, 2000—. Lectr. securities law seminars With USAF, 1959-65. Mem. ABA (securities com.), Chgo. Bar Assn., Lawyers Club (Chgo.), Phi Beta Kappa, Phi Kappa Phi. Home: 34W880 Army Trail Rd Saint Charles IL 60174 Office: Sidley Austin One S Dearborn St Chicago IL 60603-0001 Office Phone: 312-853-7416. Personal E-mail: retlaw1934@aol.com. Business E-Mail: wdelp@sidley.com.

DELPH, DONNA JEAN (MAROC), education educator, consultant, academic administrator; b. Hammond, Ind., Mar. 7, 1931; d. Edward Joseph and Beatrice Catherine (Ethier) Maroc; m. Billy Keith Delph, May 30, 1953 (div. 1967); 1 child, James Eric. BS, Ball State U., 1953, MA, 1963, EdD, 1970. Cert. in ednl. adminstrn./supervision, reading specialist, Ind.; cert. elem. sch. tchr., Ind., Calif. Elem. tchr. Long Beach (Calif.) Community Schs., 1953-54; elem. tchr., reading specialist, asst. dir. elem. edn. Hammond Pub. Schs., 1954-70; prof. edn. Purdue U. Calumet, Hammond, 1970-84, 88-90, prof. emeritus, 1990—, head dept. edn., dir. tchr. edn., 1984-88. Cons. pub. schs., Highland, Ind., 1970-88, Gary, Ind., 1983-88, East Chicago, Ind., 1987-88, Hammond, 1970-88; speaker/workshop presenter numerous profl. orgns., Hammond, 1964—; mem. exec. coun. Nat. Coun. Accreditation Tchr. Edn., 1991-97. Author: (with others) Individualized Reading, 1967; contbr. articles, monographs to profl. jours. Bd. dirs. Bethany Child Care and Devel. Ctr., Hammond, 1972-77. Recipient Outstanding Teaching award Purdue U. Calumet, 1981. Mem. Assn. Tchr. Educators, Assn. for Supervision and Curriculum Devel. (rev. coun. 1987-91, bd. dirs. 1974-85), Internat. Reading Assn., Ind. Reading Profs. (pres. 1985-86), Pi Lambda Theta. Office: Purdue Univ Calumet Dept Education Hammond IN 46323 Personal E-mail: donnajdelph@bellsouth.net.

DEL PINO, EUGENIA M., biology professor; MS, Vassar Coll., 1969; PhD in Biology, Emory U., 1972. Alexander von Humboldt fellow Cancer Rsch. Ctr., Heidelberg, Germany, 1984—85; prof. sch. biol. scis. Pontifical Cath. U. Ecuador, Quito. V.p. for Ecuador Charles Darwin Found., 1992—96, v.p. gen. assembly, 1998—2001. Contbr. articles to sci. jours. Recipient L'Oréal Helena Rubinstein prize, Women in Sci. for L.Am. and the Caribbean, 2000. Mem.: Am. Acad. Arts & Scis. (hon. fgn. mem.), Third World Acad. Scis., Latin Am. Acad. Scis., NAS (fgn. assoc.). Office: Pontifical Cath U Ecuador Dept Biol Scis Ave 12 Octubre y Patria Sect 17-01-2184 Quito Ecuador E-mail: edelpino@puce.edu.ec.

DELPY, JULIE, actress; b. Paris, Dec. 21, 1969; d. Albert Delpy and Marie Pillet. Grad., NYU. Appeared in films Détective, 1985, Mauvais sang, 1987, Beatrice, 1987, Europa, Europa, 1991, Voyager, 1991, Blue, 1993, The Three Musketeers, 1993, Killing Zoe, 1994, White, 1994, Red, 1994, Trzy kolory:Bialy, 1994, Before Sunrise, 1995, Tykho Moon, 1996, An American Wolf in Paris, 1997, Alleys and Motorways (video), 1997, LA Without a Map, 1998, The Treat, 1998, (TV) Crime and Punishment, 1998, The Passion of Ayn Rand, 1999, Sand, 2000, MacArthur Park, 2001, (voice) Waking Life, 2001, Beginner's Luck, 2001, Villa des roses, 2002, Cinemagique, 2002, Notting Hill Anxiety Festival, 2003, Before Sunset, 2004 (also writer, composer), Frankenstein, 2004, Broken Flowers, 2005, 3 & 3, 2005, The Legend of Lucy Keyes, 2006, The Hoax, 2006, The Air I Breathe, 2007, Two Days in Paris, 2007 (also writer), others; actress, dir. short film Blah, Blah, Blah, 1995; dir., casting dir., writer, prodr., editor Looking for Jimmy, 2002; guest appearances ER, 2001, Graham Norton Effect, 2004, Real Time with Bill Maher, 2004, others; singer (albums) Julie Delpy, 2003.*

DEL RASO, JOSEPH VINCENT, lawyer; b. Phila., Dec. 21, 1952; s. Vincent and Dolores Ann (D'Adamo) Del R.; m. Anne Marie McGloin, Apr. 17, 1982; children: Joseph Vincent Jr., Katherine Anne, Marianna. BS in Acctg., Villanova U., 1974, JD, 1983. Bar: Pa., 1983, Fla. 1988. Exec. v.p. Belgrade Constrn., Inc., Wayne, Pa., 1974-80; atty. SEC, Washington, 1983-85; assoc. Dechert, Price & Rhoads, Washington, 1986-88; ptnr. Holland & Knight, Ft. Lauderdale, Fla., 1988-92, Stradley, Ronon, Stevens & Young, Phila., 1992-98, Pepper Hamilton LLP, Phila., 1998—. Exec. v.p., bd. dirs. Nat. Italian-Am. Found.; chair bd. trustees Am. Univ., Rome; mem. Pres.'s Commn. White Ho. Fellowships. Co-editor-in-chief Villanova Jour. Law and Investment Mgmt. Mem. Columbus Citizens Found.; bd. dirs. Justinian Found., World Affairs Coun. Phila.; vice-chair bd. counsultors Villanova U. Sch. Law; co-chair Ctr. for Mktg. and Pub. Policy Rsch. Villanova U. Decorated knight Constantinian Order, Order of Merit Italy. Mem. ABA, Aronimink Golf Club. Republican. Roman Catholic. Office: Pepper Hamilton LLP 18th & Arch Sts 3000 Two Logan Sq Philadelphia PA 19103

DEL RIEGO, RUTILIO J., bishop; b. Valdesandinas, Spain, Sept. 21, 1940; arrived in US, 1964, naturalized, 1981; Grad., Sem. of Diocesan Labor Priests, Salamanca, Spain; ThL, Cath. U. of Am., M in Spanish. Ordained priest, 1965; Spanish language instr. St. Vincent Coll., Latrobe, Pa., 1966—69; dir. Spanish Cath. Apostolate Archdiocese of Washington, Washington, 1969—73; dir. Office of Vocations Archdiocese of San Antonio, Tex., 1975—78; dir. Office for Hispanics N.E. Pastoral Ctr., NY, 1978—92; pastor Santa Lucia Parish, El Paso, Tex., 1983—93, San Antonio Parish, El Paso, 1993—94; dir. Diocesan Laborer Priests House of Formation, Washington, 1994—99; vice rector Serra House Diocese of San Bernardino, Calif., 1999—2000; pastor Our Lady of Perpetual Help, Riverside, Calif., 2000—05; ordained bishop, 2005; aux. bishop Diocese of San Bernardino, 2005—. Office: Diocese of San Bernardino 1201 E Highland Ave San Bernardino CA 92404-4641

DEL RIO, JACK, professional football coach, former professional football player; b. Castro Valley, Calif., Apr. 4, 1963; m. Linda Del Rio; children: Lauren, Hope, Aubrey, Luke. Student, U. So. Calif., 1985. Linebacker New Orleans Saints, 1985—86, Kansas City Chiefs, 1987—88, Dallas Cowboys, 1989—91, Minn. Vikings, Eden Prairie, 1992-95; asst. strength coach New Orleans Saints, 1997, linebackers coach, 1998, Balt. Ravens, 1999—2001; def. coord. Carolina Panthers, 2002; head coach Jacksonville Jaguars, 2003—. Selected to Pro Bowl, 1994. Office: 1 ALLTEL Stadium Pl Jacksonville FL 32202

DEL RIO, KATHLEEN O., language educator; b. New Orleans, July 11, 1947; d. Richard William and Jean Erichson O'Callaghan; m. Ralph Del Rio, Sept. 20, 1969; children: Nathan M., Ross P. BA in English, Southeastern La. U., Hammond, 1969; MA in English, U. New Orleans, 1972. Cert. educator La. Tchr. English Jefferson Parish Schs., La., 1993—94, St. Elizabeth Ann Seton Sch., Kenner, La., 1994—. Mem.: Nat. Coun. Tchrs. English. Office Phone: 504-468-3524.

DEL ROSSI, CHRISTOPHER, elementary school educator; b. Camden, NJ, Aug. 21, 1973; s. Joseph F. and Maryann A. Del Rossi; m. Alisa Maria Scocca, July 7, 2000; children: Isabella C., Dominique E. BEd in Elem. Edn., Rowan U., Glassboro, NJ, 1996—99; MA in Adminstrn. & Supervision, Seton Hall U., S.Orange, 2001—03. Cert. elem. edn. tchr. NJ Dept. Ed., 1999. Mid. sch. humanities tchr. Cherry Hill Bd. Edn., NJ, 1999—; adj. prof. Seton Hall U., 2003—05. Office: Rosa Internat Mid Sch PO Box 5015 Cherry Hill NJ 08034 Home Phone: 856-435-4644. Business E-Mail: cdelrossi@chclc.org.

DEL SESTO, JANICE MANCINI, opera company executive; Grad., New England Conservatory. Dir. development and comm. New England Foundation for the Arts, 1983—89; dir. development and public relations Computer Museum, 1989—92; gen. dir. Boston Lyric Opera Co., Boston, 1992—. Office: Boston Lyric Opera Co 45 Franklin St Boston MA 02110-1301

DELSON, SIDNEY LEON, architect; b. Chgo., Apr. 10, 1932; s. Robert and Evelyn (Fistel) D.; m. Elizabeth Pfannmuller, Sept. 10, 1955; children: Karen Lee, Sara Jeanne, Matthew Robert. BArch, Pratt Inst., 1959. Registered architect, N.Y. Archtl. draftsman Irving G. Kay, NYC, 1957-59; project architect William B. Tabler Assocs., NYC, 1959-62; architect-designer Union Carbide Corp., Tarrytown, NY, 1962-64; archtl. dept. head Metcalf and Eddy Engrs., NYC, 1965-66; devel. adminstr. N.Y. State Facilities Devel. Corp., NYC, 1966-80, dir. design, 1980-91; pvt. practice architecture Bklyn., 1991-99, East Hampton, NY, 1999—. Editor: Design Procedure Manual, 1986, 2d edit., 1988, 3d edit., 1991. Mem. Community Planning Bd. Bklyn., 1968-71, vice chmn., 1971; chmn. adv. com. Bklyn. Mus. Community Gallery, 1970-73. Served as sgt. U.S. Army, 1951-53. Fellow AIA; mem. N.Y. State Assn. Architects (bd. dirs. 1982-85, 89, sec.-treas. 1988, Matthew W. DelGaudio award 1992), Am. Cons. Engrs. Coun. (peer rev. 1987—), Am. Arbitration Assn. (panelist 1971—). Home and Office: 29 Orkney Rd East Hampton NY 11937-1313

DEL TIEMPO, SANDRA KAY, sales executive; d. Charles Soloman and Lacey Marie (Webb) Eggers; m. Robert Joseph Craig, June 28, 1986 (div. Jan. 1993); 1 child, Misty Marie Mangus; m. Robert David Del Tiempo, Feb. 14, 1995; stepchildren: Jaime Brandon, Joseph David Del Tiempo. AAB cum laude, Shawnee State U., 1985; BBA summa cum laude, Ohio U., 1987; postgrad., Pepperdine U., 1998—2000. From ter. mgr. to sales mgr. ARA Cory, San Diego, 1988—90; sales rep. Rsch. Inst. Am., Riverside, Calif., 1990—92, 1996—2000, regional sales mgr. So. Calif., LA, 1992—95, leader's coun. Culver City, 1996—2000, pres. bd. dirs., 1996—97, asst. mgr., 1997, 1999—2000, corp. acct. mgr., 1997—2000; mem. sales adv. bd. RIA/CLR Group (formerly Rsch. Inst. Am.), Culver City, 1998—2000; sr. v.p. Media Strategy Lawnmower Media, Culver City, 2000; sr. account exec. SAP Am., Irvine, Calif., 2000—03; acct. mgr. CCH, Inc., 2003—04; cons. internet mktg. LexisNexis, New Providence, NJ, 2004—. Cons. Video Ave., Paradise Pizza, Chillicothe, Ohio, 1987-88; sales rep. to corp. acct. mgr. Rsch. Inst. Am. Orange County, L.A., 1990-2000 Active Girl Scouts U.S., Menifee, 1988—92, Jr. All Am. Football. Mem. NAFE, NOW, Phi Kappa Phi, Phi Theta Kappa, Delta Mu Delta. Democrat. Avocations: travel, reading, jazz. Home: 6732 E Ashler Hills Cave Creek AZ 85331-3130 Office: Martindale Hubbell 123 Chanlon Rd New Providence NJ 07974 Office Phone: 480-575-0050. Personal E-mail: sdeltiempo@yahoo.com. Business E-Mail: sandra.deltiempo@lexisnexis.com.

DEL TORO, BENICIO, actor; b. Santurce, PR, Feb. 19, 1967; Actor: (films) Licence To Kill, 1989, China Moon, 1994, The Usual Suspects, 1995, The Funeral, 1996, The Fan, 1996, Joy Ride, 1996, Cannes Man, 1996, Basquiat, 1996, Excess Baggage, 1997, Fear and Loathing in Las Vegas, 1998, Snatch, 2000, The Way of the Gun, 2000, Traffic, 2000 (Acad. award best sup. actor, 2001, BAFTA award best sup. actor, 2001, Golden Globe award best sup. actor, 2001), The Pledge, 2001, The Hunted, 2003, 21 Grams, 2003 (Acad. Award nomination for best supporting actor, 2004, Screen Actors Guild Award nomination for best supporting actor, 2004), Sin City, 2005; prodr., writer: (films) Submission, 1995. TV appearances include Miami Vice, 1987, Private Eye, 1987, Tales from the Crypt, 1994, Fallen Angels, 1995, T4, 2004. Office: IFA Talent Agy 8730 W Sunset Blvd Ste 490 Los Angeles CA 90069-2248

DEL TORO, GUILLERMO, film director; b. Guadalajara, Jalisco, Mexico, Oct. 9, 1964; Attended, U. Guadalajara. Make-up supr.; founder Necropia, Mexico, The Tequila Gang, Mexico; film teacher Mexico. Jury mem. Ind. Film Project's Spirit Awards, 1999, 2000; judge, mentor NHK Awards, 2000. Writer & dir. (films) Cronos, 1993 (Critics' Week Fripresci award, Cannes Internat. Film Festival, 1993), Mimic, 1997, The Devil's Backbone, 2001, Hellboy, 2004, Pan's Labyrinth, 2006 (named Best Picture, Nat. Soc. Film Critics, 2007, Film Not in the Eng. Lang. award, Brit. Acad. Film and TV Arts, 2007); dir.: (films) Blade II, 2002; prodr.: Dona Herlinda and Her Son, 1985; (TV series) Hora Marcada.*

DEL TORO-POLITOWICZ, LILLIAN, medical association administrator, geriatrics services professional, consultant; b. Bronx, NY, Feb. 23, 1954; d. Billie Antonio Del Toro and Eva Luz (Guasp) Toro; 1 child, Yvelise Delilah Chandler; m. Walter Politowicz, Nov. 23, 1997; 1 stepchild, Sebastian. BS in Psychology summa cum laude, Mercy Coll., 1981; postgrad., L.I. U., 1982-83, Harvard U., 1973-74, Lehman Coll., 1972-75, Nova South-Eastern U., 1998—. Lic. adminstr. adult care facilities, Fla. Mental hygiene therapist Rockland Psychiat. Hosp., Orangeburg, NY, 1975-81; office mgr. Frankart Furniture, Inc., Pelham Pkwy., NY, 1979-84; regional office mgr. W.J. Sloane, Inc., Ridgewood, NY, 1984-86; bookkeeper, asst. dir. mgmt. info. sys. Midland Lumber Supply Co., Midland Pk., NY, 1986-89; adminstr. Fla. Golden Years, Spring Hill, 1991-92, Gallo House II, River Lodge, New Port Richey, Fla., 1994-95, Ranch House, Tarpon Springs, Fla., 1993-94; co-owner Elder Care Foster Home, Spring Hill, Fla., 1992—. Grad. admissions counselor L.I. U., Bklyn., 1981-82; elder-care cons. Fla. Golden Years, Spring Hill, 1991-92. Harvard U. scholar, 1973-74; recipient outstanding achievement, health & human svcs.- cmty. svc. award YWCA and St. Petersburg Times, Tampa, 1997; undergraduate pre-medicine scholar Lehman Coll., Bronx, N.Y., 1972, 75, Harvard U., 1973-74. Mem. AAUW, NAFE, Altrusa Internat. (mem. cmty. projects com. 1997), Fla. Assisted Living Adminstrs. Assn., Alpha, Psi Chi. Avocations: world music and dance, opera, ballet, reading, nature. Home and Office: Elder Care Foster Home 6427 Mayhill Ct Spring Hill FL 34606-6028 E-mail: politowicz@yahoo.com.

DEL TORO SOTO, JAIME, psychiatrist; b. Guanica, PR, Feb. 9, 1947; s. Jaime Del Toro Rodríguez and Adoración Soto Arroyo; m. Adalina Feliciano Santiago, Aug. 8, 1970; children: Adaime, Jaime Javier, Jorge Javier. BS, U. P.R., 1969; MD, Zaragoza U., Spain, 1976. Diplomate Am. Bd. Forensic Medicine. Intern in gen. medicine Bayamon Regional Hosp., PR, 1977—78; resident in psychiatry P.R. Inst. Psychiatry, San Juan, 1979—82, clin. instr., 1982—90, co-dir. Outpatient Clin., 1985—86, asst. clin. prof., 1990—. Acting med. adminstr. Psychiat. Ctr. P.R., San Juan, 1982—92; co-dir., cliin. officer Inst. Psychaitry and Human Behavior, San Juan City Hosp., 1987—90; cons. and lectr. in field, 1992—; pvt. practice, 1992—. Mem.: Am. Psychiat. Assn., Am. Bd. Disability Analysts, Am. Coll. Forensic Examiners, Colegio Med. Cirujanos P.R., P.R. Psychiat. Soc. Avocations: saltwater sportfishing, anthropology. Office: Psychiat Ctr PR 652 Ave M Rivera Ste 3195 San Juan PR 00918-4261

DEL TUFO, ROBERT J., lawyer, former state attorney general; b. Newark, Nov. 18, 1933; s. Raymond and Mary (Pellecchia) Del T.; m. Katherine Nouri Hughes; children: Barbara, Ann, Robert, David. BA cum laude in English, Princeton U., 1955; JD, Yale U., 1958. Bar: NJ 1959. Law sec. to chief justice N.J. Supreme Ct., 1958-60; assoc. firm Dillon, Bitar & Luther, Morristown, NJ, 1960-62, ptnr., 1962-74; asst. prosecutor Morris County, NJ, 1963-65; 1st asst. prosecutor, 1965-67; 1st asst. atty. gen. NJ, 1974-77; dir. criminal justice, 1976-77; U.S. atty. Dist. of N.J., Newark, 1977-80; prof. Rutgers U. Sch. Criminal Justice, 1979-81; ptnr. firm Stryker, Tams & Dill, 1980-86, Hannoch Weisman, 1986-90; atty. gen. State of N.J., 1990-93; ptnr. Skadden, Arps, Slate, Meagher & Flom, NYC and Newark, 1993—; commr. N.J. State Commn. of Investigation, 1981-84. Instr. bus. law Fairleigh-Dickinson U., 1964; mem. N.J. State Bd. Bar Examiners, 1967-74; mem. criminal law drafting com. Nat. Conf. Bar Examiners, 1972-2002; bd. dirs. Nat. Ctr. for Victims of Crime, 1995-2003, Nat. Italian Am. Found., 1995-2003, Integrity Inc., 1995—, John Cabot U. in Rome, 1997—, Legal Svcs. N.J., 2000—; adv. bd. Yale Law Jour., 2003-05, IOLTA, 1994-99, N.J. Pub. Interest Law Ctr., 1996-99, Daytop Village Found., 1998—, Planned Parenthood, 1998-99; mem. com. on character N.J. Supreme Ct., 1982-84; mem. lawyers' adv. com. NJ Fed. Dist. Ct., 1998—; mem. adv. com. of former attys. gen. NJ Atty. Gen.; spl. master, fed. jail overcrowding litigation, Essex County, 1989-90; trustee Boys and Girls Clubs of Am., 2000—, Lawyers' Fund for Client Security, N.J., 2000-05, chmn. bd. trustees U. Med. & Dentistry NJ, 2006-; mem. bd. regents Nat. Coll. Dist. Attys., 2003—. Bd. editors Yale U. Law Jour.; contbr. articles to profl. jours. Mem. law enforcement adv. com. County Coll. of Morris, 1970-85; mem. Morris County Ethics Com., 1968-71, Morris County Jud. Selection Com., 1970-72, Essex County Jud. Selection Com., 1982-84; v.p., mem. exec. com. United Fund of Morris County, 1966-70; chmn. Morris Twp. Juvenile Conf. Com., 1963-74; bd. dirs. Nat. Found. March of Dimes, 1966-68, Vis. Nurse Assn. Morris County, 1963-70, Morristown YMCA, 1970-74; trustee Boys & Girls Club Am., 1999—, Atty.'s Fund for Client Protection, 1999-2005; trustee Newark Acad., 1976-95, 97—2002, pres. bd. dirs. 1983-87; bd. regents St. Peter's Coll., 1979-85. Fellow Am. Bar Found.; mem. Am., N.J., Morris County bar assns., Nat. Dist. Attys. Assn., Soc. Former Attys. Gen., Nat. Assn. Former U.S. Attys., Yale Law Sch. Assn. (exec. com. 1978-84), Order of Coif. Home: 13 Ober Rd Princeton NJ 08540-4917 Office: Skadden Arps Slate Meagher& Flom 4 Times Sq New York NY 10036-6522 Office Phone: 212-735-3880. Business E-Mail: rdeltufo@skadden.com.

DELTUVIA, JOHN JOSEPH, JR., systems analyst; b. New Brunswick, NJ, Dec. 9, 1962; s. John Joseph and Margaret Helen Deltuvia. AA in Humanities, Ocean County Coll., Toms River, NJ, 1982; BA in Polit. Sci., Livingston Coll., 1985; AAS in Computer Sci., Ocean County Coll., Toms River, NJ, 1987; BA in Computer Sci., Thomas Edison State Coll., Trenton, NJ, 1991, MA in Profl. Studies, 2006. Cert. Master Reiki practitioner. MIS technician N.J. Divsn. Pub. Welfare, Trenton, 1986-88; sys. mgr. Monmouth County Probation Dept., Freehold, N.J., 1988-97; programmer Dezine Healthcare Solutions, East Brunswick, N.J., 1997-99; sys. and procedures analyst Adminstrv. Office N.J. Cts., Trenton, 1999—. Media chair, bd. dirs. SpiralHeart, Inc., 2003—06. Mem.: IEEE, Assn. Bodywork and Massage Profls. (cert.), Assn. Humanistic Psychology, Assn. Computing Machinery, IEEE Computer Soc. Avocations: reading, web design. Home: 1300 Violet Ln Jackson NJ 08527 Office: Adminstrv Office NJ Cts PO Box 976 Trenton NJ 08625 Office Phone: 609-984-3370. E-mail: john.deltuvia@judiciary.state.nj.us, contact@john-deltuvia.net.

DE LUCA, ANDREA (HELEN SIGLAIN), psychoanalyst; b. Bklyn., Apr. 4, 1950; d. Wilbur Louis and Helen (Hansen) Siglain; m. June 1, 1973; children: Helena, Antoinette. BS in Edn., Wagner Coll., 1972; MSW, Fordham U., 1979; cert. sch. adminstrn., Coll. of S.I., 1993; LHD (hon.), Ignatius U., 2005. Diplomate Cert. Bd. Clin. Social Workers; cert. psychotherapist, NY; lic. N-6 tchr., spl. edn. grade advisor, sch. social worker, sch. supr., adminstr., NY; LCSW, NJ, NY; lic. marriage counselor, NJ, clin. social worker, NY, psychoanalyst, NY. Dir. spl. edn. svcs. Am. Inst. for Creative Living, SI, NY, 1976—, co-exec. dir., 1976—; bd. dirs. clin. svcs. Internat. Sch. for Mental Health Practitioners, SI, NY, 1980—. Cons. S.I. Cmty. TV. Named Tchr. of Yr. McKee Vocat. and Tech. HS, 1991. Fellow NY State Soc. Clin. Social Work Psychotherapists; mem. ACA, ASCD, Am. Assn. Marriage and Family Therapists, Am. Group Psychotherapy Assn., Nat. Assn. for Advancement Psychoanalysis, Assn. for Specialists in Group Work, Phi Delta Kappa. Office: 2295 Victory Blvd Staten Island NY 10314-6625 Office Phone: 718-698-0700.

DELUCA, ANNETTE, professional golfer; b. North Bergen, NJ, May 13, 1968; Golfer LPGA, 1989—; mem. Asian Tour, 1993; mem. Gold Coast Tour, 1994, 95; 3 Gold Coast victories, 1995; qualifier U.S. Women's Open, 1994, 95. Avocations: fishing, water sports, harley davidson motorcycles, movies, working out. Office: c/o LPGA 100 International Golf Dr Daytona Beach FL 32124-1082

DE LUCA, CARLO JOHN, biomedical engineer, educator; b. Bagnoli del Trigno, Italy, Oct. 12, 1943; came to the U.S., 1973; s. John and Josephine (De Blasio) DeL.; m. Christine M. Rafferty. B in Applied Sci., U. B.C., Can., 1966; MS, U. N.B., Can., 1968; PhD, Queen's U., 1972. Lectr. U. N.B. Computing Ctr., Fredericton, 1968; lectr. biomed. engring. unit Queen's U., Kingston, Ont., Canada, 1969-70, lab. instr. dept. anatomy, 1970-71, lectr. dept. anatomy, 1971-72, asst. prof. dept. anatomy, 1972-73; lectr. MIT, Cambridge, Mass., 1973—. Rsch. assoc. in orthop. surgery Children's Hosp. Med. Ctr., Harvard U. Med. Sch., Boston, 1973-79, prin. rsch. assoc. in orthopaedic surgery, 1979-84, dir. Neuromusclar Rsch. Lab., 1980-84; adj. assoc. prof. biomed. engring. Boston U., 1977-84, prof. biomed. engring., 1984—, rsch. prof. neurology, 1985—, dir. NeuroMuscular Rsch. Ctr., 1984—, chmn. dept. biomed. engring., 1986; dean Coll. Engring., Boston U., 1986-89; founder, pres. DelSys, Inc., 1993-, Altec Inc., 1997-; cons. Liberty Mut. Rsch. Ctr., Hopkinton, Mass., 1973-94; rsch. mem. Harvard-MIT divsn. health sci. and tech., 1978-84; affiliated scientist New Eng. Regional Primate Ctr., 1977-87; mem. nat. and internat. coms.; apptd. dir. Inst. Disability Prevention and Wellness, U. Medicine and Dentistry of N.J., 1999; mem. nat. adv. coun. Nat. Inst. Biomed. Imaging and Engring., NIH, 2002. Founding editor-in-chief Jour. Electromyography and Kinesiology, 1990; mem. editl. bds. sci. jours.; co-author: Muscles Alive; contbr. articles on biomed. engring. and neurophysiology to sci. publs. Founder, pres. Neuromuscular Rsch. Found., 1985—. Recipient Volvo award Internat. Soc. for Study of Lumbar Spine, 1989, Wartenweiler Lecture award Internat. Soc. Biomechanics, 1993, Stuart Reiner Meml. Lectr. award Am. Assn. Electrodiagnostic Medicine, 1994, United Cerebral Palsy Found. Tech. award, 1999, Tibbets award, SBA, 2006; named to Italian Cultural Ctr. Hall of Fame, Vancouver, Can., 1991; Ont. Govt. fellow, 1969-70; grantee RSA, VA, NIH, NASA, US Army, USAF. Fellow IEEE, Am. Inst. Med. and Biol. Engring. (founding fellow 1993, Basmajian Lectr. award 1998), Biomed. Engring. Soc. (founding fellow 2005); mem. AAAS, Internat. Soc. Electrophysiol. Kinesiology (sec. gen. 1976-80, sec. 1980-84, v.p. 1985-88, pres. 1988-92), Can. Med. and Biol. Engring. Soc., Soc. Neuro-Sci., Orthopaedics Rsch. Soc., Nat. Inst. Biomedical Imaging Bioengring (adv. coun. 2002-06), Dante Alighieri Soc. (bd. govs. 1986-88), Mass. Tech. Park Corp. (bd. govs. 1987-90), Harvard Club Boston, Sigma Xi. Home: 107 Livingston Rd Wellesley MA 02482-7308 Office: Boston U NeuroMuscular Rsch Ctr 19 Deerfield St Boston MA 02215-1904 Business E-Mail: cjd@bu.edu.

DELUCA, DOMINICK, medical educator, researcher; BA in Bacteriology, UCLA, 1969, PhD in Microbiology, 1974. Predoctoral fellow NIH dept. bacteriology UCLA, 1970—74, rsch. asst. dept. bacteriology, 1974; postdoctoral fellow Leukemia Soc. Am., Walter and Eliza Hall Inst., Parkville, Australia, 1974—77; scientist cancer biology program Frederick (Md.) Cancer Rsch. Ctr., 1977—80; asst. prof. biochemistry Med. U. SC, Charleston, 1980—85, assoc. prof. biochemistry, 1985—90; assoc. prof. microbiology and immunology U. Ariz., 1990—. Mem. pub. policy com. Ariz. Diabetes Control Coun., 1997—2001, chmn., 1999—2001; mem. AIDS rsch. program basic scis. rev. panel U. Calif., 1996—99; mem. brain disorders and clin. neuroscis. study sect. NIH, 1999—. Mem. editl. adv. bd.: Devel. and Comparative Immunology, 1995—2002; contbr. articles to profl. jours., chapters to books. Recipient Developing Scholar award, Health Scis. Found. Med. U. S.C., 1987, Rsch. award, NIH, 1983, 1986, 1989, 2002, 2003, NASA, 1999, 2004, Juvenile Diabetes Rsch. Found., 1988, 1998, 2001, 2003, Ariz. Disease Control Rsch. Commn., 1992, 1996, 1998, 2000, 2003, Am. Diabetes Assn., 1995, 2002. Mem.: Ariz. Cancer Ctr., Southeastern Immunology Conf. (pres.-elect 1982—83, pres. 1983—84, bd. dirs. 1985). Office: U Ariz Dept Micro Immuno PO Box 245049 Tucson AZ 85724-5049

DELUCA, FRED, food service executive; married; 1 child. Grad., U. Bridgeport. Co-founder, pres. Subway Restaurants, Milford, Conn., 1965—; founder Micro Investment Lending Enterprise (MILE), 1996. Co-author: Start Small, Finish Big: 15 Key Lessons to Start--and Run--Your Own Successful Business, 2000. Named one of Forbes' Richest Americans, 2006. Office: Subway Restaurants 325 Bic Dr Milford CT 06461 Office Phone: 203-877-4281.

DELUCA, JENNIE M., English educator; b. Scranton, Pa., Dec. 12, 1964; d. Russell Michael and Mary Ann Nowalk; m. Robert Anthony DeLuca, Sept. 23, 1989; 1 child, Nicole Marie. BS in Secondary Edn., Pa. State U., 1988, MEd in Instructional Sys., 1995; EdD in Ednl. Leadership, Immaculate U., 2000. Tchr. lang. arts Penn Wood West Jr. HS, Darby, Pa., 1988—89, Yeaden, 1989—91, Marple Newton Sr. HS, Newton Square, 1993—. Mem.: ASCD, Am. Ednl. Rsch. Assn., Phi Delta Kappa. Avocations: theater, music, art, travel, tennis. Home: 11 Smedley Dr Newtown Square PA 19073 Office: Marple Newtown Sr High Sch 120 Media Line Rd Newtown Square PA 19073 Office Phone: 610-296-7478. E-mail: dr.deluca@comcast.net.

DELUCA, PATRICK PHILLIP, pharmacist, educator, medical association administrator; b. Scranton, Pa., Sept. 7, 1935; m. Judy Beitzel, June 16, 1956; children: Paul, Thomas, Patrick, Donald, Michelle, Michael. BS in Pharmacy, Temple U., 1957, MS in Pharmacy, 1960, PhD in Pharmacy (SKF W.G. Karr fellow), 1963; Doctorate (hon.), U. Perugia, Italy, 2006. Analytical chemist SKF Co., 1957-59; instr., rsch. assoc. Temple U., 1959-62; sr. rsch. pharmacist CIBA Co., Summit, NJ, 1963-66, plant mgr., 1966-69, dir., 1969-70, Cormedics Corp., Somerville, NJ; faculty U. Ky. Coll. Pharmacy, 1970—, prof., assoc. dean, 1972-87, dir. ctr. for pharmaceutical sci. and tech., 1987-88, chmn. faculty pharm. scis., 1998-2000. Pharm. sci. adv. com. FDA, 2003-06; cons. to pharm. industry and FDA. Editor-in-chief: Jour. Pharm. Devel. and Tech., 1995—99; contbr. more than 220 articles to sci. and profl. jours. Recipient Leo G. Penn award Temple U., 1957, Lunsford-Richardson Pharmacy Rsch. award Richardson Merrell Co., 1960, 62, Best Paper Toward Advancement Indsl. Pharmacy award N.J. Pharmacy Discussion Group, 1965, Outstanding Educator award in U.S., 1974, Disting. Alumni award Temple U., 1989, Sturgill Rsch. award U. Ky., 1995, Advisory Com. Svc. award FDA, 2005; also numerous grants. Fellow: Am. Assn. Indian Pharm. Scientists, Acad. Pharm. Sci. (pres. 1979—80), Am. Assn. Pharm. Scientists (bd. dirs. 1986—88, editor-in-chief AAPS PharmSciTech electronic jour. 1999—, bd. dirs. 2005—, Rsch. Achievement award 1988, Outstanding Manuscript award in pharm. devel. and technology 1998, Outstanding Educator award 2000, Sullivan medallist at UK 2001, Ky Pharmacist of Yr. 2002, Outstanding Manuscript award in pharm. devel. and technology 2002, Swintosky Disting. lectr. 2003, Outstanding Manuscript award in pharm. devel. and technology 2006, Dale Wurster Rsch. Achievement award 2006), Inst. for Advanced Biotech. (sr.); mem.: Am. Soc. Enteral and Parental Nutrition, N.Y. Acad. Sci., Am. Soc. Hosp. Pharmacists (Rsch. award 1975), Parenteral Drug Assn. (Rsch. Achievement award 1975), Am. Pharm. Assn., Rho Chi, Sigma Chi. Achievements include research in pharmaceutical technology and novel drug delivery; co-founder Faith Pharmacy. Home: 3292 Nantucket Dr Lexington KY 40502-3269 Office: U Ky Coll Pharmacy Rose St Lexington KY 40536-0001 Office Phone: 859-257-1831. Business E-Mail: ppdelu1@email.uky.edu.

DELUCA, RONALD, former advertising agency executive, consultant; b. Reading, Pa., Oct. 28, 1924; s. Nicola and Grace (Carabello) DeL.; m. Lois Ann Hall, Nov. 27, 1952; children: Christine, Diane, Patricia, Maria, Lisa, Nicholas. Certificate comml. art, Pratt Inst., 1949; B.F.A., Syracuse U., 1951; BA, New Sch. Social Research, 1966. Artist J.C. Penney, NYC, 1951-52; designer Remington Rand, NYC, 1952-53; art dir. Roy S. Durstine (advt.), NYC, 1954-56, Kenyon & Eckhardt (advt.), NYC, 1956-66; head creative group Grey Advt., NYC, 1966-67; with Kenyon & Eckhardt Advt., NYC, 1967-85, exec. v.p., vice chmn., 1976-85; pres. Bozell Jacobs, Kenyon & Eckhardt, NYC, 1986-89, vice chmn., 1989-91; cons., 1991—. Founder, v.p. Hancock Cmty. Edn. Found., 1998—. Home and Office: PO Box 551 Hancock NY 13783-0551

DE LUCA, THOMAS GEORGE, lawyer; b. Jersey City, Dec. 28, 1950; s. Michael Anthony and Estelle Theresa (Wickiewicz) De L.; m. Annette Catherine Pandolfo, Aug. 16, 1975; children: Michele, Thomas, Rachel. BS in Econs., St. Peters Coll., Jersey City, 1972; JD, Seton Hall U., 1978. Bar: N.J. 1978, U.S. Dist. Ct. 1978, N.Y. 1981, U.S. Dist. Ct. (so. and ea. dists.) N.Y. 1981, U.S. Ct. Appeals (2d cir.) 1986, U.S. Ct. Appeals (3d cir.) 1987, U.S. Claims Ct. 1989, U.S. Dist. Ct. (we. dist.) N.Y. 1990, U.S. Dist. Ct. (no. dist.) N.Y. 1991, U.S. Supreme Ct. 1987. Supervising underwriter Fireman's Fund Ins. Cos., Newark, 1972-77; assoc. Sellar, Richardson & Stuart, Newark, 1978-80, Postner & Rubin, NYC, 1980-84, ptnr., 1985-93, De Luca & Forster, Cranford, N.J., 1994—. Mem. ABA Roman Catholic. Home: 14 Kilmer Dr Colonia NJ 07067-1213 Office: De Luca and Forster 11 Commerce Dr Cranford NJ 07016-3501 also: 45 East Shore Dr Valatie NY 12184-3904 Home Phone: 732-381-8402; Office Phone: 908-931-1100. E-mail: delucafor@aol.com.

DELUCCA, MICHAEL C., business executive; b. New Haven, Feb. 6, 1983; s. Mark A. and Mary G. DeLucca. BS in Polit. Sci., Fla. State U., Tallahassee, 2006. Dir. sales and mktg. Adams Fashion Headwear, Niceville, Fla., 2002—06; pres., CEO Inland Gear, Niceville, 2006—; pres. Vavoom Promotions, Niceville, 2007—. Named Salesman of Yr., Adams Fashion Headwear, 2005. Mem.: Destin Area C. of C., Libertarian Club (assoc.). Libertarian. Roman Catholic. Achievements include design of headwear. Avocations: travel, tennis, golf, outdoor activities. Office: Vavoom Promotions 4673 East Highway 20 Niceville FL 32578 Home Phone: 850-420-4066; Office Phone: 850-502-4325. Office Fax: 850-502-4701. Business E-Mail: info@vavoompromotions.com.

DELUCE, RICHARD DAVID, lawyer; b. Nanaimo, BC, Can., Oct. 3, 1928; came to U.S., 1929; s. Robert and Myrtle (Hickey) DeL; m. Joanne Strang, Sept. 10, 1955; children: David S., Amy Jane Eigner, Daniel R. AB, UCLA, 1950; JD, Stanford U., Palo Alto, Calif., 1955. Bar: Calif., 1955, U.S. Dist. Ct. (no. dist.) Calif. 1955, U.S. Ct. Appeals (9th cir.) 1955, U.S. Dist. Ct. (cen. dist.) Calif. 1956, U.S. Supreme Ct. 1963, U.S. Dist. Ct. (so. dist.) Calif. 1972. Rsch. atty. Calif. Supreme Ct., San Francisco, 1955-56; assoc. Lawler, Felix & Hall, LA, 1956-62, ptnr., 1962-90, Arter, Hadden, Lawler, Felix & Hall, LA, 1990—2000. Co-author: California Civil Writ Practice, 2d edit., 1987. Capt. U.S. Army, 1951-53, Korea. Fellow Am. Coll. Trial Lawyers, Am. Bar Found.; mem. Calif. Club. Home: 3617 Paseo Del Campo Palos Verdes Estates CA 90274-1161 Personal E-mail: richard.deluce@verizon.net.

DELUCIA, GENE ANTHONY, government administrator, computer company executive; b. Methuen, Mass., Feb. 20, 1952; s. Antonio Gitano and Carmen Theresa (Carpenito) DeL. BS, Boston Coll., 1973; MBA, Northeastern U., 1980. Project mgr. Delphi div. Arthur D. Little Inc., Lowell, Mass., 1975-78, gen. mgr. eastern region, 1978-80; systems devel. mgr. Wang Labs. Inc., Lowell, 1980-83; pres., CEO Computer Innovations Inc., Lowell, 1983-86; pres. Corp. Investment Bus. Brokers, North Andover, Mass., 1986-88; v.p. Maximus Inc., Falls Church, Va., 1988-90, div. pres., 1990-96; pres. Strategic Visions Inc., Indian Rocks Beach, Fla., 1996—2001; prin. Capital Assocs., Inc., Indian Rocks Beach, 2001—. Mem. AOPA. Avocations: electronics, flying, golf. Home and Office: 518 Harbor Dr N Indian Rocks Beach FL 33785-3117 Personal E-mail: gdelucia@tampabay.rr.com.

DELUGACH, ALBERT LAWRENCE, journalist; b. Memphis, Oct. 27, 1925; s. Gilbert and Edna (Short) D.; m. Bernice Goldstein, June 11, 1950; children: Joy, David, Daniel, Sharon. B.J., U. Mo., 1951. Reporter Kansas City (Mo.) Star, 1951-60, St. Louis Globe Democrat, 1960-69, St. Louis Post Dispatch, 1969-70; investigative reporter Los Angeles Times, 1970-89. Served with USNR, 1943-46. Recipient Pultizer prize for spl. local reporting, 1969, Gerald Loeb award for disting. bus. and fin. journalism, 1984 Home: 4313 Price St Los Angeles CA 90027-2815

DELUHERY, PATRICK JOHN, retired state official; b. Birmingham, Ala., Jan. 31, 1942; s. Frank B. and Lucille (Donovan) D.; m. Margaret Morris, 1973; children: Allison, Norah, Rose. BA with honors, U. Notre Dame, 1964; BSc in Econs. with honors, London Sch. Econs., 1967. Legis. asst. U.S. Senator Harold Hughes, Washington, 1969-74, U.S. Senator John Culver, Washington, 1975; asst. prof. econs. and fin. St. Ambrose U., Davenport, Iowa, 1975—2007; COO Gen. Svcs. Enterprise Iowa Dept. Adminstrv. Svcs., Des Moines, 2002—05; dir. strategic partnerships Dept. Adminstrv. Svcs., Des Moines, 2005—07. Mem. Iowa State Senate, 1979-2002. Democrat. Roman Catholic. Home: 629 Foster Dr Des Moines IA 50312-2517

DE LUNG, JANE SOLBERGER, independent sector executive; b. Anniston, Ala., July 9, 1944; d. Samuel and Margaret Polk (Oldham) S.; m. Harry Leonard De Lung, Apr. 23, 1965 (div. 1972); m. Charles F. Westoff, May 2, 1997. BA in History, Emory U., Atlanta, 1966; MA in Urban Planning, Roosevelt U., Chgo., 1972. Exec. asst. Cook County Legal Assistance, Chgo., 1967—69; asst. dir. family planning Am. Coll. Ob-gyn., Chgo., 1969—71; v.p. Ill. Family Planning Coun., Chgo., 1971—80; asst. commr. Chgo. Dept. Pub. Health, 1981—82; pres. Pub. Solutions, Princeton, NJ, 1982—88, Population Resource Ctr., NYC, 1988—. Bd. dirs. Planned Parenthood Mercer County, Trenton, NJ, 1986-96, Population Resource Ctr., 1989—, Trenton Head Start, 1993-98; adv. bd. dept. sociology Princeton U., 1991— Mem. APHA, AAUW, LWV, Internat. Union Sci. Study of Population, Population Assn. Am., UN Assn. of U.S.A. (nat. adv. com. 1998-). Democrat. Episcopalian. Office: Population Resource Ctr 1 Highland Rd Princeton NJ 08540 Home Phone: 609-895-0815; Office Phone: 609-492-7004. E-mail: janedelung@gmail.com.

DE LUTIS, DONALD CONSE, investment advisor, consultant; b. Rome, NY, Apr. 25, 1934; s. Conse R. and Mary D.; m. Ruth L.; 1 child, Dante. BS in Econs., Niagara U., 1956; MBA, Boston Coll., 1962. V.p. John Nuveen & Co., Inc., San Francisco, 1968-74; acct. exec. Dean Witter & Co., London, 1975-77; sr. investment officer Buffalo Savs. Bank, NY, 1978-80; exec. v.p. Robert Brown & Co., Inc., San Francisco, 1980-89, Capitol Corp. Asset mgmt., 1989-91; exec. v.p., dir. Pacific Securities, Inc., San Francisco, 1980-91; mng. dir. Coast Ptnrs. Securities, Inc., 1998-99; chmn. Orrell Capital Mgmt., Inc., 1991-98, 2000—. Commr. San Francisco Bay Conservation and Devel. Commn., 1983-93, State of Calif. Commn. Housing and Community Devel., 1974-77. Served with USAF, 1957-58. Mem.: San Francisco Bond Club. Republican. Roman Catholic.

DELVA, PAUL D., lawyer; b. 1962; BA, Concordia Coll.; MA Purdue U.; JD, Temple U. Bar: 1996. Former reporter Montreal Gazette; atty. Dechert, Price & Rhoads (now Dechert LLP), Phila., 1995—99; asst. gen. counsel Fairchild Semiconductor Internat., Inc., South Portland, Maine, 1999—2003, v.p., gen. counsel, 2003—05, corp. sec., 2005—. Mem.: ABA, Soc. Corp. Sec. Gov. Profl., Assn. Corp. Counsel., Maine Bar Assn. Office: Fairchild Semiconductor Internat Inc 82 Running Hill Rd South Portland ME 04106 Office Phone: 207-775-8100.

DEL VALLE, TERESA JONES, lawyer; b. Dayton, Ohio, July 20, 1965; BS, Ariz. State U., 1988; JD, U. Houston, 1993. Bar: Tex. 1993, US Dist. Ct. (so. and ea. dists.) Tex. 1994. Underwriter Prudential Property and Casualty Ins. Co., Scottsdale, Ariz., 1988-90; assoc. Doyle, Rider, Restrepo, Harvin & Robbins, LLP, Houston, 1993-97, Cash, Jones & Springhetti, LLP, Houston, 1997—99, Rios & Bain, P.C., 1999—2002; atty. Del Valle Law Firm, P.C., Houston, 2002—. Office: Del Valle Law Firm PC 2211 Norfolk St # 755 Houston TX 77098 Office Phone: 713-528-6600. Business E-Mail: teresa@delvallelawfirm.com.

DELY, STEVEN, retired aerospace company executive; b. NYC, July 16, 1943; m. Kristine Jon Kolbe, June 7, 1975; 1 child, Jonathan Laurence. BBA, CCNY, 1966; JD, Bklyn. Law Sch., 1968; postgrad. program mgmt. devel., Harvard U., 1979. Bar: N.Y. 1972, U.S. Supreme Ct. 1983. Corp. counsel, dir. pers. svcs. Grumman Allied Industries Inc., Garden City, NY, 1971-75, gen. counsel, sec., 1976-78; v.p. human resources Melville, NY, 1979-82; dir. human resources Grumman Corp., Bethpage, NY, 1982-85; v.p. resources and adminstrn. Grumman Electronics Systems divsn., Bethpage, 1985-86; v.p., asst. to chmn. bd. Grumman Corp., Bethpage, 1986-91, v.p. exec. staff, 1991-92, sr. v.p. exec. staff, corp. sec., 1993-94; co-founder Dispute Resolutions Inc., Huntington, NY, 1998—. Bd. dirs. Family Svc. League, Huntington. Capt. US Army, 1969—71.

DEMAIN, ARNOLD LESTER, microbiologist, educator; b. NYC, Apr. 26, 1927; s. Henry and Gussie (Katz) D.; m. Joanna Kaye, Aug. 2, 1952; children: Pamela Robin Demain McCloskey, Jeffrey Brian. BS, Mich. State U., East Lansing, 1949, MS, 1950; PhD, U. Calif., Berkeley, 1954; Doctorate (hon.), U. Leon, Spain, 1997, Ghent U., Belgium, 1999, Technion-Israeli Inst. Tech., 2000, Mich. State U., 2000, U. Muenster, Germany, 2003. Rsch. asst. U. Calif., Davis, 1952-54; rsch. microbiologist Merck & Co., Inc., Danville, Pa., 1954-56, Rahway, NJ, 1956-65, founder, head of dept. ferm. microbiology, 1965-69; prof. of ind. microbiology MIT, Cambridge, 1969—2001; fellow Charles A. Dana Rsch. Inst., Drew U., Madison, NJ, 2001—. Author or editor 12 books; contbr. more than 500 articles to profl. jours. With USN, 1945—47. Recipient Hotpack award Can. Soc. Microbiology, 1978, Rubro award Australian Soc. Microbiology, 1978, Indsl. Microbiology award Italian Pharm. Assn., 1989, Hans Knoll meml. award, Germany, 1990, G. Mendel award Czech Acad. Sci., 1998, Andrew Jackson Moyer award USDA, 1998, Internat. Achievement award Shanghai Inst. Pharm. Industry, 2005, Arima award in Applied Microbiology, IUMS, 2005 Mem.: NAS, Am. Chem. Soc. (Marvin Johnson biotech. award), Am. Soc. Microbiology (Waksman award N.J. br. 1975, Biotech. award 1990, Disting. Svc. award 1994, Alice C. Evans award 1998, hon. mem. N.E. br. 1999, Charles Porta award 2006), Soc. Indsl. Microbiology (pres. 1990, Charles Thom award 1978, Waksman Tchg. award 1995, Porter award 2006), Hungarian Acad. Sci., Mex. Acad. Sci., Croatian Soc. Biotech. (hon.), Czech Soc. Microbiology (hon. Patocka medal 2006), Soc. Actinomycetes Japan (hon.), French Soc. Microbiology (hon.). Achievements include 21 patents; elucidation of biosynthetic pathway to penicillins and cephalosporins; recognition of phenomenon of biochemical regulation of secondary metabolism; discovery of role of lysine and amino adipic acid in penicillin biosynthesis. Office: Drew Univ RISE HS-330 Madison NJ 07940 Office Phone: 973-408-3937. Business E-mail: ademain@drew.edu.

DEMAIN, JOHN, opera company director; b. Youngstown, Ohio, Jan. 11, 1944; m. Barbara DeMain; 1 child, Jennifer. BMus, Juilliard Sch. Music, 1966, MusM, 1968; studies in conducting with, Leonard Bernstein, Peter Adler. Assoc. condr. St. Paul Chamber Orch., 1972-74; music dir. Tex. Opera Theater, 1974-76; former music dir. Houston Grand Opera, Opera Omaha; music dir. Madison Symphony Orch., Wis., 1994—; artistic adv. Madison Opera, Wis., 1994—; artistic dir. & prin. condr. Opera Pacific, Calif., 1998—. Prin. guest condr. Chautauqua Opera Inst., 1985. Rec. performances: Piano Concerto (Frances Thorne), 1975, Porgy and Bess, 1976, Nocturnes (Miriam Gideon), 1978. Finalist Grand Prix, 1977; recipient Julius Rudel award, 1971, Grammy award, 1977; Juilliard Sch. Music scholar, 1964—68. Office: Madison Symphony Orchestra 222 W Washington Ave Ste 460 Madison WI 53703-2744 also: Opera Pacific 600 West Warner Ave Santa Ana CA 92707 E-mail: jldemain@operapacific.org.*

DEMAINE, ERIK D., computer scientist, educator; b. Halifax, Nova Scotia, Can., Feb. 28, 1981; BSc, Dalhousie U., 1995; MS in Math., U. Waterloo, 1996, PhD, 2001. Mem. Computer Sci. and Artificial Intelligence Lab. MIT, Cambridge, 2001—, asst. prof. dept. elec. engring. and computer sci., 2001—05, assoc. prof., 2005—, Esther and Harold E. Edgerton prof., 2005—. Contbr. articles to profl. jours., chapters to books;, co-editor 2 books. Named one of Brilliant 10, Popular Sci. mag., 2003; recipient Early Career Prin. Investigator award, Dept. Energy, 2004, CAREER award, NSF, 2004; fellow MacArthur Found., 2003; grantee Alfred P. Sloan Rsch. fellowship, 2006—. Mem.: Soc. Indsl. and Applied Math., Math. Assn. Am., Can. Math. Soc., Am. Math. Soc., Assn. Computing Machinery Spl. Interest Grp. on Algorithms and Computation Theory, Assn. Computing Machinery. Avocations: glass blowing, oragami, juggling, magic, painting. Office: MIT Computer Sci and Artificial Intelligence Lab 32 Vassar St Cambridge MA 02139 Office Phone: 617-253-6871. Office Fax: 617-258-5429. E-mail: edemaine@mit.edu.*

DEMAIO, DONNALEE A., bank executive; BA summa cum laude, Muhlenberg Coll. CPA, cert. internal auditor. Ptnr., banking practice Pricewaterhouse Coopers; CFO MetLife Bank, Bridgewater, NJ, 2002—05, pres., 2005—. Bd. mem. Regional Bus. Assistance Corp. Named one of 25 Most Powerful Women in Banking, US Banker mag., 2005, 2006. Mem.: Am. Inst. CPAs, NJ Soc. CPAs. Office: Met Life Bank 501 Rt 22 Bridgewater NJ 08807*

DEMAIO, MARLENE, orthopedist, surgeon; b. Phila., Dec. 18, 1958; d. Frank Joseph and Grace Marlene (Landrum) DeM. BS in Biology with honors, Brown U., 1981; MD, Hahnemann Med. Sch., 1985. Diplomate Nat. Bd. Med. Examiners, Am. Bd. Orthop. Surgeons. Resident in orthop. Yale U., New Haven, 1985-90, clin. asst., 1990; fellow in sports medicine Cin. Sports Medicine and Orthop. Ctr., 1991-92; staff dept. orthop. Naval Hosp., Oakland, Calif., 1992-95, Bethesda, Md., 1995—, asst. dept. head, 1995—. Asst. prof. dept. surgery Uniformed Svcs. U. Health Scis., Bethesda, Md., 1995—; thesis reader dept. mech. engring. Naval Postgrad. Sch., Monterey, Calif., 1994—2001; vice chmn. inst. rev. bd. Nat. Naval Med. Ctr., 1995—98; libr. com., mgr. equipment and materials dept. orthop. surgery Naval Hosp., Oakland, Calif., 1992—95, dir. resident rsch. and pub. dept. orthop. surgery, 1993—98, mem. intern edn. com., Calif., 1993—95, coord. ninth annual rsch. symposium, 1995, dir. rsch. and pub. dept. orthop. surgery, 1995—98; mem. Multidisciplinary Complex Pain Mgmt. Program, 1993—95; dept. head USNS Mercy, Oakland, 1992—95; reviewer Extramural Women's Health Def. Fund, Dept. Def. Rsch. Grants, 1996; head tissue com. for implants Nat. Naval Med. Ctr., 1995—98; dept. head USNS Comfort, Bethesda, 1995—98; bd. dirs. Am. Jour. Sports Medicine; cons. orthopedics Office of Attending Physician, U.S. Congress, 1999—2004, U.S. Pentagon, 1996—2004; dir. ballistics and biomechanics Inst. Pathology Lab. Armed Forces, 1998—2004; advisor enhanced human performance USMC, 1999—; head football team physician, dept. head orthop., sports medicine, podiatry US Naval Acad., 2002—04; dir. surg. svcs. Expeditionary Med. Facility, Kuwait, 2005—06; oral examiner Am. Bd. Orthop. Surgery, 2005—06. Reviewer: Am. Jour. Sports Medicine, 1996—, editl. bd.:, 2001, mng. editor:, 2000—02. Coord. Celebration of Women in Medicine, Am. Med. Women's Assn., Hahnemann U., Phila., 1984. Capt. USN, 1992—. Decorated Navy Achievement medal, 1992, Navy Commendation medal, 1995, 98, 2004, 06, Meritorious Svc. medal, 1998, Joint Commendation, 2004, Def. Meritorious medal, 2004; recipient Bronze award Nat. Soc. SAR, 1977, Excellence in Rsch. award Am. Orthopaedic Soc. Sports Medicine, 1997, Frank Berry award Delta Dental (Calif.) & U.S. Medicine, 2004; grantee Oakland Naval Hosp., 1993, Nat. Naval Med. Ctr., 1995-98, USMC, 1998, US Army, 1998-2003, Naval Med. Ctr. Portsmouth, 2005-06. Mem.: Am. Orthopaedic Soc. for Sports Medicine (chair edn. subcom. 2006, mem. exec. com. 2005—06, coun. of dels. 2000—06), Orthopaedic Rsch. Soc., Assn. Bone and Joint Surgeons, Am. Orthopedic Foot and Ankle Soc., Am. Coll. Sports Medicine, Soc. Mil. Orthop. Surgeons, Am. Acad. Orthop. Surgeons, Alpha Omega Alpha. Avocations: tennis, piano, cooking, swimming. Office: Naval Med Ctr Dept Orthop Surgery 620 John Paul Jones Cir Portsmouth VA 23708 Office Phone: 757-483-1885. Business E-Mail: mdemaio@mar.med.navy.mil.

DEMANE, MICHAEL F., medical products executive; BS in Chemistry, St. Lawrence U., Canton, NY; student in Engring., U. Tex.; MS in Bioengineering, Clemson U., SC. Various R & D and gen. mgmt. positions Smith & Nephew, Inc., Memphis; mng. dir. Australia and New Zealand Smith & Nephew Pty. Ltd., 1996—98; pres. spinal systems Medtronic Sofamor Danek Medtronic, Inc., sr. corp. v.p., pres. Spinal, Ear, Nose & Throat and Navigation, mem. exec. com., 2002—05, pres. Europe, Can., L.Am. and Emerging Markets, sr.v.p, 2005—07, COO, 2007—. Office: Medtronic Inc 710 Medtronic Pky Minneapolis MN 55432-5604 Office Phone: 763-514-4000. Office Fax: 763-514-4879.*

DEMANKOWSKI, LISA RENEE, architect, educator; b. Chgo., Apr. 11, 1967; d. William Minto Davis and Judith Ann Dobbs; m. Dale Alvin Demankowski, Jan. 19, 1985; children: Brittany Noel, Gabriel Adam, Collin William. AS with high honors, Charles Stewart Mott C.C., Flint, Mich., 1992; BS, U. Mich., 1994, MArch with distinction, 2000. Registered arch., Mich., 2005, Ohio, 2007, cert. Nat. Coun. Archtl. Registration Bd., 2005, endorsement, Fla., 2005. Arch. THA Archs. Engrs., Flint, 1995—2005; pres. NJB Archs., Inc., Flushing, Mich., 2005—. Adj. faculty Lansing (Mich.) C.C., 2005—. Treas. Shiawassee Twp., Bancroft, Mich., 1994—2004. U. Mich. Alumni scholar, U. Mich., Coll. Arch. and Urban Planning, 1999. Mem.: AIA (sec. Flint chpt. 2005—), Rotary Club, Golden Key Nat. Honor Soc. Democrat. Avocations: landscaping, construction renovation/restoration/adaptive reuse, reading. Office: NJB Architects Inc 105 1/2 Main St Flushing MI 48433 Home Phone: 810-730-5158; Office Phone: 810-659-7118. Office Fax: 810-659-7224.

DEMANN, FREDDY, film, play and television producer; b. 1939; married; 2 children. Mgr., Madonna, 1983—97; co-founder (with Madonna) Maverick Records, 1992—99; prin. DeMann Entertainment talent mgmt. Exec. prodr.: (TV spl.) Madonna: Blond Ambition World Tour Life, 1990; exec. prodr.: (TV films) Crazy from the Heart, 1991, Dangerous Game, 1993, Canadian Bacon, 1995; co-exec. prodr. (TV films) The Life and Death of Peter Sellers, 2004 (Critics Choice award, 2004, Golden Globe award, 2004, Prodr. Guild Am. award long-form TV, 2006); exec. prodr.: (films) All We Are Saying, 2005; prodr.: (plays) Top Dog/Underdog, 2002, Jumpers, 2004, Proof, 2004, Julius Caesar, 2005; co-prodr.: Take Me Out, 2003 (Tony award Play of Yr., 2003, Outer Critics Cir. award, 2003, Drama Desk award, 2003), Caroline, or Change, 2004. Home: Los Angeles CA

DEMANT, MARGARET H., retired interior designer; d. Walter and Erna Putzel Herz. Mgr., buyer, interior designer Walter Herz Interiors, Detroit and Southfield, Mich., 1944—85. Exec. comm. Internat. Furnishings Design Assn., Dallas, 1974—85. Author: Southern Market: A Market for Interior Designers. Mem. adv. bd. home furnishings mktg. program High Point Coll., 1980—85; chairperson subcom. for interior furnishings gen. adv. com. Detroit Pub. Schs., 1982—85; bd. mem. Detroit Inst. Arts, 1986—, mem. acquisitions comm., 1994—2006; trustee Mich. Opera Theatre, 2006—; bd. mem. Resettlement Svc., Detroit, 1987—90, Jewish Resettlement Svc., Detroit, 1987—90, Jewish Family Svc., Detroit, 1990—, Project Discovery, 2006—; coun. mem. Smithsonian Am. Art Mus., Washington, 2007. Recipient Life Time Svc. award, Detroit Inst. Arts, 2004; Fellow mem., Internat. Furnishings Design Assn., 1991. Personal E-mail: mdemant@wowway.com.

DEMANT, PETER, geneticist, researcher; Staff scientist Inst. Molecular Biology, Prague, Czech Republic, 1966—76; vis. scientist Jackson Lab., Bar Harbor, Maine, 1968—69; head, subdivision genetics Netherlands Cancer Inst., Amsterdam, 1978—97, head, divsn. molecular genetics, 1998—2002; disting. mem., prof. Roswell Pk. Cancer Inst., Buffalo, 2002—. Office: Roswell Park Cancer Inst Elm and Carlton Sts Buffalo NY 14263 Home Phone: 716-882-0570; Office Phone: 716-845-1399. Business E-Mail: peter.demant@roswellpark.org.

DEMAPAN, MIGUEL S., commonwealth supreme court justice; b. Saipan, Northern Marianas; m. Frances Tenorio; 5 children. BS in Chemistry, Seattle U., 1975; MBA with honors, Golden Gate U., 1983; JD, Santa Clara U., 1985. Gen. counsel J. C. Tenorio Enterprises, Inc.; pvt. practice; ptnr. Demapan and Atalig; assoc. judge Commonwealth Northern Mariana Islands Superior Ct., 1992—98; assoc. justice Commonwealth Northern Mariana Islands Supreme Ct., 1998—99, chief justice, 1999—. Judge pro tem Superior Ct. Guam, Supreme Ct. Guam; mem. Pacific Jud. Coun., 1998—, pres., 2000—02; chmn. Commonwealth Law Revision Commn.; bd. mem. U.S. Conference of Chief Justices, 2002—03; mem. Asia Pacific Conference of Chief Justices, Commonwealth Northern Mariana Islands Federal Bench Council. Chmn. Commonwealth Law Revision Commn.; mem. CNMI Tax Task Force. Trust Ter. scholar, Seattle U. Mem.: World Jurist Assn. Office: Supreme Ct Commonwealth Northern Mariana Islands PO Box 502179 Saipan MP 96950-2165*

DEMARA, RONALD FRANCIS, computer engineer, educator; BS, Lehigh U., 1987; MS, U. Md., College Park, 1989; PhD, U. So. Calif., 1992. Registered profl. engr., Calif., 1992. Assoc. engr. IBM Corp., Manassas, Va., 1986—89; assoc. prof., prof. U. Ctrl. Fla., Orlando, Fla., 1992—. Contbr. articles to profl. jours. Mem.: IEEE (sr.; assoc. editor Trans. VLSI), Assn. Computing Machinery. Office: University of Central Florida 4000 Central Florida Blvd Orlando FL 32816-2450 Home Phone: 407-823-5916. Business E-Mail: demara@mail.ucf.edu.

DEMARCUS, JAY (STANLEY DEMARCUS), country musician, songwriter; b. Columbus, Ohio, Apr. 26, 1971; s. Wayne and Caron; m. Allison Alderson, May 15, 2004. Performer Printers Alley, Nashville, Chely Wright Band; founder, guitarist, bass, keyboard, songwriter Rascal Flatts, Nashville, 2000—. Musician: (albums) East to West, 1993; engineer, prodr., rhythm and vocal arrangements: (albums) Gospel, 1998;; musician (bass) "It's Not Just Me", Rascall Flatts, 2000; songwriter: albums "It's Not Just Me", Rascal Flatts, 2000; musician Rascal Flatts, 2000, Melt, 2002, Feels Like Today, 2004 (Group/Duo Video of Yr., Country Music Television Music awards, 2005), Me and My Gang, 2006; performer: (songs) Walk the Llama Llama, Emperor's New Groove (Original Soundtrack), 2000; musician: (singles) Praying for Daylight/Long Slow Beautiful Dance, 2000. Recipient Vocal Group Yr., Country Music Assn., 2002, 2004—06, Song Yr. for I'm Movin On, Acad. Country Music Awards, 2002, Top Vocal Group, 2003, 2005—07, Country Song Yr. for Bless the Broken Road, Radio Music Awards, 2005, Best Country Song, Grammy Awards, 2006, Group/Duo Video of Yr. for Skin (Sarabeth), Country Music TV Awards, 2006, Group Video of Yr. for What Hurts the Most, 2007, Favorite County Band, Am. Music Awards, 2006, Favorite Song from a movie & Favorite Remake-Life is a Highway, People's Choice Awards, 2007. Office: Lyric Street Records 1100 Demonbreun St Nashville TN 37203-3108 Office Phone: 615-963-4848.*

DEMAREST, DAVID FRANKLIN, JR., banker, retired government official; b. Glen Ridge, NJ, Oct. 8, 1951; s. David Franklin Demarest and Alison (Clark) Fahrer; m. Leigh Ann Wisniewski, Feb. 5, 1977 (div. 1981); m. Sarah Tinsley, July 16, 1983; 2 children. BA, Upsala Coll., 1973. Dep. dir. local elections Republican Nat. Com., Washington, 1977-80; dir. pub. and intergovtl. affairs U.S. Trade Rep., Washington, 1981-84; asst. U.S. Trade Rep. Exec. Office of Pres., Washington, 1984; dep. undersec. U.S. Labor Dept., Washington, 1985-87, asst. sec. labor, 1987-88; dir. comm. George Bush for Pres. Com., 1988; dir. pub. affairs Presdl. Transition Office, 1988-89; asst. to pres. for comm. White House, Washington, 1989-92; sr. cons. Internat. Mgmt. and Devel. Group, Ltd., Alexandria, Va., 1993; dir. corp. comms., exec. v.p. Bank of Am., San Francisco, 1993-99; exec. v.p. global corp. rels. Visa Internat., San Francisco, 1999—. Presbyterian. Office: Visa Internat PO Box 8999 San Francisco CA 94128-8999

DEMAREST, SYLVIA M., lawyer; b. Lake Charles, La., Aug. 16, 1944; d. Edmand and Emily Demarest; m. James A. Johnston, Jr., Oct. 31, 1975 (div. Dec. 1979). Student, U. S.W. La., 1963-66; JD, U. Tex., 1969. Bar: Tex. 1969, U.S. Supreme Ct. 1973, U.S. Ct. Appeals (5th cir.) 1970, U.S. Ct. Appeals (7th cir.) 1979, U.S. Ct. Appeals (11th cir.) 1980, U.S. Dist. Ct. (no. dist.) Tex. 1970, U.S. Dist. Ct. (ea. dist.) Tex. 1970, U.S. Dist. Ct. (so. dist.) Tex. 1972. Reginald H. Smith Cmty. Lawyer fellow, Corpus Christi and Dallas, 1969-71; house counsel Tex. Inst. Ednl. Devel., San Antonio, 1972-73; staff atty. Dallas Legal Svsc. Found., Inc., 1973, exec. dir., 1973-76; sole practice Dallas, 1977-78; mgr. product litig., dir. Windle Turley, P.C., Dallas, 1978-83; sole practice Dallas, 1983-85; ptnr. Demarest & Smith, Dallas, 1985—. Mem. faculty trial advocacy program So. Meth. U. Law Sch., 1984; lectr. Contbr. articles to profl. jours. Mem. ABA, State Bar Tex., ATLA, Dallas Bar Assn., Dallas Trial Lawyers Assn. (past pres.), Dallas Inn of Ct. (master of the bar 1989—). Democrat. Home: 1812 Atlantic St Dallas TX 75208-3002 Office: Ste 800 8686 Cole Ave Dallas TX 75231

DE MARGITAY, GEDEON, acquisitions and management consultant; b. Budapest, Hungary, Mar. 6, 1924; came to U.S., 1953, naturalized, 1958; s. Joseph and Anne (de Bessenyei) de M.; m. Virginia Varet Martin, Dec. 30, 1963. Student, U. Budapest Grad. Sch. Econs., 1941-44, Ecole des Scis. Politiques, Paris, 1946-48. With N.Y. Times, 1947-50, 54-61; with European info. divsn. Mut. Security Agy., 1950-53; chief exec. Magnum Photos, Inc., NYC, 1961-63; with Time Inc., 1964-75, dir. mktg. svcs. Time/Life TV, 1975; dir. broadcast and corp. planning NBC, 1975-78; acquistions and mgmt. cons. NYC, 1978—. Co-author: Broadcasting: The Next Ten Years, 1977. Mem. Internat. Radio-TV Soc., Am. Acad. Polit. and Social Sci. Republican. Presbyterian.

DE MARIA, ALFRED ANTHONY, neurologist; b. Sewickley, Pa., Mar. 27, 1952; s. Alfred Anthony and Helen Josephine (Goray) De M.; m. Katherine Grace Bridge, June 25, 1977; children: Genevieve Camille, Gabrielle Christine. BA, Johns Hopkins U., 1973; MD, Ohio State U., 1976. Diplomate Am. Bd. Psychiatry and Neurology. Intern N.C. Baptist Hosp., Winston-Salem, 1976-77; resident in neurology N.C. Meml. Hosp., Chapel Hill, 1977-80; fellow in EEG Mayo Clinic, Rochester, Minn., 1980-81; attending physician Neurol. Assocs., Columbus, Ohio, 1981-92, Wilmington (N.C.) Health Assocs., 1993—. Med. dir. EEG lab. Riverside Meth. Hosp., Columbus, Ohio, 1981-92; med. dir. sleep lab. Cape Fear Meml. Hosp., Wilmington, 1993—. Host (TV show) Second Opinion, 1996—. Mem. Am. Acad. Neurology, Am. Sleep Disorders Assn., Am. EEG Soc., Am. Epilepsy Soc., Nat. Stroke Assn., Nat. Headache Found., Nat. Assn. Physician Broadcasters. Avocations: music, skiing. Office: Wilmington Health Assocs 1202 Medical Center Dr Wilmington NC 28401-7307 Home Phone: 910-256-5222; Office Phone: 910-341-3358. Business E-Mail: ademaria@wilmingtonhealth.com.

DE MARIA, ANTHONY JOHN, electrical engineer; b. Santa Croce, Italy, Oct. 30, 1931; came to U.S., 1935; s. Joseph and Nicolina (Daddona) De M.; m. Katherine M. Waybright, Aug. 29, 1953; 1 dau., Karla Kay. BS in Elec. Engring., U. Conn., Storrs, 1956, PhD in Elec. Engring., 1965; MS, Rensselaer Poly. Inst., 1960. Acoustic research engr. Andersen Lab., West Hartford, Conn., 1956-57; magnetic research engr. Hamilton Standard Div. United Techs. Corp., Windsor Locks, Conn., 1957-58; asst. dir. rsch. electronics and photonics United Techs. Rsch. Ctr., East Hartford, Conn., 1958-94; founder, chmn., CEO DeMaria ElectroOptics Sys., Inc., Bloomfield, Conn., 1994-2001, chief scientist Coherent Laser divsn., 2001—; rsch. prof. Photonics Rsch. Ctr. U. Conn., Storrs, 1994-98; pres. TeraBit Commns., LLC, 2001—; prof.-in-residence elec. and computer engring. U. Conn., Storrs, Conn., 2004—. Instr. electronics U. Hartford, 1957-60; adj. prof. physics Rensselaer Poly. Inst. Grad. Ctr., Hartford, 1970-77; lectr. in lasers UCLA, 1974-82; mem. adv. group on electronic devices Dept. Def., 1977-86, chmn., 1980-85; mem. evaluation com. on electromagnetic tech. Nat. Bur. Standards, 1977-79; mem. Ctr. Elec. and Electronic Engring., 1979-83; mem. LANL Adv. Com. for Chemistry and Laser Sci., 1985-92. Author: Lasers, Vol. III, 1972, Vol. IV, 1976; Contbr. articles to profl. jours. Mem. Air Force Sci. Adv. Bd., 1981-86. Recipient Disting. Alumnus award U. Conn., 1978, Disting. Engring. award, U. Conn., 1983, Davies medal and award Rensselaer Poly. Inst., 1980, Air Force Meritorious medal for civilian svc., 1986. Fellow IEEE (editor Jour. Quantum Electronics, Morris N. Liebman meml. award 1980), SPIE (bd. dirs. 1995—, v.p. 2002, pres. 2003), Optical Soc. Am. (v.p. 1979, pres. 1981, chmn. bd. editors 1986-89, Frederic Ives medal 1988), Am. Phys. Soc.; mem. NAE (Farichild Disting. scholar 1982-83, Calif. Inst. Tech.), NAS, Conn. Acad. Scis. and Engring. (pres. 1994-99). Address: Coherent DEOS LLC 1280 Blue Hills Ave Bloomfield CT 06002-5304

DEMARIA, ANTHONY NICHOLAS, cardiologist, educator; b. Elizabeth, NJ, Jan. 12, 1943; s. Anthony and Charlotte DeMaria; m. Delores Horn; children: Christine, Anthony, Jonathon. BA, Coll. Holy Cross, 1964; MD, N.J. Coll. Medicine, 1968; degree (hon.), Kagawa Med. U., Japan, U. Bordeaux, France. Diplomate Am. Bd. Internal Medicine, Am. Bd. Cardiovascular Disease, Am. Bd. Cardiovascular Medicine. Intern St. Vincent Hosp., Worcester, Mass., 1968-69; resident USPHS Hosp., Staten Island, NY, 1969-71; fellow cardiology U. Calif., Davis, 1969-73, asst. prof. medicine, 1972-77, assoc. prof. medicine, 1977-81, prof. medicine, 1977-81; prof. medicine, chief cardiology div. U. Ky., Lexington, 1981-92; dir. Ky. Heart Inst., Lexington, 1989—; prof. medicine, chief cardiology U. Calif. Sch. Medicine, San Diego, 1992—2994, vice chmn. internal medicine, 1998—2001, med. dir. Cardiovasc. Ctr., Judith and Jack White chair cardiovasc. medicine, dir. Cardiovasc. Ctr., 2004—. Mem. rev. bds. Vets. Adminstrn. Med. Research Merit in Cardiovascular Studies, Nat. Inst. Health, NSF, NIH, NHLBI, U. Calif., U.S. FDA; chmn. Diagnostic Radiology Study Sect. NIH; vice-chmn. dept. medicine U. Calif., San Diego, 1998-2001. Mem. editl. bd. Am. Heart Jour., Am. Jour. Cardiac Imaging, Circulation, Am. Jour. Cardiology, Jour. Am. Coll. Cardiology, Health News from New Eng. Jour. Medicine; editor-in-chief Jour. Am. Coll. Cardiology, 2001—; assoc. editor Jour. Am. Coll. Cardiology; editl. cons. Am. Jour. Physiology, Annals Internal Medicine, Archives Phys. Medicine and Rehab., Catheterization and Cardiovascular Diagnosis, Jour. Clin. Investigation, New Eng. Jour. Medicine; contbr. numerous articles to profl. jours.; host Cardiology Update, Lifetime Med. TV. Recipient Humanitarian award Theodore and Susan Cummings, 1978, Disting. Alumnus award Coll. Medicine and Dentistry of N.J., 1988, Echocardiography award Tufts U., 1988, award of excellence Am. Acad. Med. Adminstrs., 1994, William Harvey award Am. Med. Writers Assn., 1996; named one of Best Doctors in Am., Best Heart Specialist in U.S. Good Housekeeping mag., 1996; Golden Empire Heart Assn. grantee, Am. Heart Assn. grantee, Ky. Heart Assn. grantee, Vet. Adminstrn. grantee, Nat. Heart, Lung and Blood Inst. grantee; teaching scholar Am. Heart Assn. Fellow ACP, Am. Coll. Cardiology (chmn. 27th ann. scientific session 1978, cardiovascular procedures com., govt. rels. com., v.p. elect 1986, pres. elect 1987-88, pres. 1988—, active various coms., Young Investigator award 1976), Am. Coll. Chest Physicians; mem. Am. Heart Assn. (bd. dirs. work evaluation unit Yolo Sierra chpt., Ky. chapter, active various coms., Teaching scholar 1979-82), Am. Fedn. Clin. Rsch., Yolo County Med. Socs., Am. Inst. Ultrasound in Medicine (bd. dirs.), Am. Soc. Echocardiography (bd. dirs. 1975-87, v.p. 1983-85, pres. 1985-87, assoc. editor), N.Am. Soc. for Cardiac Radiology, Assn. U. Cardiologists. Roman Catholic. Office: U Calif Med Ctr 225 Dickinson St Ste 360 San Diego CA 92103-1910

DEMARIA, MARK, construction executive; b. 1974; Developer DeMaria Bldg. Co.; prin., co-founder Denali Devel. Grp., Royal Oak, Mich., 2003—. Named one of 40 Under 40, Crain's Detroit Bus., 2006. Office: Denali Development Group 230 E Harrison Ave Royal Oak MI 48067 Office Phone: 248-545-6800. Office Fax: 248-545-6886.

DE MARINO, DONALD NICHOLSON, federal agency administrator, diversified financial services company executive; b. Greensburg, Pa., Sept. 28, 1945; s. Thomas C. and Sue Eleanor (Nicholson) De M.; m. Caroline Mack, Dec. 27, 1967 (div. 1981); children: Christopher Tyson, Benjamin Nicholson; m. Betsy Reiver, July 18, 1981; children: Alexander Reiver, William McCurdy. BA, U. Pa., 1967. Dir. Mack & Nicholson, West Chester, Pa., 1972-76; bus. cons. The Nicholson Group, Inc., NYC, 1976-81; sr. project officer U.S.-Saudi Arabian Joint Commn. on Econ. Cooperation, Riyadh, Saudi Arabia, 1981-84, dir., 1985-87; mgr. Litton Industries Offset Investment Programs, Riyadh, 1984-85; sr. project adviser The Arab Investment Co., Riyadh, 1985; internat. bus. cons., prin. De Marino Assocs., Coatesville, Pa., 1987-88; dep. asst. sec. Africa, Near East and South Asia U.S. Dept. Commerce, Washington, 1989-90; U.S. advisor Tata Group of India, 1991—; chmn. Nat. U.S.-Arab C. of C., 1991—; prin. De Marino Ptnrs., LLC, 2004—. Lectr. Wharton Sch. Advanced Mgmt. Program, 1994-96; nat. adv. bd. Mid. East Policy Coun.; bd. dir. Rivada Networks, LLC; mem. Iraq pers. evaluation team U.S. Dept. Def., 2004. Recipient Disting. Svc. award Govt. of Saudi Arabia, 1987. Mem. Sovereign Mil. Order Temple of Jerusalem (decorated Chevalier Templars), Arab-Fgn. C. of C. (chmn. 1999-2000), Racquet Club, Mask and Wig Club. Republican. Presbyn. Home: 43 Longview Rd Coatesville PA 19320-4311 Office: PO Box 791 Unionville PA 19375-0791 Office Phone: 610-347-0701. Personal E-mail: dndemarino@aol.com.

DE MARINO, THOMAS JOHN, lawyer; b. Greensburg, Pa., Nov. 24, 1937; s. Thomas Camille and Sue Eleanor (Nicholson) De M.; m. Elizabeth Hamilton Bardsley, Aug. 22, 1959 (div. Aug. 1978); children: Jeffrey, Lynn; m. Joyce Hobson Lee, May 18, 1979 (dec. Sept. 1995); m. Wendy Hattaway, Aug. 22, 1999. BA, Dickinson Coll., 1959; JD, Pa. State U., 1962. Bar: Pa. 1963, Colo. 1965, U.S. Dist. Ct. Colo. 1965, U.S. Ct. Appeals (10th cir.) 1965, U.S. Supreme Ct. 1984. Assoc. Hamilton, Darmo, Malloy, Phila., 1963; ptnr. firm Ellison, De Marino & Knapp, Denver, 1965-76, De Marino & Knapp, Denver, 1976-77, Sheldon, Bayer, McLean & Glasman, Denver, 1978; Colo. mng. atty. law dept. litigation divsn. Travelers Ins. Co., Denver, 1979-93; dir. Weinberger & Kanan, P.C., Denver, 1994-98; adminstrv. law judge Colo. Divsn. Workers Comp., 1999—, apptd. chief prehearing judge, 1999. Author: Colorado Workers Compensation Law and Practice, 1984; contbr. articles to legal jours. Pres. Denver Lyric Opera Co., 1973; treas. Colo. Mountain Club Found., Denver, 1984. Fellow Am. Bar Found., Colo. Bar Found.; mem. Colo. Bar Assn. (bd. govs. 1985-90, 2000-01, chmn. interprofl. com. 1983, chmn. worker's compensation sect. 1983, vice chmn. litigation sect. coun. 1988), Denver Bar Assn. (pres. 1997, 1st v.p. 1988, bd. trustees 1991-94, chmn. barristers benefit ball com. 1989, Merit award 1995), Colo. Def. Lawyers Assn. (v.p. 1975, pres. 1976), Def. Rsch. Inst. (exceptional performance citation 1977), Colo. Mountain Club (bd. dirs. Denver 1974), Denver Law Club. Republican. Congregationalist. Office: Tower 2 Ste 620 1515 Arapahoe St Denver CO 80202-2117 E-mail: tom.demarino@state.co.us.

DE MARNEFFE, FRANCIS, psychiatrist, hospital administrator; b. Brussels, May 7, 1924; arrived in Eng., 1940; came to US, 1950; s. Armand Gustave and Esther Magdalen (Loveday) de M.; m. Nancy Marie Edmonds, Aug. 5, 1955 (div. Sept. 1967); children: Peter Loveday, Daphne Elizabeth, Colette; m. Barbara Rowe Hopkins, Dec. 5, 1969. MB, BS, U. London, 1950. Diplomate Am. Bd. Psychiatry Neurology. Intern Muhlenberg Hosp., Plainfield, NJ, 1950-51; asst. resident psychiatry Mass. Gen. Hosp., Boston, 1952; tchg. fellow psychiatry Med. Sch. Harvard U., Boston, 1955-56, rsch. fellow, 1955-56; resident psychiatry McLean Hosp., Belmont, Mass., 1953-54, staff psychiatrist, 1955-90, cons. psychiatrist, 1990—, gen. dir., 1962-87, gen. dir. emeritus, 1987—, pres., CEO McLean Health Svcs., Inc., 1986-89; med. dir. Holly Hill Mental Health Svcs., Raleigh, NC, 1990-93; pvt. practice, 1993—. Instr. psychiatry Med. Sch. Harvard U., 1961-66, lectr. 1966—; mem. accreditation coun. psychiat. facilities Joint Commn. Accreditation Hosps., Chgo., 1979-84, mem. tech. adv. com., 1979-84, chmn. accreditation, 1970-72, mem. coun., 1970-79; adminstr. McLean divsn. Hall-Mercer Hosp., Phila., 1969-87; v.p. Hall-Mercer Hosp., 1980-87; exec. v.p. Belmont programs Mass. Gen. Hosp., Boston, 1986-87; clin. prof. psychiatry U. NC, Chapel Hill, 1991-93; assoc. cons. prof. psychiatry Duke U. Med. Sch., 1991-93, v.p. Wake County

Mental Health Assn., 1992-93, med. staff Rex Hosp., Raleigh, NC, 1993; mem. Corp. Ptnrs. Health Care Inc., Boston, 1994—; trustee working group McLean Hosp., 1996, co-chair com. expanding svcs. revs.; cons. Exec. Svcs. Corps., Boston, 1996—; cons. Mass. Soc. Prevention of Cruelty to Children, 2004-. Author: (non-fiction) Introduction to Adolescent Patients in Transition, 1974; author: (contbg.) The Changing Mental Health Scene, 1976; author: Last Boat From Bordeaux, 2001; mem. editl. bd. (jour.) McLean (Hosp.) Jour., 1976—90. Trustee Guidance Camps, Inc., Boston, 1968-90, Preschool, Inc., Cambridge, Mass., 1961-62, Concord Acad. Mass., 1975-78, Nat. Assn. Pvt. Psychiat. Hosps., Washington, 1982-85, 93-94, McLean Hosp. Corp., Belmont, 1985-87; mem. Corp. Family Svc. Assn. Greater Boston, 1978-81; hon. trustee Concord Acad., 1978—; bd. dirs. Mass. chpt. Nat. Com. Prevention Child Abuse, Boston, 1979-81, Health Planning Coun. Greater Boston, 1972-76; chmn. med. divsn. United Way, 1986; mem. Mass. Gen. Hosp. Corp., 1988-94, coll. Des Conseillers French Libr. & Cultural Ctr., Boston, 1995-99; bd. dirs. Friends McLean, 1995—, 1st v.p., 1997-99, pres., 1999-2005, chmn. 2005—; chmn. Boston chpt. French Heritage Soc. (formerly Friends of Vieilles Maisons Françaises), 2000—; cons. Mass. Soc. Prevention of Cruelty to Children, 2004-05. Served as flying officer RAF, 1943-46. Recipient Presdl. award Nat. Assn. Pvt. Psychiat. Hosps., 1991. Fellow: Am. Coll. Mental Health Adminstrn., Mass. Med. Soc., Royal Coll. Psychiatrists, Am. Coll. Psychiatrists, Am. Psychiat. Assn. (life), Royal Coll. Physicians (licentiate); mem.: Ctrl. Neuropsychiat. Hosp. Assn. (pres. 1986—87), Royal Coll. Surgeons, The Royal Air Force Club (London), Lake (Dublin, N.H.) Club, Thames Rowing Club (London), Cambridge Boat Club, Leander (Henley-on-Thames, Eng.) Club, Somerset (Boston) Club, The Country Club (Brookline). Home: 126 Coolidge Hl Cambridge MA 02138-5522 Office: McLean Hosp 115 Mill St Belmont MA 02478-9106 Office Phone: 617-855-3802.

DE MARR, MARY JEAN, English language educator; b. Champaign, Ill., Sept. 20, 1932; d. William Fleming and Laura Alice (Shauman) Bailey. BA, Lawrence Coll., 1954; MA, U. Ill., Urbana, 1957; PhD, U. Ill., 1963; postgrad., U. Tuebingen, Germany, 1954—55, Moscow State U., 1961—62. Asst. prof. English Willamette U., 1964-65; asst. prof. English Ind. State U., 1965-70, assoc. prof., 1970-75, prof., 1975-95, prof. emerita English and women's studies, 1996—. Author: Colleen McCullough: A Critical Companion, 1996, Barbara Kingsolver: A Critical Companion, 1999, Kaye Gibbons: A Critical Companion, 2003; co-author: Adolescent Female Portraits in the American Novel, 1961-81: An Annotated Bibliography, 1983, The Adolescent in The American Novel Since 1960, 1986; Am. editor: Annual Bibliography of English Language and Literature, 1979-90; editor, contbr. In the Beginning: First Novels in Mystery Series, 1995. Recipient Fulbright assistantship, 1954—55, Dove award, Popular Culture Assn., 1996, Midam. award, Soc. for the Study of Midwestern Lit., 2000. Mem.: ACLU, AAUP, MLA, Modern Humanities Rsch. Assn., Phi Kappa Phi, Phi Beta Kappa. Home: 594 Woodbine Terre Haute IN 47803-1760 Personal E-mail: mjd594@msn.com.

DEMARS, LESLIE R., oncologist, obstetrician, gynecologist, educator; b. Ankara, Turkey, Apr. 11, 1961; MD, U. Vt. Coll. Medicine, Burlington, 1987. Cert. Gynecologic Oncology, Obstetrics & Gynecology. Intern U. NC, Chapel Hill, NC, 1987—88, resident, obstetrics & gynecology, 1988—91; fellow, gynecologic oncology U. NC Hosps., Chapel Hill, 1992—94; asst. prof. Eastern Va. Med. Sch., 1994—97; hosp. appointment Dartmouth-Hitchcock Med. Ctr., Lebanon, NH, 1997—, interim divsn. dir., gynecology oncology; asst. prof. Dartmouth-Hitchcock Med. Sch., Lebanon, NH, 1997—. Named one of Top Doctors, NH Mag., 2005. Office: Dartmouth-Hitchcock Med Ctr Gynecology Oncology One Medical Center Dr Lebanon NH 03756 Office Phone: 603-653-3530. Office Fax: 603-653-3545.*

DEMARSICO, JONNETTE M., theater educator, consultant; b. Lakewood, NJ, Sept. 4, 1949; d. John Joseph DeMarsico and Gloria June Bilenky; children: Jonnette Marie Rivenbark-Hay, Thomas Michael Hay Jr., Allison Lee Hay. BA in Theatre Edn., Montclair State U., Upper Montclair, NJ, 1971; M in Liberal Studies, Rollins Coll., Winter Park, Fla., 2003. Theatre educator New Smyrna Beach H.S., Fla., 1983—94, Atlantic H.S., Port Orange, Fla., 1994—. Theatre educator Spruce Creek H.S., Port Orange, 1986—87; drama liaison Volusia County Schs., Fla., 1991—. Performer, vol. Daytona Playhouse, Fla., 1993—. Recipient Tchr. Yr., New Smyrna Beach H.S., 1986; grantee, Atlantic H.S., 2006. Mem.: Am. Assn. Theatre Edn., Fla. State Thespians, Fla. Assn. Theatre Edn. (bd. dirs. 1993—, Educator Yr. 2000). Independent. Episcopalian. Office: Atlantic HS 1250 Reed Canal Rd Port Orange FL 32129

DEMARTINI, RICHARD MICHAEL, retired bank executive; b. San Francisco, Oct. 12, 1952; s. James G.B. and Mary (Nehls) D.; m. Jennifer Brorsen; children: Chad, Susan, Jake. BS in Mktg., San Diego State U., 1974. Account exec. Dean Witter, San Mateo, Calif., 1975-78, br. mgr. Bakersfield, Calif., 1978-80, 1st v.p. and br. mgr. Chgo., 1980-83, sr. v.p., regional dir., 1983-84, exec. v.p., nat. sales dir. NYC, 1984-85; pres., COO Dean Witter Consumer Markets Dean Witter Fin. Svcs. Group, NYC, 1985-88, pres., COO Sears Consumer Fin. Corp. Lincolnshire, Ill., 1988-89, pres., COO Dean Witter Capital NYC, 1989—98; chmn., CEO, internat. private client group Morgan Stanley Dean Witter, NYC, 1998—2001; pres., asset mgmt. group Bank Am., 2001—04. Chmn. Nasdaq, 1996—97; former vice chmn. Nat. Assoc. Securities Dealers. Trustee Cancer Rsch. Inst.; bd. dirs. Graham Windham, NYC.

DEMARTINO, ANTHONY GABRIEL, cardiologist, internist; b. Bronx, NY, Oct. 7, 1931; s. Agostino and Vincenzina (Clarizia) DeM.; m. Marlene Mignone, Aug. 8, 1964; children: Anthony Augustin, Laura Jean. BS cum laude, Iona Coll., 1953; MD, SUNY, 1957. Diplomate Nat. Bd. Med. Examiners, Am. Bd. Internal Medicine (cardiovascular disease). Intern U. divsn. Kings County Med. Ctr., Bklyn., 1957-58, med. resident, 1960-62; fellow cardiopulmonary Cornell U., NY Hosp., 1962-64; acting chief medicine Fordham divsn. Misericordia-Fordham Affiliation, Bronx, 1964-65, physician in charge cardiac lab., 1965-69; attending physician dept. medicine and cardiology Our Lady of Mercy Med. Ctr., Bronx, 1967-95, sr. physician, 1995—, mem. med. bd., 1985-93; asst. attending Presbyn. Hosp., NYC, 1998—2006. Attending physician dept. medicine and cardiology Lawrence Hosp., Bronxville, N.Y., 1977-97, sr. attending physician, 1997—, mem. med. bd., 1989-94, sec., treas. med. bd., 1996-97, assoc. dir. dept. medicine, 1993-97; practice medicine, specializing in cardiology and internal medicine, Bronxville, 1964—; v.p. med. bd. Misericordia Hosp. Med. Ctr., Bronx, 1973-75, pres., 1975-77; clin. asst. prof. medicine N.Y. Med. Coll., 1971—; hon. police surgeon N.Y.C., 1978—; asst. attending physician Presbyn. Hosp., N.Y., 1996—; asst. in medicine Columbia U., N.Y.C., 1996—. Mem. editl. bd. N.Y. Med. Quar., 1980-84; contbr. articles to profl. jours. Trustee Misericordia Hosp., 1977-83; sec., treas. med. bd. Lawrence Hosp., 1996-97. Served to capt., M.C., U.S. Army, 1958-60. Named Top Doctor Metro NY Area, 2001—; Nat. Heart Inst. fellow, 1962-64. Fellow ACP/Am. Soc. Internal Medicine, Am. Coll. Cardiology, Coun. Clin. Cardiology of Am. Heart Assn., Am. Coll. Chest Physicians, N.Y. Cardiol. Assn.; mem. AMA, Westchester County, N.Y. County Med. Soc., Am. Coll. Medicine. Roman Catholic. Home Phone: 914-779-8742; Office Phone: 914-552-1488. Personal E-mail: agdemartino@optonline.net.

DE MARTINO, RALPH VICTOR, lawyer; b. Jackson Heights, NY, Dec. 16, 1954; s. Yolanda De Martino; children: Andrew, Matthew, Kira. BSBA cum laude with honors, Bucknell U., Lewisburg, Pa., 1976; JD with honors, George Washington U., Washington, 1979. Bar: U.S. Ct. Appeals (D.C. cir.), Va., D.C., U.S. Ct. Appeals (4th cir.), U.S. Supreme Ct. Ptnr. Routier and Johnson, P.C., Washington, 1979—83; prin./mng. ptnr. De Martino Finkelstein Rosen & Virga, PC, Washington, 1983—2002; mng. ptnr./chair of securities practice group Dilworth Paxson LLP, Washington, 2003—05; mem. and vice chair, securities offerings and regulations practice group Cozen O'Connor, Washington, 2005—. Dir. Isolagen, Inc., Exton, Pa. Contbr. articles to profl. jours. Mem.: ABA (subcom. on securities regulation, subcom. on NASD pricing issues), D.C. Bar Assn. (com. on corp. banking and bus. law), Va. State Bar Assn. (licentiate). Office: Cozen O'Connor 1627 I St NW #1100 Washington DC 20006 Office Phone: 202-912-4825. Office Fax: 202-912-4830. E-mail: rdemartino@cozen.com.

DEMARY, JO LYNNE, retired school system administrator, former elementary school educator; BEd, DEd, Coll. of William and Mary; MS in Spl. Edn., U. Va. Commonwealth. Tchr. Fairfax County Schs., Va., Henrico County Schs., Va., from tchr. to asst. supt. Va.; asst. supt. pub. instruction Commonwealth of Va., 1994—99, acting supt. pub. instruction, 1999—2000, supt. of pub. instruction, 2000—06. Bd. trustee Va. Ctr. for Tchg. Internat. Studies. Recipient Va. Assn. Elementary Sch. Principals 2000-2001 Pathfinders award, Breaking the Glass Ceiling award, Assn. Va. Women Educators, 2000, Outstanding Ednl. Leadership Alumni award, Coll. William and Mary Sch. Edn., 2001, Alumni Star award, Va. Commonwealth U., 2001, State Leadership award, Nat. Assn. Fed. Edn. Prog. Adminstr., 2002, Disting. Svc. award, Va. Art Edn. Assn., 2003, Va. Assn. Test Dir. Excellence in Assessment award, 2003, Pace Humanitarian award, Nat. Assn. State Directors Spl. Edn., 2004, Frank E. Flora Lamp of Knowledge award, Va. Assn. Secondary Sch. Principals, 2005. Mem.: Edn. Commn. States, Nat. Coun. for Accreditation Tchr. Edn. (mem. task force on sch. health and safety, mem. internat. com., mem. state partnership bd.), Coun. Chief State Sch. Officers, Va. Commonwealth U. Alumni Assn.*

DEMASI, KARIN A., lawyer; b. San Francisco, July 20, 1971; BS, Northwestern Univ., 1993; JD, Univ. Pa., 1996. Bar: Pa. 1996, NY 1997. Law clk., Hon. D. Brock Hornby US Dist. Ct., Dist. of Maine; assoc. Cravath Swaine & Moore LLP, NYC, 1997—2005, ptnr., litig., 2005—. Editor: Univ. Pa. Law Rev. Office: Cravath Swaine & Moore LLP Worldwide Plz 825 Eighth Ave New York NY 10019-7475 Office Phone: 212-474-1059. Office Fax: 212-474-3700. Business E-Mail: kdemasi@cravath.com.

DE MASI, KENNETH FORREST, secondary school educator; b. Phoenix, May 11, 1950; s. Charles Armand and Delphine Edna (Fuller) de Masi; m. Josephine MacLaren Shepard (div.); children: Chauncey Adin Fuller, Michael Orlando Sage; m. Linda Ann Redburn, Dec. 13, 1943; stepchildren: Scott Aaron, Peter M., Matthew Jon, Kristen Madeleine Gundersen. BA in Edn., Ariz. State U., 1974, MEd, 2000. Std. secondary tchg. cert. Ariz., 1974. Tchr. South Mountain HS, Phoenix, 1974—78, social studies dept. chmn., 1975—78; tchr. Mesa Vista HS, Ariz., 1983—, social studies dept. chmn., 1983—2007; tchr. Riverview HS, Chandler, Ariz., 2007—. Tchr. cons. Ariz. Geog. Alliance, Tempe, 2001—05. Author: (curriculum materials-CD) Making Sense of Place: Phoenix-the Urban Desert, 2004; co-author: (curriculum package) The Panama Canal: Building the 8th Wonder of the World, 2003. Chmn. investment com. Mesa United Way, 1991—2000, chmn. neighborhood small grants, 1995—2000; com. mem. Mesa Mayor's Alliance Against Drugs. With US Army, 1970—71. Named Betty Kerr Vol. of Yr., Mesa United Way, 1998; recipient Tribune Newspapers' Ednl. Leadership award, Mesa Tribune, 1992, ambassadorship, Motorola/Mesa Pub. Schs./Industry, 1993—94; Nat. Security Coun. Tchr. fellow, 1975—76, sr. fellow, James Madison Meml. Found., 1998. Mem.: ASCD, Am. Ednl. Rsch. Assn., Nat. Coun. History Edn., Internat. Reading Assn., Nat. Reading Coun., Nat. Coun. Geog. Edn. (Disting. Tchg. Achievement award 2005), Nat. Coun. Social Studies (curriculum com. 2005—), Ariz. Coun. Social Studies (v.p. 2003—04, pres. 2004—06), Gamma Beta Phi, Kappa Delta Pi. Independent. Avocations: hiking, fishing, backpacking, woodworking, birdwatching. Office: Mesa Vista HS 1731 N Country Club Dr Mesa AZ 85201 Office Phone: 480-472-5366. E-mail: kfdemasi@mpsaz.org.

DE MASSA, JESSIE G., media specialist; b. Aliquippa, Pa. BJ, Temple U.; MLS, San Jose State U., 1967; postgrad., U. Okla., U. So. Calif. Tchr. Palo Alto Unified Sch. Dist., Calif., 1966; libr. Antelope Valley Joint Union HS Dist., Lancaster, Calif., 1966, ABC Unified Sch. Dist., Artesia, Calif., 1968—72; dist. libr. Tehachapi Unified Sch. Dist., Calif., 1972—81; media specialist, free lance writer, 1981—; assoc. Chris DeMassa & Assocs., 1988—. Author: (novel) The Haunting and Murder in Aruba, 2002; contbr. articles to profl. jours. Active Statue of Liberty Ellis Island Found., Inc., Nat. Trust Hist. Preservation; founding mem. Nat. Campaign for Tolerance Wall of Tolerance, Montgomery, Ala., 2005; charter supporter US Holocaust Meml. Mus., Washington; supporting mem. US Holocaust Meml. Coun., Washington; founder Pacific Aviation Mus. Pearl Harbor at Ford Islands, Hawaii, 2006. Named Nat. Women's Hall Fame, 1995. Fellow Internat. Biog. Assn.; mem. Calif. Media Libr. Educators Assn., Calif. Assn. Sch. Librs. (exec. coun.), AAUW (bull. editor chpt., assoc. editor state bull., chmn. publicity, 1955-68), Nat. Mus. Women Arts (charter), Hon Fellows John F. Kennedy Libr. (founding mem.), Women's Roundtable Orange County, Nat. Writer's Assn. (so. Calif. chpt.), Calif. Retired Tchrs. Assn. (Harbor Beach divsn. 77), Heritage Found., Claremont Inst., Nat. Women's History Mus. (charter mem.), Libr. Congress (nat. charter mem.), Nat. World War II Meml. Nat. Mall (charter mem.), Nat. Trust Hist. Preservation. Home and Office: 9951 Garrett Cir Huntington Beach CA 92646-3604 Office Phone: 714-962-9810. Personal E-mail: jdwriter10@verizon.net.

DE MATTEO, DREA, actress; b. Queens, NY, Jan. 19, 1973; BFA in film prodn., NYU, Tish Sch. Arts. Owner Filth Mart Clothing, NY. Actor: (TV series) The Sopranos, 1999—2004 (Emmy award Outstanding Supporting Actress in a Drama Series, 2004), Joey, 2004—; (films) Meet Prince Charming, 1999, Sleepwalk, 2000, Swordfish, 2001, The Perfect You, 2002, Deuces Wild, 2002, Love Rome, 2002, Prey for Rock & Roll, 2003, Beacon Hill, 2003, Assault on Precinct 13, 2005, Broken English, 2007.*

DEMAUSE, LLOYD, psychologist; b. Detroit, Sept. 19, 1931; s. Leon and Martha (Koren) DeM.; m. Susan Hein; children: Neil, Jennifer, Jonathan. Student, GM Inst., 1948-52; AB, Columbia U., 1957, postgrad., 1957-61, Nat. Psychol. Assn. for Psychoanalysis, 1959-60. Founder Atcom Inc. (pub.), 1959; chmn. bd., dir. Inst. for Psychohistory; pub. Psychohistory Press; mem. faculty N.Y. Center for Psychoanalytic Tng. Editor, author: Jimmy Carter and American Fantasy, The History of Childhood, The New Psychohistory, A Bibliography of Psychohistory, Foundations of Psychohistory, Reagan's America: The Emotional Life of Nations; editor: Jour. Psychohistory. With AUS, 1952-54. Mem. Internat. Psychohist. Assn. (pres.). Home and Office: Inst for Psychohistory 140 Riverside Dr New York NY 10024-2605 Office Phone: 212-799-2294. E-mail: psychhst@tiac.net.

DEMAY, MICHAEL F., secondary school educator, small business owner; b. Rochester, NY, Mar. 3, 1974; s. Marshall and Carol DeMay; m. Cyndie Nigro; 1 child, Cameron. BS in Phys. Edn., Ithaca Coll., NY, 1996, MS in Sports Pedagogy, 2000; Cert. of Advanced Study in Sch. Adminstrn., SUNY, Brockport, 2003. Cert. K-12 health edn. NY State, 1996, K-12 phys. edn. NY State, 1996, driver edn. NY State, 1997, sch. dist. adminstr. NY State, 2003. Phys. edn. tchr. Fairport (NY) Ctrl. Schs., 1997—; dir. driver edn. program Monroe #1 BOCES, Rochester, NY, 2002. Summer sch. health, driver edn. tchr. Monroe #1 BOCES, Rochester, NY, 1997—; owner East Side Driving, Inc., Suburban Driving Sch. Mem.: AAHPERD, NYSAAHPERD. Home: 140 Hamilton Rd Fairport NY 14450 Office: Fairport High School 1358 Ayrault Rd Fairport NY 14450 Home Phone: 585-739-4440; Office Phone: 585-421-2100. Business E-Mail: michael_demay@fairport.monroe.edu.

DE MAYNADIER, PATRICK D., lawyer; b. Wooster, Ohio, May 30, 1960; m. Heather de Maynadier. BA in Philosophy, U. Va., 1982, JD, 1985; student, Advanced Mgmt., Harvard U., 1999. Atty. Bracewell & Patterson, LLP, Houston; assoc. gen. counsel Falcon Seaboard Resources, Inc., Houston, 1995—96; sr. v.p., gen. counsel, sec. Sterling Diagnostic Imaging, Inc., Greenville, SC, 1996—99; pres., CEO SDI Investments LLC (spin-off of Sterling Diagnostic Imaging, Inc.), 1999—2005; exec. v.p., gen. counsel, sec. CombiMatrix Corp., Mukilteo, Wash., 2000—01; v.p., gen. counsel, sec. Hillenbrand Industries, Inc., 2002—. Mem.: DC Bar Assn., State Bar Tex. Office: Hillenbrand Industries Inc Mail Code Y-20 700 State Route 46 E Batesville IN 47006

DEMBLING, PAUL GERALD, lawyer, former government official; b. Rahway, NJ, Jan. 11, 1920; s. Simon and Fannie (Ellenbogen) D.; m. Florence Brotman, Nov. 22, 1947; children: Ross Wayne, Douglas Evan, Donna Stacy. BA, Rutgers U., 1940, MA, 1942; JD, George Washington U., 1951. Bar: D.C. 1952. Grad. asst., teaching fellow Rutgers U., 1940-42; economist Office Chief Transp., Dept. Army, 1942-45; since practiced in Washington; indsl. relations NACA, 1945-51, spl. counsel, legal adviser, gen. counsel, 1951-58; asst. gen. counsel NASA, 1958-61, dir. legis. affairs, 1961-63, dep. gen. counsel, 1963-67, gen. counsel, 1967-69, chmn. bd. contract appeals, 1958-61, vice chmn. inventions and contbns. bd., 1959-67; mem. and alt. rep. U.S. del. UN Legal Subcom. Com. on Outer Space, 1964-69; gen. counsel GAO, 1969-78; partner Schnader, Harrison, Segal & Lewis, Washington, 1978-93, sr. counsel, 1994—2002. Prin. author NASA Act, 1958; professorial lectr. George Washington U. Law Sch., 1965-86; lectr. Am. Grad. U., 1978-2000. Co-author: Federal Contract Management, 1988, Essentials of Grant Law Practice, 1991; editor in chief Fed. Bar Jour., 1962-69; contbr. articles to profl. jours. Recipient Meritorious Civilian Service award War Dept., 1945, Disting. Service medal NASA, 1968, Nat. Civil Service League award, 1973, Earl W. Kintner award FBA, 2003, Newton award Nat. Grants Mgmt. Assn., 2005. Fellow: AIAA (chmn. com. law and sociology 1969—71), FBA (life; nat. coun. 1963—, pres. Capitol Hill chpt. 1977—78, nat. sec. 1978—79, pres.-elect 1981—82, nat. pres. 1983—84, bd. dirs. bldg. corp. 1989—2005, Earl W. Kintner Disting. award 2003), Nat. Acad. Pub. Adminstrn., Nat. Contract Mgmt. Assn. (bd. advisers 1973—98), Fed. Bar Found. (life); mem.: ABA (pub. contract law sec. 1983—84, vice chmn. 1984—85, chmn. elect 1985—86, chmn. 1986—87, coun.), Internat. Inst. Space Law (pres. Am. assn. 1970—72, Internat. Astronaut. Fedn. award 1992), Procurement Roundtable (bd. dirs. 1984—, vice chmn. 1988—), D.C. Bar (mem. steering com. govt. contracts and litigation sect. 1989—95), Cosmos Club, Phi Delta Phi. Home: 11625 Pamplona Blvd Boynton Beach FL 33437-4077 Office: Schnader Harrison Segal & Lewis 2001 Pennsylvania Ave NW Washington DC 20006 E-mail: pfdemb@webtv.net.

DEMBOWSKI, PETER FLORIAN, foreign language educator; b. Warsaw, Dec. 23, 1925; arrived in U.S., 1966, naturalized, 1974; s. Wlodzimierz and Henryka (Sokolowski) D.; m. Yolande Jessop, June 29, 1954; children: Anne, Eve, Paul. BA with honors, U. BC, 1952; Doctorat d'Universite, U. Paris, France, 1954; PhD, U. Calif., Berkeley, 1960. Instr. French U. B.C., 1954-56; asst. prof. French U. Toronto, 1960-63, assoc. prof., 1963-66; mem. faculty U. Chgo., 1966-95, prof. French, 1970-95, Disting. Svc. prof., 1989-95, prof. emeritus, 1995—, dean students div. humanities, 1968-70, chmn. dept. Romance langs. and lits., 1976-83, resident master Snell-Hitchcock halls, 1973-79; vis. mem. Sch. Hist. Studies, Inst. Advanced Study, Princeton, NJ, 1979-80. Author: La Chronique de Robert de Clari, 1963, Jourdain de Blaye, 1969, Ami et Amile, 1969, La Vie de sainte Marie l'Egyptienne, 1977, Jean Froissart and his Meliador, 1983, Jean Froissart, Le Paradis d'Amour et l'Orloge Amoureus, 1986, Erec et Enide, 1994, L'Estrif de Fortune et Vertu, 1999, Christians in the Warsaw Ghetto: An Epitaph for the Unremembered, 2005. Served with Polish Army, 1944-46. Decorated Cross of Valor, Cross of Service with swords (Poland), Chevalier des Palmes Academiques (France); Guggenheim fellow, 1970-71; Danforth Found. assoc., 1976-84 Fellow Am. Acad. Arts and Scis.; mem. Société de Linguistique Romane (councillor 1995-99), Medieval Acad. Am. (councillor 1980-82). Office: U Chgo Dept Romance Langs and Lit 1050 E 59th St Rm 205B Chicago IL 60637-1559 Business E-Mail: p_dembowski@uchicago.edu.

DEMCHAK, WILLIAM S., bank executive; b. 1962; BA, Allegheny Coll.; MBA, U. Mich. Global head, structured fin. and credit portfolio JP Morgan Chase, 1997—2002; vice chmn., head corp. & inst. banking PNC Fin. Svcs. Group, Inc., Pitts., 2002—. Bd. dir. Black Rock, Inc. Office: PNC Fin Svcs Group Inc One PNC Plaza 249 5th Ave Pittsburgh PA 15222-2707*

DEMEDIO, KATHLEEN MARIE, chemistry educator; b. Norristown, Pa., June 20, 1961; d. John Patrick and Caroline Mary (Conners) Agnew; m. John Francis DeMedio, Nov. 5, 1994; children: Jacqueline, John, Joseph Francis, Kathleen Marie. AB in Biology, Immaculata U., Pa., 1983; MS in Edn., St Joseph's U., Phila., 1996. Cert. biology Pa. Dept. Edn., 1994, chemistry Pa. Dept. Edn., 2000. Tchr. US Peace Corps, Mmadinare, Botswana, 1986—88; chemistry tchr. Acad. Notre Dame de Namur, Villanova, Pa., 1990—97; sci. tchr. St. Aloysius Acad., Bryn Mawr, Pa., 1998—99; chemistry tchr. Norristown Area Sch. Dist., Pa., 1999—. Mem.: NSTA. Democrat. Roman Catholic. Avocations: piano, singing. Home: 1806 Sandy Hill Rd Plymouth Meeting PA 19462 Office: Norristown Area High School 1900 Eagle Dr Norristown PA 19401 Home Phone: 610-277-1536; Office Phone: 610-630-5090. Personal E-mail: kmd620@aol.com. Business E-Mail: kdemedio@nassd.k12.pa.us.

DE MENIL, GEORGES, economist, educator; s. John de Menil and Dominique Schlumberger; m. Lois Pattison, Aug. 3, 1968; children: John-Charles, Joy, Benjamin, Victoria. BA magna cum laude, Harvard Coll., Cambridge, Mass., 1963; PhD, MIT, Cambridge, 1968. Asst. prof. Princeton U., NJ, 1970—74; dir. quar. modelling project Ministry Fin., Paris, 1975—78; prof. Ecole des Hautes Etudes en Sciences Sociales, Paris, 1978—, dir. Ctr. for Quantitative and Comparative Econs., 1978—81. Jury mem. History Prize in Honor of Francois Guizot, Paris; sr. vis. fellow Coun. on Fgn. Rels., NYC, 1981—83; econ. advisor Prime Min. Govt. Romania, Bucharest, 1997—2000; vis. prof., scholar Kennedy Sch. Govt., Cambridge, 2001—02; vis. prof. Stern Sch., NYU, NYC, 2003—. Author: (books) Bargaining: Monopoly Power vs. Union Power, 1971, Ukrainian Economic Reform: The Unfinished Agenda, 1971, Economic Summitry, 1983, Comparative Analyses of Stabilization Policy: France and Germany, 1985, International Volatility and Economic Growth, 1991; mem. editl. bd.: Commentaire, 1978—, editor, founder: quar. rev. Economic Policy; contbr. articles to profl. jours. Pres. Am. Friends of the Paris Sch. Econs., NYC, 2006, The Brearley Sch., NYC, 1989—96; bd. mem. Schlumberger, Ltd., Paris Sch. Economics, 2006—. Recipient Chevalier, Ordre des Palmes Academiques, French Govt., 1995, Comdr., Order of Merit, Pres. Romania, 2000. Mem.: European Econ. Assn., Am. Econ. Assn., Coun. Fgn. Rels., Fishers Island Country Club, Knickerbocker Club. Episcopalian. Avocations: collecting art, fishing, skiing. Home: Box 417 Isabella Rd Fishers Island NY 06390 Office: Paris Sch Econs 48 Blvd Jourdan 75014 Paris France Home Phone: 917-496-6748; Office Phone: 212-998-0866, 33-1-43136300.

DE MENIL, LOIS PATTISON, historian, philanthropist; b. NYC, May 15, 1938; d. Charles Krone and Julia Anne (Hasson) Pattison; m. Georges

Francois Conrad de Menil, Aug. 3, 1968; children: John-Charles, Joy-Alexandra, Benjamin, Victoria. AB, Wellesley Coll., 1960; diploma, Inst. d'Etudes Politiques, Paris, 1962; Lic. in Law, U. Paris, 1962; PhD, Harvard U., 1972. Pres. D. M. Found., NYC, 1986—2001; pres., chmn. Ctr. Khmer Studies, Cambodia, 2001—. Bd. dirs. AXA Art Ins. Corp., 1998—; counsellor to Ministry of Culture, Romania, 1997—2001; mem. Coun. Fgn. Rels., 1976—, Inst. for Strategic Studies, London, 1978—, French Inst. Internat. Rels., Paris, 1980—, U.S. Coun. on Germany, NYC, 1978—, Festival d'Automne, Paris, 1997—. Author: Who Speaks for Europe?, 1978; editor, translator: The African Unity Movement, 1965, French Foreign Policy under De Gaulle, 1967. Internat. coun. Mus. Modern Art, NYC, 1975—; vis. com. to art mus. Harvard U., Cambridge, Mass., 1977—; vice-chair bd. dirs. Dia Ctr. for Arts, NYC, 1985—96; vice-chair trustees coun. Nat. Gallery Art, Washington, 1988—96; bd. dirs. World Monuments Fund, NYC, 1990—, Groton Sch., 1991—2004, NASDAQ Found., 2000—04, Coun. Am. Overseas Rsch. Ctrs., 2003—; bd. trustees Tennis Hall of Fame, 2005—. Fulbright scholar, France, 1960-62; Ford Found. fellow, 1966-68. Mem. Century Assn., Univ. Club, Harvard Club, Fishers Island Country Club, Phi Beta Kappa. Episcopalian. Avocations: art, skiing, tennis, travel. Office: D M Found 149 E 63rd St New York NY 10021-7405 Home Phone: 631-788-7394.

DEMENT, JAMES ALDERSON, JR., lawyer; b. Clinton, Okla., Sept. 11, 1947; s. James Alderson and Ruby (Weaver) DeM.; m. Sally Anne Wylder, June 6, 1970; children: Stephen, Suzanne, Jonathan. BA summa cum laude, Tex. Christian U., 1969; JD in Internat. Affairs, Cornell U., 1972. Bar: N.Y. 1973, Tex. 1974. Assoc. Alexander & Green, NYC, 1972-73, Baker Botts, LLP, Houston, 1977-85, ptnr., 1998—; ptnr., chmn. corp. tax and internat. sect. Butler & Binion, LLP, Houston, 1985-97. Adj. prof. U. Houston, 1987-88; dir. Houston World Affairs Coun. 2002-06. Mem. edtl. rev. bd. The Internat. Lawyer, 1987-94. Trustee Houston Ballet Found., 1989-96, Brazos Presbyn. Homes, Inc., 1990-96. Capt. USAF, 1973-77. Fellow Tex. Bar Found.; mem. State Bar Tex. (internat. law sect., chmn. 1989-90), Internat. and Comparative Law Ctr. Southwestern Legal Found. (adv. coun. 1986—), Houston Bar Assn. (internat. law sect., pres. 1989-90). Presbyterian. Office: Baker Botts LLP 910 Louisiana St Houston TX 77002-4995 Home Phone: 281-261-0445; Office Phone: 713-229-1816. Business E-Mail: jdement@bakerbotts.com.

DEMENT, WILLIAM CHARLES, medical researcher, educator; b. Wenatchee, Wash., July 29, 1928; s. Charles Frederick and Kathryn (Severyns) Dement; m. Eleanor Weber, Mar. 23, 1956; children: Catherine Lynn, Elizabeth Anne, John Nicholas. BS, U. Wash., 1951; MD, U. Chgo., 1955, PhD, 1957. Bd. cert. in clin. polysomography. Intern Mt. Sinai Hosp., NYC, 1957—58, rsch. fellow dept. psychiatry, 1958—63; assoc. prof. dept. psychiatry and behavioral scis. Stanford U., 1963—67, prof., 1967—; dir. Stanford Sleep Disorders Clinic and Lab., 1970—, Sleep Rsch. Lab., Stanford, Calif., 1963—. Chmn. U.S. Surgeon Gen.'s Joint Coord. Coun., Project Sleep, 1979—, Nat. Commn. on Sleep Disorders Rsch., 1990—92. Author: Some Must Watch While Some Must Sleep, 1972, The Sleep Watchers, 1992; editor-in-chief: Sleep, 1977—, mem. editl. bd.: Neurobiology of Aging, 1982—. Recipient medal, Intra-Sci. Rsch. Found., 1981, Disting. Svc. award, U. Chgo. Med. Alumni Assn., 1978. Mem.: Am. Physiol. Soc., Am. EEG Soc., Western EEG Soc., Soc. Neuroscience, Psychiat. Rsch. Found., Inst. Medicine of NAS, Assn. Sleep Disorders Ctrs. (pres. 1982, Nathaniel Kleitman prize), Sleep Rsch. Soc. (founder). Office: Stanford Sleep Disorders Ctr 701 Welch Rd Ste 2226 Palo Alto CA 94304-1711

DEMENTIEVA, ELENA, professional tennis player; b. Moscow, Oct. 15, 1981; d. Viatcheslav and Vera Dementieva. Profl. tennis player WTA Tour, 1998—. Named WTA Tour Most Improved Player, 2000; recipient Female of Yr. Award, Russia, 2001. Achievements include Winner 7 WTA Tour singles titles: Amelia Island, 2003, Bali, 2003, Shanghai, 2003, Hasselt, 2004, Toray Pan Pacific Open, 2006, JPMorgan Chase Open, 2006, Istanbul Cup, 2007; Winner 5 WTA Tour doubles titles: (with Husarova) Moscow, 2002, San Diego, 2002, Berlin, 2002, Season-Ending Championships, 2002, (with Krasnoroutskaya) Hertogenbosch, 2003, (with Pennetta) LA, 2005; winner 3 career singles titles, 3 career doubles titles, ITF; Mem. Russian Fed Cupt Team, 1999, 2001-03, Russian Olympic Team, 2000, 2004. Avocations: chess, skiing. Office: c/o WTA Tour Corp Hdqs One Progress Plz Ste 1500 Saint Petersburg FL 33701*

DEMENY, PAUL GEORGE, demographer, researcher; b. Nyiregyháza, Hungary, Dec. 24, 1932; s. József Demény and Margit Iványi; children: Lylla Carter, John. BA, U. Budapest, Hungary, 1955; PhD, Princeton U., 1961. Asst. prof., economics and rsch. assoc. Princeton U., NJ, 1961—66; assoc. to full prof. econs. U. Mich., Ann Arbor, 1966—69; prof. econs. U. Hawaii, Honolulu, 1969—73; dir. east-west population inst. East-West Ctr., Honolulu, 1969—73; v.p. The Population Coun., NYC, 1973—88, disting. scholar, 1989—. Founding editor Population and Devel. Rev., NYC, 1975—. Co-author: (book) Regional Model Life Tables and Stable Populations; co-editor: Population and Development, Encyclopedia of Population, The Political Economy of Global Population Change, 2006. Pres. Population Assn. of Am., Washington, 1986. Recipient External Mem., Hungarian Acad. of Scis., 2001, Laureate, Internat. Union for the Sci. Study of Population, Paris, 2003. Mem.: Princeton Club of NY (assoc.). Office: The Population Coun One Dag Hammarskjold Pl New York NY 10017 Home: 303 East 83rd St Apt 32E New York NY 10028 Office Phone: 212-339-0691. Personal E-mail: pauldemeny@hotmail.com. Business E-Mail: pdemeny@popcouncil.org.

DEMERDASH, NABEEL ALY OMAR, electrical engineer; b. Cairo, Apr. 26, 1943; came to U.S., 1966; s. Aly Omar and Aziza D.; m. Esther Adel Feher, Feb. 22, 1969; children: Yvonne, Omar, Nancy. BScEE with 1st class honors, Cairo U., 1964; MSEE, U. Pitts., 1967, PhD, 1971. Tchg. asst. in elec. engring. Cairo U., 1964—66, U. Pitts., 1966-68; engr. Westinghouse Electric Corp., Pitts., 1968-72; asst. prof. elec. engring. Va. Poly. Tech. Inst. and State U., Blacksburg, 1972-77, assoc. prof. elec. engring., 1977-81, prof., 1981-83; prof. dept. elec. and computer engring. Clarkson U., Potsdam, NY, 1983-94; prof., chmn. dept. elec. and computer engring. Marquette U., Milw., 1994-97, prof. dept. elec. and computer engring., 1994—. Cons. Sundstrand Corp., Rockford, Ill., 1985-98. Contbr. articles to profl. jours. Recipient Cert. of Recognition, NASA, 1979, Cert. of Tchg. Excellence, Va. Poly. Inst. and State U., 1980, Tchr. of Yr. award, Beta Omicron chpt. Eta Kappa Nu, Marquette Univ., 2003, Outstanding Rsch. award Coll. Engring, Marquette U., 2004. Fellow IEEE (subcom. chmn. 1988-92, 94-97, Nikola Tesla award 1999); mem. IEEE Power Engring. Soc. (disting. lectr. 1987—, Elec. Machinery Com. prize paper award 1993, working group award 1994, PES prize paper award 1993, working group award 1994), Indsl. Electronics Soc. (Disting. Spkr. program 1990—), Electromagnetics Acad. Achievements include development of three dimensional finite element vector potential and coupled 3D vector potential-scalar potential methods of solution of electromagnetic fields in electric devices; time-stepping coupled finite element-state space computer simulation models and design of electronically operated/controlled AC and DC motor drives. Office: Marquette Univ Elec Computer Engring Dept PO Box 1881 Milwaukee WI 53201-1881 Office Phone: 414-288-5680. Business E-Mail: nabeel.demerdash@marquette.edu.

DEMERE, ROBERT HOUSTOUN, JR., oil industry executive; b. Savannah, Ga., Feb. 15, 1924; s. Raymond McAllister and Josephine Elizabeth (Mobley) D.; m. Mary Elizabeth Bullock, Sept. 21, 1946; children— Robert H., John B., Raymond S., Sims B., Anne E. Econs. student, Yale U. From chmn. bd. Colonial Oil Industries to CEO Colonial Group, Savannah, Ga., 1958—86, CEO, 1986—; dir. Enmark Stas., Inc., Savannah, Ga., 1964—; pres., dir. Chatham Towing Co., Inc., Savannah, Ga., 1952—. Colonial Terminals, Inc., Savannah, Ga., 1991—. Bd. dirs. 1st Union Bank Savannah, 1st Union Corp. Ga. Bd. dirs. YMCA of Savannah, Mighty Eighth Air Force Mus., 1999—. Served to lt. (j.g.) USN, 1942-45. Named Indsl. Man of Yr., Internat. Mgmt. Coun., Savannah, 1972 Mem. Ind. Fuel Terminal Operators Assn. (v.p. 1986—), Ind. Liquid Terminal Operators Assn., Nat. Oil Jobbers Assn., S.C. Petroleum Marketers Assn., N.C. Oil Jobbers Assn., Ga. Oilmen's Assn., World Bus. Council, Sea Edn. Assn. (trustee 1982—), Ga. C. of C., Savannah (Ga.) Yacht Club, Century Club, Chatham Club, Cotillion Club, Oglethorpe Club. Avocations: sailing, fishing, swimming.*

DEMERS, ELIZABETH ANNE, education educator; b. Windsor, Ontario, Canada, July 13; d. Roland Joseph and Annie Hamilton (Drummond) Demers. BA in Acctg., U. of Waterloo, 1989; M in Acctg., U. Waterloo, 1990; PhD Bus. Admin., Stanford U., 2000, MS Stats., 1997. Asst. mgr. fin. adv. Price Waterhouse, Toronto, Canada, 1992—93; rsch. asst. grad. sch. of bus. Stanford U., 1994—99; asst. prof. Simon Sch. of Bus. U. of Rochester, 1999—. Contbr. articles to profl. jours. Grantee Rsch. Grant, CIMA, 2001. Fellowship, Soc. of Mgmt. Acctg. of Can., 1994—98. Mem.: Am. Fin. Assn., Am. Academic Acctg. Assoc. Office: INSEAD Boulevard de Constance 77305 Fontainebleau France Office Phone: 33 (0) 1 60 72 92 06. Business E-Mail: liz.demers@insead.edu.

DEMERTZOGLOU, PINDARO EPAMINONDA, systems administrator, educator; s. Epaminodas Pindaros and Gesthimani Prodromos Demertzoglou. BS, Am. Coll. of Thessaloniki, Greece, 1995; MBA, Rensselaer Poly. Inst., NYC, 1998, MS, 2001; postgrad. in Info. Sci., SUNY, 2001—. Network database adminstr. Am. Coll. of Thessaloniki, Greece, 1995—96; database developer Aristotelian U., Thessaloniki, Greece, 1996; bus. mgr. The Design Works, Troy, NY, 1997; database developer Rensselaer Poly. Inst., Troy, NY, 1997—98, database specialist, 1999—2001, sr. sys. adminstr., 2001—, clin. asst. prof., 2007—. Adj. mis faculty Rensselaer Poly. Inst., Troy, NY, 2000—, Union Coll., Schenectady, NY, 2003—. Scholar Tuition Scholarship, Am. Coll. of Thessaloniki, 1994—95, Rensselar Poly. Inst., 1997—98. Mem.: Am. Mgmt. Assn., AAUP, N.Y. State Sheriffs' Assn. Inst., Inc. (hon.). Home: 16 Ann Lee Ct Latham NY 12110 Office: Rensselaer Polytechnic Inst 110 8th St Pitts 4106 Troy NY 12180 Office Phone: 518-276-2753. Personal E-mail: demerp@hotmail.com. Business E-Mail: demerp@rpi.edu.

DEMETRESCU, MIHAI CONSTANTIN, research scientist, educator, computer company executive; b. Bucharest, Romania, May 23, 1929; came to U.S., 1966; s. Dan and Alina (Dragosescu) D.; m. Agnes Halas, May 25, 1969; 1 child, Stefan. M.E.E., Poly. Inst. of U. Bucharest, 1954; PhD, Romanian Acad. Sci., 1957. Prin. investigator Rsch. Inst. Endocrinology Romanian Acad. Sci., Bucharest, 1958-66; rsch. fellow dept. anatomy UCLA, 1966-67; faculty U. Calif.-Irvine, 1967-83, asst. prof. dept. physiology, 1971-78, assoc. rschr., 1978-79, assoc. clin. prof., 1979-83; v.p. Resonance Motors, Inc., Monrovia, Calif., 1972-85; pres. Neurometrics, Inc., Irvine, 1978-82, Lasergraphics Inc., Irvine, 1982-84, chmn., CEO, 1984—. Mem. com. on honor degrees U. Calif.-Irvine, 1970-72. Contbr. articles to profl. jours.; patentee in field. Postdoctoral fellow UCLA, 1966. Mem. IEEE (sr.), Am. Physiol. Soc. Republican. Home: 8 Sunset Hbr Newport Coast CA 92657-1706 Office: 20 Ada Irvine CA 92618-2303 Business E-Mail: dr.d@lasergraphics.com.

DEMETRI, KATHRYN J., civil engineer; b. Pitts., Pa., Sept. 28, 1962; d. James Ejler and Shirley Jevne Jensen; m. George John Demetri, Sept. 8, 2001; children: Athena, Sophia. BS in Civil Engring., U. Pitts., Johnstown, 1984. Engr. Westinghouse Electric Co., Pitts., 1984—. Mem. fin. com., creative tasks Mothers of Preschoolers, Fox Chapel, Pa., 2007—; bd. dirs. Forest Manor Home Assn., Harmar, Pa., 2003—04. Mem.: Women in Nuc. (leadership team). Avocations: tennis, crafts. Office: Westinghouse Electric Co PO Box 355 Pittsburgh PA 15238

DEMETRION, JAMES THOMAS, retired museum director, consultant; b. Middletown, Ohio, July 10, 1930; s. Tom and Susie Demetrion; m. Barbara Parrish, 1954; 1 child, Elaine. BS in Edn., Miami U., 1952; doctorate (hon.), Simpson Coll., 1984. Curator Pasadena Art Mus., Calif., 1964-66, dir., 1966-69, Des Moines Art Ctr., 1969-84, Hirshhorn Mus. & Sculpture Garden, Washington, 1984—2001; interm dir. Menil Collection, Houston, 2002—03; ret., 2003. Trustee Noguchi Found., 2002-03, Kampa Mus., Prague; mus. adv. panel Nat. Endowment for Arts, 1973-76, co-chmn., 1974-76; art adv. panel IRS, 1983-86; mem. adv. com. Clyfford Still Mus., 2006—; cons. in field. Mem. Assn. Art Mus. Dirs. (treas. 1976-77, pres. 1979-80). Home: 1276 N Wayne Apt 1207 Arlington VA 22201-5856

DEMETRIOS, (DEMETRIOS TRAKATELLIS), archbishop; b. Thessaloniki, Greece, Feb. 1, 1928; Degree with honors, U. Athens, 1950, ThD in Theology, 1977; PhD in Philosophy with distinction, Harvard U., 1972. Ordained deacon, 1960, priest Greek Orthodox Ch., 1964. Elected titular bishop, aux. bishop to Archbishop of Athens, Vresthena, Greece, 1967; disting. prof. Biblical studies and Christian origins Holy Cross Greek Orthodox Sch. of Theology, Brookline, Mass., 1983-93; elected Archbishop of Am., Exarch of Atlantic & Pacific Oceans Greek Orthodox Ch. in Am., 1999—. Vis. prof. New Testament Harvard Divinity Sch., 1984-85, 1988-89; abroad-residing mem. in theol., Acad. of Athens, 2003-; mem. Holy & Sacred Synod of Ecumenical Patriarchate, 2004-. Author: Authority and Passion, 1987, The Transcendent God of Eugonostos, 1991, Christ, the Pre-Existing God, 1992, The Fathers Interpret, 1996. Office: Greek Orthodox Archdiocese of Am 8-10 E 79th St New York NY 10021

DEMETRIOU, STEVEN J., metal products executive; BS, Tufts Univ. Mgmt. positions Exxon Corp., 1981—97; v.p., pres. Cytec Asia Cytec Industries Inc., 1997—99; exec. v.p., pres. IMC crop nutrients IMC Global Inc., 1999—2001; pres., CEO Noveon Inc., 2001—04, Commonwealth Industries, 2004; chmn., CEO Aleris Internat. Inc., Beachwood, Ohio, 2004—. Bd. dir. OM Group Inc.; dir. Am. Chem. Council; chmn. exec. com. Aluminum Assn. Inc. Office: Aleris Internat Inc Ste 400 25825 Science Park Dr Beachwood OH 44122*

DEMETS, DAVID L., medical educator, biomedical researcher; b. Austin, Minn., Nov. 27, 1944; married; 2 children. BA in Math., Gustavus Adolphus Coll., St. Peter, Minn., 1966; MS in Biostats., U. Minn., 1968, PhD in Biostats., 1970. Statistician, divsn. computer rsch. and tech. NIH, Bethesda, Md., 1970-72, math. statistician, Nat. Heart, Lung and Blood Inst., 1973-79, chief, mathematical and applied statistics br., 1979-82; dir. biostats. Ctr., prof. stats. and biostats. U. Wis., Madison, 1982-91, assoc. dir. Clin. Cancer Ctr., 1982-91, chair dept. biostats., prof. stats. and biostats., 1991—, assoc. dir. Comprehensive Cancer Ctr., 1991—. Lectr., cons. in field; bd. scientific counselors Nat. Cancer Inst., 1993-96. Co-author: Fundamentals of Clinical Trials, 1981, 2d edit. 1985, 3d edit. 1995; contbr. numerous articles to profl. jours., chpts. to books; presenter in field; mem. adv. bd. jour. Controlled Clin. Trials, 1993—, editl. bd. 1994—; assoc. editor Jour. Clin. Rsch. and Drug Devel., 1987-90. Recipient Disting. Alumni award Gustavus Adolphus Coll., 1990, Gaylord Anderson Leadership award U. Minn. Sch. Pub. Health Alumni Soc., 1993. Fellow Am. Statis. Assn. (bd. dirs. 1987-89), Internat. Statis. Inst.; mem. Biometrics Soc. (regional adv. bd. 1975-77, 80-82, exec. com. Ea. N.Am. region 1992-94, pres. 1993), Soc. for Controlled Clin. Trials (bd. dirs. 1983-87, program com. 1984, 85, program chmn. 1988, v.p. 1988-89, pres. 1989-90, joint program com. with Internat. Soc. Clin. Biostats., Brussels, 1991, policy com. 1993—), Internat. Soc. Clin. Biostats. Office: U Wis Clin Science Ctr Dept Biostatistics & Med In 600 Highland Ave K61446 Madison WI 53792-0001

DEMETZ, KATHLEEN SUSAN, lawyer; b. Mishawaka, Ind., Nov. 1, 1952; d. Achille and Adrienne Marie Christine (DeKesel) D.; children: Carrie Kathleen, Marc Lawrence. BA cum laude, Brandeis U., 1974; JD, U. Notre Dame, 1977. Bar: Ohio 1977. Atty. Legal Aid-Civil, Cleve., 1977-80, Legal Aid-Criminal, Cleve., 1980—. Vol. Ambassador Nursing Ctr., East Cleveland, Ohio, 1985-88, Valley Save-A-Pet, 1985—, St. Gregory the Great Parish, 1989—; active Animal Legal Defense Fund, 1986—; fund com. U. Sch., 2003— Mem. Bar Assn. Greater Cleve. (adopt-a-class 1978—), Notre Dame U., Brandeis U. Alumni Assn. Roman Catholic. Avocations: sports, walking, reading. Home: 3574 St Albans Rd Cleveland OH 44121-1552 Office: ¢uyahoga County Pub Def Office 310 Lakeside 4th Fl Cleveland OH 44113 Office Phone: 216-443-7579.

DEMEURE, MICHAEL J., surgeon, researcher; s. Joseph A. and Irma G. Demeure. MD, Hahnemann U., Phila., 1983; MBA, U. Ariz., Tucson, 2007. Prof. surgery U. Ariz., Tucson, 2002—07; adj. sr. investigator Translational Genomics Rsch. Inst., Phoenix, 2004—. Office: U Ariz 1501 N Campbell Ave Box 245063 Tucson AZ 85718 Office Phone: 520-626-9157. E-mail: mdemeure@email.arizona.edu.

DEMICHELE, DOMENIC JOHN, neurologist, neuroradiologist; b. Utica, NY, Apr. 2, 1951; s. Joseph John DeMichele and Mary JoAnn Uzgo; children: Carrie, Kristan. BS in Biology cum laude, Syracuse U., 1974; PhD, Georgetown U., 1981, MD, 1984. Cert. in nuc. medicine, positron emission, spectamise imaging, magnetic resonance imaging NIH, Bethesda, Md, lic. physician Md., NY, SC. Instr. human anatomy Syracuse U., 1972—75, instr. comparative anatomy, 1974; instr. human histology Georgetown U., Washington, 1977—78, instr. human neurobiology, 1977—80; dir. neurology critical care nursing Georgetown U. Med. Ctr., Washington, 1979—81; asst. prof. biology Cath. U., Washington, 1980—82; intern St. Joseph's Hosp., Syracuse, 1984—85; resident dept. neurology Georgetown U. Med. Ctr., Washington, 1987—90; med. staff fellow Nat. Inst. Neurol. and Communicative Disorders and Stroke, NIH neuroimaging sect., Bethesda, 1986—87; pvt. practice neurologist Florence, SC, 1990—94; founder, dir. Carolinas Hosp. Systems Sleep Disorders Ctr., Florence, 1990—. Med. dir. Open MRI of Florence; med. dir., dir. nuc. medicine In-Med; presenter in field. Author (with F. Suarez, H.K. Huang, J. Mazziotta): Cross Sectional Anatomy, 1978; editor (with Ampara Escarilla): General Chemistry: A Laboratory Experience, 1973; contbr. articles to profl. jours., chapters to books; author 9 novels, photographer. Mem. Senate subcom. Senate Majority Trust, 2004—, Senate subcom. Medicare/Medicaid Reform, 2004—; elected state chmn. Nat. Rep. Com. to Pres. for Medicare/Medicaid Reform, 2003—04. Finalist Physician of Yr., 2004; recipient Tchr. Recognition award, McLeod Regional Med. Ctr., 1990—93. Mem.: Soc. Neuroimaging, Florence County Med. Assn., SC Med. Assn., Psi Chi. Avocations: coin collecting/numismatics, stamp collecting/philately, guitar, keyboard playing, flying. Home: 2416 Windsor Forest Dr Florence SC 29501-2093 Office: Ea Carolina Medicine 2013 Second Loop Rd Florence SC 29501 Office Phone: 843-665-2600. Office Fax: 843-665-7530.

DE MICHELE, O. MARK, real estate company executive; b. Syracuse, NY, Mar. 23, 1934; s. Aldo and Dora (Carno) De M.; m. Faye Ann Venturin, Nov. 8, 1957; children: Mark A., Christopher C., Michele M., Julianne; m. Barbara Joan Stanley, May 22, 1982; 1 child, Angela Marie. BS, Syracuse U., 1955; doctorate (hon.), No. Ariz. U., 1997. Mgr. Seal Right Co., Inc., Fulton, NY, 1955-58; v.p., gen. mgr. L.M. Harvey Co. Inc., Syracuse, 1958-62; v.p. Niagara Mohawk Power, Syracuse, 1962-78, Ariz. Pub. Svc., Phoenix, 1978-81, exec. v.p., 1981-82, pres., CEO, 1982-97, also bd. dirs.; pres., CEO Greater Phoenix Econ. Coun., 1997-98; chmn., CEO Urban Realty Ptnrs. LLC, 1998—. Bd. dirs. Ont. Power Generation. Pres. Jr. Achievement, Syracuse, 1974-75, Phoenix, 1982-83, United Way Ctrl. N.Y., Syracuse, 1978, Ariz. Opera Co., Phoenix, 1981-83, Phoenix Symphony, 1984-86, United Way Phoenix, 1985-86, Ariz. Mus. Sci. and Tech., 1988-90; pres. Children's Action Alliance, 1989-92; chmn. Valley Sun United Way, 1984-86, Phoenix Econ. Coun., 1991-94; chmn. Morrison Inst. Pub. Policy at Ariz. State U.; chmn. Ariz. Cities in Schs., 1994-97, Nat. Environ. Edn. Found., 1997—; pres. Episcopal Cmty. Svc. Found. Named Outstanding Young Man of Yr., Syracuse Jaycees, 1968, Phoenix Man of Yr., Phoenix Ad Club, 1992; recipient Humanitarian award Nat. Conf., 1995. Mem. Phoenix C. of C. (chmn. bd. 1986-87), Phoenix Country Club, Ariz. Club (Phoenix). Republican. Home: 1536 Glorietta Blvd Coronado CA 92118-2306 Office: Urban Realty Ptnrs LLC 2415 E Camelback Rd Ste 700 Phoenix AZ 85016-4245 E-mail: mdemichele@aol.com.

DEMICK, BARBARA, journalist; Fgn. corr., Middle East bur. chief Phila. Inquirer, Jerusalem, 1998—2002; fgn. corr, bur. chief LA Times, Seoul, Republic of Korea, 2002—. Recipient Joe & Laurie Dine award, Overseas Press Club, 2006. Office: LA Times 202 W 1st St Los Angeles CA 90012 Office Phone: 213-237-5000. E-mail: barbara.demick@latimes.com.

DEMIDOV, VADIM V., biotechnologist, writer; MS in Phys.-Chem. Engring., Moscow Phys-Tech. Inst., 1977; PhD in Biophysics, Inst. Molecular Genetics, Moscow, 1980. Named to rank of sr. scientific worker USSR Superior Certifying Comm., 1990. Jr. rschr. Rsch. Inst. for Biol. Testing of Chem. Compounds, Moscow, 1980—85; rschr. Moscow Inst. Biotech., 1985—87; sr. rschr. Inst. Mineralogy, Geochemistry and Crystallochemistry of Rare Elements, 1987—90, Inst. Molecular Genetics, Moscow, 1990—93; vis. asst. rsch. prof. dept. biology George Mason U., Fairfax, Va., 1993; vis. rsch. prof. Panum Inst. Copenhagen U., 1993—94; sr. rsch. assoc., group leader, prin. investigator, cons. biotechnologist Ctr. Advanced Biotech. Dept. Biomedical Engring. Boston (Mass.) U., 1994—; biotechnology analyst Global Prior Art Inc., 2003—. Participant 3 sci. ecol. expeditions on peninsulas Kamchatka and Taimyr and Russian Far East, 1990—92; mem. internat. working group experts on planetary protection, 1991—92; mem. sci. bd. on problem of gene targeted drugs Russian Acad. Sci., 1992—93. Co-editor: DNA Amplification: Current Technologies & Applications, 2004; contbg. editor: Drug Discover & Development, 2004; mem. editl. bd.: Trends in Biotechnology and Expert Review of Molecular Diagnostics, 2003—07, Current Medicinal Chemistry, 2006—07, Open Medicinal Chemistry, 2007, Expert Opinion on Medical Diagnostics, 2007, reviewer: jours. in field; contbr. chapters to books, articles to profl. jours. Recipient Silver medal, All-Union Nat. Exhbn. Econ. Achievements, Moscow, 1988, Medal of Hon., Internat. Biographical Ctr., Cambridge, Eng., 2007; grantee, Russian State Com. Natural Resources and Environment, 1991—93, St. Jude Children's Rsch. Hosp., Memphis, 2006—07. Mem.: Soc. Chem. Industry, Planetary Soc., Amnesty Internat. Avocations: travel, art collecting. Office: Ctr Advanced Biotech Boston U 36 Cummington St 2d Fl Rm 204 Boston MA 02215 Business E-Mail: VVD@bu.edu.

DEMIERI, JOSEPH L., retired bank executive; b. NYC, Aug. 31, 1940; s. Leo A. and Frances (Garone) DeM.; m. Anne Patricia McCue, May 15, 1965. BBA, Tex. A&M U., 1962. C.P.A., N.Y. With Peat, Marwick, Mitchell & Co., NYC, 1962-68; v.p., controller City Investing Co., NYC and Beverly Hills, Calif., 1968-82; exec. v.p. Motown Industries, Los Angeles, 1982-84; chmn., CEO Calif. Millworks Corp., Valencia, 1985-95; sr. v.p., CFO Western Security Bank, Burbank, Calif., 1995—2002. Home: 6259 Ebbtide Way Malibu CA 90265-3608

D'EMILIO, JOHN, humanities educator, writer; BA cum laude, Columbia U., 1970, MA, 1972, PhD, 1982. Asst. prof. Dept. History U. NC, 1983—88, dir. grad. studies, 1988—93, assoc. prof., 1988—92, prof., 1992—98; vis. scholar Grad. Program in Pub. Policy George Wash. U., 1998—99; prof. Dept. History U. Ill., Chgo., 1999—, dir. Gender and Women's Studies Program, 2002—04, dir. grad. studies, 2005—06. Author: (book) The Universities and the Gay Experience: Proceedings of a Conference Sponsored by the Women and Men of the Gay Academic Union, 1974, The Civil Rights Struggle: Leaders in Profile, 1979, Making Trouble: Essays on Gay History, Politics and the University, 1992, Intimate Matters: A History of Sexuality in America, 1998, Creating Change: Sexuality, Public Plicy and Civil Rights, 2000, The World Turned: Essays on Gay History, Politics and Culture, 2002, Lost Prophet: The Life and Times of Bayard Rustin, 2003 (Nat. Book award nominee, 2003); contbr. articles to jours. Mem. Chancellor's Com. on Lesbian, Gay, Bisexual and Transgender Concerns, 2000—; co-chair Women's Studies Program Dir. Search, 1999—2000; mem. Gender and Women's Studies Program Com., 1999—; mem. adv. bd. Between Men, Between Women series, Columbia U. Press, 1995—. Nominee U. of Chgo. Press for Pulitzer prize in U.S. History, 1983; Rsch. grant, Lyndon Baines Johnson Libr. Found., 1999, fellowship, John Simon Guggenheim Meml. Found., 1998—99, Nat. Endowment for the Humanities, 1997—98, Rsch. grant, Am. Philosophical Soc., 1994, John F. Kennedy Libr., 1993. Mem.: Phi Beta Kappa. Office: U Ill at Chgo Gender and Women's Studies Program 1812 University Hall 601 S Morgan St Chicago IL 60607 Office Phone: 312-996-2502. Office Fax: 312-996-6377. E-mail: demilioj@aol.com.

DEMILLE, DAVID P., physics professor; AB in Physics, U. Chgo., 1985; MS, U. Calif., Berkeley, PhD in Physics, 1994. Postdoctoral rschr. Lawrence Berkeley Nat. Lab.; asst. prof. Amherst Coll., 1997; asst. prof. physics Yale U., New Haven, 1998—2004, prof., 2004—. Contbr. articles to sci. jours. Grantee David and Lucile Packard Found. fellowship, 1999—2004, Alfred P Sloan Found. fellowship, 2000—02. Fellow: Am. Phys. Soc. (Francis M. Pipkin award 2007). Office: Sloane Physics Lab 217 Prospect St New Haven CT 06520 Office Phone: 203-432-3833. E-mail: david.demille@yale.edu.*

DEMILLE, NELSON RICHARD, writer; b. NYC, Aug. 23, 1943; s. Huron and Antonia (Panzera) D.; m. Sandra Dillingham; children: Lauren, Alex, James. BA in Polit. Sci. and History, Hofstra U., 1970, LHD (hon.), 1989; DLitt (hon.), L.I. U., 1993; LDH (hon.), Dowling Coll., 1997. Freelance writer, 1973—. Judge Book-of-the-Month Club. Author: By the Rivers of Babylon, 1978, Cathedral, 1981, The Talbot Odyssey, 1984, Word of Honor, 1985, The Charm School, 1988, The Gold Coast, 1990, The General's Daughter, 1992, Spencerville, 1994, Plum Island, 1997, The Lion's Game, 2000, Up Country, 2002, Night Fall, 2004, Wild Fire, 2006; co-author: Mayday, 1998; contbr. short stories to mags. and anthologies. 1st lt. U.S. Army, 1966-69. Decorated Air medal, Bronze Star, Vietnamese Cross of Gallantry; recipient Estabrook award Hofstra U. Mem. Mystery Writers Am. (pres. 2007), Authors Guild, Mensa. Roman Catholic.

DEMING, CLAIBORNE PAYNE, oil industry executive; Positions in law, prodn., exploration, mktg. and land depts. Murphy Oil Corp., El Dorado, Ark., 1979, v.p. petroleum ops., 1988, pres. Murphy Oil USA, Inc., 1989, exec. v.p., COO, 1992, mem. exec. com., 1993—, pres., CEO, 1994—. With Ocean Drilling and Exploration Co. (ODECO, now Murphy Exploration & Production Co.), New Orleans. Office: Murphy Oil Corp PO Box 7000 El Dorado AR 71731-7000 Office Phone: 870-862-6411. E-mail: claiborne.deming@murphyoilcorp.com.*

DEMING, DAVID LAWSON, art educator; b. Cleve., May 26, 1943; s. Lawson Joseph and Mary Rita (Basile) D.; m. Ann Elizabeth Haldeman, Sept. 4, 1965; children: Matthew Lawson, Lisa Ann, Michael David. BFA, Cleve. Inst. Art, 1967; MFA, Cranbrook Acad. Art, Bloomfield Hills, Mich., 1970. Instr. Boston U., 1967-68, U. Tex., El Paso, 1970-72, asst. prof., assoc. prof. art Austin, 1972, prof., 1985, chmn. art dept., Marguerite Fairchild prof. art, 1991-96; interim dean Coll. of Fine Arts U. Tex., Austin, 1996-97, dean, 1997-98; pres. Cleve. Inst. Art, 1998—. Sculptures represented in permanent collection Columbus (Ohio) Mus. Art, Ark. Art Ctr., Little Rock, U. Tex. Southwestern Regional Med. Ctr. Dallas; included in White House Garden Exhbn. of Am. Sculptors, 1995. Recipient award of honor Austin chpt. AIA, 1983. Mem. Internat. Sculpture Assn. Roman Catholic. Office: Cleveland Inst of Art 11141 East Blvd Cleveland OH 44106-1700 Office Phone: 216-421-7410. E-mail: ddeming@cia.edu.*

DEMING, FREDERICK WILSON, retired economist, banker; b. St. Louis, Dec. 29, 1935; s. Frederick Lewis and Corinne Inez (Wilson) D.; m. Lynne Eve Anken, Mar. 24, 1960; children: Susanne Lyn, Frederick Lawrence. BA, Princeton U., 1957; MA, Yale U., 1958. With Fed. Res. Bank of N.Y., 1961-71; sr. staff economist Council Econ. Advisers, 1968; exec. dir. Commn. Mortgage Interest Rates, 1969; spl. asst. to Sec. of HUD, 1970-71; sr. v.p., economist Chem. Bank, NYC, 1971—89; exec. asst. to chmn. Chem. Bank/Chase Manhattan Bank, NYC, 1989—99; ret., 2000. Home: 59 Pippins Way Morristown NJ 07960

DEMING, JODY WHEELER, oceanography educator; b. Houston, July 2, 1952; d. Samuel Henry Wheeler and Laverne (Lewis) Kraft. BA in Biol. Scis., Smith Coll., 1974; PhD in Microbiology, U. Md., 1981. Rsch. asst. biology Sloan Found. Rsch. Smith Coll., Northampton, Mass., 1973; field biologist Water Quality Div. Md. State Dept. Natural Resources, Annapolis, 1974; rsch. technician Div. Infectious Diseases Tufts/New Eng. Med. Ctr. Hosp., Boston, 1974-75; rsch. assoc. Bioluminescence Lab. NASA/Goddard Space Flight Ctr., Greenbelt, Md., 1975-77; grad. teaching and rsch. asst. microbiology U. Md., College Park, 1977-81; NSF postdoctoral fellow Marine Biology Rsch. Div. Scripps Inst. Oceanography, La Jolla, Calif., 1981-82; NOAA postdoctoral fellow Office of Marine Pollution and Assessment, Rockville, Md., 1982-83; assoc. rsch. scientist Chesapeake Bay Inst. Johns Hopkins U., Shady Side, Md., 1981-86, rsch. scientist Chesapeake Bay Inst., 1986-88, asst. prof. biology, 1983-86; scientist Ctr. Marine Biotech., U. Md., Balt., 1986-88; dir. , Marine Bioremediation Program U. Wash., Seattle, 1993—99; assoc. prof. U. Wash. Sch. Oceanography, Seattle, 1988—95, prof., 1995—, U. Wash. Astrobiology Program, 1998—. Mem. nat. com. ALVIN Rev. Com., 1984-87, internat. Arctic projects and steering coms., numerous proposal review panels for NOAA, NSF and others. Contbr. numerous chpts. to books and articles to profl. jours. Recipient award for Sci. Achievement in the Biol. Scis., Wash. Acad. Scis., 1987, Presdl. Young Investigator NSF award, 1989-94. Mem. AAAS, Am. Soc. for Microbiology, Am. Acad. of Microbiology, Am. Soc. of Limnology and Oceanography, Am. Geophys. Union, The Oceanography Soc., Sigma Xi. Achievements include patents for rapid quantitive determination of bacteria and their antibiotic susceptibilities in a variety of fluid samples. Office: U Wash Sch Oceanography Box 357940 Seattle WA 98195-0001 E-mail: jdeming@u.washington.edu.

DEMING, N. KAREN, lawyer; b. Valdosta, Ga., Sept. 7, 1953; BA magna cum laude, Valdosta State Coll., 1975; JD cum laude, U. Ga., 1978. Bar: Ga. 1978, U.S. Ct. Appeals (4th, 5th and 11th cirs.), U.S. Dist. Ct. (no., mid. and so. dists.) Ga. Assoc. Troutman Sanders LLP, Atlanta, 1978—85, ptnr., 1986—, practice group leader, product liability, mem. exec. com. Mem. editorial bd. Ga. Law Rev., 1976-77, rsch. editor, 1977-78. Named a Super Lawyer, Atlanta Mag., 2004, Legal Elite in personal injury, Ga. Trends Mag., 2004. Mem. ABA, Def. Rsch. Inst., State Bar Ga., Ga. Def. Lawyers Assn., Atlanta Bar Assn., Atlanta Coun. Young Lawyers (bd. dirs. 1983-85), Lawyers Club Atlanta, Order of Coif., Phi Kappa Phi. Office: Troutman Sanders LLP 600 Peachtree St NE Ste 5200 Atlanta GA 30308-2216 Office Phone: 404-885-3124. Office Fax: 404-962-6543. Business E-Mail: karen.deming@troutmansanders.com.

DEMING, RUST M., ambassador; b. Oct. 1941; m. Kristen Deming; 3 children. Diploma, Rollins Coll., 1964; Postgrad. Diploma, Stanford U., 1981. Former polit. officer U.S. Embassy, Tunisia, 1966; dir. Office of Japanese Affairs, Washington, 1991—93; dep. chief of mission Japan, 1993—96; Charge d'Affaires, ad interim, 1996—97; prin. dep. asst. sec. for East Asian and Pacific Affairs Dept. State, Washington, 1998—2000; U.S. amb. to Rep. of Tunisia, 2001—03; prof. Johns Hopkins U., Balt., 2004—. Recipient Civilian Meritorious awards, U.S. Def. Dept., 1995—97.

DEMING, THOMAS EDWARD, publishing executive; b. Chgo., May 5, 1954; s. Anthony A. and Josephine (Andracki) Dziurdzik; m. Mary Ann Jadowic, May 15, 1976; children: Mark Thomas, Emily Marie, William Joseph. BS in Acctg., De Paul U., 1976, MBA, 1986. CPA, Ill. Acct. Arthur Andersen & Co., Chgo., 1975-81; asst. contr. Scott, Foresman & Co., Glenview, Ill., 1981-83, v.p., contr., 1983-88, v.p. fin., 1988-89, v.p. fin. and adminstrn., 1990; treas. Macmillan/McGraw-Hill Sch. Pub. Co., Lake Forest, Ill., 1990-91, v.p., treas., 1991-92, Harper Collins Pubs., NYC, 1992-95; v.p. fin. Harper Collins Pubs., Inc., NYC, 1995-96; v.p. fin. planning & ops. McDougal Littell Pub., Inc., Evanston, Ill., 1996—; corp. v.p. McDougal Littell parent co. Houghton Mifflin, 1996—. Mem. Fin. Execs. Inst., Am. Inst. CPA's, Ill. Soc. CPA's, DePaul U.'s Ledger & Quill, Beta Alpha Psi, Delta Mu Delta, Beta Gamma Sigma. Avocations: golf, target shooting. Office: McDougal Littell Inc 909 Davis St Evanston IL 60201 Office Phone: 847-424-3803. Business E-Mail: tom_deming@hmco.com.

DEMING, WILLIS RILEY, retired lawyer; b. Ada, Ohio, Nov. 28, 1914; s. Cliffe and Okla (Riley) D.; m. Dorothy Arline Hill, 1950 (div. 1971); children: Susan Elizabeth, Deborah Anne Gunst, David Riley; m. Constance S. Mori, 1971 (div. 1986); m. Olive Plunkett Rose, 1994 (dec. 1999). BA, Ohio State U., 1935, JD, 1938. Bar: Ohio 1938, Calif. 1947, D.C. 1957. Pvt. practice, Columbus, Ohio, 1938-39; casualty claim examiner Am. Surety Co., NYC, 1939-41; chief bds. and claims rev. br. San Francisco Port of Embarkation, 1946-47; atty. Treadwell and Laughlin, San Francisco, 1947-54, Brobeck, Phleger & Harrison, San Francisco, 1954-56, Washington, 1956-60; pvt. practice Washington, 1961-62; sr. v.p., gen. counsel Matson Nav. Co., San Francisco, 1962—71, 1974—92; v.p., sec., gen. counsel Alexander & Baldwin, Inc., Honolulu, 1968—74. Served to lt. col. AUS, 1941-46; col. U.S. Army, ret. Mem. ABA, State Bar Calif., Soc. for Asian Art (pres. 1995-97), Claremont Country Club (Oakland). Home: 5649 Country Club Dr Oakland CA 94618-1715

DEMINT, JIM (JAMES WARREN DEMINT), senator, former congressman; b. Greenville, SC, Sept. 2, 1951; s. Thomas Eugene and Betty (Rawlings) Batson; m. Deborah Henderson, Nov. 6, 1951; children: Jake, Ginger, Timothy, Donna. BS in Comm., U. Tenn., 1973; MBA, Clemson U., SC, 1979. Sr. sales rep. Scott Paper Co., Greensboro, NC, 1973-75; writer Henderson Advt., Greenville, 1975-81; v.p. Leslie Advt., Greenville, 1981-83; CEO, pres. The DeMint Mktg. Group, Greenville, 1983—; mem. US Congress from 4th SC dist., 1999—2005; US Senator from SC, 2005—. Mem. com. commerce, sci. and transp. US Senate, com. environment and public works, congressional exec. com. on China, joint econ. com., spl. com. aging. Chmn. bd. Greenville Vocat. Rehab. Ctr. 1986, Christian Bus. Men's Com., 1983, Mitchell Rd. Christian Acad., 1988, 1st v.p. Speech, Hear and Learning Ctr., 1986. Recipient Defender of Pvt. Property award, Executive of Yr. award, Profl. Secretaries Internat., Friend of Seniors award, 60 Plus Assn., Hero of Taxpayer award, Am. Tax Reform, Spirit Enterprise award, C. of C., Taxpayer Friend award, Nat. Taxpayer Union. Mem. Greenville C. of C., S.C. C. of C., Rotary. Republican. Presbyterian. Avocations: sailing, running, biking, tennis, music. Office: District Office 105 N Spring St Ste109 Greenville SC 29601 also: District Office 112 Customs House 200 E Bay St Charleston SC 29401 also: US Senate 340 Russell Senate Office Bldg Washington DC 20510 Office Phone: 864-233-5366. Office Fax: 202-224-6121, 202-228-5143, 864-271-8901.*

DEMIRTAS, K. OZGUR, finance educator; s. U. Kenan and S. Nuray Demirtas. PhD in Fin., Boston Coll., 2003. Prof. Baruch Coll., NYC, 2003—. Contbr. articles to profl. jours. Recipient Tchg. Excellence award, Zicklin Sch. Bus., 2005, Presdl. Excellence award for Disting. Tchg., Baruch Coll., 2006, Donald J. White Tchg. Excellence award, Boston Coll., 2002; grantee, CUNY, 2004—05, 2006; scholar, Boston Coll., 1998—2002; Grad. fellow, 1998-2002, Eugene M. Lang Rsch. fellow, Office Sponsored Programs and Rsch., 2007. Home: 1 River Ct Apt # 2103 Jersey City NJ 07310 Office: CUNY Baruch Coll One Bernard Baruch Way Box: B10-225 New York NY 10010 Office Phone: 646-312-3484.

DEMITCHELL, TERRI ANN, law educator; b. San Diego, Apr. 10, 1953; d. William Edward and Rose Annette Wheeler; m. Todd Allan DeMitchell, Aug. 14, 1982. AB in English with honors, San Diego State U., 1975; JD, U. San Diego, 1984; MA in Edn., U. Calif., Davis, 1990; MEd, Harvard U., 1997. Bar: Calif. 1985, U.S. Dist. Ct. (so. dist.) Calif. 1985; cert. elem. tchr., Calif. Tchr. Fallbrook (Calif.) Union Elem. Sch. Dist., 1976-86; adminstrv. asst. gen. counsel San Diego Unified Sch. Dist., 1984; assoc. Biddle and Hamilton, Sacramento, 1986-88; instr. U. N.H., 1990-93. Teaching asst. U. Calif., Davis, 1987. Author: The California Teacher and the Law, 1985, The Law in Relation to Teacher, Out of School Behavior, 1990, Censorship and the Public School Library: A Bicoastal View, 1991, Statutes and Standards: Has the Door to Educational Malpractice Been Opened?, 2003, You Will Come Back, 2004 (Mayhaven award Children's Fiction Mayhaven Pub., 2004) Recipient Mayhaven award for children's fiction, Mayhaven Pub. Co., 2004. Mem. Calif. Bar Assn., Am. Bar Assn.

DEMITRA, PAVOL, professional hockey player; b. Dubnica, Slovakia, Nov. 29, 1974; Right wing Ottawa Senators, 1993—96, St. Louis Blues, 1996—2005, LA Kings, 2005—06, Minn. Wild, 2006—. Mem. Slovakia Hockey Team, Olympic Games, Nagano, Japan, 1998; player NHL All-Star Game, 1999, 2000, 02. Recipient Lady Byng Meml. Trophy, 2000. Office: Minnesota Wild 317 Washington St Saint Paul MN 55102

DEMITRACK, THOMAS, lawyer; b. Denville, NJ, 1954; MusB, Univ. Hartford, 1976; JD summa cum laude, Ohio State Univ., 1979. Bar: Ohio 1979. Profl. responsibilities ptnr. and coord. of antitrust practice Jones Day, Cleve., and mem. profl. services com. Mem., profl. services com. Jones Day. Author: numerous articles in profl. publications. Named a leading lawyer in antitrust, N.E. Ohio Inside Bus. mag. and Ohio Super Lawyers. Mem.: Order of Coif. Office: Jones Day North Point 901 Lakeside Ave Cleveland OH 44114-1190 Office Fax: 216-579-0212.

DEMITRY, ELPIS HOPE, music educator; b. Trenton, NJ, Apr. 4, 1947; d. Lillian and James Demitry. MusB, Trenton State Coll., 1970, MA in Music Edn., 1976. Teacher of Music Mercer County/State of NJ., 1970, Supervisor/Principal Certification Mercer County/State of NJ., 1983, Nursery/Kindergarten Certification Mercer County/State of NJ., 1983. Internal coach,facilitator for the accelerated sch. plus program, our whole sch. reform Trenton Bd. of Edn. - Wash. Elem. Sch., NJ, 1999—; vocal/gen. elem. music tchr. Trenton Bd. of Edn., 1970—2003; pvt. piano tchr. Trenton Conservatory of Music and Home Instrn., 1966—2003; coord. of elem. music faculty meetings Trenton Pub. Schs., 1993—, coord. all city elem. music festivals. Coord. of the all city elem. music festivals Trenton Pub. Schs., Trenton, NJ, 1971—86, coord. of elem. music faculty meetings, 1993—98; acting prin. in principals absence Wash. Elem. Sch., Trenton, NJ, 1998—, profl. devel. coord., 1999—, trainor of staff, 1999—. Nat. grand gov. zone i Daughters of Penelope, 1993—95, dist. gov. NJ, 1982—83; organist St. George Greek Orthodox Ch., Trenton, NJ, 1960—2005; treas. - diocesan svc. Ea. Fedn. of Greek Orthodox Choirs and Musicians, NJ, 1993—2005. Recipient Patriarch Athenagoras I Medal for Ch. Musicians, Diocesan Svc. Award- Ea. Fedn. of Greek Orthodox Ch. Choirs and Musicians, 1999. Mem.: NEA, Assn. Supr. and Curriculum Devel. (assoc.), Am. Choral Dirs. Assn. (assoc.), Trenton Edn. Assn. (assoc.), Music Educators Nat. Conf., NJ. Music Educators Assn. (assoc.), Nat. Forum of Ch. Musicians (life). Greek Orthodox. Avocations: swimming, travel, needlecrafts. Home: 95 Beechwood Ave Trenton NJ 08618 Office: Washington Elem Sch 331 Emory Ave Trenton NJ 08611 Home Phone: 609-695-4033; Office Phone: 609-656-4960 3714. Personal E-mail: ehoped@comcast.net. E-mail: hdemitry@trenton.k12.nj.us.

DEMKO, GEORGE JOSEPH, geographer; b. Catasauqua, Pa., Apr. 10, 1933; s. George and Anna (Scarba) D.; m. Jeanette Edwina Small, Aug. 29, 1959; children: Megan, Kerstin. BS, West Chester U., 1958; MS, So. Ill. U., 1959; PhD, Pa. State U., 1964; postgrad., Moscow State U., USSR; DSc (hon.), Shawnee State U. of Ohio, 1995. Instr. Pa. State U., State College, 1963-64; asst. prof. Ind. U., Bloomington, 1964-65; prof. Ohio State U., Columbus, 1965-83; program dir. Geography and Regional Sci., NSF, Washington, 1983-84; The Geographer, dir. Office of The Geographer, State Dept., Washington, 1984-89; dir. Rockefeller Ctr. for Social Scis., Dartmouth Coll., Hanover, NH, 1989-95, prof. geography, 1989—. Cons. Internat. Research and Exchanges Bd., Princeton, NJ, 1970-95, NASA, 1979-80, Microsoft Corp., 1992—; head subcommn. on geography, US/USSR, Princeton, 1980-91; adj. prof. Charles U., Prague, Czech Republic; columnist Mystery Rev., Mysteries Online. Author: The Russian Colonization of Kazakhstan, 1966, Kazakh transl., 1998, Discovery in Geography, 1980, Regional Development in East and West Europe, 1986, Perspectives on Soviet Geography, 1980, Geography in the USSR and U.S.: A Spectrum of Views, 1992, Why In The World: Adventures in Geography, 1993, Populations at Risk in America, 1995, Reordering the World: Geopolitical Perspectives on the 21st Century, 1995; contbr. numerous articles to profl. jours. Sgt. USMC, 1951-54, Korea. Named Outstanding Alumnus, W. Chester (Pa.) U., 1980, University Fellow, Pa. State U., State College, 1986; recipient numerous grants and awards for research and teaching from the Nat. Sci. Found., Rockefeller Found., Gold Medal award for scholarly contbns. Charles U., Prague, Czech Republic, 1998, others. Mem. Assn. Am. Geographers (pres. 1986-88), Am. Assn. for Advancement of Slavic Studies (exec. dir. 1969-74), Kennan Inst. for Advanced Russian Studies (acad. advisor 1982-86), Russian Geog. Soc. (hon.). Avocations: sailing, squash, piano. Office: Dartmouth Coll Dept Geography Hanover NH 03755 E-mail: george.demko@dartmouth.edu.

DEMKOVITZ, RUSSELL BERNARD, deacon, ceremetary director; b. Elizabeth, NJ, May 21, 1949; s. Russell and Hedwig Demkovitz; m. Monica Patricia Michalski, May 8, 1976; 1 child, Abigail. BA, Rutgers U., 1967—71, MPA, 1972—74. Inside auditor Southland Corp., Parsippany, NJ, 1974—79; inside sales Naporano Iron and Metal, Newark, 1977—79; sales engr. Otis Elevator, Mahwah, NJ, 1979—84; regional mgr. Gen. Elevator, Springfield, NJ, 1984—89; v.p. sales and admin. Advance Elevator, New Brunswick, NJ, 1989—96; territory rep. Dover Elevator, Secaucus, 1996—98; dir. of cemeteries Diocese of Metuchen, Piscataway, NJ, 1998—; cemetery dir., pres. NJ Cemetery Assn., 2004—06. Mem. adv. bd. St. Peter's Cemetery Assn., New Brunswick, NJ, 1999—, NJ Allied Meml. Coun., Flemington, NJ, 2001—, NJ Legislative Commn., Westfield, NJ, 1999—. Councilman at large Franklin Township, Somerset, NJ, 1987—95, dep. mayor, 1987—90, mayor, 1990—91. Mem.: NJ Cemetery Assn. (pres.). Republican. Roman Cath. Avocations: golf, travel, automobilia collecting. Home: 15 Liberty Lane Somerset NJ 08873 Office: Diocese of Metuchen P O Box 191 Metuchen NJ 08840 Office Fax: 732-562-9650. Personal E-mail: rdemkovitz@aol.com.

DEMLING, ROBERT HUGH, surgeon, researcher; b. Grand Rapids, Mich., July 17, 1943; s. Gerry James and Margaret Helen (Boucher) D.; m. Patricia Ann Huber, Nov. 6, 1971; children: Jill, Kate. BS, Notre Dame U., 1965; MD, Med. Coll. Wis., 1969. Diplomate Am. Bd. Surgeons (cons. 1986—). Intern U. Calif., San Francisco, 1969, resident, 1970-76; dir. Burn Ctr. U. Wis., Madison, 1976-79, U. Calif., Davis, 1979-82; prof. surgery Harvard Med. Sch., Boston, 1982—; dir. Burn-Trauma Ctr. Brigham and Women's Hosp., Boston, 1982, dir. edn. & rsch.; dir. Longwood Area Trauma Ctr., Boston, 1982—; chmn. bd. med. advisors Internat. Assoc. of Fire Fighters Burn Found. Cons. NIH, 1984—. Author: 2 books; contbr. numerous articles to profl. publs. Mem. ACS (chmn. pre and post operation care com. 1987—), Univ. Surgeons (treas. 1986-89), Am. Burn Assn. (program chair 1990-94, pres. 1994-95). Republican. Roman Catholic. Avocations: rugby, weightlifting, martial arts. Home: 44 Algonquin Dr Natick MA 01760-6095 Office: Longwood Area Trauma Ctr 75 Francis St Boston MA 02115-6110*

DEMLOW, DANIEL J., lawyer; b. Ludington, Mich., Oct. 16, 1944; s. Richard M. and Nan (Jager) D.; m. Catherine M. Jerzak, Aug. 7, 1982; children: Sara Beth, Michelle Catherine. BA, Mich. State U., 1966; JD, U. Mich., 1969. Atty. Fraser Trebilock Davis & Foster, Lansing, Mich., 1969-70, Securities Bur., Lansing, Mich., 1970-71; dep. dir. Mich. Dept. Commerce, Lansing, 1971-73; commr. ins. Ins. Bur., Lansing, 1973-75; chmn. Mich. Pub. Svc. Commn., Lansing, 1975-81; assoc. Honigman Miller Schwartz & Cohn LLP, Lansing, 1985—. Fellow Mich. State Bar Found. Republican. Presbyterian. Avocations: tennis, boating, grouse hunting. Home: 3773 Yosemite Dr Okemos MI 48864-3838 Office: Honigman Miller Schwartz & Cohn LLP 222 N Washington Sq Ste 400 Lansing MI 48933-1800 Home Phone: 517-349-6360; Office Phone: 517-377-0700. Business E-Mail: ddemlow@honigman.com.

DEMME, JONATHAN, director, producer, writer; b. Baldwin, LI, NY, Feb. 22, 1944; m. Evelyn Purcell (div.); m. Joanne Howard; 3 children. Student, U. Fla.; degree (hon.), Wesleyan U., 1990. With Avco Embassy Films, 1966, Pathe Films, 1966-67; with publicity dept. United Artists, 1968-69; writer Film Daily, 1966-68. Actor: (films) The Incredible Melting Man, 1977, Into the Night, 1985; dir: Crazy Mama, 1975, Handle with Care, 1977, Last Embrace, 1979, Melvin and Howard, 1980, Swing Shift, 1984, Swimming to Cambodia, 1987, Married to the Mob, 1988, Famous All Over Town, 1988, The Silence of the Lambs, 1991 (Acad. Award for best dir., 1992, Dir.'s Guild of Am. Award for Outstanding Directorial Achievement in Motion Pictures, 1992), Cousin Bobby, 1992, The Complex Sessions, 1994, Storefront Hitchcock, 1998; (TV films) Columbo: Murder Under Glass, 1978, Who Am I This Time?, 1982; (TV series) Alive From Off Center, 1984—87, Trying Times, 1987; exec. prodr.: (films) Amos & Andrew, 1993, Household Saints, 1993, Ray Cohn/Jack Smith, 1994, Devil in a Blue Dress, 1995, Shadrach, 1998, The Opportunists, 2000, Maangamizi: The Ancient One, 2001; prodr.: Miami Blues, 1990, One Foot On a Banana Peel, the Other Foot in the Grave: Secrets From the Dolly Madison Room, 1994, That Thing You Do! (also actor), 1996, Mandela, 1996, Into the Rope, 1996, Courage and Pain, 1996, The Uttmost, 1998, Adaptation, 2002, Beah: A Black Woman Speaks, 2003; (TV films) Women & Men 2: In Love There Are No Rules, 1991; writer (films) Black Mama, White Mama, 1972, Ladies and Gentlemen, the Fabulous Stains, 1981, cinematographer, dir., prodr. The Agronomist, 2003, dir., exec. prodr. (TV films) Subway Stories: Tales from the Underground, 1997, dir., prodr. (films) Something Wild, 1986, Philadelphia, 1993, Beloved, 1998, The Manchurian Candidate, 2004, Neil Young: Heart of Gold, 2006, dir., writer Caged Heat, 1974, Fighting Mad, 1976, Stop Making Sense, 1984, dir., prodr., writer The Truth About Charlie, 2002, prodr., writer Angels Hard as

They Come, 1971, The Hot Box, 1972; dir.: (Bruce Springsteen music video) Murder, Inc., 1995; co-dir.: Streets of Philadelphia. Recipient Billy Wilder Award for Excellence in Directing, Nat. Bd. Review, 2006. Mem.: Dirs. Guild Am.*

DEMMLER, JOHN HENRY, retired lawyer; b. Pitts., June 20, 1932; s. Ralph Henry and Catherine (Hollinger) D.; m. Janet Rice, July 20, 1957; children: Richard H., Ralph W., Carol L. BA, Princeton U., 1954; LLB cum laude, Harvard U., 1959. Bar: Pa. 1960, U.S. Dist. Ct. (we. dist.) Pa. 1960. Assoc. Reed Smith Shaw & McClay, Pitts., 1959—65, ptnr., 1966—93, ret., 1995. Dir. Duquesne Light Co., Pitts., 1977-90. Trustee Shady Side Acad., Pitts., 1969-75, 77—, vice chmn., 1980-84, chmn., 1984-87; chmn. Fox Chapel Borough Zoning Hearing Bd., 1993-2005. Mem. Pa. Bar Assn. (pub. utility law sect. 1976-05), Fox Chapel Golf Club, Allegheny-HYP Club. Republican. Episcopalian. Home and Office: Two Winding Way Verona PA 15147

DEMOFF, MARVIN ALAN, lawyer; b. LA, Oct. 28, 1942; s. Max and Mildred (Tweer) D.; m. Patricia Caryn Abelov, June 16, 1968; children: Allison Leigh, Kevin Andrew. BA, UCLA, 1964; JD, Loyola U., LA, 1967. Bar: Calif. 1969. Asst. pub. defender Los Angeles County, 1968-72; ptnr. Steinberg & Demoff, LA, 1973-83, Craighill, Fentress & Demoff, L.A. and Washington, 1983-86; of counsel Mitchell, Silberberg & Knupp, LA, 1987—2002; mng. dir. Neuberger Berman LLC, LA, 2002—. Mem. citizens adv. bd. Olympic Organizing Com., L.A., 1982-84; bd. trustees Curtis Sch., L.A., 1985-94, chmn. bd. trustees, 1988-93; sports adv. bd. Constitution Rights Found., L.A., 1986—. Mem. ABA (mem. forum com. on entertainment and sports), Calif. Bar Assn., UCLA Alumni Assn., Phi Delta Phi. Avocations: sports, music, art. Office: Neuberger Berman LLC 10250 Constallation Blvd Los Angeles CA 90067 Office Phone: 310-595-9111. Business E-Mail: MDemoff@nb.com.

DE MOLINA, ALVARO G., former bank executive; b. Havana, Cuba, July 13, 1957; arrived in US, 1960; m. Donna de Molina; children: Nicolas, Rachel, Julia. BS in Acctg., Fairleigh Dickinson U.; MBA, Rutgers U. With PriceWaterhouse, 1979; CFO emerging markets grp. JP Morgan; with Bank Am. Corp., 1989—2007, dep. treas., 1998—2000, corp. treas., 2000—04, pres. capital market & investment banking, 2004, CFO, 2005—07, CEO Bank Am. Securities, 2005. Mem. bd. visitors Duke U. Fuqua Sch. Bus., 2003—; mem. dean's coun. Fla. Internat. U. Coll. Bus. Adminstrn.; bd. dirs. Fin. Svc. Vol. Corps, Opera Carolina. Named a Champion of Yr., Allegro Found., 2005; named one of Carolinas' Fathers of Yr., Nat. Father's Day Coun., 2004.*

DEMOND, WALTER EUGENE, lawyer; b. Sacramento, Oct. 15, 1947; s. Walter G. and Laura (Bartlett) D.; m. Kari; 1 child, William. BA, U. Tex., 1969, JD with honors, 1976. Bar: Tex. 1976, Nebr. 2004. With Clark, Thomas & Winters, Austin, 1976—, CFO, 1984—, sr. ptnr. energy and telecomm. sect. Mem. mgmt. com. Clark, Thomas & Winters, 1984-94, 97-99, 2002-04. Capt. USAF, 1970-74. Fellow: Austin Bar Found. (founding mem.), Tex. Bar Found. (life), Am. Bar Found. (life; vice chmn. sect. 2007—); mem.: ABA (vice chmn. gas com. 1986—91, chmn. gas com. 1991—93, long-range planning com. 1995—, vice chmn. gas com. 1997—2003, vice chmn. corp. governance com. 2003—07, chmn. program com. 2006—07, pub. utility comm. and transp. law sect.), State Bar of Tex. (adminstrv. law com. 1984—87). Office: Clark Thomas & Winters Box 1148 Austin TX 78767 Office Phone: 512-472-8800. Business E-Mail: wed@ctw.com.

DEMONG, RICHARD FRANCIS, finance and investments educator; b. Freeport, Ill., May 2, 1944; s. Maurice Dale and Ruth Jane (Kidwell) DeM.; m. Sue Ann Liddle, June 17, 1967 (div. Dec. 1983); children: Cheryl Ann, Lynn Ann; m. Linda H. Krongaard, May 15, 1988. AA, Orange Coast Coll., Costa Mesa, Calif., 1964; BA, Calif. State U., 1966; MBA, Coll. of William & Mary, 1974; PhD, U. Colo., 1977. Cert. cost analyst; chartered fin. analyst. Time keeper Douglas Aircraft Co., Long Beach, Calif., 1966; instr. U. Colo., Boulder, 1974-77; Va. Bankers prof. bank mgmt. U. Va., Charlottesville, 1977—, dir. Ctr. for Fin. Studies, 1991—97; rsch. dir. Fin. Analyst Rsch. Found., Charlottesville, 1982-85; registered investment adv. Va., 1996—. Cons. Fin. Forecasting & Svc., 1978—; fin. coord. Dalkon Shield Claimants Trust, 1989-1999. Author: (with others) 1998 Home Equity Loan Study, 1998, Principles of Financial Management, 2d edit., 1988; editor (with others) The Technology Industry: The Impact of the Internet, 2002; contbr. articles to profl. jours. Mem. Va. Small Bus. Coun., Richmond, 1981-82; chmn. U. Va. ROTC com., Charlottesville, 1981-84, 2001-05; co-chmn. Central Va. Score and Ace chpt., Charlottesville, 1981; dir. McIntire Small Bus. Inst., Charlottesville, 1978-82, Innisfree Village, 1995-98, 2002—, Charlottesville Cath. Sch. Bd., 2002-05. Capt. USAF, 1966-72, Vietnam, col. USAFR, ret. Decorated DFC; named outstanding Air Force Mobilization Augmentee (reservist), Air Tng. Comman, 1980. Mem. Fin. Mgmt. Assn., Am. Fin. Assn., CFA Inst. Roman Catholic. Avocation: gardening. Office: U Va McIntire Sch of Commerce PO Box 400173 Charlottesville VA 22904 Office Phone: 434-924-3227. Business E-Mail: rfd@virginia.edu.

DEMONTE, CLAUDIA ANN, artist, educator; b. Astoria, NY, Aug. 25, 1947; d. Joseph James and Ammeda Ellen (Heiss) DeM.; m. William Edward McGowin, May 28, 1977. BA, Coll. Notre Dame, 1969; MFA, Cath. U., 1971; D (hon.), Coll. Santa Fe, 2006. Instr. Bowie State Coll., Md., 1971—72, Prince Georges C.C., Largo, Md., 1972; prof. dept. art U. Md., Coll. Pk., 1972—2005, prof. emeritus, 2005—; dir. arts internship program SUNY, Stony Brook, 2005—. Dir. Art Workshops, New Sch. Social Rsch., NYC, 1980-94; USIA artist in residene (Sofia) Bulgaria, 1982; art bd. Queens Coll., NY. Selected exhbns.: Corcoran Gallery Art, 1976, Contemporary Arts Ctr., New Orleans, Cranbrook Acad., 1978, Marianne-Deson Gallery, 1979, Miss. Mus., Fort Worth Mus., Washington Project for Arts, 1980, Marion Locks Gallery, Miami Dade Gallery, Xochipilli, 1981, 86, 95, New Sch. Social Rsch., 1982, Queens Mus., N.Y., Stamford Mus., Conn., Gallery 121, Antwerp, Belgium, 1985, Gracie Mansion Gallery, N.Y., 1987, Brentwood Art Gallery, St. Louis, 1987, Nina Freunenheim Gallery, Buffalo, 1987, 92, 94, Internat. Rev. of Arts Arsenal, Amalfi, Italy, 1987, Esbo Mus., Helsinki, Finland, 1988, Evanston (Ill.) Art Ctr., 1989, Barbara Gillman Gallery, Miami, 1991, 92, 94, Gallery 86, Lodz, Poland, Slow Art, Painting in N.Y. Now, P.S. 1 Mus., N.Y., 1991, Haggerty Mus., Wis., 1993, Nina Freudenheim Gallery, Buffalo, 1994, Leedy Voulkos Gallery, Kansas City, Mo., 1996, Panaroma Gallery, Barcelona, Spain, Silpakorn U., Bangkok, 1997, Retrospective, Choklal-fabuken, Malmo, Sweden, 1998, Liesbeth Lip Gallery, Rotterdam, The Netherlands, 1999, Retrospective Rosemont Coll., Pa., 2000, U. New Eng., Tucson Mus., 2001, Mus. of S.W., Midland, Tex., 2002, Internat. Mus. of Women, San Francisco, 2003, Tallinn Kunsit House, Estonia, Gerdubery Cultural Ctr., Iceland, 2004, Contemporary Art Ctr., New Orleans, 2005, U. Md., 2006, MAKAN, Amman, Jordan, 2007, June Kelly Gallery, N.Y.C., 2007; pub. collections include Indpls. Mus., Stamford Mus., Miss. Mus., Prudential Life Ins., Hyatt-Regency, Chem. Bank, Best Products, U. Md., Mus. Modern Art, New Orleans Mus., Minn. Mus., Grand Rapids Mus., Mich., UCLA, Corcoran Gallery of Art, Bklyn. Mus., Mus., Bass Mus., Tucson Mus., Boca Raton Mus.; author: (with Judy Bachrach) The Height Report, 1983, (pomegranate) Women of the World: A Global Collection of Art, 2000; commd. works include: U. No.Iowa, 2003. Mem. art bd. Queens Coll., NY; bd. mem. Pollack Krasner House, 2007—. Recipient award Am.-Italian Assn., 1971, Head Balt. Bus., 1972, Creative award Me., 1974, 77, 83, 87; fellow N.Y. Found. Arts, 1989—, N.Y.C. Dept. Cultural Affairs Art in Pub. Places Sculpture Commn., 1991, N.Y.C. Dept. Cultural Affairs Mural Commn., 1993, sculpture commn. N.Y.C. Dept. Cultural Affairs, 1997, N.Mex. State Art Commn., Sculpture Commn., Socorro, 1998, U. No. Iowa Commn., 2003, N.Mex. State Hwy. Rte. 66 Commn., 2006, Ft. Lauderdale Broward County Sculpture Commn., 2006; grantee Gund Found., 1998, Ancohrage Found. Tex., 1999, Cantor Found., 2004. Democrat. Home: 96 Grand St New York NY 10013-2633 Office Phone: 212-966-4496. Business E-Mail: demonte@umd.edu.

DE MONTEBELLO, PHILIPPE LANNES, museum director; b. Paris, May 16, 1936; came to U.S., 1951, naturalized, 1955; s. Roger L. and Germaine (de Croisset) de M.; m. Edith Bradford Myles, June 24, 1961; children: Marc, Laure, Charles. BA magna cum laude, Harvard U., 1958, ArtsD (hon.), 2006; MA, NYU Inst. Fine Arts, 1963; LLD (hon.), Lafayette Coll., 1979; DHL (hon.), Bard Coll., 1981; DFA (hon.), Iona Coll., 1982; LLD (hon.), Dartmouth Coll., 2004; DFA (hon.), NYU, 2007; HHD (hon.), Savannah Coll. Art and Design, 2007. Assoc. curator European paintings Met. Mus. Art, NYC, 1963-69; dir. Mus. Fine Arts, Houston, 1969—74; vice dir. for curatorial and ednl. affairs Met. Mus. Art, 1974-77, acting dir., 1977-78, dir. NYC, 1978-99, dir., CEO, 1999—. Mem. adv. coun. depts. art and archaeology Columbia U.; fellow, Fogg Mus., Harvard U. Author: Peter Paul Rubens, 1968; mem. editorial bd. Internat. Jour. of Mus. Mgmt. and Curatorship. Trustee, NYU Inst. Fine Arts. Served to 2d lt. AUS, 1956-58. Decorated chevalier Legion d'Honneur (France), Encomienda de Numero de la Orden Isabel la Catholica (Spain), officier Ordre de Leopold (Belgium), Knight Commdr. Pontifical Order of St. Gregory the Great, Comdr. Order of Arts and Letters, 2001, Officier l'Ordre Nat. la Légion d'Hoaneur, 2005; Named to Centennial Honor Roll, Am. Assn. Mus., 2006, recipient NYU Grad. Sch. Alumni Achievement award, 1978, gold medal Nat. Inst. Soc. Sci., 1989, The Spanish Inst., 1992, Rebekah Kohut award Nat. Coun. Jewish Women, 1993, NYU Alumni Assn. Disting. Alumni award, 1998, Living Landmark award NY Landmarks Conservancy, 2001, Mayoral Proclamation, 2002, Nat. Endowment for the Arts, Nat. Medal of Arts, 2003, Amigos Museo Prado prize, 2004, Confedn. Internat. Négociants Oeuvres d'Art, 2005; Woodrow Wilson fellow, 1961-62; Gallatin fellow, 1981. Mem. Assn. Art Mus. Dirs. (works of art com.), Mus. Coun. N.Y.C., Am. Fedn. of the Arts (trustee, exec. com.), Am. Assn. Mus. Avocations: collecting old master drawings, chess, tennis. Home: 25 E 86th St New York NY 10028 Office: Met Mus of Art 1000 5th Ave New York NY 10028-0113

DE MONTEIRO, NADSA, chef; b. Cambodia; d. Longteine de Monteiro; m. Bob Perry, Dec. 1986. Studied, Cambridge Sch. Culinary Arts. Travel agt., Boston, 1986—92; owner, sous chef The Elephant Walk, Somerville, Mass., 1992—94, owner, exec. chef Boston, 1994—; owner, chef Carambola, Waltham, Mass., 1997—. Author: The Elephant Walk Cookbook. Office: The Elephant Walk 2067 Massachusetts Ave Cambridge MA 02140

DEMOPOULOS, HARRY BYRON, retired pathologist, pharmaceutical researcher; b. NYC, Feb. 14, 1932; m. Rita Margarite Iovine, July 24, 1956; children: Thomas, Laura, Richard, Byron. Student, NYU, 1949-52; MD, SUNY, NYC, 1956. Diplomate Am. Bd. of Pathology. Intern Kings County Hosp., Bklyn., 1956-57; resident, tng. fellow in rsch. NYU Med. Ctr., NYC, 1957-61; sr. asst. surgeon USPHS NIH, Bethesda, Md., 1961-63; assoc. prof. U. So. Calif., LA, 1963-67; tenured assoc. prof. NYU Med. Ctr., NYC, 1967—2000; chmn., CEO Antioxidant Pharm. Corp., Elmsford, NY, 1982—, ThyoGen Pharm., 1993—. Exec. dir. Internat. Study Ctr. for Environ. Health Scis., Rye, NY, 1980-83; founding trustee Doris Duke Charitable Found., 1996—. Editor: (book) Cancer and the Environment, 1980, Thresholds for Carcinogens, 1983; contbr. 92 sci. publs. to profl. jours. Recipient Rsch. Career Devel. award Nat. Cancer Inst., NIH, 1963-67. Mem. N.Y. Acad. Scis. Achievements include the founding of the sci. of Free Radical Pathology acknowledged by Nobel winner Dr. Gerhard Herzberg; founding of the sci. of antioxidant pharmacology. Office: ThyoGen Pharmaceuticals 7 Westchester Plz Elmsford NY 10523-1603 Office Phone: 914-261-5855. Business E-Mail: hdemopoulos@thyogen.com.

DEMOREST, ALLAN FREDERICK, retired psychologist; b. Omaha, Dec. 20, 1931; 1 child, Steven M. BA, U. Omaha, 1957; MA, U. Mich., 1959, postgrad., 1960. Lic. psychologist, Iowa, Nat. Register Health Svc. Providers. Counselor Mayor's Com. on Skid Row Problems, Detroit, 1959-61; psychologist Macomb County Schs., Mt. Clemens, Mich., 1961-64; chief psychologist Jasper County Mental Health Ctr., Newton, Iowa, 1964-68; exec. dir. North Cen. Iowa Mental Health Ctr., Ft. Dodge, 1968-75; pvt. practice Ft. Dodge, 1968-85; psychologist Iowa Luth. Hosp., Des Moines, 1985-87; clin. dir. United Behavioral Systems, Des Moines, 1987-94, sr. psychologist, 1994-96; cons. pvt. practice, Des Moines, 1996—. Adj. prof. psychology Buena Vista U., Ft. Dodge, 1974-2002; substitute tchr. Des Moines Pub. Schs., 1999-05; chief trainer AARP Iowa Driver Safety Program, 2005—. Contbr. articles on rational therapy to profl. jours. Founding bd. dirs. Rape and Sexual Assault Victim Program, Ft. Dodge, 1976-85, Family Violence Ctr., Ft. Dodge, 1976-85, Youth Shelter Svcs., Ft. Dodge, 1979. With U.S. Army, 1952-54, Korea. Recipient appreciation award Community Mental Health Ctrs. Assn., 1968, community svc. award Iowa Dept. Human Svcs., 1985. Fellow Albert Ellis Inst.; mem. APA, VFW (quartermaster 2006—), Iowa Psychol. Assn., Adminstrv. Mgmt. Soc. (pres. Ft. Dodge 1979-80, 84-85), Iowa Assn. for Advancement Psychology (pres. 1984, appreciation award 1988), Elks (exalted ruler 1979, trustee 2002, Elk of Yr. 2004). Home and Office: 4225 Hickman Rd Des Moines IA 50310-3334 Personal E-mail: Ademorest@aol.com. *Honesty and integrity are the greatest personal assets of a human being.*

DEMOREST, MARK STUART, lawyer; b. Chambley, France, Mar. 14, 1957; came to U.S., 1960; s. Raymond Phillip and Maud Jane D.; m. Patricia Louise Button, July 28, 1979; children: Melissa, Matthew, Kristin, Kevin, Ryan. AB magna cum laude, Harvard U., 1979; JD magna cum laude, U. Mich., 1983. Bar: Mich. 1983, U.S. Dist. Ct. (ea. dist.) Mich. 1983, U.S. Ct. Appeals (6th cir.) 1984, U.S. Ct. Appeals (7th cir.) 1986, U.S. Supreme Ct. 1993, U.S. Dist. Ct. (cen. dist.) Ill. 1995, U.S. Ct. Appeals (4th cir.) 1995, U.S. Dist. Ct. (we. dist.) Mich. 1996, U.S. Dist. Ct. (ea. dist.) Wis. 2003, US Ct. Appeals (fed. cir.) 2007. Assoc. Dykema Gossett, Detroit, 1983-85, Simpson & Moran, Birmingham, Mich., 1985-87; ptnr. The Robert P. Ufer Partnership, Bloomfield Hills, Mich., 1987-92, Hainer, Demorest & Berman, P.C., Troy, Mich., 1993-98; atty, mng. mem. Demorest Law Firm, PLLC, 1998—. Mem. ABA, State Bar Mich., Harvard Club Ea. Mich. (schs. com.), Order of Coif. Avocations: lacrosse, other sports. Office: 555 S Old Woodward Ave Ste 21U Birmingham MI 48009 Office Phone: 248-723-5500. Business E-Mail: mark@demolaw.net.

DEMORY-LUCE, DEBBY KAY, dietician, consultant; adopted d. Robert George and Ellen Philena Demory; m. Stephen George Luce, June 25, 1977; children: Matthew Robert Luce, Bryan George Luce. BS, Tex. Christian U., Ft. Worth, 1975; MS, Tex. Woman's U., Houston, 1990; PhD in Pub. Health, U. Tex., Houston, 1997. Registered dietitian Am. Dietetic Assn., lic. State of Tex. Dietetic intern VA Med. Ctr., Houston, 1989; instr., nutritionist Baylor Coll. Medicine, Houston, 1998—2004; adj. faculty North Harris Coll., Houston, 2005—. Ind. contractor evidence-based projects Am. Dietetic Assn., Chgo., jour. reviewer, 2003—. Contbr. articles to profl. jours. Named Outstanding Club Pres., Tex. Ea. divsn. Toastmasters Internat., 1990. Mem.: Am. Dietetic Assn., Houston Area Dietetics Assn., The Am. Dietetic Assn., Tall Pines Dietetic Assn. (v.p. 1997—98, pres.-elect and pres. 1998—2000), Tex. Dietetic Assn., Kappa Delta Pi. Methodist. Achievements include research in Pediatric Nutrition. Avocation: travel. Home: 9419 Walnut Glen Houston TX 77064 Home Phone: 281-894-9129. Personal E-mail: ddemluce@sbcglobal.net.

DEMOS, NICHOLAS JOHN, physician, surgeon, researcher; b. Tripolis, Greece, Apr. 5, 1930; came to U.S., 1949; s. John Nicholas and Vakoula (Haritopoulos) D.; chilcren: Victoria N., Stephanie N. BS, Northwestern U., 1952, MS in Pathology, 1954, MD, 1955. Cert. Gen. Surgery, thoracic Surgery, Gen. Vascular Surgery. Resident in surgery Northwestern U. Med. Sch., Chgo., 1955-58, 60-63; internship Passavant Hosp., Chgo., 1955-56; lt. commdr. USN, 1958-60; resident in thoracic surgery Seton Hall U. Med. Sch., Jersey City, N.J., 1960-63, NIH fellow surgical cardiology, 1963-64; chief cardiovascular surgery Christ Hosp., Jersey City, N.J., 1977—; chief dept. surgery St. Francis Hosp., Jersey City, N.J., 1979-84; chief thoracic surgery Meadowlands Hosp., Secaucus, N.J., 1994—; clin. prof. surgery Newark Med. Sch., 1998—. Past pres. Med. Staff Christ Hosp., Jersey City, N.J., 1980, N.J. Soc. Thoracic Surgeons, 1980, N.J. Soc. Vascular Surgery, 1980; liaison officer ACS, 1980—. Author: Stapled Gastroplasty, 1974, Surgery of Esophogus (movies), 1970—, Thorascopic Surgery of Esophogus; patentee of surgical instrument, 1987; contbr. over 100 articles to profl. jours. Fellow Am. Coll. Cardiology, ACS; mem. Soc. Thoracic Surgeons, N.J. Soc. Vascular Surgery, Am. Gastroenterological Assn. Greek Orthodox. Avocations: photography, painting. Office: 142 Palisade Ave Jersey City NJ 07306-1108

DEMOSS, HAROLD RAYMOND, JR., federal judge; b. Houston, Dec. 30, 1930; s. Harold R. and Jessy May (Cox) DeMoss; m. Judith Phelps; children: Harold R. III, Louise Holland. BA, Rice U., 1952; LLB, U. Tex., 1955. Bar: Tex. Assoc. Bracewell & Patterson, Houston, 1957—61, ptnr., 1961—91; judge US Ct. of Appeals (5th cir.), Houston, 1991—2007, sr. judge, 2007—. Dir. Panama Canal Co., 1976—77; coun. mem. Admin. Conference of US, 1990—91. Chmn. bd. Tex. Bill of Rights Found., Houston, 1969—70; pres. Tanglewood Homeowners Assn., 1987; area chmn. Bush Congl. Campaign, 1968; mem. platform group Bush for Pres., Washington, 1988; rsch. analyst Bush/Quayle campaign, 1988; dist. del.-at-large Rep. Nat. Conv., Houston, 1980, alt. del.-at-large, 1984, 1988; Harris County vice chmn. Tower Senate campaign, Houston, 1972, Ford/Dale campaign, 1976; Harris County chmn. Loeffler for Gov. Primary, 1986; Harris County co-chair Regan/Bush campaign, 1980, 1984; Tex. state chmn. Bush for Pres. Primary, 1979—80, Tex. vice chmn., 1988; del. Rep. State Conv., Houston, 1968; vestryman St. Martin's Episcopal Ch., Houston, 1968—72; mem. exec. bd. Episcopal Diocese Tex., 1983—86, chmn. planning com., 1985—88, del. Diocesan Conv., 1976—88; bd. dirs. Amigos de las Americas, 1974—76. Sgt. US Army, 1955—57. Recipient Disting. Alumni award, Rice U., 2004, George Washington Disting. Svc. award, SAR, 2006. Fellow: Tex. Bar Assn. (life); mem.: ABA, N.Mex. Trial Lawyers Assn., Tex. Assn. Def. Counsel (bd. dirs. 1972—74), Houston Bar Assn. (bd. dirs. 1969—71, 1st v.p. 1972—73), Maritime Law Assn. US, Am. Judicature Soc., Internat. Bar Assn., The Houston Club. Avocations: fishing, waterskiing. Office: Bob Casey US Courthouse 515 Rusk St Ste 12015 Houston TX 77002-2605*

DEMOSS, JON W., insurance company executive, lawyer; b. Kewanee, Ill., Aug. 9, 1947; s. Wendell and Virginia Beth DeMoss; m. Eleanor T. Thornley, Aug. 9, 1969; 1 child, Marc Alain. BS, U. Ill., 1969, JD, 1972. Bar: Ill. 1972, U.S. Dist. Ct. (cen. dist.) Ill. 1977, U.S. Supreme Ct. 1978, U.S. dist. Ct. (no. dist., trial bar) Ill. 1983. In house counsel Assn. Ill. Electric Coop., Springfield, 1972-74; registered lobbyist Ill. Gen. Assembly, Springfield, 1972-74; asst. dir. Ill. Inst. for CLE, Springfield, 1974-85; exec. dir. Ill. State Bar Assn., 1986-94; pres., CEO ISBA Mut. Ins. Co., Chgo., 1994—. Bd. dirs. Bar Plan Surety & Fidelity Co., St. Louis, 1999-2005 Bd. dirs. Springfield Symphony Orch., 1982-87, Ill. Inst. for CLE, 1986-89, Nat. Assn. of Bar Related Ins. Cos., 1989, pres., elect., 1998-99, pres. 1999-2000; bd. dirs. Lawyers Reins. Co., 1997—; bd. visitors John Marshall Law Sch., 1990—. Capt. U.S. Army, 1972. Fellow Am. Bar Found. (life, co-chmn. projects to prepare Appellate Handbook 1978, 90), Ill. Bar Found. (life, bd. dirs. 1983-85); mem. ABA (ho. of dels. 1979-85, 89, 91, 93-94), Nat. Conf. Bar Pres., Am. Judicature Soc. (bd. dirs. Ill. state chpt., treas. 2002-04), Ill. State Bar Assn. (pres. 1984-85, bd. govs. 1975-85, chmn. com. on scope and correlation of work 1982-83, chmn. budget com. 1983-85, chmn. legis. com. 1983-84, 85, chmn. com. on merit selection of judges 1977, del. long-range planning conf. 1972, 78, liaison to numerous coms. and sects.), Chgo. Bar Assn., Lake County Bar Assn., U. Ill. Coll. Dean's Club, La Chaine des Rotisseurs (Chgo.), Ordre Mondial des Gourmet Degustateurs (Chgo.). Home: 180 Norwich Ct Lake Bluff IL 60044-1914 Office: ISBA Mutual Ins Co 223 W Ohio St Chicago IL 60610-4101 Office Phone: 312-379-2000. Business E-Mail: jon.demoss@isbamic.com.

DEMOTT, DEBORAH ANN, law educator; b. Collingswood, NJ, July 21, 1948; d. Lyle J. and Frances F. (Cummings) DeM. BA, Swarthmore Coll., 1970; JD, NYU, 1973. Bar: N.Y. 1974. Law clk. U.S. Dist. Ct. (so. dist.) N.Y., 1973; assoc. Simpson, Thacher & Bartlett, NYC, 1974-75; from asst. prof. to assoc. prof. Duke U., Durham, NC, 1975-80, prof. law, 1980—, David F. Cavers prof. law, 2000—. Vis. asst. prof. U. Tex., Austin, 1977-78; Bost rsch. prof. law, 1981; vis. prof. U. Calif. Hastings Coll. Law, 1986, U. Colo., 1989, U. San Diego, 1991; James L. Lewtas vis. prof. law Osgoode Hall Law Sch., Toronto, Ont., Can., 1991; vis. fellow U. Melbourne, 1993, 95, 98; Huber C. Hurst Eminent vis. scholar U. Fla. Coll. Law, 1996; Frances Lewis Scholar-in-Residence Washington and Lee Law Sch., 1998; centennial vis. prof. law dept. London Sch. Econs., 2000-02; vis. prof. internat. faculty U. Sydney Faculty of Law, 2004, McWilliams vis. prof., 2006. Author: Shareholder Derivative Actions, 1987, Fiduciary Obligation Agency and Partnership, 1991; editor: Corporations at the Crossroads: Governance and Reform; contbr. articles to profl. jours.; bd. advisors Jour. Legal Edn., 1983-86. Trustee Law Sch. Admission Coun., 1984-88; mem. N.C. Gen. Statutes Commn., 1990-98; mem. selection com. Coif Book Award, 1988-90. Recipient Pomeroy prize NYU Sch. Law, 1971-73; AAUW fellow, 1972-73; Fulbright Sr. scholar Sydney U. and Monash (Australia) U., 1986. Mem. ABA, Am. Law Inst. (reporter restatement of agy.), The Assn. Am. Law Schs. (chmn. sect. bus. assocs. 2006). Office: Duke U Law Sch PO Box 90360 Durham NC 27708-0360 Office Phone: 919-613-7082. Business E-Mail: demott@law.duke.edu.

DEMOTTE, JOHN BUCK, educational consultant; b. Nampa, Idaho, Feb. 9, 1945; s. John (Jack) Benson DeMotte and Ruby Violet Yates DeMotte. Postgrad., Purdue U., Ind., 1981—86, U. Oreg., 1981—86. Ordained Universal Life Ch., Modesto, Calif., 2004. Educator, instr., prof., 1970—2007; pvt. cons. Boise, Idaho, 1977—. Maj. ret. US Army, 1965—91. Decorated ARCOM US Army; Tchg. fellow, Purdue U./U. Oreg., 1981—86. Mem.: Am. Mensa (corr.; mem. at large 1976—2007). Reform. Universal Unitarian. Avocations: films, travel. Home: 5723 Mineral Dr Boise ID 83716 Home Phone: 208-336-3637. Personal E-mail: valde@icehouse.net.

DEMOUY, ALYSON M., social studies educator; d. Patricia Demouy. BA in History, U. So. Miss., Hattiesburg, 2000; EdM in Curriculum and Instrn., Tex. A & M U., College Station, 2005. Cert. tchr. Tex. State Bd. Edn. World geography tchr. Westfield 9th Grade Ctr., Houston, 2002—. Student coun. sponsor Westfield 9th Grade Ctr., Houston, 2005—. Mem.: Kappa Delta Pi. Office: Westfield 9th Grade Center 1500 Southridge Houston TX 77090 Home Phone: 832-249-9029; Office Phone: 832-446-1401. Business E-Mail: alysond@springisd.org.

DEMPSEY, BERNARD HAYDEN, JR., lawyer; b. Evanston, Ill., Mar. 29, 1942; s. Bernard H. and Margaret C. (Gallagher) D.; m. Cynthia T. Dempsey; children: Bernard H. III, Matthew B., Kathleen N., Rose Maureen G., Alexandra C., Anastasia M. BS, Coll. Holy Cross, Worcester, Mass., 1964; JD, Georgetown U., Washington, DC, 1967. Bar: Fla. 1968, DC 1979. Law clk. to chief judge US Dist. Ct. (mid. dist.) Fla., 1967-69; asst. US Atty. Mid. Dist. Fla., 1969-73; pvt. practice Orlando, Fla., 1973—; spl. asst. to US Atty. Mid. Dist. Fla., 1974. Lectr. in field. Contbr. articles to profl. jours. Recipient John Marshall award US Dept. Justice, 1972, US Atty's Outstanding Performance award 1970, 71, 72, 73. Mem.: ATLA, ABA, Am. Acad. Trial Counsel, Orange County Bar Assn., Am. Arbitration Assn., Fed. Bar Assn., Fla. Bar Found., Am. Judicature Soc., Fla. Bar Assn., Nat. Employment Lawyers Assn., US Attys. Assn. for Mid. Dist. Fla., Fla. Assn. Criminal Def. Lawyers, Nat. Assn. Criminal Def. Lawyers, Winter Park Racquet Club (Fla.), Delta Theta Phi. Republican. Roman Catholic. Office: Dempsey & Assocs PA 1560 Orange Ave Ste 200 Winter Park FL 32789-5544 Office Phone: 407-422-5166. Business E-Mail: bhd@dempsey-law.com.

DEMPSEY, CECELIA See BYRNE-DEMPSEY, CECELIA

DEMPSEY, CLINTON (CLINT) DREW, professional soccer player; b. Nacogdoches, Tex., Mar. 9, 1983; Attended, Furman Univ. Midfielder New England Revolution, 2004—07, Fulham FC, London, 2007—. 21 caps, 5 goals U.S. Nat. Soccer team, 2004—; mem. U.S. World Cup team, 2006. Named Rookie of the Yr., Major League Soccer, 2004. Mailing: US Soccer Fedn 1801 S Prairie Ave Chicago IL 60616

DEMPSEY, DONALD CHANDLER, stockbroker, financial planner; b. Detroit, Nov. 13, 1951; s. Donald Chandler Sr. and Phillippa E. D.; m. Karen Lynn Petroskey, Apr. 19, 1980; 1 child, Michael Patrick. B of Bus., Cleary Coll., 1975. CFP, Coll. Fin. Planning Denver. Sr. v.p. investments E.F. Hutton, Detroit, 1977-94, Wachovia Securities, Detroit, 1994—. Roman Catholic. Home: 18134 Shelley Pond Ct Northville MI 48167-3543 Office Phone: 248-737-8468. Personal E-mail: ddempsey@ameritech.net.

DEMPSEY, EDWARD JOSEPH, lawyer; b. Lynn, Mass., Mar. 13, 1943; s. Timothy Finbar and Christine Margaret (Callahan) D.; m. Eileen Margaret McManus, Apr. 15, 1967; children: Kristen A. Stolfi, Katherine B. Aydin, Shelagh E., James P. AB, Boston Coll., 1964; JD, Cath. U. Am., 1970. Bar: D.C. 1970, Conn. 1982. Assoc. Arent, Fox, Kintner, Plotkin & Kahn, Washington, 1970-72, Akin, Gump, Strauss, Hauer & Feld, Washington, 1972-75; supervisory trial atty. EEOC, Washington, 1975-79; assoc. Whitman & Ransom, Washington, 1979-81, Farmer, Wells, McGuinn & Sibal, Washington, 1981-82; ptnr. Farmer, Wells, Sibal & Dempsey, Washington, Hartford, Conn., 1983-84; dir. indsl. rels. and labor counsel United Technologies Corp., Hartford, Conn., 1985—2006; of counsel Day Pitney, LLP, Hartford and Washington, 2007—. Editor-in-chief: Cath. U. Law Rev. Capt. USNR (ret.). Fellow Coll. Labor and Employment Lawyers; mem. ABA. Business E-Mail: ejdempsey@daypitney.com.

DEMPSEY, JAMES RAYMON, manufacturing executive; b. Red Bay, Ala., Oct. 4, 1921; s. Newman W. and Maude (Berry) D.; m. Dolores Barnes, Jan. 19, 1943 (dec. Sept. 1997); children: Susan, David Barnes, Anne. Student, U. Ala., 1937—39; BS, U.S. Mil. Acad., 1943; MS, U. Mich., 1947, D (hon.) of Engring., 1964. Commd. 2d lt. U.S. Army, 1943; advanced through grades to lt. col. USAF, 1951; with photo reconnaissance squadron Eng., France, World War II; squadron comdr., 1945; guided missiles project officer, then chief guided missile projects (Research and Devel. Directorate, Air Force Hdqrs.), 1948- 49; exec. officer to (Dep. Chief Staff for Devel.), 1950-51; chief project sect. (Air Force Missile Test Center), Patrick AFB, Fla., then operations officer missile test range, 1951-53, resigned, 1953; asst. to v.p. planning Convair div. Gen. Dynamics Corp., 1953-54; dir. Gen. Dynamics Corp. (Atlas program), 1954-57; mgr. Gen. Dynamics Corp. (Convair-Astronautics div.), 1957-58; v.p. Gen. Dynamics Corp. (Convair div.), 1958-61; sr. v.p. Gen. Dynamics Corp.; pres. Gen. Dynamics Astronautics, 1961-65, Gen. Dynamics Convair, 1965-66; v.p. missiles, space and electronics group Avco Corp., 1966-68, v.p., group exec. govt. products group, 1968-75; pres. Digital Broadcasting Corp., 1978-79; mng. partner J.J. Finnigan Industries, Duluth, Ga., 1978-85; pres. Southeastern Rail Car Co., 1986-89; pvt. investor, 1990—. Trustee Phoenix Series Fund, 1968-91, Big Edge Series Fund, 1985-91, Phoenix Multi-Portfolio Fund, 1989-91, Precious Metal Holdings, 1980-93, Keystone Internat., 1987-93; chmn. bd. Transatlantic Capital Corp., Transatlantic Investment Corp., 1984-86; spl. com. on space tech. NASA Decorated Air medal with clusters, D.F.C.; Croix de Guerre (France); recipient Disting. Grad. award U.S. Mil. Acad., 2002 Fellow AIAA, Am. Astronaut. Soc.; mem. Air Force Assn. (bd. dirs. 1958-59), Burning Tree Club, Congl. Country Club. Home and Office: 4081 Ridgeview Cir Mc Lean VA 22101-5809

DEMPSEY, JERRY EDWARD, retired service company executive; b. Landrum, SC, Oct. 1, 1932; s. Adolphus Gerald and Willie Ceyattie (Lee) D.; m. Harriet Coan Calvert; children: Jerrie E., Harriet R., Margaret. BS, Clemson U., 1954, LLD (hon.), 2001; MBA, Ga. State Coll., 1968. With Borg-Warner Corp., Chgo., 1956-84, gen. mgr. York divsn., 1972-77, exec. v.p., 1977-79, pres., COO, 1979-84; sr. v.p. Waste Mgmt. Inc., Oak Brook, Ill., 1984-93; chmn., CEO PPG Industries, Inc., Pitts., 1993-97, chmn., 1997. Bd. dirs. Navistar, Eastman Chem. Co. Dean's adv. coun. Sch. Engring. Clemson U., chmn. pres.'s adv. coun.; bd. dirs. Pitts. Theol. Sem., Greenville Symphony, Greater Greenville Forum. Named Bus. Leader of Yr., Oak Brook (Ill.) Jaycees, 1989; recipient Bronze award Fin. World, 1989, 90, Pres.'s award Clemson U., 1990, Disting. Svc. award, 1992, Horatio Alger award, 1995, Am. Heritage award Anti-Defamation League, 1995, Disting. Alumni award Ga. State U., 1999, Lifetime Achievement award Ga. State U., 2004. Mem. ASHRAE, Melrose Club, Duquesne Club (dir.), Thornblade Country Club, Greenville Country Club, Fox Chapel Golf Club. Office: PPG Industries Inc 1 PPG Pl Pittsburgh PA 15272-0001

DEMPSEY, JOAN, federal agency administrator; BA Polit. Sci., So. Ark. U.; MA Pub. Adminstrn., U. Ark. Deputy dir. Gen. Defense Intelligence Program Staff; dir. Mil. Intelligence Staff, Nat. Mil. Intelligence Prodn. Ctr.; acting asst. sec. defense Command, Control, Comm. and Intelligence; deputy asst. sec. Defense for Intelligence and Security; deputy dir. cmty. mgmt. CIA, Washington, 1997—; exec. dir. Fgn. Intelligence Adv. Bd., Office of Pres., Washington, 2003—. With USN. Mailing: c/oj President's Foreign Int Adv Board 1600 Pennsylvania Ave Washington DC 20500

DEMPSEY, LORCAN, library and information scientist; Distributed nat. electronic resource dir. UKOLN U. Bath, England, 1994—2000; with Joint Info. Systems Com., London, 2000—01; v.p. rsch. Online Computer Libr. Ctr., Inc., Dublin, Ohio, 2001—, chief strategist, 2004—. Bd. dirs. Nat. Info. Stds. Orgn.; hon. rsch. fellow U. Wales, Aberystwyth. Contbr. articles to profl. publs. Office: Online Computer Libr Ctr Inc 6565 Kilgour Pl Dublin OH 43017-3395 Office Phone: 614-761-5335. E-mail: dempseyl@oclc.org.

DEMPSEY, MARTIN E., career military officer; b. 1952; BS, US Military Acad.; MA, Duke U., 1984; MMAS, US Army Command and Gen. Staff Coll., 1988; MS in Nat. Security and Strategic Studies, Nat. Defense U., 1996. Advanced through grades to lt. gen. US Army, 2005; platoon leader B Troop, 1st Squadron, 2d Armored Cavalry US Army Europe and Seventh Army, Germany, 1975—76, support platoon leader, 1976—77, S-1, 1977—78, exec. officer 4th Battalion, 67th Armor, 3d Armored Div., 1988—89, S-3 ops to exec. officer, 1989—91, Ops. Dessert Shield/Storm, Saudi Arabia, 1989—91, comdr. 4th Battalion, 67th Armor, 1st Brigade, 1st Armored Div. Germany, 1991—93, commdg. gen. 1st Armored Div. Operation Iraqi Freedom, 2003—04, Germany, 2004—05; motor officer 1st Squadron, 10th Cavalry, 4th Infantry Div. US Army, Fort Carson, Colo., 1979—80, comdr. A Troop, 1980, S-3 ops, 1980—81, comdr. Hdqs. and Hdqs. Troop, 1981—82; chief Armor Branch, Combat Arms Div. Officer Personnel Mgmt. Directorate, US Total Army Personnel Command, Alexandria, Va., 1993—95; comdr. 3rd Armored Cavalry Regiment US Army, Fort Carson, Colo., 1996—98; asst. dep. dir. Politico-Military Affairs, Europe and Africa Joint Staff (J-5), Washington, 1998—99, spl. asst. to chmn. of Joint Chiefs of Staff, 1999—2001; program mgr. Saudi Arabian Nat. Guard Modernization Program, 2001—03; comdr. Multinational Security Transition Commd., Iraq, 2005—07; dep. comdr. US Ctr. Command, 2007—. Instr. to asst. prof. Dept. English US Military Acad., West Point, NY, 1984—87. Decorated Disting. Svc. Medal, Defense Superior Svc. Medal, Legion of Merit, Bronze Star Medal with V Device, Bronze Star Medal, Meritorious Svc. Medal, Joint Svc. Commendation Medal, Army Achievement Medal, Parachutist Badge, Joint Chiefs of Staff Identification Badge. Office: US Ctrl Command 7115 S Boundary Blvd Tampa FL 33621*

DEMPSEY, MARY A., library commissioner, lawyer; m. Philip Corboy, Sept. 4, 1992. BA, St. Mary's Coll., Winona, Minn., 1975; MLS, U. Ill., 1976; JD, DePaul U., 1982. Bar: Ill. 1982. Libr. Hillside Pub. Libr., Ill., 1976—78; assoc. Reuben and Proctor, Chgo., 1982—85; assoc. gen. counsel Michael Reese Hosp. and Med. Ctr., Chgo., 1985—86; pvt. practice Chgo., 1987—89; counsel Sidley and Austin, Chgo., 1990—93; commr. Chgo. Pub. Libr., 1994—. Adj. prof. law DePaul U. Coll. Law and Health Inst., Chgo., 1986-90; spl. counsel Chgo. Bd. Edn., 1987-89; mem. adv. bd. Dominican U. Grad. Sch. Libr. and Info. Sci., River Forest, Ill. Mem. State St. Commn., Chgo.; bd. dir. Big Shoulders Fund (for inner city Cath. sch.), Urban Libr. Coun.; trustee DePaul U., Chgo.; mem. Ill. State Libr. Adv. Coun. Named one of Pub. Officials of Yr., Governing Mag., 2006, recipient Ken Haycock award for Promoting Librarianship, ALA, 2007; state libr. scholar in Ill. Mem. Chgo. Bar Assn., Chgo. Network. Office: Chgo Pub Libr 400 S State St Chicago IL 60605-1203 Office Phone: 312-747-4090. Office Fax: 312-747-4968. E-mail: mdempsey@chipublib.org.*

DEMPSEY, PATRICK, actor; b. Lewiston, Maine, Jan. 13, 1966; m. Rocky Parker, 1987 (div. 1994); m. Jillian Fink, July 31, 1999; children: Tallulah Fyfe, Darby Galen, Sullivan Patrick. Actor: (films) Heaven Help Us, 1985, Meatballs III: Summer Job, 1986, Can't Buy Me Love, 1987, In the Mood, 1987, In a Shallow Grave, 1988, Some Girls, 1988, Loverboy, 1989, Happy Together, 1987, Coupe de Ville, 1990, Run, 1991, Mobsters, 1991, Face the Music, 1993, Bank Robber, 1993, Ava's Magical Adventure, 1994, With Honors, 1994, Bloodknot, 1995, Outbreak, 1995, Hugo Pool, 1997, Denial, 1998, The Treat, 1998, There's No Fish Food In Heaven, 1998, Me and Will, 1999, Scream 3, 2000, Rebellion, 2002, The Emperor's Club, 2002, Sweet Home Alabama, 2002, Shade, 2006, Freedom Writers, 2007, (voice) Brother Bear, 2006,: (TV films) A Fighting Choice, 1986, Merry Christmas Baby, 1991, For Better and for Worse, 1993, J.F.K.: Reckless Youth, 1993, The Right to Remain Silent, 1996, A Season in Purgatory, 1996, Odd Jobs, 1997, The Player, 1997, The Escape, 1997, 20,000 Leagues Under the Sea, 1997, Crime and Punishment, 1998, Jeremiah, 1998, Chestnut Hill, 2001, Blonde, 2001, Corsairs, 2002, About a Boy, 2003, Lucky 7, 2003, Iron Jawed Angels, 2004; (TV series) Fast Times, 1986, Grey's Anatomy, 2005— (Outstanding Performance by an Ensemble in a Drama Series, SAG, 2007), (guest appearances) Will & Grace, 2000, 2001, Once and Again, 2000, 2001, 2003, Karen Sisco, 2003, The Practice, 2004. Named Favorite Male Star-TV, People's Choice Awards, 2007; named one of Barbara Walters-10 Most Fascinating People of 2006. Office: c/o Grey's Anatomy Los Feliz Tower 4th Fl 4151 Prospect Ave Los Angeles CA 90027 also: c/o BWR Pub Rels Sixth Fl West Tower 9100 Wilshire Blvd Beverly Hills CA 90212*

DEMPSEY, RAYMOND LEO, JR., radio and television producer, moderator, writer; b. Providence, June 18, 1949; s. Raymond Leo Sr. and Louise Veronica (Gambuto) D.; m. Patricia Batchelder (div. 1984); children: Joab, Jahdeam, Deezsha, Nathaniel, Talitha. BA in Liberal Arts, R.I. Coll., 1973; cert., Blake Computer Programming Inst., 1977; cert. in Bus., U. R.I., 1979; cert., Billy Graham Sch. Evangelism, Ashville, NC, 1989; postgrad., Harvard U., Roger Williams U., Bryant U., Bristol C.C., C.C. R.I., Providence Coll. Lic. real estate agt., R.I.; lic. radio sta. operator FCC; cert. secondary tchr., videographer, contractor, R.I. Writer local and nat. publs., 1980—88; producer, moderator Chapter & Verse TV, Sta. RICA-TV, Providence, 1983—; tchr. R.I. Pub. High Schs., Providence and Cranston, 1988; producer, moderator radio programs Ch. Focus and People, Sta. WRIB, East Providence, 1989—97. Bd. dirs. Blessing, Inc., Providence; spl. corr. Songtime U.S.A. Radio Network, 1988—96, spl. reporter, spl. contbr., 1991; host Straight Talk, Sta. WKRI, 1989, dir. World Exch., 1991-93; co-host The Bible Answer Program, Sta. WARV, 1986; judge The Ace Awards, 1992, Cable Ace Awards, 1992; interviewer Gallup Poll, 1987; trainee N.E. Law Enforcement Officers Assn., 1991; elector Radio Hall of Fame, 1993, Stellar Awards, 1993; nursing asst. nursing homes, R.I., 1979; pvt. nurse's asst. R.I. Hosp., 1979; patient attendant R.I. Mental Hosp.; papers placed in permanent reference res. Brit. Libr., London, N.Y.C. Pub. Libr., Libr. Congress, Washington; preliminary judge Audio Pub. Assn. awards, 1996—. Dancer R.I. Coll. Dance Co., 1969; actor: The Wig and Mask Society of La Salle Acad., 1965. Bd. dirs. R.I. Right to Life, Cranston, 1973—95; witness R.I. Gen. Assembly, 1973—75, R.I. Bd. Health, 1973—; vol. ARC, R.I. Hosp.; registrar voters State of R.I., 1980, 91-92; del. Rep. Nat. Conv. 1980; sponsor World Vision, Pasadena, Calif., 1981—, Compassion Internat., Colo. Springs, Colo., 1989—; chief boys instr. karate Mattson Acad., Providence, 1968-71; mem. Providence Sci. Outreach of Brown U.; del. Gov.'s Conf. on Libr. and Info. Svcs., 1991; elector White House Conf. on Libr. and Info. Svcs.; Justice of Peace, 1991; regional rep. Students Against Vietnam War, 1971, Taxpayers Action Network, 1991; ptnr. Food for the Hungry, 1984—; del. Ellen McCormack for Pres., 1976; vol. U.S. Fish and Wildlife Svc., R.I. Hosp., Providence, 1975, Providence Amb. Clinic, 1975; elected Rep. City Com. and Rep. State Ctrl. Com.; chmn. Issues and Rsch. Com. Rep. party Providence; collection donations to Holy Name Sch. Libr., Archdiocese of NY; ret. dir. Ground Zero, Citizens Against Govt. Waste; donator Vt. Hist. Soc., Brattleboro, 1975, Dominican Phillips Meml. Libr., Providence Coll., 1975, U. Steubenville, Ohio, 1995, Brown U. Libr., 2001, Cranston (RI) Pub. Libr., 2001, The Master's Sem., Calif., 2001, Joseph Stanton Meml. Libr., NYC, 2001, Kinsey Libr. at Ind. U., Bloomington, 2007. Named One of Top 4 Local Cable TV Prodrs. in Nation, Nat. Assn. Local Cable Programming, 1987, ofcl. Jerusalem Pilgrim, State of Israel, 1990, Ptnr. in Philanthropy, 1995; recipient 2 Internat. Angel awards for excellence in Cable TV presentations, 1991, cert. U.S. SBA, 1990, Diamond award, 1992, 1st prize for excellence in pub. affairs in R.I. and Mass., 1992, Achievement award Dale Carnegie Orgn., 1992, 1st pl. award Mastermedia: The Spotlight award, 1993. Mem. AAAS, ASCD, NRA, Am. Math. Soc., Coll. Sci. Tchrs., Sons Union Vets., Nat. Assn. H.S. Tchrs. English, Evangel. Theol. Soc., Soc. for Coll. Tchrs., Nat. Assn. Edn. of Young Children, Nat. Assn. Tchg. Sci., Modern Poetry Assn., Am. Soc. Oriental Rsch., Archaeol. Inst. Am., R.I. Assn. for Edn. Young Children, R.I. Assn. for Supervision and Curriculum Devel., Mental Health Assn. R.I., N.Y. Acad. Scis., Internat. Press Assn. (founding mem.), Nat. Geog. Soc., Nat. Assn. Broadcasters, Modern Poetry Assn., Nat. Assn. Radio Talk Show Hosts, Nat. Acad. Cable Programming, Near East Archaeol. Soc., Internat. Platform Assn., Nat. Assn. Tchrs. Sci., Jewish TV Inst. (charter), Smithsonian Air and Space Mus., Smithsonian Instn. (assoc.), Royal Inst. Pub. Health and Hygiene London (affiliate), Bread for the World, Evangs. for Social Action, Mus. Heritage Soc., Interscholastic Inst., Libr. Co. Phila., John Russell Bartlett Soc. (Brown U.), Intertel, Mensa, USCG Aux., Golden Key, Abraham Lincoln Soc., Internet Soc., Rel. Heritage Am., Providence Athenaeum, Toastmasters Internat., R.I. Pilots Assn., Phi Theta Kappa. Avocations: scuba diving, marksmanship, archaeology. Home and Office: PO Box 41000 Providence RI 02940-1000 *Orthodoxy presumes orthopraxy, and correct knowledge must precede correct action; yet anything minus love equals zero.*

DEMPSEY, THOMAS JOSEPH, retired postmaster; b. Centralia, Pa., Mar. 16, 1945; s. William Anthony and Helen Agnes (Dewey) D.; m. Grace Mary Sewa, Nov. 24, 1973; children: Brian, Thomas Joseph Jr., Kevin. Grad., Postal Svc. Acad., Potomac, Md., 1984. Cert. postmaster trainer U.S. Postal Svc. Clk. U.S. Postal Svc., Centralia, 1968-77, mail carrier Girardville, Pa., 1977-79, postmaster Locustdale, Pa., 1979-81, Centralia, 1981-84, Girardville, 1984-2000, officer-in-charge selection bd. Lancaster, Pa., 1992-99, mem. postmaster selection bd. and customer svc. bd., 1994-99; ret., 2000. Author: History of Centralia, 1992. Sec. Centralia Ambulance Svc., 1970-73. Mem. Nat. Assn. Postmasters U.S., Nat. League Postmasters, Hist. Soc. Schuylkill County, Ancient Order Hibernians (v.p.), KC. Democrat. Roman Catholic. Avocations: genealogy, history, fishing. Home: 204 W Main St Girardville PA 17935-1706 Personal E-mail: tdemps_98@yahoo.com.

DEMPSEY, WILLIAM G., pharmaceutical executive; b. Evergreen Park, Ill., Nov. 17, 1951; B of Acctg., DePaul U. With Abbott Labs., Abbott Park, Ill., 1982—, gen. mgr. home infusion svcs., civisional v.p. critical care systems, divisional v.p. hosp. bus. sector sales, 1995—96, v.p. hosp. products bus. sector, 1996—98, sr. v.p. chem. and agrl. products, 1998—99, sr. v.p. internat. ops., 1999—2003, sr. v.p. pharm. ops., 2003—06, exec. v.p. pharm. group, 2006—. Chmn. internat. sect. exec. com. PhRMA; mem. governing coun. Adv. Good Shepherd Hosp.; chmn. supervisory bd. Knoll GmBH, Germany; bd. dirs. TAP, Dainabot. Office: Abbott Labs 100 Abbott Park Rd Abbott Park IL 60064-6400*

DEMPSTER, RYAN SCOTT, professional baseball player; b. Sechelt, BC, Can., May 3, 1977; Pitcher Fla. Marlins, 1998—2002, Cin. Reds, 2002—03, Chgo. Cubs, 2004—. Office: Chgo Cubs Wrigley Field 1060 W Addison St Chicago IL 60613 Fax: 305-626-7428.

DEMSON, PHILIP HENRY, military officer; b. Grand Junction, Colo., Feb. 6, 1983; s. Philip Leroy and Gladys Louise Demson; m. Rhianna Lynn Addyman, Nov. 29, 1980; children: Abigail Jordan, Alicia Reagan. Adminstrv. asst. to navy chief of info. for media rels. Navy Chief Info., DC, 2001—04; adminstrv. asst. leading petty officer VP-10, Brunswick, Maine, 2004—. 2d class petty officer USN, 2001—07, Omaha, Nebr. Decorated Navy and Marine Corps Achievement award Sec. Navy. Personal E-mail: philipdemsonva@gmail.com. Business E-Mail: philip.demson@navy.mil.

DEMUNBRUN-HARMON, DONNE O'DONNELL, retired family physician; b. St. Paul, Aug. 26, 1926; d. Francis Joseph and Julia (Hoffmann) O'Donnell; m. Truman Weldon DeMunbrun, Mar. 17, 1948 (dec. Aug. 1996); children: Michael J., Steven M., Julie F., Suzanne B.; m. Donald Laurance Harmon, Aug. 26, 1997. BS, U. Ky., 1948, MS, 1949; MD, U. Louisville, 1954. Diplomate Am. Bd. Family Practice. Rotating intern St. Anthony Hosp., Louisville, 1955—56; pvt. practice Louisville, 1956—85; med. dir. St. Mary and Elizabeth Hosp., Louisville, 1971—76, Parkway Med. Ctr., Louisville, 1976—99, Family Health Ctrs., Louisville, 1985—90; ret., 1999. Case reviewer Health Care Rev., Louisville, 1995-96; criteria writer Nat. Health Svcs., Louisville, 1995-96; asst. clin. prof. family practice, U. Louisville Med. Sch., 1987-90. Pres. Jacques Timothe Boucher Sieur de Montbrun Heritage Soc., Nashville, 1996-97. Recipient mayor's citation Cify of Louisville, 1990, proclamation of tribute Jefferson County, Ky., 1990. Mem.: Jefferson County Med. Soc. (life; v.p. 1976—77), Ky. Acad. Family Practice (life), Ky. Med. Assn. (life; del.), Am. Acad. Family Practice (life), Frazier Arms Mus., Filson Club, Execs. Club, Univ. Club, Sigma Pi Sigma, Pi Mu Epsilon, Alpha Lambda Delta. Avocations: gardening, reading, travel, pets. Home: 3004 Beals Branch Dr Louisville KY 40206-2902 Personal E-mail: donneharmon@bellsouth.net.

DE MUNIZ, PAUL J., state supreme court chief justice; BS, Portland State U., 1972; JD, Willamette U., 1975. Bar: (Oreg. State Bar) 1975, (U.S. Dist. Ct.) 1977, (U.S. Ct. of Appeals, Ninth Circuit) 1980, (U.S. Supreme Ct.) 1981. Atty. Garret, Seideman, Hemann, Robertson & De Muniz, P.C., 1977—90; judge Oreg. Ct. Appeals, 1990—2001, presiding judge dept. one, 1997—2000; justice Oreg. Supreme Ct., 2001—, chief justice, 2006—. Mem. Jud. Fitness & Disability Commn., Supreme Ct. Access to Justice for All Com.; chair Com. to Implement Recommendations; mem. Oreg. Supreme Ct. Task Force on Racial/Ethnic Issues in Jud. System, Defense Advisory Com. on Women in Services, 1998—2001; former prof. Nat. Jud. Coll.; former mem., chair Oreg. Criminal Justice Council. Author (with others): Immigrants in Courts, 1999. Served in USAF, 1966—70. Mem.: Oreg. State Bar, ABA. Office: Supreme Ct 1163 State St Salem OR 97301*

DEMURO, GERARD J, information technology executive; B in commn., U. Pitts., 1977; MBA, Farleigh Dickinson U. V.p., gen. mgr. GTE Govt. Systems Commn. Systems Divsn., 1997—99; pres. Gen. Dynamics Commn. Systems, 1999—2001; v.p. Gen. Dynamics Systems Corp., 1999—2003; pres. Gen. Dynamics C4 Systems, 2001—; exec. v.p., group. exec., info. sys. and tech. Gen. Dynamics Corp., 2003—. Mem.: Nat. Contracts Mgmt. Assn., Assn. of the U.S. Army, AFCEA. Office: General Dynamics Corp Ste 100 2941 Fairview Park Dr Falls Church VA 22042*

DEMURO, PAUL ROBERT, lawyer; b. Aberdeen, Md., Mar. 21, 1954; s. Paul Robert and Amelia C. DeMuro; m. Susan Taylor, May 26, 1990; children: Melissa Taylor, Natalie Lauren, Alanna Leigh. BA summa cum laude, U. Md., 1976; JD, Washington U., 1979; MBA, U. Calif., Berkeley, 1986. CPA Md.; bar: Md. 1979, U.S. Dist. Ct. Md. 1979, DC 1980, U.S. Dist. Ct. DC 1980, U.S. Tax Ct. 1981, U.S. Ct. Appeals (4th cir.) 1981, Calif. 1982, U.S. Dist. Ct. (no. dist.) Calif. 1982, U.S. Dist. Ct. (ea. dist.) Calif. 1986. Assoc. Ober, Grimes & Shriver, Balt., 1979-82; ptnr. Carpenter et al, San Francisco, 1982-89, McCutchen, Doyle, Brown & Enerson, San Francisco, 1989-93, Latham & Watkins, San Francisco, 1993—. Author: The Financial Managers Guide to Managed Care and Integrated Delivery Systems, 1995, The Fundamentals of Managed Care and Network Development, 1999; co-author: Health Care Mergers and Acquisitions: The Transactional Perspective, 1996, Health Care Executives' Guide to Fraud and Abuse, 1998; editor, contbg. author: Integrated Delivery Systems, 1994, article and rev. editor: Washington U. Law Quar., 1975—76. Mem. San Francisco Mus. Art, 1985—. Fellow: Am. Coll. Med. Practice Execs., Med. Group Mgmt. Assn. (cert. med. practice exec.), Healthcare Fin. Mgmt. Assn. (bd. dirs. No. Calif. chpt. 1990—93, nat. principles and practices bd. 1992—95, vice chair 1993—95, nat. bd. dirs. 1995—97, mem. exec. com. 1996—97, chair compliance officers forum adv. coun. 1998—2000, sec. 1999—2001, bd. dirs. No. Calif. chpt. 1999—2005, mem. nominating com. 2001—02, pres.-elect 2001—02, pres. 2002—03, mem. governance com. 2002—03); mem.: AICPA, ABA (chair transactional and bus. health care interest group 1998—2000, chair programs com. 2000—02, governing coun. 2000—, chmn. mem. and mktg. com. 2002—04, vice chair coord. com. diversity 2002—, budget officer 2003—05, chair elect 2005—06, chair 2006—07, health law sect.), Md. Assn. CPAs, San Francisco Bar Assn., Healthcare Compliance Assn. (cert. in health care compliance), Am. Coll. Healthcare Execs., Am. Health Lawyers Assn. (task force best practices in advising clients 1998—99, fraud and abuse and self-referral substantive law com. 1998—, task force on ENRON 2002), Calif. Bar Assn., LA County Bar Assn. (health law sect.). Republican. Office: Latham & Watkins LLP 505 Montgomery St Ste 2000 San Francisco CA 94111-2552 Office Phone: 415-395-8180. Business E-Mail: paul.demuro@lw.com.

DEMUTH, CHRISTOPHER CLAY, think-tank executive; b. Evanston, Ill., Aug. 5, 1946; s. Harry Clay and Ethel Marie (Schaiell) DeM.; m. Susan Ann Shultis, June 9, 1973; children: Christopher Clay, Elizabeth Ann,

Catherine Leas. AB, Harvard Coll., 1968; JD, U. Chgo., 1973. Bar: Ill. 1973, D.C. 1984. Staff asst. to Pres. Richard Nixon, Washington, 1969-70; assoc. Sidley & Austin, Chgo., 1973-76; assoc. gen. counsel Consol. Rail Corp., Phila., 1976-77; lectr., dir. regulatory studies Harvard Sch. Govt., Cambridge, Mass., 1977-81; adminstr. info. and regulatory affairs U.S. Office Mgmt. and Budget, Washington, 1981-84, exec. dir. Presdl. Task Force on Regulatory Relief, 1981-83; mng. dir. Lexecon Inc., Washington, 1984-86; editor-in-chief, pub. Regulation mag., 1986; pres. Am. Enterprise Inst. for Pub. Policy Research, Washington, 1986—. Chmn. bd. DeMuth Steel Products, 1993—, Clean Burn, Inc., 1993—; bd. dirs. State Farm Mut. Automobile Ins. Co. Republican. Episcopalian. Office: Am Enterprise Inst Pub Policy Rsch 1150 17th St NW Washington DC 20036-4603

DEMUTH, LAURENCE WHEELER, JR., lawyer, utilities executive; b. Boulder, Colo., Nov. 22; s. Laurence Wheeler and Eugenia Augusta (Roach) DeM.; m. Paula Phipps, Mar. 7, 1987; children: Debra Lynn, Laurence Wheeler III, Brant Hill. AB, U. Colo., 1951, LLB, 1953. Gen. atty. Mountain State Telephone and Telegraph Co., Denver, 1968, v.p., gen. counsel, 1968-84, sec., 1974-84; exec. v.p., gen. counsel, sec. U.S. West, Inc., Englewood, Colo., 1984-92, ret., 1992. Dist. capt. Rep. Precinct Com., 1957-70' trustee Lakewood (Colo.) Presbyn. Ch., 1965-68; bd. dirs. Colo. Epilepsy Assn., 1973-79; bd. litigation Mountain States Legal Found., 1980-89; Colo. Commr. on Uniform State of Laws, 1997—. Mem. ABA, Colo. Bar Assn. (chmn. ethics com. 1973-74, bd. govs., fellow found.), Denver Bar Assn., Am. Judicature Soc., Colo. Assn. Corp. Counsel (pres.), Order of Coif, Phi Beta Kappa, Pi Gamma Mu. Clubs: University, Metropolitan. Office: Att Broadband 183 Inverness Dr W Englewood CO 80112-5203

DEMY, TIMOTHY JAMES, military chaplain; b. Brownsville, Tex., Dec. 6, 1954; s. Millard Nile and Pauline Juanita (Owen) D.; m. Lyn Elizabeth Evans, Aug. 26, 1978. BA, Tex. Christian U., 1977; ThM, Dallas Theol. Sem., 1981, ThD, 1990; MA, U. Tex. at Arlington, 1994, Salve Regina U., 1990, PhD, 2004; MA, Naval War Coll., 1999. Commd. lt. jr. grade USN, 1981, advanced through grades to cmdr., 1993. Adj. instr. Naval War Coll., Newport, R.I., 1996—; co-dir. Ctr. for the Am. Family, Springfield, Va., 1995—. Co-author: When the Trumpet Sounds, 1995, The Coming Cashless Soc., 1996, Suicide: A Christian Response, 1998, Winning the Marriage Marathon, 1999, Genetic Engineering: A Christian Response, 1999, The Return, 1999, Politics and Public Policy: A Christian Response, 2000, In the Name of God, 2002; contbr. articles to profl. jours. Mem. Nat. Assn. Evangelicals, Evangelical Theol. Soc., Soc. Biblical Lit., Ctr. for Bioethics and Human Dignity, Orgn. Am. Historians, Naval Order U.S. Avocations: reading, cartography, animals. Office: 7 Ellen Rd Middletown RI 02842-5504 E-mail: lynd1@mindspring.com.

DENACO, PARKER ALDEN, state official, lawyer, arbitrator; b. Bangor, Maine, Apr. 19, 1943; s. Alden F. and Pauline N. Denaco; m. Gayle Gernert Denaco, May 23, 1989. BA in History and Govt., U. Maine, 1965, MBA, 1975; JD, Washington and Lee U., 1968; postgrad., Air Command and Staff Coll., 1981. Bar: Maine 1968, U.S. Dist. Ct. Maine 1968, U.S. Ct. Mil. Appeals. Assoc. Eaton & Peabody, Bangor, Maine, 1968—69; exec. officer and adj. 100 MP Bn. Ft. Bragg, NC, 1969—70; provost marshal US Army, Inchon, Republic of Korea, 1970—71; exec. dir. Maine Labor Rels. Bd., Augusta, 1972—88; state staff judge adv. Maine Air N.G., Augusta, Maine, 1973—86; legal officer 101 ARW, MeANG, Bangor, Maine, 1973—81; adj. grad. instr. Thomas Coll., Waterville, Maine, 1977—80; state staff judge adv. Maine Air N.G., Augusta, 1981—85; vis. prof. in constl. law U. Maine, 1990—91; exec. dir. N.H. Pub. Employee Labor Rels. Bd., 1991—2003; hon. faculty mem. USAF Judge Adv. Gen. Sch., Maxwell AFB, Ala. Contbr. articles to profl. jours. Bd. dirs. Acad. Collective Bargaining Info. Svc., 1979-82; bd. dirs. Pub. Employment Rels. Svcs., 1978-81; founding mem. and dir. New Eng. Consortium of State Labor Rels. Agys., 1978-2003; neutral pub. mem. Com. on Pub. Sector Bargaining, ABA, 1974—; neutral chair, 1987-01, mem. Alternate Dispute Resolution Section, ABA, 1998—; mem. Boston Adv. Coun., Am. Arbitration Assn., 1978—; elected Nat. Acad. Arbitrators, 1987; Judicial Divsn., ABA, 1998—, Nat. Conf. of Admin. Law Judges; corporator Maine Savs. Bank, 1982-84; mem. law coun. Washington and Lee U., 1988-92. Served to capt. U.S. Army, 1969-73, to col. Air NG and USAFR, 1973-95. Decorated Harmon award USAF, Legion of Merit, Meritorious Svc. medal, Inchon City medal Rep. of Korea, L'Ordre de Bon Temps Acadie Province of Nova Scotia. Fellow Coll. Labor and Employment Lawyers (chmn. First Circuit Com., 2003); mem. ABA (Disting. Svc. award 2001), Assn. Labor Rels. Agys. (pres. 1978-79), Maine Bar Assn. (labor sect. co-chmn. 1980-85), N.H. Bar Assn. (chmn. labor and employment law sect. 2002-03) Soc. Profls. in Dispute Resolution (charter), Indsl. Rels. Rsch. Assn., Nat. Acad. Arbitrators, Res. Ofcrs. Assn. (life), N.G. Assn. of U.S. (life), Phi Delta Phi, Beta Gamma Sigma. also: PO Box 227 Lincolnville ME 04849-0227 Home and Office: 48 Augusta Way Dover NH 03820 Office Phone: 603-343-5166 Personal E-mail: denaco4adr@yahoo.com.

DEN ADEL, RAYMOND LEE, classics educator; b. Pella, Iowa, Apr. 23, 1932; s. John J. and Nellie (DeGeus) D. BA, Ctrl. Coll., 1954; MA, U. Iowa, 1959; PhD, U. Ill., 1971. Latin tchr. Pella HS, 1954-55; grad. student Am. Acad., Rome, 1960, Vergilian Sch., Cumae, Italy, 1960, 73; fellow U. Iowa, Iowa City, 1957-58, tchg. asst., 1962-63; Latin and English tchr. Proviso West H.S., Hillside, Ill., 1958-62; v.p. Proviso Ednl. Assn., 1960-61; grad. student Am. Sch. Classical Studies, Athens, 1961, on-site participant, 1989, 1990; fellow, asst. and instr. in classics U. Ill., Urbana, 1963-67; dir. Ill. HS Latin Conf., 1967; faculty, chair classics dept. Rockford Coll., Ill., 1967—97, chair div. lang. and lit., 1971—74, prof., 1975—97, prof. emeritus, 1997—. Lectr. Ctr. for Learning in Retirement Rock Valley Coll., 2001—03; lectr. Beloit Coll., 1985. Bd. dirs. Rockford Cmty. Concert Assn., 1979-85; mem. Burpee Museum of Natural Hist. (life); mem. exec. com. Archaeol. Inst. Am., 1976-82, governing bd., 1990-96, trustee, 1990-94, v.p., 1994-96, Disting. Svc. award, 1997. With CIC, U.S. Army, 1955-57. Fulbright grant, Rome, 1960; named Vol. of Yr., Source Program in Rockford, 1983, Outstanding Coll. Latin Tchr. in Ill., 1987, Outstanding Fgn. Lang. Tchr. in Ill., 1989; recipient AIA Colloquium of Honor, 1997. Mem.: AAUP (pres. Rockford chpt. 1974—76, Ill. coun. 1977—80, sec. 1984—86, v.p. 1988—89), AIA (Ctrl. Ill. Soc. sec.-treas. 1966—67, mem. nat. coun. 1966—98, Rockford Soc. pres. 1968—70, 1972—74, 1991—93, sec. Rockford chpt. 1993—94, v.p. 1998—99), Classical Soc. Am. Acad. Rome (sec. 1990—93), Ill. Coun. Tchg. Fgn. Langs., Biblical Archaeol. Soc., Am. Assn. Dutch-Am. Studies, Vergilian Soc. Am. (life; sec. 1978—80), Classical Assn. Mid. West and South (life; 1st v.p. 1980—81), Fulbright Alumni Assn. (life), Ill. Classical Conf. (life; v.p. 1968—69, pres. 1969—70), Am. Philol. Assn. (life Field Scholarship award 1961), Am. Classical League (life; nat. coun. 1969—82, Scholarship award 1960), Pella Hist. Soc., Chgo. Classical Club (life; v.p. 1975—77, pres. 1977—79), Rotary (bd. dirs. Rockford chpt. 1987—89, dist. gov. rep. 1989—91, bd. dirs. Rockford chpt. 1991—95, v.p. 1992—93, pres. 1993—94, dist. gov. rep. 1994—97, gov. dist. 6420 1997—98, chmn. past dist. gov. coun. 2001, Paul Harris 711 Club, life, bd. dirs. 2002—, Svc. Above Self award Rockford Club and Dist. 6420 1989, Paul Harris fellow, benefactor 1982), Chi Gamma Iota (life), Phi Sigma Iota (life), Phi Beta Kappa (life; v.p. 1988—89, triennial coun. 1988—2003, pres. Eta Ill. chpt. 1989—92), Eta Sigma Phi (life; nat. exec. sec. 1974—78), Sigma Tau Delta. Presbyterian. Avocations: photography, travel, reading, stamp collecting/philately, music. Home: 701 Broadway St Pella IA 50219

DENAPOLI, DYAN, small business owner, educational consultant; b. Salem, Mass. d. Paul Angelo and Phyllis Carter deNapoli. AA in Liberal Arts, Colby-Sawyer Coll., New London, NH, 1981; BS in Animal Sci., Mt. Ida Coll., Newton Ctr., Mass., 1996. Cert. vet. technician N.Am. Vet. Tech. Assn., 1995. Owner, silversmith Dyan deNapoli Jewelry, Beverly, Mass., 1985—94; vet. nurse Winchester Animal Hosp., Mass., 1996—97; sr. penguin aquarist New Eng. Aquarium, Boston, 1997—2004; owner, ednl. cons. The Penguin Lady, Georgetown, Mass., 2004—. Bd. mem. vet. tech. adv. com. Mt. Ida Coll., 2003—. Jewelry exhibition, Thomas Mann Gallery, New Orleans, 1971; author: (book) The Great Penguin Rescue; contbr. chapter to book, articles to profl. jours. Vol. Spl. Olympics, Danvers, Mass., 1985—92, Animals as Intermediaries, Concord, Mass., 2005—. Mem.: N.Shore Bus. Forum, Homebased Businesswomen's Net-work (v.p. 2007—), N.Shore Women in Bus., Mass. Marine Educators Assn., Nat. Marine Educators Assn., Mensa. Avocations: skiing, sailing, scuba diving, photography, travel. Office: The Penguin Lady 7 Rock Pond Ave Georgetown MA 01833 Office Phone: 978-352-2235. Business E-Mail: dyan@thepenguinlady.com.

DENARO, ANTHONY THOMAS, psychiatrist; b. NYC, Aug. 9, 1929; s. Joseph and Maria (DeGennaro) Denaro; m. Mitsuru Suzuki, Nov. 23, 1963. BS, CCNY, 1960; MD, U. Okla., 1969; MPA, U. Hartford, 1981. Diplomate Nat. Bd. Med. Examiners, Am. Bd. Psychiatry, Am. Bd. Gen. Psychiatry and Child Psychiatry, Adminstrv. Psychiatry. Intern Nassau County Med. Ctr., East Meadow, NY, 1969-70; resident in child psychiatry U. Pa., Phila., 1970-72, resident in gen. psychiatry, 1972-74; dir. child psychiatry U. Conn. Health Ctr., Farmington, 1974-78; dir. adolescent unit Natchaug Psychiat. Hosp., Willamantic, Conn., 1978-80; assoc. dir. child and adolescent service Mt. Sinai Hosp., Hartford, Conn., 1980-82; assoc. dir. child and adolescent psychiatry Elmcrest Psychiat. Inst., Portland, Conn., 1982-84; dir. outpatient psychiatry Woodhull Med. and Mental Health Ctr., NYC, 1984-85; dir. child and adolescent psychiatry First Hosp. Wyoming Valley, Kingston, Pa., 1985-98; child and adolescent behavioral health svcs. Child Devel. Clinic, Scranton, Pa., 1998—2001; dir. child and adolescent svcs. First Hosp. Wyoming Valley, Kingston, 2001—04; with KidsPeace Nat. Ctrs., Temple, Pa., 2004—. Asst. prof. dept. psychiatry U. Conn. Sch. Medicine, Farmington, 1974-83. With U.S. Army, 1947-49. Fellow Am. Acad. Child and Adolescent Psychiatry; mem. AMA, Am. Psychiat. Assn., Am. Assn. Psychiat. Adminstrs., Northeastern Pa. Psychiat. Soc. (pres. 1990-91), Phi Beta Kappa. Republican. Office: KidsPeace Nat Ctrs 8th Ave and May Rd Temple PA 19560

DE NATALE, ANDREW PETER, lawyer; b. Bklyn., July 7, 1950; s. Peter E. and Mary (Tamberino) DeN.; m. Lynn Susan Kennedy, July 28, 1973; children: Andrew, Christopher. BS in Econs., U. Pa., 1972; JD, Fordham U., 1975. Bar: N.Y. 1976, U.S. Dist. Ct. (so. dist.) N.Y. 1976, U.S. Dist. Ct. (ea. dist.) N.Y. 1977, U.S. Ct. Appeals (2d cir.) 1978, U.S. Supreme Ct. 1979, U.S. Dist. Ct. (no. dist.) N.Y. 1982. Assoc. Krause, Hirsch & Gross, NYC, 1975-79, Stroock & Stroock & Lavan, NYC, 1980-83, ptnr., 1984-91, White & Case, NYC, 1991—. Contbr. numerous articles to newspapers and profl. jours. Mem.: ABA, INSOL Internat., Am. Bankruptcy Inst., N.Y. Yacht Club, Seawanhaka Corinthian Yacht Club. Office: White & Case LLP 1155 Avenue Of The Americas New York NY 10036-2787 Home Phone: 516-628-2002; Office Phone: 212-819-8303. Business E-Mail: adenatale@whitecase.com.

DENAULT, LEO P., energy executive; BS in Econs. and Acctg., Ball State U., Muncie, Ind., 1982; MBA, Ind. U., Bloomington, 1991. Staff acct. Cinergy Corp., Cin., 1982, various positions in tax acctg., budget and fin. analysis and strategic planning, mgr. corp. devel., 1991, v.p. corp. devel., Entergy Corp., New Orleans, 1999—2002, v.p. corp. devel. and strategic planning, 2002—04, exec. v.p., CFO, 2004—. Office: Entergy Corp 639 Loyola Ave New Orleans LA 70113 Office Phone: 504-576-4000.*

DENCE, EDWARD WILLIAM, JR., retired lawyer, bank executive; b. Newport, RI, Feb. 25, 1938; s. Edward William and Dorothea Margaret (Conway) D.; m. Claire A. Guertin, Nov. 14, 1970; children: Suzanne Lynn, Christine Anne. AB summa cum laude, Providence Coll., 1959; LL.B., Harvard U., 1963. Bar: Mass. 1963, R.I. 1965. Atty. New Eng. Electric System, 1963-68; sec., gen. counsel, v.p., mem. mgmt. com. Fleet Boston Fin. Corp. (now Bank of Am. Corp.), Providence, 1969—85; atty. Ropes and Gray Law Firm, 1985—92, Edwards Angell Palmer & Dodge Law Firm LLP, Providence, 1992—2007; ret., 2007. Mem. stockholders' adv. com. Fed. Res. Bank, Boston. Trustee, chmn. audit com., chmn. compensation com. St. Joseph Hosp., 1994-2006; trustee So. New Eng. Rehab. Ctr., 1994-2006. Named One of Outstanding Young Men in Am., 1972 Mem. R.I. Bar Found. (scholarship com.), R.I. Bar Assn., Boston Bar Assn. Home: 1485 High Hawk Rd East Greenwich RI 02818-1364

DENCH, JUDI, actress; b. York, Eng., Dec. 9, 1934; d. Reginald Arthur and Eleanora Olave (Jones) D.; m. Michael Williams, Feb. 5, 1971 (dec. Jan. 11, 2001); 1 child, Tara Cressida Frances. Student, Ctrl. Sch. Speech Tng.; LittD (hon.), Warwick U., 1978, York U., 1983, Oxford U., 2000, Trinity Coll., 2003. Theatrical appearances include: (Old Vic) Hamlet, Midsummer Night's Dream, Twelfth Night, 1957-58, The Importance of Being Earnest, As You Like It, Romeo and Juliet, 1959-61; (Venice Festival) Romeo and Juliet (Paladino d'Argentino), 1961; (Royal Shakespeare Co., Stratford) The Cherry Orchard, Measure for Measure, Midsummer Night's Dream, A Penny for a Song, 1961-62; (Oxford Playhouse) The Alchemist, The Three Sisters, Romeo and Jeanette, 1964; (Oxford and London) The Promise, 1966-67; (London) Sally Bowles in Cabaret, 1968; (Royal Shakespeare Co., London) Twelfth Night, A Winter's Tale, London (Royal Shakespeare Co., Stratford) The Merchant of Assurance, 1970; (Royal Shakespeare Co., Stratford) The Merchant of Venice, The Duchess of Malfi, 1971; tour of Japan with Twelfth Night, 1972; (London) London Assurance, 1973; (Oxford and London) The Wolf, 1974; (London) The Good Companions, 1974-75, The Gay Lord Quex, 1975; (Royal Shakespeare Co., Stratford) Much Ado About Nothing, The Comedy of Errors, Macbeth (SWET Best Actress award for Lady Macbeth), King Lear, 1976-77; Cymbeline, 1979; (Royal Shakespeare Co., London) Pillars of the Community, The Way of the World, 1977-78, (Aldwych) Juno and the Paycock (SWET Best Actress award, Evening Std. Drama award for best actress, Plays and Players award for Best Actress, Variety Club award Actress of Yr.), 1981, A Kind of Alaska, The Importance of Being Earnest (Std. Best Actress award, Plays and Players award for best actress), Pack of Lies (Plays and Players award, SWET Best Actress award, Laurence Olivier Theatre award), Mr. and Mrs. Nobody, 1988, Antony and Cleopatra (Laurence Olivier Theatre award, Evening Std. Drama award, Drama mag. award), Gertrude in Hamlet, The Cherry Orchard, 1989, 90, The Blough and the Stars, The Sea, Coriolanus, 1992, The Gift of the Gorgon, 1992-93, The Seagull, 1994, Filumena in London, 1998, Amy's View in New York, 1999, The Royal Family, 2001, The Breath of Life, 2002, All's Well That Ends Well, London and Stratford-upon-Avon, 2003-04; dir. plays Much Ado About Nothing, Look Back in Anger, The Boys from Syracuse, Romeo and Juliet; TV appearances include: Major Barbara, Talking to a Stranger (Best TV Actress of Yr. award 1967), Jackanory, Luther, Neighbours, Marching Song, Days to Come, The Comedy of Errors, Macbeth, Village Wooing, Love in a Cold Climate, A Fine Romance, The Cherry Orchard, Going Gently, Saigon, Mr. and Mrs. Edgehill, 1988 (ACE award), Ghosts, Make and Break, Behaving Badly, Can You Hear Me Thinking, Torch, Absolute Hell (Oliver award Best Actress 1996), As Time Goes By; (films): He Who Rides a Tiger, A Study in Terror, Four in the Morning (Brit. Film Acad. Most Promising Newcomer award 1965), A Midsummer Night's Dream, The Third Secret, Dead Cert, Wetherby, 1985, A Room with a View, 84 Charing Cross Road, A Handful of Dust (Brit. Acad. Film and TV Arts award 1989), Henry V, 1989, Jack & Sarah, 1994, Golden Eye, 1995, A Little Night Music, 1995 (Oliver award Best Actress in a Musical 1996), Mrs. Brown (Brit. Acad. Film and TV Arts Scotland award 1997, Critics Circle Film award 1997, Golden Globe award for best actress 1997, Acad. award nomination 1997), Amy's View, 1997 (Critics Circle Drama award 1997), Tomorrow Never Dies, 1997, Shakespeare in Love, 1998 (Acad. award Best Supporting Actress 1998), Tea With Mussolini, 1999, The World is Not Enough, 1999, The Last of the Blond Bombshells, 2000, Chocolat, 2000, Iris, 2002 (BAFTA award best actress), The Shipping News, 2002, The Importance of Being Ernest, 2002, Die Another Day, 2002, Home on the Range (voice), 2004, The Chronicles of Riddick, 2004, Ladies In Lavender, 2004, Pride & Prejudice, 2005, Mrs. Henderson Presents, 2005, (voice) Doogal, 2006, Casino Royale, 2006, Notes on a Scandal, 2006. Recipient Rothermore award for lifetime achievement, 1997, Critics Circle award for outstanding svc. to the arts, Acad. Award for Best Supporting Actress for Shakespeare in Love, 1999, Tony Award for Best Actress in Amy's View; decorated Order Brit. Empire, Dame Comdr. Brit. Empire, Order Companion of Honour, 2005; named UK Entertainment Personality of Yr. Variety, 1999, Walpole medal, NY, 2000, Benjamin Franklin medal, Royal Soc. Arts, London, 2000, Golden Globe award for best supporting actress in Chocolat, 2000, Olivier award lifetime achievement, 2004, Evening Standard Theater award, 2004; BAFTA fellow, 2001, Lucy Cavendish Coll. fellow, Cambridge, Eng., 2005. Mem. Religious Soc. Friends.

DENDA, KAYO, librarian; b. Nagoya, Japan; arrived in US, 1979; m. Mitsunori Denda; children: Yasuhiro, Kenji. BS, Federal U. of Rio de Janeiro, Brazil; MLS, Rutgers U., 1997, MA in women's studies, 2006. Asst. libr. Hist. Studies-Social Sci. Libr., Inst. Advanced Study, Princeton, NJ, 1997—2001; women's & gender studies libr. Douglass Libr., Rutgers U. Librs., New Brunswick, NJ, 2001—. Mem. NJ Hist. Commn., 2007—. Mem.: Assn. Coll. & Rsch. Librs. (Women's Studies sect., WSS sec. 2003—04, WSS Significant Achievement award 2007). Office: Rutgers U Librs Mabel Smith Douglass Libr 8 Chapel Dr New Brunswick NJ 08901 Office Phone: 732-932-9407 ext. 23. Office Fax: 732-923-6777. E-mail: kdenda@rci.rutgers.edu.

DENDINGER, WILLIAM J., career officer, chaplain; BA in Philosophy and English, Immaculate Conception Sem., 1961; MA in Theology, Aquinas Inst., 1964; MS in Counseling, Creighton U., 1969; student, Squadron Officer Sch., 1973; postgrad., Sch. Applied Theology, 1978; student, Air War Coll., 1987. Commd. capt. USAF, 1970, advanced through grades to maj. gen., 1997; base chaplain Maxwell AFB, Ala., 1970-72, Yokota Air Base, Japan, 1972-74; cadet wing chaplain USAF Acad., Colorado Springs, Colo., 1974-78; base chaplain Osan Air Base, S. Korea, 1979-80, Mather AFB, Calif., 1980-82; mem. chaplain resource bd. USAF Chaplain Svc. Inst., Maxwell AFB, 1982-85; base chaplain Hahn Air Base, W. Germany, 1985-88; plans and programs officer then chief plans/programs div. Office Air Force Chief Chaplains, Bolling AFB, D.C., 1988-93; command chaplain Hdqs. Air Combat Command, Langley AFB, Va., 1993-95; dep. chief Air Force Chaplain Svc. Hdqs. USAF, Washington, 1995-97, chief Air Force Chaplain Svc., 1997—. Decorated Legion of Merit with oak leaf cluster. Named Prelate of Honor with title of Rev. Monsignor, His Holiness Pope John Paul II, 1994. Office: HQ USAF/HC 112 Luke Ave SW Ste 316 Bolling Afb DC 20332-5113

DENENBERG, DAVID SCOTT, sports association executive, lawyer; s. Allan and Betty Denenberg; m. Marni Jill Schlissel, May 6, 1995; children: Zoe, Ethan, Madelyn. Grad. magna cum laude, Colgate U., Hamilton, NY, 1988; grad. cum laude, Harvard Law Sch., 1991. Atty. corp. dept. Paul, Hastings, Janofsky & Walker, NYC; positions up to sr. v.p. legal and bus. affairs NBA Entertainment, Secaucus, NJ, 1995—. Office: NBA Entertainment 450 Harmon Meadow Blvd Secaucus NJ 07094*

DENENBERG, HERBERT SIDNEY, journalist, lawyer, educator, retired state official; b. Omaha, Nov. 20, 1929; s. David Aaron and Fannie (Rothenberg) Denenberg; m. Naomi N. Glushakow, June 22, 1958. BS, Johns Hopkins U., 1958; JD, Creighton U., 1954; LLM, Harvard U., 1959; PhD, U. Pa., 1962; LLD, Allentown Coll. St. Francis de Sales, 1989; LHD, Spring Garden Coll., 1992. CLU, CPCU. Mem. firm Denenberg & Denenberg, Omaha, 1954—55; asst. prof. ins. U. Iowa, Iowa City, 1962, Wharton Sch. Fin. and Commerce, U. Pa., 1962—65, assoc. prof., 1965—68, Harry J. Loman prof. ins., 1968—73; commr. ins. State of Pa., 1971—74; commr. Pa. Pub. Utility Commn., 1975; columnist Phila. Bull., 1975—79; consumer columnist Phila. Daily News, 1979—81, Phila. Jour., 1981—82, Del. County Daily and Sunday Times, 1987—90, Bucks County Courier Times, 1987—90, Pottstown Mercury, 1988—94, Burlington County Daily Times, 1987—90, Reading Eagle, 1989—, Doylestown Patriot, 1991—, Citizen's Choice of Wilkes-Barre, Pa., 1992—, Mainliner, 1992—94, Auto Insider, 1992—93, Collector's Guide, 1992—93, New Chester Jour., 1992—94, Del. County Bus. Monthly, 1993—96, Hellenic News, 1993—, 1994, Phoenixville, Phoenix, 1994—96, Eastern Poconos Cmty. News, 1999—; editor The Denenberg Report Orgn., 1999—; consumer and investigative reporter Adelphia Cable Update Cable Sys., 1999—2000, Sta. WCAU-TV (NBC), Phila., 1975—98; talk show host Sta. WCAU-AM CBS, Phila., 1976—80; consumer reporter WLVT-TV (PBS), 2001—. Columnist Sales and Mktg. Mag., 1976—80, Ins. Monitor, Hyderabad, India; regular on Real People NBC-TV, 1979—80; consumer reporter Nat. Pub. Radio, 1979; spl. counsel, rsch. dir. Pres.'s Nat. Adv. Panel on Ins. in Riot-Affected Areas., 1967—68; spl. adviser to Gov. Pa. on consumer affairs, 1974—75; assoc. dir. Wis. Ins. Laws Rev. Project, 1966—71; cons. Dept. Labor, 1965—68, Coop. Devel. Adminstrn., PR, 1967—68, John F. Kennedy Ctr., Washington, 1966—71, Small Bus. Adminstrn., 1968—71, Dept. Justice, 1969, FTC, 1968, Dept. Transp., 1969—70, State of Nev., 1969—71. Alaska Legislature, 1976, U.S. Commn. Civil Rights, 1977—78, Concerned Physicians for Patient Care; spl. cons. to Mayor Washington, 1968—69; mem. Bd. of Health Promotion and Disease Prevention of Inst. Medicine NAS, 1973—74, mem., 1973—; vis. prof. law Temple U.; adj. prof. ins., info. sci. and tech. Cabrini Coll., 1999—; rsch. fellow Sapio Inst. Interactive Learning, 1999—. Author (with others): (book) Risk and Insurance, 2d edit., 1973; author: (with Spencer L. Kimball) Insurance Government and Social Policy, 1969; author: (with J.R. Ferrari) Life Insurance and/or Mutual Funds, 1967; author: (with S.L. Kimball) Mass Marketing of Property and Liability Insurance, 1970; author: The Insurance Trap, 1972, Shopper's guide to Surgery, 1972, Shopper's Guide to Dentistry, 1973, Shopper's Guide to Insurance on Mobile Homes, 1973, A Citizens Bill of Hospital Rights, 1973, Shopper's guide to Bankruptcy, 1974, Shopper's guide Book, 1974, Herb Denenberg's Smart Shopper's Guide, 1980, Shopper's guide to Medical Equipment, 1990, A Consumer's Guide to Herbal Medicines, 1999, Guide to Selecting a Pharmacist, 1999; columnist, mem. editl. bd. Caveat Emptor, 1971—79; columnist: Phila. Evening Bulletin; mem. adv. bd. medicine and health newsletter The Dr.'s People, 1989—93. Mem. adminstrv. bd. S.S. Huebner Found., 1968—71; pres. Am. Risk and Ins. Assn., 1969—70; Dem. candidate U.S. Senate, 1974; bd. dirs. Consumers Union, 1973—76; bd. trustees Ctr. for Proper Medication Use, 1994—. 1st lt. JAGC US Army, 1955—58. Named to Phila. Press Club Hall of Fame, 1995; recipient awards for articles, Jour. Risk and Ins., Lambert award, 1972, Nat. Press Club award, 1976, 1977, 1980, 1984, 1988, Journalism award, Am. Osteo. Assn., 1976, Am. Chiropractors Assn., 1977—80, 1988, citation, Columbia U., Media award, ATLA, 1986, Enterprise Reporting award, Phila. Press Club, 1986, 1987, 1999, Pub. Svc. award, 1987, 1989, 1996, 1997, 1999, Best Feature award, 1995, 1996, 1997, Spot News award, 1999, award for lifetime achievement, 1998, Gov.'s Hwy. Safety award, State of Pa., 1997, Enterprise Reporting award, Pa. AP, 1988, Nat. Headliner award, 1987—88, 1990, 1992, 40 Emmy awards, Best TV Pub. Svc. award, Soc. Profl. Journalists, 1987, 1988, 1990, 1992, 1993, 1994, 1998, 1999, TV Feature award, 1989, 1994, 1995, 1996, 1997, 1998, TV Mag. Feature award, 1989, 1992, Best Media Criticism, 1990, 1993, Best Investigation, 1990, 1992, 1993, 1994, 1995, 1996, 1997, 1998, 1999, Best Health and Sci. Report, 1995—99, Breaking News award, 1998, Outstanding Media Consumer Svc. award, Consumer Fedn. Am., 1990, Sam Beber

Disting. AZA Alumnus award, B'nai B'rith, 1990, Outstanding Citizen award, Firemen's Assn. Pa., 1991, Consumer of Yr. award, Pa. Assn. Weights and Measures, 1991, Phila. award integrity in journalism, 1988, Award of Excellence in legal reporting and analysis, Am. Bd. Trial Advocates, 1996, Award of Lifetime Achievement, Phila. Press Club, 1998, Award for Excellence in Legal Reporting and Analysis, Am. Bd. Trial Advocates, 1996, Phila. Press Club award for lifetime achievement, 1998, others, Am. Bd. Trial Advocates award, 1996. Mem.: ABA (life), Internat. Assn. Ins. Law (v.p. sci. sect. Am. chpt. 1967—71), Med. Soc. Access to Physicians (blue ribbon panel Phila. County 1998—), Am. Risk and Ins. Assn. (2nd v.p. 1967—68, bd. dirs. 1967—71, pres. 1969—70), Montgomery County Bar Assn., Pa. Bar Assn., Old Clunker Club (founder, pres. 1982—). Home: PO Box 7301 Saint Davids PA 19087-7301 Office Phone: 610-687-0293. Personal E-mail: hdenenberg@aol.com. *Our governmental system is designed to make politicians fat and special interests groups rich. Government has become our number "one" consumer fraud. As a government official, educator, and author I have attempted to make government work for people instead of for special interests and politicians only. I have been willing to make waves and rock boats. I have tried to show that government can help people.*

DENETT, PAUL ALFRED, federal official; b. 1946; m. Lucy Denett; children: Scott, Michael. MSA, George Washington U. Dir. adminstrn., sr. procurement exec. Office of Sec. U.S. Dept. Interior, vice chmn. chief acquisition officers coun.; program dir. Logistics Mgmt. Inst., 2001—02; v.p. contracting programs ESI Internat., 2003—06; counselor to dep. dir. for mgmt. Office Mgmt. and Budget, 2006, adminstr. Office Fed. Procurement Policy, 2006—. Recipient Presdl. Rank Award, E.R. "Dick" Alley, Jr. award, Com. for Purchase from People Who Are Blind or Severly Disabled, 1999. Office: Office Fed Procurement Policy 17th and Pennsylvania Ave NW Washington DC 20503

DE NEUFVILLE, PIERRE, retired brokerage house executive; b. Paris, Sept. 15, 1924; came to U.S., 1974; s. Andre and Jacqueline (de Villeneuve) de N.; 1 child, Oliver. BA, Sorbonne U., 1946. Asst. v.p. LaCruz, Linares, Spain, 1947-50; USAF liaison Coca-Cola Internat., Paris, 1950-54; mgr. sales promotion France-Presse, Paris, 1954-56; mgr. Hayden Stone, Paris, 1956-64; resident ptnr. Bache and Co., Paris, 1964-73; internat. v.p. Lehman Bros., NYC, 1973-87; mgr. internat. dept. Balis, Zorn, Gerard Inc., NYC, 1987-89; ret., 1989; writer. Author: The Half Wit, 1987, The Red Star, 1987. Counsel to co-chmn. U.S. Senate/Congress Peace Through Strength, Washington, 1987—. Served to brig. gen. Free French Army. Decorated Medaille Militaire, 3 Croix de Guerres France; recipient U.S. Presdl. Order of Merit. Sufi. Club: Yacht Club de France. Avocations: philosophy, writing, sailing.

DE NEUFVILLE, RICHARD LAWRENCE, engineering educator; b. NYC, May 6, 1939; s. Lawrence Eustace and Adeline de N.; m. Virginia Lyons; children: Robert, Julie. SB, SM, MIT, 1961, PhD, 1965; Dr. h.c (hon.), Tech U., Delft, 2002. Asst. prof. to assoc. prof. dept. civil engring. MIT, Cambridge, Mass., 1965-75, prof., chmn. Tech. and Policy Program, 1975-2000, prof. engring sys., 2000—. Vis. prof. U. Calif., Berkeley, 1974—76, London Grad. Sch. Bus., 1973, Ecole Centrale de Paris, 1981—82; adj. prof. Ecole Nationale des Ponts et Chausees of Paris, 1988—2004, U. Bristol, England, 1992—99; vis. prof. Australian Bur. Transport and Comml. Econs., 1995; mem. vis. com. U. Va., Charlottesville, 1987, Tech. U., Delft, Eindhoven and Utrecht, 1996—97, Instituto Superior Tecnico, Portugal, 2004, U.S. Army Engring. Ctr., 2005; vis. prof. Harvard U., 2000—; advisor Alta. Heritage Fund for Sci. and Engring. Rsch., 2000—, B.C. Leading Edge Found., 2003, Laing O'Rourke, PLC; adj. prof. Ecole Hassania des Travaux Publics of Casablanca, 2000—01, MBA des Ponts, 2000—05; vis. prof. Balliol Coll., Oxford U., 2001; life mem. Clare Hall Coll., Cambridge U., 2002—; mem. Netherlands Rev. on Engring. Sys., 2002—03; sr. rsch. assoc. Judge Inst. Author: Airport Systems Planning, Design and Management, 2003, Applied Systems Analysis, 1990, Airport Systems Planning, 1976, Systems Planning and Design, 1979, Systems Analysis for Engineers and Managers, 1971; editor Jour. Transp. Rsch., 1975-86, Jour. Air Transport Mgmt., 1993—, Internat. Jour. Tech. Policy and Mgmt., 1999—. Bd. dirs. Geographic Data Tech., 1982-90, Urban Data Processing, 1970-80, Ecole Bilingue, French-Am. Internat. Sch. of Boston, 1992-97; trustee Kennedy Meml. Trust (U.K.), 1993-98; Consejo del Rector, Universidad Anahuac del Sur, Mexico, 1999. 1st lt. C.E., U.S. Army, 1961-62. Decorated chevalier Ordre des Palmes Academiques (France); White House fellow, 1964-65, Guggenheim fellow, 1973, U.S.-Japan Leadership fellow, 1990, Class of 1960 fellow, 2000; recipient Sys. Sci. prize NATO, 1974, Risk and Ins. prize Risk and Ins. Soc., 1976, Alpha Kappa Psi award, 1985, Engring. Excellence award Australia Instn. Engrs., 1986, Irwin Sizer award, 1988, FAA prize for tchg. excellence, 1990, Martore prize for tchg. excellence, 2004. Mem. ASCE (life), AAAS, Ops. Rsch. Soc. Am., Brit.-N.Am. Com., Am. Alpine Club, Cambridge Boat Club, Cambridge Skating Club, Cambridge Tennis Club, Internat. House of Japan. Office: MIT Rm E40-245 Cambridge MA 02139 Office Phone: 617-253-7694. Business E-Mail: ardent@mit.edu.

DENEUVE, CATHERINE (CATHERINE DORLEAC), actress; b. Paris, Oct. 22, 1943; d. Maurice Dorleac and Renee Deneuve; m. David Bailey, 1965 (div. 1970); children: Christian Vadim, Chiara Mastroianni. Student, Lycée La Fontaine, Paris. Co-chair UNESCO campaign to protect World's Film Heritage, 1994—. Films include Les Petits Chats, 1956, Les Collegiennes, 1956, Les portes claquent, 1960, Les Parisiennes, 1961, Et Satan conduit le bal, 1962, Vacances portugaises, 1963, Le Vice et la Vertu, 1963, Les Parapluies de Cherbourg, 1964 (Golden Palm of Cannes Festival), La Chasse à l'homme, 1964, Les Plus belles escroqueries du monde, 1964, Un Monsieur de compagnie, 1964, Repulsion, 1965, Coeur à la gorge, 1965, Le Chant de Ronde, 1965, La Vie de Chateau, 1965, Les créatures, 1966, Les Demoiselles de Rochefort, 1966, Benjamin, 1967, Manon 70, 1967, Belle de Jour, 1967 (Golden Lion of Venice Festival), Meyerling, 1967, La Chamade, 1968, The April Fools, 1968, La Sirène du Mississippi, 1968, Tristana, 1969, It Only Happens to Others, 1971, Dirty Money, Hustle, 1975, Lovers Like Us, 1975, Act of Aggression, 1976, March or Die, 1977, La Grande Bourgeoise, 1977, The Last Metro, 1980, A Second Chance, 1981, Reporters, 1982, The Hunger, 1983, Fort Saganne, Scene of the Crime, Agent Trouble, 1987, FM-Frequency Murder, 1988, Drole d'endroit Pour Une Rencontre, 1988, Helmut Newton: Frames from the Edge, 1989, Indochine, 1992 (César award Best Actress, Acad. award nominee for Best Actress), Ma Saison Preferee, 1993, La Partie d'Echecs, 1994, Les Cent et Une Nuits, 1995, Les Voleurs, 1996, Place Vendome, 1997, Gènèalogies d'un Crime, 1997, Pola X, 1998, Le Temps retrouvé, La Princesse de Clèves, 1999, The Last Napoleon, 1999, Est, ouest, 1999, Le Vent de la nuit, 1999, Belle Maman, 1999, Dancer in the Dark, 2000, Je rentre à la maison, 2001, Absolument fabuleux, 2001, The Musketeer, 2001, Le Petit poucet, 2001, 8 femmes, 2002 (Berlin Film Festival Silver Bear for Individual Artistic Contbn.), Au plus près du paradis, 2002, Um Filme Falado, 2003; TV movies include Les Liaisons dangereuses, 2003, Princesse Marie, 2004; prodr. A Strange Place to Meet, 1988. Recipient Berlin Film Festival Golden Bear for Lifetime Achievement, 1998, Venice Film Festival Silver Lion for Best Actress, 1998, Bangkok Internat. Film Festival Golden Kinnaree Career Achievement award, 2006. Office: 76 Rue Bonaparte 75006 Paris France

DENEVAN, WILLIAM MAXFIELD, geographer, historical ecologist, educator; b. San Diego, Oct. 16, 1931; s. Lester W. and Wilda M. D.; m. Patricia Sue French, June 21, 1958; children: Curtis, Victoria. BA, U. Calif., Berkeley, 1953, MA, 1958, PhD, 1963. Faculty dept. geography U. Wis., Madison, 1963-94, prof., 1972-94, chmn. dept., 1980-83, dir. L.Am. Ctr., 1975-77, prof. emeritus, 1994—. Author/co-author: The Upland Pine Forests of Nicaragua, 1961, The Aboriginal Cultural Geography of the Llanos de Mojos of Bolivia, 1966, The Biogeography of a Savanna Landscape, Eastern Peru, 1970, Adaptive Strategies in Karinya Subsistance, Venezuelan Llanos, 1978, Campos Elevados en los Llanos Occidentales de Venezuela, 1979, Cultivated Landscapes of Native Amazonia and the Andes, 2001; editor/co-editor: The Native Population of the Americas in 1492, 1976, Pre-Hispanic Agricultural Fields in the Andean Region, 1987, Swidden-Fallow Agroforestry in the Peruvian Amazon, 1988, Hispanic Lands and Peoples, 1989, Las Chacras de Coporaque, 1994; contbr. 75 articles to profl. jours., chpts. to books. With USNR, 1950—55. Fulbright grantee, 1957; grantee NRC, 1961-62, Ford Found., 1965-66, NSF, 1972-73, 84-86, Nat. Geog. Soc., 1985-86, NEH, 1989-90; Guggenheim fellow, 1977-78. Mem. Assn. Am. Geographers (Honors award 1987), Am. Geog. Soc., Am. Anthrop. Assn., Soc. for Am. Archaeology, Am. Acad. Arts and Scis. Personal E-mail: sbden@saber.net.

DENG, LI, computer scientist, researcher, electrical engineer; b. Fujian, China, June 29, 1958; arrived in U.S., 1982; s. Weiqun Deng and Liqiong He. BS, U. Sci. and Tech. China, Hefei, 1982; MS, U. Wis., Madison, 1984, PhD, 1986. Asst. prof. U. Waterloo, Ont., Canada, 1989—92, assoc. prof., 1992—96, prof., 1996—99; prin. rschr. Microsoft Rsch., Redmond, Wash., 1999—. Author: Speech Processing, 2003, Dynamic Speech Models, 2006. Recipient Guo Mo Ruo prize, U. Sci. and Tech. China, 1981. Fellow: IEEE (tech. chair ICASSP 2004, gen. chair workshop 2006), Acoustical Soc. Am. Office Phone: 425-706-2719. Business E-Mail: deng629@gmail.com.

DENG, LUOL, professional basketball player; b. Wow, Sudan, Apr. 16, 1985; s. Aldo. Student, Duke U., Durham, NC, 2003—04. Draft pick Phoenix Suns, 2004; guard-forward Chgo. Bulls, 2004—. Named Most Outstanding Player, NCAA Atlanta Regional, 2004; named to Nat. All-Freshman Team, Basketball Times, Collegeinsider.com and Rivals.com, 2004, Atlantic Coast Conf.-All-Freshman Team, 2004, NBA All-Rookie First Team, 2005; recipient NBA Sportsmanship award, 2007. Mailing: Chgo Bulls United Ctr 1901 W Madison St Chicago IL 60612-2459*

DENG, PING, finance educator; arrived in US, 1993; m. Changyun Nie; children: Irwin, Amy. BA in Internat. Studies, Chongqing U., China, 1988; MS, Remin U., China, 1990; MA, Old Domion U., Norfold, Va., 1998; PhD, Old Dominion U., Norfold, Va., 1998. Vis. prof. Troy State U.-Atlantic Region, Norfolk, Va., 1998—99; with Ea. Oreg. U., 1999—2001; prof. bus. adminstrn. Maryville U., St. Louis, 2001—. Cons. in field. Contbr. articles to profl. jours. Grantee, Maryville U. and East Oreg. U., 2001, 2004, 2007. Mem.: Strategic Mgmt. Soc. (assoc.). Achievements include research in outwarf FDI from China and other East Asian countries. Home: 2306 Spyglass Summit Ct High Ridge MO 63049 Office: Maryville Univ St Louis 650 Maryville Univ Dr Saint Louis MO 63141 Office Phone: 314-529-9687. Office Fax: 314-529-9975. Business E-Mail: pdeng@maryville.edu.

DENG, SHENGLOU, chemistry professor; b. Guangshui, Hubei, China, Dec. 1, 1970; arrived in U.S., 2002; s. Daodian Deng and Dehua Chen; m. Ying Dong, July 26, 1998; 1 child, Ryan. BS, Xiaogan U., China, 1993; MS, Ctrl. China Normal U., Wuhan, 1997; PhD, Nankai U., Tianjin, China, 2000. English tchr. Dengdian Middle Sch., Guangshui, Hubei, China, 1993—94; asst. prof., assoc. chair Tiajin U., 2000—01; rsch. assoc. U. Bourgogne, Dijon, France, 2002, Fla. State U., Tallahassee, 2003—04, Utah State U., Logan, 2004—05, Brigham Young U., Provo, Utah, 2005—. Cons. Puyang's Sci. and Tech. Soc., China, 2001. Contbr. articles to profl. jours. Named Excellent Supr., Tianjin U., 2001; recipient 3rd Pl. award in vocal music contest, Tianjin Edn. Bur., 1997; Motorola scholar, Motorola Co., Tianjin, 1998. Mem.: Am. Chem. Soc. Achievements include patents in field; 28 publications. Avocations: music, swimming. Office: Chemistry Dept Brigham Young Univ Provo UT 84602 Office Phone: 801-422-4172. Business E-Mail: sdeng@chem.byu.edu.

DENGER, MICHAEL LOUIS, lawyer; b. Davenport, Iowa, Sept. 8, 1945; s. Ralph Henry and Bernice Marie (Cederberg) D.; m. Mary Elizabeth Colbert, Aug. 30, 1969; children: Lorna Marie, Mary Catherine, Rachel Anne. BS with highest distinction, Northwestern U., 1967; JD cum laude, Harvard U., 1970. Bar: D.C. 1970, U.S. Ct. Appeals (D.C. cir.) 1971, U.S. Supreme Ct. 1978. Assoc. atty. Sutherland, Asbill & Brennan, Washington, 1970-76, ptnr., 1976-92, Gibson, Dunn & Crutcher LLP, Washington, 1992—. Adj. prof. law Washington and Lee U., 2000-05; spkr. on antitrust, trade regulation numerous groups. Bd. editors Antitrust Report, 1992—; contbr. articles to profl. jours. Mem. nat. adv. coun. Northwestern U. Sch. Comm., Evanston, Ill., 1990—. 2nd lt. USAR, 1970. Mem. ABA (vice chair antitrust law sect. 1985-86, sec. antitrust law sect. 1988-91, chair-elect antitrust law sect. 1991-92, chair antitrust law sect. 1992-93, chair edit. bd. antitrust sect. Federal and State Price Discrimination Law 1991, co-editor in chief antitrust sect. State Antitrust Practice and Statutes 3 vols. 1990, vice chair edit. bd. antitrust sect. Antitrust Law Devels. 2d edit. 1984), Columbia Country Club (Chevy Chase, Md.). Republican. Roman Catholic. Avocations: tennis, collecting military miniatures, military history, bridge. Home: 5802 Kirkside Dr Chevy Chase MD 20815-7118 Office: Gibson Dunn & Crutcher LLP Ste 300 1050 Connecticut Ave NW Washington DC 20036-5306 E-mail: mdenger@gibsondunn.com.

DENGLER, ROBERT ANTHONY, management consultant; b. Upper Darby, Pa., Aug. 23, 1947; s. Anthony William and Harriet Josephine (Schneider) D.; m. Renee Faith Aird, Oct. 26, 1985. BS, Drexel U., 1970, MBA, 1972; MS in MIS, Benedictine U., 2000, PhD, 2006. Cert. assn. exec., mtg. planner; registered orgn. devel. cons. Cons. orgn devel. Abinton Hosp., Abington, 1970—73; dir. tng. & edn. Parkview Meml. Hosp., Ft. Wayne, Ind., 1973-76; dir. human resource mgmt. Americana Healthcare Corp., Chgo., 1976-82; corp. mgr. Human Resource Tng. and Devel. Means Svc. Inc., Chgo., 1982-83; dir. physician services West Suburban Hosp. Med. Ctr., Oak Park, Ill., 1983-85; assoc. dir. Assoc. Equipment Distributors, Oak Brook, Ill., 1985-88; exec. v.p. Internat. Reprographic Assn., Oak Brook, 1988-92; exec. dir. Data Processing Mgmt. Assn., Park Ridge, Ill., 1993-94, Nat. Assn. Med. Staff Svcs., Lombard, Ill., 1996-98; pres. R.A. Dengler & Assocs., 1994—; engring. leadership devel. adminstr. Commonwealth Edison/Exelon Corp., 2001—03. Adj. instr. orgn. behavior Aurora U., Ill.; adj. instr. Hawaii Pacific U., Honolulu, Benedictine U., Roosvelt Univ.; instr. grad. mgmt. Phoenix U., Nat. Louis U. Capt. USAR, 1972-80. Mem. Inst. Mgmt. Cons., Project Mgmt. Inst., Am. Soc. Assn. Execs., Acad. of Mgmt., Midwest Acad. Mgmt., Orgn. Devel. Network, Orgn. Devel. Inst., Mensa. Home and Office: 294 Lionel Rd Riverside IL 60546-2204

DENHAM, EARL LAMAR, lawyer; b. Biloxi, Miss., July 1, 1947; s. Earl Lamar and Ruby (Young) D.; children: Katherine Elizabeth, Rachel Ann, Israel Anderson, Nathan Levi, Earl Lamar III; m. N.A. Hema Malini; children: Judith Jaya, Sachika Braka, Arya Tova, Ariela Anuja. BS, U. Miss., 1969, JD, 1972. Bar: Miss. 1972, U.S. Dist. Ct. (no. and so. dists.) Miss. 1972, U.S. Ct. Appeals (5th cir.) 1978, U.S. Supreme Ct. 1978. Assoc. Hurlbert & O'Barr, Biloxi, 1972-73; ptnr. Levi & Denham, Ltd., Ocean Springs, Miss., 1973—99, Denham, Backstrom, O'Bart & Hollingsworth, Ltd., 2000—02, Denton Law Firm, Ltd., 2002—06, Denham Law Firm, PLLC, 2006—. Capt. USAR, 1970-78. Mem. ABA, ATLA (sustaining), Nat. Assn. Criminal Def. Lawyers, Miss. Trial Lawyers Assn., Miss. Bar Assn., Southern Trial Lawyers Assn. (bd. govs.). Democrat. Jewish. Avocations: farming, hunting. Office Phone: 228-875-1234. Business E-Mail: earl@denhamlaw.com.

DENHAM, ROBERT EDWIN, lawyer, investment company executive; b. Dallas, Aug. 27, 1945; s. Wilburn H. and Anna Maria (Hughes) Denham; m. Carolyn Hunter, June 3, 1966; children: Jeffrey Hunter, Laura Maria. BA magna cum laude, U. Tex., 1966; MA, Harvard U., 1968, JD magna cum laude, 1971. Bar: Calif. 1972. Assoc. Munger Tolles and Olson, LA, 1971—73; ptnr. Munger Tolles Olson, LA, 1973—85, 1992—93; mng. ptnr. Munger Tolles and Olson, LA, 1985—91; chmn., chief exec. officer Salomon Inc, NYC, 1992—97; ptnr. Munger Tolles and Olson, LA, 1998—. Pres. Pasadena (Calif.) Ednl. Found., 1977—79; trustee Poly. Sch. Pasadena, 1989—93, v.p. bd. trustees, 1991—93; trustee New Sch. U., 1995—, Natural Resources Def. Coun., 1992—2002; adv. bd. of the pres. Calif. State U., Sonoma, 1993—; trustee The Conf. Bd., 1994—2003, Russell Sage Found., 1997—; pub. mem. Ind. Stds. Bd., 1997—2000; former co-chmn. Subcoun. on Capital Allocation of the Competitiveness Policy Coun.; former mem. Bipartisan Commn. on Entitlement and Tax Reform; former U.S. rep. to the Asia Pacific Econ. Coun. Bus. Adv. Coun.; mem. bus. sector adv. group on corp. governance OECD; trustee Cathedral Corp. Diocese of L.A., 1986—92; bd. dirs. Pub. Counsel, L.A., 1981—84, United Way, NYC, 1994—97, U.S. Trust Co., AMKOR Tech., Inc., 1998—99, MacArthur Found. Mem.: ABA, L.A. County Bar (bus. and corps. exec. com. 1985—), State Bar Calif. Democrat. Episcopalian. Avocations: soccer, cooking, running. Office: Munger Tolles and Olson 355 S Grand Ave # 3500 Los Angeles CA 90071-1560

DENHARDT, DAVID TILTON, molecular and cell biology educator; b. Sacramento, Feb. 25, 1939; s. David Burton and Edith (Tilton) D.; m. Georgetta Louise Harrar, July 1, 1961; children: Laura Jean, Kristin Ann, David Harrar. BA in Chemistry with high honors, Swarthmore Coll., 1960; PhD in Biophysics, Calif. Inst. Tech., 1965. Instr. biol. labs Harvard U., 1964-66, asst. prof., 1966-70; assoc. prof. biochemistry McGill U., Montreal, Que., Canada, 1970-77, prof., 1977-80; prof. biochemistry, microbiology and immunology, dir. Cancer Research Lab., U. Western Ont., London, 1980-88; prof. biol. scis. Rutgers U., New Brunswick, NJ, 1988—, chmn., 1988-95, dir. Bur. Biol. Rsch., 1988-95, dir. cell devel. biology grad. program, 1991-94. Mem. sci. adv. bd. Ctr. for Advanced Biotech. and Medicine, Piscataway, N.J., 1988-91, 1988-91. Editor: Jour. Virology, 1977-87, Gene, 1985-93, Exptl. Cell Rsch., 1994—; assoc. editor: Jour. Cellular Biochemistry, 1994—; mem. editorial bd. Jour. Cancer Rsch. Methods and Clin. Oncology, In Vivo Internat. Jour. Fellow AAAS, Am. Acad. Microbiology, Royal Soc. Can.; mem. Am. Cancer Soc., Am. Soc. Biol. Chemists, Am. Microbiol. Soc., N.Y. Acad. Scis., Am. Soc. Cell Biology, Phi Beta Kappa. Office: Rutgers U Nelson Biol Labs 604 Allison Rd Piscataway NJ 08854-8000 Office Phone: 732-445-4569. Business E-Mail: denhardt@biology.rutgers.edu.

DEN HARTOG, GRACE ROBINSON, lawyer; b. Richmond, Va., Jan. 19, 1952; d. Eldred Hiter and Jane Haddon (Pitt) Robinson; m. Wilhelm H. King, June 14, 1997; children: Jonathan Wilhelm, Mary Douglas. BA, U. Richmond, 1974; JD, U. Va., 1980. Bar: Va. 1980, US Dist. Ct. Ea. and We. Districts Va. 1984, US Ct. Appeals 4th Cir. 1983, Tex. 1993. Assoc. Tremblay & Smith, Charlottesville, Va., 1980-83, McGuire, Woods, Battle & Boothe LLP (McGuire Woods LLP as of 2000), Richmond, Va., 1984—90, ptnr., 1990—2003, chmn., product liability litig. mgmt. group, 1994-97, mem. associates com., 1992-97; sr. v.p., gen. counsel Owens & Minor Inc., Glen Allen, Va., 2003—. Mem. allocations com. United Way, Charlottesville, 1980-83; mem. Jefferson Area Cmty. Corrections Resources Bd., 1983-84. Named one of Nation's Top 50 Women Litigators, Nat. Law Jour., 2001. Mem. Va. Bar Assn., Va. State Bar (bd. governors young lawyers com. 1983-87, chmn. cir. representatives com. 1985-87; chmn. membership com. 1983-85). Office: Owens & Minor Inc 4800 Cox Rd Glen Allen VA 23060-6292*

DENHOLM, ROBYN, information technology executive; B in Econs., U. Sydney; M of Commerce, U. New South Wales, Australia. With Arthur Andersen & Co., Toyota Australia, Sun Microsystems, Inc., 1996—, svc. dir. Shared Fin. Svcs. Asia Pacific, contr. Australia, v.p. fin., v.p., corp. contr., chief acctg. officer, sr. v.p. fin., sr. v.p. corp. strategic planning. Fellow: Inst. Chartered Accts. Australia. Office: Sun Microsystems Inc 4150 Network Cir Santa Clara CA 95054 Office Phone: 650-960-1300.*

DENICE, MARCELLA LOUISE, counselor; b. 1934; BA in English, Our Lady of the Lake U., 1973, MA in Counseling, 1990. English tchr., volleyball/basketball coach Anson Jones Mid. Sch., San Antonio, 1974—80; head basketball coach Alamo Heights H.S., 1978—80; English tchr., cross-country track coach Burbank H.S., San Antonio, 1983—90; guidance counselor Highland Park Elem. Sch., San Antonio, 1990—. Bd. dirs. Nat. Bd. for Profl. Tchg. Stds.; mem. adv. com. for counselors San Antonio Ind. Sch. Dist., mem. dist. leadership team, 2002—. Mem. spkrs. bur. Am. Cancer Soc. Nominee H.E. Butt Grocery Chain Excellence in Tchg. award, 2005; named Outstanding Counselor of Yr., Tex. Counseling Assn., 1991, Tex. Tchr. of Yr., Peer Assistance Leadership Skills, 2002, Counselor of Yr., So. Tex. Counseling Assn., 2004; recipient Remarkable Woman award, Our Lady of the Lake, 1995. Mem.: So. Tax Counseling Assn. (named counselor of yr. 2004). Office: Highland Park Elem 635 Rigsby San Antonio TX 78210 Business E-Mail: marcella@fittingadventures.com.

DE NICOLA, PETER FRANCIS, tax executive; b. NYC, Oct. 28, 1954; s. Louis Joseph and Nancy Eleanor (Maddi) DeN.; m. Charlotte Rebecca White, Sept. 2, 1998. BS, NYU, 1976, MBA, 1978. Pres., founder P.F. DeNicola, Inc., Stamford, Conn., 1976-84; acct. Main Hurdman, NYC, Conn., 1978-81; tax mgr. Gen. Signal Corp., Stamford, Conn., 1981-83, Emery Air Freight Corp., Wilton, Conn., 1983-85; dir. taxes A.I. Internat. Corp., NYC, 1985-88; tax mgr. Siemens Corp., NYC, 1989-91; sr. tax analyst FujiFilm USA, Inc., Valhalla, NY, 1991—93, assoc. tax mgr., 1994—98, tax mgr., 1999—2006; group tax mgr. FujiFilm Holdings Am. Corp., Valhalla, NY, 2007—. Iconographic cons. AP Giannini Exhibit, Rome, 2004. Author: Legal Liability of Tax Return Preparers, 1978; contbr. Palm Springs Weekend, articles to profl. jours., chapters to books. Recipient Ferdinand W. Lafrentz acctg. award, 1977 CPA, Conn., NY Mem. Tax Soc. NYU, Assn. MBA Exec., Am. Mgmt. Assn., Stamford Tax Assn. (sec.-treas. 1988-89, v.p. 1989-90, treas. 1999—), Nat. Assn. Acct., NYU Commerce Alumni Assn. (dir. 1978-96 , corr. sec. 1978-79, rec. sec. 1979-81, chmn. budget com. 1987-88, chmn. Annual Bus. Conf. 1988-89, chmn. alumni admissions coun. 1989-96), AICPA (fed. tax and tax acctg. com. 1984—), NY Soc. CPA (fed. and state tax com. 1983-85, depreciation and investment tax credit com. 1986-87), Conn. Soc. CPA, Tax Exec. Inst. (bd. dirs. 2002-, asst. sec. 2004-05, treas. 2005-06, sec. 2006-07, v.p. 2007-), Round Table Assn. of US (co-founder 1986, nat. treas. 1987-88, 90-92, nat. pres. 1988-89, del. to internat. convention, 1987, 88), Estate Planning Coun. Westchester County, Round Table 3 of Greenwich (Conn.) (dir. 1984-90, v.p. 1985-86, pres. 1986-88), Internat. Platform Assn., Princeton Club (NYC), Long Ridge Club (Stamford, treas. 2006-, dir.), Capitol Hill Club (Washington), NY Athletic Club, Rotary (v.p. Mt. Pleasant chpt. 2005-06, pres. 2006—07, Rotarian of Yr. 2006, dir. Mt. Pleasant Rotary Found. 2007-), Am. Assn. Individual Investors (dir., 2005- , treas. 2006 -). Republican. Roman Catholic. Home: PO Box 4637 Stamford CT 06907-0637 Office: FujiFilm Holdings America Corp 200 Summit Lake Dr Valhalla NY 10595 Office Phone: 914-789-8336. Personal E-mail: peterd7510@aol.com. Business E-Mail: peter_denicola@fujifilm.com.

DENICOLA, T. KEVIN, chemicals executive; Grad. in chem. engring., U. Va., 1979. Ethylene products mgr. Lyondell Chem., Houston, 1993—96, dir., investor relations, 1996—98, v.p., corp. devel., 1998—2002, sr. v.p., CFO, 2002—. Mem.: Parnership Governance Com. of Equistar and LCR. Office: Lyondell Chem 1221 McKinney St Ste 1600 Houston TX 77253-3646*

DENINNO, DAVID L., lawyer; b. Pitts., Dec. 28, 1955; BA, U. Va., 1977; JD with honors, George Washington U., 1981. Bar: Pa. 1981. Law clerk to Judge Roger Robb US Ct. Appeals for DC Cir., 1981—82; with Reed Smith LLP, Pitts., 1981—; now ptnr., mem. exec. com., chair bus. & regulatory dept. Office: Reed Smith LLP PO Box 2009 Pittsburgh PA 15230-2009 Office Phone: 412-288-3214. Office Fax: 412-288-3063. Business E-Mail: ddeninno@reedsmith.com.

DENIOUS, SHARON MARIE, retired publishing executive; b. Rulo, Nebr., Jan. 27, 1941; d. Thomas Wayne and Alma (Murphy) Fee; m. Jon Parks Denious, June 17, 1963; children: Timothy Scot, Elizabeth Denious Cessna. Grad. high sch. Operator N.W. Pipeline Co., Ignacio, Colo., 1975-90; pub. The Silverton Standard & The Miner, Colo., 1990-99. Avocations: reading, hiking. Personal E-mail: jondenious@comcast.net.

DENIRO, MARY LYN S., lawyer; b. Salt Lake City, Feb. 15, 1959; d. Ted Gordon and Marilyn Valoe (Butcher) Symes; m. Dan DeNiro. BS magna cum laude, U. Utah, Salt Lake City, 1980; JD magna cum laude, Fordham U., NYC, 1992. Bar: N.Y. 1993. Exec. asst. to chmn. ASARCO Inc., NYC, 1983-91, legal asst., 1991-92; jud. clk. US Dist. Ct. (ea. dist.), Bklyn., 1992-93; assoc. Davis Polk & Wardwell, NYC, 1993-99; v.p., legal counsel Zurich Centre Group, NYC, 1999—2003; v.p. counsel Ace Capital Re Inc., 2003—04; v.p., asst. gen. counsel Ctr. Group Holdings Ltd., NYC, 2004—. Mem. Order of Coif, Phi Kappa Phi, Phi Eta Sigma. Office: Zurich Fin Svcs 105 East 17th St New York NY 10003 Business E-Mail: mary.lyn.deniro@centresolutions.com.

DE NIRO, ROBERT, actor, film producer and director, restaurant owner; b. NYC, Aug. 17, 1943; s. Robert and Virginia De Niro; m. Diahnne Abbott, 1976 (div. 1988); 1 child, Raphael Eugene, 1 stepchild, Drina; m. Grace Hightower, June 17, 1997; 1 child, Elliot; 2 children, Aaron Kendric DeNiro, Julian Henry De Niro (with Toukie Smith). Studied acting with, Stella Adler, Lee Strasberg. Co-founder Tribeca Productions, 1988, Tribeca Film Festival, 2002; co-owner Tribeca Grill, 1990, Nobu, NYC, 1994, Rubicon, San Francisco, 1994. Actor: (films) The Wedding Party, 1969, Hi, Mom!, 1970, Bloody Mama, 1970, Jennifer On My Mind, 1971, Born to Win, 1971, The Gang That Couldn't Shoot Straight, 1971, Bang the Drum Slowly, 1973, Mean Streets, 1973, The Godfather, Part II, 1974 (Acad. award best supporting actor), The Last Tycoon, 1976, 1900, 1976, Taxi Driver, 1976, New York, New York, 1977, The Deer Hunter, 1978, Raging Bull, 1980 (Acad. award best actor), True Confessions, 1981, The King of Comedy, 1982, Once Upon a Time in America, 1984, Falling in Love, 1984, Brazil, 1984, The Mission, 1985, Angel Heart, 1987, The Untouchables, 1987, Midnight Run, 1988, Jacknife, 1989, Stanley & Iris, 1990, Goodfellas, 1990, Awakenings, 1991 (Acad. award nom.), Backdraft, 1991, Cape Fear, 1991, Guilty By Suspicion, 1991, Mistress, 1992, Night and the City, 1992, Mad Dog and Glory, 1993, This Boy's Life, 1993, Mary Shelley's Frankenstein, 1994, Casino, 1995, Heat, 1995, The Fan, 1996, Marvin's Room, 1996, Sleepers, 1996, Copland, 1997, Great Expectations, 1998, 15 Minutes, 1999, Analyze This, 1999, Flawless, 1999, The Score, 2001, Showtime, 2002, Analyze That, 2002, Godsend, 2004, (voice) Shark Tale, 2004, Hide and Seek, 2005, (voice) Arthur and the Invisibles, 2006, Stardust, 2007; actor, exec. prodr.: (films) We're No Angels, 1989, Meet the Parents, 2000; actor, prodr.: (films) Wag the Dog, 1997, Lenny Bruce: Swear to Tell the Truth, 1998, The Adventures of Rocky and Bullwinkle, 1999, Meet the Fockers, 2004, The Good Shepherd, 2006; actor, dir.: (films) A Bronx Tale, 1993; dir., actor: (films) City by the Sea, 2002; (plays) Strange Show, 1982; (documentaries) Dear America: Letters Home From Vietnam, 1987; prodr.: (films) Entropy, 1999, About a Boy, 2002, Stage Beauty, 2004, Rent, 2005; co-prodr.: Thunderheart, 1992; exec. prodr.: (TV films) Tribeca, 1993, Holiday Heart, 2000; (films) Faithful, 1996, Navy Driver, 2000, Conjugating Niki, 2000. Named Greatest Living Movie Star, Empire Mag., 2004; recipient Hasty Pudding award, Harvard U., 1979, D.W. Griffith award for best actor, 1990. Office: Creative Artists Agy 9830 Wilshire Blvd Beverly Hills CA 90212-1825*

DENISH, DIANE D., lieutenant governor; d. Libby Donley and Jack Daniels; m. Herb Denish; 3 children. Assoc. pub., bus. devel. and advt. sales Starlight Pub. Ltd., Albuquerque Living and N.Mex Monthly, Albuquerque; state chmn. N.Mex Dem. Party, 1999—2001; former owner Target Group; lt. gov. State of N.Mex, Santa Fe, 2003—. Chair Children's Cabinet, Mortgage Fin. Authority, Mil. Base Planning Commn., Ind. Devel. Advocacy Adv. Coun.; active Equal Pay Task Force, Spaceport Commn., Border Authority, Fin. Independence Task Force, Workforce Devel. Bd., Commn. on Volunteerism; trustee N.Mex. Mil. Inst. Found. Bd.; former chair N.Mex. First, N.Mex. Cmty. Found., N.Mex. Tech. Bd. Regents; former mem. N.Mex. Commn. on the Status of Women; former mem. nat. adv. bd. Small Bus. Adminstrn.; pres. N.Mex. State Senate; bd. mem. Daniels Fund. Named 2003 YWCA New Mexican of Vision; named one of Top 100 New Mexicans in honor of her cmty. leadership. Democrat. Office: Office Lt Governor State Capitol Ste 417 Santa Fe NM 87501

DENISI, ANGELO, dean; b. Bronx, NY; m. Adrienne Colella; children: Jessica, Rebecca. B in Psychology, CUNY, 1973; PhD in Indsl. and Orgnl. Psychology, Purdue U., 1977. Asst. prof. Kent State U.; prof. U. SC, 1979—89, Rutgers U., 1989—97, Texas A&M U May Bus. Sch., 1997—2005, head dept. mgmt., Paul M. and Rosalie Robertson chair in bus. adminstrn., U. Disting. prof.; dean Tulane U. A.B. Freeman Sch. Bus, New Orleans, 2005—. Co-editor Managing Knowledge for Sustained Competitive Advantage; editl. bd. mem. Acad. Mgmt. Jour., Acad. Mgmt. Rev., Jour. Applied Psychology, Jour. of Mgmt., Jour. Orgnl. Behavior. Fellow: Southern Mgmt. Assn., Soc. Indsl. and Orgnl. Psychology, APA (pres. 1999—2000, Disting. Sci. Contbn. Award 2005), Acad. Mgmt.

DENISON, MARY BONEY, lawyer; b. Wilmington, NC, June 8, 1956; d. Leslie Norwood Jr. and Lillian (Bellamy) Boney; m. John R. Clark III; children: John R. Clark IV, Andrew B.H. Clark; children: Mary Catesby Bellamy, James Wholley IV. AB, Duke U., 1978; JD, U. N.C., 1981. Bar: N.Y. 1982, U.S. Dist. Ct. (so. and ea. dists.) N.Y. 1983, U.S. Ct. Appeals (2d cir.) 1984, DC 1988, U.S. Dist. Ct. DC 1988, U.S. Ct. Appeals (DC cir.) 1988. Assoc. Law Office William G. Kaelin, NYC, 1981-82, Smith, Steibel, Alexander & Saskor, NYC, 1982-86, Graham & James, Washington, 1986-91, ptnr., 1992-96, Farkas & Manelli PLLC, Washington, 1996-2000, Manelli, Denison & Selter, PLLC, Washington, 2001—. Vol. Legal Aid Soc., NYC, 1983—86. Recipient Washington DC Super Lawyer, Key Profl. Media, Inc., 2007. Mem.: ABA, U. NC Law Alumni Assn. (bd. dirs. 2006—), Internat. Trademark Assn. (vice chair treaty analysis com. 2000—01, chair treaty analysis com. 2001—03, bd. dirs. 2003—05), French Am. C. of C. Washington (treas. 1991—97). Democrat. Episcopalian. Office: Manelli Denison & Selter PLLC 2000 M St NW Ste 700 Washington DC 20036-3364 Home Phone: 301-469-6278; Office Phone: 202-261-1000. Business E-Mail: mdenison@mdslaw.com.

DENKE, CONRAD WILLIAM, motion picture producer; b. Cottonwood, Ariz., July 23, 1947; s. Lee Ernest and Barbara Ann (Russell) D.; m. Laura Lee Nielson; children: Alexander, Elisabeth. BA in Radio-TV Communications and Psychology, U. Wash., 1969. Dir. Sta. KCTS-TV, Seattle, 1967-69; dir. prodr. Cinema Assocs., Seattle, 1973-78; pres. Am. Motion Pictures, Seattle, 1978—2002; CEO Victory Studios, Seattle, 2002—. Bd. dirs. Am. Cinema Found., Whidbey Island Films; CEO, owner Victory Studios L.A., Post Solutions, 2003—; publ., founder Highdef Mag., 2002—. Dir., producer: (indsl. documentary) Tunnels Under Chicago, 1981 (Chris award 1981, Gold award, Silver award, Cine Golden Eagle award, 1981); dir. (ednl. documentary) More Than Bows and Arrows, 1978 (Best Western Documentary 1978); producer: (TV series) Adventures on Sinclair Island, 1986, (talk show series) Teens Talk, (PBS documentary) Educations Wars, 1996, National Desk, 1997, 99. Mormon bishop, stake presidency. With USAF, 1969-73. Recipient Cine Golden Eagle award Council on Internat. Nontheatrical Events, 1977, 79, 89, 95, Silver Cindy award Info. Film Producers Am., 1977, 98, Gold Camera award U.S. Indsl. Film Festival, 1978, Telly award, 1989, 95, 97, 2 Telly's, 1998, 3 Gold awards Emerald City awards, 1997, 2000, World medal N.Y. Film Festival, 1998, 2 Aegis awards, 1998, 2 Aurora awards, 1998, Nat. ITVA award, 2000, Silver Screen award 2000. Mem. Internat. TV Assn. (dir. Seattle chpt. 1980-90, chpt. pres. 1983-84, chmn. HD Consortium for Nat. Assn. TV Program Execs., Silver Reel, 1986, Gold Reel 1997), Wash. Motion Picture Coun. (pres. 1992-96), Assn. Ind. Comml. Prodrs. (v.p. N.W. chpt. 1985-87, pres. 1987-90), Am. Cinema Found. in L.A. (bd. dirs., v.p. 1994—), Prodrs. Guild Am. Republican. Formed E Pluribus Unum Films in 2000. Office: Victory Studios 2247 15th Ave W Seattle WA 98119-2417 Home Phone: 206-789-1011; Office Phone: 206-282-1776. Business E-Mail: conrad@victorystudios.com.

DENKE, PAUL HERMAN, retired aircraft engineer; b. San Francisco, Feb. 7, 1916; s. Edmund Herman and Ella Hermine (Riehl) D.; m. Beryl Ann Lincoln, Feb. 10, 1940; children: Karen Denke Mottaz, Claudia Denke Tesche, Marilyn Denke Oliver. BCE, U. Calif.-Berkeley, 1937, MCE, 1939. Registered profl. engr., Calif. Stress engr. Douglas Aircraft Co., Santa Monica, Calif., 1940-62, mgr. structural mechanics Long Beach, Calif., 1962-65, chief sci. computing, 1965-71, chief structures engr. methods and devel., 1972-78, chief scientist structural mechanics, 1979-84, staff mgr. Boeing fellow, 1985-2000; ret., 2000. Mem. faculty dept. engring. UCLA, 1941-50. Author numerous tech. papers. Assoc. fellow AIAA; mem. Soc. Automotive Engrs. (Arch T. Colwell merit award 1966, IAE Outstanding Engr. merit award 1985), Sigma Xi, Chi Epsilon, Tau Beta Pi. Democrat. Achievements include pioneering and developing finite element method of structural analysis. Home: 1800 Via Estudillo Palos Verdes Peninsula CA 90274-1908 Personal E-mail: pauldenke@earthlink.net.

DENKER, HENRY, playwright, author, director; b. NYC, Nov. 25, 1912; s. Max and Jennie (Geller) D.; m. Edith Rose Heckman, Dec. 5, 1942. LL.B., N.Y. Law Sch., 1934. Bar: N.Y. 1935. Practiced law, NYC, 1935-38; exec. Research Inst. Am., NYC, 1936-37; tax cons. Standard Stats. subs. Standard and Poor, NYC, 1937-39. Lectr. dramatic writing Am. Theatre Wing, 1961-63, Coll. of the Desert. Writer, dir., prodr.: (radio series) The Greatest Story Ever Told, N.Y.C., 1947-57; author: (Broadway plays) Time Limit, 1956, A Far Country, 1961, Venus at Large, 1962, A Case of Libel, 1964, What Did We Do Wrong, 1968, Something Old, Something New, 1976, Horowitz and Mrs. Washington, 1979; (off-Broadway) The Name of the Game, 1967, A Sound of Distant Thunder, 1969, The Headhunters, 1974, CurtainCall, 1999, An Evening in Athens, 2006; (screenplays) The Heartfarm, 1970, The Hook, Twilight of Honor, Time Limit, A Time for Miracles, 1980, Outrage, 1984; writer, dir., prodr. numerous TV dramas, 1950-66; TV spls. include Give Us Barrabas, 1964, Neither Are We Enemies, 1971, The Choice, The Court Martial of Lietenant Calley, Mother Seton, 1980, Love Leads the Way, 1985, Outrage, 1986, Case of Libel, 1986; author: I'll be Right Home Ma, 1949, My Son, The Lawyer, 1950, Salome, Princess of Galilee, 1954, That First Easter, 1956, The Director, 1970, The Kingmaker, 1972, A Place for the Mighty, 1973, The Physicians, 1975, The Experiment, 1976, The Starmaker, 1977, The Scofield Diagnosis, 1977, The Actress, 1978, The Error Judgement, 1979, Horowitz and Mrs. Washington, 1979, The Warfield Syndrome, 1981, Outrage!, 1982, The Healers, 1983, Kincaid, 1984, Love Leads the Way, 1985, A Case of Libel, 1985, Robert, My Son, 1985, Judge Spencer Dissents, 1986, The Choice, 1987, The Retreat, 1988, A Gift of Life, 1989, Payment in Full, 1990, Doctor on Trial, 1991, Labyrinth, 1994, This Child is Mine, 1995, To Marcy, With Love, 1996, A Place for Kathy, 1997, The Third Day, 1999, Benjie, 1999, Class Action, 2000, Clarence, 2002, Final Shooting Script, 2004, It Runs in Jewish Families, 2006. Recipient Peabody award, 1949; Christopher award, 1953; Emmy award, 1948 Mem. Acad. TV Arts and Scis. (coun.), Authors League (coun.), Dramatists Guild (coun. 1967-69), Authors Guild, Writers' Guild. Jewish. Address: 241 Central Park W New York NY 10024-4530 Office Phone: 212-873-5821. E-mail: hwdenker@aol.com.

DENLINGER, DAVID LANDIS, insect biology educator; b. Lancaster, Pa., Nov. 20, 1945; s. Paul Leaman and Almeda Esbenshade (Landis) D.; m. Judith Katharine Yoder, Sept. 7, 1967; children: Michael, Jonathan. BS, Pa. State U., 1967; PhD, U. Ill., 1971. Rsch. fellow Agrl. U., Wageningen, The Netherlands, 1971-72; rsch. scientist Internat. Centre Insect Physiology and Ecology, Nairobi, Kenya, 1972-74; rsch. fellow Harvard U., Cambridge, Mass., 1974-76; prof. Ohio State U., Columbus, 1976—, chmn. dept., 1994—. Contbr. articles to profl. jours. Grantee NIH, USDA, NSF, Smithsonian. Fellow AAAS; mem. Entomological Soc. Am. (chair sect. B 1990), NAS, Royal Entomological Soc. Mennonite. Home: 6163 Olentangy Blvd Worthington OH 43085-3865 Office: Aronoff Lab 318 W 12th Ave Columbus OH 43210 Business E-Mail: denlinger.1@osu.edu.

DENLINGER, EDGAR JACOB, retired electronics engineering executive, researcher; s. Victor Jacob and Marian Alice (Shoemaker) D.; m. Cynthia Della Wilson, June 24, 1967; children— Crystal Shereen, Craig Wesley BS in Engring. Sci., Pa. State U., 1961; MSE.E., U. Pa., 1964, PhD in E.E., 1969. Research engr. Applied Research RCA, Camden, NJ, 1961—65; research assoc. Moore Sch. U. Pa., Phila., 1965—67; mem. tech. staff MIT Lincoln Lab., Lexington, Mass., 1967—73, RCA Labs, Princeton, NJ, 1973—83, group head signal conversion systems research, 1983—87; group head microwave systems rsch. David Sarnoff Research Ctr., Princeton, NJ, 1987—92, sr. mem. tech. staff, 1992—2003; ret., 2003—. Adj. prof. dept. elec. engring. Drexel U., Phila., 1982-88. Contbr. articles to profl. jours. Patentee microwave devices and circuits Mem. Hickory Acres Civic Assn., East Windsor, N.J., 1973-81 Recipient Achievement award David Sarnoff Rsch. Ctr., Princeton, 1979, 94. Fellow IEEE (treas. sect. 1980-83, vice chmn. 1984, chmn. 1985) Lodges: Mason, Tall Cedars, Shriners. Republican. Presbyterian. Avocations: music, swimming. Home: 7 Wheatston Ct Princeton Junction NJ 08550-1936 Home Phone: 609-799-3140. Personal E-mail: edenlinger@msn.com.

DENMAN, DAVID, actor; b. Calif., July 25, 1973; m. Nikki Boyer. BFA, Julliard Sch.; attended, Am. Conservatory Theatre, San Francisco. Actor: (films) The Replacements, 2000, Out Cold, 2001, The Singing Detective, 2003, Big Fish, 2003, When A Stranger Calls, 2006, The Nines, 2007, If I Had Known I Was a Genius, 2007, Cake, 2007, Take, 2007; (TV films) A Vow to Cherish, 1999, The '60s, 1999, The Perfect Husband: The Laci Peterson Story, 2004; (TV series) Angel, 2001—03, The Office, 2005— (SAG award outstanding performance by an ensemble in a comedy series, 2007), (appeared on) ER, 1997, Chicago Hope, 1997, The Pretender, 1998, The X Files, 1999, Arliss, 2000, CSI: Miami, 2002, Crossing Jordan, 2002, Without A Trace, 2004, Second Time Around, 2004, Night Stalker, 2005.*

DENMARK, BERNHARDT, manufacturing executive; b. Bklyn., June 6, 1917; s. William M. and Kate (Lazarus) D.; m. Muriel Schechter, Sept. 22, 1943; children: Richard J., Karen. AB, NYU, 1941; postgrad., Am. U., 1941-42, Nat. Inst. Pub. Affairs, 1941-42. Vice pres. sales Telecoin Corp., NYC, 1946-49; v.p. sales Internat. Latex Corp., NYC, 1949-55; mgr. mktg. Playtex Co., NYC, 1955-59, v.p., gen. mgr. family products div., 1959-63, v.p. mktg., 1963-65; pres. Playtex Co. Playtex div., 1965-67, Internat. Playtex Corp., NYC, 1968-69, chmn. bd., 1969; exec. v.p., dir., mem. exec. com. Glen Alden Corp., NYC, 1969-72; pres. Bevis Industries, Inc., White Plains, NY, 1972-76, Bus. Mktg. Corp. for N.Y.C., 1977-78; chmn. Denmark, Donovan & Oppel Inc., NYC, 1978-85; chmn. bd. dirs. Advanced Photonix, Inc., Camarillo, Calif., 1992—, Xsirius, Inc., Camarillo, 1992—. Bd. dirs. Stanley Warner Corp., Schenley Industries, BVD Corp., Kleinerts Inc., Advanced Photonics Inc. Served to capt. AUS, 1942-46. Mem.: Fairview Country (Greenwich, Conn.). Home: 870 United Nations Plz Apt 34B New York NY 10017-1820

DENMARK, FLORENCE HARRIET LEVIN, psychology professor; b. Phila., Jan. 28, 1931; d. Morris and Minnerva (Sharkis) L.; m. Stanley J. Denmark, June 7, 1953 (div. Apr. 1973); children: Valerie, Pamela (dec.) and Richard (twins); m. Robert W. Wesner, Sept. 5, 1973; stepchildren: Kathleen, Michael, Wendy. AB, U. Pa., 1952, AM, 1954, PhD, 1958; DHL, Mass. Sch. Profl. Psychology, 1985, Cedar Crest Coll., 1988; D of psychology, Ill. Sch. Profl. Psychology, 1995; DHL, Alleghany Coll., 1998. Lectr. psychology CUNY, Queens, 1959-66, instr. to prof. NYC, 1964-90, doctoral faculty psychology, 1967-87, prof. psychology, 1984-90; Robert Scott Pace Disting. prof. psychology, chair Pace U., NYC, 1988—; adj. prof. CUNY, NYC, 1990—. Editor: Who Discriminates Against Women?, 1974, Psychology: The Leading Edge Into the Unknown, 1980, (with L.L. Adler) Violence and the Prevention of Violence, 1995, (with M.B. Nadien) Females and Autonomy: A Life-span Perspective, 1999, (with V. Rabinowitz and J. Sechzer) Engendering Psychology, 2000, others; co-editor: Women: Dependent or Independent Variable?, 1975; contbr. various chpts. to books and numerous articles to profl. jours. Mellon scholar St. Olaf Coll., 1977; grantee Ctr. Human Rels. U. Pa., U.S. Office Edn., Rsch. Found. State of N.Y., N.Y. Cmty. Trust, Nat. Sci. Found., Ford Found., Nat. Endowment for Humanities, Nat. Inst. Mental Health, Muskowini Fund, Pace U. Fellow APA (com. on accreditation 1998—, pres. divsn. 52 internat. psychology 1999, pres. 1980, mem. various coms.; Centennial award 1992, disting. contbns. to psychology in pub. interest 1993, disting. contbns. to internat. psychology award 1996, 99), Am. Psychol. Soc. (charter); mem. Internat. Coun. Psychologists (pres. 1989-90), Interamerican Soc. Psychology (Interamerican award in Psychology 1997), Internat. Orgn. for Study of Group Tensions (v.p.), N.Y. State Psychol. Assn. (pres. divsn. social psychology 1989-90, acad. divsn. 1990-91; Kurt Lewin award 1978, Wilhelm Wundt award 1988, Carolyn Wood Sherif award 1992, Allen V. Williams Jr. Meml. award 1994, Margaret Floy Washburn award 1996), N.Y. Acad. Scis. (fellow 1966, v.p. 1984-87, Psychology Adv. Com. 1971—), Eastern Psychol. Assn. (pres. 1986, bd. dirs. 1988-91), Coun. Sci. Pres. (sec., exec. bd. mem. 1983-84), Internat. Coun. Psychologists, Assn. Women in Psychology (Outstanding Women in Sci. award 1980, disting. career award 1996), Soc. for Advancement of Social Psychology, Nat. Coun. of Chairs of Grad. Depts. Psychology, Soc. for Psychol. Study of Social Issues (mem. Otto Klineberg Intercultural and Internat. Rels. Award. Com.), Century Club, Chemists Club, Psi Chi (nat. pres. 1978-80). Avocations: opera, ballet, theater, travel, sports. Office: Pace U 41 Park Row Fl 13 New York NY 10038-1508 E-mail: Fdenmark@pace.edu.

DENMARK, STANLEY JAY, orthodontist; b. Queens, NY, May 26, 1927; s. Jack and Frieda (Kirschenbaum) D.; m. Florence Levin, June 7, 1953 (div. June 1973); children: Valerie, Pamela (dec.) and Richard (twins); m. Anita Goodman, Jan. 2, 1983. BS, Queens Coll., 1950; MSc, NYU, 1955; DDS, U. Pa., 1955, orthodontics cert., 1957. Diplomate Am. Bd. Orthodontics. Practice dentistry specializing in orthodontics, Westbury, N.Y., 1955-91; asst. prof. orthodontics Fairleigh Dickinson U., Hackensack, N.J., 1974-79; clin. assoc. prof. growth and devel. scis. orthodontics Sch. Dentistry NYU, 1991—. With USN, 1945-47. Mem. ADA, Am. Assn. Orthodontists, Northeastern Soc. Orthodontists, Coll. Diplomates of Am. Bd. Orthodontists, Sigma Xi. Jewish. Avocations: painting, woodcuts, tennis, cross country skiing. Home and Office: 351 E 54th St #6B New York NY 10022-4943 Personal E-mail: stanleydenmark@aol.com.

DENN, CYRIL JOSEPH, retired financial advisor; b. Mankato, Minn., Jan. 23, 1948; s. Bertram Henry and Hildegard M. (Drummer) D.; m. Sandra Lee Jones, Oct. 22, 1966 (div. 1970); m. Darlene Kay Wittrock, Apr. 19, 1974; children: Darcy Ann, Amanda Kay, Cassandra Jo. BS, Mankato State U., 1977; cert., Am. Coll., 1985. Factory laborer Kato Engring. Co., Mankato, 1971—74; sales rep. Met. Life, Mankato, 1974—76, sales mgr., 1976—79, sales rep., 1979—82, mktg. specialist Aurora, Ill., 1982—83, br. mgr. Sioux Falls, SD, 1983—84, sales rep., 1984—86; regional mgr. Cath. Aid Assn., St. Paul, 1986—89; mgr. Prudential Ins. Co., Sioux Falls, 1989—91, Aberdeen, SD, 1992—94; asst. mgr. Farm Bur. Fin. Svcs., Aberdeen, 1995—96; fin. advisor Bus., Estate, Retirement & Ins. Planning, Mankato, 1996—2000; fin. svcs. rep. Denn Ins. & Fin. Svcs., 1996—2000; fin. svcs. exec., fin. planner MetLife Fin. Svcs., Mankato, 1997—2000; ret., 2001. Mem. St. Clair (Minn.) Pub. Sch. Bd., 1981-83. With U.S. Army, 1968-71. Fellow: Life Underwriters Tng. Coun.; mem.: So. Minn. Soc. Fin. Svc. Profls., Farmamerica (devel. com. 2003—05, mktg. com. 2003—, programs com. 2003—), Ea. S.D. Soc. Fin. Svc. Profls. (pres. 1992—93, video teleconf. coord. 1992—96), Greater Mankato Area C. of C. (bus. devel. com. 1996—2001, bus. devel. chair 2000—01), Am. Legion (post 475), Leave-A-Legacy (Mankato Chpt.) (chmn. mem. com. 1997—2001), S.D. Planned Giving Coun. (steering com. 1994—95, chair 1995—2001, v.p. programs), Soc. Fin. Svc. Profls. (profl. achievement in cont. edn. com. 1991—94, midwest liaison team 1992—2000, mem. devel. com. 1994—97), Nat. Assn. Ins. and Fin. Advisors (bd. dirs. Sioux Falls chpt. 1991—92, bd. dirs. Aberdeen chpt. 1992—96, chmn. life underwriters tng. coun. state of SD 1993—96, sec.-treas. Aberdeen chpt. 1994—95, pres. elect Aberdeen chpt. 1995—96, edn. chmn. Sioux Falls chpt., co-chmn. life underwriting tng. coun. Sioux Falls chpt.), Gen. Agy. Mgrs. Assn. (career devel. award 1994), Midwest Pony of Americas Club (pres. 1988—91, horse show chmn. 1989), S.D. Ponies of Americas Club (bd. dirs. 1986—97, pres. 1987—89). Independent. Roman Catholic. Avocation: reading. Personal E-mail: cydenn@hickorytech.net.

DENN, MATTHEW P., lawyer; b. 1966; s. Morton Denn; m. Michele Denn; children: Zachary, Adam. B with high distinction, U. Calif., Berkeley; JD, Yale U., 1991. Assco. Del. Vol. Legal Svc., 1991; pvt. practice Del.; atty. Young Conaway, 1994—2001; gen. counsel to gov. Office Gov. State of Del., Dover, 2001; ins. commr. State of Del., Dover, Del. Adj. prof. Widener Law Sch. Mem Kutz Home; mem. Big Brothers/Big Sisters of Del.; vice chmn. Wilmington Civil Rights Commn.; chmn. Child Protection Accountability Commn., Del., 1998; represented Gov. Strategic Econ. Coun., Gov. Cancer Task Force; vice chmn. Del. Dems. Recipient Disting. Svc. award, Del. State Bar Assn. (Young Lawyers Sect.). Office: State of Del 841 Silver Lake Blvd Dover DE 19904 Business E-Mail: matthew.denn@state.de.us.

DENNARD, ROBERT HEATH, engineering executive, scientist; b. Terrell, Tex., Sept. 5, 1932; s. Buford Leon and Loma (Heath) Dennard; m. Jane Bridges; children: Robert(dec.) , Amy, Holly. BSEE, So. Methodist U., 1954, MSEE, 1956; PhD, Carnegie Inst. Tech., 1958. Staff engr. IBM, Yorktown Heights, NY, 1958—63; rsch. staff mem. IBM Rsch. Ctr., Yorktown Heights, NY, 1963—71, group mgr., 1971—79, fellow, Silicon Tech. Dept., 1979—. Contbr. articles to profl. jours.; patentee (scientific works) in field, including basic dynamic RAM memory cell. Named Inventor of Yr., N.Y. Intellectual Property Law Assn., 1995; named to Nat. Inventors Hall of Fame, 1997; recipient Nat. medal of Tech., Pres. U.S., 1988, Harvey prize, Technion-Israel Inst. Tech., 1990, Aachener and

Munchener prize for tech. and applied sci., 2001, Lifetime Achievement award, MIT program, Lemelson, 2005, Benjamin Franklin medal in Electrical Engring., Franklin Inst., 2007. Fellow: IEEE (Edison medal 2001); mem.: Am. Philos. Soc., NAE. Achievements include invention of the dynamitc random access memory chip in 1967; patents in field. Avocation: Scottish country dancing. Office: IBM Rsch Ctr PO Box 218 Yorktown Heights NY 10598-0218

DENNEEN, JOHN PAUL, lawyer; b. NYC, Aug. 18, 1940; s. John Thomas Denneen and Pauline Jane Ludlow; m. Mary Veronica Murphy, July 3, 1965 (dec. Dec. 2000); children: John Edward, Thomas Michael, James Patrick, Robert Andrew, Daniel Joseph, Mary Elizabeth; m. Ginger O'Brien, Feb. 21, 2004. BS, Fordham U., 1963; JD, Columbia U., 1966. Bar: N.Y. 1966, U.S. Ct. Appeals (2d cir.) 1974, U.S. Dist. Ct. (so. and ea. dists.) N.Y. 1975, Mo. 1987. Assoc. Seward & Kissel, NYC, 1966-75; sr. v.p., gen counsel, sec. GK Techs., Inc., Greenwich, Conn., 1975-83; exec. v.p., gen. counsel, sec. Chromalloy Am. Corp., St. Louis, 1983-87; ptnr. Bryan Cave LLP, St. Louis, 1987-99; exec. v.p. corp. devel. and legal affairs, sec. NuVox, Inc., St. Louis, 1999—. Mem. ABA, Internat. Bar Assn., N.Y. State Bar Assn., N.Y.C. Bar Assn., Bar Assn. Met. St. Louis. Office Phone: 636-537-7356.

DENNEHY, BRIAN, actor; b. Bridgeport, Conn., July 9, 1938; m. Judith Scheff, 1959 (div. 1974); 3 children; m. Jennifer Arnott, 1988; 1 adopted child. BFA, Columbia U.; postgrad., Yale U. Appeared in motion pictures Semi-Tough, 1977, F.I.S.T., 1978, Foul Play, 1978, Butch and Sundance: The Early Days, 1979, 10, 1979, Little Miss Marker, 1980, Split Image, 1982, First Blood, 1982, Never Cry Wolf, 1983, Gorky Park, 1983, Twice in a Lifetime, 1985, Silverado, 1985, Cocoon, 1985, F/X, 1986, Legal Eagles, 1986, Best Seller, 1987, The Belly of an Architect, 1987, Return to Snowy River, 1988, Miles from Home, 1988, Cocoon: The Return, 1988, The Last of the Finest, Seven Minutes, Presumed Innocent, 1990, F/X 2, 1991, Gladiators, 1991, Midnight Movie, 1993, Gilligan's Island: The Movie, 1997, Tommy Boy, 1995, The Stars Fell on Henrietta, 1995, Romeo and Juliet, 1996, Dish Dogs, 1998, Out of the Cold, 1999, Deep River, Finders, Keepers, Looking for Mr. Goodbar, Summer Catch, 2001, Stolen Summer, 2002, She Hate Me, 2004, Assault on Precinct 13, 2005, 10th & Wolf, 2006, Welcome to Paradise, 2006, (voice) Everyone's Hero, 2006; theatre appearances include Streamers, off-Broadway, 1976, The Rat in the Skull, Death of a Salesman (Tony award 1999), Wisdom Bridge Theatre, Chgo., 1985, The Cherry Orchard, Bklyn. Acad. Music, 1988, The Iceman Cometh, Goodman Theatre, Chgo., 1990, Says I, Says He, Sea Plays, Bus Stop, Julius Caesar, Ivanov, The Front Page, Translations, Galileo, A Touch of the Poet, Goodman Theatre, Chgo., MacBeth, Romeo & Juliet, 1996, Long Days Journey into Night (Tony award winner for best actor), 2003, Death of a Salesman (Laurence Olivier award best actor, 2006), Inherit the Wind, 2007; appeared in TV series Big Shamus, Little Shamus, 1979, Star of the Family, 1982-83, Birdland, 1993-94, (BBC series) Nostromo, 1995, A Season in Purgatory, 1996, Undue Influence, 1996, Larry McMurty's Dean Man Walk, 1996; numerous movies for TV including Annie Oakley, Showtime Cable TV Tall Tales and Legends series, 1985, Acceptable Risk, 1986, HBO prodn. The Lion of Africa, 1987, Perfect Witness, 1989 (Cable Ace nominee), The Last of the Finest, 1990, Shattered Vows, 1993, Murder in the Heartland, 1993 (Emmy nomination, Supporting Actor - Miniseries or Special, 1993), Prophet of Evil, 1993, Foreign Affair, 1993 (CableAce award, Best Actor in a movie or miniseries), Rising Son, Bloodfeud, Evergreen, Acceptable Risks, The Terrorist, A Rumor of War, In Broad Daylight, The Last Place on Earth, Teamster Boss: The Jackie Presser Story, Birdland, Leave of Absence, Jack Reed: An Honest Cop, Final Appeal, Pride and Extreme Prejudice, (miniseries) A Killing in a Small Town, 1990 (Emmy nominee for Outstanding Supporting Actor), To Catch a Killer, 1991 (Emmy nominee, Am TV awards nominee), The Burden of Proof, 1992 (Emmy nominee for Outstanding Supporting Actor), A Season in Purgatory, 1996, Nostromo, 1996, Dead Man's Walk, 1996, Day One, Undue Influence, 1996; dir., co-writer, actor, co-exec. prodr.: (TV movies) Jack Reed: Champion of the Cheap Homicide, Jack Reed: A Killer Amoungst Us, Jack Reed: One of Our Own, Shadow of A Doubt, Jack Reed: A Search for Justice, Jack Reed: Death and Vengeance, 1996, Netforce, 1999, Too Rich: The Secret Life of Doris Duke, Fail Safe, 2000, A Season on the Brink, 2002, Our Fathers, 2005; exec. prodr. (TV films) Three Blind Mice, 2001, Warden of Red Rock, 2001, Death of a Salesmean, 2000. With USMC, Vietnam. Mem.: Sigma Chi.*

DENNEHY, RAYMOND LEO, philosopher, educator; b. San Francisco, Aug. 31, 1934; s. Joseph Patrick and Mary Agnes Dennehy; m. Maryann Dennehy, Aug. 4, 1990; children: Mark, Bridget, Andrea, Rosalind. BA in Philosophy, U. San Francisco, 1962; postgrad., U. Calif., Berkeley, 1962—64; PhD in Philosophy, U. Toronto, 1973. Asst. prof. philosophy U. Santa Clara, Calif., 1966—72; instr. philosophy West Valley C.C., Saratoga, Calif., 1972—74; asst. dean, lectr. philosophy U. San Francisco, 1974—79, assoc. prof. philosophy, 1979—85, prof. philosophy, 1985—. Founding mem., tchr. St. Ignatius Inst., U. San Francisco, 1976—2001, Campion Coll., San Francisco, 2002—. Author: Reason & Dignity, 1981, Anti-Abortionist at Large, 2002; editor: Christian Married Love, 1981. With USN, 1954—58, PTO. Recipient Human Life award, San Francisco United for Life, 1999, St. Luke's award, San Francisco Guild of the Cath. Med. Assn., 2004. Mem.: Cath. Acad. Scis. USA, Nat. Assn. Scholars, Am. Soc. for Bioethics and Humanities, Fellowship of Cath. Scholars (bd. dirs. 1984—87), Am. Cath. Philos. Assn. (exec. com. 1983—86), Am. Maritain Assn. (pres. 1986—94, Humanitarian award 2003). Republican. Roman Catholic. Office: U San Francisco Philosophy Dept 2130 Fulton St San Francisco CA 94117 Home Phone: 415-753-3749; Office Phone: 415-422-6456.

DENNEN, KEITH CAMERON, lawyer; b. Savannah, Ga., Dec. 7, 1962; s. James B. and Margaret (Carey) D.; m. Leah Mead May, Sept. 12, 1987; 1 child, Hillary Claire. BBA, Memphis State U., 1984, JD, 1987. Bar: Tenn. Supreme Ct. 1987, U.S. Dist. Ct. (mid. dist Tenn. 1988). Judicial clerk to Hon. William H.D. Fones Tenn. Supreme Ct., Nashville, 1987—88; atty. Baker, Worthington, Crossley, Stansberry & Woolf, Memphis, 1987, Bone McAllester Norton PLLC, Nashville. Contbr. articles to profl. jours.; former editor Tenn. Ethics Handbook, 2nd edit., Tenn. Local Rules of Court. Bd. dir. Hendersonville Area C. of C., 1997—2001, Sumner Found., Gallatin, Tenn., 1998—, United Chambers of Commerce, Sumner County, 1998—2001; pres. Hendersonville Area C. of C., 1999—2000; bd. trustee Davidson Acad., 2001—; mem. exec. com. bd. dirs. Nashville Med. Group Mgmt. Assn., 2000—; pres. Hendersonville Chamber Found., 2001. Recipient Hendersonville Chamber's Vol. Yr. award, 1998. Mem. ABA (young lawyers divsn., chair ethics & professionalism com., 1991-93, governing bd. forum on franchising, 1993-95), Tenn. Bar Assn. (young lawyers divsn. chair publs., 1992-93, disting. svc. award, 1993), Nashville Bar assn., Sumner County Bar Assn., Rotary Club of Hendersonville, Tenn. Office: Baker Worthington Crossley Stansberry & Woolf 1700 Nashville City Ctr 511 Union St Nashville TN 37219-1733 also: Bone McAllester Norton PLLC 511 Union St Ste 1600 Nashville City Center Nashville TN 37219

DENNERY, LINDA, newspaper publishing executive; b. Phila., July 7, 1947; V.p., gen. mgr. Times-Picayune, New Orleans, 1987—97, pres., mem. of advisory bd., 1997—99; pub. Star-Ledger, Newark, 1999—2004; exec. v.p. benefits Advance Newspaper Group, 2004—. Bd. dirs. Kingsley House, Touro Infirmary, Bur. Govtl. Rsch., So. Newspaper Pub. Assn., Internat. Women's Forum. Mem.: bd. of dir. of Kingsley House, Touro Infirmary, Bureau of Governmental Research, Southern Newspaper Pub. Assoc., International Women's Forum. Office: Exec VP Benefits Advance Publications Inc 950 Fingerboard Rd Staten Island NY 10305 Office Phone: 212-286-2860.

DENNETT, DANIEL CLEMENT, philosopher, writer, educator; b. Boston, Mar. 28, 1942; s. Daniel Clement Jr. and Ruth Marjorie (Leck) D.; m. Susan Elizabeth Bell, June 8, 1962; children: Andrea Elizabeth, Peter Nathaniel. BA, Harvard U., 1963; PhD, Oxford U., 1965. Lectr. Oxford Coll. Tech., Eng., 1964-65; asst. prof. philosophy U. Calif., Irvine, 1965-70, assoc. prof. philosophy, 1970-71, Tufts U., Medford, Mass., 1971-75, prof. philosophy, 1975-85, disting. arts and scis. prof., 1985—, dir. ctr. cognitive studies, 1985—. Vis. prof. Harvard U., Cambridge, Mass., 1973, Pitts. U., 1975; co-dir. curricular software studio, Tufts U., Medford, 1985-89; John Locke lectr. Oxford U., 1983; Gavin David Young lectr. Adelaide U., Australia, 1985; Taft lectr. U. Cin., 1978; Luce disting. lectr. cognitive sci. U. Rochester, 1979; Herbert Spencer lectr. Oxford U., 1979; annual philosophy lectr. Princeton U., N.J., 1980; Sloan vis. scientist lectr. Yale U., New Haven, Conn., 1980; council philos. studies, summer inst. psychology, philosophy mind U. Wash., Seattle, 1981; Gramlich Meml. lectr. Dartmouth Coll., Hanover, N.H., 1985; vis. prof. Ecole Normale Superieure, Paris, 1985; disting. lectr. series, MIT Lab. Computer Sci., Cambridge, 1986. Author: Content and Consciousness, 1969, International Library of Philosophy and Scientific Method, paperback edit., 1986, Italian edit., 1992, Brainstorms: Philosophical Essays on Mind Psychology, 1978, Italian edit., 1990, Swedish edit., 1992, Elbow Room: The Varieties of Free Will Worth Wanting, 1984, German edit., 1986, Spanish edit., 1992, The Intentional Stance, 1987, French edit., 1990, Spanish edit., 1991, Consciousness Explained, 1991, Dutch, Italian, French, German edits., 1993, Darwin's Dangerous Idea, 1995, Kinds of Minds, 1996, BrainChildren, 1998, Freedom Evolves, 2003, Sweet Dreams, 2005, Breaking the Spell, 2006; co-author: (with Douglas R. Hofstadter) The Mind's I: Fantasies and Reflections on Self and Soul, 1981, Japanese edit., 1984, Spanish and Italian edits., 1985, German and Dutch edits., 1986, Chinese, French edits., 1987; assoc. editor: Behavioral and Brain Sciences; contbr. numerous articles and reviews to profl. jours. Santayana fellow (hon.), 1974, NEH Younger Humanist fellow, 1974, Fulbright research fellow, 1978, All Souls Coll. vis. fellow, 1979, NEH sr. fellow, 1979, Ctr. Advanced Study Behavioral Scis., 1979-80, Guggenheim fellow, 1986-87, Golden Plate award, Acad. Achievement, 2006. Mem. AAUP, Am. Acad. Arts and Scis., Am. Philos. Assn., Cognitive Sci. Soc., Coun. Philos. Studies, Soc. Philosophy Psychology (pres. 1980-81). Clubs: Kollegewidgwok Yacht (Blue Hill, Maine). Democrat. Avocations: sculpture, farming, sailing, scuba diving. Office: Tufts U Ctr for Cognitive Studies Medford MA 02155*

DENNICK, LORI ANN (L. ANNE), publicist, actress, journalist; b. Cannonsburg, Pa., Feb. 8, 1962; d. Albert William and Mary Alice (Baldwin) D. Diploma in cosmetology and salon mgmt., Pa. Beauty Acad., 1981; AS, Pa. Comml. Bus. Coll., Washington, 1987; BA, U. Md., 1992; diploma in modeling, acting and profl. devel., Barbizon Pitts., 1995. Editor, art dir. Common Ground, Pitts., 1995-96. Holdenlog guest product reviewer, 2003; publicist Pitts. Idol Publicity Team, 2006; signature sponsor A White Ho. Dinner in Pitts., 2007; publicist Am. Sleep Apnea Assn., Washington. Freelance contbr.: Observer Reporter, 1980—97, staff writer, music reviewer: Indie Music Stop, 2006—; actor: (films) The Mothman Prophecies, 2002, The Clearing, 2004, Smart People, 2007, (theater) Footloose, A Human Face, Oliver, Go Ask Alice, Fiddler on the Roof, Miracle on 34th Street, Three Penny Opera, Curse of the Starving Class, Richard III, The Seagull, The Game: It's All About Football, The Kill Point, 2007; contbr. columns in newspapers, articles to mags. and jours. Mem. daffodil days com. Am. Cancer Soc., Pitts., 1999. Named Miss 16 Plus-Model of Yr., Miami, Fla., 1995, Ms. Plus Internet World, 2002, Miss Pa. Galaxy, 2002, Miss Am. Rose McKeesport City Queen, 2003; recipient Ms. McKeesport Am. States, 2003. Mem.: NOW, AFTRA, Am. Sleep Apnea Assn. Democrat. Presbyterian. Avocations: theater arts, travel, painting, jewelry design. Office Phone: 412-927-3182. Personal E-mail: lannecarrington@publicist.com.

DENNIES, SANDRA LEE, city official; b. Buffalo, Dec. 26, 1951; d. Norman John and Shirley Edith (Dils) D.; m. Robert Francis Gilbane, Sept. 21, 1974 (div. Apr. 1987); children: Brandon Michael, Gianpatrick. AS in Dental Hygiene, U. Bridgeport, Conn., 1972, BS in Dental Hygiene Edn., 1973; MS in Health Scis., So. Conn. State U., New Haven, 1979. Dental hygienist various orgns., New Haven, 1972-73, Leonard B. Zaslow, DDS, Westport, Conn., 1973-81; lectr. U. Bridgeport, Conn., 1973—76; planner City of Bridgeport, Conn., 1977—79, planning asst., 1979—81; grants dir. City of Stamford, Conn., 1981—2007, dir. adminstrn., 2007—. Sec. Com. Emergency Med. Disaster Planning, Bridgeport, 1978-79; dir., dep. dir. Stamford Coliseum Authority, 1982-91; dep. dir. Stamford Film Commn., 1986-88; mem. Stamford Water Pollution Control Authority, 2007-. Editor, chief Hy-Light Jour., 1973-76. Mem. Stamford Youth Planning Adv. Bd., 1981-91, Stamford Youth Svc. Bur., 1991-95, 2006—, United Way Corp., Stamford, 1986-93; pres., sec. Alcohol Drug Abuse Coun., 1987-92; mem. bd. Christian Outreach North Stamford Congl. Ch., 1988-92, 1995-2000, 2006-07; mem. pastoral rels. com., 1995—; mem. Coun. Chs. Synagogues Assembly, Stamford, 1989; pres. Stamford Mcpl. Supervisory Employees Union, 1991-99, mem. 1981—; v.p., sec. Stamford Sch. Readiness Found., 1998—; advisor Stamford Sr. Ctr, 2004-2007; bd. dir. Smith House, 2007-, Conn. Conf. Munipalities, 2007-, legislative com., 2007-; mem. Conn. Coalition for Justice in Edn. Funding, 2007-. Mem.: Govt. Fraud Officer's Assn. Democrat. Avocations: piano, guitar. Home: 171 Shadow Ridge Rd Stamford CT 06905-1813 Office: City of Stamford 888 Washington Blvd PO Box 10152 Stamford CT 06904-2152

DENNIN, JOSEPH FRANCIS, former government official, lawyer; b. NYC, June 9, 1943; s. William Wilfred and Kathryn L (Sever) D.; m. Sandra Earl Peek, Dec. 28, 1968; children: Theresa Michel, Allison Kathleen, James Joseph. AB with great distinction, Stanford U., 1965, JD, 1968; postgrad., U. Helsinki, Finland, 1968-69. Bar: Calif. 1969, N.Y. 1970, D.C. 1986, U.S. Supreme Ct. 1985, U.S. Ct. Appeals (fed. cir.) 1987, Ct. Internat. Trade 1987. Assoc. Simpson, Thacher & Bartlett, NYC, 1969-75; counsel U.S. Senate Intelligence Com., Washington, 1975-76; staff asst. to Pres. White House, Washington, 1976-78; dir. ops. U.S. Internat. Trade Commn., Washington, 1978-79; dep. assoc. atty. gen. Dept. Justice, Washington, 1979-81; dep. asst. sec. for fin., investment and svcs. Dept. Commerce, Washington, 1981-82, dep. asst. sec. for Africa, the Near East and South Asia, 1982-84, asst. sec. for internat. econ. policy, 1984-86; ptnr. internat. dept. McKenna Long & Aldridge LLP, Washington, 1986—. Bd. dirs. U.S.-Taiwan Bus. Coun.; mem. bd. advisors N.Am. Free Trade and Investment Report; mem. N.Am. Free Trade Agreement Article 19 Panel. Gen. editor Law and Practice of the World Trade Orgn. Fulbright grantee Inst. Internat. Edn., 1968 Mem. ABA. Home: 5108 Nahant St Bethesda MD 20816-2336

DENNING, KAREN CRAFT, finance educator; b. Pitts., Mar. 23, 1952; d. Edward Harvey and Esther Naomi Craft; m. John Thomas Denning; children: Naomi Liza, Chloe, Lacey. AB, Cornell U., 1974; PhD, U. Pitts., 1986. Lectr., asst. prof. Case Western Res. U., Cleve., 1985—88; prof. W.Va. U., Morgantown, 1988—2003, Fairleigh Dickinson U., 2003—. Editor: e-Jour. Social Studies, 2002—; contbr. articles to profl. jours. Bd. dirs. Katz Grad. Sch. Bus. Ph.D. Alumni Bd., Pitts. Grantee Internat. Programs Instrnl. Tech. grantee, W.Va. U., 1998—99. Mem.: Am. Fin. Assn., So. Fin. Assn., Midwestern Fin. Assn., Ea. Fin. Assn., Fin. Mgmt. Assn., 20th Century Club, Beta Gamma Sigma (pres. 1998). Presbyterian. Avocations: travel, piano, reading, skiing. Office: Fairleigh Dickinson U 1000 River Rd H-DH-02-5 Ridgefield Park NJ 07660

DENNING, PETER JAMES, computer scientist, engineer; b. NYC, Jan. 6, 1942; s. James Edwin and Catherine M. D.; m. Dorothy Elizabeth Robling, Jan. 24, 1974; children: Anne, Diana. BEE, Manhattan Coll., 1964, ScD (hon.), 1985; MS in Elec. Engring., MIT, 1965, PhD, 1968; LLD (hon.), Concordia U., 1984; PhD (hon.), Pace U., 2002. Asst. prof. elec. engring. Princeton U., 1968-72; assoc. prof. computer scis. Purdue U., 1972-75, prof., 1975-84, head dept., 1979-83; dir. Rsch. Inst. Advanced Computer Sci. NASA Ames Rsch. Ctr., Mountain View, Calif., 1983-90, rsch. fellow, 1990-91; assoc. dean, chair of computer sci. dept. George Mason U., 1991-97, dir. Ctr. for New Engr., 1993-98, vice provost for continuing profl. edn., 1997-98, univ. coord. for process reengring., 1998-2000, spl. asst. to v.p. for info. tech., 2000—02, chair of technology coun., 2001—02; prof., chmn. computer sci. dept. Naval Postgrad. Sch., 2002—, dir. Cebrowski Inst. Info. Superiority and Innovation, 2003—. Co-founder CSNET, 1981; bd. dirs. Charles Babbage Inst., 2000-04, trustee, 1997—; bd. dirs. Ctr. for Nat. Software Studies, 1996—; mem. tech. adv. bd. Sequent Computer Corp., 1985-91, Hewlett-Packard Labs., 1989-93. Author: Professional Development Seminars, 1968—, also textbooks and numerous rsch. papers; columnist Am. Scientist mag., 1985-93, ACM Comm., 2001-. Bd. dirs. Philharmonic Baroque Orchestra, San Francisco, 1988—91. Recipient Outstanding Faculty award Princeton U. Engring. Assn., 1971, Best Paper award Am. Fedn. Info. Processing Socs., 1972, Disting. Svc. to Computing Rsch. award Computing Rsch. Assn., 1989, Centennial Engring. award Manhattan Coll., 1992, Commonwealth Va. Outstanding Educator award, 2003, Engring. Best Tchr. award George Mason U., 2002, Univ. Outstanding Faculty award 2002, Hall of Fame award Spl. Interest Group on Op. Sys., 2005; NSF fellow, 1964-67, NSF Disting. Edn. fellow, 2007. Fellow IEEE, AAAS, Assn. for Computing Machinery (pres. 1980-82, Karl Karlstrom Outstanding Educator award 1996, Outstanding Contbn. award 1998, Outstanding Computer Sci. Educator award 1999, Special award for Svc. 2007), Am. Soc. for Engring. Edn., Assn. for Computing Machinery (chmn. publs. bd. and leader digital libr. project 1992-98, chmn. edn. bd. 1998—2003, dir. info. tech. profession initiative 1999-2001, editor-in-chief Computing Surveys 1977-79, Comm. ACM 1983-92, Best Paper award 1968, Recognition of Svc. award 1974, Disting. Svc. award 1989), N.Y. Acad. Scis.; mem. Sigma Xi, Eta Kappa Nu, Tau Beta Pi. Achievements include development of a working set model for program behavior, an essential element of virtual memory, computer architecture and Internet caching; important extensions to operational analysis of network systems; discovery of seven foundational practices for innovation, formulation of great principles of computing. Office: Naval Postgrad Sch Code CS Monterey CA 93943 Home Phone: 831-455-0190; Office Phone: 831-656-3603. Business E-Mail: pjd@nps.edu.

DENNIS, ANTHONY JAMES, lawyer; b. Manchester, Conn., Feb. 11, 1963; BA cum laude, Tufts U., Medford, Mass., 1985; JD, Northwestern U., Chgo., 1988. Bar: Conn. 1988, DC 1989, US Dist. Ct. Conn. 1988. Assoc. Robinson & Cole, Hartford, Conn., 1988-89; atty. Aetna, Inc., Hartford, 1989-92, counsel, 1992—. Author: The Rise of the Islamic Empire and the Threat to the West, 1996, Letters to Khatami: A Reply to the Iranian President's Call for a Dialogue Among Civilizations, 2001, Osama Bin Laden: A Psychological and Political Portrait, 2002; co-author: Healthcare Antitrust: Strategies for Changing Provider Organizations, 1994, Handbook of Psychobiography, 2005; contbr. articles to profl. jours.; co-host (TV series) Able Lives (Emmy award, 2007), Able Lives Incorporated, guest commentator (Nat. Empowerment TV) Direct Line, (Court TV) Cochran & Company, guest various talk radio shows. Mem. Conn. Bar Assn. (subcom. chmn. 1990-93, exec. com. 1990—, com. chmn. 1990—, treas. 1993-94, vice-chmn. 1994-95, chmn. 1995-99), DC Bar Assn., Am. Health Lawyers Assn., KC (past grand knight). Business E-Mail: dennisaj@aetna.com.

DENNIS, DIANE JOY MILAM, retired architect; b. Jacksonville, Fla., Oct. 8, 1925; d. Robert Richerson Milam, Meriel Lapham Wilson; m. Thomas Gordon Dennis, Nov. 9, 1974 (dec. Apr. 1999). Grad., Bennington Coll., 1947; MArch, Columbia U., 1955; studied landscape arch., Harvard U., 1998. With several archtl. firms, NYC; with Edward Durell Stone on Kennedy Ctr. Mem.: AIA. Home: 47 E 64th St Apt 10A New York NY 10021

DENNIS, DONNA FRANCES, sculptor, art educator; b. Springfield, Ohio, Oct. 16, 1942; d. Donald Phillips and Helen Frances (Hogue) D. BA in Art, Carleton Coll., 1964; student, Coll. Art Studies Abroad, Paris, 1964-65, Art Students League, NYC, 1965-66. Instr. Skowhegan Sch. Painting and Sculpture, Maine, 1982, Sch. Visual Arts, NYC, 1983-90, SUNY, Purchase, 1984-85, 87, Princeton U., NJ, 1984; assoc. prof. SUNY Purchase Coll., 1990-96; prof. SUNY, 1996—, Doris and Karl Kempner disting. prof., 2001—03. One-woman shows include Holly Solomon Gallery, NYC, 1976, 80, 83, 98, Contemporary Arts Ctr., Cin., 1979, Neuberger Mus. of SUNY-Purchase, 1985, Univ. Gallery, U. Mass., Amherst, 1985, Bklyn. Mus., 1987, Del. Art Mus., Wilmington, 1988, Indpls. Mus. Art, 1991-98, Sculpture Ctr., NYC, 1993, Dayton Art Inst., 2003, Five Myles, Bklyn., 2005, Park Ave. Malls, NYC, 2007; exhibited in group shows Venice Biennale, Italy, 1982, 84, Whitney Mus., NYC, 1979, 81, Tate Gallery, London, 1983, Hirshhorn Mus., Washington, 1979, 84, Biennial of Pub. Art, Neuberger Mus., 1997, Asheville Mus. Art, NC, 1998, Palazzo Ducale, Genoa, Italy, 2004, Ctr. for Arch., NY, 2005, Margulies Collection at the Warehouse, Miami; commd. decorative fence P.S. 234, N.Y.C., I.S. 5, Queens, NY, Grey Gallery, NYU, 2006; represented in permanent collections at Wonderland Sta., MBTA, Boston, North Plaza, Klapper Hall, Queens Coll., Queens, NY, Am. Airlines Terminal, Terminal One, Kennedy Airport, NYC. Recipient Art award for excellence in design N.Y.C. Art Commn., 1987, Art award Am. Acad. and Inst. of Arts and Letters, 1984, Bessie Set Design award, 1992; grantee N.Y. State Creative Artists, 1975, 81, N.Y. Found. for Arts, 1985, 92; fiscal sponsorship, N.Y. Found. for Arts, 2002-; fellow Guggenheim Found., 1979, NEA, 1977, 80, 86, 94, Pollock-Krasner award, 2001, 05; Doris and Karl Kempner Dist. Prof. award Purchase Coll. SUNY, 2001-03. Democrat. Home: 131 Duane St New York NY 10013-3850 E-mail: tunnelsandtowers@att.net.

DENNIS, EVERETTE EUGENE, JR., foundation executive, educator, writer; b. Seattle, Aug. 15, 1942; s. Everette Eugene and Kathryn Marie (Platt) D.; m. Emily Thompson Smith, 1987. BS, U. Oreg., 1964; MA, Syracuse U., 1966; PhD, U. Minn., 1974; postdoc., Harvard U., 1978-79. Info. officer dept. mental health State of Ill., Chgo., 1966-68; asst. prof. Kans. State U., Manhattan, 1968-72; asst. prof., assoc. prof. then prof. U. Minn., Mpls., 1972-81, dir. grad. program. Sch. Journalism and Mass Communication, 1978-81; prof., dean Sch. Journalism U. Oreg., Eugene, 1981-84; founding exec. dir. Freedom Forum Media Studies Ctr. Columbia U., NYC, 1984-96; also v.p., 1989-94; sr. v.p., 1994-97; exec. dir. Internat. Consortiums Univs., 1996-97; founding pres. Am. Acad. in Berlin, 1996-2000; Felix E. Larkin disting. prof. Grad. Sch. of Bus., Fordham U., 1997—; COO Internat. Longevity Ctr., 1999—. Head Project on Future of Journalism and Mass Communication Edn.; former trustee Internat. Mus. Photography at Eastman House, Rochester, NY, Internat. Inst. Communications, London, Ctr. Internat. Journalists. Reston, Va.; councillor Am. Antiquarian Soc., Worcester, Mass.; mem. adv. bd. Fred Rogers Ctr., Latrobe, Pa.; mem. Annenberg Found. Commn. on the Press, 2005. Author, editor books including: The Magic Writing Machine, 1971, Other Voices: The New Journalism in America, 1973, Justice Hugh Black and the First Amendment, 1978, Enduring Issues in Mass Communication, 1978, The

Media Society, 1978, Reporting Processes and Practices, 1981, New Strategies for Public Affairs Reporting, 1983, Basic Issues in Mass Communication, 1984, Reshaping the Media, 1989, Media Freedom and Accountability, 1989, The Cost of Libel, 1989, Media Debates, 1991, 3rd edit., 2006, Understanding Mass Communication, 7th edit. 2002, Media and the Environment, 1991, Beyond the Cold War, 1991, Of Media and People, 1992, Demystifying Media Technology, 1993, Higher Education in the Information Age, 1993, America's Schools and the Mass Media, 1993, Radio-The Forgotten Medium, 1995, The Culture of Crime, 1995, American Communication Research, 1996, Publishing Books, 1997, Media and Public Life, 1997, Media and Children, 1996, Media-Black and White, 1996, Media and Congress, 1997, Media and Democracy, 1998, Finding the Best Business School, 2006; editor-in-chief Media Studies Jour. 1987-96; contbr. articles to profl. jours. Summer fellow Stanford U., 1969, East-West Communication Inst., Hawaii, 1976; liberal arts fellow in law, Harvard U., 1978-79, vis. Nieman fellow, 1980, John F. Kennedy Sch. Govt. rsch. fellow, 1981, John Henry Newman fellow Fordham U., 2002-03, fellow Ctr. for Journalism and Democracy, U. So. Calif.; recipient H. Kreighbaum Under 40 award, 1982, U. Oreg. Webfoot award, 1985, Disting. Svc. award U. Oreg., 2002, Global Media Rsch. award Ctr. Global Media, 2002, Eleanor Blum award for rsch. and rsch., 2004; inducted to Oreg. Journalism Hall of Achievement, 2001. Fellow Am. Orthopsychiat. Assn.; mem. Assn. Edn. in Journalism and Mass. Comms. (pres. 1983-84), Am. Polit. Sci. Assn., Internat. Comm. Assn., Soc. Profl. Journalists, Internat. Mass Comm. Rsch. Soc., Internat. Inst. Comm., Coun. Fgn. Rels., Century Assn. (NY), Harvard Club (NY). Office: ILC-USA 60 E 86th St New York NY 10028-1009 also: Fordham U 113 W 60th St New York NY 10023-7404 Home Phone: 914-271-2890; Office Phone: 212-663-6144. Business E-Mail: dennis@fordham.edu. E-mail: eedennis@optonline.net.

DENNIS, FRANK GEORGE, JR., retired horticulture educator; b. Lyons, NY, Apr. 12, 1932; s. Frank George and Corinne Isabel (Smith) D.; m. Katharine Ann Merrell, June 5, 1954. BS in Agriculture, Cornell U., 1955, PhD in Pomology, 1961. Postdoctoral fellow NSF, Gif-sur-Yvette, France, 1961-62; asst. prof. Cornell U., Geneva, NY, 1962-68, assoc. prof., 1968—, Mich. State U., East Lansing, 1968-72, prof., 1972-96; ret., 1996. Fulbright fellow, Morocco, 1990. Fellow Am. Soc. for Hort. Sci. (v.p. 1985-86, Gourley award 1985, sci. editor HortScience 1997-2000); mem. Internat. Soc. Hort. Sci. (chmn. working group 1984-90), Sigma Xi. Home: 1600 Ridgewood Dr East Lansing MI 48823-2936 Business E-Mail: fgdennis@msu.edu.

DENNIS, GARY C., neurosurgeon, educator; b. Washington, Dec. 27, 1950; s. Creed and Yvonne (Bush) C.; children: Gary Jr., Gina, Gregory. BA, Boston U., 1972; MD, Howard U., 1976. Intern Johns Hopkins Hosp., Balt., 1976-77; resident Baylor Coll. Medicine Affiliated Hosp., Houston, 1977-81; chief of neurosurgery Kern Med. Ctr., Bakersfield, Calif., 1981-83; clin. assoc. prof. U. Calif., San Diego, 1981-85; chief of neurosurgery Howard U., Washington, 1984—, asst. prof. surgery, 1984-90, assoc. prof., 1990—; attending physician DC Gen. Hosp., Washington, 1990—. Surg. cons. DC Gen. Hosp., 1986-89; mem. Mayors Commn. to oversee Med. Examiners Office, Washington, 1990, Mayors Transition Team for Health, Washington, 1990; vis. lectr. neurosurgery Johns Hopkins Sch. Med., 1990-98; mem. DC Commn. on Jud. Disabilities and Tenure, 2000—; mem. Sec.'s Adv. Com. on Regulatory Reform, 2001-02; chmn. bd. Delmarva Found. DC; mem. Bd. Med. Edn. for South African Blacks, 2002-06. Mem. Practicing Physicians Adv. Coun., Health Care Fin. Agy., Washington, 1991-99, Com. on Health Care Reform, Congl. Black Caucus, Washington, 1994—; bd. dirs. Am. Liver Found., 1999-2002; mem. DC Health Care Reform Commn. Named One of Top Drs. S.E. Area, Washingtonian Mag., 1995, Top Drs. No. Va. Mag., 2007. Fellow ACS; mem. Med. Soc. DC (pres. 1996-98, chmn. bd. dirs. 1998-99, alt. del. to AMA 2001), Nat. Med. Assn. (bd. dirs. 1992-97, 98-, pres.-elect 1997, pres. 1998-99), Am. Assn. Neurol. Surgeons (mem. chair 1994-95), Howard U. Med. Alumni Assn. (pres. 2002-04). Avocations: music, outdoor cooking, fishing. Office: Howard U Hosp 2041 Georgia Ave NW Washington DC 20060-0001 E-mail: gcdennis@pol.net.

DENNIS, GIGI (GINETTE E. DENNIS), former state official; b. Kansas City, Mo., Nov. 28, 1961; m. Dean Dennis. Student, Adams State Coll., U. So. Colo., Harvard U. With Band of Monte Vista, 1982-87; customer svc. rep. Pub. Svc. Co. Colo., Alamosa, 1987-91, Pueblo, 1991-94; mem. Colo. State Senate from dist. 5, Denver, 1995—2001; dir. rural devel USDA, Denver, 2001—05; sec. state State of Colo., Denver, 2005—07. Bd. mem. El Pueblo Boys and Girls Ranch; active Sangre de Cristo Arts Ctr., Rosemount Mus.; sec., past sec. Rio Grande County Reps.; past chair Ho. Dist. 60; mem. Local, State and Nat. Campaign Com., 1984—. Mem. Pueblo Zool. Soc., Bel Nor Rep. Women, Monte Vista C. of C., Pueblo West Rotary, Colo. Cattle Assn. Republican. Roman Catholic. Office Phone: 303-894-2200 ext. 6108. Fax: 719-547-9330; Office Fax: 303-869-8460.*

DENNIS, JACK BONNELL, computer scientist, educator; b. Elizabeth, NJ, Oct. 13, 1931; SB, SM, MIT, 1954, ScD in Elec. Engring., 1958. Asst. prof. elec. engring. MIT, Cambridge, 1959-65, assoc. prof., 1965-69, prof. computer sci. and engring., 1969-87; prof. computer sci. and engring. emeritus, 1987—; pres. Dataflow Computer Corp., 1987-2000; computer arch. Carlstedt Elektronik, 1992—94. Chief scientist Acorn Networks, 1996-2001. Recipient Eckert-Mauchly award IEEE Assn. for Computing Machinery, 1984 Fellow IEEE, Assn. for Computing Machinery. Office: Computer Sci and Artificial Intelligence Lab MIT Rm 32-G864 Cambridge MA 02139

DENNIS, JAMES L., history educator; m. Bonnie J. Hasley, June 24, 1972. BA in History, Marietta Coll., Ohio, 1975; MA in Edn., Salem Coll., W.Va., 1985; M. W.Va. U., Morgantown. Social studies tchr. Parkersburg (W.Va.) S. H.S., 1979—, chmn. dept., 2001—. Author: Washington's Darker Brother, 1986; contbr. articles to profl. jours. Named Outstanding History Tchr., DAR, Wood County, W.Va., 2007; recipient Star award, Gen. Electric, 1991, 2005. Mem.: W.Va. Profl. Educators, Nat. Coun. Social Studies. Avocations: reading, sports. Home: 1508 Lake Hills Dr Parkersburg WV 26101 Office: Parkersburg S High Sch 1511 Blizzard Dr Parkersburg WV 26101 Office Phone: 304-420-9610.

DENNIS, JAMES LEON, federal judge; b. Monroe, La., Jan. 9, 1936; s. Jenner Leon and Hope (Taylo) Dennis; children: Stephen James, Gregory Leon, Mark Taylo, John Timothy. BS in Bus. Adminstrn, La. Tech. U., Ruston, 1959; JD, La. State U., 1962; LLM, U. Va., 1984. Bar: La. 1962. Assoc. firm Hudson, Potts & Bernstein, Monroe, 1962—65, ptnr., 1965—72; judge 4th Dist. Ct. La. for Morehouse and Ouachita Parishes, 1972—74, La. 2d Circuit Ct. Appeals, 1974—75; assoc. justice La. Supreme Ct., 1975—95; coord. La. Constnl. Revision Commn., 1970—72; del., chmn. judiciary com. La. Constnl. Conv., 1973; judge US Ct. Appeals (5th cir.), New Orleans, 1995—; visiting prof. Tulane Law School, 2003. Chmn. La. Commn. on Bicentennial U.S. Constn.; mem. La. Ho. of Reps., 1968—72. With US Army, 1955—57. Mem.: ABA (com. on appellate practice), 4th Jud. Bar Assn., La. Bar Assn., Rotary. Methodist. Office: US Courthouse 600 Camp St Rm 219 New Orleans LA 70130-3425*

DENNIS, JOHN DAVISON, minister; b. Pitts., Sept. 18, 1937; s. John Wellington and Helen Isabella (Davison) D.; m. Nancy Schumacher, Jan. 7, 1967; children: Michael, Andrew. AB, Wesleyan U., 1959; BD, Princeton Theol. Sem., 1962, ThM, 1965. Ordained to ministry United Presbyn. Ch. (USA), 1962. Asst. pastor First Presbyn. Ch., Germantown, Pa., 1962—69, sr. pastor Corvallis, Oreg., 1969—2006, sr. minister emeritus, 2006—. Exch. min. St. Columba's Presbyn. Ch., Johannesburg, Republic of South Africa, 1978. Chaplain Germantown Hosp., 1965-69; west coast dean Presbyn. Young Pastors Seminars, 1983-85; pres. Madison Ave. Task Force, 1975-77, pres. Corvallis Community Improvement, Inc., pres. USSR Sister City Assn., 1989-90; founder Corvallis Fish Emergency Aid Svc., 1969-76; trustee Ecumenical Ministries of Oreg., 1989-98, chmn. bd. dirs. 1996-98; bd. dirs. United Way of Benton County, 1986-90; candidate U.S. Congress from Oreg. 5th dist., 1988; asst. squash coach Princeton U., 1959-62; fundraiser for humanitarian orgns. working with landmine victims in Cambodia, 1994—. Recipient Spl. Achievment award City of Corvallis, 2002; fellow Aspen Inst., 1987; Pacific coast doubles squash champion, 1972-73. Mem. Rotary (charter mem., dir. local club, Rotarian of Yr. 1998). Home: 2760 NW Skyline Dr Corvallis OR 97330-3168 Personal E-mail: johnddennis@comcast.net.

DENNIS, KELLY, art history professor; AB, Occidental Coll., LA, 1985; MA, UCLA, 1989, PhD, 1994. Vis. lectr. U. Calif., Santa Cruz, 1994—96; asst. prof. Sch. Art Inst. Chgo., 1996—99, U. Conn., Storrs, 2002—. Author: (book) Art/Porn: A History of Seeing and Touching. Office: Univ Conn Dept Art & Art History Storrs Mansfield CT 06269-1099 Office Fax: 860-486-3769. Business E-Mail: kelly.dennis@uconn.edu.

DENNIS, KEVIN M., lawyer; BA cum laude, Middlebury Coll., 1976; JD, Boston Coll., 1983. Bar: Mass. 1983. Assoc. Goodwin Procter LLP, Boston, 1983—90, ptnr., bus. law dept., 1990—, mem., private equity group, ptnr. in charge, profl. develop., training. Staff Boston Coll. Law Rev. Mem.: ABA, Mass. Bar Assn., Boston Bar Assn. Office: Goodwin Procter LLP Exchange Pl 53 State St Boston MA 02109 Office Phone: 617-570-1528. Office Fax: 617-523-1231. Business E-Mail: kdennis@goodwinprocter.com.

DENNIS, LAWRENCE C. (LARRY), dean, physics professor; BS, U. Mich., 1974; PhD in Nuclear Physics, U. Va., 1979. Prof. physics Fla. State U., Tallahassee, 1979—, acting dir. Supercomputer Computations Rsch. Inst., assoc. v.p. academic affairs, dir. office for distributed and distance learning, dean Coll. Info., 2004—. Mem. adv. com. on tchg. and learning EDUCAUSE. Recipient Tchg. Incentive Program award, State of Fla. Mem.: Southeastern U. Rsch. Assn. (bd. dirs.). Office: Fla State U Coll Info 101 Louis Shores Bldg 222 Magnolia Way Tallahassee FL 32306-2100 Office Phone: 850-644-5775. Office Fax: 850-644-9763. E-mail: ldennis@ci.fsu.edu.*

DENNIS, PATRICIA DIAZ, lawyer; b. Santa Rita, N.Mex., 1946; d. Porfirio Madrid and Mary (Romero) Diaz; m. Michael John Dennis, Aug. 3, 1968; children: Ashley Elizabeth, Geoffrey Diaz, Alicia Sarah Diaz. BA in English, UCLA, 1970; JD, Loyola U. LA Sch. Law, 1973. Bar: Calif. 1973, DC 1984, Tex. 1998. Law clk. Calif. Rural Legal Asst., McFarland, 1971; assoc. Paul, Hastings, Janofsky & Walker, LA, 1973—76; atty. Pacific Lighting Corp., LA, 1976—78; atty., asst. gen. atty. ABC, Hollywood, 1978—83; mem. NLRB, Washington, 1983—86; commr. FCC, 1986—89; ptnr., head comm. Jones, Day, Reavis & Pogue, 1989—91; v.p. govt. affairs US Sprint/United Telecom, 1991—92; asst. sec. State for Human Rights and Humanitarian Affairs Dept. State, Washington, 1992; special coun. comm. Sullivan & Cromwell, 1993—95; sr. v.p.and asst. gen. counsel SBC Comm., San Antonio, 1995—98, sr. v.p. regulatory and pub. affairs, 1998—2002; sr. v.p., gen. counsel and sec. SBC West, 2002—04; sr. v.p. and asst. gen. counsel AT&T (formerly known as SBC), 2004—. Bd. dir. Mass. Mut. Life Ins. Co., UST Inc.; chmn. US del. Internat. Telecomm. Union Region 2 Broadcasting Conf., Rio de Janeiro, 1988; bd. dir. Telemundo Group Inc., 1989-92, Nat. Pub. Radio, 1993-99, PR Legal Def. and Edn. Fund, 1991-92; mem. adv. bd. Ctr. Telecom. and Info. Studies, Columbia U., 1991-05, Latin Am. Inst., Loyola U. (LA Sch. Law), 1973, Bur. Nat. Affairs, Media Law Reporter, 1990-05; mem. Nat. Adv. Com. (Women Judges' Fund for Justice), 1990-93. Exec. editor Loyola Law Rev., 1972—73. Com. mem. Hispanic leadership program Coro Found., LA, 1981-82; U.S. del. UN Commn. on Status of Women, 30th session Econ. and Social Coun., Vienna, Austria, 1984, World Conf. UN Decade Women, Nairobi, Kenya, 1985; bd. dir. Resources Infant Educators, 1981-83, Nat. Network Hispanic Women, LA, 1983-92, Reading is Fundamental, 1991-98; mem. exec. com., nat. adv. bd. Leadership Am., Found. for Women's Resources, 1989-02, bd. mem.; bd. visitors Pepperdine U. Sch. Law, 1988-92; mem. adv. coun. Ctr. Pub. Utilities, N.Mex. State U., 1988-92; trustee Tomás Rivera Policy Inst., 1991-05, Radio and Television News Dirs. Found., 1993-05,; bd. dir. Women's Mus., 1998-03, Bexar County Women's Bar Assn., 1998-02, Tex. State U. Sys. Bd. Regents, 1999-05, Hispanic Scholarship Fund, 1997-00, Mex. Am. Legal Defense and Ednl. Fund, 1999-01; nat. sec. Girl Scouts US, 1999-02, first vice chair, 2002-05, chair, 2005-; trustee NHP Found., 2003-. Named Hispanic Woman Yr., Houston YWCA, 1992, Alumna Yr., UCLA Latino Alumni Assn., 1999, Corp. Exec. Yr., San Antonio Women's C. of C., 1999; named one of 100 Influentials, Hispanic Bus. mag., 1987, 1988, 1990, 1996, 80 Elite, Hispanic Women Directory, 2002, Top 25 Elite Women, Hispanic Mag., 2004, Top 100 Latinas, 2003, 2004; recipient cert. achievement, L.A. YMCA, 1979, Woman Yr. award merit, Mex. Am. Opportunity Found., 1984, Recognition Outstanding Achievements award, Nat. Coun. Hispanic Women, 1986, Woman Achievement award, City Club Cleve., 1986, Friend of Family award, The Family Place, 1987, Woman Yr. award, Hispanic Women's Coun., Inc., 1989, Exec. of Yr. award, Nat. Hispanic Employee Assn., 1999, Belva Lockwood Outstanding Lawyer award, Bexar County Women's Bar Assn., 2000, Pub. Endeavor award, Assn. Women in Comm., 2001, Leadership award, Cuban Am. Nat. Coun., 2002, Hall of Fame award, San Antonio Women, 2002, Corp. Responsibility Svc. award, MALDEF, 2003, Fortune Dir. award, Hispanic Assn. Corp. Responsibility, 2004, Legacy of Leadership award, Spelman Coll., 2006. Mem. Mex.-Am. Bar Assn. (sec. 1980-81, trustee 1979-80, 81-82), LA County Bar Assn. (child abuse subcom. chmn. barristers sect. 1980-81, exec. com. barristers sect. 1980-82), Hispanic Bar Assn. DC, ABA (com. labor arbitration and law of collective bargaining agreements, labor law sect. 1979-82), Women's Forum Wash., Am. Bar Assn. Commn. (on opportunities for minorities in the profession 1991-92, mem. nominations com., 1991-92, co-chmn. common carrier com., 1990-91), Fed. Comm. Bar Assn. Democrat. Roman Catholic. Office Phone: 210-351-3439. Business E-Mail: pdennis.1@att.com.

DENNIS, ROGER J., dean, law educator; b. Cleve., Jan. 17, 1950; BS in Speech, Northwestern U., 1971, JD, 1974. Bar: Ill. 1974. Law clk. to Hon. Richard W. McLaren US Dist. Ct., Ill.; trial atty. & spl. asst. to asst. atty. gen. Antitrust Divsn. US Dept. Justice, Washington; assoc. Skadden, Arps, Slate, Meagher & Flom, Washington; assoc. prof. law Rutgers U. Sch. of Law, Camden, NJ, 1986, assoc. dean faculty and academic affairs, 1987—90, acting dean, 1990, prof. of law, 1991—2007, dean, 1991—97, acting provost, 1997, provost, 1997; founding dean Drexel U. Coll. of Law, Phila., 2007—. Mem. Nat. Multiple Sclerosis Soc., Camden County Regional Legal Services Bd.; vice chmn. NJ Commn. on Professionalism in Law; bd. dirs. United Way of Camden County; bd. trustees Greater Camden Partnership; mem. C. of C. of Southern NJ; bd. dirs. Cooper Ferry Develop. Corp. Recipient Nathan Asbell Humanitarian award, United Way of Camden County, 2003. Mem.: Am. Law Inst., ABA (past vice chmn. accreditation com. legal edn. sect.). Office: College of Law Drexel Univ 3320 Market St Philadelphia PA 19104

DENNIS, RUTLEDGE M., sociologist, educator; b. Charleston, SC, Aug. 16, 1939; s. David and Ora Jane (Porcher) D.; children: Shay Tchaka, Imaro Marlin Aki, Kimya Nuru, Zuri Sanyika. BS, S.C. State U., Orangeburg, 1966; MA, Wash. State U., Pullman, 1969, PhD, 1975. Dir. Black studies program Va. Commonwealth U., Richmond, 1971—78, assoc. prof. dept. sociology, 1978—89; Commonwealth prof. dept. sociology George Mason U., Fairfax, Va., 1989—, prof. dept. sociology, 1992—, dir. African Am. studies, 2006—. Co.-dir. sociology grad. program George Mason U., 1993—2001; coord. Southeastern Regional African Seminar, Richmond-Charlottesville, 1973—76; del. Ea. Va. Internat. Consortium, 1972—77; pres. Assn. Black Sociologists, 1981—83; founder Rutledge Dennis Found. for Human Devel., Ctr. for African Am. Culture and Leadership; co-founder African-Am. Acad.; creator of Dennis-Weathers award for intergroup rels. George Mason U., 2004, mem. exec. com. African Am. Studies Program, 2004—; co-investigator Black Middletown Project, 1980—81. Co-author: The Politics of Annexation, 1982; editor: Elsevier Sci. Ltd. Series in Race and Ethnic Rels., 1990—, Racial and Ethnic Politics, 1994, The Black Middle Class, 1995, W.E.B. Du Bois: The Scholar as Activist, 1996, Black Intellectuals, 1997, Marginality, Power and Social Structure: Issues in Race, Class and Gender Analysis, 2005; series editor: Oliver C. Cox, 2000; co-editor: The Afro-Americans, 1976, Race and Ethnicity in Rsch. Methods, 1993, Race and Ethnicity: Comparative and Theoretical Approaches, 2003, The Racial Politics of Booker T. Washington, 2006, The New Black: New Paradigms and Perspectives for the 21st Century, 2007, The Bi-Cultural Experience, 2007, Black Conservative Thought, 2007. Housing commr. Richmond Redevel. and Housing Authority, 1977-80; bd. dirs. Housing Opportunities Made Equal, Richmond, 1976-80; participant Sea Island Voter Edn. Project, Charleston, SC, 1964. With U.S. Army, 1960-63. Fellow Fgn. Affairs scholar, 1965; recipient Cmty. Svc. award Boys Clubs Am., 1976; named Outstanding Educator of Am., 1975; Fenwick fellow George Mason U., 2005—; recipient Reise-Melton Cultural award, 1980, Disting. Leadership award Afro-Am. Studies Program, 1991, Nat. Black Monitor Family and Cmty. award 1985, Va. Commonwealth U., 1991, Pres.'s award S.C. State U., 1966, Jewish Educators award, 1998, Joseph Himes award for Disting. scholar, 2001, Ba'Alay Keriyah Soc., 2003, DuBois-Johnson-Frazier award for Disting. Scholarship, Tchg., and Svc., Am. Sociol. Assn., 2006, others; grantee Ford Found., 1970, NEH, 1978, NIMH, 1980-81; 25th Ann. lectr. African-Am. studies program Va. Commonwealth U., 1996, Faculty Devel. grantee Coll. Humanities and Social Sci. George Mason U., 2007, others. Mem. AAAS, AAUP (v.p. George Mason U. chpt. 2005—), NAACP (life, Faculty Excellence award George Mason U. chpt. 2007), Am. Sociol. Assn., Soc. Study Social Problems, So. Sociol. Soc., Ea. Sociol. Soc. (chmn. minorities com. 1992-96, mem. editl. bd. Race and Soc. 1998-2005), Assn. Black Sociologists (pres. 1981-82, 82-83, chmn. hist. and archives com., 2002—, Leadership award 1995), African Heritage Soc., Sigma Xi, Omicron Delta Kappa, Alpha Phi Alpha (Acad. Excellence award 1985), Alpha Kappa Mu, Alpha Kappa Delta. Office: George Mason U Dept Sociology Anthrop Fairfax VA 22030 Office Phone: 703-993-1431. Business E-Mail: rdennis1@gmu.edu.

DENNIS, WILLIE E., lawyer; b. Queens, NY, Mar. 30, 1962; BA in English, Columbia U., 1984, JD, 1988. Bar: NJ 1988, NY 1990, DC 1992. Assoc. Orrick, Herrington & Sutcliffe, 1988—91, Mudge Rose Guthrie Alexander & Ferdon, 1991—95; ptnr. Thelen Reid & Priest LLP, NYC, and co-chair, private equity and venture capital practice; ptnr. Kirkpatrick Lockhart Nicholson Graham LLP, 2005—. Bd. dirs. Upper Manhattan Empowerment Zone Devel. Corp. Named one of Am. Top Black Attys., Black Enterprise, 2003. Office: Kirkpatrick Lockhart Nicholson Graham LLP 599 Lexington Ave New York NY 10022 Office Phone: 212-536-4044. Office Fax: 212-536-3901. Business E-Mail: wdennis@klng.com.

DENNISON, D. BRIAN, lawyer; b. Augusta, Ga., Nov. 29, 1972; BA with hon., Univ. Ga., 1995, MBA, 1998, JD cum laude, 1998. Bar: Ga. 1998. Assoc. atty., comml. litig., criminal defense Bouhan, Williams & Levy, LLP, Atlanta. Spkr. in field. Mem. edl. bd.: Ga. Jour. Internat. Comparative Law. Mem. bd. Christ Church Children's Sch.; coach mock trial Savannah Arts Acad. Named Rising Star, Ga. SuperLawyers Mag., 2005. Mem.: ABA, Savannah Bar Assn. Office: Bouhan Willams Levy Amstrong House 447 Bull St Savannah GA 31402-2139 Fax: 912-233-0801.

DENNISON, DANIEL THOMAS, environmental compliance and lab administrator; b. Denver; s. James Thomas Dennison and Martha Elizabeth McLendon; m. Carol Lin Massey, Feb. 21, 2004; children: Kristopher Thomas, Kimberlee Dyan stepchildren: Caleb Travis Holsey, Seth James Holsey, Rachael Dené Crain. BA in Biology, Tex. Tech U., Lubbock, 1972, grad. cert. profl. study in health orgn. mgmt., 1987, MBA, 1990. Cert. asbestos hazard emergency response operations and maintenance Tex. Dept. Health, hazardous waste operations and emergency response OSHA, incident comdr., accredited clin. lab. technologist Ctrs. Disease Control, tchg. cert. sci. Tex., registered environ. health specialist Nat. Environ. Health Assn., sanitarian Tex. Dept. Health. Lab. svcs. coord., regional lab. dir. Lubbock Health Dept., 1974—88, environ. programs coord., 1988—93; mgr. communication svcs. & emergency preparedness City of Lubbock, 1993—95, environ. compliance mgr., 1995—. Mem. exec. com. Local Emergency Planning Com., Lubbock, 1994—95, vice chmn., 2004—07; mem. cmty. disaster adv. com. ARC, Lubbock, 1995; bd. dirs. Lubbock Emergency Communication Dist., 1994—95; mayor's restoration adv. bd. rep. Dept. of Def. / Reese AFB, Lubbock, 1996—2007; bd. dirs., mem. fin. com. South Plains Aids Resource Ctr., Lubbock, 1998—2001; rep. EPA Nat. Soil, Wind Erosion and Agrl. Particulates Coalition, Research Triangle Park, NC, 1992—94; air adv. panel US Sec. of Agr., Amarillo, Tex., 1999; human health workgroup state of tex. environ. priorities project Tex. Natural Resources Conservation Commn., Austin, 1994. Named MDA Camp Attendant of the Yr., Muscular Dystrophy Assn., 2002, 2005; recipient citation for exemplary work on environ. hazards, Nat. Clean Air, Clean Water and Toxic Waste Superfund Task Force, 1986, commendation, Chmn. of Tex. Natural Resources Conservation Commn., 2000, Legendary Svc. award, City of Lubbock, 2000, 2001, Outstanding Achievement award, Lubbock City Coun., 2001, Spl. recognition for enhancing quality of life in Lubbock, Tex., 2003, Breakthrough Award, Dale Carnagie, 2004. Fellow: Tex. Pub. Health Assn. (hon.; pres., vp, exec. bd., governing coun. 1980—2006, Outstanding Svc. award 1985, 1988, 1996), Tex. Environ. Health Assn. (assoc.; governing coun., west tex. chpt. pres. 1989—93, I.E. Scott award for Excellence 2000); mem.: Clin. Lab. Managers Assn. (assoc.; treas., chmn. fin. com. 1985—87), Nat. Environ. Health Assn. (assoc. Nat. cert. of Merit 2003), Lubbock Area Grotto (assoc.; chmn., environ. officer, safety officer 1993—2006), Nat. Speleological Soc. (assoc.). Achievements include development of BT Test to detect covert antibiotic use; direct glucose quantitation of patient whole blood microspecimens. Avocations: caving, backpacking, writing, hunting, travel. Home: 5718-68th St Lubbock TX 79424 Home Phone: 806-794-3440; Office Phone: 806-775-2880.

DENNISON, DONALD LEE, lawyer; b. Dec. 5, 1932; s. Robert Irving and Hannah W. Dennison; m. Tina L. Dennison, Feb. 12, 1955; children: Scott A., Carol R., David R. BSME, Carnegie Inst. Tech., Pitts., 1955; JD, George Washington U., 1961. Bar: Va. 1969, U.S. Supreme Ct. 1965, U.S. Ct. Appeals (fed. cir.) 1969, Md. 1968, D.C. 1962, U.S. Ct. Appeals (4th cir.) 1970. Examiner U.S. Patent Office, Washington, 1957-60; ptnr. Dennison & Dennison, Washington, 1960-66, Dennison, Meserole, Pollack & Scheiner, Arlington, Va., 1966-98, Dennison, Meserole, Scheiner & Schultz, 1999-2000, Dennison, Scheiner, Schultz and Wakeman, 2000—01, Dennison, Schultz, and MacDonald, Alexandria, 2002—. Past pres. Met. Washington Soccer Referees Assn., 1980-83; v.p. Mid-Atlantic D.O.G.S., Inc. Search and Rescue Unit. 1st lt. U.S. Army, 1954-57. Mem. Internat. Trademark Assn., European Cmty. Trademark Assn., Internat. Assn. Intellectual Property. Republican. Home: 11209 Farmland Dr North Bethesda MD 20852-4521 Office: Dennison Schultz & MacDonald 1727 King St Alexandria VA 22314 Office Phone: 703-837-9600. Business E-Mail: ddennison@dennisonlaw.com.

DENNISON, GEORGE MARSHEL, academic administrator; b. Buffalo, Ill., Aug. 11, 1935; s. Earl Fredrick and Irene Gladys (McWhorter) D.; m. Jane Irene Schroeder, Dec. 26, 1954; children: Robert Gene, Rick Steven. AA, Custer County (Mont.) Jr. Coll., 1960; BA, U. Mont., 1962, MA, 1963; PhD, U. Wash., 1967. Asst. prof. U. Ark., Fayetteville, 1967-68; vis. asst. prof. U. Wash., Seattle, 1968-69; asst. prof. Colo. State U., Fort Collins, 1969-73, assoc. prof., 1973-77, assoc. dean Coll. Arts, Humanities and Social Sci., 1976-80, prof., 1977-87, acting acad. v.p., 1980-82, acting assoc. acad. v.p., 1982-86, assoc. acad. v.p., 1987; provost, v.p. acad. affairs Western Mich. U., Kalamazoo, 1987-90; pres. U. Mont., Missoula, 1990—. Cons. U.S. Dept. Justice, 1976-84; bd. dirs. Inst. Medicine and Humanities, Missoula, Internat. Heart Inst. Mont., Missoula. Author: The Dorr War, 1976; contbr. articles to jours. in field. Bd. dirs. Kalamazoo Ctr. for Med. Studies, 1989-90, Missoula Rocky Mountain Coll., Billings, Mont. Campus Compact, Internat; Maureen & Mike Mansfield Found.; bd. dirs., chair Student Exchange Program; chair Mont. Commn. Cmty. Svc.; presdl. appointee Nat. Security Edn. Bd. With USN, 1953-57. ABA grantee, 1969-70; Colo. State U. grantee, 1970-75, Nat. Trust for Hist. Preservation grantee, 1976-78; U.S. Agy. for Internat. Devel. grantee, 1979—; Colo. Commn. on Higher Edn. devel. grantee, 1985. Mem. Am. Hist. Assn., Orgn. Am. Historians, Am. Assn. Higher Edn., Am. Soc. for Legal History. Avocations: handball, cross country skiing. Office: U Montana Office of The Pres Univ UH 109 Missoula MT 59812-0001 Business E-Mail: dennisongm@mso.umt.edu.*

DENNISON, LISA, auction house executive; b. NJ, May 13, 1953; d. Saul and Ellyn Dennison; m. Roderick Waywell, Sept. 9, 1983; children: Brad, Tyler. BA in Art History and French, Wellesley Coll., Mass., 1975; MA in Art History, Brown U., Providence, 1978. Intern Solomon R. Guggenheim Mus., NYC, 1973, asst. curator, 1981-89, assoc. curator, 1990-91, collections curator, 1991—94, curator of collections exhbns., 1994-96, chief curator, 1996, dep. dir., 1996—2005, dir., 2005—07; North and South Am. exec. v.p. Sotheby's, NYC, 2007—. Instr. Sch. Visual Arts, NYC, 1983—84; mem. ArtTable, NYC. Mem. NY State Coun. on Arts, NYC; founding mem. creative arts adv. bd. Brown U.; mem. NY com. Wellesley Coll. Friends of Art; mem. nat. adv. coun. visual arts Wake Forest U., Winston-Salem, NC; mem. internat. adv. bd. Louise T. Blouin Found.; bd. dirs. Byrd Hoffman Found., NYC. Office: Sothebys 1334 York Ave at 72nd St New York NY 10021 Office Phone: 212-423-3500.*

DENNISON, RONALD WALTON, engineer; b. Oct. 23, 1944; s. S. Mason and Elizabeth Louise (Hatcher) D.; m. Deborah Ann Rutter, Aug. 10, 1991; children: Ronald, Frederick. BS in Physics and Math., San Jose State U., 1970, MS in Physics, 1972. Physicist Memorex, Santa Clara, 1970—71; sr. engr. AVCO, San Jose, Calif., 1972—73; advanced devel. engr. Perkin Elmer, Palo Alto, Calif., 1973—75; staff engr. Hewlett-Packard, Santa Rosa, Calif., 1975—79; program gen. mgr. Burroughs, Westlake Village, Calif., 1979—82; dir. engring., founder EIKON, Simi Valley, Calif., 1982—85; sr. staff technologist Maxtor Corp., San Jose, 1987—90; dir. engring. Toshiba Am. Info. Sys., 1990—93, cons. engr., 1994—. Author: tech. publs. Sgt. USAF, 1963—67. Mem.: IEEE, Internat. Comanche Soc., Aircraft Owners and Pilots Assn., Internat. Disk Drive Equipment and Materials Assn., Internat. Soc. Hybrid Microelectronics, Am. Vacuum Soc. Republican. Methodist. Home: 4050 Soelro Ct San Jose CA 95127-2711 Office Phone: 408-929-7023. E-mail: ron@rondennison.com.

DENNISON, SHIRLEY ANN, publishing executive; b. Durango, Colo., Oct. 5, 1946; d. Harold Colonel and Amy Dorothy (Nelson) Thompson; m. Harry Woodrow Dennison, Apr. 23, 1974; 1 child, James Michael. Student, Colo. State U., Fort Collins, 1964—65, Ft. Lewis Coll., Durango, Colo., 1965—66. Reporter, proofreader The Dolores Star, Colo., 1981—97, editor, reporter, photographer, 1997—2003; admin. asst. I Colo. Dept. Labor and Employment, Denver, 2004—06; disability program navigator Dept. Labor and Dept. Local Affairs, Denver, 2006—; co-owner, pub. editor The Valley Voice newspaper, Dolores, 2005—. Freelance historian, Dolores, Cortez, Mancos, Colo., 1965—; freelance rschr., Colo., 1965—. Contbr. articles and photos to publs. Com. mem. Nat. Seat Belt Com., Cortez, 2000, Vocat. Coalition/Vocat. Consortium, Cortez/Durango, 2006; mem. Montezuma County Jail Ministry, Cortez, 2007; bd. mem. Montezuma County Cmty. Corrections, Cortez, 2000—05. Scholar, Dolores Re-4A Sch. Bd., 1964. Mem.: Dolores C. of C., Dolores Rotary Club. Republican. Avocations: writing, gardening, reading, dance, travel. Home Phone: 970-882-4114.

DENNISTON, BRACKETT BADGER, III, lawyer; b. Oak Park, Ill., July 23, 1947; s. Brackett Badger Jr. and Frances Ann (Jones) D.; m. Kathleen Foley, Aug. 2, 1975; children: Alexandra, Brackett Badger IV, Elizabeth. AB, Kenyon Coll., Gambier, Ohio, 1969; JD, Harvard U., Cambridge, Mass., 1973. Bar: Mass. 1974, U.S. Dist. Ct. Mass. 1975, U.S. Dist. Ct. (we. dist.) Tex. 1987, U.S. Ct. Appeals (1st cir.) 1975, U.S. Ct. Appeals (D.C. cir.) 1976, U.S. Ct. Appeals (7th cir.) 1978, U.S. Ct. Appeals (10th cir.) 1981, U.S. Supreme Ct. 1981. Law clk. to judge U.S. Ct. Appeals 9th Cir., Honolulu, 1973—74; assoc. Goodwin, Procter & Hoar, Boston, 1974—81, ptnr., 1981—82, 1986—93, mem. exec. com., 1990—93; chief major frauds unit U.S. Atty.'s Office, Boston, 1982—86; chief legal counsel Gov. of Mass., Boston, 1993—96; v.p. GE, Fairfield, 1996—2005, sr. counsel litig., 1996—2004, gen. counsel, 2004—05, sr. v.p., gen. counsel, sec., 2005—. Chair, compliance review bd. GE, 1999—. Class chmn. Kenyon Coll., Gambier, Ohio, 1979-90, trustee, 2000-04, 2005—, sec., 2005—; mem. Duxbury (Mass.) Zoning Bd. Appeals, 1980-92, chmn., 1984-90; dir. New Eng. Legal Found., 1998—, vice-chair 2003— Recipient Dir.'s award for superior achievement U.S. Dept. Justice, 1986. Mem. Am. Arbitration Assn. (bd. dirs.), Mass. Bar Assn. (chmn. coun. jud. adminstrn. sect. 1989-90, jud. adminstrv. coun. 1987-90), Boston Bar Found. (trustee 2002-04). Office: GE Corp 3137 Easton Tpke Fairfield CT 06432-1008 Office Phone: 203-373-2453. Business E-Mail: brackett.denniston@corporate.ge.com.

DENNO, DEBORAH W., law educator; b. June 6, 1952; BA, U. Va., 1974; MA, U. Toronto, 1975; Ph.D, U. Pa., 1982, JD, 1989. Bar: Pa. 1990. Rsch. assoc. Georgetown Law Ctr., Inst. Criminal Law & Procedure, 1975—76; instr. criminology, Dept. Sociology U. Pa., 1977—79; mgmt. rsch. analyst Wharton Sch., U. Pa., 1977—79, sr. rsch. assoc., lectr., & project dir. Sellin Ctr. Studies in Criminology & Criminal Law, 1979—88; assoc. Simpson, Thacher & Bartlett LLP, 1990; law clk. to Hon. Anthony J. Scirica US Ct. Appeals (3rd. Cir.), Phila., 1990—91; assoc. prof. law Fordham U. Sch. Law, NYC, 1991—97, prof. law, 1997—2006, Arthur A. McGivney prof. law, 2006—. Cons. NJ Death Penalty Project, Office Pub. Defender, 1984—91; coord., Wharton Doctoral Program in Criminology U. Pa., 1984—85; vis. prof. pub. & internat. affairs Woodrow Wilson Sch., Princeton U., 1992; mem. US Sentencing Commn. Drugs/Violence Task Force, 1994—97; vis. prof. law Vanderbilt U. Sch. Law, 2000, Columbia U. Sch. Law, 2001; vis. sr. fellow U. London, Sch. Advanced Study, Inst. Advanced Legal Study, 2001; British Acad. vis. prof. London Sch. Econ. & Polit. Sci., 2006. Co-author (with Ruth Schwarz): Biological, Psychological, & Environmental Factors in Delinquency & Mental Disorder: An Interdisciplinary Bibliography, 1985; author: Biology and Violence: From Birth to Adulthood, 1990; co-editor: Encyclopedia of Crime & Justice, vols. 1-4, 2002. Named one of The 50 Most Influential Women Lawyers in Am., Nat. Law Jour., 2007. Office: Fordham U Sch Law 140 W 62nd St New York NY 10023 E-mail: ddenno@law.fordham.edu.*

DENNY, BREWSTER CASTBERG, retired university dean; b. Seattle, Sept. 5, 1924; s. Merle Wilson and Margaraith (Castberg) D.; m. Patricia Virginia Sollitt, June 14, 1950; 1 child, Maria Janet. AB, U. Wash., 1945; MA in Law and Diplomacy, Tufts U., 1948, PhD, 1959. Instr. Mass. Inst. Tech., 1948-52; with Office of Sec. of Def., 1952-60; profl. staff mem. Sub-Com. on Nat. Policy Machinery, US Senate, 1960-61; asso. prof. pub. affairs U. Wash., 1961-64, prof. pub. affairs, 1964—, 1st dir. Grad. Sch. Pub. Affairs, 1962-68, 1st dean, 1968-80, dean emeritus, 1980—, chmn. marine affairs bd., 1972-79, prof. Am. diplomatic history, 1991—. US rep. to 23d Gen. Assembly UN, 1968; cons. RAND Corp., 1961-68; mem. vis. com. dept. govt. Harvard U., 1967-72; mem. Presdl. Adv. Coun. on Intergovtl. Pers. Policy, 1971-74; chmn. Gov. Task Force on Exec. Orgn., 1968-72; presdl. mem. US-PR Commn. on Status of PR, 1964-66; mem. bd. sci. and tech. in devel. NAS, 1976-81, co-chmn. Korean com. on sci. and tech., 1977-82; mem. Rsch. and Edn. Adv. Panel to Compt. Gen. US, 1979-2000. Author: Seeing American Policy Whole, 1985; contbr. to Am. Polit. Sci. Rev., Pub. Adminstrn. Rev.; contbr. articles to profl. jours.; chpts. to books. Trustee Century Fund, 1975—, vice chmn., 1982-86, chmn., 1986-94; co-chair Children's Budget Coalition, 1991—. Mem. AAAS (com. on new directions 1975-78, charter mem. com. on sci. and pub. policy 1968-72, com. on arms control 1980-88), ASPA, UN Assn. USA (nat. policy panel on UN capabilities in the 1970s 1970-71), Nat. Acad. Pub. Adminstrn., Am. Hist. Assn., Coun. Fgn. rels., Nat. Assn. Sch. Pub. Affairs and Adminstrn. (pres. 1968-69). Home: 2021 1st Ave Apt F12 Seattle WA 98121-3113

DENNY, COLLINS, III, lawyer; b. Richmond, Va., Dec. 5, 1933; s. Collins Jr. and Rebecca (Miller) Denny; m. Anne Carples, June 28, 1957; children: Collins IV, William R., Katharine D. Joyce. AB, Princeton U., 1956; LLB, U. Va., 1961. Bar: Va. 1961, U.S. Dist. Ct. (ea. dist.) Va. 1962, U.S. Ct. Appeals (4th cir.) 1962, U.S. Tax Ct. 1971, U.S. Ct. Claims 1976. Assoc. Denny, Valentine & Davenport, Richmond, 1961-67; ptnr. Mays & Valentine LLP, Richmond, 1967-2000, mng. ptnr., 1992-93; gen. counsel, corp. sec. Coastal Lumber Co., Weldon, NC, 1980—2003; ptnr. Troutman, Sanders, Mays & Valentine LLP, Richmond, 2001. Gen. counsel Bear Island Timberlands Co., LLC, Ashland, Va., 1985—99, Bear Island Paper Co., LLC, 1989—2000. Contbr. chapters to books, articles to profl. jours. Lt. USNR, 1956—66. Mem.: ABA (chmn. exempt orgns. subcom., tax. sect. 1971—86), Richmond Feeder Cattle Assn. (pres. 1972—77), Va. Forestry Assn., Va. Tax Rev. (adv. bd. 1978—2002), Va. State Bar (com. chmn. 1981—83), Va. Bar Assn. (chmn. jr. bar 1965—66), Princeton Alumni Assn. Va. (pres. 1974—78), Country Club Va., Deep Run Hunt Club (pres. 1987—88), Richmond-First Club (pres. 1969—70). Episcoplian. Avocations: horse sports, tree farming, agriculture. Office: Troutman Sanders LLP 1001 Haxall Point PO Box 1122 Richmond VA 23218-1122

DENNY, JAMES M., pharmaceutical and former retail executive; Former exec. v.p., chief fin. and planning officer G.D. Searle & Co.; former chmn. Pearle Heath Svcs. Inc., Dallas; former CFO & vice chmn. Sears, Roebuck & Co.; bd. dirs. Gilead Sci., 1996—, chmn., 2001—, mem. nominating, audit and corp. governance commt. Former dir. Astra AB; sr. advisor William Blair Capital Partners, LLC, 1995—2000; bd. dirs. Allstate Corp., GATX Corp., ChoicePoint, Inc. Chmn. Northwestern Memorial Found. Office: Gilead Sciences Inc 333 Lakeside Dr Foster City CA 94404

DENNY, MARY CRAVER, retired state legislator, business owner; b. Houston, July 9, 1948; d. Kenneth and Lois (Skiles) Craver; m. Henry William Denny, Jan. 26, 1969 (div. Aug. 1990); 1 child, Bryan William; m. Norman C. Tolpo, May 6, 2005. Student, U. Tex., 1966—70; BS in Elem. Edn. magna cum laude, U. North Tex., 1973. Cert. tchr. Tex. Mem. Tex. Ho. of Reps., Austin, 1993—, chair ho. com. on elections. Mem. numerous other civic orgns.; del. state and nat. Rep. convs., 1972—; chmn. Denton (Tex.) County Rep. Com., 1983—91; bd. dirs. Tex. Fedn. Rep. Women, 1988—2003, Tex. Com. Humanities, 1990, YMCA, Denton, 1985—; life mem. pres.'s coun. U. N. Tex., Denton, 1974—, chmn., 1983; mem. Denton Benefit League, 1976—, Denton Arts Coun., 1986—. Named Outstanding Rep. Vol., Denton County Rep. Com., 1985, Outstanding Alumna in Edn., U. N. Tex. Coll. Edn., 1993; named one of 10 Outstanding Rep. Women, Tex. Fedn. Rep. Women, 1991. Mem.: Nat. Conf. State Legislature, Am. Legis. Exch. Coun., Ariel Club, Delta Zeta. Episcopalian. Avocations: swimming, bridge. Address: 8684 FM 2153 Aubrey TX 76227-3029

DENNY, RICHARD ALDEN, JR., retired lawyer; b. Atlanta, Oct. 13, 1931; s. Richard Alden and Maybeth Sullivan (Graham) D.; m. Margaret Hunt, Aug. 1954; children: Margaret Denny Dozier, Richard Alden III, Dallas Hunt, Lee Denny Griffith. BA, Washington and Lee U., 1952; LLB, Emory U., 1954. Bar: Ga. 1954. Assoc. King & Spalding, Atlanta, 1954-60, ptnr., 1960-92. Chmn. bd. Met. Atlanta Crime Commn., 1972-73; bd. dirs. Woodruff Arts Ctr., 1991-97, life trustee, 1997—; bd. dirs. High Mus. Art, Atlanta, 1971-2007, chmn., 1991-94, life trustee, 2007—; bd. dirs. Lovett Sch., Atlanta, 1969—, chmn., 1980-83, emeritus trustee, 1999—; founder High Mus. Atlanta Wine Auction, 1993, chief taster, 1998—. Mem. Lawyers Club Atlanta (pres. 1972-73), Atlanta Lawyers Found. (chmn. 1976-77), Washington and Lee Alumni Assn. (pres. 1980-81), Piedmont Driving Club (pres. 1982-84), Peachtree Golf Club, Omicron Delta Kappa. Episcopalian. Office: King & Spalding Ste 3100 1180 Peachtree St Atlanta GA 30309-3531

DENNY, WILLIAM MURDOCH, JR., investment management executive; b. Schenectady, NY, June 10, 1934; s. William Murdock and Ione Elizabeth (Lundy) D.; m. Delores Gay Shillady, June 11, 1966; children: Ellen Gay, Nancy Beth, Linda Ann. ScB in Chemistry, Brown U., 1958; MBA in Fin., Drexel U., 1974. Mem. mgmt. staff chem. spltys. divsn. Pennwalt Corp., Phila., 1961-73; pres. Denny Fin. Enterprises, Paoli, Pa., 1974—. Chmn. mgmt. com. Houston-Leon County Coal Co. Interests, Crockett, Tex., 1987-2002; winegrower Clover Mill Farm Vineyards, LLC, Chester Springs, Pa., 1998—. Bd. dirs. United Way North Central Chester County, 1980—83. Lt. comdr. USN, 1959—61. Mem. Fin. Analysts Fedn., Fin. Analysts Phila., Navy League U.S., Corinthians Assn. (Phila. fleet capt. 1996-97, corp. sec. 2002-05), Phi Kappa Psi, Brown U. Club (pres. 1979-81, Phila.), Aronimink Golf Club (Newtown Square, Pa.), Yacht Club of Hilton Head Island (S.C.), Sea Pines Club. Home: Clover Mill Farm Chester Springs PA 19425 Office: PO Box 458 Paoli PA 19301-0458

DE NOTARISTEFANI, CARLO, pharmaceutical executive; DEng, U. Naples, Italy. Cert. profl. engr. With Marion Merrel Dow, Hoechst Marion Roussel; v.p. IO Internat. Aventis Pharms., 2000—01, v.p. IO Internat. L.Am. and Japan, 2001—03, sr. v.p. global finishing solids, 2003—04; sr. v.p. global mfg. ops. Bristol-Myers Squibb, 2004, pres. tech. ops., 2004—. Office: Bristol Myers Squibb 345 Park Ave New York NY 10154-0037*

DENSEN, PAUL MAXIMILLIAN, retired health facility administrator; b. NYC, Aug. 1, 1913; s. Charles Edwin and Carrie (Weinberg) Densen; m. Elizabeth A. Reed, Dec. 19, 1939; children: Rebecca E., Peter. AB, Bklyn.Coll., 1934; DSc, Johns Hopkins U., 1939; MA (hon.), Harvard U., 1968. From instr. to assoc. prof. preventive medicine Vanderbilt U. Med. Sch., 1939—46; chief div. med. research statistics VA, Washington, 1946—49; assoc. prof., then prof. biometry Grad. Sch. Pub. Health, U. Pitts., 1949—54; dir. div. research and statistics Health Ins. Plan Greater N.Y., 1954—59; dept. commr. N.Y.C. Dept. Health, 1959—66; dept. adminstr. N.Y.C. Health Services Adminstrn., 1966—69; dir. Harvard Center Community Health and Med. Care, 1968—85; prof. community health Harvard Sch. Pub. Health, 1968—85, prof. emeritus, 1985—. Fellow: AAAS, APHA, Am. Statis. Assn.; mem.: Inst. Medicine of NAS, Am. Epidemiol. Soc. Home: Apt 1019 350 Dublin Dr Iowa City IA 52246

DENSLEY, COLLEEN T., principal; b. Provo, Utah, Apr. 12, 1950; d. Floyd and Mary Lou (Dixon) Taylor; m. Steven T. Densley, July 23, 1968; children: Steven, Tiffany, Landon, Marianne, Wendy, Logan. BS in Elem. Edn., Brigham Young U., 1986, MEd in Tchg. and Learning, 1998. Cert. in elem. edn., K-12 adminstrn. Utah. Substitute tchr. Provo Sch. Dist., 1972-85, curriculum specialist, 1999-2001; tchr. 6th grade, mainstreaming program Canyon Crest Elem. Sch., Provo, 1985—94; instructional facilitator Campus Crest Elem., 1994—99; prin. Wasatch Elem. Sch., Provo, 2001—. Tchr. asst., math. tutor Brigham Young U., 1968—69; attendee World Gifted and Talented Conf., Salt Lake City, 1987, Tchr. Expectations and Student Achievement, 1988—89, Space Acad. for Educators, Huntsville, Ala., 1992; supr. coop. tchr. for practicum tchrs., 1987—90; co-chmn. accelerated learning and devel. com.; trainee working with handicapped students in mainstream classroom, 1989; mem. elem. sch. lang. arts curriculum devel. com., 90; mem. task force Thinking Strategies Curriculum, 1990—91; extensions specialist gifted and talented, 1990—91; math, 1991—; master tchr. Nat. Tchr. Tng. Inst., 1993. Co-author: (curricula) Provo Sch. Dist.'s Microorganism Sci. Kit, 1988, Arthropod Sci. Kit, 1988, Tchg. for Thinking, 1990—, PAWS Presents the Internet and the World Wide Web, 1997. Named Utah State Tchr. of the Yr., 1992; recipient Honor Young Mother of Yr. award, State of Utah, 1981, Mayor's award of Excellence, Provo, Utah, 2003. Mem.: NEA, Provo Edn. Assn. (Tchr. of the Yr. 1991—92), Internat. Space Edn. Initiative (adv. bd.), Utah Coun. Tchrs. Math., Utah Edn. Assn., Nat. Coun. Tchrs. Math. Republican. Mem. Lds Ch. Office: Wasatch Elem Sch 1080 N 900 E Provo UT 84604 Office Phone: 801-374-4910. Business E-Mail: colleend@provo.edu.

DENSLOW, DEBORAH PIERSON, primary school educator; b. Phila., May 2, 1947; d. Merrill Tracy Jr. and Margaret (Aiman) D.; m. James Tracy Grey III, Nov. 24, 1972 (div. Dec. 1980); 1 child, Sarah Elizabeth. BS, Gwynedd Mercy Coll., 1971; MA, Marygrove Coll., Detroit, 2000; M in Ednl. Adminstrn., Gwynedd Mercy Coll., Gwynedd, Pa., 2005. Tchr. Willingboro (N.J.) Bd. Edn., 1971—. Union rep. Burlington County Edn. Assn., Willingboro, 1981-82, ednl. adv. Nat. Constitution Ctr., Phila., 2002-.; mem. task force for reoganization Morrisville Sch. Dist., 1991-92. Mem. Borough Coun., Morrisville, 1988—94, pres., 1992—94, rep. candidate, 1986; borough chmn. Am. Cancer Soc., 1986—87; sec. bd. dirs. Morrisville Free Libr., 1988—90, bd. dirs., 1988—2001; mem. Morrisville Mcpl. Authority, chmn., 1994—95, 1996—2000, asst. sec., treas., 1995—96, 2001; judge City Gardens Contest The Pa. Horticultural Soc., Phila., 2002; committeewoman 1st ward Morrisville (Pa.) Rep. Com., 1986—98. Mem. NEA, N.J. Edn. Assn., Willingboro Edn. Assn. (union rep. 1981-82, alt. union rep. 1988-89), Parents without Ptnrs. (bd. dirs. Mercer County chpt. 1981-82, sec. 1982-84), Bucks County Boroughs Assn. (bd. dirs. 1989—, v.p. 1990-92, pres. 1992-93), Pa. Mcpl. Authorities Assn. (profl. devel. com. 2000-2001). Presbyterian. Avocations: swimming, sailing. Home: 1 Garrett Lane Willingboro NJ 08046

DENSMORE, DOUGLAS WARREN, lawyer; b. Jan. 30, 1948; s. Warren Orson and Lois Martha D.; m. Janet Roberta Broadley, Oct. 26, 1973; children: Bradley Wythe, Andrew Fitz Douglas. AB, Coll. of William and Mary, Williamsburg, Va., 1970; JD cum laude, U. Toledo, 1975. Bar: Ohio 1976, US Dist. Ct. (no. and so. dist.) Ohio, Va. 1980, US Dist. Ct. (ea. and we. dist.) Va. 1980, US Ct. Appeals (4th cir.) 1980, US Ct. Appeals (6th cir.) 2004, US Supreme Ct., 1997, US Bankruptcy Ct. (we. dist.) Va., 2002. Assoc. Gertner, Barkan & Robon, Toledo, 1975-77, Shumaker, Loop & Kendrick, Toledo, 1977-79; corp. counsel Dominion Bankshares Corp., Roanoke, Va., 1979-80; assoc. Woods, Rogers, Muse, Walker & Thornton, 1980-84; ptnr. Woods, Rogers & Hazlegrove, 1984-96, Flippin, Densmore, Morse and Jessee, 1996—2004, LeClair, Ryan, Flippin, Densmore, 2004—. Co-author: Examining the Increase in Federal Regulatory Requirements and Penalties: Is Banking Facing Another Troubled Decade?, 1995; contbr. articles to profl. jour. Bd. Commonwealth of Va. Treasury, 2005—. Decorated Officer Venerable Order St. John (Eng.), Knight Order of Saints Maurice and Lazarus, Italy, Companion of the O'Conor Don (Ireland), first class Order of Polonia Restituta (Poland), knight grand cross Order St. Stanislas, Poland, Royal Ukranian Order, Order Temple Jerusalem. Master: Masons (jr. deacon 1992, 32 degree); fellow: Baskerville Soc. (UK); mem.: ABA (banking law com. 1988—, Uniform Comml. Code com. 1988—), Juvenile Diabetes Rsch. Fund (bd. dirs. 2004—), The Business Leadership Fund (bd. of dir. 2003—), Roanoke Bar Assn. Found. (pres. 2002—03), Bar Assn. City of Roanoke (bd. dirs. 1998—2003, pres. 2001—02), Va. Bar Assn. (Corp. Code com. 1984—), Scottish Heraldry Soc., Greater Roanoke Valley Character Coalition (chair legal com.), Roanoke Regional C. of C. (bd. dirs. 2000—02), New Century Tech. Coun. (bd. dir. 1997—2001), Scottish Soc. Va. Highlands (bd. dir. 1992—2000), Vet. Corps Art NY, Army-Navy Union, Brit. Manorial Soc. (Lord of Stratford St. Andrew), Augustan Soc., English Speaking Union, New Century Venture Ctr. (bd. dirs. 2003—06), Rolls-Royce Owners Club, Hunting Hills Country Club, Royal Overseas Club (London), Farmington Country Club (Charlottesville, Va.), Rotary (Paul Harris fellow), Royal Order of Scotland, Shriners. Episcopalian. Avocations: golf, gardening, reading. Office: Leclair Ryan Flippin Densmore Ste 1800 Wachovia Tower Roanoke VA 24011-3315 Office Phone: 540-510-3024. Business E-Mail: douglas.densmore@leclairryan.com.

DENSON, BRYAN, reporter; Staff writer The Oregonian, Portland. Co-recipient George Polk award for Nat. Reporting, 2006. Office: The Oregonian 1320 SW Broadway Portland OR 97201 Office Phone: 503-294-7614. E-mail: bryandenson@news.oregonian.com.

DENSON, CHARLES D., apparel executive; b. Corvallis, Oreg. BA in Bus., Utah State U., Logan, 1978. Asst. store mgr. The Athletic Dept., Portland, Oreg., 1979—80; East coast sports mktg. rep. coll. basketball, pro football and pro baseball Nike, Inc., Boston, 1980—81, Futures 1 customer svc. mgr. Western US Portland, 1981—82, sales rep. footwear & apparel LA, 1982—89, So. Calif. footwear sales mgr., 1989—90, strategic accounts apparel GMM Portland, 1990—91, Foot Locker Footwear GMM, 1991, head sales tng. & devel., 1992, dir. SAI (FootAction, TSA, JCP, TFL and TAF), 1993—94, dir. USA apparel sales, 1994, dir. US sales, 1994—97, v.p. European sales Hilversum, Netherlands, 1997—98, v.p., gen. mgr. NIKE Europe, 1998—2000, v.p., gen. mgr. NIKE USA, 2000—01, pres. NIKE Brand, 2001—. Office: Nike Inc One Bowerman Dr Beaverton OR 97005-6453 Office Phone: 503-671-6453.*

DENSON, J. RUSSELL, publishing executive; b. Houston; m. Carolyn Denson; 3 children. BBA in Accounting, U. Houston. CPA. Exec. v.p. HEI Corp., 1981—87, CFO, 1983; COO Hippocrates Partners; mng. partner Denson Pub. Group, 1987—92; pres., CEO Houston Biotechnology Inc., 1992—97; exec. v.p., CFO DSI Toys Inc., 1997—99; chmn., dir. ICELEBRATE.com, 1999—2000; COO, CFO Weider Publications, 2000—01, pres., CEO, dir., 2001—03; pres., CEO Reiman Media Group, Greendale, Wis., 2003—04, Gruner + Jahr USA Pub., NYC, 2004—. Office: Gruner + Jahr Pub 375 Lexington Ave New York NY 10017-5514

DENSON, NIKKOLE, film producer, company executive; b. 1971; Grad., U. San Francisco Law Sch. Prodn. asst. Paramount, 1996—99; head movie divsn., fmr. LA Laker Earvin "Magic" Johnson, 1999—2004; dir. Bus. Devel., Starbucks Corp., 2004—. Prodr.: (films) Hair Show, 2004, Brown Sugar. Office: Starbucks Corp Entertainment Divsn Los Angeles CA 90003*

DENSON, TERRY, telecommunications industry executive; b. Rochester, NY; Grad., Harvard U.; JD, Georgetown Univ. Mgr. talent rights acquisition ABC; dir. bus. develop. for affiliate sales and marketing MTV Networks; v.p. programming Insight Comm. Co.; v.p., video programming and mktg. Verizon, 2004—06, v.p., content strategy and acquisition, FiOS TV, 2006—. Office: Verizon 1095 Ave of the Americas New York NY 10036*

DENSON, WILLIAM FRANK, III, lawyer; b. Birmingham, Ala., Aug. 1, 1943; s. William Frank Jr. and Martha Jane (Wilson) D.; m. Deborah Lynn Davis, July 6, 1974; 1 child, Patricia Lynn Pyle. BA, U. Montevallo, 1965; JD, Emory U., 1968. Bar: Ala. 1968. Atty. Spain, Gillon, Riley, Tate & Ansley, Birmingham, 1969-73; atty., asst. sec., sec. Vulcan Materials Co., Birmingham, 1973-88, sec., asst. gen. counsel, 1988-92, v.p., sec., asst. gen. counsel, 1992-94, v.p. law, sec., 1994-98, sr. v.p. law, sec., 1998-99, sr. v.p., gen. counsel, sec., 1999—. Trustee U. Montevallo, 1987-99; bd. dirs. Glenwood Mental Health Svcs., 1990-96. Mem. ABA, Ala. State Bar, Country Club of Birmingham, Willow Point Country Club (Alexander City, Ala.), Kiwanis Club Birmingham. Republican. Episcopalian. Avocations: golf, reading, travel. Home: 3215 E Briarcliff Rd Birmingham AL 35223-1304 Office: Vulcan Materials Co 1200 Urban Center Dr Birmingham AL 35242-2545 Office Phone: 205-298-3204.*

DENT, CHARLES WIEDER (CHARLIE DENT), congressman; b. Allentown, Pa., May 24, 1960; s. Walter R. and Marjorie (Wieder) Dent; m. Pamela J. Serfass, Aug. 17, 1991; children: Kathryn Elizabeth, William Reed, Charles John. BA in Fgn. Svc. and Internat. Politics, Pa. State U., 1982; MPA, Lehigh U., Bethlehem, Pa., 1993. Sales rep. P.A. Peters, Inc., Allentown; devel. officer Lehigh U., Bethlehem, Pa., 1986-90; mem. Pa. State Ho. Reps. from Dist. 132, Harrisburg, 1991-98, Pa. State Senate from Dist. 16, Harrisburg, 1998—2004, US Congress from 15th Pa. dist, 2005—, mem. transp. and infrastructure com., mem. homeland security com. Bd. dirs. Ben Franklin Partnership, Pa. Coun. Arts, Pa. Commn. on Crime and Delinquency; chair bd. dirs. task force Jt. State Govt. Commn. Studying Children and Youth Svcs. Delivery Sys. Mem. pres.'s adv. bd. Good Shepherd Rehab. Hosp.; mem. bd. ambs. Lehigh Carbon CC, Cedar Crest Coll., Allentown; active Cmty. Svcs. for Children, N.E. chpt. Pa. Cystic Fibrosis Found., Crime Victims Coun. Lehigh Valley, Prog. for Women and Families, Minsi Traisl Coun. Boy Scouts Am. Republican. Presbyterian. Office: 701 W Broad St Ste 200 Bethlehem PA 18018 Office Phone: 202-225-6411, 610-861-9734. Office Fax: 610-861-9308.*

DENT, FREDERICK BAILY, retired textiles executive, ambassador; b. Cape May, NJ, Aug. 17, 1922; s. Magruder and Edith (Baily) D.; m. Mildred C. Harrison, Mar. 11, 1944 (dec.); children: Frederick Baily, Mildred Hutcheson, Pauline Harrison, Diana Gwynn, Magruder Harrison. BA, Yale U., 1944. With Joshua L. Baily & Co., Inc., NYC, 1946-47; with Mayfair Mills, Arcadia, SC, 1947—2003, pres., 1958-88, treas., 1977—2001, chmn., 1998—2001, bd. dirs. Sec. Dept. Commerce, Washington, 1973-75; amb., spl. rep. for trade negotiations, 1975-77; bd. dirs. Joshua L. Baily & Co. Chmn. Spartanburg County Planning and Devel. Commn., 1960-72; trustee Spartanburg Day Sch., Brevard Music Ctr.; past mem. corp. Yale U.; mem. Pres.'s Commn. on an All-Vol. Army, 1969-70; mem. Pres.'s Commn. on Indsl. Competitiveness, 1982. Lt. USNR, 1943-46, PTO. Named laureate, S.C. Bus. Hall of Fame, Textile Hall of Fame. Mem. Spartanburg Area C. of C. (chmn. 1991). Episcopalian. Home: 221 Montgomery Dr Spartanburg SC 29302-3443 E-mail: dentf@bellsouth.net.

DENT, JULIE, executive director; d. Ernest and Elaine (King) Dent; m. Barry Morrow; 1 child, Christopher Dent Morrow. AAS, Borough Manhattan CC, 1988; BS in Edn., Empire State Coll.; MS with honors in Edn., CUNY, 1995. Tchr. Horace E. Greene Day Care Ctr., Bklyn., 1983—88, adminstrv. dir., 1988—97; exec. dir. Audrey Johnson Day Care, Bklyn., 1997—. Domestic violence prevention counselor Women Working for a Better Cmty., 1996—; exec. bd. 1st vice chair Woodhull Hosp., Bklyn., 1999—; exec. vice chair Cmty. Sch. Bd. Dist. # 32, Bklyn., 2002—; dir. universal pre-K program dept. of edn. Long Island U., 1994—. Recipient award for excellence in early childhood edn., Profl. Assn. Day Care Dirs. Inc., 1989, award for outstanding cmty. svc., City Coun. N.Y., 1996, Key Stone award, Fedn. Protestant Welfare Agy. Inc., 2000, Citation of Honor, Charles J. Hynes, Dist. Atty., 2002, award for dedicated svc. to children, State Senator Martin M. Dilan, 2003, Citizenship award, Assemblyman Vito Lopez, Cmty Svc. award, Hon. D. Towns, 2004, Congressional Recognition award, Hon. E. Towns, 2004. Mem.: Nat. Assn. for Female Exec., Nat. Assn. For the Edn. of Young Children, Phi Delta Kappa (mem. Beta Omicron chpt.). Avocations: reading, dance. Office Phone: 718-574-0130. Personal E-mail: julieeduc@aol.com. Business E-Mail: audreyjo272@aol.com.

DENTALI, STEVEN J., chemist; BS in Biochemistry and Human Nutrition, Evergreen State Coll.; PhD in Pharm. Sciences with a specialization in Natural Products Chemistry, U. Ariz., Tucson, 1991. Owner Dentali Associates, Troutdale, Oreg.; v.p. for scientific and tech. affairs Am. Herbal Products Assn., Silver Spring, Md. Lectr. in field; mem. US Pharmacopeia 2000-2005 Convention; reviewer Nat. Ctr. for Complementary and Alternative Medicine, NIH, Inst. Medicine, NAS, AOAC Internat., Am. Herbal Pharmacopoeia; mem. adv. bd. Am. Botanical Coun.; mem. Dietary Supplements General Chapters com. US Pharmacopeia, 2005—; works as an independent medicinal plant expert. Mem. editl. adv. bd. Nutraceuticals World, assoc. editor Medical Herbalism, mem. adv. bd. Journal of the American Herbalist Guild, written about popular herb use, published safety reviews of kava and ephedra; author: Ginkgo & Memory; contbr. chapters to books Natural Medications for Psychiatric Disorders. Am. Found. for Pharm. Edn. Fellow. Office: Am Herbal Product Assn 8484 Georgia Ave Ste 370 Silver Spring MD 20910 Office Phone: 301-588-1171 ext. 103. Business E-Mail: sdentali@ahpa.org.*

DENTEN, CHRISTOPHER PETER, lawyer; b. Oakland, Calif., Apr. 23, 1964; s. Richard and Waltraud Denten; m. Mary McLaughlin, May 18, 1996; children: Aiden, Eva. BA, U. Calif., Berkeley, 1986; JD, U. San Francisco, 1990; LLM in Tax, Golden Gate U., 2003. Bar: Calif. 1991, U.S. Dist. Ct. (no. dist.) Calif. 1991, U.S. Ct. Appeals (9th cir.) 1991; CPA, Colo.; notary pub. Tax profl. KPMG Peat Marwick, Oakland, 1988-92; sr. tax analyst Cisco Sys., Inc., San Jose, Calif., 1992-97; assoc. gen. counsel, dir. legal affairs and taxation McAfee, Inc., Santa Clara, Calif., 1997—2002; gen. counsel iManage, Inc., Foster City, Calif., 2003—04, Connection to eBay/Accenture, 2004; v.p., gen. counsel Zoran Corp., Sunnyvale, Calif., 2004—. Bd. dirs. Network Assocs. fgn. subs., 2000-02., Zoran fgn. subs., 2004—. Named to Outstanding Young Men of Am., 1982; Brother Gary Stone Meml. scholar, 1982. Mem. AICPA, Santa Clara Bar Assn., San Mateo County Bar Assn., Nat. Notary Assn., U. Calif. Berkeley Alumni Assn., U. San Francisco Law Sch. Alumni Assn., Network Assocs. Pres. Club. Republican. Roman Catholic. Avocations: marathons, golf, art, travel. Home and Office: PO Box 117932 Burlingame CA 94011-7932 Office Phone: 408-523-4370. Personal E-mail: chris@denten.com.

DENTINGER, RONALD LEE, comedian, speaker, freelance writer; b. Milw., Feb. 14, 1941; s. William Cassel and Kathryn Faye (Ritzman) D.; m. Kaylee Ann Kasten, Aug. 28, 1965; children: Ronald Lee Jr., Joann Jean. Officer Milw. Police Dept., 1962-67; dist. mgr. Am. Automobile Assn., Madison, Wis., 1967-71; gen. mgr. Don Q Inn, Dodgeville, Wis., 1971-85; comedian, spkr. Dodgeville, 1976—. Humorist quoted in comedy mags., books; jokes sold to Rodney Dangerfield Joan Rivers, The Tonight Show, Saturday Night Live, 20/20 Show, Time Mag.; author: (with others) The Art of Communication, The Great Communicators II, (joke books) Down Time, How to Argue with Your Spouse. Pres. Hidden Valley Tourism Region, Wis., 1984. Named Funniest Person in Wis., Showtime-TV Network, 1985. Mem. Nat. Spkrs. Assn., Wis. Profl. Spkrs. Assn., Wis. Soc. Assn. Execs., Dodgeville C. of C. (pres. 1984), Internat. Assn. Profl. Pranksters (founding mem. 2005). Home and Office: PO Box 151 Dodgeville WI 53533-0151 Office Phone: 608-935-2417.

DENTLER, ROBERT ARNOLD, sociologist, educator; b. Chgo., Nov. 26, 1928; s. Arnold E. and Jennie (Munsen) D.; m. Helen Hosmer, Sept. 7, 1950; children: Deborah, Eric, Robin. BS, Northwestern U., 1949, MA, 1950, Am. U., 1954; PhD, U. Chgo., 1960. Reporter Chgo. City News Bur., 1949; tchr. Pomfret Sch., 1950-52; intelligence officer U.S. Govt., 1952-54; instr. Dickinson Coll., 1954-57; fellow U. Chgo., 1957-59; rschr. U. Kans., 1959-61; asst. prof. Dartmouth Coll., 1961-62; mem. faculty Tchrs. Coll., Columbia U., NYC, 1962-72, prof. sociology, dep. dir. to dir. Ctr. for Urban Edn., 1966-72; dean Sch. Edn., Boston U., 1972-79; sr. sociologist Abt Assocs., Cambridge, Mass., 1979-83; prof. sociology U. Mass., Boston, 1983-92; sr. fellow McCormack Inst. Pub. Affairs, 1993-94; faculty assoc. Trotter Inst., 1994—2001; dir. Inst. for Learning and Teaching U. Mass., Boston, 1987, acting dean Coll. Edn., 1988. Author: (with Peter Rossi) The Politics of Urban Renewal, 1961, (with Nelson W. Polsby and Paul A. Smith) Politics and Social Life, 1963, (with Phillips Cutright) Hostage America, 1963, (with B. Mackler and M.E. Warshauer) The Urban R's: Race Relations as the Problem in Urban Education, 1967, Major American Social Problems, 1967, (with M.E. Warshauer) Big City Dropouts and Illiterates, 1967, American Community Problems, 1967, Major Social Problems, 1973, Urban Problems, 1977, (with M.B. Scott) Schools on Trial: An Inside Account of the Boston School Desegregation Case, 1981, (with D.C. Baltzell and D.J. Sullivan) University on Trial, 1983, (with A.L. Hafner) Hosting Newcomers, 1997, Practicing Sociology, 2001, The Looking-Glass Self: A Memoir, 2002; editor Sociol. Practice Rev., 1989-92. Home: 11 Childs Rd Lexington MA 02421-4517 Office: U Mass Dept Sociology Boston MA 02125-3393 Personal E-mail: robertd917@aol.com.

DENTON, D. BROCK, lawyer; b. Bowling Green, Ky., Dec. 14, 1974; BS, U. Ky., 1997; JD, Salmon P. Chase Coll. Law, Northern Ky. U., 2000. Bar: Ohio 2000, Ky. 2001. Assoc. Keating, Muething & Klekamp PLL, Cin., mem., Holding Com., coord., Summer Assoc. Prog. Mem., Bd. Dirs. Cin. Reds Cmty. Fund. Named one of Ohio's Rising Stars, Super Lawyers, 2005, 2006. Mem.: Ohio State Bar Assn., Northern Ky. Bar Assn., Ky. Bar Assn., Cin. Bar Assn. Office: Keating Muething & Klekamp PLL One E Fourth St Ste 1400 Cincinnati OH 45202 Office Phone: 513-579-6400. Office Fax: 513-579-6457.

DENTON, D. KEITH, management educator; b. Paducah, Ky., June 28, 1948; s. Derward and Bonnie Denton; children: Shane, Taylor. BS, Murray State U., 1971; M in Pub. Adminstrn., Memphis State U., 1974; PhD, So. Ill. U., 1981. Supr. Shelby Pre-Casting, Memphis, 1971-72; safety engr. Md. Casualty Corp., Memphis, 1972-76; instr. Draughn's Bus. Coll., Paducah, 1977; safety trainer Union Carbide Corp., Paducah, 1977-78; prof. So. Ill. U., Carbondale, 1978-83, Mo. State U., Springfield, 1983—. Cons. Small Bus. Research Ctr., Springfield, 1985—, Springfield Remfg. Corp., 1986. Author: Safety Management, 1982, (with others) Safety Performance, 1985, Quality Service in America, 1989, The Production Game, 1990, Handling Employee Complaints, 1990, Horizontal Management, 1991, The Service Trainer, 1992, Recruitment Retention and Employee Relations, 1992, Did You Know?, Fascinating Facts and Fallacies, 1994, Enviro-Management: How Companies Turn Pollution Cost into Profits, 1994, The Toolbox for the Mind, 1999, Empowering Intranets, 2002; contbr. over 150 articles to profl. jours. Mem. Acad. Mgmt., Nat. Assn. Purchasing, Am. Soc. Prodn. and Inventory Control, Inst. Indsl. Engrs. Office: Mo State U 901 S National Ave Springfield MO 65804-0088 Home Phone: 417-889-6763; Office Phone: 417-836-5573. Business E-Mail: dkdentonf@missouristate.edu.

DENTON, DEREK ASHWORTH, medical researcher, foundation administrator; b. Launceston, Tasmania, Australia, May 27, 1924; s. Arthur A. and Catherine (Edwards) D.; m. Margaret Catherine Scott, Mar. 13, 1953; children: Matthew, Angus. MBBS, Melbourne U., 1947. Haley Rsch. Fellow Walter and Eliza Hall Inst., Melbourne, 1948; med. rsch. fellow, sr. med. rsch. fellow Nat. Health and Med. Rsch. Coun., Melbourne, 1948—, prin. med. rsch. fellow, 1970; founding dir. Howard Florey Inst. Exptl. Physiology and Medicine, Melbourne, 1971-89, emeritus dir., 1990—; dep. chmn. Howard Florey Biomed. Found., Melbourne, 1997—. Bd. dir. David Syme Ltd. Pubs. The Age, 1984-93; invited OECD examiner of sci. and tech. policy Govt. Sweden, 1985-86; 1st v.p. Internat. Union of Physiol. Scis., 1983-89 (chmn. nominating com. and com. on commns. 1986-93), jury Albert and Mary Lasker Found. awards in med. sci., 1979-90; fgn. assoc. NAS of U.S., 1995; adj. scientist Southwest Found. Biomed. Rsch., San Antonio, 1994—; fgn. assoc. Inst. France Acad. Scis., 2000. Author: The Hunger for Salt, 1982, The Pinnacle of Life: Consciousness in Animals and Humans; editor: Olfaction and Taste, 1985, Les Emotions Primordiales et L'Eveil de la Conscience, 2005, The Primordial Emotions: The Dawning of Consciousness, 2006. Decorated companion Order of Australia. Fellow Royal Soc. London, Royal Coll. Physicians (hon.) London and Australia, Am. Physiol. Soc. (hon.), Am. Acad. Arts and Scis. (fgn.); mem. Royal Swedish Acad. Scis. (fgn. med. mem.). Avocations: wine, tennis, fly fishing. Home: 816 Orrong Rd Toorak 3142 Melbourne Australia Office: Univ Melbourne Dept Physiology Parkville 3010 Australia Home Phone: 61 3 9827 2640; Office Phone: 61 3 8344 5639. Business E-Mail: ddenton@unimelb.edu.au.

DENTON, FRANK M., publishing executive; b. Tulsa, Mar. 30, 1945; s. Frank McCray and Eydith (Langley) D.; m. April Murphy, June 18, 1983 (div. 2000); children: Langley Sara, Allegra Murphy. BA, U. Tex., 1968; MS, Columbia U., 1970; MBA, U. Wis., 1994, PhD, 1996. Sportswriter Austin Am. Statesman, 1964-66; reporter Stuart Long News Svc., Austin, Tex., 1966-69, Anniston (Ala.) Star, 1970-72, Cin. Enquirer, 1972-75; asst. lifestyle editor Detroit Free Press, 1976-78, lifestyle editor, 1978-81, asst. mng. editor, 1981-86; editor Wis. State Journal, Madison, 1986—2004; editor, v.p. Tampa Tribune, Fla., 2004; v.p. journalism Morris Comm. Co., Augusta, Ga., 2005—. Mem.: Am. Soc. Newspaper Editors, Phi Kappa Phi. Office: Morris Communications 725 Broad Street Augusta GA 30901 Home Phone: 706-731-0068; Office Phone: 706-823-3492. E-mail: frank.denton@morris.com.

DENTON, JAMES, actor; b. Nashville, Jan. 20, 1963; m. Jenna Lyn Ward (div. 2000); m. Erin O'Brien, 2002; children: Sheppard, Malin. Grad. with honors, U. Tenn., Knoxville. Actor: (films) Thieves Quartet, 1994, Hunter's Moon, 1995, That Old Feeling, 1997, Face/Off, 1997, Primary Colors, 1998, Jumbo Girl, 2004; (TV series, guest appearance) Moloney, 1996, Dark Skies, 1996, JAG, 1996, 2003, Two Guys, a Girl and a Pizza Place, 2000, Ally McBeal, 2000, The West Wing, 2000, The Pretender, 2000, Philly, 2001, The Drew Carey Show, 2002, Reba, 2005; (TV films) The Pretender 2001, 2001, The Pretender: Island of the Haunted, 2001; (TV series) Threat Matrix, 2003, Desperate Housewives, 2004— (Screen Actors Guild Award for outstanding performance by an ensemble in a comedy series, 2005, 2006, TV Choice Actor, Teen Choice Awards, 2006). Office: Desperate Housewives Touchstone Television 100 Universal City Plaza Bldg 2128 Ste G Universal City CA 91608

DENTON, JODY, chef; A in Hotel and Restaurant Ops., El Centro Coll., Dallas, 1980. Apprenticeship Dallas Country Club, 1978; cook Restaurant Gentiana, Davos Platz, Switzerland, 1979, Hotel Swiss Chalet, Merlischachen, Switzerland, 1980; sous chef Sheraton Park Central, Dallas, 1981—84, Hotel Bel Air, LA, 1984; exec. chef Eureka, LA, 1990, Red Sage, Washington, 1992, The Big Bowl Cafe, Chgo., 1993, The Eccentric, Chgo., 1993; CEO, exec. chef LuLu, San Francisco, 1995, Zibibbo, Palo Alto, 1997, Azie, San Francisco, 1999, Merenda Restaurant and Wine Bar, Bend, Oreg.; owner Restaurant LuLu Catering. Guest chef James Beard House, NYC, London, Hong Kong, Bangkok, Kuala Lumpur, New Zealand, Hawaii, Singapore, Sagebrush Classic celebrity chef event, Bend, Oreg.; owner Restaurant LuLu Gourmet Food Products. Recipient Outstanding Product Line award, NY Fancy Food Show. Office: Merenda Restaurant and Wine Bar 900 NW Wall St Bend OR 97701 Office Phone: 541-330-2304.*

DENTON, LAWRENCE A., automotive executive; Formerly with Ford Motor Co.; pres. Dow Automotive, 1996—2002; pres., CEO DURA Automotive Systems, Rochester Hills, Mich., 2003—, chmn. Rochester, Mich., 2005—. Bd. dirs. Autotemp Co. Bd. dirs. Kettering U. Mem.: Motor & Equipment Mfrs. Assn. (bd. dirs.), Original Equipment Suppliers Assn. (chmn.). Office: DURA Automotive Systems 2791 Research Dr Rochester Hills MI 48309-3575*

DENTON, NICK, publishing executive; Grad. in Econs., Oxford U., Eng. Fgn. corr., investment corr., internet media writer Fin. Times London, Silicon Valley corr. San Francisco, 1997; founder First Tuesday; founder, CEO Moreover Technologies, London, 1998—2001; publisher Gawker Media (includes Gawker and Wonkette), NYC; founder, temporary editor ValleyWag, 2006—. Co-author: All That Glitters: The Fall of Barings, 1996. Named one of 50 Who Matter Now, CNNMoney.com Bus. 2.0, 2006. Office: Gawker Media 76 Crosby St New York NY 10012 Office Phone: 646-808-0248. E-mail: nick@gawker.com.*

D'ENTREMONT, EDWARD JOSEPH, application developer, educator; b. Lynn, Mass., June 25, 1954; s. Joseph Albenie and Gertrude Grace (Flattery) D'E. BA in Math., Salem State Coll., 1976; MS in Applied Math., Northeastern U., 1982. Floor supr. Jordan Marsh Co., Peabody, Mass., 1972—76; sci. programmer Electronics Corp. Am., Cambridge, Mass., 1977, Sulivan and Cogliano, Waltham, Mass., 1977; software engr. Raytheon Svc. Co., Burlington, Mass., 1977—86, Baytheon Missile Sys. divsn., Bedford, Mass., 1986—96, Desktop Data Inc., Burlington, Mass., 1995—98; prin. software engr. Newsedge Corp., Burlington, 1998—2002, Dialog Corp., Burlington, 2002—06, Raytheon Corp., Tewksbury, 2006—. Instr. Fitchburg State Raytheon Inst., Tewksbury, Mass., 1986-96, U. Lowell, Mass., 1991-2001; sr. software engr. Raytheon Co.; instr. continuing edn. Salem State Coll., 1993-95. Campaign worker presdl. campaigns, 1968-72, city coun., state rep., Lynn, 1976, Dukakis for Gov., Lynn, 1982; vol. tech. com. Aborn Elem. Sch. Mem. IEEE, Am. Math. Soc., Math. Assn. Am., Soc. for Indsl. and Applied Math., IEEE Computer Soc., N.Y. Acad. Scis., Assn. Computing Machinery, St. Mary's H.S. Alumni Assn., Salem State Coll. Alumni Assn., Northeastern U. Alumni Assn., Lexington Racquet and Swim Club. Democrat. Roman Catholic. Home: 50 York Rd Lynn MA 01904-1130

DENUNZIO, DAVID AMES, investment banker; s. Ralph Dwight DeNunzio; m. Jocelyne Antoinette Giroux, Oct. 8, 1988. BA magna cum laude, Princeton U., 1978; MBA, Harvard U. Sr. v.p. Kidder Peabody & Co. Inc., NYC; joined Credit Suisse First Boston, NYC, 1989, various positions from co-head, transformation team to dep. global head, private equity, now vice. chmn. Americas mergers and acquisitions. Pres., bd. trustees Greenwich Country Day Sch.; adv. coun. Bendheim Ctr. for Fin., Princeton Univ. Named a Top Dealmaker, Dealmaker mag., 2006. Office: Credit Suisse M & A 11 Madison Ave New York NY 10010 Office Phone: 212-325-2000. Business E-Mail: david.denunzio@csfb.com.*

DENUZZO, RINALDO VINCENT, pharmacy educator; b. Cleve., Oct. 21, 1922; s. Luigi and Domenica Mary (Razzano) DiNuzzo; m. Lucy Bernadine Sneed, June 29, 1946; 1 child, Lisa Ann. BS, Albany Coll. Pharmacy, 1952; MS in Edn., SUNY-Albany, 1956; LHD, Union U., 2003. Registered pharmacist, N.Y., Fla., Vt. Prof. pharmacy N.Y. Coll. Pharmacy, Albany, 1952—, adminstrv. asst., 1963-80. Pharmacist N.Y., Fla., Vt., 1968-95; sr. pharmacist inspector N.Y. State Dept. Health, 1966-95; field dir. Market Measures, Inc.; chmn. tech. pharmacy adv. com., 1977-95; lectr. drug product substitution and generic drugs; notary public. Author: Ann. Albany Coll. Pharmacy Prescription Survey, 1956—84, Substitution, The New York State Experience, 1980, RX Services, XIII Winter Olympic Games, 1980, Ann. DeNuzzo Prescription Survey, 1985—96, Imapct of One-Line Prescription Form on Generic Drug Use, 1987, Cipro, Vasotec, Volatren Post Biggest Gains, 1987, Using the Right Tools to Achieve Personal Success, 1990, Personal Selling, 1991, Annual Survey Tracks Drug Prescribing Trends, 1990, Consumer Prescription Prices Increase, 1991, Changes in Dental Prescribing, 1991, How to Reduce Prescription Medical Costs, 1992, Are Dental Prescriptions a Viable Target for RPhs?, 1992, Financial Success: A Challenge for the Future, 1996, A National Drug Expert Is Needed, 1999, Down Memory Lane, 1999, 2002, What Graduates Need to Know: A Prescription for the Future Financial Success: ACP's Reflection of Progress 1881-2001; A Brief Written and Pictorial History, 2001; editor: Albany Coll. Pharmacy Alumni News, 1961—81; mem. editl. bd. MMM, 1977—80. Instr. first aid, responding to emergencies CPR ARC; mem. East Greenbush Ctrl. Sch. Dist. Bd. Edn., 1974—92, v.p., 1975—76, pres., 1976—78, 1991—92, East Greenbush Edn. Found.; chmn. Albany Coll. Pharmacy Faculty, 1987—89, com. on coms., 1984—87, promotions com., 1989—92, exec. com., grievance com., chair strategic planning steering com., 1995—96; faculty affairs chmn. and rev. Albany Coll. Pharmacy, 1990—94; sr. student status com., faculty ombudsman Albany Coll. Pharmacy Faculty, 1991—2002, mission statement com., 1995; mem. adv. bd. Merrell-Dow Hosp., 1987; sec.-treas. Union U. Pharmacy Coll. Coun., 1970—80; com. on coms., faculty senate parliamentarian Albany Coll. Pharmacy Faculty, 1996—97; mem. profl. adv. com. Albany Vis. Nurses Assn.; mem. rev. panel on prescription payment rev. commn. Office Tech. Assessment U. S. Congress, 1988; mem. ethics panel Siena Coll., 1992; mem., dir. Rensselaer County Taxpayers Assn.; cons. pharmacist, coord. pharm. svcs. XIII Olympic Winter Games, Lake Placid, NY, 1980; liaison Health Sys. Mgmt. degree Joint MS with Union Coll. With US Army, 1941—46, with USAF, 1946—47, capt. M.C., pharm. officer USAFR, 1948—63, ret. USAFR, 1982. Named Francis J. O'Brien Pharmacy Man of Yr., 1979, 2002; recipient 25 Yr. Svc. citation, ARC, 30 Yr. Svc. citation, Svc. plaque, East Greenbush Ctrl. Sch. Dist., 25 Yr. Svc. award, N.Y. State Dept. Health, Disting. Svc. citation, Rensselaer County Taxpayers Assn., established L. Sneed DeNuzzo Sch., Concord U., W.V. Mem.: AAUP (pres. 1978—), AARP, Albany Coll. Pharmacy Alumni Assn. (exec. dir. 1965—86, disting. svc. medal 1975), N.Y. State Pub. Employees Fedn., N.Y. Sch. Bd. Assn., N.Y. State Pharm. Soc., Am. Pharm. Assn., Am. Assn. Colls. Pharmacy (sec.-treas., coun. faculties 1979—80, chmn. elect 1982—83, chmn. 1984—87, dir. 1984—89, roundtable presentation ann. meeting 1996, del. ann. meeting 1997), USA Air Muse, 46th and 72nd Recon. Assn., Nat. Italian-Am. Found. (coun.), Officers Club (West Point, N.Y.), Albany Coll. Pharmacy Pres.'s Club (chmn. bd. 1962—87), Kappa Psi (dep. grand coun. Beta Delta chpt., sec.-treas., created and funded Beta Delta scholar, Albany grad.), Army Five Star, Beta Delta (ann. Rinaldo V. DeNuzzo lucnheon 1988—). Republican. Roman Catholic. Home: 19 Alva St East Greenbush NY 12061-2027 Office: 106 New Scotland Ave Albany NY 12208-3425 E-mail: denuzzor@acp.edu.

DENVER, EILEEN ANN, retired editor; b. NYC, Nov. 16, 1942; d. Daniel Joseph and Katherine Agnes (Boland) Denver; m. Duncan C. Stephens, July 2, 1988. BA, Coll. New Rochelle, 1964; certificate, Radcliffe Sch. Pub., 1964; MA, Ind. U., 1967. Editorial asst. Mass. Inst. Tech. Tech. Review, Boston, 1965-66; instr. English St. Peter's Coll., Jersey City, 1967-70; assoc. editor, writer Am. Home mag., NYC, 1971-75; asst. editor Consumer Reports, Mt. Vernon, NY, 1975-77, asst. mng. editor, 1977-79, mng. editor, 1979-91, exec. editor, 1991-96, dir. editl. ops.,

1997-2000, assoc. editl. dir./exec. editor, 2000—04; ret., 2003—. Chair Friends Glebe House and Gertrude Jekyll Garden, Woodbury, Conn., 2006—; mem. bd. dirs. Denan Project, 2004—.

DENVER, THOMAS HR, lawyer; b. NYC, Oct. 29, 1944; s. Thomas H. Rorke and Eileen Ann Boland; m. Barbara Ann Denver, Dec. 19, 1987; children: Rorke, Nate. BS, Syracuse U., 1966; MS, U. Wash., 1967; JD, U. Calif., San Francisco, 1973. Bar: Calif. 1973, U.S. Dist. Ct. (no. dist.) Calif. 1973. From assoc. to mng. ptnr. Hoge, Fenton, Jones & Appel, Inc., San Jose, Calif., 1973—99. Judge pro tem Santa Clara County Superior Ct., San Jose, 1980—; instr. Stanford U. Law Sch. Advocacy Program; mem. faculty Hastings Coll. of Advocacy; mediator, arbitrator. Contbr. articles to profl. jours. Fellow Am. Coll. Trial Lawyers; mem. Am. Bd. Trial Advocates, Santa Clara County Civil Litigation Com., Santa Clara County Bar Assn Avocations: running, fishing, reading. Office: Mediation Masters 96 N Third St # 300 San Jose CA 95112 Office Phone: 408-535-3298. Business E-Mail: tdenver@mediationmasters.com.

DENYS, SYLVIA, lawyer, researcher; d. Joseph and Louise D. BA in Philosophy and English with honors, Duquesne U., 1970, MA in English, 1977, JD, 1979. Bar: Pa. 1979, U.S. Dist. Ct. (we. dist.) Pa. 1979, U.S. Ct. Appeals (3d cir.), 1994, U.S. Supreme Ct. 2003. Atty. Neighborhood Legal Svcs. Assn., Pitts., 1979-81; jud. law clk. Superior Ct. Pa., Pitts., 1981-82; asst. prof. Duquesne U. Grad. Sch. Bus. and Sch. Bus., 1982-89; pvt. practice, Pitts., 1982-91, 93—; tchr. Acad. for Advancement Sci., Pecs, Hungary, 1992-93. Adj. prof. Duquesne U. Sch. Bus., 1990-91; vis. prof. Sch. Medicine, Pecs, 1991-92; adj. prof. Janus Pannonius Sch. Law, Pecs, Hungary, 1991-92; lectr. and presenter in field. Mem. editl. bd. Duquesne Law Rev., 1978-79; contbr. articles to profl. jours. Legal coun., bd. dir. Pitts. Deaf Theatre, Pitts., 1984-85; bd. dir. YWCA, Pitts., 1984, Blind Outdoor Leisure Devel., Pitts., 1994-95, Radio Info. Svc. for Blind and Print Handicapped, 2004—; rev. com. United Way, Pitts., 1982-86; citizens assembly mem. Health and Welfare Planning Allegheny County, Pitts., 1982-85; v.p. UN Assn. Pitts., 1984-85, bd. dirs., 1982-85; vol. atty. Legal Resources for Women, Pitts., 1997, Neighborhood Legal Svcs. Assn., Pitts., 1994—; adv. bd. Radio Info. Svc., Pitts., 1994-95, vol. atty., 1996-97, bd. dirs. 2004—; govtl. activities com. United Cerebral Palsy, Pitts., 1994-96; dir. legal project for deaf and hard of hearing Pitts. Hearing, Speech and Deaf Svcs., 1995-96; tutor goodwill literacy program Allegheny County Jail, Pitts., 1995-96; membership com. World Affairs Coun., Pitts., 1983-85; mem. Allegheny County Dem. Com.; dialogue group St. Paul Cathedral Race and Reconciliation, 2002—. Grantee Hunkele Found., Brussels, 1988, U.S. Info. Agy. grant U. Pitts., 1992-93; Fulbright-Hayes fellow Coun. for Internat. Exch. of Scholars, 1990; selected mem. Team '92 Delegation of Commn. of European Communities, 1989-91. Mem. ABA (editor-in-chief Internat. Aspects of Antitrust Law newsletter 1984-86, del. to European Union 1989), ACLU (lawyers com. 1994-98), Fed. Bar Assn. (bd. dirs. labor and employment sect. 2003-06, treas. labor and employment sect. 2004-05, sec. labor and employment sect. 2005-06, chair disability law com. 2003-06, Western Pa. chpt. 2003-04, steering com. bd. v.p. editor newsletter, 2003-04, 3d v.p., 2005-), Nat. Employment Lawyers Assn., ADA (adv. panel), Nat. Alliance for Mental Illness (nat. profl. diversity group), Am. Inns of Ct, (barrister 2006-), Pa. Bar Assn. (legal svcs. to persons with disabilities com. 1994—, civil and equal rights com. 1994-98, House of Dels., Pro Bono award 2006), Allegheny County Bar Assn. (antitrust and class action com., court rules com., editl. bd. Pitts. Legal Jour. 1982-88, pub. svc. com., civil rights com., internat. twinning com. 1994-98, Recognition for Pro Bono Svc. award 2003), Allegheny County Bar Found. (Spl. Recognition award Pitts. Aids Task Force, 2003), Womens Bar Assn. Allegheny County, Nat. Inst. Trial Advocacy, Amnesty Internat., Pitts. Aids Task Force (legal com., buddy program, spkr's. bur.), Sierra Club. Avocations: hiking, reading, arts, gourmet cooking, gardening. Office: 1220 Grant Bldg 330 Grant St Pittsburgh PA 15219-2257 Office Phone: 412-681-6554. Business E-Mail: civright@telerama.com.

DENYSYK, BOHDAN, marketing professional, consultant; b. Kornberg, Germany, Feb. 13, 1947; came to U.S., 1949; s. John and Maria (Zelenewich) D.; m. Halina Bubela, June 28, 1969; children: Maria H., Danya L., Adrienne Y., Alexis M. BS, Manhattan Coll., 1968; MS, Cath. U. Am., 1971; PhD, Union Inst. (formerly Union for Experimenting Colls. and Univs.), Cin., 1981. Project mgr. Naval Weapons Lab., Bethesda, Md., 1968-72, analyst and ops., 1972-75; program mgr. Naval Surface Weapons Ctr., 1975-78; dept. head E.G. & G. Inc., Rockville, Md., 1978-81; dep. asst. sec. U.S. Dept. Commerce, Washington, 1981—84; dir. civil programs IBM Corp., 1984—86; pres. DLR Assocs., Arlington, Va., 1972-80, 83—, Global U.S.A., 1987—, also owner, bd. dirs. Mem. Congl. Adv. Panel on China, 1985—; bd. dirs. Mazak Corp., Prokom Software SA; mem. Def. Sci. Bd., 1990—. Contbr. articles to profl. jours. Mem. Presdl. Transition Team, Washington, 1980; regional dir. Rep. Nat. Com., 1980; dir. pub. rels. Ukrainian Nat. Info. Svc., 1976-80; mem. Pres.'s Export Coun., 1981—, Presdl. Awards Commn., 1986-87, 2005; exec. dir. Md. Reagan-Bush Campaign, 1984, Bush-Quayle Campaign, 1992; mem. nat. policy forum Fgn. Affairs Coun., 1995—; pres. Phi Mu Alpha Sinfonia, 1967-68; nat. dir. for coalitions Dole for U.S. Pres. Campaign, 1987-88; dep. polit. dir. Dole for Pres., 1995-96; regional polit. dir. Gov. Bush for Pres. 2000, 1999—; mem. Bush-Cheney Transition Team, 2001; mem. sr. commn. on nat. security CSIS, 2000-01; mem. Md. State Info. Tech. Bd., 2003—, Md. Tech. Devel. Bd., 2006—. Navy fellow, 1969-72; Regents scholar, 1964-68 Fellow N.Y. Acad. Sci.; mem. AIAA, AAAS, Am. Def. Preparedness Assn., Am. Phys. Soc. Republican. Roman Catholic. Avocations: scuba, skiing, running. Office: Global USA Inc 2121 K St NW Ste 650 Washington DC 20037-1825 Office Phone: 202-296-2400.

DENZEL, NORA, information technology executive; BS in Computer Sci., SUNY, Plattsburgh; MS in bus. admin., Santa Clara U., Calif. Various engring., mktg. and exec. roles to worldwide dir. storage software products IBM, 1984—97; sr. v.p. product operations Legato Systems, 1997—2000; gen. mgr., v.p. network storage solutions orgn. Hewlett Packard Co., 2000—03, sr. v.p. and gen. mgr. adaptive enterprise and software global bus. unit, 2003—05. Spkr. about computer technology and women's advancement in technology careers; mem. tech. adv. bd. of startup co. Mem. adv. bd. Santa Clara Univ. Bus. Sch., Women in Technology Internat., several private technology companies, Calif. C. of C.; mentors young executives in high tech careers WOMEN unlimited Program. Named Most Powerful People in Computer Networking, Networking World Mag.; named one of Top 20 Storage Movers and Shakers, Storage, Inc., Top 50 Tech. Women of the Next Millennium, Feminine Fortunes Mag., 50 Most Powerful People in Networking, Network World mag., 2003; recipient Tribute to Women in Industry, YWCA, Santa Clara County. Office: Hewlett Packard Co 1428 Hamilton Ave Palo Alto CA 94301 Office Phone: 650-327-2697. E-mail: nora.denzel@sbcglobal.net.

DEO, NARSINGH, computer scientist, educator; b. Raniganj, Bihar, India, Jan. 2, 1936; s. Bihari Lal and Durga (Modi) Jee; m. Karen Ruth Baier, June 29, 1968. BS, Patna U., India, 1956; Dip. I.I.Sc., Indian Inst. Sci., 1959; MS, Calif. Inst. Tech., 1960; PhD, Northwestern U., 1965. Assoc. electronic engr. Burroughs Electro Data divsn., 1960-62; sr. engr. Jet Propulsion Lab., Pasadena, 1966-69, mem. tech. staff, 1969-71; v.p. Britt Electronics Corp., Santa Monica, Calif., 1968-69; asst. prof. elec. engring. Calif. State Coll., 1971; assoc. prof. elec. engring. Indian Inst. Tech., Kanpur, 1971-74, prof., head computer ctr., 1975-77; prof. Wash. State U., Pullman, 1977-87, chmn. dept. computer sci., 1980-84; Millican chair prof. U. Ctrl. Fla., Orlando, 1986—; dir. Ctr. Parallel Computation, 1989—. Electronics design cons. Ctr. Behavior Therapy, Beverly Hills, Calif., 1967—71; mem. faculty engring. ext. UCLA, 1965—68; vis. assoc. prof. U. Ill., Urbana; vis. prof. Wash. State U., Pullman, 1974—75, ETH, Zurich, Switzerland, 1993, Australian Nat. U., Canberra, 1996, Chuo U., Tokyo, 2002; vis. faculty IBM Thomas J. Watson Rsch., Yorktown Heights, NY, 1984, Oak Ridge Nat. Lab., 1994; pres. Forum Interdisciplinary Math., 2007—. Author: Graph Theory with Application to Engineering and Computer Science, 1974, Simulation with Digital Computers, 1979; co-author (wih E.M. Reingold and J. Nievergelt): Combinatorial Algorithms: Theory and Practice, 1977; co-author: (with M.M. Syslo and J.S. Kowalik) Discrete Optimization Algorithms: With Pascal Programs, 1983; contbr. scientific papers to profl. jours. Recipient Fla. Gov.'s award, 1989; grantee, NSF, U.S. Dept. Transp., Army Rsch. Office, U.S. Army's PM-TRADE, Fla. High Tech. and Industry Coun. Fellow: IEEE, Assn. Computing Machinery. Achievements include patents in field. Home: 3901 Orange Lake Dr Orlando FL 32817-1637 Home Phone: 407-679-6186. Business E-Mail: deo@cs.ucf.edu.

DEORCHIS, FRANKIE JUANITA, forester, writer; b. Hawkins, Tex., Dec. 10, 1920; d. E. Whitney and Bura Moseley Moore; m. M. E. DeOrchis, June 27, 1948; children: Vincent Moore, Diane Frances Vogth-Eriksen, Douglas F. BS, Columbia U., 1948. Bookkeeper Civil Svc., Washington, 1942—44; law office mgr. DeOrchis & Ptnrs., NYC; mgr. hardwood forest The Timbers, Killingworth, Conn., 1967—. Author: Breaking Bread with Friends Around the World, 2000, From Mom Mom's Kitchen, 1995. Republican. Avocations: travel, reading, cooking, entertaining, charity work. Home: 50 Shore Rd Old Greenwich CT 06870

DEORCHIS, VINCENT MOORE, lawyer; b. NYC, Aug. 25, 1949; s. Mario E. and Frankie (Moore) DeO.; children: Vincent Scott, Dana Lauren. BA, Fordham Coll., 1971, JD, 1974. Bar: N.Y. 1975, U.S. Dist. Ct. (so. and ea. dists.) N.Y. 1975, U.S. Ct. Appeals (2d cir.) 1975, U.S. Supreme Ct. 1985, U.S. Ct. Appeals (3d cir.) 1989, U.S. Dist. Ct. (so. dist.) Tex. 1992, U.S. Ct. Appeals (4th cir.) 1996. Assoc. Haight, Gardner, Poor & Havens, NYC, 1974-84; ptnr. DeOrchis, Walker & Corsa, LLP, NYC, 1997—2002; mng. and sr. ptnr., maritime law DeOrchis & Ptnrs. LLP, NYC, 1984—. Advisor on UNCITRAL transport law conv. U.S. Dept. of State; titulary del. Com. Maritime Internat. Co-author: Attorney's Practice Guide to Negotiations, 1985. Pres. North Stratmore Civic Assn., Manhasset, N.Y., 1978-82. Mem. ATLA, ABA (com. on maritime litig.), Inter-Pacific Bar Assn., Maritime Law Assn. (former bd. dirs., rep. to Comite Maritime Internat.), Assn. Transp. Practitioners, N.Y. County Lawyers Assn. (com. on maritime and admiralty law), Propeller Club U.S. Avocation: sailing. Office: DeOrchis and Ptnrs LLP 61 Broadway Fl 26 New York NY 10006-2802 Office Phone: 212-344-4700. Business E-Mail: vdeorchis@marinelex.com.

DEOUL, KATHLEEN BOARDSEN, publishing executive; b. New London, Conn., May 5, 1944; d. Harry Kostrope Boardsen and Elizabeth (Conti) Dunham; m. Neal Deoul, June 20, 1982; 1 child, Shannon Rae. Grad. high sch., New London. Br. mgr. Qwip Sys. divsn. Exxon, Balt.; br. ops. mgr. Exxon Office Sys., Pitts., 1977—82; owner, pres. Bus. Quars., Crystal City, Va., 1983—95, Wellness Alternatives, Balt., 1993—, Cassandra Books, LLC, Balt., 2001; one-star presdl. dir. Bio Pro Tech., 2005—. Author: Cancer Cover-up, 2001. With Safe Wireless Initiative; co-chair Found. Alternative and Complementary Therapies. Named Cons. of Yr., Nikken, Inc., 1999, Bio Pro Tech., 2005, 2006. Mem.: Pres.'s Club Nikken, Inc. (Distbr. of Yr. 1999), Pres.'s Club Exxon. Avocations: venture capitalist, travel, writing, interior decorating, public speaking. E-mail: kathleendeoul@comcast.net.

DEPACE, NICHOLAS LOUIS, physician; b. Nutley, NJ, Oct. 18, 1953; s. Nicholas Frank and Rose (Piro) DeP.; m. Marilyn Tomaro, Jan. 17, 1981. BS, Seton Hall U.; MD, N.J. Sch. Medicine, Mt. Sinai, NYC; internal medicine cardiology, Hahnemann U., Phila. Diplomate Am. Bd. Internal Medicine and Cardiology. Intern in internal medicine Overlook Hosp., Summit, N.J., Columbia U., NYC, 1978-79; resident internal medicine, fellow in cardiology Hahnemann Med. Coll. and Hosp., Phila., 1979—83; practice medicine specializing in internal and cardiology medicine Phila., 1982—; with radio Sta. WPEN, Phila., 1990—2001; clin. prof. medicine Thomas Jefferson U. Hosp., 1997—; chief divsn. preventive cardiology Grad. Hosp., 1996-97; dir. heart repair program Phila. Heart Inst., Presbyn. Med. Ctr., Phila., 1993-95; dir. Jefferson Heart Ctr. South, 1997—. Co-author: The Heart Repair Manual; mem. editl. bd. Am. Jour. Cardiology. Fellow Am. Coll. Cardiology, Am. Coll. Chest Physicians; mem. Phila. Coll. Physicians. Republican. Roman Catholic. Avocations: reading, writing, travel, sports. Office: 188 Fries Mill Rd Ste N2 Turnersville NJ 08012-2055 also: 2422 24 S Broad St Philadelphia PA 19145

DEPALMA, RALPH GEORGE, surgeon, educator; m. Maleva Tankard, Sept. 17, 1955; children: Ralph L., Edward F., Maleva B., Malinda G. AB, Columbia U, 1953; MD, NYU, 1956. Diplomate Am. Bd. Surgery, Am. Bd. Vascular Surgery. Resident in surgery Univ. Hosps., Cleve., 1962-64; from instr. to prof. surgery Case Western Res. U., Cleve., 1964-80; prof., chmn. surgery U. Nev., Reno, 1980-82, George Washington U. Sch. Medicine, Washington, 1982-92; Lewis B. Saltz prof. of surgery George Washington U. Med. Ctr., Washington, 1992-94; prof. surgery, vice-chmn. dept. surgery, assoc. dean U. Nev., Reno, 1994-2000; nat. dir. surgery Dept. Vets. Affairs, Washington, 2000—; prof. surgery Uniformed Svsc. U. Health Scis., Bethesda, Md., 2000—. Faculty chair surgery Inst. for Health Care Improvement, 2007. Editor: (with J.M. Giordano) Reoperative Vascular Surgery, 1987, Basic Science of Vascular Surgery, 1988, Lives and Loves in Cars XLibris, 2005, Practicing and Other Stories XLibris, 2005; assoc. editor: Haimovici Vascular Surgery: Principles and Techniques, 1989; co-editor: Basic Science in Vascular Disease, 1997, Vascular Surgery, Internat. Jour. Impotence Rsch.; mem. editl. bd. Vascular and Endovascular Surgery, 2003; contbr. articles to profl. jours. Stroke liaison nat. chpt. Am. Heart Assn., 1992-94; bd. dirs. Reno Chamber Orch., 1999-00; active Nat. Quality Found., 2004, steering com. surg. complications improvement project, 2004—, tech. adv. group venous thromboembolism. Capt. USAF, 1958-61. Grantee USPHS, 1974-82. Fellow ACS; mem. Cleve. Vascular Soc. (pres. 1977-78), Rocky Mt. Vascular Soc. (pres. 1981-82), Am. Surg. Assn., Soc. Vascular Surgery, Washington Acad. Surgery (sec. 1991-92, v.p. 1992-93, pres. 1993-94), Am. Venous Forum (sec. 1991-94, bd. dirs. found. 1992-95), Am. Coll. Healthcare Execs. (assoc.), 1996, Cosmos Club (admissions com. 1992-94, awards com. 2001, chair 2003—), Western Vascular Soc., Surgical Soc. Inst. Health Care Improvement, Prospectors Club Reno. Office Phone: 202-461-7141. Personal E-mail: docdepalma@msn.com. Business E-Mail: ralph.depalma@va.gov.

DE PALMA-IOZZI, FRANCES M., music educator, conductor; b. Montclair, NJ, Aug. 27, 1947; d. Anthony Francis De Palma and Edith I. Dilorio; m. Louis A. Iozzi, Aug. 28, 1993; m. Eugene W. McBride (div.). BA in Music, William Patterson U., NJ, 1969; MA in Liberal Studies summa cum laude, Kean U., NJ, 1987. Cert. supr. N.J. Dept. Edn. Music educator and choral condr. West Caldwell Pub. Schs., NJ, 1969—2006. Adjudicator N.J. State Honors Choirs, 1986—; mem. Clin. Schs. Network Montclair State U., 1989—96; tchg. fellow Lincoln Ctr. Inst. Arts Edn., NYC, 1995—2005; adj. prof. Montclair State U., NJ, 2001, Caldwell Coll., 2003. Pianist charity big band Reeds Rhythm and All That Brass, Caldwell, NJ, 1989—; founding mem. West Caldwell Performing Arts Com., 1994, program chair, 1994—2000, bd. mem., 1994—2000. Nominee Tchr. of Yr., N.J. Edn. Assn., 1993; named Best Master's Thesis in Humanities, Kean U., 1993; recipient Tchr. Edn. in Democracy award, Montclair State U., 1993; fellow, Cornell U. and NEH, 1989. Mem.: NJ Jazz Soc. (bd. mem.), Mensa. Avocations: quilting, cooking, winemaking.

DEPAN, HARRY JOHN, cardiothoracic surgeon; s. Harry McCarthy and Mary Elizabeth Depan; m. Ellen Taylor, Feb. 16, 1992; children: Brian James, Matthew Sean, Cara Gan Tao. BS in Chemistry, Washington and Lee U., Lexington, Va., 1974; MD, Albany Med. Coll., NY, 1978. Intern surgery NYU, 1978, resident, 1979—83, resident cardiothoracic surgery, 1983—85, asst. prof. surgery, 1985—89; attending physician St. Peters Hosp., Albany, 1989—; attending surgeon Albany Med. Ctr., 1989—, Ellis Hosp., Schenectady, 1991—, divsn. chief cardio surgery, 1994—, chief of staff, 2000—04. Bd. dirs. Ellis Hosp., 2000—. Mem.: ACS, Soc. Thoracic Surgeons. Avocations: fly fishing, skiing, sailing. Office: Schenectady CardioThoracic Surgeons 1101 Nott St Ste 4B Schenectady NY 12308 Office Phone: 518-243-3610. Business E-Mail: hdepan@nycap.rr.com.

DEPAOLA, DOMINICK PHILIP, academic administrator; b. Bklyn., Dec. 29, 1942; s. Dominick and Marie (DeStefano) DeP.; m. Rosemary Elizabeth Femiano, Aug. 2, 1969; 1 child, Alexis Jane. BS, St. Francis Coll., 1964; DDS, NYU, 1969; PhD, MIT, 1974; ScD (hon.), Baylor U., 1995; PharmD (hon.), Mass. Coll. Pharmacy and Health Scis., 2002. Assoc. prof. Va. Commonwealth U., Med. Coll. Va., Richmond, 1974-78; dean Dental Sch. U. Tex. Health Sci. Ctr., San Antonio, 1983-87, interim dean Grad. Sch. Biomed. Scis., 1986-87; dean Dental Sch. U. Medicine and Dentistry N.J., Newark, 1988-90; pres., dean Baylor Coll. Dentistry, Dallas, 1990-96; pres. Tex. A&M Univ. Sys.-Baylor Coll. Dentistry, Dallas, 1996-97; pres., CEO Forsyth Inst., Boston, 1998—; prof. Harvard U. Sch. Dental Medicine, Boston, 1999—. Mem. Nat. Adv. Dental Rsch. Coun. for Nat. Inst. Dental Rsch., 1996-2000; mem. dental adv. com. Pew Commn. for Health Professions, 1991; chair, bd. dirs. Oral Health Am., 1999-2000; bd. dirs. Block Drug Co.; mem. Commn. on Dental Accreditation, 1992-97. Recipient Presdl. award San Antonio Dist. Dental Soc., 1987, Alumni Achievement award NYU Coll. Dentistry, 1993, Kriser medal NYU Coll. Dentistry, 2003, Disting. Svc. award Am. Dental Edn. Assn., 2005. Fellow Am. Acad. Oral Medicine (hon.); mem. ADA, Am. Inst. Nutrition, Am. Assn. Dental Schs. (past pres. 1989-91), Am. Soc. for Clin. Nutrition (chair pub. info. com. 1995-2002), Am. Soc. Nutritional Scis. (chair pub. info. com. 1995-2002), Am. Assn. Dental Rsch. (pres. 2004), Internat. Assn. Dental Rsch., Hispanic Dental Assn. (hon.), Am. Dietetic Assn. (hon.), Rsch. Am (bd. dirs.). Avocations: skiing, racquetball, tennis, golf, reading. Office: Forsyth Inst 140 Fenway Boston MA 02115-3799 Business E-Mail: ddepaola@forsyth.org.

DEPAOLI, GERI M. (JOAN DEPAOLI), artist, historian; b. June 8, 1941; m. Alexander DePaoli, July 4, 1961; children: Alexander Mark, Michael Alexander. BA, U. Md., 1974, MA, 1978; student, U. Calif., Davis, 1965-68. Art history educator, artist, curator slides and photos Nat. Mus., Bangkok, Thailand, 1968-71; art prof. Montgomery Coll., Rockville, Md., 1978-82; cons. oriental slide and photo collection Princeton U., 1983-84; lectr. Princeton Sch. Visual Arts, 1986-90; curator The Mus. Art, Ft. Lauderdale, Fla., 1986; dir. Coun. for Creative Projects, NYC, 1989-91; faculty artworks Princeton Sch. Visual Arts, 1984-91; exec. dir. EducArt Projects Inc., Davis, Calif., 1991—. Cons. in field. Author: Emmy Lou Packard: A Woman and a Century, 1998, Barbara Spring, Populations from the Collective Unconscious, 1998, Donna Billick: Making Art out of Stone, 1999, Clayton Bailey: Happenings in the Circus of Life, 2000, Lisa Reinertson: Art Out of Experience, 2005; editor (exhbn. catalog): Elvis & Marilyn: 2 X Immortal, Rizzoli, 1994; author (ednl. resource guide) Elvis & Marilyn: 2 X Immortal, 1994, (ednl. program) Images of Power, 1994, video prodr. Images of Power: Balinese Paintings made for Gregory Bateson and Margaret Mead, 1994, editor/co-curator (exhbn. catalog) Transcending Abstraction, 1986, reviewer ArtMatters Newspaper, Phila., 1987—90, author-curator The Trans Parent Thread: Asian Philosophy in Recent Am. Art, 1990, contbg. author Art of Calif. Mag.; one-woman shows include E.W. Gallery, Bethesda, Md., 1978, Upstairs Gallery, Kingston, N.J., 1982, Gallery at the Purple Barge, N.Y.C., 1984, The Art Gallery, Kingston, 1985, Back Door Gallery, Princeton, 1986, Campion Gallery of Art, 1987, AT&T Corp. Gallery, Princeton, 1989, Rider Coll. Gallery, Lawrenceville, N.J., 1990; also numerous group shows. Councilor Nat. Abortion Rights Action League, 1989—. Recipient award for excellence in pub., Office of Pres. of U.S., 1969. Fellow Soc. for Arts Religion and Contemporary Culture; mem. Assn. Ind. Historians of Art (v.p. 1988—), Coll. Art Assn., Princeton Rsch. Forum, Nat. Coalition of Ind. Scholars, Sierra Club, Greenpeace. Buddhist. Avocations: skiing, philosophy discussion groups, intellectual history. Office: EducArt Projects Inc PO Box 267 Davis CA 95617-0267

DEPAOLI, LOU, professional sports team executive; m. Kathy DePaoli; children: Ryan, Emily. BA in Mgmt. of Profl. Sports Orgns., U. Mass. With Prudential Ins. Co. Am., Auburn, Mass.; owner ins. agy., Worcester, Mass.; v.p. sales Am. Hockey League Worcester IceCats, 1994—96; positions up to v.p. sales and mktg. Maj. League Baseball Fla. Marlins, 1996—2000; positions up to v.p. team mktg. and bus. devel. Team Mktg. and Bus. Ops. dept. NBA, 2000—05; exec. v.p., chief mktg. officer Atlanta Spirit, LLC (parent co. of NBA Atlanta Hawks, NHL Atlanta Thrashers and Philips Arena), 2005—. Office: Atlanta Spirit LLC 101 Marietta St NW Ste 1900 Atlanta GA 30303 Office Phone: 404-878-3802. E-mail: Lou.Depaoli@atlantaspirit.com.*

DEPAOLIS, POTITO UMBERTO, food company executive; b. Mignano, Italy, Aug. 28, 1925; arrived in U.S., 1966, naturalized, 1970; s. Giuseppe A. and Filomena (Macchiaverna) DePaolis; m. Marie A. Caronna, Apr. 10, 1965. Vet Dr, U. Naples, 1948; Libera Docenza, Ministero Pub. Istruzione, Rome, 1955. Prof. food svc. Vet. Sch., U. Naples, Italy, 1948—66; asst. prof. A Titre Benevole Ecole Veterinaire Alfort, Paris, 1956; vet. inspector U.S. Dept. Agr., Omaha, 1966—67; sr. rsch. chemist Grain Processing Corp., Muscatine, Iowa, 1967—68; v.p., dir. prod. devel. Reddi Wip, Inc., LA, 1968—72; with Kubro Foods, LA, 1972—73, Shade Foods, Inc., 1975—; pres. Vegetable Protein Co., Riverside, Calif., 1973—, Tima Brand Food Co., 1975—, Dr. Tima Natural Foods, 1977—. Contbr. articles to profl. jours. Fulbright scholar, Cornell U., Ithaca, N.Y., 1954, British Coun. scholar, U. Reading, Eng., 1959—60, postdoctoral rsch. fellow, NIH, Cornell U., 1963—64. Mem.: AAAS, Greater L.A. Press Club, Italian Press Assn., Biol. Sci. Assn. Italy, Vet. Med. Assn., Italian Assn. Advancement Sci., Inst. Food Technologists ("Seminatore D'oro" as best soccer referee for all Italy). Achievements include patents in field. Home: Bel Air 131 Groverton Pl Los Angeles CA 90077-3732 Personal E-mail: drtima@aol.com.

DEPAOLO, RONALD FRANCIS, editor-in-chief, writer; b. Jamaica, NY, July 12, 1938; s. Francis Edward and Evelyn Helen (Turck) deP.; m. Meredith Nell Mass, Aug. 12, 1967; children— Britton, Damon, Baird. BA cum laude, Moravian Coll., Bethlehem, Pa., 1964; MS, Northwestern U., 1965. Reporter, corr., writer Life mag., 1965-70; news editor, corr. Business Week mag., 1970-72; freelance writer and editor, 1972-76; editor-in-chief, asso. pub. I-AM mag., NYC, 1976-78; sr. editor Boardroom Reports, NYC, 1978-80; editor-in-chief M.D. Mag., NYC, 1980-84; editor, pub. Kirkus Revs., NYC, 1984-87. Pres. Rock Lodge Devel. Corp., 1987—; adj. prof. communications Ramapo Coll., Mahwah, N.J., 1974-75 Author: Russia and the Independent States, 1992, The Presidency from A to Z, 1998, Elections from A to Z, 1998, Guide to Congress, 1999; contbr.: Encyclopedia of American Political History, 2001. Served with AUS, 1957-59, 60-61. Home: 331 Western County Rd Penobscot ME 04476 Home Phone: 207-326-9002. E-mail: rondep@hughes.net.

DEPARLE, NANCY-ANN MIN, former federal agency administrator, lawyer; b. Cleve., Dec. 17, 1956; m. Jason DeParle. BA, U. Tenn., 1978; JD, Harvard U., 1983; BA, MA, Balliol Coll., Oxford U., Eng., 1981. Past pvt. practice in law; commr. human services State of Tenn., 1987-89; assoc. dir. health and pers. White House Office Mgmt. & Budget, Washington; administr. Health Care Financing Adminstrn. HHS, Washington,

1997—2000; now sr. advisor JP Morgan Partners LLC; also cons. on health policy and regulatory affairs. Mem. Medicare Payment Adv. Commn.; adj. prof. health care systems Wharton Sch., U. Pa.; bd. dirs. Cerner Corp., 2001—; mem. bd. DaVita, Guidant Corp., Triad Hospitals, Nat. Quality Forum. Bd. trustees The Robert Wood Johnson Found., 2002—. Rhodes scholar, 1979-81. Address: MedPAC Ste 9000 601 New Jersey Ave NW Washington DC 20001

DEPAUL, CHRISTINA, dean, artist; b. Pitts., 1959; BFA, Carnegie-Mellon U., 1981; MFA, Temple U., 1984. Assoc. prof. art in metals U. Akron, Ohio, 1986—2002, dir. Mary Schiller Myers Sch. Art Ohio, 1995—2002; dean Corcoran Coll. Art and Design, Washington, DC, 2002—. Office: Corcoran Coll Art and Design 500 Seventeenth St, NW Washington DC 20006-4804 Office Phone: 202-639-1801.

DEPAUL, MICHAEL, music educator; b. Lansdale, Pa., Mar. 24, 1977; s. Joesph DePaul and Janet DePaul-James, Melvin James (Stepfather) and Lolly Yancey (Stepmother). MusB, Temple U., Phila., 2001; MusM, Boston Conservatory, 2005. Video editor The Entertainment Source, Phila., 2000—01; prodn. mgr. Rocky Mountain Prodn. and Wildflower Records, NYC, 2002—05. Piano instr. Stuarts Music, Lansdale, Pa., 1999—2003; tchg. asst. Boston Conservatory, 2003—05. Composer: Requiem Mass, Blue Note Room, Brooklyn Love, Cadenzas to the Beethoven Violin Concerto. Scholar Esther Boyer Merit scholar, Temple U., 1998—2001. Mem.: Am. Music Ctr., Am. Composers Forum. Home Phone: 215-855-933.

DE PAULO, CRAIG J. N., priest, philosopher, educator; b. Phila., Jan. 1, 1968; s. Michael Alexander, Jr. and Maria Margaret (Florio) de Paulo; m. Catherine Conroy, Aug. 28, 1999; 1 child, Christian. BA in Philosophy, La Salle U., 1989; MA in Philosophy, Villanova U., 1991; PhL in Philosophy, Pontificia U. Gregoriana, Vatican City, 1994, PhD in Philosophy, 1995. Asst. prof. Temple U., Phila., 2000—07; assoc. prof. Wheeling Jesuit U., W.Va., 2007—. Author: Being and Conversion, 2002; editor: Ambiguity in The Western Mind, 2005, The Influence of Augustine on Heidegger: The Emergence of an Augustinian Phenomenology, 2006. Decorated knight Order of Malta, Equestrian Order of Holy Sepulchre, Constantinian Order, Savoy Order of Merit. Mem.: Am. Philos. Assn., Am. Cath. Philos Assn. Roman Catholic (Bizantine Rite). Office: Wheeling Jesuit U Dept Philosophy 316 Washington Ave Wheeling WV 26003

DEPAULO, J. RAYMOND, JR., psychiatrist, researcher; b. Charleston, W.Va., May 21, 1946; s. J Raymond and Mary Catherine DePaulo; m. Joanne M. Althoff, May 17, 1997; children: Marianne DePaulo Plant, Margaret DePaulo Kottke. MD, Johns Hopkins U. Sch. Medicine, 1972. Cert. Am. Bd. Psychiatry and Neurology, 1977. Asst. prof. to prof., psychiatry and behavioral scis. Johns Hopkins U. Sch. Medicine, Balt., 1977—2002, Henry Phipps prof. & dir. dept. psychiatry and behavioral sci., 2002—. Founder Affective Disorders Clinic Johns Hopkins Hosp., Balt., 1977. Author (teacher, lectr.): (books about depression) How To Cope with Depression, Understanding Depression (Nat. Edn. Award, Depression Awareness Recognition and Treatment, NIMH, 1992); editl. bd. Am. Jour. Psychiatry, Biol. Psychiatry, Bipolar Disorder, Psychiatric Genetics, Jour. Nervous and Mental Disease. Recipient Selo Prize, Nat. Assn. Rsch. on Schizophrenia and Depression, 1996, Disting. Investigator award, 1998, 2003, Rsch. award, Am. Found. for Suicide Prevention, 2007; grantee Genetics of Bipolar and Depressive Disorders, NIH, 1988—2005. Fellow: Am. Coll. Psychiatrists, Am. Psychopathological Assn. (pres. 2006), Am. Psychiat. Assn. (life); mem.: Internat. Soc. for Psychiat. Genetics. Roman Catholic. Achievements include principal investigator of several studies into the genetics of bipolar disorder and unipolar depression. Office: Dept of Psychiatry Johns Hopkins Hosp Meyer 4-113 601 N Wolfe St Baltimore MD 21287-7413 Home Phone: 410-321-7326; Office Phone: 410-955-3130. Office Fax: 410-955-0946; Home Fax: none. E-mail: psychchair@jhmi.edu.

DE PAUW, LINDA GRANT, historian, educator, writer; b. NYC, Jan. 19, 1940; d. Phillip and Ruth (Marks) Grant. BA, Swarthmore Coll., 1961; PhD, Johns Hopkins U., 1964. Asst. prof. history George Mason Coll.-U. Va., Fairfax, 1964-65; spl. asst. to archivist U.S. Nat. Archives, Washington, 1965-66; asst. prof. history George Washington U., Washington, 1966-69, assoc. prof., 1969-75, prof. Am. history, 1975-98, prof. emeritus, 1999—. Editor-in-chief, project dir.: (documentary) History of the First Fed. Congress, 1966-84; author: The Eleventh Pillar: New York State and the Federal Constitution, 1966, Founding Mothers: Women of America in the Revolutionary Era, 1975, Remember the Ladies, 1976, Seafaring Women, 1982, Baptism of Fire, 1993, Battle Cries and Lullabies, 1998, Sea Changes, 2003, In Search of Molly Pitcher, 2007; editor, pub.: Minerva Quar. Report on Women and Mil., 1983-2002, Minerva's Bulletin Bd., 1988-98; writer/prodr.: (armed forces radio) Minerva on Air, 1987-89; editor: H-Minerva, 1995—, Minerva Jour. Women and War, 2007—. Founder, pres. Minerva Ctr., 1983—. Woodrow Wilson fellow, 1961 Mem. Am. Hist. Assn. (Beveridge award 1964). Home and Office: 20 Granada Rd Pasadena MD 21122-2708 Office Phone: 410-437-5379. Business E-Mail: depauw@minervacenter.com.

DEPINHO, RONALD, research scientist; MD, Albert Einstein Med. Coll., 1981; postgraduate rsch., Columbia Presbyn. Hosp. Feinberg scholar Albert Einstein Med. Coll.; mem. dept. adult oncology, Dana-Farber Cancer Inst. Harvard Med. Sch., Boston, 1998—, prof. medicine (genetics), 1998—, Am. Cancer Soc. Rsch. Prof. Co-founder, scientific adv. bd. AVEO Pharm. Inc., Cambridge, Mass.; bd. dirs. Am. Assn. Cancer Rsch. Bd. dirs. Am. Assn. Cancer Rsch., 2001. Recipient Rsch. Prof., Am. Cancer Soc., 1998, Am. Soc. Clin. Investigation award, 2000, Steven and Michele Kirsch Found. Investigator award, 2000, AACR-GHA Clowes award, 2003. Mem.: Inst. Medicine. Office: Dana-Farber Cancer Inst Mayer 413 44 Binney St Boston MA 02115 Office Phone: 617-632-6086. Office Fax: 617-632-6069.

DEPINTO, DAVID J., public relations executive; BA in Polit. Sci., Brown U.; MBA, U. So. Calif. Dir. mktg., pub. rels., pub. affairs Coca-Cola Bottling Co., LA; exec. v.p. Pacific/West Comm. Group, LA; pres., CEO Stoorza Comm., Inc., San Diego. Mem. bd. dirs. L.A. Ednl. Partnership, Adopt-A-School-Coun. L.A. Unified Sch. Dist., Crescenta Youth Sports Assn.

DE PLANQUE, E. GAIL, physicist; b. Orange, NJ, Jan. 15, 1945; d. Martin William and Edna de Planque. AB, Immaculata Coll., 1967; MS in Physics, N.J. Inst. Tech., 1973; PhD in Environ. Health Scis., NYU, 1983. Physicist U.S. AEC, U.S. Dept. Energy, NYC, 1967-82; dep. dir. environ. measurement lab. U.S. Dept. Energy, NYC, 1982-87, dir. environ. measurement lab., 1987-91; commr. U.S. Nuclear Regulatory Commn., 1991—95; pres. Strategy Matters, Inc., 1998—; dir. Energy Strategists Consultancy, Ltd., 2000—. Adj. prof. NYU, N.Y.C., 1986—; pres. Pacific Nuclear Coun., 1989-91; mem. engring. sci. dept. adv. com., bd. trustees N.J. Inst. Tech., Newark, 1985-91; bd. dirs. TXU Corp. Landauer, Inc.; mem. visiting com. dept. nuclear engring. MIT, Diablo Canyon Ind. Safety Commn.; mem. TU Electric Ops. Rev. Com.; cons. in field. Contbr. articles to profl. jours. Commr. U.S. Nuclear Regulatory Commn., 1991-95; bd. trustees Northeast Utilities, 1995—; bd. dirs. British Nuclear Fuels, Inc., 1996—; Tex. Utilities Elec. Ops. Review Com., 1996—; cons. United Nation's Internat. Atomic Energy Agy., 1996—; mem. external adv. com., Amarillo Nat. Resource Ctr. for Plutonium, 1996—. Named to Hall of Fame, Women in Tech. Internat., 2004. Fellow Am. Nuclear Soc. (bd. dirs. 1977-80, 84-91, v.p. 1987-88, pres. 1988-89), Health Physics Soc., AAAS, Am. Phys. Soc., Assn. for Women in Sci. (v.p. N.Y. met. sect. 1980-82), Internat. Nuclear Energy Acad., (sec. 1996—); mem. NAE. Achievements include research in environmental radiation, radiation protection, solid state dosimetry, thermoluminescence.

DEPP, JOHNNY, actor; b. Owensboro, Ky., June 9, 1963; s. John and Betty Sue Depp; m. Lori Anne Allison Dec. 20, 1983 (div. 1985); children: Lily-Rose Melody, Jack. Guitarist; ex-member bands the Flame, the Kids, Rock City Angels, 1985; actor TV series 21 Jump Street, 1987-90; actor (films) A Nightmare on Elm Street, 1984, Private Resort, 1985, Platoon, 1986, Cry-Baby, 1990, Edward Scissorhands, 1990, Freddy's Dead: The Final Nightmare, 1991, American Dreamers, 1992, Benny & Joon, 1993, What's Eating Gilbert Grape, 1993, Ed Wood, 1994, Arizona Dreamer, Don Juan DeMarco, 1995, Dead Man, 1995, Nick of Time, 1996, Donnie Brasco, 1997, The Astronaut's Wife, 1998, L.A. Without a Map, 1998, Fear and Loathing in Las Vegas, 1998, The Source, 1999, The Ninth Gate, 1999, Just to Be Together, 1999, The Astronaut's Wife, 1999, Sleepy Hollow, 1999, The Source, 1999, The Man Who Cried, 2000, Chocolat, 2000, Blow, 2001, From Hell, 2001, Pirates of the Caribbean: The Curse of the Black Pearl, 2003 (Screen Actors Guild Award for best actor, 2004, Acad. Award nomination for best actor, 2004, Golden Globe nomination for best actor in a musical or comedy, 2004), Once Upon A Time in Mexico, 2003, Secret Window, 2004, Ils se marièrent et eurent beaucoup d'enfants, 2004, Finding Neverland, 2004, The Libertine, 2004, Charlie and the Chocolate Factory, 2005 (Choice Movie Actor: Comedy, Teen Choice awards, 2006), (voice) Corpse Bride, 2005, (narrator) Deep Sea 3D, 2006, Pirates of the Caribbean: Dead Man's Chest, 2006 (Choice Movie Actor: Drama/Action Adventure, Teen Choice awards, 2006, Best Performance, MTV Movie Awards, 2007), Pirates of the Caribbean: At World's End, 2007 (Choice Movie Actor: Action Adventure, Teen Choice Awards, 2007); writer, dir., actor: The Brave, 1997; TV movies include Slow Burn, 1986; TV guest appearances include Lady Blue, 1985, Hotel, 1987, The Vicar of Dibley, 1999, (voice) King of the Hill, 2004; (video-voice) Kingdom Hearts II, 2005. Named Favorite Male Movie Star, People's Choice Awards, 2006, Favorite Male Star, Favorite Male Action Star & On-screen matchup (Keira Knightly), 2007; named one of Time Mag. 100 Most Influential People, 2005, 50 Most Powerful People in Hollywood, Premiere mag., 2004, 2005, 2006, The 100 Most Powerful Celebrities, Forbes.com, 2007. Office: 9100 Wilshire Blvd Ste 725E Beverly Hills CA 90212-3441*

DEPPAS, LOUIS ANTHONY, financial adviser; b. Jamestown, NY, May 25, 1956; s. Anthony L. and Dominica Deppas; m. Melissa J. Harner, July 30, 1989; children: Brynne H., Morgan J., Sydney L. MMus in Edn., SUNY, Fredonia, NY, 1986. Dir. of bands Jamestown Pub. Schs., 1980—2000; registered rep. Legend Equities Corp., Jamestown, 1987—. Treas. YMCA, Jamestown, 2003—; chmn. of fin. ministry Christ First United Meth. Ch., Jamestown, 2000—; adv. bd. mem. Jamestown Jammers Minor League Baseball Team, 2005—. Mem. roundtable YMCA, Jamestown, 2004. Named YMCA Bd. Mem. of Yr., 2004; named one of Outstanding Young Men of Am., 1988. Mem.: Elks. Office: The Legend Group 305 E Fairmount Ave Lakewood NY 14750 Home Phone: 716-487-1437; Office Phone: 716-763-9380. Office Fax: 716-763-9383. E-mail: louisdeppas@legendequities.com.

DEPPERSCHMIDT, THOMAS ORLANDO, economist, consultant; b. St. Louis, Dec. 3, 1935; s. Robert O. and Marcella C. (Meier) D.; m. Bertha Marie Waldman, Nov. 28, 1957; children: M. Susan, Mark, Joel, Andrew, Amy, Joan. AB, Ft. Hays State U., Kans., 1958; PhD, U. Tex., 1965. Asst. prof., then assoc. prof. W. Tex. State U., Canyon, 1961-66; prof. econs. Memphis State U., 1966—2001, prof. emeritus, 2001—, chmn. dept., 1977-83. Research assoc. study N.Y.C. elevator industry, 1996, 2004. Author: Detritus: The SIP Initiative to Stalk Hitler, 2006; co-author: Encyclopedia of Economics, 1974, Assessing Family Loss in Wrongful Death Litigation, 1999; editor: Financial Policies in Transition, 1968; author over 40 tech. treatises. With AUS, 1954-56. Mem.: Am. Acad. Econ. and Fin. Experts, Nat. Assn. Forensic Economists, Am. Econ. Assn. Home and Office: 1957 Mt Repose Germantown TN 38139-3443 E-mail: tdpprsch@memphis.edu.

DEPRE, CHRISTOPHE, medical educator; arrived in US, 1997, permanent resident, 2003; MD, U. Louvain, Belgium, 1991, PhD, 1995. Lic. cardiologist Belgium, 1997. Resident St.-Luc Univ. Hosp., Brussels, 1995—97; asst. prof. U. Tex., Houston, 1999, Pa. State U., Hershey, Pa., 1999—2001, U. Medicine and Dentistry NJ, Newark, 2001—04, assoc. prof., 2004—. Recipient M. Marcus Young Investigator award, Am. Heart Assn., 1999, Established Investigator award, 2006; grantee, NIH, 2002—. Office: U Medicine and Dentistry NJ 185 South Orange MSB G 609 Newark NJ 07103 Office Phone: 973-972-3926. Office Fax: 973-972-7489. Business E-Mail: deprech@umdnj.edu.

DEPREIST, JAMES ANDERSON, conductor; b. Phila., Nov. 21, 1936; s. James Henry and Ethel (Anderson) DePriest; m. Betty Louise Childress, Aug. 10, 1963; children: Tracy Elisabeth DePriest, Jennifer Anne DePriest; m. Ginette Grenier, July 19, 1980. BS, U. Pa., 1958, MA, 1961, LHD (hon.), 1976; student, Phila. Conservatory Music, 1959—61; LHD (hon.), Reed Coll., 1990, Portland State U., 1993; MusD (hon.), Laval U., Quebec City, Can., 1980, Linfield Coll., 1986, Juilliard, 1993; DFA (hon.), U. Portland, 1983, Pacific U., 1985, Willamette U., 1987, Drexel U., 1989, Oreg. State U., 1990; D of Arts and Letters (hon.), St. Mary's Coll., Moraga, Calif., 1985; HHD (hon.), Lewis and Clark U., 1986. Am. specialist music for State Dept., 1962—63; condr.-in-residence Bangkok, 1963—64; condr. various symphonies and orchs., 1964—; condr., music dir. Oreg. Symphony, Portland, 1980, laureate music dir.; now permanent condr. Tokyo Met. Symphony Orchestra; and dir. of conducting and orchestral studies The Juilliard Sch., NYC. Prin. artistic adv. Phoenix Symphony. Condr.: Am. debut with N.Y. Philharm., 1964, asst. condr. to Leonard Bernstein N.Y. Philharm. Orch., 1965—66, prin. guest condr. Symphony of New World, 1968—70, European debut with Rotterdam Philharm., 1969, Helsinki Philharm., 1993, assoc. condr. Nat. Symphony Orch., Washington, 1971—75, prin. guest condr., 1975—76, music dir. L'Orch. Symphonique de Que., 1976—83, Oreg. Symphony, 1980—, prin. guest condr. Helsinki Philharm., 1993, music dir. Monte Carlo Philharm., 1994, appeared with Phila. Orch., 1972, 1976, 1984—85, 1987, 1990, 1992—94, Chgo. Symphony, 1973, 1990, 1992, 1994, Boston Symphony, 1973, 1997—99, Cleve. Orch., 1974, condr. Am. premiere of Dvorak's First Symphony, N.Y. Philharm., 1972, London Symphony, Barbican, 2005, chief condr. Malmö Symphony, 1991—94; author: (poetry books) This Precipice Garden, 1987, The Distant Siren, 1989. Trustee Lewis and Clark Coll., 1983—. Decorated Insignia of Comdr. of Order of Lion of Finland; recipient 1st prize gold medal, Dimitri Mitropoulos Internat. Music Competition for Condrs., 1964, Merit citation, City of Phila., 1969, medal, City of Que., 1983, Officer of the Order of Cultural Merit of Monaco, Nat. Medal of Arts, Nat. Endowment for the Arts, 2005; grantee, Martha Baird Rockefeller Fund for Music, 1969. Fellow: Royal Swedish Acad. Music, Am. Acad. Arts and Scis. Mailing: c/o ICM Artists Ltd Jason Bagdade 40 West 57th St New York NY 10019

DEPRIEST, C(HARLES) DAVID, engineering executive, retired military officer; b. Mount Pleasant, Pa., Oct. 18, 1938; s. Charles Leonard and Elizabeth Carolyn (Hoover) DeP.; m. Blanca Reinoso Rivas, July 1, 1960 (div.); children: Lisa Lynn Nees, Diane Cokerdem DePriest, David Eric; m. Marlena J. Brechtel, Aug. 1, 2001 (dec.). BSEE with distinction, Air Force Inst. Tech., 1974, MS in Electro-Optics, 1975. Cert. profl. logistician Soc. Logistics Engrs. Enlisted USAF, 1959, advanced through grades to col., 1984, squadron navigator Beale AFB, Calif., 1964-68, squadron radar navigator, wing flight examiner Wright-Patterson AFB, Ohio, 1968-72; chief missile guidance br. USAF armament lab., Eglin AFB, Fla., 1975-79; program element monitor, dep. chief, avionics & armament divsn. air staff HQ USAF, Washington, 1979-83; chief engring. divsn. material mgmt. directorate Warner-Robins ALC, Ga., 1984-86; dir. intercommand electronic warfare aero. systems divsn. Wright-Patterson AFB, 1986-88; dir. plans and ops. AF electronic combat office USAF, Wright-Patterson AFB, 1988-91; ret., 1991; mgr. Warner Robins applications dept. The Analytic Scis. Corp., Inc., Warner Robins, Ga., 1992-97; pres. DePriest Assocs., Inc., Warner Robins, 1997—. Decorated Legion of Merit, DFC, Air medal with silver oak leaf cluster, Meritorious Svc. medal with two bronze oak leaf clusters. Mem.: IEEE (sr.), Soc. Logistics Engrs., Air Force Assn., Mensa, Rotary, Assn. Old Crows, Tau Beta Pi. Office: DePriest Assocs Inc 110 Park Dr Warner Robins GA 31088-5167 Office Phone: 478-329-9258. Personal E-mail: cddeprie@ix.netcom.com. Business E-Mail: dave@depriest-associates.com.

DE PUGET, ALBERT BORG OLIVIER, magistrate judge; b. Valletta, Malta, Apr. 15, 1932; s. Joseph and Helen Lowell. Diploma of Legal Procurator, Royal U. Malta, Valletta, 1954, LLD, 1958. M.P. Ho. of Reps., Malta, 1966-81; mem. Parliamentary Assembly Coun. Europe, Strasbourg, France, 1966-75; magistrate Cts. of Justice, Malta, 1983-87; amb. to France, Spain, Portugal, Switzerland and UNESCO, 1987-91, U.S., Washington, 1991-97; high commr. to Can., 1992-97; amb. designate to Mex., 1996; amb.-in-residence Ctr. for Global Edn., George Mason U., 1997—2002; lectr. multilateral diplomacy Elliott Sch. Internat. Affairs, George Washington U., 1998; apptd. amb. of Malta to Brazil, 2002, to Mexico, 2003. Pvt. law practice, 1958-83; vice chmn., sr. ptnr. Washington World Group Ltd., 1998; sr. counsel Zammit Dimech and Busuttil, Advs., Malta; dir. Assn. on Third World Affairs, Inc., Washington. Editor: Studenti; mem. edit. bds. (newspapers) Patria, Il-Poplu, Malta Taghna, Encounter, In-Nazzjon Taghna; contbr. articles to profl. jours. V.p. Christian Dem. Group; mem. Bur. European Union Christian Dems.; hon. v.p. Malta Coun. European Movement; internat. sec. Nationalist Party, Malta, 1975-77; bd. gov. Internat. Student House, Washington, mem. Com. on Internat. Dialogue; bd. trustees Elsie Whitlow Stokes Cmty. Freedom Pub. Charter Sch., Washington. Mem. La Valette Phil. Soc., The Casino (1852), Cercle de L'Union Interalliée, Internat. Club, Univ. Club, Hannibal Club of Washington (founding mem.). Roman Catholic. Avocations: reading, music, walking. Home and Office: 1673 Columbia Rd NW Apt 309 Washington DC 20009-3604 Office Phone: 202-387-5435. Personal E-mail: abodepuget@aol.com.

DEPUGLIO, JOSEPH, physics educator; b. Trenton, NJ; BA, Coll. of N.J., Trenton, MA in Counseling, MA in Physics. Cert. tchg. N.J. Physics tchr. Steinert H.S., Hamilton, NJ, 1980—. Named Physics Tchr. of Yr., Mercer County Engrs. Soc., 2000, Delaware Valley Engrs. Soc., 2001; recipient Honor award, NJN-TV, 2005. Mem.: State of N.J. Mentor of Sci. Tchrs. Office: Steinert HS East 2900 Klockner Rd Trenton NJ 08690 Office Phone: 609-631-4150.

DEPUY, CHARLES HERBERT, chemist, educator; b. Detroit, Sept. 10, 1927; s. Carroll E. and Helen (Plehn) DeP.; m. Eleanor Burch, Dec. 21, 1949; children: David Gareth, Nancy Ellen, Stephen Baylie, Katherine Louise. BS, U. Calif., Berkeley, 1948; A.M., Columbia U., 1952; PhD, Yale U., 1953. Asst. prof. chemistry Iowa State U., 1953-59, asso. prof., 1959-62, prof., 1962-63; prof. chemistry U. Colo., Boulder, 1963-92, prof. emeritus, 1992—. Vis. prof. U. Ill., summer 1954, U. Calif., Berkeley, summer 1960; NIH sr. postdoctoral fellow U. Basel, Switzerland, 1969-70; cons. A.E. Staley Co., 1956-80, Marathon Oil Co., 1964-89. Author: (with Kenneth L. Rinehart) Introduction to Organic Chemistry, 1967, rev. edit., 1975, (with Orville L. Chapman) Molecular Reactions and Photochemistry, 1970, (with Robert H. Shapiro) Exercises in Organic Spectroscopy; contbr. articles profl. jours. Served wih AUS, 1946-47. John Simon Guggenheim fellow, 1977-78, 86-87; Alexander von Humboldt fellow, 1988-89, James Flack Norris Award, Am. Chem. Soc., 2001. Fellow AAAS; mem. Am. Chem. Soc. (exec. com. organic div., chmn. Colo. sect., mem. adv. bd. jour. 1987-92, gold medal), Sigma Xi, Nat. Acad of Sci., 1999, Am. Acad. of Arts and Sci., 2003. Home: 1509 Cascade Ave Boulder CO 80302-7631 Office: U Colo Boulder Dept Chemistry & Biochemistry PO Box 215 Boulder CO 80309-0215 Office Phone: 303-492-7652. Business E-Mail: charles.depuy@colorado.edu.

DE QUADROS, CIRO A., epidemiologist, educator; MD, Cath. Sch. Medicine, Brazil; MPH, Nat. Sch. Pub. Health, Rio de Janeiro, 1968. Chief epidemiologist Smallpox Eradication Prog., WHO, Ethiopia, 1970; Expanded Prog. on Immunization Pan Am. Health Orgn., 1991, dir. Div. Vaccines and Immunization Washington; dir. Internat. Progs. Sabin Vaccine Inst. (SVI), Washington, 2003—, interim pres., CEO, 2006. Assoc. adj. prof. Johns Hopkins Sch. Hygiene and Pub. Health; assoc. prof. Sch. Medicine, Case Western Reserve U.; adj. prof. Dept. Tropical Medicine Sch. Medicine, George Washington U. Author: Vaccines: Preventing Disease Protecting Health; presented papers in over 100 confs. Mem. bd. Internat. AIDS Vaccine Initiative; chmn. ind. rev. com. Global Alliance for Vaccines & Immunization; chmn. tech. adv. group on vaccines & immunizations Pan. Am. Health Orgn. Recipient Order of the Bifurcated Needle, WHO, Internat. Child Survival Award, UNICEF and the Carter Ctr., Prince Mahidol Award, Thailand, 1993, Order of Rio Branco, Govt. Brazil, 1999, Albert B. Sabin Gold Medal, 2000, Order of Pub. Health, Govt. Bolivia, 2003, Internat. Pub. Health Hero award, U. Calif., Berkeley. Mem.: AAAS, Inst. Medicine, NY Acad. Scis., Am. Soc. Tropical Medicine & Hygiene, Nat. Coun. Internat. Health, Am. Pub. Health Assn. Achievements include participating in the organization of the first national epidemiology center in Brazil. Office: Albert B Sabin Vaccine Inst Ste 200S 1889 F St NW Washington DC 20006-4400

DE QUESADA, ALEJANDRO MANUEL, film and museum consultant, writer; b. Gainesville, Fla., Oct. 1965; s. Alejandro Marcelo and Graciela Margarita de Quesada; 1 child, Caroline Grace. AA, Emory U., 1987, BA, 1988. Asst. curator Veterans Meml. Mus. & Pk., Tampa, Fla., 1992—2000; CEO, hist. rschr. AdeQ Hist. Archives & Services, Tampa, 2000—. Mus. curator El Circulo Cubano, Tampa, 1999—2001; bd. govs. Cuban Club Found., Tampa, 1999—2001; mus. collections com. mem. SS Am. Victory, Tampa, 1999—2003; v.p. adminstrn., bd. govs. The Co. Mil. Historians, 2003—. Author: (book) The Men of Fort Foster, 1996, Distant Thunder, 2005, Uniforms of the German Soldier, Volumes One & Two, 2006, A History of Florida Forts, 2006, The Mexican Revolution, 2006, The Spanish-American War and Philippine Insurrection, 1898-1902, 2007, Spring Training in Clearwater, 2007. 7th dist. historian USCG Aux., Tampa, 2002—07. Decorated Meritorious Team Commendation Ribbon USCG, Dept. Transp. 9-11 Ribbon; recipient The Robert Loren Miller Meml. award, The Co. Mil. Historians, 2002—04; Fellow, 2003. Mem.: Fla. Assn. Museums (corr.), The Soc. Army Hist. Rsch. (corr.), US Naval Inst. (life), The Navy League (life), 8th Air Force Hist. Soc. (life), Friends of Jefferson Barracks (life), Sons of Union Veterans of the Civil War (assoc. War Svc. Cross 2005), Most Loyal Legion of the US (assoc.), SCV (life; 5th brigade comdr. Tenn. army 1990—93, War Svc. Cross 1991, 2003). Conservative. Roman Catholic. Avocations: travel, scuba, writing. Office: AdeQ Historical Archives & Service 5012 West Lemon St Tampa FL 33609 Home Phone: 813-636-5077; Office Phone: 813-636-5077. Office Fax: 813-636-9327; Home Fax: 813-636-9327. Personal E-mail: adqhisres@aol.com.

DER, DAVID F., family practice physician, retired general surgeon; married. MD, Howard Univ. Sr. ptnr., chief surgeon Bay Valley Med. Group, Hayward, Calif.; ret.; exec. dir. Chinese Am. Physicians' Soc.; currently family physician Alta Bates Summit Med. Ctr., Oakland, Calif.

Asian Outreach Adv. Com. Alta Bates Summit Med. Ctr. Founder Asian Health Svcs., Oakland, 1974, Hong Fook Senior Health Care Ctr., Oakland, 1986. Recipient Benjamin Rush award for Citizenship and Comty. Svc., AMA, 2006. Mem.: Fedn. Chinese Am. and Chinese Canadian Med. Societies (sec.). Office: Prime Med Assocs Inc 817 Harrison St Oakland CA 94607 Office Phone: 510-451-8088. E-mail: daveder44@hotmail.com.

DERAISMES, ANN M., insurance company executive, human resources specialist; BA, Keuka Coll., Keuka Park, NY; MA in Human Resources, Western Conn. State U. Mgr. staffing Hartford Life, 1984—87, asst. dir. personnel, 1987—91, dir human resources, 1991—92, asst. v.p. human resources, 1992—94, v.p. human resources, 1994—97, sr. v. p. human resources, 1997—2003; group sr. v.p. human resources Hartford Fin. Svcs. Group, 2003—04, exec. v.p. HR, 2004—. Office: Hartford Fin Svcs Group Hartford Plz 890 Asylum Ave Hartford CT 06115*

DE RATO Y FIGAREDO, RODRIGO, international banking official; b. Madrid, Mar. 18, 1949; married; 3 children. Law degree, Madrid Complutense U., 1971; MBA, U. Calif., Berkeley, 1974; PhD in Econs., Universidad Complutense, 2003. Mem. Nat. Exec. Com. of AP, 1979-86; co-founder Econ. Commn. of AP, 1979; asst. gen. sec. AP, 1983-86; spokesman for the econ., 1984-86; mem. Parliament for Cádiz in the 2nd Legislature; v.p. of def. and security commn. NATO, 1987, 88, mem. spl. com. for strategy and control of armaments, 1988; asst. gen. sec. IXth Party Congress; nat. mem. Parliament for Madrid, 1982—2004; spokesman for Grupo Parlamentario Popular Parliament in the IVth and Vth Legislatures; mem. Parliament in the VIth Legislatures; vice gen. sec. of Partido Popular XIIth Nat. Congress, 1996—; 2nd v.p. of govt. Ministry Econs. and Fin., Madrid, 1996—2000; 2nd v.p. of govt. and min. of the economy, 2000—04; mng. dir., chmn. IMF, 2004—. Bd. gov. IMF, World Bank, Inter-Am. Devel. Bank, European Investment Bank, European Bank for Reconstruction and Devel.; regularly attends the European Union's Econs. and Fin. Ministers mtgs.; represented the European Union at the Group of Seven Fin. Min. meeting, Ottawa, Canada, 2002; in charge of fgn. trade rels. for the Govt. of Spain; represented Spain at the World Trade Orgn. Min. meetings, Doha, Qatar, 01, Cancún, Mexico, 03. Office: IMF 700 19th St NW Washington DC 20431*

DE RAVEL D'ESCLAPON, PIERRE F., lawyer; b. Salins-les-Bains, France; came to US, 1969. Student, U. Besancon, France; degree, U. Montreal Law Sch., Can., 1969; LLM, Harvard U., 1970. Bar: NY 1975, DC 1985, Paris 1992. Sr. ptnr. LeBoeuf, Lamb, Greene & MacRae LLP, NYC, 1992—2007, of counsel, 2007—. Bd. dirs., chmn. audit com. J&L Specialty Steel, Pitts., 1990-99; bd. dirs. Le Blanc de Nicolay, NYC, 1985-1995, bd. mem. Ctr. Bus. and Internat. Trade Law, U. Montreal Sch. Law, 2005-;bd. mem. Compagnie d'Assurance des Risques Financiers 1995-; vis. prof. corp. governance HEC-MBA, France. Contbr. articles to profl. jours. Chmn. Friends of Univ. Montreal, Quebec; bd. mem. Friends of HEC, Inc. Decorated Chevalier de la Legion d'Honneur, Chevalier de l'Ordre National du Mérite; named Super Lawyer in NY for Bus. and Commercial Law, 2006, 2007. Mem. Harvard Club, Knickerbocker Club. Avocations: chess, history, languages, golf, fencing. Office: LeBoeuf Lamb Greene & MacRae LLP 125 E 55th St New York NY 10019-5389 Office Phone: 212-424-8545. Office Fax: 212-649-9373. Business E-Mail: pderavel@llgm.com.

DE RAVIN, EMILIE, actress; b. Mount Eliza, Victoria, Australia, Dec. 27, 1981; m. Josh Janowicz, June 19, 2006 (separated). Student, Australian Ballet Sch., Melbourne, Nat. Inst. Dramatic Art, Australia. Actor: (TV films) Carrie, 2002; (TV series) BeastMaster, 1999—2000, Roswell, 2000—01, Lost, 2004— (Outstanding Performance by an Ensemble in a Drama Series, Screen Actors Guild award, 2006); (films) Brick, 2005, Santa's Slay, 2005, The Hills Have Eyes, 2006, numerous TV series guest appearances. Avocations: painting, exercise. Mailing: care Touchstone TV Prodn Bldg #343 500 S Buena Vista Burbank CA 91521

DERBES, DANIEL WILLIAM, manufacturing executive; b. Cin., Mar. 30, 1930; s. Earl Milton and Ruth Irene (Grauten) Derbes; m. Patricia Maloney, June 4, 1952; children: Donna Ann, Nancy Lynn(dec.) , Stephen Paul. BS, U.S. Mil. Acad., 1952; MBA, Xavier U., Cin., 1963. Devel. engr. AiResearch Mfg. Co., Phoenix, 1956-58; with Garrett Corp., LA, 1958-80, v.p., gen. mgr., then exec. v.p., 1975-80, dir., 1976-87; pres. Signal Cos., Inc., La Jolla, Calif., 1980—82, Signal Advanced Tech Group, 1982—85, Allied-Signal Internat. Inc., 1985-88; exec. v.p. Allied-Signal, Inc., Morristown, NJ, 1985-88; pres. Signal Ventures, Solana Beach, Calif., 1990—2004. Chmn. bd. dirs. WD-40 Co.; bd. dirs. Sempra Energy, Oak Industries. Exec. bd. nat. coun. Boy Scouts Am., 1981—95; trustee U. San Diego, 1981—2005, vice-chmn., trustee, 1990—93, chmn., 1993—96, trustee emeritus, 2006. With US Army, 1952—56. Republican. Roman Catholic. Office: PO Box 8185 Rancho Santa Fe CA 92067-8184 Personal E-mail: dwderbes@aol.com.

DERBY, DEBORAH, retail executive; BA in Econs., Harvard U.; MBA, JD, U. Notre Dame. Fin. analyst Goldman Sachs; atty. Miller, Canfield, Paddock and Stone; various human resources positions Whirlpool Corp., 1992—2000; from v.p. human resources Babies "R" Us Divsn. to exec. v.p. human resources Toys "R" Us, Inc., Wayne, NJ, 2000—03, exec. v.p. human resources, 2003—06; pres. Babies "R" Us Toys "R" US, Inc., Wayne, NJ, 2006—. Bd. dirs. Jobs for America's Graduates, Inc. (JAG). Mem.: ABA, Soc. Human Resource Profls., Mich. Bar Assn. Office: Toys R Us Inc 1 Geoffrey Way Wayne NJ 07470-2030 Office Phone: 973-617-3500.*

DERBY, ERNEST STEPHEN, retired judge; b. Boston, July 10, 1938; s. Elmer Goodrich and Lucy (Davis) D.; m. Gretel Hanauer, June 10, 1961 (dec. Oct. 2000); children: Anne Gray, Michael Stephen; m. Carolyn Schwenk, May 11, 2002. AB with distinction, Wesleyan U., 1960; LLB cum laude, Harvard U., 1965. Bar: Md. Ct. Appeals 1965, U.S. Dist. Ct. Md. 1966, U.S. Ct. Appeals (4th cir.) 1968, U.S. Supreme Ct. 1973. Law clk. to presiding justice U.S. Dist. Ct. Md. and U.S. Ct. of Appeals 4th cir., 1965-66; assoc. Piper & Marbury, Balt., 1966-71, ptnr., 1973-87; asst. atty. gen. Atty. Gen. Md., 1971-73; judge U.S. Bankruptcy Ct., Balt., 1987—2004, recalled, 2004—07, chief bankruptcy judge, 2005; ret., 2007. Adj. faculty U. Md. Sch. Law, 1987, 90-99. Pres. Dismas Ho., Balt. Inc., 1969—; trustee Enoch Pratt Free Libr., Balt., 1977-93. Fellow Am. Coll. Bankruptcy, Md. Bar Found.; mem. Md. State Bar Assn., Anne Arundel County Bar Assn., Paca/Brent Am. Inn of Ct. (pres. 1993-94). Office: US District Court US Courthouse 101 W Lombard St Ste 9442 Baltimore MD 21201-2906 Office Phone: 410-962-7801.

DERBY, SUSAN EILEEN, not-for-profit fundraiser; b. Balt., Mar. 7, 1969; d. Charles Carroll and Marian Rose Derby; m. John Eric Uggen, Apr. 27, 2002; 1 child, Liam Derby Uggen. BA, U. Md., Balt., 1992. Sr. settlement officer Columbia Nat., inc., Md., 1993—96; vol. Peace Corps, Mereni, Moldova, 1996—98; devel. coord. Am. Inst. Cancer Rsch., Washington, 1998—2000, devel. assoc., 2000—01, asst. dir. devel., 2001—02, assoc. dir. devel., 2002—06, major gift officer, 2007—. Mem.: Assn. Fundraising Profls. Avocations: travel, reading, jewelry making. Office: Am Inst Cancer Rsch 1759 R St NW Washington DC 20009 Office Phone: 202-328-7744. Office Fax: 202-328-7226. Business E-Mail: s.derby@aicr.org.

DERDARIAN, CHRISTINE ANNE, lawyer; b. Highland Park, Mich., Aug. 30, 1948; d. Samuel and Mae Margaret (Mikjian) D. BA in Sociology, U. Mich., 1970; JD, Detroit Coll. Law, 1973. Bar: Mich. 1973. Sole practice, Detroit, 1974; asst. atty. gen. Mich. Dept. Atty. Gen., Lansing, 1974-80, sr. specialist, asst. atty. gen. Detroit, 1980-85, asst. in charge labor divsn. Lansing, 1985—2003; dir. Mich. Atty. Gen. Opinion Rev. Bd., Lansing, 1985—2002; pvt. practice Sylvan Lake, Mich., 2003—. Pres. PAX Resolution Svcs., LLC; bd. dirs. Oakland County Mediation Ctr. Bd. dir. Internat. Inst. Met. Detroit, 1980-84, v.p., 1984-86, pres., 1986-88; bd. dirs. Detroit Inst. Children, 1996-98; trustee Alvin Bentley Found., 1997-03; chair Mich. Employment Rels. Commn., 2006—; bd. dirs. Oakland County Mediation Ctr. Mem. Mich. State Bar (dir. young lawyers coun. 1981-83, comm. com. young lawyers coun. 1982-86, bd. dirs. health com. 1986-91, coun. mem. adminstrv. law sect. 1994-96, assoc. mem. state bar com. on character and fitness 1997-99), Internat. Women's Forum, Mich. Women's Forum (dir. 1985—, pres. 1997-2004), Women's Econ. Club Detroit (pres. 1984-85, bd. trustees Project Discovery, 2004-, Human Spectrum Svcs., 2005—. Democrat. Home: 6952 Sandalwood Dr Bloomfield Hills MI 48301-3025 Office: 2055 Orchard Lake Rd Sylvan Lake MI 48320 Office Phone: 248-538-9737.

DERDENGER, PATRICK, lawyer; b. LA, June 29, 1946; s. Charles Patrick and Drucilla Marguerite (Lange) D.; m. Jo Lynn Dickins, Aug. 24, 1968; children: Kristin Lynn, Bryan Patrick, Timothy Patrick. BA, Loyola U., LA, 1968; MBA, U. So. Calif., 1971, JD, 1974; LLM in Taxation, George Washington U., 1977. Bar: Calif. 1974, U.S. Ct. Claims 1975, Ariz. 1979, U.S. Ct. Appeals (9th cir.) 1979, U.S. Dist. Ct. Ariz. 1979, U.S. Tax Ct. 1979, U.S. Supreme Ct. 1979; cert. specialist in tax law. Trial atty. honors program US Dept. Justice, Washington, 1974—78; ptnr. Lewis and Roca, Phoenix, 1978—2000, Steptoe and Johnson, LLP, 2000—. Adj. prof. taxation Golden Gate U., Phoenix, 1983-87; mem. Ariz. State Tax Ct. Legis. Study Commn., Tax Law Specialist Commn., Ariz. Property Tax Oversight Commn.; appt. Ariz. Property Tax Oversight Commn., 1997—. Author: Arizona State and Local Taxation, Cases and Materials, 1983, Arizona Sales and Use Tax Guide, 1990, Advanced Arizona Sales and Use Tax, 1987-96, Arizona State and Local Taxation, 1989, 93, 96, Arizona Sales and Use Tax, 1988-96. Arizona Property Taxation, 1993-96, ABA Sales and Use Tax Deskbook, Property Tax Deskbook. Past pres., bd. dirs. North Scottsdale Little League; apptd. Ariz. Property Tax Oversight Commn. Served to capt. USAF, 1968-71. Recipient U.S. Law Week award Bur. Nat. Affairs, 1974. Mem. ABA (taxation sect., various coms.), Ariz. Bar Assn. (taxation sect., former chair sect. taxation, former treas., chmn. state and local tax com., chmn. continuing legal edn. com., tax adv. com., others, mem. tax law specialist commn.), Maricopa County Bar Assn., Inst. Sales Taxation, Nat. Tax Assn., Inst. Property Taxation Met. C. of C., Ariz. C. of C. (chair tax com.), U. So. Calif. Alumni Club (past pres., bd. dirs.), Phi Delta Phi. Home: 10040 E Happy Valley Rd Scottsdale AZ 85255-2395 Office: Steptoe & Johnson LLP 201 E Washington St Fl 16 Phoenix AZ 85004-4453 Office Phone: 602-257-5209. Business E-Mail: pderdenger@steptoe.com.

DERE, WILLARD HONGLEN, medical products executive; b. Sacramento, Jan. 8, 1954; s. William Janson and Bessie Lon (Joe) D.; m. Julia Mei Lum, June 18, 1978; children: Melissa Ellen, Kathryn Elizabeth. AB, U. Calif., Davis, 1975, MD, 1980. Intern U. Utah Health Sci. Ctr., Salt Lake City, 1980-81, resident, 1981-83; instr. internal medicine, geriatrics U. Utah, Salt Lake City, 1985-87, asst. prof., 1987-89; rsch. fellow U. Calif., San Francisco, 1983-85; asst. prof. Ind. U. Sch. Medicine, Indpls., 1989-98, clin. assoc. prof., 1998—; clin. rsch. physician Lilly Rsch. Labs., Indpls., 1989-91, dir. European regulatory affairs, 1991-94, dir. endocrine rsch., 1994-98, exec. dir. global clin. rsch., 1998-2001, v.p. med., endocrine, bone and gen. medicine R & D, 2002—03; with Amgen, Inc., 2003—, v.p. inflammation and bone therapeutic area, v.p., head gen. medicine therapeutic area, sr. v.p. global devel., chief med. officer, sr. v.p., internat. chief med. officer, 2007—. Dir. emergency rm. VA Med. Ctr., Salt Lake City, 1985-86; cons. U. Utah Student Health Svc., Salt Lake City, 1985-89, acting dir., 1987-88. Editor: Practical Care of the Ambulatory Patient, 1989; Contbr. articles to profl. jours. Hon. assoc. investigator VA, San Francisco, 1984. Mem. ACP, AAAS, Am. Soc. Bone and Mineral Rsch., Assn. Osteobiology. Presbyterian. Achievements include rsch. in adrenocortical function in AIDS, oncogene regulation in thyroid cells, multi-center antibiotic trials, drug safety, health economics, selective estrogen receptor modulators, osteoporosis. Office: Amgen Inc One Amgen Center Dr Thousand Oaks CA 91320-1799 Office Phone: 805-447-1000. Office Fax: 805-447-1010.*

DEREMEE, RICHARD ARTHUR, retired internist, educator, researcher; b. Red Wing, Minn., July 4, 1933; s. Arthur Eugene and Anna Helen (Vinquist) DeR.; m. E. Lucille Fogelstrom, Mar. 17, 1956; children: Lisa C., Brita L., Bo A. BA, Gustavus Adolphus Coll., 1955; BS, MD, U. Minn., 1959. Diplomate Am. Bd. Internal Medicine. Intern William Beaumont Gen. Hosp., El Paso, 1959-60; resident, fellow in internal medicine and pulmonary disease Mayo Clinic, Rochester, Minn., 1962—66, cons. in internal medicine and pulmonary disease, 1966—96; ret., 1996. Assoc. prof. medicine Mayo Med. Sch., Rochester, 1977-83, prof. medicine, 1983-96; Friedrich Wegener Meml. lectr. Lübeck, Germany, 1992. Author: (books) Time and the Mystery of Consciousness, 2003, The Mick-Rick Debates: Controversies in Contemporary Christianity, 2007; contbr. articles to profl. jours. Pres. South Woodly Civic Assn., Va., 1960-62. Capt. med. corp. US Army, 1959—62. Recipient cert. of achievement U.S. Army, 1962; Judson Daland travel award Mayo Found., 1966; Alumni citation Gustavus Adolphus Coll., 1982; named to Red Wing H.S. Wall of Honor, 2000. Mem.: Gustavus Adolphus Alumni Assn. (pres. 1979—80), Sigma Xi (pres. Mayo chpt. 1988—89). Republican. Lutheran. discovered the use of trimethoprim/sulfa as a new treatment for Wegener's granulomatosis. Home: 2209 5th Ave NE Rochester MN 55906-4017 Personal E-mail: radrst@aol.com.

DERENZO, STEPHEN E., electrical engineering and computer science educator, researcher; b. Chgo., Dec. 31, 1941; married, 1966; 2 children. BS in Physics, U. Chgo., 1963, MS in Physics, 1965, PhD in Physics, 1968. Rsch. asst. Enrico Fermi Inst. U. Chgo., 1964-68; physicist Lawrence Berkeley Lab. U. Calif., Berkeley, 1968-82, lectr. dept. physics, 1969-70, lectr. dept. elec. engring. and computer sci., 1979-87, sr. scientist Lawrence Berkeley Lab., 1982—, prof., 1988—. Grant application reviewer U.S. Dept. Energy, U.S. Nat. Insts. Health; co-chmn. Internat. Workshop on Bismuth Germanate, Princeton U., 1982; active numerous coms. Lawrence Berkeley Lab., U. Calif., mem. recreation adv. panel, 1984-87, mem. computer svc. adv. panel, 1985-88, quality assurance coord. bio-med divsn., 1986-88, asst. dir. rsch. medicine and radiation biophysics divsn., 1990-92, safety coord. rsch. medicine and radiation biophysics divsn., 1991-92, mem. mgmt. integration group, 1990—, authorized reviewer, quality assurance rep., environ. safety and health coord., and asst. dep. life scis. divsn., 1992—. Reviewer Jour. Cerebral Blood Flow and Metabolism, Physics in Medicine and Biology, Jour. Computer Assisted Tomography. Recipient Tech. Brief award NASA, 1973; grantee NIH, 1973—, IBM, 1986, U.S. Nat. Insts. Health, 1989—; Aargonne Nat. Lab. fellow Associated Midwest Univs., 1965-66, Shell Found. fellow, 1967-68; Ill. State scholar, 1959-62, U. Chgo. scholar, 1961-63. Mem. IEEE (sr., reviewer Transactions on Nuclear Sci., guest editor 1989, chair med. imaging conf. 1991, fellow award, radiation intrumentation achievement award, 01), Nuclear and Plasma Scis. Soc. of IEEE (mem. tech. com. on nuclear med. sci. 1983—, chair 1988-91, mem. adminstrv. com. 1988-91, Merit award 1992), Am. Phys. Soc., Materials Rsch. Soc. Avocations: long distance running, photography, astronomy. Office: U Calif Lawrence Berkeley Lab Berkeley CA 94720-0001

DERESIEWICZ, HERBERT, retired mechanical engineering educator, consultant; b. Brno, Czechoslovakia, Nov. 5, 1925; arrived in US, 1939; s. William and Lotte (Rappaport) D.; m. Evelyn Altman, Mar. 12, 1955; children: Ellen, Robert, William. BME, CCNY, 1946; MS, Columbia U., 1948, PhD, 1952. Sr. staff engr. Applied Physics Lab., Johns Hopkins U., 1950-51; mem. faculty Columbia U., NYC, 1951—, prof. mech. engring., 1962-94, chmn. dept. mech. engring., 1981-87, 90-93, emeritus, 1994—. Cons. stress analysis, vibrations, elastic contact, wave propagation, mechanics of granular and porous media., Fulbright sr. rsch. scholar, Italy, 1960-61, Fulbright lectr., Israel, 1966-67; vis. prof., Israel, 1973-74. Editor Columbia Engring. Rsch., 1975-92; contbr. articles to profl. jours. Served with AUS, 1946-47. Univ. fellow, Columbia U., 1949—50. Home: 240 E Palisade Ave Apt I1 Englewood NJ 07631

DE REVERE, DAVID WILSEN, retired professional society administrator; b. Englewood, NJ, Nov. 13, 1937; s. Wilbur L. and Ethel M. (Gilchrist) De R.; m. Ellen B. Tompkins, June 7, 1958; children: Mark S., Roger T. BA, Colgate U., Hamilton, NY, 1959; MDiv, Yale U., New Haven, Conn., 1963. Cert. master chaplain Internat. Conf. Police Chaplains. Sr. pastor 1st Ch. of Christ in Saybrook, Old Saybrook, Conn., 1963-85; exec. dir. Internat. Conf. Police Chaplains, Destin, Fla., 1985—2003. Author, editor: Chaplaincy in Law Enforcement, 1989. Chaplain Old Saybrook (Conn.) Dept. Police Svcs., 1964-85, FBI, 1991-2007. Home: 110 Sussex Ln Fayetteville GA 30215 Personal E-mail: davede@comcast.net.

DERGALIS, GEORGE, artist, educator; b. Athens, Greece, 1928; s. Demetrios and Zina Dergalis; m. Margaret Murphey; 1 child by previous marriage, Alexis. MFA, Acad. Belle Arti, Rome, 1951; diploma, Boston Museum Sch., 1956-59. Instr. Boston Mus. Sch., 1961-69, De Cordova Mus., Lincoln, Mass., 1961-94; pvt. instrn. Wayland, Mass., 1969—; chmn., curator Festival Bostonians for Art and Humanity, 1976; chmn. curator prisom art Inst. Contemporary Art Boston, 1975-76; artist-in-residence Ptnrs. of Ams., Colombia, 1979; lectr. Helicon, Harvard U., 1981 One-man shows include Woodstock Gallery, London, 1974, Cámera de Comercio de Medellin, Colombia, 1980, Galesburg (Ill) Civic Art Ctr., 1985, Hotel Meridien, Boston, 1987, Wayland Art/Space, 1994; exhibited in group shows at Danforth Mus., Framingham, Mass., 1988-90, Mus. Fine Arts, Boston, 1989 (Merit award), Boston Pub. Libr., 1994-95, Boston Art, 1995-, Indpls. Art Ctr., 2000-01, Mass. State House and Commonwealth Mus., Boston, 2000, Springfield Art Mus., 2002, 2007, Foothills Art Ctr., 2003, 05, De Cordova Mus., 2003-04, No. Ky. U., 2004, Attleboro Mus., 2006, others; designer Wayland Vets. Meml., 2005; represented in permanent collections Loomis and Sayles, Boston, Novartis, Wilmer, Cutler, Pickering, Hale & Dorr, Decordova Mus. Lincoln, Mass., Print Rsch. Found., Stanford, Conn., Museo de Zea, Colombia, U.S. Army Ctr. Mil. History, Washington, also pvt. collections; contbr. It's All in Your Head, 1991, Art of War, 2002. Trustee, Graham Jr. Coll., 1971; hon. dir. Boston Ballet, 1971; mem. Attleboro Mus.; mem. nominating com. 2007 Nat. Design awards Cooper-Hewitt Nat. Design Mus., N.Y.C. With USAF, 1951-54. William Paige scholar, 1959; recipient Prix de Rome, 1951, Civilian Merit award U.S. Army Hist. Soc., 1969, Gold medal Acad. Italia delle Arte, 1980, Best of Show award Commonwealth of Mass., 2000, Juror's award Watercolor USA, 2002, Juror's Choice award Attleboro Mus., 2004; named among Wayland's Top People of Yr., Wayland Town Crier, 2005. Mem.: Attleboro Mus., Copley Soc. Boston (v.p., art chmn. 1978, Excellence in Technique award 1978), Alumni Assn. Boston Mus. Sch. (pres. 1966—67). Home: 72 Oxbow Rd Wayland MA 01778-1009

DERGARABEDIAN, PAUL, environmental services administrator, consultant; b. Racine, Wis., Jan. 19, 1922; s. John and Mary (Hirmizian) D.; m. Mary A. Jansouzian, Dec. 27, 1947; children— Celeste, Claudia, Clarice, Paul. BS, U. Wis., 1948, MS, 1949; PhD (Shell Oil fellow), Caltech, 1952. Br. head U.S. Naval Weapons Center, Pasadena, Calif., 1952-55; lab. dir. TRW Systems, Redondo Beach, Calif., 1955-72; staff dir. TRW Systems (Energy Systems group), 1974-80; dir. The Aerospace Corp., El Segundo, Calif., 1972-74, 80-89, tech. cons., 1989—. Vis. prof. aeros. Caltech, 1971-72; founder, dir. Frontier Savs. & Loan; cons. in field. Served with USAAF, 1943-46. Fellow Inst. Advancement of Engring., Am. Astron. Soc. (dir. 1971— , nat. pres. 1969-71); mem. Phi Beta Kappa, Sigma Xi. Democrat. Armenian Apostolic. Club: Stereophonic of So. Calif. (pres. 1967-69). Office Phone: 949-713-6551. E-mail: sysanalcon@compuserve.com. *As a scientist I have been moderately successful - and lucky - in doing what people in my field would consider creative work. The greatest contribution to this success, I feel, has been methodology which was gleaned from certain teachers and associates. If I have done the same for someone else, that would be the greater success.*

DE RHAM, CASIMIR, JR., lawyer; b. NYC, Sept. 5, 1924; s. Casimir and Lucy Lathrop (Patterson) de Rham; m. Elizabeth Moran Evarts, June 9, 1945; children: Elizabeth Morgan, Henry Casimir, Rufus Patterson, Jeremiah Evarts. Student, Yale U., 1943-44; AB, Harvard U., 1946, JD, 1949. Bar: Mass. 1949, U.S. Dist. Ct. Mass. 1949. Assoc. Palmer & Dodge, Boston, 1949-51, 52-55, ptnr., 1956-94, of counsel, 1994—2005, Edwards Angell Palmer & Dodge LLP, Boston, 2005—. Dir. Cambridge Trust Co., Cambridge Bancorp, 1967-99, hon. dir., 1999-2002. Trustee Mount Auburn Hosp., Cambridge, Mass., 1962-93, pres., 1966-77, chmn. bd. dirs., 1977-80, treas., 1993-, The Mount Auburn Found., Inc., 1985-91, 93-96, Commonwealth Sch., Boston, 1958-2002, chmn. bd. dirs., 1966-87, sr. adv. com., 2002- , St. Mark's Sch., Southborough, Mass., 1962-74, Cambridge Cmty. Found., 1985-; overseer, dir. Boys and Girls Clubs of Boston Inc., 1956-93, sec., 1973-93, sr. adv. bd., 1993—; dir. Ctr. Blood Rsch. Inst. Boston, 1964-90, clk., 1964-84, hon. trustee, 1990—; trustee, sec. Sterling and Francine Clark Art Inst., Williamstown, Mass., 1973-95, hon. trustee, 1995-; dir. The Women's Union, Boston, 1975-98; dir., treas. Florence Evans Bushee Found., Boston, 1982-94; trustee Campbell & Hall Charity Fund, Boston, 1981-; dir. Dino Olivetti Found. Inc., Boston, 1960-, treas., 1983-94, clk., 1960-94; trustee Little Harbor Chapel, Portsmouth, N.H., 1959-; fin. adv. com. Cambridge Hist. Soc., 1980-91, chmn., 1988-90; chmn. Cambridge Rep. City Com., 1954-58; mem. Mass. Rep. State Com., 1960-69; alt. del. Rep. Nat. Conv., 1964, 68; mem. exec. com. Permanent Fund Soc., The Boston Found., 1993-94. Capt. USMCR, 1943-46, 51-52. Mem. ABA, Mass. Bar Assn., Boston Bar Assn., Cambridge-Arlington-Belmont Bar Assn. (pres. 1982-83), Am. Bar Found., St. Botolph Club (Boston), The Country Club (Brookline, Mass.), Masons (Harvard Lodge), Am. Legion. Episcopalian. Avocations: reading, tennis, politics. Home: 47 Lakeview Ave Cambridge MA 02138-3255 Office: Edwards Angell Palmer & Dodge LLP 111 Huntington Ave Boston MA 02199-7613 Office Phone: 617-239-0124. Business E-Mail: cderham@eapdlaw.com.

DER-HOUSSIKIAN, HAIG, linguist, educator; b. Cairo, Aug. 16, 1938; s. Vagharsh and Adrine (Karalian) Der-H.; m. Gaylynne Hall, Aug. 27, 1961. Student, Am. U., Cairo, 1957-59; BA, Am. U., Beirut, 1961, MA, 1962; PhD, U. Tex., 1969. Research assoc. U. Dar-es-Salaam, Tanzania, 1966-67; asst. prof. linguistics U. Fla., Gainesville, 1967-72; dir. linguistics, 1971-72, 84-85; assoc. prof. U. Fla., Gainesville, 1972-77, dir. Ctr. for African Studies, 1973-79, prof., 1977—2003, chmn. dept. African and Asian langs. and lits., 1982-91, prof. emeritus, 2003—. Mem. grad. council U. Fla., 1988-91; sr. Fulbright lectr. Universidade de Luanda, Angola, 1972-73, Universite du Benin, Lome, Togo, 1979-81; vis. prof. African linguistics U. Zimbabwe, Harare, 1989; panelist, grant proposal reviewer U.S. Dept. Edn., Washington, 1976—; USIA Acad. Specialist Grant cons. to U. De Ouagadougou, Burkina Faso, 1981; USIA Acad. Specialist Grant lectr. U. Marien Ngouabi, Brazzaville, Congo, May-Aug. 1988; occasional grant proposal evaluator Social Sci. and Humanities Coun. Can. Author: TEM, Grammar Handbook, 1980, TEM, Communication and Culture, 1980, TEM, Special Skills, 1980; co-editor: Language and Linguistics

Problems in Africa, 1977; compiler: A Bibliography of African Linguistics, 1972, reviewer: African Book Publ. Rev., 1996—; contbr. chapters to books. ACTION grantee, 1980-81. Mem. MLA (African Linguistics bibliographer 1967-74), Linguistics Soc. Am., African Studies Assn., Southeastern Conf. on Linguistics, Phi Kappa Phi. Armenian Apostolic. Avocations: reading, hiking, travel. Business E-Mail: haig@ufl.edu.

DERICCO, LAWRENCE ALBERT, retired college president; b. Stockton, Calif., Jan. 28, 1923; s. Giulio and Agnes (Giovacchini) DeR.; m. Alma Mezzetta, June 19, 1949; 1 child, Lawrence Paul. BA, U. Pacific, Stockton, Calif., 1949, MA, 1971, LLD (hon.), 1987. Bank clk. Bank of Am., Stockton, 1942-43; prin. Castle Sch. Dist., San Joaquin County, Calif., 1950-53; dist. supt., prin. Waverly Sch. Dist., Stockton, 1953-63; bus. mgr. San Joaquin Delta Jr. Coll. Dist., Stockton, 1963-65, asst. supt., bus. mgr., 1965-77, v.p. mgmt. services, 1977-81; pres., supt. San Joaquin Delta Coll., 1981-87, pres. emeritus, 1988—. Mem. Workforce Investment Bd. With AUS, 1943-46, PTO. Mem. NEA, Calif. Tchrs. Assn., Native Sons of Golden West (past pres.), Phi Delta Kappa Home: 6847 N Pershing Ave Stockton CA 95207-2524 Personal E-mail: ldericco@sbcglobal.net.

DERICKSON, SANDY (SANDRA L.), bank executive; b. Mar. 13, 1953; With GE Capital Corp., 1976—99, officer, 1991—99; pres. GE Capital Auto Fin. Svcs., 1991—99; joined Household Internat. (now HSBC Fin. Corp.), 2000, CEO retail svcs. then Group Exec. Retail Services, Ins. Services and Refund Lending businesses, 2000—04, group exec. retail svcs., insurance svcs. and refund lending bus., vice chair, 2004—07; group gen. mgr. HSBC Holdings, plc, 2005—06; pres., CEO HSBC Bank USA, Inc., HSBC Bank USA, N.A., 2007. Bd. dirs. Hexcel Corp., 2002—.*

DERISI, JOSEPH L., biochemist, educator; BA Biochemistry, U. Calif., Santa Cruz, 1992; PhD Biochemistry, Stanford U., 1999. Asst. prof. biochemistry, biophysics U. Calif., San Francisco, 2000—04, assoc. prof. biochemistry, biophysics, 2004—. Named a MacArthur Fellow, 2004; recipient JPMorgan Chase Health award. Fellow: The David & Lucille Packard Found., 2003. Achievements include invention of microarray known as the virus chip, a glass slide embedded with 12,096 snippets of viral DNA which has advanced the diagnosis and treatment of disease; along with colleagues, identified and characterized a novel coronavirus responsible for the outbreak of Severe Acute Respiratory Syndrome (SARS) in early 2003. Office: 513 Parnassus Ave Box 0448 San Francisco CA 94143 Business E-Mail: joe@derisilab.ucsf.edu.

DE RIVAS, CARMELA FODERARO, retired psychiatrist, health facility administrator; b. Cortale, Italy, Nov. 25, 1920; arrived in U.S., 1935, naturalized, 1942; d. Salvatore and Mary (Vaiti) Foderaro; m. Aureliano Rivas, Oct. 30, 1948; children: Carmen, Norma, Sandra, David. Student, U. Pa., 1940—42; MD, Women's Med. Coll. Pa., 1946. Diplomate Am. Bd. Psychiatry and Neurology. Intern women's health Med. Coll. Pa. Hosp., 1946—47; resident gen. medicine Chestnut Hill Hosp., Phila., 1947—48; gen. practice Tex., 1948—49; mem. staff Norristown State Hosp., Pa., 1949—63, supt., 1963—70, dir. family planning, 1979—87, clin. dir. spl. assignments, 1979—82. Psychiatrist Penn Found. Mental Health, Sellersville, Pa., 1970—72; dir. intake coping svcs. Ctrl. Montgomery Mental Health/ Mental Retardation Ctr., Norristown, 1972—77, med. dir., 1977—82, psychiatrist, 1980—82; cons. surveyor Health Care Fin. Adminstrn., 1987—2001; dir. program evaluation Norristown State Hosp., 1979—82, med. dir., 1982—87; assoc. psychiatry U. Pa., 1963—75. Named to Hall of Fame S. Phila. H.S., 1968; recipient citation Women's Med. Coll. Pa., 1968, Amita achievement award, 1976, achievement award Grad. Club Phila., 1976; named Woman of Yr. Pa. Fedn. Bus. and Profl. Women, 1979. Disting. life fellow Am. Psychiat. Assn., Pa. Psychiat. Soc. (rep. assembly of dist. brs. 1979-88); mem. AMA, Phila. Psychiat. Soc. (councilor), Montgomery County Med. Soc. (bd. dir., past pres.), Pa. Med. Soc. (chmn. adv. com. to aux. 1981-88, ho. of dels., commn. med. edn. 1991-94, com. continuing med. edn. 1994-98) Home: Dunwoody Village-CH 112 3500 W Chester Pike Newtown Square PA 19073-4101

DERKSEN, CHARLOTTE RUTH MEYNINK, librarian; b. Newberg, Oreg., Mar. 15, 1944; BS in Geology, Wheaton Coll., Ill., 1966; MA in Geology, U. Oreg., Eugene, 1968, MLS, 1973. Faculty and libr. Moeding Coll., Ootse, Botswana, 1968—71, head history dept., 1970-71; tchr. Jackson Pub. H.S., Minn., 1975-77; sci. libr. U. Wis., Oshkosh, 1977-80; libr. and bibliographer Stanford U., Calif., 1980—2004. Acting chief scis., 1985-86, head Sci. and Engring. Librs., 1992-97; cons. Am. Geol. Inst., 2004-. Contbg. author: Union List of Geologic Field Trip Guidebooks of North America; contbr. articles to profl. jours. Mem. ALA, Western Assn. Map Librs., Geosci. Info. Soc. (v.p. 1997-98, pres. 1998-99; first Mary B. Ansari Disting. Svc. award, 2005), Am. Geol. Inst. (mem. soc. coun. 2000-02), Geol. Soc. Am. (publ. com. 2002-05), Geoscience World (libr. adv. com., chair 2005—). Republican. Mennonite. Office: Stanford U Branner Earth Scis Library Stanford CA 94305 Home: 12522C 26th Ave NE Seattle WA 98125-8803 Business E-Mail: cderksen@stanford.edu.

DERMAN, CYRUS, mathematical statistician; b. Phila., July 16, 1925; s. Samuel and Bessie (Segal) D.; Martha Winn, Feb. 24, 1961; children: Adam Jason Winn (dec.), Hester Beth Rebecca. AB, U. Penn., 1948, A.M., 1949; PhD, Columbia U., NYC., 1954. Instr. Syracuse U., Syracuse, NY, 1954-55; faculty Columbia U., NYC, 1955—, prof. ops. rsch. NYC., 1965-94; prof. emeritus, 1994. Vis. prof. Israel Inst. Tech., Haifa, 1961-62, Stanford, 1965-66; vis. prof. U. Calif., Davis, 1975-76, U. Calif., Berkeley, 1979 Author: (with Morton Klein) Probability and Statistical Inference for Engineers, 1959, Finite State Markovian Decision Processes, 1970, (with Leon Gleser and Ingram Olkin) A Guide to Probability Theory and Application, 1973, Probability Models and Applications, 1980, 2d edit., 1994, (with Sheldon Ross) Statistical Aspects of Quality Control, 1996. With U.S. Navy, 1943-46. Recipient John von Neumann Theory prize, INFORMS, 2002. Fellow Inst. Math. Statistics, Am. Statis. Assn. Achievements include research and publs. on theory of Markov chains, Brownian motion, statis. inference, mgmt. sci. and ops. research. Home: 15 Pond Hill Rd Chappaqua NY 10514-2531 Office: Columbia U Mudd Bldg New York NY 10027 Personal E-mail: dermancyrus@hotmail.com.

DERMANIS, PAUL RAYMOND, architect; b. Jelgava, Latvia, Aug. 2, 1932; came to U.S., 1949; s. Pauls and Milda (Argals) D. BArch, U. Wash., 1955; MArch, MIT, 1959. Registered arch., Wash. Arch. John Morse & Assocs., Seattle, 1961-62; assoc. Fred Bassetti & Co., Seattle, 1963-70; arch. Ibsen Nelsen & Assocs., Seattle, 1970-71; ptnr. Streeter/Dermanis & Assocs., Seattle, 1973-97; owner Paul Dermanis Archs., 1997—. Designs include Sunset house (citation 1984), treatment plant, 1992. Mem. Phinney Ridge Neighborhood Assn., Seattle, 1985—. With USN, 1955-57. Mem. AIA, Apt. Assn. Seattle and King County, U. Wash. Alumni Assn., MIT Club of Puget Sound, Phi Beta Kappa, Tau Sigma Delta. Democrat. Lutheran. Avocations: skiing, painting, photography. Home Phone: 206-783-3873; Office Phone: 206-783-0266. E-mail: pdermanis@comcast.net.

DERMODY, WILLIAM CHRISTIAN, biomedical consultant; b. Lompoc, Calif., Sept. 22, 1941; s. William Frederick and Ann Drusilla Dermody; m. Lynne Heringer, Sept. 19, 1964; 1 child, Christina. BS, Calif. State Polytechnic U., 1964; MS, Utah State U., 1968, PhD, 1970. Postdoctoral fellow Cornell U., Ithaca, NY, 1969-70; sr. rsch. physiologist Parke-Davis & Co., Ann Arbor, Mich., 1970-76; sect. head cancer markers Frederick (Md.) Cancer Rsch. Ctr., 1976-81; dir. biotech. Am. Dade, Miami, Fla., 1981-84; mktg. mgr. ICN Biomed./Miles Sci., Lyle, Ill., 1984-86; mgr. tech. resources Difco Labs., Ann Arbor, 1986-88; assoc. dir. sci. Am. Type Culture Collection, Rockville, Md., 1988-90; pres. Bio World Assoc., Gaithersburg, Md., 1990—. Adj. prof. U.Miami Cancer Ctr., 1982-84, Fla. Internat. U., Miami, 1982-84; proposal reviewer Advanced Tech. Program, NIST, Gaithersburg, 1995-2004, 2007—; mem. steering com. Molecular Biology Ctr., Wayne State U., Detroit, 1987-88; pub. spokesperson to civic and sci. orgns. Pres. Homeowners Assn., North Potomac, Md., 1990-92; bd. dirs. Hyde Park Condominium Assn. Grantee NSF, 1967-70. Mem. Alpha Zeta. Avocations: antiques, photography. Home and Office: 405 Christopher Ave Apt 34 Gaithersburg MD 20879-3539 Office Phone: 301-947-6914. E-mail: cldermody@comcast.net.

DERN, BRUCE MACLEISH, actor; b. Chgo., June 4, 1936; s. John and Jean (MacLeish) D.; m. Diane Ladd, 1960 (div. 1969); 2 children; m. Andrea Beckett, Oct. 20, 1969. Student, U. Pa., 1954-57. Actor: (films) Wild River, 1960, Hush, Hush Sweet Charlotte, 1964, Marnie, 1964, Wild Angels, 1966, The Trip, 1967, War Wagon, 1967, Support Your Local Sheriff, 1968, Waterhole 3, 1967, Will Penny, 1968, Number One, 1969, Castle Keep, 1969, Bloody Mama, 1970, They Shoot Horses, Don't They?, 1970, Silent Running, 1972, Drive He Said, 1971 (Nat. Soc. Film Critics award), The Cowboys, 1972, The King of Marvin Gardens, 1972, The Laughing Policeman, 1973, The Great Gatsby, 1974, Smile, 1975, Posse, 1975, Family Plot, 1976, Won Ton Ton, 1976, Black Sunday, 1977, Coming Home (nominated Acad Award for Best Supporting Actor, 1978), The Driver, 1978, Middle Age Crazy, 1980, Tattoo, 1981, That Championship Season, 1982, Harry Tracy, 1983, On the Edge, 1986, The Big Town, 1987, World Gone Wild, 1988, The 'Burbs, 1989, After Dark, My Sweet, 1990, Diggstown, 1992, Wild Bill, 1995, Mrs. Munck, 1995, Mullholland Falls, 1996, Last Man Standing, 1996, Down Periscope, 1996, The Haunting, 1999, If.Dog.Rabbit, 1999, Madison, 2000, The Glass House, 2000, All The Pretty Horses, 2000, Masked and Anonymous, 2003, Milwaukee, Minnesota, 2003, Monster, 2003, The Hard Easy, 2005, Down in the Valley, 2005, Walker Payne, 2006, Believe in Me, 2006, The Astronaut Farmer, 2007; N.Y. stage debut in Shadow of a Gunman, 1959; appeared in Broadway play Strangers, 1979; other appearances include Sweet Bird of Youth; actor (TV movies) Toughlove, 1985, A Mother's Prayer, 1995, Comfort Texas, 1996, Hard Time: The Premonition, 1999; (TV miniseries) Space, 1985, Roses Are For The Rich, 1987, Trenchcoat in Paradise, 1989, The Court-Martial of Jackie Robinson, 1990, Into the Badlands, 1991, Carolina Skeletons, 1991, It's Nothing Personal, 1993, A Mother's Prayer, 1995, Comfort Texas, 1997, (TV series) Stoney Burke, 1962-63, Big Love, 2006-; co-author: (with Christopher Fryer & Robert Crane) Things I've Said, But Probably Shouldn't Have: An Unrepentant Memoir, 2007 Named Actor of Yr., Pacific Archives, Berkeley, Calif. 1972. Mem. Santa Monica Track Club. Office: care Creative Artists Agy 9830 Wilshire Blvd Beverly Hills CA 90212-1804*

DERN, LAURA, actress; b. LA, Feb. 10, 1967; d. Bruce Dern and Diane Ladd; m. Ben Harper, Dec. 23, 2005; children: Ellery Walker, Jaya. Student, Lee Strasberg Inst., Royal Acad. Dramatic Art, London. Appeared in films Alice Doesn't Live Here Anymore, 1975, Foxes, 1980, Ladies and Gentlemen, The Fabulous Stains, 1982, Teachers, 1984, Mask, 1985, Smooth Talk, 1985, Blue Velvet, 1986, Haunted Summer, 1988, Fat Man & Little Boy, 1989, Wild At Heart, 1990, Rambling Rose, 1991 (Acad. award nomination for best actress, Golden Globe nomination for best actress in a drama), Jurassic Park, 1993, A Perfect World, 1993, Citizen Ruth, 1996, Bastard Out of Carolina, 1996, October Sky, 1999, Daddy and Them, 2001, Jurassic Park III, 2001, Novocaine, 2001, I Am Sam, 2001, We Don't Live Here Anymore, 2004, Happy Endings, 2005, The Prize Winner of Defiance, Ohio, 2005, Lonely Hearts, 2006, Inland Empire, 2006 (also co-prodr.), Year of the Dog, 2007; TV appearances include: Afterburn, 1992 (Golden Globe award for best actress in TV movie or mini series), Fallen Angels (Murder, Obliquely), 1993 (Emmy nomination, Best Actress - Drama, 1994), Ruby Ridge, 1996, The Baby Dance, 1998, Damaged Care, 2002 (also co-prodr.); exec. prodr.: (TV film) Down Came a Blackbird, 1995; dir.: (TV film) The Gift, 1994; TV guest appearances include Shannon, 1981, Fallen Angels, 1993, Frasier, 1995, Ellen, 1997, The West Wing, 2002, (voice) King of the Hill, 2003; stage appearances include The Palace of Amateurs (N.Y.), 1988, Brooklyn Laundry (L.A.).*

DE ROBERTIS, EDWARD M. F., research scientist, educator; MD, U. Uruguay; PhD in Chemistry, U. Buenos Aires. Postdoctoral tng. Med. Rsch. Coun. Lab. Molecular Biology, Cambridge, England; prof. U. Basel, Switzerland; investigator Howard Hughes Med. Inst., LA; Norman Sprague Prof. Biol. Chemistry UCLA Sch. Medicine. Fellow: Am. Acad. Arts and Scis.; mem.: Latin Am. Acad. Scis., Internat. Soc. Devel. Biology (pres.), Iberoam. Molecular Biology Orgn., European Molecular Biology Orgn. Office: Howard Hughes Med Inst 5-748 MRL Bldg 675 Charles Dr Los Angeles CA 90095-1662

DERODES, ROBERT P., consumer products company executive; b. Wooster, Ohio; BSBA, St. Louis U., 1983; MBA, U. Tex., 1993. V.p. application systems, v.p. strategic planning Centerre Bancorporation, St. Louis, 1975—83; various positions including sr. v.p. bank ops. and tech. and v.p. fin. svcs. systems US Automobile Assn., 1983—93; pres. SABRE Devel. Svcs. SABRE Grp. (subsidiary of AMR Corp., the parent co. of Am. Airlines), 1993—95; sr. tech. officer card products grp. Citibank, 1995—99; chief info. officer Delta Air Lines, Inc., 1999—2002; pres., CEO Delta Tech., Inc., 1999—2002; exec. v.p., chief info. officer Home Depot, Inc., 2002—. Named one of 25 Top Chief Tech. Officers, InfoWorld mag., 2006. Office: Home Depot Inc 2455 Paces Ferry Rd N W Atlanta GA 30339-4024*

DE ROE DEVON, The Marchioness See GERRINGER, ELIZABETH

DEROMEDI, ROGER K., food products executive; b. Calif., Aug. 18, 1953; m. Sandra Deromedi; 3 children. BA in Econ. & Math., Vanderbilt U., 1975; MBA, Stanford U., 1977. Brand mgr. Gen. Foods, 1977—88; v.p. corp. devel. Kraft Foods, 1988—89, v.p. mktg. grocery products & retail cheese, 1989—92, exec. v.p., gen. mgr. splty. products divsn., 1992—93, exec. v.p., gen. mgr. cheese divsn., 1993—95, exec. v.p., area dir. Paris, 1995; group v.p. Kraft Foods Internat, 1995—98; pres. Kraft Foods Asia Pacific, 1998—99; co-CEO Kraft Foods, Inc., 1999—2001; pres., CEO Kraft Food Internat., 2001—03; CEO Kraft Foods, Inc., 2003—06.*

DERON, EDWARD MICHAEL, lawyer; b. Detroit, Dec. 18, 1945; m. Jana Lene Berlenbach, Aug. 12, 1977. BS, Wayne State U., 1968, JD cum laude, 1972; LLM in Taxation, NYU, 1973. Bar: Mich. 1972, U.S. Ct. Appeals (6th cir.) 1973, U.S. Tax Ct. 1974. Assoc. Evans & Luptak, Detroit, 1973-79, ptnr., 1980—. Contbr. chpt. to book. With U.S. Army, 1969-71, ETO, Germany. Mem.: ABA, Met. Detroit Bar Assn. (co-chmn. taxation com. 1984—86), Fin. and Estate Planning Coun. Met. Detroit, Oakland County Bar Assn., Mich. Bar Assn. (taxation sect., chmn. estates and trusts com. 1994—96, taxation sect. coun. 1996—99, editor Mich. Tax Lawyer 1998—99, sec. 1999—2000, treas. 2000—01, vice-chmn. 2001—02, chmn. 2002—03), KC, Detroit Athletic Club. Office: Evans & Luptak 7457 Franklin Rd Ste 250 Bloomfield Hills MI 48301 also: 18720 Mack Ave Ste 220 Grosse Pointe Farms MI 48236 Office Phone: 248-406-5100. Business E-Mail: ederon@evansluptak.com.

DEROO, SALLY ANN, biology, geology and environmental science educator; BS, Eastern Mich. U., 1958; postgrad., 1958-63; MA, U. Mich., 1961, postgrad., 1963—93, Wayne State U., 1964-68, Ohio State U., 1995—, U. So. Calif., Berkeley, 1996, Washtenaw C.C., 2004—. Cert. elem. tchr., middle level, all subjects K-8; cert. high sch. level environ. scis., social studies, English, econs. 9-12; cert. tchr. mentally handicapped and emotionally impaired K-12; cert. Master Gardener cert., Mich. State U. Coop. Ext., 1997, advanced Master Gardener, 2005. Asst. prof. sci. Ea. Mich. U., Ypsilanti, 1958-63, asst. prof. biology and geology, 1968—2003, tchr. spl. edn., 1989—2003; tchr. sci. and geology Plymouth-Canton Cmty. Schs., 1963-95; curriculum specialist Ctrl. Mich. U., 1989-90; instr. dept. tchr. edn. Mich. State U., 1994-95; instr. sci. edn. Madonna U., asst. prof., mem. staff student tchr. edn. Dept. Edn., 1992—2003; pvt. practice consulting and gardening Sally's Pond/Pots & Herbs. Asst. prof., mem. staff student tchr. edn. Dept. Edn. Madonna U.; advisor Salem H.S., 1990-95, Wayne State U., Detroit, 1995-2006, Pitts. State U., Kans. at Greenbush, 1995-97, Oakland U. Sci. Edn., 1997-2003, Oakland U. Profl. Devel., 2004, Wayne State U., Detroit; ednl. cons. Scholastic, Inc., 1996-2000; mem. satellite conf. Tchrs. Making a Difference, 1990; mem. support team Sci. Teaching Edn. STEP adv. bd. Madonna U., Livonia, Mich.; mem. math. and sci. challenge grant design com. Wayne County, 1991; adv. bd. SEMSplus Mich. Envirothon, steering com. Nat. Envirothon, 1996—; mem. adv. com., issues author sci. curriculum support guides Mich. Dept. Edn., 1989-90; mem. adv. coun. Mich. Dept. Edn.; mem. Mich. curriculum frameworks joint steering com., 1992-2002, mem. writing com. H.S. proficiency exam., 1993, 94, 95—, mem. adv. com. H.S. sci. proficiency test, 1993, 94, 95-96; dist. commr. Wayne County Soil Dist. USDA, 1996-2000; mem. citizens adv. com. Stockbridge Township, Mich., 2000—; project chair Project Cattail, Tchrs. and Students Making an Environ. Difference, 1992—; project dir. Gt. Lakes-Thunderbay Gt. Lakes Basin Work Shop, Alpena, Mich., 1990-93; mem. ednl. planning com. Detroit Zool. Inst., 2000; advisor biomass curriculum Envirathon, 2004—; facilitator numerous workshops; presenter in field; cons. in field. Author: (newsletter) Fledgeling, 1990-2003, (tchg. manuals) Exploring Our Environment; contbg. writer Detroit Free Press sci. page; contbr. articles to sci. mags.; writer, dir. 26-week sci. TV series Explore with Me; sci. editor Ann Arbor Pubs., 1968-86; elem. publ. editor Mich. Sci. Tchrs.; adv. (tv waste mgmt. series) Neuton's Apple. Active Rouge River Restoration, 1988—, Friends of Matthaei Bot. Gardens Ann. Flower Show; established Model Adopt-a-Stream Project "River Watch" for Rough River Water Shed, 1994; planning asst. Cobo Ctr. 1st Annual Detroit Bloomfest, 1999—. Recipient Outstanding Educator award Mich. Jaycees, 1963, Best of West Edn. award, 1984, Outstanding Svc. Recognition award Mich. Assn. Mid. Sch. Educators, 1989, 90, Gov.'s citation State of Mich., 1990, 91, Tchr. of Yr. Program award IBM, 1990, Can Doers award Mich. Tech. Coun., 1993, Recognition of Support and Dedication dept. natural resources Builder's Assn. Southeastern Mich., 1990, 91, 92, Land Preservation Recognition award Southeastern Mich. Land Conservancy, 2002; named Outstanding Sci. Educator, Metro Detroit Sci. Tchrs. Assn., 1994; listed in Guinness Book of Records 1990-95 for snail racing. Mem. NEA, Nat. Sci. Tchrs. Assn. (presenter, local leader, chair publicity regional conf. 1999), Mich. Sci. Tchrs. Assn (dir.-at-large, chair outreach conf., bd. spl. edn. 2006—, spl. edn. dir., 2006-, Outstanding Svc. award 1997, Disting. Svc. award 1998), Nat. Mid. Level Sci. Tchrs. Assn. (treas. 1998-2000, dir. publicity-promotions 2001—), Nat. Resource Def. Coun., Mich. Sci. Leaders Assn. (bd. dirs.), Mich. Dept. Edn., Sci. Curriculum Devel. Assn. (mid. sch. goal-based curriculum), Wayne County Task Force (intermediate sch. dist. writing team 1989, bd. dirs.), Mich. Alliance for Outdoor Edn., Detroit Zool. Inst., Internat. Joint Commn. (Gt. Lakes), Mich. Reading Assn. (sci. conf. chairperson 1992-2005), Stewart Nat. Wildlife Fedn., Citizens Adv. Com., Phi Delta Kappa (editor newsletter U. Mich. chpt. 1990-2003, treas. U. Mich. chpt. 2004-2006, pres. U. Mich. chpt. 2006—). Address: Wayne State U Dept Edn Gullen Ct Detroit MI 48202 Home Phone: 734-426-8895; Office Phone: 313-577-0991.

DEROSA, CHRISTOPHER SAMUEL, history professor; b. Rockville Ctr., NY, Mar. 4, 1969; s. Joseph F. and Esther M. DeRosa; m. Katherine Joyce Parkin; children: Vivian Parkin, Quinn Parkin. BA, Columbia U., NY, 1991; PhD, Temple U., Phila., 2000. Asst. prof. history Monmouth U., West Long Branch, NJ, 2003—. Author: (book) Political Indoctrination in the U.S. Army from World War II to the Vietnam War. Mem.: Soc. Am. Baseball Rsch., Am. Hist. Assn., Orgn. Am. Historians, Soc. Mil. History. Office: Monmouth Univ West Long Branch NJ 07764 Office Phone: 732-571-4495. Business E-Mail: cderosa@monmouth.edu.

DE ROSA, CHRISTOPHER THOMAS, biomedical researcher; b. Cin., June 18, 1949; s. Frank P. and Mary Lorean De Rosa; m. Yolan Susan De Rosa, Aug. 25, 1979; children: Brian, Erin, Phillip, Joel. BA, Ohio Weslyan U., 1971; MS Ecology, Miami U., Oxford, Ohio, 1974, PhD Biology, 1977. From instr. to asst. prof. biology U. Va., Charlottesville, 1976—80; sr. scientist U.S. EPA, Cin., 1980—82, br. chief, 1984—88, dir. Nat. Ctr. Environ. Assessment, 1988—91; asst. prof. botany and zoology U. Maine, Orono, 1982—84; dep. assoc. adminstr. sci. Ctr. Disease Control, Atlanta, 1991—92, dir. divsn. toxicology, 1991—2005, dir. divsn. toxicology and environ. medicine, 2005—. Tchr. St. Bernard's Parish Sch., Cin., 1986—88; mem. steering com. risk assessment WHO, Geneva, 1992—, cons., State Dept., NASA, Dept. Energy, Dept. Def., NATO, Pan Am. Health Orgn.; reader, contbr. Ednl. Testing Svc., Princeton, NJ, mem. test devel. com.; presenter in field; credentialed mem. Sr. Biomed. Rsch. Svc. Editor: Toxicology Letters, 1995; reviewer: Jour. Ambulatory Pediat., Quar. Rev. Biology, Oxford U. Press.; contbr. articles to profl. jours.; mem. editl. bd. Environ. Rsch., Environ. Health Perspectives, Toxicology and Indsl. Health, Environ. Rsch. Mem. bd. edn. Hampden Sch. Dist., Maine, 1982—84. Recipient Bronze medal, U.S. EPA, 1981, 1986, 1988, 1998, Publ. award, Ctr. Disease Control, 1998, Hammer award, U.S. V.P. Al Gore, 2000; fellow, NSF, 1975; grantee, Am. Philos. Soc., 1977, Exxon Found., 1983, U.S. EPA, 1989, NSF, 1975, 1978; Faculty Rsch. grantee, U. Maine, 1982, Faculty Equipment grantee, 1983. Fellow: Collegium Ramazzini; mem.: AAAS, Soc. Occupl. and Environ. Health, N.Y. Acad. Scis., Animal Behavior Soc., Rsch. Soc. N.Am., Soc. Integrative and Comparative Biology, Ecol. Soc. Am., Soc. Risk Analysis, Am. Coll. Toxicology, Sigma Xi (grantee 1975). Avocations: landscape design, fly fishing, natural history. Office: CDC F32 Divsn Toxicology and Environ Medicine 1600 Clifton Rd Atlanta GA 30333 Home: 5305 Burdock Creek Acworth GA 30101

DEROSA, DONALD V., academic administrator; b. New Rochelle, NY; m. Karen DeRosa; children: Michael, David;children from previous marriage: Carol, Joseph, Lauren. BA, Am. Internat. Coll., 1963; MA, Kent State U., PhD in Psychology, 1967. Prof. to dept. chair psychology Bowling Green State U., Ohio; dean Grad. Sch. U. NC, Greensboro, 1985—89, vice chancellor academic affairs, 1989—90, provost, 1990—95; pres. Univ. of the Pacific, Stockton, Calif., 1995—. Office: U of the Pacific Office of Pres 3601 Pacific Ave Stockton CA 95211

DEROSA, FRANCIS DOMINIC, chemical company executive; b. Seneca Falls, NY, Feb. 26, 1936; s. Frank and Frances (Bruno) DeR.; m. Vivian DeRosa, Oct. 24, 1959; children: Kevin, Marc, Terri. Student, Rochester Inst. Tech., 1959—61; BS, MBA, Chadwick U.; PhD, City U. L.A. Cert. med. photographer. CEO Advance Paper & Equipment Supply Inc., Mesa, Ariz., 1974—, Pottery Plus Ltd., Mesa, 1984—, Advance Tool Supply Inc., Mesa, 1993—94. Vice chmn. bd. adjustments City of Mesa, 1983-89, bd. dirs. dept. parks and recreation, 1983-86; pres. Christ the King Mens Club, 1983-84; bd. dirs. Mesa C. of C., 1983-88. Mem. Ariz. Sanitary Supply Assn. (pres. 1983-84), Internat. Sanitary Supply Assn. (coord. Ariz. chpt. 1994-96, sec. bd. 1994-96), Gilbert, Ariz. C. of C. (bd. dirs., v.p. 1992-96, pres. 1996-97, sec. internat. bd. 1994-96), Gilbert Heights Owners Assn. (pres. 1992-93), Mesa Country Club, Calif. Yacht Club, Rotary (pres. Mesa Sunrise chpt. 1987-88, Paul Harris fellow 1988), Masons (32 degree, pres. 1973), Sons of Italy (pres. 1983-84), Shriners. Avocations: music, exercise, sailing, golf. Home: 1325 E Treasure Cove Dr Gilbert AZ 85234 Office: Advance Paper Maintenance 1826 W Broadway Rd Ste 6 Mesa AZ 85202-1132 Office Phone: 480-964-6108. Business E-Mail: frank@advancepaper.com.

DE ROSA, GUY PAUL, orthopedic surgery educator; b. Napoleon, Ohio, Oct. 25, 1939; married. BS, Notre Dame U., 1961; MD, Ind. U., 1965. Diplomate Am. Bd. Orthopedic Surgery. Resident in gen. surgery Sch. Medicine, Ind. U., Indpls., 1965—66, resident in orthopedic surgery, 1966—70; fellow in pediat. orthopedics Hosp. for Sick Children, London, 1969—70; asst. prof. orthopedic surgery Sch. Medicine, Ind. U., Indpls., 1970—76, assoc. prof., 1976—82, dir. undergrad. edn. dept. orthopedic surgery, 1972—, chief neuromuscular disease, 1972—, coord. Garceau-Wayu Lectureships dept. orthopedic surgery, 1975—, dir. Cerebral Palsy Clinic, 1978—88, orthopedic cons. Hemophilia Clinic, 1978—91, prof. orthopedic surgery, 1981—, orthopedic cons. Rheumato-Orthopedic Clinic, 1984—, chmn. dept. orthopedic surgery, 1986—95; exec. dir. Am. Bd. Orthopaedic Surgery, Chapel Hill. Attending physician Wishard Meml. Hosp., Indpls., 1970—95, Ind. U. Med. Ctr., Indpls., 1970—95, James Whitcomb Riley Hosp. for Children, Indpls., 1970—95; coord. Ctrl. Ind. and So. Ind. State Bd. Health Programs, Scoliosis and Sch. Screening, 1977; mem. orthop. surgery steering com. Children's Cancer Study Group, 1990; mem. residency rev. com. for orthop. surgery Accreditation Coun. for Grad. Med. Edn., 1990—; vis. prof. Children's Hosp., Columbus, Ohio, 1977, St. Joseph Hosp., Ft. Wayne, Ind., 1977, Miami Valley Hosp., Dayton, Ohio, 1978, Dayton, 82, Dayton, 85, Dayton, 86, Deaconess Hosp., Evansville, Ind., 1980, Bloomington (Ind.) Hosp., 1982, U. Tex., Galveston, 1982, U. Mo. Med. Ctr., Columbia, 1983, Southwestern Mich. Area Health Edn. Ctr., Kalamazoo, 1985, Newington (Conn.) Children's Hosp., 1988, Children's Hosp. Med. Ctr., Akron, Ohio, 1992; and numerous others; active Hemophilia Med. Adv. Coun., 1978—; presenter in field. Contbr. articles to profl. jours. Bd. dirs. United Cerebral Palsy, 1973—85, Hemophilia Found., 1978—, New Hope of Ind., 1984—86, mem. long range planning com., 1984—85, mem. task force on serving brain injured, 1988; bd. dirs. Ind. Found. Hand Surg. Rsch. and Edn., 1989—95; mem. adv. bd. Head Injury Found., 1995, Children's Limb Found., 1992—; mem. pub. rels. and promotion com. Ind. Gov.'s Coun. on Phys. Fitness and Sports Medicine, 1986—92, mem. promotion com., 1988—92; dir. State of Ind. Orthop. Rsch. and Edn. Found., 1993, bd. trustees, 1994. Maj. USAF, 1970—72. Recipient Ensminger award for rsch. in trauma, 1967, Willis Gatch award, 1968; grantee grantee in field. Mem.: 20th Century Orthop. Assn., Internat. Soc. Orthop. Surgery and Traumatology, Scoliosis Rsch. Soc. (mem. edn. com. 1985—), Russell Hibbs Soc., Pediat. Orthop. Soc. N.Am. (mem. com. on fellowships 1986—92, bd. dirs. 1990—92, 2d v.p. 1994, 1st v.p. 1995, pres. 1996), Mid-Am. Orthop. Assn. (chmn. program com. 1986—87, bd. dirs. 1986—, sec. 1990—93, 2d v.p. 1993—94, 1st v.p. 1994—), Marion County Med. Soc., Acad. Orthop. Soc. (mem. undergrad. edn. com. 1983—87), Clin. Orthop. Soc., Assn. Orthop. Chmn., Ind. State Med. Soc., Ind. Orthop. Soc. (mem. exec. com. 1986—95), Am. Orthop. Foot and Ankle Soc. (mem. com. biomechanics 1982—84, mem. program com. 1985—), Am. Acad. Cerebral Palsy and Devel. Medicine, Am. Acad. Orthop. Surgeons (mem. com. undergrad. edn. 1976—83, chmn. 1979—83, mem. com. pediat. orthopedics 1988—94, mem. subcom. on spine 1990, mem. subcom. on pediats. program com. 1992, mem. coun. clin. resources 1993—94), Am. Acad. Pediats., Am. Fracture Assn. (Wellmerling award 1982), Am. Orthop. Assn. (mem. nominating com. 1988—89, del.-at-large exec. com. 1988—89, mem. com. on N.Am. traveling fellowship 1989—93, mem. com. planning and devel. 1991—, 2d pres.-elect 1994—), AMA, Am. Bd. Orthopedic Surgery (oral examiner 1983—, site investigator residency rev. com. 1983—, mem. credentials com. 1990—93, bd. dirs. 1990—, mem. oral examinations com. 1990—, mem. grad. edn. com. 1990—, mem. oral recert. examination com. 1992—93, mem. practice audit com. 1992—93, rep. alt. 1992—93, ACS adv. coun. 1992—94, sec. 1993—94, mem. cert. renewal com. 1993—94, mem. fin. com. 1993—94, mem. exec. com. 1993—94, vice chmn. residency rev. com. 1994—, chmn. 1995—97, exec. dir), Spectators Orthop. Letters Club, Little Orthop. Club, Orthop. Letters Club, Alpha Epsilon Delta, Alpha Omega Alpha. Office: Am Bd Orthopedic Surgery 400 Silver Cedar Ct Chapel Hill NC 27514-1585

DEROSA, RICHARD JEROME, composer, musician, educator; b. Huntington, NY, 1955; s. Clement Richard and Shirley Ramsdell DeRosa; m. Julie Mary Geiger (div.); 1 child, Martina. MusB, Jersey City State Coll., 1977; MusM, Manhattan Sch. Music, NY, 1985. Drummer Gerry Mulligan, Darien, Conn., 1979—90, JackieCain and Roy Kral, Montclair, NJ, 1987—2001; prin., owner Blane & DeRosa Prodn., NYC, 1985—. Arranger, performer Concord (Calif.) Records, 1992—99; composer various soap operas, NYC, 1990; arranger for Wynton Marsalis Lincoln Ctr. Jazz Orch., NYC, 2002—; composer Artspower Theater Co., Montclair, 1990—; adj. prof. Jersey City (N.J.) State Coll., 1980—82, Manhattan (N.Y.) Sch. Music, NYC, 1982—98; assoc. prof. William Paterson U., Wayne, NJ, 1999—. Author: Concepts For Improvisation, 1997; composer: (songs) (suite f9r percussion) Millennium, 1999. Mem.: Am. Fedn. Musicians, Internat. Assn. Jazz Educators, Broadcast Music Inc. Office: William Paterson Univ Shea Ctr Arts 300 Pompton Rd Wayne NJ 07470 Office Phone: 973-720-3802.

DEROSE, PAUL CHRISTIAN, chemist, researcher; b. Teaneck, NJ, Sept. 26, 1966; s. Thomas Charles and Joan (Simister) DeR. BA in Chemistry, Rutgers U., 1990; PhD in Chemistry, U. Pa., Phila., 1996. NRC/Nat. Inst. Stds. & Tech. postdoctoral assoc. Nat. Inst. Stds. & Tech., Gaithersburg, Md., 1996-98, analytical rsch. chemist, 1998—. Contbr. book chpts. and articles to profl. jours. Mem. Am. Chem. Soc., Sigma Xi. Avocations: wine tasting, trumpet. Office: NIST 100 Bureau Dr MS 8394 Gaithersburg MD 20899-8394 E-mail: paul.derose@nist.gov.

DE ROSE, SANDRA MICHELE, psychotherapist, educator, administrator; b. Beacon, NY; d. Michael Joseph Borrell and Mabel Adelaide Edic Sloane; m. James Joseph De Rose, June 28, 1964 (div. 1977); children: Stacey Marie, Harrison Marquisa. Diploma in nursing, St. Luke's Hosp., 1964; BA in Child and Cmty. Psychology, Albertus Magnus Coll., 1983; MS in Counseling Psychology with honors, Century U., 1986, PhD in Counseling Psychology with honors, 1987. Gen. duty float nurse St. Luke's Hosp., Newburgh, N.Y., 1964-65; supr. nurses Craig House Hosp., Beacon, NY, 1965—70; pvt. practice New Haven, 1975—; psychotherapist, inpatient unit Conn. Mental Health Ctr., Outpatient Treatment Svc., 1970—71, psychotherapist, out-patient unit, 1971—75, head nurse, outpatient divsn., 1975—80, clin. instrn., outpatient divsn., 1980—86, dir. staff devel., team dir. divsn. New Haven, 1986-94; dir. edn. Conn. Mental Health Ctr., Outpatient Divsn., New Haven, 1994-95; clin. instr., sch. nursing Yale U., New Haven, 1979-84, clin. instr., dept. psychiatry, 1989-96. Clin. dir. Comprehensive Psychiat. Care, Norwich, Colchester and Willimantic, Conn., 1994-96; group practice Comprehensive Psychiat. Care, Norwich, Conn., 1995-2003, Alternative Paths, Yalesville, Conn., 1995-97. Mem. AAUW, ANA (cert.), Conn. Nurses Assn., Conn. Nurse Psychotherapists Assn., Western New Eng., Psychoanalytic Psychologists Soc., New Haven C. of C., Sigma Theta Tau, Delta Mu, Alpha Sigma Lambda. Avocations: music, theater, antiques, interior design/architecture, travel. Office: 129 Church St Ste 609 New Haven CT 06510 Office Phone: 203-787-5381. E-mail: phdrx10@yahoo.com.

DEROSIER, ARTHUR HENRY, JR., historian; b. Norwich, Conn., Feb. 18, 1931; s. Arthur Henry and Rose (Raymond) DeR.; m. Linda Preston Scott, Dec. 26, 1979; children: Deborah Ann, Marsha Carol, Brett Preston Scott, Melissa Estelle. BS, U. So. Miss., 1953; MA, U. S.C., 1955, PhD, 1959. Asst. prof. history The Citadel, 1956—57, Converse Coll., Spartanburg, SC, 1957—59; asst. prof. U. So. Miss., 1959-60, assoc. prof., 1960-64, prof., 1964-65; assoc. prof. history U. Okla., 1965-67, asst. dean, Grad. Coll., 1966-67; dean Grad. Sch., prof. history East Tenn. State U., Johnson City, 1967-72, v.p. for adminstrn., 1972-74; vice chancellor for acad. affairs, prof. history U. Miss., 1974-76, vice chancellor, 1976-77; pres. East Tenn. State U., 1977-80, Coll. of Idaho, Caldwell, 1980-87, Rocky Mountain Coll., Billings, Mont., 1987—2002; historian We. Heritage Ctr., Billings, 2002—, CEO and sr. fellow, 2002—. Pres. Ind. Colls. of Mont., 1992-2002; vis. prof. history U. Mass., summer 1964; ednl. TV series on Am. history, 1966-72; bd. dirs. Rocky Mountain Bank. Author: Through the South with a Union Soldier, 1969, The Removal of the Choctaw Indians, 1970, (with others) Four Centuries of Southern Indians, 1975, Forked Tongues and Broken Treaties, 1975, Appalachia: Family Traditions in Transition, 1975, Pioneer Trails West, 1985, Institutional Revival: Case Histories, 1986, Looking for Daylight, 2003; editor Gorgeous Notions Press, 2004-; contbr. articles to hist. jours. Active numerous Indian philanthropies; commr. U.S. Senate Commn. Oneline Chile Protection, 1999—2001; mem. Idaho Commn. on Pardons and Parole, 1985—87; mem. adv. com. on apprenticeship U.S. Dept. of Labor, 2003—; bd. dirs. Deaconess Med. Ctr., 1988—92. With1952 USAF, 1948. So. fellow, 1958; Am. Philos. Soc. grantee, 1964 Mem. Am. Hist. Assn., Orgn. Am. Historians, So. Hist. Assn., Western Hist. Assn., Nat. Assn. Ind. Colls. and Univs. (fin. com. higher edn. 1990-97), Coun. Ind. Colls., Western Ind. Colls. Fund, Nat. Assn. Sch. and Coll. of United Meth. Ch. (chmn. com. on internat. edn. 1993-96, bd. dirs. 1994-97), Phi Beta Kappa. Home: 1809 Mulberry Dr Billings MT 59102-0601 Office: Western Heritage Ctr 2822 Montana Ave Billings MT 59101 Office Phone: 406-248-8443. Business E-Mail: derosier@rocky.edu. *I continue to believe in higher education and note again that a college is a place where educational opportunities are available for all who treasure learning. The testing, challenging, and expanding of the mind is our primary responsibility, and we should be graded on how successfully we complete that task. A college is also an integral part of society. It helps us develop and clarify ideals and goals; it challenges us to develop a civilized set of principles; and it affords us an opportunity to test those principles and goals in the greater society. And it must teach us to approach life with a sense of humor. We are human: we are capable of significant achievements and bumbling failures. An educated person learns to live with both, allowing success and failure to meet each other with good grace and a smile.*

DEROSIER, LINDA SCOTT, psychologist, educator; b. Boones Camp, Ky., Feb. 20, 1941; d. E. Jay and Grayce Jean (Mollette) Preston; m. Brett Dorse Scott, Aug. 7, 1960(div.); 1 child, Brett Preston Scott; m. Arthur Henry DeRosier, Jr., Dec. 26, 1979; children: Deborah DeRosier, Marsha DeRosier, Melissa DeRosier. BA, Pikeville Coll., 1962; MA, Ea. Ky. U., 1968; PhD, U. Ky., 1972; EdM, Harvard U., 1995. Claims rep. Social Security Adminstrn., 1962-67; prof. Psychology Rocky Mountain Coll., Billings, Mont., 1988—; teaching asst. Ea. Ky. U., Richmond, 1967-68; instr. U. Ky., Lexington, 1968-72; asst. prof. psychology Ky. State U., Frankfort, 1972-74, 74-78, U. Louisville, 1972-74; prof. psychology, dir. rsch. ctr. Ky. State U., 1974-78; dir. Appalachian Inst. E. Tenn. State U., Johnson City, 1978-79, prof. psychology, 1978-80, Coll. of Idaho, Caldwell, 1980-88; pvt. prac., 1995—. Pres. Appalwest, Inc., Caldwell, Idaho, Billings, Mont., 1986—. Author: Creeker, 1999, Songs of Life & Grace, 2003, (textbook) Understanding Psychology, 2004, Study Guide for Understanding Psychology, 2005. Bd. dirs. Billings Symphony, Rimrock Found., Billings, 1989—. Mem. Am. Psychol. Soc., Mensa. Presbyterian. Home: 1809 Mulberry Dr Billings MT 59102-0601 Office: Rocky Mountain Coll Psychology Dept 1511 Poly Dr Billings MT 59102-1739 Office Phone: 406-657-1053. Personal E-mail: lsd@lindascottderosier.com.

DEROUCHEY, BEVERLY JEAN, investment company executive; b. Kenosha, Wis., Sept. 3, 1958; d. Dean Rodney and Doris May (Rasch) DeR. BS in Bus. Mgmt., U. Wis., 1982; MBA in Fin., Cornell U., 1984. Chartered fin. analyst, 1993; lic. NASD-series 2-7-63-65. Acctg. asst. Kenosha (Wis.)-News Pub. Corp., 1979—81; polit. intern Office of Congressman Les Aspin, Racine, Wis., 1982; teaching asst. Cornell U., Ithaca, NY, 1983; audit intern Coopers and Lybrand, Syracuse, NY, 1983; staff cons. Peterson & Co., NYC, 1984—86; assoc. Salomon Bros., NYC, 1986—90, v.p., 1991; assoc. investment officer Dartmouth Coll., Hanover, NH, 1992—94; v.p., dir. asset allocation CTC Consulting, Portland, Oreg., 1995; investment mgr. Constellation Investments, Inc., Balt., 1996—97; dir. rsch. Paradigm Cons. Svcs. LLC, Quechee VT. and Clifton NJ., 1998—2000; founder, mng. dir. Long Trail Capital LLC, Quechee, Vt., 2000—; registered rep. IIG Horizons Securities, LLC, NYC, 2000—04, APB Fin. Group, Inc., NYC, 2004—. Alumni phonathons Cornell U., Ithaca, N.Y. and N.Y.C., 1982-87, co-chair new donor com., 1985-87; active Rep. Senatorial Inner Circle. Cornell U. scholar, 1982-84, BPW scholar, 1977, 82-83, AAUW scholar, 1981. Mem. Am. Film Inst., N.Y. Soc. of Security Analysts, CFA Inst., Bus. and Profl. Women (bd. dirs. 1991-92), Film Soc. Lincoln Ctr., Quechee (Vt.)-Lakes Landowners' Assn. Republican. Lutheran. Avocations: tennis, golf, travel, writing. Home: PO Box 1309 Quechee VT 05059-1309 Personal E-mail: bderouchey@hotmail.com.

DEROUIN, JAMES GILBERT, lawyer; b. Eau Claire, Wis., July 11, 1944; BA cum laude, U. Wis., 1967, JD, 1968. Bar: Wis. 1968, Ariz. 1986. Ptnr. Steptoe & Johnson LLC, Phoenix, Ariz.; atty. Meyer, Hendricks, Victor, Osbonn & Maledon, Phoenix, Ariz.; ptnr. Dewitt, Ross & Stevens, Madison, Wis. Mem. bd. sci. counselors Agy. for Toxic Substances and Disease Registry, 2003—; mem. profl. task force Ariz. State Bar. Polychlorinatedbyphenol chair Wis. Dept. Natural Resources, 1976-78; mem. spl. com. on solid waste mgmt. Wis. Legis. Coun., 1976-79, ad hoc com. on hazardous waste mgmt., 1980-82, spl. com. on groundwater mgmt.; mem. Wis. Dept. Nat. Resources Metallic Mining Coun., 1978-85; chair Phoenix Environ. Quality Commn., 1986, Phoenix Environ. Quality Com., 1989-92; mem. Ariz. Govs. Regulatory Review Coun. 1986—; co-chair Ariz. Dept. Environ. Quality/Ariz. Dept. Water Resources Groundwater Task Force, 1996-97; mem. nat. adv. coun. superfun subcom. EPA. Chair. State Bar Ariz. (environ. and nat. resources law sect. 1989-90). Office: 201 E Washington St # 1600 Phoenix AZ 85004-2382

DEROUSIE, CHARLES STUART, lawyer; b. Adrian, Mich., May 24, 1947; s. Stuart J. and Helia I. (Juntunen) DeR.; m. Patricia Jean Fetzer, May 31, 1969; children: Jennifer, Jason. BA magna cum laude, Oakland U., 1969; JD magna cum laude, U. Mich., 1973. Bar: Ohio, 1973, U.S. Dist. Ct. (so. dist.) Ohio 1974. Ptnr. Vorys, Sater, Seymour and Pease, LLP, Columbus, Ohio, 1973—. Trustee Ballet Met., Inc., Columbus, 1978-90, pres., 1986-88; trustee Gladden Community House, Columbus, 1975-81, pres., 1979-81; mem. Children's Hosp. Devel. Bd., Columbus, 1987—, pres. 1995-96; trustee Elder Choices of Ctrl. Ohio, Columbus, 1989-95, Heritage Day Health Ctrs., Columbus, 1992-98. Fellow Columbus Bar Found.; mem. ABA, Am. Health Lawyers Assn., Columbus Bar Assn., Ohio Bar Assn., Order of Coif. Office: Vorys Sater Seymour and Pease LLP PO Box 1008 52 E Gay St Columbus OH 43215-3161

DEROW, PETER ALFRED, publishing executive; b. Boston, Apr. 18, 1940; s. Harry A. and Ruth D. (Dimond) Derow; m. Ruth C. Joffe, June 13, 1965; children: Jonathan, Polly, James. BA cum laude, Harvard U., 1963, MBA, 1965. Pres. Newsweek, Inc., NYC, 1976-77; sr. v.p., dir. CBS, Inc., NYC, 1977-78; v.p., dir. The Washington Post, NYC, 1978-81; chmn. Newsweek, Inc., NYC, 1978-81; pres. CBS Pub. Group, NYC, 1981-86; v.p. CBS, Inc., 1981-86; pres. Goldmark Industries, NYC, 1987-88; sr. v.p. Reed Pub. USA, Stamford, Conn. and Newton, Mass., 1988; pres. Instl. Investor, Inc., NYC, 1988-97; dir. Publishers Clearing House, Port Washington, NY, 1998—, E-Dialog, Lexington, Mass., 2006—, GlobalSpec, Troy, NY, 1999—, CACI, Inc., Arlington, Va., 2000—, The Motley Fool, Alexandria, Va., 2003—06, Money Media, NYC, 2004—, Aspire Media Inc., Loveland, Colo., 2005—, On Target Jobs, Ft. Worth, 2005—, WMI Holdings, Fairfield, Conn., 2005—. Bd. dirs. WMI Holdings, Fairfield, Conn. Author: Successful Publishing on Campus, 1966; mem. editl. bd. Harvard Bus. Rev., 1981—95. Avocations: tennis, sculling, reading, bicycling. Home: PO Box 534 Bedford NY 10506-0534 Office: 270 Madison Ave 15th Fl New York NY 10010

DEROY, CRAIG I., title insurance company executive, lawyer; b. 1953; BA, U. So. Calif.; JD, Loyola U.; LLM in taxation, Univ. San Diego. Dep. chief, asst. atty., LA; v.p., gen. counsel First Am. Corp., Santa Ana, 1993—96, exec. v.p., gen. counsel, 1996—2002, sr. exec. v.p., gen. counsel, 2002—04; bd. dir. First Am. Corp., First Am. Title Ins. Co., Santa Ana, Calif., 2001—; pres. First Am. Corp., Santa Ana, Calif., 2004—. Office: First Am 1 First Am Way Santa Ana CA 92707*

DERR, FREDERICK MUELLER, civil engineer; b. Plainfield, NJ, July 10, 1932; s. Ferdinand Earl Mueller and Berenice (Yeager) D.; m. Carol Membert, June 7, 1957 (div. Dec. 1987); children: Elizabeth, Katherine, Charlotte; m. Teresa Elbare, May 20, 1988. BS, U.S. Naval Acad., 1957; BCE, Rensselaer Poly. Inst., 1959; MCE, Tulane U., 1964. Registered profl. engr., NY, La., Fla. Dir. pub. works US Naval Supply Ctr., Bayonne, NJ, 1965-67; exec. v.p., pres. Wendel Kent & Co., Inc., Sarasota, Fla., 1967-91; pres., CEO Frederick Derr & Co., Sarasota, Fla., 1991—; founder, dir. shareholder Flagship Nat. Bank, 1999; dir., sec./treas. Sarasota Military Acad., 2002—. Dir. Gator Asphalt Co., Sarasota, 1983-97, Quality Aggregates, Sarasota, 1983-99. Bd. trustees Mote Marine Lab., Sarasota, 1982—, vice chmn. bd. trustees, 1998, chmn., 1999—; v.p., dir. La Musica Internat. Music Festival, Sarasota, 1986-95. Lt. comdr. USN Civil Engr. Corps, 1957-67, Capt. CEC, USNR, ret. 1987. Named Engr. of the Yr., Fla. Engring. Soc., 1989; recipient Outstanding Tech. Achievement award, Fla. Engring.Soc., 1999. Mem. ASCE, Soc. Am. Mil. Engrs. Achievements include design and construction of the first soil cement step revetment on the coastline of Fla. in order to provide erosion protection to the only access road serving north Casey Key, a barrier island. Home: 3221 Bayou Way Longboat Key FL 34228-3026 Office: Frederick Derr & Co Inc 3801 N Orange Ave Sarasota FL 34234-4755 Office Phone: 941-355-8575. Business E-Mail: fred@frederickderrcompany.com.

DERR, KENNETH T., energy executive; b. 1936; m. Donna Mettler, Sept. 12, 1959; 3 children. BSME, Cornell U., 1959, MBA, 1960. With Chevron Corp. (formerly Standard Oil Co. of Calif.), San Francisco, 1960—, v.p., 1972—85; pres. Chevron U.S.A., Inc. subs. Chevron Corp., San Francisco, 1978—84; head merger program Chevron Corp. and Gulf Oil Corp., San Francisco, 1984—85; vice-chmn. Chevron Corp., San Francisco, 1985—88, chmn., CEO, 1989—99; ret., 1999; acting CEO Calpine Corp., San Jose, Calif., 2005—, chmn., 2005—. Bd. dir. AT&T Corp., 1995—2005, Citigroup Inc., Calpine Corp., 2001—, Halliburton Co., 2001—, Am. Productivity and Quality Ctr. Trustee emeritus Cornell U. Mem.: The Bus. Coun., Pacific Union Club, Orinda Country Club, San Francisco Golf Club. Office: Calpine Corp 50 W San Fernando St San Jose CA 95113*

DERR, THOMAS SIEGER, religion educator; b. Boston, June 18, 1931; s. Thomas Sieger and Mary Ferguson (Sebring) D.; children: Peter Bulkeley, Laura Seely, Mary Williams, Erin Vincent, Philip Henry; m. Linda Vincent, Feb. 14, 1986. AB, Harvard U., 1953; MDiv, Union Theol. Sem., 1956; PhD, Columbia U., 1972. Ordained to ministry, United Ch. of Christ, 1956. Researcher World Council Chs., Geneva, 1961-62; asst. chaplain Stanford U., Calif., 1956-59, Smith Coll., Northampton, Mass., 1963-65, asst. prof. religion, 1965-71, assoc. prof., 1972-77, prof., 1977—. Cons. World Coun. Chs., 1965—; dir. Inst. on Religion in Pub. Life, NYC; mem. complemental faculty Rush Med. Coll., Chgo., 1979-84. Author: The Political Thought of the Ecumenical Movement, 1972, Ecology and Human Need, 1975, Church, State and Politics, 1981, Barriers to Ecumenism: The Holy See and the World Council of Churches on Social Questions, 1983, Believable Futures of American Protestantism, 1988, Creation at Risk? Religion, Science, and Environmentalism, 1995, Environmental Ethics and Christian Humanism, 1996; contbr. articles to profl. jours. Danforth Found. grantee, 1959-60, 65-66; Inst. for Advanced Study of Religion U. Chgo. fellow, 1981. Soc. for Christian Ethics. Home: 60 Harrison Ave Northampton MA 01060-2911 Office: Smith Coll Dept Religion Northampton MA 01063-0001 Office Phone: 413-585-3660. Business E-Mail: tderr@smith.edu.

DERR, WILLIAM JAMES, retired non-commissioned officer; b. Catawissa, Pa., Oct. 24, 1934; s. Cyrus Sylvester and Dorothy Mae Derr; m. Marie Louise Parise, Oct. 27, 1956; children: Tina Marie, Theresa Ann. Grad. with GED, 1957. Enlisted U.S. Army, 1951, served in Korea, Japan, Germany, Vietnam, Alaska, 1951—72, ret., 1972; warehouse supt. Pa. Liquor Control Bd., Harrisburg, Pa., 1972—94, ret., 1994. Author: Righteousness or Iniquity, 2001. Mem. retiree coun. U.S. Army, Carlisle Barracks, Pa., 1984—; vol. ombudsman Dept. of Aging, Carlisle, Pa., 1999—2000. Decorated Army meritorious Unit Commendation, Vietnam Gallantry Cross with bronze palm., Vietnam Civil Action medal, Army Commendation Medal with Oak Leaf Cluster, Nat. Defense Svc. Medal with Bronze Star, Korean Svc. Medal, Vietnam Service Medal with Silver Star, UN Svc. Medal (Korea), Republic of Vietnam Campaign Medal, Korean Def. Svc. medal. Mem.: AARP, VFW (life), Disabled Am. Vet. (life), Nat. Assn. for Uniformed Svc. (life), Mechanicsburg Lions Club (pres. 2000—01, 2005—06, Lion of Yr. 2001—02), Am. Legion (life). Avocations: world travel, hunting, fishing, reading, gardening. Home: 8 Cumberland Dr Mechanicsburg PA 17050

DERRICK, DEBORAH BALL, editor, writer; b. Syracuse, NY, Aug. 20, 1952; d. Thomas Martin and Joyce Virginia (DeLine) Ball; m. Thomas Charles Derrick, Sept. 29, 1978; children: Kristina, Jonathan. BA, Drake U., Des Moines, 1981; MA, U. Nebr., Omaha, 2003; postgrad., U. Nebr., Lincoln, 2003. Program specialist City of Syracuse, 1975-77; planner Ctrl. Iowa Regional Assn., Des Moines, 1977-82; MIS supr., contract mgmt. coord. Ctrl. Iowa Employment and Tng. Consortium, Des Moines, 1982-84; adminstrv. asst. Francis & Assocs., Des Moines, 1984-85; mktg. coord. Wells Engrs., inc., Omaha, 1985-90; instr. tech. writing U. Nebr., Lincoln, 2003—05, 2007—, asst. to dean Med. Ctr. Omaha, 1990-92, comms. specialist Lincoln, 1992—2005, grant writer, 1992—, grant coord. Omaha, 2005—07, grant mgr., 2007—. Presenter in field. Editor: Contacts Mag., 1997—2002 (award of excellence Pub. Rels. Soc. Am., 2002); editor: (with others) PCI Bridge Manual, 1997, Plains Song Rev., 2004—; contbr. feature articles and stories to profl. jours. Dir. Friends Loren Eiseley. Recipient Jim Raglin Media award, Am. Cancer Soc., 1995. Mem.: Soc. Rsch. Adminstrs. Internat., Am. Assn. Grant Profls., Soc. Tech. Communication (award for Merit 2003), Nat. Fedn. Press Women (dir., Mag. and Website Design award 1999). Avocations: writing, travel, reading, outdoor activities. Home: 5411 Western Ave Omaha NE 68132-2158 Office: Peter Kiewit Inst 60th and Dodge Rm 170B Omaha NE 68182 Business E-Mail: dderrick@mail.unomaha.edu.

DERRICK, GARY WAYNE, lawyer; b. Enid, Okla., Nov. 3, 1953; s. John Henry and Leota Elaine (Glenn) D.; m. Susan Adele Goodwin, Dec. 22, 1979 (div. June 1981); m. Francys Hollis Johnson, May 3, 1986; children: Meghan, Drew, Jane. BA in History, English, Okla. State U., 1976; JD, U. Okla., Norman, 1979. Bar: Okla. 1979. Assoc. Andrews, Davis, Legg, Bixler, Milsten & Price, Oklahoma City, 1979-84, ptnr., 1985-90; of counsel McKinney, Stringer & Webster, P.C., Oklahoma City, 1990-93; ptnr. Derrick & Briggs, LLP, Oklahoma City, 1994—. Active Securities

Law and Acctg. Group, Oklahoma City, 1979—; chmn. Gen. Corp. Act Commn., Okla., 1984—, chmn. Securities Liaison Com., Okla., 1985-86; lectr. sem. Okla. Corp. Act, 1986—. Contbg. author Oklahoma Business Organizations. Mem. Okla. State U. Found., Stillwater, 1983—89, Univ. Found., Norman, 1982—; mem. condr.'s cir. Okla. Symphony Orch., 1981—88, Okla. Philharm., 2001—06; chmn. constn. and canons com. Episcopal Diocese of Okla., 1999—; bd. dirs. Historic Preservation, Inc., 1990—; bd. dirs. fund policy bd. EDGE, 2006—. Mem.: ABA (taxation and corp. sect., banking and bus. law sect.), Am. Soc. Corp. Secs. (pres. Okla.-Ark. chpt. 1994—95), Oklahoma County Bar Assn. (bd. govs. young lawyers divsn. 1981—82), Okla. Bar Assn. (chmn. bus. assn. sect. 1985—87, 2004—, outstanding contbn. to continuing legal edn., Earl Sneed award 1997), Oklahoma City Boat Club, Oklahoma City Golf and Country Club. Republican. Episcopalian. Avocations: sailing, violin. Home: 500 NW 15th St Oklahoma City OK 73103-2102 Office: Derrick & Briggs LLP Chase Tower 28th Fl 100 N Broadway Ave Oklahoma City OK 73102-8831 Home Phone: 405-232-3366; Office Phone: 405-235-1900. Business E-Mail: derrick@derrickandbriggs.com.

DERRICK, KATHRYN THILL, secondary school educator; b. Rochester, Mich., Jan. 9, 1976; d. Thomas Robert Thill, Jr. and Nancy Katherine Christian Thill; m. Brian Alan Derrick, June 7, 2003. BS, U. Conn., 1997; MEd, Peabody Coll.Vanderbilt U., 2000; M in Info. Sci., U. Tenn., 2006. Cert. tchr. Tenn. Environ. scientist IT Corp., Norwood, Mass., 1998—99; tchr. St. Cecilia Acad., Nashville, 2000—01, Met. Nashville Pub. Schs., 2001—03, Pope John Paul II H.S., Hendersonville, Tenn., 2003—. Writer of credit recovery curriculum Met. Nashville Pub. Schs., 2002—03; supr./mentor Peabody Coll., 2002; sci. standards com. mem. Met. Nashville Pub. Schools, 2003. Supr. and designer of 9-11 meml. Overton H.S. - MNPS, Nashville, 2001; vol. ARC, Storrs, Conn., 1995—97, Nashville Cath. Diocese, 2003—. Fulbright Meml. Fund grantee, Japan-U.S. Ednl. Commn., 2004. Mem.: ALA, Tenn. Environ. Edn. Assn., Tenn. Acad. Scis., Nat. Assn. Biology Tchrs., Tenn. Sci. Tchr. Assn. (Tchr. of Yr. Grades 9-12 2005), Nat. Sci. Tchr. Assn., Kappa Delta Pi, Golden Key, Phi Kappa Phi. Roman Catholic. Avocations: scuba diving, travel, reading, hiking.

DERRICK, MALCOLM, physicist; b. Hull, Eng., Feb. 15, 1933; came to U.S., 1963, naturalized, 1976; s. Arthur Henry and Gladys (Hopkinson) D.; m. Kathleen Allen, 1957; 1 child, Matthew; m. Christa Zars Baumgardner; 1966; m. Eva Krebbers, 1995. B.Sc. with 1st class honours, U. Birmingham, 1954, PhD, 1959; MA, Oxford U., 1961. Instr. Carnegie Inst. Tech., 1957-60; asst. prof. Oxford U., 1960-63; asst. physicist Argonne (Ill.) Nat. Lab., 1963-67, sr. physicist, 1967—, dir. high energy physics div., 1974-81. Vis. prof. U. Minn., 1969-70, Univ. Coll., London, 1972-73; adv. com. Stanford U. Accelerator Center, Fermi Nat. Accelerator Lab.; mem. high energy physics adv. panel Dept. Energy. Author numerous research papers on high energy physics. Fellow Am. Phys. Soc. Home: 20 Equestrian Way Lemont IL 60439-9785 Office: Argonne Nat Lab Bldg 362 Argonne IL 60439 Office Phone: 630-252-6272. Business E-Mail: mxd@hep.anl.gov. *The opportunity to spend a lifetime's career investigating the Fundamental physical basis of matter is one that has been given to relatively few people. Such research requires large and expensive accelerators and particle detectors and so can only be funded by government agencies. It is to the credit of the United States that such support has been generously given, and the resulting revolution in our understanding of nature is the outstanding intellectual achievement of our times.*

DERRICK, WILLIAM DENNIS, retired physical plant administrator, consultant; b. San Diego, Feb. 7, 1946; s. Charles Woodrow and Catherine Elizabeth (McCormick) D.; m. Lynda Ray Adams, June 15, 1964 (div. 1971); children: Tod Sean, Shannon Kay, Nicole Dione, Johnathon Robert; m. Frances C. Bouck, Nov. 19, 1979; children: Kaila June Warner, Bryan Charles. Student, U. Nebr., 1971-72, 73-74, U. Mont., 1974-77, 98-99, Internat. Corr., 1966-67, 81, Battelle Meml. Inst., 1985, Project Mgmt. Inst., 1986-95, 98—. Elec. draftsman City of Lincoln (Nebr.) Light Dept., 1964-65; asst. engr. to adjutant gen. Nebr. N.G. State of Nebr., Lincoln, 1965-66; owner, mgr., archtl. draftsman Lumberman's Plan Svc., Inc., Lincoln, 1966-70; owner, mgr. Lenny's Lounge, Missoula, Mont., 1978-80; engring. technician, constrn. insp., adminstr. USDA/Helena (Mont.) Nat. Forest, 1980-83; facilities project mgr. pub. office bldgs. div. City and County of Denver, 1984-86; supt. bldgs. and grounds Denver Pub. Libr., 1986-91; dir. phys. plant Red Rocks C.C., Lakewood, Colo., 1991-94; CEO Derrick, Inc., Stevensville, Mont. Mem. Local Govt. Study Commn., Stevensville, Mont., 1974; bd. dirs. Lewis and Clark County Fair Bd., Helena, Mont., 1979-83; candidate U.S. Ho. of Reps., 1999—. Active SP5E5 US Army, 1967—70. Mem. Project Mgmt. Inst. (cert. project mgr. profl. #619, v.p. programs Denver chpt. 1986-89, pres. 1990-91, v.p. pub. rels. 1992-93, bd. dirs., ex-officio). Avocations: computers, videography, photo journalism, golf. Home: 39255 Jones Blvd 1096 Las Vegas NV 89103-7106 Office Phone: 702-487-0500. Personal E-mail: williamderrick12@peoplespc.com.

DERRICKSON, WILLIAM BORDEN, manufacturing executive; b. Milford, Del., May 30, 1940; m. Patricia Jean Hayes, Feb. 1, 1964; children: Stephen Russel, Michael Scot BSEE, U. Del., 1964; diploma, Harvard Bus. Sch., 1979. Registered profl. engr. Supr. elec. maintenance Delmarva Power, Salisbury, Md., 1964-68; instrumentation engr. Hercules, Inc., Wilmington, Del., 1968-69, Sun Shipbldg., Chester, Pa., 1969-70; dir. project Fla. Power & Light Co., Juno Beach, Fla., 1970-84; sr. v.p. Pub. Svc. Co. N.H., Manchester, 1984-85; pres. New Hampshire Yankee Electric Co., Seabrook, 1985-87; pres., COO WPD Assocs., Inc., 1986-88, Quadrex Corp., Campbell, Calif., 1988-89, chmn. bd., CEO, 1989-93; also chmn. bd. dirs.; chmn. bd., CEO QES Inc., Palm City, Fla., 1994—, IBEX Engring. Svcs., Palm City, 1995—2002. Nuclear advisor Tenn. Valley Authority Bd. Dirs., 1987. Contbr. articles to profl. publs. Named Constrn. Man of Yr. ENR/McGraw-Hill Publs., 1984 Mem. NSPE, Am. Nuclear Soc., Project Mgmt. Inst., N.H. Soc. Profl. Engrs., Internat. Platform Assn., Rep. Senatorial Inner Circle. Republican. Avocations: golf, travel, coin collecting/numismatics, piano. Home: 316 SW Atlanta Ave Stuart FL 34994 E-mail: bderricksn@aol.com.

DERRY, WILLIAM R., JR., lawyer; b. Cleve., Jan. 21, 1946; BA, Yale U., 1967; JD, U. Va., 1974. Bar: Va. 1974. Atty. Mays & Valentine (merged with Troutman Sanders), Richmond, Va.; ptnr., public fin. group leader Troutman Sanders LLP, Richmond, Va., 2001—. 1st lt. U.S. Army, 1969-71. Mem. ABA, Nat. Assn. Bond Lawyers, Va. Bar Assn., Richmond Bar Assn. Office: Troutman Sanders LLP 1111 E Main St PO Box 1122 Richmond VA 23218-1122 Office Phone: 804-697-1375. Office Fax: 804-697-1339. Business E-Mail: bill.derry@troutmansanders.com.

DERSHOWITZ, ALAN MORTON, law educator; b. Bklyn., Sept. 1, 1938; s. Harry and Claire Dershowitz; m. Carolyn Cohen; children: Elon Marc, Jamin Seth, Ella Kaille Cohen Dershowitz. BA magna cum laude, Bklyn. Coll., 1959, LLD (hon.), 2001; LLB magna cum laude, Yale U., 1962; MA (hon.), Harvard Coll., 1967; LLD (hon.), Yeshiva U., 1989; PhD (hon.), Haifa U., 1993; LLD (hon.), Hebrew Union Coll., 1993, Syracuse U., 1997, Monmouth Coll., Bar Ilan U., 2004. Bar: DC 1963, Mass. 1968, US Supreme Ct. 1968. Law clk. to Hon. David L. Bazelon US Ct. Appeals DC Cir., 1962—63; law clk. to Hon. Arthur J. Goldberg US Supreme Ct., 1963—64; fellow Ctr. for Advanced Study of Behavioral Sciences, 1971—72; asst. prof. law Harvard Law Sch., 1964—67, prof. law, 1967—, Felix Frankfurter Prof. Law, 1993—. Cons. to dir. NIMH, 1967—69, Pres.'s Commn. Civil Disorders, 1967, Pres.'s Com. Causes Violence, 1968, NAACP Legal Def. Fund, 1967—68, NIMH's Pres.'s Commn. Marijuana and Drug Abuse, 1972—73, Coun. on Drug Abuse, 1972—, Ford Found. Study on Law and Justice, 1973—76; rapporteur Twentieth Century Fund Study on Sentencing, 1975—76. Co-author: Psychoanalysis, Psychiatry and the Law, 1967, Criminal Law: Theory and Process, 1974; author: The Best Defense, 1982, Reversal of Fortune: Inside the von Bulow Case, 1986, Taking Liberties: a Decade of Hard Cases, Bad Laws and Bum Raps, 1988, Chutzpah, 1991, Contrary to Public Opinion, 1992, The Abuse Excuse, 1994, The Advocate's Devil, 1994, Reasonable Doubts: The O.J. Simpson Case and the Criminal Justice System, 1996, The Vanishing American Jew: In Search of Jewish Identity for the Next Century, 1997, Sexual McCarthyism: Clinton, Starr and the Emerging Constitutional Crisis, 1998, Just Revenge, 1999, The Genesis of Justice: Ten Stories of Biblical Injustice That Led to the Ten Commandments and Modern Law, 2000, Supreme Injustice: How the High Court Hijacked Election 2000, 2001, Letters to a Young Lawyer, 2001, Why Terrorism Works: Understanding the Threat, Responding to the Challenge, 2002, Shouting Fire: Civil Liberties in a Turbulent Age, 2002, America Declares Independence, 2003, The Case for Israel, 2003, America on Trial, 2004, Rights from Wrongs: The Origins of Human Rights in the Experience of Injustice, 2004, The Case for Peace: How the Arab-Israeli Conflict Can Be Resolved, 2005; contbr. articles to profl. jounals; editor-in-chief: Yale Law Jour., 1961—62. Chmn. civil rights com. New England region Anti-Defamation League, B'nai B'rith, 1980—85; bd. dirs. ACLU, 1968—71, 1972—75, Assembly Behavioral and Social Scis. at NAS, 1973—76. Fellow Guggenheim, 1978—79. Mem.: Order of Coif, Phi Beta Kappa. Jewish. Office: Harvard Law School Hauser Hall 520 1575 Massachusetts Ave Cambridge MA 02138 Office Phone: 617-495-4617. Office Fax: 617-495-7855. Business E-Mail: dersh@law.harvard.edu.*

DERSTADT, RONALD THEODORE, health facility administrator; b. Detroit, June 9, 1950; s. Theodore Edward and Dorothy J. (Semko) D.; m. J. Gail Adamson, June 9, 1990. BA, U. Detroit, 1971; M of Hosp. Healthcare Adminstn., Xavier U., 1975. Mgr. shared svcs. Bethesda Hosp. North, Cin., 1975-76; asst. adminstr. McCullough-Hyde Meml. Hosp., Oxford, Ohio, 1977-79; pres. Hospice of Cin., Inc., 1979-82; dir. strategic planning St. Francis-St. George Hosp., Cin., 1982-84; v.p. Mgmt. Dynamics, Inc., Cin., 1984-85; sr. v.p. St. Francis-St. George Mgmt. Co., Cin., 1986-88; v.p. Franciscan Health System of Cin., 1988-91; dir. hosp. affairs ChoiceCare, Cin., 1991-95; CEO Medquest, Owensboro, Ky., 1995-98; COO Ctr. for Chem. Addictions Treatment, Cin., 1998—. Vice-chmn., bd. dirs. Franciscan Health Network, Cin., Franciscan Health Ventures, Cin. Treas., bd. dirs. Ohio Easter Seals Soc., Columbus, 1987-93; bd. dirs. S.W. Ohio Easter Seal Soc., Cin., 1986-92; adv. bd. Dater Jr. H.S., Cin., 1984-88. Fellow Am. Coll. Healthcare Execs.; mem. Healthcare Fin. Mgmt. Assn., Am. Hosp. Assn., Ohio Hosp. Assn. Avocations: boating, golf, radio control model building. Home: 7363 Dogtrot Rd Cincinnati OH 45248 Office: 830 Ezzard Charles Dr Cincinnati OH 45214-2525 Office Phone: 513-381-6672.

DERTHICK, ALAN WENDELL, architect, architectural firm executive; b. Johnson City, Tenn., July 6, 1931; s. Lawrence Gridley and Helda Lee (Hannah) Derthick; m. Jane Bailey, Dec. 22, 1958; children: Mark Alan, Steven John. BArch, Auburn U., 1954. Registered arch., Tenn., Ga., Ala. Ptnr. Derthick, Henley & Wilkerson Archs., Chattanooga, 1960—. Prin. works include Miller Pl., 1989 (Honor award), Hunter Mus. Art, 1977 (Honor awards), 1994, 2004, 2005, Chattanooga Pub. Libr., 1977 (Honor award), 1992, Hamilton County Cts. Bldg., 1992, Alexian Village, 1993, 2003, 2005, 2007, Covenant Transport Nat. Hdqrs., 1997, 2000, 2005, 2006, Chattanoooga Conv. Ctr., 2003, 2005, EPB Garage, 2003, 2005, 2006, TVPPA, 2002, Hardy Sch., 2001. Chmn. Chattanooga Codes Rev. Bd., 1975—95, Mayor's Better Schs. Task Force, Chattanooga, 1984—85, Hamilton County Codes Appeals Bd., 1999—2007; pres. 1st Christian Ch., 1978, 1984, 1998, 1999, 2000. With USAF, 1954—56. Recipient Honor award, Nat. Concrete Reinforcing Steel Inst., 1977. Mem.: AIA (pres. Chattanooga chpt. 1966, 1972, Gulf States Regional and Nat. Honor award 1961, 1977, 1978, 1989), Tenn. Soc. Archs. (pres. 1991), Mountain City Club. Home: 602 Marr Dr Signal Mountain TN 37377-2228 Office: Derthick Henley Wilkerson 1001 Carter St Chattanooga TN 37402-5014 Office Phone: 423-266-4816. Business E-Mail: alan@dhw-architects.com.

DER TOROSSIAN, PAPKEN, engineering executive; B in Mech. Engring., MIT; M, Stanford U. Pres., CEO EVS Microsystems, Inc.; pres. Santa Cruz divsn., v.p. telephone products group Plantronics; pres. Silicon Valley Group, San Jose, Calif., 1984—, CEO, 1986—, chmn. bd. dirs., 1991—. Spkr. in field.

DERVAN, JOHN PATRICK, cardiologist; b. Boston, Aug. 3, 1950; s. Peter Brendan and Ellen (Comer) D. BS, Boston Coll., 1972; MD, St. Louis U., 1976. Diplomate Am. Bd. Internal Medicine, also Sub-bds. Cardiovascular Disease, Interventional Cardiology. Intern Faulkner Hosp., Boston, 1976-77, jr. and sr. resident, 1977-79, chief resident in internal medicine, 1979-80; fellow cardiology Beth Israel Hosp., Boston, 1980-83; instr. medicine Harvard Med. Sch., Boston, 1982-83; clin. asst. prof. medicine Jefferson Med. Coll., Phila., 1983-85, asst. prof. medicine, 1985-86, SUNY, Stony Brook, 1986-93, assoc. prof. medicine, 1993-98, clin. assoc. prof. medicine, 1998—. Dir. cardiac catheterization lab. Univ. Hosp., SUNY, Stony Brook, 1986-98, dir. interventional cardiology, 1986-98. Fellow Am. Coll. Cardiology, Soc. Cardiac Angiography and Intervention; mem. ACP, Soc. Critical Care Medicine, Am. Heart Assn. Office: Heart Assocs of LI 220 Belle Meade Rd East Setauket NY 11733 Office Phone: 631-941-2273.

DERVAN, PETER BRENDAN, chemistry professor; b. Boston, July 28, 1945; s. Peter Brendan and Ellen (Comer) D.; m. Jackqueline K. Barton; children: Andrew, Elizabeth. BS in Chemistry, Boston Coll., 1967, DSc, 1997; PhD in Chemistry, Yale U., New Haven, Conn., 1972. NIH postdoctoral fellow Stanford U., 1973; asst. prof. chemistry Calif. Inst. Tech., Pasadena, 1973-79, assoc. prof. chemistry, 1979-82, prof. chemistry, 1982-88, Bren prof. chemistry, 1988—, chmn. div. chemistry & chem. engring., 1994—99. Adv. bd. ACS Monographs, Washington, 1979-81; vis. prof. for several internat. & domestic; mem. organizing com., nineteeth reaction mechanisms conf., 1982; co-organizer, workshop on reactive intermediates, NSF, 1984-85, mem. adv. panel for chemistry of life scis., 1985, mem. adv. com. for chemistry, 1986-88, chmn. adv. com. for chemistry, 1988-89; mem. bd. on chem. scis. and tech., NRC, 1988-90, chmn. bd. on chem. scis. and tech., 1991-94; mem. coun. Gordon Rsch. Conf., 1991-94; mem. adv. bd. Chem. & Engring. News, 1992-94. Mem. adv. bd. Jour. Organic Chemistry, Washington, 1981-85, Bioorganic Chemistry, 1983-, Chem. Rev. Jour., 1984-89, Nucleic Acids Res., 1986-88, Jour. Am. Chem. Soc., 1986-92, Accounts Chem. Res., 1987-89, Bioorganic Chem. Rev., 1988—, Catalysis Letters, 1988-89, Bioconjugate Chemistry, 1989—, Jour. Med. Chemistry, 1991-93, Tetrahedron, 1992-, Bioorganic and Medicinal Chemistry, 1993-, Chemical and Engineering News, 1992- Current Opinion in Drug Discovery and Develop., 1997-, Proceedings of NAS, 1999, Am. Chem. Soc. Chem. Biology, 2006-; contbr. articles to profl. jours. Alfred P. Sloan Rsch. fellow, 1977; Camille and Henry Dreyfus Tchr.-Scholar, 1978; John Simon Guggenheim Meml. Fellow, 1983; Arthur C. Cope Scholar award, 1986; recipient Maison de la Chimie Found. prize, 1996, Max Tishler prize, 1999; named 2006 Nat. Medal Sci. Laureate, NSF, 2007. Fellow Am. Acad. Scis.; mem. NAS(Class I membership com., 1994-96, 2005, nominating com., 1997), Am. Chem. Soc. (Nobel Laureate Signature award 1985, Harrison Howe award 1988, Arthur C. Cope award, 1993, Willard Gibbs medal, 1993, Rolf Sammet prize, 1993, William H. Nichols medal 1994, Kirkwood medal 1998, Alfred Bader award 1999, Achievement in Biomimetic Chemistry award , 2005, Ronald Breslow award, 2005), Inst. Medicine (Remsen award 1998, Linus Pauling medal 1999, Richard C. Tolman medal 1999), French Acad. Scis. (fgn., Tetrahedron prize 2000); mem. Am. Philos. Soc. (Harvey prize, Israel 2002), German Acad. Natural Scientists (Wilbur Cross medal 2005, Nat. Medal of Sci., 2006). Office: Calif Inst Tech Divsn Chemisty & Chem Engring 164-30 1201 E Calif Blvd Pasadena CA 91125-0001 Business E-Mail: dervan@caltech.edu.

DERWART, GREGORY M., state agency administrator; s. John W. and Joan E. Derwart; m. Kelly J. Derwart, Apr. 19, 1997; children: Hannah E., Rachel E. BA, U. Md., College Park, 1992; MA, U. Balt., 1996. Mktg. dir. AeroMist, Inc., Bel Air, Md., 1992—93; customer svc. rep. Loyola Fed. Savs. Bank, Balt., 1993—94; membership comm. Govt. Employees Benefit Assn., Ft. Meade, Md., 1994; pub. rels. mgr., sect. adminstr. Md. State Bar Assn., Balt., 1995—96; project mgr. Aon Cons., Owings Mills, Md., 1996—99; dir. adminstrn. Md. State Bar Assn., Balt., 1999—2005, Md. Transp. Authority, Balt., 2005—. Leadership program Greater Balt. Com., 2006; bd. dirs. Chesapeake Human Resources Assn., Balt., Civic Works, Inc., Balt.; com. mem. Greater Balt. Com., 2004—; fundraising com. Live Balt. Home Ctr., 2003—; bd. dirs. Federalist Soc. Law & Pub. Policy Studies, Balt.; v.p., dir. membership Internat. Assn. Bus. Communicators, Balt., 1996—98. Mem. Rep. Ctrl. Com., Balt., 2003—04; coun. v.p., com. mem. St. Luke Luth. Ch., Balt., 2000. Mem.: Masons, Scottish Rite. Conservative. Lutheran. Office: Maryland Transportation Authority 303 Authority Dr Baltimore MD 21222 Office Phone: 410-537-7510. E-mail: gderwart@mdta.state.md.us.

DERYUGA, VYACHESLAV O., nuclear physicist; b. Krasny Liman, Ukraine, Mar. 9, 1955; s. Oleksiy D. and Polina P. Deryuga; m. Larisa P. Kolomiets, July 28, 1978 (div. Nov. 1984); 1 child, Anna Dotsenko; m. Vera B. Smirnova, Apr. 18, 1986; 1 child, Polina. BSc, Kharkiv U., Ukraine, 1978, PhD, 1982; MSc, Kharkov State U., 1978. Vis. rschr. Joint Inst. for Nucler Rsch., Dubna, Russia, 1978—81; sr. rsch. scis. Kharkov State U., 1981—86, assoc. prof., sr. rsch. scientist, 1992—97; assoc. prof., head dept. Kharkov Inst. Zootechniques and Vet. Medicine, 1986—92; cons. Computer Tech., Inc., NYC, 1997—2002; project leader Morgan Stanley, NYC, 2002—05; sr. quantitative analyst GFI Group, NYC, 2005—. Mem. coun. Soc. for Sci. Edn. Knowledge, Kharkov, 1986-91; docent USSR Bd. Edn., 1991; fellow James Beard Found. Author: Physics, 1993; contbr. articles to profl. jours. including Instruments and Exptl. Techniques, Nuclear Physics, Jour. Physics, Hyperfine Interactions. Mem. IEEE (sr.), IEEE Computer Soc. (sr.), Ukrainian Phys. Soc. Inventor of electro-hydraulic desintegrator of microorganisms; research on acoustic effects of high-current electron beams; pionering work in design computer programs for automated spectra processing; design of automated customer account transfer service. E-mail: deryuga@computer.org.

DERZAW, RICHARD LAWRENCE, lawyer; b. NYC, Mar. 6, 1954; s. Ronald Murray and Diana (Diamond) Derzaw; m. Susan Katz, 1993. BA magna cum laude, Fairleigh Dickinson U., 1976; JD, Ohio No. U., 1979. Bar: Fla. 1979, U.S. Dist. Ct. (so. dist.) Fla. 1981, U.S. Dist. Ct. Appeals (5th and 11th cirs.) 1981, N.Y. 1982, U.S. Dist. Ct. (so. dist.) N.Y. 1985, U.S. Dist. Ct. (ea. dist.) N.Y. 1986, U.S. Tax Ct. 1986, U.S. Ct. Appeals (2d cir.) 1988, U.S. Supreme Ct. 1988, N.C. 1995. Pvt. practice, Boca Raton, Fla., 1979-82, NYC, 1982—. Mem.: ABA, Fed. Bar Coun., Assn. Bar City of N.Y., Am. Arbitration Assn., Fla. Bar Assn., N.C. Bar Assn., N.Y. State Bar Assn., Lions Boca Raton (treas. 1981—82), Phi Omega Epsilon, Phi Zeta Kappa, Phi Alpha Delta. Office: 477 Madison Ave New York NY 10022 Office Phone: 212-838-4644. Business E-Mail: derzlaw@aol.com.

DERZON, GORDON M., hospital administrator; b. Milw., Dec. 28, 1934; married. BA, Dartmouth Coll., 1957; MHA, U. Mich., 1961. Adminstrv. resident Bklyn. Hosp., 1960-61, adminstrv. asst., 1961-63, asst. exec. dir., 1963-65, exec. dir., 1966-67, State U. Hosp., Bklyn., 1967-68, Kings County Hosp. Center, Bklyn., 1968-74; CEO U. Wis. Hosps. and Clinics, Madison, 1974-2000; assoc. prof. SUNY, 1967-74; clin. prof. U. Wis., now emeritus prof. Bd. dirs. MATC Found., Madison Cmty. Health Ctr. Hospice, Combat Blindness Found., Ctr. Health Emotions. Contbr. articles to profl. jours. Mem. Am. Hosp. Assn. (past chmn. pub. gen. hosp. sect.). Home: 3440 Topping Rd Madison WI 53705-1439 Office Phone: 608-238-9407. Business E-Mail: gm.derzon@hosp.wisc.edu.

DE SÁ E SILVA, ELIZABETH ANNE, secondary school educator; b. Edmonds, Wash., Mar. 17, 1931; d. Sven Yngve and Anna Laura Elizabeth (Dahlin) Erlandson; m. Claudio de Sá e Silva, Sept. 12, 1955 (div. July 1977); children: Lydia, Marco, Nelson. BA, U. Oreg., 1953; postgrad., Columbia U., 1954—56, Calif. State U., Fresno, 1990, U. No. Iowa, 1983; MEd, Mont. State U., 1978. Med. sec., 1947—49; sec. Merced Sch. Dist., Calif., 1950—51; sec., asst. Simon and Schuster, Inc., NYC, 1954—56; tchr. Casa Roosevelt-União Cultural, São Paulo, Brazil, 1957—59, Coquille Sch. Dist., Oreg., 1978—96; tchr. music Cartwheels Pre-sch., North Bend, Oreg., 1997—99, 2001. Tchr. piano, 1967—78; instr. Spanish Southwestern Oreg. C.C., Coos Bay, 1991—94; pianist/organist Faith Luth. Ch., North Bend, Oreg., 1995—2002, New Life Luth. Ch., Florence, Oreg., 2002—04; vocal soloist, 1996—; voice tchr., 1997—99. Chmn. publicity Music in Our Schs. Month, Oreg. Dist. VII, 1980-85; sec. Newcomer's Club, Bozeman, Mont., 1971. Quincentennial fellow U. Minn. and Found. José Ortega y Gasset, Madrid, 1991, Sheffield Berkshire Choral Festival, Sheffield, Mass., 2004, 05. Mem. AAUW (sec., scholarship chmn., co-pres., pres., treas., editor newsletter), Nat. Trust Hist. Preservation, Am. Coun. on Tchg. Fgn. Langs., Am. Assn. Tchrs. Spanish and Portuguese, Nat. Coun. Tchrs. English, Music Educators Nat. Conf., Oreg. Music Educators Assn., Oreg. Coun. Tchrs. English, Confedn. Oreg. Fgn. Lang. Tchrs., VoiceCare Network, Am. Guild Organists, Berkshire Choral Festival. Democrat. Avocations: swimming, walking, travel, drama. Home: 14425 SW Arabian Dr Beaverton OR 97008 Office Phone: 503-524-6036.

DESAI, DEEPAK K., lawyer; b. Cin., Dec. 19, 1968; BA, Northern Ky. U., 1988; JD, Salmon P. Chase Coll. Law, 1991. Bar: Ohio 1993, US Dist. Ct. Southern Dist. Ohio. Assoc. Santen & Hughes, Cin. Named one of Ohio's Rising Stars, Super Lawyers, 2006. Mem.: Cin. Bar Assn., Ohio State Bar Assn. Office: Santen & Hughes Ste 3100 312 Walnut St Cincinnati OH 45202 Office Phone: 513-721-4450. Office Fax: 513-721-0109.

DESAI, KIRAN, writer; b. New Delhi, Sept. 3, 1971; arrived in England, 1985, arrived in USA, 1986; d. Ashvin and Anita Desai. BA, Bennington Coll., Vt., 1993; writing workshop, Hollins Coll., Va.; MFA, Columbia U., NYC. Author: (novels) Hullabaloo in the Guava Orchard, 1998 (Betty Trask Award, Soc. Authors, 1998), The Inheritance of Loss, 2006 (The Man Booker Prize, 2006, The Nat. Book Critics Circle award for Fiction, 2006). Achievements include being youngest ever female to Win Booker Prize. Office: c/o Atlantic Monthly Press Fourth Fl 841 New York NY 10003 Office Fax: 212-614-7850.

DESAI, NITIN DAYALJI, international organization official; b. Bombay, July 5, 1941; s. Dayalji M. and Shantaben Desai; m. Aditi Gupta, Apr. 28, 1979; children: Kartikeya, Nandan. BA with honors, U. Bombay, 1962; MSc in Econs., London Sch. Econs., 1965. Econs. lectr. Liverpool (Eng.) U., 1965-67, Southampton (Eng.) U., 1967-70; cons. Tata (India) Econ. Consultancy Svcs., 1970-73; cons., adviser Planning Commn. Govt. of India, 1973-85, sr. adviser Brundtland Commn., 1985-87, spl. sec. Planning Commn., 1987-88, sec., chief econs. adviser Min. of Fin., 1988-90; dep. sec. gen. UNCED UN, Geneva, 1990-92, undersec. gen. for policy coordination and sustainable devel. NYC, 1993-97, undersec. gen. for econ. and social affairs, 1992—2003, spl. adviser to U.N. Sec.-Gen. on the

World Summit on the Info. Soc., 2003; disting. vis. fellow London Sch. of Econs. and Polit. Scis., 2003—. Office: London School of Economics Houghton Street London WC2A 2AE England

DESAI, SAMIR T., electronics executive; BS in Physics and Elec. Engring., U. India; MSEE, Ill. Inst. Tech.; MBA, Loyola U., Chgo. Joined Motorola, Inc., Schaumburg, Ill., 1973, gen. mgr. iDEN Subscriber Group Plantation, Fla., 1993—99, sr. v.p., gen. mgr., 1999—2000, sr. v.p., dir. office of e-bus. and bus. transformation Comm. Enterprise, 2000—01, sr. v.p., dep. to the pres. of personal comm. sector, 2001—02, sr. v.p., chief info. officer, 2002—04, sr. v.p., gen. mgr. iDEN Networks and Devices, 2004—. Office: Motorola Inc 1303 E Algonquin Rd Schaumburg IL 60196

DESAI, TEJAL ASHWIN, biomedical engineer, educator; BSc in Biomedical Engring., Brown U., Providence, 1994; PhD joint degree in Bioengineering, U. Calif., Berkeley and San Francisco, 1998. Asst. prof. dept. bioengineering U. Ill., Chgo., 1998—2000, Disting. asst. prof. bioengineering, 2000—02; assoc. prof. biomedical engring. Boston U., 2002—. Contbr. articles to profl. jours. Named one of 40 Under 40, Crain's Chgo. Bus., 1999, Brilliant 10, Popular Sci. mag., 2003; recipient TR100 award, MIT Tech. Rev., 1999, New Century Scholar award, NSF, 2000, CAREER award, 2000, Frontiers in Engring. award, NAS, 2001, Visionary Sci. award, BioMEMS and Nanotechnology Soc., 2001, McGowan Inst. award, Contbns. to Regenerative Medicine, 2002, Focused Giving award, Johnson & Johnson, 2002, EURAND Grand Prize award, Outstanding Rsch. in Oral Drug Delivery, 2003. Mem.: Women in Sci. and Engring., Soc. Women Engrs., Soc. Biomaterials, Materials Rsch. Soc., Internat. Soc. Optical Engring., Am. Chem. Soc., IEEE Engring. in Medicine and Biology, Biomedical Engring. Soc., Internat. Soc. BioMEMS and Biomedical Nanotechnology (bd. mem. 2001—). Office: Dept Biomedical Engring Boston U 44 Cummington St Boston MA 02215 Office Phone: 617-358-3054. E-mail: tdesai@bu.edu.*

DESAI, VEENA BALVANTRAI, obstetrician, gynecologist, educator; b. Karvan, Gujarat, India, Oct. 5, 1931; arrived in U.S., 1973; d. Balvantrai P. and Maniben (Vashl) Desai; m. Vinay D. Gandevia, Sept. 19, 1964. MBBS, Seth G.S. Med. Coll., Bombay, 1957, MD, 1961. Jr. resident Bombay U., 1957-59; house officer gyn. Chalmer's Hosp., Edinburgh, Scotland, 1962-63; registrar ob-gyn. Neath Gen. Hosp., England, 1963-64, Scunthorpe Gen. Hosp., England, 1964-66; chief resident ob-gyn. St. John Gen. Hosp., Canada, 1973-74; attending ob-gyn. Portsmouth Hosp., NH, 1975-84; assoc. prof. Boston U., 1985-86; sr. staff ob-gyn. Santa Clara Valley Med. Ctr., Calif., 1986-87; mem. staff ob-gyn. West Anaheim Med. Ctr., Calif., 1988-98, chief dept. ob-gyn., 1992-93, vice chief of gen. med. staff, 1994—95; ob/gyn Bay State Med. Ctr., Springfield, Mass., 1998—; chief ob-gyn. Mercy Med. Ctr., Springfield, 2002—03. Pres. Desai Med. Corp., Anaheim, 1989—; assoc. clin. prof. ob-gyn. U. Calif., Irvine, 1990—98. Chmn.'s advisor NSC; charter mem. Presdl. Task Force; mem. Reps. Inner Cir., 1984—2003; bd. dirs. ARC Pioneer Valley Chpt., Springfield, Mass., 2007. Named Pioneer of Healthcare Reform, Nat. Rep. Congl. Com., 2004, Merit for Life, Confedn. Chivalry, Sydney, 1989; recipient Presdl. medal of Merit, 1982, award, Spl. Congl. Adv. Bd., 1984, Order of Liberty, US Congress, 1995, medal of Freedom, US Senate, 1994, medal, Ronald Wilson Reagan Eternal Flame of Freedom, 1996, Millennium medal of Freedom, Rep. Senate, 1999, Internat. Peace prize, United Cultural Conv., 2003, Congl. Order of Merit, 2004, Dame, Confedn. Chivalry, Sydney, 1989, Outstanding Achievement in Poetry award, Internat. Soc. Poets, 2005. Fellow: ACOG, ACS, Royal Coll. Ob-Gyn. (chmn. Am. rep. com. 1997—2002), Western Mass. Ob-Gyn. Soc. (pres. 2002—), Internat. Coll. Surgeons; mem.: Buena Park Rotary (pres. 1994, chair internat. svc. 1992—93). Avocations: latchhook work, international politics, travel. Home: 35 Sean Louis Cir West Springfield MA 01089-4547 Personal E-mail: veenadesai@comcast.net.

DESAI, VISHAKHA N., professional society administrator; b. Ahmedabad, Gujarat, India, May 1, 1949; came to U.S., 1966; m. Robert B. Oxnam, 1993. BA, Bombay U., Elphinstone Coll., 1970; MA in History of Art, U. Mich., 1975, PhD in History of Art, 1984. With edn. div. Bklyn. Mus., NYC, 1972-74; head exhibit resource Mus. sect. edn. dept. Fine Arts, Boston, 1977-80; acting dir. edn. dept. Mus. Fine Arts, Boston, 1980-81, coord. acad. program, 1981-88, asst. curator, 1981-90, mus. pres.; dir. Asia Soc. Galleries, NYC, 1990—; v.p. Asia Soc., NYC, 1993—2004, pres., 2004—. Adj. asst. prof. Boston U., 1982-87; assoc. prof. U. Mass., Boston, 1986-90; adj. prof. Columbia U., 1995-96, 97; bd. dirs. Am. Com. South/S.E. Asia Art; reviewer Bunting Inst., Radcliffe Coll., Boston, 1990—; bd. dirs. Art Table, N.Y.C., 1991-94. Contbr. articles to profl. jours. Pres. Mass. Found. for Humanities, 1989-91. Outstanding Teaching fellow U. Mich., 1977, Am. Inst. of Indian Studies fellow, 1978; grantee, Nat. Endowment for the Arts, NEM, 1979—, Mus. Sabbaticatal grantee Nat. Endowment for the Arts, 1982. Mem. Coll. Art Assn. (bd. dirs. 1995—), Am. Assn. Art Mus. Dirs. (bd. dirs 1995—. pres. 1998—). Office: Asia Soc and Mus 725 Park Ave New York NY 10021-5025

DE SAINT PHALLE, THIBAUT, investment banker, financial consultant; b. Tuxedo Pk., NY, July 23, 1918; s. Fal and Marie (Duryee) de Saint P.; m. Rosamond (Frame), Jan. 12, 1946 (dec. 1960); children: Fal, Pierre, Thérèse; m. Elene Canrobert (Isles), June 21, 1965 (div. 1983); children: Marc, Diane; m. Mariana M. (Smith), April 24, 1983. Student, Harvard U., 1935—37; BA, Columbia U., 1939, JD, 1941. Bar: N.Y. 1942, U.S. Supreme Ct., 1945, D.C. 1984. Assoc. Chadbourne, Wallace, Parke, and Whiteside, NYC, 1941—50; ptnr., head corp. law dept. Lewis 1950and McDonald, NYC, 1950—58; v.p., treas. Becton, Dickinson, and Co., Rutherford, NJ, 1958—62, dir., 1958—67; sr. ptnr. Coudert Bros., NYC, 1962—66, counsel, 1966—77; of counsel Vorys, Sater, Seymour, and Pease, Washington, 1983—86. Ltd. ptnr. Dean Witter and Co., pres. Dean Witter Overseas Fin. Corp., N.Y.C., 1967-68; investment banker Stralem, Saint Phalle and Co., Inc., N.Y.C., 1968-70, vice chmn. bd. dir., 1968-70; mem. faculty, prof. internat. fin. and law Ctr. d'Etudes Industrielles, Geneva, 1971-76; dir. Export Import Bank U.S., Washington, 1977-81; Scholl chair internat. bus. Georgetown U. Ctr. Strategic and Internat. Studies, 1981-83; chmn. Saint Phalle Internat. Group, 1985—. Author: The Dollar Crisis, 1963; Multi Nat. Corporations, 1976; U.S. Productivity and Competitiveness in Internat. Trade, 1980; Trade Inflation and the Dollar, 1981, (rev. edit., 1984), The Federal Reserve, an Intentional Mystery, 1985; Saints, Sinners and Scalawags, 2004; contbg. numerous articles on internat. fin. and trade to profl. journals. Lt. comdr. USNR, 1942—46. Decorated Navy Commendation medal, Bronze Star, Legion of Honor, (France). Mem.: ABA, Jockey Club, Met. Club. Roman Catholic. Home and Office: Saint Phalle Internat Group PO Box 2038 Boca Grande FL 33921 Personal E-mail: thibaut@comcast.net.

DE SALVA, CHRISTOPHER JOSEPH, lawyer, consultant; b. Milw., June 16, 1950; s. Salvatore Joseph and Elaine Mae De S.; m. Erika Marie De Salva, May 24, 1975; 1 child, Jessica Anne. BA in Polit. Sci., St. Vincent Coll., 1972; JD summa cum laude, Am. Coll. Law, 1987; MBA, Calif. Coast U., 1993, postgrad., 1994. Bar: Calif. 1994, U.S. Dist. Ct. (ctrl. dist., so. dist.) Calif. 1995, U.S. Ct. Fed. Claims 1995, U.S. Tax Ct. 1995, U.S. Supreme Ct., 2000. Founder, owner C.J. De Salva & Assocs. Investment and Mktg. Svcs. of La Quinta (now C.J. De Salva & Assocs., La Quinta, 1979—; pvt. practice La Quinta, Calif., 1994-98, Indio, Calif., 1994—, San Diego, 1996-98. CEO, pres. The Kings Vault Gallery, Inc., 1985; adj. faculty property law Am. Coll. Law, Brea, Calif., 1989-90, 92-95; life and disability ins. agent C.J. De Salva Ins. Agency 1978—; real estate broker De Salva Realty Calif., 1980—, realtor, 1985-94; tax cons., preparer Christopher De Salva Tax Cons.; cons. Christopher De Salva Bus. and Mgmt. Cons.; lectr. property law. Am. Coll. Law. Author: NAFTA, The Hidden Agenda, 1995. 1st lt. USMC, 1974-77. Recipient Am. Jurisprudence scholarship award Am. Coll. Law. Mem. ABA, Assn. Trial Lawyers, Vietnam Era Vet., Vet. of Latin Am., Nat. Soc. Pub. Accts (cert. 1984), Calif. Bar Assn. Avocations: music, sports, writing songs, flying. Office: 45-902 Oasis St Ste D Indio CA 92201

DE SALVA, SALVATORE JOSEPH, retired pharmacologist, toxicologist; b. NYC, Jan. 14, 1924; s. Nicola Carlo and Frances Agnes (Caldarella) De S.; m. Elaine Mae Radloff, June 14, 1948; children: Salaine Claire De Salva Bonanne, Christopher Joseph, Stephanie De Salva Farrelly, Steven William, Gregory Vincent, Peter Nicholas, Philip Anthony, Deidre De Salva Berry. BS, Marquette U., 1947, MS, 1949; postgrad., U. Ill., Chgo., 1951-53; PhD, Stritch Sch. Medicine, Loyola U., Chgo., 1958. Research and teaching asst. Marquette U., Milw., 1947-49; research biochemist Milw. County Gen. Hosp., 1954; instr. U. Ill., Chgo., 1951-52; asst. prof. Chgo. Coll. Optometry, 1951-53; pharmacologist Armour Pharm. Lab., Chgo, 1953-59; sect. head Colgate Palmolive Co., Piscataway, NJ, 1959-66, sr. research assoc., 1966-72, mgr., 1972-76, assoc. dir. research for pharmacology and toxicology, 1976-83, dir. research pharmacology and toxicology, 1983-88, worldwide ops. dir., 1988-90, corp. dir. human and environ. safety worldwide, 1990-92; pres. Salva Cons. Svcs., Somerset, NJ, 1992-99; ret., 1999. Lectr. Loyola U., 1957-59; mem. technician tng. N.J. Council for Research and Devel., Rutgers U., 1969-72. Editor: Symposium for Biomedical Electronic Instrumentation, 1965; contbr. articles to profl. jours.; patentee in field; current work in pharmaco-toxicology of flourides, sequestering agts. and surfactants, nitrosamine risk assessment, alternative safety testing method devel., safety of triclosan and use in dental therapeutic products. Mem. Park Forest (Ill.) Mosquito Abatement Program, 1952-55, Franklin Twp. (N.J.) Sch. Bd., 1969-70, Somerset (N.J.) Bd. Health, 1965-67, Cath. Youth Orgn., Somerset; v.p. Cedar Hill Swim Club, Somerset; active Boy Scouts Am., Somerset, 1965-67; trustee Franklin Twp. Day Care Ctr., 1969. Served with USN, 1942-46. Mem. AAAS, Soc. Exptl. Biology and Medicine, Am. Soc. Pharmacology and Exptl. Therapeutics, Soc. Toxicology, Internat. Union Pharmacology (toxicology sect.), N.Y. Acad. Scis., Internat. Soc. Regulatory Pharmacology and Toxicology, Internat. Soc. Study of Xenobiotics, Sigma Xi. Roman Catholic. Home: 83 Demott Ln Somerset NJ 08873-1604 Home Phone: 732-545-8785. Personal E-mail: saldesalvasafety@aol.com.

DESAN, CHRISTINE, law educator; b. Washington, Mar. 20, 1959; AB in Religion, Princeton U., 1981; MALD Fletcher Sch. Law & Diplomacy, Tufts U., 1987; JD, Yale U., 1987. Bar: Mass. 1987, DC 1989. Law clk. to Judge Stephen Breyer US Ct. Appeals 11th Cir.; asst. to Solicitor Gen. Charles Fried; asst. prof. law Harvard Law Sch., Cambridge, Mass., 1992—98, prof., 1998—. Office: Harvard Law Sch 1563 Massachusetts Ave Cambridge MA 02138 Office Phone: 617-495-4613, 617-495-5156. Business E-Mail: desan@law.harvard.edu.

DESANCTIS, ROMAN WILLIAM, cardiologist, educator; b. Cambridge Springs, Pa., Oct. 30, 1930; s. Vincent and Margherita (Marini) DeSanctis; m. Ruth Ann Foley, May 7, 1955; children: Ellen Ruth, Lydia Marie, Andrea Jean, Marcia Louise. BS summa cum laude, U. Ariz., 1951, DSc (hon.), 1999; MD magna cum laude, Harvard U., 1955; DSc (hon.), Wilkes Coll., 1984, U. Ariz., 1998. Diplomate Am. Bd. Internal Medicine, Sub Bd. Cardiovasc. Diseases. Intern medicine Mass. Gen. Hosp., Boston, 1955—56, from asst. resident to sr. resident medicine, 1958—60, fellow cardiology, 1960—62; dir. CCU, 1967—80, dir. clin. cardiology, 1980—98, emeritus, 1998—, physician, 1970—. Mem. faculty Harvard U. Med. Sch., 1962—, Evelyn and James Jenks and Paul Dudley White prof. medicine, 1998—. Co-author: Cardiac Clinico-Pathological Conferences of the Massachusetts General Hospital, 1972, The Practice of Cardiology, 1989; contbr. articles to med. jours. Officer M.C. USNR, 1956—58. Decorated Order of Dynasty of Alouite Morocco; recipient Excellence in Clin. Tchg. award, Harvard U. Med. Sch., 1990, Centennial Achievement award, U. Ariz., 1989, Alumni Achievement award, 2001, Glorney-Raisbeck award, NY Acad. Medicine, 2003, Trustee's award, Mass. Gen. Physician's Orgn., 2006. Fellow: ACP (master coll. 1994), Am. Coll. Cardiology (Gifted Tchr. award 1991, Disting. Fellow award 1999); mem.: N.Y. Acad. Medicine (Glorney-Raisbeck award 2003), Am. Clin. Climatol. Soc., New Eng. Cardiovasc. Soc. (pres. 1979—80), Inst. Medicine, Assn. Am. Physicians, Am. Heart Assn. (David Littmann award 1996, Paul Dudley White award 1999, Master Clinician award 2003, Trustee's Gold medal 2006), Knights of Malta, Aesculapian Club, Winchester Country Club. Roman Catholic. Home: 5 Thoreau Cir Winchester MA 01890-3340 Office: Mass Gen Hosp Yawkey Bldg 55 Fruit St Ste 5700 Boston MA 02114 Home Phone: 781-729-1453; Office Phone: 617-726-2889.

DE SANTIAGO, DENA KALENE, investment company executive, writer; b. Council Bluffs, Iowa, Aug. 19, 1970; d. Savino Michael and Linda Lou (Hannum) De Santiago; life ptnr. Vincent William Young, Jan. 14, 1979; children: Todd Michael Roberts, Isabella Kalene De Santiago-Young. Degree in Pub. Rels./Orgnl. Comm. & Devel., Creighton U., Omaha, Nebr., 1991; degree in Liberal Arts (hon.), Bellevue U., Nebr., 2002, M in Leadership (hon.), 2003; PhD, Walden U., Balt., 2004. Lic. ins. Nebr., 1996; cert. CPR/First Aid Nebr., 2003; Child Care Nebr., 1999; Mergers and Acquisitions Columbia U., 1999, Series 7 NASD, 1996, Series 63 NASD, 1996, Series 65 NASD, 1996, Series 31 NASD and CFTC, 1996, Series 3 NASD and CFTC, 1997. Investment exec. Dain Rauscher, Omaha, 1997—98; devel. dir. First Investment Inc., Omaha, 1998—. Ops. mgr. Law Offices of S.J. Albracht, Omaha, 1991—93; rsch. and fin. coord. Dain Bosworth, Inc, Omaha, 1993—94; mktg. dir. Hawkeye Investment Ctr., Council Bluffs, Iowa, 1994—96; agt./exec. DKD Modeling, Omaha, 1995—96; account exec. Dean Witter Reynolds, Omaha, 1996—97; casting asst. Topeka Prodns., Omaha, 1995—96. Actor: (primetime mini series) Gone in the Night; contbr., vol. (cmty. leader) KPTM Fox News; author: (publs. com.) Omaha Press Club; contbr. speech (1st Pl.); contbr.: speech Why My Family is Important, 1981-1982; contbr. citywide childrens' works (Trophy and Cert., 1978), essay contest (7th Pl. out of 35,000 entries, 1982), essay (1st Pl., 2001). Vol./fundraising Muscular Dystrophy Assn., Council Bluffs, Iowa, 1974—80, Nebr. Aids Project, Omaha, 1991—2000, MADD, Omaha, 1994—2000; vol. Girl's Inc., Omaha, 1995—97; NW divsn. comm. chair Mar. of Dimes, Omaha, 2001—02. Democrat. Catholic And Christian. Achievements include research in prison reform; development of National Issues Forum. Avocations: writing, research, mentoring, public speaking. Office: First Investment Inc PO Box 31616 Omaha NE 68131-0616 Office Phone: 402-689-8792. Business E-Mail: ddesantiago@firstinvestmentinc.com.

DESANTO, JAMES JOHN, lawyer; b. Chgo., Oct. 12, 1943; s. John Joseph and Erminia Asunda (Cassano) DeS.; m. Denise Clare Caneva, Feb. 3, 1968; children: Carrie Ann, James Thomas, John Joseph. BA, U. Ill., 1965; JD, DePaul U., 1969. Bar: Ill. 1969, U.S. Dist. Ct. (no. dist.) Ill. 1969, U.S. Ct. Appeals (7th cir.) 1972, U.S. Supreme Ct. 1974; cert. mediator 19th Jud. Circuit, Ill., 1996. Asst. state's atty., Waukegan, Ill., 1969-72; assoc. Finn, Geiger & Rafferty, Waukegan, 1972-74; ptnr. Rawles, Katz & DeSanto, Waukegan, 1975-80; pvt. practice, Waukegan, 1980-88; sr. ptnr. DeSanto & Bonamarte, Waukegan, 1988-91; pvt. practice, Libertyville, Ill., 1991—, James J. DeSanto and Assocs., 1992-99; ptnr. DeSanto, Morgan & Mittelman, Libertyville, 1999—. Lectr. in trial technique and practice Ill. Inst. for CLE and Ill. Bar Assn.; lectr. in bus. law Coll. of Lake County, 1974-84; bd. dirs. Ill. State Bar Assn. Mut. Ins. Co., 1989—, chair com. on fin. and investment 1995-97, 2000-01, sec./treas., 1999—, 2d v.p., 2001-02, 1st v.p., 2002—, chmn. bd. dirs., 2003—. Co-editor Tort Trends newsletter, 1988-91. Trustee Village of Libertyville, 1991-93; chairperson parish pastoral coun. St. Joseph's Ch., Libertyville, 2000-02. Fellow Ill. Bar Inst.; mem. ATLA, State Bar Assn. (mem. ad hoc com. profl. quality in practice of law, 1995—, ins. law sect. coun., 2001—), Ill. State Bar Assn., Lake County Bar Assn. (sec. 1979-80, 2d v.p. 1991-92, pres. 1993-94), Lake County Trial Lawyers Assn. (sec. 1985—), Jefferson Inns of Ct., Libertyville Rotary (pres. 1990-91). Avocations: golf, fishing. Home: 1209 St William Dr Libertyville IL 60048-1275 Office: 712 Florsheim Dr Libertyville IL 60048-5270 Office Phone: 847-816-8100. Business E-Mail: desanto@iconnect.net.

DESANTO, JOHN A., physicist, educator, mathematics professor; b. Wilkes-Barre, Pa., May 25, 1941; s. John and Esther DeSanto; m. Beverly DeSanto; children: John, Lauren, Andrea. BS in Physics, Villanova U., Pa., 1962, MA in Math., 1962; MS in Physics, U. Mich., Ann Arbor, 1963, PhD in Physics, 1967. Rsch. scientist Naval Rsch. Lab., Washington, 1967—81; sr. scientist Electromagnetic Applications Inc., Lakewood, Colo., 1981—82; prof. math. U. Denver, 1982—83, Colo. Sch. Mines, Golden, 1983—2006, prof. physics, 2006—, dir. Ctr. for Wave Phenomena, 1988—89. Mem. rev. panel Ocean Acoustic Tomography NSF, 1980; presenter in field. Author: Scalar Wave Theory, 1992; editor: Ocean Acoustics, 1979, 1982, Mathematical and Numerical Aspects of Wave Propagation, 1998; co-editor: Mathematical Methods and Applications of Scattering Theory, 1980; contbr. articles to profl. jours. Fellow, NSF, 1962—67, Am. Physical Soc., Inst. Physics, Eng., Acoustical Soc. Am.; Woodrow Wilson fellow, 1962, Fulbright fellow, 1993, sr. postdoctoral fellow, NRC, 1994. Fellow: Am. Phys. Soc., Inst. Physics, Acoustical Soc. Am.; mem.: IEEE, Soc. for Indsl. and Applied Math. Home: 7692 S Saulsbury Ct Littleton CO 80128 Office: Colo Sch Mines Golden CO 80401 Business E-Mail: jdesanto@mines.edu.

DESAULNIERS, RENE GERARD LESIEUR, retired optometrist; b. Danielson, Conn., Oct. 21, 1922; s. Egide A. and Rose (Regis) D.; children: Suzanne Rose Bauzys, Maureen Frances Russe, Michelle Elizabeth Van Haagen, Thomas Benedict, John Christopher. Grad., U.S. Army Mil. Intel. Sch.; student, Georgetown U., 1943, Boston U., 1944; OD, Pa. Coll. Optometry, 1948; grad., Joe Brinkman Profl. Umpire Sch., Fla. Lic. optometrist Conn., Fla., R.I. Individual practice optometry, Putnam, Conn., 1948-98; ret., 1998. Externship Gessel Inst. Child Devel. Yale U., 1964-; past pres. Conn. Bd. Examiners in Optometry, 1957-91; past pres. Internat. Assn. Bd. Examiners in Optometry; past pres. Nat. Bd. Examiners in Optometry, Washington, D.C., 1975-85; cons. American League. Life mem., former nat. dir. Am. Optometric Found.; past pres. Putnam Little League; 2d pres. Quinnebaug Valley Assn. for Retarded, 1963; past mem. Putnam Sch. Bd.; chmn. DK Hosp. Devel. Fund, 1984—85. Lt. US Army, 1943—46, maj. inf. USAR, 1946—63. Recipient Sam Levitt Meml. award, 1948; named Conn. Optometrist of Yr., 1989. Fellow: Nat. Acad. Practices (Disting. Practitioner), Am. Acad. Optometry; mem.: Conn. Assn. Optometrists, Am. Optometric Assn., New Eng. Coun. Optometrists (chmn. 42nd Congress), Conn. Approved Baseball Umpires (ea. bd. past pres. 1981—82), Am. Legion (baseball com., VFW commn.), Major League Umpires Baseball (vision cons.), Elk, KC (4th degree), Omega Delta. Home: 41 Grove St Putnam CT 06260-2107 Office Phone: 860-928-6416.

DE SAVORGNANI, ADRIANE ALDRICH, healthcare administrator, nurse; d. Merritt James Aldrich and Edith Carolyn (Borrebach); m. Luciano de Savorgnani, Aug. 1, 1979 (dec. Aug. 2002); children: Andrew, Alexia, Miranda. AB, Radcliffe Coll., 1962; diploma in nursing coord. program, Radcliffe Coll./Mass. Gen Hosp, 1965; MPH, U. Hawaii, 1974; DBA, Nova U., 1992. RN Hawaii, cert. nursing adminstrn. advanced., Am. Nurses Credentialing Ctr., Silver Spring, Md. Clin. nurse Dept. Public Health, Washington, 1966-67; staff nurse pediat., obstetrics, nursery, med.-surg. US Naval Hosp., Naples, Italy, 1967-69; pub. health nurse Dept. Human Resources, Washington, 1969-72; staff nurse, ob-gyn., nursery, recovery rm. Kapiolani Hosp., Honolulu, 1972-75; rsch. nurse U. Hawaii Newborn Psychology Rsch. Lab, Honolulu, 1974-75; staff nurse, med. and gynecol. oncology Naval Regional Med. Ctr., San Diego, 1975-78; staff nurse emergency rm. Naval Aerospace Reg. Med. Ctr., Pensacola, Fla., 1978-79; charge nurse, emergency rm. outpatient-inpatient care coord. US Naval Hosp., Naples, Italy, 1979-83; charge nurse military med. dept., utilization rev., discharge planning Naval Hosp., Newport, RI, 1983-86; head, Reg./Fleet Support, Naval Med. Command N.E. Region, Great Lakes, Ill., 1986-89; head health care plans spl. projects, head preventive med. health promotion br. Bur. Medicine and Surgery, Washington, 1989—92; exec. officer Naval Med. Clinic, Key West, Fla., 1993—. Asst. dir. nursing svcs. Naval Hosp., Jacksonville, Fla., 1992—95; exec. officer Naval Hosp., Lemoore, Calif., 1995—98; comdg. officer US Naval Med. Clinics, UK, 1998—2001; head clin. plans and mgmt. , acting asst. dep. chief med. ops. support Bur. Medicine and Surgery, Washington, DC, 2001—03; adminstrv. asst. to Def. Attaché Office Am. Embassy, London, 2003—. Contbr. articles to profl. jours. Lector, lay eucharistic minister, choir accompanist; vol. local sch.; vol. tchr. ESL; vol. women's homeless shelter. Capt., Nurse Corps, US Navy, 1975-2003. Decorated Legion of Merit, Meritorious Svc. medal (5), Navy and Marine Corps Commendation medal (2), Nat. Def. medal one star, Global War on Terrorism Svc. medal, Navy and Marine Corps Overseas Svc. Ribbon (7 stars); recipient Clara Barton award, ARC, Naples, 1983, cert. of appreciation, Operation Desert Storm, Washington, 1991, Jane A. Delano award, ARC London, 2001, dir.'s award, Human Resources Svc. Ctr., Europe, 2001, incentive award, 2007. Fellow Am. Coll. Healthcare Execs.; mem. ANA, APHA, Assn. Mil. Surgeons US (life), Acad. Mgmt., Internat. Tng. in Comm., ARC (instr.), Navy Nurse Corps. Assn., Soc. Scholarship Nursing, Midwifery, Allied Health Professions, Coll. Alumnae Assns., Mensa (life), Sigma Theta Tau. Republican. Roman Catholic. Avocations: piano, theater, art, travel, exercise. Home: 14 Bardsley Ln London SE10 9RF England

DESBARATS, PETER HULLETT, journalist, educator, academic administrator; b. Montreal, Que., Can., July 2, 1933; s. Hullett John and Margaret Ogston (Rettie) D. Student, Loyola Coll., Montreal, 1951. Feature writer The Gazette, Montreal, 1953-55; local reporter Reuters, London, 1955; feature writer The Winnipeg (Can.) Tribune, 1956, legis. reporter, 1957-60; polit. reporter, feature writer The Montreal Star, 1960-65; editor Parallel Mag., Montreal, 1965; host nightly news and pub. affairs show Sta. CBC-TV, Montreal, 1966-70; Ottawa editor Toronto Star, 1970-72; Ottawa bur. chief Global TV, 1973-80; sr. cons. Royal Commn. on Newspapers, Ottawa, 1980-81; dean Sch. Journalism U. Western Ont., London, Canada, 1981-96, assoc. prof. journalism, 1981-86, prof., 1986-96, adj. prof., 2005—. Mem. comm. adv. com. Can. commn. UNESCO; cons. Task Force on Broadcasting Policy, 1985, Royal Commn. Electoral Reform, 1991, House of Commons Broadcasting com., Ottawa, 2002, others; mem. selection com. Can. News Hall of Fame, 1986—; dir. Univ. Club U. Western Ont., 1987, also chair numerous coms.; mem. Ont. Task Force Cardiovasc. Scis., 1991, Can. Observers' Mission to Romania, 1992; commr. Commn. on Inquiry into Deployment of Can. Forces to Somalia, 1995—96; columnist The Globe and Mail, Toronto, 1997—2002, The Free Press, London, 1998—2002; former Can. corr. The Nat. Observer, Washington; MacLean Hunter chair comm. ethics Ryerson U., Toronto, 2000—01; mem. social scis. and humanities rsch. coun. Can. adjudication com. Std. Rsch. Grants Program, 2005—06; spkr. on journalism and the role of the media numerous sites throughout the U.S., Can., overseas. Author: The State of Quebec, 1965, Gabrielle and Selena, 1966, René: A Canadian in Search of a Country, 1976; author: (book of poetry) The Night the City Sang, 1977; author: The Hecklers, 1979, Canada Lost/Canada Found: The Search for a New Nation, 1981, Colin and the Computer, 1985, Guide to Canadian News Media, 1990, rev. edit., 1996, Somalia Cover-up: A Commissioner's Journal, 1997, (plays) The Great White Computer, 1966, Her Worship, 2002, Lucretia, 2003, The Practical Joke, 2005; editor: What They Used to Tell About Indian Legends from Labrador, 1969, Freedom of Expression and New Communication Technologies, 1998;

mem. editl. bd. Can. Jour. Comm., 1987—, co-host PBS series The Editors, 1987—91. Mem. Ont. Task Force on Cardiovascular Svcs., 1991, Ont. Citizens Panel on Increasing Organ Donations, 2006—07; bd. dirs. Performing Arts Ctr. for Today, London, 1993—95, Orch. London, 1993—99, London Mus. Archaeology, 1993—, v.p., 2001—03, pres., 2003—05. Recipient Best News Broadcaster award Assn. Can. TV and Radio Artists, 1977, Best TV Interviewer award Assn. Can. TV and Radio Artists, 1980, 125th Anniversary Confedn. Can. medal, 1992; named officer Order of Can., 2007. Mem.: Soc. Environ. Journalists (adv. bd. 1995—), Can. Journalism Found. (bd. dirs. 1997—2005, adv. bd. 2005—), Can. Civil Liberties Assn. (bd. dirs. 1998—), Can. Assn. Journalists. E-mail: pdesbarats@sympatico.ca.

DESCH, THEODORE EDWARD, retired insurance company executive, lawyer; b. Chgo., Oct. 1, 1931; s. Louis G. and Dorothy (Prieb) D.; m. Donna K. Thorsell, Feb. 3, 1951 (dec. 2005); children: Theodore M. (dec. 1968), Steven R., Katherine S. Collins, Gregory S. AB, U. Ill., 1952, LLB, 1954. Bar: Ill. 1954; cert. employee benefits specialist, CLU, ChFC. Asst. gen. atty. C.,R.I.&P. R.R., 1956-59, gen. atty., 1959-65, gen. counsel, 1965-68, v.p. and gen. counsel, 1968-70, vice chmn. bd., 1970-73, chmn. bd., 1973-74, chief exec. officer, 1970-74, dir., 1970-75; ptnr. Kirkland & Ellis, Chgo., 1975-77; sr. v.p. law and pub. affairs Health Care Svc. Corp., a Mut. Legal Res. Co., Blue Cross and Blue Shield Ill., Chgo., 1977-86, sr. v.p. law and corp. affairs, 1986-97; sr. v.p. govt. contracts Chgo., 1997-98; ret., 1998; acting deputy gen. counsel Blue Cross and Blue Shield Assoc., Chgo., 2001—02. Chmn. Preferred Fin. Corp., Denver, 1995-98; bd. dirs. Walker Parking Cons., Inc., Elgin, Ill., Isaac Ray Ctr., Inc., Chgo. Trustee North Cen. Coll., Naperville; bd. dirs., pres. Naperville Elderly Homes, Inc.; mem. adv. bd. dirs. Salvation Army, Chgo. 1st lt., inf. U.S. Army, 1954-56. Mem. ABA, Ill. Bar Assn., Chgo. Bar Assn., Union League, Sky-Line Club, Cress Creek Country Club, Delta Sigma Phi (found. bd. trustees), Phi Alpha Delta. Home: 129 Springwood Dr Naperville IL 60540-7331

DESCHANEL, MARY JO, actress; b. LA, 1945; d. Donald L. and Elizabeth Ellen (Manchester) Weir; m. Caleb Deschanel, July 8, 1972; children: Emily, Zooey. BA, UCLA, 1967, teaching credential, 1973. Actor: (films) The Right Stuff, 1983, 2010, 1984, Twin Peaks: Fire Walk with Me, 1992, The Patriot, 2000, Bark!, 2002, Winter Passing, 2005, Breach, 2007, (TV films) A Winner Never Quits, 1986, Cameo by Night, 1987, (TV series) Twin Peaks, 1990-91.*

DESCHENES, ISABELLE, medical educator, researcher; b. Quebec, Can., Oct. 21, 1971; d. Michel Deschenes and Therese Ruelland; m. Fouad Doua. BS, U. Laval, Québec, Can., 1995, MS, 1996, PhD, 1999. Post-doctoral fellow Johns Hopkins U., Balt., 1999—2003; rsch. scientist MetroHealth Med. Ctr., Cleve., 2003—; asst. prof. medicine and biomed. engring. Case Western Res. U., Cleve., 2003—. Grantee, NIH, 2007—; Rsch. fellow, Heart and Stroke Found. Can., 1999—2001, Rsch. fellowship, North Am. Soc. of Pacing and Electrophysiology, 2001—03, Rsch. fellow, Fond de Recherche en Sante du Que., 2001—03. Mem.: Can. Cardiovasc. Soc., Cardiac Muscle Soc., Cardiac Electrophysiology Soc., Biophys. Soc., Heart Rhythm Soc., Am. Heart Assn. (sci. reviewer 2005, Louis N. and Arnold M. Katz Basic Sci. Rsch. prize 2003, Nat. Scientist Devel. grant, Student Presentation award 1999). Achievements include patents pending for use of a sodium channel based peptide to prevent cardiac arrhythmias. Office: Case Western Res Univ 2500 MetroHealth Dr Cleveland OH 44109 Home Phone: 216-526-6030; Office Phone: 216-778-5166. Office Fax: 216-778-1261. Business E-Mail: ideschenes@metrohealth.org.

DESCHRYVER, DAVID ALAN, lawyer; b. Mex. City, Mex., Aug. 21, 1972; s. Bruce and Margaret DeSchryver. JD, George Wash. U., Washington, 2003. Sr. policy analyst Ctr. Edn. Reform, Washington, 1996—99; mng. editor SchoolNet / The Doyle Report, Washington, 1999—2006; legis. dir. Brustein & Manasevit, Washington, 2005—. Author: Angela Dale and David DeSchryver. The Charter School Workbook: Your Roadmap to the Charter School Movement, 1997; contbr. articles to profl. jours. Office: Brustein & Manasevit 3105 South St NW Washington DC 20007 Home Phone: 202-232-3641; Office Phone: 202-965-3652.

DESCHUYTNER, EDWARD ALPHONSE, biochemist, educator; b. Chelsea, Mass., Sept. 3, 1944; s. Alphonso and Josephine Elizabeth (Kiewlicz) Deschuytner; m. Carolyn Ann McGraw, Aug. 1, 1971; children: Brian Charles Deschuytner, Matthew Edward Deschuytner. BA, Northeastern U., 1967; PhD, Boston Coll., 1972. Asst. in floriculture Waltham Exptl. Field Sta. U. Mass., 1963-64; lab. technician Mass. Soldiers Home, Chelsea, 1964-65; rsch. asst. New Eng. Med. Ctr. Hosps., Boston, 1965-67; asst. Cancer Rsch. Inst., Boston Coll., 1967-71; mem. faculty No. Essex C.C., Haverhill, Mass., 1971—2003, prof. biology, 2002—03, chmn. dept. natural scis., 1988—95, asst. dean math., sci., and tech., 1995—98, assoc. dean math., sci., techs. and health professions, 1998—2002, prof. emeritus natural scis., 2004—. Grant rev. panelist NSF, 1976—80; program coord. Eisenhower Title II Math. and Sci. Grant, 1989—98; project dir. Bell Atlantic Ed Link, 1998—99, 2000—01, Sci. Adventures for Everyone, 2000—03. Author: (software) Biology in Action series, 1983; author: (with others) (book) Princiles of Biology, 2d edit., 1986, A Study and Laboratory Guide for Anatomy and Physiology, 2d edit., 1990. Bd. dirs. Mass. Sci. Educators Hall of Fame, 2002—. Named Mass. Sci. Educator of the Yr. for Essex County, 1996, Sci. Educator of the Yr. for Essex County, 1996, Outstanding Sci. Educator of the Yr., Mass. Assn. Sci. Suprs., 1998; named to Mass. Sci. Educators Hall of Fame, 2001; recipient citation for Outstanding Performance, Commonwealth of Mass., 1991, Outstanding Svc. and Leadership award, Nat. Sci. Edn. Leadership Assn., 1998, 1999, award for Excellence in Tchg. and Leadership, Nat. Inst. Staff and Orgnl. Devel., 2003; Nat. Edn. Act fellow, Boston Coll., 1968—71, Eisenhower title II Math. and Sci. grantee, 1989—90, 1991—92, 1992—93, 1993—94, 1994—95. Mem.: AAAS, Sci. Edn. Leadership Assn., Nat. Assn. Biology Tchrs., N. Shore Sci. Suprs. Assn. (pres. 1995—96, 1996—97), Nat. Sci. Tchrs. Assn., Mass. Assn. Sci. Suprs., Mass. Assn. Sci. Tchrs., N.Y. Acad. Scis., Am. Soc. Microbiology. Office: No Essex Community Coll 100 Elliott St Haverhill MA 01830-2306 Office Phone: 978-556-3894. Business E-Mail: edeschuytner@necc.mass.edu.

DE SEAR, EDWARD MARSHALL, lawyer; b. Bradenton, Fla., Oct. 27, 1946; s. Robert Ashland and Shirley Ethelwyne (Griffin) De S.; m. Patricia Gail Healy, Aug. 8, 1970; children: Emily, Andrew. AB, Columbia Coll., 1968; JD, U. Va., 1973. Bar: NY 1974. Ptnr. Brown & Wood, NYC, 1973—82; v.p. Salomon Bros., Inc., NYC, 1982—88; ptnr. Milbank, Tweed Hadley & McCloy, NYC, 1988—93, Orrick, Herrington & Sutcliffe, LLP, NYC, 1993—2003, head structured fin. group, 1998—2003; ptnr. McKee Nelson LLP, NYC, 2003—. Mem. editl. bd.: Jour. Structured Fin., 2004—. Alumni recruiting comm. Columbia U., NYC, 1984—; bd. dirs. inMotion, Inc., NYC. Mem. ABA, Columbia Club (bd. govs. 2004—), Phi Gamma Delta. Republican. Episcopalian. Office: McKee Nelson LLP One Battery Park Plz 33d Fl New York NY 10004 Home Phone: 201-995-9268; Office Phone: 917-777-4565. Business E-Mail: edesear@mckeenelson.com.

DE SELDING, EDWARD BERTRAND, retired bank executive; b. Summit, NJ, June 15, 1926; s. Edward Fitzgerald and Alene (Rockwell) deS.; m. Joan Bulkley, Oct. 21, 1950; children: Peter, Ann, Edward Bertrand. BA, Yale, 1950. With Spencer Trask & Co., Inc., NYC, 1950-77, ptnr., 1962-68, sr. v.p., dir., 1968-77, Hornblower, Weeks, Noyes & Trask, Inc., NYC, 1977-78; 1st v.p. Loeb Rhoades, Hornblower & Co., 1978-79; v.p. Bruns, Nordeman, Rea & Co., NYC, 1979-81, Bache Halsey Stuart, Inc., 1981-82, Conn. Nat. Bank, 1982-91, ret. Served with USAAF, 1944-46. Mem.: NASD (chmn. dist. 12 com. 1971, gov. 1972), Tokeneke Club (pres. 1974—75), Sawgrass Country Club (gov., pres. 2001). Republican. Episcopalian (vestryman 1961-63, 67-69, 77-79, warden 1984-87). Home: 1000 Vicars Landing Way F-303 Ponte Vedra Beach FL 32082-3118

DE SENA, FERDINANDO, composer, educator; b. NYC, July 12, 1950; s. Carlo and Michelina De Sena; m. Laura Norkin, Jan. 26, 1994; children: Johan Gilbert, Samuel Gilbert. BA, Ithaca Coll., 1987; MusM, U. Miami, 1989, Dr. in Mus. Arts, 1994. Asst. prof., music theory and composition U. Miami, Coral Gables, 2002—, dir. electronic and computer music, 2003—. Composer: (computer music and chorus) Requiem for the Living, (computer music and flute) Elegy, (clarinet choir) Increase (n.), (chorus and string quartet) On These Restive Shores, (woodwind quintet) Midsummer Quintet. Mem.: Soc. Electroacoustic Music US, Internat. Computer Music Assn., Coll. Music Soc., Soc. Composers. Office: Frost Sch U Miami PO Box 248165 Coral Gables FL 33124-7610 Home Phone: 305-595-3352; Office Phone: 305-284-3110. E-mail: fdesena@miami.edu.

DESFORGES, DEBORAH WALN, music educator; b. Phillippi, W.Va., Nov. 27, 1951; d. Raymond Reeder Waln and Ann Luse Manning; m. Christopher Tracy Sylvester, July 14, 2001; 1 child, Christopher Douglas Sylvester. BA, W.Va. Wesleyan Coll., 1973; MusM, U. Fla., Gainesville, 1993. Cert. profl. educator State of Fla. Dept. of Edn. Music tchr. Collier County Pub. Schs., Naples, Fla., 1974—77, Sch. Bd. of Alachua County, Gainesville, Fla., 1977—. Music workshop cons. Sch. Bd. of Alachua County, Gainesville, mem. music curriculum devel. com., performing arts summer symposium co-dir., dist. liaison elem. music, 2006—; condr. honor choir Polk County Sch. Bd., Lakeland, Fla., 2002—03, Sch. Bd. of Columbia County, Lake City, Fla., 2003—05; dist. chair Arts for a Complete Edn., Gainesville; chair fine arts Glen Springs Elem., Gainesville, mem. placement rev. com., 2002—; dir. Glen Springs Summer Enrichment Program, Gainesville; yearbook editor Glen Springs Elem., Gainesville; co-chair Glen Springs com. So. Assn. of Colls. and Schs. Rev., Gainesville; coord. Glen Springs Summer Sci. Acad., Gainesville, 2004—; founder, dir. choir selected to perform with Vienna Boys Choir European Cultural Initiative for Young Generation, 2002. Author: (mus. play) Florida History Live! (grant Sch. Bd. of Alachua County), (computer program) Computerized Composer Information Retrieval System. Team capt. U.S. Tennis Assn. Women's 3.0 Team, Gainesville, 2000—01; founder, artistic dir. Gainesville (Fla.) Youth Chorus, Inc., 1994—; mem. worship com. 1st Presbyn. Ch., Gainesville; choir mem. 1st Presbyn. Ch. Chancel Choir, Gainesville. Named Outstanding Vol. in the Arts, City of Gainesville Cultural Affairs Bd., 2002. Mem.: NEA, Fla. Elem. Music Educators Assn. (bd. dirs., dist. chair), Alachua County Educators Assn., Am. Choral Dirs. Assn., Music Educators Nat. Conf., DB Racquet Club, Alpha Phi Gamma, Alpha Gamma Delta. Avocations: tennis, singing, gardening, photography, travel. Office: 2826 NW 31st Ave Gainesville FL 32605 Home Phone: 352-335-7327; Office Phone: 352-955-6708. E-mail: desfordw@sbac.edu.

DESFORGES, JANE FAY, retired internist, hematologist, educator; b. Melrose, Mass., Dec. 18, 1921; d. Joseph Henry and Alics Maher (Fay) Desforges; m. Gerard Desforges, Sept. 11, 1948; children: Gerard Joseph, Jane Alice. BA cum laude (Durant scholar), Wellesley Coll., 1942; MD cum laude, Tufts U., 1945; ScD (hon.), Holy Cross Coll., 1990. Diplomate Am. Bd. Internal Medicine, Am. Bd. Hematology. Intern in pathology Mt. Auburn Hosp., Cambridge, Mass., 1945—46; intern in medicine Boston City Hosp., 1946—47, resident in medicine, then chief resident, 1948—50; USPHS rsch. fellow in hematology Salt Lake Gen. Hosp., Salt Lake City, 1946—47; rsch. fellow in hematology hosp. Thorndike Lab., 1950—52; physician-in-charge RH lab., 1952—53; faculty Tufts U. Med. Sch., 1952—72, prof. medicine, 1972—92, disting. prof., 1992—94, prof. emerita, 1994—; asst. dir. Tufts Med. Svc., Boston City Hosp., 1952—67; assoc. dir. Tufts Med. Svc., 1967—68, acting dir., physician in charge, 1968—73, dir., 1968—69; ret., 1999. Sr. physician in hematology New Eng. Med. Ctr. Hosp., Boston, 1973—, rsch. assoc. blood resch. lab, 1973—92; attending physician VA Hosp., Jamaica Plain; cons. in hematology to various area hosps., 1955—72. Assoc. editor New Eng. Jour. Medicine, 1960—93, mem. editl. bd. Blood, 1976—79; contbr. numerous articles to med. jours. Bd. dirs. Med. Found., Inc., 1976—82; bd. trustees Boston Med. Libr., 1977—81; chmn. automation in med. lab. scis. rev. com. Nat. Inst. Gen. Med. Scis., 1974—76; chmn. consensus com. of infectious disease testing for blood transfusions NIH, 1995—96; mem. subcom. on hematology Am. Bd. Internal Medicine, 1976—82, bd. dirs., 1980—88, exec. com., 1984—88; chmn. blood diseases and resources adv. com. Nat. Heart, Lung and Blood Inst., 1978—81. Named to Internat. Women in Medicine Hall of Fame, Am. Med. Women's Assn., 2003; recipient Disting. Alumna award, Wellesley Coll., 1981; grantee NIH, 1955—88. Fellow: AAAS; mem.: Inst. Medicine, Am. Assn. Physicians, N.Y. Acad. Scis., Mass. Med. Soc. (mem. publs. com. 1995—99, Lifetime Achievement award 2001), Internat. Soc. Hematology, Am. Soc. Hematology (exec. com. 1975—78, adv. bd. 1980—82, v.p. 1982—83, pres. 1984—85), Am. Soc. Clin. Pathology, Am. Fedn. Clin. Rsch., ACP (chmn. med. knowledge self assessment program IX 1989—92, Master 1983, Disting. Tchr. award 1987), Alpha Omega Alpha (Outstanding Tchr. award 1994), Phi Beta Kappa. Home: 49 Lake Ave Melrose MA 02176-2701

DESHAZER, JAMES ARTHUR, biological engineer, educator, research administrator; b. Wash., July 18, 1938; s. Grant Arthur and Velma DeShazer; m. Alice Marie DeShazer, Apr. 5, 1969; children: Jean Marie, David James. BS in Agr., U. Md., Coll. Pk., 1960, BSME, 1961; MS, Rutgers U., New Brunswick, NJ, 1963; PhD, N.C. State U., Raleigh, 1967. Profl. engr., Idaho, Nebr. Assoc. prof. U. Nebr., Lincoln, 1967-75, prof., 1975-91, asst. dean, 1988-89; head agrl. engring. dept. U. Idaho, Moscow, 1991-95, head biol. and agrl. engring. dept., 1995—2001. Chair animal care and use com. U. Nebr. , 1989—90; program coord. North Cen. Sustainable Agrl., Washington, 1988—89; nat. chair Modeling Responses of Swine CSRS, Washington, 1989-90, Sys. Approach to Poultry Prodn.-CSRS, Washington, 1990-91; dir. Idaho Rsch. Found., 1996—2001. Editor procs. Optics in Agr., 1990, Optics in Agr. & Forestry, 1992, Optics in Agr., Forestry & Biol. Processing, 1994, Optics in Agr., Forestry & Biol. Processing II, 1996, Precision Agriculture and Biological Quality, 1998, vol. II, 2000; contbr. chpt. in book. Trustee ASAE Found., 1996—2002; biol. and agr. engring. adv. bd. N.C. State U., 2002—04. Recipient Livestock Svc. award Walnut Grove, Iowa, 1988. Fellow: Am. Soc. Agrl. Engrs. (chair 1984—94, nat. medal 1979); mem.: NSPE (chpt. chair 1986—87, 1993—94, bd. dirs. 1994—2001, state pres. 1998—99, Young Engring. award 1974), Internat. Soc. Biometeorology, Am. Soc. Engring. Edn. (chair 1993—94), Lions (chpt. dir. 1995—97, 2002—04, club v.p. 2005—07, club pres. 2007—, Lion of Yr. 2004—05), Alpha Gamma Rho (alumni bd. dirs. 1993—99, Alum of Yr. 2006). Home: 819 Nylarol St Moscow ID 83843-9313 Office: Biol & Agr Engring Dept Univ Idaho Moscow ID 83844-0904 Office Phone: 208-885-6182. Business E-Mail: Jades@uidaho.edu.

DE-SHAZO, RICHARD DENSON, medical educator, academic administrator; b. Birmingham, Ala., Apr. 4, 1945; s. Hyman Denson and Agnes L. (Carr) de S.; m. Gloria L. Jenkins, June 4, 1967; children: Melanie, Mollie, Matthew. BA in Chemistry, Religion, Birmingham So. Coll., 1967; MD, U. Ala., 1971. Diplomate Am. Bd. Internal Medicine, Am. Bd. Allergy and Immunology, Am. Bd. Rheumatology, Am. Bd. Geriatrics, Nat. Bd. Med. Examiners. Lt. col. U.S. Army Med. Corp., 1972-80; intern in pediat. Children's and Univ. Hosp., Birmingham, 1971-72; resident in internal medicine Walter Reed Army Med. Ctr., Washington, 1972-74, fellow in immunology, microbiology, 1974-75, fellow in clin. immunology, 1975-77; clin. asst. prof. medicine U. Colo. Sch. Med., Denver, 1977-78; asst. prof. medicine and pediatrics Uniformed Svcs. Univ. Health Scis., Bethesda, Md., 1978-80; assoc. prof. medicine and pediat. Tulane U. Sch. Medicine, New Orleans, 1980-85, prof. medicine and pediat., 1985-89; prof., chmn. dept. medicine U. South Ala. Coll. Medicine, Mobile, 1989-97; prof. medicine and pediat., chmn. dept. medicine U. Miss. Med. Ctr., Jackson, 1997—, Billy Guyton disting. prof. medicine and pediat., 2004—. Clin. immunologist Fitzsimmons Army Med. Ctr., Denver, 1977-78; staff attending internal medicine, asst. chief, clin. immunologist, dir. lab. exptl. immunology, allergy, clin. immunology Svc. Walter Reed Army Med. Ctr., Washington, 1978-80; staff internist S.E. Cmty. Hosp., Washington, 1978-80; chief allergy and rheumatology dept. pediat. Tulane U. Sch. Med., New Orleans, 1980-85, adj. assoc. prof. microbiology, 1983-85, dir. rsch. and clin. ops. dept. medicine, 1985-89, dir. immunology program AIDS clin. trials unit, 1987-89; attending physician VA and U. Hosps., New Orleans, 1980-89, St. Jude Hosp., Kenner, La., 1987-89; mem. Nat. Sci. Adv. Com. on AIDS, NIH, 1987-91, study sect. on epidemiology of AIDS, 1987-91, AIDS clin. trials group, 1987-89, reviewers res., 1990-94; chief clin. immunology and allergy VA med. Ctr. New Orleans, 1985-89, assoc. chief staff edn., 1988-89; dir. tng. program internal medicine, v.p. health svcs. found., chief divsn. allergy depts. medicine and pediat., mem. various com. U. South Ala. Hosps. and Clinics, Mobile, 1989-97; chief clin. immunology, allergy and rheumatology dept. medicine VA Med. Ctr., Biloxi, Miss., 1989-97; mem. expert panel allergenic products FDA, 1991-96; asst. clin. coord. Health Care Financing Agy. coop. cardiovasc. project Ala. Quality Assurance Found, Birmingham, 1993-94, bd. dirs., 1994-95, fin. and planning com., 1995-96; pres. UMC Faculty Practice Plan, 2001-; guest prof. Children's Hosp. Kansas City, St. Louis U. Med. Sch., Walter Reed and Brooke Army Med. Ctr., Nat. Jewish Hosp., U. South Fla., U. Tex. Med. Br. at Galveston, Houston, Boston U., others; presenter in field. Assoc. editor, editl. bd. So. Med. Jour., 1995—, Am. J. Med., 2005-; mem. editl. bd. Jour. Allergy and Clin. Immunology, 1986-89, Postgrad. Medicine, 1986-94, Jour. Investigational Allergology and Clin. Immunology, 1987-93, Am. Jour. Med. Scis., 1989—, Annals of Allergy, 1991-96, Clin. Immunotherapeutics, 1993-99; contbr. 25 chpts. to books, over 110 articles to profl. jours. Elder Cumberland Presbyn. Ch., 1986-89; mem. adminstrv. bd. Christ United Meth. Ch., Mobile, 1990-97, chmn., 1993-96, chmn. coun. on ministries 1993-95; bd. dirs. Leadership Mobile, 1994-97; bd. stewards Galloway United Meth. Ch., 1999-2002, Mission MS, 1999-; bd. adv. Millsaps Coll. Sch. Bus., 1999-. Optimist Club scholar, 1963-67; Caduceus Club Travel fellow St. George Hosp. Med. Sch., London, 1970; grantee NIH, 1981-89, NIAID, 1985-88, Cancer Assn. New Orleans, 1982, 83, La. Lung Trust, 1982, 83, others; recipient Armed Forces Meritorious Svc. medal, 1980, Cert. Merit Cmty. Svc., City New Orleans, 1983. Fellow ACP (program com. 1993-95), Am. Coll. Rheumatology, Am. Coll. Chest Physicians, Am. Acad. Allergy, Asthma and Immunology (program and workshop com. 1985, chmn. 1986, grad. edn. com. 1988-89, allergy and immunology program dirs. assn. 1989-2005, standing com. fellowship programs 1990-97, standing com. immunology in med. schs. 1993, chmn. primer adv. com. 1992-93, co-chair com. on allergy in VA Med. Ctr. 1995-96, chair com. med. sch. 1994, Young Investigators award, 1979, Special Svc. award, 1993, 1996, 2006), Am. Coll. Allergy, Asthma, Immunology (editl. bd. 1995, Bernard Burman Lectureship 2002), Am. Thoracic Soc. (program and workshop com. 1986-87, sec.-treas. 1987, nat. program com. 1988-90, vice-chmn. 1989, chmn. 1989, chair sect. immunology 1992), So. Med. Assn. (Morton Rsch. medal, 2004); mem. AMA (editor Primer on Allergy 1994), Am. Assn. Immunology, Clin. Immunology Soc. So. Med. Assn., Am. Assn. Med. Colls. (coun. acad. socs. 1994—), Am. Fedn. Clin. Rsch. (coun. so. sect. 1984-87, 93), Assn. Profs. Medicine (bd. dirs. 1995—2004, nat. manpower com. 1994-96, pres. 2001), Am. Bd. Med. Specialists (coun. bd. reps. and adminstrn. 1996-99), 2 Carnival Orgns., Am. Bd. Internal Medicine (bd. dirs. 2000-04), So. Soc. Clin. Investigation (pres. 2001, Founder's medal 2004), Am. Bd. Allergy-Immunology (bd. dirs. 1995-2004, sec., 2003). Avocations: gardening, swimming, youth work, writing. Office: U Miss Med Ctr Dept Internal Medicine 2500 N State St Jackson MS 39216-4105 Office Phone: 601-984-5600. Business E-Mail: rdeshazo@medicine.umsmed.edu.

DESHMUKH, OM DADAJI, electrical engineer, researcher; b. India; s. Dadaji Balwantrao and Prabha Dadaji Deshmukh; m. Lavanya Muthukumar; 1 child, Devdatt Om. B Engring., Birla Inst. Tech. and Sci., Pilani, Rajasthan, India, 1999; MS, Boston U., 2001; PhD, U. Md., College Park, 2006. Grad. rsch. asst. U. Md., 2001—06, postdoctoral rsch. assoc., 2006—. Royster Student scholar, Acoustical Soc. Am., 2005. Office: U Md Dept Elec and Computer Engring A V Williams Bldg College Park MD 20742

DESHMUKH, VENKATESH SURESH, education educator; b. Mumbai, Maharashtra, India, Jan. 8, 1971; s. Suresh Dattatraya and Renu Suresh Deshmukh; m. Deepali Damle, Dec. 17, 1999. PhD, Auburn U., Ala., 2000. Post-doctoral fellow U. Alaska, Fairbanks, Alaska, 2002—04; asst. prof. Villanova U., Pa., 2005—. Rsch. asst. U. Oxford, 2000—02. Home: 513 Monroe Blvd King Of Prussia PA 19406 Office: Villanova Univ 800 E Lancaster Ave Villanova PA 19085 Home Phone: 610-265-4974; Office Phone: 610-519-4949. Personal E-mail: badak2001@yahoo.com. Business E-Mail: venkatesh.deshmukh@villanova.edu.

DESHPANDE, NILENDRA GANESH, physics professor; b. Karachi, Pakistan, Apr. 18, 1938; came to U.S., 1961; s. Ganesh V. and Myna G. (Junnarkar) D.; m. Kanchan S. Karnik, May 15, 1960; children: Pranay N., Rahul N. BS with honors, U. Madras, India, 1959, MA in Physics, 1960, MS in Physics, 1961; PhD, U. Pa., 1965. Asst. prof. physics Northwestern U., Evanston, Ill., 1967-73; assoc. prof U. Tex., Austin, 1973-75, U. Oreg., Eugene, 1975-83, prof., 1983—, head dept. physics, 1992-98, dir. Inst. Theoretical Sci., 1987-92, assoc. dean scis., 1998—2001. Contbr. articles to profl. jours. Named Outstanding Jr. Investigator, U.S. Dept. Energy, 1981-86; prin. investigator High Energy Physics Grant, U.S. Dept. Energy, 1981—. Fellow Am. Phys. Soc. (organizer annual meeting div. particles and fields 1985), Sigma Xi. Office: U Oreg Inst Theoretical Sci Eugene OR 97403 Home Phone: 541-344-9152; Office Phone: 541-346-5204. Business E-Mail: desh@uoregon.edu.

DESHPANDÉ, ROHIT, business educator; b. Bombay, Dec. 7, 1951; came to U.S., 1973; s. Prabhakar and Vimala (Waglé) D.; m. Rebecca Schorin, Dec. 29, 1979; children: Jay Alexander, Neil Benjamin. BSc, U. Bombay, 1971, MMS, 1973; MBA, Northwestern U., Evanston, 1975; PhD, U. Pitts., 1979; MA (hon.), Dartmouth Coll., 1993, Harvard U., 2000. Asst. and assoc. prof. mktg. U. Tex., Austin, 1979-87; assoc. prof. mktg. Dartmouth Coll., Hanover, 1987-89, prof., 1989-93, E.B. Osborn prof. mktg., 1993-97; prof. Harvard Bus. Sch., Cambridge, Mass., 1997-98, Sebastian S. Kresge prof. mktg., 1998—. Thomas Henry Carroll Ford Found. vis. prof. bus. adminstrn. Harvard Bus. Sch., 1993, chmn. strategic mktg. mgmt. program, 2001-06; co-chmn., chief mktg. officer Summit at HBS; vis. scholar and vis. prof. Stanford Bus. Sch., 1994, 96; exec. dir. Mktg. Sci. Inst., 1997-99, mem. exec. dirs. coun., 1999—; mem. adv. coun. David Rockefeller Ctr. L.Am. Studies, Harvard U., 2000—. Author/editor: Developing a Market Orientation, 1999, Using Market Knowledge, 2001, The Global Market, 2004; mem. editl. bd. Jour. Mktg., Jour. Mktg. Rsch.; contbr. articles to profl. jours. Recipient Jack Taylor Teaching Excellence award. Fellow (consortium) Am. Mktg. Assn. (bd. dir. 2006—); mem. Assn. Consumer Rsch., Am. Sociol. Assn., Omicron Delta Kappa, Beta Alpha Phi. Office: Harvard Bus Sch Boston MA 02163

DESIATO, MICHAEL, editor-in-chief; b. Rochester, NY, Dec. 9, 1955; s. Nicholas and Jenny Desiato; m. Lauren Desiato, Nov. 5, 1983; 1 child, Anthony. BSJ, Ohio U., 1977; postgrad., NYU. With Real Estate Forum, NYC, 1978—, editor-in-chief, now group mng dir; also pub. dir. Real

Estate N.Y.; editl. dir. Globest.com. Mem. Nat. Assn. Real Estate Editors (bd. dirs., pres.). Office: Real Estate Forum 520 Eighth Ave 17th Fl New York NY 10018 Office Phone: 212-929-6900. E-mail: mdesiato@remedianetwork.com.

DESIDERIO, DOMINIC MORSE, JR., chemistry and neurochemistry professor; b. McKees Rocks, Pa., Jan. 11, 1941; s. Dominic Morse and Jewell Aline (Hull) D.; m. Julie Marie Thomas, Oct. 9, 1965; children—Annette Marie, Dominic Michael. BA, U. Pitts., 1961; MS, MIT, 1964, PhD, 1965. Organic control chemist Pitts. Coke and Chem. Co., 1958-60; research chemist U. Pitts., 1960-61; teaching asst. MIT, Cambridge, 1961-62, research asst., 1962-65; research chemist Am. Cyanamid Co., Stamford, Conn., 1966-67; asst. prof. chemistry Baylor Coll. Medicine, Houston, 1967-71, assoc. prof. chemistry and biochemistry, 1971-78; prof. neurology (chemistry) and molecular scis., dir. U. Tenn., Memphis, 1978—. Exch. student Internat. Assn. Exch. Students for Tech. Experience; polymer chemist Badische Anilin and Sodafabrik, Germany, summer 1962. Author and editor of books, chpts. in books and articles including Analysis of Neuropeptides by Liquid Chromatography and Mass Spectrometry, 1984, Mass Spectrometry of Peptides, 1990, Mass Spectrometry: Clinical and Biomedical Applications, vol. I, 1992, vol. II, 1994; co-editor (book series) Mass Spectrometry, 1997—; editor Mass. Spectrometry Rev., 1993—. Recipient 1st Ann. Internat. award Mass Spectrometry in Biochemistry and Medicine, Alghero, Italy, 1975; Intra-Sci. Research Found. fellow, 1971-75 Mem. Am. Soc. Biol. Chemistry, Am. Chem. Soc., Am. Soc. Mass Spectrometry, AAAS, Soc. for Neurosci., Memphis Neurosci. Soc. (pres, 1984-85), NIH (Metallobiochemistry study sect. 1985-89). Avocations: reading, amateur radio, fishing, travel. Office: U Tenn Health Sci Ctr Stout Neurosci Mass Spectrom Lab 847 Madison Ave Rm 117 Memphis TN 38163-0001 Home Phone: 901-683-2753. Business E-Mail: ddesiderio@utmem.edu.

DESILETS, ALICIA R., pharmacist, educator; b. Nashua, NH, Sept. 30, 1979; d. Brian W. and Nancy J. Desilets. PharmD, U. Conn., Storrs, 2004. Pharmacist CVS Pharmacy, Derry, NH, 2004—; asst. prof. pharmacy practice MCPHS, Manchester, NH, 2005—. Spkr. Pfizer Inc., NH, 2006—. Mem.: NH Pharmacist Assn. (bd. dirs. 2006—). Home Phone: 603-548-3766; Office Phone: 603-314-1711.

DESILVA, ALAN W., physics professor, researcher; b. LA, Feb. 8, 1932; s. Woodruff and Dorothy Belle (Cole) DeS.; m. Mochiko Yokoyama, July 27, 1959; children: Audrey Hope, Eric Woodruff, Eliot Gen. MS, UCLA, 1954; PhD, U. Calif., Berkeley, 1961. NSF postdoctoral rsch. fellow The Culham Lab., Abingdon, Berkshire, Eng., 1962-64; asst. prof. physics U. Md., College Park, 1964-68, assoc. prof., 1968-74, prof., 1974-97, prof. emeritus, 1997—. Cons. Los Alamos Nat. Lab., 1963-81, U.S. Naval Rsch. Lab., Washington, 1973-90. Contbr. over 30 articles to sci. jours. With U.S. Army, 1954-56. Recipient sr. U.S. scientist award Alexander von Humboldt Found., Ruhr U., Bochum, Fed. Republic Germany, 1984-85. Fellow AAAS, Am. Phys. Soc. Achievements include devel. of light scattering as a plasma diagnostic, light scattering observations of plasmas; rsch. on shock waves in plasmas and transport in strongly coupled plasmas. Office: U Md Inst Rsch Electronics/Applied Physics College Park MD 20742-0001 Office Phone: 301-405-4958.

DESILVEY, DENNIS LEE, cardiologist, educator, academic administrator; b. May 17, 1942; m. Kathleen Selkirk, Aug. 28, 1965; children: Ethan Selkirk, Caitlin O'Brian, Sarah Candace Shaw. BA in History and Religion magna cum laude, Yale U., 1964; MD, Columbia U., 1968. Lic. Vt., Va., Maine; cert. Advanced Trauma Life Support instr. Intern medicine Cornell Med. Ctr., NYC, 1968-69, resident medicine, 1969-71, resident medicine, cardiology, 1971; chief med. resident medicine North Shore U. Hosp., Manhasset, NY, 1972-73, instr. medicine, 1972-73; mem. staff Rancocas Valley Hosp., Willingboro, NJ, 1973-75; cardiologist Brachfeld Med. Assocs., Willingboro, NJ, 1974-75, Castleton (Vt.) Med. Assocs., 1975-77; attending physician Rutland Regional Med. Ctr., Rutland, Vt., 1975-92; pvt. practice Rutland, Vt., 1977-92; adj. asst. prof. clin. medicine Dartmouth Hitchcock Med. Ctr., Hanover, NH, 1979-92; asst. prof. medicine U. Vt., Burlington, 1983-92; mem. staff Dwight David Eisenhower Med. Ctr., Ft. Gordon, Ga., 1991; dir. ambulatory cardiology, dir. cardiology consult svc., mem. clin. faculty cardiovascular divsn., dept. medicine Health Scis. Ctr. U. Va., Charlottesville, 1992—2001, assoc. prof. medicine Health Scis. Ctr., 1992—. Cons. Southwestern Vt. Med. Ctr., Bennington, 1986—, Keller U.S. Army Hosp., West Point, NY, 1985—, internal medicine Veteran Affairs Med. Ctr., Salem, Va., 1993—, Consultants in Cardiology, Lexington, Va., 2001-05, Waldo CU Medicine, Belfast, Maine, 2005—; critical care com. Rutland Regional Med. Ctr., pharmacy and therapeutics com., investigational review bd., ethics com.; mem. pharmacy and therapeutics com. Health Scis. Ctr. U. Va., nutrition com., health care evaluation com., ambulatory policy com.; bd. dirs., profl. affairs com., bylaws com. Blue Cross/Blue Shield Vt.; bd. dirs., founding mem. Vt. Cardiac Network; presenter New Eng. regional meeting Am. Coll. Physicians, Hanover, N.H., 1976, Advanced Concepts Shock and Trauma, Woodstock (Vt.) Inn, 1982; dir. ACLS Tng. Ctr.; chmn. Resolution Com. Contbr. articles to profl. jours. Med. advisor skiing svcs. Killington Ski Area, 1975-92, Smokey House Found., 1975-80, Farm and Wilderness Camps, 1975-85; steering com. Vt. Med. Practice Variation Assessment Program, 1988; cardiology study sect. Vt. Program Quality Care, 1988-92, Vt. Gov.'s Coun. Phys. Fitness, 1985-88; vestry Trinity Episcopal Ch., 1986-89; bd. dirs. Vermont Diabetes Assn., 1975-79, Rutland Mental Health Svc., 1975-82, Rutland Area Vis. Nurses Assn., 1975-77, chmn. profl. affairs com., mem. utilization review com.; bd. dirs. Barstow Sch., 1986-90; town health officer Wallingford, Vt., 1975-80. Maj. U.S. Army, 1973-75; col. USAR, 1985—. Decorated Nat. Def. Svc. medal, Reserve Achievement medal, Army Commendation medal; recipient Physician Recognition award Am. Med. Assn., Exceptional Svc. award, Spiritual Aims award Kiwanis Club Am., 1983, U. Va. Pres.'s Report award, 1992. Fellow Am. Coll. Physicians, Am. Coll. Cardiology, N.Am. Soc. Pacing and Electrophysiology; mem. Am. Heart Assn. (ACLS instr., BCLS instr., nat. faculty ACLS Vt., mem. mil. tng. network ACLS, Advanced Trauma Life Support; bd. dirs. 1978-80, bd. dirs., at large appointee 1988-93, agenda planning com. 1986-89, affiliate relations com. 1986-88, sci. pub. com. 1989-93, "heart and stroke" planning com. 1989-90, participant edn. and inf. group heart guide consumer health and info. program, 1989-91, chmn. task force mission to elderly 1989-90; v.p.-elect New Eng. region 1986-87, regional v.p. 1987-88, fellow coun. clin. cardiology, bd. dirs. Charlottesville divsn. 1992—, bd. dirs. Va. affiliate 1992—, bd. dirs. Rutland, Vt. divsn. 1986-92, program coun. 1986-92, bd. dirs. Vt. affiliate 1975-92, exec. com. 1978-92, pres.-elect 1982-83, pres. 1983-85, co-chair capital campaign 1988-90, nominating com. 1984-86, cardiac rehab. com. 1982-85, program coun. 1978-90, ACLS com. 1978-90, cardiac critical care com. 1978-82, hypertension com. 1975-82, chmn. emergency cardiac care com. region V 1976-80, bd. dirs. N.J. affiliate 1973-75, BCLS com. 1973-75, mem. greater N.Y. affiliate 1966-72, BCLS instr. 1968-72, del. N.E. regional heart com. 1985-91, reaffiliation com. 1987-89, nominating com. 1987-88, Pysician of Yr. award 1992), Am. Soc. Echocardiology, N.Y. Acad. Scis., Vt. Cardiac Network (vice chmn. 1982-86), Phi Beta Kappa. Avocations: bicycling, running, cross country skiing, hiking, mountain climbing, theology. Office: Waldo Cardiovasc Medicine PO Box 287 116 Northport Ave 218 Belfast ME 04915 Home: 68 Court St Belfast ME 04915 Office Phone: 207-338-1838. E-mail: ddesilvey@wchi.com.

DESIMONE, JOSEPH M., chemist, educator; b. May 16, 1964; m. Suzanne, 1986; children: Philip, Emily. BS in Chemistry, Ursinus Coll., 1986, doctorate (hon.) in Sci., 1999; PhD in Chemistry, Va. Poly. State U., 1990. Rsch. tech. Pennwalt Corp., King of Prussia, Pa., 1986; asst. prof. chemistry U. N.C., Chapel Hill, 1990-94, Mary Ann Smith assoc. prof., 1995—, Mary Ann Smith prof., 1996—99, William R. Kenan Jr. disting. prof. chemistry, 1999—, dir. inst. advanced materials, 2003—; William R. Kenan Jr. disting. prof. chem. engring. NCSU, 1999—. Co-dir. Kenan Ctr. Utilization of CO2 in Mfg., 1997—99; dir. sci. and tech ctr. environmentally responsible solvents and processes NSF, 1999—; co-founder, mem. sci. advisory bd. BioStent; co-founder, chmn. MICELL Technologies, Inc.; mem. bd. trustees Ursinus Coll., 2001—; mem. adv. coun. dept. chemistry Va. Tech., 2001—; mem. nat. rsch. coun. bd. chem. scis. and tech., 2000—. Editl. bd. Jour. Applied Polymer Sci., 1992-99, Trends in Polymer Sci., 1993-94, High Performance Polymers, 1994-99, Jour. Polymer Sci, 1999-, Macromolecules, 2001-03, Indsl. and Engring. Chemistry Rsch., 2000-03; contbr. articles to profl. jours. Recipient Charles H. Stone award 1995, Entrepreneur of Yr. in Technology award Ernst & Young, 2001, Engring. Excellence award DuPont, 2002, John Scott award City Trusts Phila., 2002; NSF young investigator, 1992; fellow Bell Comms., 1989-90, Lord Corp., 1988-89. Mem. AAAS, NAE, Am. Chem. Soc. (Wallace H. Carothers award 2002, award Creative Invention 2005), Soc. Advancement of Material and Process Engring., Sigma Xi., Phi Lambda Upsilon. Achievements include patents in field. Office: U NC Dept Chemistry Venable Hall 300 Chapel Hill NC 27599-0001 Fax: 919-962-5467. Business E-Mail: desimone@unc.edu.

DESIO, DELORES JEAN, writer, artist, retired elementary school educator; b. Detroit, May 20, 1933; d. Thomas Matthew Lannie and Anne Charlotte Zambon; m. Anthony William Desio, June 27, 1959; children: Douglas Anthony, Darcy Desio Rouse. BS in Fine Arts and Art Edn., Wayne State U., Detroit, 1955. Life credential tchg. Calif. Art educator Clawson City Schs., Mich., 1955—56; elem. tchr. Redondo Beach Schs., Calif., 1956—57; tchr. Inglewood Schs., Calif., 1957—59, Palo Alto (Unified Schs., Palo Alto, 1959—63, Cupertino Schs., Los Altos, 1963—65, St. John's Sch., Encinitas, 1979—85; art tchr. St. Patrick's Sch., Carlsbad, 1986—87; owner, writer, illustrator Primo Publs. Trustee Interfaith Shelter Network Homeless, San Diego, 1992—, Nev. Mus. Art, Reno, 2000—06; ret., 2006. Author: Rescue of the Gem Children, 1999, Up a Tree with Mary McPhee, 2006; Distinctly Duck, 2003, periodicals. Prin. Anthony and Delores J. Desio Found., 1998—. Recipient Christian Unity award, Ecumenical Coun. of San Diego, 1995. Personal E-mail: deloresdco@aol.com.

DESIREE, LAURA, dancer; Studied with, Natalia Clare; student, Joffrey Ballet Sch. Former mem. Joffrey Ballet Concert Group; mem. Pitts. Ballet Theatre, 1982—, 1st soloist, 1986, prin. dancer, 1990. Originated role of Jordan Baker in Prokovksy's The Great Gatsby. Office: Pitts Ballet Theatre 2900 Liberty Ave Pittsburgh PA 15201-1511

DESJARDINS, CLAUDE, physiologist, dean; b. Fall River, Mass., June 13, 1938; s. Armand Louis and Marguerite Jean (Mercier) D.; m. Jane Elizabeth Campbell, June 30, 1962; children: Douglas, Mark, Anne. BS, U. R.I., 1960; MS, Mich. State U., 1964, PhD, 1967. Asst. prof. dept. physiology Okla. State U., Stillwater, 1968-69, assoc. prof., 1969-72; assoc. prof. physiology U. Tex., Austin, 1970-75; prof. physiology Inst. Reproductive Biology, Patterson Labs., 1975-86, U. Va. Med. Sch., Charlottesville, 1987-96, dir. Ctr. Rsch. Reprodn., 1990-96; prof. physiology and biophysics, sr. assoc. dean Med. Coll., U. Ill., Chgo., 1996—, dean, dir. program for rsch. in acad. medicine and clin. scholar project, 2005—. Mem. Ctr. for Advanced Studies, 1986; cons. NIH, ASA, VA, FDA. Author: Cell and Molecular Biology of the Testis, 1993, Molecular Physiology of Testicular Cells, 1996; editor-in-chief Am. Jour. physiology: Endocrinology and Metabolism, 1991-95; editor-in-chief Jour. Andrology, 1989-91, Ency. of Reprodn., 1997-98; mem. editl. bd. Biology Reprodn., Endocrinology; contbr. articles to profl. jours.; patentee techs. for male contraception, mechanisms of peptide hormone transport in the microcirculation and ligand-dependent and ligand ind. action of steroid hormones in peripheral vasculature. Fellow The Jackson Lab., Bar Harbor, Maine, 1967, NIH Sr. fellow U. Va. Med. Sch., 1983-84, Danforth Found. fellow, 1960; Cornell U. fellow, 2004-05; C.F. Wilcox Found. scholar, 1958. Mem. Am. Physiol. Soc., Soc. Neurosci., Soc. Study Reprodn. (pres. 1982-83), Endocrine Soc., Am. Soc. Cell Biology, The Microcirculatory Soc. Office: U Ill at Chgo Coll Medicine M/C 955 820 S Wood St Chicago IL 60612-4325 Office Phone: 312-355-0916. Business E-Mail: clauded@uic.edu.

DESJARDINS, RAOUL, medical association administrator, financial consultant; b. Montreal, Quebec, Can., Oct. 8, 1933; came to U.S., 1962; s. Elso and Blanche (Lemieux) D.; m. Regina Turgeon, Oct. 10, 1961; children: Bryan-Claude, John Andrew. BA, U. Montreal, 1953, MD, 1958; MS, Baylor U., 1964, PhD, 1966; MBA, Rutgers U., 1990. Diplomate Am. Bd. Medicine. Chief intern, resident St. Joan of Arc Hosp., Montreal, 1958-59; med. dir. Candiac (Can.) Med. Clinic, 1953-62, Ortho Research Found., Raritan, NJ, 1966-72; pres. Raoul Desjardins Assocs. Inc., Mendham, NJ, 1972-83, Research Cons. Inc., Mendham, 1983—, APG Internat., Inc., 1991—. Med. dirs. Iroquois Class Co., Candiac, 1959-62; asst. prof. Hahnemann Hosp. and U., Phila., 1976-80; bd. govs. Internat. Medicines Exch. and Devel., Georgetown, Ga., 1986—; chmn. bd. advisors Fed. Inst. Health, 1991—; chmn. bd. govs. Grand Masters Found., 1989—. Prodr. video: The Apgram: A New Tool to Measure Cardiovascular Performance, 1995. Recipient physician's recognition award AMA, 1969. Fellow: N.Y. Acad. Medicine, Am. Coll. Clin. Pharmacology, The Royal Soc. Health, Am. Coll. Angiology; mem.: Petroleum Club Houston, Doctors Club, Met. Club (membership com. 1991—), Med. Execs. Club, Beta Gamma Omega, Sigma Xi. Roman Catholic. Avocations: safaris, history. Office: Fed Inst Health 35 Stonecroft Pl The Woodlands TX 77381-5226 Office Phone: 281-298-9205. E-mail: doctord@fih.ky.

DES JARDINS, TRACI, chef, restaurant owner; b. Calif. Student, U. Calif., Santa Cruz. Formerly mem. staff 7th St. Bistro, LA; former apprentice Michel and Pierre Troisgros, Lucas Carton, Alain Ducasse, Alain Passard, France; former mem. staff Montrachet, NYC; former chef de cuisine Patina, Calif.; former chef Aqua, San Francisco, Elka, San Francisco; exec. chef Rubicon, San Francisco, 1993—97; ptnr., chef Jardiniere, San Francisco, 1997—. Environ. activist. Named Rising Star Chef of Yr., James Beard Found., Best Chef: Pacific, 2007, Chef of Yr., San Francisco Mag.; named one of Best New Chefs, Food & Wine Mag., Top 3 Chefs in Bay Area, San Francisco Chronicle. Office: Jardiniere 300 Grove St San Francisco CA 94102*

DESLOGE, CHRISTOPHER DAVIS, SR., real estate company, merchant banking and consulting executive; b. St. Louis, July 23, 1958; s. William Livingston and Loriel Martens (Johnson) D.; m. Mary Roberta Dubuque, May 22, 1981; children: William Livingston II, Christopher Davis Jr., Raymond Amadee Dubuque. Student, Drake U., 1977-79, Maryville Coll., 1979-80. V.p. Follman Properties, St. Louis, 1982-85; leasing mgr. Paragon Group, St. Louis, 1985-86; pres. Desloge Co., St. Louis, 1986-90; v.p. Hilliker Corp., St. Louis, 1990-92; pres. Braeburn Ptnrs., St. Louis, 1992-96; account mgr. Maritz, Stamford, Conn., 1996-98; owner Desloge Consol. Lead Co., LLC, 2001—. Pvt. investments arbitrator BBB, St. Louis, 1991—; owner Tenant Rep Agy., LLC, 2006-. Author: Tenant's Guerilla Guide to Office Leasing, 2004, Entrepreneurial Spirit, Corporate Precision, 2005; contbg. editor: St. Louis Bus. Jour., 1986—94. Mem. Real Estate Bd. Met. St. Louis, 1982—93; bd. dirs. St. Louis Psychoanalytic Inst., 1988—91, Internat. Tenant Representation Alliance, St. Louis, 1992—94, Ctr. Head Injury Svcs., 1994—96; co-chmn. disaster svcs. ARC-Bi State Chpt., St. Louis, 1992—94; pres. bd. dirs. Desloge Found., St. Louis, 1993—; founder, bd. dirs. NPO Pres.'s Coun., St. Louis, 2003—05; elected. to bd. Tax Assessment Appeals, Darien, Conn., 1999—; Nat. Disaster Relief coord. Soc. St. Vincent de Paul Coun. US, Nat. Case Mgmt. coord. Recipient Recognition award for effort St. Louis Psychoanalytic Inst., 1992, Honor award Red Cross-Bi State Chpt., St. Louis, 1994. Mem. Nat. Coun. Consumer Arbitrators, Barnes Road Luncheon Group, Noonday Club, Veiled Prophet, St. Louis Country Club, Landmark Club, Darien Boat Club (bd. dirs., fin. sec. 1998-2002). Republican. Roman Catholic. Avocations: boating, shooting, golf, tennis, automobiles. Home and Office: Sunny Hills Farm PO Box 127 Gray Summit MO 63039

DESLOGE, ROSEMARY BYRNE, otolaryngologist, educator; b. Tallahassee, Fla., Feb. 25, 1962; d. Edward Augustine and Moira Dunne Desloge; m. John M. Wassem, July 8, 2005; 1 child, Moira Wassem. BS in Biology, U. Notre Dame, 1984; MD, U. Miami, 1989. Diplomate Am. Bd. Otolaryngology, Nat. Bd. Med. Examiners. Resident in gen. surgery U. SC, Columbia, 1989—91; resident in internal medicine NYU/Bellevue Hosps., NYC, 1992—93; ENT resident/fellow Manhattan Eye/Ear/Throat Hosp., NYC, 1993—98; laryngology fellow Harvard U., Boston, 1993—99; asst. prof. dept. otorhinolaryngology Weill Med. Coll., Cornell U., NYC, 1999—2005. Contbr. articles to profl. jours. Fellow: ACS; mem.: AMA, Am. Acad. Otolaryngology Head and Neck Surgery. Office: 969 Park Ave Ste 1C New York NY 10028 Office Phone: 212-717-2700.

DESLONGCHAMPS, PIERRE, chemistry professor; b. St.-Lin, Que., Can., May 8, 1938; s. Rodolphe and Madeleine D.; 3d m. Marie-Marthe Leroux; children: Patrice, Ghyslain. BS., U. Montreal, Que., Can., 1959; PhD (hon.), U. Montreal, 1984; PhD, U. N.B., 1964, PhD (hon.), 1985, U. Pierre et Marie, 1983, Bishop's U., 1984, Laval U., 1984; DSc, U. Moncton, NB, Can., 1995. Research fellow Harvard U., 1964, postdoctoral fellow, 1965; asst. prof. chemistry U. Montreal, 1966-67; asst. prof. U. Sherbrooke, Que., 1967-68, assoc. prof., 1968-72, prof., 1972—2006, prof. emeritus, 2006—. Author: Stereoelectronic Effects in Organic Chemistry, 1983; contbr. over 225 articles to profl. jours. Decorated Officer Order of Can., 1989; recipient E.W.R. Steacie prize Nat. Rsch. Coun. Can., 1974, Can. Gold medal for sci. and engring. Nat. Scis. and Engring. Rsch. Coun. Can., 1993, Sci. prize Province Que., 1971-72, Marie-Victorian prize, 1987, Alfred Bader award Can. Soc. Chemistry, 1991, R.U. Lemieux award Chem. Soc. of Chemistry, 1994; fellow A.P. Sloan, 1970-72, E.W.R. Steacie, 1971-74, John Simon Guggenheim Meml. Found., 1979; Izaak Walton Killam scholar Can. Coun., 1976-77. Fellow AAAS, Chem. Inst. Can. (Merck, Sharp and Dohme Lectrs. award 1976), Royal Soc. Can., Royal Soc. London, World Innovation Found.; mem. Corp. Profl. Chemists Que., Am. Chem. Soc., Assn. Canadienne-Francaise pour l'Advancement des Sciences (medaille Vincent 1975, medaille Pariseau 1979), Acad. des Scis. de Paris (foreign asst.). Achievements include patents in field; inventor in field. Address: Univ Sherbrooke Inst Pharm 3001 12 North Ave Sherbrooke Canada J1H 5N4 Home: 161 de Vimy Sherbrooke PQ Canada J1J 3M6 Business E-Mail: pierre.deslongchamps@usherbrooke.ca.

DESMARAIS, CHARLES JOSEPH, museum director, writer; b. NYC, Apr. 21, 1949; s. Charles Emil and Helen Barbara (Young) D.; m. Sharon McLeod, May 1, 1970; m. Patricia Jon Carroll, June 15, 1979; m. Katherine Ann Morgan, Dec. 31, 1985 Student, Western Conn. State Coll., Danbury, 1967-71; BS, SUNY-Rochester, 1975; MFA, SUNY-Buffalo, 1977. Curator Friends of Photography, Carmel, Calif., 1973-74; asst. editor Afterimage, Rochester, 1975-77; editor Exposure, Chgo., 1977-81; dir. Art Gallery, Columbia Coll., Chgo., 1977-79, Calif. Mus. Photography, U. Calif.-Riverside, 1981-88, Laguna Art Mus., Laguna Beach, Calif., 1988-94, Contemporary Arts Ctr., Cin., 1995—2004; dep. dir. for art Bklyn. Mus., 2005—. Guest curator Mus. Contemporary Art, Chgo., 1980, L.A. Ctr. Photog. Studies, 1981; arts adv. com. Riverside County Bd. Suprs., 1981-86; chair Orange County Arts Coun., 1989-91; bd. dirs. Regional Cultural Alliance, 2000—03. Author, editor: Roger Mertin: Records 1976-1978, 1978, Michael Bishop, 1979, The Portrait Extended, 1980, Why I Got Into TV and Other Stories: The Art of Ilene Segalove, 1990, Proof: Los Angeles Art and the Photograph, 1960-1980, 1992, Humongolous: Sculpture and Other Works by Tim Hawkinson, 1996, Jim Dine Photographs, 1999, Stephan Balkenhol, 2000; arts columnist Riverside Press Enterprise, 1987-88. Art Critic's fellow Nat. Endowment Arts, 1979 Mem. Assn. Art Mus. Dirs., Soc. Photog. Edn. (dir. 1979-83), Am. Assn. Museums, Coll. Art Assn. Office: Bklyn Museum 200 Eastern Pkwy Brooklyn NY 11238-6052 Business E-Mail: charles.desmarais@brooklynmuseum.org.

DESMARAIS, JOHN M., lawyer; BS in Chem. Engring., Manhattan Coll., 1985; JD, NYU, 1988. Bar: NY 1989, DC 1989, U.S. Dist. Ct. (So. and ea. dist. NY) 1989, U.S. Ct. Appeals (2d and Fed. cir.) 1989, U.S. Supreme Ct., registered: U.S. Patent and Trademark Office. Atty. Fish & Neave, 1988—92; asst. U.S. atty. criminal divsn. U.S. Atty.'s Office So. dist., NY, 1992—95; ptnr., mem. firm com. Kirkland & Ellis, NYC. Mem. judge's intellectual property adv. com. Del. Dist. Ct., 1999—. Named one of 40 Under 40, Nat. Law Jour., 2002, The Nation's Top Litigators, 2007, 45 Under 45, Am. Lawyer mag., 2003, America's Leading Bus. Lawyers in Intellectual Poperty, Chambers & Partners, 2004. Mem.: AIChE, ABA, Del. Dist. Ct. Judges' Intellectual Property Adv. Com., Internat. Trademark Assn., Bar Assn. City of NY, NY Intellectual Property Owners Assn., NY County Lawyer's Assn., Fed. Bar Coun., NY Bar Assn. Office: Kirkland & Ellis LLP Citigroup Ctr 153 E 53rd St New York NY 10022-4675 Office Phone: 212-446-4739. Office Fax: 212-446-4900. E-mail: jdesmarais@kirkland.com.*

DESMARAIS, PAUL, diversified management and holding company executive; b. Sudbury, Ont., Can., Jan. 4, 1927; s. Jean-Noël and Lébéa Desmarais; m. Jacqueline Maranger, Sept. 8, 1953; children: Paul, André, Louise, Sophie. BComm, U. Ottawa, Canada, 1949. Chmn., CEO, Power Corp. Can., Montreal, Que., 1968—96, chmn. exec. com., 1996—, also. bd. dirs. Dir. emeritus Great-West Lifeco Inc., Investors Group Inc.; bd. dirs. Gesca Ltée, Groupe Bruxelles Lambert S.A., Power Corp. Can., Power Fin. Corp., La Presse Ltée, Power Tex. Investment Corp., Canada Life Capital Corp. Inc., Les Journaux Trans-Can. Inc.; mem. internat. adv. bd. Barrick Gold Corp. Can.; chmn., mng. dir. Pargesa Holding S.A. Mem. Queen's Privy Coun., Canada. Decorated companion Order of Can., officer Nat. Order of Que., Legion of Honor France, Ordre de Léopold II Belgium; named one of World's Richest People, Forbes mag., 2005—. Avocations: bird hunting, Canadian art collecting. Office: Power Corp Can 751 Victoria Sq Montreal PQ Canada H2Y 2J3*

DESMARAIS, PAUL LEO, critical care nurse; b. Manchester, NH, Sept. 30, 1947; s. Raymond E. and Theresa A. (Rioux) D.; m. Cecile I. Gibeau, June 11, 1966; children: Paul Jr., Roseann, Raymond, Catherine. AD, Ohio U., 1978; BA, St. Anselm's Coll., 1973, BSN, 1984; MSN, U. Mass., Lowell, 1993, PhD, 2002. Orderly Good Samaritan Med. Ctr., Zanesville, Ohio; staff nurse Nashua (N.H.) Meml. Hosp., nurse mgr., 1988—93; critical care coord. VA Med. Ctr., Manchester; nurse mgr. So. NH Med. Ctr., Telemetry, 1988—93; asst. prof. Rivier Coll., Nashua, NH, 1993—2003, U. Ctrl. Fla., Winter Pk., 2003—. With U.S. Army, 1966-69. Mem. AACCN, Sigma Theta Tau. Home: 3207 Netherwood Dr Winter Park FL 32792 Home Phone: 407-677-9754; Office Phone: 407-823-2868.

DESMARTEAU, DARRYL DWAYNE, chemistry professor; b. Garden City, Kans., May 25, 1940; s. Arthur L. and Esther P. (Deines) DesM.; m. Genie L. Hardy, Sept. 16, 1962; children: Scott (dec.), Noel, Chad. BS in Chemistry, Wash. State U., Pullman, 1963; PhD, U. Wash, 1966. Acting asst. prof. U. Wash., 1966-67; asst. prof. Northeastern U., Boston, 1967-71, Kans. State U., Manhattan, 1971-73, assoc. prof., 1973-77, prof., 1977-82; prof., chmn. dept. chemistry and geology Clemson U., SC, 1982-89, Tobey-Beaudrot prof. chemistry, 1989—; cons. Monsanto Chem. Co., St.

Louis, 1976-78, Hooker Chem. Co., Grand Island, NY, 1978-80, Ausimont, Milan, 1985—, DuPont Co., Wilmington, Del., 1986-93. Bd. editors: Jour. Flourine Chemistry, 1981-2005; contbr. articles on fluorine chemistry to profl. jours. Served with USMCR, 1960-66. Recipient award for outstanding research Clemson U. Alumni Assn., 1985, award for Contbrn. to Sci. in S.C. Drug Sci. Found., 1988, Wash. State U. Alumni Achievement award, 1995, Sr. U.S. Scientist award (Humboldt-Preis) Alexander von Humboldt Found., 1988—, Internat. Nissan Prize in Fluorine Chemistry, 2006; Sloan Found fellow, 1975-77, Alexander von Humboldt Found. Research fellow Bonn., W.Ger., 1979-80; numerous research grants Mem. Am. Chem. Soc. (chmn. div. fluorine chemistry 1979, sec.-treas. 1976-78, exec. council 1973-80, award for Creative Work in Fluorine Chemistry 1983, Charles H. Stone award 1994), Sigma Xi, Phi Lambda Upsilon, Alpha Chi Sigma Republican. Roman Catholic. Office: Clemson Univ Dept Chemistry Clemson SC 29634-0001 Home: 106 Fox Trail Ln Seneca SC 29672-8023 Business E-Mail: fluorin@clemson.edu.

DESMOND, BEVIN, investment research company executive; B in Psych., St. Mary's Coll. With Morningstar, Inc., 1993—, mgr. internat. ventures, 1998—2000, pres. internat. bus., 2001—. Named one of Top 40 Under 40, Crain's Chgo. Bus., 2006. Office: Morningstar Inc 225 W Wacker Dr Chicago IL 60606*

DESMOND, LAURA, advertising executive; b. 1965; Media assoc. Leo Burnett (now Starcom), NYC, 1987—94, v.p., 1994—2000; chief exec., Latin Am. Starcom MediaVest Group, NYC, 2000—02, CEO, USA, 2002—, CEO, the Americas, 2006—. Named a Media Exec. All Star, Mediaweek mag., 2004, Media Maven, Advt. Age mag., 2005; named one of 50 Women to Watch, Wall St. Jour., 2006; named to Dream Team of Young Executives, Business 2.0, 2004, Advt. Hall of Achievement, Advt. Fedn., 2005. Office: Starcom MediaVest Group 1675 Broadway New York NY 10019 Office Phone: 212-468-3444. Business E-Mail: laura.desmond@mediavestww.com.*

DESMOND, NED, editor, writer; Student, Amherst Coll., 1980; MA, Tufts U.; Reuters fellow, Oxford U. Writer Fgn. Affairs, NY Rev. Books; researcher, staff writer Time Mag., 1984—88, bur. chief, New Delhi, 1988—91; bur. chief, Tokyo Time Inc., 1992—96, sr. writer, Fortune Mag., 1997—98; editor, pres. eCompany Now, 1999—2001; editor, pres., Bus. 2.0 mag. Time Inc., pres., Bus. 2.0 mag., 2001—02; exec. editor Time Inc. Interactive, 2002, now pres.; with InfoSeek, Silicon Valley, 1996—97, 1998—99. Office: Time Inc Interactive 22000 Aol Way Dulles VA 20166-9032

DESMOND, SUSAN FAHEY, lawyer; b. Greenville, Miss., Feb. 24, 1961; d. Richard Paul and Bonnie Jean (Williams) Fahey; m. John Michael Desmond; May 28, 1994; children: Meghan, Kelsey. BA in English and History, U. Miss., 1982; JD, U. Tenn., 1985. Bar: Miss. 1985, Colo. 1996, La. 1998. Assoc. Robertshaw, Terney & Noble, Greenville, Miss., 1985-86, Miller, Milam & Moeller, Jackson, Miss., 1986-89, Phelps Dunbar, Jackson, Miss., 1989-92, ptnr., 1992-97, New Orleans, 1998—2003; shareholder Watkins, Ludlam, Winter and Stennis, P.A., Gulfport, Miss., 2003—. Author: Employment Issues for Hospital Supervisors, 1996; editor: Mississippi Pro Bono Material, 1989. Bd. dirs. Am. Cancer Soc. Hinds County Unit, Jackson, Miss., 1990-96, YMCA Greater New Orleans, 2002-03. Mem. Jackson Young Lawyers (dir. 1991-93, merit award 1988), Am. Bar Assn./Young Lawyers (labor com. chmn., Chgo., 1990-92), Miss. Bar Assn. (dir. 1990-92, Outstanding Young Lawyer 1997). Republican. Roman Catholic. Avocations: tennis, reading. E-mail: sdesmond@watkinsludlam.com.

DESMOND-HELLMANN, SUSAN, medical products manufacturing executive; b. 1958; BS in Pre-Medicine, U. Nev., MD; M in Epidemiology and Biostats., U. Calif. Sch. Pub. Health, Berkeley. Bd. cert. internal medicine and med. oncology. Trainee U. Calif., San Francisco; assoc. dir. clin. cancer rsch., project team leader Taxol Bristol-Myers Squibb Pharm. Rsch. Inst.; clin. scientist Genentech, Inc., South San Francisco, 1995-96, sr. dir. clin. sci., 1996, v.p. med. affairs, 1996, chief med. officer, 1996—97, v.p. devel., 1997, sr. v.p. devel., 1997, exec. v.p. devel. and product ops., 1999, pres., product devel., 2004—. Vis. faculty Uganda Cancer Inst.; asst. prof. hematology-oncology U. Calif. San Francisco, adj. assoc. prof. epidemiology and biostats; adv. com. regulatory reform, HHS, 2002; bd. dirs. Biotechnology Industry Orgn., 2001-, Am. Assn. Cancer Rsch., 2005-. Named Woman of Yr., Healthcare Businesswomen's Assn., 2006; named one of 50 Most Powerful Women in Bus., Fortune mag., 2001, 2003, 2004, 2006, 100 Most Powerful Women in World, Forbes Mag., 2005, Top 50 Women to Watch, Wall St. Jour., 2004, 50 Women to Watch, 2005, 2006, Leading Women and Minority Scientists, NY Acad. Scis., 2005, 50 Who Matter Now, CNNMoney.com Bus. 2.0, 2006. Office: Genentech Inc One DNA Way South San Francisco CA 94080-4990 Office Fax: 650-225-6000.*

DESNICK, ROBERT JOHN, human geneticist; b. Mpls., July 12, 1943; s. Theodore David and Celia Janice (Marcus) D.; Julie E. Herzig, Oct. 23, 1988; 1 child, Jonathan Phillips. BA, U. Minn., 1965, PhD, 1970, MD, 1971; DSc (hon.), Mt. Sinai Sch. Medicine/NYU, 2004. Diplomate Am. Bd. Med. Examiners, Am. Acad. Pediat., Am. Bd. Med. Genetics (bd. dirs. 1990-93, treas. 1991-93). Rsch. assoc. U. Minn., 1970-72, intern and resident dept. pediat., 1972—73, asst. prof. lab. medicine and pathology, 1973-75; asst. prof. pediat. U. Minn. Dight Inst. Human Genetics, 1973-75, assoc. prof. pediat., 1975—77; assoc. prof. genetics and cell biology U. Minn. Coll. Biol. Sci., 1975-77. Arthur J. and Nellie Z. Cohen prof. pediat. and genetics Mt. Sinai Sch. Medicine, NYC, 1977—2000, chief divsn. med. and molecular genetics, 1977—, chair dept. human genetics (renamed genetics and genomic scis. 2007), 1993—; med. adv. bd. Nat. Neurofibromatosis Found., 1978—81; dir. Mt. Sinai Ctr. Jewish Genetic Diseases, 1981—; program dir. Mt. Sinai Gen. Clin. Rsch. Ctr., 1990—99; attending physician pediat. Mt. Sinai Hosp.; cons. physician pediat. Beth Israel Med. Ctr., NYC, City Ctr. Hosp., Elmhurst, NY; med. adv. bd. Nat. Found. Jewish Genetic Diseases, 1981—2002; mem. NY Gov.'s Adv. Com. on Genetics, 1982—92; med. adv. bd. Mucolipidosis IV Found., 1984—; sci. adv. bd. Dysautonomia Found., 1990—2005, Nat. Niemann-Pick Found., 1992—; med. adv. bd. Internat. Incontinenta Pigmenti Found., 1993—; mem. mental retardation study sect. NIH, 1995—98; sci. adv. bd. Ara Parshegian Med. Rsch. Found., 1995—2002, Bachman-Strauss Dystonia & Parkinson Found., 1997—2005; chmn. organizing com. Internat. Congresses Inherited Metabolic Diseases, 1990—2006; mem. NCRR adv. coun. NIH, 2000—04; med. adv. bd. Am. Porphyria Found., 1984—; adj. prof. Tokyo Jikei U. Sch. Medicine. Editor: Enzyme Therapy in Genetic Diseases, 1973, Molecular Genetic Modification of Eucaryotes, 1978, Enzyme Therapy in Genetic Diseases, 1980, Gaucher Disease: A Century of Delineation and Research, 1982, Animal Models of Inherited Metabolic Disorders, 1982, Clinica Chemica Acta, 1984, Recent Advances in Inborn Errors of Metabolism, 1987, Treatment of Genetic Diseases, 1991, Tay-Sachs Disease, 2001; mem. editl. bd. Enzyme, 1979—98, Am. Jour. Human Genetics, 1980—84, Pediatrics, 1991—96, Human Mutation, 1991—, Biochem. Medicine and Metabolic Biology, 1991—97, Jour. Clin. Investigation, 1992—97, Jour. Inherited Metabolic Disease, 1996—, Jour. Human Genetics, 1998—, Molecular Genetics and Metabolism, 1998—, Molecular Medicine, 2002—, Human Genome, 2003—; contbr. articles to profl. jours. Pres. fifth Internat. Congress of Inborn Errors of Metabolism, 1990. Recipient Ross award Soc. Pediat. Rsch., 1972, C.J. Watson award U. Minn. Med. Sch., 1973, E. Mead Johnson award Am. Acad. Pediat., 1981, Outstanding Faculty award Mt. Sinai Sch.of Medicine, 1991, NIH Merit award, 1992, J. Lester Gabrilove award for med. rsch., 2003, Jacobi award Mt. Sinai Sch. Medicine Alumni Assn., 2003, E.H. Ahrens Jr. Disting. Rsch. award Assn. Patient-Oriented Rsch., 2004, Disting. Alumni award U. Minn. Med. Sch., 2004, Clin. Rsch. Excellence award Nat. Ctr. Clin. Rsch., NIH, 2005, Albion O. Bernstein award N.Y. State Med. Soc., 2005; USPHS fellow, 1968-70; grantee NIH, 1975-. Fellow AAAS (sr.); mem. Nat. Acad. Scis. (mem. inst. medicine 2004), Am. Soc. Human Genetics, Genetics Soc. Am., Am. Acad. Pediat., Minn. Human Genetics League (dir. 1970-77), Soc. Complex Carbohydrates, Behavior Genetics Assn., Am. Fedn. Clin. Rsch., Am. Coll. Med. Genetics (founding fellow, chair hon. membership com. 1990-98, chair biochem. and molecular resource com. 1993-2002, chmn. accreditation com. 1998-2000), Am. Coll. Med. Genetics Found. (bd. dirs. 1998—), Am. Soc. Biochemistry and Molecular Biology, Assn. Profs. Human/Med. Genetics (co-founder 1994, pres. 1996-98), Ea. Soc. Pediatric Rsch., Soc. Pediatric Rsch., Soc. Exptl. Biology and Medicine, Am. Soc. Exptl. Pathology, Ctrl. Soc. Clin. Rsch., Soc. Study Social Biology, Soc. Study Inborn Errors of Metabolism, NY Acad. Sci., European Soc. Human Genetics, Harvey Soc. (sec. 1984-89), Soc. Inherited Metabolic Diseases (bd. dirs. 1983-92, pres. 1989-91), Am. Pediatric Soc., Am. Soc. Microbiology, Assn. Am. Med. Colls. (adminstrv. bd., coun. acad. socs. 2001—, chmn.-elect, 2004, chmn., 2005), Nat. Tay-Sachs and Allied Diseases Assn. (med. adv. bd. 1975—, chmn. 1990-92), Nat. MPS Soc. (med. adv. bd. 1987—), Am. Assn. Physicians, Am. Soc. Clin. Investigation, Assn. Patient-Oriented Rsch. (founding mem. 1998—), Am. Soc. for Gene Therapy, Japanese Soc. Inherited Diseases (hon.), Societá Italiana di Pediatrica (hon.), Sigma Xi, Inst. Medicine, 2004. Office: Mt Sinai Sch Medicine Dept Human Genetics 5th Ave & 100th St New York NY 10029 Office Phone: 212-659-6700. Business E-Mail: rjdesnick@mssm.edu.

DESNOYERS, MEGAN FLOYD, retired archivist, educator; b. NYC, Oct. 31, 1945; d. Lawrence Clifford and Frances Irene Floyd; m. David George Desnoyers, Sept. 2, 1967; 1 child, Adam O'Neil. AB, Vassar Coll., 1967; MLS, Rutgers U., 1968. Libr. John Jay H.S., Wappingers Falls, NY, 1968-69; archivist Franklin D. Roosevelt Presdl. Libr., Hyde Park, NY, 1969, John F. Kennedy Presdl. Libr., Boston, 1970—2007, curator Ernest Hemingway Collection, 1987—96, 2000—01; instr. in archives adminstrn. Nat. Archives Modern Archives Inst., Washington, 1982-2000; ret., 2007. Lectr. archives adminstrn. U. Mass., Boston, 1978-80; lectr. on Hemingway, 1992—2000; mem. Archives Adv. Commn., Boston, 1977-2000; archival advisor Girl Scouts U.S., N.Y.C., 1991—2002. Contbr. chpt. to book, articles to profl. jours. Mem. adv. bd., chmn. com. Voluntary Action Ctr., Mass. Bay United Way, Boston, 1974-80; mem., chair bd. trustees Randall Libr., Stow, Mass., 1976-80; mem. Mass. Hist. Records Adv. Bd., 1979-2000. Nat. Def. fellow, 1967-68. Fellow Soc. Am. Archivists; mem. New Eng. Archivists (sec. 1976-78), Soc. Am. Archivists (workshop instr. 1978-2000), Acad. Cert. Archivists (task force on recert. 1991-92), Beta Phi Mu. Democrat. Roman Catholic.

DESOER, BARBARA J., bank executive; b. Nov. 4, 1952; BA in Math., Mt. Holyoke Coll., 1974; MBA, U. Calif., Berkeley. Various positions to mng. strategy devel. and implementation, consumer banking unit Bank Am. Corp., 1977—96, exec. v.p. Calif. retail banking grp., 1996—98, pres. No. Calif. banking, 1998, mktg. exec., 1999—2001, pres. consumer products, 2001—04, global tech., svc. & fulfillment exec., 2004—. Chmn. internat. diversity adv. coun. Bank Am. Corpn.; mem. adv. coun. Haas Sch. Bus. U. Calif., Berkeley; mem. bus. adv. coun. U. NC Belk Coll. Bus. Adminstrn., Charlotte. Bd. dirs. Providence Day Sch., Charlotte, NC Dance Theatre, Presbyn. Hosp. Found., United Way Ctrl. Carolinas. Named one of 25 Most Powerful Women in Banking, US Banker, 2006. Office: Bank Am Corp 100 N Tryon St Charlotte NC 28255*

DESOTO, LEWIS DAMIEN, artist, educator; b. San Bernardino, Calif., Jan. 3, 1954; s. Lewis Dan and Albertina (Quiroz) DeS. BA, U. Calif., Riverside, 1978; MFA, Claremont Grad. Sch., 1981. Tchr. Otis Parsons, LA, 1982-85; chmn. art dept. Cornish Coll. of Arts, Seattle, 1985-88; prof. art San Francisco State U., 1988—95; dir. grad. studies Calif. Coll. Arts and Crafts, Oakland, 1993-95; prof. art San Francisco State U., 1995—. Exhibitions include New Mus., N.Y.C., 1992, Centro Cultural De La Raza, San Diego, 1993, Moderna Museet, Stockholm, Sweden, 1993, Christopher Grimes Gallery, Santa Monica, Calif., 1994, Denver Art Mus., 1994, Columbus Mus. Art, 1994, Des Moines Art Ctr., 1995, Fundacao Serralves, Opporto, Portugal, 1995, Metronóm, Barcelona, Spain, 1997, Public Art Commn., San Francisco Courthouse, 1998, San Francisco Internat. Airport, 2000, San Jose Animal Care Ctr. Public Commn., Calif., 2004, U. Tex., San Antonio, 2003, Public Art Commn., List Visual Art Ctr., MIT, Cambridge, 1998, Bill Maynes Gallery, N.Y.C., 1999, 2000, Mus. of Contemporary Religious Art, St. Louis, 2000, Mus. Contemporary Art, San Diego, 2001, Worcester Art (Mass.) Mus., 2001, Bill Maynes Gallery, N.Y.C., 2002, Samek Art Ctr., Bucknell U., Lewisburg, Pa., 2002, N.C. Mus. Art, Raleigh, 2003, Newhouse Ctr. for Contemporary Art, S.I., 2003, Harn Mus. Art, Gainesville, Fla., 2003, Vanderbilt Art Gallery, Vanderbilt U., Nashville, 2003, San Diego Mus. Contemporary Aft, LaJolla, 2004, Columbus Mus. of Art, 2004, UCLA Fowler Art Mus., LA, 2006—, Aldrich Contemporary Art Mus., Ridgefield, Conn., 2006—, Oakland estuary channel project, Pub. Art Com., 2006—, one-man shows include Brian Gross Fine Art, San Francisco, 2006—. Mem. photo coun. Seattle Art Mus., 1987-88, Eureka Fellowship, vis. arts, 1999. Recipient New Genres award Calif. Arts Coun., 1992, NEA fellow, 1996, recipient Visual Arts award Flintridge Found., Pasadena, Calif., 2004. Mem. L.A. Ctr. for Photographic Studies (bd. dirs. 1983-85), CameraWork (exec. bd. dirs. 1991-93), Ctr. for Arts (adv. bd. 1993-95), Friends of Photography (peer award bd. 1991-96). Office: San Francisco State U Art Dept 1600 Holloway Ave San Francisco CA 94132-1722 Personal E-mail: Sotolux@sbcglobal.net.

DE SOTO, LISA, lawyer; Gen. counsel Social Security Adminstrn., dep. commr. Disability Adjudication and Rev. Office: Social Security Adminstrn Altmeyer Bldg Rm 617 6401 Security Blvd Baltimore MD 21235-0001 Office Phone: 410-965-0600. Office Fax: 410-966-3146. Business E-Mail: lisa.desoto@ssa.gov.

DESOUZA, KEVIN CLYDE, application developer, educator; BSc with dist. in acctg., info. decision, U. Ill., 2000; MBA, Stuart Grad. Sch. of Bus., Ill. Inst. of Tech., 2001; PhD, U. Ill., Chgo., 2006. Software engr. CCC Info. Services, Chgo., 1998—2001; prof. info. scis. U. Wash., 2001—. Contbr. articles various profl. jours. and papers. Home: 809B NW 97th St Seattle WA 98117 Office Phone: 206-616-0880. Personal E-mail: kev.desouza@gmail.com.

DESPINS, LUC, lawyer; b. 1960; LLL, U. Ottawa, 1981, LLB, 1982; LLM, Harvard Law Sch., 1985. Bar: Quebec 1983, NY 1986, US Dist. Ct., So. Dist. NY 1987, US Ct. Appeals, Second Circuit 1993, US Dist. Ct., No. Dist. NY 1996, US Ct. Appeals, Third Circuit 2001. Assoc. Kirkland & Ellis; ptnr. & co-chmn. Fin. Restructuring Group Milbank, Tweed, Hadley & McCloy LLP, 1999—. Named one of Top 45 Lawyers in Country Under 45, Am. Lawyer Mag., 2003. Office: Milbank Tweed Hadley & McCloy LLP 1 Chase Manhattan Plaza New York NY 10005-1413 Office Phone: 212-530-5660. Office Fax: 212-530-5219. Business E-Mail: ldespins@milbank.com.

DESPOMMIER, DICKSON DONALD, microbiology educator, parasitologist; b. New Orleans, June 5, 1940; s. Roland Medd and Beverly (Wood) D.; children— Bruce, Bradley BS, Fairleigh Dickinson U., 1962; MS, Columbia U., 1964; PhD, U. Notre Dame, 1967. Postdoctoral fellow Rockefeller U., 1967-71; Asst. prof. pub. health Columbia U., NYC, 1971-75, assoc. prof., 1975-77, prof. pub. health and microbiology, 1982—. Cons. NIH, 1980-84, Gen. Food Corp., 1976, Cordis Corp., 1973-74, Bionetics Rsch. Inc., 1986-89, Eco-Chem, Inc., 1993; Theobald Smith lectr. 1993; pres. Apple Trees Prodns., LLC, NYC; dir. Vertical Farm Project. Author: Parasitic Diseases, 5th edit., 2005, Parasite Life Cycles, 1988, West Nile Story, 2001. Bd. dirs., chmn. edn. com. Catskill Flyfishing Ctr. and Mus., 1994—, dir., 1994—. Named Tchr. of Yr. Columbia U., 1980, 81, 83, 84; recipient Career Devel. award Nat. Inst. A.I.D., 1971-75, Disting. Tchr. award Med. Coll. Ohio, 1980, Deans' Disting. Tchr. award Columbia U., 1989, Golden Apple Tchr. of Yr. award Am. Med. Students Assn., 2003. Mem. AAAS, Am. Soc. Parasitologists, Brodheads Forest and Stream Assn., Am. Soc. Tropical Medicine and Hygiene, Harvey Soc., N.Y. Soc. Tropical Medicine (pres. 1980), Internat. Commn. on Trichinellosis, Trout Unltd. (bd. dirs. 1976-78), Salmagundi Club, Anglers Club NY, Sci Barge (adv. bd.). Office Phone: 212-781-6670. Business E-Mail: ddd1@columbia.edu.

D'ESPOSITO, JULIAN C., JR., lawyer; b. NYC, Aug. 6, 1944; BS, Loyola U., 1966; JD cum laude, Northwestern U., 1969. Bar: Ill. 1969, U.S. Dist. Ct. (no. dist.) 1969. With Ross, Hardies, O'Keefe, Babcock & Parsons, 1970—76, ptnr., 1976; counsel to Gov. Ill., 1977-81; ptnr. Isham, Lincoln & Beale, 1981—87, Mayer, Brown, Rowe & Maw, 1988—, ptnr. in charge Chgo. office, 2002—. Chmn. Winnetka Plan Commn., 1985-89; mem. Ill. Med. Ctr. Commn., 1987-94; dir. Ill. Capital Devel. Bd., 1994-95, Chgo. Ctrl. Area Com., 2004-; chmn. Ill. State Toll Hwy. Authority, 1995-99. Co-editor-in-chief Jour. Criminal Law, Criminology & Police Sci., Northwestern U., 1968-69. Mem. ABA, Nat. Assn. Bond Lawyers. Office: Mayer Brown Rowe & Maw LLP 71 S Wacker Dr Chicago IL 60606

DESPRES, LEO ARTHUR, sociologist, anthropologist, educator, academic administrator; b. Lebanon, NH, Mar. 29, 1932; s. Leo Arthur and Madeline (Bedford) D.; m. Loretta A. LaBarre, Aug. 22, 1953; children— Christine, Michelle, Denise, Mary Louise, Renee. BA, U. Notre Dame, 1954, MA, 1956; PhD, Ohio State U., 1960. Research assoc. Columbia Psychiat. Inst. and Hosp., 1957-60; postdoctoral fellow Social Sci. Research Council, Guyana, 1960-61; asst. prof. Ohio Wesleyan U., 1961-63; faculty Case Western Res. U., Cleve., 1963-74, prof. anthropology, 1967-74, chmn. dept., 1968-74; prof. sociology, anthropology U. Notre Dame, Ind., 1974-97, chmn. dept., 1974-80, fellow Kellogg Inst. Internat. Studies, 1982—, prof. emeritus, 1997—. Cons. in field. Author: Cultural Pluralism and Nationalist Politics in British Guyana, 1968; editor: Ethnicity and Resource Competition in Plural Societies, 1975, Manaus: Social Life and Work in Brazil's Free Trade Zone, 1991. Fulbright scholar, U. Guyana, 1970—71, Brazil, 1986, rsch. grantee, NSF, 1984. Mem. Am. Anthrop. Assn., Am. Ethnol. Soc., Latin Am. Studies Assn., Cen. States Anthrop. Soc. (pres. 1976-77), AAUP. Office: U Notre Dame Dept Anthropology Notre Dame IN 46556 Home: PO Box 6752 South Bend IN 46660-6752 Business E-Mail: ldespres@nd.edu.

DESPRES, LEON MATHIS, lawyer, former city official; b. Chgo., Feb. 2, 1908; s. Samuel and Henrietta (Rubovits) D.; m. Marian Alschuler, Sept. 10, 1931; children— Linda Baskin, Robert Leon. PhB, U. Chgo., 1927, JD, 1929; DLitt (hon.), Columbia Coll., Chgo., 1990, U. Ill., 2000. Bar: Ill. 1929. Ptnr. Despres, Schwartz and Geoghegan, Chgo.; alderman 5th Ward Chgo. City Council, 1955-75, parliamentarian, 1979-87. Author: Challenging the Daley Machine, 2005. Mem. Chgo. Plan Commn., 1979-89. Recipient Benton medal, U. Chgo., 2005. Mem.: Phi Beta Kappa, Order of Coif. Home: 5830 S Stony Island Ave Apt 10A Chicago IL 60637-2024 Office: 77 W Washington St Chicago IL 60602-2801 Office Phone: 312-372-2511.

DESPRES, LOUISE FAY, secondary school educator; b. New Haven, Conn., Feb. 29, 1944; d. Frederick Taylor and Ruth Jean (Lowery) Fay; m. Robert Leon Despres, Feb. 16, 1974; 1 child, Frederick Leon. Studied organ with Nadia Boulanger Fontainebleau, Am. Sch. Music, France, 1965; BA, Conn. Coll., 1966; MAT, Brown U., 1968; MA, Middlebury Coll., France, 1973. Cert. secondary sch. tchr. Conn. French tchr. N. Haven HS, Conn., 1967—69, High Plains Sch., Orange, Conn., 1969—70, New Canaan HS, Conn., 1970—, Spanish tchr., 1979—, advanced placement tchr., 1980—, chair world langs., 2001—06, advisor to Internat. Club, 1986—87, ind. study advisor, 1990—2003, mentor tchr., 1991—93, 2005—06, chair ind. study, 1996—2001, mem. ind. study com., 1992—94, mem. advanced placement rev. com., 2006—07; coop. tchr. U. Conn., 1985—90. Hs tchr. liaison Am. Field Svc., New Canaan, Conn., 1979—81; sch. liaison Sch. Yr. Abroad, New Canaan, 1983—85; summer sch. tchr. Saxe Mid. Sch., 1984, New Canaan HS, 1986; rev. curriculum com. New Canaan Schs., 1989—91, chair rev. curriculum com., 1999—2001; tchr. assessor State of Conn., 1989—91. Vol. devel. tchr. LEAP, New Haven, 1968; vol. Recs. for the Blind, New Haven, 1969; participant Conn. Inst. Tchg. and Learning, 1988—90. Recipient Advanced Placement Tchr. Recognition award, New Eng. Coll. Bd., 1994, Pegasus Pride award, Conn. Orgn. Lang. Tchrs., 2001; fellow, NEH, 1983; grantee, North Haven Bd. Edn., Conn., 1968, Bd. of A Better Chance, New Canaan, Conn., 2001—06; Higher Edn. Act fellow, 1966—67, French govt. fellow, 1972—73. Mem.: PEO, Orgn. Lang. Tchrs., Am. Assn. Tchrs. French (adminstr. Conn. Nat. French Contest 1980—81). Congregationalist. Avocations: music, theater, reading, travel. Home: 3 Peters Ln Westport CT 06880-3937 Office: New Canaan High Sch 11 Farm Rd New Canaan CT 06840-6608 Home Phone: 203-227-3723. Personal E-mail: duds95@sbcglobal.net. Business E-Mail: louise.despres@newcanaan.k12.ct.us.

DESROSIER, THOMAS J., lawyer; BA, U. Vermont; JD, Wake Forrest U. Sch. Law. Bar:. Formerly with E.I. DuPont de Nemours and Co., New Eng. Nuclear Corp.; former v.p., chief patent counsel Genetics Institute Inc.; former asst. gen. counsel American Home Products Corp.; v.p., gen. counsel, chief patent counsel Genzyme Corp., 0199—. Office: Genzyme Corp 500 Kendall St Cambridge MA 02142

DESSAU, NIGEL, information technology executive; b. Nottingham, Eng. Head mktg. programs UK and Europe for S/390 brand and Server Group worldwide IBM, bus. unit exec. Virtualization Solutions; chief mktg. officer StorageTek; sr. v.p. storage mktg. & bus. ops. Sun Microsystems, Inc. Office: Sun Microsystems Inc 4150 Network Cir Santa Clara CA 95054 Office Phone: 650-960-1300.

DESSEM, R. LAWRENCE, dean, law educator; b. Berea, Ohio, May 16, 1951; s. Ralph Eugene and Jane Elizabeth (Brightbill) D.; m. Beth Ann Taylor, May 20, 1973; children: Matthew, Lindsay, Emily. BA summa cum laude, Macalester Coll., 1973; JD cum laude, Harvard U., 1976. Bar: Ohio 1976, D.C. 1979, Tenn. 1985, Mo., 2002. Law clk. to presiding judge U.S. Dist. Ct. (no. dist.) Ohio, Cleve., 1976-78; asst. gen. counsel NEA, Washington, 1978-80; trial atty. civil div. U.S. Dept. Justice, Washington, 1980-84, sr. trial counsel, 1984-85; assoc. prof. law coll. of law U. Tenn., Knoxville, 1985-92, prof. law coll. of law, 1992-95, assoc. dean, 1993-95; prof., dean Mercer U., Macon, Ga., 1995—2002; dean & prof. law U. Mo.-Columbia, Sch. Law, 2002—. Mem. faculty Legal Edn. Inst., U.S. Dept. Justice, San Francisco, 1985, Nat. Inst. for Trial Adv., Chgo., 1987-90; reporter Adv. Group on Litigation Cost and Delay, Tenn., 1991-95; mem. Tenn. Supreme Ct. Commn. on Dispute Resolution, 1992-94; mem. fed. adv. com. US Ct. Appeals (8th cir.), 2005—. Author: Pretrial Litigation, 1991, 4th edit., 2007, Pretrial Litigation in a Nutshell, 3d edit. 2001; contbr. articles to profl. jours. Nat. Merit scholar 1969. Fellow Am. Bar Found., Lawyer's Found. of Ga.; mem. ABA (co-chair dean's workshop 1998-99), Tenn. Bar Found., Am. Law Inst., Assn. Am.

Law Schs. (mem. review com., chair, 2005-07), Phi Beta Kappa. Office: U Mo 230 Hulston Hall Columbia MO 65211-4300 Office Phone: 573-882-3246. E-mail: dessemrl@missouri.edu.

DESSLER, ALEXANDER JACK, astrophysicist, educator; b. San Francisco, Oct. 21, 1928; s. David Alexander and Julia (Shapiro) D.; m. Lorraine Hudek, Apr. 18, 1952; children: Pauline Karen, David Alexander, Valerie Jan, Andrew Emory. BS, Calif. Inst. Tech., 1952; PhD, Duke U., 1956. Sect. head Lockheed Missiles & Space Co., 1956-62; prof. Grad. Rsch. Ctr., Dallas, 1962-63, prof. space physics and astronomy, 1963-82, 86-93; chmn. dept. Rice U., Houston, 1963-69, 79-82, 87-92, campus bus. mgr., 1974-76; dir. space sci. lab. MSFC NASA, Huntsville, Ala., 1982-86; sr. rsch. scientist Lunar and Planetary Lab. U. Ariz., Tucson, 1993—. Sci. adviser Nat. Aeros. and Space Coun., 1969-70; pres. Univs. Space Rsch. Assn., 1975-81. Editor Jour. Geophys. Rsch., 1965-69, Revs. of Geophysics, 1969-74, The John Wiley Space Sci. Text Series, 1968-76, Geophys. Rsch. Letters, 1986-89, Atmospheric and Space Sci. Series, 1986—; adv. bd.: Planetary and Space Sci., 1963-92; assoc. editor Space Solar Power Rev., 1980-85. Served with USN, 1946-48. Recipient Outstanding Young Scientist award Tex. Wing Air Force Assn., 1964, medal for contbns. to internat. geophysics Soviet Geophys. Com., 1984, Stellar award for acad. devel., Rotary Nat., 1988. Fellow AAAS, Am. Geophys. Union (Macelwane award 1963, John Adam Fleming medal 1993, William Kaula award for publs. 2003); mem. Am. Astron. Soc., Internat. Assn. Geomagnetism and Aeronomy (v.p. 1979-83), Royal Swedish Acad. Scis. (fgn.), Cosmos Club (Washington). Office: Tex A& M Univ Dept Atmospheric Sci College Station TX 77843-3150 Home: 4780 Stonebriar Cir College Station TX 77845 Business E-Mail: dessler@arizona.edu.

DESSUREAULT, SOPHIE, oncologist, surgeon, educator; d. Jean-Guy and Normande Dessureault. BSc, Dalhousie U., Halifax, NS, Canada, 1986, MD, 1990; PhD, U. Toronto, Ont., Canada, 1999. Diplomate Am. Bd. Surgery. Asst. prof. U. South Fla., Tampa, 2001—. Contbr. articles to med. jours. Grantee, Lymphoma Rsch. Found., 2004—. Fellow: ACS, Royal Coll. of Physicians and Surgeons of Can.; mem.: Soc. Surg. Oncology (Young Investigator award 2004—05), Am. Soc. Clin. Oncology (Career Devel. award 2004—), Am. Assn. of Cancer Rsch. Office: H Lee Moffitt Cancer Ctr 12902 Magnolia Dr Tampa FL 33612 Office Phone: 813-745-3636. Personal E-mail: sophie.dessureault@moffitt.org.

DESTAFENO, JOHN J., ophthalmologist; b. Newburgh, NY, July 30, 1975; s. Joseph DeStafeno and Barbara Rys; m. Kerri Mather, July 29, 2006. BA in Biology summa cum laude, Siena Coll., 1997; MD, Albany Med. Coll., NY, 2001. Med. intern Roger Williams Hosp. Ctr., Providence, 2001—02; resident, ophthalmology LI Jewish Med. Ctr., Great Neck, NY, 2002—05; fellow cornea and refractive surgery Duke U., Durham, NC, 2005—07. Chief resident LI Jewish Med. Ctr., Great Neck, 2004—05. Contbr. articles to profl. jours. Mem.: Am. Soc. Cataract and Refractive Surgeons, Am. Acad. Ophthalmology. Achievements include research in anti-VEGF medications for corneal neovascularization. Personal E-mail: jdestafeno@yahoo.com.

DESTEFANO, GARY M., apparel executive; b. Portsmouth, NH; married, 1978; 2 children. BS in Phys. Edn., U. NH, Durham, 1978; MBA, NH Coll., 1983. Customer svc. area mgr. Nike, Inc., 1982—84, asst. Ea. sales mgr. Footwear, 1984—88, nat. asst. Mid-West sales mgr. Apparel, 1988—89, dir. sports & fitness sales, 1989—92, divisional v.p. domestic sales, 1992—93, v.p. global sales, 1993—96, v.p. NIKE Asia Pacific, 1996—97, v.p., gen. mgr. Asia Pacific, 1997—2001, pres. USA ops., 2001—06, pres. global ops., 2006—. Avocations: running, golf, skiing, water-skiing, reading. Office: Nike Inc One Bowerman Dr Beaverton OR 97005-6453 Office Phone: 503-671-6453.*

DESTLER, I. M(AC), political scientist, foreign policy writer; b. Statesboro, Ga., Aug. 21, 1939; s. Chester McArthur and Katharine (Hardesty) D.; m. Harriett Kirkham Parsons, July 27, 1968; children: Mark Dodson, Katharine Elizabeth. BA magna cum laude, Harvard U., 1961; MPA, Princeton U., 1965, PhD, 1971. Peace Corps vol. U. Nigeria, Nsukka, 1961-63; asst. Senator Walter Mondale Washington, 1965-67; staff assoc. Pres.'s Task Force on Govt. Orgn., Washington, 1967; analyst, acting coord. for Asia Internat. Agrl. Devel. Svc., USDA, Washington, 1967-69; Internat. Affairs fellow Coun. Fgn. Rels., Washington, 1969-70; vis. lectr. Woodrow Wilson Sch., Princeton U., 1971-72; rsch. assoc. Brookings Inst., Washington, 1972-76, sr. fellow, 1976-77; sr. assoc. Carnegie Endowment for Internat. Peace, Washington, 1977-83; sr. fellow Inst. Internat. Econs., Washington, 1983-87; prof. Sch. Pub. Policy U. Md., College Park, 1987—, acting dean, 1994-95, dir. Ctr. Internat. and Security Studies, 1991-99, dir. PhD program, 2000—07; dir. Md. seminar in U.S. fgn. policymaking, 1987-95. Cons. U.S. Office Mgmt. and Budget, 1977, 79, U.S. Dept. State, 1976, 93, U.S. Agy. for Internat. Devel., Ctrl. Asia, 1999-2000; vis. prof. Internat. U. Japan (Urasa), 1986; fellow Peterson Inst. Internat. Econs., 1987—. Author: Presidents, Bureaucrats and Foreign Policy - The Politics of Organizational Reform, 1972, 74, (with others) Managing an Alliance - The Politics of U.S.-Japanese Relations, 1976, (with Fukui and Sato) The Textile Wrangle - Conflict in Japanese-American Relations, 1969-71, 1979, Making Foreign Economic Policy, 1980, (with Gelb and Lake) Our Own Worst Enemy: The Unmaking of American Foreign Policy, 1984, American Trade Politics, 1986 (Gladys M. Kammerer award Am. Polit. Sci. Assn. 1987), 4th edit., 2005, Chinese edit., 2006, (with Odell) Anti-Protection: Changing Forces in U.S. Trade Politics, 1987, (with Henning) Dollar Politics: Exchange Rate Policy Making in the United States, 1989, The National Economic Council: A Work in Progress, 1996, Renewing Fast-Track Legislation, 1997, (with Kull) Misreading the Public: The Myth of a New Isolationism, 1999, (with Balint) The New Politics of American Trade, 1999, (with others) Protecting the American Homeland, 2002, 03; co-editor: Coping with U.S.-Japanese Economic Conflicts, 1982, Beyond the Beltway: Engaging the Public in U.S. Foreign Policy, 1994. Mem. Coun. Fgn. Rels., Am. Polit. Sci. Assn., Nat. Acad. Pub. Adminstrn. Democrat. Presbyterian. Home: 701 River Bend Rd Great Falls VA 22066-2712 Office: U Md Sch Pub Policy College Park MD 20742-1811 Office Phone: 301-405-6357. E-mail: mdestler@umd.edu.

DESTLER, WILLIAM W., academic administrator; m. Rebecca Johnson; 2 children. BS, Stevens Inst. Tech., 1968; PhD, Cornell U., 1972. Former chair dept. elec. engring. U. Md., College Park, dean sch. engring., 1994—97, v.p. rsch., dean grad. sch., 1999—2001, sr. v.p. acad. affairs and provost, 2001—07; pres. Rochester Inst. Tech., 2007—. Contbr. numerous articles to profl. jours. Recipient award for excellence in engring. edn. for Mid-Atlantic states, AT&T, 1989. Fellow: IEEE, Am. Phys. Soc. Office: Rochester Inst Tech Office of Pres One Lomb Memorial Dr Rochester NY 14623-5603 Office Phone: 585-475-2396. E-mail: bill.destler@rit.edu.

DESTRI, JIMMY, musician; b. Bklyn., Apr. 13, 1954; Keyboard player with Blondie, 1975—82, 1998—. Musician: (albums) Heart on a Wall, 1982, (with Blondie) Blondie, 1976, Plastic Letters, 1977, Parallel Lines, 1978, Eat to the Beat, 1979, Autoamerican, 1980, The Hunter, 1982, No Exit, 1999, Livid, 2000, The Curse of Blondie, 2004, Best Live, 2005. Named to Rock and Roll Hall of Fame, 2006. Office: c/o 10th St Entertainment Ste G410 700 San Vicente Blvd West Hollywood CA 90069 E-mail: jimmydestri@dhbis.com.

DESUTTER, PAULA A., federal agency administrator; BA, U. Nev., Las Vegas, MA in Econs.; MS in Nat. Security Strategy, Nat. War Coll.; MA in Internat. Rels., U. So. Calif. Profl. staff mem. US Senate Select Com. on Intelligence; staff liaison to Senator Jon Kyl US Sentate; fgn. affairs specialist Bur. of Verification, Compliance, and Implementation, US Dept. State, Washington, spl. asst., asst. sec., 2002—. Sr. vis. rsch. fellow Ctr. for Counter-Proliferation Rsch. Recipient Presidentís Strategic Vision Award for Excellence in Rsch. and Writing. Office: US Dept State 2201 C St NW Washington DC 20520

DETELS, ROGER, epidemiologist, retired dean; b. Bklyn., Oct. 14, 1936; s. Martin P. and Mary J. (Crooker) D.; m. Mary M. Doud, Sept. 14, 1963; children: Martin, Edward. BA, Harvard U., 1958; MD, NYU, 1962; MS in Preventive Medicine, U. Wash., 1966. Diplomate Am. Bd. Preventive Medicine. Intern U. Calif. Gen. Hosp., San Francisco, 1962—63; resident U. Wash., Seattle, 1963—66; med. officer, epidemiologist Nat. Inst. Neurol. Diseases, Bethesda, Md., 1969—71; assoc. prof. epidemiology Sch. Pub. Health UCLA, 1971—73, prof. Sch. Pub. Health, 1973—, dean, 1980—85, head divsn. epidemiology Sch. Pub. Health, 1972—80, chair, dept. epidemiology, 2001—05. Guest lectr. various univs., profl. confs. and med. orgns., 1969—; sci. adv. com. Am. Found AIDS Rsch.; dir. UCLA/Fogarty AIDS Internat. Tng. and Rsch. Program, 1988—, Tng. Program in Epidemiology of HIV/AIDS, 1995—; cons. Ministries of Health, Thailand, Myanmar, Philippines, 1989, Global Program on AIDS, 1995, Singapore, 1996, 2006, China, 2002-, WHO, 1999, U.S. AID, 1998, 99, 2000, 01, Cambodia, 1998, 99, 2000, 02, 03, 04, 05, 06, 07, UN Devel. Program, 2001, St. Thomas Med. Sch., London, 1993-94, Myanmar, 1997, UN Devel. Program, Myanmar, 2001, UNICEF, 2005; mem. Nat. Adv. Environ. Health Scis. Coun., 1990-94; com. to study transmission of HIV through blood products Inst. Medicine, 1994-95; external examiner Nat. U. Singapore, 1994, 2004. Editor: Oxford Textbook of Public Health, 1985, 2d edit. 1991, 3d edit., 1997, 4th edit., 2002; contbr. articles to profl. jours. Lt. comdr. M.C. USN, 1966-69. Grantee in field; recipient Sahametry award, Gov. Cambodia, 2007. Fellow AAAS, Am. Coll. Preventive Medicine, Am. Coll. Epidemiology (coun. 1987-89), Faculty Pub. Health Medicine Royal Coll. Physicians of U.K. (hon.); mem. Am. Epidemiol. Soc., Soc. Epidemiologic Rsch. (pres. 1977-78), Assn. Tchrs. Preventive Medicine (chmn. essay com. 1969-75), APHA, Am. Assn. Cancer Edn. (membership com. 1978-85), Internat. Epidemiol. Assn. (exec. com. 1984-99, treas. 1984-90, pres. 1990-93), Assn. Schs. Pub. Health (sec.-treas. 1980-85), Sigma Xi, Delta Omega. Office: UCLA Dept Epidemiology Ctr for Health Scis Box 951772 Los Angeles CA 90095-1772 Office Fax: 310-206-6039. Business E-Mail: detels@ucla.edu.

DETER, RUSSELL LEE, II, obstetrical ultrasonographer; b. Dallas, Jan. 14, 1936; s. Russell Lee and Virginia (Peden) D.; m. Susan Tipery, Dec. 14, 1981. BS, Baylor U., Waco, Tex., 1958; MS, MD, Baylor U., Houston, 1963. Postdoctoral fellow Rockefeller U., NYC, 1964-66, U. Louvain, Belgium, 1966-67; asst. prof. anatomy Baylor Coll. Medicine, Houston, 1967-72, asst. prof. cell biology, 1973—, asst. prof. ob-gyn., 1975-80, dir. obstet. ultrasonography, 1977-95, assoc. prof. ob-gyn., 1981-84, prof., 1985—. Med. dir. outpatient ultrasound program Harris County Hosp. Dist., Houston, 1986-2005. Co-author: Quantitative Obstetrical Ultrasonography, 1986; editor-in-chief Jour. Clin. Ultrasound, 1982-96; contbr. articles to profl. jours., chpts. to books. Recipient rsch. grants Frankel Found., 1979-84, March of Dimes, 1979-83, 84-87, Joseph H. Holmes award Jour. Clin. Ultrasound, 1987. Mem. ACOG, Am. Inst. Ultrasound in Medicine (assoc.), Soc. Maternal-Fetal Medicine (assoc.), Internat. Soc. Ultrasound in Ob-Gyn. Home: 1721 Hawthorne St Houston TX 77098-1605 Office: Baylor Coll Medicine Dept Ob Gyn 1 Baylor Plz Houston TX 77030 Office Phone: 713-524-2877. Business E-Mail: russelld@bcm.tmc.edu.

DETERMAN, JOHN DAVID, lawyer; b. Mitchell, SD, Feb. 18, 1933; s. Alred John and Olive Gertrude (Lovinger) D.; m. Gloria Esther Rivas, Nov. 15, 1980; children by previous marriage: James Taylor, Mark Sterling. BEE cum laude, U. So. Calif., 1955; LLD magna cum laude, UCLA, 1961. Electronics engr. Hughes Aircraft Co., LA, 1955-60; sr. ptnr. Tuttle & Taylor, Inc., LA, 1961-86; gen. counsel Provena Foods Inc., Chino, Calif., 1986-92, CEO, 1992-98, chmn. bd., 1992—2004. Founder Carl D. Spaeth Scholarship Fund, Stanford U. Law Sch., 1972; mem. nat. panel arbitrators Am. Arbitration Assn., L.A., 1962—, mem. adv. coun., 1982—, mem. nat. panel of mediators, 1986—, mem. large complex case panel of arbitrators, 1993—. Mem. Am. Coll. Constrn. Arbitrators (charter 1982—), Order of Coif, Eta Kappa Nu, Tau Beta Pi. Home: 25 S El Molino St Alhambra CA 91801-4102 *Tolerate even intolerance but never cruelty.*

DETERT, MIRIAM ANNE, chemical analyst; b. San Diego, Sept. 16, 1925; d. George Bernard and Margaret Theresa Zita (Lohre) D. BS, Dominican Coll., San Rafael, Calif., 1947. Chem. analyst Shell Devel. Co., Emeryville, Calif., 1947-72, Houston, 1972-86. Photo participant Wax Rsch.: Quest, 1981; exhibited etchings Sight and Insight Art Studio, Mill Valley, Calif., 2002; contbr. poetry to books including The International Library of Poetry - Best Poems of the 90's, Spirit of the Age, The Nightfall of Diamonds, The Long and Winding Road, Through Oceans of Time. Vol. Falkirk Cultural Ctr., San Rafael, 1987-91, M.D. Anderson Tumor Inst., Houston, 1978-86, Rep. Party, San Rafael, 1990, 94; mem. Jewish Comm. Ctr. Recipient Disting. Alumni award Dominican Coll., 1994. Mem. Marin Geneal. Soc. Republican. Roman Catholic. Avocations: etching, painting, genealogy, swimming. Personal E-mail: mdetert@ix.netcom.com.

DETHERO, J. HAMBRIGHT, banker; b. Chattanooga, Jan. 2, 1932; s. Jacob Hambright and Rosalie Frances (Gasser) D.; m. Charlotte Nixon Lee, Sept. 19, 1959; children: Dinah Lee, Charles Drew. BS in Bus. Adminstrn., U. Fla., 1953; BFT, Am. Grad. Sch. Internat. Mgmt., Phoenix, 1958. With Citibank, NYC, P.R., Caracas, Venezuela, San Francisco, 1958-69; mgr. First Nat. City Bank (Internat.), San Francisco, until 1969; v.p. internat. div. Crocker Nat. Bank, San Francisco, 1969-75; sr. v.p. London, 1976-80, San Francisco, 1980-84, Bank America World Trade Corp., San Francisco, 1984-85; 1st v.p. Security Pacific Nat. Bank, Los Angeles, 1986-87; regional mgr. Calif. Export Fin. Office, Calif. State World Trade Commn., San Francisco, 1988-93; sr. v.p. Comml. Bank of San Francisco, 1994-98. Internat. bus. cons., instr., 1998—; adj. prof. Grad. Sch. Bus., St. Mary's Coll., Moraga, Calif., 1988-2000, John F. Kennedy U., Walnut Creek, Calif., 1997-2000. Author: Exporting Guide for California, 1993, 2d edit., 1999. Bd. dirs. Calif. Coun. Internat. Trade, 1972-77, 82-98, pres., 1974-76; trustee World Affairs Coun. No. Calif., 1971-77, 88-93; chmn. dist. Export Coun. No. Calif., 1983-93; dir. Internat. Diplomacy Coun., San Francisco, 1995-2002, treas., 1997-2000, pres., 2000-01; mem. San Francisco Host Com., 2000-02, chair, past pres. Com., 2005-06. Lt. USN, 1953—57, with USNR. Recipient Export Citizen of the Year award No. Calif. Export Coun./San Francisco Bus. Times, 1996. Home and Office: 694 Old Jonas Hill Rd Lafayette CA 94549-5214 Personal E-mail: hamdethero@aol.com.

DETHIER, C. BROCK, humanities educator, writer; b. North Conway, NH, June 15, 1952; s. Charles Putnam and Mary Hardenbergh Dethier; m. Melody G. Graulich, June 5, 1976; children: Corey N., Larkin K. AB, Stanford U., Calif., 1973; MA, PhD, U. Va., Charlottesville, 1978. Assoc. prof. Utah State U., Logan, 1997—. Author: First Time Up: An Insider's Guide for New Composition Teachers, From Dylan to Donne: Bridging English and Music, The Composition Instructor's Survival Guide. Named Tchr. of Yr., Coll. Humanities, Arts and Social Scis., Utah State U., 2006—07. Home: 7006 S 2400 W Wellsville UT 84339 Office: Utah State University 3200 Old Main Hill Logan UT 84322 Home Phone: 435-245-5747; Office Phone: 435-797-3546. Business E-Mail: bdethier@english.usu.edu.

DETHLOFF, HENRY CLAY, historian, educator; b. New Orleans, Aug. 10, 1934; s. Carl Curt and Camelia (Jordan) Dethloff; m. Myrtle Anne Elliott, Aug. 27, 1961; children: Clay, Carl. BA, U. Tex., Austin, 1956; MA, Northwestern State U., Natchitoches, La., 1960; PhD, U. Mo., Columbia, 1964. From instr. to assoc. prof. history U. So. La., 1962—66, assoc. prof., 1966—69; from mem. faculty to prof. emeritus Tex. A&M U., College Station, 1969—99, prof. emeritus history, 1999—. Author: (book) Our Louisiana Legacy, 1968, The Centennial History of Texas A&M University, 1976-1976, 1975, Americans and Free Enterprise, 1979, A History of the American Rice Industry 1685-1985, 1988, Suddenly, Tomorrow Came: A History of Johnson Space Center, 1993, The U.S. and the Global Economy, 1945-1995, 1997, A Bookmark: The Texas A&M University Press, 1999; co-author: A History of American Business, 1983, Timeless Heritage, A History of the Forest Service in the Southwest, 1988, Pattillo Higgins and the Search for Texas Oil, 1989, A Special Kind of Doctor: A History of Veterinary Medicine in Texas, 1991, Louisiana: A Study of Diveristy, 1998, Voyager's Grand Tour: To the Outer Planets and Beyond, 2003, Texas Aggies Go To War: In Service of Their Country, 2005; co-editor: (book) American Business History: Case Studies, 1987, Aerial Navigation, 1783-1903, 2003. Served to lt. (j.g.) USNR, 1956—58. Mem.: La. Hist. Assn., Tex. Hist. Assn., So. Hist. Assn., Econ. History Assn., Agrl. History Assn., Sigma Chi, Phi Alpha Theta, Phi Kappa Phi. Republican. Methodist. Home: 8709 Bent Tree Dr College Station TX 77845-5561

DETHOMAS, JOSEPH MICHAEL, former ambassador; b. Easton, Pa., June 1951; BA, MA, Pa. State U.; MPA, Harvard U.; Disting. Grad., Nat. War coll. Former dir. Office of European Union and Regioanl Affairs and Bur. of Polit.-Mil. Affairs; former prin. dep. asst. sec. of state Bureau of Nonproliferation US Dept. State, US amb. to Estonia, 2001—04. Recipient Meritorious Honor award for earthquake rescue work in Mexico, U.S. Dept. of State, numerous honor awards and citations.

DETJEN, DAVID WHEELER, lawyer; b. St. Louis, Jan. 25, 1948; s. Don Wheeler and Shirley (Pence) Detjen; m. Barbara Louise Morgan, Jan. 6, 1973; children: Andrea Marlene, Erika Alexandra. AB magna cum laude, Washington U., 1970, JD with honors, 1973; postgrad., Eberhard-Karls-Universitaet, Tuebingen, Germany, 1969—70. Bar: Mo. 1973, U.S. Ct. Appeals (8th cir.) 1976, U.S. Supreme Ct. 1976, N.Y. 1981. Law clk. to chief judge U.S. Ct. Appeals (8th cir.), St. Louis, 1973-75; assoc. Lewis, Rice, Tucker, Allen & Chubb, St. Louis, 1975-80, Walter, Conston, Alexander & Green, P.C., NYC, 1980-83; ptnr. Walter, Conston, Alexander & Green, NYC, 1983-2000, Alston & Bird LLP, NYC, 2001—, co-chmn. internat. practice group, 2001—04. Lectr. law Washington U., St. Louis, 1975—80; bd. dirs. Felix Schoeller Tech. Papers, Inc. Author: (book) Distributorship Agreements in the US, 1983, 2d edit., 1989, The Germans in Mo. 1900-1918: Prohibition, Neutrality and Assimilation, 1985, Licensing Tech. and Trademarks in the US, 1988, 1997, Establishing a US Joint Venture with a Fgn. Ptnr., 1988, 2d edit., 1989, 3d edit., 1993, US Joint Ventures with Internat. Partners, 2000. Sec. German Forum, NYC, 1988—2005, bd. dirs., 1995—, chmn., 2005—; co-pres. King-Merritt Cmty. Assn., Greenwich, Conn., 1997—2006; mem. Am. Coun. Germany, NYC, Atlantik-Bruecke, Berlin; bd. trustees Friends Goethe N.Y., Inc., 2005—, Arthur F. Burns Fellowship, 2006—; mem. St. Louis County Rep. Cen. Com., 1976—83, Representative Town Meeting, Greenwich, 2000—, vice-chmn. labor contracts com., 2002—; mem. nat. coun. Washington U. Law Sch., St. Louis, 1989—; trustee Washington U., 2004—, Am. Inst. Contemporary German Studies, Johns Hopkins U., 1999—, corp. sec., 2000—, vice chmn., 2004—. Recipient Disting. Alumnus award, Washington U. Law Sch., 1998, Regional Disting. Leadership award, Washington U., 2003. Mem.: ABA, Order of Coif, German Am. Law Assn., NY State Bar Assn. (exec. editor Internat. Law Practicum 1988—, mem. exec. com. internat. law and practice sect. 1999—, editor-in-chief Internat. Law Practicum 2004—, vice chmn. internat. law and practice sect. 2004—), German-Am. C. of C. (bd. dirs. 2003—, vice chmn. 2006—), German Am. Round Table, William G. Eliot Soc. Washington U. (N.Y. chmn. 1993—2006, nat. membership chair 2004—07, chmn. NY regional cabinet Washington U. 2004—), Deutscher Verein Club NYC (bd. dirs. 1994—97, 1999—2005, v.p., sec. 2000—03), Delta Phi Delta. Presbyterian. Office: Alston & Bird LLP 90 Park Ave Fl 14 New York NY 10016-1301 Office Phone: 212-210-9400. Office Fax: 212-210-9444. Business E-Mail: david.detjen@alston.com.

DETMAR-PINES, GINA LOUISE, business strategy and policy educator; b. SI, NY, May 3, 1949; d. Joseph and Grace Vivian (Brown) Sargente; m. Michael B. Pines, Sept. 11, 1988; 1 child, Drue Joseph Pines. BS in Edn., Wagner Coll., 1971, MS, 1972; MA in Urban Affairs and Policy Analysis, New Sch. for Social Rsch., 1987; MPhil, CUNY, 1995; PhD in Bus./Orgn. and Policy Studies, CUNY-Baruch Coll., 1997. Cert. adminstr. and supr., sch. dist. adminstr. Tchr. pub. schs., NYC, 1971-82; coord. spl. projects, pub. affairs N.Y.C. Bd. Edn., 1982, spl. asst. to exec. dir. pupil svcs., 1983, asst. to chancellor, 1983-84, exec. dir. tchr. Summer Bus. Industry Program, 1984-93; prof. pub. adminstrn. and mgmt. John Jay Coll. Criminal Justice CUNY, 1992-93; prof. bus. Ctrl. Conn. State U., 2000—04; assoc. prof. bus. strategy and policy U. Hartford, West Hartford, Conn., 2004—. Vs. prof. Rensselaer at Hartford, 1993—98, Fairfield U., 1998—2000; liaison for the Tech. Industry Program N.Y.C. Partnership, 1985—93; mem. editl. adv. bd. Internat. Jour. Bus. Rsch. Mem. com. to re-elect Borough pres. Lamberti, S.I., 1985-86; chairperson Crystal Ball event Greater Hartford Easter Seals Rehab. Ctr., 1994, trustee, 1994—; bd. dirs. Hartford Symphony, com. mem. 50th Anniversary Gala, 1993. Mayor's scholar, City of N.Y., 1984—96. Mem. ASPA, Fgn. Lang. Instrs. Assn., Strategic Mgmt. Soc., Acad. Mgmt., U.S. Seaplane Pilot's Assn., Internat. Orgn. for Lic. Women Pilots, Jr. League of Hartford, Hartford Task Force on Healthy Families, Chinese-Am. Soc., Am. Mgmt. Soc., Ea. Acad. Mgmt., Acad. of Internat. Bus., Cambridge Flying Group Club. Episcopalian. Avocations: flying, scuba diving, skiing. Office: Univ Hartford 200 Bloomfield Ave West Hartford CT 06117 Business E-Mail: gipines@hartford.edu.

DETMER, DON EUGENE, health informatics, management and policy researcher; b. Winfield, Kans., Feb. 3, 1939; s. Lawrence Oscar and Esther Beulah (McCormick) Detmer; m. Mary Helen McFerson, Aug. 26, 1961; children: Mary Catherine, Emily Anne. Student, U. Kans., Lawrence, 1957—59, U. Durham, NC, 1959—60; MD, U. Kans., Kansas City, 1965; MA, U. Cambridge, Eng., 2002. Intern, then resident in surgery Johns Hopkins U., Balt., 1965—67; clin. assoc. surg. br. Nat. Heart Inst. NIH, Bethesda, Md., 1967—69; resident in surgery Duke U., Durham, NC, 1969—72; Global Cmty. Health fellow Dept. HEW, Inst. Medicine/NAS, Washington, 1972—73; prof. preventive medicine and surgery U. Wis., Madison, 1973—84; v.p. health scis., prof. surgery and med. info. U. Utah, Salt Lake City, 1984—88; univ. prof. health policy, prof. surgery and health evaluation scis. U. Va., Charlottesville, 1988—93, v.p., provost for health scis., 1988—96, sr. v.p., 1996—98, Louise Nurancy prof. health scis. policy, 1996—99, prof. emeritus, prof. med. edn., 1999—; Dennis Gillings prof. health mgmt. Cambridge U., 1999—2003; dir. Cambridge U. Health, 1999—2003; sr. assoc. judge bus. sch. Cambridge U., 2004—07; pres. and CEO Am. Med. Informatics Assn., Bethesda, Md., 2004—. Mem. comm. on systemic interoperability US Dept. HHS, Washington, 2004—05, mem. Am. health info. cmty. workgroup confidentiality, privacy and security, 2006—; chmn. bd. dirs. MedBiquitious, 2006—; vice chmn. China Med. Bd. NY, Inc., 2002—04; chmn. bd. healthcare svcs. Inst. Medicine, Washington, 1994—2000; chmn. nat. com. vital health stats. HHS, Washington, 1996—99; chmn. Blue Ridge Acad. Health Group, 1997—, co-chmn., 2002—; regent Nat. Libr. Medicine, NIH, Bethesda, Md., 1987—91; trustee Nuffield Trust, 2000—06; bd. dirs., developer adminstrv.

medicine U. Wis., Madison; membership com. chmn. sect. 12 Inst. Medicine, Washington, 2002—04; chair Nat. Libr. Medicine NIH, Bethesda, 1989—91; assoc. Nat. Acads., 2002; vis. prof. Chime U. Coll. London, 2005—; health IT steering com. Agy. Healthcare Rsch. and Quality Nat. Resource Ctr., Rockville, Md., 2005—; healthcare IT adv. panel Joint Commn. Accreditation Healthcare Orgns., Oakbrook, Ill., 2005—06; cons. in field; vice chmn. Friends of Nat. Libr. Medicine, Bethesda, Md., 2006—. Contbr. articles on nat. health info. sys., compartment syndromes, health svcs. rsch. and policy to profl. jours. Chmn. pub. svc. com. bd. dir. United Way, Salt Lake City, 1986—88, Charlottesville, 1992—97; active USPHS, 1967—69; pres. Peace Luth. Ch., 1996—99. Recipient Global Cmty. Health fellowship, HEW, 1972—73; fellow, Clare Hall, Cambridge U., 2000—05. Fellow: ACS (vice chmn. com. allied health pers. 1989—90, chmn. 1990—94, internat. health com. 1996—2002, informatics com. 2004—, web portal com. 2004—), AAAS; mem.: NAS Inst. Medicine (chmn. Cecil awards com. 2004—06), Royal Soc. Medicine, Soc. Med. Adminstrs. (treas. 1997—2000), Am. Hosp. Assn. (chmn. coun. hosp. med. staffs 1984—87), Assn. Acad. Health Ctrs. (bd. dir. 1996—98), Am. Med. Informatics Assn. (bd. dir. 1996—98, chair internat. com. 2004), Am. Acad. Physician Assts. (hon.), Clare Hall Cambridge U. (life), Alpha Omega Alpha. Lutheran. Avocations: fly fishing, painting, horseback riding, crafts, reading. Home: 5245 Browns Gap Tpke Crozet VA 22932-1613 Office Phone: 301-657-1291. Business E-Mail: detmer@virginia.edu.

DE TOLEDO, CATHERINE HOLT, medical writer; b. Columbus, Ohio, May 16, 1954; d. Golden Jr. and Petrea (Giles) Holt; m. Luiz Carlos de Toledo, Mar. 10, 1979; 1 child, Laura Holt. BS, Stanford U., 1976. Med. writer Alfred I. duPont Inst., Wilmington, Del., 1976-79; tchr. English Mich. Lang. Inst., Campinas, Brazil, 1980-81; propr. Belladerme Skin Care, Campinas, 1981-84; med. writer Louisville Hand Surgery, 1984-85; freelance med. writer Ft. Worth, 1985-98. Owner MedShare Office Concepts, 1998—. Asst. editor: Reconstruction of the Child's Hand, 1989; contbr. articles to various publs. Polit. Campaign Mgmt. Bd. dirs. North Tex. Planned Parenthood, 1992—, chmn. bd. 1998-2000. Mem. NAFE, Am. Med. Writers Assn., Soc. Profl. Journalists, Texpac Alliance (dist. chmn. 1989—, exec. com. 1990-2000), Tarrant County Med. Soc. Alliance (chmn. health fair 1988, v.p. publicity 1989, rep.-at-large 1990, pres.-elect 1992, pres. 1993), Tex. Med. Assn. Alliance (publ. editor 1990-92, legis. chmn. 1992, pres. 1993, v.p. legis. 1997), Women's Club Ft. Worth, Etta Newby Club. Avocations: running, sewing, biking, reading. Home and Office: 8608 Funtier Ct Fort Worth TX 76179-2835

DE TONNANCOUR, PAUL ROGER GODEFROY, library administrator; b. Fall River, Mass., May 22, 1926; s. R. Godefroy and Emilie (St. Germain) de T.; m. Mary E. Fenno, Apr. 9, 1955; children— Paul Godefroy, Camille Marie. AB cum laude, Providence Coll., 1952; MS, Simmons Coll., 1953; postgrad., Western Res. U., U. So. Cal. Asst. librarian Enoch Pratt Library, Balt., 1953-54; chief librarian, tech. analyst Armco Steel Corp., Balt., 1954-56; dir. rsch. library Gen. Dynamics (Ft. Worth div.), 1956—, dir. tech. information programs, 1964-87, with Proposal Devel. Ctr., 1987—. Cons. MLA, U.S. Office Edn. on sci. info. pers.; John Cotton Dana lectr., 1966 Singer, Ft. Worth Opera Assn. Chorus; Author: The Exploitation of Technical Information, 1966; co-author: Science Information Personnel, 1963; Contbr. articles to profl. jours. Active United Fund and Community Council; mem. exec. com. Big Bros. Tarrant County.; Trustee Cosmopolitan Internat., 1961-63. Served with USNR, 1943-46. Named Boss of Year Am. Bus. Women's Assn., 1965 Mem. ALA, AAAS, Am., Nat. mgmt. assns., Ft. Worth Art Assn., Spl. Libraries Assn., Am. Soc. Information Sci., Delta Epsilon Sigma. Clubs: Mason, Fort Worth Boat. Episcopalian. Home: 6332 Genoa Rd Fort Worth TX 76116-2028 Office: PO Box 748 Fort Worth TX 76101-0748 *Above all, don't take yourself too seriously; Seek wisdom for itself and nurture a sense of humor. Together, they will serve you well.*

DE TORNYAY, RHEBA, nursing educator, retired dean; b. Petaluma, Calif., Apr. 17, 1926; d. Bernard and Ella Fradkin; m. Rudy de Tornyay, June 4, 1954. Student, U. Calif., Berkeley, 1944-46; diploma, Mt. Zion Hosp. Sch. Nursing, 1949; AB, San Francisco State U., 1951, MA, 1954; Ed.D., Stanford U., 1967; Sc.D. (hon.), Ill. Wesleyan U., 1974; LHD (hon.), U. Portland, 1974, Georgetown U., 1994. Mem. faculty San Francisco State U., 1957-67, prof. nursing, 1966-67, chmn. dept., 1959-67; assoc. prof. U. Calif. Sch. Nursing, San Francisco, 1968-71, prof., 1971; dean, prof. Sch. Nursing UCLA, 1971-75; dean emeritus, prof. U. Wash., Seattle, 1986—. Author: Strategies for Teaching nursing, 1971, 3rd edit., 1987, Japanese transl., 1974, Spanish edit., 1986; co-author: (with Heather Young) Choices: Making a Good Move to a Retirement Community, 2001. Trustee emeritus Robert Wood Johnson Found. Mem. ANA, Am. Acad. Nursing (charter fellow, pres. 1973-75), Inst. Medicine (governing coun. 1979-81). Home: 4540 8th Ave NE Apt 1001 Seattle WA 98105-4795 Business E-Mail: rheba@u.washington.edu.

DETRANI, JOSEPH, federal agency administrator; b. NYC; BS, NYU. Econ. analyst CIA, exec. dir. to dir., dir. European ops, dir. tech. svcs., dir. pub. affairs, dir. Crime and Narcotics Ctr., dir. East Asia ops.; spl. envoy for negotiations with Dem. People's Rep. of Korea US Dept. State, 2003—, spl. envoy for Six-Party Talks. Officer USAF. Office: US Dept State 2201 C St NW Washington DC 20520

DETSCHEL, WILLIAM FREDERICK, information scientist; b. Bklyn., Jan. 23, 1957; s. Frederick William and Margaret Detschel; m. Nanette Elaine Clerc; children: Marissa, Matthew, Michael, William Jr. AAS, SUNY, Stone Ridge, 1978; postgrad., SUNY, New Paltz, 1979—81; cert. in programming, IBM, NY, 1981; postgrad., Marist Coll., Poughkeepsie, NY, 1982—83. Computer programmer IBM, Kingston, NY, 1978—95; computer cons. Comtex Sys., NYC, 1995—98; info. tech. architect Volvo Info. Tech., Greensboro, NC, 1998—. Project team mem. Cornell U., Ithaca, NY, 1986, Los Alamos Nat. Lab., N.Mex., 1989—90; cons. Matlen Silver Group, Charlotte, NC, 1994. Mem. bronze level winners cir. NC Spl. Olympics, Raleigh, 2005—07; com. mem. troop 265 Boy Scouts Am., Gibsonville, NC, 2002—, merit badge counselor, 1999—. Recipient Informal award, IBM, 1984, 1990, 1991, 1992, 1993; scholar, NY State Bd. of Regents, 1974. Achievements include patents in field. Avocations: amateur radio, motorcycling, woodworking, model building. Home: 6905 Stella Dr W Whitsett NC 27377 Office: Volvo Info Tech AB 7821 National Service Rd Greensboro NC 27409

DETTERLINE, MILTON E., JR., minister; b. Bethlehem, Pa., Nov. 16, 1929; s. Milton Elmer Detterline, Sr. and Mary Elizabeth Detterline; m. Nancy Jane Day, June 26, 1954 (div. July 1976); children: James Lee, Jon Scott, Peter Kirk. BA, Moravian Coll., 1951; MDiv, Drew U., 1954. Ordained to ministry Evang. Congl. Ch., Pa. Conf., 1954. Pastor Pottsville Evang. Congl. Ch., Pa., 1954—57, St. John Evang. Congl. Ch., Allentown, Pa., 1957—61, St. John United Ch. of Christ, Tamaqua, Pa., 1961—69; pastoral fellow in ecumenics Yale U., New Haven, 1968; spl. asst. to pres., chaplain, alumni dir. Ursinus Coll., Collegeville, Pa., 1969—74; sr. pastor St. Peters United Ch. of Christ, Pa., 1972—. Dir. sch. methods Evang. Congl. denomina, bd. christian edn., various other offices. Contbr. articles to newspapers, reports and publs. Past pres. Allentown Area Coun. Chs.; chmn. Lehigh County Child Care Commn., Schuylkill County Child Care Commn., numerous other offices; moderator, co-founder Coventry-Warwick Ministerium; bd. Christian concern PSE Housing for Elderly, bd. Jefferson Apts.; pres., mem. bd. Orion Cmtys., Inc. Named Citizen of Yr., City of Tamaqua, 1968, Bldg. named in honor, St. Peter United Ch. of Christ, 2001; fellow, Westar Inst. Office: St Peter United Ch of Christ 1100 Mt Pleasant Rd Saint Peters PA 19470 Home: Box 156 Saint Peters PA 19470 Office Phone: 610-469-9690. Personal E-mail: medetterline@aol.com.

DETTERMAN, DOUGLAS KENWARD, psychologist, researcher; b. Lakewood, Ohio, July 24, 1942; s. Orville Kenward and Mary Louise (Knestrict) Detterman; m. Dora Jane Plunk, Aug. 21, 1965; 1 child, Damon Kenward. BA, Boston U., 1967; MA, U. Ala., 1969, PhD, 1970. Asst. prof. U. Dayton, Ohio, 1970—72; postdoctoral fellow Northwestern U., Evanston, Ill., 1972—73; from asst. prof. to prof. Case Western Res. U., Cleve., 1973—. Founder, editor Intelligence: A Multidisciplinary Jour., Cleve., 1977—; dir. Gatlinburg Conf. on Mental Retardation, Tenn., 1981—86; chmn. dept. psychology Case Western Res. U., Cleve., 1982—85, Armington prof., 1995—97, Louis D. Beaumont Univ. prof., 1998—, chair dept. psychology, 2003—05; pres. Divsn. 33, APA, Washington, 1984; vis. scientist Air Force Human Resources Lab., San Antonio, 1985—86; dir. Exptl. Psychology Program, Cleve., 1986—. Contbr. over 140 articles to profl. jours. Served with USN, 1960—63. Recipient Mensa award, 1991. Fellow: APA (Doll award Rsch. Divsn. 33 2007); mem.: Am. Psychol. Soc. (Edgar A. Doll award 2007), Internat. Soc. Intelligence Rsch. (corr.; dir., founder 2000—06). Achievements include development of battery with basic cognitive ability tasks. Home: 8520 Peppermill Run Chagrin Falls OH 44023 Office: Dept Psychology Case Western Res U 10900 Euclid Ave Cleveland OH 44106 Home Phone: 440-543-5067; Office Phone: 216-368-2681. Office Fax: 216-368-4891. Personal E-mail: detterman@case.edu.

DETTERMAN, ROBERT LINWOOD, financial planner; b. Norfolk, Va., May 1, 1931; s. George William and Jeanneille (Watson) D.; m. Virginia Armstrong; children: Janine, Patricia, William Arthur. BS in Engring., Va. Poly. Inst., 1953; PhD in Nuclear Engring., Oak Ridge Sch. Reactor Tech., 1954, postgrad., 1954; cert. in fin. planning, Coll. Fin. Planning, Denver, 1986. Registered investment advisor, Calif. Engring. test dir. Foster Wheeler Co., NYC, 1954-59; sr. research engr. Atomics Internat. Co., Canoga Park, Calif., 1959-62; chief project engr. Rockwell Internat. Co., Canoga Park, Calif., 1962-68, dir. bus. devel., 1968-84, mgr. internat. program, 1984-87; pres. Bo-Gin Fin., Inc., Thousand Oaks, Calif., 1987—; owner Bo-Gin Arabians, Thousand Oaks, 1963—. Nuclear cons. Danish Govt., 1960, Lawrence Livermore Lab., Calif., 1959. Trustee, mem. exec. com. Morris Animal Found., Denver, 1984—, chmn., 1984-88, now trustee emeritus; mem. pres.' adv. com. Kellog Arabian Ranch, U. Calif. Poly., Pomona; treas., trustee Arabian Horse Trust, Denver, 1979-94, now trustee emeritus; chmn. Cal Bred Futurity. Named to Arabian Tent of Honor, Arabian Horse Trust, 1997. Mem. Nat. Assn. Personal Fin. Advisers, Fin. Planning Assn., Acad. Magical Arts, Am. Horse Shows Assn., Am. Horse Coun., Magic Castle Club, Internat. Arabian Horse Assn. Club, Tau Beta Phi, Eta Kappa Nu, Phi Kappa Phi. Republican. Avocations: stamp collecting/philately, gardening. Office: 3609 E Thousand Oaks Blvd Ste 220 Westlake Village CA 91362-6941 Home Phone: 805-495-1788; Office Phone: 805-494-1844. Business E-Mail: boginfin@aol.com.

DETTINGER, WARREN WALTER, lawyer; b. Toledo, Feb. 13, 1954; s. Walter Henry and Elizabeth Mae (Zoll) Dettinger. BS cum laude, U. Toledo, 1977, JD magna cum laude, 1980. Bar: Ohio 1980, US Dist. Ct. (no. dist.) Ohio 1980, US Ct. Appeals (6th cir.) 1980, US Tax Ct. 1981. Law clk. to presiding judge US Ct. Appeals (6th cir.), Grand Rapids, Mich., 1980-81; assoc. Fuller & Henry, Toledo, 1981-84; atty. Sheller-Globe Corp., Toledo, 1984-87; v.p., gen. counsel, sec. Diebold, Inc., Canton, Ohio, 1987—. Mem. ABA, Ohio Bar Assn., Stark County Bar Assn., Am. Corp. Counsel Assn., Mfrs. Alliance (law coun. II), Brookside Country Club, Phi Kappa Phi. Roman Catholic. Avocations: golf, travel, photography. Home: 5237 Birkdale St NW Canton OH 44708-1825 Office: Diebold Inc 5995 Mayfair Rd PO Box 3077 North Canton OH 44720-8077 Office Phone: 330-490-5037. Business E-Mail: warren.dettinger@diebold.com.

DETTMAN, DONALD REESE, loss control inspector; b. Rockford, Ill., Apr. 4, 1937; s. Albert John and Gladys Elizabeth Dettman; m. Kathryn Mary Rossato, July 26, 1958; children: Pamela Ann Overson, Lana Marie Tollefson, Lynn Jean Berti. AA, West Valley Coll., Saratoga, Calif., 1972; BA in Social Sci., San Jose State U., Calif., 1977. Regional sales mgr. Pengo Corp., Sunnyvale, Calif., 1978—88, sales engr. Union City, Calif., 1991—93; nat. sales mgr. forged tooth divsn. Corona Clipper and Forge, Calif., 1988—91; pvt. investigator loss control insp. Index Rsch. Svcs., Inc., San Mateo, Calif., 1994—2003; ins. loss control insp. Allied Inspections, Fresno, Calif., 2004—. Tchr. San Jose Sch. Dist., Calif., 1993—2003; self employed pvt. investigator, San Jose, 1995—2007. With USAF, 1955—58. Mem.: KC (assoc.). Democrat. Roman Catholic. Avocations: golf, reading, travel. Home and Office: 15118 SE McGillivray Blvd Vancouver WA 98683 Home Phone: 360-326-3575; Office Phone: 360-510-8523. Personal E-mail: dettman0998@comcast.net.

DETTMAN, MARY, biology professor; b. Aliquippa, Pa., Feb. 22, 1970; d. James and Joann Dolnack; m. Glynn J. Dettman, June 8, 1996; children: Samantha Rose, Grant Alexander, Mason James. BS, Fla. State U., Tallahassee, 1992, U. Ctrl. Fla., Orlando, 1994, MS, 1997. Tchg. & rsch. asst. U. Ctrl. Fla., Orlando, 1993—97; front desk mgr. Marriott Corp., Orlando, 1993—98; prof. biology Seminole C.C., Sanford, Fla., 1997—. Student advisor Seminole C.C., Sanford, Fla., 2006—, faculty senate, 2005—, faculty inst. adv. com., 2006—. Mem.: Human Anatomy and Physiology Soc., Assn. Biology Lab. Edn., Nat. Assn. Biology Tchrs. Roman Catholic. Achievements include research in effects of growth hormones on underdeveloped sSrague-Dawley rats. Avocations: photography, swimming, camping, bicycling. Office: Seminole CC 100 Weldon Blvd Sanford FL 32773 Home Phone: 407-230-5801; Office Phone: 407-971-5045. Business E-Mail: dettmanm@scc-fl.edu.

DETTMANN, DAVID ALLEN, lawyer; b. Milw., Mar. 30, 1949; s. Karl F. and Beverly J. Dettmann; m. Jenee A. Nelson, June 26, 1971; children: Justin, Lisa, Jacob. BA in Acctg./Econs., Luther Coll., 1971; MBA, JD, Drake U., 1974. Bar: Iowa 1974, US Dist. Ct. (so. dist.) Iowa 1974, US Tax Ct. 1974, US Ct. Appeals (8th cir.) 1989, Ill. 1993; CPA, Iowa; accredited estate planner, Am. Coll. Real Estate Lawyers, 1994, Am. Coll. Trust and Estate Counsel, 2000. Ptnr. Lane & Waterman LLP, Davenport, Iowa, 1974—. Iowa State Bar Assn. rep. to Iowa legis. adv. com. on electronic filing of real property instruments, 2000—01; rep. to Iowa legis. county real estate electronic govt. adv. com., 2005—07. Dir., vice chair, chair Miss. Valley Regional Blood Ctr., Davenport, 1984—; mem. adult edn. adv. com. Scott CC, 1998—; mem. Presidentsrad com. Luther Coll., 2002—; former mem. ch. coun. Redeemer Luth. Ch.; bd. dirs. Cmty. Found. Great River Bend, 1996—2006, chair, 2004; bd. dirs. Am. Inst. Commerce, Davenport, 1986—98, Quad-City Estate Planning Coun., pres., 1990—91. Named Outstanding Planned Giving Profl., Ill. Quad Cities Chpt. Assn. Fundraising Profls., 2006; recipient Recognition for vol. svcs., Supreme Ct. Iowa, 1999, Disting. Svc. award, Luther Coll., 2001. Mem.: ABA, AICPA (assoc.), Scott County Bar Assn. (chmn. abstract/real estate com. 1985—95), Iowa Soc. CPAs, Iowa State Bar Assn. (title stds. com. 1985—94, chmn. title guaranty subcom. 1990—94, real estate and title law sect. coun. 1993—96, chair 1994—95, real estate and title law sect. coun. 2001—04, chmn. real estate modernization com. 2002—03). Avocations: travel, photography. Office: Lane & Waterman LLP 220 N Main St Ste 600 Davenport IA 52801-1987 Office Phone: 563-324-3246. Business E-Mail: ddettmann@l-wlaw.com.

DETTMER, ROBERT GERHART, retired beverage company executive; b. Parsons, Kans., Sept. 11, 1931; s. Ira Gerhart and Dema (Hinze) D.; m. Patricia Isabel York, Aug. 20, 1955; children: Stephanie, Constance, Robert Brantley. Student, U.S. Naval Acad., 1949-52; B in Bus. and Engring. Adminstrn., MIT, 1955; MBA, Harvard U., 1957. Engr. Lincoln Electric Co., Cleve., 1957-60; assoc. Booz, Allen & Hamilton, Cleve., 1960-64; propr. Robert G. Dettmer, Investment Mgmt., Cleve., 1964-66; v.p. ops. Tasa Corp., Pitts., 1966-68; pres. Scott Aviation div. A-T-O, Lancaster, NY, 1968-70, George J. Meyer Mfg. div. A-T-O, Milw., 1970-72, N.Am. Van Lines subs. PepsiCo, Inc., Fort Wayne, Ind., 1973-76; v.p. fin. mgmt. and planning PepsiCo, Inc., Purchase, NY, 1976-79; pres. Pepsi Cola Bottling Group subs., Purchase, NY, 1979-86; exec. v.p., CFO PepsiCo., Purchase, NY, 1986-96. Chmn. bd. Am. Movers Conf., 1974-76; trustee Miss Porter's Sch., 1978-84; trustee Manhattanville Coll., 1986-93, chmn. bd. trustees, 1988-92. Mem. Delta Tau Delta, Tau Beta Pi. Clubs: Harvard Bus. Sch. of Westchester-Fairfield County (chmn. bd. 1977-80), Harvard Bus. Sch. of Greater N.Y. (chmn. bd. 1982-83). Home: 80 Round Hill Rd Greenwich CT 06831-3743

DETWEILER, DAVID KENNETH, veterinary physiologist, educator; b. Phila., Oct. 23, 1919; s. David Rieser and Pearl Irene (Overholt) Detweiler; children: Ellen, Diane, Judith, Inge, Kenneth, David. VMD, U. Pa., 1942, MS, 1949; ScD (hon.), Ohio State U., 1966; MVD (hon.), U. Vienna, Austria, 1968; DMV (hon.), U. Turin, Italy, 1969. Asst. instr. physiology and pharmacology Sch. Vet. Medicine, U. Pa., Phila., 1942—43, instr., 1943—45, assoc. in physiology, pharmacology, 1945—47, asst. prof., 1947—51, assoc. prof., 1951—62, assoc. prof. Grad. Sch. Arts and Scis., chmn. dept. vet. med. scis. Grad. Sch. Medicine, 1956—68, dir. comparative cardiovasc. studies unit, 1960—90, prof., head lab. physiology and pharmacology, 1962—68, prof., head lab. physiology, 1968—90, prof. faculty arts and scis., 1968—90, chmn. grad. group comparative med. scis., 1971—87, prof. emeritus, 1990—. Mem. Inst. Medicine of NAS, 1974—; guest USSR Acad. Sci.; cons. cardiovasc. toxicology, 1950—. Contbr. articles to profl. jours. Named Father of Vet. Cardiology, Veterinary Sch. U. Pa., 1994; recipient Disting. Veterinarian award, Pa. Vet. Med. Assn., 1989, Disting. Practitioner award, Nat. Acads. of Practice in Vet. Medicine, 1989, D.K. Detweiler prize in cardiology established in his honor, German Group of World Vet. Med. Assn., 1982, David K. Detweiler Conf. Rm. named in honor, Veterinary Sch. U. Pa., 1993, Centennial medal, Sch. Vet. Medicine, U. Pa., 1994, cert. appreciation, FDA, 1998; fellow Guggenheim Found. Fellow: AAAS; mem.: Vet. Med. Alumni Soc. (Merit award U. Pa. 1981), Am. Coll. Vet. Internal Medicine (diplomate, cardiology group), Acad. Vet. Cardiology (pres.), Am. Heart Assn., Coun. Basic Scis., Am. Vet. Med. Assn. (Gaines award and medal 1960, Honor Roll award 1990), N.Y. Acad. Scis., Am. Assn. Vet. Physiology and Pharmacology (pres.), Am. Physiol. Soc., Phi Zeta, Sigma Xi. Home Fax: 610-645-8719.

DETWEILER, GREG JEFFREY, music educator; b. Harrisburg, Pa., Dec. 31, 1951; s. Roderick Leon and Betty Mae Detweiler; m. Rebecca Ann Finley, Mar. 3, 1985 (div. Dec. 20, 1999); children: Jaron Matthew, Aaron Nathaniel. BS, Lebanon Valley Coll., Annville, Pa., 1973; MusM, U. Ill., 1978, DMA, 1985. Vocal music tchr. Susquehanna Twp. Mid. Sch., Harrisburg, Pa., 1973—74; vis. dir. choral-vocal studies Mercer U., Macon, Ga., 1980—81; dir. choral activities Idaho State U., Pocatello, 1982—86, Southeastern La. U., Hammond, 1986—88, Albertson Coll. Idaho, Caldwell, 1989—97, Morehead State U., Ky., 1998—. Condr., artistic dir. Boise Master Chorale, 1993—95; choral dir. 1st Bapt. Ch., Morehead, 1999—; prof., choral condr. Ky. Inst. for Internat. Studies, Salzburg, Austria, 2001, 03; founder, dir. cmty. choir Idaho State Chorale, Pocatello, 1985—86, Albertson Coll. Choral Union, Caldwell, 1989—97. Specialist 6 US Army, 1974—77. Named Outstanding Young Man of Am., 1983, Ky. Coll.-Univ. Tchr. of Yr., Ky. Music Educators Assn., 2002; recipient Outstanding Svc. award, Gen. Commn. Chaplains and Armed Forces Pers., 1977. Mem.: Internat. Fedn. Choral Music, Nat. Assn. Tchrs. of Singing, Music Educators Nat. Conf. (dist. festival mgr. 2003—, Ky. Tchr. of Yr. 2002), Am. Choral Dirs. Assn. (chmn. youth and student activities N.W. divsn. 1992—96, Ky. 2003—06), Phi Kappa Phi. Southern Baptist. Achievements include research in investigation of resonance source of the singer's formant; psychoacoustic ramifications of singer's formant; laryngeal configuration in pulse register phonation: MRI and stroboscopic data; relationship of music and content area reading and writing. Avocations: mountain biking, hiking, reading, figure skating. Office: Morehead State U Dept Music Morehead KY 40351 Home: 249 Valley View Morehead KY 40351 Home Phone: 606-784-9360; Office Phone: 606-783-2480. Business E-Mail: g.detweiler@moreheadstate.edu.

DETWEILER, STANLEY BRUCE, music educator; b. Denver, May 28, 1951; s. Stanley Howe and Bernadine Marie Detweiler; m. Kelly Kathleen Lynch, Sept. 22, 1983; children: Chelsea Elise, Sonja Marie. MusB, Calif. State U., Long Beach, Calif., 1975, MA in Music, 1981. Single subject tchg. credential State of Calif., 1976. Army bandsmen U.S. Army, Fort Sill, Okla., 1976—2000, ret., 2000; sr. tech. writer, developer Armed Forces Sch. of Music, Little Creek, Va., 1986—94; prof. Ctrl. Tex. Coll., Panama City, Panama, 1995—97; instr. Pikes Peak C.C., Fort Sill, Okla., 2000—05; prof. Cameron U., Lawton, 2002—; band dir. Lawton Christian Sch., 2003—. Presenter Nat. Assn. Music Merchandisers, Anaheim, Calif., 1994—94. Lead alto saxophone player Cameron U./Lawton Ft. Sill Cmty. Jazz Band; 1st alto saxophone player Cameron U./Lawton Ft. Sill Cmty. Concert Band; vocalist Cameron U./Lawton Ft. Sill Cmty. Chorus (Messiah); sanctuary choir mem. New Post Chapel; choir mem. Calif. State U., Long Beach. Decorated Meritorious Svc. medal, First Oak Leaf Cluster US Army, Meritorious Svc. medal, Humanitarian Svc. medal, Good Conduct medal, Seventh award, Army Commendation medal, Third Oak Leaf Cluster, Army Achievement medal, Second Oak Leaf Cluster. Mem.: Okla. Music Educators Assn., Music Educators Nat. Councel, Harley Owners Group, Kappa Delta Pi, Phi Delta Gamma. Liberal. Methodist. Achievements include research in Researched, developed, and wrote a video script Rhythm Section Techniques, 42 Self Development Tests for Career Management Field 97, Army Bands. Avocations: fly fishing, fly rod building, trout fishing, hiking, motorcycling. Home: 124 SE Churchill Way Lawton OK 73501-6413 Office: Lawton Christian Sch 1 NW Crusader Dr Lawton OK 73505-9598 Home Phone: 580-351-6534; Office Phone: 580-536-6885. Office Fax: 580-536-5242. Personal E-mail: sbdetweiler@sbcglobal.net.

DETWILER, CHRISTINE WENDLER, special education educator; b. Phila., Nov. 7, 1947; d. Frederick Lawrence Wendler, Jr. and Eileen Casey Wendler; m. Barry Russell Detwiler, Dec. 9, 1967 (div. 1993); children: B.R. Brendan Jr., Benjamin Jonathan(dec.). AAS in Early Childhood Edn. summa cum laude, Montgomery County CC, Blue Bell, Pa., 1985; BS in Spl. Edn. cum laude, Gwynedd-Mercy Coll., Pa., 1990; MA in Edn., U. Arts, Phila., 1994. Cert. tchr. for mentally or physically handicapped Pa. Instrnl. asst., spl. edn. North Pa. Sch. Dist., Lansdale, 1983—90, spl. edn. tchr., all levels, 1990—99, program tchr., ann. young authors' conf., 1998—, learning support tchr., co-tchg. inclusion tchr., 1999—; tchr. elem. Walton Farm Sch., 1996—. Freelance writer Phila. Inquirer; writer, implemented various ednl. programs; presenter in field; lectr. in field. Contbr. articles to profl. jours. and newspapers. Tour guide narrator Independence Nat. Hist. Park, Phila., 1987—90; mem. cmty. forum com. North Penn Sch. Dist. Named to, Mont. County C.C. Hall of Fame, 2004; grantee, North Penn Sch. Dist. Ednl. Found., 2001—, North Penn Cmty. Health Found., 2003—05, 2006, 2007; scholar, Charlotte W. Newcombe Found., 1988, 1989, Lansdale Bus. and Profl. Women's Club, 1989. Avocations: travel, photography, writing for children, reading, antiques. Office: PO Box 453 Montgomeryville PA 18936

DETWILER, DANIEL PAUL, retired physics professor; b. Woodburty, Pa., Feb. 16, 1927; s. Clarence H. and Elsie Replogle (Stayer) Detwiler; m. Laura Buck Dennison, Mar. 10, 1989; m. Ann C. Meckes (dec.); children:

Lynn C., Paul E., Susan E. BA, Swarthmore, Pa., 1949; MS, Yale U., Conn., 1950, PhD, 1952. Rsch. Franklin Inst., Phila., 1952—54; prof. NY State Coll Ceramics, Alfred, 1954—60; dir. rsch. grad. studies Dukes Coll., Wilkesbarre, Pa., 1960—66; sci. tchr. NSF, India, 1966—69; prof. dept. chair Calif. State U., Bakersfield, 1970—74; ret., 1974. Mem.: AAAS, Am. Physics Soc. Home: 1141 Bruarcroft Rd Claremont CA 91711 Personal E-mail: ddewiler@bak.rr.com.

DEUKMEJIAN, GEORGE, lawyer, retired governor; b. Albany, NY, June 6, 1928; s. C. George and Alice (Gairdan) D.; m. Gloria M. Saatjian, 1957; children: Leslie Ann, George Krikor, Andrea Diane. BA, Siena Coll., 1949; JD, St. John's U., 1952. Bar: N.Y. 1952, Calif. 1956, U.S. Supreme Ct. 1970. Mem. Calif. Assembly, 1963-67, Calif. Senate, 1967-79, minority leader; atty. gen. State of Calif., 1979-82, gov., 1983-91, ret. gov.; former dep. county counsel Los Angeles County.; former ptnr. Sidley & Austin, 1991-2000. Served with U.S. Army, 1953-55. Republican. Episcopalian. Office: 5366 E Broadway Long Beach CA 90803-3549

DEULL, CHARLES BRIAN, lawyer, former publishing executive; b. 1959; BA, Tufts U.; JD, Boston U. Sr. v.p. legal and bus. affairs Scholastic Corp., NYC, 1995—99, sr. v.p., gen. counsel, sec., 1999—2006. Sec. bd. dirs. The Hunger Project, NYC. Office: Hunger Project 15 E 26th St New York NY 10010*

DEUPREE, MARVIN MATTOX, financial consultant; b. Woodbine, Iowa, Oct. 8, 1917; s. Archie Orin and Pearl (Mattox) D.; m. Katherine Anita Beard, Aug. 18, 1951; children: Marvin Mattox, Meredith Ann. BA with high distinction, State U. Iowa, 1941; MBA with distinction, U. Pa., 1948. C.P.A., N.Y., Ill., Mich., La., Iowa, Va., N.C. Instr. acctg. U. Pa., 1947-48; with Arthur Andersen & Co. (C.P.A.s), 1948-75, partner, 1960-75, mem. policy com. on acctg. and auditing, 1962-72; bus. cons., 1975—; pres. Emporium Specialties Co., Inc., 1977—. Adj. asso. prof. NYU Grad. Sch. Bus. Adminstrn., 1973-76 Contbr. articles to profl. jours. Served as officer USNR, 1943-46. Mem. AICPA, N.Y. State, Ill. Socs. CPA's, Nat. Assn. Accts., Am. Acctg. Assn., Execs. Club (Chgo.), Wharton Grad. Bus. Sch. Club (Chgo.), Univ. Club (Chgo.), Phi Beta Kappa. Episcopalian. Home: 5 Academy Rd Ho Ho Kus NJ 07423-1301

DEUTCH, JOHN MARK, chemistry professor, former CIA director; b. Brussels, July 27, 1938; came to U.S., 1940, naturalized, 1946; s. Michael Joseph and Rachel Felicia (Fisher) D.; m. Pat Lyons; children: Philip, Paul, Zachary. BA, Amherst Coll., 1961, DSc and Humane Letters (hon.), 1978; B Chem. Engring, M.I.T., 1961, PhD in Phys. Chemistry, 1965; DLitt (hon.), U. Lowell, 1986. System analyst Office Sec. Def., 1961-65; fellow Nat. Acad. Scis./NRC, Nat. Bur. Standards, 1966-67; asst. prof. Princeton U., 1967-70; mem. faculty MIT, 1970—, prof. chemistry, 1971—, chmn. chemistry dept., 1976—77, dean sci., 1982—85, provost, 1985—90, inst. prof., 1990—; dir. Office Energy Rsch., US Dept. Energy, Washington, 1977—79, acting asst. sec. for energy tech., 1979, under sec., 1979—80; under sec. for acquisition & tech. US Dept. Def., Washington, 1993-94, dep. sec., 1994—95; dir. CIA, Washington, 1995—96. Chmn. adv. panel on chemistry NSF, 1974; mem. Def. Sci. Bd., 1977—, Pres.'s Nuclear Safety Oversight Com., 1980-81; mem. Army Sci. Adv. Panel, 1975-78, Pres.'s Commn. on Strategic Forces, 1983, The White House Sci. Coun., 1985-89; Pres.'s Fgn. Intelligence Adv. Bd., 1990-94, Pres. Commn. on Aviation Safety & Security, 1996, Commn. on Reducing & Protecting Govt. Secrecy, 1996, Pres. Com. of Advisors on Sci. & Tech., 1997-2001; chair Commn. to Assess the Orgn. of the Fed. Govt. to Combat the Proliferation of Weapons of Mass Destruction, 1998-99; bd. dirs, Citigroup Inc., 1987-93, 1996-, Citibank, N.A., 1987-93, 1996-98 Author research articles. Sloan fellow, 1969-71; Guggenheim fellow, 1974; Disting. Intelligence medal, CIA 1996, Intelligence Community Disting. Intelligence medal, 1996, Greater Boston Fed. Exec. Bd. Speaker Thomas P. O'Neill award, 2002. Mem. Am. Phys. Soc., Am. Chem. Soc., Council Fgn. Relations, Am. Acad. Arts and Scis. Avocations: tennis, reading. Office: MIT Chemistry Dept 77 Massachusetts Ave Rm 6-208 Cambridge MA 02139-4307 E-mail: jmd@mit.edu.

DEUTSCH, ALIN BERNARD, computer scientist, educator; s. Otto and Claudette Deutsch; m. Daniela Georgescu, July 23, 1999. BS, Poly. U. Bucharest, Romania, 1993; Diplom-Informatiker, Tech. U. Darmstadt, Germany, 1995; PhD, U. Pa., Phila., 2002. Rsch. asst. U. Pa., Phila., 1996—2002; asst. prof. U. Calif., La Jolla, 2002—. Summer intern AT&T Rsch. Labs, Florham Park, NJ, 1998. Contbr. articles to profl. jours. Sgt. Romanian Mil., 1987—88. Recipient 1st prize Traian Lalescu Nat. Collegiate Math Contest, Romanian Ministry Edn., 1990, CAREER award, NSF, 2004—; fellow, U. Pa., 1996—97, Alfred P. Sloan Found., 2006. Achievements include patents in field.

DEUTSCH, AYALA, sports association executive, lawyer, educator; b. Bklyn., June 13, 1966; d. Simon and Shoshana (Salgo) D. BA cum laude, Queens Coll., 1986; JD, NYU, 1989. Bar: NY 1989, US Dist. Ct. (so. dist. NY) 1991. Assoc. Cleary, Gottlieb, Steen & Hamilton, NYC, 1989—97; with NBA, NYC, 1998—, sr. v.p., chief intellectual property counsel, 2005—. Bd. dirs. Internat. Trademark Assn., 2005; mem. trademark pub. adv. com. US Patent and Trademark Office; adj. prof. sports law Yeshiva U. Cardozo Sch. Law. Mem.: NY State Bar Assn. (co-chair sports law com.). Democrat. Jewish. Office: NBA Olympic Tower 645 5th Ave Fl 10 New York NY 10022-5986*

DEUTSCH, CLAUDIA, reporter; Industry and environ. reporter NY Times. Office: NY Times 229 W 43rd St New York NY 10036 Office Phone: 212-556-1023. Office Fax: 212-556-1448. E-mail: claudia@nytimes.com.

DEUTSCH, DAVID NEIL, investment banker; b. Newark, 1959; s. Richard and Dorothy Anita D. BA, Middlebury Coll., 1981; MBA, Columbia U., 1984. Corp. bond trader Lehman Bros. Kuhn Loeb, Inc., NYC, 1981-82; asst. to pres. Drexel Burnham Lambert Comml. Paper, Inc., NYC, 1983; assoc. corp. fin. Drexel Burnham Lambert, Inc., NYC, 1984-85; v.p. corp. fin. Bear, Stearns & Co., Inc., NYC, 1986-89; mng. dir. investment banking Congress Fin. Corp., NYC, 1990—93; founder, pres. David N. Deutsch & Co. LLC, NYC, 1993—. Author: (with others) The Mergers & Acquisitions Handbook, 1993. Mem. exec. bd. N.Y. new leadership State of Israel Bonds, N.Y.C., 1991—; mem. exec. com. Wall St. divsn. United Jewish Appeal, N.Y.C., 1991-96; patron Ballet Manhattan, N.Y.C., 1990—; mem. ann. dinner com. Grad. Sch. Bus. Columbia U., N.Y.C., 1992; trustee, chmn. nominating com. Mus. Am. Fin. History; amb. admissions Columbia Bus. Sch., mem. exec. adv. bd. Heilbrunn ctr. Grahm and Dodd investing; mem. coun. consolidated corp. fund Lincoln Ctr. Performing Arts; mem. fin. leadership forum Sci., Industry and Bus. Libr., NY. Recipient Overture award United Jewish Appeal, 1990. Mem. Assn. Corp. Growth, Comml. Fin. Assn., Columbia Bus. Sch. Club N.Y., Bonet Club NY. Avocations: running, exercise, antique collecting, thoroughbred racing, reading. Office: David N Deutsch & Co LLC 150 E 58th St Fl 16 New York NY 10155-0002

DEUTSCH, DIDIER (DELAUNOY), music producer, writer; b. Arcachon, France, Dec. 8, 1937; came to U.S., 1962; parents Ladislas Leopold and Simonne (Gruot) D. Baccalaureat, Michel Montaigne, Bordeaux, France, 1957. Dir. publicity CTI Records, 1973-77; publicity writer RCA Records, 1978-81; staff writer WEA Internat., 1983-86; record prodr. Columbia Records, NYC, 1986—, Arista Records, 1997—, Rhino Records, 1995—, RCA Records, 1994-97, Time-Life Music, 1994-97. Drama critic musicals. Contbr. articles to Stereo Review, The New York Times, After Dark, Pulse! and other mags. and newspapers. Served with French Navy, 1957-60. Recipient nomination Grammy award for Frank Sinatra: The Columbia Years, 1995, Sony Music: Soundtrack for a Century, 2000. Mem. Nat. Acad. Rec. Arts and Scis., Am. Theatre Critics Assn.

DEUTSCH, DONNY, advertising executive; s. David Deutsch; m. Stacy Josloff. Grad., U. Pa. Chmn., CEO Deutsch, Inc., NYC, 1984—; and mng. ptnr. Deutsch Open City prodn. company. Host The Big Idea with Donny Deutsch, CNBC, 2004—; mem. Clinton/Gore comm. team, 1992. Co-author (with Peter Knobler): Often Wrong, Never in Doubt: Unleash the Business Rebel Within, 2005. Bd. dir. Michael J. Fox Parkinson's Found.; exec. com. U. Pa. Sch. Social Work. Democrat. Office: Deutsch Inc 111 8th Ave Fl 14 New York NY 10011-5295

DEUTSCH, ERIC J., real estate developer, urban planner; b. Apr. 9, 1967; m. Terri Rosen-Deutsch; 2 children. With Econ. Devel. Corp., NYC, 1994—98, 1999—2002, KPMG, 1998; pres. Bklyn. Navy Yard Devel. Corp., 2002, Alliance for Downtown NY Inc., 2005—07; mng. dir. The Clarett Group, 2007—. Named one of 40 Under 40, Crain's NY Bus., 2006. Office: The Clarett Group 79 Madison Ave 17th Fl New York NY 10016*

DEUTSCH, HARVEY ELLIOT, lawyer; b. Bklyn., Aug. 18, 1940; s. Harry Deutsch and Beulah (Deutsch) Koft; m. Paula Kantor, Nov. 26, 1964; children— Stacia Francine, Steven Harold, Karen Gail. B.A., So. Methodist U., 1962; LL.B., U. Tex., 1966. Bar: U.S. Dist. Ct. Colo. 1967, U.S. Ct. Appeals (10th cir.) 1967. Assoc., Holland & Hart, Denver, 1967-69; ptnr. Isaacson, Rosenbaum, Spiegleman & Friedman, Denver, 1970-82; v.p., gen. counsel Bill L. Walters Cos., Englewood, Colo., 1982-84; ptnr. Deutsch & Sheldon, Englewood, 1984-, Deutsch, Spillane and Reutzel, PC, Denver, 1984-90; of counsel Beutzel & Assocs., Denver, 1990—; mng., owner Gateway Am. Properties LLC, Denver, 1990—; lectr. in field. Contbr. chpts. to books. Bd. dirs. Anti-Defamation League of B'nai B'rith, Denver, 1976—; commr. Colo. Civil Rights Commn., 1972-80, chmn., 1976-78. Served with USNR, 1962-70. Mem. Tex. Bar Assn., Colo. Bar Assn. Home: 255 Cook St Denver CO 80206-5304

DEUTSCH, HERBERT ARNOLD, music educator; b. Baldwin, NY, Feb. 9, 1932; s. Barnet Baruch and Miriam (Meyersburg) D.; m. Margaret Ann Carbray, Oct. 10, 1955 (dec.); children: Lisbeth Ann, Edmund Barnet; m. Nancy DiNapoli Blau, Sept. 14, 1997. BS in Edn., Hofstra U., 1956; MusM, Manhattan Sch. Music, 1961; postgrad., NYU, 1973-75. Music faculty East Meadow (N.Y.) Pub. Schs., 1959-60; freelance musician NYC area, 1960—73; lectr. music Hofstra Univ., Hempstead, NY, 1961-63, instr., 1964-68, asst. prof., 1969-73, assoc. prof., 1974-79, prof., 1983—, dept. chair, 1995—2001, prof. emeritus, 2001—; dir. mktg. Moog Music div. Norlin Corp., Buffalo, 1980-81, dir. sales/mktg., 1981-83. Cons. Pulse Concepts, L.I., NY, 1971—, Jim Henson's Muppets, NYC, 1983-86, Norlin Corp., Chgo., 1976-79; edn. cons. Music and Computer Educator, 1989-91; dir. piano festivals NY State Sch. Music Assn., 2004-07. Author: Synthesis, 1975, 2d rev. edit., 1984, Electroacoustic Music: Its First Century, 1993; composer numerous mus. works; contbr. articles to profl. jours., 1972—, Am. Record Guide, 1987-93 Mem. Huntington (N.Y.) Spl. Edn. PTA, 1976-88; bd. dirs. Huntington Symphony, 1973-75, Suffolk County (N.Y.) Family Services, 1975-77; founding tech. com. mem. NY State Sch. Music Assn., 1992-, composition adj., 1999-. Served with U.S. Army, 1956-58. Recipient grad. assistantship, Manhattan Sch. Music, 1961, Estabrook Disting. Alumni award, Hofstra U., 1995, award for alumni achievment, 2001; grantee, Meet the Composer, 1976, 1986—88, 1990—98, 2000—03. Mem.: AAUP, ASCAP (awards 1992—), Music and Entertainment Industry Edn. Assn., Am. Fedn. Musicians, L.I. Composers Alliance (bd. dirs. 1972—, v.p. 1991—95, pres. 1998—2000, archivist 2000—, founder, pres. 2003—05). Achievements include Herbert A. Deutsch award for highest music education graduate established at Hofstra University in 2001.

DEUTSCH, JAMES BERNARD, lawyer; b. St. Louis, Aug. 24, 1948; s. William Joseph and Margaret (Klevorn) D.; m. Deborah Marie Hallenberg, June 26, 1976; children: Michael, Gabriel. BA, Southeast Mo. State U., 1974; JD, U. Mo., 1978. Bar: Mo. 1978, U.S. Dist. Ct. (we. dist.) Mo. 1978, U.S. Ct. Appeals (8th cir.), 1989, U.S. Supreme Ct., 1990. Assoc. Gt. Plains Legal Found., Kansas City, Mo., 1978-79; pvt. practice, Kansas City, 1979-81; gen. counsel Mo. Dept. Revenue, Jefferson City, Mo., 1981-83; commr. Mo. Adminstrv. Hearing Commn., Jefferson City, 1983-89; dep. atty.-gen State of Mo., Jefferson City, 1989-93; ptnr. Riezman & Blitz, P.C., Jefferson City, Mo., 1993-99; Ptnr. Blitz Bardgett & Deutsch LC, Jefferson City, 2000—. Served to lance cpl. USMC, 1968-70, Vietnam. Named one of Men of Yr. in Constrn. Industry, Engring. News, McGraw-Hill Pub., N.Y.C., 1985. Mem. ABA (jud. adminstrn. com.), ASCE (hon. fellow), Mo. Bar Assn. (council mem. taxation com. 1985—, adminstrn. law and jud. adminstrn. coms., Best Lawyers in Am. 2005—), Mo. Inst. for Justice (bd. dirs. 1977—), VFW, Marine Corps League. Office: Blitz Bardgett & Deutsch LC 308 E High St Jefferson City MO 65101-3237 Office Phone: 573-634-2500. E-mail: jdeutsch@blitzbardgett.com.

DEUTSCH, JAMES I., curator; b. NYC, June 9, 1948; s. Joseph and Ethel Weiner Deutsch. BA, Williams Coll., Williamstown, Mass., 1970; MA, U. Minn., 1976; M in Librarianship, Emory U., 1979; PhD, George Washington U., 1991. Newspaper reporter The Indpls. Star, 1970—71; monorail operator Walt Disney World, Lake Buena Vista, Fla., 1971—72; park ranger-archaeologist U.S. Nat. Park Svc., Camp Verde and Clarkdale, Ariz., 1972—73; cmty. info. specialist Fairbanks North Star Borough Libr., Fairbanks, Alaska, 1973—74; forest naturalist Chugach Nat. Forest, Portage, Alaska, 1974; newspaper reporter, photographer People's Press, Yazoo City, Miss., 1977; park ranger, historian U.S. Nat. Park Svc., Vicksburg, Miss., 1977; bookmobile driver W.A. Percy Meml. Libr., Greenville, Miss., 1977—78; head ext. svcs. Parmly Billings (Mont.) Libr., 1979—82; foodways coord. Smithsonian Folklife Festival, Washington, 1991—92; hist. cons. Nat. Coun. on the Aging, Washington, 1991—94; dir. Learning Resource Ctr. Marymount U., Arlington, Va., 1995—96; census enumerator U.S. Bur. Census, Washington, 2000; program coord. Smithsonian Instn., Washington, 2001—02; acad. specialist U.S. Dept. State, Washington, 2000—03; program curator Nat. WW II Reunion, Washington, 2003—04; program curator Folklife Festival Smithsonian Instn., Washington, 2004—. Adj. prof. George Washington U., Washington, 1985—; Fulbright prof. U. Hannover, Germany, 1992—93, U. Leipzig, Germany, 1993—94, U. Veliko Turnovo, Bulgaria, 1998—99, Norwegian Ministry Edn., Oslo, 2002—03; rschr., presenter Smithsonian Folklife Festival, Washington, 1995—96; vis. prof. U. Lodz, Poland, 1997—98. Fulbright scholar, Coun. for the Internat. Exch. of Scholars, 1992—94, 1998—99, 2002—03. Office Phone: 202-275-1844. Business E-Mail: deutschj@si.edu.

DEUTSCH, KATHLEEN PILARCIK, artist; b. Chicago Heights, Ill., Nov. 21, 1960; d. Alfred and Theresa (Grzych) Pilarcik. Student, St. Mary of the Woods Coll.; AAS in Biology, St. Louis C.C., Florissant Valley, 1997, AFA in Printmaking with honors, 2006. Sr. fresh and saltwater specialist Beldt's Aquarium Hatchery, Florissant, Mo., 1994—2004; artist, printmaker, ceramicist; founder Little Dog Press, 2004—, Rose Owl Studio, 2007. Designer, preserver historically accurate clothing and crochet; editor (newsletter) Tumbleweed Connection; Ind. Edn. I-Step program; contbr. articles to profl. jours. Holistic health advocate; judge Calumet Regional Sci. Fair. Mem. AAUW, Internat. Thespian Soc., Nat. Honor Soc., Mo. Aquarium Soc. (membership chair), Quill & Scroll, Phi Theta Kappa. Avocations: music, dance, aquariums, art, writing.

DEUTSCH, MARSHALL E(MANUEL), medical products company executive, inventor; b. NYC, Aug. 17, 1921; s. David and Madeline Lea (Roth) D.; m. Judith Greene, June 27, 1947; children: Pamina Margret, Ethan Amadeus, Freeman Sarastro. BS, CCNY, 1941; PhD, NYU, 1951. Tech. dir. NEN-Picker Radiopharms., Boston, 1966-68, Picker-Hoechst Inc., Bedford, Mass., 1968-70, Mead Diagnostics, Inc., Bedford, 1970-72, CIS Radiopharms., Bedford, 1972-74, Thyroid Diagnostics Inc., Bedford, 1972-85; chmn. Marshall Diagnostics Inc., Bedford, 1985-87; tech. adv. J&S Med. Assocs., Framingham, Mass., 1989—2004, cons., 2004—. Bd. dirs., corp. sec., v.p. Health Svcs. Internat., Washington, 1983-96; contractor Joint Publs. Rsch. Svc., Arlington, Va., 1984-92. Inventor self-contained technetium generator, 1971, various radiopharm. products, 1973, various clin. chem. test kits, devices, 1953-96; contbr. articles to mags. Cons. AID, Zaire, 1979, UN Capital Devel. Fund, Benin, 1977. 1st lt. A.C., U.S. Army, 1942-45, ETO. Fellow AAAS (life); mem. Am. Assn. Clin. Chemistry (emeritus, chmn. pub. rels. com. 1962), Am. Chem. Soc. (sr., emeritus), NY Acad. Scis., Sci. Rsch. Soc. Am. Unitarian Universalist. Avocations: folk dancing, growing exotic mushrooms. Home: 41 Concord Rd Sudbury MA 01776-2328 Home Phone: 978-443-5837; Office Phone: 978-443-5837. E-mail: med41@aol.com.

DEUTSCH, MARTIN BERNARD JOSEPH, editor, publishing executive; b. Karlsruhe, Fed. Republic of Germany, Apr. 7, 1931; came to U.S., 1939, naturalized, 1948; s. Benedikt and Margarethe (Zivi) D.; 1 son, Kenneth; m. Denise Elaine Brosius, Sept. 24, 1994; 1 adopted child, Ariel Jade YunXin. Student in history and journalism, CCNY, 1953; student in Eng. lit., Columbia U., summer 1955. CCNY coll. corr. N.Y. Times, 1951-53; mng. editor The Beachcomber, Long Beach Island, NJ, summers 1952, 53; reporter Southwest American, Ft. Smith, Ark., 1954-55; mng. editor Travel Courier and Travel Weekly, 1955-67; pres., editor, pub. travel mags. divsn. Ofcl. Airline Guides, NYC, 1967-93; editor, pub. Reed Travel Mags., Secaucus, NJ, 1993-94; cons. Travel Industry Shows (Cruise Tour World), Pleasanton, Calif., 2002—; ptnr., database promotions, mktg. Morrell Wine Travel Experience, Harney Tea Tours, 2003—. CEO DB Prodns., Bedford, N.Y.; guest instr. U. Mass., 1975; cons., spkr. to travel and transp. industry. Monthly columnist: Up Front, Frequent Flyer mag., 1980-94; editor-at-large, monthly columnist Travel Agent mag., 1995-2001, pres. trade show divsn., 1995-99; pub. Selling North America, 1995-2000, CEO & columnist Travel Content on Demand, 2002—. Mem. Upper Manhattan Cmty. Planning Bd., 1965; mem. travel adv. bd. U.S. Dept. Commerce, U.S. Travel Svc., 1977-81; delegate White House Conf. on Travel and Tourism, 1995; officer Ctr. for Internat. Health and Coop., N.Y.C. With U.S. Army, 1953-55. Recipient various awards for travel journalism. Home and Office: 15 W 72nd St New York NY 10023-3402 Office Phone: 212-787-5759. E-mail: mbjdeutsch@aol.com.

DEUTSCH, NINA, pianist, vocalist; b. San Antonio, Mar. 15; d. Irvin and Freda (Smukler) Deutsch. BS, Juilliard Sch. Music, 1964; MMA, Yale U., 1973. Concert pianist internat. and U.S. tours, 1965-82; entertainer, solo pianist Holland Am. Cruise Lines, 1987, 89-90; freelance pianist, lectr. music, 1990—; pianist Royal Caribbean Cruise Lines, 2004. Exec. v.p. Internat. Symphony, NYC, 1978—82. *Nina Deutsch achieved the first musical exchange on stage in the history of the People's Republic of China in 1982. As executive vice president of International Symphony for World Peace in 1982, she represented her organization in a series of concerts on that theme. ISWP had collected musical scores on the theme of Peace, Friendship, and Humanity. Her tour was endorsed by former U.S. President George Bush, and his brother Prescott Bush. Nina is also the first woman to have recorded the massive solo piano repertoire of Charles Ives. She presents lectures on leaders in American music and lectures with musical illustrations.* Musician (pianist): (albums) Charles Ives, 1976; author: (plays) Portrait of Clara Schumann, 1987, Portrait of Liberace, 1995; contbr. articles to mags. and newspapers. Bd. dirs. Metzner Found. Overseas Relief; Ft. Lee coord. Channel 13, 1974. Recipient award for Am. music, Nat. Fedn. Music Clubs, 1975; grantee, Philips Petroleum Found., 1982; scholar, Oberlin Coll.; Tanglewood fellow, Wulsin Fellowship, 1966. Mem.: Yale Alumni Assn. Bergen County. Achievements include first American pianist to play all American music in communist China, 1982; first woman pianist to entertain for Holland America; first and only woman to record complete solo piano music of Charles Ives. Avocations: swimming, hiking, baking. Home: PO Box 405 Leonia NJ 07605-0405 Office Phone: 201-947-0087. Personal E-mail: ianist100@aol.com.

DEUTSCH, PETER R., former congressman; b. Bronx, NY, Apr. 1, 1957; m. Lori Ann Coffino; children: Jonathan Michael, Danielle Brooke. BA in Psychology, Swarthmore Coll., 1979; JD, Yale U., 1982. Atty., 1983—; mem. Fla. Ho. Reps., 1983—93, U.S. Congress 20th Fla. dist., 1993—2005; mem. energy and commerce com.; ptnr. Grant and Associates, 1990, Advantage Associates Inc., Washington. Dir., founder Medicare Info. Program, Broward County, Fla., 1981-82. Recipient Humanitarian award Deborah Hosp., 1984, Torch of Liberty award Anti-Defamation League, 1985, Appreciation award Paralyzed Vets Assn., 1987, Scroll of Hon. Jewish Fedn., 1988; named Legislator of Yr. Broward County Chiropractic Soc., 1984, 85, Man of Yr. Lauderhill Regular Dem. Club, 1990, Alzheimer's Assn., 1990; Swarthmore Nat. scholar, 1975-79; J. Roland Pennock fellow, 1979. Mem. W. Broward Dem. Club, Broward Young Dems., Lauderhill Dem. Club, Pembroke Pines Dem. Club, Davie Dem. Club, United Dem. Club, Plantation Club, Sunrise C. of C., Tamarac C. of C., Margate Knights of Pythias, B'nai B'rith (Israeli award, Sunrise 1983), Jewish Fedn., Gold Key, Phi Beta Kappa. Democrat. Office: Advantage Associates 201 Pennsylvania Ave Ste 3000 Washington DC 20004*

DEUTSCH, ROBERT WILLIAM, physicist; b. Far Rockaway, NY, Mar. 21, 1924; s. Nathan and Lena (Berger) D.; m. Florence Kadish, Sept. 11, 1949; children: Jane Lisa, David Jeffrey. BS, MIT, 1948; PhD, U. Calif., 1953; LLD (hon.), U. Balt., 1999; LHD (hon.), Towson U., 1998; DSc (hon.), U. Md. Baltimore County, 2000. Registered profl. engr., Md., Mich. Physics cons. Martin-Marietta Corp., Balt., 1962-64; prof., chmn. dept. nuclear sci. and engring. Cath. U. Am., 1963-71; chmn. bd., CEO Gen. Physics Corp., Columbia, Md., 1966-87, RWD Tech. Inc., Balt., 1988—2004, CEO, pres., chmn. bd., dir. corp. rsch. lab., 2004—. Contbr. articles to profl. jours., local newspapers Bd. visitors U. Md. Baltimore County. Fellow Am. Nuclear Soc.; mem. NAE, AAAS, Am. Soc. Engring. Edn. Achievements include the founding of world class companies dedicated to improving human performance in high technology workplaces. Office: RWD Tech Inc 5521 Research Park Dr Baltimore MD 21228 Business E-Mail: rdeutsch@rwd.com.

DEUTSCH, SID, biomedical engineer, educator; b. NYC, Sept. 19, 1918; s. Elias and Gussie (Hazen) D.; m. Ruth Appleman, Nov. 15, 1941 (div. June 1969), remarried, 1984; children: Alice, Phyllis, Naomi; m. Jane Arieti, Aug., 1969 (dec. Mar., 1978); m. Annette Page, Apr., 1979 (div. Dec., 1984). BEE, Cooper Union, 1941; MEE, Bklyn. Poly. Inst., 1947, PhD, 1955. Designer Fairchild Camera & Instrument Co., NYC, 1943-44; instr. Madison Inst., Newark, 1946-50; engr. Poly. R & D Co., Bklyn., 1950-54; mem. faculty Bklyn. Poly. Inst., 1954-72, prof. elec. engring., 1962-72; prof. bioengring. Rutgers U. Med. Sch., Piscataway, N.J., 1972-79; vis. prof. U. S.Fla., Tampa, 1983-98. Vis. prof. Tel Aviv U., Israel, 1977, prof. bioengring, 1979-84; cons. Lewyt Mfg. Corp., 1958-60; affiliate Rockefeller Inst., 1961-64. Author: Theory and Design of TV Receivers, 1951, Models of the Nervous System, 1967, Return of the Ether: When Theory and Reality Collide, 1999, Are You Conscious, and Can You Prove It? Short Science Essays, 2003, Einstein's Greatest Mistake: Abandonment of the Aether, 2006; co-author: Biomedical Instruments: Theory and Design, 1976, 2d edit., 1992, Neuroelectric Systems, 1987,

Understanding the Nervous System: An Engineering Perspective, 1993; assoc. editor: IEEE Transactions on Biomedical Engring., 1991-96; patentee pseudorandom dot scan for TV. Mem. adult edn. com. Roslyn (N.Y.) Pub. Schs., 1955-58. With USNR, 1944-46. Fellow IEEE, Soc. for Info. Display; mem. Sigma Xi, Tau Beta Pi, Eta Kappa Nu. Home: 3967 Oakhurst Blvd Sarasota FL 34233-1447 Personal E-mail: siddeutsch@ieee.org.

DEUTSCH, STANLEY, retired anesthesiologist, educator; b. NYC, Apr. 4, 1930; s. Elias and Estelle (Press) D.; m. Margaret R. Zuanic, July 11, 1971; children: Susan, Ellen, Nina, Eva. BA, NYU, 1950; MA, Boston U., 1951, PhD, 1955, MD, 1957. Diplomate Am. Bd. Anesthesiology. Rsch. and tchg. fellow in physiology Boston U. Sch. Medicine, 1951-55; intern U. Pa. Grad. Hosp., 1957-58; resident in anesthesiology Hosp. U. Pa., 1958-61; asst. prof. anesthesiology U. Pa., 1963-65; asst. prof. Harvard U., 1965-69; prof. U. Chgo., 1969-71; prof., head. dept. anesthesiology U. Okla. Health Scis. Center, 1971-82; prof. anesthesiology U. Tex. Med. Sch., Houston, 1982-89, George Washington Sch. Medicine, Washington, 1989-98, prof. emeritus, 1998—. Cons. VA Med. Center, Oklahoma City. Contbr. articles to profl. publs. Capt., M.C. USAR, 1961-63. Mem. AMA, Am. Soc. Anesthesiologists, D.C. Med. Assn., Sigma Xi, Alpha Omega Alpha. Home: 1508 Colonial Ct Arlington VA 22209-1439 Office: George Washington U Hosp 901 23rd St NW Washington DC 20037-2327 Personal E-mail: rbbs@comcast.net.

DEUTSCHMAN, LOUISE TOLLIVER, curator; b. Taylorville, Ill., Sept. 6, 1921; m. Paul Eugene Deutschman, Dec. 20, 1941 (div. 1966); 1 child, Deborah Elliott. BA, MacMurray Coll., 1937; postgrad., Northwestern U., Sorbonne, Paris, 1950—66. Assoc. dir. Waddell Gallery, NYC, 1966—74, Sidney Janis Gallery, NYC, 1975—78; dir. Alex Rosenberg Gallery, NYC, 1978—80; assoc. Sidney Janis Gallery, NYC, 1980—2000; curator PaceWildenstein, NYC, 2000—. Guest curator Nasher Sculpture Ctr., Dallas, 2004—06. Office Phone: 212-288-1174. Personal E-mail: louisetd@earthlink.net.

DEVAAN, JON S., information technology executive; BS in Math. & Computer Sci., Oreg. State U., 1985. With Microsoft Corp., Redmond, Wash., 1985—, v.p., desktop applications, 1995—99, v.p., consumer and commerce, 1999, sr. v.p., consumer and commerce, 1999, sr. v.p. TV divsn., 1999—2002, sr. v.p. engring. excellence, 2003—. Spkr. in field; panelist UN World TV Forum, 2000. Achievements include patents for simplifying user interface elements in PC applications. Office: One Microsoft Way Redmond WA 98052-6399

DEVAN, DEBORAH HUNT, lawyer; b. Allentown, Pa., Jan. 22, 1950; d. Valerio R. and Audrey (Miller) H.; m. Mark S. Devan, May 30, 1981; children: Emily, David, Eric. BA in Econs. magna cum laude, U. Md., 1972, JD cum laude, 1975. Bar: Md. 1975, D.C. 1976, U.S. Dist. Ct. Md. 1976, U.S. Dist. Ct. D.C. 1987, U.S. Ct. Appeals (4th cir.) 1988, U.S. Ct. Appeals (2d cir.) 1991, U.S. Supreme Ct. 1980, Md. Ct. Appeals 1975, D.C. Ct. Appeals 1976. Ptnr. Weinberg and Green, Balt., 1974-94; prin. Neuberger, Quinn, Gielen, Rubin & Gibber, P.A., Balt., 1994—. Bd. dirs. Lutheran Hosp. Md., Inc., 1981-86, Cystic Fibrosis Found., 1983 (Community Svc. Gold award), Lutheran Health Care Corp., 1988-91, U. Md. Law Sch. Fund, 1991, Balt. Devel. Corp., 1999—, U. Md. Sch. Law Alumni Assn., 2000—; trustee Merry-Go-Round Enterprises, Inc. Named one of Top 100 Md. Women, The Daily Record, 2005, 2007; recipient Svc. award, Md. Vol. Lawyers, 2006. Fellow Am. Coll. Bankruptcy; mem. ABA (bus. bankruptcy com., subcommittee bankruptcy litigation, subcommittee claims and priorities), Am. Bankruptcy Inst., Turnaround Mgmt. Assn., Women's Bar Assn., Assn. Comml. Fin. Attys., Md. State Bar Assn., Inc. (subcommittee creditor's rights, bankruptcy and insolvency), Bankruptcy Bar Assn. Md. (corp. sec., bd. dirs., pres. 1996-97), Exec. and Profl. Women's Coun. Md. (1st v.p. 1984), Network 2000, Comml. Real Estate Women, Bar Assn. Balt. City (profl. ethics com. 1980, publicity com. 1981). Office: Neuberger Quinn Gielen Rubin & Gibber 1 South St Fl 27 Baltimore MD 21202-3282 Office Phone: 410-332-8522.

DEVANEY, DENNIS MARTIN, lawyer, educator; b. Cheverly, Md., Feb. 25, 1946; s. Peter Paul and Alice Dorothy (Duffy) Devaney; m. Caryn Joanne; children: Jeanne Marie, Susan Theresa, Matthew Aaron. BA in History, U. Md., 1968, MA in Govt. Politics, 1970; JD, Georgetown U., 1975. Bar: Md. 1976, DC 1976, Fla. 1977, Mich. 1999, US Supreme Ct. 1980. Instr. European div. U. Md., Bremerhaven, Fed. Republic Germany, 1971-72; legis. asst. Md. Senate Jud. Commn., Annapolis, 1973-74; asst. gen. counsel US Brewers Assn., Washington, 1975-77; counsel Food Mktg. Inst., Washington, 1977-79; ptnr. Randall, Bangert & Thelen, Washington, 1979-81; assoc. Tighe, Curhan & Piliero, Washington, 1981-82; mem. US Merit System Protection Bd., Washington, 1982-88; gen. counsel Fed. Labor Relations Auth., Washington, 1988; mem. NLRB, 1988-94; commr. US Internat. Trade Commn., 2001; of counsel Winston & Strawn, 1995-97, Butzel Long, 1997—2001; ptnr. Williams, Mullen Clark and Dobbins, 2002—04; counsel Varnum, Riddering, Schmidt & Howlett, LLP, 2004—05; shareholder Strobl & Sharp, P.C., Bloomfield Hills, Mich., 2005—. Adj. prof. George Washington U., Washington, 1982—90, Boston U., 1992—94, 2002, Cornell U., 1995, Tulane U., 1995; assoc. prof. Wayne State U., 1995—2001, Thomas Cooley Law Sch., 2004. Served with USN, 1970-72, ETO. Mem. ABA, Md. Bar Assn., DC Bar Assn., Fla. Bar Assn., Mich. State Bar, Fed. Bar Assn., Phi Alpha Theta, Pi Sigma Alpha, Delta Theta Phi, Omicron Delta Kappa. Roman Catholic. Home: 5240 Buell Dr Commerce Township MI 48382 Office: Strobl & Sharp PC 300 E Long Lake Rd Ste 200 Bloomfield Hills MI 48304-2376 Office Phone: 248-205-2766. Business E-Mail: ddevaney@stroblpc.com.

DEVANEY, EARL E., federal agency administrator; b. 1947; m. Judith Devaney; 2 children. BA in Govt., Franklin & Marshall Coll., 1970; grad. exec. devel. program, George Washington U., 1990. Joined US Secret Svc., US Dept. Treasury, 1971, various positions including spl. agt. in charge Office Investigations Washington, spl. agt. in charge Fraud Divsn.; dir. Office Criminal Enforcement, Forensics and Tng. EPA, 1991—99; inspector gen. US Dept. Interior, Washington, 1999—. Recipient Meritorious Presdl. Rank award, 1998. Office: US Dept Interior Inspector Gen 1849 C St NW Washington DC 20240

DEVANEY, ROBERT L., mathematician, educator; BA, MA, Holy Cross Coll., 1969; PhD, U. Calif., Berkeley, Calif., 1973. Instr. Northwestern U., Tufts U., U. Md.; prof. Dept. Math. Boston (Mass.) U., 1980—. Dir. Dynamical Sys. and Tech. Project NSF, 1989—, dir. Regional Geometry Inst., 1990—93. Author (or editor): 10 books. Named Carnegie/CASE Mass. Prof. of the Year, 2004; recipient Deborah and Franklin Tepper Haimo award, 1994, Disting. Tchg. award, N.E. Sect. Math. Assn. Am., 1994, Dir.'s award, NSF, 2002, Excellence award, ICTCM, 2002, Trevor Evans award, Mathematical Assn. Am., 2005. Office: Dept Math Boston Univ MCS 164 111 Cummington St Boston MA 02215 E-mail: bob@bu.edu.

DEVANTIER, PAUL W., religious organization administrator, broadcast executive; b. Wausau, Wis., Mar. 25, 1946; w. Walter Herman and Ella Marie (Mundt) D.; m. Ellen Stapel, Aug. 2, 1970; children: Richard, John, Andrew, Katie, Susan. BA, Concordia Coll., 1968; MDiv, Concordia Sem., 1972; M in Mass Comm., So. Ill. U., Edwardsville, 1993; LLD, Concordia U., 1998. Radio announcer Sta. WXCO, Wausau, 1965-68, Sta. KRCH, St. Louis, 1968-72; dir. devel. Sta. KFUO-AM-FM, St. Louis, 1972-74, gen. mgr., 1974-82; exec. dir. comms. Luth. Ch.-Mo. Synod, St. Louis, 1982-2000; chief comm. officer Bethesda Luth. Homes and Svcs., Watertown, Wis., 2000—02; nat. dir. Infant Adoption Awareness Tng. Program, Washington, 2002—06; exec. dir. Nat. Luth. Alliance, 2007—. Spkr. By the Way (internat. syndicated radio program) 1974—. Author: By the Way, 1993, 2d edit., 2007, By the Way, Encore, 1999; exec. prodr.: (religious documentary film) Hymn A Celebration of Change, 1984 (Angel award), (TV spl.) Easter Alive 'Round the World, 1993 (Emmy award nomination), (TV spl.) Not Without Hope, 1994 (Angel award), Martin Luther Promo, 1998 (Telley award), Message of Hope, 1998 (Angel award DeRose Hinkhouse award), Just in Time For Christmas, 1999 (Angel award De Rose Hinkhouse award), Message of Love, 2000 (Angel award); (radio) Lutheran School Spots, 1999 (Angel award), Classical Radio Station of the Year in America, 1999 (Marconi award), (video) Free to Voice the Gospel, 2000 (Angel award), syndicated radio By The Way, 2001 (Angel award), television spl. So Much Like Us, 2002 (Angel award, Wis. Coun. on Devel. Disabilities award), television campaign, Thanks for Considering Adoption, 2004 (Angel award), Adoption Awareness, 2005 (Angel award); exec. dir. Luth. Witness mag., 1999 (Associated Ch. Press Best of Class award). Trustee, pres. Luth. Film Assocs., N.Y.C., 1982-2000; bd. dirs. Excellence in Media, Hollywood, 2001—. Recipient Outstanding Parent award, Adoption and Foster Care Coalition, 2002, Friend of Adoption award, 2006, Disting. Alumnus award, Concordia U., 2006. Office: 225 N Washington St Ste 300 Alexandria VA 22314-2520 Home Phone: 703-440-8205; Office Phone: 703-299-5131. Personal E-mail: pdevantier@blhs.com.

DE VANY, ARTHUR STACY, economics professor; b. Davenport, Iowa, Aug. 29, 1937; s. Arthur S. De Vany, Sr. and Ella G. De Vany; m. Bonnie Lenore Weiser, Apr. 19, 1958; children: Jeffrey L., Stacy Michelle, Brandon Jon. BA in Econs., MA in Econs., PhD in Econs., U. Calif., LA, Calif., 1967. Profl. baseball player Pitts. (Pa.) Pirates Minor League Sys., 1956—59; economist Gen. Electric Ctr. Advanced Studies, Santa Barbara, Calif., 1967—69; economist, dir. study Ctr. Naval Analyses, Arlington, Va., 1969—71; from assoc. prof. to prof. Tex. A&M U., College Station, Tex., 1971—80; prof. econs. Simon Fraser U., Vancouver, Canada, 1980—83, U. Houston, 1983—84; from prof. to prof. emeritus econs. U. Calif., Irvine, Calif., 1984—; pvt. practice cons. Washington, Utah, 1984—; co-founder, chief scientist Extremal Security Ptnrs. LLC. Pres., co-founder Resources Rsch. Corp., Coll. Sta., Tex., 1973—80; mem. all star baseball team Calif. Interscholastic Fedn., LA, 1955; vis. scholar U. Chgo., 1979—80; lectr. in field. Author: Hollywood Economics, The Emerging New Order in Natural Gas: Markets versus Regulation, A Property System for Market Allocation of the Electromagnetic Spectrum; contbr. articles to profl. jours. Recipient The Carol and Bruce Mallen prize for Scholarly Contbns. to Motion Picture Industry Studies, 2001. Achievements include invention of extremal securities for heavy-tailed distributions; patents pending for. Avocations: exercise, baseball, travel, softball, motorcycling. Office: Extremal Security Ptnrs LLC 3350 Broken Rock Way Washington UT 84780 Home Phone: 435-656-2469; Office Phone: 435-656-2469. Personal E-mail: asdevany@uci.edu.

DEVARD, JERRI, marketing professional; m. Gregg Smith; 2 children. BA in Econs., Spelman Coll., 1979; MBA in Mktg., Atlanta U., 1983. Mktg. asst. The Pillsbury Co., Mpls., 1983—92, group mktg. mgr. cake mixes divsn., 1992—93; dir. suites mktg. Minn. Vikings, 1993—94; v.p. mktg. Harrah's Entertainment, New Orleans, 1994—96; v.p. mktg. Color Cosmetics Revlon, 1996; v.p. new business devel. Citibank, 1998; chief mktg. officer e-Consumer line of bus. Citigroup, 2001—03; sr. v.p. brand mgmt. and mktg. comm. Verizon Comms., NYC, 2003—. Bd. dirs. Exec. Leadership Coun. Found. Named one of 50 Women to Watch, Wall St. Jour., 2006. Mem.: Nat. Black MBA Assn., Spelman Coll. Alumnae Assn. Office: Verizon Communications Inc 1095 Ave of the Americas New York NY 10036-6797*

DEVARIS, JEANNETTE MARY, psychologist; b. Burbank, Calif., Jan. 7, 1947; d. Nicholas Propper Klein and Elizabeth (Von Lichtenberg) Schaeffer; m. Robert Lee Blake, May 20, 1967 (div. 1979); 1 child: Brendon; m. Panayotis Eric DeVaris, Dec. 5, 1988. BA, Adelphi U., 1968; MA, Fairleigh Dickinson U., 1977; PhD, Seton Hall U., 1987. Lic. psychologist, N.J. Caseworker N.Y.C. Welfare Dept., 1968-72; alcohol and drug rehab. counselor U.S. Army, Ft. Monmouth, NJ, 1972-76; psychol. intern N.J. State Intern Program, Trenton, 1977-78; psychologist Greystone Psychiat. Hosp., Greystone Park, NJ, 1979; sr. psychologist R. Hall Cmty. Mental Health Ctr., Bridgewater, NJ, 1979-90; pvt. practice South Orange, NJ, 1988—. Tng. supr. Grad. Sch. Applied and Profl. Psychology; adj. prof. Seton Hall U.; sponsor and participant in Cable TV program; mem. South Orange Critical Support Team Vol. Group of Psychologists; founder One Braine Integration. Contbr. articles to profl. jours. Mem. APA, Nat. Register Health Svc. Providers, N.J. Psychol. Assn. (bd. dirs., interprofl. rels. com.), Soc. Psychologists in Pvt. Practice (bd. dirs., spkrs. bur. com.). Achievements include founding of OneBrain Integration Psychotherapy Technique. Avocations: travel, reading. Office Phone: 973-762-3149. Personal E-mail: drdevaris@yahoo.com.

DEVARIS, PANAYOTIS ERIC, architect; b. Lefkas Island, Greece, Dec. 29, 1932; came to U.S., 1960; M.Arch, Ecole des Beaux Arts, Paris, 1960; grad. cert. in bus. adminstrn., L.I. U., 1981. Registered architect; cert. Nat. Council Archtl. Registration Bds.; cert. profl. planner. Sr. corp. architect AT&T, NYC, 1972-90, PSE&G, NJ, 1990-93, cons. NJ, 1990-93; pres. DeVaris/Workspace Planning & Design, Inc., 1990-97. Prin. works include projects in N.Y.C.: World Trade Ctr., Park Lane Hotel, The Gershwin Theatre, The Sovereign Apts., The Uris Office Bldg.; in Conn.: Wesleyan U. Dormitories, 1960-72; for AT&T: Microelectronics Hdqs., Berkeley Heights, N.J., Network Software Ctr., Lisle, Ill., AT&T Corp. Ctr., Chgo., Materials Mgmt. Ctrs., Sacramento, Calif., Wichita, Kans., Ramapo, N.Y., AT&T Techs. Offices, Tokyo, 1972-90; author, internat. lectr. in field of work environments; juror furniture design competition Corp. Design mag., Annual Design Awards N.Y. State Assn. Architects; contbr. articles to trade mags. Mem. exec. com. Architects for Social Responsibility, 1988-90; trustee South Orange Village, NJ. Recipient tech. excellence award Western Electric Co., Inc., 1983. Fellow AIA (chmn. corp. architects com. N.Y. chpt. 1978, nat. chpt. 1986, N.J. chpt. 1992, mem. steering com. 1983-90, rep. to Internat. Union of Architects 1985-91). Home: 7811 Garland Ave Takoma Park MD 20912-7713

DE VARON, LORNA COOKE, choral conductor; b. Western Springs, Ill., Jan. 17, 1921; d. Vernon Walter and Hazel Mildred (Watts) Cooke; m. Jose de Varon, May 14, 1944; children: David, Joanna, Cristina, Alexander. BA, Wellesley Coll., 1942; MA, Radcliffe Coll., 1945; MusD honoris causa, New Eng. Conservatory, 1988. Asst. condr. Radcliffe Choral Soc., Radcliffe-Harvard Choir, 1942-44; condr. Bryn Mawr Coll. Choir, 1944-47; condr. chorus, chmn. choral dept. New Eng. Conservatory Music, Boston, 1947-88, condr. chorus for concerts with Boston Symphony Orch., 1952-86; concert performer New Eng. Conservatory Chorus, tours in U.S., Europe, Russia, Israel, China; condr. Israel Summer Festival, 1977-79; condr., tchr. choral conducting Tanglewood Festival Chorus, 1952-66; condr. New Eng. Conservatory Camerata, 1989—2006; prof. emerita New Eng. Conservatory; condr. Longy Chamber Chorus, 1989—2005. Guest condr. Cameron Singers, Israel, 1984, Beijing Radio Chorus and Orch., 1987; chmn. Choral Inst. of Composers Conf., 1983—85; choral adv. panel Nat. Endowment Arts; condr. New Eng. Conservatory Chamber Singers, 1982—87, Monadnock Music Festival; founder de Varonistas (small chamber chorus), 2005. Editor, arranger choral works, E.C. Schirmer and Galaxy Pubs., Boston. Mem. Cambridge Arts Council. Recipient medal for Disting. Achievement City of Boston, 1967, medal for Disting. Achievement Radcliffe Grad. Soc., 1972, medal for Disting. Achievement Wellesley Coll., 1978, medal of Israel, 1977, Ludi award New Eng. Conservatory, 1983, Harvard Glee Club medal, 1987, Disting. Achievement award New Eng. Conservatory Music Alumni, 2006. Mem. Am. Choral Condrs. Assn., Pi Kappa Lambda. Home: 94 Lake View Ave Cambridge MA 02138-3326 Office Phone: 617-547-6432. Personal E-mail: ldevaron@verizon.net.

DEVASSIE, TERRY LEE, retired publishing executive; b. Columbus, Ohio, Oct. 27, 1939; s. Robert William and Laura Belle (VanOrsdel) DeVassie; m. Lola Faye Sandifer, June 21, 1964; children: Trevor Lane, Thad Lamont. BA in Indsl. Design, Columbus Coll. Art & Design, 1964. Clk., sta. mgr. Columbus Dispatch, 1957-70, divsn. mgr., 1970-71, asst. to circulation dir., 1971-77, state circulation mgr., 1977-79, circulation mgr., 1979-81, asst. circulation dir., 1981—2001; ptnr. Preston-Strat Investments, 1993—; pres., CEO Creative Inserts Co., 1992—2006; mng. ptnr. WW Circulaton Cons. Group, 2002—05; ret. Owner, designer TLD Design, Columbus, 1964—69; arch.-designer Eagle Real Estate/Builders, Columbus, 1968—70; extrusion designer Plaskolite, Inc., Columbus, 1968—69; pub. spkr. newspaper circulation mgmt. and hosps. Designer drive-up newspaper rack, patentee graphic inserts for newspaper racks. Trustee Shriners Hosp. Children, 1996—2005; bd. govs. Lexington Unit of Shriners Hosp., Cin., 1991; endowment com. Simon Kenton Coun., Boy Scouts Am., 1998—2002; bd. govs., exec. com. Shriners Hosp. Burn Ctr., Cin., 1986—96; dir. Shriners Hosp., Ohio Donor Relations Com., Cin., 2005—; bd. dirs. St. Anthony Hosp., Columbus, 1987—91, Mercy Hosp., Columbus, 1987—91. Mem.: Press Club Ohio (pres. 1983, 1984), Circulation and Mktg. Fedn. Newspaper Assn. Am., Newspaper Assn. Am. (newspaper coun.), Internat. Circulation Mgrs. Assn. (chmn. Internat. Newspaper Carrier Day 1982—84), Ohio Newspaper Assn. (chmn. conv. 1983, Pres.'s award 1984), Ohio Circulation Mgrs. Assn. (sr. coord. and instr. circulation mgmt. 1980—2000, pres. 1982, founder Pres.'s award 1982, Pres.'s award 1986), Charity Newsies, Shriners (Illustrious Potentate Aladdin Temple 1995, imperial pub. rels. com. 1995, chmn. endowment, wills and gifts Shriners children'hosps. 1998—2000, emeritus mem. bd. trustees 2005, chmn. info. sys. com., dir. donor rels. State of Ohio), Masons (33 degree). Republican. Methodist. Avocations: landscaping, architecture, coin collecting/numismatics, golf. Home: 6330 Grassmere Dr Westerville OH 43082-8972 Personal E-mail: tdevassie@sbcglobal.net.

DEVAULT, JOHN LEE, oil industry executive, geophysicist; b. Kansas City, Mo., Aug. 4, 1937; s. Isaac Henderson and Evelyn Margaret (Rowell) DeVault; m. Janet Ann Miller, Sept. 11, 1968; children: Bryan Charles, Chris Lee. BSChE, Case Inst. Tech., 1959; BS, MacMurray Coll., 1961; MS, U. Houston, 1975. Lic. geophysicist Calif., Tex., Am. Assn. Petroleum Geologists, Soc. Ind. Profl. Earth Scientists. Geophysicist United Geophys., Europe, Africa, Middle East, Australia-Asia, Alaska, Houston, 1961—74; pres. Sercel Inc., Houston, 1974—88; chmn. bd. dirs. Jade Corp., Houston, 1988—. Contbr. articles to profl. jours. Trustee Culver Legion-Culver Academies; downstate v.p. Young Rep. Club, Springfield, 1960; bd. dirs. Jaycees, Springfield, Ill., 1960, Honors Coll., U. Houston, 1990—, McMurray Coll. Mem.: Am. Inst. Profl. Geologists (pres. Tex. sect., lic. geophysicist), Soc. Exploration Goephysics, Geophys. Soc. Houston (hon.; pres. 1987), Culver Club Greater Houston (pres.). Mem. Disciples Of Christ. Home: 703 Queensmill Ct Houston TX 77079-2411 Office: Jade Corp PO Box 218567 Houston TX 77218-8567

DEVEER, ROBERT KIPP, JR., investment banker; b. Englewood, NJ, Apr. 22, 1946; s. Robert Kipp and Patricia Ann (Mulcare) deV.; m. Sally J. Staub, Dec. 21, 1968 (dec. Jan. 1994); children: Robert Kipp III, James Britten; m. Mary Louise Leaf, Feb. 18, 1995. BA in Econs., Yale U., 1968; MBA, Stanford U., 1973. Assoc. The First Boston Corp., NYC, 1973—78, v.p., 1978—85, mng. dir., 1985—, dir. east coast investment banking, 1988—92, head natural resources group, 1992—93; alternate dir. YPF, s.a., 1993—96; dir. TheraTech Inc., 1996—2000, Palatin Techs., Inc., 1998—. Pres.deVeer Capital LLC, 1996—. Lt. USN, 1968-71. Arjay Miller scholar Stanford Bus. Sch., 1973. Mem. SC Yacht Club, Edgartown Yacht Club (Martha's Vineyard), Vail Mountain Club. Avocations: skiing, golf, sailing. E-mail: deVeer46@aol.com.

DEVELLANO, JAMES CHARLES, professional hockey manager, baseball executive; b. Ont., Can., Jan. 18, 1943; came to U.S., 1979; s. James Joseph and Jean (Piter) D. Ont. scout St. Louis Blues NHL, Toronto, 1967-72; eastern Can. scout N.Y. Islanders, Toronto, 1972-74, dir. scouting, 1974-82; asst. gen. mgr. Islanders, LI and NY, 1981-82; gen. mgr. Detroit Red Wings, 1982-90, sr. v.p., 1990—; v.p., gen. mgr. Indpls. Checkers, 1979-81; sr. v.p. Detroit Tigers, 2001—. Alternate gov. Detroit Red Wings. Winner Stanley Cup with N.Y. Islanders, 1979-80, 80-81, 81-82, with Detroit Red Wings, 1996-97, 97-98, 2001-2002, Pres.'s Trophy with Detroit Red Wings, 1994-95, 95-96, 2001-2002, 2003-04, 2005-06. Mem. Nat. Hockey League (bd. govs.). Office: Detroit Red Wings Hockey Club Joe Louis Arena 600 Civic Center Dr Detroit MI 48226-4419 Office Phone: 313-506-9885. Personal E-mail: jimdevellano@comcast.net.

DEVENISH, NICOLLE See WALLACE, NICOLLE

DEVENNY, LILLIAN NICKELL, trophy company executive; b. Chesapeake, Ohio; d. Hayes Basil and Alice Irene (Noble) Nickell; m. John Paul DeVenny Jr., Dec. 31, 1955; children: Carrie DeVenny Paganini (dec.), John Hayes. Student, Covington Bus. Sch., 1954—55, Norfolk Coll., Va., 1980—81. Office mgr., bookkeeper Nickell Electric Co., Covington, Va., 1950—55, exec., 1960—62; sec. 5th Naval Dist. Hdqs., Norfolk, Va., 1955—58, Profl. Realty, Virginia Beach, Va., 1971; pub. rels. corp. sec. Hobby Industries, Virginia Beach, 1973—74; owner, sec.-treas. Deste Corp. t/a Hobby Assoc., Virginia Beach, 1974—. Singer, actress Tidewater Dinner Theater, Norfolk, 1971-75 Writer column on Va. travel, 1978-79; editor newsletter, 1972-73. Founding mem., chair bd. dirs. Va. Opposing Drunk Driving, 1981—, state v.p., 1981—86, state pres., 1986—; adv. bd. Va. Commn. on Alcohol Safety, 1987—91; participant Va. Assembly on Future of Va.'s Cts., U. Va., Commn. Pub. Svc., 1989; mem. spl. White Ho. briefing on ways to combat tragedy of drunk driving, 1989; active Va. Civilian-Mil. Cmty. Safety Com., 1988, Va. Alcohol Safety Action Program Commn., 1991—2005; co-chair Va. Coalition Against Drunk Driving, 1989—2003; contbr. passage Omnibus Alcohol Safety Act, Va. Gen. Assembly, 1994; legis. liaison for Drive Safe Transp. Safety Coalition, 1998—; apptd. mem. Gov.'s Task Force to Combat Drunk Driving, 2002; chmn. Southeastern Task Force Drunk Driving, 1982, Virginia Beach Task Force Drunk Driving, 1982. Recipient Cmty. Svc. award J.C. Penney Co., 1985, Hometown Hero, Sta. WVEC-TV, 1986, Gov.'s Transp. Safety award, 2000, Lifetime Achievement award Civilian/Mil. Workshop, 2002. Mem.: Internat. Ceramists Assn., Modern Woodmen Am. (regional sec. 1954). Episcopalian. Avocations: singing, costume design, reading, theater, herb gardening. Office: Deste Corp t/a Hobby Assocs 5815 Hargrove St Norfolk VA 23502-4636

DEVENOT, DAVID CHARLES, human resources specialist, artist; b. Indpls., May 27, 1939; s. Charles Joseph and Pearl (Geodry) Devenot; m. Hillary Mock; children: Daniel, Mark. BBA, U. Hawaii, 1962. Dir. indsl. rels. USP Corp subs. Consol. Foods, Sara Lee, San Jose, Calif., 1964-70; mgr. human resources cons. and rsch. Hawaii Employers Coun., Honolulu, 1970. Adj. prof. U. Hawaii. Bd. dir. Hawn Humane Soc., Honolulu, 1975—, Am. Cancer Soc., 1989, pres. Pacific divsn.; active Hawaii Cmty. Svcs. Coun., 2004—. Mem.: Soc. Human Resource Mgmt., Santa Clara Valley Pers. Assn. (pres. 1968—69). Avocations: travel, photography, art, painting. Home: 2803 Puuhonua St Honolulu HI 96822-1765 Office: Hawaii Employers Coun 2682 Wai Wai Loop Honolulu HI 96819-1938 Business E-Mail: ddevenot@hecouncil.org.

DEVENS, PAUL, retired lawyer; b. Gary, Ind., June 8, 1931; s. Zenove and Anna (Brilla) Dewenetz; m. Setsuko Sugihara, Aug. 14, 1955; children: Paula, Vladimir, Mignon. BA in Econs. cum laude, Ind. U., 1954; LLB, Columbia U., 1957. Bar: N.Y. 1958, U.S. Dist. Ct. Hawaii 1960, Hawaii 1961, U.S. Ct. Appeals (9th cir.) 1962, U.S. Ct. Internat. Trade 1963, U.S. Supreme Ct. 1970. Pvt. practice law, NYC, 1958-60; ptnr. Lewis, Saunders & Key, Honolulu, 1960-69; corp. counsel City and County of Honolulu, 1969-72, mng. dir., 1973-75; ptnr. Devens, Nakano, Saito, Lee, Wong & Ching, Honolulu, 1975-94, of counsel, 1994—2006, ret., 2006. Judge Nuclear Claims Tribunal, Majuro, Republic of the Marshall Islands, 1988-90. Mem. Japan-Hawaii Econ. Coun., 1975-95, Honolulu Charter Reorgn. Com., 1979-80, Pacific and Asian Affairs Coun., 1983; trustee Japan-Am. Soc. Honolulu, 1981-2006, pres., 1987-89; chmn. bd. dirs. Nat. Assn. Japan-Am. Socs., 1989-91; mem. bd. govs. Japanese Cultural Ctr., Hawaii, 1989-94, mem. bd. dirs., v.p., 1994-96, chmn. bd. dirs., 1996-97. Decorated Imperial Order of the Sacred Treasure, Gold Rays with Neck ribbon Govt. of Japan, 1993. Mem.: Phi Beta Kappa. Democrat. Eastern Orthodox. Office: Devens Nakano Saito Lee Wong & Ching 220 S King St Ste 1600 Honolulu HI 96813-4597 Office Phone: 808-521-1456. Business E-Mail: pdevens@dnslwc.com.

DEVERAUX, JUDE (JUDE GILLIAM WHITE), writer; b. Louisville, Sept. 20, 1947; d. Harold J. and Virgina (Berry) Gilliam; m. Richard G. Sides, 1967 (div. 1969); m. Claude B. White, 1970 (div. 1993). BS Fine Arts, Murray State U., 1970; Cert. in Teaching, Coll. Santa Fe, 1973. Cert. remedial reading tchr. Tchr. elem. sch., Santa Fe, 1970-76; writer, 1976—. Author novels including: The Enchanted Land, 1978, The Black Lyon, 1980, The Velvet Promise, 1981, Casa Grande, 1982, Highland Velvet, 1982, Velvet Song, 1983, Velvet Angel, 1983, Sweetbriar, 1983, Countefeit Lady, 1984, Lost Lady, 1985, River Lady, 1985, Twin of Ice, 1985, Twin of Fire, 1985, The Temptress, 1986, The Raider, 1987, The Princess, 1987, The Maiden, 1988, The Awakening, 1988, The Taming, 1989, A Knight in Shining Armor, 1990, Wishes, 1990, Mountain Laurel, 1990, The Conquest, 1991, The Duchess, 1991, Sweet Liar, 1992, Eternity, 1992, The Invitation, 1993, Remembrance, 1994, Legend, 1996, An Angel for Emily, 1998, The Blessing, 1999, High Tide, 2000, Temptation, 2000, Twin of Fire/Twin of Ice, 2001, The Summerhouse, 2001, A Knight in Shining Armor, 2002, The Mulberry Tree, 2002, Forever, 2002, Wild Orchids, 2003, Forever and Always, 2003, Holly, 2003, Eternity, 2004, The Princess, 2004, Wishes, 2004, River Lady, 2004, Always, 2004. Mem. Costume Soc. Am. Avocations: cooking, computers, travel, collecting books on costume history, reading english history. Office: Pocket Books Simon & Schuster Inc 1230 Avenue Of The Americas New York NY 10020-1586

DEVEREUX, MARA, sculptor, artist; MFA, Otis Art Inst., LA, 1962; student, Bklyn. Mus. Art Sch.; studied with George Grosz; studied with Larry Rivers, NY; student, NY Liverpool Coll. Art, England. Numerous pvt. collections, Represented in permanent collections Lipton Tea Co., NY, Bloomingdales, Mus. Modern Art, prin. works include Millage Watch Co. faceplate design, Calif., exhibitions include LA County Mus. Art, Bklyn. Mus., Hecksher Mus., Huntington, NY, Barnsdall Gallery, LA, 2004, Asto Gallery, 2004, Gwangwhamoon Art Festival, Korea, 2006—07, Asto Mus., Long Beach, Calif., 2007, numerous others, Asto Internat. Art Festival, Seoul, 2007, LA, 2007, Barnsdall Gallery, 2007, Astogallery, 2007, Gwangwhamoon Art Festival, Republic of Korea, 2006—, Cultural Ctr., Beijing, China, 2007, Asto Mus., Long Beach, Calif., 2007—. Home: 661 Shatto Pl Unit 100 Los Angeles CA 90005 Office Phone: 310-562-2101. Personal E-mail: maradevereux@yahoo.com.

DEVEREUX, OWEN FRANCIS, retired metallurgy educator; b. Lexington, Mass., Aug. 23, 1937; s. George Francis and Mildred Anna (Gleeson) D.; m. Sally Williamson, June 15, 1957 (div. June 1969); children: Owen M., Amy L., Jonathan W., Nancy J.; m. Olivia Elaine Marin, June 13, 1969. BS, MIT, 1959, MS, 1960, PhD, 1962. Rsch. chemist Chevron Rsch. Co., La Habra, Calif., 1962-64, Corning (N.Y.) Glass Works, 1964-66, Chevron Oil Field Rsch. Co., La Habra, 1966-68; assoc. prof. metallurgy U. Conn., Storrs, 1968-76, prof., 1976-99, head dept., 1983-98; ret., 1999. Author: Topics in Metallurgical Thermodynamics, 1983; contbr. articles to profl. jours. Rsch. grantee NSF, 1970-76, U.S. Dept. Energy, 1976-86, NSF Industry/Univ. Corp. Rsch. Ctr. for Grinding Rsch. and Devel., 1990-98. Mem. AIME, AAUP, Electrochem. Soc. (div. editor 1987-90), Nat. Assn. Corrosion Engrs. Avocations: quarter horses, carriage driving, saddle making, classical guitar. Home: 99 Summit Rd Storrs Mansfield CT 06268-1421

DEVEREUX, TIMOTHY EDWARD, advertising executive; b. Chgo., Jan. 13, 1932; s. James Matthew and Nellie (Fitzmaurice) D.; m. Ann Sullivan, Apr. 2, 1956; children: Timothy Jr., Colette Marie, Jennifer Ann, Peter Gerard, Nora Marie, Matthew. BA in Communication Arts, U. Notre Dame, Ind., 1955. Copywriter Montgomery Ward & Co., Chgo., 1957-58; pub. relations dir. Victor Comptometer Corp., Chgo., 1958-60; sales promotion mgr. Bankers Life & Casualty Co., Chgo., 1960-61; dir. advt. and pub. relations Mid-America Foods, Inc., River Forest, Ill., 1961-62; mdse. mgr. Marshall John & Assos., Chgo. also Northbrook, 1962-65; acct. supr. Marshall John/Action Advt., Northbrook, Ill., 1965-70, exec. v.p., chief exec. officer, 1970-77, also dir.; pres. Devereux Direct, Ltd., 1977-79; v.p. direct response group Frankel & Co., Chgo., 1979-85; pres. Timothy E. Devereux & Assocs., Oak Park, Ill., 1985—. Served to 1st lt. USMCR, 1955—57. Home and Office: 1185 S Oak Park Ave Oak Park IL 60304-2048 Home Phone: 708-383-6256.

DEVEYDT, WAYNE S., health insurance company executive; b. 1970; m. Judith DeVeydt. Various positions PricewaterhouseCoopers LLP, 1996—2005; sr. v.p., chief acctg. officer WellPoint, Inc, Indpls., 2005—07, chief of staff, 2006—07, exec. v.p., CFO, 2007—. Office: WellPoint Inc 120 Monument Cir Indianapolis IN 46204 E-mail: wayne.deveydt@wellpoint.com.*

DE VIDO, ALFREDO EDUARDO, architect; b. NYC, Mar. 19, 1932; s. Eduardo and Maria (Zanucco) DeV.; m. Catherine Nelligan, 1962; children: Roberto, Antonio J. BArch, Carnegie Mellon U., 1954; MFA, Princeton U., 1956. Registered arch., N.J., N.Y., Conn., Mass., Pa. Arch. Archs. Collaborative, Rome, 1960-61, Marcel Breuer, NYC, 1961-62, Ernest Kump, NYC, 1963-67, McFadyen & Knowles, NYC, 1967-69, DeVido Archs., NYC, 1969—. Author: Designing Your Clients' House, 1983, Innovative Management Techniques for Architectural Design and Construction, 1984, House Design: Art and Practice, 1996, Master Architect III: Alfredo De Vido, 1999, Ten Houses/Alfredo De Vido, 1999. Recipient Solar award HUD, 1979, Bard award City Club N.Y., 1983, 89, award Am. Solar Energy Soc., 1982, Design award Interfaith Forum on Religion, Art and Arch., 1989, Design award Conn. Soc. Archs., 1991, Queens C. of C. award, 1993, Interior Design award Restaurants and Instns., 1997. Fellow AIA (honor award 1968, N.Y. chpt. design awards 1971, 77, 81, 94); mem. N.Y. State Assn. Archs. (design awards 1980, 81, 82, 86, 92, 95), Am. Inst. Steel Constrn. (award 1977), Am. Wood Coun. (award 1993). Office: Alfredo De Vido Architects 412 E 85th St New York NY 10028-6302 Business E-Mail: adevido@devido-architects.com.

DEVIGNE, KAREN COOKE, retired amateur athletics executive; b. Phila., July 31, 1943; d. Paul and Matilda (Rich) Cooke; m. Jules Lloyd Devigne, June 26, 1965; children: Jules Paul, Denise Paige, Paul Michael. AA, Centenary Coll., Hackettstown, 1963; student, Northwestern U., 1963-65; BA, Ramapo Coll., Mahwah, 1976; MA, Emory U., Atlanta, 1989. Founder GYMSET, Marietta, Ga., 1981—. Cons. Girls Club Am. Marietta, 1989; vol. Cobb County Gymnastic Ctr., Marietta, 1976-95, Ga. Youth Soccer Assn., Atlanta, 1976-95; fundraiser Scottish Rite Children's Hosp., Atlanta, 1989. Recipient recognition awards from various youth groups, Atlanta, 1976—; named Nominee Woman of Yr. ABC News, Atlanta, 1984. Avocations: skiing, tennis, bridge. Home: 4662 Wynmeade Pk NE Marietta GA 30067 also: 7 Sunrise Point Dr Breckenridge CO 80424

DEVILLE, DONALD CHARLES, accountant; b. New Roads, La., Sept. 18, 1953; s. Sterling Joseph and Barbara J. (Beaud) DeV.; m. Michelle L. Rinaudo, Apr. 14, 1984; children: Ariel Elizabeth, Stewart Charles, Olivia. BS in Acctg., La. State U., 1976. CPA, La. Auditor State of La., Baton Rouge, 1976—78; mgr. Hawthorn Waymouth & Carroll, Baton Rouge, 1978—89; pvt. practice Baton Rouge, 1989—. Pres. Baton Rouge Work Exch., 1988; publicity dir. Baton Rouge Opera, 1989-90, treas., 1991-2007; liturg. min St. George Cath. Ch., Baton Rouge, 1987—; bd. dirs. Capital Area Safety Coun. La., treas., 1994-95; bd. dirs. Baton Rouge Boys Club; chmn. fin. com. St. George Sch.; mem. Sisters of St. Joseph Congl. Devel. Com.; referee US Soccer Fedn., 2007. Recipient Freedom award La. Farm Bur. Mem. AICPA, La. Soc. CPA, SAR (sec. 1990-93, pres. 1994, treas. La. 1998—, La. Meritorious Svc. award, Silver Good Citizenship award), Soc. War of 1812. Republican. Roman Catholic. Avocations: outdoor cooking, boating. Home: 18002 Inverness Ave Baton Rouge LA 70810-5979

DEVIN, LEE (PHILLIP), researcher, consultant, dramaturg, author; b. Glendale, Calif., Apr. 28, 1938; s. Philip Lee Sr. and Bernice Hermoine (Rogers) D.; m. Barbara Kathleen Norton, June 22, 1958 (div. 1986); children: Siobhan Kathleen, Sean Michael; m. Abigail Adams, Sept. 19, 2005. AB, San Jose State Coll., 1958; MA, Ind. U., 1961, PhD, 1967. Lectr. Ind. U. extension, Indpls., 1960-62; instr., tech. dir. U. Va., Charlottesville, 1962-66; instr., assoc. dir. Exptl. Theatre Vassar Coll., Poughkeepsie, NY, 1966-67, asst. prof., assoc. dir., 1967-70; assoc. prof., dir. theatre Swarthmore (Pa.) Coll., 1970-79, prof., dir. theatre, 1979-98, prof., 1998—2003, sr. rsch. scholar, 2003—. Electrician, state mgr., prodn. stage mgr. Honey in the Rock, Beckley, W.Va., 1962-64; artist-in-residence Ball State U., Muncie, Ind., 1968, U. Calif. San Diego, La Jolla, 1973; assoc. artist People's Light and Theatre Co., Malvern, Pa., 1977—, dramaturg, 1985—. Author: (with Rob Austin) Artful Making: What Managers Need to Know About How Artists Work, 2003, (radio plays) Elegy for Irish Jack, 1973, When the Time Comes, 1978, Frankenstein, 1981 (WHA, Earplay Purchase awards); (with S. Hodkinson) (drama with music) Lament: for Guitar and Two Lovers, 1963; (active oratorio) Vox Populous, 1973; (opera) St. Carmen of the Main, 1987 actor various roles stage, film, TV; translator (with A. Adams) A Doll House, 1987, Oedipus, 1988. Recipient 1st prize WGBH Radio Drama, Boston, 1968, James S. Helms Playscript award, 1964, Calif. Olympiad of the Arts, 1965, Elliot Hayes award for dramaturgy, 2005; librettist's grantee NEA, Washington, 1974, 75, 77; grantee Mellon Found., 1973, 77; Lang fellow 1990. Mem. Actors' Equity Assn., Literary Mgrs. and Dramaturgs of the Ams. Avocation: fly fishing. Home: 603 Hillborn Ave Swarthmore PA 19081-1123 Business E-Mail: ldevin1@swarthmore.edu.

DEVINATZ, ALLEN, retired mathematician, educator; b. Chgo., July 22, 1922; s. Victor and Kate (Bass) D.; m. Pearl Moskowitz, Sep. 16, 1956; children: Victor Gary, Ethan Sander. BS, Ill. Inst. Tech., 1944; A.M., Harvard U., 1947, PhD, 1950. Instr. Ill. Inst. Tech., 1950-52; NSF Postdoctoral fellow, 1952-53; fellow Inst. Advanced Study, Princeton, 1953-54; asst. prof. U. Conn., 1954-55; mem. faculty Washington U., St. Louis, 1955-67, prof. math., 1961-67, acting chmn. dept., 1963-64; prof. math. Northwestern U., Evanston, Ill., 1967-92, prof. emeritus, 1992—, asst. chmn. dept., 1968-70, acting chmn. dept., 1991. Vis. mem. Weizmann Inst., Israel, 1980, Inst. Hautes Etudes Sci., Paris, 1982, Inst. for Applications of Calculus-Mauro Picone, Rome, 1988; vis. scholar U. Calif., Berkeley, 1985; Disting. lectr. Hebrew U., Jerusalem, 1993. Contbr. articles profl. jours. Sr. NSF Postdoctoral fellow, 1960-61 Mem. Am. Math. Soc. (translation com. for Russian 1985-88), Sigma Xi, Tau Beta Pi. Office: Northwestern U Dept Math Lunt Bldg Evanston IL 60208-0001 Office Phone: 847-467-8035. Personal E-mail: devi3@earthlink.net.

DEVINATZ, VICTOR GARY, industrial relations specialist, educator; b. St. Louis, Oct. 19, 1957; s. Allen and Pearl (Moskowitz) D. BSE, Northwestern U., 1979, MA, 1980; MS, U. Mass., 1986; PhD, U. Minn., 1990. Lectr. U. Minn., Mpls., 1990-91; asst. prof. Ill. State U., Normal, 1991-94, assoc. prof., 1994-98, prof., 1998—. Contbr. articles to profl. jours. Grantee, Henry J. Kaiser Family Found., Walter P. Reuther Libr., Wayne State U., 1989; Caterpillar scholar, 1999, 2004, Merl E. Reed fellow in so. labor history, 2003. Mem.: Labor and Employment Rels. Assn., United Assn. Labor Edn. Home: 102 S Oak St Apt 3 Normal IL 61761-3053 Office: Ill State U College of Business Bldg Dept Mgmt & Quant Methods Rm 422 Normal IL 61790-5580 Home Phone: 309-888-4596; Office Phone: 309-438-3403. Business E-Mail: vgdevin@ilstu.edu.

DEVINE, BRIAN KIERNAN, pet food and supplies company executive; b. Wash., Mar. 1, 1942; s. William John and Rita Marie (Kiernan) D.; m. Silvija Viktorija Kutlets, June 13, 1964; children— Brian Jr., Brooke BA, Georgetown U., 1963; postgrad., Am. U., 1964-65, Yale U., 1965. Statis. adv. USPHS, Washington, 1963-70; with Toys "R" Us, 1970-88; gen. mgr. San Jose, Calif., 1970-75; regional gen. mgr. Chgo., 1975-77; v.p. Saddle Brook, N.J., 1977-82; sr. v.p. Rochelle Park, N.J., 1982-88; pres. of furniture mfr./retailer Krause's Sofa Factory, Fountain Valley, Calif., 1988-89; pres. Petco, San Diego, 1990—, CEO, 1990—2004, chmn., 1994—. Bd. dirs. Nat. Retail Fedn., Students in Free Enterprise, Wild Oats Markets, Inc.; mem. coll. bd. advisers, bd. regents Georgetown U. Contbr. articles to profl. publs. Mem. Internat. Mass Retail Assn. (bd. dirs.). Republican. Roman Catholic. Office: Petco 9125 Rehco Rd San Diego CA 92121-2270 Business E-Mail: briand@petco.com.

DEVINE, DONALD J., political science professor, consultant; b. Bronxville, NY, Apr. 14, 1937; s. John and Frances M. D.; m. Ann Delia Smith, Aug. 29, 1959; children: William, J. Michael, Patricia, Joseph. BBA, St. John's U., Jamaica, NY, 1959; MA, CUNY, 1965; PhD, Syracuse U., NY, 1967. Assoc. prof. govt. and politics U. Md., 1967-81; dir. U.S. Office Personnel Mgmt., 1981-85; pres. Donald Devine Co., 1985—. Columnist Washington Times; adj. scholar Heritage Found.; Grewcock chair Bellevue U., 2001—; exec. dir. Federalist Leadership Ctr. Author: The Attentive Public, 1970, The Political Culture of the United States, 1972, Does Freedom Work? Liberty and Justice in America, 1978, Reagan Electionomics, 1983, Reagan's Terrible Swift Sword, 1991, Restoring the Tenth Amendment, 1996, In Defense of the West, 2004; editor Western Vision and American Values, 2002. Parliamentarian, exec. com. Md. Rep. Com., 1974-79; Md. chmn. Reagan for Pres., 1976, 80; sr. cons. Dole for Pres., 1988, 96; cons. Steve Forbes for pres., 1999-2000; rules com. Rep. Nat. Com., 1973-75, platform com., del., 1976-88, 96; vice chmn. Am. Conservative Union; Rep. nominee Md. State Comptroller, 1976, 5th Congl. Dist., 1994. With USAR, 1960-66. Mem. Am. Polit. Sci. Assn., Am. Assn. Public Opinion Research, Mt. Pelerin Soc., Phila. Soc. Roman Catholic. Office: 4805 Idlewilde Rd Shady Side MD 20764-9768 Office Phone: 301-261-5644.

DEVINE, EDMOND FRANCIS, retired lawyer; b. Ann Arbor, Mich., Aug. 9, 1916; s. Frank B. and Elizabeth Catherine (Doherty) DeV.; m. Elizabeth Palmer Ward, Sept. 17, 1955; children: Elizabeth Palmer, Stephen Ward, Michael Edmond, Suzanne Lee. AB, U. Mich., 1937, JD, 1940; LLM, Cath. U. Am., Washington, DC, 1941. Bar: Mich. 1940, US Dist. Ct. (ea. dist.) Mich. 1940, US Ct. Appeals (6th cir) 1974, US Supreme Ct. 1975. Spl. agt. FBI, 1941-43; chief asst. prosecutor Washtenaw County, Ann Arbor, 1947-53, prosecuting atty., 1953-58; ptnr. DeVine & DeVine, Ann Arbor, 1958-74, DeVine, DeVine, Kantor & Serr, Ann Arbor, 1974-84; sr. ptnr. Miller, Canfield, Paddock & Stone, Ann Arbor, 1984-92, of counsel, 1992—; ret., 2006. Asst. prof., adj. prof. U. Mich. Law Sch., 1949-79. Co-author: Criminal Procedure, 1960. Lt. USNR, 1943—46, PTO. Decorated Bronze Star with combat v. Fellow Am. Bar Found. Am. Coll. Trial Lawyers, Mich. Bar Found.; mem. ABA, State Bar Mich. (bd. commrs., chmn. judiciary com. 1976-85, mem. rep. assembly, chmn. rules and calendar com.1971-76, co-chair US Cts. com. 1986-87), Internat. Assn. Def. Counsel, US Supreme Ct. Hist. Soc., Ann Arbor C. of C. (chmn. bd. 1971), Detroit Athletic Club, Barton Hills Country Club, Pres.'s Club. U. Mich., Varsity M Club, Order of Coif, Barristers, Phi Delta Phi, Phi Kappa Psi. Republican. Roman Catholic. Avocations: golf, running, reading. Home: 101 Underdown Rd Ann Arbor MI 48105-1078 Home Phone: 734-668-6041.

DEVINE, EUGENE PETER, supreme court justice; b. Albany, NY, Oct. 14, 1948; s. Eugene Peter and Phyllis Jean (Albanese) D.; m. Debra Ann Ziamandanis, Apr. 11, 1992; children: Kimberly, Tracy, Adrianne, Madeline. BS, Villanova U.; JD, Union U., 1975. Bar: N.Y. 1975, U.S. Dist. Ct. (no. dist.) N.Y. 1975, U.S. Supreme Ct. 1980. Asst. N.Y. Pub. Defender, Albany County, 1976-85; ptnr. Cooper, Erving & Savage, Albany, 1975-85; chief atty. Albany County Dept. Social Svcs., 1985-88; ptnr. Devine, Piedment & Rutnik, 1985-91; chief pub. defender Albany County, 1994—2006; of counsel Girvin & Ferlazzo, 2000—06; supreme ct. justice 3rd Judicial Dist., NYS, 2007—. Bd. dirs. Ronald McDonald House, Albany, 1980—, founding mem.; committeman Albany County Dem. Com., 1979-2006; treas. com. to elect Jim Tully N.Y. State Compt., 1980; chmn. telethon Children's Hosp. Albany Med. Ctr., 1982—; vice chmn. Albany Med. Ctr. Found., 1994-2004 Mem. Wolferts Roost Country Club, Albany Sons of St. Patrick (pres. 1984), Albany Sons of Italy Office: Albany County Courthouse 16 Eagle St Rm 451 Albany NY 12211 Business E-Mail: edevine@courts.state.ny.us.

DEVINE, HUGH JAMES, JR., marketing executive; b. Buffalo, May 8, 1938; s. Hugh James Sr. and Ruth D. Devine; m. Bernice Riley Cushing, May 27, 1984; children: Hugh James III, Thomas C., Catherine D. Whitaker, Kent T., Diane C. Alleborn, Linda C. Hughes, Karen C. Krueger. AB in Econs., Bethany Coll., 1961; MBA, U. Bridgeport, 1971. Mgr. mktg. intelligence Winchester-Western Div. Olin Corp., New Haven, 1961-71; sr. v.p., dir. mktg. Rsch. Data Svcs., Inc., Princeton, NJ, 1971-75, exec. v.p., dir. mktg., 1975—93, dir., 1978-97, pres., 1993-96; COO Total Rsch. Corp., Princeton, NJ, 1996; mktg. cons.; pres. Hugh J. Devine & Assocs., 1997—. Speaker Am. Mgmt. Assn., N.Y.C., 1974-76, Assn. Nat. Advertisers, Washington, 1985, Fin. Independence Day, Princeton, 1986, U. N.C., Chapel Hill, 1989, 91, others. Author newsletter Strategic Goals Should Govern Mktg. Rsch. Budget, 1981; co-author newsletter The Value of Predictive Research, 1989; contbr. articles to mags, Sgt. USAR, 1961-67. Mem. Coun. Am. Survey Rsch. Orgn. (membership chmn. 1985, career planning chmn. 1986, survey quality com. 1990-91, 96), Am. Mktg. Assn., Inst. Mgmt. Consultants (v.p. membership 2000-02, chmn. leadership devel. 2004—05), Barbershop Harmony Soc. (mktg. task force 2002-03). Republican. Avocations: barbershop style singing, walking, reading. Home and Office: 49 Krebs Rd Plainsboro NJ 08536-1104 Home Phone: 609-799-8218; Office Phone: 609-799-8170. Personal E-mail: HJDevine@aol.com.

DEVINE, MICHAEL BUXTON, attorney, barrister, educator; b. Des Moines, Oct. 25, 1953; s. Cleatie Hiram, Jr., and Katherine Ann (Buxton) D. Student, St. Peter's Coll., Oxford U., 1975; BA cum laude, St. Olaf Coll., 1976; MPA, JD, Drake U., 1980; diploma in Advanced Internat. Legal Studies, U. Pacific, Salzburg, Austria, 1986; LLM in Internat. Bus. Legal Studies, U. Exeter, 1988, postgrad., 1997. Bar: Iowa 1980, U.S. Ct. Appeals (8th cir.) 1980, Nebr. 1985, Supreme Ct. 1985, Minn. 1986, D.C. 1986., N.Y. 1987, Wis. 1987, Colo. 1988, U.S. Dist. Ct. (so. dist.), N.Y. 1990, U.S. Ct. Appeals (fed. cir.) 1990, U.S. Ct. Internat. Trade 1990, Eng. and Wales, 1995, U.K. Ho. of Lords, 1995, Ct. Justice of European Com., 1995, No. Ireland, 2000, Ireland, 2004; mem. Gray's Inn of Ct., London, Inn of Ct. Northern Ireland, King's Inns of Ct., Dublin. Assoc. Bump & Haesemeyer, P.C., Des Moines, 1980—85; jud. law clk. Jud. Dept. State of Iowa, 1987—88; assoc. Christianson, Hohnbaum & George, Des Moines, 1989, Pavelic & Levites, P.C., NYC, 1989—92; with chambers Alan Tyrrell, Q.C., London, 1993—94; with legal dept. Philips Electronics U.K., Ltd., London, 1994; with Lafili, Van Crombrugghe & Ptnrs., Brussels, 1995; pvt. practice Des Moines/NYC/London, 1997—; tenant barrister web Internat. Chambers, England, 2001—; door tenant Rougemont Chambers, England, 2001—. Internat. legal intern Herbert Oppenheimer, Nathan & Vandyk, London, 1986; lectr. law U. Kent, Canterbury, Eng., 2000-01; lectr. law, LLM course leader Robert Gordon U., Aberdeen, Scotland, 2001-04; mem. Chartered Inst. Arbitrators, London, 2002-; asst. prof. bus. law U. Wis.-La Crosse, 2005— Asst. editor: Jour. Internat. Trade Law & Policy; contbr. articles to profl. jours. Nat. alt. U.S. Presdl. Mgmt. Intern Program, 1980. Scholar St. Olaf Coll., 1972-76 Mem. ABA (sect. internat. law), Fed. Bar Assn. (chmn. state of Iowa SBA export assistance program 1983-85, treas. Iowa chpt. 1984-85, exec. com. 1985-87), N.Y. State Bar Assn. (sec. internat. law), DC Bar (sec. internat. law), Colo. Bar Assn. (sec., internat. law), Nebr. State Bar Assn., Iowa State Bar Assn. (sec. internat. law), Minn. State Bar Assn. (sec. internat. law), Wis. Bar Assn. (sec. internat. law), Assn. of Bar of City of N.Y. (coun. internat. affairs 1990-92), Soc. Legal Scholars Gt. Britain and Ireland, Acad. Legal Studies in Bus., Phi Alpha Theta, Pi Alpha Alpha. Presbyterian. Office: 2641 Beaver Ave Des Moines IA 50310 also: Coll Bus Adminstrn Univ Wis La Crosse 1725 State St La Crosse WI 54601 Office Phone: 608-785-4679. Personal E-mail: mikedevinelawyer@aol.com. Business E-Mail: devine.mich@uwlax.edu.

DEVINE, MICHAEL J., library director, educator; b. Aurora, Ill., Jan. 5, 1945; s. Richard J. and Elayne Marie (Esser) D.; m. Maija Rhee, Nov. 7, 1970; children: Bret, Christopher, Mia, Lisa, T. Brian. BA, Loras Coll., 1967; MA, Ohio State U., 1968, PhD, 1974; LHD (hon.), Lincoln Coll., 1988. Vol. Peace Corps, 1969-70; from instr. to asst. prof. history Ohio U., Athens, 1972-74; program adminstr. Ohio Hist. Soc., Columbus, 1974-77, asst. dir., 1977-79; exec. dir. Cin. Consortium Colls., 1979-82; dep. dir. Hist. St. Mary's City, Md., 1982-85; dir. State of Ill. Hist. Preservation Agy. and Hist. Soc., Springfield, 1985-91; dir., prof. Am. Heritage Ctr., Univ. Wyo., Laramie, 1991—2001; dir. Harry S. Truman Presdl. Mus. & Libr., Independence, Mo., 2001—. Adj. lectr. history Xavier U., Cin., 1979—82; sr. lectr. Fullbright Commn., Argentina, 1983; Houghton Freeman prof Am. history Johns Hopkins U.-Nanjing U. Grad. Ctr. for Chinese and Am. Studies, Nanjing, China. Author: John W. Foster, 1981; editor: (with others) Ohio: The Next 25 Years, 1978. Mem. St. Mary's County Libr. Planning Commn., 1984-85; sec. Abraham Lincoln Assn., Springfield, 1985-91; trustee Cin. Fire Mus., 1980-82; appointed Ill., Mich. Canal Nat. Heritage Corridor Commn., 1988-91; apptd. Wyo. Commn. Parks and Cultural Affairs, 1994.; elected Wyo. Coun. Humanities, 1996. Am. Philos. Soc. grantee, 1978, NEH fellow, 1980. Mem. Am. Hist. Assn., Am. Assn. State and Local History, Nat. Coun. Pub. History (bd. dirs. 1993, v.p. 1998). Avocation: painting. Home: 3606 NE Basswood Dr Lees Summit MO 64064-1835 Office: Truman Mus and Libr 500 W US Hwy 24 Independence MO 64050-2481 Office Phone: 816-268-8210. E-mail: michael.devine@nara.gov.*

DEVINE, RICHARD A. (DICK DEVINE), lawyer; b. Chgo., July 5, 1943; m. Charlene Devine; children: Matt, Karen, Tim, Pete. BA cum laude, Loyola U., 1966; JD cum laude, Northwestern U., 1968. Bar: Ohio 1968, Ill. 1969, U.S. Dist. Ct. (no. dist.) Ill. 1973, U.S. Ct. Appeals (7th cir.) 1983, U.S. Supreme Ct. 1983. Assoc. Squire, Sanders & Dempsey, Cleve., 1968-69; adminstrv. asst. to mayor of Chgo., 1969-72; assoc. Pope,

Ballard, Shepard & Fowle, 1972-74; assoc., ptnr. Foran, Wiss & Schultz, 1974-80, ptnr., 1983-85; 1st asst. state's atty. Cook County State's Atty.'s Office, 1980-83; ptnr. Phelan, Pope, Cahill, Devine & Quinlan, Ltd., 1985-95, Shefsky Froelich & Devine Ltd., 1995-96; state's atty. Cook County, 1996—. Lectr. continuing legal edn. IIT Kent Coll. Law, John Marshall U.; co-chair courses on damages in bus. litigation Law Jour. Seminar; judge moot ct. programs Northwestern Law Sch., John Marshall Law Sch.; appointed mem. State Commn. on Accreditation of Criminal Justice; appointed mem. Spl. Commn. on Adminstrn. of Justice in Cook County, chmn. task force on misdemeanor and preliminary hearing cts., chmn. task force on jud. adminstrn.; appointed mem. profl. adv. com. Office of State's Atty. of Cook County, 1984-89; bd. dirs. Cook County Criminal Justice Project; mem. Chgo.-Cook County Criminal Justice Commn., 1971-78; hearing officer Chgo. Bd. Election Commrs., 1984. Mem. editl. bd. Northwestern U. Law Rev., 1966-68, mng. editor, 1967-68; contbr. to law jours. Bd. commrs. Chgo. Park Dist., 1989-93, pres. bd., 1990-93; bd. trustees Loyola Acad., 1982-88, St. Scholastica H.S.; bd. dirs. Chgo. Hist. Soc., 1990-93, Adler Planetarium; pro bono mem., pres. Chgo. Park Dist, 1989-93. Russell Sage fellow in law and social scis. Mem. ABA, Am. Coll. Trial Lawyers (elected), Ill. State Bar Assn., Chgo. Bar Assn. (com. jud. evaluation 1983-88, chmn. legis. assistance and evaluation com., young lawyers sect. 1973-74, vice-chmn. 1974-76, chmn. 1976-77, urban affairs com., mem. local govt. com. 1974-76, faculty young lawyers sect. trial advocacy program, lectr. on continuing legal edn.), Northwestern Law Sch. Alumni Assn. (bd. dirs. 1993—), Ill. State Attys. Assn. (bd. dirs.), Nat. Dist. Attys. Assn. (bd. dirs.). Office: Cook County State Atty 69 W Washington St Ste 3200 Chicago IL 60602 Office Phone: 312-603-5106. E-mail: stateattorny@cookcountygov.com.

DEVINEY, MARVIN LEE, JR., science administrator, director; b. Kingsville, Tex., Dec. 5, 1929; s. Marvin Lee and Esther Lee (Gambrell) D.; m. Marie Carole Massey, June 7, 1975; children: Marvin Lee III, John H., Ann-Marie K. Deviney Bowen. BS in Chemistry and Math., S.W. Tex. State U., San Marcos, 1949; MA in Phys. Chemistry, U. Tex., Austin, 1952, PhD in Phys. Chemistry, 1956. Cert. profl. chemist. Devel. chemist Celanese Chem. Co., Bishop, Tex., 1956-58; rsch. chemist Shell Chem. Co., Deer Park, Tex., 1958-66; sr. scientist, head group phys. and radio-chemistry Ashland Chem. Co., Houston, 1966-68, mgr. sect. phys. and analytical chemistry, 1968-71, mgr. sect. phys. chemistry div. rsch. and devel. Columbus, Ohio, 1971-78; rsch. assoc., supr. applied surface chemistry Ashland Ventures Rsch. and Devel., Columbus, 1978-84, supr. electron microscopy, advanced aerospace composites, govt. contracts, 1984-90; inst. scientist, mem. internal R & D com. SW Rsch. Inst., San Antonio, 1990-97; pres. MLD Polymers/Composites, Inc., 1997—; R&D dir. Nuresco Polymers, 1998—; cons. polymer divsn. Tex. State U., San Marcos, 1998—. Adj. prof. U. Tex., San Antonio, 1973-75, Ohio State U., 1990-91; mem. sci. adv. bd. Am. Petroleum Inst. Rsch. Project 60, 1968-74. Contbr. numerous articles to profl. jours.; patentee in field. Mem. ednl. adv. com. Columbus Tech. Inst., 1974-84, Cen. Ohio Tech. Coll., 1975-82, Hocking Tech. Coll., 1989-91. Lt. col., USAR, retired. Humble Oil Rsch. fellow, 1954. Fellow Am. Inst. Chemists (pres. Ohio Inst. 1978-82); mem. Tex. Acad. Sci., Am. Def. Preparedness Assn., Electron Microscopy Soc. Am., Materials Rsch. Soc., SAMPE Composites Soc., N.Am. Catalysis Soc., Am. Soc. Composites, Soc. Plastics Engrs., Soc. Automotive Engrs., Am. Chem. Soc. (chmn. chpt. exec. bd. 1969, bus. mgr. nat. div. Petroleum Chemistry, 1986-90, Best Paper award rubber div. 1967, 70, Honorable Mention awards 1968, 69, 73, symposia co-chmn., co-editor books on catalysis-surface chemistry 1985, carbon-graphite chemistry 1975), Engrs.' Coun. Houston (sr. councilor 1970-71), Sigma Xi, Phi Lambda Upsilon, Alpha Chi, Sigma Pi Sigma. Methodist. Home and Office: 106 Pecos Ct Georgetown TX 78628-4231 Office Phone: 512-864-1518. E-mail: deviney_marvin@hotmail.com.

DEVINS, ROBERT SYLVESTER, retired lawyer; b. NYC, Mar. 19, 1949; s. Arthur Sylvester and Judith Delores (Whelan) D. BA, Tulane U., 1971; JD, Emory U., 1978. Bar: Ga. 1978, Fla. 1981, U.S. Dist. Ct. (no. dist.) Ga. 1978, U.S. Tax Ct. 1978, U.S. Ct. Appeals (5th cir.) 1978, U.S. Supreme Ct. 1982, U.S. Dist. Ct. (mid. dist.) Ga. 1994. Pvt. practice, Atlanta, 1978-99; ret., 1999. Lt. USN, 1971-75. Mem. ABA, Internat. Bar Assn. (vice chmn. criminal law sect. 1985-87, chmn. 1987-89. rep. UN Conf. 1987, 89), Inter Am. Bar Assn., Nat. Assn. Criminal Def. Lawyers, Ga. Assn. Criminal Def. Lawyers, Assn. Trial Lawyers Am., Ga. Trial Lawyers Assn., Union International des Avocats. Avocation: reading. Home: Casa Ventosear 2335 S Ocean Blvd Palm Beach FL 33480-5368

DEVITA, M. CHRISTINE, foundation administrator; b. NY; BA magna cum laude, Queens Coll., 1977; grad. cum laude, Fordham U., 1980. Bar: N.Y. 1981, U.S. Dist. Ct. (so. dist.) N.Y. 1982, U.S. Supreme Ct. 1986. With legal dept. Reader's Digest Assn., Inc., 1980-87, dep/ gen. counsel, 1984, also bd. dirs.; exec. dir. DeWitt Wallace and Lila Wallace Reader's Digest Funds, NYC, 1987-89, pres., 1989—2002, also bd. dirs.; pres. Wallace Found., 2002—. Editor: Fordham Law Rev. Bd. dirs. Found. Ctr., Reader's Digest Assn., Inc., Queens Coll. Found. Office: Wallace Found 5 Penn Plaza 7th Fl New York NY 10001

DEVITA, VINCENT THEODORE, JR., oncologist; b. Bronx, NY, Mar. 7, 1935; s. Vincent Theodore and Isabel DeVita; m. Mary Kay Bush, Aug. 3, 1957; children: Ted(dec.) , Elizabeth. BS, Coll. William and Mary, 1957; MD with distinction, George Washington U., 1961; DSc (hon.), NY Med. Coll., 1987, Georgetown U., 1989. Diplomate Nat. Bd. Med. Examiners, Am. Bd. Internal Medicine (subspecialty hematology, med. oncology). Intern U. Mich. Med. Center, Ann Arbor, 1961—62; resident in medicine George Washington U. Med. Service D.C. Gen. Hosp., 1962—63; sr. resident in medicine Yale New Haven Med. Center, 1965—66; clin. assoc. Lab. Chem. Pharmacology, Nat. Cancer Inst. NIH, Bethesda, Md., 1963—65, sr. investigator solid tumor service, medicine br., 1966—68, head solid tumor service, medicine br., 1968—71, chief med. br., 1971—74, dir. div. cancer treatment, 1974—80, clin. dir. inst., 1975—80; dir. Nat. Cancer Inst., Nat. Cancer Program, NIH, 1980—88; physician-in-chief Meml. Sloan-Kettering Cancer Ctr., NYC, 1988—91, attending physician, mem., 1988—95, Benno C. Schmidt chair clin. oncology, 1988—93; prof. medicine Cornell U. Med. Coll., 1989—93; med. dir. oncology Yale Cancer Ctr., New Haven, 2000—03, chair, bd. dirs. New Haven, Conn., Conn., 2003—, chmn. adv. bd.; Amy and Joseph Perella prof. of med. Yale Cancer Ctr., Yale Sch. Med., 2004—; prof. medicine Yale U. Sch. Medicine, New Haven, 1993—, prof. internal medicine, epidemiology and pub. health, 1994—, dir. Yale Cancer Ctr., 1993—2003; attending physician Yale-New Haven Hosp., 1993—. Chmn. Institutional Securities; chmn., investment banking group Morgan Stanley; dir. ImClone Systems Inc., 1992—; scientific adv. cons. The Immunotherapy Rsch. and Treatment Inst., St. Luke's Med. Ctr., 2002—; chmn., scientific adv. bd. Am.-Italian Cancer Found., 2003—. Mem. editl. bd.: Cancer Rsch., 1981—91, Gynecologic Oncology, 1981—91, Hematol. Oncology, 1981—87, Physicians' Drug Alert, 1982—, Jour. Clin. Oncology, 1983—87; co-editor: (textbooks) Cancer: Principles and Practice Oncology, edits. 1-6, Progress in Oncology, edits. 1-4, (jours.) The Cancer Jour., 1995—; editor-in-chief The Cancer Jour., —; co-editor: (jours.) Principles and Practice Oncology updates, 1987—; assoc. editor Online Jour. Current Clin. Trials, 1991—94; assoc. editor Cancer Investigation, 1983—87, Am. Jour. Medicine, 1983—88, mem. extramural bd. assoc. editors: Physicians Desk Query (PDQ), Nat. Cancer Inst., 1989—, adv. bd.: Am. Health Mag., 1995—99, mem. editl. sci. bd.: Oncologia Clinica, 1996, mem. editl. sci. bd.: Cancer Rsch., 1997, Current Oncology Reports, 1998—, Jour. Bone and Soft Tissue Sarcomas, 1999—, mem. editl. bd. or adv. editor: numerous other med. jours.; editor-in-chief Nat. Clinical Practice Oncology, Yale. U. Sch. Medicine, 1997—2000; contbr. numerous articles to med. jours. Mem. awards assembly GM Cancer Rsch. Found., 1981—85, adv. coun., 1984—; chair med. adv. bd. CancerSource.com, 1999—; bd. advisors Breast Cancer Alliance, Inc., 1999—; mem. Armand Hammer Cancer Award Com., 1983—86. With USMC, 1955—61. Decorated Oren del Sol en el Grando de Official Govt. of Peru; named Stratton lectr., Am. Soc. Hematology, 1985, Leukemia Rsch. Fund lectr., London, 1985; named to, Conn. Acad. Sci. and Engring., 1994, Commendatore of Italian Rep. order of merit, Pres. Italy, 1998, European Acad. Scis. for outstanding and lasting contbn. to cancer rsch. edn., 2002; recipient Albert and Mary Lasker Med. Rsch. award, 1972, Superior Svc. award, HEW, 1975, Esther Langer Found. award, 1976, Alumni medallion, Coll. William and Mary, 1976, Jeffrey Gottlieb award, 1976, Bronze medal, Am. Soc. Therapeutic Radiology, 1978, Karnofsky prize and lectr., 1979, Griffuel prize, Assn. for Devel. Rsch. on Cancer, 1980, James Ewing award, Soc. Surg. Oncology, 1982, Meml. Sloan-Kettering Cancer Ctr. award, 1972, DSM, USPHS, 1983, Meyer and Anna Prentiss award, 1984, Second Emmanuel Cancer Found. award, 1984, Pierluigi Nervi award, Rome, 1985, Medal of Honor, Am. Cancer Soc., 1985, Barbara Bohen Pfeifer award, Am.-Italian Found. Cancer Rsch., 1985, Tenth Richard and Hilda Rosenthal Found. award, Am. Assn. Cancer Rsch., Inc., 1986, Stanley G. Kay Meml. award, D.C. Am. Cancer Soc., 1986, Sci. award, Brady Cancer Rsch. Inst., 1987, Prix Cino del Duca, Paris, 1988, Pezcoller award, European Soc. Oncology, Trento, Italy, 1988, Surgeon Gen.'s Exemplary Svc. medal, 1988, Armand Hammer Cancer prize, 1990, Outstanding Achievement in Clin. Rsch. award, Assn. Cmty. Cancer Ctrs., 1992, City of Medicine award, 1995, Presdl. award, New Eng. Cancer Soc., 1997, Key to Cure award, Cure for Lymphoma Found., 1997, Mary Waterman award, Breast Cancer Alliance, 1999, 50th Anniversary Leukemia Soc. Am., 1999, Saul Rosenberg Rsch. award, Lymphoma Rsch. Found. Am., 2000; Tobacco Rsch. Industry fellow, 1959. Fellow: ACP, NY Acad. Medicine; mem.: AMA, Assn. Am. Cancer Insts. (bd. dirs. 1999—, co-chmn., Nat. Cancer Legis. adv.com. 2000—02, policy and planning com. 2000—, mem., award panel for Pollin Prize in Pediatric Rsch. 2000), Internat. Coun. for Coordinating Cancer Rsch. (pres. Am. bd. 1989—92), Smith-Reed-Russel Med. Soc., Soc. Surg. Oncology, Assn. Am. Physicians, Am. Soc. Clin. Investigation, Am. Fedn. Clin. Rsch., Am. Assn. Cancer Rsch. (dir. 1976—79, Gertrude B. Elion cancer rsch. award com. 1999—2000), Am. Soc. Hematology, Am. Cancer Soc., Am. Soc. Clin. Oncology (chmn. program com. 1972, dir. 1973—76, pres. 1977—78), Alpha Omega Alpha. Achievements include development of the first successful combination cancer chemotherapy program, which ultimately led to effective regimens of curative chemotherapy for a variety of cancers; co-developer of the four combination drug, known as the acronym MOPP, which increased the cure rate of patients with advanced Hodgkin's disease; co-developer of the combination chemotherapy CMF, which still remains useful for theraphy for breast cancer. E-mail: vincent.devita@yale.edu.*

DEVITO, DANNY MICHAEL, actor, film director; b. Asbury Park, NJ, Nov. 17, 1944; s. Daniel and Julia DeV.; m. Rhea Perlman, Jan. 28, 1982; children: Lucie Chet, Gracie Fan, Jacob Daniel. Grad., Am. Acad. Dramatic Arts, 1966. Co-founder Jersey Films, 1992—; owner DeVito South Beach, Miami, Fla., 2007—. Theater appearances include The Man With a Flower in His Mouth, Sheridan Sq. Playhouse, 1969, The Shrinking Bride, 1971, One Flew Over the Cuckoo's Nest, 1971, DuBarry Was a Lady, 1972, A Phantasmagoria Historia of D. Johann Fauster Magister, Ph.D, M.D., D.D., D.L., etc., 1973, The Many Wives of Windsor (N.Y. Shakespeare Festival), 1974, Where Do We Go From Here?, 1974; motion picture appearances include Dreams of Glass, 1970, Lady Liberty, 1971, Hurry Up, or I'll Be 30, 1973, Scalawag, 1972, One Flew Over the Cuckoo's Nest, 1975, The Money, 1976, Hot Dogs for Gaugin, Goin' South, 1978, Swap Meet, 1979, Going Ape!, 1981, Terms of Endearment, 1983, Romancing the Stone, 1984, Johnny Dangerously, 1984, Head Office, 1985, Jewel of the Nile, 1985, Wise Guys, 1986, My Little Pony (voice), 1986, Ruthless People, 1986, Tin Men, 1987, (dir. debut) Throw Momma from the Train, 1987, Twins, 1988, The War of the Roses (also dir.), 1989, Other People's Money, 1991, Batman Returns, 1992, Hoffa, (also producer, dir.) 1992, Jack the Bear, 1993, Last Action Hero minor role-voice), 1993, Look Who's Talking Now (voice), 1993, Renaissance Man, 1994, Junior, 1994, Get Shorty, (also prodr.), 1995, Matilda (also prodr., dir.), 1996, Mars Attacks!, 1996, The Rainmaker, 1997, Hercules (voice), 1997, Living Out Loud (also prodr.), 1998 The Virgin Suicides, 1999, The Big Kahuna, 1999, Man On the Moon (also prodr.), 1999, Drowning Mona, 2000 (also exec. prodr.), Screwed, 2000, How High, 2001 (also prodr.), What's the Worst That Could Happen, 2001, Heist, 2001, Death to Smoochy (also dir.), 2002, Austin Powers in Goldmember, 2002, Marx Brothers, 2003, Anything Else, 2003, (voice) Big Fish, 2003, Duplex (also dir.), Family of the Year, 2004, (voice) Catching Kringle, 2004, Christmas in Love, 2004, Marilyn Hotchkiss' Ballroom Dancing Charm School, 2005, Be Cool (also prodr.), 2005, The OH in Ohio, 2006, Even Money, 2006, Relative Strangers (also prodr.), 2006, Deck the Halls, 2006, The Good Night, 2007, Reno 911!: Miami (also exec. prodr.), 2007; TV series appearances Taxi, 1978-83, It's Always Sunny in Philadelphia, 2006-; directed and appeared in cable TV movie Selling of Vince D'Angelo, 1976 (also dir.), The World's Greatest Lover, 1977, Valentine, 1979, All the Kids Do It, 1984, The Ratings Game, 1984 (also dir.); guest appearances include Starsky and Hutch, 1977, Police Woman, 1977, Amazing Stories, 1986, (voice) The Simpsons, 1989, 1991, 92, Pearl, 1997, Ed, 2002, Friends, 2004, (voice) Father of the Pride, 2004; exec. prodr.: (TV series) Kate Brasher, 2001, UC: Undercover, 2001, The American Embassy, 2002, Karen Sisco, 2003-04, Reno 911, 2003-; co-exec. prodr. Pulp Fiction, 1994; prodr.: Reality Bites, 1994, Sunset Park, 1996, Feeling Minnesota, 1996, Gattaca, 1997, Out of Sight, 1998, Erin Brokovich, 2000, The Caveman's Valentine, 2001, Camp, 2003, Along Came Polly, 2004, Freedom Writers, 2007; co-prodr. 8 Seconds, 1994; exec. prodr. Garden State, 2004, Bye Bye Benjamin, 2006. Recipient: Golden Globe award for TV series, Taxi, 1979; Emmy award 1981, Crystal Globe prize for Contribution to Cinema, Karlovy Vary Film Festival, 2007 Office: care Fred Specktor Creative Artists Agy Inc 9830 Wilshire Blvd Beverly Hills CA 90212-1804*

DEVITO, MATHIAS JOSEPH, retired real estate company executive; b. Trenton, NJ, Aug. 23, 1930; s. Charles P. and Margaret L. DeV.; m. Rosetta Kormuth, July 28, 1956; children: Ann DeVito Walker, Charles Michael. BA, U. Md., 1954, LL.B. with highest honors, 1956; L.H.D., Salisbury State Coll., 1984. Bar: Md. Asst. atty. gen. State of Md., 1963-64; ptnr. Piper & Marbury, Balt., 1965-70; sr. v.p., gen. counsel, then exec. v.p. Rouse Co., Columbia, Md., 1968-73, pres., CEO, bd. dirs., 1973-84, chmn. bd. dirs., pres., CEO, 1984-93, chmn. bd. dirs., CEO, 1993-95, chmn. bd. dirs., 1995-97, chmn. exec. com. bd., 1997-2001, chmn. emeritus, 1997—. Bd. dirs. Mars Supermarkets, Inc.; chmn. Greater Balt. Com., 1990—92. Editor Md. Law Rev., 1955-56. Chmn. bd. trustees Md. State Colls., 1970-73; trustee Johns Hopkins U., 1983-89, Md. Inst. Coll. Art, 1995—, Adirondack Mus., 2005—, Garrison Forest Sch., 2006—. Mem. Adirondack League, Elkridge Club, Order of Coif. Roman Catholic. Office: Ste 220 Village Sq II Baltimore MD 21210-1935 Personal E-mail: mnrdevito@aol.com.

DEVITRE, DINYAR S., consumer products company and corporate financial executive; b. Jamshedpur, India; BA, St. Joseph's Coll., Darjeeling, India; MBA, Indian Inst. Mgmt., Ahmedabad. With Godfrey Phillips India, Ltd., Mumbai, 1970, gen. mgr. to mng. dir., 1976; mktg. svcs. mgr. Asia Pacific Philip Morris, Melbourne, Australia, regional coord. Asia/Can. NYC, 1974, regional dir. Asia Hong Kong, 1980, v.p. Asia, 1981, pres. Asia, 1984, sr. v.p., chief adminstrv. officer NYC, 1990—92, exec. v.p., 1992, sr. v.p. corp. planning, 1995; chmn., CEO Philip Morris K.K., Tokyo, 1992; exec. v.p. Citibank Europe, 1998—2001; sr. v.p., CFO Altria Group Inc., 2002—. Bd. dirs. Kraft Foods Inc., Western Union; bd. mem. Western Union Co.; non-exec. dir., mem. audit com. SABMiller, 2007—. Office: Altria Group Inc 120 Park Ave New York NY 10017*

DEVITT, H. WILLIAM, III, treasurer, corporate financial executive; m. Deborah Herridge. BBA in Acctg., U. Notre Dame, Ind., 1981; JD, U. Pitts., 1985. Bar: NJ 1986. Treasury mgr. FL Industries (Forstmann Little), Livingston, NJ, 1986—91; dir. divisional fin. Reed Internat. p.l.c., Secaucus, NJ, 1991—92; dir. treasury and fin. Saks Fifth Ave., NYC, 1992—96; dir. corp. fin. Tommy Hilfiger, NYC, 1996—2000; treas., in-house counsel Myron Corp., Maywood, NJ, 2000—03; gen. counsel, treas. Aircast LLC, Summit, NJ, 2003—06; CFO, treas. FSS, LLC, Springfield, NJ, 2007—. Mem. Econ. Devel. Commn., New Providence, NJ, 2004—06. Mem.: Assn. Corp. Counsel Am., U. Pitts. Alumni Club NJ, Notre Dame Alumni Club No. NJ, Upper Montclair Country Club. Avocations: golf, skiing. Office: FSS LLC 871 Mountain Ave Ste 200 Springfield NJ 07081 Home Phone: 908-347-8004; Office Phone: 973-218-9601. Office Fax: 404-393-8004. Personal E-mail: bdevitt@alumni.nd.edu.

DEVIVO, ANGE, retired small business owner; b. Bay Shore, NY, Oct. 20, 1925; d. Romeo Zanetti and Karolina (Hodapp) King; m. John Michael DeVivo, Dec. 30, 1950; 1 child, Michael. Student, Washington Sch. for Secs., NYC, 1945-46. Sec. Am. Airlines, NYC, 1946-51; exec. sec. W.C. Holzhauer, NYC, 1951-52; dist. sales mgr. Emmons Jewelers, Inc., Bound Brook, N.J., 1952-53; exec. sec. NJ Rep. State Com., 1960—64; dist. office supr. 19th Decenniel census U.S. Dept. Commerce, Charlotte, NC, 1970; adminstrv. sec. Mercy Hosp., Charlotte, NC, 1973—81; pres. Secs., Plus, Convs., Plus, Charlotte, 1983—91; prin. Ange DeVivo & Assocs., Inc., Charlotte, 1991—92; ret., 1992. Editor: The North Carolina Republican Woman, 2d edit., 1994, 3d edit., 1995; author Precinct Training Manual, 1971. First woman chair Mecklenburg County Rep. Party, 1976; adminstrv. sec. Nat. Broadcast Assn. for Cmty. Affairs, 1987-90; active in local politics, NJ, 1956-64, Conn., 1964-68, NC, 1968-96; conducted polit. seminars, 1973, 74, 76; panelist Seminar for Tchrs., Robert A. Taft Inst. Govt., 1977; small bus. action coun. Greater Charlotte C. of C., 1983-89, discount com., 1985, co-chair minority and women owned bus. directory, 1988, chair Bus. Opportunity Network and Mixer Exhibit, 1987, chair Carolina Bus. Fair, 1989; active Human Svcs. Coun., Charlotte, 1984-88; conf. mgr., 8th Nat. Recycling Congress, 1989; active Emergency Med. Svc. Adv. Coun., Charlotte, 1981-92, chmn., 1988-90; active Charlotte Women's Polit. Caucus, 1972-96; chair Mecklenburg County Rep. Party, 1976-77; mem. Mecklenburg Evening Rep. Women's Club, Charlotte, 1968-2006, pres., 1973-74, 93-94; mem. Mecklenburg County Women's Commn., 1990-96, Women's Roundtable, 1994-95; citizens adv. com. Conv. and Visitors Bur., 1986-90; coord. Women's Equality Day celebration Mecklenburg County Women's Commn., 1990, coord., fin. chair, 1991-92, co-chmn., fin. chair, 1993-96, adv. bd. 1993-96, vice-chair bd., 1995; fundraiser March of Dimes and Leukemia, Ala., 1999, 02, 06; active Rep. Women Today Ala., 1997-01, tel. com., 2001; pres. Cardinal Bus. and Profl. Women's Club, 1979-81; site insp. for spl. events in Jamaica, 1987. Recipient Seal of City of Stamford, Conn., 1968, Order of Long Leaf Pine award Gov. of NC, 1974, nominee WBT Woman of Yr, Charlotte chpt. Nat. Sec. Assn., 1977, Cert. Appreciation Cardinal Bus. and Profl. Womens' Club, 1978, Woman of Yr. award Cardinal Bus. and Profl. Womens' Club, 1982, Entrepreneur of Yr. award Women Bus. Owners, 1987, Cert. Appreciation outstanding leadership and dedicated svc. Charlotte Women's Bus. Owners Assn., 1990-91, Award of Honor in recognition of outstanding svc. Mecklenburg County Women's Com., 1991, Spl. Recognition award for devotion, dedication and untiring efforts Mecklenburg County Women's Commn., 1996, Seal of Mecklenberg County, NC, 1996; honoree NC Fedn. Rep. Women, 1987; nominee Cmty. Svc. award Mecklenburg County Women's Commn., 1994, Hall Fame, NC Rep. Party, 1995. Mem.: Rep. Women of the South (telephone com. 2004—07, bd. dirs. 2006). Roman Catholic. Avocations: politics, community service. Personal E-mail: jmdevivo531@cs.com.

DE VIVO, DARRYL CLAUDE, pediatrician, neurologist; b. Everett, Mass., Aug. 28, 1937; children: Cynthia, Jessica, Kristin. BA, Amherst Coll., 1959; MD, U. Va., 1964. Diplomate Am. Bd. Psychiatry and Neurology (dir. neurology 1991-99, pres. 1999). Intern Univ. Hosp., Boston, 1964—65; resident in pediat. and neurology Mass. Gen. Hosp., Boston, 1965—67; clin. assoc. NIH, 1967—69; fellow in pediatric neurology St. Louis Children's Hosp., 1969—70; mem. faculty Wash. U. Sch. Medicine, St. Louis, 1970—78, prof. pediat. and neurology, 1977—78; Sidney Carter prof. neurology and prof. pediatrics Coll. Physicians and Surgeons, Columbia U., NYC, 1979—; dir. pediatric neurology Columbia-Presbyn. Med. Ctr., NYC, 1979—2000, assoc. chmn. child neurology and devel. neurobiology, 1998—. Mem. coun. NANDS, 1997—2000. Assoc. editor Rudolph's Textbook of Pediatrics, 17th edit., 1982, 18th edit., 1987, 19th edit., 1990, 20th edit., 1996, 21st edit., 2000, Annals of Neurology, 1979—83, Advances in Pediatrics, 1989—; contbr. articles to profl. jours. With With USPHS, 1967—69. Grantee NIH. Mem.: Soc. Neurosci., Internat. Child Neurology Assn., Am. Soc. Neurochemistry, Soc. Pediatric Rsch., Am. Pediatric Soc., Child Neurology Soc. (pres. 1989—91), Am. Acad. Neurology (sec. 1993—97, trustee Rsch. and Edn. Found. 1997—), Am. Neurol. Assn., Alpha Omega Alpha. Office: Presbyn Hosp Neurology Inst 710 W 168th St New York NY 10032-2603 Office Phone: 212-305-5244.

DEVIVO, SAL J., newspaper executive; b. Saratoga Springs, NY, Feb. 3, 1937; s. Salvatore and Sabine (Lobombardo) DeV.; m. Carolyn Ann Turney, Dec. 17, 1961; children: Sally, Karen, Michael, Darin. BA in Journalism, St. Bonaventure U., 1962. Reporter The Saratogian, Saratoga Springs, 1956-58, Schenectady Gazette, 1959, Niagara Falls Gazette, N.Y., 1962, Sunday editor Niagara Gazette, 1964, city editor, 1966-68, editor, pub., 1974-75; mng. editor The Saratogian, 1968-72, editor, pub., 1972-74; editor Camden Courier-Post, N.J., 1975, pub., 1976-79; exec. editor, assoc. pub. Binghamton Press and Sun-Bull., N.Y., 1979-80; pres., pub. Utica Observer-Dispatch and Daily Press, N.Y., 1980-85, Wilmington Morning News and Evening Jour., Del., 1985-94, The Daily Jour., Vineland, N.J., 1994-96. Pres. Saratoga County United Way, 1973; gen. campaign chmn. Niagara Falls United Givers Fund, 1975, Utica United Way, 1985; pres. adv. council St. Bonaventure U., 1978-79; bd. dirs. Cooper Med. Center, Camden, 1978-79; trustee Wilmington Coll., 1989-2005. Mem. N.Y. State Soc. Newspaper Editors (past pres.), Md., Del. , D.C. press assns., N.J. Press Assn. (dir.), Am. Newspaper Pubs. Assn., Am. Soc. Newspaper Editors. Roman Catholic. Home: 10 Summerknoll Cir Newark DE 19711-2488

DEVLIN, BARBARA JO, school district administrator; b. Milw., 1947; m. John Edward Devlin, 1973; 2 children. BA, Gustavus Adolphus Coll., 1969; MA, U. Mass., 1971; PhD, U. Minn., 1978. Cert. tchr., sch. prin., supt., Minn.; cert. supt., Ill., Minn. Tchr. Worthington (Minn.) High Sch., 1971-75; rsch. assoc. Ednl. R & D, Mpls.-St. Paul, 1975-76, 76-77; coord. edn. svcs. Ednl. Coop. Svc., Mpls.-St. Paul, 1977-79; dir. personnel Minnetonka Pub. Schs., Excelsior, Minn., 1979-85, asst. supt., 1985-87; supt. Sch. Dist. 45, Villa Park, Ill., 1987-95, Ind. Sch. Dist. 280, Richfield, Minn., 1995—. Editor working papers Gov.'s Coun. on Fluctuating Enrollments, St. Paul, 1976. Contbr. articles to ednl. jours. Bd. dir. Richfield Found., 1995—. Named Ill. Supt. of Yr., 1994, Region 9 Adminstr. of Excellence, Minn. Assn. Sch. Adminstrs., 2004; recipient Disting. Alumni award, Gustavus Adolphus Coll., 1994; Ednl. Policy fellow, George Washington U., 1977—78, mem. fellow program, Bush Found. Pub. Schs., 1984—85. Mem. Minn. Assn. Sch. Adminstrs. (Morris Bye Meml. award for Supt. Leadership 2006), Rotary Internat. (membership chair Villa Park unit 1989-91, vocat. dir. 1991-92, sec. 1992-93, pres.

1994-95), Optimists Internat. (pres. 2000-2001). Methodist. Office: Richfield Pub Schs 7001 Harriet Ave Richfield MN 55423-3061 Office Phone: 612-798-6010. E-mail: Barbara.Devlin@richfield.k12.mn.us.

DEVLIN, CYNTHIA M., air transportation executive, consultant; b. Freeport, Tex., Dec. 13, 1949; d. Kellon Sherrell and Janiece (Chambers) Marshall; m. Philip Devlin. BA in Anthropology, U. Houston, 1991; MA in History, Stephen F. Austin State U., 2005. Cert. archaeool. U. London, 1988, paralegal Southwestern Paralegal Inst., 1994. Flight attendant Trans-Tex. Airways/Tex. Internat., Houston, 1969—73; office mgr. Mark Stevens Co., Houston, 1973—76, 1981—86, Foster Testers and Oil Drilling, Odessa, Tex., 1977—80; sales sec. Sys. One/Ea. Airlines, Miami and Houston, 1987—88, Continental Ea. Sales, Houston, 1988—89; sales adminstr. Continental Airlines, Houston, 1989—91, spl. events coord., 1991—94; specialist tech. publs. Continental Express, Houston, 1995; pres. PJD Airworthiness Cons., Inc., Houston and Zavalla, Tex., 1998—. Mem. adv. bd. Tenneco Marathon, Houston, 1994—96; cons. in field; adj. prof. Stephen F. Austin State U., 2006, 07. Author: Fahrenheit 6000, 2002, When the Sun Hides the Moon, 2003. Vol. Toys for Tots, Houston, Am. Cancer Soc., Spring, Tex.; mem. USO, Washington, Friends of Archaeology, U. St. Thomas, Houston, 1999—2003. Scholar, Assn. Women in Mgmt., 1989. Mem.: Tex. Archaeology Soc., East Tex. Hist. Assn. (v.p. women's history group 2007), U. Houston Alumni Assn. (life), Golden Key, Phi Alpha Theta. Republican. Avocations: painting, gardening, sewing, cooking. Home: 421 Chambers Rd Zavalla TX 75980 Office: PJD Airworthiness Cons Inc PO Box 46 Zavalla TX 75980

DEVLIN, FRANCIS JAMES, lawyer; b. NYC, Apr. 12, 1943; dual citizen, U.S., Ireland, 2005; s. Francis James and Marie A. D.; m. Patricia Ann Scheid; children: Christopher James, Kimberley. BA magna cum laude, Providence Coll., 1964; JD, Fordham U., 1967. Bar: N.Y. 1968, Tex. 1979, U.S. Ct. Appeals (5th and 11th cirs.) 1981, U.S. Supreme Ct. 1993. Assoc. Rogers and Wells, NYC, 1967-72; counsel Standard Oil Co. N.J., NYC, 1972, Exxon Corp., NYC, 1973-78, Exxon Co., U.S.A., Houston, 1978-90, sr. counsel, 1990-99, coord. gen. comml. practice group, 1996-99; sr. counsel, coord. mktg. Exxon Mobil Corp., Fuels Mktg. Co., Fairfax, Va., 1999—2002; spl. counsel Duane Morris, LLP, Houston, 2003—04. Adj. prof. Fordham U., 1978, U. Houston Law Ctr., 2006—. Editor-in-chief The Cowl, Providence Coll., 1962-64; articles editor Fordham Law Rev., 1966-67. Bd. dirs. Our Lady of Guadalupe Sch., Houston, 1994-2000, chmn., 1998-2000. Fellow: Am. Bar Found., Coll. State Bar Tex.; mem.: ABA (vice-chmn. 1997—2003, chmn. 2003—05, vice-chmn. petroleum mktg. com. 2005—, oil and natural gas downstream com., environment, energy and resources sect.), Houston Bar Assn. (vice chmn. antitrust section 2007—), Brit.-Am. Bus. Coun., Tex. Mid-Continent Oil and Gas Assn. (chmn. mktg. subcom.legal com. 1982—2000), Am. Petroleum Inst. (chmn. 1990—92, vice-chmn. 1992—94, chmn. 1997—98, vice-chmn. 1998—99, founding chmn. subcom. on mktg. law, counsel, gen. com. on mktg. 2001—02, gen. com. law, emeritus mem.), Tex. State Bar (unauthorized practice of law com. 1989—92, Bar Jour. com. 1995—98), Soc. Friendly Sons of St. Patrick in City N.Y. Republican. Roman Catholic. Home: 12625 Memorial Dr #112 Houston TX 77024-4819 Office: 12625 Memorial Dr Ste 112 Houston TX 77024-4819 Home Phone: 713-467-0633. E-mail: francisdevlin@msn.com.

DEVLIN, JOHN GERARD, lawyer, writer; b. Phila., Apr. 26, 1955; s. John and Catherine (Flannery) D.; m. Maureen Borneman, June 17, 1978; children: Caitlin, Colin, Courtenay, Conor. BA, Temple U., 1977, JD, 1980, LLM, 1996. Bar: Pa. 1980, N.J. 1992. Assoc. Spencer, Sherr & Moses, Norristown, Pa., 1980-82, Deasey, Scanlan & Bender, Phila., 1982-84; mng. atty. Devlin Assocs., P.A., Phila., 1984—. Author: Tort Liability for Bad Faith Claims, 1995. Mem. Union League Club, Phi Beta Kappa. Office: 1515 Market St Ste 2010 Philadelphia PA 19102-1920 Office Phone: 215-564-6740. E-mail: jgd@devlinlaw.com.

DEVLIN, MICHAEL COLES, bass-baritone; b. Chgo., Nov. 27, 1942; s. John Stott and Jane (Coles) D. Mus.B., La. State U., 1965. Debut, N.Y.C. Opera, 1966, appeared with, Santa Fe Opera, Houston Opera and Symphony, San Francisco Symphony, symphonies in, Los Angeles, Phila., Boston, Chgo., New Orleans, Washington, N.Y. Philharm., opera cos. in, Boston, New Orleans, Washington, Ft. Worth, English debut, Glyndebourne Festival, 1974; appeared at, Covent Garden, 1975, 77, European debut, Holland Festival, 1977; appeared with, Frankfurt and Munich operas, 1977, Can. opera and symphony work in, Winnipeg, Toronto and Ottawa, debut, Met. Opera, 1978, San Francisco Opera, 1979, Hamburg and Paris operas, 1980, Miami and Monte Carlo operas, 1981, Dallas opera, 1983, Chgo. Opera, 1984, Los Angeles Opera, 1986.

DEVLIN, PETER J., lawyer; BS, Clarkson Coll., 1980; JD magna cum laude, Suffolk U., 1985. Bar: Mass. 1985, US Patent and Trademark Office. Elec. engr., patent atty. Raytheon Co.; with Fish & Richardson PC, Boston, 1987—, pres., prin., 1993—. Contbg. author Inside the Minds: The Innovative Lawyer, 2003. Office: Fish & Richardson PC 225 Franklin St Boston MA 02110-2804 Office Phone: 617-521-7018. Office Fax: 617-542-8906. E-mail: devlin@fr.com.

DEVLIN, PHILLIP M., radiologist, medical educator; b. London, Eng. MD, U. Va., Charlottesville, 1991. Cert. therapeutic radiologist Am. Bd. Radiology, 1996. Chief, divsn. brachytherapy Dana Farber BWH Cancer Ctr., Boston, 1997—. Course dir., cme Harvard Med. Sch., Boston, 2005—. Editor: (textbook) Brachytherapy: Applications and Techniques. Nominating com. chair Am. Brachytherapy Soc., Phila., 2000—03. Mem.: Am. Soc. Therapeutic Radiology and Oncology. Independent. Achievements include research in brachytherapy Applications. Avocations: music, golf. Office: Dana Farber Brigham and Women's Cancer Ctr 75 Francis St Boston MA 02115 Office Phone: 617-732-6331. Business E-Mail: pdevlin@lroc.harvard.edu.

DEVLIN, ROBERT MANNING, diversified financial services company executive; b. Bklyn., Feb. 28, 1941; s. John Manning and Norma (Hall) D.; m. Katharine Bareis, Sept. 13, 1961; children: Michael Hall II, Matthew Bareis. BA in Econs., Tulane U., 1964. Various positions Mut. of N.Y., 1964-77; v.p., asst. to pres. Calif. Western States Life Ins. Co., Sacramento, 1977-80, sr. v.p., 1980; exec. v.p., dir. Am. Gen. Life and Accident Ins. Co., Nashville, 1980-85; pres., CEO Am. Gen. Life Insurance Co., Houston, 1986—93; vice chmn., bd. dir. Am. Gen. Corp., Houston, 1993—95, pres., CEO, 1995—2001, chmn., bd. dirs., 1997—2001; chmn. Curragh Capital Ptnrs. LLC, 2001—. Bd. dirs. Cooper Industries Inc., LKQ, Corp.; bd. trustees Boston Coll., Tulane Coll.; exec. com., bd. dirs. Internat. Insurance Soc. Inc.; exec. com., bd. dir. Am. Irish Historical Soc. Dir. Fin. Svcs. Roundtable; mem. Bus. Roundtable; bd. dirs. America's Promise-Alliance for Youth. Mem. Saratoga Reading Rooms, N.Y., Winged Foot Golf Club, N.Y., Met. Club, N.Y., Univ. Club, N.Y., Caves Valley Golf Club, Owings Mill, Md. Roman Catholic. Office: Curragh Capital Ptnrs LLC 730 5th Ave Ste 2102 New York NY 10019

DEVLIN, THOMAS MCKEOWN, biochemist, educator; b. Phila., June 29, 1929; s. Frank and Ella Mae (McKeown) Devlin; m. Marjorie Adele Paynter, Aug. 15, 1953; children: Steven James, Mark Thomas. BA, U. Pa., 1953; PhD, Johns Hopkins U., 1957. Rsch. assoc. Merck Inst., Rahway, NJ, 1957-61, sect. head, 1961-66, dir. enzymology, 1966-67; prof., chmn. dept. biochemistry Coll. Medicine Drexel U. (formerly Hahnemann U.), 1967-94, prof., 1994-95, prof. emeritus, 1995—, acting dean, Sch. Allied Health Professions, 1972-74, 80-81. Vis. scientist U. Brussels, 1964—65, Inst. Genetics, Naples, Italy, 1965; mem. rev. panels NSF, 1976—77; mem. com. sci. and arts Franklin Inst., 1977—90; mem. test com. Nat. Bd. Med. Examiners, 1983—85; chair Med. Biochemistry Edn. Bd., 1986—93. Editor: Textbook of Biochemistry (J. Wiley), 1982, 1986, 1992, 1997, 2002; contbr. articles to profl. jours. Mem. commn. evaluation, retention and selection of judges Phila. Bar Assn., 1976—79, vice chmn., 1979; mem. selection panel for magistrate judges, 1993, 1995, 2005; mem. vis. com. Lehigh U., 1982—90; mem. tech. adv. com. Ben Franklin Tech. Ctr., 1991—2000. Mem.: Biochemical Soc., Biophys. Soc., Soc. Exptl. Biology and Medicine, Am. Soc. Cell Biology, Am. Assn. Cancer Rsch., Am. Soc. Biochemistry and Molecular Biology, Greate Bay Golf Club, Ocean City (N.J.) Yacht Club, Sigma Xi, Phi Beta Kappa. Episcopalian. Home: 159 Greenville Ct Berwyn PA 19312-2071 Office: Drexel U Coll Medicine 159 Greenville Ct Berwyn PA 19312-2071 Business E-Mail: tdevlin@drexelmed.edu.

DEVOE, ANDREW, healthcare system executive; m. Susan DeVoe; 5 children. B. in fin., Belmont Coll., Nashville, 1991. With Health Mgmt. Assn., Inc., Naples, Fla., Hosp. Corp. Am., Nashville, Tenet Healthcare Corp., 1996—2004, regional v.p. fin. Phila.; sr. v.p. & CFO UPenn. Health System, Phila., 2004—. Mem. PENN Medicine Leadership Group. Recipient Outstanding CFO award, Tenet Corp., 1999, 2001—03, 40 Under 40 award, Phila. Bus. Jour., 2006. Mem.: Healthcare Fin. Mgmt. Assn. Office: UPenn Health System 21 Penn Twr 399 S 34th St Philadelphia PA 19104-4385 Office Phone: 215-662-2992. Office Fax: 215-662-7431. E-mail: andrew.devoe@uphs.upenn.edu.

DEVOE, DAVID F., SR., publishing executive; Group internal auditor News Corp., 1983; dep. fin. dir. News Corp. Ltd., NYC, 1985—90; CFO, fin. dir. News Corp., NYC, 1990—96, sr. exec. v.p., CFO, 1996—, exec. v.p. News Am. Inc., 1991—98, sr. exec. v.p. News Am. Inc., 1998—. Dir. William Collins Holdings, Harper Collins, British Sky Broadcasting Group, NDS Group, The News Corp. Office: News Corp Ste 300 1211 Avenue Of The Americas New York NY 10036-8795*

DEVOGT, JOHN FREDERICK, management science and business ethics educator, consultant; b. Detroit, Oct. 20, 1930; s. Leo Henry and Dorothy Helen (Gibbs) D.; m. Ann Marie Berby, Aug. 29, 1959; children—Joanne Elise, Linda Christine. BS, U. N.C., 1957, PhD, 1966. Instr. Washington and Lee U., Lexington, Va., 1962-66, asst. prof., 1966-67, assoc. prof., 1967-70, prof., 1970-2000, head dept., 1968-90, prof. emeritus, 2000—; acad. dir. Washington and Lee Family Bus. Inst., 1987—89. State judge Blue Chip Enterprise Initiative, 1991-96; acad. Jonah A.Y. Goldratt Inst., 1991—; chmn. adv. bd. Lexington office CorEast Savs. Bank, Richmond, 1976-90. Chmn. Lexington City Sch. Bd., 1973; pres. Va. Sch. Bds. Assn., Charlottesville, 1974; v.p. Henry St. Playhouse, Lexington, 1985, Friends Rockbridge Choral Soc., 2000—04; deacon, elder Lexington Presbyterian Ch.; bd. dirs. Lexington Indsl. Devel., 2004—. Served to staff sgt. USAF, 1951—55. Vis. fellow, Univ. Coll., Oxford, Eng., 1983. Mem. So. Mgmt. Assn. (pres. 1975-76), Rotary, Lexington Golf and Country Club (bd. dirs. 2004-06), Phi Beta Kappa, Phi Eta Sigma, Beta Gamma Sigma. Presbyterian. Avocations: golf, amateur dramatics, singing. Home: 617 Stonewall St Lexington VA 24450-1947 Office: Washington and Lee Univ Lexington VA 24450 Personal E-mail: jdevogt@rockbridge.net. Business E-Mail: devogtj@wlu.edu.

DEVORE, C. BRENT, college president, educator; b. Zanesville, Ohio, Sept. 3, 1940; s. Carl Emerson and Helen Elizabeth (Van Atta) DeVore; m. Linda Mospens, July 2, 1966; children: Krista, Matthew. BSJ., Ohio U., 1962; MA, Kent State U., 1971, PhD, 1978. Dir. devel. Am. Heart Assn., Cleve., 1965-68; exec. dir. Kent State U. Found., Ohio, 1968-72; v.p. Hiram Coll., Ohio, 1972-82; pres. Davis and Elkins Coll., Elkins, W.Va., 1982-84, Otterbein Coll., Westerville, Ohio, 1984—. Pres. Higher Edn. Coun., Columbus, 1985; trustee Nationwide Investing Found., 1990; bd. dirs. Coun. Ind. Colleges, 2004-. Producer and moderator film series on liberal arts edn. Pres. Hiram (Ohio) Village Council, 1981; chmn. E. Cen. Colls., 1990; pres. Nat. Assn. Schs. and Colls., United Meth. Ch., 1991. Mem. Am. Assn. Advancement of Humanities, AAUP, Ohio Council of Fund Raising Execs. (pres. 1976), Ohio Coll. Assn. (pres. 1987), W.Va. Assn. Coll. and Univ. Pres. (pres. 1984), Westerville C. of C. (pres.). Clubs: University (Columbus, Ohio); University (NYC). Lodges: Rotary. Office: Otterbein Coll Pres Office 27 S Grove St Westerville OH 43081-2004*

DEVORE, DAUN ALINE, lawyer; b. Ft. Worth; Student, U. Paris IV; BA magna cum laude, U. Calif., Irvine; JD, U. San Francisco; MPA, Harvard U.; postgrad., Oxford U. Bar: Calif., US Ct. Appeals (fed. and 9th cirs.), US Ct. Internat. Trade, US Dist. Ct. (ctrl. dist.) Calif., US Ct. Vets. Appeals. Law clk. US Environ. Protection Agy. Region IX, Constitution Sub-Com., US Senate Jud. Com.; honors clk. civil rights divsn. fed. enforcement US Dept. Justice; summer atty. Office Pub. Defenders for the City and County, San Francisco; lectr. law coll. Seoul Nat. U., Republic of Korea; assoc. Cen. Internat. Law Firm, Seoul; US prin. Othniel H.K. Ltd., Cambridge, Mass., LA, Hong Kong; ptnr. Internat. Bus. Law Firm, Palm Springs, Calif. and Washington. Constitutional law expert; Fulbright fellow judge, Seoul; presenter in field Contbr. articles to profl. jours. City commr. Hist. Site Preservation Bd., Palm Springs, Appeals Bd., Palm Springs; mem. legis. com. San Francisco Commn. on Status of Women. Named America's Miss USA Beauty and Talent Queen, Miss Mass., Miss Palm Springs UN. Mem. ABA (chair internat. law com. gen. practice sect., com. internat. svcs., chmn. subcom. on Asia-Pacific sect. internat. law, chmn. internat. law com. gen. practice sect., mem. standing com. liaison to fgn. and internat. bars.), Internat. Inst. Strategic Studies, Calif. Bar Assn. (com. internat. law), Armed Forces Comm. and Electronic Assn., Harvard Club (bd. dirs. Korea), Toastmasters (numerous speech awards), Phi Delta Phi. Avocations: operatic singer, songwriter, flute. Office Phone: 760-773-2257. Personal E-mail: daundevore@yahoo.com.

DEVORE, PAUL CAMERON, lawyer; b. Great Falls, Mont., Apr. 25, 1932; s. Paul Theodore and Maxine (Cameron) DeV.; m. Roberta Humphrey, Feb. 3, 1962; children: Jennifer Ross, Andrew Cameron, Christopher Humphrey. BA, Yale U., 1954; MA, Cambridge U., 1956; JD, Harvard U., 1961. Bar: Wash. 1961. Assoc. Wright, Innis, Simon & Todd, Seattle, 1961-66; ptnr. Davis Wright Tremaine, Seattle, 1967—, chmn. exec. com., 1983-95. Mem. adv. bd. BNA Media Law Reporter, 1978—. Chmn. Seattle C.C., 1967-68, Bush Sch., Seattle, 1976-79, Virginia Mason Med. Found., 1984-85, Virginia Mason Rsch. Ctr., 1983-84, Seattle Found., 1985-87, Children's Hosp. Found., 1993—; trustee Lakeside Sch., 1995—2004, Lopez Cmty. Land Trust; chmn. bd. visitors U. Wash. Sch. Comm., 1989-98; pres. A Contemporary Theatre, Seattle, 1972-74; sec. Seattle Art Mus., 1973-2000. Mem. ABA (chmn. forum on comm. law 1981-84), Wash. State Bar Assn. (chmn. sect. corp. bus. and banking law 1981-82, bench, bar, press com. 1984-90), Seattle-King County Bar Assn. (trustee 1975-76), Seattle Tennis Club, Phi Beta Kappa, Beta Theta Phi. Home: 5740 27th Ave NE Seattle WA 98105-5512 Office: Davis Wright Tremaine 2600 Century Sq 1501 4th Ave Ste 2600 Seattle WA 98101-1688 E-mail: camdevore@dwt.com.

DE VORE, PAUL WARREN, technology educator; b. Parkersburg, W.Va., July 18, 1926; s. Harry and Eleanor Sarah (Dunn) De Vore; m. Eleanor Jean Condron, Apr. 7, 1952; children: Harry Edwin, Michelle Ann, Phillip Charles. BS, Ohio U., Athens, 1950; MA, Kent State U., Ohio, 1954; EdD, Pa. State U., University Park, 1961; postgrad., Ohio State U., Columbus, 1983. Cert. homeland security angel flight pilot first responder 2005. Postdoctoral fellow U. Md., 1965-66; instr. pub. schs. Chagrin Falls, Ohio, 1950-53; asst. prof. engring. Grove City Coll., 1953-56; asst. prof. SUNY-Oswego, 1956-60, dir. div. indsl. arts and tech., 1960-67; prof. tech. edn. W. Va. U., Morgantown, 1967-75, prof., chmn. tech. edn., 1975-85, prof., coord. rsch. project offices, dept. technology, 1985-92; dir. Appalachian Tech. Edn. Consortium, 1990-95; dir. div. edn. and tng. Nat. Tech. Transfer Ctr., 1992-93. Tech. cons., pres. PWD Assocs., Dublin, Ohio, 1974—; cons. NSF, U.S. Dept. Edn., AID, pub. schs., colls., univs.; mem. com. technol. literacy Nat. Acad. Engring., 1999—; pres. Aviation Resources Inc., 1999—; pres. Hart Field Coalition, 1998-2003; mem. Morgantown Airport Com., 2004—. Author: Technology: An Intellectual Discipline, 1964, Education in a Technological Society, 1971, Technology and the New Liberal Arts, 1976, Technology: An Introduction, 1980, Introduction to Transportation, 1983; cons. editor: Tech. Edn. Series, 1974-93. Mem. nat. commn. Tech. for All Ams., 1994—95; chmn. campaign United Fund, Oswego, 1962—63; mem. Monongalia County Devel. Authority, 2000—04. With USN, 1944—46, PTO. Named Outstanding Tchr., W.Va. U., 1970-71, 89, W.Va. U. Coll. Resources and Edn., 1988; recipient Outstanding Rsch. award Phi Delta Kappa, 1978; recognized as one of individuals who has contbd. most to tech. edn., 1985. Mem. Coun. on Tech. Tchr. Edn. (life), Internat. Tech. Edn. Assn. (Acad. of Fellows 1987), Epsilon Pi Tau (Disting. Svc. award 1976, Paul T. Hiser Exemplary Publ. award 1988, 99, Bill Hart Aviation award 2001, established Dr. Paul W. De Vore Freedom of Flight aviation scholarship 2004, established Dr. Paul W. De Vore Libr. Endowment for Technology Studies, W.Va. U. 2004). Office: W Va U Tech Edn Rsch Proj Offices Morgantown WV 26506-6680 Home: 6000 Riverside Dr Apt A 332 Dublin OH 43017-5113 *Seek quality in all you do and conduct your personal and civic affairs in a responsible and civil manner.*

DE VOS, GEORGE ALPHONSE, psychologist, anthropologist; b. Detroit, July 25, 1922; s. Medard Joseph and Marina Marie (Tack) De V.; m. Winifred Olsen, May 4, 1944 (div. 1974); m. Suzanne Lake, Nov. 18, 1974; children: Laurie, Susan, Eric, Michael. BA in Sociology, U. Chgo., 1946, MA in Anthropology, 1948, PhD in Psychology, 1951. Chief psychologist, dir. psychol. tng. Elgin (Ill.) State Hosp., 1951-53; asst. prof. psychology U. Mich., Ann Arbor, 1955-57; assoc. prof. social welfare U. Calif., Berkeley, 1957-63, prof. anthropology, 1963-91, prof. emeritus, 1991—. Vis. prof. U. Rome, 1975, U. Paris, 1979, Cath. U. Leuven, Belgium, 1986, U. Barcelona, 1992; exch. prof. U. Leningrad (now U. St. Petersburg), 1990; chmn. Ctr. for Japanese and Korean Studies U. Calif., 1965—91; cons. Family Planning Rsch., Korean Inst. Behavioral Scis., Seoul, Republic of Korea, 1970—71; rsch. assoc. Ecole des Hautes Etudes en Scis. Sociales, U. Paris, 1973—91; sr. cons. series prodn. The Japanese Film PBS, 1975; dir. NSF project The Korean Minority in Japan; cons. on Japanese culture Human Rels. Area File, New Haven, 1975—82; cons. Cultural Learning East-West Center, Hawaii, 1978—79. Author: 22 books, including Oasis and Casbah, 1960, Japan's Invisible Race, 1966, Socialization for Achievement, 1973, Ethnic Identity, 1975, 4th edit., 2006, Responses to Change, 1976, Koreans in Japan, 1981, Heritage of Endurance: Delinquency in Japan, 1984, Culture and Self, 1985, 1984, Religion and the Family in East Asia, 1986, Symbolic Analysis Cross Culturally: The Rorschach Test, 1989, Status Inequality, 1990, Social Cohesion and Alienation, 1992, Confucianism and The Family, 1998, Basic Dimensions in Conscious Thought, 2004, Cross Cultural Dimensions in Conscious Thought, 2004. Fulbright fellow, Nagoya, Japan, 1953-55, NIMH fellow French Min. Justice, 1963, NSF fellow UN Social Def. Rsch. Inst., Rome, 1972-73; Fulbright Sr. Rsch. Sch. Cath. U. Rio Grande do Sul, Brazil, 1992. Mem. APA (pres. Soc. for Psychol. Anthropology 1984-85), Assn. Asian Studies, Am. Anthropology Assn. Home: 2835 Morley Dr Oakland CA 94611-2547 E-mail: devos@berkeley.edu.

DE VOS, PAULA FRANCESCA, finance company executive, investment advisor, consultant; d. Elliot Adrian and Pauline Francis Mizelle; m. Rene A. de Vos, Apr. 9, 1992; 1 child, Adrian Anthony. Superior Degree in French Lang., U. Paris Sorbonne, 1981; BA in Internat. Econs., U. Calif., Berkeley, 1982; MBA in Fin., U. San Francisco, 1994. Cert. fin. planner. In mgmt. Madrigal Inc., San Francisco; asst. v.p. JPMorgan Pvt. Bank, San Francisco, 1983—93; v.p. Wells Fargo Pvt. Client Services, Carmel, Calif., 2001—03; pres. Synergist Wealth Advisors LLC, Carmel, 2003—, Catalyst Wealth Mgmt. LLC, Carmel, 2003—. Cons. Synergist Wealth Advisors LLC, Carmel, Calif., 2003—. Contbr. articles to profl. jours. Mem.: Fin. Planning Assn. Avocations: sports, travel, reading, tennis. Office: Synergist Wealth Advisors LLC PO Box 1844 Carmel CA 93921 Office Phone: 831-626-1442. Business E-Mail: paula@synergistwealth.com.

DE VOS, PETER JON, ambassador; b. San Diego, Dec. 24, 1938; BA, Princeton U., 1960; MA, Johns Hopkins U., 1962. Consular officer Am. Consulate, Recife, Brazil, 1962—64; fgn. service officer for Brazil Dept. State, Washington, 1964-66; polit. officer Am. Consulate, Naples, 1966-68; dep. prin. officer Am. Embassy, Luanda, 1968-70; polit. officer Am. Consulate, Sao Paulo, 1970-71, Am. Embassy, Brasilia, 1971-73; spl. asst. Bur. Inter-Am. Affairs Dept. State, Washington, 1973-75; polit. officer Am. Embassy, Athens, 1975-78, Nat. War. Coll., 1978-79; dep. dir. So. African Affairs Dept. State, Washington, 1979-80; U.S. ambassador to Republic of Guinea-Bissau and to Republic of Cape Verde, 1980-83, Mozambique, Maputo, 1983-87; dep. asst. sec. of state U.S. Dept. State, Washington, 1987-89, prin. dep. asst. sec. state Bur. Oceans and Internat. Environ. and Sci. Affairsv, 1989-90, amb. to Republic of Liberia, 1990-92, appointed U.S. spl. envoy to Somalia, 1992, amb. to Republic of Tanzania, 1992-94, amb. to Republic of Costa Rica, 1994-97. Disting. guest lectr. U. Chgo., 1997—; Rivers chair prof. East Carolina U., 2000—01; bd. dirs. Old Theater Corp. Bd. dirs. Pamlico Music Soc., Grant-Valkaria Code Enforcement Bd. Home: 3725 Laurens Ave Malabar FL 32950

DEVOS, RICHARD MARVIN, SR., professional sports team owner, former network marketing company executive; b. Grand Rapids, Mich., Mar. 4, 1926; s. Simon C. and Ethel R. (Dekker) DeV.; m. Helen J. Van Wesep, Feb. 7, 1953. Student, Calvin Coll., 1946; LLD (hon.), Oral Roberts U., 1976, Grove City Coll., Pa., Northwood Inst., Midland, Mich., 1977, Dickinson Sch. Law, Carlisle, Pa., 1980, Pepperdine U., 1980, Lubbock Christian Coll., 1981; DLitt (hon.), Hope Coll., 1982; LHD (hon.), Grand Valley State U., 1992; LLD (hon.), Regent U., 1992; D in Bus. (hon.), No. Mich. U., 1998. Ptnr. Wolverine Air Svc., 1945-48; co-founder, pres. Ja-Ri Corp., 1949, Amway Corp., 1959-92; owner, chmn. NBA Orlando Magic, Fla. Author: Believe!, Compassionate Capitalism, Hope From My Heart: Ten Lessons For Life. Chmn. Gospel Films, Muskegon, Mich.; bd. dirs., chmn. Midwest region BIPAC, Nat. Orgn. Disability; past co-chair Salvation Army Campaign, Grand Rapids, Mich., 1993; dir. Grand Rapids Econ. Club; past pres. Grand Rapids Jr. Achievement, 1966-67; past mem. bd. control Grand Valley State Coll.; past bd. dirs. United Way Kent County; past bd. dirs. Nat. Legal Ctr. Pub. Interest; chmn., past bd. dirs. Butterworth Health Corp., Grand Rapids, Nat. Adv. Bd. Coral Ridge Ministries, Fla. Bd. Govs. Northwood U.; trustee Gerald R. Ford Found.; past chmn. New Grand Rapids Com.; spl. adv. Pres. Coun. on Phys. Fitness and Sports; mem. Close-Up Found. Hon. State Bd. Adv.; mem. coun. trustees Freedoms Found.; past chmn. Nat. Adv. Bd. Nat. Rep. Com.; past fin. chmn. Rep. Nat. Com.; past mem. Presdl. Commn. AIDS; past pres. Coun. Nat. Policy; fellow World Fellowship for Duke of Edinburgh's Award; named to Jr. Achievement Nat. Bus. Hall of Fame, 1998. Served in USAAF, 1944—46. Recipient Alexander Hamilton award Econ. Edn. from Freedoms Found.; Disting. Salesman of Yr. award Grand Rapids Sales and Mktg. Assn., Bus. Leader of Yr. award Religious Heritage Am., Industry Week Excellence in Mgmt. award, Thomas Jefferson Freedom of Speech award Kiwanis Internat., Mich. Week Vol. Leadership award, Am. Spirit award, Rep. House and Senate, 1998, House of Hope Humanitarian award, 1999, Excellence in Bus. award, Davenport U., 2000, Mktg. Man of Yr. award West Mich. chpt. Am. Mktg. Assn., Edison Achievement award, 1994, Horatio Alger award, 1996, Am. Enterprise Exec. award Nat. Mgmt. Assn., Golden Plate award Acad. of Achievement,

George Washington Honor Medal award Freedoms Found., Free Enterprise award Americanism Ednl. League, Patron award Mich. Found. for the Arts, 1982, Am. Entrepreneur of Yr. award U. Mo., 1988, Disting. Alumni award Calvin Coll., 1982, Exec. of Yr. award U. Ariz., 1991, Napoleon Hill Gold medal, 1989, Outstanding Bus. Leader award Northwood U., 1983, Outstanding Am. award Nat. Future Farmers Am., 1990, Environ. Prog. Achievement award UN, 1989, William Booth award Salvation Army, 1990, Adam Smith Free Enterprise award Am. Legis. Exch. Coun., 1993, Donald J. Porter Humanitarian award YMCA Heritage Club, 1993, Inspiration award Internat. Assn. Organ Donation, 2003; named to Greater Grand Rapids Hall of Fame, 1989, Sales & Mktg. Execs. Internat. Acad. Achievement, 1990; named Socially Responsible Entrepreneur of Yr.; named one of Forbes' Richest Ams., 1999—, World's Richest People, Forbes mag., 2001—. Mem. NAM (past dir.), Direct Selling Assn. (past chmn., dir., Champion of Free Enterprise and Knights of Royal Way awards, Hall of Fame award, Circle of Honor award), Direct Selling Edn. Found., Newcomen Soc., Grand Rapids Econ. Club (dir.), Round Table Internat. (hon. knight for life 1992) , Omicron Delta Kappa (hon.). Mem. Christian Reformed Ch. (former elder, chmn. fin. com.; past pres. missionary soc.). Clubs: Econ. (Grand Rapids) (dir.), Rotary (Disting. Svc. award) (Grand Rapids); Pillars bd. dirs. Office: Orlando Magic 8701 Maitland Summit Blvd Orlando FL 32810*

DEVREOTES, PETER NICHOLAS, biochemistry educator; b. Long Branch, NJ, Apr. 22, 1948; s. Peter and Lucille (Mignon) D.; m. Aline Devreotes, Aug. 15, 1980. BS, U. Wis., 1971; PhD, Johns Hopkins U., 1977. Postdoctoral fellow U. Chgo., 1977-80; asst. prof. Sch. of Medicine, Johns Hopkins U., Balt., 1980-85, assoc. prof., 1985-87, prof. biol. chemistry, 1987—, dir. biochemistry cellular and molecular biology grad. program, 1990—2000, dir. Dept. Cell Biology, 2000—. Mem. sci. rev. com. Am. Cancer Soc., Atlanta, 1990—; dir. biochemistry, cellular and molecular biology program Johns Hopkins U. Sch. Medicine, 1990—; established investigator Am. Heart Assn. Contbr. articles to profl. jours.; assoc. editor Molecular Biology of the Cell, 1997—2004. Mem.: NAS, Am. Soc. for Cell Biology, Am. Soc. Biochemistry and Molecular Biology. Office: Johns Hopkins U Sch Med 520 WBSB 725 N Wolfe St Baltimore MD 21205-2105

DE VRIES, BRIAN, gerontologist, researcher; BA, U. BC, Vancouver, 1988, MA, PhD, U. BC, Vancouver. Vis. scholar U. of Calif., San Francisco, 1995—97; prof. Gerontology Program, San Francisco State U., 2000—. Dir. Gerontology Program, San Francisco State U., 2000—03; assoc. editor Internat. Jour. of Aging and Human Devel., San Francisco, 1998—2006, editor sexuality rsch. and social policy, 2007—. Editor: (books) End of Life Issues, Narrative Gerontology, Gay and Lesbian Aging, Kinship Bereavement in Later Life, 2006, Jour. Sexuality Rsch. and Soc. Policy, 2007—, author over 70 jour. articles, book chpts., rsch. reports. Mem. leadership com. Am. Soc. Aging. Rsch. award, Nat. Inst. on Aging, 2004—. Fellow: Gerontol. Soc. of Am.; mem.: Am. Soc. Aging (leadership coun.). Office: San Francisco State U 1600 Holloway Ave HSS 242 San Francisco CA 94132 Office Phone: 415-338-3559.

DEVRIES, DONALD LAWSON, JR., lawyer; b. Phila., May 1, 1947; s. Donald Lawson and Jeanne (Coleman) DeV.; m. Nancy Shafer, Aug. 10, 1977; children: Donald Lawson III, Emily Shafer; stepdaughter: Alison Brady Beale. BA with honors, Dartmouth Coll., 1969; JD with honors, U. Md., 1973. Bar: Md. 1973, U.S. Dist. Ct. Md. 1973, U.S. Ct. Appeals (4th cir.) 1976, U.S. Ct. Appeals (DC cir.) 1989, U.S. Dist. Ct. DC 1991. Assoc. Semmes, Bowen & Semmes, Balt., 1973-80, ptnr., chmn. med. malpractice dept., 1980-88; founding and mng. ptnr. Goodell, DeVries, Leech & Dann, Balt., 1988—. Mem. faculty Md. Inst. Continuing Profl. Edn. for Lawyers, 1984-95; gov.'s task force on Med. Malpractice Ins., 1985; master Am. Inns of Ct., 1986-90. Contbr. Md. Law Rev., 1973. Trustee Roland Pk. Country Sch., 1987-94, Woodbourne Ctr., 1981-88, Union Meml. Hosp. Found., 2003—; trustee, exec. com. South Balt. Gen. Hosp., 1983-88; mem. Canons and Other Bus. Coms. of Episcopal Diocese Md., 1984-95; vestryman St. David's Ch., 1982-85; bd. dirs. Md. affiliate Am. Heart Assn., 1986-90, co-chmn. Heart Ball, 1986, 87, 88, chmn. solicitation com. Shock Trauma Gala, 1988, 89, co-chmn., 1990, 91, bd. visitors Shock Trauma, 1989-93, chmn. 1990-93; chmn. Emergency Med. Svcs. Bd., Md., 1992—; mem. joint exec./legis. task force on med. malpractice ins., Md., 1985; mem. com. on uninsured persons Gov.'s Commn. on Health Care Policy and Financing, 1988-90. Named one of Top 10 Md. Super Lawyers, 2007; recipient Leadership in Law award, Daily Record, 2006. Fellow Am. Coll. Trial Lawyers, Internat. Acad. Trial Lawyers; mem. ABA (spkr. ann. meeting 1984, moderator, program planner ann. meeting medicine and law com. 1986, 88, vice chmn. medicine and law com. torts and ins. practice sect. 1982-89, med. adv. panel medicine and law com. 1986-87, forum com. health law 1984—, faculty nat. inst. on med. malpractice 1987, 88, 89, 90, chmn. medicine and law com., torts and ins. practice sect. 1988-89), Internat. Assn. Ins. Counsel, Internat. Assn. Def. Counsel (faculty trial acad. 1991, moderator, program planner 1992, vice chmn. med. malpractice com. for newsletters 1989-90, program chmn. 1990-92, chmn. med. malpractice com. 1992-94, chmn. def. counsel com. 1997-99, exec. com. 1999-02, George W. Yancey Meml. award 1998, The Daily Rec.'s Leadership in Law award 2006, Top 10 Md. Lawyers 2007), Internat. Soc. Barristers, Assn. Def. Trial Attys., Am. Bd. Trial Advs. (pres. Md. chpt. 1993-95, nat. bd. dirs. 1993—), Md. State Bar Assn. (spl. com. on health claims arbitration 1983), Md. Trial Lawyers Assn. (faculty 1983, 85), Md. Assn. Def. Trial Counsel, Def. Rsch. Inst. (Daily Record Leadership in Law award, 2006), Wednesday Law Club, Md. Club, Farmington Country Club, Ctr. Club, Annapolis Yacht Club. Republican. Office: Goodell DeVries Leech & Dann LLP 1 South St Ste 2000 Baltimore MD 21202-7314 Home Phone: 410-464-9063; Office Phone: 410-783-4000. Business E-Mail: dld@gdldlaw.com.

DEVRIES, JANET MARY, archivist, curator; b. Evergreen Park, Ill., June 27, 1962; d. Francis Martin and Rita Gibbens Gardner; m. William P. DeVries, Nov. 4, 1989; children: Amy Frances, Heidi Annette, Bridget Mary. AS in Bus. Adminstrn., Palm Beach Coll., Lake Worth, Fla., 2003. Credit officer Sco Hy's, Winter Haven, Fla., 1987—91; teller Barnett Bank, Boynton Beach, Fla., 1989—92; archivist Boynton Beach City Libr., 1997—; curator collections Schoolhouse Children's Mus., Boynton Beach, 2000—; staff writer Susabella's Passengers MAg., Pebble Beach, Calif., 2003—; editor The Whispered Watchword, Antelope, Calif., 2003—. Trustee Boynton Beach Hist. Soc., 1997—; advisor City of Boynton Beach Libr., 1993—97. Mem.: Am. Assn. State and Local History, Am. Assn. Archivists, Soc. Fla. Archivists, Internat. Nancy Drew Slueths (founder). Presbyterian. Avocations: snorkeling, genealogy, history, treasure hunting. Office: Boynton Beach City Libr 208 S Seacrest Blvd Boynton Beach FL 33435

DEVRIES, KENNETH LAWRENCE, mechanical engineer, educator; b. Ogden, Utah, Oct. 27, 1933; s. Sam and Fern (Slater) DeVries; m. Kay M. McGee, Mar. 1, 1959; children: Kenneth, Susan. AS in Civil Engring., Weber State Coll., 1953; BSME, U. Utah, 1959, PhD in Physics, Mech. Engring., 1962. Registered profl. engr., Utah. Rsch. engr. hydraulic group Convair Aircraft Corp., Fort Worth, 1957-58; prof. dept. mech. engring. U. Utah, Salt Lake City, 1969-75, 1976-91, disting. prof., 1991—, chmn. dept., 1970-81, pres. acad. senate, 2004—05; sr. assoc. dean U. Utah Coll. Engring., Salt Lake City, 1983-97, acting dean, 1997-98. Program dir. div. materials rsch. NSF, Washington, 1975-76, pres. academic senate, 2004-05; materials cons. Browning, Morgan, Utah, 1972—; cons. 3M Co., Mpls., 1985—; tech. adv. bd. Emerson Electric, St. Louis, 1978-2002; mem. Utah Coun. Sci. and Tech., 1973-77; trustee Gordon Rsch. Conf., 1989-97, chair, 1992-93 Co-author: Analysis and Testing of Adhesive Bonds, 1978; contbr. chpts. to books, articles to profl. jours. Fellow ASME, Am. Phys. Soc.; mem. Am. Chem. Soc. (polymer div.), Am. Soc. for Engring. Edn. (nat. officer), Adhesion Soc. Mem. Lds Ch. Office: U Utah Coll Engring 50 S Central Campus Dr Salt Lake City UT 84112-9249 Office Phone: 801-581-7101. Business E-Mail: kldevries@mech.utah.edu, kldevries@eng.utah.edu.

DE VRIES, MARGARET GARRITSEN, economist; b. Detroit, Feb. 11, 1922; d. John Edward and Margaret Florence (Ruggles) Garritsen; m. Barend A. de Vries, Apr. 5, 1952; children: Christine, Barton. BA in Econs. with honors, U. Mich., 1943; PhD in Econs., MIT, 1946. With IMF, Washington, 1946-87, sr. economist, 1949-52, asst. chief multiple currency pratices div., 1953-57, chief Far Eastern Div., 1957-59, econ. cons., 1963-73, historian, 1973-87. Professorial lectr. econs. George Washington U., 1946-49, 58-63 Author: The International Monetary Fund, 1966-71, The System Under Stress, 2 vols., 1977, The International Monetary Fund, 1972-78, Cooperation on Trial, 3 vols., 1985, The IMF in a Changing World, 1945-85, transl. into Chinese, 1986, Balance of Payments, Adjustment: The IMF Experience, 1945-86, transl. into Chinese, 1989, (with I.S. Friedman) Foreign Economic Policy of the United States in the Postwar, 1947, (with J.K. Horsefield) The International Monetary Fund, 1945-65, Twenty Years of International Monetary Cooperation, 3 vols., 1969; contbr. articles to profl. jours. Recipient Disting. Alumni award U. Mich., 1980, Cert. of Appreciation George Washington U., 1987, Outstanding Washington Woman Economist award, 1987; AAUW scholar, 1939-42; U. Mich. Univ. scholar, 1942; Phi Kappa Phi fellow, 1943; MIT fellow, 1943-46; Ford Found. grantee, 1959-62. Mem. Am. Econ. Assn. (CSWEP - Carolyn Shaw Bell award 2002), U. Mich. Alumni Assn., MIT Alumnae Assn., Phi Beta Kappa, Phi Kappa Phi. Mem. United Church of Christ. Home: 10018 Woodhill Rd Bethesda MD 20817-1218 Personal E-mail: barmar1022@comcast.net. *Probably the greatest factor in my life has been a sense of direction. Growing up in Detroit in the Great Depression of the 1930's, as a child I became aware of the problem of extensive unemployment. Then, as now, in times of recession, Detroit was one of the hardest hit cities. I knew I wanted to be an economist and to work in the public sector. Motivation, determination, a continuing interest in economics, and a feeling of the need for public service have carried me the rest of the way.*

DE VRIES, RIMMER, economist; b. Utrecht, Netherlands, Jan. 20, 1929; came to U.S., 1951, naturalized, 1957; s. Jacob and Mettje (Verburg) de V.; m. Ruth Berg, May 24, 1958; children— Rimmer D., Jacqueline R., Joyce C. BA, Netherlands Sch. Econs., 1951; MA, Ohio State U., 1952, PhD, 1955. Economist Fed. Res. Bank N.Y., 1956-61; economist, then v.p. Morgan Guaranty Trust Co., NYC, 1961-78, sr. v.p., 1978-88, chief economist, 1988-94, mng. dir., 1990-94; cons. J.P. Morgan & Co. Inc., 1994-97. Bd. dirs. AGF Cos. Ltd.; bd. economists Time Mag., 1976-86; mem. Pres. Reagan Commn. on Competitiveness, 1984-86. Founder, editor: World Fin. Markets, 1971—91. Mem. Coun. Fgn. Rels. Republican. Home: 804 Holbeck Dr Camano Island WA 98282-7366 Personal E-mail: rdevries@wavecable.com.

DEVRIES, ROBERT ALLEN, foundation administrator; b. Chgo., May 12, 1936; s. Robert and Mildred (Burgess) DeV.; m. Eleanor Rose Siems, Aug. 16, 1958; children: Susan E., Robert S., Laura H., Steven P. BS in Physiology, U. Chgo., 1958, MBA in Hosp. Adminstrn., 1961. Adminstrv. resident, asst. Miami Valley Hosp., Dayton, Ohio, 1959-61, asst. dir., 1961-67; adminstr. McPherson Community Health Ctr., Howell, Mich., 1967-71; program dir. W.K. Kellogg Found., Battle Creek, Mich., 1971-88, program dir., dir. Kellogg Internat. Fellowship Programs, 1988-90, program dir., dir. Internat. Study Grants and Exchanges, 1990-97, mem. adminstrv. coun., 1995-97, program dir., mem. fellowship com., 1997-99; ret., 1999. Cons. on domestic and internat. programs W.K. Kellogg Found., 1999—; mem. com. vis. Sch. Nursing, U. Mich., 2000—; assisting min. St. Peter Luth. Ch.; chmn. quality com. bd. trustees Battle Creek Health Sys., 2001—; bd. dirs. Lifecare Ambulance, chmn. bd., 2004—; bd. dirs. North Pointe Woods, Mich. Health Coun.; lectr. nursing orgn., adminstrn. Sch. Nursing Miami Valley Hosp., 1961-67, Grad. Sch. Pub. Health U. Mich., 1967—; adj. prof. Coll. Health and Human Svcs., Western Mich. U., 1986—; advisor Sch. Pub. Health Beijing Med. U., 1986—, Med. Coll. Health Staff, Shanghai, 1986—, 1st People's Hosp., Shanghai, 1986—; mem. nat. adv. com. on rural health U.S. Dept. Health and Human Svcs., Washington, 1988-92; mem. adv. panel acad. health scis. ctr. U.N.C., Chapel Hill, 1992-94; mem. policy coun. Nat. Inst. Rural Health Policy, 1987-90; mem. health planning and cert. of need workgroup Mich. Dept. Mgmt. & Budget, Mich. Dept. Pub. Health, 1986-87; vice chmn. adv. coun. Hosp. Rsch. & Ednl. Trust, Chgo., 1974-85; treas. coun. practice Am. Assn. Nurse Anesthetists, 1978-84; mem. Southwest Mich. Health Sys. Agy. Bd., 1980-83; guest lectr. King's Fund Coll., London, U. Leeds, Eng., French Nat. Sch. Pub. Health, Rennes, U. Toronto, Pan Am. Health Orgn., Washington and Brasilia, Brazil, Katholieke Universiteit Leuven, Belgium, Internat. Hosp. Fedn., London, Elton Mayo Sch. Mgmt., Adelaide, Australia, Ministry Pub. Health, Beijing, Indian Hosp. Assn., New Delhi, Harvard Med. Sch., Assn. Am. Med. Coll. Co-author healthcare trustee book; mem. editl. bds. Inquiry, Hosp. & Health Svcs.; contbr. articles to profl. jours., also book chpts. Counselor Baxter Am. Found. Prize in Health Svcs. Rsch., 1986—; assoc. trustee Florence Nightingale Mus. Trust, London. Recipient Disting. Svc. award Am. Soc. Allied Health Professions, 1989, Med. Group Mgmt. Assn., Denver, 1990, Ohio State U. Alumni Assn., 1998; Monsignor Griffin award for disting. writing Ohio Hosp. Assn., 1965, Civic Achievement award Jr. C. of C., Chgo., 1955, recognition award for contbns. to svcs. to handicapped Commn. on Accreditation of Rehab. Facilities, 1976, Cmty. Health Leadership award Hosp. Rsch. and Ednl. Trust, 1994, Spl. Recognition award Mich. Health and Hosp. Assn., 1999, Cert. of Honor, Peking U., China, 2003, Red Rose award for disting. cmty. svc. Gr. Battle Creek Rotary, 2004, U. Chgo. Pub. Svc. citation, 2005; named Outstanding Young Men in Am. Howell, Mich. Area C. of C. and Jaycees, 1970; Nat. Health Svcs. rsch. fellow U. Mich., 1970-71. Fellow Am. Coll. Healthcare Execs.(life), U.S. China Ednl. Inst., Can. Sch. Mgmt. (hon.); mem. APHA, Am. Hosp. Assn. (hon. life, vice chair R&D coun. 1974-85, adv. panel multi-hosp. systems 1977-85, Living the Vision award 1999, Blue Ribbon com. on healthcare governance), Internat. Hosp. Fedn., Nat. Rural Health Assn., Mich. Hosp. Assn. (assn. governance and strategic planning com. 1986-89, pub. policy and govt. com. 1981-83), U. Chgo. Hosp. Adminstrn. Alumni Assn. (pres. 1982-83), Leila Arboretum Soc. (pres. 2003-04). Lutheran. Avocations: music, writing, travel, gardening.

DEVRIES, ROBERT CHARLES, research scientist; b. Evansport, Ohio, Oct. 10, 1922; s. Charles and Rebecca (Goethe) DeV.; m. Ruth Elizabeth Wood, Oct. 30, 1943; children: David, Peter, Charles, Jonathan, Katherine. BA, DePauw U., 1948; PhD, Pa. State U., 1953. Topographer U.S. Geol. Survey, Washington, 1943-46; postdoctoral fellow Pa. State U., State College, 1953-54; staff scientist rsch. lab. GE, Schenectady, N.Y., 1954-61, staff scientist corp. R& D Ctr., 1965-88; assoc. prof. Rensselaer Poly. Inst., Troy, N.Y., 1961-65; cons. P-T-X, Burnt Hills, N.Y., 1988—. Adj. prof. Pa. State U., 1992-95; cultural exch. visitor, Japan, 1974; Coolidge fellow R&D Ctr. CE, 1981. Editor: The Reactivity of Solids, 1968, contbr. numerous articles to profl. jours.; patentee in field. With USAF, 1943. Rector scholar DePauw U., 1941; recipient Engring. Materials Achievement award Am. Soc. Metals, 1973. Fellow Am. Ceramic Soc., Am. Mineral Soc.; mem. AAAS, Am. Assn. Crystal Growth, Materials Rsch. Soc., Nat. Acad. Engring., Materials Rsch. Soc. (hon. Japan 1993), Mineral Soc. London, Sigma Xi. Avocations: gemmology, beekeeping, biking, reading, wood carving. Home and Office: P-T-X 17 Van Vorst Dr Burnt Hills NY 12027-9712 Home Phone: 518-399-5225; Office Phone: 518-399-5225. Personal E-mail: rcdvriesptx@worldnet.att.net.

DEVRIES, ROBERT K., retired publisher, consultant; b. Sully, Iowa, July 6, 1932; s. Fred G. and Selena Irene (Willetts) DeV.; m. Carolyn Jo Schroeder, June 2, 1962 (div. 1978); children: Stephen Robert, Suzanne Mishael Dahill; m. Carolyn Gail Bergmans, May 26, 1979; children: Staci Ann McKellar, Keri Gail Bailey. AB, Wheaton Coll., 1954; ThM, Dallas Theol. Sem., 1958, ThD, 1969. Asst. registrar Dallas Theol. Sem., 1959-63; editor-in-chief Moody Press, Chgo., 1963-68; dir., v.p. pubs. Zondervan Pub. House, Grand Rapids, Mich., 1968-76, exec. v.p. book div., 1976-85; exec. v.p., publisher Zondervan Book Group, Zondervan Corp., Grand Rapids, Mich., 1985-86; pub., bd. dirs. Discovery House Pubs., Grand Rapids, 1987-2000, sr. publisher, bd. dirs., 2000—07; cons., bd. dirs. Serendipity House, Littleton, Colo., 1990-99; bd. dirs. Serendipity House Found., Littleton, 1999—2003. Bd. dirs. Oswald Chambers Pub. Assn. Ltd., Eng. Bd. dirs. Ligonier Valley Study Ctr., Stahlstown, Pa., 1979-83, Bd. Publ., Evang. Covenant Ch. Am., Chgo., 1989-94, chmn., 1992-94; advisor Internat. Coun. Bibl. Inerrancy, Walnut Creek, Calif., 1978-87. Recipient Outstanding Young Men in Am. award Jaycees, 1965, Lifetime Achievement award, Evangelical Christian Publishers Assn., 2006. Republican. Mem. Evangelical Covenant Ch. Home: 7554 Lime Hollow Dr SE Grand Rapids MI 49546-7439 Office: 3000 Kraft Ave SE Grand Rapids MI 49512-2024

DEVRIES SMITH, KATE, lawyer; BS in Physics cum laude, Drake U., 1993; JD cum laude, U. Mich. Law Sch., 1996. Bar: Minn. 1996, US Patent and Trademark Office 1998. Ptnr. Merchant & Gould, Mpls.; co-founder, ptnr. Pauly, DeVries Smith & Deffner, L.L.C., Mpls. Named a Rising Star, Minn. Super Lawyers mag., 2006. Mem.: Minn. Women Lawyers, Minn. Intellectual Property Law Assn., Am. Intellectual Property Law Assn., ABA (mem. intellectual property sect.), Vol. Lawyers Network (bd. dirs., named Vol. Lawyer of Yr. 2005). Office: Pauly DeVries Smith & Defner LLC Plz VII Ste 3000 455 Seventh St Minneapolis MN 55402 Office Phone: 612-746-4784. E-mail: kds@pdsdlaw.com.

DEVRIES-WHITE, DONNA LYNN, education educator, consultant; b. Hawthorne, Calif., July 9, 1956; d. Adrian and Antoinetta Lucretia Christina (Mulder) deV.; m. Steven Eugene White, Mar. 7, 1987. Cert. in profl. edn., Seattle Pacific U., 1980, 83, 86, BA, 1980, MEd, 1987; postgrad., U. Calif., Riverside, 1989; postgrad. in ednl. adminstrn., Azusa Pacific U., 2003—. Cert. learning and severely handicapped and spl. edn. tchr., Wash., Calif; profl. adminstrv. credential.; multiple subject clear credential, specialist credential, 1980; resource specialist credential, 1989; instr. credetial, 1989. Instructional aide Garden Grove Unified Sch. Dist., Calif., 1976-77; co-tchr., aide N.W. Ctr. for Mentally Retarded, Seattle, 1978-79; intern Seattle Pacific U., 1979-80; tchr. Highline Sch. Dist., Seattle, 1981-87; tchr., resource specialist Riverside County Office of Edn., 1988-92, program devel. specialist, 1992-94, coord., 1994-95, program spec. disabilities, 1995—98; coord. adminstrv. projects Mt. San Jacinto Coll., 1998—2002; pvt. practice cons., 2000—. Mem. adv. com. LA County Office of Edn., 1988-; guest speaker pvt. and pub. colls. and confs., 1988—; early childhood assessment for LA County Office of Edn., 1988-90; instr. Mt. San Jacinto Coll., 1990-94; cons. Head Start T&TA Network, 2000-; cons. in field, 2003-. Mem. Coun. for Exceptional Children, Assn. for Childhood Edn. Internat. Achievements include developing the "pattern approach" to classroom and program data analysis for program lesson plan development, improvement and accountability. Avocations: reading, travel, drawing, outdoor sports. Home: 24446 Tuscola Cir Murrieta CA 92562-4177 Home Phone: 951-461-8054; Office Phone: 951-970-3386. E-mail: kidworks@verizon.net.

DEVYLDER, EDGAR PAUL, JR., lawyer; b. Waterbury, Conn., Jan. 7, 1945; s. Edgar Paul Sr. and Lillian (Cordett) DeV.; m. Elaine Jordan, Jan. 8, 1972; children: Joseph Steven, Jordan Edgar. AB, Yale U., 1967; JD, U. Mich., 1974. Bar: Conn. 1974, U.S. Dist. Ct. Conn. 1975, U.S. Ct. Appeals (2nd cir.) 1975, Fla. 1978, U.S. Supreme Ct. 1979. Assoc. Cummings & Lockwood, Stamford, Conn., 1974-79; counsel Gen. Signal Corp., Stamford, 1979-85, sr. atty., 1985-87; v.p., gen. counsel, sec. BTR, Inc., Stamford, 1988-99; ptnr. Cummings & Lockwood, Stamford, 2000—01, Pepe & Hazard, Southport, Conn., 2001—02; v.p. adminstrn., gen. counsel, sec. Raytech Corp., Shelton, Conn., 2002—. Lt. USN, 1967-71. Mem.: Yale Club of Stamford (pres. 2000—), Assn. Yale Alumni (del. 2000—). Office Phone: 203-952-4300. E-mail: edevylder2@aol.com.

DEW, CHARLES BURGESS, historian, educator; b. St. Petersburg, Fla., Jan. 5, 1937; s. Jack Carlos and Amy (Meek) Dew; m. Robb Reavill Forman, Jan. 26, 1968. AB, Williams Coll., 1958; PhD, Johns Hopkins, 1964. Instr. Wayne State U., 1963-64, asst. prof., 1964-65, La. State U., 1965-68; assoc. prof. U. Mo., Columbia, 1968-72, prof., 1972-78; vis. assoc. prof. U. Va., 1970-71; vis. prof. history Williams Coll., Williamstown, Mass., 1977-78, prof. history, 1978-85, Class of 1956 prof. Am. Studies, 1985-96, chmn. dept. history, 1986-92, dir. Francis C. Oakley Ctr. for Humanities and Social Scis., 1994-97; prof. social scis. W. Van Alan Clark Third Century, 1996—2002, Charles R. Keller prof. history, 2002—03, Ephraim Williams prof. Am. history, 2003—. Adviser Am. Civil War Ctr., Historie Tradegar, Richmond, Va. Author: Ironmaker to the Confederacy: Joseph R. Anderson and the Tredegar Iron Works, 1966, rev. edit., 1999, The Meanings of American History, 1972, Bond of Iron: Master and Slave at Buffalo Forge, 1994, Apostles of Disunion: Southern Secession Commissioners and the Causes of the Civil War, 2001; contbr. chapters to books. Recipient Fletcher Pratt award, N.Y. Civil War Round Table, 1966, 2001, award of merit, Am. Assn. State and Local History, 1967, hon. mention Peter Seaborg award for Civil War scholarship, George Tyler Moore Ctr. for Study the Civil War, Shepherd Coll., Shepherdstown, W.Va., 2002, Disting. Svc. award, Woodberry Forest Sch., 2004. Mem.: Orgn. Am. Historians (Elliott Rudwick award 1995), Am. Hist. Assn., Phi Beta Kappa, Delta Psi. Home: 218 Bulkley St Williamstown MA 01267-2023 Office: Williams Coll Stetson Hall History Dept Williamstown MA 01267 Office Phone: 413-597-2597. Personal E-mail: Charlesdew37@aol.com. Business E-Mail: charles.b.dew@williams.edu.

DEW, THOMAS EDWARD, lawyer; b. Detroit, Feb. 13, 1947; s. Albert Nelson and Irene Theresa (Morris) D.; m. Gail Ruth Tuesink, June 27, 1970. BA, U. Mich., 1969; JD, Detroit Coll. Law, 1974. Bar: Mich. 1974, U.S. Dist. Ct. (ea. dist.) Mich. 1974, U.S. Tax Ct. 1980. Agt. IRS, Detroit, 1969-74; trust officer Ann Arbor (Mich.) Trust Co., 1974-75, asst. v.p., 1975-78; ptnr. Conner, Harbour, Dew, Ann Arbor, 1978-83, Harris, Lax, Guenzel & Dew, Ann Arbor, 1983-87; private practice Thomas E. Dew Profl. Corp., Ann Arbor, 1987-88; prin. Dever and Dew Profl. Corp., Ann Arbor, 1988-99, Wise & Marsac, Detroit, 1999-2001, Berry Moorman, PC, Detroit, 2001—. Lectr. Am. Coll., Bryn Mawr, Pa., 1979-82, Am. Inst. Paralegal Studies, Detroit, 1982; adj. prof. Ave Maria Sch. Law, 2003—. Mem. Ann Harbor Housing Commn., 1979-81, pres. 1981; trustee Ann Arbor Area Cmty. Found. Named Law scholar, Sigma Nu Phi, 1974. Fellow Mich. State Bar Found.; mem. State Bar Mich., Washtenaw County Bar Assn., Washtenaw Estate Planning Coun. (pres. 1979-80), New Enterprise Forum. Republican. Lutheran. Office: Berry Moorman PC 900 Victors Way Ste 300 Ann Arbor MI 48108 E-mail: tdew@berrymoorman.com.

DEWAAL, CAROLINE SMITH, education and advocacy organization executive, lawyer; BA in Polit. Sci., U. Vermont, Burlington; JD, Antioch Sch. Law, Washington, DC. Supreme Jud. Ct. Mass.: 1985, US Dist. Ct.: Mass. 1988, US Ct. Appeals, 1st Cir.: 1988. Chief legis. counsel Divsn. Insurance, Commonwealth Mass., Boston, 1985—89; staff atty. Pub. Citzen's Congress Watch, Washington, 1989—91; dir., legal affairs Pub. Voice for Food and Health Policy, Washington, 1991—94; dir., food safety program Ctr. for Sci. in Pub. Interest, Washington, 1994—. Mem., food sect. Transatlantic Consumer Dialogue; task force mem. Coun. for Agrl. Sci. and Tech. Task Force on Foodborne Pathogens: Review of Recommendations; chair, H Thomas Austern Writing award com. Food and Drug Law Inst., 1994—96; mem. Nat. Adv. Com. on Meat and Poultry Inspection, 1997—2000; spkr. in field; provided several congl. testimonies; maintains and annually publishes a listing of foodbourne illness outbreaks, 1999—. Mem. editl. bd. Food and Drug Law Jour., chair adv. bd., 2004—05; contbr. to food safety publications and reports; co-author: Is Our Food Safe? A Consumer's Guide to Protecting Your Health and the Environment, 2002; guest appearances Good Morning America, Today Show, Nightline, Dateline and others. Mem.: Internat. Assn. Food Protection, Mass. Bar. Office: Ctr for Sci in the Pub Interest 1875 Connecticut Ave NW Ste 300 Washington DC 20009 Office Phone: 202-332-9110 ext 366. Business E-Mail: edewaal@cspinet.org.

DE WAAL, FRANS B.M., biologist, psychology professor; b. Netherlands, 1948; B in Biology, U. Nijmegen, Netherlands, 1970; D in Biology, U. Groeningen, Netherlands, 1973; PhD in Biology, U. Utrecht, Netherlands, 1977. Rsch. assoc., lab. comparative physiology U. Utrecht, 1973—81; vis. asst. scientist Wis. Nat. Primate Rsch. Ctr., 1981—82, asst. scientist, 1982—85, assoc. scientist, 1985—91, affiliate scientist, 1991—; assoc. prof. psychology Emory U., 1991—93, prof, psychology, 1993—96, dir. grad. studies: Program in Population Biology, Ecology, & Evolution, 1996—2000, Charles Howard Candler prof. primate behavior, dept. psychology, 1996—; affiliate scientist Yerkes Nat. Primate Rsch. Ctr., 1989—91, rsch. prof. psychobiology, 1991—, dir. Living Links Ctr., 1997—. Adj. assoc. prof., biol. sciences U. Wis., Milw., 1988—91; spkr. in field. Author: Chimpanzee Politics: Power and Sex Among Apes, 1982, Peacemaking Among Primates, 1989 (LA Times Book award, 1989), Good Natured: The Origins of Right and Wrong in Humans and Other Animals, 1996, Bonobo: The Forgotten Ape, 1997, The Ape and the Sushi Master: Cultural Reflections by a primologist, 2001, My Family Album: Thirty Years of Photgraphy, 2003, Our Inner Ape: A Leading Primatologist Explains Why We are Who We Are, 2005, Primates and Philosophers: How Morality Evolved, 2006; consulting editor Zoo Biology, 1988—93; consulting editor: Jour. of Comparative Psychology; mem. editl. nd. Jour. of Comparative Psychology, 1993—, assoc. editor Am. Jour. Primatology, 1997—2003, mem. editl. bd. De Levende Natuur (Dutch), 1980—82, Animal Behavior, 1985—88; mem. editl. bd.: Primatologie, 1987; mem. editl. bd. Politics and the Life Sciences, 1991—; mem. editl. bd.: Primates, 1998—, Evolutionary Psychology, 2001—, PloS Biology, 2003—, Internat. Jour. of Primatology, Politics, and the Life Sciences; mem. editl. bd. Internat. Jour. of Primatology, Politics, and the Life Sciences, 1995—; contbr. articles to peer-reviewed jours., chapters to books. Named one of The World's Most Influential People, TIME Mag., 2007; recipient Presdl. Citation, APA, 2001, Arthur W. Staats award, 2005; fellow, Carl Friedrich von Siemens Stiftung, 1995. Fellow: Carl Friedrich von Siemens Stiftung (Germany), Japan Soc. for the Promotion of Sci.; mem.: NAS (fgn. assoc.), Royal Dutch Acad. Scis. (corr.). Office: Living Links Ctr Yerkes Nat Primate Ctr 954 N Gatewood Rd Atlanta GA 30329 also: Dept Psychology Emory Univ Atlanta GA 30322 Office Phone: 404-727-3695, 404-727-7898. Office Fax: 404-727-3270, 404-727-0372.

DEWALD, BRUCE WAYNE, lawyer; b. Tripp, SD, Apr. 10, 1955; s. Maynard W. and Adaline (Mehihaff) Dewald; m. Sherry L. Messina, Aug. 27, 1978; children: Paul S., Melinda L. BS in Econ., U. S.D., 1977; JD, U. Chgo., 1980. Bar: Colo. 1981, US Dist. Ct. Colo. 1981, US Claims Ct. 1984, US Ct. Appeals (10th cir.) 1988. Atty. Grant, McHendrie, Haines & Crouse, Denver, 1980-82, Canges, Shaver, Volpe & Licht, Denver, 1982-83, Shaver & Licht, Denver, 1983-99, Bombardier Capital, 1999; pvt. practice Littleton, Colo., 2000—05; ptnr. Hudgins & Dewald, Greenwood Village, Colo., 2005—. Mem.: Cherry Creek Luncheon Optimists (sec.-treas. 1989—93). Avocations: bicycling, hiking. Office: 5105 DTC Pkwy Greenwood Village CO 80111 Home Phone: 303-347-9119; Office Phone: 303-347-8906. Office Fax: 303-996-1446. Business E-Mail: dewaldlaw@msn.com.

DEWALD, PAUL ADOLPH, psychiatrist, educator; b. NYC, Mar. 12, 1920; s. Jacob Frederick and Elsie (Wurzburger) D.; m. Eleanor Whitman, Sept. 1, 1961; children: Jonathan S., Ellen F. BA, Swarthmore Coll., 1942; MD, U. Rochester, 1945; cert. psychoanalysis, SUNY, 1960. Intern, Strong Meml. Hosp., Rochester, NY, 1945-46, resident, 1948-52; instr. U. Rochester, 1952-57, asst. prof. psychiatry, 1957-61; pvt. practice psychoanalysis St. Louis, 1961-99; asst. clin. prof. psychiatry Washington U., St. Louis, 1961-65, 96—; asso. clin. prof. St. Louis U., 1965-69, clin. prof. psychiatry, 1969—. Dir. treatment svc. Psychoanalytic Found. St. Louis, 1961-72, med. dir., 1972-83 St. Louis Psychoanalytic Inst., 1973-83, supervising and tng. analyst, 1973—; mem. faculty Chgo. Inst. Psychoanlysis, 1961-75, supervising and tng. analyst, 1965-73; vis. prof. U. Cin., 1968-80; mem. Mo. State Mental Health Commn., 1978-83, chmn., 1981-83; asst. prof. clin. psychiatry Washington U., 1995—. Author: Psychotherapy: A Dynamic Approach, 1964, 2d edit., 1969, The Psychoanalytic Process, 1972, Learning Process in Psycho-analytic Supervision, 1987; co-editor: Ethics Case Book of the American Psychoanalytic Assn., 2001; contbr. articles to profl. jours. Served to capt. M.C., AUS, 1946-48. Fellow Am. Psychiat. Assn. (life); mem. Mo. Psychiat. Assn. (pres. 1970-71), Eastern Mo. Psychiat. Assn. (pres. 1969-70), Am. Psychoanalytic Assn. (life), St. Louis Psychoanalytic Soc. (pres. 1970-71, 86-88) Home: Apt 3H 8600 Delmar Blvd Saint Louis MO 63124-1961 Office: 8600 Delmar Blvd Saint Louis MO 63124 Office Phone: 314-994-9608. Personal E-mail: padewald@charter.net. *I was encouraged by my parents to see my career as a potential source of creative enjoyment, fulfillment and self-esteem. I was fortunate to choose a field that encouraged those attitudes, and a wife who supported me in them. I have other interests and sources of fulfillment, but when there is nothing better or more enjoyable to do, I work.*

DEWAN, VIKRAM H., zoological park administrator; b. 1954; m. Jami Dewan; children: Adam, Maya Schaaf, Tara. Bachelor's degree, Cornell U.; MBA, U. Pa., 1978. With Phila. Nat. Bank, CoreStates Fin., Wachovia Corp., pres. Phila. and Del. region; mem. Wachovia Regional Diversity Coun., 1998—2006; pres., CEO Phila. Zoo, 2006—. Bd. dirs. Phila. Children's First Fund, Phila. Education Fund, Pa. Ballet, Brandywine Ballet, Internat. House, Mayor's Commn. on Children. Office: Zoological Soc Phila 3400 W Girard Ave Philadelphia PA 19104-1196

DEWANE, JOHN RICHARD, retired manufacturing executive, small business owner; b. Cooperstown, Wis., Mar. 4, 1934; s. Clarence John and Arvilla Anne (Gannon) D.; m. Judith Anne Arnold, Mar. 17, 1974; 1 child, Kelly Susanne. BSME, U. Wis., Madison, 1957; MBA, U. Minn., Mpls., 1973. Lic. pvt. pilot. Dir. mktg. planning Honeywell, Inc., Washington, 1974-76, dir. mktg. Mpls., 1976-78, v.p. svc. engring., 1979-81, v.p. bus. devel., 1981-82, v.p., gen. mgr., 1982-87, group v.p., 1987-92, pres. space and aviation control Phoenix, 1992-97, pres. emeritus, 1997—; pres. Dewane Investments LLC, JJR Enterprises. Mem. NASA Aeronautics Adv. Com.; adj. prof. strategy Ariz. State U. Vice chmn. Cmty. Long-Range Improvement Com., Maple Grove, Minn., 1980-81, chmn. Econ. Devel. Commn., 1982-86; mem. Polit. Action com. Honeywell, 1979-83; mem. alumni adv. coun. U. Wis., mem. dean's indsl. liaison coun., mem. capital com. Coll. Engring.; mem. tech. adv. com. on transp. equipment U.S. Dept. Commerce; bd. govs. Am. Def. Preparedness Assn., 1988-91; chmn. bd. dirs. Success By Six, 1989-98, Ariz. Cities in Schs. Inc., Honeywell Found.; chmn. Cmty. in Schs. Fund Raising; nat. bd. advisor U. Ariz. Keller Bus. Sch., mem. dean's exec. com.; mem. deans 100 bd. Ariz. State U., bd. dirs., pres.'s club, chmn. undergrad. curriculum com.; chmn. indsl. liaison coun. Embry-Riddle Aero U.; mem. State of Ariz. Gov.'s Tech. Commn., State of Ariz. Smart Beginnings Com.; mem. strategy coun. United Way of Phoenix, chair dirs. coun. conf. bd., 1995-97; bd. dirs. Asia Pacific Econ. Coun.; mem. endowment com. Habitat for Humanity; mem. APEC Satellite and Comm. Com., Honeywell Execs. Cmty. Cons.; mem. hon. bd. Phoenix Found. for the Blind, mem. State of Ariz. Coun. on Aging; vol. Ctr. Funds. Com.; bd. mem. Exec. Svc. Corp. Maricopa; mem. acad. adv. bd. Westener Internat. U.; mem. bd. Western Internat. U.; dir. Dewane Pvt. Found. With USN, 1957-60. Holder four world airplane speed records. Navy scholar, 1952-57. Mem. US Navy League, Air Force Assn., Assn. US Army, Am. Def. Preparedness Assn., Aircraft Owners and Pilots Assn., Gen. Aviation Mfrs. Assn. (dir. 1983-97, chmn. forecasting com., chmn. airport ops. com.), Mpls. C. of C. (aviation com. 1980-88), Provost Club Ariz. State U. West. Office: Honeywell Space and Aviation Control PO Box 21111 Phoenix AZ 85036-1111 Address: PO Box 42777 Phoenix AZ 85080

DEWAR, DONALD JOHN, III, property manager; married; 2 children. AA in Criminal Justice; BA in Sociology, U. Balt., 1973; MBA, Western States U., 2000, PhD in Bus. Adminstrn., 2001. Cert. real estate brokerage mgr. Realtors Nat. Mktg. Inst., lic. real estate security dealer SEC, cert. real estate appraiser Nat. Assn. Real Estate Appraisers. Police officer, 1969—70; v.p. sales Chris Coile and Assocs.; property mgr. Md. Mgmt. Co.; CEO Kenilworth Equities Property Mgmt., 1985—86; owner, broker Equitable Asset Mgmt., 1986—; pres. Equitable Asset Mgmt. Constrn. Inc. Part-time tchr. Dundalk C.C., 1985—86; lectr. in field. Contbr. articles to profl. jours. With USAR, maj. Civil Air Patrol. Recipient Nat. Leadership award, Rep. Congl. Com., 2003. Mem.: Am. Mensa, Phi Theta Kappa. Avocation: sailing. Address: 3220 Elliott St Baltimore MD 21224-5016 Office: 1920 Fleet St Baltimore MD 21231

DEWAR, JAMES MCEWEN, marketing, aerospace and defense executive, developing nations consultant; b. Williamsport, Pa., Aug. 4, 1943; s. James Livingston and Margaret Ann (McEwen) D.; m. Margaret Cawley, Feb. 27, 1982; children: Alec, Porter, Leah. BS in Internat. Affairs, Trinity U., 1965, postgrad., 1965-66. Mgr. Dash brand Procter & Gamble Corp., Cin., 1969-71; CEO, DeLair & Dewar, Inc., Tucson and Washington, 1972—2001; chmn. bd. Cabot South Asia Inc. subs. Cabot Corp., 1982-87; pres., dir.-gen. ASI, Inc. subs. Boeing Co., 1987-97; CEO, J. Dewar Indochine, Ltd., Hanoi, Vietnam, 1993—2005; CEO J. Dewar N.Am., Inc., Washington, J. Dwar Internat. Ltd., Washington. Pres., interim cons. CEO, N.Am. Automotive Project, Southfield, Mich., 1993-98; bd. dirs. Metz Constrn. Co., Marine Environ. Rsch. Corp., Computational Analysis Corp.; mem. Aerospace, Def. and Automotive Industry Devel. Commn., Detroit, 1994. Contbr. numerous articles to profl. publs. Bd. dirs. Casa de Los Ninos, Tucson, 1974-2007, Safari Club Internat., Tucson, 1974-2000, Internat. Marine Fisheries Corp.; founding mem. Dist. Atty.'s Victim/Witness Adv. Program; mem. White House Talent Pool, 1975-76, White House Nat. Cambodia Crisis Com., 1979-80, U.S. Aerospace Indsl. Reps. in Europe; adj. Mil. Order World Wars, Tucson, 1977-80, perpetual mem.; chmn. internat. bd. advs. Ariz.-Sonora Desert Mus.; bd. advs. guardian ad litem program Superior Ct. Ariz. Capt. USAF, 1966-70, Vietnam. Recipient Key to City of Seoul, 1973, citation Pres. of Korea, 1973, award for work with Mother Teresa, Cabot Found., 1982-87. Mem. Am. Soc. Agrl. Cons., Dirs. Guild Am., Assn. Old Crows, Australian/Asian Order Old Bastards (Sydney), Army Navy Club, Mountain Oyster Club, Automobile Club France, Maxim's Bus. Club (Paris), St. James Club (Paris), Chambers Club (New Delhi), Hanoi Club. Communist. Office Phone: 202-742-6640. Business E-Mail: jdewarnorthamerica@j-dewar.com.

DEWBERRY, RAYMOND ALLEN, research scientist, combat engineer; b. Fredericksburg, Va., Feb. 10, 1952; s. Raymond Allen and Florence Thomas (Watlington) Dewberry; children: Raymond, Clayton. BS in Chemistry, Va. Poly. Inst. and State U., Blacksburg, Va., 1974; PhD in Chemistry, Fla. State U., Tallahassee, 1980. Lab. rsch. asst. U. Cologne Hosp., Germany, 1975; grad. rsch. and tchg. asst. Fla. State U., Tallahassee, 1975—80; rsch. assoc. Princeton U., NJ, 1980—83; rsch. scientist Savannah River Nat. Lab., Aiken, SC, 1983—2006. Com. mem. Dept. Energy Accountability Tech. Exch., 1985—88, Nat. Materials Characterization Ctr., 1989—91, Inst. Nuc. Material Mgmt., 1999—2006; adj. prof. nuc. engring. Clemson U., 1999—2007. Contbr. articles to profl. revs., sci. publs., profl. jours. and books. Varsity baseball coach Barnwell HS, SC, 2004—05; commr. Men's Recreational Basketball League, Barnwell, 2004—07, coach, 2004—07; player Recreational Basketball and Softball, Barnwell, Augusta Sr. Men's Baseball, Ga., 1999—2000; coach Dixie Youth Baseball, Barnwell, 1995—2000. With USN, 1974, with US Army, 1985—93, combat engr. USNG. Recipient Nat. Def. medal, US Navy, 1974, V.P.'s award, Savannah River Tech. Ctr., 1995, Dir.'s award, Savannah River Nat. Lab., 2005, 2006, Spl. Compensation award, Savannah River Site, 2004. Mem.: Lion's Club (v.p., dir. 1995—2005). Conservative. Protestant. Avocations: softball, physical training, basketball, baseball. Office: Savannah River Nat Lab 773-41 A Aiken SC 29808 Home: 135 Heathwood St Barnwell SC 29812 Home Phone: 803-259-1746. Personal E-mail: radewberry@barnwellsc.com. Business E-Mail: raymond.dewberry@srnl.doe.gov.

DE WECK, OLIVER, engineering educator, researcher; b. Bern, Switzerland, 1968; Diplom Ingenieur degree, Swiss Fed. Inst. Tech., 1993; SM in Aeronautics and Astronautics, MIT, 1999, PhD in Aerospace Systems, 2001. Liaison engr. to engring. program mgr. Swiss F/A-18 program McDonnell Douglas (now Boeing), St. Louis, 1993—97; asst. prof. aeronautics, astronautics & engring. systems MIT, Cambridge, 1997—2003, Robert N. Noyce career devel. prof., 2002—05, assoc. prof. aeronautics, astronautics & engring. systems, 2006—. Contbr. articles to profl. jours. Recipient Carroll L. Wilson award, 1998; Pellegrini-Medicus Fellowship, 1997. Mem.: Am. Soc. Engring. Edn., Internat. Coun. Systems Engring., IEEE, AIAA (mem. multidisciplinary design optimization specialist com. 2002—, assoc. fellow 2006, Frank E. Perkins award 2007), Sigma Xi. Office: MIT Bldg 33-406 77 Massachusetts Ave Cambridge MA 02139 Office Phone: 617-253-0255. Business E-Mail: deweck@mit.edu.

DEWEES, DONALD CHARLES, security firm executive; b. Phila., Sept. 7, 1931; s. John Coleman and Elva (Burke) DeW.; m. Martha V. Folk, July 31, 1954; children: Donald C., Suzanne C., Gretchen F. BS in Commerce and Finance, Bucknell U., 1953; MBA, U. Pa., 1954. Data processing rep. Nat. Cash Register Co., Wilmington, Del., 1954-62; account rep. Francis I. duPont Co., Investments, Wilmington, 1962-67, br. mgr. Balt., 1968, Butcher & Singer, Wilmington, 1969-71, v.p., 1971-76, 1st v.p., 1977, sr. v.p., 1978—, resident mgr., 1969-76, ltd. ptnr., 1976-87, exec. v.p., 1987, sr. exec. v.p., 1988—, mng. dir., 1988—. Mng. dir. Butcher & Singer, 1986-98, Wheat Securities, 1998-2006; dir. Mgmt. Scis. Inc., 1978-92, Bus. Trends Inc., 1977-91, Computer Terminals and Tapes Ltd., 1970-98, Wheat Securities, mng. dir., 1986-2007, Wheat Securities Butcher & Singer, 1986-2004, Lloyds of London, 1985-2000, First Union Bank, 1998-2004, Wachovia Securities, 2005-07; underwriting mem. Lloyds of London, 1985-02; cons. in field. Author sales tng. publs. Active Wilmington YMCA; bd. dirs. Del. Ctr. of Contemporary Arts, 1992-94, Ingleside Nursing Home, 1989-2004, Ch. Home Found., 1986-92, Episcopal Home Del., 1983-90, Kalmar Nyckle Found., 2000-07, Del Marva Boy Scouts Am., 1989-2003, chmn. endowment com., 1993-2003; vice chmn. Nat. Assn. Christians and Jews, 1991-98; mem. allocation com. United Way, 1994; bd. dirs. Am. Cancer Soc., 1994-2005, Leukemia Soc., 1994-2007; chmn. Edgar A. Thronson Charitable Found., 1995—; dir. Del. Symphony, 1990-2007, Del. Art Mus., 1994-2004; pres. Donald and Martha DeWees Found., 2006—; chmn. DeWees Family Found., 2007. Served with AUS, 1952-53, 58-59, Korea. Mem. Fin. Analysts Soc., Am. Philatelic Soc., Phi Kappa Psi, Univ. Club (Wilmington), Collectors Club (N.Y.), Rodney Square Club, Masons, Shriners, Greenville Country Club, Bonita Bay Country Club. Home: 4200 Pyles Ford Rd Wilmington DE 19807-1734 also: 25 Kelly Ln Bethany Beach DE 19930-9549 Office: Wheat Securities 3801 Kennett Pike Greenville DE 19807-2321 Office Phone: 800-832-6669.

DEWEESE, JAMES ARVILLE, surgeon, educator; b. Apr. 5, 1925; s. Arville Ottis and Vergie (Jenkins) DeW.; m. Margaret Brown, June 20, 1950 (dec. 1960); children: James Arville Jr., Margaret Ann, Elizabeth Lynn, Joanne Spencer; m. Patricia Bidwell, May 5, 1962; children; Robert Bidwell, Jamie Susan. Student, Harvard U., 1942-43, Kent State U., 1943-44; MD, U. Rochester, 1949. Diplomate Am. Bd. Surgery (bd. dirs. 1986-91), Am. Bd. Thoracic and Cardiovascular Surgery (bd. dirs. 1987-91); cert. spl. qualifications gen. vascular surgery. Intern Strong Meml. Hosp., Rochester, NY, 1949-50, resident, 1950-52, 54-56; instr. surgery U. Rochester (N.Y.) Sch. Medicine and Dentistry, 1955-58, asst. prof. surgery, 1958-63, assoc. prof. surgery, 1963-69, prof. surgery, 1969-74, prof. cardiothoracic surgery, 1975—, chmn. div. cardiothoracic surgery, 1977-91, assoc. chmn. dept. surgery, 1986-90, chief sect. vascular surgery, 1987-91, acting co-chief divsn. vascular surgery, 2004—05. Bd. dirs. Jour. Vascular Surgery, 1983—; editor: Vascular Surgery, 1985; contbr. over 200 articles to sci. jours. and over 60 chpts. to books. Mem. bd. trustees Clifton Springs (N.Y.) Hosp., 1980—. Mem. Am. Heart Assn. (bd. dirs. 1982-86, chmn. coun. cardiovascular surgery 1982-84), Ea. Vascular Soc. (pres. 1988), Internat. Soc. Cardiovascular Surgery (pres. N.Am. chpt. 1984-85, sec.-gen. 1987-95, pres. 1995-97), Pan Pacific Surg. Assn. (pres. 1989-91), Soc. Vascular Surgery (pres. 1977-78), Am. Venous Forum (pres. 1993-94), Sr. Cardiovascular Surg. Soc. (pres. 1996), Oak Hill Country Club (bd. govs. 1978-81). Home: 601 Crittenden Blvd Rochester NY 14642-0001 Office: U Rochester Dept Surgery M&D Cardiothoracic Div 601 Elmwood Ave Rochester NY 14642-0001 E-mail: deweesepnj@aol.com.

DEWEESE, THEORDORE L., radiation oncologist; b. Denver, Colo., July 9, 1961; m. Bonny DeWeese; children: Alex, Tate. BA magna cum laude, Metropolitan State Coll. Denver, 1986; MD with honors, U. Colo. Sch. Medicine, 1990. Cert. Am. Bd. Radiology, Md. State Bd. Examiners. Intern, internal medicine Franklin Square Hosp. Ctr., Balt., 1990—91; resident, radiation oncology John Hopkins Hosp., Balt., 1991—93, chief resident, divsn. radiation oncology, The Oncology Ctr., 1993—94; post-doctoral rsch. fellow, urologic oncology John Hopkins Oncology Ctr. and James Buchanan Brady Urological Inst., Balt., 1994—95; instructor, oncology John Hopkins U. Sch. Medicine, Balt., 1995—97, instructor, urology, James Buchanan Brady Urological Inst., 1995—97, asst. prof., oncology, 1997—2001, asst. prof., urology, James Buchanan Brady Urological Inst., 1997—2001, dir., radiation biology program, 2000—, assoc. prof., oncology, 2002—03, assoc. prof., urology, James Buchanan Brady Urological Inst., 2002—03, prof., radiation oncology and molecular radiation sciences, 2003—, prof., oncology, 2003—, prof. urology, James Buchanan Brady Urological Inst., 2003—, chair, dept. radiation oncology and molecular radiation sciences, 2003—; joint appt., dept. environ. health sciences John Hopkins U. Bloomberg Sch. Pub. Health; radiation oncologist-in-chief John Hopkins Hosp., dir., dept. radiation oncology and molecular radiation sciences, attending physician and head of genitourinary radiation oncology, 2003—. Examiner, genitourinary sect. of oral boards Am. Bd. Radiology, 2002—; invited spkr. in field; several vis. professorships. Mem. editl. bd. The Prostate, Jour. Clin. Oncology, ad hoc reviewer International Journal of Radiation Oncology, Biology, Physics, Cancer Research, Clinical Cancer Research, Molecular Cancer Research, Journal Urology, Urology, Journal of the American Medical Association, Proceedings of NAS; contbr. articles to profl. jours. Recipient European Soc. for Therapeutic Radiology and Oncology Basic Sci. Travel Grant, 1995, Doris Duke Rsch. Scientist award, 1999. Mem.: Am. Assn. for Cancer Rsch. (mem. edn. com. 2004), Am. Coll. Radiology, Am. Soc. for Therapeutic Radiology and Oncology (mem. exec. com., cancer and radiation biology com. 2002—, Fellowship award 1994, Travel Grant 1995), Clin. Practice Assn. (bd. governor 2005—). Office: John Hopkins Cancer Ctr Weinberg Bldg 401 N Broadway Ste 1440 Baltimore MD 21231-2410 Office Phone: 410-614-3979. Office Fax: 410-502-7234. Business E-Mail: deweete@jhmi.edu.

DEWERD, LARRY ALBERT, medical physicist, educator; b. Milw., July 18, 1941; s. Anthony Lawrence and Dorothy M. (Heling) DeW.; m. Vada Mary Anderson, Sept. 14, 1963; children: Scott, Mark, Eric. BS, U. Wis., Milw., 1963; MS, U. Wis., 1965, PhD, 1970. Rsch. assoc. U. Wash., Seattle, 1970-72, rsch. asst. prof., 1973-75; vis. asst. prof. U. Wis., Madison, 1975-76, clin. asst. prof., 1976-79, clin. assoc. prof., 1979-86, prof., 1990—. Mgr. product devel. Radiation Measurements, Middleton, Wis., 1986-90; dir. Radiation Calibration Lab., Madison, 1983-86, 90—; cons. Instrumentarium, Milw., 1990; v.p. Standard Imaging, Madison, 1990—; presenter in field; cons. IAEA. Contbg. author: Brachytherapy, Ionization Chambers and Dosimetry, Thermoluminescence and Mammography; also numerous articles. Science chmn. Am. Cancer Soc. State of Wis., 1986-90. Nat. Cancer Inst. grantee, 1979-86, 94-98. Fellow Am. Assn. Physicists in Medicine (pres. 1990-92, L. Lanzl hon. award 2005), Health Physics Soc., Am. Phys. Soc., Coun. Ionizing Radiation Measurements and Standards (pres. 1995-98), Sigma Xi (bd. dirs. 1984-86). Avocations: golf, fishing, backpacking, hunting. Home: 13 Pilgrim Cir Madison WI 53711-4033 Office: U Wis 1530 Med Sci Ctr 1300 University Ave Madison WI 53706-1510 Business E-Mail: ladewerd@wisc.edu.

DEWERTH, GORDON HENRY, management consultant; b. Milw., Sept. 3, 1939; s. Henry Andrew and Elizabeth Barbara (Schlitt) DeWerth; m. Karen Lillian Overson, July 7, 1962 (div.); children: Julie, Christine, Amy. BBA, U. Wis., 1961; MBA, Bradley U., 1965. Asst. to treas. Jos. Schlitz Brewing Co., Milw., 1965—71; with ITT, NYC, 1971—76; treas. Macmillan, Inc., NYC, 1976—82; sr. v.p. fin. Cowles Media Co., Mpls., 1982—85; sr. v.p. fin., treas. U. Hartford, Conn., 1985—89; v.p., gen. mgr. Gestra Inc., West Caldwell, NJ, 1989—90; v.p. David Werner Internat. Corp., NYC, 1990—94; mng. ptnr. Round Table Ptnrs. Cons. Group, Framingham, Mass., 1994—. With U.S. Army, 1961-63. Mem. Assn. Corp. Growth, Mensa. Office: Round Table Ptnrs Cons Group 146 Maynard Rd Ste 503C Framingham MA 01701

DEWEY, ARTHUR EUGENE, former federal agency administrator; b. Mainesburg, Pennsylvania, Feb. 18, 1933; s. Glenn Cecil and Florence (Tice) D.; m. Priscilla Ann (Parce), June 24, 1956; 1 child, Elisabeth Parce Ainsworth. BSE, U.S. Mil. Acad., 1956; MSE, Princeton U., 1961; post grad., Grad. Inst. Internat. Studies, Geneva, Switzerland, 1972-73. Officer U.S. Army, 1956; White House fellow US Dept. State, Washington, 1968-69, dir. Pres. Commn. on White House Fellowships, 1971-72; advanced through grades to col. U.S. Army, 1973, ret., 1981; dep. asst. sec., Bur. Refugee Program US Dept. State, Washington, 1981-86; asst. sec. gen., dep. high commr. for refugees UN, Geneva, 1986-90; exec. dir. Congl. Hunger Ctr., 1993—97; asst. sec., Bur Population, Refugees, & Migration US Dept. State, Washington, 2002—05; US rep. Internat. Ind. Group Eminent Persons Dealing with Human Rights, Sri Lanka, 2006—. Decorated Dist. Flying Cross, Legion of Merit with two oak leaf clusters, Air medal with nine oak leaf clusters, Army Commendation medal with three oak leaf clusters. Mem.: Cosmos Club. Republican. Presbyterian. E-mail: deweyg56@hotmail.com.

DEWEY, BARBARA I., librarian, dean; BA, MLS, U. Minn. Head reference and adult svcs. Minn. Valley Regional Libr., Mankato; reference and interlibrary loan libr. Northwestern U. Libr.; dir. admissions Ind. U. Sch. of Libr. and Info. Sci.; dir. info. and rsch. svcs. to interim univ. libr. U. Iowa Librs., 1987—2000; dean of librs., prof. University of Tenn., Knoxville, 2000—. Bd. dirs. New Media Consortium, Knoxville Friends of

Literacy, Digital Library Fedn.; mem. Tenn. Coun. on Librs. Author: Achieving Diversity, 2006; contbr. articles to profl. jours. Mem.: Assn. of S.E. Rsch. Librs. (past pres., past chair Diversity Com.). Office: Adminstrv Ste 607 John C Hodges Libr 1015 Volunteer Blvd Knoxville TN 37996 Office Phone: 865-974-4127. E-mail: bdewey@utk.edu.*

DEWEY, CLARENCE FORBES, JR., engineering educator; b. Pueblo, Colo., Mar. 27, 1935; s. Clarence F. and Elsie (Hafermalz) D.; m. Carolyn Miller, Aug. 3, 1963; 1 child, Devan Forbes. BE, Yale U., 1956; MS, Stanford U., 1957; PhD, Calif. Inst. Tech., 1963. Aero. rsch. scientist NASA-AMES, Moffet Field, Calif., summer 1956; tech. staff aeronutronic divsn. Ford, Newport Beach, 1957-59; rsch. asst. Calif. Inst. Tech., Pasadena, Calif., 1959-63; asst. prof. mech. engring. U. Colo., Boulder, 1963-68; assoc. prof. MIT, Cambridge, 1968-76, prof., 1976-98, prof. mech. engring. and bioengring., 1998—, head fluid mechanics lab., 1975—83, head microfluids lab., 2001—03; assoc. in pathology Peter Brent Brigham Hosp., Boston, 1978-95. Vis. scientist Inst. Plasma Physics, Garching, Germany, 1966—67; vis. prof. Harvard U. Med. Sch., 1978—79, Hefei Poly. U., China, 1986, Imperial Coll. Ctr. Med. and Biol. Sys., London, 1992, London, 2001; biomed. engr. Mass. Gen. Hosp., Boston, 1975—76, cons. in medicine, 1976—80; founder Concurrent Computer Corp., 1981; co-dir. Internat. Consortium for Med. Imaging Tech., 1992—; path. cons. Brigham and Women's Hosp., 1982—96. Contbr. articles to profl. jours. Chmn. MIT United Way, 1996—97; trustee Fidelity Non-Profit Mgmt. Found., 2001—. Grantee NIH, Bethesda, Md., 1971—, Office Naval Rsch., San Diego 1970-75, 1987-89, Air Force Office Sci. Rsch., Washington, 1976-79, Dept. of Energy, 2003—. Fellow Am. Inst. Med. Biol. Engring. (founding), Am. Phys. Soc., Biomed. Engring. Soc. (founding). Achievements include patents in field. Avocations: trout fishing, skiing. Office: 77 Massachusetts Ave Rm 3-254 Cambridge MA 02139-4301 Home Phone: 617-742-1703; Office Phone: 617-253-2235. Business E-Mail: cfdewey@mit.edu.

DEWEY, DONALD ODELL, dean, academic administrator; b. Portland, Oreg., July 9, 1930; s. Leslie Hamilton and Helen (Odell) D.; m. Charlotte Marion Neuber, Sept. 21, 1952; children: Leslie Helen, Catherine Dawn, Scott Hamilton. Student, Lewis and Clark Coll., Portland, Oreg., 1948—49; BA, U. Oreg., Eugene, 1952; MS, U. Utah, Salt Lake City, 1956; PhD, U. Chgo., 1960. Mng. editor Condon Globe-Times, Oreg., 1952-53; city editor Ashland Daily Tidings, Oreg., 1953-54; asst. editor, assoc. editor The Papers of James Madison, Chgo., 1957-62; instr. U. Chgo., 1960-62; from asst. prof. to prof. Calif. State U., LA, 1962-96, dean Sch. Letters and Sci., 1970-84, dean Sch. Natural and Social Sci., 1984-96, dean emeritus, prof. emeritus, 1996—; v.p. acad. affairs Trinity Coll. Grad. Studies, Anaheim, Calif., 2000—06. V.p. Calif. U. Emeritus and Retired Faculty Assn., 2005—06, pres., 2006—. Author: The Continuing Dialogue, 2 vols., 1964, Union and Liberty: Documents in American Constitutionalism, 1969, Marshall versus Jefferson: The Political Background of Marbury v. Madison, 1970, Becoming Informed Citizens: Lessons on the Constitution for Junior High School Students, 1988, revised edit., 1995, Invitation to the Dance: An Introduction to Social Dance, 1991, Becoming Informed Citizens: The Bill of Rights and Limited Government, 1995, That's a Good One: Cal State L.A. at 50, 1997, The Federalist and Antifederalist Papers, 1998, Controversial Elections, 2001; contbr. chpts. to books. Recipient Outstanding Prof. award Calif. State U., 1976 Mem. Am. Hist. Assn. (exec. com. Pacific Coast br. 1971-74), Orgn. Am. Historians, Am. Soc. Legal History (adv. bd. Pacific Coast br. 1972-75), Gold Key, Calif. State U. Emeritus and Ret. Faculty Assn. (v.p. 2005-06, pres. 2006-), Phi Alpha Theta, Pi Sigma Alpha, Phi Kappa Phi, Sigma Delta Chi. Office: Calif State U Dept History 5151 State University Dr Los Angeles CA 90032-4226 Business E-Mail: ddewey@calstatela.edu.

DEWEY, ELIZABETH R., lawyer; b. Phoenix, Nov. 29, 1967; Student, Univ. Madrid, Spain, 1989; BA cum laude, Univ. Tulsa, 1990; JD summa cum laude, Am. Univ. of Washington, 1993. Bar: Md. 1993, DC 1995, US Dist. Ct. (DC, Md. dist.), Md. Ct. Appeals, US Ct. Appeals (Fed. cir.). Law clk. Hon. Noel Anketell Kramer DC Superior Ct.; pro bono ptnr. DLA Piper Rudnick Gray Cary, Washington, 1999—. Adj. prof. law Am. Univ. Wash. Coll. of Law. Founder, editorial bd. mem. Journal of Gender and the Law, Am. Univ. of Washington; contbr. articles to profl. jours. Hon. trustee AYUDA Inc. Named co-winner, Young Guns category, Washington Bus. Jour., 2004. Mem.: ABA, DC Women's Bar Assn., Mortar Board, Phi Beta Kappa. Office: DLA Piper Rudnick Gray Cary 1200 Nineteenth St NW Washington DC 20036-2412 Office Phone: 202-861-6218. Office Fax: 202-223-2085. Business E-Mail: elizabeth.dewey@dlapiper.com.

DEWEY, JOEL ALLEN, lawyer; b. Balt., Dec. 17, 1956; s. Allen Leonard and Mary Louise (Karcher) D.; m. Martha Dayle Nesbitt, Aug 25, 1979; children: Samuel Everett, Sarah Radcliffe. SBCE, MIT, 1977; JD, Harvard U., 1980. Bar: Calif. 1980, Md. 1981, D.C. 1981, U.S. Dist. Ct. Md. 1981, U.S. Ct. Appeals (4th cir.) 1981, N.Y. 1993, Va. 1994. Law clk. to presiding justice U.S. Dist. Ct. Md., Balt., 1980-81; assoc. Piper & Marbury, Balt., 1981-88, ptnr., 1989—. Mem. Chi Epsilon, Tau Beta Pi. Republican. Presbyterian. Avocation: running. Office: DLA Piper US LLP 6225 Smith Ave Baltimore MD 21209-3600 Home: 11865 Sherbourne Dr Timonium MD 21093 Office Phone: 410-580-4135. Office Fax: 410-580-3135. Business E-Mail: joel.dewey@dlapiper.com.

DEWEY, RALPH JAY, school system administrator; b. NYC, Feb. 8, 1944; s. Ralph Morris and Evelyn Elizabeth (Karle) D.; m. Vivian V. Barone Dewey, Dec. 20, 1970; children: Gabriella Maria, Meredith Elizabeth, Ralph Stephen. BS, Holy Cross Coll., Worcester, Mass., 1965; MAT, Brown U., Providence, 1968; EdS, Rutgers U., 1985. Cert. tchr., N.Y. Tchr. Moses Brown Sch., Providence, 1965-68; founding head of mid. sch. Portledge Sch., Locust Valley, N.Y., 1968-74; head of lower sch. Rutgers Preparatory Sch., Somerset, N.J., 1974-83; founding headmaster The Winston Sch., Summit, N.J., 1983-87; headmaster St. James Episc. Sch., Corpus Christi, 1987-95; headmaster, bd. dirs. Cape Fear Acad., Wilmington, NC, 1995—2001; founding dir. Schechter Regional HS, Bergen County, NJ, 2002—06; founding head Met. Schechter Acad., 2006. Regional coord. Southwestern Assn. Episcopal Schs., Corpus Christi, Tex., 1989-93, stds. com. Southwestern Assn. Episcopal Schs., 1994-95, cons., Dallas, 1990-92; presenter in field Author, editor: Winston Newsletter, 1983-87, St. James Episcopal School Newsletter, 1987-95; author: Classical Vocabulary, 1990; contbr. articles to profl. jours. Treas. Coastal Bend Soc. Friends, 1988-95; sec., v.p. Harbor Playhouse, Corpus Christi, Tex., 1989-92; mem. Com. of 100, Wilmington, 1995; mem. exec. coun. Leadership Wilmington, 1996; bd. dirs. Ea. Plains Ind. Conf. Recipient U.S. Dept. Blue Ribbon Sch. Excellence award, Salute to Prins. award Nat. Assn. Elem. Sch. Prins. Mem. NC Assn. Ind. Schs. (bd. dirs. 1998-2002, membership chmn. 1998-2001), SAR, ASCD, Nat. Coun. Tchrs. English, Assn. Leadership Educators, Internat. Leadership Assn., Loyal Order St. Andrew's Brewers, Rotary, Leadership Wilmington, Wilmington Execs. Club, City Club de Rossette. Mem. Soc. Friends. Avocations: Russian literature, furniture building. Office: Metropolitan Schechter HS 800 Broad St Teaneck NJ 07666 Home: 296 Myrtle Ave New Milford NJ 07646-1912 Office Phone: 201-837-8357. Business E-Mail: jdewey@schechter.info.

DEWEY-BALZHISER, ANNE ELIZABETH MARIE, lawyer; b. Balt., Mar. 16, 1951; d. George Daniel and Elizabeth Patricia (Mohan) Dewey; m. Richard J. Balzhiser; children: Brendan M. Barnett, Andrew P. Barnett, Meghan E. Barnett. BA, Mich. State U., 1972; JD, U. Chgo., 1975; grad., Stonier Grad. Sch. Banking, East Brunswick, NJ, 1983. Bar: DC 1976. Legal clk. and atty. FTC, Washington, 1975—78; atty. , sr. atty. Comptr. of Currency, Dallas and Washington, 1978—86; assoc. gen. counsel, gen. counsel, spl. counsel Farm Credit Adminstrn., McLean, Va., 1986—92; counsel, closed bank litig. and policy sect. FDIC, Washington, 1993—94; gen. counsel, spl. advisor Office of Fed. Housing Enterprise Oversight, HUD, Washington, 1994—2004; pres. Women Lead LLC, 2003—. Mem. DC study devel. coun. Mich. State U., 1999—; chair, govt. rels. com., Parent Tchr. Student Assn. Thomas Jefferson HS Sci. and Tech., 2005—. Mem.: FBA (bd. dirs. D.C. chpt. 1988—91, banking law com. exec. coun. 1995—2001), ABA (coun. 2002—, govt. and pub. sect. law divsn., bus. law sect., banking law com., liaison to com. on women in the profession, adminstrv. law and regulatory practice sect.), D.C. Bar Assn., Women in Housing and Fin. (bd. dirs. 1982—83, gen. counsel 1991—93, co-chair profl. devel. com. 2002—06), Exchequer Club. Roman Catholic. Office: Women Lead LLC PO Box 1414 Falls Church VA 22041 Office Phone: 703-933-2444. E-mail: womenlead@womenlead.net.

DEWHURST, CHARLES KURT, museum director, curator, language educator; b. Passaic, NJ, Dec. 21, 1948; s. Charles Allaire and Minn Jule (Hanzl) D.; m. Marsha MacDowell, Dec. 15, 1972; 1 dau., Marit Charlene. BA, Mich. State U., 1970, MA, 1973, PhD, 1983. Editorial asst. Carlton Press, NYC, 1967; computer operator IBM, NYC, 1968; project dir. Mich. State U. Mus., 1975, curator, 1976-83, dir., 1982—. Guest curator Mus. Am. Folk Art, NYC, 1978—83, Artrain, Detroit, 1980—83; dir. Festival of Mich. Folklife, 1987—95, Ctr. for Great Lakes Culture, 2000—. Author: Reflections of Faith, 1983, Artists in Aprons, 1979, Rainbows in the Sky, 1978, Michigan Folk Art, 1976 (Am. Assn. State and Local History award 1977), Art at Work: Folk Pottery of Grand Ledge, Michigan, 1986, Michigan Quilts, 1987, Michigan Folklife Reader, 1988, To Honor and Comfort: Native Quilting Traditions, 1998, MSU Campus: Buildings, Places and Spaces, 2002. Coord. South African-U.S. Partnership Project, 1967—; mem. and chair adv. com. Smithsonian Ctr. for Folklife Cultural Heritage; pres. bd. dirs. Fund for Folk Culture; bd. dirs. Am. Folklife Ctr., Libr. Congress. Recipient Disting. Svc. and Humanities award, 1994. Fellow Mich. State U.; mem. Am. Folkore Soc.(Americo Padres proze, 2004), Mich. Folklore Soc., Midwest Soc. Lit., Popular Culture Assn., Mich. Hist. Soc., Mich. Mus. Assn., Am. Assn. Mus., Internat. Coun. Mus. Home: 1804 Cricket Ln East Lansing MI 48823-1225 Office: Mich State U Mus W Circle Dr East Lansing MI 48824 Business E-Mail: dewhurs1@msu.edu.

DEWHURST, DAVID, lieutenant governor; b. Tex., Aug. 18, 1945; BA, U. Ariz. Officer CIA, U.S. State Dept.; founder Falcon Seaboard, 1981; ptnr. Falcon Seabord Diversified Energy and Investments Co.; commr. Tex. Gen. Land Office; lt. gov. State of Tex., 2003—. Chmn. Gov.'s Task Force on Homeland Security, 2001—03; mem. Gov.'s Bus. Coun., Pres.'s Commn. on Capabilities of U.S. Intelligence Cmty.; chmn. State Product Devel. Bd. Founder Falcon Seaboard. Officer USAF. Mem.: Nat. Cutting Horse Assn. Republican. Presbyterian. Avocation: horseback riding. Office: Office Lt Governor Capitol Station PO Box 12068 Austin TX 78711 Office Phone: 512-463-0001. Office Fax: 512-463-0677.

DEWHURST, MORAY P., utilities executive; BS in Naval Architecture and Marine Engring., MIT, Cambridge, MBA. Sr. ptnr. Mercer Mgmt. Consulting; co-founder, sr. ptnr., dir. Dean & Co., 1993—2001; v.p. fin., CFO FPL Group, Inc., Juno Beach, Fla., 2001—; sr. v.p. fin., CFO Fla. Power & Light Co., 2001—. Office: FPL Group Inc 700 Universe Blvd Juno Beach FL 33408-0420*

DEWILDE, DAVID MICHAEL, management consultant, lawyer, finance company executive, retired recruiter; b. Bridgeton, NJ, Aug. 11, 1940; s. Louis and Dorothea (Donnelly) deW.; m. Katherine August, Dec. 30, 1984; children: Holland Stockdale, Christian DuCroix, Nicholas Alexander, Lucas Barrymore. AB, Dartmouth Coll., 1962; LLB, U. Va., 1967; MS in Mgmt., Stanford U., 1984. Bar: N.Y. 1968, D.C. 1972. Assoc. Curtis, Mallet-Prevost, Colt & Mosle, NYC, 1967-69; assoc. gen. counsel HUD, Washington, 1969-72; investment banker Lehman Bros., Washington, 1972-74; dep. commr. FHA, Washington, 1974-76; pres. Govt. Nat. Mortgage Assn., Washington, 1976-77; mng. dir. Lepercq DeNeuflize & Co., NYC, 1977-81; exec. v.p. policy and planning Fed. Nat. Mortgage Assn., Washington, 1981-82; pres. deWilde & Assocs., Washington, 1982-84; mng. dir., dir. fin. svcs. Boyden Internat., San Francisco, 1984-88; CEO Chartwell Ptnrs. Internat., San Francisco, 1989-97; mng. dir. LAI Worldwide, San Francisco, 1998-99; mng. ptnr. TMP Worldwide, San Francisco, 1999-2001; mgmt. cons., 2001—. Bd. dirs. Berkshire Realty Investment Trust, Fritzi of Calif., Silicon Valley Bankshares; bd. dirs. St. Luke's School, San Francisco, chair, 2001-03. Editor-in-chief Va. Jour. Internat. Law, 1966-67. Lt. USN, 1962-64. Mem. Pacific Union Club (San Francisco), Villa Taverna (San Francisco), Met. Club (Washington), Belvedere Tennis Club. Republican. Personal E-mail: ddewilde@pacbell.net.

DEWINE, MIKE (RICHARD MICHAEL DEWINE), former senator, lawyer; b. Springfield, Ohio, Jan. 5, 1947; s. Richard and Jean DeWine; m. Frances Struewing, June 3, 1967; children: Patrick, Jill, Rebecca, John, Brian, Alice, Mark, Anna. BS in Edn., Miami U., Oxford, Ohio, 1969; JD, Ohio No. U., 1972. Bar: Ohio 1972, U.S. Supreme Ct. 1977. Asst. prosecuting atty. Greene County, Xenia, Ohio, 1973-75, prosecuting atty., 1977-81; mem. Ohio State Senate, 1981-82, US Congress from 7th Ohio dist., Washington, 1983-90; lt. gov. State of Ohio, Columbus, Ohio, 1991-94; US Senator from Ohio, 1995—2007; instr., Ctr. for Polit. Sciences Cedarville U., 2007—. Mem. com. intelligence US Senate, com. judiciary, com. health, edn., labor and pensions, com. appropriations. Mem. Nat. Commn. Drug Free Schools. Recipient Excellence in Public Svc. award, Am. Acad. Pediatrics, 1997, Congressional Recognition award, Internat. Assn. Fire Fighters, 2001, Nathan Davis award, AMA, Donald Santarelli award public policy, Nat. Orgn. Victim Assistance, Golden Eagle award, Nat. Coun. Defense, Guardian Small Business award, Nat. Fedn. Independent Bus., MADD award, Nat. Security Leadership award, Am. Security Coun., Spirit Enterprise award, US C. of C., Watchdog of the Treasury award, Nat. Taxpayers Union, Champion award, Campaign for Tobacco-Free Kids, 2005. Republican. Roman Catholic.*

DEWITT, CHARLES BARBOUR, federal official; b. LA, Mar. 13, 1950; s. Homer Charles and Gwenyth Deakin (Barbour) DeW.; m. Bonnie St. Clair; 1 child, Anna. BA with univ. distinction and dept. honors, Stanford U., 1972; postgrad., Cambridge U., 1972-73. Dep. sheriff City of San Jose, Calif., 1973-74, specialist regional crime bd. Calif., 1974-78, dir. justice div. Calif., 1978-84; fellow U.S. Dept. of Justice, 1984-89; advisor White House, Washington, 1989-90; dir. Nat. Inst. Justice, 1990-93; ptnr. Lafayette Group, Inc., Vienna, Va., 1993—. Faculty Nat. Acad. Corrections, Boulder, Colo., 1986-90, Nat. Inst. Corrections, Washington, 1986-90; cons. Police Found., 1993-94. Author: National Directory of Corrections, 1986, 1988, Building on Experience, 1987, Prison Expansion, 1988. Adv. coun. The Ditchley Found. With USMCR, 1968-71. Recipient Atty. Gen's Achievement award, 1993, Dist. Attys. award, 1993, Am. Jails award, 1993. Mem. Am. Correctional Assn., Internat. Assn. Chiefs Police, Nat. Sheriffs Assn., Nat. Dist. Attys. Assn. Republican. Episcopalian. Avocations: jogging, skiing, tennis. Home: 5058 Sedgwick St NW Washington DC 20016-1940 Office: Lafayette Group Inc 8150 Leesburg Pike Ste 900 Vienna VA 22182-7749 Office Phone: 703-760-8866. Business E-Mail: cbdewitt@lafayettegroup.com.

DEWITT, CHARLES BENJAMIN, III, lawyer, educator; b. Glendale, Calif., Nov. 29, 1952; s. Charles Benjamin Jr. and Lucille Ann (Johnston) deW.; m. Karen Denise Blackwood, Dec. 29, 1979. BA magna cum laude, Pacific Union Coll., 1973; JD, U. So. Calif., 1976; MA, U. Memphis, 1995. Bar: Tenn. 1984, U.S. Dist. Ct. (we. dist.) Tenn. 1984, D.C. 1989. Atty., agy. mgr., v.p. SAFECO/Chgo. Title Ins., Memphis, 1980-91; regional underwriting counsel Commonwealth Land Title Ins. Co., 1991-93. Asst. prof., instr. U. Memphis, 1986—, asst. dean paralegal, 1993-96., asst. dean law sch., 1996—; judge adv. U.S. Army Gen. Corps, CPT (Reserves). Contbr. articles to profl. jours. Registrar gen. Washington Family Descendants Mem. ABA, Memphis Bar Assn., Tenn. Land Title Assn. (sec.-treas. 1983-87), U. S.C. Alumni Assn. (life), Order Crown of Charlemagne, Kiwanis, Mensa, Phi Alpha Theta, Phi Kappa Phi, Phi Alpha Delta. Home: 2488 Cedarwood Dr Germantown TN 38138-5802 Office: U Memphis Sch Law 107 Law School Memphis TN 38152-0001 Business E-Mail: cdewitt@memphis.edu.

DEWITT, DAVID J., computer scientist; PhD, U. Mich., 1976. Prof., Romnes fellow computer scis. U. Wis., Madison. Fellow Am. Acad. Arts & Scis.; mem. NAE. Office: U Wis Dept Computer Sci 1210 W Dayton St Madison WI 53706-1685 E-mail: dewitt@cs.wisc.edu.*

DEWITT, EDWARD FRANCIS, artist; b. Jersey City, Aug. 1, 1938; s. Elmer and Linda (Kroll) DeW.; m. Cora Finn, Nov. 11, 1959 (separated 1970); children: April, Lenneice, Edward, Linda; m. Mary Golazizian, Sept. 17, 1972. Artist cons. Bronx Zoo, 1968-70, Aquarius Art Ltd., Fairview, N.J., 1971-73; artist, sculptor, v.p. Artistic Classics, Rutherford, N.J., 1974-77; artist, sculptor, Browns Mills, N.J., 1977-97. Artist 5-yr. silverplate series Anheuser Busch; commemorative works for Pub. Svc., Babe Ruth, Gen. Doolittle, Jim Thorpe PA; sculptures Ford Motor Co., GM Corp., Bicentennial Soc., Boy Scouts Am., Thomas Edison, NATO, Chesapeake Reproductions, Mappsville, Va.; award programs for Progresso Foods, Kentucky Fried Chicken; medallions John F. Kennedy, Dwight D. Eisenhower, Winston Churchill, Bobby Kennedy, Charles A. Lindbergh, Gerald Ford: President; artist prints-sculptures models and collector plates Abundant Ocean Treasures, Saddlebrook, N.J., Double Eagle Sculpture (ofcl. symbol for New Millenium chosen by U.S. Hist. Soc.); series of prints chosen for Zallies Shop-Rite chain; commd. to sculpt profiles of Am. Presidents Medallion Series, Chesapeake Reprodns., Mappsville, Va., 2003, Louis and Clark 200th anniversary sculpture, 2003; represented in numerous pvt. collections in U.S. and Europe; patentee on door striker plate. Double eagle sculpture chosen as official symbol by U.S. Hist. Soc., 2000. Avocations: the arts, music, guitar, fishing. Home: 411 N Carolina Trl Browns Mills NJ 08015-5405 Office Phone: 609-893-6527. Personal E-mail: eddewitt3@verizon.net.

DE WITT, JEANETTE MARIE, physical therapist; d. Dale Frederick and Joan Carol Brandt; m. Joel Eric De Witt, Aug. 6, 2005. BS, Xavier U., Cin., 1996; M.Phys. Therapy, Allegheny U., Phila., 1998. Cert. athletic trainer, core control cert. instr. Phys. therapist TriHealth Pavilion, Cin., 1998—2003, TriHealth Summit Woods, Cin., 2003—05, phys. therapist, supr., 2006—. Adj. prof. Coll. Mt. St. Joseph, Cin., 2003, Xavier U., Cin., 2005—; cons. in field; lead phys. therapist TriHealth-Xavier U. Sports-medicine, Cin., 2003—. Mem.: Am. Phys. Therapy Assn., Nat. Athletic Trainers Assn. Avocations: running, kayaking, reading, Bible study. Office: TriHealth Physical Therapy at Summit Woods 508 E Business Way Cincinnati OH 45241

DEWITT-MORETTE, CÉCILE, physicist; b. Paris, Dec. 21, 1922; came to U.S., 1948; d. André and Marie Louise (Ravaudet) Morette; m. Bryce S. DeWitt, Apr. 26, 1951; children: Nicolette, Jan, Chris, Abigail. BS, U. Caen, 1943; PhD, U. Paris, 1947. With Centre Nat. de la Recherche Sci., 1944-65, Maitre de Confs. prof., 1965-88. Mem. Inst. Advanced Studies, Dublin, 1946—47, Copenhagen, 1947—48, Princeton, 1948—50; lectr. U. Calif., Berkeley, 1952—55, U. N.C., Chapel Hill, 1956—71; prof. U. Tex., 1972—93, Jane and Roland Blumberg Centennial prof. physics, 1993—2000, prof. emeritus, 2000—; founder, dir. Ecole d'ete de Physique Theorique, Les Houches, France, 1951—72. Author: Particules Elementaires, 1951, (with Y. Choquet-Bruhat and M. Dillard-Bleick) Analysis, Manifolds and Physics, 1977, rev. edit., 1982, 1996, (with A. Maheshwari, B. Nelson) Path Integration in Non Relativistic Quantum Mechanics, 1979, (with Y. Choquet Bruhat) Analysis, Manifolds and Physics, Part II, 92 Applications, 1989, rev. edit., 2000, (with P. Cartier) Functional Integration, Action and Symmetries, 2006, also articles. Decorated chevalier Ordre Nat. du Mërite, chevalier Ordre des Palmes Acadēmiques; chevalier Ordre Nat. Legion d'Honneur; Rask-Oersted fellow, 1947-48, Prix des Sciences Physiques et Mathematiques (Comite du Rayonnement Français, 1992); recipient (with Bryce DeWitt) Marcel Grossman award, 2000, Disting. Achievement medal, Am. Soc. French Legion of Honor, 2007. Fellow Am. Phys. Soc.; mem. Internat. Astron. Union, European Phys. Soc., Inst. Hautes Etudes Scientific (trustee), French Soc. Physics (Membre d'honneur). Home: 2411 Vista Ln Austin TX 78703-2343 Office: U Tex Austin Dept Physics 1 University Station C1600 Austin TX 78712-0268 Business E-Mail: cdewitt@physics.utexas.edu.

DE WOLF, DAVID ALTER, physicist, educator; b. Dordrecht, The Netherlands, July 23, 1934; came to U.S., 1962; children from previous marriage: Naomi, Jiska, Sarah. BS in Physics, U. Amsterdam, The Netherlands, 1955, MS in Physics, 1959; PhDEE, U. Eindhoven, The Netherlands, 1968. Rsch. scientist Edgewood (Md.) Arsenal U.S. Army Chem. Ctr., 1962; mem. tech. staff RCA Labs.-David Sarnoff Rsch. Ctr., Princeton, NJ, 1962-82; prof. elec. engring. Va. Tech., Blacksburg, 1982—2003, prof. emeritus, 2003—. Commn. B and F U.S. Nat. Com. Internat. Union Radio Sci., sec. 1985-89. Author 2 books and contbr. numerous articles on wave propagation, electron optics to profl. jours. Fellow IEEE, Optical Soc. Am. (assoc. editor JOSA 1969-81); mem. Am. Assn. Physics Tchrs., Dutch Physics Soc., Electromagnetics Acad., Sigma Xi, Eta Kappa Nu. Avocations: music, piano, literature, tennis. Office: Va Tech Bradley Dept Elec and Computer Engring Blacksburg VA 24061-0111 Home Phone: 540-951-3073; Office Phone: 540-231-4874. Business E-Mail: dadewolf@vt.edu.

DEWOLFE, CHRIS T., Internet company executive; b. 1967; married. BA in Fin., U. Wash.; MBA in Mktg., U. So. Calif., 1997. Mgr. merchant commerce divsn. First Bank Beverly Hills, v.p. mktg., 1997—99; pres. Euniverse, Inc., LA; v.p. mktg. Xdrive Technologies, Inc., Santa Monica, Calif., 1999—2001; CEO ResponseBase, LLC, Santa Monica, Calif., 2001—02, co-founder, pres., 2002—03; pres., CEO ResponseBase Mktg., LLC, 2002—03; co-founder, CEO MySpace.com, 2003—. Bd. dirs. Fog Cutter Capital Grp., Inc., 2002—. Co-recipient with Tom Anderson, Breakout of Yr., Webby award, Internat. Acad. Digital Arts and Scis., 2006; named one of 100 Most Influential People, Time mag., 2006, with Tom Anderson, 25 Most Influential People in Web Music, Powergeek 25, 2007. Achievements include MySpace.com being the most popular social networking website on the internet. Office: MySpace.com Inc 8225 Sunset Blvd West Hollywood CA 90069

DEWOLFE, JOHN CHAUNCEY, JR., lawyer; b. Chgo., June 9, 1913; s. John Chauncey and Mabel (Spafford) DeW.; m. Dorothy Fulton, May 9, 1942; children: John Chauncey, III, George F. BS, U. Ill.; JD, U. Wis., 1939. Bar: Wis. 1939, Ill. 1940. Ptnr. firm DeWolfe, Poynton & Stevens and predecessor firms, 1946—. Contbr. articles to profl. jours. Trustee Village of Riverside, Ill., 1963-70; Chmn. West Suburban Mass Transit Dist., 1974-76. Served from lt. to maj. AUS, 1942-45, 51-52; lt. col. USAR ret. Mem. ABA, Ill. Bar Assn., Wis. Bar Assn., Chgo. Bar Assn. (chmn. corp. law com. 1973-74), Univ. Clug (Chgo.), Sigma Phi Epsilon. Republican. Episcopalian.

DE WOLFF, LOUIS, management consultant; b. NYC, Dec. 21, 1929; s. Maurice and Minnie (Konrad) De W.; m. Grace Elise Sorrentino, Apr. 27, 1957 (dec. Dec. 2000); children: Douglas Louis, Cynthia Ann. AS, Bklyn.

Coll., 1960; BS in Acctg., CCNY, 1962. Officer Lykes Bros. S.S. Co., New Orleans, 1950-57; export mgr. Cory Mann George Corp., NYC, 1957-60; dist. supt. F&M Schaefer Brewing Co., NYC, 1960-64; product and material mgr. Del Labs., Inc., Farmingdale, NY, 1965-69; exec. cons., exec. v.p. Pennington (N.J.) Industries, 1969-73; dir. ops. Alexander Proudfoot Co., Chgo., 1973-86; mgr. ops. Metra Proudfoot Ltd., Brussels, 1986-87; CEO, chmn. DeWolff Boberg & Assocs., Charleston, SC, 1987—. Lt. (j.g.) USMS and USNR, 1950-57, PTO. Mem.: U.S. Navy League, U.S. Naval Inst., Charleston Concert Assn. (bd. dirs.). Republican. Lutheran. Avocations: carpentry, sailing, gardening. Home: 53 Waterway Island Dr Isle Of Palms SC 29451 Office: DeWolff Boberg & Assocs PO Box 21989 Charleston SC 29413-1989 Home Phone: 843-886-3244. Office Fax: 843-886-5323.

DEWOODY, BETH RUDIN, film producer; b. NYC; d. Lewis Rudin; m. Jim DeWoody (div.); children: Carlton, Kyle. Studied Anthropology & Film Studies, U. Calif. Santa Barbara; BA, New Sch. Social Rsch. Pres. May & Samuel Rudin Found. Inc.; exec. v.p. Rudin Mgmt. Co.; contbg. editor Hampton's Cottages & Garden's Mag. Dir.(asst. dir.): (TV series) Born Free; prodn. asst. Annie Hall, The Front, Hair, co-prodr. Enter Juliet. Bd. dir. Creative Time Inc., Whitney Mus. Am. Art, Bklyn. Mus. Am. Art, New Sch. U.; bd. adv. Eos Music Inc. Mailing: Whitney Mus Am Art 945 Madison Ave New York NY 10021

DEWOSKIN, ALAN ELLIS, lawyer; b. St. Louis, Sept. 10, 1940; s. Samuel S. and Lillian (Sachs) DeW.; m. Iris Lynn Shapiro, Aug. 15, 1942; children: Joseph, Henry, Franklin. BA, Washington U., St. Louis, 1962, JD, 1965; postgrad., U.S. Army Command & Gen. Staff Coll., 1978, U.S. Army War Coll., 1985. Bar: Mo. 1968, Ill. 1999, U.S. Dist. Ct. (ea. dist.) Mo. 1968, U.S. Ct. Appeals (8th cir.) 1969, U.S. Ct. Appeals (Armed Forces) 1976, U.S. Supreme Ct. 1990, U.S. Ct. Claims 1997. Pvt. practice, St. Louis, 1968-82; prin. Alan E. DeWoskin, PC, St. Louis, 1982—. Active Boy Scouts Am. Ret. col. JAGC US Army. Recipient U.S. Legion of Merit, 1992. Fellow Am. Bar Found., Mo. Bar Found., St. Louis Bar Found. (disting.); mem. ABA (chmn., gen. practice sect. 1985-86, ho. of dels. 1986-87, assembly del., standing com. mil. law, standing com. assembly resolutions 1988-91, vice-chmn. task force solo and small firm practitioners), ATLA, Mo. Bar Assn. (chmn. gen. practice com. 1987-90, chmn. computer interest groups 1988-90), Bar Assn. Met. St. Louis (exec. com. 1993-94, bd. govs. 1994-95, chmn. solo and small firm sect. 1993-95), Mo. Assn. Trial Attys., Res. Officers Assn. (Mo. Dept. pres. 1979), Masons (past master, dir. 1972—, dist. dep. grand master 2006-07), Am. Legion. Home: 14030 Deltona Dr Chesterfield MO 63017-3311 Office: 225 S Meramec Ave Ste 426 Saint Louis MO 63105-3511 Office Phone: 314-727-6330. E-mail: aedewoskin@cs.com.

DEWOSKIN, MARGARET FOGARTY, real estate company executive; Grad., U. Wis. With Hilco Real Estate LLC; v.p. acquisitions Klaff Realty L.P.; exec. v.p. Builders Bank, Chgo.; trans. coord. Orix Real Estate Capital, Inc., Chgo., 2004, sr. v.p., COO. Chair real estate capital investment com. Orix Real Estate Capital, Inc. Named one of Top 40 Under 40, Crain's Chgo. Bus., 2006. Mem.: Wis. Real Estate Alumni Assn. Office: Orix Real Estate Capital Inc 100 N Riverside Plz Ste 1400 Chicago IL 60606 E-mail: margaret.dewoskin@orix.com.*

DE WREE, EUGENE ERNEST, manufacturing executive; b. Fairbanks, Alaska, June 26, 1930; s. Henry Joseph and Bertha Agnes DeWree; m. Shirley May Russo, Apr. 16, 1955 (dec. Sept. 1990); children: Angela Kathryn, Mary Rebecca, Thomas Albert, Babette Gabrielle, Jane Elizabeth; m. Jean Stanley Mack, Sept. 4, 1993 (dec. Apr. 2004); children: John Currie, Brigget Currie. ME, Cogswell Engring. Coll., 1956; MBA in Mktg., Stanford U., 1976. Project engr. Heat and Control Co., San Francisco, 1955-59; chief appliations engr., then market mgr. Wesix Electric Heater Co., San Francisco, 1959-65; account mgr. Fisher Controls, San Francisco, 1965-76; market and sales mgr. TRW Mission, Houston, 1976-80; v.p. mktg.-sales Houston Heat Exch., 1980-82; mktg. mgr. Anderson, Greenwood & Co., 1982—. Sr. ptnr. Affiliated Products, Inc.; pres. DeWree Enterprises, DeWree Rental Properties; dir. Creative Capers, San Francisco and Houston; ptnr., dir. Constrn. Info. Svcs., Cismap, TVMP; sr. v.p. Indsl. Market Rsch.; ptnr. Indsl. Info. Resource; sr. v.p. bd. dirs. strategic planning industrialinfo.com., 1984—. Mem. Belmont Pers. Bd., Calif., 1965; com. chmn. Boy Scouts Am., 1970; elected to bd. dirs. Cypress Forest Pub. Utility Dist. Harris County, Tex., 1981, 83, 85, 86-90, 92-96, Harris County Regional Water Supply; pres. Water Bd. Capt. arty. U.S. Army, 1952-53, Korea. Decorated knight Sovereign Order of St. John (Jerusalem); named Outstanding Jaycee of Yr., 1966. Mem. Am. Mgmt. Assn., Am. Nuc. Soc., Valve Mfg. Assn., Instrument Soc. Am. (sr.), Assn. Water Bd. Dirs., Water Pollution Control Fedn., Sales and Mktg. Execs., Houston Engring. and Sci. Soc., KC (3d degree, dep. Grand Knight, 4th degree trustee), Inner Circle, Pine Forest Country Club, Plaza Club, Engrs. Club (San Francisco). Republican. Roman Catholic. Home and Office: 5315B PM 1960 Rd W Unit 11 Houston TX 77069-4403 Home Phone: 281-444-8008; Office Phone: 281-444-8008. E-mail: api77069@aol.com.

DEWS, P(ETER) B(OOTH), retired pharmacology educator, physician; b. Ossett, Yorkshire, Eng., Sept. 11, 1922; s. G.A. and E. (Booth) D.; m. Grace Miller, Dec. 1949; children: Pamela, Kenneth, Alan, Michael. MBChB, U. Leeds, Eng., 1944; PhD, U. Minn., 1952; MA, Harvard U., 1959. House physician Grimsby Hosp., England, 1944-45; lectr. pharmacology U. Leeds, England, 1945-47; rsch. assoc. Wellcome Rsch. Labs., Tuckahoe, NY, 1948-49, Mayo Found., Rochester, Minn., 1950-52; from instr. to prof. Harvard Med. Sch., Boston, 1953-93, prof. emeritus, 1993—. Mem. Nat. Adv. Mental Health Coun., Washington, 1985-88, Nat. Adv. Space Coun., Washington, 1982-86; v.p. Internat. Life Scis. Inst., Washington, 1977-97. Mem.: Inst. of Medicine. Home Phone: 617-244-0663. Personal E-mail: peter_dews@hms.harvard.edu.

DEWSBURY, DONALD ALLEN, psychologist; b. Bklyn., Aug. 11, 1939; s. Edwin Leroy and Carol Wieler (Neil) D.; m.; children: Bryan Bradley, Laura Alison. AB, Bucknell U., 1961; PhD, U. Mich., 1965. NSF postdoctoral fellow U. Calif., Berkeley, 1965-66; mem. faculty dept. psychology U. Fla., Gainesville, 1966—, prof., 1973—2007, ret. prof. emeritus, 2007—. Author: Comparative Animal Behavior, 1978, Comparative Psychology in the Twentieth Century, 1984, Monkey Farm: A history of Yerkes Laboratories of Primate Biology, 1930-1965, 2006; editor (with D. Rethlingshafer): Comparative Psychology: A Modern Survey, 1973; editor: (with T. McGill, B. Sachs) Sex and Behavior: Status and Prospectus, 1978; editor: Mammalian Sexual Behavior, 1981, Foundations of Comparative Psychology, 1984, Leaders in the Study of Animal Behavior, 1985, Studying Animal Behavior, 1989, Contemporary Issues in Comparative Psychology, 1990, Unification Through Division: Histories of the Divisions of the American Psychological Association, vol. 1, 1996, vol. 2, 1997, vol. 3, 1998, vol. 4, 1999, vol. 5, 2000; editor: (with W. Pickren) Evolving Perspectives on the History of Psychology, 2002; editor: (with L.T. Benjamin, Jr. and M. Wertheimer) Portraits of Pioneers in Psychology, vol. 6, 2006. Recipient Wainwright D. Blake prize in Psychology, Bucknell U., 1961, Phi Sigma award Biological Sci., U. Mich., 1962. Fellow APA (pres. divsn. 6 1992-93, pres. divsn. 26 1997-98, Clifford T. Morgan Disting. Svc. to divsn. 6 award, 1998, pres.-elect divsn. 1 2007-), AAAS, Animal Behavior Soc. (pres. 1978-79, Exemplary award, 1998, Exceptional Svc. award, 2003); mem. Assn. Psychological Sci., History of Sci. Soc., Cheiron Soc., Phi Beta Kappa, Psi Chi, Phi Eta Sigma, Sigma Xi (U. Fla. Sr. Rsch. award 1997). Avocations: opera, baseball, photography, jazz. Home: 4004 NW 59th Ave Gainesville FL 32653-8358 Office: Univ Fla Dept Psychology Gainesville FL 32611-2250 Office Phone: 352-392-0601 279.

DEWSNUP, RALPH L., lawyer; b. Salt Lake City, Mar. 13, 1948; s. Edwin Grant and Mary Jeannette (Fairbanks) D.; m. Mary C. Dewsnup, Mar. 26, 1971; children: Emily, Rebecca, Hillary, Nathan, Heidi. BA, U. Utah, 1972; JD, Brigham Young U., 1977. Bar: Utah, 1977; U.S. Dist. Ct. Utah, 1977, U.S. Ct. Appeals (10th cir.) 1978, U.S. Supreme Ct., 1985. Asst. trust officer Tracy Collins Bank and Trust, Salt Lake City, 1971-74; brig. gen. Utah Air Nat. Guard, Salt Lake City, 1967—; law clk. Hansen & Orton, Salt Lake City, 1975-77; assoc. Hansen & Thompson, Salt Lake City, 1977-80; ptnr. Hansen, Thompson & Dewsnup, Salt Lake City, 1980-83, Hansen & Dewsnup, Salt Lake City, 1983-90; shareholder, officer Wilcox, Dewsnup & King, Salt Lake City, 1990-97; pres. Dewsnup, King & Olsen, 1998—2007. Stake pres. LDS Ch., Salt Lake City, 1988-97, bishop, 1985-88; chmn. prelitigation task force Divsn. of Occpl. and Profl. Lics., Salt Lake City, 1995-96. Mem.: ATLA, Am. Inns of Ct. Found. (trustee 1987—88, sec. 1985—96, treas. 1996—98, mem. exec. com. 1988—98), Utah Trial Lawyers Assn. (pres. 1990—92), Temple Bar Found. (trustee 1996—98), Utah State Bar (gov. 1987—2001), Aldon J. Anderson Am. Inn of Ct. (pres. 1991—92). Republican. Avocations: music (piano, banjo and guitar), woodworking, basketball. Office: Dewsnup King & Olsen 36 S State St Ste 2400 Salt Lake City UT 84111-1401 Office Phone: 801-533-0400.

DEWULF NICKELL, KAROL, editor-in-chief; m. Don Nickell; children: Lauren, Alexander. BA in Journalism, Iowa St. U. Furnishings editor Better Homes and Gardens mag., 1979—87, editor-in-chief, 2001—, Traditional Home mag., 1987—2001, Renovation Style mag., 1995—2000; columnist Country Home mag., 1987—2001. Avocations: gardening, reading, cooking. Office: 1716 Locust St Des Moines IA 50309-3023

DEXHEIMER, HENRY PHILLIP, II, insurance agency executive; b. Dayton, Ohio, Sept. 16, 1925; s. Henry Phillip and Helene Francis (Veach) D.; m. Maria DaGraca Fernandes, Nov. 21, 1988; children: James Phillip, Jana Helene. BS in Commerce, U. So. Calif., 1952; CLU, 1971. Sales acct. exec. various cos. and newspapers, 1946-51; broadcasting sales exec. Sta. KBIG, KTLA-TV, LA, 1952-58; broadcasting sales exec. Sta. KFXM, San Bernardino, Calif., 1956-57, pres., 1956-57; founder, owner, pres. Dexheimer Co., LA, 1958-89; owner, founder, pres., CEO Dexco Internat., Marina Del Rey, 1990—. Served with inf. and adj. gen.'s dept. US Army, 1943-46; PTO. Recipient Sammy award LA Sales Execs. Club, 1955, Silver Sales trophy Radio Advt. Bur. NY, 1955, Hal Parsons award, 1978, 83-88; named Agt. of Year LA Office Travelers Ins. Cos., 1978, 83-88, Nat. Agt. of Yr. Travelers Ins. Cos., 1983. Mem. Am. Soc. CLUs (nat. dir. Travelers chpt. 1972-73, 80-81), Am. Coll. Life Underwriters, Advt. Assn. West, Radio and TV Soc. Hollywood, Life Ins. and Trust Coun. LA, LA Life Underwriters Assn. (dir. 1963-65, v.p. 1967-69), Million Dollar Round Table (life, honor roll), World Affairs Coun. LA, Internat. Assn. Fin. Planners, Am. Art Coun., Decorative Art Coun. LA County Art Mus., Alpha Delta Sigma, Phi Kappa Tau (Hall of Fame 2006), Town Hall Club (LA), Beverly Hills Men's Club (Calif.), Masons (32 degree), Shriners, Legion of Honor. Republican. Presbyterian. Home: 13225 Admiral Ave Unit C Marina Del Rey CA 90292-7040

DEXTER, DONALD HARVEY, surgeon, educator; b. Maywood, Ill., Apr. 8, 1928; s. Harry Malcolm and Theodora Jane (Trelawny) D.; m. Esther Ruth Reeve, May 16, 1953; children: Donald Harvey, Scott Reeve, Bryce Malcolm, Margaret Helen. BS, Tulane U., 1948; MD, Northwestern U., 1950; LHD (hon.), Western Ill. U., 1993. Diplomate: Am. Bd. Surgery. Intern Cook County Hosp., Chgo., 1950-51; resident in surgery Ill. Central Hosp., Chgo., 1951-52, Cook County Hosp., 1955-58; practice medicine specializing in surgery Macomb, Ill., 1958—89; prof. dept. health scis. Western Ill. U., 1975—89; physician surveyor Joint Commn. on Accreditation Healthcare Orgns., 1989-93; chief of staff Beu Health Ctr., Western Ill. U., 1993-2001, physician, 2001—. Sr. mem. Macomb Clinic; team physician; coroner McDonough County, Ill., 1964-76; mem. gov. bd., chmn. devel. coun. McDonough Dist. Hosp., 1995—. Mem. Western Ill. U. Found. Served with USNR, 1953-54. Named Outstanding Citizen of Macomb Jaycees, 1972, Outstanding Citizen of Macomb Macomb Area C. of C., 1973; recipient award of recognition Devel. Center of Western Ill. U. and Macomb Area C. of C., 1977, Hon. Alumni award Western Ill. U., 2004; named to Hall of Fame Western Ill. U., 1991. Fellow ACS (pres. Ill. chpt. 1972, gov.-at-large Ill. chpt. 1983-88), state chmn. field liaison program commn. on cancer, 1983-89); mem. AMA, Ill. Med. Soc., (Outstanding Team Physician award 1985), Ill. Surg. Soc., M.W. Surg. Assn., Rotary (Paul Harris fellow 1987), Phi Beta Kappa. Republican. Episcopalian. Home: 1601 Tower Rd RR 1 Macomb IL 61455-9801

DEXTER, ROBERT PAUL, lawyer; b. Halifax, NS, Can., Dec. 11, 1951; s. Carl Edmund and Jean Rankin (Collins) D.; 1 child, Angela Elizabeth. BComm, Dalhousie U., 1973, LLB, 1976. With firm Stewart McKelvey Stirling Scales, Halifax, 1977—; chmn., CEO Maritime Travel, Halifax, Canada, 1978—; chmn. Empire Co. Ltd., Stellarton, Canada, 2004—. Vice chmn. N.S. Bus. Devel. Corp., 1992-94; bd. dirs. Empire Co. Ltd., Sobeys Inc., High Liner Foods Inc., Bell Aliant Income Fund, Wajon Income Fund; pres. Halifax Bd. Trade, 1993-94. Chmn. Metro United Way Campaign, 1997. I.W. Killam scholar, 1973, Sir James Dunn scholar, 1976. Mem. N.S. Barristers Soc., Can. Bar Assn., Young Pres. Orgn. Avocations: sailing, skiing, tennis. Home: 1028 Ridgewood Dr Halifax NS Canada B3H 3Y4 Office: Maritime Travel 2000 Barrington St Ste 202 Halifax NS Canada B3J 2X2

DEXTER, THEODORE HENRY, chemist; b. Preston, Cuba, June 1, 1923; parents Am. citizens; s. Harry Malcolm and Theodora Jane (Trelawny) D.; m. Marilyn Ann Cantara, July 26, 1952; children: Carol Dexter Villagran, Martha Dexter Rogala, John Dexter. BS, Tulane U., New Orleans, 1944, MS, 1947; PhD, U. Ill., 1950. Tchg. asst. chemistry Tulane U., New Orleans, 1943-44, 46-47; chemist E.I. du Pont de Nemours, Inc.; Okla. Ordnance Works, 1944-45; gen. aniline chem. rsch. asst. U. Ill., Urbana, 1947-49; group leader chem. rsch. Mathieson Chem. Corp., Niagara Falls, NY, 1949-55, sect. chief rsch., 1955-60; rsch. supr. Hooker Chem. Corp., Grand Island, NY, 1960-75; program leader, 1975-76; sr. rsch. chemist Hooker Indsl. and Splty. Chems div. Occidental Chem. Corp., 1976—85. Cons. Dexter Cons. Svcs., 1986—; lect., rsch. adv. Joe Berg Found., 1960-61; mem. photoreactivity task force Mfg. Chemists Assn., 1966-68; lectr. in field. Contbr. articles to profl. jours.; US, fgn. patentee inorganic chemistry and processes. Violinist Niagara Falls Philharm. Orch., 1950-72, Niagara Cmty. Orch., 1988-92, Niagara Symphony, 1992— 2001; group chmn. in-house steering com. United Givers Fund., 1970-73; mem. exec. com. Episc. Diocese We. NY, 1977-81, nursing home ministry, 1972—; lay reader, vestryman Episc. Ch., warden, 1967-68, 77-80, 92-94; vol. tax counselor AARP, 1998—06. With USN, 1945—46, with USNR, 1946—48. Mem. Am. Chem. Soc. (chmn. Western NY 1969-70, N.E. regional meeting divisional chn. 1971, founder Western N.Y. Inorganic Chemistry Group 1967, Schoellkopf Award jury chmn. 1970-72), Soap and Detergent Assn. (del. internat. conf. 1979, com. chmn.), Electrochem. Soc., Sigma Xi, Alpha Chi Sigma (Niagara Frontier pres. 1954), Phi Lambda Upsilon. Home and Office: 850 Hillside Dr Lewiston NY 14092-1828

DEY, CHARLOTTE JANE, retired community health nurse; b. Benson, Minn., Dec. 14, 1927; d. Elmer Ellsworth and Charlotte Iona (Eastman) Bowers; m. Thomas A. Dey, June 25, 1948 (dec. Mar. 1973); children: Thomas A. Jr., Scott E. (dec.). Grad., St. Luke's Hosp. Sch. Nursing, 1948; student, Kans. City CC, 1968; BS in Nursing with distinction, U. Kans., 1970; MPA, U. Mo., Kansas City, 1975. RN, Mo.; ordained deacon, Episcopal Ch., 1993. Head nurse communicable disease ward St. Luke's Children's Hosp., Kansas City, Mo., 1948-49; head nurse newborn nursery Providence Hosp., Kansas City, Kans., 1949-51; pub. health nurse Johnson County Health Dept., Olathe, Kans., 1951-52, 66-68, pub. health nurse, supr., 1970-72; evening supr. Olathe Community Hosp., 1953-55; office nurse B. Albert Lieberman, Jr., MD, Kansas City, Mo., 1960-66; coord. clin. confs. ANA, Kansas City, 1973-76; chief Bur. Community Health Nursing Mo. Dept. Health, Jefferson City, 1976-93; ret., 1993. Sem. expert panel to review and update criteria to estimate future requirements for nursing pers. div. nursing Dept. Health and Human Svcs., 1984, mem. nat. adv. coun. nursing edn. and practice div. nursing, 1998-2002; chair Mid-Am. Community Health Nursing Leadership Group. Recipient award of merit Assn. State and Territorial Dirs. Nursing, 1992. Mem. ANA (cert. nursing adminstrn. advanced, chairperson exec. com. coun. community health nursing 1989-92), APHA, Nat. League Nursing, Nat. Perinatal Assn., Am. Acad. Health Adminstrn. (pres. Mo. chpt. 1980-82), Mo. State Nurses Assn. (coun. nursing svc. facilitors exec. com. 1983-92), Mo. Pub. Health Assn., Mo. League Nursing, Mo. Perinatal Assn., Kans. State Nurses' Assn. (vice chairperson community health conf. group), Kans. Pub. Health Assn. (legislative com.), Sigma Theta Tau. Mem. Episcopal Ch. Home: 8090 Granite Falls Ct Redmond OR 97756-7389 Personal E-mail: janedey@bendcable.com.

DEY, MOUL, molecular biologist, researcher; arrived in U.S., 2001; BS in Biology and Chemistry, 1994, MS in Plant Sci., 1996, PhD in Biotechnology, 2002. Tchr. Pre-U. Sys., Calcutta, India, 1996—97; assoc. sci. editor Bharati Bhavan Nat. Pubs., Kolkata, India, 1997; rsch. scholar Internat. Rice Rsch. Inst., Metro Manila, Philippines, 1997—2000; post doctoral assoc. Cornell U., Ithaca, NY, 2001—04, rsch. assoc., 2004; rsch. faculty Rutgers U., New Brunswick, NJ, 2004—. Presenter in field. Mem. editl. bd.: Internat. Pubs., 2004—05; contbr. chapters to books, articles to profl. jours. Fellow, Rockefeller Found., 1999—2000, Danida, Denmark, 1997—99, Cornell U., 2001—04; scholar, Govt India, Edn. Ministry, 1989, 1991. Mem.: Inflammation Rsch. Assn., Philippines Assn. Plant Tissue Culture and Biotechnology (Best Poster award 1999). Achievements include research in improvement of agriculture and human health care; development of molecular tools and screens that can be used for future drug discovery; patents pending for new drug molecule. Office Phone: 732-932-8165 111.

DEY, RADHESHYAM CHANDRA, cytologist; b. Calcutta, India, Jan. 30, 1950; arrived in US, 1978; s. Bhairab and Satyabala D.; m. Indrani Roy Chowdhury, July 5, 1981; children: Smita, Anita, Ishan. BSc, Bangabasi Coll., Calcutta, 1970; MSc, U. Calcutta, 1972, cert. in life sci., 1974; CT, Brooke Army Med. Ctr., San Antonio, 1983; cert. leaderhsip mgmt., ednl. devel., quality improvement and equal opportunity, Walter Reed Army Med. Ctr., 1989; postgrad., Laval U., Quebec City, Can., 1995, Albert Einstein Sch. Medicine, NYC, 1997; student in quality assurance, Inspector's Inspection Lab., Coll. Am. Pathologists, 2005. Registered cytotechnologist, Am. Soc. Clin. Pathologists, Internat. Acad. Cytology, Calif., Md. Rsch. fellow U. Calcutta, 1975-77; with Anthropol. Survey of India Indian Mus. Calcutta, India, 1977—78; biol. sci. asst. Army Inst. Rsch., Washington, 1980—83; cytology specialist U.S. Army Hosp., Ft. Campbell, Ky., 1983-85, SHAPE Med. Ctr., Mons, Belgium, 1985—87; cytotechnologist Nat. Health Lab., Vienna, Va., 1988; supervisory cytologist Walter Reed Army Med. Ctr., Washington, 1988—. Vis. Indian Statis. Inst., Calcutta, 1999; presenter in field; mem. European Congress Cytology, Athens, Greece, 2004. Contbr. articles to profl. jours. Decorated U.S. Army Commendation medal, Achievement medal, Good Conduct medals; recipient Decree of Merit for outstanding contbn. to medicine and health care, 1995, Excellence in Tchg. award Nat. Capital Region Consortium Pathology Residency, 1997, Comdr.'s award US Army Walter Reed Med. Ctr., 1997; Anthrop. Survey of India fellow U. Calcutta, 1976. Fellow: Internat. Acad. Cytology; mem.: AAAS, Md. Assn. Cytopathology, Washington Met. Assn. Cytology, Indian Anthropol. Soc., Ind. Sci. Congress, Md. Assn. Cytopathology, Belge de Cytologie Clinique (del. visit to People's Republic China 1987, internat. team cytologists exch. sci. knowledge with USSR 1990, del. visit to People's Republic China 1991, vis. and inspected cytopathology and histopathology lab. 2005, vis. Athens, Greece for European Congress of Cytology, 2005), Soc. of Armed Forces Med. Lab. Scientists, N.Y. Acad. Scis., Am. Soc. for Cytotech., Am. Soc. Clin. Pathologists, Am. Soc. Cytopathology, Am. Anthropol. Assn., Am. Legion. Avocations: soccer, swimming, running, travel, theater. Home: 10110 Treble Ct Rockville MD 20850 Office: Walter Reed Army Med Ctr Dept Pathology Cytology Lab Washington DC 20307-0001 Home Phone: 301-838-0341; Office Phone: 202-782-1126. Personal E-mail: dey_rad@hotmail.com.

DEYO, RUSSELL C., health products executive, lawyer; BA, Dartmouth Coll.; JD, Georgetown U. With Johnson & Johnson, New Brunswick, NJ, 1985—, assoc. gen. counsel, 1991—96, v.p. adminstrn., 1996—2004, v.p., gen. counsel, chief compliance officer, 2004—, mem. exec. com. Office: Johnson & Johnson 1 Johnson & Johnson Plz New Brunswick NJ 08933-0001*

DEYOE, DAVID P., lawyer; b. Muskegon, Mich., July 18, 1948; s. Frank A. and Mildred E. (Jensen) DeY.; m. Ilene L. Nevel, May 26, 1979; children: Andrew, Mary, Emily, Peter. BA in Econs., U. Mich., 1970; JD, Stanford U., 1973. Bar: Ill. 1973, U.S. Dist. Ct. (no. dist.) Ill. 1973, Cal. 1975. Assoc. McDermott, Will & Emery, Chgo., 1973-79, ptnr., 1979—. Contbr. articles to profl. jours. Office: McDermott Will & Emery 227 W Monroe St Ste 4700 Chicago IL 60606-5096 Office Phone: 312-984-7659. Office Fax: 312-984-7700. E-mail: ddeyoe@mwe.com.

DEYONKER, ALEX J., lawyer, food products executive; BS, Mich. State U.; JD cum laude, Wayne State U. Mng. ptnr. Warner Norcross & Judd LLP, 1988—2006; gen. counsel Spartan Stores Inc., Grand Rapids, Mich., 1995—, sec., 2000—, bd. mem., 1999—2003, exec. v.p., 2006—. Mem.: ABA, Grand Rapids Bar Assn., State Bar of Mich. Office: Spartan Stores Inc 850 76th St, SW PO Box 8700 Grand Rapids MI 49518*

DE YOUNG, DAVID SPENCER, astrophysicist, educator; b. Colorado Springs, Nov. 29, 1940; s. Henry C. and Zona L. (Church) DeY.; m. Mary Ellen Haney. BA, U. Colo., 1962; PhD, Cornell U., 1967. Rsch. physicist Los Alamos (N.Mex.) Nat. Labs., 1967-69; astronomer Nat. Radio Astronomy Obs., Charlottesville, Va., 1969-80, Kitt Peak Nat. Obs., Tucson, 1980—, assoc. dir., 1983-88, dir., 1988-94. Organizer numerous sci. confs.; mem. adv. bd. Aspen (Colo.) Ctr. Physics, 1977—, trustee, 1992—, pres., 2001-05; mem. exec. com. steering com. San Diego Supercomputer Ctr., 1985-98, chmn., 1989-91; mem. steering com. Nat. Virtual Obs., 2000—, project scientist, 2001-, exec. com., 2001—; mem. Nat. Optical Astronomy Obs., Tucson, 1982—, assoc. dir., 1988-94, 2007—; bd. dirs. WIYN Telescope Consortium, Tucson; mem. exec. com. Internat. Virtual Obs. Alliance, 2001—, vice chair, 2006—; mem. sci. adv. com. European Virtual Observatory, 2006—. Contbr. articles to profl. jours. NASA grantee. Fellow Am. Phys. Soc.; mem. Astron. Soc. Pacific, Am. Astron. Soc., Internat. Astron. Union, Internat. Union Radio Soc., Phi Beta Kappa. Office: Nat Optical Astronomy Observatory 950 N Cherry Ave Tucson AZ 85719-4933

DEYOUNG, MARILYN BRANT-CHANDLER, retired urban planner, farmer; b. LA, June 24, 1931; d. Robert Alston and Jane Mann Brant; m. Patrick Lyons DeYoung, Aug. 23, 1997; stepchildren: Daniel, Alice, Gloria, Linda, Patrick Jr.;children from previous marriage: Norman Brant Chandler(dec.) , Harry Brant Chandler, Michael Otis Chandler, Carolyn Chandler, Cathleen Chandler Eckhardt. Attended, Stanford U., Palo Alto, Calif., 1949—51; student, U. Calif., Berkeley, 1951, Occidental Coll., 1959; MA, UCLA, 1975; student, Claremont Grad. Sch. Cert. A.I.C.P. Asst. urban planner Archistystems of Summa Corp., Van Nuys, Calif., 1975—79; founder, pres. Urban Design Disciplines, Pasadena, 1979—82, Marilyn Brant & Assoc., LA, 1982—84, Population Edn. Com., LA, 1984—95; ret., 1995. Dir., sec. , treas. L.A. Hdqrs. Assn., 1974—84; dir. ACT Inc. Snowbird Devel. Corp., Utah; dir. adv. bd. and transp. chair So. Calif. Assn. of Govt., 1981—85. Dir. Population Assn. Internat., Washington, Population Comm. Internat., NYC; mem. bd. Otis Art Inst., LA; dir. and fin. chair Santa Barbara Hist. Soc., 1995—; pres. L.A. County Bd. Suprs. Apptd., Commn. Population Growth, Pres. Nixon, 1970—72, White House Fellowship Commn., Pres. Carter, 1977—82. Mem.: Coral Casino Club, Birnam Wood Golf Club. Independent. Episcopalian. Achievements include development of an avocado farm. Avocations: tennis, painting, fly fishing, reading, exercise.

DEYSHER, PAUL EVANS, retired management consultant; b. Reading, Pa., Oct. 16, 1923; s. Paul Stauffer and Ida Estelle (Evans) D.; m. Myrtle Constance Stover, June 17, 1950 (dec. Feb. 2003); children: David Paul, Mark Edward. BS, Albright Coll., 1945; M in Ednl. Adminstrn., Temple U., 1949. Math. and sci. tchr. Lebanon City (Pa.) Sch. Dist., 1950-56; asst. h.s. prin. Ocean City Sch. (N.J.) Dist., 1956-57; h.s. prin. Yeadon Sch. (Pa.), Dist., 1957-60; mgr. pers. adminstrn. Philco Corp., Phila., 1960-66; tng. specialist AMP, Inc., Harrisburg, Pa., 1966-80, supr. mgmt. tng., 1980-85, mgr. mgmt. tng. and devel., 1986, ret., 1986. Cons. and lectr. in field. Author: (poems) Anthologies of International Library of Poetry, 1999, 00, 07; co-author: Transistor Fundamentals, 1962; contbr. chpts. to books and articles to profl. jours. Pres. Albright Coll., Lebanon County Alumni chpt., 1979—; trustee Albright Coll., Reading, Pa., 1985-89. Mem. NEA (life), Am. Soc. Pers. Adminstrn. (cert., sr. prof. in human resources), ASTD (past pres.), Internat. Soc. Poets (Disting. mem.), Phi Delta Kappa. Republican. Lutheran. Home: 39 S Mill St Lebanon PA 17042-3124

DE ZAFRA ATWELL, DOROTHEA ELIZABETH, retired government agency administrator; b. Rochester, NY, Apr. 8, 1942; d. Carlos de Zafra, Jr. and Dorothea Schwartz (Michelsen) de Zafra; m. Wilbur Munroe Atwell, Aug. 11, 2001. BA magna cum laude in Non-Western Civilizations, U. Rochester, NYC, 1963; M of Pub. and Internat. Affairs, U. Pitts., 1965; diploma in info. resources mgmt., Nat. Def. Univ., Washington, 1994. New Eng. regional exec. World Univ. Svc., NYC, 1965—67; study abroad program asst. CUNY, Queens, 1967—69; mgmt. intern, legis. analyst USPHS, Rockville, Md., 1969—74, privacy act officer, health agys. info. practices analyst, 1974—84, info. sys. security program mgr., 1984—95; sci. edn. program dir. NIH, Nat. Inst. Alcohol Abuse and Alcoholism, Bethesda, Md., 1995—2002; ret. Workgroup chair, author Info. Tech. Security Tng. Requirements: A Role and Performance-Based Model, 1998; archaeology cons., guest instr. gifted and talented enrichment Alexandria City Schs.; mem. diversity coun. NIH; EEO counselor USPHS. Mem. adv. coun. U. Pitts. Alumni Assn. and Internat. Alumni Liason, 2004—06; excavation vol. Alexandria Archaeology, Va., 1990—91, Earthwatch, Nev., 1974, Honduras, 1985—86. Named Fed. 100 award, Fed. Computer Week mag., 1995; recipient Vol. Svc. award, Grad. Sch. Pub. and Internat. Affairs, U. Pitts., 2006, EEO Spl. Achievement award, Nat. Inst. Alcohol Abuse and Alcoholism, 1998, Exemplary Svc. award, Office of Asst. Sec. for Health, U.S. Dept. Health and Human Svcs., 1994, Spl. Recognition award, 1982. Mem.: Computer Security Program Mgrs. Forum (exec. bd. dirs. 1990—93), Fed. Info. Sys. Security Educators Assn. (v.p., pres. 1987—94, Educator of Yr. 1998), Am. Soc. Access Profls. (exec. bd. dirs. 1978—82, editor newsletter), Mensa, Red Hat Soc., Phi Beta Kappa. Democrat. Unitarian Universalist. Avocations: archaeology, history and current events, educational travel. Home: 2020 Cradock St Silver Spring MD 20905

DEZENHALL, ERIC B., management consultant, writer; b. Camden, NJ, 1962; married; 2 children. Grad., Dartmouth Coll., 1984. Damage control cons.; founder, CEO Denzenhall Resources, 1987—. Lectr. in field; guest commentator various TV and radio networks including CNN, Fox, CNBC and NPR. Author: Nail 'em, Confronting High-Profile Attacks on Celebrities and Business, 1999, (novels) Money Wanders, 2002, Jackie Disaster, 2003, Shakedown Beach, 2004, Turnpike Flameout, 2005. Bd. dirs. Nat. Ovarian Cancer Coalition. Office: Dezenhall Resources 1130 Connecticut Ave NW Ste 600 Washington DC 20036 Office Phone: 202-296-0263. E-mail: contactDC@dezenahll.com.

DEZHNYUK, SERGEY FEDOROVICH, business executive, minister; b. Rokitne, Ukraine, Jan. 5, 1976; s. Fedir Ivanovich Dezhnyuk and Raisa Nikolaevna Koloteva; m. Yelena Maksimovna Zherebylo, Sept. 27, 1997; children: Olesya Westlie, Maksim Fred. MDiv, Rivne Spiritual Sem., Ukraine, 1997; MA, Okla. Bapt. U., Shawnee. Ordained min. SHBC, 2003; cert. family counselor Okla., 2002. V.p. Ind. Am. Ctr. of Polit. Monitoring, Oklahoma City, 2005—; exec. dir. Traveling Treasures Expo, Inc., Oklahoma City, 2006—. Min. edn. First Slavic Bapt. Ch. of Tulsa, 1998—2001; pastor First Slavic Bapt. Ch., Oklahoma City, 2001—05; religious news editor Piligrim, Pensacola, Fla., 2000—04; columnist Max Internat., Tulsa, 2002—05; chair Coun. of Ethic Chs., Oklahoma City, 2003—05. Independent. Episcopalian. Home: 5012 Brookdale Dr Oklahoma City OK 73135 Home Phone: 405-672-8814. Personal E-mail: dezhnyuk@gmail.com.

DHALL, ROHIT, neurologist; b. Jalandhar, Punjab, India, Sept. 4, 1977; arrived in U.S., 2001; s. Harish Chander and Usha Rani Dhall; life ptnr. Suzanne Jay Roseman. MB BChir, All India Inst. Med. Scis., New Delhi, 2001; MS in Epidemiology, U. Tex., Houston, 2001. Resident physician dept. psychiatry All India Inst. Med. Scis., Delhi, 2001; grad. rsch. asst. Mickey Leland Nat. Urban Air Toxics Rsch. Ctr., Houston, 2001—03; resident physician PGY1 dept. internal medicine U. Tex., Houston, 2003—04; resident physician dept. neurology U. Ala., Birmingham, 2004—. Recipient Nat. Talent Search scholarship, Nat. Coun. for Edn., Rsch. and Tng., India, 1993—2000. Mem.: Am. Assn. Neuromuscular and Electrodiagnostic Medicine (jr. mem. 2006), Am. Acad. Neurology (jr. mem. 2004). Hindu. Avocation: reading. Office: U Ala 1530 3rd Ave S Birmingham AL 35294 Home Phone: 205-261-1324; Office Phone: 205-975-0447.

DHAM, VINOD K., Indo-US venture capitalist company executive; b. Pune, 1950; arrived in US, 1975; BEE, Delhi Coll. Engring., 1971; MEE in Solid State, U. Cinn., 1977. With Delhi for Continental Devices; mem. memory design group Nat. Cash Register, Dayton, Ohio, 1977; with Intel Corp., 1979—95; COO, exec. v.p. Nexgen, Inc. (acquired by Advanced Micro Devices, Inc.), 1995—96; group v.p., oversaw the launch of the K6 (world's fastest windows processor) Advanced Micro Devices, Inc., 1996—97; chmn., pres., CEO Silicon Spice, Inc. (acquired by Broadcom Corp.), Mountain View, Calif., 1997—2000; v.p., gen. mgr., carrier access bus. unit Broadcom Corp., 2000—02; co-founder, mng. dir. NewPath Ventures LLC, Santa Clara, Calif., 2002—. Advisor HelloSoft, Inc.; bd. dir. Satyam, Sasken, InSilica, Nevis Networks, Inc., Telsima, Montalvo; served on US President's Adv. Comm. on Asian Americans and Pacific Islanders, 2000. Co-author technical papers. Bd. dir. TIE-a not; trustee Am. Indian Found. Named one of Top 25 Executives in the Computer Industry in Am., 1993, Top 100 Most Influential Asian Americans of the Decade, 1999. Achievements include co-inventor of flash memory; being best known as the Father of the Pentium Processor; patents in field. Avocation: carpentry. Office: NewPath Ventures LLC 3945 Freedom Cir Ste 1050 Santa Clara CA 95054 Address: NewPath Ventures LLC 26 Cunningham Rd Bangalore 560 052 India Office Phone: 408-919-9900. Business E-Mail: vin@newpathventures.com.

DHARA, VENKATA RAMANA, physician, educator; b. Gudivada, India, Nov. 14, 1953; came to U.S., 1985; s. Venkateswarlu and Sarojini Devi D.; m. Rosaline James Dodda, Feb. 16, 1979; children: Rahul, Vishal. MBBS, Armed Forces Med. Coll., 1976; MPH, U. Medicine Dentistry N.J., 1987; DSc, U. Mass., 2000. Diplomate Am. Bd. Preventive Medicine. Intern Sion Hosp., Bombay, 1976—77; med. dir. People's Clinic, Hyderabad, India, 1979—85; resident, fellow occupl. and environ. medicine Robert Wood Johnson Med. Sch., Piscataway, NJ, 1985—89; cons. Envirotech Cons., New Delhi, 1990—92; med. officer Agy. Toxic Substances Disease Registry, Atlanta, 1992—96; dir. occupl. medicine Choice Care, Atlanta, 1997—2000; adj. clin. assoc. prof. Morehouse Sch. Medicine, Atlanta, 1998—, adj. clin. prof., 2006—; med. dir. Emory Eastside Med. Ctr., Snellville, Ga., 2000—03; adj. clin. assoc. prof. Rollins Sch. Pub. Health Emory U., Atlanta, 2000—. Cons. World Environment Ctr., NYC, 1992—96, Internat. Labor Office, Geneva, 1992—; mem. Internat. Med. Commn. Bhopal, Toronto, Canada, 1994—; cons. U.S. Dept. Energy, 2001—05; med. cons. U.S. Dept. Labor, 2006—. Contbr. articles to profl. jours. Active Forum Protection Environment, Hyderabad, 1982-85. Recipient Disting. Svc. award Meridian Med. Group, 1997; grantee Nat. Inst. Environ. Health Scis., 1998-2000. Mem. Am. Coll. Occpl. Environ. Medicine. Avocations: writing, reading, snorkeling, yoga. Personal E-mail: rdhara@pol.net. Business E-Mail: vdhara@emory.edu.

DHARAN, HARI, mechanical engineer, educator; PhD, U. Calif., Berkeley. Chief scientist Ford Aerospace & Comm. Corp., Palo Alto, Calif., 1978—80; mgr. dept. Comm. Satellite Orgn., Palo Alto, 1980—82; assoc. prof. U. Calif., Berkeley, 1982—89, prof., 1990—. Fellow: ASME (chair, materials divsn. 1986—87). Office: University of California Department of Mechanical Engineering Berkeley CA 94720-1740 Office Phone: 510-642-4933. Office Fax: 510-643-5599. E-mail: dharan@me.berkeley.edu.

DHAWAN, ATAM PRAKASH, engineering educator, dean; b. Moradabad, India, Mar. 30, 1956; came to U.S., 1985; s. Chandar Bhan Dhawan and Shanti Devi Kapoor; m. Nilam Dhawan, Mar. 5, 1982; children: Anirudh, Akshay. B of Engring., U. Roorkee, India, 1977, M of Engring., 1979; PhD, U. Man., Winnipeg, Can., 1985. Asst. prof. elec. engring. U. Houston, 1985-88; from asst. prof. elec. and computer engring. to assoc. prof. U. Cin., 1988-95, prof. elec. engring., computer engring. and computer sci., 1995-96, dir. Ctr. Intelligence Vision Sys., 1994-96; prof./chmn. elec. engring. U. Tex., Arlington, 1996-97; adj. prof. radiol. scis. U. Tex. S.W., Dallas, 1996-98; prof. bioengring. U. Toledo, 1998-2000, asst. dean grad. studies/coll. engring., 1998-99, assoc. dean rsch. and grad. studies/coll. engring., 1998-2000; prof., chmn. elec. and computer engring. N.J. Inst. Tech., Newark, 2000—, prof. biomed. engring., 2001—. Adj. assoc. prof. radiology U. Cin., 1990-95; mem. sci. adv. com. Life Spec Inc., Houston, 1997-99; mem. nat. adv. com. Rsch. Resource for Pharmacokinetic Studies, U. Wash., Seattle, 1999-2001; mem. external adv. com. Ohio Aerospace Inst., Cleve., 2000-01; dir. N.J. Ctr. for Multimedia Rsch., 2000-02; dir. NSF-NJ Inst. Tech. Industry Univ. Coop. Rsch. Ctr. Next Generation Video, 2000-02, N.J. Ctr. for Wireless Networking and Internet Security, 2002-06. Author: (textbook) Medical Image Analysis, 2003; editor Internat. Jour. Computing Info. and Tech., 1997—, Internat. Jour. Pattern Recognition, 2006—; assoc. editor Internat. Jour. Pattern Recognition, 1999—; contbr. articles to profl. jours. Recipient NIH F.I.R.S.T. award Nat. Cancer Inst., 1988-93, Martin N. Epstein award Student Paper Competition at Symposium of Computer Applications in Med. Care, 1984; Can. Commonwealth fellow U. Man., 1982-85. Fellow IEEE (assoc. editor Transactions on Biomed. Engring. 1996-2001, 04—, asst. editor Transactions on Rehab. Engring. 1994-2001, workshop chair 1996-97, Engring. in Medicine and Biology Early Career Achievement award 1995), IEEE Engring. in Medicine and Biology (chmn. emerging techs. com. 1998-2000, chair workshop on Intelligent Med. Image Analysis: Principles to Recent Advances, Cancun, Mex. 2003, San Francisco 2004, internat. program com. Shanghai 2005, conf. chair 28th internat. conf. 2006, tech. advisor 29th internat. conf., 2007), World Congress on Med. Physics and Biomed. Engring. (chmn. New Frontier in Med. Physics and Biomed. Engring. Track 1999-2000), Eta Kappa Nu Avocations: swimming, music, reading. Office: Chair ECE Dept NJ Inst Tech University Heights Newark NJ 07102 Business E-Mail: dhawan@adm.njit.edu.

DHAWAN, VIKAS, plastic surgeon; s. Satpal and Sudershan Dhawan; 1 child, Kalinda. MD, Moscow Med. Stomatological Inst., 1994, PhD, 1997. Rsch. fellow in plastic surgery U. Louisville, 1997—99; clin. fellow in hand and microsurgery Christine M. Kleinert Inst., U. Louisville, 1999—2000; cons. plastic surgeon European Med. Ctr., Am. Med. Ctr., Moscow, 2000—01; clin. fellow in brachial plexus surgery Ogori Daiichi Gen. Hosp., U. Yamaguchi, Japan, 2001—02; clin. instr. Ctrl. Inst. Stomatology, Moscow, 2003—; vis. fellow Plastic Surgery Ctr., Buffalo, 2004—. Contbr. articles to profl. jours. Mem.: Japanese Soc. for Surgery of the Hand, Am. Soc. for Surgery of the Hand (assoc.), Assn. Plastic Surgeons India (life), Indian Soc. for Surgery of the Hand (life). Office: Plastic Surgery Ctr 405 E Mich Ave 4 Au Gres MI 48703 Mailing: 719 Farnum Rd Lititz PA 17543 Home Phone: 7-095-5717766. E-mail: dr_vikasdhawan@hotmail.com.

D'HEURLE, FRANÇOIS MAX, research scientist, engineering educator; b. Paris, Nov. 23, 1925; came to U.S., 1946; s. Albert Emile and Odette (Valentini) d'H.; m. Adma Jeha, May 6, 1950; children: Amal, David, Alain. BSc Arts et Metiers, U. Paris, 1946; MS, Mich. Tech. U., 1948; PhD, Ill. Inst. Tech., 1958; D honoris causa, Royal Inst. Tech., Stockholm, 1995. Rsch. asst. U. Chgo., 1948-55; scientist IBM, Yorktown Heights, NY, 1958—. Prof. Royal Inst. Tech., Stockholm, 1995. Contbr. numerous articles to profl. jours.; holder 10 patents. Recipient award Am. Inst. Physics, 1991, Theory to Practice Prize Minerals, Metals and Materials Soc., 1998. Fellow IEEE (Cledo-Brunetti award 1989); Am. Vacuum Soc. (Gaede-Langmuir award 1990); mem. Minerals, Metals and Materials Soc., Materials Rsch. Soc. Home: Spring Valley Rd Ossining NY 10562 Office: IBM Rsch PO Box 218 Yorktown Heights NY 10598-0218 Home Phone: 914-941-2216; Office Phone: 914-945-1701. Business E-Mail: dheurle@optonline.net.

DHIB-JALBUT, SUHAYL S., physician; b. Khiam, Lebanon, Oct. 2, 1954; came to U.S., 1980; s. Samih and Nahia (Gaith) Dhib-J.; m. Mary Maral Mouradian, June 29, 1982; 1 child, Marla. MD, Am. U. Beirut, 1980. Diplomate Am. Bd. Psychiatry and Neurology. Resident in medicine Am. U. Beirut Hosp. and Med. Sch., 1980-81; resident in neurology Am. U. Beirut Hosp. and Med. Sch. & U. Cin. Hosp., 1981-84; fellow neuroimmunology NIH, Bethesda, Md., 1985-90, sr. staff fellow, 1989-90; asst. prof. neurology U. Md., Balt., 1990-94, assoc. prof., 1994-99, prof., 1999—2003; prof., chmn. dept. neurology U. Med. Dentistry N.J., Robert Wood Johnson Med. Sch., New Brunswick, NJ, 2003—. Guest rschr. NIH, Bethesda, 1990—; prin. investigator awards from NIH and Dept. Vets. Affairs, 1991—. Assoc. editor Jour. Neuroimmunology, 2003—; contbr. articles to profl. jours., chpts. to books. Recipient Career Devel. award Dept. Vets. Affairs, Washington, 1992—, Merit Rev. award, 1992—; NIH Ctr. grantee, Bethesda, 1992—; NIH Mid-Career Investigator awardee 1999-2006. Mem. Am. Acad. Neurology, Am. Neurol. Assn., Am. Assn. Immunologists, Internat. Soc. Neuroimmunology. Achievements include research interest in the cause and treatment of Multiple Sclerosis. Office: U Medicine Dentistry NJ-Robert Wood Johnson Med Sch 97 Paterson St Rm 205 New Brunswick NJ 08901 Office Phone: 732-235-7732.

DHILLON, JANET L., lawyer, air transportation executive; Grad., Occidental Coll., 1984, UCLA, 1991. With Skadden, Arps, Slate, Meagher & Flom LLP, Washington; mng. dir. legal dept. U.S. Airways Group, Inc., Tempe, Ariz., 2004—05, dep. gen. council, 2005—06, sr. v.p., gen. counsel, 2006—. Recipient Order of Coif. Office: US Airways Group Inc 111 W Rio Salado Pkwy Tempe AZ 85281*

DHILLON, UTTAM, federal agency administrator; BA, Calif. State U.; MA, U. Calif. San Diego; JD, U. Calif. Berkeley, 1987. Asst. U.S. atty. (ctrl. dist.) Calif. US Dept. Justice; counsel to vice chmn. Com. Govt. and Oversight U.S. Ho. of Reps., sr. investigative counsel; dir. Rep. party com. US Ho. of Reps.; dep. staff dir. Select Com. Homeland Security U.S. Ho. of Reps., majority chief counsel; atty. Milbank, Tweed, Hadley & McCloy, LLP; assoc. dep. atty. gen. US Dept. Justice, 2003—06; dir. counternarcotics enforcement US Dept. Homeland Security, 2006—. Office: US Dept Homeland Security Washington DC 20528 Office Phone: 202-305-1712.

DHINDSA, HARINDER SINGH, emergency physician, educator; BS, U. Md., Princess Anne, 1985; MD, U. Md., Balt., 1989; MPH, George Washington U., Washington, 1994; MBA, Va. Commonwealth U., Richmond, 2007. Faculty Georgetown U. Med. Ctr. and Med. Sch., Washington, 1993—98, Va. Commonwealth U., Med. Coll. Va., Richmond, 1996—. Med. dir. Va. LifeEvac Air Med. Svc., Richmond, 2001—. Recipient Partners in Caring award, Va. Commonwealth U., Chaplain Svcs. Fellow: Am. Acad: Emergency Medicine, Am. Coll. Emergency Physicians; mem.: Air Med. Physicians Assn. (edn. com. mem. 2005—07, cert. med. transport exec. 2004). Office: Va Commonwealth Univ-MCV 1201 E Marshall St PO Box 980401 Richmond VA 23298-0401 Home Phone: 804-559-0535; Office Phone: 804-828-7738. Business E-Mail: hdhindsa@vcu.edu.

DHIR, ANIR, surgeon; BS in Elec. Engring., U. Tex., Austin, 1985—90; MD, Baylor Coll. Medicine, Houston, 1990—94. Lic. dr. Ky., 1999. Mohs surgeon Dermatology Assocs. Ky., Lexington, 1999—. Del. Ky. Med. Assn., 2004—06. Fellow: Am. Coll. Mohs Micrographic Surgery & Cutaneous Oncology; mem.: Alpha Omega Alpha. Office: Dermatology Assocs Ky PSC 250 Fountain Ct Lexington KY 40502

DHIR, VIJAY K., mechanical engineering educator; b. Giddarbaha, Panjab, India, Apr. 14, 1943; arrived in US, 1969; s. Harnand Lal and Parsinni Devi (Sofat) D.; m. Komal Lata Khanna, Aug. 31, 1973; children: Vinita, Vashita. BScME, Punjab Engring. Coll., India, 1965; MTechME, Indian Inst. Tech., 1969; PhD in Mech. Engring., U. Ky., 1972. Asst. devel. engr. Jyoti Pumps, Ltd., Baroda, India, 1968-69; postgrad. engr. Engring. Rsch. Ctr. Tata Engring. & Locomotive Co., Poona, India, 1969; rsch. asst. U. Ky., Lexington, 1969-72, rsch. assoc., 1972-74; asst. prof. chem., nuclear & thermal engring. dept. UCLA, 1974-78, assoc. prof., 1978-82, prof. mech., aerospace & nuclear engring. dept., 1982—, vice chmn. mech., aerospace & nuclear engring. dept., 1988-91, chmn. dept., 1994-2000, assoc. dean Henry Samueli Sch. Engring. and Applied Sci., 2001—02, interim dean, 2002—03, dean, 2003—. Cons. Nuclear Regulatory Commn., Seabulk Corp., Ft. Lauderdale, Fla., Argonne (Ill.) Nat. Lab., Pickard, Lowe & Garrick, Inc., Irvine, Calif., Rockwell Internat., Canoga Park, Calif., GE Corp., San Jose, Calif., Battelle N.W. Lab., Richland, Wash., Phys. Rsch., Inc., Torrance, Calif., Nat. Bur. Stds., Gaithersburg, Md., Los Alamos (N.Mex.) Nat. Lab., Sci. Applications Inc., El Segundo, Calif., Brookhaven Nat. Lab., Upton, N.Y.; chmn. numerous conf. sessions. Contbr. over 130 articles to profl. jours., over 130 papers to procs./conf. & symposia records; assoc. editor Applied Mechs. Rev., 1985-88, Jour. Heat Transfer, Transactions ASME, 1993-96, editor, 2000—; assoc. editor ASME Symposium Vol., 1978; referee numerous jours. Recipient Max Jakob award, ASME/AIChE, 2004. Fellow: AIChE (Donald Q. Kern award 1999), ASME (sr. tech. editor Jour. Heat Transfer 2000—05, Heat Transfer Meml. Award Sci. Category 1992), Am. Nuclear Soc.; mem.: NAE. Office: Sch of Engring & Applied Sci Univ Calif 7400 Boelter Hall Los Angeles CA 90095 Business E-Mail: vdhir@seas.ucla.edu.

DHONDT, STEVEN THOMAS, development officer; b. Xenia, Ohio, Aug. 4, 1944; s. Maurice Bernard and Madeline (Pierson) D.; m. Elizabeth Ann Emrick, June 11, 1966 (div. June 1972); 1 child, Jennifer Elizabeth; m. Patty Ruth Bayley, Jan. 9, 1982. BA, Adrian Coll., 1966; MA, Utah State U., 1967; Phd, Bowling Green State U., 1968, SUNY, Buffalo, 1971. Instr. English SUNY, Buffalo, 1968-74, assoc. dean of faculty, 1969-74; assoc. acad. dean Salem State Coll., Salem, Mass., 1974-77; dir. pub. Am.-Scandinavian Found., NYC, 1977-79; prin. Dhondt Enterprises, NYC, 1978-81; mgr. corp. comm. Merck & Co., Inc., Rahway, NJ, 1981-83; sr. v.p., asst. dir. creative resources Shearson Lehman Bros. Inc., NYC, 1983-93; sr. cons. Nagdeman & Co., Inc., NYC, 1993-95; ind. mktg. cons., 1994-96; univ. dir. corp. and found. rels. LI U., Brookville, NY, 1996-99; dir. corp. and found. rels. NYU, NYC, 1999—2002; dir. instl. giving Meml. Sloan-Kettering Cancer Ctr., 2002—05; pvt. practice mktg. cons. NYC, 2005—; dir. corp. and found. rels. Poly. U., 2007—. Trustee N.J. Coun. on Econ. Edn., Trenton, 1981-83, Borough of Manhattan Community Coll. Fund, Inc., N.Y.C., Poets House, N.Y.C., Ctr. Philanthropy and Fundraising, NYU; cons. Bayley, Leighton & Ryan, Inc., N.Y.C., 1988—. Author: First Reading, 1972, London Bridge, 1998, Yellow Monkey, 1999; mng. editor Coll. English Assn., Buffalo, 1972-74. Democrat. Methodist. Avocations: tennis, snorkeling, travel. Home: 175 W 93rd St Apt 14C New York NY 10025-9340

DHUE, STEPHANIE, television producer, reporter; BA in Comm., George Mason U. Prodr. The Insiders with Jack Anderson, Fin. News Network; prodr. CNBC, Ft. Lee, N.J.; sr. prodr., reporter Nightly Bus. Report, Washington. Office: NBR 1325 G St NW Ste 1005 Washington DC 20005-3126 Office Phone: 202-682-9029.

DHURANDHAR, NIKHIL V., biomedical researcher, educator; MS in Nutrition and Foods, ND State Univ., Fargo, 1988; PhD in Biochemistry, Univ. Bombay, India, 1992. Assoc. dir., Clinical Nutrition Clinic Univ. Wis. Dept. Medicine; assoc. prof., infection and obesity Pennington Biomedical Rsch. Ctr., La. State Univ., 2005—. Contbr. articles to profl. jours. Mem.: Obesity Soc. Achievements include discovery of the first human virus to be associated with human obesity, AD-36 (adenovirus 36), the obesity virus. Invented the term infectobesity. Office: Pennington Biomedical Rsch Ctr La State Univ 6400 Perkins Rd Baton Rouge LA 70808 Office Phone: 225-763-2741. Office Fax: 225-763-3030.*

DI, FRANCINE, music educator, writer; b. Houston, Tex., Jan. 7, 1981; d. Zong Cheng and Xiao Fan Di. BA in English, Rice U., Houston, Tex., 2003, MusB in Piano Performance, 2003; MusM, U. Fla., Gainesville, 2005. Telemarketer Artsmarketing Services, Inc., Houston, 1999; libr. asst. Brown Fine Arts Libr., Rice U., Houston, 2000—01; sec., translator Vanguard Acad., Houston, 2000—03; grad. tchg. asst. U. Fla. Sch. of Music, Gainesville, 2003—05; piano tchr. Peggy's Sch. of Music, Gainesville, Fla., 2005—; content prodn. Gleim Publications, Inc., Gainesville, 2005—. Co.-curator, writer Diverseworks, Houston, 2002. Musician: (musical) Hello, Hamlet; actor: (musical) A Funny Thing Happened on the Way to the Forum; musician: (charity) Artemis Rice; singer: (performance competition) Chinese International New Singing Talent Championship (Second Pl., 2002), (band performances) Rice Jazz Band. Recipient President's Honor Roll, Rice U., 2002, Commended scholar, Nat. Merit scholarship, 1999, Smith Coll. Book award, Smith Coll. and the H.S. for Performing and Visual Arts, 1999, Most Outstanding Sr. Girl, Houston Ind. Sch. Dist., 1999; scholar Miss Chinatown Houston, Chinese Am. Citizens Alliance, 1998; Mary Gibbs Jones scholarship, Houston Endowment, 1999, James Swearingen scholarship, H.S. for the Performing and Visual Arts, 1999, Radio Shack Tandy scholarship, Radio Shack/Tandy Inc., 1999. Mem.: Nat. Piano Guild. Home Phone: 713-828-4256.

DI, XU, education educator; arrived in U.S., 1985; d. Xingshi Zheng and Zhengyuen Xu. BA in English and Tchg., Beijing Normal U., 1982; EdM in Ednl. Found. and English, Wake Forest U., 1987; EdD in Curriculum and Instrn., Harvard U., 1992. Tchg. asst. history dept. Wake Forest U.,

Winston-Salem, NC, 1986—87; fellow Harvard U. Sch. Edn., Cambridge, Mass., 1988—91; asst. prof. secondary edn. U. N.D., Grand Forks, 1991—93; asst. prof. U. W. Fla., Pensacola, 1993—96, assoc. prof., 1996—99, prof. edn. found., 2000—. Vis. prof. Peking U., Beijing, 1997; exchg. prof. dept. edn. Nat. Kaohsiung Normal U., Taiwan, 1998; vis. scholar, rsch. assoc. Harvard U., 1999—2000; tchr. edn. cons. World bank, Ministry Edn., Maseru, Lesotho, 2001; instl. tech. cons. World Bank, Ministry Edn. of Rep. Azerbaijan, Baku, 2001; spkr. in field. Contbg. author: A Comparison of the Educational Ideas and Practices of John Dewey and Mao Zedong in China, 1998; contbr. chapters to books. Mem.: Nat. Women's Assn., Philosophy Soc. Edn., Am. Ednl. Rsch. Assn. Avocations: travel, ballroom dancing, gardening. Office: Univ West Fla Divsn Tchr Edn 11000 University Pkwy Pensacola FL 32514

DIAKOS, STEPHEN SAMUEL, billing and insurance specialist; b. Naples, Fla., June 4, 1979; s. Peter and Sylvia Diakos. BS in Computer Engring., U. Ctrl. Fla., Orlando, 2002. Cert. sys. engr. Microsoft, 2004. Computer technician Pelican Wire Co., Inc., Naples, 1999—2002; billing and ins. specialist Dr. Dennis C. Close, DDS, Tallahassee, 2002—. Mem.: Am. Mensa. Home Phone: 850-514-0144. Personal E-mail: stephendiakos@yahoo.com.

DIAKUNCHAK, IHOR S., retired mechanical engineer; arrived in US, 1994; s. Georgij and Katherine Diakunchak; m. Christina M. Barahura, Sept. 7, 1967; children: Yuriy W., Ksenia M. Evans. BSME, U. Man., Winnipeg, Can., 1957; MME, McGill U., Montreal, Que., Can., 1960. Cert. profl. engr. Analytical engr. Pratt & Whitney Can., Longueuil, Que., Canada, 1960—63, sr. engr., 1967—73, staff engr., 1973—78; aerodynamic engr. Orenda Engines, Ltd., Malton, Ont., Canada, 1963—67; aero-thermo design mgr. Westinghouse Can., Hamilton, Ont., Canada, 1978—90, GT devel. mgr., 1990—93; adv. engr. Westinghouse Power Generation, Orlando, Fla., 1993—98, Siemens Power Generation, Orlando, 1998—2003, cons., 2005—. Mem. adv. com. propulsion Nat. Rsch. Coun., Ottawa, Ont., Canada, 1979—85. Contbr. articles to profl. jours. Mem.: Profl. Engrs. Ont., Assn. Profl. Engrs. Ont. (mem. nurbomachinery and electric power com. 1995—, cert., Project of the Yr. award 1986). Achievements include patents in field.

DIAL, ELLEN CONEDERA, lawyer; b. Chgo., July 19, 1946; AB in English magna cum laude, Cornell U., 1968, JD magna cum laude, 1977. Bar: Washington 1979. Law clk. to Hon. Charles Horowitz Supreme Ct. Washington, 1977—79; ptnr. Perkins Coie LLP, Seattle. Named one of Washington's Super Lawyers, Washington Law & Politics, 2003—06, Seattle's Top Lawyers, Seattle Mag., 2003. Fellow: Am. Bar Found.; mem.: King County Bar Assn. (co-chair awards com. 2004), Washington State Bar Assn. (chair ethics com. 2003, pres.-elect 2006, pres. 2007, chair legis. com 1996—98, chair character and fitness com. 1994—95, com. on code of profl. responsibility, chair emeritus exec. com. real property probate adn trust sect. 1994—95, Award of Merit 2004). Office: Perkins Coie LLP Ste 4800 1201 Third Ave Seattle WA 98101-3099 Office Phone: 206-359-8438. Office Fax: 206-359-9000. E-mail: edial@perkinscoie.com.

DIAMA, BENJAMIN, retired secondary school educator, artist, composer, writer; b. Hilo, Hawaii, Sept. 23, 1933; s. Agapito and Catalina (Buscas) D. BFA, Sch. Art Inst. Chgo., 1956. Cert. tchr., Hawaii. Tchr. art, basketball coach Waimea (Kauai, Hawaii) High Sch., 1963-67; tchr. music and art Campbell High Sch., Honolulu, 1967-68; tchr. math. and art Waipahu High Sch., Honolulu, 1968-69; tchr. art and music Palisades Elem. Sch., Honolulu, 1969-70; tchr. typing, history, art and music Honokaa (Hawaii) High Sch., 1970-73; tchr. music Kealakehe Sch., Kailua, 1973-74; ret., 1974. Spkr. Big Island Sci. Conf. State of Hawaii Govt., U. Hawaii, Hilo, 2003. Author, writer, composer: Hawaii, 1983; author: Poems of Faith, 1983-88, School One vs. School Two On The Same School Campus, 1983, The Calendar-Clock Theory of the Universe with Faith-Above and Beyond, 1984-90, Phonetic Sound-Musical Theory, 1990; contbg. author: Benjamin Diama-The Calendar Clock Theory of the Universe, 1991, 92, (poetry) Celebration of Poets, 1998, Poets Elite, Internat. Soc. of Poets, 2000, Labours of Love, Song of Honour, 2005; prodr., composer (Cassette) Hawaii I Love You, 1986; inventor universal clock, double floater boat, Gardener's Water Box, Full Court Half Court 6 vs. 6, 3 Offense-3 Defense Basketball Game. Recipient Achievement award Waimea Dept. Edn., 1964-67, Purchase award State Found. Arts on Culture and the Arts, 1984, State Found. Arts and Culture Acquisition Painting Art award State of Hawaii Govt. Art Collection, Lifetime Achievement award Internat. Biog. Ctr., 2005. Mem. NEA, Hawaii Tchrs. Assn., Hawaii Edn. Assn., AAAS, Nat. Geog. Soc., Smithsonian Assocs., ASCAP, N.Y. Acad. Scis., Nat. Libr. Poetry (assoc.), Internat. Soc. Poets, Am. Geophysical Union. Mem. Salvation Army. Achievements include design of slip on-pull a step lace walking aid foot or shoe slipper supporter. Avocations: singing, writing, basketball. Home: PO Box 2997 Kailua Kona HI 96745-2997 Home Phone: 808-329-9789.

DIAMANDIS, PETER H., foundation administrator, entrepreneur; b. Bronx, NY, May 20, 1961; Undergraduate and graduate degree in Aerospace Engring., MIT; MD, Harvard Med. Sch. Founder, CEO Intenat. MicroSpace, Inc. (acquired by CTA Inc.), 1989—93; v.p., commercial space CTA Inc.; founder, pres., chmn., CEO X PRIZE Found., Inc., (originally in Rockville, Md., but now in St. Louis), 1995—; pres., COO Angel Technologies Corp.; CEO BlastOff! Corp. Founder SpaceFair, 1983, chair, 83, 85, 87; co-founder, trustee Internat. Space U., Strasbourg, France, 1987—, co-chair, bus. & mgmt. dept., 1992—94, also served as mng. dir., CEO; co-founder, bd. dir. Space Adventures, Ltd., 1998—; co-founder Zero Gravity Corp. (ZERO-G); co-founder, past chmn. Starport.com (acquired by Space.com in 1990); founder, dir. Constellation Communications, Inc (sold to E-Systems then to Orbital Sciences), 1991; formed Rocket Racing League, 2005; bd. trustee Foresight Inst. Founded Students for the Exploration and Development of Space (SEDS), 1980; co-founder, chmn. Space Generation Found., 1985—. Named one of Top 25 Stars of Space, Nat. Space Soc., 1994; recipient MIT William L. Stewart, Jr. award, 1984, Kresge award, MIT, Space Industrialization Fellowship award, 1986, Aviation Week and Space Technology Laurel, 1988, Pioneer award, Space Frontier Found., 1993, K.E. Tsiolkovsky award, 1995, World Technology award, World Tech. Counsel, 2002, WIRED Rave award for Sci., 2006, Robert & Virginia Heinlein prize for Advances in Space Commercialization, 2006, Lindbergh award, Lindbergh Found., 2006. X PRIZE Foundation developed the X PRIZE in May, 1996. This prize is a $10,000,000 prize to jumpstart the space tourism industry through competition among the most talented entrepreneurs and rocket experts in the world. In 2004, the X PRIZE was officially re-named the ANSARI X PRIZE. Office: X Prize Found Inc 722-A Spirit of St Louis Blvd Chesterfield MO 63005 Address: X Prize Found inc Sonnenschein Laura L Carley One Metropolitan Sq Ste 3000 Saint Louis MO 63102*

DIAMANDOPOULOS, PETER, philosophy professor; b. Irakleion, Crete, Greece, Sept. 1, 1928; came to U.S., 1948, naturalized, 1964; s. Theodore George and Rita (Mouzenides) D.; m. Maria Stanton, 1980; children: Theodoros, Cybele, Ariadne, Patricia. Diploma with honors, Athens Coll., 1947; AB cum laude, Harvard U., 1951, MA, 1956, PhD, 1957; LHD (hon.), Am. Internat. Coll., 1988. Instr. philosophy Bates Coll., 1958; instr., then asst. prof. philosophy U. Md., 1958-62; mem. faculty Brandeis U., 1962-77, prof. philosophy, 1964-77, dean faculty, 1965-71, chmn. dept. philosophy and history of ideas, 1972-76, faculty mem. bd. trustees, 1974-77; pres. Calif. State U.-Sonoma, Rohnert Park, 1977-83, pres. emeritus, 1983—; univ. trustees' prof. Calif. State U., San Francisco, 1983-85; pres., trustee Adelphi U., Garden City, NY, 1985—97; prof. philosophy and humanities Boston U., 1998—2008. Dir. internat. studies Adlai Stevenson Inst., Chgo., 1969-74; cons. history of Sci. Smithsonian Inst., 1959-62; bd. dirs. Atlantic Bank of NY; lectr. to profl., learned socs., acad. instns. Contbr. articles to profl. jours. Trustee Adelphi Acad., Athens Coll., 1987—; chmn., bd. advisers US Command and Gen. Staff Coll., 1987. Recipient Cum Laude Soc. award Am. Internat. Coll., 1988,; named Outstanding Tchr. Confucius Inst. Am., 1983; Teschemacher fellow in classics and philosophy Harvard U., 1954-57; sr. fellow Adlai Stevenson Inst. for Internat. Studies, 1969-74. Mem. AAAS, Am. Philol. Assn., Am. Philos. Assn., MIND Assn. (Oxford, Eng.), Aristotelian Soc., Hellenic Soc., Assn. Am. Colls., Soc. for Promotion Hellenic Studies (London), Coun. for Greek Am. Affairs (dir. 1986—), Assn. Governing Bds. Univs. and Colls., NY Acad. Scis., Nat. Assn. Scholars (bd. Advisors), The Links, Union League Club, Harvard Club of Boston, Harvard Club of NYC. Avocations: minoan archaeology, art criticism, theater. Office: Boston Univ 704 Commonwealth Ave Ste 104 Boston MA 02215 Home: 525 E 72nd St Apt 45H New York NY 10021-3174 Office Phone: 617-358-0611.

DIAMANDUROS, TERRY DAVIS, psychology professor, director; d. James B. and Betty C. Davis; m. Andrew William Diamanduros, July 28, 1985; children: William James, Elizabeth Aspasia. AS, U. SC, Lancaster, 1980; BS, Clemson U., SC, 1982; MA, NYU, NYC, 1991, PhD, 2004. Cert. sch. psychologist NY, 2000. Group psychotherapist spl. needs clinic NY Presbyn. Med. Ctr., NYC, 1999—2003, neurodevelopmental examiner, 1999—2004; asst. prof. Ga. So. U., Statesboro, 2004—, program dir. sch. psychology program, 2006—. Cons. adv. bd. assessments for cert. of educators Ga. Profl. Stds. Commn. and Nat. Evaluations Sys., Atlanta; mem. of the faculty senate Ga. So. U., Statesboro, Ga., 2006—. Viola Bernard Rsch. grantee, NY State Psychiat. Inst., Columbia Presbyn. Med. Ctr., 1995. Mem.: NASP, APA, Ga. Ednl. Rsch. Assn., Ga. Assn. Sch. Psychologists. Office: Ga Southern U 237 Forest Dr Box 8131 Statesboro GA 30460 Home Phone: 912-489-1853; Office Phone: 912-871-1548. Office Fax: 912-486-7104. Business E-Mail: tdiamanduros@georgiasouthern.edu.

DIAMANT, ANITA, writer; b. NYC, June 27, 1951; d. Maurice and Helene Diamant; m. James R. Ball, June 11, 1982; 1 child, Emilia. AB, Washington U., St. Louis, 1973; MA, SUNY, Binghamton, 1975. Sr. staff writer Boston Mag., 1986-88; columnist Boston Globe mag., 1988-95; freelance writer, 1988—; columnist Jewishfamily.com., Boston, 1998-99; commentator WBUR-FM, Boston, 1994-96; contbg. editor Parenting Mag., 1994-95. Author: The New Jewish Wedding, 1985, Living a Jewish Life, 1991, The New Jewish Baby Book, 1994, Bible Baby Names, 1996, Choosing a Jewish Life: A Handbook for People Converting to Judaism and Their Family and Friends, 1997, The Red Tent, 1997, Saying Kaddish: How to Mourn as a Jew, 1998, How to be a Jewish Parent, 2000, Good Harbor, 2001, Pitching My Tent, 2003, The Last Days of Dogtown, 2005; editor: Equal Times, 1977—78; contbr. to profl. publs. and mags. Founder, pres. Mayyim Hayyim Living Waters and Cmty. Mikveh and Edn. Ctr., 2000—. Recipient Book of Yr. award Boston Author's Club, 1998, Significant Jewish Book of Yr. award UAHC Reform Judaism Mag., 1999, Booksense Book of Yr. award, 2001. Jewish. E-mail: anitaweb@aol.com.

DIAMANTIS, JENNIFER, lawyer; d. George and Rhea Diamantis; m. David E. Tawes, Oct. 23, 1999; 1 child, Alexander Charles Tawes. BA, U. Fla., Gainesville, 1996; JD, U. Mich. Law Sch., Ann Arbor, 1999. Atty. Schnader Harrison Segal & Lewis LLP, Phila., 1999—. Named Pro Bono Atty. of Yr., Ctr. Gay and Lesbian Civil Rights Phila., 2005. Mem.: Phila. Bar Assn., Pa. Bar Assn. Office: Schnader Harrison Segal and Lewis LLP Ste 3600 1600 Market St Philadelphia PA 19103 Office Phone: 215-751-2000.

DIAMOND, BERNARD ROBIN, lawyer; b. Bronx, NY, July 3, 1944; m. Elizabeth Heimbuch, Oct. 20, 1976; children: Jessica, Carey, Erin. BA, Rutgers U., 1966; JD, Bklyn. Law Sch., 1972. Bar: N.Y. 1973, U.S. Dist. Ct. (so. and ea. dists.) N.Y. 1973, U.S. Ct. Appeals (2d cir.) 1974. Gen. counsel The Trump Orgn., NYC, 1995—. Mem. Assn. of the Bar of the City of N.Y. Office: Trump Orgn 725 5th Ave Fl 26 New York NY 10022-2520

DIAMOND, BRIAN, lawyer; b. Jan. 17, 1956; BA, SUNY, Stony Brook, 1978; JD, Bklyn. Law Sch., 1982. Bar: NY 1983. Ptnr., real estate practice Stroock & Stroock & Lavan LLP, NYC, 1991—, mem., operating exec. com. Editor-in-chief Bklyn. Law Rev. Mem.: Pension Real Estate Assn., Comml. Mortgage Securities Assn., NY State Bar Assn. Office: Stroock & Stroock & Lavan LLP 180 Maiden Ln New York NY 10038-4982 Office Phone: 212-806-5569. Office Fax: 212-806-6006. Business E-Mail: bdiamond@stroock.com.

DIAMOND, CASEY See DAMJANOVICH, CHASLAV

DIAMOND, DAVID HOWARD, lawyer; b. NYC, June 24, 1945; s. Philip and Betty (Resnikoff) D.; m. Barbara R. Jacobs, Sep. 6, 1969; children: John, Andrew, Jill. BA, SUNY, Binghamton, 1967; JD, Georgetown U., DC, 1970. Bar: Va. 1970, D.C. 1971, N.J. 1972, N.Y. 1973, U.S. Supreme Ct. 1982, U.S. Dist. Ct. Asst. gen. counsel Nat. Treas. Employees Union, Washington, 1970-71; trial atty. Nat. Labor Relations Bd., Newark, 1971-73; assoc. Putney, Twombly, Hall & Hirson, NYC, 1973-76; ptnr. Guggenheimer & Untermeyer, NYC, 1976-86, Summit, Rovins & Feldesman, NYC, 1986-89, Patterson, Belknap, Webb & Tyler, NYC, 1989-91, Proskauer, Rose LLP, NYC, 1991—. Contbg. editor: Developing Labor Law, 1975-82, The Fair Labor Standards Act, BNA, 2000. Pres., dir. Birchwood Civic Assn., Jericho, N.Y., 1985-95; trustee Jericho Libr. Bd., 1994—, pres. 2004—. Mem. ABA (sect. labor and employment law, com. fed. labor standards), N.Y. State Bar Assn. (com. on individual and employee rights). Avocations: biking, tennis, whitewater rafting. Home: 18 Briar Ln Jericho NY 11753-2212 Office: Proskauer Rose LLP 1585 Broadway Fl 27 New York NY 10036-8299 Office Phone: 212-969-3775. Business E-Mail: ddiamond@proskauer.com.

DIAMOND, DIANA LOUISE, editor, journalist; b. Floral Park, NY, Feb. 4, 1937; d. Louis Bartholomew and Helen Stephanie (Strzelecki) Chmielewski; m. Horace Williams Diamond, Jr., June 29, 1958 (div. 1975); children: Bruce Williams, Scott Kenneth, Kent Christopher, Mark Patrick. BA in English, U. Mich., Ann Arbor, 1958. Reporter Lerner Newspapers, Highland Park, 1970-72, mng. editor, 1972-78, suburban coord., 1974-78; part-time corr. NY Times, 1975-78; prof. journalism fellow Stanford U., 1978-79, sr. writer, editor, spl. asst. to pres., 1983-88, exec. asst. to v.p. and dean Sch. of Medicine, 1988-89; writer, editl. bd. San Jose Mercury News, Calif., 1979—81; editor, sect., spl. projects editor Sunday Opinion, 1981; editor-in-chief Calif. Lawyer, 1981—83; spl. asst. to pres. Stanford U. Hosp., 1990-93, mgr. publs., 1993-94; pres. Diamond Comm. and Design, Palo Alto, Calif., 1994—2005; columnist Palo Alto Daily News, 2001—; exec. editor Daily News Newspaper, 2005—06; columnist Palo Alto Weekly, Calif., 2006—; editor Valley Life Quar., 2006—. Bd. dirs. Midpeninsula Citizens for Fair Housing, pres., 1983—86; bd. dirs. New Forum, 1985—90, Pacific Art League, 1989—94, Palo Alto Centennial '94, 1990—94, Palo Alto chpt. ARC, 2000—; founder, chmn. bd. dirs. RotaCare Internat., 1992—; bd. dirs. Palo Alto Red Cross, Peninsula Press Club, 2007—. Recipient 3d pl., Ill. Editor of the Yr. contest, 1974, Nat. Blue Ribbon Newspaper award, 1976—78, 1st pl. for Best Feature Story, Ill. Press Assn., 1976, Suburban Newspapers Assn., 1977, 2d pl. for Best Column, Nat. Newspaper Assn., 1977, Maggie award, Western Pubs. Assn., Silver Six award, Internat. Bus. Comm., 1996, Crystal award, Communicators Group, 1998, 1st pl. for Best Column, Pa. Press Assn., 2002, 2005, 2006. Mem.: Rotary (pres. Palo Alto chpt. 1999—2000). Home: 2512 Cowper St Palo Alto CA 94301-4218 Office: Silicon Valley San Jose Bus Jour 96 N Third St San Jose CA 95112 Personal E-mail: diana@dianadiamond.com.

DIAMOND, EUGENE CHRISTOPHER, lawyer, health facility administrator; b. Oceanside, Calif., Oct. 19, 1952; s. Eugene Francis and Rosemary (Wright) D.; m. Mary Theresa O'Donnell, Jan. 20, 1984; children: Eugene John, Kevin Seamus, Hannah Rosemary, Seamus Michael, Maeve Therese. BA, U. Notre Dame, 1974; MHA, St. Louis U., 1978, JD, 1979. Bar: Ill. 1979. Staff atty. AUL Legal Def. Fund, Chgo., 1979-80; adminstrv. asst. Holy Cross Hosp., Chgo., 1980-81, asst. adminstr., 1981-82, v.p., 1982-83, counsel to adminstr., 1980—, exec. v.p., 1983-91; exec. v.p., COO, St. Margaret Mercy Healthcare Ctrs., Hammond, Ind., 1991-93, pres., CEO, 1993—2004, regional COO, 2001—04, regional CEO, 2004—. Cons. Birthright of Chgo., 1979—, mem. benefit com., 1981—; bd. dirs. Hammond C. of C., 1993, North West Ind. Forum. Mem.: Chgo. Bar Assn. Roman Catholic. Office: St Margaret Mercy Healthcare Ctrs 5454 Hohman Ave Hammond IN 46320-1999 Home Phone: 708-361-5866; Office Phone: 219-933-2178. Business E-Mail: gene.diamond@ssfhs.org.

DIAMOND, GUSTAVE, federal judge; b. Burgettstown, Pa., Jan. 29, 1928; s. George and Margaret (Solinsky) D.; m. Emma L. Scarton, Dec. 28, 1974; 1 dau., Margaret Ann; 1 stepdau., Joanne Yoney. AB, Duke U., 1951; JD, Duquesne U., 1956. Bar: Pa. bar 1958, U.S. Ct. Appeals bar 1962. Law clk. to judge U.S. Dist. Ct., Pitts., 1955-61; 1st asst. U.S. atty. Western Dist. Pa., 1961-62, U.S. atty., 1963-69; partner firm Cooper, Schwartz, Diamond & Reich, Pitts., 1969-75; formerly individual practice law Washington, Pa.; former solicitor Washington County, Pa.; judge U.S. Dist. Ct. Western Dist. Pa.; chief judge U.S. Dist. Ct. (we. dist.) Pa., 1992-94, sr. judge, 1994—. Chmn. Jud. Conf. Com. on Defender Svcs. Mem. ABA, Fed. Bar Assn., Pa. Bar Assn., Allegheny County Bar Assn., Washington County Bar Assn. Office: US Dist Court Ste 8270 US Courthouse 700 Grant St Pittsburgh PA 15219 Office Phone: 412-208-7390.

DIAMOND, HEIDI JANICE, marketing professional; b. Washington, Dec. 8, 1958; d. Lawrence David and Vicky (Katz) D. BS, U. Md., 1979; postgrad., Boston U., 1976-78; MBA, Am. U., 1989. Account exec. Abramson Assocs., Washington, 1980-82; account exec., media dir. KMD Media, Arlington, Va., 1982-83; mktg. mgr. Hardee's Food Systems, Annapolis, Md., 1983-84, sr. mktg. mgr., 1984-86; dir. field advt. planning and devel. Erols, Inc., Springfield, Va., 1986, dir. advt., planning and devel., 1986-88, dir. mktg., 1988—; sr. v.p. mktg., creative and bus. develop. The Food Network, 1998—2000, sr. v.p. strategic network planning/develop., 2001; exec. v.p. AMC Networks and Rainbow Media, 2001—02; exec. v.p., pres. TV Martha Stewart Living Omnimedia, NYC, 2002—05, cons., 2005—. Named Washington Woman of Yr. Washington Woman Mag., 1986, 87; recipient Viddies award, 1989. Mem. Women in Advt. and Mktg. (bd. dirs. 1983-86). Democrat. Jewish. Office: Martha Stewart Living Omnimedia Inc 11 W 42nd St New York NY 10036

DIAMOND, JARED MASON, biologist, writer; b. Boston, Sept. 10, 1937; m. Marie Cohen; children: Max, Joshua. BA in biochemical sciences, Harvard U., 1958; PhD in physiology, Cambridge U., Eng., 1961. Jr. fellow, Soc. Fellows Harvard U., 1962—65; assoc. in biophysics Harvard Med. Sch., 1965—66; assoc. prof. physiology UCLA Med. Sch., 1966—68, prof., 1968—; now prof. geography UCLA. Rsch. assoc. ornithology Am. Mus. Natural History, 1973—, LA County Mus. Natural History, 1985—; contbg. editor Discover mag., 1984—; bd. dirs. World Wildlife Fund, 1993—. Author: The Avifauna of the Eastern Highlands of New Guinea, 1972, The Third Chimpanzee: The Evolution and Future of the Human Animal, 1992 (Rhone-Poulenc Science Book Prize, 1992), Why is Sex Fun? The Evolution of Human Sexuality, 1997, Guns, Germs, and Steel: The Fates of Human Societies, 1997 (Phi Beta Kappa Sci. Book Prize, 1997, Pulitzer Prize, 1998, Cosmos Prize, Japan, 1998, Rhone-Poulenc Science Book Prize, 1998), Collapse: How Societies Choose to Fail or Succeed, 2004; co-author: Birds of New Guinea, 1986, The Birds of Northern Melanesia: Speciation, Ecology, and Biogeography, 2001; co-editor (with M.L. Cody) Ecology and Evolution of Communities, 1975; co-editor: (with T.J. Case) Community Ecology, 1986. Recipient Disting. Achievement Award, Am. Gastroent. Assn., 1975, Bowditch Prize, Am. Physiol. Soc., 1976, Burr Medal, Nat. Geog. Soc., 1979, Carr Medal, 1989, Coues Award, Am. Ornithologists' Union, 1998, Nat. Medal Science, 1999, Tyler Prize for Environ. Achievement, 2001; MacArthur Found. Fellowship, 1985. Fellow: Am. Acad. Arts and Scis.; mem.: NAS, Inst. Medicine, Am. Philos. Soc. Office: UCLA Med Ctr Dept of Physiology 10833 Le Conte Ave Los Angeles CA 90095-3075

DIAMOND, JASON BRETT, facial plastic surgeon, otolaryngologist; b. NJ, Dec. 21, 1970; MD, U. Rochester Sch. Medicine, 1997. Diplomate Am. Bd. Facial Plastic and Reconstructive Surgery, Am. Bd. Otolaryngology. Pvt. practice, Beverly Hills. Featured facelift, rhinoplasty and eyelid expert on Dr. 90210, 2005—, guest appearances Discovery Health Channel, Entertainment Tonight, NBC, and E! Channel, ABC, CBS, Access Hollywood, others, featured in Harpers Bazaar, Life & Style, People. Fellow: ACS. Office: 9201 Sunset Blvd Los Angeles CA 90069 Office Fax: 310-859-9815. Business E-Mail: drdiamond@jasonbdiamond.com.

DIAMOND, JOSEF, lawyer; b. LA, Mar. 6, 1907; s. Michael and Ruby (Shifrin) D.; m. Violett Diamond, Apr. 2, 1933 (dec. 1979); children: Joel, Diane Foreman; m. Ann Dulien, Jan. 12, 1981 (dec. 1984); m. Muriel Bach, 1986. BBA, U. Wash., 1929, JD, 1931. Bar: Wash. 1931, U.S. Dist. Ct. (we. dist.) Wash. 1932, U.S. Ct. Appeals (9th cir.) 1934, U.S. Supreme Ct. 1944. Assoc. Caldwell & Lycette, Seattle, 1931-35; ptnr. Caldwell, Lycette & Diamond, Seattle, 1935-45, Lycette, Diamond & Sylvester, Seattle, 1945-80, Diamond & Sylvester, Seattle, 1980-82, of counsel, 1982-88, Short, Cressman & Burgess, Seattle, 1988—2002; pvt. practice Seattle, 2002—. Chmn. bd. Diamond Parking Inc., Seattle, 1945-70; cons. various businesses. Bd. dirs. Am. Heart Assn., 1960; chmn. Wash. Heart Assn., 1962. Col. JAGC, U.S. Army, WWII. Decorated Legion of Merit. Mem. Wash. Bar Assn., Assn. Trial Lawyers Wash., Seattle Bar Assn., Mil. Engrs. Soc., Wash. Athletic Club, Bellevue Athletic Club, Harbor Club. Office: Diamond Bldg Ste 200 3161 Elliott Ave Seattle WA 98121 Office Phone: 206-284-3100.

DIAMOND, LARRY, political scientist; BA, Stanford U., 1974, MA, 1978, PhD, 1980. Prof. Vanderbilt U., 1980—85; sr. fellow Hoover Inst., Stanford, Calif., 1985—; prof. Stanford U., 1985—. Coord., Democracy Prog. Inst. for Internat. Studies, Stanford U.; co-dir. Forum Dem. Studies, Nat Endowment for Democracy; Fulbright vis. lectr. Bayero U., Kano, Nigeria, 1982—83; vis. scholar Academia Sinica, Taiwan, 1997—98; cons. US Agency for Internat. Devel., 2001—02; sr. advisor Coalition Provisional Authority, Iraq, 2004. Co-editor: Journal of Democracy, 1990—; author: Developing Democracy: Toward Consolidation, 1999, Promoting Democracy in the 1990s: Actors and Instruments, Issues and Imperatives, 1999, Class, Ethnicity and Democracy in Nigeria: The Failure of the First Republic, 1988, Squandered Victory: The American Occupation and Bungled Effort to Bring Democracy to Iraq, 2005; contbr. articles to profl jours. Office: Hoover Institution Room 1202 Hoover Tower Stanford CA 94305-6010 Business E-Mail: diamond@hoover.stanford.edu.

DIAMOND, M. JEROME, lawyer, retired state attorney general; b. Chgo., Mar. 16, 1942; s. Leo and Sonya (Pevsner) D.; m. Carol English Robinson; 8 children. AB, George Washington U., Washington, DC, 1963;

MA, U. Tenn., 1965, JD, 1968. Bar: Vt. 1968, US Supreme Ct. 1975. Law clk. US Dist. Judge Ernest Gibson, 1968-69; assoc. Kristensen, Cummings & Price, Brattleboro, Vt., 1969-70; state's atty. Windham County, Vt., 1970-74; atty. gen. State of Vt., 1975-81; atty., sr. ptnr. Diamond & Robinson, PC, Montpelier, Vt., 1981—. Trustee Brooks Meml. Libr., 1970-73, Vt. Law Sch., 2004—; chmn. Putney Zoning Bd. Adjustment, 1971-74; mem. Vt. Criminal Justice Tng. Council, 1974-81, Vt. Commn. Adminstrn. of Justice, 1975-81; mem. Vt. Adv. Group, US Civil Rights Commn.; gen. campaign chmn. United Way Washington County, 1986-87, 88-89; bd. dirs. Nat. Coun. on Aging, 1990-93, Vt. Bar Found., 1997—, Vt. State Employees Credit Union, 1997—, chmn. bd., 2004—; internat. commr. Anti-Defamation League, 1988-93; bd. trustees Vt. Law Sch., 2004-. Mem. Vt. State's Attys. Assn. (past pres.), Vt. Bar Assn., Vt. Bar Found. (bd. dirs. 1997—), Washington County Bar Assn., Nat. Assn. Atty. Gens. (v.p. 1978-79, pres. 1980), Ea. Regional Conf. Attys. Gen. (chmn. 1975-76), B'nai B'rith (internat. commr. anti-defamation league 1988-93, internat. bd. govs. 1990-92), Jewish Inst. for Nat. Security Affairs (bd. dirs. 1993—), Am. Judicature Soc. (bd. dirs., Vt. rep. 1994-00), Vt. State Employees Credit Union, 1997 (bd. dirs., v.p. bd. 2000-03, pres. bd. dirs. 2004-), Shriners, Masons, Montpelier Rotary Club (bd. dirs. 1998—, v.p. 2001-02, pres.-elect 2002-03, pres. 2003-04). Democrat. Jewish. Office: Diamond & Robinson PC PO Box 1460 Montpelier VT 05601 Office Phone: 802-223-6182. Business E-Mail: mjd@diamond-robinson.com.

DIAMOND, MARIAN CLEEVES, neuroscientist, educator; b. Glendale, Calif., Nov. 11, 1926; d. Montague and Rosa Marian (Wamphler) Cleeves; m. Richard M. Diamond, Dec. 20, 1950 (div.); m. Arnold B. Scheibel, Sept. 14, 1982; children: Catherine, Richard, Jeffrey, Ann. AB, U. Calif., Berkeley, 1948, MA, 1949, PhD, 1953. With Harvard U., Cambridge, 1952-54, Cornell U., Ithaca, NY, 1954-58, U. Calif., San Francisco, 1959—62, prof. anatomy Berkeley, 1962—. Asst. dean U. Calif., Berkeley, 1967-70, assoc. dean, 1970-73, dir. The Lawrence Hall of Sci., 1990-95, dir. emeritus, 1995—; vis. scholar Australian Nat. U., 1978, Fudan U., Shanghai, China, 1985, U. Nairobi, Kenya, 1988. Author (with J. Hopson): Magic Trees of the Mind, 1998; author: Enriching Heredity, 1989; co-author: The Human Brain Coloring, 1985; editor: Contraceptive Hormones Estrogen and Human Welfare, 1978; contbr. over 155 articles to profl. jours. V.p. County Women Dems., Ithaca, 1957; bd. dirs. Unitarian Ch., Berkeley, 1969. Recipient Calif. Gifted award, 1989, C.A.S.E. Calif. Prof. of Yr. award, Nat. Gold medalist, 1990, Woman of Yr. award Zonta Internat., 1991, U. medal La. U. Del Zulia, Maricaibo, Venezuela, 1992, Alumna of the Yr. award U. Calif., Berkeley, 1995; Calif. Acad. Scis. fellow, 1991, Calif. Soc. Biomedical Rsch. Dist. Svc. award, 1998, Alumnae Resources-Women of Achievement Vision and Excellence award, 1999, Benjamin Ide Wheeler award 1999, Achievement award Calif. Child Devel. Adminstrs. Assn., 2001; named Disting. Scholar America, Am. Assn. U. Women, 1997; named to Internat. Educators Hall of Fame, 1999. Fellow AAAS, AAUW (sr.; fellowship chair 1970-85); mem. Am. Assn. Anatomists, Soc. Neurosci., Philos. Soc. Washington, The Faculty Club (Berkeley, v.p. 1979-85, 90-95). Avocations: hiking, sports, painting. Home: 2583 Virginia St Berkeley CA 94709-1108 Office: U Calif Dept Integrative Biology 3060 Valley Life Sciences Bldg Berkeley CA 94720-3116 Office Phone: 510-642-4547. Business E-Mail: diamond@berkeley.edu.

DIAMOND, MATTHEW C., media and marketing company executive; b. 1969; With GE Co.; co-founder, chmn. & CEO Alloy, Inc., NYC, 1997—. Bd. dirs. Genesco Inc., Nashville. Active in Ad Coun., Office Nat. Drug Control Policy, Am. Prepared, Nat. Heart Found., Pub. Edn. Needs Civic Involvement in Learning (PENCIL). Office: Alloy Inc 11th Fl 151 W 26th St New York NY 10001 Office Phone: 212-244-4307. Office Fax: 212-244-4311.

DIAMOND, MIKE (MIKE D), recording artist; b. NYC, Nov. 20, 1966; m. Tamra Davis; 2 children. Founder, mem. The Beastie Boys, 1981—. Owner Grand Royal, Grand Royal mag., 1984—. Albums include Licensed to Ill, 1986, Paul's Boutique, 1989, Check Your Head, 1992, 94, Ill Communication, 1994, Some Old Bullshit, 1994, In Sound from Way Out, 1996, Def & Dumb, 1996, Hello Nasty, 1998, To the 5 Boroughs, 2004, The Mix Up, 2007, (extended play singles) Pollwog Stew, 1982, Cooky Puss, 1983, Rock Hard, 1984, Tour Shot, 1994, Sure Shot, 1994, Get It Together, 1994, Root Down, 1995, Aglio E Olio, 1995, (singles) Jimmy James, 1992, Gratitude, 1992, So What'cha Want, 1992, Sabotage, 1994, Hey Ladies, 1997, (video) Skills to Pay the Bills, 1992; contbg. rap artist Heart to Soul, 1988, Rap Rap Rap, 1996, Rap: Most Valuable Players, 1996; vocalist Rap's Biggest Hits, 1990; prodr. Rap Declares War, 1992, Cb4, 1993, Rebirth of Cool (vol. 3), 1995, Music for Our Mother Ocean, 1996. Office: care Capitol Records 1750 Vine St Hollywood CA 90028-5209*

DIAMOND, PAMELA M., science educator; d. Adolph Gilbert Holdren and Eloise Roberta Freshwater; children: Aaron Michael, Jeffery Asa. BA, Carnegie Mellon U., Pitts., 1967; MA, Tex. Women's U., Denton, 1986; PhD, U. Tex., Austin, 1992. Rsch. assoc. Hogg Found. for Mental Health, Austin, 1988—95; dir. program evaluation Tex. Tech. U. Health Sc. Ctr. Correctional Managed Care, Lubbock, 1995—99; asst. prof. criminal justice Sam Houston State U., Huntsville, Tex., 1999—2002; asst. prof. behavioral sciences and biostatistics U. Tex. Houston Sch. Pub. Health, 2002—. Statis. cons. Fed. Bur. Prisons, Washington, 2003—. Fellow, U. Tex., 1986—87; grantee, Centers for Disease Control, 2004—07, Hogg Found. for Mental Health, 2005—07; Evaluation Rsch. fellow, 1987—88. Mem.: APHA, APA. Avocations: reading, travel. Office: UT Houston School Public Health 7000 Fannin Suite 2614 Houston TX 77030 Home Phone: 713-541-5460; Office Phone: 713-500-9979. Business E-Mail: pamela.m.diamond@uth.tmc.edu.

DIAMOND, PAUL STEVEN, federal judge, lawyer, educator; b. Bklyn., Jan. 2, 1953; s. George and Anna (Jaeger) D.; m. Robin Nilon. BA magna cum laude, Columbia U., 1974; JD, U. Pa., 1977. Bar: Pa. 1977, U.S. Dist. Ct. (ea. dist.) Pa. 1979, U.S. Ct. Appeals (3d cir.) 1979, U.S. Supreme Ct. 1983. Asst. dist. atty. Phila. Dist. Atty. Office, 1977-83; law clk. Supreme Ct. Pa., Phila., 1980; assoc. Dilworth, Paxson, Kalish & Kauffman, Phila., 1983-85, ptnr., 1986-91, Obermayer, Rebmann, Maxwell & Hippel, Phila., 1992—2004; judge U.S. Dist. Ct. (ea. dist.) Pa, 2004—. Lectr. Temple U. Sch. Law, Phila., 1990—92; mem. civil procedural rules com. Supreme Ct. Pa., 1995—98, treas. Pa. lawyers fund for client security bd., 1999—, chmn. Pa. lawyers fund for client security bd., 2002—; mem. civil procedural rules com. fed. jud. nominating commn., 1993, 1995—2000; vice chmn., chmn. Amicus Curiae Briefs Com., 1995—99. Author: Federal Grand Jury Practice and Procedure, 1990, rev. 4d edit., 2001. Mem. ABA (criminal justice sect., Amicus Curiae briefs subcom. 1984-99, grand jury subcom. 1991-93), Am. Law Inst., Pa. Bar Assn., Phila. Bar Assn. Republican. Jewish. Office: US Courthouse 601 Market St Rm 2609 Philadelphia PA 19106-1797

DIAMOND, RICHARD, retired educator; b. NYC, June 23, 1936; s. Oscar and Frieda (Rosenfeld) D.; m. Donna Jean Berkshire Wilson, June 14, 1961 (div. June 1974); m. Betty Ruth Jane Foster, Nov. 17, 1975; children: Thomas, Laura, Rick, Jeff. BA, U. Calif., Berkeley, 1958. Cert. tchr., Calif. Tchr. Riverside Unified Schs., Calif., 1959-67, 73-99, coord. social studies, 1967-69, program dir. compensatory edn., 1969-72, attendance officer, 1972-73; project mgr. Biotech. Sch., 1999—2002. Creator curriculum programs Afro-Am. history and Chicano studies, 1968; developer law and youth HS course, 1978, track coach, 1975-88. Contbr. articles and photographs to profl. jours.; sports reporter North Coast Citizen, 2005—; free lance journalist. Co-creator h.s. vol. program, h.s. svc. learning coord., 1995-99; active Riverside County Hist. Commn., 1997-2003; Dem. Party worker, 1964-72; Rep. Party worker, 1992—98; historic commn. liaison Riverside County Archives Commn., 1998-2002; bd. dirs. Calif. Citrus Hist. State Park, 2000-02, sec., 2000-03; pres. Vail Ranch Restoration Assn., Inc., Temecula, Calif., 2000-02; budget com. Bay City, Oreg., 2005-06; mem. Pre-Disaster Mitigation Com., Bay City, Oreg., 2005. Named Social Studies Tchr. of Yr. Inland Empire Social Studies Assn., 1980, Tchr. of Yr. Arlington HS, Riverside, 1992; recipient Hon. Svc. award Dist. Coun. PTA, Riverside, 1993, Johnny Harris Youth Action award City of Riverside, 1998. Mem. NEA, Calif. Tchrs. Assn., Riverside County Tchrs. Assn., Calif. Retired Tchrs. Assn., Masons. Presbyterian. Avocations: gardening, travel, reading, gourmet cooking. Office Phone: 503-812-9585. Business E-Mail: diamond@where-eagles-soar.com.

DIAMOND, RICHARD MARTIN, nuclear chemist; b. LA, Jan. 7, 1924; divorced; 4 children. BS, UCLA, 1947; PhD in Nuclear Chemistry, U. Calif. Berkeley, 1951. Instr. chemistry Harvard U., 1951-54; asst. prof. Cornell U., 1954-58; mem. sr. staff Lawrence Berkeley Lab., U. Calif., 1958—, sr. scientist emeritus, 1995—. Mem. U.S. Physics del. to Russia, 1966, rev. com. physics divsn. Oak Ridge Lab., 1972-74, Dept. of Energy rev. com. Brookhaven (n, gamma) Facility and Isotope Separator, 1983, 8pi Gamma Spect. Com., Chalk River, Canada, 1983, adv. com. Ind. Cyclotron Facility, 1980-83, Tandem-Linac Facility Argonne Nat. Lab., 1983-86, Holifield Rsch. Facility, 1988-90, Holifield Radioactive Ion Beam Facility, 1994-97; chmn. Gordon Conf. on Nuclear Chemistry, 1965, Gordon Conf. on Ion Exch., 1969, rev. com. UNISOR, Oak Ridge Nat. Lab., 1974-75, subcom. high spin and nuclei far from stability Dept. Energy-NSF, 1983; vis. fellow Japan Soc. for Promotion of Sci., 1981; co-organizer Int. Conf. Nuclear Physics, 1980, workshop on nuclear str., 1986, workshop Nat. Gamma-Ray Facility, 1987. Guggenheim fellow, 1966-67, Fullbright fellow, 1977. Fellow AAAS, Am. Phys. Soc. (shared Tom W. Bonner award 1980); mem. Am. Chem. Soc. (award in nuclear chemistry 1993). Achievements include research in nuclear spectroscopy, coulomb excitation, high-spin nuclear structure. Home: The Berkshire 2235 Sacramento St Berkeley CA 94702 Home Phone: 510-524-9794; Office Phone: 510-486-5720. Business E-Mail: rmdiamond@lbl.gov.

DIAMOND, RICHARD S., lawyer; b. Newark, June 26, 1960; BA in Econs./Bus. Adminstrn., Rutgers U., 1981; JD, Seton Hall U., 1985. Bar: N.J. 1985, Fla. 1991, U.S. Dist. Ct. N.J. 1991; cert. matrimonial trial, Laywer by the N.J. Supreme Ct. cert. divorce mediator; ct. apptd. econ. mediator N.J. Supreme Ct. Law sec. to Hon. Burton J. Ironson State of N.J., Union County, NJ, 1985-86; assoc. Law Firm of Robert Diamond, Springfield, NJ; ptnr. Diamond Hodes & Diamond, Springfield, Diamond & Diamond P.A., Millburn, NJ. Spkr., guest lectr. TV and radio broadcasts. Contbr. articles to profl. jours. Mem.: N.J. Bar Assn. (lectr., spkr.), Essex County Bar (matrimonial practice), Union County Bar Assn. Office: Diamond & Diamond PA 225 Millburn Ave Ste 208 Millburn NJ 07041-1712 also: 1545 Rt 206 Bedminster NJ 07921 Office Phone: 973-379-9292. Fax: 973-379-9210.

DIAMOND, ROBERT MACH, higher education administrator; b. Schenectady, NY, Mar. 5, 1930; s. Henry Gordon and Ruth Ada (Mach) D.; m. Dolores Lou Jacobs, Apr. 14, 1957; children: Harli Fait, H. Gordon. AB, Union Coll., Schenectady, 1951; MA, NYU, 1953, PhD, 1962. Secondary sch. tchr. math., TV tchr., TV project dir. Schenectady Pub. Schs., 1956-59; assoc. prof. edn., instructional TV prodn. supr. San Jose State U., 1959-63; dir. instructional rsch., vis. prof. U. Miami, Coral Gables, Fla., 1963-66; dir. instructional resources ctr., prof. edn. SUNY, Fredonia, 1966-71; asst. vice chancellor instrnl. devel., dir., prof. edn. Syracuse (N.Y.) U. Ctr. for Instructional Devel., 1971-97, rsch. prof., dir. Inst. Change in Higher Edn., 1998-99; rsch. prof. Syracuse U., 1999—; pres. Nat. Acad. Academic Leadership, St. Petersburg, Fla., 1999—. Nat. adv. bd. Bur. of Handicapped, Office of Edn.; dir. Focus in Tchg. Project, Fund for Improvement of Postsecondary Edn., Washington; Fulbright sr. lectr., 1976; dir. Nat. Project on Instnl. Priorities and Faculty Rewards, Lilly Endowment and Pew Charitable Trusts, Indpls., Phila., 1989-95; cons. NIH, NSF, Office of Edn., various colls., univs. and assns.; scholar Ctr. Advancement Scholarship Engring. Edn. Nat. Acad. Engrs., 2005—; lectr. in field. Author: A Guide to Instrnl. Television, 1964, Designing and Improving Courses and Curricula in Higher Edn., 1989, Serving on Promotion Tenure, and Faculty Review Coms., A Faculty Guide, 1994, 2002, Preparing for Tenure Promotion and Ann. Rev., 1995, 2004; co-author: Instrnl. Development for Individualized Learning in Higher Edn., 1975, Nat. Study of Tchg. Assts., 1987, A Nat. Study of Rsch. Univs. on the Perceived Balance Between Rsch. and Undergraduate Tchr., 1991, 93, 95; editor: Field Guide to Academic Leadership, 2002; co-editor: Recognizing Faculty Work: Reward Systems for the Year 2000, 1993, Changing Priorties at Rsch. Univs., 1997, Designing & Assessing Courses and Curriculum, 1998, Aligining Faculty Records With Inst. Mission, 1999, The Disciplies Speak, Vol. I, 1995, Vol. II, 2000; mem. editl bd. Jour. Higher Ednl. Rsch. and Devel., South African Jour. Edn.; contbr. chpts. to books and articles to profl. jours. Bd. dir. Temple Adath, 1990-94, Jewish Family Svcs., Syracuse, 1975-83. With U.S. Army, 1973-75. Recipient Outstanding Practice in Instructional Devel. award Assn. Ednl. Comm. and Tech. Mem. Am. Assn. Higher Edn. (cited innovations in the improvement of higher edn. 1994). E-mail: r.m.diamond@verizon.net.

DIAMOND, ROBERT MICHAEL, lawyer; b. NYC, Dec. 23, 1948; s. Meyer and Libby (Leventhal) Diamond; m. Amy B. Pullman, July 5, 1987; children: Michael Israel, Philip Brenner, Julia Rose. Student, Vassar Coll., 1969—70; AB, Colgate U., 1970; JD, Columbia U., 1974. Bar: DC 1974, Va. 1976, Md. 1982. Assoc. Fried, Frank, Harris, Shriver & Kampelman, Washington, 1974-75; from assoc. to ptnr. Reed Smith, LLP, Falls Church, Va., 1975—. *Robert Diamond practices real property law, with special emphasis on the planning, development, and financing of condominiums, mixed-use projects and planned unit developments, he prepares community association documents for developers and builders, reviews documents for lenders, ensures compliance with secondary mortgage market requirements, negotiates and litigates warranty and construction defect claims, and represents community associations. He has been active in the development of legislation concerning condominiums and planned communities since 1975. He is one of four drafters of the Uniform Condominium Act, and he also drafted portions of the Virginia and D.C. Condominium Acts. He also has authored a number of articles in the field.* Contbr. articles to profl. jours. and industry publs. Trustee Cmty. Assns. Inst., Alexandria, Va., sec., 1993, treas., 1994, pres.-elect, 1995, pres., 1996; liaison to joint editl. bd. Uniform Real Estate Acts, 1997—. Named Superlawyer, Va., 2006, Washington, DC, 2006; recipient Oustanding Leadership award, Cmty. Assns. Inst., 1989, Pres.'s award for outstanding leadership, 1989—90, others. Mem.: Coll. Cmty. Assn. Lawyers, Urban Land Inst. Avocations: scuba diving, classic automobiles. Office: Reed Smith LLP 3110 Fairview Park Dr Ste 1400 Falls Church VA 22042-4536 Home Phone: 703-790-0222; Office Phone: 703-641-4273. Business E-Mail: rdiamond@reedsmith.com.

DIAMOND, SEYMOUR, physician; b. Chgo., Apr. 15, 1925; s. Nathan Avruum and Rose (Roth) D.; m. Elaine June Flamm, June 20, 1948; children: Judi, Merle, Amy. Student, Loyola U., 1943-45; MB, Chgo. Med. Sch., 1948, MD, 1949. Intern White Cross Hosp., Columbus, Ohio, 1949-50; gen. practice medicine Chgo., 1950—; founder, dir. Diamond Headache Clinic, Ltd., Chgo., 1970—; dir. inpatient headache unit St. Joseph Hosp., Chgo.; prof. neurology Chgo. Med. Sch. at Rosalind Franklin U. Medicine and Sci., 1970-82, 85—, adj. prof. cellular and molecular pharmacology, 1985—, clin. prof. family medicine, 1999—; clin. prof. dept. family medicine U. Medicine and Dentistry N.J. Sch. Osteo. Medicine, Stratford, NJ, 1994-98; cons. mem. FDA Orphan Products Devel. Initial Rev. Group. Lectr. dept. cmty. and family medicine Loyola U. Stritch Sch. Medicine, 1972-78; lectr. Falconbridge lecture series Laurentian U., Sudbury, Ont., Can., 1987; disting. lectr. neurology U. Tenn., 1992; AMA cons. on drug evaluation, 1993; mem. sci. com. neurology Internat. Jour. Pain Therapy, 1993; mem. panel Nat. Ctr. on Addiction and Substance Abuse, Columbia U., N.Y.C., 2003. Author: A Pain Specialist's Approach to the Headache Patient, 1994; (with Bill and Cynthia Still) The Hormone Headache, 1995; Diagnosing and Managing Headaches, 1994, 4th edit., 2004; (with Donald J. Dalessio) The Practicing Physician's Approach to Headache, 5th edit., 1992, More Than Two Aspirin: Help for Your Headache Problem, 1976, (with Judi Diamond-Falk) Advice from the Diamond Headache Clinic, 1982, (with Mary Franklin Epstein) Coping with Your Headaches, 1982, 2d edit., 1987, (with Arnold P. Friedman MD) Headache in Contemporary Patient Management series, 1983; (with Amy Diamond Vye) Headache and Diet, 1990; (with Michael Maliszewski) Sexual Aspects of Headaches, 1992; (with Mary A. Franklin) Conquering Your Migraine, 2001; (with Amy Diamond) Headache and Your Child, 2001; (with Merle L. Diamond) Contemporary Diagnosis and Management of Headache and Migraine, 2d edit., 2000, (with Mary A. Franklin) Headache Through the Ages, 2005; contbg. author: Wolff's Headache and Other Head Pain, 6th edit., 1993, Handbook of Pain Management, 2d edit., 1994, Nonsteroidal Anti-Inflammatory Drugs, 2d edit., 1994, Current Review of Pain, 1994, New Advances in Headache Research, 1994, Conn's Current Therapy, 1998, Advanced Therapy of Headache, 1999, Diamond and Dalessio's Practicing Physician's Approach to Headache, 6th edit., 1999; editor: Migraine Headache Prevention and Management; editor-in-chief Headache Quar., 1990-02; editor-in-chief Headache and Pain, 2003-; mem. internat. editl. bd. Pediat. Drugs, 2001-; editl. cons. BIOSIS, 1986-90; contbr. numerous articles on headache and related fields to profl. jours. Bd. govs. Chgo. Med. Sch. at Rosalind Franklin U. Medicine & Sci. Recipient Disting. Alumni award Chgo. Med. Sch., 1977; Nat. Migraine Found. lectureship award, 1982, award Headache Consortium of New Eng., 1997, Cert. Appreciation, Chgo. Med. Soc., 1998, Presdl. award Alumni Assn. Chgo. Med. Sch., 2002; 1st recipient Migraine Trust lectureship, 1988; Brit. Migraine Trust 7th Internat. Migraine Symposium, London; Nat. Headache Found. Seymour Diamond fellow, 1993; Disting. lectr. in neurology U. Tenn., 1992. Fellow Royal Soc. Medicine; mem. AMA (Physicians Recognition awards 1970-73, 74, 77, 79, 82, 87, del. sect. clin. pharmacology and therapeutics 1987-89, mem. health policy agenda for Am. people, mem. cost effectiveness conf., del. reference com. "C" on edn., reference com. C, 1988), Am. Coun. on Sci. and Health (bd. sci. and policy advisors), Am. Assn. Study of Headache (exec. dir. 1971-85, pres. 1972-74, #1 regent mem. 1984, svc. award 1971-85, Lifetime Achievement award 1999), Nat. Headache Found. (pres. 1971-77, exec. dir. 1977-95, exec. chmn. 1995—, 1st recipient cert. of added qualification in headache mgmt. Nat. Bd. Cert. in Headache Mgmt. 2001), Assn. Applied Psychophysiology and Biofeedback (Presidl. Recognition award 2005), World Fedn. Neurology (exec. officer 1980-95, research group on migraine and headache), Ill. Acad. Gen. Practice (chmn. mental health com. 1966-70), Ill. Med. Soc., Chgo. Med. Soc., Assn. for Applied Psychophysiology and Biofeedback, Internat. Assn. Study of Pain, Am. Soc. Clin. Pharmacology and Therapeutics (chmn. headache sect. 1982-89, mem. com. coordination sci. sects. 1983-89), Postgrad. Med. Assn. (pres. 1981). Office: 467 W Deming Pl Ste 500 Chicago IL 60614-1726 Home Phone: 312-337-0360; Office Phone: 773-388-6390. Personal E-mail: MACF48@aol.com. Business E-Mail: clinic@diamondheadache.com. *I derive great satisfaction from helping a person who is totally disabled from pain to again lead a normal, functional life.*

DIAMOND, SHARI SEIDMAN, law and psychology professor; b. Chgo., Mar. 17, 1947; d. Leon Harry and Rita (Wolff) S.; m. Stewart Howard Diamond, Nov. 1, 1970; 1 child, Nicole. BA in Psychology, Sociology, U. Mich., 1968; MA in Psychology, Northwestern U., 1970, PhD in Social Psychology, 1972; JD with honors, U. Chgo., 1985. Bar: Ill. 1985. Rsch. assoc. Sch. Law U. Chgo., 1972-73; asst. prof. psychology and criminal justice U. Ill., Chgo., 1973-79, assoc. prof., 1979-90, prof., 1990-2000; assoc. Sidley & Austin, Chgo., 1985-87; sr. rsch. fellow ABF, Chgo., 1987—; lectr. U. Chgo. Law Sch., 1994-96; prof. law and psychology Northwestern U., 1999—, Stanton Clinton sr. rsch. prof., 2000-01, Howard J. Trienens prof. law, 2002—. Cons. govtl. and pub. interests groups including Rsch. Adv. Panel US Sentencing Commn., 1987-91; acad. visitor dept. law London Sch. Econs., 1981; hon. fellow Ctr. Urban Affairs Northwestern U., Evanston, Ill., 1973-73; hon. rsch. assoc. U. London, 1970; mem. NAS panel sentencing rsch., 1981-83, panel forensic DNA evidence, 1994-96; vis. prof. Harvard Law Sch., 2006; speaker, lectr. in field. Editor Law and Soc. Rev., 1988-91; past mem. editorial bd. Law and Soc. Rev., 1983-88, Law and Human Behavior, Crime and Justice Annual, Evaluation Rev.; reviewer NSF; contbr. articles to profl. jours. Chair Coll. Edn. Policy Com., 1979-80; dir. tng. grant NIMH Crime and Delinquency, 1979-80. Fellow Northwestern U., 1968-69, NIMH, 1969-71; grantee Spencer Found., 1972-74, disting. scholar, grantee, U. Ill., 1995-98, Law Enforcement Assistance Adminstrn., 1974-76, Ctr. for Crime and Delinquency NIMH, 1976-81, NSF, 1980-83, 90-92, 99—; B. Kenneth West U. scholar, 1995-98. Fellow APA (Award for Disting. Contbns. to Rsch. in Pub. Policy 1991), ABA, Am. Psychol. Soc.; mem. Am. Psychology-Law Soc. (pres. 1987-88), Law and Soc. Assn. (trustee 1979-82). Office: Northwestern U Law Sch 357 E Chicago Ave Chicago IL 60611 Business E-Mail: s-diamond@law.northwestern.edu.

DIAMOND, SIDNEY, chemist, educator; b. NYC, Nov. 10, 1929; s. Julius and Ethel D.; m. Harriet Urish, May 2, 1953; children: Florence, Julia. BS, Syracuse U., 1950; M.F., Duke U., 1951; PhD, Purdue U., 1963. Research engr. U.S. Bur. Public Rds. (now Fed. Hwy. Adminstrn.), Washington, 1953-61, research chemist, 1961-65; assoc. prof. engring. materials Purdue U., 1965-69, prof. Ind., 1969—2002, prof. emeritus Ind., 2002—; pres. Sidney Diamond and Assocs., Inc. Mem. Nat. Materials Adv. Bd. Com. on Status of Research in U.S. Cement and Concrete Industries; chmn. Internat. Symposium on Durability of Glass Fiber Reinforced Concrete, Chgo., 1985; mem. adv. com. NSF Ctr. for Advanced Cement-Based Materials, 1989—. Contbr. numerous articles on cement and concrete to profl. jours.; editor: Cement and Concrete Research. Served with U.S. Army, 1951-53. Fellow Am. Ceramic Soc. (past trustee, Copeland award), Am. Concrete Inst., Am. Concrete Inst. (anderson award 1993); mem. ASTM, Internat. Congress on Chemistry of Cement (pres. sect. 6 of 8th congress), Materials Rsch. Soc. Home: 819 Essex St West Lafayette IN 47906-1534 Office: Purdue U Sch Civil Enging West Lafayette IN 47907 Business E-Mail: diamond@ecn.purdue.edu.

DIAMOND, STANLEY JAY, lawyer; b. LA, Nov. 27, 1927; s. Philip Alfred and Florence (Fadem) D.; m. Lois Jane Broida, June 22, 1969; children: Caryn Elaine, Diana Beth. BA, UCLA, 1949; JD, U. So. Calif., 1952. Bar: Calif. 1953. Practiced law, LA, 1953—; dep. Office of Calif. Atty. Gen., LA, 1953; ptnr. Diamond & Tilem, LA, 1957-60, Diamond, Tilem & Colden, LA, 1960-79, Diamond & Wilson, LA, 1979—. Lectr. music and entertainment law UCLA; mem. nat. panel arbitrators Am. Arbitration Assn. Bd. dirs. LA Suicide Prevention Ctr., 1971-76. Served with 349th Engr. Constrn. Bn. AUS, 1945-47. Mem. ABA, Calif. Bar Assn., Los Angeles County Bar Assn., Beverly Hills Bar Assn., Am. Judicature Soc., Calif. Copyright Conf., Nat. Acad. Rec. Arts and Scis., Zeta Beta Tau, Nu Beta Epsilon. Office: 12304 Santa Monica Blvd Fl 3D Los Angeles CA 90025-2551 Office Phone: 310-820-7808. E-mail: standimond@aol.com.

DIAMOND, STUART, lawyer, educator, business executive, writer; b. Camden, NJ, June 20, 1948; s. Irving H. and Ruth (Safran) D. BA in English, Rutgers U., 1970; JD, Harvard U., 1990; MBA, U. Pa., 1992. Bar: N.J. 1990, N.Y. 1991. Mcpl., investigative, polit., energy, tech. and fin. reporter Home News, New Brunswick, NJ, 1969—73, Newsday, LI, NY, 1973—84, The N.Y. Times, NYC, 1984—88; assoc. Morgan Stanley, NYC, 1989, Sullivan & Cromwell, NYC, 1989; assoc. dir. Harvard negotiation project, exec. dir. Conflict Mgmt. Group Harvard U. Sch. Law, Cambridge, Mass., 1990—92; v.p. MerOil, 1990—92; CEO Global Strategy Group, L.I., L.A., Phila., NY, 1991—; prof. Wharton Sch. U. Pa., Phila., 1993—, adj. law prof., 1994—; pres., CEO First Manhattan Capital Group, 1996—2004; pres. The Andean Group, 1997—2002; chmn., CEO i-Luxury.com, 2000—01; chmn. Summus, Inc., 2001, First Phila. Capital Group, 2003—; CEO Four Star Aviation, 2005—. Lectr., TV commentator, 1978—, cons. U.N., 1991-97. Author: It's In Your Power, 1978, No-Cost, Low-Cost Energy Tips, 1980; documentary films: The Energy War, 1980, The Future is Now, 1981. Recipient Amos Tuck award nat. econ. reporting, 1978, 80, 82, Polk award nat. reporting, 1980, Pulitzer Prize, 1987, Tchg. award Wharton, 1997, 98, 2001, 02, 05. Mem. ABA. Business E-Mail: sd@gsg.bz.

DIAMOND, SUSAN ZEE, management consultant; b. Okla., Aug. 20, 1949; d. Louis Edward and Henrietta (Wood) Diamond; m. Allan T. Devitt, July 27, 1974. AB, U. Chgo., 1970; MBA, DePaul U., 1979. Dir. study guide prodn. Am. Sch., Chgo., 1972—75; supr. publs. Allied Van Lines, Broadview, Ill., 1975—78, sr. account svcs. rep., 1978—79; pres. Diamond Assocs. Ltd., Bensenville, Ill., 1978—. Author: Records Management: A Practical Guide, 3d edit., 1995, Seventeen Steps to Slimness: A Sherlockian Guide to Dieting, 2002; editor: The Serpentine Muse, 1996—, Serpentine Muse-ings, 2004, 2005; condr. seminars Am. Mgmt. Assn., —, Can. Mgmt. Ctr., —. Mem.: Inst. Mgmt. Accts., Baker St. Irregulars, Adventuresses of Sherlock Holmes.

DIAMONSTEIN-SPIELVOGEL, BARBARALEE, writer; b. NYC; d. Rubin Robert and Sally H. Simmons; m. Alan A. Diamonstein, July 22, 1956; m. Carl Spielvogel, Oct. 27, 1981. BA, BC, MA, Doctorate, NYU, 1963; DHL (hon.), Md. Inst. Coll. Art, 1990, Longwood U., 1995. Staff asst. The White House, Washington, 1963—66; 1st dir. Dept. Cultural Affairs City of NY, 1966—67; dir. of forums McCall Corp., 1967—69; editor spl. supplements, columnist Harper's Bazaar, 1969—71; spl. project dir., guest editor Art News, 1971—93. Columnist Ladies Home Jour., 1979-84; contbr. to Saturday Rev., Vogue, Ms., Partisan Rev., NY Times, Condé Nast Traveller, House and Garden, NY News, others; faculty Hunter Coll., CUNY, 1974-76, New Sch., 1976-84, Duke U. Inst. Policy Sci., 1978; arts cons. Sunday Morning CBS-TV, 1978-82; curator Buildings Reborn, Collaborations, Visions and Images, Remaking America, The Landmarks of NY I, II, III and IV, 1978—, others. Author: Open Secrets: 94 Women in Touch With Our Time, 1972, The World of Art, 1902-77, 75 Years of Art News, 1977, Buildings Reborn: New Uses, Old Places, 1978, Inside New York's Art World, 1979, Collaboration: Artists and Architects, 1981, Visions and Images: American Photographers on Photography, 1981, Interior Design: The New Freedom, 1982, Handmade in Am., 1983, Fashion: The Inside Story, 1985, American Architecture Now, 1985, Remaking America, 1986, The Landmarks of N.Y., 1988, 18 Wonders of the N.Y. World, 1992, The Landmarks of N.Y.: Vol. II, 1993, Inside the Art World: Conversations with Barbaralee Diamonstein, 1994, Skills, Values, Dreams, 1995, Singular Voices: Americans Who Make a Difference, 1997, The Landmarks of N. Y.: Vol. III, 1998, Barbaralee's Rules of the Road: 59 Simple Ways to Cope with a Complex World, 2001, The Landmarks of New York: An Illustrated Record of the City's Historic Buildings, 2005, The Landmarks of New York, 2006; editor: Our 200 Years: Tradition and Renewal, 1975, MOMA at 50, 1980; traveling exhibit to 72 countries, Landmarks of NY II, US Dept. State; TV interviewer, prodr. ABC-TV Arts, 1980—88, A and E Network, 1980—89; TV interviewer, prodr.: CBS-TV, 1978—97. Nat. juror Vietnam Vet. Meml. Edn. Ctr. Competition, 2004; juror High Line Competition, 2004; mem. Caramoor Ctr. for Music and Arts, 1981—92; chair Hist. Landmarks Preservation Ctr., 1995—; co-chair NGO Assn. Culture, Edn. and Comm., 2001—; chair Nat. Competition for Low Cost Housing, NYC, 2004; mem. US Commn. Fine Arts, 1996—2005, vice chmn., 2001—02; commr. NYC Landmarks Preservation Commn., 1972—87, NYC Arts Commn., 1991—94; bd. dir. NYC Bicentennial Commn., 1973—77; commr. NYC Cultural Commn., 1975—86; mem. NY State Travel and Tourism Bd.; bd. advisors Film Anthology Archives, 1969—; bd. dir. PEN Am. Ctr., 1980—96, Mcpl. Art Soc., 1973—83, Am. Coun. Arts, 1982—89, Bklyn. Acad. Music, 1969—74, NY Landmarks Conservancy, 1973—97, Fresh Air Fund, 1983—, Big Apple Circus, 1989—92, Corcoran Gallery Art, Washington, 1992—99, NY State Hist. Archive's Partnership Trust, 1994—, White House Endowment Fund, 1995—98, Friends of the High Line, 2001—; vice-chmn. NY Landmarks Conservancy, NYC, 1983—87; pres. coun. Rockefeller U., NYC, 1987—; bd. visitors Pub. Policy Inst. Duke U., Durham, NC, 1987—93; bd. mem. US Holocaust Meml. Mus., NYC, 1987—93, chair art pub. spaces com., 1987—96; commr. NY Landmarks Preservation Found., NYC, 1987—95; drawing com. Met. Mus. Art, NYC, 1990—, Whitney Mus. Am. Art, 1995—98; trustee Ctrl. Pk. Conservancy, 1993—95; bd. trustee NY Hist. Soc., 1993—95; bd. trustees Leadership Ctr. Mus. of Women, NYC, 1999—. Recipient Founder's Day award Pratt Inst., 1994, Outstanding Citizen award Citizen Ctr., 1996, Visionary in Arts award, Mus. Contemporary Crafts, 1996, Heritage Trails award, 1998, Spirit of the City award Women's City Club, 1998, Manhattan award, 1999, New Millenium Humanitarian award HELP, 1999, Gen. Milan R. Stefanik award Slovak Am. Cultural Ctr., 2002, Aging in Am. Humanitarian award, 2003, Gold medal of the Ministry of Fgn. Affairs of Slovakia, 2004, Humanitarian award Jewish Women's Found. N.Y., 2005. Mem.: Nat. Am. Inst. Architects (hon.). Home: 720 Park Ave New York NY 10021-4954

DIAN, JIANWEI, mathematician; PhD, U. La., Lafayette, 2000. Asst. prof. Chongqing Inst. Comm., China, 1992—96; engr. software design Hewlett-Packard Co., Richardson, Tex., 2000—. Grantee, Sun Microsystems, Inc., 1997—98, NSF, 1999. Mem.: Soc. Indsl. and Applied Math. Achievements include patents pending for heterogeneous parallel processing based on processor performance; first to discover theory and design corresponding algorithm for existence verification of singular solutions to complex and real nonlinear systems; propose a meaning based information theory. Office: Hewlett-Packard Co 3000 Waterview Pky Richardson TX 75080 Office Phone: 972-497-3057.

DIANA, JOHN NICHOLAS, physiologist; b. Lake Placid, NY, Dec. 19, 1930; s. Alphonse Walton and Dolores (Mirto) D.; m. Anita Louise Harris, May 8, 1966; children: Gina Sue, Lisa Ann, John Nicholas. BA, Norwich U., 1952; PhD, U. Louisville, 1965. Asst. prof. physiology Mich. State U. Med. Sch., 1966-68; assoc. prof., then prof. U. Iowa Med. Sch., 1969-78; prof. physiology, chmn. dept. La. State U. Med. Ctr., Shreveport, 1978-85; dir. cardiovasc. rsch. ctr. U. Ky., 1985-87, assoc. dean rsch. and basic sci., 1987-88, prof. emeritus, 1997—. Dir. T&H Rsch. Inst., 1988—; cons. Nat. Inst. Neurol. Diseases and Stroke, 1973-75, Nat. Heart, Lung and Blood Inst., 1974—, mem. cardiovasc. and renal study sect., 1980-85, mem. clin. scis. study sect., 1986-91, chmn. 1989-91; rsch. com. Iowa Heart Assn., 1974-77, bd. dirs., 1977-79; mem. cardiovasc. study sect. Am. Heart Assn., 1981-84. Author papers, abstracts in field. Served with AUS, 1952-54; Served with USAR, 1961-62. NIH postdoctoral fellow, 1965-67 Mem. Am. Fedn. Clin. Research, Am. Physiol. Soc. (editorial bd. jour. 1974-78), Microcirculation Soc. (pres. 1977-78, editorial bd. jour. 1979-85), Am. Heart Assn. (fellow council circulation), N.Y. Acad. Scis., La. Heart Assn. (dir. 1979-81, research com. 1978-82), Sigma Xi. Democrat. Achievements include patent for coronary vasodilator. Home: 7332 Saint Georges Way Bradenton FL 34201-2353 *Progress related to the health and welfare of any nation can only be accomplished by programs directed at the development of human thought and human thought processes. The ultimate fate of man will rest upon the success of all societies to stimulate human vital curiosity, talents. energies. basic scholarship and research to address those factors which will preserve man's natural cultural heritage and his ability to lead a free and independent existence.*

DIANA, JOSEPH A., retired foundation executive; b. New Castle, Pa., June 26, 1924; s. Joseph Anthony and Emma (Eardly) D.; m. Kathryn June Matthews, June 26, 1946; children: Mark Steven, Chris Joseph, Todd Francis, Paul Jeffrey. Student, Notre Dame U., 1942; BA, U. Mich., 1950, postgrad., 1950-51. Mem. adminstrv. staff U. Mich., 1950-56, sec. to faculty Med. Sch., 1956-69, asst. controller, 1969-70; v.p. fin. and mgmt. SUNY, Stony Brook, 1970-75; vice chancellor adminstrv. affairs, assoc. v.p. bus. affairs U. Ill., Champaign-Urbana, 1975-79; v.p., treas. emeritus John D. and Catherine T. MacArthur Found., Chgo.; pres. Dianaid Ltd., 1985-91. Interim pub. Harper's mag.; sec., treas. Harper's Mag. Found., 1980-82. Republican. Roman Catholic. Home: 2310 Saint Francis Dr Ann Arbor MI 48104-4807

DI ANGELO, CHRISTOPHER J., lawyer; b. Poughkeepsie, NY, Mar. 24, 1957; BA, Williams Coll., 1979; JD, Columbia Univ., 1984. Bar: N.Y. Staff N.Y. State Housing Fin. Agency; assoc. Dewey Ballantine LLP, NYC, 1984—92, ptnr. & chmn. structured fin. group, 1992—. Office: Dewey Ballantine LLP 1301 Ave of the Americas New York NY 10019-6092 Office Phone: 212-259-6718. Office Fax: 212-259-6333. Business E-Mail: cdiangelo@dbllp.com.

DIAS, FIONA P., retail executive; m. Floyd Dias. Grad., Harvard U., 1987; MBA, Stanford U. Sr. fin. analyst Merrill Lynch Capital Markets, Inc.; sr. asst. brand mgr. Fixodent and Fasteeth denture adhesives Proctor and Gamble Co., 1996; v.p., corp. develop. Pennzoil Quaker State Co., 1996—99; v.p., mktg. and develop. Frito-Lay Co., 1999—2000; chief mktg. officer Stick Networks, Inc., 2000; sr. v.p., mktg. Circuit City, 2000—05; pres. Circuit City Direct, 2003—; chief marketing officer Circuit City Stores, Inc., 2005—, exec. v.p., 2006—. Office: Circuit City 9950 Mayland Dr Richmond VA 23233-1464

DIAS, JERRY RAY, chemistry professor, researcher; s. Francis Frederic and Margurette Ruth Dias; m. Barbara Jean Turner, July 13, 1958; children: Rene Barbara, Harvey William, Jennifer Jean Birriel. BS in Chemistry with honors, San Jose State U., Calif., 1965; PhD, Ariz. State U., Tempe, 1970. EIT Mo., 1975. Fellow Stanford U., Calif., 1970—72; prof. chemistry U. Mo., Kansas City, 1972—; Fulbright lectr. U. Ljubljana, Slovenia, Serbia and Montenegro, 1980. Chem. cons. EPA, Kansas City, Kans.; lectr. in field. Author: Handbook of Polycyclic Hydrocarbons, 1987, Molecular Orbital Calculations Using Chemical Graph Theory, 1993; contbr. articles to profl. jours. Faculty Rsch. fellow, U. Kansas City, 1995—96, 2002—03. Fellow: Am. Inst. Chemists; mem.: Internat. Soc. for Polycyclic Aromatic Compounds, Am. Chem. Soc. Republican. Roman Catholic. Achievements include first to organize benzenoid hydrocarbons into a unified framework; research in synthesized bile acid related molecules having novel architectures. Office: Univ Mo 5100 Rockhill Rd Kansas City MO 64110-2499 Home Phone: 913-962-7548; Office Phone: 816-235-2284. Office Fax: 816-235-5502. Business E-Mail: diasj@umkc.edu.

DIAS GRIFFIN, ANNE, investment advisor; MBA, Harvard Bus. Sch.; grad. summa cum laude, Georgetown U. Analyst, Banking Dept. Goldman Sachs; investment analyst Fidelity Investment Ltd., London; analyst & portfolio mgr. Soro Fund Mgmt.; analyst Viking Global Investors; founder, v.p., mng. ptnr. Aragon Global Investors. Trustee Chgo. Symphony Orchestra, Whitney Mus. Am. Art. Named to Top 200 Collectors, ARTnews Mag., 2006. Mailing: c/o Whitney Mus Am Art 945 Madison Ave New York NY 10021

DIASIO, ILSE WOLFARTSBERGER, volunteer; b. Linz, Austria, Nov. 12, 1946; came to U.S., 1967; d. D.I. Gottfried and Elfriede (Stuchlik) Wolfartsberger; m. Robert B. Diasio, July 4, 1970; children: Christoph, Thomas, Michael. Grad. in Phys. Therapy, U. Vienna, 1967. Phys. therapist Yale-New Haven Hosp., 1968—71, Vis. Nurse Assn., Rochester, NY, 1971—72; symposium coord. dept. pharmacology U. Ala., 1988. Vol. tchr. German, Pemberton Elem. Sch., Richmond, Va., 1980-84, Vestavia Hills Elem. and H.S., 1985-93; organizer student exch. program between Vestavia Hills H.S. and Seebacher Gymnasium, Graz, Austria, 1990, 91, 94. Bd. dirs. Pemberton Elem. Sch. PTA, Va., 1979-84, pres., 1982-84; bd. dirs. Va. Commonwealth U. Faculty Woman's Club, 1978-84, Greater Birmingham Ministries, chmn. direct svcs. work group, 1999-2002, Ala. chpt. Fulbright Assn., 1999—; pres. Childrens Svc. League, 1992-93, treas. 1991-92, asst. treas. 1990-91, 2d v.p., rec. sec., 1998-99; vol. Our Lady Queen of the Universe and Sacred Heart of Jesus Cath. Chs., 1988-90; St. Peter's rep. Ala. Arise, diocesan rep., rec. sec., 1988-94; mem. Peace and Justice Commn. of the Cath. Diocese of Birmingham, 1989-95, chair of commn., 1994-95; bd. dirs. Be an Apostle of Christ, vice chair, 2003-06; chair human concerns com. St. Peter's Outreach Commn., 1988-2006; active Direct Svc. Network, 1989—2006, Greater Birmingham Ministries, 1989-2006, treas. Greater Birmingham UNA-USA chpt., 1982-2004, pres., 2005—, CCD steering com. South Atlantic region rep., 2002—07; mem. COMPEER Bd., Birmingham, Ala., 1990-99; active WOC, Call to Action, Bread for the World, CALC, Pax Christi, Amnesty Internat., Nat. Conf. of Cmty. and Justice, Smithsonian Inst., UNICEF, Coalition Against Hate Crimes, 1997—, Birmingham Com. on Fgn. Rels., 1998—; organizer Angel Tree project St. Peter's Cath. Ch., 1988-2006; bd. dirs., sec. World of Opportunity, 2002-06; vol. tchr. for GED preparation. Recipient resolution City of Birmingham, 1999. Mem. AAUW, Nat. Mus. of Women in the Arts, U.S. Holocost Mus., Vereinigung Ehemaliger Körnerschülerinnen, LWV (bd. dirs. Greater Birmingham 1999-2000). Roman Catholic. Avocations: reading, music, skiing, cooking, travel. Home: 1225 Branchwater Ln Birmingham AL 35216-2001 Personal E-mail: idiasio@aol.com.

DIAZ, ALPHONSO VINCENT, federal agency administrator; b. Bklyn. m. Angela Phillips. BS in Physics, St. Joseph U.; MS in Physics, Old Dominion U.; MS in Mgmt., MIT, 1986; Ph.D in Sci. (hon.), Md. Capital Coll., 2004; Ph.D in Aerospace Engrng. (hon.), U. Rome, 2005. Dep. assoc. adminstr., chief engineer Office of Space Sci. and Applications NASA, Washington, 1989-93, dep. assoc. adminstr. for space sci., 1994-96, dep. dir. Goddard Space Flight Ctr. Greenbelt, Md., 1996-98, dir., 1998—2004, assoc. adminstr. for sci. Washington, 2004—; divsn. v.p. space and aeronautics svcs. GE Govt. Svcs. Divsn., Cherry Hill, NJ, 1988-89. Named one of 50 Most Important Hispanics in Govt., Edn., Hispanic Engineer and Info. Tech. mag., 2005; recipient Exceptional Scientific Achievement medal, NASA, 1976, Presdl Rank award as Meritorious Exec., 1990, 1995, 2003, Exceptional Svc. medal, NASA, 1999, Outstanding Leadership medal, 1994, 2002, 2004, Lifetime Achievement award, Hispanic Bus. mag., 2005. Fellow AIAA (assoc.). Office: NASA 300 E St SW Washington DC 20546

DIAZ, ANGELA, pediatrician, educator; b. Dominican Republic, Oct. 2, 1954; MD, Columbia Coll. Physicians and Surgeons, 1994. Diplomate Am. Bd. Pediatrics with subspecialty in adolescent medicine. Intern Mt. Sinai Med. Ctr., NYC, 1981—82, resident in pediats., 1982—84, fellow, 1984—85, prof. dept. pediats., 1985—. Mem.: SAM, Am. Acad. Pediats. (Founders of Adolescent Health award 2001). Office: Mount Sinai Med Ctr 320 E 94th St New York NY 10128-5604

DIAZ, CAMERON, actress; b. San Diego, Aug. 30, 1972; d. Emilio and Billie Diaz. Grad. high sch., Long Beach, Calif. Appeared in (films) The Mask, 1994, Feeling Minnesota, 1996, She's the One, 1996, The Last Supper, 1996, Keys to Tulsa, 1996, Head Above Water, 1996, My Best Friend's Wedding, 1997 (Blockbuster Entertainment award), a Life Less Ordinary, 1997, (TV) Space Ghost Coast to Coast, 1994, Very Bad Things, 1998, Fear and Loathing in Las Vegas, 1998, There's Something About Mary (Golden Globe nomination Best Performance by an Actress in a Comedy or Musical Motion Picture), 1998 (N.Y. Film Critics Cir. award, MTV Movie award, Am. Comedy award), Invisible Circus, 1999, Being John Malkovich (Golden Globe nomination Best Supporting Actress in a Motion Picture), 1999, Any Given Sunday, 1999, Charlie's Angels: The Movie, 2000, Things You Can Tell Just by Looking at Her, 2000, Shrek (voice), 2001, Vanilla Sky, 2001, The Sweetest Thing, 2002, Gangs of New York, 2002, Charlie's Angels: Full Throttle, 2003, Shrek 2 (voice), 2004, In Her Shoes, 2005, The Holiday, 2006, Shrek the Third (voice), 2007; exec. prodr., host (TV series) Trippin, 2005. Named Female Star of Tomorrow, Nat. Theatre Owners Assn., 1996, Boston Soc. of Film Critics best supporting actress award, 2001, Chicago Film Critics Award for best supporting actress, 2002, Favorite Leading Lady, People's Choice award, 2007.*

DIAZ, DIANE LINDA, library director; 1 child, Marc Paul. Libr. svcs. supr. Hialeah Pub. Librs., Fla., acting dir. Fla., 2007—. Mem.: ALA (mem. bus. reference and svcs. sect.). Office: Hialeah Pub Librs 190 W 49th St Hialeah FL 33012 Office Phone: 305-818-9140. Office Fax: 305-818-9144. E-mail: ddiaz@hialeahfl.gov.

DIÁZ, ELENA R., community health nurse; b. Albuquerque; d. Mariá E. Lopes. BSN, U. Ariz., 1975. RN Ariz., cert. cmty. health nurse, Ariz. Cmty. health nurse Pima County Health Dept., Tucson, 1975—. Mem. ad hoc com. minority recruitment and retention Coll. Nursing U. Ariz., Tucson. Recipient St. Cyril's Clari Dunn/Judith Lovchick award, Peace and Justice Com., 1987, La Esperanza award, 1987. Mem.: Phi Beta Kappa. Office: Pima County Health Dept South Office 175 W Irvington Tucson AZ 85714 Office Phone: 520-889-9543.

DIAZ, FERNANDO GUSTAVO, neurosurgeon; s. Fernando Diaz Calderon and Susana (Barriga) D.; children: Fernando Austin, David Frederick, Sean Christopher, Patrick Aaron, Johnathan Paul. BS, Centro Universitario Mex., 1963; MD, Univ. de Mex., 1969; MA, U. Kans., Kansas City, 1973; PhD, U. Minn., 1979; MA in Bus., Cen. Mich. U., Mt. Pleasant, 1987; JD, Wayne State U., 1995. Diplomate Am. Bd. Neurol. Surgery; bar: Mich. 1995. Intern Regina Gen. Hosp., Sask., Can., 1969-70, resident in anethesia Sask., 1971; resident in gen. surgery U. Kans., Kansas City, 1971-73; resident in neurosurgery U. Minn. Hosps., Mpls., 1973-78; staff neurosurgeon Henry Ford Hosp., Detroit, 1978-87; chmn. Neurosci. Inst. Santa Fe, Gainesville, Fla., 1987-90; prof., chmn. dept. neurol. surgery Wayne State U., Detroit, 1990—; chief med. officer Detroit Med. Ctr., 2000—; cert. physician exec. ACPE, 2002. Neurosurg. nat. cons. to U.S. Surgeon Gen., USAF, 1991; coord. neurosurgery resident edn. Henry Ford Hosp., 1979—; clin. assoc. prof. surgery U. Mich., 1986—; mem. working group in neurosurgery WHO. Mem. editl. bd. Neurosurgery Jour.; contbr. articles to profl. jours. Lt. col. USAFR. Recipient awards Lily Pharms., Merck, Sharp & Dome Pharms., Organon Labs. Fellow Am. Chem. Soc., Interam. Coll. Physicians, Internat. Coll. Surgeons (vice regent U.S. sect. 1985); mem. AMA, Neurosurg. Soc. Am., Soc. Neurol. Surgeons, Mich. Med. Soc., Wayne County Med. Soc., Am. Assn. Neurol. Surgeons (cerebrovascular sect.), Congress Neurol. Surgeons, Mich. Assn. Neurol. Surgeons (sec.-treas. 1984-86, v.p. 1986, pres. 1997-98), Detroit Neurosurg. Acad. (v.p. 1986-90), Soc. Critical Care Medicine, Mich. Heart Assn. (chmn. stroke com. 1984-86, cmty. site ad-hoc com. 1984, cmty. programs and edn. com. 1986), Mich. Assn. Neurosurgery (chmn. bd.), L.Am. Fedn. Neurosurgery (sec. gen., 1999-2002), Coun. State Neurol. Soc. (vice chair) U. Minn. Alumni Assn. Roman Catholic.

DIAZ, JOSÉ J., surgeon; b. Guadalajara, Mexico, May 24, 1965; m. Dinah Diaz; children: Gabriella, Veronica, Alejandro. MD, U. Tex., Houston, 1992. Diplomate Am. Bd. Surgery, surg. critical care Am. Bd. Surgery, cert. bd. nutrition specialty Am. Coll. Nutrition. Surg. co-dir. adult nutritional support svcs. Vanderbilt U. Med. Ctr., Nashville, 1999—, dir. emergency gen. surgery, 2002—, assoc. prof. surgery and medicine, 2004—. Dir. emergency gen. surgery Vanderbilt U. Med. Ctr., surg. co-dir. adult nutritional support svcs., clin. assoc. prof. nursing. Fellow, Vanderbilt U. Med. Ctr., Nashville, 1998—99. Fellow: ACS, Southeastern Surg. Congress, Soc. Critical Care Medicine; mem.: Surg. Infection Soc., Ea. Assn. for the Surgery of Trauma, Am. Soc. for Parental and Enteral Nutrition, Am. Coll. Nutrition, Am. Coll. Chest Physician, Soc. Am. Gastrointestinal Endoscopic Surgeons, Western Surg. Assn., Am. Assn. for the Surgery of Trauma, Pan Am. Trauma Soc., H. William Scott, Jr. Soc. Office: Vanderbilt University Medical Center 1211 21st Ave S 404 MAB Nashville TN 37212 Office Phone: 615-936-0175.

DIAZ, MAGNA M., librarian, educator; b. NYC, Mar. 20, 1951; d. Jose Enrique Rodriguez and Juanita (Diaz) Rodriguez Garcia; m. Ramon A. Diaz, Jr., May 1, 1976. 1 child: Joana Marie. BA, U. P.R., 1972; postgrad. CC Phila., 1978, Temple U., 1979-80; MLS, Rutgers U., 1980; postgrad. Gratz Coll., U. Arts. Tchr. English Pub. Sch. Bd., P.R., 1972-76; bilingual cataloger Temple U., Merit Ctr., Phila., 1980; bilingual librarian Camden (N.J.) Free Pub. Library, 1980-81; children's libr. Free Libr. Phila., 1981-82; bilingual libr., 1983-93, bilingual storyteller, 1984—, tchr. libr. sci., developer multi-cultural program Vare Mid. Sch., Phila., 1988-92; bilingual libr. Kensington HS, Phila., 1993—, Frankford HS, 1999—; curriculum specialist Latino-Am. studiessch. libr. Phila.; reference libr. CC Phila., 1982; chair Spanish com. Free Libr. Phila., treas. Coord. Coun. Human Svcs., 1986-88, AMR (Hispanic Adv. Com. 1986-88), coord. Nat. Assn. to Promote Library Svcs. to the Spanish Speaking; presenter in field. Author: What We Want to Tell You, 2005, The Writings on the Wall, 2005; contbr. articles to profl. jours. HEW scholar, 1980. Mem. ALA (assoc.), Assn. Phila. Sch. Librs. Lutheran. Home: 464 Woodhaven Plz Philadelphia PA 19116-2409 Office: Sch Dist Phila Frankford High Sch Amber & Cumberland St Philadelphia PA 19116 Office Phone: 215-537-2519. Business E-Mail: mdiaz@phila.K12.pa.us.

DIAZ, MANUEL A., mayor; b. Havana, Cuba, Nov. 5, 1954; arrived in U.S., 1961; m. Robin Smith; children: Manny, Natlie, Bobby, Elisa. Grad. with high honors, Miami-Dade C.C., 1975, Fla. Internat. U., 1977; JD, U. Miami. Bar: Fla., U.S. Ct. Appeals (5th cir.), U.S. Dist. Ct. Appeals (11th cir.), U.S. Dist. Ct. (so. dist.) Fla., U.S. Supreme Ct. With Coopers & Lybrand; founder, mng. ptnr. Berkowitz & Diaz; former exec. v.p., gen. counsel Terremark Investment Svcs., Inc., Fla.; v.p., gen. counsel Monty's Restaurant Holdings; gen. counsel Fla. Worker's Compensation Ins. Guaranty Assn.; ptnr. Diaz & O'Naghten, L.L.P.; mayor City of Miami, 2001—. Cons. U. Chgo. Law Sch., Nat. Assessment of Ednl. Progress. Founding bd. mem. State Bd. C.C.'s, Fla.; apptd. mem. Fla. Residential Property & Casualty JUA, chmn. investment com.; chmn. Dade County Com. for Fair Representation; bd. mem. numerous cmty. orgns.; founding mem. Little Havana Activities and Nutrition Ctr.; past mem. Little Havana Devel. Authority; founding mem. Coalition Hispanic Am. Women; past chmn. Spanish Am. League Against Discrimination; founding mem. Gtr. Miami United; co-chair Music Fest Miami; past bd. dirs. United Way Hispanic Leadership Devel. Program, Miami's for Me Com. of 100; Leadership Miami; City of Miami Bds. & Coms. Rev. Com.; City of Miami City Atty. Selection Com.; City of Miami Bond Underwriters Selection Com. Named a Outstanding Am. by Choice, U.S. Citizenship and Immigration Svc., 2007; named Urban Innovator of the Yr., Manhattan Inst.,

2004; named one of Top 25 Most Powerful Hispanics, Hispanic Mag., 2006; recipient Bus. Leader of Yr. award, So. Fla. CEO Mag., 2004, Govt. Achiev. award, Hispanic Mag., 2006, Nat. Pub. Ldrshp. in Arts award, Am. for Arts & U.S. Conf. Mayors, 2006, Aguila Ldrshp. award, Latino Leaders Network, 2007. Office: City Hall 3500 Pan American Dr Miami FL 33133*

DIAZ, MARIA G., lawyer; BA, Stanford U., 1991, JD; MPP, Harvard U., 1994. Bar: Calif. Assoc., employment law practice Allred Maroko & Goldberg, LA. Named a Rising Star, So. Calif. Super Lawyers, 2005—06; recipient Wiley W. Manuel award, State Bar Calif., Outstanding Legal Services award, San Diego Volunteer Lawyer Program, Outstanding Service award, US Senator Barbara Boxer; Woodrow Wilson Nat. Fellow. Mem.: Calif. Employment Lawyers Assn., Mexican-Am. Bas Assn. LA, Latina Lawyers Bar Assn. LA, Nat. Employment Lawyers Assn., LA County Bar Assn. Office: Allred Maroko & Goldberg Ste 1500 6300 Wilshire Blvd Los Angeles CA 90048 Office Phone: 323-653-6530. Office Fax: 323-653-1660.

DIAZ, NELSON A., lawyer; b. NYC, May 23, 1947; s. Luis Diaz and Maria (Cancel) Rodriguez; children: Vilmarie, Nelson M.V., Delia Lee. AAS, St. John's U., 1967, BS, 1969; JD, Temple U., 1972; LLD (hon.), LaSalle Coll., 1982, St. John's U., 1987, Temple U., 1990, Albright Coll., 1995, Lincoln U., 1996. Bar: Pa. 1972, DC 1978, US Supreme Ct. 1978, NY 1998. Legal intern Camden (NJ.) Regional Legal Svcs., 1970-71; asst. defender Defender Assn. Phila., 1972-73; assoc. counsel Temple U. Legal Aid Office, Phila., 1973-75; assoc. Fell, Spalding, Goff & Ruben, Phila., 1976-77; exec. dir. Spanish Mchts. Assn., Phila., 1973-77; White House fellow Office of V.P. The White House, Washington, 1977-78; assoc. Wolf, Block, Schorr & Solis-Cohen, Phila., 1978-81; adminstrv. judge Phila. Ct. Common Pleas, 1981—93; gen. counsel US Dept. Housing & Urban Devel., Washington, 1993-97; ptnr. Blank, Rome, Comisky & McCauley LLP, Phila., 1997—2001, Blank Rome LLP, Phila., 2004—07; solicitor City of Phila., 2001—04; of counsel Cozen O'Connor, Phila., 2007—. Lectr. Sch. Law Temple U., Phila., 1983—; bd. dirs. Exelon, 2004-; adv. bd. PNC. Columnist Phila. Sun and Evening Bull., 1973-75; contbr. articles on Japanese, Peruvian legal system to various publs. Founder Phila. Leadership Prayer Breakfast, 1984-93; bd. dirs., com. chmn. Revitalized Neighborhood, 1983-87; participant, hon. chair Soviet Jewry Coun., 1985; com. mem. Charter Rev. Phila., 1986; chmn. Nat. Assn. Hispanic Elderly, LA, 1978-93, 97—; trustee Young Life, 1989-93, Temple U., 1997—; trustee com. chair Phila. Mus. Art; bd. govs. Temple Hosp., Phila., 1975-93; founder, bd. dirs. Nat. P.R. Coalition, 1978-86; co-chmn., bd. dirs. Urban Affairs Partnership, Phila., 1984-90; bd. dirs. USHLI, Chgo., 1982-93, 97—. World Affairs Coun., 1997-01, Phila. (Pa.) Indsl. Corp., Red Cross Phila., 2002-04, Pa. Convention Ctr.; vice chair multicultural affairs coun. Pa. Conv. and Visitors Bur., 2004-; chair Greater Phila. Billy Graham Crusade, Nat. Bar Assn. Jud. Coun., 1993, Frederick Douglass Soc. Fund., 1995, Salvation Army, 1995, Boricua Coll., 1995; Mayor's St. Police Discipline Task Force, Phila., Pa.; bd. dirs. Nat. Orgn. African Am. Housing, 2006-. Recipient Life Achievement award Nat. Puerto Rican Coalition, Washington, 1988, Judge of the Yr. award Pa. Trial Lawyers Assn., 1989, Man of the Yr., NAACP, North Phila., 1990, Found. Improvement Justice award, 1992, Cesar Chavez award, 1995, Spirit of Excellence award ABA, 2001, William Hall award Barristers, 2003, Lifetime Achievement award Pa. Minority Bar, 2003, Learned Hand award Am. Jewish Com., 2003, Outstanding Recognition award Phila. (Pa.) Multicultural Congress, 2004, Thurgood Marshall award TAIG Found., 2007; named Grand Marshall, P.R. Milburne (Fla.) Parade; named to Super Lawyer Phila. mag., 2004, 05, 06, 07; named one of Boardroom Elite, Hispanic Bus. Mag., 2007; Japan Soc. fellow, Fulbright fellow, 1990. Mem. Pa. Bar Assn. (chair DNC Hispanic Caucus, exec. com., bylaws and rules com., Martin Luther King Barrister award 2003), Phila. Bar Assn., DC Bar Assn., Pa. Trial Lawyers Assn., State Conf. Trial Judges, Hist. Soc. (bd. dirs.), Lawyers Club, Phila. Mus. Art. Democrat. Avocation: sports. Office: Cozen O'Connor 1900 Market St Philadelphia PA 19103 Home Phone: 215-242-4230; Office Phone: 215-665-5514. Business E-Mail: ndiaz@cozen.com.

DIAZ, NILS JUAN, federal agency administrator; b. Moron, Cuba, Apr. 7, 1938; came to US, 1961; s. Rafael Octavio Diaz and Rosa Dalia (Rojas) Chao; m. Zenaida G. Gonzalez, Oct. 9, 1960; children: NIls, Ariadne, Allene. BSME, U. Villanova, Havana, 1960; MS in Nuclear Engring. Sci., U. Fla., 1964, PhD in Nuclear Engring. Sci., 1969. Rsch. assoc. nuclear engring. sci. U. Fla., Gainesville, 1965-69, asst. prof., reactor supr., 1969-74, assoc. prof., dir. nuclear facilities, 1974-79, prof., dir. nuclear facilities, 1979-84; assoc. dean for rsch. Sch. of Engring. Calif. State U., Long Beach, 1984-86; prof. nuclear engring. scis. U. Fla., Gainesville, 1986-96; dir. Innovative Nuclear Space Power and Propulsion Inst., Calif. and Fla., 1985-96; commr. Nuclear Regulatory Commn., Washington, 1996—, chmn., 2003—. Sr. cons. Exxon Nuclear, Fla. Power and Light-Fla. Power Corp., Bellevue, Wash. and Fla., 1974-79; pres., chief engr. Fla. Nuclear Assocs., Inc., Gainesville, 1976-96; prin. advisor Nuclear Safety Coun., Madrid, 1981-83; internat. energy cons., Argentina, Brazil, Mex., Santo Domingo, Spain; commr. U.S. Nuclear Regulatory Commn. Contbr. articles to profl. jours. Chmn. Minority Engr. Program Adv. Bd., Long Beach, 1984-86. Recipient Disting. Svc. Award Math. Engring. Sci. Achievements and Minority Engring. Program State of Calif., Long Beach, 1983, Hispanic Bus. Fed. Elite award, HispanicBusiness.com, 2002; named Hispanic Engr. of Yr. for Outstanding Tech. Contbns., Hispanic Engr. Nat. Achievement Com., Houston, 1990, Top 50 Hispanics in Business and Tech., Hispanic Engr. & Information Tech., 2003, 2005. Fellow AAAS, ASME, Am. Nuclear Soc.; mem. Am. Soc. for Engring. Edn., Cuban-Am. Engring. Soc. (Engr. of Yr. 1993), Hispanic Assn. Profl. Engrs. Republican. Roman Catholic. Achievements include patents for heterogeneous gas core reactors, gamma ray flaw detection system; invention of vapor core nuclear rocket propulsion system. Office: US Nuclear Regulatory Commn Offices Of The Commr Washington DC 20555-0001

DIAZ, NINA ISABEL, industrial engineer; b. Queens, NY, Sept. 24, 1980; d. Edward Joseph Diaz and Teresa Isabel Badillo. BS in Indsl. Engring., MS in Indsl. Engring., U. Miami, Coral Gables, Fla., 2003; PhD in Indsl. Engring., U. Okla., Norman, 2007. Rsch. asst., program coord. U. Okla. Sch. Indsl. Engring., Norman, 2003—07; indsl. engr. FAA, Oklahoma City, 2005—. Alumnae Delta Delta Delta, Coral Gables, 2000—07. Mem.: INFORMS (student chpt. pres. 2005—07), Tau Beta Pi, Golden Key. Personal E-mail: ninadiaz80@hotmail.com.

DIAZ, OLIVER E., JR., state supreme court justice; b. Biloxi, Miss., Dec. 16, 1959; s. Oliver E. Sr. and Sylvia (Fountain) D. AA, Miss. Gulf Coast Jr. Coll., 1979; BA, U. S. Ala., 1982; JD, U. Miss., 1985. Bar: Miss., U.S. Dist. Ct. (no. and so. dists.) Miss., U.S. Ct. Appeals (5th cir.). Assoc. Holkins Logan Vaughn & Anderson, Gulfport, Miss., 1985-86, Gerald R. Emil PA, Gulfport, 1986-88; mem. Miss. House of Reps., 1988—94; ptnr. Diaz Davis & Emil, Gulfport, 1988—95; judge Miss. Ct. of Appeals, Jackson, 1995—2000; justice Miss. Supreme Court, Jackson, 2000—. Mem. Harrison County Rep. exec. com., 1987—; treas. Miss. State Young Reps., 1987-88; pres. Miss. Gulf Coast Young Reps., Harrison County, 1987-88. Mem. Assn. Trial Lawyers Am., Miss. Trial Lawyers Assn., Am. Legis. Exchange Com., Jaycees. Office: Mississippi Supreme Ct Gartin Justice Bldg PO Box 249 Jackson MS 39205*

DIAZ, PAUL J., health products executive; With Arthur Andersen LLC; atty. pvt. practice; CEO Allegis Health Svcs., Inc.; exec. v.p., COO Mariner Health Group, Inc., 1996—98; chmn., CEO Capella Sr. Living, LLC; mng. mem. Falcon Capital Partners, LLC; pres., CEO Kindred Healthcare, Louisville, 2002—. Mem.: Johns Hopkins Bloomberg Sch. Pub. Health. Office: Kindred Healthcare 680 S Fourth St Louisville KY 40202*

DIAZ, ROMULO L., JR., lawyer; b. Tex., 1946; BA, Univ. Tex. at Austin; JD, Univ. Tex. Sch. Law, 1972. Bar: Pa., NJ, DC, Tex. Dir. Internat. Ops. Office Emergency Planning & Ops. Dept. Energy, Washington, 1981—92, dep. chief staff & counselor sec., 1993—95, dir. office regulatory coordination, 1995—98; chair Petroleum Planning Commn. NATO, Washington, 1992—95; asst. adminstr. mgmt. EPA, Washington, 1998—2002; mem. Comml. and Regulatory Law Dept., Phila., 2002—; city solicitor Law Dept., Phila., 2005—. Mem. Phila. Energy Devel. Authority, 2004—, Phila. Bd. Ethics, 2005—. Dir. Svc. Mem. Legal. Def. Network, Sapphire Fund; Pan Am. Assoc. Phila. Recipient Gold Award, Sec. Energy. Fellow: FBA (charter fell.); mem.: Hispanic Bar Assn. of Pa. (treas.). Office: Law Dept City Phila 1515 Arch St 16th Fl Philadelphia PA 19102-1595 Office Phone: 215-683-5186. E-mail: romulo.l.diazjr@phila.gov.

DIAZ, SHARON, education administrator; b. Bakersfield, Calif., July 29, 1946; d. Karl C. and Mildred (Lunn) Clark; m. Luis F. Diaz, Oct. 19, 1968; children: Daniel, David. BS, San Jose State U., 1969; MS, U. Calif., San Francisco, 1973; PhD (hon.), St. Mary's Coll. Calif., 1999. Nurse Kaiser Found. Hosp., Redwood City, Calif., 1969-73; lectr. San Jose (Calif.) State U., 1969-70; instr. St. Francis Meml. Hosp. Sch. Nursing, San Francisco, 1970—71; pub. health nurse San Mateo County, 1971—72; instr. Samuel Merritt Hosp. Sch. Nursing, Oakland, Calif., 1973—76, asst. dir., 1976—78, dir., 1978—84; founding pres. Samuel Merritt Coll., Oakland, 1984—; interim pres. Calif. Coll. Podiatric Medicine, 2001. V.p. East Bay Area Health Edn. Ctr., Oakland, 1980-87; mem. adv. com. Calif. Acad. Partnership Program, 1990-92; mem. nat. adv. com. Nursing Outcomes Project; bd. dirs. Calif. Workforce Initiative, U. Calif. San Francisco Ctr. for the Health Professions, 2000-. Bd. dirs. Head Royce Sch., 1990-98, vice-chair, 1993-95, chair, 1995-97; bd. dirs. Ladies Home Soc., 1992-2007, sec. 1994-95, treas., CFO 1995-97, 2d v.p. 1997-99, pres., 2006-07; bd. dirs. George Mark Children's House, 2001-07; adv. bd. Ethnic Health Inst., 1997—; com. minorities higher edn. Am. Coun. Edn., 1998—. Named Woman of Yr., Oakland YWCA, 1996. Mem. Am. Assn. Pres. Ind. Colls. and Univs., Sigma Theta Tau (bd. dirs. Nu Xi internat. chpt. at-large 2005-07, Leadership award Nu Xi chpt. 2001, Philanthropy award 2005). Office: Samuel Merritt Coll 450 30th St Oakland CA 94609-3302 E-mail: sdiaz@samuelmerritt.edu.

DIAZ, TERESITA PEREZ, chemist; b. Placetas, Las Villas, Cuba, Sept. 2, 1956; arrived in U.S., 1974; d. Pedro Angel and Gladys (Teresita) Perez; m. Luis Diaz, Jr., Sept. 2, 1984; children: Tiffany Marie, Luis III. BS in Chemistry, Monclair U., NJ, 1979. Asst. scientist baby products Johnson & Johnson, Raritan, NJ, 1979—81, assoc. scientist, 1981—84, assoc. scientist toiletries Skillman, NJ, 1984—86, scientist R & D, 1986—96, sr. scientist rsch, devel. and engring., 1996—2001, staff scientist, 2001—02, group leader, 2002—05, mgr., 2006—. Piano tchr., Perth Amboy, NJ, 1975—; coach, trainer Johnson & Johnson Skillman U., 2001—04. Class mother Perth Amboy Cath. Schs., 1989—2003. Recipient Grandview award, Johnson & Johnson, 2000, 2002, 2004, Engring. Excellence award, 2002. Mem.: Nat. Guild Piano Tchrs., Soc. Cosmetic Chemists. Achievements include co-inventor skin toning formulation; co-inventor relaxing personal care composition; co-inventor delivery system for topical skin care agents. Avocations: art, theater, museums, music, films. Office: Johnson and Johnson 199 Grandview Rd Skillman NJ 08558 Office Phone: 908-874-1415. Personal E-mail: tdiaz7@cpcus.jnj.com.

DIAZ-BALART, LINCOLN, congressman, lawyer; b. Havana, Cuba, Aug. 13, 1954; m. Cristina Fernandez; children: Lincoln Gabriel, Daniel. BA in Internat. Rels., New Coll. of U. So. Fla., 1976; diploma in Brit. Politics, Cambridge U., Eng.; JD, Case Western Res. U., 1979. Lawyer Legal Svcs. of Greater Miami, Fla.; asst. state atty. State of Fla.; mem. Fla. Ho. of Reps. from 110th Dist., 1986-89, Fla. State Senate from Dist. 34, 1989-92, U.S. Congress from 21st Fla. dist., 1993—, Select Com. on Homeland Security; mem. Rules com. Mem. rules com.; vice chmn. subcom. on rules of the house. Mem. exec. com. Congl. Human Rights Caucus; vice chmn. Nat. Rep. Congl. Com. Mem. ABA, Fla. Bar Assn., Dade County Bar Assn., Cuban-Am. Bar Assn., Rep. Nat. Lawyers Assn., Lions. Republican. Roman Catholic. Office: US Ho of Reps 2244 Rayburn Ho Office Bldg Washington DC 20515-0921*

DIAZ-BALART, MARIO, congressman; b. Ft. Lauderdale, Fla., Sept. 25, 1961; m. Tia Diaz-Balart. Student, U. South Fla., 1979—82. Pres. Gordeon, Sloan and Diaz-Balart; adminstrv. asst. to Mayor Xavier Suarez City of Miami, 1985-88; mem. Fla. Ho. of Reps., Tallahassee, 1988-92, 2001—03, Fla. State Senate, Tallahassee, 1992—2000, US Congress from 25th Fla. dist., 2003—, mem. com. on sci., 2006—. Vice chmn. Rules and Calendar Com.; chmn. Banking and Ins. Com.; mem. Subcom. E Fin. and Tax Ways and Means Com., Natural Resources Com., Edn. Com. Commerce and Econ. Opportunities Com., Hispanic Adv. Bd., Republican Nat. Com., South Fla. Young Republicans Mem. consultive com. Children's First; mem. Dade Ptnrs. for Safe Neighborhoods, Spanish-Am. League Against Discriminations, advisor Nat. Human Rights Commn. Municipios en el Exilio; bd. dirs. Fla. Entertainment Commn., Spl. Olympics Recipient award Pub. Svc. award Am. League Against Discrimination, 1992, Leadership award Fla. Assn. of State Troopers, 1993, 1996, Furtherance of Justice award Fla. Attys. Assn., 1994, Legis. Courage award Dade County Fla. Chapter Labor Coun. for Latin Am. Advancement, 1996, Top Forty award Fla. C of C, 1996, 2000, Disting. Leadership award Fla. Police Benevolent Assn., 1996, Govt. Recognition award Am. Assn. Poison Control Centers, 1996, Disting. Leadership award Nat. Alliance for the Mentally Ill, 1997, Senator of the Yr. Fla. Assn. of Life Underwriters, 1998, Conservationist of the Yr. award Biscayne Bay Found., 1999, Claude Pepper Meml. award United Homecare Services, 2000, Legis. of the Yr., Fla. Assn. Realtors, 2000, Legis of the Yr., Fla. Optometrics Assn., 2000, Golden Shovel award Miami River Marine Group, 2000, Legis. award of Distinction MADD, 2000, Lifetime Legis. Achievemnt award Fla. Assn. CC Bd. Dirs., 2000, Top Pillar award, Fla. Internat. U., 2000 Mem. Am. Legis. Exch. Coun., Nat. Assn. Latino Elected Officials, Dade Partners for Safe Neighborhoods, Asociacion Integral Mambisa, Westchester Lions Club, Nat. Conf. of State Legislatures, Commerce & Comm. Com., Spanish Am.League Against Discrimination Republican. Roman Catholic. Avocations: reading, biking, diving. Office: 313 Cannon Ho Office Bldg Washington DC 20515-0925

DIAZ-CRUZ, MARIO, III, lawyer; b. Havana, Cuba, 1946; BBA cum laude, Univ. Miami, 1967; JD, Harvard Univ., 1970. Bar: NY 1971. Ptnr., corp. dept., chair, Latin Am. dept. Dorsey & Whitney LLP, NYC, 1995—. Chmn., pres. Spain-US C of C, Girls' Vacation Fund. Mem.: ABA, Assn. of Bar City NY, NY State Bar Assn. Office: Dorsey & Whitney LLP 250 Park Ave New York NY 10177-1500 Office Phone: 212-415-9250. Office Fax: 212-953-7201. Business E-Mail: diaz.cruz.mario@dorsey.com.

DIAZ-FUENTES, GILDA, pulmonologist; d. Bernardino Diaz and Graciela Fuentes; m. Wilfredo Mellado, Nov. 23, 1983. MD, U. Austral, Chile, 1983. Chief pulmonary and critical care divsn. Bronx Lebanon Hosp. Ctr., NY, 2006—, dir. pulmonary fellowship program, 2006—. Recipient Best Tchr. award, Bronx Lebanon Hosp. Ctr., 2001, 2002, 2004, 2005, 2006. Fellow: Am. Coll. Chest Physicians (assoc.). Office: Bronx Lebanon Hospital 1650 Grand Concourse Bronx NY 10457 Office Phone: 718-960-2003.

DIAZ-MONTES, TERESA P., oncologist, obstetrician, gynecologist; b. Rio Piedras, PR, May 21, 1973; d. Eduardo Diaz and Carmen T. Montes; m. Alberto A. Alejandro, June 19, 1999. BS in Biology, U. PR, 1995, MD, 1999; MPH, Johns Hopkins U., 2004. Lic. physician PR, Md.; control substance cert. Md., cert. DEA. Resident in ob-gyn. U. PR, Rio Piedras, 1999—2003; fellow in gynecologic oncology Johns Hopkins Med. Instns., Balt., 2003—06; asst. prof. gynecologic oncology Johns Hopkins Hosp., Balt., 2006—. Presenter in field. Contbr. articles to profl. jours. Recipient Nat. Collegiate Natural Scis. award, 1994, All-Am. Scholar Collegiate award, 1995, 1998, Pres. Achievement award, U. PR, 1995, 1999, Nat. Collegiate Med. Professions award, 1997, Dept. Ob.-Gyn. award, U. PR Sch. Medicine, 1999; summer rsch. fellow, 1996, Mayo Clinic, Rochester, Minn., 1997, Diversity scholar, 1998, Graber Vis. fellow, Cleve. Clinic, 2001. Mem.: PR Med. Assn., Am. Coll. Ob-gyn., Soc. Gynecologic Oncolgy, Beta Beta Beta, Golden Key, Alpha Omega Alpha. Avocations: reading, movies, cooking, rafting, walking. Office: The Kelly Gynecologic Oncology Svc 600 N Wolfe St Phipps 281 Baltimore MD 21287-1281 Mailing: PO Box 1499 Owings Mills MD 21117-1403 Office Fax: 410-614-8718. Business E-Mail: tdiazmo1@jhmi.edu.

DIAZ-VERSON, SALVADOR, JR., investment advisor; b. Havana, Cuba, Dec. 31, 1951; s. Salvador and Metodia Diaz-V.; children: Salvador III, Patricia Elizabeth. BA in Fin., Fla. State U., Tallahassee, 1973. Chief investment officer Am. Family Life Assurance, Columbus, Ga., 1977-79; exec. v.p. Am. Family Corp., Columbus, 1980-83, pres., 1983-91, also dir.; pres. Diaz-Verson Capital Investment, 1991—. Bd. dirs. Regions Bank, Ga.; pres., CEO Diaz-Verson Capital Investment Inc., 1992. Trustee St. Francis Hosp., United Way, Columbus, 1983—2000, Boys and Girls Club, 1989—; chair United Americas Bank, 1999—; chmn. DVA Sports, 2003—. Mem. Columbus C. of C. (bd. dirs. 1983—), Green Island Country Club, Country Club of Columbus. Roman Catholic.

DIAZ-ZUBIETA, AGUSTIN, nuclear physicist, engineering executive; b. Madrid, Mar. 24, 1936; came to U.S., 1953; s. Emilio Diaz Cabeza and Maria Teresa Zubieta Atucha; m. Beth Lee Fortune, Sept. 6, 1958; children: Walter Agustin, Michael Joel, Anthony John. B, U. Madrid, 1953; BSc in Physics, U. Tenn., 1958; MSc in Mech. Engring., Duke U., 1960; PhD in Nuclear Engring., U. Md., 1981. Nuclear engr. Combustion Engring., Tenn., 1954-58; instr. engring. Duke U., Durham, NC, 1958-60; nuclear physicist Allis Chalmers Co., Washington, 1960-64, country mgr. South Africa, 1964-66; mgr. internat. power generation projects GE, NYC, 1966-69, mgr. Europe and Middle East strategic planning, 1969-71, dir. internat. constrn. planning Westport, Conn., 1971-75, dir. constrn., 1975-83; CEO GE Affiliate, Westport, 1983-87; v.p. internat. sales, devel. Internat. Tech. Corp., LA, 1987-94. Mng. dir. IT Italia S.P.A., IT Spain, S.A. Author: Measurement of Subcriticality of Nuclear Reactors by Stocastic Processes, 1981. Pres. Fairfield (Conn.) Assn. Condo Owners, 1983-87. Named Astronomer of Yr. Barnard Astronomical Soc., Chattanooga, 1957; fgn. exchange scholar U.S. Govt., 1953-58; grantee, NSF, 1958-60, U.S. Office of Ordinance Rsch. U.S. Army, 1958-60. Mem. Am. Nuclear Soc., Am. Soc. Mech. Engrs., Am. Soc. Profl. Engrs., Sigma Xi. Republican. Roman Catholic. Avocations: golf, tennis, swimming, sailing, music. Home: 47 Country Meadow Rd Rolling Hills Estates CA 90274

DIB, NABIL, cardiologist, researcher; b. Toumin, Syria, Nov. 24, 1961; U.S. m. Cheryl A. Brandt, Apr. 12, 1996; children: Dib, Lauren. MD, U. Damascus, Syria, 1985; cardiologist, U. Wis., Milw., 1997; MSc, Harvard U., 1999. Lic. Mass., Wis., Ariz., diplomate Am. Bd. Internal Medicine, Am. Bd. Cardiovasc. Disease, Am. Bd. Interventional Cardiology. Dir. cardiovasc. rsch. Ariz. Heart Inst., Phoenix, 1998—; investigational interventional cardiology fellow Harvard Med. Sch., Boston, 1999; also dir., cardiovascular rsch. Mercy Gilbert (Ariz.) Hosp., Phoenix; and assoc. physician diplomate, dir. clin. cardiovascular cell therapy Univ. Calif., San Diego. Spkr. in field; advisor Radi Med., 1995—, Possis Med., Minn., 1998—; cons. in field. Contbr. articles to profl. jours.; editl. cons.: Catheterization and Cardiovasc. Jour., 1996—. Recipient Med. Staff Sci. award, Tufts U., Boston, 1994; Med. scholar, Damascus U., 1985. Fellow: Am. Coll. Cardiology; mem.: ACP, Internat. Soc. Endovascular Interventionists. Avocations: swimming, fishing, travel. Office: Ariz Heart Inst 2632 N 20th St Phoenix AZ 85028 also: Perlman Ambulatory Care Ctr 9350 Campus Point Dr La Jolla CA 92037*

DIBACCO, NADINE LOUISE, retired library director, photographer, writer; b. Biloxi, Miss., Nov. 2, 1952; d. Keith Royce and Ira Jean Allen; m. T. Jay DiBacco, June 1, 1976. AA, Laramie County C.C., 1972; BA in English Edn., U. Wyo., 1974; MS in Mgmt., Regis U., 2000. Cert. pub. librarian, tchr. Nebr. Serials libr. Laramie County C.C., Cheyenne, Wyo., 1974—76; tchr., english St. Agnes Acad., Alliance, Nebr., 1976—77; exec. sec. Gering Police Dept., Nebr., 1977—85; asst. dir. Gering Pub. Libr., Gering, Nebr., 1985—90, libr. dir., 1990—2005; adj. instr. Western Nebr. C.C., Scottsbluff, Nebr., 1991—96. Bd. pres. Panhandle Libr. Sys., Scottsbluff, Nebr., 1991—93, author tour com., 1990—. Com. mem. Scottsbluff/Gering United C. of C., Nebr., 1987—2005, United Way of Scotts Bluff County, Nebr., 1989—90; treas. Mar. of Dimes, Scottsbluff, Nebr., 1983—84; active Nebr. N.G. Civilian Leadership Coun., Lincoln, 2004—05; vice chair, chair-elect pub. libr. sect. Nebr. Libr. Assn., Lincoln, 2005—06. Recipient Individual Devel. Nat. Panel Participant, Bus. and Profl. Women, USA, 1988. Mem.: Soroptimist Internat. of Scotts Bluff County (corr. sec. 2005—06), Nebr. Bus. and Profl. Women (state pres. 2002—03), Soc. for Creative Anachronism (treas. local chpt. 1997—2005, regional pres. 1998—2000, Order of the Pelican 1996). Avocations: photography, music, travel. Office: PO Box 68 Boys Town NE 68010 Home Phone: 402-991-5433; Office Phone: 402-991-5433. Personal E-mail: nadinedibacco@yahoo.com.

DIBACCO, T. JAY, financial services executive, retired military officer; b. Casper, Wyo., June 8, 1954; s. Albert Joseph and Evelyn DeBacco; m. Nadine Louise Allen, June 1, 1976. MusB, cert. in edn., U. Wyo., 1976; MBA, Almeda Coll. and U., 2003; diploma, US Army Command and Gen. Staff Coll., Ft. Leavenworth, Kans., 1994. Life Underwriter Tng. Coun. fellow Nat. Assn. Life Underwriters, cert. sr. advisor Soc. Cert. Sr. Advisors; registered rep. Nat. Assn. Securities Dealers. Music tchr. St. Agnes Acad., Alliance, Nebr., 1976-77; instrumental music Gering (Nebr.) Pub. Schs., 1977-79; sales assoc. Panhandle Co-op, Scottsbluff, 1980-81; advanced underwriter Security Mut. Life Nebr., Scottsbluff, 1981-99; sr. assoc. Hi-Plains Fin. Svcs. Inc., Scottsbluff, 1985-99; pres., CEO DiBacco & Assoc.-WealthMaker$ Ltd., Scottsbluff, 1999—2005; regional v.p. Ohio Nat. Fin. Svcs., 2005—. Adj. faculty Western Nebr. C.C., Scottsbluff, 1989—90; gen. agt. Ohio Nat. Fin. Svcs., 2000—05; gen. practitioner Cir. of Wealth Sys., 2000—; rep. Ohio Nat. Equity Sales Co., 1999—. Contbr. articles to profl. jours.; writer local newspaper column, 2000-05. Mem. adv. bd. Regional West Med. Ctr. Found., Scottsbluff, 1989-2005; MBA catalyst group U. Nebr. Panhandle Sta., Scottsbluff, 1990-92; dist. commr. Longs Peak Coun. Boy Scouts Am., 1980-83; active emergency comms. Amateur Radio Emergency Svc., Scottsbluff, 1990-2005; founding pres., bd. dirs. Panhandle Estate Planning Coun., Scottsbluff, 1982-92; chmn. bus. adv. coun., Nebr.; co-chmn. nat. rep. congl. com., Nebr., 2002, chmn. 2003-04; co-chmn. presidl. bus. round table, Nebr., 2005. Lt. col. U.S. Army N.G., 1975-2004. Decorated Meritorious Svc. medal, Army Commendation medal with oak leaf cluster, named Nebr. Comdr. of Yr., Am. Spirit Honor medal Ancient and Hon. Order St. Barbara; named Nat. Rookie of Yr., Security Mutual Life, 1981; recipient Scouter Tng. award, Longs Peak coun. Boy Scouts Am., 1977, Vigil Honor award, 1977, Assn. Achievement award, Nebr. Assn. Life Underwriters, 1988. Mem.: Gen. Agts. and Mgrs. Assn., Soc. Fin. Svc. Profls., Nat. Assn. Ins. and Fin. Advisors (past local pres., Nat. Mgr. award 2005, Nat. Sales Achievement award, Nat. Quality award, named to Million Dollar Round Table), Fin. Planning Assn. (named to Million Dollar Round Table), Nebr. N.G. Officers Assn. (life), N.G. Officers Assn. of US (life; Nebr. del. 1990—92), Sugar Valley Singers (pres. 2002—04, Barbershopper of Yr. 1997), Barbershp Harmony Soc., Soc. Creative Anachronism (regional safety officer 1995—99, Regional Svc. award 1995), Valley Vintners (pres. 2002—06), Elks, Am. Legion. Avocations: music, history, archery, travel, wine making. Home: PO Box 68 Boys Town NE 68010 Office: PO Box 40 Boys Town NE 68010 Office Phone: 402-697-0264. E-mail: tjay_dibacco@ohionational.com.

DIBATTISTE, CAROL A., military officer; b. Phila., Dec. 28, 1951; d. Peter Martin DiBattiste and Hilda Yolanda (Battilana) Mignogna. BA magna cum luade, LaSalle U., 1976; JD, Temple U., 1981; LLM, Columbia U., 1986. Bar: Pa. 1982, U.S. Ct. Mil. Appeals 1982, U.S. Supreme Ct. 1985, N.Y. 1989, D.C. 1989, Fla. 1990, U.S. Dist. Ct. (so. dist.) Fla. 1991, U.S. Ct. Appeals (11th cir.) 1991. Commd. 2d lt. USAF, 1976, advanced through grades to maj., 1987, cir. trial counsel Pacific Region, 1982—85; mem. faculty USAF JAG Sch., Maxwell AFB, Ala., 1986—89; chief recruiting atty. Office of Judge Advocate Gen. USAF, Washington, 1989—91; asst. U.S. atty. (So. Dist.) Fla. US Dept. Justice, Miami, 1991—92, dir. Office of Legal Edn., 1992—93; prin. dep. gen. coun. USN, 1993—94; dir. Exec. Office for U.S. Attys., Washington, 1994—98; dep. U.S. atty. (So. Dist.) Fla. US Dept. Justice, Miami, 1998—99; undersec. USAF, Arlington, Va., 1999—2001; ptnr. Holland & Knight, LLP, 2001—03; chief of staff Transp. Security Adminstrn., 2003—04, dep. adminstr., 2004—05; chief credentialing compliance and privacy officer ChoicePoint Inc., McLean, 2005—06, gen. counsel, chief privacy officer Alpharetta, Ga., 2006—. Adj. faculty U. Miami Sch. Law Trial Skills, 1998—99; bd. dirs. Alpha Security Group. Editor: The Reporter, Air Force JAG Sch., 1986—87; mem. editl. bd.: Air Force Law Rev., 1984. Bd. visitors Temple U. Sch. Law, 1996-99; trustee USAF JAG Sch. Found., 1993-96, Air Force Falcon Found., 2004—. Mem. ABA (chmn. standing com. on mil. law 1989-91), Fed. Bar Assn. (Young Fed. Lawyer award 1985), Nat. Inst. for Trial Advocacy (faculty 1986-92), USAF Assn. Roman Catholic. Home: 24014 Gardner Dr Alpharetta GA 30004 Business E-Mail: carol.dibattiste@choicepoint.net.

DIBBLE, DAVID VAN VLACK, visually impaired educator, lawyer; b. San Francisco, Feb. 5, 1928; s. Oliver and Isabelle (Bishop) D.; m. Frances Bauer, May 3, 1984; 1 child, T.C. Clark. AA, San Mateo Jr. Coll., 1948; student, Mexico City Coll., 1950; BA, U. Calif., Berkeley, 1952; JD, U. Calif., San Francisco, 1962; grad. in Edn., Calif. State U., Hayward, 1969; MA, San Francisco State U., 1981. Bar: Calif., 1962; cert. elem. tchr., spl. edn. visually impaired, Calif. Tchr. Marine Corps Inst., Washington, 1953-54; purser Am. Pres. Lines, San Francisco, 1955, passenger agt. Honolulu, 1956-58, San Francisco, 1958-60; trial lawyer Barfield, Barfield & Dryden, San Francisco, 1963-65; ptnr. Thorpe & Dibble, Hayward, Calif., 1966-69; part time tchr. various Calif. sch. dist., 1970-74; lawyer and vision tchr. pvt. practice, San Francisco, 1974-82; sec., dir. Original Sixteen to One Mine, Inc., Alleghany, Calif., 1978-81; vision tchr. Oakland Pub. Sch., Calif., 1982-89; cons. vision edn. pvt. practice, Oakland, 1989—. Author: The Pelton Wheel, 2003; contbr. articles on Art of Seeing to various pubs. Pub. defender Legal Aid Soc., San Francisco, 1965-66; bd. dir. Healing Ctr., San Francisco, 1974-78; vol., 1974-90; bd. dir., v.p. Calif. Heritage Coun., 1970—, Telegraph Hill Dwellers, 1979-88, pres., 1976, San Francisco; bd. dirs., v.p. Diamond Improvement Assn., Oakland, 1987-88; vestry and warden St. Paul's Episcopal Ch., Oakland, 1989-92; dir. Internat. Maritime Ctr., Oakland, 1995—; docent Oakland Mus., 1992, presdl. yacht. U.S.S. Potomac, Jack London Mus., Hugenot Soc. Calif., Thomas Jefferson chpt. SAR. Recipient Cert. Appreciation, Calif. Heritage Coun., San Francisco, 1990. Mem. Bar Assn. Calif., Oakland Tchrs. Assn., Calif. Assn. Orientation and Mobility Specialists, Calif. Alumni Assn., Nat. Audubon Soc., Bay Area Assn. Disabled Sailors, San Francisco Bay Wildlife Soc., E.C.V. YB#1, History Soc., Sierra Club, Calif. Mus. History (docent coun.), Calif. Hist. Soc., Alameda County Hist. Soc., Bates-Corbett Tchr. Assn., Phi Gamma Delta. Republican. Episcopalian. Home: 2806 Bellaire Pl Oakland CA 94601-2010 Office Phone: 510-536-5609. Personal E-mail: daviddibble@aol.com.

DIBBLE, FRANCIS DANIEL, JR., lawyer; b. Holyoke, Mass., Mar. 1, 1947; s. Francis Daniel and Rita (Egan) D.; m. Mary Harris Dibble, June 26, 1971. AB, Amherst Coll., 1971; JD magna cum laude, Suffolk U., 1974. Bar: Mass. 1974, U.S. Dist. Ct. Mass. 1975, U.S. Dist. Ct. Conn. 1978, U.S. Dist. Ct. (ea. dist.) Mich. 1984, U.S. Ct. Appeals (1st cir.) 1987, U.S. Ct. Appeals (D.C. cir.) 1981, U.S. Supreme Ct. 1984. Law clk. to justice Supreme Jud. Ct. of Mass., Boston, 1974-75; from assoc. to mng. ptnr. Bulkley, Richardson and Gelinas, Springfield, Mass., 1975-94, chmn., exec. com., 1997—. Instr. Western New Eng. Law Sch., Springfield, 1979. Contbr. articles to profl. jours. Mem. civil justice adv. bd. U.S. Dist. Ct. Mass.; spl. counsel. Fellow Mass. Bar Found. (life); mem. ABA (antitrust law sect.), Mass. Bar Assn., Hampden County Bar, Boston Bar Assn., The Colony Club, Longmeadow Country Club, East Chop Assn., East Chop Yacht Club, East Chop Tennis Club. Office: Bulkley Richardson and Gelinas LLP 1500 Main St Ste 2700 Springfield MA 01115-0001 Office Phone: 413-781-2820. E-mail: fdibble@bulkley.com.

DIBELLA, RUSSELL THOMAS, federal investigator; b. Phila., Mar. 21, 1934; s. Carmen and Erina (Louden) DiB.; m. Mary Sarah McGivern, Feb. 9, 1957; children: Diane Hanna, Carole Yates, Kathleen Tower, Russell Carmen, Michael Bernard. BS in Bus., LaSalle U., 1962. Bank clk. 1st Pa. Bank, Phila., 1951—62; spl. agt. U.S. Treasury Dept., Phila., 1962—87; criminal investigator N.J. Atty. Gen., Trenton, 1987—89; state investigator N.J. Taxation, Trenton, 1989—97; investigator Def. Security, Tabernacle, NJ, 2002—04; spl. investigator FBI - Background Investigations Contract Svcs., Tabernacle, 2000—. Ch. organist St. Mary of the Lakes Ch., Medford, NJ, 1980—85; accordionist Aqua String Band, Phila., 1949—50. Musician USN, 1952—56. Mem.: DAV, Fed. Criminal Investigators (regional v.p. 1984—86, pres. 1986—87), Assn. Former Spl. Agts. (nat. pres. 2001—02), Tabernacle Rep. Club (treas. 2001—02), KC, VFW, Am. Legion. Republican. Roman Catholic. Avocations: piano, accordion, competitive pistol shooting. Home: 30 Powell Place Rd Tabernacle NJ 08088 Office: FBI-BICS 30 Powell Place Rd Tabernacle NJ 08088

DIBELLO, JOSEPH NICHOLAS, plastic surgeon; b. Phila., Pa., Feb. 12, 1962; MD, Jefferson Med. Coll., 1989. Cert. Surgery, diplomate Am. Bd. Plastic Surgery. Resident, surgery Thomas Jefferson U. Hosp., 1989—95; resident, plastic surgery Wright State U., Dayton, Ohio, 1995—97; chief, plastic surgery Jeanes Hosp., Phila.; staff, plastic surgery Holy Redeemer Hosp., Meadowbrook, Pa., Fox Chase Cancer Ctr.; adj. clin. asst. prof., surgery Temple U. Sch. Medicine, Phila., faculty plastic surgery, 1997—2000, clin. faculty, plastic surgery, 2000—. Contbr. several articles to peer-reviewed publications. Fellow: ACS; mem.: Robert H. Ivy Soc. Plastic Surgeons, Northeastern Soc. Plastic Surgery, Am. Soc. Aesthetic Plastic Surgeons, Am. Soc. Plastic Surgeons. Office: DiBello Plastic Surgery 2361 Huntingdon Pike Huntingdon Valley PA 19006 Office Phone: 215-947-4990. Office Fax: 215-947-7660.*

DI BENEDETTO, ANN LOUISE, retired accounting administrator; b. Knoxville, Tenn., Jan. 26, 1954; d. William Brown and Louise (Emerson) Nixon; m. Raymond Peters, July 11, 1975 (dec.); m. Robert Di Benedetto, Sept. 22, 2002. BBA, Miami U., Oxford, Ohio, 1976; MBA, Xavier U., 1985. Cert. internal auditor. Acctg. officer Soc. Bank (formerly Citizens Bank), Hamilton, Ohio, 1977—85; internal auditor Procter & Gamble Co., Cin., 1985—86, mgr. audit sect., 1986—88, sr. cost analyst, beauty care, 1988—90; mgr. plant fin. Procter & Gamble Mfg. Co., Phoenix, 1990—92; sr. fin. analyst, beauty care Procter & Gamble Co., Cin., 1992—93, group mgr., gen. acctg., 1993—96, group mgr. R&D fin., 1996—99, group mgr., global fin., paper divsn., 1999—2002, group mgr. global fin. governance, 2002—03, group mgr., fin., global bus. svcs., 2003—06; ret., 2006. Mem. Inst. Internal Auditors, Inst. Mgmt. Accts. Republican. Congregationalist. Avocations: golf, swimming. Home: 5316 Grove Manor Lady Lake FL 32159

DI BENEDETTO, C. ANTHONY, marketing educator; b. Windsor, Ont., Can., June 23, 1957; arrived in U.S., 1984; BSc with great distinction, McGill U., 1978, MBA, 1980, PhD, 1985. New product profl. cert. Asst. prof. U. Ky., Lexington, 1985—88, Temple U., Phila., 1990—91, assoc. prof., 1991—98, prof., 1998—. Co-author: (with R. Calantone) The Product Manager's Toolbox, 1993, (with Merle Crawford) New Products Management, 8th edit., 2006; contbr. articles to profl. jours. Recipient Steven J. Shaw Best Paper award, So. Mktg. Assn., 1992. Mem.: Product Devel. and Mgmt. Assn. (acad. news and book rev. editor Visions 1991—93, editor nat. newsletter Visions 1992—96, v.p. publs. 1994—95, abstracts editor Jour. Product Innovation Mgmt. 1996—2003, bd. dirs. 2001—03, editor Jour. Product Innovation Mgmt. 2004—), Am. Mktg. Assn. (treas. Phila. chpt. 1991—93, dir. Phila. chpt. 1993—95). Office: Temple U Fox Sch Bus and Mgmt 1810 N 13th St Philadelphia PA 19122-6012 Office Phone: 215-204-8147. Business E-Mail: anthony.dibenedetto@temple.edu.

DI BENEDETTO, STEPHEN ANTHONY, performing arts educator; s. Anthony T. and RoseMarie DiBenedetto; m. Juliet T. Di Benedetto. BFA, DePaul U., Chgo., Ill., 1993; MA, U. Mich., Ann Arbor, 1995; PhD, U. London, Eng., 2000. Asst. prof. U. Miami, Fla., 2005—, U. Houston; asst. lectr. U. Coll. Dublin. Editor: Theater Rsch. Internat. North Am. Book Rev. Mem.: Performance Studies Internat., Internat. Fedn. for Theatre Rsch., Am. Soc. for Theatre Rsch. Office Phone: 305-284-5669. E-mail: sdibenedetto@miami.edu.

DIBERARDINO, MARIE ANTOINETTE, developmental biologist, educator; b. Phila., May 2, 1926; d. Henry and Adelina (Belfi) DiB. BS in Biology, Chestnut Hill Coll., 1948, JD (hon.), 1990; PhD in Zoology, U. Pa., 1962. Rsch. asst. Fox Chase Cancer Ctr. (formerly Inst. Cancer Rsch.), 1948-58, rsch. assoc., 1960-64, asst. mem., 1964-67; assoc. prof. anatomy Drexel U. Coll. Medicine, Phila., 1967-71, prof. anatomy, 1971-81, prof. physiology, 1981-92, prof. biochemistry, 1992-96, prof. emerita, 1996—. Adv. bd. Internat. Rev. of Cytology, 1976-2000, Differentiation, 1981—, Series: Developmental Biology, A Comprehensive Synthesis, 1982-94; assoc. editor Jour. Exptl. Zoology, 1984-86; Contbr. articles on devel., genetics and cell biology to sci. jours.; contbr. book revs. in field. Mem. NIH Fogarty Internat. Fellowship Study Group, 1984. NSF grantee, NIH grantee; recipient Jean Brachet Meml. award. Fellow AAAS; mem. Am. Soc. Cell Biology (emerita), Soc. for Devel. Biologists (emerita, treas., trustee 1975-78), Internat. Soc. Devel. Biologists, Internat. Soc. of Differentiation (emerita, exec. com. 1978-85, 87-90, bd. dirs. 1980-94). Home: The Quadrangle 7311 #3300 Darby Rd Haverford PA 19041 E-mail: mdiberar@drexelmed.edu.

DIBIAGGIO, JOHN A., university president; b. San Antonio, Sept. 11, 1932; s. Ciro and Acidalia DiBiaggio; married; children: David John, Dana Elizabeth, Deirdre Joan; m. Nancy Cronemiller, May 27, 1989. AB, Eastern Mich. U., 1954, D (hon.) of Edn., 1985; DDS, U. Detroit, 1958, LHD (hon.), 1985; MA, U. Mich., 1967; DSc (hon.), Fairleigh Dickinson U., 1981; LLD (hon.), Sacred Heart U., Bridgeport, Conn., 1984; LLD (hon.), U. Md., 1985; DHL (hon.), U. New Eng., 1987; DHL (hon.), Tokyo U. Agr., 1991; LLD (hon.), U. Nigeria, Nsukka, 1992; LHD (hon.), Fitchburg State Coll., 1994; LHD (hon.), Amer. Coll. Greece, 1998; LLD (hon.), Tufts U., 2002. Pvt. practice, New Baltimore, Mich., 1958—65; asst. prof., asst. to dean, dept. chmn. sch. dentistry U. Detroit, 1965—67; asst. dean student affairs U. Ky., Lexington, 1967—70; prof., dean sch. dentistry Va. Commonwealth U., Richmond, 1970—76; v.p. for health affairs, exec. dir. health ctr. U. Conn., Farmington, 1976—79, pres. Storrs, 1979—85, Mich. State U., East Lansing, 1985—92, Tufts U., Medford, Mass., 1992—2001, now pres. emeritus, 2001—; bd. trustees U. Mass., 2003—. Bd. dirs. Kaman Corp.; mem. Knight Found. Commn. on Intercollegiate Athletics, 1990—2001, PEW Health Professions Commn., 1990—93; cons. in field. Author (with others): Applied Practice Management: A Strategy for Stress Control, 1979; contbr. articles to profl. jours. Bd. nominators Am. Inst. Pub. Svc., 1989—92; bd. dirs. Nat. Italian Am. Found., 1988—94; active Bus. Higher Edn. Forum, 1996—2002, WGBH Ednl. Found., 1992—2001, chmn. governance com., 1997—98; trustee U. Detroit, 1979—86, Am. Film Inst., 1988—, Forsyth Dental Ctr., 1993—, Am. Cancer Soc. Found., 1993—, pres., 1999; trustee Oral Health Am., 1995—97; chmn. adv. com. dental scholars R.W. Johnson Found.; pres. com. Argonne Nat. Lab. 6, 1986—92; coun. pres. Univs. Rsch. Assn., 1989—92; bd. dirs. Black Child and Family Inst., 1990, Coun. for Aid to Edn., 1994—96, Mass. Nat. and Cmty. Svc. Commn., 1994—97, Am. Coun. on Edn., 1995—2001, vice-chmn., 1998, chmn., 1999; exec. com. Mass. Campus Compact, 1995—2001, exec. dir. search com., 1996—2000, chmn. devel. com., 1996—, governance com., 1996—98, chmn., 1998; bd. assocs. Whitehead Inst. for Biomed. Rsch., 1995—2001. Decorated Order of Merit Italy; named Disting. Profl. of Yr., Mich. Assn. Profls., 1985, Disting. Alumni, Ea. Mich. U., 1986, Man of Yr., City of Detroit, 1985; recipient Leadership award, Sacred Heart U., Pierre Fauchard Gold Medal award, 1989. Fellow: Internat. Coll. Dentists, Am. Coll. Dentists; mem.: NCAA (found. bd. dirs. 1988—2001, found. divsn. III pres.'s coun. 1997—2001), APHA, ADA, Nat. Assn. State Univs. and Land Grant Colls. (chmn. 1986—87), Internat. Assn. Dental Rsch., Am. Assn. Dental Schs., Mass. Automobile Assn. (bd. dirs. 1992—2002), Am. Automobile Assn. (bd. dirs. 1994—2002), Am. Film Inst., Phi Beta Kappa, Golden Key, Alpha Lambda Delta, Alpha Sigma Chi, Alpha Omega Alpha (Achievement award 1993), Beta Gamma Sigma, Omicron Kappa Upsilon, Phi Kappa Phi. Avocations: golf, antique automobiles, skiing. Home: PO Box 5346 Snowmass Village CO 81615-5346 Business E-Mail: john.dibiaggio@tufts.edu.

DIBIAGIO, THOMAS MICHAEL, lawyer, former prosecutor; b. Balt., June 1960; BA, Dickinson Coll., 1982; JD, U. Richmond, 1985. Bar: Md. 1985, DC 1986. Assoc. Semmes, Brown and Semmes, Balt., 1986—91; asst. US atty. US Dept. Justice, Balt., 1991—2000, US atty., 2001—05; ptnr. Dyer, Ellis & Joseph, Washington, 2000—01; shareholder Beveridge & Diamond P.C., Balt., 2005—. Contbr. articles to profl. jours. Office: Beveridge & Diamond PC 201 N Charles St Ste 2210 Baltimore MD 21201 Office Phone: 410-230-1340.

DIBIASIO, ADOLF R., entertainment company executive; BS in elec. engring., U. Rhode Island; MBA, Wharton Bus. Sch. Sr. dir. McKinsey & Co., 1969—2000; exec. v.p., strategy and investments Time Warner, Inc., 2001—. Past trustee Brunswick Sch., Greenwich, Conn., New Canaan Country Sch.; past chmn. Fairfield County March of Dimes; trustee A Better Chance; dir. Wharton Exec. Bd. of Pa. Office: Time Warner Inc 75 Rockefeller Plaza New York NY 10019

DIBLASI, GANDOLFO VINCENT, lawyer; b. Bklyn., July 7, 1953; s. Rudolph Francis and Theresa (Restivo) DiB.; m. Roberta Wilson, Sept. 13, 1980; children: Richard, William. BA, Yale Coll., 1975, JD, 1978. Bar: N.Y., 1979, U.S. Ct. Appeals (2d cir.), 1982, U.S. Ct. Appeals (4th cir.), 1991, U.S. Ct. Appeals (9th cir.), 1981, U.S. Supreme Ct., 1990, U.S. Dist. Ct. (so. dist.) N.Y., 1979, U.S. Dist. Ct. (ea. dist.) N.Y., 1982, U.S. Dist. Ct. (no. dist.) Calif., 1989. Assoc. Sullivan & Cromwell, NYC, 1978-85, ptnr., 1985—. Home: 200 E End Ave Apt 15I New York NY 10128-7887 Office: Sullivan & Cromwell 125 Broad St Fl 28 New York NY 10004-2489 Office Phone: 212-558-3836.

DIBNER, DAVID ROBERT, architect, writer; b. NYC, May 29, 1926; s. Harry Jesse and Masha Leah (Goldberg) D.; m. Dorothy Joyce Siegel, June 22, 1947; children: Mark Douglas, Amy Lauren. B.Arch., U. Pa., 1949. Registered architect, N.Y., Md., Va., D.C. Ptnr. Fordyce & Hamby Assocs., NYC, 1956-66, The Grad Ptnrship., Newark, 1966-77; pres. Grad-Hoffman, Inc., 1971-75; v.p. Walker-Grad, NYC, 1972-77; exec. v.p. Grad Assocs. P.A., Newark, 1975-77; asst. commr. design and constrn. GSA, Washington, 1977-82; sr. v.p. Bernard Johnson Inc., Bethesda, Md., 1982-89; v.p. and prin. architect Sverdrup Corp., Arlington, Va., 1989-92. Adj. prof. Seton Hall U., South Orange, N.J., 1972-77; mem. Bldg. Rsch. Bd. of Nat. Acad. Sci., com. chmn., 1984-92. Author: Joint Ventures for Architects and Engineers, 1972, You and Your Architect, 1973, (with Amy Dibner-Dunlap) Building Additions Design, 1985; editor (with Andrew Lemer) The Role of Public Agencies in Fostering New Technology and Innovation in Building, 1992, Dreams and Schemes: Stories of People and Architecture, 2001; chmn. editorial bd. Architecture/N.J., 1968-71; contbr. articles to profl. jours. Mem. West Orange Bd. of Adjustment, N.J., 1970-77, Nat. Trust for Historic Preservation. Served with USN, 1944-46, PTO. Fellow AIA (Washington chpt.). Personal E-mail: drdibs@cox.net.

DIBONA, CHARLES JOSEPH, retired trade association administrator; b. Quincy, Mass., Feb. 26, 1932; s. Guido Ralph and Helen Elizabeth (Pangraze) DiB.; m. Evelyn Rauch, July 2, 1959; children: Caroline Anne, Charles J. BS, U.S. Naval Acad., 1956; MA (Rhodes scholar), Oxford U., Eng., 1962. Pres., chief exec. officer Center for Naval Analyses, 1967-73; spl. cons. to Pres. U.S., dep. dir.; White House Energy Policy Office, 1973-74; exec. v.p., chief oper. officer Am. Petroleum Inst., Washington, 1974-78, pres., chief exec. officer, 1979-98; ret., 1998. Hon. dir. Am. Petroleum Inst., 1998—; mem. Fed. City Coun.; chmn. Sentienl Coun. Lt. comdr. USN, 1956-67. Mem. Cosmos Club, Met. Club, Chevy Chase Country Club. Roman Catholic. Home: 9306 Georgetown Pike Great Falls VA 22066-2725 Personal E-mail: dibonac@cox.net.

DIBUONO, EILEEN ELIZABETH, artist; b. Framingham, Mass., July 21, 1948; d. Michael Angelo and Mary Anna (Brennan) DiBuono; m. Alan Marshall Hebditch, Feb. 5, 1971; children: Christian Phillip Hebditch, Davies Leigh. BA, U. Mass., Boston, 1995. Goldsmith Ross Coppelman Goldsmiths, Yarmouthport, Mass., 1975—88. Author: (novel) Paris, Maine; composer: (book of songs) Between the Keys; performer: Damn Yankees; prodr.: (music promotion) The Third Fret Coffee House. Active Rep. Party Campaign for Pres. Bush, Sandwich, Mass., 2003—04; set up vol. One Light Ctr. for Spiritual Transformation, West Yarmouth, Mass., 2004—07. Recipient 1st Prize for artwork, Archdiocese of Boston, 1959; scholar, Marlborough Women's Club, 1994. Independent. Avocations: travel, swimming, tennis, walking. Home Phone: 508-888-1922; Office Phone: 508-274-2856. Personal E-mail: edib@comcast.net.

DICAMILLO, GARY THOMAS, manufacturing executive; b. Niagara Falls, NY, Dec. 10, 1950; s. Joseph John and Olga Marie (Parenti) DiC.; m. Susan Christine Whitaker, Sept. 13, 1975; children: David, John, Benjamin. BSChemE, Rensselaer Poly. Inst., 1973; MBA, Harvard U., 1975. Brand mgr. Procter & Gamble, Cin., 1975-80; mgr. Mckinsey & Co., Chgo., 1980-83; v.p., gen. mgr. Culligan Internat. Co., Northbrook, Ill., 1983-86; pres. Worldwide Power Tools Group Black & Decker Corp., Towson, Md., 1986-95; chmn., CEO Polaroid Corp., Cambridge, Mass., 1995—2002; pres., CEO TAC Worldwide Cos., 2002—05, Am. Crystal Inc., Dedham, Mass., 2005—. Bd. dirs. Whirlpool Corp., Pella Corp., Sheridan Group, 3Com Corp. Mem. bd. govs. New Eng. Aquarium, 1996-2003; commr. Md. Pub. Broadcasting Commn., 1988-93; trustee St. Paul's Sch., 1988-95, Greater Balt. Com., Md. Sci. Ctr.; bd. dirs. Leadership Balt., 1991-93; trustee Mus. of Sci., Boston, Rensselaer Poly. Inst.; mem. bd. trustees The Conf. Bd., 1999-2002. Recipient Albert Demers medal, Livingston Houston prize, Rensselaer Poly. Inst., 1973; Buffalo Alumni scholar Buffalo area Rensselaer Poly. Inst. Alumni, 1969; Chirurg Advt. fellow Harvard U. Bus. Sch., 1974; recipient Rensselaer Poly. Inst. Dirs. award, 1989. Mem. Water Quality Assn. (bd. dirs. 1985-86), Md. Acad. Scis. (bd. dirs. 1991-96), Rensselaer Poly. Inst. Club (bd. dirs. 1987-91, pres.), Rensselaer Alumni Assn. (bd. dirs. 1989-93, Alumni Key award 1990), Hardware Mktg. Coun., DIY Rsch. Inst. (bd. dirs. 1989-90), Skokie Country Club, Elkridge Club, Md. Club, L'Hirondelle Club, Willowbend Club, Wianno Club, Brae Burn Country Club, Harvard Club, Ocean Reef Club, Caves Valley Golf Club. Republican. Avocations: golf, squash, antique furniture, italian cooking. Home: 113 Cliff Rd Wellesley MA 02481-3017 Home and Office: Am Crystal Inc PO Box 9100 Dedham MA 02027-9100

DICAMILLO, KATE, writer; b. Phila. Degree, U. Fla., Gainesville, Fla. Author: (children's books) Because of Winn-Dixie, 2000 (named Newbery Honor Book, 2001, Dorothy Canfield Fisher Children's Book award, 2002, NY Times Bestseller, Publishers Weekly Bestseller children's fiction list, 2005), The Tiger Rising, 2001 (Nat. Book award finalist, 2000), The Tale of Despereaux: Being the Story of a Mouse, a Princess, Some Soup, and a Spool of Thread, 2003 (Newbery medal, 2004, NY Times Bestseller, USA Today Bestseller, Book Sense Bestseller, Publishers Weekly Bestseller), Mercy Watson to the Rescue, 2005, The Miraculous Journey of Edward Tulane, 2005. Grantee McKnight Artist fellowship, 1998. Office: Candlewick Press Inc 2067 Massachusetts Ave Cambridge MA 02140

DICANDILO, MICHAEL D., corporate financial executive, accountant; BSc in Acctg., U. Pa. Wharton Sch. CPA. With Ernst & Young, 1982—90; regional v.p. fin. AmeriSource, Thorofare, NJ, 1990—95, v.p., 1995—2001; v.p., corp. contr. AmerisourceBergen Corp., 2001—02, sr. v.p., CFO, 2002—05, exec. v.p., CFO, 2005—. Office: AmerisourceBergen Corp 1300 Morris Dr Ste 100 Chesterbrook PA 19087 Office Phone: 610-727-7000, 800-829-3132. Office Fax: 800-829-3132.

DICAPRIO, LEONARDO, actor; b. Hollywood, Calif., Nov. 11, 1974; s. George and Irmelin DiC. Actor: (films) Critters III, 1991, This Boy's Life, 1993, What's Eating Gilbert Grape?, 1993 (Academy award nomination best supporting actor 1993), The Quick and the Dead, 1995, The Basketball Diaries, 1995, Total Eclipse, 1995, Romeo and Juliet, 1996, Marvin's Room, 1996, Titanic, 1997, The Man in the Iron Mask, 1998, Celebrity, 1998, The Beach, 2000, Dons Plum, 2001, Gangs of New York, 2002, Catch Me If You Can, 2002, The Departed, 2006, Blood Diamond, 2006; actor, prodr., The Aviator, 2004 (Golden Globe award for best actor, 2005); exec. prodr. The Assassination of Richard Nixon, 2004; writer, narrator The 11th Hour, 2007; (TV series) Parenthood, 1990, Growing Pains, 1991-92. Founder The Leondardo DiCaprio Charitable Found., 1998—. Named Commdr. Order of Arts & Letters, Govt. France, 2005; named one of 50 Most Powerful People in Hollywood, Premiere mag., 2003—06, The World's Most Influential People, TIME mag., 2007; recipient Green Cross Millenium award for Entertainment Ind. Environ., Global Green USA, 2003, Platinum award, Santa Barbara Internat. Film Festival, 2005.*

DI CARLO, ARMANDO, Italian language educator; b. Magliano dei Marsi, Italy, Apr. 2, 1948; came to U.S., 1974; s. Carlo and Costanza (Marini) Di C.; m. Marie A. Morelli, Aug. 29, 1974; children: Carlo, Dino. Doctoral degree, U. Rome, 1972; PhD, U. Mich., 1983. Tchg. asst. U. Mich., Ann Arbor, 1975-79; instr. Miami U., Oxford, Ohio, 1979-82; instr., lang. specialist, dept. chief Def. Lang. Inst., Monterey, Calif., 1982-91, acad. advisor, 1984-87; lectr., dir. Italian lang. program U. Calif., Berkeley, 1991—. Co-author: Italian Basic Course, 1988; contbr. articles to profl. jours. Named Instr. of Yr., Def. Lang. Inst., 1988, recipient exceptional performance award, 1989. Mem. MLA, Dante Soc., Italica, Silarus, Fgn. Lang. Assn. North Calif., Amici dell'Italia (bd. dirs. 1994—). Avocations: travel, gardening, walking, reading, cooking.

DICE, BRUCE BURTON, gas industry executive; b. Grand Rapids, Mich., Dec. 24, 1926; s. William and Wilma (Rose) D.; children: Karen, Kevin, Kirk. BS in Geology, U. Mich., 1950; MS in Geology, Mich. State U., 1956. With El Paso Natural Gas, 1956—62, Drilling and Exploration Co., 1962—63, Ocean Drilling and Exploration, New Orleans, 1963—75; pres. Transco Exploration Co., Houston, 1975—82, Dice Exploration Co., Inc., Houston, 1982—95, Wadi Petroleum, Inc., Houston, 1996—. Cons. in field. Mem.: Shepherd Soc., Houston Geol. Soc., Am. Assn. Petroleum Geologists. Home: 1907 Grand Valley Dr Houston TX 77090-1052 Office: Wadi Petroleum Inc 4355 Sylvanfield Ste 200 Houston TX 77014 Business E-Mail: sgc@wadipetroleum.com.

DI CECCO, JAMES, real estate company executive; b. Westchester, Pa., May 12, 1945; s. Thomas and Blanche Di Cecco. Student, Jacksonville U., Fla., 1964, Goldey Beacom Coll., Wilmington, Del., 1967; Food Technologist, Rutgers U., 1973; student, Gulfstream Coll., Fla., 1978. Sales mgr. Avondale Mushroom Co., Pa., 1966—68, v.p., 1968—70, pres., 1970—72; CEO Avondale Industries, Pa., 1972—74, Superior Wholesale Foods, Pa., 1976—78; v.p., nat. sales mgr. Silverbrook Foods, Del., 1974—76; v.p. investment divsn. Gulfstream Realty, 1978—82. Treas., dir. Hollywood Bd. Realtors, 1987—90; cons. to banking and fin. com. Ho. of Reps., State of Del., 1981. Mem.: Fla. Assn. Realtors (dir. 1987—90), KC (brother 2005).

DICE-K, See **ENOMOTO, DAISUKE**

DICELLO, CARMEN CHARLES, health educator; b. Pottsville, Pa., Nov. 3, 1959; s. Carmen Anthony and Katherine Elizabeth DiCello; m. Marilyn Elizabeth Dee, May 22, 1987; children: Luke, Jacob. BS, Pa. State U., 1984; MDiv, Columbia Evang. Sem., Longview, 2001, Dr. of Theol. Studies, 2004. Tchr. Pottsville Area H.S., Pa., 1984—. Asst. pastor Word of Life Bapt. Ch., Pottsville, 1992—2000; lead pastor New Hope Ch., Pottsville, 2000—05; adj. prof. Columbia Evang. Sem., Longview, 2004—. Author: Dangerous Blessing: The Emergence of a Postmodern Faith, 2005, Why? Reflections on the Problem of Evil, 2007; contbr. New Dictionary of Christian Apologetics. Avocation: running.

DICELLO, FRANCIS P., lawyer; b. Waukegan, Ill., May 5, 1941; s. Anthony M. and Mary Dicello; m. Mary Janice Dicello; children: Anthony, Andrew, Carlotta. BA, U. Notre Dame, 1963; JD, Fordham U., 1966. Bar: Conn. 1966, D.C. 1967, Md 1984, Va 1982. Trial atty. U.S. Dept. Justice, Washington, 1970-76; dep. asst., gen. counsel U.S. Railway Assn., Washington, 1976-78; asst., chief trial & settlement rev. sects. tax divsn. U.S. Dept. Justice, Washington, 1978-79; U.S. trustee ea. dist. Va. and D.C., 1979—82; ptnr., owner Hazel & Thomas, P.C., Washington, 1982-94; ptnr. Reed Smith, LLP, Washington, 1994—. Fellow Am. Coll. Bankruptcy; mem. Am. Bankruptcy Inst. Office: Reed Smith LLP 1301 K St NW Ste 1100E Washington DC 20005-3373 Office Phone: 202-414-9200. E-mail: fdicello@reedsmith.com.

DICELLO, JOHN FRANCIS, JR., physicist, researcher; b. Bradford, Pa., Dec. 18, 1938; s. John Francis and Nicolina Camille (Costello) D.; m. Shirley Ann Rodgers, Aug. 25, 1962; children: John Francis III, Paul T. BS, St. Bonaventure U., 1962-63; MS, U. Pitts., 1962; PhD, Tex. A&M U., 1968. Instr. St. Bonaventure U., 1962-63; Univ. grad. fellow Tex. A&M U., College Station, 1963-65; AEC-Assoc. Western Univs. grad. fellow Los Alamos Nat. Lab., 1965-67, staff scientist, 1973-84; rsch. assoc., rsch. scientist Columbia U., NYC, 1967-73; faculty U. N.Mex., Los Alamos, 1980-82; faculty fellowship Northwest Coll. and Univ. Assn. for Sci., Pacific N.W. Labs., 1989; prof. physics Clarkson U., Potsdam, N.Y., 1982-95; dir. med. physics and prof. radiation, oncology, joint appointment Johns Hopkins U., Balt., 1995—. Mem. peer rev. panel NASA specialized ctrs. of rsch. and tng., 1991—; mem. ad hoc com. NIH/Dept. Energy, 1991—; vis. prof. Johns Hopkins Oncology Ctr., 1992-93. Bd. dirs. N.Mex. divsn. Am. Cancer Soc., 1978-82; mem. sci. com. #88 and #93, Nat. Coun. on Radiation Protection and Measurements, 1992—; mem. task group on biol. effects of space radiation NRC NAS, 1996. Mem. AAUP, IEEE (nuc. and plasma scis. divsn.), Am. Assn. Physicists in Medicine, Radiation Rsch. Soc. (editl. bd., assoc. editor Radiation Rsch. jour. 1992-96), Am. Inst. Biol. Scis. (radiation health peer rev. panel to NASA 1990-94), Am. Phys. Soc. (com. on space rsch.), Sigma Xi (pres. Clarkson U. chpt. 1991-92), Sigma Pi Sigma. Roman Catholic. Achievements include research in field of physics, dosimetry, microdosimetry, radiation biology, cancer research, integrated circuits, accelerator and nuclear physics, heavy-particle radiation therapy. Office: Johns Hopkins U Sch Medicine Oncology Ctr Divsn Radiation Oncology 600 N Wolfe St Baltimore MD 21287-0005

DICERCHIO, RICHARD D., wholesale distribution executive; b. 1945; V.p. ops. Costco Distbn. Corp., Issaquah, Wash., 1983—86, sr. v.p. merchandising, 1986—92, exec v.p., dir., 1992, exec. v.p., COO No. Divsn., 1992—94, now COO merchandising, distbn., constrn., also sr. exec., v.p., 1997—. Office: Costco Corp 999 Lake Dr Issaquah WA 98027*

DICHIERA, DAVID, opera company director; b. McKeesport, Pa., Apr. 8, 1935; s. Cosimo and Maria (Pezzaniti) DiC.; m. Karen VanderKloot, July 20, 1965 (div. 1992); children: Lisa Maria, Cristina Maria. BA in Music summa cum laude, UCLA, 1956, MA in Composition (scholar), 1958, PhD in Musicology, 1962; certificate in composition and piano (Fulbright Research grantee), Naples Conservatory of Music, 1959; D (hon.), U. Mich., 1998. Instr. music U. Calif., Los Angeles, 1960-61; asst. prof. music, asst. dean Oakland U., Rochester, Mich., 1962-65, chmn. music dept., 1966-73; founding gen. dir. Mich. Opera Theatre, Detroit, 1971—; founding dir. Music Hall Center for the Performing Arts, Detroit, 1973—. Artistic dir. Dayton Opera Assn., 1981-92; founding gen. dir. Opera Pacific, Costa Mesa, Calif., 1985-97; trustee Nat. Opera Inst.; adj. prof. Oakland U., Wayne State U. Producer, dir.: Overture to Opera series for, Detroit Grand Opera series, 1963-71; Composer various works for piano, violin, orch., voice; author articles on Italian opera for various encyclopedias; contbr. revs. and articles to music jours. Mem. Arts Com. New Detroit, Inc.; trustee, mem. exec. com. Music Center for Performing Arts; mem. Arts Task Force City of Detroit. Recipient Atwater Kent award U. Calif., Los Angeles, 1961; Certificate of Appreciation City of Detroit, 1970; citation Mich. Legislature, 1976; Michaelangelo award Boys' Town of Italy, 1980; award Arts Found. of Mich., 1981; President's Cabinet award U. Detroit, 1982; George Gershwin fellow, 1958; named A Michiganian of Yr., 1980; cavaliere della Repubblica Italiana. Mem. Am. Arts Alliance (exec. com.), Nat. Opera Assn., Internat. Assn. Lyric Theatre (v.p.), Am. Symphony League, Am. Musicol. Soc., OPERA Am. (pres. 1979-83), AAUP, Phi Beta Kappa, Phi Mu Alpha Sinfonia. Clubs: Detroit Athletic. Office: Mich Opera Theatre 1526 Broadway St Detroit MI 48226-2115 Office Phone: 313-237-3420. E-mail: ddd@motopera.org.*

DICHTER, MARC ALLEN, physician; b. NYC, Dec. 1, 1943; m. Carole Dichter; children: Harold, Eric. BS, Queen Coll. CUNY, 1964; MD, PhD, NYU, 1969. Asst. prof., assoc. prof. neurology Harvard Med. Sch., Boston, 1975-86; prof. neurology U. Pa., Phila., 1986—. Lt. comdr. USPHS, 1970-72. Office: Hosp U Pa Dept Neurology 3400 Spruce St Philadelphia PA 19104-4206 Office Phone: 215-349-5166.

DICHTER, MARK S., lawyer; b. Phila., Jan. 22, 1943; s. Harry B. and Mollie (Silverstein) D.; m. Tobey Gordon, Aug. 17, 1969; children: Aliza, Melissa. BSEE, Drexel U., 1966; JD magna cum laude, Villanova U., 1969. Bar: Pa. 1969, U.S. Ct. Appeals (3d cir.) 1969, U.S. Supreme Ct. 1979. Assoc. Morgan, Lewis & Bockius, LLP, Phila., 1969-76, ptnr., 1976—, chmn. labor and employment law practice group. Co-author: Employee Dismissal Law: Forms and Procedures, 1986-91; editor-in-chief Ann. Supplement Employment Discrimination Law, 1984-89; co-editor: Employment-at-will, 1985, 86, State-by-State Survey, 1984-89; adv. bd. Disability Law Reporter. Bd. dirs. Urban League Phila.; bd. dirs., chmn. Wilma Theater; bd. consultors Villanova U. Sch. Law; bd. dirs. Pub. Interest Law Ctr. Phila. Mem. ABA (labor and employment law sect., chmn. 2000-01, mem. governing coun. 1991-2000, co-chmn. equal opportunity com. 1986-89, employment law com. litigation sect.), FBA (vice chmn. equal employment com. 1983-86), Nat. Employment Law Inst. (adv. bd. 1984—), Am. Employment Law Counsel (bd. dirs.), Am. Coll. Employment Lawyers, Def. Rsch. Inst. (chmn. employment law com. 1989-93). Office: Morgan Lewis & Bockius LLP 1701 Market St Philadelphia PA 19103-2903 Home Phone: 215-922-1633; Office Phone: 215-963-5291. Office Fax: 215-963-5001. Business E-Mail: mdichter@morganlewis.com.

DICK, BARRY LEE, surgeon; b. Cin., Feb. 23, 1954; MD, U. Cin., 1987. Diplomate Am. Bd. Surgery with added qualifications in vascular surgery. Intern U. Cin., 1987-88, resident in gen. surgery, 1988-92; fellow in vasc. surgery St. Louis U., 1992-93; attending Good Samaritan Hosp., Cin., 1993—; attending, v.p. med. staff St. Elizabeth Hosps., Edgewood, Ky., 1993-95, bd. trustees, 2000—. Chmn. surgery St. Luke's Hosps., Florence, Ky., 1997-99. Fellow ACS; mem. Ohio Med. Assn., No. Ky. Med. Assn., Ky. Med. Assn., Mid West Vascular Surg. Soc. Office: Cranley Surg Assocs Inc 3747 W Fork Rd Cincinnati OH 45247-7548

DICK, BERTRAM GALE, JR., physics professor; b. Portland, Oreg., June 12, 1926; s. Bertram Gale and Helen (Meengs) D.; m. Ann Bradford Volkmann, June 23, 1956; children— Timothy Howe, Robin Louise, Stephen Gale. BA, Reed Coll., 1950, Wadham Coll., Oxford U., Eng., 1953, MA, 1958; PhD, Cornell U., 1958. Rsch. assoc. U. Ill., 1957-59; mem. faculty U. Utah, 1959-98, prof. physics, 1965-98, prof. emeritus, 1998—, Univ. prof., 1979-80, chmn. dept., 1964-67, dean grad. sch., 1987-93. Cons. Minn. Mining and Mfg. Co., 1960-67; vis. prof. Technische Hochschule, Munich, 1967-68; vis. scientist Max Planck Institut für Festkörperforschung, Stuttgart, Fed. Republic Germany, 1976-77; faculty Semester at Sea, fall 1983, 86. Mem. Alta Planning and Zoning Commn., 1972-76; pres. Chamber Music Salt Lake City, 1974-76; bd. trustees Citizen's Com. to Save Our Canyons, 1972—, Coalition for Utah's Future Project 2000, 1989-96. Served with USNR, 1944-46. Rhodes scholar, Oxford U., 1950—53. Fellow Am. Phys. Soc.; mem. Am. Alpine Club, Phi Beta Kappa, Sigma Xi. Achievements include research in solid state theory. Home: 1377 Butler Ave Salt Lake City UT 84102-1803 Home Phone: 801-359-5764. E-mail: gdick@xmission.com.

DICK, HAROLD LATHAM, manufacturing executive; b. Wichita, Kans., Oct. 24, 1943; s. Harold G. and Evelyn (Spines) D.; m. Jeanne Marie Luczai, Aug. 25, 1973; children: Harold Campbell, Edward Latham. BA, Washburn U., 1966; MBA, Harvard U., 1968. Exec. asst. to treas. Skelly Oil Co., Tulsa, 1968-70; mgmt. cons. McKinsey & Co. Inc., Chgo., Dallas, Houston, 1970-77; dir. planning Frito-Lay Inc., Dallas, 1977-80; v.p. Norton Simon Inc., NYC, 1980-83; founder Summit Ptnrs., Wichita, Kans., 1983-85; pres., chief exec. officer Doskocil Cos. Inc., Hutchinson, Kans., 1985-88; founder, pres. The Summit Group, Hutchinson, 1988—. Adv. bd. dirs. Garvey Industries, Wichita, 1987-94, Petroleum Inc., Wichita, 1993—. Trustee Kanza coun. Boy Scouts Am., 1989-97, exec. bd., 1995-97, v.p. 1997—, exec. bd. dirs. Quivira coun., 1997—, v.p., 1997-98, coun. commr., 1998-2002, coun. pres., 2002-04, nat. coun. rep., 2004-; Stephen minister, 1987-94; mem. bd. regents Washburn U., 1995—2003, chmn. bd. regents, 2001-02, chmn. fin. com., 1998-2001, mem. presdl. search com., 1987-88; chmn. Washburn Regents Soc., 2003—; trustee Washburn Endowment Assn., 1990-. Mem. Washburn Alumni Assn. (bd. dirs. 1986-89, Disting. Svc. award), Washburn Regents Soc. (chmn. fin. com. 2004—), Former Regents Soc. (chmn. 2004—). Republican. Episcopalian. Office: The Summit Group PO Box 3216 Hutchinson KS 67504-3216 Personal E-mail: hldick@yahoo.com.

DICK, HENRY HENRY, minister; b. Russia, June 1, 1922; s. Henry Henry and Mary (Unger) D.; m. Erica Penner, May 25, 1946; children— Janet (Mrs. Arthur Enns), Judith (Mrs. Ron Brown), James, Henry. Th.B., Mennonite Brethren Bible Coll., 1950. Ordained to ministry Mennonite Brethren Ch., 1950; pastor in Orillia, Ont., Canada, 1950-54, Lodi, Calif., 1954-57, Shafter, Calif., 1958-69; faculty Tabor Coll., 1954-55; gen. sec. Mennonite Brethren Conf. of U.S.A., 1969-72; pres. Mennonite Brethren Bibl. Sem., Fresno, Calif., 1972-76; vice moderator Gen Conf. Mennonite Brethren Ch., 1975-78, moderator, 1979-84; pastor Reedley Mennonite Brethren Ch., 1976-88; ret., 1989; dir. ch. and constituency relations Mennonite Brethren Biblical Sem., 1987-89; dist. min. emeritus Mennonites, 2002—; min. pastoral care Mennonite Brethren, Dinuba, Calif., 2003—. Moderator Pacific Dist. Conf., 1959-60, 61-63, 75-77; mem. exec. com. Mennonite Central Com. Internat., 1967-75, mem. bd. reference and counsel, 1966-69, 72-75, mem. bd. missions and services, 1969-72; exec. sec. Bd. Edn. Mennonite Brethren, 1969-72; chmn. Bd. Missions and Services, 1985-91; pastor emeritus Reedley Mennonite Brethren Ch., 1987. Columnist bi-weekly publ. Christian Leader, 1969-75. Bd. dirs. Bob Wilson Meml. Hosp., Ulysses, Kans., 1969-72; dist. minister Pacific Dist. Conf. Mennonite Brethren, 1989—. Recipient Humanitarian award Shafter C. of C., 1969, Citation bd. dirs. Bibl. Sem. Mem.: Kiwanis, Reedley Rotary. Mem. Mennonite Brethren Ch. Home: 5710 W Herbert # 36 Reedley CA 93654 Office: 1632 L St Reedley CA 93654-3340

DICK, JAMES CORDELL, concert pianist; b. Hutchinson, Kans., June 29, 1940; s. George Gerhard and Dorothy Lois (Ulsh) Dick., 1958-63; studied with, Dalies Frantz; MusB with spl. honors, U. Tex., 1963; studied with Sir Clifford Curzon, 1963-65; postgrad., Royal Acad. Music, London, 1963-65. Concert pianist Sol Hurok Presents, NYC, 1968-70, Shaw Concerts, NYC, 1970-75, Columbia Artists, NYC, 1975-89, A.G. Declert and Assocs., Round Top, Tex., 1989—. Founder, artistic dir. Internat. Festival-Inst., Round Top, 1971—; judge internat. rec. competition Nat. Guild Piano Tchrs., 1970—71; nat. cons. music com. Inst. Internat. Edn., NYC, 1971—72; mem. internat. jury Tschaikovsky Competition, Moscow, 1974, Van Cliburn Competition, Ft. Worth, 1975, Ft. Worth, 78; chmn. Fulbright Panel in Music, NYC, 1978. Commd. (Am. piano concerto) Shiva's Drum, (nominated Pulitzer Prize in music), 1994. Recipient First Prize award Shreveport Symphony Competition, 1958-60, San Angelo Symphony Competition, 1958-60, Dallas Symphony, 1961-62, Nat. Guild Piano Tchrs., 1961-62, Tschaikovsky Internat. Competition, 1965-66, Leventritt Piano Competition, 1965-66, Busoni Internat. Piano Competition, 1965-66, Citation cert. Tex. Ho. Reps., 1975, award Japan Soc. Houston, 1975, Presdl. citation Nat. Fedn. Music Clubs, 1979, Round Top award Gov. William. P. Clements, Tex., 1980, Headliner of Yr. award Headliners Club, 1983, Tex. State Musician award, 2003; honoree Pres. Lyndon B. Johnson, 1965-66; nominee Pulitzer Prize in Music, 1974; commd. Amb. of Goodwill, State of Tex., 1978; named Hon. Texan, Gov. Dolph Briscoe, 1978, Chevalier des Arts et Lettres French Ministry Culture, 1994; Fulbright scholar, Tobias Matthay fellow, Royal Acad. Music, Hon assoc., 1969, recipient Merit cert., 1965, Beethoven prize, Recital medal, Chevalier des Arts et Lettres, French Ministry of Cult., 1994; named Tex. State Musician, 2003. Mem.: Tex. Lyceum Assn. (adv. dir. 1978—), Tex. Fedn. Music Clubs (hon. life), Philos. Soc. Tex. (treas. 1976—), English Speaking Union, Bohemians Club (N.Y.C.), Tuesday Mus. Club (hon.), Rotary Internat. (hon. life), Sigma Alpha Iota (hon. nat. patron 2001). Avocations: architecture, landscaping, literature, poetry, woodworking. Office Phone: 979-249-3129. Office Fax: 979-249-5078. Business E-Mail: jamesd@festivalhill.org.

DICK, JOHN R., bank executive; m. Mary Valenta; 2 children. Grad., U. Va., 1979. Chief info. officer N.Am. GMAC, Detroit; exec. v.p., chief info. officer Regions Fin. Corp., Birmingham, Ala., 2001—. Named one of Premier 100 IT Leaders, Computerworld, 2005. Office: Regions Fin Corp 417 N 20th St Birmingham AL 35202 Office Phone: 205-944-1300.

DICK, RAYMOND DALE, psychologist, educator; b. Toledo, Ohio, July 16, 1930; s. Floyd Edward and Clara Belle (Spilker) D.; m. Beverly Ann Sparks, June 18, 1955; children: Gregory Dale, Jeffrey Clayton. BS, Northwestern U., 1952; MA, U. Mo., 1955, PhD, 1958. Asst. prof. psychology Ft. Hays (Kans.) State Coll., 1958-62; assoc. prof. Fort Hayes (Kans.) State Coll., 1962-64, prof., 1964-66, acad. chmn. psychology dept., 1959-66; prof. psychology U. Wis., Eau Claire, 1966-98, dean Sch. Grad Studies, 1966-81, prof. emeritus, 1998—. Assoc. Danforth Found., 1962-84, also chmn. Upper Midwest selection com., 1969-72; mem. com. liberal arts edn. North Central Assn. Colls. and Secondary Schs., 1963-66, coordinator liberal arts com., 1965-68, cons-examiner, 1971— Contbr. profl. jours. Mem. APA, AAAS. Home: 2823 Irene Dr Eau Claire WI 54701-6692 E-mail: rddick@uwec.edu.

DICK, RICHARD IRWIN, environmental engineer, educator; b. Sanborn, Iowa, July 18, 1935; s. Laurence Irwin and Lillian Marie (Riesser) D.; m. Delores Kay Den Beste, Aug. 31, 1958; children: Natalie Ann, Kevin Irwin, Laura Lynn, Craig David. BS, Iowa State U., 1957; MS, State U. Iowa, 1958; PhD, U. Ill., 1965. Sanitary engr. USPHS, Kansas City, Mo., 1958-60; sanitary engr. Clark, Daily and Dietz (Cons. Engrs.), Urbana, Ill., 1960-62; instr. to prof. civil engring. U. Ill., 1962-72; prof. civil engring. U. Del., Newark, 1972-77; Joseph P. Ripley prof. engring. Cornell U., Ithaca, NY, 1977—2002, Joseph P. Ripley prof. emeritus, 2002—; Thomas R. Camp lectr. Boston Soc. Civil Engrs., 1981. Disting. vis. scientist U.S. EPA Water Engring. Rsch. Lab., Cin., 1986-89; vis. engr. Water Pollution Rsch. Lab., Stevenage, Eng., 1970-71; hon. rsch. fellow Univ. Coll. London, 1990; vis. prof. U. B.C., Vancouver, 1991, McGill U., Montreal, 1991. Contbr. over 200 articles to profl. jours. Served with USPHS, 1958-60. Recipient Disting. Alumnus award, U. Ill., 1996, Daniel M. Lazar '29 Excellence in Tchg. award, Cornell U., 1996, James M. and Martha D. McCormick Excellence Advising award, 1999. Mem.: ASCE (Rudolph Hering medal 1986), Charted Instn. Water and Environ. Mgmt., Am. Water Works Assn., Water Environment Fedn. (Harrison Prescott Eddy medal 1968), Internat. Water Assn. (past mem. exec. com., bd. govs.), Assn. Environ. Engring. Profs. (past pres., Disting. lectr. 1980, Outstanding Pub. award 1986, 1987, Founder's award 1998), Phi Kappa Phi, Chi Epsilon (U. Ill. Chpt. Honor mem. 1980, Cornell U. Prof. of Yr. 1995, 2002), Tau Beta Pi, Sigma Xi. Home: 115 W Upland Rd Ithaca NY 14850-1415 Office: Cornell U 105 Hollister Hall Ithaca NY 14853-3501 Business E-Mail: rid1@cornell.edu.

DICKE, CANDICE EDWARDS, librarian, educator; b. Elmhurst, Ill., Aug. 5, 1949; d. Frederick Francis and Bernice Pauline (Bartels) Cramer; m. Mark Edwin Edwards, June 19, 1971 (div. 1981); 1 child, Kristin Paige; m. Timothy Lee Dicke, Aug. 5, 1984; 1 child, Elizabeth Ann. BA, U. Iowa, 1971; MLS, George Peabody Coll. Tchrs., 1974. Media specialist, Ohio; cert. tchr., libr., tchr. educably mentally retarded Durant Cmty. Sch. Dist., Iowa, 1971-72, Peabody Demonstration Sch., Nashville, 1972-75; reading tchr. Edgewood Ind. Sch. Dist., San Antonio, 1975-76; libr. Northside Ind. Sch. Dist., San Antonio, 1976-79; childrn's libr. DeKalb Libr. System, Decatur, Ga., 1979-80; media specialist DeKalb County Bd. Edn., Decatur, 1980-84, 86-88; libr. Elida (Ohio) Local Schs., 1988-91; tchr. 3rd grade Elida Elem. Sch., 1991-96, tchr. Title I reading and math., 1996—2006; pastor Botkins United Meth. Ch., Ohio, 1997—2000; assoc. pastor Wayne St. United Meth. Ch., St. Mary's, Ohio, 2000—02; pastor family ministries Westside United Meth. Ch., Lima, Ohio, 2002—05. Title 1/Hosts coord., 2003-06; adviser Elida H.S. Quiz Bowl, 1992-93; bookseller Back in Time, Inc. (formerly Everychild Bookstore), Duluth, Ga., 1984-86; treas. S.E. Advocates of Lit. for Young People, Athens, Ga., 1986-88. Author: The Reference Point, 1983. Advisor Jr. High Youth Fellowship Wayne State United Meth. Ch., 1991—93; coord. Christian Personhood Lima Mission Dist., 1995—97, West Ohio Conf. United Meth. Ch.; leader Girl Scout Troop 3050, 1986—88; Sunday sch. tchr. mentally handicapped adults, 1989—; Chancel Choir; v.p. United Meth. Women, 1994—95, pres., 1996—; bd. dirs. Harbor House Maternity Home and Elizabeth Pregnancy Svcs, 2005—07; exec. dir. Family Life Ctr. Augharze County, 2007. Mem. NEA, Ohio Edn. Assn., Elida Edn. Assn. Methodist. Home: 1815 Fenway Ct Saint Marys OH 45885-1366 E-mail: cadicke@aol.com.

DICKE, JAMES FREDERICK, II, manufacturing executive; b. San Angelo, Tex., Nov. 9, 1945; s. James Frederick and Eilleen (Webster) D.; m. Janet St. Clair, July 6, 1968; children: James F. III, Jennifer S. BS, Trinity U., 1968. Intern U.S. Ho. of Reps., Washington, 1966; sales coord. Crown Controls Corp., New Bremen, Ohio, 1968-69, v.p. internat., 1970-78; exec. v.p. Crown Equipment Corp., New Bremen, Ohio, 1979-80, pres., CEO, 1980—2002, chmn., CEO, 2003—. Chmn. Crown Australia Pty. Ltd., Sydney, 1980—, Crown Ltd., Galway, Ireland, 1980—; bd. dirs. Dayton (Ohio) Power and Light Co. Chmn. bd. trustees Dayton (Ohio) Art Inst., 1998—; trustee, v.p., sec. Culver (Ind.) Ednl. Found., 1981-2001; Midwest dir. Boys and Girls Clubs Am., Chgo., 1987-2001; co-chmn. Ohio Rep. Fin. Com., 1995—. Recipient Disting. Svc. award Culver Acads., 1989, Disting. Alumnus award Trinity U., 1991; honoree Nat. Acad. Design, 1999. Mem. Young Pres.' Orgn. (bd. dirs. 1985-94, internat. pres. 1992-93), Cum Laude Soc. Culver Acads., Key Largo Anglers CLub (chmn. bd. dirs. 1999-2001). Mem. United Ch. of Christ. Office: Crown Equipment Corp PO Box 97 New Bremen OH 45869-0097

DICKEL, DAVID I., III, financial analyst; b. Phila., Sept. 26, 1967; adopted s. David I. Dickel, Jr. and Dorothy R. (Tripp) Dickel, s. Wanda (Kyle) and Stephen G. Barone (Stepfather); m. Paula Sue Crabb, Sept. 23, 1988; 1 child, David I. Dickel, IV. Degree in mgmt., Elizabethtown Coll., Pa., 1987, Stroehmann U., Montgomery, Pa., 1990. Gen. mgr. Kreider Farms, Inc., Manheim, Pa., 1982—87; transp. adminstr. Wenger Feeds, Inc., Rheems, Pa., 1987—89; mktg. account mgr. George Weston, Inc., Toronto, Ontario, Canada, 1989—94; pres. Dickel Enterprises, Elizabethtown, Pa., 1989—; fin. officer Keller Bros, Inc., Lititz, Pa., 1994—; bd. dirs. Naaman Ctr., Elizabethtown, Pa., 1995—97; mktg. dir. Skyline Corp., Elkhart, Ind., 1997—2000. Supt. edn. Conoy Brethren in Christ, Elizabethtown, 1988—95. Recipient 2d Pl. award, NRA Pa. State Rifle Championship, 1985, 1st Pl. Individual & Team award, NRA US Regional Rifle Championship, 1985—86. Mem.: Mensa (life). R-Consevative. Brethren In Christ. Avocations: auto racing, hunting. Home and Office: Dickel Enterprises 37 Foxfield Ln Elizabethtown PA 17022-1776 Home Phone: 717-314-3769. Home Fax: 413-460-0644. Personal E-mail: didiii@comcast.net. Business E-Mail: didickel@comcast.net.

DICKEN, ERIC L., academic administrator; b. Salem, Ohio, Sept. 21, 1969; s. Richard and Nancy Dicken; life ptnr. Paul Putman, Dec. 31, 1990. BA, Hiram Coll., Ohio, 1991; EdM in Higher Edn., Kent State U., Ohio, 1993; cert. in human resource mgmt., Baldwin-Wallace Coll., Berea, Ohio, 2000; postgrad., Case Western Res. U., Cleve., 2004—. Coord. coop. edn. Emporia State U., Kans., 1995—97; assoc., asst. dir., career advisor, career services Baldwin-Wallace Coll., Berea, 1997—2003; asst. dir. student preparation Case Western Res. U. Career Ctr., Cleve., 2003—05; dir. campus events Case Western Res. U., Cleve., 2005—. Recipient Gerald Saddlemire Mentor award, Ohio Coll. Pers. Assn., 2003; Grad. fellow, Ohio Bd. Regents, 1991—93. Home: 7414 Franklin Blvd Cleveland OH 44102 Office: Case Western Reserve University 10900 Euclid Ave Cleveland OH 44106-7035 Office Phone: 216-368-3189. Office Fax: 216-368-6872.

DICKENS, CHARLES HENDERSON, retired social sciences educator; b. Thomasville, NC, Nov. 22, 1934; s. Argie Marshall and Edna (Sullivan) D.; m. Jane McClung, Aug. 27, 1965; children: Martha Jane, Anne Elizabeth. BS, Duke U., 1957, MEd, 1964, ED, 1966. Asst. prof. Wake Forest U., Winston-Salem, NC, 1965-67; planning specialist NSF, Washington, 1967-69, assoc. program dir. undergrad. instrnl. program, 1969-73, study dir. sci. edn. studies group, 1973-83, sect. head scientific and tech. pers. studies sect., 1983-86, sect. head surveys and analysis sect., 1986-90; sr. policy analyst Fed. Coordinating Coun. for Sci., Engring., and Tech., Washington, 1990-92, exec. sec., 1992-93, ret., 1993. Mem. adv. bd. Am. Men and Women of Sci., New Providence, NJ, 1991—, C.C. Cameron Applied Rsch. Ctr., U. NC, Charlotte, 1994—99; cons. Stanford Rsch. Internat., 2002—, Sr. Tar Heel Legis., 2005—. Adv. bd. Buncombe County Coun. on Aging, 2000—06; active Buncombe County Aging Coordinating Consortium, 2005—, co-chmn., 2006—; active Friends of NC Sr. Tar Heels, Inc., 2005—, v.p., 2007—. With US Army, 1958—59. Recipient Angier B. Duke prize Duke U., 1953-57; Woodrow Wilson fellow Woodrow Wilson Fellowship Found., 1963, James B. Duke fellow Duke U., 1963-64. Fellow: AAAS; mem.: Nat. Active and Ret. Fed. Employees Assn. (v.p. chpt. 156 1995—96, pres. 1996—97, v.p. N.C. area I 1997—2001). Republican. Presbyterian. Avocations: computing, reading. Home: 4 Arrow Pl Asheville NC 28805-9748 E-mail: chas34@juno.com.

DICKENS, JOYCE REBECCA, addictions therapist, educator; b. Roanoke Rapids, NC; d. Leslie and Lydia Marie Dickens. M in Addiction Psychology with honors, Capella U., 2000, PhD in Psychology with honors, 2003. Cert. addiction profl. Adj. instr. Broward CC, Ft. Lauderdale, Fla., 1991—; primary therapist addictions Treatment Works, Ft. Lauderdale, 2002—. Mem.: AAUW, Phi Theta Kappa, Alpha Chi. Avocations: tennis, travel, public speaking. Office Phone: 954-761-3420. Personal E-mail: joyced@bellsouth.net.

DICKENS, JUSTIN KIRK, nuclear physicist; b. Syracuse, NY, Nov. 2, 1931; s. Milton Clifford and Jennette Martin (Holmes) D.; m. Marcay Cosette Jordan, Dec. 21, 1957; children: Alan Russell, Leonard Raymond, Steven Kenneth, Michael Loren. AB in Physics, U. So. Calif., LA, 1955, PhD in Physics, 1962; MS in Physics, U. Chgo., 1956. Engring. assoc. Collins Radio Co., Burbank, Calif., 1955; electronic technician Enrico Fermi Inst. for Nuclear Studies, Chgo., 1956-57; grad. teaching asst. U. So. Calif., LA, 1957-61, rsch. assoc., 1961-62; rsch. staff mem. Oak Ridge (Tenn.) Nat. Lab., 1962-78, sr. rsch. staff mem., 1978-94, cons., 2000—; private cons., 1995; rsch. prof. physics U. Tenn., Knoxville, 1996-99, 2001; cons. Oak Ridge Nat. Lab., 2000—. Gen. chmn. Internat. Conf. on Nuclear Data for Sci. and Tech., Gatlinburg, Tenn., 1994. Author: The Descendants of Ephraim Dickens (Jr.) and Thomas Dickens, 1992, rev. edit., vol. I, 2005, vol. II, 2005, Memoirs and Memories, 2002; co-author (tech. standard) Am. Nat. Standard on Decay Heat, rev. edit., 2005; contbr. 200 articles to profl. jours. Bd. dirs. Oak Ridge Community Playhouse, 1972, 85. With U.S. Army, 1950-52. Recipient Lifetime Achievement award Oak Ridge Comty. Playhouse, 1996, Lockheed Martin Energy Rsch. Tech. Achievement award, 1997. Mem. Am. Phys. Soc., Am. Nuclear Soc., Phi Beta Kappa, Sigma Xi. Office Phone: 865-482-1920. Personal E-mail: jkdickens@aol.com.

DICKENS, WILLIAM THEODORE, economic researcher; b. Chgo., Dec. 31, 1953; s. William James and Estelle Geraldine (Schmidt) D.; m. Maureen Ellen Finegan, June 18, 1982; 1 child, Christopher James. BA, Bard Coll., 1976; PhD, MIT, 1981. Econometric computing cons. MIT, Cambridge, Mass., 1978-80; from asst. to assoc. prof. econ. U. Calif., Berkeley, 1980-95, prof. econ., 1995. Vis. asst. prof. MIT, Cambridge, 1985-86; sr. economist, pres. Coun. Econ. Advisors, 1993-94; vis. fellow The Brookings Instn., 1994-95, sr. fellow, 1995—; faculty rsch. fellow NBER, 1982-86, rsch. assoc., 1986-97; cons. N.Y. Fed. Res. Bank, 2005—. Editor, author: (with Laura Tyson) Dynamics of trade and Employment, 1988, (with Lloyd Ulman and Barry Eichengreen) Labor and an Integrated Europe, 1993, The U.S. Labor Market Effects of European Economic Integration, 1993, (with Kent Weaver) Looking Before We Leap: Social Science and Welfare Reform, 1995, (with Ronald Ferguson) Urban Problems and Community Development, 1999; contbr. articles to profl. jours. including The Brookings Papers on Econ. Activity, 1996, Psychol. Rev., 2001. Grad. fellow NSF, 1976; recipient numerous grants. Mem. Am. Econs. Assn. Democrat. Avocation: flying. Home: 9813 Ashburton Ln Bethesda MD 20817-1723 Office: The Brookings Instn 1775 Massachusetts Ave NW Washington DC 20036-2103 Home Phone: 301-530-8773; Office Phone: 202-797-6113. E-mail: wdickens@brookings.edu.

DICKENSON, KATHARINE HORN, historic preservationist; b. Newburgh, NY, Oct. 31, 1945; d. John Harold and Eleanor (Hamway) Horn; m. David Blaine Dickenson, July 12, 1969; children: Blaine, John David, Daniel. BEd, U. Miami, Coral Gables, Fla., 1967; MEd, U. Miami, 1968. Pres., trustee Boca Raton (Fla.) Hist. Soc., 1974; pres. Boca Raton Jr. League, 1980; chmn. Fla. Historic Preservation Adv. Coun., Tallahassee, 1985, Palm Beach (Fla.) County Preservation Bd., 1986-88; dir. Bonnet House, Ft. Lauderdale, Fla., 1984—, Seaboard Rwy. Sta., West Palm Beach, 1988—, Preservation Action, Washington, 1986—. Trustee Nat. Trust Hist. Preservation, Washington, 1991—2000; chmn. bd. Boca Raton (Fla.) Hist. Soc.; mem. Fla. Arts Coun., 2001—. Recipient Disting. Svc. in Historic Preservation award, Fla. Trust, 1989, Judge Knott Hist. award. Roman Catholic. Avocations: gardening, tennis. Office: Dickenson & Co Inc 980 N Federal Hwy Ste 410 Boca Raton FL 33432-2704 Office Phone: 407-391-1900. Personal E-mail: lkatboca@aol.com.

DICKENSON, LARRY, aerospace transportation executive; b. 1943; BBA, Calif. State U.; attended, U. So. Calif. V.p. comml. sales Europe, Middle East and Africa McDonnell Douglas; v.p. aircraft programs Tex. Air Corp.; with Boeing Comml. Airplanes, 1983—, head Asia/Pacific sales, v.p. sales, 2006—. Bd. dirs. Fred Hutchinson Cancer Rsch. Ctr. Holiday Gala, Nat. Econ. Devel. Bd. Calif. State U. Fellow: Royal Aeronautical Soc. Office: Boeing Comml Airplanes PO Box 3707 Seattle WA 98124*

DICKERMAN, SERAFINA POERIO, real estate broker, consultant; b. Camden, NJ, Sept. 20, 1920; d. Giuseppe Francesco Poerio and Christina Audia; m. John M. Dickerman, Oct. 27, 1956; 1 child, Dorothea Wilhelmina. Attended, Seton Hill Coll., 1938—39, St. Vincent Coll., Latrobe, Pa., 1939—40, Barnard Coll., 1941, Northwestern U., 1943, Strayer Coll., 1951, U. Md., 1971, Am. U., 1953—73. Lic. pvt. pilot, radio operator, meteorologist, radio tel. operator, real estate agt. Md., D.C., Va., N.Y., Fla., Fedn. Internat. Professions Immobilieres, France, cert. internat. property specialist Nat. Assn. Realtors. Mem. Civil Air Patrol Civil Aeronautics Authority, Latrobe, 1939—41; operator control tower radio TWA, Columbus, Ohio, 1941—42; meteorologist Pan Am. Airlines and Colonial Airlines, NYC, 1942—43; stewardess Ea. Airlines, NYC, 1943—45; part-time high fashion model Harry Conover Agy., NYC, 1943—45; negotiator, organizer Airline Stewards and Stewardesses Assn. U.S., Chgo., 1944—46; pres. Dickerman Real Estate/Investment Co., Potomac, Md., 1972—. Participant European Bldg. and Real Estate Study Nat. Assn. Home Builders and European builder orgns., 1963. Contbr. articles to mags. in field. Driver blood mobile, life saver swimmer Nat. Red Cross, Washington, 1955; hostess USO, NYC, 1941; mem. Young Rep. Club, NYC, 1941, Potomac Women's Rep. Club, 1960. First Woman recipient Civil Air Patrol Silver Wings, FAA World War II, 1939—40. Mem.: Nat. Mus. Women in Arts (charter), Italian Culture Soc. Washington, Capital Spkrs. Club (Washington), Women's Golf Assn. of Congl. Country Club, Congl. Country Club (hon. life). Presbyterian. Avocations: music, art, golf, tennis, swimming. Office: Dickerman Real Estate/Investment Co 9030 Bronson Dr Potomac MD 20854 Office Phone: 301-983-2546.

DICKERSON, CLAIRE MOORE, lawyer, educator; b. Boston, Apr. 1, 1950; d. Roger Cleveland and Ines Idelette (Roullet) Moore; m. Thomas Pasquali Dickerson, May 22, 1976; children: Caroline Anne, Susannah Moore. AB, Wellesley Coll., 1971; JD, Columbia U., 1974; LLM in Taxation, NYU, 1981. Bar: N.Y. 1975, U.S. Dist. Ct. (ea. and so. dists.) N.Y. 1975, U.S. Ct. Appeals (2d cir.) 1975, U.S. Supreme Ct. 1980. Assoc. Coudert Brothers, NYC, 1974-82, ptnr., 1983-86, Schnader, Harrison, Segal & Lewis, N.Y., 1987-88, of counsel N.Y., 1988—; assoc. prof. law St. John's U., Jamaica, N.Y., 1986-88, prof., 1989-2000; prof law Rutgers U., Newark, 2000—. Author: Partnership Law Adviser; contbr. articles to profl. jours. Scholar Arthur L. Dickson scholar. Mem.: ABA, Soc. for Advancement of Socio-Econs., Law and Soc. Assn., Assn. of Bar of City of N.Y., Shenorock Club. Democrat. E-mail: cmdckrsn@rci.rutgers.edu.

DICKERSON, DENNIS CLARK, SR., historian, educator; b. McKeesport, Pa., Aug. 12, 1949; s. Carl O'Neal and Oswanna (Wheeler) D.; m. Mary Anne Eubanks, Aug. 6, 1977; children: Nicole Denise, Valerie Anne, Christina Marie, Dennis Clark Jr. BA, Lincoln U., 1971; MA, Washington U., Mo., 1974, PhD, 1978; LHD (hon.), Morris Brown Coll., 1990; postgrad., Hartford Sem., Memphis Theol. Seminary; postgrad. in Divinity, Vanderbilt U., 2005—. Instr. history Forest Park C.C., St. Louis, 1974, Pa. State U. Ogontz, Abington, 1975-76; from asst. to assoc. prof. history Williams Coll., Williamstown, Mass., 1976-85, assoc. prof., 1987-88, prof., 1988-99, Stanfield prof. history, 1992-99; assoc. prof. history Rhodes Coll., Memphis, 1985—87; James M. Lawson Jr. prof. history Vanderbilt U., Nashville, 1999—. Mem. com. examiners GRE History test Ednl. Testing Svc., Princeton, 1990-96; corporator Williamstown Savs. Bank, 1992-99; vis. prof. Payne Theol. Sem., Wilberforce, Ohio, 1992, 96, 98, 2002, 04; vis. prof. Am. religious history Yale Div. Sch., 1995. Author: Out of the Crucible, 1986, Religion, Race and Region: Research Notes on A.M.E. Church History, 1995, Militant Mediator: Whitney M. Young, Jr., 1998, A Liberated Past: Explorations in A.M.E. Church History, 2003; historiographer, exec. dir. rsch. and scholarship, editor A.M.E. Ch. Rev., 2000—; contbr. articles to profl. jours. Historiographer, African Meth. Episcopal Ch., 1988—, min. 1977—; trustee Mass. Coll. Liberal Arts, 1992-95. Rockefeller Found. fellow U. Va., 1987-88. Mem. Am. Bible Soc. (chmn. bd. trustees 2006—), Am. Soc. Ch. History (pres. 2004), Elks, Alpha Phi Alpha. Office: Vanderbilt U Dept History Nashville TN 37235-0001 Business E-Mail: dennis.c.dickerson@vanderbilt.edu.

DICKERSON, JILL LOUISE, elementary school educator; b. Kansas City, Mo., Nov. 13, 1965; d. Richard Eugene and Lois Jean (Holzhauser) Markley; m. Daniel Sean Dickerson, July 1, 1989. BS in Edn., S.W. Mo. State U., 1989, Diploma in Voice, 1989; M Mus. Edn., U. Mo., Kansas City, 1992. Elem. music tchr. Raymore-Peculiar Sch. Dist., Raymore, Mo., 1989—. Mem. cultural arts com. Raymore-Peculiar Schs., 1989-93, curriculum com., 1992, bldg. leadership team, 1992-93, O.B.E. com., 1992-93, Am. 2000 com., 1992-93; performer Meistersingers, Kansas City, Mo., 1989-92, Wyandotte Players, Kansas City, Kans., 1992, Theater Under the Stars, Kansas City, Mo., 1991, Kans. Opera Theater, Overland Park, 1991-93, MCC Players, 1993. U. Mo.-Kansas City Women's Coun. rsch. fellow, 1991-93. Mem. NEA, Mo. Music Educators Assn. (rsch. presenter), Mo. Tchrs. Assn., Pi Kappa Lambda. Avocations: equitation, theater, fast-pitch softball, travel. Home: 2105 W 72nd Ter Prairie Village KS 66208-3344 Office: Raymore Elem Sch 500 S Madison St Raymore MO 64083-9007

DICKERSON, JOHN ROBERT, retired automotive engineer; b. Detroit, Oct. 8, 1930; s. James Eldridge and Edith Barrie Dickerson; m. Jacqueline Bowman, June 14, 1952 (div. Sept. 1967); children: Robert Floyd, Diane Lynn; m. Barbara Marie Gannon, Feb. 7, 1969; 1 child, Edward Michael Gannon. Cert., Wayne State U., 1950, N.D. State U., 1951, Chrysler Inst. Engring., 1956, Cert., 1964. Sr. stylist designer Chrysler Corp., Highland Park, Mich., 1957—61, 1961—64, sr. stylist designer, engr., 1964—69, engr. product devel., 1978—84, mgr. vehicle build ops., 1984—88; owner, CFO J. Robert Dickerson & Assocs., Detroit, 1969—72; supr. fleet engring. Am. Motors Corp., Detroit, 1972—78. Stylist designer cons. Creative Industries, Detroit, 1970—71; cons. Wayne State U. Consortium, Detroit, 1971—72; design cons. J. Robert Dickerson & Assocs., Detroit, 1969—73; chmn. adv. com. Tech. Comms., 2001—02; engring. rep. to G.S.A. Automotive Vehicle Bid Consortium, Washington, 1974—78; signatory party to UN for Am. Motors Corp., 1974—78. Author: One Goal is Not Enough, 2001, How to Build a 50 Foot Yacht, 1972. Contbr., organizer 100th Anniversary Auto., Detroit Hist. Mus., 2000; charter mem. Rep. Nat. Com., Washington, 2000—; mem. Rep. Presdl. Task Force, Washington, 2000—. With USAF, 1950—52. Recipient Design award, GSA, 1980. Mem.: Am. Soc. Body Engring., NRA, Sr. Mens Club of Grosse Pointe. Republican. Achievements include patents for automotive design; first to introduce and homologatie the first Pacer vehicle and American Motors Automotive Products into European markets; managed, directed and created concept engineering test and show vehicle development from tooling to complete running vehicles; prototype vehicle build coordinator in Italy for Chrysler Maserati Program; first to style, design and name Dodge Charger, 1963; development of show cars from preproduction vehicles for Nat. Press Shows. Avocations: flying, boating, golf, travel, gardening.

DICKERSON, LON RICHARD, library administrator; b. Ypsilanti, Mich., Dec. 16, 1941; s. Lon E. and Maxine A. (Merryfield) D.; m. Anne Elizabeth Bryan, Aug. 24, 1968; children: Robert Lon, Sarah Elizabeth, Peter Bryan. AB, Albion Coll., 1964; MLS, U. Pitts., 1968. Dir. U. Liberia Librs., Monrovia, 1968-72, Lake Agassiz Regional Libr., Moorhead, Minn., 1972-85, Timberland Regional Libr., Olympia, Wash., 1985-92, Omaha Pub. Libr., 1993—96, Chatham-Effingham-Liberty Regional Libr., Savannah, Ga., 1996—2000, Jefferson Parish Libr., Metairie, La., 2004—. Pres. Adv. Coun. State Libr., Minn., 1977-78, Minn. Regional Pub. Libr. Sys. Adminstrs., 1980, No. Lights Libr. Network Adv. Coun., Minn., 1981-82; v.p. Ga. Coun. Pub. Librs., 1998-00, pres., 2000. Contbr. articles to profl. jours. Libr. vol. Peace Corps Sierra Leone Libr. Bd., Freetown, 1964-67; mem. planning commn. City of Lacey, Wash.,1985-93; vice-chair planning commn. City of Lacey, 1991-93, mem. various sch. dist. coms.; bd. dir. Clay-Wilkin Opportunity Coun., Moorhead, Minn., 1982-85; mem. steering com. Omaha 2000, 1993-96, Omaha Free-Net, 1994-96, United Way of the Midlands Com., Omaha, 1996. Mem. ALA (internat. rels. com. 1974-75), Wash. Libr. Assn. (co-chmn. legis. planning com. 1987-92, Pres.'s award 1988), La. Libr. Assn., Pub. Libr. Assn. (nominating com. 1989-90), Tau Kappa Epsilon. Democrat. Presbyterian. Office: Jefferson Parish Libr 4747 W Napoleon Ave Metairie LA 70001-2310 Office Phone: 504-838-1133. Business E-Mail: ldickerson@jefferson.lib.la.us.

DICKERSON, MARTIN LEE, principal; b. Wilson, NC, Mar. 30, 1961; s. Joelene Armwood; m. Barbara Gail Lutterloh; 1 child, Lamont Lee. BS, Rutgers U., 1983; MA, Montclair State U., 1997; EdD, U. Pa., 2006. Cert. tchr. N.H., prin. N.H., supt. N.J. Tchr. Newark Bd. Edn., 1986—99; vice prin. Sampson G. Smith Sch., Somerset, NJ, 1999—2005. Track and field coach Arts H.S., Newark, 1986—94; prin. Walter O. Krumbiegel Mid. Sch., Hillside, NJ, 2005—. Vol. United Way, Newark, 2003—05; v.p. Fairview Apt. Tenant Assn., East Orange, NJ, 1994. Named Track and Field Coach of Yr., Newark Star Ledger, 1990, Cross Country Coach of Yr., Nat. Fedn. Interscholastic Athletics, Kansas City, 1991. Mem.: Am. Ednl. Rsch Assn., N.J. Prin. and Supervisors Assn. (com. mem. 1999—2005), Gideons (camp pres. 1997—2000). Independent. Avocations: reading, fishing, basketball. Office: Walter O Krumbiegel Mid Sch 145 Hillside Ave Hillside NJ 07205 Business E-Mail: mdickerson@hillsidek12.org.

DICKESON, ROBERT CELMER, retired foundation administrator, management consultant; b. Independence, Mo., June 28, 1940; s. James Houston and Sophie Stephanie (Celmer) Dickeson; m. Ludmila Ann Weir, June 22, 1963; children: Elizabeth Ann, Cynthia Marie. AB, U. Mo., 1962, MA, 1963, PhD, 1968; postgrad., U. No. Colo., 1971-72; postgrad. inst. ednl. mgmt., Harvard U., 1973. Adminstrv. asst. U. Mo., Columbia, 1962-64, dir. student activities, 1964-68, asst. dean students, 1968-69; dean student affairs No. Ariz. U., Flagstaff, 1969-70, assoc. prof. polit. sci., 1970-76, prof., 1976-81, v.p. student affairs, 1970-79, v.p. univ. rels., 1973-79; dir. Ariz. Dept. Adminstrn., Phoenix, 1979-81; pres. U. No. Colo., Greeley, 1981-91, prof. polit. sci., 1981-87, 88-91; chief of staff to gov., exec. dir. Office of State Planning and Budgeting State of Colo., 1987; pres. Noel/Levitz Ctrs. Inc., Iowa City, 1991-97; divsn. pres. USA Group Found., Indpls., 1995—97; sr. v.p. Ludmina Found. Edn., 1997—2005; cons., 2005—. Adj. prof. U. Colo., Denver, 1987, Ariz. State U., Tempe, 1979—81; nat. vice chmn. Cert. Pub. Mgr. Policy Bd., 1980—81; mem. univ. adv. coun. Am. Coun. Life Ins.; mem. Pres. Commn. NCAA, 1989—91, Nat. Commn. Minorities Higher Edn., 1989—91; nat. cons. Office Women Higher Edn., Am. Coun. Edn., 1989—97; mem. rsch. adv. coun. Assn. Governing Bds., 2007—; dir. United Bank Greeley; planning and mgmt. cons. Author: Prioritizing Academic Programs and Services, 1999, others; contbr. articles to profl. jours. Mem. nat. coun. Boy Scouts Am., 1976—81; internat. trustee Sigma Alpha Epsilon Found., 1993—97; active Boy Scouts Am., v.p. Grand Canyon coun. Flagstaff, 1974—76, pres., 1976—79, mem. T. Roosevelt coun., 1979—81, mem. Long's Peak coun., 1981—87; chmn. Gov.'s Commn. Merit Sys. Reform, 1979—80, Gov.'s Regulatory Rev. Coun., 1980—81, Gov.'s Commn. Higher Edn., 1983—86; mem. Gov.'s Commn. Excellence Edn., 1983—86, Gov.'s Coun. Creative Schs., 1989—91; commr. Colo. Edn. Commn. of States, 1987—91; mem. state com. Ariz. Dem. Com., 1970—72; pres. bd. trustees United Meth., 1974; bd. fellow Rocky Mountain Leadership Inst., 2006—. Named to N. Ctrl. Athletic Conf. Hall of Fame, 1991; recipient Disting. award. of Merit, 1973, Silver Beaver award, 1975, Disting. Svc. award, Sigma Alpha Epsilon, 1969, Merit Key award, 1997, Disting. Alumnus award, U. Mo., Columbia, 1988, Outstanding Pres. award, Am. Assn. Colls. Tchrs. Edn., 1991, Bus. Excellence award, U. No. Colo., 1996, Faculty-Alumni U. Mo. award, 1999, Disting. Svc. award, Am. Coun. Edn., 2000; vis. scholar, U. Mich., 2003. Mem.: ASPA (Ariz. exec. bd., Superior Svc. award 1981), Am. Assn. State Colls. and Univs. (chmn. coun. doctoral granting instns., Meritorious Svc. award 1991), Nat. Assn. Student Adminstrs. (regional coun. 1974—79), Assn. Pub. Coll. and Univ. Pres. (pres. 1985—87), Coll. Student Pers. Inst. (acad. coun. 1969—73), Am. Acad. Polit. and Social Sci., Am. Polit. Sci. Assn., Columbia Club (Indpls.), Rotary, Kiwanis (pres. 1975—76), Newcomen Soc., Phi Kappa Phi. Home Phone: 970-586-9409; Office Phone: 970-586-9409. Personal E-mail: rdickeson@beyondbb.com.

DICKEY, BETTY C., former state supreme court justice; b. 1940; m. Jay Dickey, 1960 (div. 1987); 1 adopted child, John 1 foster child, Cindy children: Laura, Ted, Rachel. BA in English, U. Ark., 1962, JD, 1985; attended, Nat. Coll. Dist. Attorneys Executive Program, 1994, FBI Nat. Law Inst., 1994. Former tchr. Pine Bluff High Sch., Ark., Watson Chapel Elementary Sch., Ark.; pvt. practice atty. Pine Bluff, Ark., 1985—86, Little Rock, 1990—91; asst. atty., 1986—90, 1993—94; city atty., 1988—94; atty. State Soil and Water Commn., Ark., 1991—93; prosecutor 11th Jud. Dist., 1995—99; commr. Ark. Pub. Svc., 1999—2003; chief legal counsel Ark. Gov.'s Office, 2003; chief justice Ark. Supreme Ct., 2004, assoc. justice Ark., 2004—07. Recipient Atty. Gen.'s Top Prosecutor award, 1997, Top 100 Women in Ark. award, 1998, 1999. Mem.: Jefferson County Bar Assn., Pulaski County Bar Assn., Texas Bar Assn., Ark. Bar Assn. Office Phone: 501-682-6861. E-mail: bcdickey@arkansas.gov.*

DICKEY, DAVID HERSCHEL, lawyer, accountant; b. Savannah, Ga., Dec. 31, 1951; s. Grady Lee and Sara (Leon) D.; children: David Bradford, Carolyn Amanda. BBA in Acctg. and Fin., Armstrong State Coll., 1974; M in Accountancy, U. Ga., 1977, JD, 1977. CPA; bar: Ga. 1978, U.S. Dist. Ct. (no. dist.) Ga. 1980, U.S. Ct. Claims 1978, U.S. Tax Ct. 1978, U.S. Ct. Appeals (5th and 11th cirs.) 1978, U.S. Supreme Ct. 1981. Assoc., acct. Thompson and Benken, Attys., Savannah, 1977-79; pub. acct. Arthur Andersen & Co., Atlanta, 1979-81; assoc. Oliver Maner & Gray, LLP, Savannah, 1981—82, ptnr., 1982—. Pres. Savannah Estate Planning Coun., 1986-87, chmn. bd., 1987-88; bd. dirs. Chatham-Savannah Citizen's Advocacy; mem. legal adv. bd. Small Bus. Coun. Am., Inc., 1989—; pres. Seminar Group, Inc., 1989—. Hist. Investment Properties, Inc., 1991—. Pres. L'Alliance Francaise de Savannah, 2001—03; bd. dirs. Savannah Theatre Co., 1984, Savannah chpt. Am. Cancer Soc., 1986—91, Hist. Savannah Found., Inc., 1988—94, Candler Hosp. Found., 2003; chmn., trustee Armstrong State Coll. Alumni Endowment Fund, Inc., 1991; chmn. lawyers divsn. Chatham County United Way, 1992; dir., v.p. Armstrong Atlantic State U. Found., 2001—03; bd. trustees The Candler Found., 2001—03. Recipient Outstanding Svc. award Am. Cancer Soc., 1987, Outstanding Alumni Svc. award Armstrong State Coll., 1992; named to Leadership Savannah, Savannah C. of C., 1984-86. Fellow: Am. Coll. Trust and Estate Counsel; mem.: S.R. (pres. Ga. chpt. 2001—03), SAR (pres. Ga. 1999), AICPA, ABA (estate and gift tax com. taxation sect. 1990—), Mil. Order of the Stars and Bars (Lafayette McLaws chpt. comdr. 2005—07), Am. Assn. Atty.-CPAs, Ga. Soc. CPAs, Savannah Bar Assn., Ga. Bar Assn., St. Andrew's Soc., Soc. Colonial Wars, Sons Confederate Vets (comdr. Francis S. Bartow camp no. 93 1997—98), Chatham Club, First City Club (bd. dirs. Savannah 1987—90). Avocations: history, genealogy, music, computers, historic rehab. Home: 4 Springfield Pl Savannah GA 31411 Office: Oliver Maner & Gray LLP 218 W State St Savannah GA 31401-3232 Home Phone: 912-598-0275; Office Phone: 912-236-3311. Business E-Mail: ddickey@omg-law.com.

DICKEY, GEORGE EDWARD, economist, educator, lobbyist, federal official; s. George Otto and Frances Marie (Dougherty) D.; m. Susan Emma Veigel, July 14, 1966; children: Paul Edward, George Louis. BA, Johns Hopkins U., 1961; MA, Northwestern U., 1964, PhD, 1968. Operation rsch. analyst Office Sec. Def., Washington, 1967-69; asst. prof. U. Md., Balt., 1969-73; mem. staff Office Sec. of Army, Washington, 1973-75, econ. advisor, 1976-83; dep. for policy and evaluation Office of Asst. Sec. of Army for Civil Works, Washington, 1983-90, acting prin. dep., 1990-93; acting asst. sec., 1993-94; chief planning divsn. US Army Corps of Engr., Washington, 1994-98; affiliate prof. econ. Loyal Coll., Md., 1998—; sr. advisor Dawson & Assocs., 1998—. Vis. prof. Indsl. Coll. Armed Forces, Washington, 1967-70; cons. in field of water resources. Author: Money, Prices and Growth: The American Experience 1869-1896, 1977; contbr. articles to profl. publ. Exec. bd., v.p. Mother Seton House, 2004—. Capt. US Army, 1965—67. Recipient award for Meritorious Civil Svc., 1981, Presdl. Rank award for Meritorious Svc., 1988, Presdl. Rank award for Disting. Svc., 1993, award for Exceptional Civilian Svc., 1998, Silver Order of the deFluery medal, 1998; Harold E. Stonier fellow, 1964-65; decorated Knight of Magisterial Grace, Sovereign Military Order of St. John of Jerusalem, Rhodes and Malta, 2005-. Mem. SAR, Soc. of colonial Wars, Soc. of Sons of Revolution in State of Md., Cath. League for Religious and Civil Rights, Engring. Soc. Balt., Soc. Mil. Engrs., Md. Hist. Soc., Sovereign Mil. Order Malta (named Knight Magisterial Grace), Johns Hopkins Club, Omicron Delta Epsilon. Roman Catholic. Avocations: gardening, genealogy, hiking, bicycling. Home and Office: 3 Stratford Rd Baltimore MD 21218-1145 Office Phone: 410-467-9545, 202-289-2060. Business E-Mail: gedickey@jhu.edu.

DICKEY, GLENN ERNEST, JR., sportswriter; b. Virginia, Minn., Feb. 16, 1936; s. Glenn Ernest and Madlyn Marie (Emmert) D.; m. Nancy Jo McDaniel, Feb. 25, 1967; 1 son, Kevin Scott. BA, U. Calif., Berkeley,

1958. Sports editor Watsonville (Calif.) Register-Pajoronian, 1958-63; sports writer San Francisco Chronicle, 1963-71, sports columnist, 1971—. Author: The Jock Empire, 1974, The Great No-Hitters, 1976, Champs and Chumps, 1976, The History of National League Baseball, 1979, The History of American League Baseball, 1980, (with Dick Berg) Eavesdropping America, 1980, America Has a Better Team, 1982, The History of Professional Basketball, 1982, The History of the World Series, 1984, (with Jim Tunney) Impartial Judgment: The Dean of NFL Referees Calls Football As He Sees It, 1988, San Francisco Forty-Niners: The Super Year, 1989; (with Bill Walsh) Building a Champion, 1990; Just Win, Baby, Al Davis and His Raiders, 1991; Sports Hero Kevin Mitchell (juvenile), 1993, Sports Hero Jerry Rice (juvenile), 1993, San Francisco 49ers: 50 Years, 1995, San Francisco Giants: 40 Seasons, 1997, Glenn Dickey's 49ers, 2000, Champions: The History of the Oakland A's; contbr. stories to Best Sports Stories, 1962, 68, 71, 75, 76. Home: 120 Florence Ave Oakland CA 94618-2249 Office: Chronicle Pub Co 901 Mission St San Francisco CA 94103-2905

DICKEY, JOSEPH WILLIAM, utilities executive, engineer; b. Decatur, Ill., Sept. 20, 1944; s. Lawrence Wayne and Helen Marie (Van Horn) D. BS in Chem. Engring., MIT, 1966, MS in Civil Engring., 1967; postgrad., U. Va., 1978. Registered profl. engr., Tenn., Fla. Plant mgr. Fla. Power & Light Co., Miami, 1973-76, mgmt. positions in nuclear energy and power resources, 1976-85, v.p. nuclear energy and nuclear ops., 1985-88, v.p. power resources, 1988-91; sr. v.p. fossil and hydro power TVA, Chattanooga, 1991-94, chief operating officer Knoxville, 1994-98; pres., CEO FGS & Assocs. LLC, 1999—. Mem. subcom., chmn., officer EEI Prime Movers Com., Washington, 1980-85; mem. subcom., officer S.E. Electric Exch., Atlanta, 1988-91; speaker in field. Contbr. numerous articles to jours. and trade mags. Chmn. for Broward County MIT Ednl. Coun., 1978-91; bd. govs. Dept. Energy Robotics Program, 1987-88; mem. industry adv. coun. U. Fla. Coll. Engring., Gainesville, 1987-91; trustee, chmn. FPL Polit. Action Com., 1981-85, 83-84. Recipient Ishikawa medal Am. Soc. Quality Control, 1996. Fellow Fla. Engring. Soc.; mem. NSPE, ASCE (br. pres. 1974-75).

DICKEY, NANCY WILSON, chancellor, physician; b. Watertown, SD, Sept. 10, 1950; m. Franklin Champ; children: Danielle, Wilson, Elizabeth. BA, Stephen F. Austin State U.; MD, U. Tex., 1976. Diplomate Am. Bd. Family Practice. Resident family medicine Meml. Hosp. System, Houston, 1976-79; pres., vice chancellor health affairs TAMUS Health Sci. Ctr.; prof. family medicine TAMUS Coll. Med., College Station, Tex., 1996—, pres., 2006—. Hon. staff Polly Ryon Meml. Hosp., Richmond; active staff Coll. Sta. (Tex.) Med. Ctr., St. Josephs Hosp., Bryan, Tex. Reviewer Jour. of AMA; editl. adv. bd. Patient Care, Med. World News, Med. Ethics Advisor, Archives of Family Medicine. Coach youth soccer, 1986-88; sponsor United Meth. Youth Fellowship, 1991-95; bd. dirs. Hastings Ctr., Office of Early Childhood Devel., Am. Heart Assn.; mem. Christ United Meth. Ch., College Station. Recipient Disting. Alumni award U. Tex. Med. Sch., Citation of Merit Tex. Soc. of Pathologists, 1995. Mem. AMA (pres. elect 1997, pres. 1998, chair bd. trustees 1995-97, vice chair 1994-95, bd. trustees 1989-97, sec. treas. 1993-94, exec. com. 1991, other coms.), Tex. Acad. of Family Physicians, Tex. Med. Assn., Alpha Omega Alpha. Office: 301 Tarrow St #7th Flr College Station TX 77840-7896

DICKEY, ROBERT J., publishing executive; m. Lori Dickey; 1 child, Megan. With Daily Tidings, Ashland, Oreg., 1981; retail advt. mgr. to advt. dir. Reno Gazette-Jour., Nev., 1989—93; pres., pub. Desert Sun, 1993—2005; and v.p., Pacific Newspaper Group Gannett Newspapers, 1997—2005, sr. group pres., Pacific Newspaper Group, Inc. Escondido, Calif., 2005—, chmn., Phoenix Newspapers, Inc. Phoenix, 2005—. Bd. dir. Downtown Phoenix Partnership, Agua Caliente Devel. Authtority, Desert Health Care Dist., United Way of the Desert, Palm Springs Art Mus., Coachella Valley Econ. Partnership, Palm Springs Internat. Film Festival. Office: Arizona Republic 200 E Van Buren St PO Box 1950 Phoenix AZ 85001 Office Phone: 602-444-8000.

DICKEY, ROBERT PRESTON, writer, educator, poet; b. Flat River, Mo., Sept. 24, 1936; s. Delno Miren D. and Naomi Valentine (Jackson) D.; children: Georgia Rae, Shannon Ezra, Rain Dancer. BA, U. Mo., 1968, MA, 1969; PhD, Walden U., 1975. Instr. U. Mo., 1967-69; asst. prof. English and creative writing U. So. Colo., 1969-73; assoc. mem. faculty Pima Coll., Tucson, 1975-78. Author: (with Donald Justice, Thomas McAfee, Donald Drummond) poetry Four Poets, 1967, Running Lucky, 1969, Acting Immortal, 1970; Concise Dictionary of Lead River, Mo., 1972, The Basic Stuff of Poetry, 1972, Life Cycle of Seven Songs, 1972, McCabe Wants Chimes, 1973, Admitting Complicity, 1973; opera librettos Minnequa, 1976, The Witch of Tucson, 1976; Jimmie Cotton!, 1979, Way Out West, 1979, The Poetica Erotica of R.P. Dickey, 1989, The Little Book on Racism and Politics, 1990, The Way of Eternal Recurrence, 1994, Ode on Liberty, 1996, The Lee Poems, 1998, Self-Liberation, 1998, Exercise Anytime, 1998, Collected Poems, 1999, (with Lee Foster) Taos and Other Works of Art, 2002; contbr. poetry to popular mags., Poetry, Saturday Rev., Commonwealth, Prairie Schooner; founder, editor: The Poetry Bag quar., 1966-71; poetry editor: So. Colo. Std., 1973-74. With USAF, 1955-57. Recipient Mahan award for poetry U. Mo., 1965-66 Home: PO Box 87 Ranchos De Taos NM 87557-0087

DICKFELD, TIMM-MICHAEL, electrophysiologist, cardiologist, educator; s. Lutz Heiner and Renate Dickfeld. MD, J.W. v.G-University, Frankfurt, Germany, 1995, PhD, 1997. Asst. prof. medicine U. Md., Balt., 2005—; dir. electrophysiology VA Balt., 2005—. Adj. asst. prof. Johns Hopkins U., Balt. Recipient Silverman Award for Creative Rsch., Johns Hopkins U., 2001. Mem.: AMA, Soc. Cardiovasc. Magnetic Resonance (Best Abstract award 2003), Am. Heart Assn. (Melvin Judkins Young Investigator award 2002, grant 2002, Scientist Devel. grant 2006). Achievements include research in the feasibility of image integration for real-time guidance of radiofrequency ablations; visualization of ablation lesions using magnetic resonance imaging; real-time CT guidance for percutaneous placement of left ventricular leads; validation of image integration for clinical ablation procedures; patents pending for visualization of radiofrequency ablation lesions and novel methods to guide ablation procedures. Office: Univ Maryland 22 S Greene St Baltimore MD 21201 Office Phone: 410-328-6056.

DICKIE, MARTHA S., lawyer; b. July 14, 1956; d. Alex and Marilyn Dickie; m. James Rader; children: Clark, Joey. BA in Economics with spl. honors, U. Tex., Austin, 1977, JD, 1980. Bar: Tex. 1980, US Ct. Appeals (5th Cir.), US Dist. Ct. (So. Dist. Tex.), US Dist. Ct. (We. Dist. Tex.). Law clk. to Hon. Jack Roberts US Dist. Ct., 1980—82; atty., mng. ptnr. Minton Burton Foster and Collins PC, Austin, 1982—2004; of counsel Akin & Almanza, Austin, Tex., 2004, ptnr., 2005—. Bd. mem. Tex. Alcoholic Beverage Commn., 1994—2000; mem. Tex. Bd. Legal Specialization, 1995—2001. Fellow: Tex. Bar Found. (trustee 1992—95, chair of fellows 2003—04); mem.: State Bar Tex. (dir. 1989—92, pres. 2006—07, Pres. Citation 1997, 1998, Outstanding Third Yr. Dir. 1992), Travis County Bar Assn. (pres. criminal law and procedure sect. 1985—86, pres. 1988—89). Office: AKin & Almanza Bldg H 2301 S Capital of Texas Hwy Austin TX 78746 Office Phone: 512-474-9486. Office Fax: 512-478-7151. E-mail: mdickie@akin-almanza.com.

DICKIE, RENEE, physiologist, researcher; b. Canada; d. R. T. Dickie and C. L. Belec. BSc, U. Toronto, 1993; PhD, U. Calif., Berkeley, 1999. Lectr. U. Calif., Berkeley, 2000; postdoctoral rsch. fellow sch. pub. health, physiology Harvard U., Boston, 2001—04, rsch. assoc. sch. pub. health, physiology, 2004—06, rsch. scientist sch. pub. health, molecular and integrative physiol. scis., 2006—. Contbr. articles to profl. jours. Fellow, NIH, 2001—04. Mem.: New Eng. Soc. Microscopy (pres. 2007—), Internat. Soc. Vertebrate Morphologists, Soc. Integrative and Comparative Biology.

DICKIE, ROBERT BENJAMIN, lawyer, educator; b. Glendale, Calif., Sept. 10, 1941; s. John A. and Dorothy C. Dickie; m. Susan J. Williams, Jan. 28, 1967 (div. 1987); children: Amy, John, Thomas. BA, Yale U., 1963; JD, U. Calif., Berkeley, 1967. Bar: Calif. 1967, N.Y. 1970, Mass. 1971. Assoc. Shearman & Sterling, NYC, 1969-71, Sullivan & Worcester, Boston, 1971-77; asst. prof. mgmt. policy Boston U., 1977-83, tenured assoc. prof., 1983-94; prin The Dickie Group, 1994—. Cons. World Bank, Washington, Fortune 100 Cos., leading law firms in U.S., Europe and Asia. Author: Financial Statement Analysis and Business Valuation for the Practical Lawyer, ABA, 1999, 2d edit., 2006; contbr. numerous articles to Nat. Law Jour., Strategic Mgmt. Jour., Columbia Jour. World Bus., others. Mem.: ABA, Calif. Bar Assn., Boston Bar Assn., Longwood Cricket Club, Yale Club Boston. Office: The Dickie Group 545 Boylston St Boston MA 02116 Office Phone: 617-262-6800.

DICKINSON, CAROL RITTGERS, art historian, writer; b. Des Moines, Apr. 16, 1933; d. Robert Johnson and Cecil Marjorie (Snyder) Rittgers; m. Donald Ira Dickinson, June 6, 1959; 1 child, Lauren Lucy. BA in English with honors, Drake U., 1954; MA in Art History, U. Hawaii, 1964. Lydia Roberts fellow Columbia U., NYC, 1954-56; instr. Iowa State U., U. Hawaii, Colo Women's Coll., U. Petroleum and Minerals, Dhahran, Saudi Arabia, Colo. Sc. Mines, Golden, 1956-76; dir. pub. programs Denver Art Mus., 1980-83; dir. publicity and edn. Mus. Western Art, Denver, 1985-86; freelance writer, 1979—. Lectr., panelist numerous mus., univs. and profl. groups, Colo., 1980—. Co-editor, contbg. author: Colorado and the American Renaissance, 1980, Walking in Beauty, 1990, The Art of Dean Mitchell, 1999; founding editor Denver Urban Design Forum Newsletter, 1984, 85; contbr. more than 500 articles to nat. and regional newspapers and mags.; art critic Denver Rocky Mountain News, 1990-92. Exec. dir. Foothills Art Ctr., Golden, 1992-2003. Recipient Denver Mayor's Award for Excellence in Arts, 2000, 1st Cultural award, Jefferson Symphony, 2000, medal, Colorado Sch. Mines, 2000, Living Landmarks award, Golden Landmarks Assn., 2005, 1st pl. awards, revs./features, Colo. Press Women; Honoree in naming of The Carol and Don Dickinson Sculpture Garden, Foothills Art Ctr., Golden, Colo., 2005. Mem. Golden Fortnightly Club, Asian Art Assn. Democrat. Episcopalian. Avocations: Asian philosophies and history, Chinese brush painting, films. Home: 1908 Pinal Rd Golden CO 80401-1744 Office Phone: 303-278-1357. Business E-Mail: ddickins@mines.edu.

DICKINSON, DONALD CHARLES, library science professor; b. Schenectady, NY, June 9, 1927; s. Charles William and Stella Barney (Sheldon) D.; m. Colleen Eleanor Schindler, Aug. 7, 1954; children: Ann, Jean, Ellen, Mary, Kathleen, Sheila. AB, SUNY, Albany, 1949; MLS, U. Ill., 1951; PhD, U. Mich., 1964. Reference librarian Cen. Mo. State Coll., Warrensburg, 1951-53, Eastern Mich. U., Ypsilanti, 1953-56; asst. acquisitions U. Kans., Lawrence, 1956-58; head librarian Bemidji (Minn.) State Coll., 1958-66; dir. reader service U. Mo., Columbia, 1966-69; dir. grad. libr. sch. U. Ariz., Tucson, 1969-78, prof. grad. libr. sch., 1979-96, prof. emeritus, 1996—. Author: Bio-bibliography Langston Hughes, 1967, 2d edit., 1972, Hellmut Lehmann-Haupt, 1975, Dictionary of American Book Collectors, 1986, George Watson Cole, 1990, Henry E. Huntington's Library of Libraries, 1995, Dictionary of American Antiquarian Bookdealers, 1998, John Carter, Taste and Technique of a Bookman, 2004. Am. Philos. Assn. grantee, 1969; Andrew W. Mellon fellow Henry E. Huntington Libr., 1989; Helm fellow Ind. U., 1999; C.P. Snow travel fellow U. Tex., 2000; Huntington/Brit. Acad. fellow, 2000. Mem. ALA (coun. 1972-73, travel grantee 1960), Bibliographic Soc. Am., Ariz. Libr. Assn. (pres. 1978-79), Grolier Club (N.Y.C.), Zamorano Club (L.A.). Democrat. Business E-Mail: dickinsd@u.arizona.edu.

DICKINSON, ELEANOR CREEKMORE, artist, educator; b. Knoxville, Tenn., Feb. 7, 1931; d. Robert Elmond and Evelyn Louise (Van Gilder) C.; m. Ben Wade Oakes Dickinson, June 12, 1952; children: Mark Wade, Katherine Van Gilder, Peter Somers. BA, U. Tenn., 1952; postgrad., San Francisco Art Inst., 1961—63, Académie de la Grande Chaumière, Paris, 1971; MFA, Calif. Coll. Arts, Crafts, 1982, Golden Gate U., 1984. Cert. Recognition El Consejo Mundial de Artistas Plasticos, 1993. Escrow officer Security Nat. Bank, Santa Monica, Calif., 1953-54; mem. faculty Calif. Coll. of the Arts, Oakland, 1971—2001, assoc. prof. art, 1974—84, prof., 1984-2001, prof. emerita, 2001—, dir. galleries, 1975-85. Artist-in-residence U. Tenn., 1969, Ark. State U., 1993, Fine Arts Mus. of San Francisco, 2000, U. Alaska, 1991; faculty U. Calif. Ext., 1967-70; lectr. U. Calif., Berkeley, 1990—; interviewer Hatch, Billops, Collin, NY State Coun. for Arts, 2004; juror Interfaith Forum, Magnes Mus., 1986, Crocker Mus. Art, 1987, Sun Gallery, 1990, Caligraphy Rev., 1991, U. Alaska, 1991, San Francisco Women Arts, 1993, Pleasanton Art League, 1993, U. Tenn. Ann., 1997, Sierra Coll. Ann., 2000, Costal Art League, 2006, Commn. Status Women, 2006, Pacific Art League, 2006-07; lectr., juror in field. Author, illustrator: Elkmont: The Heart of the Great Smoky Mountains National Park, 2005; co-author, illustrator: Revival, 1974, That Old Time Religion, 1975; also mus. catalogs; illustrator: The Complete Fruit Cookbook, 1972, Human Sexuality: A Search for Understanding, 1984, Days Journey, 1985; commissions: U. San Francisco, 1990-2001; one-woman shows include San Francisco Mus. Modern Art, 1965, 68, Santa Barbara Mus., 1966, Corcoran Gallery Art, Washington, 1970, 74, Fine Arts Mus. San Francisco, 1969, 75, J.B. Speed Art Mus., 1972, Poindexter Gallery, NY, 1972, 74, U. Tenn. Downtown Gallery, 1976 Smithsonian Inst., 1975-81, U. Tenn., 1976, 2005, Galeria de Arte y Libros, Monterrey, Mex., 1978, Oakland Mus., 1979, Interart Ctr., NY, 1980, Tenn. State Mus., 1981-82, Hatley Martin Gallery, San Francisco, 1986, 89, Michael Himovitz Gallery, Sacramento, Calif., 1988-89, 91, 93, 97-98, Gallery 10, Washington, 1989, Diverse Works, Houston, 1990, Ewing Gallery, U. Tenn., 1991, G.T.U. Gallery, U. Calif., Berkeley, 1991, Mus. Contemporary Religious Art, St. Louis, 1995, Coun. Creative Projects, NY, 1996, Thacher Gallery, U. San Francisco, 2000, Retrospective U. Tenn, 2005, Tenn. Regional Art Ctr., 2006, Retrospective Peninsula Mus. Art, Calif., 2007; represented in permanent collections Nat. Collection Fine Arts, Corcoran Gallery Art, Libr. of Congress, Smithsonian Instn., San Francisco Mus. Modern Art, Butler Inst. Am. Art, Oakland Mus., Santa Barbara Mus., Nat. Mus. Women in Arts, Washington, Achenbach Found. Fine Arts Mus., San Francisco; prodr. (TV) The Art of the Matter-Professional Practices in Fine Arts, 1986—. Bd. dirs. Calif. Confedn. of the Arts, 1983-85; bd. dirs., v.p. Calif. Lawyers for the Arts, 1986—; mem. coun. bd. San Francisco Art Inst., 1966-91, trustee, 1964-67; sec., bd. dirs. YWCA, 1955-62; treas., bd. Westminster Ctr., 1955-59; bd. dirs. Children's Theater Assn., 1958-60, 93-94, Internat. Child Art Ctr., 1958-68. Recipient Disting. Alumni award San Francisco Art Inst., 1983, Master Drawing award Nat. Soc. Arts and Letters, 1983, Pres.'s award Nat. Women's Caucus for Art, 1995, Allgemeines Kunstlerfexidon, 2001, Lifetime Achivement award Nat. Women's Caucus for Art, 2003; grantee Zellerbach Family Fund, 1975, NEH, 1978, 80, 82-85, Thomas F. Stanley Found., 1985, Bay Area Video Coalition, 1988-92, PAS Graphics, 1988, San Francisco Cmty. TV Corp., 1990, Skaggs Found., 1991. Mem.: NOW, Nat. Women's Caucus for Art (nat. Affirmative Action officer 1978—80, nat. bd. dirs. 2000—, Pres.'s award 1995), Arts Advocates, Artists Equity Assn. (nat. v.p., dir. 1978—92), San Francisco Art Assn. (sec., dir. 1964—67), Calif. Lawyers for Arts (v.p. 1986—2004, bd. dirs. 1986—), Calif. Confederation of Arts (bd. dirs. 1983—89), Coll. Art Assn. (chair com. of Women in the Arts 2004—06), Coalition Women's Art Orgns. (dir. 1978—80, v.p. 2000—01), AAUP. Democrat. Episcopalian. Office: Calif Coll of the Arts 1111 8th St San Francisco CA 94107-2247 Personal E-mail: eleanordickinson@mac.com.

DICKINSON, GAIL KREPPS, library science educator; b. Lewistown, Pa., June 10, 1956; d. Harold and Esther (Bourdess) Krepps; m. Willis H. Dickinson, Dec. 22, 1979 (div. 1998); children: Margaret Lee, Elizabeth Ann; m. Michael G. Colson, Sr., June 9, 2003. BS, Millersville U. Pa., 1977; MSLS, U. N.C., 1987; PhD, U. Va., 2000. Libr. Cape Charles (Va.) Pub. Sch., 1977-81, Broadwater Acad., Exmore, Va., 1981-85; instrnl. supervisor Union-Endicott Sch. Dist., Endicott, NY, 1987-96; asst. prof. U. N.C., Greensboro, 2000—04, Old Dominion U., Norfolk, Va., 2004—. Adj. prof. James Madison U., Harrisonburg, Va., 1997-99. Mem. AAUW, ASCD, Am. Ednl. Rsch. Assn., Am. Assn. Sch. Librs. (bd. dirs. 1994-97), N.Y. Libr. Assn. (pres. sch. libr. media sect. 1994), Phi Delta Kappa. Avocations: reading, word and video games.

DICKINSON, JANE W., retired executive secretary, volunteer; b. Sept. 27, 1919; d. Charles Herman and Rachel (Whaler) Wagner; m. E. F. Sherwood Dickinson, Oct. 23, 1943; children: Diane Jane Gray Clem, Carolyn Dickinson Vane. BA, Duke U., 1941; MEd, Goucher Coll., 1965. Exec. sec. Petroleum Industry Com., Balt., 1941-43, Sherwood Feed Mills Inc., Balt., 1943-79. Mem. exec. com. Children's Aid Md., 1960-61; mem. bd. women's aux. Balt. Symphony Orch., 1958-60; dist. chmn. Balt. Cancer Drive, 1957; co-chmn. Balt. United Appeal, 1968; bd. mgrs. Pickersgill Retirement Home. Mem. Three Arts Club (Balt., sec. 1958-60, bd. govs. 1960-64, 67-70, pres. 1970-72), Women's Club of Roland Park (bd. govs. 1960-64, 86-88, 92-94), Cliff Dwellers Garden Club, Alpha Delta Phi Home and Office: Apt 609 1055 W Joppa Rd Baltimore MD 21204-3748 Office Phone: 410-321-1030.

DICKINSON, JESS H., state supreme court justice; b. Charleston, Miss., 1947; m. Janet Holiman; 4 children. BS, Miss. State U., 1978; JD cum laude, U. Miss. Sch. of Law, 1982. Bar: Miss. 1982. Atty. priv. practice, Jackson, Miss., 1982—83, Gulfport, Miss., 1984—2003; judge Forrest and Perry County Circuit Ct.; justice Miss. Supreme Ct., 2004—. Ed. bd. mem. Miss. Law Jour. Mem.: Miss. Bar Assn. (Ethics Com., Professionalism Com.). Office: Miss Supreme Ct PO Box 249 Jackson MS 39205*

DICKINSON, JOSHUA CLIFTON, JR., museum director, educator; b. Tampa, Fla., Apr. 28, 1916; s. Joshua Clifton and Mary (Martin) D.; m. Lucy Jackson, Apr. 13, 1936 (wid. June 10, 1997); children: Joshua Clifton III, Martin Freeman, Susan Ellissa; m. Sarah Donnovin Hadley, Nov. 1, 1997. Student, U. Va., 1936-39, Cornell U., 1938; BS, U. Fla., 1940, MS, 1946, PhD, 1950. Faculty U. Fla., 1946—, asst. prof. biology, 1950-55, assoc. prof. biology, 1955, prof. zoology, 1973-79; curator Fla. State Mus. (name changed to Fla. Mus. of Natural History-U. Fla.), 1952-79, chmn. natural scis., 1953-60, acting dir., 1959-61, dir., 1961-79, dir. emeritus, 1979—. Vis. investigator Woods Hole Oceanographic Inst., 1952; expdns. to, Honduras, 1946, Bahamas, 1958-62, 66-67, Jamaica, 1946, Baffin Island, 1955, Sombrero Island, 1964, Navassa Island, 1967, Turks and Caicos Islands, 1974. Contbr. articles to profl. jours. Chmn. Fla. Bd. Archives and History, 1967-69; mus. adv. panel Nat. Endowment for Arts, 1970-72, co-chmn., 1972-74; panelist fellowship program NSF, 1966-68; mem. Nat. Council on Arts, 1976-82, chmn. com. planning and policy; bd. dirs. Fla. Arts Celebration, 1984-92, vice chmn., 1985-86. Comdr. USCGR, 1942—46, ret. Grantee Nat. Park Service, 1954, NSF, 1955-57; Rsch. fellow Harvard U., 1951-52; recipient Disting. Alumnus award U. Fla., 1977, Presdl. Medallion U. Fla., 1979; Dickinson Hall named in his honor U. Fla. Mem. Am. Ornithologists Union, Am. Soc. Naturalists, Am. Assn. Museums (chmn. sci. mus. sect. 1961, mem. council 1964-70, sec. 1970), Am. Soc. Zoologists, Wilson Ornithol. Soc., Am. Assn. Sci. Mus. Dirs. (v.p. 1967-69), Assn. Systematic Collections (pres. 1972-75, bd. dir. 1974-76, chmn. membership com. 1976-79), Bahamas Nat. Trust, Assn. S.E. Biologists (sec. 1955-58), Fla. Acad. Scis. (chmn. biology sect. 1952, editor quar. jour. 1955-63), Conf. Dirs. Systematics Collections (pres. 1976-78), Fla. Audubon Soc. (bd. dir. 1958-64, 79-84), S.E. Museums Conf. (v.p. 1971-72, pres. 1972, James L. Shortt award 1987), Internat. Council Museums (exec. com. 1974-77), Am. Assn. Museums (vis. accreditation team 1973-75), Sigma Xi, Phi Sigma, Alpha Tau Omega. Democrat. Presbyterian. Home: 9517 SW 40th Ln Gainesville FL 32608-4647 Office Phone: 352-392-1721.

DICKINSON, MARGERY ELSIE, missionary, clinical psychologist; b. Petoskey, Mich., Oct. 29, 1940; d. David Eugene and Beryle Mae (Herrington) L.; m. Hugh Dickinson, July 30, 2005. BS with honors, Taylor U., Upland, Ind., 1962; MA with high honors, Wheaton Coll., Ill., 1983; student, U. Paris Sorbonne, 1970. Lic. psychologist, Pa., limited lic. psychologist, Mich. Tchr. Waterford (Mich.) Sch. Sys., 1962-64; ednl. missionary, county dir. BCM Internat., Union County, NJ, 1965-69; ednl. missionary BCM Internat. and AIM Internat., Albertville and Paris, France, 1969-70, ednl. missionary, technician Watsa, Democratic Republic of Congo, 1970-81; counselor, therapist BCM Internat./AIM Internat. Amani Counseling Ctr., Nairobi, Kenya, 1983-84; organizer, dir. counseling dept., counselor, cons. BCM Internat., Upper Darby, Pa., 1985-97, psychol. testing and assessment of mission candidates, 1986—95, organizer, dir. mem. care ministries, 1998—2000, mem. care ministries, cons., 2000—. Organizer/facilitator Missions and Mental Health-East, Mt. Bethel, Pa., 1995-97; lectr. in field; spkr. in field. Editor: Commit Thy Way, 1994; author: (bible study series) Living in Community, 1980, translator (illustrator) Bible lessons from English to Lingala for use in Congo; contbr. articles to profl. jours. Facilitator Bible Club work, Democratic Republic of Congo, 1985—; fundraiser, facilitator printing and distbn. Christian lit., 2001—; leader grief support group First Congl. Ch., Rockford, Mich., 2003; Bible study leader Rockford (Mich.) Bapt. Ch., 2004; cons. Congo Internat. Mission, Grand Rapids, Mich., 2004—. Billy Graham Evangelistic Assn. scholar, 1981-83. Mem.: APA (assoc.), Midwest Mem. Care Network (charter), Christian Therapists Bible Study, Assn. N.Am. Missions, Am. Assn. of Christian Counselors (charter, spkr. regional conf. 1999). Baptist. Avocations: writing, clarinet, walking, weightlifting, swimming. Office: 309 Colonial Dr Box 249 Akron PA 17501-0249 also: BCMI Western Mich 710 Baldwin St Jenison MI 49428-9706 Business E-Mail: membercare@bcmintl.org.

DICKINSON, RICHARD DONALD NYE, clergyman, theology studies educator; b. Monson, Mass., Aug. 1, 1929; s. Richard Donald Nye and Phoebe Abigail (Naylor) D.; m. Nancy Leland Stone, Nov. 26, 1955; children: Elizabeth Stone, Richard Donald Nye III, Edward David McCrea. BA, Am. Internat. Coll., 1950, MA, 1951; STB, Boston U., 1954, PhD, 1959; cert., Institut Oecumenique, Geneva, 1955. Ordained to ministry United Ch. of Christ; chaplain, instr. Wheaton Coll., Norton, Mass., 1957-62; assoc. dir. Quaker Confs. in So. Asia, 1962-64; sr. research officer Inst. for Social Studies, The Hague, Netherlands, 1964-67; sec. for specialized assistance World Council Chs., 1967-68; now cons.; prof. Christian social ethics Christian Theol. Sem., Indpls., 1968-74, v.p., dean, 1974-86, acting pres., 1986-87, pres., 1987-97. Chmn. devel. commn. World Coun. Chs.; mem. edn. commn. Nat. Coun. Chs., 1972-74; mem. ch. world service com.; incorporating mem. Center for Exploration Values and Meaning.; bd. dirs. internat. affairs div. Am. Friends Service Com., div. overseas ministries of Christian Ch. Author: The Christian College and National Development, 1967, Line and Plummet, 1968, The Christian College in Developing India, 1969, To Set at Liberty the Oppressed, 1975, Poor, Yet Making Many Rich, 1983, Economic Globalization: Challenge for Christians. Bd. dirs. Ind. Opera Theatre, Internat. Ctr. Indpls., The Gemmer Found., Ind. Com. Econ. Edn., Martin Luther King Multiservice Ctr., Ind.-Ky. Conf. United Ch. of Christ, bd. dirs., chair fin. com.; mem.

Greater Indpls. Progress Com.; moderator First Congl. Ch.; chmn. Ch. World Svc. Bd. Ind.-Ky. Mem. Am. Soc. for Christian Ethics, Soc. for Sci. Study Religion, Econs. Club of Indpls. (bd. dir.), Rotary. Mem. United Ch. Of Christ. Home: 5173 N Kenwood Ave Indianapolis IN 46208-2619 E-mail: rdndjnsd@aol.com, rdndjnsd@earthlink.net.

DICKINSON, ROBERT EARL, atmospheric scientist, educator, retired science administrator; b. Millersburg, Ohio, Mar. 26, 1940; s. Leonard Earl and Carmen L. (Ostby) D. AB in Chemistry and Physics, Harvard U., 1961; MS in Meteorology, MIT, 1962, PhD in Meteorology, 1966. Rsch. assoc. MIT, Cambridge, 1966-68; scientist Nat. Ctr. Atmospheric Rsch., Boulder, Colo., 1968-73, sr. scientist, 1973-90, head climate sect., 1975-81, dep. dir. A.A.P. divsn., 1981-86, acting dir., 1986-87; prof. atmospheric physics U. Ariz., 1990-93, regents prof., 1993-99; prof. earth and atmospheric scis. Ga. Inst. Tech., Atlanta, 1999—; chair Ga. Power/Ga. Rsch. Alliance. Mem. climate rsch. com. NRC, Washington, 1985-90, chmn., 1987-90, com. earth sci., 1985-88, global change com., 1985-92; mem. WCRP sci. steering group GEWEX, 1988-92; UNU steering com. Climatic, Biotic and Human Interactions in Humid Tropics, 1984-88, steering com. Internat. Satellite Land Surface Climatology project, 1984-89. Editor: The Geophysiology of Amazonia, 1986; contbr. articles to profl. jours. Recipient G. Unger Vetlesen prize, 1996. Fellow AAAS, Am. Meteorol. Soc. (chmn. com. biometeorol. and aerobiol. 1987-89, Meisinger award 1973, Editors award 1976, Jule Charney award 1989, Walter Orr Roberts lectr. in interdisciplinary sci. 1995, Carl-Gustaf Rossby award 1997), Am. Geophys. Union (atmospheric sci. sect. 1986-88, pres.-elect 1988-90, pres. 1990-92, pres.-elect 2000-02, pres. 2002-04, Revelle medal 1996); mem. NAS, NAE, European Geoscis. Union (hon.), Chinese Acad. Scis. (fgn.). Democrat. Home: 1074 Peachtree Walk B311 Atlanta GA 30309 Office: Ga Inst Tech EAS 311 Ferst Dr Atlanta GA 30332-0340

DICKINSON, WADE, oil industry executive, educator; b. Sharon, Pa., Oct. 29, 1926; s. Ben Wade Orr and Gladys Grace (Oakes) D.; m. Eleanor Creekmore, June 12, 1952; children: Mark, Katherine, Peter. Student, Carnegie Inst. Tech., 1944-45; BS, U.S. Mil. Acad., 1949; postgrad., Oak Ridge Sch. Reactor Tech., 1950-51. Commd. 2d lt. USAF, 1949, advanced through grades to capt., 1954, resigned, 1954; cons. physicist RAND Corp., Santa Monica, Calif., 1952-54; engring. cons. Bechtel Group, Inc., San Francisco, 1954-87; tech. advisor U.S. Congress, Washington, 1957-58; pres. Agrophysics, Inc., San Francisco, 1968—, Petrolphysics Inc., San Francisco, 1975—; ptnr. Radialphysics Ltd., San Francisco, 1980—, Robotphysics Ltd., San Francisco, 1983—. Lectr. engring. and bus. U. Calif., Berkeley, 1984—2004; cardiology cons. Mt. Zion Med. Ctr. U. Calif., San Francisco, 1970—99; chmn. bd. Calif. Med. Clin. Psychotherapy; mng. mem. The Spark Group, 2000—, Petro Jet, LLC, Solid Gas Techs., 2005—, Petrol Physics, Inc., Sequestration Co. LLC, 2007—. Contbr. articles to profl. jours; patentee in field. Trustee World Affair Coun., 1958-62; mem. San Francisco Com. Fgn. Rels., Young Republicans, Calif. Mem. Am. Phys. Soc., Am. Soc. Petroleum Engrs. Clubs: Bohemian (San Francisco), Chit Chat (San Francisco). Lodges: Masons, Guardsmen. Episcopalian. Home and Office: Petrolphysics Inc 2125 Broderick St San Francisco CA 94115-1627 Office: Petrolphysics Inc 2125 Broderick St San Francisco CA 94115 Office Phone: 415-922-3733.

DICKINSON, WILLIAM BOYD, JR., media consultant; b. Kansas City, Mo., Feb. 21, 1931; s. William Boyd and Aileen (Robinson) D.; m. Betty Ann Landree, Feb. 1, 1953; children: William Boyd IV, David Alan. AB, U. Kans., 1953; student, George Washington U. Law Sch., 1957-58. With U.P.I., 1955-59, mem. staff overnight desk Washington, 1957-59; staff writer Editorial Research Reports, Washington, 1959-66, editor, 1966-73; editor, v.p. Congl. Quar., Inc., 1972-73; gen. mgr., editorial dir. Washington Post Writers Group, 1973-91; cons., 1991-96, Biocentric Inst., 1991—. Resident profl. Journalism Sch. U. Kans., 1993-99; manship chair Journalism Sch. La. State U., 1999-2003, disting. prof., 2003—; Winston Churchill Traveling fellow, summer 1968. Supervisory editor: Congl. Quar.'s Complete Guide to Congress. Served with AUS, 1953-55. Press fellowship Knight Internat., 1998. Mem. William Allen White Found. (trustee), Alpha Tau Omega, Omicron Delta Kappa. (Washington). Home and Office: 1617 Alvamar Dr Lawrence KS 66047-1715 also: LSU 221B Journalism Bldg Baton Rouge LA 70803-0001 Office Phone: 785-832-1899.

DICKINSON, WILLIAM TREVOR, hydrologist, educator; b. Toronto, Ont., Can., Aug. 30, 1939; s. Clarence Heber and Katie Isobel (Kneen) D.; m. Sharon Lucille Tutt, Aug. 24, 1963; children: Michael Trevor, Cathryn Ruth. BSA., U. Toronto, 1961, BASci., 1962, MSA., 1964; PhD, Colo. State U., 1967. Research assoc. Colo. State U., 1964-67; asst. prof. engring. U. Guelph, Ont., 1967-70, assoc. prof. Ont., 1970-78, prof. Ont., 1978-94, prof. emeritus Ont., 1995—, coordinator instructional devel. Ont., 1979-82, Soc. Tchg. and Learning Higher Edn. and 3M teaching fellow, coord. univ. teaching program, 1991—93; pvt. cons. water resources engring. Contbr. articles to profl. jours. Recipient Conservation Pioneer award, Conservation Ont., 2000. Mem. Assn. Profl. Engrs. Ont., Can. Assn. Univ. Tchrs., Soc. Tchg. Learning High Edn. Mem. United Ch. of Can. Home: 68 Pine Ridge Dr Guelph ON Canada N1L 1J1 Office: Univ Guelph Guelph ON Canada N1G 2W1 E-mail: wdickins@ucguelph.ca.

DICKMAN, FRANCOIS MOUSSIEGT, former foreign service officer, educator; b. Iowa City, Dec. 23, 1924; s. Adolphe Jacques and Henriette Louise (Moussiegt) D.; m. Margaret Hoy, June 3, 1947; children: Christine, Paul. BA, U. Wyo., 1947; MA, Fletcher Sch. Law & Diplomacy, 1948; student, U.S. Army War Coll., Carlisle, Pa., 1968—69. Rsch. asst. Brookings Instn., Washington, 1950; with U.S. Fgn. Svc., 1951-84, consular/comml. officer Barranquilla, Colombia, 1952-54, Arabic lang. trainee Beirut, 1955-57, econ., comml., consular officer Khartoum, Sudan, 1957-60; Egyptian-Syrian affairs desk officer Dept. State, 1961-65, econ. officer Tunis, Tunisia, 1965-68; econ. counselor Jidda, Saudi Arabia, 1969-72; dir. Arabian Peninsula affairs Dept. State, 1972-76, amb. to United Arab Emirates, 1976-79, amb. to Kuwait, 1979-83; diplomat in residence Marquette U., 1984; adj. prof. polit. sci. U. Wyo., Laramie, 1985—2004. Lectr. in field. Served with AUS, 1943-46, 50-51. Recipient Dept. State Meritorious Honor award, 1965, Disting. Alumni award U. Wyo., 1980; named Exemplary Alumnus U. Wyo., 1993. Mem. VFW, U.S. Army War Coll. Alumni Assn., U. Wyo. Alumni Assn., Phi Beta Kappa, Phi Kappa Phi. Office: U Wyo Polit Sci Dept Laramie WY 82071-3197 Personal E-mail: fmdmhd@aol.com.

DICKMAN, JAMES BRUCE, photojournalist; b. St. Louis, Mar. 25, 1949; s. Joseph Edward and Isabel Catherine (Brown) D.; m. Mary Kay Thomas, Sept. 23, 1968 (div.); children: Kristi Michele, Gavin Thomas; m. 2d Rebecca Lauren Skelton, Sept. 16, 1983; children: Matthew Benjamin, Margaret Catherine Anne. Student, U. Tex., 1967-69. Photographer McKinney Job Corps., Tex., 1969-70, Dallas Times Herald, 1970-86. Founder First Light photography workshops, France, 2003, Scotland, 04, Chesapeake Bay, 05, Dubois, Wyo., 06; Olympus visionary, 02; Lexar Elite photographer, 03. Worked on photo projects Day in the Life of Can., Day in the Life of Am., Day in the Life of Spain, Day in the Life of the Soviet Union, Day in the Life of China; co-author: Perfect Digital Photography, 2005; (book and CD-ROM) Passage to Vietnam, 1994, Day in the Life of Africa, 2002; contbg. editor Am. Way Mag. Recipient Pulitzer prize for photography Columbia U., 1983, World Press Photo of Yr. award World Press Photo Orgn., Holland, Amsterdam, 1983, 89, awards Dallas Press Club, AP and UPI, Tex. Headliners, Damascus Syria, Internat. Orgn. of Photography, 1st place, Sigma Delta Chi Disting. Service award, Bronze Medallion, others; named Disting. Alum, North Dallas H.S. Mem. Am. Soc. Mag. Photographers. Home Phone: 303-730-2894; Office Phone: 303-730-2894. Personal E-mail: jaybec@comcast.net. *I've always felt that I've had a guardian angel pointing me in the correct directions. But it's always been up to me to do something with the opportunities once they're presented.*

DICKMAN, MARTIN J., federal agency administrator; b. Chgo. BS, U. Ill., 1966; JD, DePaul U., 1969. Asst. corp. counsel City of Chgo., 1970—72; counsel to minority leader Ill. Ho. Reps., 1972—73; mem. Bd. Trade, Chgo., 1972—91; asst. Peter Ftizpatrick and Assocs., 1973—89; hearings ref. Ill. Dept. Revenue, 1976—80; prosecutor Cook County Ill. State's Atty.'s Fin. and Govtl. Crimes Task Force, 1991—94; inspector gen. Railroad Retirement Bd., 1994—. Office: US Railroad Retirementt Bd 4th Fl 844 N Rush St Chicago IL 60611-2092 Office Phone: 312-751-4690. Business E-Mail: mdickman@oig.rrb.gov.

DICKMAN, ROBERT S., aerospace institute administrator, retired military officer; b. Bklyn. BS in Physics, Union Coll., 1966; MS in Space Physics, Air Force Inst. Tech., 1968; MA in Mgmt., Salve Regina Coll.; grad. (dist.), Naval War Coll., 1983. 2nd. lt. USAF, 1966, advanced through grades to major gen., 1966-2000; prog. mgr. USAF Office Sci Rsch., Arlington, Va., 1968-72; prog. element monitor USAF Hdqs., Washington, 1972-73; terminal sys. mgr. USAF, Los Angeles AFB, Calif., 1973-75; operational mgr. USAF Hdqs., Washington, 1976-79; space Def. Opers. Ctr. Hdrs. Aerospace Def. Command, Cheyenne Mtn. AFB, Colo., 1979-82; dir. space sys., dep. chief staff ops. Hdqs. Air Force Space Command, Peterson AFB, Colo., 1983-84; chief comdr. group Hdqs. N.Am. Aerospace Def. Command, Space Command, Peterson AFB, Colo., 1984-85; vice comdr. 2d space wing Schriever AFB, Colo., 1985—86; asst. to dir. ops., then dir. missile warning Space Command, Colo., 1986-87; chief Space Sys. Divsn., Washington, 1987-89; dep. dir. space progams Office of Asst. Sec. USAF for Acquisition, Washington, 1987-92; dir. plans Hdqs. USAF Space Command, Peterson AFB, Colo., 1992-93; comdr. 45th Space Wing, Patrick AFB, Fla., 1993-95; dir. Eastern Range, Cape Canaveral Air Sta., Fla., 1993-95; dir. space programs Office Asst. Sec. USAF for Acquisition, Washington, 1995; space architect US Dept. Def., Washington, 1995-98; dir. Office Plans and Analysis and Sys. of Sys. Architect Nat. Reconnaissance Office, Washington, 1998-2000, dir. corp. ops., chief info. officer, 2000; aerospace cons., 2001—01; dep. for military space, Office of Under-Sec., USAF, Washington, 2002—05; exec. dir. Am. Inst. Aeronautics & Astronautics Inc., Reston, Va., 2005—. Decorated Def. D.S.M., Air Force D.S.M., Def. Superior Svc. Medal, Legion of Merit; recipient Astronautics award Nat. Space Club, master space badge. Office: Am Inst Aeronautics & Astronautics Inc 1801 Alexander Bell Dr Reston VA 20191

DICKS, NORMAN DE VALOIS, congressman; b. Bremerton, Wash., Dec. 16, 1940; s. Horace D. and Eileen Cora Dicks; m. Suzanne Callison, Aug. 25, 1967; children: David, Ryan. BA, U. Wash., 1963; JD, U. Wash. Sch. Law, 1968; LLD (hon.), Gonzaga U., 1987. Bars: Wash. 1968, DC, 1978. Salesman Boise Cascade Corp., Seattle, 1963; labor negotiator Kaiser Gypsum Co., Seattle, 1964; legis. asst. Staff of US Senator Warren Magnuson of Wash., 1968-73, adminstrv. asst., 1973-76; mem. US Congress from 6th Wash. dist., 1977—, mem. homeland security com., mem. appropriations com., ranking minority mem. interior and environment and related agencies subcommittee. Mem. U. Wash. Alumni Assn., Puget Sound Naval Bases Assn., Sigma Nu, Rotary (hon.), Kiwanis (hon.). Democrat. Lutheran. Office: US Reps 2467 Rayburn Ho Office Bldg Washington DC 20515-0001 Office Phone: 202-225-5916.*

DICKSHEET, SHARADKUMAR, plastic surgeon; b. Pandharpur, Mumbai, India, Dec. 13, 1930; s. Sitaram Ganpat and Malathibai Dixit; children: Shari, Sharad, Supriya. BMus, Bhatkhande U., 1943; BS, Osmania U., Hyperabad, India, 1951; MBBS, Naqpur U., India, 1956. Pvt. practice, Fairbanks, Ala., 1969—78; fellow cosmetic surgery Guadalahara Inst. of Plastic Surgery, Mexico, 1979—80, Manhattan EET Hosp., NYC, 1980—81, Trudi Vogt Inst., Zurich, Switzerland, 1981—82; resident plastic surgery Downstate Med. Ctr., Bklyn., 1982—84; pvt. practice Bklyn., 1984—94. Residency tchg. Downstate Med. Ctr., Bklyn., 1984—94; classical music vocalist, India, 1948—58; founder Plasti Surgery India Project, 1968. Contbr. articles to profl. jours. Recipient Internat. award for child advocacy, Hannah Neil Ctr. Found. Bd., 2001, Sheikh Hamdan Bid Rashid Al Maktoum award for volunteers in humanitarian medical services, 2001—02, Dr. Nathan Davis Internat. Humanitarian award in medicine, AMA Found., 2005, Internat. Humanitarian award, Am. Soc. Plastic Surgeons, 2005, award, Rotary Internat., 2005. Mem.: Bhavatiya Jaih Soc., Giants Club, Lions Club, Rotary Club. Hindu. Avocation: music. Business E-Mail: murphy.pianoman@att.net.

DICKSON, BRENT E., state supreme court justice; b. July 18, 1941; m. Jan Aikman, June 8, 1963; children: Andrew, Kyle, Reed. BA, Purdue U., 1964; JD, Ind. U., Indpls., 1968; LittD, Purdue U., 1996. Bar: Ind. 1968, U.S. Ct. Appeals (7th cir.) 1972, U.S. Supreme Ct. 1975; cert. civil trial adv., NBTA. Pvt. practice, Lafayette, Ind., 1968-85; sr. ptnr. Dickson, Reiling, Teder & Withered, 1977-85; assoc. justice Ind. Supreme Ct., Indpls., 1986—. Adj. prof. Sch. of Law Ind. U., 1992-. Past pres. Tippecanoe County Hist. Assn.; mem. dean's adv. coun. Sch. Liberal Arts Purdue U., 1990-94; mem. adv. bd. Heartland Film Festival, 1995-2000. Mem. Am. Inns Ct. (founding pres. Sagamore chpt.), Am. Law Inst. Office: Ind Supreme Ct 313 Ind Statehouse Indianapolis IN 46204-2213*

DICKSON, CONSTANCE PIERCE, retired law librarian; b. Boston; d. Lorin Edward and Kathryn (Josephs) Pierce; m. William Simmonds Dickson; children: Mark Pierce, Carol Anne. AB, Tufts U., Medford, Mass., 1956; MLS, U. Md., 1973. Law libr. Dow, Lohnes & Albertson, Washington, 1973-74, Dewey Ballantine Bushby Palmer & Wood, Paris, 1974-78, Y.B. Kim & Assocs., Seoul, 1978-81, Brownstein Zeidman & Schomer, Washington, 1982-84, Gibson, Dunn & Crutcher, Washington, 1984—2005, Duane Morris LLP, Washington, 2005—07; ret., 2007. Mem. Am. Assn. Law Librs. (membership com. 1987-88, stats. com. 1988-89, PLL survey 1989-91, CRIV 1993-95, gov. rels. com. 1996-98, AMPS com. 1999-2001, AMPS spl. com. 2001-03, salary survey rev. 2002-03), PLL program com. 1996-99), Law Librarians Soc. Washington (PLL sec. 1984-85, v.p. 1989-90, pres. 1990-91, chair bylaws com. 1992-93), Phi Kappa Phi, Beta Phi Mu. Personal E-mail: dicksoncw@netzero.net.

DICKSON, JAMES FRANCIS, III, surgeon; b. Boston, May 4, 1924; s. James Francis Jr. and Mary Elizabeth (Rich) Dickson; m. Vivian Joan Franco, Dec. 23, 1977. AB, Dartmouth Coll., 1944; MD, Harvard Med. Sch., 1947. Diplomate Am. Bd. Surgery. Intern and resident Boston City Hosp., 1947—51; practice in thoracic and cardiovascular surgery Boston, 1951—61; NIH spl. fellow MIT, Cambridge, 1961—65; dir. engring. in biology and medicine program NIH, Bethesda, Md., 1965—75; asst. surgeon gen. HHS, Washington, 1976—89. Sr. advisor to dean Harvard Med. Sch., 1992—2001, vis. com., 1992—2001; bd. overseers Dartmouth Med. Sch., 1990—2003, C. Everett Koop Inst., 1992—. Fellow: IEEE, ACS; mem.: Inst. Medicine of NAS. Home Phone: 508-487-3962.

DICKSON, JIM, writer, theater producer; b. Chgo., Mar. 25, 1949; s. Vincent Brackley and Carol Lois (Schaffner) D.; m. Helen Denise McEachrane , Feb. 11, 1984 (div. 1988). BA, Harvard U., 1970. Artistic adminstr. Santa Fe Opera, 1978-80; mng. dir. Chamber Opera Theatre, 1982; gen. mgr. Opera Festival of N.J., 1982-85; mng. dir. N.J. State Opera, 1985-89; exec. dir. Newark Arts Coun., 1989-95. Propr. The Dickson Office, 1991—. Author: Monmouth, 1968, Fear of Success, 1971, Summer in the Midwest, 1975, Chiliasm, 1972, The Princess of the Suburbs, 1973, Banjo, 1981, A Couple Interviews With A Couple Czars, 1991; (musical) Pippin, 1969, Appetite and Embarrassment, 1998. Recipient Phyllis Anderson award, 1969 Office: PO Box 1337 Newark NJ 07101-1337

DICKSON, JOHN T., information technology executive; b. Sheffield, Eng. Degree in Elec. Engring. (hon.), U. Sheffield, 1966, postgrad. in Bus. studies. With ICL, plc., bd. dir.; with Texas Instruments (UK and France); pres. microelectronics group Lucent Tech., COO, v.p. integrated circuits divsn., v.p., CEO; CEO Headland Tech., Inc., bd. dir.; CEO SHOGraphics, Inc., Sunnyvale, Calif., bd. dir.; joined Agere Systems, Inc., Allentown, Pa., 1993, pres., CEO. Bd. dir. Tandon Computer Corp., Inc., LSI Logic Europe, Inc., Internat. Network Svcs. Ltd., EO, Inc., Mettler-Toledo Internat., Inc., 2000—; bd. dir. (current) Semiconductor Industry Assn. Recipient Mensforth medal, Inst. Elec. Engrs., 1990. Office: Agere Systems Inc 1110 American Pkwy NE Allentown PA 18109-9138

DICKSON, LANCE E., former law librarian, educator; b. 1939; BA, U. Cape Town, 1960, LLB, 1962, B.Com., 1969; MLS, U. Tex., 1971. Magistrate's clk. Dept. Justice, Cape Town, 1961-62; legal asst. Mobil Oil, Cape Town, 1963-69, corp. sec., legal counsel, 1970; assoc. libr. U. Tex., 1973-75; libr., assoc. prof. La. State U., 1975-78, libr., prof., 1978-87; dir. Robert Crown Law Libr. Stanford U. Sch. Law, Calif., 1987—2005, prof emeritus law, 2005—. Mem. Am. Assn. Law Librs., Brit. and Irish Assn. Law Librs., Calif. Libr. Assn. Office: Robert Crown Law Libr Stanford Law Sch 559 Nathan Abbott Way Stanford CA 94305-8612 Office Phone: 950-723-2740. E-mail: lance@law.stanford.edu.

DICKSON, PAUL WESLEY, JR., physicist; b. Sharon, Pa., Sept. 14, 1931; s. Paul Wesley and Elizabeth Ella (Trevethan) D.; m. Eleanor Ann Dunning, Nov. 17, 1952; children: Gretchen Ann, Heather Elizabeth, Paul Wesley. BS in Metall. Engring., U. Ariz., Tucson, 1954, MS, 1954; PhD in Physics, NC State U., Raleigh, 1962. With Westinghouse Electric Corp., Large, Pa., 1963-84, mgr. weapon systems, 1965-68, mgr. advanced projects, 1969-72, mgr. reactor analysis and core design Madison, Pa., 1972-79, tech. dir. Oak Ridge, 1979-84; with EG & G Idaho, Idaho Falls, 1984-89, mgr. new tech. devel., 1984-87, mgr. reactor projects and programs, 1987-88; dir. Ctr. for Nuc. Engring. and Tech., 1988-89; tech. dir. reactor restart div. Westinghouse Savannah River Co., 1989-92; chief engr. nuclear materials processing div. Westinghouse, 1992-95; pvt. cons., 1995—. Mem. adv. com. on advanced propulsion systems NASA, Washington, 1970-72; mem. adv. com. reactor physics AEC/Dept. Energy, 1974-79; mem. rev. com. applied physics Argonne (Ill.) Nat. Lab., 1978-83, chmn., 1980; mem. rev. com. engring. physics Oak Ridge Nat. Lab., 1982-86, chmn., 1986; mem. fellow selection com. Dept. Energy, 1981-82; mem. rev. com. EBR II Argonne Nat. Lab., 1984, sci. and tech. adv. com., 1985-91. Contbr. numerous sci. articles to profl. publs. Capt. USAF, 1955-63. Fellow Am. Nuc. Soc.; mem. Am. Phys. Soc., NY Acad. Scis., AIME , AAAS, Scabbord and Blade, Sigma Xi, Phi Kappa Phi, Tau Beta Pi, Phi Lambda Upsilon, Sigma Pi Sigma. Republican. Home: 4005 Woodvalley Dr Aiken SC 29803-8421 Personal E-mail: pwdickson@bellsouth.net.

DICKSON, THOMAS WALTER, textile company executive; b. Charlotte, NC, Aug. 17, 1955; s. Rush Stuart and Joanne (Shoemaker) D.; m. Billie Cecelia Seddinger, Sept. 22, 1984; children: William Thomas, Michael Alan. BA in Econs., U. Va., 1977, MBA, 1980. Project mgr. spinning div. Am. & Efird, Inc., Mount Holly, N.C., 1980-81, project mgr. internat. Manchester, Eng., 1981-82, plant mgr. spinning div. Gastonia, N.C., 1982-84, mgr. Far East ops. Hong Kong, 1984-87, v.p. internat. ops. Mount Holly, 1987—91, exec. v.p., 1991—94, pres., 1994—96; exec. v.p. Ruddick Corp., Charlotte, NC, 1996—97, pres., CEO, 1997—2006, chmn., pres., CEO, 2006—. Bd. dirs. Am. & Efird (Hong Kong) Ltd., Am. & Efird Mills Singapore, Am. & Efird (Great Britain) Ltd. Bd. dirs. Dickson Found., Charlotte, 1983—. Mem. Charlotte Country Club, Linville Golf Club. Republican. Baptist. Office: Ruddick Corp Ste 1800 301 S Tryon St Charlotte NC 28202 Office Phone: 704-372-5404. Office Fax: 704-372-6409.*

DICKSTEIN, HARVEY LEONARD, pharmaceutical executive, researcher; b. Springfield, Mass., Jan. 19, 1936; s. David and Ruth (Stein) D.; m. Judith Marie Barton, Mar. 26, 1966; children: Jason Adam, Debra Ann. BA in Biology, Am. Internat. Coll., 1957; MD, Tufts U., 1961. Diplomate Nat. Bd. Med. Examiners. Intern then resident Bronx Mcpl. Hosp. Ctr., 1961-63; surg. resident Springfield (Mass.) Hosp., 1963-64; surg. resident, then chief resident Boston U. Med. Ctr., 1964-66; med. monitor Baxter Labs., Morton Grove, Ill., 1968-69; assoc. dir. hosp. products div. Abbott Labs., North Chgo., Ill., 1969-72, assoc. dir. exptl. therapy, 1972-73; dir. clin. rsch. Johnson & Johnson, New Brunswick, NJ, 1973-83; group leader surg. anesthetic and dental products FDA, Rockville, Md., 1983-85; dir. regulatory med. affairs E.R. Squibb, New Brunswick, 1985-87; v.p. regulatory affairs Parke-Davis Div. of Warner-Lambert, Morris Plains, NJ, 1987-89, v.p. med. rsch., 1989-91, v.p. med. affairs, 1992-93, v.p. med. and regulatory affairs, consumer products R&D, 1993-96; v.p., med. dir. Metaworks, Inc., Boston, 1996-97; v.p. clin. rsch. Transcend Therapeutics, Inc., Cambridge, Mass., 1997-98. Pharm. cons., Cohasset, Mass., 1999—. Lt. comdr. USPHS, 1966-68. New England Arthritis and Rheumatism Found. summer scholar, 1959. Avocations: weightlifting, skiing, jogging. Home: 393 Beechwood St Cohasset MA 02025-1521 Home Phone: 781-383-7058; Office Phone: 781-383-7058. Personal E-mail: Harveydickstein@comcast.net.

DICKSTEIN, JACK, chemist; b. Phila., Dec. 14, 1925; s. Harry and Anna A. (Anselevitz) D.; m. Pauline M. Gotheif, Dec. 24, 1950; children: Jeffrey L., John F., Andrea E. BS in Biochemistry, Pa. State U., 1946; MA in Organic Chemistry, Temple U., 1951; PhD in Polymer Chemistry, Rutgers U., 1958. Rsch. assoc. E.R. Squibb & Sons, New Brunswick, NJ, 1951—56; mgr. lab. Borden Chem. Co., Phila., 1958—61, devel. mgr. thermoplastics divsn. Leominster, Mass., 1961—67, dir. R&D Phila., 1967—74; group mgr. R&D Haven Chem. Co., Phila., 1974—77; v.p., dir. R&D Seal Inc., Naugatuck, Conn., 1977—79; pres. Kibow Biotech Inc., Phila., 1997—, Monomer-Polymer & Dajac Labs., Inc., Feasterville, Pa., 1979—. Tech. cons. Avery Internat., Pasadena, Calif., 1978-81, Painesville, Ohio, 1981-83, Avmor Inc., Montreal, Can., 1982-84, Wesley Jessen, Chgo., Ill., 1980-90. Patentee in field; contbr. articles to profl. jours. Mem. AAAS, Am. Chem. Soc., Am. Inst. Chemists, N.Y. Acad. Scis., Franklin Inst., Sigma Xi, Phi Lambda Upsilon, Phi Eta Sigma. Jewish. Avocations: sports statistics, photography. Office: Monomer-Polymer & Dajac Labs 1675 Bustleton Pike Feasterville Trevose PA 19053 Home Phone: 215-947-4008; Office Phone: 215-364-1155. Personal E-mail: featherpoo@comcast.net, monomerpolymer@comcast.net. Business E-Mail: info@monomerpolymer.com.

DICKSTEIN, MICHAEL ETHAN, mediator, arbitrator, lawyer; b. Montreal, Can., Sept. 8, 1959; s. Joseph and Barbara Dickstein AB, Harvard U., 1981, JD, 1985. Bar: Calif. 1985. Assoc. Heller, Ehrman, White & McAuliffe, San Francisco, 1985-91, ptnr., 1992; mediator, arbitrator, atty., cons. in pvt. practice dispute resolution, 1993—. Judge pro tem/mediator San Francisco and Alameda Superior and Mcpl. Cts., 1992—; adj. prof. U. San Francisco, 2003-04; mediation and negotiation instr. Stitt, Feld et al, 1996—; lectr. Stanford Law Sch. Mem.: Assn. Conflict Resolution (nat. co-chmn. workplace sect. 2001—04, adv. bd. 2004—).

DICKSTEIN, MORRIS, language educator, writer; b. NYC, Feb. 23, 1940; s. Abraham and Anne (Reitman) D.; m. Lore Willner, Jan. 3, 1965; children: Jeremy Elliot, Rachel Ariela. AB, Columbia U., NYC, 1961; MA,

Yale U., New Haven, Conn., 1963, PhD, 1967; postgrad., Cambridge U., Eng., 1963-64. Instr. English Columbia U., NYC, 1966-67, asst. prof. English, 1967-71; assoc. prof. English Queens Coll., CUNY, 1971-75, prof. English, 1976—, CUNY Grad. Ctr., 1974—, dir. Humanities Ctr., 1993—2000, sr. fellow Humanities Ctr., 2000—, disting. prof. English, 1994—. Vis. prof. U. Paris VIII, 1980-81; humanities cons. Basic Books, Inc., N.Y.C., 1972-80; adv. bd. Revue Francaise d'Etudes Americaines, Paris, 1986-2003; vice chmn. N.Y. Coun. Humanities, 1997-2001. Author: Keats and His Poetry, 1971, Gates of Eden, 1977, Double Agent, 1992, Leopards in the Temple: The Transformation of American Fiction, 1945-1970, 2002, A Mirror in the Roadway: Literature and the Real World, 2005; editor: The Revival of Pragmatism, 1998; co-editor: Great Film Directors, 1978; contbg. editor Partisan Rev., Boston, 1972-2003. Fellow, J.S. Guggenheim Found., 1973-74, ACLS, 1977, Rockefeller Found., 1981-82, NEH, 1986-87, Nat. Humanities Ctr., 1989-90. Mem. MLA, PEN Am. Ctr., Nat. Soc. Film Critics, Am. Studies Assn., Nat. Book Critics Circle (bd. dirs. 1983-89), Assn. Literary Scholars and Critics (v.p. 2005-06, pres. 2006-07). Office Phone: 212-817-7210. Business E-Mail: mdickstein@gc.cuny.edu.

DICKSTEIN, SIDNEY, lawyer; b. Bklyn., May 13, 1925; s. Charles and Pearl (Stahl) D.; m. Barbara H. (Duke), Sept. 20, 1953; children: Ellen Simeon, Matthew Howard, Nancy Joy. BA, Franklin and Marshall Coll., Lancaster, Pa., 1947; JD, Columbia U., 1949; LLD (hon.), Franklin and Marshall Coll., Lancaster, Pa., 2003. Bar: N.Y., 1949; D.C., 1959. Law clk. Joseph Richter, NYC, 1949-50; assoc. law office Herman E. Cooper, 1950-53; founder Dickstein and Shapiro, NYC, 1953; sr. ptnr. successor firm Dickstein, Shapiro, Morin, and Oshinsky, Washington, 1953-97, sr. counsel, 1998—. Mem. bd. advisors and article contbr., Jour. of Wealth Mgmt. Contbr. articles to profl. jours including Jour. Wealth Mgmt., 2003. Trustee Franklin and Marshall Coll., 1978—. Served with AUS, 1943-44; USNR, 1944-46. Mem.: Am. Jewish Com. (pres. Washington chpt., 1999-2001, mem. nat. bd. gov.), Bar Assn., D.C., ABA. E-mail: dicksteins@dsmo.com.

DICLERICO, JOSEPH ANTHONY, JR., federal judge; b. Lynn, Mass., Jan. 30, 1941; s. Joseph Anthony and Ruth Adel (Cummings) DiC.; m. Laurie Breed Thomson, July 27, 1975; 1 child, Devon Thomson. BA, Williams Coll., Williamstown, Mass., 1963; LLB, Yale U., 1966. Bar: NH 1967, US Dist. Ct. NH 1967, US Ct. Appeals (1st cir.) 1973, US Supreme Ct. 1975. Law clk. to presiding justice US Dist. Ct. NH, Concord, 1966—67, NH Supreme Ct., Concord, 1967—68; assoc. Cleveland Waters & Bass, Concord, 1968—70; asst. atty. gen. State of NH, Concord, 1970—77; assoc. justice NH Superior Ct., Concord, 1977—91, chief justice, 1991—92; chief judge US Dist. Ct. NH, Concord, 1992—97. Chmn. Superior Ct. sentence rev. disvn., 1987-92. Fellow Am. Bar Found. (life), NH Bar Found. (jud.); mem. NH Bar Assn (nat. conf. state trial judges 1986-92, nat. conf. fed. trial judges, 1992-96, mem. com. on codes of conduct jud. conf. of US 1994-2002, dist. judge rep. from 1st cir. to Jud. Conf. of US 1997-2000, 1st cir. jud. coun. mem. 1992-94, 98-2004, mem. com. to review circuit coun. conduct and disability orders, Jud. Conf. of US 2006-), Phi Beta Kappa. Independent. Roman Catholic. Avocation: gardening. Office: 55 Pleasant St Concord NH 03301-3954

DI COLA, JOAN BARBARA, lawyer; d. John Schiano and Viola Grace Di Cola. AB magna cum laude, Brown U., 1977; JD, Boston U., 1981, LLM in Taxation, 1986. Bar: Mass. 1981, R.I. 1981. Assoc. Fine & Ambrogne, Boston, 1983—85, Parker Coulter Daley & White, Boston, 1985—90; pvt. practice Boston, 1990—. Contbr. articles to law jours. Recipient Barnard Farr prize in Estate Planning, Boston U. Sch. Law, 1980. Mem.: Mass. Bar Assn., Boston Bar Assn. (co-chair estate planning com. 2000—02, mem. edn. com. 2003—05), Brown U. Club Boston (bd. dirs. 1983—96), Phi Beta Kappa. Office: Law Office of Joan Di Cola 63 Atlantic Ave Boston MA 02110 Office Phone: 617-227-8886.

DICONTI, MICHAEL ANDREW, not-for-profit executive; b. Glendale, Calif., Aug. 19, 1958; s. Andrew Raphael Jr. and Diane Rose (Carlotti) DiConti; m. Veronica Donahue, Aug. 6, 1988; children: Nolan James, Jason Andrew, Aidan Michael. AB in Psychology magna cum laude, Occidental Coll., 1980; MBA in Acctg./Fin., UCLA, 1983; MA in Polit. Sci., Johns Hopkins U., 1987, PhD in Polit. Sci., 1990. Tax advisor Arthur Young, LA, 1983-85; instr. C.C. of Balt., 1985-90, Johns Hopkins U., Balt., 1987-90; exec. asst. to pres. The Bus. Roundtable, Washington, 1990-93, dir. ops. & pub. policy, 1993—2004; dir. strategic partnerships Am. Coun. for Tech., Fairfax, Va., 2005—06; COO Nat. Commn. Energy Policy, Washington, 2006—07; dir. strategic ops. fin. Bipartisan Policy Ctr., Washington, 2007—. Author: Entrepreneurship in Training, 1992. Mem. Fairfax County Info. Tech. Policy Adv. Com., 2004—. Fellow Inst. for Study of World Politics, Washington, 1987-88. Mem. Phi Beta Kappa, Psi Chi (pres. Occidental Coll. chpt. 1979-80). Home: 4172B Lochleven Trl Fairfax VA 22030-8582 Office: Bipartisan Policy Ctr 1225 Eye St NW Ste 1000 Washington DC 22030 Address: 4172B Lochleven Trail Fairfax VA 22030 Home Phone: 202-468-1165; Office Phone: 202-204-2406. Personal E-mail: mdiconti@cox.net. Business E-Mail: mdiconti@energycommission.org.

DICOSMO, NINO, engineering company executive; b. 1968; B in Polit. Sci., Oakland U., 1990; M in Info. Systems Mgmt., Carnegie Mellon U., 2005. Account exec. EDS Grp., Germany, England, Italy; dir., Bus. Devel., Info. Systems and Services Gen. Motors Corp.; chmn., pres., CEO Autoweb.com, Rochester Hills, Mich., 2004—. Named one of 40 Under 40, Crain's Detroit Bus., 2006. Office: Autoweb.com 1688 Star Batt Dr Rochester Hills MI 48309

DICUS, STEPHEN HOWARD, lawyer; b. Kansas City, Mo., Mar. 3, 1948; s. Clarence Howard and Edith Helen (George) D.; m. Jolene Purcell; children: Brett S., Adam J. AB, U. Mo., 1970; JD, U. Mo., Kansas City, 1973. Bar: Mo. 1973, U.S. Dist. Ct. (we. dist.) Mo. 1973. Ptnr. Dietrich, Davis, Dicus, Rowlands, Schmitt & Gorman, Kansas City, 1979—89; shareholder Dicus Davis Sands & Collins, P.C., Kansas City, 1991—2004, Farchmin Dicus PC, 2005—. Mem. Kansas City Met. Bar Assn., Mo. Bar, Estate Planning Soc. Kansas City, Rotary Club. Meth. Avocations: tennis, golf. Home: 14011 Pawnee Leawood KS 66224-1069 Office: Farchmin Dicus PC 4520 Madison Ave Ste 110 Kansas City MO 64111 Office Phone: 816-931-1984. Business E-Mail: sdicus@farchmindicus.com.

DIDDY, See COMBS, SEAN

DIDIER, ELAINE K., library director, educator; m. Gordon Didier. BA, AMLS, PhD, U. Mich., Ann Arbor; student, U. Oxford. With U. Mich., Ann Arbor, 1977—99, interim dir. academic outreach, assoc. dean to dean Rackham Sch. Grad. Studies, dir. info. resources Stephen M. Ross Sch. Bus., adj. assoc. prof. Sch. Info., dir. Erasmus/Mich. Master of Bus. Info. Program; dean, prof. Kresge Libr., Oakland U.; dir. Gerald R. Ford Presdl. Libr. and Mus., Ann Arbor, 2005—. Mem. bd. trustees Libr. of Mich., 2001, chair, 2003—04. Mem.: Assn. of Coll. and Rsch. Libraries (exec. bd. mem., rep. to Am. Libr. Assn. Coun.), Mich. Libr. Assn. (past pres.). Office: Gerald R Ford Libr 1000 Beal Ave Ann Arbor MI 48109-2114 Office Phone: 734-205-0566. E-mail: elaine.didier@nara.gov.*

DIDION, JOAN, writer; b. Sacramento, Calif., Dec. 5, 1934; d. Frank Reese and Eduene (Jerrett) D.; m. John Gregory Dunne, Jan. 30, 1964 (dec. Dec. 30, 2003); 1 child, Quintana Roo (dec. Aug. 26, 2005). BA, U. Calif., Berkeley, 1956. Assoc. feature editor Vogue mag., 1956-63; former columnist Saturday Evening Post, Life, Esquire; now contbr. The NY Rev. of Books. Author: (novels) Run River, 1963, Play It As It Lays, 1970, A Book of Common Prayer, 1977, Democracy, 1984, The Last Thing He Wanted, 1996; (essays) Slouching Towards Bethlehem, 1968, The White Album, 1979, After Henry, 1992; (non-fiction) Salvador, 1983, Miami, 1987, Political Fictions, 2001, Fixed Ideas, 2003, Where I Was From: A Memoir, 2003; (plays) The Year of Magical Thinking, 2005 (Nat. Book award for non-fiction 2005), We Tell Ourselves Stories in Order to Live: Collected Nonfiction, 2006; co-author: (with John Gregory Dunne) Screenplays for films The Panic in Needle Park, 1971, Play It As It Lays, 1972, A Star Is Born, 1976, True Confessions, 1981, Hills Like White Elephants, 1991, Broken Trust, 1995, Up Close and Personal, 1996, (play) The Year of Magical Thinking, 2007. Recipient 1st prize Vogue's Prix de Paris, 1956, Morton Dauwen Zabel prize AAAL, 1978, The Edward MacDowell medal, 1996, Columbia Journalism award, 1999, George Polk award, 2001, Golden Plate award, Acad. Achievement, 2006, Evelyn F. Burkey award for contributions bringing honor and dignity to writers everywhere, Writers Guild Am., East, 2007. Mem. Am. Acad. Arts and Letters (Gold medal in Belle Lettres and Criticism, 2005), Am. Acad. Arts and Scis., Coun. Fgn. Rels. Mailing: care Janklow & Nesbit 445 Park Ave New York NY 10022-2606

DIDKOVSKY, LEONID V., engineer; s. Vladimir B. Didkovsky and Polina F. Didkovska; m. Vira F. Didkovska; children: Vladimir, Tanya, Alex. PhD in Astronomy, Main Astron. Obs., Kiev, 1990. Electronics Devices and Techniques, Lviv Poly. Inst., Ukraine, 1970. Engr. Electropribor, Kamenets Podolsky, Ukraine, 1970—75; lead engr. Crimean Astrophys. Obs., Nauchny, Ukraine, 1975—87, rsch. scientist, 1987—96, sci. dep. dir., 1996—2000; rsch. scientist Big Bear Solar Obs., Calif., 2000—04, project engr., 2002—04; rsch. scientist U. So. Calif., LA, 2004—. Mem.: Internat. Astron. Union (corr.). Office: U of Southern Calif 835 W 37th St Los Angeles CA 90089-1341 Home Phone: 909-585-1860; Office Phone: 213-740-6343.

DI DOMENICA, ROBERT ANTHONY, musician, composer; b. NYC, Mar. 4, 1927; s. Angelo and Philomena (Mosca) DiD.; m. Leona Knopf, Feb. 6, 1951 (dec. 1998); children— David, Peter Josef, Claude Robert; m. Ellen Bender, Apr., 1999. BS, N.Y. U., 1951. Mem. theory-composition faculty New Eng. Conservatory, 1969-92, assoc. dean performing orgns., 1973-76, dean, 1976-78. Flutist, N.Y.C. Ctr. Opera, N.Y. Philharm., Symphony of Air, soloist, Composers Forum, 20th Century Innovations, rec. artist, RCA, Columbia, Colpix, MGM, Atlantic, Deutsche Grammophon records; recs. include Leona DiDomenica In Live First Performance of the Solo Piano Music of Robert DiDomenica, GM/200/CD; compositions include Symphony, 1961, Concerto for Violin and Chamber Orch., 1962, Quintet for Clarinet and String Quartet, 1965, Sonata for Violin and Piano, 1966; opera The Balcony, 1972, Black Poems (baritone, piano and tape), 1976, The Holy Colophon for Orch., Chorus, Soprano and Tenor, 1980, Piano Concerto No. 2, 1982, Dream Journeys for Orch., 1984, The Scarlet Letter (opera), 1986, Opera The Balcony given its world premier by The Opera Co. of Boston, 1990, performed at Moscow's Bolshoi Theater, 1991, (operatic trilogy) Francesco Cenci, 1996, Beatrice Cenci, 1993, The Cenci, 1995. Served with USNR, 1944-46. Guggenheim fellow, 1972-73; grantee Rockefeller Found., 1965; commd. by Goethe Inst., Boston, 1975 Mem. Broadcast Music Inc. Home: 159 Valley Rd Needham MA 02492-4724 Office Phone: 781-455-9175. Personal E-mail: esbender@verizon.net.

DIDOMENICO, MAURO, JR., communications executive; b. Bronx, NY, Jan. 12, 1937; s. Mauro and Elizabeth DiD.; m. Angela M. Carracino, Aug. 29, 1964; children— Catherine Lee, David M. BS, Stanford U., 1958, MS, 1959, PhD, 1963. Mem. tech. staff Bell Labs., Murray Hill, NJ, 1962-66, supr., 1966-70, head optical device dept., 1970-80, dept. head integrated circuit customer service dept., 1980-82; divsn. mgr. strategic planning AT&T, Basking Ridge, NJ, 1982-84; divsn. mgr. applied rsch. BellCore, Morristown, NJ, 1984-85; exec. dir. tech. liaison office Bell Comms. Rsch., Morristown, NJ, 1985-92, ret., 1992; pres. CommTech Internat., Bernardsville, NJ, 1993-95; pres., founder FreeLinQ Comm., NYC, 1995—99; founder, exec. v.p. eVideo Incorporated, 2000—; prin. UltraPro Internat., 2000—03; program. mgr. NineSigma Corp., 2005—. Contbr. numerous articles to profl. lit. Fellow IEEE, Am. Phys. Soc.; mem. N.Y. Acad. Scis., Sigma Xi, Tau Beta Pi. Roman Catholic. Home Phone: 239-947-5694. Personal E-mail: maury.dido@verizon.net.

DIDRIKSEN, CALEB H., III, lawyer; b. Cleve., Nov. 3, 1955; s. Caleb H. Jr. and Eleanore Ann (Hoepli) D.; m. Sondra L. Brown, Apr. 21, 1993; children: Severin, Spencer, Luke. BS in Engring., U. Ill., 1977; JD, Tulane U., 1982. Bar: La. 1982, Tex. 1995, US Dist. Ct. (ea., mid. and we. dists.) La. 1982, US Ct. Appeals (5th cir.) 1982, US Supreme Ct. 1987. Assoc. McGlinchey, Stafford, New Orleans, 1982-84, Monroe & Lemann, New Orleans, 1984-88; pvt. practice New Orleans, 1988-89; sr. ptnr. Didriksen & Carbo, New Orleans, 1989—98, Didriksen Law Firm, 1998—. Mem. Boy Scouts-Eagle; scout leader; soccer coach; mem staff parish rels. com. Munholland United Meth. Ch; bd. mem. Raintree Svcs. Inc. Mem. ABA, La. Bar Assn. (asst. grader), New Orleans Bar Assn., Tau Beta Pi, Gamma Epsilon. Home: 231 Garden Rd River Ridge LA 70123 Office Phone: 504-586-1600, 225-644-0444.

DIEBOLD, FRANCIS X., economist, educator; b. Nov. 12, 1959; m. Susan S. Diebold; 3 children. BS in Fin. and Econs., U. Pa., 1981, PhD in Econs., 1986. Rsch. economist, mem. bd. govs. FRS, 1986—89; asst. prof. econs., J.M. Cohen term chair U. Pa., 1989—92, assoc. prof., 1992—96, prof., 1996—99, prof. stats. Wharton Sch., 1996—, dir. Inst. Econ. Rsch., Lawrence R. Klein prof. econs., 1999—; faculty rsch. fellow Nat. Bur. Econ. Rsch., 1993—99, rsch. assoc., 1999—2001; prof. fin. Wharton Sch. U. Pa., 2001—, W.P. Carey prof. econs., 2000—. Charter mem. Oliver Wyman Inst., 1996—; vis. prof. fin., econ., stats. Stern Sch. Bus., NYU, 1998-2000; vis. prof. Cambridge U., 1998, Princeton U., 1997, Johns Hopkins U., 1995, U. Chgo., 1993, London Sch. Econs., 1992, U. Minn., 1990; Benedum lectr. W.Va. U., 1992; mem. organizing com. Computational Fin., 1999—; mem. econs. panel NSF, 1998-2000, chmn. forecasting seminar, 1995—. Author: (with G. Rudebusch) Business Cycles: Durations, Dynamics and Forecasting, 1999, Elements of Forecasting, 1998, Empirical Modeling of Exchange Rate Dynamics, 1988; assoc. editor Rev. Econs. and Stats., 1993—, Jour. Bus. and Econ. Stats., 1993—, Jour. Forecasting, 1994—, Stata Tech. Bull., 1994—, Econometrica, 1994-97, Jour. Applied Econometrics, 1991-97, Jour. Empirical Fin., 1992-95, Econometric Revs., 1989-92; mem. adv. bd. Econ. Policy Rev., Fed. Res. Bank N.Y., 1997—, Macroecon. Dynamics, 1996—; co-editor Internat. Econ. Rev., 1993-99, Jour. Forecasting, 1990-94; contbr. articles to econ. and bus. jours.; spkr. at many profl. meetings and confs. Mem. bd. sr. scholars Nat. Ctr. for Ednl. Quality of Workforce, 1993-95. Fellow Wharton Fin. Instns. Ctr., 1997—; Alfred P. Sloan Found. rsch. fellow, 1992-94; grantee NSF, 1989-92, 92-94, 95-98, 98—, Pew Found., 1995-96, NSF and Cornell Super Computer Ctr., 1992-92, Alexander von Humboldt award, Fed. Rep. Germany, 2004, Guggenheim fellow, 2003-2004, Fellow, Am. State. Assn., 2004. Fellow Econometric Soc. (program com. N.Am. winter mtg. 1999, program com. time-series econometrics 1993); mem. Am. Statis. Assn. (mem. editl. selection com. Jour. B sec., Econ. Stats., 1994, 2000, Zellner award selection com. 1995, sec./treas. bus. and econ. stats. sect. 1994, program chair 1991), Am. Econ. Assn., Am. Fin. Assn. Office: U Pa Dept Econs 3718 Locust Walk Philadelphia PA 19104-6297

DIEDERICHS, JANET WOOD, public relations executive; b. Libertyville, Ill. BA, Wellesley Coll, 1950. Sales agt. Pan Am. Airways, Chgo., 1951-52; regional mgr. pub. relations Braniff Internat., Chgo., 1953-69; pres. Janet Diederichs & Assocs., Inc.; pub. rels. cons. Chgo., 1970—. Com. mem. Nat. Trust for Historic Preservation, 1975—79, Marshall Scholars (Brit. Govt.), 1975—79; trustee Sherwood Conservatory Music, 2000—04, Northwestern Meml. Hosp., 1985—2005, mem. exec. com., 1995—2000, life trustee; founder Com. of 200; chmn. Field Mus., 2003—, founders coun., 1999—; mem. exec. com. Vatican Art Coun., Chgo., 1981—83; pres. Jr. League Chgo., 1968—69; trustee Fourth Presbyn. Ch., mem. bd. dirs., 1990—93; bd. dirs., mem. exec. com. Chgo. Conv. and Visitors Bur., 1978—87; bd. dirs. Internat. House, U. Chgo., 1978—84; bd. dirs. Latino Inst., 1986—89, Albert Pick Jr. Found. Bd. Trustees. Mem. Chgo. Assn. Commerce and Industry (bd. dirs. 1982-89, exec. com. 1985-88), Internat. Women's Forum, Woman's Athletic Club of Chgo., Comml. Club of Chgo., The Casino Club (Chgo.), Wellesley Coll. Bus. Leadership Coun.

DIEDRICH, RICHARD JOSEPH, architect; b. South Bend, Ind., May 8, 1936; s. Arthur Joseph and Lucille D.; m. Francyne L. Diedrich (div. 1980); children: Dawn Marie, Lisa Lee, Andrea Lynn; m. Linda P. Diedrich. BArch, U. Ill., 1961, MArch, 1962. Archtl. designer Richardson Severns Scheeler & Assocs., Champaign, Ill., 1961-62; design critic U. Ill. Sch. Architecture, Champaign, 1961-62; archtl. designer Swensson & Kott, Nashville, 1963-64; architect, v.p. Miller Waltz Diedrich, Architects, Milw., 1965-77; pres. MWD Archs., Atlanta, 1978-80, Diedrich Archs., Atlanta, 1980-97; pres., exec. v.p. Diedrich/NBA, Atlanta, 1997—2002; pres. Diedrich LLC, Atlanta, 2002—. Instr. profl. devel. course Harvard Grad. Sch. Design, 1990-2004, 06. Author: Building Type Basics for Recreational Facilities, 2005; co-author: Golf Course Development and Real Estate; archtl. works include: Avondale Sta., Med. Ctr. Sta., Atlanta Rapid Transit, S. Miami Sta. of Miami Rapid Transit, Vt. Sunset Sta., L.A. Rapid Transit, Student Ctr., U. Ga., Bloomingdale's Stores, Boca Raton, Palm Beach Gardens, Mall of Am., Neiman Marcus Stores, Scottsdale, Ariz., Troy, Mich., Honolulu, Short Hills, N.J., King of Prussia, Pa., Paramus, N.J., Tampa, Fla., Coral Gables, Fla., Plano, Tex., Orlando, Fla., Grand Cypress Clubhouse, Orlando, English Turn Clubhouse, New Orelans, Golf Club Ga., Atlanta, Country Club North, Dayton, Old Overton Club House, Birmingham, Cherokee Country Club, Atlanta, Naples Nat. Golf Club, Sun City Hilton Head amenity facilities, Aerial Tram, Stone Mountain Park, Atlanta, Village Clubhouse, Kapaulua, Maui, Hawaii. Mem. Whitefish Bay Bd. Appeals, 1968-71; v.p. North Decatur Youth Assn., 1975-76; bd. dirs. Lake Burton Civic Assn., 2002-05; bd. govs. Urban Land Inst. Found., 2006. Margaret T. Biddle scholar, 1960. Mem. AIA (past pres. Milw. chpt., six design awards, two S.E. regional awards, four Ga. AIA awards), Wis. Architect (past pres.). Home and Office: 8 Brookhaven Dr Atlanta GA 30319 Office Phone: 404-231-3350.

DIEDRICHS, CAROL PITTS, library director, dean; b. New Orleans, Mar. 8, 1958; d. Leland Bascom and Mae Nell (Harper) Pitts; m. Frank M. Diedrichs. BA, Baylor U., Waco, Tex., 1980; M of Libr. and Info. Sci., U. Tex., Austin, 1981. Serials cataloger U. Houston Librs., 1981-82, head acquisition dept., 1982-87, Ohio State U., Columbus, 1987-97, asst. dir. tech. svcs. and collections, 1997—2003; dean librs. U. Ky., Lexington, 2003—. Mem. editl. bd. Libr. Collections, Acquisitions and Tech. Svcs., 1989-90, U. Press, Ky.; editor-in-chief, 1990-2003; contbr. articles to profl. jours. Chair acquisitions serial control com. OhioLink, asst. dir. policy devel., 1991-92, chair database mgmt. and stds. com.; mem. OCLC Mems. Coun., 2001-03, SOLINET Bd. Dirs., 2005—07, chair nominating com., 2006. Mem. ALA (chairperson discussion group, com. mem., sec. mem.-at-large, chmn. sect., pres., Esther J. Piercy award 1991, Leadership in Acquisitions award 1999), N.Am. Serials Interest Group (mem.-at-large), INNOVATIVE Users' Group (com. mem.), Assoc. Libr. Collections and Tech. Svcs. (pres.), Assn. Rsch. Librs. (mem. scholarly comm. com. 2005-07, nominating com. 2006). Office: William T Young Libr U Ky 500 S Limestone St Lexington KY 40506-0456 Office Phone: 859-257-0500 ext. 2087. E-mail: diedrichs@uky.edu.

DIEFENBACH, DALE ALAN, retired law librarian; b. Cleve., Aug. 14, 1933; s. Walter Ewald and Alice Naomi (Austin) D.; m. Olga Maspaitella, Jan. 20, 1973; 1 stepson, Andrew Ivan Ward. BA, Baldwin-Wallace Coll., 1955; MLS, U. Hawaii, 1970. Fgn. svc. officer U.S. Dept. State, 1961-68; reference libr. Cornell U. Law Libr., Ithaca, N.Y., 1970-87; sr. reference libr. Harvard U. Law Libr., Cambridge, Mass., 1987-97, ret., 1997; reference libr., adj. assoc. prof. law libr. Barry U. Sch. Law Euliano Law Libr., 1998—2003. Lt. (j.g.) USNR, 1956-60, Philippines. Recipient Ficken Meml. award Baldwin-Wallace Coll., Berea, Ohio, 1988. Mem. ALA, Am. Assn. Law Librs. Democrat. Home: 500 Windmeadows St Altamonte Springs FL 32701-3572 E-mail: deepbrook@embarqmail.com.

DIEFENDERFER, DAN, filmmaker; s. Raymond Gernard Diefenderfer, Jr. and Jean Francis Magerstadt. Student, U. Miami, 1972. Prodr.(director, co-writer): (5 hour PBS documentary series) Uniquely Kansas City; editor (post- production supervisior): (motion picture) Ninth Street (Ind. Film Channel award, 1999); prodr.: (U.S. EPA film) Dioxin Destruction, (director, co-writer) (motion picture) Timesweep. Recipient Press Club award, Kans. City Star newspaper, 2000, EMMY award for Best Direction-Documentary, NATAS, 2001, 2d pl. documentary category, Kan Film Fest-Kansas City, Mo., 2001, PBS Series of Yr., Nat. Ednl. Telecom. Assn., 2001, Preservation award, Kans. City Hist. Found., 2001, Gold award, The Aurora Awards, 2002, 2-Platinum Best of Show, 2002, 2 Gold finalist awards, The Telly Awards, 2002, Gold finalist, 2003. Mem.: KC Screenwriters. Achievements include produced, directed and co-wrote Uniquely Kansas City, the first locally originated PBS series shot and nationally broadcast in High Definition video; produced & directed the motion picture Timesweep, documented by The New York Times: first use of new film stock specifically designed for conversion of 16mm film to 35mm theatrical exhibition prints. Home Phone: 816-390-9089; Office Phone: 816-294-8735.

DIEFFENBACH, OTTO WEAVER, III, real estate company executive; b. Key West, Fla., Aug. 4, 1953; s. Otto, Jr. and Alice Jean Thompson D.; m. Susan S., Jan. 16, 1982 (div. May 1997); children: Otto Weaver IV, Claire T., Bryan V.; m. Elisabeth I., June 12, 1997 (div. Sept. 2002). BSEM, USAF Acad., 1975; MBA, Golden Gate U., 1977; MS in Aeronautics, USAF Test Pilot Sch., 1978. With USAF, 1975-81, advanced through ranks to capt., 1979; flight test engr. Air Force Flight Test Ctr., Edwards AFB, Calif., 1975-78; sys. test engr. USAF Armament Divsn., Eglin AFB, Fla., 1979-81; sr. staff engr. Martin Marietta, Denver, 1981-83; regional ops. mgr. air traffic control divsn. Lockheed Martin, LA, 1984-93; mgr. bus. devel. Advanced Devel. Ops., San Diego, 1993-96; dir. bus. devel. L3 Comm., Anaheim, Calif., 1997-99; dir. mktg. Racal Comm., Bonn, Germany, 1999—2000; v.p. mktg. Spirent Comm., Calabasas, Calif., 2000—01; dir. Lockheed Martin, Lawndale, Calif., 2002—03; ptnr. Dieffenbach Real Estate, Rancho Santa Fe, Calif., 2003—. CEO Ariel Ltd., San Diego, 1988-90. Developer autonomous precision approach and landing sys. (Best of Whats New award Popular Sci. 1997). Vol. Children's Hosp. and Health Ctr. Recipient Nat. Conservation award Dept. of Energy, 1980, Industry Leadership award Dubai-Partnership 21, 1995, Outstanding Tech. Paper award Air Traffic Control Assn., 1995, Aviation & Space award Popular Sci., 1996. Mem.: Rotary Internat. Avocations: sailing, car restoration, water-skiing. Home: PO Box 990 Rancho Santa Fe CA 92067 Office: Dieffenbach Real Estate 6013 La Granada Rancho Santa Fe CA 92067 Office Phone: 858-756-2345. Personal E-mail: otto3@sbcglobal.net.

DIEHL, DEBORAH HILDA, lawyer; b. Troy, NY, Feb. 13, 1951; d. Warren S. and Norma K. (Apple) D.; 1 child, Alexandra Ellen. Student, U. de Rouen, France, 1971-72; BA, St. Lawrence U., 1973; JD, Syracuse U., 1976; postdoctoral, George Washington U., 1978-79. Bar: N.Y. 1977, D.C. 1981, Ohio 1982, Md. 1987. Atty. USDA, Washington, 1976-81; assoc.

Thompson, Hine & Flory, Columbus, Ohio, 1981-87, Semmes, Bowen & Semmes, Balt., 1987-90, ptnr., 1990-95, Whiteford, Taylor & Preston, Balt., 1995—. Pres. Mt. Royal Improvement Assn., 1995—97; chair Midtown Cmty. Benefits Dist. Mgmt. Authority, 1998—2000, dir., 1995—2001, Midtown Devel. Corp., 2000—; participant Leadership Md., 1997; mem. U. Md. Baltimore County Tech. Ctr. Adv. Bd., 2001—; mem. vision coun. United Way, 2006—; bd. dirs. Jenkins Meml. Hist. Trust, Corpus Christi, Tex. Mem.: ABA, Bar Assn. City Balt., Md. State Bar Assn. (bus. law sect. coun. 1998—, chair 2002—03). Avocations: bicycling, travel, economic development. Office Phone: 410-347-8766.

DIEHL, DOLORES, performing company executive; b. Salina, Kans., Dec. 28, 1927; d. William Augustus and Martha (Frank) Diehl. Student pub. schs., Kans. Bus. rep. Southwestern Bell Telephone Co., St. Louis and Kansas City, Mo., 1948-49, Mountain States Telephone Co., Denver, 1949-50; edn. coord. pub. rels. Pacific Telephone/AT&T, L.A. and San Diego, 1950-83; cons. Bus. Magnet High Sch., L.A. Unified Sch. Dist., 1977-79; pres. First Calif. Acad. Decathlon, 1979; owner Community Connection, LA, 1983—; mgr., dir. DelMar Media Arts, Burbank, Calif., 1985-89; mgr. Susan Blu workshops Blupka Prodns., LA, 1989—; ptnr., dir. animation and commls. voiceover workshops Elaine Craig Voicecasting, Hollywood, Calif., 1989—; freelance performer, voiceover LA, 1990—; mgr. Sounds Great Film Looping Workshops, LA, 1992-93; owner Voiceover Connection, LA, 1994-95; pres. Voiceover Connection, Inc., LA, 1995—. V.p. pub. rels. San Diego Inst. Creativity, 1965—67. Pub. rels. dir. Greater San Diego Sci. Fair, 1963—68; mem. exec. com. San Diego's 200th Anniversary Celebration, 1967; mem. Better Bus. Bur. Named one of Seven Top Voiceover Trainer, Animation Mag., 1999; recipient Dedication to Edn. award, Industry Edn. Coun., Calif., 1964. Mem.: Industry Edn. Coun. Calif., L.A. and San Diego (past pres.), Magnet Sch. Consortium Cities (chairperson), L.A. Area C. of C. (bd. dirs. women's coun.), Bus. and Profl. Women's Club, Delta Kappa Gamma (hon.). Republican. Methodist. Home and Office: 691 Irolo St Apt 212 Los Angeles CA 90005-4110 Home Phone: 213-384-9251; Office Phone: 213-384-9251. E-mail: doloresdiehl@speakeasy.net.

DIEHL, DONNA RAE See GARDNER, DONNA

DIEHL, JACKSON KEMPER, journalist; b. San Antonio, Aug. 8, 1956; s. Kemper Wilson and Mary Suzanne Diehl; m. Jean Frances Heilprin, Jan. 3, 1987; children: Sanford L., Caroline K. BA, Yale U., 1978. Metro reporter Washington Post, Washington, 1978-81, bur. chief Buenos Aires, 1982-85, Warsaw, 1985-89, Jerusalem, 1989-92, asst. mng. editor fgn. divsn. Washington, 1994-99, asst. mng. editor nat. divsn., 1999-2000, dep. editl. page editor, 2001—. Recipient Inter-Am. Press award Inter-Am. Press Club, 1984, Bob Considine award Overseas Press Club, 1989. Mem. Coun. on Fgn. Rels. Office: The Washington Post 1150 15th St NW Washington DC 20071 E-mail: diehlj@washpost.com.

DIEHL, JAMES HARVEY, church administrator; m. Dorothy Diehl; 4 children. BA, Olivet Nazarene U., 1959; DD, N.W. Nazarene U., 1990. Adminstr. MidAm. Nazarene U., 1973-76; dist. supt. Ch. of Nazarene, Nebr. and Colo., 1979-89; pastor Atlanta First Ch., 1976-79, Nazarene chs. in Iowa, Denver First Ch. of Nazarene, 1989-93; gen. supt. Ch. of the Nazarene, Kansas City, Mo., 1993—. Contbr. articles to Herald of Holiness, Preacher's Mag., Bread, World Mission, others; condr. daily radio program, weekly TV broadcast. Bd. trustees MidAm. Nazarene U., Nazarene Theol. Sem., Nazarene Bible Coll., N.W. Nazarene U.; chmn. bd. N.W. Nazarene U. Mem. Ch. Of Nazarene. Office: Ch of the Nazarene 6401 Paseo Blvd Kansas City MO 64131-1213 Office Phone: 816-333-7000.

DIEHL, LOUIS F., hematologist; b. Trenton, NJ, Apr. 8, 1948; s. Louis and Anna D.; m. Anna Mae, Dec. 3, 1973; children: Megan, Erin. BS, Georgetown U., 1970, MD, 1975. Oncologist Johns Hopkins Oncology Ctr., Balt., 1999—2004, Duke U. Med. Ctr., 2004—.

DIEHL, NANCY J., lawyer; b. 1953; d. Robert and Anne Diehl. B, Western Mich. Univ.; JD, Wayne State Univ., 1978. Trial prosecutor Recorder's Ct., Detroit, 1981—84; spl. assignment trial prosecutor Cir. Ct., 1984—87; dir. Child Abuse Unit, 1987—94; dep. chief Child and Family Abuse Bur., 1994—2000; chief projects and tng. divsn. Wayne County Prosecutor's Office, Detroit, 2000—04, chief felony trial divsn., 2004—. Mem. Gov. Task Force on Children's Justice (exec. com.), State Bar Rep. Assembly, 1992—96, 1996—2005. Author, illustrator with Lynda Baker (booklet) It is Good to Tell the Truth, 1988, Kids and Secrets, 1992, author, photographer with Lynda Baker Kids Go to Court, 1988; author (with Lynda Baker): (booklet) Sometimes It Is Sad to Be at Home, What Is a Kid to Do About Domestic Violence, 1997. Recipient Leonard Gilman award, 1999. Mem.: Detroit Met. Bar Assn. (Champion of Justice award 2004), State Bar of Mich. (pres. 2004). Office: Wayne County Prosecutor's Office 1441 St Antoine Detroit MI 48226-2302 Office Phone: 313-224-5742. Business E-Mail: ndiehl@co.wayne.mi.us.

DIEHL, RICHARD KURTH, retail executive, consultant; b. Chgo., July 6, 1935; s. George Henry and Agnes Martha (Kurth) D.; m. Barbara Louise Clark, June 9, 1957; children— Clark Kurth, Scott Richard, Stacy Louise. BA, Beloit Coll., 1957; postgrad., Harvard U., 1957-58; MBA, U. Chgo., 1959. With brand mgmt. staff Procter & Gamble, Cin., 1959-62; v.p., account supr. Needham, Harper & Steers, Chgo., 1963-68; Dir. mktg. Kimberly-Clark Corp., Neenah, Wis., 1968-70; pres., chief exec. officer Purnell, Inc., Santa Monica, Calif., 1970-72; v.p., chief operating officer Theta Cable TV, Santa Monica, 1972-74; exec. v.p., chief savs. officer Western Fed. Savs. and Loan Assn., Los Angeles, 1974-80; exec. v.p., a founding officer Centurion Savs. and Loan Assn., Century City, Calif., 1980-82; founder Diehl & Assocs., Los Angeles, 1983—; pres., CEO Stockwell and Binney/Royale, La Habra, Calif., 1992—. Mem. Citizens Adv. Council Los Angeles Schs., 1970-72. Woodrow Wilson fellow, 1957-58; Harvard Austin fellow, 1957-58; Sears Roebuck Found. fellow, 1958-59 Mem. Phi Beta Kappa, Sigma Alpha Epsilon. Clubs: Riviera Tennis, Santa Monica Tennis Patrons. Lodges: Rotary. Home: 17117 Ave Herradura Pacific Palisades CA 90272-2002

DIEHL, RICHARD PAUL, lawyer; b. Toledo, Dec. 25, 1940; s. Clair Bertrand and Josephine Frances (Kwiatkowski) D.; m. Laura Gean Carpenter, Mar. 26, 1966; children: Michelle, Michael. BSME, U. Mich., 1963; MBA, Tulane U., 1972; JD, U. Detroit, 1983. Bar: Mich. 1983, U.S. Dist. Ct. (ea. dist.) Mich. 1983, U.S. Supreme Ct. 1988, U.S. Ct. Fed. Claims 1990, U.S. Ct. Appeals (6th cir.) 1991, U.S. Ct. Appeals (fed., D.C. cirs.) 1992), U.S. Dist. Ct. (we. dist.) Mich. 1996. Commd. 2d lt. U.S. Army, 1963, advanced through grades to col., ret., 1986; pres. Diehl & Sobczak, PC, Troy, Mich., 1986-99; with Inst. for Def. Analyses, Alexandria, Va., 1999—. Adj. prof. bus. Am. Tech. U., Killeen, Tex., 1977-78; adj. prof. law U. Detroit, 1987-89. Contbr. articles to profl. jours. Decorated 2 Silver stars, five Bronze stars, 2 Purple Hearts, 2 Legions of Merit Meritorious Svc. medal, Army Commendation medal, 3 Air medals, Cross of Gallantry. Mem. Am. Def. Preparedness Assn., Assn. U.S. Army, U. Mich. Alumni Assn., Elks. Avocations: hunting, fishing, sports. Address: 125 Birdie Dr Suffolk VA 23434-9283 E-mail: rpdiehl@aol.com.

DIEHL, STEPHEN ANTHONY, human resources consultant; b. NYC, Mar. 15, 1942; s. Anthony Stephen and Paula (Kula) D.; m. Barbara Lynn Marschman, Aug. 3, 1968. BS, LI U., 1963; postgrad. in bus., NYU, 1967-73. V.p. mktg. dir. Green Point Savs. Bank, Bklyn., 1969—77; sr. v.p., human resources dir. Green Point Bank, NYC, 1977—95. Dir. Human Resources NY Road Runners Club (NY City Marathon), 1996-2001; officer, dir. Soc. for Human Resources Mgmt., NY chpt., 1995-2001. Mem. Savs. Banks Mktg. Forum NY State (chmn. 1973-74), NYC Mktg. Forum (chmn. 1975-76), Human Resources Officers Forum (chmn. 1980-81), Savs. Banks Officers Forum (pres. 1986-87). Avocations: photography, video, stereo. E-mail: sadiehl@aol.com.

DIEHM, JAMES WARREN, lawyer, educator; b. Lancaster, Pa., Nov. 6, 1944; s. Warren G. and Verna M. (Hertzler) D.; m. Cathleen M. Hohmeier; children: Elizabeth Ann, Rebecca Jane. BA, Pa. State U., 1966; JD, Georgetown U., 1969. Bar: D.C. 1969, V.I. 1975, Pa. 1988. Asst. U.S. atty., Washington, 1970-74; asst. atty. gen. Atty. Gen.'s Office U.S. V.I., St. Croix, 1974-76; from assoc. to ptnr. Isherwood, Hunter & Diehm, St. Croix, 1976-83; U.S. atty. U.S. V.I., 1983-87; prof. law Widener U., Harrisburg, 1987—. Bar examiner U.S. V.I. Bar, 1979-87. Mem. ABA. Republican. Lutheran. Office: Widener U Sch Law 3800 Vartan Way PO Box 69382 Harrisburg PA 17106-9382 Office Phone: 717-541-3939.

DIEHR, BEVERLY HUNT, lawyer; b. Tampa, Fla., Aug. 19, 1954; d. Carl William Jr. and Helen Fern (Rouse) Hunt; children: Erin Elizabeth, Sara Katherine, Dana Marie. BA with high honors, U. So. Fla., 1975; JD with high honors, U. Fla., 1978. Bar: Fla. 1978, U.S. Dist. Ct. (mid. dist.) Fla. 1979. Staff atty. Three Rivers Legal Svcs. Inc., Gainesville, Fla., 1979-82; assoc. Sessums and McCall, Tampa, 1982-83; asst. dist. legal counsel dist. 6 Fla. Dept. Health and Rehab. Svcs., Tampa, 1983-84; pvt. practice law Tampa, 1984—2004; sr. atty. Fla. Dept. Children and Families, 2004—. Mem. Fla. Bar Assn., Hillsborough County Bar Assn., Fla. Assn. Women Lawyers, Hillsborough Assn. Women Lawyers, Order of Coif. Home: 4301 W Cleveland St Tampa FL 33609-3867 Office: State Fla Dept Children and Families 9393 North Florida Ave Ste 902 Tampa FL 33612 Office Phone: 813-558-5510.

DIEKEMA, ANTHONY J., college president, consultant; b. Borculo, Mich., Dec. 3, 1933; m. Jeane Waanders, Dec. 20, 1957; children: Douglas, David, Daniel, Paul, Mark, Maria, Tanya. BA, Calvin Coll., Grand Rapids, Mich., 1956; MA in Sociology and Anthropology, Mich. State U., 1958, PhD in Sociology, 1965. Field interviewer Bur. Bus. Research Mich. State U., East Lansing, 1955-56, asst. dir. housing, 1957-59, instr., lectr. sociology and anthropology, 1959-64, admissions counselor, 1959-61, asst. dir. admissions and scholarships, 1961-62, asst. registrar, 1962-64; asst. dean admissions and records, research assoc. in med. edn. and asst. prof. sociology U. Ill. Med. Center, Chgo., 1964-66, dir. admissions and records, asst. prof. sociology and edn., 1966-70, asso. chancellor, asso. prof. med. edn., 1970-76; pres. Calvin Coll., 1976-96, pres. emeritus, 2003—; interim pres. Trinity Christian Coll., Palos Heights, Ill., 2002—03. Adv. bd. NBD Grand Rapids, 1983-95; chmn. bd. Russian-Am. Christian U., Moscow, 2005-. Trustee Blodgett Meml. Med. Center, Grand Rapids, 1979-91; bd. dirs. Met. YMCA, 1979-93, Project Rehab, 1978-84; treas. Back-to-God Hour Radio Com., 1970-76; chmn. Synodical Com. on Race Relations, 1973-75; pres. Strategic Christian Ministry Found., 1969-73; mem. bd. curators Trinity Christian Coll., 1969-73, chmn., 1972-73, mem. presdl. search com., 1972-73, NCAA coun. 1983-87, Pres'. commn. 1987-91. Mem. Am. Assn. Pres.'s Ind. Coll. and Univs. (bd. dirs. 1978-84, 88-91), Nat. Assn. Ind. Colls. and Univs. (bd. dirs. 1991-94), Assn. Ind. Colls. and Univs. Mich. (exec. com. 1979-84), Am. Assn. Higher Edn., Am. Sociol. Assn., Soc. Health and Human Values, Soc. Values in Higher Edn., Nat. League Nursing (accreditation com. 1974-79), Alpha Kappa Delta, Rotary. Office: Calvin Coll Grand Rapids MI 49546 Office Phone: 616-402-6898. Personal E-mail: ajdiek@aol.com.

DIEKHOFF, BILLY HERMAN, retired music educator; b. Terre Haute, Ind., July 29, 1936; s. Herman M. and Rosemary Diekhoff; children: James Bryan, John William. BS in Music Edn., Ind. State U., Terre Haute, 1958; MS in Music Edn., Ind. State U., 1963. Tchr. Terre Haute Pub. Schs., 1958—60, Martinsville Pub. Schs., Ind., 1960—69, Kokomo Pub. Schs., Ind., 1969—70, Racine Unified Sch. Dist., Wis., 1970—93; ret., 1993. Founding mem. Comprehensive Musicianship Wis. Dept. Pub. Instrn., 1976—84. Recipient Outstanding Young Educator, Jaycees Club, 1968. Mem.: Chorus Am., Nat. Assn. Tchrs. Singing, Am. Choral Dirs. Assn. (nat. chair cmty. choirs 1986—97). Avocations: boating, fishing, travel. Home: 5019 Hermitage Anderson SC 29625

DIEKMAN, CONNIE, nutritionist; BA food and nutrition, Fontbonne Coll.; MA edn., U. Mo. - St. Louis. Dietetic internship Barnes Hospital, St. Louis; private instructor Fontbonne U., St. Louis; former television nutrition reporter St. Louis NBC, FOX; former chair Am. Heart Assn., Mo. affiliate; Professional Issues Del. for Community; staff mem. Wash. U., St. Louis, 1994—, dir. U. Nutrition. Pres. Am. Dietetic Assn., 2007—08. Named Young Dietitian of Yr., Mo.; recipient Alumni Disting. Svc. Award, Fontbonne Coll., Outstanding Dietitian of Yr. Award, Mo. Dietetic Assn., Dr. Arthur Strauss Award, Am. Heart Assn., St. Louis. Office: Campus Box 1092 6515 Wydown Saint Louis MO 63105 Office Phone: 314-935-4439. Office Fax: 314-935-8935. Business E-Mail: connie_diekman@aismail.wustl.edu.*

DIEKMANN, GILMORE FREDERICK, JR., lawyer; b. Evansville, Ind., Jan. 14, 1946; s. Gilmore Frederick Sr. and Mabel Pauline (Daniel) K.; children: Anne Westlake, Andrew Gilmore, Matthew Frederick. BSBA, Northwestern U., 1968, JD, 1971. Bar: Calif. 1972, U.S. Dist. Ct. Calif. (no., ea., cen. and so. dists.) Calif. 1972, U.S. Ct. Appeals (9th cir.) 1972, U.S. Supreme Ct. 1978. Assoc. Bronson, Bronson & McKinnon, San Francisco, 1971-78, ptnr. labor and employment law, 1979-99, chmn., mng. ptnr., 1991-93, chmn. labor, employment dept., 1993-99; ptnr. Seyfarth Shaw, San Francisco, 1999—, chmn. no. Calif. labor dept., 1999—2005. Author and speaker in field. Mem. ABA, Def. Rsch. Inst., Am. Employment Law Coun., Order of Coif. Republican. Lutheran. Home: 901 Powell St # 6 San Francisco CA 94108 Office: Seyfarth Shaw 560 Mission St Fl 31 San Francisco CA 94105-2907 Office Phone: 415-544-1070. Business E-Mail: gdiekmann@seyfarth.com.

DIEMER, EMMA LOU, composer, educator; b. Kansas City, Mo., Nov. 24, 1927; d. George Willis and Myrtle (Casebolt) D. MusB, Yale U., 1949, MusM, 1950; PhD, Eastman Sch. Music, 1960; LHD (hon.), Ctrl. Mo. State U., 1999. Composer-in-residence Arlington (Va.) Schs., 1959-61; composer, cons. pub. schs., Arlington and Balt., 1964-65; prof. theory and composition U. Md., College Park, 1965-70, U. Calif., Santa Barbara, 1971-91. Organist Ch. of the Reformation, Washington, 1962—71, Ch. of Christ, Santa Barbara, 1973—84, 1st Presbyn. Ch., Santa Barbara, 1984—2001. Composer including Music for Woodwind Quartet, 1976, Four Poems of Alice Meynell for soprano and chamber ensemble, 1977, Symphony No. 2, 1980, Suite for Orchestra, 1981, Suite of Homages, 1985, Church Rock, 1986, Variations for Piano, 4 Hands, 1987, String Quartet No. 1, 1987, Serenade for string orch., 1988, Concerto for Marimba, 1990, Concerto for Piano, 1991, Sextet, 1992, Four Biblical Settings for organ, 1992, Fantasy for piano, 1993, Kyrie for mixed chorus, organ, and piano - 4 Hands, 1993, Santa Barbara Overture, 1995, Gloria for Mixed Chorus, 2 Pianos and Percussion, 1996, Psalm 122 for bass trombone and organ, Psalm 121 for organ, brass and percussion, Psalms for flute and organ, Psalms for trumpet and organ, Psalms for percussion and organ, 1998, Latin Mass, 2000, Homage to Tschaikovsky, 2000, Piano Trio, 2000, Quartet for piano and brass, 2001, Songs for the Earth, 2002, Toccata for Six, 2004, Requiem for woodwind quintet and string quintet, 2004, Chumash Indian Dance Celebration, 2004, Homage to Poulenc, Mozart, and MacDowell, 2004, Oxford Town Hall for organ, 2005, Poem of Remembrance for clarinet and chamber orch., 2006, others; composer-in-residence Santa Barbara Symphony, 1990-92. Fulbright scholar, 1952-53; grantee Ford Found. Young Composers, 1959-61, Kindler Found. Commn., 1963, Nat. Endowment Arts, 1980-81; Kennedy Ctr. Friedheim award, 1992. Mem. ASCAP (ann. awards 1962—), Am. Guild Organists (Composer of Yr. 1995), Internat. Alliance for Women in Music, Am. Music Ctr., Mu Phi Epsilon (award of merit 1995). Democrat. Presbyterian. Avocations: reading, electronic and computer music. E-mail: eldiemer@cox.net. *A composer who succeeds in some measure must have talent, encouragement, strong self-motivation, an almost obsessive need for self-expression through music, a belief in the importance of one's own contribution, the ability to appraise one's own work, the desire, at least part of the time, to communicate.*

DIENELT, JOHN F., lawyer; b. Alexandria, Va., Nov. 24, 1943; BA, U. Va., 1965; MA, Fletcher Sch. Law and Diplomacy, Tufts Univ., 1966; LLB, Yale U., 1969. Law clk. to Hon. G.A. Gesell U.S. Dist. Ct. D.C., 1969-70; asst. to Solicitor Gen. U.S. Dept. Justice, 1970-71; ptnr., chmn. Franchise Litigation practice group DLA Piper Rudnick Gray Cary, Washington, 1996—. Mng. editor Yale Law Jour., 1968-69; contbr. articles to profl. jours. Mem. ABA (chmn. Forum on Franchising 2000-2001), DC Bar, Order of Coif, Phi Beta Kappa. Office: DLA Piper 1200 19th St NW Washington DC 20036-2412 Office Phone: 202-861-3880. Office Fax: 202-223-2085. Business E-Mail: john.dienelt@dlapiper.com.

DIENER, BETTY JANE, business educator; b. Washington, Sept. 15, 1940; d. Edward George and Minnie (Feild) Diener; m. Robert D. Bell, 1987 (dec. 1993). AB, Wellesley Coll., 1962; MBA, Harvard U., 1964, DBA, 1974. Account exec. Young & Rubicam, Inc., NYC, 1964-70; product mgr. Am. Cyanamid Co., Wayne, NJ, 1970-72; asst. dean Sch. Bus. Case Western Res. U., Cleve., 1974-79; dean Sch. Bus. Adminstrn. Old Dominion U., Norfolk, Va., 1986-87; provost, vice-chancellor acad. affairs U. Mass., Boston, 1987-88, prof. mktg., 1987—2002, spl. asst. to chancellor econ. devel., 1993-94; prof., mgmt. Barry U., Miami Shores, Fla., 2002—. Pres. Environ. Bus. Coun. New Eng., Inc., 1995—97. Contbr. articles to profl. publs. Mem. Citizens Coun. Chesapeake Bay, 1986—87; adviser Jr. League, 1963—64, Plans for Progress, 1968—70, Leadership Met. Richmond, 1980—82; mem. Mass. Gov.'s Adv. Com. Sci. and Tech., 1988—90, Mayor's Task Force Empowerment Zones, 1994; mem. cmty. working group Mass. Mil. Reservation, 1997—2000; pres. Provincetown (Mass.) Repertory Theater, 2002, bd. dirs., 2001—03; commr. Norfolk Indsl. Devel. Authority, 1979—82; bd. dirs. Norfolk Conv. and Visitors Bur., 1979—82, Norfolk C. of C., 1979—82, Greater Norfolk Corp., 1986—87, Va. Orch. Group, 1982—87, Va. Stage Co., 1986—87, Karamu Ho., 1975—79, Woodruff Hosp., 1975—79, Women's City Club Cleve., 1976—79, Coun. Sustainable Fla., 2003—, Bainbridge Grad. Inst., 2003—05; mem. adv. com. state and local govt. programs John F. Kennedy Sch. Govt., Harvard U., 1986—88. Named Outstanding Working Woman, Glamour Mag., 1979; named one of 10 Outstanding Career Women of Decade, 1984; recipient Honor award, Soil Conservation Soc., 1984; Fulbright scholar, 2001. Democrat. Home: 4000 Towerside Terr #1108 Miami FL 33138 Office: Barry Univ Andreas Sch of Business Miami Shores FL 33161 Personal E-mail: bejade@aol.com.

DIENER, ERWIN, immunologist; b. Lucerne, Switzerland, Jan. 6, 1932; arrived in Can., 1970; s. Reinhold and Alice (Treichler) D.; m. Eva Schaufelberger, 1957. PhD, U. Zurich, 1963. Rsch. fellow Inst. for Radiobiology, Zurich, 1960-64; Roche fellow Walter and Eliza Hall Inst., Melbourne, Australia, 1964-67, rsch. fellow, 1967-70; prof. U. Alta., Edmonton, Can., 1970-73, prof., head dept. immunology, 1973-88, prof. emeritus, 1989—. Fellow Royal Soc. Can.

DIENER, ROYCE, retired health products executive; b. Mar. 27, 1918; s. Louis and Lillian (Goodman) Diener; m. Jennifer S. Flinton; children: Robert, Joan, Michael, Dianne. BA, Harvard U.; LLD (hon.), Pepperdine U. Comml. lending officer, ivnestment banker, various locations, 1972; pres. Am. Med. Internat., Inc., Beverly Hills, Calif., 1972—75, pres., CEO, 1975—78, chmn., CEO, 1978—85, chmn. bd., chmn. exec. com., 1986—89. Bd. dirs. Calif. Econ. Devel. Corp., Acuson, Inc., Advanced Tech. Venture Funds, Am. Health Properties, AMI Health Svcs., plc., Constorium 2000. Author: Financing a Growing Business, 1966, 4th edit., 1995. Mem. bd. visitors Grad. Sch. Mgmt., UCLA Med. Ctr.; mem. vis. com. Med. Sch. and Sch. Dental Medicine, Harvard U.; bd. dirs. L.A. Philharm. Assn.; bd. dirs. L.A. chpt. ARC; bd. dirs. Heritage Sq. Mus., Santa Monica, Calif.; trustee Contemporary Mus., Honolulu; chmn. bd. UCLA Med. Ctr. Capt. USAF, 1942—46, PTO. Decorated D.F.C. with oak leaf cluster. Mem.: Calif. Bus. Round Table (bd. dirs.), Calif. C. of C. (bd. dirs.), L.A. C. of C. (bd. dirs.), Outrigger Canoe Club (Honolulu), Marks Club (London), Riviera Country Club (L.A.), Calif. Yacht Club, Regency Club, Harvard Club.

DIENER, THEODOR OTTO, plant pathologist, researcher; b. Zurich, Switzerland, Feb. 28, 1921; arrived in 1949, 1949, naturalized, 1955; s. Theodor Emanuel and Hedwig Rosa (Baumann) D.; m. Sybil Mary Fox, May 11, 1968; children from previous marriage: Theodor W., Robert A., Michael S. Diploma, Swiss Fed. Inst. Tech., 1946; DSc, Nat. Swiss Fed. Inst. Tech., 1948. Asst. Swiss Fed. Inst. Tech., Zurich, 1946—48; plant pathologist Swiss Fed. Exptl. Sta., Waedenswil, 1949—50; asst. prof. plant pathology RI State U., Kingston, 1950; asst. plant pathologist Wash. State U., Prosser, 1950—55, assoc. plant pathologist, 1955—59; rsch. plant pathologist agr. rsch. svc. USDA, Beltsville, Md., 1959—88, collaborator agr. rsch. svc., 1988—97; prof. botany, sr. staff sci. Ctr. Agr. Biotech., dept. Botany U. Md., College Park, 1988—98, acting dir. Ctr. Agr. Biotech., 1991—92, Disting. Univ. prof., 1994—98; Disting. prof. U. Md. Biotech. Inst., 1998, Disting. Univ. prof. emeritus, 1999—. Univ. lectr., rsch. instr.; Regent's lectr. U. Calif., Riverside, 1970; A.W. Dimock lectr. Cornell U., 1975, Andrew D. White prof.-at-large, 1979—81; James Law disting. lectr. NY State Coll. Vet. Medicine, 1981; disting. lectr. Boyce Thomson Inst. for Plant Rsch., 1987, Hong Kong U. Sci. and Tech., 1992; Ernest Everett Just Meml. lectr. Howard U., Washington, 1990; guest lectr. Israel Soc. for Microbiology, Rehovot, 1994, Royal Swedish Acad. of Scis., Stockholm, 1997, Swedish Agrl. U., Uppsala, 1997, Royal Netherlands Acad. Arts and Scis., Amsterdam, 1998, Alexander von Humboldt Assn., Washington, 1999. Author: Viroids and Viroid Diseases, 1979; editor: The Viroids, 1987; assoc. editor: Virology, 1967—71, mem. editl. com.: Ann. Rev. Phytopathology, 1970—74, Annales de Virologie, 1980—88; contbr. articles to profl. jours. Named to USDA Sci. Hall of Fame, 1989, Cir. Discovery, U. Md. Coll. Chem. and Life Scis., College Park, 2007; recipient Campbell award, Am. Inst. Biol. Scis., 1968, Superior Svc. award, USDA, 1969, Disting. Svc. award, 1975, Alexander von Humboldt award, 1975, Wolf prize in agr., Wolf Found., Israel, 1987, U.S. Nat. medal of Sci., 1987, Gov.'s citation, State of Md., 1988, E.C. Stakman award, U. Minn., 1988. Fellow: Am. Acad. Arts and Scis., NY Acad. Scis., Am. Phytopath. Soc.; mem.: AAAS, NAS, German Acad. Natural Scientists, Leopoldina. Achievements include discovery of novel class of pathogens (viroids), 1971. Home: 11711 Battersea Dr PO Box 272 Beltsville MD 20704-0272 Office: U Md Biosystems Rsch Ctr College Park MD 20742-0001 Home Phone: 301-937-3591. Personal E-mail: todiener@verizon.net. E-mail: diener@umbi.umd.edu.

DIENES, LOUIS ROBERT, lawyer; b. New Brunswick, NJ, Apr. 17, 1966; s. Louis S. and Rosemary T. D. AB, U. Calif., Berkeley, 1990; JD, Stanford U., 1994. Bar: Calif. 1994. Ptnr. Alschuler Grossman Stein & Kahan, LLP, LA, 2005—06, Jeffer Mangels Butler & Marmaro LLP, 2006—. Mem. adv. bd. L.A. Bus. Tech. Ctr., LA, 2002—. Mem.: Century City Bar Assn. (treas. 2006—), Pasadena Angels. Office: 1900 Ave of the Stars Los Angeles CA 90067 Home Phone: 310-487-3503; Office Phone: 310-785-5345. Business E-Mail: ldienes@jmbm.com.

DIENES, TIMOTHY PAUL, mathematician, educator; b. Cleve., Apr. 18, 1960; s. William and Ruth Marilyn Dienes. BA in Math., U. NC, Chapel Hill, 1982; MS in Applied Stats., U. NC, Charlotte, 1992. Prodn. control Absorba, Inc., Hendersonville, NC, 1983—89; rate auditor United Parcel Svc., Charlotte, NC, 1993—97; tchr. math. Resurrection Christian Sch., Charlotte, 1997—99; document control Bechtel Corp., Charlotte, 2000—02; instr. math. Carolinas Coll. Health Scis., Charlotte, 2003—, Ctrl. Piedmont C.C., Charlotte, 2003—, Cabarrus Coll. Health Scis., Concord, 2004—05. Author: (poetry) Song of Silent Reliance, Take and Eat. Nat. Merit scholar, Bendix Corp., 1978—82. Mem.: Am. Mensa. Lutheran. Office: Carolinas College of Health Sciences 1200 Blythe Blvd Charlotte NC 28203 Office Phone: 704-355-0981. Business E-Mail: timothy.dienes@cpcc.edu. E-mail: tim.dienes@carolinascollege.edu.

DIENST, DANIEL W., metal products executive; BA, Wash. Univ.; JD, Brooklyn Law Sch. Positions through v.p. corp. fin. Jeffries and Co., Inc., 1995—98; exec. dir. high yield & fin. restructuring CIBC World Markets Corp., 1999—2000, mng. dir. corp. & leveraged fin., 2000—04; chmn. Metal Mgmt. Inc., Chgo., 2003, chmn., pres., CEO, 2004—. Office: Metal Management Inc Ste 550 325 N LaSalle St Chicago IL 60610*

DIENSTAG, JULES LEONARD, dean, hepatologist, researcher; b. NYC, Dec. 10, 1946; m. Judy Iris Gordon, Feb. 3, 1974; children: Josh, Jonathan. AB magna cum laude, Columbia Coll., 1968; MD, Columbia U., 1972. Diplomate Am. Bd Internal Medicine. Intern in medicine U. Chgo., 1972-73, resident in medicine, 1973-74; postdoctoral fellow, rsch. assoc. NIH, Bethesda, Md., 1974-76; clin. and rsch. fellow Mass. Gen. Hosp., Boston, 1976-78, clin. asst. medicine, 1978-79, asst. in medicine, 1979-82, asst. physician, 1983-87, assoc. physician, 1988-93, physician, 1993—; asst. prof. of medicine Harvard Med. Sch., Boston, 1978-82, assoc. prof., 1982—2002, faculty assoc. dean for admissions, 1998—2004, prof. medicine, 2002—, assoc. dean Academic and Clin. Programs, 2003—05, dean Med. Edn., 2005—, Carl W. Walter prof. medicine, 2005—. Expert panelist on viral hepatitis Lister Hill Nat. Ctr. Biomed. Comm., Nat. Libr. Medicine, 1980-82, advisor, 1982-86; numerous tchg. appointments; lectr. in field Mem. editl. bd. Jour. Clin. Microbiology, 1977-86, Hepatology, 1980-86, Infectious Disease Series, Marcel Dekker Med. divsn., 1981-85, Gastroenterology, 1981-86, Jour. Viral Hepatitis, 1993—; editor: Gastroenterology Series, Marcel Dekker, 1983-86, Mass. Gen. Hosp. Liver-Biliary-Pancreas Ctr. Newsletter, 1990-05; assoc. editor: Gastroenterology, 1986-91, 96-01. Recipient Clin. Investigator award USPHS, 1978-79. Fellow ACP; mem. AAAS, Internat. Assn. Study of the Liver, European Assn. Study of the Liver (corr.), Am. Soc. Microbiology, Am. Fedn. Clin. Rsch. Am. Assn. Immunologists, Am. Assn. Study Liver Diseases, Am. Gastroent. Assn., Mass. Med. Soc., Phi Beta Kappa. Office: Harvard Med Sch Off Dean for Med Edn / Gordon Hall 25 Shattuck St Boston MA 02115 also: Mass Gen Hosp 55 Fruit St Boston MA 02114-2696 Office Fax: 617-432-6253. Personal E-mail: jdienstag@partners.org. Business E-Mail: jdienstag@hms.harvard.edu.

DIERAUF, LESLIE ANN, wildlife veterinarian, conservation biologist, consultant; b. Boston, Feb. 7, 1948; d. Curtis John and Adeline M. (Kirk) D. BS in Microbiology, English cum laude, U. Mass., 1970; VMD, U. Pa., 1974; postdoctoral, U. Calif., Davis, 1974-77. Lic. vet., N.Mex., Calif., DC, Nev., NY, Vt., Va.; cert. community coll. tchr., Calif. Instr. physiology U. Calif., Davis, 1976-77; staff vet. Elk Grove (Calif.) Vet. Clinic, 1977, Midtown Animal Hosp., Sacramento, 1978-79, Marin County Vet. Emergency Clinic, San Rafael, Calif., 1979-87; ind. contractor, 1988-93; staff vet. Calif. Marine Mammal Ctr., Ft. Cronkhite, 1979-82, dir. vet. services, 1982-84, bd. sci. advisors, 1984—; instr. animal health tech. Western Sch. Allied Health Professions, Sacramento, 1977-79; cons. Marine Mammal Cons. Services, Novato, Calif., 1985-90; mem. profl. staff fisheries and wildlife conservation issues, sci. advisor Merchant Marine and Fisheries Com. US Ho. of Reps., 1990-93; policy analyst Assn. Am. Vet. Med. Colls. and Am. Vet. Med. Assn., Washington, 1993; vet Wyoming Animal Hosp., Albuquerque, 1993; worked on the endangered species program for the Southwest US Fish and Wildlife Svc.; dir. Nat. Wildlife Health Ctr., US Geological Soc., Madison, Wis., 2004—. Cons. Nat. Marine Fisheries Svc., Animal and Plant Health Inspectia Svc., Envirovet, 1993—, Naval Ocean Systems Ctr., 1984-90, Calif. Marine Mammal Ctr., 1984—, Pribilof Island Fur Seal Program, 1981-84, San Francisco Zoo, 1979-84, Calif. State U., Hayward, 1979-84; mem. bd. sci. advisors West Quoddy Marine Rsch. Sta., Lubec, Maine, 1979-90; bd. examiners Calif. Dept. Consumer Affairs, 1978-85.; mem. exec. com. Consortium for Conservation Medicine.; mem. coordinating com. US Geological Survey Human Health; mem. US Dept. Interior Partnership and Collaboration Team.; mem. working group Nat. Marine Fisheries Service Marine Mammal Unusual Mortality Editor: Handbook of Marine Mammal Medicine: Health, Disease and Rehabilitation, 1990, 2nd edit. 2001; mem. editorial bd. Diseases of Aquatic Organisms, 1985—; contbr. articles to profl. jours. Mem. com. to Save Squaw Valley Meadow; dir. Calif. Marine Mammal Ctr. Run for Seals; mem. Wildlife Care Assn., Sacramento, Sacramento Jr. Sci. Mus., Sacramento Community Orch., Sacramento Intramural Softball and Volleyball; vol. Belchertown State Hosp., Vet. Assistance, Nicaragua, 1988, Pakistan, 1989; bd. dir. U. Calif. Davis Wildlife Health Ctr. Recipient Erickson Ednl. Found. award 1982-83; Thouron scholar U. Pa., 1974, U. Pa. scholar 1970-73; U. Calif., Davis grantee 1974-76; U. Calif. fellow, 1974-75, Teaching fellow U. Calif., 1975-77. Mem. AAAS (Congl. Sci. Fellow, 1990), Washington, DC, 1990, AVMA (editorial asst. 1986, 88-90, mem. environ. affairs com., Animal Welfare award, 1998), Internat. Assn. Aquatic Animal Medicine (pres. 1986-87, chair sci. govt. com. 1989-91, chair govt. rels. 1991—), Soc. Marine Mammalogy, Am. Assn. Wildlife Vets., Women's Vet. Med. Assn., Wildlife Disease Assn., Calif. Acad. Scis., Marine Mammal Ctr., Friends of Sea Otter, Marine Ecosystem Health SeaDoc Soc. (mem. adv. bd.) US Animal Health Assn. (mem. exec. bd.), Internat. Assn. of Fish and Wildlife Agencies Fish and Wildlife Health Com., Alliance of Veterinarians for the Environment (co-founder, mem.) Democrat. Episcopalian. Avocations: skiing, bicycling, climbing, writing, running. Office: Nat Wildlife Health Ctr 6006 Schroeder Rd Madison WI 53711-6223 Office Phone: 608-270-2401. Business E-Mail: ldierauf@usgs.gov.

DIERBERG, JAMES F., bank executive; b. 1937; s. William and Genevieve Dierberg; m. Mary Dierberg; 2 children. BS, BA, Univ. Mo.; JD, Univ. Wash. Pres. First Bank, Inc., St. Louis, 1966—99, former CEO, chmn.; owner Hermanhoff Winery, Hermann, Mo., 1978—, Dierberg Vineyards, Santa Barbara, Calif., 1996—. Served U.S. Air Nat. Guard, France. Office: First Bank Inc 11901 Olive Blvd Saint Louis MO 63141

DIERCKS, WALTER ELMER, lawyer; b. Irvington, NJ, July 6, 1945; s. Elmer Jules and Evelyn Sophie (Lauster) D.; m. Mary-Jane Atwater, Apr. 16, 1977; children: Emily Jane, Gillian Ruth. B.Chem. Engring., Rensselaer Poly. Inst., 1967; JD, U. Va., 1972. Bar: Va. 1972, DC 1973, US Supreme Ct. 1984. Engr. Bethlehem Steel Corp., Balt., 1968-69; Devel. engr. Diamond Shamrock Corp., Balt., 1969-70; pub. Charlottesville (Va.) Consumer, 1970-72; atty. FTC, Washington, 1972-76; dep. asst. dir. compliance Bur. Consumer Protection, 1976-77; gen. counsel, sec. Washington Star Co., 1977-81; ptnr. Rubin, Winston, Diercks, Harris & Cooke, LLP, Washington, 1981—. Chmn. Alexandria (Va.) Landlord-Tenant Relations Bd., 1976; mem. Alexandria Charter Rev. Commn., 1980-81, Alexandria Democratic Com., 1979-81, 83-85. Recipient award excellence FTC, 1977 Master: Fed. Am. Inn of Ct. (pres. 2007—); mem.: ABA. Home: 304 Lamond Pl Alexandria VA 22314-4907 Office: 6th Fl 1155 Connecticut Ave NW Washington DC 20036-4306 Office Phone: 202-861-0870. E-mail: wdiercks@rwdhc.com.

DIERCKSEN, JOHN W., telecommunications industry executive; BBA in Fin., Iona Coll.; MBA, Pace U.; postgraduate student, NYU, Columbia U. With Ins. Co. N.Am., 1971, Lever Bros. Co., NYC; dir. internat. costs and budget Internat. divsn. Internat. Playtex, 1975—79; dir. fin. planning and control Am. Can Co. Technologies Divsn., 1979—82; corp. contr. Coleco Industries, 1982; v.p. fin. and adminstrn. Bus. Info. Systems Co. NYNEX, 1986—91, v.p. fin., treas. Telecom. Grp., 1991—97; CFO Bell Atlantic Directory Grp., 1997—2000, chief info. officer, 1998—2000; acting grp. pres. directory Bell Atlantic, 2000; sr. v.p. investor rels. Verizon Comm., Inc., NYC, 2000—03, exec. v.p. strategy, devel. and planning, 2003—. Office: Verizon Comm 140 West St New York NY 10007*

DIERDORF, DANIEL LEE (DAN DIERDORF), sports commentator, football analyst, former professional football player; b. Canton, Ohio, June 29, 1949; m. Debbie D.; children: Dana, Kelly(dec.) , Katherine; children: Dan, Kristen. Student, U. Mich. Football player St. Louis Cardinals, 1971—83; with Sta. KMOX, St. Louis, 1974—; sports dir. Sta. KMOV-TV, St. Louis, 1987—; football analyst CBS NFL broadcasts, 1985—87, ABC Monday Night Football broadcasts, 1987—99; NFL football analyst CBS Sports, 1999—. Named to NFL Pro-Bowl Team, 1974—78, 1980, Pro Football Hall of Fame, 1996. Office: CBS Sports 51 W 52nd St New York NY 10019-6119

DIERICKX, CONSTANCE RICKER, psychologist, management consultant; b. Evanston, Ill, June 26, 1952; d. Benjamin Franklin Ricker and Betty June Caldwell; m. Michael James Dierickx; children: Amy Steinlight, April Gambill. PhD, Ga. State U., Atlanta, GA, 1998. Psychologist self employed, Marietta, Ga., 1990—98; cons. RHR Internat.Co. , Atlanta, 1998—. Spkr. in field; presenter in field. Vol. Save the Park , Marietta, 2001; member, vol., adv. Ga. Coun. for Hearing Impaired., Atlanta, 1995—98; vol. Citizens to Rescind the Resolution, Marietta; Chair, Selection Com/ Habitat for Humanity , Asheville , NC, 1989—90. Grantee, Undergraduate Research Council - University of North Carolina - Asheville, NC, 1989. Mem.: APA, Soc.for Consulting. Psychology, Bd. Dirs. Network (bd. mem.), National Assn. Corp. Dirs. Unitarian Universalist. Avocations: cooking, reading, walking, boxing fan. Office Phone: 404-870-9160. Business E-Mail: cdierickx@rhrinternational.com.

DIERKER, DAVID F., bank executive; Strategic fin. officer SunTrust Banks, Inc., 2000—04, corp. exec. v.p., chief adminstrv. officer, 2004—. Bd. dirs. Young Audiences, Woodruff Arts Ctr., Atlanta. Office: SunTrust Banks Inc PO Box 4418 Atlanta GA 30302-4418 Office Phone: 404-588-7711. Office Fax: 404-827-6173.*

DIERKING, LYNN D., educational administrator; m. John H. Falk. BA with honors, magna cum laude, U. Miami, 1978; MA in Edn., U. Fla., Gainesville, 1981, PhD, 1987. Assoc. Smithsonian Off. Ednl. Rsch.; mem. faculty U. Md. Coll. Edn.; dir. Sci. in Am. Life project Nat. Mus. Am. History, Smithsonian Inst.; sr. rsch. assoc. Inst. for Learning Innovation, Md., 1993—. Sea Grant prof. Oreg. State U., Corvallis, 2006—; mem. editl. bd. Sci. Edn., Jour. Mus. Mgmt. & Curatorship. Co-author: The Museum Experience, 1992, Collaboration: Critical Criteria for Success, 1997, Learning from Museums, 2000, Questioning Assumptions, 1998; co-editor: Public Institutions for Personal Learning. Named to Centennial Honor Roll, Am. Assn. Mus., 2006. Office: Inst for Learning Innovation Ste 280 3168 Braverton St Edgewater MD 21037 Office Phone: 410-956-5144. Office Fax: 410-956-5148. E-mail: dierking@ilinet.org.*

DIERKS, MELINDA ADAIR, science educator; b. Hutchinson, Kans., Aug. 20, 1944; d. Joseph Burton and Edith May (Griffin) Ward; m. LaRue Theodore Dierks, Nov. 27, 1970; 1 child, Jason Laredo. BA in biology, Sterling Coll., Kans., 1971; M in Edn., Wichita State U., Kans., 1978, Post Masters Studies, 1981, U. Tex., 1991. Cert. Teacher Kans. State Bd. of Edn., 2005. Secondary sci. tchr. Unified Sch. Dist. 285, Cedar Vale, Kans., 1971—75, Unified Sch. Dist. 462, Burden, Kans., 1975—80; tchr., facilitator of gifted Cowley County Spec. Services Coop., Winfield, Kans., 1980—2000; tchr., cons. of v.i. & blind Cowley County Spec. Services Coop, Winfield, Kans., 1990—2000; natural sci. instr. Cowley Coll., North Campus, Wichita, Kans., 1998—. Project leader 4-H, Grenola, Kans., 1979—87. Tuition, Materials, Living Accommodations scholar, Cowley County Spec. Services Coop, 1990, 1991. Mem.: Alpha Tau Ch., Delta Kappa Gamma. Protestant. Avocations: woodcarving, travel. Home: 744 Blackjack Grenola KS 67346 Office: Cowley Coll Southside Edn Ctr 4501 East 47th St South Wichita KS 67210 Home Phone: 620-358-3271.

DIERKS, RICHARD ERNEST, veterinarian, academic administrator; b. Flandreau, SD, Mar. 11, 1934; s. Martin and Lillian Ester (Benedict) D.; m. Eveline Carol Amundson, July 20, 1956; children— Jeffrey Scott, Steven Eric, Joel Richard. Student, S.D. State U., 1952—55; BS, U. Minn., 1957, DVM, 1959, MPH, PhD, U. Minn., 1964; MBA, U. Ill., 1985. Diplomate Am. Coll. Vet. Microbiologists, Am. Coll. Vet. Preventive Medicine. Supervisory microbiologist Communicable Disease Ctr., Atlanta, 1964-68; prof. coll. veterinary medicine Iowa State U., Ames, 1968-74; head dept. veterinary sci. Mont. State U., Bozeman, 1974-76; dean Coll. Veterinary Medicine U. Ill., Urbana, 1976-89, prof., dean emeritus, 1989—; dean Coll. Veterinary Medicine U. Fla., Gainesville, 1989-97, prof., dean emeritus, 1997—. Mem. tng. grant rev. com. Nat. Inst. Allergy and Infectious Diseases, 1973-74 Contbr. articles on virology, immunology and epidemiology to profl. jours. Served with USPHS, 1964-67. Career Devel. awardee Nat. Inst. Allergy and Infectious Diseases, 1969-74, Nat. Acad. Practitioners, 1995. Mem. Am. Vet. Medicine Assn., Am. Soc. Virology, Am. Soc. Microbiologists, Am. Assn. Immunologists, Am. Assn. Vet. Lab. Diagnosis, Colo. Vet. Medicine Assn., Soc. Exptl. Biology and Medicine, Gamma Sigma Delta, Phi Kappa Phi, Phi Zeta. Clubs: Rotary. Republican. Lutheran. Office: 2409 Tyrrhenian Dr Longmont CO 80501 Home Phone: 303-774-1897; Office Phone: 303-774-1897. Personal E-mail: dierksrichardcar@msn.com, richcaro6@mesanetworks.net.

DIERNA, JOSEPH BIAGIO, construction company executive, land development consultant; b. Bklyn., June 19, 1959; s. Joseph Michael and Anna (DeVito) D.; children: Andrea Lynn, Tina Marie, Nicole Suzanne; m. Anastasia Peters, Oct. 14, 2004. Student, Orange County Coll., 1979. Supr. Steverand, Inc., Builders, Monroe, NY, 1978-84; project mgr. Sherman Builders, Monroe, 1984-86, Solart Builders, Monroe, 1984-86; treas./gen. mgr. Pine Tree Lake Corp., Developers, Monroe, 1986-89; project mgr. Fieldcrest Corp., home builders, Chester, NY, 1989—; owner, pres. Orange & Rockland Bldg. Corp., 1994—, Orange & Rockland Realty, 1994—, also bd. dirs.; v.p., owner Maple Tree Assocs., Washingtonville, NY. Sec. Weathervane Condo I, Washingtonville, NY, 1981-84; cons. D.E. P. Resources, Monroe, 1985—, US One Corp., NYC, 1986—, NY Archdiocese Bldg. Commn., 1991. Mem. Interact, Monroe, 1977; jr. varsity hockey coach Washingtonville HS, 1998—2002. Mem.: Bear Mountain Hockey Coub (Highland Falls, NY, coach), Builders Assn. Hudson Valley, NY State Builders Assn., Nat. Assn. Builders. Republican. Roman Catholic. Avocations: gardening, tennis, hockey. Office: 371 Orchard Dr Monroe NY 10950 Office Phone: 914-447-2026. Personal E-mail: jbdierna94@aol.com.

DIERWECHTER, DAVID C., retired elementary school educator, theater director; b. Ephrata, Pa., Oct. 2, 1946; s. Clarence and Leone Dierwechter; m. Marcia L. Stoner, Aug. 26, 2000; m. Donna J. Buffenmyer (div.); 1 child, Scott A. BS in Edn., Millersville U., Pa., 1968, MEd in Edn., 1972. Tchr. Ephrata Area Sch. Dist., 1968—2003; ret., 2003. Theater dir. Ephrata Area Sch. Dist., 1968—, Ephrata Area Comty. Theater, 2000—, Ephrata Performing Arts Ctr., 1980—, bd. dirs. Home: 422 Swamp Rd Morgantown PA 19543 Personal E-mail: ddwechter@aol.com.

DIESCH, STANLEY LA VERNE, veterinarian, educator; b. Blooming Prairie, Minn., May 16, 1925; s. John Herman and Emma Lillian (Erickson) D.; m. Darlene Ardis Witty; July 22, 1956; children: Lauren, Stephanie. BS, U. Minn., 1951, DVM, 1956, MPH, 1963. Diplomate Am. Coll. Vet. Preventive Medicine and Epidemiology. Asst. prof. Coll. Vet. Med., U. Iowa, Iowa City, 1963-66; asst. prof. U. Minn. Coll. Vet. Medicine, St. Paul, 1966-69, assoc. prof., 1969-73, prof., 1973-95, prof. emeritus, 1995—, dir. internat. programs, 1985-98; prof. Sch. Pub. Health, U. Minn., Mpls., 1973-95. Advisor Pan Am. Health Orgn., Washington, 1971— Contbr. more than 100 articles to profl. jours., 4 chapters to books. Mem. East Buchanan County Sch. Bd., Winthrop, Iowa, 1960; Rep. del., Minn., 1970-85; co-chair nat. Outdoor Speedskating, St. Paul, 1973; dir. CENSHARE, Mpls., 1981-82; chmn. Veterinarians for Re-election of Durenberger, Minn., 1982, 88; bd. dirs. Minn.-Uruguay Ptnrs. Ams., 1981—, pres., 1990-94, chmn. bd., 1995-99; hon. consul of Uruguay in Minn., 1991-96. Recipient Am. Express award Nat. Assn. Ptnrs. Ams., 1984, Internat. Castricone U. Linkage award Nat. Assn. Ptnrs. Ams., 1998, Dummond Peck Hill Lifetime Achievement award Ptnrs. Ams., 2002; WHO travel fellow, 1974; grantee EPA, 1968-71, USDA, 1978. Mem. AVMA (Pub. Svc. award 1987, Internat. Vet. Congress award 1998), APHA (coun. 1971-84), U.S. Animal Health Assn. (com. chair, Appreciation award 1986), Internat. Soc. Animal Hygiene (exec. bd. 1988-2000, pres. 1991-94, Honor award 2000), Minn. Vet. Medicine Assn. (com. chair 1970-75, Disting. Svc. award 1996). Lutheran. Avocations: fishing, hunting, boating. Home and Office: 743 Heinel Dr Saint Paul MN 55113-2152 Home Phone: 651-484-8635; Office Phone: 651-484-8635. Business E-Mail: diesc001@umn.edu.

DIESEL, VIN (MARK VINCENT), actor; b. NYC, July 18, 1967; Student, Hunter Coll. Actor, dir., prodr., writer: (films) Multi-facial, 1994; Strays, 1997; actor, exec. prodr. XXX, 2002; A Man Apart, 2003; actor, prodr. The Chronicles of Riddick, 2004; actor: Saving Private Ryan, 1998, (voice) The Iron Giant, 1999, Boiler Room, 2000, Pitch Black, 2000, The Fast and the Furious, 2001, Knockaround Guys, 2001, Be Cool, 2005; (TV films) Into Pitch Black, 2000. Office: Endeavor Talent Agency 9601 Wilshire Blvd Ste 300 Beverly Hills CA 90210-5200

DIETEL, JAMES EDWIN, lawyer, consultant; b. Dallas, Sept. 14, 1941; s. Bernhard Herman and Gladys Ellen D.; m. Elizabeth Nathan, May 9, 1964; 1 child, Elizabeth Lindsay. BSME, So. Meth. U., 1964; JD, George Washington U., 1969; LLM in Internat. Trade, Georgetown U., 1977; MBA, U. Pa., 1992. Bar: D.C. 1971, U.S. Dist. Ct. D.C. 1971, U.S. Ct. Appeals (D.C. cir.) 1975, U.S. Supreme Ct. 1975, Va. 1990. Engr. CIA, Washington, 1964—70, program evaluation officer, 1970—73, assoc. gen. counsel, 1979—80, assoc. dep. gen. counsel, 1980—82, dep. gen. counsel, 1982—90, insp., office exec. dir., 1990—94, counsel for info. policy, 1994—95; pvt. practice, 1995—. Participant ann. jud. conf. U.S. Ct. Appeals (D.C. cir.), 1986; spkr. and presenter in field. Author: Leading a Law Practice to Excellence, 1992, Sustaining Law Practice Excellence, 1992, Designing Effective Records Retention Compliance Program, 1993, Leaders' Digest: A Review of the Best Books on Leadership, 1995; chmn. bd. Law Practice Quar.; contbr. articles to profl. jours. Mem. ABA (coun. law practice mgmt. sect., chmn. govt. and pub. sector lawyers divsn.), Coll. Law Practice Mgmt., Cosmos Club, Pi Tau Sigma, Kappa Mu Epsilon, Kappa Alpha.

DIETEL, WILLIAM MOORE, former foundation executive; b. Islip, NY, Aug. 14, 1927; s. Frederick William and Zillah Yolanda (Vannuccini) D.; m. Linda Remington, June 16, 1951; children: Elizabeth Lynn, Cynthia Lyon, Lisa Remington, John Frederick, Victoria Moore. AB, Princeton U., 1950; MA, Yale U., 1952, PhD, 1959; postgrad., London U. Inst. Hist. Research, 1953-54. Instr. history U. Mass., Amherst, 1954-59; asst. dean of coll., asst. prof. humanities Amherst Coll., 1959-61; prin. Emma Willard Sch., Troy, NY, 1961-70; pres. Rockefeller Bros. Fund, NYC, 1975-87. Pres. Pierson-Lovelace Found., L.A.; chmn. FB Heron Found., N.Y.C., Brain Mapping Med. Rsch. Orgn., L.A.; adv. counsel Inst. for Philanthropy, London, Princeton U. Dept. Astrophys. Sci.; internat. adv. com. Johns Hopkins UN; co-chair pres.'s adv. coun. Am. Farmland Trust; chmn.Civil Soc. Sys., London, Williamsburg, Va. Mem. Univ. Club (N.Y.C.), Cosmos Club (Washington). Office: PO Box 309 Flint Hill VA 22627-0309

DIETER, GEORGE ELWOOD, JR., academic administrator; b. Phila., Dec. 5, 1928; m. Nancy Joan Russell, June 21, 1952; children: Carol Joan, Barbara June. BS in Metall. Engring, Drexel Inst. Tech., 1950; ScD, Carnegie Inst. Tech., 1953. Research engr. E.I. duPont Engring Research Lab., Wilmington, Del., 1955-59, research supr., 1959-62; prof., head dept. metall. engring. Drexel Inst. Tech., 1962-69; dean Coll. Engring. Drexel U., 1969-73; dir. Processing Research Inst., Carnegie-Mellon U., 1973-77; dean Coll. Engring. U. Md., College Park, 1977-94, dir. continuous quality improvement, 1994-2000, Glenn L. Martin prof. engring., 2000—. Cons. in field. Author: Mechanical Metallurgy, 1961, 3d edit., 1986, Engineering Design, 1983, 3d edit., 1999. Mem. 1953-55, AUS. Recipient Pres. medal, U. Md., 2004. Fellow AAAS, Am. Soc. Metals (A.E. White award 1986, Sauver award 1992), Am. Soc. Engring. Edn. (pres. 1993, Lamme award 1996), Minerals, Metals and Materials Soc. (educator award 1994); mem. NAE, AIME, Soc. Mfg. Engrs. (educator award 1987), Fedn. Materials Socs. (pres. 1990-92), Sigma Xi, Tau Beta Pi. Home: 1 Locksley Ct Silver Spring MD 20904-6321 Office: U Md Dept Mech Engring College Park MD 20742-0001 Office Phone: 301-405-5248. Business E-Mail: gdieter@eng.umd.edu.

DIETER, MELVIN EASTERDAY, retired minister, educator; b. Cherryville, Pa., Oct. 12, 1924; s. Harold David Dieter and Laura Esther Easterday; m. Hallie Arline Kirtz, Dec. 27, 1945; 1 child, Judith Patrice. Grad. Cantonese, Naval Oriental Lang. Sch., U. Colo., 1946; AB in Modern Langs. summa cum laude, Muhlenberg Coll., 1947; BTh in Bible and Theology summa cum laude, Ea. Pilgrim Coll., 1950; MA in Am. History, Lehigh U., 1951; STM in Church History and Sacred Theology, Temple U., 1953; LLD (hon.), Houghton Coll., 1964; PhD in Religion, Temple U., 1973. Ordained to ministry Wesleyan Ch., 1952. From instr. to pres. Ea. Pilgrim Coll., Allentown, Pa., 1946-65; acad. dean Houghton (N.Y.) Coll., 1968; pastor Chichester Wesleyan Ch., Boothwyn, Pa., 1965—67; gen. sec. edn. The Wesleyan Ch., Marion, Ind., 1968-75; prof. ch. history and hist. theology, provost, v.p. Asbury Theol. Sem., Wilmore, Ky., 1975-90. Dir. Pew Charitable Trusts' Wesleyan Holiness Study Project Asbury Theol. Sem., 1987-90; pres. Wesleyan Theol. Soc., 1977; chair Houghton Coll. Bd. Trustees, 1992-99. Author: The Holiness Revival of the Nineteenth Century, 1980; co-editor: The Church, 1984; (with Hallie Dieter): God is Enough, 1986; editor: The Christian's Secret of a Holy Life, 1994, The 19th Century Holiness Movement, 1998; contbr.: Mandate for Mission, 1970, Aspects of Pentecostal- Charismatic Origins, 1975, Five Views on Sanctification, 1987, John Wesley:Contemporary Perspectives, 1988, Reformers and Revivalists, 1992, Theological Education in the Evangelical Tradition, 1996, Christianity in Appalachia, 1999; contbr. articles to profl. jours. Pres. William J. Harley Found., Allentown, 1961-85, Lehigh Valley Pub. Rels. Club, 1965; treas. Allentown Sch. Bd. Authority, 1963-65, Rotary, Waynesboro, Va.; chaplain Kiwanis Club, Allentown, Pa.; trustee Kiwanis Found. Lt. J.G. USNR, 1942—51. Recipient Outstanding Alumnus award, United Wesleyan Coll., 1976. Mem.: Wesleyan Theol. Soc. (pres., Disting. Lifetime Svc. award 1996—), Conf. on Faith and History, Am. Soc. Ch. History, Pi Gamma Mu, Eta Sigma Phi. Independent. Wesleyan. Avocations: genealogy, gardening. Home: 400 Chinquapin Dr Lyndhurst VA 22952-2911 Personal E-mail: meldie@ntelos.net.

DIETER, RAYMOND ANDREW, JR., physician, thoracic and vascular surgeon; b. Chebanse, Ill., June 19, 1934; s. Raymond Augustus Sr. and Emma Rose Mayme (Witt) D.; m. Bette René Myers, Sept. 29, 1961; children: Raymond III, David, Lisa, Lynn, Deanna, Robert. Student, U. Ill., 1952-56, Olivet Nazarene Coll., 1954; MA in Physiology, U. Ill., Chgo., 1966; BS in Chemistry, U. Ill., Champaign, 1994; MD, Loyola U., 1960. Diplomate Am. Bd. Thoracic Surgery, Am. Bd. Surgery. Intern Cook County Hosp., Chgo., 1960-61; resident in gen. surgery VA Hosp., Hines, Ill., 1963-67, sr. resident in cardiopulmonary surgery, 1967-69; practice specializing in thoracic, cardiovascular surg. DuPage Med. Group, 1969—, Glen Ellyn (Ill.) Clinic, 1969—, pres., 1982-85, also bd. dirs.; mem. staff Hines (Ill.) VA Hosp., 1963-74, Cen. DuPage Hosp., Winfield, Ill., 1969—, pres. staff, 1987-89; mem. staff Loyola U. Med. Ctr., Maywood, Ill., 1969-80, Meml. Hosp. DuPage County, Elmhurst, Ill., 1969—, Delnor Hosp., St. Charles, Ill., 1970—, Community Hosp., Geneva, Ill., 1970—79, Alexian Bros. Med. Ctr., Elk Grove Village, Ill., 1975-79, 93—, Good Samaritan Hosp., Downers Grove, Ill., 1976—, pres. staff, 1979; mem. staff Glendale Heights (Ill.) and Glen Oaks Cmty. Hosp., 1980—, St. Mary's Hosp., Streator, Ill., 1997—. Clin. instr. Stritch Sch. Medicine Loyola U., 1966-71, clin. asst. prof., 1971-80; trustee Ctr. Bank, Glen Ellyn, 1978-90, Lake Shore Bank, Glen Ellyn Found.; internat. lectr. on med. topics; chmn. Glen Ellyn Clinic Facilities, 1987-98, Physicians Benefit trust, 1988-92; pres., chmn. bd. No. Ill. Surg. Ctr., 1989—; pres. DuPage Doctors, Inc., Ctr. for Surgery; co-founder Cmty. Banks of Wheaton Glen Ellyn, 1993-05, bd. dirs., vice chmn., 2005—; co-founder, pres. Northeast DuPage Surgicenter, 1997—; chmn. bd. dirs., CEO, pres. Masterile, Inc., 1997-99; mem., chmn. negotiating com. Glen Ellyn Clinic, 1999; officer Internat. Healthcare Cons., LLC, 2002—. Author: (with B.R. Dieter and A.C. Mickelson) Mickelson and Peterson Family Sketch, 1970, (with M.C. Sorensen and E.R. Dieter) A Sorensen and Jensen Family Tree, 1975, (with B.R. Dieter, C. Myers, U. Myers, and D. Dieter) A Myers and Remley Family Tree, 1978, (with others) A Witt and (von) Ruehle Family Sketch, 1976, A Hofeling, Janssen, Lehnert, and Meier Family Sketch, 1979, A Dieter Family Tree: Sketches of German Families, 1981, Thoracoscopy for Surgeons, 1994; editor: Thoracoscopy for Surgeons-Diagnostic and Therapeutic, 1995; contbr. numerous articles to profl. jours. and chpts. in med. book. Mgr. Glen Ellyn baseball team, 1970, 71, 78-82; asst. leader 4-H Club, 1975-83; mem. Glenbard South High Sch. Boosters, World Fedn. Drs. Who Respect Human Life, 1980—; pres., bd. dirs. DuPage Med. Found.; mem. Econ. Devel. Coun. Glen Ellyn, sec., 2000, v.p., 2001-02, pres., 2003; bd. dirs. Farm Safety Just 4 Kids, 2004-07. Served with USPHS, 1961-63, with Res., 1982—. Named Hon. Citizen, Quito Ecuador, La Paz, Bolivia; recipient Key to City of Manila, Philippines. Fellow ACS, Internat. Coll. Angiology (editl. bd. 1995—), Internat. Coll. Surgeons (exec. com. 1991—, treas. 1993-94, pres. elect 1995-96, pres. 1997-98, U.S. sect., corp. sec. 1997-2000, pres.-elect 2001-02, pres. 2003-04, immediate past pres. 2005-06, chmn. internat. surg. teams. program 2005-06, World body, del. 2001-06); mem. AMA (Physician's Recognition awards, mem. ho. dels.), Internat. Mus. Surg. Sci. (chmn. bd. dirs. 1991—), Internat. Soc. Circumpolar Health, Internat. Soc. Outdoor Health, Global Acad. for Tropical Surgery (co-founder 2004), Am. Coll. Angiology, Am. Coll. Chest Physicians, Assn. Acad. Surgeons, Am. Soc. Circumpolar Health (charter), Assn. Mil. Surgeons, Assn. Res. Officers, Am. Heart Assn. (coun. 1974—), Soc. Med. Hist. Chgo., Soc. Critical Care Medicine, Soc. Thoracic Surgeons (membership com.), Ill. State Med. Soc. (trustee 1983-92, chmn. Ill. hosp. med. staff sect. 1985-87, pres., med. adminstrs. ctr. for surgery 1994—), Ill. Thoracic Surg. Soc. (sec. 1981-83, pres. 1984-85), DuPage County Med. Soc. (pres. 1977, mem. govtl. com., numerous others), Chgo. Med. Soc., Charles B. Puestow Surg. Soc. (sec., treas. 1966-67, v.p. 1968), Good Samaritan Soc., Ala. Geographic Soc., Kankakee Valley Geneal. Soc., Ill. Geneal. Soc., U. Ill. Alumni Assn. (bd. dirs. 2002-), Am. Rabbit Breeders Assn., Silver Marten Club, Century Club (Elmhurst), Chebanse Lions (charter), Resurrection Bay (Alaska) Lions. Internat. lions Club (50 yr. mem.). Republican. Roman Catholic. Avocations: exercise, farming, fishing, hunting. Office: Glen Ellyn Clinic 454 Pennsylvania Ave Glen Ellyn IL 60137-4496 Office Fax: 630-545-7853.

DIETERT, RODNEY REYNOLDS, immunology and toxicology educator; b. Ft. Lee, Va., Dec. 6, 1951; s. Ralph O. and Beverly (Reynolds) D.; children: Grant C., Matthew W; m. Janice M. Dietert. BS, Duke U., 1974; PhD, U. Tex., 1977. Asst. prof. immunogenetics Cornell U., Ithaca, NY, 1977-83, assoc. prof., 1983-89, prof., 1989—, prof. immunotoxicology, 1997—; adj. prof. N.C. State U., 1992—; head grad. program in immunology Cornell U., Ithaca, NY, 1989-92, dir. Inst. for Comparative and Environ. Toxicology, 1992-97, prof. immunotoxicology, 1997—, dir. program on breast cancer and environ. risk factors, 2000—04; sr. fellow Ctr. for the Environment, 1993-96. Cons. pesticide program EPA, Washington, 1984-86, Embrex, Inc., Research Triangle Park, N.C., 1991-95; panelist Nat. Inst. Environ. Health Scis. (AIDS Therapeutics), Research Triangle Park, 1988, mem. oxidative damage panel, 1997; USDA grant panel mgr., Washington, 1993-94; mem. Am. Inst. Biol. Scis.-Gulf War Illnesses panel Dept. Def., 1995, 97; invited testimony U.S. Congress Clean Water Act, 1995; spkr. at profl. confs. Jour. editor CRC Press, Inc., Boca Raton, Fla., 1986-90, editor book series, 1990—; editor jour. Elsevier Sci. Publs., Ltd., Oxford, U.K., 1990-95; contbr. to profl. publs. Bd. dirs. Wesley Found., Ithaca, 1979-84; chmn. Minority Edn. Com., Ithaca, 1980; chmn. Environ. Com. on Native Americans, Ithaca, 1994-95. Mem. Am. Assn. Immunologists, Soc. Toxicology. Office: Cornell U Dept Microbiology/Immunol Coll Vet Med C5-135 UMC Ithaca NY 14853-5601 Home Phone: 607-257-1156; Office Phone: 607-253-4015. Business E-Mail: rrd1@cornell.edu.

DIETHELM, ARNOLD GILLESPIE, surgeon; b. Balt., Jan. 13, 1932; s. Oskar Arnold and Grace (Gillespie) D.; m. Nancy Lee Lane, June 21, 1951; children: Nancy Elizabeth, Linda Lane, Eugene Arnold (dec.), Ellen Jeanette, Richard Gillespie. AB, Wash. State U., 1953; MD, Cornell U., 1958; DSc (hon.), U. Ala., 1993. Intern, then resident in surgery NY Hosp., 1958-65; asst. in surgery, research fellow Peter Bent Brigham Hosp., Boston, 1965-66; research fellow surgery Harvard U. Med. Sch., 1966-67; instr. Cornell U. Med. Sch., 1964-65; mem. faculty U. Ala. Med. Center, Birmingham, 1967—, prof. surgery, 1973—, vice chmn. dept., 1973-82, chmn. dept. surgery, 1982-2000; prof. emeritus dept. surgery U. Ala. Sch. Medicine. Mem. residency rev. com. for surgery Accreditation Coun. for Grad. Med. Edn., 1994—, chmn., 1997-99. Contbr. articles med. jours. Mem. AAAS, ACS, AMA, Am. Soc. Nephrology, Am. Soc. Transplant Surgeons (pres. 1991-92), Am. Surg. Assn., Am. Bd. Surgery (dir. 1987-93), Assn. Acad. Surgery, Transplantation Soc., So. Surg. Assn. (pres. 1989). Home: 3248 Sterling Rd Birmingham AL 35213-3508 Office: U Ala Hosp Dept Surgery 619 19th St S Birmingham AL 35233-0001

DIETHELM, KAI, mathematician, researcher; b. Braunschweig, Germany, Nov. 10, 1967; Diploma in Math., Tech. U. Braunschweig, 1992; D in Computer Scis., U. Hildesheim, Germany, 1994. Rsch. scientist U. Hildesheim, Germany, 1992-98, Tech. U., Braunschweig, Germany, 1998—2004; software developer GNS mbH, Braunschweig, Germany, 2004—. Adj. prof. math. Tech. U., Braunschweig, Germany, 2002—. Contbr. articles to profl. jours. Office: GNS mbH Am Gaussberg 2 38114 Braunschweig Germany

DIETHRICH, EDWARD BRONSON, heart institute executive, cardiovascular surgeon; b. Toledo, Aug. 6, 1935; m. Gloria Baldwin, June 17, 1956; children: Lynne, Edward Bronson II. AB, U. Mich., 1956, MD, 1960. Diplomate: Am. Bd. Surgery, Am. Bd. Thoracic Surgery. Intern. St. Joseph Mercy Hosp., Ann Arbor, Mich., 1960-61; resident in surgery St. Joseph Mercy Hosp. and U. Mich. Med. Ctr., Ann Arbor, 1961-62, 64-65, Henry Ford Hosp., Detroit, 1963-64; resident in thoracic and cardiovascular surgery Baylor Coll. of Medicine Hosp., Houston, 1965-66, instr., 1966-67, asst. prof. surgery, 1967-71; founder, pres., CEO Ariz. Heart Inst., Phoenix, 1971—, med. dir., 1971—; and chief, cardiovascular surgery Ariz. Heart Hosp., Phoenix, 1997—. Dir., chmn. dept. cardiovascular services, dir. and chief cardiovascular surgery and heart, lung transplantation, Healthwest Regional Med. Ctr., 1987—; bd. dir. Endologix, Inc. 1997-2002. Author: Heart Test, 1981; editor: Noninvasive Cardiovascular Diagnosis, 197i, 80, Noninvasive Assessment of the Cardiovascular System, 1982, Women and Heart Disease, 1992. Mem. Pres.'s Council for Phys. Fitness and Sports. Recipient U. Mich. Regents Alumni Honor award, 1953-54; recipient Med. Research award St. Joseph Mercy Hosp., 1963, 64, San Francisco Film Festival 1st prize, 1967, Cardiovascular Surgery Adv. Panel citation Ethicon, Inc., 1976 Fellow Am. Coll. Cardiology, Am. Coll. Chest Physicians (merit cert 1970, Outstanding Film award 1973, 77); mem. AMA (Hektoen Gold Medal award 1970), Am. Coll. Angiology, ACS, Am. Fedn. for Clin. Research, Am. Heart Assn. (council on cardiovascular diseases), Am. Trauma Soc., Assn. for Acad. Surgery, Denton A. Cooley Cardiovascular Surg. Soc. (exec. com. 1977-78), Frederick A. Coller Surg. Soc. (award 1963), Internat. Cardiovascular Soc., Michael E. DeBakey Internat. Cardiovascular Soc., Samson Thoracic Surg. Soc., Surg. Soc. Chile, Soc. for Vascular Surgery, Soc. Thoracic Surgeons, Soc. Acad. Surgeons, Southwestern Surg. Congress, Jordanian Surg. Soc., Nu Sigma Nu Office: Ariz Heart Inst 2632 N 20th St Phoenix AZ 85006-1339*

DIETL, BO (RICHARD A. DIETL), private investigator, former police officer; b. Dec. 4, 1950; s. Richard and Sally Dietl; m. Regina Dietl, 1973; children: Richard, Jaclyn. Police officer, NYC; ret., 1985; founder Beau Dietl & Assocs., 1985—. Co-founder How Good Is This Prodn. Co.; cons. to dir. security Nat. Rep. Convention, Houston, 1992; chmn. NY State Security Guard Adv. Coun. Author: One Tough Cop: The Bo Dietl Story, 1988, Business Lunchatations: How an Everyday Guy Became One of America's Most Colorful CEOs.and How You Can Too!, 2005; assoc. prodr.: The Bone Collector, 1999; actor, exec. prodr.: (films) One Tough Cop, 1998; exec. prodr.: The Lucky Ones, 2003; actor: Maniac Cop 2, 1990, Goodfellas, 1990, This Is My Life, 1992, Whispers in the Dark, 1992, Bad Lieutenant, 1992, Carlito's Way, 1993, Dead Man's Curve, 1998; (TV films) Casualties of Love: The Long Island Lolita Story, 1993, Exiled, 1998. Office: Beau Dietl & Assocs Daily News Bldg 220 E 42nd St New York NY 10017-5806*

DIETMEYER, DONALD LEO, retired electrical engineering educator; b. Wausau, Wis., Nov. 20, 1932; s. Henry Joseph and Erna M. (Zastrow) D.; m. Carol White, Jan. 26, 1957; children: Karl Peter, Elizabeth Mary, Anne Katherine, Diana Lee. BSEE, U. Wis., Madison, 1954, MS, 1955, PhD, 1959. Mem. faculty U. Wis., Madison, 1958-63, 64-98, prof. elec. and computer engring., 1967-98, prof. emeritus, 1998—, assoc. dean Coll. Engring., 1983-95. Sr. engr. IBM Corp., Poughkeepsie, N.Y., 1964 Author: Logic Design of Digital Systems, 1978, 3rd rev. edit., 1988, Conlan Report, 1983. With AUS, 1957. Recipient Western Electric Fund award, 1972 Fellow IEEE; mem. Computer Soc., Assn. Computing Machinery, Sigma Xi. Home: 2211 Waunona Way Madison WI 53713-1619 E-mail: dld@engr.wisc.edu.

DIETRICH, BRUCE LEINBACH, museum administrator, astronomer, educator; b. Reading, Pa., Oct. 10, 1937; s. Harold Richard and Emily Jeannette (Leinbach) Dietrich; m. Renee Carol Long, Nov. 25, 1959; children: Dodson Bruce, Katie Ellen. BS, Kutztown U., 1960; MS, SUNY, Oswego, 1969. Tchr. Reading Pub. Schs., 1960-67; curator space sci. Reading Mus., 1967-69, dir. planetarium, 1969-92, dir., 1976-92, dir. emeritus, 1992—; instr. astronomy Reading Area C.C., 1972-75, asst. prof., 1975-82, prof., 1982—. Contbr. articles to profl. jours. Trustee Berks County Hist. Soc., 1994—, pres., 1996—98; sec. Interactive Video Sci. Consortium, Reading Musical Found., 1980—88, trustee, hon. trustee, 1998—. Named Kellogg Mus. Profl., 1987; NSF grantee, 1965—67. Fellow: Internat. Planetarium Soc.; mem.: SAR, AAAS, Pa. Soc., Am. Assn. Mus., Mid-Atlantic Planetarium Soc., Torch Club (Reading, pres. 1987). Home and Office: 1546 Dauphin Ave Reading PA 19610-2118 Office Phone: 610-374-7381. E-mail: commefflvia@comcast.net.

DIETRICH, DEAN FORBES, academic administrator; b. Davenport, Iowa, Jan. 10, 1966; s. Dean Willis and Carolyn (Brandhorst) Dietrich. AB summa cum laude, Dartmouth Coll., 1988; MA, U. Va., 1990, PhD, 1997. Viewer info., ednl. svcs. asst. C-SPAN, Washington, 1988, 89; grad. instr. U. Va., Charlottesville, 1990-97, computer, video cons. Law Sch., 1995-97; vis. asst. prof. English Hanover (Ind.) Coll., 1998-99; sr. rschr. advancement SUNY, Stony Brook, 2000—03; prospect rsch. mgr. U. Nev., Reno, 2003—. Gov.'s fellow U. Va., 1990-91, 92-93. Mem. Assn. Profl. Rschrs. Advancement, Coun. Advancement and Support Edn., Greater N.Y. Assn. Profl. Rschrs. Advancement (sec. 2002-03), Phi Beta Kappa. Office: U Nev Devel & Alumni Rels Mail Stop 007 Reno NV 89557

DIETRICH, RICHARD VINCENT, geologist, educator; b. LaFargeville, NY, Feb. 7, 1924; s. Roy Eugene and Mida Amy (Vincent) D.; m. Frances Elizabeth Smith, Dec. 28, 1946; children: Richard Smith, Kurt Robert, Krista Gayle Brown. AB, Colgate U., 1947; MS, Yale U., 1950, PhD, 1951. Geologist Iowa Geol. Survey, 1947, N.Y. State Sci. Service, summers 1949-50; asst. prof. geology Va. Poly. Inst., Blacksburg, 1951, assoc. prof., 1952-56, prof., 1956-69, mineral technologist Va. Engring. Exp. Sta., 1951-58; Fulbright rsch. prof. Oslo U., Norway, 1959-60; asso. dean arts and scis. Va. Poly. Inst., 1966—68, dean, 1968—69; prof. geology Central Mich. U., Mt. Pleasant, 1969-86, prof. emeritus, 1986—, dean arts and scis., 1969-75. Dir. Econ. Geol. Pub. Co., 1966-72. Author or co-author over 23 sci. books and textbooks in field (transl. into German, Malaysian, Russian, and Japanese); also poems, haiku, essays, cartoons; editor Mineral Industries Jour., 1953-61; mng. editor Bull. Econ. Geology, 1966-73; exec. editor Rocks and Minerals, 1980-88, petrology adv. editor, 1988—; mem. editl. bd. Mineral Record, 1969-74; contbr. over 300 articles to profl. jours.; composer, performer music. Organizer N. Am. for Mineral. Abstracts. 1976-80. Served with U.S. Air Corps, 1943-46. Recipient Acad. Citation Mich. Acad. Sci., Arts and Letters, 1978, Children's Sci. Book award N.Y. Acad. Scis., 1981; Fulbright rsch. prof. U. Oslo, 1958-59; Pres.'s scholar, 1941-42, Austin Colgate scholar Colgate U., 1943, Newton Lloyd Andrews scholar, 1943, Colgate U. scholar, 1946; Edward S. Binney fellow, 1948-49, James Dwight Dana fellow Yale U., 1950-51. Fellow Am. Mineral. Soc. (assoc. life), Soc. Econ. Geol. (sr.); mem. Norsk Geologisk Forening (life), Geol. Soc. Finland (life), Am. Geol. Inst. (gov. 1972-74), Assn. Earth Sci. Editors (pres. 1972-73), Phi Beta Kappa, Sigma Xi, Phi Kappa Phi, Sigma Gamma Epsilon. Independent. Presbyterian. Avocations: birdwatching, illustrations, peach pit carving. Home: 1323 Center Dr Mount Pleasant MI 48858-4103 Business E-Mail: dietr1rv@cmich.edu. *My parents were supportive although they had hoped for a different direction. Education, the work ethic, and retention of individualism and imagination were promoted.*

DIETRICH, ROBERT ANTHONY, pathologist, consultant, medical association administrator; b. Buffalo, May 24, 1933; s. Charles Thomas and Mary Evelyn (Shoecraft) D.; m. Alison Elinor D'Arcy, June 13, 1959; children— Anne Marie, Alison D'Arcy, Karen Elizabeth, Kathleen Murray, Patricia Evelyn, Ellen Kiley BS, Canisius Coll., Buffalo, 1955; MD, Georgetown U., Washington, 1959; MS in Surg. Pathology, U. Minn., Mpls., 1964; JD, George Washington U., Washington, 1974. Diplomate Am. Bd. Pathology, Am. Bd. Nuclear Medicine. Intern D.C. Gen. Hosp., Washington, 1959-60; resident Mayo Clinic, Rochester, Minn., 1960-64; chief pathology svc. U.S. Army Hosp., Fort Gordon, Augusta, Ga., 1964-66; pathologist O.B. Hunter Meml. Lab., Washington, 1966-78; chmn. dept. pathology, chief div. nuclear medicine Montgomery Gen. Hosp., Olney, Md., 1972-78; vice chmn. dept. pathology, chief divsn. nuclear medicine Sibley Meml. Hosp., Washington, 1978-89; sec. Am. Soc. Clin. Pathologists, Chgo., 1981-88, exec. v.p./chief staff, 1982-92; cons., 1992—. Served to capt. U.S. Army, 1964-66. Noble Found. grantee Mayo Clinic, 1964 Fellow Am. Coll. Legal Medicine, Coll. Am. Path., Am. Soc. Clin. Path.; mem. Med. Soc. D.C. (sec. 1984-86, pres. 1988). Home and Office: 5506 Parkston Rd Bethesda MD 20816-3326

DIETRICH, WILLIAM ALAN, reporter, writer; b. Tacoma, Sept. 29, 1951; s. William Richard and Janice Lenore (Pooler) D.; m. Holly Susan Roberts, Dec. 19, 1970; children: Lisa, Heidi. BA, Western Wash. U., 1973. Reporter Bellingham (Wash.) Herald, 1973-76, Gannett News Svc., Washington, 1976-78, Vancouver (Wash.) Columbian, 1978-82, Seattle Times, 1982-97, 2002—; freelance writer, 1998—. Asst. prof. Western Wash. U., 2006—. Author: The Final Forest, 1992, Northwest Passage, 1995, Ice Reich, 1998, Getting Back, 2000, Dark Winter, 2001, Natural Grace, 2003, Hadrian's Wall, 2004, The Scourge of God, 2005, Napoleon's Pyramids, 2007. Recipient Paul Tobenkin award Columbia U., 1986, Pulitzer prize for nat. reporting, 1990; Nieman fellow Harvard U., 1987-88. Office Phone: 206-464-2373.

DIETRICH, WILLIAM GALE, lawyer, real estate developer, consultant; b. Kansas City, Mo., Mar. 6, 1925; s. Roy Kaiser and Gale (Gossett) D.; m. Marjorie Nell Reich, July 14, 1945; children: Meredith G. Dietrich Steinhaus, Ann E. Dietrich Cooling, Walter R. AB with high honors, Yale U., 1948, LLB, 1951. Bar: Mo. 1951. Ptnr. Dietrich, Davis, Dicus, Rowlands, Schmitt & Gorman (and predecessors), 1953-73; project dir., gen. counsel Blue Ridge Shopping Ctr., Inc., Kansas City, 1955-73, pres., gen. mgr., 1964-73, Blue Ridge Tower, Inc., Kansas City, 1967-73; sec.-treas. A. Reich & Sons, Inc., Kansas City, 1973-88, chmn., 1988—; pvt. practice law Kansas City, 1973—; sec., treas. A. Reich & Sons Gardens, Inc., 1973-89; pres. J&D Devel., Inc., 1987—; gen. ptnr. J & D Enterprises, 1986—2006; gen. mgr. The Farm Shopping and Office Ctr., 1994-98; pres. BBJ Treats, L.L.C., 1994-98; mem. WGD Properties, LLC, 1999—. Sec., bd. dirs. Rsch. Med. Ctr., Kansas City, 1977, vice-chmn., 1980-83, chmn., 1983-87; bd. dirs. The Rsch. Found., 1980-91, vice-chmn., 1989-91; bd. dirs. Rsch. Health Svcs., 1980-81, vice chmn., 1983-87, chmn. 1987-89; bd. dirs. Mahana Condominium Assn., Maui. Hawaii, 1977-96, Blue Ridge Bank and Trust Co., Kansas City, 1982-94; vestry mem. Grace & Holy Trinity Cathedral, Kansas City, 1972-95, former treas. 1st lt. AUS, 1943-46, PTO. Recipient Army Commendation Ribbon, 1946. Mem. ABA, Mo. Bar Assn., Kansas City Bar Assn., Blue Ridge Mall Mchts. Assn. (dir. 1958-73), Internat. Coun. Shopping Ctrs. (past dir. for Mo., Kans, Iowa, cert. shopping ctr. mgr.), Lawyers Assn. Kansas City, Mission Hills Country Club, Yale Club, Kansas City (Mo.) Club, Rotary (bd. dirs., sec. found. Kansas City 1978—), Phi Beta Kappa (pres. Kansas City chpt. 1989-91), Phi Delta Phi. Home: 1000 Huntington Rd Kansas City MO 64113-1346 Office: 6155 Oak St Profl Bldg Ste A Kansas City MO 64113-2266 Office Phone: 816-822-2600. E-mail: wgdlo@sbcglobal.net.

DIETTE, KELLY A., psychologist; b. New Bedford, Mass., Aug. 8, 1974; d. Randall R. Desroches and Debra A. Moniz; m. Jonathan Diette, Aug. 21, 1999; children: Nicholas, Patrick. BA Psychology, U. Mass., 1997, MEd Sch. Psychology, 1999, cert. advanced grad. study, 2000. Sch. psychologist, chairperson spl. edn. team Sudbury Pub. Schs., Mass., 2000—. Grantee Lit. and English Lang. Learner, Sudbury Edn. Resource Fund, 2002, Elem. Peer Mediation, 2002. Mem.: Mass. Sch. Psychology Assn., Nat. Assn. Sch. Psychologists. Avocation: bicycling. Office: Ephraim Curtis Mid Sch 22 Pratts Mill Rd Sudbury MA 01776 Office Phone: 978-443-1071. E-mail: kelly_diette@sudbury.k12.ma.us.

DIETZ, ARTHUR TOWNSEND, investment counseling company executive; b. Mt. Vernon, NY, Oct. 30, 1923; s. William Arthur and Adele Townsend (Dods) D.; m. Mary Archer, June 29, 1947 (dec. 1980); children: Adele Archer Dietz, Laura Townsend Burke, Amelia Edmunds Williams; m. Mary Laura Peavy, Sept. 16, 1982 (dec. 1992); m. Margie Nell Lee Baghose, Oct. 4, 1992. AB, Wesleyan U., Middletown, Conn., 1946; MA, Princeton U., 1948, PhD, 1953. Instr. Princeton U., 1948-49; asst. prof. Wesleyan U., 1949-54; Mills Bee Lane prof. fin. and banking, dir. MBA program Emory U., Atlanta, 1954—88; dir. Alpha Fund, Atlanta, 1972-85. Enterprise Funds, Atlanta, 1985—. Enterprise Accumulation Trust, 1995—, Car Trax Security Systems, 2000—. Pres. ATD Adv. Corp., 1996-2003, Strategic Portfolio Mgmt., 1988-95; trustee Emory U. Resolution in Honor, 1983, Amherst Coll., 1953-54; vis. prof. Internat. Inst. Mgmt. Devel., 1965-66; Robert Morris prof., Va., 1984-85. Author books; mem. editl. bd. Jour. of Mktg., 1950, Jour. of Pub. Law, 1950; contbr. articles to profl. jours. Pres. Fernbank PTA, DeKalb County, Ga., 1959-60; mem. DeKalb County Inflation com., 1974, DeKalb County Devel. Authority, 1980-84; Retirement Facility for Elderly Authority, DeKalb County, 1982-84. Staff sgt. AUS, 1942-45, ETO. Named one of Outstanding Educators of Am., 1972; recipient Emory Williams Disting. Tchg. award Emory U., 1983, Disting. Achievement award Emory Bus. Alumni Assn., 1985; Woodrow Wilson fellow, 1946. Fellow Fin. Analysts Soc.; mem. Phi Beta Kappa (pres. Gamma chpt. 1964-65). Methodist. Avocations: tennis, bridge.

DIETZ, ROBERT BARRON, lawyer; b. San Diego, May 14, 1942; s. J. Thomas and Mary Agnes (Barron) D.; m. Grace Louise Purcell, Aug. 19, 1967; children: Thomas E., Michael B., Denis P., M. Alison. AB, Coll. Holy Cross, 1964; JD, Cornell U., 1968. Bar: NY 1968, US Dist. Ct. (no. dist.) NY 1968, US Dist. Ct. (so. and ea. dists.) NY 1973, US Supreme Ct. 1974. Asst. dist. atty. County of Dutchess, Poughkeepsie, N.Y., 1969-70, confidential law clk. to surrogate of Dutchess County, 1970-73; corp. counsel City of Poughkeepsie, 1973-75; assoc. Garrity & Dietz, Poughkeepsie, 1969-73, ptnr., 1973-75; assoc. Gellert & Cutler, P.C. and predecessor firms, Poughkeepsie, 1975-78, ptnr., 1978-86; pvt. practice law Poughkeepsie, 1986-94; ptnr. Dietz & Dietz LLP, Poughkeepsie, 1995—. Lectr. Dutchess C.C., Poughkeepsie, 1985-98, practical skills course N.Y. State Bar Assn. Bd. dirs. Mid Hudson Workshop for Disabled; former mem. Sports Mus. Dutchess County; chmn. Mid Hudson adv. bd. Salvation Army, 1998-2000; bd. trustees Vassar-Warner Home, 1997-2001; bd. counsellors The Children's Home of Poughkeepsie, Inc., 1997-2006; past bd. dirs. Dutchess County coun. Boy Scouts Am., 1997; former mem. City of Poughkeepsie Recreation Commn.; bd. dirs. Greystone Programs, Inc., 1999-2005, pres. endowment com., 2006-; mem. Pastoral Coun. Ch. Holy Trinity, 1999-2001. Fellow Dist. 721 Rotary, Poughkeepsie, 1964-65. Mem. ABA, N.Y. State Bar Assn. (lectr. practical skills course, probate, elder), Dutchess County Bar Assn., Poughkeepsie C. of C., Kiwanis (pres. Poughkeepsie club 1974-75). Republican. Roman Catholic. Avocations: golf, tennis, reading, baseball card collecting. Office: 2 Cannon St Poughkeepsie NY 12601-3224 Office Phone: 845-452-4000. Business E-Mail: rdietz@dietzllp.com.

DIETZ, WILLIAM HARRY, pediatrician; b. Phila., Oct. 6, 1944; s. William H. and Margaret (Shoemaker) Dietz; m. Nancy Fenn, May 6, 1966. BA, Wesleyan U., 1966; MD, U. Pa., 1970; PhD, MIT, 1981. Diplomate Am. Bd. Pediatrics. Intern Children's Hosp. Phila., 1970-71; resident Upstate Med. Ctr., Syracuse, NY, 1974-76; rsch. assoc. NIH, 1971-74, MIT, Cambridge, 1976-81; assoc. prof. Tufts U. Sch. Medicine, Boston, 1986-96, prof., 1996-98; dir. clin. nutrition New England Med. Ctr., Boston, 1983-97. Adj. prof. Tufts U. Sch. Medicine, Boston, 1998—. Fellow: Am. Acad. Pediat. (chmn. task force on children and TV, Elk Grove Village, Ill. 1984—87); mem.: Nat. Acad. Scis., Inst. Medicine, Am. Dietetic Assn. (hon.), N.Am. Assn. Study Obesity (pres. 1993—94), Am.

Soc. Clin. Nutrition (v.p. 1998—99, pres. 1999—2000, counselor). Office: CDC Divsn Nutrition/Phys Act 4770 Buford Hwy NE # MS-K24 Atlanta GA 30341-3717 Office Phone: 770-488-6042. Business E-Mail: wcd4@cdc.gov.

DIETZ, WILLIAM RONALD, corporate management professional; b. Seattle, Nov. 25, 1942; s. William Phillip and Helen Mae (Wilson) D.; m. Carol Jean Gies; 1 child, David Phillip. BA, U. Wash., 1964; MBA, Stanford U., 1968. Fin. cons. 1st Nat. City Bank, NYC, 1968-70; v.p., mgr. Citicorp Subs. Mgmt. Office, Citicorp, NYC, 1971-74; chmn. Citicorp Factors, Inc., NYC, 1974-75; v.p., mgr. N.Y., N.J. and Conn. comml. banking Citibank N.A., NYC, 1976-78, sr. v.p., gen. mgr. Eastern region corp. banking, 1978-81, sr. v.p., head Caribbean Basin div., 1982-84; pres. Charter Assocs. Ltd., 1985-89; chmn. and chief exec. officer CorEast Savs. Bank, Richmond, Va., 1989-91; pres., CEO Am. Savs. Bank, White Plains, NY, 1991-92, Mo. Bridge Bank, Kansas City, 1992-93, Anthem Fin., Inc., Indpls., 1993-96; ptnr. Concord Ptnrs., 1997—2003; mng. ptnr. Customer Contact solutions, LLC, 1999—; pres., CEO W.M. Putnam Co., 2001—. Bd. dirs. Capital One Fin. Corp., Stratis Corp., W.M. Putnam Co.; mem. policy com. Bank Mgmt. Inst., SUNY-Buffalo. Contbg. author: Customer-Focused Marketing of Financial Services. Trustee Children's Mus. Dupage County, Children's Mus. of Indpls., 1994-2006; bd. advisors Ind. U./Purdue U., Indpls., 1995-2003. Lt. USNR, 1964-66. Mem. Delta Tau Delta. Office: WM Putnam Co 1625 Commerce Pky Bloomington IL 61704 Personal E-mail: contactsolutions@earthlink.net. Business E-Mail: rdietz@officereal.com.

DI FALCO, GERARD A., artist; b. Camden, NJ, Sept. 26, 1952; s. Horace Giovanni Robilotta-Di Falco and Marie Ann Mazur-Di Falco. BA in Visual Art, Rutgers U., 1974; MS in Arts Adminstrn., Drexel U., Phila., 1985. Tchg. certificate in art Dept. Edn., NJ, 1977. Visual artist DiFALCO Studios, Phila., 1978—; visual artist: juried into group Nexus Gallery/Found. for Today's Art, Phila., 1984—98; mus. curator The Port of History Mus., Phila., 1988—90; visual artist: juried into group Creative Artists Network, Phila., 1994—96; resident artist art futures project Phila. Mus. of Art, 2002—03. Ind. curator, 1973—; curator, chair, group and exch. show com. Nexus Gallery/Found. for Today's Art, Phila., 1984—90. One-man shows include The Midas Touch, The Spanish Paintings, Phila., The Madrid Paintings, Societal Genres, Art Golf Installation, Paintings and Installations by Di Falco, Paintings: A Thirteen Year Retrospective, U. Pa., The Strega Dance, Davinci Art Alliance, Phila., Installation Called Relics, 2000—, exhibited in group shows at CAN Artists In Soho, Majority Rules, Scotland, State Mus. Harrisburg, Pa., 2004, Del. Ctr. Contemporary Art, Wilmington, 2004, Phila. City Hall, 2004, BoxHeart Gallery, Pitts., 2005 (Best of Show award), 2006, The Free Libr., Phila., 2006, Nat. Episcopal Ch. Gen. Convention Exhibit of Sacred Art, Columbus, Ohio, 2006, Rutgers U. Alumni and Faculty Exhibit, Camden, NJ, 2006, Art Ability X, Bryn Mawr, Pa., 2006 (Best of Show award, 2006), Bryn Mawr Rehab. Gallery, Pa., 2006, Visions X, Cathedral of Convention, Ky., 2006, MUSE Gallery, Phila., 2006, Phila. Episcopal Cathedral, 2007, Stedman Gallery, Rutgers U., Camden, NJ, 2007, altar painting, My Crucifixion, Phila. Episcopal Cathedral, 2007, 6 juried shows, Borowsky Gallery, Phila., 65 juried group shows, Across USA and Madrid, show of furniture, 10 Couturier, LA, Represented in permanent collections DaVinci Art Alliance, Phila., Nexus Gallery. Donating artist for ann. auction MANNA Met. AIDS Neighborhood Nutrition Alliance, Phila., 1994—2007; mem. Episcopal Ch. and Visual Artists, 2005—, St. Clements Episc. Ch., Phila., 2004—; bd. mem. World AIDS Day/Day With(out) Art Com., Phila., 1995—2003. Grantee Individual Artist's Grant, Pa. Coun. on the Arts, 1992, Fellowship Grant, The Pollock-Krasner Found., Inc., NYC, 2002; scholar Grad. Assistantship in Arts Adminstrn., Drexel U., 1984—85. Mem.: DaVinci Art Alliance. Independent. Avocations: researching folklore, herbology, paranormal investigation, reading art history/literature, lecturing/workshop presentation. Home and Office: Art Studio Di Falco 2201 Cherry St #902 Philadelphia PA 19103 Office Phone: 215-640-0765. Personal E-mail: gerarddifalco@msn.com.

DIFFIE, WHITFIELD (WHIT), computer and communications engineer; b. June 5, 1944; m. Mary L. Fischer. BS in Math., MIT, 1965; postgrad. in elec. enging., Stanford U., 1975-78; D in Tech. Scis. honoris causa, Swiss Fed. Inst. Tech., Zurich, 1992. Rsch. asst. The Mitre Corp., Bedford, Mass., 1965-69; rsch. programmer artificial intellingence lab. Stanford U., Palo Alto, Calif., 1969-73, rsch. asst., 1975-78, rsch. programmer, 1975; self-supported researcher in cryptography, 1973-74; mgr. secure syss. rsch. No. Telecom, Mountain View, Calif., 1978-91; disting. engr., adv. computer and comm. security Sun Microsystems, Palo Alto, Calif., 1991—, v.p., Sun fellow and chief security officer. Organizer conf. Crypto '81, '83; mem. program com. Crypto 89; mem. program com. Status and Prospects of Rsch. in Cryptography '93, First ACM Conf. on Comms. and Computer Security, 1993; mem. adv. bd. Electronic Privacy Info. Ctr.; presenter in field. Author (with Susan Landau) Privacy on the Line (Donald McGannon award for Social and Ethical Relevance in Comm. Policy Rsch. and the IEEE-USA award for Disting. Literary Contbn. Furthering Public Understanding of the Profession); Contbr. numerous articles to scientific jours.; featured in Sci.Am., Sci., Time, Omni, Newsweek, NY Times mag., others. G.C. Steward fellow Gonville and Caius Coll., 1996; recipient award for Disting. Contbn. to Consumer Protection Calif. State Psychol. Assn., 1978, Nat. Computer Sys. Security award Nat. Inst. Stds. and Tech. and Nat. Security Agy., 1996, Louis E. Levy medal Franklin Inst., 1997, First Paris Kanellakis award ACM, 1997, Fellow Marconi Found, 2000, Chairman's award for Innovation and Fellow Internat. Assn. for Cryptologic Rsch. 2004. Mem. IEEE (Info. Theory Soc. Paper award 1979, Donald G. Fink award 1981, conf. organizer 1983). Achievements include discovery of the concept of public key cryptography, 1975; devel. of Mathlab symbolic manipulation sys., of Lisp 1.6 sys.; rsch. on interactive debugging and extensible compiling, proof of correctness of programs, proof checking and extensible compilers, on cryptography and its applications; patents (with Martin E. Hellman and Ralph Merkle) for cryptographic apparatus and method, 1980, (with Ashar Aziz) on security of mobile comm., 1993. Office: Sun Microsystems MAK 15-214 901 San Antonio Rd Palo Alto CA 94303-4900

DIFFINE, SUZANNE MICHELE, language educator; d. Edward Chester and Betty Ann Diffine. BA in English, SUNY, Buffalo, 1970, MA in English, 1974. Tchr. English, dept. chair Frederick Law Olmsted Sch. Gifted, Buffalo, 1981—2003; coord. home sch. Buffalo Bd. Edn., 1988—89; curriculum writer Buffalo Pub. Schs., 1989—91; student coord. Manchester Music Festival, Vt., 1996—2003; tchr. English, team coord. North Broward Prep. Sch., Coconut Creek, Fla., 2004—. Trainer Pulse Pilates, Boca Raton, Fla., 2005—; trainer Pilates Bally Total Fitness, Buffalo, 1998—2004, Ft. Lauderdale, 2004—. Mem. Chautauqua Lit. and Scientific Cir., Boca Raton Mus. Art; mem. bd. Just Buffalo Lit. Ctr., Am. Acad. Ballet, Amherst Youth Ballet. Office: North Broward Prep Sch 7600 Lyons Rd Coconut Creek FL 33073

DIFIORE, DAVID GERARD, musician; b. Seattle; s. Herman DiFiore and Maria Fiorito Ciarla. MusB, U. Wash., Seattle, 1975, MusM in Organ Performance, 1981; studied with, Odile Pierre, 1983—92. Dir. music ministries Univ. United Meth. Ch., Seattle, 1971—. Performer internat. organ festivals, debut Notre Dame Cathedral, Paris; vis. faculty Cath. U., Ruzomberok, Slovakia, 2007—. Musician: (CD) Les Amoureux del l'orgue, 1997, Grand Organ of the Castle Church in Kremnica, 2001, 2003, 2005. Named Disting. Grad., Nat. Cath. Edn. Assn., 1997. Mem.: Am. Guild Organists. Personal E-mail: dgdif98@hotmail.com.

DIFORIO, ROBERT GEORGE, literary agent; b. Mamaroneck, NY, Mar. 19, 1940; s. Richard John and Mildred (Kuntz) Diforio; m. Birgit Rasmussen; children: Stephen Christopher, Danielle Alexandra. BA, Williams Coll., 1964; student Advanced Mgmt. Program, Harvard U. Bus. Sch., Cambridge, Mass., 1978. From book sales rep. to v.p. book Kable News Co., 1964—72; with New Am. Libr./E.P. Dutton, NYC, 1972—80, exec. v.p., 1980—81, chmn., CEO, 1983—89; sr. v.p. book sales and mktg. Arcata Graphics Co., 1990-91; founder, prin. D4EO Lit. Agy., 1991—. Served USCGR. Mem.: Conn. Golf Club. Avocations: reading, golf. Home: 7 Indian Valley Rd Weston CT 06883-1018 Office Phone: 203-544-7180. Business E-Mail: d4eo@optonline.net.

DIFRANCO, ANI, music executive, musician; b. Buffalo, Sept. 23, 1970; 1 child, Petah Lucia. Founder Righteous Babe, 1990—. Albums include: Ani DiFranco, 1989, Not So Soft, 1991, Imperfectly, 1992, Puddle Drive, 1993, Out of Range, 1994, Like I Said, 1994, Not A Pretty Girl, 1995, More Joy Less Shame, 1996, Dilate, 1996, Living in Clip, 1997, Little Plastic Castle, 1998, Up, 1999, Little Plastic Remixes, 1999, Fellow Workers, 1999, To the Teeth, 1999, Swing Set, 2000, Revelling/Reckoning, 2001, So Much Shouting, So Much Laughter, 2002, Evolve, 2003, Educated Guess, 2003, Knuckle Down, 2005, Carnegie Hall, 2006, Reprieve, 2006, Canon, 2007. Office: Righteous Babe Records PO Box 95 Ellicot Sta Buffalo NY 14205-0095 also: c/o Tracy Mann at MG Ltd 6th Fl 355 W 52nd St New York NY 10019*

DIGANCI, TODD T., financial regulatory service executive; b. 1960; BS in Acctg. & Computer Info. Systems, Drake U., 1982, MS in Fin., 1984; grad., Advanced Mgmt. Program at Harvard U. Bus. Sch. Various sr. fin. positions Marriott Corp., corp. controller Host-Marriott operating group; corp. controller NASD, Washington, 1995—99, named sr. v.p., controller, 1999, exec. v.p., CFO, 1999—2007, Fin. Industry Regulatory Authority, Washington, 2007—. Mem. bd. dirs. Securities Dealers Insurance Co., Ltd. (SDIC); mem. NASD Mgmt. Com. Office: Financial Industry Regulatory Authority 1735 K St NW Washington DC 20006*

DIGANGI, FRANK EDWARD, academic administrator; b. West Rutland, Vt., Sept. 29, 1917; s. Leonard and Mary Grace (Zafonti) DiG.; m. Genevieve Frances Colignon, June 27, 1946; children: Ellen (Mrs. Philo David Hall), Janet (Mrs. W. Dale Greenwood). BS in Pharmacy, Rutgers U., 1940; MS, Western Res. U., 1942; PhD, U. Minn., 1948. Asst. prof. U. Minn. Coll. Pharmacy, 1948-52, asso. prof., 1952-57, prof. medicinal chemistry, 1957—, also asso. dean adminstrv. affairs. Author: Quantitative Pharmaceutical Analysis, 7th edit, 1977, The History of the Minnesota Pharmacists Association, 1883-1983, 2004; Contbr. articles to pharm. jours. Served with USNR, 1943-46, PTO. Recipient Alumni Assn. Disting. Pharmacist award, 1977, Faculty Recognition award Coll. of Pharmacy Alumni Soc., 1981, Lawrence and Delores M. Weaver medal, 1997. Mem. Am. Pharm. Assn., Minn. Pharm. Assn. (pres. 1971, chmn. bd. 1972-73, Pharmacist of Yr. award 1972, Harold R. Popp Meml. award 1979, hon. mem. 1994), Mpls. Soc. Profl. Pharmacists (hon.), AAUP, Am. Chem. Soc., Am. Assn. Colls. Pharmacy, Univ. Campus Club (Mpls.), Univ. Faculty Golf Club (Mpls., Gownin-Town Club (Mpls.), Sigma Xi, Phi Beta Phi, Phi Lambda Upsilon, Rho Chi. Home: 1666 Coffman St Apt 234 Saint Paul MN 55108-1343 Office: Univ Minn Coll of Pharmacy Minneapolis MN 55455

DIGBY, PAMELA ANNETTE, elementary school educator; d. Joe and Annette Tripp; m. William E. Digby, Jan. 2, 1972; children: Donterio, Tamija children: Shaquala Thurman, Tevin. BS, Ga. Coll. and State U., Milledgeville. Cert. middle sch. educator Ga., 1990. 5th grade tchr. Putnam County Elem. Sch., Eatonton, Ga., 1990—. Vacation Bible sch. tchr. Springfield Bapt. Ch., Monticello, Ga., 2002—05; inclusion tchr., 2003—06. Mem.: NEA (assoc.). Home: 9836 Ga Hwy 83 Monticello GA 31064 Office: Putnam County Elementary School 162 Old Glennwood Spring Rd Eatonton GA 31024 Home Phone: 706-468-6769; Office Phone: 706-485-5141. Business E-Mail: pamtri@yahoo.com.

DIGENOVA, JOSEPH E., lawyer; b. Wilmington, Del., Feb. 22, 1945; s. Egidio Joseph and Elizabeth (Castelline) diG.; m. Victoria Toensing, June 27, 1981; children: Todd, Brady, Amy. BA, U. Cinn., 1967; JD, Georgetown U., 1970. Bar: D.C. 1970, U.S. Dist. Ct. D.C. 1970, U.S. Ct. Appeals (D.C. cir.) 1972. Law clk. to assoc. judge D.C. Ct. Appeals, 1970-71; dir., gen. counsel U. Cin. Project, 1971-72; asst. U.S. atty. Office of U.S. Atty., Washington, 1972-75, prin. asst. U.S. atty., 1982-83; U.S. atty. Washington, 1983-88; counsel on intelligence matters Office of U.S. Atty. Gen., Washington, 1976; counsel for select com. on intelligence U.S. Senate, Washington, 1975-76, counsel for subcommittee on D.C., com. govt. affairs, 1976, counsel for com. on judiciary, 1978, chief counsel, staff advisor for com. on rules and adminstrn., 1981; adminstrv. asst., legis. counsel U.S. Senator Charles Mathias, Washington, 1979; U.S. Atty. for D.C., 1983-88; ptnr. Bishop, Cook, Purcell & Reynolds, 1988-90, Manatt Phelps & Phillips, 1991-95; founding ptnr. diGenova & Toensing, 1996—. Ind. counsel Clinton passport file search matter, 1992-95; apptd. grievance com. U.S. Dist. Ct. D.C., 1994. Contbr. articles to profl. jours. Mem.: ABA (com. grand jury 1983—87, criminal justice sect. 1982—, white collar crime com. 1988—), Gridiron Club. Republican. Roman Catholic. Avocations: golf, music, singing. Office: diGenova & Toensing 901 15th St NW Ste 430 Washington DC 20005-2327 Home Phone: 301-951-6142; Office Phone: 202-289-7701.

DIGGES, EDWARD S(IMMS), business management consultant; b. Pitts., June 30, 1946; AB, Princeton U., NJ, 1968; JD, U. Md., 1971; MBA, U. Pitts., 1994. Bar: Md. 1972, US Supreme Ct. 1975. With staff of gov. State of Md., Annapolis, 1973; ptnr. Piper & Marbury, Washington and Balt., 1977-84; founding ptnr. Digges, Wharton & Levin, Annapolis, 1984-89; corp. cons. various corps., NYC, 1990—2006. Bd. dirs. Camtucket LLC, Chilham, LLC, Interlude Fin., LLC, ZBP, LLC; instr. advanced bus. law Johns Hopkins U., 1975—78; lectr. fed. jurisdiction U. Md. Law Sch., 1976—78; lectr. civil procedure U. Balt. Law Sch., 1976—78; mem. Gov.'s Commn. to Revise Md. Code, 1978—90. Contbr. articles to profl. jours. Mem. alumni coun. Mercersburg Acad., 1982-88, pres. 1987-88; bd. advisors Indian Creek Sch., 1982-88, chmn. 1986-88; pres. Beacon Hill Cmty. Assn., 1978-86. ROTC, U.S. Army, 1970-71. Mem. Md. State Bar Assn. (bd. govs. 1978-84), Am. Law Inst., Am. Bd. Trial Adv. (pres. Md. chpt. 1984-89), Inn XIII, Am. Inns of Ct. (Master of the Bench 1986-89), Scribes. Clubs: So. Md. Soc. (bd. govs., pres. 1988), Mid Ocean (Bermuda), Princeton Club of NY. Democrat. Roman Catholic. Home and Office: One Sandy Acres Rd Cambridge MD 21613 Personal E-mail: ed.digges@gmail.com.

DIGGINS, PETER SHEEHAN, arts administrator; b. Rochester, NY, June 23, 1938; s. Bartholomew A. and Mona (Sheehan) D. BA in English, Georgetown U., 1959. guest artist cons. San Francisco Opera, 1997. Staff reporter Washington Post, 1960-65; asst. artistic adminstr. Met. Opera, NYC, 1965-72; dir. dance programs NY State Coun. on the Arts, 1972-75; gen. adminstr. The Joffrey Ballet, NYC, 1975-79; pres. Peter S. Diggins Assocs., 1979—; Am. entertainment coord. Winter Olympics, Nagano, Japan, 1998; artistic adminstr. Ballet Pacifica, 2004—06. Cons. in arts mgmt. dance and opera cos.; cons. for guest dancers San Francisco Opera, 1996; casting cons. Broadway and tour prodns. of Carousel, Titanic, Victor/Victoria, Cats, Red Shoes, Christmas Carol, 1993-98. Contbr. articles to Opera Mag. Recipient grant for European work-study tour Met. Opera, 1968 Home: 133 W 71st St New York NY 10023-3834 Office Phone: 212-874-4534. Personal E-mail: Festspiel@aol.com.

DIGGS, DAVID B., music educator; b. Lubbock, Tex., Mar. 20, 1947; s. Bill H and Adele Diggs; m. Grace Louise Meade, Jan. 2, 1982; children: Christina Susan, Gordon Meade. MusB, Okla. City U., 1965—69; MusM, SUNY at Stony Brook, 1972—74. Tchg. asst. SUNY at Stony Brook, NY, 1972—74; woodwind specialist (oboist) NYC Musical Organizations, 1974—; dir. of winds Lehigh U., Bethlehem, Pa., 1998—. Cons. Moravian Music Found., Winston-Salem, NC, 2002—; rschr. Band of HM Coldstream Guards, London, 2003—. Prodr.(condr.): (cd) Lehigh Glory, Rhapsody; author: (book) The Dalton Recorder Book; composer: (musical suite) Echoes of Glory; transcriber (overture) Henry the Fifth Overture; editor (transcriber): (music) The Eley Project; composer: (musical suite) Trooping the Colour Suite, Highland Pipes Medley, The Jamestowne Jubilee of 1807; prodr. (condr.): (cd) American Overture; prodr.(condr.): (cd) Incantation, Tempered Steel, Pipes & Band:Music of Ireland & Scotland, H.M. Qeen Elizabeth II State Dinner, 2006; composer: (albums) Jamestown Jubilee 1607-2007, 2007. Grantee, Henry Lawrence Gipson Inst., 2004—05, Lehigh U., 2001—03, Mary Gordon Roberts Fund, 1999—. Mem.: Am. Fedn. of Musicians, Coll. Band Directors Nat. Assn. Achievements include research in band music of the civil war era; music of the 18th century foot guards bands. Avocation: computers. Office: Lehigh Univ 420 East Packer Ave Bethlehem PA 18015 Home Phone: 212-410-2288; Office Phone: 610-758-3831. Office Fax: 610-758-6470. Personal E-mail: dbd2@lehigh.edu.

DIGGS, TAYE (SCOTT DIGGS), actor; b. Rochester, NY, Jan. 2, 1972; m. Idina Menzel, Jan. 11, 2003. BFA in Musical Theatre, Syracuse U. Actor: (Broadway plays) Carousel, 1994—95, Rent, 1996, Chicago, 1997, Wicked, 2004, (Off-Broadway) A Soldier's Play, 2005; choreographer (ballets) Loose Change, 2007; actor: (films) How Stella Got Her Groove Back, 1998, Go, 1999, The Wood, 1999, The Best Man, 1999, House on Haunted Hill, 1999, The Way of the Gun, 2000, New Best Friend, 2002, Just A Kiss, 2002, Brown Sugar, 2002, Equilibrium, 2002, Chicago, 2002, Basic, 2003, Malibu's Most Wanted, 2003, Drum, 2004, Rent, 2005, 30 Days, 2006; (TV series) Ally McBeal, 2001, Day Break, 2006; actor & prodr. (TV series) Kevin Hill, 2004—05, guest appearances Law & Order, 1996, New York Undercover, 1996, Ed, 2003, The West Wing, 2003. Recipient Blockbuster Entertainment award for Favorite Supporting Actor, 2000, Chgo. Internat. Film Festival award for Excellence in Filmmaking, 2003, SAG award for Outstanding Performance by the Cast of a Theatrical Motion Picture, 2003. Office: c/o Kevin Hill UPN 9 9 Broadcast Plaza Secaucus NJ 07096 Mailing: c/o Second Stage Theatre A Soldier's Play 307 West 43rd St @ 8th Ave New York NY 10036*

DIGGS, WALTER WHITLEY, health science facility administrator; b. Memphis, Tenn., June 8, 1932; s. Lemuel Whitley and Beatrice (Moshier) D.; m. Ann C. Thobae, Nov. 29, 1958; children: Jennie, Thomas, Andrew. BS, Washington and Lee U., 1954; MHA, U. Minn., 1956. Adminstrv. resident Stormont-Vail Hosp., Topeka, 1955-56; asst. dir. The Johns Hopkins Hosp., Balt., 1959-66; adminstr. Med. Coll. Ga. Hosp., Augusta, 1966-70; asst. prof. Med. Coll. Ga., Augusta, 1970-71, U. Tenn. and U. Memphis, 1971-97; field rep. Joint Commn. Hosps., Chgo., 1981-88, 93—; supt. Memphis Mental Health Inst., 1987-93. Cons. Tenn. Dept. Mental Health, 1993-95. Pres. Delta Found., Miss., 1987—, Ballet South, Memphis Ballet, Augusta Civic Ballet. Lt. USNR, 1956-59. Recipient Peter Cooper award, Unitarian Ch., Memphis, 1975, Forrest Fletcher, Washington and Lee, Lexington, Va., 1954. Fellow Am. Coll. Healthcare Execs. (life). Avocation: seniors track and field. Home: 5282 Shady Grove Rd Memphis TN 38120-2404 Personal E-mail: cordovawwd@aol.com.

DIGHAM, FADEL, research and development company executive, director; b. Mahallet Zayyad, Gharbia, Egypt, Feb. 17, 1972; s. Fadel Abdel Aziz Digham and Fatma Abdel Rahman Khalil; m. Najwan Tayel, June 22, 2000; 1 child, Maryam Fadel. BSc with distinction, Cairo U., 1995, MSc, 1999; MEE, U. Minn., Mpls., 2002; PhD, U. Minn., 2005. Gsm switching team leader Alcatel-Telecom, Cairo, 1996—2000; rsch. asst., tchg. asst. U. Minn., 2000—05; internship Mitsubishi Electric Rsch. Lab., Cambridge, Mass., 2004—05; postdoctoral fellow, instr. U. Minn., 2005—06. rsch. & devel. dir. Nat. Telecom Regulatory Authority, Cairo, 2007—. Contbr. articles to profl. jours. Head Province HS Union, Mahallet-Zayyad, Gharbia, Egypt, 1989; mem. Commonwealth Ter. Coop., St. Paul, 2002—03. Recipient Travel award, Intelligent Transp. Sys., Dept. Transp., Mpls., 2002—03; grantee Dept. Travel grant, Dept. Elec. & Computer Enging., U. Minn., 2002. Mem.: IEEE (Travel grant 2002). Achievements include patents for joint pilot and data loading for multiple input multiple output antenna systems; research in data packet transmission over fading channels; adaptive wireless transceivers; unknown signal detection over fading channels; wireless sensor networks. Avocations: soccer, travel, poetry, ping pong/table tennis. Home: 5 Sokkar Bldg Elkoom Alakhdar Ahram St Giza 12111 Egypt Personal E-mail: fdigham@yahoo.com.

DI GIACOMO, FRAN, artist; b. Miami, Ariz., Oct. 24, 1944; d. B.J. and LaVenia Marilyn (Beavers) Fain; m. Len DiGiacomo, May 9, 1970; children: Marc, Eric. Student, Scottsdale Artist's Sch., 1985—2000; studied with, David Leffel, with Joe Anna Arnette, with Greg Kreutz, with Howard Terpning. Commissions include portraits of Supreme Court Chief Justice Warren E. Burger, Dist. Atty., 1994, Henry Wade, 1995, Haggar Apparel, Dallas Cowboys' Emmitt Smith, 1993; author: I'd Rather Do Chemo Than Clean Out the Garage, 2003; subject of numerous articles. Recepient 2nd place, 1993, Hon. Mention, 1994, 1st place, 1996, Plano Art Assn.,1st place, 1994, Assoc. Creative Artists, Grumbacher Gold, 1997, 2nd place, 1994, Trinity Arts Guild, 1st place, 1998, 3rd place, 1999, Richardson Civic Art, 3rd place, 1995, Tex. and Neighbors 5 state. Mem. Oil Painters Am. (assoc., signature), Am. Soc. (assoc.), Classical Realism, Portrait Soc. Am., Assoc. Creative Artists (signature). Avocation: tennis.

DIGICAYLIOGLU, MURAT HAYDAR, medical educator; PhD, U. Zurich, Switzerland, 1994. Postdoctoral fellow Harvard U., Children's Hosp., Boston, 1997—2000; sr. postdoctoral fellow Burnham Inst., La Jolla, Calif., 2000—03, rsch. asst. prof., 2003—06; asst. prof. U. Calif., San Diego, 2006—07, UTHSCSA, San Antonio, 2007—. Grantee rsch. grantee, NIH/NINDS. Achievements include patents for nNeuroprotective synergy of erythropoietin and insulin-like growth factors. Office: UTHSCSA Dept Neurosurgery 7703 Floyd Curl Dr (MC 7843) San Antonio TX 78229-3900 Office Phone: 210-567-5625.

DI GIOVANNI, ANTHONY, retired coal mining company executive; b. Phila., May 10, 1919; s. Charles and Josephine (Giacobbe) Di Giovanni; m. Rose Persichetti, July 28, 1946 (dec. Mar. 2003); children: Joanne, Diane, Rosemary, Charles. BS in Bus. Adminstrn, St. Joseph's U., 1940. CPA Pa. Acct. Service Supply Corp., Phila., 1940-42; account supr. Ernst & Ernst, 1942-51, mgr. Phila., 1952—65; former v.p., dir. United Eastern Coal Sales Corp.; exec. v.p. finance and adminstrn. Barnes & Tucker Co., Valley Forge, Pa., 1965-72, pres., 1972-84; group pres. resources div. Alco Standard Corp. (now Ikon Office Solutions, Inc.), 1973-85, v.p., 1976-85; pres. Alco Standard Canadian Coal Corp., 1976-85; v.p. Tri County Ventures, Inc., Ebensburg, Pa., 1986—. Dir. Upshur Coals Corp. Bd. dirs. St. Joseph U., 1983—85. Mem.: AICPA, Pa. Inst. CPA (past bd. dirs., chmn. com.), Nat. Coal Assn. (bd. dirs. 1973—85, fin. com. 1978—83), Sons of Italy (treas., policy com. Commonwealth Lodge #1949 1989—91), Phoenixville Country Club. Roman Catholic.

DIGIOVANNI, ELEANOR ELMA, scaffold installation company executive; b. L.I., NY, May 14, 1944; d. Charles and Josephine (Laureni) DiGiovanni. Student, Queensboro Coll. Collector Atlas/Re/Sun Ins. Co., NYC, 1965-69; instr. Oak Manor Equitation, Weyers Cave, Va., 1970-76; dispatcher, salesperson Safway Steel Products, LI, NY, 1977-83; ops. mgr.

York Scaffold, LI, 1983—95; scaffold sales rep. Safway Steel Prod., Bklyn., 1977—83; ptnr. E-Z Scholarship Data Svs., 1992-94; scaffold sales rep. R&R Scaffolding, Moonachie, NJ, 2001—02, Highrise Hoisting and Scaffolding Inc., L.I. City, NY, 2002—04; sales mgr. Swing Staging Inc., L.I. City, 2004—. Mem.: NAFE, Women in Constrn., Mus. Natural History, Internat. Platform Assn. Democrat. Roman Catholic. Avocations: reading, horseback riding, needlepoint. Home: 14-34 30th Rd Astoria NY 11102-3640 Office: Swing Staging Inc 49-47 31 St Long Island City NY 11101 Personal E-mail: ellie2002@aol.com.

DIGIUSTINI, ANTONETTA ANNA, educational association administrator, educator; b. Boston, July 10, 1961; d. Luigi and Elisa Carolina (Castrucci) DiGiustini. AB, Harvard U., Cambridge, Mass., 1997. Tchr., writer, arts adminstr. Charles River Creative Arts Program, Dover, Mass., 1977—92; program asst. Nazzaro Cmty. Ctr., Boston, 1989—90; asst. dir. pub. programs and edn. Bostonian Soc., Boston, 1991—93; stewardship coord. Radcliffe Inst. for Advanced Study, Cambridge, Mass., 1995—2003; co-founder, dir., tchr. LearningBOSTON Advent Sch., 1999—; master tchr., mem. faculty Saturday Course at Milton Acad., Mass., 2000—. Contbr. poetry to anthologies, 1976—. Account mgr., loaned exec. United Way Mass. Bay, Boston, 2004—05; pvt. writing tutor Boston, 2005—; rsch. analyst joint com. mental health and substance abuse Rep. Ruth B. Balser, House Chair, Commonwealth Mass., 2007—; tchr., tutor, mentor in writing Trinity Edn. for Excellence Program Trinity Ch., Boston, 2006—. Recipient Am. Registry of Outstanding Profl., 2002—. Mem.: Assn. Fundraising Profls., Orgn. Am. Historians, Am. Hist. Assn. Avocations: poetry, photography, running, reading. Home: 107 Beacon St Apt 6 Boston MA 02116 Personal E-mail: antonetta_digiustini@yahoo.com.

DIGIUSTO, ELAINE BESSIE, science educator; b. Joliet, Ill., Nov. 1, 1952; d. Phillip and Bessie Frances (Lestina) DiGiusto. BS in Biology, U. St. Francis, Joliet, Ill., 1975; M in Sci. Edn., Olivet Nazarene U., Ill., 1990. 6th grade sci./social studies tchr. Coal City (Ill.) Mid. Sch., 1979—89, 5th grade sci./social studies tchr., 1989—, 6th grade sci./social studies tchr., coord. 6th grade chemist challenge program, 1999—. Mid. sch. coord. Sch. Improvement Team, Coal City, Ill., 1990—. Mem.: NEA, ASCD, Nat. Middle Sch. Assn., Ill. Edn. Assn., Ill. Sci. Tchrs. Assn., Nat. Coun. Social Studies Tchrs. Roman Catholic. Avocations: reading, travel, crafts. Home: 152 E 1st St Braidwood IL 60408 Office: Coal City Mid Sch 500 S Carbon Hill Rd Coal City IL 60416

DIGMAN, LESTER ALOYSIUS, management educator; b. Kieler, Wis., Nov. 22, 1938; s. Arthur Louis and Hilda Dorothy (Jansen) Digman; m. Ellen Rhomberg Pfohl, Jan. 15, 1966; children: Stephanie, Sarah, Mark. BSME, U. Iowa, Iowa City, 1961, MSIE, 1962, PhD, 1970. Registered profl. engr., Mass. Mgmt. cons. U.S. Ameta, Rock Island, Ill., 1962-67; mgmt. instr. U. Iowa, Iowa City, 1967-69; head applied math. dept. US Ameta, Rock Island, Ill., 1969-74, head managerial tng. dept., 1974-77; assoc. prof. mgt. U. Nebr., Lincoln, 1977-84, dir. grad. studies in mgmt., 1982—, prof. mgmt., 1984-87, Leonard E Whittaker Am. Charter disting. prof. mgmt., 1987-93, Met. Fed. Bank disting. prof. mgmt., 1993-95, First Bank disting. prof. mgmt., 1995-98, US Bank disting. prof. mgmt., 1998—2002, Harold J. Laipply coll. prof., 2002—; dir. Ctr. for Tech. Mgmt. and Decision Scis., 1992-94; interim dir. Gallup Rsch. Ctr., 1994-95; mem. adv. bd. Ctr. for Albanian Studies, 1992—. Cons. various orgns., 1963—72; sec., treas. Mgmt. Svcs. Assocs. Ltd., Davenport, Iowa, 1972—77; owner L. A. Digman and Assocs., Lincoln, 1977—; gen. ptnr. Letna Properties, Madison, Wis., 1978—. Author: Strategic Management: Concepts, Decisions, Cases, 1986, 3d edit., 1990, Strategic Management: Concepts, Processes, Decisions, 1995, Strategic Management: Cases, 1995;: 2d edit., 1999, Network Analysis for Management Decisions, 1982, Strategic Management: Cases for the Global Information Age, 2002, 3d edit., 2007, Strategic Management: Competing in the Global Information Age, 2002, 3d edit., 2006; contbr. articles to profl. jours. Recipient Disting. award, SBA, 1980, certs. of Appreciation, Dept. Def., 1972, Disting. Faculty award, Coll. Bus. Adminstrn., 2006. Fellow: Pan Pacific Bus. Assn., Decision Scis. Inst. (program chmn. 1986, pres. 1987—88, coord. doctoral consortium 1989, strategy/policy track chmn. 1991, v.p. 1992—94, strategic mgmt. track chmn. internat. meeting 1993, chair long-range planning com. 1995—96, mem. adv. com. internat. meeting 1997, chair fellows com. 1999—2000, charter); mem.: IEEE, MBA Roundtable (charter, mem. steering com.), Inst. Ops. Rsch. and Mgmt. Scis. (founding), Strategic Leadership Forum, Acad. Mgmt., Strategic Mgmt. Soc. (founding), Confrerie de la Chaine Rotisseurs, Firethom Country Club, Nebr. Club. Roman Catholic. Avocations: gardening, photography, wine tasting. Home: 7520 Lincolnshire Rd Lincoln NE 68506-1635 Office: U Nebr 277 CBA Lincoln NE 68588 Business E-Mail: ldigman1@unl.edu.

DIGNAC, GENY (EUGENIA M. BERMUDEZ), sculptor; b. Buenos Aires, June 8, 1932; came to U.S., 1954; d. Jose Victor Marenco and Margarita Eugenia D.; m. Jose Y. Bermudez, Apr. 7, 1958; children—Alexander, Melanie. Student, U. Buenos Aires, 1952-54. Lectr. in field. Exhibited in one-woman shows at Galeria 22, Caracas, Venezuela, 1967, Michael Berger Gallery, Pitts., 1969, Cinema 2, Caracas, 1971, Pyramid Gallery, Washington, 1971; exhibited in numerous group shows including Corcoran Gallery of Art, Washington, 1958, 59, Inst. Contemporary Arts, Washington, 1967, Bklyn. Mus., 1968, Mus. Modern Art, Buenos Aires, 1971, Mus. Fine Arts, Boston, 1971, Palais des Beaux Arts, Brussels, 1974, Inst. Contemporary Arts, London, 1974; represented in permanent collections including Fundacio Joan Miro, Barcelona, Spain, Palazzo Dei Diamanti, Ferrara, Italy, Museo La Tertulia, Cali, Colombia, Galeria del Banco Central, Guayaquil, Ecuador, The Latinoamerican Art Found., San Juan, P.R., and others in Argentina, Chile, Germany, Italy, Ireland, Spain, U.S. and Venezuela; works include 27 Fire Gestures-, 1970-2000; radio and TV interviews, U.S. and abroad; works with lights, fire and temperatures; subject of profl. articles, films. Recipient prize for light sculpture IX Festival of Art, 1969 Home: 4109 E Via Estrella Phoenix AZ 85028-4515 Office: Osuna Art 7200 Wisconsin Ave Bethesda MD 20814 Office Phone: 602-996-1555. E-mail: gdignac@aol.com.

DIGNAN, THOMAS GREGORY, JR., lawyer; b. Worcester, Mass., May 23, 1940; s. Thomas Gregory and Hester Clare (Sharkey) D.; m. Mary Anne Connor, Sept. 16, 1978; children: Kellyanne E., Maryclare E. BA, Yale U., 1961; JD, U. Mich., 1964. Bar: Mass. 1964, U.S. Supreme Ct. 1968. Assoc. Ropes & Gray, Boston, 1964—74, ptnr., 1974—2000, of counsel, 2001—. Spl. asst. atty. gen. State of Mass., 1974-76; trustee NSTAR. Asst. editor: Mich. Law Rev., 1963-64; contbr. articles to profl. jours. Bd. dirs. Family Counseling and Guidance Ctrs., Inc., 1967-76, 78-94, v.p., 1983-87, pres., 1987-89; trustee Cath. Charitable Bur. of Boston, Inc., 1994-97, Dana Hall Sch., 1994-2005; bd. dirs. Gov.'s Mgmt. Task Force, 1979-81, Mass. Moderator's Assn., 1994-2000; mem. fin. com. Town of Sudbury, 1982-85, moderator, 1985-2003; bd. advisors Environ. Law Ctr., Vt. Law Sch., 1981—; mem. vis. com. U. Mich. Law Sch.; corporator Emerson Hosp., 1989-2004. Mem. Nashawtuc Country Club, Shadow Wood Country Club, Order of the Coif, Phi Delta Phi. Republican. Roman Catholic. Home: 9053 Windswept Dr Bonita Springs FL 34135 Personal E-mail: Tdignanjr@aol.com.

DIGORGIO, KENNETH, lawyer; MBA, JD, UCLA. Regulatory counsel First Am. Title Insurance Corp. (now The First Am. Corp.), Santa Ana, Calif., 1999—2003; exec. v.p., gen counsel First Advantage Corp. (subsidiary of First Am. Corp), 2003—04; gen. counsel The First Am. Corp., Santa Ana, Calif., 2004—. Office: First American Corp 1 First American Way Santa Ana CA 92707*

DIGREGORIO, AMANDA ELIZABETH, medical products executive; b. Boulder, Colo., Dec. 2, 1981; d. Milton Ralph and Beverly Alice DiGregorio. BSc in Athletic Tng., Xavier U., Cin., Ohio, 2004; MSc in Health Adminstrn. and Mgmt., Regis U., Denver, 2005. Cert. athletic trainer Nat. Athletic Tng. Bd. Certification. Asst. athletic trainer Xavier U., Cin., 2000—04; med. asst. sports medicine Colo. U., Boulder, Colo., 2004—05; coord. med. equipment distibn. Colo. Prof. Med., Golden, Colo., 2005—. Med. interpreter Internat. Interpreting, Denver, 2004—; med. translator Wellness Coaches USA, Bluebell, Pa., 2004—; cons. in field. Counselor RAAP, Denver, 2000—. Mem.: Colo. Athletic Trainers Assn., Nat. Athletic Trainers Assn. Avocations: singing, triathlons, volleyball.

DIKE, RAD (EDWARD CONRAD DIKE), artist; b. Maywood, Nebr., June 9, 1945; s. Raymond Hadyn and Mary Dorothy (Popp) D.; m. Laurel Ellen Rathbun, 1970 (div. 1971); m. Ann Doherty Langenbach, Feb. 14, 1985. Think tank dir. Henry Dreyfuss Assn., N.Y.C., 1970-72; vis. prof. Pratt Inst. Sch. of Architecture, N.Y.C., 1970-72, adj. prof., 1972-77; organizer Nat Indsl. Design Conf., Pa., 1971; mentor prof. PhD leadership program NYU, 1974-77; guest lectr. CCNY, Cooper Union, N.Y. Sch. Interior Design, 1975-77; vis. prof. Parsons Sch. Design, 1976-77; spkr. Harvard Grad. Sch. Design, 1983. Exhibited in shows at Pratt Inst., N.Y.C., 1968, 69, U.S. Embassy, Stockholm, 1970, Smithsonian Air & Space Mus., Washington, 1971, Gotham Book Mart Gallery, N.Y.C, 1973, Field Taos, N.Mex., 1976, Nat. Peace Garden Travelling Show, 1989-92, Boston Athenaeum, 1992, 94, 96, Nat. Arts Club (Pres. award), 1995, Flickinger Arts Ctr., 1995, HGTV Arts Video, 1995, Virtuosity Art Internat. 3D CD ROM Mus., 1996; author: Architectural Common Sense, 1983; represented in permanent collections; inventor Mr. McCogitator robot, 1959, balcony-autogyro/boat/car balcony, 1969, naturally refined architecture, gesso/metal dusts paint tech.; prin. archtl. works include N.Y.C. Dept. Gen. Svc. Gardens, 1981, Hell's Kitchen Seedling Greenhouse, 1983, Whole Tree Cottage, 1988, Trussed Arched Tree Branches (Vt. Gov.'s Spl. Merit award), 1989, Arch Keystone Tree, 1990, Suspension Tree Facade, 1991, Chez Ploix, France, 1994—, others. Cons., organizer First Earth Day, N.Y.C, 1970; laborer Green Guerillas, 1976-82; regional planning commr. So. Windsor (Vt.) County, 1989-90; bd. dirs. Hist. Windsor, 1991-93, trustee, 1994-95; founder Conservation Commn., West Windsor, 1990; commr. Vt. Road & Bridges Agy., 1990, Vt. Assn. Planners & Developers Agys., 1990; bd. advisors Preservation Inst. Bldg. Crafts, 1994—; bd. dirs. Am Inst. Wine & Food New England, 1993-95. Batchelder grantee, 1964-70, Ford Motor grantee, 1967-70, Travel grantee U.S. Dept. Commerce, Pratt Inst., 1969; recipient Armco Steel prize, 1969, Merit award NEA, 1984, Outstanding Electronics award USAF, 1959, Poetry award Quill & Scroll USA, 1960. Mem. Nat. Arts Club, Vt. Land Trust (life). Achievements include scientific research and demonstration on Squared Circle of da Vinci's Man, Disproof of Le Corbusier's Modular Man, Human Golden Trinity, Skyscraper as Garden-Engine, Heat chimney Skyscraper Cooling, Laws of Branches, Natural Refinement. Home: Dike Outlook Reading VT 05062 Office Phone: 802-484-3339.

DIKER, CHARLES M., investment advisor; b. NYC; m. Valerie Diker. B, Harvard U., 1956, MBA, 1958. Mng. ptnr. Diker Mgmt. LLC. Dir. Loews Corp.; mem. fund reunion gift steering com. Harvard U., com. on U. resources, visiting com. to art mus.; dir. Cantel Medical Corp., 1985—, chmn. bd., 1986—. Named one of Top 200 Collectors, ARTnews Mag., 2004. Mem.: Antique Tribal Art Dealers Assn. Inc., George Gustav Heye Ctr. (co-chmn. bd., mem. nat. bd.), Nat. Mus. Am. Indian. Avocation: Collector of Native Am. Art; Modern & Contemporary Art. Home: 745 5th Ave Ste 1409 New York NY 10151-1406 Office Phone: 212-904-0321. Office Fax: 212-308-6891. Business E-Mail: charles.diker@wpginvest.com.

DIKET, MARY READ M., academic administrator, educator; b. Oak Ridge, Tenn., Aug. 2, 1944; d. Edmund Warren and Jeanne (Howie) Montgomery; m. Merrill Edward Diket, Feb. 12, 1966; children: Cameron, Melissa, Tally. B in Art Edn., U. Miss., 1965; M in Art Edn., U. So. Miss., 1988; PhD in Art, U. Ga., Athens, 1991. Art and English instr. Murrah High Sch., Jackson, Miss., 1965-66; art instr. St. John's Day Sch., Laurel, Miss., 1971-73, 86; ptnr. Art Assocs. Studio, 1987-89; grad. teaching asst. U. So. Miss., 1987-89, U. Ga., 1989-90, rsch. affiliate, 1991-92; dir. creativity workshop William Carey U., Laurel, Miss., 1992—, dir. honors program, 1992—, prof. art and edn., 1992—. Prodr., instr. workshops U. Ga. Family Housing, 1989; humanities instr. and testing cons. creative scholars program Lamar U., Beaumont, Tex., 1990-93; adj. prof. William Carey Coll., 1992; vis. prof. art dept. U. So. Miss., 1992; dir. Apple Edn. Seed Grant, 1995-96; presenter in field. Co-editor: Trends in Art Education From Diverse Cultures, 1995; editor: Miss. Assn. for Gifted Children, 1993; contbr. articles to profl. jours.; exhbns. U. Miss., 1964-65, Protective Paint Co. Jackson, Miss., 1965, McComb Juried Art Show, 1966, Jones County Jr. Coll., 1987, YWCA, Laurel, Miss., 1988, U. So. Miss., 1988, U. Ga., 1990; costume designer, set designer for 10 plays Laurel Little Theatre, 1981-87; cartoonist: (campus newspaper) Mississippian, 1963. Recipient Nat. Historian award Delta Delta Delta, 1984, Faculty Excellence award William Carey Coll., 1993, Outstanding Humanities Faculty, 1995, Miss. Legis. HEADWAE award for Faculty, 2001, Miss. Alliance for Arts Excellence in Higher Edn., 2002, Nat. Higher Educator of Yr., 2003; grantee Task Force for Edn. Govt. Elect Kirk Fordice, 1991, Lauren Rogers Mus., 1986. Fellow Nat. Art Edn. Assn. (disting., presenter); mem. Internat. Soc. Edn. Through Art, Am. Ednl. Rsch. Assn. (reviewer 1992, presenter 1992—, co-chmn. arts and learning 1993, 94, editor arts and learning rsch. 1995, 96), Brain, Neuroscience Edn. (pres. 2002-04), Siminar Rsch. Art Edn. (pres. 1999-2000), Women's Caucus (pres.-elect 2006-), Nat. Art Edn. Assn.(Manual Barkan award for Pub. of Yr., 2003), Internat. Mind, Brain, Neuroscience Soc. (charter), Miss. Art Edn. Assn., Nat. Assn. for Gifted, Miss. Assn. for Gifted Children, Laurel Arts League, Colonial Dames Am., DAR, Affiliate Garden Clubs Am., Phi Delta Kappa, Alpha Chi (Nat. advisor award 2003). Avocation: theater. Home: 805 N 6th Ave Laurel MS 39440-2710 Office: William Carey Coll 498 Tuscan Ave Hattiesburg MS 39401-5461 E-mail: diketwcc@netdoor.com.

DIKKERS, SCOTT, editor; b. 1965; Student, Univ. Wis. Co-founder, cartoonist The Onion parody newspaper, Madison, Wis., 1988—89, co-owner, 1989—, editor-in-chief, 1989—2000, 2005—. Co-author (with Onion Staff): Our Dumb Century, 1999 (Thurber prize for Am. Humor, 1999); co-author: (with Robert Siegel) The Onion's Finest News Reporting, Vol. 1, 2000; author: You Are Worthless, 1999; writer, dir., prodr. (films) Spaceman, 1999 (Audience award Austin Film Festival, 1998), writer, dir. Bad Meat, 2003, writer, prodr. The Astounding World of the Future, 2001. Named one of Top 10 Favorite Writers in Am., Rolling Stone mag., Top 50 Movers and Shakers in the Digital Realm, Time mag.; named to It List of 100 Most Talented People in Entertainment Industry, Entertainment Weekly, 1998. Office: The Onion 10th Fl 536 Broadway New York NY 10012 also: The Onion #270 33 University Sq Madison WI 53715

DIKTAS, CHRISTOS JAMES, lawyer; b. June 17, 1955; s. Christos James and Elpiniki D. Student, U. Salonika, Greece, 1976, U. Copenhagen, Denmark, 1976; BA, Montclair State U., 1977; JD, Calif. Western Sch. Law, 1981; diplomate, Rutgers U., 1992. Bar: N.J. 1982, U.S. Dist. Ct. N.J. 1982, N.Y. 1989, U.S. Supreme Ct. 1989. Law sec. to Hon. James F. Madden Superior Ct., Hackensack, NJ, 1981-82; sr. assoc. Klinger, Nicolette, Mavroudis & Honig, Hackensack, 1982-85; ptnr. Montecallo & Diktas, Hackensack, 1985-86, Biagiotti, Marino, Montecallo & Diktas, Hackensack, 1986-89, Diktas & Habeeb, North Bergen, NJ, 1989-94, Diktas Gillen, 1995-99, Diktas Schandler Gillen, Cliffside Park, NJ, 2000—. Asst. counsel Bergen County, 1986-87; atty. zoning bd. adjustment Borough of Cliffside Park, 1986-94, Borough atty., 1994—, Borough Administrator, 2007-; planning bd. Borough of Ridgefield, NJ, 1987-99, 2001-2002, borough atty., 2000-01; borough atty., Bogota, NJ, 1989-91, Fairview, NJ, 1994-95; bd. edn. atty., Bogota, 1992-95; labor counsel Bergen County, NJ, 1990-2001; atty. planning bd. City of Garfield, NJ, 1994-2003; atty., sec. Garfield Redevel. Agy., 2002—; spl. tax coun., Fairview, NJ, Creskill, NJ, 2003—; adj. prof. law Montclair (NJ) State U., 1988-2001. Editor lead articles Calif. Western Internat. Law Jour., 1980-81. Campaign dir. Kingman for Senate Com., Bergen County, N.J., 1983; mcpl. coord. Kean for Gov. campaign, 1985; asst. treas. Arthur F. Jones for Congress, 9th Congl. Dist., 1986. Mem. Bergen County Bar Assn., Order of Am. Hellenic Edn. Progressive Assn., Phi Alpha Delta (parliamentarian Campbell E. Beaumont chpt. 1978-81), Sons of Pericles (5th dist. gov. 1976-77, supreme gov. 1977-78). Greek Orthodox. Home: 445 Oncrest Ter Cliffside Park NJ 07010-2814 Office: Diktas Schandler Gillen 596 Anderson Ave Cliffside Park NJ 07010-1831 Office Phone: 201-943-8020. Personal E-mail: cdiktas@weblawnj.net.

DILBECK, CHARLES STEVENS, JR., real estate company executive; b. Dallas, Dec. 2, 1944; s. Charles Stevens Sr. and Betty Doris (Owens) D.; 1 child, Stephen Douglas; m. Carolyn Jane DeBoer, Sept. 4, 1994. BS, Wichita State U., 1968; MS, Stanford U., 1969, postgrad., 1970-71. Engr. United Tech. Ctr., Sunnyvale, Calif., 1971-72; cons. Diversicom, Inc., Santa Clara, Calif., 1972-73; engr. Anamet Labs., San Carlos, Calif., 1973-75; cons. real estate investment Cert. Capital Corp., San Jose, Calif., 1975-82; pvt. practice in real estate, San Jose, 1981—; prin. Am. Equity Investments, San Jose, 1982—. Mem. Los Gatos (Calif.) Rent Adv. Com., 1988. Mem. Nat. Apt. Assn., San Jose Real Estate Bd., Tri-County Apt. Assn., Gold Key Club, Tau Beta Pi (pres. 1968), Sigma Gamma Tau. Republican. Avocation: ocean yacht racing. Office: Am Equity Investments 301 Alta Loma Ln Santa Cruz CA 95062-4620

DILCHER, DAVID LEONARD, paleobotany educator, researcher; b. Cedar Falls, Iowa, July 10, 1936; m. Katherine Swanson, 1961; children: Peter, Ann. BS in Natural History, U. Minn., 1958, MS in Botany, Geology and Zoology, 1960; postgrad., U. Ill., 1960-62; PhD in Biology, Geology, Yale U., 1964; participant OTS course field dendrology, Costa Rica, 1968; doctorate (hon.), Lyon U. 1, France, 2007. Teaching asst. U. Minn., Mpls., 1958-60, U. Ill., Urbana, 1960-62, Yale U., New Haven, Conn., 1962-63, Cullman-Univ. fellow, 1963-64, instr. biology, 1965-66; NSF postdoctoral fellow Senckenberg Mus., Frankfurt am Main, Fed. Republic of Germany, 1964-65; asst. prof. botany Ind. U., Bloomington, 1966-70, assoc. prof., 1970-76; Guggenheim fellow Imperial Coll., Univ. London, 1972-73; assoc. prof. geology Ind. U., Bloomington, 1975-77, prof. paleobotany, 1977-90, adj. prof. biology, adj. prof. geology, 1990—; grad. rsch. prof. Fla. Mus. Natural History, U. Fla., Gainesville, 1990—. Panel mem. for systematic biology program, NSF, 1977-79, panel mem. for selecting NATO postdoctoral fellow, 1982, mem. adv. com. Earth Sys. History, 1997-2000, bd. mem. on earth scis. and resources NRC, 2001-04; vis. lectr. to People's Republic of China Nat. Acad. Sci. com. on scholarly communications with China, 1986; corr. mem. Senckenberg Mus., Frankfurt, Fed. Republic Germany, 1989; hon. prof. Nanjing Inst. Geology and Paleontology, Acad. Sinica, China, 1998—, Jilin U., Changchau, China, 2001—; adj. prof. biology U. Tenn., Martin, 2000—; hon. prof., vice chmn. sci. com. rsch. ctr. paleontoloty and stratigraphy Jilin U., Changchun, China, 2001—; bd. dirs. Smithsonian Inst., 1998-2006; prof. Rsch. Found. Univ. Fla., 2004—. Author: (with D. Redmon, M. Tansey and D. Whitehead) Plant Biology Laboratory Manual, 1973, 2d edit., 1975; editor: (with Tom Taylor and Theodore Delevoryas) Plant Reproduction in the Fossil Record, symposium vol., 1979; (with T. Taylor) Biostratigraphy of Fossil Plants: Successional and Paleoecological Analysis, 1980; (with William L. Crepet) Origin and Evolution of Flowering Plants, Symposium Volume, 1984; (with Michael S. Zavada) Phylogeny of the Hamamedidae, symposium vol., 1986; (with Patrick S. Herendeen) Advances in Legume Systematics Part 4, The Fossil Record, 1992; mem. edilt. bd. Taxon, 2004—; contbr. over 200 articles to profl. jours. Mem. utilities bd. City of Bloomington, 1974-76; ruling elder First Presbyn. Ch. Bloomington, 1975-77; bd. dirs. United Campus Ministries, 1971-72, Smithsonian Mus. Natural History, 1998—; mem. coun. Monroe County United Ministries, 1975-77. Dist. Vis. Rsch. scholar U. Adelaide, Australia, 1981, 88; Vis. Rsch. scholar Birbal Sahni Palaeonbot. Inst., Lucknow, India, 1992; grantee Sigma Xi, 1961-62, 66, Ind. U., 1967-68, Orgn. Tropical Studies, 1971, Travel grantee Ind. U., 1968, 71, 77, 80, Rsch. grantee NSF, 1966-89, 96—, Amax Coal Found., 1980-81, NATO Coop, 1991-93; Eaton-Hooker fellow, 1963, Cullman-Univ. fellow, 1963-64, Guggenheim fellow, Giessen, Fed. Republic of Germany, 1972-73, Ind. U., 1972-73, Brit. Mus. Natural History, London, 1988-89; recipient Tracey M. Sonneborn award for disting. rsch. and excellence in tchg. Ind. U., 1978-88, Bot. Soc. Am. Merit award, 1991, Birbal Sahni Found. award, 1998, U. Fla. Rsch. Found. Professorship award, 2004-06, Outstanding Palaeobotanist award Indian Palaeontological Soc., 2005, Mt. Changbai Friendship cup, Jilin Province China, 2006; hon. prof. Honzhou U., China, 2007. Fellow Ind. Acad. Sci.; mem. NAS, AAAS, Bot. Soc. Am. (chmn. paleobot. sect. 1974, sec.-treas. 1975-77, rep. to jour. editl. bd. 1978-79, jour. editl. bd. 1981-82, conservation com. 1978-81, chmn. conservation com. 1981, 82, program dir. 1982-84, exec. bd. 1982-91, sec. 1984-88, pres.-elect 1988-89, pres. 1989-90), Paleontol. Soc., Paleontol. Assn., Internat. Orgn. Paleobotany (N.Am. rep. 1975-81, v.p. 1987-93), Assn. Tropical Biology, Am. Inst. Biol. Scis., Am. Assn. Stratigraphic Palynologists, Internat. Assn. Angiosperm Paleobotany (pres. 1977-80), Geol. Soc. Am. (com. on collection and collecting 1978-85), Ky. Acad. Scis., Senckenberg Natur Mus. und Forschungsgeshellshaft Frankfurt am Main (corr. mem. 1990), Sigma Xi (pres.-elect Ind. chpt. 1985-86, pres. 1986-87). Office: U Fla Dept Natural Sci Fla Mus Natural History PO Box 117800 Gainesville FL 32611-7800 Business E-Mail: dilcher@flmnh.ufl.edu.

DI LELLA, ALEXANDER ANTHONY, biblical studies educator; b. Paterson, NJ, Aug. 14, 1929; s. Alessandro and Adelaide (Grimaldi) Di L. BA, St. Bonaventure U., NY, 1952; S.T.L., Cath. U. Am., Washington, DC, 1959, PhD, 1962; S.S.L., Pontifical Bibl. Inst., Rome, 1964. Entered Franciscan Order, Roman Catholic Ch., 1949; ordained priest, 1955. Lectr. O.T. and bibl. Greek Holy Name Coll., Washington, 1964-67; asst. prof. Semitic lang. Cath. U. Am., 1966-68, assoc. prof., 1968-76, assoc. prof. Bibl. studies, 1976-77, prof., 1977-92, Andrews-Kelly-Ryan disting. prof. bib. studies, 1992—2004, prof. emeritus, 2004—. Adj. prof. O.T., Washington Theol. Union, 1969-72; vis. prof. O.T., Theol. Faculty of Sicily, 2005; mem. Rev. Standard Version Bible Com., 1982—; chmn. bd. of control New Am. Bible, 1988—. Assoc. editor, translator New American Bible, 1965-87; editor New Revised Standard Version Bible Cath. Edit., 1993; author: The Hebrew Text of Sirach: A Text-Critical and Historical Study, 1966, The Book of Daniel, 1978, Proverbs in the Old Testament in Syriac According to the Peshitta Version, 1979, The Wisdom of Ben Sira, 1987, Il Libro di Daniele (1-6), 1995, (7-14), 1996, Daniel: A Book for Troubling Times, 1997, El libro de Daniel (1-6), 2000, (7-14), 2001; contbr. articles and revs. to scholarly and popular publs. Mem. instnl. rev. bd. Dubroff Eye Ctr., Silver Spring, Md., 1982-94; cancer care continuum group Washington Hosp. Ctr., 1995-96. Am. Sch. Oriental rsch. fellow, 1962-63; Guggenheim fellow, 1972-73. Mem. Soc. Bibl. Lit. (pres. Chesapeake Bay region 1972-73), Cath. Bibl. Assn. (pres. 1975-76, del. Coun. on Study of Religion 1971-72) Home: Curley Hall Cath U Am Washington DC 20064-0001 Office: Cath U Am Rm 420 Caldwell Hall Washington DC 20064 Business E-Mail: dilella@cua.edu. *Most of my adult life I have been a student of Biblical languages and literatures,* *interpretation and theology. Teaching, research and publications enable me to convey to others the value of the Bible as a primary document of Judaism and Christianity and as a significant factor in Western culture and civilization.*

DILENGE, THOMAS, lawyer; BA summa cum laude, Fordham Univ., 1988; JD, Univ. Va., 1993. Bar: Va. 1993, D.C. 1994. Spl. asst. Office of the Mayor, New York, 1988—89; spl. asst. rsch. Giuliani for Mayor campaign, New York, 1989; assoc. Mayer Brown & Platt, 1993—97; dep. chief counsel, oversight & investigations Com. on Energy & Commerce, U.S. Ho. Rep., Washington, 1997—2003; chief counsel & policy dir. Select Com. on Homeland Security, U.S. Ho. Rep., Washington, 2003—. Mem.: Order of the Coif. Republican. Roman Catholic. Office: Select Committee Homeland Security 176 Ford HOB Washington DC 20515

DILEO, TONY, professional sports team executive; m. Anna DiLeo; children: T.J., Max. Student, Tenn. Tech U.; grad., LaSalle U. Coach men's and women's teams West Germany, 1979—90; Nat. Coach West German fedn., 1981—85; with Phila. 76ers, 1990—, asst. coach, dir. scouting, dir. player pers., 1999—2003, sr. v.p. basketball ops., asst. gen. mgr., 2003—. Author: European Basketball Handbook, 1984. Recipient Coach of Yr., West Germany, 1987. Office: Phila 76ers 3601 S Broad St Philadelphia PA 19148*

DILER, RASIM SOMER, psychiatrist, researcher; s. Kemal and Leman Cerrcel Diler; m. Hacer Aytas, Sept. 3, 1995; 1 child, Simge Su. MD, Istanbul U., Turkey, 1993. Cert. specialist in child and adolescent psychiatry Child and Adolescent Psychiatry Bd., 1999, Crisis Mgmt. in Psychiatry U. of Pitts., 2000, eye movement desensitization and reprocessing Internat. Soc. EMDR, 2001, Autism Diagnostic Interview Turkish Soc. of Child and Adolescent Psychiatry, 2003, Treatment of Pervasive Developmental Disorders Turkish Soc. of Child and Adolescent Psychiatry, 2003. Asst. prof. psychiatry Cukurova U. Faculty of Medicine, Child and Adolescent Psychiatry, Adana, Turkey, 1999—2003, assoc. prof. psychiatry, 2003—. Dir. outpatient svcs. Cukurova U. Faculty of Medicine, Child and Adolescent Psychiatry, Adana, Turkey, 1999—, co-dir. and supr. of rsch. studies, 1999—, co-dir. residency tng., 1999, web dir. of ofcl. child psychiatry univ. homepage, 1998—; bd. mem., Ctr. Hearing and Communication Disabilities Cukurova U. Faculty of Medicine, Adana, Turkey, 2003—; site coord. tech. and rsch. cooperation Xi'an U. (China) and Cukurova U., 2003—; bd. mem. and cons. Gov. Oguz Kaan Koksal Residential Treatment Ctr.(the first juvenile residential treatment ctr. of Adana city), Turkey, Adana, Turkey, 2002—; bd. mem. Bridging Ea. and Western Psychiatry Orgn., Pisa, Italy, 2002—. Co-dir. Commn. Planning Core Edn. For Grad. Students, Adana, Turkey, 2002—03; cons., bd. mem., and policy maker State Coun. for Preventing Youth from Harmful Environment and Activities, Adana, Turkey, 2001—03; coord. Commn. Planning Core Edn. For Grad. Students, Adana, Turkey, 2002—03. Named Hon. Prof. and Prof. Emeritus, Xi'an (China) Jiaoton U., 2003—; recipient Young Minds in CNS (Ctrl. Nervous Sys.) Award in Depressionand Anxiety category, AstraZeneca, 2001; fellow XII. World Congress of Psychiatry, World Psychiat. Assn., 2002; Disting. Rsch. grantee, Sci. and Tech. Rsch. Coun. of Turkey (TUBITAK), 2003—. Mem.: AAAS, Pa. Med. Soc. (licentiate), Bridging Ea. and Western Psychiatry (corr.; site coord. 2001), Turkish Psychiatry Soc. (life), Turkish Soc. of Child and Adolescent Psychiatry (life). Achievements include research in Pharmacotherapy and changes in regional cerebral blood flow in children with obsessive compulsive disorder; Emotional and behavioral problems in migrant children; Efficacy of Risperidone in Children with Autism; Efficacy of paroxetine in children with obsessive compulsive disorder; discovery of presence of selective serotonin reuptake inhibitor discontinuation syndrome in children; selective serotonin reuptake inhibitors induced mania in children with obsessive compulsive disorder; an atypical antipsyhotic agent which may be used adjunctively for obsessions, can induce obsessive compulsive symptoms in children; research in efficacy of moclobemide in young adolescents with major depressive disorder. Avocations: music, dance, travel, international cuisine, movies. Office: Cukurova U Faculty Medicine Balcali 01130 Adana Turkey also: 3811 O'Hara St Pittsburgh PA 15213 Home Phone: +90.322.2348918; Office Phone: +90.322.3386060/3246. Personal E-mail: dilerrs@yahoo.com.

DILG, JOSEPH CARL, lawyer; b. Dallas, Apr. 1, 1951; s. Millard John and Helen Mary (Gill) D.; m. Alexandra Gregg, Aug. 5, 1972; children: Helen Lane, Mary Saunders. BA in economics, So. Meth. U., 1973; JD with high honors, U. Tex., 1976. Bar: Tex. 1976. Assoc. Vinson & Elkins, Houston, 1976—83, ptnr., 1983—2002, mng. ptnr., 2002—. Editor U. Tex. Law Rev., 1976. Trustee U. Tex. Law Sch. Found.; dir. Bus. Com. for the Arts Inc., Greater Houston Partnership, Ctrl. Houston Inc. Named Outstanding Editor, U. Tex. Law Rev., 1976; named one of The Top 100 Tex. Super Lawyers, Tex. Monthly, 2003—04. Mem. ABA, Tex. Bar Assn., Houston Bar Assn., Order of Coif. Office: Vinson & Elkins LLP 3401 First City Tower 1001 Fannin St Ste 2300 Houston TX 77002-6760 Business E-Mail: jdilg@velaw.com.

DILIBERTO, RICHARD ANTHONY, JR., lawyer; b. Hazleton, Pa., July 19, 1961; s. Richard A. Sr. and Marija (Vukcevich) D.; m. Faith Ann Petrovich, Sept. 4, 1982. BS in Edn. cum laude, Bloomsburg U. of Pa., 1982; JD cum laude, Widener U., Wilmington, Del., 1986. Bar: Del. 1986, Pa. 1987, N.J. 1987, U.S. Dist. Ct. Del. 1987. Law clk. Superior Ct. Del., Wilmington, 1986-87; ptnr. Young, Conaway, Stargatt & Taylor, Wilmington, 1987—. Adj. prof. paralegal program Widener U., 1987-90; rep. Del State House of Reps., 1992-2002. Contbr. articles to profl. jours. Coach basketball YMCA, softball, 1994—. Recipient Advocacy award ATLA, Outstanding Alumni Svc. award Widener U. Law Sch., 1999. Mem. ABA, Del. Bar Assn. (Disting. Legis. award 1999), Del. Trial Lawyers Assn. (pres. 2005—). Roman Catholic. Home: 311 Winterthur Ln Newark DE 19711-4136 Office: Young Conaway Stargatt & Taylor LLP PO Box 391 Wilmington DE 19899-0391 Office Phone: 302-571-6657. Fax: (302) 576-3290. E-mail: rdiliberto@ycst.com.

DILL, ELLEN RENÉE, minister, educator, writer; b. Detroit, Jan. 2, 1949; d. Clarence Lorenzo and Melvin Elizabeth (Knowles) D.; divorced; children: Christopher Edward Brown, Crystal Elizabeth Brown. BA, Nazareth Coll. Mich., 1972; MDiv, Garrett Evang. Sem., Evanston, Ill., 1979; postgrad., Northwestern U., Evanston, Ill., 1979-82; DMin, Chgo. Theol. Sem., 1999. Lic. ministry United Meth. Ch. 1974, ordained 1985, lic. missionary Meth. Ch. 2003, ordained 2003. Teaching asst. Head Start St. Agnes Ch., Detroit, 1966-68; tchr. Eastside Vicariate Sch., Detroit, 1972-77; pastor St. Luke United Meth. Ch., Chgo., 1980-82; assoc. pastor First United Meth. Ch., Chgo., 1982-84; pastor Clair-Christian United Meth. Ch., Chgo., 1984-88, Community United Meth. Ch., Markham, Ill., 1988-90, Woodlawn United Meth. Ch., Chgo., 1990-93, Immanuel United Meth. Ch., 1993-99; pastor United Campus Ministry Winona (Minn.) State U., 1995-99; tchr. Tracy McGregor Elem. Sch., Detroit, 1999—2005, webmaster, 2000—05. Condr. seminar on women in ministry Garrett Evang. Sem., 1981, condr. seminar on ch. and soc., 1980, instr. continuing edn. seminar for clergy in adminstrn., 1987; bd. dirs. So. Dist. Bd. Ordained Ministry, Bd. Ch. Bldg. Location; mem. So. Dist. Coun. on Ministries, So. Dist. Strategy Com.; former chmn. No. Ill. Conf. Bd. Edn., So. Dist. Bd. Edn.; former asst. chmn. bd. edn. United Meth. Ch.; mem. Detroit Conf. Elders Orders, 1985; min. Internat. Missionary Ch., 2003; asst. spiritual dir. Walk to Emmaus, 1988-90, 92, spiritual dir. men's walk, 1991; mem. No. Ill. Conf. Commn. on Status and Role of Women, 1991-93, United Meth. Found., U. Chgo., 1990-93; mem. monitoring com. Ill. Conf. Configuration; mem. planning com. Western Dist. Lab. Sch.; invocation Chgo. City Coun. meetings, 1990, 91, 93; chairperson Minn. Conf. Commn. on Religion and Race, 1995; mem. Minn. Conf. Coun. on Ministries, 1995—; mem. Ethics Minority Concerns Commn., Minn. Conf., 1993—; mem. med. ethics com. Cmty. Meml. Hosp., Winona, Minn., 1995—; active Winona Area Ministerium, 1995—, Winona Cultural Diversity Task Force, 1997—; bd. mem. Project Fine, 1997—; adj. prof. Winona State Univ., Minn., 1998—. Co-author: Teachers Guide: Two Hundred Years of American Methodism, 1981; editorial advisor The Christian Ministry jour., 1987—; webmaster Tracy McGregor Elem. Sch., 2000-05; contbr. articles to profl. jours. Bd. dirs. Carroll M. Felton Jr. Housing Found., 1992-93; asst. dean Pembroke Inst., 1992; bd. dirs. Austin Christian Law Ctr., 1983-93, Child Serve Cmty. Coun., Chgo., 1984-88, Garrett-Evang. Sem., 1978; area chair Mayor's Com. to Keep Detroit Beautiful, 1965. Recipient citation Mayor's Com. To Keep Detroit Beautiful, 1966, citation for excellence in journalism Mich. Press Assn., 1978; Hartman scholar, 1979; Dempster Grad. fellow, 1980, Hartman fellow, 1981. Mem. NAFE, Nat. Assn. Bus. and Profl. Women, Internat. Platform Assn., Black United Meths. for Ch. Renewal (citation for svc. 1982, planning com. jurisdictional meeting, bd. dirs.), Clergy Cluster, Ecumenical Ministerial Assn., Women of the 90s (exec. com. 1992-93), Minn. Coun. of Chs. (bd. dirs. 1994-99), Mpls. Initiative Against Racism, Mpls. Coun. Ch. (ministries divsn. 1993-95), Northeast Optimist Club of Detroit, Mich. Reading Assn. Avocations: reading, sewing, teaching, writing, studying. Office: 3151 Soaring Gulls Dr Unit 1019 Las Vegas NV 89128 Home Phone: 702-465-9054. *In my life I have found that the power of evil is impotent when confronted by that which is good.*

DILL, ELLIS HAROLD, university dean; b. Pittsburg County, Okla., Dec. 31, 1932; s. Harold and Mayme Doris (Ellis) D.; m. Cleone June Granrud, Sept. 12, 1953; children: Michael Harold, Susan Marie. AA, Grant Tech. Jr. Coll., 1951; BS in Civil Engring, U. Calif., Berkeley, 1954, MS in Civil Engring, 1955, PhD, 1957. Asst. prof. to prof. aeros. and astronautics U. Wash., 1956-77, chmn. dept. aeros. and astronautics, 1976-77; dean engring. Rutgers U., New Brunswick, NJ, 1977-98, univ. prof., 1998—. Mem. Soc. Natural Philosophy, Am. Acad. Mechanics. Achievements include research, numerous publications on mechanics of solids. Home: 436 Brentwood Dr Piscataway NJ 08854-3608 Office: Rutgers U Coll Engring 98 Brett Rd Piscataway NJ 08854-8058

DILL, GARY A., academic administrator; BA in Philos. and Religion, Houston Bapt. U.; PhD in Philosophy, U. Tex.; Doctorate in Ministry, Southern Theological Seminary; MDiv., Princeton Theol. Seminary. Pastor Price of Peace Ch. Brethren, South Bend, Ind., 1975—79; adj. staff Bethany Theological Seminary, 1978—82; pastor York Ctr. Ch. Brethren, Lombard, Ill., 1979—82; sr. v.p., prof. Schreiner Coll., Kerrville, Tex., 1991—96; pres. McPherson Coll., 1997—2002, Coll. S.W., N.Mex., 2002—. Former chmn. Tex. Arts and Crafts Ednl. Found.; mem. bd. dirs. Ptnrs. in Parenting Edn. Bd.; dir. cmty. svc. Noon Rotary Club, Kerrville. Office: Coll SW 6610 Lovington Hwy Hobbs NM 88240*

DILL, KENNETH AUSTIN, pharmaceutical chemistry educator; b. Oklahoma City, Dec. 11, 1947; s. Austin Glenn and Margaret (Blocker) D. SB, SM, MIT, 1971; PhD, U. Calif., San Diego, 1978. Fellow Damon Runyon-Walter Winchell Stanford (Calif.) U., 1978-81; asst. prof. chemistry U. Fla., Gainesville, 1981-82; asst. prof. pharm. chemistry and pharmacy U. Calif., San Francisco, 1982-85, assoc. prof., 1985-89, prof., 1989—, co-dir. program in quantitative biology, assoc. dean rsch. Sch. Pharmacy, 2001—. Adj. prof. pharmaceutics U. Utah, 1989—. Contbr. numerous sci. articles to profl. publs.; patentee in field. Recipient Hans Neurath award Protein Soc., 1998; PEW Found. scholar. Fellow AAAS, Am. Phys. Soc. (physics policy coun. 2002—), Biophys. Soc. (nat lectr. 1996, pres. 1998, Disting. Svc. award, 2007); mem. Am. Chem. Soc., Protein Soc. Office: Univ Calif San Francisco 600 16th St MC 2240 San Francisco CA 94158-2517

DILL, WILLIAM RANKIN, college president; b. Sewickley, Pa., Aug. 18, 1930; s. Frederick Hayes and Caroline (Rankin) D.; m. Jean McLeod, June 13, 1953; children: Jens McLeod, Holly Ruth, Harrison Rankin, Cynthia Wightman. AB, Bates Coll., 1951, LLD (hon.), 1987; MS, Carnegie Inst. Tech., 1953, PhD, 1956; postgrad., U. Oslo, 1953-54; LHD (hon.), Babson Coll., 1991. Faculty mem. Carnegie-Mellon U., Pitts., 1955—65; program dir. edn. R & D IBM, White Plains, NY, 1965-70; dean Grad. Sch. Bus. Adminstrn., NYU, NYC, 1970-80, U.S.-Chinese Nat. Ctr. for Mgmt. Devel., Dalian, China, 1980-81; pres. Babson Coll., Wellesley, Mass., 1981-89; dir. Office of Global Enterprise U. So. Maine, Portland, 1989-91, cons., 1991-94; pres. Anna Maria Coll., 1995-96, Boston Arch. Ctr., 1996-97, trustee, 2005—06; bd. dirs. Maine Coll. Art, Portland, 1999—2005, pres., 2005—06, trustee, 2007—. Overseer Boston Architectural Ctr. Author: The New Managers, 1962, The Carnegie Tech. Management Game, 1964, The Organizational World, 1973, Running the American Corporation, 1978, Planning in the US and USSR, 1978. Fulbright scholar, 1953-54; recipient Disting. Achievement award Carnegie-Mellon U., 1989. Fellow AAAS; mem. Phi Beta Kappa, Sigma Xi, Delta Sigma Rho, Beta Gamma Sigma. Unitarian Universalist. Home: 25 Birch Ln Cumberland Foreside ME 04110-1225 Office: Maine Coll Art 97 Spring St Portland ME 04101 E-mail: wdill1@maine.rr.com.

DILLARD, ANNIE, writer; b. Pitts., Apr. 30, 1945; d. Frank and Pam (Lambert) Doak; m. R.H.W. Dillard, 1965 (div.); m. Gary Clevidence, 1980 (div.); 1 child, Cody Rose; stepchildren: Carin, Shelly; m. Robert D. Richardson, Jr., 1988. BA, Hollins Coll., 1967, MA, 1968. Contbg. editor Harper's Mag., NYC, 1974-81, 83-85; scholar-in-residence Western Wash. U., Bellingham, 1975-78; disting. vis. prof. Wesleyan U., 1979-83, adj. prof., 1983—, writer-in-residence, 1987—98, writer emeritus, 1998—, bd. dirs. Writers Conf., 1984—, chmn., 1991—. Fellow Calhoun Coll., Yale U., New Haven, Conn.; Phi Beta Kappa orator Harvard-Radcliffe U., 1983; mem. U.S. writers del. UCLA US.-Chinese Writers Conf., 1982; mem. U.S. cultural del. to China, 1982; bd. dirs. The New Press, Key West Writers Conf., Wesleyan Writers Conf., Key West Literary Seminars; mem. usage panel Am. Heritage Dictionary. Author (poems): Tickets for a Prayer Wheel, 1974, 3d edit., 2002, Pilgrim at Tinker Creek, 1974 (Pulitzer prize for gen. non-fiction 1975, Best Fgn. Book Pub. in France 1990), Holy the Firm, 1978, Living by Fiction, 1982, Teaching a Stone to Talk, 1982, Encounters with Chinese Writers, 1984, An American Childhood, 1987 (Nat. Book Critics award finalist 1987), The Writing Life, 1989 (English-speaking union Amb. Book award 1990), The Living, 1992, The Annie Dillard Reader, 1994, Mornings Like This, 1995, For the Time Being, 1999 (Maurice Coindreau prize 2001); editor: (with Robert Atwan) Best Essays, 1988; (with Cort Conley) Modern American Memoirs, 1995. Mem. Nat. Com. on U.S.-China Rels., 1982—, St. Mary's Soup Kitchen, Key West, Fla.; bd. dirs. Milton Ctr., Authors League Fund, Key West Literary Seminars, Wesleyan Writers Conf. Recipient N.Y. Presswomen's award for excellence, 1975, Wash. Gov.'s award for contbn. to lit., 1978, Appalachian Gold medallion U. Charleston, 1989, Found. award St. Botolph's Club, 1989, History Maker award Hist. Soc. Western Pa., 1993, Conn. Gov.'s award in the arts, 1993, Milton Ctr. prize, 1994, Campion award Am. Mag., 1994, Am. Acad. Arts and Letters award in Lit., 1998; grantee NEA, 1980-81, Guggenheim Found., 1985-86. Mem. NAACP, Soc. Am. Historians, Authors Guild, Am. Acad. Arts and Letters, Key West Volleyball Assn.,Phi Beta Kappa. Democrat. Address: c/o Timothy Seldes Russell & Volkening 50 W 29th St New York NY 10001-4227

DILLARD, DEAN INNES, English language educator, academic administrator; b. Melvern, Kans., Aug. 13, 1947; s. Alva Everett and Dorothy Marie (Whitney) D. BS in Edn., Emporia State U., Kans., 1969, MA, 1975, postgrad., 1977, Ft. Hays State U., Hays, Kans., 1980. Tchr. English, Unified Sch. Dist. 379, Clay Center, Kans., 1969-70; tchr. English and social studies Unified Sch. Dist. 208, WaKeeney, Kans., 1972-84; instr. English, Neosho County C.C., Chanute, Kans., 1984—, chair divsn. liberal arts, 1996-99, interim v.p. acad. and student affairs, 1997-98, 99-00, faculty senate pres., 2004—06. Fine arts task force Neosho County C.C., Chanute, 1990-91. With U.S. Army, 1970-71. Mem.: MLA, VFW (life), Nat. Acad. Advising Assn., Neosho County C.C. Educators Assn., Kans. Assn. Tchrs. English (exec. bd. 1981—84), Assn. Lit. Scholars and Critics (life), Nat. Coun. Tchrs. English, Kans. Assn. Scholars, Nat. Assn. Scholars, Assembly on Lit. for Adolescents (life), Vietnam Vets. Am., Kans. Acad. Advising Network, Chanute Lions Club (zone chmn. 1988—90), Am. Legion, Kappa Delta Pi. Republican. Home: 732 S Washington Ave Chanute KS 66720-2713 Office: Neosho County C C 800 W 14th St Chanute KS 66720-2639 Office Phone: 620-431-2820 235.

DILLARD, JOHN MARTIN, lawyer, pilot; b. Long Beach, Calif., Dec. 25, 1945; s. John Warren and Clara Leora (Livermore) D.; m. Patricia Anne Yeager, Aug. 10, 1968; children: Jason Robert, Jennifer Lee. Student, U. Calif., Berkeley, 1963-67; BA, UCLA, 1968; JD, Pepperdine U., 1976. Bar: Calif. 1976. Instr. pilot, Norton AFB, Calif., 1973-77; assoc. Magana, Cathcart & McCarthy, LA, 1977-80, Lord, Bissell & Book, LA, 1980-85; of counsel Finley, Kumble, Wagner, 1985-86, Schell & Delamer, 1986—94, Law Offices of John M. Dillard, 1985—, mediator, arbitrator, 1994—; v.p., gen. counsel, dir. Resort Aviation Svcs., Inc., Calif., 1988—93; mng. ptnr. Natkin & Weisbach, Calif., 1988—89; arbitrator Orange County Superior Ct. Atty. settlement officer U.S. Dist. Ct. Ctrl. Dist. Calif.; trained mediator Straus Inst. Active Am. Cancer Soc.; bd. dirs. Placentia-Yorba Linda Ednl. Found., Inc. Capt. USAF, 1968-73, Vietnam. Mem. ATLA (aviation litigation com.), Am. Bar Assn. (aviation com.), Orange County Bar Assn., Fed. Bar Assn., L.A. County Bar Assn. (aviation com.), Century City Bar Assn., Internat. Platform Assn., Res. Officers Assn., Orange County Com. of 100, Sigma Nu. Home: 19621 Verona Ln Yorba Linda CA 92886-2858 Office: 313 N Birch St Santa Ana CA 92701-5263 Office Phone: 714-953-9936. Personal E-mail: leeegal1@aol.com. Business E-Mail: dillardlawcal@aol.com.

DILLARD, MARILYN DIANNE, property manager; b. Norfolk, Va., July 7, 1940; d. Thomas Ortman and Sally Ruth (Wallerich) D.; m. James Conner Coons, Nov. 6, 1965 (div. June 1988); 1 child, Adrienne Alexandra Dillard Coons (dec.). Studied with, Alexandra Danilova, Russia, 1940—49; student with honors, UCLA, 1958—59; BA in Bus. Adminstrn. with honors, U. Wash., Seattle, 1962. Modeling-print work Harry Conover, NYC, 1945; ballet instr. Ivan Novikoff Sch. Russian Ballet, 1955; model Elizabeth Leonard Agy., Seattle, 1955-68; mem. fashion bd., retail worker Frederick & Nelson, Seattle, 1962; retail worker I. Magnin & Co., Seattle, 1963-64; property mgr. Kirkland, Wash., 1961—; antique and interior designer John J. Cunningham Antiques, Seattle, 1968-73; owner, interior designer Marilyn Dianne Dillard Interiors, Seattle, 1973—. Rsch. bd. advisors Am. Biog. Inst., Inc., 1990—. Author: (poetry) Flutterby, 1951, Spring Flowers, 1951; contbr., asst. chmn. (with Jr. League of Seattle) Seattle Classic Cookbook, 1980-83. Charter mem., pres. Children's Med. Ctr., Maude Fox Guild, Seattle, 1965—, Jr. Women's Symphony Assn., 1967-73, "200+1" Org., 1967-70, Virginia Mason Med. Ctr. Soc., 1990—, Nat. Mus. of Am. Indian, Smithsonian Instn., 1992—; mem. Seattle Jr. Club, 1962-65, 97—; mem. Friends of the Pike Place Market (saved the market from demolition), 1971; bd. dirs. Patrons N.W. Civic, Cultural and Charitable Orgns., chmn. various coms., Seattle, 1976—, prodn. chmn., 1977-78, 84-85, auction party chmn., 1983-84, v.p. party/prodn., 1984-85, exec. com., 1984-85, chmn. bd. vols., 1990-91, adv. coun., 1991—; mem. U. Wash. Arboretum Found. Unit, 1966-73, pres., 1969; bd. dirs. Coun. for Prevention Child Abuse-Neglect, Seattle, 1974-75; bd. dirs., v.p., mem. coms. Seattle Children's Theatre, 1984-90, asst. in lighting main stage plays, 1987-93, adv. coun., 1993—2004, asst. in lighting main stage plays Bathhouse Theatre, 1987-90; adv. bd. N.W. Asian Am. Theatre, 1987-2001, Co-Motion Dance Co., 1991—; organizer teen groups Episcopal Ch. of Epiphany, 1965-67; provisional class pres. Jr. League Seattle, 1971-72, next to new shop asst. chmn., 1972-73, bd. dirs., admissions chmn., 1976-77, exec. v.p., exec. com., bd. dirs. 1978-79, sustaining mem., 1984—; charter mem. Jr. Women's Symphony Assn., 1967-73; mem. Seattle Art Mus., 1975-90, Landmark, 1990—, Corp. Coun. for Arts, 1991-2003; founding dir. Adrienne Coons Meml. Fund, 1985, v.p. 1985-92, 95—, pres. 1992-95; mem. steering com. Heart Ball Am. Heart Assn., 1986, 87, auction chmn., 1986; mem. steering com. Bellevue Sch. Dist. Children's Theatre, 1983-85, pub. rels. chair, 1984, asst. stage mgr., 1985; mem. Hist. Seattle Preservation and Devel. Authority, 1997—; mem. Eastlake Cmty. Coun., 1997—; mem. Steamship Virginia V. Found., 1997—; mem. Floating Homes Assn., Seattle, 1999—; mem. Queen Anne Hist. Soc., 2000—; com. chmn. Rep. Precinct, 2000; mem. Kirkland Downtown on the Lake Orgn., 1999—; apptd. City of Kirkland Downtown Strategic Planning Action Com., 2001—; mem. City of Kirkland Transit Ctr. location com., 2001-03. Named Miss Greater Seattle, 1964; honored for leadership in the arts Jr. League of Seattle, 2002; charter mem. Nat. Cowgirl Hall of Fame, 2002. Mem. U. Wash. Alumnae Assn. (life), Pacific N.W. Ballet Assn., Progressive Animal Welfare Soc., Associated Women U. Wash.(student coun. 1962), Husky Honeys (U. Wash. rep. 1961-62, chair fashion bd. U. Wash. 1961-62, Sr. Honor Woman award U. Wash. 1961-62), Seattle Tennis Club. Republican. Episcopalian. Avocations: needlepoint, horseback riding, theater, travel, antique restoration. Home and Office: 2053 Minor Ave E Seattle WA 98102-3513 Office Phone: 206-328-0322.

DILLARD, MICHAEL E., lawyer; b. Shreveport, La. BA summa cum laude, So. Meth. Univ., Dallas, 1979, JD cum laude, 1982. Bar: Tex. 1982. Co-chair firmwide mergers and acquisitions practice group and head of corp. practice Houston Akin Gump Strauss Hauer & Feld LLP, Houston, 1989—, ptnr. Mng. editor Jour. of Air Law and Commerce, 1981—82. Mem.: Dallas Bar Assn., State Bar of Tex. (former sec., venture capital com. of Bus. Law Sect.), Phi Beta Kappa, Order of Coif. Office: Akin Gump Strauss Hauer & Feld LLP 44th Fl 1111 Louisiana St Houston TX 77002-5200 Office Phone: 713-220-5821. Office Fax: 713-236-0822. Business E-Mail: mdillard@akingump.com.

DILLARD, RODNEY JEFFERSON, real estate executive; b. Short Hills, NJ, Jan. 1, 1939; s. Albert Jefferson and Anne E. (Willingham) D.; m. Anne Palfrey Lanston, June 10, 1961 (div.); children: Courtney Lanston, Carter Jefferson. BA, Rollins Coll., 1961. Account exec. A.M. Kidder Co., NYC, 1961-62; v.p. Previews, Inc, Palm Beach, Fla., 1963-76; pres., chmn. bd. Illustated Properties, Inc., Palm Beach, Fla., 1976-79; sr. v.p., bd. dirs. Sotheby's Internat. Realty Corp., Palm Beach, Fla., 1979-91; pres. John's Island Real Estate Co., Vero Beach, Fla., 1991-95, vice chmn., 1995-97; pres. The Dillard Investment Corp., Palm Beach, Fla., 1996, Illustrated Properties Internat. Inc., 1998—. Mem. Bath and Tennis Club (Palm Beach), Spouting Rock Club (Newport, R.I.), The Travellers Club (Paris). Office: Illustrated Properties Real Estate Inc 249 Royal Palm Way Palm Beach FL 33480 Personal E-mail: rodneyipi@aol.com. Business E-Mail: rdillard@ipintl.com.

DILLARD, STEPHEN C., lawyer; b. Tyler, Tex., Nov. 1, 1946; BA, Baylor U., 1968, JD, 1971. Bar: Tex. 1971. Ptnr. Fulbright & Jaworski LLP, Houston, 1978—, chair, firmwide litig. dept., 2004—, mem. exec. com. Named a Tex. Super Lawyer, Tex. Monthly Mag., 2003, 2004, 2005, 2006. Fellow: Am. Bd. Trial Advs. (adv.), Internat. Assn. Def. Counsel, Am. Coll. Trial Lawyers (life), Tex. Bar Found. (life); mem.: ABA, Houston Bar Assn., Tex. Assn. Def. Counsel, State Bar Tex., Phi Alpha Delta (v.p. 1984—87). Office: Fulbright & Jaworski LLP 1301 McKinney St Ste 5100 Houston TX 77010-3031 Office Phone: 713-651-5507. Office Fax: 713-651-5246. Business E-Mail: sdillard@fulbright.com.

DILLARD, SUZANNE, interior designer, actress; d. Jerome Wallace and Mary Mae (Price) Sorenson; m. Warren Marcus Dillard; 1 child, Jeremy Blake. Student, Tex. A&M U., 1961—65; BS, U. Tex., 1965; student, Pepperdine U., 1974, UCLA, 1977-78. Interior designer Pepperdine U., Malibu, Calif., 1982—2005, exec. bd. dirs. Ctr. Arts, 1993—2006; cons., interior design Neptune and Thomas, Architects, Pasadena, Calif., 1979—; pres. Suzanne Dillard Interiors, Beverly Hills, Calif., 1984—. Prin. on camera designer TV pilot, Dream House, Forecast Group Prodns., 1983; speaker in field. Actor: Cattle Call, 2006, Harbinger, 2006. Treas. Nat. Arts Assn., LA, 1982—83, benefit chair, 2001; pres. Fine Arts aux. Assistance League So. Calif., LA, 1984; patron, sponsor, prodn. chmn. The Footlighters, LA, 1992—93, pres., 1992—, League for Children, 1991—93, benefit chair, 2002; pres. Achievement Awards Coll. Scientists, 1994—96; bd. dirs. Ctr. for Arts, Pepperdine U.; pres. Freedoms Found., 1998—2000, 2004—. Mem.: NATAS (Acad. Emmy Blue Ribbon panel 2001—05), AFTRA, SAG (nominating com. Acad. awards 2003—05), Internat. Found. for Ednl. and Performing Arts (adv. bd.), Acad. TV Arts and Scis., Delta Delta Delta (pres. L.A. chpt. 1970—72, pres. sleighbell 1993—94). Republican. Mem. Ch. of Christ. Avocations: piano, voice, painting, reading, skiing. Personal E-mail: suzannedillard@hotmail.com.

DILLARD, W. THOMAS, lawyer; b. Dothan, Ala., Nov. 28, 1941; s. William T. and Gladys (Harris) D.; m. Susan Jean Jakuboski, Oct. 26, 1974. BA, U. Tenn., 1963, JD, 1964. Bar: Tenn. 1965; cert. criminal trial specialist Nat. Bd. Trial Advocacy. Asst. U.S. atty. Dept. Justice, Knoxville, Tenn., 1967-76, chief asst. U.S. atty., 1978-83, U.S. atty., 1981, Tallahassee, 1983-86; ptnr. Ritchie, Fels, and Dillard, P.C., Knoxville, 1987—; U.S. magistrate, 1976-78. Adj. prof. East Tenn. State U., Knoxville, 1979-80, U. Tenn. Coll. Law, 1993—; instr. Knoxville Police Acad., 1979-82, Nat. Inst. Trial Advocacy, Chapel Hill, N.C. and Boulder, Colo., 1985-2001, U. Tenn. Trial Advocacy Program, 1992-2001 mem. Tenn. Bar Profl. Stds. com.; pres. Fed. Def. Svcs., 2001; mem. Tenn. Supreme Ct. Adv. Commn. on Rules of Practice and Procedure. Deacon Presbyn. Ch., Knoxville, 1972-76, elder, 1978-82, 88-91, 95-98, 2000-03; mem. Mayor's Commn. on Police; mem. Leadership Knoxville, 1998; bd. dirs. Helen Ross McNabb Ctr. Fellow Am. Coll. Trial Lawyers, Tenn. Bar Found.; mem. ABA, Am. Judicature Soc., Knoxville Young Lawyers (pres. 1972-73), Nat. Assn. Criminal Def. Lawyers, Tenn. Assn. Criminal Def. Lawyers (bd. dirs.), Nat. Assn. Former U.S. Attys. (bd. dirs.), Knoxville Bar Found. (bd. govs.). Avocations: reading, hiking, travel. Home: 8667 Ellijay Way Strawberry Plains TN 37871 Office: Ritchie Dillard & Davies PC 606 W Main St Knoxville TN 37902-2617 Home Phone: 865-933-9649; Office Phone: 865-637-0661. E-mail: dillard@rddlawfirm.com.

DILLARD, WILLIAM, II, department store chain executive; b. 1945; married. Grad., U. Ark.; MBA, Harvard U. With Dillard Dept. Stores, Little Rock, 1967—, dir., 1968—, exec. v.p., 1973-77, pres. and COO, 1977—98, CEO, 1998—, chmn., 2002—. Nat. adv. bd. JPMorganChase & Co., Dallas Region adv. bd.; dir. Acxiom Corp. Office: Dillard Dept Stores Inc 1600 Cantrell Rd Little Rock AR 72201-1110*

DILLE, JOHN ROBERT, retired physician; b. Waynesburg, Pa., Sept. 2, 1931; s. Charles Emanuel and Ruth Emma (South) D.; m. Joan Marie Sirtosky, Dec. 17, 1955 (wid. Mar. 1996); children: Paul Andrew, John Alan. BS, Waynesburg Coll., Pa., 1952; MD, U. Pitts., 1956; M in Indsl. Health, Harvard U., Canbridge, Mass., 1960. Diplomate Am. Bd. Preventive Medicine. Intern Akron City Hosp., 1956-57; resident in aerospace medicine USAF Sch. Aerospace Medicine, San Antonio, 1960-62; program adv. officer FAA Civil Aeromed. Rsch. Inst., Oklahoma City, 1961-64; western region flight surgeon FAA, LA, 1965; chief FAA Civil Aeromed. Inst., US Dept. Transp., Oklahoma City, 1966-87, ret., 1987; med. dir. Okla. Dept. Corrections, Oklahoma City, 1990-93. Assoc. prof. U. Okla., 1961-98, dir. tng. residency in aerospace medicine, 1967-72; state surgeon Okla. Army N.G., 1990-91; surveyor Nat. Commn. on Correctional Health Care, 2000-04. Assoc. editor: Ag Pilot Internat. mag., 1980-98, Conservation Aeronautics mag., 1989-92, Above All mag., 1992; mem. editorial bd. Aviation, Space and Environ. Medicine, 1987-94; contbr. chpts. to textbooks and articles to profl. jours. With USAF, 1957-59; col. M.C., US Army N.G., 1976-91. Recipient Meritorious award William A. Jump Found., 1968; named Army N.G. Flight Surgeon of Yr. 1987, Master Flight Surgeon, 1987. Fellow: Am. Coll. Preventive Medicine (regent 1974—77), Aerospace Med. Assn. (mem. exec. coun. 1978—81, chmn. history and archives com. 1982—90, chmn. sci. program com. 1985, 1st v.p. 1990—91, pres. 1992—93, mem. exec. coun. 1993—98, chmn. nominating com. 1997—98, Theodore C. Lyster award 1978, Harry G. Moseley award 1987, Armstrong lectr. 1997); mem.: Civil Aviation Med. Assn., Am. Soc. Aerospace Medicine Specialists, Res. Officers Assn. (state surgeon Okla. dept. 2002—07), Am. Air Mail Soc. (bd. dir. 1990—92), Soc. US Army Flight Surgeons (bd. govs. 1990—92, Order Aeromed. Merit), Internat. Acad. Aviation and Space Medicine, Mil. and Hospitaller Order St. Lazarus of Jerusalem (knight hospitaller, commandery of the Midwest 2007—), Sigma Xi, Nu Sigma Nu. Presbyterian. Home: 335 Merkle Dr Norman OK 73069-6429 Personal E-mail: jrobtdille@aol.com.

DILLE, ROLAND PAUL, college president; b. Dassel, Minn., Sept. 16, 1924; s. Oliver Valentine and Eleanor (Johnson) D.; m. Beth Hopeman, Sept. 4, 1948; children: Deborah, Martha, Sarah, Benjamin. BA summa cum laude, U. Minn., 1949, PhD, 1962, LHD (hon.), 1995. Instr. English U. Minn., 1953-56; asst. prof. St. Olaf Coll., Northfield, Minn., 1956-61; asst. prof. English Calif. Lutheran Coll., Thousand Oaks, Calif., 1961-63; mem. faculty Moorhead (Minn.) State U., 1964-94, pres., 1968-94; ret., 1994. Author: Four Romantic Poets, 1969; contbr. numerous articles and revs. to profl. jours. Treas. Am. Assn. State Colls. and Univs., 1977-78, bd. dirs., 1978-80, chmn., 1980-81; mem. Nat. Coun. for Humanities, 1980-86; vice-chair Commn. on Higher Edn., North Cen. Assn., 1989-91, chair, 1991-93. With inf. AUS, 1944-46. Disting. Svc. to Humanities award given by Minn. Humanities Commn. named in his honor; named one of 100 most effective Am. coll. pres., 1987. Mem. Phi Beta Kappa. Home: 516 9th St S Moorhead MN 56560-3519 Office: Minn State U Moorhead 11th St S Moorhead MN 56560-9980 Office Phone: 218-477-2612. Business E-Mail: dille@mnstate.edu.

DILLEHAY, TOM D., anthropologist, educator; Disting. prof., chair anthropology dept. Vanderbilt Univ., Nashville; and prof. extraordinaire Universidad Austral de Chile. Author: 15 books, 200 refereed jour. articles. Fellow: Am. Acad. Arts & Scis.; mem.: Am. Anthropological Assn. Office: Dept Anthropology Vanderbilt Univ Sta B #356050 2301 Vanderbilt Pl Nashville TN 37235 Business E-Mail: tom.d.dillehay@vanderbilt.edu.*

DILLENBERG, JACK, dean; b. NYC, Nov. 22, 1945; m. Marianna Dillenberg. BA in Psychology, Tulane U., 1967; DDS, NYU, 1971; MPH, Harvard Sch. Pub. Health, 1978. Dental officer USN, 1971—73; dentist Southbury (Conn.) Tng. Sch., 1973-75; mgr. dental clinic, Jamaica, 1975-77; vis. lectr. Cape Cod C.C., 1978-84; tutor dept. population scis. Harvard Sch. Pub. Health, 1978-81; cons. Mass. Dept. Mental Health, 1978-84; pvt. practice Beacon St. Dental Assocs., Brookline, Mass., 1980-84; instr. Harvard Sch. Dental Medicine, 1980-84; cons. Pan Am. Health Orgn., 1993-97; acting dir. Ariz. Dept. Health Services, 1993—94, dir., 1994—97; area health officer west area L.A. County Dept. Health Services, Santa Monica, Calif., 1997-99; assoc. dir. pub. health programs Calif. Dept. Health Services; dean Ariz. Sch. Dentistry and Oral Health A.T. Still U. of Health Sciences, 2001—; pres. Dillenberg & Friends Health Services Consulting. Cons. Dillenberg & Friends, Inc., 1979-84; pres. Dentanomics, Inc., 1984-86; pub. health cons. World Bank, 1978-99. Recipient Presdl. Citation ADA, 1992, Nat. Fluoridation award CDC, 1991, Alumni award of Merit, Harvard Sch. Pub. Health, 1997; named Marketer of the Yr., Am. Mktg. Assn., 1997, CEO of Yr., Am. Pub. Adminstrn. Assn., 1997. Mem. ADA, Assn. State and Territorial Dental Dirs., Ariz. Pub. Health Assn. Office: AT Still U Health Scis Ariz Sch Dentistry & Oral Health 5850 East Still Cir Mesa AZ 85206 E-mail: jdillenberg@dhs.co.la.ca.us.

DILLENBURG, CAROLYN EVA LAUER, retired secondary school educator; b. Adair County, Iowa, May 13, 1934; d. Harvey Francis and Lorna Orilda (Gilbert) Lauer; m. Dale Everett Dillenburg, May 29, 1954; children: Candace Dee Brotherton, Shari Sue Eivins, Jeffrey Dale Dillenburg. AA, Creston Jr. Coll., 1954; BS, Iowa State Coll., 1956; MSEd., Drake U., 1968. Cert. secondary tchr. Engr.'s aide GM, Indpls., 1955; math. and sci. tchr. Afton Ind. Sch., Iowa, 1957—58, Runnells Ind. Sch., Iowa, 1958—59; math. and English tchr. Winterset Cmty. Sch., Iowa, 1959—61; math. and sci. tchr. O-M Cmty. Sch., Orient, Iowa, 1961-63; math. and English tchr. Creston Cmty. Sch., Iowa, 1964—65; math. tchr. Lenox Cmty. Sch., Iowa, 1968—94; ret., 1994. Adj. math. tchr. Southwestern CC, Creston, 1977-81; curriculum coord. Green Valley AEA 14 Schs., 1994-2006. Treas. Iowa Town and Country YWCA, southwest Iowa, 1981-2001; pres. Creston YWCA Coun., 1981—2001; bd. trustees Greater Regional Med. Ctr., 1997—. Mem. NEA (life), SW Uniserv (bd. dirs. 1988-92, mem. contract advancement cadre 1992-94, mem. ret. tchrs. cadre 1994—2000), Iowa State Edn. Assn. (life, ret., mem. standing com. for ret. tchrs. 1994—2000), Creston Area Ret. Sch. Personnel Assn., P.E.O., Iowa Town and Country YWCA (treas. 1981-2001), Elzivirs Women's Reading Group, Delta Kappa Gamma, Pi Mu Epsilon, Psi Chi. Congregationalist. Avocations: antiques, travel. Home: 1392 150th St Creston IA 50801-8406 Business E-Mail: cdillenburg@aea14.k12.ia.us.

DILLER, BARRY, Internet company executive; b. San Francisco, Feb. 2, 1942; s. Michael and Reva (Addison) D.; m. Diane Von Furtstenburg, Feb. 2, 2001 Student, UCLA, 1959. Asst. to v.p. programming ABC, 1966—68, exec. asst. to v.p. in programming & dir. feature films, 1968—69, v.p. feature films & program devel, 1969—71, v.p. feature films & movies of week, 1971-73, v.p. prime time TV, 1973-74; chmn. Paramount Pictures Corp., 1974-84; pres. Gulf & Western Entertainment and Comm. Group, Simon and Schuster, Inc., Madison Sq. Garden Corp., SEGA Enterprises, Inc., 1983-84; chmn., CEO Twentieth Century Fox Film Corp., TCF Holdings, LA, 1984-85, Fox, Inc., 1984-92, QVC Network, Inc., 1992-94, Silver King Comm., Inc., 1995-98, Home Shopping Network, Inc., 1996-98, IAC / InterActiveCorp (formerly USA Networks, Inc., USA Interactive), NYC, 1995—; chmn. Expedia, Inc., 2005—; co-CEO Vivendi Universal, 2002—03. Bd. dirs. Washington Post Co., 2000-, Coca-Cola Co., 2002-, Brightcove, Inc., 2005-, FCC Adv. Com. on Advanced TV Svcs., N.Y. Pub. Libr., Conservation Internat., Mus. TV & Radio, Calif. Inst. Arts, Acad. Arts and Scis. Found., Ticketmaster Online-Citysearch, Inc., Seagram Co. Ltd., Channel 13/WNET; bd. councilors Sch. Cinema-TV U. So. Calif.; exec. bd. med. scis. UCLA; bd. trustees NYU.; dean's coun. Tisch Sch. Art; mem. adv. bd. Ctr. Health Comm. Harvard U. Sch. Pub. Health. Mem. Pres. Export Coun. Named an 50 Who Matter Now, CNNMoney.com Bus. 2.0, 2007; named one of Forbes' Richest Ams., 2006, 50 Who Matter Now, CNNMoney.com Bus. 2.0, 2006. Office: IAC / InterActiveCorp 152 W 57th St Fl 42 New York NY 10019-3310*

DILLER, EDWARD DIETRICH, lawyer; b. Pandora, Ohio, Aug. 7, 1947; s. Hiram D. and Selma G. (Warkentin) D.; m. Karen Esmonde, June 1, 1968; children: Jason, Anna. BA, Bluffton Coll., 1969; postgrad., U. Oreg., 1969-70; JD cum laude, Harvard U., 1976. Assoc. Taft, Stettinius & Hollister, Cin., 1976-84, ptnr., 1984—, chmn. dept. bus. & fin., 1998—. Chmn. Gen. Conf. Coun. on Higher Edn., 1990-93, 96-2001, vice chmn., 1993-94; lectr. numerous seminars; mem. women's initiative adv. bd. Deloitte & Touche, Cin., 2000—. Tchr. Mennonite Ctrl. Com., Frankfield, Jamaica, 1970-73; chmn. edn. integration com. Mennonite Ch. USA, 1997-2001; trustee Mental Health Svcs. East, 1977-85, Bluffton Coll., 1979-2002, mem. exec. com., 1987-2002, chmn. bd., 1991-2002; mem. Family Svc. of Greater Cin. Area, 1989-96, chmn., 1992-95; trustee Habitat for Humanity (Southwestern Ohio and No. Ky. affiliate), 1995-2000; trustee Working in Neighborhoods, 1991-94, Dan Beard Coun. Boy Scouts of Am., 1996-, chmn. 2003-04, Leadership Cin. Alumni Assn., 2001-02; mem. Leadership Cin. Class XVI; trustee Found. Family Svc., 1997-, chmn. 2002—; bd. dirs. Cin. Mus. Ctr., 2005—, Cin. Playhouse, 2005—. Mem. Ohio State Bar Assn., Cin. Bar Assn., Ohio Harvard Law Sch. Assn. Office: Ste 1800 425 Walnut St Cincinnati OH 45202-3923 Office Phone: 513-357-9313. Business E-Mail: diller@taftlaw.com.

DILLER, ELIZABETH E., architect, educator, artist; b. Poland, 1954; m. Ricardo Scofidio. B in Arch., Cooper Union Sch. of Arch., 1979. Ptnr. Diller & Scofidio (now Diller Scofidio & Renfro), NYC, 1979—; assoc. prof. arch. design Princeton U., NJ, 1990—, prof. arch. Works include Inst. of Contemporary Art, Boston, Seagrams, NY, Mus. of Art & Tech., NY, Blur Bldg. (Progressive Architecture Design award), media pavillion for Swiss EXPO 2002, designed viewing platform for Ground Zero, NYC, Brasserie Restaurant, NY (James Beard Found. award for Best New Restaurant Design), Slither, Gifu, Japan, Loophole, Mus. Contemporary Art, Chgo., 1992, Apparatus Drawing, Mus. of Modern Art, NY, 1993, Case#00-17164, New Mus., 1993, Dysfunction, Ctr. d'Art Contemporian de Castres, France, 1993, Desiring Eye, I' dentity and Difference, Triennale, Milan, 1994, Pelts, Thaddeus Ropac Gallery, Paris, France, 1997, Non-Place, San Francisco Mus. Modern Art, 1997, Slow House, At the End of the Century: One Hundred Years of Architecture, Mus. Contemporary Art, LA, 1998, The American Lawn: Surface of Everyday Life, Canadian Centre for Architecture, Montreal, 1998, Public Faces/Private Places, Pusan Internat. Arts Festival, Korea, 1998, His/Her Bathroom, Thomas Healy Gallery, NY, 1998, Dress Code, Landesmuseum, Linz, Austria, 1998, (permanent collections) Travelogues, Internat. Arrivals Terminal 4, JFK Airport, NY, (installation) The Desiring Eye: Reviewing the Slow House, Gallery MA, Tokyo, 1992, Master/Slave, Fondation Cartier, Paris, Inter-Clone Hotel, Ataturk Airport for Istanbul Biennial, 1997, (dance collaborations with the Lyon Ballet Opera of France and Charlerol/Danses of Belgium (touring exhbn.) EJM1:Man Walking at Ordinary Speed and EJM2: Inertia, 1998, (web project) Refresh, Dia Art Found., (video installation) Pageant, Johannesburg Biennial & Rotterdam Film Festival, 1997, (permanent installation) X,Y, Kobe, Japan, 1997, (multi-media work for stage in collaboration with Builders Assn.) Jet Lag, 1998 (Obie award for Creative Achievement), (pub. art commn., permanent video marques) Jump Cuts, United Artists Cineplex, San Jose, Calif., (collaborative dance work with Charlerol/Danses) Moving Target, (collaborative theater work with Dumb Type and Hotel Pro Forma) Business Class, Copenhagen Cultural Capital, (interactive video installation) Indigestion, Barbican Art Gallery, London, Walter Phillips Gallery, Banff, Canada, Biennial Nagoya, Japan, 1997, (electronic project) Subtopia, ICC Gallery, Tokyo, 1997, and several others, installations commissioned by Mus. of Modern Art, Whitney Mus., New Mus. of Contemporary Art, Walker Art Ctr., Minn., Cartier Found., Palais des Beaux-Arts Brussels, and Gallery Ma Tokyo, works are in the permanent collections of Mus. of Modern Art, Mus. Modern Art San Francisco, Fond Nat. d'Art Contemporain, several FRACs in France, Musee de la Mode in Paris, and many private collections, co-pub. with Ricardo Scofidio Back to the Front: Tourisms of War, FRAC Basse-Normandie, 1994, Flesh: Architectural Probes, Princeton Architectural Press, 1995, Blur: The Making of Nothing, Abrams, 2002. Recipient Chrysler award for Innovation in Design, 1988—89, MacArthur Found. award, 1999, Brunner prize in Arch., AAAL, 2003, MacDermott award for Creative Achievement, MIT; Graham Found. Fellowship, 1998—99, Chgo. Inst. for Architecture and Urbanism Fellowship. Office: Princeton U Sch Architecture 5116 Architecture Princeton NJ 08544-0001 also: Diller Scofidio & Renfro 36 Cooper Sq New York NY 10003 Office Phone: 212-260-7971.*

DILLER, PHYLLIS (PHYLLIS ADA DRIVER DILLER), actress, writer; b. Lima, Ohio, July 17, 1917; d. Perry Marcus and Frances Ada (Romshe) Driver; m. Sherwood Anderson Diller, Nov. 4, 1939 (div. Sept. 1965); children: Peter III, Sally, Suzanne Diller Mills, Stephanie Diller Waldron, Perry; m. Warde Donovan, Oct. 7, 1965 (div. July 1975). Student, Sherwood Music Conservatory, Chgo., 1935-37, Bluffton Coll., Ohio, 1938-39; DHL, Nat. Christian U., 1973; PhD (hon.), Bluffton Coll., 1993. (Best TV Comedienne award TV Radio Mirror 1965); Author: Phyllis Diller Tells All About Fang, 1963, Phyllis Diller's Housekeeping Hints, 1966, Phyllis Diller's Marriage Manual, The Complete Mother, The Joys of Aging and How to Avoid Them, 1981, (with Richard Buskin) Like A Lampshade in a Whorehouse: My Life in Comedy, 2005; Accompanied Bob Hope entertainment group to, South Vietnam, Christmas, 1966, symphony appearances soloing on piano.; Theatrical prodns. include Dark at the Top of the Stairs, 1961, Wonderful Town, 1962, Happy Birthday, 1963, Hello, Dolly!, 1970, Everybody Loves Opal, 1972, What Are We Going to Do With Jenny, 1977, Nunsense, 1989, The Wizard of Oz, 1990-92; numerous appearances TV and radio, concerts, supper clubs and hotels, 1955-; producer, writer: Phyllis Diller Shows, 1963, 64; rec. artist, Verve Records, Columbia Records, pres., BAM Prodns., Ltd., from 1965, PhilDil Prodns., Ltd., 1966-; motion pictures include Eight on the Lam, 1967, The Private Navy of Sergeant O'Farrell, Hungry Reunion, 1981, Pink Motel, 1983, The Nutcracker Prince, 1990, The Boneyard, 1991, The Perfect Man, 1993, The Silence of the Hams, 1994, A Bug's Life (voice), 1998, The Debtors, 1999, Everything's Jake, 2000, The Last Place on Earth, 2002, Hip! Edgy! Quirky!, 2002, West From North Goes South, 2002, Motocross Kids, 2004, West From North Goes South, 2004, Forget About It, 2005; star: TV series The Pruitts of Southampton, 1966-67, Beautiful Phyllis Diller Show, 1968-69 (Recipient honors including Star of Year award Nat. Assn. Theatre Owners), The Bold and the Beautiful (recurring role), 1995-, Titus, 2002; video appearance: How to Have a Moneymaking Garage Sale, 1987. Recipient Minuteman award U.S. Treasury Dept., Disting. Service citation Ladies Aux. VFW, Woman of Year award Variety Club Women Balt.; Golden Apple Hollywood Women's Press Club, 1967, Woman of Year award St. Louis chpt. Nat. Bus. and Profl. Women's Club, 1971; named hon. mayor Brentwood, Calif., 1971; Hon. life mem. San Francisco Press and Union League Club; named Walk of Fame Star on Hollywood Blvd., 1975, Hon. Chair for Outstanding Svc. to Calif. State U. at Los Angeles, Friends of Music Scholarship Auction, 1982; recipient Doctor of Comedy award Kent State U., 1980, AMC Cancer Rsch. Ctr. Humanitarian award, 1981, Child-Help USA Woman of Yr. award, 1989; City of Los Angeles Proclamation of Phyllis Diller Week Mayor Tom Bradley, 1979; named to Ohio's Hall of Fame, 1981; Commonwealth scholar, 1964. Office: c/o The Sychin Co Ste 208 12747 Riverside Dr Valley Village CA 91607-3303

DILLIN, ANDREW, medical researcher, educator; b. Reno, Nev. B in Biochemistry, U. Nev., Reno; PhD in Molecular and Cellular Biology, U. Calif., Berkeley. Postdoctoral rsch. fellow U. Calif., San Francisco; with Salk Inst. for Biol. Studies, La Jolla, Calif., 2002—, Pioneer Develop. chair, assoc. prof. molecular and cell biology lab. Contbr. articles to profl. jours. Recipient Jr. Faculty award, Am. Diabetes Assn., 2004—06, Larry L. Hillblom Jr. Faculty award, 2003—06, Ellison Med. Found. award, 2004—06, McKnight Neuroscience Brain Disorders award, 2007; Damon Runyon-Walter Winchell Postdoctoral Fellowship, Univ. Calif. San Francisco, 1999—2002. Achievements include using the tiny roundworm C. elegans to study the process of aging and age-related diseases. Office: Salk Inst for Biol Studies Molecular and Cell Biology Lab 10010 N Torrey Pines Rd La Jolla CA 92037 Office Phone: 858-453-4100 ext. 1771.*

DILLIN, JOHN WOODWARD, JR., retired editor, reporter; b. Miami, Fla., July 6, 1936; s. John Woodward and Alberta (Thompson) D.; m. Gay Andrews, Oct. 1, 1966 (div. 1988); 1 child, Katherine. BSJ. with honors, U. Fla., 1958, postgrad. in U.S. history, 1961-63. Reporter St. Augustine Record, Fla., 1958, Tampa Tribune, Fla., 1960-61; with Christian Sci. Monitor, 1964—, reporter Boston, 1964-66, corr. Saigon, Vietnam, 1966-67, city editor Boston, 1967-71, corr. Atlanta and Washington, 1971-79, mng. editor for news Boston, 1979-83, nat. polit. corr. Washington, 1983-94, mng. editor Boston, 1994-99, assoc. editor, Washington bur. chief Washington, 1999—, ret., 2001. Mem. advd. bd. UF Florida/Today, 2004—. Served with AUS, 1958-59 Recipient Sigma Delta Chi award for Washington Corr., 1993; named Alumnus of Distinction, Coll. Journalism and Comms., U. Fla., 2002. Christian Scientist. Home: 5525 15th St N Arlington VA 22205-2712 Office: 910 16th St NW Washington DC 20006-2903 Personal E-mail: jdillin7@excite.com.

DILLINGER, SUSAN ALICE, reading specialist; b. Oyster Bay, June 16, 1950; d. Gerard Thomas and Martha Alice Soper; m. Edwin Thaine Dillinger, Nov. 5, 1988. M Curriculum and Instrn., Kans. State U., 1977, M Spl. Edn., 1986. Tchr.'s lic. Kans. State Dept. Edn. Tchr. 2d-6th grade Unified Sch. Dist. 450 Shawnee Heights, Tecumseh, Kans., 1973—83, tchr. spl. edn., 1983—93; title I reading specialist Unified Sch. Dist. 329 Mill Creek Valley, Alma, Kans., 1993—96; tchr. 4-5th grade lang. arts Unified Sch. Dist. 320, Wamego, Kans., 1996—99; title I reading specialist Unified Sch. Dist. 322, Onaga, Kans., 1999—. Exch. tchr. Washburn U., Topeka, 1992—; conf./ inservice presenter, at-risk coord. Unified Sch. Dist. 322, Onaga, 1999—, dist. chairperson comm. curriculum, 2004—, mem. dist. steering com., 2004—; instr. Kans. State U., Manhattan, 2000—, reading specialist, adj. prof.; trainer Kans. Reading First, 2005—. Membership rep. Jr. League, Topeka, 1989—90, vol. trainer, 1990—91. Named to East Asian Studies Tchr. Program, 2003; recipient Curriculum Devel. in Econs., Kans. Bankers' Assn., 1976. Mem.: Delta Kappa Gamma (rec. sec. 1998—99). Republican. Episcopalian. Avocations: travel, raising, training and showing morgan horses, raising bison, volunteering. Home: 17455 Pauling Run Rd Westmoreland KS 66549 Office: USD 322 400 High St Onaga KS 66521 Home Phone: 785-456-9465; Office Phone: 785-889-7101. E-mail: lhdranch@wamego.net.

DILLINGHAM, JOHN ALLEN, marketing professional; b. Kansas City, Mo., Jan. 9, 1939; s. Jay B. and Frances (Thompson) D.; m. Nancy Jane Abbott, Sept. 4, 1965; children: Allen Edwards, William Kemp. AS, Wentworth Mil. Acad., 1958; AB in Polit. Sci., U. Mo., 1961, MS in Pub. Adminstrn., 1962. Br. mgr. Rudy-Patrick divsn. W.R. Grace Co., Mt. Vernon, Ill., 1964-68; pres. Sho-Hawk Industries, Kansas City, Mo., 1968-72; v.p. comml. loans Traders Nat. Bank, Kansas City, 1972-79; sr. v.p. sales and mktg. Garney Constrn. Co., Kansas City, 1979-95; pres., bd. dirs. Jo Dill, Inc., 1985—, Dillingham Enterprises, 1997—. Bd. dirs. Waddell and Read Advisor Funds 1997-00, Inc., Kansas City; chmn. Clay County Indsl. Devel. Authority, 1980-2003, Clay County EDC, 1972-74; adv. bd. for extension U. Mo., 1972-80; cons. CMSU Grad. Sch., Warrensberg, Mo., 1996-97; dir., cons. McDougal Constrn., Kansas City, 1996-97; adv. dir. Northland Bd. United Mo. Bank, 1998—, Synergy Svcs. Trustee Wentworth Mil. Acad., Lexington, 1978-80, 93-00; state chmn. Mo. 4H Found., Columbia, 1985-90; mem. ctrl. governing bd. Children's Mercy Hosp., Kansas City, 1987-92; bd. dirs. Kansas City Conv. and Vis. Bur., 1976-80, Northland Cmty. Fund, Kansas City, 1988-97, Kansas City Sports Commn., 1990-93; treas. Harry S. Truman Scholarship Nat. Alumni Assn., 1979-90; mem., v.p. Kansas City Bd. Police Commrs., 1990-95; chmn. Kansas City Mcpl. Asst. Corp., 1984—, Alex Doniphan Meml. Hwy. Naming, 1998, Naming I635 Harry Darby Meml. Pkwy; hon. co-chair St. Plus X H.S. Capital campaign, 1997-98; coordinating bd. task force on affordability of higher edn. State of Mo., 1999; mem. Nat. 4H Resource Devel. Com., 1990-92, mem., pres. Kansas City Mayor's Fast Forward Commn., 1996—; mem. exec. com. Metro C. C. Found., Kansas City, 1996—; exec. bd. Heart of Am. coun. Boy Scouts Am., 1993-01; 1st bd. dirs. alumni assn. U.S. Command and Gen. Staff Coll., Ft. Leavenworth, Kans., 1993—; dir. DARE of Greater Kansas City, 1995-98, CMSU Found. Warrensburg, 1995-97, Am. Royal, Kansas City, Mo., 1997-03; co-chmn. K.C. Storm runoff campaign, 1998. With U.S. Army, 1964. Recipient Faculty Alumni award U. Mo., Columbia, 1981, Silver Beaver award Boy Scouts Am. Heart Am. coun., 1992, Harry S. Truman Scholarship Appreciation plaque, 1993, Cmty. Svc. award Park Coll., 1993, Pub. Svc. award Ctrl. Mo. State Univ., 1994; named one of 100 Most Influential Kans. Citizens, Ingrams Mag., 1993, Spirit award Kansas City, 1999. Mem. SAR, VFW, Am. Legion, Sons of the Confederate Officers, Decendents of Magna Charta, Plantenegent Soc., Northland C. of C. (Quality of Life award 1990), KC Kings, Gold Coaters (pres. 1979-89), Mt. Vernon Ill. C. of C. (pres. 1968), Native Sons Kansas City (bd. dirs., pres., 1991-92, 98—), Sigma Alpha Epsilon (KC Alumni Assn. pres. 1976, Honor Man 1988, trustee Nat. Found. 1987-93, Nat. Disting. Svc. award 1993). Democrat. Mem. Christian Ch. Avocations: fishing, landscaping, genealogy. Home: 4040 NW Claymont Dr Kansas City MO 64116-1751 Office: 924 Livestock Exch Bldg Kansas City MO 64102 Office Phone: 816-842-5504. Office Fax: 816-842-6803.

DILLINGHAM, LEE, social studies educator; m. Janet Dillingham; children: Rebekah, Bradley. BS in Bible, Phila. Bibl. U., 1989; BS in Edn., Millersville U. Pa., 1993; EdM in Edn., Kutztown U., Pa., 1997. Tchr. and dept. head social studies Pennridge Sch. Dist., Perkasie, Pa., 1993—. Girls' softball coach Pennridge Sch. Dist., Perkasie, Pa., 1997—2003, Crusader team leader, 1999—, ski club dir., 2001—. Sunday sch. supt. First Bapt. Ch. Perkasie, Pa., 2003, youth club leader, 2004—. Mem.: NEA, Alpha Epsilon Lambda. Office: Pennridge Sch Dist 1506 N Fifth St Perkasie PA 18944 Office Phone: 215-258-0946 217.

DILLINGHAM, WILLIAM BYRON, literature educator, author; b. Atlanta, Mar. 7, 1930; s. Cornelius Howard and Emerald (Storey) D.; m. Marion Elizabeth Joiner, July 3, 1952; children: Rebecca Lynn, Judith Ann, Paul Christopher. BA, Emory U., 1955, MA, 1956; PhD, U. Pa., 1961. Instr. Emory U., Atlanta, 1956-62, asst. prof., 1962-66, assoc. prof., 1966-68, prof., 1968-84, chair. dept. English, 1979-82, 85-86, 90-91, Charles Howard Candler prof. Am. lit., 1984-96; prof. emeritus, 1996—. Author: Frank Norris: Instinct and Art, 1969, An Artist in the Rigging, 1972, Melville's Short Fiction, 1977, Melville's Later Novels, 1986, Melville and His Circle: The Last Years, 1996, Rudyard Kipling: Hell and Heroism, 2005; co-author: Humor of the Old Southwest, 1964, 3d edit., 1994, Practical English Handbook, 10th edit., 1996; mem. editl. bd. Nineteenth-Century Lit., 1990-97, South Atlantic Rev., 1986-89, Frank Norris Studies, 1986-94. With US Army, 1950—52. Recipient Fulbright award, U.S. Govt., 1964—65, award of distinction, Emory U., 2000, Disting. Emeritus award, 2004; fellow, Guggenheim Found., 1982—83; Sr. fellow, NEH, 1978—79, Heilbrun Disting. Emeritus fellow, 2002—03. Mem. MLA (mem. adv. coun. Am. lit. sect. 1988-90), Nat. Assn. Scholars, Soc. Lit. Scholars and Critics, Frank Norris Soc., Melville Soc. (pres. 1987), Kipling Soc., Phi Beta Kappa, Omicron Delta Kappa. Home: 1416 Vista Leaf Dr Decatur GA 30033-2012 also: 3258 Esperanza Ave Daytona Beach FL 32118-6231 Business E-Mail: wdillin@emory.edu.

DILLMAN, FREDERICK, information technology executive; BS in Computer Sci., Math., SUNY, Albany; MS in Computer Sci., Rensselaer Poly. Inst., MSEE. Ops. sys., infrastructure developer Unisys Corp., Blue Bell, Pa., mng. prin., sys. integration tech., v.p. tech., architecture, solution devel., chief tech. officer, 2005—. Named one of Top 25 Chief Tech. Officers, InfoWorld mag., 2006. Mem.: IEEE, Phi Beta Kappa. Office: Unisys Corp M/S E8 —108 Unisys Way Blue Bell PA 19424-0001 Office Phone: 215-986-3052.*

DILLMAN, LINDA M., retail executive; b. Ft. Wayne, Ind., June 29, 1956; BS, U. Indpls., 1976. With Hewlett-Packard, 1982—87, Wholesale Club (acquired by Wal-Mart Stores, Inc.), Indpls., 1987—91; application devel. mgr. Wal-Mart Stores, Inc., 1991—97, dir. applications devel., 1997—98, v.p. applications devel., 1998—99, v.p. internat. sys., 1999—2002, sr. v.p., CIO info. sys. divsn., 2002—03, exec. v.p., CIO, 2003—06, exec. v.p. risk mgmt. and benefits adminstrn., 2006—. Bd. trustees U. Indpls., 2005—. Bd. dirs. Northwest Ark. Community Coll. Named one of The Top 50 Most Powerful Women in Bus., Fortune mag., 2003—06. Mem.: Uniform Code Council (bd. mem.). Office: Wal-Mart Stores Inc 702 SW Eighth St Bentonville AR 72716*

DILLON, ADRIAN T., financial executive; BA summa cum laude, Amherst Coll. Sr. economist Eaton Corp., 1979-82, chief economist, 1982-86, mgr. corp. strategy, 1984-86, dir. fin. strategy, chief economist, 1986-88, asst. treas., 1988-91, v.p. planning, 1991-95, v.p., chief fin. and planning officer, 1995-97, exec. v.p., chief fin. and planning officer, 1997—2001; exec. v.p. fin. & adminstrn., CFO Agilent Technologies, Palo Alto, Calif., 2001—. Non-exec. chmn. Verigy Ltd.; bd. dir. Williams-Sonoma Inc. Chmn. Eaton's United Way Campaign, 1993, 94; exec. bd. mem. Boy Scouts Greater Cleve. Coun.; past chmn. bd. trustees Beech Brook; past vice-chmn. WVIZ & WCPN public radio, Cleve.; bd. mem. Castilleja Sch. Mem. Am. Econ. Assn., Conf. Bus. Economists, Coun. Fin. Execs. (mem. conf. bd.); past chmn. Conference Bd. Council of Fin. Executives. Office: Agilent Technologies 395 Page Mill Rd Palo Alto CA 94306*

DILLON, ANDREW PATRICK, dean, library and information science educator; b. Buckinghamshire, Eng., Mar. 19, 1962; came to U.S., 1994; s. Thomas Joseph and Rita Dillon. BA, Univ. Coll. Cork, 1984, MA with 1st class honors, 1987; PhD, Loughborough U., Eng., 1991. Rsch. fellow Loughborough U., 1986-93; vis. prof. Dept. Psychology and Inst. for Study of Human Capabilities Ind. U., Bloomington, 1992—93, assoc. prof. info. sci. & informatics Sch. Libr. and Info. Sci., 1994—2002, dir. Program in Human-Computer Interaction, 2000—02; dean, prof. Sch. Info., U. Tex., Austin, 2002—. Cons. software industry, 1989—. Author: Designing Usable Electronic Text, 1994; editor: Hypertext and Cognition, 1996; editl. bd. mem. Internat. Jour. Human Computer Studies, 1994—, Jour. Digital Info., 1996—; contbr. articles to profl. jours. Grantee European Commn., 1990-93. Mem. AAUP, Assn. Computing Machinery, Am. Soc. Info. Sci. (guest editor jour. 1997), Human Factors Soc. Achievements include design team member for world's first hypertext-based academic journal. Home: 841 E 37th St Austin TX 78705-1805 Office: U Tex at Austin Sch Info SZB 564 1 University Station, D7000 Austin TX 78712-1276 Office Phone: 512-471-3821. E-mail: adillon@ischool.utexas.edu.*

DILLON, COREY, professional football player; b. Oct. 24, 1975; s. Jerline; m. Desiree Dillon; 1 child, Cameron. Student, U. Wash. Football player Cin. Bengals, 1997—2003, New England Patriots, 2004—07. Founder Corey Dillon Youth Found. Named Am. Football Conf. Rookie Yr., NFL Players Assn., 1998; named to NFL Pro-Bowl, 1999—2001, 2004. Achievements include being a member of Super Bowl XXXIX Champion New England Patriots, 2004; holding several rushing records at U. Wash., including single season rushing yards, 1995-1996. Office: c/o New England Patriots 1 Patriot Place Foxboro MA 02035*

DILLON, DAVID ANTHONY, editor, educator; b. Fitchburg, Mass., Aug. 24, 1947; s. John Joseph and Lauretta Irene (Morris) D.; m. Sally Ann Hall, June 5, 1971; children: Christopher, Catherine. BA, Boston Coll., 1963; MA, Harvard U., 1965, PhD, 1972. Asst. prof. So. Meth. U., Dallas, 1970-77; mag. editor D Mag., Dallas, 1978-81; archtl. editor Dallas Morning News, 1983—. Author: Experience and Expression, 1976, Dallas Architecture, 1986, Extending the Legacy: Planning America's Capital in the 21st Century, 1997, The Architecture of O'Neil Ford, 1999; contbg. editor Texas Architect, Landscape Architecture, 1990—, Archtl. Record, 1996—. Loeb fellow Harvard U., 1986-87; NEA Critic's grantee, 1980; recipient AP award for criticism, 1988, 90, 91, 2002. Democrat. Roman Catholic. Home: PO Box 3323 Amherst MA 01004-3323 Office: The Dallas Morning News 508 Young St Dallas TX 75202-4828 Home Phone: 413-256-4858; Office Phone: 214-977-8471. Business E-Mail: ddillon@dallasnews.com.

DILLON, DAVID BRIAN, retail grocery executive; b. Hutchinson, Kans., Mar. 30, 1951; s. Paul Wilson and Ruth (Muirhead) D.; m. Dee A. Ehling, July 29, 1973; children: Jefferson, Heather, Kathryn. BS, U. Kans., 1973; JD, So. Meth. U., 1976. V.p. Fry's Food Stores of Ariz. Inc. div. Dillon Cos. Inc., Phoenix, 1978-79, exec. v.p., 1979-83; v.p. Dillon Cos. Inc. (subs. of Kroger Co.), Hutchinson, 1983-86, pres., 1986-95; exec. v.p. Kroger Co., Cin., 1990-95; chmn. bd. Dillon Cos., Inc. (subs. Kroger Co.), Cin., 1993—95; pres., COO The Kroger Co., Cin., 1995—99, pres., 1999—2000, pres., COO, 2000—03, CEO, 2003—, chmn., 2004—. Bd. dirs. Convergys. Chmn. Leadership Hutchinson, 1986-87, Leadership Kans., 1988; bd. dirs. Bethesda Hosp., Cin., 1996—; trustee U. Kans. Endowment Assn., 1993—, U. Cin. Found., 1997—, Dan Beard coun. Boy Scouts Am., 1996—; bd. advisors U. Kans. Bus. Sch., 1990—. Recipient Brotherhood-Sisterhood award Kans. region NCCJ, 1992. Mem. U. Kans. Alumni Assn., Urban League of Greater Cin. (trustee 1998—), Order of Coif, Sigma Chi (Balfour award 1973). Republican. Presbyterian. Office: The Kroger Co 1014 Vine St Cincinnati OH 45202-1100*

DILLON, DONALD F., data processing executive; Positions through sr. v.p. Nat. Bank of Commerce, Lincoln, Nebr., 1966—76; co-founder, pres. Info. Tech., Inc., 1976—95; vice chmn. Fiserv, Inc., Brookfield, Wis., 1995—2000, chmn. bd., 2000—. Chmn. bd. Info. Tech., Inc. Chmn. bd. trustees Doane Coll.; trustee Univ. Nebr. Office: Fiserv Inc 255 Fiserv Dr Brookfield WI 53045*

DILLON, DONALD WARD, management consultant; b. Wichita, Kans., Jan. 31, 1936; s. Maurice B. and Helen M. (Ward) D.; m. Jacquelyn A. Hicks, Dec. 28, 1958; m. Brenda Marie Rager, July 9, 1983. B.Music Edn., Wichita State U., 1959, M.Music Edn., 1961; D.Music. Edn., U. Okla., 1970. Tchr. music Derby (Kans.) public schs., 1959-66; mem. faculty Southeastern La. U., Hammond, 1968-69; exec. dir. Okla. Arts and Humanities Council, 1969-73; asst. dir. fed.-state partnership Nat. Endowment Arts, Washington, 1973-79, dir. grants office, 1979; exec. dir. Music Educators Nat. Conf., Reston, Va., 1979-83; pres. Don Dillon Assocs. Inc., Dallas, 1983—2006, Dillon Exec. Svcs. LLC, 2006—. Exec. mgmt. cons., bd.dirs. Fund Advancement Music Edn., 1979—. Exec. editor: Music Educators Jour, 1979— , Design for Arts Edn, 1980—; Contbr. articles profl. jours. Bd. dirs. Nat. Com. Arts for Handicapped, 1980—. Mem. Am. Soc. Assn. Execs., Inst. Assn. Mgmt. Cos., Meeting Planners Internat. Methodist. Home: 6204 Trailwood Dr Plano TX 75024-6023 Office: 5960 W Parker R Ste 278 Number 233 Plano TX 75093-7792 Office Phone: 972-625-0110. Business E-Mail: don@dondillon.com.

DILLON (KENOFER), DORIS, artist, historian, educator, interior designer; b. Kansas City, Mo., Dec. 1, 1929; d. Joseph Patrick and Geraldine Elizabeth (Galligan) D.; m. Calvin Louis Kenofer, Aug. 25, 1950; children: Wendy Annette Kenofer Barnes, Bruce Patrick Kenofer. BA in Art, U. Denver, 1950, MA in Art History, 1965. Stewardess United Air Lines, 1950-51; founder, chmn. fine arts dept. Regis Coll., Denver, 1970-74; cons. Sarkisian's Oriental Imports, Denver, 1975-93; curator Van Vechten-Lineberry Taos Art Mus., Taos, N.Mex., 1995. Coord. Inter-Relationship Between the Fine Arts and Science Seminars, 1970-74, Colo. Coun. on Arts & Humanities, Denver, 1980, adv. panel, 1981; permanent consular rep. United Cultural Conv., 2004; dep dir. gen. Internat. Biog. Ctr., Eng., 1997-2004; rsch. bd. advisors Am. Biog. Inst., 1997; lectr. Outer Space and Inner Man, Mensa Chpts., Asheville, NC, 2003; permanent US amb. gen. World Forum; lectr. in field. One-woman shows include Heard Mus., Dallas, 1984, El Pueblo Art Gallery/Mus., Colo., 1970, Nelson Rockefeller Collection, N.Y.C., 1984, Amparo Gallery, Denver, 1985, Veerhoff Gallery, Washington, 1986, Colo. Gallery the Arts Mus., Littleton, 1987, Highland Gallery, Atlanta, 1988, The Earth Sci. Mus., Asheville, N.C., 2003, Turchin Ctr. for Visual Arts, Appalachian State U., Boone, N.C., 2005, two-person shows, E Margo Gallery, N.Y.C., 2003, 2006, exhibited in group shows at U. Denver, 1970, Denver Art Mus., 1970, Denver Mus. Natural History, 1976, U. Colo., 1986, Denver C. of C., 1987, Cadme Gallery, Phila., 1987, Internat. Platform Assn., Washington, 1998—2001, Internat. Exhbn. Gallery, Lisbon, 2000, Turchin Ctr. for Visual Arts, Boone, N.C., 2005, exhibitions include St. Johns Coll., Cambridge, Eng., 2001, Vancouver, Can., 2002, 30th Internat. Congress on Sci., Culture and Arts in the 21st Century, Dublin, Ireland, 2003 (Congress Medallion for distinctive participation), Oxford U., Eng., 2006, Palomar Hotel, Washington, 2007. Named Woman of Yr., ABI, 1998; recipient 1st place drawing award, 4 States Conf. Ctr., Colo., 1960, Salute to Women award, AAUW, 1997, Key award, Excellence Arts, Rsch., Tchg., 1997, Best of Show award, Internat. Platform Assn., Washington, 2001—02, Internat. Visual Artist of the Yr., 2004, Congress medallion, Dublin Congress. Mem.: Denver Art Mus., Asian Art assn. (bd. dirs. 1982—84, treas. 1985), Fine Arts Guild (v.p. 1982), Soc. for Arts, Religion and Contemporary Culture, Nat. Mus. for Women in the Arts (assoc.), Mensa (scholarship juror 1993—94). Avocations: piano, travel, bridge, swimming, hiking. Home and Office: 315 Delphia Dr Brevard NC 28712 Office Phone: 828-883-3623.

DILLON, EVA A., publishing executive; d. Paul Leo Dillon. BA in Music, Va. Commonwealth U., Richmond. With The New Yorker, Harper's Bazaar, Vogue, Adweek; NY regional mgr. TV Guide; NY mgr. YM; advt. dir. Glamour, assoc. pub., 1999; pub. Jane mag. Fairchild Publs., 1999—2005, v.p. Jane mag., 2000—05; v.p., pub. Cookie mag. Condé Nast, 2005—07; pres., group pub. Reader's Digest Mag., NYC, 2007—. Named a Woman to Watch, Advt. Age, 2002. Office: Readers Digest Readers Digest Rd Pleasantville NY 10570 Office Phone: 914-238-1000.*

DILLON, FRANCIS PATRICK, retired human resources specialist; b. Long Beach, Calif., Mar. 15, 1937; s. Wallace Myron and Mary Elizabeth (Land) D.; m. Vicki Lee Dillon, Oct. 1980; children: Cary Randolph, Francis Patrick Jr., Randee, Rick. BA, U. Va., 1959; MS, Def. Fgn. Affairs Sch., 1962; MBA, Pepperdine U., 1976. Traffic mgr., mgr. pers. svcs. Pacific Telephone Co., Sacramento and Lakeport, Calif., 1966-69; asst. mgr. manpower planning and devel. Pan-Am. World Airways, NYC, 1969-71; mgr. pers. and orgn. devel. Continental Airlines, LA, 1971-74; dir. human resources Bourns, Inc., Riverside, Calif., 1974-80; v.p. employee and cmty. rels. MSI Data Corp., 1980-83; pres. Pavi Enterprises, 1983—2003; ret., 2003. Cons. mgmt. Pers. Outplacement Counseling/Sales/Mgmt., fin. svcs., ins., tax oriented strategies, retirement planning for srs., and estate planning, 1983—; pres., CEO Pers. Products & Svcs., Inc., 1984-91; v.p. Exec. Horizons, Inc., 1988-94; sr. profl. svcs. cons. Right Assocs., 1994-97; pres. Meditrans Inc., 1977-80. Bd. dirs. Health Svcs. Maintenance Orgn., Inc., Youth Svcs. Ctr., Inc.; vol. precinct worker. Lt. comdr. USN, 1959-66; asst. naval attaché, Brazil, 1963-65. Recipient Disting. Svc. award Jaycees, 1969, Jack Cates Meml. Vol. of Year award Youth Svc. Ctr., 1977. Mem. ASTD, Assn. Internal Mgmt. Cons., Am. Soc. Pers. Adminstrn., Pers. Indsl. Rels. Assn., Am. Electronics Assn. (human resources com., chmn. human resources symposium), Lake Mission Viejo Assn. (sec., bd. dirs. 1990-94), Mission Viejo Sailing Club, YMCA Bike Club, Mission Viejo Ski Club, Caving Club, Toastmasters (pres. 1966-67), Have Dirt Will Travel, Capo Valley 4 Wheelers. Republican. Episcopalian.

DILLON, JAMES JOSEPH, lawyer; b. Rockville Ctr., NY, June 18, 1948; s. James Martin and Rosemary (Peter) D.; m. Martha Stone Wiske, Mar. 19, 1977; 1 child, Eleanor. BA, Fordham U., 1970; JD, Harvard U., 1975; MA, Oxford U., 1982. Bar: Mass. 1975, U.S. Dist. Ct. Mass. 1976, N.Y. 2000, D.C. 2004, U.S. Ct. Appeals (1st cir.) 1978, U.S. Ct. Appeals (5th cir.) 1986, U.S. Ct. Appeals (6th cir.) 1996, U.S. Ct. Appeals (11th cir.) 1995, U.S. Ct. Appeals (D.C. cir.) 2005, U.S. Supreme Ct. 1990. Assoc. Goodwin Procter LLP, Boston, 1975-83, a ptnr., 1983—2002; ptnr. Foley Hoag LLP, 2002—. Dir. Beth Israel Deaconess Med. Ctr. Obstetrics and Gynecology Found., Inc.; trustee Huntington Theatre Co. Mem. ABA, Boston Bar Assn. Democrat. Office: Foley Hoag LLP 155 Seaport Blvd Boston MA 02210 Home Phone: 617-738-1775; Office Phone: 617-832-1109. Business E-Mail: jdillon@foleyhong.com.

DILLON, JOSEPH FRANCIS, lawyer; b. Bklyn., Oct. 15, 1938; s. Joseph and Elizabeth (Sullivan) D.; m. Pamela Margaret Higbee, May 15, 1966 (div. Feb. 1972); children: Elizabeth Margaret, J. Alexander; m. Diane K. Long, Mar. 17, 1978. BBA, St. John's U., 1960; LLB, U. Va., 1963. Bar: Va. 1963, N.Y. 1964, U.S. Tax Ct. 1965, Mich. 1968, Ohio 1975, Fla. 1983. Tax trial atty. IRS, Washington and Detroit, 1963-68; mem. Raymond & Dillon, P.C., Detroit, 1969-93, Dykema Gossett PLC, Detroit, 1993-97, Giarmarco, Mullins & Horton, P.C., Detroit, 1997—. Adj. prof. taxation U. Detroit Law Sch., 1977-87; spkr., planning chmn. Inst. CLE Programs; mem. magistrates merit selection panel and profl. assistance com. U.S. Dist. Ct. for Ea. Dist. Mich.; mem. U.S. Ct. Internat. Trade. Bd. dirs., exec. com. Met. Ctr. for High Tech., Detroit, 1993-96. Cpl. USAR, 1958-64. Fellow Mich. State Bar Found.; mem. ABA (taxation and internat. sects. 1963—), FBA (officer, pres. Detroit chpt. 1978-82), Mich. Bar Assn. 1988—, (taxation counsel 1979-82, internat. sec. 1990—), Detroit Bar Assn. (taxation com. 1973—), Ohio Bar Assn., Fla. Bar Assn., Am. Judicature Soc., Am. C. of C. in Japan, London Ct. of Internat. Arbitration, Inter-Pacific Bar Assn., Internat. Bar Assn., Greater Detroit-Windsor Japan Am. Soc. (bd. dirs. 1992—, exec. com. 1999—), Japanese Bus. Soc. Detroit Found. (v.p. 1992—), Detroit Regional Chamber (nominating com. for dirs.), French-Am. C. of C. of Detroit (bd. dirs. 1997-2000), Detroit Athletic Club, Lochmoor Club, Vineyards Country Club, World Trade Club, Econ. Club (Detroit). Republican. Roman Catholic. Avocations: golf, squash, skiing. Office: Giarmarco Mullins Horton PC 10th Fl Columbia Ctr 101 W Big Beaver Rd Troy MI 48084-5280 Business E-Mail: jdillon@gmhlaw.com.

DILLON, MARY, food products executive; married; 4 children. Grad., Univ. Ill., Chgo. Dir., product offerings, Snapple Quaker Foods (a PepsiCo subs.), Chgo., 1995—96, sr. v.p., mktg., Gardenburger, 1996—2000, v.p., mktg., Gatorade, Propel Fitness Waters, 2000—02, v.p., mktg., 2002—04, divsn. pres., 2004—05; exec. v.p., global chief mktg. officer McDonald's Corp., Oak Brook, Ill., 2005—. Named one of 50 Women to Watch, Wall St. Jour., 2006. Avocation: running. Office: McDonald's Corp 2111 McDonald's Dr Oak Brook IL 60523*

DILLON, MATTHEW, chef; b. San Bernardino, Calif., 1973; Grad., Seattle Ctrl. Cmty. Coll. Chef Salish Lodge, Snoqualmie, Wash., Supreme, The Herbfarm, Woodinville, Wash., Stumbling Goat Bistro, Seattle; owner, chef Sitka & Spruce, Seattle, 2006—. Named one of Best New Chefs, Food and Wine Mag., 2007. Avocation: foraging. Office: Sitka and Spruce 2238 Eastlake Ave E Seattle WA 98102 Office Phone: 206-324-0662.*

DILLON, MERTON LYNN, historian, educator; b. nr. Addison, Mich., Apr. 4, 1924; s. Henry J. and Cecil Edith (Sanford) D. BA, Mich. State Normal Coll., 1945; MA, U. Mich., 1948, PhD, 1951. Asst. prof. history N.Mex. Mil. Inst., Roswell, 1951-56; asst. prof. Tex. Tech. Coll., Lubbock, 1956-59, asso. prof., 1959-63, prof., 1963-65; asso. prof. Northern Ill. U., DeKalb, 1965-67; prof. Ohio State U., Columbus, 1967-91, prof. emeritus, 1991—. Author: Elijah P. Lovejoy, Abolitionist Editor, 1961, Benjamin Lundy and the Struggle for Negro Freedom, 1966, The Abolitionists, the Growth of a Dissenting Minority, 1974; Ulrich Bonnell Phillips, Historian of the Old South, 1985, Slavery Attacked: Southern Slaves and Their Allies, 1619-1865, 1990; contbr. articles to profl. jours. NEH fellow, 1973-74 Mem.Orgn. Am. Historians, So. Hist. Assn. (bd. editors 1959-63). Home: 10460 Addison Rd Jerome MI 49249-9723 Personal E-mail: mertondillon@yahoo.com.

DILLON, MICHAEL A. (MIKE), lawyer, information technology executive; BA in Comm. and Sociology, U. Calif., San Diego; JD, U. Santa Clara, Calif., 1984. Various positions Sun Microsystems, Inc., Santa Clara, Calif., 1993—99, v.p. products law group, 2002—04, sr. v.p., sec., 2004, gen. counsel, 2004—, exec. v.p.; v.p., gen. counsel ONI Systems Corp., San Jose, Calif., 1999—2002, sec., 2000—02. Office: Sun Microsystems Inc 4150 Network Cir Santa Clara CA 95054 Office Phone: 650-960-1300.*

DILLON, MICHAEL EARL, mechanical engineering executive, educator; children: Bryan Douglas, Nicole Marie, Brendon McMichael. BA in Math., Calif. State U., Long Beach, 1978, postgrad. Registered profl. engr., Ala., Alaska, Ariz., Ark., Calif., Colo., Conn., Del., Fla., Ga., Hawaii, Idaho, Ill., Ind., Iowa, Kans., Ky., La., Md., Maine, Mass., Mich., Minn., Miss., Mo., Mont., Nebr., Nev., N.Mex., NJ, NY, NC, Ohio, Okla., Oreg., Pa., SC, Tenn., Tex., Utah, Va., Wash., W.Va., Wis., Wyo., chartered engr., U.K. Journeyman plumber Roy E. Dillon & Sons, Long Beach, 1967—69, ptnr., 1969—73; field supr. Dennis Mech., San Marino, 1973—74; chief mech. official City of Long Beach, 1974—79; mgr. engr. Southland Industries, Long Beach, 1979—83; v.p. Syska & Hennessy, LA and NY, 1983—87; prin. Robert M. Young & Assoc., Pasadena, Calif., 1987—89; pres. Dillon Cons. Engrs., Long Beach, 1989—. Mech. cons. in field; instr. in field; lectr. in field UCLA, U. Calif. San Diego, U. Calif., Irvine, U. So. Calif., U.S. Mil. Acad., West Point. Author: numerous poems; contbr. articles to profl. jours., chapters to books. Former chair Mechanical, Plumbing. Elec. and Energy CodeAdv. Commn. of Calif. Bldg. Stds. Commn.; former vice chmn. bd. examiners Appeals and Condemnations, Long Beach; mem. adv. bd. City of LA; mem. bus. adv. bd. City of Long Beach. Recipient Environ. Ozone Protection award, U.S. EPA, 1993, John Fies award, Internat. Conf. Bldg. Ofcls., 1995. Fellow Chartered Inst. Bldg. Svc. Engrs. Gt. Britain and Ireland, Inst. Refrigeration, Heating, Air Conditioning Engrs. of New Zealand, Inst. Advancement Engring.; mem. ASCE, ASME, IEEE, ISA, Internat. Soc. Fire Safety Sci., Nat. Inst. for Engring. Ethics, Nat. Fire Protection Assn., Internat. Assn. Bldg. Ofcls., Internat. Fire Code Inst., Internat. Code Coun., Soc. Fire Protection Engrs., Tau Beta Pi, Pi Tau Sigma, Chi Epsilon, others. Avocation: poetry. Office: Dillon Cons Engrs Inc 671 Quincy Ave Long Beach CA 90814-1818 Office Phone: 562-434-4640. Business E-Mail: medillon@dillon-consulting.com. *Rather I live and love in coventry than lust and rust in the public reign of insouciant sycophancy.*

DILLON, ROBERT SHERWOOD, retired diplomat; b. Chgo., Jan. 7, 1929; s. Dale Crowell and Viola May (Sherwood)D.; m. Caroline Sue Burch, June 16, 1951; children: Dale, Robert Jr., John, Elizabeth, Thomas. BA, Duke U., 1951; postgrad., Princeton U., 1958-59. Ops. officer CIA, 1951-56; fgn. svc. officer (including US Amb. Lebanon, 1981-83) Dept. State, Washington, 1956-84; asst. sec. gen. UN, Vienna, Austria, 1984-88;

pres. Am.-Mideast Ednl. & Tng. Svcs., Washington, 1988-95. UN spl. envoy for Rwanda and Burundi, 1994; advisor Dept. of State, 1995-96. Cpl. U.S. Army, 1947-48. Recipient Presdl. Honor award, White House, 1983.

DILLON, VERONICA, publishing executive, lawyer; b. 1949; BA cum laude, St. John's U., 1971; JD, Fordham U., 1976. Bar: NY 1977. Assoc. Simpson Thacher & Bartlett, 1976—80; staff atty. NY regional office FTC, 1980—82; asst. gen. counsel MacMillan, Inc., 1982—90; corp. counsel, gen. counsel Kaplan, Inc., 1991—2002, exec. v.p., gen. counsel, chief adminstrv. officer, 2002—03, chief adminstr. officer, chief legal officer, 2003—07, vice chmn., 2006—07; v.p., gen. counsel, & corp. sec. The Wash. Post Co., 2007—. Office: The Washington Post Co 1150 15th St NW Washington DC 20071*

DILLON, WILLIAM HENRY, retired secondary school educator; b. Pearisburg, Va., Nov. 4, 1941; s. Ernest Henry and Mary (Robertson) D.; m. Doris Jean Elliott, Jan. 3, 1964; 1 child, Mary Elliott. BA, Emory and Henry Coll., 1973; MS, Radford U., 1979. Cert. tchr., Va. English educator Castlewood (Va.) H.S., 1973—81, Riverheads H.S., Staunton, Va., 1981—2001. Adj. English instr. Blue Ridge C.C., Weyers Cave, Va., 1984-92. With USAR, 1966-72. Fellow Masons; mem. Schola Cantorum (pres. 1996-2000). Avocations: reading, herb and flower gardening. Home: 1501 Tuckahoe Rd Waynesboro VA 22980-3520

DILLON, WILTON STERLING, anthropologist, foundation administrator; b. Yale, Okla., July 13, 1923; s. Earl Henry and Edith Holland (Canfield) D.; m. Virginia Leigh Harris, Jan. 20, 1956; 1 child, James Harris BA, U. Calif. Berkeley, 1951; postgrad., Inst. Ethnology, U. Paris, U. Leyden, 1951—52; PhD, Columbia U., 1961. News reporter Holdenville Daily News, Okla., 1936—41; info. specialist, civilian mem. Civil Info. and Edn. Sect. SCAP, Tokyo, 1946—49; vis. lectr. sociology and anthropology Hobart and William Smith Colls., Geneva, NY, 1953—54; staff anthropologist Japan Soc. N.Y.; also lectr. Japanese studies Fordham U., 1954; dir. Clearinghouse for Rsch. in Human Orgn., Soc. Applied Anthropology, NYC, 1954—56; exec. sec., dir. rsch. Phelps-Stokes Fund N.Y.; dir. rsch. project on higher edn. and African nationhood U. Ghana, 1957—63; vis. lectr. Columbia U., New Sch. Social Rsch., 1957—63; staff dir. Nat. Acad. Scis., 1963—69; dir. symposia and seminars Smithsonian Instn., Washington, 1969—85, dir. interdisciplinary studies, 1986—90, sr. scholar, 1990—; sr. scholar emeritus. Dir. internat. commemoration of 250th anniversary of birth of Thomas Jefferson, 1992—; adj. prof. U. Ala., 1971—; chmn. Oxford U.-Smithsonian Seminars, 1985 Author: Gifts and Nations, 1968; editor: (with John F. Eisenberg) Man and Beast: Comparative Social Behavior, 1971, The Cultural Drama, 1974, (with Neil G. Kotler) The Statue of Liberty Revisited: Making a Universal Symbol, 1993; contbr. articles to profl. jours.; editl. bd. Ala. Heritage Del. internat. confs. including UNESCO, Pugwash; adv. coun. Africa Dept. State, 1964-68; hon. commr. Internat. Year of Child, 1979-80; pres. bd. dirs. Inst. Intercultural Studies, NYC; trustee emeritus Phelps-Stokes Fund, 1985—; sec.-treas., bd. dirs. Inst. Psychiatry and Fgn. Affairs; bd. visitors Wake Forest U., 1978-81; adv. com. Hubert Humphrey Inst. for Pub. Affairs, 1988-94; bd. dirs. Delta Rsch. and Ednl. Found., 1987-95; trustee Friends of Raoul Wallenberg Found., 1995-97, Lives and Legacies Inc., 1995—; advisor Nation's Capital Bicentennial Celebration 1999-2000, Margaret Mead Centenary 2001, Historic Mt. Vernon 1999, Benjamin Franklin Creativity Found., 2002; lay reader NY Episc. Diocese, 1958-60. With USAAF, 1943-46 Decorated Chevalier de l'ordre des arts et lettres; Woodrow Wilson Internat. Center for Scholars guest scholar, 1970. Fellow AAAS, Am. Anthrop. Assn., Royal Soc. Arts; mem. NY Acad. Scis., Lit. Soc. Washington (pres. 1990), Anthrop. Soc. Washington, Cosmos Club Washington. Home: 1446 Woodacre Dr Mc Lean VA 22101-2536 Office: Smithsonian Instn Nat Mus Natural History MRC 124 PO Box 37012 Washington DC 20013-7012 Office Phone: 202-633-1081. Business E-Mail: dillonwi@si.edu.

DILLON RYDMAN, LINDA GAY, nurse, consultant; d. Vannessa Dillon; children: Kate Dillon, Estlin Robert Rydman. BA, BSN, No. Ill. U., DeKalb, Ill., 1973; MS, Univ. Ill. Chgo. Med Cntr., Chgo., 1986. RN Ill., 1973, Mass., 1990; Ccm CCMC, 2001, Cpur McKesson HBOC, 2000, Type 73 Sch. Nursing DuPage County, Ill., 1982, Family Therapist Inst. Juvenile Rsch., 1980. Clin. nursing cons./instr. U. Ill. Med. Ctr., Chgo., 1974—81; dir. of profl. services Home Health of Chgo. South, Inc., Chgo., 1983—85; clin. nurse specialist/staff nurse Loyola U., Maywood, 1985—89; don Linden Oaks Hosp., Naperville, Ill., 1989—90; clin. nurse specialist Ctrl. DuPage Hosp., Behavioral Health, Winfield, Ill., 1992—94; dir. ops. Staff Builders Health Care Svcs., Chgo., 1994—98; utilization mgmt. specialist Marianjoy Rehablink, Wheaton, Ill., 1998—2000; cons. ImageMasters, Clarendon Hills, Ill., 1990—; dir. patient care svcs. Univ. Ill. at Chgo. Med. Cntr., Chicago, Ill., 2001—05. Mem., children's theater bd.,mktg. Theater of Western Springs, Western Springs, Ill., 1994—99. Author (presenter): (monograph) The Affective Disorders Clinic; contbr. presentation, chapters to books. Deacon Cmty. Presbyn. Ch., Clarendon Hills, Ill., 1997—99. Grantee Ann. grant funding Affective Disorders Clinic, Ill. Dept. of Mental Health, 1976-1981. Mem.: Am. Assoc. of Managed Care Nurses, Case Mgmt. Soc. of Am. Home Phone: 802-280-1970. Office Fax: 603-448-1599.

DILLOW, JOHN DAVID, lawyer; b. Bremerton, Wash., Aug. 17, 1946; s. Garold Maurice and Margaret (Roediger) D.; m. Alison Wenke, Sept. 19, 1977; children: Gwen, Jake, Claire BS magna cum laude, U. Wash., 1968; JD, Duke U., 1971. Bar: Calif. 1972, Wash. 1975, U.S. Dist. Ct. (Ctrl. Dist.) Wash. 1972, U.S. Dist. Ct. (We. Dist.) Calif. 1975, U.S. Ct. Appeals (9th Cir.) 1972, U.S. Supreme Ct. 1975, N.Y. 1981. Assoc. O'Melveny and Meyers, LA, 1971-75, Perkins Coie, LLP, Seattle, 1975-77, ptnr., Product Liability Area, 1977—. Editor Duke Law Jour. Bd. dirs. ARC King County, Seattle, 1987—; mem. coun. fund raising Duke U., Durham, N.C., 1975—. Mem. ABA (aviation & space law com.), Wash. State Bar Assn., King County Bar Assn., Barristers Club, Seattle Tennis Club, Order of Coif, Tau Beta Pi. Avocations: tennis, skiing. Office: Perkins Coie LLP 1201 3rd Ave Fl 40 Seattle WA 98101-3029 Office Phone: 206-359-8476. Office Fax: 206-359-9000. Business E-Mail: jdillow@perkinscoie.com.

DILLS, JAMES ARLOF, retired publishing executive; b. Guelph, Ont., Can., Aug. 11, 1930; s. George Arlof and Isma Marie (MacPherson) D.; m. Shirley Jean Elliott, Aug. 16, 1952; children— Steven George, James Mark, Paul David, Catherine Jane, Carolyn Shirley. Grad. in journalism, Ryerson Poly. Inst., 1951. Pub. The Can. Champion, Milton, Ont., 1966-78, The Georgetown (Ont.) Ind., 1973-78; sec.-treas. Dills Printing and Pub. Co. Ltd., Acton, Ont., 1954—; exec. dir. Can. Community Newspapers Assn., Toronto, Ont., 1979-87; mem. adv. com. journalism program Sheridan Coll., 1965-78; pres. Ont. Weekly Newspapers Assn., 1975-76; pub. County Chronicles Press, 1992—2003; ret., 2003. Dir. Milton Evergreen Cemetery Co., 1997. Author: Moments in History, 1993; editor: Time Capsules from Milton's Past 1890-1894, 2002; co-author: Milton Remembers World War I, 2006. Pres. Milton Hist. Soc., 1977-80; dir. emeritus Mackenzie Printery and Newspaper Mus, 2004. Named Citizen of Yr., Milton, 1978; recipient Lifetime Achievement Cmty. award, Milton C. of C., 1999, Lifetime Achievement cert., Ont. Heritage Found., 2005. E-mail: jdills@idirect.com.

DILORENZO, FRANCIS X., bishop; b. Phila., Apr. 15, 1942; s. Samuel and Anna (Porrino) DiLorenzo. Student, St. Charles Borromeo Sem.; STD, Pontifical U. of St. Thomas Aquinas, 1975. Ordained priest, 1968; served Archdiocese Phila., 1968—71; chaplain & instr. theology St. Pius X H.S., Pottstown, Pa., 1975—77; chaplain & assoc. prof. moral theology Immaculata Coll., Pa., 1977—83; vice rector St. Charles Borromeo Sem., Wynnewood, Pa., 1983—85, rector, 1985—88; Titular Bishop of Tigia, 1988—93; Aux. Bishop of Scranton Pa., 1988—93; apostolic adminstr. Diocese of Honolulu, Hawaii, 1993-94; Bishop of Honolulu, 1994—2004; Bishop of Richmond Va., 2004—. Mem.: US Conf. Cath. Bishops (mem. adminstrv. com., chmn. com. on sci. & human values). Roman Catholic. Office: Diocese of Richmond 811 Cathedral Pl Richmond VA 23220-4801

DI LORENZO, JOHN FLORIO, JR., retired lawyer; b. Paterson, NJ, May 18, 1940; s. John F. and Ida (Cona) Di L.; m. Ernestine R. De Rose, Nov. 15, 1969; children: Christina P., Roberta J. BA, Seton Hall U., 1962; LLB, MBA, Columbia U., 1966. Bar: N.J. 1967, N.Y. 1968, Ohio 1981. Assoc. Stryker, Tams & Dill, Esqs., Newark, 1966-68; atty. Am. Electric Power Svc. Corp., NYC, 1968-79, asst. gen. counsel, asst. v.p., exec. asst. to pres., 1979-81, assoc. gen. counsel, v.p., sec. Columbus, Ohio, 1981-2001; ret., 2001. Sec. various Am. Electric Power Sys. cos., 1987-2001, asst. sec. 1979. Trustee Ballet Met. Columbus, 1981-87. Mem. ABA (chmn. subcom. on pub. utility holding co. act of fed. regulation of securities com. 1985-94), Knights of Malta, Knights of the Holy Sepulchre of Jerusalem, Scioto Country Club. Roman Catholic. Avocations: skiing, travel. Home: 2756 Elginfield Rd Columbus OH 43220-4248 Office Phone: 614-459-0047. E-mail: jfdilorenzo@att.net.

DILORENZO, LOUIS PATRICK, lawyer; b. Waterloo, NY, Nov. 3, 1952; s.Luigi and Theresa Marie (Grieco) D.; m. Deborah Joan Boudreau, Aug. 18, 1973; children: Louis Patrick, Lisa Marie, Laura Gabriel. Student, US Mil. Acad., West Point, 1970—72; BA, Syracuse U., NY, 1973; JD, SUNY, Buffalo, 1976. Bar: NY 1977, US Dist. Ct. (no., ea., so. we. dists.) NY, US Supreme Ct. 1988. Assoc. Bond, Schoeneck & King, Syracuse, 1976-84, ptnr., 1985—, chair recruiting com., chair labor and employment law dept., founder, co-chair employment law litig. group, mng. ptnr. NY office, 1988—; gen. counsel Agway, Inc., 2002—04, chair compensation com., 2004—; adj. prof. Syracuse U., 1988—. Participant NYU Ann. Conf. on Labor, 1989; mem. dean's adv. coun. Buffalo Law Sch. Author: Syracuse Law Jour., 1978, Jour. of Coll. and U. Law Jour., 1980, NY State Bar Jour., 1982; author: (with others) Compliance with Federal Labor and Employment Laws, Corporate Counseling, 1988, Public Sector Labor Law, 1988, Duke Journal of Gender Law and Policy, 1999, Fordham Urban Law Jour., 2002; mem. editl. bd. NY State Bar Jour., 1998-06, NY Civil Practice Before Trial, 2001; contbr. articles to profl. publs. Bd. dirs. Syracuse Opera Co., 1986. Fellow: Am. Acad. Trial Counsel, NY State Bar Found., Am. Coll. Employment and Labor Law Lawyers; mem.: ABA, NY State Bar Assn. (mem. ho. of dels. 1984—90, 1999—, chmn. young lawyers sect. 1987, chmn. labor rels. com. 1988, chmn. CLE com. 1990—93, chmn. labor and employment law sect. 1994), Fedn. Def. and Corp. Counsel, Nat. Assn. Coll. and Univ. Attys. Republican. Roman Catholic. Avocations: golf, gardening, reading. Home: 150 E 44th St New York NY 10017 Office: Bond Schoeneck & King 330 Madison Ave New York NY 10017 Office Phone: 646-253-2315. Business E-Mail: ldilorenzo@bsk.com.

DILTS, JON PAUL, law educator; b. Monterey, Ind., Sept. 7, 1945; s. Charles Albert and Janet Cecilia (Keitzer) D.; m. Anne Williams Avirett, Aug. 21, 1971; children: Christopher, Andrew. BA, Saint Meinrad Coll., 1967; MA, Ind. U., 1974; JD, Valparaiso U., Ind., 1981. Bar: Ind. 1981, US Dist. Ct. (so. dist.) Ind. 1981, US Supreme Ct. 2000. Reporter Peru (Ind.) Daily Tribune, 1972-73, wire editor, 1973-76, city editor, 1976-78; law clk. Ind. Ct. Appeals, Indpls., 1981-82; asst. prof. Ind. U., Bloomington, 1982-88, assoc. prof., 1988—, asst. dean, 1982—85, assoc. dean, 1985-2000. Author: The Magnificent 92 Indiana Courthouses, 1992; co-author: Media Law, 1994, 2d edit., 97; mem. editl. bd. Comms. Law & Policy, 1998—. Bd. overseers St. Meinrad Coll. Sch. Theology, 1992-, trustee 1996-98, 2003-06, chmn., 2004-06; exec. bd. dirs. Hoosier Trails coun. Boy Scouts Am., Bloomington, 1992-93. With US Army, 1968—71. Nat. Press Club First Amendment fellow, 2002. Mem. Assn. for Edn. in Journalism and Mass Comm. (head law divsn. 1987-88), Soc. Profl. Journalists, AP Mng. Editors Assn., Rotary (bd. dirs.). Democrat. Roman Catholic. Avocations: skiing, hiking, backpacking, canoeing, sailing. Office: Ind U Sch Journalism 940 E 7th St Bloomington IN 47405-7108 Business E-Mail: dilts@indiana.edu.

DILWORTH, ROBERT LEXOW, career military officer, educator; b. Chgo., Aug. 19, 1936; s. Robert Oliver and Linda Agnes (Lexow) D.; m. Doris Elthea Smith, Sept. 1, 1981; children by previous marriage: Alexa, Robert. BS in Advt., U. Fla., 1959; MS in Mil. Sci., U.S. Army Command and Gen. Staff Coll., 1971; MA in Pub. Adminstrn., U. Okla., 1975; MEd, EdD, Columbia U., 1993. Commd. 2nd lt. U.S. Army, 1959, advanced through grades to brig. gen., 1986, chief adminstrn. div. office chief of staff Washington, 1968-70, chief mgmt. analysis br. office chief of staff, 1971-75, chief of staff 2nd infantry div. Republic of Korea, 1975-76, chief mgmt. div. adj. gen. ctr. Washington, 1976-77, chief compt. div. Nat. Guard Bur., 1978-81, dep. comdr. 1st pers. command Schwetzingen, Fed. Republic of Germany, 1981-84, dir. resource mgmt. U.S. Mil. Acad. West Point, NY, 1984-86, adjutant gen. army Alexandria, Va., 1986-88, dep. chief of staff base ops. support tng./doctrine command Ft. Monroe, Va., 1988-91; assoc. prof. emeritus adult edn., human resource devel. Va. Commonwealth U., Richmond, 1993—. Guest lectr. Hungarian Mil. Acad., 1989. Contbr. articles to profl. jours. Mem. ASPA (exec. com. mgmt. sci. and policy analysis sect. 1992-96), ASTD (chair nat. rsch. to practice com. 2000-2002), Acad. Human Resource Devel., Assn. U.S. Army, Mil. Officer Assn., Internat. Soc. Quality Govt. (nat. dir. 1992-93). Mem. Lds Ch. Avocation: writing for publication. Home: PO Box 29 Gum Spring VA 23065-0029 Personal E-mail: lexter@earthlink.net.

DIMAGGIO, DEBBI, realtor; b. Oakland, July 14, 1964; d. Vincent S. and Marietta DiMaggio; m. Adam R. Betta, July 25, 1992; children: Bianca Betta, Chase Betta. BS in Polit. Sci., U. Calif., Berkeley, 1987. Lic. realtor Calif. Realtor San Francisco Real Estate Svcs., 1992—96, Grubb Co., Oakland, 1996—. Owner, ptnr. Rock Star Confidential LLC, 2006—. Fundraising chair Children's Support League, Oakland, 1998—2007; mem. Jr. League Oakland, 2000—07; mem. mother/daughter vol. organ. Nat. Charity League, 2005—07. Mem.: Piedmont Baseball and Softball Found. (fundraising chair 2005—07). Avocations: tennis, travel, swimming, writing. Office: The Grubb Co 1960 Mountain Blvd Oakland CA 94611 Office Phone: 510-339-0400 ext. 227. Business E-Mail: debbi@debbidimaggio.com.

DIMAGGIO, FRANK LOUIS, civil engineering educator; b. NYC, Sept. 2, 1929; s. Serafino and Maria (Barbuto) DiM.; m. Irene C. Koehn, Dec. 15, 1963 (dec. June 1998); children: Samuel, Peter. BS, Columbia U., 1950, MS, 1951, PhD, 1954. Registered profl. engr., N.Y. Prof. civil engring. Columbia U., 1956—, chmn. dept., 1975-78, Carleton prof., 1978—. Cons. in field, 1956— Served with AUS, 1954-56. Recipient Mel Baron medal Shock and Vibration Info. Analysis Ctr., 2006; NSF sr. postdoctoral fellow, 1962-63; guest scholar Kyoto U., Japan, 1986. Fellow ASCE (chmn. exec. com. engring. mech. div. 1982-83, chmn. adv. bd. engring. mechanics div. 1985-86); mem. Sigma Xi. Home: 138 Van Orden Ave Leonia NJ 07605-1521 Office: Columbia Univ Dept Civil Engring and Engring Mechanics New York NY 10027 Office Phone: 212-854-3751. E-mail: dimaggio@civil.columbia.edu.

DIMAIRA, ANN B., medical/surgical nurse; b. Newark, July 21, 1959; d. Bernard C. and Clair Ellen (Kirchner) Welch; m. Frank C. Dimaira, June 26, 1982; children: Peter Sean, Jennifer Ann, Kathleen Ellen. BSN, Seton Hall U., 1982. Cert. intravenous nurse. Asst. clin. coord. Riverview Med. Ctr., Red Bank, NJ, 1985—90; primary case mgmt. nurse Vis. Nurse Assn. Ctrl. Jersey, Red Bank, 1990—91; asst. to supr. level III MCOSS Nursing Svcs., Red Bank, 1991—92, clin. nursing supr., 1992—95, clin. nurse mgr., 1995—97; staff nurse geriatric care Regency Park Nursing Ctr., 1998—; staff nurse, adminstrv. supr. Riverview Med. Ctr., 2001—. Active in PTA and ch.; vol. Barn for the Poorest of the Poor. Recipient State Recognition for Nor'Easter Disaster Care and Coordination, 1992, Galaxy award, Riverview Med. Ctr., 2005. Personal E-mail: ab721@aol.com.

DIMANCESCU, MIHAI D., neurosurgeon, researcher, educator; b. Maidenhead, Berkshire, Eng., Mar. 27, 1940; arrived in US, 1956, naturalized, 1963; s. Dimitri D. and Alexandra Irina (Radulescu) D.; m. Joan E. Brenner, Mar. 17, 1966; children: Stefan, Marc-Mihai. BA, Yale U., 1962; MD, U. Toulouse, France, 1968. Diplomate Am. Bd. Neurol. Surgery. Rotating intern Purpan Hosp., Toulouse, 1968-69; jr. resident in gen. surgery Hartford Hosp., Conn., 1969-70; jr. resident neurosurgy Albert Einstein-Montefiore Hosp., Bronx, NY, 1970-72; rsch. fellow in spasticity and movement disorders U. Miami VA Hosp., Miami, Fla., 1972-74; sr. resident in neurosurgery U. Miami, 1972-76, asst. instr. in neurol. surgery, 1975-76; pvt. practice Freeport, NY, 1976—2003, Garden City, 1976—2003; v.p. med. affairs OmniCorder Tech., Inc., Bohemia, NY, 2004—06; pres. Gogosh, Inc., Lake Success, NY, 2006—. Dir. Internat. Coma Recovery Inst., Garden City, 1977—2006; faculty, dir. brain studies Internat. Sch. Evan Thomas Inst., Phila., 1980—; staff, dir. dept. neurosurgery Franklin Hosp. Med. Ctr., Valley Stream, NY; staff neurosurgery South Nassau Cmtys. Hosp., Oceanside, NY, Mercy Med. Ctr., Rockville Ctr., NY, St. Francis Hosp., Rockville Ctr., NY, Winthrop U. Hosp., Mineola, NY, North Shore U. Hosp., Manhasset, NY, continuing med. edn. lectr., 1977—2003; cons. neurosurgery Inst. Achievement Human Potential, Phila., 1977—; surg. core faculty Health Sci. Ctr., Sch. Medicine, SUNY Stony Brook, 1980—2003; med. coun. LI Health Network; v.p. med. affairs Advanced BioPhotonics, Inc., Bohemia, NY, 2004—06; bd. dirs. South Nassau Cmty. Hosp.; adj. faculty Molloy Coll., Rockville Centre, NY, 2007—; mem. faculty Leeds U. Touro Coll. Campus, Bayshore, NY, 2007—. Contbr. articles profl. jours. Bd. dirs. Inst. Achievement Human Potential, 1990—, Princess Margarita Romania Found., chmn., 1998—. Recipient Golden medal, World Orgn. Human Potential, 1978; grantee, VA, 1972—74. Fellow: Royal Soc. Arts, ACS; mem.: Nassau Physicians' Rev. Orgn., Nassau County Med. Soc., World Med. Assn., NY State Head Injury Providers' Council (rotating chmn. 1986—87), Med. Soc. State NY (neurosurg. de. intersplty. com. 1983—88), NY State Neurosurg. Soc. (bd. dirs. 1983—88, pres. elect 1986—87, pres. 1988), Coma Recovery Assn. (chmn. bd. dirs. Garden City chpt. 1983), Congress Neurol. Surgeons (Sci. Exhibit award 1974), Am. Assn. Neurol. Surgeons, AMA. Personal E-mail: mihaidimancescu@aol.com. Business E-Mail: mihaidimancescu@aya.yale.edu.

DI MARCO, BARBARANNE YANUS, principal; b. Jersey City, Nov. 16, 1946; d. Stanley Joseph and Anne Barbara (Dalack) Yanus; m. Charles Benjamin DiMarco, Mar. 15, 1986; 1 child, Charles Garrett. BA in Music Edn., Trenton State Coll., 1968; MA in Spl. Edn., Kean Coll., 1971, elem. edn. cert., 1974, adminstrv. cert., 1976. Cert. elem., music, adminstrn., spl. edn., N.J. Vocal music educator Roselle (N.J.) Bd. Edn., 1968-69, tchr. trainable mentally retarded, 1969-76, tchr. multiple handicapped, 1976—95, tchr. neurologically impaired, 1995—2003; prin. Grace Wilday Jr. H.S., Roselle, 2003—. Color guard instr. Roselle Bd. Edn., 1973—88, elem. tutor, 1976—92, adminstrv. asst. to supt., 1980—85; program dir., sec. Expanded Dimensions in Gifted Edn., Westfield, NJ, 1978—85. Vestryperson St. Luke's Ch., Roselle, 1989-91. Recipient Govs. Tchr. Recognition award, Gov. Florio, N.J., Trenton, 1992-93. Mem. NEA, N.J. Edn. Assn., Roselle Edn. Assn., N.J. Assn. for Retarded Children, Eastern Star (25-yr award 1991), Delta Omicron. Republican. Episcopalian. Avocations: skiing, flying, painting, travel, swimming. Home: 13 Gentore Ct Edison NJ 08820-1029 Office: Grace Wilday Jr HS 400 Brooklawn Ave Roselle NJ 07203 Office Phone: 908-298-2066 2105. Personal E-mail: btdtbarb@aol.com.

DIMARCO, DAVID, mathematician, educator; s. Jeanette Mary and Joseph Paul DiMarco. BS, Stevens Inst. of Tech., Hoboken, NJ, 1975—79; MS, Stevens Inst Tech., Hoboken, NJ, 1981, PhD, 1988; MS, Iona Coll., New Rochelle, NY, 1995—95. Instr. math. Various Colleges, 1983—; adj. asst. professor-math NYC Tech. Coll., Brooklyn, NY, 1994—2002; adj. instr. math Fairleigh Dickinson U., Teaneck, NJ, 1997—2002; asst. prof. math Neumann Coll., Aston, Pa., 2002—. Contbr. articles to profl. jours. Mem.: Am. Math. Soc. Avocations: cross training, jogging. Office: Neumann Coll Div of Arts and Sci One Neumann Dr Aston PA 19014

DIMARZIO, NICHOLAS ANTHONY, bishop; b. Newark, June 16, 1944; s. Nicholas Anthony and Grace (Grande) DiMarzio. BA, Seton Hall U., 1966; STB, Catholic U., 1970; MSW, Fordham U., 1980; PhD, Rutgers U., 1985. Ordained to ministry Roman Cath. Ch., 1970, ordained to bishop Roman Cath. Ch., 1996. Divsn. dir. spl. svcs. Cath. Cmty. Svcs., Newark, 1976-85, assoc. exec. dir., 1991-92, exec. dir., 1992-97, Migration & Refugee Svcs. U.S. Cath. Conf., Washington, 1985-91; bishop Camden, NJ, 1999—2003; pontifical coun. pastoral care of migrants and itinerant people, 1999—; bishop Brooklyn Diocese, 2003—. Vicar human svcs. Archdiocese of Newark, 1991—99; global commn. internat. migration, 2004—05; cons. in field. Co-author: (book) Profiling Unapprehended Undocumented Aliens in the New York Metropolitan Area: An Exploration into Their Social and Labor Market Incorporation, 1986; contbr. articles to profl. jours., mags., and newspapers. V.p. Internat. Cath. Migration Commn., 1989—92; chmn. bd. dirs. Nat. Immigration, Refugee and Citizenship Forum, Washington, 1986—89; bd. dirs. Ctr. Migration Studies, Washington, 1988—93, Am. Com. Italian Migration, 1989—91, Cath. Relief Svcs. Decorated Knight of the Italian Republic N.Y., Prelate of Honor Pope John Paul II, Vatican; recipient Spl. award, N.Y. Assn. New Ams. Mem.: NASW. Office: Brooklyn Diocese 75 Greene Ave PO Box C Brooklyn NY 11202

DIMASCIO, JOHN PHILIP, lawyer; b. Bklyn., Feb. 4, 1944; s. Eugenio and Stella (Scheuermann) DiM.; m. Angela Piccininni, Apr. 2, 1967 (div. 1980); children: John Philip, Jr., Christine Pagano, Thomas; m. Linda Nick, Oct. 19, 1997. BA, C.W. Post Coll., 1975; MA, L.I. U., 1976; postgrad., NYU, 1976-79; JD, St. John's U., 1983. Bar: N.Y. 1984, U.S. Dist. Ct. (ea. and so. dists.) N.Y. 1984, U.S. Ct. Appeals (2d cir.) 1984, U.S. Supreme Ct. 1997, U.S. Ct. Appeals for Armed Forces 1997, U.S. Ct. of Fed. Claims, 1997, U.S. Ct. Appeals (fed. cir.) 1997. Sr. ct. officer N.Y. State Supreme Ct., Mineola, 1970-82; assoc. Joel R. Brandes, PC, Garden City, NY, 1984; pvt. practice NY, 1984-87; ptnr. Di Mascio, Meisner & Koopersmith, Carle Place, 1987-93; pvt. practice Garden City, 1993—2004; ptnr. John P. DiMascio & Assocs., Garden City, 2004—. Lectr. Nassau Acad. Law; barrister, NY family law chpt. Am. Inns of Ct. With USN, 1962—69. Recipient acad. awards. Fellow: Am. Bar Found.; mem.: Nassau County Bar Assn. (family ct. com. 1984—, past chmn. matrimonial com., bd. dirs., past editor Recent Decisions, contbg. author, dir.), N.Y. State Bar Assn. (family law com. 1982—). Office: John P DiMascio & Assoc LLP 300 Garden City Plz Garden City NY 11530-3302 Office Phone: 516-747-4343. Business E-Mail: jpdlawoff@msn.com.

DI MASSA, ERNANI VINCENZO, JR., communications executive, television producer, writer; b. Phila., Sept. 12, 1947; s. Ernani Vincenzo and Rita C. (Iacovoni) Di M.; divorced; 1 child, Michael Colin. BA, La Salle Coll., Phila., 1970; MS, Temple U., Phila., 1972. Producer, writer Mike Douglas Show, Phila. and L.A., 1969-81, Regis Philbin Show, NBC-TV, 1981, Fantasy NBC-TV, LA, 1981-83; exec. producer, writer Thicke of the Night, LA, 1983-84, Tony Orlando Show, 1985-86; supervising producer Hollywood Squares, LA, 1987-89; sr. v.p. programming and devel. King World Prodns., LA, 1989-97; pres. DiMassa Prodns.,

1998—. Supervising prodr. Candid Camera; exec. in charge prodn. Rolonda; exec. prodr. Terry Bradshaw-Fox TV; exec. in charge of programming and devel. The Oprah Winfrey Show, Wheel of Fortune, Jeopardy, Inside Edition, Am. Jour., Instant Recall, The Arts and Entertainment Rev. Recipient Emmy award NATAS, 1982. Mem. Producers Guild Am., Writers Guild Am. Roman Catholic. Avocations: auto restoration, photography. Office Phone: 949-548-1510. E-mail: ernani-d@usa.net.

DIMBERG, LENNART AXEL, medical researcher, physician; b. Vanersborg, Sweden, Aug. 28, 1947; arrived in U.S., 1998; s. Sven Ingvar and Eva Ingrid Dimberg; m. Kerstin Aline Dimberg, Mar. 31, 1973; children: Asa, Ida, Emelie. DMS in Occpl. Health, Arbet Arskydds Styrelsen, Stockholm, 1973; diploma in Gen. Medicine, Norra Alvsborgs Stukhus, Trollhattan, Sweden, 1978; PhD in Orthop. Surgery, Goteborg U., Sweden, 1991. Intern then resident Trollhattans Sjulhns, Trollhattan, Sweden, 1975—78; mgr. health promotion Volvo Flygmotor, 1978—98; corp. medical dir. Volvo AB, Goteborg, 1989—94; occpl. health specialist World Bank, Washington, 1998—. Chmn. Assn. Volvo Physicians, Goteborg, Sweden, 1993—98; Swedish coord. Volvo-Renault Heart Study, 1993—2004; assoc. prof. Sahlgrenska Acad., 2004; co-task mgr. first symposium on travel and stress World Bank, Washington, 2004. Contbr. chapters to books, articles to profl. jours. Coord. table tennis team Volvo AG, Goteborg, Sweden, 1980—90; vol. instr. Tennis Club, Vanersborg, 1988—89; bd. mem PTA, Vanersborg, 1997—98. Mem.: Swedish Med. Assn. (sec. 1982—85), Am. Coll. Occpl. and Environ. Medicine. Avocations: tennis, ping pong/table tennis, guitar, piano. Office: World Bank Occpl Health Svcs 1818 H St NW Washington DC 20433-0001 Office Phone: 202-458-0849. Personal E-mail: ldimberg@aol.com.

DIMEGLIO, DAVID J., lawyer; b. San Pedro, Calif. BA, U. Calif., Los Angeles, 1984; JD, Stanford U., 1987. Bar: Calif. 1987, Calif. Ninth Circuit Ct. of Appeals. Ptnr., civil litigation Jones Day, Los Angeles, Calif. Mem.: ABA, Calif. State Bar Assn. Office: Jones Day 555 S Flower St # 50 Los Angeles CA 90071-2300 Office Phone: 213-243-2551. Office Fax: 213-243-2539. Business E-Mail: djdimeglio@jonesday.com.

DI MEO, DOMINICK, artist, sculptor, painter; b. Niagara Falls, NY, Feb. 1, 1927; s. Antonio and Michelina (Sandonato) Di M.; m. Judith S. Cousins, Dec. 26, 1963. B.F.A., Sch. Art Inst., Chgo., 1952; M.F.A., State U. Iowa, 1953. Vis. artist Sch. of Art Inst. Chgo., 1977; instr. Chgo. Acad. Fine Arts, 1967-69 One man shows include Lake Forest (Ill.) Coll., 1955, Bemidji (Minn.) Coll., 1963, Fairweather-Hardin Gallery, Chgo., 1964, 68, 71, Barat Coll., Lake Forest, 1966, Chgo. Public Libr., 1966, Kendall Coll., Evanston, Ill., 1967, Westbroadway Gallery, NYC, 1973, 75-76, Project Studios One, Long Island City, NY, 1982, group exhbns. include, Albright-Knox Art Gallery, Buffalo, 1953-54, Art Inst. Chgo, 1959-61, 63, 65-68, 71, 76, 79, 89-90, Whitney Mus. Am. Art, NY, 1967-68, Mus. Contemporary Art, Chgo., 1969, Joan Miro Internat. Drawing Prize Competition, Barcelona, Spain, 1977-80, Centro Cultural/Arte Contemporaneo, Mexico City, 1986-1987, Art Inst. Chgo., 1989-90, Pa. Acad. Fine Arts, 2006; represented in permanent collections Art Inst. Chgo., Whitney Mus. Am. Art, NYC, U. Mass., Amherst, Nat. Collection Fine Arts, Smithsonian Instn., Elmhurst (Ill.) Coll. Fellow Guggenheim Found., 1972, sculpture fellow Nat. Endowment for Arts, 1983. Mem. Momentum (founding mem.), Participating Artists Chgo.), Artists Collaborative. Address: 429 Broome St New York NY 10013-2686 Office Phone: 212-966-6037.

DIMICCO, DANIEL R., manufacturing executive; BS in Engring., Metallurgy and Materials Sci., Brown U., Providence, 1972; MS in Metallurgy and Materials Sci., U. Pa., Phila., 1975. Rsch. metallurgist, project leader Republic Steel, Cleve., 1975—82; plant metallurgist, mgr. quality control Nucor Steel, Plymouth, Utah, 1982—88, mgr. melting and casting Utah divsn., 1988—91; gen. mgr. Nucor-Yamato, Blytheville, Ark., 1991—92, v.p., 1992—99, exec. v.p., 1999—2000; pres., CEO Nucor Corp., Charlotte, NC, 2000—, vice chmn., 2001—06, chmn., 2006—. Office: Nucor Corp 1915 Rexford Rd Charlotte NC 28211 Office Phone: 704-366-7000. Office Fax: 704-362-4208.*

DIMICK, BARBARA L., library director; Dir. Madison Pub. Libr., Wis. Ex-officio mem. bd. Madison Pub. Libr. Found. Office: Madison Pub Libr 201 W Mifflin St Madison WI 53703 Office Phone: 608-266-6363. E-mail: bdimick@cityofmadison.com.

DI MINO, ANDRÉ ANTHONY, manufacturing executive, consultant; b. Bklyn., Aug. 24, 1955; s. Alfonso and Nancy (Zarbo) DiM.; m. Jenny DiCapua, May 30, 1981. BS in Indsl. Engring., Fairleigh Dickinson U., Teaneck, NJ, 1978, MBA in Fin., 1981. Engr. ADMTronics Inc., Emerson, NJ, 1977—79, dir. tech., 1979—82, sec./treas. Northvale, NJ, 1982—86, exec. v.p. and dir., 1986—2001; pres. ADMTronics, Northvale, NJ, 2002—; founder, dir. Enviro-Pack Devel. Corp., Northvale, 1991—2002. Ptnr., cons. Tech. Mgmt. Cons., Woodcliff Lake, NJ, 1978-94; v.p., dir. Pegasus Labs., Inc., Northvale, NJ, 1989—, Sonotron Med. Sys., Inc., Northvale, 1988—, VET-Sonotron Sys., Inc., Northvale, 1988-2002; pres. AANorthvale Med. Assocs., Inc., 1998-2004, chmn. bd. dirs., 2004—; pres. Ivivi Tech., Inc., 2004-. Inventor in field. Mem. coun. Borough of Woodcliff Lake, 1984-97, pres., 1987-93, 97, cable adv. com., 1999-; corr. sec. Office N.E. Rep. Orgn., 1989-93, treas., 1992-93, vice chmn., 1993; co-chmn. privatization subcom. Bergen County Cost Containment Rev. Team, 1991; open space com. Bergen County, 1997, 98; fundraising dir. Our Lady Mother of the Ch., Woodcliff Lake, 1990-99; founding mem., 1st v.p. Woodcliff chpt. Unico Nat. Svcs. Orgn., 1990-92, pres., 1992-94, 97-00; dep. dist. gov., 1993-94, dist. gov., 1994-96, nat. treas., 2002—05, 3d v.p. 2005-; founder, pres. Cmty. Access TV studio WCL-TV, 1990—; pres. Woodcliff Lake Rep. Club, 1994-96; devel. chmn. NW Bergen chpt. Am. Heart Assn. (vice chmn. 1995-96), 1994; founder, chmn. Woodcliff Lake Sr. Assn., 1989-99; trustee Pascack Hist. Soc., 1995-99; vice chmn. Pascack Valley Region Cmty. Devel. com., 1997; computer sci. adv. bd. Fairleigh Dickinson U., Madison, NJ, 2000-; chmn. Marconi Sci. Award Com., 2000—. Named Vol. of Yr. Bergen County, NJ, 1991, 93, Citizen of Yr. Pascack Valley C. of C., 1993. Mem. Woodcliff Lake Vol. Fire Assn. (hon.). Republican. Roman Catholic. Avocations: classic cars, antiques, video and photography. Office: ADMTronics Inc 224S Pegasus Ave Northvale NJ 07647-1904 Business E-Mail: andre@admtronics.com.

DIMINO, JOSEPH C., lawyer; b. Rochester, NY, 1952; BA summa cum laude, U. Rochester, 1973; JD, U. Va., 1976. Aty. Norfolk So. Corp., Va., corp. gen. counsel, 2000—02, sr. gen. counsel, 2002—05, v.p., corp. counsel, 2005—. ABA Office: Norfolk Southern Corp 3 Commerical Pl Norfolk VA 23510-2191 Office Phone: 757-629-2816.*

DI MITRI, PIERO, fashion designer; b. Palermo, Italy, July 1, 1933; came to U.S., 1963, naturalized, 1970; s. Raffaele and Michelangela (Mirabella) Dimitri; m. Maria Parisi, Nov. 9, 1955; children: Rafael, Michele, Robert, Peter. Diploma, Milan Fashion Inst., Italy, 1956. Designer, tailor Caraceni, Rome, 1950-52, Litrico, Rome, 1953-56; owner, mgr. Custom and Design Studios, Milan, 1957-63, Palermo, Sicily, 1957-63, DiMitri of Italy, NYC, 1964—, DiMitri Couture, Ltd., NYC, 1980—. Designer, cons. Am. Fashion, Inc., 1975—, Melbo Clothing Co., Osaka, Japan, 1976—, Matsuzakaya, Tokyo, 1976—, Pacific Shirt Co., 1980—, Ithaca Industries, Inc., 1980—, Syd Levethan Shoes, 1985—, Itokin Am., Inc., Tokyo, 1988—, Tokyo Itokin Co., Ltd., 1989—, Standard Shoe Co., Ltd., 1990—, Nishijin Necktie Co., Ltd., Shin-Ei Sangyo Co., Ltd., 1990—, Elite Co., Ltd., 1990—, Sun-Maruka Co., Ltd. 1990—. Creator: Pia by DiMitri (women's cologne and perfume), 1978, DiMitri (men's cologne), 1978. Recipient Coty Fashion Critics award for menswear, 1973, Coty Return award, 1974, Coty Hall of Fame award, 1975 Mem. Coun. Fashion Designers Am., Inc., Mens' Fashion Assn. Clubs: Jockey (Miami); Atrium (N.Y.C.), Le Club (N.Y.C.); Club A. Roman Catholic. Office: DiMitri of Italy Inc-Mailbox Etc 666 5th Ave # 311 New York NY 10103-0001 also: 8981 W Sunset Blvd Ste 105 Los Angeles CA 90069-1838

DIMITRIADIS, ANDRE C., health care executive; b. Istanbul, Turkey, Sept. 29, 1940; s. Constantine N. and Terry D. BS, Robert Coll., Istanbul, 1964; MS, Princeton U., 1965; MBA, NYU, 1967, PhD, 1970. Analyst Mobil Oil Internat., NYC, 1965-67; mgr. TWA, NYC, 1967-73; dir. Pan Am. Airways, NYC, 1973-76, asst. treas., 1976-79; v.p., chief fin. officer Air Calif., Newport Beach, 1979-82; exec. v.p. fin. and adminstrn., chief fin. officer Western Airlines, Los Angeles, 1982-85, dir.; sr. v.p. (fin) Am. Med. Internat., from 1985, chief fin. officer, 1985-89, exec. v.p., 1988-89; dir., exec. v.p. fin., chief fin. officer Beverly Enterprises Inc., Ft. Smith, Ark., 1989-92; chmn., CEO LTC Properties, Inc., 1992—. Bd. dirs. Assisted Living Concepts, Inc. Democrat. Greek Orthodox. Home: 4470 Vista Del Preseas Malibu CA 90265-2540 Office: Ltc Properties Inc 31365 Oak Crest Dr Ste 200 Westlake Village CA 91361-5693

DIMITRIJEVIC, MARKO, finance company executive; Grad., U. of Lausanne, Switzerland; MBA, Stanford Bus. Sch. Chartered finl. analyst. Analyst Wall Street; founder, pres. Everest Capital, 1990—. Trustee Stanford Bus. Sch. Trust, Miami Mus. of Sci. and Planetarium. Featured (Investing with the Hedge Fund Giants), spkr. in field. Office: Everest Capital Inc 2601 S Bayshore Dr Ste 1700 Miami FL 33133 Office Phone: 305-666-1700. Office Fax: 305-666-1919.*

DIMITRIOU, DOLORES ENNIS, computer consultant; b. Phila., Apr. 7, 1932; d. Charles Adair and Rubye Stanton (Greene) Ennis; m. John Alexander Dimitriou, Sept. 25, 1954 (div. Aug. 1983); 1 child, Sandra Irene Dimitriou Falor. BS in Math., U. Miami, 1954; MA in Linguistics, U. Tex., 1994. Jet engine supr. GE, Evendale, Ohio, 1954-58; rsch. aide Marine Lab. U. Miami, Coral Gables, 1959-65; supr. tests Weathering Rsch. Svc., Princeton, Fla., 1959-87; income tax preparer H&R Block, Homestead, Fla., 1981-83; small bus. cons., pres., co-founder Facts & Figures Svcs., Homestead, 1983-87; computer cons., trainer Wycliffe Bible Translators, Orlando, Fla., 1987-97. Sec., treas., co-founder Weathering Rsch. Svcs., Princeton, Fla., 1959—95; treas. GILLBT, Ghana, 1994—96. Tax aide Am. Assn. Ret. Persons, 1998—, instr., 2002—; long-term care ombudsman state coun., 2000—01, 2003—05; dist. chmn., 2000—01, 2003—04; ombudsman Fla., 1998—2006; bd. dirs. Ch. Women United, 1999—2003; ch. rels. Wycliffe Bible Translators, 1998—2003. Named Outstanding Woman in Religion YWCA, U. Miami, 1953-54. Mem.: Cutler Ridge Woman's Club, Mortar Board, Phi Mu Epsilon. Democrat. Avocations: computers, travel, reading, crafts. Home and Office: 10381 SW 209 Ln Miami FL 33189-3612 Personal E-mail: dolores-dimitriou@att.net.

DIMITRIUS, JO-ELLAN, trial consultant; BS, Scripps Coll., Claremont, Calif., 1975; M, Claremont Grad. Sch., 1977, PhD in Criminology, 1984. With Litig. Scis. Inc., FTI, Vinson & Dimitrius, Dimitrius & Assocs., Pasadena, Calif. Co-author: Reading People, 1998, Put Your Best Foot Forward, 2000. Achievements include consulting on jury selection for the following high-profile trials: Night Stalker (Richard Ramirez), Rodney King, Reginald Denny, O.J. Simpson, Ken Lay, and Jeff Skilling. Office: Dimitrius & Assocs Ste 305 201 S Lake Ave Pasadena CA 91101 Office Phone: 626-431-2700. Office Fax: 626-431-2702. Business E-Mail: jed@dimita.com.

DIMITROV, NIKOLAY, chemistry professor; b. Shumen, Bulgaria, 1962; s. Georgi Petrov Dimitrov and Kitka Nikolava Dimitrova; m. Biliana Staneva-Dimitrova; 1 child, Nikolay Nikolaev. PhD, Bulgarian Acad. Scis., Sofia, 1993. Asst. prof. rsch. Ariz. State U., 2000—02; asst. prof. SUNY, Binghamton, 2003—. Grantee, NSF-DMR, 2006—. Mem.: Electrochem. Soc. Office: SUNY at Binghamton Dept Chemistry PO Box 6000 Binghamton NY 13902-6000 Office Phone: +1-607-777-4271. Business E-Mail: dimitrov@binghamton.edu.

DIMLING, JOHN ARTHUR, marketing executive; b. Pitts., Apr. 9, 1938; s. John Arthur and Elizabeth (Powell) D.; m. Marilyn Jean O'Connor; children: Courtney O'Connor, Meredith O'Connor. AB, Dartmouth Coll., 1960; MS, Carnegie Mellon U., 1962; JD, George Washington U., 1977. Bar: Md. 1977, D.C. 1978. Group mgr. Spindletop Rsch. Corp., Lexington, Ky., 1965-69; v.p. rsch. analysis Nat. Assn. Broadcasters, Washington, 1969-79; v.p. rsch., planning and analysis Arbitron Co., 1979; dir. planning & policy Corp. Pub. Broadcasting, Washington, 1979-82; exec. dir., CEO Electronic Media Rating Coun., NYC, 1982-85; sr. v.p. A.C. Nielsen Co., NYC, 1985-88, exec. v.p., 1988-93, pres., 1993—2001, chmn., 2001—. Chmn. Coltram, NYC, 1969-79; asst. treas. Broadcasting Rating Coun., NYC, 1971-79; cons. Western Broadcasting Corp., Missoula, Mont., 1981; sec., treas. Electronic Media Rating Coun., NYC, 1970-72; bd. dirs. Advt. Rsch. Found., 1989-95, sec., 1992, chmn., 1993-94; exec. com. Market Rsch. Coun., 1995-96; chmn. bd. dirs. NetRatings, Inc. Author: (with others) The Role of Analysis in Regulatory Decision Making-The Case of Cable Television, 1973; contbr. articles to profl. jours. Bd. dirs. Ctr. for Comm., 1994—, St. Christopher's Sch., 2002—; trustee Masters Sch., 2000—. 1st lt. U.S. Army, 1963-65. Mem. ABA, Radio-TV Rsch. Coun., Ardsley Country Club (bd. govs. 1987-94, 2003-), Dartmouth Club (NY). Avocation: tennis. Home: 198 Judson Ave Dobbs Ferry NY 10522-3028 Office: Nielsen Media Rsch 770 Broadway New York NY 10003 E-mail: dimling@tvratings.com.

DIMMA, WILLIAM ANDREW, real estate executive; b. Montreal, Que., Can., Aug. 13, 1928; s. William Roy and Lillian Norine (Miller) D.; m. Katherine Louise Vacy Ash, May 13, 1961; children: Suzanne Elizabeth Irene, Katherine Lillian Louise. BA in Sci., U. Toronto, Can., 1948; postgrad., Harvard U., 1956, DBA, 1973; MBA, York U., Toronto, 1969; LLD (hon.), York U., 1998; D of Commerce (hon.), St. Mary's U., 1991. Registered profl. engr., Ont. With Union Carbide Can Ltd., 1948-70, exec. v.p., bd. dirs., 1967-70; prof., dean faculty adminstrv. studies York U., 1974-76; pres., bd. dirs. Torstar Corp., Toronto Star Newspapers Ltd., Toronto, 1976-78; pres. A.E. LePage Ltd., Toronto, 1979-84; pres., CEO Royal LePage Ltd., Toronto, 1984-86, dep. chmn., 1986-93. Bd. dirs. Brookfield Asset Mgmt. Inc., Home Trust Co., Magellan Aerospace Corp., York U. Devel. Corp.; chmn. bd. dirs. Decision Dynamics Tech. Ltd., Home Capital Group; dir. adv. group Inst. Chartered Accts.; jury Best Bus. Book of Yr., Best Bds. of Yr., Bus. Hall Fame. Author: Canada Development Corporation: Diffident Experiment on a Large Scale, 1973, Excellence in the Boardroom, 2002, Tougher Boards for Tougher Times, 2006. Hon. dir. Niagara Inst., chmn. 1983-86; hon. gov. York U., chmn., 1992-97; hon. trustee Hosp. for Sick Children, Jr. Achievement of Met. Toronto, chmn., 1992-93; gov. Can. Journalism Found. Decorated Order of Can., Order of Ont.; knight comdr. Order of St. Lazarus of Jerusalem; Elmslie Meml. scholar, 1944; Stevens gold medal Harvard Bus. Sch., 1971; Can. Coun. fellow, 1970-73; recipient York U. award Outstanding Corp. Leadership, 2001, Schulich Sch. Bus. Outstanding Leadership award, 1992, Queen's Golden Jubilee medal, 2002. Fellow Inst. Corp. Dirs.; mem. Toronto Club, Toronto Golf Club, York Club, Harvard Club Toronto, Bellair Country Club, Beta Theta Pi. Avocations: swimming, bicycling, writing. Home: Apt 302 407 Walmer Rd Toronto ON Canada M5R 3N2 Personal E-mail: wdimma@brookfield.com.

DIMMICK, CAROLYN REABER, federal judge; b. Seattle, Oct. 24, 1929; d. Maurice C. and Margaret T. (Taylor) Reaber; m. Cyrus Allen Dimmick, Sept. 10, 1955; children: Taylor, Dana. BA, U. Wash., 1951, JD, 1953; LLD, Gonzaga U., 1982, CUNY, 1987. Bar: Wash. 1953. Asst. atty. gen. State of Wash., Seattle, 1953-55; pros. atty. King County, Wash., 1955-59, 60-62; sole practice Seattle, 1959-60, 62-65; judge N.E. Dist. Ct. Wash., 1965-75, King County Superior Ct., 1976-80; justice Wash. Supreme Ct., 1981-85; judge U.S. Dist. Ct. (we. dist.) Wash., Seattle, 1985-94, chief judge, 1994-97, sr. judge, 1997—. Mem. Jud. Resources Com., 1987—94, chmn., 1991—94; mem. Jud. Conf. Com. to Rev. Cir. Coun. Conduct and Disability Orders, 2001—. Recipient Matrix Table award, 1981, World Plan Execs. Coun. award, 1981, Vanguard Honor award King County of Wash. Women Lawyers, 1996, Disting. Alumni award U. Wash. Law Sch., 1997, Outstanding Jurist award King County Bar Assn., 2003; named Wash. Women of Yr. Seattle U. Women's Law Caucus, 2004. Mem. ABA, Am. Judges Assn. (gov.), Nat. Assn. Women Judges, World Assn. Judges, Wash. Bar Assn., Am. Judicature Soc., Order of Coif (Wash. chpt.). Office: US Dist Ct 16134 US Courthouse 700 Stewart St Seattle WA 98101 Office Phone: 206-370-8850. E-mail: carolyn_dimmick@wawd.uscourts.gov.

DIMMICK, JOHN W., communications educator; b. Williamsport, Ind., Oct. 26, 1944; s. Arthur Dimmick and Clara Janet Miller; m. Judith Robinson; 1 child, Jennifer Megan; m. Karen Ann Larson, Mar. 9, 1991. BA, Ind. U., Bloomington, 1966, MA, 1968; PhD, U. Mich., Ann Arbor, 1973. Announcer, newscaster Sta. WBIW Radio, Bedford, Ind., 1964—65; prodn. asst. Sta. WLWI TV, Indpls., 1963; announcer Sta. WTTS-WTTV Radio, Bloomington, 1965—66; announcer, narrator U. of Mich. TV Ctr., Ann Arbor, 1970—72; mem. faculty U. Ill., Chgo., 1972—77, Ohio State U., Columbus, 1977—. Author: Media Competition and Coexistence: The Theory of the Niche, 2003 (award, 2004); contbr. articles to profl. jours. Mem. Air Force ROTC, 1962—64. Mem.: Assn. Edn. Journalism and Mass Communication (mem. mgmt. and econs. divsn. 1990—). Independent. Lutheran. Avocations: shooting sports, English and American history. Office: Ohio State U Sch Comms 3045 A Derby Hall 154 N Oval Columbus OH 43210 Office Phone: 614-292-0168. Office Fax: 614-292-2055. Business E-Mail: dimmick.1@osu.edu.

DIMMITT, LAWRENCE ANDREW, lawyer, educator; b. Kansas City, Kans., July 20, 1941; s. Herbert Andrew and Mary (Duncan) Dimmitt; m. Lois Kinney, Dec. 23, 1962; children: Cynthia Susan, Lawrence Michael. BA, Kans. State U., 1963, MA, 1967; JD, Washburn U., 1968. Bar: Kans. 1968, U.S. Dist. Ct. Kans. 1968, U.S. Ct. Appeals (10th cir.) 1969, Mo. 1973, N.Y. 1975, U.S. Supreme Ct. 1986. Atty. Southwestern Bell Tel. Co., Topeka, 1968-73, gen. atty. Kans., 1979-94, atty. St. Louis, 1973-74, gen. atty. regulation, 1979; atty. AT&T, NYC, 1974-79; ret., 1994. Adj. prof. telecom. law Washburn U. Sch. Law, 1996—2005; mem. polit. sci. adv. coun. Kans State U., 2003—. Mem. master planning com. Hist. Ward-Meade Pk., 1998—2004; bd. dirs. 1st United Meth. Ch., Topeka, 1979—84, mem. nominating com., 1985—87; bd. dirs. Sunflower Music Festival, 1993—94. Recipient commendation, Legal Aid Soc. Topeka, 1986, 1990, 1993. Mem.: Topeka Bar Assn., Kans. Bar Assn. (pres. adminstrv. law sect. 1985—86, bd. editors newsletter), Jayhawker Lit. Club, Rotary (pres. 2001, asst. gov. 2003—05, dist. gov. 2006), Phi Alpha Delta (alumni bd. 1986—88, 1993—97). Home: 3123 SW 15th St Topeka KS 66604-2515 Office Phone: 785-232-9933. E-mail: LLDimmitt@aol.com.

DIMMOCK, VIRGINIA ELLEN, literature and language educator, consultant; d. Howard Gerald and Janet Allen Glabau; m. Donald James Dimmock, Aug. 30, 1985; children: Brett Howard Miller, Ryan Frederick Miller. BA cum laude, Conn. Coll., New London, 1988, MA in Tchg., 1992; 6th-Yr. Cert. in Reading and Lang. Arts, U. Conn., Storrs, 1993. Emergency svcs. dispatcher Waterford (Conn.) Police Dept., 1976—90; tutor lang. arts East Lyme (Conn.) Bd. Edn., 1989—93; cons. lang. arts Chaplin (Conn.) Bd. Edn., 1993—97, Old Saybrook (Conn.) Bd. Edn., 1997—2006, Coventry Bd. Edn., Conn., 2006—. Adj. prof. U. New Haven, New London, Conn., 1999. Comdr. New London (Conn.) Power Squadron, 2000—02, instr. boating safety, 1995—. Fellow: Conn. Writing Project; mem.: Internat. Reading Assn., Conn. Reading Assn. (conf. presenter 1995, cons. 1993—99). Avocations: art, animal rescue, boating, piano. Office: Capt Nathan Hale Mid Sch 1776 Main St Coventry CT 06238

DIMON, JAMIE (JAMES L. DIMON), diversified financial services company executive; b. NYC, Mar. 13, 1956; s. Theodore and Themis Dimon; m. Judith Kent, May 21, 1983; children: Julia, Laura, Kara. BA, Tufts U., 1978; MBA, Harvard U., 1982. V.p., asst. to pres. Am. Express Co., NYC, 1982-85; sr. v.p., CFO Comml. Credit Co., Balt., 1986-88; exec. v.p., CFO Primerica Corp., NYC, 1989—90, pres., 1990—93; pres., COO, CFO The Travelers Group Inc, 1993—98; chmn, co-CEO Salomon Smith Barney Holdings Inc., 1998—2000; pres. Citigroup Inc., 1998—2000; chmn., CEO Bank One Corp., Chgo., 2000—04; pres., COO JPMorgan Chase & Co., NYC, 2004—05, pres., CEO, 2006, chmn., CEO, 2007—. Former bd. dirs. Yum! Brands, Inc.; bd. dirs. Fed. Res. Bank NY, 2007—. Mem. Coun. Fgn. Rels.; bd. dirs. Nat. Ctr. Addiction and Substance Abuse, United Negro Coll. Fund; trustee U. Chgo., NYU Med. Ctr.; civic com. Comml. Club Chgo.; bd. dirs. Econ. Club Chgo., Mt. Sinai Med. Ctr. and Health Systems; mem. trustees com. Chgo. Community Trust. Named one of 100 Most Influential People, Time Mag., 2006; recipient Golden Plate award, Acad. Achievement, 2006. Mem.: Fin. Services Roundtable (bd. dirs.). Office: JPMorgan Chase & Co 270 Park Ave New York NY 10017 E-mail: jamie.dimon@jpmchase.com.*

DIMOND, EDMUNDS GREY, medical educator; b. St. Louis, Dec. 8, 1918; s. Edmunds Grey and Gertrude Ruth (Schmidt) D.; m. Mary Dwight Clark, Nov. 28, 1968 (dec. June 1983); children: Sherri Grey Byrer, Lea Grey Dimond, Lark Grey Dimond-Cates. Student, Purdue U., 1938—39; BS, Ind. U., 1942, MD, 1944. Mem. faculty Med. Ctr., U. Kans., Kansas City, 1950-60, prof., chmn. dept. medicine, 1953-60, dir. cardiovasc. lab., 1950-60; mem., dir. Inst. for Cardiopulmonary Diseases, Scripps Clinic and Rsch. Found., 1960-67; rsch. assoc. physiology Scripps Inst. Oceanography, La Jolla, Calif., 1960-68; prof. in residence Sch. Medicine, U. Calif., San Diego, 1967-68; scholar in residence Nat. Libr. Medicine, 1967; spl. asst. to asst. sec. HEW, Washington, 1968; Disting. univ. prof. medicine U. Mo., Kansas City, 1968-98, provost for health scis., 1968-79. Fulbright prof., The Netherlands, 1956; vis. prof., Israel, 1978; scholar in residence Rockefeller Found. Study Ctr., Bellagio, Italy, 1978; chmn. overseas edn. team Dept. State, 1962, 64-66, 73; guest lectr. Chinese Med. Assn., 1971-73, 76-80, 82-92; pres. Edgar Snow Fund, Inc., Diastole-Hospital Hill, Inc. Author: Electrocardiography, 1952, rev. edits., 1955, 60, 64, Digitalis, 1957, Exercise Electrocardiograms, 1961, More Than Herbs and Acupuncture, 1975, Inside China Today, 1981, Take Wing, 1991, Dr. Horse of China, 1992, Reverend Whitehead, Mississippi Pioneer, 1987, Letters from Forest Place, 1993, Essays By An Unfinished Physician, 1995, Milepost Eighty, 2000, Milepost Eighty-Five, 2005; editor: Diastole on Hospital Hill Audiotape, 1980-86; editor-in-chief Accel, 1968-77; contbr. articles to profl. jours. Bd. dirs. Truman Med. Ctr., Kansas City, Mo., Eye Found., Kansas City, Sci. Edn. Partnership, Kansas City. With M.C., AUS, 1945-47. Paul Dudley White Traveling scholar, 1956-57. Master Am. Coll. Cardiology (pres. 1962, Disting. Svc. award 1969). Home and Office: 2501 Holmes St Kansas City MO 64108-2742 Office Phone: 816-235-8855. Personal E-mail: gdimond@kc.rr.com.

DIMOPOULOS, VASSILIOS GEORGIOS, physician, researcher; s. Georgios Vassilios and Chrysoula Dimopoulos; m. Polyxeni Mouhtouri, Jan. 6, 2001; children: George, Aris-Christian. MD, U. Patras, 1995. Gen.

practitioner Kalamata Hosp., Androusa, Greece, 1996—97, gen. surgery resident Greece, 1999—2000; neurosurgical resident U. Hosp. Patras, Greece, 2001; neurosurgical fellow Med. Ctr. Ctrl. Ga., Macon, 2001—06; neurosurgical resident Strong Meml. Hosp., Rochester, NY, 2006—. Contbr. articles to profl. jours.; sci. reviewer: Med. Sci. Monitor. Mem. Young Neurosurgeons Forum. Flight surgeon Hellenic Air Force, 1997—98, Athens, Kalamata. Mem.: AMA, World Fedn. Neurosurgical Soc., Arbeitsgemeinschaft Osteosynthesedragen Spine N.Am., Soc. Neurosci., Hellenic Med. Assn., Patras Med. Assn., Gen. Med. Coun., So. Med. Assn. Achievements include research in the use of transintracranial ultrasound in neurosurgery; the proposal of third nerve palsy scale; the proposal of recurrent laryngeal nerve intraoperative irritation scale. Avocations: travel, weightlifting, movies, track and field. Office: Strong Meml Hosp 601 Elmwood Ave Box 670 Rochester NY 14642-8670

DIMSDALE, JOEL EDWARD, psychiatry educator; b. Sioux City, Iowa, Apr. 16, 1947; s. Lewis J. and Phyllis (Green) D.; m. Nancy Kleinman, Sept. 17, 1978; 1 child, Jonathan Jared. BA in Biology, Carleton Coll., 1968; MA in Sociology, Stanford U., 1970, MD, 1973. Diplomate Am. Bd. Psychiatry. Resident in psychiatry Mass. Gen. Hosp., Boston, 1973-76; instr. psychiatry Harvard U. Sch. Medicine, Boston, 1976-80, asst. prof., 1980-84, assoc. prof., 1984-85; assoc. prof., now prof. psychiatry U. Calif., San Diego, 1985—, chair acad. senate, 2002—03. Cons. to Pres.'s Commn. on Mental Health, Washington, 1977-78, NIH, Washington, 1980—. Editor: Survivors, Victims and Perpetrators, 1980, Quality of Life in Behavior Medicine Rsch., 1995; editor-in-chief Psychosomatic Medicine, 1992-02; mem. editl. bd. Internat. Jour. Behavioral Medicine, 1993—, Applied Biobehavioral Rsch., 1994—, Am. Jour. Human Biology, 1994-2003, Psychosomatics, 1996—; contbr. articles to profl. jours. Fellow Am. Psychopathol. Assn., Acad. Behavioral Med. Rsch. (coun. 1988-91, 2004—, pres. 1991-92), Soc. of Behavioral Medicine (pres. 2000), Disting. fellow Am. Psychiat. Assn., Sleep Rsch. Soc. (chmn. rsch. com. 2005—); mem. Am. Psychosomatic Soc. (coun. 1982-85, pres. 1999), Sigma Xi. Home: 4435 Ampudia St San Diego CA 92103 Office: Dept Psychiatry 0804 9500 Gilman Dr UCSD La Jolla CA 92093-0804 Office Phone: 619-543-5592. Business E-Mail: jdimsdale@ucsd.edu.

DI MUCCIO, MARY-JO, retired librarian; b. Hanford, Calif., June 16, 1930; d. Vincent and Theresa (Yovino) DiMuccio. BA, Immaculate Heart Coll., LA, 1953, MA, 1960; PhD, US Internat. U., San Diego, 1970. Tchr. parochial schs., Los Angeles, 1949-54, San Francisco, 1954-58; tchr. Govt. of Can., Victoria, B.C., 1958—60; asst. libr. Immaculate Heart Coll. Libr., Los Angeles, 1960-62, head libr., 1962—72; adminstrv. libr. City of Sunnyvale, Calif., 1972-88; ret., 1988. Instr. Foothill C.C., Los Altos, 1977—95. Mem. exec. bd., past pres. Sunnyvale Cmty. Svcs.; chair for Chefs Who Care, Cmty. Svcs. Agy., 1999— Mem. ICF (past pres.), Cath. Libr. Assn. (past pres.), Sunnyvale Bus. and Profl. Women, Peninsula Dist. Bus. and Profl. Women (past pres.). Home: 736 Muir Dr Mountain View CA 94041-2509 E-mail: JO736@aol.com. *My goal has been to become a universal person, and that is my responsibility as a professional person-to see that the society we are building for tomorrow is appropriate to the needs of the people we serve.*

DIMUCCIO, ROBERT A., insurance company executive; b. Providence; Grad., Providence Coll. CPA; cert. CPCU. With KPMG Peat Marwick, Providence, 1978—92; v.p., sr. v.p., treas., to CFO Amica Mutual Ins. Co., Lincoln, RI, 1992—2004, exec. v.p., 2004—05, pres., CEO, 2005—. Bd. dir. Inst. Bus. & Home Safety, 2005—, RI Pub. Expenditure Coun. Phi Class Leadership RI, 2001. Office: Amica Mutual Ins Co 100 Amica Way Lincoln RI 02865 Office Phone: 800-652-6422.*

DINAN, CURTIS L., gas industry executive; Grad., Drury Univ. CPA. Sr. acctg. positions Arthur Andersen LLP; ptnr., audit practice Grant Thornton LLP; sr. v.p., chief acctg. officer ONEOK Inc., Tulsa, Okla., 2004—07, sr. v.p., CFO., treas., 2007—. Past. pres., treas., dir. Tulsa Court Appointed Spl. Advocates; past. treas., dir. Child Abuse Network; mem. adv. bd. Breech Sch. Bus. Drury Univ. Mem.: Am. Inst. CPAs, Okla. Soc. CPAs. Office: ONEOK Inc 100 W Fifth St Tulsa OK 74103*

DINAN, DONALD ROBERT, lawyer; b. Nashua, NH, Aug. 28, 1949; s. Robert J. and Jeanette F. (Farland) D.; m. Amy Littlepage, June 24, 1978; 1 child: Emma. BS in Econs., U. Pa., 1971; JD, Georgetown U., 1974; LLM, London Sch. Econs., 1975. Bar: Mass. 1976, D.C. 1977, N.Y. 1986, U.S. Ct. Appeals (1st, 2d, D.C. and fed. cirs.), U.S. Supreme Ct. 1979, U.S. Ct. Internat. Trade 1982. Atty. advisor US Internat. Trade Commn., Washington, 1976-81, chief patent br., 1981-82, chief unfair imports investigation div., 1981-82; ptnr. Adduci Dinan & Mastriani, 1982-88, Fitzpatrick, Cella, Harper & Scinto, 1988-90, O'Connor & Hannan, 1990-98, Hall Estill, 1998—2006, Roetzel & Andress, 2006—. Prof. internat. trade Georgetown U., Wharton Econs. Soc.; prin. Coun. for Excellence in Govt. Mem. Mayor's Internat. Adv. Coun., Washington, D.C. Regulatory Reform Com.; mem. Washington Dem. State Com., gen. counsel, 1988-92, 94-2000; chmn. D.C. Affirmative Action Com. for Dem. Conv. 2004; chmn. D.C. Dem. Campaign Victory Fund, 2004. Mem. ABA, Fed. Bar Assn., ITC Trial Laywers Assn., Am. Intellectual Property Law Assn. (chmn. internat. trade com., export lic. com.). Democrat. Roman Catholic. Home: 221 9th St SE Washington DC 20003-2112 Office: Roetzel & Andress 1300 Eye Dr NW Ste 400 East Washington DC 20005 Office Phone: 202-625-0600. Business E-Mail: ddinan@ralaw.com.

DINAN, ROBERT MICHAEL, lawyer; b. Quebec City, Que., Can., Aug. 12, 1956; s. John H.T. and Lorraine (Matte) D.; m. Alicia Soldevila, June 11, 1983; children: Karina, Philippe, John. LLB, U. Laval, 1978. Bar: Que., 1980. Assoc. Pothier Begin et al, Quebec City, 1980—87, ptnr., 1987—94, Lepage Dinan, Quebec City, 1994—2002; chmn. bd. TeleFilm Can., Montreal, 1993—98; ptnr. O'Brien, Avocats, Quebec City, 2003—. Mem. exec. com., v.p., pres. Jeffery Hales Hosp., Quebec City, 1992-95, bd. dirs., chmn. bd. dirs., 1996—; bd. dirs. Duke of Edinburgh's award, 1998-2000, Voice of English Que., 1992-98, mem. exec. com., 1995-98, v.p., 1997-98, v.p. St. Brigid's Home, 1985-89, pres., 2002-; v.p. Danse Partout, 1989-91; v.p. Morrin Coll. Found., 1997-2000, fin. com. 1997-2000, bldg. com. 1997-2000; mem. Centre Aide Que., 1985—, Assemblée Regie Régional Santé et Svcs. Sociaux, 1992-97, appt. Queen's Coun., 1992; bd. dirs. Can. TV and Cable Prodn. Fund, 1996-98, Que. Garrison Club, 2006—. Recipient Bursery award Minister of Justice, Can., 1978. Mem.: Que. Bar Assn. (external rels. com. 1993—96, libr. com. 1986—88), Can. Bar Assn., Que. Garrison Club (bd. dirs. 2006—), Que. C. of C. Avocations: gardening, painting, skiing, bicycling. Home: 2391 Marie-Victorin Quebec City PQ Canada G1T 1K2 Home Phone: 418-682-6849; Office Phone: 418-648-1511. Personal E-mail: rdinan@obrienavocats.qc.ca.

DINAPOLI, THOMAS PETER, state official, former state legislator; b. Rockville Centre, NY, Feb. 10, 1954; s. Nicholas and Adeline DiNapoli. BA in History magna cum laude, Hofstra U., 1976; MA in Human Resources Mgmt., New Sch. U., 1988. Mem. N.Y. State Assembly from Dist. 16, 1987—2007; mem. standing com. children & families, edn. com., environ. conservation com., higher edn. com., tourism, arts & sports devel. com. N.Y. State Assembly, co-chmn. legis. com. water resource needs of L.I., chmn. bucom. marine resources & task force L.I. Sound; comptr. State of NY, Albany, 2007—. Truste mineola Bd. Edn., 1972-82; legis. asst. Assenblyman Angelo Orazio; Dem. candidate North Hempstead Town Coun., 1975, town supr., 1982; dist. rep. COngressman Robert Mrazek, 1983-85; pres. Reform Dem. Assn. Great Neck; mem. Great Neck United Cmty. Fund Bd.; pres., bd. dirs. Big Bros. & Big Sisters Nassau County; bd. dirs. Herricks Cmty. Life Ctr. Mem. Sierra Club, Cellini Lodge-Sons of Italy. Office: Office State Comptr 110 State St Albany NY 12236*

DINARDO, DANIEL N., archbishop; b. Steubenville, Ohio, May 23, 1949; BA, Cath. U. Am., Master's degree; BST, Gregorian U., Rome, 1975. Ordained priest Roman Cath. Ch., 1977. Asst. pastor St. Pius X Ch., Brookline, Pa., 1977-80; asst. chancellor Diocese of Pitts., 1980-83; mem. staff Congregation of Bishops, Rome, 1983-89; asst. sec. edn. Diocese of Pitts., 1991; pastor Sts. John and Paul Parish; consecrated bishop, 1997; co-adjutor bishop Diocese of Sioux City, Iowa, 1997-98, bishop, 1998—2004, Archdiocese of Galveston-Houston, 2004—06, archbishop, 2006—. Office: Archdiocese of Galveston Houston 1700 San Jacinto Houston TX 77001-090

DINCECCO, JENNIE ELIZABETH WILLIAMS SWANSON, health-care administrator, mentor, educator, volunteer; b. Atlanta, Aug. 5, 1932; d. Chester Arthur and Cleo Annie Williams; m. Richard Edward Swanson, Apr. 24, 1954 (dec. 1994); children: Laurel Dee Swanson, Jeffrey Richard Swanson, Scott Edward Swanson; m. Thomas M. Dincecco, Aug. 26, 2000. BS, Northwestern U., 1954; MS, No. Ill. U., 1972, EdD, 1976. Pub. sch. tchr., 1954-69; psycho-ednl. diagnostician, 1969-72; faculty Loyola U., Chgo., 1976-82, asst. prof. ob-gyn and pediat., 1979-82; dir. pre-start project depts. ob-gyn and pediat. Stritch Sch. Medicine, 1978-82; dir. spl. svcs. Cmty. Unit Sch. Dist. 220, 1982-92. Hospice bereavement vol., 1997—; coun. mem., mentor Cong. Unitarian Ch.; antique dealer; mem. Gov. Ill. Com. Preventive Svcs., 1979-80; chair B-3 subcom. First Chance Consortium, 1978-80; chair INTER-ACT, 1979-80; cons. in field. Author: Dying With Open Eyes: Alzheimer's Disease, 2005, (with others) Wise Words From Women of a Certain Age, 2006; co-author: Partners in Child Development, 1978; columnist: Woodstock Ind. Newspaper, 2006-07. Vol. Latino Coalition, Alzheimer's Assn. Grantee HEW, 1973-76, 78-82. Mem.: Rep. Tchrs. McHenry County, Nat. Assn. Edn. Young Child, Nat. Acad. Neuropsychology, Nat. Perinatal Assn., Assn. Maternal and Child Health, Coun. Exceptional Children, Golden Cir., Woodstock Opera House Commn. (chairperson 2001—), Northwestern U. Alumni Assn., Nu Alumni Club, Delta Kappa Gamma (scholar 1974), Delta Delta Delta (life; golden cir.). Unitarian Universalist.

DINCULEANU, NICOLAE, mathematician, educator; b. Padea, Romania, Feb. 26, 1925; came to U.S., 1976. s. Nicolae and Frusina (Lusca) Dobrescu; m. Elena Constantinescu, Feb. 9, 1959. Engr., Poly. Inst., Bucharest, 1950; licencie math., U. Bucharest, 1951; PhD in Math, U. Bucarest, 1957; Doctor honoris causa, U. Craiova, 1995, U. Bucharest, 2001. Prof. math. U. Bucharest, 1950-77; vis. prof. Queen's U., Kingston, Ont., Canada, 1966-67, U. Rennes, France, U. Erlangen, Germany, 1970; Disting. vis. prof. U. Pitts., 1970-71; vis. research prof. U. Fla., Gainesville, 1972-77, prof. math., 1977—2003. Author: Vector Measures, 1967, Integration on Locally Compact Spaces, 1974, Textbook of Mathematical Analysis, 2 vols, 1962, Vector Integration and Stochastic Integration in Banach Spaces, 2000; also articles. Mem.: Romanian Acad. (hon.). Mem. Romanian Orthodox Ch. Club: Torch. Office: U Fla Math Dept Little Hall # 450A Gainesville FL 32611-2082 Business E-Mail: nd@math.ufl.edu.

DINE, JEFFREY MALCOLM, lawyer; b. Cin., Oct. 26, 1966; BA, U. Mich., Ann Arbor, 1988, JD, 1995. Bar: NY 1996. Assoc. Weil, Gotshal & Manges LLP, NYC, 1995—98, Seward & Kissel LLP, NYC, 1998—. Note editor (jour.) Michigan Jour. of Internat. Law. V.p., treas., bd. mem. The Barrow Group, Inc., NYC, 1999—. Mem.: ABA, NYC Bar, U. Mich. Gilbert & Sullivan Soc., Blue Hill Troupe, Ltd., Lotos Club. Avocations: theatrical design, photography, film. Office: Seward & Kissel LLP 1 Battery Park Plz New York NY 10004 Home Phone: 646-329-5145; Office Phone: 212-574-1547. Business E-Mail: dine@sewkis.com.

DINEEN, JOHN C., manufacturing executive; m. Gina Dineen; 2 children. BS, Univ. Vt. Mgmt. positions GE, 1986—2005, telecommunications engr. Rockville, Md., gen. mgr. power equip. Plainville, Conn., gen. mgr. meter bus. Somersworth, NH, gen. mgr. microwave & a.c. Louisville; mgr. of fin. GE Asia, Hong Kong; pres. GE Plastics Pacific; v.p. & gen. mgr. plastics & resins GE Advanced Materials; pres., CEO GE Infrastructure-Rail, 2005—. Office: GE 3135 Easton Tpke Fairfield CT 06431*

DINEEN, JOHN K., lawyer; b. Gardiner, Maine, Jan. 21, 1928; s. James J. and Eleanor (Kelley) D.; m. Carolyn Foley Reardon (dec. 1982); children: Jane, Martha, Louisa, Jessica, John; m. Susan Lowell Wales, Aug. 15, 1986; children: Theodore, Ralph, Andrew. BA, U. Maine, 1951; JD, Boston U., 1954; DHL (hon.), Cambridge Coll., 2001. Bar: Maine 1954, Mass. 1954. Ptnr. Weston, Patrick & Stevens, Boston, 1954-67, Gaston & Snow, Boston, 1970-91, Peabody & Arnold, Boston, 1967—70, ptnr., 1991—2000, counsel, 2000—02; sr. counsel Nutter McClennen & Fish, 2002—. Spl. asst. atty. gen. Commonwealth of Mass., Boston, 1965-67; dir. Dingle Am. Properties Ltd., Dingle, County Kerry, Ireland, 1973—; pres., trustee Boston Local Devel. Corp., 1982—. Trustee emeritus Waring Sch., Beverley, Mass., 1981—. Cambridge (Mass.) Coll.; life trustee U.S.S. Constn. Mus., 1993—; trustee, chmn. Nahant (Mass.) Pub. Libr., 1996—; former trustee Boston U. Med. Ctr., Winsor Sch. Emmanuel Coll., Boston, Hebron Acad., Maine, Boston Aid to the Blind, 1994-2000. With U.S. Army, 1946-48. Mem. Boston Bar Assn., Mass. Bar Assn., Boston Law Sch. Alumni Assn. (exec. com. 1989-91), Marshall Street Hist. Soc., Tavern Club, Union Club, Cary Street Club, Apollo Club, Norway Weary Club. Republican. Roman Catholic. Home: 40 Pleasant St Nahant MA 01908-1632 Office: Nutter McClennen & Fish LLP World Trade Ctr West 155 Seaport Blvd Boston MA 02210-2604 Office Phone: 617-439-2804 E-mail: jdineen@nutter.com.

DINEL, RICHARD HENRY, lawyer; b. LA, Sept. 16, 1942; s. Edward Price and Edith Elizabeth (Rheinstein) D.; m. Joyce Ann Korsmeyer, Dec. 26, 1970; children: Edward, Alison. BA, Pomona Coll., 1964; JD, Stanford U., 1967. Bar: Calif. Owner Richard H. Dinel, Profl. Law Corp., LA, 1971-79; ptnr. Richards, Watson & Gershon, LA, 1979-92, of counsel, 1992-93; pres. R.H. Dinel Investment Counsel, Inc., LA, 1992—. Chmn. bd. Pomona Coll. Assocs., 1987-89; ex-officio trustee Pomona Coll., 1987-89; arbitrator Chgo. Bd. Options Exch., 1978—, Pacific Stock Exch., 1979—; bd. govs. Western Los Angeles County coun. Boys Scouts Am., 1993—. Mem. Securities Ind. Assn. (speaker compliance and legal div. 1978-92), Pomona Coll. Alumni Assn. (chmn. alumni fund and continuing edn. com. 1972-73), Nat. Assn. Securities Dealers (mem. nat. bd. arbitrators 1978-90). Office: 11661 San Vicente Blvd Ste 400 Los Angeles CA 90049-5112

DINER, BRYAN C., lawyer; b. Livingston, NJ, Dec. 22, 1962; BSChemE, NJ Inst. Tech., 1984; JD, Seton Hall U., 1987. Bar: DC 1988, NJ, US Dist. Ct. (Dist. NJ), US Patent & Trademark Office. Resident & mng. ptnr. Brussels Office Finnegan, Henderson, Farabow, Garrett & Dunner LLP, 1998—2003, ptnr. Washington, mem. exec. com. Spkr. in field. Mem.: NJ State Bar Assn., DC Bar Assn., Am. Inst. Chem. Engrs., Am. Chem. Soc., Am. Intellectual Property Law Assn., ABA. Fluent in French. Office: Finnegan Henderson Farabow Garrett & Dunner LLP 901 New York Ave NW Washington DC 20001-3315 Office Phone: 202-408-4000. Office Fax: 202-408-4400. Business E-Mail: bryan.diner@finnegan.com.

DINERMAN, MIRIAM, social work educator; b. NYC, Apr. 13, 1925; d. Abraham J. and Frances (Shostac) Goldforb; m. Harold Dinerman, June 12, 1951 (dec. June 1976); children: David, Ellen, Ruth. BA with honors, Swarthmore Coll., 1945; MSW, Columbia U., 1949, D of Social Welfare, 1972. Youth dir. Jewish Assn. for Neighborhood Ctrs., NYC, 1949-50, program dir., 1951-54; various social work part time positions, 1955-60; asst. prof. Rutgers U. Grad. Sch. Social Work, New Brunswick, NJ, 1961-72, assoc. prof., 1972-76, prof., 1976-99, asst. dean for acad. planning, 1973-75, assoc. dean, 1975-81, acting dean, 1978, chmn. health care sequence, mem. New Brunswick faculty coun., 1989-93, chair, 1991-92; dir. PhD program Rutgers U. Sch. Social Work, 1992-97, emerita, 1999—. Mem. grants rev. panel Office Human Devel. Svcs., HHS, 1986—90; cons. on health and social svcs. N.J. Legis. Task Force on 21st Century; mem. task force on std. of need N.J. Divsn. Econ. Assistance, 1989—91; manuscript rev. editor Longman's Press, Methuen Press; dir. Ctr. for Internat. and Comparative Social Work, 1977—99; adj. prof. Yeshiva U. Sch. Social Work, 1999—. Editor: Social Work Futures, 1983; mem. editl. bd. Affilia: Jour. Women and Social Work, 1985-94, 1995—, book rev. editor., 1995-00, editor-in-chief, 2000-06, mem. corp. bd., 2006-; contbr. articles to profl. jours., chpts. to books. Bd. dirs. Def. for Children Internat., 1980—88; steering com. Nat. Jobs for All Campaign, 2005—; bd. dirs. Friend to Advance Social Svc., 2006. Grantee NIMH, 1966-67, Rutgers U. Rsch. Coun. and Samuel Silberman Fund, 1979-80. Mem.: NJ AAUP (task force on health care policy), NASW (chpt. pres. 1984—86, nat. com. on nominations and leadership identification 1988—97, editl. com. 1991—95, steering com. polit. action for candidate election NYC chpt. 1996—, bd. dirs. NYC chpt. 1999—), Group for Advancement of Doctoral Edn. (sec. steering com. 1990—96), Coun. on Social Work Edn. (program planning com. 1984—89, ednl. policy and planning commn. 1989—94), Internat. Assn. Schs. Social Work (agt. 1988—95, bd. dirs.), Acad. Cert. Social Workers. Home: 353 W 29th St New York NY 10001-4784 Office Phone: 212-960-5289.

DINERSTEIN, ROBERT CHARLES, lawyer, former bank executive; b. Bklyn., Aug. 4, 1942; s. Benjamin and Frances Dinerstein; m. Martha Lay. BA cum laude, Harvard U., 1963; JD, U. Mich., 1966. Bar: NY 1966, US Dist. Ct. (so. dist.) NY, US Ct. Appeals (2nd cir.), US Supreme Ct. Asst. to corp. counsel law dept. City of NY, 1966-70; litig. assoc. Debevoise, Plimpton, Lyons & Gates, NYC, 1970-73; corp. sec., assoc. gen. counsel Am. Airlines, Inc., NYC, 1973-79; gen. counsel Citicorp, NYC, 1982-87; exec. v.p., gen. counsel Shearson Lehman Bros., Inc., NYC, 1987-90; mng. dir., gen. counsel Union Bank Switzerland AG, NYC, 1991—2006; co-chair, global fin. institutions grp. Greenberg Traurig, NYC, 2006—, chair, fin. institutions practice, 2006—. Chmn., nominating and governance com. bd. dirs. Medarex, Inc. Trustee ARC Greater NY, NYC, 1996—, Phipps Houses, NYC, 1997—, Jewish Mus., NYC, 1999—, Stamford (Conn.) Symphony Orch., 1999—; bd. chmn. Everybody Wins! Found., NY Chpt. Mem. Securities Industries Assn. (mem. fed. regulation com. 1997, chmn. holding co. regulatory com. 1999—, 2005 Disting. Leadership award), Coun. Fgn. Rels., Coun. Sr. Internat. Legal Officers (mem. conf. bd.), Swiss-Am. C. of C, Assn. Bar of City NY, ABA, Fgn. Policy Assn. (assoc.), Econ. Club NY, Inst. Internat. Bankers (exec. com. of Bd. Dirs.) Home: 15 W 81st St New York NY 10024-6022 Office: Greenberg Traurig LLP Metlife Bldg 200 Park Ave New York NY 10166 Office Phone: 212-801-2212. Fax: 212-821-5804; Office Fax: 212-805-5592.*

DINES, DAVID MICHAEL, surgeon, educator; b. NYC, Feb. 4, 1948; s. Aaron and Yvette Harriet Dines; m. Judith Lori Dines, Jan. 29, 1973; children: Joshua Scott, Alison Kate. BA in Biology, Lehigh U., Bethlehem, Pa., 1970; MD, NJ Coll. Medicine, 1974. Diplomate Am. Bd. Surgery. Resident in orthop. surgery NY Hosp. Cornell, NYC, 1974—76, Hosp. Spl. Surgery, NYC, 1976—79, fellow, 1980, Am. Acad. Orthop. Surgery, Chgo., 1981; adj. Cornell U. Med. Coll., NYC, 1983—; clin. prof. orthop. surgery Albert Einstein Coll. Medicine, NYC, 1998—, chmn. dept. orthop. surgery, 1996—; sr. orthop. attending Hosp. for Spl. Surgery, NYC. Team physician NY Mets, 1991—97, USTA, 1999—; med. advisor Assn. Tennis Profls., Punte Verde, Fla., 1994—, dir. med. svcs. (Men's Profl. Tennis), 2004—; team physician US Davis Cup Tennis Team, 2000—04; trustee bd. Jour. Shoulder and Elbow Surgery, 2005—; presenter in field. Contbr. more than 100 articles to profl. jours. Fund raiser Hosp. Spl. Surgery, NYC, 1979—. Named one of Best Drs. in NY, NY Mag., 1997—, 2002, 2005, Best Drs in Am., 1999—2002, 2005; recipient John Chanley Meml. award, U. Liverpool, Eng., 1996. Fellow: Am. Acad. Orthop. Surgeons (mem. publs. com. 2005—, mem. bd. edn. com. 2005—); mem.: Assn. Tennis Profls. (med. dir. 2005—), Assn. Team Profl. Med. Soc. (assoc. dir. 1991), Am. Orthop. Assn. (mem. membership com. 1998—), Acad. Orthop. Soc. Am., Am. Shoulder and Elbow Soc. (mem. exec. com. 1999—, pres. 2005, pres.-elect, Neer award 2004). Avocations: tennis, golf, politics. Office: Albert Einstein Coll Med 935 Northern Blvd Ste 303 Great Neck NY 11021 Home Phone: 516-997-8514; Office Phone: 516-482-1037. Personal E-mail: ddinesmd98@aol.com.

DING, JIANCHI, embryologist, researcher; b. Jiangyin, Jiangsu, Peoples Republic of China, Oct. 24, 1957; came to U.S., 1996; s. Xufu and Xiujin (Gao) D.; m. Mingxian Shen, Nov. 15, 1983; children: Helen Guangning, Jennifer Guangting. BSc, Jiangsu Agrl. Coll., Yangzhou, 1982, MSc, 1985; PhD, U. Alta., Edmonton, Can., 1993. Cert. high complexity lab. dir. Am. Bd. Bioanalysis. Instr. Jiangsu Agrl. Coll., Yangzhou, 1985-87; Natural Sci. and Engring. Rsch. Coun. postdoctoral fellow U. Guelph, Guelph, Ont., Can., 1993-95, rsch. assoc., 1993-96; sr. rschr. Inst. for the Study and Treatment of Endometriosis, Oak Brook, Ill., 1996—; lab. dir. Oak Brook Fertility Ctr., 1996—. Contbr. articles to profl. jours. including Biology of Reprodn., Molecular Reprodn. Devel., and Human Reprodn.; assoc. editor: New Technics to Animal and Poultry Production, 2003. Recipient scholarship Jiangsu Edn. Com., China, 1987-88. Mem. Am. Assn. Bioanalysts, Am. Soc. for Reproductive Medicine, Am. Soc. Andrology, Soc. for Study Reprodn., Coll. Reproductive Biology. Home: 117 Hawkins Cir Wheaton IL 60187-8564 Office: Oak Brook Fertility Ctr 2425 W 22nd St Ste 102 Oak Brook IL 60523-4643 Home Phone: 630-665-8959; Office Phone: 630-954-0054. E-mail: jianchiding@sbcglobal.net.

DING, JINWEN, biomedical researcher; MD, Tongji Med. U., Wuhan, China, 1983; PhD, Lund U., Sweden, 1993. Rsch. scientist U. of Toronto, Ont., Canada, 1993—99; asst. prof. Loyola U. Med. Ctr., Maywood, Ill., 1999—2004, U. Chgo., 2004—. Recipient Rsch. award, Am. Cancer Soc., 2004; grantee, Can. Assn. Gastroenterology, 1997, Ill. Transplant Soc., 2002; Sheila Sherlock Basic Rsch. grant, The U. of Toronto, 1997. Mem.: World Assn. of HPB Surgery, Am. Gastroent. Assn. Achievements include research in immunological and molecular mechanisms of liver injury. Home Phone: 630-321-1660.

DINGELL, JOHN DAVID, congressman; b. Colorado Springs, Colo., July 8, 1926; s. John D. and Grace (Bigler) D.m. Deborah Insley; 4 children. BS in Chemistry, Georgetown U., 1949, JD, 1952. Bar: DC 1952, Mich. 1953. Pk. ranger U.S. Dept. Interior, 1948-52; asst. pros. atty. Wayne County, Mich., 1953-55; mem. U.S. Ho. of Reps. from 15th Mich. dist., 1955-65, 2003—, U.S. Ho. of Reps. from 16th Mich. dist., 1965—2002. Ranking minority mem. energy and commerce com. US Congress. Served to 2nd lt. US Army, 1944—46. Recipient Bryce Harlow award, Bryce Harlow Found., 1996, Legis. of Yr. award, Independent Insurance Agents Am., 1997, Nat. Congressional award, Nat. Recreation and Park Assn., 1999, Leadership in Govt. award, The Keystone Ctr., 2000, Golden Carrot award, Consumer Fedn. Am., 2003, Congressional Am. Spirit Medallion, Nat. D-Day Mus., 2004, Connie Mack award, Susan G. Komen Breast Cancer Found., 2004, Esther Peterson Sr. Adv. award, United Seniors Health Cooperative, Frank J. Kelley Public Svc. award, State Bar Mich., 2005. Mem.: Mich. Bar. Assn. Democrat. Roman Catholic. Office: US Ho of Reps 2328 Rayburn Bldg Washington DC 20515-2216 also: District Office 19855 W Outer Dr Ste 103-E Dearborn MI 48124 Office Phone: 202-225-4071, 313-278-2936. Office Fax: 313-278-3914.*

DINGES, RICHARD ALLEN, entrepreneur; b. Englewood, NJ, June 17, 1945; m. Kathie A. Headley; children: Kelly, Courtney, Daniel. Grad., Jersey City State Coll., 1967; MEd, U. Hawaii, 1972; postgrad., William Peterson Coll., 1974-79. Cert. sch. adminstr.; cert. sch. spl. services dir., N.J., Ariz., Hawaii. Pres. Def. Industry Assocs., Sierra Vista, Ariz., 1979—, Fed. Career Cons., Sierra Vista, Ariz., 1985; dir. Nat. Scholarship Locators, Sierra Vista, 1985—. Spl. needs counselor Pinelands Regional Sch. Dist. Editor: Guide to U.S. Defense Contractors, 1985, 87, 10 Step Guide to College Selection, Salary Negotiations for Military, How to Survive the Job Interview. Vice prin. Little Egg Harbor Primary Sch.; founder Families in Touch, 1992. Mem. Cochise County Merit Commn. (vice-chmn.), Platform Soc. Speakers' Assn. Office: 37 Olena St Hilo HI 96720-1867 Home Phone: 808-935-9121. E-mail: Richard_Dinges@hotmail.com.

DINGLE, CAROL A., state agency administrator, writer; b. Winchester, Mass., May 12, 1943; d. Leon B. and Lillian Dingle; m. Melvin Green (dec. Mar. 1989). BA, Merrimack Coll., North Andover, Mass., 1965. English tchr. Springbrook H.S., Silver Spring, Md., 1965—67; program dir. USO, Okinawa, Japan, 1967—69, dir. vols. Frankfurt, Germany, 1970—72, dir. fleet canteens Athens, Greece, 1973—74; bus. owner D&D Advertising, Arlington, Mass., 1975—92; grant adminstr. Commonwealth of Mass., Boston, 1992—; owner Memorable Quotations.com, Intelligentsia Network.com. Editor: (books) Memorable Quotations: Philosophers of Western Civilization, 2000, Memorable Quotations: English Writers of the Past, 2000, Memorable Quotations: French Writers of the Past, 2000, Memorable Quotations: Irish Writers of the Past, 2001, Memorable Quotations: Massachusetts Writers of the Past, 2001, Memorable Quotations: Jewish Writers of the Past, 2003; co-author: (screenplays) Megan McShane, 2003, Escape from Quiet Desperation, 2003, Tina Toscano, 2004, The Carriage House, 2004, That Year in Saigon, 2004, Mel's Boarding House, 2004, The Family Firm, 2006, Return to Saigon, 2006, My Name is Anna Busch, 2007. Personal E-mail: caroladingle@aol.com.

DINGLE, PHILIP, retired oil industry executive; BSCE, U. Calgary, Can., 1970. With drilling and prodn. Imperial Oil Ltd., 1970, v.p. corp. planning, v.p. exploration and prodn.; engring. mgr. Esso Prodn. Malaysia, Inc., 1981, offshore divsn. mgr., 1984; mng. dir. Esso Exploration and Prodn. UK, 1993; chmn. and CEO Esso Malaysia, 1995; pres., gen. mgr. Mobil Oil Can., 1999; pres. ExxonMobil Saudi Arabia, 2001—04; v.p. ExxonMobil Prodn. Co. for Africa, Afghanistan, 2001; chmn., prodn. dir. ExxonMobil Internat. Ltd., 2003—04; pres. ExxonMobil Gas and Power Mktg., 2004—06; v.p. ExxonMobil Production Co., 2004—06. Office: ExxonMobil Gas & Power Mktg 5959 Las Colinas Blvd Irving TX 75039-2298

DINGMAN, MICHAEL DAVID, manufacturing executive, investor; b. New Haven, Sept. 29, 1931; s. James Everett and Amelia (Williamson) D.; children from 1st marriage: Michael David, Linda Channing Cady, James Clifford; m. 2d, Elizabeth G. Tharp; children: James Tharp, David Ross, Patrick Michael. Student, U. Md., DSc Bus. Mgmt. (hon.). Various mgmt. positions Sigma Instruments, Inc., Braintree, Mass., 1954-64; gen. and ltd. ptnr. Burnham & Co., NYC, 1964-70; pres., CEO, bd. dirs. Wheelabrator-Frye Inc., Hampton, NH, 1970-83, chmn. bd., 1977-83; pres., bd. dirs. The Signal Cos., Inc., La Jolla, Calif., 1983-85, AlliedSignal, Morristown, NJ, 1985-86; chmn. bd., CEO The Henley Group, Inc. and affiliates, Hampton, NH, 1986-92; chmn. bd. Fisher Sci. Internat. Inc., Hampton, 1991-98; chmn. bd., CEO Abex Inc., Hampton, 1992-95; pres., CEO Shipston Group Ltd., Nassau, The Bahamas, 1994—. Former bd. dirs. Ford Motor Co., Fisher Sci. Internat. Inc., Timer Warner, Inc., Mellon Fin. Corp., Teekay Shipping Corp. Trustee The John A. Hartford Found. Mem. IEEE (adv. bd.). Clubs: Links, Yacht (N.Y.C.); Union (Boston); Cruising of Am. (Conn.); Bohemian (San Francisco); Lyford Cay (Nassau); La Jolla Country, San Diego Yacht. Office: Shipston Group Ltd Beijing Rep Office LG Twin Towers E 10th Fl B-12 Jianguomenwai Ave Beijing 100022 China Office Phone: 603-929-6800.

DINH, HAI QUANG, mathematics professor, researcher; s. Huynh Van Dinh and Lien Bich Phung; m. Trang Diem Vu, Dec. 28, 2003; 1 child, Anthony Hieu Quang. BS summa cum laude, Ohio U., Athens, 1998, MS, 2000, PhD, 2003. Vis. prof. dept. math. N.D. State U., Fargo, 2003—04; asst. prof. math. Kent State U., Warren, Ohio, 2004—. Contbr. over 15 articles to profl. jours. Recipient Graselli Undergrad. Rsch. award, Ohio U., Dean of Coll. of Arts and Scis., 1998, Rsch. awards, Ohio U., Ctr. of Ring Theory and Its Application, 2001-2002, 2002-2003, Disting. Prof. fellowship, Ohio U. Disting. Prof., 2003, Outstanding Rsch. Accomplishments award, Ohio U., Dept. of Math., 2003. Mem.: Am. Math. Soc. (assoc.). Office: Kent State Univ Trumbull 4314 Mahoning Ave Warren OH 44483 Home Phone: 330-766-3183; Office Phone: 330-675-8924. Business E-Mail: hdinh@kent.edu.

DINH, VIET D., law educator; b. Saigon, Vietnam, Feb. 22, 1968; came to U.S., 1978; s. Phong Hong Dinh and Thunga Thi Nguyen. AB, Harvard U., 1990, JD, 1993. Legal methods instr. Harvard Law Sch., Cambridge, Mass., 1991-93; law clk. to Hon. Laurence Silberman U.S. Ct. Appeals, Washington, 1993-94; law clk. to Justice Sandra Day O' Connor U.S. Supreme Ct., Washington, 1994-95; assoc. spl. counsel Whitewater Com. U.S. Senate, Washington, 1995-96; prof. law Georgetown U., Washington, 1996—; asst. atty. gen. legal policy U.S. Dept. Justice, Washington, 2001—03. Pres. Viet D. Dinh, LLC, Alexandria, Va., 1996—; bd. dirs. News Corp. Ltd., 2004- Contbr. articles, essay to profl. publs. Dep. issues dir. legal policy Wilson for Pres., 1996; mem. Dole/Kemp Econ. Policy Adv. Com., 1996. Republican. Roman Catholic. Avocations: tennis, golf, chess. Office: Georgetown U Law Ctr 600 New Jersey Ave NW Washington DC 20001-2075 E-mail: dinhv@law.georgetown.edu.

DINICH, MICHAEL ANDREW, financial planner; b. Norristown, Pa., Jan. 17, 1981; s. Michael Robert and Kellie Marie Dinich (Stepmother); m. Elizabeth Ann Harding. Registered fin. cons. Internat. Assn. Registered Fin. Consultants, 2006, chartered retirement plans specialist Coll. for Fin. Planning, 2006. Fin. planner Your Money Matters, Sayre, Pa., 1998—. Donor Carbonfund.org, Silver Springs, Md., 2007. With US Army, 1998—2004. Mem.: Million Dollar Round Table (Ct. of the Table 2006). Libertarian. Roman Catholic. Office: Your Money Matters 2382 Elmira St Sayre PA 18840 Home Phone: 570-882-7413; Office Phone: 800-729-1564.

DINICOLA, ROBERT J., consumer products company executive; b. 1948; Grad., St. Peter's Coll. With Macy's Dept. Store, NYC, 1973-89, Federated Stores, NYC, 1989-91; chmn. bd., CEO Bon, Seattle, 1991-94; chmn., CEO Zale Corp., Irving, Tex., 1994—2000, CEO, 2001—02, chmn., 2001—04; exec. chmn. GNC Corp., Pitts., 2004—06, interim CEO, 2005; chmn., CEO Linens Holding Co. (Linens 'n Things), Clifton, NJ, 2006—. Office: Linens Holding Co 6 Brighton Rd Clifton NJ 07015*

DINITZ, SUSAN MARIE, language educator; d. Joseph Frederick and Joyce Marie Cook; m. Jeffrey Howard Dinitz, Aug. 3, 1980; children: Michael Henry, Amy Elizabeth, Thomas James. BA, Ohio Wesleyan U., Delaware, 1974; MA, PhD, Ohio State U., Columbus, 1981. Sr. lectr. U. Vt., Burlington, 1980—, writing ctr. dir., 1983—88, 1998—. Author, editor with Toby Fulwiler: The Letter Book: Assigning and Assessing Letters in the College English Classroom; contbr. articles to profl. jours. Named Vt. Prof. of Yr., Carnegie Found. for the Advancement of Tchg., 2004; recipient Kroepsch-Maurice Excellence in Tchg. award, U. Vt., 1995. Mem.: United Academics (v.p., grievance officer 2003—05), NE Writing Ctrs. Assn. (mem. steering com., v.p., pres.), Internat. Writing Ctrs. Assn., Nat. Coun. Tchrs. English, Phi Beta Kappa. Jewish. Home: 152 Forests Edge Hinesburg VT 05461 Office: University of Vermont 244 Commons L/L Burlington VT 05405 Home Phone: 802-482-3835; Office Phone: 802-656-7963. Business E-Mail: susan.dinitz@uvm.edu.

DINKEL, JOHN GEORGE, automotive executive, consultant; b. Bklyn., Aug. 1, 1944; s. Charles Ernst and Loretta Gertrude D.; m. Leslie Hawkins, Oct. 25, 1969; children: Meredith Anne, Kevin Carter. BS in Mech. Engring, U. Mich., 1967, MS in Mech. Engring, 1969. Staff engr. Chrysler Corp., Highland Park, Mich., 1967-69; engring. editor Car Life Mag., Newport Beach, Calif., 1969-70, Road & Track Mag., Newport Beach, 1972-79, editor, 1979-88, editor in chief, 1988-91, editor at large, 1991-92; dir. product communications Hill-Holliday, 1991-92; pres. John Dinkel & Assocs., 1991—; editor-at-large Sports Car Internat., 1992—; v.p. editl. ops. Calcar, 1995-97; group mgr. member info. and comm. svcs. Automobile Club So. Calif., Costa Mesa, 1998-2000; pub. Westways, 1998-2000; v.p. pub. Driving Media, Inc./Driving.com, 2000—02; asst. pub. relations dir. Pirelli Tire and Saleen, Inc., 2002—05; exec. v.p. product planning, devel. and testing Visionary Vehicles, 2005—; L.A. bur. chief Auto Aficionado Mag., 2005—. Commencement spkr. U. Mich., Dearborn, 1987; hon. judge Meadow Brook Hall Concourse D'Elegance, 1985-86, Hillsborough Concourse D'Elegance, 1989, Palo Alto Concours D'Elegance, 1990; spkr. Direct Mktg. Club So. Calif., 1992; SCCA competition driving instr., 2000—. Author: Road & Track Auto Dictionary, 1977, Road & Track Illustrated Auto Dictionary, 2000; co-author: RX-7: Mazda's Legendary Sports Car, 1991, Mazda MX-5 Miata, 1998, The Mazda RX-8: World's First 4-Door, 4-Seat Sports Car, 2003; editor-at-large Westways, 2003—; contbg. editor No. New Eng. Journey, 2000—, European Car, 2003—; co-host daily radio show Auto Report, 1986-88; host weekly radio show Drive Time, 1996—; contbr. articles to profl. jours.; patentee method and sys. for adjusting settings of vehicle functions, 2000 Nat. chmn. U. Mich. Ann. Fund, 1988—; commr. Irvine (Calif.) Baseball Assn.; sec. Irvine Pony Baseball-Softball, 1995—; organizer clothing drive victims of Armenia earthquake, 1988; soccer coach AYSO, 1984-90, Irvine Soccer Club, 1991—; baseball coach Northwood Little League, 1994—; basketball coach Irvine Boys and Girls Club, 1993—; vol. mem. corp. alliance com. Orange County chpt. Nat. Multiple Sclerosis Soc., 2002. Honored by Colden Ctr. for the Performing Arts, Queens Coll., N.Y.C., 1990. Mem. SAE (panelist conf. on impacts of intelligent vehicle hwy. systems 1990, organizer, chmn. sessions on fuel economy and small cars 1978-79, chmn. pub. affairs Future Transp. Conf. 1997), Am. Racing Press Assn., Internat. Motor Press Assn., Sports Car Club Am., Internat. Motor Sports Assn., Motor Press Guild (pres. 1991), Road Racing Drivers Club (hon.)Pi Tau Sigma. Achievements include being the Four-time winner of SCCA Nelson Ledges 24-hour endurance auto race. E-mail: eleven-tenths@cox.net.

DINKINS, CAROL EGGERT, federal official, lawyer; b. Corpus Christi, Tex., Nov. 9, 1945; d. Edgar H. Jr. and Evelyn S. (Scheel) Eggert; m. Bob Brown; children: Anne, Amy. BS, U. Tex., 1968; JD, U. Houston, 1971. Bar: Tex. 1971. Prin. assoc. Tex. Law Inst. Coastal and Marine Resources, Coll. Law U. Houston, Tex., 1971-73; assoc., ptnr. Vinson & Elkins LLP, Houston, 1973-81, 83-84, 85—, mem. mgmt. com., 1991-96, chair Adminstrv. and Environ. Law practice; asst. atty. gen. environ. & natural resources US Dept. Justice, Washington, 1981-83, dep. atty. gen., 1984-85. Chmn. Pres.'s Task Force on Legal Equity for Women, 1981-83; mem. Hawaiian Native Study Commn., 1981-83; dir. Nat. Consumer Coop. Banks Bd., 1981; chair Pres. Oversight Bd. on Privacy and Civil Liberties, 2006- Contbr. articles to profl. jours. Chmn. Gov.'s Conservation Task Force, 2000, Tex. Gov.'s Flood Control Action Group 1980-81; commr. Tex. Parks and Wildlife Dept., 1997-2001; bd. govs. The Nature Conservancy, 1996—, chmn. 2003-04; dir. Oryx Energy Co., 1990-95, U. Houston Law Ctr. Found., 1985-89, 96-98, Environ. and Energy Study Inst., 1986-98, Houston Mus. Natural Sci., 1986-98, 2000—; mem. exec. com., bd. dirs. Tex. Nature Conservancy, 1985—, chmn., 1996-99, 2003. Mem. ABA (ho. of dels., past chmn. state and local govt. sect., past chair sect. nat. resources, energy, and environ. law, standing com. on fed. judiciary 1997-98, chair 2002—, bd. editors ABA Jour., chair 2003—, bd. govs. 2005—), Fed. Bar Assn. (bd. dirs. Houston chpt. 1986), State Bar Tex., Houston Bar Assn., Tex. Water Conservation Assn., Houston Law Rev. Assn. (bd. dirs. 1978). Republican. Lutheran. Office: Vinson & Elkins 2300 First City Tower 1001 Fannin St Houston TX 77002-6706 Business E-Mail: cdinkins@velaw.com.*

DINKINS, JANE POLING, management consultant, application developer; b. Van Wert, Ohio, Oct. 11, 1928; d. Doyt Carl and Kathryn (Sawyer) Poling. BBA, So. Meth. U., 1974. Stewardess, acting chief stewardess Am. Airlines, 1946—50; exec. sec., adminstrv. asst. Southland Royalty Co., Ft. Worth, 1956—63; exec. sec. Charles E. Seay, Inc., C. W. Goyer Jr., Dallas, 1964—68; sys. analyst, programmer Southland Life Ins. Co., Dallas, 1968—69, 1st Nat. Bank, Dallas, 1969—72, Occidental Life Ins. Co., LA, 1972—73, Pacific Mut. Life Ins. Co., Newport Beach, Calif., 1973—74, mgr. mut. fund subs., 1975; sys. analyst, programmer Info. Svcs. divsn. TRW, Orange, Calif., 1975—79; EDP auditor Union Bank, LA, 1979; sr. EDP auditor Security Pacific Nat. Bank, Glendale, Calif., 1979—80, asst. v.p. LA, 1981; mgmt. cons. Automation Program Office, Fed. Res. Bank, Dallas, 1982—85; pres. Poling & Assocs., Inc., 1985—; adv. auditor Peer Svcs., Inc., Dallas, 1986—88; sr. computer auditor Merabank, Phoenix, 1988—89; quality assurance analyst Am. Airlines, Carrollton, Tex., 1989—91; assoc. DFW Airport, 1991—2001; quality assurance sr. software programmer Experian, Allen, Tex., 1998—99. Vol. Presbyn. Hosp., C.R. Smith Mus. Mem.: Quality Assurance Inst. (Cert. Quality Analyst award), Flight Attendants Lunch Bunch, Kiwi Club (founding mem.), Sigma Kappa. Republican. Methodist. Home and Office: 10019 Regal Park Ln Apt 206 Dallas TX 75230-5543

DINNEEN, GERALD PAUL, electrical engineer, retired federal official; b. Elmhurst, NY, Oct. 23, 1924; s. Walter James and Anna Constance (Costello) D.; m. Mary Purington, June 28, 1947; children: Patricia Dinneen Mooney, Barbara Dinneen Sehr, Michael. BS, Queens Coll., 1947; MS, U. Wis., 1948, PhD, 1952. Teaching asst. U. Wis., 1947-51; sr. devel. engr. Goodyear Aircraft, 1951-53; with MIT, Lexington, 1953-77, prof. elec. engring., dir. Lincoln Lab.; asst. sec. of def., 1977-81; corp. v.p. sci. and tech. Honeywell Inc., Mpls., 1981-89; fgn. sec. NAE, Washington, 1988-95; chair policy and global affairs divsn. Nat. Rsch. Coun., Washington, 1997—2004. Cons. Def. Dept. NASA, USN, USAF. Served with AC, AUS, 1943-46. Recipient Disting. Pub. Service award Dept. Def., 1981. Mem. NAE, Engring. Acad. Japan, Swiss Acad. of Engring. Scis., Royal Acad. of Engring. (U.K.), Am. Math. Soc., Math. Assn. Am., Cosmos Club (Washington), Sigma Xi, Phi Beta Kappa. Home: 1010 Waltham St Apt D434 Lexington MA 02421 Personal E-mail: gdinneen@comcast.net.

DINNERSTEIN, HARVEY, artist; b. NYC, Apr. 3, 1928; s. Louis and Sarah (Kobilansky) D.; m. Lois Behrke, May 25, 1951; children: Rachel, Michael. Student of, Moses Soyer, 1944-46; student, Art Students League, 1946-47, Tyler Art Sch., Temple U., 1950; D (hon.), Lyme Acad. Fine Arts, 1998. Instr. drawing and painting Sch. Visual Arts, NYC, 1963—80, N.A.D., 1974-92, Art Students League, 1980—. One-man shows include Davis Galleries, NYC, 1955, 60-61, 63, Kenmore Galleries, Phila., 1964, 66, 69-70, F.A.R. Galleries, NYC, 1972, 79, Sindin Galleries, 1983, Deutsch Galleries, 1989, Capricorn Galleries, 1990, Butler Inst. Am. Art, Youngstown, Ohio, 1994, Gerold Wunderlich Galleries, 1997, Frey Norris Gallery, San Francisco, 2003, 05; exhibited in group shows at Whitney Mus. Am. Art, NYC, 1955, New Britain (Conn.) Mus. Am. Art, 1964, Am. Acad. and Inst. Arts and Letters, NYC, 1974, Pa. State U. Mus. Art, 1974, others; works represented in collections Met. Mus. Art, Lehman Coll., Whitney Mus. Am. Art, Martin Luther King Labor Ctr., NYC, New Britain Mus. Art, Fleming Mus. at U. Vt., Burlington, de Young Mus., San Francisco; author: A Portfolio of Drawings, 1968, Harvey Dinnerstein-Artist at Work, 1978. Served with U.S. Army, 1951-53. Recipient Temple Gold medal Pa. Acad. Fine Art, 1950; Allied Artist Gold medal, 1977; President's award Audubon Artists, 1978; Arthur Ross award Classical Am., 1983; others; Tiffany Found. grantee, 1948, 61 Mem. N.A.D. (Samuel F.B. Morse medal 2003). Home: 933 President St Brooklyn NY 11215-1603

DINNERSTEIN, LEONARD, historian, educator; b. NYC, May 5, 1934; s. Abraham and Lillian (Kubrik) D.; m. Myra Anne Rosenberg, Aug. 20, 1961; children: Andrew, Julie. B of Social Scis., CCNY, 1955; MA, Columbia U., 1960, PhD, 1966. Instr. N.Y. Inst. Tech., NYC, 1960-65; asst. prof. Fairleigh Dickinson U., Teaneck, NJ, 1967-70; dir. Judaic studies U. Ariz., Tucson, 1993-2000, prof. Am. history, 1970—2004; ret. Adj. prof. Columbia U., summers 1969, 72, 74, 81, 87, 89, NYU, summers 1969-70, 82, 86. Author: The Leo Frank Case, 1968 (Anisfield-Wolf award 1969), America and the Survivors of the Holocaust, 1982, Uneasy at Home, 1987; (with David M. Reimers) Ethnic Americans: A History of Immigration and Assimilation, 1987, 4th edit., 1999; (with R.L. Nichols, D.M. Reimers) Natives and Strangers, 1996, 4th edit., 2003, Antisemitism in America, 1994 (Nat. Jewish Book prize 1994); contbr. articles to profl. jours.; editor: (with Fred Jaher) The Aliens, 1970; (with Kenneth T. Jackson) American Vistas, 1971, 7th edit., 1995; (with Mary Dale Palsson) Jews in the South, 1973; (with Jean Christie) Decisions and Revisions: Interpretations of 20th Century American History, 1975, America Since World War II, 1976. Mem. Orgn. Am. Historians, Am. Hist. Assn., Am. Jewish Hist. Assn. Democrat. Jewish. Home: 1981 E Miraval Cuarto Tucson AZ 85718-3032 Office Phone: 520-615-8585. Business E-Mail: dinnerst@u.arizona.edu.

DINNERSTEIN, SIMON ABRAHAM, artist, educator; b. Bklyn., Feb. 16, 1943; s. Louis and Sarah (Kobalansky) Dinnerstein; m. Renée Sudler, Aug. 28, 1965; 1 child, Simone. BA, CCNY, 1965; postgrad., Bklyn. Mus. Art Sch., 1964-67, Hochschule für Bildende Kunst, Kassel, Fed. Republic Germany, 1970-71. Instr. in fine arts New Sch. Social Rsch., Parsons Sch. of Design, NYC, 1975—2005; pvt. tchr. Bklyn., 1996—. Adj. lectr. N.Y.C. Tech. Coll., Bklyn., 1979—88; vis. prof. Pratt Inst., Bklyn., 1986—87; vis. artist Calhoun Sch., NY, 1988—89; lectr. Am. Acad. Rome, 1977—78, USIS, Barcelona and Madrid, Spain, 1979, Pa. State U., 1984, Pt. Washington Pub. Libr., 1990, St. Paul's Sch., Concord, N.H., 1991, Nassau County C.C., 1994, NAD, 2000, Walton Arts Ctr., Fayetteville, Ark., 1999, U. Richmond, Va., 2000. One-man shows include Staempfli Gallery, N.Y.C., 1975, 1979, 1988, Inst. Internat. Edn., 1976—77, 1979, Am. Acad. Rome, 1977, Pratt Inst., 1987, New Sch. Social Rsch., 1981, 1993, Martin Luther King, Jr., Labor Ctr., N.Y.C., 1985, St. Paul's Sch., Concord, 1991, N.J. Ctr. for Visual Art, Summit, 1994, ACA Galleries, N.Y., Bread and Roses Gallery, N.Y. and St. Peter's Church, N.Y., 1999, Walton Arts Ctr., Fayetteville, Texarkana Regional Arts Ctr., Tex./Ark., Marsh Art Gallery, U. Richmond, 2000, Arnot Art Mus., 2003; subject of monographs: The Art of Simon Dinnerstein, 1991, Simon Dinnerstein: Paintings and Drawings, 2000; included in anthology Drawing from Life, 1992, Drawing from Life (Clint Brown), 1997, Centennial Directory of Fellows, Am. Acad. Rome, 1995, Hooked on Drawing: Illustrated Lessons and Exercises for Grades 4 and up, 1996, Community of Creativity, A Century of MacDowell Colony Artists, 1996, Drawing Dimensions, 1999, Ont. Rev., 1998, St. Ann's Rev., 2000, Rattapallax Jour., 2000, Bklyn. Jews, 2001, Great Am. Writers, 2001, City Secrets, Rome, 2000, City Secrets, Florence, Venice and the Towns of Italy, 2001, City Secrets, New York, 2002, Hanging Loose, 2003, 100 New York Painters, 2006; represented, ACA Galleries, N.Y.C. Recipient Rome prize Am. Acad. in Rome, 1976-78, Ingram Merrill Found. award for painting, 1978-79, Cannon prize NAD, 1988, Ralph Fabri prize NAD, 1997, Bertelsen award NAD, 1998; Childe Hassam purchase award Am. Acad. Arts and Letters, 1976-78; fellow Fulbright Found., Germany, 1970-71, Louis Comfort Tiffany Found., 1976, MacDowell Colony, 1969, 79, N.Y. Found. for Arts, 1987; grantee E.D. Found., 1977-78, 78-79, Robert Lehman Found., 1999; composer Gabriela Lena Frank composed a quintet based on his art; to premiere, Trinity Ctr. for Performing Arts, Phila., 2005. Mem.: NAD, Soc. Fellows Am. Acad. Rome. Democrat. Jewish. Avocations: reading, films, walking, travel, dreaming. Home: 415 1st St Brooklyn NY 11215-2507 Office Phone: 718-788-4387. Personal E-mail: pturtle58@aol.com. E-mail: simondinnerstein@aol.com.

DINNERSTEIN, SIMONE, pianist; b. Bklyn., 1973; d. Simon Abraham Dinnerstein and Renée Sudler; married; 1 child, Adrian. Grad., Juilliard Sch. Solo pianist Piatigorsky Found., NYC, 1996—. Musician: (albums) J.S. Bach: Goldberg Variations, 2007, (with Zuill Bailey) Beethoven: Complete Works for Piano & Cello, Vol. 1, 2006 (Classical Recording Found. award, 2006, 2007). Recipient Chopin award; fellow, Tanglewood Music Ctr.; William Petschek piano scholarship, Vladimir Horowitz scholarship, Nat. Auditions winner, Astral Artistic Svcs. Office: c/o Tanja Dorn at IMG Artists Carnegie Hall Tower 152 W 57th St 5th Fl New York NY 10019 also: Christina Jensen PR LLC St George Tower 111 Hicks St Ste 7A Brooklyn NY 11201*

DINNIMAN, ANDREW ERIC, international studies and history professor, state senator; b. New Haven, Oct. 10, 1944; s. Harold and Edith (Stephson) D.; m. Margo Portnoy, June 8, 1969; 1 dau., Alexis. BA, U. Conn., 1966; MA, U. Md., 1969; EdD, Pa. State U., 1978. Student pers. worker U. Md., 1969-71, U. Denver, 1971-72; prof. West Chester (Pa.) State U., 1972—, dir. Ctr. for Internat. Programs, 1986-2001; commissioner Chester County, 1992—2006; senator Commonwealth of Pa., 2006—. Author: Book of Human Relations Readings, 1980, Education for International Competence in Pennsylvania, 1988; contbr. articles to profl. jours. Chmn. Chester County Dem. Com., 1979-85; mem. Pa. Dem. State Com., 1982-89, mem. exec. com., 1984-89; chmn. Eastern Pa. Dem. County Chmn. Assn., 1982-85; mem. Dem. Nat. Com., 1984-89; del. Dem. Nat. Conv., 1984, 88, 92, 96; pres. Pa. Coun. on Internat. Edn., 1989-91; v.p. Downingtown Area (Pa.) Sch. Bd., 1975-79; mem. Ctrl. Chester County Vocat.-Tech. Sch. Bd., 1978-79; mem. Chester County Conservation Dist., 1992—; mem. Pa. State Transp. Adv. Com., 1992-95, mem. Chester County Econ. Devel. Bd., 1992-96; mem. Nat. Assn. Counties Com. on Globalization, 1997-98, Chester County Internat. Trade Coun., 1999—, Pa. Emergency Mgmt. Coun., 2007-, Ben Franklin Tech. Devel. Authority, 2007-, Pa. Abraham Lincoln Bicentennial Comm., 2007-. Recipient Bicentennial award Pa. Sch. Bds. Assn., 1976, Outstanding Acad. Svc. award Commonwealth Pa., 1977, Human Rights award W. Chester State U. chpt. NAACP, 1980, Cmty. Svc. award Coatesville NAACP, 1997, Mil. Order of Purple Heart Nat. citation for outstanding svc., 1998, Excellence in Local Govt. award Commonwealth of Pa., 1998, Grange award for pub. svc., 1999, Regional Leadership award Exton Regional C. of C., 1999, Leadership award Chester County Water Resources Authority, 2003, Cmty. Builder award, Melton Arts and Edn. Ctr, 2004, Cert. Appreciation, Borough West Chester, 2004, People That Make A Difference award, Hutchinson UAME Ch., 2004; Proclamation for Dedicated Svc., City of Coatsville, 2004, Appreciation Inspirational Moments award, 2004, Building Better Cmtys. award, Housing Partnership Chester County, 2004, Hunger Awareness award Chester County CARES, 2006, Appreciation award Phoenixville Religious Coun., 2007, Ann. Svc. award Safe Harbor Homeless Shelter, 2007. Mem. Chester County Hist. Soc., Pa. Soc., Pa. Emergency Mgmt. Coun., Ben Franklin Tech. Devel. Authority, Pa. Abraham Lincoln Bicentennial Commn. Jewish. Home: 471 Spruce Dr Exton PA 19341-2025 Office: 183 Main Capital Harrisburg PA 17120 Office Phone: 610-692-2112. Business E-Mail: adinniman@pasenate.com.

DINNING, WOODFORD WYNDHAM, JR., lawyer; b. Demopolis, Ala., Aug. 15, 1954; s. Woodford W. and Gladys (Brown) D.; m. Tammy E. Cannon, May 27, 1994. AS, U. Ala., 1976, JD, 1979. Bar: Ala. 1979, U.S. Dist. Ct. (so. dist.) Ala. 1980. Mcpl. judge City of Demopolis, 1980-93, 98—; ptnr. Lloyd & Dinning, LLC, Demopolis, 1979—; mcpl. judge City of Linden, Ala., 1997—. Atty. Marengo County Commn. and City of Linden, Ala., 1997—. Mem.: U. Ala. Alumni Assn. Avocations: water-skiing, marathon running. Office: Lloyd & Dinning LLC PO Drawer Z Demopolis AL 36732

DINOVI, DENISE, producer; b. Can. Journalist, reporter, film critic, Toronto, Can.; unit publicist, 1980; co-producer, assoc. producer, prodn. exec. Montreal's Film Plan; exec. v.p. prodn. New World Cinema; head Tim Burton Prodns., 1989-92; prodr. Warner Bros. Studios, 1996—. Movie prodns. include: Heathers, 1989, Edward Scissorhands, 1990, Meet the Applegates, 1991, Batman Returns, 1992, The Nightmare Before Christmas, 1993, Cabin Boy, 1994, Ed Wood, 1994, Little Women, 1994, James and The Giant Peach, 1996, Almost Heros, 1998, Practical Magic, 1998, Message in a Bottle, 1999, Happy Campers, 2001, Original Sin, 2001, A Walk to Remember, 2002, What a Girl Wants, 2003, New York Minute, 2004, Catwoman, 2004, The Sisterhood fo the Traveling Pants, 2005, Lucky You, 2007.

DINRSTEIN, CHARLES ROBERT, vascular surgeon; b. LA, Sept. 26, 1950; m. Catherine Dolan; children: Michael Dinerstein, Nicholas Dinerstein. BA, UCLA, 1972; MMS, RW Johnson Med. Sch., Piscataway, NJ, 1976; MD, R W Johnson Med. Sch., Piscataway, NJ, 1976. Bd. Cert. Gen. Surgery Am. Bd. Surgery, Bd. Cert. Vascular Surgery Am. Bd. Surgery. Attending surgeon RW Johnson U. Hosp., New Brunswick, NJ, 1986—2006, CentraState Med. Ctr., Freehold, NJ, 1991—. Office: 501 Iron Bridge Rd Ste 9 Freehold NJ 07728 Home Phone: 732-297-6802; Office Phone: 732-238-9030.

DINSDALE, CAROL ELLEN, special education educator; b. Dallas, May 22, 1953; d. Calvin Anderson Loving and Mims Ellen Brinker; m. Paul Francis Dinsdale, Oct. 19, 1996; children: Kelley Ann Tuggle, Keith Robert Tuggle. Student, George Peabody Coll. for Tchrs., Nashville, 1972; AA in Edn., St. Petersburg Jr. Coll., Clearwater, Fla., 1988; BS in Spl. Edn. magna cum laude, U. South Fla., 1990, MA in Behavior Disorders, 1994. Nat. bd. certification for tchrs.: mid. childhood generalist Nat. Bd. Profl. Tchg. Stds., educator emotional handicaps, specific learning disabilities Fla., educator varying exceptionalities Fla., educator elem. edn. Fla., educator exceptional student edn. Fla., educator English spkrs. of other langs. Fla. Tchr. pre-sch. and kindergarten Highland Pk. Sch., Clearwater, Fla., 1982—88; tchr. of emotionally handicapped students Pinellas County Schs., Mt. Vernon Elem. Sch., St. Petersburg, Fla., 1991—; adj. prof. for spl. edn. U. South Fla. Coll Edn., St. Petersburg, 2001—, St. Petersburg Coll., 2001—. Presenter Internat. Conf. for Adolescents with Behavior Disorders, 1994—; supervising tchr. for interns U. South Fla., St. Petersburg, 1994—, St. Petersburg Coll., 1994—; mentor nat. bd. cert. process State of Fla., 2004—; sch.-based coord. minority students Students Targeted Ednl. Performance, Fla., 1999—2006; v.p. Fla. Coun. for Children with Behavior Disorders, Fla.; site-based coach, new tchr. mentor Pinellas County Sch. Bd., Fla., 2001—; presenter, spkr. in field. Presenter, spkr. Fla. Children's Ministry Conf., St. Petersburg, 2001—; tchr. children's ministry Calvary Chapel, St. Petersburg, 1999—; vol. ministry for children of incarcerated adults Angel Tree through Calvary Chapel, St. Petersburg, 1997—; vol. prison ministry to area correctional facilities Prison Ministry through Calvary Chapel, St. Petersburg, 2004—. Named Marjorie Crick Tchr. of the Yr., Fla. Coun. for Exceptional Children, 2003; recipient Balanced Literacy Grant and Materials, B.A.L.A.N.C.E. Literacy Instrn., Collaborative Consultation Initiative, 1993—94, Peace Garden School-wide Project award, Radiant Peace, 2001, Fla. Watershed Environment grant water resource edn., SW Fla. Water Mgmt., 2002—03, Tampa Bay's Channel 10, Sci. in the Classroom grant, Pinellas Edn. Found., 2003—04, Grant for Profl. Devel., Increasing Tchg. Competencies, Citigroup Team Mentor Grant, 2003—04, Outstanding Profl. Performance award for Children with Behavior Disorders, 2007, Nat. Profl. Practitioner award, Nat. Coun. for Children with Behavior Disorders, 2007. Mem.: Fla. Coun. Children Behavior Disorders (v.p. 2006, pres.-elect 2006—07), Pinellas Reading Coun., Coun. for Exceptional Children (chpt. membership chair 1989—90, chpt. historian newsletter 1990—91, exec. bd. 2004—, mem. nat. bd. profl. standards 2005—, mem. nat. honors com. 2006, profl. devel. grant 2002—03, Exceptional Student Educator award 2003, grant for profl. devel. 2003—04, grants for classroom, sci., and reading chpt. 176 2003—05, Clarissa Hug Tchr. of Year, USA and Can. 2005), U. South Fla. Alumni Assn., Internat. Assn. Spl. Educators, PTA, Phi Kappa Phi, Kappa Delta Phi. Avocations: herpetology, advocating for literacy, gardening. Office: Mount Vernon Elem Sch 4629 13th Ave N Saint Petersburg FL 33713 Office Phone: 727-893-1815.

DINSE, JOHN MERRELL, lawyer; b. Rochester, NY, June 26, 1925; s. Frank John and Lois Vanlora (Merrell) D.; m. Ann Thompson (Goodenough), Dec. 27, 1948; children— Jeffrey P., Pamela D. Johnston AB, U. Rochester, 1947; LL.B., Cornell U., 1950. Bar: N.Y. 1950, Vt. 1951, U.S. Dist. Ct. Vt. 1952, U.S. Ct. Appeals (2d cir.) 1957. Assoc. firm Austin & Edmunds, Burlington, Vt., 1950-57; ptnr. Dinse, Erdmann, & Clapp (and predecessor firms), Burlington, 1957-90; of counsel Dinse, Knapp, & McAndrew (and predecessor firms), Burlington, 1990—. Mem. Med. Ctr. Hosp. Assocs.; dir. Vt. Mcpl. Bond Bank, 1980—83; past trustee Burlington (Vt.) YWCA; past bd. govs. Med. Ctr. Hosp. Vt.; past bd. dirs. Vt. Diabetes Assn., Arthritis Found.; bd. dirs. Vt. Symphony Orch., v.p., 1995—, chmn. bd., 2001—05; mem. Vt. Waterways Commn., 1962—63; chmn. Jud. Nominating Bd., 1967—77; campaign chmn. Gov. Deane C. Davis, 1968, 1970; mem. Waterways Commn. on Champlain Basin. With USAR, 1943—46. Decorated Bronze Star U.S. Army. Fellow Am. Coll. Trial Lawyers, Am. Bar Found., Am. Coll. Trust and Estate Counsel; mem. ABA, New Eng. Bar Assn. (bd. dirs. 1977-80), Chittenden County Bar Assn., Vt. Bar Assn. (bd. mgrs. 1974— , pres. 1978-79), Am. Bd. Trial Advs. (bd. dirs. 1990-92), Am. Judicature Soc. (dir. 1975-79), Am. Acad. Hosp. Attys., No. New Eng. Def. Counsel Assn. (pres. 1971-72), Assn. Def. Attys., Internat. Assn. Def. Counsel, Def. Research Inst. (dir. 1975-81, pres. 1980, chmn. bd. 1981), Am. Law Inst., Nat. Assn. Coll. and Univ. Attys. Clubs: Lake Champlain Yacht (commodore 1961-62); Malletts Bay Boat (master 1957-58). Home: Harbor Rd Shelburne VT 05482 Office: Dinse Knapp & McAndrew PO Box 988 209 Battery St Burlington VT 05402 Office Phone: 802-864-5751.

DINSMORE, ROBERTA JOAN MAIER, library director; b. Phila., Sept. 30, 1934; d. Bert Faust and Emma Baker (Keen) Maier; m. Ray W. Dinsmore, Sr., Oct. 20, 1956; children: Ray Wilson Jr., Jeffrey Maier, Debra Joan, Matthew Bert. BA, Pa. State U., 1956; MLS, Clarion U. Pa., 1990. Proofreader Aluminum Co. Am., Pitts., 1957-60; office mgr. Dinsmore, Lithographer, Punxsutawney, Pa., 1969—; dir. Punxsutawney Meml. Libr., 1978—. Freelance writer Greenburg Tribune Rev., 1980—81; adult edn. tchr. Jeff Tech., Reynoldsville, Pa., 1981—82; freelance writer Punxsutawney Spirit, 2003—; dist. 3 coord. Kiskiminetas Presbytery; sec. Jefferson County Libr. Sys. Mem. Jefferson County Constrn. Com., Jefferson County Heritage Com.; mem. sch. dist. strategic planning com.; chair Police Civil Svc. Commn., Punxsutawney; exec. bd. Theatre Arts; sec. Punxsutawney Youth Commn., 2006—; ch. libr. Punxsutawney Presbyn. Ch., 1985—, pres. investment com.; elder Presbyn. Ch.; mem. com. on ministry Kiskiminetas Presbytery; head hostess Welcome Wagon Internat., Memphis, 1976—80; mem. libr. sci. accreditation team Clarion U., Pa.; mem. exec. bd. Punxsutawney Theatre Arts Guild; hospice vol.; tchr. adult discussion class; mem. coun., vice chair Cmty. Action Svc. Corp.; vice chair numerous orgns. Mem.: AAUW (pres., Woman of the Yr. 1987), ALA, Goschenhoppen Historians, Punxsutawney Area Hist. and Geneol. Soc. (charter), Clarion Dist. Libr. Assn. (pres. 1984—86), Pa. Libr. Assn. (past chair pub. libr. divsn.), Punxsutawney Hosp. Aux., Friends of Libr., Pa. Citizens for Better Librs., Irving Club (past pres., v.p.), Garden Club (past pres. Punxsutawney chpt.), PEO. Republican. Avocations: reading, making and selling crafts in small, self-owned business, genealogy. Home: 808 E Mahoning St Punxsutawney PA 15767-2320 Office: Punxsutawney Meml Libr 301 E Mahoning St Punxsutawney PA 15767-2198 Office Phone: 814-938-5020. E-mail: punxlib@adelphia.net.

DIODOSIO, CHARLES JOSEPH, lawyer; b. Pueblo, Colo., Apr. 27, 1951; s. Warren Joseph and Lucille Julia Diodosio. BSChemE, U. Colo., 1973; JD, Northwestern U., 1976. Assoc. McDermott, Will & Emery, Chgo., 1976-80; internat. counsel Beatrice Co., Chgo., 1980-84, v.p. Asia devel., 1984-88; chmn. TMGC Ltd., Chgo., 1988—, Meadow Gold Investment Holding Co., Beijing, 1993—; chmn. L&D International Corp., Beijing, 1993—. Chmn. L&D Internat. Corp., Beijing, China, 1993—. Mem. ABA, Ill. Bar. Home: 1387 Calle de Maria Palm Springs CA 92264-8503 Fax: 760-327-1200. E-mail: meadgo@aol.com.

DION FAUST, DEBRA, secondary school educator; b. Pottstown, Pa., Nov. 8, 1951; m. Joseph Edward Dion, Sept. 18, 1982; children: Andrea Renee Dion Jacobs, Joanne Theresa Dorgan. BA in Music and French, Moravian Coll., Bethlehem, Pa., 1973; MFA in Theatre Edn., Boston U., 1978. Tchr. English, theatre, advisor drama Saugus H.S., Mass., 1979—81; tchr. English, theatre Ipswich H.S., 1983—. Contbr. articles to profl. jours. Recipient Fine Arts Tchr. Yr., Mass. Alliance Arts Edn., 1994. Mem.: Mass. H.S. Drama Guild (v.p. 2002—04, pres. 2004—06, treas. 2004—, past pres. 2005—06, treas. 2005—), Nat. Coun. Tchrs. English. Office: Ipswich High School 134 High Street Ipswich MA 01938-1247 Home Phone: 781-233-9290; Office Phone: 978-356-3137 ext. 138. Office Fax: 978-356-5720. Business E-Mail: dfaust@ipswichschools.org.

DIONISOPOULOS, GEORGE ALLAN, lawyer; b. Santa Monica, Calif., July 31, 1954; s. P. Allan and Christine (Nassios) D.; m. Sandra Doreen Jordan, June 11, 1977; children: Sarah, Elaina. BA summa cum laude, U. Ill., 1976; JD cum laude, Harvard U., 1980. Bar: Wis. 1980, U.S. Dist. Ct. (ea. and we. dists.) Wis. 1980. Ptnr. Foley & Lardner LLP, Milw., 1980—, co-chmn. estates & trusts practice group. Mem. ABA (real property and probate sect., taxation sect.), Wis. Bar Assn. (speaker 1984—), Milw. Young Lawyers Assn., Phi Beta Kappa. Greek Orthodox. Office: Foley & Lardner LLP 777 E Wisconsin Ave Ste 3800 Milwaukee WI 53202-5367 Office Phone: 414-297-5750. Office Fax: 414-297-4900. Business E-Mail: gdionisopoulos@foleylaw.com.

DIONNE, E. J., JR., columnist; b. Boston, Apr. 23, 1952; m. Mary Boyle; children: James, Julia, Margot. BA summa cum laude, Harvard Univ, 1973; DPhil, Oxford Univ, 1982. Correspondent New York Times, 1977—89, Washington Post, 1990—92, columnist, 1993—; sr fellow Brookings Inst, Washington, 1996—. Prof Georgetown Univ; co-founder & co-chmn Pew Forum on Religion & Public Life, 2000—. Contbr. articles to polit jours, columns in newspapers, commentary on TV & radio programs; author: Why Americans Hate Politics, 1991 (Los Angeles Times Book prize, National Book Award nominee), They Only Look Dead: Why Progressives Will Dominate the Next Political Era, 1996, Community Works: The Revival of Civil Society in America, 1998, What's God Got to Do with the American Experiment, 2000, Bush v Gore: The Court Cases and the Commentary, 2000, Sacred Places, Civic Purposes: Should Government Help Faith-Based Charity?, 2001, United We Serve: National Service and the Future of Citizenship, 2003. Rhodes scholar. Mem.: Phi Beta Kappa. Office: The Brookings Institution 1775 Massachusetts Ave NW Washington DC 20036 Business E-Mail: edionne@brookings.edu.

DIONNE, GERALD FRANCIS, research physicist, educator, consultant; b. Montreal, Can., Feb. 5, 1935; arrived in U.S., 1964, naturalized, 1980; s. Louis Philip and Clare Isabel (Flood); m. Claudette Leblanc, June 29, 1963; 1 child, Stephen. BS in Physics, summa cum laude, Loyola Coll., U. Montreal, 1956; B in Engring. Physics, magna cum laude, McGill U., Montreal, 1958, PhD in Physics, 1964; MS in Physics, Carnegie-Mellon U., 1959. Jr. engr. IBM Corp., Poughkeepsie, NY, 1959-60; sr. engr. Sylvania Electric Products, Woburn, Mass., 1960-61; fellow NRC, 1961—63; rsch. asst., lectr. McGill U., 1964; sr. rsch. assoc. Pratt & Whitney Aircraft, North Haven, Conn., 1964-66; rsch. staff Lincoln lab. MIT, Lexington, Mass., 1966—96, expert, svcs. pers. Lincoln lab., 1996—, rsch. affiliate, dept. materials sci. and engring., 2005—. Cons. in field; rsch. advisor. Contbr. articles to sci. jours. Fellow IEEE, Am. Phys. Soc.; mem. Materials Rsch. Soc., Corp. Profl. Engrs. Que., Sigma Xi. Achievements include patents for microwave, superconducting, and magnetic devices; research in magnetism and magnetic materials, magnetoelastic and magneto-optic phenomena, magnetic spin transport, magnetoresistance, superconductivity theory and devices; microwave and submillimeter-wave physics and instrumentation, physics of electron emission. Home: 182 High St Winchester MA 01890-3366 Office: 244 Wood St Lexington MA 02421-9108

DIONNE, KAREN MARIE, veterinary technician, educator; b. New Haven, Conn., Mar. 26, 1975; d. Gary Anthony and Barbara Carrie Dionne. M of Biomedical Sci., Quinnipiac U., Hamden, Conn., 2003. Cert. veterinary technician AVMA, Conn., 2006; lab. animal technologist Am. Assn. of Lab. Animal Sci., Tenn., 2001, biology tchr. Bd. of Edn., Conn., 2007. Vet. technician Shakespeare Vet. Hosp., Stratford, Conn., 2006—, Bristol-Myers Squibb, Wallingford, Conn., 1998—99; rsch. scientist Bayer Corp., West Haven, Conn., 1999—2006; adj. prof. Quinnipiac U., Hamden, Conn., 2001—. Avocations: running, reading, poetry, music. Home: 37 Tremper Dr Wallingford CT 06492 Home Phone: 203-265-9808; Office Phone: 203-378-8276. Business E-Mail: karen.dionne@quinnipiac.edu.

DIORIO, EILEEN PATRICIA, retired medical technologist, philosophy educator; b. Pitts., Mar. 17, 1938; d. Charles Frederick and Elizabeth (Maturkanich) Kozlowski; m. David Robert Kaslewicz, June 21, 1958 (div. May 1965); m. Alfred Frank Diorio, June 11, 1983; children: Suzanne C. Kaslewicz Ickes, Fredric C. Kaslewicz, Warren G. Kaslewicz, Jennifer Kaslewicz Dalessandro. Student, Duquesne U., 1956-58. Reg. Med. Technologist, Pa. Microbiology technician Presbyn. U. Hosp., Pitts., 1967-70; supr. virology/immunology lab. Allegheny Gen. Hosp., Pitts., 1970-90. Co-dir. Himalayan Inst. Yoga Science & Philosophy of Pitts., 1977-96. Vol. med. lab. mgr. Himalayan Inst. Hosp., India, 1992-96. Avocations: violin, cooking, meditation.

DI PALMA, JOSEPH ALPHONSE, investment company executive, lawyer; b. NYC, Jan. 17, 1931; s. Gaetano and Michela May (Ambrosio) Di P.; m. Joycelyn Ann Engle, Apr. 18, 1970; children: Joycelyn Joan, Julianne Michelle. BA, Columbia U., 1952; JD, Fordham U., 1958; LLM in Taxation, NYU, 1959. Bar: NY 1959. Tax atty. CBS, NYC, 1960-64; v.p. tax dept. TWA, NYC, 1964-74; pvt. practice law NYC, 1974-87; investor, exec. dir. Di Palma Family Holdings, Las Vegas and NYC, 1987—. Cons. in field; head study group Comprehensive Gaming Study, NYC and Washington, 1990—; think tank exec. dir. Di Palma Position Papers; founder Di Palma Forum, U. Nev., Las Vegas; established The Di Palma Ctr. for Study of Jewelry and Precious Metals at Cooper-Hewitt, Nat. Design Mus., Smithsonian Instn., NYC Contbr. articles to profl. jours. Bd. dirs. Friends of the Henry St. Settlement, NYC, 1961-63, Outdoor Cleanliness Assn., NYC, 1961-65; chmn. Air Transport Assn. Taxation Com., 1974. With US Army, 1953-54. Recipient Disting. Svc. and Valuable Counsel commendation award, Air Transport Assn., 1974, spl. commendation, NYC mayor Rudolph Giuliani, 1997, U. Nev., Las Vegas, 1999, Tiffany Smithsonian Benefactors Circle award, 2001, WNET/Thirteen Pub. Spirit award, 2002. Mem. Internat. Platform Assn., NY State Bar Assn., NY Athletic Club. Roman Catholic. Home: 3111 Bel Air Dr Apt 21B Las Vegas NV 89109-1506 Office: 930 5th Ave # 4 J&H New York NY 10021-2651 Office Phone: 212-861-1945.

DIPALMA, JOSEPH RUPERT, pharmacology educator, dean; b. NYC, Mar. 21, 1916; s. Frank and Anna (Attanasio) DiP.; m. Mary Solowey, June 26, 1948; children: Maria, Dorothea, Joan, Yvonne, Mary-Jo. BS, Columbia U., 1936; MD, SUNY, Bklyn., 1941; DSc (hon.), Hahnemann U., 1980. Intern, resident in internal medicine Kings County Hosp., Bklyn., 1942-44; asst. prof. medicine and pharmacology State U. N.Y. Downstate Med. Sch., 1946; prof. pharmacology, chmn. dept. Hahnemann Med. Coll. and Hosp., Phila., 1951-67, dean, 1967-82, v.p., 1971-82, sr. v.p., 1972-82, prof. pharmacology and medicine, 1982-86, emeritus prof. pharmacology and medicine, 1986—, emeritus dean, 1986—. Bd. dirs. Regional Med. Program Southeastern Pa., 1967-75, Health Sys. Agy., 1977-82, Hahnemann Hosp., 2000-, St. Davids Instnl. Rev., 1975-. Author: Decanus Maximus, The Life and Times of a Medical School Dean, 2004; editor: Pharmacology in Medicine, 1971, Basic Pharmacology in Medicine, 1976, 4th edit., 1994; contbr. articles to med. jours. Bd. dirs. Hahnemann Univ. Hosp., 2003—. Recipient Alumni medallion SUNY, Downstate Med. Sch., 1966, Corp. medal Hahnemann U., 1990 Mem. Coll. Physicians Phila. (council 1969-78), AMA, Pa., Phila. County Med. socs., Am. Physiol. Soc., Am. Soc. Pharmacology and Exptl. Therapeutics, Am. Soc. Clin. Investigation, Am. Soc. Clin. Pharmacology, Alpha Omega Alpha. Home: 100 Pembroke Ave Wayne PA 19087-4819 Office: 235 N 15th St Philadelphia PA 19102-1101 Personal E-mail: josephdipalma@yahoo.com. *The creation of new ideas and approaches is always the ultimate goal.*

DIPAOLA, ROBERT, internist; b. Bklyn., Nov. 13, 1961; MD with honors, U. Utah, 1988. Diplomate Am. Bd. Internal Medicine, Am. Bd. Medical Oncology, Am. Bd. Hematology. Intern, medicine Duke U. Med. Ctr., Durham, NC, 1988-89, resident, internal medicine, 1989-91; fellow, hematologic oncology Hosp., U. Pa., Phila., 1991-94; assoc. prof. Cancer Inst. NJ, U. Medicine Dentistry NJ-Robert Wood Johnson Med. Sch.; exec. dir. Dean and Betty Gallo Prostrate Cancer Ctr. Mem. Merck Oncology Adv. Bd., Aventis Oncology Adv. Bd.; mem. PDQ com. Nat. Cancer Inst.; chmn. rsch sect. NJ Prostate Summit Com.; mem. Prostate Rsch Adv. Bd.; chmn. Prostate Task Force, 1998—; co-dir. Genitourinary Tumor Study Group, Cancer Inst. NJ. Named CaRelations Physician Yr., 2000; named one of Best Doctors in Am., 1998. Mem. ACP, AMA. Office: Cancer Inst of NJ 195 Little Albany St New Brunswick NJ 08903 Office Phone: 732-235-2465. Office Fax: 732-235-7355. Business E-Mail: dipaolrs@umdnj.edu.*

DI PAOLO, JOSEPH AMEDEO, geneticist; b. Bridgeport, Conn., June 13, 1924; s. John Anthony and Nancy (Montagano) Di P.; m. Arleta Mae Schreib, June 14, 1952; children: Nancy, John. BA, Wesleyan U., 1948; MS, Western Res. U., 1949; PhD, Northwestern U., 1951; MD (hon.), U. Cagliari, Italy, 1991. Instr. genetics bacteriology dept. biology Loyola U., Chgo., 1951-53; instr. clin. and exptl. pathology Northwestern U. Med. Sch., Chgo., 1953-55; sr. cancer research scientist Roswell Park Meml. Inst., Buffalo, 1955-63; research pharmacologist, cell biologist biology br., div. chem. and phys. carcinogenesis program Nat. Cancer Inst., Bethesda, Md., 1963-76, chief lab. biology, divsn. basic scis., 1976—99; emeritus, 1999. Assoc. prof., lectr. anatomy George Washington U., Washington, 1973-96; chmn. U.S.-Germany Cancer Program Area for Environ. Carcinogenesis, 1979-85, U.S.-USSR Mammalian Sometic Cell Genetics Relation to Neoplasia Program, 1973-76; cons. U.S.-Poland Cancer Program, 1979-91; mem. Coun. of the European Rsch. Orgn. on Genital Infection and Neoplasia, 1994; co-chmn. Cervical Cancer Prevention and Therapy Symposium UICC, New Delhi, 1994; co-organizer 16th Internat. Papillomavirus Conf., Siena, Italy, 1997; mem. sci. com. European Environ. Hygiene, 1996, mem. scientific com. 23d Internat. Papilloma Conf., Prague, 2006; sci. advisor divsn. biol. scis. NCI Frontiers in Sci., 1999—. Editor, co-author: Chemical Carcinogenesis, 1974; assoc. editor: Jour. of Nat. Cancer Inst., 1968-71, Cancer Rsch., 1970-78, Teratogenesis, Carcinogenesis, Mutagenesis, 1982-92; editl. acad. Internat. Jour. Oncology, 1992—; guest editor Cancer Investigation, 2000-01; sci. adv. mem. CCR Frontiers in Sci., 2000-. With USN, 1943-46 Fellow N.Y. Acad. Sci., AAAS; mem. Am. Assn. Cancer Rsch. (bd. dirs. 1983-86), Coun. of European Rsch., Orgn. Genital Infection and Neoplasia, Am. Soc. Human Genetics, Am. Soc. for Investigation of Pathology, Genetics Soc. Am., Teratology Soc., Hamster Soc., Tissue Culture Assn., Am. Assn. Pathology, European Assn. for Cancer Rsch., Sigma Xi. Achievements include research on ribozyme and antisense patents for cervical cancer; patent for identification of transforming fragment of HSV-2 and its detection in clinical specimens. Home: 6605 Melody Ln Bethesda MD 20817-3154 Office: Nat Cancer Inst 37-2014 Convent Dr Bethesda MD 20892-4256 Home Phone: 301-469-7003; Office Phone: 301-496-6441. Business E-Mail: jd8la@nih.gov.

DIPASQUALE, JOHN, real estate developer; Former real estate broker; CEO Elliott Bldg. Group, Langhorne, Pa., 1998—. Recipient 40 Under 40 award, Phila. Bus. Jour., 2006. Office: Elliott Bldg Group Ste 200 3000 Cabot Blvd W Langhorne PA 19047 Office Phone: 267-852-4500. Office Fax: 267-852-4522. E-mail: info@ebgmail.com.

DIPAUL, CHRISTOPHER, psychologist; b. Upper Darby, Pa., June 5, 1966; s. John and Irene DiPaul. BA, U. Pa., 1988; MA, Tufts U., 1994. Cert. sch. psychologist Nat. Assn. Sch. Psychologists. Sch. psychologist Seattle Pub. Schs., 1994—99, Palos Verdes Peninsula Unified Sch. Dist., Palos Verdes Estates, Calif., 2000—. Mem. bd. sch. psychology doctoral program Seattle Pacific U., 1997—99. Mem.: Calif. Assn. Sch. Psychologists, Nat. Assn. Sch. Psychologists. Avocation: travel. Office: Palos Verdes Peninsula Unified Sch Dist 3801 Via La Selva Palos Verdes Estates CA 90274 Office Phone: 310-378-9966.

DIPENTIMA, RENATO ANTHONY, information technology executive; b. Jan. 17, 1941; s. S. Victor and Mary DiP.; m. Patricia Ellen Gillespie, July 24, 1965; children: Margaret Ellen, Katherine Alice. BA, NYU, 1963; MA, George Washington U., 1979; PhD, U. Md., 1984. With Social Security Adminstrn., NYC, 1963—95, exec. officer Nat. Commn. Social Security Reform Balt., 1979—82, dep. commr. sys., 1990—95; v.p., chief info. officer Sys. Rsch. and Applications Corp., Arlington, Va., 1995-97; pres. SRA Fed. Sys., 1997-98, SRA Govt. Sector, 1999—2000, SRA Cons. and Sys. Integration, 2001—03, pres., COO, 2003—05, pres., CEO, 2005—07. Bd. dirs. ITAA, SRA, UMBC Poly Sci., Brocade Corp., Redshift. Mem. Coun. on Excellence, vice-chmn. industry adv. coun., 2002-04; mem. Nat. Acad. Social Ins. Recipient Under Sec.'s Spl. citation HEW, 1972, Sec.'s citation, 1974, Commr.'s citation Social Security Adminstrn., 1974, Dir.'s citation, 1979, Dep. Commr.'s citation, 1984, Commr.'s citation, 1991, Sec.'s Exec. Mgmt. citation Health and Human Svcs., 1987, Presdl. Meritorious Rank award, 1989, Presdl. Disting. Rank award, 1990. Mem. Nat. Acad. of Soc. Ins. Business E-Mail: renny_dipentima@sra.com.

DIPERNA, FRANK PAUL, photographer, educator; b. Pitts., Feb. 4, 1947; s. Frank Paul and Virginia Carmella (DeRenna) DiP. BS in Mech. Engring., Va.Polytech. Inst., 1970; student, Visual Studies Workshop, 1971-72; MA in Photography, Goddard Coll., 1977. Assoc. prof. art and photography Corcoran Coll. Art and Design, Washington, 1974-94, prof., 1994—, chmn. photography dept., 1978—81, 1984—87, 1999—2002.

Instr. photography No. Va. C.C., Alexandria, 1973-78, George Washington U., Washington, summer 1974; lectrs. and workshops Smithsonian Inst., 1976, Maine Photog. Inst. Rockport, 1977, Am. U., Washington, 1977, 78, 79, Internat. Ctr. Photography, N.Y.C., 1979, U. Del., 1981, James Madison U., Harrisonburg, Va., 1982, Rice U., Houston, No. Va. C.C., Sterling, 1991; resident Vt. Studio Ctr., Johnson, Vt., 2002; vis. prof. U. Ga, Study Abroad Program, Cortona, Italy, 2005. Solo exhbns. include Kathleen Ewing Gallery, Washington, 1982, 84, 89, 95, 98, 2000, 06, Diane Brown Gallery, Washington, 1977, 78, 80, Bird in Hand Gallery, Alexandria, 1973, Corcoran Gallery Art, 1974, 77, Recontres Internationales de la Photographie, Arles, France, 1981, Rice U., Houston, 1986; group exhbns. include Athenaeum Mus., Alexandria, 1972, Photo Impressions Gallery, Washington, 1974, Va. Mus. Fine Arts, Richmond, 1973, 75, 80, The Franklin Inst., Phila., 1978, Susan Spiritus Gallery, Newport Beach, Calif., 1979, Mus. Fine Arts, Houston, 1979, Decordova Mus., Lincoln, Mass., 1979, Mpls. Inst. Arts, 1979, L.A. Inst. Contemporary Art, 1979, Denver Art Mus., 1979, Art Inst. Chgo., 1979, Phila. Coll. Art, 1980, Brown U., Providence, 1980, Arlington (Va.) Arts Ctr., 1981, Everson Mus. Art, Syracuse, N.Y., 1985, Comfort Gallery Haverford (Pa.) Coll., 1986, Washington Ctr. Photography, 1992, Nat. Mus. Am. Art, 1992, Smithsonian Inst., 1992, Carnegie Mus. Art, 1992, New Orleans Mus. Art, 1992, Corcoran Gallery Art, 1994, 96, 98, Virginia's Photographers, Longwood Ctr. for the Visual Arts, Farmville, Va., 1997, Kathleen Ewing Gallery, Washington, 1999, Art Mus. Western Va., Roanoke, 2002, Smithsonian Am. Art Mus., 2003, 1708 Gallery, Richmond, Va., 2003, Room Full of Mirrors, U. Md., 2004, Images of Italy, Kathleen Ewing Gallery, 2004, Road Trip Gallery, Smithsonian Mus. Am. Art, many others; represented in permanent collections Chrysler Mus., Norfolk, Va., Recontres Internationale de la Photographie, Arles, France, Bibliotheque Nationale, Paris, Libr. Cong., Washington, Polaroid (Euopa) Amsterdam, The Netherlands, Corcoran Gallery Art, Va. Mus. Fine Arts, Smithsonian Inst., Balt. Mus. Art, Nat. Mus. Am. Art, Washington, Met. Mus. Art, N.Y., Ctr. for Creative Photography, U. Ariz. Artist-in-Residence Lightwork, Syracuse, N.Y., 1982, Camargo Found., Cassis, France, 1980, Vt. Studio Ctr., Johnson, 2002; Grad. fellow Va. Mus. Fine Arts, 1975. Avocations: tennis, fishing, playing guitar, birdwatching, furniture making. Office: Corcoran Coll Art & Design 500 17th St NW Washington DC 20006-4804 E-mail: bluebirdfd@aol.com.

DIPERSIO, JOHN F., oncologist; b. Boston; BA (magna cum laude) in Biology, Williams Coll., 1973; MD, PhD in Microbiology, U. Rochester, 1980. Cert. Am. Bd. Internal Medicine, Am. Bd. Internal Medicine (Med. Oncology), Am. Bd. Internal Medicine (Hematology). Intern, medicine Parkland Meml. Hosp., UT Southwestern, Dallas, 1980—81, resident, 1981—83, chief resident, 1983—84; fellow, divsn. hematology-oncology UCLA Sch. Medicine, 1984—87, instr. medicine, divsn. hematology-oncology, 1987—88, asst. prof. medicine, divsn. hematology-oncology, 1988—90; asst. prof. oncology U. Rochester Sch. Medicine and Dentistry, NY, 1990—94; dir., bone marrow transplant program Strong Meml. Hosp., Rochester, NY, 1990—94; asst. prof. medicine, hematology unit U. Rochester Sch. Medicine, Rochester, NY, 1990—94; assoc. prof. medicine, pediatrics and pathology Washington U. Sch. Medicine, St. Louis, 1994—97, chief, divsn. bone marrow transplantation & stem cell biology, 1994—2000, prof. medicine, pediatrics and pathology, 1997—, acting dir., divsn. med. oncology, 2000—03, dir., sect. bone marrow transplantation & leukemia, 2000—06, chief, divsn. oncology, 2000—, dep. dir., Siteman Cancer Ctr., 2000—. Bd. dir. Barnard Free Skin and Cancer Hosp., 1998, 2003; career develop. award study sect. mem. Leukemia and Lymphoma Soc. Am., 2000—06; mem. med. adv. bd. Bone Marrow Found., 2005. Mem. editl. bd. Journal of Experimental Hematology, 1993; guest editor Blood Hournal, 1998-2001; contbr. articles to profl. jours. Recipient Jr. Faculty Rsch. award, Am. Cancer Soc., 1989, Lewis T. and Rosalind B. Apple Chair in Oncology, 1997; Spl. Fellow, Leukemia Soc. Am., 1986. Mem. Internat. Soc. for Exptl. Hematology (councilor, 1997, mem. nomating com. 1995, chmn. nominating com. 1997), Am. Soc. Hematology (study sect. mem. faculty and fellow scholar award, 2003-05), Am. Soc. for Biochemistry and Molecular Biology, Internat. Soc. for Hematotherapy and Graft Engring.(mem. stem celkl evaluation com., 1997, Am. Soc. for Blood and Marrow Transplant (bd. dir. 2003, chmn. coun. edn. and standards, 2003), Am. Soc. Clin. Investigation, Am. Soc. Clin. Oncology, Am. Soc. Clin. Investigation, Alpha Omega Alpha. helping pioneer stem cell transplants and focuses research efforts on improving the success of bone marrow and stem cell transplants for the treatment of cancer and disorders of the blood. Office: Divsn Oncology Campus Box 8007 Washington U Med Sch 660 S Euclid Ave 14th Fl Northwest Tower Saint Louis MO 63110 Office Phone: 314-454-8306. Office Fax: 314-454-7551. Business E-Mail: jdipersi@im.wustl.edu.*

DIPIAZZA, MICHAEL CHARLES, insurance company executive; b. NYC, Aug. 22, 1953; s. Carmelo and Grace (Vassallo) DiP.; m. Lillian Dugan, Dec. 21, 1979. CLU. Asst. v.p. sales Nat. Benefit Life Ins. Co., NYC, 1975-79, asst. v.p. product devel., 1979-81; pres. Wm. B. Smith Agy., NYC, 1979; cons. Ins. Sales Support Systems, Piscataway, N.J., 1981-82; asst. v.p. merchandising MONY, NYC, 1982-86; v.p. merchandising Home Life Ins. Co., NYC, 1986-92; asst. v.p. product devel. and mktg. MetLife, Bridgewater, N.J., 1992-97; v.p. mktg. MONY Group, NYC, 1998—2004; v.p. advanced markets and merchandising AXA Equitable Life Ins. Co., NYC, 2005—. Mem. Nat. Assn. Life Underwriters, Am. Soc. CLU's. Avocations: music, railroads, woodworking, American history. Business E-Mail: michael_dipiazzza@mony.com.

DIPIAZZA, SAMUEL A., JR., finance company executive; m. Melody DiPiazza; 2 children. BS in Acctg./Economics, U. Ala.; MS in Tax Acctg., U. Houston, 1973. Joined Coopers & Lybrand, 1973, named ptnr., 1979, elected to firm coun., 1986, head Birmingham, Alabama and Chicago offices, named midwest regional mng. ptnr., 1992, regional mng. ptnr. NY metro region, client svc. vice chmn., 1994—98; Americas leader tax and legal services PricewaterhouseCoopers, 1998—2000, chmn, sr. ptnr. US firm, 2000—02, global CEO, 2002—. Trustee Fin. Acctg. Found. Author: (books) Building Public Trust: The Future of Corporate Reporting, 2002. Mem. exec. coun. Inner City Scholarship Fund; mem. exec. com. Nat. Corp. Theatre Fund; mem. internat. adv. bd. Jr. Achievement; mem. bd. dirs. NYC Ballet; pres. Big Bros./Sisters, NYC., 2001; bd. visitors U. Ala. Culverhouse Coll. Commerce and Bus Adminstrn. Named Acct. of Yr., Beta Alpha Psi Soc.; recipient Ellis Island medal of honor, INROADS Leadership award. Mem.: Mergers and Acquistions Group (Frankfurt). Office: PricewaterhouseCoopers 300 Madison Ave New York NY 10017-6204 Office Phone: 646-471-4000.*

DIPIETRO, JOSEPH A., dermatologist; b. New Rochelle, NY, May 28, 1947; s. Joseph and Concetta DiPietro; m. Mary Lynne Ricigliano; children: Joseph, Stephen. BS in Biology cum laude, Boston Coll., Newton, Mass., 1969; MD, Loyola Med. Sch., Maywood, Ill., 1973; cert. in Dermatology, Cornell U. Med. Sch., NYC, 1978. Pvt. practice, New Rochelle, NY, 1979—. Author: History of New Rochelle, NY. Mem. Westchester County Bd. Health, 1991. Named one of Best Doctors in Westchester County, Westchester mag., 2001. Mem.: Wstchester County Acad. Medicine, Am. Acad. Dermatology. Roman Catholic. Avocations: gardening, cooking, sports, history, foreign languages.

DIPIETRO, RALPH ANTHONY, management and marketing consultant, educator; b. NYC, Oct. 27, 1942; s. Joseph and Marie (Borelli) DiP. BBA, CUNY, 1964, MBA, 1966; PhD, NYU, 1972. Chmn., prof. mktg. and internat. bus. dept. Sch. Bus. Montclair State U., Upper Montclair, NJ, 1972—. Adj. prof. mgmt. NYU, 1976-97, mgmt. tng. dir. Inst. Retail Mgmt., 1976-86; cons. Mfrs. Hanover Trust, N.Y.C., 1979-85, Sharp Electronics, N.Y.C., 1980-94, Battus Corp., N.Y.C., 1982-85, AT&T Bell Labs., 1989-91; program dir. Bally of Switzerland, N.Y.C., 1981-93, Fortunoff's, N.Y.C., 1984-86. Author: Managerial Effectiveness: A Review and an Empirical Testing of a Model, 1973; contbr. articles to profl. jours. Mem. Am. Mktg. Assn., Acad. Mktg. Scis., Internat. Assn. Applied Psychology, Omicron Delta Epsilon. Avocations: tennis, swimming, opera. Home: 12 Manor Dr Warren NJ 07059 Office Phone: 973-655-7218. Business E-Mail: dipietror@mail.montclair.edu. E-mail: ralphd01@optonline.net.

DIPIETRO, RALPH JOHN, lawyer; b. York, Pa., June 11, 1963; s. Richard Ralph DiPietro and Jacqueline Caroline Sova. BA, Boston U., 1986; JD, George Washington U., 1989. Bar: Pa. 1990, U.S. Ct. Appeals (D.C. cir.) 1991, U.S. Dist. Ct. D.C. 1994, N.Y. 1997, U.S. Dist. Ct. (ea. dist.) N.Y. 1997, U.S. Dist. Ct. (so. dist.) N.Y. 1998, Md. 2002, U.S. Dist. Ct. Md. 2002. Atty. David E. Fox & Associates, Washington, 1990—94, Andrew Maloney, NYC, 1994—96; atty./ptnr. Ralph J. DiPietro, P.C., Great Neck, NY, 1997—2001; atty. Bierman, Geesing & Ward, LLC, Bethesda, Md., 2001—. Adj. prof. Mercy Coll., NYC, 1998—2001; adj. prof. paralegal program Queens Coll., Flushing, NY, 1999—2001. Mem.: ABA (assoc.), Bar Assn. Montgomery County (assoc.), Bar Assn. D.C. (assoc.). Democrat. Avocations: travel, writing, tennis, piano. Home: Ste 315E 7315 Wisconsin Ave Bethesda MD 20814 Home Phone: 301-469-3513; Office Phone: 301-961-6555. Office Fax: 301-961-6545; Home Fax: 301-961-6545. Business E-Mail: ralph@bgw-llc.com.

DIPIETRO, RICK, professional hockey player; b. Lewiston, Maine, Sept. 19, 1981; s. Rick and Cheryl DiPietro. Attended, Boston U., 1999—2000. Goalie NY Islanders, 2001—. Mem. USA Olympic Hockey Team, Torino, Italy, 2006. Named Rookie of Yr., Hockey East, 2000; named to Second All-Star Team, 2000, All-Rookie Team, 2000. Achievements include being the first goaltender in NHL draft history to be selected first overall, 2000. Office: c/o NY Islanders Nassau Veterans Meml Coliseum 1255 Hempstead Turnpike Uniondale NY 11553

DIPILLO, PATRICIA ANNE, language educator, researcher; b. Boston, Aug. 13, 1951; d. Alfred N. and Louise M. DiPillo. BA, Boston Coll., 1973; EdM, Lesley U., 1995; EdD, U. Mass., Lowell, 2005. Cert. Latin and classical humanities Mass. Dept. Edn., Spanish Mass. Dept. Edn., supr./dir. Mass. Dept. Edn. Latin/Spanish tchr. Weymouth (Mass.) Pub. Schs., 1975—77, Ashland (Mass.) Pub. Schs., 1977—81, Acton (Mass.) Pub. Schs., 1981—2004; Latin tchr. Marlborough (Mass.) Pub. Schs., 2004—. Assessor Nat. Bd. Profl. Tchg. Stds., 2002—; adj. Merrimack Edn. Collaborative/Fitchburg State Coll., Chelmsford, Mass., 2006—; tchr. edn. licensure scorer Mass. Dept. Edn.; reviewer Nat. Coun. Tchr. Accreditation Am. Coun. Tchg. of Fgn. Langs., Am. Edn. Rsch. Jour.; invited spkr. Am. Edn. Rsch. Assn., China, 2007, Nat. Coun. Tchg. Fgn. Langs., NYC, 2007; presenter in field; pvt. tutor for fgn. langs. Co-author: The Ancient City of AB-urbe SUBurbe (Gold Chalice award, 2000); author: Gods and Heroes of the Odyssey, 2006 (Gold Chalice award, 2007); contbr. articles to profl. jours.; corr.: Boston Coll. mag. Neighborhood coord. Boston City Coun., 2003—05. Recipient Reader Star Schools Program, Office Ednl. Rsch. and Improvement, 1999, Nat. Tchg. award, Nat. Honor Roll; fellow, Nat. Endowment for the Humanities, 1983; scholar, Inst. Spanish Lang. and Culture, 1994; Fulbright scholar, US Dept. Edn., 1985, Profl. Devel. grantee, U. Mass., 1985. Mem.: Am. Ednl. Rsch. Assn., Mass. ASCD (mem. devel. pubs. com.), Classical Assn. Mass. (pres. 1991—95). Democrat. Achievements include design of WebQuest Curriculum. Avocation: travel. Home: 19 Hartlawn Rd Boston MA 02132 Office: MEC 84 Brick Kiln Rd Chelmsford MA 01824 Office Fax: 978-937-5585. Personal E-mail: perseus813@aol.com.

DIPINO, RAYMOND KIM, psychologist; s. Raymond and Patricia DiPino. MA, Loyola Coll., 1984; PhD, George Mason U., 1992. Neuropsychologist VA Med. Ctr., Balt., 1994—99, Hampton, Va., 1999—2001; dir. psychol. assessment W.Va. U. Sch. Medicine, Charleston, 2001—. Asst. prof. U. Md., Balt., 1994—99, Coll. of William And Mary, Williamsburg, Va., 1999—2001; assoc. prof. W.Va. U. Sch. of Medicine, Charleston, 2001—. Contbr. articles to profl. jours. Mem.: Am. Psychol. Assn., W. Va. Psychol. Assn., Nat. Acad. of Neuropsychology, APA, Nat. Register of Health Svc. Providers in Psychology. Office: WVa Univ Sch Medicine Charleston Divsn 501 Morris St 4 West Charleston WV 25326-1547 Home Phone: 304-342-0189; Office Phone: 304-341-1555. Office Fax: 304-341-1570. Business E-Mail: raymond.dipino@camc.org.

DIPKO, THOMAS EARL, retired minister, religious organization administrator; b. St. Michael, Pa., June 26, 1936; s. John and Sarah Jane (Gittins) D.; m. Sandra Jane Faust, Nov. 19, 1960; children: Lisa Renee, Sarah Marie. BA, Otterbein Coll., 1958; MDiv, United Theol. Sem., 1961; PhD in Ecumenical Theology, Boston U., 1969; LLD (hon.), Heidelberg Coll., 1987; DD (hon.), United Theol. Sem. of the Twin Cities, 1992; LHD (hon.), The Defiance Coll., 1992; DD (hon.), Elmhurst Coll., 1993, Ursinus Coll., 1994. ordained min. Youth min. First United Methodist Ch., Dayton, Ohio, 1958-61; ecumenical intern social action office Ch. Rhineland-Westphalia, Germany, 1962; asst. pastor First Ch. Congregational, Swampscott, Mass., 1963-64; pastor First United Methodist Ch., East Conemaugh, Pa., 1964-66; asst. pastor South Ch. Congregational, Andover, Mass., 1966-68; sr. pastor Christ Ch. United in Lowell, Mass., 1969-77, Grace Congregational Ch., Framingham, Mass., 1977-84; conf. min. and exec. Ohio conf. United Ch. of Christ, Columbus, 1984-92; exec. v.p. United Ch. Bd. for Homeland Ministries, Cleve., 1992-2000. Mem. bd. trustees The Defiance Coll., 1985—; mem. exec. com. Consultation on Ch. Union, 1989-02; del. Seventh Assembly World Coun. Chs., Canberra, Australia, 1991; mem. bd. dirs. Ryder Meml. Hosp., Humacao, Puerto Rico, 1993-96; interim dir. Chs. Uniting in Christ, Clev., 2005-06. Author: (first draft, book) United Church of Christ Book of Worship, 1986; contbr. chpts. to books, articles to profl. jours. Chmn. Lowell Drug Action Com., 1971-74; mem. bd. dirs. Internat. Inst., 1971-77. Samaritans (suicide intervention), 1983-84; del. gen. coun. World Alliance Reformed Chs., Debrecen, Hungary, 1997; bd. trustees LeMoyne-Owen Coll. Fellow Coll. Preachers, 1983. Mem. N.Am. Acad. Ecumenists (mem. exec. com. 1981-83), Christians Associated for Rels. in Eastern Europe, Consultation on Common Texts. Avocations: swimming, perennial gardening, canoeing. Personal E-mail: stdipko@aol.com.

DIPRIMA, RICHARD JOSEPH, neuropsychologist; s. Michael T. and Kathleen M. DiPrima; m. Erin Kathleen Cashin, Aug. 14, 1999; 1 child, Joseph Michael. BA, Marquette U., 1995; MA, Argosy U., 1999, D Psychology, 2002. Lic. psychologist NY. Job coach supportive rehab. and tng. Lifetime Asst., Rochester, NY, 1997; psychologist Alexian Bros. No. Mental Health Ctr., Palatine, Ill., 1998—99; psychotherapy/day ctr. practice in neuropsychology Neuropsychol. and Rehab. Cons., Chgo., 1999—2000; cons., diagnostician U.S. Family Counseling Ctr., Chgo., 1999—2001; predoctoral intern U. Rochester Med. Ctr., 2001—02, postdoctoral resident in neuropsychology, 2002—04, faculty mem., sr. instr., 2004—05; neuropsychologist Gillette Childrens, 2005—. Program aide in support rehab. and tng. Crestomathy Ctr., Mpls., 1996; program counselor Dungarvin, St. Paul, 1996. Acad. scholar, Marquette U., 1991, Dean's Acad. scholar, Argosy U., 1999, APA Conf. Student Rep. scholar, 1999. Mem.: APA, Psi Chi. Avocations: soccer, tennis, golf, writing.

DIR, DAVE, professional soccer coach; b. June 23, 1959; Student, Western Ill. U. Profl. soccer player Chgo. Sting, 1980-84; soccer coach Trinity Prep Luth. Sch., Orlando, Fla., 1984-90; coach Regis U., Denver, 1990-92; head coach Colo. Foxes, 1992-93; dir. player devel. Major League Soccer, 1993-95; head coach Dallas Burn, 1995—. Goalkeeper coach U.S. Youth Soccer Assn. Region IV Olympic Devel. Program. Named Coach of the Yr., Colo. Athletic Conf., 1991. Office: c/o Dallas Burn 14800 Quorum Drive #300 Dallas TX 75254

DIRECTOR, STEPHEN WILLIAM, electrical and computer engineering educator, academic administrator; b. Bklyn., June 28, 1943; s. Murray and Lillian (Brody) D.; m. Lorraine Schwartz, June 20, 1965; children: Joshua (dec.), Kimberly, Cynthia, Deborah. BS, SUNY, Stony Brook, 1965; MS, U. Calif., Berkeley, 1967, PhD, 1968. Prof. elec. engring. U. Fla., Gainesville, 1968-77; vis. scientist IBM Rsch. Labs., Yorktown Heights, NY, 1974-75; prof. elec. and computer engring. Carnegie-Mellon U., Pitts., 1977-96, U.A. and Helen Whitaker Univ. prof. electrical and computer engring., 1980-96, prof. computer sci., 1981-96, head dept. elec. and computer engring., 1982-91, univ. prof., 1992-93, dean Carnegie Inst. Tech., 1991-96; Robert J. Vlasic dean of engring. U. Mich., Ann Arbor, 1996—2005, prof. elec. engring. and computer science, 1996—2005; provost, sr. v.p. Drexel U., Phila., 2005—. Advisor info. and comm. tech. Techno Venture Mgmt., 1999—2002; sr. rsch. fellow IC2 Inst., 1996—; sr. cons. editor McGraw-Hill Book Co., NYC, 1976—; dir. Rsch. Ctr. Computer-Aided Design, Pitts., 1982—89; mem. tech. adv. bd. Nextwave, Inc., 1990—95, CAD Framework Initiative, 1991—93, Aspect Devel. Corp., 1991—92, JW2 Inc., 1991—94, LSI Logic, 1994, Autogate Logic, 1994—96, EDF Ventures, 1999—, MobileWebSurf Inc., 2002—; bd. dirs. Job Gravity, 1999—; hon. prof. Shanghai Jiao Tong U., 2003; mem. adv. coun. Lutron Electronics Inc., 1999—; cons. in field. Author: Introduction to System Theory, 1972, Circuit Theory, 1975, VLSI Design for Manufacturing: Yield Enhancement, 1989, Principles of VLSI System Planning: A Framework for Conceptual Design, 1991; editor: Computer-Aided Design, 1974; co-editor: Advances in Computer-Aided Design for VLSI: vol. 8, Statistical Approach to VLSI, 1994. Chair bd. dirs. Am. Soc. Engring. Edn., Engring. Deans Coun., 1999-2001. Named Distinguished Alumnus, SUNY, Stony Brook, 1984; Recipient Aristotle award Semicondr. Rsch. Corp., 1996, Outstanding Alumnus award in Elec. Engring. U. Calif., Berkeley, 1996, Berkeley Disting. Engring. Alumnus award U. Calif., 1999; fellow Am. Soc. Engring. Edn., 2004. Fellow IEEE (W.R.G. Baker prize 1979, Edn. Soc. Outstanding Achievement award 1995, Edn. medal 1998, Millennium medal 2000), Am. Soc. Engring Edn. (Frederick Emmons Terman award 1976, Benjamin Garver Lamme award 2004); mem. NAE (chair com. on engring. edn.), IEEE Cirs. and Sys. Soc. (pres. 1981, assoc. editor jour. 1973-75, best paper award 1970, 85, 89, 92, Centennial medal 1984, soc. award 1992, Golden Jubilee medal 1999). Office: Drexel Univ Office of Provost 3141 Chestnut St Philadelphia PA 19104 E-mail: director@drexel.edu.

DIRENZO, GORDON JAMES, sociologist, psychologist, educator; b. North Attleboro, Mass., July 19, 1934; s. Santo and Giulia (Petti) DiR.; m. Mary Kathleen Ryan, July 6, 1968; children: Maria Giulia, Chiara Veronica, Marco Santo. BA, U. Notre Dame, Ind., 1956, MA, 1957, PhD, 1963; postgrad., Harvard U., Cambridge, Mass., 1959, Columbia U., NYC, 1963-65, U. Colo., Boulder, 1964. Lic. psychologist, Del.; cert. social psychologist. Instr. Coll. of St. Rose, Albany, NY, 1957-59; Instr. U. Portland, Oreg., 1961-62; asst. prof. Fairfield U., Conn., 1962-66; assoc. prof. Ind. U., South Bend, 1966-70; prof. sociology U. Del., Newark, 1970—; mem. faculty Siena Coll., Albany Med. Ctr., NY, 1958-59, U. Notre Dame, 1960-61, Coll. White Plains, 1963-65, Bklyn. Coll., 1965, Western Conn. State U., 1964, SUNY, Stony Brook, 1980, Cortland, 1966; affiliate mem. med. and dental staff Med. Ctr. Del., Wilmington, 1976-80, St. Francis Hosp., Wilmington, 1980—, Northeastern Hosp., Phila., 1982-85, Rockford Ctr., Wilmington, 1995—, Pres. Behavior Cons., Newark, Del., 1975—; dir. Sociol. Cons. Group, North Attleboro, Mass., 1963-75; Fulbright-Hays prof. U. Rome, 1968-69, U. Bologna, Italy, 1980-81; mem., bd. examiners psychologists State of Del., 1991-99, 2003—, exec. sec. 1992-99, 2007—. Author: Concepts, Theory and Explanation in the Behavioral Sciences, 1966, Personality, Power and Politics, 1967, Personalità Potere Politico, 1967, Personality and Politics, 1974, We, the People: American Character and Social Change, 1977, Sociological Perspectives, 1987, Human Social Behavior, 1990, Personality and Society, 2001, The Social Individual, 2002, Individuo e Società, 2003, Conoscenza e Spiegazione, 2004, La Persona Sociale, 2007; contbr. articles to profl. jours. Recipient Disting. Svc. award Am. Assn. Family Practice, 1980, 82, 84, Excellence in Teaching award U. Del., 1991; fellow U. Notre Dame, 1959-60, Italian Ministry Edn., 1960, NSF, 1964; grantee Ford Found., 1960, NEH, 1975, Del. Inst. Med. Edn. and Rsch., 1975, Hon. Comdr. USAF, Dover AFB, 2005. Fellow Am. Sociol. Assn., Assn. State and Provincial Bds. Psychology; mem. APA, AAUP, AAAS, Assn. Behavioral Scis. in Med. Edn., Soc. Personality and Social Psychology, Soc. for Advancement Social Psychology (bd. dirs. 1988-94), Am.-Italian Hist. Assn. (nat. exec. council 1977-80), Fulbright Alumni Assn., Internat. Sociol. Assn., Clin. Sociology Assn., Internat. Soc. Polit. Psychology (charter), Soc. Psychologists in Medicine, Internat. Polit. Sci. Assn., Soc. for Study Social Problems, Soc. Psychol. Study Social Issues, Eastern Sociol. Soc., Am. Sociol. Assn., Nat. Assn. Scholars, Alpha Kappa Delta. Home: 28 Deer Run Little Baltimore Farms Newark DE 19711 Office: U Del Dept Sociology Newark DE 19716 Office Phone: 302-239-4975. Business E-Mail: gdirenzo@udel.edu.

DIRESTA, GENE ROBERT, biomedical researcher, director; s. Pasqualino and Assunta DiResta; m. Ursula Mary Fallahay, Jan. 3, 1976; children: Renee Adelina, Lauren Nicole. BS, Mich. State U., East Lansing, 1970; MEng, NYU, NYC, 1973; PhD, Poly. U., Bklyn., 1981. Registered profl. engr., N.Y., 1991; diplomate Am. Bd. Radiology, 1997. Biochem. engr. Novo Labs., Inc., 1970—77; rsch. assoc. Cornell U. Med. Coll., 1981—84; dir. pre-clin. rsch. orthop. Meml. Sloan Kettering Cancer Ctr., NYC, 1984—. Consulting MicroFlow Assocs., Pleasantville, NY, 1982—. Judge Tri-County Sci., NY, 1996—2007. Grantee, NIH, 1999—2002, Orthopaedic Rsch. and Edn. Found., 2000—02, MusculoSkeletal Transplant Found., 2006—. Democrat. Roman Catholic. Achievements include patents for device for measuring blood flow; artificial lymphatic system; Antiresorptive Bone Cement; patents pending for high pressure cell culture device; research in elevated IFP on tumor cell culture and solid tumor treatment response; verifying adverse influence of elevated IFP on drug transport into tumors. Avocations: piano, gardening, skiing. Office: Memorial Sloan Kettering Cancer Center 1275 York Avenue New York NY 10021-6007 Home Phone: 914-769-4820; Office Phone: 212-639-7405.

DIRITA, DAVID M., lawyer, manufacturing executive; BA, JD, U. Mich., Ann Arbor. Corp. atty. Dickinson-Wright, Detroit; gen. counsel N.Am. and S.Am. Johnson Controls, Inc.; with Visteon Corp., 2000—05, dep. gen. counsel; sr. v.p., gen. counsel Tower Automotive, Inc., Novi, Mich., 2005—. Office: Tower Automotive, Inc 27175 Haggerty Rd Novi MI 48377 Office Phone: 248-675-6000.*

DI RITA, LARRY (LAWRENCE T.), bank executive, former federal agency administrator; b. Detroit; Grad., U.S. Naval Acad.; master's degree, Johns Hopkins U. Dep. dir. fgn. policy and def. studies Heritage Found., 1994—96; legis. dir., chief of staff to Sen. Kay Bailey Hutchison US Senate, 1996—2001; spl. asst. to sec. US Dept. Def., 2001—06, prin. dep. asst. sec., 2001—06; comm. exec. Bank Am. Corp., 2006—. Policy dir. Presdl. Campaign for Sen. Phil Gramm, 1996. Former officer USN.*

DIRKS, KENNETH RAY, medical educator, army officer; b. Newton, Kans., Feb. 11, 1925; s. Jacob Kenneth and Ruth Viola (Penner) Dirks; m. Betty Jean Worsham, June 9, 1946; children: Susan Jan, Jeffrey Mark, Deborah Anne, Timothy David, Melissa Jane. MD, Washington U., St. Louis, 1947. Diplomate Am. Bd. Pathology. Rotating intern St. Louis City

Hosp., 1948, asst. resident in gen. surgery, 1948-49; resident in pathology VA Hosp., Jefferson Barracks, Mo., 1951-53, resident in pathology, asst. chief lab. service Indpls., 1953-54; resident in pathology Letterman Army Hosp., San Francisco, 1956-57; fellow in tropical medicine and parasitology La. State U., Central Am., 1958; asst. in pathology Washington U. Sch. Medicine, 1952-53; asst. chief lab. service VA Hosp., Jefferson Barracks, 1953; instr. pathology U. Ind. Med. Center, Indpls., 1953-54; commd. capt. M.C. U.S. Army, 1954, advanced through grades to maj. gen., 1976; dir. research Med. Research and Devel. Command, Washington, 1968-69, dep. comdr., 1969-71, comdr., 1973-76; asst. surgeon gen., research and devel. U.S. Army, 1973-76; dep. comdr., comdr. Med. Research Inst. Infectious Diseases, Ft. Detrick, Frederick, Md., 1972-73; comdr. Fitzsimons Army Med. Center, Denver, 1976-77; supt. Acad. Health Scis., Ft. Sam Houston, Tex., 1977-80; assoc. prof. to prof. pathology and lab. medicine Coll. Med. Tex. A&M U., College Station, 1980-95; interim head dept. Coll. Medicine, Tex. A&M U., College Station, 1990-91; prof. emeritus pathology, 1995—; asst. dean coll. Coll. Medicine, Tex. A&M U., College Station, 1985-88; dir. dept. student health svcs. and A.P. Beutel Health Ctr. Tex. A&M U., College Station, 1989-95; dir. student health svcs. emeritus, 1995—. Contbr. articles to profl. jours. Decorated DSM, Legion of Merit with oak leaf cluster, Meritorious Svc. medal, Army Commendation medal with oak leaf cluster. Fellow: Am. Soc. Clin. Pathology (emeritus), Internat. Acad. Pathology, Coll. Am. Pathologists. Republican. Baptist. Address: 2513 Oak Cir Bryan TX 77802-2009 Personal E-mail: kdemeritus@verizon.net. *1) Know your job and work hard. 2) Respect all persons. 3) Be candid and honest always. 4)Persevere in the face of adversity. 5) Love God, country, and other people. 6) Help others.*

DIRKS, LEE EDWARD, newspaper executive; b. Indpls., Aug. 4, 1935; s. Raymond Louis and Virginia Belle (Wagner) Dirks; m. Barbara Dee Nutt, June 16, 1956 (div. Jan. 1985); children: Stephen Merle, Deborah Virginia, David Louis; m. Judith Ann Putman, Dec. 28, 2001. BA, DePauw U., 1956; MA, Fletcher Sch. Law and Diplomacy, 1957. Reporter Boston Globe, 1957, Nat. Observer, Washington, 1962-65, news editor, 1966-68; securities analyst specializing in newspaper stocks Dirks Bros., Ltd., Washington, 1969-71, Delafield, Childs, Inc., Washington, 1971-75, C.S. McKee & Co., Washington, 1975-76; asst. to pres. Detroit Free Press, 1976-77, v.p., gen. mgr., 1977-80; chmn. Dirks, Van Essen & Murray, Santa Fe, N.Mex., 1980—. Author: Religion in Action, 1965; pub. Newspaper Newsletter, 1970-76. Bd. dirs. Nat. Ghost Ranch Found., Santa Fe, 1973-97, Santa Fe Opera, 1998-2004; pres. Georgia O'Keeffe Mus., Santa Fe, 2000-04. Named Religion Writer of Yr. Religious Newswriters Assn., 1964. Mem. Phi Beta Kappa, Lambda Chi Alpha, Nat. Press Club (Washington), Oakland Hills Country Club (Detroit), Las Campanas(Santa Fe). Presbyterian. Home: 11 E Arrowhead Cir Santa Fe NM 87506-8248 Office: 119 E Marcy St Ste 100 Santa Fe NM 87501-2046 Office Phone: 505-820-2700. E-mail: lee@dirksvanessen.com.

DIRKS, ROGER L., mathematics educator; s. Harry H. and Henrietta H. Dirks; m. Cynthia E. Capellari, Oct. 8, 1988; children: Renee L. May, Marla J. BS, Bethany Coll., Lindsborg, Kans., 1963; MS, Kans. State U., Manhattan, 1966. Lic. tchr. Kans., 2005. Math. tchr. HS Topeka Pub. Schs., 1964—70, asst. prin. Topeka West HS, 1970—76, dir. continuing edn., 1976—88, dir. staff devel. and grant procurement, 1988—97, prin. Topeka edn. ctr., 1997—2000, dir. student support svcs., 2000—01; tchr. math. Rossville Jr. Sr. HS, Kans., 2001—. Math. tutor Menninger Found., Topeka, 1965—66; tchr. emotionally disturbed Capital City HS Topeka State Hosp., Topeka, 1965; instr. math. Washburn U., Topeka, 1965—66; mayor's commn. literacy City Topeka, 1987—2001; mem. making the grade task force United Way Topeka; chmn. juvenile correction adv. bd. Kans. Third Jud. Dist., Topeka, 1997—. Co-author: (book) Training Manuel for ABE/GED Teachers, Training Manuel for Experienced ABE/GED Instructors. Com. study city govt. City Topeka. Named one of Outstanding Am. Tchrs., Nat. Honor Roll, 2006; recipient Spl. Merit award, Topeka Pub. Schs., 1962. Mem.: NEA (life), Mo. Valley Adult Edn. Assn. (rep. Kans. chpt., treas., Achievement award 1989), Kans. Adult Edn. Assn. (pres., v.p., treas.), Nat. Coun. Tchrs. Math., Kaw Valley Edn. Assn. (bldg. rep. 2002—06). Avocations: travel, reading, collecting books, the arts. Home Phone: 785-272-7157; Office Phone: 785-584-6193. Personal E-mail: rogdirks@yahoo.com.

DIRNT, MIKE (MICHAEL RYAN PRITCHARD), musician, singer; b. Berkeley, Calif., May 4, 1972; m. Anastasia Dirnt, 1999 (div.); 1 child, Estelle Desiree. Played with the bands Screeching Weasel, Crummy Musicians, Squirtgun; currently bassist with side band The Frustrators; co-founder, musician, back-up vocals Sweet Children (name changed to Green Day in 1989), 1988—. Musician (bassist): How to Make Enemies and Irritate People (with Screeching Weasel); musician, back-up vocals (first EP) 1,000 Hours, (albums) 1,039/Smoothed Out Slappy Hour, 1991, Kerplunk, 1992, Dookie, 1994 (Grammy award for Best Alternative Music Performance, 1994), Insomniac, 1995, Nimrod, 1997, Warning, 2000, American Idiot, 2004 (Viewers Choice award, MTV Video Music Awards, 2005, Am. Music Awards Favorite Rock Album, 2005), voice (films) Live Freaky Die Freaky, 2003; composer: (films) Angus, 1995, Godzilla, 1998, Varsity Blues, 1999, Austin Powers: The Spy Who Shagged Me, 1999; guest appearances Saturday Night Live, 1994, 2005, Mad TV, 2001, (voice) King of the Hill, 1997, and several others. Recipient Video of Yr., Best Group Video, Best Rock Video, Best Editing in a Video, Best Direction in a Video for Boulevard of Broken Dreams, MTV Video Music Awards, 2005, Pop Group of Yr., Rock Artist of Yr., Modern Rock Artist of Yr., Hot 100 Artist of Yr., Billboard 200 Album Group of Yr., Billboard Music Awards, 2005, Rock Song of Yr. for Boulevard of Broken Dreams, 2005, Favorite Group, People's Choice Awards, 2006, Record of Yr. for Boulevard of Broken Dreams, Grammy Awards, 2006.

DIROSA, STEVEN JOSEPH, primary and secondary school educator; b. Phila. s. Joseph and Patricia (Bealer) D. BS, Temple U., 1989; MS in Ednl. Technologies, Rosemont Coll., 1996. Cert. elem., secondary tchr., Pa. Tchr., dept. head Chester-Upland (Pa.) Sch. Dist., 1989-2000; spl. assignmnet middle sch. tchr. Penn-Delco Sch. Dist., 2000—. Tech. dir. STEP Summer Student Prog., Chester, Pa., 1990-95; intramural sports asst. dir. Chester-Upland Sch. Dist., 1993-96. Author: Travel Tales (Billy the Shoe), 1989 (best children's short story award Pa. Tchr. Pages 1990). Recipient Pres.' award Pres.' Acad. Excellence Com., Rosemont, Pa., 1992, outstanding svc. award S.E. Pa. STEP Prog., Chester, Pa., 1994. Fellow Smithsonian Instn.; mem. World Wildlife Fund, Nat. Coun. Tchrs. Math., Sierra Club, Audubon Soc. Home: 232 Talbot Dr Broomall PA 19008-3729 Office: EDCO 232 Talbot Dr Broomall PA 19008

DIRSCHL, DOUGLAS RAY, surgeon, educator; b. Klamath Falls, Oreg., May 16, 1962; s. Raymond Bernard and Sandra Helen Dirschl; m. Virginia Lee Pereira, July 27, 1985; children: Katherine Cord, Douglas Kirk, Margaret Alexandra. BS, Stanford U., 1984; MD, Oreg. Health Scis. U., 1988; cert., Kenan Flagler Grad. Sch. Bus., 1998, MIT, 2000, Northwestern U., 2005. Diplomate U.S. Med. Licensing Exam., Am. Bd. Orthopedic Surgery. Resident in orthop. surgery U. N.C. Sch. Medicine, Chapel Hill, 1988—93, asst. prof. orthops., 1993—99, assoc. prof., 1999—2001, prof., chmn. dept. orthop., 2003—; dir. dept. orthop. Wake Area Health Edn. Ctr., Raleigh, NC, 1996—2001, exec. dir., 1998—2001; prof., chmn. dept. orthops. Oreg. Health & Sci. U., Portland, 2001—03. Chief orthops. VA Med. Ctr., Portland, 2001—03; cons. surgeon EBI Med. Sys., Parsippany, NJ, 1996—. Author: Orthopaedics: PreTest, Self-Assessment, and Review, On Call Orthopaedics: Principles and Protocols; mem. editl. bd. Jour. Orthop. Trauma, Jour. Am. Acad. Orthop. Surgeons, cons. reviewer Jour. Bone and Joint Surgery; contbr. articles to profl. jours., chapters to books. Mem., bd. dirs. Thomas Dameron Found. Orthop. Edn., Raleigh, 1996—2001; mem. exec. com. OHSU Med. Group, Portland, 2001—03; mem. fin. com., mem. exec. com., manged care com. UNC Physicians and Assocs., Chapel Hill, 2003—05; specialist site visitor Accreditation Coun. Grad. Med. Edn., Chgo., 2002—05. Named Edwin J. Bovill Jr. MD Meml. lectr., Orthopaedic Trauma Assn., 1998; recipient Lange Book award for Academic Excellence, Oreg. Health & Scis. U., 1986, Tchg. award for Resident Instrn., U. N.C. Dept. Orthops., 1990, Musculoskeletal cup for Outstanding Faculty Instrn., 2004, Frank C. Wilson Faculty Tchg. award, 1998, Musculoskeletal Cup for Outstanding Faculty Instrn. to med. students, 1994, Jr. Faculty Devel. award, U. N.C., 1994; Nathan Womack scholar, U. N.C. Dept. Surgery, 1993, Tchg. scholar, U. N.C. Sch. Medicine, 1997—99. Fellow: Am. Acad. Orthop. Surgeons (mem. edn. com., mem. program com. 1995—2005); mem.: Interurban Orthop. Soc. (mem. edn. com., mem. program com. 2001—05), Am. Orthop. Assn. (mem. various coms., program chair 2001—05, Travelling fellow 2001), Orthop. Trauma Assn. (mem. various coms., bd. dirs. 1996—2005), Nathan Womack Surg. Soc., Alpha Omega Alpha, Tau Beta Pi. Avocations: baseball, reading, tennis, bicycling. Office: U NC Dept Orthop CB #7055 3147 Bioinformatics Bldg Chapel Hill NC 27599-7055 Office Phone: 919-966-9072. Office Fax: 919-966-6730.

DIRSMITH, RONALD, architect; m. Suzanne Roe Dirsmith. BS in Archtl. Engring., U. of Il., MA in Archtl. Design. Cert. Il., Fl., NCARB. With Perkins & Will; principal Ed Dart & Assoc.; founder, principal architect Dirsmith Group, 1971—. Named Nat. Academician, Nat. Academy of Design, 1999; fellow Rome Prize in Architecture. Office: c/o The Dirsmith Group 318 Maple Avenue Highland Park IL 60035

DIRUSCIO, LAWRENCE WILLIAM, advertising executive; b. Buffalo, Jan. 2, 1941; s. Guido Carmen and Mabel Ella (Bach) DiR.; m. Gloria J. Edney, Aug. 19, 1972; children: Lawrence M., Lorie P., Darryl C., Teresa M., Jack D. With various broadcast stas. and instr., adminstr. Bill Wade Sch. Radio and TV, San Diego, San Francisco, LA, 1961-69; acct. exec. Sta. KGB Radio, San Diego, 1969, gen. sales mgr., 1970-72; pres. Free Apple Advt., San Diego, 1972-94, Fin. Mgmt. Assocs., Inc., San Diego, 1979-84, Self-Pub. Ptnrs., San Diego, 1981—, Media Mix Assocs. Enterprises, Inc., 1984-86; pres. Press-Courier Pub. Co., Inc., 1985-86; pres. Media Mix Advt. and Pub. Rels., 1985—, Taking Care of Bus. Pub. Co., 1990—; pres. Formula Mktg. Co., 1993. Chmn. bd. Quicksilver Enterprises, Inc., A Pub. Corp., 1992-93; lectr., writer on problems of small bus. survival. Author: How SOB's Succeed and Nice Guys Fail in Small Business, 2007. 5 Emmy nominations for T.V. comml. writing and prodn. With USN, 1958-60. Mem. Nat. Acad. TV Arts and Scis. Democrat. Roman Catholic. Office: Media Mix Advt and Pub Rels 726 W Kalmia St San Diego CA 92101-1311

DIRVIN, GERALD VINCENT, retired consumer products company executive; b. Phila., Mar. 28, 1937; s. Vincent A. and Mary (Fitch) D.; m. Polly Burnett, June 27, 1959; children: John, David, Barbara. BA, Hamilton Coll., Clinton, NY, 1959. With Procter & Gamble Co., 1959-94, sales mgt., then v.p. coffee divsn., 1975-80, group v.p. Cin., 1980-89, exec. v.p., 1990-94, dir., 1981-94. Bd. dirs. Cintas Corp. Bd. trustees Hamilton Coll. Mem. Comml. Club, Plantation Golf Club, Commonwealth Club, Camargo Club, Pine Valley Golf Club, Double Eagle Golf Club, Confrerie des Chevaliers du Tastevin, Pablo Creek Golf Club, Kingsley Golf Club. Republican. Roman Catholic. E-mail: gdirvin@aol.com.

DIRZO, RODOLFO, biologist, educator, researcher; b. Cuernavaca, Mex., June 26, 1951; s. Felix and Antonia (Minjarez) D.; m. Bertha Guillermina Gomez, Dec. 18, 1986; 1 child, Arturo. BSc in Biology, U. Morelos, Cuernavaca, 1974; MSc in Ecology, U. Wales, Bangor, UK, 1977, PhD in Ecology, 1980. Rsch. asst. Nat. U. Mex., Mexico City, 1974-80, assoc. prof. ecology, 1980-83, prof. ecology, 1983-85; dir. Tropical Rsch. Sta., Veracruz, Mex., 1985-87; dep. chair Inst. Ecology, Nat. U. Mex., 1994-97, full prof. ecology, 1990—; Bing prof. environ. sci., dept. biol. scis. Stanford U., 2004. Prof., instr. Orgn. Tropical Studies, Costa Rica and U.S., 1982-; conservation & environment scholar Pew Charitable Trust, U.S., 1993; nat. rschr. Mex. Coun. Sci., Mexico City, 1990-; cons. Nat. Geographic Soc., Washington, 1995. Author, editor: Perspectives on Plant Population Ecology, 1984, Mexico Faces the Biodiversity Crisis, 1992, Tropical Forests: Biodiversity, 1996; mem. editl. bd. Trends in Ecology and Evolution, 1993—. Mem. Mex. Acad. Sci. (chair biology 1996-97), Ecol. Soc. Am. (mem. pub. affairs com. 1996-98, governing bd. 1999—), Internat. Geosphere-Biosphere Program (mem. scientific com. 1997—), Assn. Tropical Biology (pres. 1993-94), NAS (fgn. assoc.), Am. Acad. Arts & Sciences (hon. fgn.). Avocations: children's education, hiking, soccer, music, movies. Office: Stanford U Dept Biol Sciences Gilbert Hall Stanford CA 94305-5020 Business E-Mail: rdirzo@stanford.edu.

DISA, JOSEPH JAMES, plastic surgeon; s. Rose and Ralph Disa; m. Julie Lynn Stebbins, Oct. 2, 1961. MD, U. Mass. Sch. Medicine, Worcester, MA, 1988. American Board of Plastic Surgery Am. Bd. of Med. Specialties, 1999, American Board of Surgery Am. Bd. of Med. Specialties, 1995. Intern, gen. surgery U. Md. Med. Ctr., Balt., 1988—89, resident, 1989—94, John Hopkins U., Balt., 1994—96; fellow, plastic surgery Meml. Sloan-Kettering Cancer Ctr., 1996, attending surgeon, plastic and reconstructive surgery New York, NY, 1997—; assoc. prof., plastic and reconstructive surgery Cornell Weill Sch. of Medicine, New York, NY, 1997—. Co-author: 100 Questions & Answers About Breast Surgery, 2006. Fellow: ACS; mem.: Northeastern Soc. Plastic Surgeons (bd. dir. historian 2006—07), Plastic Surgery Edn. Found., Am. Soc. of Reconstructive Microsurgery, Am. Soc. of Plastic Surgeons. Achievements include research in Microsurgical Reconstruction. Office: Memorial Sloan-Kettering Cancer Center 1275 York Avenue New York NY 10021 Office Phone: 212-639-5022. Office Fax: 212-717-3677. Business E-Mail: disaj@mskcc.org.*

DISAIA, PHILIP JOHN, obstetrician, gynecologist, radiology educator; b. Providence, Aug. 14, 1937; s. George and Antoinette (Vastano) DiS.; children: John P., Steven D.; m. Patricia June; children: Dominic J., Vincent J. BS cum laude, Brown U., 1959; MD cum laude, Tufts U., 1963; MD (hon.), U. Genoa, Italy, 1999. Diplomate Am. Bd. Ob-Gyn. (examiner 1975—, bd. dirs. 1994, v.p. bd. dirs. 1997—), Am. Bd. Gynecologic Oncology (bd. dirs. 1987—). Intern Yale U. Sch. Medicine, New Haven Hosp., 1963-64, resident in ob-gyn., 1964-67, instr. ob-gyn., 1966-67; fellow in gynecologic oncology U. Tex. M.D. Anderson Hosp. and Tumor Inst., Houston, 1969-70, NIH sr. fellow, 1969-70, instr. ob-gyn., 1969-71; asst. prof. ob-gyn. and radiology U. So. Calif. Sch. Medicine, LA, 1971-74, assoc. prof., 1974-77; prof., chmn. dept. ob-gyn. U. Calif. Irvine Med. Ctr., Calif. Coll. Medicine, 1977-88, prof., 1977—, prof. radiology, radiation therapy div., 1978—, assoc. vice chancellor for health scis. Irvine Coll. Medicine, 1987-89, Dorothy Marsh chair of reproductive biology, 1989—; dep. dir. cancer ctr. U. Calif, Irvine Med. Ctr., Calif. Coll. Medicine, 1989—; pres. med. staff U. Calif. Irvine Med. Ctr. , Calif. Coll. Medicine, 1993-97; pres. UCI Clin. Practice Group, 1994—. Dir. div. gynecol. oncology Am. Bd. Obstetrics & Gynecology, 1995—, bd. dirs., 1994—, past chair, current pres.; bd. dirs. U. Calif. Irvine Med. Ctr., 1995, chair health sys. steering com., 1995, chair health sys. capital planning group, 1995, health sys. bd. dirs., 1995; clin. enterprise adv. coun. to pres. U. Calif., 1995; academic planning task force U. Calif. Irvine, 1994, continuing med. edn. com., 1991-94; cancer liaison commn. on cancer Am. Coll. Surgeons, 1981-94; bd. dirs., dir. at large Am. Cancer Soc., 1985—; clin. prof. dept. ob-gyn. U. Nev. Sch. Medicine, Reno, 1985—; chmn. site visit team for surgery br. Nat. Cancer Inst. NIH, 1983, subcom. surg. oncology rsch. devel., 1982-83, mem. sci. counselors div. cancer treatment, 1979-83; mem. gov.'s adv. coun. on cancer State of Calif., 1980-85; vis. prof., lectr., speaker various sci. meetings, confs., courses. Recipient Disting. Alumnus award M.D. Anderson Hosp. and Tumor Inst. U. Tex., 1980, Silver Apple award U. Calif. Med. Students, 1983, Lauds and Laurels Profl. Achievement award U. Calif. Alumni Assn., 1983, Hubert Haussel's award Long Beach Meml. Hosp., 1983, Dist. Faculty Lectureship award for Teaching, U. Calif. Irvine Acad. Senate, 1993-94, Robert Wood Johnson award, 2003, medal for excellence UIC, 2003, IGS award for excellence in gynecologic oncology Bristol Myers Squibb, 2004, Arise award UCI, 2005, award Women's Cancer Symposium, Amman, Jordan, 2005, Frederick Naptolin award SGI, 2007, also various rsch. awards. Fellow Am. Coll. Obstetricians and Gynecologists (com. on human rsch. for cancer 1979—, chmn. 1984—, chmn. subcom. on gynecologic oncology 1984-85, prolog editorial and adv. com. 1986—, v.p. 1997-99, various others), ACS (bd. govs. 1998—), Commn. on Cancer Liaison, Western Assn. Gynecologic Oncologists (founder 1971, pres. 1978-79), Am. Gynecol. and Obstet. Soc. (exec. coun. 1986—), Am. Gynecologic Soc., Pacific Coast Ob/Gyn Soc., South Atlantic Assn. Obstetricians and Gynecologists (hon.); mem. AMA, Am. Cancer Soc. (bd. dirs. L.A. County unit 1975-77, Orange County 1979, unit pres. 1993—; bd. dirs. Calif. div. 1985—, chmn. med. scientific com. 1993-94), Nat. Am. Cancer Soc. (dir.-at-large, bd. dirs. 1985—, chmn. program com. for nat. conf. 1986, vice-chmn. detection and treatment adv. group gynecol. cancer 1993-94, active in others), Am. Coll. Radiology (commn. on cancer 1984-85), Am. Soc. Clin. Oncologists, Soc. Gynecologic Oncologists (exec. coun. 1975-80, pres. 1982-83), Internat. Gynecologic Oncology Cancer Soc., Italian Soc. Ob-Gyn. (Camillo Golgi prof. U. Brescia 1991), Calif. Med. Assn., NCI, Ctrl. IRB, Academic Senate, (chair 2000-), Gynecologic Oncology Group, (chair 2002-), ABOG, (pres.2002-06, chmn. bd. 2006—), Alpha Omega Alpha. Office: U Calif Irvine Med Ctr 101 The City Dr S Bldg 56 Rm 265 Orange CA 92868-3201 E-mail: pjdisaia@uci.edu.

DISALVATORE, WILLIAM P., lawyer; b. 1966; BA cum laude, Hofstra U., 1987; JD cum laude, Pace U., 1991. Bar: Ct. 1991, NY 1992. Ptnr. Wilmer, Cutler, Pickering, Hale, and Dorr, LLP, New York. Named one of Top 40 Under 40, Nat. Law Journal, 2002. Mem.: Am. Intellectual Property Law Assoc., Federal Circuit Bar Assoc., N.Y. City Bar Assoc., Am. Bar. Assoc. Office: Wilmer Cutler Pickering Hale and Dorr LLP 399 Park Ave New York NY 10022

DISANTIS, LINDA KATHERINE, lawyer; b. Chgo., Oct. 22, 1946; m. G. Robert Kerr. RN, Luth. Gen. Sch. of Nursing, 1967; BA summa cum laude, Ga. State U., 1985, JD summa cum laude, 1988. Bar: Ga. 1988, U.S. Dist. Ct. (no. dist.) Ga. 1988. RN emergency rm. Cook County Hosp., Chgo., 1967-68; asst. head nurse med. unit Oak Park (Ill.) Hosp., 1968-69; RN neurology unit Case Western Res. Hosp., Cleve., 1970-72; rsch. asst. legis. monitor Ga. Conservancy, Atlanta, 1982-86; intern, researcher Ga. Dept. of Community Affairs, Atlanta, 1986; assoc. Smith, Currie & Hancock, Atlanta, summer 1987, Alston & Bird, Atlanta, 1987—91; environ. coun. UPS, 1991—96, Corp. Compliance Com., 1996—2001, mgr. Corp. Compliance Dept., 2000—01; city atty. Law Dept., Atlanta, 2001—06. Contbr. articles to profl. jours. Mem. consumer adv. coun. Ga. Power Co., Atlanta, 1983-86; mem. econ. devel. task force Gov.'s Growth Strategies Commn., Atlanta, 1987-88. Named Woman of Distinction, Com. on Women, State Bar Ga., 2003; recipient Ben F Johnson Svc. award, Ga. State Coll. Law, 2006. Mem. ABA, Ga. Bar Assn., Atlanta Bar Assn., Ga. State U. Alumni Assn. (bd. dirs. 1989—). Avocations: camping, canoeing. Office Phone: 404-330-6400. Office Fax: 404-658-6894. E-mail: lawdepartment@atlantaga.gov.

DISCIULLO, ALAN MICHAEL, lawyer; b. Long Branch, NJ, Mar. 18, 1950; s. Peter Michael and Marion (Kaney) DiS.; m. Mary Jo Coppola, Oct. 13, 1979; children: Megan Eileen, Corinne Leigh. AB cum laude, Georgetown U., 1972, JD, 1977; MBA, NYU, 1986; M in Corp. Real Estate with honors, NACORE Inst., 1997. Bar: N.J. 1977; U.S. Dist. Ct. N.J. 1977, D.C. 1980, N.Y. 1980. Law clk. to presiding justice U.S. Tax Ct., Washington, 1975-76; assoc. Shanley & Fisher, Newark, 1977-78; asst. v.p. Paine Webber Jackson, NYC, 1978-83; v.p., 1st v.p. Morgan Stanley, NYC, 1983—2005; of counsel Sills, Cummis, Epstein & Gross, P.C., Newark, 2005—06; sr. v.p. Citi Group Inc., NYC, 2006—07; dir. global real estate Shearman & Sterling LLP, NYC, 2007—. V.p., dir. Wall St. Realty, NYC, 1981—83; bd. dirs., gen. counsel, sec. Dean Witter polit. action com., NYC, 1986—91; prof. masters real estate program NYU, 1991—; v.p. North Brunswick Tenants Assn., NJ, 1979—81; mem. task force Pres.'s Pvt. Sector Survey on Cost Control, Grace Commn., Washington, 1982—83; land use adv. com. 12th Congl. Dist. NJ, 1999—2005; lectr. Practicing Law Inst., 1996—, Strategic Rsch. Inst., 1996—98, NACORE Inst. for Corp. Real Estate, Corenet Global, 2002—; adv. bd. Corenet Learning, 2002—05; vice chmn. Negotiating Comml. Leases Panel, 2000—; spkr. in field. Co-author: (treatise) Negotiating and Drafting Office Leases, 1995; co-editor: Met. Corp. Counsel Real Estate Corner column, corp. counsel adv. com., 1997—99; bd. editors: Jour. of Corp. Real Estate Mgmt., 1998—2007, exec. mem.:, 2003—07, mem. edtl. bd.: Comml. Leasing Law and Strategy, 1999—2007, Comml. Tenant's Lease Insider, 2003—07; contbr. articles to profl. jours., book chpt. Treas., dir., coach West Windsor Plainsboro Soccer Assn., 1990—97; mgr. West Windsor Little League, 1993—2000; coach West Windsor Wildcats Traveling ASA Team, 1998—2001; dir. Princeton Soccer Assn., 2001—02; lectr. Sobelsohn Sch.; advisor site plan rev. com. West Windsor Twp., 1987—88, mem. growth mgmt. planning com., 1988—90, mem. growth mgmt. adv. com., 1991—93, zoning bd., 1997—98; chmn. West Windsor Planning Bd., 1993—97; co-chair Mayor's West Windsor Bus. Task Force, 2003—05; mem. West Windsor Plainsboro sch. redistricting com., 1995; trustee West Windsor Plainsboro Sch. Dist. Edn. Found., Inc., 1996—2002, v.p., 1999—2001; mem. Mayor's (NYC) Bldg. Industry Adv. Com., 2003—05; dir. N.J. Planning Ofcls., 1997—. Recipient O'Connor award for disting. legal writing, 1987, 89, 91, Individual Achievement in Planning award NJ Planning Ofcls., 1996, Outstanding Svc. award NYU, 1998, Outstanding Tchr. award NYU, 2002, Corenet Top Faculty award, 2001, 04. Fellow: Am. Coll. Real Estate Lawyers, Am. Bar Assn. Found.; mem.: ABA (chmn. young lawyers divsn. 1985—86, vice chair office lease sect. 1994—98, chmn. task force bldg. safety 1995—2004, chair 1998—2005, office lease assignment sect. 2006—, v.p. securities law divsn., corp. banking and bus. law sect., comml. leasing subcom., exec. com. mem., chmn.coms. on tenant equity participation, subrogation, idemnification), Georgetown U. Wall Street Alliance (adv. bd. 2003—), Practising Law Inst. (real estate adv. bd. mem. 1996—), N.Y. County Lawyers Assn. (exec. com. corp. law sect. 1994—95, co-chair 1996—98), Internat. Assn. Attys. in Corp. Real Estate, NACORE Internat. (dir. N.Y. chpt. 1996, pres. N.Y.C. chpt. 1997—98, internat. bd. dirs. 1997—2002, dir. NACORE Inst. 1999—2002, pres.-elect 2001—02, pres. 2002), Young Lawyers of N.Y.C. (treas. 1982—83, chmn. 1983—85), Georgetown U. Alumni Admissions Program, Mensa, Gavel Club, Princeton (N.J.) Athletic Rugby Club, Carnegie Lake Rowing Club (chair nominating com. 2004), Pi Sigma Alpha. Democrat. Roman Catholic. Avocations: athletics, photography, reading. Home: 19 Taunton Ct Princeton Junction NJ 08550-2164 Office: Shearman & Sterling LLP 850 3d Ave New York NY 10022 Office Phone: 212-848-4137. Personal E-mail: adisciu9@comcast.net. Business E-Mail: alan.disciullo@shearman.com.

DISESSA, ANDREA A., education educator; b. June 3, 1947; m. Melinda M. diSessa; children: Kurt, Nicholas. AB in Physics, Princeton U., 1969; PhD in Physics, MIT, 1975. Mem. A.I. lab. logo group MIT, Cambridge, Mass., 1972—82, spl. lectr. edn., 1975—77, from asst. prof. to assoc. prof. edn., 1977—82, prin. scientist lab. for computer sci., 1982—84, sr. scientist lab. for computer sci., leader ednl. computing group, 1984—85; assoc. prof. edn. U. Calif., Berkeley, 1985—88, prof. edn., 1988—, chmn.

SESAME grad. program, 1988—89, assoc. dean for acad. affairs Grad. Sch. Edn., 1989—91, chair cognition and devel. edn., 1998—2000. Vis. rschr. World Ctr. for Computers and Human Resources, Paris, 1982; spkr. divsn. edn. and math., sci. and tech. edn. U. Calif., Berkeley, 1992—93; vis. prof. media lab. MIT, Cambridge, 1993—94; convenor Ctr. for Study of Critical Transitions, 1997—2002; fellow Ctr. for Advanced Study in Behavioral Scis., 1997—98; cons. in field; founding mem. adv. bd. SIG in Edn. in Sci. and Tech., 1989—; mem. adv. bd. Handheld Assessment Project, 1999—. Contbg. editor: Jour. Math. Behavior, 1982—; editor: Instructional Science, 1984—89; mem. editl. bd.: Jour. Learning Scis., 1990—, Interactive Learning Environments, 1990, Jour. Sci. Edn. and Tech., 1993—. Recipient grants in field. Mem.: NAE, Math. Assn. Am., Jean Piaget Soc., Internat. Soc. of Learning Scis., Cognitive Sci. Soc., Am. Ednl. Rsch. Assn., Nat. Consortium on Uses of Computers in Math. Scis. Edn. (steering com. 1984—86), Phi Beta Kappa. Achievements include research in computers in education; learning genetic epistemology; instruction in physics and mathematics; programming languages for non-professionals. Office: 4533 Tolman Hall #1670 Grad Sch Edn U Calif Berkeley CA 94720-1670

DISHER, DAVID ALAN, lawyer, consultant; b. Chgo., Apr. 15, 1944; s. Hugh George and Beatrice Rose (Selmanovitz) D.; children: Karl Theodore, Carol Ann, Kathy; m. Clara Hoffman, Sept. 17, 1991. BSEE, MIT, Cambridge, 1965, MSEE, 1966; JD, U. Houston, 1983. Bar: Tex. 1984, US Ct. Appeals (5th cir.) 1984, US Tax Ct. 1984, US Dist. Ct. (so. dist.) 1986, US Supreme Ct. 1987. Mathematician Shell Devel., Houston, 1966—68; sr. engr. Tex. Instruments, Stafford, 1968; dir. rsch. GEOCOM, New Orleans, 1969—70; cons., inventor Disher Consulting Svc., Houston, 1970—73; pres., chmn. bd. Seismic Programming Internat., 1973—84; pvt. practice law LaMarque, Tex., 1994—99; pvt. practice Houston, 1999—. Ind. geophys. rsch. cons. Contbr. articles to Geophysics. Mem. crime control com. Houston C. of C., 1974—76. Mem. ACLU, Coll. State Bar Tex., Tex. Criminal Def. Lawyers Assn., Galveston County Bar Assn., Houston Geophys. Soc., Houston Bar Assn., Bar Assn. of Fifth Fed. Cir. Office: 16 North Heights La Marque TX 77568 Office Phone: 409-908-0875. Office Fax: 409-908-0459. Personal E-mail: disherdave@aol.com.

DISHEROON, FRED RUSSELL, lawyer; b. Hot Springs, Ark., Nov. 21, 1931; s. Andrew Russell and Ruth Fayrene (Bearden) D.;children: Terri Suzanne, John Frederick; m. Diane L. Donley, Apr. 8, 1989; 1 child, Travis William. AB, Hendrix Coll., 1953; JD, So. Meth. U., 1956; LLM in Environ. Law, George Washington U., 1976. Bar: Tex. 1956, Va. 1974, U.S. Ct. Appeals (1st, 4th, 5th, 6th, 8th, 9th, 10th, 11th, D.C. and fed. cirs.), U.S. Supreme Ct. 1964. Atty. Superior Ins. Co., Dallas, 1960-64; claims atty. Sentry Ins. Co., Dallas, 1964-67; litigation counsel Stigall, Maxfield & Collier, Dallas, 1967-69; sole practice Dallas, 1969-70; asst. gen. counsel for litigation C.E. U.S. Army, Washington, 1970-75; spl. litigation counsel Dept. Justice, Washington, 1975—. Instr. environ. law U. Ala.-Huntsville, 1979-82; lectr. law George Washington U., 1981-86; vis. rsch. specialist U. Calif., Davis, 1990. Co-author: Sustainable Environmental Law, 1993, Water Law, Trends, Policies and Practice, 1995; editor Southwestern Law Jour., 1955-56. Col. JAGC, USAR. Recipient Sr. Exec. Svc. Meritorious award Dept. Justice, 1984, Outstanding Civilian Svc. medal Dept. Army, Disting. Svc. award Atty. Gen., 2004, John Marshall award disting. svc., 2005. Mem. Sr. Execs. Assn. Home: 3508 Riverwood Rd Alexandria VA 22309-2720 Office: Dept Justice Environ & Natural Resources Divsn 601 D St NW Washington DC 20004 Business E-Mail: fred.disheroon@usdoj.gov.

DISHMAN, ROSE MARIE RICE, academic administrator, researcher; BS in Physics with honors, U. Mo., 1966; MS in Physics, U. Calif., Riverside, 1968, PhD, 1971; MBA, San Diego State U., 1979. Physics instr., elem. particle rsch. assoc. U. Tenn., Knoxville, Oak Ridge, 1968-71; computer programmer, analyst Signal Processing Divsn. Sys. Ctrl., Inc., Palo Alto, Calif., 1971-72; instr. physics San Diego State U., 1974-75; instr. algebra, calculus, physics San Diego C.C., Navy Tng. Ctr., Marine Corps Recruit Depot, 1975-78; instr. Grossmont Coll., San Diego, 1976-77; prof., dept. head Sch. Engring. and Applied Sci. U.S. Internat. U., San Diego, 1977-92, dean Sch. Engring. and Applied Sci., 1989-92, acting provost, v.p. acad. affairs, 1991-92; dean acad. affairs DeVry Inst. Tech., Pomona, Calif., 1992-94, pres. Pomona, Long Beach, Calif., 1994—. Supr. world-wide acad. progs. including campuses in Mex., Eng., Kenya, U.S. Internat. U., primary supr. deans Schs. of Edn., Bus., Visual and Performing Arts, Human Behavior, Hotel and Restaurant Mgmt., Libr., Learning Resource Ctr., developer civil engring., engring. mgmt., electronics tech., elec. engring. progs. resulting in Engring. Accreditation Commn. of the Accreditation Bd. for Engring. and Tech. accreditation for civil engring. prog. for San Diego, London campuses, mem. curriculum coun. for all univ. progs., advisor U.S. Internat. U. Engring. Club; elected mem. Calif. Engring. Liaison Com., pres. pvt. univ. segment. Named outstanting engring. educator Am. Soc. Engring. Edn., 1989; rsch. grantee Fulbright-Hayes, 1972-73, grantee Am. Soc. Engring. Edn., NASA, 1979, Am. Soc. Engring. Edn., Dept. Energy, 1981, 82, 1984-85, Fed. Emergency Mgmt. Agy., 1983, 86. Office: DeVry Inst Tech Univ Ctr 901 Corp Ctr Dr Pomona CA 91768-2642 Fax: 909-623-5666.

DISHONG, MORRIS WILLIAM, forensic specialist, nurse; b. Canton, Ohio, Aug. 13, 1953; s. Morris W. and Vera M. Dishong; m. Rebecca S. Coburn, Nov. 2006; 1 child, Jeffery. Cert. death investigator, St. Louis U., 1997. Firefighter Plain Twp. Fire Dept., North Canton, Ohio, 1975-85; staff nurse emergency rm. Massillon Cmty. Hosp., Ohio, 1986—; forensic investigator Stark County Coroner, Massillon, 1997—. Mem.: Am. Assn. Critical Care Nurses. Republican. Avocations: travel, land exploration. Office: Stark County Coroner 1967 Easton St NW #103 North Canton OH 44720 Personal E-mail: kristine2@hotmail.com.

DISHY, BOB, actor; b. Bklyn. s. Nathan and Amy (Barazani) D.; m. Judy Graubart; 1 child, Samuel Nathan. Student in Drama, Syracuse U. Appeared in Broadway plays Damn Yankees, 1955, From A to Z, Flora The Red Menace, The Unknown Soldier and His Wife, Something Different, The Goodbye People, A Way of Life, The Creation of the World and Other Business, An American Millionaire, Sly Fox, Murder at the Howard Johnsons, Grown Ups, Cafe Crown (revival), The Tenth Man (revival), The Price (revival), Morning's at Seven (revival), Sly Fox (revival); off-Broadway plays Chic, There Is A Play Tonight (revival), Can-Can (revival), By Jupiter (revival), The Shawl; actor, dir. N.Y. Second City Co., 70 Girls 70; also appeared in various regional theaters, Stratford Shakespeare Festival, Mark Taper Forum, Am. Repertory Theatre, The Public Theatre, Berkshire Theatre Festival, Williamson Theatre Festival, Westport Country Playhouse, Bay Street Theatre, Vineyard Playhouse; appeared in films including The Tiger Makes Out, Lovers and Others Strangers, The Big Bus, Last Married Couple in America, First Family, Author, Author, Brighton Beach Memoirs, Critical Condition, Stay Tuned, Used People, My Boyfriend's Back, Don Juan DeMarco and the Centerfold, Jungle 2 Jungle, The Fish in the Bathtub, Judy Berlin, Labor Pains, Along Came Polly, The Wackness; (TV) Frasier, Columbo, Law and Order, Jonny Zero, All in the Family, Mary Tyler Moore, Barney Miller, The Good Doctor, The Cafeteria; mem. TV series co. That Was The Week That Was; actor, dir. TV series Story Theatre. Served with U.S. Army 1957-59. Winner All-Army Entertainment Contest; Tony award nomination; recipient Drama League award, Chancellor's medal for disting. achievement Syracuse U., Outer Critics Cir. award. Mem. Acad. Motion Picture Arts and Scis.

DISILVIO, MARILENA, lawyer; b. Vasto, Italy, June 1, 1967; arrived in U.S., 1972; d. Giuseppe and Grazia DiSilvio; m. David A. Young, Jan. 16, 1999; children: Samuel, Alexander. BSN, U. Pa., Phila., 1989; JD, Clev.-Marshall Coll., 1995. Pediat., neonatal nurse Children's Hosp., Phila., 1989—90, Rainbow Batnes Children's Hosp., Cleve., 1990—91; legal nurse cons. Weisman Kennedy, Cleve., 1991—95, atty., 1995—97, Reminger and Reminger, Cleve., 1995—. Contbr. articles to profl. jours. Named one of Ohio's Rising Stars, Cin. Mag., Ohio's Super Lawyer, Inside Bus. Mem.: Inns of Court, Cuyahoga County Bar Assn., Am. Trial Lawyers Assn., Cleve. Bar Assn., Ohio Women's Bar Assn., Ohio State Bar Assn., Justinian Forum. Office: Reminger and Reminger 101 Prospect Ave W Ste 1400 Cleveland OH 44115 Office Fax: 216-687-1841. Business E-Mail: mdisilvio@reminger.com.

DI SIMONE, ROBERT NICHOLAS, radiologist, educator; b. Canton, Ohio, Nov. 15, 1937; s. Nicholas Joseph and Margaret Elizabeth (Karas) DiS.; m. Patricia Anne Zwigard, June 22, 1963; children: Christopher, Angela, Elizabeth BSc summa cum laude, Ohio State U., 1959, MSc, 1963, MD cum laude, 1963. Diplomate Am. Bd. Radiology, Am. Bd. Nuclear Medicine. Intern, fellow Johns Hopkins U. Hosp., Balt., 1963-64, asst. resident, fellow in internal medicine, 1964-65, asst. resident, fellow in radiology, 1967-70, instr., radiologist, 1970-71; dir. nuclear medicine Aultman Hosp., Canton, 1971-95, pres., med. staff, 1986-87, vice-chmn. dept. radiology, 1988-96, sec.-treas. med. staff, 1977-79; chmn. nuclear medicine sect. Northeastern Ohio Univs. Coll. Medicine, Rootstown, 1979-97; chmn. dept. radiology Northeastern Ohio Univs. Coll. of Medicine (NEOUCOM), Rootstown, 1992-93; diagnostic radiologist Aultman Health Found., Canton, Ohio, 1971-2000; radiology cons. North Canton, Ohio, 2000—. Author: Imaging of the Endocrine System in Organ System Radiology, 1984; contbr. articles to profl. jours Fellow Am. Coll. Radiology; mem. AMA, Soc. Nuc. Medicine (emeritus), Ohio State Med. Soc. (del. 1983-95), Radiol. Soc. N.Am., Stark County Med. Soc. (trustee 1979-95, chmn. bd. censors 1980-82, pres. 1993), Unique Club Stark County, Phi Beta Kappa, Sigma Xi, Alpha Omega Alpha, Phi Lambda Upsilon Avocations: playing bluegrass guitar music, collecting antique old trains, travel, hiking, gardening. Home and Office: 2465 Oakway St NW North Canton OH 44720-5886

DISIPIO, ROCCO THOMAS, writer; b. Phila., Dec. 17, 1949; s. Rocco Benjamin and Rita Elizabeth DiSipio. BS in Police Adminstrn., Mich. State U., 1971. Dir. tours Mich. State U., 1970—71; probation, parole officer Pa. Ct. Common Pleas, 1971-79; gen. mgr. Poniard Books, Inc., Broomall, Pa., 1980-82; ops. mgr. Myles Med. Equip., Ardmore, Pa., 1982-85; editor-in-chief Merit Industries, Bensalem, Pa., 1985-87; freelance writer, 1987—. Guest lectr. creative writing Haven House, Smith Coll., Northhampton, Mass., 1987; prodr. Fgn. Films Enterprises, L.A., 1995—. Author: (world's 1st internet novel) Arcadia Ego, 1996 (USA Today award), (novel) Darkness. Paradise. 1997. Avocation: target shooting. Office: PO Box 405 New Kingstown PA 17072-0405 Office Phone: 717-691-8150.

DISKANT, GREGORY L., lawyer; b. Phila., June 7, 1948; s. Robert and Eda (Grunberg) D.; m. Sandra S. Baron, Feb. 29, 1980; children: Edward, Benjamin. AB, Princeton U., 1970; JD, Columbia U., 1974. Bar: N.Y. 1975. Law clk. to Hon. J. Skelly Wright, U.S. Ct. Appeals for D.C. Cir., Washington, 1974-75; law clk. to Hon. Thurgood Marshall, U.S. Supreme Ct., Washington, 1975-76; asst. U.S. atty. for so. dist. N.Y., Dept. Justice, NYC, 1976-80, chief appellate atty., 1980; assoc. Patterson, Belknap, Webb & Tyler, NYC, 1981—82, ptnr., 1982—, co-chmn., 1997—2002, chmn., 2003—07. Editor-in-chief Columbia Law Rev., 1973-74. Kent scholar, 1972, Stone scholar, 1973, 74. Fellow Am. Coll. Trial Lawyers; mem. ABA, N.Y. State Bar Assn., Assn. Bar of City of N.Y. Office: Patterson Belknap Webb & Tyler Rm 2400 1133 Avenue of the Americas Fl 22 New York NY 10036-6731 Home Phone: 216-874-4258; Office Phone: 212-336-2710. Business E-Mail: gldiskant@pbwt.com.

DISKIN, MICHAEL EDWARD, plastics company and food service executive; b. Dallas, Aug. 8, 1946; s. William Michael and Edna Patricia (Loughran) Diskin; m. Mary Jean Fraser, Oct. 8, 1972; children: Robyn Kristine, Karyn Marie, Michael Alexander, Stephen James, Alisyn Krystal. BS in Bus. Adminstrn & Econs., No. Mich. U., 1971. Sales rep. Lincoln Nat. Life, Fort Wayne, Ind., 1971-73, Durkee Foods, Dayton, Ohio, 1973-75, sales mgr. Cleve., 1975-78, from product mgr. asst. to sr. mktg. mgr. Westlake, Ohio, 1978-87; bus. mgr. Engelhard Corp., Cleve., 1987-88; dir. mktg. Master Builders Technologies, Cleve., 1988-92; exec. v.p. Specrete-Ip, Inc., Cleve., 1992-98; pres., owner Four Seasons Industries, Garretsville, Ohio, 1998—, Durajoint Concrete Accessories, Garretsville, 2001—. V.p. Put In Bay (Ohio) Property Owners Assn.; mem., bd. dirs. Put In Bay Twp. Port Authority. With USMC, 1966—68. Mem.: Lake Erie Islands Hist. Soc., Crews Nest Club, Put-In-Bay Yacht Club. Republican. Roman Catholic. Avocations: trap and target shooting, boating, fishing, travel. Home: 1745 Halls Carriage Path Westlake OH 44145-2030 Office: Diskin Enterprises Inc 10426 Industrial Dr Garrettsville OH 44231-9764 Office Phone: 330-527-4308. Business E-Mail: mediskin@fourseas.net.

DISMUKES, CAROL JAEHNE, county official; b. Giddings, Tex., July 17, 1938; d. Herbert Emil and Ruby (Alexander) Jaehne; m. Harold Charles Schumann, Feb. 7, 1959 (div. May 1970); children: Timothy, Michael, Keith, Gregory; m. Milton Brown Dismukes, Mar. 19, 1971. Student Tex. Lutheran Coll., 1958. Dep. Lee County Clk., Giddings, Tex., 1970-74, chief dep., 1975-77; accounts receivable clk. Invader Inc., Giddings, 1977-79; prodn. sec. Humble Exploration, Giddings, 1979-80; county clk. Lee County, Giddings, 1980—2006. Mem., Dime Box Ind. Sch. Dist. Trustees, Tex., 1972-80, pres., 1977-80; chmn. Dime Box Homecoming and Mini-Marathon, 1978—2000; chmn. scholar com. Lee Co. Jr. Livestock Show, 1982-2000; v.p. coun. St. John's Luth. Ch., 1982-84, sec., 1986, treas., 1987-89, chmn., 1991-93, 97-99. Mem. County and Dist. Clks Assn. Tex., Dime Box Lions Club (charter, pres. 1996-97, sec. 1999-2003). Democrat. Avocations: reading; sewing. Office: Lee County Clk PO Box 419 Giddings TX 78942-0419 Office Phone: 979-542-3684.

DISNEY, ANTHEA, publishing executive; b. Dunstable, Eng., Oct. 13, 1946; naturalized, U.S., 1973; d. Alfred Leslie and Elsie (Wale) Disney; m. Peter Robert Howe, Jan. 28, 1984. Ed., Queen's Coll., Eng. Fgn. corr. London Daily Mail, NYC, 1973-75, features editor London, 1975-77, bur. chief NYC, 1977-79; columnist London Daily Express, NYC, 1979-84; dep. mng. editor N.Y. Daily News, NYC, 1984-87; editor Sunday Daily News, 1984-87, US Mag., 1987-88; editor-in-chief Self mag., 1988-89; mag. developer Murdoch Mags., 1989-90; exec. producer Fox TV's A Current Affair, 1990-91; editor-in-chief TV Guide mag., NYC, 1991-95; editorial dir. Murdoch Mags., 1993-95; editor-in-chief I-Guide, News-corp's Internet Svc., 1995-96; pres., CEO Harper Collins Publishers, 1996-97; chmn., CEO News Am. Pub. Group, NYC, 1997—99, TV Guide, Inc., 1999; exec. v.p. content The News Corp Ltd., NYC, 1999—; exec. chmn. Gemstar-TV Guide International Inc., LA, 2004—. Bd. dirs. Household Internat. Inc., 2001—. Office: The News Corp Ltd Ste 300 1211 Avenue Of The Americas New York NY 10036-8795

DISNEY, RALPH L(YNDE), retired industrial engineering educator; b. Balt., Feb. 27, 1928; BE, Johns Hopkins U., 1952, MSE, 1955, DEng., 1964. Engr. Industrial Diecraft Inc., 1953-55, rsch. analyst Ops. Rsch. Office, 1955-56; asst. prof. Lamar State Coll., Beaumont, 1956-59; assoc. prof. U. Buffalo, 1959-63; vis. assoc. prof. U. Mich., Ann Arbor, 1963-64, assoc. prof., 1964-68, prof. indsl. engring., 1968-77; Charles O. Gordon prof. indsl. engring. Va. Polytech Inst. & State U., Blacksburg, 1977-87; prof. indsl. engring. dept. Tex. A&M U., College Station, 1988-96; ret., 1996. OAS vis. prof. Inst. Aeron. Tech., Brazil, 1970-71; disting. vis. prof. Grad. Sch. Ohio State U., Columbus, 1974-75; vis. prof. dept. math. and stats. U. São Paulo, Brazil. Contbr. articles to profl. jours.; co-author (with A.B. Clarke): Probability and Random Processes for Engineers and Scientists, 1970, Probability and Random Processes: And Introduction to Applications, 1985; co-author: (with Peter C. Kiessler) Traffic Processes in Queueing Networks, 1987; co-editor (with T. Ott): (symposium proceedings) Applied Probability- Computer Science: The Interface, 1982. Erskine fellow Canterbury U., Christchurch, New Zealand, 1995. Fellow Am. Inst. Indsl. Engrs. (A.G. Holzman award 1986, David Baker award 1972, Frank and Lillian Gilbreth Indsl. Engring. award 1993), INFORMS (founder sect. on applied probabilities, sect. pres. 1979); mem. ORSA (mem. coun. 1978-82), NAE Home (Summer): 1313 Woodside Ter Blacksburg VA 24060 Personal E-mail: rdisney@warmhearthva.org.

DISNEY, ROY EDWARD, broadcasting company executive; b. LA, Jan. 10, 1930; s. Roy Oliver and Edna (Francis) D.; m. Patricia Ann Dailey, Sept. 17, 1955; children: Roy Patrick, Susan Margaret, Abigail Edna, Timothy John. BA, Pomona Coll., 1951. Apprentice film editor Mark VII Prodns., Hollywood, 1942; guest relations exec. NBC, Hollywood, Calif., 1952; asst. film editor, cameraman prodn. asst., writer, producer Walt Disney Prodns., Burbank, Calif., 1954-77, dir., 1967—77; pres. Roy E. Disney Prodns. Inc., Burbank, 1978—; chmn. bd. dir. Shamrock Broadcasting Co., Hollywood, 1979—; chmn. bd. dir., founder Shamrock Holdings Inc., Burbank, 1980—; chmn. Walt Disney Animation, 1984—2003; vice chmn. Walt Disney Co., Burbank, 1984—2003, dir. emeritus, cons., 2005—. Trustee Calif. Inst. of the Arts, Valencia, 1967—. Author: novelized adaptation of Perri; producer (film) Pacific High, Mysteries of the Deep exec. producer Cheetah, 1989, The Little Mermaid, 1989, Beauty and the Beast, 1991, The Lion King, 1994, Pocahontas, 1995, Fantasia 2000;(TV show) Walt Disney's Wonderful World of Color, others; writer, dir., producer numerous TV prodns. Bd. dirs. Big Bros. of Greater Los Angeles, U.S. com. UNICEF, Ronald McDonald House charities, chmn. emeritus, Peregrine Fund; mem. adv. bd. dirs. St. Joseph Med. Ctr., Burbank; mem. U.S. Naval Acad. Sailing Squadron, Annapolis, Md.; fellow U. Ky. Recipient Acad. award nomination for Mysteries of the Deep, Mort Walker award for Outstanding Contbn. to the Cartoon Industry, Boca Raton Internat. Mus. of Cartoon Art, 1997, Internat. Creative Achievement award, Cinema Expo, 1997, Elizabeth Ann Seton award, Nat. Catholic Edn. Assn. 1999, Henry Bergh Humane award, ASPCA, 1999, Inaugural Environ. Leadership award, Audubon Soc. 2000, Lifetime Achievement in Animation, Santa Clarita Internat. Film Festival, 2002; named one of Forbes' Richest Americans, 2006. Mem. Dirs. Guild Am. West, Writers Guild Am. Clubs: 100, Confrerie des Chevaliers du Tastevin, St. Francis Yacht, Calif. Yacht, San Diego Yacht, Transpacific Yacht, Los Angeles Yacht. Republican.

DISPENZA, MARY CATHERINE, director, educator, photographer; d. Nicholas Joseph Dispenza and Catherine Viola Cox; life ptnr. Mary Ann Woodruff. BA in Art, Loyola Marymount, 1965; MA in Human Behavior, U.S. Internat. U., 1973. Cert. edn. adminstrn. U. Puget Sound, Seattle, 1978, elem. and secondary tchg. credential U. Puget Sound, 1978. Sister in religious cmty. Religious of the Sacred Heart of Mary, LA, 1958—73; prin. St. Alphonsus Sch., LA, 1970—73, St. Mary's Sch., Aberdeen, Wash., 1973—84, St. Louise Elem. Sch., Bellevue, Wash., 1985—99; dir. pastoral life svc. dept. Cath. Archdiocese Seattle, 1989—92; dir. Propect Enrichment Presch., Seattle, 1997—2005; ESL coord. Entre Hermanos, Seattle, 2005—. Co-founder TEN, Bellevue, Wash., 1993—; exec. bd. mem., co-chair Hands off Wash., Seattle, 1993—98; chair Lesbian and Gay Child Care Task Force, King County, 1993—2005; ednl. cons. Seattle Hebrew Acad., 1994—96; lead rschr. report Our Families, Our Children, 1999. Illustrated book, Non-Verbal Communication Between Nurse and Patient, LGBT Family Poster Kit for Schools, 2006. Chair br. juvenile jud. sys. Family Conf. Com., Aberdeen, Wash., 1973—79; mem., spkr. Hands off Wash., Seattle, 1993—97; vol. cook, homeless gay youth Lambert Ho., Seattle, 1993—; creator travelling exhibit LGBT Youth, Seattle, 2001—; photographer ann. calendar highlighting LGBT families Lesbian and Gay Child Care Task Force, Seattle, 2001—; editor, continuum Religious of the Sacred Heart of Mary, LA, 1965—70. Recipient Nat. Disting. Prin., NEA, 1988, Disting. Cath. Sch. Prin., Nat. Cath. Edn. Assn., 1988; grantee, PRIDE found, 2001—02. Mem.: Nat. Assn. Edn. of Young Children (assoc.). Avocations: photography, art. Office Phone: 425-644-2468. Personal E-mail: mcdispenza@earthlink.net.

DI SPIGNO, GUY JOSEPH, industrial psychologist, international management consultant; b. Bklyn., Mar. 6, 1948; s. Joseph Vincent and Jeanne Nina (Renna) DiS.; m. Gisela Riba, May 23, 1979; children: Michael Paul, Abie Francis. BS, Carroll Coll., 1969; MA, No. Ill. U., 1972; MEd, Loyola U., 1974; PhD, Northwestern U., 1977. Instr. No. Ill. U., DeKalb, 1969-70; chmn. humanities dept. Quincy (Ill.) Boys' H.S., 1970-71; dir. religious edn. St. Mary's Ch., DeKalb, 1971-72; dir. edn. Immaculate Conception Parish, Highland Park, Ill., 1972-77; dir. human resources Am. Valuation Cons., Des Plaines, Ill., 1977-79; psychologist Hay Assocs., Chgo., 1979-80; v.p. mktg. Exec. Assets Corp., Chgo., 1980-82; dir. mgmt. devel. and pers. svcs. Borg-Warner Corp., Chgo., 1982-84; ptnr., cons. psychologist Medina & Thompson, Chgo., 1984-91; pres. Exec. Synergies, Inc., Northbrook, Ill., 1991—. Coun. regents Loyola U., Chgo., 2004—, student affairs com., 2006—; adv. bd. Northwestern U. Sch. Continuing Studies, 2005—. Contbr. articles to profl. jours. Mem. Highland Park Human Rels. Commn., 1975-77, Home Owners and Businessmen's Assn., Highland Park, 1976-77; mem. legis. com. Vernon Hills (Ill.) Sch. Bd., alumni coun. Carroll Coll., 1981-83; soccer coach Am. Youth Soccer Orgn., Glenview, Ill.; chmn.'s cabinet Ill. Dem. Party, 1988-92; benefactor Jesuit Partnership, Chgo. province, 1995—. Clifford B. Scott scholar, 1967; fellow No. Ill. U., 1970-72; named to Order Ky. Cols. Mem. APA, Cmty. Religious Edn. Dirs. (nat. vice chmn. 1971-73), Ill. Psychol. Assn., Nat. Registry Health Svc. Providers in Psychology, Am. Pers. and Guidance Assn., Soc. Indsl. and Orgnl. Psychology, Carroll Coll. Alumni Counsel, Phi Alpha Theta, Sigma Phi Epsilon. Office: 555 Skokie Blvd Ste 260 Northbrook IL 60062-2889 Office Phone: 847-272-3420. Business E-Mail: guyd@executivesynergies.com.

DISPIRITO, ROCCO, restaurant owner, chef; Degree, Culinary Inst. Am., 1986; student, Jardin de Cygne, Paris; BA, Boston U., 1990. Chef under Jean-Michel Diot and Jacques Chibois Adrienne, NYC; chef de partie Aujourd'hui, Boston, Lespinasse, NYC; exec. chef Dava Restaurant, 1995, Union Pacific, NYC, 1997—2004; founder, exec. chef Rocco's, NYC, 2003—04. Stagiere with Dominique Cecillon, with David Bouley, with Charles Palmer, with Gilbert Le Coze, with Gray Kunz. Reality show: The Restaurant, 2003—04; radio host WOR, 2004—05; author: Flavor, 2003, Rocco's Italian-American, 2004, Rocco's Five Minute Flavor, 2005. Named Best New Chef, Food and Wine, 1999; recipient 3-star rev., NY Times, favorable cooking revs., NY Mag., Crain's NY Bus., NY Observer, Food Arts. Avocations: guitar, mountain biking, collecting wine and cookbooks.*

DISSEN, JAMES HARDIMAN, lawyer; b. Pitts., Jan. 26, 1942; s. William Paul and Kathryn Grace (Reilly) D.; m. Shirley Ann Stark, Dec. 17, 1976; children: Elizabeth Ann, William Stark, Anna Kathryn. BS, Wheeling Jesuit U., W.Va., 1963; MBA, Xavier U., Cin., 1966; JD, Duquesne U., Pitts., 1972. Bar: Pa. 1972, U.S. Dist. Ct. (we. dist.) Pa. 1972, W.Va. 1973, U.S. Dist. Ct. (so. dist.) W.Va. 1973, U.S. Supreme Ct. 1976. Spl. agent Counter Intelligence U.S. Army Intelligence Corps, 1963-66; personnel mgr. Columbia Gas of Pa., Inc., Uniontown, 1969-73; dir. labor rels. Columbia Gas Transmission Corp., Charleston, W.Va., 1973-84, dir. personnel and labor rels., 1984-87, dir. employee rels., 1987-96; v.p. Columbia Natural Resources, Charleston, W.Va., 1996-2001; v.p., ptnr. Triana Energy, Charleston, W.Va., 2001—03; sr. v.p. Columbia Natural Resources, LLC, Charleston, 2003—06; v.p., ptnr. Triana Energy LLC, 2006—. Adj. prof. W.Va. Grad. Coll., 1996-97, Wheeling Jesuit U., 1997,

U. Charleston, 1998; chmn., exec. com., bd. dir. Star U.S.A. Fed. Credit Union. Chmn. bd. trustees Highland Hosp., 1991—; chmn. bd. dir. Inroads/W.Va., 1995-2001, Christmas in April, 2000-01; pres. Cath. Bus. Network, 2002—. Mem. ABA, W.Va. State Bar, Soc. Human Resource Mgmt., W.Va. C. of C. (chmn. human resource com., bd. dir.), St. Thomas Moore Soc., Berry Hills Country Club. Republican. Roman Catholic. Avocation: golf. Home: 1501 Brentwood Rd Charleston WV 25314-2307 Office: Triana Energy LLC Ste 700 500 Va St E Charleston WV 25301 Home Phone: 304-344-3038; Office Phone: 304-353-5112, 304-380-0112. E-mail: jdissen@trianaenergy.com.

DISSMORE, LARRY DAVID, musician, educator, conductor; b. Kenosha, Wis., May 3, 1960; s. David Arne and Sarah Viola Dissmore; m. Gayle Donna Gunderson, Aug. 14, 1982; children: Anthony David, Gregory Paul. MusB Edn., U. Wis., Eau Claire, 1983; MusM in Violin Performance, Wichita State U., Kans., 1985; D Mus. Arts in Orchestral Conducting, U. Mo., Kansas City, 2003. Cert. violin instr. Suzuki Assn. Am. Sect. violin Rochester Symphony Orch., Minn., 1982—83, Wichita Symphony Orch., 1983—85; instr. music Vitterbo U., La Crosse, Wis., 1985—88; sect. violin Springfield Symphony Orch., Mo., 1988—90, prin. 2d violin, 1988—90, 1990—; concertmaster Springfield Regional Opera Orch., 1995—; prof. music Evangel U., 1988—. Music dir. Springfield Youth Symphony, 2002—; concertmaster La Crosse (WI) Symphony Orch., La Crosse, Wis., 1985—88; asst. prin. 2d violin Symphony Sch. Am., La Crosse, 1985; prin. 2d violin Springfield Regional Opera Orch., 1989—95, concertmaster, 1995—. Bd. dirs. Springfield Symphony Assn., 1996—2002. Cohen scholar, U. Wis. Eau Claire Found., 1978—82. Mem.: Coll. Orch. Dirs. Assn. (treas. north ctrl. dist. 2004—06), Music Tchrs. Nat. Assn. (v.p. 1993—2006), Am. String Tchrs. Assn., Internat. Condrs. Guild, Music Educators Nat. Conf., Phi Kappa Phi, Pi Kappa Lambda, Phi Eta Sigma. Republican. Mem. Assemblies Of God. Avocations: hunting, golf, fishing. Office: Evangel U 1111 N Glenstone Springfield MO 65802 Home Phone: 417-886-2810; Office Phone: 417-865-2815. Office Fax: 417-865-9599. Personal E-mail: ldissmore@atlascomm.net. Business E-Mail: dissmorel@evangel.edu.

DISTAD, B. JANE, neurologist; d. Paul and Laverne. BA, Northwestern U., Evanston, Ill., 1989; MD, Med. Coll. Ohio, Toledo, 1994. Asst. prof. U. Wash., Seattle, 2001—. Contbr. chapters to books. Mem.: Am. Acad. Neurology. Office: U Wash Box 356465 1959 NE Pacific Seattle WA 98195

DISTEFANO, PHILIP, academic administrator; BA in Humanities Edn., Ohio State U., 1968, PhD in Humanities Edn., 1974; MA in English Edn., W.Va. U., 1971. Joined U. Colo., Boulder, 1974, dean, 1986—96, vice chancellor, 1998—2000, exec. vice chancellor, provost, 2000—05, 2006—, interim chancellor, 2005—06.*

DISTELHORST, GARIS FRED, trade association administrator; b. Columbus, Ohio, Jan. 21, 1942; s. Harold Theodore and Ruth (Haywood) D.; m. Helen Cecilla Gillen, Oct. 28, 1972; children: Garen, Kristen, Alison. BSc, Ohio State U., 1965. V.p. Smith, Bucklin & Assocs., Washington, 1969-80; chief staff exec., CEO, pres. Nat. Assn. Coll. Stores, Oberlin, Ohio, 1980-98; pres. Assn. Initiatives, Inc., Westlake, Ohio, 1998—2002; pres., CEO Conv. Industry Coun., 1999—2001, Marble Inst. Am., 2002—. Mem. book and libr. adv. com. USIA, 1990-93; bd. dirs. FirstMerit Bank, N.A., Holcombs, Inc. Pres. Oberlin Cmty. Improvement Corp., 1985-88; bd. dirs. Leadership Lorain County, 1988-89, Access Program, 1994-97, Conv. and Visitors Bur. Greater Cleve., 1994-2003, Lorain County C.C. Found., Lorain County United Way, 1991-97, v.p., 1993-94, pres., 1994-96, campaign chmn., 1993; bd. dirs. Project Love, 2003-05, Avon Lake Cmty. Improvement Corp., 2003—. Decorated USN Achievement medal, 1969 Mem. Inst. Assn. Mgmt. Soc. (treas. 1979-80, award of merit), Am. Soc. Assn. Execs. (bd. dirs. 1981-84, vice chmn. 1985, chmn.-elect 1994, chmn. 1995-96, bd. dirs. found. 1990-94, vice chmn. found. 1991-92, chmn. found. 1992-93, Key award 1984, chmn. Assn. Advance Am. 1993-94), Oberlin Area C. of C. (pres. 1987-90, bd. dirs. 1987-90), Greater Cleve. Soc. Assn. Execs. (bd. dirs. 2003—). Republican. Roman Catholic. Office: Marble Inst Am 28901 Clemens Rd Ste 100 Cleveland OH 44145 Office Phone: 440-250-9222. Business E-Mail: gdistelhorst@marble-institute.com. *Leadership isn't about having followers, but rather about providing an inspiring vision of a better future for your associates & colleagues.*

DI SUVERO, MARK, sculptor; b. Shanghai, Sept. 18, 1933; s. Vittorio and Matilde (Millo) Di Suvero. BA, U. Calif., Berkeley, 1957. Co-founder Park Place Gallery, NYC, 1963. Founder Socrates Sculpture Pk., N.Y.C., 1986; one-person shows include Green Gallery, N.Y., 1960, Park Place Gallery, N.Y., 1966, Van Abbemuseum, Eindhoven, Netherlands, 1972, City of Chalon-sur-Saone, France, 1974, Jardin des Tuileries, Paris, 1975, Whitney Mus., N.Y.C., 1975, Oil and Steel Gallery, N.Y.C., 1983, Storm King Art Ctr., 1985, 95, 96, Wurttembergischer Kunstverein, Stuttgart, 1988, City of Valence, France, 1990, Musee d'Art Moderne et d'Art Contemporain de Nice, France, 1991, City of Chalon/Saône, France, 1992, IVAM Centre Julio Gonzalez, Valencia, Spain, 1994, XLVI Venice Biennial, 1995, City of Paris, 1997, Hiroshima Mus. Contemporary Art, 1998, Gagosian Gallery, N.Y.C., 2001, Peace Tower, Day for Night, Whitney Biennial, 2006, others; represented in permanent collections, Art Inst. Chgo., Whitney Mus., N.Y.C., Museum of Modern Art, N.Y.C., Nat. Gallery Art, Washington, Hirshhorn Mus. and Sculpture Garden, Washington, Mus. of Contemporary Art, L.A., others. Recipient Art Inst. Chgo. award, 1963, Creative Arts award, Brandeis U., 1969, Skowhegan Sch. award, 1974, Heinz Award in the Arts and Humanities, 2005; grantee Longview Found., Walter K. Gutman Found. Business E-Mail: disuvero@spacetimecc.com.

DITELBERG, JOSHUA L., lawyer; b. Newton, Mass., Feb. 14, 1966; s. Dennis L. and Frances D. Ditelberg; m. Jane H. Gorham, Nov. 9, 1996; 1 child, Claire F. BA in Philosophy and History, U. Pa., Phila., 1987; MA in History, U. Pa., 1987; JD, U. Mich., Ann Arbor, 1991. Law clk. Hon. Joseph R. Weisberger, Providence, 1991—92, Hon. Ralph B. Guy, Jr., Ann Arbor, 1992—93; assoc. Edwards & Angell, LLP, Boston, 1993—96, Seyfarth Shaw, LLP, Chgo., 1997—2002, ptnr., 2002—. Mem., bus. advice & planning com. Ill. Inst. Continuing Legal Edn., Chgo., 2006—. Contbr. articles to profl. jours. Named Leading Lawyer, Leading Lawyers Network, 2006—07, Ill. Super Lawyer, Law & Politics, 2006; recipient Order of the Coif, Order of the Coif & U. Mich. Law Sch., 1991; Younger Scholar fellow, Nat. Endowment Humanities, 1986. Mem.: ABA, Order of the Coif, Labor and Employment Rels. Assn. (pres., Chgo. chpt. 2006—), Phi Alpha Theta, Phi Beta Kappa. Office: Seyfarth Shaw LLP 131 S Dearborn St Ste 2400 Chicago IL 60603 Office Fax: 312-460-7000. Business E-Mail: jditelberg@seyfarth.com.

DI TERLIZZI, ROBERTA, pathologist, educator; d. Francesco Di Terlizzi and Donata Spilotros. DVM, U. Bari, Italy, 1996. Cert. vet. pathology Italy, 1999. Resident in vet. clin. pathologist Kans. State U., Manhattan, 2004—07; lectr. clin. pathology Coll. Vet. Medicine Iowa State U., Ames, 2007—. Recipient Young Investigator award, Am. Coll. Vet. Clin. Pathologist, 2005. Home: 1418 McCain Ln Apt 346 Manhattan KS 66502 Office: Kans State U Vet Med 1800 Denison Ave Manhattan KS 66506 Home Phone: 785-317-0316; Office Phone: 7855324891. Personal E-mail: robertaditerlizzi@hotmail.com. Business E-Mail: rterlizz@vet.ksu.edu.

DITHRIDGE, ELIZABETH, civic worker; b. L.A., Sept. 11, 1920; d. Thomas Edward and Louise (Miles) Mitchell; m. Andrew Morrison Dithridge, May 11, 1940; 1 child, Andrew Morrison Jr. Student, UCLA, 1937-39. Boy scout and cub scout leader L.A. Orphan's Home Soc., 1952-69, sec. extension com., 1959-61, chmn., 1966-68; vol. worker USO; mem. L.A. Jr. Philharmonic Com., 1949—; active Symphonies for Youth Concerts, 1958-59; founder, chmn. San Marino Protection Com., 1971-72; sec. L.A. County Grand Jury, 1974-75; bd. dirs. Pasadena chpt. ARC, 1961-62, Vol. Service Bur. Pasadena; bd. dirs., treas. Wilshire Community Police Coun., 1979-81; mem. citizens adv. com. L.A. Olympics Organizing Com., 1982-84; dir. Capistrano Bay Community Svcs. Dist., 1987—; receptionist Welfare Office, USMC, Camp Pendleton, 1992-98; vol. computer room for swimmers and divers, Olympics; guide Doheny State Beach Interpretive Assn. Recipient awards for work with local youth groups. Recipient award Comdr. Camp Pendleton, 1998. Mem. Wilshire C. of C. (chmn. women's bur. 1957-59), L.A.C. of C. Assocs. L.A. City Coll., Orange County Marine Inst., Friends of Huntington Libr., D.A.R., Friends of San Juan Capistrano Libr., San Juan Capistrano Hist. Soc., L.A. Grand Jurors Assn., Alpha Phi, Sigma Alpha Iota. Home: 35411 Beach Rd Capistrano Beach CA 92624

DITKA, MIKE (MICHAEL KELLER DITKA JR.), sports commentator, former professional football coach; b. Carnegie, Pa., Oct. 18, 1939; s. Mike and Charlotte (Keller) D.; m. Margery Ditka, Jan. 21, 1961 (div. 1973); children: Michael, Mark, Megan, Matthew; m. Diana S. Ditka, July 8, 1977. Grad, U. Pitts., 1961. Profl. football player Chgo. Bears, 1961-66, Phila. Eagles, 1967-68, Dallas Cowboys, 1969-72, asst. coach, 1973-81; head coach Chgo. Bears, 1982-93, New Orleans Saints, 1997-99; owner Ditka's Restaurant, Chgo., 1986—; studio analyst, NFL Today CBS, 2000—01; commentator, NFL Live ESPN. Actor: (films) Up, Michigan!, 2001, Kicking & Screaming, 2005; (TV films) Maxiumum Surge Movie, 2003; host (TV series) Mike Ditka Show, 1982, guest appearances L.A. Law, 1990, Cheers, 1993, Coach, 1996, 3rd Rock from the Sun, 1996, 1997, Becker, 2001, According to Jim, 2002, ESPN Sports Century, 2001—05. Named NFL Rookie of Yr., 1961; named to Pro Bowl, 1962-66, named Coach of the Yr, AP, 1988; inducted into NFL Hall of Fame, 1988 Head coach, Superbowl Champion Chgo. Bears, 1985; mem. Sigma Chi Fraternity Roman Catholic.

DITKOWSKY, KENNETH K., lawyer; b. Chgo., July 12, 1936; s. Samuel J. and Lillian (Plavnik) Ditkowsky; m. Judith Goodman, Sept. 9, 1959; children: Naomi, Deborah, R. Benjamin. BS, U. Chgo.; JD, Loyola U., Chgo. Bar: Ill. 1961, U.S. Dist. Ct. (no. dist.) Ill. 1962, U.S. Ct. Appeals (7th cir.) 1973, U.S. Tax Ct. 1973, U.S. Supreme Ct. 1975. Ptnr. Ditkowsky & Contorer, Chgo., 1961—. Mem.: Ill. Bar Assn. Home: 5940 W Touhy Ave Ste 230 Niles IL 60714-4614 Office Phone: 847-600-3421. Personal E-mail: kenditkowsky@yahoo.com.

DITMARS, JAMES EVERETT, social worker, actor; b. Geneva, NY, June 5, 1959; s. James Ford and Shirley Jane Ditmars; m. Lynn Ann Baily, Sept. 19, 1993; 1 child, Heather Lynn Williams. BFA, SUNY, Fredonia, 1981; MSW, Syracuse U., NY, 1992. LCSW NY. Therapist Ontario County Mental Health Ctr., Canandaigua, NY, 1993—. Actor: Bristol Valley Theatre. Office: Ontario County Mental Health Ctr 3019 County Complex Dr Canandaigua NY 14424

DI TORO, DOMINIC M., engineering educator; BE with honors, Manhattan Coll., 1963; MA in Elec. Engring., Princeton U., 1965, PhD in Civil and Geological Engring., 1967. Rsch. assoc. Environ. Engring. and Sci. Program, 1967—69; sr. rsch. cons. engr. Hydroscience, Inc., 1969—80; prin. cons. HydroQual, Inc., 1980—; rsch. prof. environ. engring. Manhattan Coll., 1986—99, Donald J. O'Connor prof. environ. engring., 1999—2003; Edward C. Davis prof. civil and environ. engring. U. Del., Newark, 2003—. Author: Sediment Flux Modeling, 2001; contbr. articles to profl. jours. Named Inst. of Scientific Info. Highly Cited Rschr., 2003. Mem.: NAE, IEEE, Am. Chemical Soc., Am. Geophysical Union, Am. Soc. of Civil Engrs. (Wesley W. Horner Award 1980), Am. Soc. of Limnology and Oceanography, Assn. Environ. Engring. and Sci. Profs., Estuarine Rsch. Fedn., Internat. Assn. for Great Lakes Rsch. (Chandler Misener Award 1983), Internat. Water Assn., Soc. Toxicology and Environ. Chemistry, Geochemical Soc. Office: U Del Dept Civil and Environ Engring 356 DuPont Hall Newark DE 19716 Office Phone: 302-831-4094. Office Fax: 302-831-3640. E-mail: dditoro@ce.udel.edu.

D'ITRI, FRANK MICHAEL, environmental research chemist; b. Flint, Mich., Apr. 25, 1933; s. Dominic and Angelina D'Itri; m. Patricia Ann Ward, Sept. 10, 1955; children: Michael Payne, Angela Kathryn, Patricia Ann, Julie Lynn. BS in Zoology, Mich. State U., 1955, MS in Analytical Chemistry, 1966, PhD, 1968. Lab. technician Dow Industry Service Labs., Midland, Mich., 1960-62; research asst. dept. chemistry Mich. State U., East Lansing, 1963-68, asst. prof. dept. fisheries and wildlife, 1968-72, assoc. prof. dept. fisheries and wildlife, 1973-76, prof. dept. fisheries and wildlife, 1977—; assoc. dir. Inst. Water Rsch., 1987—; asst. dir. Mich. Agrl. Exptl. Sta., 1996—2000; internat. studies and programs, 2004—. Cons. U.S. Dept. Energy, Washington, 1983-85, EEC, UN, Geneva, 1982—; vis. prof. U. Bahia, Brazil, 1978, Tokyo U. Agr., 1980, 84-85, 87, 94, 2000, 01; mem. adv. bd. Lewis Pubs., Inc., Springer-Verlag. Author: The Environmental Mercury Problem, 1972, (with P.A. D'Itri) Mercury Contamination: A Human Tragedy, 1977, (with A.W. Andren, R.A. Doherty, J.M. Wood), Assessment of Mercury in the Environment, 1978, Acid Precipitation, 1982, Artificial Reefs, 1985; editor (with J. Aguirre M., M. Athie L.), Municipal Wastewater in Agriculture, 1981, Land Treatment of Municipal Wastewater: Vegetation Selection and Management, 1982, Acid Precipitation: Effects on Ecological Systems, 1982, (with M.A. Kamrin) PCBs: Human and Environmental Hazards, 1983, Artificial Reefs: Marine and Freshwater Applications, 1985, A System Approach to Conservation Tillage, 1985, (with H.H. Prince) Coastal Wetlands, 1985; (with L.G. Wolfson) Rural Groundwater Contamination, 1987, Chemical Deicers And The Environment, 1992, (with H.W. Belcher) Subirrigation and Controlled Drainage, 1995, Zebra Mussels and Aquatic Nuisance Species, 1997, (with Y. Itakura) Integrated Environmental Management, 1999; contbr. numerous articles to profl. jours. Mem. critical materials adv. subcom. Mich. Water Resources Commns. Mich. Dept. Natural Resources, 1971-79, mem. solid waste com., 1971-79; mem. subcom. Mich. State U. Waste Control Authority Chem. Waste, 1971—; mem. tech. adv. com. Great Lakes Protection fund tech. adv. com., 1990-93; mem. Great Lakes Commn., 1992—; mem. subirrigation steering com. Mich. Soil Conservation Svc., 1986—; mem. fluctuating lake levels com. Internat. Joint Commn., 1992-93; mem. internat. rsch. group mercury pollution in Amazon, Brazil, 1992—. NIH summer fellow, 1964-67, Socony-Mobil fellow Mich. State U., 1967-68, Japan Soc. Promotion Sci. fellow, 1980; Rockefeller Found. Bellagio Resident scholar, 1972, 75. Mem. Am. Chem. Soc., Am. Soc. Limnology and Oceanography, Assn. Analytical Chemists, Water Pollution Research Soc., Midwest Univs. Analytical Chemists Conf., Mich. Acad. Sci., Arts and Letters, Sigma Xi, Setac. Office: Mich State U 4A Internat Ctr East Lansing MI 48824-1035 Office Phone: 517-432-8244. Business E-Mail: ditri@msu.edu.

DITTENHAFER, BRIAN DOUGLAS, banker, economist; b. York, Pa., Aug. 15, 1942; s. Nathaniel Webster and Evelyn Romaine (Myers) D.; m. Miriam Marcy, Aug. 22, 1964; 1 child. BA, Ursinus Coll., 1964; MA, Temple U., 1966, postgrad., 1967—71. Pers. asst. Philco Corp., Phila., 1965—66; tchg. asst. Temple U., Phila., 1966—67, rsch. assoc., 1968—69; bus. economist Fed. Res. Bank of Atlanta, 1971—76; v.p., chief economist Fed. Home Loan Bank of N.Y., NYC, 1976—79, sr. v.p., CFO, 1979—80, exec. v.p., 1980—85, pres., 1985—92, Collective Fed. Savs. Bank, 1992—94, Collective Bancorp, 1992—94; chmn. MBD Mgmt. Co., 1994—. Vice chmn. Fin. Instns. Thrift Plan, 1991-92, chmn., 1992; trustee Fin. Instns. Retirement Fund, 1985-92, vice chmn., 1991, chmn., 1992; bd. dirs. Investors Savs. Bank, 1997—. Bd. dirs. Social Compact, 1990-99, sec., 1995-99; mem. FNMA Found. Adv. Group, 1994; deacon Ctrl. Presbyn. Ch., 1981-84; bd. dirs. N.Y. Coun. Econ. Edn., 1983-89; chmn. Resolution Funding Corp., 1989-92. Temple U. fellow, G.E. Found. fellow Temple U. Mem. Nat. Assn. Bus. Economists, Forecaster's Club N.Y. (sec.-treas. 1982-84), Suntree Country Club (dir., treas. 2000-03), Omicron Delta Epsilon.

DITTENHAFER, DANIEL WEBSTER, II, computer scientist; b. Ga., Feb. 2, 1975; m. Jennifer Dittenhafer. Cert. profl. Microsoft Corp. Systems arch. Identitech, Inc., Melbourne, Fla., 1996—2004; prin. solutions arch. Global 360, Inc., Melbourne, Fla., 2004—06; sr. software developer AgCert Internat., Melbourne, Fla., 2006—. Chief software cons. Dittenhafer Solutions, Melbourne, 2004—. Named Most Valuable Programmer, Identitech, Inc., 2001. Mem.: Project Mgmt. Inst.

DITTER, J. WILLIAM, JR., federal judge; b. Phila., Oct. 19, 1921; m. Verna B. Ditter (dec. 2005); children: J. William III, George B., Robert V., David B. *Father, a congressman from 1933 until his death in 1943, lead the efforts before World War II to obtain legislation for a two ocean navy. The USS J. William Ditter (DM31), a destroyer mine-layer, was named in his honor as is the chapel at the Naval Air Station, Willow Grove, Pennsylvania. Cousin, Dorothy Gondos Beers, was full professor and dean of women at American University, Washington, DC. Cousin, Edward G. Biester, was a state judge, 1949-70, and his son, Edward G. Biester, Jr., a member of congress, Attorney General of Pennsylvania, and is now a retired state judge.* BA, Ursinus Coll., 1943, LLD, 1970; LLB, U. Pa., 1948. Bar: Pa. 1949. Clk. Ct. Common Pleas, Montgomery County, Pa., 1948-51; asst. dist. atty. Montgomery County, 1951, 53-55; 1st asst. dist. atty., 1956-60; mem. firm Ditter and Jenkins and predecessor firm, Ambler, Pa., 1953-63; judge Ct. Common Pleas, Montgomery County, 1964-70, U.S. Dist. Ct. Ea. Dist. Pa., Phila., 1970-86, sr. judge, 1986—; lectr. Villanova U. Past pres. bd. trustees Calvary Methodist Ch.; charter pres. Ambler Jaycees, 1954-55; bd. dirs. Riverview Osteo. Hosp., Norristown, Pa., 1964-71; bd. consulters Villanova U. Sch. Law, 1977—. Served to capt. USNR, 1943-68. Recipient Disting. Alumnus award Ambler High Sch., 1986; named Alumnus of Yr., Ursinus Coll., 1980. Mem. Am., Fed., Pa., Montgomery County bar assns., Hist. Soc. U.S. Dist. Ct. Eastern Dist. Pa. (incorporator, bd. dirs.) Office Phone: 215-597-9640.

DITTMER, FRANCES R., curator; m. Thomas Henry Dittmer (div.). Former curator Refco Collection; pvt. cons.; curator of modern & contemporary art Art Inst. Chgo. Bd. dir. Drawing Ctr. Inc., Whitney Mus. Am. Art, NYC; bd. trustees Menil Collection, Dia Art Found., Art Inst. Chgo., 1988—. Named one of Top 200 collectors, ARTnews Mag., 2004. Avocation: Collector of Contemporary Art. Mailing: Art Inst Chicago 111 S Michiagn Ave Chicago IL 60603-6110

DITTMER, H. ROBERT, music educator, director; b. Manitowoc, Wis., June 9, 1956; s. Roderick Townsend and Lois Ann Dittmer. MusB in Edn., Olivet Coll., Mich., 1978; MusM, U. Wis., Madison, 1986. Dir. bands Rosholt HS, Wis., 1979—84; band dir. Madison Holy Name HS, 1985—86; dir. bands West Bend, Wis., 1986—. Musician (mgr.): (profl. horn quartet) Quattro Horns, 1995—. Recipient Tchg. award, Rolf's Edn. Found., 1997. Mem.: Wis. Bandmaster Assn., Wis. Sch. Music Assn. (dir. music publ. com. 1995—). Avocations: travel, photography, motor scooters, aviation, architecture. Office: West Bend HS 1305 E Decorah Rd West Bend WI 53095 Office Phone: 262-335-5557. Business E-Mail: rdittmer@wi.rr.com.

DITTMER, JOHN AVERY, history professor; b. Seymour, Ind., Oct. 30, 1939; s. J. Avery and Melba Roberta (Ahlbrand) D.; m. Ellen Ann Tobey, June 3, 1961; children: Julia Susan, John David. BS in Edn., Ind. U., 1961, MA in History, 1964, PhD in History, 1971. Asst. prof. Tougaloo (Miss.) Coll., 1967-68, acad. dean, 1968-70, assoc. prof., 1971-79; assoc. prof. history DePauw U., Greencastle, Ind., 1985-92, prof., 1993—2004, prof. emeritus, 2004—. Vis. assoc. prof. Brown U., Providence, 1979-80, 81-82, 83-84, MIT, Cambridge, 1982-84; cons. NEH, Washington, 1980-83, PBS Series, Eyes on the Prize, Boston, 1986. Author: Black Georgia in the Progressive Era, 1900-1920, 1977, Local People: The Struggle for Civil Rights in Mississippi, 1994 (Lillian Smith book award, 1994, Bancroft prize Columbia U. 1995); contbr. articles to profl. jours. Younger Humanist fellow NEH, 1973-74, fellowship-in-residence NEH, 1976-77, fellow Rockefeller Found., 1980-81, Am. Coun. Learned Socs., 1983-84, Ctr. Study Civil Rights U. Va., 1988-89, NEH, 2000-01, Nat. Humanities Ctr., 2001-01; grantee Ford Found., 2005—. Mem. Orgn. of Am. Historians (Frederick Jackson Turner award finalist 1972), So. Hist. Assn., Am. Hist. Assn. Avocations: tennis, golf, jazz music. Home: 230 Westwood Rd Fillmore IN 46128-9621 Office: DePauw U Dept History Greencastle IN 46135 Office Phone: 765-658-4590. Business E-Mail: rip@depauw.edu.

DITTRICK, WILLIAM G., lawyer; b. 1947; BBA, Univ. Neb., 1969, JD, 1974. Bar: US Dist. Ct. (Dist. Nebr.) 1972, Nebr. 1974, US Ct. Appeals (8th Cir.) 1982, Iowa 1998, US Supreme Ct. 1999. Law clerk Hon. Warren K. Urbom, Chief US Dist. Judge, 1974—76; mem. Baird Holm LLP, 1976—. Exec. ed.: editorial bd. Neb. Law Review, 1973—74. Past pres., bd. dirs. Big Brothers/Big Sisters, Midlands. Fellow: Am. Coll. of Trial Lawyers; mem.: ABA, Nebr. Assn. Trial Lawyers, Robert M. Spire Inns of Ct., Neb. State Bar Assn. (pres.-elect 2005, pres. 2006). Office: Baird Holm LLP 1500 Woodmen Tower Omaha NE 68102-2068 Office Phone: 402-636-8205. Business E-Mail: wdittrick@bairdholm.com.

DIVAKARAN, VIJAY GANESH, medical researcher; MBBS, Madras Med. Coll., Chennai, India, 2000; baccalaureate, Tamil Nadu MGR Med. U., India, 2001; MPH, U. Tex., Houston, 2003; MD, SUNY, Bklyn., 2006. Diplomate Am. Bd. Internal Medicine, 2006. Grad. rsch. asst. Human Genetics Ctr., U. Tex. Sch. Pub. Health, Houston, 2002—03; rsch. assoc. U. Tex. MD Anderson Cancer Ctr., Houston, 2003; resident SUNY Downstate Med. Ctr., Bklyn., 2003—06; clin. postdoctoral fellow Baylor Coll. Medicine, Houston, 2006—. Recipient Dr. R.K. Thirupad Meml. Endowment prize, Madras Med. Coll., 1999, Dr. A. Lakshmanaswami Mudaliar medal, MGR Med. U., 1999, T. Rajagopal Meml. prize, 1999, Dr. Avvai Meml. Endowment prize, 1999, A.C. Asirvada Nadar Meml. prize, 1999; fellow in molecular cardiology, Bugher Found., 2005. Mem.: ACP, Am. Assn. Physicians of Indian Origin, Am. Coll. Cardiology. Home Phone: 281-412-2795; Office Phone: 713-798-4951.

DIVELY, JUSTIN MATTHEW, psychologist; s. Bruce and Gayle Dively; m. Tara Hostetter, Oct. 29, 2005. MS in Edn., Bucknell U., Lewisburg, Pa., 2000. Sch. psychologist Lincoln Intermediate Unit, New Oxford, Pa., 2000—02, Lewisburg Area Sch. Dist., 2002. Mem.: NASP (assoc.). Avocation: coaching soccer. Office: Lewisburg Area School District 1951 Washington Ave Lewisburg PA 17837 Home Phone: 570-837-1421; Office Phone: 570-523-3220 3276. Personal E-mail: jdively@gmail.com.

DIVENERE, ANTHONY JOSEPH, lawyer; b. Bari, Italy, June 20, 1941; s. Joseph and Donna (Montini) DiV.; m. Sylvia Kathleen Scarnati, June 19, 1965; children: Anthony, Diana, John. AB, John Carroll U., 1964; JD, Ohio State U., 1967. BAr: Ohio 1967. Atty. in charge Cleve. Legal Aid Soc., 1967-70; prin., v.p. Burke Haber & Berick Co., L.P.A., Cleve., 1971; shareholder McDonald, Hopkins, Burke & Haber. Recipient Claude E.

Clark award Cleve. Legal Aid. Soc., 1968, Cmty. Svc. aard North Olmsted Jaycees, 1972. Mem. ABA, Ohio Bar Assn., Cleve. Bar Assn. (Appreciation award 1979-80), Cleve. Assn. Trial Attys. (pres. 1979-80), Def. Rsch. Inst., Vermilion Yacht Club. Avocations: sailing, marathon running, squash, opera. Home: 310 Rye Gate St Cleveland OH 44140-1272 Office: McDonald Hopkins Co 600 Superior Ave Ste 2100 Cleveland OH 44114 Business E-Mail: adivenere@mcdonaldhopkins.com.

DIVER, COLIN S., academic administrator, educator; b. 1943; BA, Amherst Coll., 1965; LLB, Harvard U., 1968; MA, U. Pa., 1989; LLD, Amherst Coll., 1990. Bar: Mass. 1968. Spl. counsel Office of the Mayor, Boston, 1968-71; asst. sec. consumer affairs Exec. Office Consumer Affairs, Boston, 1971-72; undersec. adminstrn. Exec. Office Adminstrn. and Fin., Boston, 1972-74; assoc. prof. Boston U., 1975-81, prof., 1981-89, from assoc. dean to dean, 1985-89; dean, Bernard G. Segal prof. U. Pa., Phila., 1989—99, Charles A. Heinbold, Jr., prof., 1999—2002; pres. Reed Coll., Portland, Oreg., 2002—. Cons. Adminstrv. Conf. of U.S., 1980-88. Chmn. Mass. State Ethics Com., 1983-89; mem. adv. com. on enforcement policy NRC, 1984-85. Office: Reed Coll 3203 SE Woodstock Blvd Portland OR 97202 Office Phone: 503-777-7500. Office Fax: 503-777-7701. E-mail: presidentsoffice@reed.edu.

DIVERS, KEVIN SAMUEL, aerospace physiologist; b. Biloxi, Miss., June 26, 1975; s. Walter Alfred and Rita Gonzales Divers; 1 child, Zachary Allan. BS in Human Factors Engring., USAF Acad., Colo., 1998; MBA, Webster U., Miss., 2002. Squadron adj. 48th Ops. Support Squadron, RAF Lakenheath, Suffolk, England, 1998—99; student pilot 37th Flying Tng. Squadron, Columbus AFB, Miss., 1999—2001; pilot vehicle interface, life support test officer F-22 Combined Test Force, Edwards AFB, Calif., 2001—03, chief human sys. integration sect., 2003—04; officer in charge human performance enhancement 1st Aerospace Medicine Squadron, Langley AFB, Va., 2004—06, officer in charge, standardization and evaluation, 2006—. Co-designer, attenuating custom comm. earpiece sys. Air Force Rsch. Lab., Wright-Patterson AFB, Ohio, 2002—; asst. prof., med. resource mgmt. U. Ky., Lexington, 2005—; test condr., advanced mil. freefall oxygen sys. Naval Spl. Warfare Devel. Group, Little Creek, Va., 2006—. Capt. USAF, 1993. Decorated Commendation medal USAF. Mem.: Aerospace Physiol. Soc., Aerospace Med. Assn. Achievements include design of aircrew customized earplugs, attenuating custom communication earpiece system. Office: 1 Aerospace Medicine Squadron 76 Holly St Hampton VA 23665 Business E-Mail: kevin.divers@langley.af.mil.

DIVINEY, CRAIG DAVID, lawyer; b. Keokuk, Iowa, July 19, 1953; s. William Thomas and Ella (Michel) D.; m. Astrid Maria Kost, Oct. 6, 1975; children: Adam Thomas, Elliot Michel, Lisa Anne. BA, Augustana Coll., Rock Island, Ill., 1975; JD, U. Iowa, 1979. Bar: Minn. 1979, U.S. Dist. Ct. Minn. 1980, U.S. Ct. Appeals (8th cir.) 1984, U.S. Ct. Appeals (7th cir.) 1987, U.S. Ct. Appeals (fed. cir.) 1990. Assoc. Dorsey & Whitney, Mpls., 1979-84, ptnr., trial, intellectual property litig., 1985—, and chmn., life sci. and health care group. Adj. prof. William Mitchell Coll. Law, 1983-85; faculty Minn. Advocacy Inst., 1989—. Mem. fed. practice com. Dist. Minn., 1990-91; mem. adv. com. U.S. Dist. Ct., 1991—. Mem. ABA, Order of Coif. Office: Dorsey & Whitney 50 S 6th St Minneapolis MN 55402-1498 Office Phone: 601-340-2873. Office Fax: 612-340-2868. Business E-Mail: diviney.craig@dorsey.com.

DIVINEY, NANCY LYNN, elementary school educator; d. Thomas Peter and Marguerite Lillian Diviney; children: Andrew Thomas DiOrio, Emily Katherine DiOrio. BS in Edn., U. Kans., 1974, MS in Edn., 1988; grad. in ESL, Emporia State U., Kans., 2006. Cert. elem. tchr. Kans., reading specialist Kans., ESL Kans. Tchr. Sacred Heart Sch., Bonner Springs, Kans., 1974—75, St. Ann's Sch., Prairie Village, Kans., 1975—77, 1984—89, Queen of the Holy Rosary, Overland Park, Kans., 1978—79; substitute tchr. Shawnee Mission (Kans.) Sch. Dist., 1979—84, tchr., 1993—95, reading specialist, 1995—; tchr. Arlington (Tex.) ISD, 1990—92. Ednl. trainer SRA, McGraw Hill, NYC, 1996—; dist. trainer Shawnee Mission Sch. Dist., Kans., 1995—; publr. KC Star, 2004; presenter in field. Vol. Kansas City Hands On, Mo., 2002—, 40 Hour Club; coord. U. Kans. Juniper Garden Grant for Ruston; v.p. Celtic Fringe, Kansas City, Mo., 2004—05; vol. Cath. Charities, Kansas City, Kans., 2002—06. Nominee Phoebe Apperson Hearst award, Nat. PTA; recipient Dist. Employee Recognition, Shawnee Mission Sch. Dist., 1997, Literacy award, Internat. Reading Assn., Kans., 2000, cert. of appreciation, Kansas City, 2002, Action Rsch. Project award, Shawnee Mission Sch. Dist., 2002, Project Best Grant award, Emporia State U., 2005; Shawnee Mission Ednl. grantee, 1998, 2000. Mem.: Kans. Reading Assn. (assoc.; conf. presenter 1997, 1998, chmn. READ Week 1999—2000, conf. presenter 2000, 2001, Literacy award 2000), Internat. Reading Assn. (assoc.), Breakfast Reading Club (founder), Alpha Phi (alumna officer 1977—78), Delta Kappa Gamma (assoc.). Avocations: reading, travel, volunteering. Home Phone: 913-341-3143.

DIVITA, JAMES J., retired social studies educator, writer, researcher; b. Chgo., Jan. 20, 1938; s. Charles V. and Theresa Rohde Divita; m. Mary Frances Beckmeyer, Aug. 22, 1964; children: Lawrence, Mary Theresa, Michael, Anne. BA, DePaul U., Chgo., 1959, AM, 1960; PhD, U. Chgo., 1972. Instr. history Marian Coll., Indpls., 1961—64, asst. prof. history, 1964—70, assoc. prof. history, 1970—76, prof. history, 1976—2003, prof. emeritus history, 2003—, chmn. dept. history and polit. sci., 1974—75, 1983—2002. Pres. Ind. Religious History Assn., Indpls., 1987—97; chmn. Am. Cath. Hist. Assn. Regional Meeting, Indpls., 1998. Author: Slaves to No One, 1981, The Italians of Indianapolis, 1984, Indianapolis Cathedral, 1986, History of St. Christopher Speedway, 1987, Ethnic Settlement Patterns in Indianapolis, 1989, Rejoice and Remember, 1992, Workers' Church, 1994 (IRHA Excellence award, 1995), Splendor of the South Side, 2000 (IRHA Excellence award, 2001), Return to Splendor, 2003, Indianapolis Italians, 2006; contbr. chapters to books, articles pub. to profl. jour., encyclopedia. Recipient Franciscan Values award, Marian Coll., 2003, Tchg. Excellence award, 1998, Fadely History award, Marion County-Indpls. Hist. Soc., 2006; grantee, NEH, 1977, 1981, 1984. Mem.: Ind. Hist. Soc. (libr. com. chmn. 1983—94), Am. Hist. Assn. (life), Italian Heritage Soc. Ind. (v.p. 1998—2004, pres. 2004—06), Indpls. Literary Club (asst. sec. 1989—92). Roman Catholic. Home: 3208 Acacia Dr Indianapolis IN 46214 Office: Marian Coll Dept History 3200 Cold Springs Rd Indianapolis IN 46222-1997

DIVON, MICHAEL Y., obstetrician and gynecologist; b. Cheb, Czechoslovaki, Oct. 6, 1947; s. David and Friei D.; m. Ruth Divon Barkai, Jan. 3, 1956 (div.). BS summa cum laude, Northrop Inst. Tech., 1973; MD cum laude, Technion Israel Inst., 1978. Dir. ob-gyn Albert Einstein Coll. Medicine, Bronx, N.Y., 1989-97, Lenox Hill Hosp., NYC, 1997—. Maj. USAF, 1966-83. Office: 130 E 77th St Fl 2 Black Hall New York NY 10021

DIWAN, ABHINAV, medical educator, researcher; b. Raipur, Chattisgarh, India, May 5, 1973; s. Shridhar and Shachi Diwan; m. Anupam Mishra, Oct. 25, 1975; 1 child, Aaradhya. MBBS, All India Inst. Med. Scis., New Delhi, 1997. Diplomate Am. Bd. Internal Medicine, 2000, in cardiovascular disease Am. Bd. Internal Medicine, 2004, adult comprehensive echocardiography Nat. Bd. Echocardiography, 2004. Jr. resident (non-academic) dept. microbiology All India Inst. Med. Scis., 1997; housestaff, internal medicine Baylor Coll. Medicine, Houston, 1997—2001, housestaff, cardiology, 2001—04; asst. prof. clin. medicine U. Cin., 2004—. Asst. dir. echocardiography lab. Cin. Vet.'s Affairs Med. Ctr., 2004—; dir. echocardiography lab. U. Hosp., Cin., 2005. Author: articles in profl. jours. Recipient Inst. Medal for Best Grad., All India Inst. Med. Scis., 1997, Best All Round Med. Student, Delhi Med. Assn., 1997, Richard Van Reet award, Divsn. Cardiology, Baylor Coll. Medicine, 2004. Fellow: Am. Soc. Echocardiography (hon.), Am. Coll. Cardiology (hon. Merck Fellowship Rsch. award 2003); mem.: AMA (assoc.), Am. Heart Assn. (assoc.). Achievements include research in mechanisms of LV remodeling as a cause of heart failure. Office: Univ Cin 231 Albert Sabin Way ML0542 Cincinnati OH 45267 Home Phone: 513-336-2238.

DIX, ROLLIN C(UMMING), mechanical engineering educator, consultant; b. NYC, Feb. 8, 1936; s. Omer Houston and Ona Mae (Cumming) D.; m. Elaine B. VanNest, June 18, 1960; children: Gregory, Elisabeth, Karen. BSME, Purdue U., 1957, MSME, 1958, PhD, 1963. Registered profl. engr., Ill. Asst. prof. mech. engring. Ill. Inst. Tech., Chgo., 1964-69, assoc. prof., 1969-80, prof., 1980—2004, assoc. dean for computing, 1980-96; pres. Patpending Mktg., Inc., 1996—. 1st lt. US Army, 1960—61. Fellow: ASME. Achievements include patents in field. Home: 10154 S Seeley Ave Chicago IL 60643-2037 Office: Ill Inst Tech 10 W 32d St Chicago IL 60616-3729 Office Phone: 773-239-9778. Personal E-mail: rcd9778@sbcglobal.net.

DIXIT, AVINASH KAMALAKAR, economics professor; b. Bombay, June 8, 1944; s. Kamalakar Ramachandra and Kusum Dixit. BA, Cambridge U., Eng., 1965; PhD, MIT, 1968. Acting asst. prof. U. Calif., Berkeley, 1968-69; fellow Balliol Coll., Oxford, Eng., 1970-74; prof. econs. U. Warwick, Coventry, Eng., 1974-80; prof. economics Princeton U., 1981—. Author: (books) Thinking Strategically, 1991, Investment Under Uncertainty, 1994, Games of Strategy, 1999, Theory of International Trade, 1980. Guggenheim fellow, 1991-92, Am. Acad. Arts and Scis., 1992. Fellow Econometric Soc. (pres. 2001); mem. NAS, Am. Econ. Assn. (v.p. 2002, pres.-elect 2007), Indian Econometric Soc. (Mahalanobis Internat. medal 1985), Am. Acad. Arts and Sciences (economics membership panel chair, 1999-2000, nominating com. 2001-03). Office Phone: 609-258-4013. Business E-Mail: dixitak@princeton.edu.

DIXIT, BALWANT NARAYAN, pharmacology and toxicology educator; b. Kerawade, India, Jan. 7, 1933; came to U.S., 1962; s. Narayan V. and Janakibai N. (Gokhale) D.; m. Vidya B. Ghanekar, Dec. 26, 1969; children: Sunil, Sanjay. BS in Chemistry and Biology, Fergusson Coll., Poona, India, 1954; BS in Chemistry with honors, U. Poona, 1955; MS in Biochemistry with honors, U.Poona, 1956; MS in Pharmacology with honors, U. Baroda, India, 1962; PhD, U. Pitts., 1965, MBA, 2001. Sr. research fellow Baroda U., 1960-61; asst. prof. pharmacology U. Pitts., 1965-68; assoc. prof., 1968-74; prof., 1974—; asst. chmn., 1969-74; acting dean, 1976-78; chmn., 1974-87; assoc. dean, 1974-84; dir. Ctr. for the Performing Arts of India, 1992—. Recipient Disting. Alumnus award U. Pitts. Sch. Pharmacy, 1982; fellow Internat. Union Physiological Scis., 1962 Mem. Am. Soc. Pharmacology and Explt. Therapeutics, Soc. Neurosci., Internat. Soc. Xenobiotic Metabolism Home: 608 Ravencrest Rd Pittsburgh PA 15215-1120 Office: U Pitts 559 Salk Hall Pittsburgh PA 15261-1905 Fax: (412) 648-8475. E-mail: bdixit@pitt.edu.

DIXNER, ARNE WILFRED, environmental services administrator; b. Boris, Sweden, Jan. 2, 1924; s. Einar David and Elise Gulbrensen Dixner; m. Cecile Deschenes Dixner, May 5, 1978 (div.); children: Karen Lee, Kenneth Arne. Masters, U. Calif., San Diego, 1947; BA in Biology, Pacific Union Coll., Mich., 1951. Clin. lab. tech. Paradise Valley Hosp., Nat. City, Calif., 1943—44, 1946—47, 1951—59, 1959—72; staff County San Diego, Dept. Health Svcs., 1959—91; tchr. San Diego State U., 1975—88; cons. food handling San Diego, 1996—2000; ednl. program dir. Food & Beverage Assn., San Diego, 1997—2002. Program coord. evaluation com. San Diego Environ. Health, 1991. With US Army, 1944—46, India. Mem.: Calif. Environ. Health Assn., Nat. Environ. Health Assn. Avocations: baseball, basketball, swimming, jogging, walking.

DIXON, ALBERT TRUMAN, mathematician, educator; b. Springfield, Mo., June 4, 1956; s. Truman Albert and Juanita Louise Dixon; m. Anita S. Grogan. PhD, U. Mo., Columbia, 1987. Prof. math. Coll. Ozarks, Point Lookout, Mo., 1987—. Recipient Profl. Achievement award, Coll. Ozarks, 1999. Mem.: Coll. Ozarks Assocs. (bd. dirs. 2000—06, chmn. 2000—06), Branson-Hollister Rotary (past dir.). Business E-Mail: dixon@cofo.edu.

DIXON, ANDREW DERART, retired academic administrator; b. Belfast, No. Ireland, Oct. 27, 1925; arrived in came to U.S., 1963, naturalized; s. Andrew and Martha (Stewart) Dixon; m. Mary Elizabeth Hernderson, Oct. 14, 1948; children: Penelope Jane, Melinda Sara, Alison Mary. Licentiate in Dental Surgery, Queens U., Belfast, 1948, B in Dental Surgery, 1949, M.Dental Surgery, 1953, BS (Nuffield Found. dental fellow), 1954, D.Sc., 1965; PhD, U. Manchester, 1958. Asst. lectr. anatomy U. Manchester, 1954—56, lectr., 1956—62, sr. lectr., 1962—63; 1vis. assoc. prof. anatomy U. Iowa, 1959—61; prof. dental sci. U. N.C., Chapel Hill, 1963—65, prof. dental sci., anatomy, 1965—69, prof. oral biology and anatomy, 1969—73, asst. dean, coordinator research Sch. Dentistry, 1966—69, dir. Dental Research Ctr., 1967—73, assoc. dean research, 1969—73; prof., dean UCLA, 1973—80, assoc. dean for faculty affairs, 1985—92, assoc. dean adminstrn., 1989—92; prof. emeritus, 1993—. Chmn. dental tng. com. Nat. Inst. Dental Rsch., 1972—73; mem. No. Ireland Partnership. Author sci. texts; contbr. articles to profl. jours.; Studies on early devel. and growth of the jaws, sex chromatin in oral smears as a diagnostic tool, nerve supply to oral mucous membrane, facial tissues and temporomandibular joint, craniofacial skeletal growth, trigeminal pathway. Grantee Fulbright Sr. Fellow award, 1959—61, Commonwealth Fund Travel fellow, 1961. Fellow: AAAS, Internat. Coll. Dentists, Am. Coll. Dentists; mem.: Pierre Fauchard Acad., Internat. Soc. Craniofacial Biology, N.Y. Acad. Sci., Am. Soc. Cell Biology, AAAS, Internat. Assn. Dental Rsch., Am. Assn. Anatomists, Anat. Soc. Gt. Britain and Ireland (sr.), Western Conf. Dental Examiners and Dental Deans, Pacific Coast Soc. Orthodontists (hon.), Inst. of Medicine, ADA, Psi Omega, Omicron Kappa Upsilon, Sigma Xi. Home: 2213 Quail Point Terr Medford OR 97504 Personal E-mail: addixRVM@charter.net.

DIXON, ARMENDIA PIERCE, school program administrator; b. Laurel, Miss., July 15, 1937; d. L.E. and Denothras (Pickens) Pierce; m. Harrison D. Dixon Jr., Aug. 28, 1971; 1 child, Harrison D. III BS in Edn., Jackson State U., Miss., 1960; postgrad., No. Ill. State U., 1965-66; MEd, Edinboro U., Pa., 1978; PhD, Kent State U., 1994. Cert. English and secondary edn., Miss. Tchr. English, libr. Laurel City Schs., 1962-67; tchr. English, dir. summer pre-sch. Erie (Pa.) Pub. Schs., 1967-72; tchr. English, drama, journalism, forensic coach Crawford Cen. Schs., Meadville, Pa., 1972-85, asst. prin., facilitator sch. improvement coun., 1985-89, coord. successful student partnership, 1988—; prin. Meadville Area Sr. High, 1993; prof. Edinboro U., Pa., 2002—. Chair acad. support svcs. Edinboro U. Pa., 2005—; exec. dir. Meadville Latch-Key Program, 1985—; coord. Urban Tchrs. Project, Kent State U., adj. asst. prof., 1989—, dir. Prospective Tchrs. Program for Phi Delta Kappa; charter mem. Results chpt., Kent State U., 1990; dir. HS edn. Sch. dist. City of Erie, 1993-2001; chair acad. support svcs. Edinboro U. Pa. Fundraiser Cystic Fibrosis Found., Pitts., 1976. 79, 81, Sickle Cell Anemia, Erie, 1978-83; pres. Martin Luther King Jr. Scholarship Fund, Inc., 1979-89, 2000-; bd. dirs. ARC, Erie, 1996—, Villa Marie Coll., Erie, 1995—, Internat. Inst., 19, 2000—94—; mem. adv. bd. Am. Enterprise, Erie, 1993—; mem. alumni bd. dirs. Edinboro U. Alumni, 1997—. Named to Oak Park Hall of Fame, Laurel, Miss., 2004. Mem.: NAACP (pres. Meadville chpt. 1984—), Nat. Assn. Secondary Sch. Prins., Pa. Assn. Secondary Sch. Prins., Navy Mothers, Rainbow Ill, Burres, Order Eastern Star (worthy matron), Phi Delta Kappa, Alpha Kappa Alpha. Methodist. Avocations: doll collecting, writing, gardening. Office: Crawford Ctrl Schs 847 N Main St Meadville PA 16335-2655 Home: 716 Jefferson Street Meadville PA 16335 Office Phone: 814-732-2218. Personal E-mail: armendia1@alltel.net. Business E-Mail: adixon@edinboro.edu.

DIXON, BARBARA BRUINEKOOL, academic administrator; b. Sparta, Wis., June 14, 1943; MusB magna cum laude in Applied Piano, Mich. State U., 1966, MusM, 1969; MusD, U. Colo., 1991. Instr. vocal music K-12 Capac (Mich.) Cmty. Schs., 1970-71; tchr. dept. music Ctrl. Mich. U., Mt. Pleasant, 1971-89, assoc. dean coll. arts and scis., 1989-95, interim dean coll. arts and scis., 1995-97; provost, v.p. acad. affairs SUNY, Geneseo, 1997—2003; pres. Truman St. U., Kirksville, Mo., 2003—. Rep. acad. senate exec. bd., acad. senate liaison com., univ. acad. planning coun. Ctrl. Mich. U., 1986-89; dir. tchr. edn. search com., 1990, 95; chair faculty load equity study com., 1988-89, undergrad. curriculum com., 1992-93, formal hearing com. for grievance under senate rules, 1988-89; mem. profl. edn. coun., 1990-95, honors coun., 1989-94, task force on distance learning, 1992-93, piano search com., 1989, 90, 92, 95, music awards policy com., 1980-81, numerous others. One-woman performances include Kirtland C.C., Roscommon, Mich., 1986, Lansing (Mich.) C.C. Artist Series, 1987, Wurlitzer Hdqs., Holly Springs, Miss., 1989, Benefit for Cmty. Arts Coun., Pigeon, Mich., 1991, Beethoven Festival, Lansing, 1993, and others; accompanying performances include Backstage Recital Series, Jasper, Ind., 1984, Bridgeport (Mich.) Voice Symposium, 1986, Manistee (Mich.) Opera House, 1986, Saginaw (Mich.) Choral Soc., 1987, Alma (Mich.) Coll. Faculty, 1995, Black Forest Music Festival (Broadway rev.), Harbor Springs, Mich., 1995, and others. Active Art Reach Mid-Mich. (gallery com. 1995-96, chamber music com. 1995-97, fund drive com. 1996-97, bd. dirs. 1995-97, treas. 1996-97), Lions Club (chair spl. events com., bd. dirs. 1995-97), United Way (liaison to campus campaign); vol. Mich. Spl. Olympics. Mem. Mich. Music Tchrs. Assn. (bd. of certification 1976-79, 84-90, 95-97, chair 1996-97, pres. local chpt. 1991-92; chmn. collegiate activities 1979-81; mem. spkrs. bur. 1974-97, adjudicators bur. 1975-97, exec. bd. 1979-81, 96; rep. Mich. Youth Arts Festival bd. 1976-81, Mich. Alliance for Arts in Edn. 1988-89), Dalcroze Soc. Am., Delta Omicron, AAUW, Am. Assn. Higher Edn., Phi Beta Delta, Pi Kappa Lambda, Phi Kappa Phi Mortar Bd. Office: Truman St U 100 E Normal St MC200 Kirksville MO 63501 E-mail: dixon@truman.edu.

DIXON, BEN HAROLD, musician, educator; b. Gaffney, SC, Dec. 25, 1934; s. O.C. Marcus Dixon and Evelyn Pinder Pryor; m. Minnie Cordelia Davis (dec. 1960); children: Dawnelle, Beneé, Velori; m. Ollie Olivia Priester, Oct. 27, 1972; children: Richard, Qadir, Kameelah. Diploma, Armstrong Tech. High, 1953. Drummer Real Jazz Sextet, Bklyn., 1997—. Musician Jacksonville (Fla.) Jazz Festival, 2005, St. Albans (NY) Jazz Festi, 2005. Musician: (albums) numerous recordings since 1961 with Blue Note Records including most recently, Lost Sessions, 1999, Blues For Lou, 1999, Man With A Horn, 1999, Have Guitar Will Travel, 1999, Party Jazz, 1999, 32 Gems From 32 Jazz, 1999; musician, arranger, composer (albums) Say Yes To Your Best, 2000. Basketball coach Say Yes to Success Found., Bklyn., 1990—93, Crown Heights Youth Collective and Peace Acad., Bklyn., 1992—95, EKB Scouting Svc., East Orange, NJ, 1991—97. Recipient 6 Gold Records, Gold Album, Devotion to Jazz award, Greater Jamaican Devel. Corp., 2001, You Make A Difference award, Masjid Abdul Muhsi Khalifah, 2004, coaching award, Say Yes to Success Found., 1990, Crown Heights Youth Collective and Peace Acad., 1994; Basketball scholar, Ctrl. State U., Wilberforce, Ohio, 1955. Mem.: Internat. Assn. Approved Basketball Ofcls. (cert. pub. sch. athletic league ofcl.), African Am. Jazz Caucus, Internat. Assn. Jazz Educators. Democrat. Islamic.

DIXON, BILLY GENE, academic administrator, educator; b. Benton, Ill., Oct. 25, 1935; s. John and Stella (Prowell) D.; m. Judith R. McCommons, June 7, 1957; children: Valerie J., Clark A. BS, So. Ill. U., 1957, MS, 1960, PhD, 1967; MS, Ill. Wesleyan U., 1961. Tchr. math., chmn. dept. Cahokia (Ill.) High Sch., 1960-61; tchr. Univ. Sch., So. Ill. U., Carbondale, 1961-67, chmn. dept. math., 1963-67; dir. rsch. and evaluation ESEA Title II Project Uplift, Mt. Vernon, Ill., 1967-69; coordinator profl. edn. experiences Coll. Edn. So. Ill. U., Carbondale, 1968-75, mem. faculty, coord. grad. program in secondary edn., 1975-78, departmental exec. officer curriculum and instrn., 1978—2001, asst. to dept. exec. officer for spl. projects, 2001—04, asst. to dean profl. devel. Coll. Edn. and Human Svcs., 2004—06. Bd. dirs. Holmes Partnership. Pres. Benton Cmty. Pk. Dist., 1974—95; bd. dirs. United Meth. Children's Home, 2004—. Named Citizen of Yr., Benton C. of C., 1982; recipient Liberty Bell award, 1995. Mem. Ill. Assn. Tchr. Educators (pres. 1973, exec. coun. 1976-79, Disting. mem. 1984), Assn. Tchr. Educators (chmn. nat. rev. panel Disting. Program in Tchr. Edn. 1976-86, exec. bd. 1983-86, pres. 1988-89, Pres.'s award 1983, 84, 95, 99, 2004, 05, 07, Disting. mem. 1992, named Disting. Tchr. Educator, 2007), Pi Mu Epsilon, Phi Kappa Phi, Phi Delta Kappa, Kappa Delta Pi. Democrat. Methodist. Home: 9793 Stuyvesant St Benton IL 62812-5916 Office: So Ill U Coll Edn Human Svcs Carbondale IL 62901-4610 Business E-Mail: bgdixon@siu.edu.

DIXON, DAVID ADAMS, chemistry professor, researcher; b. Houston, Dec. 3, 1949; s. John Wilburn Dixon and Nancy Eddy Wilder; m. Christine Diane Powless-Dixon, June 2, 1983; children: Michelle Dawes, Nicole Dawes, Jessica Dawes. BS in Chemistry, Calif. Inst. Tech., 1971; PhD in Phys. Chemistry, Harvard U., 1976. Asst. prof. chemistry dept. U. Minn., Mpls., 1977—83; mem. rsch. staff ctrl. rsch. and devel. dept. E.I. du Pont de Nemours and Co., Inc., Wilmington, Del., 1983—95, rsch. leader, 1990—95; assoc. dir. theory, modeling & simulation Environ. Molecular Sci. Lab., Pacific Northwest Nat. Lab., 1995—2002; prof. chemistry U. Ala., Tuscaloosa, 2004—, Robert Ramsay chair dept. chemistry, 2004—. Vis. assoc. chemistry Calif. Inst. Tech., Pasadena, 1977; adj. faculty chemistry dept. U. Pa., Phila., 1986; adj. prof. chemistry dept. U. Del., Newark, 1989—99, U. Utah, Salt Lake City, 1997—2003. Contbr. articles to profl. jours. Recipient ACS award for Creative Work in Fluorine Chemistry, 2003; fellow, DuPont Ctrl. Sci. and Engring. Labs., Exptl. Sta., Wilmington, 1992—95; scholar, Autonomous Met. U., Mexico City, 1997; Jr. fellow, Harvard U., 1975—77, Alfred P. Sloan Rsch. fellow, 1977—81, Battelle fellow, Pacific Northwest Nat. Lab., 2002—03, Camille and Henry Dreyfus Tchr. scholar, 1978—83. Fellow: AAAS, Am. Phys. Soc.; mem.: Mat. Assn. Am., Soc. Indsl. & Applied Math., Assn. Computing Machinery, Am. Chem. Soc. (Leo Hendrik Baekeland award 1989). Avocations: art collecting, swimming, reading, surfing. Office: U Ala Chemistry Dept Shelby Hall Box 870336 Tuscaloosa AL 35487-0336 Office Phone: 205-348-8441. Business E-Mail: dadixon@bama.ua.edu.

DIXON, E. A., JR., lawyer; b. Bryn Mawr, Pa., Dec. 12, 1939; m. Margaret Kennedy Cortright; children: Thomas W.W., Abigail C., Marion W., Meghan. AB, Princeton U., 1962; JD with honors, George Washington U., 1967. Bar: Pa. 1968, U.S. Dist. Ct. (ea. dist.) 1968. Assoc. Montgomery, McCracken, Walker & Rhoads, Phila., 1967-69; assoc. resident counsel Industrial Valley Bank, Phila., 1970-73; ptnr. Hepburn, Ross, Wilcox & Putnam, Phila., 1974-78; owner wholesale nursery business, 1979-85; atty. Monumental Title Corp., Severna Park, Md., 1985-86; mgr. comml. divsn. The Sentinel Title Corp., Balt., 1987-89; regional underwriting counsel Nations Title Ins. (formerly Nat. Attys and TRW Title), Trevose, Pa., 1989-96; sr. title counsel Lawyers Title Ins. Corp., Phila., 1996, N.J. area counsel Iselin, 1997; counsel Stewart Title Guaranty Co., Wayne, Pa., 1998—2004, Ticor Title Ins. Co., Malvern, Pa., 2004—. Seminar spkr. Nat. Bus. Inst., N.J., 1995-96, Title Acad. N.J., 1995—. Contbr. articles to profl. jours. 2d lt. USAF, 1963—64. Mem. Pa. Land Title Assn. (exec. com. 1993—, chmn., legis. and jud. com.), Pa. Bar Assn., Del. State Bar Assn. (assoc.), Rittenhouse Club, St. Andrew's Soc. (Phila.).

Libertarian. Episcopalian. Avocations: horticulture, sailing, fly fishing, tennis. Office: Ticor Title Ins Co 7 Great Valley Pkwy Ste 150 Malvern PA 19355 Office Phone: 610-722-5969. Personal E-mail: grumpyfungus@comcast.net.

DIXON, FRANK JAMES, pathologist, educator; b. St. Paul, Mar. 9, 1920; s. Frank James and Rose Augusta (Kuhfeld) Dixon; m. Marion Edwards, Mar. 14, 1946; children: Janet Wynne, Frank, Michael. BS, U. Minn., 1941, MB, 1943, MD, 1944; DS (hon.), Med. Coll. Ohio, 1983; DSc (hon.), Washington U., 1992. Diplomate: Am. Bd. Pathology. Intern U.S. Naval Hosp., Great Lakes, Ill., 1943-44; research asst. dept. pathology Harvard, 1946-48; instr. dept. pathology Washington U., 1948-50, asst. prof., 1950-51; prof., chmn. dept. pathology U. Pitts. Med. Sch., 1951-60; chmn. dept. exptl. pathology Scripps Clinic and Research Found., La Jolla, Calif., 1961-74, chmn. biomed. research depts., 1970-74, dir. research inst., 1974-86, dir. emeritus, 1987—. Rsch. assoc. dept. biology U. Calif., San Diego, 1961-64, prof. in residence dept. biology, 1965-68, adj. prof. dept. pathology, 1968-96; sci. advisor NIH, Nat. Found., Helen Hay Whitney Found., St. Jude's Med. Ctr., Christ Hosp. Inst., Cin.; mem. expert adv. panel on immunology WHO; sci. adv. bd. Nat. Kidney Found.; Pahlavi lectr. Ministry of Sci. and Higher Tech., Iran, 1976: mem. adv. com. Lupus Rsch. Inst., Nat. Multiple Sclerosis Soc., Harold C. Simmons Arthritis Rsch. Ctr., Irvington House Inst.; bd. dirs. La Jolla Inst. Allergy and Immunology, 1996-2005. Editor: Advances in Immunology; mem. editorial bd. Excerpta Medica, Jour. Exptl. Medicine, Am. Jour. Pathology, Cellular Immunology, Kidney Hosp. Practice, Perspectives in Biology and Medicine, Jour. Exptl. Clin. Cancer Rsch., Springer Seminars in Immunopathology, Immunological Revs.; contbr. articles to profl. jours. Served with M.C. USNR, 1943-46. Recipient Theobald Smith award, 1952, Parke-Davis award in exptl. pathology, 1957, Disting. Achievement award Modern Medicine, 1961, Martin E. Rehfuss award in internal medicine, 1966, Von Pirquet medal Ann. Forum on Allergy, 1967, Bunim medal Am. Rheumatism Assn., 1968, Internat. award Gairdner Found., 1969, Mayo Soley award Western Soc. Clin. Research, 1969, Albert Lasker Basic Med. Research award, 1975, Dickson prize U. Pitts., 1975, Homer Smith award NY Heart Assn., 1976, Rous-Whipple award Am. Assn. Pathologists, 1979, So. Calif. Permanente Med. Group Immunology award, 1979, Regents award U. Minn., 1985, H.P. Smith award Am. Soc. Clin. Pathologists, 1985, Gold-Headed Cane award, 1987, Distinguished Service award Lupus Found. Am., 1987, 88; Flame of Hope award Terri Gotthelf Rsch. Inst., 1987, Paul Klemperer award NY Acad. Medicine, 1989, Jean Hamburger award Internat. Soc. Nephrology, 1990. Fellow Am. Coll. Allergists, Am. Acad. Allergy, Royal Coll. Pathologists (hon.); mem. NAS, NY Acad. Scis. Western Assn. Physicians, Western Soc. Clin. Research, Soc. Exptl. Biology and Medicine, Transplantation Soc., AAAS, Am. Soc. Clin. Investigation, Am. Acad. Allergists, Interurban Path. Soc., Harvey Soc. (lectr. 1962), Am. Soc. Exptl. Pathology (pres. 1966), Am. Assn. Immunologists (pres. 1972), Am. Assn. for Cancer Research, Assn. Am. Physicians, Am. Acad. Arts and Scis., Am. Heart Assn., Coun. on the Kidney in Cardiovascular Disease, Fedn. Am. Scientists, Internat. Acad. Pathology, U.S. Acad. Pathologists, Can. Acad. Pathologists, Scandinavian Soc. for Immunology (hon.), Japanese Nephrology Soc. (hon.), Sigma Xi, Nu Sigma Nu, Alpha Omega Alpha. Office: Scripps Rsch Inst 10550 N Torrey Pines Rd La Jolla CA 92037-1000

DIXON, FREDERICK DAIL, architect; b. Raleigh, NC, Dec. 18, 1942; s. Frederick Dail (dec.) and Mary Isabel (Richbourg)(dec.) D.; m. Artemis Markatos, July 7, 1968; children: Frederick Markatos. BArch, Clemson U., SC, 1966; MFA in Sculpture, U. NC, 1970. Intern Leslie Boney, Architects, Wilmington, NC, 1966—68; arch. John D. Latimer & Assocs., Durham, NC, 1968—72, Cogswell/Hausler Assocs., Chapel Hill, NC, 1972—74; founding ptnr. Designworks, Carrboro, NC, 1974—82; dir. Dixon Weinstein Architects, PA, Chapel Hill, 1982—. Instr. Boston Archtl. Ctr., 1970-71; vis. prof. arch. NC State U. Coll. Design, Raleigh, 1983-2005; studio instr. Penland Sch. of Crafts, 2007. Recipient 1st Place award (with sculptor Patrick Dougherty) Pines Portico Competition, Penland Sch. Crafts, 2005; HUD grantee. Fellow AIA, South Atlantic Region AIA (firm awards for Excellence in Arch. 1991, 92, Merit award 1998), NC AIA (Merit award 1991, 92, 95, 98, Honor award 2002, 2006, Outstanding Firm award 2003). Democrat. Office: Dixon Weinstein Architects PA #25 The Courtyard 431 W Franklin St Chapel Hill NC 27516-2319 Home Phone: 919-933-0020; Office Phone: 919-968-8333. Business E-Mail: dail@dixonweinstein.com.

DIXON, GORDON HENRY, biochemist, educator; b. Durban, South Africa, Mar. 25, 1930; naturalized, Can., 1951; s. Walter James and Ruth (Nightingale) Dixon; m. Sylvia W. Gillen, Nov. 20, 1954; children: Frances Anne, Walter Timothy, Christopher James, Robin Jonathan. MA with honors, U. Cambridge, Eng., 1951; PhD, U. Toronto, 1956. Rsch. assoc. U. Wash., 1954-58, U. Oxford, England, 1958-59; asst. prof. biochemistry U. Toronto, 1959-61, assoc. prof., 1961-63; prof. U. B.C., 1963-72; prof., chmn. dept. biochemistry U. Sussex, England, 1972-74; prof. med. biochemistry U. Calgary, Alta., Canada, 1974-94; emeritus, 1994—; chmn. U. Calgary, Alta., Canada, 1983-88. Contbr. over 250 articles to prof. jours. Flying officer Royal Can. AFR 5001 Air Intelligence, 1952—54. Decorated officer Order of Can.; recipient Steacie prize, Steacie Found., 1966, Killam Meml. prize, Can. Coun., 1991, Queens Golden Jubilee medal, 2002. Fellow: Royal Soc. Can. (Flavelle medal 1980), Royal Soc. London; mem.: Internat. Union Biochemistry (mem. exec. coun. 1988—94), Pan-Am. Assn. Biochem. Socs. (v.p. 1984—87, pres. 1987—90), Can. Biochem. Soc. (pres. 1982—83, Ayerst award 1966). Avocations: hiking, gardening. Personal E-mail: gordon.dixon@shaw.ca.

DIXON, HARRY D., JR., (DONNIE DIXON), lawyer, former prosecutor; b. Waycross, Ga., Nov. 6, 1953; s. Harry D. Sr. and Ruth (Starling) D.; m. Elizabeth Tonning, Apr. 19, 1980; 2 children. AB in History, Valdosta State Coll., 1974; JD, U. Ga., 1977. Bar: Ga. 1977, U.S. Dist. Ct. Ga. 1978, U.S. Ct. Appeals 1979. Law clk. to Hon. Marvin Hartley, Jr. Superior Ct. for Mid. Jud. Cir., 1977-78; asst. dist. atty. Waycross Jud. Cir, 1977-79, dist. atty., 1983-94; atty. Bennett, Pedrick and Bennett, 1979-83; U.S. atty. for so. dist. Ga. U.S. Dept. Justice, Savannah, 1994—2001; atty. Oliver Maner & Gray LLP, Savannah, Ga., 2002—04, Donnie Dixon Atty. at Law, 2004—. His profl. assoc. include the Nat. Assoc. of Former US Atty., the Nat. Assoc. of Criminal Defense Lawyers, the fGa. Assoc. of Criminal Defense Lawyers, the Savannah Bar Assoc. and the Savannah Assoc. of Criminal Defense Lawyers.

DIXON, JACK EDWARD, biological chemistry professor, consultant; b. June 16, 1943; BA, UCLA, 1966; PhD, U. Calif., Santa Barbara, 1971. NSF Found. postdoctoral rsch. fellow U. Calif., San Diego, 1971—73; from asst. prof. to assoc. prof. biochemistry Purdue U., West Lafayette, Ind., 1973—82, prof. biochemistry, 1982—86, Harvey W. Wiley disting. prof. biochemistry, 1986—91; Minor J. Coon prof. biol. chemistry, chmn. dept. U. Mich., Ann Arbor, 1991—2003, co-dir. Life Scis. Inst., 2001—02, dir. Life Scis. Inst., 2002—03; prof. pharmacology, cellular medicine, chemistry and biochemistry U. Calif., San Diego, 2003—, dean sci. affairs Sch. Medicine, 2003—. Nathan O. Kaplan lectr. U. Calif., San Diego, 1991; Edmund Fischer lectr. U. Wash., Seattle, 1993; adj. prof. Salk Inst., 2003—; Baker lectr. U. Calif., Santa Barbara, 2003; Merck Award lectr. ASBMB, 2005; Dyer lectr. NIH, 2005. Recipient Merit award, NIH, 1987, 1996, 2004, William Rose award, ASBMB, 2003, Biochemistry and Molecular Biology award, Merck, 2003. Fellow: AAAS, Am. Acad. Arts and Sci., Mich. Soc. Fellows U. Mich. (sr.); mem.: Inst. Medicine, Nat. Acad. Sci., Am. Soc. Cell Biology, Am. Soc. Biochemistry and Molecular Biology (program chmn. 1994—, pres. 1996—97), Sigma Xi. Office: U Calif San Diego 9500 Gilman Dr 0602 La Jolla CA 92093-0602 Office Phone: 858-822-3529.

DIXON, JAMIE (P.), (II), men's college basketball coach; b. Burbank, Calif., Nov. 10, 1965; s. Jim and Marge Dixon; m. Jacqueline Corteway Dixon; children: Jack Connor, Shannon Iwalani. BBA in Fin., Tex. Christian U., Ft. Worth, 1987; MS in Econs., U. Calif., Santa Barbara, 1992. Draft pick NBA Washington Bullets, 1987; profl. basketball player Continental Basketball Assn. Lacrosse Catbirds, New Zealand; head coach TeAute Coll., New Zealand, 1989; asst. coach LA Valley Jr. Coll., 1989—91, U. Calif., Santa Barbara, 1991—92, U. Hawaii, 1992—94, 1998—99, No. Ariz. U., 1994—98; assoc. head coach, recruiting coord. U. Pitts., 1999—2003, head coach, 2003—. Named Big East Coach of Yr., 2004, Person of Yr., YMCA, 2004. Office: Mens Basketball Athletics Dept U Pitts Pittsburgh PA 15260 Office Phone: 412-648-8350. E-mail: jdixon@athletics.pitt.edu.*

DIXON, JANE FRAZIER, elementary school educator, consultant; b. Wilbreforce, Ohio, Oct. 23, 1936; d. G. Thurston Frazier and E. Anne (Robinson) Frazire; 1 child, Elizabeth Yawn Ivy. BS in Math, Ctrl. State U., Wilberforce, 1957, BS in Elem Edn., 1960, MEd in Elem. Edn., 1969. Developer City Day Cmty. Sch., Dayton, 1998—2003; founder, dir., master tchr. Oasis Edn. Ctr., Ft. Worth, 1985—96, early childhood reading cons., 2003—. Author: (books) Kasa Is Sound and a Little More, 1995, Locking The Lock On Literacy, 1998. Named to Hall of Fame, Ctrl. State U., 1994.

DIXON, JO-ANN CONTE, management consultant; b. Orange, NJ, Aug. 5, 1942; d. Rocco Louis and Antoinette (DeRosa) Conte; m. Michael Eugene Dixon, July 26, 1964; children: Christopher Michael, Peter Eugene. Student, Paterson State Coll., 1960—63; AA, Thomas A. Edison Coll., 1976, BA, 1978; MA, Drew U., 1985. Tchr. St. Raphael's Sch., Livingston, NJ, 1963—68; owner Orgn. Unltd., Glen Ridge, NJ, 1972—78; market rsch. analyst Harkness & Assoc., San Francisco, 1976—78; adminstr. corp. tng. dept. Rapidata, Inc., Fairfield, NJ, 1978—79, mgr. corp. tng. dept., 1979—80, dir., 1980—81; pres., prin. cons. Q, Inc., Essex Fells, 1980—89; pres. MatchPlay Internat., Inc., 1989—96; regional dir. Am. Mgmt. Assoc., 1996—2007; CEO Home Health Svc. and Staffing Assn. NJ, 2007—. Trustee Mt. St. Dominic Acad., 1989-95; dir. alumni rels. NJ Inst. Tech., Newark, 1981-83, West Essex Cmty. Health Svcs., devel. chair, 1988-93, pres. 1993-95; dir. mgmt. devel. Rutgers U. Grad. Sch. Mgmt., 1983-84; bd. dir. alumni affairs/devel. officer Seton Hall Law Sch., Newark, 1984-85; chmn. bd. trustees Nat. Inst. for Orgnl. and Mgmt. Rsch., Essex Fells, NJ, 1987-92. Chmn. bd. Passaic River Coalition, Basking Ridge, NJ, 1976-83, vice chmn. bd., 1983-88, regional coord., 1971-76; chmn. mayor's com. on environ., Glen Ridge, 1974-75; mem. NJ Gov.'s Task Force for Passaic River, 1976-78; mem., pres. Home and Sch. Bd., Glen Ridge, 1978-79. Recipient citation Borough of Glen Ridge; Nat. Trust Hist. Preservation scholar, 1977; named Woman of Distinction Girl Scouts Am., 2004. Mem.: ASTD (v.p. comms. profl. excellence award, Charles T. Morgan award for excellence in tng. and devel. 1989), LWV, Exec. Women of NJ (strategic planning chair 1996—99, pres.-elect 1999—2002, pres. 2002—04), West Essex C. of C. (bd. dirs. 1988—89, v.p. 1990—91, pres. 1991—92, Bus. Person/Cmty. Leader of Yr. 2001), Exec. Women's Golf Assn. of No. NJ (founder, comms. chair 1997—98, v.p. 1999—2000, sectional dir. Metro N.E. 2001—02, leadership chair 2004, pres. 2004—), Glen Ridge Hist. Soc. (founder), Kiwanis (N.J. found. bd. trustees 1990—92, sec. bd. dirs. 1990—93, v.p. Caldwell/West Essex chpt. 1996—97, sec. 1996—98, pres. elect 1997—98, pres. 1998—99, chair pediat. trauma program N.J. dist. 1999—2001, lt. gov. divsn. 12 2002—03, Hixson fellow 2001), Knights of Malta-Order St. John of Jerusalem (Dame of Malta 1986). Home and Office: 97 Lane Ave West Caldwell NJ 07006-7426 Office Phone: 973-403-8800. Personal E-mail: joanndixon@comcast.net, joanncdixon@aol.com. Business E-Mail: joann@hhssanj.com.

DIXON, JOHN JAMES, music educator; b. Rockford, Ill., Oct. 26, 1953; s. John Henry Dixon and Sarah Rosemary Intravaia; m. Debra Ann Flanders-Dixon, Aug. 8, 1981. MusB, Northern Ill. U., DeKalb, 1975, MusM, 1979. Cert. tchr. elem. and secondary Ill. State Tchr. Cert. Bd., tchr. music Ill. State Tchr. Cert. Bd. Tchr. instrumental music, band, jazz band and orch. Rockford (Ill.) Sch. Dist. #205, 1975—. Mem. Rockford Wind Ensemble, 2002—, SPHear Saxaphone Quartet, 2000—. Nominee Golden Apple award, Golden Apple Found. Rockford, 2002; recipient Alumnus of Month, Rock Valley Coll., 1981. Mem.: Internat. Clarinet Soc., Music Educators Nat. Conf., Ill. Music Educators Assn. Home: 5420 Pebble Creek Trl Loves Park IL 61111-4329 E-mail: dixon.john@ingishtbb.com.

DIXON, JOHN MORRIS, magazine editor; b. Long Branch, NJ, June 22, 1933; s. Abram C. and Emily (Minton) D.; m. Carol Ruth Nipomnich, Dec. 27, 1959; children: Peter, Susannah. B.Arch., MIT, 1955. From asst. editor to sr. editor Progressive Architecture, 1960-65, editor, 1971-96; assoc. editor Archtl. Rsch. Quar., 1999—2002. Sr. editor Archtl. Forum, 1965-71 Author: Architectural Design Preview, U.S.A, 1962, (with N. White and E. Willensky) A.I.A. Guide to New York City, 1967, Urban Spaces, 1999, Urban Spaces No. 2, 2001, Urban Spaces No. 3, 2004, Urban Spaces No. 4, 2006, The World Bank, 2002. Served to 1st lt. AUS, 1955-57. Fellow A.I.A. (chmn. exhibits com. N.Y. chpt. 1964-65, co-chmn. visitors com. N.Y. chpt. 1965-66, chmn. pub. relations com. N.Y. chpt. 1970-71, mem. design com. 1978—, chmn. 1983), Gen. Svcs. Adminstrn. (peer rev. panelist 2001—). Home: 382 Sound Beach Ave Old Greenwich CT 06870-2223 E-mail: jmdixon@optonline.net.

DIXON, JOHN MORRIS, JR., retired judge, lawyer; b. Gulf Shores, Ala., Apr. 3, 1940; s. John Morris Sr. and Margaret (Herndon) D.; children: John M. III, Kathryn D. BS, U. Ky., 1962, JD, 1965. Bar: Ky. 1965, Ark. 1968. Assoc. Bridges, Young, Matthews & Davis, Pine Bluff, Ark., 1968-70; ptnr. Turner & Dixon, Hopkinsville, 1970-75, Turner, Dixon, Kemp & Fletcher, Hopkinsville, 1975-77, Turner, Dixon & Kemp, Hopkinsville, 1977-89; prin. John M. Dixon Jr., Atty., Hopkinsville, 1989; ptnr. Dixon & Kemp, Hopkinsville, 1989-91; U.S. magistrate judge Bowling Green, Ky., 1971—98; of counsel Corrhott and Willen, Hopkinsville, 1999—, Resolute Systems, Inc., 1998—; pres. John M. Dixon Jr., P.S.C., 2004—. Capt. U.S. Army, 1965-68. Mem. Ky. Bar Assn.

DIXON, JOHN SPENCER, performing arts association administrator; b. London, Apr. 23, 1957; s. Richard Kennedy and Elizabeth Ann (Flaxman) D.; m. Karen Beth Swanson, Aug. 18, 1984; children: Katherine Elizabeth, John Spencer Jr. BA with honors, Oxford U., 1979, MA, 1985; MBA, Harvard U., 1982. Supply exec. Hi-Tec Sports Ltd., Essex, England, 1982-86; pres. Hi-Tec Internat. Ltd., Taichung, Taiwan, 1983-84; founder, ptnr. Transatlantic Mktg. Co., Essex, England, 1985-2000; exec. v.p. Decipher, Inc., Norfolk, Va., 1988-90; pres. Waller Whittemore & Co., Virginia Beach, Va., 1992—, PH Internat., Virginia Beach, Va., 1997—2001; organist, composer-in-residence Providence Presbyn. Ch., Virginia Beach, Va., 1998—; exec. dir. Acad. of Music, Norfolk, Va., 2003—. Mem.: Am. Guild Organists. Presbyterian. Avocations: music, sports. Home: 4829 Berrywood Rd Virginia Beach VA 23464-5874 Office: 5497 Providence Rd Virginia Beach VA 23464

DIXON, KEITH W., meteorologist; married; 1 child. undergraduate degree, graduate degree, Rutgers U., New Brunswick, NJ. Radio broadcast meterologist; tchr. Rutgers U., NJ; with NOAA Geophysical Fluid Dynamics Lab. Princeton U. Forrestal Campus, Princeton, NJ, 1983—, sr. rsch. meteorologist, climate dynamics & prediction group, NOAA Geophysical Fluid Dynamics Lab. Presenter in field; participates in ednl. outreach programs; prepares exhibits for NAS Marian Koshland Sci. Mus., Washington. Develops graphics and text for popular publications Newsweek, Time and Discover. Co-recipient US Dept Commerce Silver medal as mem. Geophysical Fluid Dynamics Lab. IPCC modeling team, 1993; recipient Am. Meteorological Soc. Father James B. Macelwane award for undergraduate rsch., 1982. Mem.: AAAS, Am. Geophyical Union, Am. Meteorological Soc. Office: GFDL/NOAA PO Box 308 Princeton University Princeton NJ 08542-0308 Address: Geophysical Fluid Dynamics Lab/NOAA Princeton Forrestal Campus 201 Forrestal Rd Princeton NJ 08542 Office Phone: 609-987-5063. Business E-Mail: Keith.Dixon@noaa.gov.

DIXON, LARRY DEAN, state legislator; b. Aug. 31, 1942; s. Chesley Lafayette and Charlene (Walker) D.; m. Gaynell Kimbrough, Dec. 23, 1967; children: Katherine Dixon Hert, Elizabeth Walker. AAS, Columbia Basin Jr. Coll., 1966; BS in Police Sci., Wash. State U., 1968, MA in History, 1970. Cons. Ala. State Dept. Edn., 1970-72; dir. dept. edn. Med. Assn. State of Ala., Montgomery, 1972-76; dir. Montgomery Family Practice Residency Program, 1976-78, Jackson Hosp. Found., Montgomery, 1978-81; exec. dir. Ala. Bd. Med. Examiners, Montgomery, 1981—. Mem. Montgomery City Coun., 1975-78, Ala. Ho. of Reps., 1978-82, Ala. Senate, 1982—; past mem. steering com. Nat. Clearinghouse on Licensure, Enforcement and Regulation; presdl. appointee Intergovt. Agy. Coun. on Edn., 1986-90, 90-94, 2002-06, 06—; mem. legis. adv. bd. So. Regional Edn. Bd., 1986-90; mem. Med. Scholarship Bd., State of Ala., 1988-98; past trustee Tuskegee U.; commr. So. Assn. Colls. and Schs., 1998-01. With U.S. Army, 1961-64. Mem. Nat. Conf. State Legislatures, Adminstrs. in Medicine Soc. (pres. 1984-85), Edn. Commn. of the States, Fedn. State Med. Bds. (mem. bd. dirs. 2006-), Ala. Ex POWs (hon.), Blue Gray Assn., Lions. Republican. Methodist. Home and Office: 820 E Fairview Ave Montgomery AL 36106-1818 also: PO Box 946 Montgomery AL 36101-0946

DIXON, LUGENIA, psychology educator; b. Columbus, Ga., Jan. 20, 1949; d. Sam and Ola (Bowman) Dixon; m. Willie Cornelius Ladner, 1969 (div. Aug. 1973); children: Dexteralan Keith Ladner, Craig Jeffrey Ladner, Olivia Dara Young. Student, Harris Jr. Coll., Meridian, Miss., 1967-68, Columbus Coll., Ga., 1971-78; BA in Psychology, U. Ga., Athens, 1980, MEd in Early Childhood Edn., 1982, PhD in Ednl. Psychology, 1985; postgrad., Ft. Valley Coll., Ga., 1989; grad. course, Art Instrn. Schs., Mpls., 1997. Medicare claims approval clk. Blue Cross/Blue Shield, Columbus, 1969-71, Medicare unit leader, 1975-77; collector Sears, Columbus, 1971-75; substitute tchr. Clarke County Sch. Dist., Athens, Ga., 1981, instrnl. aide, substitute tchr., 1984-85; work/study (rschr.) U. Ga., Athens, 1981-83; substitute tchr. Ga. Retardation Ctr., Athens, 1983-84; asst. prof. psychology Gordon Coll., Barnesville, Ga., 1985-89; assoc. prof. psychology Bainbridge Coll., Ga., 1989—2001, prof. Ga., 2001—, chair CEPO Ga., 2005; E.T.S. reader AP in psychology, 2004—07. Coord. judging Social Sci. Fair, Bainbridge Coll., 1992—, dir., 1997—; coord. minority achievement program Bainbridge Coll., 1992-97; mem. adv. com. on psychology Regents Acad.; presenter Nat. Inst. Tchg. of Pyschology, 2006. Co-author: Living Psychology: An Introduction, 1995, Handbook for Living Psychology: An Introduction, 1995, Introduction to Psychology: A Combination Text and Study Guide 5th Edit., 2007, NSF Tried & True: Investigative Psychophysiology Activities for Introductory Psychology Courses Workshop, 2007; textbook reviewer Wadsworth Publishing, 2007. Sec. Decatur County Artists Guild, 1994, v.p., program chair, 2005—06; mem. Acad. for Learning through Performance Stds. and Assessment, 2005—06. Recipient cmty. svc. cert. Athens Recreation Dept., 1984, internat. scenario writing contest award 5th World Conf. on Children, Youth and Adults, Athens, 1984; mini-grant Bainbridge Coll., 1996;, Regents minority scholar U. Ga., 1983-84; Univ. Sys. Ga. grantee Summer Inst., Brazil. Mem.: Coun. Tchrs. Undergrad. Psychology, Ga. Assn. Educators, AAUW (gender equity liason, Bainbridge br. 1995—96, Ga. Coll. U. rep.). Democrat. Roman Catholic. Avocations: gardening, drawing and painting. Home: 261 Dollar Dr Bainbridge GA 31717-6438 Office: Bainbridge College Hwy 84 Bainbridge GA 31717 Office Phone: 229-248-2571. Business E-Mail: ldixon@bainbridge.edu.

DIXON, PATRICK RICHARD, prosecutor; m. Diane Dixon; 1 child, Colleen. Grad., U. So. Calif., LA, 1971; law degree, U. San Diego. Bar: Calif. 1976. Dep. dist. atty., asst. head major crimes divsn. LA County Dist. Atty.'s Office, dep. dist. atty., head major crimes divsn. Spl. counsel to com. bar examiners State Bar Calif., 1986—89, 1999, mem. Commn. on Jud. Nominees Evaluation, 1990—92, mem. com. bar examiners, 1993—97, chair com. bar examiners, 1997, bd. govs. for LA County, Dist. 7, 2000—03. Named Prosecutor of Yr., Assn. Dep. Dist. Attys., 1994. Mem.: LA County Bar Assn. (vice chair jud. elections evaluation com. 1984—89, trustee 1993—95, chair criminal justice sect. 1994, mem. jud. appointments com. 1998—99, Prosecuting Atty. of Yr. (criminal justice sect.) 1998). Office: LA County Dist Attys Office 210 W Temple St Ste 18000 Los Angeles CA 90012 Office Phone: 213-974-3926.

DIXON, PHILLIP RAY, SR., lawyer; b. Wake Forest, NC, Mar. 26, 1949; s. Milton R. Dixon and Lottie Belle (Tippett) Larson; m. Candace (Mamie) Cicerone, Nov. 26, 1977; children: Phillip Ray Jr., Joseph David, Jonathan Scott. BSBA, East Carolina U., 1971; JD, U. NC, 1974. Bar: NC 1974, US Dist. Ct. (ea. dist.) NC 1976, US Ct. Appeals (4th cir.) 1981, US Supreme Ct. 1981. Law clk. to assoc. judge NC Ct. Appeals, Raleigh, 1974-75; assoc. Gaylord & Singleton, Greenville, NC, 1975-78; ptnr. Dixon, Duffus & Doub, Greenville, 1978-90; with Dixon Doub Conner and Foster PLLC, Greenville, 1990—2006, Dixon, Conner, Allen & Garcia, PLLC, 2006—. Instr. police sci. paralegal program Pitt CC and Pitt Tech. Inst., 1975-79, advisor 1982—; 981; bd. dirs., counsel RBC Ctr. Bank and Trust Co., Greenville, bd. dirs. RBC Centura Bank. Editor-in-chief NC Law Record, 1972-73, assoc. editor 1973-74. Atty. Greenville City Schs. and Greenville City Bd. Edn., 1978-86, Pitt County Schs. and Bd. of Edn., 1986-; local and state hearing officer NC Dept. Pub. Instrn.; atty. Greenville Utilities Commn., 1981—; mem. Pitt County Area Mental Health Mental Retardation and Substance Abuse Bd., 1983-87, chmn. bd. dirs. 1984-86; chancel choir mem. 1st Christian Ch. of Greenville, 1975-77, Sunday sch. supt., 1977, deacon, 1978-82, elder, 1983-87, guest minister, 1984, vice chmn. bd. dirs. 1981, chmn. 1982; bd. dirs., trustee Pitt-Greenville Arts Coun., Inc., 1979-81; exec. bd. Pitt County United Way, Inc., 1981, sec., campaign chmn., pres. 1982, 1986; mem. Downtown Greenville Assn., 1980—, Greenville Mus. Art, 1980—, treas. 1986-87, v.p., 1987-88, trustee, 1986—; pres. 1988—; bd. dirs. Greenville Jaycees 1975-77; past pres. East Carolina U. Ednl. Founds., Inc., 1987; del. county, dist. and state Dem. Convs., 1984, del. NC State Dem. Conv., Pitt. County campaign chmn. lt. gov.'s race, 1983-84; bd. govs. U. NC, 2005-; local adv. bd. Wachovia Bank N.Am. Named one of Outstanding Young Men of Am., 1974-83. Mem. ABA, NC Bar Assn. (sustaining mem., family law sect., criminal law sect., real estate sect., probate sect., practical tng. com., instr. and seminar spkr. on topic appeals, practical skills course 1975-81, bd. govs.), Pitts County Bar Assn. (sec. law libr. com. 1976-77, chmn. 1976-82), NC Acad. Trial Lawyers, NC Coll. Advocacy, NC Coun. Sch. Bd. of Attys. (bd. dirs. 1982—, chmn. 1984-85, v.p. 1983-84, chmn. ins. com. 1983-84, Disting. Svc. award 2003), Nat. Coun. Sch. Bd. Attys., Greenville C. of C. (chmn.), Greenville-Pitt County Home Builders Assn. (chmn.), East Carolina Univ. Alumni Assn. (Outstanding Alumnus award 1984), Phi Sigma Pi (Outstanding Alumnus 2006), Greenville Sports Club (chartered, sec., treas. 1975-77, pres. 1979-80), Rotary (chartered, bd. dirs. Greenville chpt. 1981-83, dist. sec. 1982, v.p. 1983, pres. 1986-87, Paul Harris fellow 1982), East Carolina U. (sec. 1995-97, vice chair, 1997-99, chair, bd.

trustees, 1999-01, Disting. Svc. award 2006), Pitts. CC (vice chmn., 1989-91, chmn. 1992-99, bd. trustees, 1991-99), NC Ctr. Pub. Policy Rsch. (chmn., 2002-03), Greenville City Bond Advocacy Com (co-chair, 2004). Democrat. Office: Dixon Allen Conner and Garcia PLLC PO Box Drawer 8668 110 Arlington Blvd Greenville NC 27835 Office Phone: 252-355-8100. E-mail: phildixon@dcaglaw.com.

DIXON, RICHARD ARTHUR, botanist, educator, researcher; b. Capetown, South Africa, Dec. 29, 1951; came to US, 1988; s. Arthur and Ena (Parrott) D.; m. Rachel Corfield, Aug. 5, 1978; children: Lois Mary, Arthur Malcolm. BA in Biochemistry, U. Oxford, Eng., 1973, MA, 1976, DPhil in Botany, 1976; DSc (hon.), U. Oxford, 2004. Postdoctoral rsch. asst. dept. biochemistry U. Cambridge, 1976-78; lectr. dept. biochemistry U. London Royal Holloway and Bedford New Coll., 1978-85, reader plant biochemistry, 1985-88, hon. rsch. fellow, 1988—90; prof., dir. plant biology divsn. Samuel Roberts Noble Found., Ardmore, Okla., 1988—, sr. v.p. Adj. prof. biochemistry and molecular biology Okla. State U., Stillwater, 1988-2005; mem. adv. bd. botany vis. com. U. Tex., Austin, 1990, adj. prof. botany, 1993-98, adj. prof. molecular, cell and devel. biology, 1998-; mem. adv. panel on cellular biochemistry NSF, Washington, 1990-93; mem. adv. bd. Plant Jour., 1990-2003; mem. applied rsch. com. Okla. Ctr. Advancement Sci. and Tech., Oklahoma City, 1992-96; adj. prof. botany and microbiology U. Okla., Norman, 1994—; hon. vis. rsch. prof. Norman Borlaug Inst. Plant Sci. Rsch. De Montfort U., Leicester, UK, 1995-2003; adj. prof. Inst. Biol. Chemistry Wash. State U., Pullman, 1997-2005; adj. prof. biochemistry and cellular biology Rice U., Houston, 2003-; vis. chair phytochemical genomics U. York Ctr. Novel Agrl. Products, UK, 2003-06. Contbr. articles to sci. jours.; editor: Plant Cell Culture: A Practical Approach, 1985, 96, Transgenic Rsch., 1991-96, Biotechnology for Aridland Plants, 1993; mem. editl. bd. Archives Biochemistry and Biophysics, 1991—; assoc. editor: Plant Molecular Biology, 1994—. Grantee Agr. and Food Rsch. Coun., Eng., 1979-88, Sci. and Engring. Rsch. Coun., Eng., 1982-88. Fellow AAAS; mem. Am. Soc. Plant Physiologists (publs. com. 1991-96), Internat. Soc. Plant Molecular Biology, Phytochemical Soc. N.Am., Phytochemical Soc. Europe (com. 1983-86), NAS. Avocations: classical music, opera, hiking, swimming, growing cacti and succulents. Office: Samuel Roberts Noble Found 2510 Sam Noble Pky Ardmore OK 73401 E-mail: radixon@noble.org.*

DIXON, RICHARD DEAN, lawyer, educator; b. Columbus, Ohio, Nov. 6, 1944; s. Dean A. and Katherine L. (Currier) D.; m. Kathleen A. Manfrass, June 17, 1967; children: Jennifer, Lindsay. BSEE, Ohio State U., 1967, MSEE, 1968; MBA, Fla. State U., 1972, JD, 1974. Bar: Fla. 1975, Colo. 1985, Mich. 1992, U.S. Dist. Ct. (mid. dist.) Fla., U.S. Dist. Ct. Colo. 1985, U.S. Patent and Trademanrk Office 1975. Telemetry sys. engr. Pan Am. World Airways, Patrick AFB, Fla., 1968-72; sole practice Melbourne and Orlando, Fla., 1975-80; sr. counsel Harris Corp., Melbourne, 1980-85; corp. counsel, dir. strategic and bus. planning Ford Microelectronics, Inc., Colorado Springs, Colo., 1985-89; mgr. strategic alliances electronics divsn. Ford Motor Co., Dearborn, Mich., 1989-90, assoc. counsel intellectual property, 1991-93, dep. chief patent counsel, 1994—2000; with Dixon Mediation Svcs., 2001—. Adj. prof. bus. law U. Cen. Fla., Cocoa, 1977, Fla. Inst. Tech., Melbourne, 1980-84. Cooper Industries Engring. scholar Ohio State U., 1964-67. Mem. ABA, Licensing Execs. Soc., Am. Intellectual Property Law Assn., Am. Corp. Counsel Assn., Sigma Iota Epsilon, Eta Kappa Nu, Phi Eta Sigma. Home and Office: 8162 Old Tramway Dr Melbourne FL 32940-2183

DIXON, RICHARD WAYNE, retired communications company executive; b. Hubbard, Oreg., Sept. 25, 1936; s. Harlow C. and Mabel (Nilsson) D.; m. Rosina O. Berry, July 4, 1970; children: Erica, Douglas, Andrew. BA summa cum laude, Harvard U., 1958, MA, 1960, PhD, 1964. Tech. staff mem. AT&T Bell Labs., Murray Hill, N.J., 1965, supr. lightwave lasers group, 1968-79, head optoelectronics devices dept., 1979-83, dir. lightwave devices lab., 1983-90, dir. platforms and new products labs., 1991-93; now expert witness and tech. cons., Bernardsville, N.J. Contbr. articles to various publs. Nat. scholar Harvard U., 1955-58; NSF fellow, 1959-63. Fellow IEEE (editor Electronic Device Letters 1980-90, Medal of Engring. Excellence 1993); mem. AAAS, Am. Phys. Soc. Home: 43 Old Wood Rd Bernardsville NJ 07924-1416 Home Phone: 908-766-3558. Personal E-mail: rdixon@worldnet.att.net.

DIXON, ROSINA BERRY, physician, pharmaceutical executive, consultant; b. Columbus, Ohio, Dec. 3, 1942; d. Loren C. and Florence H. (Bateson) Berry; m. Richard W. Dixon, July 4, 1970; children: Erica H., Douglas R., Andrew D. BA in Chemistry, Radcliffe Coll., Cambridge, Mass., 1964; MD, Columbia U., NYC, 1968. Diplomate Am. Bd. Internal Medicine. Intern, resident, and chief med. resident Roosevelt Hosp., NYC, 1968-72; from sr. assoc. to exec. dir. Ciba-Geigy, Summit, N.J., 1972-81; med. dir. Schering Labs., Kenilworth, N.J., 1981-84; v.p. Med. Market Spltys., Boonton, N.J., 1985-86; cons. pharm. devel. Bernardsville, NJ, 1986—2006; sr. dir. global pharmacovigilance and epidemiology Sanofi-Aventis, Bridgewater, NJ, 2006—. Bd. dirs. Cambrex Corp., East Rutherford, N.J., Church & Dwight Co., Inc., Princeton, N.J.; instr. medicine Columbia U. Coll. P&S, 1972-99; preceptor in family practice Overlook Hosp., Summit, 1979—; governing bd. Daytop, N.J., 1991—; bd. advisors Fairleigh Dickinson Silberman Coll., 2003— Mem. Am. Coll. Clin. Pharmacology, Am. Soc. Clin. Pharmacology and Therapeutics, Nat. Assn. Corp. Dirs. Home and Office: 43 Old Wood Rd Bernardsville NJ 07924-1416

DIXON, SHEILA, mayor; b. Balt., Dec. 27, 1953; d. Phillip and Winona Dixon; m. Thomas E. Hampton; children: Joshua, Jasmine. BA in Early Childhood Edn., Towson State U., 1976; MS in Ednl. Adminstrn., Johns Hopkins U., 1982. Internat. trade specialist, Dept. Bus. & Econ. Devel. Office Internat. Bus. City of Balt., 1986—2002, mem. Dem. State Century Com. Dist 40, 1986-87; city councilwoman Dist 4 Balt. City Coun., 1987—99, pres, 1999—2007; mayor City of Balt., 2007—. Mem., exec. appointments com., Balt. City Coun., 1992-99, health & environ. com., 192-93, land use com. & econ. devel. subcom., 1992-93, housing com., 1992-93, urban & inter-govtl. affairs com., 1994-99, edn. & human resources com., 1994-99; chair, taxation & fin., com., 1992-93, mktg. subcom., Balt. City/Balt. County Coun. Task Force on Waste Stream Mgmt. & Reduction, pres., Balt. City Coun. African Am. Coalition, 1992-93; bd. dirs., Revitalizing Balt. Adv. Panel, 1994-96, Women of Tomorrow, 1992-93 Bd. mem. Balt. City Tobacco Cmty. Health Coalition, 1993—99, Walters Art Mus., 1999—, Balt. Pub. Markets Corp., 1996—, Balt. Mus. Art, 1999—; bd. dirs. Marble Hill Assn., 1989—97, Action for the Homeless, 1990—99, Md. Food Com., 1992—99; bd. trustees Living Classroom Found., 1990—99, Bethel A.M.E. Church, 1992—99; mem. Retired Sr. Volunteers Program Adv. Coun., 1999—, Prince George's County Internat. Econ. Adv. Bd., 2001—02; fellow Urban Health Intiative, 2001—. Recipient: Legis. Achievement award Greater Balt. Bd. Realtors, 1991, Enolia P. McMillan Women in NAACP award, 1993, Unsung Hero award, Minority Contractors Assn., 2000, Md. Women for Responsive Govt. Shero award, 2000, Svc. Above Self award, Rotary Club, 2001, David Horner Ednl. AIDS Project Founders award, 2001; named one of Md. Top 100 Women, The Daily Record, 1996, 1999, Balt. Most influential Leaders, Balt. Bus. Jour., 2000 Mem. NAACP, African Am. Women's Caucus, Women Power, Assn. Study Afro-Am. Life and History Inc., Rainbow Coalition, Nat. Forum Black Pub. Adminstrn. Democrat. Achievements include first woman mayor of Baltimore. Office: City Hall 100 N Holliday St Rm 250 Baltimore MD 21202 E-mail: mayor@baltimorecity.gov.*

DIXON, SHIRLEY JUANITA, retired restaurant owner; b. Canton, NC, June 29, 1935; d. Willard Luther and Bessie Eugenia (Scroggs) Clark; m. Clinton Matthew Dixon, Jan. 3, 1953; children: Elizabeth Swanger, Hugh Monroe III, Cynthia Owen, Sharon Henson. BS, Wayne State U., 1956; postgrad., Mary Baldwin Coll., 1958, U. N.C., 1977. Acct. Standard Oil Co., Detroit, 1955-57; asst. dining room mgr. Statler Hilton, Detroit, 1958-60; bookkeeper Osborne Lumber Co., Canton, N.C., 1960-61; bus. owner, pres. Dixon's Restaurant, Canton, 1961-99; ret. Judge NC Assn. Distributive Edn. Assn., state and dist., 1982—; owner Halbert's Family Heritage Ctr., Canton; dir. rep. Avon. Past Pres. Haywood County Assn. Retarded Citizens Bd., 1985-94, past v.p., chmn. bd. dirs.; bd. commrs. Haywood Vocats. Opportunities, 1985-94, treas. bd. dirs.; Haywood Sr. Leadership Council; dist. dir. 11th Congl. Dist. Dem. Women, 1982-85; state Teen-Dem. advisor State Dem. party, 1985-90; del. 1988 Dem. Nat. Conv., Atlanta; alderwoman Town of Canton, NC; vice-chair Gov.'s. Adv. Coun. on Aging, State NC, 1982-89; 1st v.p. crime prevention Community Watch Bd., State NC, 1985, 86; mem. Criminal Justice Bd., NC Assembly on Women and the Economy; chair Western NC Epilepsy Assn., Haywood County NC Mus. History, 1987—; bd. dirs. W. NC Women's Coalition, 1999-00; co-chair Haywood County Commn. on the Bi-Centennial of Constn., 1987-92; Haywood County Econ. Strategy Commn.; v.p., bd. dirs. Haywood County Retirement Coun., Region A Coun. on Aging; bd. dirs. Haywood County Sr. Housing, C.B.C. United Way (mem. chair); chair bd. Canton Sr. Citizen's Ctr.; mem. Haywood County Ease Retirement Com.; pres., chairwoman bd. Haywood County Assn. Retarded Citizens; pres. NC coun. Alzheimer's Disease and Related Disorders Assn.; bd. dirs. Canton Recreation Dept., Western NC Alzheimer's Disease and Related Disorders Assn., 1987-91, v.p., C.B; bd. dirs. Haywood Literary Coun., Haywood Sr. Leadership Coun., Haywood County Block Grant Com., W. NC Econ. Devel. Com., United Way, 1991—, drive chmn.; mem. legis. subcom. Alzheimer's-NC; bd. dirs. NC Conf. for Social Svcs., 1987-91; v.p. bd. W. NC Alzheimer's Assn., 1987-91; pres. State Coun. on Alzheimer's; apptd. mem. Legis. Study Com. on Alzheimer's; apptd. mem. State of NC Adv. Bd. on Cmty. Care and Health; mem. Habitat for Humanity Haywood County; bd. chair Pigeon Valley Optimist Club; apptd. by Senate Western NC Econ. Devel. Commn.; appointee Haywood County Econ. Devel. Commn., Canton Hist. Commn.; judge U.S. Olympic Torch Bearers; mem. Bd. Mount. Area Resource Ctr., 2004—, Bd. Haywood Cty. Coun. on Aging, 2004—; dist. rep. NC Sr. Dems.; pres. Haywood County Sr. Dems.; chairperson Steedy Commn., Tourism Devel. Assn., Haywood County Sr. Advocacy Coun. Recipient Outstanding Svc. award Crime Prevention from Gov., 1982, Gov.'s Spl. Vol. award, 1983, Outstanding Svc. award NC Cmty. Watch Assn., 1984, Cmty. Svc. award to Handicapped, 1983-84, Outstanding Svc. award ARC, 1988; named Employer of Yr. Hiring Handicapped NC Assn. Retarded Citizens, 1985, Cmty. Person of Yr. Kiwanis Club, 1991, Citizen of Yr. in Western NC, 1995, Rec. Outstanding award Haywood Co. Sr. Games, 1992, Roy A. Taylor award for disting. svc., 1999, Smoky Mtn. Mental Health Hero award, 2004, Liston B. Ramsey award, 2005, NC Dem. Women Star, 2005; inducted into NC Softball Hall of Fame, 1997; Canton Sr. Ctr. dedicated in her honor, 2007. Mem. AAUW, NAFE, Women's Polit. Caucus (So. Women's Leadership award 1998) , Internat. Platform Assn., Women's Forum N.C., Nat. Bd. Alzheimers Assn. (regional del.), Canton Bus. and Profl. Assn. (pres. 1974-79, Woman of Yr. 1984), Altrusa (Woman of Yr. in N.C. 1989). Democrat. Episcopalian. Avocation: softball club. Home and Office: 104 Skyland Terr Canton NC 28716-3718 Personal E-mail: sjdixon28716@yahoo.com.

DIXON, STEPHANIE BELL, elementary school educator; d. Clarence Marshall and Leola Robinson Bell; m. Bruce Dixon III, June 26, 1993; children: Bruce Justice IV, Braylen Jarrod. MEd, U. NC, Charlotte, 2000. Cert. Nat. Bd. Profl. Tchg. Stds. Tchr. Charlotte-Mecklenburg Schs., 1992—. Dir.: (play) The Christmas Toy Shop. Rep. Kids Voting of Mecklenburg County, Charlotte, 2001—. Named Tchr. of Yr. Mem.: CTA (sch. rep. 2004—06). Democrat. Office: Davidson IB Mid Sch 251 South St PO Box 369 Davidson NC 28036 Home Phone: 704-794-2111; Office Phone: 980-343-5185. Office Fax: 980-343-5187. Personal E-mail: stephanie.dixon@cms.k12.nc.us. E-mail: bruceandstephanie.dixon@netzero.net.

DIXON, STEWART STRAWN, lawyer, consultant; b. Chgo., Nov. 5, 1930; s. Wesley M. and Katherine (Strawn) D.; m. Romayne Wilson, June 24, 1961 (dec. July 1993); children: Stewart S. Jr., John W., Romayne W. Thompson; m. Ann Wilson Grozier, Sept. 15, 1997. BA, Yale U., 1952; JD, U. Mich., 1955. Bar: Ill. 1957, U.S. Dist. Ct. 1957, U.S. Ct. Appeals 1974, U.S. Supreme Ct. 1974. Ptnr. Kirkland & Ellis, Chgo., 1957-67, Wildman, Harrold, Allen & Dixon, Chgo., 1967—. Dir. Lord, Abbett & Co. Managed Mut. Funds, N.Y.C., 1976-2002, ret. Dec. 31, 2002; dir. Otho Sprague Inst., Chgo. Trustee, past chmn. Chgo. Hist. Soc., 1982-87. 1st lt. U.S. Army, 1955-60. Mem. Am. Bar Assn., Am. Law Inst., Ill. Bar Assn., Chgo. Bar Assn. Clubs: Chgo., Commonwealth, Commercial, Met., Univ., Old Elm, Onwentsia, Rolling Rock. Republican. Episcopalian. Office: Wildman Harrold Allen & Dixon 225 W Wacker Dr Chicago IL 60606-1229 Office Phone: 312-201-2604. Business E-mail: dixon@wildmanharrold.com.

DIXON, WENDY L., pharmaceutical executive; B in Natural Scis., M in Natural Scis., U. Cambridge, Eng., PhD in Biochemistry. Biochemist SmithKline, various regulatory, mktg. and strategy positions; with Centocor; v.p. mktg. Merck & Co., Inc., 1996—2001, sr. v.p. mktg., 2001; with Bristol-Myers Squibb, 2001, pres. global mktg., chief mktg. officer, 2001—. Bd. dirs. DENTSPLY Internat. Inc. Office: Bristol Myers Squibb 345 Park Ave New York NY 10154-0037*

DIXON, WHEELER WINSTON, film and video studies educator, writer; b. New Brunswick, NJ, Mar. 12, 1950; s. Percival Vincent and Hilda-Barr (Wheeler) D.; m. Gwendolyn Audrey Foster, Dec. 23, 1985. AB, Livingston Coll., 1972; MA, MPhil, Rutgers U., 1980, PhD, 1982. Instr. English Rutgers U., New Brunswick, 1974-84; lectr. film studies The New Sch. for Social Rsch., 1983, 97, 98; asst. prof. English and art U. Nebr., Lincoln, 1984-88, assoc. prof. English, 1988—92, chmn. film studies program, 1988—2003, prof. English, 1992—2002; series editor Cultural Studies in Cinema Video Series SUNY Press, 1995—2004, endowed chair, Ryan prof. of film studies, 2000—. Guest programmer, lectr. Nat. Film Theatre of Brit. Film Inst. and Mus. of Moving Image, London, 1991; guest programmer Nat. Film Theatre of Brit. Film Inst., London, 1992; mem. ad hoc curriculum rev. com. dept. English, U. Nebr., Lincoln, 1992, mem. faculty devel. fellowship com., 1992-95, chmn. Robinson Prize com., spring 1994, chmn. faculty devel. fellowship com., 1994, mem. various MA thesis and PhD coms.; panelist NEH, 1993—; presenter papers in field; lectr. Lincoln Ctr., Mus. Modern Art, N.Y.C., New Sch. Univ., N.Y.C., 1997; guest lectr. on digital theory, U. Amsterdam, 1999. Author: The "B" Directors: A Bibliographical Directory, 1985, The Cinematic Vision of F. Scott Fitzgerald, 1986, The Films of Freddie Francis, 1991, The Charm of Evil: The Films of Terence Fisher, 1991, The Films of Reginald Le Borg: Interviews, Essays and Filmography, 1992, The Early Film Criticism of François Truffaut, 1993, Re-Viewing British Cinema 1900-1992: Essays and Interviews, 1994, It Looks at You: The Returned Gaze of Cinema, 1995, The Films of Jean-Luc Godard, 1997, The Exploding Eye: A Re-visionary History of 1960s Experimental Cinema, 1997, The Transparency of Spectacle, 1998, Disaster and Memory, 1999, The Second Century of Cinema, 2000, Film Genre 2000, 2000, Collected Interviews: Voices from 20th Century Cinema, 2001, Experimental Cinema: The Film Reader, 2002, Straight: Constructions of Heterosexuality in the Cinema, 2003, Visions of the Apocalpyse: Spectacles of Destruction in the American Cinema, 2003, Film and Television after 9/11, 2004, Lost in the Fifties, 2005, American Cinema of the 1940s, 2006, Visions of Paradise, 2006, Film Talk: Directors at Work, 2007; editor-in-chief Quarterly Review of Film and Video, 1999—; guest editor Film Criticism, Fall-Winter 1991-92, mem. editl. bd., 1991—, article reviewer 1991—; article reviewer Jour. of History of Sexuality, 1991-93, Cinema Jour., 1993—; mem. adv. bd. Jour. Popular Brit. Cinema; manuscript reviewer SUNY Press, 1993—; contbr. articles and revs. to profl. jours. and essays to various publs., including Film Criticism, Films in Rev., Cineaste, Interview, others; writer, dir., prodr. Coming Attractions: A History of the Motion Picture Trailer, 1986-88, (feature film) What Can I Do?, 1993 (Layman Fund award 1993-94); co-prodr., co-dir., co-writer: Women Who Made The Movies, 1988-90; dir./prodr.: (feature film) Squatters, 1994; exhibited in group shows at U. Nebr.-Lincoln, 1985-86, 87-88, 89-90, Syracuse U., 1986, W.Va. U., 1986, Lincolnshire Coll. Art, Lincoln, Eng., 1988-89; performances include That's Different: Tales of Nebraska, 1987; exhibitions of films include Whitney Mus. Am. Art, 1972, Mus. Modern Art, 1994, Mus. Moving Image, London, 1994, Millennium Film Workshop, 1997, Mus. Modern Art, 2003; complete films archived exclusively at Mus. of Modern Art, 2003, Career Retrospective, 2003; author (notes) Home Vision DVDs, 2004-05. Recipient Outstanding Rsch. and Creative Achievement award, 2003; grantee Royal Film Archive of Belgium, 1974, N.J. State Arts Coun., 1972, Rsch. Coun., U. Nebr., 1984-85, Ind. Filmmaker, S.W. Alt. Media Project, 1985, Interdisciplinary Arts Fellowship Program, Rockefeller Found. and NEA, 1987, Rsch. Coun., 1987, 89, S.W. Alt. Media Project Ind. Prodn. Fund, 1993, John C. and Nettie V. David Meml. Trust, 2003, Maude Hammond Flip Fellowship, 2006. Mem.: Soc. for Cinema Studies (exec. coun. 2004—). Office: U Nebraska Dept English 202 Andrews Hall Lincoln NE 68588-0333 Home Phone: 402-423-2105; Office Phone: 402-472-6064. Business E-Mail: wdixon@unlserve.unl.edu.

DIXON, WILLIAM ROBERT, musician, educator; b. Nantucket, Mass., Oct. 5, 1925; s. William Robert and Louise Ann (Wade) D.; children: William, Claudia Gayle, William. Diploma, Hartnette Conservatory Music, 1951. Clk., internat. civil servant UN Secretariat, NYC, 1956-62; free lance musician, composer NYC, 1962-67; mem. faculty Columbia U. Tchrs. Coll., 1967-70; composer-in-residence George Washington U., Washington, 1967; dir. Conservatory of Univ. of the Streets, NYC, 1967-68; guest artist in residence Ohio State U., 1967; mem. faculty dept. dance Bennington (Vt.) Coll., 1968-95, chmn. dept. black music, 1973-86. Vis. prof. U. Wis., Madison, 1971-72; lectr. painting and music Mus. Modern Art, Verona, Italy, 1982, Palast, Nuremberg, Fed. Republic Germany, 1990; lectr. workshop on contemporary music Pori, Finland, 1991, Jerusalem, Tel Aviv, Israel, 1990; lectr. in Black Art Music Maison du Livre et du Son, Villeurbanne, France, 1994; tchr. Master Classes in Improvisation Ecole Nationale de Musique, Villeurbanne, France, 1994, Master Class Composition and Performance NYU, 1996; in residence Wesleyan U., 2005. Recs. include Archie Shepp-Bill Dixon Quartet, 1962, Bill Dixon 7-Tette, 1963, Intents and Purposes: The Bill Dixon Orchestra, 1967, For Franz, 1976, New Music, Second Wave, 1979, Bill Dixon in Italy, 2 vols., 1980, considerations 1 and 2 Bill Dixon, 1980, 82, November: 1981, 1982, Bill Dixon in the Labyrinth, 1983, Collection, 1985, Thoughts, 1986, Son of Sisyphus, 1990, Bill Dixon: Vade Mecum, 1994, Vade Mecum II, 1996, (6-CD set) Bill Dixon: Solo Trumpet, 1998, PAPYRUS vol. 1 and 2, compositions for trumpet, percussion & piano, 1999, Berlin Abbozzi, 2000; retrospective of music compositions 1963-91 by Radio Sta. WKCR, Columbia U., 1991-92; trumpet soloist Celebration Orchestra, Berlin, Germany, 1994; concert performance of original compositions Espace Tonkin, Villeurbanne, France, 1994, Teatro Colosseo, Rome, Italy, 1996, Nickelsdorf, Austria, 1997; new composition quintet perfomace Vision Festival, NYC, 2005, trio performance Pompidou Ctr., Paris, 2006; guest trumpet soloist in ensemble Que., Can., 2006; composed orch. piece Cologne (Germany) Radio Sta., 1998; performer new compositions Festival of New Music for Trumpet, 2004, Donaueschingen, Guiramers and Royal Festival Hall, London, 2004; exhbns. include Ferrari Gallery, Verona, Italy, 1982, Multimedia Contemporary Art Gallery, Brescia, Italy, 1982, Uferpalast, Nuremberg, Germany, 1990, Cite de la Musique, Paris, 2002, Columbia U., 2005, Sons d'Hiver Festival, 2006; lithograph exhbns. Villeurbanne, France, 1994, Chittenden Bank, Bennington, Vt., 1994-95, Skoto Gallery, N.Y.C., 1996, Rogue Art Gallery, 2006; retrospective of paintings 1968-91, So. Vt. Coll., 1991; author: L'Opera, (bio-discography by Ben Young) Dixonia, 1998; prodr. lithographs Union Regionale pour le Devel. de la Lithographie d'Art, Lyon, France, 1994; orchestral work Index, 2000; artist album cover, 2002; artist in residence Wesleyan U., 2005. Mem. adv. com. New Eng. Found. of the Arts. Served with U.S. Army, 1944-46. Recipient Disting. Visitor in the Arts Middlebury Coll., 1986. Fellow Vt. Acad. Arts and Scis.; mem. Am. Fedn. Musicians, Duke Ellington Jazz Soc. (hon.) Office Phone: 802-442-4490. Personal E-mail: bill-dixon@comcast.net. *Were it possible to live for three thousand years, one could lay around the house and do nothing for the first five hundred years, go to school for the next five hundred and then have two thousand years left to find a way to do work, etc., of substance. Since that is NOT the case (and even if one crosses with the green and not in between and manages to live to be one hundred--in cosmic or universal time akin to attempting to spit in the Atlantic Ocean from a height of 50,000 feet and expecting a ripple to follow) there is another reality extant. And from the time THAT reality dawned on me, I have endeavoured (albeit not always with success) to do everything one hundred percent. Those things I felt I COULDN'T (for whatever reason) expend that kind of energy upon, I have left alone.*

DIXON, W(ILLIAM) ROBERT, retired psychologist; b. Hudson, Pa., Sept. 16, 1917; s. William Robert and Mary (George) D.; m. Carol Everson Lewis, Dec. 20, 1940; children: William R., Barbara Ann. AB, Syracuse U., 1938, MA, 1939; PhD (Horace H. Rackham fellow 1947-48, Burke Aaron Hinsdale scholar 1948), U. Mich., 1948. Tchr., prin. W. Canada Valley Central Schs., Middleville, NY, 1940-42; asst. prof. U. Ill., 1948-49, U. Mich., 1949-52, asso. prof., 1952-56, prof. ednl. psychology, 1956-86, ret., 1986. Vis. prof. edn. U. Bombay, India, 1964-65 Contbr. articles to profl. jours. Dir. Mich. Interdisciplinary Research Tng. Program, 1967-72. Served with USAAF, 1942-45. Decorated Air Medal with 10 oak leaf clusters, D.F.C. Fellow Am. Psychol. Assn., AAAS; mem. Am. Ednl. Research Assn. Achievements include being nationally ranked tennis player Men's Singles, 1945, Vets. Singles, 1962. Home: 2793 W Fairway Loop Dunnellon FL 34434-4829

DIXSON, J. B., communications executive; b. Norwich, NY, Oct. 19, 1941; d. William Joseph and Ann Wanda (Teale) Barrett. BS, Syracuse U., 1963; postgrad. in bus. adminstrn., Wayne State U., 1979-81; MBA, Ctrl. Mich. U., 1984. Pub. rels. editl. asst. Am. Mus. Natural History, NYC, 1963-64; writer, prodr. Norman, Navan, Moore & Baird Advt., Grand Rapids, Mich., 1964-67; prin. J.B. Dixson Comm. Cons., Detroit, 1967-74; dir. Pub. Info. Svcs. divsn. Mich. Employment Security Commn., Detroit, 1974-82; news rels. mgr. Burroughs Corp., 1982-83, dir. creative svcs., 1983-85, dir. pub. rels., 1985-86; prin. Dixson Comm., Detroit, 1986-93, Durocher Dixson Werba, LLC, Detroit, 1994—. Lectr., spkr. in field at colls, univs., cmty. orgns. Author: Guidelines for Non-Sexist Verbal and Written Communication, 1976, Sexual Harassment on The Job, 1979, The TV Interview: Good News or Bad?, 1981. Mem. Detroit Mayor's Transition Com. of 100, 1972; mem. bd. mgmt. Detroit YWCA, 1974; chmn. Detroit Women's Equality Day Com., 1975; bd. dirs., founding mem. Feminist Fed. Credit Union, Detroit, 1976; centennial chair Indian Village Assn., 1993-95; founding mem. Mich. Women's Campaign Fund, 1980; active Mich. Task Force on Sexual Harassment in Workplace, Mich. Women's Com. of 100, Mich. Women's Polit. Caucus, Mich. Women's Found. Named Outstanding Sr. Woman in Radio and TV, Syracuse U., 1963; recipient Five Watch award Am. Women in Radio and TV, Mich., 1969, 75, Outstanding Women in Comm. Women's Advt. Club, 1998, cert.

of recognition Detroit City Coun., 1976, Feminist of Yr. award NOW, 1977, City of Detroit Human Rights Commn., 1988, Design in Mich. award Mich. Coun. of Arts/Gov. William G. Milliken, 1977, Achievement award U.S. Dept. Labor, 1979, Spirit of Detroit award Detroit City Coun., 1980, PR Casebook, 1983, PR News Case Study, 1986, Pinnacle award Mich. Hosp. Pub. Rels. Assn., 1987, award Nat. Sch. Pub. Rels. Assn., 1992, 21st Century award Corp. Detroit Mag., 1995, Creativity in Advt. award Detroit Newspapers Assn., 2000; subject of Mich. Senate Resolution 412, 1979. Fellow Pub. Rels. Soc. Am. (accredited, pres. chpt. 1983-84, Dist. award and citation 1984, 86, 87, 93, exec. com. corp. sect. 1996-2001, Disting. Svc. award 1999, named to Pub. Rels. Hall Fame 2004), Internat. Assn. Bus. Communicators (Silver Quill award chpt. 1987, 88, 91, 93, dist. 1987, Renaissance award 1988, 91, Mercury award 1987), Nat. Assn. Govt. Communicators (Blue Pencil award 1977, Gold Screen award 1980), Automotive Press Assn., Women's Advt. Club (Top 75 Women in Comm. 1999), Econ. Club Detroit, Maple Grove Gun Club, Detroit Athletic Club. Home: 3000 N Ocean Dr Apt 28b Singer Island FL 33404-3249 Personal E-mail: dixson@ddwpr.com.

DJANG, ARTHUR H.K., pathologist, preventive medicine physician; b. Beijing, Feb. 12, 1925; arrived in U.S., 1948; s. Wei-Fang DJang and Sujen Liu; m. Mary Helen Winston; divorced; children: Philipp, Douglas, Lincoln, David; m. Tina Marie Barone, 1980-98; 1 child, Anna Claire. MD, Harbin Med. U., China, 1944; MPH, U. Minn., 1951; PhD in Infectious Diseases, UCLA, 1955. Cert. specialist in Clin. Pathology, Anatomic Pathology, Nuclear Medicine Clin. Faculty UCLA Sch. Medicine, 1955. Chief state epidemiologist, dir. chronic & communicable diseases State Dept. Pub. Health, Santa Fe, 1956-58; pres., dir. Biomedical Sci. Labs., Albuquerque, 1962-74; chmn. dept. pathology & nuclear med. Jamestown Gen. Hosp., NY, 1975-85; clin. prof. of molecular biology SUNY, Fredonia, NY, 1977-86; pres. Internat. Health Inc., Jamestown, 1987—90; pres., CEO Santé Internat. Inc., Jamestown (NY) and Tianjin, China, 1994—; pres. Environ. Scis. Internat., Jamestown and Tianjin, China, 1993—. Cons. prof. in pathology N. Mex. State U., University Park, 1962-74; cons. physician NASA White Sands Facility, N. Mex., 1966-74; med. dir., cons. physician Medina Meml. Hosp., 1991—93; disting. vis. prof. Grad. Sch. Health Scis. Dalian (China) U., 1988—, bd. dirs.; hon. chmn. Sci. and Tech. Commn., Zhuhai. Author monographs in field; cons. editor Jour. Gerontology, 1988—. Bd. dirs. Am. Heart Assn., Albuquerque, 1965-75, Am. Cancer Soc., 1965-74, Chautauqua Bd. Health, Mayville, NY, 1976-84; coun. mem. SUNY, Fredonia, 1978-86. Named hon. chmn. Scis. Tech. Commn., hon. pres. Yantai Internat. Red Cross Hosp., hon. pres. Dalian Inst. Gerontology, 1988, hon. prof. Harbin Med. U., 1981; recipient First Nation Gold Medal award outstanding contbn. health scis., 2004. Fellow Am. Coll. Pathologists, Am. Coll. Nuclear Med. (chmn. Internat. com. 1984-85), Am. Coll. Preventive Med. (mem. by-laws com. 1983-85); mem. AAAS, Am. Coll. Physician Execs., NY Acad. Scis., Sigma Xi. Achievements include discovery of main ingredients used in Lysol, 1955; holder of 5 patents related to Anti-Aging and Cancer Prevention and Treatment (3 U.S., 1 Canadian, and 1 European) and 1 U.S. pending patent; inventor of Oncolyn (anti-cancer plant extract); Longevity Crystal (for life extension); Nasbesilin (for particle and inhalation injury and respiratory diseases); Mellinol (for blood sugar and weight balance); Evergreen (for protection of UV damage and antimutation); Memory Gold+ (for prevention and treatment of pre-dementia and Alzheimer); Cardio-CP (for cardiovascular health); Bariatol (weight management); Rejuvenin (skin anti-aging and UV damage); Viranox (HIV and other viral infections); Pomecran (anti-cancer); Mégrani (anti-aging). Avocations: coins, stamps, paintings. Office: Santé Internat Inc 111 W Second St Ste 4000 Jamestown NY 14701 Office Phone: 716-664-7255. E-mail: santedjang@netscape.net.

DJANG, DAVID S.W., physician; b. Seattle, Jan. 24, 1970; s. Mary Helen Surovik; m. Eleanor Yu-Chen Lo, Mar. 3, 2001; 1 child, Luke. BA, U. Tex., 1992; MD, U. Tex. S.W. Med. Sch., 1998. Diplomate Am. Bd. Nuc. Medicine. Intern U. Wash. Med. Ctr., Seattle, 1998—99, resident, 1999—2003; staff physician Swedish Hosp., Seattle, 2003—, med. dir. divsn. nuc. medicine, 2004—. Bd. dirs. Brain Imaging Coun. Vol. US Peace Corp., Malawi, Africa, 1992—94. Recipient Rsch. in Tng., RSNA, 2002, WRSNM, 2002. Mem.: Brain Imaging Coun., Soc. Nuc. Medicine, AMA.

DJAWAD, SAID TAYEB See JAWAD, SAID

DJ CRAZE, (ARISTH DELGADO), disc jockey; b. Managua, Nicaragua, Nov. 19, 1977; 1 child, Angelee. Performer: (albums) Crazee Musick, 1999, United DJs of Am., Vol. 16, 2000, Scratch Nerds, 2002, Rugged Radio Saturday, Live in Puerto Rico: Hip Hop Drum n Bass Turntablism, 2003, Miami Heat, 2005, (with The Allies) D-Day, 2000. Named Zulu Nat. champion, 1995, 1996, East Coast Rap Sheet champion, 1996, Winter Music Conf. Scratch Off champion, 1996—99, East Coast DMC champion, 1997, ITF Western Hemisphere Scratch Off champion, 1998, World ITF Scratch Off champion, 1998, USA DMC champion, 1998, World DMC champion, 1998—2001, America's Best DJ, Time mag., 2001. Office: Contagious Musiq Ste 4251 1717 N Bayshore Dr Miami FL 33132 Office Phone: 305-416-9330. Office Fax: 305-416-9331. E-mail: craze@djcraze.com.*

DJERASSI, CARL, writer, retired chemistry professor; b. Vienna, Oct. 29, 1923; s. Samuel and Alice (Friedmann) Djerassi; m. Virginia Jeremiah (div. 1950); m. Norma Lundholm (div. 1976); children: Dale, Pamela(dec.); m. Diane W. Middlebrook, 1985. AB summa cum laude, Kenyon Coll., 1942, DSc (hon.), 1959; PhD, U. Wis., 1945, DSc (hon.), 1995, Nat. U. Mex., 1953, Fed. U., Rio de Janeiro, 1969, Worcester Poly. Inst., 1972, Wayne State U., 1974, Columbia U., 1975, Uppsala U., 1977, Coe Coll., 1978, U. Geneva, 1978, U. Ghent, 1985, U. Man., 1985, Adelphi U., 1993, U. S.C., 1995, Swiss Fed. Inst. Tech., 1995, U. Md.- Balt. County, 1997, Bulgarian Acad. Scis., 1998, U. Aberdeen, 2000, Polytechnic U., 2001, Cambridge U., 2005. Rsch. chemist Ciba Pharm. Products, Inc., Summit, NJ, 1942—43, 1945—49; assoc. dir. rsch. Syntex, Mexico City, 1949—52, rsch. v.p., 1957—60; v.p. Syntex Labs., Palo Alto, Calif., 1960—62, Syntex Rsch., 1962—68, pres., 1968—72, Zoecon Corp., 1968—83, chmn. bd. dirs., 1968—86; prof. chemistry Wayne State U., 1952—59, Stanford (Calif.) U., 1959—2002; ret., 2002. Founder Djerassi Resident Artists Program, Woodside, Calif. Author: The Futurist and Other Stories, 1988; author: (novels) Cantor's Dilemma, 1989, The Bourbaki Gambit, 1994, Marx Deceased, 1996, Menachem's Seed, 1997, NO, 1998; author: (poetry) The Clock Runs Backward, 1991; author: (plays) An Immaculate Misconception, 1998, BBC World Svc. Play of Week, 2000, ICSI--a pedagogic wordplay for 2 voices, 2002, Calculus, 2003, (musical version) Music Werner Schulze, 2005, Ego, 2003, Three on a Couch, 2004, Phallacy, 2005, Taboos, 2006, Four Jews on Parnassus, 2007; author: (with Roald Hoffmann) Oxygen, 2001, BBC World Svc.Play of Week, 2001; author: (with Pierre Laszlo) NO--a pedagogic wordplay for 3 voices, 2003; author: (autobiography) The Pill, Pygmy Chimps and Degas' Horse, 1992; author: (memoir) This Man's Pill, 2001; author: (with D. Pinner) Newton's Darkness: Two Dramatic Views, 2004; author: 9 other books; mem. editl. bd. Jour. Organic Chemistry, 1955—59, Tetrahedron, 1958—92, Steroids, 1963—2001, Procs. NAS, 1964—70, Jour. Am. Chem. Soc., 1966—75, Organic Mass Spectrometry, 1968—91, contbr. numerous articles to profl. jours., poems, memoirs and short stories to lit. publs. Decorated Austrian Cross of Honor 1st class, Great Cross of Merit Germany; named to Nat. Inventors Hall of Fame; recipient Intrasci. Rsch. Found. award, 1969, Freedman Patent award, Am. Inst. Chemists, 1970, Chem. Pioneer award, 1973, Nat. medal of Sci. for first synthesis of oral contraceptive, 1973, Wolf prize in chemistry, Wolf Found., 1978, John and Samuel Bard award in Sci. and Medicine, 1983, Roussel prize, Paris, 1988, Discovers award, Pharm. Mfg. Assn., 1988, Nat. medal Tech. for new approaches to insect control, 1991, Nev. medal, 1992, Thomson medal, Internat. Soc. Mass Spectroscopy, 1994, Prince Mahidol award, Thailand, 1995, Sovereign Fund award, 1996, Othmer Gold medal, Chem. Heritage Found., 2000, Author's prize, German Chem. Soc., 2001, Erasmus medal, Acad. Europeae, 2003, Gold medal, Am. Inst. Chemists, 2004, Serono prize fiction, Rome, 2005, Lichtenberg medal, Göttingen Acad., 2005. Mem.: NAS (Indsl. Application of Sci. award 1990), Acad. Europeae, Bulgarian Acad. Scis. (fgn. mem.), Mex. Acad. Scis., Brazilian Acad. Scis., Royal Swedish Acad. Engring. (fgn. mem.), Royal Swedish Acad. Scis. (fgn. mem.), German Acad. Leopoldina, Am. Acad. Arts and Scis., Royal Soc. Chemistry (hon. fellow, Centenary lectr. 1964), Am. Chem. Soc. (award pure chemistry 1958, Baekeland medal 1959, Fritzsche award 1960, award for creative invention 1973, award in chemistry of contemporary tech. problems 1983, Esselen award 1989, Priestley medal 1992, Gibbs medal 1997), NAS Inst. Medicine, Am. Acad. Pharm. Scis. (hon.), Sigma Xi (Proctor prize for sci. achievement 1998), Phi Beta Kappa, Phi Lambda Upsilon (hon.). Office: Stanford U Dept Chemistry Stanford CA 94305-5080 Business E-Mail: djerassi@stanford.edu.

DJERASSI, ISAAC, medical researcher; b. Sofia, Bulgaria, July 27, 1925; came to U.S., 1954, naturalized, 1962; s. Rahamim and Adela (Tadjer) D.; m. Nira Eskenazy, Jan. 31, 1954; children— Ram Isaac, Ady Lynn. Student, Sofia U. Med. Sch., 1944-49; MD, Hebrew U., Jerusalem, 1952; DH (hon.), Villanova U., 1977. Intern Hadassah Hosp., Tel Aviv, 1951-52, resident, 1953-54; rsch. assoc. Med. Sch. Harvard U., Boston, 1955-60; asst. prof. pediats. U. Pa., Phila., 1960-69; dir. rsch. oncology-hematology Mercy Cath. Med. Ctr., Phila., 1969-98. Prof. oncology Med. Sch. U. Tel Aviv, Israel, 1986, dir. Djerassi-Elias Oncology Inst., 1987. Contbr. articles to profl. jours. Mem. med. advisory bd. Nat. Hemophilia Found., Phila., 1964-75; mem. med. advisory bd. Leukemia Soc., 1970-75. Recipient Albert Lasker Found. award, 1972, E. Cohn-De Laval award, 1990. Mem. Am. Soc. Cancer Rsch., Am. Soc. Clin. Oncology, Am. Assn. Blood Banks. Inventor filtration leukopheresis system and machine for white blood cell transfusions, 1970; discoverer high methotrexate-citrovorum rescue chemotherapy of cancer, 1964-77; developer platelet and white cells transfusions and supportive care, 1955-71; developed curative treatments for acute childhood leukemia, non-Hodgkin lymphoma, 1964-68, osteogenic sarcoma, 1971, effective brain gliomas, 1983-99. Home: 1820 Rittenhouse Sq Philadelphia PA 19103 Office: Mercy Cath Med Ctr PO Box 19709 Philadelphia PA 19143-0709

DJEREJIAN, EDWARD PETER, academic administrator, retired diplomat; b. NYC, Mar. 6, 1939; s. Peter Minas and Mary (Yazudjian) D.; m. Francoise Andrée Haelters, July 31, 1971; children: Gregory, Francesca. BS in Fgn. Svc., Georgetown U., 1960, doctorate (hon.), 1992; LLD (hon.), Middlebury Coll., 2004. Staff asst. to sec. of state U.S. Dept. of State, 1963-64; Political officer Am. Embassy, Beirut, 1965-69; political/labor officer Am. Consulate Gen., Casablanca, Morocco, 1969-72; spl. asst. Under Sec. of State, Washington, 1973-75; prin. officer Am. Consulate Gen., Bordeaux, France, 1975-77; political counselor Am. Embassy, Moscow, USSR, 1979-81, dep. chief of mission Amman, Jordan, 1981-84; dep. spokesman & dep. asst. sec. Dept. of State, Washington, 1984-85; spl. asst. to the pres., dep. press sec. The White House, 1985-86; prin. dep. asst. sec. for Near East/South Asia, 1987-88; Am. ambassador Am. Embassy, Damascus, Syria, 1988-91; asst. sec. Near Eastern and South Asian Affairs bur. Dept. State, Washington, 1991-93; amb. to Israel Tel Aviv, 1993-94; dir. James A. Baker III Inst. for Pub. Policy Rice U., Houston, 1994—; chmn. adv. group Pub. Diplomacy for the Arab and Muslim World, 2003; sr. advisor Iraq Study Group, 2006; mng. ptnr. Djerejian Global Consultants, LLP. Bd. dirs. Occidental Petroleum Corp., Global Industries, Ltd., Baker Hughes. 1st Lt. U.S. Army, 1961-62 (Korea). Recipient Presdl. award, Presdl. Meritorious Svc. award, 1988, Superior Honor award Dept. State, 1984, Disting. Honor award, 1993, Presdl. Disting. Svc. award, 1994, Ellis Island medal of honor, Moral Statesman award ADL, 1994. Mem. Coun. on Fgn. Rels. Armenian Apostolic. Avocations: writing, skiing. Office: Baker Inst Pub Policy Rice Univ - MS40 6100 Main St Houston TX 77005-1827 Office Phone: 713-348-4981. Business E-Mail: epd@rice.edu.

DJOKIC, WALTER HENRY, lawyer; b. Schwaforden, Germany, Sept. 12, 1947; came to U.S., 1951, naturalized, 1959; s. Radovan and Martha (Schulenburg) D.; married; 1 child, Joshua David. B.A., U. Ill., 1969; J.D., DePaul U., 1972. Bar: Ill. 1972, Ariz. 1980, Fla. 1994. Assoc. Wachowski & Wachowski, Chgo., 1972-73; atty. Pretzel & Stouffer, Chartered, Chgo., 1973-79, ptnr., 1979-85; ptnr. Wood, Lucksinger & Epstein, Chgo., 1985-86, Finley Kumble Wagner, Heine, Underberg, Manley, Myerson & Casey, Chgo., 1986-88; of counsel McCullough, Campbell & Lane, 1988-93, Conrad, Scherer & James, 1994-95, Miller, Kagan, Rodriguez & Silver, 1995-2000; atty. McIntosh, Sawran Peltz & Cargaya, 2000-02, ptnr., 2002—. Mem. Chgo. Bar Assn., Ill. State Bar Assn., State Bar of Ariz., State Bar of Fla. Office: 625 N Flagler Dr Ste 502 West Palm Beach FL 33401 Home: 2077 Carambola Rd West Palm Beach FL 33406-5314 Home Phone: 561-547-3307; Office Phone: 561-655-7520. Business E-Mail: wdjokic@mspcesq.com.

DJORDJEVIC, DIMITRIJE, historian, educator; b. Belgrad, Yugoslavia, Feb. 27, 1922; came to U.S., 1970, naturalized, 1977; s. Vladimir and Jelena (Rasic) D.; m. Nan Fletcher, June 1981; 1 child, Jelena Grad., U. Beograd, 1954, PhD, 1962. Sr. staff mem. Inst. History, Serbian Acad. Scis. and Arts, 1958-69, Inst. Balkan Studies, 1969-70; prof. U. Calif., Santa Barbara, 1970-91, prof. emeritus, 1991—, chmn. Russian area studies, 1976-82. Mem. Nat. Com. to Promote History of Habsburg Monarchy, 1973-79 Author: Austro-Serbian Customs War 1906-1911, in Serbian, 1962, Revolutions nationales des peuples balkaniques, 1804-1914, 1965, Scars and Memory, 1997; co-author: The Balkan Revolutionary Tradition, 1981, also papers, essays, revs.; editor: The Creation of Yugoslavia, 1914-1918, 1980; editorial bd. profl. jours. Mem. Am. Hist. Assn., Am. Assn. Advancement Slavic Studies, Conf. Slavic and East European History (pres. 1984), Serbian Acad. Scis., N. Am. Assn. Serbian Studies (pres. 1986-88). Serbian Orthodox. Personal E-mail: vmarkovic@msn.com.

DJORDJEVICH, MIROSLAV-MICHAEL, bank executive; b. Belgrade, Yugoslavia, 1936; arrived in U.S., 1956; s. Dragoslav and Ruzica Georgevich; m. Marie Louise Hohman, 1963; children: Marie, Alexander, Michelle. BS, U. Calif., Berkeley, 1960; MBA, San Francisco State U., 1963; cert. advanced fin., U. Stanford. Fin. analyst Fireman's Fund Ins. Co., San Francisco, 1962-68, asst. v.p. investments, 1972-76, v.p. investments, 1976-78, v.p., treas., 1978-84; pres., CEO U.S. Fidelity and Guaranty Fin. Co., San Francisco, 1985-86; chmn., pres., CEO Capital Guaranty Ins. Co., San Francisco, 1986-94; pres., CEO Monad Fin., San Rafael, Calif., 1994-97, Bank S.E. Europe Internat., San Juan, 1997—2004; chmn. Devel. Bank of South-East Europe, Bosnia-Herzegovina, 2002—05; pres. Monad Fin. Co., San Rafael, Calif., 2005—, CEO, 2005—. Pres. Studenica Found., 1993—. Author: About Happy Living, 1985, Moral Society and Modern State, 2003. State pres. Calif. Young Reps., 1965-66; commr. Statue of Liberty Ellis Island Centennial Commn., 1986; pres. Serbian Unity Congress, 1990-93, Coun. for Dem. Changes, 1998-01, Studenica Found., 1995-; dir. World Affairs Coun. of Am., 2002-04. With U.S. Army, 1961-63. Recipient Excellence award Am. Security Coun., 1967, Americanism medal Nat. Soc. DAR, 1969, medal of Yuboslav Flag II degree, 2003, medal of Nemanja, II degree, 2005. Mem.: First Serbian Benevolent Soc. (treas. 1978—82). Avocations: reading, tennis, politics. Office: Monad Fin 535 4th St Ste 203 San Rafael CA 94901-3314 Business E-Mail: info@monadfinancial.com.

DLAB, VLASTIMIL, mathematics professor, researcher; b. Bzi, Czech Republic, Aug. 5, 1932; arrived in Can., 1968; s. Vlastimil Dlab and Anna (Stuchlikova) Dlabova; m. Zdenka Dvorakova, Apr. 27, 1959 (div.); children: Dagmar, Daniel Jan; m. Helena Briestenska, Dec. 18, 1985; children: Philip Adam, David Michael. R.N.Dr., Charles U., 1956, C.Sc., 1959, Habilitation, 1962, DSc, 1966; PhD, U. Khartoum, 1962. Rsch. fellow Czechoslovak Acad. Sci., Prague, 1956—57; lectr., sr. lectr. Charles U., Prague, 1957—59, reader, 1964—65, dir. Grad. Inst., 1992—94; lectr., sr. lectr. U. Khartoum, Sudan, 1959—64; rsch. fellow, sr. rsch. fellow Inst. Advanced Studies, Australian Nat. U., Canberra, 1965—66; prof. math. Carleton U., Ottawa, Ont., Canada, 1968—98, chmn. dept., 1971—74, 1994—97, disting. rsch. prof., 1998—, prof. emeritus; professorem hospitem Charles U., 1995—. Vis. prof. U. Paris VI, Brandeis U., U. Bonn, Monash U., U. Tsukuba, U. Sao Paulo, U. Stuttgart, U. Poitiers, Nat. U. Mex., U. Essen, U. Bielefeld, Hungarian Acad. Sci., Budapest, U. Warsaw, U. Normal Beijing, U. Vienna, UCLA, U. Va., Czechoslovak Acad. Sci., U. Trondheim, U. Paderborn, U. St. Petersburg, U. Reims, U. Sao Paulo, Osaka U., Yamaneashi U., Shinshu U., Eotvos U., Budapest, Charles U., Prague, U. Murcia, Spain, Erdos Rsch. Ctr., Budapest, Australian Nat. Univ., Canberra, Gadjah Mada U., Jogjakarta, U. Kron Kaen, Mahidol, U.; presenter in field. Author: Representations of Valued Graphs, 1980, An Introduction to Diagrammatical Methods, 1981, Quasi-hereditary Algebras, 1994; editor: procs. internat. confs., 1974, 1979, 1984, 1987, 1990, 1992, 1993, 1994, 1996, 2004, Algebra and Representation Theory, 1998—, procs. internat. confs., 2002, Algebra and Discrete Mathematics, 2002—, Southeast Asian Bulletin of Mathematics, Czechoslovak Math. Jour., 2007—; contbr. numerous articles to profl. jours. Recipient Diploma of Honour Union Czechoslovak Mathematicians, 1962; Can. Coun. fellow, 1974; Japan Soc. Promotion of Sci. sr. rsch. fellow, 1981; sci. exch. grantee Nat. Sci. and Engring. Rsch. Coun. Can., 1978, 81, 83, 85, 88, 91. Fellow Royal Soc. Can. (convenor 1977-78, 80-81, coun. 1980-81, editor-in-chief Comptes rendus mathematiques-Math. Reports 1997-2005); mem. Am. Math. Soc., Math. Assn. Am., Can. Math. Soc. (coun., chmn. rsch. com. 1973-77, editor-in-chief Can. Jour. Math. 1988-93), European Math. Soc., London Math. Soc., Czech Math. Union. Roman Catholic. Avocations: sports, music. Home: 277 Sherwood Dr Ottawa ON Canada K1Y 3W3 Office: Carleton U Sch Math & Stat Math Dept Ottawa ON Canada K1S 5B6 Office Phone: 613-520-2600 ext 2616. E-mail: vdlab@math.carleton.ca.

DLOTT, SUSAN JUDY, judge, lawyer; b. Dayton, Ohio, Sept. 11, 1949; d. Herman and Mildred (Zemboch) D.; m. Stanley M. Chesley, Dec. 7, 1991. BA, U. Pa., 1971; JD, Boston U., 1973. Bar: Ohio 1973, U.S. Dist. Ct. (so. dist.) Ohio 1975, U.S. Ct. Appeals (6th cir.) 1976, U.S. Supreme Ct. 1980, U.S. Dist. Ct. (ea. dist.) Ky. 1984, U.S. dist. Ct. (no. dist.) Ohio 1989, Ky. 1990. Law clk. Ohio Ct. of Appeals, Cleve., 1973-74; asst. U.S. atty. U.S. Dist. Ct. (so. dist.) Ohio, Dayton, 1975-79; ptnr. Graydon, Head & Ritchey, Cin., 1979-95; dist. judge U.S. Dist. Ct. for So. Dist. Ohio, Cin., 1995—. Legal reporter Multimedia Program Prodn., Inc., 1982-84; instr. trial advocacy workshop, Harvard Law Sch., 2000. Mem. Ohio Bldg. Authority, 1988-93, vice chmn., 1990-93, Jewish Fedn. Cin., trustee and mem. com. 1979-93, Jewish Cmty. Rels. Coun. Cin., 1980-90, Hamilton County Park Dist. Vol. in Parks, 1985-86 Named a Career Woman of Achievement, YWCA, 1996, Cin. Leading Woman, 1998; recipient commendation, US Postal Svc., 1977, Svc. award, Dayton Bar Assn., 1975—76, Gift of Appreciation award, Downtown Residents' Coun., 2000, Fair and Courageous award, NAACP, 2006. Mem. ABA, FBA (asst. treas. 1981-82, treas. 1982-83, sec. 1983-84, v.p. 1984-86), Ohio Bar Assn., Ky. Bar Assn., Cin. Bar Assn., Leadership Cin. Alumni Assn., Queen City Dog Tng. Club, 6th Cir. Jud. Conf. (life), NAACP (life), Hadassah (life), Potter Stewart Inn of Ct. (pres. 1997—), Cavalier King Charles Spaniel Club Jewish. Office: 100 E 5th St Cincinnati OH 45202-3927 Office Phone: 513-564-7630.

DLUGOFF, MARC ALAN, lawyer; b. NYC, Oct. 6, 1955; s. Arnold M. and Ruth B. (Schnall) D. AB, Colgate U., 1976; JD, Hofstra U., 1980; LLM in Taxation, NYU, 1981. Bar: N.Y. 1981, D.C. 1985, Calif. 1988. Law clk. to presiding justice U.S. Tax Ct., Washington, 1981-83; assoc. Mudge, Rose, Guthrie, Alexander & Ferdon, NYC, 1983-85, Milbank, Tweed, Hadley & McCloy, NYC, 1985-89, ptnr., 1989—92; counsel Roberts & Holland, NYC, 1993-94; pres., CEO, Atlantic Adv. Corp., NYC, 1995—; mng. editor The Scenographer Mag., 2003—. Fundraiser lawyers divsn. United Jewish Appeal, N.Y.C. chpt., 1986-90; chmn. adv. bd. arts and media Tikva Children's Home, 2005—. Charles Dana scholar Colgate U., 1976. Mem. ABA, N.Y. State Bar Assn., Assn. Bar City N.Y., State Bar Calif., Phi Beta Kappa. Jewish. Home and Office: 130 Water St Ste 5-G New York NY 10005-1625 Personal E-mail: marcnyc130@hotmail.com.

DLUHOS, ANDRE, artist; b. Spisske Podhradie, Slovakia, June 7, 1940; m. Yary Svabova, July 27, 1963; 1 child, Peter. BA, Graphic Design Bratislava Art Acad., Slovakia, 1959; MA, Uherski Hradiste Sch. Fine Arts, Czech Republic, 1961. Paintings, sculptures, mosaics, Oil Paintings, Portraiture, exhibitions include Robert Wright Fine Art Gallery, Escondo, Calif., Design Consortium, Cin., Ohio, Ordover Gallery, Solana Beach, Calif. Home Phone: 760-638-0504; Office Phone: 760-638-0504. Home Fax: 760-749-8646. Personal E-mail: andre@dluhosarts.com.

DLUHY, DEBORAH HAIGH, dean; b. Summit, NJ, Mar. 4, 1940; d. Richard Hartman Haigh and Elin Frederika Anderson Neumann; m. Robert George Dluhy, June 11, 1962; 1 child, Leonore Alexandra. BA, Wheaton Coll., 1962; postgrad., Boston U., 1962—63, U. Heidelberg, Germany, 1963—65; PhD, Harvard U., 1976. Instr. fine arts Wheaton Coll., Norton, Mass., 1975—76, Radcliffe Coll., Cambridge, Mass., 1977, Boston Coll., Newton, Mass., 1976—78; devel. officer Mus. Fine Arts, Boston, 1978—84, asst. dir. devel., 1984—86; assoc. dean adminstrn. Sch. Mus. Fine Arts, Boston, 1986—87, dean acad. programs and adminstrn., 1987—93, dean, 1993—; dep. dir. Mus. Fine Arts, Boston, 1999—. Trustee Cultural Edn. Collaborative Boston, 1987—90, Wheaton Coll., Norton, Mass., 1988—, mem. exec. com., vice chair fin. and facilities, 2001—02, chair faculty/staff com., mem. governance bd., 2004—, vice chair presdl. search com., 2003—04, chair bd. trustees, 2005—; pres. Wheaton Coll. Alumni Assn., Norton, Mass., 1994—2000; visitor Walnut Hill Sch., Natick, Mass., 1996—; pres. Pro Arts Consortium, 1999—2000; bd. dirs. Boston Arts Acad., 1999—. Fellow, Woodrow Wilson fellow, 1963. Mem.: Assn. Ind. Coll. Art and Design (program com. 1995—2001, bd. dirs., exec. com., chair), Copley Soc. Boston (hon. trustee 1997—), Nat. Assn. Schs. Art and Design (rsch. com. 1990—96, evaluator 1996—, bd. dirs. 1996—, sec. bd. dirs. 2001—, exec. com. 2001—). Office: Sch Mus of Fine Arts 230 Fenway Boston MA 02115-5534 Home Phone: 617-484-8770, 617-416-1125; Office Phone: 617-369-3611. Business E-Mail: ddluhy@mfa.org.

D'LUHY, JOHN JAMES, investment banker; b. Passaic, NJ, Sept. 18, 1933; s. John George and Leonora (Fila) D'L.; m. Gale Rainsford, Dec. 7, 1968; children: Amanda, Pamela. AB, Trinity Coll., 1955; MBA, The Wharton Sch., U. Pa., 1959. Lic. amateur radio operator K2EXI, comml. pilot (instrument-rated). Jr. exec. trainee Merrill Lynch, NYC, 1956—58, with over-the-counter rsch. dept., 1959—60; assoc. syndicate dept., investment mgmt., investment banking Lazard Freres & Co., NYC, 1960—68; sr. v.p., ptnr., dir. money mgmt. and venture capital divsn. R.W. Pressprich & Co., NYC, 1968—72; dir. money mgmt. and pvt. placements Wood Walker & Co., NYC, 1972—73; pres. U.S. Oil Co., 1973—83, founder, pres., 1983—84; pvt. investor Dominick & Dominick, NYC, 1983—86; fin. advisor Robert Thomas Securities divsn. Raymond James Assocs., NYC, 1990—2002; pvt. investor Spring Lake, NJ, 2002—. Trustee Collier Svcs. Found., Marlboro, N.J., 1986-92; bus. coun. Monmouth Univ., West Long

Branch, N.J., 1994-98; sr. analyst NY Soc. Security Analysts. Hon. usher St. Patrick's Cath., NYC, 1969—, chief hon. usher, 1975-76; founding mem. US Naval War Coll. Found., 1969, Newport, RI, trustee, 2001—, fin. com. 2002-06, chmn. audit com, chmn., 2004-05, treas., 2005-06, chmn. fin. com., 2005-06, strategic planning com., 2001-03, capital campaign com., 2001-03, chmn. bd. trustees 2006—; co-chmn. Spring Lake Centennial Com., 1990-92; pres. Spring Lake Chorus, 1990-92; active Chorus of Atlantic, 2000—, barbershop chorus; 1st pilot, aux. air arm, U.S. Coast Guard Aux., flotilla air officer, 2001-03, vice comdr., 2003-04. With USN, 1955. Mem. Investment Assn. N.Y. (bd. dirs. 1967, chmn. capital and money mktgs. com.), Assn. Investment Mgmt. and Rsch., N.Y. Soc. Security Analysts (sr. analyst, high net worth investors com. 2000-02, career devel. com. 2000-02), Am. Radio Relay League, Aircraft Owners and Pilots Assn., Univ. Club N.Y.C. (coun. 1977-83, exec. com., treas. 1979-83), Spring Lake Bath and Tennis Club, Jersey Aero Club (chmn. rules com. 1992), Blue Hill (N.Y.C.) Troupe, Penn Club N.Y., Clayton (N.Y.) Yacht Club. Roman Catholic. Home: 115 Ludlow Ave Spring Lake NJ 07762-1547 Home (Summer): Club Island Clayton NY 13624 E-mail: johngale@worldnet.att.net.

DLUHY, ROBERT GEORGE, physician; b. Montclair, NJ, Jan. 23, 1937; s. John George and Leona (Fila) D.; m. Deborah Haigh; 1 child, Leonore Alexandra. AB magna cum laude, Princeton U., 1958; MD, Harvard Med. Sch., 1962. Intern/resident Peter Bent Brigham Hosp., Boston, 1962, 65-67, endocrine fellow, 1967-69; instr. med. Harvard Med. Sch., Boston, 1969-74, asst. prof. med., 1974-80, assoc. prof. med., 1980-98, prof. med., 1998—. Assoc. editor New Eng. Jour. Medicine. Capt. med. corp. U.S. Army, 1964-66, Germany. Fellow: Endocrine Soc., Hypertension Coun. AHA; mem.: Phi Beta Kappa. Office: Endocrine Hypertension Divs 221 Longwood Ave # Rfb2 Boston MA 02115-5804 Office Phone: 617-732-5011. E-mail: rdluhy@partners.org.

DMITRIEV, DMITRY A., entomologist, researcher; b. Voronezh, Russia, Feb. 3, 1975; arrived in US, 2002; s. Alexandr N. Dmitriev and Lyudmila M. Dmitrieva; m. Yulia Y. Fomenko (div.); 1 child, Anna Dmitrieva; m. Margarita D. Mikhailova, Jan. 20, 2005; 1 child, Vladislav. MA, Voronezh State U., 1997; PhD, Zool. Inst. Russian Acad. Scis., 2001. Tchr. Sch. 70, St. Petersburg, Russia, 1999—2000; rsch. scientist Zool. Inst. Russian Acad. Scis., St. Petersburg, 2002—05; asst. rsch. scientist Ill. Natural History Survey, Champaign, 2002—. Recipient Herbert H. Ross Meml. award, Ill. Natural History Survey, 2003. Mem.: Russian Entomol. Soc. (presidium, dep. sec.). Avocation: tennis. Office: Ill Natural History Survey 1816 S Oak St Champaign IL 61820 Office Phone: 217-244-9578. Office Fax: 217-244-0729.

DMITROVSKY, ETHAN, oncologist, medical educator, researcher; b. Phila., 1954; BS, Harvard Coll., 1976; MD, Cornell U. Med. Coll., 1980. Intern NY Hosp. - Meml. Sloan-Kettering Cancer Ctr., NYC, 1980—81, resident in internal medicine, 1981—83; med. staff fellow Nat. Cancer Inst., NIH, Bethesda, Md., 1983—86, fellow in biotechnology, Molecular Genetics Section-Navy Med. Oncology Br., 1986—87; clin. asst. physician Meml. Sloan-Kettering Cancer Ctr., 1987—89, asst. prof., 1989—92, named head lab. molecular medicine, 1992, named assoc. mem. Sloan Kettering Inst. molecular pharmacology and therapeutics program, 1994; named assoc. prof. medicine Cornell U., 1992; Andrew G. Wallace Prof., chmn. dept. pharmacology and toxicology Dartmouth Med. Sch., 1998—, acting dean, 2002—03. Spkr. in field. Contbr. articles to profl. jours., more than 100 pubs.; mem. editl. bds. (major oncology jours.) Jour. Nat. Cancer Inst., Cancer Rsch., Clin. Cancer Rsch., Jour. Clin. Oncology, Molecular Cancer Therapeutics; assoc. editor: Encyclopedia of Cancer. Mem.: Am. Soc. Clin. Investigation, Am. Soc. Clin. Oncology (young investigator award), Am. Assn. Cancer Rsch., Am. Cancer Soc. Achievements include research on mechanisms of human tumor cell growth and differentiation helping to advance cancer therapy and prevention; helped clone the abnormal retinoid receptor found in acute promyelocytic leukemia and led the team that developed the molecular test used to diagnose this disease. Office: Dartmouth Med Sch 1 Rope Ferry Rd Hanover NH 03755-1404

DMOCHOWSKI, ROGER, urologist, educator; s. Sheila Dmochowski and Leon; m. Suzanne Sykora, Nov. 10, 1986; children: Colin Edward, Nicolas Roman. MD, U. Tex., Galveston, 1983. Diplomate Am. Bd. Urology. Staff urologist Naval hosp. U.S. Navy, Portsmouth, Va., 1989—93; dir. of resident edn. Ea. Va. Med. Sch., Norfolk, 1990—93; clin. instr. in surgery Uniformed Svcs. U. of Health Scis., Bethesda, Md., 1990—91, clin. asst. prof. in surgery, 1991—2006; asst. prof. dept. of urology U. Tenn., Memphis, 1994—95, assoc. prof. depts. of urology/gynecology, dir. divsn. of neurourology, 1996—98; med. dir. North Tex. Ctr. for Urinary Control, 1998—2001; prof. dept. of urology Vanderbilt U. Med. Ctr., Nashville, 2001—. Admissions com. Vanderbilt U. Sch. of Medicine, Nashville, 2004—; vis. prof. Walter Reed Army Med. Ctr., Tulane U. Med. Ctr., Kans. Med. Ctr.; lectr. in field. Contbr. chapters to books, articles to profl. jours. Recipient Zimskind award, Urodynamics Soc., 1999. Fellow: ACS; mem.: Internat. Continence Soc. (sci. com. 2003—06, edn. com. 2003—06), Am. Urogynecologic Soc., Cociete' Internationale d'Urologie, Soc. of Genitourinary Reconstructive Surgeons, Urodynamicc Soc., Soc. of Govt. Svcs. Urologists, Southeastern Sect. Am. Urologic Assn., Soc. of Female Urology and Urodynamics (v.p. 2003—06, pres. 2006—), Am. Urologic Assn. (safety com. 2003—, Blue Ribbon com. 2005—06, chair practice parameters and guidelines com. 2005—06, pub. rels. com. 2005—06). Office: Vanderbilt Univ Med Ctr A-1302 Medical Ctr N Nashville TN 37232-2765 Office Phone: 615-343-5602.

DMYTRYSHYN, BASIL, historian, educator; b. Poland, Jan. 14, 1925; arrived in U.S., 1947, naturalized, 1951; s. Frank and Euphrosinia (Senchak) Dmytryshyn; m. Virginia Roehl, July 16, 1949; children: Sonia, Tania. BA, U. Ark., 1950; MA, U. Ark, 1951; PhD, U. Calif., Berkeley, 1955; diploma (hon.), U. Kiev-Mohyla Acad., 1993. Asst. prof. history Portland (Oreg.) State U., 1956-59, assoc. prof., 1959-64, prof., 1964-89, prof. emeritus, 1989—, assoc. dir. Internat. Trade and Commerce Inst., 1984-89. Vis. prof. U. Ill., 1964-65, Harvard U., 1971, U. Hawaii, 1976, Hokkaido U., Sapporo, Japan, 1978-79; adviser U. Kiev-Mohyla Acad., 1993. Author books including: Moscow and the Ukraine, 1918-1953, 1956, Medieval Russia, 900-1700, 4th edit., 2000, Imperial Russia, 1700-1917, 4th edit., 1999, Modernization of Russia Under Peter I and Catherine II, 1974, Colonial Russian America 1817-1832, 1976, A History of Russia, 1977, U.S.S.R.: A Concise History, 4th edit., 1984, The End of Russian America, 1979, Civil and Savage Encounters, 1983, Russian Statecraft, 1985, Russian Conquest of Siberia 1558-1700, 1985, Russian Penetration of the North Pacific Archipelago, 1700-1799, 1987, The Soviet Union and the Middle East, 1917-1985, 1987, Russia's Colonies in North America, 1799-1867, 1988, The Soviet Union and the Arab World of the Fertile Crescent, 1918-1985, 1994, Imperial Russia, 1700-1917, 1999, Medieval Russia, 850-1700, 2000; contbr. articles to profl. jours. U.S., Can., Yugoslavia, Italy, South Korea, Fed. Republic Germany, France, Eng., Japan, Russia, Ukraine. State bd. dirs. PTA, Oreg., 1963-64; mem. World Affairs Coun., 1965-92. Named Hon. Rsch. Prof. Emeritus, Kyungnam U., 1989—; Fulbright-Hays fellow W. Germany, 1967-68; fellow Kennan Inst. Advanced Russian Studies, Washington, 1978; recipient John Mosser award Oreg. State Bd. Higher Edn., 1966, 67; Branford P. Millar award for faculty excellence Portland State U., 1985, Outstanding Retired Faculty award, 1994; Hillard scholar in the humanities U. Nev., Reno, 1992. Mem. Am. Assn. Advancement Slavic Studies (dir. 1972-75), Am. Hist. Assn., Western Slavic Assn. (pres. 1990-92), Can. Assn. Slavists, Oreg. Hist. Soc. (hon. mem. coun.), Nat. Geog. Soc., Conf. Slavic and East European History (nat. sec. 1972-75), Am. Assn. for Ukrainian Studies (pres. 1991-93), Ctr. Study of Russian Am. (hon.), Assn. Study Nationalities (bd. mem.-at-large USSR and Ea. Europe 1993—), Czechoslovak Soc. Arts and Scis., Soc. Jewish-Ukraine Contacts Assn., Salem City Club. Home: 5291 Woodscape Dr SE Salem OR 97306

DO, TWEE T., orthopedist; BS in Microbiology, U. Iowa, 1989, MD, 1993. Diplomate Am. Bd. Orthop. Surgeons. Resident in orthop. surgery U. Colo., Denver, 1993—98; fellow in pediat. orthopedics Hosp. for Spl. Surgery, NYC, 1998—99; asst. prof. orthop. surgery Children's Hosp. Med. Ctr., Cin., 1999—; clin. affiliate U. Cin. Orthopedics, 1999—. Mem. adv. bd. Girls on the Run, Cin., 2002—03; dir. neuromuscular orthop. Children's Hosp., Cin., 2002—. Contbr. articles to profl. jours., chapters to books. Mentor Cin. Youth Collaborative, 2003—. Fellow Travelling fellow, Japanese Orthop. Assn., 2004; grantee Allergon Rsch. grantee, Allergon Corp., 2003, Rsch. grantee, U. Cin. Orthop. Rsch. and Edn. Fund, 2003. Fellow: Am. Acad. Orthop. Surgeons, Am. Acad. Pediats.; mem.: Pediat. Orthop. Soc. N.Am. Avocations: camping, gardening, baking, running, mountain biking. Office: Cincinnati Children's Hosp 3333 Barnet Ave Cincinnati OH 45229 Office Phone: 513-636-4785. E-mail: twee.do@cchmc.org.

DOAK, NANCY ANN, mathematics educator; b. Phila., Feb. 4, 1960; d. Joseph Robert and Marie Florence Doak; 1 child, Michael Christopher. BS in Math/Secondary Edn., Millersville U., Pa., 1982; MA in Edn., Arcadia U., Glenside, 2002. Cert. tchr. N.J., 1984, Pa., 1982. Tchr. math. Lakewood H.S., NJ, 1984—. Creator (power point presentations) Probability and Statistics. Recipient Tchr. of Yr., Lakewood Bd. Edn., 2000. Mem.: N.J. Edn. Assn. Achievements include development of several programs that could help students pass the HSPA. Home: 66 Schoolhouse Rd Chalfont PA 18914 Office: Lakewood HS 855 Somerset Ave Lakewood NJ 08701 Home Phone: 215-822-2387; Office Phone: 732-905-3525. Personal E-mail: goldeneagle2m@verizon.net. Business E-Mail: ndoak@piners.org.

DOAN, GERALD XUYEN VAN, lawyer; b. Hadong, Vietnam, Apr. 1, 1949; s. Quyet V. Doan and Binh T. Kieu; m. Binh Thanh Tran, 1980; children: Quy-Bao, Ky-Nam. Licence en droit, U. Saigon Law Sch., Vietnam, 1971; MBA, U. Ark., 1977; JD, U. Calif., Hastings, 1982. Bar: Saigon 1972, Calif. 1982. Sole practice, Costa Mesa and San Jose, Calif., 1982-84; ptnr. Doan & Vu, San Jose, 1984-90; prin. Law Offices of Xuyen V. Doan, 1990-95; ptnr. Doan & Tran, San Jose, 1995—2003; prin. Law Offices of Xuyen V. Doan, San Jose, 2003—. Author: Of the Seas and Men, 1985, other publs. in English and Vietnamese. Named Ark. Traveler Ambassador of Good Will, State of Ark., 1975. Office: 300 S First St Ste 320 San Jose CA 95113 Personal E-mail: xvdoan@yahoo.com. Business E-Mail: doanesq@yahoo.com.

DOAN, KIRK HUGH, lawyer; b. Independence, Iowa, Jan. 30, 1953; s. Arthur Nelson and Kathlyn (Kingsley) D.; m. Laura Leah Brown, M.D., Sept. 25, 1982. BS, Iowa State U., 1975; JD, U. Iowa, 1978. Bar: Mo. 1978, Kans. 2006, U.S. Dist. Ct. (we. dist.) Mo. 1978, U.S. Dist. Ct. Kans. 1998, U.S. Dist. Ct. Appeals (8th cir.) 1989, U.S. Supreme Ct. 1990. Assoc. Stinson Morrison Hecker, LLP, Kansas City, Mo., 1978-83, ptnr., 1983—. Contbr. articles to profl. jours. Advisor Heart of Am. coun. Boy Scouts Am., 1982—; counsel Met. Med. Soc. Greater Kansas City; capt. U.S. CAP. Mem. Mo. Bar Assn., Kansas City Met. Bar Assn., Lawyers Assn. Kansas City (pres. young lawyers sect. 1984-85, treas. sr. sect. 1991-94, bd. dirs. 2004-), Greater Kans. City Soc. Health Care Attorneys (pres. 2004), Am. Heart Assn. (bd. dirs. Kans. City divsn. 2007—), Order of Coif, Lakewood Oaks Country Club. Republican. Methodist. Home: 4300 NW Lake Dr Lees Summit MO 64064-1425 Office: Stinson Morrison Hecker LLP 1201 Walnut Ste 2600 Kansas City MO 64106-2150 Home Phone: 816-478-1627. Business E-Mail: kdoan@stinson.com.

DOAN, LURITA ALEXIS, federal agency administrator; b. New Orleans, 1958; m. Douglas C. Doan. BA, Vassar Coll.; M in Renaissance Lit., U. Tenn. Knoxville. Founder, pres., CEO New Technology Mgmt., Inc., 1990—2005; adminstr. U.S. Gen. Svcs. Adminstrn., 2006—. Mem. steering com. Women's Majority Network; mem. presdl. search com. Vassar Coll., mem. bd. trustees; mem. Com. of 200, Coun. on Competitiveness, No. Va. Technology Coun. Mem. bd. trustees Shakespeare Theatre. Mem.: Minority Bus. Network, Women in Technology Internat., Nat. Assn. Female Execs., Nat. Assn. Women Bus. Owners. Office: 1800 F St NW Washington DC 20405-0002 Office Phone: 202-501-0800. E-mail: lurita.doan@gsa.gov.*

DOAN, MARY FRANCES, advertising executive; b. Vallejo, Calif., Apr. 16, 1954; d. Larry E. and Dudley (Harbison) D.; m. Timothy Warren Hesselgren, Mar. 19, 1988; children: Edward Latimer, Clinton Robert. BA in Linguistics, U. Calif., Berkeley, 1976; M in Internat. Mgmt., Am. Grad. Sch. Internat. Mgmt., 1980. Trading asst. The Capital Group, LA, 1980-81; fin. analyst Litton Industries, Beverly Hills, 1981-82; account exec. Grey Advt., San Francisco, L.A., 1982-84, J. Walter Thompson, San Francisco, 1984-85, Lowe Marshalk, 1985-86; account supr. Young & Rubicam, 1986-89; acct. mgr. Saatchi & Saatchi, 1989—95, CEO, pres., 1995—96, worldwide dir. client svc. applications, 1997—98; cons., 1999; v.p. mktg. Roundl, San Francisco, 1999-2000; cons., 2001—02; v.p. mktg. and advt. Good Guys, 2002—04, cons., 2005—. Office Phone: 415-504-6977. Personal E-mail: mfdoan@hotmail.com.

DOAN, MICHAEL FREDERICK, editor; b. Oakland, Calif., Feb. 5, 1942; s. Philip Melville and Agnes Blair (Gee) Doan; m. Mary Pickett Craddock, May 11, 1985; 1 child, Sara. BA in Journalism, U. Calif., Berkeley, 1963. Corr. AP, Las Vegas, 1968-69, econs. corr. Washington, 1970-79; assoc. editor U.S. News and World Report, Washington, 1979-87; editor Satellite Orbit mag., Vienna, Va., 1987-92; sr. assoc. editor Kiplinger Washington Editors, 1992-99; editor Kiplinger Calif. Letter, 2000—. Treas. United Meth. Ch., Washington. With USAR, 1964—70. Mem.: Washington Press Club (chmn. membership, sec. 1980—87). Methodist. Avocations: skiing, biking, jazz piano. Home: 3316 21st Ave N Arlington VA 22207-3821 Office: Kiplinger Washington Editors 1729 H St NW Washington DC 20006-3925 E-mail: mdoan@kiplinger.com.

DOAN, SHANE, professional hockey player; b. Halkirk, Alta., Can., Oct. 10, 1976; s. Bernie; m. Andrea Doan; children: Gracie, Joshua. Right wing Winnipeg Jets (now Phoenix Coyotes), 1995—96, Phoenix Coyotes, 1996—, capt., 2003—. Player Team Can., World Championships, 2003, Team Can., World Cup of Hockey, 2002. Charity work United Blood Svcs. Named to, Western Conf. All-Star Team, 2004. Achievements include winning gold medal with team Canada, World Championships, 2003; being a member of World Cup Champion Team Can., 2004. Avocations: golf, horseback riding. Office: Phoenix Coyotes Hockey Club 5800 W Glenn Dr Ste 350 Glendale AZ 85301-2471

DOANE, EILEEN MALONEY, learning disabilities teacher consultant; b. Welcome, Md., Dec. 5, 1933; d. John Laurence and Lillian Marion (Posey) Maloney; m. Allan Hammond Doane, June 12, 1954; children: Kathleen, Sharon, Elizabeth. BA in Speech Arts, George Washington U., 1955; MA in Edn., Seton Hall U., 1983; postgrad. studies Learning Disabilities, Kean Coll., 1987; PhD, Berne U., 2002. Cert. tchr. of handicapped, speech correction, prin., supr., learning cons., N.J. Mem. child study team Elizabeth (N.J.) Bd. Edn. Spl. Svcs., 1990-95; learning disability tchr. cons., instrnl. supr. Matheny Sch. and Hosp., Peapack, NJ, 1995—; owner, dir. Randolph Denville Ednl. Ctr., Denville. Mem. Outreach Com. St. Peter's Epsicopal Ch., Mountain Lakes, N.J., adult edn. com. Mountain Lakes. Recipient cert. appreciation Vol. Action Ctr., Morristown, N.J, Mental Health Players, Morris County Mental Health Assn., Madison, N.J., 1987, Benefactor award Rotary Found., Evanston, Ill., 1995; named Paul Harris fellow Rotary Found., 1984. Mem. AAUW, N.J. Assn. Learning Cons., Coun. Exceptional Children, Kappa Delta Pi. Democrat. Avocations: bridge, reading, travel. Office: Randolph Denville Ednl Ctr 3125 Rt 105 Denville NJ 07834 Office Phone: 973-328-8088.

DOANE, TIM, travel company executive; BBA in Mktg. and Mgmt., U. Cin., 1979; MBA in Mktg. and Fin., Miami U., Ohio. With Travel Centers of Am., Westlake, Ohio, 1995—, sr. v.p., mktg., pres., COO, 2003—05, pres., CEO, 2005—. Office: Travel Centers of Am 24601 Center Ridge Rd Westlake OH 44145

DOANE, W. ALLEN, water transportation executive; b. Jan. 17, 1948; BA, Brigham Young Univ., 1969; MBA, Harvard Univ., 1975. Mgmt. positions C. Brewer Co., 1975—85; group v.p. IU Internat. Corp., 1985—88; COO The Shidler Group, 1988—90; exec. v.p., COO A&B Hawaii Inc., Honolulu, 1991—95, pres., 1995—99, CEO, 1997—99; exec. v.p. Alexander & Baldwin Inc., Honolulu, 1998, pres., CEO, 1998—, chmn., 2006—, Matson Navigation Co. Inc. Bd. dir. First Hawaiian Bank, BancWest Corp., Pacific Guardian Life Ins. Co. Officer USN. Office: Alexander & Baldwin Inc 822 Bishop St Honolulu HI 96813*

DOBBERPHUL, DANIEL, engineering company executive; BS, U. Ill. Engr. Digital Equipment Corp., SiByte Inc.; v.p., gen. mgr. processor div. Broadcom Corp.; co-founder, pres., CEO P.A. Semi Inc., Santa Clara, Calif., 2003—. Named one of 40 forces to shape the future of the Semiconductor Industry, EE Times, 1998; recipient Solid State Circuits Award, IEEE, 2003. Mem.: NAE. Office: PA Semi, Inc 3965 Freedom Cir, 8th Fl Santa Clara CA 95054-1203

DOBBIN, EDMUND J., former academic administrator; b. Bklyn., 1935; BA in Philosophy, Villanova U., 1958; MA, Augustinian Coll., 1962; SDT, U. Louvain, Belgium, 1971. ordained priest Roman Cath. Ch., 1962. Tchr. math. and religion, prefect of students Malvern Prep. Sch., 1962-67; tchr. systematic theology Washington Theol. Union, 1971-87, asst. prof., assoc. prof.; assoc. prof. Villanova U., Pa., 1987—, pres., 1988—2006. Trustee Villanova U., 1979-87, Merrimack Coll., North Andover, Mass., 1971-89, chmn. bd., 1986-89; mem. provincial coun. Augustinian Province of St. Thomas of Villanova, 1982-89. Mem. Am. Acad. Religion, Cath. Theol. Soc. Am. Office: Villanova U 3rd Middleton Hall 800 E Lancaster Ave Villanova PA 19085 Office Phone: 610-519-6856. E-mail: edmund.dobbin@villanova.edu.

DOBBINS, BENJAMIN KNOX, lawyer; b. Decatur, Ga., Jan. 12, 1951; m. Carolyn Black; 1 child, Amanda. AB magna cum laude, Cornell U., 1973; JD cum laude, Harvard U., 1976. Bar: Ga. 1976. Ptnr. Sutherland, Asbill & Brennan, 1983—. Spkr. in field. Bd. dirs. Atlanta Preservation Ctr.; alumnus Leadership Atlanta; mem. Midtown Alliance bd. dir's. Named Best Lawyers Am., 2003—04, 2006—07, Ga. Super Lawyer, 2006; recipient H. Sol Clark award, by State Bar, 2001. Mem. State Bar Ga. (mem. com. indigent def., pro bono com.), Atlanta Bar Assn., Lawyers Club Atlanta, Phi Beta Kappa, ABA (pro bono exec. com. bus. law sect.). Office: Sutherland Asbill & Brennan 999 Peachtree St NE Ste 2300 Atlanta GA 30309-3996 Office Phone: 404-853-8053. Business E-Mail: knox.dobbins@sablaw.com.

DOBBINS, DAVID FOSTER, lawyer; b. Cleve., Aug. 22, 1928; s. Verne Foster and Ida Wells (Smith) D.; m. Iris McKee, Sept. 27, 1953 (div. 1983); children: David Jr., Carol, James. BA, Yale U., 1950; LLB, Columbia U., 1956. Bar: N.Y. 1957, U.S. Ct. Appeals (2nd cir.) 1957, U.S. Dist. Ct. (so. and ea. dists.) N.Y. 1958, Ohio 1961, U.S. Ct. Appeals (9th cir.) 1978, U.S. Ct. Appeals (1st cir.) 1980, U.S. Ct. Appeals (5th cir.) 1980, U.S. Ct. Appeals (3rd cir.) 1981, U.S. Ct. Appeals (8th cir.) 1982, U.S. Supreme Ct. 1983, U.S. Ct. Appeals (10th cir.) 1985. Assoc. Dwight, Royall, Harris, Koegel & Caskey, NYC, 1956-57; law clk. to Hon. Leonard P. Moore U.S. Ct. Appeals (2nd cir.), NYC, 1957-58; assoc. Dwight, Royall, Harris, Koegel & Caskey, NYC, 1958-60, Lane, Krotinger & Santoka, Cleve., 1961-62; assoc. to ptnr. Royall, Koegel, Rogers & Wells, Cleve., 1962-77; ptnr. Patterson, Belknap, Webb & Tyler LLP, Cleve., 1977—2000, of counsel, 2001—. Bd. dirs. All-O-Matic Inds., Jackson Heights, N.Y., 1988. Mem. bd. govs. Young Republican Club, N.Y.C., 1962-68. Lt. (j.g.), USN, 1950-53. Mem. ABA, Assn. of Bar of City of N.Y., Ken Court Club, Phi Delta Phi. Republican. Episcopalian. Avocations: jogging, climbing, skiing. Office: Patterson Belknap Webb & Tyler LLP 1133 Ave Americas New York NY 10036

DOBBINS, JIM (JAMES FRANCIS DOBBINS JR.), think-tank executive, former federal agency administrator; b. NYC, May 31, 1942; s. James Francis and Agnes Ann (Bent) D.; m. Toril Kleivdal, Dec. 31, 1969; children: Colin, Christian. BSFS, Georgetown U., 1963. Commd. fgn. svc. officer US Dept. State, 1967; staff U.S. del. Paris Peace Talks, 1968; mem. policy planning staff US Dept. State, Washington, 1969-71; consul Am. Embassy, Strasbourg, France, 1971-73; spl. asst. to U.S. rep. UN, NYC, 1973-75; spl. asst. to counselor US Dept. State, Washington, 1975-76, officer in charge French affairs, 1976-78; polit.-mil. officer Am. Embassy, London, 1978-81; dir. office theatre military policy US Dept. State, 1981-82, dep. asst. sec. Washington, 1982-85; dep. chief mission Am. Embassy, Bonn, Fed. Republic Germany, 1985-89; prin. dep. asst. sec. for European/Can. affairs US Dept. State, 1989-91, amb. to the European Communities, 1991-93, acting asst. sec. for European/Can. affairs, 1991, spl. coord. for Somalia Washington, 1993, spl. Haiti coord., 1994-96; sr. dir. Inter-Am. affairs The White House, Washington, 1996-99, spl. adv. to Pres., 1999-2000, spl. adv. sec. state for Kosovo and Dayton Implementation, 1999-2000; asst. sec. for European affairs US Dept. State, Washington, 2000—01, spl. envoy to Afghan opposition, 2001—02; dir. internat. security and def. policy centre The RAND Corp., Arlington, 2002—. Lt. (j.g.) USN, 1963-66. Recipient Superior Honor award, US Dept. State, 1982, Presdl. award 1989, 92, 97, Expeditionary medal Vietnam, 7 sr. performance awards US Dept. State, 1993. Office: The RAND Corp Internat Security & Def Policy Centre 1200 S Hayes St Arlington VA 22202-5050 E-mail: James_Dobbins@rand.org.

DOBBS, DAN BYRON, lawyer, educator; b. Ft. Smith, Ark., Nov. 8, 1932; s. George Byron and Gladys Pauline (Stone) D.; m. Betty Jo Teeter, May 31, 1953 (div. 1978); children: Katherine, George, Rebecca, Jean. BA, LL.B., U. Ark., 1956; LL.M., U. Ill., 1961, J.S.D., 1966. Bar: Ark. 1956. Partner firm Dobbs, Pryor & Dobbs, Ft. Smith, 1956-60; asst. prof. law U. N.C., Chapel Hill, 1961-63, assoc. prof., 1963-66, prof., 1967, Aubrey L. Brooks prof. law, 1975-77; Rosenstiel prof. law U. Ariz., 1978—, Regents prof., 1992—. Vis. asst. prof. U. Tex., summer 1961; vis. prof. U. Minn., 1966-67, Cornell Law Sch., 1968-69, U. Va. Law Sch., 1974, U. Ariz. Law Sch., 1977-78 Author: Handbook on the Law of Remedies, Damages, Equity, Restitution, 1973, Problems in Remedies, 1974, The Law of Remedies, 3 vols., 2d edit., 1993, The Law of Torts, 2000; co-author: Prosser and Keeton on Torts, 5th edit., 1984, Torts and Compensation, 1985, 5th edit., 2005, (with Paul Hayden), 1997, (with Ellen Bublick) Economic and Dignitary Torts, 2006; contbr. articles to legal jours. Office: U Ariz Law Coll Tucson AZ 85721-0001 Business E-Mail: dobbs@law.arizona.edu.

DOBBS, GREGORY ALLAN, journalist; b. San Francisco, Oct. 9, 1946; s. Harold Stanley and Annette Rae (Lehrer) D.; m. Carol Lynn Walker, Nov. 25, 1973; children: Jason Walker, Alexander Adair. BA, U. Calif., Berkeley, 1968; MSJ, Northwestern U., 1969. Assignment editor, reporter Sta.

KGO-TV, San Francisco, 1966-68; news dir. San Francisco Tourist Info. Program Service, 1968; editor ABC Radio, Chgo., 1969-71; prodr. ABC News, Chgo., 1971-73, corr., 1973-77, London, 1977-82, Paris, 1982-86, Denver, 1986-92; host The Greg Dobbs Show/Sta. KOA Radio, 1992—98; corr. Nat. Geographic TV, 2001—03; host The Greg Dobbs Morning Show KNRC Radio, Denver, 2002—04; host Colo. State of Mind Rocky Mt. PBS, 2003—; chief corr. HDNet TV, 2004—. Adj. prof. Northwestern U. Sch. Journalism, 1975, 76; prof. U. Colo. Sch. Journalism, 1996—; chief corr. Nat. Geog. TV, HD Net TV. Columnist The Denver Post, 1996—2001, Rocky Mountain News, 2001—05, nationally syndicated columnist Scripps Howard, 2001—05. Recipient Sigma Delta Chi Disting. Svc. award for TV reporting Soc. Profl. Journalists, 1980, Emmy award for the best news reporting on a network 1980, outstanding documentary, 1989, award of excellence Colo. Broadcasters Assn., 1993, 94, award for best talk show Colo. Soc. Profl. Journalists, 1994, Emmy Best Interview/Discussion program, 2003; Lippmann fellow Ford Found., 1975; named Best Talk Show Host in Denver, Westword Mag., 2002 Office: 1153 Bergen Pkwy Ste M150 Evergreen CO 80439-9501 Office Phone: 303-670-1977. E-mail: dobbs@newslike.com.

DOBBS, HERBERT HOTALING, automotive executive, consultant, research scientist, retired military officer; b. Mpls., July 5, 1931; s. Willis Clark and Mary Evalyn (Hotaling) D.; m. Joyce Belle Roberts, Mar. 20, 1954; children: Herbert H., Jr., Douglas Edwin, Graeme Clark. BSME, U. Minn., 1954; MSME, U. Mich., 1961, PhD in Mech. Engring., 1972; grad., U.S. Army Command and Gen., 1972, U.S. Army War Coll., 1977. Registered profl. engr., Mich. Commd. 2d. lt. U.S. Army, 1954, advanced through grades to col., 1977, assigned to Italy, 1955-57, assigned to Vietnam, 1966—67, assigned to Taiwan, 1975—76, ret., 1983; tech. dir. U.S. Army Tank-Automotive Command, 1983-85; dir. Torvec, Inc., Pittsford, NY, 1998—, chmn., 1998—2002, sec. bd. dir., 2005—. Design engr. Aerojet Gen. Corp., Sacramento, 1957; mem indsl. adv. bd. mech. engring. dept. Wayne State U., 1986—, Oakland U. Sch. Engring. and Computer Sci., 1986-; cons. Dobbs Assocs., Rochester Hills, Mich., 1986—; cons. Office Naval Rsch. USN, 1997; mem. or cons. U.S. Army Sci. Bd., 1994-2006; various govt. adv. bds., 1986-; mem. adv. bd. Nat. Jr. Sci. and Humanities Symposium, 1995—. Contbr. articles to profl. jours.; patentee for turbulent flow research work and military research and development work. State chmn. MSPE Mathcounts, 1986—. Decorated Legion of Merit, US Army, 1983, Bronze Star, 1966, Meritorious Svc. Medal, 1975, 1981; Joint Svcs. Commendation Medal, US Mil. Adv. and Assistance Group, Taiwan, 1976; recepient Silver Medal, Am. Defense Preparedness Assn. (now Nat. Defense Industrial Assn.), 1992. Fellow Mich. Soc. Profl. Engrs. (named Engr. of Yr. 1995), Soc. Automotive Engrs. Internat; mem. AIAA, ASME, AAAS, NSPE, Soc. Automotive Engrs., Soc. Mfg. Engrs., Assn. Unmanned Vehicle Systems Internat., Res. Officers Assn., Assn. U.S. Army, Detroit chpt., exec. bd. 1985-99, chmn. jr. sci. and humanities seminar 1988-99, Armor Assn., Nat. Def. Indsl. Assn. Avocations: reading, mathematics, woodworking, opera. Home: 448 Maryknoll Rd Rochester Hills MI 48309 Office: Torvec Inc Powder Mills Office Pk 1169 Pittsford-Victor Rd Ste 125 Pittsford NY 14534-9501 Office Phone: 248-375-2558. Business E-Mail: dr.hh.dobbs@earthlink.net.

DOBBS, JOHN BARNES, artist, educator; b. Nutley, NJ, Aug. 2, 1931; s. John Montgomery and Catherine (Barnes) D.; m. Anne Baudement, 1959; children: Nicolas, Michel. Student, R.I. Sch. Design, 1949, Bklyn. Mus. Art Sch., 1950-52, Skowhegan Sch., 1952. Prof. studio art John Jay Coll. CUNY, NYC, 1974-96. Over 30 one-man shows in U.S. and France; group exhbns. include Am. Acad. Arts and Letters (Childe Hassam purchase prize 1972, Art award 1994), Whitney Mus., Nat. Acad. Design (Ranger Fund purchase prize 1966, 90, Benjamin Altman prize 1980, Edwin Palmer prize 1991, Obrig prize 2003), Mus. Modern Art, Butler Inst. Am. Art, Salon des Independents. Cpl. U.S. Army, 1952-54, ETO. Louis Comfort Tiffany grantee, 1967 Mem. NAD (academician), Century Club. Home: 463 West St Apt B339 New York NY 10014-2032

DOBBS, JOHN MCGREGOR, physicist, mechanical engineer; b. Hankow, China, June 30, 1936; arrived in U.S., 1942; s. Francis Edward Litton Dobbs and Alice Gibb; children: Candlin Hamilton, Alexander Cathcart, Charlotte Litton. BSME, U. Pa., 1959, MS in Physics, 1960, PhD in Particle Physics, 1965. Asst. prof. Washington U., St. Louis, 1966—73; pvt. practice cons. engr. St. Louis and Boston, 1973—75; prin. engr., divsn. mgr. Analogic Corp., Wakefield, Mass., 1975—80, v.p., chief scientist, 1981—84, Peabody, Mass., 1992—; v.p., tech. dir. Gen. Ionex, Newburyport, Mass., 1980—81; pres., CEO Ion Beam Tech., Beverly, Mass., 1984—86; pvt. practice cons. product devel. Boston area, 1986—88; chmn., chief tech. officer Autogen Instruments, Beverly, 1988—89; dir. bioinstrumentation devel. Milligen Divsn. Millipore, Burlington and Milford, Mass., 1989—92. Contbr. articles to profl. publs. Fellow: IEEE; mem.: Am. Assn. Physicists in Medicine, Am. Phys. Soc. Achievements include research in particle physics and engineering; 24 patents in field. Avocations: kayaking, wood and metal working, home repair. Office: Analogic Corp 8 Centennial Dr Peabody MA 01960 Office Phone: 978-326-4715. Business E-Mail: jdobbs@analogic.com.

DOBBS, JOHNNIE, retail executive; BBA, East Tex. State U. Various civilian logistic related positions US Army, 1978; distbn. ctr. gen. mgr. Service Merchandise; joined Wal-Mart Stores Inc., 1990, gen. mgr., regional mgr., dir. distbn. and logistics for SAM'S CLUB, v.p. membership and sales SAM'S CLUB, v.p. specialty distbn. and transportation, divisional v.p. logistics, divisional sr. v.p. logistics, exec. v.p. logistics and supply chain, 2006—. Mem.: Retail Industry Leaders Assn. (chmn. logistics steering com.). Office: Wal-Mart Stores Inc Bentonville AR 72716-8611

DOBBS, LOU (LOUIS EARL DOBBS), commentator, former broadcast executive; b. Childress, Tex., Sept. 24, 1945; m. Debi Segura; children: Chance, Jason, Hilary, Heather. Degree in econs., Harvard U., 1967. Copy reader LA Times; chief econs. corr., anchor Moneyline CNN, NYC, 1980-81, anchor Primenews, 1981, v.p., mng. editor bus. news, 1984-97, pres. news, exec. v.p., 1997-98, anchor Moneyline Tokyo, 1989; host TV spl. Nobel Minds Stockholm, 1993; anchor Moneyline Chgo., 1992-1999; sr. v.p., 1992-97; exec. v.p., 1997-98; founder, CEO., chmn. space.com, 1999—2001; pres. CNNfn, 1995—99; exec. v.p. CNNfn.com, 1995—99; anchor, mng. editor CNN's Lou Dobbs Tonight, 2001—; anchor syndicated fin. news radio report Lou Dobbs Fin. Report, 2001—. Mem. Loeb Award judges com.; bd. mem. Soc. Profl. Journalists Found., Horatio Alger Assn., Nat. Space Found., Space.com. Columnist Money mag., NY Daily News, US News and World Report; author: Exporting America: Why Corporate Greed is Shipping American Jobs Overseas, 2004, Space: The Next Business Frontier, 2005, War on the Middle Class: How the Government, Big Business and Special Interest Groups are Waging War on the American Dream and How to Fight Back, 2006. Recipient George Foster Peabody award for coverage of 1987 stock market crash, Luminary award Bus. Journalism Rev., 1990, CableAce award, Front Page award, NY Film Festival award, Janus award, Daniel Webster award, Emmy awards, Award for Disting. Am., Horatio Alger Assn., 1999, Media award, Nat. Space Club, 2000, Eugene Katz award For Excellence in the Coverage of Immigration, Ctr. for Immigration Studies, 2004, Alexis de Tocqueville Instn. Statesmanship award, 2005; named Father Yr., Nat. Father's Day Com., 1993. Mem. NATAS, Investigative Reporters and Editors Assn., Am. Econ. Assn., Nat. Acad. TV Arts and Scis., Overseas Press Club, Planetary Soc., Sigma Delta Chi.

DOBBS, MICHEAL W., lawyer; b. Houston, Feb. 18, 1973; BS, Tex. A&M U., 1995; JD magna cum laude, U. Houston, 1999. Bar: Tex. 1999, US Dist. Ct. (no. and so. dists. Tex.), US Dist. Ct. (ea. and we. dists. Ark.). Assoc. McFall, Sherwood & Breitbeil, P.C., Houston, Cowles & Thompson, P.C., Dallas, Connelly, Baker, Maston, Wotring & Jackson LLP, Houston, 2001—. Named a Rising Star, Tex. Super Lawyers mag., 2006. Mem.: Houston Bar Assn., Houston Young Lawyers Assn., Tex. Young Lawyers Assn.*

DOBELL, BYRON MAXWELL, magazine consultant; b. Bronx, NY, May 30, 1927; s. Jacob and Marie (Schaeffer) D.; m. Edith Spielberg, 1952 (div. 1957); m. Ande Rubin, 1958 (dec. 1967); 1 dau., Elizabeth; m. Elizabeth Rodgers Dempster, 1969 (dec. 1992); m. Alexandra Mayes Birnbaum, 1999. AB, Columbia U., 1947. Picture editor U.S. Camera, 1952-55; assoc. editor Popular Photography, 1956-57; feature editor Pageant, 1957-58, This Week, 1958-60; sr. editor Time-Life Books, 1960-62, assoc. dir. editl. planning, 1971-72; mng. editor Esquire mag., NYC, 1962-67, 79-82, editor-in-chief, 1977, Book World (weekly lit. supplement Chgo. Tribune and Washington Post), 1967-69; editor-in-chief book divsn. McCall Pub. Co., 1969-71; editl. dir. New York mag., 1972-77; sr. editor Life mag., NYC, 1978-79; editor-in-chief Am. Heritage mag., 1982-90, Am. Heritage of Invention & Tech. mag., 1984-90; mag. cons. NYC, 1990—. Bd. dirs. Am. Soc. Mag. Editors, 1987-91. Editor: Life Guide to Paris, A Sense of History. Bd. advisors Libr. of Am., 2003—07. With US Army, 1946—47. Named to Am. Soc. of Mag. Editor's Hall of Fame, 1998. Mem.: Century Assn. Home and Office: 145 E 76th St New York NY 10021-2843 Home Phone: 212-861-0256; Office Phone: 212-861-0256.

DOBERENZ, ALEXANDER R., retired nutrition educator, chemist; b. Newark, Aug. 17, 1936; s. Alexander J. and Marie (Zink) D.; m. Angela Rajoppi, June 7, 1958; children: Annamarie Wexler, Judith Lynn, Hoke Jr. BS in Chemistry, Tusculum Coll., 1958; MS, U. Ariz., 1960, PhD in Biochemistry and Nutrition, 1963. Rsch. assoc. dept. physics U. Ariz., Tucson, 1963-69; vis. assoc. prof. nutrition U. Hawaii, 1969; assoc. prof. nutritional scis. U. Wis., Green Bay, 1969-71, prof., 1971-76, assoc. dean Coll. and Sch. Profl. Studies, 1969-76, prof. growth and devel., 1975-76; prof. food sci. and human nutrition U. Del., Newark, 1976-97, dean Coll. Human Resources, 1976-93, coord. home econs. rsch., 1978-93, spl. asst. to the pres., 1993, interim v.p. for student life, 1994-95, prof. nutritional scis., Coll. of Health and Nursing Scis., 1997-99, prof. emerita, 1999—. Cons. food industry, 1976-93; nat. steering com. new initiatives for home econs. U.S. Dept. Agr., 1979-81, USDA Planning com. Workshops on Improving Health Maintenance, 1984-87. Contbr. numerous articles on food chemistry and nutrition to profl. publs. Head underwater recovery unit Pima County Sheriff's Dept., 1966-68; warrant officer CAP, 1965-69; mem. Brown County Comprehensive Health Planning Coun., 1973-76; bd. dirs. Pima County Sheriff's Search and Rescue, 1968. Recipient Rsch. Career Devel. award NIH, 1966-69; named Outstanding Educator Am., 1971-72. Fellow Am. Inst. Chemists; mem. Am. Chem. Soc., Am. Home Econs. Soc., Am. Inst. Nutrition (Mead Johnson award nominating com. 1973-76), Nutrition Soc. Today, Soc. for Nutrition Edn., Nutrition Soc. London Soc. Exptl. Biology and Medicine, Am. Soc. Clin. Nutrition, AAAS, Assn. Adminstrs. of Home Econs., Del. Gerontol. Soc. (exec. com. 1978), Nat. Coun. Adminstrs. Home Econs. (exec. bd. 1982-83), APHA, Del.-Panama Ptnrs. of Ams., Assn. for Devel. Computer Based Instruction, Del. Acad. Sci., Univ. and Whist Club, Sigma Xi, Phi Lambda Upsilon., Phi Kappa Phi. Roman Catholic. Business E-Mail: ard@udel.edu.

DOBERSEN, MICHAEL JOSEPH, pathologist, researcher; b. Bay Village, Ohio, May 13, 1949; s. Arthur Joseph and Dolores (Warnock) Dobrzeniecki; m. Deborah Ann Thomas, Sept. 28, 1985; children: Andrew Thomas, Amy Kathryn. BS, Kent State U., 1971; PhD magna cum laude, U. Miami, 1976; MD with honors, U. Colo., Denver, 1989. Cert. med. technologist Am. Soc. Clin. Pathologists. Teaching asst. dept. biology Kent (Ohio) State U., 1971-72; rsch. asst. dept. microbiology U. Miami (Fla.) Sch. Medicine, 1972-76, postdoctoral investigator, 1976-77; staff fellow Nat. Inst. Dental Rsch., NIH, Bethesda, Md., 1977-82, sr. staff fellow Nat. Inst. Neurol.-Communicative Disorders and Stroke, 1982-84; asst. prof. dep. microbiology and Barbara Davis Ctr. for Childhood Diabetes U. Colo. Sch. Medicine, 1985-5, resident in pathology, 1989—. Mem. animal care com. NIH, 1977-82, mem. trans.-NIH diabetes coordinating com., 1980-82; cons. Devel. Psychobiology Rsch. Group, Denver, 1986-87. Co-author: Understanding Gestational Diabetes: A Practical Guide To a Healthy Pregnancy, 1989; contbr. numerous articles on virology and autoimmune diseases to sci. jours., also chpts. to books in field. Mem. So. Poverty Law Ctr., Community for Creative Nonviolence, Union Concerned Scientists. Mem. AMA, Coll. Am. Pathologists, Am. Soc. Clin. Pathologists. Democrat. Avocations: pottery, guitar, skiing, sports. Office: U Colo Sch Med Dept Pathology 4200 E 9th Ave Denver CO 80220-3706

DOBEY, JAMES KENNETH, banker; b. Vallejo, Calif., June 20, 1919; s. Austin E. and Margaret (Hansen) D.; m. Jean Smith, Apr. 18, 1942 (dec. Feb. 2007); children: James A., Peter M. AB, U. Calif., Berkeley, 1940; postgrad., Rutgers U., 1956. With Shell Oil Co., Comml. Credit Corp., 1940-42, Wells Fargo Bank, San Francisco, 1946-72, exec. v.p., 1965-72, vice chmn. bd., 1973, chmn. bd., 1977-80, ret. Capt. airborne inf. AUS, 1942-46. Mem. Delta Chi. Mailing: Carmel Valley Manor 8545 Carmel Valley Rd Carmel CA 93923-9556

DOBKIN, JAKE, online publishing executive, blogger; b. Bklyn. Student, Columbia Univ.; MBA, NYU. Co-founder, pub. Gothamist online blog. Featured (articles) LA Times, NY Observer, NY Sun, NY Times, Village Voice, San Francisco Bay Guardian, others, appearances (networks) UPN, Fox TV. Nominee Best NY Blog, NY mag., 2004; recipient Best NY Blog award, NY Press, 2004, RAVE award for blogs, Wired mag., 2007. Office: Gothamist Prince St Sta PO Box 510 New York NY 10012 Business E-Mail: jake@gothamist.com.*

DOBLER, DONALD WILLIAM, retired procurement and materials executive, dean; b. Rocky Ford, Colo., Apr. 18, 1927; s. William L. and Anna (Nelson) Dobler; m. Elaine Carlson, Dec. 27, 1951; children: Kathleen, David, Daniel. BS in Engring., Colo State U., 1946-50; MBA, Stanford U., 1958, PhD, 1960. Application and sales engr. Westinghouse Elec. Corp., Pitts. and Phila., 1950-53; mgr. procurement and materials FMC Corp., Green River, Wyo., 1953-57; guest lectr. Stanford Sch. Bus., 1960; asst. prof. mgmt. State U. Utah, Logan, 1960-63, assoc. prof., 1964-66, head dept. bus. adminstrn., 1964-66; vis. prof. mgmt. Dartmouth Coll., 1963-64; dean Coll. Bus., Colo. State U., Ft. Collins, 1966-86; ind. mgmt. cons. Ft. Collins, 1986-91; corp. v.p. for cert. and program devel. Inst. Supply Mgmt., Tempe, Ariz., 1990-94. Pres. Parklane Arms, Inc., 1967—77; part-time mgmt. cons., 1960—86; cons. European Logistics Mgmt. Program, 1970, 72, 77, European Fedn. Purchasing, 1970; faculty Mgmt. Ctr. Netherlands, 1972; mem. dean's adv. coun. logistics mgmt. program Ariz. State U., 1991—94; mem. adv. bd. Mgmt. Inst. U. Wis., 1992—97; past bd. dirs. U. Nat. Bank, Home Fed. Savs. Bank. Sr. author: Purchasing and Supply Management, 1965, 6th edit., 1996; co-author: The Purchasing Handbook, 1993; mem. editl. bd. European Jour. Purchasing and Supply Mgmt., 1993—; contbr. articles to profl. jours., chapters to books. Mem. Colo. Gov.'s Adv. Com., 1968—77, Ft. Collins Mayor's Budget Com., 1968—71; dist. chmn. Boy Scouts Am., 1974—77; mem. adv. coun. Colo. region SBA, 1973—79, mem. adv. coun. no. region Colo. divsn. employment, 1975—77; bd. dirs., divsn. chmn. Ft. Collins United Way, 1973—80, pres., 1977; bd. dirs. Ft. Collins Jr. Achievement, 1973—87, Colo. Assn. Commerce and Industry Ednl. Found., 1988—91. With USNR, 1945—46. Mem.: Am. Assn. Collegiate Schs. Bus. (nat. com. continuing accreditation 1972—78, nat. stds. commn. 1978—81, dir. 1980—83, chmn. fin. and audit com. 1983), Acad. Mgmt., Am. Prodn. and Inventory Control Soc., Denver Purchasing Mgmt. Assn. (dir. 1975—83, v.p. 1977, pres. 1979), Nat. Assn. Purchasing Mgmt. (assoc. editor Internat. Jour. Purchasing and Materials Mgmt. 1975—80, chmn. nat. acad. plan com. 1976—81, editor Jour. 1980—97, profl. cert. bd. 1981—86, chmn. 1985—86, Shipman medalist 1987), Green River Jr. C. of C. (pres. 1955), Rotary, Beta Gamma Sigma (nat. gov. 1975—78), Phi Kappa Phi (editl. cons. Nat. Forum 1988—94), Sigma Tau. Methodist.

DOBOSIEWICZ, ELIZABETH J., lawyer; m. Kurt R. Saccone, June 3, 2000; children: Alexandra, Christopher, Katherine. BA with hons., cum laude, Canisius Coll., Buffalo, NY, 1986—90; JD cum laude, SUNY Buffalo Sch. Law, NY, 1990—93. NY Supreme Ct., Appellate Divsn., 2nd Dept.: 1994. Gen. atty. US Dept. of Justice, Immigration & Naturalization Svc., New York, NY, 1993—95, asst. dist. counsel Philadelphia, Pa., 1995—97, dep. dist. counsel, 1997—99; assoc. atty. Jaeckle Fleischmann & Mugel LLP, Buffalo, 1999—2001, Phillips Lytle LLP, Buffalo, 2001—04; ptnr. Saccone & Dobosiewicz LLP, Buffalo, 2005—. Sec., upstate NY chpt. Am. Immigration Lawyers Assn., Buffalo, 2000—02, treas., upstate NY chpt., 2002—04, vice-chair, upstate NY chpt., 2004—06, chair, upstate NY chpt., 2006—. Recipient Robert J. Connelly Award for Excellence in Trial Practice, Western NY Trial Lawyers Assn., 1992, Commissioner's Atty. of the Yr. award, Immigration and Naturalization Svc., 1996. Mem.: Am. Immigration Lawyers Assn., Alpha Sigma Nu (life). Office: Saccone & Dobosiewicz LLP 300 International Drive Williamsville NY 14221 Office Phone: 716-810-9220.

DOBRANSKI, BERNARD, dean, law educator; b. Sept. 3, 1939; s. Walter John and Helen Dolores (Rudnick) Dobranski; m. Caroll Sue Wood, Aug. 31, 1963; children: Stephanie, Andrea, Christopher. BBA in Fin., U. Notre Dame, 1961; JD, U. Va., 1964. Bar: Va. 64, U.S. Supreme Ct. 68, U.S. Ct. Appeals (DC cir.) 71. Legal advisor to bd. Nat. Labor Rels. Bd., 1964—67; profl. staff mem. Pres.'s Adv. Commn. on Civil Disorders, 1967—68; adminstrv. asst. U.S. Ho. of Reps., 1968—71; gen. counsel Washington Met. Area Transit Commn., 1971—72; mem. faculty Creighton U. Sch. of Law, Omaha, 1972—77, U. Notre Dame, 1977—83; prof., dean U. Detroit Sch. of Law, 1983—95, Cath. U. Am. Sch. of Law, 1995—99; prof., pres., dean Ave Maria Sch. of Law, Ann Arbor, Mich., 1999—. Contbr. articles to profl. jours. Mem.: ABA, Detroit Athletic Club, Hurlingham Club, Frank Murphy Honor Soc. Roman Catholic. Office: Ave Maria Sch of Law 3475 Plymouth Rd Ann Arbor MI 48105 Home Phone: 734-424-2376; Office Phone: 734-827-8043. Business E-Mail: bdobranski@avemarialaw.edu.

DOBRASKO, REBEKAH, cultural organization administrator, historian; b. Akron, Ohio, June 1, 1979; d. Michael and Mary Dobrasko. BA cum laude with departmental honors in History, Tulane U., New Orleans, 2001; MA in Pub. History, U. SC, Columbia, 2005. Edn. asst. Hermann-Grima/Gallier Hist. Houses, New Orleans, 2001—02; intern City of Columbia Planning Dept., Preservation Office, Columbia, SC, 2004—04; info. mgmt. specialist State Hist. Preservation Office, Columbia, 2003—05, rev. and compliance coord., 2005—. Historian/cons. SC. Civil/Human Rights Anthology, Columbia, 2004—. Contbr. archive collection, scientific papers to profl. jour. Hist. preservation vol. Hist. Columbia, SC, 2003—06. Fellow, Keepers Preservation Edn. Fund, 2004, Joseph P. Logsdon Fellowship, Amistad Rsch. Ctr., 2000. Mem.: Palmetto Trust Hist. Preservation, Southeastern Soc. Archtl. Historians, SC Hist. Assn., Nat. Coun. Pub. History, Nat. Trust Hist. Preservation. Office: SC Dept Archives and History 8301 Parklane Rd Columbia SC 29223 Office Phone: 803-896-6169. Business E-Mail: dobrasko@scdah.state.sc.us.

DOBRAY, ALAN MICHAEL, theoretical physicist, research scientist; b. Waukegan, Ill., Aug. 25, 1954; s. Michael Dobray and Ann Davis Ziezel; 1 son, Shane Alan. Mech. engr. Texaco Oil, Lake Forest, Ill., 1975-79; fabricating engr. Connor Gear Machine and Transmission Svcs., Highland Park, Ill., 1983-84; elec. engr. Inland Marine, Waukegan, 1985; theoretical physicist N.Y. Acad. Scis., NYC, 1996—; rsch. scientist AAAS, Washington, 1998—. Mem. Nat. Space Soc., 1996. Co-author: (textbook) Gang Delinquency in an American Suburb, 1983; inventor in field of ice boats. Active Duff Olympics, 1982-83, Silver Moon Blues Oasis, 1995—; mem. Secular Humanist Soc., Chgo. Recipient Hon. Mem., MIT Alumni Assn., 1996; scholar Milw. Sch. Engring., 1970. Mem. Union of Concerned Scientists, Planetary Soc., Wilderness Soc., Libr. of Congress. Democrat. Achievements include helping solve the telemetry problem for NASA and having name engraved on computer chip used on Cassini space probe to Saturn and all subsequent missions leaving earth's orbit. Avocations: ice sailing, planting trees, playing horse-shoes, drums. Home: N 3325 Jute Rd Lake Geneva WI 53147 Home Phone: 262-249-0791; Office Phone: 262-249-0791.

DOBRIANSKY, LEV EUGENE, economics professor, diplomat; b. NYC, Nov. 9, 1918; s. John and Eugenia (Greshchuk) Dobriansky; m. Julia Kusy, June 29, 1946; children: Larisa Eugenia, Paula Jon. BS (Charles Hayden Meml. scholar), NYU, 1941, MA, 1943, Hirshland polit. sci. fellow, 1943—44, PhD, 1951; LLD, Free Ukrainian U. at U. Munich, 1952. Mem. faculty NYU, 1942—48; from asst. prof. econs. to prof. Georgetown U., Washington, 1948—86; prof. emeritus, 1986—; chmn. dept. Georgetown U., 1953—54; exec. mem. Inst. Ethnic Studies, 1957—65; dir. Inst. Comparative Econ. and Polit. Sys., 1970—86; grad. faculty Nat. War Coll., 1957—58; U.S. ambassador to Bahamas, 1982—86; pres. Global Economic Action Inst., 1987—92; chmn. Victims of Communism Meml. Found., Inc., 1994—2003. Lectr. on Soviet Union, Communism, U.S. Fgn. Policy; chmn. Nat. Captive Nations Com., Inc., 1959—; pres. Ukrainian Congress Com. Am., 1949-82, Am. Coun. for World Freedom, 1976-79; mem. Economists Nat. Com. on Monetary Policy; strategy staff Am. Security Coun., 1962-70; econs. editor Washington Report; mem. Pres.'s Commn. on Population, 1974-75; cons. Corpus Instrumentation, Kreber Found., Dept. State, 1971-75, USIA, 1971-74; mem. Am. Com. to Aid Katanga Freedom Fighters, Emergency Com. Chinese Refugees; Internat. mem. Pacific Rim Cmty. Inst., 1992-96; hon. pres. Ukrainian Congress com. Am., 1992—. Author: A Philosophico-Economic Critique of Thorstein Veblen, 1943, The Social Philosophical System of Thorstein Veblen, 1950, Free Trade Ideal, 1954, Communist Takeover of Non-Russian Nations in USSR, 1954, Veblenism: A New Critique, 1957, Captive Nations Week Resolution, 1959, Shevchenko Statue Resolution, 1960, Vulnerabilities of USSR, 1963, The Vulnerable Russians, 1967, U.S.A. and the Soviet Myth, 1971; co-author: The Great Pretense, 1956, The Crimes of Khrushchev, 1959, Decisions for a Better America, 1960, Nations, Peoples, and Countries in the USSR, 1964, PL 103-199, Victims of Communism Memorial, 1993; pub.: Revista Americana, 1977; editor: Europe's Freedom Fighter: Taras Shevchenko, 1960, Tenth Anniversary of the Captive Nations Week Resolution, 1969, The Bicentennial Salute to the Captive Nations, 1977, Twentieth Observance and Anniversary of Captive Nations Week, 1980; assoc. editor: (1946-62) Ukrainian Quar., chmn. editorial bd., 1962-94, The Making of a Memorial, 2007; contbr.: Peace and Freedom Through Cold War Victory, 1964, Nationalism in the USSR and Eastern Europe, 1977, Ukraine in a Changing World, 1978; contbr. articles to profl. jours. Planning mem. Freedom Studies Center, Boston; asst. sec. Republican Nat. Conv., 1952; adviser Rep. Nat. Com., 1956; mem. Com. on Program and Progress of Rep. Party, 1959; asst. to chmn. Rep. Nat. Conv., 1964; vice chmn. nationalities div. Rep. Nat. Com., 1964; sr. adviser United Citizens for Nixon-Agnew, 1968; exec. mem. ethnic div. Com. to Reelect the Pres., 1972; advisor to Gov. Reagan, 1980; issues dir. Republican Nat. Com., 1980; chmn. Ukrainian Catholic Studies Found., 1970-73; bd. govs. Charles Edison Youth Fund, 1976-87; mem. expert adv.

bd. NBC, Washington, 1977-80. chmn. Victims of Communism Meml. Found. Inc., chmn. emeritus, 2003-. Lt. col. (res.) 352d Mil. Govt. Civil Affairs 1958; col. U.S. Army Res., 1966. Recipient Freedoms Found. award, 1961, 73; Shevchenko Freedom award Shevchenko Meml. Com., 1964; Shevchenko Sci. Soc. medal, 1965; Hungarian Freedom Fighters' Freedom award, 1965; Latvian Pro Merito medal, 1968; Freedom Acad. award Korea, 1969; Wisdom award of honor Calif., 1970; named Outstanding Am. Educator, 1973; decorated M.S.M., 1973; Georgetown U. Centennial medal of honor, 1982; Ellis Island medal of honor, 1986; Thomas C. Corcoran award, 1987; Lifetime Achievement award, 2005; Truman, Reagan Freedom award, 2005. Mem. Free World Forum (exec. com.), Citizens for Democracy, Acad. Polit. Sci., Nat. Acad. Econs. and Polit. Sci., AAUP, Am. Acad. Polit. and Social Sci., Am., Cath. econ. assns., Am. Finance Assn., Nat. Soc. Study Edn., Shevchenko Sci. Soc., U.S. Global Strategy Council, Social List of Washington, Council Am. Ambassadors, NYU Alumni Assn., Georgetown U. Alumni Assn. (hon.), Reagan Alumni Assn., Internat. Cultural Soc. Korea (hon.), Am. Legion, Res. Officers Assn., Nat. War Coll. Alumni Assn., University Club of Washington (hon.), Capitol Hill Club, Internat. Club, Gold Key Soc., Beta Gamma Sigma, Delta Sigma Pi. Achievements include helped in the unveiling of the Goddess of Democracy memorial in Washington.

DOBRIANSKY, PAULA JON, federal agency administrator, ambassador; b. Sept. 14, 1955; d. Lev Eugene and Julia Kusy Dobriansky. BS summa cum laude, Georgetown U., 1977; MA, Harvard U., 1980, PhD, 1991; LHD (hon.), Fairleigh Dickinson U., 2002, Westminster Coll., 2005, Roger Williams U., 2005; LLD (hon.), Flagler Coll., 2003. Adminstrv. aide Dept. Army, Washington, 1973-76; staff asst. Am. Embassy, Rome, 1976; rsch. asst. joint econ. com. U.S. Congress, Washington, 1977-78; NATO analyst Bur. Intelligence and Rsch. US Dept. State, Washington, 1979; staff mem. NSC, White House, Washington, 1980-83, dep. dir. European and Soviet affairs, 1983-84, dir. European and Soviet affairs, 1984-87; dep. asst. sec. of state Human Rights and Humanitarian Affairs, 1987-90; dep. head U.S. Del. to Conf. on Security and Cooperation in Europe, Copenhagen, 1990; assoc. dir. for policy and programs U.S. Info. Agy., 1990-93; co-chair internat. TV coun. Corp. Pub. Broadcasting, 1993-94; sr. internat. affairs and trade advisor Hunton and Williams, Washington, 1994-97; sr. v.p., dir. Washington Office Coun. on Fgn. Rels., 1997—2001; under sec. for global affairs US Dept. State, 2001—05, under sec. for democracy and global affairs, 2005—, spl. envoy to No. Ireland, 2007—. Commr. U.S. Adv. Commn. on Pub. Diplomacy, 1997-2001; adj. fellow Hudson Inst., 1993-2001. Host: Freedom's Challenge, Nat. Empowerment Television, 1994-96; co-host: Worldwise, 1997. Bd. dirs. Congl. Human Rights Found., 1994-95, Freedom House, 1999-2001, Western NIS Enterprise Fund, 1994-2001, Am. Com. for Aid to Poland, 1994-95, ABA Ctrl./East European Law Initiative, 1994-99; mem. bd. visitors George Mason U., 1994-98; mem. adv. bd. Horton Internat. Inc., 1998-99. Decorated Grand Cross of Comdr. Order of Lithuanian Grand Duke Gediminas, Star of Romania; named Ethnic Woman of Yr., 1990; named to Order of Merit, Hungary's Commander's Cross, 2007; recipient Georgetown U. Alumni Achievement award, 1986, State Dept. Superior Honor award, 1990, Poland's Highest medal of Merit, 1998, Dialogue on Diversity Internat. award, 2001, Democracy Svc. medal, Nat. Endowment Democracy, 2002; fellow, Rotary Found., 1979, Ford Found., 1980; scholar Fulbright-Hays scholar, 1978. Mem. Internat. Inst. Strategic Studies, Coun. Fgn. Rels., Am. Polit. Sci. Assn., Fulbright Assn., Nat. Endowment for Democracy (bd. dirs. 1993-2001, vice-chmn. 1995-2001), Am. Coun. on Young Polit. Leaders (trustee 1993-2001), U.S. Environ. Tng. Inst. (bd. adv. 1992-93), Harvard Club (bd. dirs. 1982-85), Univ. Club, Phi Beta Kappa, Phi Alpha Theta, Pi Sigma Alpha. Office: US Dept State 2201 C St NW Washington DC 20520

DOBRIN, TORY, performing company executive, dancer; b. LA; Student, Stanley Holden Dance Ctr., LA, Harkness Ballet Sch., NYC. Dancer Les Ballets Trockadero de Monte Carlo, NYC, 1980—, asst. to dirs., 1989—93, assoc. dir., 1993—98, artistic dir., 1998—; sec., treas. Les Ballets Trockadero de Monte Carlo, Inc. Recipient Company prize for Outstanding Classical Repertoire, Nat. Dance Awards, 2007. Office: Les Ballets Trockadero de Monte Carlo Box 46 Cathedral Sta New York NY 10025 E-mail: info@trockadero.org.*

DOBROF, ROSE WIESMAN, gerontology educator; b. Denver, Nov. 11, 1924; d. Jerome and Mildred (Hornbein) Wiesman; m. Alfred Dobrof, June 8, 1948 (dec. Mar. 2001); children: Marilyn, Joan, Susan, Judy. BA, U. Colo., 1945; MSW, U. Pitts., 1948; DSW, Columbia U., 1976; DHL (hon.), SUNY, 1996, Hunter Coll., 2000, Hebrew Union Coll., 2002. Lect. div. social svcs. Ind. U., Bloomington, 1952-60; dir. group svc. and vol. dept. The Hebrew Home for the Aged at Riverdale, Bronx, N.Y., 1961-63, asst. dir., 1966-70; assoc. prof. Hunter Coll. CUNY, 1975-78, Brookdale prof. gerontology NYC, 1979—, prof. Hunter Coll., 1979-96, prof. emeritus, 2000—; exec. dir. Brookdale Ctr. on Aging Hunter Coll., NYC, 1974-93, acting v.p., 1993-94. Doctoral faculty grad. ctr. CUNY, 1979-96; profl. lectr. in cmty. medicine Mt. Sinai Sch. Medicine, 1982—, co-dir. long-term gerontol. ctr., 1979-81, co-dir. geriatric edn. ctr., 1985-96; chair gov.'s task force on long term care in year 2000, 1986; mem. gov.'s task force on older women, 1986-87; adv. com. sr. citizen affairs for Congresswoman Nita M. Lowey, 1990—; mem. N.Y. State Pub. Health Coun., 1991-95, Gov.'s Health Care Adv. Bd., 1991-94; mem. policy com. White Ho. Conf. Aging, 1995, Fed. Coun. on Aging, 1994-96; del. White Ho. Conf. Aging, 2005; adv. bd. Ctr. Aging, U. Miami, 2003. Editor-in-chief Jour. Gerontol. Social Work, 1977—. Trustee Jewish Assn. for Svcs. of the Aged, NYC, 1977-83, NY Found., trustee emerita, 2003—; bd. dirs. NYC chpt. Nat. Caucus and Ctr. for the Black Aged, 1982—, New York Found., 1996—, sec., 1999-2002, Young Adult Inst., 2004—; sr. fellow The Brookdale Found., 1985—; co-chair U.S. Com. for Celebration of UN Yr. of Older Persons, 1997-99; mem. adv. coun. Nat. Inst. Aging, 1998-2002; trustee The Dekay Found., 1999—, Burden Ctr. for the Aged, 1990— Named One of Five Outstanding Alumni, U. Pitts., 1979; recipient Outstanding Alumnus award U. Pitts., 1981, Robert Ray Parks award, 1986, Alice Brophy award The Burden Ctr., 1987, The Gift of Life award Parker Jewish Geriatric Inst., 1989, The Walter M. Beattie Jr. award N.Y. State Assn. Gerontol. Educators Inst., 1989, 1990, The Pres.'s medal Hunter Coll., 1991, Gerontology Educator Merit award, 1991, Merit award Older Women's League Greater N.Y., 1993, Elinor Guggenheimer award Coun. Sr. Ctrs. and Svcs., 1995, Lifetime Achievement award Sr. Action in a Gay Environment, 1997, Lifetime Achievement award Presbyn. Sr. Svcs., 1999, Katherine Engel award Nat. Coun. Jewish Women, 2001, Coalition Leadership award Continuing Care Leadership Coalition, 2004, Burton Blatt Disting. Leadership award Yai Nat. Inst. People with Disabilities, 2004; named to Social Work Hall Fame, Columbia U., 2002 Fellow N.Y. Acad. Medicine; mem. Acad. for the Humanities and Scis., Nat. Assn. Social Workers (Outstanding Leadership award 1983, Social Worker in Aging award 1990, Knee/Whitman award 2002), Nat. Coun. on Aging (Claude Pepper award 2000), N.Y. Acad. Sci., Am. Soc. on Aging (Sr. Achievement award 2000, Lifetime Achievement award 2005), Gerontological Soc., Am. Fedn. Aging Rsch. (bd. dirs. 1996-2004, trustee emerita 2004—), Phi Beta Kappa, Delta Sigma Rho, Pi Gamma Mu Democrat. Jewish. Avocations: bridge, swimming, gardening. Office: Brookdale Ctr on Aging Hunter College 425 E 25th St New York NY 10010 Home: 377 E 33rd St Apt 10H New York NY 10016-9478 Office Phone: 212-481-3780. Business E-Mail: rdobrof@hunter.cuny.edu.

DOBRY, RICARDO, engineering educator; b. Santiago, Chile, Dec. 7, 1937; arrived in US, 1977, naturalized; BS in Civil Engring., U. Chile, Santiago, 1963; MS in Soil Mechanics, Nat. U. Mex., 1964; ScD in Civil Engring., MIT, 1971. Cert. civil engr., Colegio de Ingenieros de Chile, 1964. Prin. Solum Assocs., Chile, 1965—68; instr. MIT, Cambridge, Mass., 1970—71; prof., head soil mechanics group U. Chile, 1971—73; assoc. prof. civil engring. Rensselaer Polytechnic Inst., Troy, NY, 1977—81, prof., 1981—. Vis. prof. U. Tex., Austin, 1984—85; dir. Geotechnical Centrifuge Rsch. Ctr., 1988—2005; dir. Ctr. Earthquake Engring. Simulation Rensselaer Polytechnic Inst., 2005—. Contbr. articles to profl. jours. Mem.: NAE, Earthquake Engring. Rsch. Inst., Network for Earthquake Engring. Simulation, Am. Soc. Civil Engrs. (J. James Croes medal 1985). Jewish. Office: Dept Civil Engring Rensselaer Polytechnic Inst 110 8th St Troy NY 12180-3590 Office Phone: 518-276-6934. Office Fax: 518-276-4833. Personal E-mail: rdobry1@nycap.rr.com.

DOBRZYNSKI, JUDITH HELEN, journalist, commentator; b. Rochester, NY, Mar. 8, 1949; d. Francis Anthony and Theresa (Contino) Dobrzynski. BS cum laude, Syracuse U., 1971. Corr. McGraw-Hill, San Francisco and NYC, 1971—75, Bus. Week, Washington, 1976—79, London, 1979—83, corp. strategies editor, assoc. editor NYC, 1983—88, sr. writer, 1988—91, sr. editor, 1991—94; bus. reporter N.Y. Times, NYC, 1995—97, culture reporter, 1997—2000, dep. bus. editor and editor Sunday Money and Bus. sect., 2000—03; mng. editor CNBC, Englewood Cliffs, NJ, 2003—05, exec. editor, 2005—. Adj. instr. Columbia U. Sch. Journalism, 2002—; mem. New Founds. Corp. Governance Group Harvard U., Boston, 1992—95; adv. panel Corp. Investment Project U.S. Coun. on Competitiveness, Washington, 1990—92. Contbr. articles to profl. jours. and book revs. Trustee CEC Internat. Ptnrs., NYC, 1993—96; bd. dirs. City Lights Youth Theatre, NYC, 1994—96. Recipient Nat. Headliner award 1st Pl. in Bus. and Consumer TV Journalism, 2004, 2005; Knight Found. fellow, Salzburg Seminar, 2002. Mem.: Syracuse U. Newhouse Sch. Alumni Assn. (bd. dirs. 1991—94, pres. 1992—93), Century Assn. Office: CNBC 900 Sylvan Ave Englewood Cliffs NJ 07632 Office Phone: 201-735-3001. E-mail: jhdobrzynski@nyc.rr.com.

DOBS, ADRIAN SANDRA, endocrinologist, educator; b. June 27, 1952; m. Martin Auster; children: Nina Auster, Becky Auster, Harry Auster, Paul Auster. BS in Nutrition Scis., Cornell U., 1973; MD, Albany Med. Coll., 1978; MHS in Cardiovascular Epidemiology, Johns Hopkins U., 1990. Diplomate Nat. Bd. Med. Examiners, Am. Bd. Internal Medicine, Am. Bd. Endocrinology and Metabolism. Resident in internal medicine Montefiore Hosp. Med. Ctr./Albert Einstein Coll. Medicine, Bronx, NY, 1978-81, chief resident, 1981-82; instr. medicine, physicians asst. program CCNY, NYC, 1981-82; endocrinology fellow Johns Hopkins U., Balt., 1982-84, instr. divsn. endocrinology and metabolism, 1984-87, asst. prof. medicine, 1987-93, assoc. prof. medicine, 1993—2005, prof. medicine, 2006—, vice chair dept. medicine, clin. rsch., 1996—. Mem. study sect., adv. com. Nat. Inst. Aging, 1992, NIH, 1993, 94; lectr. in field. Reviewer Am. Jour. Clin. Nutrition, Am. Jour. Medicine, Diabetes Care, Jour. AMA, Jour. Clin. Endocrinology and Metabolism, New Eng. Jour. Medicine; contbr. articles, abstracts to profl. jours., chpts. to books. Recipient Rsch. award Women Physicians Stetler Found., 1986-87; scholar Leopold Schepp Found., 1975, Vanderbilt U., 1976, Carnegie-Mellon Found., 1984-85, Robert Glassner Found. Diabetes Rsch., 1985-86; grantee Merck, Inc., 1991-93, TheraTech, Inc., 1991-94, NIH, 1992-93, 92—, Diabetes Rsch. and Edn. Found., 1992-93, Johns Hopkins Out-patient Clin. Rsch. Ctr., 1992-93. Mem. ACP, Am. Coll. Nutrition, Am. Diabetes Assn. (award Md. chpt. 1986-87), Am. Fedn. Clin. Rsch. (Johns Hopkins rep. 1990—, sch. coun. 1990—), Am. Heart Assn. (epidemiology coun. 1985, grantee 1990-94), Endocrine Soc. Home: 3510 Anton Farms Rd Baltimore MD 21208-1703 Office: Johns Hopkins Hosp 1830 Monument St Baltimore MD 21287-0005 Office Phone: 410-955-2130. Business E-Mail: adobs@jhu.edu.

DOBSON, DONALD ALFRED, retired electrical engineer; b. Evanston, Ill., Feb. 19, 1928; s. Alfred Topping and Agnes Lucille (Park) D. BSEE, Northwestern U., 1950, PhD, 1955; MSEE, MIT, 1951. Research assoc. Northwestern U., Evanston, 1951-54; engr. Indsl. Research Products, Franklin Park, Ill., 1952; sr. engr. Sperry Gyroscope Co., Great Neck, NY, 1954-59; sr. tech. specialist N.Am. Aviation, Columbus, Ohio, 1959-63; research staff mem. Inst. for Def. Analyses, Arlington, Va., 1963-90, adj. staff mem., 1990-98, ret., 1998. Instr. physics Adelphi Coll., Garden City, N.Y., 1956 Mem. IEEE, Sigma Xi, Tau Beta Pi, Eta Kappa Mu, Pi Mu Epsilon Home: 6800 Fleetwood Rd Apt 420 Mc Lean VA 22101-3607

DOBSON, DOROTHY LYNN WATTS, retired elementary school educator; b. Santa Monica, Calif., Nov. 29, 1954; d. Seymour Locke and Margaret (Cheeseman) Watts; m. J. Cody Dobson, June 5, 1982; children: Jeremiah, Hannah. BS, Utah State U., 1975; MEd, U. Utah, 1982. Cert. tchr. intellectually handicapped and behaviorally handicapped, elem., Utah. Tchr. San Juan Sch. Dist., Blanding, Utah, 1974-76; behavioral specialist Salt Lake Sch. Dist., Salt Lake City, 1976-77; tchr. Granite Sch. Dist., Salt Lake City, 1977-82; instr. Utah State U., Logan, 1981—2003; tchr. Edith Bowen Lab. Sch., Logan, 1982—2004. Team coord. First Amendment Schs., Bowen Lab. Sch., Logan, 2002—. Author: Utilizing Newspapers in Social Studies, Math. and Science and Language Arts, 1983; also articles. Mem. Nat. Coun. for Social Studies (bd. dirs. 1996-99, Nat. Elem. Tchr. of Yr. 1992, State Farm Good Neighbor award 1993), Utah Coun. for Social Studies (State Elem. Tchr. of Yr. 1991), Nat. Assn. Lab. Schs. Episcopalian. E-mail: dordob@direcway.com.

DOBSON, JAMES CLAYTON, psychologist, author; b. Shreveport, La., Apr. 21, 1936; s. James Clayton Sr. and Myrtle Georgia (Dillingham) D.; m. Shirley Mae Deere, Aug. 27, 1960; children: Danae A., J. Ryan. BA in Psychology, Pasadena City Coll., Calif., 1958; MS, U. So. Calif., 1962, PhD in Child Devel., 1967; LLD, Pepperdine U., 1983; DHum (hon.), Franciscan U., 1988; DHL, Seattle Pacific U., 1988, Liberty U., 1993, Biola U., 1995; others. Lic. psychologist, marriage, family and child counselor. Psychometrist, tchr. Hudson Sch. Dist., Hacienda Heights, Calif., 1962-63; psychometrist, counselor Charter Oak H.S., Covina, Calif., 1963-64; sch. psychologist, coord. pers. svcs. Charter Oak Unified Dist., Covina, 1964-66; asst. prof. pediatrics U. So. Calif. Sch. Medicine, LA, 1969-77, assoc. clin. prof., 1978-83; attending staff div. med. genetics Childrens Hosp. of L.A., 1969-83; pres., chmn Focus on the Family, Colorado Springs, Colo., 1977—2004, chmn., 2004—. Author, speaker, radio and TV host shows relating to successful family living, 1965—; bd. dirs. Focus on the Family/Can., Vancouver, B.C., 1982—; bd. dirs. Family Rsch. Coun., 1992—. Author: Dare to Discipline, 1970, Hide or Seek, 1974, The Strong Willed Child, 1978, Preparing for Adolescence, 1978, Love Must Be Tough, 1983, Straight Talk, 1991, When God Doesn't Make Sense, 1994, Life of the Edge, 1995, Heart of the Family, 1996, Solid Answers, 1997, Bringing Up Boys:Practical Advice and Encouragement for Those Shaping the Next Generation of Men, 2001, Marriage Under Fire: Why We Must Win This Battle, 2004, The New Strong-Willed Child: Birth Through Adolescence, 2004, 5 Essentials for Lifelong Intimacy (Home Counts), 2005, others; contbr. chpts. to books, articles to profl. jours. Del. White House Conf. on Families, 1980; mem. Nat. Adv. Commn. on Juvenile Justice and Delinquency Prevention, 1982-84; mem. U.S. Army Task Force on Families, 1986-87, chmn., 1988; mem. Atty. Gen.'s Adv. Bd. on Missing and Exploited Children, 1987-88; mem. Sen. Dole Commn. on Child and Family Welfare, 1994, Nat. Gambling Impact Study Commn., 1997. Served with U.S. Army, 1958-59. Recipient Humanitarian award Calif. State Psychol. Assn., 1988, Alumni Merit award U. So. Calif. Gen. Alumni Assn., 1989; HHS grantee; NIH grantee, 1975-80; named one of 25 Most Influential Evangelicals in Am. Time mag., 2005. Office: Focus on the Family 8605 Explorer Dr Colorado Springs CO 80920-1051*

DOBSON, PARRISH, photographer, educator; d. Peyton Hoge and Parrish Cummings Houston; m. Eugene H. Pool, May 9, 1943; 1 child, Miranda Parrish Pool. BA, Yale U., 1971; MA, Brandeis U., Waltham, Mass., 1980. Dir. careers for girls W.I.S.E., Hanover, NH, 1973—75; dir. women's studies programs Colby-Sawyer Coll., New London, NH, 1975—78; English tchr. Philips Acad., Andover, Mass., 1980—84; photograhy tchr. Buckingham, Browne and Nichols Sch., Cambridge, 1986—. Bd. mem. Kendall Ctr. for Arts, Belmont, Mass., 1996—99; mem. adv. bd. North Haven (Maine) Arts and Enrichment, 1999—; chair arts dept. Buckingham, Browne and Nichols Sch., Cambridge, 2001—. Exhibitions include DoMaine Gallery, Portland, Maine, Cambridge Ctr. for Arts, 1999—2005, The Gallery at 357 Main St., Rockland, Maine, 2003, Botolph Club, 2004. Artist grantee, Mass. Cultural Coun., 1998. Mem.: New Eng. Women in Photography Steering Com., St. Botolph Club (artist assoc. hon. mem.). Avocations: travel, walking, gardening. Home: 263 Payson Rd Belmont MA 02478 Office: Buckingham Browne and Nichols Sch Gerry's Landing Rd Cambridge MA 02138 Studio: 4 Bradley St Somerville MA Office Phone: 617-800-2291.

DOBSON, RICHARD LAWRENCE, dermatologist, educator; b. Boston, Apr. 12, 1928; s. Joseph William and Celia Beatrice (Siegler) D.; children: Richard Lawrence, Pamela Blair, Lisa Marie; m. Rhoda H. Freda, Feb. 14, 2004. MD, U. Chgo., 1953; BS, U. N.H., 1981. Diplomate Am. Bd. Dermatology (v.p. 1987-88, pres. 1988-89). Intern Cin. Gen. Hosp., 1953-54; resident Hitchcock Clinic, Hanover, NH, 1954-57; asst. prof. dermatology U. N.C., Chapel Hill, 1957-61; prof. U. Oreg., Portland, 1961-72, SUNY-Buffalo, 1972-79, Med. U. S.C., Charleston, 1980-98, acting dean, 1985-86, chmn. dept. anatomy and cell biology, 1991-92, prof. emeritus, 1998—. Vis. prof. U. Nijmegen, The Netherlands, 1969-70; hon. prof. Shanghai 2d Med. U.; hon. cons. Royal Prince Alfred Hosp., Sydney, Australia. Editor: Year Book of Dermatology, 1979-82, Clinical Dermatology, 1972-82, Contemporary Review, 1973-87; asst. editor: Jour. Am. Acad. Dermatology, 1979-87, editor, 1988-98; mng. editor Arch. Dermatol. Research, 1982-87. Served with USN, 1946-47. Fellow ACP, Am. Acad. Dermatology (pres. 1983-84); mem. Am. Dermatologic Assn. (treas. 1977-82), Soc. Investigative Dermatology (pres. 1975-76), Oreg. Dermatol. Soc. (pres. 1971-72); hon. mem. Brit. Assn. Dermatology, Spanish Assn. Dermatology, French Dermatology Soc., Polish Dermatology Soc., Finnish Dermatology Soc., Dutch Dermatology Soc., German Dermatology Soc., N.Am. Dermatology Soc., Ga. Dermatology Soc., Iowa Dermatology Soc., Snee Farm Club. Republican. Roman Catholic. Office: Med U SC 171 Ashley Ave Charleston SC 29425-0001 Home Phone: 843-884-7550; Office Phone: 803-792-5858. Personal E-mail: rowda@aol.com.

DOBSON, RICK, metals company executive; BS in bus. admin., U. Wis.; MBA in fin., U. Nebr. Cert. CPA. Audit mgr. Arthur Andersen, 1981—89; v.p., contr. Aquila Merchant Svcs., 1989—95; v.p., risk mgmt. acctg. Aquila, Kans. City, Mo., 1997, interim CFO, 2002—03, CFO, 2003—06; CFO, sr. v.p. Novelis, Inc., 2006—. Office: Novelis Inc 3399 Peachtree Rd NE Ste 1500 Atlanta GA 30326

DOBSON, ROBERT ALBERTUS, III, lawyer, volunteer; b. Greenville, SC, Nov. 27, 1938; s. Robert A. Jr. and Dorothy (Leonard) D.; m. Linda Josephine Bryant, Nov. 18, 1956; children: Robert, William, Michael, Daniel, Jonathan, Laura (dec.); m. Catherine Elizabeth Cornmesser, Sept. 17, 1983; children: Andrew, Thomas, Juana. BS in Acctg. summa cum laude, U. S.C., 1960, JD magna cum laude, 1962; DPS, Limestone Coll., 2002. Asst. dean of students U. S.C., 1960-62; pvt. practice pub. acctg. Greenville, 1962-64; ptnr. Dobson & Dobson, Greenville, 1964-93. Chmn., bd. trustees Limestone Coll., 1987-89, founder Christian edn. and leadership program; trustee The King's Coll., 2003—. Contbr. articles to profl. jours. Sr. warden St. Francis Episcopal Ch., Greenville; chmn. bd. Dobson Tape Ministry, Homeless Children Internat., Inc.; bd. dirs. A Child's Haven, Inc.; chmn. Walker Found. for the SC Sch. for the Deaf and Blind, Spartanburg, SC; adv. bd. Salvation Army, Greenville; chmn. bd. Sch. Ministries, Inc.; active History's Handful Campus Crusade for Christ; founder Dobson Vol. Svc. Program, U. SC; mem. bd. commrs. SC Sch. for the Deaf and Blind. Recipient Algernon Sydney Sullivan award for disting. svc. as alumnus, U. SC, 2005. Mem. ABA, S.C. Bar Assn., AICPAs, Am. Assn. Attys. and CPAs, S.C. Assn. Pub. Accts., Block C Assn. The Group, U. S.C. Alumni Assn. (cir. v.p.), Kappa Sigma (chmn. legal com. 1989-93, dist. grand master 1971-2002, Nat. Dist. Grand Master of the Yr. 1986, John G. Tower Disting. Alumni award 2000, Stephen Alonzo Jackson award 1998), Phi Beta Kappa. Lodges: Sertoma Internat. (dist. treas.), Sertoma Sunrisers (pres. Greenville club). Episcopalian.

DOBSON, SUZANNE, science educator; MS in Curriculum Instrn. and Tech., Nova Southeastern U., Ft. Lauderdale, Fla.; MA in Edn., Jacksonville State U., Ala. Tchr. Bartow County Bd. of Edn., Adairsville, Ga., 1991—; tchr. curriculum, sci. Ind. Wesleyn U., Marion, Ind., 2004—. Mem. Nat. Coun. Tchrs. Math. Tutor, lectr. Internat. Dyslexia Assn., Atlanta, 1998—2005. Recipient Tchr. of Promise award, Sci. and Engring. Fair, 1998, grants for innovative programs to be implemented in Adairsville schs., Etowah Edn. Found., 1995, 1996, 1997; scholar NASA Tchr. Enhancement Program, 1999. Fellow: Nat. Sci. Tchrs. Assn.; mem.: Internat. Reading Assn., Ga. Sci. Tchrs. Assn., Internat. Dyslexia Assn. Office: Bartow County Bd Edn 100 College St Adairsville GA 30103

DOBSON, WENDY KATHLEEN, economics professor; BSN, U. B.C., 1963; MPA, Harvard U., 1971, SM, 1972; PhD in Econs., Princeton U., 1979. Pres. C.D. Howe Inst., Toronto, 1981—87; assoc. dep. min. Dept. Fin. Govt. Can., Ottawa, Ont., 1987—89; prof., dir. Inst. Internat. Bus. Rotman Sch. Mgmt. U. Toronto, 1993—. Author: Japan in East Asia: Trade and Investment Strategies, 1993, Multinationals and East Asian Integration, 1997 (Ohira prize, 1998), Financial Services Liberalization in the WTO, 1998, Shaping the Future of North American Economic Space: A Framework for Action, 2002, Taking a Giant's Measure: Canada, NAFTA and an Emergent China, 2004, Governance, Multinationals and Growth, 2005, The Elephant Sheds Its Past, The Implications for Canada, 2006, The Contradictions in Arena's Banking Reforms, 2006; co-editor: Shaping Comparative Advantage, 1987, East Asian Capitalism: Diversity and Dynamism, 1996, Managing U.S. Japanese Trade Disputes, 1996, The People Link, 1997, Fiscal Framework and Financial Systems in East Asia, 1998, East Asia in Transition, 1999; contbr. chapters to books, articles to profl. jours. Steering com. Pacific Trade Devel. Network; adv. com. Inst. Internat. Econs., Washington; mem. Trilateral Commn.; bd. dirs. Toronto-Dominion Bank, TransCan. Pipelines, Can. Pub. Accountability Bd. Office: Rotman Sch Mgmt U Toronto 105 St George St Toronto ON M5S 3E6 Canada Business E-Mail: dobson@rotman.utoronto.ca.

DOBY, JOHN THOMAS, social psychologist; b. Gray, Ky., May 29, 1920; s. Daniel W. and Minnie (Farris) D.; m. Rose Catherine Hopper Doby, Dec. 21, 1942; children: Mary Catherine, Nancy H. AB cum laude, Union Coll., Barbourville, Ky., 1946; MS, U. Wis., 1950; PhD, 1956. From assoc. prof. to prof. sociology and anthropology Wofford Coll., Spartanburg, SC, 1950-57; assoc. prof. sociology and anthropology Emory U., Atlanta, 1958-63, prof., 1963-85, chmn. dept. sociology and anthropology, 1960-69, chmn. dept. sociology, 1980-85, prof. emeritus sociology, 1985; cons. engring. Ga. Inst. Tech., Atlanta, 1960-62; cons. Ednl. Testing Svc., Princeton, N.J., 1969; mem. faculty Grad. Sch. Consumer Banking, U. Va., summer 1972-75. Vis. scientist/lectr. NSF, 1965-66; chair tech. sci. adv. com. on mental retardation Ga. Dept. Health, 1965-66; dir. NSF Summer Inst. for Coll. Tchrs. of Sociology, Emory U., 1965-66; mem. sci. faculty panel Am. Coun. Learned Socs., Nat. Sci. Postdoctoral Panel, 1976-77. Author: Introduction to Social Research, 1954, Introduction to Social Psychology, 1966, Introduction to Social Research, 1967; editor, author: Sociology: A Study of Man in Adaptation, 1973; contbr. articles to profl. jours., chpt. to book. Maj. USAF, 1941-46. Grantee NIMH, 1960, NSF,

1964, 65, 71, OEO, 1966-67, NICHD, 1979-80. Mem.: So. Sociol. Assn. (pres. 1969—70), Am. Sociol. Assn. Methodist. Home: 473 Ky-1629 Corbin KY 40701-9469 Office Phone: 606-523-0850.

DOBYNS, BROWN MCILVAINE, retired surgeon, educator; b. Jacksonville, Ill., May 14, 1913; s. Henry D. and Leah (McIlvaine) D.; married; children— Mary Meredith, Courtney Sara, Brown McIlvaine. BA with hons., Ill. Coll., 1935; MD, Johns Hopkins, 1939; MS, U. Minn., 1944, PhD, 1946; LHD, Ill. Coll., 2005. Diplomate: Am. Bd. Surgery. Intern surgery Johns Hopkins Hosp., 1939-40; fellow surgery Mayo Found., 1940-43; resident surgery Kahler Hosp., Mayo Clinic, 1943-45, 1st asst. surgery, 1945-46, asst. surg. staff, 1946; research fellow surgery, med. sch. Harvard, 1946-48, asst. prof. surgery, 1948-51; grad. asst. surgery Mass. Gen. Hosp., 1946-48, asst. surgery, 1946-51; assoc. prof. surgery Case Western Res. U. Med. Sch., 1951-58, prof. surgery, 1958—88, prof. emeritus, 1984—88; ret., 1988. Asst. chief surg. service Cleve. Met. Gen. Hosp., 1951-88, assoc. chief surg. service, 1967-88; asst. surgeon Univ. Hosp., Cleve., 1951-88; Fulbright lectr., Australia, 1966. Mem. fellowship subcom. Com. on Growth NRC, 1950-54; mem. fellowship com. NSF, 1954-61, chmn., 1955-61; adv. screening com. med. scis. Fulbright, 1955-58; adv. com. research on etiology cancer Am. Cancer Soc., 1956-59, chmn. adv. com. on instnl. grants, 1963-65; mem. Dernham Scholarship com. Calif. Cancer Soc., 1964-74; cons. Markle Found. Selection Com., 1961-62. Recipient citation for disting. pub. svc. Ill. Coll., Outstanding Achievement award U. Minn., 1964; elected to Cleve. Med. Hall of Fame, 1997. Fellow ACS; mem. AAAS, Soc. Univ. Surgeons, Am. Soc. Clin. Investigation, Am. Surg. Assn., Ctrl. Surg. Assn., Am. Thyroid Assn. (pres. 1956-57, Van Meter prize, 1946, award of merit, 1954, Disting. Sevc. award, 1978), Cleve. Surg. Soc. (pres. 1966-67), Halstead Soc., Société Internationale de Chirurgie, Endocrine Soc., Internat. Assn. Endocrine Surgeons, Sigma Xi, Phi Beta Kappa. Home: 9930 Kirtland Rd Chardon OH 44024-9746 *Try to have a new experience every day.*

DOCKERY, J. LEE, retired medical school administrator; b. Amity, Ark., 1932; MD, U. Ark., 1957. Rotating intern Jackson Meml. Hosp., Miami, Fla., 1957—58; resident in ob-gyn. U. Miami, 1958—61; active attending staff Jackson Meml. Hosp., Miami, Fla., 1963—75; active staff Doctor's Hosp. Miami, 1963—75; active staff, chmn. dept. ob-gyn. Bapt. Hosp. Miami, 1972—73; staff Shands Hosp., Gainesville, Fla., 1975—91; prof. ob-gyn. U. Fla., Gainesville, 1980—92, assoc. dean, 1980—86, exec. assoc. dean, 1986—88, interim dean, assoc. v.p. clin. affairs, 1988—91; exec. v.p. Am. Bd. Med. Specialties, 1991—97. Clin. adj. prof. dept. ob-gyn. Northwestern U. Med. Sch., 1992—; clin. prof. dept. ob-gyn. U. Fla. Coll. Medicine, 1992—2000; trustee McKnight Brain Rsch. Found., 1999—; prof. emeritus U. Fla. Coll. Medicine, 2000—; mem. Accreditation Coun. for Grad. Med. Edn., 1984—89, Liaison Com. for Med. Edn., 1989—91, Fla. Bd. Medicine, 1988—92; mem. exam. bd. Fed. State Med. Bds., 1991—94; mem. U.S. Med. Licensing Exam. Composite Com., 1996—2002, Nat. Com. on Fgn. Med. Edn. and Accreditation, 2001—04, chair, 2006—. Mem.: AMA (mem. coun. med. edn. 1983—92, chmn. 1987—88), Fla. Med. Assn. (pres. 1983—84), So. Med. Assn. (pres. 1987—88), Alpha Omega Alpha.

DOCKING, THOMAS ROBERT, lawyer, former state lieutenant governor; b. Lawrence, Kans., Aug. 10, 1954; s. Robert Blackwell and Meredith (Gear) D.; m. Jill Sadowsky, June 18, 1977; children: Brian Thomas, Margery Meredith BS, U. Kans., 1976, MBA, JD, 1980. Bar: Kans. 1980. Assoc. Regan & McGannon, Wichita, Kans., 1980-82, ptnr., 1983-90, Ayesh, Docking, Herd & Theis, Wichita, 1990, Morris, Laing, Evans, Brock & Kennedy, Wichita, 1990—; lt. gov. State of Kans., Topeka, 1983-87. Dem. nominee for Gov. of Kans., 1986; chmn. adv. bd. Docking Inst. Pub. Affairs, Ft. Hays State U. Mem. steering com. Campaign Kans.; chmn. campaign com. Coll. Liberal Arts and Sci., 1988—91; trustee Emporia State U. Sch. Bus.; chmn. Wichita Water Conservation Task Force, 1991—; mem. Wichita/Brookes Water Task Force, 1997; bd. govs. U. Kans. Sch. Law, 1998—2000; bd. dirs. Kans. Easter Seals-Goodwill Industries, 1987—93, chmn. 1989 Telethon, vice-chair, 1991—93; bd. dirs. Wichita Conv. and Visitors Bur., 1988—2002; chmn., bd. dirs. St. Francis Found., 1988—94; bd. dirs. Wichita Downtown Devel. Corp., 2001—, Fin. Fitness Found., 1999—; chmn. allocation com. United Way of the Plains, 2003, bd. dirs., 2004—, vice chmn., 2006, chmn., 2007. Recipient Bob Brock award, Kansas Dem. Party, 2003. Mem. ABA, Kans. Bar Assn., Pi Sigma Alpha, Beta Gamma Sigma, Beta Theta Pi. Presbyterian. Home: 125 S Crestway St Wichita KS 67218-1309 Office: Morris Laing Evans Brock & Kennedy 300 N Mead St #200 Wichita KS 67202-2744 Office Phone: 316-262-2671.

DOCKSTADER, DEBORAH RUTH, minister; b. Elmira, NY, Oct. 12, 1948; d. E. Stanley and Ruth Emery Dockstader. BA, Mercyhurst Coll., 1974; MDiv, Princeton Theol. Sem., 1977. Ordained to ministry Presbyn. Ch., 1977. Pastor Lake Champlain Islands Parish, North Hero, Vt., 1977—79, East Greene Presbyn. Ch., Erie, Pa., 1979—84; dir. edn. St. Stephen's Ch., Fairview, 1984—85; assoc. exec. dir. Inter-Ch. Ministries Northwestern Pa, Erie, 1985—93; interim pastor Ross Meml. Presbyn. Ch., Binghamton, NY, 1993—96; pastor Southside Presbyn. Ch., Niles, Ohio, 1997—, First Presbyn. Ch., Girard, 1997—. Perm. jud. commn. Eastminster Presbytery, Youngstown, Ohio, 1999—2005, com. ministry, 2000—04, comms. com., 2005—06; commr. synod assembly Covenant Synod, 1997—2001. Bd. dirs. WQLN Pub. TV & Radio, Erie, 1987—90; active Erie Tanzania Project Bd., 1987—90, Allegany Nature Pilgrimage Bd., 1988—93; trustee Erie Rotary Club Scholarship Found., 1990—93; sec. bd. dirs. Niles Cmty. Svcs., 1997—; treas. Friends McKinley Libr., 2000—01; active Presbyn. Media Mission Bd., 1983—87, Ecumenical Theol. Ctr. Bd., 1987—90; trustee Susquehanna Valley Presbytery, 1994—96; bd. dirs. Manhoning Valley Assn. Chs., 2000—02, Emmanuel Cmty. Care Ctr., 2005—; active Presbytery Self Study Com., 2001—02; vice moderator Eastminster Presbytery, 2005—06, moderator, 2007. Mem.: Lions Club. Avocations: reading, birdwatching. Office Phone: 330-505-1192. Personal E-mail: drdockstader@sbcglobal.net.

DOCKSTADER, EMMETT STANLEY, civil engineer, construction executive; b. Elmira, NY, Nov. 7, 1923; s. Roy S. and Gertrude (Everts) D.; m. Ruth Norma Emery, May 11, 1946 (dec.); children: Deborah Ruth, David Stanley; m. Muriel Thomas Fearnot, Oct. 31, 1999. BCE cum laude, Syracuse U., 1947. Registered profl. engr. RI, Pa., W.Va., Ga., NC. Engr., Am. Bridge Co., Elmira, 1948-50; field engr. Sessinghaus & Ostergaard, Inc., Erie, Pa., 1950-53; project mgr., 1953-58; v.p., 1958-69; sr. v.p., sec. Pa., 1972-79; pres., 1984-86; gen. mgr. constrn. divsn. H.H. Roberston Co., Ambridge, 1969-71; constrn. exec. Gilbane Bldg. Co., Providence, 1979-84; pres. Dockstader Constrn. Assocs., Erie, 1986—. Dir. Erie Constrn. Coun.; mem. Erie Port Commn., 1967—69; chmn. NW Pa. Rail Authority; mem. Erie City Water Authority. Dir. Erie Civic Music Assn.; trustee Ch. of the Covenant. Inductee Hall of Achievement, Thomas A. Edison HS Alumni Assn., 2000. Mem. NSPE (life), Am. Arbitration Assn. (arbitrator), Soc. Profls. in Dispute Resolution, Nat. Railway Hist. Soc. (bd. dirs. Lakeshore chpt.), Erie Mannerchor (life), SAR, Pa. Soc., Torch Soc., Masons (32d degree), Rotary (Paul Harris fellow), Erie Yacht Club, Y Mens Club (past pres.), Tau Beta Pi. Office: 125 Lincoln Ave Erie PA 16505-2441

DOCKSTEADER, KAREN KEMP, marketing professional; b. Salisbury, Md., Feb. 11, 1953; d. Robert George and Laverne (Briggs) Kemp; m. Gerald Hugh Docksteader, Apr. 3, 1997; children from previous marriage: Daniel Richard Arrington IV, James William Arrington. BS, Iowa State U., 1975; MEd, Salisbury U., 1979. Dir. horticultural project Chesapeake Rehab. Ctr., Easton, Md., 1975-76; mgr. greenhouses Bountiful Ridge Nurseries, Inc., Princess Anne, Md., 1976-77; instr. horticulture Dorchester Bd. Edn., Cambridge, Md., 1978-80, Fredrick (Md.) Bd. Edn., 1980-87; instr. agronomy Frederick C.C., 1985; treas. Kemp's Ltd., Inc., Martinsburg, W.Va., 1985-87, pres. Frederick, 1987—2001; mgr. U.S. retail sales Kord Products, Ltd., Brampton, 1995-98; sales and mktg. dir. Angelica Nurseries, Inc., Kennedyville, Md., 2001—; published photographer, author Garden Writers Assn., 2003—. Keynote spkr. Vocat. Counseling Orgn., Md., 1980—88; cons. retail and comml. mktg. groups, 1977—91; dir. Russian-Georgian Rose Project, Tblissi, Georgia, 1993. Editor: (newsletter) The Spreader, 1990; featured narrator: (documentaries) Our Land, Our Future, 1980; exhibitor Assn. Nurserymen, Balt. and King of Prussia, Pa., 1986—2003. Coach 4-H, FFA, NJHA, and other youth orgns., 1977—98; state chair Soil Conservation Poster Competition, Md., 1990—91; judge horticulture county fairs, state and nat. 4-H and FFA activities, 1977—91; co-founder Windows of Opportunity Found., 2000—. Named Conservation Tchr. of the Yr., State Soil and Water Conservation Svc., 1984. Mem.: DAR, Somerset Pa. Hist. Soc., Hackers Creek Hist. Soc., Md. Hist. Soc., New Market Grange, Md. Greenhouse Growers Assn. Avocations: genealogy, writing, needlepoint, gardening, history. Office: Hortgraphics Inc 26875 Mallard Rd Chestertown MD 21620 Business E-Mail: kkemp@hortgraphics.com.

DOCKTERMAN, MICHAEL, lawyer; b. Davenport, Iowa, Dec. 14, 1954; s. Jerome and Elaine (Epstein) D.; m. Laura Di Giantonio, Sept. 25, 1983; 1 child, Eliana. BA, Yale U., 1975; JD, Duke U., 1978. Bar: Ill. 1978, US Dist. Ct. (no. dist. Ill.) 1978, US Ct. Appeals (7th cir.) 1978, US Dist. Ct. (ea. dist. Mich.) 1986, US Dist. Ct. (ctrl. dist. Ill.) 1988, US Ct. Appeals (4th, 6th and fed. cir.) 1990, US Dist. Ct. (so. dist. Ill.) 1991, US Supreme Ct. 1992, US Ct. Appeals (2nd cir.) 1993, US Dist Ct. (we. dist. Mich.) 1995, US Dist. Ct. (ea. dist. Mo.) 1996, US Ct. Appeals (9th cir.) 2004; registered fgn. lawyer UK, 2004—. Ptnr. Wildman, Harrold, Allen and Dixon, LLP, Chgo., 1978—, mem. exec. com. Chmn. bd. visitors Sch. Law Duke U., 2007—. Co-author: IICLE Class Actions, 1986, 92, 2000, 07; contbr. articles to profl. jours. Active Chgo. Vol. Legal Svc., 1983—, The Chgo. Com., Am. Refugee Com., Chgo. Coun. Global Affairs, mem. President's Cir.; bd. dir. KAM Isaiah Israel Congregation, 1993-96, 2002-03; bd. dir. Duke Law Alumni Assn., 1994-2003, pres., 2000-02, bd. visitors, 2003-; trustee Max and Gretel Janowski Fund, Chgo., 1992-99; chmn. bd. visitors Duke U. Sch. Law, 2007. Recipient Award for Advocacy Internat. Acad. Trial Lawyers, Charles A. Dukes award for vol. svc., Leadership Devel. award B'nai B'rith Youth Orgn.; named one of Top 10 Trial Lawyers in Am., Nat. Law Jour., 2006, 500 Leading Litigators, Lawdragon, 2006. Mem. Am. Bar Found.; mem. ABA (chair corp. governance subcommittee Corp. Counsel com. Bus. Law Sect. 1997-2003), Chgo. Bar Assn., Lawyers Club Chgo., B'nai B'rith Justice Lodge. Office: Wildman Harrold Allen Dixon LLP 225 W Wacker Dr Ste 3000 Chicago IL 60606-1229 Office Phone: 312-201-2652. Business E-Mail: dockterman@wildman.com.

DOCTOR, KENNETH JAY, digital content consultant; b. LA, Jan. 5, 1950; s. Joseph and Ruth (Kazdoy) D.; m. Katherine Conant Francis, June 14, 1971; children: Jenika, Joseph, Katy. BA in Sociology, U. Calif., Santa Cruz, 1971; MS in Journalism, U. Oreg., 1979. Editor, pub. Willamette Valley Observer, Eugene, Oreg., 1975-82; mng. editor Oreg. Mag., Portland, 1982-84; mng. editor, features Boulder (Colo.) Daily Camera, 1984-86; assoc. editor, features St. Paul Pioneer Press, 1986-90, mng. editor, features, 1990-94, mng. editor, 1994-97; v.p. editl. Knight Ridder New Media, San Jose, Calif., 1997-99; v.p. strategy Knight-Ridder.com., 1999-2001; v.p. content svcs. Knight-Ridder Digital, 2001—05; pres. Content Bridges, LLC, 2005—; lead news industry analyst Outsell, Inc., 2006—. Chair Knight-Ridder Task Force on Family Readers, Miami, Fla., 1991, Knight-Ridder mgmt. devel. program, Harvard U., 1993. Pres. Alumni Assn. U. Calif., Santa Cruz. Recipient Achievement award Oreg. Civil Liberties Union, Eugene, 1982. Mem. Soc. Newspaper Design, Am. Soc. Newspaper Editors, U. Calif. Santa Cruz Alumni Assn. (pres. 2003-05), Santa Cruz Found. (trustee 2006-). Avocations: baseball, travel. Personal E-mail: kdoctor@gmail.com.

DOCTOROFF, DANIEL L., municipal official; b. July 11, 1958; m. Alisa Doctoroff; children: Jacob, Ariel, Jenna. BA, Harvard Coll.; JD, Law Sch. U. Chgo. Investment banker Lehman Bros.; mng. ptnr. Oak Hill Capital Ptnrs.; dep. mayor for econ. devel. and rebuilding NYC, 2002—. Founder, pres. NYC2012, 2000; bd. mem. NYC and Co., NYC Partnership. Bd. mem. YMCA Greater NY. Office: 1 Liberty Plz 34th Fl New York NY 10006 also: City Hall New York NY 10007 Office Phone: 212-953-2012, 212-788-3000. Office Fax: 212-788-2460.*

DOCTOROW, CORY, blogger, writer; b. Toronto, Can., July 17, 1971; Co-founder free software co. Opencola (sold to Open Text Corp.), 1999—2003; dir. European Affairs Electronic Frontier Found., London, 2002—06, fellow, 2006—; co-editor BoingBoing.com blog; host, creator Craphound.com blog. Canadian Fulbright chair in Public Diplomacy UCLA Ctr. on Public Diplomacy, 2006—07; bd. dir. Technorati, Inc., Onion Networks. Co-author (with Karl Schroeder): Complete Idiot's Guide to Publishing Science Fiction, 2000; author: Essential Blogging, 2002, Eastern Standard Tribe, 2005, Down and Out in the Magic Kingdom, 2003 (Locus Award for Best First Novel, 2003), Someone Comes to Town, Someone Leaves Town, 2006, Overclocked: Stories of the Future Present, 2007, (short stories) A Place So Foreign and Eight More, 2003 (Sunburst award for best Canadian Sci. Fiction Book, 2004). Bd. dir. Participatory Culture Found., Open Rights Group, MetaBrainz Found. Named one of Top 25 Web Celebs, Forbes mag., 2007; recipient John W. Campbell award for Best New Writer, 2000. Mem.: Science Fiction and Fantasy Writers of Am. (Canadian Regional Dir. 1999). E-mail: doctorow@craphound.com.*

DOCTOROW, E.L. (EDGAR LAWRENCE), writer, English educator; b. Bronx, NY, Jan. 6, 1931; s. David Richard and Rose (Levine) D.; m. Helen Esther Setzer, Aug. 20, 1954; children: Jenny, Caroline, Richard. AB in Philosophy with honors, Kenyon Coll., 1952; student, Columbia U., 1952-53; LHD (hon.), Kenyon Coll., 1976; LittD (hon.), Hobart and William Smith Coll., 1979; LHD (hon.), Brandeis U., 1989. Script reader Columbia Pictures, Inc., NYC; assoc. editor to sr. editor New Am. Libr., NYC, 1959-64; editor-in-chief Dial Press, NYC, 1964-69, v.p., pub., 1968-69; writer-in-residence Univ. Calif., Irvine; mem. faculty Sarah Lawrence Coll., Bronxville, NY, 1971-78; creative writing fellow Sch. Drama Yale U., New Haven, 1974-75; Glucksman Prof. English and Am. Letters NYU, 1982—. Writer-in-residence U. Calif, Irvine, 1969-70; vis. prof. U. Utah, 1975; vis. sr. fellow Coun. on Humanities Princeton U., 1980. Author: (novels) Welcome to Hard Times, 1960, Big as Life, 1966, The Book of Daniel, 1971 (Nat. Book award nominee 1972), Ragtime, 1975 (Nat. Book Critics Circle award 1976, Arts and Letters award 1976), Loon Lake, 1980 (Nat. Book award nomiee 1980), Lives of the Poets: Six Stories and a Novella, 1984, World's Fair, 1985 (Nat. Book award 1986), Billy Bathgate, 1989 (Nat. Book award nominee 1989, Nat. Book Critics Circle award 1990, PEN/Faulkner award 1990, William Dean Howells medal Am. Acad. and Inst. Arts and Letters 1990), The Waterworks, 1994, City of God, 2000, The March, 2005 (PEN/Faulkner award 2006, 2005 Nat. Book Critics Circle's award for fiction); (plays) Drinks Before Dinner, 1979; (screenplay) Daniel, 1983; (essays) Jack London, Hemingway, and the Constitution: Selected Essays 1977-92, 1993, Creationists: Selected Essays 1993-2006, 2006 With AUS, 1953-55. Recipient Arts and Letters award Am. Acad. and Nat. Inst. Art, 1976; Guggenheim fellow, 1973, Creative Artists Program Svc. fellow, 1973-74; Edith Wharton citation of merit for fiction and N.Y. State Author, 1989-91, Nat. Humanities medal, 1998, Commonwealth award, 2000. Mem. Authors Guild, Am. Acad. Arts and Letters, Am. Acad. Arts and Scis., Am. PEN, Writers Guild Am. East, Century Assn. Office: NYU English Dept Rm 221 Faculty Arts and Scis 19 University Pl New York NY 10003-6607

DODANI, SUNITA, physician, educator; MD, MSc, U. Pitts., PhD, 2006. Diplomate. Asst. prof. Aga Khan U., Karachi, Sindh, Pakistan, 2000—02, U. Pitts., 2003—. Achievements include research in heart diseases in young population. Home: 1423 Fernledge Dr Allison Park PA 15101 Home Phone: 412-383-1453. Home Fax: 412-383-1974. Personal E-mail: sud9@pitt.edu.

DODD, CHRISTOPHER JOHN, senator; b. Willimantic, Conn., May 27, 1944; s. Thomas J. and Grace (Murphy) D; m. Jackie Marie Clegg; two children. BA in English Lit., Providence Coll., 1966; JD, U. Louisville, 1972. Bar: Conn. 1973. Vol. Peace Corps, Dominican Republic, 1966-68; atty. Suisman, Shapiro, Wool & Brennan, New London, Conn., 1973-74; mem. 94th-96th Congresses from 2d Conn. Dist., 1975-80; US Senator from Conn., 1981—. Chmn. Dem. Nat. Com.; mem. Whitewater com. Served with USAR, 1969—75. Recipient Hubert H. Humphrey Pub. Svc. award Hubert H. Humphrey Inst. Public Affairs Univ. Minn., Outstanding US Senator award, Nathan Davis award AMA, Head Start Senator of Decade award, Excellence in Public Svc. award Am. Acad. Pediatrics, 1987, High Tech Legis. of Yr. Info. Tech. Industry Coun., 2000, Congressional Recognition award Internat. Assn. Fire Fighters, 2001, Nat. Family Week award Alliance for Children and Families, 2002, Gerald Solomon Legis. of Yr. award Independent Insu. Agents adn Brokers of Am., 2002. Democrat. Roman Catholic. Office: US Senate 448 Russell Senate Bldg Washington DC 20510-0001 also: District Office Putnam Park 100 Great Meadow Rd Wethersfield CT 06109 Office Phone: 202-224-2823, 860-258-6940. Office Fax: 202-224-1083, 860-258-6958.*

DODD, GERALD DEWEY, JR., radiologist, educator; b. Oaklyn, NJ, Nov. 18, 1922; s. Gerald Dewey and Anne Aloysius (Keveney) D.; m. Helen Carolyn Glenzing, Apr. 5, 1946; children: Patricia, Michael, Barbara, Gerald Dewey III, Anne, Susan, Thomas. AB, Lafayette Coll., 1945; MD, Jefferson Med. Coll., 1947; DSc (hon.), Lafayette Coll., 1991. Diplomate Am. Bd. Radiology. Intern Fitzgerald Mercy Hosp., Darby, Pa., 1947; resident Jefferson Med. Coll., Phila., 1948—50; asst. radiologist, asst. in radiology Thomas Jefferson Med. Coll. and Hosp., Phila., 1952—54, assoc. in radiology, 1954—55; asst. radiologist, clin. prof. radiology Thomas Jefferson Med. Coll., 1961—66; assoc. radiologist, assoc. prof. radiology U. Tex. M.D. Anderson Cancer Ctr., Houston, 1955—61, prof., 1966—89, chmn. dept. diagnostic radiology, 1966—89, prof., head divsn. diagnostic imaging, 1984—92, Robert D. Moreton Chair Diagnostic Radiology, 1988—93, chair emeritus, 1996—; prof. radiology U. Tex. Med. Sch., Houston, 1971—, chmn. dept. radiology, 1971—74, prof. radiology Sch. Allied Health Scis., 1971—94. Cons. radiologist St. Luke's Hosp., Tex. Children's Hosp., Houston, 1966—, Singleton Prof. Radiology, 1995-99; vis. mem. grad. faculty Tex. A&M U., College Station, 1969-93; adj. prof. radiology Baylor Coll. Medicine, 1983—. Cons. to editor Radiology, 1977—86, cons. editor The Cancer Bull., 1979—89, assoc. editor Cancer, 1991—2000; editor: Breast Diseases, 1993—2004; referee CRC Critical Revs. in Radiol. Scis., 1969—95; contbr. articles to profl. jours. Dir.-at-large Am. Cancer Soc., 1977-90, pres., 1990-91, past officer dir.; mem. coun. Nat. Coun. Radiation Protection and Measurement, 1979-91, bd. dirs., 1981-91. Fellow Am. Coll. Radiology (bd. chancellors, 1971-80, pres. 1984-85, Gold medal 1989); mem. Radiol. Soc. N.Am. (Gold medal 1986), Am. Roentgen Ray Soc. (Gold medal 1992), Soc. Gastrointestinal Radiologists (Cannon medal 1995), Assn. Univ. Radiologists, Tex. Med. Assn., Tex. Radiol. Soc. (Gold medal 1988), Soc. Breast Imaging (Gold medal 1995), Harris County Med. Soc., Houston Radiol. Soc., Phila. Roentgen Ray Soc. (hon.), Alpha Omega Alpha, Phi Delta Theta, Phi Chi. Republican. Roman Catholic. Office: M D Anderson Hosp 1515 Holcombe Blvd Houston TX 77030-4009

DODD, JACK GORDON, JR., physicist, researcher; b. Spokane, Wash., June 19, 1926; s. Jack Gordon and Mary Ida (Stuart) D.; m. Mary Ann Howell, June 11, 1951 (dec. Jan. 2007); children: Jeffrey John, Laura Jean. Student, State Coll. Wash., 1946-48; BS in Physics, Ill. Inst. Tech., 1951; MS in Physics, U. Ark., 1957, PhD in Physics, 1965. With Argonne (Ill.) Nat. Lab., 1951-53; tchr. Fourche Valley High Sch., 1953-55, 56-57; asst. prof. Drury Coll., 1957-60; assoc. prof. Ark. Poly. Coll., 1960-65, U. Tenn., Knoxville, 1965-69; Charles A. Dana prof. physics and astronomy Colgate U., Hamilton, NY, 1969-87, ret., 1988; v.p. Spectrum Sq., Ithaca, NY, 1987—; bd. trustees McCrone Rsch. Inst., Chgo., 1999—. Cons. on phys. optics, microscopy, detonation theory, spectral and image data processing Served with USN, 1944-46. Mem. Am. Assn. Physics Tchrs., Am. Phys. Soc., Am. Astron. Soc., Optical Soc. Am., Sigma Xi. Office: 213 Sears Pond Rd Sherburne NY 13460-5018 Business E-Mail: jgdodd@gmail.com.

DODD, JAMES B., Internet executive; BA in Econs., Stanford U.; MBA, Harvard U. CPA. With Sprint; pres., CEO Nat. Info. Consortium Inc., Overland Park, Kans. Office: National Information Center 10540 S Ridgeview Rd Olathe KS 66061-6440

DODD, JAN EVE, lawyer; b. Kansas City, Mo., May 24, 1964; d. Raymond Thomas and Eva Faith (McCorkle) D. BA in Polit. Sci. & Journalism, U. Mo., Columbia, 1985; JD, U. Mo., Kansas City, 1988. Bar: Mo. 1988, Ill. 1989, U.S. Dist. Ct. (so. dist.) Ill. 1989, U.S. Dist. Ct. (ea. dist.) Mo. 1989, U.S. Ct. Appeals (7th cir.) 1991, U.S. Ct. Appeals (8th cir.) 1994. Rsch. asst. Prof. Jack M. Balkin, Kansas City, Mo., 1986-87; jud. law clk. Judge Edward D. Robertson Jr. Mo. Supreme Ct., Jefferson City, Mo., 1988-89; sr. assoc. def. litigation Sandberg, Phoenix & Von Gontard, St. Louis, 1989—; former special state atty gen. State of Mo.; now ptnr., litigation dept. Kaye Scholer, Los Angeles, Calif. Named one of Litigation's Rising Stars, The Am. Lawyer, 2007; recipient diploma Nat. Inst. for Trial Adv., Mid-Am. Regional, 1994. Mem. Def. Rsch. Inst., Bar Assn. Met. St. Louis, Tower Grove Neighborhood Assn. Office: Kaye Scholer 1999 Ave of Stars Ste 1700 Los Angeles CA 90067 Office Phone: 310-788-1000. Office Fax: 310-788-1200. Business E-Mail: jdodd@kayescholer.com.*

DODD, JEFF C., lawyer; b. St. Louis, 1955; BA magna cum laude, U. Houston, 1976, JD summa cum laude, 1979. Bar: Tex. 1979. Ptnr., Corp./Securities Practice Andrews Kurth LLP, Houston, mem. mgmt. com. Adj. prof. law U. Houston, 1994, 95, 99, 2000, 01, S. Tex. Coll. Law, 1989, 90. Editor: Houston Law Rev., 1978—79. Adv. bd. Honors. Coll. U. Houston. Mem.: ABA (Bus. Law Sect., Taxation Sect., Sci. & Tech. Sect., Forum on Franchising), State Bar Tex. (Bus. Law Sect., electronic com. subcom.), Houston Bar Assn. (Bus. Law Sect., electronic commerce subcom.), Phi Kappa Phi. Office: Andrews Kurth LLP 600 Travis St Ste 4200 Houston TX 77002-3090 also: Andrews Kurth LLP 111 Congress Ste 1700 Austin TX 78701 Office Phone: 713-220-4736, 512-320-9252. Office Fax: 713-220-4285. Business E-Mail: jeffdodd@andrewskurth.com.

DODD, JERRY LEE, lawyer; b. Bakersfield, Calif., Nov. 16, 1953; s. James Luther and Juanita Louise (Holmes) D.; m. Phena Fite, Jan. 9, 1972; children: Jody, Kimberly, Kristy, Julie, Timothy, Andrew, Matthew, Lindsey, Allison, Daniel. BS magna cum laude, U. Ark., 1975; MBA, Monmouth Coll., 1978; JD, Rutgers U., 1979. CPA; bar: NJ 1979, Pa. 1983, Minn. 1988. Commd. 2d. lt. USAF, 1975, advanced through grades to capt., auditor A.F. Audit Agy. Wrightstown, NJ, 1975-78, base counsel Alexandria, La., 1979-81, def. counsel, 1981-82, contract trial atty. A.F. Contract Law Ctr. Dayton, Ohio, 1982-86, ret., 1986; govt. contracts counsel US Army 7th Signal Command, Ft. Richie, Md., 1986-87; group counsel Honeywell, Mpls., 1987-90; divsn. counsel Harsco-BMY Wheeled Vehicles Divsn., Marysville, Ohio, 1990—2006; counsel Converga Enterprises, 2006—. Mem.: ABA (com. mem.), Nat. Contract Mgmt. Assn. (chpt. pres.), Ark. Soc. CPAs. Home: 700 Kirkpatrick Rd Malvern AR 72104 Office: Converga Enterprises 700 Kirkpatrick Rd Malvern AR 72104 Office Phone: 501-332-7173. Personal E-mail: jerryleedodd@yahoo.com.

DODD, JOHN ROBERT, non-profit organization administrator; b. Dallas, Oct. 15, 1951; s. Carlos Lestor and Betty (Ayers) D.; m. Mary Teresa Parsons, Nov. 12, 1983; children: Katherine Howard, Mary Alexandra. BA, Coll. William and Mary, 1975; MA, U. N.C., 1980. Tchr. Cinnaminson (N.J.) H.S., 1975-78; grad. asst. U. N.C., Chapel Hill, 1978-80; PAC coord. Nat. Congl. Club, Raleigh, NC, 1981-82; v.p. Coalition for Freedom, Raleigh, 1982-85; pres. J & T Dodd Assocs., Fairfax, Va., 1985-94, Jesse Helms Ctr, Wingate, NC, 1994—. Cons. to various mems. of Congress. Bd. dirs. Fellowship of Christian Athletes, Washington, 1991-94, Turning Point Women's Shelter, 2005—; del. Rep. Nat. Conv., 2000, 04; pres. Lacrosse Camps, Inc., 1993— Named Deep South Conf. Coach of Yr., 2001, coach North-South Coll. All-Star Game, 2001. Fellow: Am. Leadership Forum (sr.). Republican. Office: Jesse Helms Ctr PO Box 247 Wingate NC 28174-0247 Office Phone: 704-233-1776.

DODD, MEGHAN P., mathematics educator; d. William A. and Patricia Dodd. BA in Math., Sacred Heart U., Fairfield, Conn., 2004. Cert. secondary math. edn. Conn. State Dept. Edn., 2004. Math. tchr. Stamford Pub. Schs., Conn., 2004—. Mem.: Nat. Coun. Tchrs. Math., Pi Lambda Theta. Home: 18 Kennedy Ln Stamford CT 06906 Home Phone: 203-355-1076; Office Phone: 203-977-4260.

DODDS, JUDY B., curator, consultant, artist; b. New Orleans, Nov. 19, 1927; d. Earle Canney Crumb and Emily Guillemet Crumb Brett; m. James Henry Dodds, Sept. 1, 1973; m. Jacob Jean Seidenberg (div.); children: Eugenie Brett Seidenberg Delaney, Brett Jonathan Seidenberg. AA in Art, Newcomb Art Sch. Tulane U., New Orleans, 1947, continuing study in Arts, 1969—2007, U. Vt., Burlington, 1968. Curator decorative arts La. State Mus., New Orleans, 1955—64, chief curator, 1964—70; program and exhibit developer Boston Children's Mus., 1971—73; owner, craftsperson Tulip Tree Crafts, Waitsfield, Vt., 1973—2003; acting dir. Waitsfield Hist. Soc., 1989—91, pres., 1991—94, curator, exhibit designer, 2007—. Design cons. La. State Mus., New Orleans, 1970—74; New Eng. rep. Am. Crafts Coun., 1977—80; mem. Gov.'s Commn. Crafts, Montpelier, Vt., 1980—82; oral historian, videographer Waitsfield Hist. Soc., 2003—. Murals, Washington Corey Elderly Housing, Boston, 1978, exhibitions include Stratton Arts Festival, Vt., 1979 (Elinor Janeway award); author: (exhibition catalogue) Playthings of the Past, 1969; prodr.: (films) Heart of Rug Hooking, 2006 (Merit award in Oral History); contbr. articles to profl. jours. Vol. Valley Players Theatre Group, 1975—85, Mountain Gardeners, 1979—, Sugarbush C. of C., 1973—2003, Vt. Festival of Arts; mem. Green Mountain Rug Hooking Guild, 1999—. Mem.: Vt. Mus. and Gallery Alliance, Green Mountain Rug Hooking Guild. Avocations: gardening, genealogy. Home: 112 Dugway Rd Waitsfield VT 05673 Office: Waitsfield Hist Soc PO Box 816 Waitsfield VT 05673

DODDS, MICHAEL BRUCE, lawyer; b. Spokane, Wash., June 27, 1952; s. Bruce Alison and Janet Lorraine (Swanbeck) D.; m. Karen Lynn Sifford, Jan. 5, 1972; children: Jennifer Ann, Stephanie Marie, Alexander Michael, Matthew Tyler. BA, Gonzaga U., 1974, JD, 1979. Bar: Wash. 1980, U.S. Dist. (ea. dist.) Wash. 1983, U.S. Dist. Ct. (we. dist.) Wash. 1987, U.S. Ct. Appeals (9th cir.) 1994, U.S. Supreme Ct. 1987. Dep. prosecutor Okanogan (Wash.) County, 1980-87, Clark (Wash.) County, 1987—. Served to 2d lt. U.S. Army, 1974-76. Recipient Excellence in Performance award, Clark County, 1995, Silver Beaver award, Cascade Pacific coun. Boy Scouts Am., 2004. Mem.: Clark County Bar Assn., Wash. State Bar Assn., Nat. Dist. Attys. Assn., Phi Alpha Delta. Republican. Home: 2104 NE Cranbrook Dr Vancouver WA 98664-2960 Office: Clark County Prosecutor's Office PO Box 5000 Vancouver WA 98666-5000 Home Phone: 360-892-5132; Office Phone: 360-397-2261.

DODDS, ROBERT JAMES, III, lawyer; b. San Antonio, Sept. 19, 1943; s. Robert James Jr. and Kathryn (Bechman) D.; m. Deborah N. Detchon, June 25, 1966 (div. Mar. 1989); children: Zachary Bechman, Seth Detchon; m. D.J. Knowles, Dec. 27, 1990. BA, Yale U., 1965; LLB, U. Pa., 1969. Assoc. Reed Smith Shaw & McClay, Pitts., 1969-77, ptnr., 1978-91, Davenport & Dodds, LLP, Santa Fe, 1992—. Bd. dirs. ATP Inc., Davison Sand & Gravel Co., Pitts.; pres. Homewood Cemetery, Pitts., 1980-91, bd. dirs. Trustee Mus. Art, Carnegie Inst, 1974-84, Westmoreland Mus. Art, Greensburg, Pa., YMCA of Pitts., Carnegie-Mellon U.; dir., pres. Pitts. Plan for Art, 1981-85; dir., chmn. West Pa. Hosp. Found., Carnegie Mellon Art Gallery; bd. dirs. Western Pa. Hosp., Western Pa. Healthcare Systems Inc., Pitts. Athletic Assn., Inst. Am. Indian Arts Found., Santa Fe; mus. panel Pa. Coun. on the Arts. Mem.: Yale Club (N.Y.C.), Duquesne Club (Pitts.). Democrat. Episcopalian. Home: 3101 Old Pecos Trl Unit 687 Santa Fe NM 87505-9547 Office: Davenport & Dodds LLP 721 Don Diego Ave Santa Fe NM 87505 Office Phone: 505-982-0080. E-mail: dod@newmexico.com.

DODEZ, DIANE M., principal; b. Sioux Falls, SD, Mar. 4, 1950; d. Phillip John and Theresa Margaret Sandblade; m. Orin Dodez, June 7, 1981; children: Phillip, Rebekah. BS, Kans. State U., 1974; MS, Ft. Hays State U., 1985. Lic. elem., English, social studies tchr., edn. adminstr. Curator exhbns. Grand Ctrl. Art Gallery, NYC, 1974—76; editor Women's Page Tiller and Toiler Newspaper, Larned, Kans., 1977—80; tchr. Esbon (Kans.) Grade Sch., 1980—81, Wellington (Kans.) Unified Sch. Dist. 495, 1981—94; prin. Sacred Heart Sch., Larned, 1994—99, Chase County Elem., Cottonwood Falls, Kans., 1999—. Dir. religious edn., catechist, Wellington, Larned, Cottonwood Falls, 1991—. Mem.: ASCD, Cottonwood C. of C. (com. chair 1999—), Phi Delta Kappa. Home: Box 34 Cottonwood Falls KS 66845 Office: Chase County Elem Box 370 Cottonwood Falls KS 66845

DODGE, ARTHUR BYRON, JR., b. Lancaster, Pa., June 13, 1923; s. Arthur Byron and Marion Frances (Cochran) D.; m. Margaretha Gerbert, Dec. 28, 1954; children: Arthur B., Andrew Nikolaus. Student, Williams Coll., 1942; BS in Econs., Franklin and Marshall Coll., 1947. With Dodge Cork Co., 1947-89, product mgr., 1947-50, factory mgr., 1952-57, mgr. fgn. divsn., 1958-61, v.p., sec., 1961-81, pres., 1981-90. Bd. dirs. Dodge-Regupol, Inc., 1989—, chmn., 1990—; bd. dirs., sec. Gerbert, Ltd., Lancaster, 1979—, Intertrade, Inc., Lancaster, 1979-91. Trustee Episcopal Ch. Sch. Found., 1958-85, Lancaster Theol. Sem., 1998—; pres. Friends of SOS Children's Villages, 1979-85, bd. dirs., 1979-93; bd. dirs., treas. SOS Children's Villages USA, 1993-98; bd. dirs. 88th Inf. Divsn. Assn., 1988—, pres., 1996-97; bd. dirs. Meml. Trust, 1992—. Capt. AUS, 1942-45, 50-52. Decorated Bronze Star with cluster, Purple Heart with cluster, Meritorious Svc. award; battlefield commn. Italy, 1944. Mem. ASTM, Cork Inst. Am. (treas. 1980—), Newcomen Soc., Pa. Soc., Pa. Commn. Employment of Handicapped, Delta Upsilon, Hamilton Club, Lancaster Country Club. Republican. Office: 715 Fountain Ave Lancaster PA 17601-4547 E-mail: gwd@regupol.com.

DODGE, CLEVELAND EARL, JR., retired manufacturing executive, director; b. NYC, Mar. 7, 1922; s. Cleveland Earl and Pauline (Morgan) D.; m. Phyllis Boushall, Dec. 19, 1942 (dec. Jan. 2004); children: Alice Berkeley, Sally Mole, Cleveland Earl III. BS in Mech. Engring., Princeton U., 1943; D in Humanics, Springfield Coll., 1996. With DeLaval Steam Turbine Co., 1942, GE, 1946-51; v.p., dir. Warren Wire Co., Pownal, Vt., 1951-55; pres., dir. Dodge Industries, Inc., Hoosick Falls, NY, 1955-67; v.p., dir. Engineered Yarns, Inc., 1962-68; pres., dir. Circuit Materials Corp., 1962-68; pres., treas., dir. Internat. Dodge, Inc., 1968—2005; pres., dir. Dodge Machine Co., 1968—2005; pres., bd. dirs. Alta Energy Corp., 1980-89, Amex Plastics Inc., 1972-74, Am. Hydride Corp., 1991—2005; ret., 2005. Bd. dirs. Display Sys., Inc., Imetrix Corp., Internat. Dodge, Inc., Cleeland Corp., Am. Hydride Corp., Dodge Machine Co., Inc., Wild Goose Island Corp., Imetrix, Inc.; bd. dirs. emeritus Phelps Dodge Corp., Atlantic Mut. Ins., Key Bank. Patentee in field. Chmn., bd. dirs. Cleveland H. Dodge Found.; vice chmn. emeritus YMCA Retirement Fund; bd. dirs. emeritus Springfield Coll., Bennington Mus., Antique Boat Mus., Brisbee Coun. on Arts and Humanities, Silver City Mus., YMCA Retirement Fund. Lt. USNR, 1943-45. Mem. Princeton Engring. Assn., Princeton Rowing Assn., Laurentian Lodge (Shawbridge, Que., Can.), Taconic Golf Club (Williamstown, Mass.), Kiwanis. Congregationalist. Avocations: skiing, golf, travel. Office: Internat Dodge Inc PO Box 178 Hoosick Falls NY 12090-0178 Office Phone: 518-686-7841.

DODGE, EDWARD JOHN, retired insurance company executive; b. Malone, NY, Mar. 28, 1935; s. Harry Gilman and Marjorie Dietz (Wright) Dodge; m. Ann Louise Cupps. Grad. hs, 1953. Map clk. N.Y. Underwriters, San Francisco, 1956-57; underwriter Reliance Ins., San Francisco, 1957-58; agt. Am. Hardware Mut., San Francisco, 1958; investigator Retail Credit Co., 1963-68; claims adjuster Allstate Ins., Arlington Heights, Ill., 1968-70, Epiic Ins., Phoenix, 1974; claims examiner GEICO, Chgo., 1970-73; multi-line adjuster Ariz. Adjustment, Phoenix, 1973-74; investigator Equifax, Chgo., 1974-78; sales br. mgr. Hooper Holmes, Chgo., Springfield, Ill., 1978-80; multi-line agt. Met. Ins., Springfield, 1980-81; subrogation examiner Horace Mann Ins., Springfield, 1982-97; ret., 1997. Spkr. in field. Author: Relief is Greatly Wanted, The Battle of Fort William Henry, 1998; contbr. articles to hist. publs. Commr. Boy Scouts Am., Arlington Heights, Ill., 1971—78, vice chmn. scouting, 1977—79, vice chmn. exploring, 1988—90, commr. Springfield, 1981—92, Phoenix, 1983—84. Recipient Dist. Commrs. award, Boy Scouts Am., 1978, Scouter of the Month award, 1978, Bronze Big Horn award, 1989. Mem.: Masons, Princess of Wale's Royal Regtl. Assn. (licentiate), Queen's Regtl. Assn. (life). Republican. Methodist. Avocations: historical research, historical writing. Home: 1223 N Rutledge St Springfield IL 62702-2524 Personal E-mail: sprngflddodge@att.net.

DODGE, GEOFFREY A., publishing executive; b. Newburyport, Mass., Aug. 14, 1960; s. Edward and Sandra (Whitley) D. BA, Babson Coll., Wellesley, Mass., 1983. Ad sales rep. IDG, Boston, 1985-86; pub. Boston Computer News, 1986; sales rep. Fortune, NYC, 1987-89, Washington mgr., 1989-92, N.Y. advt. dir., 1992-94, eastern advt. dir., 1994-95; pub. Money mag., NYC, 1995—2000; CEO mediospacebank.com, 2000—02; assoc. pub., v.p. U.S. advt. BusinessWeek mag. The McGraw Hill Cos., NYC, 2002, pub. North Am., v.p. BusinessWeek mag., 2006—. Mem. exec. com. Jr. Achievement, N.Y.C., 1988—. Mem. N.Y. Athletic Club, Rockefeller Center Club, Sleepy Hollow Country Club (Scarborough, N.Y.). Office: Business Week The McGraw Hill Cos Bldg 1221 Avenue of the Americas New York NY 10020 Office Phone: 212-412-4611. Office Fax: 212-512-2277. E-mail: geoff_dodge@businessweek.com.*

DODGE, PAUL CECIL, academic administrator; b. Granville, NY, Mar. 25, 1943; s. Cecil John Paul and Elsie Elizabeth Dodge Rogers; m. Margaret Mary Kostyun, June 6, 1964 (div. Sept. 1985); 1 child, Cynthia Ruth; m. Cynthia Dee Bennett, Apr. 26, 1986; children: Michelle Lynn, Jason Paul, Benjamin Charles. BA in Math., U. Vt., 1967. Mgr. data processing Thermal Wire & Electronics, South Hero, Vt., 1967-70, DDSV divsn. Vt. Cos., Burlington, 1970-73, Revere Copper & Brass, Clinton, Ill., 1973-78, Angelica Corp., St. Louis, 1978-81; pres. chief ops. officer Dodge Mgmt., St. Louis, 1981-82; mgr. systems and programming Terra Internat., 1982-87; pres., COO Mo. Tech, 1987—. Mem. Mo. Assn. Pvt. Career Schs. (pres. 1993-94), Nat. Rehab. Assn., Mo. Rehab. Assn. Republican. Presbyterian. Avocations: amatuer radio, chess. Office: Mo Tech Sch 1167 Corporate Lake Dr Saint Louis MO 63132-1716

DODGE, PHILIP ROGERS, neurologist, educator; b. Beverly, Mass., Mar. 16, 1923; s. Israel R.; children: Susan, Judith. Student, U. N.H., 1941-43, Yale, 1943; MD, U. Rochester, 1948. Diplomate Am. Bd. Psychiatry and Neurology. Intern Strong Meml. Hosp., 1948-49; asst. resident neurology Boston City Hosp., 1949-50, resident, 1950, sr. resident, 1951-52; practice medicine, specializing in child neurology Boston, 1956-67, St. Louis, 1967—; teaching fellow neurology Harvard Med. Sch., 1950, 51-53, instr. neurology, 1956-58, assoc. in neurology, 1958-61, asst. prof., 1962-67; asst. neurologist Mass. Gen. Hosp., 1956-59, dir. pediatric neurology program, 1958-67, assoc. neurologist, 1959-63, neurologist, 1963-67, assoc. pediatrician, 1961-62, pediatrician, 1962-67; investigator Joseph P. Kennedy, Jr. Meml. Labs. for Study Mental Retardation, 1962-67; pediatric neurologist Boston Lying-In Hosp., 1961-67; cons. in neurology Walter E. Fernald State Sch. for Retarded Children, 1963-67; med. dir. St. Louis Children's Hosp., 1967-84, pediatrician-in-chief, 1967-86; assoc. neurologist Barnes Hosp., 1967—; chmn. Mallinckrodt Dept. Pediatrics, Washington U. Sch. Medicine, 1967-86, prof. pediatrics and neurology, 1967-93; prof. emeritus pediatrics and neurology Washington U. Sch. Medicine, 1993—; lectr. in pediatrics, 1993-99. Cons. collaborative project cerebral palsy Nat. Inst. Neurol. Diseases and Blindness, 1958; vis. scientist Cin. Rsch. Ctr., U. PR, 1965—66, hon. vis. prof. physiology, 1967; bd. dirs., chmn. rsch. adv. com. Mass. Soc. Prevention Cruelty to Children, 1961—67; mem. sci. rsch. adv. bd. Nat. Assn. Retarded Children, 1963—67; bd. dirs. Ctrl. Midwestern Regional Lab., Inc., 1968—70; mem. gen. clin. rsch. ctrs. adv. com. USPHS, 1971—74; chmn. Mo. Mental Health Commn., 1974—78; mem. nat. adv. child health and human devel. coun. NIH, 1974—77; chmn. panel neurol. disorders, devel., long-range program strategies NINCDS, 1977—79; panel chmn., consensus devel. conf. diagnosis and treatment Reye's Syndrome, 1981; vis. prof. pediat. and adolescent medicine Royal Post-grad. Med. Sch., U. London, 1986—; hon. vis. fellow dept. pathology U. Western Australia, Nedlands, 1986—87; vis. prof. neurology Columbia U. Coll. Physicians and Surgeons, NYC, 1987—88; sPl. asst. to dir. mental retardation Nat. Inst. Child Health and Human Devel., NIH, Washington, 1987—88. Author (with others): Nutrition and the Developing Nervous System, 1975; mem. editl. bd. Jour. Devel. Medicine and Child Neurology, 1965—, Jour. Pediat., 1970—80, Pediatric Rsch., 1970—78, Current Problems in Pediat., 1969—84, Neurology, 1973—76; contbr. articles to profl. jours. Maj. M.C. US Army, 1950—56. Mem.: Assn. Med. Sch. Pediatric Dept. Chmn. (pres. 1975—77), St. Louis Soc. Neurol. Scis., Soc. Biol. Psychiatry, Soc. Pediatric Rsch., Assn. Rsch. Nervous and Mental Disease, Child Neurology Soc., Am. Neurol. Assn., Am. Acad. Neurology (past com. chmn.), Am. Pediatric Soc. (coun. 1972—78, chmn. coun. 1978—79), Alpha Omega Alpha. Home: 410 N Newstead Ave Saint Louis MO 63108-2654 Office: 1 Childrens Pl Saint Louis MO 63110-1002 Office Phone: 314-454-6042, 314-454-2699.

DODGE, R(ALPH) EDWARD, JR., physician; b. Salamanca, NY, Jan. 14, 1936; s. Ralph Edward and Eunice Elvira (Davis) D.; m. Nancy Lou De Lay, Aug. 14, 1957 (dec. 1999); children: Randall, Jeffrey, Amy; m. Carol Marie Fitzgerald, Dec. 17, 1999. BA, Taylor U., 1958; MD, Ind. U., 1962; MPH, Johns Hopkins U., 1967. Diplomate Am. Bd. Preventive Medicine, Am. Bd. Family Practice. Rotating intern L.A. County Gen. Hosp., 1962—63; resident gen. preventive medicine sch. hygiene & pub. health Johns Hopkins U., Balt., 1966—69; asst. prof. pub. health Haile Sellassie U., Gondar, Ethiopia, 1967—69; staff physician Frontier Nursing Svc., Hyden, Ky., 1970—71; med. dir. Citrus-Levy County Health Dept., Inverness, Fla., 1971—74; physician emergency dept. Waterman Meml. Hosp., Eustis, Fla., 1974—75; pvt. practice Inverness, 1975—96. Clin. asst. prof. U. Fla., 1994-98; med. dir. Citrus Primary Care Network, 1994-96. Author: Tim's Story-A Spiritual Perspective of Health, 2005; contbr. articles to med. jours.; editor Fla. Family Physician, 1991-95, 97-99; newspaper columnist: Health Simplicity, 1988-90, Life and Health, 1990-2000, A Passion for Health, 2005— Bd. dirs. Marion-Citrus Mental Health Ctrs., Ocala, Fla., 1972—74, North Ctrl. Fla. Health Planning Commn., Gainesville, 1979—80, Fla. divsn. Am. Cancer Soc., 1988—90, Citrus Meml. Health Found., Inverness, 1988—94, Citrus County Edn. Found., 1998—2002, Citrus County Assn. for Retarded Citizens, v.p., 1999—; trustee Old Courthouse Heritage Mus., 1999—2000; active Citrus County Hist. Soc.; chmn. bd. dirs. George A. Dame. Cmty. Health Ctr., 2005—; trustee Unity Ch. of Citrus County, 2000—03, pres., 2001—03. Lt comdr. USPHS, 1964—66. Recipient Disting. Svc. award Fla. Assn. Emergency Med. Technicians, 1976, Cmty. Svc. award Seventh Day Adventist Ch., Inverness, 1978, Citizen of Yr. award Citrus County Chronicle, 1987, Svc. Above Self award Rotary Club Inverness, 1998 Mem. AMA, Am. Coll. Preventive Medicine, Am. Acad. Family Physicians, Fla. Acad. Family Physicians (bd. dirs. 1994-96), Fla. Med. Assn., Citrus County Med. Soc. (pres. 1977, sec.-treas. 1981-86) Democrat. Avocations: tennis, chess, gardening.

DODGE, TIMOTHY DE K., school librarian; b. Boston, Apr. 15, 1957; s. Peter and Renata de Kanicky Dodge. BA, Swarthmore Coll., Swarthmore, Pa., 1979; MS, Columbia Univ., NYC, 1980; MA, Univ. N.H., Durham, PhD, 1992. Cemetery maintenance man Town of Lee, Lee, NH, 1971—77, 1981—83, 1988; gen. asst. Butler Libr., Columbia Univ., NYC, 1979—80; spl.collections libr. Dimond Libr., Univ. N.H., Durham, NH, 1982—84; serials and reference libr. Barry Univ. Libr., Miami Shores, Fla., 1984—87; spl. collections libr. Dimond Libr., Univ. N.H., Durham, NH, 1987—92; reference libr. Draughon Libr., Auburn Univ., Auburn, Ala., 1992—. Author: Crime & Punishment in N.H. 1812-1914, 1995, Poor Relief in Durham, Lee & Madbury N.H., 1995; contbr. articles to profl. jour. Mem.: Ala. Libr. Assn. (sec. 2000—01, pres. 2004—05), Ala. Assn. of Coll. & Rsch. Libr. (pres. 2000—01). Democrat. Avocation: radio broadcaster. Office: Ralph Brown Draughon Libr Auburn Univ 231 Mell St Auburn University AL 36849-5606 Office Phone: 334-844-1729. Business E-Mail: dodgeti@auburn.edu.

DODGE, WILLIAM DOUGLAS, risk management consultant; b. Savannah, Ga., Sept. 26, 1937; s. Kenneth Douglas and Bettie Wilbur (Sadler) D.; m. Susan Penny, Dec. 27, 1958 (div. 1976); children: Gregory D., Phillip C., Warren D., Andrew L.; m. Marian Elizabeth Monroe, Apr. 2, 1983. BS, Ga. Inst. Tech., 1959; MBA, Ga. State U., 1966. CPCU, ARM. Underwriter Liberty Mutual Ins. Co., Atlanta, 1960-66; ins. adminstr. Lockheed Corp., Marietta, Ga., 1966-78; risk mgr. Schlumberger Ltd., Atlanta, 1978-79; v.p. ins. Fuqua Industries, Inc., Atlanta, 1979-90, v.p. ins. and benefits, 1991-92; pres. Fuqua Ins. Co. Ltd., Hamilton, Bermuda, 1978-92, Fuqua Risk Retention Group, Atlanta, 1989-92; ind. risk mgmt. cons. Atlanta, 1992-95. Adv. bd. Risk Mgmt. Inc., N.Y.C., 1978-92; chmn. bd., mem. investment com. J&H WF Syndicate B., N.Y. Ins. Exch., N.Y.C., 1984-88. Co-author: The Hold Harmless Agreement, 1968. Mem. Exec. Com. Reorgn. and Mgmt. Improvement State of Ga., 1971, Agts. Licensing Exam. Revision Bd. State Ga., 1970; bd. dirs. Ga. State U. Ednl. Found., 1980-88; lt. comdr. USPS/Tybee Light Power Squadron, 1999, comdr., 2000—. Republican. Methodist. Avocations: gardening, boating. Office: Mickey Dodge & Assocs Inc 12 Pipers Pond Ln Savannah GA 31404-1122 Personal E-mail: savdodges@aol.com.

DODGEN, DANIEL W., health policy advisor, psychologist; s. David W Dodgen and Marye Dodgen Settles. BA in Psychology, U. So. Calif., L.A., 1986, BA in Spanish, 1986; MA in Clin. Psychology, U. Houston, 1990, PhD in Clin. Psychology, 1995. Lic. clin. psychologist D.C., 2000. Clin. psychologist Didi Hirsch CMHC, L.A., 1992—96; congl. fellow U.S. Ho. of Reps., Washington, 1996—97; sr. fed. affairs officer APA, Washington, 1997—2003; emergency mgmt. coord. Office of the Sec., U.S. Dept. HHS, Washington, 2003—. Chair Pentagon Mental Health Response Coalition, Washington, 2001—03, Nat. Child and Adolescent Mental Health Coalition, Washington, 1997—2003; mental health steering com. Met. Wash. Coun. of Govts., Washington, 2003—05. Recipient Early Career Contbn. award, APA, 2005, Scholar in Rehab. Policy, Mary Switzer Found., 2000; fellow Congl. Sci. fellow, APA. Mem.: APA, Smithsonian Instn., US Holocaust Meml. Mus., Phi Beta Kapa. Office: US Dept HHS 200 Independence Ave Washington DC 20201 Home Phone: 202-518-0151; Office Phone: 240-276-2237.

DODGEN, JOHN N., manufacturing executive; b. Sapulpa, Okla., June 22, 1926; s. Claude W. and Pearl M. (Glass) D.; m. Wanda Lou Edwards; children: James, Mary Lou, John C.T., Lori. BA, Ottawa U., 1956; PMD, Harvard U., 1961. V.p. distbn. farm equipment Dodgen & Co., Fort Dodge, Iowa, 1947-56; v.p. mfg. and distbn. farm equipment Dodgen Associated Mfrs., Sioux City, Iowa, 1956-58; pres. mfg. and distbn. farm equipment Silbaugh Mfg., Humboldt, Iowa, 1958-61; pres. mfg. farm and indsl. equipment Dodgen Industries, Inc., Humboldt, 1961—; pres., owner Rib Case, Ft. Dodge. Pres., founder John N. Dodgen Found., 1960—; pres. Dodgen Leasing Corp., Humboldt, 1964—, Born Free, Inc., Humboldt, 1969—, Fiberglass Fabricators, Inc., Humboldt, 1984—, Dodgen Mobile Technologies, Humboldt, 1990—, Custom Cabinets, Humboldt, Born Free Fla., 1998—, Born Free Kans., 1999—, Born Free Calif., 1999—; owner, pres. The Rib Cage, Fort Dodge, Iowa; trustee Ottawa (Kans.) U., 1964-99; bd. dirs. Iowa Assn. Bus. and Industry. Licensed Bapt. lay min., 1954—, trustee Ctrl. Bapt. Sem., 1963-73; chmn. campaign Humboldt Area Family Aquatic Ctr; pres. Humboldt County Taxpayers Assn., 2002. Named one of One Thousand Gt. Ams., 2003. Mem. Rotary. Avocations: hunting pheasants, geese and ducks, golf, fishing, public speaking. Office: Dodgen Industries Inc Hwy 169 N Humboldt IA 50548 Office Phone: 515-332-3755.

DODGEN, LARRY J., career military officer; b. New Orleans, June 12, 1949; BS, La. State U., 1972; MBA in Pub. Adminstrn., U. Mo.; MS in Nat. Security and Strategy, US Navel War Coll. Advanced through grades to lt. gen. US Army, 2003; comdr. 8th Battalion, 43d Air Defense Artillery, 1989—91, 69th Air Defense Artillery Brigade, Germany, 1993; comdr.-in-chief U.S. Army Europe; brigadier gen., 1996; dep. asst. sec. def. for policy and missions US Dept. Def.; dir. Joint Theater Air Missile Def. Orgn., Washington, 1998—2001; commdg. gen. U.S. Army Aviation and Missile Command, 2001—03, U.S. Army Space and Missile Defense Command / U.S. Army Forces Strategic Command, Arlington, Va., 2003—. Decorated Defense Disting. Svc. Medal with Oak Leaf Cluster, Legion of Merit (two Oak Leaf Clusters), Meritorious Svc. Medal (four Oak Leaf Clusters), Army Commendation Medal, Army Achievement Medal. Office: Commdg Gen USASMDC/ARSTRAT PO Box 15280 Arlington VA 22215-0280 Office Phone: 703-607-1874. Office Fax: 703-607-1879.

DODGE ROBBINS, DOROTHY ELLIN, language educator; b. Aug. 16, 1958; MA, U. S.D., 1991; PhD, U. Nebr., 2000. Lectr. Tex. A&M, College Station, 1987—88; asst. prof. English Dakota Wesleyan U., Mitchell, SD, 1995—99; instr. speech comm. La. Tech. U., Ruston, 1999—2000, asst. prof. English, 2000—. Co-editor: Christmas Stories from Louisiana, 2003, Christmas on the Great Plains, 2004, Christmas Stories from Georgia, 2005. Office: PO Box 3162 Ruston LA 71272-0001 Office Phone: 318-257-5488. Business E-Mail: drobbins@latech.edu.

DODIN, ILYA, research scientist; arrived in US, 1999; m. Yevgeniya Ilyunina. BS in Physics, Nizhniy Novgorod State U., Russia, 1998; MS in Physics, Princeton U., NJ, 2000, PhD, 2005. Rsch. asst. Princeton U.,

1999—2005, rsch. assoc., 2005—. Lectr. Nizhniy Novgorod State U., 2001—02. Recipient 1st prize, 7th Nizhniy Novgorod Session of Young Scientists, 2002; fellow Harold W. Dodds Fellowship, Princeton U., 2003—04; grantee, Russian Found. for Basic Rsch., 2002. Mem.: Am. Phys. Soc. Achievements include discovery of method of directing plasma flows along magnetic discontinuities; asymmetric ponderomotive current drive with reduced cyclotron heating; invention of storing, retrieving, and processing optical information by Raman backscattering in plasmas; current drive in a ponderomotive potential with sign reversal.

DODSON, ARLEEN CECILIA, language educator; b. Alhambra, Calif., Mar. 18, 1953; d. Moses and Olivia Beatrice (Potts) Baca; m. Walter Anthony Dodson, June 24, 1979; children: Robert, Elizabeth. AA, East Los Angeles Coll., 1973; BA in Spanish, Calif. State U., Los Angeles, 1978. Cert. life tchr., Calif. Bilingual aide Alhambra High Sch., 1977-78; tchr. 4th grade St. Anthony's, San Gabriel, Calif., 1982-84; bilingual tchr. 1st and 2d grades Garvey Sch. Dist., Rosemead, Calif., 1984-86; bilingual tchr. 3d-6th grades Wing Lane Sch., Hacienda La Puente Unified Sch. Dist., 1986—. Spanish interpreter Fed. Bldg. Immigration Ct., Los Angeles, 1977, 1987. Mem. adult choir St. John Vianney Cath. Ch., choir dir., 1986—; club staff rep. Friend to Friend Say No To Drugs; spokesperson Nat. Kidney Found. Recipient Outstanding Service award Garvey Sch. Dist., 1986, 1st place softball games San Luis Obispo Transplant Games, 1992; named Outstanding Woman of Achievement, YMCA, 1992. Mem. NEA, Calif. Edn. Assn., Calif. Tchrs. Assn., Assn. Curriculum Devel. Democrat. Roman Catholic. Avocation: teaching music. Home: 15320 Pintura Dr Hacienda Heights CA 91745-4406 Office: Hacienda La Puente Unified Sch Dist 15959 Gale Ave Hacienda Heights CA 91745-1604 Office Phone: 626-933-5300. E-mail: dracula318@aol.com.

DODSON, CARL EDWARD, nuclear engineer, real estate agent, minister, assistant superintendent; b. Chgo., July 8, 1956; s. John Eddie and Birdie (Dodson) Allen; m. Peggy E. Dodson; children: LaTreesa, Letiticia, LaTonya, Carl Jr., Barry. A in Engring., State Tech. Inst. at Memphis, 1980. Cert. plant engr.; lic. FCC 3d class, lic. Tenn. Bd. Realtors; ordained elder. Engring. aide Spl. Design, Knoxville, Tenn., 1980-82, Sequoyah Nuclear Plant, Knoxville, Tenn., 1982-84, design engr. Soddy, Tenn., 1985-88; real estate agt. Holmes Real Estate Co., Knoxville, Tenn., 1989-91; pres., CEO, Ezra Inc., Knoxville, 1990-91; sr. technician, analyst Weston Gulf Coast, University Park, Ill., 1992-94; pharm. technician Centeon, Kankakee, Ill., 1994-96; assoc. pastor (ordained) Shiloh Full Gospel Bapt. Ch., Kankakee; asst. supt. pub. works City of Kankakee, 1996—2002, mgr. bldg. maintenance, 2002—06; facility mgr. Dept. State, Fgn. Svcs., Kuala, Lumpar, 2006—. Author (software): New Student, 1980. Mem. Nat. Inst. Certification in Engring. Technologies, Jaycees (Chattanooga), Mem. Cert. in Plant Engring., Nat. Fire Protection Assn., Assn. Plant Engrs. Avocations: chess, reading, computer programming, bowling, photography. Office: US Dept State 4210 Kuala Lumpar Pl Dulles VA 20189-4210 Office Phone: 302-168-4894. Personal E-mail: carled@prodigy.net.

DODSON, DARYL THEODORE, ballet administrator, consultant; b. Warrensburg, Mo., Oct. 9, 1934; s. Theodore and Ada Marie (Ayres) D. BS, Ctrl. Mo. State U., 1956. Mem. Gov. S.C.'s Coun. of the Arts, 1974; mem. adv. panel Vt. Coun. on Arts, 1978; mgr. Am. tour 1st cultural exch., People's Republic of China and U.S., 1978, Nat. Ballet Cuba, 1979, Royal Ballet Eng., 1981; pres. Pine Cone Enterprises, Ltd., 1977-81; propr. Pine Cone Inn, Haverhill, N.H., 1978-81; mgr. Opera House, John F. Kennedy Ctr., Washington, 1981; mgr. U.S. and Can. tour Sweeney Todd, 1982; mgr. U.S. tours Amadeus, 1982-83, The Wiz, 1983-84, Les Miserables, 1988-92, Phantom of the Opera, 1992-2003; mgr. N.Y. engagement The Golden Land, 1985; mgr. Porgy and Bess, 1986-87, La Cage Aux Folles, 1987, N.Y. and U.S. tour Paris Opera Ballet, 1988; gen. mgr. John Curry Skating Co., 1984. Asst. dir. The Mikado, N.Y.C. Opera, 1959; regisseur Chgo. Opera Ballet, 1960, asst. stage mgr. Am. Ballet Theatre, N.Y.C., 1960, stage mgr., 1961, prodn. stage mgr., 1961, prodn. mgr., 1963, gen. mgr., 1968-77. Served with U.S. Army, 1957-59. Recipient Nat. Touring Broadway Achievement award, 2003. Mem. Theta Chi, Theta Alpha Phi. Episcopalian.

DODSON, HOWARD, research center administrator; b. Chester, Pa., June 1, 1939; m. Jualynne e. White; children: Alyce Christine, David Primus Luta. BS, West Chester State Coll., 1961; postgrad., UCLA, 1964; MA, Villanova U., 1964; ABF, U. Calif., Berkeley, 1977; DHL (hon.), Widner U., 1987, Adelphi Univ., 2004. Recruiter Peace Corps, 1966-67, dir. spl. recruiting, 1967-68, tng. officer, 1968; assoc. prof. Calif. State Coll., 1970; adj. prof. Shaw U., 1975; lectr. Emory U., 1976; program dir. Inst. of the Black World, 1973-74, exec. dir., 1974-79; asst. to chmn. NEH, 1980-82; dir. The Schomburg Ctr. for Rsch. in Black Culture, NYC, 1984—. Volunteer Peace Corps, 1964-66; cons. NEH, 1979-80; chmn., CEO Black theology Project, 1982-84; bd. mem. Inst. of the Black World, Apollo Theater Found., UNESCO Save the Route Project, Tougaloo Coll., Eugene Lang Coll., New Sch. for Social Rsch.; trustee Inst. Internat. Edn. Editor-in-chief Black World View, 1977; co-author Jubilee: The Emergence of African-American Culture, 2003, Black New Yorkers: The Schomburg Illustrated Chronology, 1999, Urban Physical Environments, 1995; editor Ideology, Identity and Assumptions, 2007, In Motion: The African-American Migration Experience, 2005. Mem. Oakland Black Caucus, 1969-73; mem. Edn. Brain trust Congl. Black Caucus, Atlanta U. Sch. Social Work, Nat. Commn. for Citizens in Edn., Nat. Credit Union Fed. Ecuador; bd. overseers Lang Coll./New Sch. for Social Rsch.; bd. dirs. NCBS, AHSA, Caribbean Rsch. Ctr. PICCO scholar, 1959-61; U. Calif.-Berkeley Grad. fellow, 1969-73, Inst. of the Black World Rsch. fellow, 1970-71; recipient Cmty. Leadership award, NY Assn. of Black Journalists, 2002. Mem. S.C. Hist. Soc., Atlanta Assn. for Internat. Edn., Ga. Assn. Black Elected Ofcls., ESEA, African Heritage Studies Assn., Assn. for Study of Afro-Am. History, So. Hist. Assn., Alpha Phi Alpha. Office: New York Public Libr 515 Malcolm X Blvd New York NY 10037-1801

DODSON, JOHN THOMAS, orchestra conductor; b. Dayton, Ohio, Jan. 17, 1957; s. James Henry and Anita Faye Dodson; m. Amy Elizabeth Simpson, June 14, 1990. MusM in Orchestral Conducting, Johns Hopkins U., 1981. Music dir. Philharmonia Orch. of Tucson, 1984—89, Coronado Music Festival, Tucson, 1985—87, Orch. N.Y., NYC, 1990—93; faculty Tenn. Technol. U., Cookeville, 1993—2001; music dir. Bryan Symphony Orch., Cookeville, Tenn., 1993—2001; faculty Adrian Coll., Mich., 2001—; music dir. Adrian Symphony Orch., Mich., 2001—. Guest condr. Budapest Philharm., Hungary, 1987; adminstrv. dir. The Yard: A Colony for Performing Artists, NYC, 1990—93; guest condr. Rochester Philharm., NY, 1994; cover condr. St. Louis Symphony Orch., 1995—97; condr. Sewannee Summer Music Ctr., Tenn., 1995—98, Tenn. Gov.'s Sch. for Arts, Murphreesboro, 1996—; guest condr. Rochester Philharm. Pops, NY, 1997; condr. Colo. Symphony Orch. Summer Orch. Tng. Program, Denver, 1997; guest condr. Albany Symphony Orch., Ga., 1998, Orquesta Sinfonica UANL, Monterrey, Mexico, 1998—99, Nat. Philharm. Orch. of Russia, Tomsk, 1999, Irkutsk Philharm., Russia, 1999; faculty condr. Okla. Arts Summer Inst., Norman, 1999; guest condr. Omsk Philharm., Russia, 1999—2004, Nat. Symphony Orch. of Bashkortostan, Ufa, Russia, 2000—04, Bialystok Symphony Orch., Poland, 2002. Recipient Outstanding Young Alumni award, Tenn. Technol. U., 1985, Golden Book award, Budapest Philharm., 1987, Sally Parker Edn. award, Am. Symphony Orch. League, 1995, 1998; Music Club of Am. scholarship, Peabody Conservatory of Music, 1981 - 1983, Conducting fellowship, Aspen Music Sch., 1983. Home: 1117 College Ave Adrian MI 49221 Office: Adrian Symphony Orch Rush Hall 110 S Madison St Adrian MI 49221 Home Phone: 517-264-5414; Office Phone: 517-264-3121. Office Fax: 517-264-3833. Personal E-mail: jdodson@adrian.edu. E-mail: john@aso.org.

DODSON, ROBERT WAYNE, surgeon; b. Hugoton, Kans., Dec. 10, 1957; s. Tollie Lones Dodson and Oma Jo Dodson-Boyte; m. Connie Gail Bowdre, Dec. 27, 1975; children: Jared Wayne, Amber Renee, Elizabeth Anna. BS, Okla. State U., Stillwater, 1982; MD, Uniformed Svcs. U., Bethesda, Md., 1986. Diplomate Am. Bd. Surgery, Am. Bd. Colon and Rectal Surgery. Surgery resident Keesler AFB, 1986—91; colon and rectal surgery fellow U. Ill., Carle Found. Hosp., Urbana Champaign, 1991—92; cons. surgeon USAF Surgeon Gen., Bolling AFB, DC, 1997—99; pvt. practice Crescent City, Calif., 1999—2001, Grove, Okla., 2001—04; pvt. practice, trauma dir. St. John's Med. Group, Joplin, Mo., 2004—. Lt. col., staff surgeon USAF, 1992—97. Fellow: ACS, Am. Soc. Colon and Rectal Surgery. Office: Saint Johns Med Group 2817 McClelland Ste 256 Joplin MO 64804

DODSON, SAMUEL ROBINETTE, III, retired investment banker; b. Nashville, Feb. 24, 1943; s. Samuel Robinette and Helen Elizabeth (Maiden) D.; m. Marsha Robertson Moody, Aug. 2, 1969; children—Bradley John, Andrew Caldwell. Student, Yale U., 1961-63; BS, Vanderbilt U., 1966; MBA, U. Chgo., 1968; MS, London Sch. Econs., 1968. Various fin. and planning positions Exxon Corp. and Affiliates, Houston, 1968-81; v.p. First Boston Corp., 1981-84, mng. dir., 1984-93, Merrill Lynch, Houston, 1993—2004; ret., 2004. Served to 1st lt. U.S. Army, 1963-64 Home Phone: 713-468-5353. E-mail: sam_dodson@ml.com.

DODSWORTH, ROY W., pharmaceutical company executive; b. Norwood, Mass., Sept. 6, 1948; s. James W. and Beulah G. Dodsworth; m. Genevieve Dodsworth, June 26, 1971; children: Dawn Terri, Roger H. Whitford Jr. BA, Drew U., 1970. Asst. dir. Ayerst Labs. Inc., NYC, 1983-86; dir., N.Am. head regulatory affairs Organon, Inc., West Orange, NJ, 1986-94; sr. assoc. dir. Sandoz, East Hanover, NJ, 1995-97, dir. N.Am. head, Regulatory CMC, 1995-97; from dir., regional area head-asthma, hormone replacement therapy, bone to v.p. global therapeutic area head neurosci. Novartis Pharm. Co., East Hanover, NJ, 1997—2004, v.p. global therapeutic area head neurosci., 2004—06; ret. Cons. in field to numerous pharm. cos. Contbr. numerous tech. publs. Active Budd Lake Rescue Squad, 1992-93; adv. com. Mt. Olive Township Multiple Family Dwelling, Budd Lane, 1980-83. Fellow Am. Inst. Chemists; mem. Regulatory Affairs Profl. Soc., Am. Chem. Soc., Drug Info. Assn., Parenteral Drug Assn. Republican. Methodist. Avocations: raquetball, basketball, football, softball, fishing. Home: 10 Crossing Dr Flanders NJ 07836-4709 Office: Novartis Pharm Co 1 Heatlh Plz East Hanover NJ 07936 Home Phone: 973-927-7496; Office Phone: 973-598-5324. Personal E-mail: dodsworthrw@optonline.net.

DOEBBLER, CURTIS F.J., lawyer; b. Buffalo, 1961; BA, BFA, So. Meth. U., 1983; JD, NYU Law Sch., 1988; LLM, U. Nijmegen, 1993; PhD in Internat. Law, London Sch. Econs. & Polit. Sci., 1998; diploma, Hague Acad. Internat. Law, 2000. Bar: Washington, DC, U.S. Ct. Appeals, 4th Cir., U.S. Ct. Fed. Claims. Internat. human rights lawyer, 1988—; legal asst. Van Driel & Verraats, Netherlands, 1993; legal cons. UNICEF, Sudan, 1997; of counsel Law Office of Ghazi Suleiman, Khartoum, Sudan, 1997—2002; advisor Adv. Coun. Human Rights Min. Justice, Govt. Sudan, 1997—99. Cons. on humanitarian projects Former Yugoslavia, 1992—97; instr. London Sch. Econs. and Polit. Sci., 1995—97; vis. prof. U. Tuzla, Bosnia-Herzegovina, 1996, Khartoum U., Sudan, 1997—98, U. Pristina, Kosovo, 2002—03, Tashkent State Inst. Law, Uzbekistan, 2004—05, An-Najah Nat. U., Nablus, Palestine, 2005—; disting. lectr. Dept. Polit. Sci. Am. U., Cairo, 2000—02. Author: International Human Rights Law: Cases and Materials, 2004, Introduction to International Humanitarian Law, 2005; contbr. numerous articles. Recipient Human Rights award, Acad. Internat. Human Rights and Humanitarian Law, 2001; Rsch. fellow, Hague Acad. Internat. Law, 1988, Law Dept. fellow, London Sch. Econs., 1995—97. Office: 1003 K St NW Ste 640 Washington DC 20001 Office Phone: 206-984-4734. Personal E-mail: human_rights_lawyer@writeme.com, cdoebbler@gmail.com.

DOEBERT, SANDRA L., school system administrator; b. Chicago Heights, Ill., June 5, 1957; d. William Jeremiah Teed and Barbara Ione (Stead) Allen; m. Edward Eugene Doebert, Apr. 20, 1984; children: Jeremiah Eugene, Justin Edward. M in Comm. Studies, No. Ill. U., Dekalb, 1984; cert. advanced studies, Nat. Louis U., Evanston, Ill., 1994; EdS, No. Ill. U., Dekalb, 2002, EdD, 2004. Supt. endorsement Ill., cert. type 75 adminstr. Ill., tchr. Ill. Tchr. Downers Grove (Ill.) South H.S., 1979—85, dean of students, 1985—94; asst. prin. Lemont (Ill.) H.S., 1994—2001, asst. supt. dist. 210, 2001—02, supt. dist. 210, 2002—. Assoc. Sch. Exec. Connect, Highland Park, Ill., 2005—06; pres. Fellowship Ednl. Leadership, DePere, Wis., 2003—06, Three Rivers Edn. for Employment Sys.; bd. dirs. Will County Area Vocat. Ctr. Choir mem. Bethany Luth. Ch., Lemont, 1987—2006. Mem.: Ill. Assn. Sch. Bus. Ofcls., Ill. Assn. Sch. Adminstrs., Ill. H.S. Dist. Orgn. (bd. dirs. 2004—06), S.W. Cook County Coop. Assn. for Spl. Edn. (chairperson), Lemont C. of C., Nat. Assn. Federally Impacted Schs. (bd. dirs. 2003—06), Lemont Jr. Womans Club. Avocations: fitness, singing, travel. Office: Lemont H S Dist 210 800 Porter St Lemont IL 60439

DOEBLER, BETTIE ANNE, language educator, researcher, poet; b. Atlantic City; d. Willoughby Foster and Ann (Ratledge) Young; m. John W. Doebler, Sept. 1, 1954 (dec. Aug. 26, 1994); 1 child, Mark B. BA, Duke U., 1953, MA, 1955; PhD, U. Wis., 1961. From instr. to assoc. prof. Dickinson Coll., Carlisle, Pa., 1961-70; assoc. prof. Ariz. State U., Tempe, 1971, prof., 1975, prof. emeritus, 1994—, dir. interdisciplinary humanities program, 1989-94. Vis. prof. English Grand Canyon U., Ariz., 2002—03; vis. prof. Ariz. State U., 2006. Author: The Quickening Seed: Death in the Sermons of John Donne, 1974, Rooted Sorrow: Dying in Early Modern Eng., 1994; co-author: Book of the Mermaid: Poems by Doebler, Slotten, Thiem, 2001, Breathing Between Dreams, 2007, Nine Waves: Poems by Doebler, Slotten, Thiem, 2003; co-editor: Funeral Sermons Publ. for Women (1600-1630), 8 vol., 2006; contbr. poetry in Passages North, The Awakenings Rev., articles to profl. jour. Angier B. Duke Grad. fellow Duke U., 1954; recipient Faculty Rsch. award Ariz. State U., 1984. Episcopalian. Personal E-mail: bettiea.doebler@aol.com.

DOEDE, JOHN HENRY, investment company executive; b. Chgo., Sept. 29, 1937; s. Clinton Milford and Dorothy Ruth (Hagemeyer) D.; m. Jean Anne Dabbs, May 6, 1983; children: Danna, Tina, Timothy. AB in Chemistry, Harvard U., 1959; MS in Phys. Chemistry, U. Chgo., 1962, PhD in Phys. Chemistry, Physics, 1963. Physicist Argonne Nat. Lab., Ill., 1963-65; mgr. EMR computer div. (electro magnetic rsch). Schlumberger Corp., Mpls., 1965-67; pres. Data Internat. Inc., Mpls., 1967-70; v.p. Heizer Corp., Chgo., 1970-72; v.p., dir. 1st Chgo. Investment Corp., 1972-83; pres. Polaris Capital Group, San Diego, 1983—88; chmn. JDJD, Inc., Palm Beach, Fla., 1992-97, Blue Eagle Golf Ctrs., Inc., Wayne, Pa., 1996-98, AIG Silk Road Fund, NYC, 1997—2006, Am. European Industries, Inc., 1999—2004, Answer System, Inc., 1999—2004; mng. mem. Bitter Inc. LLC, 2004—. Republican. Home: 7525 E Gainey Ranch Rd Unit 197 Scottsdale AZ 85258-1610 E-mail: john@johndoede.com.

DOERFLER, RONALD JOHN, publishing executive; b. Jersey City, July 15, 1941; s. Louis S. and Ann E. (Dubiak) D.; m. Beatrice Mary Corbett, Jan. 4, 1942; children: Stephanie, Nicholas. B in Acctg., Fairleigh Dickinson U., 1967, MBA magna cum laude, 1972. CPA N.Y., 1967. Fin. analyst ITT, NYC, 1966—69; asst. contr. Capital Cities Comm., NYC, 1969—76, treas., 1977—80, sr. v.p., CFO, 1980—85, Capital Cities/ABC, NYC, 1986—98, HEARST, NYC, 1998—, also bd. dirs. Trustee Fairleigh Dickinson U.; bd. dirs. Arts and Bus. Coun. Named one of Ams. Best CFO's, Instnl. Investor mag., 1986. Mem. AICPA, Internat. Radio and TV Soc., Inst. Newspaper Fin. Execs., Broadcast Cable Fin. Mgmt. Assn. (pres. 1979-80, former chmn. bd.). Office: Hearst 1345 Sixth Ave New York NY 10105*

DOERKSEN, ROBERT JOHN, pharmacy educator; s. Daniel William and Nettie Nan Doerksen; m. Yu-Chu Chen, July 3, 1993; children: Rosalie Shinwei, Edmund Siwei. BS, U. NB, Fredericton, NB, Can., 1986; diploma in Christian studies, Regent Coll., Vancouver, 1988; PhD, U. NB, Fredericton, NB, Can., 1998. Postdoctoral fellow U. Calif., Berkeley, 1999—2001, U. Pa., Phila., 2001—04; asst. prof. U. Miss., University, 2004—; rsch. asst. prof. Rsch. Inst. Pharm. Sci., University, 2004—. Hon. editl. bd. Perspectives in Medicinal Chemistry, North Harbour, Auckland, New Zealand, 2006—. Contbr. articles to profl. jours. Scholar, Natural Scis. Engring. Rsch. Coun., Can., 1995—97. Mem.: ONE, Am. Assn. Colls. Pharmacy, Am. Chem. Soc. (symposium co-chair 2005—). Achievements include patent pending for methods, systems, and computer program products for computational analysis and design of amphiphilic polymers. Office: Univ Miss Department of Medicinal Chemistry 421 Faser Hall University MS 38677-1848 Office Phone: 662-915-5880. Office Fax: 662-915-5638. Business E-Mail: rjd@olemiss.edu.

DOERMANN, HUMPHREY, writer, consultant; b. Toledo, Nov. 13, 1930; s. Henry John and Alice (Robbins Humphrey) D.; m. Elisabeth Adams Wakefield, Jan. 7, 1956; children: Elisabeth M., Eleanor H., Julia L. AB, Harvard U., 1952, MBA, 1958, PhD, 1967; LLD (hon.), Xavier U., La., 1990, U. Minn., 1997; LHD (hon.), Coll. St. Scholastica, 1993, U. St. Thomas, 1996, Ctrl. Coll., 1998. Asst. to com. on admissions and scholarships Harvard, 1955-56; reporter Mpls. Star, 1958-60; asst. to bus. mgr. Mpls. Star & Tribune Co., 1960-61; dir. admissions Harvard, 1961-66; asst. to dean Harvard (Faculty of Arts and Scis.), 1966-69, asst. dean for financial affairs, 1970-71; lectr. on edn. Harvard (Grad. Sch. Edn.), 1967-71; exec. dir. Bush Found., St. Paul, 1971-78, pres., 1978-97; vis. prof. Macalester Coll., 1997-2000, rsch. assoc., 2000—. Cons. Coun. Higher Edn. Va., 1969, W.Va. Bd. Regents, 1970; bd. overseers Harvard Coll., Harvard U., 1973-79; trustee St. Paul Acad. and Summit Sch., 1997-2006; bd. dirs. Coun. on Founds., Washington, 1985-92, chmn. bd. 1990-92; trustee Found. Ctr., N.Y.C., 1975-83, chmn. bd. 1982-83; chmn. Minn. Coun. on Founds., 1981-85, Coll. Bd., N.Y.C., 1994-99; chmn. Minn. Legis. Task Force on Student Aid, 1993; chair regents candidate adv. coun. U. Minn., 1997-99; chmn. Minn. Humanities Commn., 2004-06. Author: Crosscurrents in College Admissions, rev. edit, 1970, Toward Equal Access, 1978; co-author (with Henry N. Drewry) Stand and Prosper, 2001. Mem. Belmont (Mass.) Town Meeting, 1969-70. Served to lt. (j.g.) USN, 1952-55. Home: 736 Goodrich Ave Saint Paul MN 55105-3524 Office: Macalester Coll 1600 Grand Ave Saint Paul MN 55105-1801 E-mail: doermann@macalester.edu.

DOERPER, JOHN ERWIN, journal editor, publishing executive; b. Würzburg, Germany, Sept. 17, 1943; came to U.S., 1963, naturalized resident, 1973; s. Werner and Theresa (Wolf) Doerper; m. Victoria McCulloch, Dec. 2, 1970. BA, Calif. State U., Fullerton, 1968; postgrad., U. Calif., Davis, 1972. Writer/author, Seattle, 1984—; food columnist Washington, Seattle, 1985-88, Seattle Times, 1985-88; food editor Wash.-The Evergreen State Mag., Seattle, 1989-94, Pacific Northwest mag., 1989-94, Seattle Home and Garden, 1989-91; pub., editor, founder Pacific Epicure, Quarterly Jour. Gastronomy, Bellingham, Wash., 1988—. Dir. Annual N.W. Invitational Chef's Symposium. Author: Eating Well: A Guide to Foods of the Pacific Northwest, 1984, The Eating Well Cookbook, 1984, Shellfish Cookery: Absolutely Delicious Recipes from the West Coast, 1985, Pacific Northwest Wine Country, 2001, author: Washington: A Compass Guide, 2002, Fodor's Pacific Northwest, 2002, Fodor's Seattle, 2000, California Wine Country, 2004, Oregon Wine Country, 2004, Washington Wine Country, 2004; author, illustrator: The Blue Carp, 1994, Wine Country: California's Napa and Sonoma Valleys, 1996, Pacific Northwest, 1997, Coastal California, 1998, 3d edit, 2005 (Lowell Thomas Travel Journalism Competition Gold medal 1999), 3d edit., 2005; contbr. articles to profl. jours., intro. and chpts. to books. Recipient Silver medal, White award for city and regional mags. William Allen White Sch. Journalism, U. Kans., Lowell Thomas award Gold medal for best guide book, 1999. Mem. Oxford Symposium Food and Cookery (speaker 26th Ann. Pacific N.W. Writer's Conf. 1982, 92). Avocations: travel, painting, printmaking. Business E-Mail: jdoerper@mac.com.

DOERR, HARVEY, oil industry executive; With Hudson's Bay Oil & Gas (formerly Dome Petroleum Ltd., Calgary, Alta., Husky Oil Ops. Ltd., Lloydminster, Alta., Murphy Oil Co. Ltd., 1989—2006, various positions including mgr. dist. ops., sr. engr., mgr. fgn. ops. and gen. mgr. fgn. ops. & spl. projects, pres., 1997—2006; exec. v.p. Murphy Oil Corp., 2007—. Former chair bd. dirs. C-Core; former bd. mem. Syncrude Can. Mem.: Assn. Profl. Engrs., Geologists and Geophysicists Alta. Office: Murphy Oil Corp PO Box 7000 El Dorado AR 71731-7000 Office Phone: 870-862-6411.*

DOERR, (L.) JOHN, venture capitalist; b. St. Louis, June 29, 1951; m. Ann Doerr; 2 children. BS in Electrical Engring., Rice U., 1973, MSEE in Electrical Engring., 1974; MBA, Harvard U. Joined Intel Corp., 1974; ptnr. Kleiner Perkins Caulfield & Byers, Menlo Park, Calif., 1980—; founder, CEO Silicon Compilers, 1981—. Bd. dirs. Intuit, Amazon.com, Drugstore.com, Homestore.com, PalmOne, Sun Microsystems, 1982—2006, Google, Good Tech., Segway, Elance, EndForce. Named one of 400 Richest Ams., Forbes mag., 2006. Office: Kleiner Perkins Caufield and Byers 2750 Sand Hill Rd Menlo Park CA 94025-7020 E-mail: johnd@kpcd.com.*

DOERR, PATRICIA MARIAN, elementary and special education educator; b. Rochford, Essex, Eng., Mar. 14, 1947; came to U.S., 1976; d. Edward Earnest and Winifred May (Daniels) Earl; m. Hans Joachim Doerr, Dec. 17, 1983; children: Daniel, Nicholas, Carla. Cert. of Edn., Sussex U., 1968; Diploma in Edn. of Handicapped, London U., 1974; MS, Calif. Luth. U., 1986. Tchr. Long Road Jr. Sch., Canvey Island, Eng., 1968-70; tchr. scale 1 Belvedere Jr. Sch., Kent, England, 1970-71; tchr. scale 2 Bostal Manor Jr. Sch., Kent, England, 1971-73; tchr. scale 3, head remedial Warren Wood Boys Comprehensive Sch., Rochester, Kent, 1974-76; ednl. therapist Westvalley Ctr. for Ednl. Therapy, Canoga Park, Calif., 1977-79; tchr. K-2 Sundance Sch., Simi Valley, Calif., 1977-78; spl. tchr. Conejo Valley Unified Sch. Dist., Thousand Oaks, Calif., 1979-94; elem. tchr. Meadows Elem. Sch., Thousand Oaks, Calif., 1994—98; tchr. on leave (lang. arts specialist) Ventura County, 1998—2004; 7th grade tchr. Los Cerritos Mid. Sch., Thousand Oaks, Calif., 2004—. Ednl. cons., Ventura County, 1998-2004; mem. London Panel of Art Tutors, ILEA Evening Inst., 1969-73; mentor spl. edn. and lang. arts Conejo Valley Unified Sch. Dist., 1988-95. Recipient Award of Tchr. Excellence, AMGEN, 1996; Scwrip fellow Santa Barbara U., 1988. Mem. Calif. Assn. Mediated Learning (bd. dirs. 1991-95). Episcopalian. Home: 1933 Tamarack St Westlake Village CA 91361-1841

DOERRIE, BOBETTE, secondary school educator, consultant; b. Albuquerque, June 22, 1944; d. Neill and Dorothy Madelyn (Jones) Patterson; m. Edward Lewis Horton, Aug. 21, 1966 (div. 1990); children: Leah, James, Carol, Neill; m. Jerome Lee Doerrie, July 28, 1991; children: Jennifer, Elena. BA, McMurry Coll., 1966; MEd, DePaul U., 1977. Cert. sec. broadfield sci. Tchr. physics and phys. sci, environ. edn., TAKS remed. G/T coord. Perryton HS, Tex.; tchr. Summit Sch., Dundee, Ill., 1974-77, Lamesa Mid. Sch., 1980—85, Lamesa HS, 1968—69, 1985—91, Perryton HS, 1991—2005; ednl. cons. adult edn. Frank Phillips CC, Borger, 2005—06; dir. ednl. svcs. Frank Philipps CC, 2006—. Co-dir. Dawson County Sci. Fair, 1981-91; coach Odyssey of the Mind, 1988-91; mem.

McMurry U. Ednl. Adv. Bd., 1991-97, engring. team faculty advisor, 1993-2004, sci. olympiad coach, 1998-2000, sci. bowl advisor, 2001-05; instr. astronomy Frank Phillips Coll., 2006—; rsch. dir., Duck Pond Creek Exptl. Farms. Bd. dirs. Mus.Dawson County, 1983—90, Libr. Ochiltree County, 1993—95, v.p., 1993—95; bd. dirs. Perrytown Crisis Ctr., 2005—. Recipient Excellence in Teaching award Tex. State Assn. for Physics Tchrs., 1992, Nat. Tchg. award RadioShack, 2001; NSF/Tex. Edn. Assn. Christa McAuliffe grantee, 1993, Outstanding Sci. Educator, Tex. Acad. Sci., 2002, Nat. Tchg. award Health Physics Soc., 2002; named Tchr. of Yr., Region XVI Gifted and Talented Tchrs., 1994, Perryton H.S., 2004. Mem.: Sci. Tchrs. of Tex. (treas. 1998—2001), South Plains Sci. Soc. (pres. 1988, Sharon Christa McAuliffe Tchr. of Yr. 1987), Delta Kamma Gamma (past pres.). Avocations: amateur radio, painting, astronomy, reading, writing. Home: 13925 County Rd B Booker TX 79005-4125 Office Phone: 806-648-1450. Business E-Mail: bdoerrie@fpctx.edu.

DOERRIES, REINHARD RENÉ, historian, educator; b. Berlin, Sept. 25, 1934; came to U.S., 1954; s. Hermann and Annemarie (Kochendoerffer) D.; m. Elaine Sulli, Jan. 20, 1963; 1 child, Chantal-Aimée. BA, Concordia Coll., 1958; MFA, Ohio U., 1960; MA, Yale U., 1962; MBA, Inst. Europèen d'Adminstrn. des Affaires, Fontainebleau, France, 1965; PhD, Bochum U., 1971; habilitation, U. Hamburg, 1982. With internat. divsn. 1st Nat. Bank of Boston, 1962-64; internat. mgmt. cons. Booz Allen & Hamilton Internat., Zurich, Switzerland, 1965-68; asst. prof. modern history Hamburg U., Germany, 1970-73, 75-83, prof., 1983-86, U. Kassel, Germany, 1986-88, U. Erlangen-Nuremberg, Germany, 1988—. Guest prof. U. Southampton, Eng., 1986; internat. fellow Am. Coun. Learned Socs., N.Y.C., 1973-75; lectr. in field. Author: Washington-Berlin 1908/1917, 1975, Iren und Deutsche in der Neuen Welt, 1985, Imperial Challenge, 1989, Prelude to the Easter Rising, 2000, Hitler's Last Chief of Foreign Intelligence, 2003; editor: Memoirs of Erika von Watzdorf-Bachoff, 1997, Diplomaten und Agenten, 2001; co-editor: Amerikastudien, 1990—2003, American Studies Book Series, 1990—; adv. editor: Perspectives in Intelligence History, 1991—95; contbr. articles to profl. jours. Bd. dirs. Internat. Sch., Hamburg, 1979-80; bd. dirs. Am. House Nuremberg, 1995—, vice chmn., 1996—. Danforth Found. fellow Yale U., 1962. Mem. German Soc. for Am. Studies (dir. 1976-84, pres. 1987-90, dir. 1990-98), Am. Hist. Assn., German Soc. for Can. Studies, Immigration History Soc., Internat. Intelligence History Study Assn. (dir. 1993-00), Soc. Historians of Am. Fgn. Rels., German Hist. Assn., Group 65 Club (founder), Yale Club. Avocation: painting. Office: U Erlangen-Nuremberg Findelgasse 9 90402 Nuremberg Germany

DOERSAM, CHARLES HENRY, JR., engineer, educator, entrepreneur, writer; b. NYC, Nov. 1, 1921; s. Charles Henry, Sr. and Mary Emily (Davenport) D.; m. Cynthia Ann Wick, Dec. 7, 1954 (div. dec. 1980); children: Charles Henry III, Donna Davenport, Dean Robert. BS in Engring., Columbia U., NYC, 1942, MSME, 1944; postgrad., MIT, Cambridge, Mass., U. Mich., Ann Arbor, NYU. Registered profl. engr., N.Y. Indsl. engr. Pratt & Whitney, East Hartford, Conn., 1941-42; mem. tech. staff Bell Telephone Labs, NYC, 1942-44; with Combined Rsch. Group, Naval Rsch. Lab., 1944—46; sr. project engr Spl. Devices Ctr., Sands Point, NY, 1946-53; project mgr. Sperry Gyroscope Co., Lake Success, N.Y., 1953-60; new product planning mgr. Potter Instrument Co., Plainview, N.Y., 1960-62; dir. mktg. chief engr. Instruments for Industry, Hicksville, N.Y., 1962-64; prof. Poly. Inst. Bklyn., 1964-69; pres. Com Comp Inc, Hauppauge, N.Y., 1969-71; chmn., CEO Fiber Optic Sensors, Inc., Old Lyme, Conn., 1983—, Pres. DOERCO Cons., CUB Computer Co., NUTEK Corp., Princeton Automated Labs., Pedagogy Rsch. Inst.; nat. chmn. IRE Profl. Group on Space Electronics, 1950. Pantentee in field; contbr. articles to profl. jours. Bd. Advisors Waldorf Sch., Garden City, N.Y., 1964-68, Portledge Sch., Locust Valley, N.Y., 1977. Lt. (j.g.) USNR, 1944-46. Mem. North Shore Yacht Club (commn. 1968-69), Point O'Woods Club. Republican. Congregationalist. Avocations: tennis, sailing, woodworking, gardening, construction. Home and Office: 67 Shore Rd PO Box 927 Old Lyme CT 06371-0927 Office Phone: 860-434-0666 ext. 7. Personal E-mail: fosicharlie@yahoo.com.

DOETSCH, VIRGINIA LAMB, former advertising executive, writer; b. NYC, Oct. 12, 1920; d. Andrew Thomas and Cameola Weeden (Burns) Lamb; m. Gunter H. Doetsch, Oct. 12, 1953 (div. Feb. 1972); 1 child, Hugo. BS, Northwestern U., 1941; postgrad., Columbia U., 1943—44, postgrad., 1946—47. Writer, dir. pub. rels. J. Walter Thompson, Frankfurt, Germany, 1953-56; creative group head, v.p. to ptnr. Tatham-Laird & Kudner (now Euro RSCG), Chgo., 1959—76; v.p. Needham Harper & Steers (now DDB Chgo.), Chgo., 1976-83; free-lance advt. writer and prodr. Chgo., 1983—; writer, rschr. OmniTech Cons. Group, Chgo., 1992-99. Mem. Chgo. Symphony Orch. Women's Assn., 1992—2006; fundraiser, subscription sales Goodman Theatre, Chgo., 2003—; bd. dirs. Better Bus. Bur., Chgo., 1973—76, Jr. Achievement, Chgo., 1973, Chgo. Symphony Orch. Women's Assn., 2002—06. With ARC, 1944—46, China, Burma, India. Decorated Bronze Star; named Woman of Yr., Am. Advt. Fedn., 1973. Mem. Women's Advt. Club Chgo. (Woman of Yr. award 1973), Chgo. Advt. Club (bd. dirs. 1973-76). Home: 400 E Randolph St Apt 828 Chicago IL 60601-7309

DOFT, BERNARD HARVEY, ophthalmologist; b. NYC, Aug. 13, 1946; children: Michelle, Amy, Jennifer. Student, Cornell U., 1964—67; MD, NYU, 1971. Diplomate Am. Bd. Internal Medicine, Am. Bd. Ophthalmology. Intern, asst. resident in internal medicine Barnes Hosp., Washington U. Sch. of Medicine, St. Louis, 1971—73; rsch. assoc. NIH, Nat. Heart & Lung Inst. and Bur. of Biologics, Bethesda, Md., 1973—75; resident in ophthalmology Bascom Palmer Eye Inst., U. Miami Sch. Medicine, 1975—78, fellowship in diseases and surgery of retina and vitreous, 1978—79; asst. prof. ophthalmology U. Pitts. Sch. Medicine, 1979—84, clin. assoc. prof. ophthalmology, 1984—99, clin. assoc. prof. epidemiology, 1989—99, clin. prof. ophthalmology, 1999—; pvt. practice Retina Vitreous Cons, Pitts., 1984—. Cons. vision rsch. rev. com. NIH Nat. Eye Inst., 1985, protocol rev. com, 2003; apptd. ophthalmic steering com., diabetic control and complications trial NIH, 1983; quality assurance com. Bascom Palmer Eye Inst., Ann Bates Leach Eye Hosp., U. Miami Sch. Medicine, 1977—78; co-dir., retina svc. Eye and Ear Hosp., U. Pitts., 1979—84, operating rm. com., 1982—87, chmn. com. on lasers, 1982—85; clinic coord. com. Eye and Ear Hosp., Pitts., 1982—85, ad hoc. com. for adminstrn./staff rels., 1983—85, chmn. oversight com. outpatient testing and laser ctr., 1983—85, med. staff nursing oversight com., 1983—98; study chair the endophthalmitis vitrectomy study Nat. Eye Inst., Bethesda, 1989—99; SurgiCenter task force U. Pitts. Med. Ctr., 1995, ophthalmology search com. dept. of ophthalmology chmn., 95; network cons. Diabetic Retinopathy Clin. Rsch. Network, 2003; rsch. adv. com. for steroids in ctrl. vein occlusion study NIH, 2003—. Vitreoretinal Surgery and Technology, 1989—99; contbr. articles to profl. jours. Parent coun. Emory U., Atlanta, 1998—2002. With USPHS, 1973—75. Named one of Best Drs. in Am., 1999, 2002, 2003, 2004, 2005, 2006; recipient Disting. Tchg. award Dept. Ophthalmology, U. Pitts. Sch. Medicine, 1998, 2000, 2007; grantee in field. Fellow: ACS, Am. Acad. Ophthalmology; mem.: AMA, Pa. Acad. Ophthalmology (coun. mem. 1990—91), Retina Soc. (chmn. nominating com. 2006—07), Am. Soc. Retnal Specialists, Macula Soc., Allegheny County Med. Soc., Pa. Med. Soc., Pitts. Ophthalmology Soc. (exec. com. 1980—91, program co-chmn. 1982—83, program chmn. 1983—87, v.p., pres.-elect 1987—88, pres. 1989—91, chmn. nominating com. 1991—93), Bascom Palmer Eye Inst. Alumni Assn., Alpha Omega Alpha. Avocation: tennis. Home: 123 South Dr Pittsburgh PA 15238-2313 Office: Retina-Vitreous Cons Ste 500 3501 Forbes Ave Pittsburgh PA 15213-3317 Office Phone: 412-683-5300.

DOGANÇAY, BURHAN C., artist, photographer, sculptor; b. Istanbul, Turkey, Sept. 11, 1929; s. Adil and Hediye Dogançay; m. Angela Hausmann, Dec. 11, 1978. Student in Art, Acad. de la Grande Chaumière, Paris, 1955; PhD in Econs., U. Paris, 1955. Artist, NYC, 1964—. Dir. dept. tourism Govt. of Turkey, Ankara, 1959-62, dir. Turk Info. NYC, 1962-64; founder Dogançay Mus., Istanbul, Turkey, 2004. One-man exhibitions, Ctr. Georges Pompidou, Paris, 1982, Mus. St.-Georges, Liége, Belgium, 1982, Mus. Art Contemporain, Montreal, 1983, Seibu Mus. Art, Tokyo, 1989, State Russian Mus., St. Petersburg, 1992, Artists' Union, Moscow, 1992, JFK Internat. Airport, 1998—2000, Inst. Francais d'Istanbul, 2005; contbr. art to profl. pubs. Recipient Cert. of Appreciation, City of NY, 1964, Appreciaiton medal Ministry of Culture Russia, 1992, Nat. Medal of Arts for Lifetime Achievement and Cultural Contbn., Pres. of Turkey, 1995; fellow Tamarind Lithography Workshop, 1969; design selected for UNICEF cards, 1974, 1996. Mem.: NY Artists' Equity Assn. Avocations: travel, photography. Personal E-mail: gogancay@aol.com. *Mostly unshattered self-confidence, hard work and the willingness to meet new challenges are the basis of my success and happiness.*

DOGANDZIC, ALEKSANDAR, electrical engineer, educator; b. Uzice, Yugoslavia, Nov. 7, 1971; s. Ljubodrag and Radmila Dogandzic. PhD, U. Ill., Chgo., 2001. Asst. prof. Iowa State U., Ames, Litton Industries asst. prof. elec. and computer engring., 2006—. Contbr. articles to profl. publs. Career grantee, NSF, 2006—. Mem.: IEEE. Orthodox Christian. Office: Iowa State U ECpE Dept 3119 Coover Hall Ames IA Home Phone: 515-292-4495; Office Phone: 515-294-0500. Office Fax: 515-294-8432. Business E-Mail: ald@iastate.edu.

DOGGETT, JOHN MARTIN, JR., (MARTY DOGGETT), headmaster; m. Patti Doggett. BA in Am. Civilization, Williams Coll., 1973; MA in History, NYU, 1981. History and econs. tchr., housemaster and coach to assoc. headmaster and dean students Lawrenceville Sch., Lawrenceville, NJ, 1974—98; headmaster Gov. Dummer Acad., Byfield, Mass., 1999—. Mem. bd. dirs. City Prep, Inc. Office: Gov Dummer Acad 1 Elm St Byfield MA 01922*

DOGGETT, LLOYD ALTON, II, congressman, retired judge; b. Austin, Tex., Oct. 6, 1946; s. Lloyd A. and Alyce (Freydenfeldt) Doggett; m. Elizabeth Belk, 1969; children: Lisa, Catherine. BBA in Bus., U. Tex., Austin, 1967; JD with honors, U. Tex. Sch. Law, 1970. Bar: Tex. 1971, US Ct. Appeals (5th cir.) 1972, US Dist. Ct. (we. dist.) Tex. 1972. Mem. Tex. State Senate from Dist. 14, 1973-85; ptnr. Doggett and Jacks, Austin, Tex., 1975-88; justice Tex. Supreme Ct., Austin, 1989-94; mem. US Congress from 25th Tex. dist., 1995—, mem. ways and means com., mem. Green Scissors Caucus. Adj. prof. U. Tex. Sch. Law, 1989-94; chair Supreme Ct. Task Force on Jud. Ethics, 1992-94; co-founder Info. Tech. Working Grp.; mem. Congl. Task Force on Tobacco and Health. Named one of Five Outstanding Young Texans Tex. Jaycees, 1977, Best Legislators, Tex. Monthly, 1979, 81; named Outstanding Young Lawyer of Austin, 1978, Outstanding State Senator, Common Cause, 1980, Disting. Alumnus, Bus. Adminstrn. Honors prog. U. Tex., 1989, Outstanding Jurist in Tex., Mex. Am. Bar Assn., 1993, Hispanic Bus. Adv. of Yr. Tex. Assn. Mex.-Am. Cs. of C.; recipient James Madison award Freedom of Info. Found. Tex., 1990, First Amendment award Nat. Soc. Profl. Journalists, 1990, Arthur B. DeWitty award for outstanding achievement in human rights Austin NAACP, Pub. Interest Champion award Pub. Interest Rsch. Grp., 2003, Environ. Champion award Tex. League of Conservation Voters, 2006. Mem. Consumers Union US (bd. dirs. 1976-79, 80-81, 86-89), Tex. Consumer Assn. (pres. 1973). Democrat. Methodist. Office: US Ho Reps 201 Cannon Ho Office Bldg Washington DC 20515-4310 Office Phone: 202-225-4865.*

DOGGRELL, HENRY PATTON, lawyer; b. Memphis, July 3, 1948; s. Frank Ernest Doggrell Jr. and Martha (Patton) Brown; m. Beverly Gay Rhoda, Jan. 22, 1983; children: Henry Patton Jr., Dana Scott, Adrian Edward. BS in Commerce, U. Va., 1970; JD, Vanderbilt U., 1976. Bar: U.S. Dist. Ct. (mid. dist.) Tenn. 1977, U.S. Ct. Appeals (6th cir.) 1977, U.S. Dist. Ct. (we. dist.) Tenn. 1978, U.S. Ct. Appeals (fed. cir.) 1985. Law clk. to Judge Harry W. Wellford, U.S. Dist. Ct., 1975; assoc. Boult, Cummings, Conners & Berry, Nashville, 1976-78; ptnr. Burch, Porter & Johnson, Memphis, 1978-88, Baker, Donelson, Bearman & Caldwell, Memphis, 1988—96; gen. counsel Buckeye Techs., Inc., 1996—97, sr. v.p. corp. devel., 1998—2001; v.p. gen coun. GTx, Inc., Memphis, 2001—, sec., 2001—. Chmn. ad hoc com. Citizens on Govtl. Consolidation, Memphis, 1978; chmn. Brooks Mus. Art, 2000-02; bd. dirs. Calvary St. Ministry, 1996—, Nature Conservancy Tenn. Lt. (j.g) USN, 1970—71. Mem. ABA, Tenn. Bar Assn. (chmn. real estate sect., sec. com. on real estate 1988-90). Republican. Unitarian. Avocations: backpacking, fishing, hiking, skiing, reading, golf. Home: 1657 Peabody Ave Memphis TN 38104-3829 Office: GTx Inc 3 N Dunlap 3rd FL Memphis TN 38163 Home Phone: 901-726-6544; Office Phone: 901-507-6916. Business E-Mail: hdoggrell@gtxinc.com.

DOGLIONE, ARTHUR GEORGE, data processing executive; b. Bklyn., May 24, 1938; s. Francis and Georgia (Smith) D.; m. Maryann Laurette Bonfanti, Sept. 3, 1960; children: Dana Ann, Arthur Todd, Lora Michele. AA, Scottsdale CC, Ariz., 1978; AAS, Maricopa Tech. Coll., Phoenix, 1984; BS, Ariz. State U., 1985. Salesman Columbus Realty Co., Trenton, N.J., 1962-65; appraiser J.H. Martin Appraisal Co., Trenton, 1965-68; office mgr. Mcpl. Revaluations, Avon-by-the-Sea, N.J., 1968-69; pres., broker Area Real Estate Agy., Wall, N.J., 1969-76; property appraiser Ariz. Dept. Revenue, Phoenix, 1976-78; investment appraiser Continental Bank, Phoenix, 1978-79; appraisal systems specialist Ariz. Dept. Revenue, Phoenix, 1979-80; project dir. Ariz. Dept. Adminstrn., 1980-83; pres. Logical Models, Scottsdale, Ariz., 1983-95; founder GENUS Technology, Scottsdale, 1989—. Tax assessor Upper Freehold Twp., N.J., 1974-75, Borough of Bradley Beach, N.J., 1975; lectr. in field. Author various software; pantentee infield. Counselor SCORE, SBA, Mesa, Ariz., 1986-90. Mem. Phi Theta Kappa. Republican. Roman Catholic. Achievements include patents for system and method for defining and creating surrogate addresses for township and range quarter sections. Office: GENUS Technology PO Box 725 Scottsdale AZ 85252-0725 Office Phone: 480-990-2470. Personal E-mail: genustech@msn.com.

DOHAN, ANDREW H., lawyer; b. Phila., 1952; BA in Econs., Yale U., New Haven, 1974; JD cum laude, Villanova U., Pa. Bar: Pa. 1977, US Dist. Ct. (ea. dist. Pa.) 1980, US Tax Ct. 1980. Shareholder Lentz, Cantor & Massey, Ltd., Malvern. Author: The Dictionary of Paperweight Signature Canes, 1997. Named one of Top 100 Attys., Worth mag., 2005—06. Mem.: Pa. Bar Assn., Chester County Bar Assn., Paoli Malvern Berwyn Rotary Club, Order of the Coif. Office: Lentz Cantor & Massey 460 E King Rd Malvern PA 19355 Office Phone: 610-722-5800. Office Fax: 610-647-6714. E-mail: dohan@lentzlaw.com.*

DOHANIAN, DIRAN KAVORK, art historian, educator; b. Somerville, Mass., Mar. 26, 1931; s. Hagop Mardiros and Esther (Babigian) D. BFA, Mass. Sch. Art, 1952; MA in Tchg., Harvard U., 1953, MA, 1955, PhD, 1964. Instr. art Ea. Nazarene Coll., Wollaston, Mass., 1952—55; reader in fine arts Harvard U., Cambridge, Mass., 1954—57, tchg. fellow fine arts, 1955—57; vis. asst. prof. history art U. Ala., 1957—58; vis. asst. prof. history Oriental art U. Hawaii, 1959—60; asst. prof. fine arts, dir. course in Oriental humanities U. Rochester, NY, 1960—65, assoc. prof. fine arts NY, 1965—71, prof. NY, 1971—87, prof. art history NY, 1988—2001, acting chmn. dept. fine arts NY, 1977—78, chmn. dept. fine arts NY, 1980—83, mem. faculty coun. Coll. Arts and Sci. NY, 1991—94, sec. faculty coun. NY, 1992—94, prof. art history emeritus NY, 2002—. Cons., curator Oriental art The Meml. Art Gallery, Rochester, 1976—88, bd. mgrs., 1977—78, 1980—83; Cooke-Daniels Meml. lectr. Cooke-Daniels Found. and Denver Art Mus., 1965; Louise Weiser lectr. Mt. Holyoke Coll., 1983; ind. scholar, cons. to art collections, 2003—. Author: The Mahayana Buddhist Sculpture of Ceylon, 1977; contbr. articles to profl. jours. C.R.B. fellow Belgian Art Seminar, Brussels and Antwerp, 1956, Fulbright fellow India, 1958-59, sr. rsch. fellow Am. Inst. Ceylonese Studies, Colombo, 1968, Am. Coun. Learned Socs. fellow India, 1973; fine arts rsch. scholar, 2002—. Fellow Am. Philos. Soc.; mem. Am. Inst. Indian Studies (trustee 1964-65), Am. Com. for History South Asian Art (dir. 1969-71). Home: 269 Payson Rd Belmont MA 02478-3406 Office Phone: 781-933-0157. E-mail: dkdn@netzero.com.

DOHENY, DANIEL P., corporate financial executive; B accountancy, Univ. Ill. CPA. Ptnr. transp. practice & Audit Com. Inst. KPMG, 1984—2000; sr. v.p., CFO Reyes Holdings LLC, Rosemont, Ill., 2000—. Mem. Pres. Council Univ. Ill.; chmn. Spl. Olympics Ill., Jr. Achievement Ill.; pres. Chgo. chpt. Lumen Inst.; mem. Illini Leadership Council. Mem.: Am. Inst. CPAs, Econ. Club Chgo., Fin. Executives Internat. Office: Reyes Holdings LLC Ste 700 9500 W bryn Mawr Ave Rosemont IL 60018*

DOHERTY, BRIAN GERARD, alderman; b. Chgo., Oct. 25, 1957; s. Daniel Joseph and Kathleen (McDonagh) D.; m. Rose Mary Gillespie, 1986; children: Kathleen Marie, Kevin Michael. BA, U. N.E. Ill., 1984; MA in Urban Studies, Loyola U., Chgo., 2005. Alderman 41st Ward, Chgo., 1991—. Boxing champ Chgo. Pk. Dist., 1972, 73, Chgo. Golden Gloves champion Tribune Charities, 1973. Mem. Alpha Chi Honor Soc. Roman Catholic. Home: 7805 W Catalpa Ave Chicago IL 60656-1640 Office: 6650 N Northwest Hwy Chicago IL 60631-1307 Office Phone: 773-792-1991.

DOHERTY, CHARLES VINCENT, investment advisor; b. Pitts., Dec. 17, 1933; s. Charles V. and Emma (Lager) D.; m. Marilyn Bongiorno, Oct. 17, 1964; children: Charles, Michelle, Kristen. BS, U. Notre Dame, Ind., 1955; MBA, U. Chgo., 1967. CPA, Ill. Tax specialist Haskins & Sells, CPA, Chgo., 1960-67; ptnr. Lamson Bros. & Co., Chgo., 1968-73; pres. Doherty Zable & Co., Chgo., 1974-85, Chgo. Stock Exch., Inc., 1986-92; mng. dir. Madison Adv. Group, Chgo., 1993—. Bd. dirs. Lakeside Bank, Howe Barnes Hoefer Arnett Securities, Inc., Banc of Am. Fin. Products. Personal E-mail: milfordtrek@msn.com.

DOHERTY, EDMOND JOHN, retired librarian; b. NYC, Dec. 9, 1933; s. George and Marie Eloise (Ducote) D.; m. Frances Jeffreys, Aug. 1, 1959; children: Jon, Elizabeth, Margaret, Katharine. BA, St. Martin's Coll., Lacey, Wash., 1955; MLS, Rutgers U., 1960. Adult svcs. libr. East Orange (N.J.) Pub. Libr., 1958-61; br. libr. Free Libr. of Phila., 1961-66; libr. dir. Reading (Pa.) Pub. Libr., 1966-90; libr. Reading Alloys, Inc., Robesonia, Pa., 1990-98. Contbr. articles to profl. jours. Chmn. planning com. United Way of Berks County, Reading, 1972-74, active mem., 1968-90; pres. Fellowship House of Reading, 1978—, LWV of Berks County, 1992-93; pres., founder Friends Hopewell Furnace Nat. Historic Site, 1995-98, treas. 1999—; mem. ethics bd. City of Reading, 1996-2000, chair, 1997-00. Recipient Doran award United Way of Berks County, 1979. Mem. Middle Atlantic Regional Libr. Fedn. (pres. 1977-79), Pa. Libr. Assn. (treas. 1973-75), Interlibr. Delivery Svc. of Pa. (treas. 1980-82). Avocations: travel, hosting cable tv programs. Home: 855 N Park Rd Apt BB103 Wyomissing PA 19610-3405

DOHERTY, EVELYN MARIE, data processing consultant; b. Phila., Sept. 26, 1941; d. James Robert and Virginia. Diploma, RCA Tech. Inst., Cherry Hill, NJ, 1968. Freelance data processing programmer, NJ, 1978-81; data processing cons. NJ, 1981—. Cons. in main frame & PC field; lectr., mgr. data processing Camden County (NJ) Coll. Contbr. articles to profl. jours.; author: numerous poems. Organizer Earlton South Town Watch; budget com. Cherry Hill Sch. Dist.; adv. for vol. firefighters; vol. tech. lab. learning ctr. Cherry Twp. Libr.; vol. Classroom Computer Learning Ctr. Cherry Hill Schs.; mem. Southhampton Zoning Bd., 2004—07; mem. bd. edn. Southampton Schs., 2004—07, chair cmty. rels. com., 2005—06, bus. and fin. com., 2004—06; active Year 2000 Cherry Hill Schs. Tech. Design Com.; trustee Leisure Towne Home Owners Assn., 2007—; founder Babe Didrikson Collingswood Softball Team Women. Mem.: Data Processing Mgmt. Assn. (chmn., mem. ednl. com.), Leisure Curtain Callers, Leisure Towne Harmonizers, Leisure Towne Singers. Roman Catholic. Avocations: tennis, bridge, chess, charitable activites.

DOHERTY, KATHERINE MANN, librarian, writer; d. Jack Howard Mann and Glenn (Ellis) Andrews; m. Craig A. Doherty, June 16, 1973; 1 child, Meghan Corinne. BA, U. N.Mex., 1973; MSLS, Simmons Coll., 1976. Cataloger Mass. Hist. Soc., Boston, 1976-79; libr. media specialist Zuni (N.Mex.) Pub. Sch.s, 1982-86; libr. dist. Zuni Pub. Schs., 1985-86; unified media specialist Nantucket (Mass.) Elem. Sch., 1986-87; dir. learning resources Fortier Libr., N.H. Cmty. Tech. Coll., Berlin, 1987—. Author: (children's books) Apaches and Navajos, 1989, Iroquois, 1989, (young adult books) Benazir Bhutto, 1990, The Zunis, 1993, Arnold Schwarzenegger, 1993, The Huron, 1994, The Narragansett, 1994, The Chickasaw, 1994, The Ute, 1994, The Chuilla, 1994, The Sioux, 1994, The Golden Gate Bridge, 1995, Hoover Dam, 1995, Mount Rushmore, 1995, Washington Monument, 1995, Gateway Arch, 1995, The Wampanoag, 1995, The Penobscot, 1995, The Astrodome, 1996, The Erie Canal, 1996, the Empire State Building, 1997, The Alaska Pipeline, 1997, Richard I and the Crusades, 2002, New Hampshire, 2005, Massachusetts, 2005, Rhode Island, 2005, others; pub. Field Trial Mag. Office: NH Com Tech Coll Coll Libr 2020 Riverside Dr Berlin NH 03570-3717 Home Phone: 603-449-3419; Office Phone: 603-752-1113. Business E-Mail: kdoherty@nhctc.edu.

DOHERTY, PETER CHARLES, immunologist; b. Brisbane, Australia, Oct. 15, 1940; s. Eric C. and Linda Doherty; m. Penelope Stephens, 1965; children: James, Michael. BSc, U. Queensland, Australia, 1963, MSc, 1966; PhD, U. Edinburgh, Scotland, 1970; doctorates (hon.). Vet. officer Animal Rsch. Inst., Brisbane, Australia, 1963—67; sci. officer Moredun Rsch. Inst., Edinburgh, 1967—71; postdoctoral fellow John Curtin Sch. Med. Rsch., Canberra, Australia, 1972—75, prof., head dept. exptl. pathology, 1982—88; from assoc. prof. to prof. The Wistar Inst., Phila., 1975—82; mem., chmn. dept. immunology St. Jude Children's Rsch. Hosp., Memphis, 1988—2001; laureate prof. dept. microbiology and immunology U. Melbourne, Australia, 2002—. Bd. dirs. Internat. Lab. Animal Diseases, Nairobi, 1986—92; mem. exptl. virology study sect. NIH, 1982—83, 1990—; hon. prof. U. Tenn. Contbr. chapters to books, articles to profl. jours. Co-recipient Nobel Prize for medicine, 1996; named Australian of Yr., Nat. Australia Day Coun., 1997; recipient Paul Ehrlich prize, Fed. Republic Germany, 1983, Gairdner Internat. award for med. sci., Can., 1986, Lasker award for Basic Med. Rsch., 1995. Fellow: Australian Acad. Sci., Royal Soc. London. Avocations: walking, reading. Office Phone: 61-3-8344-7968. Office Fax: 61-3-8344-7990. E-mail: pcd@unimelb.edu.au.

DOHERTY, ROBERT CHRISTOPHER, lawyer; b. Elizabeth, NJ, Sept. 3, 1943; s. Christopher Joseph and Marie Veronica (McLaughlin) D.; m. Sarajane Frances Doherty, June 12, 1965; children: Dennis Michael, Amy Elizabeth, Tracey Carolan. AB, St. Peter's Coll., 1965; JD, Seton Hall U., 1970. Bar: N.J. 1970, U.S. Ct. Appeals (3d cir.) 1982, U.S. Supreme Ct. 1977. Asst. prosecutor Union County, Elizabeth, 1971-72; mem. firm Schumann, Hession, Kennelly & Dorment, Jersey City, 1972-73, Robert D. Younghans, Westfield, N.J., 1973-76; ptnr. Doherty & Kopnicki, Westfield, 1976—87; county counsel, Union County, 1981-88; assoc. Nelinson,

Roche & Carter, East Orange, N.J., 1988-92, Stanley Marcus, Newark, 1992-98, Weiner Lesniak, Parsippany, N.J., 1998-2000; dep. atty. gen. N.J. Divsn. Law, Trenton, 2000—. Mem. ABA, N.J. Bar Assn., Union County Bar Assn., N.J. Assn. County Counsels. Republican. Roman Catholic. Home: 771 Fairacres Ave Westfield NJ 07090-2027 Office: RJ Hughes Justice Complex PO Box 112 Trenton NJ 08625-0112

DOHERTY, ROBERT CUNNINGHAM, retired advertising executive; b. NYC, Sept. 30, 1930; s. Francis Joseph and Helen (Utley) D.; m. Brucie Rial (div. 1961); children: Michael Bruce, Robert Kelly; m. Kerstin Brigetta Karlsson; children: Andrew Seger, Thomas Nils. BA, Princeton U., 1952. Account exec. Needham Harper Steers, NYC, 1958-62, v.p., account supr., 1962-65; exec. v.p. John Rockwell and Assocs., NYC, 1965-73, ptnr., chmn. bd., 1973-75; v.p. mgmt. group Wells, Rich & Greene, NYC, 1975-79; sr. v.p. McKinney & Silver, Raleigh, NC, 1979-83, exec. v.p., 1983-87, pres., 1987-90, chief exec. officer, 1991-97, chmn., 1993-98; ret., 1998. Trustee, mem. exec. com. N.C. Symphony, 1991—, chmn. bd. 2001-03; trustee, mem. exec. com. NC Mus. History, 1997—; trustee, sec. NC Mus. History Found., 2004-. Served to 1st lt. USMC, 1952-54, Korea. Mem. Figure Eight Yacht Club (Wilmington, NC), Ivy Club (Princeton, NJ), Cardinal Club (Raleigh, NC). Episcopalian. Office: 5 W Hargett St Raleigh NC 27601 Office Phone: 919-831-4761.

DOHERTY, ROBERT FRANCIS, JR., aerospace engineer; b. North Quincy, Mass., Aug. 7, 1954; s. Robert Francis and Rose Virginia (Wheeler) D. BS in Mgmt., U. Mass., Dartmouth, 1977. Sales mgr. Jordan Marsh Co., Boston, 1977-78; ops. mgr. Cramer Electronics, Newton, Mass., 1978-79; from d/e supr. to sect. mgr. nat. accts. Data Gen. Corp., Westboro, Mass., 1979-84; sales ops. mgr. Printronix, Inc., Malden, Mass., 1984-87; sales-contracts adminstrn. mgr. M/A-COM, Inc., Burlington, Mass., 1987-89, mktg. mgr. Chelmsford, Mass., 1989-92, mgr. customer satisfaction Lowell, Mass., 1992-94, internal cons. sys. applications products, 1994-95, program mgr., 1995—99; dir. program mgmt., sr. program mgr. M/A-COM divsn. Tyco Internat., Lowell, Mass., 1999—. Bd. dirs. MA-com Fed. Credit Union Active human rights groups, health founds. Mem. Nat. Contract Mgmt. Assn., Assn. of Old Crows, Nat. Def. Indsl. Assn., Air Force Assn. Roman Catholic. Avocations: jogging, swimming, skiing, antiques, travel. Home: 84 Berkeley St Ste 1 Boston MA 02116-6262 Office Phone: 978-442-4801. E-mail: dohertyb@tycoelectronics.com.

DOHERTY, STEVE, lawyer, state legislator; b. Great Falls, Mont., May 5, 1952; s. Arthur Frederick and Myra M. Doherty. BA, U. Pa., 1975; JD, Lewis & Clark Law Sch., 1984. Assoc. Spears, Lubersky, Campbell, Bledsoe, Anderson & Young, Portland, 1984-86; from assoc. to ptnr. Graybill, Ostrem, Warner & Crotty, Great Falls, Mont., 1986-92; assoc. Smith & Guenther, Great Falls, Mont., 1992-97; mem. Mont. Senate, Dist. 24, Great Falls, 1991—2003; majority whip, chmn. jud. com. Mont. Senate, Great Falls, Mont., 1993-94, mem. taxation and nat. resources com., 1991-94, mem. environ. quality coun. com., 1991-94, mem. edn. com., 1995, mem. fish and game and ethics com., 1997, minority leader, 1999-2001, mem. rules com., 1999—2001; ptnr. Smith & Doherty, Great Falls, 1998—2002, Smith, Doherty & Belcourt, P.C., Great Falls, 2003—06, Smith & Doherty PC, Great Falls, 2006—. Chmn. Mont. Fish, Wildlife, and Parks Commn., 2005—. Mem. legis. del. to Taiwan, 2000, Mont. del. to Mnsfield Ctr. Conf. on Environment, Kumamoto, Japan, 2000; trainer Nat. Dem. Inst., Guiyang Province, China, 2004; bd. dirs. Rural Employment Opportunities, Helena, 1990—92. Recipient Conservation Eagle award, N.W. Energy Coalition, 1999, Pub. Svc. award, Mont. Trial Lawyers Assn., 2001; Flemming fellow, Ctr. for Policy Alts., 1998, Eleanor Roosevelt Global fellow, Chile, 2001. Mem. Great Falls Pub. Radio Assn. (bd. dirs. 1986-91). Democrat. Avocations: hunting, fishing, hiking, skiing, western history. Office: Smith Doherty PC 410 Central Ave Ste 608 Great Falls MT 59401-3128 Office Phone: 406-721-1070. Fax: 406-721-1799.

DOHERTY, THOMAS, publisher; b. Hartford, Conn., Apr. 23, 1935; Thomas and Elizabeth (Story) D.; m. Barbara Slocum, Feb. 14, 1958 (dec.); children: Thomas, Kathleen, Linda; m. Tatiana Pachina, July 19, 1991; 1 stepchild, Elena. Student, Trinity Coll., 1953-57. From salesman to divsn. sales mgr. Pocket Books, 1958—68; nat. sales mgr. Simon & Schuster, 1968—70; pub. Tempo Books, 1971-75; pub., gen. mgr. Ace and Tempo divsns. Grossett & Dunlap Inc., 1976-80; founder, pres. Tom Doherty Assocs., Inc., NYC, 1980-87; pres., pub. Tor & Forge Imprints of Tom Doherty Assocs. LLC, A Holtzbrinck Co., NYC, 1987—, Tor and Forge Books. Winner Skylark award, Locus award for best pub. sci. and fantasy, annually, 1987—, World Fantasy Life Achievement award, 2005, Raymond Z. Gallan Sci. Fiction award ICON, 2006. Mem. World Sci. Fiction Assn. (charter), Nat. Space Inst. Roman Catholic. Office: Tor Books 175 Fifth Ave New York NY 10010-7703 Home Phone: 212-995-2028; Office Phone: 646-307-5503. Personal E-mail: tom.doherty@tor.com.

DOHERTY, WILLIAM THOMAS, JR., historian, retired educator; b. Cape Girardeau, Mo., Mar. 30, 1923; s. William Thomas and Kittie (Baird) D.; m. Dorothy Ashley Huff Zienowicz, Aug. 13, 1947; children: Victor Sargent, Dorothy Ashley, Catherine Baird, Julia Holbrook, William Thomas III. AB, BS, S.E. Mo. State U., 1943; MA, Am. U., 1950; PhD, U. Mo., 1951. Instr. history Westminster Coll., Fulton, Mo., 1947-48, Christian Coll., 1949-50, U. Mo., 1948-49, 50-51; asst. prof. history U. Miss., 1951-53, assoc. prof. history, 1956-58, prof., chmn. dept. history, 1958-61; asst. prof., then assoc. prof. history U. Ark., 1953-56; prof. history, dir. Ford Found. 3 yr. Master's program Kan. State U., Manhattan, 1961-63; prof. history, chmn. dept. W.Va. U., Morgantown, 1963-79, univ. historian, 1979-88, prof. emeritus, 1988—. Author: Louis Houck: Missouri Historian and Entrepreneur, 1960, Berkeley, U.S.A.: A Bicentennial History of a Virginia and West Virginia County 1772-1972, 1972, West Virginia History, 1974, West Virginia University: Symbol of Unity in a Sectionalized State, 1982, West Virginia Studies, 1984, West Virginia: Our Land, Our People, 1990; editor: Minerals, Vol. IV in Conservation History of the United States, 1971; editor in chief West Virginia History Jour., 1979-88; contbr. numerous articles to profl. jours. Served with AUS, 1943-46. Decorated Bronze star medal, 1946. Mem. Am. Hist. Assn., So. Hist. Assn., Orgn. Am. Historians, AAUP, Kappa Delta Pi, Sigma Tau Delta, Phi Alpha Theta. Democrat. Home: 15115 Interlachen Dr Apt 214 Silver Spring MD 20906-5638

DOHMEN, MARY HOLGATE, retired primary school educator; b. Gary, Ind., July 28, 1918; d. Clarence Gibson and Margaret Alexander (Kinnear) Holgate; m. Frederick Hoeger Dohmen, June 27, 1964 (dec. Apr. 2006); children: William Francis, Robert Charles. BS, Milw. State Tchrs. Coll., 1940; M in Philosophy, U. Wis., 1945. Cert. tchr. Wis. Tchr. primary grades Baraboo Pub. Schs., Wis., 1940-43, Whitefish Bay Pub. Schs., Wis., 1943-64; ret., 1964. Author short stories, numerous poems; contbr. articles to profl. jours. Bd. dirs. Homestead HS chpt. Am. Field Svc., Mequon, Wis., 1970-80; mem. Milw. Aux. VNA, 1975—, 2d v.p., 1983-85, Milw. Pub. Mus. Enrichment Club, 1975—, Boys and Girls Club of Greater Milw., 1986—; vol. Reading is Fun program, 1987—, Milw. Symphony Orch. League, 1960—, Ptnrs. in Conservation, World Wildlife Fund, Washington, 1991—, Milw. Art Mus. Garden Club, 1979—, com. chmn., 1981-86; mem. Chancellor's Soc. U. Wis.-Milw., 1991—; travel lectr. various orgns., 1980—. Mem. AAUW, Milw. Coll. Endowment Assn. (v.p. 1987-90, pres. 1991-93), Bascom Hill Soc. (U. Wis.), Woman's Club Wis., Alpha Phi (pres. Milw. alumnae 1962-64), Pi Lambda Theta (pres. Milw. alumnae 1962-64), Delta Kappa Gamma. Republican. Presbyterian. Avocations: writing, travel, nature.

DOHN, JULIANNE, child protective services specialist; d. William Henry and Geraldine Mae Dohn. BA, SUNY, Buffalo, 1971. Child protective svcs. supr. Erie County Child Protective Svcs., Buffalo, 1974—2006; coord. Erie County Child Fatality Review Team, Buffalo, 1997—2006. Cons. in field. Recipient Cert. of Hon. Recognition, Erie County, 1999; grantee, N.Y. State Office of Child and Family Svcs., 1997, 1998. Mem.: U.S. Equestrian Fedn. Avocation: riding and showing horses. Office: PO Box 133 East Aurora NY 14052 Home: 20 Warner Ln Orchard Park NY 14127 Office Phone: 716-998-9202.

DOHNAL, DENNIS WILLIAM, judge; b. Cleve., Oct. 4, 1945; s. William Edward and Alta Louella Dohnal; m. Alecia Faye Woofter, Dec. 20, 1986; 1 child, Kelly Elizabeth;children from previous marriage: Todd Andrew, Mark Alan. BA, Bucknell U., Lewisburg, Pa., 1967; JD, George Washington U., 1970. Bar: Va. 1971. Asst. US atty. US Dept. Justice, Richmond, Va., 1971—74; ptnr. Brenner, Baber & Janus, Richmond, 1974—96, Brenner, Dohnal, Evans & Yoffy, Richmond, 1996—2000; US magistrate judge US Dist. Ct., Richmond, 2000—. Bd. dirs. Hanover Assn. Retarded Citizens, Va., 1995—2000, Cmty. Based Svcs., Hanover, 1999—2005. Fellow: Va. Law Found.; mem.: John Marshall Inn Ct., Richmond City Bar Assn. (pres. 1988—89), Va. State Bar Assn. (chmn. criminal law sect. 1983—84, Harry L. Carrico Professionalism award 1999). Avocations: gardening, fishing, boating, reading. Office: US Dist Ct 1000 E Main St Richmond VA 23219

DOHNÁNYI, CHRISTOPH VON, musician, conductor; b. Berlin, Sept. 8, 1929; s. Hans and Christine (Bonhoeffer) Von Dohnányi. Student, U. Munich, Hochschule fuer Musik, Munich, Fla. State U., Berkshire Music Ctr.; doctorate (hon.), Oberlin Coll., Cleve. Inst. Music, Kent State U., Case Western Res. U., Eastman Sch. Music, 1998. Coach, condr., asst. to Sir George Solti Frankfurt (Germany) Opera, 1952-57, gen. music dir., artistic dir., 1968-77; gen. music dir. Lubeck, Germany, 1957-63, Kassel, Germany, 1963-66; chief conductor West German Radio Symphony Orch., Cologne, 1964-70; artistic dir., chief condr., intendant Hamburg (Germany) State Opera, 1977-84; music dir. designate Cleve. Orch., 1982-84, music dir., 1984—2002; prin. guest conductor Philharmonia Orch., London, 1995—97, prin. condr., 1997—. Guest conductor Salzburg Festival, Chatelet Paris, Zurich Opera House, Israel Philharm., Orchestre de Paris, Vienna Philharm., Berlin Philharm. Recordings with Vienna Philharmonia include opera Wozzeck, Lulu, Fidelio, Flying Dutchman, Salome, 5 Mendelssohn symphonies, works by Stravinsky, Tschaikovsky, Glass, Schnittke, recordings with Cleve. orch. include symphonies of Beethoven, Brahms, Schumann, Bruckner, Dvorak, Mahler, Mozart, Schubert, orchestral works by Bartok, Lutoslawski, R. Strauss, Webern, Ives, Ruggles, Birtwistle, opera Rheingold, Walkure. Recipient Scopus award, Am. Friends of Hebrew U. in Jerusalem, 1996, Scroll of Remembrance for Von Dohnányi and Bonhoeffer Families in German resistance U.S. Holocaust Mus., Washington, 1995, Condr. of Yr. award Musical Am., 1992, Comdr.'s Cross Republic of Austria, 1992, Comdr. de L'Ordre des Arts et des Lettres, France, Cross Order of Merit, Cross Order of Merit, Germany, Bartok prize, Hungary, 1982, Goethe medal City of Frankfurt, 1979, Richard Straus prize Munich, 1951, Torch of Liberty award Anti Defamation League, 2001. Address: Colbert Artists Mgmt 111 W 57th St Ste 1416 New York NY 10019-2211 Office: Philharmonia Orch 125 High Holborn 1 FL London WCIV6QA England

DOHNER, RUSSEL ROWLAND, physician; b. Astoria, Ill., Feb. 8, 1925; s. David Royer and Ethel Mae Dohner. BA, Northwestern U., Chgo., 1950, MD, 1953; MD (hon.), Western Ill. U., Macomb, Ill., 2006. Med. Dr. gen. practice, Rushville, Ill., 1955—. Hosp. staff Culbertson Hosp., Rushville, 1953—. Staff sgt. US Army, 1944—46, Washington. Named Dr. Dohner Day, Gov. Ill., 2005, Rushville, Ill., 2005. Mem.: Masonic Lodge, Am. Legion, Rushville Rotary Club (past. pres., Paul Harris fellow 1960). Avocations: fishing, gardening. Office: Med Office 103 W Wasington Rushville IL 62681

DOHOHUE, JOHN FRANCIS, secondary school educator; b. Passaic, NJ, May 15, 1952; s. James Joseph and Dorothy Catherine Donohue; m. Teri Susan Mefford, Mar. 11, 1988; children: April Donohue, Joshua Donohue;children from previous marriage: Joyce Donohue, John Donohue, Robert Donohue. BS, U. SC, Columbia, 1977, MEd, 1980, postgrad., 1994. Cert. tchr. SC. Tchr., coach Newberry HS, SC, 1990—97, Ridge View HS, Columbia, 1997—99, 2006—; asst. prin. Blythe Wood Mid. Sch., SC, 1999—2006. With USN, 1970—76. Mem.: SC Soccer Coaches Assn., SC Coaches Assn. Avocation: coaching indoor and outdoor soccer. Home: 405 Angus Dr Columbia SC 29223

DOHRENWEND, BRUCE PHILIP, epidemiologist, social sciences educator; b. NYC, July 26, 1927; s. Gustav John and Gertrude Elise (Funke) D.; m. Barbara Anne Snell, Sept. 21, 1951 (dec. June 1982); m. Catherine J. Douglass, June 1, 1985 BA, Columbia U., 1950, MA, 1952; PhD, Cornell U., 1955. Cert. psychologist, N.Y. Research assoc. Cornell U., Ithaca, NY, 1954-58; research assoc. Columbia U., NYC, 1958-63, asst. prof., 1963-67, assoc. prof., 1967-70, prof., 1970—; chief of rsch. dept. social psychiatry N.Y. State Psychiat. Inst., NYC, 1979—. Mem. task panel on problems, scope and boundaries Presl. Commn. on Mental Health, Washington, 1977-78; head task group on behavioral effects Presl. Commn. on Accident at Three Mile Island, Washington, 1979; mem. tech. evaluation bd. Vietnam Era Veterans study, VA, Washington, 1983-89. Author: (with others) Social Status and Psychological Disorder, 1969, Mental Illness in the United States, 1980, (with others) Socioeconomic Status and Psychiatric Disorders, 1992; editor: (with others) Stressful Life Events, 1974, Stressful Life Events and Their Contexts, 1981 Served with USNR, 1945-46 Recipient Research Scientist award NIMH, 1971, 76, 81, 86, 91, Emily Mumford award Columbia U., 1992; NIMH grantee, 1964-82, 77—. Fellow AAAS (co-recipient prize for behavioral rsch. 1990); APA (co-recipient disting. contbns. div. community psychology award 1980), Am. Psychopathol. Assn. (Hamilton award 1994); mem. Am. Pub. Health Assn. (co-recipient Rema Lapouse Mental Health Epidemiology award 1981), Am. Sociol. Assn. (Leo G. Reeder award for disting. contbn. med. sociology sect. 1999), Soc. for Study of Social Problems (Disting. Contbrs. award divsn. psychiat. sociology 1994). Home: 1056 5th Ave New York NY 10028-0112 Office: NY State Psychiat Inst 1051 Riverside Dr Unit 8 New York NY 10032-1013

DOHRMANN, RUSSELL WILLIAM, retired manufacturing executive; b. Clinton, Iowa, June 29, 1942; s. Russell Wilbert and Anita Doris (Miller) D.; m. Rita Marie Meade, Dec. 26, 1964 (dec. Feb. 1978); m. M. Jean Stapleton, Aug. 18, 1979. BS, Upper Iowa U., 1965; MBA, Drake U., 1971. Acct. Chamberlain Mfg. Corp., Clinton, 1965-66, plant controller Derry, Pa., 1967-68; fin. analyst Frye Copysystems Inc., Des Moines, 1968-71, v.p., controller, 1971-77, pres., 1980-97, also bd. dirs.; internat. controller Wheelabrator-Frye, NYC, 1977-78; pres. FryeTech, Inc., Des Moines, 1997-98; group controller Wheelabrator-Frye, Des Moines, 1978-80; cons., 1998—. Mem. Des. Moines C. of C. Republican. Methodist. Personal E-mail: windyridge@mchsi.com.

DOI, ROY HIROSHI, biochemist, educator; b. Sacramento, Mar. 26, 1933; s. Thomas Toshiteru and Ima (Sato) D.; m. Joyce Takahashi, Aug. 30, 1958 (div. 1992); children: Kathryn E., Douglas A.; m. Joan M. Saul, Feb. 14, 1992. BA in Physiology, U. Calif., Berkeley, 1953, BA in Bacteriology, 1957; MS in Bacteriology, U. Wis., Madison, 1958, PhD in Bacteriology, 1960. NIH postdoctoral fellow U. Ill., Urbana, 1960-63; asst. prof. Syracuse U., NY, 1963-65, U. Calif., Davis, 1965-66, assoc. prof., 1966-69, prof. biochemistry, 1969-92, chmn. dept. biochemistry and biophysics, 1974—77, dir. biotechnology prog., 1989-92, prof. molecular biology, 1992—. Cons. NIH, Bethesda, Md., 1975-79, 82-84, Syntro Corp., San Diego, 1983-88; treas. Internat. Spores Conf., Boston, 1980-89; mem. recombinant DNA adv. com. NIH, 1990-94; eminent scientist Riken Inst., Wako, Japan, 1998. Contbr. articles sci. jours.; editor: Microbiol. and Molecular Biology Revs., 1998—2006. With U.S. Army, 1953-55. Fellow NSF, 1971-72; recipient Sr. Scientist award, Alexander von Humboldt Found., Munich, 1978-79, vis. scholar award Naito Found, Tokyo. Fellow AAAS, Am. Acad. Microbiology; mem. NAS. Democrat. Avocations: photography, sports. Office: U Calif Molecular and Cellular Biology 2251 Life Sci Davis CA 95616

DOIG, JAMESON WALLACE, political science professor; b. Oakland, Calif., June 12, 1933; s. James Rufus and Mary (Jameson) D.; m. Joan Nishimoto, Oct. 8, 1955; children: Rachel, Stephen, Sean. AB, Dartmouth Coll., Hanover, NH, 1954; M.P.A., Princeton U., NJ, 1958, MA, 1959, PhD, 1961. Research asst. N.J. Republican Com., 1957; staff mem. Brookings Instn., 1959-61; from asst. prof. to prof. politics and pub. affairs Princeton U., 1961—2004, prof. emeritus, 2004—, sr. scholar, 2004—; assoc. dean Woodrow Wilson Sch., Princeton U., 1972-73, dir. univ. research program in criminal justice, 1973-93. Dir. grad. studies dept. polit. sci. Princeton U., 1988—90, chair undergrad. studies, 1991—94, chair dept. polit. sci., 1997—2000; dir. Mamdouha S. Bobst Ctr. for Peace and Justice, 2000—04, chair Can. studies, 2002—04, chair athletics com., 2002—03; cons. Fels Fund, 1966—68, Daniel and Florence Guggenheim Found., 1970—, Nat. Prison Overcrowding Project, 1983, Lavenburg Found., 1983—90; vis. prof. John Jay Coll. Criminal Justice, 1967—68, 1970—72; mem. adv. com. Gov. N.J., 1965—71, Vera Inst. Justice, 1986—92; mem. NRC/Trans. Rsch. Bd., 1990—92, 2006—; mem. adv. coun. N.J. Dept. Corrections, 1974—82; mem. adv. com. Rockefeller Ctr., Dartmouth Coll., 1990—96, Taubman Ctr., Harvard U., Cambridge, Mass., 1996—2005; vice-chmn. N.J. Dept. Corrections, 1980—82, cons. on parole to gov. of N.J., 1975—78; dir. Guggenheim Summer Internship Program, 1997—. Author: Metropolitan Transportation Politics and the New York Region, 1966, (with D.E. Mann) The Assistant Secretaries, 1965, (with D.T. Stanley and D.E. Mann) Men Who Govern, 1967, (with M. Danielson) New York: The Politics of Urban Regional Development, 1982, Empire on the Hudson, 2001; co-author, editor: Criminal Corrections: Ideals and Realities, 1983, Leadership and Innovation, 1987, 90, Combating Corruption/Encouraging Ethics, 1990; contbr. Governing the States and Localities, 1969, Agenda for a City, 1970, Metropolitan Politics, 1971, Urban Politics and Policy-Making, 1973, Crime and Criminal Justice, 1975, Public Administration of Law Enforcement Policies, 1979, Politics of Urban Development, 1987, Public Authorities and Public Policy, 1991, Landscape of Modernity, 1992, Studies in American Political Development, 1993, Technology and Culture, 1994, 06, Building the Public City, 1995, Seaport, 2001, Innovation, 2002, Art of Structural Design, 2003, Textual Studies in Canada, 2004, Multiculturalism and The Canadian Constitution, 2007, Canadian Diversity, 2007. Served to lt. (j.g.) USNR, 1954-56. Recipient Herbert Kaufman award, 1989, A.P. Usher prize, 1995, A. Wildavsky award, 1997, Abel Wolman award, 2001, Humanities Honor award, 2002. Mem. Am. Correctional Assn., Am. Polit. Sci. Assn., Am. Soc. Pub. Adminstrn., Law and Soc. Assn., Soc. History of Technology, Policy Studies Orgn., Pub. Works Hist. Soc. (bd. dirs. 2003—05), Can. Studies Assn., Phi Beta Kappa. Office: Princeton U 5252 Main St Newbury VT 05051 Office Phone: 609-258-4808. Business E-Mail: jimdoig@princeton.edu.

DOKE, MARSHALL J., JR., lawyer; b. Wichita Falls, Tex., June 9, 1934; s. Marshall J. and Mary Jane (Johnson) D.; m. Betty Marie Orsini, June 2, 1956; children: Gregory J., Michael J., Laetitia Marie. BA magna cum laude, Hardin-Simmons U., 1956; LLB magna cum laude, So. Meth. U., 1959. Bar: Tex. 1959. Founding ptnr. Rain Harrell Emery Young & Doke, Dallas, 1965-87; assoc. Thompson, Knight, Wright & Simmons, Dallas, 1959, 62-65; founding ptnr. Doke & Riley, Dallas, 1987-92; ptnr. McKenna & Cuneo, 1993-96, Gardere Wynne Sewell L.L.P., Dallas, 1996—. Gen. counsel Tex. Rep. Party, 1976-77; mem. adv. coun. U.S. Ct. Fed. Claims, 1982—; mem. fed. acquisitions adv. panel U.S. OMB, 2005-06. Author: Ann. Procurement Rev., Govt. Contractor Briefing Papers, Contract Changes, Fed. Contract Mgmt., 1982—, also articles; editor-in-chief: Southwestern Law Jour., 1958-59. Pres. Hope Cottage-Children's Bur., Inc., 1969-70, Hope Cottage Found., 1997-2002, pres., 1998-2002; bd. visitors Law Sch., So. Meth. U., 1966-69, McDonald Obs., U. Tex., 1990—; dir. Tex. Hist. Found., 1993—, v.p., 1996-98, pres. 2000-2004, chmn., 2004—; law com., bd. trustees So. Meth. U., 1977-78; bd. dirs., pres. World Trade Assn., Dallas-Ft. Worth, 1979-80; chmn. bd. dirs. Internat. Trade Assn. Dallas/Ft. Worth, 1993-94; bd. dirs., sec. Mayor's Internat. Com., City of Dallas, 1984-87, mem. Judicial Nominating Commn., Dallas, 1997-2005, vice chair, 1998-2000, chair, 2000-2005. 1st lt. JAGC, U.S. Army, 1959-62. Fellow Am. Bar Found., Tex. Bar Found.; mem. ABA (chmn. sect. pub. contract law 1969-70, ho. of dels. 1970-72, 74-2003, bd. govs. 1980-82, nominating com. 1988-91, 2000-2003, chmn. conf. sect. dels. 1991-2003, standing com. on audit 2003—), Tex. Bar Assn., U.S. Ct. of Fed. Claims Bar Assn. (bd. govs. 1987-2001, pres. 1996, adv. com. 2006-), Bd. of Contract Appeals Bar Assn. (pres. 1988-90, bd. govs. 1988—), Am. Bar Retirement Assn. (bd. dirs., trustee 1980-84, pres 1982-84), Nat. Conf. Lawyers and CPAs (co-chmn. 1983-85), Nat. Contract Mgmt. Assn. (nat. bd. advisors 1983—), Dallas C. of C. (chmn. internat. com. 1979-83). Home: 11 Glenmeadow Ct Dallas TX 75225 Office: Gardere Wynne Sewell LLP Thanksgiving Tower 1601 Elm Ste 3000 Dallas TX 75201-7254 Office Fax: 214-999-3733. Business E-Mail: mdoke@gardere.com.

DOKOS, DANIEL S., lawyer; b. Apr. 8, 1957; BA, Dartmouth Coll., 1979; JD, U. Va., 1982. Ptnr. Weil, Gotshal & Manges, NYC, 1998—, chmn. banking & fin. practice. Recipient Dealmaker of Yr. award, Am. Lawyer mag., 2007. Mem.: Order of the Coif. Office: Weil Gotshal & Manges 767 5th Ave New York NY 10153 Office Phone: 212-310-8576. Office Fax: 212-310-6862. E-mail: daniel.dokos@weil.com.*

DOKURNO, ANTHONY DAVID, lawyer; b. Gardner, Mass., Mar. 14, 1957; s. Anthony Chester and Damey Anteena (Aleson) D. BA, Holy Cross Coll., 1979; JD, Vt. Law Sch., 1982; postgrad., Johns Hopkins U., 1993-94. Bar: Mass. 1982, U.S. Ct. Appeals for the Armed Forces 1986, U.S. Supreme Ct. 1987. Pvt. practice, Fitchburg, Mass., 1982-86; appellate counsel Navy-Marine Corps Appellate Rev. Activity, Navy JAG, Washington, 1986-88; atty. admiralty law divsn. Navy JAG, Washington, 1988-90, atty. ops. and mgmt., 1991-93. Assoc. counsel, bd. vets. appeals Dept. Vets. Affairs, 1994-96; analyst Dept. Def., 1996—. Comdr. USNR, 1998-06. Mem.: Nat. Cryptologic History Found., Maritime Law Assn., Amnesty Internat., Am. Legion, Mensa, Phi Beta Kappa.

DOLACKY, SUSAN K., music educator; d. Richard T. Davis and Olga E. Johnson; m. David Dolacky, Feb. 26, 1972; children: Jon David, Andrea Sue. BA in Vocal Music Edn., Ctrl. Washington U., 1970; MusM, U. So. Calif., 1972. Prof., head vocal divsn., acad. advisor Shoreline (Wash.) C.C., 1972—, prodr., music dir. opera, Broadway musical, 1972—. Adjudicator Met. Opera Nat. Coun. Dist Auditions, 2002—06. Mem.: Music Educators Nat. Conf. (adjudicator 1983—), Nat. Assn. Tchrs. Singing (adjudicator 1988—). Office: Shoreline CC 16101 Greenwood Ave N Shoreline WA 98133 Office Phone: 206-546-4617. Business E-Mail: sdolacky@shoreline.edu.

DOLAK, FRITZ, librarian, information administrator; b. Cleve., Ohio, Mar. 27, 1946; s. Frank and Barbara Stephie Dolak; m. Deborah Ann Perry, May 18, 1980. MusB, Cleve. Inst. Music, 1968; MusM, Ball State U., 1974, ArtsD, 1979, MLS, 1985. Head, ednl. resources pub. svcs. Ball State

U., Muncie, Ind., 1990—97, copyright digital resources libr., 1998—2004, copyright intellectual property mgr., spl. asst. to dean, 2004—, rsch. fellow Digital Policy Inst., 2004—. Chair Annual Univ. Libr. Copyright Conf.; chair, ind. partnership statewide copyright com. Ind. Higher Edn. Telecommunication Sys., Idpls., 2000—; mem. copyright and rights mgmt. com. Ind. State Libr., 2006—; advisor Intellectual Property Resource Ctr. Knowledge Pt. Acad., Slippery Rock, Pa., 2007—; intellectual property presenter and workshop facilitator. Composer: (contemporary clarinet etudes) Augmenting Clarinet Technique; contbr. articles various profl. jours. Worship com. chair Riverside UMC, Muncie, 2004—07; mem. lung transplant recipient resource various hosps., Muncie. Sgt. USAF, 1968—72, Philippine Islands. Decorated Marksman, Sharpshooter USAF; recipient Recognition award, Ball State U., 2006; Doctoral Tchg. fellowship, 1975—78, scholarship, Ford Found., 1964-1968. Mem.: Phi Mu Alpha Sinfonia (alumni adv. 1977—). Meth. Achievements include development of copyright forum for Ball State University; University copyright center; nationally recognized, 30-second, info. videos for copyright education at Ball State U; provided fed. testimony at public hearings on "Licensing in Distance Education" at U. Ill. Chicago, February 12, 1999; development of Bracken Library Matinee Musicales. Avocations: photography, baroque music, reading, biblical studies, hiking. Office: Ball State U Copyright & Intellectual Property Office Muncie IN 47306 Home Phone: 765-288-2514; Office Phone: 765-285-5330. Office Fax: 765-285-2008. Business E-Mail: fdolak@bsu.edu.

DOLAN, ANDREW KEVIN, lawyer; b. Chgo., Dec. 7, 1945; s. Andrew O. and Elsie Dolan; children: Andrew, Francesca, Melinda. BA, U. Ill., Chgo., 1967; JD, Columbia U., 1970, MPH, 1976, DPH, 1980. Bar: Wash. 1980. Asst. prof. law Rutgers-Camden Law Sch., N.J., 1970-72; assoc. prof. law U. So. Calif., LA, 1972-75; assoc. prof. pub. health U. Wash., Seattle, 1977-81; ptnr. Bogle & Gates, Seattle, 1988-93; pvt. practice law, 1993—. Commr. Civil Svc. Commn., Lake Forest Park, Wash., 1981; mcpl. judge City of Lake Forest Park, 1982-98. Russell Sage fellow, 1975. Mem. Order of Coif, Washington Athletic Club. Avocation: book collecting. Office: Ste 2006 480 S Marion Pkwy Denver CO 80209

DOLAN, CHARLES FRANCIS (CHARLES "CHUCK" DOLAN), media and entertainment company executive; b. Cleve., Oct. 16, 1926; m. Helen Ann Burgess; children: Patrick, Tom, James, MariAnne, Kathleen, Deborah. Student, John Carroll U. Founder Sterling Manhattan Cable, 1961, Teleguide, Inc., HBO, 1971, Cablevision, Sterling Manhattan Cable, 1973; mng. gen. ptnr. Cablevision and predecessor firms, 1973—85; chmn. Cablevision Systems Corp., Woodbury, NY, 1985—. Mng. dir. Met. Opera, NYC; majority owner Madison Square Garden Properties, 1995—, also bd. dirs. Bd. dirs., bd. govs. St. Francis Hosp., LI, NY; bd. dirs. Cold Spring Harbor Lab.; trustee Fairfield U., Conn. Served USAF. Named one of Forbes' Richest Americans, 2006. Avocation: sailing. Office: Cablevision Systems Corp 1111 Stewart Ave Bethpage NY 11714-3581 Office Phone: 516-803-2300. Office Fax: 516-803-2273.*

DOLAN, DENNIS JOSEPH, pilot, lawyer; b. St. Louis, Mar. 19, 1946; s. Robert Glennon and Lucille Anne (Stanley) D.; m. Aura Maritza Vargas, June 8, 1974; children: Dennis J. Jr., Rebecca and Robert (twins). BSc, Spring Hill Coll., Mobile, Ala., 1967; JD cum laude, St. Louis U., 1985. Bar: Mo. 1985, U.S. Dist. Ct. (ea. dist.) Mo. 1987. Commd. 2nd lt. USMC, 1967, advanced through grades to capt., 1970, resigned, 1976; served to maj. USMCR; flew in numerous combat missions, 2 combat tours Vietnam; airline pilot Western Air Lines, LA, 1976-87, Delta Air Lines, Inc., Atlanta, 1987—; pvt. practice law Clayton, Mo., 1985-88. Mem. ABA, ATLA, Air Line Pilots Assn. (bd. dirs. 1992-94, exec. v.p. 1994-96, chmn. Delta Master exec. coun. 1996-98, 1st v.p. 1999-2006), Internat. Fedn. Airline Pilot Assns. (prin. v.p. profl. affairs 2000-03, pres., 2003-07). Roman Catholic. Avocations: skiing, woodworking. Home: 13065 Addison Rd Roswell GA 30075-6305

DOLAN, EDWARD FRANCIS, writer; b. Oakland, Calif., Feb. 10, 1924; s. Edward Francis Sr. and Zelda Olympia (Vieira) D.; m. Rose Esther Puddefoot, Nov. 17, 1945 (dec.); children: Timothy L. (dec.), Wendy Anne Irving. Student, U. So. Calif., LA, 1942-43, U. San Francisco, 1958-59. Free-lance writer KRON-TV, Bay Area Pub. Schs. TV Coun., Pub. Svc. telecasts for Archdiocese, San Francisco, 1949-53; instr. dept. speech and drama Monticello Coll., Alton, Ill., 1953-56; writer, 1957—. Author: Pasteur and the Invisible Giants, 1958, White Battleground: The Conquest of the Arctic, 1961, Disaster 1906: The San Francisco Earthquake and Fire, 1967, Legal Action: A Layman's Guide, 1972; A Lion in the Sun: The Rise and Fall of the British Empire, 1973, Amnesty: The American Puzzle, 1976, Gun Control: A Decision for Americans, 1978, Child Abuse, 1980, revised edit., 1992, Adolf Hitler: A Portrait in Tyranny, 1981, History of the Movies, 1983, The Simon & Schuster Sports Question and Answer Book, 1984, Hollywood Goes to War, 1985, Drugs in Sports, 1986, revised edit., 1992, The Old Farmer's Almanac Book of Weather Lore, 1988, MIA: Missing in Action, 1989, America after Vietnam: Legacies of a Hated War, 1989, (with M.M. Scariano) Nuclear Waste: The 10,000-Year Challenge, 1990, Our Poisoned Sky, 1991, America in World War II: 1941, 1991, America in World War II: 1942, 1992, America in World War II: 1943, 1992, Animal Folklore: From Black Cats to White Horses, 1992, The American Wilderness and Its Future, 1992, America in World War II, 1944, 1993, Folk Medicine: Cures and Curiosities, 1993, America in World War II: 1945, 1994, Your Privacy: Protecting It in a Nosy World, 1994, Teenagers and Compulsive Gambling, 1994, (with M.M. Scariano) Illiteracy in America, 1995, The American Revolution: How We Fought the War of Independence, 1995, America in World War I, 1996, (with M.M. Scariano) Shaping U.S. Foreign Policy, 1996, In Sports, Money Talks, 1996, Our Poisoned Waters, 1997, The Civil War: A House Divided, 1997, America in the Korean War, 1998, Beyond the Frontier: The Story of the Trails West, 1999, The Spanish-American War, 2001, The Irish Potato Famine, 2003, The American Indian Wars, 2003, George Washington: Presidents and Their Times, 2007, 120 non-fiction titles. With U.S. Army, 1943-45, ETO. Mem.: Calif. Writers Club (pres. Redwood br. 1976—77, 1983—84). Avocation: golf.

DOLAN, JAMES L., communications executive, professional sports team owner; m. Kristin Dolan; 5 children. Advt. sales v.p. Cablevision Systems Corp., advt. corp. dir. Rainbow Advt. Sales Corp., CEO Rainbow Programming Holdings, Inc. (now Rainbow Media Holdings, LLC), CEO, pres. Woodbury, NY, 1995—, bd. dirs.; creator Rainbow Advt. Sales Corp. Chmn. Madison Sq. Garden (presiding over NBA NY Knicks and NHL NY Rangers); creator, mgr. Sta. WKNR-AM, Cleve. Trustee WNET; bd. dirs. Lustgarten Found. Pancreatic Rsch., Allan Houston Found. Avocations: music, sailing. Office: Cablevision Systems Corp 1111 Stewart Ave Bethpage NY 11714-5310 Office Phone: 516-803-2300. Office Fax: 516-803-2273.*

DOLAN, JOHN E., retired utilities executive, consultant; b. NYC, May 9, 1923; s. John A. and Marie C. (Comiskey) D.; m. Anne Dolan, Feb. 16, 1952; children— John E., Bryan, Vincent, Robert, Raymond, Philip, Lawrence, Paul. Student, Rensselaer Poly. Inst., 1946-47; BSM.E., Columbia U., 1950. With Am. Electric Power Service Corp., Columbus, Ohio, 1950-88, chief mech. engr., 1966, chief engr., 1967, sr. exec. v.p. engring., 1975-79, vice chmn. engring. and constrn., 1979-88; ret.; bd. dir., v.p. subs. cos. and Am. Electric Power Service Corp.; cons., 1988—. Bd. dirs. Dravo Corp. Served to 1st lt. USAAF, 1942-46. Decorated Air medal (4). Fellow ASME (James N. Landis medal 1990); mem. NAE, Tau Beta Pi. Roman Catholic. Home: 14448 Mark Dr Largo FL 33774-5102

DOLAN, JOHN RALPH, retired electronics executive; b. Peabody, Mass., Apr. 20, 1926; s. John L. and Ethel M. D.; m. Lois M. Burkhart, Jan. 24, 1948 (dec.); children: Mary Ellen, Geraldine, Dorothy, John, Peter; m. Barbara C. Gleason, Dec. 22, 1995; stepchildren: Janet Rogers, Barry, David, Julie Doyle. Student, Boston Coll., 1943, Bryant and Stratton Coll., 1945-46, Bentley Coll., 1948-50. Passenger accountant Cunard Steamship Co., 1947-50; office mgr. Dolan Tanning Co., 1950-56; gen. mgr. Flash Sportswear, 1957-59; budget mgr. CBS Electronics Co., 1959-62; contr./treas. Am. Polymer & Chem. Co., 1962-63; dir. fin. planning E.G. & G., Inc., Bedford, Mass., 1963-71, corp. contr., 1971-86; sr. v.p., CFO, EG&G Inc., Wellesley, Mass., 1986-91. Mem. Town Meeting, Danvers, Mass., 1964-70, Sch. Bldg. Com., Danvers, 1966-69. Served with USNR, 1943-45. Mem. Financial Execs. Inst. Home: 56 Summer St Danvers MA 01923-1549

DOLAN, LOUISE ANN, physicist; b. Wilmington, Del., Apr. 5, 1950; BA, Wellesley Coll., 1971; PhD in Physics, MIT, 1976. Jr. fellow in physics Harvard U., 1976-79; asst. prof. physics Rockefeller U., NYC, 1979-82, assoc. prof., 1983-90, lab. head, 1990; prof. physics U. N.C., Chapel Hill, 1990—. Program dir. for theoretical physics NSF, 1995. Recipient Wellesley Alumna Achievement award, 2004; John Simon Guggenheim fellow, 1988. Fellow Am. Phys. Soc. (Maria Goeppert-Mayer award 1987).

DOLAN, MARY ANNE, journalist, columnist; b. Wash., May 1, 1947; d. William David and Christine (Shea) D. BA, Marymount Coll., Tarrytown, NY, 1968; HHD (hon.), Marymount Coll., %, 1984; student, Queen Mary, Royal Holloway colls., U. London, London Sch. Econs., Kings Coll., Cambridge U., 1966-68. Reporter, editor Washington Star, 1969-77; asst. mng. editor, 1976-77; mng. editor L.A. Herald Examiner, 1978-81, editor, 1981—, now commentator. Mem. Pulitzer Prize Journalism Jury, 1981—82; bd. selectors for Neiman Fellows Harvard U. Recipient Golden Flame award, Calif. Press Women, 1980, Woman Achiever award, Calif. Fed. Bus. and Profl. Women's Clubs, 1981. Mem.: Am. Soc. Newspaper Editors, NOW. Office: MAD Inc 1033 Gayley Ave Ste 205 Los Angeles CA 90024-3417

DOLAN, MICHAEL J., former multi media company and advertising executive; b. NY, Nov. 9, 1946; m. Dorothy F. Dolan; 2 children. BA in English, Fordham U., 1968; PhD in English, Cornell U., 1975; MBA, Columbia U., 1977. With Morgan Guaranty Trust; ptnr. strategy practice Booz Allen & Hamilton, 1985—87; exec. v.p. ops. Nat. Can Co. Inc. subs. Peter Kienist Sons Inc., Norwalk, Conn., 1987-91; sr. v.p. Worldwide ops. PepsiCo Foods Internat., 1991—95, pres., CEO, Snack Ventures Europe, 1992—95; vice chmn., CFO Young & Rubicam Inc., NYC, 1996—2000, pres., COO, 2000, chmn., CEO, 2000—03; sr. adv. Kohlberg Kravis Roberts & Co. pvt. investment co., 2003—05; exec. v.p., CFO Viacom Inc., NYC, 2005—06. Non-exec. chmn. America's Choice; bd. dir. Mattel, Inc. Bd.dir. USA Swimming Found., United Way NY, Northside Ctr. Child Devel.

DOLAN, MICHAEL WILLIAM, lawyer; b. Kansas City, Mo., Dec. 13, 1942; s. William Michael and Vivian (Bush) D.; m. Laurel C. Cummings, June 13, 1964 (div. 1984); children: Matthew, Abigail. BA, U. Kans., 1964; JD with honors, George Washington U., 1969; LLM, Georgetown U., 1981. Bar: Va. 1969, D.C. 1970, U.S. Ct. Claims 1981, U.S. Tax Ct. 1981, U.S. Supreme Ct. 1973. Atty. Dept. Justice, Washington, 1971-73, dep. legis. counsel, 1973-79, dep. asst. atty. gen., 1979-85; with Fed Exec. Devel. Program, 1978-79; law clk. to hon. Catherine B. Kelly DC Ct. Appeals, 1981; assoc. Winthrop, Stimson, Putnam & Roberts, Washington, 1985-94; chief Article III Judges divsn. Adminstrv. Office of U.S. Cts., Washington, 1994—2002; atty. Michael W. Dolan, PLLC, 2003—. Contbr. numerous articles to profl. jours. 1st lt. U.S. Army, 1964-66. Recipient John Marshall award Dept. Justice, 1978 Democrat. Office: 2021 L St NW Ste 204 Washington DC 20036 Home Phone: 202-462-5957; Office Phone: 202-293-2776. E-mail: mwdolan@att.net.

DOLAN, PETER BROWN, lawyer; b. Bklyn., Mar. 25, 1939; s. Daniel Arthur and Eileen Margaret (Brown) D.; m. Jacqueline Elizabeth Gruning, Sept. 9, 1961; children: Kerry Anne, Peter Brown Jr. BS, U.S. Naval Acad., 1960; JD, U. So. Calif., 1967. Bar: Calif. 1967, U.S. Ct. Appeals (9th cir.) 1967, U.S. Dist. Ct. (no. and ctrl. dists.) Calif. 1967, U.S. Dist. Ct. (ea. dist.) Calif. 1972, U.S. Dist. Ct. (so. dist.) Calif. 1973, U.S. Claims Ct. 1982, U.S. Supreme Ct. 1986. Dep. L.A. County counsel, 1967-69; assoc. Macdonald, Halsted & Laybourne, LA, 1969-71, ptnr., 1972-77, Overton, Lyman & Prince, LA, 1977-87, Morrison & Foerster, LA, 1987-93, Morgan, Lewis & Bockius LLP, LA, 1993-99; prin. The Dolan Law Firm, LA, 1999—. Active Pasadena (Calif.) Tournament Roses Assn., 1973-05; pres. West Pasadena Residents Assn., 1979-81. Served to lt. USN, 1960-64, comdr. USNR, 1964-86. Mem.: L.A. County Bar Assn., Assn. Bus. Trial Lawyers, State Bar Calif., Chancery (LA), Bel-Air Bay Club, Phi Delta Phi. Roman Catholic. Office Phone: 213-689-0333. Fax: 213-680-9889. Personal E-mail: peterbdolan@yahoo.com. Business E-Mail: dolanlaw@yahoo.com.

DOLAN, RAYMOND BERNARD, insurance company executive, director; b. Chgo., Feb. 13, 1923; s. Christopher P. and Florence M. (Taylor) D.; m. Theresa, May 25, 1946; children— Paul, Ronald, Donald, Sharon. Student, No. Mich. U., 1942; DArts and Scis. (hon.), Mt. Marty Coll., Yankton, SD, 1980. With Equitable Life Assurance Soc. U.S., 1946—, v.p., chief line ops. NYC, 1971-74, sr. v.p. corp. communications, 1974-79, exec. v.p., chief agy. officer, 1979—; chmn. bd. Equitable of Del., 1985—. Inst. Life Ins. prof. in residence, econs. dept. St. Olaf Coll., 1975; dir. Equitable Variable Life Ins. Co., Equitable Capitol Mgmt. Corp., Equitable Life Leasing Corp., Equico Securities Corp., Donaldson, Lufkin & Jennette Inc., U.S. Marshalls Found. Vice chmn. Holy Spirit Ch. Parish Council, Stamford, Conn., 1968-71; chmn. Stamford dist. Boy Scouts Am., 1970-73; past trustee, vice chmn. bd. dirs. Teledaga Coll., Ala.; chmn. bd. dirs. Nat. Council Better Bus. Burs. Served to lt. col. USAF, 1942-45, 51-52, 61-62. Decorated D.F.C., Air medal with 4 oak leaf clusters. Mem. Nat. Assn. Life Underwriters, C.L.U.'s N.Y., Nat. Guard Assn. (life), Consumer Council, Am. Council Life Ins., Res. Officers Assn., Conf. Bd., Pub. Affairs Research Council. Clubs: K.C. (4th deg.). Republican. Roman Catholic. Home: 5 Kings Grant 377 Main St New Canaan CT 06840-5941 Office: Equitable Life Assurance Soc US 787 7th Ave Fl 38 New York NY 10019-6018 Personal E-mail: raydolan@aol.com.

DOLAN, ROBERT J., dean; b. Peabody, Mass. m. Kathleen Splaine-Dolan; children: Hilary, Nicholas. BA in Math., magna cum laude, Boston Coll., 1969; MS in Bus. Adminstrn., U. Rochester, 1976, PhD in Bus. Adminstrn., 1977; MA (hon.), Harvard U., 1986. Asst. prof. mgmt. sci. and mktg. U. Chgo., 1976—80, assoc. prof., 1980; assoc. prof. bus. adminstrn. Harvard U. Grad. Sch. Bus. Adminstrn., 1980—85, prof. bus. adminstrn., 1985—90, mktg. area chmn., 1986—94, mktg. tchr. Advanced Mgmt. Program, 1990—95, Edward W. Carter prof. bus. adminstrn., 1990—2001, faculty chmn. MBA program, 1996—97; pres. William David Inst. U. Mich. Ann Arbor Ross Sch. Bus., 2001—, Gilbert and Ruth Whitaker prof. bus. adminstrn., 2001—, dean, 2001—. Vis. prof. IESE, Barcelona, 2001; editor Field Studies Sect. Marketing Science, 1989—94, mem. editl. rev. bd., 1982—88, Jour. Marketing, 1978—84, 1990—98. Author: (books) Managing the New Product Development Process, 1993, Marketing Management: Text and Cases, 2001; co-author (with John Quelch and Benson Shapiro): Marketing Management Readings: From Theory to Practice, 1985, Marketing Management: Strategy, Planning and Implementation, 1985, Marketing Management: Principles, Analysis, and Application, 1985; co-author: (with John Quelch and Thomas Kosnik) Marketing Management, 1993; co-author: (with Hermann Simon) Power Pricing: How Managing Price Transforms the Bottom Line, 1996; editor: Strategic Marketing Management, 1992; contbr. articles to numerous jour. Mem.: Am. Mktg. Assn. (mem. Faculty Consortium 1990, 1992, mem. Doctoral Consortium 1984, 1986, 1988, 1990, coord. Doctoral Consortium 1989). Office: Univ Michigan Business School 701 Tappan St Ann Arbor MI 48109-1234 Office Phone: 734-764-1363. Office Fax: 734-763-0671. Business E-Mail: rjdolan@umich.edu.*

DOLAN, TERESA A., dean, educator, researcher; MPH, UCLA; BA Zoology, Rutgers U., 1979; DDS , U. Tex., 1983; cert. gen. practice, L.I. Jewish Med. Ctr., 1985; cert. geriatric dentistry, Vets. Adminstrn., 1989; cert. dental pub. health, U. Fla., 1991; grad., Pub. Health Leadership Inst. Fla., 1998; grad. cert., U. Fla., 2001. Diplomate Am. Bd. Dental Pub. Health, 1994. Resident in gen. dentistry dept. dentistry L.I. Jewish Med. Ctr., 1983—84, chief resident in gen. dentistry dept. dentistry, 1984—85; fellow geriatric dentistry Vets. Adminstrn. Med. Ctr., Sepulveda, Calif., 1987—89; asst. prof. U. Fla. Coll. Dentistry, 1989—93, assoc. prof. with tenure, 1993—98, acting assoc. dean acad. affairs, 1996—97, assoc. dean acad. affairs, 1997—2001, prof. with tenure, 1998—, assoc. dean edn., 2001—03, interim dean, 2002—03, dean, 2003—. Rschr., tchr., spkr. in field, lectr. various seminars; vis. asst. prof. U. Calif., 1985—87, adj. asst. prof., 1987—89; faculty discipline com. Fla. Dept. Edn., Statewide Course Numbering Sys., 1998—; reviewer grants in field; participant NIH Summer Inst. Rsh. on Minority Aging, 1991; pres. Am. Bd. of Dental Pub. Health, 2005—06. Contbr. articles to profl. jours.; exec. prodr.: (ednl. satellite videoconf.) Dental Care for the Developmentally Disabled Patient, 1991, Challenges in Geriatrics: Moving on- Rehabilitation After Stroke, 1991, How Much is Enough? Dental Tretament Decisions for Older Adults, 1992; author (dir.): Five Steps to Improving the Oral Health of Your Older Patients: A Guide for Non-dental Health Professionals, 1994. Adv., treating dentist cmty. nursing homes, 1989—96; dentist to low income elderly participants U. Fla. Geriatric Dental Demonstration Project, Jacksonville, 1990—92; dir. dental svcs. to older and medically compromised patients U. Fla. Geriatric Dental Group, 1990—95. Named honorable mention AARP Healthy Order Adults, 2000 Recognition Programs Exemplary Contbns. to Healthy Aging, 1992; recipient numerous grants and awards; fellow Vets. Adminstrn. Geriatric Dentistry; scholar Rsch., Robert Wood Johnson Found. Dental Health Svcs., 1985—87, L.I. U., 1984—85. Mem.: APHA, Am. Coll. Dentists, Phi Beta Kappa, Am. Soc. Geriatric Dentistry (ad hoc reviewer Spl. Care in Dentistry 1992—93, judge Saul Kamen Sci. Report award competition 1993—, chmn. ann. sci. session 1996), Fla. Coun. Aging, Fla. Pub. Health Assn., Am. Assn. Pub. Health Dentistry (abstract reviewer 1987, co-chmn. local arrangements ann. meeting 1992, ad hoc reviewer Jour. Pub. Health Dentistry 1994, session co-chmn. ann. meeting 1996, judge grad. student merit award projects 1997, mem. at large exec. coun. 1997—2000, mem. awards and nominations com. 2000, Pres.'s award 1999), Am. Dental Assn. (com. G Coun. Dental Edn. and Licensure 1999—, Geriatric Dental Care award 1991), Internat. Assn. Dental Rsch. (v.p. abstract reviewer geriat. oral rsch. sect. 1992—93, dir. behavioral sci. and health svcs. rsch. sect. 1992—95, pres.-elect program chmn. geriat. oral rsch. sect. 1993—94, pres. symposium organizer geriat. oral rsch. sect. 1994—95), Am. Assn. Women Dentists (chmn. com. student and component chpts. 1986—88, trustee dist. XIII Calif. 1986—89, contbg. editor Chronicle 1986—91), Acorn Clinic (v.p., acting pres. 1996—97, pres. 1997—99, past pres. 1999—2000), Fla. Coun. Aging (bd. trustees 1993—95), U. Health Sci. Ctr., Edn. Task Force, U. Curriculum Com., Geriatric Rsch., Edn. and Clin. Ctr., ACORN Clinic, Internat. Assn. Dental Rsch. (session co-chmn., abstract reviewer geriat. oral rsch. sect. 1991—92, immediate past-pres., chmn. nominations com. geriat. oral rsch. sect. 1995—96, mem. awards com. geriat. oral rsch. sect. 1996—97, constn. and bylaws com. 1996—), Am. Bd. Dental Pub. Health (dir.-elect 2000—01, pres. 2005—), Am. Dental Edn. Assn. (chair-elect spl. interest group in geriatric dentistry 1991—92, editl. rev. bd. Jour. Dental Edn. 1991—94, chmn. spl. intertest group in geriatric dentistry 1992—93, immediate past chmn. sect. on gerontology and geriat. edn. 1993—94, abstract reviewer ann. session 1998—2000, ann. session planning com. 2002—), Beta Beta Beta, Omicron Kappa Upsilon (Xi Omicron chpt. 1998), Phi Beta Kappa. Office: U Fla Coll Dentistry 1600 SW Archer Rd D 4-6B Box 100405 JHMH Gainesville FL 32610-0405 Office Phone: 352-392-2911. Office Fax: 352-392-3070. E-mail: tdolan@dental.ufl.edu.

DOLAN, THOMAS CHRISTOPHER, professional society administrator; b. Chgo., Dec. 31, 1947; s. Thomas Christopher and Bernice Mary (Doyle) D.; m. Georgia Ann Siebke, Feb. 14, 1983; children: William, Barbara, Lauren. BBA, Loyola U., Chgo., 1969; PhD, U. Iowa, 1977. Instr. U. Iowa, Iowa City, 1971-72; vis. fellow U. Wash., Seattle, 1973-74; asst. prof. U. Mo., Columbia, 1974-79; assoc. prof., dir. St. Louis U., 1979-86; v.p. Am. Coll. Healthcare Execs., Chgo., 1986-87, exec. v.p., 1987-91, pres., CEO, 1991—. Mem. Accrediting Commn. on Edn. for Health Svcs. Adminstrn., Washington, 1985-86; chmn. Assn. Univ. Programs in Health Adminstrn., Washington, 1983-84; cons. HEW, Kansas City, Mo., 1974-79, State of Mo., Jefferson City, 1974-79. Author: Systems for Health Care Administration: A Model for the Education of Health Manpower, 1975; contbr. articles to profl. jours. Pres. Mental Health Assn. Boone County, Columbia, Mo., 1977—78, Mental Health Assn. Mo., Jefferson City, 1980—82; chair Inst. Diversity in Health Mgmt., 2002, Assn. Forum, 1999—2000, Am. Soc. Assn. Execs. Found., Washington, 2000—01; bd. dirs. Alexian Bros. Hosp., St. Louis, 1980—86, Internat. Hosp. Fedn., 2005—. Fellow: Am. Soc. Assn. Execs. (chmn.-elect 2006—07, cert. assn. exec., bd. dirs.), Am. Coll. Healthcare Execs. Roman Catholic. Avocations: golf, motorcycling, photography. Office: Am Coll Healthcare Execs 1 N Franklin St Ste 1700 Chicago IL 60606-4425

DOLAN, THOMAS J., printing company executive; b. Rockville Centre, NY, July 7, 1944; B in Econs., Manhattan Coll. Sales rep. Xerox Corp., Phila., 1970, v.p. maj. account mktg. Stamford, Conn., 1988—92, pres. Xerox Bus. Svcs., 1997—99, pres. North Am. solutions group, 1999, corp. sr. v.p., 1999—, pres. Xerox Global Svcs., 2001—07, pres. Xerox Global Accounts, 2007—. Exec. bd. mem. Otetiana Coun., Inc., Boy Scouts of Am. Mem.: Integic, Inc. (bd. dirs.), INROADS, Inc. Office: Xerox Corp 800 Long Ridge Rd Stamford CT 06904 Office Phone: 203-968-3000.*

DOLAN, THOMAS JOSEPH, judge; b. Bronx, NY, Oct. 24, 1943; s. Joseph William and Helen Winnifred (Hannigan) D.; m. Barbara Louise Nuesell, Apr. 6, 1968; children: Claire Jean, Claudia Barbara. BS, Fordham U., 1965; JD, St. John's U., 1968. Bar: N.Y. 1968, U.S. Ct. Mil. Appeals 1969, U.S. Dist. Ct. (so. and ea. dists.) N.Y. 1975, U.S. Supreme Ct. 1980. Asst. dist. atty. Office of Dist. Atty., Dutchess County, Poughkeepsie, NY, 1973-92; county ct. judge Dutchess County, 1993—; acting judge N.Y. State Supreme Ct., 2001—. Served to capt. JAGC, U.S. Army, 1968-73. Decorated Bronze Star (2); Army Commendation medal (2). Mem. NY State Bar Assn., Dutchess County Bar Assn., So. Dutchess Exchange Club(Fishkill, NY). Republican. Home: Neville Rd Wappingers Falls NY 12590 Office: County Court 10 Market St Ste 7 Poughkeepsie NY 12601-3233 Office Phone: 845-486-2210. Business E-Mail: tdolan@courts.state.ny.us.

DOLAN, TIMOTHY MICHAEL, archbishop; b. Feb. 6, 1950; s. Robert and Shirley Radcliffe Dolan. BA in Philosophy, Cardinal Glennon Coll.; attended, Pontifical N. Am. Coll., Rome; License in Sacred Theology, Pontifical U. of St. Thomas; PhD in Am. Church History, Catholic U. Am. Ordained to priesthood, 1976; assoc. pastor Immaculata Parish, Richmond Heights, Mo., 1976—79; served in parish ministry, liaison for Archbishop John L. May St. Louis, 1983—87; secretary Apostolic Nunciature, Washington, 1987—92; vice rector, dir. of spiritual formation & prof. of church history Kenrick-Glennon Seminary, St. Louis, 1992—94; rector Pontifical N. Am. Coll., Rome, 1994—2001; auxiliary bishop St. Louis, 2001—02; archbishop of Milwaukee, 2002—. Former adjunct prof. of theology St. Louis U.; visiting prof. of church history Pontifical Gregorian U., Rome; faculty mem. dept. of ecumenical theology Pontifical U. of St. Thomas Aquinas, Rome. Office: Archdiocese of Milwaukee 3501 S Lake Dr PO Box 070912 Milwaukee WI 53207

DOLAN, WILLIAM D., III, lawyer; b. Washington, Nov. 20, 1943; AB, Marquette U., 1967; JD, Cath. U. Am., 1972. Bar: Va. 1972, D.C. 1974. Ptnr., commercial litigation Venable LLP (formerly Venable, Baetjer and Howard), McLean, Va. Adj. prof. med. malpractice law Georgetown U., 1982-, former pres., Va. Com. on Women & Minorities in Legal System. Fellow Am. Bar Found., Am. Coll. Trial Lawyers, Internat. Acad. Trial Lawyers, Va. Law Found.; mem. ABA (former deleg.), Am. Law Inst., Va. State Bar (pres. 1984-85, chair criminal law section), D.C. Bar, Assn. Trial Lawyers Am., Va. Trial Lawyers Assn. Office: Venable LLP 8010 Towers Crescent Dr Ste 300 Vienna VA 22182 Office Phone: 703-760-1680. Office Fax: 703-821-8949. Business E-Mail: wddolan@venable.com.

DOLBERG, DAVID SPENCER, lawyer; b. LA, Nov. 28, 1945; s. Samuel and Kitty (Snyder) D.; m. Katherine Blumberg, Feb. 22, 1974 (div. 1979); 1 child, Max; m. Sarah Carnochan, May 23, 1992 (div. 1995); m. Elana Mann, June 15, 1997; children: Kayla, Sophia. BA in Biology with honors, U. Calif., Berkeley, 1974; PhD in Molecular Biology, U. Calif., San Diego, 1980; JD, U. Calif., Berkeley, 1989. Bar: Calif. 1989, U.S. Dist. Ct. (no. dist.) Calif. 1989, U.S. Patent and Trademark Office, 1990. Staff biologist, postdoctoral fellow Lawrence Berkeley Lab. U. Calif., 1980-85; assoc. Irell & Manella, Menlo Park, Calif., 1989-91; v.p. EROX Corp., Menlo Park, Calif., 1991-92; v.p. sci. and patents Pherin Corp., Menlo Park, Calif., 1992-94; pvt. practice Berkeley, 1994-98, NYC, 1996-97, Richmond, Calif., 1998—; dir. intellectual property Sanaria Inc., Rockville, Md., 2004—, Protein Potential LLC, Rockville, Md., 2004—. Speaker in field. Contbr. articles to Jour. Gen. Virology, Jour. Virology, Nature, Science, Psychoneuroendocrinology. Address: 37 Terrace Ave Richmond CA 94801-3937 Office Phone: 510-685-6405. Business E-Mail: david@dolberg-law.com.

DOLBY, RAY MILTON, electrical engineer, company executive; b. Portland, Oreg., Jan. 18, 1933; s. Earl Milton and Esther Eufemia (Strand) Dolby; m. Dagmar Baumert, Aug. 19, 1966; 1 child, Thomas Eric; 1 child, David Earl. Student, San Jose State Coll., 1951-52, 55, Washington U., St. Louis, 1953—54; BSEE, Stanford U., 1957; PhD in Physics (Marshall scholar 1957-60, Draper's studentship 1959-61, NSF fellow 1960-61), Cambridge U., Eng., 1961, ScD (hon.), 1997; Doctor of the U. (hon.), U. York. Lic. Comml. pilot instrument rating FAA. Electronic technician/jr. engr. Ampex Corp., Redwood City, Calif., 1949—53, engr., 1955—57, sr. engr., 1957; PhD research student in physics Cavendish Lab., Cambridge U., 1957—61, research in long wavelength x-rays, 1957—63; fellow Pembroke Coll., 1961—63; cons. U.K. Atomic Energy Authority, 1962—63; UNESCO adviser Central Sci. Instruments Orgn., Chandigarh, Punjab, India, 1963—65; owner, chmn., CEO Dolby Labs., Inc., San Francisco and Wootton Bassett, U.K., 1965—. Mem. Marshall Scholarship selection com., 1979—85; Trustee Univ. High Sch., San Francisco, 1978—84; bd. dirs. San Francisco Opera; bd. govs. San Francisco Symphony. With US Army, 1953—54. Decorated officer Most Excellent Order of Brit. Empire; named Man of Yr., Internat. Tape Assn., 1987, Nat. Inventors Hall of Fame, U.S. Patent and Trademark Office, 2004; named one of Forbes' Richest Americans, 2006; recipient Beech-Thompson award, Stanford U., 1956, Emmy award, 1957, 1989, Trendsetter award, Billboard, 1971, Emile Berliner Maker of the microphone award, Emile Berliner Assn., 1972, Lyre award, Inst. High Fidelity, 1972, Top 200 Execs. Bi-Centennial award, 1976, Sci. and Engring. award, Acad. Motion Picture Arts and Scis., 1979, Pioneer award, Internat. Teleprodn. Soc., 1988, Edward Rhein Ring award, Edward Rhein Found., 1988, Oscar award, 1989, Life Achievement award, Cinema Audio Soc., 1989, Grammy award, NARAS, 1995, Nat. medal Tech., U.S. Dept. Commerce, 1997, medal of Achievement, Am. Electronics Assn., 1997, Festival medal Cannes, Cannes Internat. Film Festival, 2004; fellow Pembroke Coll., Cambridge U., 1983. Fellow: Inst. Broadcast Sound, Soc. Motion Picture and TV Engrs. (Samuel L. Warner award 1979, Alexander M. Poniatoff Gold medal 1982, Progress award 1983), Brit. Kinematograph, Sound and TV Soc. (Outstanding Tech. and Sci. award 1995), Audio Engring. Soc. (bd. govs. 1972-74 1979—84, Silver medal 1971, Gold medal 1992); mem.: NATAS (Charles F. Jenkins Lifetime award 2003), Consumer Electronics Assn. (Consumer Electronics Hall of Fame 2000), Internat. Broadcasting Conv. (John Tucker award 2000), IEEE (Ibuka award 1997), Pacific Union Club, St. Francis Yacht Club, Tau Beta Pi. Achievements include research in Achievements include inventing Dolby Stero, rsch., publs. in video tape recording, x-ray microanalysis, noise reduction and quality improvements in audio and video systems; more than 80 patents. Office: Dolby Labs 100 Potrero Ave San Francisco CA 94103-4886

DOLCE, CARL JOHN, education administration educator; b. New Orleans, June 3, 1928; s. John and Nina (Puglia) D.; m. Nancy Lockwood, July 27, 1955; children: Carla, John. BA, Tulane U., 1947; MEd, Loyola U., New Orleans, 1955; EdD, Harvard U., 1963. Elem. sch. tchr. New Orleans Pub. Schs., 1948-54, secondary sch. tchr., 1954-55, jr. high sch. prin., 1955-63, supt. schs., 1965-69; rsch. assoc., lectr. Harvard Grad. Sch. Edn., Cambridge, Mass., 1963-65; dean Coll. Edn. and Psychology, N.C. State U., Raleigh, 1969-88, dean emeritus, prof. edn. adminstrn., 1989—. Chair adv. com. aesthetic edn. Cen. Midwest Regional Lab., St. Louis, 1968-71; chair exptl. schs. selection com. Office Edn., Washington, 1971-72; pres. Coun. Basic Edn., Washington, 1972-79; vice chmn. nat. assn. Elem. and Secondary Edn. Act Title IV state adv. councs., 1978-79 Editorial bd. Ednl. Forum, 1988; author book chpts., monograph, articles. Chmn. Wake County (N.C.) Sch. Study Com., Raleigh, 1978-79; chmn. tech. advisors Durham City/County Merger Task Force, 1988. Sgt. U.S. Army, 1950-52. Grantee U.S Office Edn. grantee, 1981—82, 1986—87;, 1971—78. Mem. Raleigh Chamber Music Guild (pres. 1978-1980, Phi Kappa Phi (pres. N.C. State U. chpt. 1982-83). Avocations: gardening, reading, mysteries, puzzles. Home: 801 Macon Pl Raleigh NC 27609-5552

DOLCE, DOMENICO, fashion designer; b. Polizzi Generosa, Sicily, Sept. 13, 1958; Studied fashion design in Italy. Worked in his family's small clothing factory; asst. in an atelier in Milan, 1980—82; cons. in field, 1982; co-owner Dolce and Gabbana, Milan, 1982—. First collection established in 1986; first boutique opened in Japan in 1989; established first men's collection and opened first women's boutique in Milan in 1990; co-designer La Maglie di Dolce & Gabbana (knitwear), 1986, Dolce & Gabbana Beachwear, 1989, L'intimo di Dolce & Gabbana (lingerie), 1989, Complice line for the Genny Group in Milan, 1990, scarves, ties, beachwear, perfume, and accessories added in 1992; D&G (diffusion), manufactured by Ittierra S.p.A., 1994, jeans, 1995, Basic women's line, Dolce & Gabbana Occhialli, 1996; co-author with Stefano Gabbana (book) Dolce & Gabbana: Animal, 1998; co-author with Stefano Gabbana and Eve Claxton (book) Hollywood, 2003; recorded Compact Disc. Recipient Woolmark award, 1990. Office: Dolce & Gabbana Via Santa Cecilia 7 20122 Milan Italy Office Phone: 02 79 50 15 or 79 50 16. Office Fax: 02 78 44 36.*

DOLCH, GARY D., health products executive; BS in Chemistry, Ursinus Coll.; MS in Chemistry, Fairleigh Dickinson U.; PhD in Med. Chemistry, Purdue U. Quality mgr. Ayerst Labs., Am. Home Products, 1979—85, asst. v.p., 1986—88; various mgmt. positions quality control Genetech, Inc., Boehringer-Ingelheim Pharms., 1988—92; v.p. quality affairs and tech. ops. Knoll Pharms., BASF, 1992—2001; sr. v.p. quality and regulatory affairs ARC, 2001—02; exec. v.p. quality and regulatory affairs Cardinal Health, Inc., 2002—. Mem. dean's coun. Sch. Pharmacy Purdue U., 2004—; dir. PDA Found., 1987—94. Office: Cardinal Health Inc 7000 Cardinal Pl Dublin OH 43017 Home Phone: 740-548-5333; Office Phone: 614-757-5697.*

DOLD, ROBERT BRUCE, journalist; b. Newark, Mar. 9, 1955; s. Robert Bruce and Margaret (Noll) Dold; m. Eileen Claire Norris, July 10, 1982; children: Megan, Kristen. BS in Journalism, Northwestern U., 1977, MS in Journalism, 1978. Reporter Suburban Tribune, Hinsdale, Ill., 1978—83, Chgo. Tribune, 1983—90, mem. editl. bd., 1990—95, dep. editl. page editor, columnist, 1995—2000, editl. page editor, 2000—. Pulitzer Prize juror, 1997—98; columnist Chgo. Enterprise, 1991—95; critic Downbeat Mag., 1980—84; commentator Chgo. Week in Rev., 1987—. Bd. dirs. Jazz Inst. Chgo., 1980—83. Recipient Peter Lisagor award, Sigma Delta Chi, 1988, Pulitzer Prize for editl. writing, 1994, Scripps Howard Found. Nat. award for commentary, 1999. Mem.: Am. Soc. Newspaper Editors, Econ. Club of Chgo. Roman Catholic. Avocations: golf, basketball, jazz. Home: 501 N Park Rd La Grange Park IL 60526-5516 Office: Chgo Tribune 435 N Michigan Ave Chicago IL 60611-4066 Home Phone: 708-352-1777; Office Phone: 312-222-4438. Business E-Mail: bdold@tribune.com.

DOLE, ARTHUR ALEXANDER, former psychology professor, department chairman; b. San Francisco, Oct. 25, 1917; s. Arthur Alexander and Ella Elizabeth (Duncan) D.; m. Marjorie Elizabeth Welsh, Mar. 19, 1949; children: Peter, Steven, Barbara. BA, Antioch Coll., 1946; MA, Ohio State U., 1949, PhD, 1951; MA (hon.), U. Pa., 1973. Diplomate Am. Bd. Examiners Profl. Psychology. Asst. psychology, edn. Antioch Coll., 1946-48; counselor Ohio State U., 1948-51; dir. Bur. Testing and Guidance, U. Hawaii, 1951-60, asst. prof., prof. psychology, 1951-67; prof. psychology edn. U. Pa., 1967-88, chmn. divsn., 1967-88, prof. emeritus, 1988—. Mem. internat. adv. bd. Univ MSG, Romero, El Salvador. Author articles in field.; cons. editor profl. jours. Bd. dirs. PEACE, Internat. Cultic Studies Assn Fellow APA, AAUP, ACA, Am. Ednl. Rsch. Assn., Internat. Coun. Psychologists, Internat. Assn. Applied Psychology, Nat. Rehab. Assn. Home Phone: 207-667-9237. E-mail: aadole@adelphia.net.

DOLE, BOB (ROBERT JOSEPH DOLE), lawyer, retired senator; b. Russell, Kans., July 22, 1923; s. Doran R. and Bina Dole; m. Phyllis Holden, 1948 (div. 1972); 1 child, Robin; m. Elizabeth Hanford, Dec. 6, 1975. Student, U. Kans., 1941—43, U. Ariz., 1948—49; AB, LLB, Washburn Mcpl. U., Topeka, 1952; LLD (hon.), Washburn U., Topeka, 1969. Bar: Kans. 1952. Mem. Kans. Ho. of Reps., 1951—53; sole practice Russell, Kans., 1953—61; atty. Russell County, 1953—61; mem. US Congress from 6th Kans. dist., 1961—63, US Congress from 1st Kans. dist., 1963—69; US Senator from Kans., 1969—96; majority leader, 1985—87, 1995—96; minority leader, 1987—95; chmn. Rep. Nat. Com., 1971—73; of counsel Verner, Liipfert, Bernhard, McPherson & Hand, 1997—2002; spl. counsel Alston & Bird, 2003—. Advisor US Del. to the UN Food & Agrl. Orgn., 1965, 68, 74, 75, 77, 79, President's Del. to Study the Food Crisis in India, 1966, US Del. to Study the Arab Refugee Problem, 1967, GATT Ministerial Trade Conf., 1982; mem. US Nat. Commn. for the UN Ednl., Scientific, & Cultural Orgn., 1970, 73, Commn. on Security & Cooperation in Europe, 1977, Nat. Commn. on Social Security Reform, 1983, Martin Luther King Jr. Fed. Holiday Commn., 1984; chmn. Internat. Commn. on Missing Persons in the Former Yugoslavia, 1997—2001; co-chair Pres. Commn. on Care for Am. Returning Wounded Warriors, 2007—; Rep. vice-presdl. candidate, 1976; Rep. presdl. candidate, 96. Author: Great Political Wit: Laughing (Almost) All the Way to the White House, 1998, Great Presidential Wits (.I Wish I Was in the Book): A Collection of Humorous Anecdotes and Quotations, 2001, One Soldier's Story: A Memoir, 2005 (NY Times Bestseller list, 2005); co-author (with George McGovern, Donald Messer): Ending Hunger Now: A Challenge to Persons of Faith, 2005; co-author: (with Elizabeth Dole Richard Norton Smith and Kerry Tymchuk) (autobiography) Unlimited Partners: Our American Story, 1996. Chmn. Nat. WWII Meml., 1997—2004, Dole Found. With US Army, WW II. Decorated Purple Heart (2), Bronze Star with oak cluster; recipient Horatio Alger award, Horatio Alger Assn. Disting. Ams., 1988, Presdl. Medal of Freedom, 1997. Mem.: DAV, VFW, 4-H Fair Assn., Am. Legion, Kiwanis, Elks, Shriners, Masons, Kappa Sigma. Methodist. Office: Office of Sen Dole c/o Alston & Bird 601 Pennsylvania Ave NW Washington DC 20004 Business E-Mail: bdole@alston.com.*

DOLE, ELIZABETH HANFORD (LIDDY), senator, former federal agency administrator; b. Salisbury, NC, July 29, 1936; d. John Van and Mary Ella (Cathey) Hanford; m. Robert Joseph Dole (former U.S. Senator from Kans.), Dec. 6, 1975. BA in Polit. Sci., with honors, Duke U., 1958; postgrad., Oxford U., Eng., summer 1959; MA in Edn. and Govt., Harvard U., 1960, JD, 1965. Bar: DC 1966. Staff asst. to asst. sec. for edn. HEW, Washington, 1966-67; practiced law Washington, 1967-68; assoc. dir. legis. affairs, then exec. dir. Pres.'s Com. for Consumer Interests, Washington, 1968-71; dep. asst. to Pres. The White House, Washington, 1971-73; commr. FTC, Washington, 1973-79; chmn. Voters for Reagan-Bush, 1980; dir. Human Services Group, Office of Exec. Br. Mgmt., Office of Pres.-Elect, 1980; asst. to Pres. for pub. liaison, 1981-83; sec. U.S. Dept. Transp., 1983-87; with Robert Dole Presdl. Campaign, 1987-88; participant 1988 Presdl. and Congl. campaigns; sec. U.S. Dept. Labor, 1989-90; pres. AM. Red Cross, 1991-99; U.S. senator from N.C., 2003—; mem. armed services, banking and aging coms.; chair Nat. Rep. Senatorial Com., 2005—. Mem. nominating com. NC Consumer Coun., 1972; mem. com. armed forces, US Senate, com. banking, housing and urban affairs, spl. com. aging. Author (with Bob Dole Richard Norton Smith and Kerry Tymchuk): (autobiography) Unlimited Partners, 1996; author: Hearts Touched With Fire, 2006. Trustee Duke U., 1974-88; mem. coun. Harvard Law Sch. Assocs., mem. vis. com. Harvard Sch. Pub. Health, 1992-95; mem. bd. overseers Harvard U., 1989-95; hon. chair, Project RoundHouse, 2001. Recipient Arthur S. Flemming award U.S. Govt., 1972, Humanitarian award Nat. Commn. Against Drunk Driving, 1988, Disting. Alumni award Duke U., 1988, N.C. award, 1991, Lifetime Achievement award (Breaking The Glass Ceiling) Women Execs. in State Govt., 1993, North Carolinian of the Yr. award N.C. Press Assn., 1993, Radcliffe medal, 1993, Leadership award LWV, 1994, Maxwell Finland award Nat. Found. Infectious Diseases, 1994, Disting. Svc. award Nat. Safety Coun., 1989, Raoul Wallenberg award for Humanitarian Svc., 1995, Christian Woman of Yr. award, 1996; named one of Am.'s 200 Young Leaders, Time mag., 1974, one of World's 10 Most Admired Women, Gallup Poll, 1988, one of 10 most fascinating people 1996 Barbara Walter's Spl., most inspiring polit. figure 1996 MSNBC, 3rd most admired woman in Am. Good Housekeeping, 1996, 98, one of most powerful women, Forbes mag., 2005; selected for Safety and Health Hall of Fame Internat., 1993; inducted into Nat. Women's Hall of Fame, 1995. Mem. Phi Beta Kappa, Pi Lambda Theta, Pi Sigma Alpha. Republican. Methodist. Office: US Senate 555 Dirksen Office Bldg Washington DC 20510 also: District Office Ste 122 310 New Bern Ave Raleigh NC 27601 Office Phone: 202-224-6342, 919-856-4630. Office Fax: 202-224-1100, 919-856-4053.*

DOLE, JANICE GAIL ARNOLD, literacy educator; b. Boston, Jan. 31, 1947; d. Walter Francis and Jenny Clare (Sapuppo) Arnold; m. Patrick John Brennan, Dec. 30, 1992; 1 child, Melissa Erin. BA, U. Mass., Boston, 1969; MA, U. Colo., 1974, PhD, 1977. Cert. elem. tchr., Mass., Calif. Elem. tchr. Medford (Mass.) Sch. Sys., 1969-70, Ridgecrest (Calif.) Sch. Dist., 1970-73; rsch./tchg. asst. U. Colo., Boulder, 1974-77; asst. prof. U. Denver, 1978-84; asst. vis. prof. Ctr. for Study of Reading U. Ill., 1984-86; asst. prof. Mich. State U., East Lansing, 1986-88, U. Utah, Salt Lake City, 1988—. Adv. bd. Reading Rsch. Quarterly, Contemporary Edn. Psychology, Jour. Lit. Rsch.; mem. devel. panel Nat. Assessment Ednl. Progress, Princeton, N.J., 1992—; co-dir. Utah Reading Excellence Act, 1999-2001; mem. Rand Panel Reading, 2000—, cons. to numerous sch. dists. Author: Elementary Language Arts, 1984; contbr. articles to profl. publs. Mem. Am. Edn. Rsch. Assn., Nat. Reading Conf., Internat. Reading Assn., Soc. for Sci. Study of Reading. Avocations: skiing, hiking, reading, running. Office: U Utah 1705 E Central Campus #120 Salt Lake City UT 84112-1169 E-mail: dole@ed.utah.edu.

DOLEAC, CHARLES BARTHOLOMEW, lawyer; b. New Orleans, Sept. 20, 1947; s. Cyril Bartholomew and Emma Elizabeth (St. Clair) D.; m. Denise Kilfoyle, Feb. 2, 1972; children: Keith Gabriel, Jessa Lee. BS cum laude, U. N.H., 1968; JD, NYU, 1971. Bar: Mass. 1972, N.H. 1972, Maine 1973. Law clk. to Justice Grimes N.H. Supreme Ct., Concord, 1972-73; assoc. Boynton, Waldron, Dill & Aeschliman, Portsmouth, NH, 1973-76; ptnr. Boynton, Waldron, Doleac, Woodman & Scott, Portsmouth, 1977—. Apptd. mediator N.H. Superior Ct., 1992—; del. to tour Chinese legal system Chinese Ministry Justice, 1982; del. to People's Republic of China/U.S. joint session on trade investments and econ. law Chinese Ministry Justice/U.S. Dept. Justice, Beijing, 1987; propr. Portsmouth Athenaeum; moderator seminars on ethics for Leaders & Comparative Cultures and Values/East & West and Exec. Seminar Aspen Inst., 1990-95; moderator exec. sem. Aspen Inst., 1997-2000; mem. faculty Southwestern Legal Found. Internat. & Comparative Law Ctr., 1997—; ofcl. guest Fgn. Ministry Japan, Tokyo, 1998; developed Asian Seminar, Aspen Inst., 2000; spkr. ethics Ann. Nat. Conf. Appellate Ct. Clks., 1999-2000. Contbr. articles to profl. jours. Citizens adv. coun. Portsmouth Cmty. Devel. Program, 1976-77; incorporator NH Charitable Found.; pres., bd. dirs. Seacoast United Way; chmn. Portsmouth Bd. Bldg. Appeals, 1976-77; chmn. stewardship com. Soc. Preservation New Eng. Antiquities, 1980-84, trustee; pres. bd. trustees Strawbery Banke Mus., 1985-88; founder Daniel Webster Inn of Ct., 1993, Charles C. Doe Inn of Ct., 1994, Portsmouth Peace Treaty Forums I-IV, 1994-2000; chmn. Portsmouth Peace Treaty 100th Ann. Com., 1993-; founder, pres. Japan-Am. Soc. NH, 1988; develop Asian seminar, Aspen Inst., 2000. Named Citizen of Yr., Portsmouth, N.H., 1991, 2005; recipient John E. Thayer III award, Japan Soc. Boston, 2001, Henry E. Thayer award, Portsmouth Peace Treaty Forums, 2002, citation for chairing Portsmouth Peace Treaty Centennial, Fgn. Minister Japan, 2005. Fellow N.H. Bar Found; mem. Mass. Bar Assn., Maine Bar Assn., N.H. Bar Assn., N.H. Trial Lawyers Assn., Maine Trial Lawyers Assn. Avocation: swimming. Home: Little Harbor Rd Portsmouth NH 03801 Office: Boynton Waldron Doleac Woodman & Scott PA 82 Court St Portsmouth NH 03801-4414 Home Phone: 603-431-8782; Office Phone: 603-436-4010. Business E-Mail: cdoleac@nhlawfirm.com.

DOLEN, WILLIAM KENNEDY, allergist, immunologist, pediatrician, educator; b. Memphis, Oct. 16, 1952; s. William Smith and Dorothy DeWitt (Kennedy) D.; m. Carolyn Canon, Dec. 21, 1974; children: John William, Susan Elizabeth. BS in Biology with distinction and honors, Rhodes Coll., 1974; MD, U. Tenn., 1977. Cert. Nat. Bd. Med. Examiners, Am. Bd. Pediatrics, Am. Bd. Allergy and Immunology. Commd. 2d lt. U.S. Army, 1974, advanced through grades to maj., 1982; intern in pediatrics U. Tenn. Hosp., Knoxville, 1977-78; med. officer SHAPE Med. Ctr., Belgium, 1978-79; comdr. U.S. Army NATO Health Clinic, Belgium, 1979-80; resident in pediatrics Letterman Army Med. Ctr., San Francisco, 1980-82; pediatrician Bassett Army Community Hosp., Ft. Wainwright, Alaska, 1982-84; fellow allergy and clin. immunology Fitzsimons Army Med. Ctr., Aurora, Colo., 1984-86; allergist, immunologist Ochsner Clinic, New Orleans, 1988-89, Allergy Respiratory Inst. Colo., Denver, 1989-92; chief pediatric allergy sect. allergy-immunology svc. Fitzsimons Army Med. Ctr., Aurora, Colo., 1986-88; clin. assoc. prof. medicine Ctr. for Health Scis. U. Colo., Denver, 1990-92; assoc. prof. pediatrics and medicine Med. Coll. Ga., Augusta, 1992-98, prof., 1998—. Presenter in field. Author: (with others) Rhinolaryngoscopy, 2d edit., 1989; mem. editl. bd. Annals of Allergy, 1993-99; contbr. articles to profl. jours., chpts. to books. Assoc. dir. Augusta Choral Soc. Fellow Am. Coll. Allergy, Asthma and Immunology (bd. regents 1993-96, exec. com. 1995-96, chair comm. coun. 1993-96, disting. fellow, pres. 2005-2006), Am. Acad. Allergy and Immunology (com. computers and tech. 1994-97, workshop com. 1993-96), Am. Acad. Pediats.; mem. AMA, Allergy, Asthma and Immunology Soc. of Ga. (pres. 2001-2003), Southeastern Allergy, Asthma and Immunology Soc. (pres. 2002-03), European Acad. Allergology and Clin. Immunology, Am. Guild of Organists. Episcopalian. Office: Sect Allergy Immunology Med Coll GA Augusta GA 30912

DOLENZ, MICKEY (GEORGE MICHAEL DOLENZ, MICKEY BRADDOCK), entertainer, actor, television producer; b. LA, Mar. 8, 1945; s. George and Janelle (Johnson) Dolenz; m. Samantha Just, 1967-1975 (div.) 1 daughter, m. Trina Dow, 1977-91 (div.) 3 daughters, m. Donna Quinter, 2002-. Student, Valley Coll., Los Angeles Tech. Inst. Ind. actor, musician, 1958-66; mem. The Monkees, 1966-70, 85—, star TV series, 1966-68; cartoon voice-over artist, actor, musician, 1970-77; TV dir., producer England, 1977-85; solo artist, 1990—92; actor theater productions; morning host CBS-FM 101.1, NYC, 2005. Rec. artist: (The Monkees: Dolenz, Mike Nesmith, Davey Jones, Peter Tork) The Monkees, 1966, More of the Monkees, 1967, Headquarters, Pisces, Aquarius, Capircorn & Jones Ltd., 1967, The Birds, the Bees & the Monkees, 1968, (film soundtrack) Head, 1968, Instant Replay, 1969, The Monkees Present, 1969, Changes, 1969, The Monkees Greatest Hits, 1969, The Monkees Golden Hits, (The Monkees: Dolenz, Jones, Tork) Then and Now, 1986, Missing Links, 1987, vol. 2, 1990, Listen To The Bard, 1991, JustUs, 1996; hit singles include Last Train to Clarksville, Daydream Believer, Valerie, Peter Percival and his Pet Pig Porky, I'm a Believer, Steppin' Stone, Pleasant Valley Sunday; other TV series appearances include My Three Sons, Adam 12, Pacific Blues, 1995; (cartoon series) Scooby Doo, Devlin, The Funky Phantom, 1971, The Tick, 1995; (TV movies) 33 1/3 Revolutions per Monkee, 1969, Hey, Hey, It's the Monkees, 1997, The Love Bug, 1997; (films) Head, 1968, Keep off my Grass!, 1971, Night of the Strangler, 1972, Keep Off! Keep Off!, 1975, Linda Lovelace for President, 1976, Deadfall, 1993, The Brady Bunch Movie, 1995, Mom, Can I keep Her?, 1998; stage appearances include Tom Sawyer, Sacramento, 1976, The Point by Harry Nilsson, London; author: I'm a Believer: My Life of Monkees, Music and Madness, 1993.

DOLEV, JACQUELINE, physician, researcher; b. Feb. 25, 1975; d. Sharon and Mark Dolev. BA, U. Calif, Berkeley; MD, Yale U. Sch. Medicine. Lic. Calif. Internal medicine resident Stanford U. Hosp., Calif.; dermatology resident and fellow UCSF, San Francisco. Dir. Looking with Care; med. observational skills curriculum, Stanford Med. Sch., The Cantor Center for Visual Arts, Calif.; healthcare fellow U.S Senate, Washington; co-founder Med. observational skills curriculum, Yale Ctr. for Brit. Art, New Haven; eDerm co-dir. UCSF online curriculum. Contbr. articles various profl. jours. and chpts. to books; author: (resolution) AMA Policy Compendium; author: (illustrator) (children's book) Around the World. Mem.: AMA, San Francisco Med. Soc. (editor), Calif. Med. Assn., Psi Chi Nat. Honor Soc. in Psychology.

DOLEY, HAROLD EMANUEL, JR., securities company executive; b. New Orleans, Mar. 8, 1947; s. Helena C. Doley; children: Harold E. III, Aaron M. BS, Xavier U., New Orleans, 1968; DHL (hon.), Bishop Coll., Dallas, 1983; DL (hon.), Clark Atlanta U., 1984; postgrad. bus. sch. mgmt. program, Harvard U., 1987-90; DHL (hon.), Shaw U. Div. Sch., 1992. Account exec. Bache & Co., NYC and New Orleans, 1968-73; mem. N.Y. Stock Exchange, 1973—; v.p. Howard, Weil, Labouisse & Fredericks, New Orleans, 1973-76; pres. Doley Securities Inc., New Orleans, 1976-82,

85-86, chmn., 1986—; dir. minerals mgmt. service Dept. Interior, Washington, 1982-83; U.S. rep. to African Devel. Bank and Fund, 1983-85. Instr. So. U., 1970-77; mem. La. Mineral Bd., Baton Rouge, chmn. royalty acctg. com., 1980-81. Treas. Greater New Orleans Ednl. TV, 1975-81; trustee Clark Atlanta U., 1985—, Shaw U., 1992—, African Am. Inst., 1992. Named Outstanding Stockbroker of Yr. Shareholders Mgmt. Co., 1972; winner Stock Pickers' Choice contest Wall Street Jour., 1989. Mem. N.Y. Options Exchange, Lloyds of London, Population Resource Ctr. (bd. dirs.), U.S.-Africa C. of C., Sigma Phi Phi. Republican. Office: Doley Securities 616 Baronne St New Orleans LA 70113

DOLEZAL, DALE FRANCIS, truck manufacturing company executive; b. Ronan, Mont., Apr. 9, 1936; s. Henry Lewis and Regina Marie (Nedjelski) D.; m. Patricia Louise Johnson, Aug. 27, 1960 (div. Dec. 1980); children: Craig, Kelly, Kathleen, Kari. BS in Indsl. Engring., Mont. State U., 1961; student Exec. Program for Mgmt. Devel., Bus. Sch., Harvard U., 1974. Registered profl. engr., Oreg. Indsl. and methods engr. Westinghouse Electric Corp., Sunnyvale, Calif., 1962—63; chief indsl. engr. Clarke Equipment Corp., Spokane, Wash., 1963—65; mgr. materials Freightliner Corp., Portland, Oreg., 1965—67; dir. purchasing and inventory mgmt. Internat. Harvester Co., Chgo., 1977—80, dir. materials and ops. planning, 1980—81; gen. mgr. parts and retail Indsl. Trucks div. Eaton Corp., Phila., 1981—84; pres. Modern Group, Phila., 1984—86; group v.p., gen. mgr. Holland Atlantic Hitch. Co. of Denmark, Whitehouse Sta., NJ, 1986—2001; COO Holland U.S.A., 2001—03; pres., CEO Road Guard Systems, LLC, 2003—. Bd. dirs. Real Am. Corp.; mem. bd. bus. and indsl. advisers U. Wis., Madison; bd. dirs. Ops. Tng. Inst., Ea. Leadership Mgmt., Inc. Contbr. articles to trade jours. Mem. parents adv. bd. Naperville (Ill.) Central High Sch., 1977—; mem. adv. bd. Sch. Dist. 203, Naperville, 1978—; mem. New Hope (Pa.) Solebury Sch. Bd., 1982-87; mem. bd. dirs "Am. Moisture Monitoring Sys. LLC, Westland Seed, Inc., Mission Mountain Country Club. Served with USMC, 1954-57. Mem. Am. Inst. Indsl. Engrs., Am. Prodn. and Inventory Control. Soc. (pres. 1968-74), Am. Soc. Indsl. Engrs., Rotary (Paul Harris fellow 1992, bd. dirs. 1988—, pres. 1989-90), K.C. (pres.), Harvard Club. Republican. Avocations: golf, hunting, fishing. E-mail: jmartin512@aol.com, nedjelskidfd@ronan.net, ddolezal@roadguardsystems.com.

DOLFI, CHIP, publishing executive; s. William George and Sarah Louise Dolfi; m. Lisa Dolfi, Sept. 17, 2005; children: William Clark, Marshall Collins. Pres., CEO Consol. Holding, Investment & Philanthropic Grp., Inc., Pitts., 1990—. Dir. Hist. News Journals Gifting Program, Pitts., 2006—07. R-Conservative. Achievements include development of historical news journals. Avocations: sailing, golf, travel, skiing. Office: Consol Holding Investment & Philanthropic Grp 461 Cochran Rd Pittsburgh PA 15228 Home Phone: 724-328-8205. Business E-Mail: thechipgroupinc@hotmail.com.

DOLGEN, JONATHAN L., former motion picture company executive; b. NYC, Apr. 27, 1945; m. Susan Dolgen; children: Tamar, Lauren. Grad., Cornell U., 1966; JD, N.Y.U. Law Sch., 1969. Lawyer Fried, Frank, Harris, Shriver & Jacobson, NYC, 1969-76; asst. gen. counsel, deputy gen. counsel Columbia Pictures Industries, 1976-85, sr. v.p. Worldwide Bus. Affairs, 1979, exec. v.p., 1980, pres. Pay Cable & Home Entertainment Group, 1983—85; sr. exec. v.p. Fox Inc., 1985—88, pres. Beverly Hills, 1988—90, chmn. Twentieth Century TV, 1988—90; pres. Columbia Pictures, 1990-94; pres. motion picture group Sony Pictures Entertainment, 1991—94; chmn., CEO Viacom Entertainment Group, NYC, 1994—2004. Bd. fellows Claremont U. Ctr. and Grad. Sch.; founder Friends of the Cornell U. Theater Arts Ctr.; mem. Alumni Coun. N.Y.U. Law Sch.; founding mem. Edn. First; adv. Calif. State Summer Sch. for the Arts.; bd. dirs. Sony Pictures, Charter Comm. Named Pioneer of Yr., Will Rogers Motion Picture Pioneers Found., 2002.

DOLGIN, STEPHEN MARK, secondary school educator, retired social worker; b. San Francisco, Dec. 22, 1949; s. David Aubrey and Ruth (Ogurak) D. BA, U. Minn., 1972, MSW, 1976; MBA in Health Svcs. Mgmt., Golden Gate U., 1982; postgrad., San Francisco State U., 1987—. Social worker US Army, 1976—79; social caseworker Contra Costa County Social Svcs. Dept., Richmond, Calif., 1979-81; social ins. claims examiner Social Security Adminstrn., Richmond, Calif., 1982-84; vets. svc. officer Dakota County, Minn., 1987; substitute tchr. Laguna Salada, South San Francisco Sch. Dist., 1987-88; tchr. Fresno Unified Sch. Dist., Calif., 1989, San Francisco Unified Sch. Dist., 1989—90, 1992—, Oakland Unified Sch. Dist., Calif., 1990—91, Fremont Unified Sch. Dist., Fremont, Calif., 1991—92. Intern Lawrence Livermore Nat. Lab., summer 1991. Admissions ptnr. program vol. USCG Acad., 2005-. Tutor, Learning Ctr., Coast Guard Island, Alameda, Calif. With US Army, 1976—79, lt. col. (ret.) USAR. Decorated Meritiorious Svc. medal US Army, Army Commendation medal, Sea Cadet Disting. Svc. ribbon US Naval Sea Cadet Corps. Mem. CAP (lt. col. cadet program officer, Squadron Officer of Yr. award 1980), Assn. U.S. Army, Am. Philatelic Soc., Res. Officers Assn. (v.p. med. svc. dept. Calif. 1983-84, chpt. sec.), U.S. Naval Sea Cadets (lt. comdr. assoc., sr. regional dir. 2002-05), Coast Guard Aux., Navy League, Naval Order, Assn. of US Army, Air Force Assn., Am. Legion. Avocations: running, history, computers, stamp collecting/philately. Home: Ste 306 1400 Carpentier St Apt 306 San Leandro CA 94577-3657 Office Phone: 510-501-2607. Personal E-mail: ltcdolgin@aol.com.

DOLGON, COREY, sociology educator, political activist; b. Bklyn., Dec. 13, 1961; s. Fred Stewart and Arlene (Fromberg) D.; m. Deborah Millbauer; children: Bailey Maya, Ruby Hannah. BA in English/Sociology, Boston U., 1984; MA in Am. Studies, Baylor U., 1986; PhD in Am. Culture, U. Mich., 1993. Organizer Pub. Interest Rsch. Group, Ann Arbor, Mich., 1986-87; instr. U. Mich., Ann Arbor, 1987; asst. prof., Am. Studies Southampton Coll, Long Island Univ.; vis. asst. prof., social studies Worcester State Coll., Mass., dir. Ctr. Svc. Learning and Civic Engagement. Coord. Wade McCree Scholar Incentive program, Ann Arbor, 1990-92; vis. prof. sociology Harvard U. Author: The End of the Hamptons: Scenes from the Class Struggle in America's Paradise, 2005; editor: Humanity and Society, jour. of Assn. for Humanist Sociology. Organizer Students Against US Intervention in Mid. East, Ann Arbor, 1990, Homeless Action Com., Ann Arbor, 1990-92; chair Mich. Student Assemby, Students Rights Commn., Ann Arbor, 1989-90; steering com. Grad. Employees Orgn. MFT Local 3550; bd. dirs. Oak Hill CED; mem. planning com. Comprehensive Homeless Access Initgration Network. Recipient Book award, Assn. Humanist Sociology, 2005. Mem. Homeless Action Com., Grad. Employees Orgn. Avocations: music, sports. Office: Sociology Dept Worcester State Coll 486 Chandler St Worcester MA 01602-2597 Office Phone: 508-929-8534. Business E-Mail: cdolgon@worcester.edu.

DOLIBOIS, JOHN MICHAEL, surgeon; b. Waynesboro, Pa., May 14, 1944; s. John Ernest and Winifred Englehart Dolibois; m. Alison Millar Hodgson, July 1, 1967; children: Kristen Dolibois Naughton, Lauren Dolibois Sheahan. BA in Zoology, Miami U., Oxford, Ohio, 1962—66; MD, U. Cin., 1966—70. Lic. orthopaedic surgeon Am. Bd. Orthopaedic Surgery, 1976, Ohio, 1970, Ill., 1993, Iowa, 1997, Wis., 2001. Internship Christ Hosp., Cin., 1970—71; orthopaedic resident Mt. Carmel Med. Ctr., Columbus, Ohio, 1971—75; orthopaedic surgeon Hamilton Orthopaedic Clinic, Inc., Ohio, 1975—93, Danville Polyclinic, Ltd., Ill., 1993—95, Family Orthopaedics, Ltd., Bloomington, Ill., 1995—96, Gundersen Luth. Med. Clinic, Decorah, Iowa, 1997—2001, Cmty. Meml. Hosp., Oconto Falls, Wis., 2001—. Orthopaedic cons. dept. intercollegiate athletics Miami U., 1975—90, orthopaedic cons. Student Health Svc., 1975—91; chmn. dept. surgery Mercy Hosp., Hamilton, 1980—81, chief of staff, 1983—84; pres. med. & dental staff Ft. Hamilton Hosp., 1988—89; councilor Hamilton-Fairfield Area Acad. Medicine, 1990—; mem. physician advisor bd. Nat. Rep. Congl. Com., DC, 2005—. Ohio 8th dist. congl. awards council US Congress, DC, 1985—89; mem., bd. trustees Butler County Alcoholism Coun., Hamilton, 1987—99. Recipient Wis. Physician of Yr. award, Nat. Rep. Congl. Com., 2005—06. Fellow: ACS, Internat. Coll. Surgeons, Am. Acad. Orthopaedic Surgeons; mem.: AMA, Wis. State Med. Soc., Mid-America Orthopaedic Assn., Phi Beta Kappa. R-Liberal. Presbyn. Avocations: woodworking, computers, photography, videography. Office: Cmty Meml Hosp 855 S Main St Oconto Falls WI 54154 Home Phone: 920-846-8376. Office Fax: 920-846-2073. Personal E-mail: jmdmd@ez-net.com. Business E-Mail: miked@cmhospital.org.

DOLICH, ANDREW BRUCE, professional sports team executive; b. Bklyn., Feb. 18, 1947; s. Mac and Yetta (Weiselter) D.; m. Ellen Andrea Fass, June 11, 1972; children: Lindsey, Caryn, Cory. BA, Am. U., 1969; MEd, Ohio U., 1971. Adminstrv. asst. to gen. mgr. NBA Phila. 76ers, 1971—74; v.p. Md. Arrows Lacrosse, Landover, 1974—76; mktg. dir. NHL Washington Capitals, Landover, 1976—78; exec. v.p., gen. mgr. Washington Diplomats Soccer, 1978—80; v.p. bus. ops. Oakland A's Baseball, Calif., 1980—92, exec. v.p. bus. ops., 1993—95; pres., COO NBA Golden State Warriors, Oakland, 1994—95; pres. Dolich & Assocs. Sports Mktg., Alameda, Calif., 1996—97; exec. v.p. sales and mktg. Tickets.com, 1998—2000; pres. bus. ops. Memphis Grizzlies, 2000—. Nat. fundraising chmn. sports adminstrs. prog. Ohio U., Athens, dir., 1978-82; lectr. sports mktg. U. Calif. Ext. Bd. dirs. Bay Area Sports Hall of Fame, 1982, Grizzlies Found, Sports Exec. Leadership Coun., 2000-04, MIFA, Memphis Art Coun.; mem. Greater Memphis Arts Coun. Recipient Alumni of Yr. award Ohio U. Sports Adminstrs. Prog., Athens, 1982, Clio award Am. Advt. Fedn., 1982; Woodard fellow U. Oreg. Mem.: Memphis Sports Commn., Memphis C. of C. Office: Memphis Grizzlies FedEx Forum 191 Beale St Memphis TN 38103 Office Phone: 901-205-1234. E-mail: adolich@grizzlies.com.*

DOLICH, BARRY H., plastic surgeon, educator; m. Carol Lagin Dolich, July 26, 1964; children: Matthew, Scott. BA, Alfred U., NY, 1962; MD, Upstate Medical Ctr., Syracuse, 1966. Lic. Nat. Bd. Medical Examiners, 1967, cert. Am. Bd. Plastic Surgery, 1975. Intership Albert Einstein Coll. Medicine, Bronx, NY, 1966—67, resident general surgery, 1967—70; clin. instr. plastic surgery Einstein Coll. Medicine, 1973—74, asst. clin. prof. plastic surgery, 1974—85, assoc. clin. prof. plastic surgery, 1985—; attending surgeon Bronx Mcpl. Hosp. Ctr., 1973—96. Cons. Hand Surgery & Plastic & Reconstructive Surgery Children's Aid Soc., NYC, 1980—86; mem. faculty senate Albert Einstein Coll. Medicine, 1989—94, mem. medical exec. com., 1992—95; presenter in field. Contbr. articles to profl. jours. Mem. Pub. Edn. Needs Civic Involvement Learning, 2003; medical advisor Rye Youth Coun. Lt. commr. USN, 1967—76. Named one of Best Doctors NY, NY Mag., 2002, Top Doctors NY, Castle Connolly Guide, 2003—05. Fellow: NY Acad. Medicine, Am. Coll. Surgeons; mem.: Lipoplasty Soc., Am. Soc. Aesthetic Plastic Surgery, NY State Medical Soc., NY Soc. Surgery Hand (treas. 1989—90), Am. Cleft Palate Assn., Am. Soc. Surgery Hand (pres.-elect 1990—91, pres. 1992—93), Am. Soc. Plastic & Reconstructive Surgery. Avocations: fly fishing, skiing, tennis, photography. Office: 1200 Waters Pl M106 Bronx NY 10461 Office Phone: 718-430-0942.

DOLIGOSA, ANNIE LUMAMPAO, elementary school educator, researcher; b. Iloilo, Philippines, June 1, 1949; d. Ananias Balbanido Lumampao and Erlinda Vargas Caliston; m. Luis Doligosa, Dec. 24, 1973; children: Anil, Louie. BS in elem. edn., West Visyas State U., Philippines, 1969; MA in reading edn., West Visayas State U., Philippines, 1994, PhD in curriculum, instrn. and evaluation edn., 2001. Cert. CCT, CCTC-CLAD, CSTE Philippines. Elem. tchr. Banate Elem. Sch., Philippines, 1969—75; master tchr. Barotac Viejo Elem. Sch., Philippines, 1975—82; supr. tchr. West Visayas State U. Lab. Sch., Ibilo City, Philippines, 1982—2001; prof. West Visayas State U., Ibilo City, Philippines, 1989—2001, grad. sch. prof., 1994—2001; second grade tchr. C.P. Kelly Elem. tchr., Compton, Calif., 2002—03; first grade tchr. W.J. Clinton Elem. Sch., Compton, Calif., 2003—. Sch. paper advisor West Visayas State U. Lab. Sch. Pen Blazers, Ibilo City, Philippines, 1996—2001; peer coach CUSD, Clinton Elem. Sch., Compton, Calif., 2004—; support provider Begining Tchr. Support and Assessment, Compton, Calif., 2005—06. Author: (book) Developmental Reading for College Students, 1998, Learning to Write for Grade One, 2000, (articles) Philippine Jour. Edn., 1996. Sec. Kiwanettes, Barotac, Philippines, 1976—77; donor Am. Heart Soc., Calif., 2003, Am. Vets., Calif., 2005, Cancer Soc., Calif., 2005. Recipient Outstanding Nat. Sch. Paper Advisor, Dept. Edn., 1967; grantee Academic Scholarship, West Visayas State U., 1960—68, Faculty Devel. Scholarship, 1993—94, 2000—01. Mem.: Calif. Reading Assn., World Coun. for Curriculum and Instrn., Calif. Tchrs. Assn., Nat. Assn. for Asian and Pacific Am. Edn., Internat. Reading Assn. Roman Catholic. Avocations: reading, music, gardening, writing, poetry.

D'OLIMPIO, JAMES THOMAS, oncologist; b. Quincy, Mass., June 3, 1950; s. Orlando James D'Olimpio and Marie Johanna Ricciuti; m. Mary Suzanne Clifford, Dec. 30, 1995; 1 child, John; children: Matthew, Christopher. BA, Boston U., 1972; MD, Autonomous U. Guadalajara, 1978. Diplomate Am. Bd. Internal Medicine and Med. Oncology, Am. Bd. Internal Medicine and , and Hospice/Palliative Medicine. Intern, resident Mt. Sinai Hosp. and Svcs., NYC, 1979—82; resident Oncology, fellow Montefiore Med. Ctr., Bronx, NY, 1982—84; rsch. fellow Albert Einstein Coll. Medicine, Bronx, 1984—85; dir. Hospice Care Network North Shore L.I. Jewish Health Sys., Westbury, NY, 1992—97, dir. Supportive Oncology and Palliative Oncology Program Manhasset, NY, 1997—; dir. Montery Cancer Ctr., Lake Success, NY. Asst. prof. medicine NYU Sch. Medicine. Contbr. articles to profl. jours. Grantee, United Hosp. Fund, 2000—02. Mem.: Cancer and Leukemia Group B, Multinat. Assn. Supportive Care in Cancer, Am. Acad. Hospice and Palliative Medicine (cert. 1997), Am. Pain Soc., Am. Soc. Clin. Oncology. Avocations: jazz, painting, golf. Office: N Shore U Hosp 300 Cmty Dr Manhasset NY 11030 Office Phone: 516-562-8935.

DOLIN, MITCHELL F., lawyer; b. Augusta, Ga., Feb. 6, 1956; s. Martin and Harriet Dolin; m. Monica P. Dolin; 2 children. BA, Tufts U., 1978; JD, NYU, 1981. Bar: DC 1982, registered: US Supreme Ct. 1986. Clk. to chief judge U.S. Ct. Appeals (5th cir.), 1981-82; assoc. Covington & Burling LLP, Washington, 1982-89, ptnr., 1989—, chmn. Arbitration & Alternative Dispute Resolution Practice Group, chmn. client devel. com. Mem.: ABA, Human Rights First (past bd. dir.), Am. Judicature Soc. (past bd. dir.), Am. Law Inst. Office: Covington & Burling LLP 1201 Pennsylvania Ave NW Washington DC 20004-2401

DOLIN, RAPHAEL, medical educator; b. Kaunas, Lithuania, Aug. 31, 1941; came to the U.S., 1950; s. Simon and Sara (Zolkov) D.; m. Kelly Millar, June 17, 1989; children: Eric, Nathaniel, Brooke, Allison. BS, Harvard U., 1963, MD, 1967. Intern Boston City Hosp., 1967—68, resident, 1968—69; rsch. assoc. Nat. Inst. Allergy and Infectious Diseases, NIH, Bethesda, Md., 1969-72, fellow in infectious disease, 1972-73, head med. virology sect., 1972-78; prof. medicine U. Vt., Burlington, 1978-82; prof. medicine, head infectious disease unit U. Rochester, NY, 1982-91, prof. microbiology and immunology, 1982-98, Charles A. Dewey prof., chair dept. medicine, 1991-98; physician in chief Strong Meml. Hosp., Rochester, NY, 1991—97; dean for clin. programs Harvard Med. Sch., 1997—2003, dean for academic and clin. programs, 2003—, Maxwell Finland prof. medicine. Editor: Principles and Practice of Infectious Disease, 1995, AIDS Therapy, 1999. Fellow Infectious Disease Soc. Am.; mem. Am. Soc. for Clin. Investigation, Assn. Am. Physicians. Office: Harvard Med Sch 25 Shattuck St Rm 101 Boston MA 02115-6027

DOLINER, NATHANIEL LEE, lawyer; b. Daytona Beach, Fla., June 28, 1949; s. Joseph and Asia (Shaffer) D.; m. Debra Lynn Simon, June 5, 1983. BA, George Washington U., 1970; JD, Vanderbilt U., 1973; LLM in Taxation, U. Fla., 1977. Bar: Fla. 1973. Assoc. Smalbein, Eubank, Johnson, Rosier & Bussey, PA, Daytona Beach, Fla., 1973-76; vis. asst. prof. law U. Fla. Law Sch., Gainesville, 1977-78; assoc. Carlton, Fields, Ward, Emmanuel, Smith & Cutler, PA, Tampa, Fla., 1978-82; shareholder Carlton Fields, P.A., Tampa, 1982—, chair bus. trans. practice group, 1984—2006, mng. shareholder, 2006—. Spkr. in field. Adv. bd. Mergers and Acquisitions Law Report, pub. Bur. Nat. Affairs. Dist. commr. Gulf Ridge coun. Boy Scouts Am., 1983—84; bd. dirs. Kol Ami Synagogue, Tampa, 2003—04, Big Bros./Big Sisters Greater Tampa, Inc., 1980—82, Child Abuse Coun., Inc., 1986—95, asst. treas., 1987—88, treas., 1988—89, pres.-elect, 1989—90, pres., 1990—91; bd. dirs. Tampa Jewish Fedn., 1988—91, 2005—06, Mus. Sci. and Industry, Tampa, 1994—2002, exec. com., 1994—2002, sec., 1995—97, first vice-chmn., 1997—99, chair, 1999—2001; mem. alumni bd. Vanderbilt Law Sch., 1999—2000; bd. dirs. Hillel Sch., Tampa, 1998—, first v.p., 1999—2000, pres., 2001—03. Fellow: Am. Coll. Tax Counsel, Am. Bar Found.; mem.: ABA (chmn. task force preliminary and ancillary agreements 1992—95, acquisition rev. task force 1992—95, chmn. programs subcom. 1995—98, vice-chmn. 1997—98, chmn. 1998—2002, panelist confs., mem. negotiated acquisitions com., bus. law sect., negotiated acqusitions com., mem. bus. law sect., sec. 2006—), Tampa C. of C. (chmn. Ambassadors Target Task Force of Com. of 100 1984—85, 1987—88, vice-chmn. govt. fin. and taxation coun. 1987—88, chmn. 1988—89, chair geographic task force 1989—90, bd. govs. 1991—93, exec. com. 1992, chmn. govtl. affairs com. 1992), Fla. Bar Assn. (exec. coun. tax sect. 1980—82, tax cert. com. 1987—88, vice-chmn. 1988—89, chmn. 1989—90), Am. Law Inst., Anti-Defamation League (regional bd. dirs. 1986—90, exec. com. 1987—90), Tampa Club (sec. 1987—89, bd. dirs. 1987—92, pres. 1990—91). Home: 13341 Golf Crest Cir Tampa FL 33624-4648 Office: Carlton Fields PA 4221 W Boy Scout Blvd Tampa FL 33607-5736 Office Phone: 813-229-4208. Business E-Mail: ndoliner@carltonfields.com.

DOLINKO, ROBERT A., lawyer; b. NYC, Oct. 9, 1953; married; 2 children. BS in Indsl. & Labor Relations, Cornell U., 1974; JD, NYU, 1977. Bar: Calif. 1977. Assoc. Littler Mendelson, San Francisco, 1977—80; labor atty. Merck & Co. Inc., Whitehouse Station, NJ, 1980—82; assoc. Epstein, Becker & Green, San Francisco, 1982—86, ptnr., 1986—94; ptnr., labor & employment dept. Thelen Reid & Priest LLP, San Francisco. Lectr. Cornell U. Sch. Indsl. & Labor Relations, Ithaca, NY, 1980—82. Bd. trustees Seven Hills Sch., Walnut Creek, Calif., 1992—. Mem.: ABA (Labor Sect.), State Bar Calif. (Labor Sect.). Office: Thelen Reid & Priest LLP 101 Second St Ste 1800 San Francisco CA 94105-3606 Office Phone: 415-369-7180. Office Fax: 415-371-1211. Business E-Mail: radolinko@thelenreid.com.

DOLL, LYNNE MARIE, public relations agency executive; b. Glendale, Calif., Aug. 27, 1961; d. George William and Carol Ann (Kennedy) Doll; m. David Jay Lans, Oct. 11, 1986. BA in Journalism, Calif. State U., Northridge, 1983. Freelance writer Austin Pub. Rels. Systems, Glendale, 1978-82; asst. account exec. Berkhemer & Kline, LA, 1982-83; pres., ptnr. Rogers & Assocs., LA, 1983—, head, Mgmt. and Crisis Comm. Practice Group, head, Pub. Sector Dept. Exec. dir. Suzuki Automotive Found. for Life, Brea, Calif., 1986—91; mem., strategic planning com. Gateway to Indian Am. Corp. for Am. Devel., San Francisco, 1988—90. Pub. rels. cons. Rape Treatment Ctr., LA, 1986; regional bd. dir. Nat. Conf. for Cmty. and Justice, LA, nat. bd. dir.; cmty. adv. com. LA Fire Dept.; mem. adv. coun. for pres. Calif. State U., Northridge. Named Pub. Rels. Profl. of Yr.; named one of Women Who Make A Difference, LA Bus. Jour.; recipient Disting. Alumni Award, Calif. State U. Northridge. Mem.: Internat. Motor Press Assn., Pub. Rels. Soc. Am. (Outstanding Profl. (LA chpt.) 1999), Nat. Conf. for Cmty. and Justice (LA region bd. dir. 1996, nat. bd. dir. 2002), So. Calif. Assn. Philanthropy, Coun. on Foundations, Ad Club LA (bd. dir., pres. 1994—95). Democrat. Office: Rogers & Assocs 1875 Century Park E Ste 300 Los Angeles CA 90067-2504 Office Phone: 310-552-6922. Office Fax: 310-552-9052.

DOLL, ROBERT C., investment company executive; B in Acctg., Lehigh U., B in Econs.; MBA, U. Pa. Wharton Sch. CPA; cert. CFA. Chief investment officer OppenheimerFunds, Inc.; chief investment officer equities Merrill Lynch Investment Mgrs. Ams. Merrill Lynch, 1999, co-head Merrill Lynch Investment Mgrs., 1999—2001, global chief investment officer, 2001—, sr. v.p., pres. and chief investment officer Merrill Lynch Investment Mgrs., 2001—. Office: Merrill Lynch Investment Mgrs PO Box 9011 Princeton NJ 08543-9011

DOLLAR, DAVID, chemistry professor; s. Bill and Alta Dollar. BS, Tex. Wesleyan U., 1985; MS, U. North Tex., Denton, 1998, PhD in Higher Edn., 2003. Tchg. cert. Tex., 1985. Chemistry educator Ft. Worth ISD, Tex., 1986—2000; chemistry asst. prof. Tarrant County Coll. SE, Arlington, Tex., 2000—. Recipient Tandy Tech. Scholar, Tandy Corp., 2000. Mem.: Assn. Study Higher Edn. Office: Tarrant County Coll SE 2100 SE Pwy Arlington TX 76018

DOLLARHIDE, MARY C., lawyer; b. Long Beach, Calif., Jan. 28, 1957; BA with distinction, Occidental Coll., 1979; OTH, Circle Sq. Theatre Sch., NYC, 1981; JD, U. So. Calif., 1988. Bar: Calif. 1988, D.C. 1991, Conn. 1996. Ptnr. Paul, Hastings, Janofsky & Walker LLP, San Diego. Master Wallace Inn of Ct., sec. Co-author: Reductions-in-Force Treatise; editor-in-chief: So. Calif. Law Rev. Named a San Diego Super Lawyer, 2007; named one of Top Employment Lawyers in San Diego, 2005—06. Master: Wallace Inn Ct.; mem.: Assn. Bus. Trial Lawyers (bd. govs.), ABA. Avocations: baseball, sailing. Office: Paul Hastings Janofsky & Walker LLP 3579 Valley Center Dr San Diego CA 92130 Office Phone: 858-720-2660. Office Fax: 858-847-3660. Business E-Mail: marydollarhide@paulhastings.com.

DOLLENS, RONALD W., pharmaceutical executive; b. Ind., Dec. 17, 1946; s. William Franklin and Louise Anna (Davis) D.; m. Susan Stanley, Aug. 30, 1969; children: Stephanie, Grant. BS, Purdue U., 1970; MBA, Ind. U., 1972. From sales rep. to dir. bus. devel. Eli Lilly & Co., Indpls., 1972-85; sr. v.p. Advanced Cardiovasc. Sys., Santa Clara, 1985—88, pres., CEO, 1988—94; pres. med. devices divsn. Eli Lilly & Co., 1991-94; pres., CEO Guidant Corp., Indpls., 1994—2005; ret., 2005. Mem., Adv. Com. on Regulatory Health US Dept. Health & Human Svcs., 2002—; mem. bd. Ind. Health Industry Forum, Kinetic Concepts Inc., Beckman Coulter Corp. Bd. dir. Butler U., Indpls., Eiteljorg Mus., Indpls., St. Vincent Hosp. Found. Mem.: AdvaMed, Alliance for Aging Rsch., Healthcare Leadership Coun. (chmn. 2003—05, bd. trustees).

DOLMAN, JOHN PHILLIPS, JR., (TIM DOLMAN), communications company executive; b. Phila., May 22, 1944; s. John Phillips and Dodie Lewis (Porter) D.; m. Rebecca Critchlow, Oct. 29, 1977; children— John P. III, Timothy Chadwick (dec.). AB in History, Wagner Coll., 1966; MBA. in Internat. Bus, U. Pa., 1971. Asst. account exec. Benton & Bowles Inc., NYC, 1971-72, account exec., 1972-73, account dir Amsterdam and London, 1973-75, v.p., account supr., 1975-78; pub. Motor Boating & Sailing mag., 1978-80; gen. mgr. mag. devel. Hearst Mags., NYC, 1980-82; v.p., asst. pub. Pub. div. Playboy Enterprises, Inc., Chgo.,

1983-84, sr. v.p., 1984-88; pres. Dolman & Co., New Canaan, Conn., 1988-92; sr. v.p. mktg. Championship Auto Racing Teams, Inc. dba IndyCar, 1992-94; v.p. mktg. and bus. devel. OCC Sports Inc. subs. ESPN, Inc. subs. ABC, Inc. subs. Walt Disney Co., 1994-99; v.p. dir., bus. ops. ESPN, ABC Sports Mktg. and Sales, 1999—2005; v.p. strategy and bus. devel. ESPN New Media, 2005—. Contbr.: Marine Bus. mag, 1977-78. 1st lt. U.S. Army, 1966-69, Vietnam; lic. capt. USCG, 1988. Decorated Bronze Star. Mem. VFW, N.Y. Yacht Club. Republican. Episcopalian. Office Phone: 212-448-4814. E-mail: TDolman@aol.com.

DOLMATCH, THEODORE BIELEY, management consultant; b. NYC, Apr. 22, 1924; s. Aaron and Diana (Bieley) D.; m. Blanche Ormont, Dec. 28, 1948; children: Karen Ann, Stephen Joseph. BA, NYU, 1947, MA, 1948; student, Columbia U., NYC, 1948-50. Tchr. Queens Coll., 1948-50; asst. supr. Sch. Gen. Studies, Bklyn. Coll., 1950-55; publs. bus. mgr. Am. Mgmt. Assn., 1955-62; pres. Pitman Pub. Corp., NYC, 1962-71, Intext Publishers Group, N.Y.C., also Intext Ednl. Devel. Group, NYC, 1971-75, Info. Please Pub., Inc., NYC, 1976-80, Dolmatch Publs., Inc., NYC, 1979-85; cons. to govt. agys. and corps., 1981—; chmn. ISD/Shaw, Inc., Washington, 1986-2000. Author (sometimes under pseudonym Stephen Josephs) books and articles. Home: 15 Pond View Ln Ossining NY 10562 Personal E-mail: t.dolmatch@verizon.net.

DOLPH, WILBERT EMERY, lawyer; b. Palatka, Fla., Dec. 29, 1923; s. Wilbert Emery and Ophelia (Reynolds) D.; m. Roberta Hundley; children: Wilbert Emery III, Kenneth Alan, Scott Marshall, Cheryl Karlsson. Student, U. Ariz., 1941-42, LL.B., 1949. Bar: Ariz. 1949. Asst. city atty., Tucson, 1949-50; asst. atty. gen. Ariz., 1950-51; pvt. practice Tucson, 1951—93; counsel. jud. com. Ariz. Senate, 1952; shareholder Bilby & Shoenhair, P.C., 1953-89; ptnr. Snell & Wilmer, Tucson, 1989-93, of counsel, 1992-93; ret., 1993. Pres. Pima County Young Dems., 1952-53; v.p. Ariz. Young Dems., 1952-53; trustee Tucson Med. Ctr., pres., 1973-75; mem. U. Ariz. Found., U. Ariz. Pres.'s Club; past chmn. bd. dirs. Friends of Libr., U. Ariz., 1995-97; past bd. visitors U. Ariz. Law Coll.; past bd. dirs. Ariz. Sonora Desert Mus., Ariz. Heart Assn., So. Ariz. Heart Assn., Tucson Festival Soc., Ariz. Children's Home Assn., Tucson YMCA, Ariz. Coun. Econ. Edn.; past vestryman, parish warden St. Phlips in the Hills Episcopal Ch., 1974-76. With USNR, 1942-44, to capt. USMCR, 1944-46. Decorated Air medal. Mem. ABA, Ariz. Bar Assn., Pima County Bar Assn. (exec. com., pres. 1974-75), Coronado Hosp. Found., Rotary Club, Coronado Roundtable, Coronado Yacht Club, Coronado Crown Club, Phi Delta Phi, Sigma Chi. Personal E-mail: wedolph@san.rr.com.

DOLUCA, TUNC, electronics executive; b. 1957; Attended, Middle East Tech. U., Ankara; BSEE, Iowa State U.; MSEE, U. Calif., Santa Barbara. Mem., integrated cir. design devel. staff Maxim Integrated Products, Inc., Sunnyvale, Calif., 1984, v.p., rsch. and devel., 1994—2005, founder, vertical bus. unit, sr. v.p., group. pres., portable, computing, instrumentation electronics group., 2005—07, pres., CEO, 2007—. Bd. dirs. Maxim Integrated Products, Inc., 2007—. Achievements include patents in field of mixed signal design. Office: Maxim Integrated Products Inc 120 San Gabriel Dr Sunnyvale CA 94086 Office Phone: 408-737-7600. Office Fax: 408-737-7194.*

DOLUISIO, JAMES THOMAS, dean, pharmacy educator; b. Bethlehem, Pa., Sept. 28, 1935; s. Dominic and Sue (Powell) D.; m. Phyllis M. Sabolski, June 20, 1959; children— Thomas, James, Rebecca. BS in Pharmacy, Temple U., 1957, MS, 1959; PhD, Purdue U., 1962; DSc, Phila. Coll. Pharmacy and Sci., 1983; DSc (hon.), Purdue U., 1995, Wilkes U., 2000. From asst. prof. to assoc. prof. pharmacy Phila. Coll. Pharmacy and Sci., 1961-67, also assoc. dir. dept., 1965-67; prof., chmn. dept. pharmacy U. Ky., Lexington, 1967-73; prof., dean U. Tex., Austin, 1973-98. Bd. dirs. Eckerd Corp., 1986-96, COR Therapeutics, 1994-02; cons. Smith Kline & French Labs., Phila., 1962-67, McNeil Labs., Ft. Washington, Pa., 1967-72, Hoechst Labs., Somerville, N.J., 1973-93, Nat. Inst. Drug Abuse, 1976-78, HEW, U.S. Surgeon Gen., 1975-83; cons. Merck-Medco, Franklin Lakes, N.J., 2000-2001. Contbr. to profl. and sci. jours. Active Pharmacists Against Drug Abuse Found, 1984; chmn. U.S. Pharmacopeial Conv., Inc., 1990-95; v.p. Fedn. Internat. Pharmaceutique, 1994-98. NSF fellow, 1959-61; Am. Found. Pharm. Edn. fellow, 1957-59 Mem. Am. Pharm. Assn. (pres. 1982, Remington Honor medal 1995), Am. Assn. Colls. Pharmacy, Am. Soc. Hosp. Pharmacy, Am. Assn. Pharm. Scientists (pres. 1988), Fed. Internat. Pharmacists (Lifetime Achievement award 2000), Rho Chi. Office: U Texas College of Pharmacy Austin TX 78712 Home Phone: 512-261-8319. Business E-Mail: doluisio.jt@mail.utexas.edu.

DOMAN, ELVIRA, retired science administrator; b. NYC; d. Andrew and Lillian (McClary) Hand; m. John H. Holder (div.); children: Paula Holder Simpkins, Rodney M. BA in Chemistry, CUNY, 1955; MA in Biochemistry, Columbia U., 1959; MS in Molecular Biology, NYU, 1960; PhD in Physiology and Biochemistry, Rutgers U., 1965. Jr. tech. U. Hosp. N.Y.U. Bellevue Med. Ctr., 1955; rsch. asst. Coll. Physicians and Surgeons, NYC, 1959-60, Sloan-Kettering Inst. Cancer Rsch., NYC, 1959-60, postdoctoral assoc., postdoctoral fellow, 1965; rsch. assoc. Rockefeller U., NYC, 1965-68; lectr. Douglass Coll. Rutgers U., New Brunswick, N.J., 1970-73; asst. prof. Seton Hall U., South Orange, N.J., 1973-77; assoc. program dir. NSF, Washington, 1978-92, program dir., 1992-99; ret., 1999. Vis. scientist Rutgers U., 1989; reader Gates Millenium Scholars, Fairfax, Va., 2002—; sci. fair judge pub., pvt. schs., colls. Bd. dirs. Math. Sci., Computer Learning Ctr. of Shiloh Bapt. Ch., Washington, 1989-99. Recipient Achievement award NSF, 1986, 92, Outstanding Mentor award U. Md. Balt. County, 2000, 06; grantee Seton Hall U., 1975; elected Hunter Coll. Hall of Fame, 2006. Fellow Am. Inst. Chemists; mem. AAAS, Am. Chem. Soc., Assn. Women Sci., Minority Women Sci., Orgn. Black Sci. (pres. 1990-93).

DOMAN, JANET JOY, professional society administrator; b. Phila., Dec. 16, 1948; d. Glenn J. and Hazel Katie (Massingham) D. Student, U. Hull, England, 1969-70; BA, U. Pa., 1971. Cert. tchr. Clinician Inst. Achievement Human Potential, Phila., 1971-74; dir. English Early Devel. Assn., Tokyo, 1974-75; dir. Evan Thomas Inst. Early Devel., Phila., 1975-77, Inst. Achievement of Intellectual Excellence, 1977-80; vice dir. The Inst. of Achievement and Human Potential, 1980-82, dir., 1982—. Internat. lectr. treatment of brain injured children and superiority. Chair Child Brain Devel., United Steelworkers Am., 1987. Recipient Gold medal Centro de Reabilitacion Nosa Senhora da Gloria, Rio de Janeiro, 1974, Brit. Star Brit. Inst. Achievement Human Potential, 1976, Sakura Korosho medal Japanese Inst. Achievement Human Potential, 1977, statuette with pedestal Internat. Forum Human Potential, 1980. Office: The Inst of Achievement and Human Potential 8801 Stenton Ave Glenside PA 19038-8319

DOMANSKIS, ALEXANDER RIMAS, lawyer; b. Chgo., June 3, 1952; s. Van and Alina Alexandra (Tamasauskas) Domanskis; m. Frances Laucka, May 6, 1978; children: Maria Laucka, John Joseph Laucka. AB, U. Mich, 1973; JD, U. Mich., 1977. Bar: Ill. 1977, U.S. Dist. Ct. (no. dist.) Ill. 1977, U.S. Ct. Appeals (7th cir.) 1978, U.S. Supreme Ct. 1985. Law clk. U.S. Dist. Ct. (no. dist.) Ill., Chgo., 1977—79; assoc. Ross & Hardies, Chgo., 1979—84, ptnr., 1985—87, 1993—94, of counsel, 1987—92; ptnr. Shaw, Gussis, Domanskis, Fishman & Glantz, 1994—2002, Boodell & Domanskis, LLC, 2002—. Assoc. gen. counsel and v.p. Intercounty Title Co. of Ill., 1987—91, bd. dir., 1990—91. Editor (adminstrv.): (jour.) U. Mich Jour. Law Reform, 1976—77. Pres. Lithuanian World Ctr., 1988—92, bd. dir., 1988—95, chmn. bd., 1994—95; bd. dir. Intercounty Credit Corp., Chgo., 1988—91, Lithuanian Montessori Soc., Chgo., 1987—90. Mem.: ABA, Lithuanian Roman Cath. Fedn. Am. (bd. dir. Chgo. 1980—87), Lithuanian Am. Coun. (bd. dir. Chgo. 1981—88, sec. found. 2006—), Chgo. Bar Assn. Home: 4236 Hampton Ave Western Springs IL 60558-1310 Office: Boodell & Domanskis LLC 205 N Michigan #4307 Chicago IL 60601 Home Phone: 708-246-0049; Office Phone: 312-540-1075. Office Fax: 312-540-1162. Business E-Mail: domanskis@boodlaw.com.

DOMANSKIS, EDWARD, plastic surgeon; s. Van Domanskis; m. Kiesha Miller, Oct. 6, 2001; children: Andrew Jonas, Julia Alina. MD, U. Ill., Chgo., 1971. Diplomate Am. Bd. Plastic Surgery, 1978. Plastic surgeon Am. Soc. Plastic Surgery, Newport Beach, Calif., 1978—; pvt. practice Newport Beach. Maj. US Army, 1976—78. Home: 1441 Avocado Ave 307 Newport Beach CA 92660 Home Phone: 949-640-6324. Home Fax: 949-640-7347. Personal E-mail: drdomanskis@surgery-plastic.com.

DOMBECK, HAROLD ARTHUR, insurance company executive; b. Bronx, NY, Mar. 23, 1941; s. Max J. and Rose R. (Schefren) D.; m. Cynthia E. Kofoed, May 14, 1983; children: Mark J., Glenn D., David S. BCE, NYU, 1962, MCE, 1963. Profl. engr., N.Y., N.J., Conn., Ga. Instr. San Antonio Coll., 1964-65, SUNY, Farmingdale, 1965-68; project mgr. H2M Group, Melville, NY, 1965-74, dir. environ. engring., 1971-81, dir. mktg., 1982-85, exec. v.p., 1986-88, pres., 1989-91, pres., CEO, chmn., 1991-94; CEO Dombeck Assocs. Inc., Duluth, Ga., 1995—. CEO Archs. and Engrs. Ins. Co., Naperville, Ill., 1987-2007, chmn. 1987—; v.p., CFO, Dod/Pritchard Comms. Inc., Norcross, Ga., 1998-2001; dir., Perceptive Solutions, Inc., Norcross, 2001-03; chmn. bd. dirs. Am. Cons. Engrs. Pension Trust, St. Louis, 1991-94; chmn. ACEC Bus. Inst. Trust, St. Louis, 1994-96. Pres. High Woods Civic Assn., St. James, N.Y., 1971-73, River Plantation Homeowners Assn., 1999-2001. 1st lt. USAF, 1963-65. Fellow ASCE, Am. Cons. Engrs. Coun. (pres. L.I. 1982-84); mem. Am. Acad. Environ. Engrs. (diplomate), NSPE (dir. 1982-85), N.Y. State Water Pollution Control Assn. (dir. 1980-83), N.Y. State Soc. Profl. Engrs. (pres. 1983-84, pres. Suffolk County chpt. 1978-80, Engr. of Yr. 1989, 90, Outstanding Svc. awards 1988, 89). Avocations: reading, golf, history. Office: AEIC 2056 Westings Ave Naperville IL 60563 Home Phone: 770-623-8384. Personal E-mail: hadombeck@yahoo.com.

DOMBROWSKI, ANNE WESSELING, retired microbiologist; b. Cin., Jan. 26, 1948; m. Allan Wayne Dombrowski, Apr. 17, 1982; children: Amy, Alicia. BA summa cum laude, Xavier U., 1970; MS, U. Cin., 1972, PhD, 1974. Fellow Scripps Clinic and Rsch. Found., La Jolla, Calif., 1974-76; sr. rsch. microbiologist Merck & Co., Inc., Rahway, NJ, 1976-87, rsch. fellow, 1987-96, sr. rsch. fellow, 1996—2003, ret., 2003. Contbr. articles to profl. jours. Mem.: Am. Soc. Microbiology, Soc. Indsl. Microbiology (sec. 1982—85, dir. 1998—2001). Achievements include patents in field. Avocations: reading, gardening. Home: 51 Landsdowne Rd East Brunswick NJ 08816-4156 Personal E-mail: annewd@aol.com.

DOMBROWSKI, BOB, artist, writer; b. Buffalo, Feb. 16, 1944; s. Edward A. and Mary Ann Dombrowski. BS, SUNY, Buffalo, 1965; postgrad., Cornish Inst., Seattle, 1975-76. Artist, NYC, 1976—; owner, mgr. GB Art Co., NYC, 1994—2005. Cons. Cementex Corp., NYC, 1989—. Creator, prodr. Ode to Birth of Shiva, 1987, Elegy for the Republic, 1991, Hwy. 17, 1993, On Thinking Thoughts, 1997; author: Theme Show, 2002, A Delicate Membrane, 2002; contbr. chpts. to books; author numerous poems; exhibited in group shows at Albright-Knox Art Mus., Buffalo, 1980, Ashford Hollow Found., NY, 1980, Storefront for Art and Architecture, NYC, 1985, Franklin Furnace, NYC, 1986, Nelson-Atkins Mus., Kansas City, 1989, Shedhalle (Rote Fabrik), Zurich, 1989, Barking Legs Dance Theater, Chattanooga, 1995 (Daimler-Chrysler Spirit of the Word award 1999), Mus. of New Art, Detroit; represented in permanent collections including Bruce Kaplan Collection, Chattanooga, Tenn., NYC Cmty. Bd. #3, Nico Smith Gallery, NYC, Mus. Modern Art Libr., NYC, Bettina Riedel Ltd., Phila., Pernod Corp., NYC, La Perla Garden, NYC, Francis Pratt Usui, Nicholson, Pa., Dorah Rosen Birmingham, Ala., Cleve. Art Inst., Linda Woodall, Chattanooga, Jim and Linda Allen, Chattanooga. Bd. dirs., treas. Keep Dade Beautiful Com.; chair design com. Better Hometown Cmty., Trenton, Ga; coord. Picture Dade County project; chmn. Trenton Arts Coun.; bd. dirs. Downtown Devel. Authority, Trenton. Mem. NY Artists Equity (bd. dirs. 1989-90). Avocations: photography, walking. Home and Office: 19740 Hwy #11N Wildwood GA 30757 Home Phone: 706-657-8858; Office Phone: 706-657-8858. Business E-Mail: d.p.productions@earthlink.net.

DOMBROWSKI, DAVID, baseball team executive; b. Chgo., July 27, 1956; s. Ronald Edward and Laurie Bernadine Dombrowski. B of Adminstrn., Western Mich. U., 1979. Adminstrv. asst. Chgo. White Sox, 1978-79, asst. dir. player devel. and scouting, 1979-80, asst. gen. mgr., 1980-85, v.p. baseball ops., 1985-86; dir. player devel. Montreal Expos, 1986-87, asst. gen. mgr., 1987-88, gen. mgr., 1988-91; exec. v.p., gen. mgr. Fla. Marlins, Miami, 1991—2003; pres., gen. mgr. Detroit Tigers, 2004—. Bd. dirs. Chgo. Baseball Cancer Charities, 1981—. Named Exec. of Yr., UPI, 1990. Avocations: sports, jogging, movies, theater. Office: Detroit Tigers 2100 Woodward Ave Detroit MI 48201*

DOMBROWSKI, KAREN S., social studies and education educator; d. Harold L. and Katherine M. Anders; m. Steven M. Dombrowski, June 14, 1975; children: Jaclyn M., Jared M., Joseph S. BS Edn., Ohio U., 1973. Cert. tchr. Ohio. Tchr. 4th grade Lancaster City Schs., Ohio, 1973—75; tchr. grades 5-8 St. Louis Sch., Louisville, Ohio, 1976—77; tchr. grades 3 and 4 Sacred Heart of Mary Sch., Louisville, Ohio, 1978—80; ednl. asst. Pickerington Local Schs., Ohio, 1989—94; tchr. grades 7 and 8 social studies Berne Union Mid. Sch., Sugar Grove, Ohio, 1994—. Tchr. mentor trainer Ohio Dept. Edn., Columbus, 1999—, mem. rangefinding com. grade 8 achievement testing; pol. action liaison Berne Union Edn. Assn. and Ohio Edn. Assn., 2006—; master tchr. Think History Program Ohio Hist. Soc. Mem.: NEA, Berne Edn. Assn. (v.p.), Ohio Ctr. Law Related Edn., Ohio Coun. Social Studies, Nat. Coun. Social Studies, Ohio Edn. Assn., Delta Kappa Gamma. Avocations: travel, cross-stitch. Home: 684 Manchester Cir N Pickerington OH 43147 Office: Berne Union Mid Sch 506 North Main St Sugar Grove OH 43155 Home Phone: 614-837-0891; Office Phone: 740-746-9738. Office Fax: 740-746-9824. Personal E-mail: mumof9@hotmail.com. Business E-Mail: karen_dombrowski@berne-union.k12.oh.us.

DOMBROWSKI, MITCHELL PAUL, obstetrician, researcher; b. Detroit, Apr. 24, 1953; s. Mitchell Stanley and Dorothy Julia (Silarski) D.; m. Jocelyn McKinley, Mar. 7, 1981; children: Michael, Jacqueline, David, Elizabeth. BS, U. Mich., 1975; MD, Wayne State U., 1979. Diplomate Am. Bd. OB-Gyn, Am. Bd. Perinatology. Resident in obstetrics and gynecology, Detroit, 1979-84; fellow in perinatology, 1984-86; from asst, to assoc. prof. Wayne State U. Sch. Medicine, Detroit, 1986-98, prof., 1998, chmn., chief, 1996-98; chief St. John Hosp., 2002. Prin. investigator maternal fetal medicine network units Nat. Inst. Child Health and Human Devel., 1996. Contbr. articles to med. publs.; patentee fetal blood sampling device, reagent test strip, digital medication device, self-capping needle assemblies, amnicentesis needle. Recipient Research award Nat Insts Hlth. Recipient Nat. Inst. Alcohol Abuse and Alcoholism award, AMA; grantee Nat. Heart, Lung and Blood Inst./NICHD, 1994; fellow Am. Coll. Obstetrics and Gynecologists, Soc. Perinatal Obstetricians; Diabetes Rsch. Office: St John Hosp & Med Ctr 22151 Moross Rd Detroit MI 48236-2114 Office Phone: 313-343-7798. Personal E-mail: wsuserver@hotmail.com.

DOMBY, ARTHUR H., lawyer; b. Lafayette, Ind., 1951; BA, Hamilton Coll., 1973; MS, Univ. Ga., 1976; JD, Union Univ., 1973. Bar: Ga. 1979, NY 1980. Assoc. Troutman Sanders LLP, Atlanta, 1979—86, ptnr., environ. and natural resources, 1987—, and group practice leader, nuclear regulation. Adj. prof., natural resources law Emory Univ., Atlanta, 1987, 89. Mem.: ABA, Nuclear Energy Inst. Lawyers' Com. (chmn. 2000—01), State Bar Ga. (past chmn., environ. law sect.). Office: Troutman Sanders LLP Bank of Am Plz Ste 5200 600 Peachtree St NE Atlanta GA 30308-2216 Office Phone: 404-885-3130. Office Fax: 404-962-6546. Business E-Mail: arthur.domby@troutmansanders.com.

DOMECK, BRIAN C., insurance company executive; b. Apr. 1959; BA in Mgmt. Sci. and Acctg., Duke U., Durham, NC; MBA in Fin. and Mktg., Northwestern U., Ill. Staff acct. Ernst & Whinney, Cleve.; contr. Ctrl. States Divsn. Progressive Corp., 1987, various positions including product mgr. for several midwestern states, gen. mgr. Kans., Mo. and Fla. and contr. Progressive Direct, sr. contr. agy. bus., demand mgr. direct bus., 2003—06, v.p., CFO, 2007—. Office: Progressive Corp 6300 Wilson Mills Rd Cleveland OH 44143-2109 Office Phone: 440-461-5000. Office Fax: 440-603-4420.*

DOMENECH, EDGAR A., federal agency administrator; b. 1946; BS in Pub. Adminstrn., John Jay Coll. Criminal Justice. Spl. agent Bur. Alcohol, Tobacco, Firearms & Explosives, US Dept Justice, Ft. Lauderdale, Fla., 1985, supr. firearms enforcement group, supr. High Intensity Drug Trafficking/Organized Drug Enforcement Task Force, various positions Washington, 1995—2004, spl. agent in charge spl. programs br.; asst. to spl. agent in charge office of inspection Bur. Alcohol, Tobacco, and Firearms, Washington; asst. spl. agent in charge NY field divsn. Bur. Alcohol, Tobacco, Firearms & Explosives, US Dept Justice, Washington, 1998, dep. asst. dir. field ops., 2002—03, acting dep. dir., 2003—04, dep. dir., 2004—. Apptd. sr. exec. svc. Fed. Govt., 2001; founder, former pres. Hispanic Agents Assn. Office: Bur Alcohol Tobacco Firearms and Explosives Office Pub and Govtl Affairs 650 Massachusetts Ave NW Rm 8290 Washington DC 20226

DOMENICI, (PETE) VICHI, senator; b. Albuquerque, May 7, 1932; s. Cherubino and Alda (Vichi) D.; m. Nancy Burk, Jan. 15, 1958; children: Lisa, Peter, Nella, Clare, David, Nanette, Helen, Paula. Student, U. Albuquerque, 1950-52; BS, U. N.Mex., 1954; LLB, Denver U., 1958; LLD (hon.), U. N.Mex., Georgetown U. Sch. Medicine; HHD (hon.), N.Mex. State U. Bar: N.Mex. 1958. Tchr. math. pub. schs., Albuquerque, 1954-55; ptnr. firm Domenici & Bonham, Albuquerque, 1958-72; chmn., ex-officio mayor Albuquerque, 1967; city commr., 1966-68; US Senator from N.Mex., 1973—. Mem. com. appropriations US Senate, com. budget, chmn. energy and natural resources, com. homeland security and governmental affairs, com. Indian affairs. Author: A Changing America: Conservatives View the '80's from teh US Senate, 1980; author: (with Sam Nunn) Ctr. Strategic and Internat. Studies, 1992. Mem. Gov.'s Policy Bd. for Law Enforcement, 1967-68; chmn. Model Cities Joint Adv. Com., 1967-68. Recipient Nat. League of Cities award Outstanding Performance in Congress; Disting. Svc. award Tax Found., 1986, Legislator of Yr. award Nat. Mental Health Assn., 1987, public sector leadership award, 1996, Award for Leadership in Reducing Threat of Nuclear Proliferation in former Soviet Union Ctr. Non-Proliferation Studies Monterey Inst. Internat. Studies, 1999, Champion Sci. and Engring. Rsch. award, Sci. Coalition, 1999, Erna and John Steinbruck award mental illness leadership N Street Village, 1999, Whitney Clinic award extraordinary public svc., 1999, Good Neighbor award US-Mexico C. of C., 2000, Henry DeWolfe Smyth Statesman award Am. Nuclear Soc. 2000, Public Svc. award, Am. Astronomical Soc., 2003, Pick and Gavel award Assn. Am. State Geologists, 2004, Public Svc. award Am. Chem. Soc., 2005. Mem. ABA, N.Mex. Bar Assn., Kiwanis, Nat. Sch. Bd. Assn., Nat. League Cities, Middle Rio Grande Council Govts. Republican. Roman Catholic. Office: US Senate 328 Hart Senate Office Bldg Washington DC 20510-0001 also: Albuquerque Plaza Ste 710 201 3rd St NW Albuquerque NM 87102 Office Phone: 202-224-6621, 505-346-6791. Office Fax: 202-228-3261, 505-346-6720.*

DOMEÑO, EUGENE TIMOTHY, elementary education educator, principal; b. LA, Oct. 22, 1938; s. Digno and Aurora Mary (Roldan) D. AA, Santa Monica City Coll., Calif., 1958; BA, Calif. State U., 1960, MA, 1966. Cert. elem. tchr., gen. sch svcs, special secondary tchr. Elem. tchr. L.A. Unified Sch. Dist., 1960-70; asst. prin. Pomona (Calif.) Unified Sch. Dist., 1970-71, prin., 1971—. Cons. testing and evaluation Pomona Unified Sch. Dist., 1990—. With USNR, 1958-65. Recipient PTA Hon. Svc. award Granada Elem. PTA, Granada Hills, Calif., 1960, Armstrong Sch. PTA, Diamond Bar, Calif., 1990, Calif. Disting. Sch. Calif. Dept. Edn., 1989, Nat. Blue Ribbon Sch. U.S. Dept. Edn., Washington, 1990, Prin. and Leadership award, 1990. Mem. ASCD, Nat. Assn, Elem. Sch. Prins. (Prin. of Leadership award with Nat. Safety Com., 1991), Nat. Assn. Year Round Sch., Assn. Calif. Sch. Administrs., Diamond Bar C. of C. (edn. com.). Avocations: golf, dance, church, flute. Office: Neil Armstrong Elem Sch 22750 Beaverhead Dr Diamond Bar CA 91765-1566 E-mail: auroratlc@aol.com.

DOMENZAIN, ANTONIO, statistician, consultant; b. San Antonio, Oct. 14, 1975; m. Patricia Vera, May 12, 2000; 1 child, Gabriela. MS in Engring., U. Mich., Ann Arbor, 2005. Assoc. cons. Tarifar Consulting, Mexico City, 1998—2003; ops. rsch. analyst Raytheon Aircraft Co. / Flight Options LLC, Cleve., 2005—07; sr. modeling analyst Key Bank, Cleve., 2007—. Fellow, Mex. Coun. Sci. and Tech., 2003—05. Mem.: Inst. Ops. Rsch. and Mgmt. Scis. (assoc.). Achievements include first to implemented optimization theory into artificial intelligence routines to identify text patterns; design of statistical tests to address data quality issues in marketing databases; application to optimize allocation of resources within a retail distribution network; development of applications to calculate air/drive distance for over 5 billion latitude-longitude data points. Office: Key Bank 800 Superior Ave Cleveland OH 44114 Home Phone: 216-255-6745. Personal E-mail: adomenzain@marketre.com. Business E-Mail: antonio_domenzain@keybank.com.

DOMIANO, JOSEPH CHARLES, lawyer; b. Cleve., Oct. 21, 1928; s. Charles Joseph and Mary Grace (Santora) D.; m. Julie Ann Birinyi, Sept. 9, 1950; children: Joseph, Jr., Laura, John. BBA, Case We. Res. U., 1951; LLD, Cleve. State U., 1956. Bar: Ohio 1957. Ptnr. Mandanici & Domiano, Cleve., 1957—84, Sindell, Rubenstein, Cleve., 1984—87, Friedman, Domiano & Smith, Cleve., 1987—. Prosecutor City of Maple Heights (Ohio), 1963-65; solicitor Village of Bentleyville (Ohio), 1974-94; law dir. City of Olmsted Falls (Ohio), 1992-93; mem. (life) 8th Dist. Jud. Law Conf., Cleve., 1994—. Contbr. articles to law jours.; presenter in field. Bd. dirs. Maple Heights Little Theatre, 1962-65, Transitional Housing, Cleve., 1994-2004; mem. parish coun. Ch. of Resurrection, Solon, Ohio, 1992-94, mem. fin. coun., 1996—. Fellow Nat. Coll. Adv.; mem. ATLA, Ohio State Bar Assn., Ohio Acad. Trial Lawyers, Cleve. Bar Assn., Cleve. Acad. Trial Lawyers, Cuyahoga County Bar Assn. (pres. 1993-94, torts personal injury, employer intentional torts, product liability), KC (exec. com. 1985-86) Avocations: skiing, water-skiing, sailing, golf. Office: Friedman Domiano & Smith 55 Public Sq Ste 109 Cleveland OH 44113 Office Phone: 216-621-0070. Business E-Mail: joedomiano@fdslaw.com.

DOMINGO, CORA MARIA CORAZON ENCARNACION, minister; b. Urdaneta City, Philippines, Mar. 25, 1917; arrived in US, 1961, naturalized, 1967; d. Martin Cantaoe and Casimira Agbanlog Echalas; m. Nicanor Barrientos Domingo, Oct. 29, 1950; m. Teofilo Alonzo Manzano, July 8, 1935 (div. Sept. 26, 1950); children: Don Leonardo Manzano, Teddy Teofilo Manzano. BMin. in Practical Theology, Word of Faith Leadership & Bible Inst., Dallas, 1985. Ordained minister Ministry Salvation Ch., 1986. Tchr. Public Sch., Urdaneta City, Philippines, 1939—46; assoc. pastor The Assembly of the First Born, Kahului, Hawaii, 1993—; pres./founder Christ Tabernacle of Praise, Cabuloan, Urdaneta

City, Philippines, 1999—; missionary pastor Cabuloan Village Chapel, Cabuloan, Philippines, 1971—99; child evangelist Child Evangelism Fellowship, Honolulu, 1980—92; pastor Maui Evang. Ch., Kahului, Hawaii, 1970—74; landlord and bus. woman Kahului, Hawaii, 1962—. Dir. of Filipino lang. radio program KNUI/KMVI, Kahului, Hawaii. Mem. Friendship Bible com., coord. Maui Christian Women's Club; pres., host Great Commn. Fellowship, 1980—95; mem. Maui Retarded Children's Assn., Big Bros./Big Sisters of Hawaii, Humane Soc.; treas., bd. dirs. Maui Adult Day Care Ctr., 1974—94; pres. Filipino Mins. Fellowship Maui, 1976—98; mem. Maui Christian Mins. Assn.; leader Girls Scout Am. Troop 78, 1953—63; bd. dirs. Status of Women, Com. on Aging, Wailuku, Hawaii. Named one of Maui's Filipino Heroes, 1998; recipient Outstanding Citizen of Filipino Ancestry, Maui Filipino Cmty. Assn., 1965, Milady of the Valley Isle award, 1968, Worthy Matron of Order, Maui Chpt. 5 Order of the Ea. Star of Maui Hawaii, 1975, 1980, 1993, Conservative Patriotic award, Young Am. Found., 2003. Mem.: Maui Filipino Ladies Cir., Bus. & Profl. Women's Club (vp & chmn. 1965—69). Republican. Avocations: reading, sewing, gardening, travel. Home and Office: 739 Iluna Pl Kahului HI 96732

DOMINGO, PLACIDO, tenor, opera company director; b. Madrid, Jan. 21, 1941; s. Placido and Pepita (Embil) Domingo; m. Marta Ornelas; children: Jose, Placido, Alvaro Maurizio. Student, Conservatory in Mexico City; degree (hon.), Royal Coll. Music, 1982, Complutense de Madrid, 1989; doctorate (hon.), Oxford U. Gen. dir. Washington Nat. Opera, 1994—, L.A. Opera, 2000—. Singer: (Operas) made operatic debut in La Traviata, 1961, debut Met. Opera, 1968, (star tenor with opera cos. including) La Scala, Covent Garden, Hamburg State Opera, Vienna State Opera, N.Y.C. Opera, San Francisco Opera, Nat. Hebrew Opera in Tel-Aviv, (leading roles 120 opera including) Don Rodrigo, Ofello, Walkure, Tosca, Andrea Chenier, Don Carlo, Carmen, La Boheme, Errani, Parsifal, Idomeneo, (films) Traviata, 1983, Carmen, 1984, Otello, 1986, (made more than 100 recs. including 93 full-length opera) BMG (formerly RCA), DGG, Sony, Decca/London, Philips, Time Warner, EMI (Angel), made more than 50 videos, (performed in concert) PBS TV spl. (with José Carreras & Luciano Pavorotti) The Three Tenors, 1994; condr. numerous performances at major opera houses including: Met. Opera, London's Covent Garden, Vienna State Opera, music dir.: Seville World's Fair, active: Operalia internat. vocal competition. Performed concerts to benefit victims of 1985 Mexican earthquake. Named Kennedy Ctr. honoree, 2000; recipient 9 Grammy awards, 2 Latin Grammy awards, Legion of Honor, France, 2002, Medal of Freedom, U.S., 2002, Gran Cruz de la Orden del Merito Civil, 2002, Knight Comdr. of the Brit. Empire, 2002. Address: care Vincent & Farrell Assocs 165 E 83d St Apt 5E New York NY 10028 Mailing: Washington National Opera Ste 104 2600 Virginia Ave NW Washington DC 20037; Los Angeles Opera 135 North Grand Ave Los Angeles CA 90012*

DOMINGUE, GERALD JAMES, medical researcher, microbiologist, immunologist, educator, clinical bacteriologist; b. Lafayette, La., Mar. 2, 1937; s. Edgar Paul and Sarah Ann (Prejean) D.; m. Marie H. Dugas, Aug. 30, 1958 (div. 1980); children: Andrea, Yvonne, Michelle, Gerald Jr., Marcel; m. Kathryn H. Colbert, June 20, 1981 (div. 1985). BS in Bacteriology, U. La., Lafayette, 1959; PhD in Med. Microbiology and Immunology, Tulane U., 1964. Post-doctoral research fellow Children's Hosp., asst. research instr. pediatrics SUNY, Buffalo, 1965-66; dir. microbiol. Snodgras Lab. of Pathology and Bacteriology, St. Louis, 1966-67; instr. microbiology St. Louis U., 1966-67; asst. prof. microbiology, immunology and urology Tulane U., New Orleans, 1967-70, assoc. prof. microbiology, immunology and urology, 1970-74, prof. microbiology, immunology and urology, 1974-97, prof. emeritus, 1997—. Lectr. microbiology sch. dentistry Washington U., St. Louis, 1966-67; vis. prof., lectr. Peruvian Urol. Assn., Lima, 1973, First Internat. Congress Bacteriology, Jerusalem, 1973, Internat. Convocation Immunology, Buffalo, 1974, World Health Orgn. Conf. on Sperm Immunology, Aarhus, Denmark, 1974, European Soc. Exptl. Urol. Research, Wurzburg, Fed. Republic Germany, 1976, Internat. Seminar L-Forms, Montpellier, France, 1976, U. Melbourne, Royal Melbourne Hosp., Australia, 1978, XII Internat. Congress Microbiology, Munich, 1978, Internat. Symposium Vaccines and Vaccinations, Institut Pasteur, Paris, 1985; speaker U. Montpellier Sch. Medicine, 1985, 4th Internat. Congress on Pyelonephritis, Goteborg, Sweden, 1986, Orion Diagnostica, Helsinki, Finland, 1986, Nat. Inst. Hygiene, Warsaw, Poland, 1986, Symposium on Molecular Biology and Infectious Diseases, Institut Pasteur, 1987; com. for infection control So. Bapt. Hosp., 1971-75, Charity Hosp. La., 1977—, Tulane U. Hosp., 1977—; infectious disease com. St. Louis City Hosp., 1966-67; reviewer, visitor project sites NIH Grant Review Study Sects., 1967-97, NSF, Kaiser Rsch. Found., Kidney Found. Can.; cons. bacteriology So. Bapt. Hosp., New Orleans, 1968-84, Tulane U. Hosp., 1978-83, Med. Tech. Corp., Somerset, NJ, 1983—; rsch. cons. VA Hosp., New Orleans, 1970-78; cons., tech. adv. bd. Analytab Products, Inc., NYC, 1972-77; expert witness to subcom. on dept. investigation oversight and rsch. for Animal Cancer Rsch. Act, U.S. Ho. of Reps., 1980; cons. in field Author, editor: Cell Wall-Deficient Bacteria, 1962; author numerous poems; contbr. over 160 articles to profl. jours. and chpts. to books. Pres. France-Louisiane de la Nouvelle Orleans, 1985—, pres. fondateur, 1988; apptd. mem. Gov.'s Council for Devel. of French Lang. in La., 1985, 88; mem. Met. Area Com., New Orleans, 1987, Bur. Govtl. Research, New Orleans, 1987; mem. Mayor's Com. New Orleans-Paris Cultural Exchange, 1988; chmn. scholar's com. La. Com. on French Revolution, 1988; mem. Alliance for Good Govt., 1980-84; mem. Greater New Orleans French Bd., 1987—; rep. Coun. for Devel. French and France Louisiane for celebration of French Bicentennial, Paris, 1989. Served with La. N.G., USAR, 1955-63. Guaranty scholar U. Southwestern La., 1958; grantee NIH, 1970-97, Schlieder Found., Armour Pharm. House, VA, Cadwallader Family Found., Med. Tech. Corp., Orion Diagnostica; decorated chevalier Order of Palmes Academiques (France); recipient French Medal, 1996. Fellow Am. Acad. Microbiology, Infectious Disease Soc. Am.; mem. Am. Soc. Microbiology (divisional lectr. 1978, found. lectr. 1979-80, symposium lectr. 1994), Soc. Basic Urologic Rsch. (state of art lectr. 1994), Soc. for Exptl. Biology and Medicine, AAAS, AAUP, Fedn. Am. Scientists, Southwestern Assn. Clin. Microbiology (editor newsletter 1983-85, pres. 1985-86), N.Y. Acad. Scis., Am. Assn. Lab. Animal Sci., Soc. Basic Urological Rsch. (nominating com. 1988), Am. Urol. Assn. (affiliate mem.), French-Am. Bus. Assn., Am. Acad. Poets (assoc.), Sigma Xi. Roman Catholic. Avocations: painting, writing. Home and Office: Kronleinstrasse 14 8044 Zurich Switzerland Personal E-mail: geralddomingue7526@msn.com.

DOMINGUE, JAMES NEAL, neurologist; MD, La. State U., New Orleans, 1974. Lic. La. State Bd. Med. Examiners, 2005. Resident in neurology U. Calif., San Francisco, 1974—78; fellow in clin. neurophysiology Mass. Gen. Hosp., Boston, 1979—81. Office: 501 W St Mary Blvd 304 Lafayette LA 70506 Office Phone: 337-269-5840.

DOMINGUEZ, CARI M., former federal official; b. Havana, Cuba, 1949; married; 2 children. BA, Am. U., 1977; MA Am. U., 1977; fellow advanced study Program in Pub. Mgmt., MIT; D in Humanitarian Svc. (hon.), Loma Linda U., 2003. Devel. specialist Office Fed. Contract Compliance, US Dept. Labor, 1974—79, spl. asst. to dir., 1980—84, dir., 1989—91; v.p., corp. mgr., Equal Opportunity Employment & Affirmative Action Bank Am. Corp., 1984—86, v.p., dir. exec. programs, 1986—89; asst. sec. for employment standards US Dept. Labor, Washington, 1991—93; dir. Spencer Stuart, San Francisco, 1993—95; ptnr. Heidrick & Struggles, 1995—98; prin. Dominguez & Associates, 1999—2001; chair US Equal Employment Opportunity Comm., Washington, 2001—06. Bd. dirs. Manpower Inc., 2007—. Named one of 80 Elite Hispanic Women, Hispanic Bus. mag., 100 Most Influential Hispanics in the Country; recipient Eagle Award, Bank America CEO, Award for Excellence, Nat. Image, Inc., 2002, Legacy of Leadership award, Spelman Coll., 2005. Mem.: Human Resources Planning Soc. (bd. mem.), Leadership Found. Internat. Women's Forum (bd. mem.). Seventh Day Adventist.*

DOMINGUEZ, DANIEL R., judge; b. San Juan, 1945; BA, Boston U., 1967; LLB cum laude, U. P.R., 1970. Bar: P.R. Atty. Hector M. Laffitte Law Offices, 1970—72; ptnr. Laffitte, Dominguez & Totti, 1973—84, Dominguez & Totti, 1983—94; judge U.S. Dist. Ct. P.R., San Juan, 1994—. Gov. Adv. Com. on Labor Policy, 1984; mem. bd. Fed. Bar Examiners U.S. Dist. Ct. P.R., 1989—94; mem. Civil Justice Reform Act Adv. Group, 1991—94; mem. merit selection com. Appointment of U.S. Magistrate Judge, 1993; mem. com. for jud. reform Gov. P.R., 1993—94. With USAR, 1967. Mem.: Hyatt Dorado Beach Country Club, Berwind Country Club. Office: US Dist Ct PR US Courthouse CH-129 150 Ave Carlos Chardon San Juan PR 00918-1703

DOMINGUEZ, EDDIE, artist; b. Tucumcari, N.Mex., Oct. 17, 1957; BFA, Cleve. Inst. Art, 1981; MFA, Alfred U., 1983. Grad. asst., ceramics and visual design courses Alfred (N.Y.) U., 1981-83; artist-in-residence, lectr. Ohio State U., Columbus, 1984; artist-in-edn. N.Mex. Arts Divsn., Santa Fe, 1985-86; artist-in-residence Cleve. Inst. Art, 1986; artist-in-residence, lectr. U. Mont., Missoula, 1988; asst. prof. art U. Nebr., Lincoln, 1998—. Lectr., presenter workshops, mem. panels Ill. Arts Coun., Chgo., 1994, NEA, Washington, 1994, Ariz. Commn. on the Arts, 1994, Concordia U., Montreal, Que., Can., 1994, Mass. Coll. Art, Boston, 1994, Bennington (Vt.) Coll., 1994, 95, 96, Peters Valley, Layton, N.J., 1994, Firehouse Art Ctr., Norman, Okla., 1994, Haystack Mountain Sch. Arts & Crafts, Deer Isle, Maine, 1994, Ghost Ranch, Abiquiu, N.Mex., 1995, We. States Arts Fedn., Santa Fe, 1995, Colo. Coun. on the Arts, Boulder, 1995, Durango (Colo.) Art Ctr., 1995, Tamarind Inst., Albuquerque, 1995, 96, Kansas City (Mo.) Ar Inst., 1995, Hallmark Cards, Kansas City, 1996, Wichita (Kans.) Ctr. Arts, 1996, La. State U., Baton Rouge, 1996, Idaho State Arts Coun. Grants, Boise, 1996, Mattie Rhodes Counseling and Art Ctr., Kansas City, 1996, Southwest Ctr. Crafts, San Antonio, 1997, Very Spl. Arts, Albuquerque, 197, Topeka (Kans.) and Shawnee County Pub. Libr., 1997, U. Alaska, Anchorage, 2000, Craft Guild of Tex., Dallas, RISD, 2001, S.W. Ctr. for Crafts, San Antonio, 2002, numerous others; mem. fellowship panelist Colo. Coun. on the Arts, Denver, Penland Sch. of Crafts, N.C., 2001. Solo exhbns. include Pro Art Gallery, St. Louis, 1990, Mobilia Gallery, Cambridge, Mass., 1990, Munson Gallery, Santa Fe, 1990, 92, 94, 95, 97, 99, 2001, Mariposa Gallery, Albuquerque, 1990, Joanne Rapp Gallery, Scottsdale, Ariz., 1991, 93, 95, Felicita Found., Escondido, Calif., 1991, Tucumcari (N.Mex.) Area Vocat. Sch., 1992, Manchester Art Ctr., Pitts., 1993, Wetsman Collection, Detroit, 1993, Clovis (N.Mex.) C.C., 1993, Firehouse Art Ctr., 1994, Kavesh Gallery, Sun Valley, Idaho, 1995, Jan Weiner Gallery, Kansas City, 1995, 96, 2000, Jan Weiner Gallery, 2000, Gallerymateria, Scotsdale, Ariz., 2001, Munson Gallery, Santa Fe, 2001, Univ. Tulsa, Okla., 2001, Roswell (N.Mex.) Mus. and Art Ctr., 2002, Mus. Nebr. Art, Kearny, 2005, Allene Lapides Gallery, Santa Fe, 2005numerous others; group exhbns. include Fred Jones Mus. Art, U. Okla., Norman, 1995, Roswell (N.Mex.) Mus. & Art Ctr., 1995, Nancy Margolis Gallery, N.Y.C., 1995, Sharadin Art Gallery, Kutztown (Pa.) U., 1995, Richard Kavesh Gallery, 1995, Jan Weiner Gallery, 1995, Ariz. State U. Art Mus., Tempe, 1995, Islip (N.Y.) Mus., 1995, Bruce Kapson Gallery, Santa Monica, Calif., 1996, Site Sante Fe Gallery, 1996, Johnston County C.C., Overland Parks, Kans., 1996, Jane Haslem Gallery, Washington, 1996, Karen Ruhlen Gallery, Santa Fe, 1996, Margo Jacobson Gallery, Portland, Oreg., 1996, Very Spl. Arts Gallery, Albuquerque, 1997, Joanne Rapp Gallery, 1997, Munson Gallery, 1999, numerous others; pub. art project include, among others, murals at Great Brook Valley Health Ctr., Worcester, Mass., 1994, Mass. Gen. Hosp., 1996, (mural) Island Nursing Home, Deer Isle, 2000, (mural) Big Red, Lincoln, Nebr., 2000, Washington Park, Albuquerque, 2002; represented in many permanent collections, including Sheldon Meml. Art Mus, Lincloln, Nebr., Mus. Nebr. Art, Kearney, Nebr., Cooper-Hewitt, N.Y.C., Mus. Fine Arts, Santa Fe, Cleve. Inst. Art, Fed. Reserve Bank, Dallas, Roswell Mus. and Art Ctr., Albuquerque Mus. Fine Arts, City of Tucson (Ariz.), Phoenix Airport, Renwick Gallery Nat. Mus. Am. Art Smithsonian Inst., Washington, Detroit Inst. Art, Hallmark Cards Corp., Kansas City, State Capitol Art Collection, Santa Fe, pvt. collections. Recipient numerous grants, including NEA fellowships, 1986, 88, Kohler Arts-in-Industry grant, Sheboygan, Wis., 1988, 2000, Percent for Art Project grant, Phoenix Arts Coun., 1990, 1992, artist-in-residence grantee Roswell (N.Mex.) Mus. and Art Found., 1986, 2001; recipient Govs. award for excellnece in the arts in sculpture State N.Mex., 2006. Office Phone: 402-472-5919. Business E-Mail: edominguez2@unl.edu.

DOMINGUEZ, JORGE IGNACIO, political scientist, educator; b. Havana, Cuba, June 2, 1945; arrived in US, 1960; s. Jorge Jose and Lilia Rosa (de la Carrera) D.; m. Mary Alice Kmietek, Dec. 16, 1967; children: Lara Lisa, Leslie Karen. AB, Yale U., 1967; AM, Harvard U., 1968, PhD, 1972. From asst. prof. to prof. govt. Harvard U., Cambridge, Mass., 1972—93, Frank G. Thomson prof. govt., 1993—96, chmn. Latin Am. and Iberian studies, 1979—83, 1990—93, acting dir. ctr. for internat. affairs, 1995, Clarence Dillon prof. internat. affairs, 1996—, dir. Weatherhead Ctr. for Internat. Affairs, 1996—2006, Harvard Coll. prof., 1998—2003, vice provost for internat. affairs, 2006—. Antonio Madero prof. govt., 2006—; chmn. Harvard Acad. for Internat. and Area Studies, 2004—. Active Coun. on Fgn. Rels., Club de Madrid, Inter-Am. Dialogue, 1982—, sr. fellow, 1993-94, assoc. fellow, 1995—. Author: Cuba: Order and Revolution, 1978, Insurrection or Loyalty, 1980, To Make the World Safe for Revolution: Cuba's Foreign Policy, 1989, Democratic Politics in Latin America and the Caribbean, 1998, Cuba Hoy: Analizando Su Pasado, Imaginando Su Futuro, 2006; editor: Democracy in the Caribbean, 1993, Technopols: Freeing Politics and Markets in Latin America in the 1990s, 1997, Democratic Transitions in Central America, 1997, The Future of Inter-American Relations, 2000, Mexico, Central and South America: New Perceptions, 5 vols., 2001, Constructing Democratic Governance in Latin America, 2003, The Cuban Economy at the Start of the Twenty-First Century, 2004, Mexico's Pivotal Democratic Election: Candidates, Voters, and the Presidential Campaign of 2000, 2004, Between Compliance and Conflict: East Asia, Latin America, and the "New" Pax Americana, 2005; co-author: Democratizing Mexico: Public Opinion and Electoral Choices, 1996, The United States and Mexico: Between Partnership and Conflict, 2001; mem. editl. bd. Am. Polit. Sci. Rev., 1979—81, Foreign Affairs en español, Polit. Sci. Quar., 1984—, Cuban Studies, 1991—, Latin Am. Rsch. Rev., 2003—, series editor Crisis in Central America: A Four-Part Special Report, Frontline, PBS (Peabody award), 1985—, chief editl. adv. 3-part spl. report Mexico, 1988. Chmn. bd. trustees Latin Am. Scholarship Program of Am. Univs., Cambridge, Mass., 1981-82. Recipient Joseph Levenson Meml. Tchg. award, Harvard U., 1991; jr. fellow, 1969—72, Fulbright-Hays fellow, 1983, 1988. Mem. Latin Am. Studies Assn. (pres. 1982-83), New Eng. Coun. Latin Am. Studies (pres. 1980), Inst. Cuban Studies (pres. 1990-94). Office: Harvard U Ctr Weatherhead Internat Affairs 1737 Cambridge St Cambridge MA 02138

DOMINGUEZ, KATHRYN MARY, economist, educator; b. Santa Monica, Calif., Nov. 26, 1960; d. Frederick A. and Margaret M. (McGauren) D. AB, Vassar Coll., 1982; MA, Yale U., 1984, M in Philosophy, 1985, PhD, 1987. Rschr. Congl. Budget Office, Washington, 1984; rsch. scholar bd. of govs. FRS, Washington, 1985—86; asst. prof. pub. policy Kennedy Sch. Govt. Harvard U., Cambridge, Mass., 1987—91, assoc. prof. pub. policy, 1991—97; assoc. prof. pub. policy and econs. U. Mich., Ann Arbor, 1997—2004, prof., 2004—. Rsch. cons IMF, Washington, 1989; vis. asst. prof., asst. dir. internat. fin. sect. dept. econs. Princeton U., 1990-91; Nat. Bur. Econs. Rsch. Olin fellow, 1991-92. Author: (monograph) Oil and Money, 1989; Exchange Rate Efficiency and the Behavior of International Asset Markets, 1992; (with Jeff Frankel) Does Foreign Exchange Intervention Work?, 1993. Mem. Nat. Bur. Econ. Rsch. (rsch. assoc. 2000—), Am. Econ. Assn., Phi Beta Kappa. Democrat. Office: Univ Mich Sch Pub Policy Weill Hall 735 S State St Ann Arbor MI 48109-1220 Office Phone: 734-764-3490.

DOMINGUEZ, MICHAEL L., federal agency administrator, former civilian military employee; b. 1953; BS, U.S. Mil. Acad., West Point, NY, 1975; MBA, Stanford U., 1983; program for sr. ofcls. in nat. security, Harvard U., 1989. Commd. 2d lt. U.S. Army, 1975; program analyst for program analysis and evaluation US Dept. Def., Washington, 1983—88, exec. asst. to asst. sec. for program analysis & evaluation, 1988—91, dir. for planning and analytical support for program analysis and evaluation, 1991—94; assoc. dir. for programming Dept. of Navy, US Dept. Def., Washington, 1994—97, asst. dir. for space, info. warfare, and command and control, 2001; gen. mgr. Tech 2000 Inc., Herndon, Va., 1997—99; rsch. project dir. Ctr. for Naval Analyses, Alexandria, Va., 1999—2001; asst. sec. for manpower & reserve affairs Dept. of Air Force, US Dept. Def., Washington, 2001—06, acting sec., 2005; dep. under sec. for pers. & readiness US Dept. Def., Washington, 2006—. Decorated Army Commendation medal, Def. Meritorious Civilian Svc. medal, , Def. medal for Civilian Svc., Medal for Superior Civilian Svc. Dept. Navy, Presdl. Meritorious Exec. Rank award.

DOMINGUEZ, SYLVIA MARGARITA, electrical engineer, researcher; d. Salvador Dominguez and Maria Aguayo. BSEE magna cum laude, U. Tex., El Paso, 1985; MSEE (hon.), N.Mex State U., Las Cruces, 1989; degree in Elec. Engring. (hon.), U. Calif., LA, 2002, PhD (hon.) in Elec. Engring., 2006. Design engr. Hewlett-Packard, Guadalajara, Jalisco, Mexico, 1986—87; lectr., elec. engring. dept. U. Tex., El Paso, 1989—91; tchg. assoc., elec. engring. dept. U. Calif., LA, 1991—97, lectr. Ctr. for Excellence in Engring. and Diversity, 1994—2001; rsch. scientist HRL Laboratories LLC, Malibu, Calif., 2000—02; sr. patent engr. Tope-McKay & Assoc., Malibu, Calif., 2002—. Contbr. articles to profl. jours., scientific papers to profl. confs. Vol. Pet Adoption Fund, Canoga Park, Calif., 1995—2007. Recipient Outstandign Tchg. award, Elec. Engring. Dept. UCLA, 1993—94, Tchg. Excellence award, Ctr. for Excellence in Engring. and Diversity, 1998; grantee, Mexican Am. Engring. Soc., 1984, 1985. Mem.: Eta Kappa Nu, Tau Beta Pi, Phi Kappa Pi, Alpha Lambda Delta. Roman Catholic. Achievements include patents for vision-based pointer tracking and object classification method and apparatus; patents pending for pupil tracking and wearable computer system. Avocations: snowboarding, rock climbing, tennis, racquetball, travel. Office: Tope-McKay and Assocs 23852 Pacific Coast Hwy 311 Malibu CA 90265 Office Phone: 818-399-4560. Business E-Mail: sdominguez@topemckay.com.

DOMINGUEZ-BENDALA, JUAN, medical educator; b. Sevilla, Sevilla, Spain, Oct. 12, 1970; s. Juan Dominguez Galiano and Lina Bendala Rodriguez; m. Xiomara Mordcovich, May 1, 2003. BS in Biology, U. Seville, Spain, 1993; MS in Applied Molecular Biology and Biotech., U. Coll. London, 1997; PhD in Cell and Molecular Biology, U. Edinburgh, Scotland, 2000. Postdoctoral assoc. Diabetes Rsch. Inst., U. Miami Leonard M. Miller Sch. Medicine, Fla., 2001—04, lectr., 2004—06, rsch. asst. prof., 2006—. Dir. stem cell & translational rsch. lab. Diabetes Rsch. Inst., U. Miami Leonard M. Miller Sch. Medicine, 2004—. Contbr. articles to profl. jours. Spokesperson stem cell rsch., therapeutic cloning and diabetes Diabetes Rsch. Inst. Found., Miami, 2000; advisor Genetics Policy Inst., Miami. 2d lt. Spanish Air Force, 1994—95. Grantee, Found. Diabetes Rsch., 2004—07, Juvenile Diabetes Rsch. Found., 2006—07, Peacock Found., 2006—; scholar, Biotech. and Biol. Sciences Rsch. Coun., England, 1997—2000. Mem.: Cell Transplantation Soc., Internat. Soc. Stem Cell Rsch., Transplantation Soc. Achievements include research in protein transduction strategies for the differentiation of pancreatic beta cells; strategies for improved gene targeting frequency in mammalian cells; strategies for the efficient differentiation of human embryonic stem cells into insulin-producing cells; patents pending for enhanced oxygenation for the differentiation of pancreatic beta cells. Avocations: music, piano, basketball. Office: Diabetes Research Institute U of Miami 1450 NW 10th Ave Miami FL 33136 Office Phone: 305-2434092.

DOMINI, AMY LEE, portfolio manager; b. NYC, Jan. 25, 1950; d. Enzo Vice and Margaret Cabot (Colt) D.; m. Peter D. Kinder, Sept. 28, 1980 (div.); 1 child, Peter D. CFA. Stockbroker Tucker Anthony & RL Day, Cambridge, Mass., 1975-80, Moseley Securities, Cambridge, 1980-85; portfolio mgr. Franklin R & D Corp., Boston, 1985-87; pvt. trustee Loring, Wolcott & Coolidge, Boston, 1987—. Pres. Domini Social Equity Fund, N.Y.C., 1996—; chair of bd. Linder, Lydenberg, Domini & Co., Cambridge, 1991—; ptnr. Domini Social Investments LLC, Boston, 1997—. Co-author: (books) Ethical Investing, 1984, Challenges of Wealth, Social Investment Almanac, 1992, Investing for Good. Bd. dirs. Social Investment Forum, Washington, 1994—, ch. pension fund Episcopal Ch., N.Y.C., 1994—; governing bd. Interfaith Ctr. on Corp. Responsibility, N.Y.C., 1985-95; mem. social responsibility investments com. Episcopal Ch., N.Y.C., 1985-91. Recipient Accioniste award Accion Internat., 1992, Money's 100 Best Mut. Funds award Money Mag., 1998, SRI Svc. award 1st Affirmative Fin. Network, 1996; named one of World's 100 Most Influential People, Time Mag. 2005. Mem. Nat. Comty. Capital Assn. (assoc., bd. dirs. 1987-91), Boston Security Analysts Soc., Social Investment Forum, Somerset Club, Cambridge Boat Club. Democrat. Episcopalian. Avocations: day-sailing, gardening. Office: Loring Wolcott & Coolidge 230 Congress St Fl 12 Boston MA 02110-2437

DOMINIAK, GERALDINE FLORENCE, retired accounting educator; b. Detroit, Sept. 28, 1934; d. Benjamin Vincent and Geraldine Esther (Davey) D. BS, U. Detroit, 1954, MBA, 1956; PhD, Mich. State U., 1966. CPA Mich. Audit supr. Coopers & Lybrand, 1958-63; asst. prof. U. Detroit, 1965-68; assoc. prof. Mich. State U., 1968-69; prof. acctg. Tex. Christian U., Ft. Worth, 1969-97, chmn. dept. acctg., 1974-83, prof. emeritus, 1997; Arthur Young prof. acctg. Fla. A&M U., 1977. Author: (with J. Edwards and T. Hedges) Interim Financial Reporting, 1972; (with J. Louderback) Managerial Accounting, 1975, 9th edit., 2000. Ford Found. fellow, 1964-65. Mem. AICPA, Am. Acctg. Assn., Tex. Soc. CPAs, ACLU, Beta Alpha Psi, Beta Gamma Sigma. Roman Catholic. Home: 4401 Cardiff Ave Fort Worth TX 76133-3513 *To teach is to learn.*

DOMINICK, PAUL ALLEN, lawyer; b. Orangeburg, SC, Feb. 13, 1954; s. Allen Etheredge and Ruby Estelle (Pardue) D.; m. Sharon Norment, May 15, 1982. BA, U. S.C., 1976; JD, Washington & Lee U., 1979. Bar: S.C. 1979, U.S. Dist. Ct. S.C. 1980, U.S. Ct. Appeals (4th cir.) 1982. Assoc. Nexsen, Pruet, Jacobs & Pollard, Columbia, SC, 1979-85, ptnr., 1985—91, Nexsen Pruet, Charleston, SC, 1991—. Bd. dirs., Columbia Forum; bd. dirs., participant Leadership Columbia-Columbia C. of C., 1986. Mem. ABA (chair bus. torts com. tort and ins. practice sect. 1995-96), SC Bar Assn., Charleston County Bar Assn., Columbia Forum, Com. of 100, Columbia 100 (pres. 1983-84), Sertoma (pres. 1987-88), Phi Beta Kappa. Presbyterian. Home: 670 Hobcaw Bluff Dr Mount Pleasant SC 29464 Office: Nexsen Pruet PO Box 486 Charleston SC 29402-0486

DOMINICK, PETER HOYT, JR., architect; b. NYC, June 9, 1941; s. Peter Hoyt and Nancy Parks D.; m. Philae M. Carver, Dec. 9, 1978; children: Philae M., James W. BA, Yale U., 1963; MArch, U. Pa., 1967. Registered architect, Colo. Project designer John R. Wild, Pty., Ltd., Papau, New Guinea, 1968-69, Spence Robinson, Hong Kong, 1969-71, W.C. Muchow & Ptnrs., Denver, 1971-74; pres. Wazee Design/Devel., Denver,

1973-75; prin. Dominick Architects, Denver, 1975-88; sr. prin. Urban Design Group, Inc. (now 4240 Arch., Inc.), Denver, 1988—. Pres., chmn. bd. Urban Design Group, Inc., 2001—. Trustee Downtown Denver, Inc., Civic Ventures, 1984-94, Met. Denver Arts Alliance, 1983-84; active Mayor's Commn. on the Arts, 1983; juror Gov.'s awards, Denver, 1982; nat. com., exec. com. Whitney Mus. Am. Art.; bd. trustees Denver Art Mus., 2002. Fellow AIA (nat. com. on design, bd. dirs.); mem. Colo. Soc. Architects, Yale Arch. Coun., Cactus Club, Arapahoe Tennis Club. Republican. Episcopalian. Office: 4240 Arch Inc 4240 Architecture Inc 1621 18th St Ste 200 Denver CO 80202-1267 Office Phone: 303-292-3388. E-mail: pdominick@4240arch.com.

DOMINO, FATS (ANTOINE DOMINO), pianist, singer, songwriter; b. New Orleans, Feb. 26, 1928; Pianist since youth; performer: with groups in clubs, for dances, in theaters, composer (blues); recording artist (albums) Here Comes Fats Domino, 1963, Fats on Fire, 1965, Fats '65, Getaway With Fats Domino, Fats Domino, 1966, Stompin' Fats Domino, 1967, Trouble in Mind, Fats is Back, 1968, Live in Montreux, 1973, Sleeping on the Job, 1978, The Best of Fats, 1990, All Time Greatest Hits, Fats Domino, 1991, Best of Fats Domino Live, Antoine "Fats" Domino, 1992, The Fat Man, 1995, Live in Concert, Early Imperial singles 1950-52, 1996, Fabulous Mr. D./Swings, 1998, Here Stands/this is, vol. 3 Imperial Singles, 1998, Live at Gilleys, 1999, Collector's Edition, 2000, toured Britain, 1967, appeared (films) Shake, Rattle & Rock, Disc Jockey Jamboree, The Big Beat, The Girl Can't Help It, Any Which Way You Can, appeared on TV spl (TV films) Fats Domino & Friends, 1987. Named to Rock and Roll Hall of Fame, 1986; recipient Nat. Medal Arts, 1998, Grammy Lifetime Achievement award, 1987. Office: care Atlantic Records 1290 Ave of the Ams New York NY 10104-0101 also: SMS Records 14134 NE Airport Way Portland OR 97230-3443

DOMJAN, LASZLO KAROLY, journalist; b. Kormend, Hungary, Apr. 19, 1947; arrived in U.S., 1956; s. Frank and Violet Domjan; m. Louise Replogle, June 6, 1969; children: Andrew P., Eric S. BJ, U. Mo., 1969. Copy editor St. Louis Globe-Democrat, 1969; reporter, bureau chief UPI, St. Louis, 1969-81; reporter, night city editor St. Louis Post-Dispatch, 1981-87, exec. city editor, 1987-96, projects editor, 1996-97, asst. mng. editor, 1997-99, sr. editor, 1999—2005. Author, editor: Dioxin: Quandary for the 80s, 1983; author: (reporter series) Hungary: Thirty Years After, 1986; editor: (series) Prosecutorial Corruption (1993 Pulitzer prize finalist). Active Leadership, St. Louis. Recipient Herb Trask award Sigma Delta Chi, St. Louis, 1968. Mem. Press Club of Met. St. Louis, Investigative Reporters and Editors. Avocations: reading, freelance writing, music. Personal E-mail: ldomjan@hotmail.com. *Always do right. Always do your best. Always make time for romance.*

DOMKE, DAVID S., communications educator; PhD in Mass Comm., U. Minn., 1996. With Orange County Register, Atlanta Jour.-Constn.; asst. prof. to assoc. prof. communication U. Wash., 1998—. Contbr. articles to profl. publs.; author: God Willing? Political Fundamentalism in the White House, the "War on Terror," and the Echoing Press, 2004. Recipient Catherine Covert award for Yr.'s Outstanding Article in Journalism and Mass Communication Hist., 1998, Hillier Krieghbaum Under-40 award for Outstanding Achievement in Rsch., Tchg. and Pub. Svc., Assn. Edn. in Journalism & Mass Communication, 2006, US Prof. of Yr. award, Carnegie Found. for Advancement of Tchg. and Coun. for Advancement and Support of Edn., 2006. Office: Dept Communication U Wash Box 353740 Seattle WA 98195-3740 Office Phone: 206-685-1739. Office Fax: 206-616-3762. E-mail: domke@u.washington.edu.*

DOMMEN, MARK, chef; Grad., Calif. Culinary Acad.; BBA, U. San Francisco. Cook Fleur de Lys, San Francisco, Park Avenue Café, NYC, Lespinasse, NYC; sous chef Palladin, NYC; opening exec. chef Julia's Kitchen, Napa Valley; exec. chef One Market, San Francisco, 2004—; with Lark Creek Restaurant Grp., 2004—. Named one of San Francisco's Rising Stars, StarChefs.com, 2007. Avocations: skiing, golf, fishing, winemaking. Office: One Market 1 Market St San Francisco CA 94105 Office Phone: 415-777-5577.*

DOMMERMUTH, WILLIAM PETER, marketing consultant, educator; b. Chgo. s. Peter R. and Gertrude Dommermuth; m. H. Joan Hasty, June 6, 1959; children: Karin, Margaret, Jean. BA, U. Iowa; PhD, Northwestern U., 1964. Advt. copywriter Sears, Roebuck & Co., Chgo., sales promotion mgr.; asst., then asso. prof. mktg. U. Tex., Austin, 1961—67; assoc. prof. U. Iowa, Iowa City, 1967—68; prof. So. Ill. U., Carbondale, 1968—86, U. Mo., St. Louis, 1986—; CEO Optiphonics, Inc. Cons. in field. Author (with Kernan and Sommers): Promotion: An Introductory Analysis, 1970, (with Andersen) Distribution Systems, 1972, (with Marcus and others) Modern Marketing, 1975, Modern Marketing Management, 1980, Promotion: Analysis, Creativity and Strategy, 1984, 2d edit., 1989; contbr. articles to profl. jours. Mem. Am. Mktg. Assn., Phi Beta Kappa, Beta Gamma Sigma, Theta Xi, Delta Sigma Pi. Home: 11 Paris Ct Lake Saint Louis MO 63367-1506 Personal E-mail: willdo@mail.com. Business E-Mail: optomizer@consultant.com.

DOMOWITZ, IAN, finance company executive; b. NYC, Nov. 29, 1951; s. Jacob and Marilyn (Raffer) D.; m. Marguerite Morton, Sept. 25, 1984. BA, U. Conn., 1977; PhD, U. Calif., San Diego, 1982. Asst. prof., assoc. prof., prof. econs. Northwestern U., Evanston, Ill., 1982-98, mem. rsch. faculty Inst. for Policy Rsch., 1987-98; Mary Jean and Frank P. Smeal chaired prof. fin. Pa. State U., University Park, 1998—2002; mng. dir. analytical products and rsch., global head rsch. ITG, Inc., 2001—; CEO, ITG Solutions Network, Inc., 2006—. Rsch. dir. K2 Capital Mgmt., 1992-94; cons. IMF, 1992, World Bank, 1993-96, 98-99, to various internat. fin. markets with respect to automated exch. structures, 1991-97; cons. U.S. Commodity Futures Trading Commn., 1991, 95-96; mem. sci. adv. bd. ITG, Inc., 1997-, mem. sci. adv. bd. ITG Europe, 2003—; bd. mgrs. Inference Group LLC, 2002-04. Contbr. more than 80 articles to profl. jours., chpts. to books. Sgt. U.S. Army, 1972-75, Germany. NSF grantee, 1984, 85, 87, 90. Mem. Am. Fin. Assn., Fin. Mgmt. Assn., Nat. Assn. Securities Dealers (econ. adv. bd. 1998-2000, chair 1998-2000, bond market transparency com. 1998-99). Home: 684 Broadway # 4E New York NY 10012 Office Phone: 212-588-4000. Business E-Mail: ian.domowitz@itg.com.

DOMZELLA, JANET, retired library director; b. Marquette, Mich., Mar. 22, 1935; d. Jack Carl and Alice Margaret (Blom) Messenger; m. Theodore S. Wodzinski (div. 1974); children: Christopher, Joseph, Daniel; m. Perry Landon Domzella, July 15, 1977; stepchildren: Perry, Pamela. BS, No. Mich. U., 1973; MLS, U. Buffalo, 1979. Sch. libr. media specialist Niagara Falls Bd. Edn., NJ, 1974-75, Iroquois Ctrl. Sch., Elma, NY, 1975-77; dir. Lewiston Pub. Libr., NY, 1977-2000, libr. emeritus, 2001—; mgr. LaSalle br. Niagara Falls Pub. Libr., NY, 2002—07; ret., 2007. Co-author: Lewiston: Self Guided Tour, 1986. Vol. firefighter Upper Mountain Vol. Fire Co., Lewiston, 1980—90, treas., 1984—90; mem. Town of Lewiston Bur. Fire Prevention, 1988—90; mem. adv. bd. Documentary Heritage Program, 1991—93; mem. pub. libr. program Coll. of Charleston (S.C.) Conf., 1998, 2000, 2001. Democrat. Roman Catholic. Avocation: painting.

DON, MANUEL, medical researcher; s. Chun and Shee Chin Don; m. Margery Mai Yeung, Aug. 20, 1967; children: Kendra Marie D'Ercole, Erica Lynn Chien, Angela Noelle. BA, U. Calif., Berkeley, 1964; MA, U. Ariz., Tucson, 1966; PhD, Stanford U., Calif., 1971. Asst. rschr. U. Calif., Irvine, 1973—76; dept. head, rschr. House Ear Inst., LA, 1976—. Study sect. mem., chair NIH, Bethesda, Md., 1988—91. Contbr. articles to profl. jours. Ch. officer Cornerstone United Meth. Ch., Placentia, Calif., 1980—2002. Grant, NIH, 1990—94, 2000—04. Mem.: Internat. Evoked Response Audiometry Study Group (treas. 1991—). Achievements include patents for sininger YS, hyde ML: method for detection of auditory evoked potentials using point optimized variance ratio; acoustic tumor detection using stacked derived-band ABR amplitude; method for aligning derived-band responses based on integration of detrended derived-band ABRs; patents pending for diagnosis of the presence of cochlear hydrops using observed auditory brainstem responses. Avocations: crossword puzzles, bowling, tennis, guitar. Office: House Ear Inst 2100 W Third St Los Angeles CA 90057 Office Phone: 213-353-7095. Office Fax: 213-413-6739. Business E-Mail: mdon@hei.org.

DONABEDIAN, AVEDIS, physician, educator; b. Beirut, Jan. 7, 1919; arrived in U.S., 1955, naturalized, 1960; s. Samuel and Maritza (Der Hagopian) Donabedian; m. Dorothy Salibian, Sept. 15, 1945; children: Haig, Bairj, Armen. BA, Am. U., Beirut, 1940, MD, 1944; MPH, Harvard U., 1955. Physician, acting supt. English Mission Hosp., Jerusalem, 1945—47; instr. physiology, clin. asst. dermatology and venereology Am. U. Med. Sch., 1948—51, univ. physician, dir. univ. health service, 1949—54; med. assoc. United Community Services Met. Boston, 1955—57; asst. prof., then assoc. prof. preventive medicine N.Y. Med. Coll., 1957—61; mem. faculty U. Mich. Sch. Pub. Health, Ann Arbor, 1961—, prof. med. care orgn., 1964—79, Nathan Sinai disting. prof. public health, 1979—89, emeritus. Author: A Guide to Medical Care Administration: Medical Care Appraisal--Quality and Utilization, 1969, Aspects of Medical Care Administration, 1973, Benefits in Medical Care Programs, 1976, The Definition of Quality and Approaches to Its Assessment, 1980, Medical Care Chartbook, 1986, The Criteria and Standards of Quality, 1982, Methods and Findings of Quality Assessment and Monitoring, 1985; co-author: Striving for Quality in Health Care: An Inquiry into Policy and Practice, 1991. Recipient Dean Conley award, Am. Coll. Hosp. Adminstrs., 1969, Norman A. Welch award, Nat. Assn. Blue Shield Plans, 1976, Elizur Wright award, Am. Risk and Ins. Assn., 1978, Nat. Merit award, Delta Omega, 1978, Richard B. Tobias award, Am. Coll. Utilization Rev. Physicians, 1984, Outstanding Contbns. in Health Svcs. Rsch. award, Assn. Health Svcs. Rsch., 1985, Baxter Am. Found. Health Svcs. Rsch. prize, 1986, Gold medal award, Med. Alumni Assn., Am. U. Beirut, 1986, The Ernest A. Codman award, Joint Commn. on Accreditation of Healthcare Orgns., 1997. Fellow: APHA (Sedgewick Meml. medal 1999), Am. Coll. Med. Quality, Am. Coll. Healthcare Execs. (hon.), Am. Coll. Utilization Rev. Physicians (hon.), Royal Coll. Gen. Practitioners (hon.); mem.: Inst. Medicine NAS, Internat. Soc. Quality Assurance in Health Care (hon.), Nat. Acad. Medicine of Mex. (hon.), Avedis Donabedian Found. (Barcelona, hon. pres. 1990—, Buenos Aires, hon. pres. 1994—). Office: HMP-SPH II 109 Observatory St Ann Arbor MI 48109-2029

DONADIO, DONALD A., lawyer; b. Hampton, Va., Jan. 3, 1943; BA cum laude, Wake Forest U., NC, 1965; JD cum laude, Wake Forest U. Law Sch., 1967. Bar: NC 1972, US Eastern and Middle District Courts, NC. Mem. mgmt. com. Womble Carlyle Sandridge & Rice, PLLC, NC, mem. recruiting com. NC, mng. mem. Raleigh, NC. Counsel NC Partnership for Econ. Development; lectr. in field. Assoc. editor Wake Forest Law Review, 1966—67; contbr. articles to profl. jours. Bd. dir. Greater Raleigh CofC. Capt., Judge Advocate General's Corp (JAGC) US Army, 1967—72. Mem.: Wake Country Econ. Development Bd., NC Econ. Developers Assn., Am. Coll. of Real Estate Lawyers, Nat. Ass. of Bond Lawyers, ABA (mem. bus. sect.), NC Bar Assn. (mem. bus. sect.), Wake County Bar Assn., Phi Delta Phi. Office: Womble Carlyle Sandridge & Rice PLLC 150 Fayetteville St Mall Ste 2100 Raleigh NC 27601 Mailing: Womble Carlyle Sandridge & Rice PLLC PO Box 831 Raleigh NC 27602 Office Phone: 919-755-2102. Office Fax: 919-755-6049. Business E-Mail: ddonadio@wcsr.com.

DONAGHY, HENRY JAMES, literature educator, academic administrator; b. NYC, Apr. 11, 1930; s. Joseph Peter and Catherine (McQuaid) D.; m. Joyce Aasen, Dec. 7, 1968 (div. Oct. 1986); children: Nora, Martin. BA in Philosophy and Classics magna cum laude, Stonehill Coll., 1954; theology student, Holy Cross Coll., 1954-58; MA in English, Fordham U., 1960; PhD in English, NYU, 1966. Priest Roman Catholic Ch., NYC, Bridgeport, Conn., 1958-1966; asst. prof. Ga. State U., Atlanta, 1966-69; assoc. prof. SUNY-Oswego, 1969-71, dir. grad. studies English, 1970-71; assoc. prof. Calif. State U., Fresno, 1971-73, supr. student tchrs., 1972-73; assoc. prof. to prof. English, chmn. dept. Idaho State U., Pocatello, 1973-83, assoc. dean Coll. Liberal Arts, 1982-83, dir. Dr. Arts teaching internship, 1973-75, dir. grad. studies English, 1975-76, vice chmn. Univ. Grad. Council, 1977-79, chmn. Dept. English and Philosophy, 1977-82; prof., head English Dept. Kans. State U., Manhattan, 1983-88, Miss. State U., Miss. State, 1988—97; ret., 1997. Dir. NEH grant offering interdisciplinary courses in sci. and humanities, Idaho, 1980-81; sr. Fulbright lect. U. Damascus, Syria, 1979-80; vis. prof. Meisei U., Tokyo, 1995-96. Author: James Clarence Mangan, 1974, Graham Greene: An Introduction to His Works, 1982; editor: Opposing Visions: Byron's and Southey's Vision of Judgement, 1976, Conversations with Graham Greene, 1992, Vessels of Clay: The Seductive Life of the Priesthood (a memoir), 2003; contbr. articles and revs. to profl. jours. and publs. Recipient Founders Day award NYU, 1966, Grand prize for fiction Memphis Mag., 1996. Mem.: MLA, Miss. Philological Assn. (pres. 1989—91). Democrat. Avocations: jazz, baseball, reading, writing, football. Mailing: 7612 Hudson Ln Las Vegas NV 89128 Personal E-mail: hdonaghy@cox.net.

DONAGHY, JAMES K., construction executive, contractor; m. Colleen Donaghy; 1 child, James Kieran. Chmn. Structure Tone, NYC. Bd. dirs. Exenet Technologies. Bd. dirs. Boy Scouts of Am., St. Thomas Aquinas Coll., Covenant House, Nat. Multiple Sclerosis Soc. Office: Structure Tone Inc 770 Broadway Fl 9 New York NY 10005-9511 Office Fax: (212) 685-9267.

DONAHE, PEGGY YVONNE, gifted and talented educator, librarian; b. Bismarck, ND, May 5, 1940; d. Fred Rattei and Austie Maire Porter; m. Robert Charles Donahe, June 17, 1967; 1 child, Noel Charles. BA in Elem. Edn., U. ND, 1964; MA, Northern U., 1970; bilingual endorsement degree, libr. media degree, Utah State, 1998. Reading and gifted edn. endorsement degrees ND, Utah. Fifth grade tchr. Ashley Sch. Dist., ND, 1964—67; fourth grade tchr. Hesla Sch. Dist., SD, 1967—89; 4th-8th lang. arts tchr. Abercrombee Sch., ND, 1989—94; title I and English tchr. Standing Rocks B/A, Fort Yates, ND, 1989—94; libr., gifted tchr. Aneth Cmty. Sch., Aneth, Utah, 1994—2006; academic dept. head B/A Sch., Skiprock Agy., 2003—05. Pres. ND Reading Assn., Wahpeton, 1977—89; pres. bd. Tao Dine Libr. Assn., Shiprock, N.Mex., 1995—2006; chief fin. leader Aneth Comm. Sch., Utah, 2000—05. Paintings and chalk, displayed at the ND Capital, 1964. Reporter ABC Election, 1981—89; scout master Cub Scouts Am., Girl Scouts Am. Recipient Educator award, NASA's Educator Program, 2000—06. Mem.: Tao Dine Libr. Assn., Delta Kappa Gamma. Avocations: reading, watercolor painting, knitting, computer design. Home: 1608 N 10 1/2 St Wahpeton ND 88075

DONAHOO, WILLIAM TROY, medical educator; s. Darrell Donahoo and Rose Dafoe; m. Julie Johnson, July 31, 1994; 1 child, Carissa Nicolle. MD, U. Colo., 1991. Diplomate Am. Bd. Internal Medicine, 1995. Asst. prof. UCHSC, Denver, 1999—2004, U. Vt., Burlington, Vt., 2004—. Dir. weight mgmt. clinic UCHSC, 1999—2002. Office: University of Vermont Given C331 89 Beaumont Ave Burlington VT 05405 Office Phone: 802-656-2530.

DONAHUE, ANN M., television producer; Student, Ohio State U. Legal asst., Century City, Calif.; writer China Beach, Picket Fences, Murder One; prodr. 21 Jump St., Street Justice; writer CSI NBC, LA, 2000—. Author: (plays) Home Fires, (films) Those Beaumont Girls, Three Girls in the Air Force, Three Girls Pose for Playboy.

DONAHUE, CHARLES, JR., law educator; b. NYC, Oct. 4, 1941; s. Charles James and Rosemary (Spang) Donahue; m. Sheila Finn, Aug. 22, 1964; 1 child, Sarah. AB in Classics & English, Harvard Coll., 1962; LLB, Yale U., 1965. Bar: NY 1966, Mich. 1969, US Supreme Ct. 1971. Atty.-adv. Office Gen. Counsel of Air Force, Washington, 1965-67; asst. gen. counsel Pres.'s Commn. on Postal Orgn., Washington, 1967-68; asst. prof. law U. Mich., 1968-70, assoc. prof., 1970-73, prof., 1973-79; prof. law Harvard Law Sch., Cambridge, Mass., 1980—, Paul A. Freund prof. law, 1995—. Acad. vis. law dept. London Sch. Economics and Polit. Sci., 1972-73; vis. prof. law Vrije Universiteit Brussel, 1975, Columbia U., 1976, U. Calif. Boalt Hall, 1976, Harvard U., 1978-79, Boston Coll., 1987; articles editor Yale Law Jour., 1963-65; bd. editors Am. Jour. Legal History, 1977-82. Editor: The Records of the Medieval Ecclesiastical Courts Part I: The Continent, 1989, The Records of the Medieval Ecclesiastical Courts Part II: England, 1994, Samuel Edmund Thorne: 1907-1994, 1995; co-editor: Lex Mercatoria and Legal Pluralism: A Late Thirteenth-Century Treatise and Its Afterlife, 1998; author (commentary): Year Books of Richard II: 6 Richard II, 1382-83, 1996; co-author: A Course in Basic Property, 1975, 1993, Cases and Materials on Property: An Introduction to the Concept and the Institution, 1974, 1993; mem. editl. bd.: Law and History Rev., 2001—. Served with USAF, 1965-68. Mem. Am. Law Inst., Am. Soc. Legal History (dir. 1977-79, v.p. 1981-85, 2002-05, pres. 2005—), Selden Soc. (v.p. 1985-87, Am. treas. 1987—, councillor 1987—), Société d'histoire du droit, Société pour l'histoire des droits de l'antiquité, Medieval Acad. Am. Roman Catholic. Office: Harvard Law Sch 1563 Massachusetts Ave Cambridge MA 02138 Office Phone: 617-495-2944. Office Fax: 617-496-4913.

DONAHUE, J. KEVIN, electrophysiologist, researcher; b. Kans. City, Mo. s. John and Martha Donahue; m. Jennifer Donahue. MD, Wash. U., St. Louis, 1987—92. Lic. cardiology Am. Bd. Internal Medicine, 1999, clinical cardiac electrophysiology Am. Bd. Internal Medicine, 2001. Assoc. prof. medicine Johns Hopkins U., Balt., 2004—05, Case We. Res. U., Cleve., 2005—. Named one of Top 10 Rsch. Advances of 2000, Am. Heart Assn., 2000. Fellow: Am. Heart Assn.; mem.: Am. Soc. Gene Therapy, Heart Rhythm Soc. Achievements include patents for gene therapy for cardiac arrhythmias.

DONAHUE, JOHN DAVID, federal agency administrator, educator; b. Alexandria, Ind., June 17, 1956; s. Thomas Edward and Judith Ann (Wheatley) D.; m. Margaret Ann (Pax), Aug. 23, 1986; children: Kathleen, Benedict. BA, Ind. U., 1979; M in Pub. Policy, Harvard U., 1982, PhD, 1987. Asst. prof. to assoc. prof. Harvard U., Cambridge, Mass., 1987—93; asst. sec. U.S. Dept. Labor, Washington, 1993—94, counselor to sec., 1994—95; assoc. prof. pub. policy Harvard U., Cambridge, Mass., 1995—99, Raymond Vernon lectr. in pub. policy, 1999—; dir. Weil Program on Collaborative Governance, 2003—, faculty chmn. healthcare delivery program, 2007—. Econ. cons., Cambridge, Mass., 1985-2002; adv. com. on shareholder responsibiity, Harvard U., 1998—. Editor: Cost Benefit Analysis and Project Design, 1980; co-author: New Deals: The Chrysler Revival, 1985; author: The Privatization Decision, 1989, Disunited States, 1997, Hazardous Crosscurrents, 1998; editor: Making Washington Work: Tales of Innovation in the Fed. Govt., 1999; co-editor: Governance in a Globalizing World, 2000, Governance Amid Bigger, Better Markets, 2001, Market Based Govt. Supply Side, Demand Side, Upside, and Downside, 2002, For the People, 2003; book rev. editor Jour. Policy Analysis and Mgmt., 2002—06. Advisor Clinton presdl. transition, Washington, 1993. Doctoral fellow NSF, 1980, fellow Dively Found., 1984. Office: Harvard Univ 79 JFK St Cambridge MA 02138-5801

DONAHUE, JOHN EDWARD, lawyer; b. Milw., Aug. 22, 1950; s. Joseph Robert and Helen Ann (Kelly) D.; m. Maureen Dolores Hart-Donahue, Sept. 20, 1974; children: Timothy Robert, Michael John. BA with honors, Marquette U., 1972; JD, U. Wis., Madison, 1975. Bar: Wis. 1975, US Dist. Ct. (we. and ea. dists.) Wis. 1975. Assoc. Weiss, Steuer, Berzowski and Kriger, Milw., 1975-80; ptnr. Weiss, Berzowski, Brady & Donahue LLP, Milw., 1981-2001; shareholder Godfrey & Kahn, S.C., Milw., 2001—. Guest lectr. Marquette U. Law Sch., Milw., 1976-90; presenter programs Wis. Inst. CPAs, 1984—, Minn. Soc. CPAs, 1992-97; expert witness. Past chmn. bd. trustees, past chmn. bd. dirs., past chmn. bd. govs., trustee, exec. com., com. chmn. Mt. Mary Coll., Milw., 1984-2001, past pres., bd. dirs. com. chmn. Met. Milw. Civic Alliance, 1980—, Children's Hosp. Found., Milw., 1984—; mem. steering com. Greater Milw. Initiative, 1989-92; v.p., bd. dirs. Future Milw., 1984-88; v.p., bd. dirs., com. chmn., scoutmaster Boy Scouts Am., 1990—. Recipient citation Milwaukee County Bd. Suprs., 1990, spl. svc. award Met. Milw. Civil Alliance, 1990, silver beaver award Boy Scouts Am., 1995; named outstanding instr. AICPA, 1991. Mem. ABA, Wis. Bar Assn., Milw. Bar Assn. (chmn. employee benefits sect.), Wis. Retirement Plan Profls., ESOP Assn., Greater Milw. Employee Benefits Coun., Kiwanis Club (pres. Milw. unit 1989-90, Outstanding Kiwanian 1989-97, Kiwanian of Yr. 1993). Office: Godfrey & Kahn SC 780 N Water St Milwaukee WI 53202-3590 Home Phone: 414-964-8330; Office Phone: 414-273-3500. Business E-Mail: jdonahue@gklaw.com.

DONAHUE, JOHN EDWARD, physician; b. Revere, Mass., Apr. 27, 1966; s. Edward Francis and Camille (Santoro) D BS summa cum laude, Tufts U., Medford, 1988, MD, 1992. Diplomate Am. Bd. Psychiatry and Neurology, Am. Bd. Pathology, Nat. Bd. Med. Examiners. Intern St. Elizabeth's Med. Ctr., Boston, 1992—93; resident New Eng. Med. Ctr., Boston, 1993—96; fellow R.I. Hosp., Providence, 1996—99; dir. neuropathology NJ Neurosci. Inst., Edison, 1999—2003, asst program dir. neurology residency program, 2001—03; asst. prof. neuroscience Sch. Grad. Med. Edn. Seton Hall U., South Orange, NJ, 1999—2003; attending neuropathologist RI Hosp., 2003—, dir. neuropathology rotation, 2007—. Asst. prof. pathology Brown U. Sch. Medicine (now Warren Alpert Med. Sch. Brown U.), 2003—; dir. neuropathology rotation RI Hosp., 2007—. Mem. editl. bd. Jour. Neuropathology and Exptl. Neurology, 2007—; contbr. articles to profl. jours Recipient David L. Kasdon prize Tufts U. Sch. Medicine, 1992, Second Pl. award Gustaf Retzius Neuroanatomy Competition, 1997, 98, champion 1999, Dean's Tchg. Excellence award Brown Med. Sch., 2004, 05, 06, 07, Alzheimer's Disease Clin. Scientist Devel. award NIH, 2006—. Mem.: AAAS, NY Acad. Scis., Neuroplex Inc., Soc. Neurosci., Am. Assn. Neuropathologists, Am. Acad. Neurology, Mass. Med. Soc., Phi Beta Kappa. Roman Catholic. Achievements include research in breakthroughs in Alzheimer's disease rsch. Avocations: swimming, computers. Office: RI Hosp Dept Pathology 593 Eddy St APC12115 Providence RI 02903 Home Phone: 508-226-5990; Office Phone: 401-444-5057. Business E-Mail: JDonahue3@Lifespan.org.

DONAHUE, JOHN FRANCIS, investment company executive; b. Pitts., 1924; Grad., U.S. Mil. Acad., 1946. Chmn. Federated Investors, Inc., Pitts. Office: Federated Investors Federated Investors Tower 1001 Liberty Ave Pittsburgh PA 15222-3779

DONAHUE, JOHN JOSEPH, parks director; b. Bklyn., Nov. 20, 1952; s. John and Anna Donahue; m. Sarah Grassi, July 2, 1977; 1 child, John Vincent. Degree in natural resource mgmt., Calif. State U., Sonoma, 1986. Instr. Bklyn. Bot. Garden, 1977-78; supr. N.Y.C. Parks Dept., 1978-79; gardener Cape Cod Nat. Seashore, 1980-83, John Muir Nat. Hist. Site,

1983-86; specialist nat. resource mgmt. Morristown (N.J.) Nat. Hist. Park, 1986-89; specialist environ. protection Nat. Park Svc., Washington, 1989-94; supt. Thomas Stone Nat. Hist. Site, Charles County, Md., 1994—, George Washington Birthplace Nat. Monument, Washington's Birthplace, Va., 1994—. Adv. bd. mem. Olmsted Ctr. Landscape Preservation, Valley Forge Archeol. Ctr.; bd. dirs., treas. George Wright Soc.; chief visitor protection and resource mgmt. Cape Cod Nat. Seashore, 1993. Spkr. in field; contbr. articles to profl. jours. Fax: 804-224-2142.

DONAHUE, LISA J., corporate financial executive, consultant; BA, Fla. State Univ. Sr. v.p. Boston Fin. & Equity Corp.; fin. cons. The Recovery Group, Boston; mng. dir., head turnaround & restructuring practice Alix Partners, NYC, 1998—; CFO Exide Technologies, 2001—03, chief restructuring officer, 2001—04; CEO World Pasta Corp., 2004—05; sr. v.p., CFO Calpine Corp., San Jose, Calif., 2006—. Mem. NY adv. bd. Am. Bankruptcy Inst. Bd. mem. InMotion Inc. Mem.: Assn. for Corporate Growth, Internat. Women's Insolvency & Restructuring Confederation, Turnaround Mgmt. Assn. (past bd. mem.). Office: Alix Partners Ste 3240 9 W 57th St New York NY 10019 also: Calpine Corp 50 W San Fernando St San Jose CA 95113*

DONAHUE, MARTHA, retired librarian; b. Danville, Ky., Jan. 5, 1936; d. Thomas E. and Mary Louise (Craig) D. BA, Centre Coll., 1958; MA, Ind. U., 1961; 6th Yr. Specialist's Cert., U. Wis., 1971. Tchr. Pompano Beach (Fla.) Jr. H.S., 1958-60; post libr. U.S. Army, Europe, Bad Tölz, Germany, 1961-65; instr. library Centre Coll., Danville, Ky., 1966-67, U. Wis., Whitewater, 1967-70; assoc. prof. library Mansfield (Pa.) U., 1971-93. Bd. dirs. Mansfield Free Pub. Libr., 1995-97, vol., 1998—; vol. Area Agy. on Aging, Towanda, Pa., 1993—, Sr. Citizen Meals Delivery, 1993—; mem. Parish Coun., Mansfield, 1994-97; bd. dirs. Ctr. Coll. Alumni Bd., 1996-98. Recipient Higher Edn. Act fellowship U. Wis., 1970. Mem. ALA, Pa. Libr. Assn. (chair various coms. 1971—93), Friday Club of Wellsboro, Mansfield Garden Club, Columbia Lit. Exchange, The Book Group, Tioga County Hist. Soc., 1901 Soc. (pres. 2001-02). Roman Catholic. Avocations: reading, gardening, travel, cross country skiing, bicycling. Home: 146 S Main St Mansfield PA 16933-1522

DONAHUE, MARY LEE, literature and language professor, editor; children: Michael G., Elizabeth C. children: Catherine A., John J. BA in English, U. Tenn., Knoxville, 1965; MA in English, U. Conn., Storrs, 1972; post-grad., Rutgers U., New Brunswick, NJ, 1997—2004. Instr. comm. Rowan U., Glassboro, NJ, 1983—; asst. editor South Jersey News Co., Woodbury, NJ, 2003—. Cons. advanced placement English Ednl. Testing Svc., Princeton, NJ, 1998—. Recipient 2d pl. Breaking News, NJ Press Assn., 2004, 1st pl. commentary, 2006, 1st Pl. award, 2007. Fellow: Am. Fedn. Tchrs. (negotiator 2005—07); mem.: Nat. Coun. Tchrs. English, MLA Am., Greater Glassboro Group, Inc. (founding pres. 1987—2000, dir., founder). Achievements include design of general academic skills proficiency examination. Office: Rowan U 201 Mullica Hill Rd Glassboro NJ 08028 Office Phone: 856-256-4500.

DONAHUE, MAURA W., construction executive; b. La. m. Jack Donahue; 6 children. BA, U. So. La. Pres. DonahueFavret Contractors Holding Co.; v.p. bus. devel. DonahueFavret Contractors, Inc. Bd. dirs. US C. of C., 1997—. past chair coun. small bus., chmn. bd. dirs., 2005—06; mem. bd. Greater New Orleans, Inc., Resource Bank, St. Tammany Parish Econ. Devel. Found. Office: DonahueFavret Contractors Inc 3030 E Causeway Approach Mandeville LA 70448

DONAHUE, THOMAS REILLY, trade union official; b. NYC, Sept. 4, 1928; s. Thomas Reilly and Mary E. (Purcell) D.; children: Nancy Angela, Thomas Reilly III. BA, Manhattan Coll., 1949; JD, Fordham U., 1956; LLD (hon.), U. Notre Dame, 1980, Loyola U., Chgo., 1984, SUNY, 1988, Manhattan Coll., 1988, U. Mass., 1990, Nat. Labor Coll., 2001. Dir. edn., bus. agt. local 32B Bldg. Svc. Employees Internat. Union, AFL-CIO, 1949-52, dir. contract dept., 1952-57; European labor program coord. Free Europe Com., Paris, 1957-60; asst. to pres. Bldg. Svc. Employees Internat. Union, AFL-CIO, 1960-67; asst. sect. for labor-mgmt. rels. U.S. Dept. Labor, 1967-69; exec. sec. Svc. Employees Internat. Union, 1969-71, v.p., 1971-73; exec. asst. to pres. AFL-CIO, 1973-79, sec.-treas., 1979-95, pres., 1995. Chmn. adv. com. to Sec. of State and Pres. on Labor Diplomacy, 1999-05; co-chmn. Found. Prevention and Early Resolution of Conflict, 1996-97; mem. bd. dirs. Nat. Endowment Democracy, 1996-2006, vice chmn., 1999-2006; chmn. bd. dirs. Am. Heavy Lift Shipping Co., 2001—. Former mem., bd. dirs. U.S. Cath. Conf. Com. on Social Devel., Coun. on Fgn. Rels., Carnegie Corp., Nat. Urban League, Brookings Instn., Muscular Dystrophy Assn., African Am. Inst., Work in Am. Inst., Nat. Planning Assn., Inst. Multi-Track Diplomacy. With USNR, 1945-46. Sr. fellow Work in Am. Inst., 1997—. Democrat. Office: AFL-CIO 1717 K St NW Ste 707 Washington DC 20036-5331 Home: 2425 L St NW Washington DC 20036

DONAHUE-MATHOV, SARA HEATHER, radiologist, educator; b. Mpls., Sept. 4, 1976; d. Thomas Christopher and Louise Mary Donahue; m. Israel Mathov, Aug. 28, 2006. BS, Mont. State U., Bozeman, 1999; D of Chiropractic, N.W. Health Scis. U., Mpls., 2003. Resident diagnostic imaging So. Calif. U. Health Scis., Whittier, 2004—06, asst. prof., 2007—. Mem.: Coun. Diagnostic Imaging (Rsch. grant 2004—06), Am. Chiropractic Assn. Personal E-mail: sarad-76@hotmail.com.

DONALD, AIDA DIPACE, retired publishing executive; d. Victor E. and Bessie DiPace; m. David Herbert Donald; 1 child, Bruce Randall. AB cum laude, Barnard Coll.; MA, Columbia U.; PhD, U. Rochester. Instr. history dept. Columbia U., NYC; cons. and series editor Hill and Wang Pubs., NYC, 1959—69; editor Mass. Hist. Soc., Boston, 1960-64, Johns Hopkins U. Press, Balt., 1972-73; social sci. editor Harvard U. Press, Cambridge, Mass., 1973-79, exec. editor, 1979-89, editor in chief, 1989—2000, asst. dir., 1990—2000; ret., 2000. Editor: John F. Kennedy and the New Frontier, 1966, (with David Herbert Donald) Charles Frances Adams Diary, 2 vols., 1965, Lion in the White House: A Biography of Theodore Roosevelt, 2007. Pres. Wellfleet Non-Resident Taxpayers Assn., 2005—. Columbia U. Dibblee fellow, 1952-53, U. Rochester fellow, 1953-55, 56-57, Oxford U. Fulbright fellow, 1959-60 Fellow AAUW; mem. Am. Hist. Assn., Orgn. Am. Historians. Avocations: tennis, first editions, antique silver, coins, miniature books.

DONALD, ALEXANDER GRANT, psychiatrist, educator; b. Darlington, SC, Jan. 24, 1928; s. Raymond George and Chesnut Evans (McIntosh) Donald; m. Emma Louise Coggeshall, Oct. 25, 1958; children: Sandy, Mary Chesnut, Marion Lide. BS, Davidson Coll., 1948; MD, Med. U. S.C., 1952. Diplomate Am. Bd. Psychiatry and Neurology. Intern Jefferson Med. Coll., 1952-53; resident in psychiatry Walter Reed Hosp., 1956-59; dir. Mental Health Clinic, Florence, SC, 1962-66; dept. commr. S.C. Dept. Mental Health, 1966-67; dir. William S Hall Psychiat. Inst., Columbia, 1967-90; prof., chmn. dept. neuropsychiatry and behavioral scis. Sch. Medicine, U. S.C., Columbia, 1975-90, Disting. prof. neuropsychiatry, assoc. dean ednl. planning, 1990-91, Disting. prof. emeritus, 1991—. Bd. dirs. Health Resource Found.; trustee Richland Meml. Hosp., 1993—2002, vice-chmn., 1997, chmn., 1999; bd. dirs. S.C. Inst. Med. Edn. and Rsch., pres., 1992—96; trustee Palmetto Health Alliance, 1999—2004, vice-chmn., 2003; steward United Way of the Midlands, 2003—. Fellow: Am. Psychiat. Assn. (pres. S.C. chpt. 1967), Am. Coll. Psychiatrists; mem.: AMA, So. Psychiat. Assn. (v.p.), Columbia Med. Soc. (v.p. 1981, del. 1981, pres. 1989—90), Evening Music Club, Alpha Omega Alpha. Presbyterian. Office: U SC Sch Medicine 3555 Harden St Ext Ste 104 Columbia SC 29203-6894 Personal E-mail: grantd@bellsouth.net. *Accepting responsibility for ones' actions - using one's mind to understand one's self is the highest function of mankind.*

DONALD, ARNOLD W., health science association administrator, former food products executive; b. New Orleans; m. Hazel Donald; children: Radiah, Alicia, Zachary. BA, Carleton Coll.; BSME, Washington U., St. Louis; MBA, U. of Chgo. Grad. Sch. Bus. From indsl. chem. sales to positions of increasing responsibility Monsanto Co., St. Louis, 1977—98, sr. v.p., 1998-99; CEO Merisant Co., 2000—03, chmn., 2000—05; pres., CEO Juvenile Diabetes Rsch. Found. Internat., NYC, 2005—. Apptd. President's Export Coun. internat. trade; bd. dirs. Crown Cork & Seal Co., Oil-Dri Corp. Am., Belden Inc., Carnival Corp., Laclede Group, Scotts Co., St. Louis Sports Commn. Bd. dirs. United Way of Greater St. Louis, Carleton Coll., Dillard U., Wash. U., St. Louis Art Museum, Mo. Botanical Garden, St. Louis Sci. Ctr., Opera Theatre of St. Louis, Boy Scouts of Am., Greater St. Louis Area Coun. Named one of 50 Most Powerful Black Executives in Am., Fortune mag., 2002; recipient Exec. of the Year, Black Enterprise mag., 1997, Disting. Alumni award, Wash. U., 1998, Eagle award, Nat. Eagle Leadership Inst., 1999, Black Engineers President's award, 2000. Office: Juvenile Diabetes Rsch Found 120 Wall St New York NY 10005-4001 Office Phone: 800-533-2873. Office Fax: 212-785-9595.

DONALD, DAVID HERBERT, writer, history professor; b. Goodman, Miss., Oct. 1, 1920; s. Ira Unger and Sue Ella (Belford) D.; m. Aida DiPace, 1955; 1 son, Bruce Randall. Student, Holmes Jr. Coll., 1937-39; AB, Millsaps Coll., 1941, LHD, 1976; AM, U. Ill., 1942, PhD, 1946, LHD (hon.), 1992; MA (hon.), U. Oxford, 1959, Harvard U., 1973; LittD (hon.), Coll. Charleston, 1985; D in History, Lincoln U., 1996; LHD, U. Calgary, 2000; LLD, Ill. Coll., 2002; LittD, Middlebury Coll., 2003. Teaching fellow U. N.C., 1942; research asst. history U. Ill., 1943-45, research assoc., 1946-47; fellow Social Sci. Research Council, 1945-46; instr. history Columbia U., 1947-49; assoc. prof. history Smith Coll., 1949-51; asst. prof. history Columbia U. Grad. Faculty, 1951-52, assoc. prof., 1952-57, prof. history, 1957-59, Princeton U., 1959-62; prof. Am. history Johns Hopkins U., Balt., 1962-73, Harry C. Black prof., 1963-73, dir. Inst. So. History, 1966-72; Charles Warren prof. Am. history and prof. Am. civilization Harvard U., 1973-91, prof. emeritus, 1991—, chmn. grad. program in Am. civilization, 1979-85. Vis. assoc. prof. Amherst Coll., 1950; Fulbright lectr. Am. history U. Coll. North Wales, 1953-54; mem. Inst. Advanced Study, 1957-58; Harmsworth prof. Am. history Oxford U., 1959-60; John P. Young lectr. Memphis State U., 1963; Walter Lynwood Fleming lectr. La. State U., 1965; Benjamin Rush lectr. Am. Psychiat. Assn., 1972; Commonwealth lectr. Univ. Coll., London, 1975; Samuel Paley lectr. Hebrew Univ. of Jerusalem, 1991; mem. U.S. del. to UNESCO, 2003. Author: Lincoln's Herndon, 1948, Divided We Fought, A Pictorial History of the War, 1861-65, 1952, Inside Lincoln's Cabinet: The Civil War Diaries of Salmon P. Chase, 1954, Lincoln Reconsidered: Essays on the Civil War Era, 1956, rev. 3d edit., 2001, A Rebel's Recollections, (G.C. Eggleston), 1959, Charles Sumner and the Coming of the Civil War, 1960 (Pulitzer prize in biography), Why the North Won the Civil War, 1960, rev. edit., 1996, (with J.G. Randall) The Civil War and Reconstruction, 2d edit., 1961, rev., enlarged edit., 1969, (with Jean H. Baker and Michael F. Holt) rev. edit., 2001, The Divided Union, 1961, The Politics of Reconstruction, 1863-67, 1965, The Nation in Crisis, 1861-1877, 1969, Charles Sumner and the Rights of Man, 1970, (with Sidney Andrews) The South Since the War, 1970, Gone for a Soldier, 1975, (with others) The Great Republic, 1977, rev. edit., 1981, 3rd edit., 1985, 4th edit., 1992, Liberty and Union, 1978, Look Homeward: A Life of Thomas Wolfe, 1987 (Pulitzer prize 1988), Lincoln, 1995 rev. edit., 1996, Charles Sumner, 1997, Lincoln at Home: Two Glimpses of Abraham Lincoln's Domestic Life, 1999, We Are Lincoln Men: Abraham Lincoln and His Friends, 2003; editor: War Diary and Letters of Stephen Minot Weld, 1979; gen. editor: Documentary History of American Life, The Making of America Series, 6 vols.; co-editor: (with wife) Diary of Charles Francis Adams, 2 vols., 1964, (with Harold Holzer) Lincoln in the Times: The Life of Abraham Lincoln as Originally Reported in The New York Times, 2004; contbr. articles to periodicals. Recipient Abraham Lincoln Lit. award Union League Club N.Y.C., 1977, C. Hugh Holman prize MLA, 1988, Joseph R. Levenson award Harvard U. 1993, Benjamin L.C. Wailes award Miss. Hist. Soc., 1994, Barondess-Lincoln prize, 1996, Award of Achievement, Lincoln Group N.Y.C., 1995, 03 Christopher award, 1996, Lincoln prize Gettysburg Coll., 1996, Jefferson Davis award Mus. of Confederacy, 1996, Nevins/Freeman award Chgo. Civil War Round Table, 1999, Life-time Achievement award Abraham Lincoln Presdl. Mus., Springfield, 2005, Bruce Catton Lifetime Achievement award Soc. Am. Historians, 2006, Lincoln medal Ford's Theatre, 2007; Guggenheim fellow, 1964-65, 85-86, fellow Am. Coun. Learned Socs., 1969-70, Ctr. for Advanced Study Behavioral Scis., 1969-70, George A. and Eliza G. Howard fellow, 1957-58, sr. fellow NEH, 1971-72. Fellow Am. Acad. Arts and Scis.; mem. Orgn. Am. Historians, Am. Hist. Assn., So. Hist. Assn. (v.p. 1968, pres. 1969), Soc. Am. Historians, Mass. Hist. Soc., Am. Antiquarian Soc., Phi Beta Kappa, Phi Kappa Phi, Pi Kappa Delta, Pi Kappa Alpha, Omicron Delta Kappa. Clubs: Harvard (N.Y.C.); Cosmos, Signet, Fox. Episcopalian. Home: 41 Lincoln Rd PO Box 6158 Lincoln MA 01773-6158 Business E-Mail: donald@fas.harvard.edu.

DONALD, JACK C., gas industry executive; b. Edmonton, Alta., Can., Nov. 29, 1934; s. Archibald Scott and Margaret Catherine (Cameron) D.; m. Joan M. Schultz, Oct. 29, 1955. Student, Southern Alta. Inst. Tech., 1959. Owner, operator Parkdale Auto Svc., Edmonton, 1959—62; sales mgr. Sanford Oil Ltd., Edmonton, 1962—64, Pacific Petroleums, Edmonton, 1964—71; pres., gen. mgr. Parkland Oil Products, Red Deer, Alta., 1971—76; v.p. mktg. Turbo Resources, Calgary, Alta., 1977—2002; chmn. Parkland Industries Ltd., Red Deer, 1977—2004. Chmn., bd. dirs. Can. Western Bank, Edmonton, Can. Western Trust; v.p., bd. dirs. Deermart Equipment Sales Ltd., Red. Deer, Sifton Energy Inc., Calgary; bd. dirs. Ensign Energy Svcs., Inc., Can. Direct Ins.; past coun. Inst. Chartered Accts. Alta. Alderman City of Red Deer, 1971-77. Mem.: Rotary. Office: Parkland Properties Ltd Bridgeview Pl Ste 110 5102 58th St Red Deer AB Canada T4N 2L8 Business E-Mail: jackdonald@telus.net.

DONALD, JAMES EDWARD, retired career officer, government agency executive; b. Jackson, Miss., Apr. 20, 1949; m. August S. Green; children: Jeff, Cheryl. BA in Polit. Sci. and History, U. Miss., 1970; MPA, U. Mo., 1983; grad., Command Gen. Staff Coll., Nat. War Coll. Commd. 2nd lt. US Army Inf., 1970, advanced through grades to maj. gen., bn. adj./comdr. C Co. 1st Bn., 87th Inf. Regiment Baumholder, Germany, inf. advisor Readiness Group Stewart NY, inspector gen., inspection team chief 101st Airborne Divsn. Ft. Campbell, Ky., bn. exec. officer 2d Bn., 502d Inf. Regiment, bn. comdr. 1st Bn., 502d Inf. Regiment, chief forces team War Plans divsn., Office Dep. Chief Staff, comdr. 1st Brigade, 101st Airborne divsn., chief mil. support divsn., dep. dir. ops./JE U.S. Pacific Command Camp Smith, Hawaii, asst. divsn. comdr. ops. 25th Inf. Divsn. Schofield Barracks, Hawaii; dep. commdg. gen. US Army Pacific, Ft. Shafter, 1998—2000; dep. chief of staff over personnel and installations (ret.) US Army Forces Command, Fort McPherson, Ga., 2000—03; corrections commr. Ga. Dept. of Corrections, Ga. State Gov., Atlanta, 2003—. Decorated Def. Superior Svc. medal, Legion of Merit with oak leaf cluster, Bronze Star, Meritorious Svc. medal with four oak leaf clusters, Army Commendation medal with oak leaf cluster, Nat. Def. Svc. medal with svc. star, Armed Forces Expeditionary medal, Kuwait Liberation medal, S.W. Asia Svc. ribbon. Office: Off of Commissioner GA Dept of Corrections 2 Martin Luther King Jr Dr Atlanta GA 30334

DONALD, JAMES L., food service executive; BBA, Century U. Trainee Publix Super Mkts., Inc., 1971-76; mgmt. exec. Fla., Ala. and Tex. divsns. Albertson's, 1976-91; key exec. Wal-Mart, 1991-94; sr. v.p., mgr. 130 store ea. divsns. Safeway, Inc., 1994-96; CEO, pres., chmn. Pathmark Stores, Inc., Carteret, NJ, 1996—2002, also chmn. bd. dirs.; pres, North Am. div. Starbucks Corp., Seattle, 2002—05, pres., CEO & dir., 2005—. Bd. dirs. Modells. Bd. dirs. Rumson Country Sch. Office: Starbucks Corp 2401 Utah Ave S Seattle WA 98134*

DONALD, JAMES ROBERT, federal agency administrator, writer, economist; b. Omega, Ga., Dec. 31, 1933; s. Clinton Ernest and Lorena (Branan) D.; m. Nancy Ripple, Sept. 16, 1961; children: James Gordon, Mary Carol. Cert., Abraham Baldwin Agrl. Coll., 1952; BS, U. Ga., 1954; MS, N.C. State U., 1956; cert. in govt. tng., Mich. State U., 1975. Economist Econ. Rsch. Svc. USDA, Washington, 1957—76; outlook officer World Agrl. Outlook Bd. USDA, 1977—81, chair, 1982—94; ret., 1994. Freelance writer on fishing affairs, 1972—. With U.S. Army, 1957-63. Recipient Superior Svc. award USDA, 1968, Presdl. rank award, 1989. Mem. Am. Agrl. Econs. Assn. (Best Info. Bull. award 1976), Bass Anglers Soc. Am. Home: 584 Laurelwood Dr Mineral VA 23117-4734 E-mail: nrd33@ns.gemlink.com.

DONALD, NORMAN HENDERSON, III, lawyer; b. Denver, Nov. 1, 1937; s. Norman Henderson Jr. and Angelene (Pell) D.; m. Alice Allen, Oct. 31, 1970 (div. Aug. 1980); children: Norman H. IV (dec.), Helen P.; m. Kathryn Akers, Sept. 26, 1981 (div. Jan. 1998). AB, Princeton U., 1959; LLB, Harvard U., 1962. Bar: N.Y. 1962. Assoc. Davis, Polk & Wardwell, NYC, 1962-67, Skadden, Arps, Slate, Meagher & Flom, NYC, 1967-68, ptnr., 1968-94. Chmn. bd. dirs. Norwil Holdings, Inc., N.Y.C., Atlanta and Sarasota. Mem. Assn. of Bar of City of N.Y., Practising Law Inst. (editor Reit Restructuring 1977—), St. Paul's Sch. Alumni Assn. (v.p., bd. dirs. 1984-86), Union Club (N.Y.C.), Rotary, Gold Creek Club (Dawsonville, Ga.). Republican. Episcopalian. Home: Mistral Farms 1544 Bailey Waters Rd Dawsonville GA 30534-1807 Office: care Brock & Silverstein 800 3d Ave New York NY 10022 Fax: 706-265-2810. E-mail: mistral@syclone.net.

DONALDSON, COLEMAN DUPONT, retired aeronautical engineer, aerospace engineer, consultant; b. Phila., Sept. 22, 1922; s. John W. and Renee (duPont) Donaldson; m. Barbara Goldsmith, Jan. 17, 1945; children: B. Beirne, Coleman duPont, Evan F., Alexander M., William M. BS in Aero. Engring., Rensselaer Poly. Inst., 1943; MA, Princeton U., 1954, PhD, 1957. Staff, NACA, Langley Field, Va., 1943-44, head aerophysics sect., 1946-52; gen. aerodynamics USAC, Wright Field, Ohio, 1945-46; aerodynamic evaluation Bell Aircraft, Niagara Falls, NY, 1946; sr. cons., pres. Aero Research Assos. of Princeton, NJ, 1954-79, chmn. bd. NJ, 1979-86; group gen. mgr. Aero Research Assocs. Princeton Inc., 1986-87; v.p. Titan Systems, Inc., 1986-87; ret., 1987. Cons. missile guidance and control Gen. Precision Equipment Corp., 1957—68; cons. magnetohydro-dynamics Thompson Ramo Woolridge, Inc., 1958—61; cons. aerodynamic heating, gen. aerodynamics Martin Marietta Corp., 1955—72, adv. devel. and tech. ops., 1989—96; gen. editor Princeton series on high speed aerodynamics and jet propulsion, 1955—64; cons. boundary layer stability, aerodynamic heating, missile and ordnance sys. dept. GE, 1956—72; cons. Grumman Aerospace Corp., 1959—72; Robert H. Goddard vis. lectr. with rank of prof. Princeton (N.J.) U., 1970—71, chmn. adv. coun. dept. aerospace and mech. scis., 1973—78; mem. rsch. tech. adv. coun. panel rsch. NASA, 1969—76, hypersonic tech. com., 1986—90; indsl. profl. adv. com. Pa. State U.; mem. Pres.' Air Quality Adv. Bd., 1973—74; chmn. lab. adv. bd. for air warfare Naval Rsch. Adv. Com., 1986—89, DARPA Tech. Adv. Panel on Hydrodynamics and Acoustics, 1991—94; cons. Ctr. Naval Analysis, 1990—98; adv. panel NASA Ctr. Turbulence Rsch., 1993—95. Contbr. articles to profl. jours. Recipient Meritorious Pub. Svc. award, Chief Naval Rsch., 1990. Fellow: AIAA (gen. chmn. 13th aerospace scis. meeting 1975, Dryden Rsch. lectr. award 1971); mem.: NAE, Am. Phys. Soc., Delta Phi, Sigma Xi. Home: Apt 1066 955 Harpersville Rd Newport News VA 23601-1093

DONALDSON, DAVID, pathologist; b. Birmingham, England, Feb. 13, 1936; s. Henry and Esther Donaldson. MB, ChB, U. Birmingham, Eng., 1959. House physician Selly Oak Hosp., Birmingham, 1959—60; house surgeon Children's Hosp., Birmingham, 1960; sr. house officer in clin. pathology Queen Elizabeth Hosp., Birmingham, 1960—61; asst. resident med. officer, registrar in gen. medicine Gen. Infirmary, Leeds, England, 1961-62; registrar in gen. medicine Victoria Hosp., Keighley, England, 1963-64; lectr., hon. sr. registrar in chem. pathology Inst. Neurology, Nat. Hosp Nervous Diseases, London, 1964—70; cons. chem. pathology East Surrey Hosp., Redhill, Surrey, England, 1970—2001, clin. dir. pathology, 1991—94; cons. in chem. pathology BUPA Gatwick Park Hosp., Horley, Surrey, England, 1984—2006. Vice chmn. med. sub-com. Marie Curie Meml. Found., London, 1978—83; chmn. South West Thames Chem. Pathology Adv. Group South Thames Regional Health Authority, London, 1995—2000; lectr. clin. biochemistry London South Bank U., 1997—. Author: Psychiatric Disorders with a Biochemical Basis, 1998; co-author: Essential Diagnostic Tests in Biochemistry and Haematology, 1971, Diagnostic Function Tests in Chem. Pathology, 1989; contbr. chapters to books, articles to over 100 profl. jours.; dep. hon. editor, mem. editl. bd. Jour. Royal Soc. for the Promotion of Health, 1997—2004. Fellow: Hunterian Soc., Med. Soc. London, Internat. Coll. Nutrition (life, Mori Felicitation award 2002), Royal Soc. Medicine, Inst. Biology, Royal Soc. for the Promotion of Health, Royal Geog. Soc. (life), Royal Soc. Chemistry, Royal Coll. Pathologists, Royal Coll. Physicians; mem.: AAAS, Brit. Med. Assn. (chmn. East Surrey divsn. 1992—93), N.Y. Acad. Sci., Brit. Assn. Advancement Sci., HEART UK (Hyperlipidaemic Edn. and Rsch. Trust UK), Assn. Clin. Pathologists, Assn. Clin. Biochemists, Harveian Soc. London, Worshipful Soc. of Apothecaries, London (faculty of history and philosophy of medicine and pharmacy). Avocations: piano, music, history of medicine. Home: 5 Woodfield Way Redhill Surrey RH1 2DP England

DONALDSON, EDWARD MOSSOP, research scientist, marine biologist, consultant; b. Whitehaven, Cumbria, Eng., June 19, 1939; arrived in Can., 1961; s. Edward and Margaret (Mossop) D.; m. Judith Selwood, Aug. 8, 1964; 1 child, Heather. BSc with honors, Sheffield U., Eng., 1961, DSc, 1975; PhD, U. B.C., Vancouver, Can., 1964. Rsch. scientist Dept. Fisheries and Oceans, West Vancouver, B.C., 1965-97, sect. head fish culture rsch., 1981-89, sect. head biotech., genetics and nutrition, 1989-97, head Ctr. of Disciplinary Excellence for Biotech. and Genetics in Aquaculture, 1987-97, scientist emeritus, 1997—; cons. in aquaculture and the environment, 1997—; dir. Ed Donaldson & Assocs. Ltd. Aquaculture and Fisheries Cons., 2001—. Hon. rsch. assoc. U. B.C., 1979-88, adj. prof., 1988—; cons. finfish aquaculture FAO, UN Devel. Program, Can. Internat. Devel. Agy., Internat. Devel. Rsch. Ctrs., U.S. AID, Office of Tech. Assessment of the U.S. Congress, Can. Exec. Svc. Overseas, Sci. Com. on Problems of Environment, WHO, U.S. Seagrant, Portugese Ministry Sci. and Tech., 2002; mem. Nat. Scis. and Engring. Rsch. Coun. Can., mem. strategic grant selection com. for food agr. and aquaculture, 1988-93; mem., active in strategic planning for applied rsch. and knowledge com. biotech. B.C. Sci. Coun. Mem. editl. bd. Gen. and Comparative Endocrinology, 1971-78, Can. Jour. Fisheries and Aquatic Sci., 1985-88, Aquaculture, 1983—, physiology sect. editor, 1999—; mem. editl. bd. Can. Jour. Zoology, 1986-91, Revista Italiana de Acquacoltura, 1991-96; contbr. over 400 articles to sci. jours. and conf. procs.; contbr. to books on endocrinology, biotech. and aquaculture; patentee in field. Bd. dirs. Vancouver Aquarium Marine Sci. Ctr., 1992—. Recipient award for best publs. in Transactions of Am. Fisheries Soc., 1977, Ministerial Merit award Min. of Fisheries and

Oceans, 1989, B.C. Sci. Coun. Gold medal, 1992, Commendation award Dep. Minister, 1997, Murray A. Newman award for Lifetime Achievement in Aquatic Rsch. and Conservation, Vancouver Aquarium Marine Sci. Ctr., 2006; B.C. Sugar Co. scholar, 1961; NIH fellow, 1964-65; recipient Thomas W. Eadie medal Royal Soc. Can., 1995. Fellow Acad. Sci. of Royal Soc. Can. (mem. Rowmanoswky medal com. 1994, Thomas W. Eadie medal com. 1995-96, life sci. fellowship selection com., 2001-04); mem. Can. Soc. Zoologists (councilor 1980-83), Aquaculture Assn. Can. (Rsch. Excellence award 2004). Office: Dept Fisheries & Oceans 4160 Marine Dr Vancouver BC Canada V7V 1N6 Office Phone: 604-666-7928. Business E-Mail: donaldsone@pac.dfo-mpo.gc.ca.

DONALDSON, EVA G., chemist, writer; b. Henderson, NC, Mar. 19, 1927; d. William and Annie Green; m. Kenneth Donaldson, Feb. 9, 1952 (dec.); children: Sonya D. Bates, Kenneth A., Keith. BS cum laude, Johnson C. Smith U., Charlotte, NC, 1948; MS in Chemistry with honors, Howard U., Washington, 1953; postgrad., U. Washington, Howard U., Cath. U. Am., Am. U., George Washington U., LaSalle U. Coll. Engring., U. Md. Lic. tchr. Washington, 1954. Tchr. chemistry, phys. sci. Spingarn Sr. H.S., Washington, 1954—59; tchr. chemistry, biology and math Dunbar Sr. H.S., 1962—93; author, 1993—; chemist, cancer rschr. NIH. Del., sci. profl. Russia Joint Edn. Conf., St. Petersburg, Russia, 2006—; lectr. in field; founder Dr. James P. Green Sr. and Atty. James P. Green Jr. endowment scholarship fund. Author: A Science Incentive Program, A Summer Enrichment Curriculum For Chemistry Students, A Revised Curriculum for the Teaching of Advanced Placement Chemistry. Mem. Howard U. Century Club/U. Capstone Socs. Donors, Washington. Grantee, NSF. Fellow: Wash. Acad. Sci. (Bernice Lamberton award Initiatives Providing Learning Success and Sci. Career Awareness Students); mem.: Washington Nat. Cathedral's Literacy Program, Nat. Sci. Found., Nat. Profl. Orgn. Devel. Black Chemists and Chem. Engrs. (life), Nat. Sci. Tchrs. Assn., Myers Soc., Legacy Soc., Smithsonian Instn., Kiwanis. Avocations: swimming, ice skating, travel, growing cyrstals. Home Phone: 202-396-7674.

DONALDSON, JAMES NEILL, banker; b. Washington County, Pa., Mar. 25, 1940; s. James Reed and Mary Alice (Neill) D. BA in Polit. Sci., Westminster Coll., 1962; MEd, U. Pitts., 1965, postgrad. in law, 1962-64. cert. trust and fin. advisor, corp. trust specialist; accredited estate planner. Trust adminstr. Bankers Trust Co., NYC, 1967-70, asst. trust officer, 1970-73, trust officer White Plains, NY, 1973-76, officer-in-charge Trust Adminstrv. Unit, 1976, v.p., 1976-78, head trust office, 1978-82, with Trust Adminstrn. Unit, 1982-83; head new bus. devel., trust and estates group Chem. Bank, NYC, 1983-88, head trust and estates adminstrn. mgmt., 1989-90; sect. head mgr. trust and estates adminstrn. Chase Manhattan Bank, NYC, 1990-2001, personal trust sales Global Trust and Fiduciary Unit, 1996-2000; wealth transfer and succession planning J.P. Morgan Chase & Co., NYC, 2001; sr. v.p. regional mgr. wealth mgmt. TD Banknorth (formerly Hudson United Bank), 2002—06, sr. v.p., sr. wealth advisor wealth mgmt. group, 2006—. Chase rep. to Corp. Fiduciaries Assn. of N.Y.C.; editl. mini-adv. bd. Trusts & Estates Mag., 1997-2002; lectr. Bank Mktg. Assn. Conf., 1995, 99; mem. Estate Planning Coun. Westchester County (N.Y.), 1975—, bd. dirs., 1980-85, treas. 1986-87, v.p., 1988-89, pres. 1989; mem. Estate Planning Coun. Rockland County (N.Y.), 1973—, pres., 1984-85; mem. Estate Planning Coun. N.Y.C., 1983—, bd. dirs., 1988-91, 97-2000, sec., 2001-02, treas., 2002-03, v.p., 2003-04, pres., 2004-06, estate adminstrn. Trust Div., N.Y. State Bankers Assn., 1975, 90, 93, 96, mem. estate planning com., 1980-83, mem. mktg. com., 1984—, chmn. 1989-94. Contbr. articles to profl. publs. Mem. Planned Giving Com., U. Pitts.; mem. planned giving com. N.Y. chpt. Arthritis Found. Mem. Am. Bankers Assn. (adv. com. for trust, asset mgmt. and mktg. conf. 2001—03), Phi Kappa Tau (Leadership Hall of Fame). Office: TD Banknorth Wealth Management 90 Post Rd E 3d Flr Westport CT 06880 Office Phone: 203-291-6705.

DONALDSON, JAMES OSWELL, III, neurologist, educator; b. Butler, Pa., July 19, 1942; s. James Oswell Jr. and Estelle Mathilda (Unverzagt) D.; m. Mary Hoopingarner, Aug. 23, 1969 (div. Dec. 1983); 1 child, Andrew Robert; m. Susan McKernin, Nov. 3, 1984; stepchildren: Brendan McDonald, Ian McDonald. BS, Haverford Coll., 1964; MD, U. Pa., 1968. Diplomate Am. Bd. Psychiatry and Neurology, Am. Bd. Internal Medicine. Intern in medicine Hosp. of U. Pa., Phila., 1968-69, resident, 1969-70, resident in neurology, 1974-76; hon. house physician Nat. Hosp. for Nervous Diseases, London, 1973-74, sr. vis. fellow, 1991; asst. prof. neurology U. Conn. Sch. Medicine, Farmington, 1977-82, assoc. prof., 1982-88, prof., 1988—. Author: Neurology of Pregnancy, 1978, 2nd edit., 1989. Maj. M.C., U.S. Army, 1970-73. Fellow ACP, Am. Acad. Neurology; mem. Am. Neurol. Assn. Office: U Conn Health Ctr 263 Farmington Ave Farmington CT 06030-1840 Home Phone: 860-521-8842; Office Phone: 860-679-3186.

DONALDSON, JOHN CECIL, JR., consumer products company executive; b. Bklyn., Dec. 8, 1933; s. John Cecil and Josephine (Greason) D.; m. Marilyn J. Smith, Aug. 29, 1959; children: Susan, John III. AB, Brown U., 1956; MBA, U. Pa., 1959; postgrad., Bentley Sch. Acctg., 1957, LaSalle Law Sch., 1959. Various positions Gen. Motors Corp., Flint, Mich., 1960-71, zone mgr. Buffalo, 1971-76, Newark, 1976-77, mgr. forward product planning, 1977-78; from dir. sales and mktg. to v.p. Corbin Ltd., 1979-85; exec. v.p. and gen. mgr. TMG Corp., NYC, 1986—. Pres. Gen. Motors Exec. Club, Newark, N.J., 1977-78. Mem. Am. Mktg. Assn. Republican. Avocations: ice skating, tennis, golf. Home: 36 Nottingham Way Millington NJ 07946-1917 Office: TMG Corp 1290 Avenue Of The Americas New York NY 10104-0101 Address: 101 Baxters Neck Rd Marstons Mills MA 02648

DONALDSON, MARCIA JEAN, lay worker; b. Wilmington, Del., June 20, 1925; C. Aubrey Smith and Marcia Allen (Hall) Whitman; m. Robert Donald Donaldson, Jan. 8, 1944; children: Robert Gary, Pamela Lynn, David Keith. Student pub. schs., Wilmington. Sunday Sch. tchr., Del., N.J., 1943-70; tchr. Child Evangelism Fellowship, Wilmington, 1943-55, tchr., bd. dirs. NJ, 1955-64, dir. Ocean County, NJ, 1964-73; pres. Christian Children's Assocs., Toms River, NJ, 1964—2005, 2005—. Writer radio and TV syndicated programs worldwide for children; author: (booklet) A 30 Year Adventure; producer, hostess radio and TV program Adventure Pals. Mem. Nat. Religious Broadcasters Assn., Gideons Aux. Office: Christian Children's Assn Inc PO Box 446 Toms River NJ 08754-0446 Office Phone: 732-240-3003. Personal E-mail: bj@donald.com. *Of all the important achievements one can accomplish in this life I believe the most rewarding is to be able to introduce another person to the one true and living God, who alone can give us real joy and hope and peace.*

DONALDSON, MICHAEL CLEAVES, lawyer; b. Montclair, NJ, Oct. 13, 1939; s. Wyman C. and Ernestine (Greenwood) D.; m. Diana D., Sept. 12, 1969 (div. 1979); children: Michelle, Amy, Wendy. BS, U. Fla., 1961; JD, U. Calif., Berkeley, 1967. Bar: Calif. 1967, U.S. Dist. Ct. (cen. dist.) Calif. 1967, U.S. Ct. Appeals (9th cir.) 1967. Assoc. Harris & Hollingsworth, LA, 1969-72; ptnr. McCabe & Donaldson, LA, 1972-79; pvt. practice Law Office of M.C. Donaldson, LA, 1979-90; ptnr. Dern & Donaldson, LA, 1990-94, Donaldson & Hart (formerly Berton & Donaldson), Beverly Hills, Calif., 1994—. Lectr. in field; judge, preliminary and finalist judge Internat. Emmys; preliminary judge Night Time Emmys; gen. counsel FIND Film Ind., Writers Guild Found.; past pres. Internat. Documentary Assn. Author: EZ Legal Guide to Copyright and Trademark, 1995, (booklet) A Funny Thing Happened on the Way to Dinner, 1976; contg. author: Conversations with Michael Landon, 1992, Negotiating for Dummies, 1996, 2d edit., 2007, Clearance & Copyright What the Independent Filmmaker Needs to Know, 1997, 2d edit., 2003. Bd. dirs. Calif. Theatre Coun., L.A. 1st lt. USMC, 1961-64. Mem. ABA (entertainment and sports sect.), ATAS, Beverly Hills Bar Assn. (chmn. entertainment sect.), LA Copyright Soc., Internat. Documentary Assoc. (pres.). Independent. Avocations: photography, writing, gardening, hiking, skiing. Home: 1057 20th St Santa Monica CA 90403 Office: Donaldson & Hart 9220 W Sunset Blvd Ste 224 Los Angeles CA 90069-3501 Office Phone: 310-273-8394 ext. 23. E-mail: mcd@donaldsonhart.com.

DONALDSON, MYRTLE NORMA, musician, educator; b. Priddy, Tex., Feb. 9, 1923; d. Emil Otto and Brunhilda Eleanore (Riewe) Schneider; m. Fletcher William Donaldson, Feb. 12, 1943; children: Patricia Annette, Rebecca Joyce. BA, U. Ariz., Tucson, 1970; MA, Middle Tenn. State U., Murfreesboro, 1982. Cert. profl. piano tchr. Tenn. Music Tchrs. Assn., profl. piano tchr.'s cert. Nat. Music Tchrs.' Assn. Organist Luth. chs., Aleman and Austin, Tex., 1937-42, 43-50, Kinston, NC, 1943, Los Alamos, N.Mex., 1951-53; Ft. Worth, 1954-56; organist Tullahoma, Tenn., 1969-81; piano tchr., 1972-2001. Composer: sonata, 1981, theme and variations, 1980. Active Cmty. Concert Bd., Tullahoma, 1973-99, Cmty. Concert Membership Ch., 1974-78, pres., 1978-80, 89-93 Mem. Music Tchrs. Nat. Assn. (cert., com. mem. 1983-99), Mid. Tenn. Music Tchrs. Assn. (sec. Murfreesboro chpt. 1975-77, chair membership state 1977-78, pres. Mid. Tenn. chpt. 1979-81, 87-89, Music Tchr. of Yr. 1992), Delta Phi Alpha. Republican. Lutheran. Avocations: knitting, sewing, creative memories album, national background of grandparents.

DONALDSON, ROBERT HERSCHEL, university administrator, educator; b. Houston, June 14, 1943; s. Herschel Arthur and Vera Edith (True) D.; m. Judy Carol Johnston, June 27, 1964 (div. Apr. 30, 1984); children: Jennifer Gwynne, John Andrew; m. Sally Susan Abravanel, Mar. 31, 1985; children: Mark Elliot, Ryan Scott. AB, Harvard U., 1964, A.M., 1966, PhD, 1969. Prof. polit. sci. Vanderbilt U., 1968-81, assoc. dean Coll. Arts and Sci., 1975-81; provost, v.p. acad. affairs, prof. polit. sci. Herbert H. Lehman Coll. CUNY, 1981-84; pres. Fairleigh Dickinson U., Rutherford, NJ, 1984-90, U. Tulsa, 1990-96, trustees prof. polit. sci., 1996—. Vis. research prof. U.S. Army War Coll., 1978-79; pres. Am. coms. fgn. rels., 2002-. Author: Stasis and Change in Revolutionary Elites, 1971, Soviet Policy toward India, 1974, The Soviet-Indian Alliance: Quest for Influence, 1979, The Soviet Union in the Third World: Successes and Failures, 1981, Soviet Foreign Policy since World War II, 1981, 85, 88, 92, The Foreign Policy of Russia: Changing Systems, Enduring Interests, 1998, 2002, 05. Council Fgn. Relations fellow, 1973-74 Mem. Coun. on Fgn. Rels., Phi Beta Kappa. Methodist. Home: 6449 S Richmond Ave Tulsa OK 74136-1669 Office: Univ Tulsa 600 S College Ave Tulsa OK 74104-3126 Office Phone: 918-631-2409. Business E-Mail: robert-donaldson@utulsa.edu.

DONALDSON, SAMUEL ANDREW, journalist; b. El Paso, Tex., Mar. 11, 1934; s. Samuel Andrew and Chloe (Hampson) Donaldson; m. Billie Kay Butler, Nov. 30, 1963 (div. 1981); children: Samuel, Jennifer, Thomas, Robert; m. Janice Claire Smith, Apr. 16, 1983. BA, Tex. Western Coll. (now UTEP), 1955; postgrad., U. So. Calif., 1955—56. Radio/TV news reporter/anchorman WTOP, Washington, 1961—67; Capitol Hill corr. ABC News, Washington, 1967—77, White House corr., 1977—89; panelist This Week With David Brinkley, 1981—96; co-anchor This Week With Sam Donaldson and Cokie Roberts, 1996—2002, Prime Time Live, ABC, 1989—98; chief White House corrs. ABC News, 1998—99; co-anchor 20/20 ABC, 1998—99; anchor SamDonaldson@abcnews.com, 1999—2002, The Sam Donaldson Show, ABC Radio Network, 2001—04; co-anchor ABC News Now, 2004—. Bd. mem. Acad. Achievement, 2003—. Author: (book) Hold On, Mr. President, 1987 (internat. best seller). Chmn. adv. bd. Moffitt Cancer Ctr.; mem. Ariz. Meml. Bd.; chmn. Woodrow Wilson Ctr. Adv. Coun. Capt. US Army, 1956—59. Named a UTEP Distinguished Alumnus, 1976; named Best TV White House Corr. in Bus., The Washington Journalism Rev., 1985, Best TV Corr. in Bus., 1986; recipient, 1987, 1988, 1989, 4 Emmy awards, 3 George Foster Peabody awards, others, Broadcaster of Yr. award, Nat. Press Found., 1998; UTEP's Ctr. for Comm. Studies named in his honor, 2002. Mem.: AFTRA (past pres. Washington-Balt. chpt.), Nat. Acad. of Achievement. Office: ABC 1717 Desales St NW Washington DC 20036

DONALDSON, SARAH SUSAN, radiologist; b. Portland, Oreg., Apr. 20, 1939; BS, RN, U. Oreg., 1961; MD, Harvard U., 1968. Intern U. Wash., 1968—69; resident in radiol. therapy Stanford Med. Ctr., Calif., 1969—72; fellow in pediatric oncology Inst. Gustave-Roussy, 1972—73; prof. radiol. oncology Stanford U. Sch. Medicine., 1973—, Catherine and Howard Avery prof., dept. radiation. Recipient Elizabeth Blackwell medal, Am. Med. Women's Assn., 2005. Mem.: NIH. Office: Stanford U Med Ctr Dept Radio/Oncology 875 Blake Wilbur Dr Stanford CA 94305-5847

DONALDSON, STEPHEN REEDER, author; b. Cleve., May 13, 1947; s. James R. and Mary Ruth (Reeder) D. BA, Coll. of Wooster, 1968; MA, Kent State U., 1971; LittD (hon.), Coll. of Wooster, 1993. Asst. dispatcher Akron City Hosp., 1968-70; tchg. fellow Kent State U., 1971; acquisitions editor Tapp-Gentz Assos., West Chester, Pa., 1973-74; instr. Ghost Ranch Writers Workshops, N.Mex., 1973-77. Author: Lord Foul's Bane, 1977, The Illearth War, 1977, The Power That Preserves, 1977, The Wounded Land, 1980, The One Tree, 1982, White Gold Wielder, 1983, Daughter of Regals, 1984, The Mirror of Her Dreams, 1986, A Man Rides Through, 1987, The Real Story, 1991, Forbidden Knowledge, 1991, A Dark and Hungry God Arises, 1992, Chaos and Order, 1994, This Day All Gods Die, 1996, Reave The Just, 1999, The Man Who Fought Alone, 2001, The Runes of the Earth, 2004, The Man Who Killed His Brother, 1980, repub. 2002, The Man Who Risked His Partner, 1984, repub. 2003, The Man Who Tried to Get Away, 1990, repub. 2004; editor: Strange Dreams, 1993. Recipient John W. Campbell award best new writer World Sci. Fiction Conv., 1979, Best Novel award Brit. Fantasy Soc., 1979, Balrog award for best novel, 1981, 83, for best collection, 1985, Saturn award for best fantasy novel, 1983, Book ofYr. award Sci. Fiction Book Club, 1987, 88, World Fantasy award, Best Collection, 2000. Mem. Am. Contract Bridge League, Internat. Assn. for the Fantastic in the Arts, N.M. Shotokan, Life - Dance Kajukenbo. Office: care Howard Morhaim 30 Pierrepont St Brooklyn NY 11201 Office Phone: 718-222-8400.

DONALDSON, THOMAS, business educator; b. Wichita, Kans., July 23, 1945; s. Paul J. and Louisene (Sadler) D.; m. Sally Leisure, May, 1970 (div. 1973); m. Jean Shephard, Sept. 3, 1977 (dec. June 2002); children: Paul, Keith, Paige. Student, US Naval Acad., 1963-65; BS, U. Kans., 1967, PhD, 1976. Asst. prof. Loyola U., Chgo., 1976-81, assoc. prof., 1981-84, Henry J. Wirtenberger prof. ethics, 1984-88; C. Stewart Sheppard vis. prof. bus. adminstrn. U. Va., Charlottesville, 1988-89; John F. Connelly prof. bus. ethics Georgetown U., Washington, 1989—96; Mark O. Winkelman endowed prof. Wharton Sch. U. Pa., Phila., 1996—, dir. PhD program in ethics and legal studies, 2004—. Testified in US Congress (Senate Judiciary Com.) on Sarbanes-Oxley legis., 2002; participant World Econ. Forum, Davos, Switzerland, 2003. Editor: Issues in Moral Philosophy, 1986, Case Studies in Business Ethics, 1987, Ethical Issues in Business, 2002; author: The Ethics of International Business, 1989, Corporations and Morality, 1982, (with Thomas W. Dunfee) Ties That Bind: A Social Contracts Approach to Business Ethics, 1999; assoc. editor Acad. Mgmt. Rev., 2002-07; contbr. articles to profl. jours. Chair US com. FTSE4Good, 2003—; mem. Haverford Friends Meeting, 1998—; vice chmn. bd. trustees Carnegie Coun. Ethics and Internat. Affairs, 2006—. With USN, 1963—68. Mem.: Acad. Mgmt. (pres. social issues in mgmt. divsn. 2006—), Phila. Country Club. Avocations: music, skiing. Home: 518 Lynmere Rd Bryn Mawr PA 19010-2818 Office: U Pa Wharton Sch Philadelphia PA 19104 Business E-Mail: donaldst@wharton.upenn.edu.

DONALDSON, WILLIAM HENRY, investment banker, former federal agency administrator; b. Buffalo, June 2, 1931; s. Eames and Guida (Marx) Donaldson; m. Jane Phillips Donaldson; children: Matthew, Kimberly, Adam. BA, Yale U., 1953, MA (hon.), 1970; MBA with distinction, Harvard U., 1958; LLD (hon.), Webster U., 1992; DPhil (hon.), St. Lawrence U., 1995; DHL (hon.), Alfred U., 1995, Weslyan U.; DD (hon.), Gen. Theol. Sem. Episcopal Ch.; DHL (hon.), Baruch U. Chmn., CEO Donaldson, Lufkin & Jenrette, Inc., NYC, 1959-73; under sec. US Dept. State, Washington, 1973—75; spl. cons. to v.p. of U.S. The White House, Washington, 1975; dean, Beinecke prof. mgmt. Yale Grad. Mgmt. Sch., New Haven, 1975-80; chmn., CEO Donaldson Enterprises, Inc., NYC, 1980-90, 2001—; chmn., chief exec. NY Stock Exch., NYC, 1990-95; sr. adv. Donaldson, Lufkin and Jenrette, Inc., 1996-2000; chair., pres., CEO Aetna Inc., Hartford, 2000—02; chmn. SEC, NYC, 2003—05; former chmn. adv. coun. Perella Weinberg Partners LP, NYC. Bd. dirs. Aetna Life & Casualty, Phillip Morris, Honeywell Inc., Bright Horizons Family Solutions, Inc. Trustee, chmn. fin. com. Ford Found., NYC, 1968-80; trustee Yale U., New Haven, 1970-75; ptnr. NYC Partnership; bd. dirs. Bus. Coun. of State of NY, 1990-96, Lincoln Ctr. for Performing Arts, NYC; trustee NY Police Found., Marine Corps Univ. Found., Aspen Inst.; gov. Fgn. Policy Assn.; chmn. Carnegie Endowment for Internat. Peace, 1999-2003. 1st lt. USMC, 1953-55. Recipient Pres.'s Disting. Svc. award SUNY, 1976; named Businessman of Yr., AP, 1969. Mem. Inst. CFAs, Yale Mgmt. Sch. (chmn. bd. advisors 1995-2003), Coun. on Fgn. Rels. Business E-Mail: bdonaldson@denterprise.com.

DONALDSON, WILMA CRANKSHAW, elementary school educator; b. Havre de Grace, Md., Aug. 28, 1942; d. John Hamilton and Wilma Chaffee (Thurlow) Crankshaw; m. James Neill Donaldson, Aug. 5, 1967. BA in Edn. cum laude, Westminster Coll., 1964; MA in Edn., Fairfield U., 1976. Educator Hurlbutt Elem. Sch., Weston, Conn., 1964-78, 92—, Weston Mid. Sch., 1979-91; tchr. Greek Mythology Elem. Sch., 1999—. Team leader Hurlbutt Elem. Sch., 1967—68, 1976—78, sci. rep., 1992—99, developer of curriculum; judge Odyssey of the Mind, Conn., 1995—2001; presenter of photography and Greek myth courses elem. sch., 2002—; tchr. pvt. student art courses; tchr. Music/Lit./Theater Workshop, 1997—; presenter in field; sci. cons. Greenwich Pub. Schs., 2002—. Author: (filmstrip script) Sci. Series, 1972, Metric Math Series, 1973. Chair fine arts New England Sch. Accreditation Com., Weston, 1990-91; trainer Project CHEM, Exxon Corp., 1991—; state planning com., program and site chmn. Conn. Elem. Sci. Day Conf., 1994—; organizer, advisor Student Elem. Sch. Environ. Orgn., 1992-2003, sci. cons. Pub. Schs. Greenwich, Conn., 2002-04; co-organizer, co-founder Elem. Family Sci. Night, Weston, 2000; dir., tchr. Camp Invention, Weston, 2002-04; active Silvermine Arts Enrichment Com. Recipient Faculty Mem. Presdl. Recognition Sch. award U.S. Dept. Edn., 1987-88, Celebration of Excellence award State of Conn., 1989, 92, 95, 98, Laurence Ohmes Meml. award Weston Bd. Edn., 1995. Mem. NEA, CEA, Nat. Sci. Tchrs. Assn. (workshop presenter Moscow 1991, NASA-NEWEST award 1997, Laurence P. Ohmes Meml. award 1995), ASCD, Conn. Edn. Assn., Conn. Alliance Arts Edn. (Weston Tchr. of Yr. 1994-95, Conn. Alliance for Art Edn. Disting. Tchr. of Yr. 1995), Coun. Elem. Sci. Internat. (com. chmn. 1991-98), Delta Zeta. Avocations: art, theater, photography, travel.

DONATONI, ROBERT J., lawyer; b. Oct. 16, 1954; BA, U. Mass.; JD, Temple U. Ptnr. Donatoni & Kratsa, West Chester, Pa. Founder Phila. Gospel Outreach Ctr. Mem.: Am. Coll. Trial Lawyers, Pa. Assn. Criminal Defense Lawyers (bd. mem. 2005). Republican. Office: Donatoni & Kratsa 17 W Gay St, Ste 102 West Chester PA 19380 also: 995 Meadowview Lane West Chester PA 19382 Office Phone: 610-719-0500. Office Fax: 610-719-0475.

DONBERGER, KAREN SHEPARD, special education and elementary school educator; b. Malcolm Grow, Md., June 7, 1968; d. Ernest A. and Elaine B. Shepard; m. Anthony Paul Donberger, Dec. 18, 1992; children: Allyson, Anthony Jr. BS, U. Md., Coll. Pk., 1991, MEd, 1994. Advanced profl. cert. Md. State Dept. Edn., 2004, postgrad. profl. lic. Commonwealth of Va. Dept. Edn., 2005. Early childhood spl. tchr. Prince George's County Pub. Schs., Upper Marlboro, Md., 1991—97, child find evaluator, 1995—96, infants and toddlers spl. tchr., 1998—99; elem. spl. tchr. Calvert County Pub. Schs., Port Repub., Md., 1997—98; child find tchr. and screener Loudoun County Pub. Schs., Ashburn, Va., 1999—. Sub. inclusion specialist The Lt. Joseph P. Kennedy Inst., Washington, 1995—96. Mem.: Coun. Exceptional Children.

DONDANVILLE, PATRICIA, lawyer; b. Anchorage, Alaska, Mar. 21, 1956; d. Leo John and Ann Louise (Mosey) D.; m. James F. Berman; children: Emily Grace, Edward James. BA in Am. Studies, U. Notre Dame, 1978; JD, U. Va., 1981. Bar: Ill. 1981. Assoc. Schiff Hardin LLP (formerly Schiff Hardin & Waite), Chgo., 1981—87, ptnr., 1998—. Bd. dir. Nat. Ctr. Laity, Chgo., 1986-98 Mem. ABA, Chgo. Bar Assn., Notre Dame Club Chgo. (bd. govs., scholarship found. 1988—), Econ. Club Chgo. Office: Schiff Hardin LLP 6600 Sears Tower Chicago IL 60606 Office Phone: 312-258-5709. Business E-Mail: pdondanville@schiffhardin.com.

DONEGAN, CHARLES EDWARD, lawyer, educator; b. Chgo., Apr. 10, 1933; s. Arthur C. and Odessa (Arnold) D.; m. Patty Lou Harris, June 15, 1963; 1 son, Carter Edward. BSc, Roosevelt U., 1954; MS, Loyola U., 1959; JD, Howard U., 1967; LL.M., Columbia, 1970. Bar: NY 1968, DC 1968, Ill. 1979; cert. bus. counselor, lic. real estate broker. Pub. sch. tchr., Chgo., 1956-59; with Office Internal Revenue, Chgo., 1959-62; labor economist US Dept. Labor, Washington, 1962-65; legal intern US Commn. Civil Rights, Washington, summer 1966; asst. counsel NAACP Legal Def. Fund, NYC, 1967-69; lectr. law Baruch Coll., NYC, 1969-70; asst. prof. law SUNY at Buffalo, 1970-73; assoc. prof. law Howard U., 1973-77; vis. assoc. prof. Ohio State U., Columbus, 1977-78; asst. regional counsel U.S. EPA, 1978-80; prof. law So. U., Baton Rouge, 1980—; sole practice law Chgo. and Washington, 1984—. Arbitrator steel industry, 1972, US Postal Svc., New Orleans, DC Superior Ct., 1987—, Fed. Mediation and Conciliation Svc., 1985—, NY Stock Exch.; vis. prof. law La. State U., 1981, NC Cen. U., Durham, 1988—, So. U., Baton Rouge, spring 1992; real estate broker; mem. bd. consumer claims Dist. DC, 1988—; mem. Mayor's Transition Task Force, Washington, 1995; moot ct. judge Georgetown U. Law Sch., Washington, 1987—, Howard U. Law Sch., Washington, 1987—, Balsa, 1987—; spkr. in field. Author: Discrimination in Public Employment, 1975, (essay) Roosevelt University, Memories of the First 60 Years, 2006; editor Nat. Bar Assn. Arbitration Section newsletter. 1997—; contbr. articles to profl. jours. Active Ams. for Dem. Action; adv. com. DC Bd. Edn. Named one of Top 42 Lawyers in Washington Area, Washington Afro-Am. Newspaper, 1993-96; Ford Found. scholar, 1965-67. Columbia U., 1972-73, NEH Postdoctoral fellow in Afro-Am. studies Yale U., 1972-73. Mem. ABA (vice-chmn. edn. and curriculum com. local govt. law sect. 1972-80, pub. edn. com. sect. local govt. 1974-84, chmn. liaison com. AALS, 1984, chair arbitration sect., editor arbitration sect. newsletter 1997-), Nat. Bar Assn. (labor and employment law sect., steering com.), DC Bar Assn., Washington Bar Assn. (chmn. legal edn. com.), Chgo. Bar Assn., Fed. Bar Assn., Cook County Bar Assn., Am. Arbitration Assn. (arbitrator), DC Fee Arbitration Bd. (bd. govs. 1990—), Nat. Conf. Black Lawyers (bd. organizers), Nat. Futures Assn. (arbitrator), Nat. Assn. Securities Dealers (arbitrator), Assn. Henri Capitant, Roosevelt U. Alumni Assn. (rep. at George Washington U. 175th anniversary charter day convocation 1996), Loyola U. Alumni Assn. (v.p. Washington), Howard U. Alumni Assn. (rep. at Hunter Coll. Centennial 1970), Columbia U. Alumni Assn. (v.p. law Washington), Alpha Phi Alpha (life), Phi Alpha Kappa, Phi Alpha Delta. Home: 4315 Argyle Ter NW Washington DC 20011-4243 Office: 601 Pennsylvania Ave NW Ste 900 Washington DC 20004-3615 also: 10 S Riversie Plz Ste 1800 Chicago IL 60606 Office Phone: 202-434-8210. *I have always tried to do my best and never give in to obstacles. I have also been blessed with wonderful parents, relatives, friends, teachers and mentors who had confidence in me.*

DONEGAN, MARK, metal products executive; Pres., airfoil divsn. Precision Castparts Corp., pres., structural divsn., pres., Wyman-Gordon, 1999, pres., COO Portland, Oreg., 1999—2002, pres., CEO, dir., 2002—03, chmn., CEO, 2003—. Office: Precision Castparts Corp 4650 SW Macadam Ave Ste 440 Portland OR 97239-4262*

DONELAN, MARK ANTHONY, physicist; b. Grenada, West Indies, Mar. 27, 1942; came to Can., 1960, naturalized, 1969; s. William Gregory and Ivy (Payne) D.; B.Engring., McGill U., 1964; Ph.D., U. B.C., 1970; m. June Lynch, June 10, 1967; children: Laura, Maxwell. Project engr. Procter & Gamble Can., Hamilton, Ont., 1964-66; Killam postdoctoral fellow Cambridge (Eng.) U., 1970-71; rsch. scientist Environ. Can., Burlington, Ont., 1971-96; prof. Rosenstiel Sch. Marine and Atmospheric Sci. U. Miami, 1996—; asso. prof. civil engring. McMaster U., Hamilton, Ont., 1979-85, prof. civil engring., 1985-93; adj. prof. Waterloo (Ont.) U., 1979—, Laval U., Que., 1990-94, U. Miami, Fla., 1992-96; emeritus scientist Environ. Can., Burlington, Ont., 1997—. Humboldt research fellow Max-Planck-Institut für Meteorologie, Germany, 1984. Fellow Am. Meteorol. Soc. (Sverdrup Gold medal 1994), Royal Soc. Can.; mem. AAAS, Can. Meteorol. and Oceanographic Soc., Am. Geophys. Union, The Oceanography Soc. Office: U Miami Rosenstiel Sch Marine/Sci 4600 Rickenbacker Cswy Miami FL 33149-1031

DONELSON, JOHN EVERETT, biochemistry professor, molecular biologist; b. Ogden, Iowa, May 23, 1943; s. Mervin E. and Christine (James) D.; m. Linda Meyers, Sept. 16, 1966; children: Christina, Loren, Lyn, Emory. BS, Iowa State U., 1965; PhD, Cornell U., 1971. Postdoctoral fellow MRC Lab. Molecular biology, Cambridge, Eng., 1971-74, Stanford (Calif.) U., 1974; from asst. prof., assoc. prof. to prof. biochemistry U. Iowa, Iowa City, 1975-89, Disting. prof. biochemistry, 1989—, chmn. dept. biochemistry, 1998—; investigator Howard Hughes Med. Ctr. Howard Hughes Med. Inst., Iowa City, 1989-97. Contbr. numerous articles to profl. jours., sci. mags. Vol. Am. Peace Corps, Dormaa, Ghana, 1965-67. Recipient Molecular Parasitology award Burroughs-Wellcome Found., N.C., 1983, Medal of Sci. Achievement award Iowa Gov., 1990. Office: U Iowa Dept Biochemistry Iowa City IA 52242

DONELY, GEORGE ANTHONY THOMAS, III, retired economist; b. New Orleans, Aug. 14, 1934; s. George A.T. and Valerie Clare (Burmaster) D.; m. Lisa Suzanne Young, June 30, 1963; 1 child, Valerie Jennie Young. AB in Econs. cum laude, Williams Coll., 1956; MA in Econs., Columbia U., 1958; PhD, U. Mashad, Iran, 1967. Economist Lionel D. Edie & Co., NYC, 1959-60; instr. La. State U., New Orleans, 1960-61; joined Fgn. Svc., Dept. State, 1961-69; economist IMF, Washington, 1969-91; mng. dir. sr. vol. program St. Mary's County, Md., 2000—05, ret., 2005. Cons. Miss Lisa's Sugarless Foods, Inc., Washington, 1985-92. Contbr. articles to profl. jours. Mem. steering com. Friends of Music at Smithsonian, Washington, 1972—; vol. Md. Hist. Trust, Annapolis, 1982—85; mem. restoration adv. bd. Patuxent River NAS; bd. dirs., treas. Chamber Orch. So. Med., 1998—2000; bd. dirs. St. Mary's County Arts Coun., 2002—. Ford Found. fellow Columbia U., 1958. Mem. Am. Econ. Assn., Econ. History Assn., Round Table, St. Mary's River Yacht Club, Met. Club, Williams Club, Rotary (Paul Harris fellow). Home: St Richard's Manor 22880 Old Manor Ln Lexington Park MD 20653-2146 also: Résidence Panorama Rte Du Village CH 1884 Villars sur Ollon Switzerland Business E-Mail: george_columbia@hotmail.com.

DONENFELD, KENNETH JAY, management consultant; b. Nov. 2, 1946; s. Israel James and Anne (Puretz) D.; m. Sharon Etta Kamer, June 23, 1968; children: Elissa Meredith, Jonathan Lloyd. BA, CUNY, 1967; MA, Syracuse U., 1968; postgrad., N.Y. Inst. Fin., 1971. Mgmt. cons. Georgeson & Co., NYC, 1969-79; exec. v.p., dir. investor rels. divsn. Robert Marston and Assocs., NYC, 1979-89; pres. Robert Marston Investor Rels., Inc., NYC, 1988; exec. v.p. D.F. King and Co., Inc., NYC, 1989-91; pres. The Donenfeld Group, Inc., NYC, 1991—, DGI Investor Rels., Inc., NYC, 1996—. N.Y. State Regents scholar, 1963-67. Merm. Nat. Investor Rels. Inst. (adv. bd. IR mag.), N.Y. Assn. for Internat. Investment, Swedish C. of C., N.Y. Soc. Security Analysts, Media Club. Republican. Home: 15 Maplewood Dr Northport NY 11768-3431 Personal E-mail: donfgroup@aol.com. Business E-Mail: kdonenfeld@dgiir.com.

DONES, DARVIS DARELL, government agency administrator; s. Charles Darvis Dones and Johnnie Katheryn Lewis. Degree, Prairieview A&M U., Tex., 1981, MS in Counseling Psychology, 1983; MEd in Applied Psychology, U. Va., Charlottesville, 2004; postgrad. in Microbiology, George Mason U., Fairfax, Va., 2007—. Spl. agt. FBI Field Divsn., Mobile, Ala., 1988—92, FBI Newark Field, 1992—96; supervisory spl. agt. sensitive ops. unit FBI Acad., Washington, 1996—97, supervisory spl. agt. undercover safeguard unit, 1997—2002, supervisory spl. agt. investigative tng. unit Quantico, Va., 2002—04, supervisory spl. agt. behavioral sci. unit, 2004—. Adjunct prof. U. Va. (FBI Acad.), 2007—. Capt. US Army, 1983—87. Mem.: ACA, Am. Legion, Phi Beta Sigma. Avocations: scuba diving, running, jet skiing, community service, travel. Office: FBI Hoover Rd Quantico VA 22195

DONFRIED, KARL PAUL, theologian, clergyman; b. NYC, Apr. 6, 1940; s. Paul and Else (Schmuck) D.; m. Katharine E. Krayer, Sept. 10, 1960; children: Paul Andrew, Karen Erika, Mark Christopher. AB, Columbia U., 1960; BD, Harvard U., 1963; STM, Union Theol. Sem., 1965; ThD, U. Heidelberg, Germany, 1968. Ordained to ministry Lutheran Ch. in Am., 1963; named ecumenical canon Christ Ch. Cathedral, Springfield, Mass., 1977. Assoc. pastor ch., NYC, 1963-64; acting Luth. chaplain (Columbia U.), 1963-64; mem. faculty Smith Coll., Northampton, Mass., 1968—, prof. New Testament and early Christianity, 1968—2000, chmn. dept. religion, 1980-83, 97-00, dir. ancient studies, 1994-95, Elizabeth A. Woodson prof. religion and bibl. lit., 2000—05, Elizabeth A. Woodson prof. emeritus religion and bibl. lit., 2005—; Joseph Gregory McCarthy prof. Pontifical Bibl. Inst., Rome, 2006. Mem. New Testament panel Nat. Luth.-Roman Cath. dialogue 1971-73, 75-78, vis. prof. Assumption Coll., Worcester, Mass., 1975, Amherst Coll., 1976, 78, 85, 2002, St. Hyacinth Coll. and Sem., Granby, Mass., 1976, Brown U., 1979, Mt. Holyoke Coll., 1983, U. Hamburg, 1985, Yale U. Div. Sch., New Haven, 1993, U. Geneva, 2001; Fulbright vis. prof. Hebrew U., Jerusalem, 1997; guest chaplain Ho. of Reps., 1999; Fulbright vis. prof. Freie U. Berlin, 2004, Humboldt U. Berlin, 2004; pres. Colloquium Oecumenicum Paulinum, Benedictine Abbey St. Paul, 2006. Author: (with R.E. Brown, J. Reumann) Peter in the New Testament, 1973, The Setting of Second Clement in Early Christianity, 1974, (with others) Mary in the New Testament, 1978, The Dynamic Word, 1981; editor: The Romans Debate, 1977, The Romans Debate: New and Expanded Edition, 1991, (with I.H. Marshall) The Shorter Pauline Epistles, 1993, (with Peter Richardson) Judaism and Christianity in First-Century Rome, 1998, (with Johannes Beutler) The Thessalonians Debate: Methodological Discord or Methodological Synthesis?, 2000, Paul, Thessalonica and Early Christianity, 2002, Who Owns the Bible? Toward the Recovery of a Christian Hermeneutic, 2006; mem. editl. bd. Jour. Bibl. Lit., 1975-81. Bd. dir. Am. Acad. Religion, 1971—73; pres. Harvard Club Heidelberg, 1966—68; mem. Ratzinger Conf. on Bible and Ch., NYC, 1988; fellow Orion Ctr. for Study of Dead Sea Scrolls and Associated Lit., 1997; official rep. of Evangelical Luterhan Ch. in Am. Joint Declaration on Justification, Augsburg, Germany, 1999. Mem. Am. Acad. Religion (dir. 1972-73, pres. New Eng. region 1971-72), Studiorum Novi Testamenti Societas (chmn. Paul seminar 1975-78, exec. com. 1979-83, chmn. New Testament Texts in Their Cultural Environment seminar 1990-94, chmn. Thessalonian Correspondence seminar 1995-2000), Soc. Bibl. Lit. (pres. New Eng. region 1975-76), Cath. Bibl. Assn. (participant internat. congresses scholars in Aberdeen, Basel, Bern, Bielefeld, Bonn, Cambridge, Canterbury, Copenhagen, Edinburgh, Einhoven, Göttingen, Heidelberg, Frankfurt, Jerusalem, Louvain, Milan, Montreal, Newcastle, Oxford, Prague, Rome, Sigtuna, Strasbourg, Toronto, Tubingen). Office: Smith Coll Dept Religion Northampton MA 01063-0001 Business E-Mail: kdonfrie@smith.edu. *As the son of immigrant parents, I learned early the value of hard and honest work, the necessity for integrity in all human relations and the blessings of generosity to those less fortunate. These values, together with my commitment to Christianity, have shaped, and continue to shape, my life.*

DONG, KUI, music educator, composer; d. Naixing Dong and Jiaxin Sun; m. Duo Huang, June 1990. BA, Ctrl. Conservatory of Music, Beijing, China, 1983—87; MA, Ctrl. Conservatory of Music, 1988—89; MusD, Stanford U., 1991—97. Prof. of music Dartmouth Coll., Hanover, NH, 1997—. Composer: The Blue Melody (1st prize Alea III Internat. Composition Competition for Chamber Music, 1994), (3-act ballet) Imperial Concubine Young (Commd. by Ctrl. Ballet Group of China, 1988), Flying Apples (Hon. mention, Prix Ars Electronica Internat. competitions for Computer Music and Art, Linz, Austria, 1996), Pangu's Song (League of Composers/Internat. Soc. of Contemporary Music Internat. composition competition, 2001), Three Voices (Internat. Music Competitions of the Val Tidone, Italy, 1999), Shui Tiao Ge To (Dale Warland Singers New Chorus Music Competition, 2000), Four Image Songs (The Nat. Ann. Collegiate Art Song Competition, first prize, Beijing, China, 1990), Three Piano Pieces (3d prize 1st Nat. Piano Works Competition, 84), Zhan Jing Tang (The Third Nat. Dance & Music Competition, First Music award, Beijing, China, 1989). Recipient Commissioning Award, Koussevitsky Music Found. & Libr. of Congress, 2001, Commissioning award, Mary Cary Flagler Trust Fund, 1999, Commissioning Program Award, Meet The Composer/USA, 1997, ASCAP Award for Young Composers, the Am. Soc. of Composers, Authors and Publishers., 1995; fellow Fellowship for Composers, Santa Clara Art Coun., 1995, Composer Resident Program, Djaressi Found., Bellagio Artist Residency Program, Rockefeller Found., 2000, Gerald Oshita Stipend Fellowship, Djaressi Found., 1995; grantee Rsch. Grant, Asia-Pacific Ednl. Rsch. Grant, Md., ME, 1993, Dickey Ctr. for Internat. Understanding, Dartmouth Coll., Dickey Fundation, 1998, Short-term Travel grant, Internat. Rsch. & Exch. Bd., 2000. Office: Music Dept Dartmouth Coll 6187 Hopkins Ctr Hanover NH 03755 E-mail: kui.dong@dartmouth.edu.

DONG, MICHAEL HON, toxicologist; b. Hong Kong, China, Dec. 17, 1948; arrived in U.S., 1963; adopted s. Henry and L-G Dong; m. Ivy Tze-Wah To, Apr. 15, 1977; children: Jennifer Ivy, Stephanie Michelle. BSc, U. Calif. Riverside, 1972; MPH, UCLA, 1973; BSc, Calif. State U., Sacramento, 1976; D in Pub. Adminstrn., U. So. Calif., 1981; PhD in Pub. Health, U. Pitts., 1984. Diplomate Am. Bd. Toxicology, NC, 1999; cert. nutrition specialist Am. Coll. Nutrition, Fla., 1994. Commd. officer US Army Med. Svc. Corps, San Francisco, 1977—80, Fort Gordon, Ga., 1980—81; rsch. asst. U. Pitts., 1981—84; occupl. toxicologist, epidemiologist US Occupl. Health and Safety Adminstrn., Washington, 1985; lt. comdr. US FDA, Rockville, Md., 1986—89; staff toxicologist Calif. Dept. Pesticide Regulation, Sacramento, 1989—. Lectr. in field. Assoc. editor: Jour. Environ. Geochemistry and Health, 2005—. Mem.: Am. Bd. Toxicology (bd. dirs. 2005—), Am. Soc. Toxicology. Office: Calif Dept Pesticide Regulation 1001 I St Sacramento CA 95812 Office Phone: 916-445-4263. Business E-Mail: mdong@cdpr.ca.gov.

DONG, NELSON G., lawyer; b. 1949; AB, Stanford U., 1971; JD, Yale U., 1974. Bar: Calif. 1974, Minn. 1992. Ptnr., corp. dept, chair, Asian dept. Dorsey & Whitney LLP, Seattle. Legal counsel IEEE. Bd. trustees Stanford U., 1978—82; bd. dir. Com. 100, NYC, 1998—, gen. counsel, sec., 1999—2003; bd. dir. White House Fellows Assn., 2004—06. Grantee White House Fellow, 1978—79. Mem.: Asian Am. Bar Assn. (secy. 1984, bd. mem. 1985). Office: Dorsey & Whitney LLP Ste 3400 US Bank Ctr 1420 Fifth Ave Seattle WA 98101-4010 Office Phone: 206-903-8871. Office Fax: 206-903-8820. Business E-Mail: dong.nelson@dorsey.com.

DONGHI, TULIO HALPERIN, history professor; b. Buenos Aires, 1926; Ed., U. Turin, Ecole Practique des Hautes Etudes de Paris; PhD, U. Buenos Aires, 1955; doctor honoris causa (hon.), Universidad Nacional de Luján, 1992, Universidad Nacional de Córdoba, 1993. Prof. faculty philosophy and letters U. Buenos Aires, 1955—66; prof. faculty humanities U. Nat. Litoral, dean faculty humanities; prof. Cambridge U., Universidad de la Republica, Montevideo, Harvard U., Oxford U., 1966—71; prof. Dept. History U. Calif., Berkeley, 1971—94, Muriel McKevitt Sonne prof. Latin American history, emeritus. Author: The Contemporary History of Latin America, 1967. Named profesor-ad-honorem, Universidad de la Republica, Montevideo, Alfonso Casos Chair, Nacional Autonoma de Mexico City; recipient Clarence Haring prize, Am. Historical Assn., 1976, Disting. Svc. award, Conf. Latin Am. History, 1994, University Medal, U. Santiago, Chile. Fellow: Am. Acad. Arts and Sciences. Office: Dept History Univ Calif Berkeley 3321 Dwinelle Berkeley CA 94720 Office Phone: 510-642-1971. Office Fax: 510-642-9850. E-mail: halperin@socrates.berkeley.edu.

DONILON, THOMAS E., lawyer, former federal agency administrator; b. Providence, May 14, 1955; m. Catherine Russell, Dec. 14, 1991. BA summa cum laude, Cath. U., 1977; JD, U. Va., 1985. Bar: D.C. With Office Congl. Liaison The White House, 1977-79; nat. del. selection coord., nat. conv. dir. Carter-Mondale Presdl. Campaign, 1979-80; lectr. politics Cath. U. Am., 1981; nat. campaign coord. Mondale for Pres. Campaign, 1983-84; assoc. O'Melveny & Myers LLP, Washington, 1985-92, ptnr., 1992-93; asst. sec. pub. affairs US Dept. State, Washington, 1993—96, chief of staff to sec., 1994-99; sr. v.p., gen. counsel Fannie Mae, Washington, 1999—2005, mem. Office Chmn., 2003—05; ptnr. O'Melveny & Myers LLP, Washington, 2005—. Cons. CBS News, 1988; presdl. debate coord. Clinton-Gore Presdl. Campaign, 1992; mem. Clinton-Gore Presdl. Transition Team, 1992-93. Mem. editorial bd. U. Va. Law Rev., 1982-83. Recipient Disting. Svc. award, US Dept. State, 1996. Mem. ABA, Coun. on Fgn. Rels., Phi Beta Kappa., Aspen Strategy Group, Miller Ctr. Pub. Affairs Governing Coun., US Dept. Justice Competition Adv. Com., 1997-2000; bd. trustees Brookings Instn., US C. of C. Office: O'Melveny & Myers LLP 1625 Eye St NW Washington DC 20006 E-mail: tdonilon@omm.com.*

DONKERVOET, RICHARD CORNELIUS, architect; b. Detroit, Oct. 8, 1930; s. Cornelius and Anna Eva Hendrika (Boer) D.; m. Carolyn Eugenia Moore, May 4, 1957; children: Carolyn Daralice Donkervoet Boles, Sharon Elisabeth Donkervoet Credit, John Cornelius. BArch, U. Mich., 1952; MArch, MIT, 1953. Fulbright fellow Tech. U., Delft, Holland, 1954-55; arch. Cochran, Stephenson & Wing, Balt., 1957-63; ptnr. Cochran, Stephenson & Donkervoet, Inc., Balt., 1963-68, exec. v.p., 1968-83, pres., 1983-96, chmn., 1996—. Trustee Roland Park Country Sch., Balt., 1968-75, Balt. Mus. Art, 1970—; pres. bd. trustees Westminster House, Balt., 1975—; pres. bd. dirs. Citizens League Balt., 1980-82. With U.S. Army, 1956-58. Fellow AIA (pres. Balt. chpt., treas. 1966, bd. dirs. 1973, Disting. Svc. awards 1977, 99); mem. Hamilton St. Club (mem. steering com. 1983-88). Avocations: reading, travel, tennis. Home: 13801 York Rd Unit M-12 Cockeysville Hunt Valley MD 21030- Office: C S & D Inc 323 W Camden St Ste 700 Baltimore MD 21201-8601 Home Phone: 410-584-8233; Office Phone: 410-539-2080. E-mail: csd@csdarch.com.

DONLEAVY, JAMES PATRICK, writer, artist; b. Bklyn., Apr. 23, 1926; m. Valerie Heron (div.); children: Philip, Karen; m. Mary Wilson Price (div.); children: Rebecca, Rory. Student, Trinity Coll., Dublin, Ireland. Author: novel, later adapted as play The Ginger Man, 1955; drama Fairy Tales of New York, 1960; A Singular Man novel, later adapted as play, 1963, Meet My Maker the Mad Molecule, short stories, sketches, 1964, The Saddest Summer of Samuel S, novella, later adapted as play, 1966, The Beastly Beatitudes of Balthazar B, novel, later adapted as play, 1968, The Onion Eaters, 1971, The Plays of J.P. Donleavy, 1972; novel A Fairy Tale of New York, 1973; The Unexpurgated Code, A Complete Manual of Survival and Manners, 1975, The Destinies of Darcy Dancer, Gentleman, 1977; novel Schultz, 1979, Leila, 1983, Are You Listening Rabbi Löw, 1987; De Alfonce Tennis, The Superlative Game of Eccentric Champions: Its History, Accoutrements, Rules, Conduct and Regimen, 1984, J.P. Donleavy's Ireland: In All Her Sins and in Some of Her Graces, 1986 (Gold award Worldfest Houston 1993, Cine Golden Eagle award), A Singular Country, 1989, That Darcy, That Dancer, That Gentleman, 1990, The History of The Ginger Man, 1994, Wrong Information is Being Given Out at Pinceton, 1998, (novella) The Lady Who Liked Clean Rest Rooms, 1996, An Author and His Image, 1997, (novella) The Dog On the Seventeenth Floor, 2007; contbr. to numerous mags. and jours. including Times of London, NY Times, Washington Post, Atlantic Monthly, The Daily Telegraph, The New Yorker, Rolling Stone, others; art exhbns. include: Painter's Gallery, St. Stephen's Green, Dublin, 1950, 51, Bronxville, N.Y., 1959, Langton Galleries, London, 1975, Godolphin Gallery, Dublin, 1986, Caldwell Galleries, Belfast, 1987, Anna Mei Chadwick Gallery, London, 1989, 91, 94, Alba Fine Art Gallery, London, 1991, Front Lounge Gallery, 1995, Walton Gallery, London, 2002, Molesworth Gallery, Dublin, 2006. Served with USNR, WWII. Recipient Creative Arts award Brandeis U., 1961-62; AAAL grantee, 1975. Home: Levington Park Mullingar County Westmeath Ireland

DONLEVY, JOHN DEARDEN, lawyer; b. Chgo., May 29, 1933; s. Frank and Alice Genevieve (O'Connor) D.; m. Kristin Bach Minnick, Apr. 20, 1963 (div. Sept. 1985); 1 son, John Dearden. Student, Stanford U., 1950-52; BS, Northwestern U., 1954; JD, U. Chgo., 1957; postgrad., Northwestern U., 1958. Bar: Ill. 1957, US Dist. Ct. (no. dist.) Ill. 1957, US Ct. Appeals (7th cir.) 1969, US Supreme Ct. 1972. Asst. state's atty. Cook County Criminal Divsn., Chgo., 1958-61; city prosecutor City of Evanston, Ill., 1961; assoc. Mayer, Brown & Platt, Chgo., 1962-73, ptnr., 1973-90; pvt. practice law Chgo., 1990—. Participant Hinton Moot Ct. Competition U. Chgo., 1955-56, judge, 1972. Contbr. articles to profl. pubs. Active Rep. Orgn., 1958—60; bd. dirs. English-Speaking Union, Chgo., 1964—65. Recipient Disting. Legal award Am. Legion, Chgo., 1960; named spl. prosecutor-labor racketeering Cook County State's Atty., Chgo., 1959-61; profiled in Lindberg "Summerdale--35 Year Anniversary", 1995. Mem. ABA, Ill. Bar Assn., Chgo. Bar Assn. (criminal law com., sr. trial atty. of Defense of Prisoners com., chair Def. of Prisoners com., mem. nom. com. for slating of officers and dir. 1994-94, chair criminal law and in-court criminal def. panels), Fed. Trial Bar, Chgo. Athletic Assn. Office: Ste 2040 30 N La Salle St Chicago IL 60602-2506 Office Phone: 312-201-0227. Office Fax: 312-236-6906. Business E-Mail: jdonlevy@core.com. *I always try to examine problems carefully to obtain a good understanding of them, as with understanding, nothing in life need be feared.*

DONLEY, DOUGLAS E., retail executive; Auditor KPMG Peat Marwick, 1992—94; internal auditor Harsco Corp., 1994—96; fin. analyst to dir. fin. analysis, asst. contr. Rite Aid Corp., Camp Hill, Pa., 1996—99, v.p., corp. contr., 1999—2000, group v.p., corp. contr., 2000—05, sr. v.p., chief acctg. officer, 2005—. Office: Rite Aid Corp 30 Hunter Ln Camp Hill PA 17011 Office Phone: 717-761-2633.*

DONLEY, JAMES WALTON, management consultant; b. Cleve., June 27, 1934; s. Howard Russell and Mary Louise (Mullikin) D.; m. Frances Elizabeth Jordan, July 5, 1963 (div. Oct. 1983); children: Dana, Elizabeth; m. Mary Todd Mann Goodspeed, May 25, 1985; children: Bennett, Mary Todd, Emily, Jonathan Goodspeed. BA, Denison U., 1958; MBA, U. Pa., 1960. Asst. to pub. Time Mag., NYC, 1960-67; sr. v.p. Thomas J. Deegan Co., NYC, 1967-71; asst. commr. N.Y.C. Dept. Commerce, 1971-72; asst. sec. U.S. Dept. Treasury, Wash., 1972-74; chmn. Donley Comm., NYC, 1974—; country dir. Bulgaria Internat. Exec. Svc. Corps, Sofia, 1995—2003. Mem. bd. advisors Internat. Exec. Svc. Corps, Stamford, Conn., TechnoServe, Inc., Washington. With U.S. Army, 1954-56, Germany. Mem.: St. Andrews Club, Round Hill Club, Belle Haven Club. Republican. Congregationalist. Home: 609 West Lyon Farm Greenwich CT 06831-3824 Personal E-mail: james_w_donley@hotmail.com.

DONLEY, RUSSELL LEE, III, small business owner, former state legislator; b. Salt Lake City, Feb. 3, 1939; s. Lee and Leona (Sherwood) Donley; m. Karen Kocherhans, June 4, 1960; children: Tammera Sue, Tonya Kay, Christina Lynn. BSCE with honors, U. Wyo., 1961; MS in Engring., U. Fla., 1962. From mem. to spkr. of house Wyo. Ho. of Reps., 1969-84; chmn. bd. Nat. Ctr. Constl. Studies, Wyo. region, 1983-87; CEO Constitution Schs. Inc., Casper, 1987—; owner Russell L. Donley & Assocs., 1988—2005. Chmn. appropriations com. Wyo. Ho. of Reps., 1975—78, chmn. legis. mgmt. coun., 1983—84. Pres. bd. dirs. YMCA, Casper, 1976—77; chmn. western region Coun. State Govts., 1982—83; Rep. candidate for Gov. Wyo., 1986; precinct committeeman Rep. Ctrl. Com., 1987—96, 2006—; chmn. Wyo. Young Reps., 1968; fin. chmn. Natrona County Rep. Ctrl. Com., 1970; state chmn. Initiative 3 dr. Invest in Wyo. not Wall St., 1994; missionary LDS Ch., 2005—06. Named Wyo. Outstanding Young Engr., Sigma Tau, 1974, Disting. Wyo. Engr., Tau Beta Pi, 1976; recipient award for engring. excellence, Am. Cons. Engrs. Coun., Legislator of the Yr. award, Nat. Rep. Legislators Assn., 1981. Republican. Mem. Lds Ch. Personal E-mail: russ-rlda@bresnan.net.

DONLON, CLAUDETTE, performing company executive; Gen. mgr. Am. Ballet Theatre, finance dir.; exec. v.p. Kennedy Center for the Performing Arts. Office: Kennedy Center for the Performing Arts 2700 F St NW Washington DC 20566

DONLON, JAMES D., III, controller, corporate financial executive; b. Seattle, Wash., Oct. 1, 1946; BSc in bus. adminstrn., Calif. State U., 1968; MBA, U. So. Calif., 1969. Mgr., investment analysis Chrysler Corp., 1979; dir., internat. planning and new venture develop. Chrysler Motor Internat. Ops., 1989—90; v.p., fin. controls Chrysler Fin., 1990—92; corp. contr. Chrysler Corp., 1992—94, v.p., contr., 1994—98; sr. v.p., corp. controlling and acctg. Daimler Chrysler, Stuggart, Germany, 1998—2000, sr. v.p., contr., 2000—03; sr. v.p., CFO Kmart Corp., 2003—05, ArvinMeritor Inc., Troy, Mich., 2005—. Office: ArvinMeritor Inc 2135 W Maple Rd Troy MI 48084*

DONLON, WILLIAM JAMES, retired lawyer; b. Colorado Springs, Colo., Apr. 22, 1924; s. John Andrew and Kathleen M. D; m. Josephine A. Janssen, July 19, 1946; children: William James, Gregory A., Michele, Dru Ann Gazelle. Student, Colo. Coll., 1941-43; BS, U. Denver, 1949, JD, 1950. Bar: Colo. 1950, Ohio 1964, Ill. 1969, US Dist. Ct. Colo. 1956, US Dist. Ct. (no. dist.) Ill. 1974, US Ct. Appeals (10th cir.) 1957, US Ct. Appeals (5th cir.) 1970, US Ct. Appeals (7th cir.) 1974, US Ct. Appeals DC 1979, US Supreme Ct. 1965. Dep. clk. Dist. Ct., Denver, 1949-50; pvt. practice Denver, 1953-63; gen. counsel Brotherhood Ry. Airline & S.S. Clks., Freight Handlers, Express & Sta. Empl., Rosemont, Ill., 1963-84, Rockville, Md., 1963-86; ret., 1985. Instr. labor U. Ill., 1972-78. With USAAF, 1942-45. Decorated Air medal with 2 oak leaf clusters; named Ky. Col. Mem. ABA (coun. sect. labor and employment law 1977-86, co-chmn. railroad and airline com., 1974-76, co-chmn. equl employment com.,

1976-77), Ill. Bar Assn., DC Bar Assn., Am. Legion, VFW, KC (Grand Knight coun. 10329, 1991-93, 2005-06), 34th Bomb Group Assn., Phi Alpha Delta, Phi Delta Theta. Democrat. Roman Catholic. E-mail: donlonw@aol.com.

DONNALLY, PATRICIA BRODERICK, writer; b. Cheverly, Md., Mar. 11, 1955; d. James Duane and Olga Frances (Duenas) Broderick; m. Robert Andrew Donnally, Dec. 30, 1977; 1 child, Danielle Christine. BS, U. Md., 1977. Fashion editor The Washington Times, 1983-85, The San Francisco Chronicle, 1985-2000; sr. fashion and beauty editor eLuxury.com, 2000; mng. editor PaperCity mag., 2002—04; co-editor Washington Spaces mag., 2004—05, editor-in-chief, 2005—. Recipient Atrium award U. Ga., 1984, 87-89, 90, 94-98, 99, Lulu award U. Ga., 1985, 87, award Am. Cancer Soc., 1991, Aldo award, U. Ga., 1994, George A. Hough III award, U. Ga., 1999. Avocation: travel. Office Phone: 703-992-1196. Business E-Mail: tdonnally@washingtonspaces.com.

DONNALLY, ROBERT ANDREW, lawyer; b. Washington, July 10, 1953; s. Reaumur Stearnes and Katherine Ann (Sutliff) D.; m. Patricia Kane Broderick, Dec. 30, 1977; 1 child, Danielle Christine BA Psychology, U. Md., 1976; JD, U. Balt., 1980; cert. in bus., Stanford U., Calif., 1996. Bar: Md. 1980, Calif. 1986. Pvt. practice, Oxen Hill, Md., 1980—81; rsch. contract staff officer Dept. Def., Ft. Meade, Md., 1981—85; asst. dir. Inst. Def. Analyses, San Diego, 1990—91; with legal and contractual ops. ARGOSys., Inc., Sunnyvale, Calif., 1985—90, dep. chief counsel, 1991—93, chief counsel, corp. sec., 1993—98; chief counsel comm. and info-mgmt. divsn. Boeing Co., 1997—98; gen. counsel, mng. ptnr. BT Comml. Real Estate, Palo Alto, Calif., 1998—99; assoc. gen. counsel Inhale Therapeutic Sys. Inc., San Carlos, Calif., 1999—2003; mng. dir. rsch. svcs. and ops. George Washington U., 2004—. Editor-in-chief The Forum, 1979-80 Active The Pillars Soc./United Way, 1991-98 Waxter Legal scholar U. Balt., 1978 Mem. Am. Corp. Counsel, Nat. Contract Mgmt. Assn., Md. Bar Assn., Calif. Bar Assn., Assn. Silicon Valley Brokers, Tae Kwon Do Assn. (Black Belt Kukkiwon World), KC Avocations: martial arts, marathons and triathlons, hiking, travel, reading. Home: 14720 Georgia Ave Rockville MD 20852 E-mail: robertdonnally@hotmail.com.

DONNANGELO, DAVID MICHAEL, artist; s. Frank and Marie Donnangelo. BA, Moravian Coll., Bethlehem, Pa., 2003. Artist, curator Gallery Enterprises, Bethlehem, 1980—95, Contemporary Fine Art, Bethlehem, 1995—2005; artist Wegmans Co., Bethlehem, 2002—. Represented in permanent collections Lehigh U. Newman Ctr., Holy Family Manor, Allentown, Pa., others. Mem. govs. prayer team, Pa., 2006—; state coord Eagles Wings Ministries, NY, 2005—. Scholar, Bucknell U., Lewisburg, Pa. Mem.: Zeta Psi, Alpha Sigma Lambda. Home: 1881 Abington Rd Bethlehem PA 18018

DONNELL, CAROLYN FAYE, music educator; b. Dallas, Tex., Dec. 31, 1949; d. Theodore Sr. and Lena Mae Roberts; m. Larry Donnell, July 6, 1974; children: Larry, Chimeka, Carlena, Lanard. BS in Music, Tex. So. U., Houston, 1976; BS in Secondary Math., U. Tex., Dallas, 1986. Cert. tchr. music all levels Tex. Tchr. music Zumwalt Mid. Sch., Dallas, 1975—76, Boude Storey Mid. Sch., 1976—85, Umphrey Lee Elem. Sch., 1985—. Workshop coord. St. Paul Ch., Dallas, 2001—02. Named Tchr. of Yr., Umphrey Lee Elem. Sch., 1996—97, K104 Tchr. of Yr., Dallas, 2001—03. Mem.: Delta Sigma Theta. Office: Umphrey Lee Elem Sch 7808 Racine Dr Dallas TX 75232-4302

DONNELL, HAROLD EUGENE, JR., retired professional society administrator; b. Balt., Mar. 12, 1935; s. Harold Eugene and Ruth Elizabeth (Meeth) D.; m. Rosemary Gatch, Apr. 25, 1959; children— David Crawford, Laurette Butler. BA, Amherst Coll., 1957. Field asst., agt. Equitable Life Assurance Soc., Balt., 1958-61; salesman Eastern Products Corp., Balt., 1961-64, asst. nat. sales mgr., 1964-66; exec. dir. Md. State Dental Assn., Towson, 1966-74, Acad. Gen. Dentistry, Chgo., 1974—2003; ret. Trustee Am. Fund for Dental Health, 1976-84. Served with U.S. Army, 1957-58. Recipient Disting. Service award N.C. Acad. Gen. Dentistry, 1980; ann. Walter E. Levine Meritorious Service award Alpha Omega, 1970, 93. Fellow Acad. Gen. Denistry (hon.); mem. ADA, Am. Soc. Assn. Execs. (cert. assn. exec.), Assn. Forum, Acad. Gen. Dentistry (Albert Borish award 2003). Republican. Luth. *Any degree of success I have achieved in this life is a result of dedicatedly applying the talents I have been given or acquired with single minded drive to accomplish specific goals.*

DONNELL, WILLIAM RAY, small business owner, communications executive; b. Lewiston, Maine, Oct. 3, 1931; s. William Thomas and Gladys Mae (Spinney) Donnell; m. Mayra Cintia Colon, June 16, 1962 (div. Jan. 1996); children: William Thomas, Jose Ismael, Ariadne Elizabeth. BA, U. Maine, 1959. Comml. capt. lic. Comml. fisherman, Maine, 1948-52, 55-60; tchr. Bath (Maine) Jr. HS, 1962, substitute tchr., 1963; tchr. Deer Isle (Maine) HS, 1965, 71, tchr. adult edn., 1976; tchr. St. Jude Integrated HS, St. Fintons, Nfld., Canada, 1972, Stonington (Maine) Elem. Sch., 1973; v.p., bd. dirs. Fisheries Comm., Inc., 1977—; owner, operator Donnell's Clapboard Mill, Sedgwick, Maine, 1983—. Recreational dir. City of Bath, 1963; capt. prin. comml. passenger schooner, 1965—71; remedial instr. Harpwell Islands Sch., Maine, 1965; farmer, Deer Isle, 1968—71, Deer Isle, 1972—78, Highlands, Nfld., 1971—72, Sedgwick, 1978—; lectr. in field; guest spkr. TV Can.-U.S. offshore boundary issue. Contbg. editor: Comml. Fisheries News, 1981—83; editor: Maine Comml. Fisheries, 1979—80, Fisheries Fed. Register Rev., 1981—82; author: numerous poems. Active Gov.'s Lobster Adv. Coun., Maine, 1980—85, Downeast Resource Conservation & Devel. Coun., 1994—, Sedgwick Budget Com., 1995—; co-chmn. Hancock County 4-H Citizenship Com., 1987—88; exec. com. Hancock County Extension, 1988—; moderator Sedgwick Town Meeting, 1993—94, 2002—; v.p. Brooklin Sedgwick Hist. Soc., 2000—02, 2004—05, hon. trustee, 2005—; candidate state legis. from Bath area Sagadahoc County, Maine, 1969; charter mem., bd. dirs. Maine Fishermen's Forum, Inc., 1985; lectr. discussion team Thelme's, Laguna Beach, Calif., 1985. Sgt. US Army, 1952—54, Korea. Decorated Bronze Star, Korean Svc. medal with 2 bronze stars, Combat Infantryman's Badge; recipient Poetry award, Nfld. and Labrador Arts and Letters Contest, 1972. Mem.: Sigma Chi (pres.). Avocations: antique vehicles, vessels and machinery. Home and Office: Donnells Clapboard Mill Box 205 County Rd Sedgwick ME 04676 Office Phone: 207-359-2036.

DONNELLEY, JAMES RUSSELL, printing company executive; b. Chgo., June 18, 1935; s. Elliott and Ann (Steinwedell) D.; m. Nina Louis Herrmann, Apr. 11, 1980; children: Niel J., Nicole C. BA, Dartmouth Coll., 1957; MBA, U. Chgo., 1962. With R.R. Donnelley & Sons Co., Chgo., 1962-2000, v.p., 1974-75, group pres. fin. svcs. group, 1985-87, group pres. corp. devel., 1987-90, vice chmn. bd., 1990-2000, also bd. dirs. Bd. dirs. Sierra Pacific Resources, PMP Inc., Melbourne, Australia. Office: Stet & Query LTD Partnership Ste 1009 360 N Michigan Ave Chicago IL 60601-3803 E-mail: james.donnelley@stetandquery.com.

DONNELLEY, STRACHAN, philosopher; b. Chgo., Mar. 22, 1942; s. Gaylord and Dorothy Ranney Donnelley; m. Vivian Hilst, Aug. 24, 1968; children: Inanna, Naomi, Aidan, Ceara, Tegan. BA, Yale U., 1964; MA, New Sch. for Social Rsch., 1972, PhD, 1977. Mem. faculty Valparaiso (Ind.) U., 1967—69, Seminar Coll., New Sch., NYC, 1978-85; dir. edn. Hastings Ctr., Garrison, NY, 1986-96, assoc. environ. ethics, 1989-96, pres., 1996-99, dir. humans and nature program, 1999—2002; pres. Ctr. for Humans and Nature, NYC, 2003—. Animal care and use com. Cornell Med. Sch., 1990-96; advisor Ctr. for Biodiversity, Am. Mus. Natural History, NYC, 1995—, Inst. Biospheric Studies, Yale U., 1995—. Editor spl. supplements Hastings Ctr. Report, 1990-98; contbr. articles to profl. jours. Trustee The Rehab. Inst. Chgo., 1983—, Hotchkiss Sch., Lakeville, Conn., 1988-98, Nat. Humanities Ctr., Raleigh, NC, 1993-2003, U. Chgo., 1994-2007, The Land Inst., Salina, Kans., 2005-, The New Sch., 1994—, Am. Mus. Natural History, 2005—; chmn. Gaylord and Dorothy Donnelley Found., Chgo., 1992-2003, vice chmn., 2003—. Recipient Pres.' award, Union Inst., 1999, Disting. Alumni award, New Sch., 2001, Disting. Svc. award, 2006. Mem. Am. Philos. Assn., World Conservation Union, Defenders of Wildlife, Nat. Wildlife Fedn. Democrat. Avocations: music, fly fishing, collecting. Home Phone: 212-799-8111; Office Phone: 212-362-7170. Business E-Mail: strachandonnelley@humansandnature.org.

DONNELLY, BARBARA SCHETTLER, retired medical technologist; b. Sweetwater, Tenn., Dec. 2, 1933; d. Clarence G. and Irene Elizabeth (Brown) Schettler; children: Linda Ann, Richard Michael. AA, Tenn. Wesleyan Coll., 1952; BS, U. Tenn., 1954; cert. med. tech., Erlanger Hosp. Sch. Med. Tech., 1954; postgrad., So. Meth. U., 1980-81. Med. technologist Erlanger Hosp., Chattanooga, 1953-57, St. Luke's Episcopal Hosp., Tex. Med. Ctr., Houston, 1957-58, 62; engring. R&D SCI Systems, Inc., Huntsville, Ala., 1974-76; cons. hematology systems Abbott Labs., Dallas, 1976-77; hematology specialist Dallas, Irving, Tex., 1977-81; tech. specialist microbiology systems Irving, Tex., 1981-83; coord. tech. svc. clin. chemistry systems, 1983-84; coord. customer tng. clin. chemistry systems, 1984-87; supr. clin. chemistry tech. svcs., 1987-88; supr. clin. chemistry customer support ctr., 1988-93; supr. clin. chemistry and x-systems customer support ctr., 1993-97; ret., 1997. Contbr. articles on cytology to profl. jours. Mem. Am. Soc. Clin. Pathologists (cert. med. technologist), Am. Soc. Microbiology, Nat. Assn. Female Execs., U. Tenn. Alumni Assn., Chi Omega. Republican. Methodist. Home: 204 Greenbriar Ln Colleyville TX 76034-8616

DONNELLY, GERARD KEVIN, marketing and retail executive; b. NYC, July 2, 1933; s. Joseph R. and Margaret M. (Siefert) D.; m. Maria McAllister, Aug. 29, 1964; children: Gerard K., Peter F., Deirdre A., Patrick J., James V. BBA in Acctg., Pace U., 1957; cert. in Indsl. Rels., Colgate U., 1966. Asst. contr. Allied Stores Corp., NYC, 1957-65; gen. auditor Lone Star Industries, NYC, 1965-67; contr., asst. sec. Computer Applications Inc., NYC, 1967-70; pres. Rhodes S.W., Phoenix, 1970-75; sr. v.p. Hart Schaffner & Marx, Chgo., 1975-81; CEO, chmn. bd. dirs. Hughes & Hatcher Inc., Phila., 1981-83; sr. v.p., dir. Macys-N.E. Inc., NYC, 1983-90; pres., CEO H.C. Prange Co., Green Bay, Wis., 1990-94; mng. cons. Houlihan, Lokey, Howard & Zukin, NYC, 1994—99; mng. dir. GeKayDee Assocs., 1994—. Bd. dirs. Frederick Atkins, Inc., N.Y.C., Younkers Inc., Des Moines, Mottahedeh & Co., N.Y.C., H.C. Prange Co., Green Bay, Saks, Inc., Birmingham, Ala. Mem. County Com., Queens County, N.Y., 1955-64; commr. pks. and recreation, Manalapan Twp., N.J., 1967-68; bd. dirs. Ctrl. Bus. Dist. Assn., Detroit, 1981-83, U. Wis. Green Bay Founders Assn., 1991-94. With USN, 1951-53. Mem.: Menswear Retailers Am., Internat. Coun. Shopping Ctrs., Am. Mgmt. Assn., Nat. Retail Fedn., Due Process Golf Club, Celtic Soc. Football (referee), N.Y. Athletic Club, U.S. Power Squadron, Cherry Valley Country Club, KC (4th degree). Roman Catholic. Home: 160 Spring Hill Rd Skillman NJ 08558-1418 Office: 2490 Pennington Rd Ste 201 Pennington NJ 08534 Office Phone: 609-737-2077.

DONNELLY, GLORIA FERRARO, university dean; b. Phila. Grad., Villanova U., U. Pa.; PhD in Human Devel., Bryn Mawr Coll., 1985. With Eastern Pa. Psychiat. Hosp., Inst. Pa. Hosp.; mem. faculty U. Pa. Sch. Nursing, Trenton (N.J.) State Coll., Villanova U.; founding dean of nursing La Salle U.; dean Sch. Nursing MCP Hahnemann U., Phila., 1996—98, Col. Nursing and Health Professions Drexel U., Phila., 1998—. Editor Holistic Nursing Practice Jour.; author 4 books. Recipient Am. Jour. Nursing Book of Yr. awards. Fellow Am. Acad. Nursing; mem. Nat. League for Nursing (bd. govs. 1995-97, chmn. coun. baccalaureate and higher degree programs, mem. exec. com.). Office: Drexel U Coll Nursing and Health Professions 245 N 15th St # 501 Philadelphia PA 19102-1192 Business E-Mail: gloria.donnelly@drexel.edu.

DONNELLY, JAMES CORCORAN, JR., lawyer; b. Newton, Mass., June 10, 1946; s. James C. and Margery J. (MacNeil) D.; m. Carol R. Burns, June 28, 1968; children: James C. IV, Sarah Y. BA, Dartmouth Coll., 1968; JD, Boston Coll., 1973. Bar: Mass. 1973, U.S. Dist. Ct. Mass. 1974, U.S. Ct. Appeals (7th cir.) 1979, U.S. Ct. Appeals (1st cir.) 1983, U.S. Tax Ct. 1988, U.S. Dist. Ct. (no. dist.) Ohio 1991, U.S. Ct. Appeals (2d cir) 1994, U.S. Ct. Appeals (3d cir.) 1999. From assoc. to ptnr. Hale & Dorr, Boston, 1973-84; sr. ptnr. Mirick, O'Connell, DeMallie & Lougee, Worcester, Mass., 1985—, chmn. litig. dept., 1993-97. Mem. selective panel US Dist. Ct. Magistrate, 2002; mem. bus. lit. session adv. com. Mass. Superior Ct., 2007—. Editor-in-chief 1972 Ann. Survey of Mass. Law. Corporator Greater Worcester Cmty. Found., 1986—, monitoring and evaluation com., 1997-2003; trustee Higgins Armory Mus., Worcester, 1985—, corporator, 1985—, pres. 1994-97, capital campaign steering com., 2006—; corporator Worcester Art Mus., 1986—, pres., mem. coun., 1987-88; councilor Am. Antiquarian Soc., 1996—, treas., 1999-2005; active Supreme Jud. Ct. Hist. Soc., 2004—; club officers exec. com. Dartmouth Coll., 1997-2005, pres., 1999-2002, alumni coun., 2000-05, coll. rels. group, 2002-05, com. on alumni orgn., 2000-05, chmn. 2002-03; trustee Worcester Craft Ctr., 2005—, devel. com. chair, 2005—. Lt. U.S. Army, 1968-70. Decorated Army Commendation medal for meritorious svc., 1970. Fellow Mass. Bar Found. (life); mem. ABA, Mass. Bar Assn. (appellate bench bar com. 1994-1995, bus. law sect. coun. 2003-06, jud. adminstrn. sect. coun. 2006—), Worcester County Bar Assn. (co-chmn. fed. ct. com. 1995-98), Dartmouth Lawyers Assn., Worcester Club (bd. dirs. 1995-98), Worcester Fire Soc. (clk. 2004-05), Dartmouth Club Ctrl. Mass. (exec. com. 1996—, pres. 1997-2002), Shakespeare Club of Worcester. Avocations: sailing, bicycling, hiking, history. Home: 285 Salisbury St Worcester MA 01609-1661 Office: Mirick O'Connell DeMallie & Lougee LLP 100 Front St Worcester MA 01608-1425

DONNELLY, JOSEPH, congressman, lawyer; b. Massapequa, NY, Sept. 29, 1955; m. Jill Donnelly; children: Molly, Joe Jr. BA in Govt., U. Notre Dame, 1977; JD, U. Notre Dame Law Sch., 1981. Of counsel Nemeth, Masters & Feeney Law Firm; owner Mktg. Solutions, Mishawaka, Ind., 1996—; mem. US Congress from 2nd Ind. dist., 2007—, mem. agrl. com., fin. svcs. com., vets affairs com. Mem. Ind. State Election Bd., 1988—89. Mem. St. Anthony de Padua Parish, chmn. Bishop's Appeal Campaign, 1994—96; mem. Mishawaka Marian High Sch. Bd. Edn., 1997—2001, pres., 2000—01. Mem.: ABA, Ind. State Bar Assn. Democrat. Roman Catholic. Office: 1218 Longworth House Office Bldg Washington DC 20515 also: 207 W Colfax St South Bend IN 46601*

DONNELLY, KEVIN WILLIAM, lawyer; b. Rockville Centre, NY, Sept. 25, 1954; s. William Lorne and Marie Grace (Busch) D.; m. Judith Marcia Brier, July 19, 1986; children: Lisa, Jennifer. BS, Boston Coll., 1976, JD, 1979; MBA, Dartmouth Coll., 1982. Bar: N.Y. 1980, Mass. 1980, U.S. Supreme Ct. 1999. Tax atty. Exxon Corp., NYC, 1979-80; assoc. Hemenway & Barnes, Boston, 1982-83; v.p., gen. counsel The Yankee Cos. Inc., Boston, 1983-88; v.p., gen. counsel, sec. Nortek, Inc., Providence, 1989—. Mem. ABA, Mass. Bar Assn. Office: Nortek Inc 50 Kennedy Plz Ste 1700 Providence RI 02903-2393 Home: 123 Abbott Rd Wellesley Hills MA 02481-6124 E-mail: donnelly@nortek-inc.com.

DONNELLY, ROSEMARIE, lawyer; b. Dallas, 1956; BA cum laude, Tex. A&M U., 1978; JD, U. Houston, 1988. Bar: Tex. 1988, admitted to practice: US Ct. Appeals (5th Cir.), US Dist. Ct. (No. Dist.) Tex., US Dist. Ct. (So. Dist.) Tex., US Dist. Ct. (Ea. Dist.) Tex., US Dist. Ct. (We. Dist.) Tex. With Andrews Kurth LLP, Houston, 1988—, ptnr., litig. dept. Contbr. articles to profl. jour. Mem.: State Bar Tex., Houston Bar Assn., Order of Barons. Office: Andrews Kurth LLP 600 Travis St Ste 4200 Houston TX 77002-3090 Office Phone: 713-220-4004. Office Fax: 713-238-7253. Business E-Mail: rdonnelly@andrewskurth.com.

DONNELLY, RUSSELL JAMES, physicist, educator; b. Hamilton, Ont., Can., Apr. 16, 1930; naturalized 2000; s. Clifford Ernest and Bessie (Harrison) D.; m. Marian Card, Jan. 21, 1956 (dec. 1999); 1 son, James. BSc, McMaster U., 1951, MSc, 1952, LLD, 1999; MS, Yale U., 1953, PhD, 1956. Faculty U. Chgo., 1956-66, prof. physics, 1965-66, U. Oreg., Eugene, 1966—, chmn. dept., 1966-72, 82-83; vis. prof. Niels Bohr Inst., Copenhagen, Denmark, 1972; co-founder Pine Mountain Obs., 1967. Cons. GM Co. Rsch. Labs., 1958—68, NSF, 1968—76, mem. adv. panel for physics, 1970—73, chmn,., 1971—72, mem. adv. coms. on materials rsch., 1979—84; mem. task force on fundamental physics and chemistry in space, space sci. bd. NRC; cons. Jet Propulsion Lab., Calif. Inst. Tech., Pasadena, 1973—82; chmn. Sci. Adv. Com. Low Temp. Facilities in Space, 1990—91; mem. fluid dynamics discipline working group NASA, 1992—95; gen. chmn. 20th Internat. Conf. on Low Temp. Physics, 1993; Chia-Shun Yih lectr. U. Mich., 1995; Fritz London meml. lectr. Duke U., 1996; Howard Vollum award Reed Coll., 1997. Author: (with Parks, Glaberson) Experimental Superfluidity, 1967, (with Francis) Cryogenic Science and Technology: Contributions of Leo Dana, 1985, Quantized Vortices in Helium II, 1991; editor: (with Herman, Prigogine) Non-Equilibrium Thermodynamics Variational Techniques and Stability, 1966, High Reynolds Number Flows Using Liquid and Gaseous Helium, 1991, Procs. 20th Internat. Conf. Low Temperature Physics, Physica B, 1994; editor: (with Sreenivasan) Flow at Ultra-High Reynolds and Rayleigh Numbers, (with Barenghi and Vinen) Quantized Vortex Dynamic and Superfluid Turbulence; mem. editl. bd. Physics of Fluids, 1966-68, Phys. Rev. E, 1978-84, assoc. editor, 1987-93; mem. editl. bd. Jour. Phys. and Chem. Ref. Data, 1989-92, Handbook of Chemistry and Physics, 1989-98, Royal Soc. London; contbr. articles to profl. jours. Bd. dirs. U. Oreg. Found., 1970-72, 88-91, investment com., 1990-91; bd. dirs. Oreg. Mus. Park Commn., 1975-87, chmn., 1975-82; bd. dirs. Oreg. Bach Festival, 1975-87, Oreg. Mozart Players, 1990-93. Recipient Disting. Alumnus award, McMaster U., 1992, Lars Onsager medal, Norwegian U. Sci. and Tech., 1996, Fritz London prize, Internat. Union Pure and Applied Physics, 2002; Alfred P. Sloan fellow, 1959—63, sr. vis. fellow, Sci. Rsch. Coun., Eng., 1978. Fellow: AAAS, Inst. of Physics (London), Am. Phys. Soc. (exec. com. divsn. fluid dynamics 1966—72, 1980—84, 1988—91, sec.-treas. 1967—70, 1988—91, chmn. 1971—72, 1983—83, Otto Laporte award 1974), Am. Acad. Arts and Scis.; mem.: Soc. Archtl. Historians, Nat. Trust for Scotland, Cosmos Club. Episcopalian. Achievements include research on physics of fluids, especially hydrodynamic stability, turbulence and superfluidity. Office: Univ Oreg Dept Physics Eugene OR 97403-1274 Home: 1975 Olive St #502/504 Eugene OR 97401 Office Phone: 541-346-4226. Business E-Mail: russ@vortex.uoregon.edu.

DONNELLY, SCOTT C., manufacturing executive; BEE, U. Colo., 1984. With GE Aerospace, Syracuse, NY, 1989—95; gen. mgr. GE Indsl. Sys. Tech., 1995—97; v.p. global tech. sys. GE Med. Sys., 1997—2000; sr. v.p. corp. R & D GE, Schenectady, NY, 2000—05; pres., CEO GE Infrastructure, Aviation, 2005—. Mem. engring. adv. com. Stanford Univ., Cornell Univ., Ctr. for Innovation in Minimally Invasive Therapy, Mass. Gen. Hosp. Office: GE 3135 Easton Tpke Fairfield CT 06828*

DONNELLY, SHARLOTTE K. B. NEELY, anthropology educator, writer; b. Savannah, Ga., Aug. 13, 1948; d. Joseph Bowden and Kathleen Bell Neely; m. Thomas Christian C. Donnelly, June 21, 1980; 1 child, Bridgette. BA, Ga. State U., 1970; MA, U. NC, 1971, PhD, 1976. Prof. of anthropology No. Ky. U., Highland Heights, 1974—, anthropology coord., 1992—2000, 2004—. Author: Snowbird Cherokees, 1991, Kasker, 2005; co-author: This Land Was Theirs, 1996, 1999; contbr. articles to profl. jours., chapters to books. Pres. League for Animal Welfare, Cincinnati, Ohio, 1984—85. Recipient Strongest Influence Award, No. Ky. U. Alumni Assn., 1996. Fellow: Am. Anthrop. Assn.; mem.: Anthropologists and Sociologists of Ky. (pres. 1979—80). Democrat-Npl. Roman Catholic. Avocations: writing, travel. Office: No Ky U Nunn Dr Highland Heights KY 41099 Office Phone: 859-572-5259. Personal E-mail: donnelly@one.net, neelys@nku.edu.

DONNELLY, SHAUN EDWARD, government agency administrator; b. Culver, Ind. m. Susan Buesing; children: Alex, Eric. BA in Econs., Lawrence U., Appleton, Wis., 1968; MA in Econs., Northwestern U., 1971. With U.S. Fgn. Svc., 1972—, econ./comml. officer Senegal, Ethiopia, Egypt, fin. economist Office of Devel. Fin. Washington; dep. asst. sec. for energy and econ. sanctions State Dept. Bur. of Econ. and Bus. Affairs, Washington, 1994—95, dep. asst. sec. for trade policy, 1996—97; amb. to Sri Lanka and Republic of Maldives U.S. Dept. State, Colombo, 1997—2000, prin. dep. asst. sec. for econ. and bus. affairs Washington, 2001—05; asst. US trade rep. for Europe and Middle East US Trade Rep. Office, Washington, 2005—. Office: US Trade Rep Office Europe and Mid East Office 600 17th St Room 323 Washington DC 20508 Office Phone: 202-647-5991.

DONNELLY, THOMAS M., lawyer; BA summa cum laude, Tufts U., 1985; JD, Harvard U., 1988. Bar: Calif., Am. Bar Assoc. Atty., shareholder Heller Ehrman LLP, San Francisco, 1988—; co-chair, Consumer and Environ. Litigation Heller, Ehrman, White, & McAuliffe LLP, San Francisco. Office: Heller Ehrman 333 Bush St San Francisco CA 94104 Office Phone: 415-772-6611. Office Fax: 415-772-6268. Business E-Mail: tdonnelly@hewm.com.

DONNELLY, TRISHA, artist; b. San Francisco, Apr. 22, 1974; BFA, U. Calif., LA, 1995; MFA, Yale U. Sch. Art, 2000. Vis. faculty, New Genres dept. San Francisco Art Inst. One-woman shows include Air de Paris, 2002, Gallery Modern Art, Bologna, 2006, Casey Kaplan, NYC, 2002, 2004, Art Positions, Art Miami Beach, 2003, The Wrong Gallery, NYC, 2004, Art Pace, San Antonio, 2005, Kunsthalle Zürich, 2005, Special Project Portikus, Frankfurt am Main, 2006, exhibited in group shows at Minty, Richard Telles Gallery, LA, 1999, Found. Louis-Jeantet de Médecine, Geneva, 1999, Echo, Artist's Space, NYC, 2000, The Wedding Show, Casey Kaplan, NYC, 2001, The Dedalic Convention, MAK Mus., Vienna, 2001, Moving Pictures, Solomon R. Guggenheim Mus., 2002, Hello, My Name Is., Carnegie Mus. Art, Pitts., 2002, 54th Carnegie Internat., 2004, 50th Internat. Exhbn. Art, Venice Biennial, 2003, C'est arrivé demain, Biennial Lyon, 2003, Peripheries become the center, Prague biennial, 2003, Atto Primo, galleria Massimo de Carlo, Milan, 2004, Biennial Contemporary African Art, Obrist, Dakar, 2004, Collection (or How I Spent a Year), PS1 Contemporary Art Ctr., Long Island City, 2004, Moscow Biennial Contemporary Art, 2005, The imaginary number, Kunst Werk, Berlin, 2005, 4th Berlin Biennial Contemporary Art: Of Mice and Men, 2006, Hans Ulrich Obrist, Astrup Fearnley Mus. Modern Art, Oslo, 2005, Day for Night, Whitney Biennial, 2006, projection, Untitled (Jumping), Centre Georges Pompidou, Paris, 2003, performances, Echo, Artist's Space, NYC, 2000, Angel Heart, Air de Paris, 2001, A Little Bit of History Repeated, Kunst-Werke, Berlin, 2001, Casey Kaplan, NYC, 2002, 50th Venice Biennial, 2003, 54th Carnegie Internat., Pitts., 2004, Where is Adventure? What is Culture?, Frieze Art Fair, London, 2004, Represented in permanent collections Walker Art Ctr., Mpls., FRAC Poitou Charentes, Mus. Contemporary Art, LA, Carnegie Mus., Pitts., Guggenheim Mus., NYC, Western Bridge Found., Seattle. Recipient Central-Kunstpreis, Cologne, Germany, 2004. Office: San Francisco Art Institute 800 Chestnut St San Francisco CA 94133*

DONNEM, SARAH LUND, financial analyst, non-profit and political organization consultant; b. St. Louis, Apr. 10, 1936; d. Joel Y. and Erle Hall (Harsh) Lund; m. Roland W. Donnem, Feb. 18, 1961; children: Elizabeth Prince Donnem Sigety, Sarah Madison Ashe-Donnem. BA, Vassar Coll., 1958. Tech. aide, computer programmer Bell Labs, Whippany, N.J., 1959-60; chmn. placement vol. opportunities N.Y. Jr. League, 1972-73, asst. treas., 1974-75, chmn. urban problems relating to mental health, 1967-69, mem. project rsch. com., 1967-70, chmn., 1973-74, mem. bd. mgrs., 1973-74. Chmn. cmty. rsch. Washington Jr. League, 1970-71, mem. bd. mgrs., 1970-71; mem. Stratford Hall (N.Y.) Com., 1970—; bd. dirs. East Side Settlement House, Bronx, N.Y., 1972-04, hon., 2005—, v.p., 1975-76, chmn. Nat. Horse Show Benefit, 1976, winter antiques show com., 1994—, co-chmn. adv. com., 1991-94, chmn. VIP Day, 1999—, mem. nominating com., 1990-00, mem. investment com., 1993-03, mem. fin. com., 2004-05; bd. dirs. Stanley M. Isaacs Neighborhood Ctr., N.Y.C., 1973-76, v.p., 1975-76; bd. dirs. Presbyn. Home for Aged Women, N.Y.C., 1974-76, v.p., 1976; mem. exec. bd. N.Y. Aux. of Blue Ridge Sch., 1971-75, sec. 1965-67, pres., 1973-75; budget and benevolence com. Brick Presbyn. Ch., N.Y.C., 1973-76, mem. social svc. com., 1973-74, chmn. fgn. students com., 1963-64; bd. dirs. Search and Care, N.Y.C., 1973--76, Project LEARN, Cleve., 1990-96, 2000—, trustee, 2000-06; chmn. Literacy Fund, 1991-95, mem., 1995—; mem. Friends of Project LEARN, 1986—, mem. Fedn. Cmty. Planning, Cleve., coun. on Older Persons, 1978-82, mem. future Planning task Force, 1980-81, commn. on social concerns, 1982-84; trustee Golden Age Ctrs. Greatr cleve., 1979-92, investment com., 1993, 1st v.p., 1980-81, pres. 1981-85, chmn. Western Res. Antiques show, 1979, 80; chmn. cleve. antiques Show Silver Anniv., 2000; mem. women's adv. coun. Westrn Res. Hist. Soc., 1977—, coord. sec., 1978; mem. women's com. Cleve. Orch., 1979-85, Vassar Coll. cleve. sec. 1980-82, v.p., 1983, pres. 1984-86, leadership gift chair 50th reunion; mem. AAVC Club Liaison com., 1986-89, chmn. regional program com., 1987-89; bd. dirs. Cleve. Ballet, 1980-01, exec. com. 1981, fin. com. 1982-88, 95-98, nominating com., 1988-90, 95-00, co-chmn. 1997-99; co-chmn. Yale Ball, 1983; bd. advisors Ret. Sr. Vol. Program, 1982, trustee, 1983-90, chmn. long range planning comm., 1986, sec. 1987-89; mem. Family Friends Adv. Coun., 1987-89; trustee Fairmount Presbyn. Ch., 1985-88; mem. long range planning com. United Way, Cleve., 1985-87; coord. Friends of Voinovich, 1987-89; womens adv. com. Voinovich for Gov., 1990, Voinovich for Senate, 1997-98, chmn. Voinovich Task Force on Aging, 1990-91, Ohio Adv. Coun. on Aging, 1991-02, legis. com., 1994-00; chmn. legis. com. Cuyahoga County Rep. Party, 1994-00, mem. policy com., mem. fin. com., 1999—, Plain Dealer adv. counsel for elderly coverage, 1991-93; chmn. Johns Hopkins Parents Fund, 1986-88, Project LEARN 15th Anniversary celebration (with Barbara Bush, hon. chmn.), 1989-90; coord. Decorative Arts Trust Cleve. Symposium, 1996; mem. Leadership Cleve. Class 1992; bd. trustees Gibbes Mus. Art, 2007-; del. White House Conf. on Aging, 1995. Named Vol. of Yr. N.Y. Jr. League, 1975; recipient Sustainer Svc. award Jr. League Cleve., 1990. Mem. Nat. Inst. Social Scis. (membership com. 1972-92, trustee 1984-96), Nat. Soc. Colonial Dames (com. regional conf. III 2007), Colony Club (NYC), Chevy Chase Club (Washington), Intown club, Vassar Club, Kirtland Club (Cleve.), Historic Charleston Found. (hon. com. Internat. Antiques Show, 2004, 05, 06, 07). Home (Winter): 1 King St Apt 307 Charleston SC 29401 Home (Summer): 2945 Fontenay Rd Shaker Heights OH 44120

DONNER, LUDVIK RAFAEL, pathologist, educator; b. Prague, Czechoslovakia, Oct. 24, 1941; came to U.S., 1976; s. Theodor and Ruzena (Desort) D.; m. Vera M. Kupka; children: John N., Timothy P., Veronica M. MD, Charles U., Prague, 1965; PhD, Czechoslovakia Acad. Scis., Prague, 1969. Diplomate Am. Bd. Pathology. Researcher Czechoslovakia Acad. Scis., Prague, 1965-75, Baylor Coll. Medicine, Houston, 1976-77; vis. scientist Nat. Cancer Inst., Bethesda, Md., 1977-81; resident George Washington U., Washington, 1981-85; fellow M.D. Anderson Cancer Ctr., Houston, 1985-86; assoc. prof. Pathology Scott & White Clinic, Temple, Tex., 1986—. Mem. edit. bd., spl. assoc. editor Cancer Genetics and Cytogenetics, 1990—; contbr. 54 articles to profl. jours. Eleanor Roosevelt Am. Cancer Soc. fellow, 1973. Mem. Soc. Pediatric Pathology, European Assn. of Hematopathology, Nat. Fedn. Cath. Physicians Guilds. Roman Catholic. Avocations: gardening, travel. Office: Scott & White Clinic 2401 S 31st St Temple TX 76508-0001 Office Phone: 254-724-4730.

DONNER, RICHARD, film director, producer; b. NYC, Apr. 24, 1930; m. Lauren Shuler Donner, 1985. Dir.: X-15, 1961, Salt and Pepper, 1968, The Omen, 1976, Superman, 1978, Inside Moves, 1981, Radio Flyer, 1991 16 Blocks, 2006; exec. prodr.: The Final Conflict, The Lost Boys, 1991, Delirious, 1991, Free Willy, 1993, Free Willy 2: The Adventure Home, 1995, Demon Knight, 1995, Free Willy 3: The Rescue, 1997, Any Given Sunday, 1999, X-Men, 2000; dir., exec. prodr.: The Toy, 1982; dir., prodr.: Ladyhawke, 1985, Goonies, 1985, Lethal Weapon, 1987, Scrooged, 1988, Lethal Weapon 2, 1989, Lethal Weapon 3, (MTV movie award, best action sequence) 1992, Maverick, 1994, Assassins, 1995, Lethal Weapon 4, 1998, Timeline, 2003; prodr.: Blackheart, 1999, The Final Conflict, 1981 (exec.), 1981, The Lost Boys (exec.), 1987, Double Tap, 1997, Ritual, 2001 (TV); dir., prodr.: Made Men, 1999, W.E.I.R.D. World, (exec.) 1995, Perversions of Science, 1997, Matthew Blackheart: Monster Smasher, 2001; dir. (TV episodes) Wanted: Dead or Alive, 1958, Sam Benedict, 1962, The Nurses, 1962, Combat, 1962, The Fugitive, 1963, The Wild Wild West, 1965, The Trials of O'Brien, 1965, Get Smart, 1965, The FBI, 1965, Its About Time, 1966, Felony Squad, 1966, Cannon, 1971, Cade's County, 1971, The Six Sense, 1972, Ghost Story, 1972, The Streets of San Francisco, 1972, The Six Million Dollar Man, 1974, Petrocelli, 1974, Twilight Zone, Have Gun Will Travel, Perry Mason, Cannon, Get Smart, The Fugitive, Kojak, 1973, Bronk, 1975, Lucas Tanner, Gilligan's Island, Man From U.N.C.L.E., Twilight Zone, The Banana Splits, 1968, Combat, Tales from the Crypt, 1989-91, Two Fisted Tales, 1991, Conspiracy Theory, 1997; (TV movies) Statutory Affair, 1969, Twinky, 1969, Lola, 1972, London Affair, 1972, Portrait of a Teenage Alcoholic, 1975, Senior Year, 1974, A Shadow in the Streets, 1975, A Very Special Place, 1977. also: Creative Artists Agy 9830 Wilshire Blvd Beverly Hills CA 90212-1804

DONNER, TED A., lawyer; b. NYC, Nov. 22, 1960; s. Robert A. and Barbara (Wood) Donner; m. Leslie Lynn Wasserman, Sept. 16, 1990; children: Alexandra Sofia, Samuel Joseph. BA, Roosevelt U., 1987; JD, Loyola U., 1990. Bar: U.S. Dist. Ct. Ill. 1990. Assoc. Rock, Fusco, Reynolds & Garvey, Chgo., 1990-94; of counsel Altheimer & Gray, Chgo., 1994-2000; ptnr. Bischoff Ptnrs. LLC, Chgo., 2000—02; mgr. Donner & Co. Law Offices LLC, 2002—. Adj. prof. Loyola U. Chgo. Sch. Law, 1990—. Author: Attorney's Practice Guide to Negotiations, 2d edit., 1995, Jury Selection Strategy & Science, 3d edit., 2000, Jury Selection Handbook, 1999. Mem.: ABA, ATLA, Alpha Sigma Nu, Chgo. Bar Assn., DuPage County Bar Assn., Am. Soc. Legal Writers, Am. Bar Found., Am. Soc. Trial Cons., Internat. Platform Assn. Office: 203 N LaSalle St # 2100 Chicago IL 60601 also: 1131 Wheaton Oaks Ct Wheaton IL 60187 Home Phone: 630-469-5384; Office Phone: 630-588-1131. E-mail: tdonner@donnerco.com.

DONNESON, SEENA SAND, artist; b. NYC; d. Max and Ann (Silber) Sand; children: Erika, Lisa. Student, Pratt Inst., Art Students League. Art staff NYU, Nassau County Office Cultural Devel., New Sch. for Social Rsch., N.H. Coll.; guest artist Tamarind Lithography Workshop; vis. artist Clayworks, NYC. One-woman shows include Laruen Rogers Mus. Art, Laurel, Miss., Greenville (N.C.) Mus. Art, Galerie #836, Santa Fe, Lehigh U., Princeton U., Portland (Maine) Mus. Art, Piertrantonio Gallery, N.y.C., U. Calif., LI U., George Washington U., Danville (Va.) Mus. Fine Arts and History, others, exhibited in group shows at SUNY, N.Y.C., Quietude Sculpture Garden, N.J., A.F.A. Pier/92, N.Y.C., Sculpture in Color, Ft. Lauderdale (Fla.) Mus., Norfolk Mus. Arts and Scis., Bklyn. Mus., San Francisco Mus. Art, DeCordova Mus., Alternate Spac, Belgrade Lakes, Maine Mod Art Foundry, N.Y.C., USIS, Mcpl. Art Mus., Tokyo, various, Japan, Musseo de Belles Artes, Buenos Aires, Scotland, Represented in permanent collections Va. Mus. Fine Art, Bklyn. Mus., Doris Freidman Sculpture garden, Albright U., Reading, Pa., Norfolk Mus., USIA Art in Embassies, Los Angeles County Mus. Art, Mus. Modern Art, N.Y.C., Smithsonian Mus., Ft. Lauderdale Mus. Fine Art, Snug Harbor Cultural Ctr., N.Y.C., N.Y. Pub. Libr., Cornell Med. Sch., N.Y.C., others, pvt. collections; contbr. revs. to publs. Recipient numerous art awards; fellow, Edward MacDowell Found.; grantee, Mcpl. Art Soc., N.Y. Art in Pk., 1974, Queens Coun. Arts, 1992; Creative Artists Pub. Svc. grantee, N.Y. State Coun. Arts, 1983—84. Mem.: L.I.C. Artists (bd. dirs.), Nat. Assn. Women Artists (bd. dirs.), Artists Equity. Studio: 20 Sutton Pl S New York NY 10022 Office Phone: 212-753-5328. Home Fax: 212-753-4967. Personal E-mail: Elaici@aol.com.

DONOFF, R. BRUCE, dean, oral surgeon, dental educator; BSc cum laude, Bklyn. Coll., 1963; DMD, Harvard U., 1967, MD, 1973. Clin. fellow in oral surgery Harvard U. Sch. Dental Medicine, Boston, 1969-71, asst. prof. oral surgery, 1974-78, assoc. prof. oral and maxillofacial surgery, 1978-83, acting chmn. dept. oral and maxillofacial surgery, 1982-83, chmn., 1983-93, prof., 1983—, dean and Walter C. Guralnick disting. prof. oral and maxillofacial surgery, 1991—. Bd. mem. Friends of the Nat. Inst. of Dental and Craniofacial Rsch. Contbr. articles to profl. jours.; editor: MGH Manual of Oral and Maxillofacial Surgery. Mem. of editl. bd. Jour. of Oral and Maxillofacial Surgery, Mass. Dental Soc. Jour. Recipient William J. Gies Found. award, 1993, 2d place award Am. Soc. Oral Surgeons, 1969, Disting. Alumni and Faculty awards from the Harvard Sch. of Dental Medicine. Fellow AAAS; mem. Omicron Kappa Upsilon. Office Phone: 617-432-1401. Office Fax: 617-432-4266. Business E-Mail: bruce_donoff@hsdm.harvard.edu.

DONOFRIO, JOHN, lawyer; BSChemE, Rutgers U.; JD, George Washington U., 1987, LLM. Law clk. US Ct. Appeals (fed. cir.); ptnr. Kirkland & Ellis; assoc. gen. counsel Honeywell Internat., 1996—98, dep. gen. counsel, 1998—2000, v.p., gen. counsel Honeywell Aerospace Phoenix, 2000—05; sr. v.p., gen. counsel Visteon Corp., Van Buren Twp., Mich., 2005—. Adj. prof. Seton Hall U. Sch. Law. Contbr. articles to profl. publs. Office: Visteon Corp 1 Village Ctr Dr Van Buren Township MI 48111-5711*

D'ONOFRIO, JUSTIN MICHAEL, information technology manager, consultant; b. Secaucus, NJ, Jan. 27, 1984; BA in Info. Tech., Rutgers Coll., New Brunswick, NJ, 2006. Cert. developer Hyperion, 2007. Info. tech. mgmt. devel. program LOreal, Clark, NJ, 2006—. Freelance web applications cons., 2004—. Mem.: Project Mgmt. Inst. (cert. assoc. in project mgmt. 2007), Am. Mensa Soc. Office: L'Oreal USA Clark NJ Home Phone: 201-407-9961; Office Phone: 7324996657. Personal E-mail: justinru@gmail.com.

DONOFRIO, NICHOLAS M., information technology executive; BEE, Rensselaer Polytechnic Inst., 1967; MSEE, Syracuse U., 1971; ED (hon.), Polytechnic U., 1999; DSc (hon.), U. Warwick, United Kingdom, 2002; D Tech. (hon.), Marist Coll., 2005. Designer IBM Corp., 1967—83, dir. Semiconductor Devel. Lab. Burlington, Vt., 1983—85, sec., exec. mgmt., 1985—86, gen. mgr. site ops., 1986—87, dir. hardware devel., 1987—88, v.p., corp. v.p., pres. Personal Computer Prod. Devel., 1988—91, sr. v.p., group exec. Server Group Internat. Bus. Mach., 1995—97, sr. v.p. tech. and mfg. Armonk, NY, 1997—2005, exec. v.p. innovation & tech., 2005—. Bd. dir. Bank of NY; bd. trustee Rensselaer Polytechnic Inst.; chmn. bd, gov. IBM Acad. Tech. Chmn. Nat. Action Coun. for Minorities in Engring., 1997—2002; mem. Sec. of Edn.'s Commn. on Future of Edn., 2005; bd. dir. Council for U.S. and Italy. Named Tech. Leader Yr., Industry Week mag., 2003, Tech. Exec. Yr., Ariz. Coll. of Engring. & Eller Coll. of Bus.& Pub. Adminstrn., 2003; named one of 25 Masters of Innovation, BusinessWeek, 2006; recipient Mensforth Internat. Gold Medal, 2002, Rodney D. Chipp Meml. award, Soc. Women Engrs., 2003, George Arents Pioneer Medal, Syracuse U., 2005, Tech. Leadership award, CNBC, 2005. Fellow: Royal Acad. Engring., UK, IEEE (Mensforth Internat. Gold medal 2002); mem.: Am. Acad. Arts and Scis., NY Acad. Sci., NAE, Sigma Xi. Achievements include patents in field. Office: IBM Corp New Orchard Rd Armonk NY 10504*

DONOFRIO, PETER DANIEL, neurology educator; b. Syracuse, NY, June 5, 1950; s. Carmin Peter and Donna Marie (Powers) D.; m. Kathleen Ann Fitzgerald, May 29, 1976; children: Molly, Emily, Julie. BS, U. Notre Dame, 1972; MD, Ohio State U., 1975. Diplomate Am. Bd. Internal Medicine, Am. Bd. Neurology, Am. Bd. Emergency Medicine. Resident internal medicine Good Samaritan Hosp., Cin., 1978; resident neurology U. Mich. Med. Ctr., Ann Arbor, 1981, instr., 1982-84, V.A. Hosp., Ann Arbor, 1982-84, asst. prof., 1984-85, U. Mich. Med. Ctr., Ann Arbor, 1984-85; asst. prof. neurology Wake Forest U. Sch. Medicine, Winston-Salem, NC, 1986-89, assoc. prof., 1989-97, prof., 1997—, vice chmn. dept., 1993—. Cons. in neurology, Winston-Salem, 1984—. Contr. articles to profl. jours. Dept. rep. United Way, Winston-Salem, N.C., 1989— Scholar U. Notre Dame U., 1968. Fellow Am. Acad. Neurology; mem. Am. Assn. Electrodiagnostic Medicine, Am. Neurological Assn. Roman Catholic. Avocations: woodworking, piano, hi-fidelity, landscaping. Home: 3509 Donegal Dr Clemmons NC 27012-8678 Office: Wake Forest Univ Medical Center Blvd Winston Salem NC 27157-0001 Business E-Mail: donofrio@wfubmc.edu.

DONOGHUE, ANN MARIE, museum administrator, consultant; b. Oswego, NY, July 26, 1950; d. Edward Daniel Perry and Eveline Anna Murray; m. John Charles Donoghue, Dec. 20, 1969; children: John Charles Donoghue, II, Kelly Anne. AA in Bus. Adminstrn., San Bernardino Valley Coll., Calif., 1983—89; BA in Anthropology, Calif. State U., San Bernardino, 1989—93. Cert. museum studies Calif. State U., 1993, Latin Am. studies Calif. State U., 1993, mktg. mgmt. San Bernardino Valley Coll., 1989, collateral duty safety tng. State of Wyo., 2002. Curatorial asst. Southwest Mus., LA, 1997—98, asst. curator, nagpra coord., 1998—99; nagpra cons. Pomona Coll. Montgomery Gallery, Claremont, Calif., 1997—98, nagpra cons., consulting curator, 1999; pvt. nagpra cons. Fontana, Calif., 1998—2000; assoc. registrar Buffalo Bill Hist. Ctr., Cody, Wyo., 2000—. Archaeology field asst. Chaffey Coll., Rancho Cucamonga, Calif., 1991—92; student adv. coun. mem. Calif. State U, 1992—93; guest lectr. anthropology dept. Calif. State U., 1995—97, LA, 1995—97, data analyst dept. social work, 1996; curriculuum specialist vol. Inland Empire W Resource Conservation Dist., Rancho Cucamonga, Calif., 1994; guest instr. Pomona Coll., 1999—99; co-program dir. ann. meeting Southwestern Anthrop. Assn., LA, 1997, panel mem. ann. meeting, Pasadena, Calif., 1997—97; guest lectr. Assn. Calif. Cmty. Coll. Tchrs., LA, 2000; safety com. mem. Buffalo Bill Hist. Ctr., Cody, Wyo., 2002—; Wyo. rep. registrars' com. Mountain Plains Mus. Assn., Cody, Wyo., 2003. Photographer Chaco Canyon, Calif. State U. art show, 1993; editor: Calif. Anthropologist, 1996—97; co-editor: Southwestern Anthropological Assn. Newsletter, 1996—97; contbr. articles. Organizer Neighborhood Watch Program, Colton, Calif., 1982—89; pres. Parent Teachers Assn., Colton, 1983; parent to parent support group Kaiser Permanente Hosp., Fontana, Calif., 1983—85; organizer Block Parent Assn., Colton, 1983—88; vol. Humane Soc. Pk. County, Cody, 2006—; mem. powwow com. Plains Indian Mus., 2003—. Mem.: Colo. Wyo. Assn. Mus., Registrars' Com., MPMA (assoc.), Mountain Plains Mus. Assn. (assoc.), Registrars' Com., AAM (assoc.), Am. Assn. Museums (assoc.), Pahaska Corral of Westerners (assoc.; editor 2002—06, Svc. award 2005), Alpha Gamma Sigma, Phi Kappa (assoc.). Avocations: southwestern art, decorating, antiques, travel, fishing. Home: PO Box 3074 Cody WY 82414 Office: Buffalo Bill Hist Ctr 720 Sheridan Ave Cody WY 82414 Office Phone: 307-578-4024. Personal E-mail: annmarie@wyoming.com. Business E-Mail: annmaried@bbhc.org.

DONOGHUE, DENIS, language professional, educator; b. Tullow, County Carlow, Ireland, Dec. 1, 1928; came to U.S., 1979; s. Denis and Johanna (O'Neill) D.; m. Frances Rutledge, Dec. 1, 1951; children—David, Helen, Hugh, Celia, Mark, Barbara, Stella, Emma. BA, Univ. Coll., Dublin, 1949, MA, 1952, PhD, 1957; MA, Cambridge U., Eng., 1964. Adminstrv. officer Dublin Dept. Fin., 1951-54; fellow King's Coll., univ. lectr. English Cambridge U., England, 1964-65; prof. modern English and Am. lit. Univ. Coll., England, 1965-79; Henry James prof., English, Am. Letters NYU, 1979—. Author: The Third Voice, 1959, Connoisseurs of Chaos, 1964, Jonathan Swift, 1965, Emily Dickinson, 1966, The Ordinary Universe, 1968, Thieves of Fire, 1973, The Sovereign Ghost, 1976, Ferocious Alphabets, 1981, The Arts without Mystery, 1983, The Practice of Reading, 1998, Words Alone: The Poet T.S. Eliot, 2000, Adam's Curse, 2001, Speaking of Beauty, 2003, The American Classics: A Personal Essay, 2005; editor: An Honoured Guest, 1965, Yeats, Memoirs, 1967. Mem. Internat. Assn. U. Profs. English (exec. com.), Roman Catholic. Office: Dept of English NYU 19 University Pl New York NY 10003-4556 Office Phone: 212-998-8800. Business E-Mail: dd1@nyu.edu.

DONOGHUE, JOHN CHARLES, application developer, consultant; b. Oswego, NY, Sept. 19, 1950; s. James Charles and Marian Louise (Farrell) Donoghue; m. Ann Marie Perry, Dec. 20, 1969; children: John Charles II, Kelly Anne. BS in Electronic Tech., Chapman Coll., 1981; postgrad., U. Calif., Irvine, 1981-82, Western State U. Coll., 1988-89, Azusa Pacific U., 1991-93; MA, U. Redlands, 1987. Enlisted USAF, 1969, advanced through grades to staff sgt., 1977, resigned, 1979; mgr. Lockheed Aircraft, Ontario, Calif., 1979-85; project engr. Northrop Corp., Pico Rivera, Calif., 1985-99; sr. prin. software engr. Raytheon Missile Syss., Tucson, 1999—; Raytheon cert. Six Sigma expert, 2001—. Cons., Fontana, Calif., 1981—2001; mem. software coun. Northrop Corp., Hawthorne, Calif., 1987—97; mem. software improvement network U. Calif., Irvine, 1988—2000; mem. capability maturity model coop. group Software Engring. Inst., Pitts., 1993—98; mem. LA software improvement network U. So. Calif, 1994—2000; mem. Tucson Software Process Improvement Network, 2000—. Active PTA, 1975—85; mem. Block Parent Assn., 1981—87, Parent to Parent Support Group, 1982—87; vol. cons. S.W. Anthrop. Assn., Calif. State U., LA, 1996—97, Resource Conservation Dist., Rancho Cucamonga, Calif., 1996—2000, S.W. Mus., LA, 1997—2000. Decorated USAF Commendation medal; named to Outstanding Young Men of Am., 1983. Mem.: IEEE Computer Soc., IEEE, Nat. Space Soc., N.Y. Acad. Scis. Avocations: motorcycling, snorkeling, photography. Office: Raytheon Missile Systems Bldg 805/K4 PO Box 11337 Tucson AZ 85734-1337 Office Phone: 520-794-3239. Personal E-mail: jcd28@cox.net.

DONOGHUE, JOHN FRANCIS, archbishop; b. Washington, Aug. 9, 1928; s. Daniel and Rose (Ryan) Donoghue. Student, St. Charles Coll., Catonsville, Md., St. Mary's Sem., Balt., Cath. U. Ordained priest St. Matthew Cathedral, Washington, 1955; asst. pastor St. Bernard's Ch., Riverdale, Md., 1955—61, Holy Face parish, Great Mills, Md., 1961—64; chancellor and vicar gen. Archdiocesan Chancery, Washington, 1965—84; given papal rank of Chaplain to his Holiness with the title Monsignor, 1970; given rank of Prelate of Honor, 1971; elevated to bishop, 1984; bishop Diocese of Charlotte, 1984—93; archbishop Diocese of Atlanta, 1993—2004, archbishop emeritus, 2004—. Roman Cath.

DONOGHUE, JOHN PHILLIP, neuroscience educator, neurotechnology company executive; b. Cambridge, Mass., Mar. 22, 1949; s. John P. and Nanette L. (Maxwell) D.; m. Karen L. Kerman, Oct. 9, 1982; children: Jacob, Noah. AB, Boston U., 1971; MS in Anatomy, U. Vt., 1976; PhD in Neurosci., Brown U., 1979. Asst. prof. Brown U. Ctr. Neural Sci., Providence, 1984-88, assoc. prof., 1988-91; chmn., dept. neuroscience Brown U., Providence, 1991—, Henry Merritt Wriston prof., exec. dir., Brain Science Program, 1998—; founder, chief scientific officer, dir. Cyberkinetics Neurotechnology Systems, Inc., Foxborough, Mass., 2001—. Mem. advisory panel NIH Neurology and Mental Health Inst.; mem., space med. panel NASA. Assoc. editor Jour. Neurosci., 1995—, Metabolic Brain Disease, 1989-93; contbr. articles to profl. jours. Basil O'Connor fellow March of Dimes Found., 1985; nominee Rave award in Medicine, WIRED, 2005. Mem. AAAS, Am. Physiological Soc., Soc. Neurosci., Internat. Brain Rsch. Orgn, Fedn. Am. Socs. for Exptl. Biology. Office: Brown U Dept Neurosci PO Box 1953 Providence RI 02912-1953 also: Cyberkinetics Neurotechnology Systems Inc 100 Foxborough Blvd Ste 240 Foxboro MA 02035 Office Phone: 508-549-9981, 401-863-2701. Office Fax: 508-549-9985. Business E-Mail: John_Donoghue@brown.edu.

DONOGHUE, MICHAEL JOHN, biologist, educator; b. Chgo., June 14, 1952; BS in Botany and Plant Pathology, Mich. State U., 1976; PhD in Biology, Harvard U., 1982. Asst. prof. biology San Diego State U., 1982—85; asst. prof. Dept. Ecology and Evolutionary Biology U. Ariz., 1985—88, assoc. prof., 1988—90, prof., 1990—92, adj. prof., 1993—99; prof. biology Harvard U., 1993—2000; dir. Harvard U. Herbaria, 1995—99; vis. prof. Stanford U., 1998—99; G. Evelyn Hutchinson prof. Dept. Ecology and Evolutionary Biology Yale U., 2000—, joint faculty, Sch. Forestry and Environment. Studies, 2000—, chmn. Dept. Ecology and Evolutionary Biology, 2001—02; cur. botany Peabody Mus. Natural History, 2000—, dir., 2003—. Mem.: NAS. Office: Yale Univ Environ Sci Ctr 21 Sachem St PO Box 208105 New Haven CT 06520-8105 Mailing: Peabody Mus Natural History Yale Univ 170 Whitney Ave PO Box 208118 New Haven CT 06520-8118 Office Phone: 203-432-2074, 203-432-3752. Office Fax: 203-432-3758, 203-432-5176. E-mail: michael.donoghue@yale.edu.

DONOGHUE, MILDRED RANSDORF, education educator; b. Cleve. d. James and Caroline (Sychra) Ransdorf; m. Charles K. Donoghue (dec.); children: Kathleen, James. EdD, UCLA, 1962; JD, Western State U., 1979. Asst. prof. edn. and reading Calif. State U., Fullerton, 1962-66, assoc. prof., 1966-71, prof., 1971—. Founder, dir. Donoghue Children's Lit. Ctr., Calif. State U., Fullerton, Calif., 2001—. Author: Foreign Languages and the Schools, 1967, Foreign Languages and the Elementary School Child, 1968, The Child and the English Language Arts, 1971, 75, 79, 85, 90, Using Literature Activities to Teach Content Areas to Emergent Readers, 2001; co-author: Second Languages in Primary Education, 1979; contbr. articles to profl. jours. and Ednl. Resources Info. Ctr. U.S. Dept. Edn. Mem. AAUP, AAUW, Nat. Network for Early Lang. Learning, Nat. Coun. Tchrs. English, Nat. Coun. Tchrs. Math., Nat. Coun. Social Studies, Nat. Sci. Tchrs. Assn., Am. Ednl. Rsch. Assn., Nat. Soc. for Study of Edn., Internat. Reading Assn., Nat. Assn. Edn. Young Children, Assn. for Childhood Edn. Internat., Phi Beta Kappa, Phi Kappa Phi, Pi Lambda Theta, Alpha Upsilon Alpha. Address: Calif State U 800 State Coll Blvd Fullerton CA 92834

DONOHO, TIM MARK, not-for-profit executive; b. St. Louis, Sept. 25, 1955; s. James O. and Jean (Dace) D.; m. Deborah Ann Peeples, Feb. 26, 1981; children: Drew Morgan, Jourdan Alexis. BABA, Columbia Coll., 1979. Editor U.S. Army, Okinawa, Japan, 1973-77; sales mgr. Unival Investments, Okinawa, 1975-77; nat. dir. mktg. Pyramid Life Ins. Co., Springfield, Mo., 1978-82; chmn., owner Ins. Mktg. Group, Springfield,

1982-90; pres., owner Am. Dental Program, Inc., Ft. Lauderdale, Fla., 1984-97, Donoho Gruppe Cos., Ft. Lauderdale, 1982—; owner Advantage Dental Health Plans, Ft. Lauderdale, Fla., 1984-97; pub., editor, owner Prime Years News Mag., Ft. Lauderdale, 1985-92; chmn., owner Bus. Healthcare Coalition Inc., 1995-98; chmn. Express Bakery, 1998—2006. Bd. dirs. So. Fla. chpt. Nat. Multiple Sclerosis Soc., 1996-97; founder, chmn. bd. dirs. Pastors Closet, 2000—, chmn., founder, Film the Bible, Inc., 1996—; bd. govs. Graves Archael. Mus., 1998-2000, chmn. founder Pasters Golf Tour, 2004—, chmn. founder World's Largest Choir Project, 2004-. With US Army, 1973—77. Mem.: Nat. Assn. Dental Plans (chmn. bd. dirs. 1996—97). Republican. Baptist. Avocations: tennis, golf, loudspeaker design. Home: 1075 Hillsboro Mile Hillsboro Beach FL 33062

DONOHOE, CATHRYN MURRAY, journalist; b. Bronx, NY; d. Harry and Helen (Crowley) Murray; m. Thomas W. Donohoe. BA cum laude in Am. Lit., Middlebury Coll., 1958; student in Russian lit., Columbia U., 1958—60; student in journalism, American U., 1983—84; cert. in Russian Lang. and Culture, Gornyi Inst., St. Petersburg, Russia, 1993. Rsch. and policy coord. Radio Liberty, NYC, 1963—74; freelance journalist, 1977—84; reporter Potomac Almanac, Potomac, Md., 1985, Washington Times, Washington, 1985—94, deputy editor, features, 1994—. Recipient Nat. Mag. award for pub. svc., 1985. Office: Washington Times 3600 New York Ave NE Washington DC 20002-1996

DONOHOE, JEROME FRANCIS, lawyer; b. Yankton, SD, Mar. 17, 1939; s. Francis A. and Ruth D. Donohoe; m. Elaine Bush, Jan. 27, 1968; 1 child, Nicole Elaine. BA, St. John's U., 1961; JD cum laude, U. Minn., 1964. Bar: Ill. 1964, S.D. 1964. Atty. Atchison, Topeka & Santa Fe Ry. Co., Chgo., 1967-73, gen. atty., 1973-78; gen. counsel corp. affairs Santa Fe Industries Inc., Chgo., 1978-84; v.p. law Santa Fe Industries, Inc., Chgo., 1984-90, Santa Fe Pacific Corp., Chgo., 1984-94; ptnr. Mayer, Brown, Rowe & Maw, Chgo., 1990-99, sr. counsel, 1999—. Capt. JAGC US Army, 1964—67. Fellow: Ill. Bar Found.; mem.: ABA (pub. utility, comm. and transp. law sect.), Northwestern U. Assocs., Mich. Shores Club (Wilmette, Ill.), Chgo. Athletic Assn., Chgo. Club. E-mail: jdonohoe@mac.com.

DONOHUE, ANDREW JOHN, lawyer, securities executive; b. Roslyn, NY, Aug. 22, 1950; s. Thomas Aloysius and Ellen Kathryn (McDermott) D.; m. Patricia Ann Cowley, Nov. 1971; children: Andrew Jr., Kerry, Erin. BA, Hofstra U., 1972; JD, NYU, 1975. Bar: N.Y. 1976, N.J. 1988. Sec., gen. counsel 1st Investors Consolidated Corp. and Subs., NYC, 1976; sec. 1st Investors Group Funds, NYC, 1979, pres., bd. dirs., 1984; sec., bd. dirs. 1st Investors Life Ins. Co., NYC, 1984; exec. v.p. gen. counsel, dir., mem. exec. com. Oppenheimer Funds, Inc., 1991—2001; retired, 2001—03; v.p., gen. counsel Merrill Lynch Investment Managers, 2003—. Office: Merrill Lynch Investment Managers PO Box 9011 Princeton NJ 08543-9011

DONOHUE, CLAIRE P., retired school librarian; b. Glen Cove, NY, Mar. 6, 1941; d. Hubert Aloysius Donohue and Catherine Teresa Scarlett; m. John T. Sexton, Aug. 30, 1975 (div. Apr. 1, 1983). BA, St. John's U., Jamaica, NY, 1965, MA, 1967; MLS, L.I. U., 1974. Cert. secondary English tchr. NY, 1967, sch. libr. media specialist NY, 1974, sch. dist. adminstr. NY, 1995. Tchr. English St. Peter Alcantara Sch., Port Washington, NY, 1966—68; dir. libr. media St. Agnes Acad. H.S., College Point, NY, 1969—77; libr. media specialist Bethpage Union Free Sch. Dist., NY, 1977—91, chair libr. media, 1991—2003; part-time reference libr. St. Joseph's Coll., Patchogue, NY, 2004—. Adj. instr. N.Y.C. Tech. Coll., Bklyn., 1975—79, Palmer Sch. L.I. U., Greenvale, NY, 1991—95; acting interim dir. Nassau BOCES Sch. Libr. Sys., Massapequa, NY, 2003. Mem.: ALA, Nassau Sch. Libr. Sys. Adv. Coun. (chair 1992—94), L.I. Sch. Media Assn. (bd. mem. 1991—93), N.Y. Libr. Assn. Home: 15 Tojan Dr East Islip NY 11730 Personal E-mail: clairedonohue@optonline.net.

DONOHUE, CRAIG S., mercantile exchange executive; b. Oct. 9, 1961; married; 3 children. BA in Polit. Sci. & History, Drake U., 1983; LLM in Fin. Svcs. Regulation, Ill. Inst. Tech., Chgo.; JD, John Marshall Law Sch., 1987; M in Mgmt., Northwestern U., 1995. Bar: Ill. Assoc. McBride, Baker & Coles, Chgo.; corp. atty. Chgo. Merc. Exch., Inc., 1989—95, v.p., assoc. gen. counsel, 1995—97, v.p. market regulation, 1997—98, sr. v.p., gen. counsel, 1998—2000; mng. dir. bus. devel. & corp./legal affairs Chgo. Merc. Exch. Inc., 2000—01, mng. dir., chief adminstrv. officer, 2001—02, exec. v.p., chief adminstrv. officer, 2002—03; CEO Chgo. Merc. Exch. Holdings Inc., 2004—07, CME Group Inc. (formerly Chgo. Merc. Exch. Holdings Inc.), 2007—. Chmn. bd. Nat. Coun. Econ. Edn.; mem. global markets. adv. com. Commodity Futures Trading Commn. Mem. adv. coun. Youth Svcs. of Glenview/Northbrook. Mem.: Chicagoland C. of C., Execs. Club Chgo. (bd. dirs.). Office: CME Group Inc 20 S Wacker Dr Chicago IL 60606*

DONOHUE, DAVID PATRICK, engineering executive, retired military officer; b. NYC, May 7, 1931; s. Patrick Joseph and Beatrice Anna (Bligh) D.; m. Dolores Theresa Bowen, Nov. 24, 1956; children: Christine, David, Steven, Joanne, Denise. AB, Holy Cross Coll., 1953; MSEE, U.S. Naval Postgrad. Sch., 1961; postgrad., Harvard Bus. Sch., 1969, Kennedy Sch. Nat. Security, 1986. Design advisor Vietnam Naval Shipyard, Saigon, Vietnam, 1965-66; plan/estimating supt. Puget Sound Naval Shipyard, Bremerton, Wash., 1966-69; ship projects officer, supr. shipbuilding USN, Seattle, 1969-71; ship systems engr. Staff Naval Air Forces Pacific, San Diego, 1971-75; exec. dir. surface platforms Naval Sea Systems Command, Washington, 1975-77; prodn., planning officer Pearl Harbor (Hawaii) Naval Shipyard, 1977-80; shipyard commdr. Norfolk Naval Shipyard, Portsmouth, Va., 1980-83; rear adm., dir. maintenance U.S. Atlantic Fleet USN, Norfolk, Va., 1983-89; engring. mgr. The Jonathan Corp., Norfolk, 1989-91, program mgr., 1991-93, v.p., gen. mgr. shipyard Norfolk, 1993-95; corp. tech. dir. Integrated Sys. Analysts, Inc., Chesapeake, Va., 1995—2002; chmn. bd. dirs. Cen. Mgmt. Sys., 2000—01; corp. tech. dir. Thermal Spray & Machine, Inc., Norfolk, 2002—. Exec. adv. coun. Old Dominion U. Coll. Bus. and Pub. Adminstrn., 1996-99; bd. dirs. Unitech Corp., Hampton. Va., Lockring Corp. Pres. Portsmouth Area United Way, 1981-82, com. mem. South Hampton Roads chpt., Norfolk, 1983-88; chmn. Portsmouth Armed Svcs. YMCA, 1981-82. Mem. Am. Soc. for Quality Control (vice-chmn. Tidewater, Va. sect. 1995-97, chmn. 1997-98, sec. 1998-2000), Am. Soc. Naval Engrs. (councillor Tidewater sect. 1981-84, 2005—, chmn. Tiewater sect. 2004-2005, nat. councillor 1990-93, 2002-06, nat. v.p. 2006-), Soc. Naval Architects and Marine engrs. (Hampton Rds. sect. chmn. 1985-86, chmn. ship prodn. com. nat. shipbuilding rsch. program 1990-95, Va. gov.'s commn. on base retention 1995), Norfolk Naval Shipyard Portsmouth Assn. (pres. 1998-2000), Town Point Club (bd. govs. 1994-2002). Republican. Roman Catholic. Home: 216 Brackenridge Ave Norfolk VA 23505-4322 Office: Thermal Spray and Machine Inc 2400 Hampton Blvd Norfolk VA 23517-1004 Home Phone: 787-440-9161; Office Phone: 757-623-6484. E-mail: donohued6@cox.net, dave.donohue@tsmnorfolk.com.

DONOHUE, GEORGE L., mechanical engineer, educator; b. Wichita, Kans., July 8, 1944; s. George Edward and Dorothy Mae (Cunningham) Custer; m. Andreana Grillis, June 7, 1969; children: Carmen, Kathleen, Georgiana, Caroline. Student, Ga. Inst. Tech., Atlanta, 1962-64; BSME, U. Houston, 1967; MS, Okla. State U., 1968, PhD, 1972. Coop student NASA, Clear Lake, Tex., 1963-67; postdoctoral fellow Naval Undersea Ctr., Pasadena, Calif., 1972-73; br. head Naval Ocean Sys. Ctr., San Diego, 1973-76, divsn. head, 1977-79; prog. mgr. Def. Adv. Rsch. Project Agy., Arlington, Va., 1976-77, office dir., 1988-89; v.p. Dynamics Tech. Inc., Torrance, Calif., 1979-84; prog. mgr. Rand Corp., Santa Monica, Calif., 1984-88, v.p., 1989-94; assoc. adminstr. rsch. and acquisition FAA, Washington, 1994-98; prof. George Mason U., Fairfax, Va., 2000—. Vis. prof. air transp. tech. and policy Sch. IT & Engring. George Mason U., Fairfax, 1998—2000, prof. sys. engring., 2000—. Author: Air Transportation Systems Engineering, 2001; contbr. articles to profl. jours. Treas. YMCA Girls Gymnastics Team, San Pedro, Calif., 1983; adult advisor Girl Scouts U.S., Torrance, 1987—88. Recipient Merit Civil Svc. medal, Dept. of Def., 1977, Pinnical award, ERAV, 2007; NDEA fellow, 1967, NRC fellow, 1972. Fellow: AIAA (mem. policy com. 1990—94); mem.: Chesapeake Yacht Club (treas. 2005—07), Elks, Sigma Xi, Pi Tau Sigma, Omicron Delta Kappa, Tau Beta Pi. Roman Catholic. Avocations: flying, skiing, sailing, backpacking. Office Phone: 703-993-2093.

DONOHUE, JAMES J., lawyer; b. NYC, Dec. 3, 1947; s. Joseph P. and Constance (Anderson) D.; m. Carol A. Mager, July 29, 1973; children: Jay Mager, Megan Constance. AB, Dartmouth Coll., 1969; JD, U. Pa., 1972. Atty. Fed. Defender Phila., 1972-76; ptnr. White and Williams, Phila., 1976—. Mem.: ABA (chair trial evidence com., litigation sect. 1995—99, judiciary task force 2000—03, fed. practice task force 2004—05), Phila Bar Found. (trustee 1992—97), WYCK (bd. dirs. 1996—, treas. 1998—2004), Rotary Club Phila. (bd. dirs. 1993-95), (bd. dirs. 1993—95), Phila. Cricket Club, Phila. Racquet Club. Avocations: skiing, golf. Office: White and Williams 1800 One Liberty Pl 1650 Market St Philadelphia PA 19103-7395 Home Phone: 215-248-5156; Office Phone: 215-864-7037. Business E-Mail: donohuej@whiteandwilliams.com.

DONOHUE, JOHN JOSEPH, law educator; b. Alexandria, Va., Jan. 30, 1953; s. Mildred (Sileo) Donohue; m. Marijke Rijsberman, Dec. 27, 1986 (div.); 1 child, Lauren Elizabeth; m. Maureen O'Kicki, Oct. 25, 1995; children: Aidan John, Patrick John. BA, Hamilton Coll., 1974; JD, Harvard U., 1977; PhD, Yale U., 1986. Bar: Conn. 1977, D.C. 1978. Assoc. Covington & Burling, Washington, 1978-81; fellow Civil Liability Program, Law Sch. Yale U., New Haven, 1985-86; rsch. fellow Am. Bar Found., Chgo., 1986-95; Class of 1967 James B. Haddad prof. law Northwestern U., Chgo., 1994-95; prof. Stanford (Calif.) Law Sch., 1995—2004, William H. Neukom prof. law, 2002—04; Leighton Homer Surbeck prof. law Yale Law Sch., New Haven, 2004—. Vis. prof. Harvard Law Sch., 2003. Contbr. articles to profl. jours. Mem. ABA, Am. Econ. Assn., Phi Beta Kappa. Office: Yale Law Sch PO Box 208215 New Haven CT 06520-8215 Office Phone: 203-432-1994. Business E-Mail: j.donohue@yale.edu.

DONOHUE, JOHN PATRICK, lawyer; b. NYC, Sept. 16, 1944; s. Joseph Francis and Catherine Elizabeth (Feeney) D.; m. Patricia Ann Holly, June 11, 1977; children: Eileen Mary, Anne Catherine. BA, Providence Coll., 1966; JD, Catholic U. Am., 1969. Bar: N.Y. 1973, U.S. Ct. Appeals (2d cir.) 1973, U.S. Ct. Appeals (fed. cir.) 1974, N.J. 1975, U.S. Dist. Ct. N.J. 1975, U.S. Dist. Ct. (so., ea. dists.) N.Y. 1975, U.S. Supreme Ct. 1978, D.C. 1981, Pa. 1986. Spl. agt. FBI, Washington, 1969-71; assoc. Donohue & Donohue, NYC, 1971-74, ptnr., 1974—; of counsel Kittredge Donley Elson Fullem & Embick. Adj. prof. law internat. bus. transactions Seton Hall U. Sch. Law, Newark, 1986-94, 2002—. Author book sect. Customs Fraud Section on Business Crimes, 1982; co-author: The Prevention and Prosecution of Computer and High Technology Crime. Bd. dirs. Maritime Exch. Delaware River and Bay, 1989—; mem. bd. regents Cath. U. Am., 1990-2000, chmn., 1997-2000; trustee Rosemont (Pa.) Sch., 1995—, chmn., 1996-2001; mem. bd. visitors Cath. U. Sch. Law, 1998—; mem. Congress of Fellows, Ctr. for Internat. Legal Studies, Salzburg, Austria. Named Man of Yr., Phila. Customs, Brokers and Forwarders Assn., 1984. Mem. Customs and Internat. Trade Bar Assn., Pa. State Bar Assn.; Republican. Roman Catholic. Office: Kittredge Donley Elson Fullem & Embick 400 Market St Ste 200 Philadelphia PA 19106 Office Phone: 215-829-9900. Business E-Mail: Jdonohue@kdefe.com.

DONOHUE, MARC DAVID, chemical engineering professor; b. Watertown, NY, Sept. 10, 1951; s. Paul Francis and Beverly Gertrude D.; m. Mary Ann Chamberlain, July 20, 1974; children: Paul, Megan, Ian. BS, Clarkson Coll. Tech., 1973; PhD, U. Calif., Berkeley, 1977. Asst. prof. chem. engring. Clarkson Coll. Tech., Potsdam, NY, 1977-79; asst. prof. Johns Hopkins U., Balt., 1979-83, assoc. prof., 1983-87, prof., 1987—, chmn. dept., 1984-95, assoc. dean, 1999—. Treas. Coun. Chem. Rsch., 1993—. Recipient Adminstr.'s Pollution Prevention award for Region III, U.S. EPA, 1992, Md. sect. Outstanding Engring. Achievement award, NSPE, 1989. Mem. Am. Inst. Chem. Engrs., Am. Chem. Soc. (Md. chemist 1999), Am. Soc. Engring. Edn. (Outstanding Young Engr. award 1984), Tau Beta Pi.

DONOHUE, MARY O., judge, former lieutenant governor; b. Rensselaer County, NY, Mar. 22, 1947; children: Sara, Justin. B.Edn., Coll. New Rochelle, 1968; MS in Edn., Russell Sage Coll., Troy, NY, 1973; JD, Union U., 1983. Bar: NY 1983. Tchr. elem., jr. h.s. Rensselaer and Albany County (N.Y.) sch. dists., Albany, 1969-78; law clk., intern U.S. Atty.'s Office, Albany, 1980-83; assoc. O'Connell & Aronowitz, Albany, 1983-88; pvt. practice Troy, 1988-92; asst. county atty. Rensselaer County, 1990-92, dist. atty., 1992-96; justice NY Supreme Ct., 3rd Jud. Dist., 1996-98; lt. gov. State of N.Y., Albany, 1998—2006; judge NY State Ct. Claims, Albany, 2007—. Chair Govs. Task Force on Sch. Violence, 1999—, Task Force on Quality Cmtys., 2000—, Govs. Task Force on Small Bus. Chair Capital Dist. Women's Adv. Coun., 1996; mem. Gov.-elect Pataki's Transition Team for Criminal Justice, 1994-96. Republican. Office: NY State Ct Claims PO Box 7344 Capitol Station Albany NY 12224*

DONOHUE, PATRICIA CAROL, academic administrator; b. St. Louis, Jan. 11, 1946; d. Carroll and Juanita Donohue; m. James H. Stevens Jr., Aug. 27, 1966 (div. Mar. 1984); children: James H. Stevens III, Carol Janet Stevens. AB, Duke U., 1966; MA, U. Mo., 1974, PhD, 1982. Tchr. math. in secondary schs., Balt., St. Louis and Shawnee Mission, Kans., 1966-71; lectr. U. Mo., Kansas City, 1975-76, rsch. asst. affirmative action, 1976-79, coord. affirmative action, 1979-82, instl. rsch. assoc., 1982-84, acting dir. affirmative action and acad. pers., 1984; dir. instl. rsch. Lakeland CC, 1984—86; asst. dean acad. affairs, math., engring. and tech. Harrisburg Area CC, 1986—89, dean sch. bus., engring., and tech., 1989—93, dean Lebanon campus, v.p. cmty. devel. and external affairs, 1993; vice chancellor edn. St. Louis CC, 1993—2002, acting pres. Florissant Valley campus, 1998—99; pres. Luzerne County CC, 2002—07, Mercer County CC, 2007—. Chairperson Pa. Occupl. Deans, 1988—93; active Pa. Coun. on Vocat. Edn., 1989—93; v.p. St. Louis Sch. to Work, Inc., 1994—96, pres., 1996—2002; bd. dirs., chmn. edn. com. Humane Soc. Mo., 1997—2002; cons. evaluator North Ctrl. Assn., 2000—; pres. Greater Wilkes-Barre Chamber Bus. and Industry, Pa., 2003—06; bd. dirs. F.M. Kirby Ctr., 2003—07, The Luzerne Found., 2004—07, Northeastern Pa. Tech. Inst., 2004—07, pres., 2004—05. Bd. dirs., v.p. Am. Cancer Soc. Jackson County, 1975—84; mem. adv. coun. Ben Franklin Partnership, 1988—93; mem. steering com. New Baldwin Corridor Coalition, 1991—93, chair edn. task force, 1992—93; mem. Leadership St. Louis, 1996—97; mem. strategic planning com. Penns Woods Girl Scout Coun., 2003—04, bd. dirs., 2004—07; chair pers. com. Penns Woods Girl Scouts Coun., 2005—07; bd. dirs. PTA, 1975—77, Cmty. Lebanon Assocs., Ctrl. Pa. Tech. Coun., 1989—93, sec., 1992—93; bd. dirs. Mantec, 1988—93, Delta Gamma Ctr. for Children with Visual Impairments, 2001—03, Osterhout Libr., 2003—07, Hemlock coun. Girl Scouts U.S.A., 1987—92, Mercer Regional C. of C., 2007—. Recipient Outstanding Service and Achievement award U. Mo. Kansas City, 1976, Outstanding Svc. award Ctrl. Pa. Tech. Coun., 1993; Jack C. Coffey grantee, 1978; named Outstanding Woman AAUW, 1989, one of Outstanding Leaders Nat. Inst. Leadership Devel., 1986, Exec. Leadership Inst., 1990, Exec. Leadership Wilkes Barre, 2003, Exec. Leadership Lackawanna, 2004, Cmty. Woman of Yr. Wilkes-Barre, Am. Bus. Women Assn., 2005, Athena award Wilkes-Barre Chamber Bus. and Industry, 2006 Mem.: Assn. Comm. Coll. Trustees (pres. adv. bd. 2005—), Assn. Inst. Rsch., Women's Network, Nat. Assn. Student Pers. Adminstrs., Women's Equity Project, Soc. Mfg. Engrs. (chmn. 1989—90), Am. Assn. Women in C.C. (Pa. state coord. 1988, bd. dirs. Region 3 1989—91, 2005—06, pres. elect 2006—07, pres. 2007—), Nat. Coun. for Occupl. Edn. (chairperson diversity task force 1991, chairperson job tng. 2000 task force 1992, v.p. programs 1992—93, bd. dirs. 1992—2000, v.p. membership 1993—94, pres. 1995—96, past pres. 1996—97), Am. Assn. Cmty. Colls. (bd. dirs. 1988—91, coun. affiliated chairpersons 1994—2000, commn. on cmty. and workforce devel. 1995—97, chairperson coun. 1996—2000, commn. on cmty. and workforce devel. 1998—2001, acad. pres. 2003, commn. diversity 2006—), Am. Vocat. Assn., Math. Assn. Am., Nat. Coun. Tchrs. of Math., ASCD, Delta Gamma (v.p., del. nat. conv. 1988, pres. 1989-91, bd. dirs. Delta Gamma Ctr. for Children with Visual Impairment 2001-03) (del. nat. conv. 1988, pres. 1989—91, v.p., Cream Rose Outstanding Svc. award 1970), Pi Lambda Theta, Phi Kappa Phi, Phi Delta Kappa (pres. 1975, Read fellow 1989). Office: Mercer County CC 1200 Old Trenton Rd Trenton NJ 08550 Home: 1 Cook Rd Trenton NJ 08690 Office Phone: 609-570-3613. Business E-Mail: donohuep@mccc.edu.

DONOHUE, PETER M., academic administrator, priest, theater educator, director; b. Bronx, NY, 1952; s. Mary and Morgan Donohue. BA, Villanova U., 1975; MA, Cath. U. of Am., 1983; MDiv, Washington Theol. Union, 1985; PhD in Theater, U. Ill., 1992. Ordained priest Roman Cath. Ch., 1979. Assoc. prof. Villanova U., Pa., chair Theater Dept. Pa., 1992—2006, chaplain Navy ROTC program Pa., 1993—, pres., 2006—. Adv. bd. mem. Augustinian Inst.; mem. NCAA Certification Self-Study Com., 1996—97, 2001—02. Dir.: (plays) Evita, 1996, Into the Woods, 1998, Children of Eden, 2001, Chicago, 2002 (Barrymore award for Outstanding Direction of a Musical, 2002), Parade, 2004 (Phila. Inquirer Critics award, Best Dir. award, named Best Musical, Best Dir., Phila. Weekly, 2004), Urinetown, 2006. Recipient Cert. of Merit, Am. Coll. Theatre Festival. Mem.: Phi Kappa Phi. Office: Villanova U Office of the Pres Tolentine Hall 1st 800 Lancaster Ave Villanova PA 19085-1603 Office Phone: 610-519-4511. E-mail: peter.donohue@villanova.edu.*

DONOHUE, RICHARD WILLIAM, musician, conductor; b. Cromwell, Conn., June 19, 1936; s. Robert Francis and Marguerite Elizabeth (Meyer) Donohue; m. Lois Franklin Donohue, June 27, 1959; children: Linda Maria, Katherine Marguerite, Robert Lawrence, Richard Franklin. BA, Wesleyan U., Middletown, Conn., 1958; MusM, Yale U., New Haven, 1960. Founder, pres. The Richard Donohue Studio of Music, Cromwell, Conn., 1951—. Choral dir., organist St. John's Roman Cath. Ch., Cromwell, Conn., 1954—60, South Congl. Ch., Hartford, Conn., 1960—67, Hartford, 1974—96, St. Peter Roman Cath. Ch., Higganum, Conn., 1996—; pvt. tchr. Yale U., New Haven, 1962; prof. Wesleyan U., Middletown, Conn., 1967—74; founder, condr. New Eng. Chamber Choir and Orch., Portland, Conn., 1996—. Pres. Cromwell Hist. Soc., 1964—66. Mem.: Delta Tau Delta, Phi Beta Kappa. Home: PO Box 211 Cromwell CT 06416

DONOHUE, SUSAN K., information technology executive, researcher; BA in Polit. Sci., Marquette U., Milwaukee, Wis., 1980; M Engring., U. Va., Charlottesville, 2000, PhD in Sys. Engring., 2006. Pres. TechWrite, Inc., Charlottesville, Va., 1995—. Tech. writer, edn. materials developer CC Workforce Alliance, Richmond, Va., 2001—; vol. rschr. Ctr. Diversity Engring., U. Va., Charlottesville, 2004—; postdoctoral engring. edn. rschr. U. Va., Charlottesville, 2007—. Mem. at large Nat. Soc. Daughter of Am. Revolution; founding mem., feline safehouse Indian Rivers Humane Soc., Aylett, Va., 1995. Mem.: IEEE, ASEE, Omega Rho, Alpha Sigma Nu, Phi Beta Kappa, Alpha Delta Pi. Achievements include provisional patent for a knowledge elicitation methodology. Home Phone: 434-953-5190.

DONOHUE, THERESE BRADY, artistic director, choreographer, costume and set designer; b. Wash., Jan. 13, 1937; d. John Bernard and Mary Catherine (Rupert) B.; m. Joseph W. Donohue Jr., June 13, 1959 (div. 1987); children: Sharon Marie, Maura Cathleen (dec.), Sheila Patricia. BA, Coll. of Notre Dame Md., 1958. Cert. tchr. ballet Royal Acad. Dance London. Advt. artist Kronstadt Advt. Agy., Washington, 1958; instr. art The Maret Sch., Washington, 1958-60, Princeton U., NJ, 1967-71; artist dir. Amherst Ballet Centre, Mass., 1971—99, Amherst Ballet Theatre Co., Mass., 1977—2000. Co-dir., founder Pioneer Valley Ballet, Northampton, 1972—77; dancer, tchr. Princeton Ballet, 1962—71; animal masks Charleston (SC) Ballet, 1985—90; choreographer Roanoke (Va.) Ballet theatre, 1983; chair NE Region Craft Choreography Conf., Amherst, 1979; artist, choreographer Nat. Gallery Art, 1986, 88, Guggenheim, 1986, Nat. Mus. Am. Art, 1969, Hirshhorn Mus. and Sculpture Garden, 1993; sch. adminstr. Amherst Ballet, 1999—2004; artist-in-residency programs based on works of Eric Carle, 2006—; artist in-res. Greenwood Elem. Sch., Brookville, Md., 2006. Choreographer (ballets for children) Peter & the Wolf, 1973, One Thousand Cranes, 1974, Punch & Judy, 1975, Amherst Poets, 1977, Uncle Wiggily & the Duck Pond, 1979, (Springfield Symphony) History of Dance, 1983, (Project Opera) Hansel & Gretel, 1983, Sea Study (included in Aberdeen Internat. Youth Festival in Scotland), 1994, Peter Pan Amherst Cmty. Theater, 1995, Aida Commonwealth Opera, 1996, Flower Fairy Ballet, 1997, Ribbon Festival Ballet, 1997; rechoreographed Matisse's Circus, Dancing with Dubuffet; toured Maui Hawaii Elem. Schs. (Amherst Ballet Theatre Co.), 1996; spl. projects dir. Amherst Ballet, 2003-05; prodr., costumer Eric Carle's The Very Lonely Firefly, 2003, Russian Nat. Dances, 2003, Eric Carle's The Honeybee and the Robber, 2004, The Eric Carle Museum of Picture Book Art; costumer Amherst Ballet's Shim Chung, 2005; ind. prodr.: (puppets and dance) Eric Carle's A House for the Hermit Crab, 2006, Picture Book Theatre, 2007, Leo Lionni's Tico and the Golden Wings, 2007. Mem. Amherst Arts Coun., 1983-89. Recipient Town of Amherst Arts and Supplemental Edn. award, 1997, Mass. Senate Citation, 2002, C.C. Dakin Medallion award in edn., 2002. Mem. Amherst Club. Avocation: travel. Home and Office: 17 Juniper Ln Amherst MA 01002-1227 Business E-Mail: tbd@crocker.com.

DONOHUE, THOMAS JOSEPH, business association administrator; b. NYC, Aug. 12, 1938; s. Thomas Joseph Sr. and Ruth (Ahern) D.; m. Elizabeth Schulz, June 29, 1963; children: Thomas, Keith, John. BA, St. John's U., 1963, PhD (hon.), 1985; MBA, Adelphi U., 1965; PhD (hon.), Marymount U., 1991. V.p. Fairfield U., Conn., 1967-69; dep. asst. postmaster gen. US Postal Svc., Washington, 1969-71, asst. regional postmaster gen. San Francisco, 1971-73, dist. mgr. NYC, 1973-75, asst. regional postmaster gen., 1975-76; group v.p. US C. of C., Washington, 1976-84, pres., CEO, 1997—, Am. Trucking Associations, Alexandria, Va., 1985—97. Pres. Ctr. Internat. Pvt. Enterprise; bd. dirs. Union Pacific Corp., Qwest, XM Satellite Radio, Sunrise Sr. Living Corp.; mem. Pres.'s Coun. 21st Century Workforce, Pres.'s Adv. Com. Trade Policy and Negotiations. Bd. dirs. Marymount U. Office: US C of C 1615 H St NW Washington DC 20062-2000 Office Phone: 202-659-6000.*

DONOHUGH, DONALD LEE, physician; b. LA, Apr. 12, 1924; s. William Noble and Florence Virginia (Shelton) D.; m. Virginia Eskew McGregor, Sept. 12, 1950 (div. 1971); children: Ruth, Laurel, Marilee, Carol, Greg; m. Beatrice Ivany Redick, Dec. 3, 1976. BS, U.S. Naval Acad., 1946; MD, U. Calif., San Francisco, 1956; MPH and Tropical Medicine, Tulane U., 1961. Diplomate Am. Bd. Internal Medicine. Intern U. Hosp., San Diego, 1956—57; resident Monterey County Hosp., 1957—58; dir. med. svc. U.S. Dept. Interior, Am. Samoa, 1958—60; instr. Tulane U. Med. Sch., New Orleans, 1960—63; resident Tulane Svc. VA and Charity Hosp., New Orleans, 1961—63; cons. Internat. Ctr. for Rsch and Tng., Costa Rica, 1961—63; asst. prof. medicine and preventive medicine La. State U. Sch. Medicine, 1962—63, assoc. prof., 1963—65; vis. prof. U. Costa Rica, 1963—65; faculty advisor, head of AID program U. Costa Rica Med. Sch., 1965—67; dir. med. svcs. Med. Ctr. U. Calif. (formerly Orange County Hosp.), Irvine, 1967—69; assoc. clin. prof. U. Calif., Irvine, 1967—79, clin. prof., 1980—85; pvt. practice Tustin, Calif., 1970—80; with Joint Commn. on Accreditation of Hosp., 1981; cons. Kauai, Hawaii, 1981—. Author: The Middle Years, 1981, Practice Management, 1986, Kauai, 1988, 4th edit., 1992, Our Ancestors, 1995, The Story of Koloa, 2001, (second edition, 2002); co-translator; Rashomon (Ryonosuke Akutagawa), 1950; also numerous articles. Lt. USN, 1946-52, capt. USNR, 1966-84. Fellow ACP (life); mem. Delta Omega. Republican. Episcopalian. Home: 4890 Lawai Beach Rd Koloa HI 96756-9675 E-mail: dldondhugh1@hawaiiantel.net.

DONOVAN, ANDREW JOSEPH, financial consultant; b. NYC, Nov. 22, 1952; s. Andrew Joseph and Marion (Cooley) D.; m. Margaret Mary Dowd, June 17, 1984; children: Andrew, John, Daniel. BA, Fordham U., 1974, MA, 1976, PhD, 1983; grad., Coll. Fin. Planning, 1996, Naval War Coll., 2000. Adj. instr. Fordham U., Bronx, N.Y., 1976-78; ops. mgr. Merrill Lynch, Pierce, Fenner & Smith, NYC, 1978-79, stockbroker Mt. Kisco, N.Y., 1984-88, Kidder Peabody, White Plains, N.Y., 1988-89; dir. devel. N.Y. Med. Coll., Valhalla, 1989-93, U.S. Merchant Marine Acad. Found., Inc., Kings Point, N.Y., 1993-96; fin. cons. Chase Investment Svcs. Corp., 1996-2001, Donovan Fin., 2001—. Chmn. N.Y. State 4-H Found., Inc., 1990-92. Author: The Political Clock, 1983. Councilman Town of Yorktown, N.Y., 1990-93; legislator Westchester County, N.Y., 1994-97. Lt. cmdr. USNR, 1979—. Fellow H.B. Earhart Found., 1976. Republican. Roman Catholic. Avocation: collecting books. Home: 168 Country Club Rd Hopewell Junction NY 12533 Office Phone: 914-526-7288. E-mail: andrew-donovan@lpl.com.

DONOVAN, ANNE, professional basketball coach; b. Ridgewood, NJ, Nov. 1, 1961; Grad., Old Dominion U., 1983. Profl. basketball player Shizuoka, Japan, 1983—88, Modena, Italy, 1988—89; asst. coach Old Dominion U., 1989—95; head coach women's basketball East Carolina U., Greenville, 1995—97; head coach Am. Basketball League Phila. Rage, 1997—98; interim head coach WNBA Ind. Fever, Indpls., 2000; head coach WNBA Charlotte Sting, 2001—02, WNBA Seattle Storm, 2002—, dir. player pers., 2003—. Head coach WNBA Ea. Conf. All-Star Team, 2002; asst. coach US Women's Sr. Nat. Team World Championships, China, 2002; asst. coach US Women's Olympic Team, Athens, Greece, 2004; head coach U.S.A. Basketball Women's Sr. Nat. Team, 2006—. Recipient Naismith Player of Yr. award, 1983, Olympic Team Gold medal, 1984, 88, World Championship Team Gold medal, 1986; named to Naismith Basketball Hall of Fame, 1995. Mem. USA Basketball Com. (exec. bd. dirs. 1996—). Achievements include being a three time All-Am. selection; led nation in rebounding, 1982; all-time leading scorer, blocker and rebounder Old Dominion U.; Olympian, 1980, 84, 88; World Championship team member, 1983, 86. Office: Seattle Storm 351 Elliott Ave W Ste 500 Seattle WA 98119*

DONOVAN, BILLY (WILLIAM JOHN), men's college basketball coach; b. Rockville Centre, NY, May 30, 1965; m. Christine D'Auria; children: William, Hasbrouck, Bryan, Connor. BA in Gen. Social Studies, Providence Coll., 1987. Profl. basketball player Wyo. Wildcatters, Continental Basketball Assn., 1987, NY Knicks, NBA, 1987-88; grad. asst. coach U. Ky., Lexington, 1989-90, asst. coach, 1990-93, assoc. coach, 1993-94; head coach Marshall U., 1994-96, U. Fla., Gainesville, 1996—2007, 2007—, Orlando Magic, 2007. (as player) named Honorable Mention All-Am. (UPI), 1987, All Big East, 1987, NABC All Dist., 1986 (second team), 1987 (first team), All Big East, 1986 (third team), 1987 (first team), New Eng. Player of Yr., 1987, Providence Male Athlete of Yr., 1986, 1987, Providence MVP, 1986, 1987, NCAA S.E. Region Most Outstanding Player, 1987, Big East All Tournament Team, 1987, All-Time Providence Civic Ctr. Team, 1999; named to Providence Hall of Fame, 1999; (as coach) named Nat. Rookie Coach of Yr., Basketball Times, 1994, W.Va. Coll. Coach of Yr., 1994, So. Conf. Coach of Yr., 1994, Gainesville Sun Sportsperson of Yr., 1999, NABC Dist. VI Coach of Yr., 2000, 2003, ESPN.com Nat. Coach of Yr., 2001. As coach of Marshall U., he was the youngest head coach in college basketball; only one of two people ever to serve as head coach in a Final Four, as an assistant coach in the Final Four and reach Final Four as a player; one of only five coaches to have reached the Final Four both as a head coach and as a player; holds record for most wins by a University of Florida head basketball coach; University of Florida Gators accomplishments include: an appearance in the National Championship game in 2000, No. 1 ranking team in the nation in consecutive years, seven straight 20-win seasons, seven consecutive NCAA appearances, SEC Tournament title in 2005, NCAA tournament championship, 2006, 07. Office: U Fla Basketball Office PO Box 14485 Gainesville FL 32604-2485*

DONOVAN, BRIAN, freelance/self-employed journalist; b. Syracuse, NY, Mar. 11, 1941; m. Ellen B. Kanner; children: Gregg, Becky. BA, Syracuse U., 1963. With Dem. and Chronicle, Rochester, NY, 1964—67; investigative reporter Newsday, Melville, NY, 1967—2001. Recipient Pulitzer Prize for investigative reporting, 1995, George Polk award for Nat. Reporting, 1980, John Hancock award for Fin. Reporting, 1985, others. Achievements include being EMRA Vanderbilt Cup auto-racing champion. E-mail: briandonovan26@hotmail.com.

DONOVAN, BRUCE ELLIOT, literature educator, dean; b. Lawrence, Mass., Mar. 8, 1937; s. Harry Albert and Ruth Hannah (Kent) D.; m. Doris Louise Stearn, Sept. 7, 1959; children: Gregory Stearn, Erika Ruth. AB, Brown U., 1959; postgrad., U. Bristol, Eng., 1959-60; MA, Yale U., 1961, PhD, 1965; postgrad., Rutgers U., 1976. Instr. Yale U., 1962-65; from instr. to prof. classics Brown U., Providence, 1965—2003, assoc. dean for chem. dependency, 1977—2003, dean freshmen and sophomores, 1981-87, assoc. dean coll., 1977—2003. Instr. summer sch. alcohol studies Rutgers U.; cons. on collegiate alcoholism and other drug abuse. Author: Euripides Papyri from Oxyrhynchus, 1969, A Bunch of Characers: An Alliterative ABC to Captivate Children, 2004; author articles and revs. on ancient Greek lit. and alcohol and other drug issues. Bd. dirs. Vols. in Action, 1975-90, RI Coun. on Alcoholism and Other Drug Dependence, 1973-94, New Eng. Inst. Alcohol Studies, 1978-91; founding mem. New Eng. Coll. Alcohol Network, Academics Recovering Together, Assn. Recovery Schs., 2006-, Meml. Soc. of RI, 2007-; steering com. Network Colls. and Univs. Committed to the Elimination of Substance Abuse, 1988-93. Fulbright fellow, 1959-60; Woodrow Wilson fellow, 1960-61; fellow Center for Hellenic Studies, Washington, 1971-72, Visionary award Assn. Recovery Schs., 2006. Mem. Am. Philol. Assn., Assn. Recovery Sch., Meml. Soc. RI. Home: 229 Medway St Apt 307 Providence RI 02906-5300

DONOVAN, CHARLES STEPHEN, lawyer; b. Boston, Feb. 28, 1951; s. Alfred Michael and Maureen (Murphy) D.; m. Lisa Marie Dicharry, Apr. 21, 1979 (div. 2005); children: Yvette, Martine, Neal. BA, Haverford Coll., 1974; JD, Cornell U., 1977. Bar: Mass. 1977, La. 1977, Calif. 1982, U.S. Supreme Ct. 1988. Atty. Phelps, Dunbar, Marks, Claverie & Sims, New Orleans, 1977-81, Dorr, Cooper & Hays, San Francisco, 1981-84, Walsh, Donovan & Keech LLP, San Francisco, 1984-2000, Schnader Harrison Segal & Lewis, LLP, San Francisco, 2000—03, co-chmn. internat. practice group, 2002—03, Sheppard Mullin Richter & Hampton LLP, San Francisco, 2003—. Instr. maritime law Calif. Maritime Acad., Vallejo, 1982—98, U. So. Calif., 2004—; spl. advisor U.S. State Dept., 1996—96. Contbr. numerous articles to profl. jours. Recipient Gustavus H. Robinson prize, Cornell Law Sch., 1977. Mem.: ABA (chmn. admiralty and maritime law com. Chgo. 1989—90, chmn. marine fin. com. 2005—), Marine Exch. (bd. dirs. San Francisco Bay region 1993—96), Tulane Admiralty Inst. (permanent adv. bd.), Maritime Law Assn. U.S. (chmn. subcom. on maritime liens and mortgages 1994—2001, chmn. com. on maritime criminal law 1998—2001), Internat. Bar Assn. Avocations: skiing, hiking, mandolin, guitar, soccer. Office: Sheppard Mullin Richter & Hampton LLP 4 Embarcadero Center 17th Fl San Francisco CA 94111-4106 Home Phone: 510-339-2623; Office Phone: 415-434-9100. Business E-Mail: cdonovan@sheppardmullin.com.

DONOVAN, DAVID P., lawyer; b. June 26, 1958; BS with honors, Iowa State Univ., 1980; JD magna cum laude, Georgetown Univ., 1984. Bar: DC 1984, Va. 2002, US Supreme Ct. Law clk. Judge Thomas A. Flannery, US Dist. Ct. (DC dist.), 1984—85; ptnr., comml. litigation, product liability practices, co-chmn. recruiting com. Wilmer Cutler Pickering Hale & Dorr, McLean, Va. Editor (in chief): Georgetown Univ. Law Jour.; contbr. articles to profl. jours. Recipient Pro Bono award, NAACP Legal Def. & Edn. Fund, 1992. Mem.: ABA, Def. Rsch. Inst., DC Bar Assn., Phi Beta Kappa. Office: Wilmer Cutler Pickering Hale & Dorr Suite 1000 1600 Tysons Blvd Mc Lean VA 22102 Office Fax: 703-251-9760, 703-251-9797. Business E-Mail: david.donovan@wilmerhale.com.

DONOVAN, DENNIS DALE, priest; b. Nyack, NY, Feb. 26, 1954; s. Thomas A. and Helen I. (Rudolph) D. BA in Philosophy, Don Bosco Coll., 1977; MA in Theology, MDiv in Theology, Pontifical Coll. Josephinum, 1983. Joined Soc. St. Francis de Sales, Roman Cath. Ch., 1973, ordained priest, 1983; cert. tchr. N.Y., N.J. Asst. adminstr. Salesian Sch., Goshen, N.Y., 1983-85; adminstr. Salesian Ctr., Columbus, Ohio, 1985-94, vicar, 1998—2004; dir. devel. Salesians of Don Bosco Province of St. Philip the Apostle, New Rochelle, N.Y., 1994-98; assoc. pastor St. Anthony Ch., Nanuet, N.Y., 1994-98; vicar Salesian Provincial House, New Rochelle, N.Y., 1994-98, Salesian Ctr., Columbus, Ohio, 1998—2004; assoc. pastor St. Joseph Cathedral, Columbus, Ohio, 1998—2004, St. Catherine Ch., Bexley, Ohio, 2002—04. Assoc., youth min. St. Andrew Parish, Upper Arlington, Ohio, 1985-94; mem. Nat. Cath. Devel. Conf., 1995—2004; chmn. Ea. province Salesian Centennial Com., 1995-98; mem. youth commn. adv. bd. City Columbus, Ohio, 2001-04, youth adv. commn. Cath. Diocese of Columbus, Ohio, 2003-04. Chaplain Ohio Senate, Columbus, 1987-94, 2002-04, Don Bosco Ladies Guild, Larchmont, NY, 1994-98; trustee Salesian Boys and Girls Club Columbus, 1993-04, Boys & Girls Club, Tampa Bay, 2004-; active Juvenile Delinquency Task Force, Franklin County, 1988-90, Westchester chpt. Crohn's and Colitis Found. Am., 1980-2000, Ctrl. Ohio chpt., 2000-04; exec. dir. Salesian Boys and Girls Club, Columbus, Ohio, 1998-2004; mem. Profl. Adv. Coun. United Way Franklin County, Columbus, 1998-2004, Ohio Alliance of Boys & Girls Clubs, 1998-2004; growth and measurement best practices task force Boys & Girls Clubs Am., Atlanta, 2002-07; bd. trustees Discovery Dist. Devel. Corp., Columbus, 1998-2004; race rels. vision coun. United Way Franklin County, 1999-2003, Columbus Met. Area Ch. Coun., 1999-2004; mem. Columbus Truancy Task Force, 2000-02; blue ribbon panel Jefferson Awards, Columbus, 2003-04, treas. Mary Help of Christians Sch., Tampa, 2004-06, dir. Mary Help of Christians Boys & Girls Club, Tampa, 2006—; assoc. pastor Good Shepherd RC Ch., Tampa, 2005-; dir. Mary Help of Christians Ctr., 2006-, exec. dir. Garry and Mavis Smith Salesian Boys and Girls Club, Tampa, 2007-. Recipient Senate Resolution award Ohio Senate, 1988. Mem. Acad. Boys & Girls Club Profls., Nat. Soc. Fundraising Execs., Am. Guild Organists (bd. dirs., chaplain 1986-2004), KC (chaplain 1987—), Assn. Boys and Girls Clubs Profls. (disting. exec. level); mem. cmty. adv. bd. Jr. League of Columbus, 2001-04).

DONOVAN, DIANNE FRANCYS, journalist; b. Houston, Sept. 30, 1948; d. James Henry and Doris Elaine (Simerly) D.; m. Anthony Charles Burba; children: Donovan Anthony, James Donovan. Student, Trinity Coll., Dublin, Ireland, 1969; BA, Spring Hill Coll., 1970; MA, U. Mo., 1975, U. Chgo., 1982. Fgn./nat. copy desk supr. Chgo. Tribune, 1979-80, asst. editor for news/features, 1980-83, lit. editor, 1985-93, mem. editl. bd., 1993-99, sr. editor for recruitment, 2000—02; v.p., editl. page editor The Balt. Sun, 2002—. Vis. prof. U. Oreg. Sch. Journalism, Eugene, 1983-85; adj. faculty Northwestern U. Sch. Journalism, 1980-81, 89-90; bd. dirs. Chgo. Tribune Found. Bd. dirs. Nelson Algren/Heartland lit. awards, Chgo., 1986-93; judge Nat. Headliners' Club Awards, Atlantic City, N.J., 1983. Recipient award for editl. writing Am. Soc. Newspaper Editors, 1999, Media award Chgo. Bar Assn., 1999. Episcopalian. Office: 501 N Calvert St Baltimore MD 21278

DONOVAN, GEORGE JOSEPH, transportation executive, consultant; b. Jersey City, Apr. 15, 1935; s. Matthew T. and Jean (Wilson) D.; m. Susan M. Tamborini; children— Marybeth, George Joseph Jr., Amy BS in Chemistry, St. Peter's Coll., Jersey City; postgrad. in organic chemistry, Seaton Hall U.; postgrad. in fin. and mktg., NYU; postgrad. in internat. relations, U. Pa. Research chemist Reaction Motors, Inc., Denville, NJ, 1956-58; research and devel. tech. rep. Thiokol Corp., Washington, 1961-63, asst. mgr. midwest regional office, 1963-65, mgr., dir. aerospace mktg., 1965-74, asst. to pres., 1974-75, corp. dir. mktg., 1975-77, v.p., 1977-82; dep. asst. sec. for systems Office of Asst. Sec. Air Force for Research Devel. and Logistics, Washington, 1983-85, prin. dep. asst. sec., 1985-86; pres. Prime Resources, 1986-87; v.p. Washington ops. Tex. Instruments Inc., 1988-91; v.p. govtl. rels. Smiths Industries, 1991—2003, Prime Resources, 2003—. Cons. to industry and govt., Def. Sci. Bd.; mem. Naval Rsch. Adv. Com.; bd. dirs. USO Capital, Smith Aerospace. Patentee liquid and solid propellant ingredients and formulations (13); contbr. articles to profl. jours. Recipient Exceptional Civilian Svc. award USAF. Mem. AIAA, Navy League, Air Force Assn. (bd. dirs.), Navy League (exec. com.), Assn. US Army, Navy League (bd. dirs.), Nat. Def. Indsl. Assn. (bd. dirs., chmn. pub. policy com.), Congl. Country Club. Avocations: hunting, fishing, golf, boating, reading. Home: 4632 Charleston Ter NW Washington DC 20007-1900 Business E-Mail: g.gjdonovan@verizon.net.

DONOVAN, GERALD ALTON, retired academic administrator, dean; b. Hartford, Conn., Feb. 10, 1925; s. Gerald Joseph and Alice Gertrude (Gleason) D.; m. Barbara Ann Hue, Feb. 1, 1948; children: Deborah E., Clayton H., Bruce G. BA, U. Conn., 1950, MS, 1952; PhD, Iowa State U., 1955. Poultry nutritionist Charles Pfizer & Co., Inc., Terre Haute, Ind., 1955-60; prof., chmn. poultry sci. dept. U. Vt., 1960-66; asso. dir. U. Vt. (Vt. Agrl. Expt. Sta.); asso. dean Coll. Agr. and Home Econs., U. Vt., 1966-73; dean Coll. Resource Devel., U. R.I., Kingston, 1973-89, dir. Internat. Ctr. Marine Resource Devel., 1975-89, ret., 1989—; exec. dir. Northeastern Region Aquaculture Ctr., Southeastern Mass. U., 1988-90, ret., 1990. Mem. U.S. AID/BIFAD Joint Research Council, 1979-83. Contbr. articles to profl. jours. Bd. dirs. Vt. C.C., 1970-73, Operation Clean Govt., 1997—; tech. specialist AARP-Tax Aide Program, 1993-2001; chairperson Narragansett Rep. Com., 1991-93; vol. tax cons. to the elderly. With USN, 1943-46. Mem. Am. Inst. Nutrition, Agrl. Research Inst., Assn. Agrl. Expt. Sta. Dirs., Sigma Xi, Alpha Zeta, Alpha Gamma Rho.

DONOVAN, JAMES M., librarian, anthropologist; b. Chattanooga, Ten., June 6, 1959; s. Dennis Howard Donovan and Yvonne Marie Fino. BA, U. Tenn., Chattanooga, 1981; M of Libr. Info. Scis., La. State U., 1989; PhD U., Tulane U., 1994; JD, Loyola University, New Orleans, LA, 2000—03; MA, La. State U., 2000. Libr. asst. Chattanooga-Hamilton County Bicentennial Libr., Chattanooga, 1978—84; libr. Tulane Law Libr., New Orleans, 1985—96; libr. Law Library U. Ga., 2003—. Contbr. articles to profl. jours.; author: Anthropology and Law, 2003. Chair Mayor's Adv. Com. for Lesbian, Gay, Bisexual and Transgender Issues, New Orleans, 1998—99; bd. dirs. AIDSLaw of La., New Orleans, 2001—03. Mem.: Am. Assn. Law Librs., Am. Anthropol. Assn., Pi Kappa Alpha. None. Home: 2360 W Broad St Apt R1 Athens GA 30606 Office: U Ga Law Libr Athens GA 30602 Office Phone: 706-542-5077. Personal E-mail: JamesMDonovan@aol.com.

DONOVAN, JAMES ROBERT, business equipment company executive; b. Wichita, Kans., Apr. 11, 1932; s. Karl Genevay and Louise (Silcott) D.; m. Ottille Schreiber, July 2, 1955; children: Amy Louise, Robert Silcott; m. Margaret Jones Esty, Ot. 31, 1981 AB, Harvard U., 1954, MBA, 1956. Mgr. sales adminstrn., market rschr. Hickok, Inc., Rochester, NY, 1956—59, mgr. reginal sales, 1959—62, asst. mgr. nat. sales, 1963—65; mgr. group program Xerox Corp., Stamford, Conn., 1965—68, mgr. mktg. spl. products, 1968—70, mgr. copier products, 1970—72, dir. corp. pricing and competitive activity, 1972—78, dir. corp. mktg. strategy and planning, 1978—83; sr. v.p. corp. mktg. McDonnell Douglas Automation Co., St. Louis, 1983—84; v.p. mktg. and planning info. sys. group McDonnell Douglas Corp., St. Louis, 1984—87; pres. Bus. Adv. Svcs., Inc., Naples, Fla., 1987—. V.p. Family Svc., Rochester, 1971-72; dir. Family and Children's Svcs., Stamford, 1972-79; mem. mktg. adv. bd. Columbia U. Bus. Sch., 1978-86; v.p. United Way New Canaan, 1982-83; bd. dirs. Family Svc. Am., 1986-91 Mem. Harvard U. Alumni Assn. (bd. dirs. 1978-83), Harvard U. Bus. Sch. Alumni Assn. (bd. dirs. 1982-85), Pelican Bay Property Owners Assn. (bd. dirs. 1994-97), Harvard Club (pres. Rochester 1971-72, pres. Fairfield County 1976-78, pres. St. Louis 1986-87, pres. Naples 1991-93), Harvard Bus. Sch. Club (pres. Rochester 1972, chmn. Westchester/Fairfield 1973-74), Hole-in-Wall Golf Club Naples.

DONOVAN, JOHN ARTHUR, lawyer; b. NYC, Apr. 11, 1942; children: Lara, Alex. AB, Harvard U., 1965; JD, Fordham Law Sch., 1967. Bar: N.Y. 1967, U.S. Tax. Ct. 1968, U.S. Ct. Appeals (2nd cir), 1968, U.S. Dist. Ct. (so., no. dists.) N.Y. 1969, U.S. Supreme Ct. 1971, U.S. Ct. Appeals (10th cir.) 1972, U.S. Ct. Appeals (9th cir.) 1976, Calif. 1982, U.S. Dist. Ct. (so., no. dists.) Calif. 1982, U.S. Ct. Appeals (5th cir.) 1983, Alaska 1993. Assoc. Hughes, Hubbard & Reed, NYC, 1967-74, ptnr. NYC, L.A., 1974-85, Skadden, Arps, Slate, Meagher & Flom, LA, 1985—. Mem. adj. faculty law sch. U. So. Calif., L.A., 1986-87. Office: Skadden Arps Slate Meagher & Flom 300 S Grand Ave Ste 3400 Los Angeles CA 90071-3109

DONOVAN, LANDON, professional soccer player; b. Ontario, Calif., Mar. 4, 1982; Midfielder/forward Bayer Leverkusen, Germany, 1999—2001, San Jose Earthquakes, 2001—04, Bayer Leverkusen, Germany, 2005, LA Galaxy, 2005—. 81 caps, 26 goals U.S. Nat. Soccer Team, 2000—; mem. U.S. World Cup Team, 2002, 06. Named MVP MLS Cup, Major League Soccer, 2003, Best MLS Athlete, ESPY awards, 2006; named to High Sch. All-Am. Team, Parade Mag., 1999, All-Star Team, Major League Soccer, 2001—05, MLS All-Time Best XI, 2005, Gold Cup All-Tournament Team, CONCACAF, 2002. Mailing: US Soccer Fedn 1801 S Prairie Ave Chicago IL 60616

DONOVAN, NOWELL, academic administrator; BS, King Edwards VII Sch.; PhD, U. Newcastle-upon-Tyne. Faculty U. Newcastle-upon-Tyne, Okla. State U.; joined faculty Tex. Christian U., Ft. Worth, 1986, provost, vice chancellor, 2004—. Contbr. articles to profl. jours. Recipient I. Leverson award, Am. Assn. Petroleum Geologists. Office: Provost and Vice Chancellor Acad Affairs TCU Box 297040 Fort Worth TX 76129*

DONOVAN, RICHARD EDWARD, lawyer; b. Cleve., Dec. 3, 1952; s. Richard A. and Eileen (Karthaus) D.; m. Ellen Brode, June 16, 1979; children: Colin, Ryan Michael, Patrick. BS, U. Notre Dame, 1974; JD, Rutgers U., 1977. Bar: N.Y. 1978, U.S. Dist. Ct. (ea. dist.) N.Y. 1978, N.J. 1985, U.S. Dist. Ct. N.J. 1985, U.S. Ct. Appeals (2d cir.) 1987, U.S. Supreme Ct. 1990. Assoc. Breed, Abbott & Morgan, NYC, 1977-80, Kelley, Drye & Warren LLP, NYC, 1980-86, ptnr., 1987—. Mem. ABA, Assn. Bar City N.Y. (com. prof. and jud. ethics 1996-99), N.J. Bar Assn., Rutgers Alumni Coun., N.Y. State Bar Assn. (sec. comml. and fed. litigation sect. 1988-90), Fed. Bar Coun., Assn. Fed. Bar N.J. Home: 61 Oak Ridge Ave Summit NJ 07901-4306 Office: Kelley Drye & Warren LLP 101 Park Ave New York NY 10178 Office Phone: 212-808-7800. E-mail: rdonovan@kelleydrye.com.

DONOVAN, ROBERT ALAN, language educator; b. Chgo., Sept. 27, 1921; s. John Elmer and Dorothy (Dickey) D.; m. Hope Elaine Taussig, Sept. 15, 1942; children: Faith, Peter Alan, Brian Roger. PhB, U. Chgo., 1948, MA, 1950; PhD, Washington U., St. Louis, 1953. Instr. English Cornell U., Ithaca, NY, 1953-56, asst. prof., 1956-62; prof. English SUNY, Albany, 1962-91, prof. emeritus, 1991—, chmn. dept. English, 1981-84. Author: The Shaping Vision: Imagination in the English Novel from Defoe to Dickens, 1966; contbr. articles to profl. jours. Sgt. U.S. Army, 1942-46, ETO. Mem.: MLA, Phi Beta Kappa. Office: SUNY Dept English Albany NY 12222-0001 Home: 214 Glen Eddy Dr Niskayuna NY 12309

DONOVAN, THOMAS JOHN, retired humanities educator; b. Vancouver, Wash., Dec. 14, 1917; s. Joseph J. and Louise (Padden) D.; m. Helen F. Murphy, Dec. 29, 1953; children: Joseph, Teresa, Marcella, Elizabeth. AB, St. Edward's Coll., Seattle, 1939; MA, U. So. Calif., LA, 1948; cert., Am. Acad. Rome, 1963. Cert. life profl. tchr., Wash. Tchr. Providence Acad., Vancouver, Wash., 1957-61, Hudson's Bay H.S., Vancouver, 1962-83, Vancouver Sch. Dist., 1983-91, U. Portland, Oreg., 1991—2006, prof. emeritus, 2006—. Cons. nat. humanities faculty, Eugene, Oreg., 1978. Sgt. M.C. U.S. Army, 1941-45, ETO. U. Chgo. fellow, 1950-52. Mem. AAUP, Classical Assn. Pacific Northwest, Classical Soc. of Am. Acad. Rome, Pi Epsilon Theta. Home: PO Box 61567 Vancouver WA 98666-1567 Home Phone: 360-693-7142. Personal E-mail: donovan130@gmail.com.

DONOVAN, TIMOTHY R., lawyer; b. 1955; BS, Ohio State U.; JD cum laude, Capital U., Columbus, OH, 1981. Bar: 1981. Assoc. Jenner & Block, ptnr., 1989—99, chmn. corp. securities group; sr. v.p. Tenneco Corp. (formerly Tenneco Automotive Inc.), Lake Forest, Ill., 1999—2001, gen. counsel, 1999—2007, exec. v.p., 2001—07, mng. dir. internat. group, 2001—07; exec. v.p., sec., gen. counsel Allied Waste Industries Inc., Phoenix, 2007—. Dir. John B. Sanfilippo Sons Inc. Mem.: Chgo. Bar Assn. (securities law com.), ABA. Office: Allied Waste Industries 18500 N Allied Way Phoenix AZ 85054*

DONOVAN, WILLIAM ALAN, retired librarian; b. Rochester, NY, Jan. 29, 1937; s. Joseph Leo and Wilhelmina (Fawcett) D. BA, St. John Fisher Coll., 1958; MA, U. South Fla., 1981. Libr. Chgo. Pub. Libr., 1961—93. Cartoon gagwriter; contbr. articles and book revs. to profl. jours. With U.S. Army, 1958-61. Mem. ALA, Phi Kappa Phi, Beta Phi Mu. Roman Catholic. Home: 2233 Ednor St Port Charlotte FL 33952-4314 E-mail: proficient@myway.com.

DONZIS, PAUL BENNETT, lawyer, finance educator, ophthalmologist; b. LA, Calif., July 7, 1956; s. Harold Kritt and Julia Bernice Donzis; m. Robin Carla Donzis, Aug. 29, 1999; children: Elizabeth, Lauren. BA, Princeton U., Princeton, NJ, 1978; MD, Washington U., Saint Louis, Mo., 1982; MBA, William Howard Taft U., Santa Ana, Calif., 1999; JD with honors, Law Office Judges Chamber Study Program, LA, 2000. Bar: Calif. 2000, US Dist. Ct. (ctrl. dist. Calif.) 2000, US Ct. Appeals (9th Cir.) 2000, US Supreme Ct. 2006. Ophthalmologist Eye Inst. Marina Del Rey, Calif., 1988—; atty. Vialla & Donzis, LA, 2000—. Assoc. clin. prof. medicine UCLA, Calif., 1986—; prof. bus. William Howard Taft U., Santa Ana, Calif., 2002—. Contbr. over 40 sci. articles, papers, book chpts. in field. Heed fellowship, Heed Opthalmic Found., 1987. Mem.: ABA, Am. Trial

Lawyers Assn., Am. Acad. Ophthalmology. Avocations: photography, tennis, golf. Office: Paul Donzis MD ESQ 4644 Lincoln Blvd Ste 102 Marina Del Rey CA 90292 Office Phone: 310-822-0022. Business E-Mail: pdonzis@donziseye.com.

DOODY, GREGORY L., lawyer, energy executive; BS in Mgmt., Tulane U., 1987; JD, Emory U. Staff acct. Price Waterhouse & Co., 1987—89; asst. mgr. Schlumberger Ltd., 1989—91; assoc. Walston Stabler Wells & Bains, Birmingham, Ala., 1994—96, Maynard Cooper & Gale, Birmingham, Ala., 1996—98; ptnr., CFO Hungry Man LLC, 1998—2000; ptnr. Balch & Bingham LLP, Birmingham, Ala., 2000—03; exec. v.p., gen. counsel, sec. HealthSouth Corp., 2003—06, Calpine Corp., San Francisco, 2006—. Mem.: ABA, Birmingham Bar Assn., Ala. Bar Assn. Office: Calpine Corp 50 W San Fernando St San Jose CA 95113 Office Phone: 800-359-5115.*

DOODY, JOHN, lawyer; b. Bklyn., 1964; BS, Bklyn. Coll. CUNY, 1989; JD, Fordham U., 1992. Bar: NY 1993, Conn. 1993, US Dist. Ct. So., Ea., & No. Districts NY, US Ct. Appeals 2nd Cir. Ptnr. Wilson, Elser, Moskowitz, Edelman & Dicker LLP, NYC. Office: Wilson Elser Moskowitz Edelman & Dicker LLP 23rd Fl 150 E 42nd St New York NY 10017-5639 Office Phone: 212-490-3000 ext. 2107. Office Fax: 212-490-3038. Business E-Mail: doodyj@wemed.com.

DOODY, JOSEPH G., retail executive; Various positions including pres. North Am. office imaging Eastman Kodak; v.p. Sutherland Group, 1998; pres. contract and comml. Staples, Inc., Framingham, Mass., 1998—2002, pres. North Am. delivery, 2002—. Office: Staples Inc 500 Staples Dr Framingham MA 01702*

DOODY, LOUIS CLARENCE, JR., retired accountant; b. New Orleans, Feb. 5, 1940; s. Louis Clarence and Elsie Clair (Connors) D.; m. Barbara Virginia Pettett, Oct. 9, 1982; children by previous marriage: Dana Lori, Mary Lyn, Kathleen Louise. BCS, Tulane U., 1963. CPA, La. Acct. Louis C. Doody, CPA, 1963-68; ptnr. Doody and Doody, CPA's, Metairie, La., 1969—2005. Mem. AICPA, La. Soc. CPA's. Home: 36 Cypress Rd Covington LA 70433-4306 Address: PO Box 1000 Covington LA 70434

D'OOGE, BENJAMIN WAYNE, emergency physician; b. Ridgecrest, Calif., May 9, 1955; BSEE, U. Calif., Davis, 1977; MD, Uniformed Svcs. U. Health Sci., Bethesda, Md., 1982. Diplomate Am. Bd. Emergency Medicine. Intern Darnall Army Cmty. Hosp., Ft. Hood, Tex., 1982-83, resident in emergency medicine, 1983-85; chief emergency med. svc. 121 Evacuation Hosp., Seoul, Korea, 1985-88, Tripler Army Med. Ctr., Hawaii, 1988-91, Blanchfield Army Cmty. Hosp., Ft. Campbell, Ky., 1991-97; dep. comdr. for clin. svcs. 86th Combat Support Hosp., Port-Au-Prince, Haiti, 1995; asst. chief emergency med. svc. Landstuhl Regional Med. Ctr., Germany, 1997—; chief EMS 212th Mobile Army Surg. Hosp., Wiesbaden, Germany, 1997—. Mem. Am. Coll. Emergency Physicians.

DOOGE, JAMES CLEMENT IGNATIUS, civil engineer, hydrologist; b. Birkenhead, Eng., July 30, 1922; s. Denis Patrick and Veronica Catherine (Carroll) D.; m. Roni O'Doherty, Nov. 25, 1946 (dec. Nov. 1991); children: Colm, Diarmuid, Clíona, Dara, Meliosa (dec. Feb. 2000). CBS, Dun Laoghaire; BE, BSc., Univ. Coll., Dublin, 1942, ME, 1952; MS, U. Iowa, 1956; DrAgrSci (hon.), U. Wageningen, 1978, DrTech (hon.), 1980; DSc (hon.), U. Birmingham, Eng., 1985, U. Dublin, 1988; D Engring. (hon.), Heriot-Watt U., 2000; Dr. (hon.), Cracow Tech. U., 2000; DSc (hon.), Nat. U., Ireland, 2001, Madrid, 2001. Jr. civil engr. Irish Office Pub. Works, 1943-46; design engr. E.S.B., 1946-58; prof. civil engring. Univ. Coll., Cork, Ireland, 1958-70, Dublin, 1970-81, 82-84; minister for fgn. affairs Ireland, 1981-82; leader Irish Senate, 1983-87; mem. Coun. of State, 1973-77. Recipient Horton award Am. Geophys. Union, 1959, Bowie medal, 1986, Ven Te Chow award ASCE, 1993, John Dalton medal European Geophys. Soc., 1998, Internat. Meteorology prize WMO, 1999. Fellow Instn. Civil Engrs. Ireland (pres. 1968-69, Kettle Premium and Plaque awards 1948, Mullins medal 1951, 62, Lifetime Achievement award 2006), Royal Irish Acad. (pres. 1987-90, Gold medal in engring. 2006), Polish Acad. Sci. (fgn.), Russian Acad. Scis. (fgn.), Spanish Acad. Sci. (fgn.), Internat. Assn. Hydrological Scis. (pres. 1975-79), Internat. Coun. Sci. Unions (pres. 1993-96), Royal Acad. Engring. (fgn., Prince Philip Gold medal 2005). Roman Catholic. Home: 2 Belgrave Rd Monkstown County Dublin Ireland Office: U Coll Earlsfort Terr Dublin 2 Ireland

DOOHER, DONNA, chef; Grad., Algonquine Coll., Can. Chef The Parrot, Toronto; owner, exec. chef Avant-gout Catering, Mildred Place Restaurant, 1986—, The Cookworks with Donna Dooher, Toronto, 1997—. Author: Out to Brunch (Cookbook of Yr., Cuisine Can., 2003); guest appearances (TV series) Breakfast TV, City Cooks, Vicki Gabereau, Fanny Kiefer, Rogers Daytime, food editor (mag.) WISH. Office: The Cookworks 99 Sudbury St Ste 8 Toronto ON M6J 3S7 Canada Office Phone: 416-537-6464. Office Fax: 416-537-2653.

DOOLEY, ANN ELIZABETH, freelance writers cooperative executive, editor; b. Mpls., Feb. 19, 1952; d. Merlyn James and Susan Marie (Hinze) Dooley; m. John M. Dodge, May 8, 1983; children: Christopher Dooley Dodge, Kathryn Dooley Dodge. BA in Journalism, U. Wis., 1974. Free-lance journalist, 1974-75; photo editor C.W. Communications, Newton, Mass., 1975-77, writer, photographer, 1977-79; editor Computerworld O A, Framingham, Mass., 1979-83; editorial dir. Computerworld Focus, Framingham, 1983-92; pres. freelance writers coop. Dooley & Assocs., West Newbury, Mass., 1992—. Speaker, chmn. mem. editorial adv. bd. various computer confs. Mem. Pub. Relations Soc. Am., Women in Communications (sec. 1982-84). Democrat. Home and Office: 1 Old Parish Way West Newbury MA 01985-1222

DOOLEY, BRENDAN DAVID, criminologist, researcher; b. Evansville, Ind., Feb. 19, 1979; s. David Donald and Helen Dooley. BS, Loyola U., Chgo., 1998, MA, 2001. Rsch. analyst Ill. Criminal Justice Info. Authority, Chgo., 2002—03; rsch. asst. Chapin Hall Ctr. Children, U. Chgo., Chgo., 2003—04; grad. rsch. asst. U. Mo., St. Louis, 2004—. Home Phone: 314-775-5949; Office Phone: 314-516-5041. Personal E-mail: bddqk6@umsl.edu.

DOOLEY, CALVIN MILLARD, former congressman; b. Visalia, Calif., Jan. 11, 1954; m. Linda Phillips; children: Brooke, Emily. BS, U. Calif., Davis, 1977; MA, Stanford U., 1987. Mem. U.S. Congresses from 17th Calif. dist., 1991-93, U.S. Congresses from 20th Calif. dist., 1993—2005; mem. agriculture com.; mem. natural resources com.; pres., CEO Nat. Food Processors Assn., Washington, 2005—. Democrat. Methodist. Office: Nat Food Processors Assn 1350 I St NW Ste 300 Washington DC 20005

DOOLEY, DONALD JOHN, retired publishing executive; b. Des Moines, Aug. 16, 1921; s. Martin and Anne Marguerite (Barger) D.; m. Beverly Frederick, Dec. 21, 1955 (div. 1977); children: Nancy Elizabeth, Katherine Anne(dec.) , Mary Bridget, Robert Frederick; m. Patricia Connell, Dec. 28, 1996. BA, U. Iowa, 1947; postgrad., Drake U., 1949-50. Gen. Promotion and pub. relations mgr. Meredith Corp., Des Moines, 1953-59, dir. pub. relations, 1960-65; art and editorial dir. Better Homes & Gardens Books & Spl. Interest Publs., Des Moines, 1965-77; dir. editorial planning and devel. Better Homes and Gardens Books (Meredith Corp.), Des Moines, 1977-84; cons., 1985. Chmn. bd. adv. com. Sch. Vol. Program, Des Moines; steering com. Intercultural Affairs program to Desegregate Dist. Schs., 1975-77; treas. Iowa U. Parents Assn., 1977-79; bd. dirs. Iowa Cystic Fibrosis Found., 1979-87, v.p., 1981-85; trustee Citizens Scholarship Found. Am., 1976-85, Iowa Freedom of Info. Council, 1977-87; adv. bd. Adult and Community Edn., Des Moines Pub. Sch., 1982—99; cons. White House Conf. on Families, 1981. Officer USAAF, 1942-46. Decorated 2 battle stars; recipient Dorothy Dawe award Home Furnishings Industry, 1973. Mem. Pub. Rels. Soc. Am. (accredited, pres. chpt. 1969, dir. chpt. 1965-76), ACLU, Beyond War (co-dir. Iowa office 1987-88), Friendship Force, Ams. for Dem. Action, Sigma Nu (comdr. chpt. 1946-47), Found. for Global Community, 1991—. Clubs: Echo Valley Country. Democrat. Home and Office: 3711 Oak Creek Pl West Des Moines IA 50265-7968

DOOLEY, DOUGLAS JOHN, bank executive; b. Lakeview, Oreg., June 9, 1955; s. Delmer John and Thalia (Doty) D.; m. Stephanie Snyder McClain, May 20, 1978 (dec. Sept. 1996); children: Carolyn J., Justin S.; m. Cynthia Stix, Aug. 20, 2000; step-children: JC, Brittany Bennett. BS, Am. U., 1977; MBA, Columbia U., 1979. Investment rsch. Morgan Guaranty Trust Co., N.Y.C., 1979-84, v.p., 1983-94, portfolio mgr., 1984—, dir. internat. rsch., 1986-90, emerging internat. markets mgr., co-founder, head emerging internat. equity mgmt., 1990-2000, lead adv. global trusts JP Morgan Pvt. Bank, N.Y.C., 2000—, dir. external due diligence, 2002-05, portfolio mgr. internat. clients pvt. bank, 2005—; mng. dir. J.P. Morgan Investment Mgmt., N.Y.C., 1994—. Mem. N.Y. Soc. Security Analysts. Office: JP Morgan Private Bank 345 Park Ave New York NY 10154 Home Phone: 203-966-1632. E-mail: doug@douglasdooley.com.

DOOLEY, J. GORDON, food scientist; b. Nevada, Mo., Nov. 15, 1935; s. Howard Eugene and Wilma June (Vanderford) D. BS in Biology with honors, Drury Coll., Springfield, Mo., 1958; postgrad., U. Mo., Rolla, 1961, Kirksville State Coll., Mo., 1959; MS in Biology, Brown U., 1966; postgrad. in bus mgmt., Alexander Hamilton Inst., 1973-75. No. Ill. U., 1964. Tchr. sci. Morton West H.S., Berwyn, Ill., 1963-64; dairy technologist Borden Co., Elgin, Ill., 1964-65; project leader Cheese Products Lab., Kraft Corp., Glenview, Ill., 1965-73; sr. food scientist Wallerstein Co. div. Travenol Labs., Inc., Morton Grove, Ill., 1973-77; mgr. food sci. GB Fermentation Industries, Inc., Des Plaines, Ill., 1977-79, mgr. product devel., 1979-82; group leader Food Ingredients divsn. Stauffer Chem. Co., Clawson, Mich., 1982-84; sr. rsch. scientist Schreiber Foods, Inc., Green Bay, Wis., 1984-87, DMV/Ridgeview, LaCrosse, Wis., 1987-92; mgr. regulatory affairs, info. svcs. DMV USA, LaCrosse, 1992-95; rsch. scientist AMPC Inc., Ames, Iowa, 1996-98; regulatory compliance officer Colo. Biolabs, Inc., Aurora, Colo., 1999—. Sci. lectr. seminars, Mex., 1975; assoc. mem. Ad Hoc Enzyme Tech. Com., 1978—; dairy rsch. adv. bd. Utah State U.; del. in field; spkr., mem. delegation to China, China Ass. for Sci. and Tech., 1989. Patentee in food and enzyme tech.; contbr. sci. articles to profl. jours. Recipient Spoke award Nevada (Mo.) Jr. C. of C., 1960; NSF grantee. Mem. Am. Dairy Sci. Assn., Inst. Food Technologists, Am. Chem. Soc., Cousteau Soc., Am. Inst. Biol. Scis., Nat. Sci. Tchrs. Assn., Whey Products Inst., Toastmasters Internat. (pres. club 1976-77), Brown U. Club (Chgo.), Beta Beta Beta, Phi Eta Sigma. Republican. Presbyterian. Home: 4208 30th St Greeley CO 80634-8738 Office: Colo Biolabs Inc PO Box 6296 Aurora CO 80045-0296

DOOLEY, JOHN AUGUSTINE, III, state supreme court justice; b. Nashua, NH, Apr. 10, 1944; s. John A. and Edna Elizabeth (Elwell) D.; m. Sandra C. Sapp, Dec. 19, 1970 BS, Union Coll., 1965; LLB, Boston Coll., 1968. Bar: Vt. 1968. Law clk. to presiding judge U.S. Dist. Ct. Vt., 1968-69; asst. dir. Vt. Legal Aid, 1969-72, dir., 1972-78; legal counsel to gov. of Vt., 1985; sec. of adminstrn. State of Vt., 1985-87; assoc. justice Vt. Supreme Ct., 1987—. Part-time U.S. magistrate for Vt., from 1971. Co-author: Cases and Materials on Urban Poverty Law, 1974. Mem. Vt. Bar Assn. Office: Vt Supreme Ct 109 State St Montpelier VT 05609-0001*

DOOLEY, KATHLEEN ANN, elementary school educator; d. Raymond and June Dooley. BA in Edn., We. Wash. U., Bellingham, Wash., 1974; MEd, U. Idaho, Moscow, 1983. Cert. tchr. K-12 Wash., 1974. Tchr. grades 9-12, head coach volleyball, gymnastics and softball Renton H.S., Wash., 1977—91. Healthy sch. leadership project Comprehensive Health Edn. Found., Seattle, 2000—. Site coun. mem. Kulshan Mid. Sch., Bellingham, Wash., 1993—99. Named Wash. State Softball Coach of Yr.; recipient Tchr. Leadership Project grantee, NW ESD 189, 2003. Mem.: Nat. C. Sci. Partnerships (assoc.; tchr. leader 2006—). Avocations: guitar, art, volleyball, badminton. Office: Kulshan Middle School 1250 Kenoyer Dr Bellingham WA 98229 Home Phone: 360-424-7846; Office Phone: 360-676-4886. Office Fax: 360-647-6892. Business E-Mail: kdooley@bham.wednet.edu.

DOOLEY, MICHAEL P., law educator; b. Iowa City, 1939; BA, U. Iowa, 1960, JD, 1963. Bar: Iowa 1963, N.Y. 1964, Ill. 1971, Va. 1979. Assoc. Dewey, Ballantine, Bushby, Palmer & Wood, 1963-68; assoc. prof. U. Ill., 1968-71, prof., 1971-72; vis. prof. U. Va., 1971-72, prof., 1972-80, Doherty prof., 1980-90, William S. Potter prof. and dir. grad. studies, 1990—. Mem. Saltzburg Seminar in Am. Studies, 1986; mem. legal adv. com. N.Y. Stock Exch. Author: Fundamentals of Corporation Law, 1995, A Practical Guide for Corporate Directors, 1996, Model Business Corporation Act Annotated, 1997. Named Ruby R. Vale Disting. Academic, Widener U. Sch. Law, 1996. Mem.: Am. Assn. Law Sch. (chmn. bus. sect., formerly), ALI, ABA (com. corp. laws 1983—91, corp. practice com. 1995—, com. corp. laws 1996—, reporter Model Bus. Corp. Act 1996—). Office: U Va Sch Law 580 Massie Rd Charlottesville VA 22903-1738 Office Phone: 434-924-3864. E-mail: mpd@virginia.edu.

DOOLEY, PATRICK JOHN, graphic designer, educator; b. Cleve., May 29, 1950; s. John William and Edna Ann (Mellick) D.; m. Mary Leah Spicer, Apr. 3, 1982; children: Claire Adele, Grace Ellen, James Joseph. BFA, U. Iowa, 1975, MA, 1977, MFA, 1978. Designer J. Paul Getty Mus., LA, 1980-89; design mgr. J. Paul Getty Mus., J. Paul Getty Trust, LA, 1987-89; designer, owner Patrick Dooley Design, Santa Monica, Calif., 1989-93, Lawrence, Kans., 1993—; mem. faculty Otis Parsons Sch. Art and Design, LA, 1988-93; prof. dept. design Sch. Fine Art U. Kans., Lawrence, 1993—, Gretchen Van Bloom Budig tchg. prof., 1997. Freelance graphic designer, LA, 1978-80, designer, cons. Walt Disney Co., Burbank, Calif., 1989-93, Lannan Lit. Found., LA, 1991—, The Lapis Press, Venice, Calif., 1989-93, Nelson-Atkins Mus., Kansas City, Mo., 1995-96; spkr. Assn. Am. U. Presses ann. conf., 1994, Art Dirs. Club Tulsa, 1996; judge 42nd Art Dirs. Club LA Show, 1988. Designer: (poster) Illuminated Manuscripts, 1984 (NY Type Dirs. Club award of excellence 1985), (books) Whisper of the Muse, 1986 (NY Art Dirs. Club award of merit 1987), Pierre Dubreuil, 1988 (Am. Inst. Graphic Arts Book Show cert. of excellence 1989), The Surrealists Look at Art, 1990 (NY Art Dirs. Club award of merit 1991), Explorations, 1992 (Am. Inst. Graphic Arts 50 Books of 1992), Pacific Wall, 1992 (Am. Inst. Graphic Arts Cover Show 1994), Walter Evans: The Getty Museum Collection, 1996 (Assn. Am. Univ. Presses cert. of excellence 1996). Recipient over 70 awards from Comm. Arts Mag., Print Mag., Am. Assn. Museums, Art Mus. Assn. Am., Am. Fedn. Arts, Univ. and Coll. Designer's Assn., others; Fulbright sr. scholar Fachhochschule, Trier, Germany, 2003. Mem.: Am. Inst. Graphic Arts. Office: U Kans Dept Design 300 Art And Design Bldg Lawrence KS 66045-0001 Business E-Mail: pdooley@ku.edu.

DOOLEY, THOMAS E., multi media company executive; b. 1957; BS, St. John's U., 1978; MBA, NYU, 1984. From sr. v.p. corp. devel. to deputy chmn. Viacom, Inc., NYC, 1980—2000; co-chmn., CEO DND Capital Partners, 2000—06; sr. exec. v.p., chief adminstrv. officer Viacom, NYC, 2006—, CFO, 2007—. Bd. dirs. Starsight Telecomms., Inc., LaBranche & Co., 2000—, Viacom, Inc., 1996—2000, 2006—. Bd. dirs. Laurie Strauss Leukemia Found. Mem.: Internat. Radio and TV Soc., Am. Mgmt. Assn., Mus. TV and Radio, Cable TV Adminstrn. Assn. Office: Viacom 1515 Broadway New York NY 10036-8901*

DOOLITTLE, JESSE WILLIAM, JR., lawyer; b. Wheaton, Ill., May 19, 1929; s. Jesse William and Selma Caroline (Schacht) D.; m. Annette Danforth Bush, May 5, 1962; children: Danforth Bush, Alice Walters. AB, DePauw U., 1951; LLB magna cum laude, Harvard, 1954. Bar: D.C. 1954. Law clk. to U.S. Supreme Ct. Justice Felix Frankfurter, 1957-58; assoc. firm Covington & Burling, Washington, 1958-61; asst. to solicitor gen. of U.S. Dept. Justice, Washington, 1961-63, 1st asst. civil div., 1963-66; gen. counsel Dept. Air Force, Washington, 1966-68, asst. sec. for manpower and res. affairs, 1968-69; partner firm Prather Seeger Doolittle & Farmer, Washington, 1969-94. Editl. cons. Lexis-Nexis, 1995-98; comml. arbitrator, 1992-2005. Mem.: Harvard Law Rev, 1952-54. Pres. bd. trustees Nat. Child Rsch. Ctr., Washington, 1972-74; mem. bd. overseers com. to visit ROTC programs Harvard, 1967-69; com. to visit Law Sch., 1969-75; mem. governing bd. Nat. Cathedral Sch. for Girls, Washington, 1979-85, vice-chmn., 1981-82, chmn., 1982-85; mem. chpt. Washington Nat. Cathedral, 1982-85; mem. policy bd. Legal Counsel for the Elderly, Washington, 1992-97; bd. dirs. Westchester Corp., Washington, 2000-2003. 1st lt. AUS, 1954-57. Recipient Career Service award Nat. Civil Service League, 1968, Exceptional Civilian Service award Dept. Air Force, 1969 Mem. Am. Law Inst., Harvard Law Sch. Assn. (coun. 1964-68), Harvard Law Rev. Assn. (bd. overseers 1967-72, 92-98), Phi Beta Kappa, Delta Chi. Democrat. Episcopalian (sr. warden 1973-75, past vestryman). Clubs: Metropolitan, Chevy Chase. Home: 4000 Cathedral Ave NW Apt 444B Washington DC 20016-5282

DOOLITTLE, JOHN TAYLOR, congressman; b. Glendale, Calif., Oct. 30, 1950; s. Merrill T. and Dorothy Doolittle; m. Julia Harlow Doolittle, Feb. 17, 1979; children: John Taylor, Jr., Courtney A. BA with hons. in History, U. Calif., Santa Cruz, 1972; JD, U. Pacific, 1978. Mem. Calif. State Senate, 1980—90, U.S. Congress from 4th Calif. dist., 1991—; mem. appropriations and house adminstrn. coms., joint com. on printing. Mem. agr. com. U.S. Congress; sec. House Rep. Conf. Com. on House Adminstrn.; vice chair Subcom. on Energy and Water Devel.; mem. Subcom. on Interior, Environ. and Related Agencies. Republican. Mem. Lds Ch. Office: Ho Reps 2410 Rayburn Ho Office Bldg Washington DC 20515-0504*

DOOLITTLE, KENNETH HERBERT, retired urologist; b. Honolulu, Hawaii, Mar. 8, 1930; s. Stewart Edward and Portia Walker Doolittle; m. Shirley Jean Doolittle; children: Kenneth Herbert II, William Winfield, Jonathan Stewart, Holly Kay. BA, Ealham Coll., Richmond, Ind., 1952; MD, U. Rochester Sch. Medicine, NYC, 1956; MMS, Ohio State U., Columbus, 1963. Cert. Bd. Urology. Intern Ohio State U., Columbus, 1956—57; surg. resident Mt. Carmel Hosp., Columbus, 1959—60; urology resident Ohio State U., Columbus, 1960—63; ret., 1994. Pres. Ctrl. Ohio Urol., 1973; chmn. clin. dept. Mt. Carmel Hosp, 1981, 82, pres. staff, 84. Mem. found. bd. Luth. Sch. Theology Chgo., 2000—. Capt. USMC, 1952—59, Capt. 101st airborne divsn. USMC, 1957—59. Lutheran. Home: 1450 Arlington Columbus OH 43212

DOOLITTLE, WARREN T., retired federal official; b. Webster City, Iowa, July 24, 1921; s. Edward and Rhoda Leone (McGuire) D.; m. Jane Anne Beddow, Dec. 29, 1942; children: Linda Jane, Randolph James, Steven Eric. BS in Forestry, Iowa State U., 1946; MS in Forestry, Duke U., 1950; PhD in Forestery, Yale U., 1955. Enlisted USAF, 1943, advanced through grades to lt. col., 1969, navigator Europe, 1943-45, South Korea, 1951-52; rsch. scientist USDA Forest Svc., Asheville, NC, 1946-57, Washington, 1957-59, from asst. dir. to dir. Upper Darby, Pa., 1959-74, assoc. dep. chief Washington, 1974-80, ret., 1980. Contbr. articles to profl. jours. Moderator Congrl. Ch., Asheville, N.C., 1956-57. Lt. col. USAF, 1943-69. Decorated DFC; recipient Disting. Alumni award Yale U., 2005. Fellow Soc. Am. Foresters (pres. 1986, John Beale Meml. award 1983); mem. Am. Forests (B.E. Fernow award 1993), Internat. Soc. Tropical Foresters (pres. 1984-01), Res. Officers Assn. Republican. Avocations: golf, skiing. Home: 5328 Trevino Drive Haymarket VA 20169

DOONAN, SIMON, window dresser, creative director; Former window dresser Maxfield, Los Angeles; former apprentice under Diana Vreeland Costume Inst. of the Metropolitan Museum of Art; window dresser then creative dir. Barney's NY, 1985—; columnist NY Observer. Author: (books) Confessions of a Window Dresser: Tales from a Life in Fashion, 2001, Wacky Chicks: Life Lessons from Fearlessly Inappropriate and Fabulously Eccentric Women, 2003, Nasty: My Family and Other Glamorous Varmints, 2005. Office: Barney's NY 660 Madison Ave New York NY 10021

DOONER, HUGO K., plant pathologist, educator; BS, U. Notre Dame; PhD, U. Wis., Madison. Prof. plant biology and pathology Waksman Inst. Microbiology Rutgers U., Piscataway, NJ. Contbr. articles to sci. jours. Mem.: NAS. Achievements include patents in field. Office: Waksman Inst Microbiology Rutgers U 190 Frelinghuysen Rd Piscataway NJ 08854-8020 Office Phone: 732-445-4684. Office Fax: 732-445-5735. E-mail: dooner@waksman.rutgers.edu.

DOONER, JOHN JOSEPH, JR., advertising executive; b. Mt. Vernon, NY, Aug. 3, 1948; s. John Joseph and Elizabeth Ann (Forrest) D.; m. Cynthia Ann Stewart, Aug. 16, 1975; children: Jaclyn. BA, St. Thomas Villanova U., Miami, Fla.; postgrad., Iona Coll. Advt. media supr. Grey Advt., NYC, 1970-73; assoc. media dir. The Marschalk Co., NYC, 1973-74, account mgr., 1974-84; sr. v.p., worldwide acct. coord. McCann-Erickson, 1984—85; exec. v.p., gen. mgr. McCann-Erickson N.Y., 1985—88; pres. McCann-Erickson N. Am., NYC, 1988-94; pres., COO McCann-Erickson Worldwide, NYC, 1992-94, pres., CEO, 1994—95; chmn., CEO McCann Worldgroup, NYC, 1995—2000; pres., COO The Interpublic Group of Companies, Inc., NYC, 2000—00, chmn., CEO, 2001—03, McCann Worldgroup, NYC, 2003—. Bd. dirs. The Interpublic Group. Bd. trustees Sound Shore Med. Ctr., 1993—, Coll. New Rochelle; trustee Irish Coun., U. Notre Dame; mem. pres. adv. coun., CARE. Mem. Pelham Country Club, Lago Mar Club (Ft. Lauderdale, Fla.). Avocations: tennis, boating. Office: McCann Worldgroup 622 3rd Ave New York NY 10017-2798 Office Phone: 646-865-2000.

DOONER, MARLENE S., communications executive; b. May 28, 1961; m. Brian C. Dooner. BA in Econs., St. Joseph's U.; MS in Fin., Drexel U. V.p. Comms. Lending Group PNC Bank; dir. investor rels. Comcast Corp., v.p. investor rels. Phila., 2000—07, sr. v.p. investor rels., 2007—. Bd. dirs. Phila. Hospitality, Haub Sch. Bus., St. Joseph's U. Named a Woman to Watch, Women in Cable & Telecommunications Found., 2005. Office: Comcast Corp 1500 Market St Philadelphia PA 19102*

DOORES, STEPHEN CURTIS, manufacturing executive; b. Wurzburg, Germany, Oct. 28, 1973; s. Michael Alan and Patricia Joann Doores; m. Sandra Gillespie Wallgren, Apr. 12, 2003. BS, Millikin U., Decatur, Ill., 1995; MBA, Keller Grad. Sch. Mgmt., Lincolnshire, Ill. and Tampa, 2006. Cert. Cmty. Assn. Mgr. DBPR, Fla., 2006. Grad. pub. svc. intern environ. dept. Ill. Dept. Transp., Springfield, 1995—97; environ. specialist BRW, Inc., Rolling Meadows, Ill., 1997—99; QA lab. technician Abbott Labs., Ill., 2000—02, mfg. specialist, 2002—05; hoa mgr. Lennar, Sarasota, Fla., 2005—. Conservative. Methodist. Avocations: travel, swimming, reading, music. Office: Lennar Cmtys 551 N Cattlemen Rd Ste 202 Sarasota FL 34232 Home Phone: 941-531-3287; Office Phone: 941-377-1222. Personal E-mail: snsdoores@hotmail.com.

DOORLEY, THOMAS LAWRENCE, III, management consultant; b. Sewickley, Pa., Aug. 15, 1944; s. Thomas Lawrence and Emma Lou (Sage) D.; m. Gail Lynn Schwartz, Feb. 3, 1968; children: Christopher Sage, Scott Frederick. BSChemE, Pa. State U., BA in Arts and Sci., 1967; MBA in Mktg., Columbia U., 1969. Cons. Westvaco, NYC, 1968-69; sr. cons. A D Little, Cambridge, Mass., 1969-74, bus. unit mgr., 1974-76; founder, exec. v.p. Braxton Assocs., Boston, 1977-84; sr. ptnr. Deloitte Consulting, 1984-99, Deloitte Consulting Braxton Assocs., Boston, 1996; chmn., CEO Sage Ptnrs., Wellesley Hills, Mass. Author: Teaming up for the 90's, 1991, Value-Creating Growth, 1999; contbr. articles to profl. jours. Chmn., bd. dirs. The Soccer Network, Boston, 1987—; mem. leadership club United Way Mass., Boston, 1986-90; coach Wellesley (Mass.) United Soccer Club, 1977-90; deacon Wellesley Congregational Ch., 1970's, sr. high youth advisor, 1970's. Woodrow Wilson fellow Columbia U., 1969. Mem. Columbia Bus. Sch. Club, Wellesley Country Club, Alliance Analyst and World Econ. Found. (advisory bd.). Avocations: running, exercise, reading, children. Home: 34 Arnold Rd Wellesley MA 02481-2841 Office: Sage Ptnrs PO Box 81295 Wellesley Hills MA 02481-0003

DOORY, ANN MARIE, legislator; married; 2 children. BA in Polit. Sci., Towson State U., 1976; JD, U. Balt., 1979. Bar: Md. Counsel to majority leader Md. State Senate, 1980—81; vol., arbitrator Better Bus. Bur., 1984-86; dep. spkr. pro tem Md. Ho. of Dels., 1999—2003, parliamentarian, 1993—94; mem. Ho. Econ. Matters Com. Md. Gen. Assembly, 1987—94, vice-chair Ho. Judiciary Com., 1995—2003, vice-chair Ho. Econ. Matters Com. Md., 2003—. Mem. Dem. State Ctrl. Com. 43d Legis. Dist., Baltimore City, 1982-86; mem. bd. Ho. of Ruth, 1999-. Named Md.'s Top 100 Women Cir. of Excellence Daily Rec. Mem. Women's Bar Assn., Md. Bar Assn. Democrat. Roman Catholic. also: Md Ho of Dels State Capitol Annapolis MD 21401 Office Fax: 410-841-3558. Business E-Mail: annmarie_doory@house.state.md.us.

DOPF, GLENN WILLIAM, lawyer; b. NYC, June 6, 1953; s. William Bernard and Doris Virginia (Roxby) D. BS cum laude, Fordham Coll., 1975; JD, Fordham U., 1979; LLM, NYU, 1983. Bar: N.J. 1979, U.S. Dist. Ct. N.J. 1979, N.Y. 1980, U.S. Dist. Ct. (so. and ea. dists.) N.Y. 1980, U.S. Ct. Appeals (2d cir.) 1980, U.S. Ct. Internat. Trade 1981, U.S. Supreme Ct. 1983. Assoc. Martin, Clearwater & Bell, NYC, 1980-81; ptnr. Kopff, Nardelli & Dopf LLP, NYC, 1982—. Named one of NY Area's Best Lawyers, NY Mag., 2006, 2007, NY Super Lawyers, 2006, 2007, Best Lawyers in Am., 2007. Mem. ABA, Assn. Bar City N.Y. Office: Kopff Nardelli & Dopf LLP 440 9th Ave Fl 15 New York NY 10001-1688

DOPPELT, AVA K., lawyer; b. Pitts., July 8, 1950; d. Morris Behr and Sylvia Joy Kirshenbaum; m. Art Doppelt. AB, Northwestern U., Ill., 1972; JD, NYU, 1976. Counsel Reader's Digest Assn., Englewood, NJ, 1976—78, Prentice-Hall, Inc., Pleasantville, NY, 1979—82; shareholder Allen, Dyer, Doppelt, Milbrath, & Gilchrist, P.A., Orlando, Fla., 1983—. Bd. mem. Orlando Ballet, Preserve the Eatonville Cmty., Fla. Mem.: ABA, Orange County Bar Assn. (William Trickel Jr. Professionalism award 2002), Fla. Bar Assn., Fla. Exec. Women, Ctrl. Fla. Assn. for Women Lawyers (Golden Star award 2001), Internat. Trademark Assn., Copyright Soc. U.S., Phi Beta Kappa. Office: Allen Dyer Doppelt Milbrath & Gilchr 255 S Orange Ave Orlando FL 32801 Office Phone: 407-841-2330. Office Fax: 407-841-2343. Business E-Mail: adoppelt@addmg.com.

DOPPMANN, WILLIAM, composer, pianist; s. William George Doppmann and Ida Ubertalli; m. Willa Starkey, May 4, 1966; children: Karla Watson, Jeff, Catherine Dolan, Paul, Gregory William. MusB, U. Mich., 1956, MusM, 1958. Pianist-in-residence/asst. prof. Iowa State U., Ames, 1960—61; pianist-in-residence/assoc. prof. U. Iowa, Iowa City, 1961—67; artist-in-residence/prof. U. Tex., Austin, 1967—73; artist faculty mem. Peabody Conservatory, Baltimore, 1987—90; freelance composer, musician Gig Harbor, Wash., 1990—. Artistic dir./ann. music festival Centrum Found., Port Townsend, Wash., 1975—99; vis. pianist/composer various univs./festivals. Musician concert performances & compositions. Pfc US Army, 1958—60, Germany & France. Recipient Gold medal, Walter Naumburg Internat. Competition, 1954, Michaels Found. internat. Competition, 1954, medal, Leventritt Found. Internat. Competition, 1957, composition award, Wash. State Arts Commn., 1980, Disting. Alumni award, U. Mich., 1987, Ann. Composition award, ASCAP, 1993—; fellow, Guggenheim Meml. Found., 1988; grantee, Martha Baird Rockefeller Found., 1957, 1961, 1966, Nat. Endowment for the Arts, 1983, 1986. Mem.: Am. Ctr. for New Music, ASCAP, Sigma Alpha Iota (hon.), Phi Kappa Lamda, Phi Beta Kappa. Home Phone: 206-529-4221.

DOR, GEORGE W. K, music educator; b. Alavanyo Wudidi, Ghana, July 11, 1954; s. Seth Kwasi and Lucia Afua Dor; m. Rose Ama Nimo; children: Dzidefo Kokutse, Nyuiemedi Yawa, Mozart Nuku, Lilian Seyram, Senyoagbe Koku. MusB, U. of Ghana, Legon, Accra, Ghana, 1982—86; MPhil, U. of Ghana, 1989—92; PhD, U. of Pitts., 1996—2001. Certified Teacher Ghana Edn. Svc., 1977. Music master Kadjebi Secondary Sch., Kadjebi, Volta Region, Ghana, 1977—80, St Aquinas Secondary Sch., Accra, Greater Accra Region, Ghana, 1980—82; tchg. asst. U. of Ghana, Music Dept., Legon, Accra, Greater Accra Region, Ghana, 1986—88; lectr. U. of Edn., Winneba, Central Region, Ghana, 1992—96; tchg. fellow and part time faculty U. of Pitts., Music Dept., 1996—2001; chair in ethnomusicology and asst. prof. of music U. of Miss. (Sally McDonnell-Barksdale Honors Coll., and Dept. of Music), Oxford, 2001—. Resident dir./condr. Ghana Nat. Symphony Orch., Accra, Ghana, 1996; music dir. Cmty. of Reconciliation Ch., Pitts., 1999—2001; nat. choir dir. Evang. Presbyn. Ch., Ghana, 1995—96; founder and dir. Goethe Inst. Choir, Accra, Ghana, 1993—96; choir dir./organist North La E. P. Ch., Accra, Ghana, 1980—96; first row cellist Ghana Nat. Symphony Orch., Accra, 1988—96; 2nd v.p. Ghana Assn. of Choral Conductors, Accra, Ghana, 1984—86; founder and dir. Ole Miss African Drum and Dance Ensembel, U. of Miss., Oxford, Miss., 2003—. Editor, contbr.: Dynamics of Creativity and Knowledge in African Music Traditions: A Festschrift in Honor of Aidn Euba; contbr. article, ency.; composer Ghanian art music. Mem. of hymbook rev. com. Evang. Presbyn. Ch., Ghana, 1992—2003; adjucator of singing competitions Ministry of Edn. and Culture, Ghana. Summer Rsch. grant, U. of Pitts., 1998, Grad. scholarship, U. of Ghana, 1989—91, Andrew Mellon GraduateTeaching fellowship, U. of Pitts., 1996—98, 2000, Summer Rsch. grant, U. of Miss., 2002, 2003. Mem.: Soc. for Ethnomusicology (life; intercultural music arts 2002). Christian. Achievements include introduce the field of ethnomusicology at the University of Mississippi, formed the first african and drum ensemble in a college in the state of Mississippi. Avocations: reading, travel, music. Office: Univ of Miss Music Dept Scruggs Hall University MS 38677 Home Phone: 662-234-1454; Office Phone: 662-915-7269. Office Fax: 662-915-1230. Personal E-mail: gwkdor@olemiss.edu. E-mail: gwkdor1@olemiss.edu.

DORADO, MARIANNE GAERTNER, retired lawyer; d. Wolfgang Wilhelm and Marianne L. Gaertner; m. Richard Manuel Dorado, Oct. 1, 1982; children: Marianne Christine, Kathleen Gina. BA, Yale U., 1978; JD, U. Mich., 1981. Bar: N.Y. 1982, U.S. Supreme Ct. 1993. Ptnr. The Dorado Law Group, LLC, NYC, 1998—2007; ret., 2007. Contbr. articles to profl. jours. Extern office legal advisor U.S. Dept. State, Washington, 1980. Republican. Roman Catholic.

DORAN, CHARLES FRANCIS, political scientist, consultant; b. Mankato, Minn., Jan. 31, 1943; s. George Francis and Harriet Jennetta (Wallace) Doran; m. Barbara Giusti, Dec. 30, 1967; children: Charles Francis, Brent Richard, Kirk Bennett, Connemara. AB in History and Sci., Harvard U., 1964; MA in Internat. Rels., Johns Hopkins U., 1966, PhD in Polit. Sci., 1969. Asst. prof. Tex. A&M U., 1968—70; from asst. prof. to prof. Rice U., Houston, 1970—79; prof. dir. Canadian studies, internat. rels., global theory and history Johns Hopkins U., Washington, 1979—90, Andrew W. Mellon prof. internat. rels., 1991—. Founder, dir. internat. programs Jones Grad. Sch. Adminstrn., 1977—79; sr. assoc. Ctr. for Strategic and Internat. Studies, Washington, 1995—; Claude T. Bissell chair U. Toronto, 1985—86; working group, standing com. on the Western Hemisphere, congrl. and dept. briefings NSF, 1981—83; vis. scholar Harvard U.; lectr. in field. Author: Politics of Assimilation: Hegemony and Its Aftermath, 1971, Myth, Oil and Politics, 1976, Forgotten Partnership, 1984, Systems in Crisis, 1991, Why Canadian Unity Matters, 2001, Power Cycle Theory and Global Politics, 2003; contbr. articles to profl. jours. Elected Can.-Am. Com., 1982; trade dipute resolution mechanisms Jt. C. of C., 1985—86; N.Am. com. Atlantic Coun. US, 1982. Recipient Gov. Gen. Internat. award, Can., 1999, medal, Internat. Soc. Scholars, Mex., 2001; Rsch. grantee, Woodrow Wilson Found., 1968, NSF, 1981—83, MacArthur and Ford Found., 1988—91, Donner Found., 1990—95, ACLS/DAAD, 1993—95. Mem.: Internat. Polit. Sci. Assn., Internat. Commn. of the History Internat. Rels., Internat. Studies Assn. (editl. bd., Disting. Scholar award 2006), Am. Polit. Sci. Assn., German Studies Assn., Mid. East Studies Assn., Assn. for Canadian Studies in the US (v.p. 1985—87, pres. 1987—89), Coun. Fgn. Rels., Harvard Club, Cosmos Club. Achievements include research in power cycle theory of historical change and fgn. policy behavior, principles of relative power dynamics. Avocations: sailing, skiing. Home: 8544 Brickyard Rd Potomac MD 20854-4833 Office: Johns Hopkins SAIS 1740 Massachusetts Ave NW Washington DC 20036 Office Phone: 202-663-5715. Office Fax: 202-663-5717. Business E-Mail: cfdoran@jhu.edu.

DORAN, CHARLES FRANCIS, JR., mathematician, mathematics professor; b. Houston, Sept. 6, 1971; s. Charles Doran, Sr. and Barbara Giusti Doran; m. Carissa Chan Escober. AB, Harvard Coll., Cambridge, Mass., 1992; AM, Harvard U., Cambridge, Mass., 1993, PhD, 1999. S. Chowla rsch. postdoctoral fellow Pa. State U., Univ. Park, Pa., 1999—2000; Ritt asst. prof. Columbia U., NYC, 2000—04; asst. prof. U. Wash., Seattle, 2003—. Mng. editor Advances in Theoretical and Math. Physics, 2004—. Recipient Faculty Excellence award, U. Wash. Dept. of Math., 2005; Royalty Rsch. Fund scholar, U. Wash. Office of Rsch., 2006. Mem.: Am. Math. Soc. Roman Catholic. Achievements include research in geometry, string theory, and number theory. Office: U Wash Dept Math Box 354350 Seattle WA 98195-4350 Personal E-mail: doran@math.washington.edu.

DORAN, DORIS JEANNE, librarian; b. Chambersburg, Pa., July 19, 1932; d. John Franklin and Kathleen Elmira (Cooke) Fraker; m. Francis Joseph Doran, Feb. 5, 1955 (div. Sept. 1991); children: Brenda Lou, Polly Ann. BS, Wilson Coll., 1954; MLS, U. Md., 1970, postgrad., 1976-77. Asst. buyer Joseph Horne Co., Pitts., 1955-56; dir. rsch. library Sears Roebuck & Co., Chgo., 1956-58; project officer contracts John I. Thompson Co., Washington, 1967-69, staff asst. to v.p. info. sci. divsn., 1969-70; program officer grants divsn. Nat. Library Medicine, Bethesda, Md., 1970-79, program analyst Office of Dir., 1980-82; project dir. Nat. Med. Audiovisual Ctr., 1979; asst. for network devel. VA, Washington, 1982-84; co-owner, treas., gen. mgr. Gilran Lighting Products, Springfield, Va., 1970-90; project mgr. Preservation Microfilm Project, REMAC Info. Corp., 1987-88, Nat. Library Medicine; acquisitions specialist Nat. Tech. Info. Svc., 1988—. Mem. Am. Library Assn., Med. Library Assn. Home: Unit # 410 8340 Greensboro Dr Apt 410 Mc Lean VA 22102-3544 Office: 5285 Port Royal Rd Springfield VA 22161-0001 Home Phone: 703-847-2963; Office Phone: 703-605-6532. Business E-Mail: ddoran@ntis.gov.

DORAN, KATHLEEN BREWER, dean, consultant; b. Glen Ridge, NJ, Mar. 5, 1955; d. Ambrose Benedict and Marjorie Westgate Doran. AB, Dartmouth Coll., 1976; MBA, U. of Va., 1978; PhD, McGill U., Montreal, Que., Can., 2000. Sr. sales rep. Internat. Paper Co., Chgo., 1978—80, sr. fin. analyst Dallas, 1980—81, strategic planning specialist, 1981—82; sr. assoc. Harbidge House, Denver, 1982; owner Eagle Valley Aviation, Vail, Colo., 1982—86, Condor Aviation, Oceano, Calif., 1986—90; lectr. Calif. Poly. State U., San Luis Obispo, 1986—90, McGill U., Montreal, Que., 1991—95; asst. prof. Babson Coll., Wellesley, Mass., 1995—2000; dean Sch. Bus. and Info. Sci. Lasell Coll., Newton, Mass., 2000—05; dean Bertolon Sch. Bus. Salem State Coll., Mass., 2005—. Instr. Tsinghua U., Beijing, 2001—02; prin. Nanod Enterprises Consulting, Vail, 1982—86; Fulbright sr. specialist, 2003. Contbr. articles to profl. jours. Commr. Essex Nat. Heritage Area, 2005—; dir. Mass. Orgn. Older Ams., 2006—. Named Outstanding Scholar in Chinese Mktg., Soc. for Mktg. Advances, Chinese Golden Tripod Com., 2002; recipient Sr. fellowship, Dartmouth Coll., 1975—76, Rsch. fellowship, U. of Nairobi, Inst. of African Studies, 1975—76, Rsch. scholarship, McGill U., 1990—91, Rsch. fellowship, McGill and Renmin Univs., 1994—95, Babson Coll., 1997—99, Sr. Specialist grant, Fulbright Fgn. Scholarship Bd., 2003. Mem.: Assn. for Consumer Rsch., Acad. of Internat. Bus. Liberal. Episcopalian. Avocations: travel, skiing, cooking. Home: 60 Dodge St Apt 10 Beverly MA 01915-1789 Office: Salem State Coll Bertolon Sch Bus 352 Lafayette St Salem MA 01970 Home Phone: 978-232-1258; Office Phone: 978-542-6640. Office Fax: 978-524-6027; Home Fax: 978-232-1258. Personal E-mail: kbdoran@gmail.com. Business E-Mail: kdoran@salemstate.edu.

DORAN, LINDSAY, film producer, executive; b. LA, 1948; V.p. creative affairs Embassy Pictures; exec. v.p. prodn. Paramount Pictures; pres. Mirage Enterprises; pres., COO United Artists Pictures. Exec. in charge of prodn.: This is Spinal Tap, 1984; exec. prodr.: The Firm, 1993, Sabrina, 1995; prodr.: Dead Again, 1991, Leaving Normal, 1992, Sense and Sensibility, 1995 (Golden Globe award 1995, Best Adapted Screenplay 1995, 6 Acad. award nominations), Sabrina, 1995, Nanny McPhee, 2005, Stranger Than Fiction, 2006. Office: United Artist Pictures 2500 Broadway Santa Monica CA 90404-3065*

DORAN, MARK RICHARD, real estate financial executive; b. Chgo., June 17, 1954; s. Paul George and Mae (Olson) D.; m. Wendy Carole Beckham, Dec. 17, 1977; children: Blake, Barrett, Hayley. BBA in Acctg., Baylor U., Waco, Tex., 1975, MBA, 1976. From asst. acct. to supr. Peat, Marwick, Mitchell & Co., Dallas, 1977-81; sr. v.p. fin. Lincoln Property Co., Dallas, 1982-89; exec. v.p., CFO Prentiss Properties Trust, Dallas, 1990-98, Transwestern, 1999—2002, COO, 2002—. Vice chmn., bd. trustees Cambridge Sch. of Dallas. Deacon Park Cities Bapt. Ch., Dallas, 1988—. Mem. The Urban Land Inst., Baylor U. Alumni Assn. Avocations: basketball, golf, skiing. Office: Transwestern 5001 Spring Valley Ste 600W Dallas TX 75244 Business E-Mail: mark.doran@transwestern.net.

DORAN, ROBERT STUART, mathematician, educator; b. Winthrop, Iowa, Dec. 21, 1937; s. Carl Arthur D. and Imogene (Ownby) Doran Nodurft; m. Shirley Ann Lange, June 27, 1959; children: Bruce Robert, Brad Christopher. BA with hons., U. Iowa, Iowa City, 1962, MA, 1964; MS, U. Washington, Seattle, 1967, PhD, 1968. Instr. U. Wash., 1968; asst. prof. U. No. Iowa, Cedar Falls, 1968-69; asst. to prof. math. Tex. Christian U., Ft. Worth, 1969—, chmn. dept. math., 1990—, John William and Helen Stubbs Potter prof. math., 1995—. Vis. prof. U. Tex., Austin, 1979; cons. in field. Author: Approximate Identities and Factorization in Banach Modules, 1979, Characterizations of C*-Algebras: The Gelfand-Naimark Theorems, 1986, Representations of Locally Compact Groups and Banach *-Algebraic Bundles, 1988; editor: Cambridge U. Press, 1987, Selfadjoint and Nonselfadjoint Operator Algebras and Operator Theory, 1991, C*-Algebras: A Fifty Year Celebration, 1994, Automorphic Forms, Automorphic Representations and Arithmetic, 1999, The Mathematical Legacy of Harish-Chandra, 2000, Operator Algebras, Quantization, and Noncommutative Geometry, 2004; contbr. articles to profl. jours. Chmn. bd. deacons Birchman Bapt. Ch., Ft. Worth, 1987; vol. Van Cliburn Internat. Piano Competition, 1984—, Am. Cancer Soc., 1987—. Recipient Burlington No. award for Disting. Tchg., 1988, Top Ten Prof. award Ho. of Reps., 1986, 87, 91, Mortar Bd. Preferred Prof. award, 1983, 87, 91, 93, 95, Gold medal for Prof. of Yr. Coun. for Advancement and Support of Edn., 1989, Honors Prof. of Yr. award, 1993, Coll. Sci. and Engring. Chancellor's award for disting. rsch., 2003; vis. scholar MIT, 1981, Oxford U., 1988; Minnie Stevens Piper prof., 1989, Chancellor's Dist. Rsch. award Coll. Sci. Engring., 2003. Mem. Inst. Advanced Study (chmn. we. U.S. 1984—), Assn. Mems. Inst. for Advanced Study (pres. bd. trustees 1990-99), Am. Math. Soc., Math. Assn. Am. (vis. lectr. 1990—, Beckenbach Book award prize com. 1990-94), Phi Beta Kappa, Sigma Xi, Pi Mu Epsilon. Republican. Avocations: chess, running, swimming. Home: 4204 Ridglea Country Club Dr Fort Worth TX 76126-2224 Office: Tex Christian U Dept Math Fort Worth TX 76129-0001 Office Phone: 817-257-7335. Business E-Mail: r.doran@tcu.edu.

DORAN, THOMAS GEORGE, bishop; b. Rockford, Ill., Feb. 20, 1936; Licentiate in Sacred Theology, Pontifical Gregorian U., Rome, 1962, PhD in Canon Law, 1978. Ordained priest Roman Cath. Ch. 1961, bishop 1994. Asst. pastor St. Joseph Parish, Elgin, Ill., St. Peter Parish, South Beloit; various admin. duties Diocese of Rockford, Ill., rector diocesan cathedral; prelate auditor Roman Rota, 1986—94; bishop Rockford, 1994—. Mem. Supreme Tribunal of the Apostolic Signatura, 2000. Mem.: Congregation for the Clergy. Roman Catholic. Office: Diocese of Rockford PO Box 7044 Rockford IL 61125-7044 Office Phone: 815-399-4300. Business E-Mail: officeofthebishop@rockforddiocese.org.

DORAN, TIMOTHY PATRICK, academic administrator; b. NYC, July 1, 1949; s. Joseph Anthony and Claire (Griffin) D.; m. Kathleen Matava, Aug. 1, 1981; children: Claire Marie, Bridget Anne. BA in Econs., Le Moyne Coll., 1971; MA in Tchg., U. Alaska, 1984, Edn. Specialist, 1990. Cert. type A secondary, econs., type B K-12 prin., supt. Svc. rep. Emigrant Savs. Bank, NYC, 1971-72; exec., dir. Project Equality Northwest, Seattle, 1972-73, Jesuit Vol. Corps., Portland, Oreg., 1973-75, adminstv. advisor Kaltag City (Alaska) coun., 1975-77; program developer Diocese Fairbanks, Alaska, 1978-81, adminstr., supt. St. Mary's Cath. H.S., 1981-83; prin. intern U. Alaska, Fairbanks, 1984, vis. instr., 1990-94; tchr. Anthony A. Andrews Sch., St. Michael, Alaska, 1984-86; prin., tchr. James C. Isabell Sch., Teller, Alaska, 1986-88; prin. Unalakleet (Alaska) Schs., 1988-90, Denali Elem. Sch., Fairbanks, 1992—. Acad. coord. U. Alaska, Fairbanks, summers, 1984—86; instr. Elderhostel, 1991—; docent U. Alaska Mus., 1991—; sch. edn. adv. bd. U. Alaska, 1998—, adj. instr., Anchorage, 2001—. Active nat. com. Campaign for Human Devel., 1980-83; mem. manpower planning coun. Tanana Chiefs Conf., 1976-77, parish coun. Sacred Heart Cathedral, 1979-81; Sunday Sch. tchr. St. Mark's Univ. Parish, 1990-97, adv. coun., 1998-2001; mem. com. chair Fairbanks Arts and Culture in Edn., 1995—; bd. dirs., v.p., pres. Literacy Coun. Alaska, 1997-2002. Recipient Merit awards Alaska Dept. Edn., 1986-90; named Alaska Disting. Prin., 1998, Fairbanks Elem. Prin. of Yr., 2003. Mem. ASCD, Nat. Assn. Elem. Sch. Prins., Alaska Assn. Elem. Sch. Prins. (v.p., pres.-elect, past pres. 2000-02, state rep. 2004-), Fairbanks Prins. Assn. (v.p. 1998-99, pres. 1999-00), Alaska Math. Consortium (bd. dirs. 1992-99), Alaska Coun. Sch. Adminstrs. (bd. dirs. 1998-2002, 04). Home: 512 Windsor Dr Fairbanks AK 99709-3439 Office: Denali Elem Sch 1042 Lathrop St Fairbanks AK 99701-4124 Office Phone: 907-452-2456. Business E-Mail: tdoran@northstar.k12.ak.us.

DORAND, FREDA J., music educator; b. Waynesboro, Pa., Dec. 7, 1957; d. Verdeen K. and Esther J. Beaver; m. Jeffrey E. Dorand, Aug. 15, 2004; children: John D. Saunders, Isaac R. Saunders, Catherine M. Saunders. BS in Music Edn., Millersville U., Pa., 1979; MA in Ministerial Studies, Gettysburg Luth. Theol. Sem., Pa., 1996. Assoc. in ministry Pa.; cert. level I tchg. Pa., level II tchg. Pa. Organist, pianist United Meth. Chs., Mercersburg, Pa., 1982—87; pvt. music instr. Cumberland Sch. of Music and Dorands Music Studio, Chambersburg, 1982—; organist St. John's Luth. Ch., Mercersburg, 1987—89; dir. music Christ Luth. Ch., Hagerstown, Md., 1989—94; dir. music and youth ministry St. Paul's Luth. Ch., Biglerville, Pa., 1994—2001; music tchr. Fannett-Metal Sch. Dist., Willow Hill, Pa., 1998—; min. ch. music 1st Luth. Ch., Chambersburg, Pa., 2001—. Woodwind clinician James Buchanan H.S. Band, Mercersburg, 1990—2003; instr. woodwind and pit percussion Waynesboro Sr. H.S. Band, Waynesboro, 2001—03. 4-H leader Franklin County 4-H Program, Chambersburg, 1981—89; troop com. mem. Boy Scouts Am., Chambersburg, 2001—04, merit badge counselor music and religion, 1995. Recipient 1-Yr. Svc. pin, Franklin County 4-H Program, 1981, 5-Yr. Svc. pin, 1986. Mem.: Am. Guild English Handbell Ringers (assoc.), Franklin/Fulton County Music Edn. Assn. (assoc.), Fannett-Metal Edn. Assn. (assoc.), Music Educators Nat. Conf. (assoc.), Pa. Music Educators Assn. (assoc.), Am. Guild Organists (assoc.), Lower Susquehanna Synod (assoc.), Phi Lambda Sigma (pres. 1977—79). Evangelical. Avocations: sewing, reading, swimming, travel. Office: Fannett-Metal Sch Dist 14823 Path Valley Rd Willow Hill PA 17271 Home Phone: 717-264-5163; Office Phone: 717-349-2513. Personal E-mail: fjdorand@pa.net. E-mail: dorandf@fmsd.k12.pa.us.

DORATO, PETER, electrical and computer engineering educator; b. NYC, Dec. 17, 1932; s. Fioretto and Rosina (Lachello) D.; m. Marie Madeleine Turlan, June 2, 1956; children: Christopher, Alexander, Sylvia, Veronica. BEE, CCNY, 1955; MSEE, Columbia U., 1956; DEE, Poly. Inst. N.Y., 1961. Registered profl. engr., Colo. Lectr. elec. engring. dept. CCNY, 1956-57; instr. elec. engring. Poly. Inst. N.Y., Bklyn., 1957-61, prof., 1961-72; prof. elec. engring., dir. Resource System Analysis U. Colo., Colorado Springs, 1972-76; Gardner-Zemke prof. elec. and computer engring. U. N.Mex., Albuquerque, 1984—2004, chmn. dept., 1976-84, prof. emeritus, 2005—. Hon. chaired prof. Nanjing Aero. Inst., 1989; vis. prof. Politecnico di Torino, Italy, 1991-921 dir. Ctr. for Intelligent Systems Engring. U. N.Mex., 2001. Author: Analytic Feedback Systems Design, 2000; co-author Linear Quadratic Control, 1995, Robust Control for Unstructured Perturbations, 1992, Robust Control-System Design, 1996, Italian Culture—A View from America, 2001; editor: Robust Control, Recent Results in Robust Control and Advances in Adaptive Control, reprint vols., 1987, 90, 91, IEEE Press Reprint Vol. Series, 1989-90; assoc. editor Automatica Jour., 1969-83, 89-92, editor rapid publs., 1994-98; assoc. editor IEEE Trans on Edn., 1989-91; contbr. articles on control systems theory to profl. jours. Recipient John R. Ragazzini edn. award Am. Automatic Control Coun., 1998 Fellow IEEE (3rd Millenium medal); mem. IEEE Control Systems Soc. (Disting. Mem. award)., World Automation Congress (Life Achievement award 2002). Democrat. Home: 1514 Roma Ave NE Albuquerque NM 87106-4513 Office: U NMex Dept Elec Computer Eng Albuquerque NM 87131-1356 Business E-Mail: peter@ece.unm.edu.

DORDELL, TIMOTHY PAUL, lawyer; b. Mpls., June 26, 1962; BA summa cum laude, St. Olaf Coll., Northfield, Minn., 1984; student, Cambridge U., Eng., 1983; JD cum laude, U. Minn., 1987. Bar: Ariz. 1987, Minn. 1989, U.S. Dist. Ct. Ariz. 1987, U.S. Dist. Ct. Minn. 1991. Atty. Streich Lang, Phoenix, 1987-89; v.p., gen. counsel Twin Star Prodns., Inc., Scottsdale, Ariz., 1989-91; atty. Fredrikson & Byron, Mpls., 1992-96; assoc. gen. counsel Ecolab Inc., St. Paul, 1996—2006; v.p., gen. counsel, sec. The Toro Co., Bloomington, Minn., 2006—. Bd. dirs. Minn. AIDS Project, Mpls., 1996-2002. Mem. Phi Beta Kappa, Phi Alpha Theta. Office: The Toro Co 8111 Lyndale Ave S Bloomington MN 55420-1196 Business E-Mail: tim.dordell@toro.com.*

DORDELMAN, WILLIAM FORSYTH, food company executive; b. Glen Ridge, NJ, Oct. 18, 1940; s. Wilbert E. and Dorothy F. (Forsyth) D.; m. Barbara Ann Gaddis, Sept. 16, 1959; children: Dorothy Ann, William Edward, Patricia Lynne, Lauren Forsyth. BA in Econs, U. Va., 1962; MBA, Harvard U., 1964. With Gen. Foods Corp., White Plains, N.Y., 1965—, advt. and merchandising mgr. Birdseye divsn., 1972-73, gen. mgr. main meal strategic bus. unit, 1973-77, v.p. corp., pres. food products divsn., 1977-80, corp. group v.p., 1980-86; pres. Fairfield Capital, Rowayton, Conn., 1986-92; co-CEO B. Manischewitz Co., 1992-93; chmn., CEO Colo. Prime Foods, 1993-98; prin. Kohlberg & Co., Mcht. Bankers, 1998—. Bd. dirs. Bailey & Alling Lumber Co., Oscar Mayer, Entemanns, B. Manischewitz Co., Color Spot Nursery, United Signature Foods, Colo. Prime Food, S.W. Supermarket, Urgrocer.com., Internat. Cancer Screening Lab., Nielsen Bain, Critical Homecare Supplies; chmn. Am. Homecare Supply, Orion Food Supply. Innotek Inc. Bd. dirs. Mid-Fairfield Youth Hockey Assn., 1973-77, St. Vincent's Hosp. Mem. Am. Mgmt. Assn., Am. Mktg. Assn., Young Pres. Orgn. (bd. dirs. N.Y. chpt. 1982), Weeburn Country Club, Ocean Reef Club, Westchester/Fairfield County Club, Harvard Bus. Sch. Club (dir. 1978—), Zeta Psi. Episcopalian. Home: 9 Woodley Rd Darien CT 06820-2622

DORE, PATRICIA ANN, psychologist; b. Chgo., Mar. 2, 1944; d. Robert Patrick Dore and Anne Elizabeth Bruen; m. Peter Ruben Romero, Oct. 16, 1967; 1 child, Peter Anthony Romero. BA Spanish Lang. & Lit., St. Xavier U., 1966; MA in Applied Linguistics, Bilingualism and Math., Northeastern Ill. U., 1977; MS in Psychology, Bilingualism and Lang. Memory, Ill. Inst. Tech., 1981, PhD in Psychology, 1990; postgrad., Oral Roberts U., 2002—. Lic. sch. psychologist State Tchr. Cert. Bd., 1984, cert. Nat. Sch. Psychology Certi. Bd., 1988, sch. psychology State of Calif. Commn. on Tchr. Credentialing, 1987. Primary tchr. Chgo. Pub. Sch., 1968—83, ESL tchr., 1977—83, sch. psychologist internship, 1983—84, bilingual sch. psychologist, 1984—87; bilingual sch. psychologist, counselor San Jose Unified Sch. Dist., 1987—88; bilingual sch. psychologist Palatine (Ill.) Sch. Dist. #15, 1989—99, North Suburban Spl. Edn. Orgn., Arlington Heights, Ill., 1999—2002; ret., 2002. Instr. Vandercook Coll. Music, Chgo., 1979—80; cons. therapist Roth Group, Northbrook, Ill., 1981—93; instr. St. Augustine Coll., Chgo., 1983—85; bilingual sch. psychologist cons. Chgo. Pub. Sch., 1987—2005; bilingual sch. psychologist Glenview (Ill.) Sch. Dist. #34, 1998—, cons., 2001—, Palatine Sch. Dist. #15, 2002—05, cons. bilingual sch. psychologist, 2002—05; cons. North Suburban Spl. Edn. Orgn., Arlington Heights, 2002—, bilingual sch. psychologist, 2002—07. Singer: Soprano in Gospel Choir. Election judge Election Bd. Chgo., 1990—92; prayer warrior Ptnr. Benny Hinn Min., 2000—. Mayor Daley Youth Found. scholar, City of Chgo., 1962. Mem.: Nat. Assn. Sch. Psychologists (assoc.), Gamma Beta Phi. Achievements include development of language fluency examination for college entrance examination. Avocations: singing, dance, design and decorating, playing organ. Office Phone: 847-702-0321. Home Fax: 847-808-7493. Personal E-mail: pattyann28@comcast.net.

DOREN, ROBERT ALAN, lawyer; b. Buffalo, Mar. 11, 1949; m. Teri B. Shaffer, Aug. 27, 1978; children: Lee Michael, Lindsey Maria. BS, SUNY, Buffalo, 1972; JD, U. Buffalo, 1975. Bar: N.Y. 1976, Ohio 2002, Pa. 2002, U.S. Dist. Ct. (we. dist.) N.Y. 1976, U.S. Ct. Appeals (2d cir.) 1978. Assoc. Brizdle & Hankin, P.C., Buffalo, 1975-76; ptnr. Flaherty, Cohen, Grande, Randazzo & Doren, Buffalo, 1976—97, Bond, Schoeneck & King, LLP, Buffalo, 1997—, regional office mng. mem. Home: 252 Ranch Trl Buffalo NY 14221-2340 Office: Bond Schoeneck & King PLLC 40 Fountain Plz Ste 600 Buffalo NY 14202-2200 Office Phone: 716-566-2833. E-mail: rdoren@bsk.com.

DORENKAMP, THEODORE, III, lawyer; b. Detroit, Feb. 28, 1970; s. Theodore Dorenkamp II and Marcia Riopelle; m. Pomy Ketema, May 27, 2000. JD, U. Minn., Mpls., 2000. Bar: US Dist. Ct. (Minn.), US Dist. Ct. (We. Dist. Wis.). Lawyer Saliterman & Siefferman, PC, Mpls., 2000—02, Bowman and Brooke LLP, Mpls., 2003—. Internat. rels. intern Ibaraki (Japan) City Office, 1993—94; ESL instr. Takatsuki (Japan) YMCA, 1994—96. Mem.: Def. Rsch. Inst., Minn. State Bar Assn. Home: 1300 Dunkirk Ln North Plymouth MN 55447 Office: Bowman and Brooke LLP Ste 2600 150 S Fifth St Minneapolis MN 55402 Home Phone: 763-473-3211; Office Phone: 612-656-4067. Personal E-mail: ted.dorenkamp@earthlink.net. Business E-Mail: ted.dorenkamp@bowmanandbrooke.com.

DORET, PETER, state agency administrator, lawyer; b. Bklyn., July 18, 1943; s. Bernard Doret and Frances Weintraub; m. Rosa Arguelles, Nov. 2, 1986. BA, Hostra U., Uniondale, NY, 1966; JD, Bklyn. Law, 1969. Parole officer NYS Divsn. Parole, Albany, 1969—77, sr. atty., 1977—85, adminstrv. law judge, 1985, bureau chief, 1985—2004. Office Phone: 516-374-6600. Personal E-mail: pdlaw@verizon.net.

DOREY, WILLIAM G., construction executive; BS in Constrn. Mgmt., Ariz. State U. Br. mgr. Granite Constrn., Inc., Santa Barbara, Calif., 1973-83, asst. divsn. mgr., br. divsn. mgr., sr. v.p., mgr. br. divsn., 1983—87; exec. v.p., COO Granite Constrn. Inc., 1998—2003, pres., COO, 2003—04, pres., CEO, 2004—. also: PO Box 50085 Watsonville CA 95077-5085 Office: Granite Constrn Inc PO Box 50085 Watsonville CA 95077-5085*

DORFAN, JONATHAN MANNIE, physicist, researcher; b. Cape Town, South Africa, Oct. 10, 1947; came to U.S., 1969; s. Charles Archie and Esther (Levine) D.; m. Renee Bing, Dec. 15, 1969; children: Nicole Michelle, Rachel Lauren. BS, U. Cape Town, 1969; PhD, U. Calif., Irvine, 1976. Rsch. assoc. Stanford (Calif.) Linear Accelerator Ctr., 1976-78, staff physicist, 1978-83, assoc. prof., 1984-88, prof. physics, 1989—, assoc. dir., 1994-99, dir., 1999—. Mem. high energy physics adv. panel U.S. Dept. Energy, 1991—94; mem. exec. bd. BaBar, 1994—99; mem. adv. coun. Princeton Plasma Physics Lab., 2000—; mem. sci. adv. bd. Max Planck Inst., 2000—; mem. Internat. Com. Future Accelerators, 2000—. Fellow: Am. Phys. Soc., Am. Acad. Arts & Scis. Office: Stanford Linear Accelerator Ctr Mail Stop 75 2575 Sand Hill Rd Menlo Park CA 94025 E-mail: jonathan.dorfan@slac.stanford.edu.

DORFF, BARBARA L., elementary and secondary school educator; b. Sweetwater, Tex., Feb. 12, 1947; d. Earnest Lee Langley, Jr. and Helen Estelle (Richter) Langley; m. Jim Dorff, Apr. 4, 1975; children: John, Michael. BS in Art Edn., Tex. Tech. U., Lubbock, Tex., 1969; MEd, Tex. A&M U., Commerce, Tex., 1986. Tchr. art Austin Ind. Sch. Dist., 1969—72, Dallas Ind. Sch. Dist., 1972—73, 1975—79, tchr., curriculum specialist, 2001—06; tchr. kindergarten, art Gainesville Ind. Sch. Dist., 1973—75; tchr. McKinney Ind. Sch. Dist., 1995—2001; tchr., curriculum specialist Region 10 Edn. Svc. Ctr., Richardson, Tex., 2006—. Named Tex. Secondary Tchr. of Year, 2002, OELA Rising Star of Year, US Dept. Edn., 2002. Home: 2907 Oakwood Ct Mc Kinney TX 75070 E-mail: barbaradorff@yahoo.com.

DORFF, ELLIOT, rabbi; b. June 24, 1943; PhD in Philosophy, Columbia U., 1971. Ordained Rabbi Jewish Theological Seminary, 1970. Rector, prof. Jewish Theology, Sol & Anne Dorff Distinguished Service Prof. In Philosophy U. Judaism, Calif., also co-chmn. Bioethics dept. Vis. lectr. Jewish Theological Seminary; mem. Rabbinical Assembly's Comm. on Jewish Law and Standards; mem. health care com. First Lady Hillary Rodham Clinton's Health Care Task Force, 1993—96. Contbr. articles to numerous profl. jours. Bd. mem. Inst. Review Bd. Midway; ethics com. mem. Jewish Homes for the Aging, UCLA Med. Ctr. Named one of The Top 50 Rabbis in America, Newsweek Mag., 2007. Mem.: Bd. Jewish Family Svc. (former v.p.). Office: U Judaism 15600 Mulholland Dr Los Angeles CA 90077*

DORFF, STEPHEN, actor; b. Atlanta, July 29, 1973; s. Steve Dorff. Actor: (TV series) In Love and War, 1987, The Absent-Minded Professor, 1988; (TV films) Quiet Victory: The Charlie Wedemeyer Story, 1988, A Son's Promise, 1990, I Know My First Name is Steven, 1998, Do You Know the Muffin Man?, 1998, Earthly Possessions, 1999; (TV series) What A Dummy, 1990; (films) The Gate, 1987, The Power of One, 1992, Judgment Night, 1993, Rescue Me, 1993, Backbeat, 1993, S.F.W., 1994, Les Cent et une nuits, 1995, Halcyon Days, 1995, Reckless, 1995, I Shot Andy Warhol, 1996, The Audition, 1996, Space Truckers, 1997, Blood and Wine, 1997, City of Industry, 1997, Blade, 1998, Entropy, 1999, Cecil B. DeMented, 2000, Zoolander, 2001, The Last Minute, 2001, All for Nothin', 2002, Riders, 2002, FearDotCom, 2002, Den of Lions, 2003, Cold Creek Manor, 2003, Alone in the Dark, 2005, Tennis, Anyone.?, 2005, Shadowboxer, 2005, World Trade Center, 2006, numerous appearances on TV series. Mailing: 9350 Wilshire Blvd # 4 Beverly Hills CA 90212

DORFMAN, ALLEN BERNARD, international management consultant; b. NYC, Mar. 30, 1930; s. Harry and Jean (Schreiber) Dorfman; m. Elaine Turbé, Jan. 9, 1955; children: Nancy Ann, Jeffrey David. BBA summa cum laude, 1952; postgrad. mgmt. studies, Harvard Bus. Sch. From mem. exec. tng. squad to sr. mgmt. R.H. Macy's, NYC, 1954-67; asst. gen. mdse. mgr., v.p., mem. mgmt. com. NY div. Allied Stores Corp., NYC, 1967-69; v.p., gen. mdse. mgr. hard and soft goods, mem. exec. com. Town & Country Full Line Discount Stores div. Lane Bryant Corp., NYC, 1969-71; pres., dir. Nat. Bellas Hess Inc., Kansas City, Mo., 1971-73; corp. sr. v.p. and pres., CEO retail div. Jewelcor, Inc., NYC, 1973-77; corp. sr. v.p., dir. corp. ops., mem. exec. com. Vornado, Inc., Garfield, NJ, 1977-78; chmn. bd. dirs., CEO Allen B. Dorfman, Mgmt. Consulting Co., 1978—. Prof. Grad. Sch., LI U., NY. Bd. dirs., exec. v.p. Am. Cancer Soc., LI; bd. dirs. Kings Point Civic Assn., LI. With US Army, 1952—54. Recipient award, Advt. Club NY, Torch of Liberty award, Nat. Anti-Defamation League. Mem.: Nat. Assn. Catalog Showroom Merchandisers, Nat. Retail Mchts. Assn., Mass. Retailing Inst., Police Athletic League, Philharmonics Assn., Boys Club, Boy Scouts Am., Adelphi Coll. Found., Wildwood Country Club (Kings Point) (pres., bd. dirs.), Polo Club (Boca Raton) (adv. bd. govs.-exec. com., chmn. coun. pres., chmn. emeritus coun. pres.), Sigma Alpha, Eta Mu Pi, Beta Gamma Sigma. Achievements include patents pending for zippered ice and roller skates. Office: Allen B Dorfman Mgmt Consulting Co, Polo Club-Penthouse Villa 17588 Ashbourne Ln Ste C Boca Raton FL 33496-4434 Office Phone: 561-241-4642. Business E-Mail: AllenDorfman@webtv.net.

DORFMAN, CYNTHIA HEARN, government agency administrator; BA in English with honors, Skidmore Coll., 1970; M in English, Middlebury Coll. Sr. exec. fellow Kennedy Sch. Govt., Harvard U.; dir. OCRI Found.; mgr. Dept. Publs. and Outreach Programs and Projects U.S. Dept. Edn., Washington, dir. media and info. svcs. Office Ednl. Rsch. and Improvement, comm. & develop. dir., Office Innovation and Improvement. Office: US Dept Edn IES Capital Place 555 New Jersey Ave NW Washington DC 20208

DORFMAN, HOWARD DAVID, pathologist, educator; b. NYC, July 20, 1928; s. Louis and Helen (Weingarten) D.; m. Esther Novick, June 21, 1952; children: Richard H., Peter W., Leslie Jane. BA, NYU, 1947; MD, SUNY, Bklyn., 1951. Cert. in pathologic anatomy Am. Bd. Pathology, 1958. Resident in pathology Mt. Sinai Hosp., NYC, 1952-54, Columbia Presby. Medical Ctr., NYC, 1954-58; dir. pathology Sharon (Conn.) Hosp., 1958-60; assoc. pathologist Sinai Hosp. Balt., Baltimore, Md., 1960-64; dir. pathology Hosp. Joint Diseases, NYC, 1964-74; pathologist-in-chief Sinai Hosp. Balt., 1974-85; prof. orthopedic pathology Johns Hopkins Sch. of Medicine, Balt., 1985; prof. pathology, radiology and orthopaedic surgery Albert Einstein Coll. Medicine, Bronx, NY, 1985—. Walter Putschar lectr. Mass. Gen. Hosp. Harvard Med. Sch., 1983; vis. prof. Wayne State U. Sch. Medicine, 1984, Baylor Coll. Medicine, Houston, 1984, Cleve. Clinic, 1984, SUNY, Stonybrook, 1994, Johns Hopkins U. Sch. Medicine, 1995, U. Mich. Sch. Medicine, 1997, Cornell U. Sch. Medicine, Meml.-Sloan Kettering Cancer Ctr., 1998, U. Pitts. Sch. Medicine, 1998, Brigham and Women's Hosp., Harvard Med. Sch., 1998, Yale U. Sch. Medicine, 2003; Stembridge lectr. Tex. Soc. Pathologists, 2006; lectr. in field. Author: Bone Tumors, 1998; co-author: Tumors of Bone and Cartilage, 1971. Recipient Henry Jaffe award Hosp. Joint Diseases, 1984. Mem. N.Y. Pathological Soc. (pres. 1989-91), Internat. Skeletal Soc. (pres. 1986-88). Democrat. Home: 201 E 79th St Apt 10G New York NY 10021-0836 Office Phone: 718-920-5622. Business E-Mail: hdorfman@montefiore.org.

DORFMAN, JOHN CHARLES, lawyer; b. Wilkinsburg, Pa., Feb. 3, 1925; s. Leo O. Dorfman; m. Ruth B. Davison; children: Beverly Dorfman Lenci, Laura Carolyn, Bradley. BE in Elec. Engring., Yale U., 1945; JD, Cornell U., 1949. Bar: N.Y. 1949, U.S. Patent & Trademark Office 1949, Conn. 1950, Pa. 1956, U.S. Dist. Ct. (ea. dist.) Pa. 1957, U.S. Ct. Appeals (3d cir.) 1957, U.S. Supreme Ct. 1959, U.S. Ct. Appeals (fed. cir.) 1982. Patent counsel Machlett Labs. Inc., Springdale, Conn., 1950-54; assoc. Pennie & Edmonds, NYC, 1949-55, Howson & Howson, Phila., 1955-59, ptnr., 1960-73; ptnr., chmn. Dann, Dorfman, Herrell & Skillman, Phila., 1974—. Elder Wayne Prebyn. Ch. Served to lt. (j.g.) USNR, 1943—46. Mem.: ABA (chmn. sect. patent, trademarkand copyright law 1984—85, hon. mem. coun.), Nat. Inventors Hall of Fame Found. (pres. 1977—78, bd. dirs. 1979—99, mem. joint bd. NIHF and Inveture Pl. 1997—2000, hon. mem. coun. 1999—), Phila. Patent Law Assn. (pres. 1974—76), Am. Intellectual Property Law Assn. (bd. dirs. 1973—76), Nat. Coun. Patent Law Assns. (chmn. 1978—79), Yale Club (Phila.) (pres. 1982—84), Union League Club (Phila.), St. David's Golf Club (Wayne), Phi Alpha Delta, Delta Tau Delta (bd. dirs. Cornell U. ho. corp. 1969—), Tau Beta Pi. Republican. Avocations: skiing, golf, travel. Home: 215 Midland Ave Wayne PA 19087-4108 Office: Dann Dorfman Herrell & Skillman 1601 Market St Ste 2400 Philadelphia PA 19103-2307 Office Phone: 215-563-4100. Business E-Mail: jdorfman@ddhs.com.

DORFMAN, MARC, lawyer; b. Washington, Feb. 3, 1952; s. David and Irene Blanche (Sheinuk) D.; children: Jennifer, Emily; m. Lisa Korngut AB, Yale U., 1973; JD, Harvard U., 1976. Bar: D.C. 1976, Md. 1989. Assoc. Ginsburg, Feldman & Bress, Washington, 1976-78; trial atty., spl. counsel U.S. SEC, Washington, 1978-81; assoc. Freedman, Levy, Kroll & Simonds, Washington, 1981-85, ptnr., 1986—2001, Foley & Lardner LLP, 2001—. Adj. prof. law Georgetown U., 2002—. Mem. ABA, D.C. Bar. Democrat. Jewish. Avocations: jogging, bicycling, travel. Office: Ste 500 3000 K St NW Washington DC 20007-5101 Office Phone: 202-295-4007. Business E-Mail: mdorfman@foley.com.

DORFMAN, RICHARD, bank executive; BA, Hofstra U.; JD, Syracuse U. Atty. FDIC; regulatory counsel NY Bank for Savings; numerous sr. exec. positions, including head of orgn., U.S. govt. and agency bus. Lehman Brothers Inc., 1983—96; mng. dir., head US Agencies & Mortgages ABN Amro, Inc., 1997—2005; strategic & operational cons., adv. work Fed. Home Loan Banks, 2005—07, Fed. Home Loan Bank System's Office of Fin., 2005—07; pres., CEO Fed. Home Loan Bank, Atlanta, 2007—. Office: Fed Home Loan Bank Atlanta 1475 Peachtree St NE PO Box 105565 Atlanta GA 30348-5565*

DORFMAN, WILLIAM M., dentist; children: Anna, Charlotte, Georgia. Grad., UCLA, 1980; DDS, U. of the Pacific, San Francisco, 1983. Dental resident, Lausanne, Switzerland, 1983—85; pvt. practice aesthetic and gen. dentistry LA, 1985—; founder Discus Dental, Inc., LA, 1989—; pvt. practice Century City Aesthetic Dentistry, LA. Dental cons. ABC's Extreme Makeover, NBC's The Today Show, NBC's Entertainment Tonight, NBC's EXTRA, NBC's The Rosie O'Donnell Show, E! Entertainment TV; founder, program coord. P.A.C.-live, U. Pacific Dental Sch., San Francisco; lectr. in field. Author (and lectr.): The Smile Guide; past editor Jour. Am. Acad. Cosmetic Dentistry; contbr. articles to profl. jours.; guest appearances Channel 4 News, LA, Channel 7 News. Judge Miss S.C. beauty pageant; raised and donated with Crown Coun. of Dentists to St Jude's Children Rsch. Hosp., Children's Dental Ctr., & Garth Brooks' Teammates for Kids Found. Named Best Aesthetic Dentist in L.A., L.A. Mag.; recipient Lifetime Achievement awards (2). Fellow: Am. Acad. Cosmetic Dentistry; mem.: ADA. Recognized as one of the country's leading dentists and is responsible for creating smiles for famous Hollywood stars; developed products such as: Nite White, Day White, Zoom!, Breath Rx. Office: Discus Dental Inc Century City Aesthetic Dentistry 2080 Century Park E Ste 1601 Los Angeles CA 90067 Office Phone: 310-277-5678. Office Fax: 310-277-3294.

DORGAN, BYRON LESLIE, senator; b. Dickinson, ND, May 14, 1942; s. Emmett P. and Dorothy (Bach) D.; m. Kimberly Olson Dorgan; children: Scott, Shelly (dec.), Brendon, Haley. BS, U. ND, 1965; MBA, U. Denver, 1966. Exec. devel. trainee Martin Marietta Corp., Denver, 1966-67; dep. tax commr., then tax commnr. State of N.D., 1967-80; mem. 97th-102nd congresses from N.D., Washington, 1981-92; US Senator from ND Washington, 1992—; asst. Dem. floor leader U.S. Senate, Washington, 1996—. Mem. commerce, sci. and transp. com., select com. on Indian affairs, appropriations com., energy and natural resource com., chmn. Dem. policy com., 1999—, instr. econs. Bismarck (N.D.) Jr. Coll., 1969-71. Contbr. articles to profl. jours. Recipient Nat. Leadership award Office Gov. N.D., 1972 Mem. Nat. Assn. Tax Adminstrs. (exec. com. 1972-75) Democrat. Lutheran. Office: US Senate 322 Hart Senate Off Bldg Washington DC 20510-0001 also: District Office 312 Federal Bldg PO Box 2579 Bismarck ND 58502 Office Phone: 202-224-2551, 701-250-4618. Office Fax: 701-250-4484, 202-224-1193. E-mail: senator@dorgan.senate.gov.*

DORGAN, KELLY M., marine biologist; BS in Marine Biology, U. Calif., Santa Cruz, 2001; PhD candidate in Oceanography, U. Maine, 2002—. REU intern Summer Systematics Inst. Calif. Acad. Scis., San Francisco, 1999; NSF REU intern Bermuda Biol. Sta., 2000, U. Maine Darling Marine Ctr., 2000, Nat. Def. Sci. and Engring. grad. fellow Darling Marine Ctr., 2002—04, NSF grad. rsch. fellow, 2002—. Contbr. articles to sci. jours. Named one of Brilliant 10, Popular Sci. mag., 2006. Office: Darling Marine Ctr U Maine 193 Clark's Grove Rd Walpole ME 04573 E-mail: kelly.dorgan@umit.maine.edu.

DORIA, MARILYN L., lawyer; b. Boston, Jan. 15, 1944; AB, Brandeis U., 1965; MPA, Syracuse U., 1967; JD, Temple U., 1974. Bar: Pa. 1974, US Dist. Ct. (ea. dist.) Pa. 1974, Tex. 1986, US Dist. Ct. (so. dist.) Tex. 1986, US Ct. Appeals (5th cir.) 1986, US Ct. Appeals (DC cir.) 1986, DC 1993. Dep. asst. to asst. gen. counsel for enforcement FERC, 1980—83, dep. gen. counsel, 1983—85; former ptnr. oil and gas litig. Reynolds Allen & Cook, Houston; now ptnr. Akin, Gump, Strauss, Hauer & Feld, L.L.P., Washington, 1983—, and sect. mgr. energy, land use and environ. practice group. Mem.: Pa. Bar Assn., Tex. Bar Assn., DC Bar Assn., Fed. Energy Bar Assn. Office: Akin Gump Strauss Hauer & Feld Ste 400 1333 New Hampshire Ave NW Washington DC 20036-1564 Office Phone: 202-887-4000. Business E-Mail: mdoria@akingump.com.

DORIO, MARTIN MATTHEW, JR., real estate company executive, investor; b. Bklyn., Nov. 12, 1945; s. Martin M. and Josephine V. (Marsala) D.; m. Gayle M. Morris, June 16, 1968; children: Paul, Jay. BS, SUNY, Stony Brook, 1967; PhD, U. Mass., 1975. Rsch. chemist Diamond Shamrock Corp., Painesville, Ohio, 1975-76, group leader, 1977-79; venture mgr. Gen. Electric Lighting Bus., Cleve., 1979-81, quality and mfg. tech. mgr., 1981-87; dir. quality and productivity FMC Corp., Chgo., 1987-90; v.p. worldwide product mgmt. and market strategy Case Corp., Racine, Wis., 1990-91; v.p. corp. planning and devel. J.I. Case Corp., Racine, Wis., 1992-95; pres., CEO, dir. CLARK Material Handling Co., Lexington, Ky., 1995-99, chmn., CEO, dir., 1999—2001. Mem. adv. com. Dept. Energy, Washington, 1977-79, Am. Productivity and Quality Ctr., Houston, 1988-90; mem. adv. com. on quality Ency. Brit., 1988-90; mem. bd. examiners Malcolm Baldrige Nat. Quality Award, 1988-90; mem. adv. bd. Bioblend Lubricants Internat., Inc., 2001-03, Forintell Inc., 2002—; counselor Sr. Corps of Ret. Execs., 2002-03. Author: Multiple Electron Resonance Spectroscopy, 1979; contbr. articles to profl. jours.; patentee in field. Adv. bd. dirs. Mus. Culture and Diversity, 1997-99; bd. dirs. Lexington Arts & Cultural Coun., 1996-99; co-chair advanced divsn. Lexington: Strides Ahead, 1998-99, counselor SCORE chpt. 573, 2002-2003; chmn. endowment com. Temple Shalom, 2003-05. Capt. USAF, 1968-71. Recipient Nat. Svc. award Nat. Inst. Sci. and Tech., 1988-90. Mem. Am. Soc. Quality Control (exec. com. 1984-85), Am. Mgmt. Assn. Avocations: tennis, raquetball, photography, reading, writing. Home and Office: 1472 Palma Blanca Ct Naples FL 34119-3368 Office Phone: 239-272-2279. E-mail: Marty@MartyDorio.com.

DORION, ROBERT CHARLES, entrepreneur, investor; b. NYC, Dec. 28, 1926; s. William J. and Adelaide (Bacardi) D.; m. Ana Maria Ferber, Nov. 26, 1954; children: Robert Patrick, Marianne Michelle, Nicholas Christian, Kristel Alexia. Student, Columbia U., 1943-44; B of Naval Scis., Dartmouth Coll., 1946. Buyer Balfour, Guthrie and Co. Ltd., 1948-49; capt. M/V Assault Shark Industries div. Borden & Co., 1950-51; pres. Dorion, Rubio and Cia, 1952-57; mgr., ins., mining and chem. dept. Grace & Co., 1954-59; sales mgr. Gen. Tires, Guatemala, 1960-61; chmn. El Salto, S.A., 1962-78; pres. Tecnicos En Seguros, S.A., 1974—, Marcas Mundiales, S.A., 1978-99. Dir. emeritus Bacardi Ltd., Bermuda; pres. Marcas Mundiales S.A.; dir. Industrias Rio Dulce S.A.; pres. Fancap Found. of Inst. Nutricion de Centroamerica y Panama. Contbr. articles to profl. jours. Friend Am. Mus. of Nat. History, NYC; field assoc. Fla. Mus., Gainesville, Mote Marine Lab., Sarasota, Fla., Interamer. Scout Found., 1978-2004. Fellow Internat. Oceanographic Found. (life); mem. Rotary (Paul Harris fellow), World Scout Orgn. (Baden-Powell fellow), Internat. Scout Found. (dir. 1980-2004), US Navy Meml. Found. (dir.), US Naval Inst. (life), Audubon Soc. (life), Internat. Wildlife Soc., Order of The Bronze Wolf. Avocations: pre-columbian archaeology, cryptozoolical studies, shark research, deep sea fishing. Office: PO Box 25339 Miami FL 33102-5339 Address: Kristel SA Apt 195A Guatemala City Guatemala Office Phone: (502)2339-0960. Personal E-mail: kristel@terra.com.gt.

DORIS, ALAN S(ANFORD), lawyer; b. Cleve., June 18, 1947; s. Sam E. and Rebecca D.; m. Nancy Rose Spitzer, Jan. 10, 1976; children: Matthew, Lisa. AB and BS in Bus. cum laude, Miami U., Oxford U., 1969; JD cum laude, Harvard U., 1972. Bar: Ohio 1972, U.S. Dist. Ct. (no. dist.) Ohio 1972, U.S. Tax Ct. 1972, U.S. Ct. Appeals (6th cir.) 1972. Assoc. Stotter, Familo, Cavitch, Elden & Durkin, Cleve., 1972-77; ptnr. Elden & Ford, Cleve., 1978-79, Benesch, Friedlander, Coplan & Aronoff, Cleve., 1980-2000, Squire, Sanders & Dempsey, 2000—. Editor: Ohio Transaction Guide. Treas. Hawthorne Valley Country Club, Cleve., 1984-85; chmn. Cleve. Tax Inst., 1994. Mem. ABA (chmn. capital recovery com. taxation sect. 1994-96). Avocation: golf. Office: Squire Sanders & Dempsey LLP 4900 Key Tower Cleveland OH 44114

DORIS, CAROLE R., rail transportation executive; b. 1948; m. Peter Doris. BA, Mundelein Coll.; JD, DePaul U. Chief dep. atty. DuPage County, Atty. Gen. Jim Ryan; DuPage County rep. Commuter Rail Board (Metra), 2003—06; chmn. Metra, 2006—. Named one of 25 Women to Watch, Crain's Chgo. Bus., 2007. Office: Metra Offices 547 W Jackson Blvd 13th Fl Chicago IL 60661 also: Dupage County State's Attorney 503 N County Farm Rd 2nd Fl Wheaton IL 60187-3907 Office Phone: 312-322-6777.*

DÖRKEN, UWE R., finance company executive; b. Schwelm, NRW, Germany, July 29, 1959; MBA, St. Gall U., Switzerland. With McKinsey & Co., Amsterdam, Netherlands, 1986—90, Zurich, Switzerland, Dusseldorf, Germany, Madrid, NYC, Tokyo; mng. dir. internat. divsn. Deutsche Post, 1991; mem. bd. mgmt. DPWN, 1999; CEO, chmn. DHL Worldwide Express, Ft. Lauderdale, Fla., 2001—. Mem. exec. bd. Deutsche Post World Net. Named one of Elite for the Future, Wirtschaftswoche, 1995, Global Leader of Tomorrow, World Econs. Forum, 1997. Office: DHL Worldwide Express De Kleetlaun 1 1831 Diegen Belgium

DORKEY, CHARLES E., III, lawyer; b. Phila., June 23, 1948; s. Charles Edward and Peggy O'Neal D.; children: Charles Edward IV, John Hilliard, Marjorie Lyddon. AB cum laude, Dartmouth Coll., Hanover, NH, 1970; JD, U. Pa., Phila., 1973. Bar: Pa. 1974, NY 1975, DC 1977. Law clk. to hon. Samuel J. Roberts Supreme Ct. of Pa., 1973-74; assoc. Sullivan & Cromwell, NYC, 1975-81; ptnr. Reboul, MacMurray, Hewitt, Maynard & Kristol, NYC, 1981-84, Richards & O'Neil, NYC, 1984-91, Haythe & Curley, NYC, 1992-99, Torys LLP, NYC, 1999—2007, McKenna Long & Aldridge LLP, NYC, 2007—. Chair Hudson River Park Trust; mem. adv. bd. St. Lawrence Seaway Devel. Corp., 2006. Trustee Citizens Budget Commn., 1993—98, NY Hist. Soc., 1998—, NY Interest Lawyers Acct. Fund, 2001—03; overseer U. Pa. Law Sch., 1993—99; nat. chmn. Law Annual Giving, 1991—93; trustee Hist. Hudson Valley, 2002—, The Beacon Inst., 2005—; mem. alumni coun. Dartmouth Coll., 1990—93, pres. class 1970, 1991—95; mem. mayor's jud. screening com. 1st Jud. Dept., 2002—03; trustee Pks and Trails NY, 1996—; mem. State Ct. of Claims Jud. Screening Com., 1995—99, 2005—06; housing ct. adv. coun. 1st Jud. Dept., 2002—04, 2005—06, mem. departmental disciplinary com., 1995—99, 2005—06; bd. dir. Empire State Devel. Corp., NYC Water Fin. Authority, NY State Job Devel. Authority, Harlem Cmty. Devel. Corp., 42d St. Devel. Project, NY State Mortgage Loan Enforcement and Adminstrn. Corp., Liberty Devel. Corp. Fellow ABA, NY State Bar Assn. (exec. com. comml. and fed. litigation sect. 1986—, fed. judiciary com. 1989—, internat. law and practice sect., com. internat. dispute resolution 1987—); mem. Assn. Bar City NY (products liability com. 1983-86. fed. legis. com. 1990-93, state cts. of superior jurisdiction 1993-96, coun. jud. adminstrn. 1996-99, fed. judiciary 2000-03, com. NYC affairs 2005-06, judiciary 2006—), NY Athletic Club, Univ. Club. Republican. Congregationalist. Home: 205 E 69th St Apt 6C New York NY 10021-5431 Office: McKenna Long & Aldridge LLP 230 Park Ave Ste 1700 New York NY 10169 Office Phone: 212-880-6300, 212-905-8330. Business E-Mail: cdorkey@torys.com.

DORKIN, FREDERIC EUGENE, lawyer; b. Bridgeport, Conn., Feb. 1, 1932; s. William and Selma (Kraus) D.; m. Harriette A. Garfinkel, June 14, 1959; children: Rosalyn Gail, David Ira, Deborah Ruth. AB, Dartmouth Coll., 1953; LLB, Duke U., 1956; LLM, George Washington U., 1968. Bar: Conn. 1956, D.C. 1968, Wash. 1979. Atty. SEC, Washington, 1956-57; pvt. practice Bridgeport, 1960-61; asst. sec. CT Corp. Sys., NYC, Washington, 1961-68; assoc. counsel, asst. sec. Susquehanna Corp., Alexandria, Va., 1968-69; sec., counsel Microdot Inc., Greenwich, Conn., 1969-72; gen. counsel Boeing Computer Svcs., Inc., Morristown, NJ, 1972-78; corp. counsel Boeing Co., Seattle, 1978-82, sr. corp. counsel, 1982-83, asst. gen. counsel, 1984-85; divsn. chief counsel Boeing Electronics Co., 1985-90; sr. counsel Boeing Def. & Space Group, Seattle, 1991-93, ret., 1993; legal cons., arbitrator-mediator Seattle, 1993—. With JAGC, U.S. Army, 1957-60. Mem. Phi Delta Phi, Tau Epsilon Phi.

DORLEAC, CATHERINE See DENEUVE, CATHERINE

DORMAN, ALBERT A., engineering executive, consultant, architect; b. Phila., Apr. 30, 1926; s. William and Edith (Kleiman) D.; m. Joan Bettie Heiten, July 29, 1950; children: Laura Jane, Kenneth Joseph, Richard Coleman. BS, Newark Coll. Engring., 1945; MS, U. So. Calif., 1962; ScD (hon.), N.J. Inst. Tech., 1999. Registered profl. engr., Calif., N.Y., Ill., Oreg., Ariz., Pa., Nev., registered architect, Calif., Oreg. Owner firm Albert A. Dorman, Hanford, Calif., 1954-66; v.p. Daniel, Mann, Johnson & Mendenhall, Los Angeles, 1967-73, pres., chief oper. officer, 1974-77, pres., chief exec. officer, 1977-84, chmn., chief exec. officer, 1984-91, chmn., 1991-99; chmn., chief exec. officer AECOM Tech. Corp., LA, 1984-91, chmn., 1991-92; founding chmn. AECOM Tech Corp., LA, 1992—; chmn. Holmes & Narver, Inc., Orange, Calif., 1991-97, Frederic R. Harris, Inc., NYC, 1988-91, Consoer, Townsend and Assocs., Inc., Chgo., 1988-91. Pres., chmn. bd. dirs. Hanford Savs. & Loan Assn., 1963-72; chair com. on bus strategies for pub. capital investment NRC, 2002-04; rsch. prof. U. So. Calif., Viterbi Sch. Engring., 2005—. Contbr. articles to profl. jours. Pres. Cmty. Concerts Assn., 1962-64; past mem. bd. councilors Sch. Urban and Regional Planning, U. So. Calif., Viterbi Sch. Engring., U. So. Calif., 2004—; trustee Harvey Mudd Coll., 1988-2005, J. David Gladstone Found., 1988—, Nat. Found. Advancement in Arts, 1988-99; bd. overseers N.J. Inst. Tech., 1989—; vice chmn. Los Angeles County Earthquake Fact-Finding Commn., 1980. With U.S. Army, 1945-47. Recipient Civil Engring. Alumnus award U. So. Calif., 1976, Edward F. Weston medal N.J. Inst. Tech., 1986, Golden Beaver Engring. award, 1991, Eponym, Albert Dorman Honors Coll., N.J. Inst. Tech., 1993, Disting. Award of Merit, ACEC, 1996, Medal, U. Calif., San Francisco, 1996. Fellow AIA, ASCE (hon. mem., Harland Bartholomew award 1976, Opal Outstanding Lifetime Achievement award 2000, Parcel-Sverdrup Civil Engring. Mgmt. award 1987, pres. L.A. sect. 1984-85), Am. Cons. Engrs. Coun. (life); mem. NAE (elected mem.), Real Estate Constrn. Industries (Humanitarian award 1986), Am. Pub. Works Assn. (life), Cons. Engrs. Assn. Calif. (bd. dirs. 1982-88, pres. 1985-86), Am. Water Works Assn. (life), Water Pollution Control Fedn. (life), Calif. C. of C. (bd. dirs. 1986-94), L.A. Area C. of C. (bd. dirs. 1983-88, exec. com. 1985-87), Calif. Club, Met. Club, Kiwanis (pres. 1962), Tau Beta Pi, Chi Epsilon. Office: AECOM Tech Corp Ste 3700 555 S Flower St Los Angeles CA 90071-2300

DORMAN, D. DOUGLAS, human resources specialist, hospital administrator; b. NYC, Dec. 22, 1953; s. David Dorman and Ruth Gammage Russell; m. Lyn Conrad, July 21, 1973 (div.); children: Jay Kenneth, Rebecca Lyn; m. Vesta Lee Elliott, Aug. 8, 1998 (dec. July 24, 2005); 1 child, Jade Elizabeth. BA, Middlebury Coll., Vt., 1978; MBA, Plymouth State Coll. U. Sys. NH, 1982. Cert. sr. profl. human resources Human Resources Certification Inst. Dir. pers. svcs. Alice Peck Day Meml. Hosp., Lebanon, NH, 1980—82; exec. v.p. Shenango Valley Med. Ctr., Farrell, Pa., 1982—93; v.p. human resources Horizon Hosp. Sys., Farrell, 1993—95, Greenville Hosp. Sys., SC, 1995—. Instr. Pa. State U., Sharon, 1988—92. Celtic traditions singer, songwriter:, musician: (recordings) First Take, 1998, 3D, 2004. Mem. Met. Arts Coun., Greenville; chair Greenville County Workforce Investment Bd.; mem. bd. dir. YMCA, Greenville. Fellow: Am. Coll. Healthcare Execs.; mem.: BMI, Am. Soc. Healthcare Human Resources Adminstrn. (chpt. pres., Outstanding Chpt. Officer award, Outstanding Contbn. award), Am. MENSA. Avocation: music. Home: 108 Cranmore Ct Greer SC 29650 Office: Greenville Hosp Sys 701 Grove Rd Greenville SC 29605 Home Phone: 864-292-5156; Office Phone: 864-455-8940. Personal E-mail: dddmusic@yahoo.com.

DORMAN, DAVID W., former telecommunications industry executive; b. Atlanta, Jan. 1954; m. Susan P. Dorman, 1971; 3 children. BS in Indsl. Mgmt., Ga. Inst. Tech., 1975. Pres. Sprint Bus. Services, 1990—94; pres., CEO, chmn. Pacific Bell, 1994—97; exec. v.p. SBC Comm., 1997; chmn., pres., CEO PointCast Inc., 1997—98; CEO Concert Comm. Co., 1998—2000; pres. AT&T Corp., 2000—02, chmn., CEO, 2002—05; pres., bd. dir. AT&T Inc. (merger of SBC Comm. & AT&T Corp.), San Antonio, 2005—06. Bd. dir. AT&T Corp., 2002—05, Sci. Applications Internat. Corp., YUM! Brands, Inc., 2005—, AT&T Inc. (merger of SBC Comm. & AT&T Corp.), 2005—06, Motorola Inc. Bd. dirs. Episcopal H.S., Alexandria, Va.; Ga. Tech. Found. Office: AT&T Inc 175 E Houston San Antonio TX 78205*

DORMAN, JANET LEE VOSPER, elementary school educator; d. Stanley R. and Chester H. Vosper; children: Elizabeth Randolph Worth, Philip Hamilton Worth. BS, Radford Coll., 1969; EdM, Va. Poly. Inst., 1976. Trainer U. Kans., Lawrence, 1991—; sci. lead tchr. Kenmore Mid. Sch., Arlington, Va., 2000—. Ordained elder Old Presbyn. Meeting Ho., Alexandria, Va., 2005—. Named Tchr. of Yr., Chesterfield County H.S., 1999—2000. Mem.: AAUW, Va. Edn. Assn. (bd. dirs., exec. com. 2004—), Arlington Edn. Assn. (exec. bd. 2000—, v.p.), Delta Kappa Gamma. Home: 419 Jackson Pl Alexandria VA 22302 Office: Arlington County Public Schools 200 S Canlin Springs Rd Arlington VA 22204 Home Phone: 703-548-7627; Office Phone: 703-228-6800. Business E-Mail: lee_dorman@apsva.us.

DORMAN, JOHN FREDERICK, genealogist; b. Louisville, July 25, 1928; s. John Frederick and Sue Carpenter (Miller) D. BA, U. Louisville, 1950; MA, Emory U., 1955. Asst. archivist Coll. William and Mary, 1953-55; genealogist, 1955—; editor The Virginia Genealogist, 1957—2006; compiler, editor Adventurers of Purse and Person, Virginia, 1607-1625, 2004—07; lectr. Nat. Inst. Geneal. Research, 1963-74, 77-93, Inst. Geneal. and Hist. Research Samford U., 1977-88. Trustee Bd. for Cert. of Genealogists, 1964-84, pres., 1979-82, exec. dir., 1983-96. Recipient Coddington award of merit, New Eng. Hist. Geneal. Soc., 2006. Fellow Am. Soc. Genealogists (treas. 1959-66, pres. 1982-85), Nat. Geneal. Soc. (v.p. 1958-59, 68-70, libr. 1959-60), Va. Geneal. Soc.; mem. Soc. Cincinnati, Soc. Colonial Wars (dep. registrar gen. 1969-81, D.C. gov. 1980-82), SR (gen. registrar 1976-85, pres. D.C. chpt. 1982-84), SAR (D.C. pres. 1967-68), Children Am. Revolution (sr. nat. registrar 1960-62, sr. nat. treas. 1962-64, 66-68, sr. nat. 2d v.p. 1968-70), Descs. Colonial Govs. (gov. gen. 1973-76), Descs. Lords Md. Manors (pres. 1985-89), Sovereign Mil. Order Temple Jerusalem, Cosmos Club (Washington). Republican. Episcopalian. Home: 175 Hulls Chapel Rd Fredericksburg VA 22406-5218

DORMAN, LINNEAUS CUTHBERT, retired chemist; b. Orangeburg, SC, June 28, 1935; s. John Albert and Georgia D.; m. Phae Louise Hubble, June 21, 1958; children: Evelyn Suzanne, John Albert III. BS, Bradley U., 1956; PhD, Ind. U., 1961; DSc (hon.), Saginaw Valley State U., 1988. Chemist No. Regional Lab., U.S. Dept. Agr., Peoria, Ill., summers 1956-59; research chemist Dow Chem. Co., Midland, Mich., 1960-68, research specialist, 1968-76, research assoc., 1976-83, assoc. scientist, 1983-93, sr. assoc. scientist, 1993-94; ret., 1994. Lawrence lectr. Bradley U., 1990, mem. adv. bd., 1994, 2005; active Centurion Soc., 1993, Burgess award selection com., 1996-2000, chemistry dept. adv. bd.; cmty. adv. panel Dow Corning Midland Plant, 1995-2005. Contbr. articles to profl. jours.; patentee in field. Active NAACP, Midland Commn. on Cmty. Rels., 1963-73, vice-chmn., 1967; active Black Exec. Exch. Program, Urban League, 1971, 75; trustee Midland Found., 1980-90, v.p., 1987-90; dir.-at-large Midland Ctr. for the Arts, 1984, 85; bd. fellows Saginaw Valley State Coll., 1975-87, emeritus mem., 1987, v.p., 1981-83, pres., 1983-85, ann. fund drive, 1985-95, presdl. search com., 1989; chmn. Cen. Rsch. and Devel. Scientists Orgn., 1992; exec. coun. Ind. U. Alumni Assn., 2002—; bd. dirs. Hidden Harvest, 2004. Paul Harris fellow Rotary, 1989; co-recipient Bond award Am. Oil Chemists Soc., 1960; recipient Cen. Rsch. Inventor of Yr. award Dow Chem. Co., 1982, Saginaw Valley State Univ. Disting. Svc. Medallion (with wife Phae), 2002. Mem. AAAS, Nat. Orgn. Black Chemists and Chem. Engrs. (Percy L. Julian award 1999), Am. Chem. Soc. (sect. treas. 1966, sec. 1967, dir. 1968-70, councilor 1971-76, 80-81, 84-92), Midland Rotary (sec. 1980-81, v.p. 1981-82, pres. 1982-83), Midland County Hist. Soc. (bd. adv. 2002), Little Forks Conservancy, Sigma Xi (chpt. treas. 1969, sec. 1970, pres. 1975), Phi Lambda Upsilon, Pi Kappa Delta, Omega Psi Phi. Mem. United Ch. of Christ. Home: PO Box 1732 Midland MI 48641-1732 Personal E-mail: lcdorman@aol.com.

DORMAN, MARGARET K., corporate financial executive; BA in Econ. and Bus., Hendrix Coll. Sr. mgr. Ernst & Young; corp. contr. Landmark Graphics Corp.; v.p., contr. Smith Internat., Houston, 1995-2000, sr. v.p., CFO, treas., 2000—. Office: Smith Internat PO Box 60068 Houston TX 77205-0068*

DORMAN, RICHARD FREDERICK, JR., association executive, consultant; b. Peoria, Ill., June 3, 1944; s. Richard Frederick and Pauline Elizabeth (Dryfus) D.; children: Richard F., Kevin M.; m. Anne Marie Carlton, May 28, 1976. Student, Franklin U., Columbus, Ohio, 1963—65, student, 1968—69, New Sch. Social Reform, NYC, 1979—80, U. Md., 1982. Field rep. Ohio Civil Svc. Employees Assn., Columbus, 1972-75; regional dir. St. Jude Children's Rsch. Hosp., NYC, 1975-80; exec. dir. Assembly Govtl. Employees, Washington, 1980-85; with Quality Mgmt. Inst., Washington, 1985-86; exec. dir. Am. Congress on Surveying and Mapping, Falls Church, Va., 1986-90, Ohio Coun. for Home Care, 1991-93; exec. v.p., COO Assn. for Profls. in Infection Control and Epidemiology Inc., Washington, 1993-95; v.p. Assn. Mgmt. Group, Arlington, Va., 1995-96. Ptnr. McIntoch & Dorman, Washington, 1982-86; pres. Catalyst Group, Alexandria, 1996—. Founder, pres. Columbus Ind. Jr. High Football League, Ohio, 1970. Recipient Recognition for Contbn. to Women's Sports award Ohio Ho. of Reps., 1975, 76. Fellow Am. Soc. Assn. Execs. (cert.); mem. Alexandria C. of C. (bd. dirs., chair). Republican. Presbyterian. Office Phone: 703-598-2724. Personal E-mail: rfdorman@aol.com.

DORMANN, HENRY O., magazine publisher; b. NYC, Mar. 5, 1932; s. Henry Maroni and Ivara (Soberg) D.; m. Alice Andreasen, Apr. 7, 1958; children: Kaari, Kristi. Chmn. bd. Nat. Enquirer, 1971-72, chmn. exec. com., 1987-89; chmn. Internat. Bd. Indsl. Advisors, 1964—; pres., editor-in-chief S.I.P.A. News Service, NYC, 1966—; pres. U.S. Tech. Devel. Co., 1969-70; pres., editor-in-chief Holiday Mag., 1976-77; chmn. editor-in-chief Leaders Mag., 1977—. Adv. council Joint Legis. Com. on Met. and Regional Areas Study N.Y. State, 1969-72; chmn. N.Y. State Assembly Council on Econ. Devel., 1972-80. Author: A Millionaire's Guide to Europe or How to Save Money Like the Rich People Do, 1967, A Millionaire's Guide to Exotic Places or How to Save Money Like the Rich People Do, 1973, A Millionaire's Guide to Fun Places or How to Save Money Like the Rich People Do, 1978, The Speaker's Book of Quotations, 1987, 2000. Founder Libr. Presdl. Papers, Inst. for Study of Presidency; bd. dirs. Inst. Edn. Affairs, Washington; trustee IATA Internat. Airline Tng. Fund, 1988-2003, Am. U., Washington, 1981-92; founder, pres. Found. for Family Values, 1990-93. With USCG. Office: 59 E 54th St New York NY 10022-4211

DORMINEY, HENRY CLAYTON, JR., allergist; b. Tifton, Ga., May 15, 1949; s. Henry Clayton and Virgina (Petty) D. BS, Davidson Coll., 1971; MD, U. Iowa, 1975. Diplomate Am. Bd. Internal Medicine, Am. Bd. Allergy and Immunology; lic. physician, Ga. Med. intern U. Iowa Hosps. and Clinics, Iowa City, 1975-76, med. resident, 1976-78, allergy and immunology fellow, 1978-80; practice medicine specializing allergy and clin. immunology Allergy & Dermatology Assocs. of Tifton, Ga., 1981—99, Allergy, Asthma and Sinus Clinic of Tifton, 1999—. Mem. staff Tift Regional Med. Ctr.; bd. dirs. Brumby's Crossing, Dorminey Enterprises; chmn. and founder Tifton Mus. Arts and Heritage, 1991; mem. Allergy, Asthma & Sinus Clinic of Tifton; pres. ZapAds, Inc., 2006—. Assoc. editor, contbg. author Vital Signs, 1969-71. Bd. dirs. Tift County Found. Ednl. Excellence, 1996—, chmn. investment com., 1998—, v.p., 2004-05, pres., 2005-06; bd. dirs. Tifton Heritage Found., pres., 1992; bd. dirs. Tifton Mus. Arts and Heritage, 1991—2006. Recipient Physician's Recognition award AMA, 1979, 85, Lee Willingham III trophy Davidson Coll., 1987, Tifton Main Street Program award, 1989, Best Adaptive Re-Use Project, Tifton Historic District, The Coca Cola Bldg., 1993; grantee Am. Coll. Allergy, 1980. Mem. Am. Acad. Allergy (travel grantee 1980), Tift County Med. Soc. (sec., treas. 1983-84, v.p., 1984-85, pres. 1985-86), Med. Assn. Ga., Am. Numismatic Soc., Forward Tifton, Tifton C. of C. Lodges: Rotary (Spl. Merit award, founder Tifton Directory, bd. dirs. 1988-93, 2006-07, pres.-elect 1989-90, pres. 1990-91, Paul Harris fellow 1993). Democrat. Home: 21 Duck Dr Tifton GA 31794-3953 Office: 820 Love Ave Tifton GA 31794-4071 Office Phone: 229-382-3720. Personal E-mail: dorminey@friendlycity.net.

DORN, DIANE M., science educator; b. Chilton, Wis., Jan. 11, 1966; d. Dennis and Marian Dorn; m. William Dowell, Feb. 13, 1993. AS in electronics, McHenry C.C., 1990; BS in natural environ. sys., No. Ill., 1994; MEd, Nat. Louis U., 1998. Sci. tchr. Woodstock HS, Woodstock, Ill., 1994—2001, Marian Ctrl. HS, Woodstock, Ill., 2001—. Bd. mem. Ringwood Planning Bd., Ringwood, Ill., 2000—05. Recipient monetary award, Earth Watch, 2000. Mem.: Nat. Sci. Tchrs. Assn., Ill. Sci. Tchrs. Assn. Avocations: soccer, snowboarding, bicycling, backpacking, travel. Office: Marian Cath Ctrl HS 1001 McHenry Ave Woodstock IL 60098 Office Phone: 815-338-4220. E-mail: ddorn@marian.com.

DORN, GEORGETTE MAGASSY, library official; b. Budapest, Hungary, Aug. 13, 1934; arrived in U.S., 1955; d. Gabriel Luis and Georgette Gyorko Magassy; m. Paul Austin Dorn Jr., June 9, 1961; children: Georgette, Elizabeth, Susan, Paul Gabriel. Degree in pub. translation, U. Buenos Aires, 1955; BS, Creighton U., 1959; MA, Boston Coll., 1961; PhD, Georgetown U., 1981. Tchg. asst. Boston Coll., 1960—61; specialist in Hispanic culture Libr. of Congress, Washington, 1964—69, head Hispanic reading rm., 1969—94, chief Hispanic divsn., 1994—. Lectr. Ctr. Am. Studies, Georgetown U., Washington, 1982—; mem. adv. com. L.Am. project Ctr. Rsch. Librs., Chgo., 1994—; asst. editor Am. Quar. Rev., Washington, 1979—; chmn. history com. Pan Am. Inst. Geography and History, Washington, 2002—; cons. Andrew Mellon Found., 2001, 05; rec. L.Am., Caribbean and Latino authors Archive of Hispanic Literature on Tape. Translator (by Jose Francisco Ruiz): Report on the Indian Tribes of Texas, 1972; assoc. editor: Encyclopedia of Latin American History and Culture, 1996 (Waldo Leland award, 97); editor: Works by Miguel de Cervantes, 1994; contbr. articles to profl. publs. Organizer L.Am. Book Fair, Washington, 1984—85; curator archive Hispanic literature on tape Libr. of Congress, Washington, 1969—; chmn. disting. award com. Conf. on L.Am. History, 1998; chmn. U.S. History Commn., Pan Am. Inst. Geography and History, 2002—05; mem. exec. com. Conf. L.Am. History, 1991—96; mem. steering com. Consortium, L.Am. Studies Programs, 1992—96; mem. adv. com. D.C. Latino Cmty. Festival Exhibit, Washington, 1989; mem. adv. bd. Mex.-Am. Lit. Archives, UCLA, 1989—91; archivist Holy Trinity Ch., Washington, 1988—94. Travel grantee, Fulbright Commn., 1988. Mem.: Am. Cath. Hist. Assn., L.Am. Studies Assn. (mem. exec. coun. 1985—87, chmn. Bryce Wood Prize Com. 1990—91, regional liaison 1975—77), Am. Hist. Assn. (Premio de Rey prize 2004, Franklin Jameson prize 1995), Intern Am. Coun. Washington (pres. 1985—86), Phi Alpha Theta, Alpha Sigma Nu. Roman Catholic. Avocations: swimming, yoga, painting, films. Home: 4702 Essex Ave Chevy Chase MD 20815 Office: Libr Congress Hispanic Divsn 101 Independence Ave SE Washington DC 20540-4850 Office Phone: 202-707-2003. Office Fax: 202-707-2005. Business E-Mail: gdor@loc.gov.

DORN, GORDON JOSEPH, artist, educator; b. Sheboygan, Wis., Dec. 5, 1943; s. Frank and Olive G. (Rollman) D. BA in Edn., Wis. State U., 1966; MFA in Painting, U. Wis., 1969. Prof. art No. Ill. U., Dekalb, 1969-2000; prof. emeritus, 2000—. State v.p. AAUP of Ill., 1990-92, state pres., 1992-96. One-man shows include Roy Boyd Gallery, Chgo., 1977, 79, 82, 85, 88, 91, 95, 97, 98, 2000; group exhbns. include Art Inst. Chgo., 1977, 79, Chgo. Internat. Art Exposition, 1997, 98, 99; patentee in field. Recipient prize Art Inst. Chgo., 1977; exhbns. reviewed in Chgo. Tribune, 1991, 95, 98, Chgo. Sun Times, 1982, 84. Avocations: writing education materials, inventing. Office Phone: 305-864-9825.

DORN, JACOB HENRY, history professor; b. Chicago, Sept. 21, 1939; s. Francis Jacob and Mary Elizabeth Dorn; m. Carole Ruth Johnson, Aug. 15, 1964; children: Jonathan Andrew, Elizabeth Ann Lublin. BA, Wheaton Coll., Ill., 1960; PhD, U. Oreg., Eugene, 1965. Prof. history Wright State U., Dayton, 1965—. Chair Dayton Area Campus Ministry Bd., 1972; dir., honors program Wright State U., Dayton, 1973—87; pres. Wright State U. Faculty, Dayton, 1977—78, Ohio Bd. United Ministries Higher Edn., Columbus, 1983—84; bd. mgrs. Am. Bapt. Hist. Soc., Valley Forge, Pa., 1987—99; pres. Dayton Coun. World Affairs, 1988—90; editl. cons. Am. Bapt. Quar., Valley Forge, Pa., 1993—2007. Author: (biography) Washington Gladden: Prophet of the Social Gospel, 1967 (Ohioana Libr. Assn. Ann. Book award, 1968); editor: Socialism and Christianity in Early 20th Centry America, 1998. Chair, bd. deacons and Christian edn. First Bapt. Ch., Dayton, 1966—85. Recipient Disting. Tchr. award, Wright State U. Coll. Liberal Arts, 1977, Outstanding Tchr. award, Ohio Acad. History, 1986, Disting. Svc. award, 1987, Faculty Mem. Yr., Wright State U. Student Govt., 1993—94; NDEA fellowship, U. of Oreg., 1960—63, Tchg. fellow, U. Oreg., 1963—64. Mem.: Mid-East Honors Assn. (Leadership award 1988), Ohio Acad. of History (life), Orgn. of Am. Historians (life). Liberal. Baptist. Avocations: travel, classical music, reading. Home: 7041 Rosecliff Pl Dayton OH 45459 Office: Wright State Univ 3640 Colonel Glenn Hwy Dayton OH 45435 Home Phone: 937-291-9818; Office Phone: 937-775-2281. Business E-Mail: jdorn1@woh.rr.com.

DORN, JAMES ANDREW, editor; b. Buffalo, Aug. 26, 1945; s. Andrew William and Mary Carol (Gannon) D.; m. Carol Evans Cronmiller, Sept. 5, 1970; children: Andrea Yvonne, Heather Katherine. BS in Econs., Canisius Coll., 1967; MA in Econs., U. Va., 1969, PhD, 1976. Prof. Towson (Md.) U., 1973—; editor Cato Jour. Cato Inst., Washington, 1982—, v.p. for acad. affairs, 1989—; rsch. fellow Inst. Humane Studies George Mason U., Fairfax, Va., 1986-95. Editor: The Future of Money in the Info. Age, 1997, China in the New Millennium, 1998; co-editor (with Henry G. Manne): Econ. Liberties and the Judiciary, 1987; co-editor: (with Anna J. Schwartz) The Search for Stable Money, 1987; co-editor: (with William A. Niskanen) Dollars, Deficits and Trade, 1989; co-editor: (with Wang Xi) Econ. Reform in China, 1990; co-editor: (with Roberto Salinas-León) Money and Markets in the Americas, 1996; co-editor: (with Steve Hanke and Alan Walters) The Revolution in Devel. Economics, 1998; co-editor: (with T.G. Carpenter) China's Future, 2000; co-editor: (with D. Artana) Internat. Fin. Crises (in Spanish), 2004; contbr. articles to profl. jours. Mem. White House Commn. on Presdl. Scholars, Washington, 1984-90. Recipient Regent's Faculty Award for Excellence in Rsch./Scholarship Univ. Sys. Md., 1998; Hayek Fund grantee Inst. for Humane Studies, 1986-87, Earhart grantee 1969-70, 81; Thomas Jefferson Ctr. fellow U. Va., 1969-70. Mem.

Am. Econ. Assn., Mont Pelerin Soc., West Side Rowing Club (Buffalo). Avocations: alpine hiking, photography, geology, jogging. Office: Cato Inst 1000 Massachusetts Ave NW Washington DC 20001-5400 Business E-Mail: jdorn@cato.org.

DORN, JENNIFER LYNN, professional association executive, former federal agency administrator; b. Grand Island, Nebr., Dec. 7, 1950; d. Harold Clarence and Ethel Agnes D.; 2 children BA, Oreg. State U., 1973; MPA, U. Conn., 1977. Legis. asst. to Senator M. Hatfield US Senate, Washington, 1977-81; com. staff Senate Appropriations, Washington, 1981-83; spl. asst. to sec. US Dept. Labor, Washington, 1983-84; dir. Comml. Space Transp., Washington, 1984-85; assoc. dep. sec. US Dept. Transp., Washington, 1985-87; asst. sec. for policy US Dept. Labor, Washington, 1989-91; sr. v.p. pub. support ARC, Washington, 1991-98; pres. Nat. Health Mus., 1998—2001; adminstr. Fed. Transit Adminstrn. US Dept. Transp., Washington, 2001—05; alt. exec. dir. Internat. Bank for Reconstruction & Devel. (The World Bank), US Dept. Treasury, Washington, 2005—06; pres., CEO Nat. Acad. Pub. Adminstrn., Washington, 2007—. Mem. Washington Women's Forum, Cosmos Club. Republican. Lutheran. Office: Nat Acad Pub Adminstrn 1100 New York Ave Ste 1090 E Washington DC 20005*

DORN, LOUIS OTTO, retired minister; b. Detroit, July 1, 1928; s. Theodore Herman and Thekla Maria (Frederking) Dorn; m. Erna Ruth Koessel, June 14, 1953; children: Margaret Ligaya Dorn White, Peter Bayani, Martin Louis, Judith Anne. BA, Concordia Theol. Sem., St. Louis, 1951, BD, 1962; MA in Linguistics, Ateneo de Manila U., Quezon City, The Philippines, 1974; PhD, Luth. Sch. Theology, Chgo., 1980. Ordained to ministry Luth. Ch.-Mo. Synod, 1953. Missionary Luth. Ch. in The Philippines, Manila, 1953-74; candidate Ohio dist. Luth. Ch. -Mo. Synod, 1975-80; candidate N.J. dist. Luth. Ch.-Mo. Synod, 1980-99; transls. rsch. assoc. Am. Bible Soc., NYC, 1979-90; transl. cons. United Bible Socs., NYC, 1990-99; ret., 1999. Chmn. Luth. Philippine Mission, Manila, 1962—63, Manila, 1971—72; sec. Luth. Ch. in the Philippines, Manila, 1962—63, commn. ecumenical affairs, 1964—74, dir. transls. dept., 1966—74; bd. dirs. Interchurch Lang. Sch., Quezon City, 1964—74, chmn. bd. dirs., 1967—74; hon. transls. advisor Philippine Bible Soc., Manila, 1968—74. Contbr. articles and revs. to religious publs. Grantee, Ctr. Dist. Luth. Ch.-Mo. Synod, 1944—53, Luth. Sch. Theology, Chgo., 1974—78. Mem.: Soc. Bibl. Lit. Home: 1414 N Gregson St Durham NC 27701-1110 Personal E-mail: ldorn@nc.rr.com. *People often don't know how to live under God's grace because they can't forgive themselves and know only God's law. To accept God's grace, to be willing to be forgiven, results in an amazing life of freedom that honors the Savior.*

DORN, MARY ANN, retired auditor; b. Overland, Mo., May 1, 1933; d. Bernard J. and Marie (Kunkler) Engler; children: Glennon (dec.), Pat Michael, Michelle; m. Donald Patrick Dorn, June 3, 2002. Student, Fontbonne Coll., 1951-52; AA, Sacramento City Coll., 1975; BS in Bus., Calif. State U., 1981. CPA, Calif.; cert. fraud examiner; cert. govt. fin. mgr. From asst. to acct. Mo. Rsch. Labs., Inc., St. Louis, 1953-55, adminstrv. asst., 1955-60; sec. western region fin. office Gen. Electric Co., St. Louis, 1960-62; credit analyst Crocker Nat. Bank, Sacramento, 1962-72; student tchr. Sacramento County Dept. Edn., 1979-81; acctg. technician East Yolo Community Services Dist., 1983; mgmt. specialist USAF Logistics Command, 1984; auditor Office Insp. Gen. U.S. Dept. Transp., 1984-92; auditor-in-charge Adminstrn. for Children and Families U.S. Dept. Health and Human Svcs., 1992—. Mem. Sacramento Community Commn. for Women, 1978-81, bd. dirs., 1980—; planning bd. Golden Empire Health Systems Agy. Mem. AARP (tax counselor), AAUW (fin. officer 1983—), AICPA, Nat. Assn. Accts. (dir., newsletter editor), Fontbonne Coll. Alumni Assn., Calif. State Alumni Assn., Assn. Govt. Accts. (chpt. officer), Calif. Soc. CPAs, German Geneological Soc. (bd. dirs. 1990—, publicity dir. 1994—), Sun City Lincoln Hills Assn., Beta Gamma Sigma, Beta Alpha Psi. Roman Catholic. Home: 815 Magnolia Ln Lincoln CA 95648-8429

DORN, NORMAN PHILIP, management consulting firm executive; b. Ithaca, NY, Jan. 29, 1945; s. Saul James and Pearl Dorn; children: Paul, Ian, Nathan, Mark. BS, Carnegie-Mellon U., 1966; MS, U. Pitts., 1969. Engr. Westinghouse Electric, Pitts., 1969-78; sr. engr. GPU Svc. Corp., Forked River, NJ, 1978-79; mng. dir. Accountable Sys. Co. Internat. Inc., Coll. Pk., Md., 1979—. Mem. Md./Del./D.C. Staff of Navy-Marine Corps Mil. Affiliate Radio Sys., Telephone Pioneers, Masons, Toastmasters. Achievements include inventions, quality improvements, requirements process engrng., process controls devel., instruction, system stability analysis procedures, telecommunications tech., systems (applications) architecture and mfg. mgmt. Office: Accountable Sys Co Internat Inc 9116 49th Pl College Park MD 20740 Office Phone: 888-607-6267.

DORNBUSCH, ARTHUR A., II, lawyer; b. Peru, Ill., Nov. 8, 1943; s. Arthur A. Sr. and Genevieve C. (Knudtson) D.; children: Kimberly, Brendan, Courtney, Eric; m. Jacqueline Bahrs Montanus, Feb. 10, 1996. BA, Yale U., 1966; LLB, U. Pa., 1969. Bar: N.Y. 1970, U.S. Ct. Appeals. (2d cir.) 1971, U.S. Dist. Ct. (so. and ea. dists.) N.Y. 1971. Assoc. Dewey, Ballantine, Bushby, Palmer & Wood, NYC, 1969-72; asst. gen. counsel Boise Cascade Corp., NYC, 1972-75, Teleprompter Corp., NYC, 1975-76, Engelhard Industries divsn. Engelhard Minerals and Chem. Corp., Edison, NJ, 1976-80; v.p., gen. counsel minerals and chems. divsn. Engelhard Corp., Edison, 1980—84, v.p., gen. counsel, sec. Iselin, NJ, 1984—. Mem. Pelham (N.Y.) Union Free Sch. Bd., 1979-82. Mem. ABA, N.Y. State Bar Assn., Assn. Bar City N.Y., Am. Corp. Counsel Assn., Am. Intellectual Property Law Assn., Am. Soc. Corp. Secs., Mfrs. Alliance for Productivity and Innovation. Office: Engelhard Corp PO Box 770 101 Wood Ave S Iselin NJ 08830-0770 Office Phone: 732-205-5527. Business E-Mail: arthur.dornbusch@engelhard.com.

DORNBUSH, K. TERRY, former ambassador, consulting company executive, educator; b. Atlanta, Oct. 31, 1933; m. Marilyn Pierce; 3 children. BA magna cum laude, Vanderbilt U.; postgrad., Emory U., N.Y. Inst. Fin. Former CEO, Hipolex Corp.; former pres. DOAG USA Inc.; former vice chmn. Am. Western Corp.; former ptnr. Courts & Co. & Investment Bankers; amb. to The Netherlands, Am. Embassy, The Hague, 1994-98; CEO Nalim Holdings BV, 1998—2003; mem. supervisory bd. RODAMCO Europe. Former prof. Nijenrode U., The Netherlands; bd. dirs. Schroders Hedge Funds. Bd. dirs. Aspen Cancer Conf.

DORNE, DAVID J., lawyer; b. Chgo., Dec. 9, 1946; BS magna cum laude, U. Ill., 1969; MSc, London Sch. Econs., 1970; JD cum laude, Boston U., 1973. Bar: N.Y. 1973, U.S. Ct. Appeals (2d cir.) 1973, U.S. Tax Ct. 1973, U.S. Dist. Ct. (so. dist.) N.Y. 1975, Calif. 1978. Mem. Seltzer Caplan McMahon Vitek P.C., San Diego. Mem. City of San Diego Charter Rev. Commn., 1989—. Mem. ABA (taxation sect., corp., banking and bus. law sect.), State Bar Calif. (taxation sect., real property law sect., chmn. personal income tax subcom. 1982-84), San Diego County Bar Assn., Assn. of Bar of City of N.Y. (taxation sect.), Beta Gamma Sigma. Office: Seltzer Caplan McMahon Vitek PC 2100 Symphony Tower 750 B St San Diego CA 92101-8114 Office Phone: 619-685-3003.

DORNE, HOWARD LESLIE, radiologist; b. Chgo., Apr. 1, 1956; BS in Math. Biomed. Scis. with high distinction, U. Mich., Ann Arbor, MD, 1980. Diplomate diagnostic radiology Am. Bd. Radiology, 1985, Can. Bd. Radiology, 1985, Quebec, 1985, cert. diagnostic radiology, vascular and interventional radiology 1995, lic. Nat. Bd. Med. Examiners, 1981, Ill., 1981, Mich., 1985, Med. Coun. Can., 1987, Calif., 1986. Intern St. Joseph Mercy Hosp., Ann Arbor, 1980—81; resident ophthalmology U. Ill. Med. Ctr., Chgo., 1981; resident diagnostic radiology McGill U. Sir. Mortimer B. Davis Jewish Gen. Hosp., Montreal, Quebec, Canada, 1982—85, chief resident diagnostic radiology; fellow cardiovasc. interventional radiology U. Mich. Hosp., Ann Arbor, 1985—86; instr. diagnostic radiology U. Mich., Ann Arbor, 1985—86; staff St. Joseph Hosp., and Children's Hosp. Orange County, Calif., 1986—. Contbr. numerous articles and sci. papers to profl. jours. Mem.: Royal Coll. Physicians ad Surgeons Can., Orange County Radiology Soc., Calif. Radiol. Soc., Am. Roentgen Ray Soc., Soc. Interventional Radiologists, Am. Coll. Radiology, Radiol. Soc. N.Am., Am. Soc. Interventional and Therapeutic Neuroradiology. Office: St Joseph Hosp Dept Radiology 1100 Stewart Dr Orange CA 92868

DORNER, PETER PAUL, retired economist, educator; b. Luxemburg, Wis., Jan. 13, 1925; s. Peter and Monica (Altmann) Dorner; m. Lois Cathryn Hartnig, Dec. 26, 1950. BS, U. Wis.-Madison, 1951; MS, U. Tenn., Knoxville, 1953; PhD, Harvard U., 1959. Asst. prof. agrl. econs. U. Tenn., 1953-54; asst. prof. U. Wis.-Madison, 1954-56, assoc. prof., 1959-62, prof., 1962-89, dir. Land Tenure Center, 1965-66, 68-71, chmn. dept. agrl. econs., 1972-76, dean internat. studies and programs, 1980-89, prof., dean emeritus, 1989—. Prof. U. Chile, Santiago, 1963—65; sr. staff economist Pres.'s Coun. Econ. Advisors, Washington, 1967—68; cons. UN, UN Food, Agrl. Orgn., World Bank, U.S. Govt., State Govtl. Agys., InterAm. Devel. Bank. Author: Land Reform and Economic Development, 1972, Latin American Land Reforms in Theory and Practice: a Retrospective Analysis, 1992; editor: Cooperative and Commune: Group Framing in the Economic Development of Agriculture, 1977, Resources and Development: Natural Resource Policies and Economic Development in an Interdependent World, 1980; contbr. numerous articles to profl. jours., popular mags. Inf. US Army, 1944—46. Mem.: AARP. Home: 3111 Pheasant Branch Rd #109A Middleton WI 53562 Personal E-mail: ppdorner@facstaff.wisc.edu.

DORNETTE, W(ILLIAM) STUART, lawyer, educator; b. Washington, Mar. 2, 1951; s. William Henry Lueders and Frances Roberta (Hester) D.; m. Martha Louise Mehl, Nov. 19, 1983; children: Marjorie Frances, Anna Christine, David Paul. AB, Williams Coll., 1972; JD, U. Va., 1975. Bar: Va. 1975, Ohio 1975, U.S. Dist. Ct. (so. dist.) Ohio 1975, D.C. 1976, U.S. Ct. Appeals (6th cir.) 1977, U.S. Supreme Ct. 1980. Assoc. Taft, Stettinius & Hollister, Cin., 1975-83, ptnr., 1983—. Instr. law U. Cin., 1980-87, adj. prof., 1988-91. Co-author: Federal Judiciary Almanac, 1984-87. Mem. Ohio Bd. Bar Examiners, 1991-93, Hamilton County Rep. Exec. Com., 1982—; bd. dirs. Zool. Soc. Cin., 1983-94, 06-, Cin. Parks Found., 1995-04; bd. visitors U. Cin. Law Sch., 2002-06. Mem. FBA, Ohio State Bar Assn., Cin. Bar Assn., Am. Phys. Soc., Nat. Assn. Coll. and Univ. Attys. Methodist. Home: 329 Bishopsbridge Dr Cincinnati OH 45255-3948 Office: 1800 US Bank Tower 425 Walnut St Cincinnati OH 45202-3923 Office Phone: 513-357-9353. E-mail: dornette@taftlaw.com.

DORNFELD, DAVID ALAN, engineering educator; b. Horicon, Wis., Aug. 3, 1949; s. Harlan Edgar and Cleopatra D.; Barbara Ruth Dornfeld, Sept. 18, 1976. BS in Mech. Engrng. with honors, U. Wis., 1972, MS in Mech. Engrng., 1973, PhD in Mech. Engrng., 1976. Asst. prof. dept. sys. design U. Wis., Milw., 1976-77; asst. prof. mfg. engrng. U. Calif., Berkeley, 1977-83, assoc. prof. mfg. engrng., 1983-89, vice-chmn. instrn. dept. mech. engrng., 1987-88, dir. Engrng. Sys. Rsch. Ctr., 1989-98, prof. mfg. engrng., 1989—, Will C. Hall Family prof. engrng., 1999—, assoc. dean interdisciplinary studies Coll. Engrng., 2001—; assoc. dir. rsch. Ecole Nationale Superieure des Mines de Paris, Berkeley, 1983-84. Invited prof. Ecole Nationale Superieure D'Arts et Metiers, Paris, 1992-93; cons., expert witness for intellectual property issues, sensor systems, mfg. automation, sustainable mfg. Contbr. articles to profl. jours., chpts. in books; presenter numerous seminars, confs.; patentee in field. Recipient Dist. Svc. citation U. Wis. Coll. Engrng, Madison, 2000. Fellow ASME (past editor, mem. editl. bd. Mfg. Rev. Jour., pres advisory com., Blackall Machine Tool and Gage Award 1990), Soc. Mfg. Engrs. (fellow editl. bd. Jour. Mfg. Systems, Outstanding Young Engr. award 1982, Frederick W. Taylor Rsch. medal 2004); mem. Am. Soc. Precision Engring., Acoustic Emission Working Group, N.Am. Mfg. Rsch. Inst. (past pres., scientific com.), Japan Soc. Precision Engring. (Takagi award 2005), Coll. Internat. pour l'Etude Scientifique des Techniques de Production Mechanique (CIRP). Avocations: hiking, travel, reading. Office: U Calif Dept Mech Engring Berkeley CA 94720-1740 Home Phone: 510-524-8890; Office Phone: 510-642-0906. E-mail: dornfeld@berkeley.edu.

DORNFEST, BURTON SAUL, anatomy educator; b. NYC, Oct. 31, 1930; s. Irving and Yetta (Rosengarten) D.; m. Eveline Drucker, June 13, 1954; children; Michael Barry. BA, NYU, 1952, MS, 1954, PhD, 1960. Rsch. asst. dept. biostats. Sloan-Kettering Inst. and Meml. Hosp., NYC, 1952-53; rsch. asst. dept. biology NYU, 1953-54, 56-58, instr. gen. sci., 1958-63; instr. anatomy N.Y. Med. Coll., 1963-64, SUNY Health Sci. Ctr., Bklyn., 1964-67, asst. prof., 1967-73; assoc. prof., 1973-91; cons. study sect. Nat. Heart and Lung Inst., 1975; adj. prof. Med. Sch. CUNY, 1974-97; adj. prof. hematology sch. health scis. Hunter Coll., 1978-82, 90-91; adj. prof. anatomy Inst. Continuing Biomed. Edn., 1979-86, N.Y. Med. Coll., 1982-85, 91-96, Touro Coll. Ctr. Biomed. Edn., 1983-88, Einstein Coll. Medicine, 1991-99. Contbr. articles to profl. jours. Served with U.S. Army, 1954-56. NIH fellow, 1958-60, 61-63; Leukemia Soc., 1960-61; Nat. Inst. Arthritis and Metabolic Diseases grantee, 1964-71; Nat. Cancer Inst. grantee, 1973-75; Mildred Werner League for Cancer Research grantee, 1976-77; co-prin. investigator NIH Heart, Blood and Lung Inst., 1982-85. Mem. AAAS, Am. Soc. Hematology, Am. Assn. Clin. Anatomists, Sigma Xi. Jewish. Home and Office: 96 Everett Rd Demarest NJ 07627-1225 Personal E-mail: bureve35@aol.com.

DORNING, JOHN JOSEPH, nuclear engineering, physics, and applied mathematics educator; b. Bronx, NY, Apr. 17, 1938; s. John Joseph and Sarrah Cathrine (McCormack) D.; m. Helen Marie Driscoll, July 27, 1963; children: Michael, James, Denise. BS in Marine Engrng., US Mcht. Marine Acad., 1959; MS in Nuc. Sci. and Engrng., Columbia U., NYC, 1963, PhD in Nuc. Sci. and Engrng., 1967. Marine engr. US Mcht. Marine, 1960-62; asst. physicist Brookhaven Nat. Lab., Upton, NY, 1967-69, assoc. physicist, grp. leader, 1969-70; assoc. prof. nuc. engring. U. Ill., Urbana, 1970-75, prof., 1975-84; Whitney Stone prof. nuc. engrng., engring. physics and applied math. U. Va., Charlottesville, 1984—. NRC vis. prof. math. physics U. Bologna, Italy, 1975-76, 81, 85, 87; internat. prof. nuc. engring. Italian Ministry of Edn., 1983, 84, 86; physicist plasma theory grp., divsn. magnetic fusion energy Lawrence Livermore Nat. Lab., Calif., 1977-78; cons. to US nat. labs. and indsl. rsch. labs., 1970—. Contbr. articles to various publs. Served as ensign USN, 1959-60. Recipient Ernest O. Lawrence award US Dept. Energy, 1990, NAE, 2007. Fellow AAAS, Am. Phys. Soc., Am. Nuc. Soc. (Mark Mills award 1967, Arthur Holly Compton award 1998, Eugene P. Wigner award 1999, Glenn T. Seaborg medal 2002); mem. Am. Soc. Engring. Edn., (Glenn Murphy award 1988), Soc. Indsl. and Applied Math., NY Acad. Scis., NAE, Sigma Xi. Office: Dept Materials Sci & Engring U Va PO Box 400745 116 Engineer's Way Charlottesville VA 22904-4745 Office Fax: 434-982-5660. Business E-Mail: dorning@virginia.edu.

DOROCKE, LAWRENCE FRANCIS, lawyer; b. Chgo., Oct. 4, 1946; s. Walter P. and Effie M. (Gillis) D.; m. Diane L. Roberts, June 22, 1968; children: Todd D., Rob L., Jill A. BS in Econs., Purdue U., 1968, MS in Indsl. Relations, 1970; JD magna cum laude, Ind. U., 1973. Bar: Ind. 1973, U.S. Dist. Ct. (so. dist.) Ind. 1973, Iowa 1974, U.S. Ct. Appeals (7th cir.). Asst. mgr. personnel Comml. Solvents Corp., Terre Haute, Ind., 1970-71; law clk. to chief justice U.S. Dist. Ct. (so. dist.) Iowa, Des Moines, 1973-75; ptnr. Dann, Pecar, Newman & Kleiman P.C., Indpls., 1975—. Mem. ABA, Ind. Bar Assn., Indpls. Bar Assn. Roman Catholic. Office: Dann Pecar Newman & Kleiman PO Box 82008 Indianapolis IN 46282-2008 Home Phone: 317-574-0305; Office Phone: 317-632-3232. Business E-Mail: ldorocke@dannpecar.com.

DOROFTEI, MUGUR GIDEON, music educator, conductor, composer, musician; b. Bucharest, Romania, Oct. 11, 1943; arrived in US, 1980; s. Aristide and Venera Alexandrina Doroftei; m. Cornelia Mesinschi, Mar. 6, 1969; children: Andrei, Gabriel, Rebecca. MusM, Conservtorul Ciprian Porumbescu, Romania, 1970; PhD, Acadmia de Muzica, Romania, 1994. Violinist Opera and Operetta, Constaniza, Romania, 1960—61, Philharm. Orch., Ploiesti, Romania, 1961—62, Ciocirlia, Opera, Radio Orch. Operetta, Bucharest, Romania, 1962—70; prof. de Vioara Liceul de Muzica, Botosani-Suceava, Romania, 1970—80; instr. strings, orch. Southwestern U., Keene, Tex., 1981—2006, Dallas Ind. Sch. Dist., 2001—04. Author: Music Theory Made Clear, Music Theory Made Clear Workbood, Music Theory For The Young Musician, Music Theory For The Young Musician Workbook, Ear Trining Intervals & Chords, Solfeggio Sight Singing, Violin Method for Beginners Book On, with companion CD, Violin Method for Beginners Book Two with companion CD. Named Personalities of the South, Am. Biog. Inst., 1983. Achievements include development of metrical rhytmical transposition; the classification of measures, abbreviations and ornaments, classification of tempo marks, scales with fewer than seven sounds, ch. modes (analysis of the scales diatonic, mixed, chromatic); formation of major and minor scales, relationship between tonalities, chromatic system, classification of intervals. Home: PO Box 711 Keene TX 76059

DOROSHOW, JAMES HALPERN, federal agency administrator, oncologist; b. Lynwood, Calif., 1948; MD, Harvard Med. Sch., 1973. Cert. internal medicine, oncology. Intern Mass. Gen. Hosp., Boston, 1973-74, resident, 1974-75; fellow in med. oncology Nat. Cancer Inst., Bethesda, Md., 1975-78; chmn. Dept. Med. Oncology and Therapeutics Rsch. City of Hope Nat. Med. Ctr., Duarte, Calif.; assoc. dir. clin. rsch. City of Hope Comprehensive Cancer Ctr., Duarte, 1981—2004; dir. Divsn. Cancer Treatment & Diagnosis Nat. Cancer Inst., Bethesda, 2004—, chmn. Clin Trials Working Group. Mem. Am. Assn. for Cancer Rsch., Am. Soc. for Clin. Oncology, Am. Soc. Hematology, Am. Fedn. for Clin. Rsch. Office: Nat Cancer Inst Divsn Cancer Treatment & Diagnosis 31 Center Dr Bldg 31 Rm 3A44 Bethesda MD 20892-2440 Office Phone: 301-496-4291. E-mail: doroshoj@mail.nih.gov.

DORR, LAWRENCE D., orthopedic surgeon; b. Storm Lake, Iowa, 1941; m. Marilyn Dorr. BA in English, Cornell Coll., 1963; MS, U. Iowa, 1965, MD, 1967. Cert. Orthopaedic Surgery, 1978. Intern, orthopedics LA County, U. So. Calif. Sch. Med., 1967—68, resident, joint replacement surgery, 1974—76; fellow Hosp. Spl. Surgery, NYC, 1976—77; founder (Calif. based inst.), med. dir. Dorr Inst., Centinela Hosp. Med. Ctr., Inglewood, Calif., 2001—; prof. U. So. Calif. Sch. Medicine, LA. Founder, med. staff mem. Operation Walk, 1994—; lectr. in field; researcher in field. Featured on Miracle Workers (ABC), 2006; contbr. articles to profl. jours. Bd. trustee Cornell Coll. Recipient Humanitarian Yr. award, Am. Acad. Orthopedic Surgeons for work with Operation Walk, 2005, Cornell Coll. Disting. Achievement award, 2003, Disting. Alumni award, U. Iowa, 2006. Mem.: Hip Soc. (pres. elect 2006). Office: Centinela Freeman Health Systems Arthritis Inst Centinela Campus 555 E Hardy St Inglewood CA 90301 Home Phone: 818-952-1281; Office Phone: 310-695-4800. E-mail: patriciajpaul@yahoo.com.

DORR, MARJORIE W., healthcare insurance company executive; BBA, U. Iowa; MBA, U. Chgo. Grad. Sch. Bus.; grad., Stanley K. Lacy Exec. Leadership Prog. With SEC, Washington, Algemene Bank Nederland, N.V., Chgo.; v.p. Houlihan, Lokey, Howard & Zukin, Inc., San Francisco; v.p. corp. fin. Anthem, Inc., 1991, pres. Blue Cross and Blue Shield's East region, 2000—04, CFO Anthem Casualty Ins. Grp., CEO, pres., dir. Prescription Mgmt., 1995—98, COO Blue Cross and Blue Shield Conn. operation; pres., CEO N.E. Region SBU Wellpoint, Inc., 2004—05, exec. v.p., chief strategy officer Indpls., 2005—. Bd. dirs. New Eng. Healthcare Inst. Bd. dirs. Lead Like Jesus. Mem.: CEO Forum, Com. of 200, Young Pres.'s Orgn. Office: Wellpoint Inc 120 Monument Cir Indianapolis IN 46204*

DORR, ROBERT CHARLES, lawyer; b. Denver, Jan. 7, 1946; s. Owen and Rose Esther (Tudek) Dorr; m. Sandra Leah Gehisen, Feb. 26, 1972; children: Bryan, Aric. BSEE, Milw. Sch. Engring., 1968; MSEE, Northwestern U., 1970; JD, U. Denver, 1975. Bar: Colo. 1975, US Dist. Ct. Colo. 1975, US Patent Office 1975. Mem. tech. staff Bell Labs, Naperville, Ill., mem. patent staff Denver, 1975; shareholder Dorr, Carson & Birney, P.C., Denver. Seminar spkr. various profl. orgns. Mem.: AAAS, IEEE, Sigma Xi. Roman Catholic. Home: 6101 Muddy Creek Rd Pueblo CO 81004-9747 Office: Dorr Carson & Birney PC Ste 800 501 Cherry St Denver CO 80246

DORR, STEPHANIE TILDEN, psychotherapist; b. Orlando, Fla., Sept. 21, 1950; d. Luther Willis Tilden II and Lillian Murfee (Grace) Owen; m. Darwin Dorr, May 21, 1986. AA, El Camino Coll., 1975; BA, U. N.C., 1985; MA, Western Carolina U., 1991. Lic. clin. psychotherapist State Kans. Behavioral Scis. Regulatory Bd., 2000. Cons. psychologist Sylva (N.C.) Psychol. Assocs., 1991-92; staff psychologist Park Ridge Hosp., Naples, N.C., 1992, Blue Ridge Ctr., Asheville, N.C., 1991-93; pvt. practice psychology Asheville, 1991-93; project mgr. Sedgwick County Dept. Mental Health, Wichita, Kans., 1993-95; pvt. practice psychotherapy and psychol. assessment Counseling and Mediation Ctr., Wichita, Kans., 1995-98; therapist United Meth. Youthville Clinic, Wichita, 1998—2001; clin. therapist Wichita (Kans.) Pub. Schs. Greiffenstein Spl. Edn. Ctr., 2001—. Adj. faculty Kans. Newman Coll., Wichita, 1995—, Butler County (Kans.) Cmty. Coll., 1996-97; Assertive Cmty. Treatment (ACT) team clinician United Meth. Youthville, Wichita, 1997-98; presenter in field. Contbr. articles to profl. publs. Recipient Excellence in Tchg. award Butler County C.C., 1997, Outstanding Faculty Mem. award Butler County C.C., 1998. Mem. APA (assoc.), Psychoanalytic Study Group (sec. 1989-93, award 1993), We. N.C. Psychol. Assn. (mem.-at-large 1985-93, pres.-elect 1993), Kans. Assn. Masters Psychologists (bd. mem. 2005, pres. 2006), Psi Chi, Pi Gamma Mu. Democrat. Episcopalian. Avocations: sewing, rock collecting, gardening. Office: Wichita Pub Schs Greiffenstein Spl Edn Ctr 1221 E Galena Wichita KS 67216 Office Phone: 316-973-6400. Personal E-mail: sdorr@usd259.net, stdorr@cox.net.

DORR, THOMAS C., federal agency administrator; BS, Morganside U. Mem. Iowa State Bd. Regents, 1991—97; pres., CEO Pine Grove Farm Co.; sr. advisor to sec. USDA, Washington, under sec. agr. & rural devel., 2005—, bd. dirs. Commodity Credit Corp. Mem.: Nat. Corn Growers. Assn. (officer), Iowa Corn Growers Assn. (officer). Office: USDA Jamie L Whitten Fed Bldg 14th and Independent Ave SW Rm 205W Washington DC 20250 Office Phone: 202-720-4581. Office Fax: 202-720-2080.

DORRANCE, BENNETT, real estate company executive; married; 2 children. Grad., U. Ariz. Founding ptnr., mng. dir. DMB Assocs., Scottsdale, Ariz., 1984—. Bd. dirs. Campbell Soup Co., Camden, NJ, Larson Co., Tucson, Am. Grad. Sch. Internat. Mgmt. Governance com. Big Bros. Big Sisters; established scholarship Ariz. State U., Ariz.; sponsor Dorrance Merit Scholarship, Ariz.; bd. dirs. Ariz. Cmty. Found., Desert Bot. Garden. Named one of 400 Richest Ams., Forbes mag., 2006. Office: DMB Assocs 7600 E Doubletree Ranch Rd Number 300 Scottsdale AZ 85258-2137

DORRELL, KARL, college football coach; b. Dec. 18, 1963; m. Kim Dorrell; children: Chandler, Lauren. Bachelor's degree, UCLA, 1986. Grad. asst. UCLA, 1998; receivers coach Ctrl. Fla. Univ., 1989; wide receivers coach Ariz. State, 1994; offensive coord., receivers coach No. Ariz., 1990—91, Univ. Wash., 1999; wide receivers coach Denver Broncos, 2000—02; head football coach UCLA, 2003—. Office: UCLA Football JD Morgan Ctr PO Box 24044 Los Angeles CA 90024

DORRILL, JEFF W., lawyer; b. Shawnee, Okla., May 13, 1961; BA with honors, Baylor U., Waco, Tex., 1983; JD cum laude, Baylor U., 1985. Bar: Tex. 1985. Ptnr. Hughes & Luce, LLP, Dallas. Named one of Tex. Super Lawyers, Law & Politics mag. and Tex. Monthly, 2004—06, Best Lawyers in Dallas, D Mag., 2005. Mem.: Dallas Bar Assn. (mem. Employee Benefits Com.), ABA. Office: Hughes & Luce LLP 1717 Main St Ste 2800 Dallas TX 75201 Office Phone: 214-939-5425. Office Fax: 214-939-5849. E-mail: jeff.dorrill@hughesluce.com.*

DORRILL, WILLIAM FRANKLIN, political scientist, educator; b. Dallas, July 25, 1931; s. William Cumbie and Ruth (Esther Webb) D.; m. Martha Jeanne Brawley, Mar. 3, 1951; children: Jennifer Ruth, William Sidney, Rebecca Jeanne, Lisa Kathryn. BA, Baylor U., 1952; MA, U. Va., 1954; postgrad., Australian Nat. U., Canberra, 1954; PhD, Harvard U., 1972. Fgn. affairs analyst U.S. Govt., Washington, 1961-63; polit. scientist RAND Corp., Santa Monica, Calif., 1963-67; project chmn., sr. staff mem. Rsch. Analysis Corp., McLean, Va., 1967-68; dir. Asian Studies Ctr., assoc. prof. polit. sci. U. Pitts., 1969-77, chmn. dept. East Asian langs. and lits., 1972-77; dean Coll. Arts and Sci., prof. polit. sci. Ohio U., Athens, 1977-84; provost, prof. polit. sci. U. Louisville, 1984-88; pres. Longwood U., Farmville, Va., 1988-96, pres. emeritus, 1996—, prof. polit. sci. and history, 1988-96, bd. visitors, disting. prof., 1996—. Mem. faculty coll. mgmt. program Carnegie-Mellon U. and Nat. Ctr. for Higher Edn. Mgmt. Systems, summer, 1980; mem. com. on internat. edn. Am. Coun. on Edn., 1990, U.S. AID Univ. Ctr. Program Adv. Group, 1991; lectr. in field; higher edn. cons. U.S. Dept of State, China, 2000—01, Libya, 2004. Contbr. articles on East Asian politics and internat. relations to profl. jours., chpts. on Chinese politics and history to scholarly books. Mem. Athens County Bd. Mental Retardation and Devel. Disabilities, Ohio, 1982-84; chmn. bd. dirs. Kentuckiana Metroversity, 1986-88. Recipient Disting. Achievement medal Baylor U., 1980; Fulbright scholar, 1954; Soc. for Values in Higher Edn. Kent fellow, 1957-58; Ford Found. fgn. area fellow Taiwan, Hong Kong, 1959-61; Longwood U. Dorrill Dining Hall named in his honor, 2004. Fellow: Soc. for Values in Higher Edn.; mem.: Coun. on Postsecondary Edn. Environ. Task Force, Coun. for Internat. Exch. of Scholars (bd. dirs. 1992—96), Gov.'s Bus. Edn. Commn., Nat. Assn. State Univs. and Land Grant Colls. (acad. coun., exec. com. 1987—88), Southside Va. Bus. and Edn. Com. (exec. coun. 1992—2000), So. Assn. Colls. and Schs. (commn. on colls. 1986—88, chair vis. coms. 1990—, commn. on colls. 1991—96), Am. Assn. State Colls. and Univs. (com. on accreditation and instl. assessment 1989—96, chmn. 1990—96, gov.'s commn. econ. devel. in Southside Region Commonwealth Va. 1990—96, nominating com. 1993—94), Nat. Com. on U.S.-China Rels., Asia Soc. (adv. com. performing arts 1977—85), Assn. Asian Studies, Am. Conf. Acad. Deans (bd. dirs. 1980—84, vice chmn. 1981—82, chmn. 1982—83), Va. C. of C. (Va. emissary 1993—96), Rotary Internat. (gov.-elect dist. 7600 2002—03, gov. 2003—04). Democrat. Presbyterian. Achievements include Longwood U. building, Dorrill Dining Hall, named in honor of, 2004. Home: 1007 Fayette St Farmville VA 23901-2029 Office: Longwood U Dept History and Polit Sci Farmville VA 23909-0001 Personal E-mail: wdorrill@kinex.net.

DORRIS, WILLIAM E., lawyer; b. Dublin, Ga., Apr. 10, 1955; BA with high distinction, U. Ky., 1976, JD with high distinction, 1979. Bar: Ga. 1979, Ky. 1979. Mem. Smith, Currie & Hancock, Atlanta; ptnr. constrn. and pub. contracts grp. Kilpatrick Stockton, LLP, Atlanta, co-mng. ptnr., 2007—. Contbr. articles to profl. jours.; co-author: Construction Disputes: Practice Guide with Forms. Mem. ABA, Ky. Bar Assn., State Bar Ga., Atlanta Bar Assn., Order of Coif, Phi Beta Kappa. Office: Kilpatrick Stockton LLP Ste 2800 1100 Peachtree St NE Atlanta GA 30309-4530 Office Phone: 404-815-6104. Office Fax: 404-541-3183. E-mail: bdorris@kilpatrickstockton.com.*

DORROUGH, VICKI LEE, theater educator; b. Oklahoma City, Mar. 8, 1953; d. Clarence Leroy and Ruby Anne Lewis; m. Bryce Coleman Dorrough, Dec. 23, 1977; children: Matthew Aaron, Kristopher Shawn. BA in Speech Edn., Okla. State U., Stillwater, 1971—75; MA in Ednl. & Cmty. Renewal, U. Okla., Norman, 2003—05. Cert. tchr. Okla. Dept. Edn. Speech/journalism/English tchr. Watonga HS, Okla., 1975—77; speech/acting/stagecrafts tchr. Norman HS, 1977—82; speech & drama tchr. Longfellow Mid. Sch., Norman, 1993—97; speech & acting tchr. Norman N. HS, 1997—99; speech & drama tchr. Whittier Mid. Sch., Norman, 2000—. Internat. thespian troupe Ednl. Theatre Assn., Cin., 1975—; bd. mem. Sooner Theatre, Norman; gifted site goal com. Whittier Mid. Sch., 2000—, exploratory team leader, 2007—; coun. mem. Norman Arts & Humanities. Founding mem. IMPACT Okla., Greater Oklahoma City, 2005; mem. Sam Noble Okla. Mus. Natural History; mem., former bd. mem. Assistance League of Norman, 1991—; bd. mem. Transition House, Inc., Norman, 2006, adv. bd. mem., 2007—. Finalist Tchr. of Yr., Whittier Mid. Sch., 2004. Mem.: NEA, Profl. Educators of Norman, Okla. Edn. Assn., S.W. Theatre Conf., Okla. Theatre Edn. Assn. (pres. elect., sec. 1975—82). Methodist. Avocations: gardening, water-skiing, scuba diving, dance, reading. Home: 2023 Morning Dew Trl Norman OK 73072 Office: Whittier Mid Sch 2000 W Brooks Norman OK 73069 E-mail: vickild@cox.net.

DORSA, CAROLINE, software company executive; b. 1960; BA in History, Colgate U., 1981; MBA in Finance and Acctg., Columbia U., 1987. Promoted economic devel. Mayor's Office NYC, 1981—85; joined Merck & Co., Whitehouse Station, NJ, 1987, exec. dir. US pricing and strategic planning Human Health Divsn., 1992—94, exec. dir. US mktg. Human Health Divsn., 1992—94, treas., 1994—96, v.p., treas., 1996—2007; sr. v.p., CFO Avaya Inc., Basking Ridge, NJ, 2007—. Bd. dirs. PSE&G, 2003—. Office: Avaya Inc 211 Mt Airy Rd Basking Ridge NJ 07920*

DORSA, GENE J., secondary school educator; b. San Jose, Calif., July 29, 1949; s. George J. and Celia Rose Dorsa; life ptnr. Dafne Ines Miller. BA, San Jose State U., Calif., MS, 1972. Tchr. h.s., jr. coll. East Side Union H.S. Dist., San Jose, Calif., 1973—. Office: William C Overfelt High Sch 1835 Cunningham Ave x San Jose CA 95122 Home Phone: 408-799-6776; Office Phone: 408-347-5900. Office Fax: 408-347-5915. E-mail: dorsag@esuhsd.org.

DORSEN, NORMAN, lawyer, educator; b. NYC, Sept. 4, 1930; s. Arthur and Tanya (Stone) D.; m. Harriette Koffler, Nov. 25, 1965; children: Jennifer, Caroline Gail, Anne. BA, Columbia U., 1950; LLB magna cum laude, Harvard U., 1953; postgrad., London Sch. Econs., 1955-56; LLD (hon.), Ripon Coll., 1981, John Jay Coll. Criminal Justice, 1992. Bar: DC 1953, NY 1954. Law clk. to chief judge Calvert Magruder U.S. Ct. Appeals, Boston, 1956-57; law clk. to Justice John Marshall Harlan U.S. Supreme Ct., Washington, 1957-58; assoc. Dewey, Ballantine, Bushby, Palmer & Wood, NYC, 1958-60; prof. law NYU Sch. Law, NYC, 1961-81, Stokes prof., 1981—, dir. Hays civil liberties program, 1961—, dir. global law sch. program, 1994-96, chmn., 1996—2002; counselor to pres. NYU, 2002—. Vis. prof. law London Sch. Econs., 1968, U. Calif., Berkeley, 1974-75, Harvard U., 1980, 83, 84; cons. U.S. Commn. on Violence, 1968-69, Random House, 1969-73, B.B.C., 1969-73, U.S. Commn. on Social Security, 1979-80, Native Am. Rights Fund, 1978-89; exec. dir. spl. com. on courtroom conduct Assn. Bar N.Y.C., 1970-73; chmn. Com. for Pub. Justice, 1972-74; vice chmn. HEW sec.'s rev. panel on new drug regulation, 1975-76, chmn., 1976-77; mem. N.Y.C. Commn. on Status of Women, 1978-80; chmn. Sec. of Treasury's Citizen Rev. Panel on Good O' Boy Round-up, 1995-96. Author (with others): Political and Civil Rights in U.S., 3rd edit., 1967, Political and Civil Rights in U.S., 4th edit., Vol. I, 1976, Political and Civil Rights in U.S., 4th edit., Vol. II, 1979, Frontiers of Civil Liberties, 1968, Discrimination and Civil Rights, 1969, Comparative Constitution, 2003; author: (with L. Friedman) Disorder in the Court, 1973; author: (with S. Gillers) Regulation of Lawyers, 1985, Regulation of Lawyers, 2d edit., 1989; author: (with others) Constitutionalism Cases and Materials, 2003; editor: The Rights of Americans, 1971; editor: (with S. Gillers) None of Your Business, 1974; editor: Our Endangered Rights, 1984, The Evolving Constitution, 1987; editor: (with others) Human Rights in Northern Ireland, 1991, The Unpredictable Constitution, 2001, with P. Gifford: Democracy and the Rule of Law, 2001;; editor: (with others) Comparitive Constitutionalism, 2003; editl. dir. Internat. Jour. Constl. Law, 2002—. 1st lt. JAGC US Army, 1953—55. Recipient medal French Minister of Justice, 1983, Presdl. Eleanor Roosevelt Human Rights award 2000, First Triennial award Assn. Am. Law Schs., 2007; Fulbright Disting. prof., Argentina, 1987, 88. Fellow Am. Acad. Arts and Scis.; mem. ABA (chmn. com. free speech and press 1968-70), ACLU (gen. counsel 1969-76, pres. 1976-91), Am. Law Inst., Coun. on Fgn. Rels., Lawyers Com. Human Rights (chmn. bd. dirs. 1995-2000), Lawyer Com. Civil Rights, Internat. Assn. Constnl. Law (exec. com. 1999-2003), U.S. Assn. Constnl. Law (pres. 1996-2003), Internat. Assn. Law Schs. (bd. govs. 2005—), Soc. Am. Law Tchrs. (pres. 1972-74, Tchg. award 1997), Thomas Jefferson Ctr. for Free Expression (trustee 1995—). Home: 146 Central Park W New York NY 10023-2005 Office: NYU Sch Law 40 Washington Sq S New York NY 10012-1005 Business E-Mail: norman.dorsen@nyu.edu.

DORSETT, BURT, investment company executive; b. Chgo., Nov. 8, 1930; s. Burton and Della (Reader) D.; m. Judith Martin, Dec. 14, 1952 (div.); children: Mark, Deborah, Jeffrey, Cindy (dec.); m. Trixie Landsberger, Mar. 1, 1981. BA, Dartmouth Coll., 1953; MBA, Harvard U., 1959. Indsl. engr. E.I. duPont de Nemours, Seaford, Del., 1953-57; cons. Booz-Allen & Hamilton, NYC, 1959-62; v.p. U. Rochester, 1962-70; exec. v.p., trustee Coll. Retirement Equities Fund, NYC, 1970-79; chmn., pres. Westinghouse Pension Investment Corp., NYC, 1979-86, Dorsett-McCabe Capital Mgmt. Inc., 1987—2007. Chief investment officer Money Growth Inst., 1999-2002; bd. dirs. Legg Maron Funds, N.Y.C. Author: (with others) Epoxy Resins, Market Survey and Users Reference, 1959. Budget com. Cmty. Chest, Rochester, 1967-70; trustee Convalescent Hosp. for Children, Rochester, 1967-70, Hillside Children's Home, Rochester, 1968-70, Keuka Coll., N.Y., 1968-71; mem. com. Boys Club of N.Y.C., 1970-80; investment com. Am. Psychol. Assn., 1969-87. William J. Cook scholar, 1953. Mem. Dartmouth Club, Harvard Bus. Sch. Club, WeeBurn Country Club (Darrien, Conn.). Office: Ste 5700 500 5th Ave New York NY 10110-3199

DORSETT, JAMES K., III, lawyer; b. Raleigh, NC, Nov. 10, 1951; BA, Davidson Coll., 1974; JD, Wake Forest U., 1977. Bar: N.C. 1977. Atty. Smith, Anderson, Blount, Dorsett, Mitchell & Jernigan, LLP, Raleigh, NC. Fellow: Am. Bar Found., Internat. Soc. Barristers (bd. govs., chair N.C. fellowship); mem.: ABA (del. ho. dels.), Wake County Bar Assn. (bd. dirs. 1982—84, 1988—90, vol. lawyers program 1990—93), Am. Bd. Trial Advs., N.C. Assn. Def. Attys., Am. Counsel Assn. (pres. 2005—06), N.C. State Bar (councilor 1992—, pres. 2002—03, chmn. grievance com.), N.C. Bar Assn., Phi Delta Phi. Office: Smith Anderson Blount Dorsett et al 2500 Wachovia Capitol Ctr PO Box 2611 Raleigh NC 27602-2611 Home Phone: 919-787-0323; Office Phone: 919-821-6649. Business E-Mail: jdorsett@smithlaw.com.

DORSEY, DOLORES FLORENCE, retired corporate treasurer, finance company executive; b. Buffalo, May 26, 1928; d. William G. and Florence R. D. BS, Coll. St. Elizabeth, 1950. With Aerojet-Gen. Corp., 1953—, asst. to treas. El Monte, Calif., 1972-74, asst. treas., 1974-79, treas., 1979—2001, ret., 2001. Mem. adv. bd. Scripps Ctr. for Integrative Medicine, 2001—. Mem. Cash Mgmt. Group San Diego (past pres.), Nat. Assn. Corp. Treas., Fin. Execs. Inst. (v.p.). Republican. Roman Catholic.

DORSEY, JAMES FRANCIS, JR., naval officer; b. Balt., May 28, 1934; s. James Francis Sr. and Elizabeth Rosalee (MacNamara) D.; m. Jeanne Lynch Hobbs, Aug. 16, 1958; children: James Francis III, Timothy Walker. Grad. in naval aviation, USN, Pensacola, Fla., 1956; degree in Polit. Sci., Naval Postgrad. Sch., Monterey, Calif., 1967. Commd. ensign USN, 1956, advanced through grades to VADM, 1991, comdg. officer 3 fighter squadrons, 1971-76, exec. officer USS Midway, 1976-78, comdg. officer USS Caloosehatchee, 1978-80, comdg. officer USS America, 1981-82, dir. joint program office, undersec. def. policy, dep. dir. def. mobilization systems planning activity, 1982-84, comdr. carrier group FOUR, and NATO comdr. carrier striking force Atlantic, 1984-85, dir. ops. U.S. European Command, 1985-87, dep. asst. chief naval ops. for plans, policy and ops., dep. ops. dep. for joint chief staff matters, 1987-89, comdr. 3d Fleet, 1989-91, ret., 1991; CEO Flag Ltd., Alexandria, Va., 1991—. Mem. Assn. Naval Aviation, U.S. Naval Inst., Chesapeake Bay Soc., Harbor Pt. Hoa (v.p.), Golden Eagle--The Early Pioneer Naval Aviators Assn. Office: PO Box 1119 Solomons MD 20688-1119

DORSEY, JEREMIAH EDMUND, pharmaceutical company executive; b. Worcester, Mass., Oct. 15, 1944; s. Jeremiah Edmund and Mary Theresa D.; m. Nadia S. Vidach, Dec. 6, 1970; children: Todd Edmund, Jaime Erin, Megan Elizabeth, Kelly Ann. AB, Assumption Coll., 1966; MBA, Farleigh Dickinson U., 1978. With Johnson & Johnson, New Brunswick, NJ, 1969-88, nat. indsl. engring. mgr., 1975-76, supt. ops. and maintenance, 1976-88, dir. ops., mem. mgmt. bd., 1976-88; v.p. mktg., ops., gen. mgr. sales Johnson & Johnson Dental Products Co., New Brunswick, 1976-88; exec. v.p. The Kaelin Group, Bridgeton, NJ, 1988; pres. Towle Housewares Co., Newburyport, Mass., 1988-90; pres., CEO Foster Med. Supply, Inc., Dedham, Mass., 1990-92; group pres. Carvel Hall Corp., Crisfield, Md., 1990—; pres., COO West Pharm. Svcs. Inc., Lionville, Pa., 1992—. Corp. officer J.E. Dorsey Co., Carvel Hall Corp., Crisfield, Md.; bd. dirs. West Co. de Mex., Daikyo Seiko, Tokyo, Schubert Seals, Horsens, Denmark, DanBioSyst, Nottingham, Eng., Geschaftsfuherer West Co., Europe, Cardiotech Internat., Wilmington, Mass; mem. bd. dirs. Associated Internat. Corp., Wilmington, Mass., audit com., compensation com.; chmn. nominating com. Cardiotec Internat. Editor: Spl. Forces Assn. News. Active N.J. Commn. for Discharge Upgrade, Appalachian Trail Conf.; mem. alumni bd. dirs. Assumption Coll., adv. com. U. PR Sch. of Pharmacy; mem. mil. acad. selection com. U.S. Senate; vice chmn. NJ Vietnam Vets Leadership Program; mem. Mercer County (NJ) Pvt. Industry Coun., NJ SR-92 Coalition. With U.S. Army, 1966-69, Vietnam. Decorated Silver Star, Bronze Star with 2 oak leaf clusters, Purple Heart with 4 oak leaf clusters, Army Commendation medal, Air medal with oak leaf cluster, Medal of Honor, Gallantry Cross, Vietnam; recipient Corp. Affirmative Action award 1981. Mem. DAV, KC, Sierra Club, Spl. Forces Assn., Smithsonian Assocs., Soc. First Divsn., Tiger Karate Soc. (Black Belt), Johnson & Johnson Mgmt. Club, Delta Epsilon Sigma. Roman Catholic. Home: PO Box 910 Quechee VT 05059-0910

DORSEY, JOHN RUSSELL, journalist; b. Balt., Dec. 17, 1938; s. Charles Howard and Emma (Deputy) D. AB, Harvard U., 1961. Mem. staff Balt. Sun, 1962-81, 83-99, Sunday Sun book rev. editor, 1967-69, Sunday Sun restaurant critic, 1971-81, 84-86, Sun art critic, 1983-84, 86-99. Author: (with James D. Dilts) A Guide to Baltimore Architecture, 1973, Mount Vernon Place, 1983, (with James DuSel) Look Again in Baltimore, 2005; editor: On Mencken, 1980. Mem. Md. Club, 14 West Hamilton Street Club, Harvard-Radcliffe Club. Home: 600 Edgevale Rd Baltimore MD 21210-1904 Personal E-mail: JRDinMD@comcast.net.

DORSEY, JOHN WESLEY, JR., retired academic administrator, economist; b. Hagerstown, Md., June 13, 1936; s. John Wesley and Abbie Virginia (Wy) D.; m. Jeanne Ascosi; 1 child, Rachel Lynette. BS, U. Md., 1958; cert., London Sch. Econs., 1959; MA, Harvard U., 1962, PhD, 1964. Teaching fellow Harvard U., 1961, 62-63; asst. prof. econs. U. Md., 1963-66, asso. prof., dir. Bur. Bus. and Econ. Rsch., 1966-70, vice chancellor for adminstrv. affairs College Park, 1970-77, acting chancellor, 1974-75, prof. econs., 1976-2001, prof. emeritus, 2001—; chancellor U. Md. Baltimore County, 1977-86; asst. to pres. U. Md. System, 1986-89. Cons. to govt. Md. Employees Credit Union Bd., 1975—. Rotary Found. scholar, 1958-59; Brookings research fellow, 1961-63 Mem. Phi Beta Kappa, Phi Kappa Phi, Omicron Delta Kappa. Home: 8234 Bubbling Spg Laurel MD 20723-1079 Personal E-mail: jwd8234@comcast.net.

DORSEY, PETER COLLINS, federal judge; b. New London, Conn., Mar. 24, 1931; s. Thomas F., Jr. and Helen Mary (Collins) D.; m. Cornelia McEwen, June 26, 1954; children: Karen G., Peter C., Jennifer S., Christopher M. BA, Yale U., 1953; JD, Harvard U., 1959. Ptnr. Flanagan, Dorsey & Flanagan, New Haven, 1963-74; U.S. atty. Dept. Justice, New Haven, 1974-77; ptnr. Flanagan, Dorsey & Mulvey, New Haven, 1977-83; judge U.S. Dist. Ct. Conn., New Haven, 1983-99, chief judge, 1994-98, now sr. judge. Mem. Jud. Conf. of U.S. Cts., 1995-98; adj. prof. Quinnipiac U. Sch. Law, 1999—. Councilman Town of Hamden, Conn., 1961-69; town atty., 1973-74; commr. Bd. of Police, Hamden, 1977-81. Served to lt. comdr., USNR, 1953-56 Recipient Judiciary award, Conn. Trial Lawyers Assn., 1991, Baldwin Pub. Svc. award, Quinnipiac U. Sch. Law, 2005. Fellow Am. Coll. Trial Lawyers; mem. ABA (mem. house of dels. 1974-78), Conn. Bar Assn. (bd. govs. 1968-70, 74-78, pres. 1978, Judiciary award 2001), Am. Coll. Trial Lawyers, Conn. Def. Lawyers Assn. (pres. 1974), Am. Inns of Ct. Hartford (pres. 1991-93). Roman Catholic. Office: US Dist Ct 141 Church St New Haven CT 06510-2030 Office Phone: 203-773-2427.

DORSEY, RICHARD J., lawyer; b. NYC, Dec. 30, 1927; s. Daniel A. and Edna J. Dorsey; m. Patricia A. Craig, June 26, 1954; children: Mary C., Richard F., Susanne M., John J., Paul C., Ann R. AB, Harvard Coll., Cambridge, Mass., 1949; JD, U. Mich., Ann Arbor, 1952. Bar: Mich. 1952, N.Y. 1956. Assoc. Gualtieri Law Practice, Rome, NY, 1956—62; prin. Dorsey Law Practice, Rome, 1962; asst. atty. gen. Dept. Law, Albany, 1963—68; assoc. counsel Environ. Facilities Corp., Albany, 1968—72; asst. atty. gen. Dept. Law, Albany, 1972—90; prin. Dorsey Law Practice, Valatie, NY, 1991—. V.p. Riders Mills Hist. Area, NY, 1998—; past pres. bd. Cath. Charities of Columbia Greene Counties, Hudson, NY, 1989—93. Lt. USNR, 1952—55, PTO. Mem.: ABA. Office: 1052 Kinderhook St Valatie NY 12184

DORSEY, SUSAN G., neuroscientist, educator; PhD, U. Md., Balt., 2001. Postdoctoral fellow Nat. Cancer Inst. Frederick, Md., 2001—04; asst. prof. U. Md. Sch. Nursing, Balt., 2004—. Office: U Md Balt Sch Nursing Baltimore MD 21201 Office Phone: 410-706-7250. Office Fax: 410-706-0344. Business E-Mail: sdorsey@umaryland.edu.

D'ORSI, CARL JOSEPH, medical educator, radiologist, researcher; b. Bklyn., Apr. 16, 1941; s. Anthony and Florence D'Orsi; m. Ellen Margaret Liberty, May 24, 2003; children: Michael Scott, Jonathin Liberty, Jenifer Liberty. BS, Downstate Med. Ctr. SUNY, Bklyn., 1964, MD, 1966. Cert. diagnostic radiology Am. Bd. Radiology, 1971. Asst. prof. radiology Harvard Med. Sch., Boston, 1970—80; prof. radiology and vice chair dept. radiology U. Mass. Med. Ctr., Worcester, 1980—2002; prof. radiology and hematology-oncology Emory U., Atlanta, 2002—. Vice chair breast cancer com. Am. Coll. Radiology, Reston, Va.; rev. editor RSNA, Chgo.; contbg. editor Breast Diseases, Phila.; pres. Soc. Breast Imaging, Reston, Va.; cons. Hologic Corp., Bedford, Mass., 2004—; com. mem. tech. assessment panel FDA, Washington, 2005—; lectr. in field. Contbr. articles to profl. jours. Lt. USNR, 1967—74. Named Alumnus of Yr., Harvard Med. Sch., 2002; recipient Radiology Editor's Recognition award with Distinction, Radiological Soc. N.Am., 1989, 1990, 1993, 1994, 2003, 2004, 2005, Disting. Svc. award, Am. Bd. Radiology, 2003. Fellow: Am. Coll. Radiology (Disting. Com. Svc. award 2003), Soc. of Breast Imaging (life; pres. 1989—90). Independent. Achievements include founder Soc. of Breast Imaging; author of BI-RADS method for reporting mammographic findings. Avocations: golf, woodworking, target shooting, travel. Home: 2271 Valley Brook way Atlanta GA 30319 Office: Emory Univ Winship Cancer Ctr 1701 Uppergate Dr Atlanta GA 30322 Home Phone: 404-467-8433; Office Phone: 404-778-4446. Business E-Mail: carl_dorsi@emoryhealthcare.org.

DORSKY, NATHANIEL, filmmaker; b. NYC, 1943; Student, Antioch Coll., 1961, NYU, 1962. Instr. U. Calif. , Berkeley, Stanford U. Filmmaker Bend in the River, 1955, Ingreen, 1964, A Fall Trip Home, 1965, Summerwind, 1965, Hours for Jerome, 1966—82, Gaugerion in Tahiti, 1968 (Emmy award), Triste, 1974—96, Revenge of the Cheerleaders, 1976, Pneuma, 1976—83, Alaya, 1976—87, Ariel, 1983, 17 Reasons Why, 1985—87, What Happened to Kerouac?, 1985 (Emmy award), Vacations, 1992—98, Night Waltz: The Music of Paul Bowles, 1999 (Emmy award), The Visitation, 2002, Monumental: David Brower's Fight for Wild America, 2004; editl. cons.: Hope Along the Wind: The Story of Harry Hay, 2002; actor: (films) Rembrandt Laughing, 1988. Grantee, NEA, Calif. Arts Coun.; Guggenheim fellow, 1997.

DORTON, TRUDA LOU, medical/surgical and geriatrics nurse; b. Elkhorn Creek, Ky., Aug. 26, 1949; d. Clair Otis Parsons and Joyce Kidd; m. Eugene Anderson, Nov. 26, 1966 (dec. Apr. 1971); children: Gena Lynn, Richard Eugene; m. Leon Dorton, Dec. 15, 1972; children: Leondra Michelle, Jerald Thomas, Jonathan Layne. AS, student, Pikeville Coll., 1993. RN, Ky.; cert. ACLS, PALS. Instr. computer usage Lookout Elem. Sch., Ky., 1983; water/sewage technician McCoy & McCoy Environ. Cons., Pikeville, Ky., 1984; owner Signs of the Times, Elkhorn City, Ky., 1979-89; sec.'s asst. humanities and social scis. divsns. Pikeville Coll., 1989-92; nurse aide Mud Creek Clinic, Grethel, Ky., 1992-93; charge nurse Jenkins Cmty. Hosp., Ky., 1993-94; case mix coord. Parkview Manor Nursing Home, 1994-95, minimum data set and nursing care plan coord., 1995; acute care nurse Harrison Meml. Hosp., Cynthiana, Ky., 1996—2002; dir. nursing Robertson County Health Care Facility, Mt. Olivet, Ky.; long-term care charge nurse Trilogy Health Ctr. at Harrison Meml. Hosp., Cynthiana; med. inpatient svcs. Floyd Meml. Hosp., New Albany, Ind. Vol. nurse aide Mud Creek Clinic, Grethel, 1989-92. Founder free blood pressure clinic H.E.L.P.S. Community Action Program, Hellier, Ky., 1983; co-founder H.E.L.P.S. Community Action Group, Hellier, 1983; mem. Ellis Island Centennial Commn., N.Y., 1986. Appalachian Honors scholar Pikeville Coll., 1989-92. Mem. Nat. Geog. Soc., Ky. Nursing Assn., Order Ky. Cols. (Honorable Ky. Col. 1989), Smithsonian Inst., Nat. Trust Hist. Preservation, World Wildlife Fund, Pikeville Coll. Alumni Assn. Democrat. Mem. Worldwide Ch. of God. Avocations: creating Indian jewelry and wall hangings, classical music, reading. Home: 901 Santa Fe Rd Brooksville KY 41004

DORWART, BONNIE BRICE, historian, retired rheumatologist; b. Petersburg, Va., Jan. 27, 1942; d. Gratien Bertrand and Myrtle Elizabeth (Houser) Brice; m. William Villee Dorwart, Jr., June 22, 1963; children: William Bertrand, Brice Burdan, Michael Walter. AB, Bryn Mawr Coll.,

1964; MD, Temple U., 1968. Diplomate Am. Bd. Med. Examiners, Am. Bd. Internal Medicine, Am. Bd. Rheumatology. Intern then resident in internal medicine Lankenau Hosp., Jefferson Med. Coll., Phila., 1968-72; instr. medicine Hosp. U. Pa., Phila., 1972-74; fellow rheumatology U. Pa. Sch. Medicine, Phila., 1974; instr. medicine Jefferson Med. Coll., Phila., 1974-76, asst. prof., 1976-81, assoc. prof., 1981-95, clin. prof., 1995—2003; assoc. investigator divsn. rsch. Lankenau Hosp., Wynnewood, Pa., 1978—88, chief arthritis clinic, 1982—86, chief connective tissue disorders, 1982—97; Civil War med. historian, writer, 2001—. Assoc. dir. Greater Delaware Valley Arthritis Control Program, 1975; mem. Gov.'s adv. bd. on Systemic Lupus Erythematosus, Phila., 1981-88. Author: Carson's Materia Medica of 1851: An Annotation, 2003; contbr. articles to med. jours., chpts. to books. Med. career advisor, active cells workshop Merion Elem. Sch., Pa., 1984-90; fund raiser Arthritis Found., Am. Cancer Soc., Phila., 1974-97; mem. resources com. Bryn Mawr Coll., 1985-90; historian Conf. Ctr. for Med. Edn., Lankenau Hosp., 2006. Named Physician of Yr., 32 Carat Club, Phila., 1986; Janet M. Glasgow scholar Temple U. Sch. Medicine, 1968. Fellow ACP, Coll. Physicians Phila.; mem. AMA, Am. Coll. Rheumatology, Phila. Rheumatism Soc. (pres. 1981-82), Pa. Med. Soc., Philadelphia County Med. Soc. Lutheran. Avocations: cooking, gardening. Home and Office: 124 Maple Ave Bala Cynwyd PA 19004-3031 Office Phone: 610-667-3849. Personal E-mail: dorwart@verizon.net.

DORWART, DONALD BRUCE, lawyer; b. Zanesville, Ohio, Dec. 12, 1949; s. Walter G. and Katherine (Kachmar) D.; children: Claire Lauren, Hillary Beth. BA, Vanderbilt U., 1971; JD, Washington U., St. Louis, 1974. Bar: Mo. 1974, U.S. Dist. Ct. (ea. dist.) Mo. 1974. Assoc. Thompson Coburn LLP, St. Louis, 1974-79, ptnr., 1980—; dir. New Energy Corp. Ind., 1992-95. Contbr. articles to profl. jours. Named to, Mo. & Kans. Super Lawyers, 2005—, Best Lawyers in Am., 2007. Mem.: ABA, FOCUS St. Louis (mem. selection com. 1990—91, mem. fin. com. 1990—2002, mem. cmty. policy com. 2000—02, bd. dirs. 2000—06, treas. 2001—02, pres. 2002—04), Bar Assn. Met. St. Louis (chair securities regulation com. 1979), Maritime Law Assn. U.S. (mem. maritime fin. com. 1980—, proctor), The Met. Forum (mem. mgmt. com. 2003—05), Noonday Club. Office: Thompson Coburn LLP One US Bank Plz Ste 3300 Saint Louis MO 63101-1643 Office Phone: 314-552-6000. Business E-Mail: ddorwart@thompsoncoburn.com.

DOSLUOGLU, HASAN HALDUN, surgeon; s. Zeki and Nebahat Dosluoglu; m. Mine Melek Igmen, Feb. 19, 1987; children: Deniz, Ates. MD, Istanbul U., Capa, Turkey, 1986. Med. diploma Ministry Health, Ankara, 1986. Surgery resident Marmara U., Istanbul, 1987—92; surg. oncology fellow Med. Ctr. Del., Wilmington, 1992—93; surgery resident Morristown Meml. Hosp., NJ, 1993—95, SUNY, Buffalo, 1995—98, vascular surgery fellow, 1998—2000, asst. prof. of surgery, 2002—; attending vascular surgeon Am. Hosp., Istanbul, 2000—01; chief divsn. vascular surgery VA Western NY Healthcare Sys., Buffalo, 2001—. Contbr. articles to profl. jours. Mem.: ACS (Western NY chpt.), Vascular Surg. Soc. Western NY (pres.-elect 2005), Assn. VA Surgeons, Internat. Soc. Endovascular Specialists, Ea. Vascular Soc., Soc. for Clin. Vascular Surgery, Soc. for Vascular Surgery, European Soc. Vascular and Endovascular Surgery (corr.). Office: VA Western NY Healthcare System 3495 Bailey Ave Buffalo NY 14215 Home Phone: 716-883-4435; Office Phone: 716-862-8937. Office Fax: 716-862-8600. Business E-Mail: hasan.dosluoglu@med.va.gov.

DOSS, DELIA L., mathematics educator; d. Norman E. and Mary F. LaPlante; life ptnr. Richard D. Antonio; children: Chasity L. Thornton, Adam L. Thornton. BEd in Secondary Math., BA in History, BS in Math., U. Alaska, Anchorage, 1994; MS in Ednl. Adminstrn., Nat. U., LaJolla, Calif., 2006. Cert. dental hygienist USAF, 1977; driver's lic. hazard material Calif., 1979, secondary math., history tchr. Alaska, 1995. Cross-country truck driver Tri State, Joplin, Mo., 1979—87; tchr. math., history Matanuska Sch. Dist., Palmer, Alaska, 1991—; adj. prof. Matanuska C.C., Palmer, Alaska, 1997—2001. Advisor, nclb coach Valley Pathways H.S., Palmer, Alaska, 2002—. Sec./treas. Goose Creek Cmty. Ctr., Talkeetna, Alaska, 1989—95; mem. Cmty. Clinic, Talkeetna, Alaska, 1989—91; pres. PTO, Talkeetna, Alaska, 1989—92. Mem.: NEA, MSEA (assoc.; rights com. 1999—2000), Profl. Math. Tchrs. (assoc.). Avocations: motorcycling, hiking, reading, writing. Home Phone: 907-376-5377; Office Phone: 907-745-2158.

DOSS, JESSICA YARINA, financial analyst; b. Johnstown, Pa., Aug. 1, 1974; d. Robert George and Karen Mastovich Yarina; m. Kenneth E. Doss, May 4, 2003. BA in Sociology, U. Calif., LA, 1995; postgrad., Pepperdine U., Irvine, Calif., 2004—. Statis. analyst Circuit City Stores, Inc., Walnut, Calif., 1994—99; sr. fin. analyst Roth Staffing Svcs., Inc., Orange, 1999—2004, IBM Corp., Costa Mesa, 2004—. Mem. com. customer satisfaction Roth Staffing, 1999—2004. Vol. Dem. Nat. Conv., LA, 2004. Mem.: NOW, Internat. Thespian Soc., Am. Mensa, UCLA Alumni Assn. Independent. Avocations: creative writing, travel, reading.

DOSS, SYLVIA M., psychologist, educator; b. Houston, Dec. 11, 1953; d. George Weston and Nancy George Doss. BA in Psychology and Rehab. Counseling, U. N.Tex., 1977; MEd in Rehab. Counseling, U. Mo., 1979; MA in Neuropsychology, Fielding Grad. Inst., 1994, PhD in Clin. Psychology, 1996. Lic. psychologist, cert. rehab. counselor. Rehab. counselor Neurol. Disabilites Support Svcs., Tucson, 1987—95; pvt. practice Phoenix, 1996—. Dir., tng. cons. Cath. Cmty. Svc. So. Ariz., Tucson and Yuma, 1981—86; surveyor Commn. Accreditation Rehab. Facilities, 1983—89; master faculty U. Phoenix, 1992—; cons. Rehab. Svcs. Admin. Dept. Econ. Security, Tucson and Yuma, Ariz., 1998; adj. faculty Glendale C.C., Phoenix, 2001—; spkr. in field. Mem. Commn. for Handicapped, Tucson, 1981—82; mentor Fresh Start, 2003—. Recipient Disability Rights award, Ctr. for Disability Law, 1998. Mem.: APA, Am. Psychol. Soc., Psi Chi. Democrat. Methodist. Avocations: exercise, movies. Office: 515 E Carefree Hwy 110 Phoenix AZ 85085 Business E-Mail: smdoss1211@aol.com.

DOSSETT, ANDREW BIENVENU, orthopedic and spine surgeon; b. Shreveport, La., Apr. 30, 1961; married; 4 children. BS in Exercise Sci. (summa cum laude), U. So. Calif., LA, 1983; MD, U. Tex. Southwestern Med. Sch., Dallas, 1988. Cert. Am. Bd. Orthop. Surgeons, lic. Tex., Calif. Intern, gen. surgery U. Tex. Southwestern Med. Sch., Dallas, 1988—93, resident, orthop. surgery, 1989—93, clin. asst. prof., orthop. surgery, 1994—; fellow, spine surgery Kerlan-Jobe Orthop. Clinic, Inglewood, Calif., 1993—94; staff orthop. surgeon Presbyn. Hosp. Dallas, Dallas, Baylor U. Med. Ctr., Dallas, Mary Shield Hosp., Dallas, Carrell Clinic, Dallas, 1996—. Asst. team physician Tex. Rangers Profl. Baseball Club, 1994—, Dallas Cowboys Football Club, 2000—, spine cons., 1996—, Profl. Rodeo Cowboys Assn. Rodeo Cowboys, 1994—, Dallas Ind. Sch. Dist. Injury Clinic, 1994—, Dallas Mavericks Basketball Club, 1996—, Dallas Stars Hockey Club, 1996—, Tex. A&M, So. Methodist U., La. State U., U. Tex. Arlington; cons. privileges HealthSouth Med. Ctr., Dallas, Parkland Meml. Hosp., Dallas; courtesy privileges St. Paul Med. Ctr., Dallas; presenter in field. Contbr. articles to profl. jours., chapters to books. Mem.: Profl. Baseball Team Physicians Soc., AMA, Tex. Orthop. Assn., Tex. Med. Assn., Dallas County Med. Soc., Am. Acad. Orthop. Surgeons, N.Am. Spine Soc., Phi Beta Kappa. Avocation: golf. Office: W B Carrell Meml Clinic 9301 N Central Expy Ste 400 Dallas TX 75231 Office Phone: 214-220-2468. Office Fax: 214-953-1483.*

DOSSIN, ERNEST JOSEPH, III, credit manager; b. Detroit, May 24, 1941; s. Ernest Joseph and Jean (Dickson) D.; m. Mary Jane Mortimore, July 24, 1965; children: Ernest Joseph IV, Tobias Alfred. BA in Bus., Valparaiso U., 1963; MBA in Fin., Fairleigh Dickinson U., 1978; postgrad., Walden U., 1995-98. Asst. store mgr. W.T. Grant, Norfolk, Va., 1967-68; dir. acctg. Am. Express, Trenton, NJ, 1968-69; asst. to chmn. Americana Hotels, NYC, 1969, dir. casinos, 1970-72, corp. dir. credit, 1972-79; v.p. Myers Group, Rouses Point, NY, 1979-92; exec. v.p. Global Collections Inc., Plattsburgh, NY, 1985-93; pres. Dossin's Consulting Assocs., Plattsburg, NY, 1993—. Guest lectr. Plattsburgh State U., 1995; leader seminars in improving credit practices, 1985-91; adj. faculty SUNY, Plattsburgh, 1993—, C.C. of Vt., 1993—. Author: Strictly Business, 1991. Corp. bd. mem. Champlaine Valley Physicians Hosp., 1998—; treas. New Eng. Synod Evang. Luth. Ch. Am., 1997—; congl. pres. Redeemer Luth. Ch., Plattsburh, 1985-8 9, congl. v.p., 1990-93; bd. dirs. Oratorio Soc., pres. 1996-98; bd. dirs. Plat tsburgh, 1986-90; treas. Luth. Coll., Teaneck, N.J., 1975-79; mem. exec. com. Boy Scouts Am., Clinton County, 1994—. Mem. Nat. Assn. Credit Mgrs. (cited 1984, 85), Internat. Credit Assn. (exec.), Soc. Cert. Consumer Credit Execs. (cert. exec.), Plattsburgh C. of C., Soc. for Preservation Barbershop Quartet Singing (v.p. 1990-93), Mgmt. Club Plattsburgh (bd. dirs. 1987-91). Republican. Lutheran. Avocations: boating, barbershop quartet singing, football. E-mail: ernieD3@aol.com.

DOST, MARK W., lawyer; b. Attleboro, Mass., May 22, 1955; s. Raymond and A. Louise (Fraser) D.; m. Karen M. Sullivan, Aug. 1976; children: Christopher, Stephen, Gregory, Isaac. AB summa cum laude, U. Mass., 1978; JD cum laude, Boston Coll., 1981. Bar: Conn. 1981, U.S. Tax Ct. 1985, U.S. Dist. Ct. Conn. 1986. Atty. Gager & Henry, Waterbury, Conn., 1981-95; ptnr. Tinley, Nastri, Renehan & Dost, Waterbury, 1995—. Author: (with John V. Galiette) Planning for Retirement Benefit Distributions, 1995, 3rd edit., 2006. Fellow Am. Coll. Trust and Estate Counsel; mem. ABA, Conn. Bar Assn. (exec. com., elder law sect. 1991—, exec. com., estates and probate sect. 1991—, chair elder law sect. 1994-96, chair publs. com. 1997-2000), Nat. Acad. Elder Law Attys. Office: Tinley Nastri Renehan Dost 60 N Main St Waterbury CT 06702-1403 Office Phone: 203-596-9030. Business E-Mail: mdost@tnrdlaw.com.

DOSTAL, DAVID EUGENE, education educator, researcher; s. Deward Lawrence and Marie Jean Dostal; m. Barbara Jean McClintock, May 21, 1983; children: Joseph Aaron, Jonathan Allen. BS in Chemistry, U. SD, Vermillion, 1976, MA in Biology, 1978; PhD, U. Mo., Columbia, 1986; postdoctoral in Pharmacology, U. Va., Charlottesville, 1986—90. Rsch. scientist Geisinger Clinic, Danville, Pa., 1990—97; asst. prof. Pa. State U. Coll. Medicine, 1997—98, assoc. prof., 1998—99, Tex. A&M U. Sys., Temple, 1999—. Grantee Rsch. award, NIH, 2004—. Mem.: Am. Heart Assn. Office: Texas A&M Univ Sys - COM 1901 S 1st St Temple TX 76504 Office Phone: 254-743-2464. Office Fax: 254-743-0165. Business E-Mail: ddostal@medicine.tamhsc.edu.

DOSTART, THOMAS J., lawyer; b. 1955; BS, Iowa State U., 1977; JD, U. Iowa, 1980. CPA; bar: 1981. Law clk. Iowa Supreme Ct.; atty. Arter & Hadden, Jones, Day, Reavis & Pogue, Diamond Shamrock, Inc., Amoco Corp., Chgo.; gen. counsel Lachman Tech. Corp., Interactive Systems Corp., Naperville, Ill., 1992—95; v.p., gen. counsel, sec. Nat. Auto Credit, Inc. (formerly Agency Rent-A-Car), 1995—97; gen. counsel, asst. sec. Alliance Coal, LLC, Lexington, Ky., 1997—2003; v.p., gen. counsel, sec. Massey Energy Co., Purchase, NY, 2003—. Former mng. editor: Iowa Law Review. Office: Massey Energy Co 4 N 4th St Richmond VA 23219 Office Phone: 804-788-1800. Office Fax: 804-788-1870.*

DOSTOURIAN, DICK, computer systems executive; b. LA, Oct. 30, 1948; s. John and Elizabeth (Cholakian) D.; m. Jeanette Adrienne Torigian; children: Leslie Ann, Christopher Scott. AA in Engring., East L.A. Coll., 1968; BS in Math., Calif. State U., LA, 1970, MS in Math., 1972; MBA, Pepperdine U., 2005. Computer engr. McDonnell Douglas, LA, 1973-76, computing specialist, 1976-80, sect. mgr. engring. sys., 1980-83, mgr. product definition sys., 1983-89, mgr. info. tech., 1989-94; sr. mgr. software devel. Keane, Inc., LA, 1994-95; software devel. mgr. Home Savings Am., Irwindale, Calif., 1995-96; prin. computing specialist The Boeing Co., Long Beach, Calif., 1997-99, mgr. product data sys., 1999—2006, sr. mgr. enterprise flight engring. sys., 2006—. Mem. St. James Armenian Ch., L.A., 1989-2000. Mem. IEEE, Assn. for Computing Machinery, Nat. Computer Graphics Soc., Data Processing Mgmt. Assn., Calif. State U. Alumni Assn. Avocations: tennis, railroading. Home: 10781 Via Jacara Stanton CA 90680-1926 Office: The Boeing Co 5301 Bolsa Ave Huntington Beach CA 92647 Office Phone: 714-654-4396. Business E-Mail: dick.dostourian@boeing.com.

DOSWALD, HERMAN KENNETH, language educator, retired academic administrator; b. Oakland, Calif., Mar. 24, 1932; s. Herman and Caroline Josephine (Mello) D.; m. Ruth Eugenie Hannes, Dec. 21, 1956; children: Caroline Susan, Stephanie Ann. AA, U. Calif., Berkeley, 1952, BA, 1955; MA, U. Wash., 1959, PhD, 1965. Instr., dept. German and Russian Oberlin (Ohio) Coll., 1959-60; instr., dept. German U. Wash., Seattle, 1960-61; instr., dept. fgn. langs. Seattle U., 1961-62; asst. prof. German U. Kans., Lawrence, 1964-67; asst., then assoc. prof., dept. fgn. langs. Fresno (Calif.) State U., 1967-72; prof., chmn. dept. German and Russian Kent (Ohio) State U., 1972-79; head dept. fgn. langs. Va. Poly. Inst. and State U., Blacksburg, 1979-84, assoc. dean adminstrn., Coll. Arts & Scis., 1984-86, interim dean Coll. Arts & Scis., 1986-87, dean, 1987-93, prof. German, 1993-96, prof. German, dean Coll. Arts & Scis. emeritus, 1996—. Adj. lectr. in German Cmty. HS, Roanoke, Va., 2006—07. Contbr. articles to profl. jours. Served to 1st lt. U.S. Army, 1962-64. Adenauer scholar, Munich, Fed. Republic Germany, 1953-54; Fulbright fellow, Vienna, Austria, 1958-59. Mem. Phi Beta Kappa, Phi Kappa Phi, Omicron Delta Kappa. Home: 4592 Preston Forest Dr Blacksburg VA 24060-8660 Personal E-mail: doswald@vt.edu.

DOSWELL, MARY CUMMINGS, energy executive; b. Atlanta, June 9, 1958; d. Robert Emery Cummings and Catherine Brierly Longyear; m. John Cabell Doswell II, July 3, 1982; children: Lindsay Cummings, Catherine Carter. BA in Physics, Mt. Holyoke Coll., South Hadley, Mass., 1980; MS in Engring., MIT, 1982. Sr. staff adminstrn. sr. coord. regulation, dir. demand-side analysis Va. Power Dominion, Richmond, dir. market rsch. Va. Power, v.p. billing and credit Dominion Delivery, sr. v.p., chief adminstrv. officer, 2003—, pres. and CEO Dominion Resources Svcs., 2004—. Contbr. articles to profl. jours. Regional dir. admissions Mt. Holyoke Coll. Mem. Soc. Women Engrs., Elec. Utility Mkt. Rsch. Coun., Richmond C. of C. (chmn. bus. rsch. advisors), Women's Club, Tuckahoe Woman's Club, Sigma Xi. Office: Dominion PO Box 26532 Richmond VA 23261-6532*

DOTO, IRENE LOUISE, statistician; b. Wilmington, Del., May 7, 1922; d. Antonio and Teresa (Tabasso) D. BA, U. Pa., 1943; MA, Temple U., 1948, Columbia U., 1954; M in Quantitative Sys., Ariz. State U., 1986. Engring. asst. RCA-Victor, 1943-44; rsch. asst. U. Pa., 1944; actuarial clk. Penn Mut. Life Ins. Co., 1944-46; instr. math. Temple U., 1946-53; commd. lt. health svcs. officer USPHS, 1954, advanced through grades to capt., 1963; statistician Communicable Disease Ctr., Atlanta, 1954-55, Kansas City, Kans., 1955-67; chief statis. and publ. svcs., ecol. investigations program Ctr. for Disease Control, Kansas City, 1967-73, chief statis. svcs., divsn. hepatitis and viral enteritis Phoenix, 1973-83; statis. cons., 1984—. Mem. adj. faculty Phoenix Ctr., Ottawa U., 1982-98. Mem. APHA, Am. Statis. Assn., Ariz. Pub. Health Assn., Ariz. Coun. Engring. and Sci. Assn. (officer 1982-90, pres. 1988-89), Primate Found. Ariz. (mem. animal care and use com. 1986—), Bus. and Profl. Women's Club Phoenix, Mil. Officers Assn. Am. (state sec.-treas. 1995-96), Ariz. SPCA (bd. dirs. 2000-01), Sigma Xi, Pi Mu Epsilon. Office: PO Box 22197 Phoenix AZ 85028-0197

DOTO, PAUL JEROME, retired accountant; b. Newark, July 22, 1917; s. Anthony and Edith Margaret (Mascellaro) Doto. BS, NYU, 1947. CPA N.J., N.Y., registered mcpl. acct., N.J., pub. sch. acct., N.J. Acct. John Hewitt Foundry Co., East Newark, 1941—43, S.D. Leidesdorf & Co., NYC, 1947—56; CPA Peat Marwick Mitchell & Co., NYC, 1956—64; asst. controller Lincoln Ctr. for Performing Arts Inc., NYC, 1964—69; controller Seton Hall U., So. Orange, NJ, 1969—74, Belart Products, Applied Coatings, Maddock, Inc., NJ, 1974—80, Internat. Trading Sales, Inc., Pan Atlantic Paper Co., NYC, 1980. Cons. Controller's Office, City N.Y., 1966; bd. dirs. Parkway, Ltd., 1973—78. Mem. Nat. Police Hall of Fame. Served AUS, 1943—46. Mem. N.Y. State Soc. CPA's (chmn. govtl. acctg. com. 1963-64, chmn. internat. control quest on aid of municipalities, N.Y. State), AICPA, Cath. Accts. Guild (bd. govs. 1961-64), N.J. Soc. CPA's, Fin. Exec. Inst. Am. Acctg. Assn., N.Y. Assn. Profs., Smithsonian Assocs. (charter mem.), Nat. Wildlife Fedn., Am. Legion, Am. Mus. Nat. Hist. (assoc.).

DOTRICE, ROY LOUIS, actor; b. Guernsey Channel Isles, U.K., May 26, 1929; came to U.S., 1967; s. Louis and Neva (Wilton) D.; m. Kay Newman, May 8, 1947; children: Michele, Karen, Yvette. Student, Elizabeth Coll., Guernsey Channel Isles. Actor in leading roles Royal Shakespeare Co., Eng., 9 yrs.; actor (plays) A Life (Tony award nomination), Moon for the Misbegotten (Tony, Critics Circle, Drama Desk, Jefferson awards), others; actor: (TV series) Beauty and the Beast, Going to Extremes, Picket Fences, Mr. and Mrs. Smith, Sliders, Madigan Men. With RAF, 1940-45, ETO. Recipient award Guiness Book of World Records for World's Longest Running One-Person Show "Brief Lives", Best Actor award "B.A.F.T.A.", 1969, Emmy award "Caretaker", 1966. Mem. Garrick Club (London). Avocations: fishing, riding. Office: Award Assocs Ste 130 280 N Westlake Blvd Westlake Village CA 91362 Office Phone: 805-557-0414. Personal E-mail: RoyDotrice06@aol.com.

DOTSON, ALBERT, not-for-profit fundraiser; b. Detroit; m. Gail Ash Dotson; children: Ashley, Albert. BS econ., Dartmouth Coll.; JD, Vanderbilt Univ. Bar: Fla. With 100 Black Men of America, Inc., 1994—, vice-pres., chmn., 2004—; ptnr. Bizlin Sumberg Baena Price & Axelrod LLP. Lectr. Nat. Law Inst.; chmn. bd. trustees Miami Dade Coll. Found.; pres. Orange Bowl Com. Named one of Cmty. Leader Award, Wilke D. Ferguson, Jr. Bar Assn., 1999, corporate elite in practice of law in So. Fla., Fla. Bus. Jour., 1999, So. Fla. Top Lawyers, Miami Metro, 2001, 100 Most Influential Black Americans, Ebony mag., 2006; recipient Cmty. Excellence in Real Estate award, March of Dimes, 2002. Office: 100 Black Men of America 141 Auburn Ave Atlanta GA 30303

DOTSON, DONALD L., lawyer; b. Rutherford County, NC, Oct. 8, 1938; s. Herman A. and Lottie E. (Hardin) D. AB, U. NC, 1960; JD, Wake Forest U., 1968. Bar: NC, Pa., DC, US Supreme Ct. Atty. NLRB, 1968-73, chmn., 1983-87; labor counsel Westinghouse Electric Corp., 1973-75; labor atty. Western Electric Co., 1975-76; chief labor counsel Wheeling-Pitts. Steel Corp., 1976-81; asst. sec. labor, 1981-83, 2001—; pvt. practice law, Washington, 1987-91; sr. v.p. Beverly Enterprises, 1991—2001; pvt. practice, 2001—. Served with USN, 1960-65. Episcopalian. Office: PO Box 4905 Charlottesville VA 22905 Office Phone: 800-227-7140.

DOTSON, GEORGE STEPHEN, retired oil industry executive; b. Okemah, Okla., Dec. 25, 1940; s. Hilmer C. and Alma Lucille (McGee) D.; m. Phyllis A. Nickerson, Aug. 17, 1963; children: Sarah, Grant. BS, M.I.T., 1963; MBA, Harvard U., 1970. Asst. to pres. Helmerich & Payne, Inc., Tulsa, 1970-73; v.p. Helmerich & Payne (Peru) Drilling Co., 1974-75, Helmerich & Payne Internat. Drilling Co., 1976-77, pres., COO, 1977—2006; v.p. drilling Helmerich & Payne, Inc., 1977—2006, ret., 2006. Bd. dirs. Atwood Oceanics, Inc.; chmn. Internat. Assn. Drilling Contractors, 1995. Served to capt. U.S. Army, 1964-68. Decorated Bronze Star. Office: Helmerich Payne 1437 S Boulder Ave Ste 1400 Tulsa OK 74119-3628

DOTSON, ROBERT CHARLES (BOB DOTSON), news correspondent; b. St. Louis, Oct. 3, 1946; s. William Henry and Dorothy Mae (Bailey) D.; m. Linda Gay Puckett, July 1, 1972; 1 child, Amy Michelle. BS in Journalism and Polit. Sci., Kans. U., 1968; MS in TV, Syracuse U., 1969. News dir. Sta. KANU-FM, Lawrence, Kans., 1966-68; reporter, photographer, documentary producer KMBC-TV, Kansas City, Mo., 1968; dir. spl. projects WKY-TV, Oklahoma City, 1969-75; corr. WKYC-TV, Cleve., 1975-77; network corr. NBC News, Dallas, 1977-79; corr. Prime Time Saturday Atlanta, 1979-80; corr. Today Show, 1980-85; nat. corr. NBC Nightly News, Atlanta, 1985-2000, Dateline NBC, 1985—; spl. nat. corr. NBC News Today Show, NYC, 2000—. Vis. prof. journalism U. Okla., 1969-73; faculty affiliate Colo. State U., Ft. Collins; writer, host Bob Dotson's Am., travel channel and NBC Superchannel, 1996-98. Author: ...in Pursuit of the American Dream, 1985 (George Washington Honor medal Freedom Found. 1985), Make it Memorable, 2000; documentaries include Through the Looking Glass Darkly, 1974 (Emmy award, RFK award), The Urban Reservation, 1975 (RFK award DuPont-Columbia Journalism award), Still Got Life to Go, 1972, (Emmy nomination), Smoke and Steel, 1973 (Emmy nomination), The Sunshine Child, 1983 (Emmy nomination), People Who Make a Difference, 1987 (Emmy nomination), Bob Dotson's NBC Nightly News Stories, 1987 (Gabriel award 1987), Bob Dotson, 1987 (Media Acess award 1987), Assignment Am., 1989 (Nat. Headliners award 1990, Emmy nomination, 1989, Ohio State award 1989), El Capitan's Courageous Climbers, 1990 (Cine Golden Eale, Italian Film Festival grand prize, Union of Mountain Climbers grand prize, Wilbur award U.S. Film Festival 1990, 91, Cine Grand Prize Best Am. Non-Fiction Film, 1991, Bombay, India Internat. Film Festival Grand Prize, 1991, Japan, Spain Internat. Sprots Film Fest. Grand Prize, 1991, Juan Antonio Samaranch Spl. Citation, 1991), The River's Edge, Dateline NBC, 1994 (Emmy award), Susan Smith Coverage, 1994 (Clarion award), Bob Dotson's America Closeup, 1994 (Clarion award), The River's Edge, 1994 (Emmy award), Bob Dotson's Am., 1996. Recipient numerous awards including Elec. Media Grand Prize Nat. Assn. Yr. Round Edn., 1993, Gabriel Grand Prize Bob Dotson's Am. Diary, 1992, TV of Merit award DAR, 1985, Gabriel award Nat. Cath. Assn. Broadcasters, 1984, Clarion award Women in Communications, 1983, Epilepsy Found. Am. award, 1977, Silver medal Internat. Film and TV Festival of N.Y., 1976, Nat. Headliner award, NBC Today Show, 2001, Edward R. Murrow award for best network news writing Radio and TV News Dirs. Assn., 1999, for best reporting, 2001, 03, Diversity award, Columbia U., 2001, Emmy award for best story in regularly scheduled broadcast, 2003. Mem. Nat. Acad. TV Arts and Scis., Nat. Press Photographers Assn. (The Sprague Meml. award 1989), Writers Guild Am., Internat. Platform Assn., Radio and TV News Dirs., Explorers Club (N.Y.C.), Sigma Delta Chi. Avocation: writing. Office: NBC News-Today Show Ste 1028W 30 Rockefeller Plz New York NY 10112-0002 E-mail: dotson@nbc.com.

DOTT, JOHN R., marine life administrator; b. Bristol, Pa., Apr. 15, 1976; s. John R. and Karen M. Dott; m. Jennifer M. Hopkins, Oct. 17, 1998; children: John K., Kiersten N., Ryan J. Student, Edinboro U., Pa., 1995—96; diploma in marine surveying, Lloyds Maritime Acad., 2004. Marine surveyor J.M. Hughes Co., Ltd., Richboro, Pa., 1996. Firefighter Newport Fire Co., Bensalem, Pa., 1996—2002. Mem.: Nat. Assn. Marine

Surveyors. Office: JM Hughes Co Ltd PO Box 736 Richboro PA 18954 Home Phone: 215-651-8920; Office Phone: 856-456-8989. Office Fax: 856-456-7916. E-mail: office@hughessurvey.com.

DOTT, ROBERT HENRY, JR., geologist, educator; b. Tulsa, June 2, 1929; s. Robert Henry and Esther Edgerton (Reed) Dott; m. Nancy Maud Robertson, Feb. 1, 1951; children: James, Karen, Eric, Cynthia, Brian. Student, U. Okla., 1946-48; BS, U. Mich., 1950, MS, 1951; PhD, Columbia U., 1956. Exploration geologist Humble Oil & Refining Co., Ariz., Oreg., Wash., 1954-56, Calif., 1958; mem. faculty U. Wis.-Madison, 1958-94, prof. geology, 1966-84, Stanley A. Tyler Disting. prof., 1984—, chmn. dept. geology and geophysics, 1974-77, emeritus prof., 1994—. Vis. prof. U. Calif., Berkeley, 1969; Cabot disting. vis. prof. U. Houston, 1986—87; NSF sci. faculty fellow Stanford U. and U.S. Geol. Survey, 1978, U. Colo., 1979; acad. visitor Imperial Coll., London, 1985—86, Oxford U., 1985—86, Adelaide U., Australia, 1992; cons. Roan Selection Trust, Ltd., Zambia, 1967, Atlantic-Richfield Co., 1983—85, Hubbard Map Co., 1984—86; lectr. Bur. Petroleum and Marine Geology, China, 1986; Erskine fellow, vis. prof. Canterbury U., New Zealand, 1987; Woodford-Ellis lectr. Pomona Coll., 1994. Co-author: Evolution of the Earth, 7th edit., 2003, Roadside Geology of Wisconsin, 2004; contbr. articles to profl. jours. 1st lt. USAF, 1956—57. Recipient Outstanding Tchr. award, Wis. Student Assn., 1969, Ben. H. Parker award, Am. Inst. Profl. Geologists, 1992; AEC fellow, Columbia U., 1951—55. Fellow: Edinburgh Geol. Soc. (hon. corr. 1997), Geol. Soc. Am. (chmn. history of geology divsn. 1990, councilor 1992—94, History of Geology award 1995, L.L. Sloss award 2001); mem.: AAAS, History of Earth Sci. Soc. (pres. 1990), Internat. Assn. Sedimentologists, Soc. Econ. Paleontologists and Mineralogists (sec.-treas. 1968—70, v.p. 1972—73, pres. 1981—82, hon., William H. Twenhofel medal 1993), Am. Assn. Petroleum Geologists (Pres.'s award 1956, Disting. Svc. award 1984, Disting. lectr. 1985), Sigma Xi (Disting. lectr. 1988—89). Unitarian Universalist. Office: U Wis Dept Geology and Geophysics 1215 W Dayton St Madison WI 53706-1600 E-mail: rdott@geology.wise.edu. *To understand the earth's past, which no human could witness, has been for me the most exciting challenge imaginable. It is like a great Sherlock Holmes mystery story.*

DOTTEN, MICHAEL CHESTER, lawyer; b. Marathon, Ont., Can., Feb. 23, 1952; arrived in US, 1957, naturalized; s. William James and Ona Adelaide (Sheppard) D.; m. Kathleen Curtis, Aug. 17, 1974 (div. July 1991); children: Matthew Curtis, Tyler Ryan; m. Cheryl Calvin, Apr. 16, 1994. BS in Polit. Sci., U. Oreg., 1974, JD, 1977. Bar: Idaho 1977, Oreg. 1978, Washington. 2005, US Dist. Ct. Idaho 1977, US Dist. Ct. Oreg. 1978, US Ct. Appeals (9th cir.), US Ct. Appeals (DC cir.) 1987, US Ct. Claims 1986, US Supreme Ct. 1996. Staff asst. to Senator Bob Packwood, U.S. Senate, Washington, 1973-74; asst. atty. gen. State of Idaho, Boise, Idaho, 1977-78; chief rate counsel Bonneville Power Adminstrn., Portland, Oreg., 1978-83; spl. counsel Heller, Ehrman, White & McAuliffe, Portland, 1983-84, ptnr., 1985-98, 99—; gen. counsel PG&E Gas Transmission, N.W. Corp., Portland, 1998-99; co-chair Energy Nat. Practice Group, 2003—06. Utility com. mem. Ctr. for Pub. Resources, N.Y.C., 1992—; Nat. Panel Arbitrators, Am. Arbitration Assn., 2005-; Panel Arbitrators and Mediators, U.S. Arbitration and Mediation Oreg., 2005-. Coun. Emanual Hosp. Assocs., Portland, 1988-92; bd. dirs. William Temple House, 1995-99, chmn. devel. com., 1996-98, v.p., 1997-98, pres., 1998-99; active Portland Interneighborhood Trans. Rev. Commn., 1986-88; vestryman Christ Episcopal Ch., Lake Oswego, Oreg., 1999-03, sr. warden, 2001-03; bd. dirs. Health Bridges Internat., Inc., 2006-, treas., 2007—; pres. Arlington Club Toastmasters, 2006. Hunter Leadership scholar U. Oreg., 1973, Oreg. scholar, 1970. Mem. ABA (chmn. electric power com. sect. natural resources 1985-88, coun. liaison energy com. 1990-93, coordinating group on energy law 1992-96), Fed. Bar Assn. (pres. Oreg. chpt. 1989-90, Chpt. Activity award 1990, Pres. award 1988-89), Oreg. State Bar (chmn. dispute resolution com. 1986-87), U. Oreg. Law Sch. Alumni Assn. (pres. 1989-92), Am. Arbitration Assn., Arlington Club, Multnomah Athletic Club. Democrat. Episcopalian. Avocations: skiing, golf, hiking, travel, racquetball. Office: Heller Ehrman White & McAuliffe 701 Fifth Ave Seattle WA 98104 Office Phone: 206-389-6111, 503-795-7420. Business E-Mail: michael.dotten@hellerehrman.com.

DOTTERWEICH, PATRICK TIMOTHY, social studies educator; b. Balt., June 2, 1961; s. Andrew Henry and Patricia Lee Dotterweich. BA, U. Md., Catonsville, 1983; MEd, Loyola Coll., Balt., 1992. Cert. advanced profl. Md. State Dept. Edn., 2004. Tchr., team leader Westminster (Md.) West Mid. Sch., 1984—2000, Shiloh Mid. Sch., Hampstead, Md., 2000—. On-line libr. adv. com. Md. Hist. Soc., Balt., 2004—; Md. state social studies task force mem. MSDE, Balt., 2005—. Parishioner Our Lady of Grace Roman Cath. Ch., Parkton, Md., 1978—2006. Recipient Md. State Social Studies Educator of the Yr., Md. Coun. for the Social Studies, 2003. Mem.: NEA, MSTA, Carroll County Edn. Assn., Nat. Coun. for the Social Studies. Roman Catholic. Avocations: travel, genealogy, antique restoration and research. Home: 19 Old Forge Garth Sparks MD 21152-8801 Office: Shiloh Mid Sch 3675 Willow St Hampstead MD 21074 Home Phone: 410-472-1297; Office Phone: 410-386-4570. Office Fax: 410-386-4579. Personal E-mail: ptdotte@k12.carr.org.

DOTTO, PETER ATTILIUS, retired marine corps officer, defense consultant; b. Milan, June 30, 1949; s. Gianni Abraham and Renata Carla (Zagni) D.; m. July 15, 1978 (div. May 1994); children: John, Nicole, Regina, Anthony, Donna, Joseph; m. Marilyn Anne Capotosto, Sept. 12, 1999. BS in Biology, U. Dayton, 1971; MS in Govt., Campbell U., 1984; MA in Nat. Security-Strategic Studies, Naval War Coll., Newport, RI, 1991. Commd. 2d lt. USMC, 1971, advanced through grades to col., 1992; dir. future ops. Unified Task Force, Somalia, 1992-93; comdr. Hdqs. Bn., 1st Marine Divsn., Camp Pendleton, Calif., 1993-94; vice dir. strategy, plans and policy U.S. So. Command, Panama, 1994-95; asst. chief staff for spl. ops. tng., exercises-simulations I Marine Expeditionary Force, Camp Pendleton, 1996-98, chief staff, 1998; ret., 1998; sr. exec. officer Avatar Sentry, Ltd., Hollywood, Fla., 1998; program dir. M2 Techs., Inc., West Hyannisport, Mass., 1999—2005; sr. analyst Marine Corps Ctr. for Lessions Learned, Quantico, Va., 2006—. Adj. prof. Marine Corps U., San Diego, 1999-2006; cons. Naval Sea Sys. Command, Corona, Calif., 1999, Sierra Cybernetics, Yorba Linda, Calif., 1999. Contbr. articles to profl. jours. Decorated Def. Superior Svc. medal; recipient merit award U.S. Dept. State, 1993. Mem.: DVA (life), Marine Corps Assn., Am. Legion, 1st Marine Divsn. Assn. (legal officer 1999—2000), Mil. Officers Assn., Sec. Navy Retiree Coun. Republican. Roman Catholic. Avocations: hiking, travel. Office: Marine Corps Ctr for Lessions Learned 1776 Elliot Rd Quantico VA 22134 Home: 120 Rachels Point West End NC 27376 Home Phone: 910-673-3459; Office Phone: 910-850-4834. Personal E-mail: dottop@embarqmail.com.

DOTY, ANGELA JOY, emergency physician, military officer; b. Royal Oak, Mich., Oct. 12, 1977; d. Allen Clark and Margie Ellen Doty; m. Ashraf Saud Harahsheh, Aug. 31, 2003; 1 child, Maryan Alina Harahsheh. BA, Albion Coll., Mich., 1999; MD, Wayne State Sch. Medicine, Detroit, 2003. EMT Albion Cmty. Ambulance, Mich., 1996—2000; resident emergency medicine Sinai- Grace Hosp. Detroit Med. Ctr., Detroit, 2003—06; capt. USAF, Andrews AFB, Md., 2006—. With USAF, 1999—. Mem.: AMA, Am. Coll. Emergency Physicians. Muslim. Avocations: bicycling, outdoor activities. Home: 3215 N Conn Ave Royal Oak MI 48073-3586

DOTY, DAVID SINGLETON, federal judge; b. Anoka, Minn., June 30, 1929; BA, JD, U. Minn., 1961; LLD (hon.), William Mitchell Coll. Law. Bar: Minn. 1961, U.S. Ct. Appeals (8th and 9th cirs.) 1976, U.S. Supreme Ct. 1982. V.p., dir. Popham, Haik, Schnobrich, Kaufman & Doty, Mpls., 1962-87, pres., 1977-79; instr. William Mitchell Coll. Law, St. Paul, 1963—64; judge U.S. Dist. Ct. for Minn., Mpls., 1987—. Mem. Adv. Com. on Civil Rules, 1992-98, Adv. Com. on Evidence Rules, 1994-98; trustee Mpls. Libr. Bd., 1969-79, Mpls. Found., 1976-83. Fellow ABA Found.; mem. ABA, Minn. Bar Assn. (gov. 1976-87, sec. 1980-83, pres. 1984-85), Hennepin County Bar Assn. (pres. 1975-76), Fed. Bar Assn. (pres. br. 1996-97), Am. Judicature Soc., Am. Law Inst. Office: US Dist Ct 14 W US Courthouse 300 S 4th St Minneapolis MN 55415-1320 Home Phone: 612-332-7853; Office Phone: 612-664-5060. Business E-Mail: dsdoty@mnd.uscourts.gov.

DOTY, DONALD D., retired bank executive; b. Independence, Kans., June 30, 1928; s. Laton L. and Dorothy (Russell) D.; m. Cheri F. Montgomery, June 14, 1952; children: John Scott, Susan Dorothy, Mark Montgomery. BS, Okla. State U., 1950; postgrad., U. Wis. Grad. Sch. Banking, 1963. Rancher, nr. Bartlesville, Okla., 1950-94; asst. cashier First Nat. Bank, Bartlesville, 1956-58, asst. v.p., 1958-60, v.p., 1964-69, exec. v.p., 1969-74; pres. WestStar Bank, n.a. (formerly First Nat. Bank), Bartlesville, 1974-93; also bd. dirs.; retired, 1993. Pres. First Bancshares, Inc., Bartlesville, 1974-93, bd. dirs.; chmn. S.W. Cattlemen's Credit Corp., 1979-90; pres. Bartlesville Credit Bur., 1972—; pres. Bartlesville-Area Indsl. Devel. Co., 1970—; chmn. First Okla. Life Ins. Co., Oklahoma City, 1990-95; chmn. Coll. Bus. Assocs., Okla. State U., 1991-92. Chmn., trustees Jane Phillips Episcopal Meml. Med. Ctr., 1970—; trustee Washington County Indsl. Devel. Trust Authority, 1973-80; chmn. Frank Phillips Found., Bartlesville, 1975—2003; trustee St. John Hosp., Tulsa, 1995-2004; bd. dirs. St. John Health Sys., 2004. Capt. USAF, 1953-55. Named to Okla. State U., Coll. of Bus. Hall of Fame, 1994; recipient Disting. S c. award Bartlesville, 1957, Disting. Alumni award Okla. State U., 2000. Mem. Am. Bankers Assn., Okla. Bankers Assn. (pres. 1984-85), Bartlesville C. of C. (v.p., bd. dirs. 1965-81, pres. 1981-82), Jaycees (Outstanding Young Man Bartlesville 1957, Okla. 1958), Masons, Shriners, Rotary, Sigma Alpha Epsilon. Republican. Episcopalian. Avocations: skiing, hunting, golf. Home: 2407 Kyle Ct Bartlesville OK 74006-6340 E-mail: dotyd@sbcglobal.net.

DOTY, DUANE HAROLD, business educator; b. Wichita, Kans., July 5, 1960; s. David H. and Martha (Parker) D.; m. Susan Michal Smith, Dec. 30, 1991; children: Lindsey, Michala, Zachary, David. BA with honors, Tex. State U., San Marcos, 1982; MBA, U. Tex., Austin, 1987, PhD, 1990. Asst. prof. U. Ark., Fayetteville, 1990—95; chair dept. strategy and human resources Syracuse U. Sch. Mgmt., 1995; dean Coll. Bus. U. So. Miss., Hattiesburg, 2003—. Contbr. articles. Mem.: Acad. Mgmt. (Best Article award 1993, Scholarly Achievement award human resouces divsn. 1997). Avocations: fishing, hunting. Office: Univ So Miss Coll Bus PO Box 5021 Hattiesburg MS 39406 Office Phone: 601-266-4659. Business E-Mail: harold.doty@usm.edu.

DOTY, ELMER, aeronautical engineer; BS in Nuclear Engring., Univ. Mo., MS in Mech. Engring. Mfg. mgr. Gen. Elec. Co., 1975—79; engring. mgr., agrl. divsn. FMC, 1979—86, corp. dir., mfg. engr., 1986—88, gen. mgr., Energy and Transportation Group Material Handling Sys. Divsn., 1988—94, v.p., gen. mgr., Steel Prods. Divsn., 1994—2001; gen. mgr. BAE Sys., 2001—05; pres., CEO Vought Aircraft Indus., 2006—. Office: Vought Aircraft 9314 W Jefferson Blvd Dallas TX 75211

DOTY, GRESDNA ANN, theatre historian, educator; b. Oelwein, Iowa, Feb. 22, 1931; d. James William and Gresdna (Wood) D.; m. James G. Traynham, Nov. 28, 1980. AA, Monticello Coll., Alton, Ill., 1951; BA, U. No. Iowa, 1953; MA, U. Fla., 1957; PhD, Ind. U., 1967. Instr. S.W. Tex. State U., San Marcos, 1957—61, asst. prof., 1964—65, La. State U., Baton Rouge, 1967-73, assoc. prof., 1973-79, dir. theatre, 1973-77, 81-91, prof., 1979-84, Alumni prof., 1984—, Alumni prof. emeritus, 1996—, chair dept. theatre, 1991-93. Author: Anne Brunton Merry in the American Theatre, 1971; co-editor: (with Billy J. Harbin) Inside the Royal Court Theatre, 1956-81: Artists Talk, 1990; contbr. articles to profl. jours. Bd. dirs. Arts Coun. Greater Baton Rouge, 1987-92, pres., 1990-91; mem. exec. com. Swine Palace Prodns. Rsch. grantee Nat. Endowment Humanities, 1981, Exxon Edn. Found., 1981. Fellow S.W. Theatre Assn.; mem. Am. Theatre Assn. (bd. dirs. 1977-80), Am. Coll. Theatre Festival (nat. chmn. 1976-79), Am. Soc. Theatre Rsch. (mem. exec. com. 1988-91, v.p. 1994-97), Nat. Theatre Conf. (sec. 1999-02), Coll. Fellows of Am. Theatre (dean-elect 2003-04, dean 2004-06). Home: 122 Highland Trace Baton Rouge LA 70810-5061

DOTY, JAMES EDWARD, minister, psychologist; b. Lakewood, Ohio, May 8, 1922; s. Ordello Luce and Margaret (McCurdy) D.; m. Mary Merciel Smith, Sept. 8, 1943; children: Mark Allen, David Wesley, Martha Suzanne. AB, Mt. Union Coll., Alliance, Ohio, 1944, DD (hon.), 1965; MDiv cum laude, Boston U., 1947, PhD, 1959; postgrad., Harvard U., Oxford U.; DD (hon.), DePauw U., 1966. Ordained to ministry Meth. Ch., 1945. Pastor in, Salem, Mass., 1947-51, Lynn, Mass., 1951-57; founder, dir. Greater Lynn Pastoral Care and Counselling Ctr., 1954-57; dir. pastoral care and counselling Ind. Area Meth. Ch., 1957-66; pres. Baker U., 1966-73; pvt. practice pastoral psychology Corpus Christi, Tex., 1973—2000; exec. dir. Corpus Christi Pastoral Counselling Ctr., 1973-84; interim sr. pastor First United Methodist Ch., Corpus Christi, 1988-89; interim pastor 1st Presbyn. Ch., Portland, Tex., 1991-98; pastor New Franklin (Ohio) United Meth. Ch., 2000—01; interim pastor Sebring (Ohio) Presbyn. Ch., 2001—03, Ch. of Silver Lake, Ohio, 2003—06. Mem. staff Boston Ctr. Adult Edn., 1949—53; spl. lectr. Union Theol. Sem., Buenos Aires, 1962, Meth. Theol. Sem., Sao Paulo, Brazil, 1962, Epworth Theol. Sem., Salisbury, Rhodesia, 1963, Meth. Theol. Sem., Mulungwishi, Congo, 1964, Trinity Theol. Coll., Singapore, 1967, Union Theol. Sem., Manila, 1967, Cbanga Meth. Theol. Sem., Monrovia, Liberia, 1975, Meth. Theol. Sem., Suva, Fiji, 1986; mem. First Student Christian Movement Conf. in postwar Germany Heidelberg U., 1947; del. World Family Life Consultation, Birmingham, England, 1966; chmn. World Family Life, 1981—86; mem. World Meth. Coun., London, 1966, Denver, 71, Dublin, 76, Honolulu, 81, del., Nairobi, Kenya, 86, Singapore, 1991—2001; chmn. exec. com., chmn. bd. visitors Sch. Theology Boston U. Author: The Pastor as Agape Counselor, 1964, Postmark Lambarene: A Visit with Albert Schweitzer, 1965; editor: Authentic Man Encounters God's World, 1967, Students Search for Meaning, 1971, (with Merciel S. Doty) For Heaven's Sake, 1993, Albert Schweitzer: Reverence for Life, 1993, With Schweitzer in Africa, 1994; producer, moderator weekly program Focus, Sta. KEDT-TV, 1984-95. V.p. Pike Twp. Sch. Bd., Marion County, Ind., 1960-66. Recipient Alumni of Yr. award, Mt. Union Coll., 1963, Alumni award of merit, Boston U., 1969. Mem. APA, S.W. Conf. United Meth. Ch., Tex. Bd. Profl. Counselors, Am. Bd. Sexology (diplomate), Am. Assn. Pastoral Counselors (diplomate, bd. dirs.), Am. Assn. Marriage and Family Therapy, Rotary, Sigma Alpha Epsilon, Zeta Chi. Home: 800 S 15th St Sebring OH 44672-2050 Office Phone: 330-930-7902.

DOTY, JAMES ROBERT, lawyer; b. Houston, May 14, 1940; s. Robert Earl and Vivian (Weaver) D.; m. Joan Stewart Richardson, June 10, 1972; children: Katherine Brooks, Robert Daniel. BA, Rice U., 1962; AB, Oxford U., Eng., 1964; MA, Harvard U., 1966; LLB, Yale U., 1969. Bar: Tex. 1969, DC 1988, US Supreme Ct., US Ct. Appeals (DC cir.). Ptnr. Baker & Botts LLP, Washington, 1977-90, sr. ptnr., 1992—; gen. counsel SEC, Washington, 1990-92. Contbr. articles to profl. jours. Named one of Top Ten Securities Lawyers in the DC area, Legal Times, 2003, Washington's Best SEC Lawyers, Washingtonian mag., 2004; Rhodes scholar Oxford U., 1962-64. Mem. ABA (Task Force on GATS Legal Svcs. Negotiations), Fed. Bar Assn. (exec. bd.), State Bar Tex., Houston Bar Assn., DC Bar Assn., Am. Law Inst., DC Bar Ct. Office: Baker & Botts LLP Ste 1200 1299 Pennsylvania Ave NW Washington DC 20004-2408*

DOTY, PAUL MEAD, biochemist, educator, arms control specialist; b. Charleston, W.Va., June 1, 1920; s. Paul Mead and Maud (Stewart) D.; m. Margaretta Elenor Grevatt, Oct. 31, 1942 (div. Aug. 1953); 1 child, Gordon Sutherland; m. Helga Boedtker, Feb. 27, 1954; children: Marcia, Rebecca, Katherine. BS, Pa. State Coll., 1941; MA, Columbia U., 1943, PhD, 1944; DSc, U. Chgo., 1966. From instr. to asst. prof. chemistry Poly. Inst. Bklyn., 1943-46; Rockefeller fellow Cambridge (Eng.) U., 1946-47; asst. prof. chemistry U. Notre Dame, South Bend, Ind., 1947-48, Harvard U., Cambridge, Mass., 1948-50, prof. chemistry, 1950-68, Mallinckrodt prof. biochemistry, 1968-88, prof. pub. policy Kennedy Sch., 1988-90, prof. biochemistry emeritus, 1988—, prof. pub. policy emeritus, 1990—. Founder, dir. Ctr. for Sci. and Internat. Affairs, Harvard U., 1973-85, dir. emeritus, 1985—; mem. Pres.'s Sci. Adv. Commn., White House, Washington, 1961-64; mem. gen. adv. com. on arms control to Pres., White House, 1976-80; bd. dirs., vice chmn. Mitre Corp., Bedford, Mass., 1975-92; bd. dirs. Internat. Sci. Found., Washington, 1993-97. Editor: Defending Deterrence: Managing the ABM Treaty, 1989; founder, editor quar. jour. Internat. Security, 1975-85; author more than 350 articles. Bd. dirs. Aspen Inst. Berlin, 1981-2005, Harriman Inst., Columbia U., 1986-98; mem. Aspen Inst. for Humanitsic Studies, Wye, Md., 1969-85; mem. Pugwash Confs., 1957-97. Recipient Pure Chemistry award Am. Chem. Soc., 1956. Mem. Am. Acad. Arts and Sci. (commn. on internat. security), Nat. Acad. Sci. (com. on internat. security and arms control), Am. Philos. Soc. Office: Kennedy Sch Govt Harvard U 79 Jfk St Cambridge MA 02138-5801 Home: 130 Mt Auburn St Unit 411 Cambridge MA 02138-5773 Business E-Mail: pauldoty@fas.harvard.edu.

DOTY, RICHARD L., medical researcher; b. Boulder, Colo., Oct. 14, 1944; s. George David and Frances Amelia (Bradley) D. BS, Colo. State U., 1966; MA, Calif. State U., 1968; PhD, Mich. State U., 1971; postgrad., U. Calif., Berkeley, 1973. Instr. dept. psychology Calif. State U., San Francisco, 1971-72, U. San Francisco, 1971-72; U. asst. mem. Monell Chem. Senses Ctr., Phila., 1974-76, assoc. mem., head human olfaction sect., 1976-78; dir. smell and taste ctr. Hosp. U. Pa., Phila., 1979—, Sch. Medicine, U. Pa., Phila., 1980—, asst. prof. dept. otorhinolaryngology, human communication, 1983-89, assoc. prof., 1989-93; prof. dept. otorhinolaryngology U. Pa., Phila., 1994—. Cons. in field; lectr. in field; editorial cons. for numerous profl. jours.; external adv. bd. Taste and Smell Ctr. U. Conn./Yale U., 1982-84, Rocky Mountain Taste and Smell Ctr., U. Colo. Sch. Medicine, 1985, Mayo Found. Project, 1989; internat. adv. bd. 1st Internat. Congress on Food and Health, Salsomaggiore Terme, Italy, 1985. Author: The Smell Identification Test (TM) Administration Manual, 1983, 2d edit., 1989, 3d edit., 1995; editor: Mammalian Olfaction, Reproductive Processes and Behavior, 1976; co-editor: (with T.V. Getchell, E.P. Koster) Chemical Senses, spl. edit., 1981, (with D.G. Laing, W. Breopohl) Human Olfaction, 1990, (with L.M. Bartoshuk, T.V. Getchell and J.B. Snow) Smell and Taste in Health Disease, 1991, (with D. Muller-Schwartze) Chemical Signals in Vertebrates VI, 1992, Handbook of Olfaction and Gustation, 1995, 2d edit., 2003. NIH postdoctoral rsch. fellow, 1973-75; grantee Nat. Inst. on Aging, 1989-91, 2000-05, Nat. Inst. Deafness and Other Comm. Disorders, 1980—. Mem. European Chemoreception Rsch. Orgn. (mem. organizational com. 1981), Assn. for Chemoreception Scis. (mem. program com. 1985, 87, mem. elections com. 1987), AAAS, N.Y. Acad. Scis., Assn. for Rsch. in Otolaryngology, Am. Acad. Otolaryngology (head and neck surgery), Am. Psychol. Assn., Internat. Soc. for Chem. Ecology, Phila. Coll. Physicians (mem. adv. com., sect. on geriatrics and gerontology). Home: 125 White Horse Pike Haddon Heights NJ 08035-1909 Office: U Pa Smell & Taste Ctr 5 Ravdin Bldg 3400 Spruce St Philadelphia PA 19104-4206 Office Phone: 215-662-6580. Business E-Mail: doty@mail.med.upenn.edu.

DOTY, ROBERT WALTER, lawyer; b. Aliquippa, Pa., Sept. 19, 1942; s. David Lucien and Iona (Fox) D.; m. Joyce Marie Shaffalo, Sept. 10, 1961; children: Genie, Merrie Beth. BA cum laude, Wheaton Coll., 1963; JD, Vanderbilt U., 1966. Bar: Pa. 1966, U.S. Supreme Ct. 1982. Assoc. Eckert Seamans Cherin & Mellot, Pitts., 1966-74; solicitor Crescent Township, Allegheny County, Pa., 1969—; ptnr. Eckert Seamans Cherin & Mellott, Pitts., 1975-91; dir. Cohen & Grigsby, P.C., Pitts., 1991—2003, of counsel, 2004—. Arbitrator Am. Arbitration Assn., nat. panel, 1978—, spkr. in field; lectr. Westinghouse Internat. Sch. Environ. Mgmt., Ft. Collins, Colo., 1980-82. Mem. nat. com. on wills and trusts centennial campaign Vanderbilt U., 1977-81. Recipient Archie B. Martin Meml. scholarship medal Vanderbilt U., 1964, Robert F. Jackson Meml. scholarship prize, 1965, Founder's medal, 1966; 3 Am. Jurisprudence awards in contracts, civil procedure and criminal law The Lawyers Co-operative Pub. Co., Rochester, N.Y., 1964, 65; Mark Woodworth Walton scholar Vanderbilt U., 1965. Mem. Pa. Bar Assn., Allegheny County Bar Assn. (governing coun. civil litigation sect.), Wheaton Club (past pres.), Fox Chapel Racquet Club, Breckenridge Golf and Tennis Club, Estero Country Club, Racquet Club Memphis, Order of Coif, Phi Kappa Delta, Phi Alpha Delta. Avocations: swimming, tennis. Office: 11 Stanwix St 15th Floor Pittsburgh PA 15222 Office Phone: 412-297-4866. Business E-Mail: rdoty@cohenlaw.com.

DOTY, ROBERT WILLIAM, neuroscientist, physiologist, educator; b. New Rochelle, NY, Jan. 10, 1920; s. Earle Birdsell and Ethel Laurette (Mack) D.; m. Elizabeth Natalie Jusewich, Aug. 30, 1941; children—Robert William, Mary E., Cheryl A., Richard M. BS, U. Chgo., 1948, MS, 1949, PhD, 1950. Postdoctoral fellow U. Ill., Chgo., 1950-51; asst. prof. U. Utah, Salt Lake City, 1951-56; from asst. to assoc. prof. U. Mich., Ann Arbor, 1956-61; prof. U. Rochester, NY, 1961—. Vis. prof. U. Mex., 1975, U. Osaka, Japan, 1981; sci. adviser NIMH, Bethesda, Md., 1975-79, Yerkes Inst., Atlanta, 1975-78 Author: (with E.N. Doty) Man and Woman, War and Peace, 1941-1951, A Dual Auto Biography, 2004; assoc. editor: Acta Neurobiologiae, Warsaw, 1971—; contbr. articles to profl. jours. Served to capt. U.S. Army, 1942-46 Recipient Javits award, Nat. Inst. Neurol. and Communicative Disorders and Stroke., NIH, 1986. Fellow AAAS; mem. Am. Psychol. Soc. (pres. div. 6, 1984), Internat. Brain Research Orgn., Current Anthropology (assoc.), Soc. for Neurosci. (pres. 1975-76, councilor 1970-74) Avocations: photography, history, langs. Office: U Rochester Med Ctr Dept Neurobiology And Anatomy Box 603 Rochester NY 14642-0001 Office Phone: 585-275-1922. Business E-Mail: robert_doty@urmc.rochester.edu.

DOTY, VICTORIA SKOWER, elementary school educator; b. Stafford, Conn., Sept. 25, 1946; d. Frank Albert Jr. and Emily Marie (Jedziniak) Skower; m. Edwin Wilfred Doty, Oct. 14, 1978 (dec. Feb. 2007); 1 child, Peter Edwin. BA, Am. Internat. Coll., Springfield, Mass., 1969; MA, Elms Coll., 1991. Cert. elem. tchr., Mass., Conn. Coord. inventory control Hallmark Cards Inc., Enfield, Conn., 1969-89; substitute tchr. Enfield and Longmeadow, Mass., 1991—98; tchr., chair mid. sch. reading and lang. arts St. Gabriels Sch., Windsor, Conn., 1998—. Sec. Thompsonville Little League, 1991-94, fin. sec., 1988-89, 93-94; elected to parish coun. St. Adalbert Ch., 1994-98; coord. local and county dist. Modern Woodmen of Am. Oration Contest, 2000—. Mem. St. Adalbert Home and Sch. Assn. (historian 1991-93, fin. sec. 1988-89, 93-94, treas. 1987-88). Republican. Roman Catholic. Avocations: folk art, crafts, crocheting, reading. Home: 45 Alden Ave Enfield CT 06082-2866

DOUB, WILLIAM OFFUTT, lawyer; b. Cumberland, Md., Sept. 3, 1931; s. Albert A. and Fannabelle (Offutt) D.; m. Mary Graham Boggs, Sept. 12, 1959; children: Joseph Peyton, Albert A., II. AB, Washington and Jefferson Coll., 1953; LLB, U. Md., 1956. Bar: Md. 1956, D.C. 1974. With law dept.

B. & O. R.R., 1955-57; assoc. Bartlett Poe & Claggett, Balt., 1957-61; ptnr. Niles Barton & Wilmer, Balt., 1961-71; commr. AEC, 1971-74; ptnr. LeBoeuf, Lamb, Leiby & MacRae, Washington, 1974-77, Doub, Muntzing and Glasgow, Washington, 1977-91, Newman & Holtzinger, P.C., Washington, 1991-94, Morgan Lewis & Bockius, Washington, 1995-2000. Chmn. Minimum Wage Commn., Balt., 1964-66; peoples' counsel Md. Pub. Service Commn., 1967-68, chmn., 1968-71; vice chmn. Washington Met. Area Transit Commn., 1968-71; mem. President's Air Quality Adv. Bd., 1970-71; mem. exec. adv. com. FPC, 1969-71, Nat. Gas Survey, 1975-78; pres. Great Lakes Conf. Pub. Utility Commrs., 1971; mem. nat. adv. bd. Am. Nat. Standards Inst., 1975-80; mem. Md. Adv. Com. Retardation, 1969-71 Mem. Adminstrv. Conf., U.S., 1973-75; chmn. U.S. Energy Assn., Inc., World Energy Conf., 1978-80, U.S. del., 1974, 77, 80, 83, 86, 89, 92, 95, 98; vice chmn. World Energy Conf., 1986-88, hon. vice chmn., 1988—; mem. adv. groups Nat. Acad. Pub. Adminstrn., NSF; presdl. appointee as rep. to So. States Energy Bd., 1983-90; bd. govs. Mid. East Inst. of U.S., 1982-86, 88-94, 95-2000; mem. exec. com. Thomas Alva Edison Found., 1983-90, 85-90; presdl. appointee 33d Ann. Conf. of Internat. Atomic Energy Agy., 1989. Recipient Nat. Energy award U.S. Energy Assn., 1998. Mem. Met. Club. Home (Winter): 512 Neapolitan Ln Naples FL 34103 Home (Summer): Box 449 Keedysville MD 21756 Personal E-mail: fudoub@aol.com.

DOUBLEDAY, CHARLES WILLIAM, dermatologist, educator; b. Houston, Oct. 1, 1954; s. Leonard Charles and Margaret (Walker) D.; m. Verlinde Van den Berge Hill, June 22, 1985; children: George Marchant, Julia Van den Berge, Walker Hill. BA with honors, U. Tex., Austin, 1976; MD, U. Tex., Houston, 1981. Diplomate Am. Bd. Dermatology, 1987. Rotating intern John Peter Smith Hosp., Ft. Worth, 1981-82; resident in dermatology U. Tex. Med. Sch., 1982-83, 85-87, fellow in dermatology, 1985, clin. asst. prof. dermatology, 1988—; pvt. practice, Houston, 1987—. Bd. dirs. The Park People. Contbr. articles to profl. jours. Recipient high sci. quality award Soc. for Investigative Dermatology, 1986; Rsch. fellow Dermatology Found., 1985. Fellow Am. Acad. Dermatology; mem. Tex. Med. Assn., Harris County Med. Soc., Tex. Dermatol. Soc., Houston Dermatol. Soc. (pres. 2005), U. Tex. Houston Health Sci. Ctr. (devel. coun. 1994-96, devel. bd., 2007-), Houston Country Club. Republican. Episcopalian. Avocations: tennis, golf. Office: 515 Post Oak Blvd Ste 535 Houston TX 77027-9494

DOUCET, JENNIFER, research scientist; MA, Calif. State U., Carson, 2003. Rsch. asst. U. RI, Kingston, 2003—. Home Phone: 401-789-5145. Personal E-mail: jdoucet@mail.uri.edu.

DOUCETTE, DAVID ROBERT, information technology executive; b. Pitts., Feb. 2, 1946; s. Adrian Robert and Mary Alyce (Newland) D. BSEE cum laude, Poly. Inst. Bklyn., 1968, MSEE, 1970, PhD, 1974. Asst. prof. elec. engring. Poly. Inst. NY (now Poly. U.), 1973-74, assoc. prof. computer sci., 1975-82, prof., 1982—, dir., 1994—2002, assoc. dean, 1997—2002; sr. staff specialist advanced planning Gruman Data Sys. Corp., Bethpage, NY, 1979-80, program mgr., 1979-80, mgr. graphics sys., 1980-84, from asst. dir. to dir. interactive sys. support, 1984-86, dir. interactive sys., 1986-94; pres., CEO D3Software Corp., 1994—. Active Nassau County Hist. Soc., Garden City Hist. Soc. Recipient Achievement award Engrs. Joint Coun. L.I., 1999. Mem. IEEE (past sect. chmn., Centennial medal, Third Millennium medal), Assn. Computing Machinery (past chpt. chmn.), Nat. Space Soc., Planetary Soc., Nat. Eagle Scout Assn. (chpt. bd.), Sigma Xi, Tau Beta Pi, Eta Kappa Nu, L.I. Early Fliers Club. Office: Poly U Dept Computer/Info Sci 6 Metrotech Ctr Brooklyn NY 11201

DOUCETTE, JOHN J., manufacturing executive; B, magna cum laude, Boston Coll. Mgmt. positions through CIO GE Plastics GE, 1980—98; CIO Otis bus. unit United Technologies Corp., Hartford, Conn., 1998—2000, v.p., CIO, 2000—. Office: United Technologies United Technologies Bldg Hartford CT 06101*

DOUCETTE, MARY-ALYCE, computer company executive; b. Pitts., Feb. 12, 1924; d. Andrew George and Alice Jane (Sloan) Newland; m. Adrian Robert Doucette, Feb. 6, 1945 (dec. June 1983); children: David Robert, Regis Robert. BS cum laude, U. Pitts., 1945. Mgr. Newland Bros., Millvale, Pa., 1946-53; gen. mgr. Newland-Ludlo, Pitts., 1953-72; mgmt. cons. D3 Software, Garden City, NY, 1972-80, sec., corp. officer, 1980—. Fin. sec. Cerebral Palsy Assn., Garden City, Helen Keller Svcs. for Blind, Garden City; mem. Winthrop-U. Hosp. Aux., Mercy League, Friends of Adelphi Univ. Libr., Friends of Hist. St. George Ch. of Hempstead, N.Y., Adv. Coun. for Continuing Edn., Garden City Sch. Dist., 1988—. Mem. AAUW, LI Panhellenic, Univ. Club LI, Nassau County Hist. Soc. (life), Garden City Hist. Soc., Cmty. Club Garden City-Hempstead, Woman's Club Garden City, Alpha Delta Pi, Pi Lambda Theta. Home: 146 Washington Ave Garden City NY 11530-3013 Office: D3 Software PO Box 8051 Garden City NY 11530-8051

DOUD, GUY R., motivational speaker, former secondary education educator; Degree summa cum laude, Concordia Coll., 1975; LHD (hon.), Judson Coll., 1992. Tchr. lang. arts Brainerd (Minn.) Sr. High Sch.; motivational spkr. Author: Molder of Dreams, Teacher of the Year, Classroom of the Heart. Recipient Nat. Tchr. of Yr. award, 1986.*

DOUD, RANDALL H., lawyer; b. Muncie, Ind., 1955; BA, U. N.C., 1977; JD, Harvard U., 1980. Bar: NY 1982. Assoc. Skadden, Arps, Slate, Meagher & Flom LLP, NYC; atty. Skadden, NYC. Contbr. articles to profl. jour. Office: Skadden 4 Times Sq Fl 24 New York NY 10036-6595 Office Phone: 212-735-3000, 212-735-2524. Office Fax: 917-777-2524. Business E-Mail: rdoud@skadden.com.

DOUD, WALLACE C., retired information technology executive; b. Bellingham, Wash., Feb. 25, 1925; s. Forrest Roy and Florence (Pollock) D.; m. Marjorie K. Fenton, Oct. 25, 1949 (dec. 1962); children: Forrest J., Mary, Margaret, Barbara, Melissa; m. Janice F. Freudenberg, June 15, 1963 (dec. 1978); children: Michael, Karen; m. Jean A. Kennedy, Aug. 25, 1979. BBA, U. Wis., 1948; DHL (hon.), Mercy Coll., 1983. Salesman IBM Corp., Milw., St. Paul, Detroit, dir. patent relations Armonk, N.Y., 1960-71, v.p. services staff, 1971-77, v.p. comml. and industry rels., 1977-85. Chmn. Bd. Parks and Recreation White Plains, N.Y., 1983-84; chmn., pres. United Way, White Plains, 1975-80. Recipient Youth Services award B'nai B'rith, 1972, Medallion Westchester Community Coll., 1980. Mem.: Rockland Golf Club, Meguntícook Golf Club. Republican. Presbyterian.

DOUGAL, ARWIN ADELBERT, electrical engineer, educator; b. Dunlap, Iowa, Nov. 22, 1926; s. Adelbert Isaac and Goldya (White) D.; m. Margaret Jane McLennan, Sept. 3, 1951; children: Catherine Ann, Roger Adelbert, Leonard Harley, Laura Beth. BS, Iowa State U., 1952; MS, U. Ill., 1955, PhD, 1957. Registered profl. engr., Tex. Radio engr. Collins Radio Co., Cedar Rapids, Iowa, 1952; research asst., research asso., asst. prof., asso. prof. U. Ill., Urbana, 1952-61; prof., mem. grad. faculty, dir. labs. for electronics and related sci. research U. Tex., Austin, 1961-67, prof., 1969—91; dir. Electronics Research Center, 1971-77, sec. grad. assembly, 1972-74; dir. Austron, Inc., 1977-82; prof. emeritus U. Tex., 1992—. Asst. dir. def. rsch. and engring. for rsch. Office Sec. Def., Washington, 1967-69; cons. Tex. Instruments, Inc., Dallas, Gen. Dynamics Corp., Ft. Worth, U. Calif. Los Alamos Sci. Lab., Battelle Meml. Inst. Contbr. articles to profl. jours Faculty sponsor U. Tex. Conservative Democrats Club, 1966-67; sr. mem. CAP, 1984—; elder local Presbyn. Ch.; commr., Mission Presbyn. With USAAF, 1946—49, with USAF, 1946—49, Airways & Air Commn. Svc. Recipient Teaching Excellence awards U. Tex. Students Assn., 1962, 63, Spl. award for outstanding service as program chmn. S.W. IEEE Conf. and Exhbn., 1967; Outstanding Grad. Adviser award Grad. Engring. Council, U. Tex., 1971; Disting. Advisor award Grad. Engring. Council, U. Tex., 1977, 84; Teaching Achievement award Grad. Engring. Council, U. Tex., 1977; Profl. Achievement citation in engring. Iowa State U. Alumni Assn., 1975 Fellow Am. Phys. Soc., IEEE (dir. 1980-81, Centennial medal 1984, Student Br. citation 1988, Outstanding Br. Counselor award, 1991, chmn. ctrl. Tex. sect. 1993-94); mem. Am. Soc. Engring. Edn., Aircraft Owners and Pilots Assn., Exptl. Aircraft Assn., Sigma Xi, Phi Kappa Phi, Tau Beta Pi, Eta Kappa Nu, Pi Mu Epsilon, Phi Eta Sigma, Rockport Yacht Club Avocation: aviation. Home: 6115 Rickey Dr Austin TX 78757-4437 E-mail: aadougal@att.net.

DOUGALL-SIDES, LESLIE K., lawyer; b. Washington, Sept. 5, 1953; d. George Malcolm Richardson and Kathleen (Cahill) Dougall; m. Kenneth Jacob Sides, Feb. 19, 1994. BA, New Coll., Sarasota, Fla., 1975; JD cum laude, Florida State U., Tallahassee, 1978. Bar: Fla. 1981, DC 1981, Oreg. 1986, cert.: in city, county and local govt. law 1996, cert. profl. human resources 2001, bar: U.S. Dis. Ct. (middle and southern dist.) Fla., U.S. ct. appeals (11th cir.), U.S. Supreme Ct. Staff atty. Ctrl. Fla. Legal Svcs., Cocoa, 1982—85, dir. atty. Handicapped Law Ctr., 1985—87; asst. city atty., acting city atty. City of Key West (Fla.), 1987—95; asst. city atty. City of Clearwater (Fla.), 1995—; bd. dirs. IRRA, 2000—02; sec. West Ctrl. Fla. Chpt., Indsl. Rels. Rsch. Assn., 2003. Mem.: Indsl. Rels. Rsch. Assn. (sec. West Ctrl. Fla. chpt. 2003, bd. dirs. 2000—02), Soc. Human Resources, Clearwater Bar Assn., ABA. Avocation: sailing. Office: City of Clearwater City Atty's Office PO Box 4748 Clearwater FL 33758 Home Phone: 813-930-0491; Office Phone: 727-562-4010. Business E-Mail: leslie.dougall-sides@myclearwater.com.

DOUGAN, BRADY W., diversified financial services company executive; b. Urbana, Illinois, Aug. 30, 1959; 2 children. AB in Economics, U. Chgo., 1981, MBA in Fin., 1982. With derivatives group to mng. dir. long term fin. Bankers Trust, Tokyo; joined Credit Suisse First Boston LLC, 1990, co-head, fin. products' marketing effort in the Americas, co-head, global debt capital markets group, head equities divsn., 1996—2001, global head securities divsn., 2001—02, co-pres. institutional securities NYC, 2002—04, CEO investment banking divsn. London, 2004; CEO Credit Suisse, 2004—07; mem. exec. bd. Credit Suisse Group, 2003—, CEO investment banking divsn., 2004—07, CEO, 2007—. Office: Credit Suisse Group Paradeplatz 8 9070 Zurich Switzerland also: Credit Suisse Group 11 Madison Ave New York NY 10010 Office Phone: 212-325-2000. Office Fax: 212-325-6665. E-mail: brady.dougan@credit-suisse.com.*

DOUGHERTY, BRIAN JAMES, lawyer; b. Bristol, Pa., Apr. 23, 1955; BS summa cum laude, Bucknell U., 1977; JD cum laude, Harvard U., 1980. Bar: Pa. 1980. Ptnr. Ballard, Spahr, Andrews & Ingersoll, Phila., Post & Schell PC. Spkr. in field. Contbr. articles to profl. jours. Named Pa. Super Lawyers, 2004—07, Best Lawyers Am., 2005—07. Mem. ABA, Pa. Bar Assn., Phila. Bar Assn. (tax sect.), fellow Am. Coll. Employee Benefits Counsel. Office: Post & Schell PC 4 Penn Ctr 1600 John F Kennedy Blvd Philadelphia PA 19103-2808 Office Phone: 215-587-5919. Office Fax: 215-587-1444. Business E-Mail: bdougherty@postschell.com.

DOUGHERTY, CHARLES HAMILTON, pediatrician; b. St. Louis, June 1, 1947; s. Charles Joseph and Suzanne Louise (Hamilton) D.; m. Mary Laverty Peckham, July 7, 1972; children: Bridget, Matthew, Erin, Kelly. BA in Biology, Coll. of the Holy Cross, 1969; MD, U. Rochester Sch. of Medicine, NYC, 1973. Pediatric resident St. Louis Children's Hosp., 1973-76, pres. med. staff, 2005—; pvt. practice pediatrics Primary Pediatric Care Group, St. Louis, 1976-86, Esse Health, St. Louis, 1986—. Fellow Am. Acad. Pediatrics. Roman Catholic. Avocations: running, travel, computers, water sports. Office: Esse Health 13303 Tesson Ferry Rd Saint Louis MO 63128-4062 Office Phone: 314-842-5239. Personal E-mail: cdoughe103@aol.com. Business E-Mail: cdougher@essehealth.com.

DOUGHERTY, CHARLES JOHN, academic administrator; b. NYC, June 28, 1949; s. Charles Aloysius and Mary Elizabeth (Quinn) D.; m. Sandra Lee Drabik; children: Constance Marie, Justin Charles. BA, St. Bonaventure U., 1971; MA, U. Notre Dame, 1973, PhD in Philosophy, 1975. Prof. philosophy Creighton U., Omaha, 1975-88, dir., Ctr. for Health Policy and Ethics, 1988-95, v.p. acad. affairs, 1995-2001; pres. Duquesne U., Pitts., 2001—. Author: Ideal, Fact, and Medicine, 1985, (with R.P. Heaney) Research for Health Professionals, 1988, American Health Care: Realities, Rights and Reforms, 1988, (with Jerry Cederblom) Ethics at Work, 1990, (with A. Haddad and B. Edwards) Ethical Dilemmas in Perioperative Nursing, 1990, Back to Reform, 1996; contbr. articles to profl. jours.; mem. bd. editors Health Progress, 1989—. Chmn. Nebr. Com. for the Humanities, Lincoln, 1987-88; bd. dirs. Fedn. of State Humanities Couns., 1986-89; mem. disciplinary rev. bd. Nebr. Supreme Ct., 1988—, Nebr. Accountability and Disclosure Commn., 1991—; bd. dirs. Sisters of Charity Health Sys. of Cin., 1994-96; bd. trustees Cath. Health Assn., 1995—. Mem. Am. Philos. Assn., Am. Catholic Philos. Assn. (exec. council mem. 1987-90), Alpha Sigma Nu. Democrat. Roman Catholic. Office: Duquesne U Office of Pres 600 Forbes Ave Pittsburgh PA 15282 E-mail: president@duq.edu.*

DOUGHERTY, CHARLOTTE ANNE, financial planner, insurance and securities representative; b. Canton, Ohio, Nov. 9, 1947; d. Myron Martin and Wilma Rose Brown; m. John Edwin Dougherty, Jr., Feb. 14, 1976; 1 child, John Edwin. BA, Miami U., Oxford, Ohio, 1969; powtgrad., Kent State U., 1971-73. Cert. fin. planner. Social worker Summit County Welfare, Akron, Ohio, 1971-73; rsch. coord. Tufts U., Medford, Mass., 1973-74; corp. recruiter Lincoln Nat. Sales Corp., Ft. Wayne, Ind., 1976-79; registered rep. Lincoln Nat. Life, Cin., 1980—, Lincoln Fin. Advisors, Cin., 1989—. Contbr. articles to profl. jours. Mem. Inst. Cert. Fin. Planners, Internat. Assn. Fin. Planners (v.p. Cin. chpt. 1990—), Internat. Assn. for Fin. Planning (pres.-elect Cin. chpt. 1991, pres. 1992-93), Nat. Assn. Life Underwriters, Cin. Assn. Life Underwriters. Office: Dougherty and Assocs CFP 4030 Smith Rd Ste 400 Cincinnati OH 45209 Office Fax: 513-745-9708.

DOUGHERTY, DAVID FRANCIS, business process outsourcing executive; b. Syracuse, NY, Aug. 19, 1956; s. Francis Edward and Mary (Kelley) D.; m. Kimberly Ann Slattery, Sept. 6, 1986. BBA in Fin., U. Mich., 1978. Brand asst. Procter & Gamble, Cin., 1978-79, asst. brand mgr., 1979-81, brand mgr., 1982-86; gen. mgr. Goggles Div. Lenscrafters, Cin., 1986-87, pres., 1987—90; pres., CEO MATRIXX Mktg. Inc. (a Convergys predecessor), 1990; pres., customer mgmt. group Convergys Corp., Cin., 1995—2000, chief develop. officer, 2000—02, exec. v.p. global info. mgmt. group, 2003—, pres., COO, 2005—07, pres., CEO, 2007—. Bd. dirs. Convergys Corp., 2006—. Author: Financial Policies & Procedures for Student Organizations, 1978. Mem. East Walnut Hills Assembly, Cin., 1988-89. Mem. Am. Mktg. Assn., President's Club Univ. Mich., Tribe of Michigama, Cin. Country Club. Democrat. Roman Catholic. Office: Convergys Corp 201 E Fourth St Cincinnati OH 45202*

DOUGHERTY, ELMER LLOYD, JR., retired chemical engineering professor, consultant; b. Dorrance, Kans., Feb. 7, 1930; s. Elmer Lloyd and Nettie Linda (Anspaugh) Dougherty; m. Joan Victoria Benton, Nov. 25, 1952 (div. June 1963); children: Sharon, Victoria, Timothy, Michael(dec.); m. Ann Marie Da Silva (dec.). Student, Ft. Hays State Coll., 1946-48; BS in Chem. Engring., U. Kans., 1950; MS in Chem. Engring., U. Ill., 1952, PhD in Chem. Engring., 1955. Chem. engr. Esso Standard Oil Co., Baton Rouge, 1951-52; chem. engr. Dow Chem. Co., Freeport, Tex., 1955-58; research engr. Standard Oil of Calif., San Francisco, 1958-65; mgr. mgmt. sci. Union Carbide Corp., NYC, 1965-68; cons. chem. engring. Stamford, Conn. and Denver, 1968-71; founder and owner Maraco, Inc., Monarch Beach, Calif., 1980—; prof. chem. engring. U. So. Calif., LA, 1971-95, prof. emeritus, 1995—. Cons. OPEC, Vienna Austria, 1978-82, SANTOS, Ltd., Adelaide, Australia, 1980—, Kuwait Oil Co., 1995—, many others. Contbr. articles to profl. pubs. Named to, Kans. U. Hall of Fame, 2006. Mem. Soc. Petroleum Engrs. (Disting. mem., chmn. Los Angeles Basin sect. 1984-85, Ferguson medal 1964, J.J. Arps award 1989), Am. Inst. Chem. Engrs., Internat. Assn. Energy Economists, Inst. Mgmt. Sci., El Niguel Country (founder 1976, bd. dirs. 1976-78). Republican. Avocation: golf. Home and Office: Maraco Inc 33531 Marlinspike Dr Monarch Beach CA 92629-4426 Office Phone: 949-388-6193. Business E-Mail: eld@maraco.com.

DOUGHERTY, F(RANCIS) KELLY, data processing executive; b. Lubbock, Tex., May 15, 1953; s. Francis Kelly and Mary Ann (Odell) D.; m. Bonnie Lee Burch, June 14, 1975; children: Anne Katherine, Margaret Erin, Mary Bridget, Kerry Meaghan, Frances Cara. BA in Math. and Physics summa cum laude, U. Dallas, 1975; MS in Computer Sci., U. Tex., Dallas, 1998; cert. assoc. customer svc., Life Office Mgmt. Inst., 1992. CLU; cert. computing profl.; chartered fin. cons.; Microsoft cert. programmer. Actuarial trainee Ranger Nat. Life Ins., Houston, 1976-77; mgr. time sharing svcs. Phila. Life Ins. Co., Houston, 1977-81; sys. engr. Electronic Data Sys., Dallas, 1981-85; IT analyst AEGON Direct Mktg. Svcs., Inc., Plano, Tex., 1985—. Pres. St. Elizabeth Seton Parish Bd. Edn., 1989-92. U. Dallas scholar, 1971-75; Rice U. fellow, 1975-76. Fellow Life Mgmt. Inst. (master); mem. IEEE, Assn. for Computing Machinery, K.C. Republican. Roman Catholic. Home: 2713 S Cypress Cir Plano TX 75075-3154 Office: AEGON Direct Mktg Svcs Inc 2700 W Plano Pky Plano TX 75075-8200 Home Phone: 214-929-6167; Office Phone: 972-881-6572. Business E-Mail: fdougher@aegonusa.com.

DOUGHERTY, JAMES, retired orthopedist; b. Lawrence, Mass., July 31, 1926; s. James A. and Maude D. (Dillard) D.; m. Marilyn Hays (dec.); m. Rita Buchman (dec.); children: James (dec.), Charles, Janice, Jonathan, Christopher. BS, Trinity Coll., Hartford, Conn., 1950; MD, Albany Med. Coll., NYC, 1951. Diplomate, examiner and monitor Am. Bd. Orthopaedic Surgery, 1965-82; diplomate Am. Bd. Forensic Examiners, Am. Bd. Forensic Medicine. Intern U. Chgo. Clinics, 1951-52, resident, 1951-56, instr., 1955-56; founding chmn. divsn. orthop. surgery SUNY, Syracuse, 1958-60; prof. clin. surgery Albany Med. Coll., 1960-96, attending surgeon, 1961-94, chief of staff, 1987-89, prof. emeritus, 1996—. Trustee Albany Med. Ctr., 1993-95; cons. Subacute Care Alternative Project, Washington. Author: Ponies in The Window, 1998, (hymns) Life's Narrow Pathways, A Babe Was Born; mem. editl. bd.: Techniques in Orthops.; proponent and architect Fla. state program for pro-bono volunteerism of ret. physicians for medically disadvantaged, 2001; contbr. articles to profl. jours. and Ency. Brittanica. Mem. bd. edn. Ravena-Coeymans-Selkirk Ctrl. Schs., Ravena, NY, 1960—75; med. dir. NY Sr. Games, 1986—89, Catskill Children's Orthop. Clinic, 1960—95; trustee Schaeffer Meml. Libr., 1990—92, Albany Med. Ctr., 1993—95; vol. coord. We Care Program, Lee County, Fla.; bd. dirs. Inst. for Study of Aging, 1990—95. With US Army, 1944—46. Recipient Alumni medal Albany Med. Coll., 1951. Fellow: Am. Acad. Orthopaedic Surgeons; mem.: Sr. and Ret. Physicians' Assn. of Lee County Fla. (founder, pres. 1997—98), Albany Med. Coll. Alumni Assn. (trustee 1990—99, pres. 1994—96, Meritorious Svc. award 1996), Northeastern Regional Assn. Sports Medicine (chmn. 1984—89), Asean Orthop. Soc. (hon.), We. Orthop. Soc. (hon. honored guest, Scottsdale, Ariz. 2000), U. Chgo. Surg. Soc., Crawford Campbell Soc. (founder, pres. 1978—88), Welsh Pony Soc. Am. (life), Sigma Nu, Sigma Psi, Alpha Omega Alpha. Presbyterian. Home: 3510 Pine Fern Ln Bonita Springs FL 34134-1918 *As an orthopaedic surgeon I have sometimes been tempted to exaggerate my role and massage my ego. But then I am reminded that I merely treated. The surgeon operates. God heals. and the patient makes it work.*

DOUGHERTY, JOHN C., lawyer; b. Louisville, Nov. 30, 1963; BA, Catholic Univ., 1988, JD, 1991. Bar: Md. 1991, DC 1994. Ptnr., co-chmn. Patent Litigation practice group DLA Piper Rudnick Gray Cary, Balt. Editor (mng.): Jour. of Contemporary Health Law & Policy. Mem. bd. vis. Columbus Sch. Law, Catholic Univ. Named one of Top 15 Intellectual Property Lawyers in Md., Balt. Bus. Jour., 2001. Office: DLA Piper Rudnick Gray Cary 6225 Smith Ave Baltimore MD 21209-3600 Office Phone: 410-580-4140. Office Fax: 410-580-3001. Business E-Mail: john.dougherty@dlapiper.com.

DOUGHERTY, JOHN CHRYSOSTOM, III, retired lawyer; b. Beeville, Tex., May 3, 1915; s. John Chrysostom and Mary V. (Henderson) D.; m. Mary Ireland Graves, Apr. 18, 1942 (dec. July 1977); children: Mary Ireland Mozzy, John Chrysostom IV; m. Bea Ann Smith, June 1978 (div. 1981); m. Sarah B. Randle, 1981 (dec. June 1997). BA, U. Tex., 1937; LLB, Harvard U., 1940; diploma, Inter-Am. Acad. Internat. and Comparative Law, Havana, Cuba, 1948. Bar: Tex. 1940. Atty. Hewit & Dougherty, Beeville, 1940-41; ptnr. Graves & Dougherty, Austin, Tex., 1946-50, Graves, Dougherty & Greenhill, Austin, 1950-57, Graves, Dougherty & Gee, Austin, 1957-60, Graves, Dougherty, Gee & Hearon, Austin, 1961-66, Graves, Dougherty, Gee, Hearon, Moody & Garwood, Austin, 1966-73, Graves, Dougherty, Hearon, Moody & Garwood, Austin, 1973-79, Graves, Dougherty, Hearon & Moody, Austin, 1979-93, sr. counsel, 1993—97; ret., 1997. Spl. asst. atty. gen., 1949-50; Hon. French Consul, Austin, 1971-86; lectr. on tax, estate planning, probate code, cmty. property problems; mem. Tex. Submerged Lands Adv. Com., 1963-72, Tex. Bus. and Commerce Code Adv. Com., 1964-66, Gov.'s Com. on Marine Resources, 1970-71, Gov.'s Planning Com. on Colorado River Basin Water Quality Mgmt. Study, 1972-73, Tex. Legis. Property Tax Com., 1973-75; adv. com. Mex. Ctr. Inst. of Latin-Am. Studies U. Tex., 1997—. Co-editor: Texas Appellate Practice, 1964, 2d edit., 1977; contbr. Bowe, Estate Planning and Taxation, 1957, 65; Texas Lawyers Practice Guide, 1967, 71, How to Live and Die with Texas Probate, 1968, 7th edit., 1995, Texas Estate Administration, 1975, 78; mem. bd. editors: Appellate Procedure in Tex., 1964, 2d edit., 1982; contbr. articles to profl. jours. Bd. dirs. Tex. Beta Students Aid Fund, 1949-84, Grenville Clark Fund at Dartmouth Coll., 1976-90, Umlauf Sculpture Garden, Inc., 1990-91, New Life Inst., 1993-2001; past bd. dirs. Advanced Religious Study Found., Holy Cross Hosp., Sea Arama, Inc., Nat. Pollution Control Found., Austin Nat. Bank; trustee St. Stephen's Episcopal Sch., Austin, 1969-83, Tex. Equal Access to Justice Found., 1986-90, U. Tex. Law Sch. Found., 1974-2002; mem. adv. com. Legal Assts. Tng. Inst., U. Tex., 1990-98; mem. vis. com. Harvard Law Sch., 1983-87. Capt. C.I.C., AUS, 1941-44, JAGC, 1944-46, maj. USAR. Decorated Medaille Française, France, medal d'honneur en Argent des Affairs Etrangeres, France, chevalier l'Ordre Nat. du Merite; recipient Wm. Reece Smith Spl. Svcs. to Pro Bono award Nat. Assn. of Pro Bono Coords., 2000. Fellow Am. Bar Found., Tex. Bar Found., Am. Coll. Trust and Estate Counsel, Am. Coll. Tax Counsel; mem. ABA (ho. of dels. 1982-88, standing com. on lawyers pub. responsibility 1983-85, spl. com. on delivery legal svcs. 1987-91, com. legal problems of the elderly 1997-2000, Sr. Lawyers divsn. Pro Bono Lawyer of 1999), Am. Arbitration Assn. (nat. panel arbitrators 1958-90), Travis County Bar Assn. (bd. dirs. 1974-76, pres. 1976-77), Internat. Acad. Estate and Trust Law (exec. coun. 1988-90), State Bar Tex. (chmn. sect. taxation 1965-66, pres. 1979-80, com. legal svcs. to the poor 1986-94), Am. Judicature Soc. (bd. dirs. 1985-87), Am. Law Inst. (adv. com. project law governing lawyers 1990-97), Tex. Supreme Ct. Hist. Soc. (trustee 1997—, chmn. 1999-2002), Philos. Soc. Tex. (pres. 1989, bd. dirs. 1989—), Harvard Law Sch. Assn.

(com. on pub. svc. law 1990-95, chmn. 1990-95, coun. 1991-95, exec. com. 1992-95), Tex. Appleseed, Inc. (bd. dirs. 1996—), The Austin Project (bd. dirs. 1999—), Rotary. Presbyterian. Business E-Mail: cdougherty@gdhm.com.

DOUGHERTY, JUDE PATRICK, philosopher, educator, dean; b. Chgo., July 21, 1930; s. Edward Timothy and Cecilia Anastasia (Loew) D.; m. Patricia Ann Regan, Dec. 28, 1957; children: Thomas, Michael, John, Paul. BA, Cath. U. Am., 1954; MA, Cath. U. Am., DC, 1955, PhD, 1960; LHD (hon.), Thomas More Coll., Crestview Hills, NY, 1995, Cath. U. Lublin, Poland, 2000. Instr. Marquette U., 1957-58; instr. Bellarmine Coll., 1958-60, asst. prof., 1960-63, assoc. prof., 1963-66, Cath. U. Am., 1966-76, prof., 1976—; dean Cath. U. Am. (Sch. Philosophy), 1967-99. Vis. assoc. prof. Georgetown U., summer, 1965; vis. prof. Katholieke Universiteit te Leuven, Belgium, 1974-75 Author: Recent American Naturalism, 1960, Western Creed; Western Identity, 2000, The Logic of Religion, 2002, Jacques Maritain: An Intellectual Profile, 2003, Religion-Gesellschaft-Demokratie, 2003; co-author: Approaches to Morality, 1966; editor: (books) Theological Directions of the Ecumenical Movement, 1964, The Impact of Vatican II, 1966, The Good Life and Its Pursuit, 1985; editor Rev. of Metaphysics, 1971; gen. editor: Studies in Philosophy and the History of Philosophy, 1978-. Mem. bd. advisors Franklin J. Matchette Found., 1971—; trustee Bellarmine Coll., 1972-75, U. Bridgeport, 1995-99; mem. Pontifical Acad., St. Thomas, Rome, 1981—; mem. Academia Scientiarum et Artium Europae, Salzburg, 1991—. Decorated Knight of St. Gregory the Great, Pope John Paul II, 1999. Mem. Am. Philos. Assn. (program chmn. ea. divsn. 1988, exec. com. ea. divsn. 1989-93), Am. Cath. Philos. Assn. (pres. 1974-75, Aquinas medal 1994), Washington Philosophy Club (pres. 1968-69), Soc. for Philosophy Religion (pres. 1978-79), Metaphys. Soc. Am. (pres. 1983-84), Fellowship Cath. Scholars (exec. sec. 1994-97, treas. 1994-97, Cardinal Wright award 1994), Am. Maritain Assn. (scholarly achievement award 2000, Fides et Ratio Lifetime Achievement award 2005). Home: 9036 Rouen Ln Potomac MD 20854-3130 Office: Cath U Am Sch Philosophy 620 Michigan Ave NE Washington DC 20064-0001 Home Phone: 301-299-7886; Office Phone: 202-319-5589. Business E-Mail: dougherj@cua.edu.

DOUGHERTY, JUNE EILEEN, librarian; b. Union City, NJ, Mar. 27, 1929; d. Robert John and Jane Veronica (Smith) Beyrer; m. Donald E. Dougherty, Dec. 2, 1946; 1 child, Glen Allan. BA in Edn., Peterson State Coll., 1967; postgrad., Rutgers U., 1959—69. With A. B. Dumont, Paterson, N.J., 1950-54; sch. libr. St. Paul's Elem. Sch., Prospect Park, N.J., 1957—. Dir. North Haledon (N.J.) Free Pub. Libr., 1957—92; sec.-treas. Dougherty & Dougherty, Inc., North Haledon, 1968—73. Den mother Boy Scouts Am., 1954—57; mem. Gov. N.J.'s Tercentenary Com., 1962—64. Mem. Am. Libr. Assn., N.J. Libr. Assn., North Haledon Libr. Assn., Cath. Libr. Assn., N.J. Librs. Roundtable, Bergen-Passaic LIbr. Club, Friends N. Haledon Publ. Libr., St. Paul's Social Club. Roman Catholic. Home: 155 Westervelt Ave Haledon NJ 07508-3074 Office: 129 Overlook Ave Haledon NJ 07508

DOUGHERTY, NEIL JOSEPH, physical education educator, consultant; b. Elizabeth, NJ, Apr. 7, 1943; s. Neil Joseph and Doris Burnett (Lindsay) D.; m. Margaret Ruth Quaranta, July 17, 1965; 1 child, Margaret Elizabeth. BS, Rutgers U., 1964, EdM, 1965; EdD, Temple U., 1970. Tchr. phys. edn. St. Joseph's Sch., Bound Brook, N.J., 1964-65; teaching assoc. Temple U., Phila., 1967-70; prof. Rutgers U., New Brunswick, N.J., 1970—. Mem. adv. bd. Youth Sports Rsch. Coun., New Brunswick, 1987—; nat. faculty mem. U.S. Sports Acad., 1988—. Co-author: Understanding and Assessing Human Movement, 1980, Management Principles in Sport and Leisure Scis., 1985, Contemporary Approaches to the Teaching of Physical Edn., 1979, 87, Sport, Physical Activity and the Law, 1993, 2002; editor: Physical Edn. and Sport for Secondary Sch. Students, 1983, 93, 2002, Principles of Safety in Physical Edn. and Sport, 1987, 93, 2002, Outdoor Recreation Safety, 1998, (jour.) The Reporter, 1977-81, (monograph series) Briefings, 1974-75; mem. editl. bd. Leisure Times Focus, 1984-88, Jour. of Tchg. in Phys. Edn., 1981-85, Safety Notebook, 1998—2006; contbr. to profl. jours. 1st lt. U.S. Army, 1965-67. Recipient Merit award Ea. Assn. for Health, Phys. Edn., Recreation and Dance, 1980, Honor award, 1982, Leadership award Soc. for Study of Legal Aspects of Sport and Phys. Activity, 1998. Fellow N.Am. Soc. Health Edn., Phys. Edn, Recreation, Sport and Dance (charter); mem. Am. Assn. Active Lifestyles and Fitness (pres. 2001-03, Honor award 2005), Nat. Assn. Phys. Edn. Higher Edn. (pres. 1984-86), Sch. and Comty. Safety Soc. Am. (pres. 1996-98, Profl. Svc. award 1991, 97, Scholar award 1994, hon. award 2004), N.J. Assn. of Dirs. of Health, Phys. Edn. and Recreation (pres. 1976-78), N.J. Assn. for Health, Phys. Edn., Recreation and Dance (pres. 1979-80, Honor fellow award 1983, Disting. Leadership award 1982), Coll. and Univ. Phys. Edn. Coun. (chmn. 1985-88), Am. Alliance for Health Physical Edn., Recreation and Dance (honor award, 2006). Avocations: fishing, water sports, golf. Home: 1655 East Dr Point Pleasant NJ 08742-5117 Office: Rutgers U Dept Exercise Sci/Sport Stu New Brunswick NJ 08903 Office Phone: 732-932-8673. Business E-Mail: njd@rci.rutgers.edu.

DOUGHERTY, PETER JOSEPH, publisher; b. Phila., Feb. 25, 1949; s. Joseph Aloysius and Vera (Grohowski) D.; m. Elizabeth Rogers Hock, May 13, 1983; 1 child, Colman Rogers. AB, LaSalle Coll., 1971. Sales rep. Harcourt Brace Jovanovich, Balt., 1972-79, editor NYC, 1979-82, McGraw-Hill, NYC, 1982-83, W.H. Freeman, NYC, 1983-84; sr. editor St. Martin's Press, NYC, 1984-85; editorial dir. Basil Blackwell Inc., NYC, 1985; sr. econ. editor to group publ. social sci. Princeton Press, Princeton, NJ, 1992—2005, dir., 2005—. Author: Who's Afraid of Adam Smith, 2002; contbr. articles to profl. journals. Mem.: Am. Assn. Univ. Presses, Am. Econ. Assn. Democrat. Roman Catholic. Office: Princeton Press 41 William St Princeton NJ 08540-5237 Office Phone: 609-258-6778. Office Fax: 609-258-6305. Business E-Mail: peter_dougherty@pupress.princeton.edu.

DOUGHERTY, RICHARD HAMLEN, management and healthcare consultant; b. Boston, Dec. 15, 1952; s. John Bruce and Jean (MacDill) D.; m. Charlotte Louise Perry, Sept. 6, 1975; children: Cyra Perry, Alexa Starr. BA with honors, Colgate U., 1974; M in Social Services Admin., U. Chgo., 1977; PhD, Boston U., 1990. Counselor Phila. Child Guidance Clinic, 1974-75; clin. coord. Communities for People, Inc., Boston, 1977-79; evaluation specialist Mass. Dept. Pub. Welfare, Boston, 1979-80, rate liaison, 1980; program mgr. Mass. Dept. Social Services, Boston, 1980-82; CFO Nat. Mentor, Inc., Boston, 1982-85; sr. mgmt. cons. Seidman & Seidman, Boston, 1985-87; CEO DMA Health Strategies, Lexington, Mass., 1987—. Cons. health systems change; bd. dirs. Mass. Council Human Service Orgns., Boston, 1982-85. Ct. receiver Coastal Cmty. Counseling Ctr., Braintree, Mass., 1987-91; asst. treas. Cmty. Music Ctr. Boston, 1985-91, treas., 1991-95, pres., 1995-99, bd. dirs., 1995-2003; bd. dirs. Hole in the Sock Prodns., 1988-90; allocations com. United Way Massachusetts Bay, 1989-91, chmn. allocations coord. com., 1992-94; mem. Lexington Human Svcs. Com., 1989-91, Childrens Outcomes Roundtable, CMHS 2001—, Children in Managed Care Advisory Com., Ctr. for Healthcare Strategies, 2000—, Deacon and Sr. Deacon, Hancock United Ch. of Christ, congl. 1997-2000, treas. 2002—; treas. VanGo Prodns., Inc., 2001—; co-chmn. Lexington Health Benefits Adv. Com., 2005; bd. dirs. Consumers for Health Care Choices, 2005—. Mem. Acad. Health, Am. Coll. Mental Health Adminstrn. (bd. dirs. 2002-05, treas. 2003-05), Boston Athenaeum Avocations: skiing, fishing, guitar. Office: DMA Health Strategies 9 Meriam St Ste 4 Lexington MA 02420-5312 Office Phone: 781-869-6990. E-mail: rhdphd@gmail.com.

DOUGHERTY, RICHARD MARTIN, library and information science professor; b. East Chicago, Ind., Jan. 17, 1935; s. Floyd C. and Harriet E. (Martin) D.; m. Ann Prescott, Mar. 24, 1974; children— Kathryn E., Emily E.; children by previous marriage— Jill Ann, Jacquelyn A., Douglas M. BS, Purdue U., 1959, LHD honoris causa, 1991; M.L.S., Rutgers U., 1961, PhD, 1963; LHD honoris causa, U. Stellenbosch, South Africa, 1995. Head acquisitions dept. Univ. Library, U. N.C., Chapel Hill, 1963-66; assoc. dir. libraries U. Colo., Boulder, 1966-70; prof. library sci. Syracuse U., NY, 1970-72; univ. librarian U. Calif-Berkeley, 1972-78; dir. univ. library U. Mich., Ann Arbor, 1978-88, acting dean. Sch. Library Sci., 1984-85, prof. sch. info., 1978-98, prof. emeritus, 1999—; pres. Dougherty & Assocs., 1994—. Founder, pres. Mountainside Pub. Corp., 1974—; co-host live teleconferences Coll. DuPage. Author: Scientific Management of Library Organizations, 2d edit., 1982; co-author: Preferred Futures for Libraries II, 1993; editor Coll. and Research Libraries jour., 1969-74, Jour. Acad. Librarianship, 1975-94, Library Issues, 1981—. Trustee Ann Arbor Dist. Libr., 1995—2002, pres. bd. trustees, 1998—2000. Recipient Esther Piercy award, 1968, Disting. Alumnus award Rutgers U., 1980, Acad. Librarian Yr., Assn. Coll. and Research Libraries, 1983, ALA Hugh C. Atkinson Meml. award, 1988, Blackwell Scholarship award, 1992, Joseph Lippincott medal, 1997; fellow Council on Library Resources. Mem. ALA (coun. 1969-76, 89-92, exec. bd. 1972-76, 89-92, endowment trustee 1986-89, pres. 1990-91), Assn. Rsch. Librs. (bd. dirs. 1977-80), Rsch. Librs. Group, Inc. (exec. com. 1984-88, chmn. bd. govs. 1986-87), Soc. Scholarly Pub. (bd. dirs. 1990-92, exec. com. 1991-92), Internat. Fedn. Libr. Assns. (round table of editors of library jours. 1985-87, standing com. univ. libr. sect. 1981-87). Home: 6 Northwick Ct Ann Arbor MI 48105-1408 Office: Dougherty & Assoc PO Box 8330 Ann Arbor MI 48107-8330 Office Phone: 734-665-4547. E-mail: rmdoughe@umich.edu.

DOUGHERTY BUCHHOLZ, KAREN, communications executive; m. Carl Buchholz; 2 children. BS, Dickinson Coll., 1988; MS, U. Pa., 1997. Mem. staff U.S. Sen. John Heinz, Gubernatorial candidate Barbara Hafer, 1990; supr. devel. Pyramid Club, Phila., 1991—93; sales exec. Comcast-Spectacor, 1993—97; pres. Phila. Host com. Rep. Nat. Convention, 1997—2000; v.p. corp. comms. Comcast Corp., Phila., 2000—03, v.p. adminstrn., 2003—. Bd. govs. Pyramid Club; deans coun. U. Pa. Sch. Arts and Scis.; co-chair Alexis de Tocqueville Soc. Campaign, United Way Southeastern Pa.; bd. trustees Abington Meml. Hosp. Found., Penn. Ballet, Crohn's & Colitis Found.; adv. bd. PNC Advisors Women's Fin. Svcs. Network; bd. dirs. People's Emergency Ctr. Named PENJERDEL Coun. Citizen of Yr.; recipient Women of Distinction, Phila. Bus. Jour., 2000, Headliner award, Greater Phila. Hotel Assn., 2000, Cradle of Liberty Couns. Summit award, Boy Scouts of Am., 2000, Take the Lead award, Girl Scouts U.S.A., Comcast Newsmaker of Year award. Mem.: Forum of Exec. Women, Nat. Assn. Women Bus. Owners (hon.). Office: Comcast 1500 Market St Philadelphia PA 19102

DOUGHTEN, MARY KATHERINE (MOLLY), retired secondary school educator; b. Belvidere, Ill., Apr. 26, 1923; d. Edwin Albert and Theora Teresa (Tefft) Loop; m. Philip Tedford Doughten, Oct. 15, 1947; children: Deborah Doughten Hellriegel, Susan Doughten Myers, Ann Doughten Fickenscher, Philip Tedford Jr., David, Sarah Doughten Wiggins. BA, DePauw U., 1945; MS, Western Res. U., 1947. Social worker Children's Svcs., Cleve., 1947, San Antonio, 1948-49; tchr. English Indian Valley High Schs., Gradenhutten, Ohio, 1962-66; tchr. English and sociology New Philadelphia (Ohio) High Sch., 1966-86; ret., 1986. Mem. Tuscarawas County Juvenile Judges Citizen's Rev. Bd., 1980—2003, United Way, 1960—67, ARC, PTA, 1955—58, coun. pres., 1960—62, mental health chmn. state bd., 1963—65, libr. chmn., 1966—68; mem. Hospice, 1987—; founding com. Kent State U. Tuscarawas campus, 1961—62; leader Girl Scouts, 1959—68; vol. Ohio Reads, 2000—06; vol. Reach for Recovery, Tell a Friend Am. Cancer Soc., 2002—; mem. Tuscarawas Arts Coun.; vol. Tuscarawas County Job and Family Svcs., 2003—; mem. Tuscarawas Philharm. League, Dem. Women, 1986—; co-pres. Presbyn. Women, 2007—; bd. dir. Tuscarawas Valley Guidance Ctr., 1950—62, Cmty Mental Health Care, Inc., 1974—82, 1984—92, pres., 1979—81; bd. dir. Alcohol, Drug and Mental Health Svcs. bd., Tuscarawas-Carroll County, 1992—2001, v.p., 1996—98; bd. mem. State CC, 1965—68; founder, bd. dir. Ohio Cmty. Mental Health Svcs., Columbus, Ohio, 1970—80; bd. dir. Mobile Meals, 1992—; bd. dirs. Kent-Tuscourty U. Found., 1996—, pres., 1998—2000, sec., 2006—. Named WJER Woman of the Yr., 2002, Ret. Tchr. of Yr., Quaker Found., 2005; recipient Mental Health award, Cmty. and Profl. Svcs., 1978; Martha Holden Jennings scholar, 1975—76. Mem. AAUW (sec. 1962, v.p. 1996-98), New Phila. Edn. Assn., Friends of Libr., Chestnut Soc. (bd. dirs. 1987-89, 01—), Tuscarawas County Med. Aux. (pres. 1959-60, 86-87, state bd. 1960-64), Union Hosp. Aux. (bd. dirs. 1986-98, editor 1986-98), DAR, Tuscarawas County Ret. Tchrs. Assn. (bd. dirs. 1999—), Coll. Club (scholarship chair 1989-91, 99-01), Union Country Club, Atwood Yacht Club, Lady Elks, Mortar Bd., Phi Beta Kappa, Alpha Chi Omega, Theta Sigma Phi. Democrat. Presbyterian. Avocations: travel, golf, sailing, reading, photography. Home: 204 Gooding Ave NW New Philadelphia OH 44663-1727 Personal E-mail: philmoll@tusco.net.

DOUGHTY, A. GLENN, minister; b. Somers Point, NJ, Aug. 30, 1942; s. Alfred and Irene Dorothy (Colhouer) D.; m. Carole True, June 17, 1967; children: Matthew Glenn, Lynn Carole. BS in Bible Studies, Phila. Coll. of Bible, 1965; MDiv, Faith Theol. Sem., 1968. Ordained to ministry Fellowship Fundamental Bible Chs., 1970. Pastor Community Bible Ch., Barrington, NJ, 1968-70, The Bible Ch. of Westville, NJ, 1970—. Chmn. Bible Protestant Ch. Ext., 1970-73; sec. Fellowship of Fundamental Bible Chs., 1976-95, 2001—04, mem. ministerial qualifications com., 1980-95, Fundamental Bible Inst., 2001. Chmn. Cmty. Dispute Resolution Com., Westville, 1986—. Named Outstanding Vol. of Yr., Gloucester Co., 2003. Mem. Am. Coun. Christian Chs. (mem. exec. com. 1990—), Fellowship of Fundamental Bible Chs. (trustee 1985-95, pres. trustees 1985-91, chmn. trustees 1993-95, sec. Fundamental Bible Missions 1996-98, pres. 1998—2002). Home and Office: 142 Hess Ave Woodbury NJ 08096 Office Phone: 856-456-3791. Personal E-mail: gcdoughty@prodigy.net.

DOUGHTY, GEORGE FRANKLIN, airport administrator; b. Wheeling, W.Va., Mar. 11, 1946; s. Ernest Heyward and Elizabeth Gertrude (Dei) D.; m. Jennifer L. Tyma; children: Susan Elizabeth, Jennifer Anne, Patrick George, Shannon Marie. BS in Aerospace Engring., W.Va. U., 1968. Asst. mgr. Cedar Rapids Mcpl. Airport, Iowa, 1975-78; dep. dir. Balt.-Washington Internat. Airport State of Md., 1978-80; dir. port control City of Cleve., Ohio, 1980-84; dir. aviation Stapleton Internat. Airport City and County of Denver, 1981-92; exec. dir. Lehigh-Northampton Airport Authority, Allentown, Pa., 1992—. Recipient Laurels award Aviation Week and Space Tech., 1988. Mem. Am. Assn. Airport Execs. (dir. 1980), Airports Coun. Internat. N.Am. (chmn. govtl. affairs com. 1985-86, bd. dirs. 1986-89, 1st vice chmn. 1992, chmn. 1993). Home: 2131 Stonewall Dr Macungie PA 18062-9064 Office: Lehigh Valley Intl Airport 3311 Airport Rd Ste 4 Allentown PA 18109-3040 Home Phone: 610-366-1045; Office Phone: 610-266-6001. E-mail: george@lnaa.com.

DOUGHTY, MARK ANTHONY, lawyer; b. Pasadena, Calif., Aug. 18, 1951; s. Lawrence Richard and Bertha Lou D.; children: Matthew James, Luke Anthony. BA in Bus. Law, Calif. State U., Chico, 1976; JD, U. Pacific, Sacramento, Calif., 1979. Bar: Calif. 1979, U.S. Dist. Ct. (ea. dist.) Calif. 1979; lic. real estate broker, cert. comml. investment mem, real estate developer. Law clk. Calif. Ct. Appeals (5th cir.), Fresno, Calif., 1979-80; assoc. Ashby and Guth, Yuba City, Calif., 1980-82; ptnr. Ashby, Guth and Doughty, Yuba City, 1982-86, Ashby & Doughty, Yuba City, 1986-92; prin. Law Offices of Mark A. Doughty, Yuba City, 1992—. Pres. Russian Radio Bible Inst. Mem. Consumer Attys. of Calif. (bd. govs. 19th dist.), Fellowship of Christian Businessmen, Yuba Sutter Bar Assn. (pres. 2001), Consumer Attys. Gold Country (pres. 1999—). Republican. Avocations: fathering, golf, private pilot, hunting, reading. Office: Law Offices of Mark A Doughty PO Box 3420 1528 Poole Blvd Ste A Yuba City CA 95992-3420 Home: 1528 Poole Blvd Ste A Yuba City CA 95993 Fax: 530-674-1180. E-mail: mark@golaw.com.

DOUGHTY, NIKEDRA, academic administrator; b. Balt., May 17, 1980; d. Glenn and Janice Doughty. BA in Comms., U. Mo., St. Louis, 2002; MA in Internat. Rels., Webster U., St. Louis, 2006. Spl. events coord. Churchill Sch., St. Louis, 2003—04; student advisor, devel. asst. U. Mo., St. Louis, 2004—05; dir. devel. and edn., cons. Stetin Ctr., St. Louis, 2005—06; asst. dir. devel., vol. coord. City Acad., St. Louis, 2005—07, dir. admissions, placement and cmty. rels., 2007—; regional campaign dir. Dem. Party of Ga., Atlanta, 2002—03. Leadership instr. Delta Program, St. Louis, 2005—07; class instr. Girls, Inc., St. Louis, 2006; mem. scholarship awards com. Carpenters Dist. Coun. St. Louis, 2005; fundraiser Ptnr. with Youth Campaign, YMCA, St. Louis, 1998—2007; cons., fundraiser Dem. Party, St. Louis, 2002—07. Recipient Dedication and Svc. award, YMCA Greater St. Louis, 1998, 2002. Mem.: ACLU (chmn. devel. com., membership cultivation com., bill of rights com.), Assn. Fundraising Profls. (assoc. fellowship 2006). Avocations: travel, political writing. Office: City Academy 4175 North Kingshighway Saint Louis MO 63115 Office Phone: 314-382-0085. Business E-Mail: ndoughty@cityacademyschool.org.

DOUGHTY-JENKINS, BONNIE-MARIE, middle school educator; b. New Britain, Conn., Mar. 12, 1967; d. Dennis John and Patricia Anne Doughty; m. John C. Jenkins, July 4, 2001. BS in Spl. Edn. and Elem. Edn., St. Joseph Coll., 1989, MA in Spl. Edn., 1995; EdD in Ednl. Leadership, Ctrl. Conn. State U., 2005. Tchr. 5th - 8th grades spl. edn. Plymouth Bd. Edn., Terryville, Conn., 1990—99, tchr. 8th grade sci., 1999—. Mem. sch. bd. St. Matthew Sch., Forestville, Conn., 2001—; adminstrv. intern Harry S. Fisher Mid. Sch., Terryville, 2003—04. Mem., scholar com. Harry S. Fisher Mid. Sch. PTA, Terryville, 1990—; mem. Nutmet Artists, Plymouth, 2004—; mem. exec. bd. dirs. Conn. Jr. Women, Inc., 1992—99; mem., chmn. Intersvc. Club Coun., Bristol, 1990—99. Named Jr. Woman of Yr., 1992; named to Subaru Tchr. Hall Fame, 2003; recipient Heart Saver award, Am. Heart Assn., 2003, 2005, Spirit of Am. award, Conn. PTA, 2005; grantee, Shopa Found., 2000, Thomaston Savs. Bank, Conn., 2001, Main St. Cmty. Found., Bristol, 2002. Mem.: ASCD, Plymouth Sch. to Career Action Com., Am. Edn. Rsch. Orgn. Roman Catholic. Avocations: travel, crafts, cooking. Office: Harry S Fisher Mid Sch 79 N Main St Terryville CT 06786

DOUGLAS, ASHANTI SHEQUOIYA See ASHANTI

DOUGLAS, BARRY K., plastic surgeon; b. NYC, June 15, 1954; s. Leonard S. and Elaine K. Douglas; m. K. K. Koenigsberg, Mar. 27, 1983; children: Marc children: Lauren, Robert. BA, Trinity Coll., Conn., 1976; MD, Wake Forest U., 1980. Diplomate Am. Bd. Plastic Surgery. Residency in gen. surgery and plastic surgery Mt. Sinai Hosp., NYC, 1980—87; fellowship in pediat. plastic surgery Children's Hosp. Akron, 1987; attending physician plastic surgery L.I. Plastic Surg. Group, Garden City, 1991—. Covers for art jours. and programs. Fellow, MEDCOM, 1987. Fellow: Am. Acad. Pediats., Am. Coll. Surgeons; mem.: N.Y. State Med. Soc., Am. Cleft Palate Assn., Am. Soc. Plastic Surgeons, Northeastern Soc. Plastic Surgeons, NY Regional Soc. Plastic Surgeons, Nassau Surg., Nassau County MAD Soc., Phi Beta Kappa. Avocation: concert pianist. Office: LI Plastic Surg Group 999 Franklin Ave Garden City NY 11530 Office Phone: 516-742-3404. E-mail: bdouglas@lipsg.com.

DOUGLAS, BRUCE LEE, oral and maxillofacial surgeon, occupational and geriatric health educator, consultant; b. NYC, July 14, 1925; s. William and Carrie (Basescu) D.; m. Janet Ramsden; children: Clifford, Steven, Jennifer, Sarah, Sandra. AB, Princeton U., 1947; DDS, NYU, 1948; postgrad. in oral surgery, Columbia U., 1949-51, MA in Edn, 1955, diploma in higher edn, 1957; MPH, U. Calif., Berkeley, 1962. Diplomate Am. Bd. Oral and Maxillofacial Surgery. Prof. oral medicine and community dentistry Coll. Dentistry U. Ill., 1962-72, prof. preventive medicine Coll. Medicine, 1962-72; prof. health adminstrn. Sch. Pub. Health, 1972-98; prof. dental and oral surgery Rush Med. Coll., 1970-76; clin. prof. environ. and occupl. medicine Sch. Pub. Health, U. Ill. at Chgo., 1998—, health policy rsch., 2001—. Chief dentistry and oral surgery Rush-Presbyn.-St. Luke's Med. Ctr., Chgo., 1968-75; chief divsn. dental health, Ill. Dept. Pub. Health, 1976-78; chief sect. dentistry and oral surgery Lincoln Park Hosp. Chgo. (formerly Grant Hosp.), 1980-90, attending oral and maxillofacial surgeon, 1967—; attending oral and maxillofacial surgeon Vista Med. Ctr. Waukegan, Ill., 2005—; Fulbright prof. oral surgery and anesthesiology Okayama (Japan) U. and Tokyo Med.-Dental U., 1959-61; WHO cons. to U. Antioquia, Colombia, Nat. U. and U. Zulia, Venezuela, 1964-69, Mahidol U., Bangkok, Thailand, 1973, Nat. Health Svc., Gt. Britain, 1977. Mem. Ill. Ho. of Reps., 11th Dist., 1971-72, 12th Dist., 1973-74; chmn. Ill. Coalition Against Tobacco, 1991-93; chief med. advisor, Sedgwick Claims Mgmt. Svcs., 1998-2002; sr. scholar in residence Wash. Bus. Group on Health, 2002-04. With USN, 1951—53, Japan, Korea, with USNR, 1943—53, lt. dental corps. USN, 1951—53. Fellow Chgo. Inst. Medicine (bd. dirs. 1970-80), Am. Dental Soc. Anesthesiology (past pres.); mem. Am. Assn. Hosp. Dentists (past pres., editor), Am. Assn. Oral and Maxillofacial Surgeons (assoc. editor Jour. Oral Surgery), Fulbright Assn. (pres. Chgo. chpt. 1990-92). Address: 2401 Duffy Ln Riverwoods IL 60015 Personal E-mail: brucedouglas@comcast.net. *A health professional career can be the portal through which an educated person can pass to a fuller and richer life. My health professional, education, and public health degrees have made it possible for me to broaden my involvement in the affairs of my community, my nation, my world, the world of business, and to serve individuals in need as well.*

DOUGLAS, CHARLES W., lawyer; b. Chgo., Apr. 1, 1948; BA, Northwestern U., 1970; JD, Harvard U., 1974. Bar: Ill. 1974, U.S. Dist. Ct. (no. dist.) Ill. 1974, U.S. Dist. Ct. (ea. dist.) Wis. 1997, U.S. Ct. Appeals (6th cir.) 1978, U.S. Ct. Appeals (9th cir.) 1981, U.S. Ct. Appeals (2nd cir.) 1983, U.S. Ct. Appeals (7th cir.) 1984, U.S. Ct. Appeals (11th cir.) 1999. Ptnr. Sidley Austin Brown & Wood LLP, Chgo., 1980—, exec. com., 1989—, mgmt. com. (chmn., 1999-), 1993—, and mng. ptnr. Chgo. office. Mem.: Phi Beta Kappa. Office: Sidley Austin Brown & Wood LLP Bank 1 Plz 10 S Dearborn St Chicago IL 60603 Office Phone: 312-853-7706. Office Fax: 312-853-7036. Business E-Mail: cdouglas@sidley.com.

DOUGLAS, CINDY HOLLOWAY, financial consultant; b. Queens, NY, Aug. 8, 1960; d. Richard Stephen and Beverly Bunny (Harris) Tannenbaum; m. David Milton Holloway (div. Mar. 1986); 1 child, Benjamin Jerome; m. Michael William Douglas, Mar. 21, 1998. BA, Calif. State U., Fullerton, 1981. Lic. real estate broker. Waitress Bob's Big Boy, San Bernardino, Calif., 1984-85; receptionist RNG Mortgage Co., San Bernardino, 1985; loan processor Quality Mortgage Co., Colton, Calif., 1985-88, loan officer, 1988-91, RNG Mortgage, 1991-92; v.p., br. mgr. Mountain West Fin., 1992-97; prodn. and mktg. mgr. South Pacific Fin., 1997-97; real estate loan mgr. Arrowhead Credit Union, 1998-2000; cons. mortgage banking, brokerages and credit unions, 2000—. Mem. San Bernardino Bd. Realtors (spl. events com. 1988—, comm. com. 1990—), Nat. Trust for Hist. Preservation, San Bernardino Execs. Assn., Assn. Profl. Mortgage Women (bd. dirs. 1989-90, v.p. 1992-93, Affiliate of Yr. award 1990), San

Bernardino Execs. Group (bd. dirs. 1994—). Home: PO Box 3366 Crestline CA 92325-3366 Address: PO Box 336C Crestline CA 92325-3366 Office Phone: 951-312-7112. Business E-Mail: cindyd@cindydouglas.com.

DOUGLAS, DAISY HOWARD, retired elementary school educator, writer, consultant; b. Morgan City, La., Aug. 12, 1939; d. Linzy John and Julia (Royal) Howard; m. James Allen Douglas, Oct. 26, 1963; 1 child, Jewel. BS Elem. Edn., Grambling State U., La., 1962; MA Early Childhood Edn., Va. Commonwealth U., Richmond, 1978; cert. endorsement prin. elem. and mid. sch., Va. Commonwealth U., 1993. Cert. writer Inst. Children's Lit. Hartford, 1989. Tchr. 3d grade Sumpter Williams Elem. Sch., Morgan City, 1962—67; tchr. 5th grade Callao Elem. Sch., Va., 1967—72; tchr. 4th grade Eugene Meyer Elem. Sch., Washington, 1972—76; tchr. kindergarten Cople Elem. Sch., Hague, Va., 1976—85, tchr. 2d grade, 1985—87; tchr. 4th grade Fairfield Elem. Sch., Richmond, 1987—97; ret., 1997. Cons. African culture Richmond City Pub. Schs., 1989—; founder, dir., storyteller Westmoreland County Storytellers, Sandy Point, Va., 1998—; mem. adv. bd. Westmoreland Sch. Sys., Montross, Va., 2004—; bd. dirs. Va. Storytelling Alliance, Richmond. Author: History of St. Paul's Catholic Church, 1977, Jad and Old Annanias, 1997 (Club award, 1998), Daisy's Bayou Tales, 2000 (Club award, 2001), The Descendants of the First Mitchell Wilson of Westmoreland County, Va. 1824-2002, 2002, Africa - My Secret Dream, 2003 (Club award, 2003), China - My Historical Journey, 2003 (Club award, 2003), They Came From Virginia, 2004 (Club award, 2004), Daisy's Delightful Delicacies, 2005. Vol. deliver meals Meals On Wheels Assn., Heathsville, Va., 2000—; judge sci. fair Colonial Beach Sch. Sys., Va., 2000—; amb. Va. State Fair, Richmond, 1998—; leader, life mem. Girl Scouts U.S.; reporter Phi Delta Kappa, 1990—2004, Alpha Kappa Alpha, 1989—97. Named Outstanding Tchr. Am., Fuller and Dees, 1975, Tchr. of Yr., Fairfield Elem. Sch., 1994; recipient Tchr. Excellence award, Va. Edn. Assn., 1989, Svc. award, Alpha Kappa Alpha, 1997, Phi Delta Kappa, 2004. Mem.: NEA, NAACP (life Golden Heritage award). Avocations: reading, travel, cooking, gardening. Home: 447 Wilson Dr PO Box 37 Sandy Point VA 22577

DOUGLAS, DIANE MIRIAM, museum director; b. Harrisburg, Pa., Mar. 25, 1957; d. David C. and Anna (Barron) D.; m. Steve I. Perlmutter, Jan. 23, 1983; 1 child, David Simon. BA, Brown U., 1979; MA, U. Del., 1982. Oral history editor Former Members of Congress, Washington, 1979-80; assoc. curator exhibitions John Michael Kohler Arts Ctr., Sheboygan, Wis., 1982-83; dir. arts ctr. Lill Street Gallery, Chgo., 1984-88; exec. dir. David Adler Cultural Ctr., Libertyville, Ill., 1988-91; dir. Bellevue (Wash.) Art Mus., 1992—. Program chair, exec. bd. nat. Coun. for Edn. in Ceramic Arts, Bandon, Oreg., 1990-93; nat. adv. bd. Friends of Fiber Art, 1992; artists adv. com. Pilchuck Glass Sch., 1993—; mem. bd. dirs. Archie Bray Found., Helena, Mont., 1995—.

DOUGLAS, FRANK FAIR, architect, graphic designer; b. Mansfield, La., Oct. 27, 1945; s. Edward Osler and Minnie Merle (Flanders) D.; m. Judith Catherine Wainwright, Sept. 6, 1969; 1 child, Samuel Wainwright. Student, NYU; BArch, La. State U., 1968. Registered architect. Designer Eggers & Higgins, NYC, 1968-69, Neuhaus & Taylor, Houston, 1969-70, dir. graphics, 1970-72, assoc., 1972-75, sr. assoc., 1975-77; v.p. 3D/Internat., Houston, 1977-81, sr. v.p., 1981-86, exec. v.p., 1986-87; chmn., pres. Douglas/Gallagher, Houston, Washington, Nashville, 1987—. Exhibit design and environ. prgaphic projects include Miss. Pavilion/Expoo '84, Singapore Pavilion/Expo '86, Conoco Retail Facilities Studies, 1987, Hotel Cheyenne and Santa Fe Disneyland Park, 1992, Environ. Graphics Stds. Entergy, Inc., 1994, Rangers Ballpark, 1994, N.Y. Yankees Spring Home Facility, 1996, Philippine Centennial Internat. Environ. Graphic, Anaheim Stadium for Disney Sports, Urban Graphics Syss. for cities of Mobile, Ala., San Antonio, San Juan, P.R., Salt Lake City, Galveston, Tex.; image cons. GM at Renaissance Ctr., Detroit, Mus. of Jewish Heritage, N.Y., 1997; Janet Annenberg Hooker Hall of Fame, Smithsonian, Independance Hall Visitors Ctr., Phila., Triple A Stadium for Oklahoma City Redhawks, Memphis Redbirds. Bd. dirs. Tex. Film Commn., Austin, 1982—; multi-media panelist Cultural Arts Coun. Houston, 1982-84; co-chair visual com. Houston Econ. Summit Host Com., 1990. Recipient awards for exhbns., 1985, 86, 88. Fellow AIA (bd. dirs. 1997—, exec. com. Houston chpt. 1989-90, pres. 1992, honor award 1985), Tex. Soc. Architects (v.p. 1994-96); mem. Soc. Environ. Graphic Designers (bd. dirs. 1971-72, Design award 1974), Rice Design Alliance (pres., bd. dirs. 1981-88, 91—), Soc. Mktg. Profl. Svcs. (bd. dirs. Houston chpt. 1982-92, Design award 1980O, Ind. Design Soc. Am., Houston City Club, Houston Club. Republican. Presbyterian. Home: 3822 Olympia Dr Houston TX 77019-3032 Office: Douglas Gallagher 3040 Post Oak Blvd Ste 510 Houston TX 77056-6521

DOUGLAS, GEORGE HALSEY, language educator, writer; b. East Orange, NJ, Jan. 9, 1934; s. Halsey M. and Harriet Elizabeth (Goldbach) D.; m. Rosalind Braun, June 19, 1961; 1 son, Philip. AB with honors in Philosophy, Lafayette Coll., 1956; MA, Columbia U., 1966; PhD, U. Ill., 1968. Tech. editor Bell Tel. Labs., Whippany, NJ, 1958—59; editor Agrl. Exptl. Sta. U. Ill., Urbana, 1961—66; instr. dept. English Agrl. Expt. Sta., U. Ill., Urbana, 1966—68, asst. prof. English, 1968—77, assoc. prof. English, 1977—88, prof. English, 1989—. Author: H.L. Mencken Critic of American Life, 1978, The Teaching of Business Communication, 1978, Rail City: Chicago and Its Railroads, 1981, Edmund Wilson's America, 1983, Women of the Twenties, 1986, The Early Days of Radio Broadcasting, 1987, The Smart Magazines, 1991, All Aboard: The Railroad in American Life, 1992, Education Without Impact: How Our Universities Fail the Young, 1992, Skyscraper: A Social History of the Tall Building in America, 1996, Postwar America, 1998, The Golden Age of the Newspaper, 1999; editor numerous books; contbr. articles to profl. jours., reference books, television documentaries. Mem. MLA, Am. Studies Assn., Am. Bus. Comm. Assn. (editor jour. bus. comm. 1968-80). Home: 809 Mendota Dr Champaign IL 61820-7566 Personal E-mail: georgehdouglas@earthlink.net.

DOUGLAS, J. ALEXANDER M. (SANDY), beverage company executive; BA, U. Va., 1983. Dist. sales mgr. Coca-Cola Fountain, 1988—94; v.p. sales mktg. group Coca-Cola Enterprises, 1994—2000; exec. v.p., COO Coca-Cola N. Am. divsn., pres., 2000—03, 2006—; sr. v.p., chief customer officer The Coca-Cola Co., 2003—06. Bd. dirs. The Coca-Cola Co., 2004—, Radiant Systems, Transora. Bd. dirs. Atlanta YMCA; mem. Anglican studies advisory bd. Candler Sch. Emory U. Office: The Coca Cola Co One Coca Cola Plaza Atlanta GA 30313*

DOUGLAS, JAMES, construction engineering educator; b. Uvalde, Tex., Oct. 1, 1914; s. Raymond C. and Mae (Savage) D.; m. Sarah Maria Bisset, July 22, 1941; children— Sarah A., Susan E., Bonnie B., James A. BS, US Naval Acad., 1938; BCE, Rensselaer Poly. Inst., 1942; MCE, 1943; PhD, Stanford U., Calif., 1963. Registered profl. engr., DC, Calif. Commd. ensign USN, 1938, advanced through grades to capt., 1956, in charge constrn. Cubi Point Naval Air Sta. Philippines, 1951-54, dir. Seabee div., 1954-58, in charge constrn. Antarctic bases Internat. Geophys. Yr., 1956-58; prof. constrn. engrng. Stanford, 1963—. Cons. constrn. engrng. Stanford Rsch. Inst., various corps., US and fgn. govts., 1963—; chmn. com. constrn. mgmt. Transp. Rsch. Bd., NRC, 1969-76 Author: Construction Equipment Policy, 1975, also numerous tech. articles. Active Boy Scouts Am., 1946—. Served with Armed Forces, World War II. Decorated Bronze Star; recipient Thomas Fitch Rowland prize ASCE, 1969, Constrn. Mgmt. award, 1975 Fellow ASCE (chmn. constrn. equipment com. 1960-65); mem. Tau Beta Pi, Sigma Xi, Chi Epsilon, Chi Phi. Republican. Episcopalian. Home and Office: 100 Thorndale Dr Apt 272 San Rafael CA 94903-4567 Office Phone: 415-492-2572. Personal E-mail: jdouglas38@juno.com. *In retrospect I realize that the most important things in life are your friends and your relations with other people. Regardless of wealth or status, life cannot be wholly satisfactory without agreeable human relations, and these are not dependent on race, creed, color, age or sex but on the quality of the individuals.*

DOUGLAS, JAMES (BUSTER), boxer; b. Columbus, Ohio; s. Billy and Lula Douglas; m. Bertha M. Douglas; children: Lamar, Cardaé, Arthur. Profl. boxer 1981—; defeated Mike Tyson, Feb. 1990 to become undisputed heavyweight champion. E-mail: mommiedog@cham-cor.com.

DOUGLAS, JAMES MATTHEW, law educator, dean; BA in Math., Tex. So. U., 1966, JD, 1970; MS Law, Stanford U., 1971. Bar: Tex. 1970. Programmer analyst Singer Gen. Precision Co., Houston, 1966-70, 71-72; asst. prof. law Tex. So. U., Houston, 1972—74, dean, prof. law, 1981-95, provost, v.p. acad. affairs, 1995, pres., 1995—99, prof., 1995—2005, disting. prof., 1999—; asst. prof. Cleve.-Marshall Coll. Law, Cleve. State U., 1974—75, asst. prof., asst. dean student affairs, 1974-75; assoc. prof., assoc. dean Coll. Law Syracuse U., NY, 1975-80; prof. Northeastern U. Sch. Law, Boston, 1980-81; dean, prof. coll. law Fla. A&M U., Orlando, 2005—07; disting. prof. law Tex. So. U., 2007—. Contbr. articles to profl. jours. Mem. steering com. Houston Campaign Homeless, 1988—89; bd. dirs. Sickle Cell Found. Tex., 1988—94, pres., 1990—91; bd. dirs. Boy Scouts Am., 1993—, Greater Houston Partnership, 1996—99. Mem.: Nat. Bar Assn., Houston Bar Assn. (chair law practice mgmt. sect. 1995—), Tex. Supreme Ct. Hist. Soc. (trustee 1990—), State Bar Tex., ABA, Houston C. of C. Home: 5318 Calhoun Rd Houston TX 77021-1714 Office: Tex So U 3100 Cleburne St Houston TX 77004-4501 Office Phone: 713-313-7352. Business E-Mail: jdouglas@tmslaw.tsu.edu.

DOUGLAS, JAMES MCCRYSTAL, lawyer; b. Wantagh, NY, 1956; Student, Bucknell U.; BA, SUNY, Binghamton, 1978; JD cum laude, Fordham U., 1981. Bar: N.Y. 1982. Ptnr. Skadden, Arps, Slate, Meagher & Flom LLP, NYC, head banking & instl. investing group. Mem. Fordham Law Rev., 1980-81. Office: Skadden Arps Slate Meagher & Flom LLP 4 Times Sq New York NY 10036-6595 Office Phone: 212-735-2868. Business E-Mail: jdouglas@skadden.com.

DOUGLAS, JANICE GREEN, physician, educator; b. Nashville, July 11, 1943; d. Louis D. and Electa Green. BA magna cum laude, Fish U., 1964; MD, Meharry Med. Coll., 1968. Intern Meharry Med. Coll., 1968-71; NIH tng. fellow in endocrinology, instr. internal medicine Vanderbilt U., Nashville, 1971-73; sr. staff fellow sect. on hormonal regulation NIH, 1973-76; asst. prof. medicine Case Western Res. U. Sch. Medicine, Cleve., 1976-81, assoc. prof. medicine, 1981-84, prof. medicine, 1984—; dir. hypertension renal ambulatory care svc. Univ. Hosps. Cleve., 1976-80; dir. divsn. endocrinology and hypertension dept. medicine Univ. Hosps. Cleve. and Case Western Res. U., 1988-93, vice chair acad. affairs dept. medicine, 1991-99, dir. divsn. hypertension dept. medicine, 1993—. Mem. numerous grant rev. coms.; lectr., presenter in field; atteding physician in medicine and endicrinology U. Hosps., 1987; vis. prof. SUNY, Kings County Hosp. and Health Sci. Ctr., Bklyn., 1987, Med. U. S.C., 1989, Harlem Hosp., N.Y.C., 1993, N.Y. Med. Coll., Valhalla, 1994. Mem. editl. rev. bd. Jour. Clin. Investigation, 1990—, Am. Jour. Physiology, Renal Fluid and Electrolytes, 1989-91; editl. bd. Hypertension, 1994—, Am. Soc. Clin. Investigation, 1990—, Ethnicity and Disease, 1990—, Circulation, 1993—; guest editor Jour. Clin. Investigation, U. Calif., San Diego, 1992—; assoc. editor Jour. Lab. and Clin. Medicine, 1986-90; reviewer numerous manuscripts and abstracts.; contbr. numerous articles, abstracts to profl. publs., chpts. to books. Fellow High Blood Pressure Coun., Am. Heart Assn., 1993—. Mem. Assn. Am. Physicians, Cleve. Med. Assn., Am. Soc. Hypertension, Kidney Found. Ohio, Women in Endocrinology, Inter-Am. Soc. Hypertension, Women in Nephrology, Assn. for Acad. Minority Physicians, Am. Physiology Soc., Endocrine Soc., Ctrl. Soc. for Clin. Rsch., Internat. Soc. Hypertension in Blacks, Inst. Medicine of NAS, Internat. Soc. Nephrology, Am. Soc. Nephrology, Am. Soc. Clin. Investigation, Am. Fedn. Clin. Rsch., Am. Heart Assn., Phi Beta Kappa, Alpha Omega Alpha (pres. Meharry chpt. 1968), Beta Kappa Chi.

DOUGLAS, JIM (JAMES HOLLEY), governor; b. Springfield, Mass., June 21, 1951; s. Robert James and Cora Elizabeth (Holley) D.; m. Dorothy Foster, May 24, 1975; children: Matthew James, Andrew Foster. AB, Middlebury Coll., 1972. Gen. mgr. Credit Bur. of Middlebury, Vt., 1972-76; exec. dir. United Way of Addison County, 1976-79; exec. asst. to Gov. of Vt., 1979-80; sec. of state State of Vt., Montpelier, 1981-93, treas., 1994—2002, gov., 2003—. Mem. Vt. Ho. of Reps., 1973-79, majority leader, 1975-77, 77-79 Mem. Nat. Assn. Secs. State (pres.). Lodges: Masons. Republican. Congregationalist. Office: Office of the Governor Pavilion 109 State St Montpelier VT 05609 Office Phone: 802-828-3333. Office Fax: 802-828-3339.*

DOUGLAS, JOHN LEWIS, lawyer; b. Atlanta, Sept. 23, 1950; s. Charles Lewis Jr. and Bettye Lee (Phelps) D.; m. Rebecca Ann Peterson, Aug. 16, 1974; children: Amber Lynne, Dianna Michelle, John Lewis Jr., Scott Foster, Charles Tillman, Alexander Peterson, Michael Lawrence, Jolanta Kuuzik, Tomas Kuuzik. BA in Econs., Davidson Coll., NC, 1972; JD, U. Ga., 1977. Bar: Ga. 1977. Assoc. Alston and Bird, Atlanta, 1977-83, ptnr., fin. inst. regulation, mergers, acquistions Atlanta and Washington, 1990—; gen. counsel FDIC, Washington, 1987-89. Mem. bd. dirs. Fin. Svcs. Vol. Corp., Providian Fin. Corp., 2003-05. Contbr. articles to profl. jours. Republican. Mem. Lds Ch. Office: Alston & Bird LLP 1 Atlantic Ctr Atlanta GA 30309-3400 Office Phone: 404-881-7880. Business E-Mail: john.douglas@alston.com.

DOUGLAS, JON DAVID **See OETJEN, DAVID**

DOUGLAS, KARIN NADJA, engineer; b. Berlin, Sept. 2, 1931; came to U.S., 1963; d. Fritz and Irma (Rutke) Kruse; m. Karl Vonmoos, May 21, 1955 (div. Dec. 1961); m. Robert P. Douglas, Dec. 13, 1969. AS in Legal Adminstrn. magna cum laude, Sacred Heart U., Fairfield, Conn., 1984. Apprentice in tech. drafting and design Hasler AG., Bern, Switzerland, 1961-63; elec. designer UOP Air Correction Divsn., Norwalk, Conn., 1968-83; engrng. cons. various engring. corps., Fairfield County, Conn., 1983-87; agy. compliance coord. ITT Flygt Corp., Trumbull, Conn., 1987—2005. Mem. univ. coll. coun. Sacred Heart U., 2000—. Sec. Friends of Boothe Park, Inc., mus. and rose garden, Stratford, Conn., 1985—; bd. dirs. Nat. Lympedema Network; Oakland, Calif., 1997—2002; creator Evelyn Conley scholarship for Sacred Heart U., 1988; also patient adv./activist, 1996—97; creator Dr. M. Palliser Endowment for Phys. Therapy for Sacred Heart U., 2001. Named Woman of Substance, Conn. Post, 1997; recipient D-Day award, Nat. Lymphedema Network, 1996, Disting. Alumni award, Sacred Heart U., 2002, Harold S. Geneen Cmty. Svc. award, ITT Industries, 2002. Achievements include invention of pink wristband for hospitals; lymphedema alert bracelet; design of lymphedema Awareness pin with turquoise ribbon. Avocations: sailing, fishing, cooking.

DOUGLAS, KATHLEEN MARY HARRIGAN, retired psychotherapist, educator; b. Boston, Apr. 24, 1950; d. John Joseph and Kathleen Margaret (Connolly) Harrigan; m. Dr. Robert E. Douglas, Feb. 24, 1977; children: David, Pamela, Elizabeth. Student, Uxbridge, England; BA in Psychology, Sophia U., Tokyo, 1972; MA in Counseling Psychology, Chapman U., Orange, Calif., 1983; PhD in Counselor Edn., U. Fla., 1990. Elem tchr. Marymount Prep Sch., Palos Verdes, Calif., 1973-99; pvt. practice Orlando, Fla., 1985-95; psychology prof. Valencia C.C., Orlando, Fla., 1989-93; prof. Fla. Inst. Tech., 1990-94; asst. prof., grad. acad. advisors, clin. internship supr. Troy State U., Orlando, Fla., 1993-97; software developer of clinically oriented software, 1994—; assoc. prof. Barry U., Orlando, 1999—2002; ret., 2002. Drug/alcohol counselor , Ft. Belvoir, Va., 1981—82; counselor Orange County Mental Health Ctr., Winter Park, Fla., 1982—83; victims of child abuse therapist Thee Door, Orlando, 1983—84; presenter in field. Author: The Therapeutic Superhighway, 1995. Counselor Winter Park Towers Nursing Home, 1985; vol. group counselor Hillcrest Halfway House, Orlando, 1985. 1st Lt. U.S. Army, 1976-80. Recipient Marion medal Cath. Ch., Boston, 1966, Civic award Spouse Abuse, Inc., Orlando, 1984. Mem.: Fla. Assn. Mental Health Counselors (elected counselor edn.), Am. Assn. for Counseling and Devel., Chi Sigma Iota, Pi Lambda Theta, Kappa Delta Phi. Roman Catholic. Home: 1781 Lake Berry Dr Winter Park FL 32789-5911 E-mail: drkathyd@msn.com.

DOUGLAS, KATIE (KATHRYN ELIZABETH DOUGLAS), professional basketball player; b. Indpls., May 7, 1979; m. Vasilis Giapalakis, Sept. 2005. Grad. in Comm., Purdue U., West Lafayette, Ind., 1971. Player Conn. Sun (formerly Orlando Miracle), 2001—. Named WNBA All-Star Game MVP, 2006; named one of Top 25 Women's Coll. Basketball Players of Past 25 Yrs., ESPN.com; named to WNBA All-Defensive First Team, 2005, 2006, 2007, WNBA All-Star Team, 2006—07, All-WNBA First Team, 2006; recipient Jim Valvano Award for Comeback Player of Yr., 2001. Mailing: Conn Sun 1 Mohegan Sun Blvd Uncasville CT 06382*

DOUGLAS, KENNETH JAY, food products executive; b. Harbor Beach, Mich., Sept. 4, 1922; s. Harry Douglas and Xenia (Williamson) D.; m. Elizabeth Ann Schweizer, Aug. 17, 1946; children: Connie Ann, Andrew Jay. Student, U. Ill., 1940-41, 46-47; JD, Chgo. Kent Coll. Law, 1950; grad., Advanced Mgmt. Program, Harvard, 1962. Bar: Ill. 1950, Ind. 1952. Spl. agt. FBI, 1950-54; dir. indsl. relations Dean Foods Co., Franklin Park, Ill., 1954-64, v.p. fin. and adminstrn., 1964-70, chmn. bd., chief exec. officer, 1970-87, chmn. bd., 1987-89, vice-chmn., 1989-92. Bd. dirs. Andrew Corp. Mem. Chgo. Com. With USNR, 1944-46. Mem. Chgo. Club, Econ. Club, Execs. Club, Comml. Club (Chgo.), Oak Park Country Club, River Forest Tennis Club, Old Baldy Country Club (Wyo.). Republican. Home: 1207 Jackson Ave River Forest IL 60305-1107 E-mail: kenmilk@aol.com.

DOUGLAS, KIMBERLY, university librarian; MA, Freie U., Germany, 1976; MS in Libr. Sci., Long Island U., Greenvale, NY, 1978. Position at Bigelow Lab. of Ocean Sci., Boothbay Harbor, Maine; dir. Hancock Libr. Biology & Oceanography U. So. Calif., LA, 1982—85, head Sci. & Engrng. Libr., 1985—88; libr. staff Calif. Inst. Tech., Pasadena, 1988—, acting libr. dir., 2003—04, univ. libr., 2004—. Libr. adv. coun. IEEE; mem. vis. com. Goddard Space Flight Ctr. Libr. Mem.: Nat. Info. Std. Orgn., Libr. Info. and Tech. Assn. Office: Building 1-43 Calif Inst Tech 1200 E California Blvd Pasadena CA 91125 Office Phone: 626-395-6414. Office Fax: 626-431-2681. E-mail: kdouglas@caltech.edu.*

DOUGLAS, KIRK (ISSUR DANIELOVITCH), actor, motion picture producer; b. Amsterdam, NY, Dec. 9, 1916; s. Harry and Bryna (Sanglel) Danielovitch; m. Diana Dill (div. Feb. 1950); children: Michael, Joel; m. Anne Buydens, May 29, 1954; children: Peter, Eric (dec. 2004) Anthony. AB, St. Lawrence U., 1938, DFA (hon.), 1958; student, Am. Acad. Dramatic Arts, 1939-41. Appeared on Broadway in Spring Again, Three Sisters, Kiss and Tell, Wind is Ninety, Alice in Arms, Man Bites Dog; producer, star Broadway play One Flew over the Cuckoo's Nest; appeared in films: The Strange Love of Martha Ivers, 1946, Morning Becomes Electra, 1947, I Walk Alone, 1947, Out of the Past, 1947, Walls of Jericho, 1948, My Dear Secretary, 1948, A Letter to Three Wives, 1948, Champion, 1949, Young Man with a Horn, 1950, The Glass Menagerie, Ace in the Hole, Along the Great Divide, Detective Story, 1951, The Big Sky, 1951, The Big Trees, The Bad and the Beautiful, 1952, Equilibrium, 1952, The Story of Three Loves, The Juggler, 1953, Act of Love, Ulysses, 20,000 Leagues Under the Sea, 1954, Man Without a Star, The Racers, 1954, Lust for Life, 1956, Top Secret Affair, Gunfight at O.K. Corral, Paths of Glory, 1957, Last Train for Gunhill, 1958, Strangers When We Meet, 1958, The Devil's Disciple, 1959, Town Without Pity, Spartacus, 1960, The Last Sunset, 1961, Two Weeks in Another Town, 1962, The List of Adrian Messenger, For Love or Money, The Hook, 1963, In Harm's Way, Heroes of Telemark, 1965, Cast a Giant Shadow, Is Paris Burning?, 1966, War Wagon, The Way West, 1967, A Lovely Way to Die, 1968, The Arrangement, 1969, There Was a Crooked Man, 1970, The Light at the Edge of the World, Catch Me A Spy, 1971, A Man To Respect, 1972, Master Touch, 1972, Scalawag, 1973, Jekyl & Hyde, 1973, Posse, 1975, Once is Not Enough, 1975, Holocaust 2000, 1977, The Fury, 1978, The Villain, Saturn 3, Home Movies, 1979, The Man from Snowy River, 1982, Eddie Macon's Run, 1983, Tough Guys, 1986, Oscar, 1991, Greedy, 1994, Welcome to Veraz, 1990, A Song for David, 1996, (documentary) Once Upon A Time in Hollywood, 2004, Illusion, 2004; producer, dir. films Scalawag, 1973, Posse, 1975; pres. Bryna Co.; producer, actor films: The Final Countdown, Indian Fighter, 1955, Vikings, 1964, Spartacus, 1960, The Last Sunset, 1961, Lonely are the Brave, 1962, Summertree, 1963, Seven Days in May, 1964, The Brotherhood, 1968, A Gunfight, 1971, Oscar, 1991, The Secret, 1991, Take Me Home Again, 1994, Diamonds, 1999, It Runs in the Family, 2003; co-producer film One Flew Over the Cuckoo's Nest, 1975, The Final Countdown, 1979; TV miniseries appearance: Queenie, 1987; TV film appearance: Mousy (also dir.), 1973, The Money Changers, Victory at Entebbe, 1976, Remembrance of Love, 1982, Draw!, 1984, Amos, 1985, Inherit the Wind, 1988, Touched by An Angel, 2000; author: (autobiography) The Ragman's Son, 1988, Climbing the Mountain, 1997, My Stroke of Luck, 2002, Let's Face It, 2007; (novels) Dance with the Devil, 1990, The Gift, 1992, Last Tango in Brooklyn, 1994, The Broken Mirror, 1997, (juvenile) Young Heroes of the Bible, 1999. Nominated for Acad. Award, 1949, 52, 56; nominated for Emmy, 1985, 98, 2000; recipient N.Y. Film Critics award, 1956, Hollywood Fgn. Press award, 1956, Heart and Torch award Am. Heart Assn., 1956, Splendid Am. award of merit George Washington Carver Meml. Found., 1957, cited in Congl. Record for service as goodwill ambassador, 1964, Cecil B. DeMille award for contbns. in entertainment field, 1967, Presdl. Medal of Freedom, 1981, elected to Cowboy Hall of Fame, 1984, Lifetime Achievement award Am. Film Inst., 1991; decorated Legion of Honor (France), 1985, Chevalier de la Legion d'Honneur, 1985, Officer de la Legion d'Honneur, 1990; Kennedy Center Honor, 1994; Honorary Oscar, Lifetime Achievement, 1996, Meltzer award for breaking blacklist Writers Guild Am., 1999, Lifetime Achievement SAG, 1999, Golden Boot award, 1999, Spencer Tracy award Outstanding Achievement in Drama, 1999, Lifetime Achievement Jerusalem Film Festival, 2000, Golden Bear award Berlin Film Festival, 2001, Nat. medal of Arts, 2002, Excellence in Film award, Santa Barbara Internat. Film Festival, 2006. Mem. UN Assn. (dir. Los Angeles chpt.) Achievements include making State Dept.-USIA tours around world; Kirk Douglas High School named in his honor, 2000, Kirk Douglas Theatre named in his honor, 2004, Kirk Douglas Way named in his honor, 2004. E-mail: mnewberger@warrencowan.com.*

DOUGLAS, LESLIE, investment banker; b. Enon Valley, Pa., Mar. 14, 1914; s. Robert R. and Margaret M. (Mc Anlis) D.; m. Jean Wallace, Oct. 12, 1946; children— David, Ann and Joan (twins). BS, Geneva Coll., Beaver Falls, Pa., 1935; MBA, Harvard U., 1937. Investment mgr. Royal Liverpool Group, NYC, 1937-41; investment banker Folger Nolan Fleming Douglas, Inc., Washington, 1946—, v.p., 1955—; bd. govs. Assn. Stock Exchange Firms, 1969-72, Securities Industry Assn., 1972-75. Trustee Holton Arms Sch., Washington, Landon Sch., Vis. Nurses Assn., Washington. Served to lt. comdr. USN, 1941-46. Mem.: Chevy Chase; Met.

(Washington), Met. Club. Republican. Presbyterian. Home: 4733 Woodway Ln NW Washington DC 20016-3240 Office: 725 15th St NW Washington DC 20005-2109 Office Phone: 202-626-5271.

DOUGLAS, MICHAEL LAWRENCE, state supreme court justice; b. LA, Mar. 13, 1948; s. Elmer Walter and Lottie Lee (Nelson) D.; m. Frankie Haws, 1968 (div. Dec. 1970); 1 child, Christine; m. A. Martha Douglas, Jan. 13, 1971. BA in Polit. Sci., Calif. State U., Long Beach, 1971; JD, U. Calif., San Francisco, 1974. Bar: Pa. 1981, US Dist. Ct. (ea. dist.) Pa. 1981, US Ct. Appeals (2d cir.) 1983, Nev. 1983, US Dist. Ct. Nev. 1983. Pvt. practice, Phila., 1981-82; directing atty. Nev. Legal Svcs., Las Vegas, 1982-84; dep. dist. atty. Clark County Dist. Atty., Las Vegas, 1984-96; dist. ct. judge State of Nev. 8th Dist. Ct., Las Vegas, 1996—2004, chief dist. ct. judge, 2003—04; justice Nev. Supreme Ct., 2004—. Instr. in law LA C.C. Dist., 1975-77; spkr. in field. Bd. dirs. Temporary Assistance for Domestic Crisis, 1983-85; mem. task force For Kids Sake/KLAS-TV, 1987-88; vol. Bridge Counseling, 1990-92; coach Ctrl. Valley Little League, 1991-95; bd. dirs. Nev. Law Found., 1991-93; mem. program com. H.P. Fitzgerald Sch., 1994-96. Recipient Svc. to Youth award YMCA LA, 1971, Proclamation for Svc. to Youth award City of LA, 1980, 81, Cmty. Svc. award Calif. State Assembly, 1981, Martin Luther King Com., LA, 1980, Proclamation for Cmty. Svc. award Clark County, 1989, Mark of Excellence award Nat. Fedn. Black Pub. Adminstrs., 1996. Mem. ABA, NAACP (fundraising com. 1990-96, freedom fund budget com. 1990-93), State Bar Nev.(atty. grievance rev. com. 1986-95, mem. disciplinary bd. 1988-95), Clark County Bar Assn., Nat. Bar Assn. (sec. Las Vegas chpt. 1985-87, pres. 1987-88, scholarship chmn. 1989-95, scholarship budget com. 1987-94, Las Vegas Svc. award 1987, 91, Pres. Appreciation award 1988, 89, 90), Pa. Bar Assn., Phila. Bar Assn., Nat. Dist. Atty.'s Assn., Nev. Gaming Attys., Hastings Coll. of Law Alumni Assn., Calif. State U.-Long Beach Alumni Assn., Sigma Pi Phi, Alpha Phi Alpha. Presbyterian. Avocations: outdoor sports, camping, coaching youth sports. Office: Nev Supreme Ct 200 Lewis Ave 17th Fl Las Vegas NV 89101 Home Phone: 702-521-4949; Office Phone: 702-486-3225, 775-684-1755. Office Fax: 702-486-3231. Business E-Mail: mdouglas@nvcourts.state.nv.us.

DOUGLAS, P C, producer, director, reporter, editor; b. Houston; s. Hilda Florence Carrithers. BA in Broadcast Journalism, Tex. Tech. U., 1994. Reporter/photographer KCBD-TV, Lubbock, Tex., 1992-93; copy editor La Ventana, Tex. Tech. U., Lubbock, 1993-94; reporter The Ind., Gallup, N.Mex., 1994, Del Rio News-Herald, 1994; radio announcer KDLK/KLKE, Del Rio, Tex., 1994, KQRX-FM, Odessa, 1996; reporter/photographer KOSA-TV, Odessa, Tex., 1994-96; flight attendant Southwest Airlines, Dallas, 1996-97; polit./govtl. reporter Houston News Today Online, 1997—98; media coord. Motivators, Inc., Houston, 1998-99; prodr., dir., reporter, editor, anchorperson Houston Internat. Bus. Ch., 1999—2000; video editor KTRK-TV ABC, Houston, 2000; prodr. TV Guide Channel, Tulsa, 2000—02; freelance journalist Houston Chronicle, 2002—03; account coord. L'Oréal USA, Houston, 2002—06, 2003—04; media coord. Opera in the Heights, 2003—04; market mgr. Gemini Cosmetics, Inc., Houston, 2006—. Co-prodr.: (TV documentary) Lubbock Hispanic Women Leaders, 1993 (1st place award 1993). Media vol. Make-A-Wish Found. West Tex., Odessa, 1994-96. Recipient 1st Pl. award, Soc. Profl. Journalists, 1993. Avocations: Hawaiian culture and history research, travel, stamp collecting/philately, running, bicycling. Office Phone: 713-443-5630. Personal E-mail: rprtpc1@aol.com. Business E-Mail: pcdouglas@qeminicos.com.

DOUGLAS, PETER RODERICK, lawyer; b. Northampton, Mass., June 3, 1950; s. John Woolman and Mary Evans (St. John) D. AB, Harvard U., 1972, JD, 1975. Bar: NY 1976. Assco. Davis Polk & Wardwell, NYC, 1975, ptnr., 1982—. Shareholder Daimler-Benz; bd. of dir. (bankers trust) Deutsche Bank. Office: Davis Polk & Wardwell 450 Lexington Ave New York NY 10017-3982 Office Phone: 212-450-4336. Office Fax: 212-450-3336. Business E-Mail: peter.douglas@dpw.com.

DOUGLAS, ROBERT GORDON, JR., physician; b. NYC, Apr. 17, 1934; s. Robert Gordon and Alice (Lewis) D.; m. Ann Castle Moses, Dec. 22, 1956; children: Robert Gordon, 3d, Timothy Stuart, Catherine Lewis. AB, Princeton U., 1955; MD, Cornell U., 1959. Diplomate Am. Bd. Internal Medicine. Successively intern, asst. resident in internal medicine, resident N.Y. Hosp., 1959-61, 62-63; asst. resident Johns Hopkins Hosp., 1961-62; USPHS clin. assoc., clin. investigator Nat. Inst. Allergy and Infectious Disease, 1963-66; asst. prof. microbiology and medicine Baylor Coll. Medicine, Houston, 1966-70; mem. faculty Sch. Medicine and Dentistry U. Rochester, NY, 1970-82, prof. medicine and microbiology Sch. Medicine and Dentistry NY, 1974-82, head infectious disease unit Sch. Medicine and Dentistry NY, 1970-82, sr. assoc. dean edn. Sch. Medicine and Dentistry NY, 1979-82; prof., chmn. dept. medicine Med. Coll. Cornell U., 1982-90; physician in chief N.Y. Hosp., 1982-90; sr. v.p. medi. and sci. affairs Merck Sharp & Dohme Internat., 1990-91; pres. Merck Vaccines, 1991-99; dir. strategic planning Vaccine Rsch. Ctr. NIAID, 1999—2004. Bd. dirs. Elusys Inc., Iomai Inc., VaxInnate Inc., Internat. AIDS Vaccine Initiative, 1997-03; chmn. bd. dirs. Vical Inc., 1999—, Middlebrook Pharm. Corp., 2006—; adj. prof. medicine Cornell U. Med. Coll., 1990—; hon. attending physician N.Y. Hosp., 1990—; chmn. Aeras Global TB Vaccine Found., 2001—; cons. in field. Editor: Principles and Practices of Infectious Diseases, 1979, 2d edit., 1985, 3d edit., 1990; contbr. articles to profl. jours. Recipient Hawkins award Assn. Am. Pubs., 1980. Fellow ACP, Infectious Diseases Soc. Am. (pres. 1991-92, Feldman award); mem. Inst. Medicine, Am. Soc. Clin. Investigation, Assn. Am. Physicians, Am. Clin. Climatol. Assn. (pres. 1999-2000), Nat. Found. for Infectious Disease (Maxwell Finland award 2000). Home and Office: 265 Old Black Point Rd Niantic CT 06357

DOUGLAS, STEVEN DANIEL, immunologist, educator, director; b. Jamaica, NY, Feb. 28, 1939; s. Albert H. and Felice (Berner) D.; m. Mary Ann Forciea, Feb. 29, 1980; children: Hope Felice, Anne Genevieve. BA, Cornell U., Ithaca, NY, 1959; MD, Cornell U. Med. Sch., NYC, 1963; MA (hon.), U. Pa., 1982. Intern Mt. Sinai Hosp., NYC, 1963-64; resident Mt. Sinai Sch. Medicine, NYC, 1966-67; staff assoc. NIH, Bethesda, Md., 1964-66; rsch. fellow U. Calif., San Francisco, 1967-69; from asst. prof. to assoc. prof. medicine Mt. Sinai Sch. Medicine, NYC, 1969-74; from assoc. prof. to prof. medicine and microbiology U. Minn., Mpls., 1974-80; prof. pediatrics and microbiology U. Pa., Phila., 1980—; dir. allergy-immunology-pulmonology Children's Hosp., Phila., 1980-89, dir. immunology lab., 1980—, dir. divsn. allergy-immunology-bone marrow transplantation, 1981-87, chief sect. immunology, 1989—, dir. clin. immunology labs., 1980—, dir. immunogenetics lab. Phila., 1996—; assoc. chmn. acad. affairs dept. pediatrics Sch. Medicine U. Pa., 1994—; chair AIDS immunology and pathogenesis study sect. Ctr. Sci. Rev. NIH, 2005—. Editor-in-chief: Clin. and Diagnostic Lab. Immunology, 1993—2005; editor: Jour. Clin. Microbiology, 1983—93, Jour. Leukocyte Biology, 1980—89; adv. bd.: Diagnostic Immunology, 1984—; editl. bd. Jour. Immunology, 1984—, Clin. Immunology Immunopathology, 1975—, Jour. Clin. Lab. Analysis, 1988—93; contbr.: over 410 articles in cellular and clin. immunology, particularly mononuclear phagocytes and immune deficiencies to profl. publs. With USPSH, 1964-66. Recipient Career Devel. award NIH, 1969-74, Abbott Labs. award, 1997, Erwin Neter award, 2000. Fellow: AAAS; mem.: Reticuloendothelial Soc. (sec. 1980—82, program chmn. 1981, councilor 1984—87, pres. 1988—89), Am. Soc. Hematology, Am. Soc. Clin. Investigation, Am. Pediatric Soc., Soc. Pediatric Rsch., Am. Acad. Microbiology, Am. Soc. Cell Biology, Am. Assn. Immunologists, Soc. Leukocyte Biology (hon. life), Interurban Clin. Club (pres. 1994—95). Jewish. Home: 2122 Delancey St Philadelphia PA 19103-6512 Business E-Mail: douglas@email.chop.edu.

DOUGLAS, THOMAS JOHN, finance educator; b. St. Louis, Dec. 21, 1946; s. Ernest Vetal and Helen Catherine Douglas; m. Linda Mary Schmid, Apr. 28, 1990; 1 child, Cassandra Elizabeth; m. Mary Eleanor Horvath, Oct. 13, 1967 (div.); children: Timothy James, Matthew John. BS in Math., St. Louis U., 1964—68; MBA, So. Ill. U., Edwardsville, 1977; PhD in Strategic Mgmt., U. Tenn., Knoxville, 1997. Dir. mktg. rsch. SBC Comm., St. Louis, 1967—93; asst. prof. U. Evansville, Ind., 1997—2000, Clemson (S.C.) U., 2000—05, So. Ill. U., Edwardsville, 2005—. Contbr. to profl. jours. Mem. Sertoma Internat., Clemson, 2004. Lt. USN, 1970—73, Holyloch, Scotland. Recipient All Conf. Best Paper award, So. Mgmt. Assn., 2002. Mem.: Strategic Mgmt. Soc., Acad. Mgmt. Avocations: cooking, sailing, yoga. Home: 3457 Wilderness Dr Edwardsville IL 62025 Office: So Ill U 2134 Founders Hall Edwardsville IL 62026 Home Phone: 618-692-7811; Office Phone: 618-650-2731. Business E-Mail: thdougl@siue.edu.

DOUGLAS, VICTORIA JEAN, marketing professional, communications executive, educator; b. Wilmington, Del., Sept. 1, 1972; d. Richard Otto and Genevieve Douglas. Student, U. Caen, France, 1993, Oxford U., Eng., 1995, NYU Paris, 1996; BA in English/French, U. Del., 1996, MA in French Lit., 1999. Dir. comm. Mayor's Office, Wilmington, 1993—2001; mktg. and comm. chief cons. Met. Wilmington Urban League, 2001—; CEO Barracuda Comm., Wilmington, 2000—. Founder, chair Fgn. Lang. and Lit. Assn. Grad. Students, Newark, 1996—97; mem. mktg. com. Dept. Youth and Families, Wilmington, 1999—2000; supporting mem. Del. Ctr. for Contemporary Arts, Wilmington, 2001—; bd. mem. Kuumba Acad., Wilmington, 2001—; curriculum devel. staff, instr. English U. Caen Sch. Law, France, 1997—98; account supr. Saatchi and Saatchi, Rowland, NY, 2001. Organizer Nat. Night Out, Wilmington, 1993—95, Mayor's Breast Cancer Awareness Campaign, Wilmington, 2001; mem. ball com. Am. Diabetes Assn., 2002, mem. leadership coun., 2002—; v.p. sales Wilmington Drama League. Recipient Tomorrow's Leaders Today award, Pub. Allies, 1994, proclamation, City of Wilmington, 2000, Apex Award for Excellence in Mktg. and Pub. Rels. Brochures, 2002, APEX award Design & Layout, 2003, Comm. award, 2003. Mem.: AAUW, Pub. Rels. Soc. Am., Met. Wilmington Urban League, Pi Delta Phi, Golden Key Nat. Honor Soc., Phi Sigma Tau, Sigma Tau Delta.

DOUGLAS, WILLIAM ERNEST, retired commissioner; b. Charleston, SC, Nov. 26, 1930; s. William Ernest and Helen A. (Fortune) D.; m. Nancy Anne (Gibson), July 18, 1980. BA cum laude, The Citadel, 1956; postgrad., U. SC, 1956—59. With IRS, 1959—80, divsn. chief Newark dist., 1970—72, asst. dir. Jackson (Miss.) dist., 1972-73, asst. dir. Atlanta dist., 1973-74, asst. commr. S.E. region, 1974-78, dir. Regional Svc. Ctr. S.E. region, 1978-80; commr. fin. mgmt. svc. U.S. Treasury Dept., Washington, 1980-91. Served in U.S. Army, 1948-52, Korean War, 1950-51. Recipient Exec. Excellence award Fed. Interagency Com. on Info. Resources Mgmt., 1985; Exec. Achievement award Sr. Exec. Svc., 1985; Am. Univ. Roger W. Jones Fed. Exec. Leadership award, 1986; Sec. of Treasury's Disting. Svc. award, 1991; Presdl. Exec. Disting. award, 1991. Home: 205 Settlers Rd Saint Simons Island GA 31522

DOUGLAS, WILLIAM W., food products executive; m. Lisa Douglas; 2 children. BBA, Univ. Ga., 1983. With Ernst & Whinney, 1983—85, Coca Cola Enterprises, Atlanta, 1985—; corp. controller Coca Cola Beverages plc, London; CFO Coca Cola HBC, Greece, 2000—04; v.p., controller, chief acctg. officer Coca Cola Enterprises, Atlanta, 2004—05, sr. v.p., CFO, 2005—. Office: Coca Cola Enterprises Ste 900 2500 Windy Ridge Pkwy Atlanta GA 30339 Mailing: Coca Cola Enterprises PO Box 723040 Atlanta GA 31139-0040*

DOUGLASS, BRUCE E., physician; b. Berwyn, Ill., Sept. 26, 1917; s. Frank Lionel and Helen Mary (Eccles) D.; m. Charlotte Maurer Natwick, Oct. 14, 1942; children: Jean N., Bruce G., John F. BA, U. Wis., 1938, MD, 1942; MS in Medicine, U. Minn., 1949. Intern Med. Coll. of Va., Richmond, 1942-43; resident in internal medicine Mayo Clinic, Rochester, Minn., 1947-50, mem. staff, 1949—, chmn. divsn. preventive medicine, 1962—; dir. Mayo Clinic (Mayo sect. of Patient and Health Edn.), 1976—. Dir. Occupational Health Inst., Chgo., 1968— Author: Anatomy of the Portal Vein and Its Tributaries, 1949, The Problem of Benign Bronchial Obstruction, 1954, Predicting Disease: Is It Possible? 1971, Health Problems of Hospital Employees, 1971, Examining Healthy Persons: How and How Often? 1980. Chmn. Rochester Music Bd., 1960-70; v.p. Minn. Zool. Soc., 1974-77. Served to capt. M.C. AUS, 1944-47. Fellow Am. Acad. Occupational Medicine (Keogh award 1981), Am. Occupational Med. Assn. (pres. 1977-78, Meritorious Service award 1979); mem. AMA (Physician's Recognition award 1974-77, chmn. sect. council on preventive medicine 1978-80, del. for occupational med. to ho. of dels. 1978-85), Minn. Med. Assn. (chmn. com. on public health edn. 1979), Ramazzini Soc., Assn. Tchrs. Preventive Medicine, Am. Coll. Preventive Medicine, Minn. Zool. Soc., Sigma Xi, Phi Kappa Phi, Sigma Phi, Nu Sigma Nu. Office: Mayo Clinic Rochester MN 55905-0001 Home: Charter House 211 2d St NW #1306 Rochester MN 55901 Office Phone: 507-284-2511.

DOUGLASS, CRAIG BRUCE, computer technology executive; b. Santa Monica, Calif., July 3, 1956; s. W. Bruce and Frances A. (Ellingwood) D. AB, Dartmouth Coll., 1978; MBA, U. Chgo., 1980. Sr. bus. devel. analyst Bell & Howell Co., Chgo., 1980-82, product mgr., 1982-83, sr. product mgr., 1983, mgr. product and market devel., 1983-86, v.p. product and market devel. Torrance, Calif., 1986-89, Bell & Howell Quintar Co., 1989-94; v.p. mktg. & product devel. Quintar Co., Torrance, Calif., 1995-96, v.p. sales and bus. devel., 1996-98; mng. dir. Multifunction Peripherals Assn., 1998—; CEO Converging Systems, Inc., 1999—. Inventor digital film recording. Mem. Nat. Computer Graphics Assn. (pres. Ill. chpt. 1985-86, v.p. Los Angeles Orange County chpt. 1986—, nat. com. 1986—), Dartmouth Club of Chgo. (v.p. 1984-85), Dartmouth Club of L.A. (bd. dirs. 1986-95, pres. 1993-99). Avocations: yacht racing, skiing, scuba diving, wind surfing. Office: Converging Systems Inc 32420 Nautilus Dr Rancho Palos Verdes CA 90275-6002 Fax: 310-544-4787.

DOUGLASS, FRANK RUSSELL, lawyer; b. Dallas, May 29, 1933; s. Claire Allen and Caroline (Score) D.; m. Carita Calkins, Feb. 5, 1955 (div. 1983); children: Russell, Tom, Andrew, Cathy; m. Betty Elwanda Richards, Dec. 31, 1983. BBA, Southwestern U., 1953; LLB, U. Tex., 1958. Bar: Tex. 1957, U.S. Dist. Ct. (we. dist.) Tex. 1960, U.S. Dist. Ct. (so. dist.) Tex. 1981, U.S. Dist. Ct. (no. dist.) Tex. 1985, U.S. Dist. Ct. (ea. dist.) Tex. 1987, U.S. Supreme Ct. 1964, U.S. Ct. Appeals (5th cir.) 1985; cert. in civil trial law, and oil, gas and energy law. Various positions to ptnr. McGinnis, Lochridge & Kilgore, Austin, Tex., 1957-76; sr. ptnr. Scott, Douglass & McConnico, Austin, 1976—. Contbr. articles to profl. jours. City atty., Westlake Hills, Tex., 1968. Served as airman USAF, 1953-55. Named Dist. Alumus Southwestern U., 1999. Fellow Am. Coll. Trial Lawyers; mem. ABA (natural resources law sect., coun. 1987-90), Am. Bar Found., Am. Inns of Ct., State Bar of Tex., Tex. Bar Found., The Tex. Ctr. for Legal Ethics and Professionalism (founding), Dallas Bar Assn., The Littlefield Soc. U. Tex. (charter). Office Phone: 214-352-9189. Office Fax: 214-352-4588.

DOUGLASS, JANE DEMPSEY, retired theology educator; b. Wilmington, Del., Mar. 22, 1933; d. Hazell Brownlie and Ethel Katherine (Smith) Dempsey; m. Gordon Klene Douglass, Aug. 23, 1964; children: Alan Bruce, Anne Lorine, John Gordon. AB, Syracuse U., 1954; postgrad., U. Geneva, Switzerland, 1954-55; AM, Radcliffe Coll., 1961; PhD, Harvard U., 1963; ThD (hon.), U. Geneva, 1994; LHD (hon.), Franklin and Marshall Coll., 1992; DD (hon.), U. St. Andrews, Scotland, 1992; STD (hon.), MacMurray Coll., 2000. Assoc. dir. Presbyn. Student Ctr., Columbia, Mo., 1955-58; teaching fellow Harvard Divinity Sch., Cambridge, Mass., 1959-62; from instr. to prof. Sch. of Theology at Claremont and Claremont Grad. Sch., Claremont, Calif., 1963-85; Hazel Thompson McCord prof. hist. theology Princeton (N.J.) Theol. Sem., 1985-98, emerita, 1998—. Pres. Am. Soc. Ch. History, 1983; v.p. World Alliance of Reformed Chs., 1989-90, pres. 1990-97, hon. mem. exec. com., 1997-2004. Author: Justification in Late Medieval Preaching: A Study of John Geiler of Keisersberg, 1966, 2d edit., 1989, Women, Freedom and Calvin, 1985; editor: (with Jack L. Stotts) To Confess the Faith Today, 1990, (with James F. Kay) Women, Gender and Christian Community, 1997, (with Páraic Réamonn) Partnership in God's Mission in the Middle East, 1998; contbr. articles to profl. jours. Presbyterian.

DOUGLASS, JOHN JAY, lawyer, educator; b. Lincoln, Nebr., Mar. 9, 1922; s. Edward Lyman and Edna Marie (Ball) D.; m. Margaret Casteel Pickering, Aug. 31, 1946; children: Carrie Bess, Timothy Pickering, Margaret Marie. AB with distinction, U. Nebr., 1943; JD with distinction, U. Mich., 1952; MA, George Washington U., 1963; LLM, U. Va., 1973; postgrad., Army War Coll., 1963. Bar: Nebr. 1952, Mich. 1952, Tex. 1975. Inf. officer U.S. Army, 1943-52, advanced through grades to col., 1966, judge adv., 1952-74, Vietnam, 1968-69, mil. judge Ft. Riley, Kans., 1969-70; comdt. U.S. Army JAG Sch., Charlottesville, Va., 1970-74; ret. U.S. Army, 1974; dean Nat. Coll. Dist. Attys., Houston, 1974-94; prof., dir. trial advocacy U. Houston, 1974—. Advisor on criminal law to Albania, 1991; advisor on elections to Ukraine, 1993; advisor Russian procuracy, 1994, Ukraine procuracy, 1995; named dist. mem. JAGC, 1994. Author: Ethical Concerns in Prosecution, 1988, 93; contbr. articles to profl. jours. Judge Harris County Absentee Voting, Houston, 1980-92; apptd. mem. Houston Ethics Commn., 2006. Decorated D.S.M., Legion of Merit, Bronze Star, Army Commendation medal; recipient U. Nebr. Alumni Achievement award, 2003. Fellow Am. Bar Found. (life); mem. ABA (ho. of dels. 1980-96, chmn. standing com. on law and electoral process 1987-90, Nelson award 2001), Tex. Bar Assn. (penal code and criminal process com. 1988-90), Houston City Club, Army and Navy Club, Order of Coif, Eagle Scout, Alpha Tau Omega. Avocation: tennis. Home: 25 T 14 E Greenway Plz Houston TX 77046-1406 Office: Univ Houston Law Ctr 100 Law Center Houston TX 77204-6060 Home Phone: 713-871-0696; Office Phone: 713-743-1831. Business E-Mail: jdouglass@uh.edu.

DOUGLASS, MELVIN ISADORE, school system administrator, humanities educator, composer; b. NYC, July 21, 1948; s. Isadore Douglass and Esther L. Tripp. AS in Early Childhood Edn., Vincennes U., 1970; BS in Early Childhood and Elem. Edn., Tuskegee Inst., 1973; MS in Urban Elem. Edn., Morgan State U., 1975; MA in Orgn. Adminstrn. Supervision, NYU, 1977; MEd in Curriculum and Teaching, Columbia U., 1978, DEd, 1981; cert. in Urban Sch. Leadership, Harvard U., 2003. Ordained to ministry Baptist Ch., 1987; cert. social studies tchr. NY, sch. dist. adminstr. and supr. NY, elem. tchr. NY, in improving schs., the art of leadership Harvard U., 2007, in Am. History Clare Coll., Cambridge U., 2007. Tchr., dean students Bronx Pub. Sch., NY, 1973-75; sch. age program dir. Amistad Child Day Care Ctr., Jamaica, 1976-77; head track and field coach CUNY, NYC, 1981—83; adminstrv. dir. Beck Meml. Day Care Ctr., Bronx, 1983—84; primary sch. dept. chair City of N.Y. Dept. Juvenile Justice, 1984-85, ombudsman, 1985-88; chmn. depts. English, reading and social studies Stimson Jr. High Sch., Huntington Station, NY, 1988—; prin. facilitator Harvard Grad. Sch. Edn., 2007—. Adj. instr. sociology and African Am. studies Coll. New Rochelle, NY, 1992-2004, adj. asst. prof. Bklyn. Coll. Grad. Sch. of Edn., NY, 2000—, adj. prof. Metropolitan Coll NY, 1999-2005; coord. various edn. confs., 1986—; CEO Minority Educators' Network, NY, 1999—, mem. community adv. bd. City of NY Dept. of Correction, Queens House of Detention Men, 1991-95; ednl. liaison NY State Senator Alton R. Waldon, Jr., 1991-2000; co-founder Prof. Hobart S. Jarrett Lecture Series Medgar Evers Coll. CUNY, 2006-. Author: Black Winners: A History of Spingarn Medalists, 1915-1983, 1984, Carter G. Woodson: A Biography, 1987, Famous Black Men of Harvard, 2005; composer (songs) Carter Woodson Song, 2006, Thanks Dr. King.Thanks Mrs. King, 2006; contbr. articles to profl. jours. Assisting minister Calvary Bapt. Ch., 1987-91; co-chair edn. com. NYC Black Leadership Coun., 1987-88, NY State Conf. NAACP, 1986-89; chmn. anti-drug com. Met. Coun. NAACP Brs., 1986-89; cons. Jamaica East/West Adolescent Pregnancy Consortium, 1986-89; area policy bd. #12 subunit 2, 1987—97; Queens adv. bd. NY Urban League, 1988-93, adv. bd. Gerald W. Deas Professorship SUNY Downstate Med. Ctr., 2002— pres. bd. dir. NYC Transit br. NAACP, 1984-89; bd. dir. Queens Coun. on Arts, 1983-86, Black Exptl. Theatre, 1982—, United Black Men Queens County Inc., 1986-90, Dance Explosion, 1987-89, nat. adv. bd. Principals' Ctr., Harvard Grad. Sch. Edn., 2004-07; cmty. adv. bd. Pub. Sch. 40, Queens, 1992-95; peer rev. com. Jour. Nat. Med. Assn., 2003—; co-chair youth com. Ptnrs. of the Ams., 2004-07; social policy advisor on children and families NY State Assemblyman William Scarborough; bd. dir. LI Child and Family Devel. Svcs., Inc., 2004—, USO Met. NYC, 2005-06; cmty. bd. unit 12 City of NY Borough of Queens, 2007—. Recipient Cmty. Svc. citation NY State Gov. Mario Cuomo, 1986, citation award NYC Mayor Edward Koch, 1986, citation of honor Queens Borough Pres. Claire Shulman, 1986, Svc. award N.Y.C. Transit br. NAACP, 1986, Jefferson award Am. Inst. for Pub. Svc. TV Sta. WNYW, 1987, Civil Rights award NYC Transit br. NAACP, 1988, citation NYC Coun., 1988, Alumni Faculty citation Vincennes U., 1991, resolution Senator A.R. Waldon, Jr., 1991, Svc. award Ea. Shore chpt. Links, 2001, Svc. award Suffolk County Human Rights Commn., 2004, citation Congressman Steve Israel, 2003, Proclamation, Legislator Allan Binder, 2003, Cert. Excellence Jour. Nat. Med. Assn., 2003, cert. spl. recognition Oxford Round Table, U. Oxford, 2005, citation Senator Carl Marcellino, 2006, cert. recognition Town Supr. Frank Petrone, 2006, cert. appreciation Suffolk County Exec. Steve Levy, 2006, cert. merit Assemblyman James Conte, 2006, Black History Maker award Huntington Beach NAACP, 2006, Svc. award Prin.s' Ctr. Harvard Grad. Sch. Edn., 2007, Man of the Yr., One Hundred Black Men of LI, 2007; Henry M. Minton fellow, 2003; Gilder Lehrman fellowship, 2007. Mem. NEA, Nat. Black Child Devel. Inst., St. Albans C. of C., Nat. Soc. for Study of Edn., Am. Fedn. Sch. Adminstrs., Coun. Adminstrs. and Suprs., South Huntington Chairmen's Assn., Assn. study African Am. Life and History, Am. Hist. Assn., Orgn. Am. Historians, L.I. Tuskegee Alumni Assn. (v.p. bd. dir. 1987-89), Jamaica Track Club (pres., founder 1973—), Masons, Shriners, Kappa Delta Pi, Phi Alpha Theta, Omega Psi Phi (basileus Nu Omicron chpt. 1986-89, bd. dirs. chpt. Early Childhood Learning Ctr. 1984—, chpt. Omega Man of Yr., 1987), Phi Delta Kappa, Sigma Pi Phi, One Hundred Black Men, Comus Club. Address: 395 Stuyvesant Ave Brooklyn NY 11233 Business E-Mail: mdouglass@shufsd.org.

DOUMANI, LISSA, chef; m. Hiro Sone. Pastry apprentice Spago Hollywood, 1982, pastry chef, 1982; designer, pastry programs Sydney, Australia, 1983; pastry chef 385 North, LA; owner, pastry chef Terra, Napa Valley, 1988—, Ame, San Francisco, 2005—. Co-author: Cooking from the Heart of Napa Valley, 2000. Office: Ame 689 Mission St San Francisco CA 94105*

DOUMATO, LAMIA, librarian, historian; b. Aug. 26, 1947; d. A.G. and Victoria (Peters) D. BA, R.I. Coll., 1969; MA, Pa. State U., 1971; MLS, Simmons Coll., 1974; student, Columbia U., 1976-78. Intern Providence Pub. Library, 1970-71; reference asst. Boston U. Libraries, 1971-74; reference librarian Mus. of Modern Art, NYC, 1974-78; from asst. prof. to dir. art and architecture U. Colo. Library, Boulder, 1978-81; reference librarian Nat. Gallery of Art, Washington, 1981-88, head rsch. svcs., 1988—. Cons. George Sand Festival, Boulder, 1980, Nat. Mus. Women in the Arts, Washington, 1982; project reviewer Nat. Endowment for Humanities, Washington, 1987—. Author: American Drawings, 1979, Women and

American Architecture, 1988, History of American Architecture, 1988, Artist's Book Librarians, 1990, The Art of Bishop Dioscorus Theodorus, 1999, England Collection of Artists Books, 2000, Opening the Door to Paradise, 2000, Michael the Great: Iconoclast or Art Patron, 2002, Pontifical of Ignatius II, 2004; contbr. Architecture: A Place for Women, 1989, Graphic Studio, 1991. Mus. Modern Art grantee, 1977-78, Coun. on Rsch. grantee U. Colo., 1979; recipient Performance award Nat. Gallery Art, 1989, Wilson award ARHS, NA, 2001; Robert H. Smith fellow 1997-98, 98-99, Bibliographical Soc. Am. fellow, 1999-2000, Ailsa Mellow Bruce fellow CASVA, 2001-02, Worldwide art fellow, 2002, Oxford rsch. fellow, 2002, Smith fellow 2005—. Mem. ALA (serials adv. com. 1980, N. Am. chpt. pubs. com. 1996-97, rsch. com. 1999-2000), Art Librarians, Assn. Archtl. Librarians (chair 1988, adv. com. 1988-91), Art and Architecture Thesaurus (adv. com. 1982-84, George Wittenborn award com. 1995, pubs. com. 1997, Gerdt Muesham award 2004). Home: 3001 Veazey Ter NW Washington DC 20008-5454 Office: Nat Gallery of Art 6th And Constitution Ave Washington DC 20565-0001 Business E-Mail: l-doumato@nga.gov.

DOURDAN, GARY, actor; b. Phila., Dec. 11, 1966; children: Nyla, Lyric. Actor: (TV films) The Good Fight, 1992, Laurel Avenue, 1993, Keys, 1994, Rendezvous, 1999, King of the World, 2000; (films) Weekend at Bernie's II, 1993, Sunset Park, 1996, Fool's Paradise, 1997, Get That Number, 1997, Playing God, 1997, Alien: Resurrection, 1997, Scar City, 1998, New Jersey Turnpikes, 1999, The Weekend, 1999, King of the World, 2000, Trois, 2000, Dancing in September, 2000, Impostor, 2002, Perfect Stranger, 2007; (TV series) A Different World, 1991—92, The Office, 1995, Swift Justice, 1996, Soul Food, 2000—01, CSI: Crime Scene Investigation, 2000— (Outstanding Supporting Actor in a Drama Series, NAACP Image Awards, 2006). Office: c/o Brillstein-Grey Entertainment 9150 Wilshire Blvd Ste 350 Beverly Hills CA 90212*

DOUT, ANNE JACQUELINE, manufacturing and sales company executive; b. Detroit, Mar. 13, 1955; d. George Edwin and Virginia Irene Boesinger; m. James Edward Dout, July 16, 1977; 1 child, Brian Ross Student, Macomb C.C., 1972—74; BBA, We. Mich. U., 1976; MBA, Duquesne U., 1982. Cert. cash mgr. Internal auditor Koppers Co. Inc., Pitts., 1976—78, cash analyst, 1978—79, supr. cash ops., 1979—80, mgr. cash ops., 1980—81, mgr. cash ops., asst. treas., 1981—87, dir. treasury svcs., asst. treas., 1987—88; corp. staff v.p., asst. treas. IMCERA Group Inc., Northbrook, Ill., 1988—91; v.p., treas. IMCERA Group, Inc., Northbrook, 1991—94; exec. v.p., CFO Champion Enterprises, Inc., Auburn Hills, Mich., 1994—98; pres. JJB Enterprises, Inc., Rochester Hills, Mich., 1998—2001; sr. v.p., CFO Pella Corp., Iowa, 2002—. Bd. dirs. Cavco Industries Inc., Iowa State Bd. Edn., Iowa Coll. Found. Bd. Mem. allocations com. United Way, Pitts., 1979-83; bd. dirs. N.E. Lake County Coun. Boy Scouts Am., v.p. adminstrn., 1989-92; bd. dirs. Barat Coll., Lake Forest, Ill., 1992-94, U. Mich. Cancer Found.; bd. visitors Sch. Bus., Oakland U., 1994-2004; devel. com. Mich. Womens Found, 1996-2000 Mem. Treas. Mgmt. Assn. (exec. com. 1988-90, govt. rels. com. 1984-86, bd. dirs. 1986-89, strategic plan com. 1987-90), Gov. Coun. Edn., Fin. Exec. Inst., Mid Am. Com., Econ. Club, Exec. Club, Womens Econ. Club Office: Pella Corp 102 Main St Pella IA 50219

DOUTHAT, REBECCA ARLENE, retired secondary school educator; b. Norfolk, Va., Feb. 10, 1946; d. Thomas Alexander and Lena Faye Douthat. BS, Radford Coll., 1967, MA, 1974; MEd, Coll. of William and Mary, 1990, EdS, 1994. Lic. tchr. Commonwealth of Va. Tchr. Fincastle County Pub. Schs., Daleville, Va., 1967—68, Newport News Pub. Schs., Newport News, Va., 1968—72, York County Pub. Schs., Yorktown, Va., 1976—2004; ret., 2004. Sponsor Students Against Drunk Driving, Tabb, Va., 1999—; sponsor food drive York County Social Svcs., York County, Va., 1995—2000. Mem.: Am. Counseling Assn., York Edn. Assn., Va. Edn. Assn., Nat. Edn. Assn., Colony Pines Residents Assn. (mem. membership drive 1995—), Kappi Delta Pi. Avocations: bowling, bicycling, reading, weightlifting. Home: 4555 Mountain View Dr Dublin VA 24084-3860 Personal E-mail: mzbad@msn.com.

DOVE, RITA FRANCES, poet, language educator; b. Akron, Ohio, Aug. 28, 1952; d. Ray A. and Elvira E. (Hord) Dove; m. Fred Viebahn, Mar. 23, 1979; 1 child, Aviva Chantal Tamu Dove-Viebahn. BA summa cum laude, Miami U., Oxford, Ohio, 1973; postgrad., Universität Tübingen, Fed. Republic Germany, 1974-75; MFA, U. Iowa, 1977; LLD (hon.), Miami U., Oxford, Ohio, 1988, Knox Coll., 1989, Tuskegee U., 1994, U. Miami, Fla., 1994, Washington U., St. Louis, 1994, Case Western Res. U., 1994, U. Akron, 1994, Ariz. State U., 1995, Boston Coll., 1995, Dartmouth Coll., 1995, Spelman Coll., 1996, U. Pa., 1996, U. NC, 1997, U. Notre Dame, 1997, Northeastern U., 1997, Columbia U., 1998, Washington & Lee U., 1999, SUNY, Brockport, 1999, Pratt Inst., 2001, Howard U., 2001, Skidmore Coll., 2004. Asst. prof. English Ariz. State U., Tempe, 1981-84, assoc. prof., 1984-87, prof., 1987-89, U. Va., Charlottesville, 1989-93, Commonwealth prof. English, 1993—; U.S. poet laureate, cons. in poetry Libr. of Congress, Washington, 1993-95, spl. cons. in poetry, 1999-2000; columnist Washington Post, 2000—02. Writer-in-residence Tuskegee Inst., Ala., 1982; lit. panelist Nat. Endowment Arts, Washington, 1984-86, chmn. poetry grants panel, 1985; judge Walt Whitman award Acad. Am. Poets, 1990, Pulitzer prize in poetry, 1991, Ruth Lilly prize 1991, Nat. Book award in poetry 1991, 98, Anisfield-Wolf Book awards, 1992—, Shelley Meml. award, 1997, Amy Lowell fellowship, 1997; poetry panel chmn. Pulitzer prize, 1997; final judge Brittingham and Pollack prizes, 1997; juror Christopher Columbus Fellowship Found., 1998-02, Duke Ellington awards, 1999; bd. dir. Poetry Daily, 2002; chancellor Acad. Am. Poets, 2006-. Author: (poetry) Ten Poems, 1977, The Only Dark Spot in the Sky, 1980, The Yellow House on the Corner, 1980, Mandolin, 1982, Museum, 1983, Thomas and Beulah, 1986 (Pulitzer Prize in poetry 1987), The Other Side of the House, 1988, Grace Notes, 1989 (Ohioana award 1990), Selected Poems, 1993 (Ohioana award 1994), Lady Freedom Among Us, 1994, Mother Love, 1995, Evening Primrose, 1998, On the Bus with Rosa Parks, 1999 (Ohioana award 2000), American Smooth, 2004; (verse drama) The Darker Face of the Earth, 1994 (W. Alton Jones Found. grant 1994, Kennedy Ctr. Fund for New Am. Plays award 1995, Geraldine Dodge Found. grant, 1997), completely rev. 2d edit., 1996, expanded 3d edit., 2000 (first performance Oreg. Shakespeare Festival 1996); (novel) Through the Ivory Gate, 1992 (Va. Coll. Stores Book award 1993); (short stories) Fifth Sunday , 1985 (Callaloo award 1986); (essays) The Poet's World, 1995, (song cycle) Seven for Luck (music by John Williams), 1st performance Boston Symphony Orch., Tanglewood, 1998; mem. editl. bd. Nat. Forum, 1984-89, Iris, 1989—; mem. adv. bd. Ploughshares, 1992—, NC Writers Network, 1992-99, Civilization, 1994-97, Am. Poetry Rev., 2005-; assoc. editor Callaloo, 1986-98; adv. and contbg. editor Gettysburg Rev., 1987—, TriQuarterly, 1988—, Ga. Review, 1994—, Bellingham Rev., 1996—, Internat. Quarterly, 1997—, Callaloo, 1998—, Mid-Am. Rev., 1998—; editor Best Am. Poetry, 2000. Commr. The Schomburg Ctr. Rsch. in Black Culture, NY Pub. Libr., 1987—; mem. Renaissance Forum Folger Shakespeare Libr., 1993-95, Coun. Scholars Libr. of Congress, 1994—; mem. nat. launch com. AmeriCorps, 1994; mem. awards coun. Am. Acad. Achievement, 1994-2001; mem. adv. bd. Thomas Jefferson Ctr. Freedom of Expression, 1994—, US Civil War Ctr., 1995-99, Va. Ctr. Creative Arts, 1995—, Student Achievement and Advocacy Svcs., 2002—, DuBois Ctr. Am. History and Culture, 2005-, The Givens Found. African Am. Lit., 2005-; The Poets Corner elector Cathedral Ch. St. John the Divine, NYC, 1991-2002; bd. govs. Humanities Rsch. Inst. U. Calif., 1996-99; bd. dir. Poetry Daily, 2004—; chancellor Acad. Am. Poets, 2006—. Presdl. scholar, 1970, Nat. Achievement scholar, 1970-73; Fulbright/Hays fellow, 1974-75, rsch. fellow U. Iowa, 1975, teaching/writing fellow U. Iowa, 1976-77, Guggenheim Found. fellow, 1983-84, Mellon sr. fellow Nat. Humanities Ctr., 1988-89, fellow Ctr. Advanced Studies, U. Va., 1989-92, fellow Shannon Ctr. for Advanced Studies, U. Va., 1995—; grantee NEA, 1977, 89; recipient Lavan Younger Poet award Acad. Am. Poets, 1986, GE Found. award, 1987, Bellagio residency Rockefeller Found., Italy, 1988, Ohio Gov.'s award 1988, Literary Lion citation NY Pub. Libr., 1991, Women of Yr. award Glamour Mag., 1993, NAACP Great Am. Artist award, 1993, Golden Plate award Am. Acad. Achievement, 1994, Disting. Achievement medal Miami U. Alumni Assn., 1994, Renaissance Forum award leadership in the literary arts Folger Shakespeare Libr., 1994, Carl Sandburg award Internat. Platform Assn., 1994, Heinz award in arts and humanities, 1996, Charles Frankel prize/Nat. Humanities medal Pres. of US and NEH, 1996; inducted Ohio Women's Hall of Fame, 1991, Nat. Assn. Women in Edn. Disting. Woman award, 1997, Sara Lee Frontrunner award, 1997, Barnes & Noble Writers Writers award, 1997, Levinson prize Poetry mag., 1998, John Frederick Nims Translation prize, 1999, Libr. Lion award NY Pub. Libr., 2000, Duke Ellington Lifetime Achievement award, 2001, Emily Couric Women's Leadership award, 2003, Common Wealth award, 2006, Writing Today Grand Master award, 2006; named Phi Beta Kappa poet Harvard U., 1993, Poet Laureate of Commonwealth of Va., 2004-06. Fellow Am. Acad. Arts & Scis.; mem. PEN, ASCAP, Am. Philos. Soc., Poetry Soc. Am., Associated Writing Programs (bd. dir. 1985-88, pres. 1986-87), Am. Acad. Achievement (mem. golden plate awards coun. 1994—2001), Phi Beta Kappa (senator 1994-2001), Phi Kappa Phi. Office: U Va Dept English 219 Bryan Hall PO Box 400121 Charlottesville VA 22904-4121 Business E-Mail: rfd4b@virginia.edu.

DOVER, SIR KENNETH JAMES, chancellor, retired classicist; b. Croydon, Eng., Mar. 11, 1920; s. Percy Henry and Dorothy Valerie (Healey) D.; student Balliol Coll., Oxford (Eng.) U., 1938-40, 45-47, MA, 1946, DLitt, 1974, student Merton Coll., 1948, hon. fellow; LLD, Birmingham U., St. Andrews U.; DLitt, U. Bristol, U. Liverpool, U. London, St. Andrews U., U. Durham; DHL, Oglethorpe U.; m. Audrey Ruth Latimer, Mar. 17, 1947; children: Alan Hugh, Catherine Ruth. Fellow, tutor Balliol Coll., Oxford (Eng.) U., 1948-55, hon. fellow, pres. Corpus Christi Coll., 1976-86, hon. fellow; prof. of Greek, St. Andrews U., 1955-76; chancellor St. Andrews U., 1981—; prof.-at-large Cornell U., 1983-89; vis. lectr. Harvard U., 1960; Sather vis. prof. U. Calif., 1967; prof. Stanford U., winter quarter, 1987-92. Served with artillery Brit. Army, 1940-45; mentioned in dispatches. Created Knight, 1977. Fellow Brit. Acad. (pres., 1978-81, Kenyon medal 1993); mem. Hellenic Soc. (pres., 1971-74), Classical Assn. (pres., 1975), Am. Acad. Arts and Scis., Netherlands Acad. Arts and Scis. Author: Greek Word Order, 1960; Lysias and the Corpus Lysiacum, 1968; Aristophanic Comedy, 1972; Greek Popular Morality in the Time of Plato and Aristotle, 1974; Greek Homosexuality, 1978; The Greeks, 1980; Greek and the Greeks (Collected Papers I), 1987; The Greeks and Their Legacy (Collected Papers II), 1988, Marginal Comment (memoirs), 1994, The Evolution of Greek Prose Style, 1997; contbr. to other books and articles; editor: Aristophanes' Clouds, 1968; Theocritus, 1971; Plato, Symposium, 1980, Perceptions of the Ancient Greeks, 1992, Aristophanes' Frogs, 1993. Home: 49 Hepburn Gardens Saint Andrews KY16 9LS Scotland

DOVRING, KARIN ELSA INGEBORG, writer, poet, playwright, media specialist; b. Stenstorp, Sweden, Dec. 5, 1919; arrived in US, 1953, naturalized, 1968; m. Folke Dovring, May 30, 1943. Grad., Coll. Commerce, Gothenburg, Sweden, 1936; MA, Lund U., Sweden, 1943, PhD, 1951; Phil. Licentiate, Gothenburg U., 1947. Journalist several Swedish daily newspapers and weekly mags., 1940-60; tchr. Swedish colls.; rsch. assoc. of Harold Lasswell Yale U., New Haven, 1953-78; fgn. corr. Swedish newspapers, Italy, Switzerland, France and Germany, 1956-60; freelance writer, journalist, 1960—; rsch. prof. comms. and media studies U. Ill., Urbana, 2002. Vis. prof. Internat. U., The Vatican, Rome, 1958-60, Gottingen (W.Ger.) U., 1962; lectr. U.S. Army, Peace Corps, Yale U., U. Wis., McGill U., U. Iowa; rsch. assoc. U. Ill., Urbana, 1968-69, guest lectr., 2001-05; invited contbr. Social Sci. Rsch. Coun., 1988; speaker Conf. Law and Policy, Yale U. Law Sch., 1992-93, 99—; hon. mem. Profl. Women's Adv. Bd. Am. Biograph. Inst., Raleigh, NC, 2003; adv. coun. Internat. Biographical Ctr., Cambridge, Eng.; interviewee radio and TV programs; writer Ill. Alliance to Prevent Nuclear War, radio, theater; prof. comm. and media studies U. Ill. Coll. Comm., 2002—; moderator series U.S.A. Faces the World-Markets in Communications, 2004—; songwriter Hollywood and Nashville; plays for TV movies. Author: Songs of Zion, 1951, Land Reform as a Propaganda Theme, 3d edit., 1965, Road of Propaganda, 1959, Optional Society, 1972, Frontiers of Communication, 1975, English as Lingua Franca: Double Talk in Global Persuasion, 1997, (short stories) No Parking This Side of Heaven, 1982, Harold D. Lasswell: His Communication with a Future, 1987, 2d edit., 1988; (novel) Heart in Escrow, 1990; (poems) Faces in a Mirror, 1995, In the Service of Persuasion: English as Lingua Franca Across the Globe, 2001, Changing Scenery, 2003, Propaganda Is the Poetry of Politics, 2002, Propagandists: The Artists, 2004, (collection of poems) On This and That, 2006; contbr. chpts. to books, articles to mags.; author numerous poems. Named Poet of Yr., Internat. Libr. Poetry, 2000—06; named to, Internat. Poetry Hall of Fame, 1996; recipient Swedish Nat. award for short stories, Bonniers Pub. Ho., Stockholm, 1951. Mem. Soc. Jean Jacques Rousseau of Geneva (hon. life), Acad. Am. Poets. Democrat. Home: 613 W Vermont Ave Urbana IL 61801-4824 Office: U Ill Coll Comm 119 Gregory Hall 810 South Wright St Urbana IL 61801

DOW, DAVID SONTAG, retired ophthalmologist; b. Ann Arbor, Mich., Feb. 15, 1934; s. William Gould and Edna Lois (Sontag) Dow; m. Gail Anita Bade, Feb. 11, 1961 (dec. Feb. 2000); children: Steven Michael, Bonnie Jean, William Herbert, James Patrick; m. Figes Flaherty, Mar. 17, 2001. BS with distinction, U. Mich., 1956, MD, 1958, MS in Ophthalmology, 1964. Diplomate Am. Bd. Ophthalmology. Intern Denver Gen. Comm. Hosp., 1958-59; psychiatrist USAF Med. Svc., Wichita Falls, Tex., 1959-61; resident in ophthalmology U. Mich. Med. Ctr., Ann Arbor, 1961-64; pvt. practice ophthalmology Scruggs, Dow, and Kannwischer ptnr., Waco, Tex., 1964-88, Cen. Tex. Eye Clinic, Waco, 1988-97; pres. Woodway Found., 2006—. Contbg. editor: Waco Tribune Herald, 1983—; author: pamphlets in field. City coun. mem., mayor Waco City Con., 1977—81; mem. Woodway City Coun., 1997—2001; bd. dir. Waco Symphony Assn., 1970—89, 1994—2001, 2006—, pres., 1982—83; bd. dir. Tex. Med. Polit. Action Com., Austin, 1973—82; founding bd. dirs., chmn. Greater Waco Arts Coun., 1986—, chmn., 1992, 1994—2000. Capt. USAF, 1959—61. Mem.: Tex. Med. Assn., Am. Acad. Ophthalmology, Ridgewood Country Club, Rotary. Episcopalian. Avocations: politics, gardening, singing, musical theater.

DOW, GARNETT MCCORMICK, geologist, consultant; b. Biddeford, Maine, Aug. 5, 1934; s. Derry Walter Fogg and Charlotte Adelade (Cousens) D.; m. Sigrid Irene Dow, May 26, 1972; children: Michael Eric, Tod McCormick, Erin Renee. BA, U. Maine, 1959; MS, U. Ill., 1962, PhD, 1965. Geophysicist, geologist Amoco, Oklahoma City, 1964-67; sr. rsch. scientist Amoco Rsch. Ctr., Tulsa, 1967-73; geol. supr. Amoco Internat., Chgo., 1973-76; regional chief geologist Amoco Europe, London, 1976-80; exploration mgr. Amoco Indonesia, Jakarta, 1980-83; sr. geol. assoc. Amoco, Houston, 1983-92; exploration cons. Noble Energy, Inc., Houston, 1995—2004, sr. geol. advisor, 2004—. Cons. in field. Sustaining mem. Repu. Nat. Com., 1990's. With U.S. Army, 1954-56. Mem. Am. Assn. Petroleum Geologists, Am. Geophys. Union, Assn. Internat. Petroleum Negotiators, Houston Geol. Soc., Planetary Soc., N.Y. Acad. Scis., Soc. Econ. Geophysicists. Avocations: sailing, photography, astronomy. Office Phone: 281-876-6500.

DOW, MARTHA ANNE, academic administrator, biology professor; b. Little Rock, Jan. 3, 1939; d. Clarence Edgar and Gretchen Devron (Gable) Eudy; m. Gary Eugene Dow, Aug. 28, 1960; children: Julie, Kevin, Jerilyn. BS in Biology, No. Mont. Coll., 1961; MS in Microbiology, Mont. State U., 1969; PhD in Microbiology, U. Hawaii, 1989. Registered microbiologist. Prof., chair biology No. Mont. Coll., Havre, 1986-90, v.p. acad. affairs, 1990-92; provost Oreg. Inst. Tech., Klamath Falls, Oreg., 1992—98, pres., 1998—. Dir. Mont. Environ. Tng. Ctr., EPA, No. Mont. Coll., 1989; pres. Nat. Environ. Tng. Assn., Phoenix, Oreg., 1990-92. Recipient Disting. Svc. award, Klamath County C. of C., 2000, Candice Richard award, Klamath County Econ. Develop. Corp., 2000. Mem. Am. Assn. for Advancement of Sci., Am. Assn. State Coll. & Univ., Am. Soc. for Engring. Edn., Am. Soc. Microbiology, Am. Water Works Assn., Water Environment Fedn. Methodist. Office: Oreg Inst Tech 3201 Campus Dr Klamath Falls OR 97601-8801*

DOW, MARY ALEXIS, auditor; b. South Amboy, NJ, Feb. 19, 1949; d. Alexander and Elizabeth Anne (Reilly) Pawlowski. BS with honors, U. R.I., 1971. CPA Oreg. Staff acct. Deloitte & Touche, Boston, 1971-74; sr. acct. Price Waterhouse, Portland, Oreg., 1974-77, mgr., 1977-81, sr. mgr., 1981-84; CFO Copeland Lumber Yards Inc., Portland, 1984-86; pvt. practice, 1986—94; elected auditor Metro, Portland, 1995—2007. Past bd. dirs. Oreg. Health Sci. U. Med. Group. Past. chmn. bd. dirs., exec. com. Oreg. Trails chpt. N.W. Regional Blood Svcs. ARC; past. bd. dirs., exec. com., treas. Oreg. Mus. Sci. and Industry. Mem.: AICPA, Fin. Execs. Internat. (nat. chmn., past nat. treas., past pres. Portland chpt., past v.p. western area), Oreg. Soc. CPAs (past bd. dirs.), Am. Woman's Soc. CPAs, Multnomah Athletic Club (past treas., past trustee), City Club (past bd. govs.). Roman Catholic.

DOW, PETER ANTHONY, advertising executive; b. Detroit, Oct. 7, 1933; s. Douglas and Mary Louise (Murray) D.; m. Jane Ann Ottaway, Mar. 21, 1959; children— Jennifer Dow Murphy, Peter Kinnersley, Thomas Anthony BA, U. Mich., 1955. Account exec. Campbell-Ewald Co., Detroit, 1958-66, exec. v.p., 1979-82, pres., 1982-93, vice chmn., 1993-95, ret., 1995; account supr. Young & Rubicam, Detroit, 1966-68; advt. dir. Chrysler Corp., Detroit, 1968-77, dir. mktg., 1977-79. Bd. dirs. Techno Brands, Inc., Masco Corp. Trustee emeritus Lawrenceville Sch., N.J. Served to lt. (j.g.) USNR, 1955-58. Mem. Mich. Advt. Industry Alliance (past pres.), Grosse Pointe Club, Detroit Athletic Club, Adcraft Club (past pres.), Country Club Detroit, Old Club. Republican. Presbyterian.

DOW, RONALD F., librarian, dean; b. Deadwood, SD, Jan. 26, 1949; s. Fay Ellsworth and Aldeen Faye (Decker) D.; m. Susan White, Apr. 24, 1982; children: Wesley E., Eleanor W. BA, Augustana Col., 1971; MLS, Syracuse U., 1972; PhD, Penn. State U., 1997. Asst. reference librarian Hamilton Col., Clinton, NY, 1972-76; asst. bus. and engring. librarian Dartmouth Col., Hanover, NH, 1976-80; dir. grad. bus. adminstrn. libr. NYU, 1980-83; first v.p. & dir. libraries Shearson Lehman Am. Express, NYC, 1983-90; assoc. dean of libraries Penn. State U., 1990-96; dean River Campus Libraries U. Rochester, NY, 1996—. Mem. editl. bd. U. Rochester Press; contbr. articles to profl. jours. Mem. ALA, Am. Assn. Higher Edn. Office: U Rochester Rush Rhees Library Rochester NY 14627 Office Phone: 585-275-4461.

DOW, SIMON, artistic director, choreographer; b. Australia; Diploma, Australian Ballet Sch. Joined Australian Ballet, Stuttgart (Germany) Ballet; joined, prin. dancer Wash. Ballet, 1979; prin. dancer Australian Ballet, 1982-85, San Francisco Ballet, 1985-88, Boston Ballet, 1988-90; freelance guest artist and master tchr., 1990; assoc. artistic dir. Wash. Ballet, 1992-93, 96-97; art dir. Milw. Ballet Co., 1999—2002; artistic dir. West Australian Ballet, Perth, Australia, 2003—. Master tchr. Australian Ballet, Australian Ballet Sch., Sydney Dance Co., NSW Coll. Dance, Am. Ballet Theatre, Boston Ballet, Met. Opera Ballet, Feld Ballet, Milw. Ballet, Internat. Tanz Wochen, Vienna, Austria, Frankfurt Ballet, Germany, Les Grands Ballet Cans.; tchr. Wash. Sch. Ballet, David Howard Sch. Dance, NY; jury mem. 4th Internat. Ballet Competition, Helsinki, USA Internat. Ballet Competition, 2006; bd. dirs. Ausdance WA; apptd. to dance bd. Australia Coun., 2004—; choreographer Milw. BAllet, West Australia Ballet, Theaterhaus, Stuttgart, Joyce Soho, NYC, Steps Beyond, NYC, St. Mark's Ch., NYC, NY Festival Ballet, Florentine Opera, Milw., Jackson Internat. Ballet Competition. Guest appearances include Mann Performing Arts Ctr., Phila., Spoleto Festival, Wolf Trap Farm park, Jacob's Pillow Dance Festival, Pendleton Music Festival, Detroit Symphony; choreographer (ballets) Wash. Ballet, N.Y. Festival Ballet, Boston Ballet, Theater Artaud, San Francisco, Cin. Dance Pl., Theaterhaus, Stuttgart, Germany, St. Mark's Ch., N.Y.C., The Joyce Soho. Recipient Cecchetti Jr. medal, Best Ptnr. award, Internat. Ballet Competition, 1981. Office: West Australian Ballet PO Box 7228 Cloisters Sq Perth 6850 Australia Office Phone: 08-9481-0407.

DOWBEN, ROBERT MORRIS, physiologist, researcher; b. Phila., Apr. 18, 1927; married, June 20, 1950; 3 children. AB, Haverford Coll., 1946; MS, U. Chgo., 1947, MD, 1949. Intern U. Chgo. Clinics, 1949-50; rsch. fellow U. Oslo, 1950-51; fellow Johns Hopkins Hosp., 1951-52; resident in medicine U. Pa. Hosp., 1952-53; instr. medicine U. Pa. and dir. radioisotope unit VA Hosp., Phila., 1953-55; asst. prof. medicine Northwestern U. Med. Sch., 1957-62; asso. prof. biology MIT, 1962-68; lectr. medicine Harvard U. Med. Sch., 1962-68; prof. med. sci. Brown U., 1968-72; prof. biochemistry U. Bergen, Norway, 1972; prof. physiology and neurology, dir. grad. program in biophysics U. Tex. Health Sci. Ctr., Dallas, 1972-88, prof. neurology, 1988-93; dir. Med. Cell Biology Lab. Baylor Rsch. Inst., Dallas, 1987-93; prof. physiology Brown U., Providence, 1993—. Cons. neurologist Children's Hosp., Dallas, Scottish Rite Hosp., Dallas, Presbyn. Hosp., Dallas, Baylor Hosp, Dallas, 1972-93; mem. corp. Haverford Coll., Pa., 1979-2001, Marine Biol. Lab., Woods Hole, Mass., 1964-79; trustee Mt. Desert Island Biol. Lab., 1994-98; adv. com. to the pres., Haverford Coll., 1997-2001; bd. dirs. Greenhill Sch., Dallas, 1974-77. Author: Biological Membranes, 1969, General Physiology, 1971, Cell Biology, 1972, also numerous articles; editor: Cell and Muscle Motility. Served to capt. M.C. USAF, 1955-57. Lalor fellow; recipient Disting. Svc. award Assn. Neuromuscular Diseases, 1964, Disting. Svc. award Alumni Assn. U. Chgo., 1980. Mem. Am. Physiol. Soc., Am. Soc. Biol. Chemists, Am. Chem. Soc., Soc. Exptl. Biology and Medicine, Biophys. Soc., Soc. Clin. Investigation, Ctrl. Soc. Clin. Rsch., Mass. Med. Soc., So. Med. Soc., Dallas County Med. Soc., Tex. Med. Assn., Biochem. Soc. London, Faraday Soc. (London), Phi Beta Kappa, Sigma Xi. Mem. Soc. Of Friends. Office: Brown U Physiology Dept PO Box G-B3 Providence RI 02912-9107

DOWD, CAROLYN LAY, social worker; b. Hagerstown, Md., May 1, 1940; d. James S. Jr. and Emily Graham (Miller) Lay; m. William J. Dowd, Sept. 1, 1962 (dec.); children: William J. Jr., James P. AB, Meredith Coll., 1962; MSW, Catholic U., 1987. Cert. social worker, clin. social worker. Social work cons. Bethesda (Md.) Fellowship House, 1987-89; social worker Family Svcs. Agy., Gaithersburg, Md., 1987-98, dir. svcs. for srs., 1991-98, clin. dir., 1996-98; pvt. practice Gaithersburg, 1991-98; clin. care mgr. Falls Church, Va., 1998—. Presenter in field. Past mem. bd. dirs. Alzheimer's Assn. of Greater Wash. Mem. NASW (register of clin. social work, diplomate), Acad. Cert. Social Workers. Home: 21913 Foxlair Rd Gaithersburg MD 20882-1306 Address: 12369 C Sunrise Valley Dr Reston VA 20191 E-mail: cnldowd@verizon.net.

DOWD, DAVID JOSEPH, banker, construction executive; b. Long Island City, NY, June 6, 1924; s. David Joseph and Elsie (Schaeffler) B.; children— Laury, David, Patrick, Carol. BS in Bus. Adminstrn, NYU,

1949. Asst. v.p. Irving Trust Co., NYC, 1952-64; v.p. Franklin Nat. Bank, NYC, 1964-66; sr. v.p. Security Nat. Bank, Huntington, NY, 1966-72; pres. Nassau Trust Co., Glen Cove, NY, 1972-75, Bankers Service Co., 1975—; pub. Long Island Financial Newsletter, 1976-82; pres. Victorian Homes, Inc., 1980-97. Pres. Suffolk County council Boy Scouts Am., 1969-70; chmn. Suffolk Community Devel. Corp., 1973-74; Trustee Stony Brook Found., State U. N.Y., 1972. Served with USMCR, 1942-45, 51-52. Mem. N.Y. State Bankers Assn. (chmn. group VII 1972-75), L.I. Bankers Assn. (dir. 1969-74), Suffolk County Bankers Assn. (pres. 1971-72), Empire State C. of C. (dir. 1969-75) Address: PO Box 1057 Shelter Island NY 11964

DOWD, EDWARD L., JR., lawyer, former prosecutor; s. Edward L. Dowd; m. Jill Goessling; 3 children. JD with distinction, St. Mary's Univ. With Dowd, Dowd & Dowd; from asst. U.S. atty. to chief narcotics sect., regional dir. south cen. region Pres.'s Organized Crime Drug Enforcement Task Force U.S. Atty.'s Office, 1979-84; pvt. practice, 1984-93; U.S. atty. ea. dist. of Mo. U.S. Dept. Justice, St. Louis, 1993-99; dep. spl. counsel to John C. Danforth Spl. Counsel Waco Investigation, 1999; ptnr. Bryan Cave LLP, St. Louis, 1999—2006, Dowd Bennett LLP, St. Louis, 2006—. Office: Dowd Bennett LLP 7733 Forsyth Blvd Ste 1410 Saint Louis MO 63105 Office Phone: 314-889-7300. Business E-Mail: edowd@dowdbennett.com.

DOWD, JOHN MAGUIRE, lawyer; b. Brockton, Mass., Nov. 2, 1941; s. Paul L. and Mary (Maquire) Dowd; m. Carole L. Folts, June 12, 1965; children: Thomas P., Anne M., Sarah E., Michael T., Daniel M. AB cum laude, St. Bernard Coll., Cullman, Ala., 1963; JD, Emory U., 1965. Bar: DC 1967, admitted to practice: US Ct. Appeals (DC Cir.) 1967, US Ct. Appeals (4th Cir.) 1967, US Ct. Appeals (5th Cir.) 1967, US Ct. Appeals (10th Cir.) 1967, US Ct. Appeals (11th Cir.) 1967, US Dist. Ct. (DC) 1967, US Ct. Internat. Trade 1967, US Supreme Ct. 1970, US Dist. Ct. (So. Dist.) Ga. 1987. Trial atty. Tax div. US Dept. Justice, Washington, 1969-72; chief strike force 18 Criminal div. US Dept. Justice, Washington, 1972-78; ptnr. Whitman & Ransom, Washington, 1978-84, Heron, Burchette, Ruckert & Rothwell, Washington, 1984-90; ptnr., head criminal litig. group, mem. mgmt. com. Akin, Gump, Strauss, Hauer & Feld, L.L.P., Washington, 1990—. Arbitrator Internat. C. of C., Internat. Ct. Arbitration, 1994—; spl. counsel Commr. of Baseball, 1989—92; lectr. Nat. Inst. for Trial Adv. Georgetown U., 1979—81, lectr. continuing legal edn., 1987—88. Co-author: (profl. law text) U.S. Laundering, Forfeiture Laws Now Reach All Points on Globe, 2002; contbr. articles to profl. jours. Trustee Flint Hill Sch., Oakton, Va.; bd. dirs. Injured Marine Semper Fi Fund. Capt. USMC, 1965—69. Named one of 75 Best Lawyers, Washingtonian mag., 2002. Master: Edward Bennett Williams Inn of Ct.; fellow: Fellows of Young Lawyers of the Am. Bar; mem.: DC Bar Assn., ABA. Avocations: golf, swimming, walking, reading, teaching. Office: Akin Gump Strauss Hauer & Feld LLP Ste 400 1333 New Hampshire Ave NW Washington DC 20036-1564 Home Phone: 703-759-4793; Office Phone: 202-887-4386. E-mail: jdowd@akingump.com.

DOWD, MAUREEN, columnist; b. Washington, Jan. 14, 1952; d. Michael and Peggy D. BA English Lit., Catholic U., DC, 1973. From editl. asst. to feature writer The Washington Star, 1974-81; from corr. to writer Time mag., 1981-83; metro reporter N.Y. Times, 1983-86, D.C. reporter, 1986-95, opinion-editl. columnist, 1995—. Author: Bushworld: Enter at Your Own Risk, 2004 (Publishers Weekly Bestseller), Are Men Necessary?: When Sexes Collide, 2005. Finalist Pulitzer Prize for nat. reporting, 1992; named one of Glamour's Women of the Yr., 1996; recipient Breakthrough Award, "Women, Men and Media", Columbia U., 1991, Matrix Award, NY Women in Comm., 1994, Pulitzer Prize for commentary, 1999, Damon Runyon Award, Denver Press Club, 2000, Golden Plate award, Acad. Achievement, 2004. Office: NY Times 1627 I St NW Washington DC 20006-4007*

DOWD, MORGAN DANIEL, retired political science professor, dean; b. Boston, Feb. 21, 1933; s. Joseph Francis and Marion Caroline (Calcari) D.; m. Dianne May Robichaud, Aug. 29, 1959; children: Megan Eileen, Sean Morgan, Colin Martin, Blaine Christopher, Roarke Terence. BA cum laude, St. Michael's Coll., Winooski Park, Conn., 1955; JD, Cath. U. Am., Washington, DC, 1958; MA, U. Mass., Amherst, 1962, PhD, 1964. Instr. U. Maine, 1959-60, U. Mass., 1960-61; asst. prof. polit. sci. SUNY-Fredonia, 1963-67, assoc. prof., 1967-76, prof., 1976—, dean grad. studies and research, 1969-78, dean faculty for natural and social scis., 1978-84, joint prof. bus. and polit. sci., 1984—98, dist. svc. prof., 1995—, ret., 1998; sr. assoc. Mendez Eng. and Assocs., Bethesda, Md., 1998—. Cons. Mid. States Assn. Colls. and Univs., 1977—; project dir. USIA grant, Albania, 1992-94, 95-96. Contbr. articles to law jours., 1956-78; co-editor: World Dictionary of Environmental Research Centers, 2d edit., 1974. Bd. dirs. com. Health Systems Agy. Western NY, 1986-87, mem. exec. com.; regional member NY state commn. Bicentennial of Constn., 1987; convocation speaker West Chester U. Pa., 1991. Recipient Pres.'s Medallion award, West Chester U. Pa., 1991, Extraordinary Svc. to Commn. on Higher Edn. U. Rochester, 1994. Mem. Columbia U. Seminar on History of Legal and Polit. Theory, Torch Club, Delta Epsilon Sigma, Pi Sigma Alpha, Delta Theta Phi, Phi Eta Sigma Democrat. Roman Catholic. E-mail: dowd@fredonia.edu.

DOWD, NED, film producer; b. Boston, May 26, 1950; BA, Bowdoin Coll., 1972; MA in Teaching, McGill U., Montreal, Que., Can., 1973. Asst. dir. Dirs. Guild Am., LA, 1981; producer Orion, Paramount, HBO, LA, 1987. Assoc. prodr: (films) Things Change, 1987; prodr.: (TV films) Lip Service, 1988 (Acad. Cable Excellence award 1989), (films) Let It Ride, 1989, State of Grace, 1990, The Last of the Mohicans, 1992, The Three Musketeers, 1993, The 13th Warrior, 1999, Shanghai Noon, 2000, The Count of Monte Cristo, 2002, Reign of Fire, 2002; exec. prodr.: (films) Wonder Boys, 2000, Veronica Guerin, 2003, King Arthur, 2004, Apocalypto, 2006. Mem. Dirs. Guild Am. Office: Dean Avedon Inc 29169 Heathercliff Rd Malibu CA 90265-6107*

DOWD, PETER JEROME, public relations executive; b. Bklyn., Oct. 5, 1942; s. Jerome Ambrose and Mary Agnes (Young) D.; m. Brenda Badura, Nov. 25, 1972; 1 child, Kelly Ann. AB, Fordham U., 1964. Reporter UPI, NYC, 1964-66; account exec. Hill and Knowlton, NYC, 1966-71, v.p., 1971-74; sr. v.p., mgr. Hill and Knowlton (Los Angeles office), 1974-78, mng. dir. Western region, 1978-80, exec. v.p., 1980; ptnr. Haley, Kiss & Dowd, Inc., Los Angeles, 1980-83; group v.p. Am. Med. Internat., 1983-88; v.p. pub. rels. Texaco Inc., White Plains, NY, 1989-96; sr. v.p. corp. affairs Fidelity Investments, Boston, 1996-99; pub. affairs cons., 1999—2006; chmn. Marshall Consultants, 2006—. Instr. U. So. Calif., Calif. State U., Fullerton. Bd. dirs. Cath. Big Bros., Nature Conservancy (Lower Hudson chpt.). Mem. Pub. Rels. Soc. Am., Alan Page Soc., Town Hall West (v.p., dir.), Westchester County Assn. (bd. dirs.), Nature Conservancy (bd. dirs. Lower Hudson chpt.), U.S. Mil. Acad. Pub. Affairs (adv. com.). Republican. Roman Catholic. Office: Fidelity Investments 82 Devonshire St Boston MA 02109-3605

DOWD, THOMAS F., lawyer; b. Boston, 1943; AB, Harvard U., 1965; JD, Case Western Reserve U., 1974. Bar: Ohio 1974, DC 1989, Mo. 1999. Ptnr. Baker & Hostetler, Washington; named ptnr. Bryan, Cave, McPheeters & Roberts, Washington, 1989; sr. v.p., gen. counsel, sec. Graybar Electric Co. Inc., St. Louis, 1997—. Adv. coun. Nat. Assn. Minority and Women-Owned Law Firms, 2004—. Editor articles Case Western Reserve Law Review, 1973-74. Mem. Order of Coif. Office: Graybar Electric Co Inc 34 N Meramec Ave Saint Louis MO 63105

DOWDELL, RODGER B., JR., electronics executive; BSEE cum laude, Brown Univ., 1971; MSEE, Univ. Rhode Island, 1975. With Texas Instruments, Brown & Sharpe, Naval Underwater Sys. Ctr.; founder, pres. Independent Energy Inc.; cons. Am. Power Conversion (APC), W. Kingston, RI, 1985, pres., CEO, 1985—, chmn., 1988—. Bd. dir. Ctr. for Quality Mgmt., Cambridge, Mass. Named Entrepreneur of Yr., New England region, Ernst & Young, 1990, Merrill Lynch, 1990; named to Hall of Fame, Univ. RI Coll. Engring., 1998; recipient Thomas H. Lee Meritorious Svc. award, Ctr. for Quality Mgmt., 2001. Office: APC 132 Fairgrounds Rd West Kingston RI 02892 Office Phone: 401-789-5735. Office Fax: 401-789-3710.

DOWDEN, THOMAS CLARK, telecommunication executive; b. Ridgetop, Tenn., May 6, 1935; s. James Robert and Anna Mary (Hunter) D.; m. Wendy Ellen Vereen, Jan. 27, 1962; children: Anna V. Dowden Tschetter, Constance H. Cobbs, John T. BA in Journalism, U. Ga., 1962, MA in Polit. Sci., 1963. Account exec. Corinthian Broadcasting, Houston, 1963-65; v.p., sec. Cox Cable Comm., Atlanta, 1965-76; owner, CEO Dowden Comm., Atlanta, 1977—. Mem. bd. dirs. Ga. Dept. Industry, Trade and Tourism, 1994-97; bd. dirs., chmn. George Foster Peabody Radio-TV-Cable awards, 1991-93. Organizer Cable TV's Role in 1976 Presdl. Election, Atlanta, 1975-76; trustee U. Ga., 1998-2004. Mem. Wade Hampton Golf Club (Cashiers, N.C.), Royal St. George's Golf Club (Sandwich, Kent, Eng.), Royal County Down Golf Club (Newcastle, No. Ireland), U.S. Sr. Golf Assn. Republican. Episcopalian. Avocations: golf, photography, travel. Office: Dowden Communications 650 Blackberry Ln Clarkesville GA 30523-4461 Home (Winter): 79655 Mandarina La Quinta CA 92253 Office Phone: 706-754-6703.

DOWDLE, PATRICK DENNIS, lawyer; b. Denver, Dec. 8, 1948; s. William Robert and Helen (Schraeder) D.; m. Eleanor Pryor, Mar. 8, 1975; children: Jeffery William, Andrew Peter. BA, Cornell Coll., Mt. Vernon, Iowa, 1971; JD, Boston U., 1975. Bar: Colo. 1975, U.S. Dist. Ct. Colo. 1975, U.S. Ct. Appeals (10th cir.) 1976, U.S. Supreme Ct. 1978. Acad. dir. in Japan Sch. Internat. Tng., Putney, Vt., 1974; assoc. Decker & Miller, Denver, 1975-77; ptnr. Miller, Makkai & Dowdle, Denver, 1977—. Designated counsel criminal appeals Colo. Atty. Gens. Office, Denver, 1980-81; guardian ad litem Adams County Dist. Ct., Brighton, Colo., 1980-83; affiliated counsel ACLU, Denver, 1980—. Mem. Colo. Bar Assn., Denver Bar Assn. (various coms.), Porsche Club of Am. Avocations: scuba diving, photography, wine making, travel, skiing. Home: 3254 Tabor Ct Wheat Ridge CO 80033-5367 Office: Miller Makkai & Dowdle 2325 W 72nd Ave Denver CO 80221-3101 Home Phone: 720-837-5060; Office Phone: 303-427-7584. Business E-Mail: pdowdle@mmdlaw.us.

DOWDY, ROBERT ALAN, retired lawyer, director; b. June 12, 1941; s. Andrew Hunter and Helen Marie (Brandes) Dowdy; m. Lynne Bryant, June 18, 1966; children: Roger Alan, Douglas John. BA, U. Calif., Berkeley, JD, 1966. Bar: D.C. 1967, Calif. 1968, Wash. 1974. Atty. Am. Airlines, NYC, 1969—72, Weyerhaeuser Co., Tacoma, 1972—74, sr. legal counsel, 1974—86, asst. gen. counsel, 1986—91, dep. gen. counsel, 1991—97, v.p., gen. counsel, 1997—2004, sr. v.p., gen. counsel, 2004—06; ret., 2006. Dir. Green Arrow Motor Co., Tacoma; mem. Wash. Bd. Bar Examiners, 1982—; arbitrator King County Superior Ct., 1986—; vis. com. U. Wash. Sch. Law, Seattle, 1986—. Contbr. articles to profl. jours. Bd. dir. N.W. Chamber Orch., Seattle, 1975—76; trustee St. James Sch., Kent, Wash., 1982—84; elder St. Elizabeth Episcopal Ch., Burien, Wash., 1976—78. Capt. US Army, 1966—69. Decorated Army Commendation medal. Mem.: Am. Forest Products and Paper Assn. (gen. counsel com. 1997—), Assn. Gen. Counsel, Wash. Bar Assn. (exec. com. corp. sect. 1977—79, mem. legal edn. sect. 1982—84). Republican.

DOWDY, WILLIAM CLARENCE, JR., retired lawyer; b. McKinney, Tex., Feb. 27, 1925; s. William C. and Emily Harryette (Gilson) D.; m. Ann Atkinson, Aug. 31, 1947; children: William Clarence III, Jill Ann, Daniel Andrew. Student, North Tex. Agrl. Coll., Arlington, 1942-43; BBA, U. Tex., Austin, 1949, JD, 1951. Bar: Tex. 1951, U.S. Supreme Ct. 1957, U.S. Dist. Ct. (no. dist.) Tex. 1960, U.S. Ct. Appeals (5th cir.) 1974. Asst. dist. atty. Dallas County, 1951-54; atty. Tex. & Pacific Ry. Co., Dallas, 1954-59; gen. atty. Tex. & Pacific Ry. Co./Mo. Pacific R.R. Co., Dallas, 1959-82; gen. solicitor Mo. Pacific R.R. Co./Union Pacific R.R. Co., Dallas, 1982-86, sr. counsel, 1986-87; ret., 1987. Dir. Great S.W. R.R.; v.p., asst. sec., dir. Weatherford, Mineral Wells & Northwestern R.R. Elder, trustee Presbyn. Ch. With field arty., 24th divsn. AUS, 1943-46; PTO. Mem. Tex. Bar Assn., Dallas Bar Assn., Collin County Bar Assn., Nat. Assn. R.R. Trial Counsel (exec. com., regional v.p.), Tower Club (Dallas), Eldorado Club (McKinney, Tex.), Phi Alpha Delta, Kappa Sigma. Home: 510 Tucker St Mc Kinney TX 75069-2714

DOWELL, DAVID RAY, library administrator; b. Trenton, Mo., Nov. 14, 1942; s. Clarence Ray and Ruth Lucille (Adams) D.; m. Arlene Grace Taylor, May 9, 1964 (div. 1983); children: Deborah Ruth, Jonathan Ray; m. Denise Jaye Christie, Aug. 19, 1983; stepchildren: David Lee Smithey, Jason Alan Smithey. BA in History, Okla. Bapt. U., 1964; AM in History, U. Ill., 1966, MLS, 1972; PhD, U. NC, Chapel Hill, 1986. Tchr. Wilson Jr. High Sch., Tulsa, 1964-65; head library adminstrv. services Iowa State U., Ames, 1972-75; asst. univ. librarian Duke U., Durham, N.C., 1975-81; dir. libraries Ill. Inst. Tech., Chgo., 1981—90; libr. dir. & asst. dean Pasadena City Coll., Calif., 1991—95; dir. libr./learning resources Cuesta Coll., San Luis Obispo, Calif., 1995—. Cons. County Commr.'s Library Planning Com., Durham, 1976, Gov.'s Conf. on Libraries and Info. Services, Raleigh, NC, 1978, Biblioteca do Centro Batista, Goiania, Brazil, 1978. Contbr. articles to profl. jours. Trustee Glenwood-Lynwood Pub. Library Dist., Ill., 1985-87. Served to capt. USAF, 1967-71 Mem. ALA (chmn. profl. ethics com. 1977-78, chmn. election com. 1982-83, chmn. libr. personnel adv. com. 1979-80, career pathways task force, 2000-02, awards com. 2001-05, Libr. of Future award jury, 2002-03, chmn. 2003-04, edn. com., 2003-04, scholarship taskforce, 2004-05), Assn. Coll. and Research Libraries (nominat ing com. 1979-80, libr. tech. asst. training com., 1992-2005, chair 1993-95, academic status com., 1993-, instnl. priorities & faculty rewards task force, 1997, profl. devel. com, 1997-2001, Learning Resources Leadership award, 2007), Libr. Adminstrn. & Mgmt. Assn. (bd. dirs. 1981-83, membership com.& govtl. affairs task force, 1983-84, alternative finance task force, 1984-85, orientation com., 1985-87). Democrat. Baptist. Avocations: tennis, genealogy. Home: 2627 Laurel Ave Morro Bay CA 93442-1723 Office: Cuesta Coll PO Box 8106 San Luis Obispo CA 93403-8106 Office Phone: 805-546-3159. E-mail: ddowell@cuesta.edu.

DOWELL, EARL HUGH, dean, aerospace and mechanical engineering educator; s. Earl S. and Edna Bernice (Dean) D.; m. Lynn Cowell; children: Marla Lorraine, Janice Lynelle, Michael Hugh. BS, U. Ill., 1959; SM, MIT, 1961, ScD, 1964. Rsch. engr. Boeing Co., 1962-63; rsch. asst. MIT, 1963-64, rsch. engr., 1964, asst. prof., 1964-65; asst. prof. aerospace and mech. engring. Princeton U., 1964-68, assoc. prof., 1968-72, prof., 1972-83, assoc. chmn., 1975-77, acting chmn., 1979; William Holland Hall prof. mech. engring. and materials sci. Duke U., Durham, NC, 1983—, dean, 1983-99. Cons. to industry and govt. Author: Aeroelasticity of Plates and Shells, 1974, A Modern Course in Aeroelasticity, 1978, 4th edit., 2004, Nonlinear Studies in Aeroelasticity, 1988, Dynamics of Very High Dimensional Systems, 2003; editl. bd.: AIAA Jour., 2000-, Jour. Sound and Vibration, 1988—, Jour. Fluids and Structures, 1987—, Jour. Nonlinear Dynamics, 1990—; contbr. articles to profl. jours. Chmn. NJ Noise Control Coun., 1972-76. Named outstanding young alumnus U. Ill. Sch. Aero. and Astronautical Engring., 1973, disting. alumnus, 1975; recipient Alumni Honor award Coll. Engring. U. Ill. Fellow: ASME, AIAA (hon.; v.p. publs. 1981—83, Structures, Structural Dynamics and Material award 1980, Theodore Von Karman lectr. 2002, Walter J. and Angeline H. Crichlow Trust prize 2007), Am. Acad. Mechanics (pres. 1991, Disting. Svc. award 1994); mem.: NAE, NAE, Acoustical Soc. Am., Am. Helicopter Soc. Office: Dept Mech Engring and Materials Sci Duke U Box 90300 Hudson Hall Durham NC 27708-0300 Office Phone: 919-660-5302. Business E-Mail: dowell@ee.duke.edu.

DOWELL, JAMES DALE, lawyer; b. Goose Creek, Tex., July 17, 1932; s. James Dale and Margaret (King) D.; m. Patricia Jo Skaggs, Feb. 2, 1957; children: Terry Dowell Owens, James Dale III. BA, Tex. A&M U, 1954; LLB, U. Tex., 1957. Bar: Tex. 1956, U.S. Dist. Ct. (ea. dist.) Tex. 1958, U.S Ct. Appeals (5th cir.) 1964, U.S. Supreme Ct. 1969. Assoc. King, Sharfstein & Rienstra, Beaumont, Tex., 1957-63, ptnr., 1963-68, Rienstra, Rienstra & Dowell, Beaumont, 1968-85, Rienstra, Dowell & Flatten, Beaumont, 1985—. Mem. Tex. Dem. Exec. Com., 1966-68, del. Nat. Conv., 1976—. Mem. ABA, State Bar Tex., Tex. Bar Found., Jefferson County Bar Assn. (pres. 1978-79, Blackstone award 2000), Def. Rsch. Inst., Tex. Assn. Def. Counsel, Beaumont Country Club, Beaumont Club (bd. dirs. 1975-77), Rotary (Paul Harris fellow 2000), Phi Gamma Delta. Methodist. Avocation: reading. Home: 6275 Wilchester Ln Beaumont TX 77706-4328 Office: 595 Orleans St Beaumont TX 77701-3214 Personal E-mail: riendf@aol.com.

DOWELL, JAMES THOMAS, artist, filmmaker; b. Greenville, Tex., Sept. 11, 1949; s. Cam Franklin and Evelyn Pruitt Dowell; life ptnr. John Kolomvakis. BFA, So. Meth. U., 1972; MFA, U. Iowa, 1974. V.p. Symbiosis Films Inc., NYC, 1995—. Exhibitions include San Angelo Mus. Art, Tex., Meadows Mus., Dallas, Tyler (Tex.) Mus. Art; dir.: (documentary film) Sleep in a Nest of Flames (to be aired RAI (Italian Pub. Tv), 2006), Ned Rorem: Word & Music. Democrat. Home: 6010 Desco Dr Dallas TX 75225 Office: Symbiosis Films Inc 777 West End Ave New York NY 10025 Home Phone: 214-368-4420; Office Phone: 212-666-0724. Business E-Mail: symbiosisfilms@msn.com.

DOWELL, MICHAEL BRENDAN, chemist; b. NYC, Nov. 18, 1942; s. William Henry and Anne Susan (Cannon) D.; m. Gail Elizabeth Renton, Mar. 16, 1968; children: Rebecca S. Hall, Margaret A. Scott. BS, Fordham U., 1963; PhD, Pa. State U., 1967. Physicist U.S. Army Frankford Arsenal, Phila., 1967-69; rsch. scientist Parma Tech. Ctr., Union Carbide Corp., Ohio, 1969-74, devel. mgr. carbon fiber applications, 1974-76, group leader metals and ceramics rsch., 1976-80, sr. group leader process rsch., 1980-82, mgr. market devel., 1982-92, Praxair Advanced Ceramics Inc. (formerly Union Carbide Corp), Ohio, 1992-93, Advanced Ceramics Corp., Cleve., 1993—, v.p. tech., 1999—2002; v.p. 5iTech, LLC, Cleve., 2003—06; engring. mgr. Powdermet Inc., Euclid, Ohio, 2007—. Mem. materials tech. adv. com. U.S. Dept. Commerce, 1994—2001; lectr. ops. mgmt. Case Western Res. U., 2001—03. Contbr. articles to profl. jours. Capt. ordnance AUS, 1967—69. Mem. Am. Chem. Soc., Am. Phys. Soc., U.S. Advanced Ceramics Assn. (bd. dirs. 1988-96), Am. Soc. Metals Internat. (govt. and pub. affairs com. 1989—), Soc. Prof. Fellows Case Western Res. U., Phi Lambda Upsilon. Roman Catholic. Home: 368 N Main St Hudson OH 44236-2246 Office: Powdermet Inc 24112 Rockwell Dr Euclid OH 44117 Office Phone: 216-404-0053 ext. 112. Personal E-mail: mbdowell@alltel.net.

DOWER GOLD, CATHERINE ANNE, music history educator; b. South Hadley, Mass., May 19, 1924; d. Lawrence Frederick Dower and Marie (Barbieri) Barber; m. Arthur Gold, Mar. 24, 1994 (dec. Oct. 1998). AB, Hamline U., 1945; MA, Smith Coll., 1948; B in Liturgical Music, U. Mont., Gregorian Inst. Am., 1949; PhD, The Cath. U. Am., 1968. Organist St. Theresa Chapel of Little Flower, South Hadley, Mass., 1937—42; New England rep. Gregorian Inst. Am., Toledo, 1948-49; tchr. music, organist St. Rose Ch. and Sch., Meriden, Conn., 1949-53; supr. music Holyoke Pub. Schs., Mass., 1953-55; instr. music U. Mass., Amherst, 1955-56; prof. music Westfield State Coll., Mass., 1956-90, prof. emerita, 1991—; columnist and freelance writer Holyoke Transcript Telegram, 1991-93. Vis. assoc. prof. music Herbert Lehman Coll. CUNY, 1970—71; concert series presenter Westfield State Coll., 1987—91, rschr. tchr. *Catherine Gold, author of 5 books and numerous published articles, received many awards from the college where she taught. She was not married and had no dependents, therefore the college president said she did not need equal salary to the male faculty members. She sued the State of Massachusetts to receive better pension. A federal judge heard the suit and determined in her favor. She won the case! This is her contribution to the women on the state college faculties. When she won the case, those who had been members for a certain length of time recieved a stipend raising their salaries.* Author: Puerto Rican Music Following the Spanish American War, 1898-1910, 1983, Alfred Einstein on Music, 1991, Yella Pessl: First Lady of the Harpsichord, 1992, Fifty Years of Marching Together, 2001, Actividades Musicales en Puerto Rico: después de la guerra hispanoamericana 1898-1910, 2006, numerous poems; editor: (newsletter) Westfield State Coll., 2000—; presenter Irish Concert Springfield Symphony Orch., 1981—(plaque, 1982); contbr. articles to profl. jours. Pres. Coun. for Human Understanding Holyoke, 1981—83, Friends of Holyoke Pub. Libr., 1990—91; bd. dirs., chmn. nominating com. Holyoke Pub. Libr., 1987—89; bd. dirs. Holyoke Pub. Libr. Corp., 1991—94, Springfield Symphony Orch., 1992—94, Fla. Philharm. Orch., 2000—03, trustee, 2002—03; presiding officer inauguration Dr. Irving Buchman pres. of Westfield State Coll.; mem. ethics com. Holyoke Hosp., 1988—94; sec. Haiti Mission, 1982—94; bd. overseers Mullen U., 1993; hon. mem. bd. Coun. Human Understanding, 1994—; hon. mem. WSC Found., 1994—; co-chair United Jewish Appeal/Jewish Fed. Boca Lago Women's Divsn., South Palm Beach County, 1996—97; mem. St. Patrick's Com., Holyoke, Mass., 1991—; 1st v.p. fin. and adminstrn. Temple Beth El Women in Reformed Judaism, Boca Raton, 1997—99; organist St. Theresa's Ch., South Hadley, 1937—41, St. Michael's Ch., NY, 1945—46. Named Career Woman of Yr., Quota Internat. Holyoke, 1988—, Westfield State Coll. concert series named Catherine A. Dower Performing Arts Series in her honor, 1991; recipient citation, Academia InterAmericana de P.R., 1978, plaque, Mass. Tchrs. Assn., Boston, 1984, medal, Equestrian Order Holy Sepulchre of Jerusalem, Papal Knighthood Soc., Boston, 1984, Performance award, Gov. Dukakis, Mass., 1988, award, P.R. Jour. Al. Margens, 1992, Human Rels. award, Coun. for Human Understanding, Holyoke, 1994, 1st prize, Raddock Eminent Scholar Chair Essay Contest, Fla. Atlantic U., 1996, Internat. Poet of Merit Silver Bowl award, Internat. Libr. Poetry, 2002—07, 1st prize, Essay Contest on World Peace by Brotherly Love Press, Mass., 2002, Outstanding Achievement in Poetry award, Internat. Soc. Poets, 2003; vis. scholar, U. So. Calif., 1969. Mem.: Acad. Arts and Scis. PR (medal 1977), Ch. Music Assn. Am. (journalist), Coll. Mus. Soc., Am. Musicol. Soc., Nat. Soc. Arts and Letters (chmn. violin competition 2005, master ceremonies NSAL piano competition 2006, chairperson 2d Nat. Violin Competition 2007, 1st v.p.), Equestrian Order of the Holy Sepulchre (named Lady Comdr. 1987, Lady Comdr. with star 1990), Holyoke Quota (v.p. 1976—79, pres. 1979—81, chmn. speech and hearing com. 1987—94, pres. 1990—92), Friends Holyoke Pub. Libr. (pres. 1990—91), Women's Symphony League (life), Friends Music Lynn U. (life; bd. dirs., editor music newsletter), Lifelong Learning Soc. Fla. Atlantic U. (life; sec. 1994—97, bd. dirs. 1994—98, 2003—07), Internat. Platform Assn., Irish Am. Cultural Inst. (chmn. bd. dirs. 1981—89), Westfield State Coll. Found., Philharm. Assn. Boca (pres. 2002—03), Univ. Club Fla. Atlantic U. (parliamentarian 2003—05, chmn. bylaws 2005—07), B'nai B'rith Boca Lago (sec. bd. dirs. 1994—99, newsletter editor 1999—2000), Phi Beta Kappa. Democrat. Home: 60 Madison Ave Holyoke MA 01040 Personal E-mail: cdowergold@comcast.net.

DOWERS, LOIS ANN, writer; d. Emerence and Francesca; m. Paul A. Dowers; children: Lania, Lauriel, McKelette. BA in Anthropology, U. SC, Columbia, 2004. Coord. pub. rels. Uleher Mgmt. Co., Schaumburg, Ill., 1987—87; resource coord. McDonald's Corp., Oak Brook, 1987—92; educator Unit Dist. 301, Burlington, 1991—99; writer, 2004—.

DOWIS, LENORE, lawyer; b. NY, Nov. 7, 1934; d. Thomas and Julianna (Csitkovits) Esteves; children: Daniel, Lenore, Denise, Jonathan. AAS, Suffolk County Community Coll., 1981; BA, SUNY, Stony Brook, 1983; JD, Touro Coll., 1987. Bar: N.Y. 1988, N.J. 1988, U.S. Dist. Ct. N.J. 1988, U.S. Dist. Ct. (so. and ea. dists.) N.Y. 1992, U.S. Ct. Mil. Appeals 1993, U.S. Ct. Claims 1993, U.S. Ct. Appeals (fed. cir.) 1993, U.S. Ct. Appeals (2d cir.), 2004, U.S. Supreme Ct. 1993. Tel. operator N.Y. Tel. Co., LI, 1951-58; real estate sales agt. Gen. Devel. Corp., Hauppauge, N.Y, 1974-75; student law clk. to assoc. judge appellate div. U.S. Supreme Ct. N.Y., Bklyn., 1986; staff atty. Nassau/Suffolk Law Svcs., Bay Shore, N.Y., 1988; pvt. practice, Smithtown, N.Y., 1988—. Mem. ABA, Suffolk County Bar Assn., N.Y. State Bar Assn., Phi Theta Kappa, Alpha Beta Gamma. Republican. Home and Office: 33 Beverly Rd Smithtown NY 11787-5324

DOWLEY, JOSEPH KYRAN, lawyer, congressman; b. LA, Apr. 23, 1946; s. Michael F. and Charlotte (Moore) D.; m. Carol Walsh, Jan. 22, 1972; children: Kristin, Michael, Patricia. BA, Georgetown U., Washington, 1968, JD, 1976. Bar: Va. 1976, D.C. 1980. Adminstrv. asst. to Honorable Dan Rostenkowski U.S. Ho. of Reps., Washington, 1977-81, asst. chief counsel Com. on Ways and Means, 1981-84, chief counsel Com. on Ways and Means, 1985-87; ptnr. Dewey Ballantine, 1987—. 1st lt. U.S. Army, 1969-71. Mem. Bar Assn. Va., Bar Assn. D.C., Georgetown Univ. Alumni Club (pres. 1984-85). Roman Catholic.

DOWLING, BARBARA R., elementary school educator; Tchr., 1971—, Hawthorne Elem. Sch., Sioux Falls, SD. Named SD Tchr. of Yr., 2006. Office: Hawthorne Elem Sch 601 N Spring Sioux Falls SD 57104 Business E-Mail: dowlingb@sf.k12.sd.us. E-mail: brdowling@aol.com.*

DOWLING, DANIELLE, writer; b. Bronx, NY, Dec. 11, 1969; d. Mary Ann Dowling and Stephen Radcliffe. BA, U. Mass., Amherst, 1988—91. Copy chief Budget Living Mag., NYC, 2003—05, mng. editor, 2005; dep. copy chief Life Mag., NYC, 2005—. Freelance writer Sports Illus., Mensa Rsch. Jour., newsweek.com, NY, Time Out NY, Paper, Interview, among others, NYC, 1988—; freelance copy editor Mensa Rsch. Jour., InStyle, Glamour, Vanity Fair, Martha Stewart Living, Nat. Geog. Adventure, among others, NYC, 1994—. Musician (backing vocals): (album) Out of Aferica, by the Heroine Sheiks. Mem.: MENSA. Libertarian. Home: 1871 Putnam Ave Flushing NY 11385 Office: Life Mag 1271 Ave of the Americas New York NY 10020 Home Phone: 917-676-0956; Office Phone: 212-522-1019. Personal E-mail: evilbunnyink@aol.com. Business E-Mail: danielle_dowling@timeinc.com.

DOWLING, DEAN EDWARD, information scientist, educator; b. Daytona Beach, Fla., Feb. 17, 1942; s. Edward Moore and Josephine Frances Dowling; m. Brenda Graham Cameron, Aug. 15, 1976; children: Brian Edward, Julie Cameron children: Jo Anne Cameron Russo, Keith Robert; m. Karen Jorgensen Jorgensen, Feb. 29, 1964 (div. Nov. 0, 1975). BS, U.S. Mil. Acad., 1963; MA, Columbia U., 1970, PhD, 1972. Commd. lt. U.S. Army, 1963, advanced through grades to lt. col., 1979, ret., 1983; v.p. MUSE Technologies, Inc., Albuquerque, 1998—2001; pres. MUSE Fed. Systems Group, Inc., Arlington, Va., 1999—2001; prof. U. Phoenix (Ariz.) Online, 2003—. Adj. prof. Park U., Parkville, Mo., 1990—; cons. in field. Contbr. chapters to books. Decorated Cross of Gallantry Republic of Vietnam, Silver Star U.S. Army, Bronze Star, Purple Heart, Def. Superior Svc. medal, Meritorious Svc. medal, Army Commendation medal. Mem.: No. Va. Assn. Realtors. Republican. Avocations: golf, music. Home: 5904 Mt Eagle Dr 1210 Alexandria VA 22303 Home Phone: 703-329-8033, 703-329-8033. Personal E-mail: dean63@msn.com.

DOWLING, EDWARD THOMAS, economics professor; b. NYC, Oct. 22, 1938; s. Edward Thomas and Mary Helen (Finegan) D. BA, Berchmans Coll., Philippines, 1962, MA in Philosophy, 1963; M.Div., Woodstock Coll., Md., 1969; PhD, Cornell U., Ithaca, NY, 1973. Asst. prof. econs. Fordham U., Bronx, 1973-79, assoc. prof., 1979-85, prof., 1985—, dean, 1982-86, chmn. dept., 1979-82, 88-94. Author: Development Economics, 1977, Mathematics for Economists, 1980, Calculus for Business, Economics, and the Social Sciences, 1990, Introduction to Mathematical Economics, 1992, 3d edit., 2000, Mathematical Methods for Business and Economics, 1993, Intermediate Statistics for Business and the Social Sciences, 2000. Mem. Am. Econ. Assn. Office Phone: 718-817-4260. Business E-Mail: dowlingsj@fordham.edu.

DOWLING, JOHN ELLIOTT, biology professor; b. Pawtucket, RI, Aug. 31, 1935; s. Joseph Leo and Ruth W. (Tappan) D.; children by previous marriage: Christopher, Nicholas.; m. Judith Falco, Oct. 18, 1975; 1 dau., Alexandra. AB, Harvard U., 1957, PhD, 1961; MD (hon.), U. Lund, Sweden, 1982. Asst. prof. biology Harvard U., Cambridge, Mass., 1961—64, prof., 1971—87, Maria Moors Cabot prof. natural sci., 1987—2001, Llura and Gordon Gund prof. neurosci., 2001—; assoc. prof. Johns Hopkins Sch. Medicine, Balt., 1964—71. Pres. Marine Biol. Lab., 1998—. Author: The Retina: An Approachable Part of the Brain, 1987, Neurons and Networks: An Introduction to Neuroscience, 1992, 2d edit., 2001, Creating Mind: How the Brain Works, 1998, The Great Brain Debate: Is it Nature or Nurture, 2004; contbr. numerous articles on vision to profl. jours. Recipient ann. award N.E. Ophthal. Soc., 1979, award of merit Retina Rsch. Found., 1981, Prentice medal Am. Acad. Optometry, 1991, Von Sallman prize, 1992, The Helen Keller prize for vision rsch., 2000, Gund award Found. Fighting Blindness, 2001. Fellow Am. Acad. Arts and Scis., AAAS; mem. Am. Philos. Soc., Assn. Rsch. in Vision and Ophthalmology (Friedenwald medal 1970), NAS, Neurosci. Soc., Soc. Gen. Physiologists. Home: 135 Charles St Boston MA 02114-3264 Office: Harvard U Biology Labs Cambridge MA 02138 Office Phone: 617-495-2245. Business E-Mail: dowling@mcb.harvard.edu.

DOWLING, MICHAEL PAUL, think-tank executive; b. Norwalk, Conn., Feb. 28, 1953; s. Thomas Edward Dowling and Marion Frances Burke. BS, Yale U., 1975, M in Pub. and Pvt. Mgmt., 1982, M in Forest Sci., 1982. Project mgr. York Rsch. Corp., Stamford, Conn., 1976-78; environ. cons. Envirosphere Co., NYC, 1978-79, energy cons. Newport Beach, Calif., 1980; mgmt. cons. Mgmt. Analysis Ctr., Inc., Cambridge, Mass., 1981, McKinsey & Co., Inc., NYC, 1982-85; sr. v.p., dir. Gen. Atlantic Resources, Inc., Denver, 1985-95; pres. Dowling Found., Denver, 1997—; ptnr. We. Ranchland Investors, 2004—. Chmn., bd. dirs. Colo. Wildlife Fedn., Lakewood, 1998-2000, Colo. Conservation Trust, Boulder, 2000—; bd. dirs. Colo. Coalition Land Trusts, Golden, 1999-2001; trustee Colo. Symphony Orch., 2006—.

DOWLING, RODERICK ANTHONY, investment banker; b. NYC, Dec. 29, 1940; s. John Joseph and Anne (Chisholm) D.; m. Lavinia Seibels, May 6, 1977; children: Lavinia Crosby, Roderick A.; children by previous marriage: Anne Chisholm, Katherine Burke. BS, Fairfield U., 1962; JD, Fordham U., 1965. Bar: N.Y. 1965, Ga. 1974. Assoc. Cahill, Gordon & Reindel, NYC, 1965-72; v.p., gen. counsel U.S. Industries N.E. Corp., NYC, 1972-73, Fugua Industries, Inc., Atlanta, 1973-81; chmn. Sun Trust-Robinson Humphrey Inc., Atlanta, 1981—, also bd. dirs. Mem. ABA, Bar Assn. City NY, Ga. Bar Assn., Atlanta Bar Assn., S.R., Piedmont Driving Club (Ga.), University Club (NY), Union Club (NY), Capitol City Club, Buckhead Club, Golf Club Ga., Palmetto Club (SC), Seabrook Island Club (SC), Kiawah Club. Home: 3038 Bakers Meadow Ln SE Atlanta GA 30339-4815 Office Phone: 404-926-5074. E-mail: rod.dowling@rhco.com.

DOWLING, THOMAS ALLAN, mathematics professor; b. Little Rock, Feb. 19, 1941; s. Charles and Esther (Jensen) D.; m. Nancy Lenthe D.; children: Debra Lynn, David Thomas. BS, Creighton U., 1962; PhD, U. N.C., 1967. Research assoc. U. N.C.-Chapel Hill, 1967-69, asst. prof., 1969-72; assoc. prof. math. Ohio State U., Columbus, 1972-82, prof., 1982—. Ops. researcher U.S. Govt., Patrick AFB, Fla., 1963-64; conf. organizer U. N.C., 1967, 70, Ohio State U., 1978, 82, 88, 92, 94, 98, 00, 02, 03, 05. Editor: Combinatorial Mathematics and its Applications, 1967, 70; contbr. article to profl. jours.; discoverer Dowling lattices. NSF grantee, 1972-80; fellow NASA, 1968 Mem. AAUP, Am. Math. Soc., Math. Assn. Am., Inst. Combinatorics and Applications. Democrat. Home: 2565 Sandover Rd Columbus OH 43220-2848 Office: Ohio State U Dept Math 231 W 18th Ave Columbus OH 43210-1101 Office Phone: 614-292-5013. E-mail: tdowling@math.ohio-state.edu, tdowling@columbus.rr.com.

DOWLING, VINCENT JOHN, retired lawyer; b. NYC, Dec. 20, 1927; s. Victor Hurlin and Joan Agnes (Reardon) D.; m. Jane Cooney, Apr. 16, 1958; children: Vincent John Jr., Douglas J., S. Colin, Joseph G. BS, Lehigh U., 1949; JD, U. Conn., 1957. Bar: Conn. 1957, Mass. 1985, Fla. 1986, U.S. Dist. Ct. Conn. 1958, U.S. Ct. Appeals (2d cir.) 1960, U.S. Ct. Claims 1986. Chief mfg. engr. Veeder-Root, Inc., Hartford, Conn., 1949—58; ptnr. Dowling & Dowling, Hartford, Conn., 1958—65, Cooney, Scully & Dowling, Hartford, Conn., 1965—2002; ret., 2001. Lectr. constrn. law. Capt. U.S. Army, 1951-53. Mem. ASME, ABA, Conn. Bar assn. (liaison com. with ctrs., constrn. law com., alt. dispute resolution com., chmn. specialization com.), Am. Arbitration Assn., Nat. Panel Constrn. Arbitrators and Mediators, Nat. Arbitration and Mediation (panel), Fed. Bar Assn., Mass. Bar Assn., Fla. Bar Assn., Internat. Bar Assn., Diocesan Attys. Assn., Hartford Golf Club, Hartford Club, John's Island Club (Vero Beach, Fla.), Quail Valley Club (Vero Beach), Kappa Alpha Soc. Roman Catholic. E-mail: vin@dowling.com.

DOWLUT, ROBERT, lawyer; b. 1945; BS, Ind. U.; JD, Howard U., Washington, 1979. Bar: DC 1980, Va. Corp. Counsel. Gen. counsel NRA. Sec. NRA Civil Rights Def. Fund. Contbr. articles to prof. legal jours. Staff sgt. US Army, 82nd Airborne Divsn. and 12th Spl. Forces. Office: NRA South Tower 6N 11250 Waples Mill Rd Fairfax VA 22030-7400 Office Phone: 703-267-1250. Office Fax: 703-267-3985.*

DOWNEN, ROBERT LYNN, international affairs analyst and political consultant, editor, writer; b. Wichita, Kans., Apr. 18, 1951; s. Lyndall and Ruth Downen; m. Holly Hutchens, Sept. 1, 1980; children: Heather, Lindsey. BA cum laude, Washington U., St. Louis, 1973; MA, George Washington U., Washington, 1975. Legis. asst. to Bob Dole, U.S. Senate, Washington, 1973-79; dir. Pacific stds. Ctr. for Strategic and Internat. Studies/Georgetown U., Washington, 1979-84; dir., spl. projects U.S. State Dept./Asia, Washington, 1984-89; v.p. Neill and Co., Washington, 1989-94, The Jefferson Group, Washington, 1994-98; pres. Downen Consulting, 1998—2004; v.p. APCO Worldwide, Washington, 2004—. Author: The Taiwan Pawn, 1979, To Bridge the China Strait, 1984; editor: Multi-System Nations and International Law, 1982, The Emerging Pacific Community, 1984. Mem. adv. group Dole for Pres., Washington, 1996, Reagan for Pres., Washington, 1980. Named Kans. DeMolay of Yr., Order of DeMolay, 1969, DeMolay Legion of Honor award, 1983; recipient Wolcott Scholar award Internat. High Twelve Clubs, Mo., 1974, Hon. Mem. award Sojourners Lodge AF & AM, Panama Canal Zone, 1978. Mem. Masons, Phi Beta Kappa, Sigma Nu. Republican. Baptist. Avocations: photography, genealogy, study of american history and government, travel.

DOWNER, ROBERT NELSON, lawyer; b. Newton, Iowa, July 15, 1939; s. Lowell William and Mabel Mary (Hannon) Downer; m. Jane Alice Glafka, May 29, 1971; children: Elise Michele Downer Frisella, Andrew Nelson. BA, U. Iowa, 1961, JD, 1963. Bar: Iowa 1963, U.S. Dist. Ct. (so. dist.) Iowa 1963, U.S. Dist. Ct. (no. dist.) Iowa 1964, U.S. Supreme Ct. 1995, U.S. Ct. Appeals (8th cir.) 2001. Assoc. Meardon Law Office, Iowa City, 1963-68; mem. Meardon, Sueppel & Downer PLC and predecessor firms, Iowa City, 1969—. Dir., sec. KZIA, Inc., Cedar Rapids, Iowa, 1975—, Iowa City Tennis & Fitness Ctr., 1987—93; trustee The Oaknoll Found., Iowa City, 1990—98, Herbert Hoover Presdl. Libr. Assn., West Branch, Iowa, 2000—06; dir. Christian Retirement Svcs., Inc., Iowa City, 1967—82, Iowa State Bar Found., 1996—2002, Iowa Law Sch. Found., 2000—; bd. regents State of Iowa, 2003—, pres. pro tem, 2004—06; commr. Midwest Higher Edn. Compact, 2005—. Mem. Iowa Supreme Ct. Task Force on Domestic Abuse, 1993—94; bd. dirs. Iowa City Area Devel. Group, 1993—2001, chmn., 1996—97, co-chair, 2000—01; bd. dirs., sec. Cmty. Found. Johnson County, Iowa, 2000—03; del. Rep. Nat. conv., New Orleans, 1988; mem. Iowa Supreme Ct. comm. Continuing Legal Edn., 1975—83; chair adminstrv. bd. First United Meth. Ch., Iowa City, 1985—87; pres. Greater Iowa City Area C. of C., 1979; bd. trustees Iowa City Pub. Libr., 1971—75, chair, 1973—74. Named to Iowa Legal Aid Hall Fame, Iowa Legal Aid, 2005; recipient Excellence in Svc. award, Legal Svcs. Corp. Iowa, 1996. Fellow: Iowa State Bar Found., Am. Bar Found., Am. Coll. Trust and Estate Counsel (state chair 2000—05); mem.: ABA, Johnson County Bar Assn. (pres. 1976), Iowa State Bar Assn. (chair probate sect. 1990—93, v.p. 1993—94, pres.-elect 1994—95, pres. 1995—96, Merit award 2001), Rotary (pres. 1989—90). Republican. Methodist. Home: 2029 Rochester Ct Iowa City IA 52245-3246 Office: Meardon Sueppel & Downer PLC 122 S Linn St Iowa City IA 52240-1830 Office Phone: 319-338-9222. Business E-Mail: bobd@meardonlaw.com.

DOWNES, LAURENCE M., gas industry executive; b. Hackensack, NJ, Sept. 27, 1957; s. Laurence F. and Helene L. (Hart) D.; m. Mary Caroline Oliva, Oct. 3, 1981; 1 child, Thomas A. BBA, Iona Coll., 1979, MBA, 1981. Asst. v.p. Midlantic Nat. Bank, Edison, N.J., 1979-84; treas. NJ Resources Corp., Wall, NJ, 1985—90, sr. v.p., CFO, 1990—95, pres., CEO, NJ Nat. Gas, 1995—, pres., CEO, dir., 1995—96, chmn., CEO, 1996—. Chmn., dir. Am. Gas Assn.; chmn. Natural Gas Council; trustee Am. Gas Found. Trustee Iona Coll.; chmn. Safe Child Consortium; dir., chmn. audit com. NJ Schools Construction Corp.; chmn. fin. council Diocese of Trenton. Republican. Roman Catholic. Office: NJ Resources Corp 1415 Wyckoff Rd Belmar NJ 07719*

DOWNES, LAWRENCE, editor; BA in English, Fordham Univ., 1986; student, Univ. Mo. Sch. Journalism, 1987—89. Copy editor Chgo. Sun-Times, 1989—92, Newsday, 1992—93, NY Times, 1993—98, dep. weekend editor to weekend editor, 1998—2000, dep. polit. editor, 2000—03, nat. desk enterprise editor, 2003—04, mem., editl. bd., 2004—. Office: Enterprise Editor NY Times 229 W 43rd St New York NY 10036 Office Fax: 212-556-3815.

DOWNES, RACKSTRAW, artist; b. Pembury, Kent, Eng., Nov. 8, 1939; came to U.S., 1961; s Henry Alfred and Rosa Kathleen (Rackstraw) D. BA, Cambridge U., 1961; MFA, Yale U., 1964. Asst. prof. U. Pa., Phila., 1967-78; mem.faculty Skowhegan Sch., Maine, 1975; mem. faculty N.Y. Studio Sch., NYC, 1980-82. Editor Fairfield Porter: Art in Its Own Terms, 1979; bd. govs. Skowhegan Sch. Painting and Sculpture, 1981-95. One-man shows Kornblee Gallery, N.Y.C., 1972-82, Hirschl & Adler Modern, N.Y.C., 1982-94, Marlborough Galleries, N.Y.C., London, Madrid, 1996-99, Chinati Found., Marfa, Tex., 1999, Robert Miller Gallery, N.Y.C., 2000-04, Betty Cuningham Gallery, N.Y.C., 2004-; exhibited in group shows San Antonio Mus., 1981, Pa. Acad., Phila., 1981, Carnegie Internat., Pitts., 1983, Whitney Biennial, N.Y.C., 1981, Mus. Modern Art, N.Y.C., 2000, Snug Harbor Cultural Ctr., S.I., 2001; represented permanent collections, Mus. Modern Art, N.Y.C., Houston Mus. Fine Arts, Whitney Mus. Am. Art, N.Y.C., Hirschhorn Mus., Washington, Pa. Acad. Fine Art, Met. Mus. Art, N.Y.C., Phila. Mus. Art, Carnegie Inst., Pitts., Corcoran Gallery Art, Smithsonian Mus., Washington, Art Inst. Chgo., Nelson-Atkins Mus. Art, Kansas City, Ludwig Mus., Cologne; author: In Relation to the Whole, 2000; author Under the Gowanus and Razor-Wire Jour., 2000. Ingram Merrill fellow, 1974; grantee Nat. Endowment for Arts, 1980; recipient Creative Artist's Pub. Svc. award State of N.Y., 1978, Nat. Acad. Arts and Scis. award, 1989; Guggenheim fellow, 1998. Mem. Am. Acad. Arts and Letters. Office Phone: 212-334-8410.

DOWNES, WILLIAM F., federal judge; b. 1946; BA, U. North Tex., 1968; JD, U. Houston, 1974. Ptnr. Clark and Downes, Green River, Wyo., 1976-78; mem. Brown & Drew, Casper, Wyo., 1978-94; dist. judge US Dist. Ct. Wyo., Casper, Wyo., 1994—, chief judge. Capt. USMC, 1968—71. Mem.: Natrona County Bar Assn., Wyo. State Bar. Office: US Dist Ct 111 S Wolcott St Rm 210 Casper WY 82601-2534

DOWNEY, ARTHUR HAROLD, JR., lawyer, mediator; b. NYC, Nov. 21, 1938; s. Arthur Harold Sr. and Charlotte (Bailey) D.; m. Gwen Vanden Berg, May 28, 1960; children: Anne Leigh, Neal Arthur, Drew Thomas. BA, Cen. Coll., Pella, Iowa, 1960; LLB, Cornell U., 1963. Bar: Colo. 1963, Wyo. 1991, U.S. Dist. Ct. Colo. 1963, U.S. Dist. Ct. Wyo. 1993, U.S. Ct. Appeals (10th cir.) 1963; diplomate Am. Bd. Forensic Examiners. From assoc. to ptnr. Weller, Friedrich, Ward & Andrew, Denver, 1963-82; ptnr., chief exec. officer Downey Law Firm P.C., Denver, 1982—. Trustee panel Colo. Hosp. Assn., 1988-93; del. Nat. Congress Hosp. Trustees, Am. Hosp. Assn., 1988-93. Contbr. articles to profl. jours. Past pres. Columbine Village Homeowners Assn., Trails End Homeowners Assn., Upper Village Homeowners Assn., Powderhorn Condo. Homeowners Assn., Breckenridge, Colo.; chmn. Promontory Point Homeowners Com., 2004—; vice moderator Presbytery of Denver, 1972; chmn. bd. trustees Bethesda Psychealth Sys., Inc., 1990—93. Fellow Internat. Soc. Barristers (emeritus); mem. Colo. Bar Assn., Larimer County Bar Assn., Wyo. Bar Assn., Def. Rsch. Inst. (disting. svc. award), Nat. Inst. Trial Advocacy (teaching faculty, team leader 1973—), Colo. Def. Lawyers Assn. (pres. 1977-78), Am. Coll. Legal Medicine (assoc. in law), Nat. Bd. Trial Advocacy (cert.), Am. Arbitration Assn. Republican. Mem. Christian Reformed Ch. In Am. Avocations: photography, woodworking, skiing. Office: Downey Law Firm PC 7688 Promontory Dr Windsor CO 80528-9305 Home Phone: 970-267-0921; Office Phone: 970-267-0925. E-mail: downeypc@comcast.net.

DOWNEY, ARTHUR THOMAS, III, lawyer; b. NYC, Aug. 17, 1937; s. Arthur T. and Beatrice (Fortune) Downey; m. Mary S. Downey; children: Thomas, Allison, Paul stepchildren: Christopher, Sarah, Matthew. BA, St. Vincent, 1959; LLB, Villanova U., 1962; LLM, Georgetown U., 1963. Bar: D.C. 1964. Atty. U.S. Dept. State, Washington and Berlin, 1964-69; prof. staff The Nat. Security Coun., The White House, Washington, 1969-72; assoc. Morgan, Lewis & Bockius, Washington, 1972-75; dep. asst. sec. U.S. Dept. Commerce, Washington, 1975-77; ptnr. Sutherland, Ashill & Brennan, Washington, 1977-90; shareholder Johnson & Gibbs, 1990—92; v.p. Baker Hughes Inc., Washington, 1992—2004. Adj. prof. Georgetown U. Law Sch., Washington, 1978—90; interim v.p. Dresser Inc., Dallas, 2005. Co-author: Freedom From Federal Establishment, 1964. Trustee Am. Univ. Sharjah, 2002—06, Fgn. Bondholders Protective Coun., 2002—05; bd. dirs. Springfield Hosp. Ctr., Md., 2004—. Mem.: ABA (vice chmn. sec. internat. law 1984), UN Assn. of USA (bd. govs. 1985—90). Home and Office: 9119 Aldershot Dr Bethesda MD 20817-1901 Office Phone: 301-767-1787. Personal E-mail: atdowney@comcast.net.

DOWNEY, BRIAN PATRICK, lawyer; b. Pitts., Sept. 1, 1964; s. Edmond John and Mary Elizabeth (Wallace) D.; m. Linda Alice McKay, Oct. 9, 1993. BA, Dartmouth Coll., 1987; JD, Dickinson Sch. of Law, 1990. Bar: Pa. 1990, U.S. Dist. Ct. (we. dist.) Pa. 1991, U.S. Dist. Ct. (ea. and mid. dists.) Pa. 1994, U.S. Ct. Appeals (3rd cir.) 1994. Assoc. counsel Eckert Seamans Cherin & Mellott, Pitts., 1990-92; asst. counsel Pa. Dept. of Labor, Harrisburg, 1992-94; ptnr. Pepper Hamilton, LLP, Harrisburg, 1994—. Mem. Friends of Tom Foley Com., Harrisburg, 1994; bd. dirs., pres. Open Stage Harrisburg, 2001—. Mem. ABA, Pa. Bar Assn., Dauphin County Bar Assn. Democrat. Roman Catholic. Avocations: creative writing, golf, reading fiction. Office: Pepper Hamilton LLP 200 One Keystone Plz Harrisburg PA 17108 Home Phone: 717-795-0543; Office Phone: 717-255-1192. Business E-Mail: downeyb@pepperlaw.com.

DOWNEY, JOHN ALEXANDER, physician, educator; b. Sept. 16, 1930; BSc in Medicine, U. Man., MD with honors, 1954; PhD, Oxford U., 1962. Diplomate Am. Bd. Phys. Medicine and Rehab. Intern Vancouver Gen. Hosp., B.C., Canada, 1953—54; resident phys. medicine and rehab. Columbia Presbyn. Med. Ctr., NYC, 1954—56, resident, 1957—58; asst. resident internal medicine Peter Bent Brigham Hosp., Boston, 1956—57; asst. to med. dir., cons. phys. medicine Blythedale Children's Hosp., Valhalla, NY, 1957—59; rsch. assoc. Columbia U., 1958—59; vis. fellow Presbyn. Hosp., NYC, 1958—59; sr. resident internal medicine Peter Bent Brigham Hosp., 1959—60; vis. worker Med. Rsch. Coun. Group for Body Temperature Control, Oxford, England, 1960—62; assc. prof. rehab. medicine Columbia U. Coll. Physicians ans Surgeons, 1962—64, assoc. prof., 1964—67, prof., 1967—74, Simon Baruch prof., 1974—, chair dept. rehab. medicine, 1974—90, asst. prof. medicine, 1963—64. Asst. attending Presbyn. Hosp., NYC, 1962—64, assoc. attending, 1964—68, attending, 1968—, dir. rehab. medicine svc., 1974—90; vis. prof. dept. human physiology and pharmacology U. Adelaide, Australia, 1969. Author: Stroke: Two to Recover, 1969; co-editor: Physiological Basis of Rehabilitation Medicine, 1971, Physiological Basis of Rehabilitation Medicine, 2d edit., 1994, The Child with Disabling Illness: Principles of Rehabilitation, 1974, The Child with Disabling Illness: Principles of Rehabilitation, 2d edit., 1982, Bereavement of Physical Disability: Recommitment to Life, Health and Function, 1982; mem. editl. bd.: Benneman's Practice of Pediatrics, 1974; contbr. articles to profl. jours.; (films) Rehabilitation: A Patient's Perspective, 1973; I Had a Stroke, 1978; Physiatry: A Physician's Perspective, 1981. Fellow: Royal Coll. Physicians (Can.; mem.: AAAS, APA, AMA, NAS, N.Y. Acad. Medicine, N.Y. Acad. Scis., N.Y. Rheumatism Assn., Am. Rheumatism Assn. Office: Columbia U Dept Rehab Medicine 630 W 168th St New York NY 10032-3795

DOWNEY, KAY, librarian; b. Cleve., May 14, 1956; d. Adriana van de Klashorst-Endeveld and Tom van de Klashorst; 1 child, Michael J. BFA, Kent State U., 1990, MLA, 1993. Libr. Akron (Ohio) Art Mus., 1993—96; serials libr. Cleve. Mus. Art, Ingalls Libr., 1996—. Mem.: Art Libr. Soc. N.Am. Avocation: art. Office: Cleve Mus Art Ingalls Libr 11150 East Blvd Cleveland OH 44106-1797 Office Phone: 216-707-2550. Office Fax: 216-421-0921. E-mail: kdowney@clevelandart.org.

DOWNEY, MATTHEW T., history professor, writer; b. Washington, Ind., Jan. 23, 1936; s. Matthew Walter Downey and Mary Cleophus Doyle; m. Rhett Adams, Dec. 24, 1979; children: Jonathan Adams, Elizabeth Ann Gibb, Sarah Adams, Thomas Matthew. BA, Ind. U., Bloomington, 1957, MA, 1958, Princeton U., NJ, 1960, PhD, 1963. Asst. prof. La. State U., Baton Rouge, 1963—67; vis. postdoctoral fellow Smithsonian Instn., Washington, 1966—67; assoc. prof. U. of Colo., Boulder, 1968—75, prof., 1975—87; dir. Clio project U. of Calif., Berkeley, 1989—96; prof. U. of No. Colo., Greeley, 1996—. Vis. asst. prof. UCLA; vis. prof. U. Calif., Berkeley. Author: (textbook) United States History, 1997, The American Century, 1999, Colorado: Crossroads of the West, 1999, American History, 2005. Mem. policymaking com. Social Sci. Edn. Consortium, Boulder,

1996—99; mem. ednl. policy com. Nat. Commn. on Social Studies in Schs., Washington, 1988—90, Calif. History/Social Sci. Framework Com., Sacramento, 1986—87. Recipient Doing History/Keeping the Past grants, Colo. State Hist. Fund, 1997—2003, Profl. Devel. Schs. Project grant, U.S. Dept. of Edn., 1995—97, Sheltered History for Ltd. English Spkrs. grant, Calif. History/Social Sci. Project, 1993—95, Writing to Learn History grant, Nat. Ctr. for the Study of Writing and Literacy, 1990—95, Tchr. Edn. in History of Sci. and Tech. grant, NSF, 1989—91, Early Nat. Period of Am. History grant, NEH, 1984, Inservice Tchr. Edn. in Local History grant, 1982. Mem.: Colo. Coun. for the Social Studies, Calif. Coun. for the Social Studies (Hilda Taba award 1993), Nat. Coun. for the Social Studies. Home: 376 Dexter St Denver CO 80220 Office: U No Colo 501 20th St Greeley CO 80639 Home Phone: 303-881-2374; Office Phone: 970-351-2929. Office Fax: 970-351-3159. E-mail: matthew.downey@unco.edu.

DOWNEY, MICHAEL PATRICK, lawyer; b. St. Louis; m. Elizabeth R. Downey. BA, Georgetown U., 1992; JD, Washington U., St. Louis, 1998. Bar: Mo. 1998, Ill. 1999, U.S. Ct. Appeals (8th cir.) 1998, U.S. Dist. Ct. (ea. dist.) Mo. 1999, U.S. Dist. Ct. (so. dist.) Ill. 1999, U.S. Dist. Ct. (cen. dist.) Ill. 2003, U.S. Dist. Ct. (we. dist.) Mo. 2004, U.S. Dist. Ct. (ea. dist.) Ark. 2005, U.S. Ct. Appeals (7th cir.) 2004, U.S. Supreme Ct. 2006, cert.: George Washington U., Wash. (in law practice mgmt.) 2006. Law clk. to Chief Judge Pasco M. Bowman U.S. Ct. Appeals (8th cir.), Kansas City, Mo., 1998—99; atty. Stinson Mag & Fizzell PC, 1999—2001, Fox Galvin LLC, St. Louis, 2001—, ptnr., 2006—. Adj. prof. Washington U. Sch. of Law, 2000—. Exec. articles editor: Washington U. Law Quar., 1997—98. Mem.: ABA (leadership mentee law practice mgmt. sect. 2004—06, chair ethics and tech. com. 2006—), Ill. State Bar Assn. (standing com. on profl. conduct 2003—), Mo. Bar Assn. (spl. com. on lawyer advt. 2004—, spl. com. on ethics 2005—), Bar Assn. Metro St. Louis (chmn. ethics com. 2003—06). Office: Fox Galvin LLC 1 Memorial Dr Saint Louis MO 63102 Home Phone: 314-961-7316; Office Phone: 314-588-7000. Business E-Mail: mdowney@foxgalvin.com.

DOWNEY, RICHARD LAWRENCE, lawyer; b. Washington, Apr. 3, 1948; s. William G. and Laufey A. D.; m. Pamela L. Drewry, July 10, 1971; children: Anna Christine, Laura Michele, Richard Lawrence, Patricia Kathleen. BA, Randolph-Macon Coll., 1970; JD, Hamline U., 1977. Bar: Va. 1978, U.S. Dist. Ct. (ea. dist.) Va. 1978, U.S. Ct. Appeals (4th cir.) 1978, U.S. Supreme Ct. 1983, U.S. Tax Ct. 1990, U.S. Claims Ct. 1990; diplomate Nat. Bd. Trial Advocacy; bd. cert. civil trial advocacy. Assoc. Downey & Lennhoff, Springfield, Va., 1978-80; pvt. practice Fairfax, Va., 1980-82; sr. ptnr. Duvall, Blackburn, Hale & Downey, Fairfax, Va., 1982-92; prin. Richard L. Downey & Assocs., 1992—. Lt. col. US Army. Named Outstanding Young Man of Am. U.S. Jaycees, 1982. Mem. ABA, ATLA, Va. State Bar Assn., Va. Trial Lawyers Assn., Fairfax Bar Assn. (gen. dist. cts. com. 1984-86, cir. ct. com. 1988-89), Nat. Lawyers Assn., Christian Legal Soc., Fairfax County C. of C. (internat. trade com., planning and land use com., legis. com. 1984), Phi Alpha Delta, Rotary. Republican. Office: 4126 Leonard Dr Fairfax VA 22030-5118 Office Phone: 703-273-8800. Personal E-mail: rldesq@aol.com.

DOWNEY, ROBERT, JR., actor, singer, musician; b. NYC, Apr. 4, 1965; s. Robert Downey and Elsie Ford; m. Deborah Falconer, May 29, 1992 (div. Apr. 26, 2004); 1 child, Indio; m. Susan Levin, Aug. 27, 2005. Appeared in plays American Passion, 1983, Alms for the Middle Class, 1983, Fraternity, 1984; TV series Saturday Night Live, 1985-86; TV miniseries Mussolini: The Untold Story, 1985; films include Pound, 1970, Greaser's Palace, 1972, Up the Academy, 1980, Baby It's You, 1983, Firstborn, 1984, Deadwait, 1985, To Live and Die in L.A., 1985, Tuff Turf, 1985, Weird Science, 1985, America, 1986, Back to School, 1986, Less Than Zero, 1987, The Pick-Up Artist, 1987, Johnny Be Good, 1988, Rented Lips, 1988, 1969, 1988, True Believer, 1989, Chances Are, 1989, That's Adequate, 1990, Air America, 1990, Too Much Sun, 1991, Soapdish, 1991, Chaplin, 1992 (Acad. award nomination best actor), Heart and Souls, 1993, Short Cuts, 1993, The Last Party, 1993, Natural Born Killers, 1994, Only You, 1994, Restoration, 1994, Hail Caesar, 1994, Richard III, 1995, Home for the Holidays, 1995, Danger Zone, 1996, One Night Stand, 1997, Hugo Pool, 1997, Two Girls and a Guy, 1997, The Gingerbread Man, 1998, U.S. Marshals, 1998, In Dreams, 1999, Friends & Lovers, 1999, Bowfinger, 1999, Black and White, 1999, Wonder Boys, 2000, Auto Motives, 2000, Lethargy, 2002, The Singing Detective, 2003, Whatever We Do, 2003, Gothika, 2003, Eros, 2004, Game 6, 2005, Kiss, Kiss, Bang, Bang, 2005, Good Night and Good Luck, 2005, A Guide to Recognizing Your Saints, 2006, The Shaggy Dog, 2006, A Scanner Darkly, 2006, Fur: An Imaginary Portrait of Diane Arbus, 2006, Zodiac, 2007, Lucky You, 2007, Charlie Bartlett, 2007; (TV films) Mr. Willowby's Christmas Tree, 1995; (TV series) Ally McBeal, 2000-2001; singer, musician Man Like Me, 2004, The Futurist, 2004; featured singer (movie and TV soundtracks) Chaplin, 1992, Heart and Sould, 1993, Ally McBeal-A Very Ally Christmas, 2000, Ally McBeal-For Once In My Life, 2001, The Singing Detective, 2003; featured in (music video) I Want Love by Elton John, 2001*

DOWNEY, SUSAN, film company executive; b. Nov. 6, 1973; m. Robert Downey, Jr., Aug. 27, 2005. Grad., U. So. Calif. Asst. to prodr. Threshold Entertainment; co-pres. Dark Castle Entertainment; v.p. prodn. to exec. v.p. prodn. Silver Pictures, 1999—. Co-prodr.: (films) Ghost Ship, 2002, Cradle 2 the Grave, 2003; prodr.: Gothika, 2003, House of Wax, 2005, The Reaping, 2007; exec. prodr.: Kiss Kiss Bang Bang, 2005. Office: Silver Pictures c/o Warner Bros Pictures 4000 Warner Blvd Bldg 90 Burbank CA 91522-0001*

DOWNIE, LEONARD, JR., editor, writer; b. Cleve., May 1, 1942; s. Leonard and Pearl Martha (Evenheimer) Downie; m. Barbara Lindsey, July 15, 1960 (div. 1971); children: David Leonard, Scott Leonard; m. Geraldine Rebach, Aug. 15, 1971 (div. 1997); children: Joshua Mark, Sarah Elizabeth; m. Janice Galin, Sept. 12, 1997; stepchildren: Brian Zachary, Sara Allison. BA, Ohio State U., 1964, MA, 1965, LLD (hon.), 1993. Reporter, editor Washington Post, 1964-74, met. editor, 1974-79, London corr., 1979-82, nat. editor, 1982-84, mng. editor, 1984-91; dir. L.A. Times-Washington Post News Svc., 1991—; exec. editor Washington Post, 1991—; dir. Internat. Herald Tribune, 1985—2002. Author: Justice Denied, 1971, Mortgage on America, 1974, The New Muckrackers, 1976; author: (with Robert G. Kaiser) The News About the News, 2002. Trustee Georgetown Day Sch., 1988-93. Recipient Gavel award ABA, 1967; Alicia Patterson Found. fellow, 1971-72, Goldsmith award for the News About the News, Joan Shorenstein Ctr., Harvard U. John F. Kennedy Sch. of Govt., 2003. Fellow Soc. Profl. Journalists; mem. Am. Soc. Newspaper Editors. Office: Washington Post Co 1150 15th St NW Washington DC 20071-0002*.

DOWNIE, RICHARD DUNCAN, government agency administrator, retired military officer; BS, U.S. Mil. Acad., 1976; M In Internat. Rels., U. So. Calif., 1983, D in Internat. Rels., 1995. Fgn. area officer, Latin Am., Colombia, Panama, Mexico and Germany; exch. officer to Colombian Army; comdt. Western Hemisphere Inst. for Security Coop., 2001—04; dir. Ctr. Hemispheric Def. Studies USCG, Washington, 2004—. Author: Learning From Conflict: The U.S. Military in Vietnam, El Salvador and the Drug War, 1998; contbr. articles. Decorated Def. Superior Svc. Legion of Merit; named to Order Peruvian Cross; recipient Orden de Merito Academico, Colombia, Bosnia/Former Yugoslavia NATO medal; fellow, MIT. Office: Ctr Hemispheric Defense Studies USCG HQ Bldg Ste 118 2100 2d St SW Washington DC 20593-0001 Office Phone: 202-685-4670.

DOWNING, DANIEL LEON, agricultural studies educator; b. Troy, Mo., Sept. 29, 1961; s. Louie B. and Doris E. Downing; m. Cindy J. Brock, Mar. 2, 2002; m. Janelle Leah Heimann, 1993 (dec. 1998). BS in Agr., U. Mo., Columbia, 1983, MS in Edn., 1991. Cert. in issues framing conflict resolution Kettering Found., 1997, trainer project W.E.T. Mo. Dept. Natural Resource, cert. trainer project learning Mo. Dept. Natural Resources, trainer project wild Mo. Dept. Conservation. Asst. youth edn. U. Mo., Columbia, 1985—91, devel. specialist 4-h youth, 1991—96, water quality assoc., 1996—. Adj. prof. agr. sys. mgmt. U. Mo., 2007—. Named Outstanding Cooperator, Mo. Cmty. Devel. Specialist Assn., 2006; recipient Outstanding Svc. award, 1993. Mem.: Assn. 4-H Youth Workers (treas. Mo. chpt. 1998—99), Nat. 4-H Agents Assn., Nat. Soil & Water Conservation Soc., Nat. Assn. County Agrl. Agents (vice chmn. com. 2004—06), Mo. Assn. Ext. Agrl. Profls., Mo. Environ. Edn. Assn. Avocations: hunting, fishing, travel. Home Phone: 573-634-3357; Office Phone: 573-882-0085.

DOWNING, HUDSON UROQUHART, retired securities trader, bank executive; b. Phenix City, Ala., Feb. 26, 1923; s. Lemuel Tyler Downing and Frances Ruth Hudson; m. Frances Ruth Hudson, Oct. 11, 1953. Tchr. U. Ala., Phenix City; stockbroker First S.E. Co., Columbus, Ga.; banker, dir, organizer Phenix Nat. Bank. Sgt. USAF, 1943—46. Decorated Purple Heart US Army, Air medal, Disting. Flying Cross medal. Mem.: Hump. Avocation: Am. Indian culture.

DOWNING, JANE KATHERINE, psychiatric nurse, lawyer; b. Miami Beach, Fla., Aug. 17, 1944; d. William Edward Cuffe and Mary Eileen McManus. ASN, Palomar Coll., 1973; BS in Law, Western State U., 1981, JD, 1981. Bar: Calif. 1983; RN Tex., 1991. Obstetrics, neonatal and ICU nurse Tri City Hosp., Oceanside, Calif., 1973—79; part-time emergency dept./hosp. nursing supr., 1979—83; part-time cert. law clk. San Diego, 1979—83; pvt. practice atty., 1983—90; emergency dept. nurse San Antonio, 1991—92; disaster health coord. ARC, San Antonio, 1992—94; clin. wound mgmt. cons. Hill-Rom, Inc., Batesville, Ind., 1994—96; psychiat. nurse The Brown Schs., Austin, Tex., 1997—98, Austin State Hosp., 1998—99; part-time nurse case mgr. South Austin Hosp., 2000; nurse case mgr. intermediate trauma care unit Brackenridge Hosp., Austin, 2001; home health nurse Progressive Home Care, Inc., San Antonio, 2002—03; crisis unit charge nurse Ctr. Health Care Svcs., San Antonio, 2003—04, crisis unit, 2005—; charge nurse acute adult psychiat. inpatient admitting unit Laurel Ridge Treatment Ctr., 2005—06. Contbr. articles to publs. Inveterate nursing vol. ARC, San Antonio, 1993—2006. Recipient SW Star award, ARC, 2001. Mem.: Am. Mensa. Democrat. Roman Catholic. Home: 303 Serna Park San Antonio TX 78218 Home Phone: 210-650-4144. Personal E-mail: jkdrnjd@hotmail.com.

DOWNING, KATHRYN M., former newspaper publishing executive, lawyer; b. Portland, Oreg., Mar. 24, 1953; BA in Econs., Lewis and Clark Coll., 1973; JD, Stanford U., 1979. Various positions Mead Data Ctrl., 1981—90, sr. dir. legal info. pub., 1988; pres., COO Electronic Pub. divsn. Thomson Profl. Pub., 1990—93; pres., CEO Lawyers Coop. Pub. divsn. Thomson Legal Pub., 1993—95, Mathew Bender, 1995—97; pres., CEO Mosby Matthew Bender unit, sr. v.p. Times Mirror, NYC, 1997—99, vice pres., 1996—97, sr. v.p., 1997—98, exec. v.p., 1998—99; pres., CEO L.A. Times, 1998—99, pres., CEO, publisher, 1999—2000; CEO My Potential Inc., Santa Monica, Calif., 2000—01. Bd. dirs. Women's Found. Calif. Mem. Times Mirror Found., Jim Murray Meml. Found.; mem. bd. visitors Sch. Law Stanford U.; trustee Friends of Law Libr. of Congress; bd. visitors UCLA Anderson Sch. Bus.; pres. L.A. Times Fund; bd. trustees Lewis & Clark Coll. Fellow: Broad Urban Supt. Acad.; mem.: Newspaper Assn. Am., Am. Inns of Ct. (past pub. trustee), Am. Assn. Pubs. (bd. dirs.), L.A. C. of C.

DOWNING, MARGARET MARY, newspaper editor; b. Altoona, Pa., June 3, 1952; d. Irvine William and Iva Ann (Regan) D.; m. Gary Beaver; children: Ian Downing-Beaver, Timothy Downing-Beaver, Abby Downing-Beaver. BA magna cum laude, Tex. Christian U., 1974. Reporting intern Corpus Christi Caller Times, 1973; reporter, bur. chief Beaumont (Tex.) Enterprise & Jour., 1974-76, Dallas Times Herald, 1976-80; reporter, asst. city editor, asst. bus., met. editor, mng. editor Houston Post, 1980—93; mng. editor Jackson (Miss.) Clarion-Ledger, 1993-97; editor-in-chief The Houston Press, 1998—. Jurist Pulitzer Prize Awards, 1992, 93; bd. dirs. News Media Credit Union, 1993, Santa's Helpers, 1992-93; mem. membership com. Assn. Alternative Newspapers, 2000- Respite foster parent vol. Harris County Children's Protective Svcs., 1993; chmn. landscape com. Windsor Hills Homeowners Assn.; active Madison Sta. Elem. PTA, 1993—98; coach South Madison County Soccer Orgn., 1997—98, First Colony Soccer Club, 2002—06; mem. runners club YMCA, 1994, mem. activities adv. bd., 1994, youth soccer and t-ball coach; coach Quail Valley Soccer Assn., 1999—2005; vol. Houston Taping for the Blind, 2000—02; vestry Grace Episcopal Ch., 2002—05, children's edn. bd., 2003, worship com., 2005—06; bd. dirs. Alvin-Manvel Helping Hands Fund, 2001, Leadership Jackson, 1996—98. Recipient Rick Nelson soccer coaching award, 2001. Mem.: Nat. Soc. Newspaper Columnists, Investigative Reporters and Editors, Inc., Nat. Edn. Writers Assn., Nat. Youth Sports Assn. (cert. coach), Press Club Houston (bd. dirs. 1982—85, pres. 1984, bd. dirs. 2000—04), AP Mng. Editors Assn. (2d v.p. La./Miss. chpt. 1995—96, 1st v.p. 1996—97, pres. 1997—98), Quota Club (bd. dirs. 1996—97). Episcopalian. Home: 3215 Breckenridge Ct Missouri City TX 77459-4907 Office: The Houston Press 1621 Milam St Ste 100 Houston TX 77002-8017 Home Phone: 281-416-1819; Office Phone: 713-280-2470. Personal E-mail: downingmargaret@yahoo.com. Business E-Mail: margaret.downing@houstonpress.com.

DOWNING, PAUL R., sports science educator; s. Richard M. and Catherine T. Downing; m. Patricia A. Jensen, May 7, 1994; children: Casey N., Brooke L., Zachary J. BS of Edn., Ashland U., Ohio, 1983; M of Sports Sci., US Sports Acad., Daphne, Ala., 1986; postgrad., Kent State U., Ohio, 1994—. Cert. athletic trainer Nat. Athletic Trainer's Assn., 1984, strength and conditioning specialist Nat. Strength Coaches Assn., 1986, lic. athletic trainer Iowa, 2005. Head athletic trainer Ky. Wesleyan Coll., Owensboro, Ky., 1983—85; asst. athletic trainer Murray State U., Ky., 1985—86, Old Dominion U., Norfolk, Va., 1986—87; head athletic trainer Winthrop U., Rock Hill, SC, 1987—91; athletic trainer, rehab. supr. Seattle Mariners, 1991—92; athletic trainer & dir. of pub. rels. Tri-City Chinook, Kennewick, Wash., 1991—95; grad. asst. Kent State U., Ohio, 1995—97; instr. & program dir. Ashland U., Ohio, 1995—98; asst. chair & asst. prof. Towson U., Md., 1998—2005; instr. Western Ill. U., Macomb, Ill., 2005—06; asst. prof. Loras Coll., Dubuque, Iowa, 2006—. Site visitor Accreditation Commn. of Athletic Training Edn. programs, Round Rock, Tex., 2002—; presenter in field. Contbr. chapters to books. Com. mem. Area-Wide Sports Medicine Adv. Com., Kennewick, Wash., 1994—95; dir. Hot Hoops Basketball Tournament, Richland, Wash., 1995; vol. Vol. Svcs. Spl. Olympics, Ames, Iowa, 2006, NCAA Divsn. III Wrestling Championship, Dubuque, Iowa, 2007. Recipient Outstanding Achievement award, Kent State U., 1997, Recognition award, Towson U. Disabilities Support Svcs. Office, 2003—04; Project grant, Towson U. Assessment Office, 2004—05, Meml. scholar, Ohio Assn. Health, Phys. Edn., Recreation, and Dance, 1983, Living Meml. Postgrad. scholar, Gt. Lakes Athletic Trainer's Assn., 1983. Mem.: Nat. Assn. Colls. & Employers, Sport and Recreation Law Assn., Am. Alliance Health, Phys. Edn., Recreation, and Dance, Nat. Assn. Kinesiology and Phys. Edn. in Higher Edn., Nat. Strength Coaches Assn., Nat. Athletic Trainer's Assn., N.Am. Soc. for Sports Mgmt., Kappa Delta Pi, Phi Epsilon Kappa. Home: 1122 West Scott Ct Eldridge IA 52748 Home Phone: 563-285-6008; Office Phone: 563-588-7216. Business E-Mail: paul.downing@loras.edu.

DOWNS, ANTHONY, economist, real estate consultant; b. Evanston, Ill., Nov. 21, 1930; s. James Chesterfield and Florence Glassbrook (Finn) D.; m. Katherine Watson, Apr. 7, 1956 (dec.May 27, 1998); children: Katherine, Christine, Tony, Paul, Carol; m. Darian Olsen, Nov. 6, 1999. BA, Carleton Coll., 1952, LLD (hon.), 2002; MA, PhD, Stanford U., 1956. With Real Estate Rsch. Corp., Chgo., 1959-77, chmn. bd. dirs., 1973-77; asst. prof. econs. and polit. sci. U. Chgo., 1959-62; econ. cons. Rand Corp., Santa Monica, Calif., 1963-65; sr. fellow Brookings Instn., Washington, 1977—; visiting fellow Pub. Policy Inst. of Calif., 2004. Bd. dirs. NAACP Legal and Ednl. Def. Fund., Inc., Gen. Growth Properties; mem. Nat. Commn. on Urban Problems, 1967—68, Adv. Commn. on Regulatory Barriers to Affordable Housing, 1990—91; adv. bd. Inst. for Rsch. on Poverty, 1970—78. Author: An Econ. Theory of Democracy, 1957, Inside Bureaucracy, 1967, Urban Problems and Prospects, 1970, 2d edit., 1976, Opening Up the Suburbs, 1973, Fed. Housing Subsidies, 1973, Racism in Am., 1970, Neighborhoods and Urban Devel., 1981, Rental Housing in the 1980s, 1983, The Revolution in Real Estate Fin., 1985, Stuck in Traffic, 1992, New Visions for Met. Am., 1994, A Re-Evaluation of Residential Rent Control, 1996, Polit. Theory and Pub. Choice, 1998, Urban Affairs and Urban Policy, 1998, Still Stuck in Traffic, 2004; co-author: Urban Decline and the Future of the Am. Cities, 1982, Costs of Sprawl, 2000, 2003, Sprawl Costs, 2005; co-editor: Do Housing Allowances Work, 1981, Energy Costs, Urban Devel. and Housing, 1984; editor: Growth Mgmt. and Affordable Houring: Do they Conflict. Served with USNR, 1956-59. Mem. Am. Econ. Assn., Am. Soc. Real Estate Counselors, Am. Acad. Arts and Scis., Urban Land Inst., Nat. Acad. Pub. Adminstrn., Anglo Am. Real Property Inst., Phi Beta Kappa, Lambda Alpha. Democrat. Roman Catholic. Home: 8483 Portland Pl Mc Lean VA 22102-1730 Office: 1775 Massachusetts Ave NW Washington DC 20036-2103 Home Phone: 703-821-0038; Office Phone: 202-797-6132. Business E-Mail: anthonydowns@csi.com.

DOWNS, CLARK EVANS, lawyer; b. Boston, July 30, 1946; s. Willis A. and Josephine Joyce (Evans) D.; m. Emilie Louise Hartnett, Aug. 17, 1968; children: Elizabeth Morgan, Julia Clark. AB in English Lit., Boston U., 1968, JD cum laude, 1973. Bar: Ill. (inactive) 1973, DC 1981. Assoc. Isham Lincoln & Beale, Washington, 1973-80, ptnr., 1981-87, Jones Day, Washington, 1988—. Trustee, sec. Found. Energy Law Jour., Washington, 1989-93; trustee Mt. Ida Coll., Newton Centre, Mass., 1989-98, chair, 1994-98; trustee Nat. Presbyn. Sch., Washington, 1986-90, Nat. Presbyn. Ch., Washington, 1991-93, Chevy Chase Presbyn. Ch., Washington, 1981-84; bd. visitors Boston U. Sch. Law, 2000-02. Fellow Am. Bar Found.; mem. ABA (ho. of dels. 1995-97), Energy Bar Assn. (chmn. program com. 1985-86, bd. dirs. 1986-89), FERC (Practice Procedure Manual editl. adv. bd. 1996—), D.C. Bar (chmn. lawyers counseling com. 1989), Order of St. John. Avocations: cello, folk music, choral music. Office: Jones Day 51 Louisiana Ave NW Washington DC 20001-2113

DOWNS, DOROTHY RIEDER, art historian, consultant, writer; b. Miami, Fla., May 14, 1937; d. William Dustin Rieder and Mary Katherine Thomas; m. R Maurice Downs, July 12, 1955; children: Craig Thomas, Gary Steven. BA, Emory U., 1959; MA in Art History, U. Miami, 1976. Registrar Lowe Art Mus., U. Miami, Coral Gables, Fla., 1977—78; dir. 4 Corners Gallery, Coral Gables, 1978—79, New Gallery, U. Miami, 1986—87; mgr. Ctr. Art Store, Ctr. Fine Arts, Miami, 1982—84; instr. dept. art & art history U. Miami, Coral Gables, 1996; guest curator Lowe Art Mus., U. Miami, Coral Gables, 1999, curatorial cons., 2001—. Cons. Miccosukee Mus., Miami, 1983; instr. art history Fla. Keys CC, Key West, 1995, St. Leo's Coll., Key West, 1995; lectr. in field. Author: Art of the Florida Seminole and Miccosukee Indians, 1995, Patchwork: Seminole & Miccosukee Art and Activities, 2005; prodr., writer: (documentaries) Patterns of Power, 1990. Pres. Tribal Arts Soc. Lowe Art Mus., Coral Gables, 2001—03. Mem.: Native Am. Art Studies Assn.

DOWNS, FLOELLA MCINTYRE, retired ferry pilot, instructor, flight examiner; b. Selmer, Tenn., Sept. 19, 1921; d. Edward N. and Ella Pearle (Byrd) McIntyre; m. James Harold Downs, May 27, 1946; children: Linda Downs Ulmer, William Edward, James Patrick. BA, LaVerne U., 1969. Flight instr., comml. pilot FAA, Memphis, 1945-46, pilot flight examiner, 1946; owner, mgr. Basic Tutoring Svc., Ventura, Calif., 1982-86. Civil air patrol pilot, 1956-57 Pres. Naval Officer's Wives, Patuxent River, Md., 1957; active charitable orgns., Md., Italy, Ventura, Calif., 1946—; vol. Children's Home Soc., Ventura and Carpenteria, Calif., 1962-70. Ferry pilot WASP, USAF, 1943-44, WWII, 1st lt. USAFR, 1952-56. Mem. AAUW (area rep. community issues VTA l980-82), Women's Air Force Svc. Pilots, Toastmistress (pres. Ventura l982-83). Democrat. Avocations: piano, painting, reading, gardening, theater. Home: 751 Montgomery Pl Ventura CA 93004-2169

DOWNS, HARTLEY H., III, chemist; b. Ridgewood, NJ, Oct. 21, 1949; s. Hartley Harrison and Jennie Mae (Smith) D.; m. Cindy Marie Millen, June 19, 1976; children: Kathryn Marie, Jennifer Anne, Susanna Jayne. BS, Grove City Coll., 1971; MS, Indiana U. of Pa., 1973; PhD, W. Va. U., 1978; postgrad., U. Colo., 1976-77. Postdoctoral rsch. assoc. chemistry dept. U. So. Calif., LA, 1977-78; staff chemist corp. rsch. labs. Exxon Rsch. and Engring. Co., Linden, NJ, 1978-81, Houston, 1981-83, Annandale, NJ, 1983-86; rsch. scientist, surface chemistry and corrosion sci. group supr. Baker Performance Chems., Houston, 1986-91, rsch. mgr., 1991-92, tech. dir., 1992-97; tech. dir. fluids conditioning tech. Baker Petrolite, Houston, 1997—2004, dir. tech. worldwide oilfield ops., 2004—05, dir. R&D, 2005—. Contbr. articles to profl. jours., chpt. to book Recipient Award for Grad. Rsch., Sigma Xi, 1973, Union Carbide award W.Va. U., 1975, Stan Gillman award U. Colo., 1977, Tech. Merit award Baker-Hughes, 1989, 91, 93. Mem. Am. Chem. Soc., Soc. Petroleum Engrs., Offshore Operators Com. (task force on environ. sci.), NACE Internat. (chmn. task force on oil industry biocides 1996—, symposium chmn. mineral scale deposit control in oilfield ops. 1994, 98, chmn. corrosion/94 and corrosion/98 symposia, vice-chmn. microbiol. control in oil industry ops. corrosion/2000 symposium), Phi Lambda Upsilon. Achievements include patents in field. Office: Baker Petrolite 12645 W Airport Blvd Sugar Land TX 77478

DOWNS, HUGH MALCOLM, retired radio and television broadcaster; b. Akron, Ohio, Feb. 14, 1921; s. Milton Howard and Edith (Hick) D.; m. Ruth Shaheen, Feb. 20, 1944; children— Hugh Raymond, Deirdre Lynn. Student, Bluffton Coll., Ohio, 1938-39, Wayne State U., 1940-41, Columbia, 1955-56. Staff announcer radio sta. WLOK, Lima, Ohio, 1939, program dir., 1939-40; staff announcer radio sta. WWJ, Detroit, 1940-42, NBC, Chgo., 1943-54; co-host 20/20 ABC News, 1978-99; with ABC-News.com. Spl. cons. UN on refugee problems Middle East, 1961-64; cons. Center for Study Democratic Instns.; chmn. bd. Raylin Prodns., Inc., 1960— Free-lance radio and TV broadcaster, 1954—; programs include Home Show, 1954-57, Sid Caesar's Hour, 1956-57, Concentration, 1958-68, Jack Paar show Tonight, 1957-62; host: programs include Today Show, 1962-72, TV Mag. of Air 20/20, 1979-99, ABC; PBS daily series Over Easy; author: Fifty to Forever, 1994, Hugh Downs years Book (with Richard J. Roll), 1982, My Ten Thousand Hours on Television, 1986, Yours Truly, Rings Around Tomorrow, A Shoal of Stars, Potential, Thirty Dirty Lies about Old, Perspectives, 1995, Greater Phoenix: The Desert in Bloom, 1999, Pure Gold: A Lifetime of Love and Marriage, 2001, Letter to a Great Grandson: A Message of Love, Advice, and Hopes for the Future, 2004. Chmn. bd. govs. Nat. Space Soc.; chmn. U.S. com. for UNICEF. Office: Care ABCNews com 77 W 66th St New York NY 10023-6201

DOWNS, JON FRANKLIN, drama educator, director, writer; b. Bartow, Fla., Sept. 15, 1938; s. Clarence Curtis and Frankie (Morgan) D. Student, Ga. State Coll., 1956-58; BFA, U. Ga., 1960, MFA, 1969. Drama dir. Ga.

Perimeter Coll. (formerly DeKalb Coll.), Clarkston, 1969-99. Dir., author The Beastly Purple Forest (marionettes) U. Ga., 1968, Dracula: A Horrible Musical, DeKalb Coll., 1971; dir. A Streetcar Named Desire, DeKalb, 1974, Brigadoon, DeKalb, 1981, West Side Story, 1983, Amadeus, 1984, Noises Off, 1986, The Three Musketeers, 1988, A Midsummer Night's Dream, 1990, A Little Night Music, 1991, Hamlet, 1993, over 200 others; actor Wedding in Japan, N.Y.C., 1960, Dark at the Top of the Stairs, N.Y.C. and on tour, 1961, A Life in the Theatre, DeKalb Coll., 1981, numerous others; designer Sweeney Todd, DeKalb Coll., 1970, Romulus, 1971, Grass Harp, 1972, A Funny Thing Happened on the Way to the Forum, 1998, many others; writer, dir. plays Tokalitta, Gold!, The Vigil; on tour of Ga. summers 1973-76; author: The Illusionist, 1979, Rapunzel, 1997; film reviewer Southernflair mag., 1994-2005, arts editor, 2000-2005. Grantee arts sect. Ga Dept. Planning and Budget, 1973, 74, State Bicentennial Commn., 1975, Nat. Bicentennial Commn., 1975. Mem. Southeastern Theater Conf. (state rep. 1971-73), Ga. Theater Conf. (exec. bd. 1970-73, 79-82).

DOWNS, ROBERT K., lawyer; BA, Grinnell Coll.; JD, Stetson U. Bar: Ill., Fla., US Supreme Ct. Ptnr. Downs Law Offices PC. Elected Ill. Ho. of Reps. 79th Gen. Assembly; chmn. emeritus Wednesday Journal Inc. Recipient Alumni Achievement award, Grinnell Coll., 1998, Ethel Parker award, Independent Voters of Ill., Best Legislator award. Mem.: Assn. of Family and Conciliation Cts., Justinian Soc. of Lawyers, North Suburban Bar Assn., DuPage County Bar Assn., West Suburban Bar Assn., Chgo. Bar Assn., Ill. Trial Lawyers Assn., Am. Bar Assn. (Pro Bono svc. award 1995), admitted to practice U.S. Supreme Ct., Fla. State Bar Assn., Ill. State Bar Assn. (bd. of gov. 1996—2002, pres.-elect 2004, pres. 2005—). Office: Downs Law Offices PC Ste 1870 150 N Wacker Dr Chicago IL 60606 Office Phone: 312-781-1963. Office Fax: 312-781-1962. Business E-Mail: bob@downslaw.com.*

DOWNS, THOMAS EDWARD, IV, lawyer; b. South Amboy, NJ, Sept. 27, 1950; s. Thomas Edward III and Theresa Mary (Jaje) D.; children: Thomas Edward VI, Lauren Ann. BA, St. Peter's Coll., 1972; JD, Seton Hall U., 1975. Bar: N.J. 1975, U.S. Dist. Ct. N.J. 1975, U.S. Dist. Cts. (so. and ea. dists.) N.Y. 1981. Law clk. to presiding judges Middlesex County, N.J., 1975; assoc. Irving Tabman, Old Bridge, N.J., 1975-76; ptnr. Tabman, Downs & McDonnell, Old Bridge, 1976-77, Tabman & Downs, Old Bridge, 1978-82; pvt. practice Old Bridge, 1982—; South Amboy Mcpl. prosecutor, 1977—; Sayreville Mcpl. prosecutor, 1987—90, 1994—2000; Carteret Mcpl. prosecutor, 2002. Atty. Old Bridge Econ. Devel. Bd., 2002—; gen. counsel South Amboy Housing Authority, 1981—, Old Bridge Housing Authority, 2004—. Sec. South Amboy Shade Tree com., 1974; co-chmn. South Amboy Blood Bank; pres. South Amboy Young Dem. Orgn.; dep. chmn. Sayreville Dem. Orgn., 1992-2003; asst. bd. counsel Middlesex County Social Svcs., 2001-. Mem. ATLA, N.J. State Trial Lawyers Assn., Middlesex County Bar Assn., N.J. State Bar Assn., Lions (pres. South Amboy chpt. 1984). Roman Catholic. Home: 118 S Stevens Ave South Amboy NJ 08879 Office: PO Box 498 Old Bridge NJ 08857-0498

DOWNS, THOMAS K., lawyer; b. New Albany, Ind., Jan. 10, 1949; BA, Ind. U., 1977, JD magna cum laude, 1980. Bar: Ind. 1980. Ptnr., mcpl. fin. chmn. Ice Miller, Indpls. Mem. editl. bd. Mcpl. Fin. Jour., 1999—; editor Fundamentals of Mcpl. Bond Law: General Law and Professional Responsibility sects., 1994—; exec. editor Ind. Law Jour., 1979-80; contbr. author various books, including Inside the Minds: Government Contract Litigation Best Practices; contbr. articles to profl. jours. Pres. Ind. Assn. Cities and Towns Found., 1994—; mem. Lt. Gov.'s Jobs Coun. Fellow Am. Coll. Bond Counsel (founding mem., bond buyer midwest pub. fin. conf. 1998); mem. Nat. Assn. Bond Lawyers (steering com. 1985-86, 90, 92, 2000, 01, 02, chmn. bond banks workshop 1985-86, tax increment workshop 1989, panelist various workshops, faculty fundamentals mcpl. bond law, opinions and profl. responsibility 1989-90, chair Ann. Washington Conf. 1996, chmn. prof. responsibility com. 2001-03), Ind. Continuing Legal Edn. Forum (chmn. mcpl. law seminars 1984-92, practical impact tax reform act of 1986, panelist mcpl. utility fin. 1988, pub. law 10 1991), Ind. Mcpl. Lawyers Assn., Inc. (bd. dirs. 1983—), Order of Coif, Assn. Ind. Counties (adv. com., gen. counsel), Ind. Assn. Cities and Towns (exec. com., special counsel), Ind. Comn. for the Purchase of Products and Svcs. of Persons with Disabilities (bd. dirs.). Office: Ice Miller LLP Ste 3100 1 American Sq Indianapolis IN 46282-0200 Office Phone: 317-236-2339. Business E-Mail: Thomas.Downs@icemiller.com.

DOWNS, THOMAS MICHAEL (TOM DOWNS), transportation executive; b. Kansas City, Mo., Apr. 21, 1943; s. Lawrence Joseph and Margaret Elizabeth (McDaniel) D.; m. Lorrene LaForge, Dec. 27, 1965; 1 child, Luke LaForge. BA, Rockhurst Coll., 1964; MA, U. Mo., 1965; MPA, U. Kans., 1970. White House fellow U.S. Dept. Transp, Washington, 1977-78; assoc. adminstr. U.S. Fed. Hwy. Adminstrn., Washington, 1978-80; exec. dir. U.S. Urban Mass Transit Adminstrn., Washington, 1980-81; dir. transp. City of Washington, 1981-83, adminstr., 1983-88; pres. Triborough Bridge and Tunnel Authority, NYC, 1988-90; commr. N.J. Dept. of Transp., Trenton, 1990-93; pres., chmn. RR Passenger Corp. (Amtrak), Washington, 1994-96, chmn., CEO, 1996-98; chmn. The Alliance for Ctr. Washington, 1998—2003; pres., CEO Eno Transp. Found., 2003—. Bd. dirs. Ctr. for Excellence in Govt., Washington, 1985-86; mem. adv. coun. MIT Ctr. for Transp. Studies, 1994—. Chmn., Washington Viet Nam Vets. Leadership Program, Washington, 1983-85; bd. dirs., vice chmn. Pub. Technology, Inc., 1986-88; trustee Ptnrs. for Livable Cmtys., 1994—. Fellow Nat. Acad. Pub. Adminstrn.; mem. Internat. City Mgmt. Assn. (v.p. 1987-89), Am. Soc. Pub. Adminstrs. (nat. coun. 1986). Democrat. Roman Catholic. Avocations: reading, sailing. Office: Eno Transp Found 1634 I St, NW, Ste 500 Washington DC 20006 Office Phone: 202-879-4700. E-mail: tdowns@enotrans.com.

DOWS, DAVID ALAN, chemistry professor; b. San Francisco, July 25, 1928; s. Samuel Randall and Rita M. (Bowers) D.; m. Wena Hunt Waldner, July 29, 1950; children— Janet Louise, Carol Marie, Joyce Ellen. BS, U. Calif., Berkeley, 1952, PhD, 1954. Instr. chemistry Cornell U., 1954-56; instr. U. So. Calif., Los Angeles, 1956-57, asst. prof., 1957-59, assoc. prof., 1959-63, prof. chemistry, 1963—, chmn. dept., 1966-72; NATO prof., 1970. Contbr. articles profl. jours. NSF fellow, 1962-63 Mem. Am. Chem. Soc., Am. Phys. Soc., Phi Beta Kappa. Office: U So Calif Dept Chemistry University Park Los Angeles CA 90089-0482 Office Phone: 213-740-4121. Business E-Mail: dows@usc.edu.

DOWTIN, AMANDA ELIZABETH, elementary school educator; d. James Morgan and Susan Leemon Dowtin. BE in Elem. Edn., Furman U., Greenville, SC, 1997—2001; MEd in Instrnl. Tech., U. Ga., Athens, 2001—03. 3d grade tchr. Mountain Pk. Elem. Sch., Lilburn, Ga., 2002—03; 2d grade tchr. Jefferson Elem. Sch., Greensboro, 2003—05, Greensboro Day Sch., 2005—. Asst. varsity girls soccer coach Greensboro Day Sch., 2004—. Mem. Jr. League, Greensboro, 2003—. Mem.: ASCD.

DOWTY, ALAN KENT, political scientist, educator; b. Greenville, Ohio, Jan. 15, 1940; s. Paul Willard and Ethel Lovella (Harbaugh) D.; m. Nancy Ellen Gordon, Sept. 8, 1961 (div. 1972); children: Merav Aurli, Tamar Eliea, Gidon Yair; m. Gail Gaynell Schupack, Jan. 1, 1973; children: Rachel Miriam, Rafael Jonathan; 1 stepchild, David Freeman. BA, Shimer Coll., 1959; MA, U. Chgo., 1960, PhD, 1963. Lectr. Hebrew U., Jerusalem, 1965-72, sr. lectr., 1972-75; assoc. prof. U. Notre Dame, Ind., 1975-78, prof. polit. sci. Ind., 1978—2004; Kahanoff chair Israeli studies U. Calgary, 2003—06. Exec. dir. Leonard Davis Inst., Jerusalem, 1972-74; editl. bd. Middle East Rev., N.Y.C., 1977-90; project dir. Twentieth Century Fund, N.Y.C., 1983-85; reporter experts meeting Internat. Inst. Human Rights, Strasbourg, France, 1989. Author: The Limits of American Isolation, 1971, Middle East Crisis, 1984 (Quincy Wright award 1985), The Arab-Israel Conflict (with others), 1984, Closed Borders, 1987, The Jewish State, 1998, Israel/Palestine, 2005; book reviewer Jerusalem Post, 1964-75; contbr. articles to profl. jours. Exec. com. Am. Profs. for Peace in Mid. East, 1976-90; witness U.S. Senate Fgn. Rels. Com., Washington, 1976; nat. adv. com. Union of Couns. for Soviet Jews, Washington, 1980-91. Woodrow Wilson fellow, 1959-60; Rothschild fellow Hebrew U., 1963-64; resident fellow Adlai Stevenson Inst., Chgo., 1971-72; Skirball fellow Oxford Ctr. for Hebrew and Jewish Studies, 2000; recipient Charles W. Ramsdell award So. Hist. Assn., 1966; grantee Twentieth Century Fund, N.Y.C., 1983. Mem. Am. Polit. Sci. Assn., Internat. Polit. Sci. Assn., Internat. Studies Assn. (exec. com. 1977-79, Quincy Wright award 1985), Assn. Israel Studies (pres. 2005-07). Jewish. Avocations: travel, jewish studies. Office: 615 S Greenlawn Ave South Bend IN 46615

DOYLE, A. PATRICK, lawyer; b. Pitts., Sept. 6, 1948; BA, SUNY, Oswego, 1971; JD, Syracuse U., 1975. Bar: N.Y. 1976, D.C. 1985. Counsel multinational banking divsn. Office of Comptr. of Currency, 1979-81; dep. gen. counsel, acting gen. counsel Fed. Home Loan Bank Bd., 1982-83; mem. Arnold & Porter, Washington, 1983—93, ptnr., Fin. Svc. Practice Group, 1993—: Adj. prof. Morin ctr. banking law studies, sch. law Boston U., 1985-1993; mem bd. adv., Banking Law Inst, Univ N.C., 1998-. Mng. editor Syracuse Jour. Internat. Law and Commerce, 1974-75; contbr. articles to profl. jours. Mem. Fed. Bar Assn. (mem. exec. com., savs. instns. law com. 1984—). Office: Arnold & Porter Thurman Arnold Bldg 555 12th St NW Washington DC 20004-1206 Office Phone: 202-942-5949. Office Fax: 202-942-5999. Business E-Mail: a.patrick.doyle@aporter.com.

DOYLE, ANTHONY PETER, lawyer; b. Washington, July 13, 1953; s. Francis X. and Anna (Klekotka) D.; m. Maria H. Duda, Aug. 13, 1977; children: Jeffrey Anthony, Joseph Edward, Natalie Maria, Andrew Michael. AA, Berkshire Community Coll., Pittsfield, Mass., 1972-75; BS magna cum laude, Worcester State Coll., 1977; JD, Western New Eng. Coll., 1980. Bar: Mass. 1980; U.S. Dist. Ct. Mass. 1981; U.S. Ct. Appeals (1st cir.) 1981, U.S. Supreme Ct. 1999. Pvt. practice, Pittsfield, 1980-84; ptnr. Doyle & Cormier, Pittsfield, 1985-88, Barry, Doyle & Cormier, Pittsfield, 1989, Barry & Doyle, Pittsfield, 1989—. Pres. Hospice of Ctrl. Berkshire, Pittsfield, 1988-90; v.p. HospiceCare of the Berkshires, Pittsfield, 1990-92, pres. 1992-02, bd. dirs., 2005—; bd. dirs. Dalton (Mass.) Youth Ctr., 1986-89, Community Recreation Assn., Dalton, 1989-95; exec. com. Appalachian Trails Dist. Boy Scouts Am., Dalton, 1989-96; mem. Zoning Bd. Appeals, Dalton, 1995—, chmn., 1997—, Dalton Coun. Aging, 1997—; bd. dirs. Berkshire Fund, 2002—. Recipient commendation Western Mass. Pro Bono Referral Svc., 1983-87. Mem. Mass. Bar Assn., Berkshire Bar Assn. (exec. com. 1989-91, v.p. 1997-99, pres. 1999-2001, Cmty. Svc. award 2004). Roman Catholic. Avocations: skiing, tennis, running. Home: 108 Barton Hill Rd Dalton MA 01226-2005 Office: Barry & Doyle 8 Bank Row Ste 2 Pittsfield MA 01201-6224 Office Phone: 413-499-1701. E-mail: doyleam@aol.com.

DOYLE, CHRISTINE ELLEN, museum researcher, educator; b. Jersey City, Oct. 21, 1975; d. Stanley F. and Margaret Rzeczkowski; m. Thomas Doyle, June 11, 2005. BA, Kean U., 1999, MA, 2002. Rsch. cons. Am. Mus. of Natural History, NYC, 1998—; rsch. assoc. Union County Coll., Cranford, NJ, 2001—06; adj. tchr. Kean U., Union, NJ, 2005—. Rsch. cons. to museums, NYC, 1997—; spkr. in field, 2005. Mem.: Grad. Psychology Soc. (v.p. 1999—2000), APA (assoc. Best Master's Thesis of Yr., N.J. chpt. 2002), Psi Chi Honor Soc., Order of Omega, Kappa Delta Tau (pres. 1997—99, Sister of Yr. 1995, 1999). Home Phone: 201-935-8552.

DOYLE, CONSTANCE TALCOTT JOHNSTON, physician, educator, medical association administrator; b. Mansfield, Ohio, July 8, 1945; d. Frederick Lyman IV and Nancy Jean Bushnell (Johnston) Talcott; children: Ian Frederick Demsky, Zachary Adam Demsky. BS, Ohio U., 1967; MD, Ohio State U., 1971. Diplomate Am. Bd. Emergency Medicine; bd. cert. in emergency crisis response. Intern Riverside Hosp., Columbus, Ohio, 1971—72; resident in internal medicine Hurley Hosp., U. Mich., Flint, 1972—74; emergency physician Oakwood Hosp., Dearborn, Mich., 1974—76, Jackson County Emergency Svcs., Mich., 1975—95; cons. Region II EMS, 1978—79, disaster cons., 1983—95, St. Joseph Mercy Hosp., Ann Arbor, 1995—, med. flight physician helicopter life support svcs., 1996—; core faculty St. Joseph Mercy Hosp./U. Mich. Emergency Residency, Ann Arbor, 1995—; survival flight physician helicopter rescue svc. U. Mich., 1983—91; course dir. advanced cardiac life support and chmn. advanced life support com. W.A. Foote Meml. Hosp., Jackson, 1979—95; dep. dir. emergency svcs. med. ctrl. bd. Washtenaw Livingston County, 2000—; core faculty St. Joseph Mercy Hosp., Ann Arbor, 1996—. Clin. instr. emergency svcs., dept. surgery U. Mich., 1981—; faculty combined emergency medicine residency St. Joseph Mercy Hosp.-U. Mich., Ann Arbor, 1995—; EMS rotation dir., asst. med. dir. Region 2 South Biodef. Network, 2002-03, co-med. dir., 2003-05, dep. med. dir., 2005-06; instr. EMT refresher courses, Jackson County, Jackson C.C.; MedFlight physician, 1996-99; Washtenaw County Subcom. on Bioterrorism, 2000—; Washtenaw County Local Emergency Planning Com., 1998—; dep. med. dir. Washtenaw/Livingston County Med. Control Authority, 2000—. Contbg. author: Clinical Approach to Poisoning and Toxicology, 1983, 89, 97, May's Textbook of Emergency Medicine, 1991, Schwartz Principles and Practice of Emergency Medicine, 1992, Reisdorff Pediatric Emergency Medicine, 1993; contbr. articles to profl. jours. Mem. Disaster Med. Assistance Team, 2000—; served Ground Zero, 2001, Hurrican Francis, 2004, Hurrican Katrina/Rita, 2005, Hurricane Ernesto. Fellow Am. Coll. Emergency Physicians (life, pres. Mich. disaster com. 1987-88, bd. dirs. Mich. 1979-88, chmn. Mich. disaster com. 1979-85, mem. nat. disaster med. svcs. com. 1983-85, chmn. 1987-88, cons. disaster mgmt. course Fed. Emergency Mgmt. Agy. 1982, treas. 1984-85, emergency med. svcs. com. 1985, pres. 1986-87, councillor 1986-87, chair steering com. policy sect., 1994—, mem. disaster sect., 1995—, exec. com. disaster sect. 1997—, chair policy sect. disaster 1995—, vice chair sect. careers in emergency medicine 1997—, chair, 2000-02, past chair 2002-04), Nat. Am. Coll. Emergency Physicians (vice chair sect. of disaster med. svcs. 1990-92, nat. disaster subcom. 1989-90, chair subsect. psychol. rehab. svcs., disaster med. svcs. 1992-94, chair policy and legis. 1994-96, task force on hazardous materials 1993-97, steering com. sect. disaster medicine 1994-2002, exec. com. sect. disaster medicine 1995); mem. ACP, Am. Med. Women's Assn., Am. Assn. Women Emergency Physicians, Mich. Assn. Emergency Med. Technicians (bd. dirs. 1979-80), Mich. State Med. Soc., Washtenaw County Med. Soc., Sierra Club. Jewish. Office: 1251 King George Blvd Ann Arbor MI 48108 also: St Joseph Mercy Hosp Dept Emergency Medicine Ann Arbor MI 48109 Personal E-mail: cjdoyle@pol.net.

DOYLE, DELORES MARIE, retired principal; b. Madison, SD, July 24, 1939; d. Martin N. and Pearl M. (Anderson) Berkelo; m. Patrick J. Doyle; children: Kathleen, Shawn, Tamara, Timothy. AS, Dakota State Coll., Madison, 1959; BS, Mid. Tenn. State U., 1966, MEd, 1968, EdS, 1975; PhD, Peabody/Vanderbilt U., 1980. Cert. career ladder III tchr. Tchr. 4th grade Meriden-Cleghorn Schs., Meriden, Iowa, 1960-62; tchr. 1st grade Hanover (Ill.) Sch., 1963-66; tchr. 2d grade Hobgood Sch., Murfreesboro, Tenn., 1969-70; tchr. 1st grade Reeves-Rogers Sch., Murfreesboro, 1972-80, tchr. 2d grade, 1981-97, prin., 1997-2000; ret., 2000. Cooperating tchr. Mid. Tenn. State U. Student Tchrs., Murfreesboro, 1972—97, mem. task force edn., 1992—93; summer sch. dir. Murfreesboro City Schs., 1986—98; lead project tutor Reeves-Rogers Sch., Murfreesboro, 1987—90. Active Edn. 2000 Com., Murfreesboro C. of C., 1993; trustee Mid Tenn State U. Found., 1995—2001; bd. dirs. Grace Luth. Ch., Murfreesboro, 1991—93, 2001—03, mem. choir, 1975—. Named Career Ladder III Tchr., Dept. Edn., Nashville, 1984; named to Tenn. Tchrs. Hall of Fame, 2001; recipient Tenn. Tchr. of the Yr. award, Dept. Edn., Nashville, 1992, Murfreesboro City Tchr. of the Yr. award, Murfreesboro City Schs., 1991, Mid-Cumberland Dist. Tchr. of the Yr. award, Dist. Dept. Edn., 1991, Trailblazer award, 1995; Creative Tchg. grantee, State Dept. Edn., 1992, 1993. Mem.: Murfreesboro Edn. Assn. (pres. 1981—82), Tenn. Edn. Assn. (Disting. Classroom Tchr. award 1992, Disting. Adminstr. award 2000), Tenn. State Tchr. of Yr. Orgn. (v.p. 2000—), Nat. State Tchr. of Yr. Orgn., Delta Kappa Gamma. Democrat. Avocations: bridge, travel, reading, ballroom dancing. Home: 1710 Sutton Pl Murfreesboro TN 37129-6513 Personal E-mail: pandddoyle@comcast.net.

DOYLE, DENNIS T., lawyer; b. White Plains, NY, Apr. 9, 1943; BA, Boston Coll., 1965; JD, Fordham U., 1968. Bar: N.Y. State 1968, U.S. Dist. Ct. (so. and ea. dists.) N.Y. 1978, U.S. Supreme Ct. 1978. Ptnr. O'Connor, McGuiness, Conte, Doyle & Oleson, White Plains, 1969—. Author: You Haven't Got a Prayer. Mem. ABA, Am. Trial Lawyers Assn., N.Y. State Trial Lawyers Assn., Fedn. Ins. and Corp. Counsel, Appalachian Mountain Club, Adirondeck Mountain Club, Adirondeck Coun. Avocations: bicycling, religious education, hiking, golf. Office: O'Connor McGuiness Conte Doyle & Oleson One Barker Ave Ste 675 White Plains NY 10601-1517 Fax: 914 948-0645. E-mail: ddoyle@omcdoc.com.

DOYLE, DONALD VINCENT, retired state legislator, lawyer; b. Sioux City, Iowa, Jan. 13, 1925; s. William E. and Nelsine E. (Sparby) D.; m. Jant E. Holtz, Aug. 9, 1963; 1 child, Dawn Renee. BS, Morningside Coll., Sioux City, 1951; JD, U. S.D., 1953. Bar: S.D. 1953, Iowa 1953, U.S. Supreme Ct. 1976. Pvt. practice, Sioux City, 1953—2006; mem. Iowa Ho. of Reps., 1956-80, Iowa Senate, 1981-93, chmn. judiciary com., 1982-90. Mem. law and justice com. Nat. Conf. State Legis., 1987-89, chmn., 1988-89; chmn. Iowa Boundary Commn., 1991, 92; mem. Commn. Accreditation Law Enforcement Agys., Inc., 1988-95. With USAF, 1943—46. Recipient award Woodbury County Peace Officers, 1974, Restoration Club Sioux City, 1964, Outstanding Elected Ofcl. award Iowa Corrections Assn., 1979. Mem. Iowa Bar Assn., S.D. Bar Assn. (50-Yr. plaque 2003), Woodbury County Bar Assn., CBI Vets. Assn. (past nat. judge adv., Iowa comdr. 1965), Am. Legion, VFW (comdr. post 1997-2001), DAV, 40 and 8 (chef de gare 1999-2001). Office: PO Box 941 Sioux City IA 51102-0941

DOYLE, EUGENIE FLERI, pediatrician, cardiologist, educator; b. Bklyn., Oct. 19, 1921; d. Paul Charles and Antoinette (Giovannetti) Fleri; m. Joseph Anthony Doyle, Aug. 19, 1944; children: Christopher, Stephen, Eugenie, Jane Marie, Richard. BS, Marymount Coll., Tarrytown, NY, 1943, DSc (hon.), 1993; MD, Johns Hopkins U., 1946; DSc (hon.), Coll. New Rochelle, 1975. Intern in pediatrics Johns Hopkins Hosp., Balt., 1946-47; pediatric resident Bellevue Hosp., NYC, 1947-49; fellow pediatric cardiology NYU Med. Ctr., 1949-53, dir. pediatric cardiology, 1958-93; asst. prof. pediatrics NYU Sch. Medicine, 1953-58, assoc. prof., 1959-70, prof., 1970-92, prof. emerita, 1993—, clin. prof. pediatrics, 1994—. Mem. cardiac adv. com. N.Y. State Health Dept., 1983-92; dir. Vis. Nurse Svc., N.Y.C., 1984—. Editor: Pediatric Cardiology, 1985; contbr. articles to profl. jours. Trustee Marymount Coll., 1983-91, vice chair bd., 1988-91. Mem. Am. Acad. Pediatrics, Am. Pediatric Soc., Am. Coll. Cardiology, Am. Heart Assn., N.Y. Heart Assn. (bd. dirs. 1977-84, pres. 1979-81), Cosmopolitan Club. Roman Catholic. Avocations: gardening, travel, ballet. Home: 32 Washington Sq W New York NY 10011-9156 Office: NYU Med Ctr 550 1st Ave New York NY 10016-6402

DOYLE, FIONA MARY, dean, metallurgical engineer, educator; b. Newcastle upon Tyne, Eng., Sept. 27, 1956; came to the U.S., 1983; d. Vincent Thomas and Teresa Mary (Lockey) D.; m. Stephen Craig Blair, Aug. 5, 1990; children: Katherine Nicole Blair, Ian James Blair. BA in Metallurgy and Materials Sci., U. Cambridge, 1978, MA in Natural Sci., 1982; MSc in Extractive Metallurgy, Imperial Coll., 1979, PhD in Metallurgy, 1983. Chartered engr., Great Britain. Grad. trainee metals and minerals div. Davy McKee, Stockton-on-Tees, United Kingdom, 1983; asst. prof. materials sci. and mineral engring. U. Calif., Berkeley, 1983-88, assoc. prof., 1988-94, prof., 1994—, acting assoc. dean coll. engring., 1990, dir. Inst. Environmental Sci. and Engring., 2001—02, chair dept. materials sci. and engring., 2002—05, exec. assoc. dean Coll. Engring., 2005—. Cons. Placer Dome, U.S., San Francisco, 1989-90. Co-editor: Innovations in Materials Processing Using Aqueous Colloids and Surface Chemistry, 1989, Biotechnology in Minerals and Metal Processing, 1989, Mineral Processing and Extractive Metallury Rev., 1990—; editor: Mining and Mineral Processing Wastes, 1990; contbr. articles to profl. jours. Tech. cons. Sierra Club Legal Def. Fund, San Francisco, 1991. Grantee NSF, 1984, U.S. Dept. Interior, 1987, 91, U.S. Dept. Energy, 1990. Mem. Minerals, Metals and Materials Soc., Am. Inst. Mining, Metall. and Petroleum Engrs. (chair aqueous processing com. 1988-90), Instn. Mining and Metallurgy, Electrochem. Soc., Materials Rsch. Soc. Office: U Calif Berkeley Dept Materials Sci 325 Hearst Mining Bldg Berkeley CA 94720-1760 Home Phone: 510-451-0318; Office Phone: 510-642-7594.

DOYLE, FREDERICK JOSEPH, retired government research scientist; b. Oak Park, Ill., Apr. 3, 1920; s. John Frederick and Mary Elizabeth (Meyers) D.; m. Mary Blaskovich, June 18, 1955; children: Frederick J., Margaret, Mary Ellen, George. BCE, Syracuse U., NY, 1951; postgrad., Internat. Tng. Ctr. Aerial Sur, Delft, The Netherlands, 1952; D in English (hon.), Tech. U., Hannover, Germany, 1976; DSc (hon.), Ohio State U., Columbus, 1986, U. Bordeaux, France, 1987; D in Tech., Royal Tech. U., Sweden, 1987. Assoc. prof. geodetic sci. Ohio State U., 1952-60, chmn. dept., 1959-60; chief scientist Raytheon Autometric Co., Alexandria, Va., 1960-69; sci. advisor Nat. Mapping divsn. U.S. Geol. Survey, Reston, Va., 1969-89, dir. Earth Resources Observation Sys. program, 1978—80; ret., 1989. Geodesy cartography adv. com. NAS, 1967-69; chmn. Apollo Orbital Sci. photo team NASA, 1969-73, planetary cartography com., 1974-95; exec. com. divsn. earth sci. NRC, 1973-76. With C.E., AUS, 1943-48, PTO. Recipient Meritorious Svc. award Dept. Interior, 1977, Disting. Svc. medal, 1981, Silver medal City of Paris, 1978; Fulbright fellow Internat. Tng. Ctr. Aerial Survey, 1952, Internat. Tng. Ctr. fellow, 1986. Fellow AAAS; Internat. Soc. Photogrammetry Remote Sensing (hon., pres. 1980-84, Brock award 1984), Am. Congress Surveying Mapping, Am. Geophys. Union, Am. Soc. Photogrammetry (hon., pres. 1969-70, contbg. author, editor publs., Fairchild Photogrammetric award 1968, Alan Gordon award 1985, Chancellors medal U.Calif. Santa Barbara 2000); mem. Nat. Acad. Engring. Home: 1591 Forest Villa Ln Mc Lean VA 22101-4132 Personal E-mail: freddoyle@aol.com.

DOYLE, GERARD FRANCIS, lawyer; b. Needham, Mass., Oct. 25, 1942; s. John Patrick and Catherine Mary (Lawler) D.; m. Paula Marie Dervay, may 14, 1983; children: Laura Dervay, Meredith Lawler, Philip John. BS in Indsl. Adminstrn., Yale U., 1966; JD, Georgetown U., 1972. Bar: D.C. 1973, U.S. Dist. Ct. D.C. 1973, U.S. Ct. Fed. Claims 1976, U.S. Ct. Appeals (fed. cir.) 1982, U.S. Supreme Ct. 1982, Va. 2000. Group head for operating submarine reactors and reactor tech Div. Naval Reactors AEC, Washington, 1970-72; atty. Morgan, Lewis & Bockius, Washington, 1972-76; legal counsel Am. Nuclear Energy Coun., Washington, 1975-76; ptnr. Cotten, Day & Doyle, Washington, 1976-87, Doyle & Savit, Doyle, Simmons & Bachman, Doyle & Bachman LLP, Washington, 1987-99, Arlington, Va., 1999—. Legal counsel Assn. Fed. Data Peripheral Suppliers, Washington, 1979; dir. M Internat., Inc.; author and lectr. in field; columnist Federal Computer Week, 1989. Served in USN, 1966-71. Recipient outstanding young man of yr. award, 1976. Mem. ABA (coun.

publ. contract law sect. 1989-92), D.C. Bar Assn., Fed. Bar Assn., Am. Arbitration Assn. (panel arbitrators), Nat. Contract Mgmt. Assn., Met. Club (Washington), Yale Club (Washington), Washington Golf & Country Club. Republican. Roman Catholic. Home: 901 Whann Ave Mc Lean VA 22101-1570 Office: Doyle & Bachman LLP 4350 N Fairfax Dr Arlington VA 22203-1637 Office Phone: 703-465-5440. Business E-Mail: gdoyle@doylebachman.com.

DOYLE, GILLIAN, actress; b. Maidenhead, Berkshire, Eng. came to U.S., 1977; d. John Joseph and Joan (Walker) D. BA in Theatre magna cum laude, Am. U., Washington. Appeared in (off Broadway) Ernest in Love, NYC, 1980; (plays) No Exit, Washington, 1985, Fefu and Her Friends, 1985, The Winters Tale, 1987, A Christmas Carol, 1987, Erpingham Camp, 1989, Turn of the Screw, 1989, Season's Greetings, 1986, Terra Nova, 1987, Mountain, 1990, Old Favorites, 1991, What the Butler Saw, 1993, Fawlty Towers, 1994, Last of the Red Hot Lovers, 1995, The Musical Comedy Murders of 1940, 1996, Move Over Mrs. Markham, 1997, Declarations: Love Letters of the Great Romantics, 1998, Present Laughter, 1999, Two, 1999, U.S.A., 2000, Blithe Spirit, 2002, A Midsummer Night's Dream, 2002, What The Butler Saw, 2003, Homebody/Kabul, 2003, Under Milkwood, 2004, My Boy Jack, 2004, The Fourth Wall, 2005, The Miser, 2006, Romeo and Juliet, 2006, Pterodactyles, 2007; (musical) The Cradle Will Rock, 2001; (films) Chances Are, 1989, Born Yesterday, 1993, North, 1993, Decade of Love, 1994, Wild Bill, 1994, The Tie That Binds, 1995, Independence Day, 1996, Play Me Again Sam, 1999, Love, 2000, Being Doctor Jack, 2005, In a Different Key, 2005, When Henri Came to Stay, 2005, Seven Shivas, 2006; (TV) Ancient Prophecies III, 1995, Friends, 1995, The Martin Short Show, 1995, Days of Our Lives, 1996, Love's Deadly Triangle: The Texas Cadet Murder, 1996, General Hospital, 1997, Port Charles, 1999, The Man Show, 1999, Titus, 2001, Passions, 2005; (music video) Johnny Sportcoat and the Casuals, 1987; (voiceover) Books on Tape Audio Narrator, 2006; (comml.) United Way, 1988. Mem. SAG, AFTRA, Actors Equity Assn., Phi Kappa Phi. Democrat. Roman Catholic. Avocations: golf, swimming, music, scuba diving. Personal E-mail: gilliandoyle@hotmail.com.

DOYLE, GLORIA THORPE, secondary school educator; b. St. Louis, Dec. 25, 1951; d. Earlie Endris and Martha Vivian (Branch) Thorpe; m. Jerry Nelson Doyle, Jan. 19, 1978; children: Keyar Jawaan, Jemauri George. BS, Hampton Inst., 1973, MA, 1975; cert. computer programmer, N.C. Ctrl. U., 1987. Jr. HS tchr. math. Hampton City Schs., Va., 1973-80; computer edn. specialist, workshop leader Durham City Schs., NC, 1980-84, HS tchr. math., 1984-93; high sch. tchr. math. Durham Pub. Schs., 1993-95; tech. coord. Hillside HS, Durham, 1995—2004; adj. prof. in math. and computer info. sys. Mt. Olive Coll. at the Triangle, Durham, 2006—. Vis. prof. Hampton U., 1976, 77, 78, 79; assoc. prof. Ctr. Alternative Programs Edn. Shaw U., 1996-2004; lead tchr. for several programs Durham Pub. Schs., 1993-2006; freelance tax preparer, 2001—. Editor: (brochure) Computer Programming in Basic & Math, 1980. Mem. Nat. Coun. Tchrs. of Math., Internat. Soc. Tech. in Edn., Leadership in Urban Math Reform, Realizing Achievement in Math Performance (lead tchr. 1995-2006), Phi Delta Kappa. Democrat. Mem. United Ch. of Christ. Avocations: reading, travel, working on computer. Home: 1811 Primrose Pl Durham NC 27707-4333 Office: Mt Olive Coll at Triangle 5001 South Miami Blvd Durham NC 27703 also: Mt Olive Coll at Triangle PO Box 12142 Research Triangle Park NC 27709 Office Phone: 919-308-9123. Personal E-mail: doyleget@yahoo.com. Business E-Mail: gloria.doyle@moc.edu.

DOYLE, JAMES DONALD, JR., librarian; b. Memphis, Jan. 11, 1947; s. James Donald and Helen Myers Doyle. BA in History, Berry Coll., 1969; MA in History, West Ga. Coll., 1974; MLS, Emory U., 1982. Bus. libr. Tri-County Regional Libr., Rome, Ga., 1980—89; reference libr. Sara Hightower Regional Libr., Rome, 1989—2004. Book reviewer Libr. Jour., NYC, 1996—. Coach Boys and Girls Club, Rome, 1967—95. Named Libr. Jour. Reviewer of Yr.-Nonfiction, 2007. Mem.: Am. Hist. Assn. (assoc.). Democrat. Roman Catholic. Avocations: fishing, reading, farming. Home: 603 McGrady Rd Rome GA 30165 Personal E-mail: doylej2@juno.com. E-mail: doylzjz@bellsouth.net.

DOYLE, JAMES THOMAS, electronics engineer; b. Bklyn., Apr. 11, 1950; s. Leo James Doyle and Mary Ruth Welton; m. Baxanne Lowrance Hunt, June 9, 1995; children: Sheila Mary, Kory Lowrance, Michael James, Kelly Kegan Lowrance, John Patrick, MaryClaire Elizabeth. BSEE, U. Nebr., 1972; MBA, Nova Southeastern, Ft. Lauderdale, Fla., 1991. Registered profl. engr., Fla., 1978. Elec. engr. Honeywell, Freeport, Ill., 1973—76; staff rsch. engr. Motorola, Ft Lauderdale, Fla., 1976—85; mgr. cmos design BurrBrown/Tex. Instruments, Tucson, 1985—87; mem. tech. staff Motorola, Chandler, Ariz., 1987—89; acting pres. and chief engr. MCE Semiconductor, West Palm Beach, Fla., 1988—90; chief technologist, prin. engr. Intel Corp., Chandler, Ariz., 1990—2001; chief technologist pps and smts Nat. Semiconductor, Longmont, Colo., 2001—. Contbr. articles to profl. jours. Vol. Dairy Ctr. of Arts, Boulder, Colo., 2003—05. Engring. Honor scholarship, U. Miami, 1968. Master: IEEE; mem.: Profl. Engr. FES (Mem. #PE024719). Achievements include over 35 patents. Office: Nat Semiconductor 1820 Lefthand Cir Longmont CO 80466 Home Phone: 303-443-2162; Office Phone: 303-845-4064. Office Fax: 303-845-4005; Home Fax: 303-443-2418. Personal E-mail: jbkkdoyle1@aol.com. Business E-Mail: jim.doyle@nsc.com.

DOYLE, JIM (JAMES EDWARD), governor, former state attorney general; b. Washington, Nov. 23, 1945; s. James E. and Ruth (Bachhuber) Doyle; m. Jessica Laird, Dec. 21, 1966; children: Augustus, Gabriel. Student, Stanford U., 1963—66; AB in History, U. Wis., 1967; JD cum laude, Harvard U., 1972. Bar: Ariz. 1973, Wis. 1975, U.S. Dist. Ct. N.Mex. 1973, U.S. Dist. Ct. Ariz. 1973, U.S. Dist. Ct. Utah 1973, U.S. Dist. Ct. (we. dist.) Wis. 1975, U.S. Dist. Ct. (ea. dist.) Wis. 1976, U.S. Ct. Appeals (10th cir.) 1974, U.S. Ct. Appeals (7th cir.) 1985, U.S. Supreme Ct. 1989. Vol. Peace Corps, Tunisia, 1967—69; atty. DNA Legal Svcs., Chinle, Ariz., 1972—75; ptnr. Jacobs & Doyle, Madison, Wis., 1975—77; dist. atty. Dane County, Madison, 1977—83; ptnr. Doyle & Ritz, Madison, 1983—90; of counsel Lawton & Cates, Madison, 1990—91; atty. gen. State of Wis., Madison, 1991—2002, gov., 2003—. Mem.: ABA, 7th Cir. Bar Assn. (chmn. criminal law sect. 1988—89), Wis. Bar Assn. (bd. dirs. criminal law sect. 1988). Democrat. Roman Catholic. Office: Office of Governor PO Box 7863 Madison WI 53707 also: Office of Governor Rm 560 819 North 6th St Milwaukee WI 53203 Office Phone: 608-266-1212, 414-227-4344. Office Fax: 608-267-8983.*

DOYLE, JOHN, artistic director, designer; b. Inverness, Scotland; Assoc. artistic dir. Watermill Theatre, Berkshire, 1996—. Dir., designer Sweeney Todd, 2005— (Tony award, best direction of a musical, 2006, Drama Desk award, outstanding dir. of a musical, 2006, Drama Desk nominee, outstanding set design of a musical, 2006, Outer Critics' Cir. award, outstanding dir. of a musical, 2006), artistic dir. of four major regional theatres in the UK, dir. more than 200 profl. productions. Address: Eugene O'Neill Theatre 230 W 49th St New York NY 10036 also: Watermill Theatre Bagnor Newbury Berkshire RG20 8AE England

DOYLE, JOHN LAWRENCE, artist; b. Chgo., Mar. 14, 1939; s. John W. and Cecelia M. (Tarkowski) D.; children: Lynn, Sean, Morgan. BA, Sch. of Art Inst. Chgo., 1962; MA, No. Ill. U., 1967. Tchr. art Forest View High Sch., Arlington Heights, Ill., 1962-72; pres. Yancey Crafted Tile. Bd. dirs. Toe River Arts Coun., Yancey Libr., Amy Regional Libr. Sys., Yancey History Assn., Yancey Evening Sch. Program, Steering Com., Yancey Mus./Visitor Ctr. Project. One-man shows of prints and/or paintings include: Denver Natural History Mus., Natural Am. Indian Mus., Spokane, Wash., Allen Galleries, Milw., U. N.D., U. S.D., Black Gallery, Taos, N.Mex., Vanderbilt U., Nashville, Tenn., Johns Hopkins U., Balt., Jockey Club Gallery, Miami, Fla., New West Whitney Gallery Western Art, Cody, Wyo., Harvard Med. Library, Lesch Gallery, Mpls., Clev. Clinic, Mayo Clinic, MGM Grand, Las Vegas, Yale U. Hosp., Now and Then Gallery, N.Y.C., Fine Print Unltd., Miami, Grand Gallery, Nev., Galerie Une, Puerto Vallarta, Mex., Welnetz Studio, Wis., Gallery G, Wichita, all 1981; group shows, latest being: U. Miami, Fla., Tex. Tech U., Amarillo and Lubbock, U. Iowa Hosp. and Clinic, Loma Linda U., Calif., Art Resources, Denver, Hayden Hayes Gallery, Colorado Springs, Colo., Southwestern Gallery, Dallas, Nat. Library of Medicine, Bethesda, Md., Cornell Med. Coll., N.Y.C., Columbia U., N.Y.C., U. Kans., Harvard Law Library, Denver Nat. Hist. Mus., William Mitchell Law Sch., Mpls., United Bank of Austin, Tex., others, 1982-85, Inter Art, Nice, France, Loyola U. Sch. Law, New Orleans, Fine Arts Ltd., Miami, U. Dubuque, Iowa, Art Expo Los Angeles, Art Expo N.Y., Degan Bella Gallery, San Antonio, U. Ariz., Tempe, Midwest Mus. Am. Art, Ind., 1986, U. Ill., Chgo., 1987, R. Volid Gallery, Chgo., 1987, Royce Gallery, Denver, 1987, Denver Mus. Nat. History, 1987, No. Ill. U., DeKalb, 1987, Art Expo, N.Y.C., 1987, U. Ill. Chgo., 1988, R. Volip Gallery, Chgo., 1988, Ramses II Denver Mus., N.H., 1988, Royce Gallery, Denver, 1988, Hayden-Hayes Gallery, Colorado Springs, 1988, World Trade Ctr., Mpls.-St. Paul, 1988, Bergren Gallery, Rockford, Ill., 1988, Red Carpet Gallery, Minn., 1988, Yancey County Hist. Mus., N.C., 1988, Minn. World Trade Ctr., St. Paul, 1989, U. Ill., Champaign, 1989, U. Wis., Madison, 1989, Jean Stephen Gallery, Mpls., 1989, New West Cont. Art, Buffalo Bill Hist. Ctr., Cody, Wyo., 1990, White Thunder World Gallery, Milw., 1990, D. Ehrlein Gallery, Milw., 1990, Bank One, Milw., 1990, White Hart Gallery, Steamboat Springs, Colo., 1991, Suzanne Brown Gallery, Scottsdale, Ariz., 1991, Midwest Mus. Am. Art, Elkhart, Ind., 1991, Scripps Meml. Hosp. Schaetzel Ctr., La Jolla, Calif., 1991, Suzanne Brown Gallery, Scottsdale, Ariz., 1992, Walker Art Ctr., Asheville, N.C., 1992; represented in permanent collections: Library of Congress, Washington, Art Inst. Chgo., Indpls., Mus. Art, Carnegie Inst., Pitts., Norton Gallery of Art, West Palm Beach, Fla., Birmingham (Ala.) Mus. Art, Canton (Ohio) Art Inst., Columbus Mus. Fine Art, Columbus, Ohio, Fort Lauderdale (Fla.) Mus. Art, Miss. Art Mus., Whitney Gallery Western Art, Jackson, Nat. Gallery of Art, Washington, U. Mich., Ann Arbor, Savannah (Ga.) Coll. Art and Design, Scripps Meml. Hosp., La Jolla, Appalachian State U., Boon, NC, U. NC, Asheville, Dunedin (Fla.) Fine Arts. Bd. dirs. Family Violence Coalition Yancey County Vol. Coop, Toe River Arts Coun., Yancey Libr., Amy Regional Libr., Healthy Yancy; pres. Yancey History Assn.; sec., treas. Mus. Visitor Ctr. Project; chair subcom. Land Use Planning Commn.; mem. 21st century cmtys. action com. Yancey County Cultural Resource Commn., now pres.; chmn. Yancey Arts; mem. Sch. Cir. Devel. Com. Recipient Hon. Mention Internat. Printmakers, 1971; George Brown Travelling fellow, 1962 Address: PO Box 715 Burnsville NC 28714-0715 Personal E-mail: jdoyle@yancey.main.nc.us.

DOYLE, JOHN ROBERT, lawyer; b. Chgo., May 12, 1950; s. Frank Edward and Dorothy (Bolton) D.; m. Kathleen Julius, June 14, 1974; children: Melissa, Maureen. BA magna cum laude, St. Louis U., 1971; JD summa cum laude, DePaul U., 1976. Bar: Ill. 1976, U.S. Dist. Ct. 1976, U.S. Dist. Ct. (no. dist.) Ill. 1982, Ill. Trial Bar 1982, U.S. Ct. Appeals (7th cir.) 1982. Ptnr. McDermott, Will & Emery, Chgo., 1976—. Mem. Chgo. Bar Assn. (jud. investigative hearing panel 1986-88), Phi Beta Kappa. Office: McDermott Will & Emery 227 W Monroe St Ste 3100 Chicago IL 60606-5096 Office Phone: 312-984-7735. Business E-Mail: jdoyle@mwe.com.

DOYLE, JOSEPH ANTHONY, retired lawyer; b. NYC, June 13, 1920; s. Joseph A. and Jane (Donahue) D.; m. Eugenie A. Fleri, Aug. 19, 1944; children: Christopher, Stephen, Eugenie, Jane, Richard. BS, Georgetown U., 1941; LLB, Columbia U., 1947. Bar: N.Y. 1948. Assoc. Shearman & Sterling, NYC, 1947-57, ptnr., 1957-79, 81-97; asst. sec. for manpower, res. affairs and logistics USN, Washington, 1979-81. Bd. dirs. The Fuji Bank and Trust Co. Bd. dirs. USO of Met. N.Y., 1982-90. Lt. USNR, 1941-45. Decorated Navy Cross, D.F.C. with 3 gold stars, Air medal with 7 gold stars; recipient Disting. Pub. Service award Sec. of Navy, 1980. Mem. Met. Club (Washington). Democrat. Roman Catholic. Home: 32 Washington Sq W New York NY 10011-9156

DOYLE, JOSEPH E., lawyer, manufacturing executive; BA, U. Ill.; JD, U. Minn. Atty. Sonnenschein Nath & Rosenthal; ptnr. Jenner & Block LLP; ptnr. Corp. and Securities Practice Mayer, Brown, Rowe & Maw LLP, 2001—07; v.p., gen. counsel, sec. Pactiv Corp., Lake Forest, Ill., 2007—. Office: Pactiv Corp 1900 W Field Ct Lake Forest IL 60045*

DOYLE, JUSTIN P., lawyer; b. Rochester, NY, Oct. 26, 1948; s. Justin Joseph and Jane Martha (Kreag) Doyle; children: Mary, Joe. BA, Dartmouth Coll., 1970; JD, Cornell U., 1974. Bar: N.Y. 1974. From assoc. to ptnr. Nixon, Hargrave, Devans & Doyle, Rochester, 1974-99; ptnr. Nixon Peabody LLP (formerly Nixon, Hargrave, Devans & Doyle), Rochester, 1999—. Mem.: Monroe County Bar Assn., N.Y. Bar Assn. Home: 252 Overbrook Rd Rochester NY 14618-3648 Office: Nixon Peabody LLP 1100 Clinton Sq Rochester NY 14603 Office Phone: 585-263-1359. Office Fax: 585-263-1600. Business E-Mail: jdoyle@nixonpeabody.com.

DOYLE, KEVIN MICHAEL, otolaryngologist; b. Rockville Center, NY, Apr. 7, 1965; s. Robert Warren and Claire Marie Doyle; m. Ellen Marie Hart, Sept. 7, 1996; children: Caroline Margaret, Claire Elisabeth. BA, U. Va., Charlottesville, 1987; MD, Duke U., Durham, NC, 1991. Diplomate Am. Bd. Otolarngology. Resident in otolaryngology Duke U., Durham, 1991—96, facial plastic fellow, 2000—01; otolarngygologist Winn Ava Hosp., Ft. Stewart, Ga., 1996—2000; otolarngygologist, ptnr. Raleigh ENT, NC, 2001—. Maj. US Army, 1996—2000. Fellow: ACS; mem.: Phi Beta Kappa. Roman Catholic. Office: Raliegh ENT 3010 Anderson Dr Raleigh NC 27619

DOYLE, L. F. BOKER, retired trust company executive; b. NYC, Apr. 23, 1931; Luke Cantwell and Rita (Boker) D.; m. Susanna Stone, Jan. 31, 1959; children: Katharine, Nancy, Victoria, Jessica. BA, Yale U., 1953; postgrad., NYU, 1956-63. 1st v.p., dir., mgr. capital mgmt. dept. Smith Barney & Co., NYC, 1956-74; exec. v.p. Fiduciary Trust Co. Internat., NYC, 1974-83, pres., 1983-94, chmn. exec. com., 1994-96, also dir., 1978-96, cons., 1996. Dir. U.S. LIfe Ins. Co., 1996-97. Trustee Margaret Sanger Rsch. Bur., N.Y.C., 1962-68, N.Y.C. Sch. Vol. Program, 1979-90, New Sch. for Social Rsch., N.Y.C., 1983-91, Taconic Found., N.Y.C., 1989—, Hudson River Found., 1997—; trustee Am. Mus. Natural History, N.Y.C., 1968-2002, hon. trustee, 2003—; bd. dirs. Cultural Instns. Retirement Sys., N.Y.C., 1971-96, chmn. bd., 1980-96; trustee Nature Cons., N.Y. State, 1990-2003, chmn., 1993-96; trustee Frick Collection, N.Y.C., 1990, treas., 1992—; trustee Ea. N.Y. chpt. Nature Conservatory, 1998—, chmn., 2003-04. 1st lt. USMC, 1953-55. Mem. Century Assn., Anglers Club N.Y. (pres. 1976-77). Avocations: fishing, birdwatching, natural history, conservation, antiques.

DOYLE, MARCUS H., computer technology educator; s. James C. and Genie F. Doyle. BA, N.Mex Highland U., 1970; MA, N.Mex. Highlands U., 1979. Cert. educator Tex., lic. N.Mex, Colo. Elem. sch. tchr. Raton Pub. Schs., N.Mex., 1973—89, mid. sch. tchr. math. and computers, 1989—97; computer tech. educator Austin Ind. Sch. Dist., Tex., 1997—. Contbr. articles to profl. jours. Youth polit. organizer N.Mex Dem. Party, 1966—70; campaign organizer Texan Dem. Party, Austin, 2000—05; organizer and leader Raton Interfaith Ministries, 1973—95, organizer, leader jail ministry, 1973—89. Mem.: Edn. Austin, Internat. Soc. Tech. in Edn., N.Mex Sci. Tchrs. Assn. (sec. 1978—84, 1978—83, recognition for outstanding svc. 1989, Sci. Fellow Award 1984), Raton Edn. Assn. (pres., v.p., state offices, others 1976—97, pres. 1976—97, Tchr. Hall of Fame - N.Mex 2001), Tex. Computer Educators Assn. (life), NEA (life; none 1997—2005, leader and organizer at local, state and nat. levels 1976—96, Tchr. Hall of Fame for N.Mex. 2001). Democrat. Avocations: health issues, refurbishing computers for disadvantaged youth, exercise, nature excursions. Office: Austin Ind Sch Dist 2206 Prather Ln Austin TX 78704 Home Phone: 512-587-9000; Office Phone: 512-414-3368. Personal E-mail: writermhd@aol.com.

DOYLE, MARY E., lawyer; B in Biology and Econs., U. Calif. Santa Cruz; JD, U. Calif. Berkeley, 1978. Litigator Manatt, Phelps & Phillips, LA, 1978—84; various positions including gen. counsel Teledyne Inc., 1984—96; gen. counsel Magic Inc., 1996—2003; sr. v.p., gen. counsel Palm Inc., Sunnyvale, Calif., 2003—. Office: Palm Inc 950 W Maude Ave Sunnyvale CA 94085*

DOYLE, MATHIAS FRANCIS, academic administrator, political scientist, educator; b. Malone, NY, Nov. 18, 1933; s. Francis J. and Madeline L. (Donnelly) D. BA, Siena Coll., 1955; MA, Cath. U. Am., 1965; PhD, U. Notre Dame, 1968; diploma, Pres. Assn. Am. Mgmt. Assn, Inst. Edn. Mgmt., Harvard U. Lectr. St. Francis Coll., Rye Beach, NH, 1963-65; assoc. prof. polit. sci. Siena Coll., Loudonville, NY, 1968-75; pres. St. Bonaventure (N.Y.) U., 1975-90, also trustee., prof. polit. sci., 1992—; Adminstr.'s fellow AID, Washington, 1990-92; dir. human svcs. St. Anthony Shrine, Boston. Trustee Commn. on Ind. Colls. and Univs. Contbr. articles periodicals. Trustee Siena Coll. Arthur Schmidt fellow, 1966-68 Mem. Am., Northeastern polit. sci. assns., Pi Gamma Mu, Delta Epsilon Sigma. Roman Catholic. Home and Office: Siena Coll 515 Loudon Rd Loudonville NY 12211 *A lifetime spent in education and ministry has taught me how true it is that it is better to give then to receive.*

DOYLE, MATTHEW BRIAN, computer graphics designer; b. Fort Worth, Texas; s. Pashia Arlene and Richard Garcia (Stepfather), Dale Waldrup; m. Kathryn Merci Wells, Aug. 29, 2000; 1 child, Deacon Patrick. Creative dir., studio head Plutonium Games, Houston, 2001—04; environ. artist Destineer Studios, Plymouth, Minn., 2004—05; lead world designer Mythic Entertainment, Fairfax, Va., 2005—06; sr. gameplay designer Midway Games, Moorpark, Calif., 2006—07; sr. world builder Cheyenne Mt. Entertainment, Mesa, Ariz., 2007—. Creative dir. (video game) Cleric, contributing author (game development textbook) Business And Legal Primer for Game Development; 3D Game, Close Combat: First to Fight; lead world designer (video game) Warhammer Online: Age of Reckoning, senior gameplay designer TNA Wrestling; author: (game review writer) Gamersinfo.net Online Game Reviews. Fellow: Mensa Internat. Achievements include design of copyrighted video game design - Cleric. Office: Cheyenne Mt Entertainment 4140 E Baseline Rd Ste 208 Mesa AZ 85206 Home Phone: 703-673-6794; Office Phone: 480-656-6500. Personal E-mail: matthewbriandoyle@gmail.com.

DOYLE, MICHAEL A., lawyer; b. Atlanta, Nov. 4, 1937; children: John, David, Peter.; m. Bernice H. Winter, Nov. 12, 1977. BA, Yale U., 1959, LLB, 1962. Bar: Ga. 1961, D.C. 1967, U.S. Dist. Ct. D.C. 1967, U.S. Dist. Ct. (no. dist.) Ga. 1962, U.S. Ct. Appeals (5th cir.) 1962, U.S. Ct. Appeals (11th cir.) 1982, U.S. Ct. Appeals (D.C. cir.) 1968, U.S. Supreme Ct. 1972, U.S. Ct. Appeals (4th cir.) 1985. Assoc. Alston, Miller & Gaines, Atlanta, 1962-67; ptnr. Alston & Bird and predecessor, Atlanta, 1967—; of counsel Alston & Bird LLP, Atlanta. Bd. dirs. Atlanta Legal Aid Soc., 1969-84, pres., 1975-76; bd. dirs. Ga. Legal Services Program; mem. Leadership Atlanta, 1974. Served to lt. USNR, 1964-69. Mem. ABA, State Bar Ga., Atlanta Lawyers Club, Assn. Yale Alumni, Yale Law Sch. Assn. (nat. v.p. 1982-85, mem. exec. com. 1978-85, chmn. planning com. 1988-90, pres. 1991-92, chmn. exec. com. 1992-94). Piedmont Driving Club, Commerce Club, Yale Club Ga. (pres. 1982-84), Yale Club N.Y. Office: Alston & Bird 4200 One Atlantic Ctr 1201 W Peachtree St NW Atlanta GA 30309-3424 Home Phone: 404-355-7796; Office Phone: 404-881-7340.

DOYLE, MICHAEL F. (MIKE), congressman; b. Swissvale, Pa., Aug. 5, 1953; s. Michael Sr. and Rosemarie (Fusco) Doyle; m. Susan Erlandson; children: Mike Jr., David, Kevin, Alexandra. BS in Cmty. Devel., Pa. State U., 1975. Exec. dir. Turtle Creek Valley Citizens Union, Pa., 1977-79; chief of staff Staff of State Senator Frank Pecora, Harrisburg, Pa., 1979-94; co-founder Eastgate Ins. Agy., Pitts., 1983-94; mem. US Congress from 14th Pa. dist., 1995—, mem. energy and commerce com., founder, co-chair Autism Caucus, mem. stds. of ofcl. conduct com., mem. vets.' affairs com. Mem. Swissvale Borough Coun., Pa., 1977-81. Mem.: Nat. Dem. Club, Italian Sons and Daughters of Am., Ancient Order of Hibernians, Lions. Democrat. Roman Catholic. Avocations: golf, Italian cooking, piano. Office: US House Reps 401 Cannon House Office Bldg Washington DC 20515-3814 Office Phone: 202-225-2135. Office Fax: 202-225-3084. E-mail: doyle@mail.house.gov.*

DOYLE, MICHAEL PATRICK, microbiologist, educator, director; b. Madison, Wis., Oct. 3, 1949; s. Donald Vincent and Evelyn (Bauer) Doyle; m. Annette Marie Ripple, Dec. 27, 1971; children: Michael Patrick, Patrick Matthew, Kristen Anne. BS in Bacteriology, U. Wis., 1973, MS in Food Microbiology, 1975, PhD in Food Microbiology, 1977. Sr. project leader Ralston Purina Co., St. Louis, 1977-80; asst. prof. U. Wis., Madison, 1980-84, assoc. prof., 1984-88, prof., 1988-91; prof., dir. U. Ga., Griffin, 1991—, dept. head Athens, 1993-99. Mem. sci. bd. U.S. FDA, 2000—03; regents prof. Bd. Regents Ga. U. Sys., 1997—; nat. adv. com. on microbiol. criteria for foods USA, Washington, 1988—90, 1994—2000; trustee Internat. Life Scis. Inst.-N.Am., Washington, 1992—, sci. advisor, 1987—96; mem. Internat. Commn. on Microbiol. Specifications for Foods, 1989—2000; Wis. Disting. prof. bd. regents U. Wis., Madison, 1988—91; James M. Craig Meml. lectr. Oreg. State U., Corvallis, 1990; sci. lectr. Am. Soc. Microbiology Found., 1991—93, 1999—2001; Peter J. Shields lectr. U. Calif., Davis, 1993; G. Malcolm Trout vis. scholar Mich. State U., Lansing, 1994; sci. adv. coun. Refrigeration Rsch. and Edn. Found., 1997—2002; York Disting. lectr. Auburn U., 1999; bd. dirs. Cooperating Food Safety, 2006—. Editor: Food Microbiology: Fundamentals and Frontiers, 1997, 3rd edit., 2007, Foodborne Bacterial Pathogens, 1989, Emerging Issues in Food Safety, 2004—; contbr. articles to profl. jours. Named one of Top 100 Most Cited Rschrs. Agrl. Scis., Inst. Sci. Info., 2002; recipient award for Profl. Excellence, Am. Agrl. Econs. Assn., 1992, Silver Plow Honor award, USDA, 1998, Ptnrs. in Pub. Health award, Ctrs. Disease Control and Prevention, 2001, Commrs. citation, FDA, 2006. Fellow: World Innovation Found., Am. Acad. Microbiology, Inst. of Food Technologists (Fred W. Tanner lectr. 1986, sci. lectr. 1987—90, exec. com. 2000—03, Samuel Cate Prescott award for rsch. 1987, Nicholas Appert award for preeminence in and contbns. to field of food tech. 1996), Internat. Assn. Food Protection (pres. 1992—93, Norbert F. Sherman article excellence award 1993, NFPA food safety award for outstanding contbn. to food safety rsch. and edn. 1999); mem.: NAS (assoc.), Inst. Medicine NAS (food and nutrition bd. 1991—97, com. to ensure safe food from prodn. to consumption 1998, chmn. rev. com. USDA E. coli O157:H7 in ground beef risk assessment 2001—02, chmn. food forum 2003—, com. nat. needs rsch. in vet. scis. 2004—05, vice chmn. food and nutrition bd. 2005—), Am. Soc. for Microbiology (chmn. food microbiology divsn. 1987—89, pub. and sci. affairs bd. 2003—, P.R. Edwards award for outstanding career achievements 1994), Gamma Sigma Delta, Phi Kappa Phi. Roman Catholic. Achievements include patents for for monoclonal antibody to enterohemorrhagic E. coli; competitive exclusion bacteria to reduce carriage of enterohemorrhagic E. coli by cattle and Listeria in floor drains; development of methods to control and detect foodborne pathogens. Office: U Ga Ctr Food Safety 1109 Experiment St Griffin GA 30223-1797 Home Phone: 770-487-4377; Office Phone: 770-228-7284. Business E-Mail: mdoyle@uga.edu.

DOYLE, MICHAEL W., international official, educator; b. Honolulu, 1948; Student, USAF Academy; AB, Harvard U, 1970; PhD, Harvard U., 1977. Lectr. internat. studies U. Warwick, England, 1975—76; asst. prof. pub. and internat. affairs Woodrow Wilson Sch. Princeton U., 1977—84, from assoc. prof. to Edwards S. Sanford prof. politics and internat. affairs, 1987—2003, dir. Ctr. Internat. Studies, 1997—2001; from asst. to assoc. prof. polit. sci. John Hopkins U., 1984—97; v.p. Internat. Peace Acad., NY, 1993—94; asst. sec.-gen. spl. adviser to sec. gen. Kofi Annan UN, 2001—03; Harold Brown prof. U.S. fgn. and security policy, prof. internat. and pub. affairs and law Columbia U., NYC. Mem. adv. coms. UN High Commr. for Refugees, Lessons Learned Unit, UN Dept. Peacekeeping Ops.; mem. Inst. for Advanced Study, Princeton, 1982-83; chmn. com. editors World Politics, 1997-2001; fellow Ctr. for Advanced Study in the Behavioral Scis., Stanford, 2000-01. Author: Empires, UN Peacekeeping in Cambodia: UNTAC's Civil Mandate, Ways of War and Peace; co-author: Alternatives to Monetary Disorder, (with Jean-Marc Coicaud and Anne-Marie Gardner) The Globalization of Human Rights, 2003, (with Nicholas Sambanis) Making War and Building Peace, 2006; co-editor: Escalation and Intervention, Keeping the Peace, Peacemaking and Peacekeeping for the New Century, New Thinking in Internat. Relations Theorys. With Mass. National Air Guard. U Harvard awards include Detur Prize, John Harvard Scholar, Atherton Prize Fellowship; Ford Foundation Rsch. Fellowship, SSRC/MacArthur Found. Fellowship, Membership of the Inst. of Advanced Studies, Ctr. for Advanced Study in the Behavioral Scis. Fellow: Am. Acad. Arts and Scis. Office: Columbia Sch of Law 13th Fl IAB 420 West 118th St New York NY 10027 Office Phone: 212-854-3061. Office Fax: 212-854-7946.

DOYLE, PATRICK JOHN, otolaryngologist, department chairman; b. Moose Jaw, Sask., Can., Nov. 17, 1926; s. William E. and Bertha L. (Fisher) D.; m. Irene Strilchuk, May 21, 1949; children: Sharon, Patrick, Robert, Barbara, Joseph, Kathleen. BSc, U. Alta., 1947, MD, 1949. Diplomate Am. Bd. Otolaryngology (bd. dirs., v.p. 1986-88, pres. 1988-90). Intern U. B.C. Hosp., 1949-50; resident in medicine and pediatrics, 1950-51; resident in otolaryngology U. Oreg. Hosp., 1958-61; asst. prof., then asso. prof. U. Oreg. Med. Sch., 1965-70; mem. faculty U. B.C. Med. Sch., 1963—, prof. otolaryngology, 1972-91, prof. otolaryngology emeritus, 1992—, head dept., 1972-91, program dir. residency tng. program, 1972-91. Head div. otolaryngology St. Paul's Hosp., mem. numerous nat. med. coms. Author numerous articles in field; mem. editorial bds. profl. jours. Fellow Royal Coll. Surgeons Can., Am. Laryngol., Rhinol. and Otol. Soc. (v.p. western sect. 1988, pres. 1994), Am. Laryngol. Soc., Am. Acad. Otolaryngology-Head and Neck Surgery (v.p. 1984, bd. dirs. 1985-87), Am. Otol. Soc.; mem. Can. Soc. Otolaryngology-Head and Neck Surgery (pres. 1987), Pacific Coast Oto-Ophthal. Soc. (pres. 1977), Soc. Univ. Otolaryngologists, U. Oreg. Otolaryngology Alumni Assn. (pres. 1968-70), Am. Otological Soc., Centurion Club, Tinnitus Rsch. Found. Roman Catholic. Office: # 301-5704 Balsam St Vancouver BC Canada V6M 4B9

DOYLE, PATRICK T., broadcast executive; Dir. taxes Hughes Electronics Corp., 1992; v.p. taxes DIRECTV Group, El Segundo, Calif., 1996—2000, v.p. corp. devel., 1997—2000, corp. v.p., 2000, contr., 2000—, treas., 2001—, sr. v.p., chief acctg. officer. Office: DIRECTV Group 2230 E Imperial Hwy El Segundo CA 90245 Office Phone: 310-964-5000.*

DOYLE, PAUL FRANCIS, lawyer; b. NYC, Sept. 3, 1946; s. Paul Francis and Rita Lilian (Mulcahy) D.; m. Margaret Mary Sullivan, Aug. 23, 1969; children: Karen, Lynn. BA in English, Holy Cross Coll., 1968; JD cum laude, NYU, 1973. Bar: Mass. 1973, N.Y. 1975, U.S. Dist. Ct. (so. and ea. dists.) N.Y. 1975, U.S. Ct. Appeals (2d and 3d cirs.) 1975, U.S. Supreme Ct. 1991, U.S. Dist. Ct. Mass. 1992, U.S. Dist. Ct. (no. dist.) N.Y. 1995. Law clk. Superior Ct. Commonwealth of Mass., Boston, 1973-74; assoc. Kelley, Drye & Warren, NYC, 1974-82, ptnr., 1983—. Instr. Nat. Inst. Trial Advocacy, 1994; mem. departmental disciplinary com. Supreme Ct. of N.Y., 1st Jud. Dept., 2003—; lectr. N.Y. State Bar Assn., 2001, 03. Assoc. editor Ann. Survey Am. Law, 1972-73. Mem. Planning Bd., Croton-on-Hudson, N.Y., 1989-92, mem. Comprehensive Plan Com., 1999—; mem. pres.'s coun. Holy Cross Coll. With U.S. Army, 1968-70, Vietnam. Mem. Am. Inns of Ct., Order of Coif. Roman Catholic. Office: Kelley Drye & Warren LLP 101 Park Ave New York NY 10178-0062

DOYLE, RICHARD HENRY, IV, lawyer; b. Elgin, Ill., Aug. 8, 1949; s. Richard Henry and Shirley Marian (Ohms) D.; m. Debbie Kay Cahalan, Aug. 2, 1975; children: John Richard, Kerry Jane. BA, Drake U., 1971, JD, 1976. Bar: Iowa 1976, U.S. Dist. Ct. (no. and so. dists.) Iowa 1977, U.S. Ct. Appeals (8th cir.) 1977, U.S. Supreme Ct. 1986. Asst. atty. gen. Iowa Dept. Justice, Des Moines, 1976-77; assoc. Lawyer, Lawyer & Jackson, Des Moines, 1977-79, Law Offices of Verne Lawyer & Assocs., Des Moines, 1979-93, Reavely, Shinkle, Bauer, Scism, Reavely & Doyle, Des Moines, 1993, Michael J. Galligan Law Firm, P.C., Des Moines, 1994-96, Galligan, Tully, Doyle & Reid, P.C., Des Moines, 1996—2003, Galligan, Doyle & Reid P.C., 2003—. Contbr. articles to profl. jours. With U.S. Army, 1971-73. Fellow Iowa Acad. Trial Lawyers; mem. ABA, ATLA, SAR (registrar Iowa 1983-94, 2001-05, v.p. 1994-97, chancellor 1997-01, 2005—), Iowa Trial Lawyers Assn., Iowa Bar Assn., Iowa State Bar Assn., Polk County Bar Assn., Order of the Founders and Patriots of Am., Phi Alpha Delta (chpt. pres. 1975). Home: 532 Waterbury Cir Des Moines IA 50312-1316 Office: Galligan Doyle & Reid PC The Plaza 300 Walnut St Ste 5 Des Moines IA 50309-2233 Office Phone: 515-282-3333. E-mail: rdoyle@galliganlaw.com.

DOYLE, TOM, sculptor; b. Jerry City, Ohio, May 23, 1928; s. John Thomas and Kathleen (Solether) D.; m. Natalie N. Burdette (div. 1957); m. Eva Hesse (dec. 1970); m. Jane Miller. Student, Miami U., Oxford, Ohio, 1948-50; BFA, Ohio State U., 1952, MFA, 1953. Sculptor, NYC, to date. Artist-in-residence La Napoule Art Found., France, 1989. One-man shows include Dwan Gallery, NYC, 1966, 67, 55 Mercer Gallery, NYC, 1972, 1974, 1976, Picker Art Gallery, Colgate U., Hamilton, NY, 1976, Sculpture Now, Inc., NYC, 1978, The Sculpture Ctr., NYC, 1988, Bill Bace Gallery, NYC, 1991, 93-94, Long House Found., East Hampton, NY, 1995, Mattatuck Mus., Waterbury, Conn., 1996, Kouros Gallery, NYC, 1999, Nicolaysen Art Mus., Casper, Wyo., 2001, New Arts Gallery, Litchfield, Conn., 2003, 2005, Shirley Jones Gallery, Yellow Springs, Ohio, 2006; exhibited in group shows at Whitney Mus., NYC, 1967, Los Angeles County Mus., 1967, Taft Mus., Cin., 1974, Indpls. Mus. Art, 1974; permanent collections include New Britian Mus. Am. Art, Conn. Recipient commendation GSA, Fairbanks, Alaska, 1980, Jimmy Ernst Lifetime Art Achievement award AAAL, 1994, Ohioana Career award for Lifetime Achievement, 1996; Guggenheim fellow, 1982, Nat. Endowment for the Arts fellow, 1990-91; rsch. grantee CUNY, 1989-90. Mem. Am. Abstract Artists, Nat. Acad. Design. Personal E-mail: tjmdoyle@charter.net.

DOYLE, WILLIAM THOMAS, physicist, retired educator; b. New Britain, Conn., Dec. 5, 1925; s. Thomas William and Kathleen (McConn) D.; m. Barbara May Grant, June 16, 1951; children— Peter, Jeffrey. Sc.B. in Physics, Brown U., 1951; MA, Yale, 1952, PhD, 1955. Mem. faculty Dartmouth, 1955-97, prof. physics, 1964-97, chmn. dept., 1967-71. Served with USNR, 1943-46. NSF predoctoral fellow, 1953-54, 54-55; postdoctoral fellow, 1958-59 Mem.: Am. Assn. of Physics Tchrs., Sigma Xi. Home: 6 Tyler Rd Hanover NH 03755-2232

DOZE, MAUREEN ADELE (MAUREEN ADELE MEE), social studies educator; b. Denver, June 11, 1953; d. James Robert and Mary Louise Mee; m. John Burtis Doze, Mar. 24, 1979; children: Laura Kathryn, Sarah Jocelyn. BA, U. Colo., Boulder, 1976; MA, U. Colo., Denver, 1985. Tchr. mid. sch. social studies Cherry Creek Schs., Englewood, Colo., 1988—. Chief proctor Nat. Evaluation Sys., Conn., 1998—2002. Mem.: Phi Beta Kappa. Avocations: quilting, gardening, reading, travel. Office: Horizon Comty Mid Sch 3981 S Reservoir Rd Aurora CO 80013 Home Phone: 303-766-4747; Office Phone: 720-886-6100. E-mail: mdoze@cherrycreekschools.org.

DOZIER, DAVID CHARLES, JR., advertising and public relations executive; b. Santa Fe, Dec. 4, 1938; s. David Charles Sr. and Zelma (Martin) D.; m. Dianne Flusche, June 1, 1960; children: Deborah, Mary Rebecca, Michael, Constance. BA, U. Dallas, 1960. Editor sports Tex. Cath., Dallas, 1960-70, gen. sales mgr., 1964-70; dir. classified advt. Dallas Times Herald, 1970-74; pres., chmn. DBG&H Unltd. Inc., Dallas, 1974-88; chmn. Dozier Co., Dallas, 1989—. Innovator, ptnr. Navi Pesanda Indian Blanket Creations, 1992. Author: A Compendium of Endurance, 1989. Mem. Am. Indian, Santa Clara Pueblo Tribe, N.Mex.; cert. athletic trainer Downtown YMCA, 1990-2003. Recipient Disting. Svc. award Pres. U.S. and HUD, 1984. Republican. Roman Catholic. Achievements include completed more than 137 marathons. Home: 7102 Wabash Cir Dallas TX 75214-3532 Office: 2547 Farrington St Dallas TX 75207-6607 Home Phone: 214-324-3562; Office Phone: 214-744-2800. Business E-Mail: david@thedoziercompany.com.

DOZIER, JAMES LEE, former army officer; b. Arcadia, Fla., Apr. 10, 1931; s. Joseph B. and Leota (Caruthers) D.; m. Judith I. Stimpson, June 30, 1956; children— Cheryl Lyn, Scott Lee BS, U.S. Mil. Acad., 1956; MS in Aerospace Engring., U. Ariz., 1964. Commd. 2d lt. U.S. Army, 1956, advanced through grades to maj. gen., 1984, comdr. 1st Squadron, 1st Cav., 1st Armored Div. Germany, 1971-73, staff officer Office of Dep. Chief of Staff for Research, Devel. and Acquisition Washington, 1974-76, also mil. asst. to asst. sec. of army, 1974-76, comdr. 2d Brigade, 2d Armored div. Fort Hood, Tex., 1976-78, chief of staff 2d Armored div., 1978-79, chief of staff III Corps and Ft. Hood, 1979-80, dep. chief of staff logistics and adminstrn. Allied Land Forces So. Europe Verona, Italy, 1980-82, asst. comdt. Armor Sch. Ft. Knox, Ky., 1982-83, dep. comdg. gen. III Corps and Fort Hood Fort Hood, Tex., 1983-85, ret., 1985; pres. Golden Grove Mgmt. Corp., Arcadia, Fla., 1985-87, Suncoast Media Group, Venice, Fla., 1987; gen. mgr. David C. Brown Enterprises, 1988-93; owner JCS Group, Ft. Myers, 1993—. Lectr., condr. seminars on kidnapping experience. Contbg. author: Winter of Fire, 1990; contbr. articles to mil. jours. Decorated Silver Star, Legion of Merit, Bronze Star with V device and 2 oak leaf clusters, Air medals, Purple Heart Avocations: fishing, boating, woodworking, tropical plants. Personal E-mail: dozier@comcast.net.

DOZIER, KIMBERLY, news correspondent; b. Honolulu, Hawaii, July 6, 1966; BA in Human Rights and Spanish (magna cum laude), Wellesley Coll., 1987; MA in Fgn. Affairs, U. Va., 1993. Washington, DC-based reporter Energy Daily, New Technology Week and Environment Week, Washington, 1988—91; reporter Christian Sci. Monitor, Cairo, 1992—95, Washington Post, Cairo, 1993, CBS News Radio News and Voice of Am., Cairo, 1994—95, San Francisco Chronicle, Cairo, 1995; anchor BBC Radio World Service's, World Update, London, 1996—98; London bur. chief and chief European corr., reporter CBS News, CBS Radio News, London, 1996—2002; chief corr., Middle East Bur. WCBS-TV, NYC, 2002—03; news corr. CBS News, Iraq, 2003—; also reporter CBS Evening News, CBS Evening News (weekend editions), The Early Show and , CBS 24-hour news svc. Recipient Alumnae Travel award, U. Va., 1993, Grand Gracie award, Am. Women in Radio and TV, 2000, Gracie award, 2000, 2001. assignments include the War in Iraq, the War in Afghanistan and the Hunt for Osama bin Laden, the Crisis and Refugee Exodus in the Balkans, Vladimir Putin's election, the Death of Princess Diana, Northern Ireland's Peace Process and the Khobar barracks bombing in Dhahran. Office: CBS TV 51 W 52nd St New York NY 10019-6188

DOZIER, THERESE KNECHT, department of education advisor, former education association administrator; BA in Social Studies Edn., U. Fla., 1974, MEd in Secondary Social Studies, 1976; EdD in Curriculum and Instrn., U. S.C., 1995; LHD (hon.), Winthrop Coll., 1985, U. S.C., 1985. Tchr. Lincoln Mid. Sch., Gainesville, Fla., 1974—76, Miami Edison Mid. Sch., Fla., 1976—77, Singapore Am. Sch., Singapore, 1986—89, Irmo HS, Columbia, SC, 1977—85, 1989—90, 1992—93; instr. and coord. profl. devel. schs. U. SC, Columbia, 1991—92; spl. advisor on tchg. to US Sec. Edn. Richard W. Riley US Dept. Edn., Washington, 1993—97, sr. advisor on tchg. to US Sec. Edn. Richard W. Riley, 1997—2001, sr. adv. on tchg. to US Sec. Edn.; nat. tchr.-in-residence and assoc. prof., dir. Ctr. Tchr. Leadership Sch. Edn. Va. Commonwealth U., Richmond, 2001. Mem. Nat. Conf. State Legislatures Taskforce on Sch. Leadership, Nat. Com. on Tchr. Mobility, Com. to Enhance K-12 Tchg. Profession in Va., Va. State Action for Ednl. Leadership Consortium; mem. adv. bd. Nat. Tchr. Recruitment Clearinghouse; mem. adv. panel SRI Internat.'s Study of Alt. Cert. of Tchrs.; mem. meritorious new tchr. com. Mid-Atlantic Regional Tchr. Project; advisor rural initiative Nat. Bd. Profl. Tchg. Stds.; mem. policy and planning coun. Met. Ednl. Rsch. Consortium; advisor DeWitt-Wallace Reader's Digest Found. Tchr. Leadership Initiative; mem. acad. coun. Nat. Inst. Cmty. Innovations Internat. Grad. Ctr.; sr. counsel on tchr. quality issues Widmeyer Comm.; cons. N. Ctrl. Regional Lab. Profl. Devel. Ctr., Asian-Pacific Econ. Coun. Tchr. Devel. Web Portal Project, NBPTS Prin.'s Initiative; presenter in field; bd. dirs. Coun. Basic Edn. Named Nat. Tchr. of Yr., 1985, S. Carolinian of Yr., 1985, Alumna of Outstanding Achievement, U. Fla., 1997; recipient Disting. Alumnus award U. Fla., 1985, Nat. Jefferson award for outstanding pub. svc. benefiting local communities, 1986, Hammer award for helping to make govt. more efficient and effective V.P. Gore, 1995; named to the Order of the Palmetto, 1985; Fulbright-Hays fellow to China, 1985; Holmes scholar U. S.C., 1991-93.*

DRABBLE, MARGARET, writer; b. Sheffield, England, June 5, 1939; d. John Frederick and Kathleen Marie (Bloor) D.; m. Clive Swift, June 27, 1960 (div. 1975); children: Adam, Rebecca, Joseph; m. Michael Holroyd, 1982. BA with honors, Newnham Coll., Cambridge, 1960; DLitt (hon.), U. Sheffield, 1976, U. Manchester, 1987, U. Keele, 1988, U. Bradford, 1988, U. East Anglia, 1994, U. York, 1995. Author: (novels) A Summer Bird-Cage, 1963, The Garrick Year, 1964, The Millstone, 1965 (John Llewelyn Rhys Meml. award 1966), Jerusalem the Golden, 1967 (James Tait Black Meml. book prize 1968), The Waterfall, 1969, The Needle's Eye, 1972 (Yorkshire Post Book of Yr. award 1972), The Realms of Gold, 1975, The Ice Age, 1977, The Middle Ground, 1980 (ALA notable book citation 1981), The Radiant Way, 1987, A Natural Curiosity, 1989, Gates of Ivory, 1991, The Witch of Exmoor, 1996, Angus Wilson: A Biography, 1995, The Peppered Moth, 2001, The Seven Sisters, 2002, The Red Queen, 2004, The Sea Lady, 2006; (short stories) Hassan's Tower, 1966, The Reunion, 1968, The Gifts of War, 1970; (non-fiction) Arnold Bennett, A Biography, 1974, For Queen and Country: Britain in the Victorian Age, 1978, A Writer's Britain, 1979; (play) Bird of Paradise, 1969; (screenplays) Laura, 1964, Isadora, 1968, Thank You All Very Much, 1969; (criticism) Wordsworth, 1966; editor: Jane Austen, Lady Susan, The Watsons, and Sanditon, 1975, The Genius of Thomas Hardy, 1976, Oxford Companion to English Literature, 1985, 6th edit., 2000, The Concise Oxford Companion to English Literature, 1987, Angus Wilson a Biography, 1995. Mem.: Am. Acad. Arts and Letters (hon.; fgn. mem., E.M. Forster award 1973). Office: care Peters Fraser & Dunlop Drury House 34-43 Russell St London WC2B 5HA England

DRABKIN, MURRAY, lawyer; b. NYC, Aug. 3, 1928; s. Max Drabkin and Minnie Masin; m. Mary Elizabeth Hooper, Nov. 27, 1971. AB, Hamilton Coll., 1950; LLB, Harvard U., 1953. Bar: D.C. 1953, U.S. Ct. Appeals (D.C. cir.) 1954, N.Y. 1966, U.S. Supreme Ct. 1972. Counsel com. on judiciary U.S. Ho. of Reps., Washington, 1957-66; spl. asst. to mayor City of N.Y., 1966-68; pvt. practice NYC and Washington, 1968-82; ptnr. Cadwalader, Wickersham & Taft, Washington, 1983-92; ret., 1992; of counsel Hopkins & Sutter, Washington, 1992-2000. Dir. Conn. State Revenue Task Force, 1969-71; mem. adv. com. FRS, 1970-71, D.C. Tax Revision Com., 1976-77; trustee Auto-Train Corp. Contbr. articles to profl. jours. Served with USN, 1953-57, to lt. comdr. USNR. Fellow Am. Coll. Bankruptcy, Phi Beta Kappa (bd. dirs. 1996—, pres. 2001—); mem. Nat. Bankruptcy Conf. (chmn. com. on R.R. reorgn. 1984-2000, chmn. com on bankruptcy crimes, 1994-98), Nat. Conf. Bankruptcy Judges (hon.), Harvard Club Washington (pres. 2000-02, bd. dirs. 1996-2004), Harvard Alumni Assn. (com. nomination overseers and dirs. 2006—), Harvard Club N.Y.C., Chesapeake Bay Bermuda 40 Assn., Cosmos Club, Nat. Press Club. Office Phone: 202-862-2408.

DRACH, JOHN CHARLES, research scientist, educator; b. Cin., Sept. 25, 1939; s. Charles Louis and Edrie B. Drach; m. E. Jean Flamm, June 20, 1964; children: Laura J., Diane E. BS in Pharmacy, U. Cin., 1961, MS in Pharm. Chemistry, 1963, PhD in Biochemistry, 1966. From assoc. rsch. scientist to rsch. scientist Parke, Davis and Co., Ann Arbor, Mich., 1966-70; asst. prof. U. Mich. Dental Sch., Ann Arbor, 1970-74; assoc. prof. U. Mich., Ann Arbor, 1974-80; assoc. prof. medicinal chemistry U. Mich. Coll. Pharmacy, Ann Arbor, 1978-80; prof. U. Mich., Ann Arbor, 1980—; chmn. dept. oral biology U. Mich. Dental Sch., Ann Arbor, 1985-87, chmn. dept. biologic and materials scis., 1987-95; vis. prof. divsn. virology Burroughs Wellcome Co., Research Triangle Park, NC, 1994. Cons. Adria Labs., Am. Inst. Chem., Am. Pharm. Assn., AMA, Chartwell, Kimberly-Clark, 1976-83. Author: Clinical Pharmacology, 1986; mem. editorial bd. Elsevier Sci. Pubs., 1984—, Antiviral Chemistry & Chemotherapy, 1996—; contbr. articles to profl. jours.; patentee antiviral drugs. NSF summer fellow, 1963; NIH grad. fellow, 1964-66; NIH grantee, 1970—. Fellow: AAAS; mem.: Internat. Soc. Antiviral Rsch. (archivist 1992—, chmn. travel grants com. 1998—2002, pres. 2002—04, chmn. nomination com. 2006—, chmn. conf. com. 2004—06), Am. Soc. Microbiology (mem. editl. bd. 1982—91), Am. Chem. Soc., Am. Assn. Oral Biology, Dental Edn. Assn. (pres. oral biology sect. 1990—91), Am. Assn. Dental Rsch., Sigma Xi, Omicron Kappa Upsilon, Rho Chi. Home: 1372 Barrister Rd Ann Arbor MI 48105-2875 Office: U Mich 1011 N University Ave Ann Arbor MI 48109-1078 Office Phone: 734-763-5579. E-mail: jcdrach@umich.edu.

DRACHMAN, DANIEL BRUCE, neurologist, educator; s. Julian Moses and Emily (Deitchman) D.; m. Jephta Piatigorsky, Aug. 28, 1960; children: Jonathan Gregor, Evan Bernard, Eric Edouard. AB summa cum laude (N.Y. State scholar), Columbia Coll., 1952; MD (N.Y. State med. scholar), NYU, 1956. Cert. Neurology and Psychiatry 1962. Intern in internal medicine Beth Israel Hosp., Boston, 1956-57; asst. resident in neurology Harvard neurol. unit Boston City Hosp., 1957-58, resident in neurology, 1958-59; resident in neuropathology Harvard neurol. unit. and Mallory Inst. Pathology, 1959-60; teaching fellow in neurology Harvard U., 1957-60; clin. assoc. Nat. Inst. Neurol. Diseases and Blindness, NIH, Bethesda, Md., 1960-62, research asso. lab. neuroanat. scis., 1962-63; clin. instr. Georgetown U., 1961-63; asst. prof. neurology Tufts U., 1963-69; assoc. prof. Johns Hopkins U., 1969-73, prof., 1974—, prof. neurosci., 1980—, W.W. Smith Charitable Found. prof. neuroimmunology, 2003—. Attending neurologist Johns Hopkins Hosp.; adv. bd. Multiple Sclerosis Soc., 1981-85; pres. med. adv. bd. Myasthenia Gravis Found.; adv. bd. Familial Dysautonomia Found.; bd. sci. councillors Nat. Inst. Neurol. and Communicative Disorders and Stroke, NIH, 1985-90; med. adv. com. Muscular Dystrophy Assn., 1994-99. Clarinetist; mem. editl. bd. Muscle and Nerve jour., Exptl. Neurology, Autoimmunity; appeared in (film) Two Hands (nominatee Acad. Award 2007); author over 200 publs. on myasthenia gravis, muscular atrophy, muscular dystrophy, clubfoot, devel. disorders, neurology, amyotrophic lateral sclerosis, chamber music. Served with USPHS, 1960-63. Recipient Founders' Day award NYU, 1956, Jacob Javits award, 1986, Berson Disting. Alumnus award NYU Sch. Medicine, 1999; NIH grantee, 1963—, Muscular Dystrophy Assn. grantee, 1969—. Fellow Am. Acad. Neurology, N.Y. Acad. Scis.; mem. AAAS, Internat. Soc. Devel. Biology, Balt. Neurol. Soc., Phi Beta Kappa, Alpha Omega Alpha. Achievements include defining pathogenesis of clubfoot (most common human congenital malformation) and arthrogryposis (rare form of similar disorder); first described the only currently useful treatment for Duchenne Muscular Dystrophy; basic work on botulinum toxin demonstrated its use to paralyze individual muscles, and led to the widespread clinical use of Botox; first defined pathogenic abnormalities in myasthenia gravis; development of several immunosuppressive treatments for Myasthenia. Avocations: clarinet, fly fishing, bicycling. Office: Johns Hopkins U Sch Medicine Dept Neurology 600 N Wolfe St Baltimore MD 21287-7519 Office Phone: 410-955-5406. Personal E-mail: dandrac@aol.com.

DRACHMAN, DAVID ALEXANDER, neurologist; b. NYC, July 18, 1932; s. Julian Moses and Emily Drachman; m. Eleanor Betsy Derby, Nov. 26, 1959; children: Laura Jeanne, Jessica Gail, Douglas Emmet. AB with highest honors, Columbia U., 1952; MD, NYU, 1956. Diplomate: Am. Bd. Psychiatry and Neurology. Intern Duke U. Med. Center, 1956-57; resident in neurology Mass. Gen. Hosp., Boston, 1957-60; clin. assoc. NIH, 1960-63; clin. instr. neurology Georgetown U. Med. Sch., 1961-63; mem. faculty Northwestern U. Med. Sch., 1963-77, dir. neurology clinics, 1963-77, prof. neurology, 1971-77, assoc. chmn. dept., 1972-75; attending physician Passavant Meml. Hosp., Chgo., 1964-72, Northwestern Meml. Hosp., 1972-77; prof. neurology, chmn. dept. neurology U. Mass.-Meml. Med. Ctr., 1977—2002, prof. neurology, chmn. emeritus dept. neurology, 2002—, prof. physiology, 2005—. Attending physician U. Mass. Med. Center, Worcester Med. Ctr., Worcester; mem. med. adv. bd. Chgo. Multiple Sclerosis Soc., 1971-77, Mass. Multiple Sclerosis Soc., 1979-87; mem. FDA adv. panel on control and peripheral nerve system drugs, 1996—2000; mem. working group on presdl. disability, 1994-96. Mem. editl. bd. Neurobiology of Aging, 1979-93, Neurology, Archives of Neurology, 1979-91, Jour. Geriat. Psychiatry and Neurology, Jour. Rehab. and Health; contbr. articles to profl. jours. Fellow Am. Acad. Neurology; mem. AAAS, Am. Neurol. Assn. (hon. mem., pres. 1994-95), Alzheimer's Disease Assn. (chmn. sci. adv. bd. 1986-90, trustee), Am. Neuro-otology Soc., Assn. Univ. Profs. Neurology, Assn. Rsch. Nervous and Mental Diseases, Mass. Assn. Neurology, N.Y. Acad. Scis., Boston Soc. Psychiatry and Neurology (pres. 1980-81), Phi Beta Kappa, Sigma Xi, Alpha Omega Alpha (counselor). Home: 111 Barretts Mill Rd Concord MA 01742-5519 Office: U Mass Med Sch Dept Neurology 55 Lake Ave N Worcester MA 01655-0002 Office Phone: 508-856-3081. Business E-Mail: david.drachman@umassmed.edu.

DRACHNIK, CATHERINE MELDYN, recreational therapist, artist, counselor; b. Kansas City, Mo., June 7, 1924; d. Gerald Willis and Edith (Gray) Weston; m. Joseph Brennan Drachnik, Oct. 6, 1946; children: Denise Elaine, Kenneth John. BS, U. Md., Coll. Park, 1945; MA, Calif. State U., Sacramento, 1975. Lic. family and child counselor; registered art therapist. Art therapist Vincent Hall Retirement Home, McLean, Va., Fairfax Mental Health Day Treatment Ctr., McLean, Arlington Mental Health Day Treatment Ctr., Va., 1971-72, Hope for Retarded, San Jose, Calif., Sequoia Hosp., Redwood City, Calif., 1972-73; supervising tchr. adult edn. Sacramento Soc. Blind, 1975-77; ptnr. Sacramento Divsn. Mediation Svcs., 1981-82; instr. Calif. State U., Sacramento, 1975-82, 92-93, 1999, Coll. Notre Dame, Belmont, Calif., 1975-96; art therapist, mental health counselor Psych West Counseling Ctr. (formerly Eskaton Am. River Mental Health Clinic), Carmichael, Calif., 1975-93; instr. Sacramento City Coll., 1997—2006; pvt. practice, 2006—. Instr. U. Utah, Salt Lake City, 1988—89; lectr. in field. Author: Interpreting Metaphors in Children's Drawings, 1995; contbr. chapters to books; one-woman shows include Vacaville Art Gallery, Calif., 1995, Dublier Gallery, Sacramento, 1997, Thistle Dew Gallery, 1998, Jeffery Bldg. Gallery, 2001, Oldham Gallery, 2001, Juno Gallery, Auburn, Calif., 2004, Taylors Nouveau Art Gallery, 2005, Doiron Gallery, Sacramento, 2006, exhibited in group shows at Art of Calif. Mag., 1993, Haggin Art Mus., Stockton, Calif., 1994, 1995, 1996, 1997, 1998, 1999, 2000, 2002, 2003, 2006, Calif. State Fair, Sacramento, 1995, 1997, 1998, 2000, 2001, 2005, Watercolor West, Brea, Calif., 1998, Rocky Mountain Nat. Watercolor, Golden, Colo., 1999, West Valley Art Mus., Phoenix, 1999, Elliot Fouts Art Gallery, Sacramento, 1999—2004, Am. Watercolor Soc., NY, 2000, Triton Mus. Art Biennial, Santa Clara, Calif., 2000, 2002, 2007, Calif. Watercolor Assn., San Francisco, 1999, 2001, 2005, Dorian Gallery, 2006, C.J.'s Gallery, 2006. Active charitable orgns. Mem.: Calif. Watercolor Assn. (signature status), Am. Assn. Marriage and Family Therapists, Nat. Art Edn. Assn., No. Calif. Arts, Inc. (master painter), No. Calif. Art Therapy Assn. (hon.; life), Am. Art Therapy Assn. (hon.; life, pres. 1987—89), Omicron Nu, Alpha Psi Omega, Kappa Kappa Gamma Alumnae Assn. (pres. Sacramento Valley chpt. 1991—92). Republican. Avocations: swimming, golf, theater. Home and Office: 4124 American River Dr Sacramento CA 95864-6025 Office Phone: 916-489-5138. Personal E-mail: cdrach@surewest.net.

DRACHTMAN, RICHARD ALLAN, pediatrician, educator; MD, U. Chgo, 1984. Diplomate Am. Bd. Pediat. Intern Northshore U. Hosp., Manhasset, NY, 1984—85, resident in pediat., 1987—88; fellow in pediat. hematology/oncology Mt. Sinai Med. Ctr., NYC, 1988—91; physician divsn. pediat. hematology & oncology Cancer Inst. N.J., New Brunswick, NJ, 1998—. Office: Cancer Inst NJ 195 Little Albany St New Brunswick NJ 08903 Home Phone: 732-613-8795; Office Phone: 732-235-8862. Office Fax: 732-235-8234.

DRACOS, THEODORE MICHAEL, journalist, television producer; b. Boston, June 30, 1945; s. Harry M. and Helen C. (Dore) D.; m. Mary Jill Moore, Oct. 28, 1969 (div. June 1979); 1 child, Erin. BA in History, U. Wis., 1969. Host WMFM Radio, Madison, Wis., 1970—72; founder, CEO, dir. Small Planet Rsch. Assocs., Seattle, 1973-76; contbg. writer Seattle Weekly Mag., 1977-80; investigative reporter Harte-Hanks TV, San Antonio, 1980-82, editl. commentator, 1992-93; dir. investigative reporting Gannett Broadcast Group, Mpls., 1983; investigative reporter, prodr. McGraw-Hill TV, San Diego, 1984—89; S.W. bur. chief Orion Nat. Telepictures, San Antonio, 1990; journalism instr. Incarnate Word Coll., San Antonio, 1991; documentary prodr., writer San Antonio, 1994—. Author: Ungodly: the Passions, Torments and Murder of Atheist Madalyn Murray O'Hair, 2003; writer, prodr. (documentary) One Moment of Madness, 1981 (Best Nat. Reporting award Nat. Headliners 1982, Charles Green Best Feature award Tex. Headliners 1982), Poisoning Paradise, 1987, Johnny Massingale, 1986, Stanley Stress, 1985. Exec. com. Puget Sound Sierra Club, Seattle, 1974-76; citizen activity coord. U.S. EPA Region 10, Seattle, 1974-75; med. dir. Jimmy Carter Presdl. Campaign, Washington, 1976; vol. Child Advocates of San Antonio, 1993. Recipient Golden medallion for best legal reporting Calif. State Bar, 1986. Mem.: Aus. Guild.

DRACUP, KATHLEEN ANNE, dean, nursing educator; b. Santa Monica, Calif., Sept. 28, 1942; d. Paul Joseph and Lucy Elizabeth (Milligan) Molloy; children: Jeffrey, Jonathan, Joy, Jan, Brian. BS in Nursing, St. Xavier's Coll., Chgo., 1967; M of Nursing, U. Calif., LA, 1974; D of Nursing Sci., U. Calif., San Francisco, 1982. Clin. nurse Little Co. of Mary Hosp., Chgo., 1967-70, UCLA Med. Ctr., 1970-74; asst. clin. prof. U. Calif., 1974-78, rsch. fellow dept. medicine, 1979-81, asst. prof. to prof., 1982-99, dean Sch. Nursing San Francisco, 2000—; clin. nurse Sch. Nursing U. Calif. San Francisco Med. Ctr., 1979; pvt. practice psychotherapist, 1980—95. Editor Heart and Lung Jour., 1981-91, Am. Jour. Critical Care, 1991—; editor Critical Care Nursing Series; contbr. chpts. to books, articles to profl. jours. Recipient Eugene Brunwald Acad. Mentorship award Am. Heart Assn., 2003; Disting. Practitioner Nat. Acad., Washington, 1987; Fulbright Sr. scholar, 1995. Fellow Coun. Cardiovascular Nursing, Am. Heart Assn., Am. Assn. Cardiopulmonary Rehab.; mem. Inst. of Medicine, Am. Nurses' Assn., Am. Assn. Critical Care Nurses (life), Sigma Theta Tau. Office: U Calif San Francisco Sch Nursing 2 Koret Way Rm N319 San Francisco CA 94143-0604 Office Phone: 415-476-1805. Business E-Mail: kathydracup@nursing.ucsf.edu.

DRAELOS, ZOE DIANA, dermatologist, consultant; b. Milw., Oct. 13, 1958; d. Dimitri Basil and Lorene June (Legan) Kececioglu; m. Michael Draelos, June 14, 1980; children: Mark, Matthew. BSME, U. Ariz., 1979, MD, 1983. Diplomate Am. Bd. Dermatology. Physician in solo dermatology practice, High Point, NC, 1988—. Cons., owner Dermatology Cons. Svcs., High Point, 1990—. Author: Cosmetics in Dermatology, 1995, Atlas of Cosmetic Dermatology, 2000. Rhodes scholar, Oxford, Eng., 1979. Office: Zoe Diana Draelos MD PA 2444 N Main St High Point NC 27262-7833 Office Phone: 336-841-2040.

DRAFT, HOWARD CRAIG, advertising executive; b. 1953; m. Elvy L. Leake; children: Andrew, Anna, Margaret. BA in Philosophy and Art History, Ripon Coll., 1974. With Draft Worldwide, Chgo., 1978—, gen. mgr. NY, 1982-86, pres., 1986-88, chmn., CEO, 1988—2006, Draftfcb, Chgo., 2006—. Bd. mem. Direct Mgtg. Assn. Edn. Found.; bd. dirs. Ad Coun., 2007—; spkr. in field. Trustee Pedia. AIDS Chgo., Herbert G. Birch Svcs.; bd. mem. Chgo. Old Town Sch. Folk Music; trustee Ripon Coll.; bd. dirs. Chgo. After Sch. Matters. Named one of 100 Best and Brightest, Advt. Age, one of The Best, The Brightest, The Most Powerful, Target Mktg., One of 50 Who Matter Now, Business 2.0, 2007, named Direct Marketer of the Yr., Chgo. Assn. Direct Mktg., 1999. Office: Draftfcb 633 N Saint Clair St Chicago IL 60611-3234 Office Phone: 312-944-3500.*

DRAGO, JOSEPH ROSARIO, urologist, educator; b. Jersey City, Oct. 28, 1947; m. Diane Lavacca; children: Andrea, Daniella, Denise. BS, U. Ill., 1968, MD, 1972. Diplomate Nat. Bd. Med. Examiners, Am. Bd. Urology; cert. Yag Laser, laparoscopic surgery. Intern Pa. State U. Milton S. Hershey Med. Ctr., 1972-73, resident in urology, 1973-77, instr. urology, 1976-77; asst. prof. urology, dir. urology oncology U. Calif., Davis, 1977-79, Milton S. Hershey (Pa.) Med. Ctr., 1979-80, assoc. prof. to prof. of surgery, dir. urologic oncology, 1980-85; assoc. staff Children's Hosp., Columbus, Ohio, 1985—; interim chief of staff elect, prof., dir. urologic oncology Ohio State U. Arthur G. James Cancer Hosp., Columbus, Ohio, 1990-92; with Easton (Pa.) Warren Urology, Easton, Pa., 1992-95; pvt. practice Washington, N.J., 1995—. Mem. editl. bd. In Vivo Jour.; advisor Internat. Urologic Svcs., Inc., 1987; cons. in field; vis. prof. more than 30 univs. and hosps. Author 12 book chpts.; reviewer various profl. jours., 1979—; contbr. articles to profl. jours. Recipient various rsch. grants, 1978-81. Fellow Internat. Coll. Surgeons in Urology; mem. AMA, Am. Coll. Surgeons, Am. Fertility Soc., Am. Inst. Ultrasound in Medicine, Am. Soc. Andrology, Am. Urologic Assn., Assn. Academic Surgery, Assn. Surgical Edn., Hershey Surgical Soc. (sec.-treas. 1983-85), Pa. Med. Soc., Phila. Urologic Soc., others. Home: 6680 Mossy Glen Dr Fort Myers FL 33908 Office: 224 Roseberry St Phillipsburg NJ 08865-1632 Office Phone: 239-826-2151. Personal E-mail: igotalife@aol.com.

DRAGO, VALERIA, neurologist, researcher; b. Messina, Italy, Nov. 7, 1977; d. Gulino and Drago. Lic. Medicina e Chirurgia Italy, 2001. Fellow U. Fla., Gainesville, 2004—. Contbr. articles to profl. jours. Office: Univ Fla McKnight Brain Ins 100 S Newell Dr Rm L3-100 Gainesville FL 32610-0236 Home Phone: 352-494-4770; Office Phone: 352-376-1611 ext. 6924. Business E-Mail: valeria.drago@neurology.ufl.edu.

DRAGOI, GEORGE, research scientist; m. Elena Dragoi; children: George, Andrei. MD, 1994, PhD, 2002. Postdoctoral fellow MIT, Cambridge, 2003—. Contbr. articles to profl. jours. Fellow, Fedn. European Neuroscience Soc.; Excellence Fellowship, Johnson and Johnson. Achievements include research in plasticity and coding in the brain; temporal coordination of cell assemblies in the brain. Home Phone: 617-738-4705.

DRAGON, WILLIAM, JR., footwear and apparel company executive; b. Lynn, Mass., Dec. 1, 1942; s. William and Anne (Stavru) D.; m. Suzanne Gail Behlmer, Feb. 24, 1968; children: Todd Christopher, Heather Anne, Paige Katherine (dec.). BS in Engring. Mgmt., Norwich U., Northfield, Vt., 1964; MS in Mgmt. Scis., Rensselaer Poly. Inst., Troy, NY, 1965. With mfg., sales and mktg. staff Gen. Electric Co., Mass. and Ky., 1967-73; dir. product planning and design Samsonite div. Beatrice Corp., Denver, 1973-75, dir. mktg. Samsonite div., 1975-78, v.p. mktg. and sales Buxton div. Springfield, Mass., 1978-81; gen. mgr. Johnston & Murphy Div. Genesco Inc., Nashville, 1981-85, exec. v.p., pres. U.S. Footwear Group, 1985-88, also dir.; v.p. Reebok Internat. Ltd., 1989-92; pres. Avia Group Internat. Inc., Portland, Oreg., 1989-92, Promotion Products Inc., Portland, 1992-94; dir. Deja, Inc., Portland, 1993-94; exec. v.p. DEJA Inc., Portland, 1994-95; pres. Pacific Trail divsn. London Fog Industries, 1995-99; pres., CEO London Fog Industries, 1999—2004, dir., 1999—2004; chmn., CEO Pacific Trail, 1999—2004; dir. Lucy, Inc., 2002. Dean's adv. coun. Oreg. State U., 1994-98. Bd. dirs. Nashville Youth Hockey League, 1983-85, Two/Ten Charity Found., 1988-92; vice chmn. Nashville United Way, 1985; mem. men's adv. bd. Cumberland Valley coun. Girl Scouts U.S., 1985-86; mem. adminstrv. bd. Brentwood United Meth. Ch., 1986. 1st lt. U.S. Army, 1965-67, Vietnam. Decorated Bronze Star medal. Recipient Superior Achievement Recognition award Genesco Inc., 1984 Presbyterian. Personal E-mail: billdsuzanned@msn.com.

DRAGONE, FRANCO, performing company executive; b. Cairano, Italy, Dec. 12, 1952; s. Giuseppe Dragone; married; 2 children. Attends, Conservatoire Royal of Mons. Employee Gulf Co.; with Theatre-Action Co., Compagnie du Campus; host Haine St. Pierre; dir. creation and devel. Cirque du Soleil, 1989—; founder DRAGONE, 2000—. Dir.: Nouvelle experience, 1990, Saltimbanco, 1992, Mystère, 1993, Alegria, 1994, Quidam, 1996, O, 1998, La Nouba, 1998, (Celine Dion): A New Day, 2003,: La Rêve, 2005. Mailing: Dragone Rue de Belle Vue 23 7100 La Louviere Belgium

DRAGONETTE, RITA HOEY, public relations executive; b. Chgo., Nov. 4, 1950; d. Louis D. and Edith M. (Finnemann) Hoey; m. Joseph John Dragonette, Sept. 4, 1982 (dec.). BA in English and History, No. Ill. U., 1972. Asst. dir. Nat. Assn. Housing and Human Devel., Chgo., 1975; pub. rels. account exec. Weber Cohn & Riley, Chgo., 1975-76; publicity coord. U.S. Gypsum Co., Chgo., 1976-77; with Daniel J. Edelman, Inc., Chgo., 1977-84, sr. v.p., 1981-84; exec. v.p. Dragonette, Inc., Chgo., 1984-91, pres., 1991-99, GCI Dragonette, Chgo., 1999—2002; prin. Dragonette Cons., 2002—. Home: Ste 422 680 North Lake Shore Dr Chicago IL 60611 E-mail: rmdragonette@ameritech.net.

DRAGOUMIS, PAUL, electric utility company executive; b. NYC, Sept. 19, 1934; s. Andrew and Theologie (Pavlou) D.; m. Maria William, Sept. 15, 1957; children— Ann Marie Murtlow, Andrew Paul. BSEE, Poly. Inst. Bklyn., 1956; MS in Nuclear Engring., Internat. Sch. Nuclear Sci. and Engring., Argonne, Ill., 1959; MA in Philosophy, Georgetown U., 1986. Asst. v.p. Am. Electric Power Co., NYC, 1956-70; gen. mgr. corp. exec. staff Allis Chalmers Corp., W. Allis, Wis., 1970-71; v.p. nuclear projects and fossil fuel supply group Potomac Electric Power Co., Washington, 1971-75, v.p. policy, 1976-78, sr. v.p., mem. exec. policy com., 1978-89, exec. v.p., 1989-95; dir. nuclear affairs USFEA, Washington, 1975-76; exec. dir. Pres. Ford's Energy Resources Coun., 1975-76. Mem. mgmt. com. PJM Interconnection, 1980-95; pres. PDA, Inc., 1995-2002. Chmn. emeritus Concert Soc. at Md.; trustee, mem. exec. com. The Washington Opera, 1980—, pres., 1990-94; trustee, mem. exec. com. Greater Washington Rsch. Ctr., 1978-97. Named U.S. Outstanding Young Elec. Engr. Eta Kappa Nu, 1964, Outstanding Young Man of Am. Jaycees, 1966; recipient award for meritorious service USFEA, 1976. Mem. Univ. Club (Washington). Republican. Greek Orthodox. Avocation: sailing. E-mail: dragoum@attglobal.net.

DRAGT, ALEXANDER JAMES, physicist, educator; b. Lafayette, Ind., Apr. 7, 1936; s. Gerrit and Beulah (Westra) D.; m. Lavonne Ann Wolters, Nov. 28, 1957; children: Alison Ann, Alexander James Jr., William David. AB, Calvin Coll., 1958; PhD in Physics (NSF fellow), U. Calif., Berkeley, 1964. Sr. scientist Lockheed Missiles & Space Corp., Palo Alto, Calif., 1961-62; staff scientist Aerospace Corp., Los Angeles, 1963; mem. Inst. Advanced Study, Princeton, NJ, 1963-65; asst. prof. physics U. Md., 1965-68, assoc. prof., 1968-74, prof., 1974—, chmn. dept. physics and astronomy, 1975-78. Mem. vis. staff Los Alamos Sci. Lab., 1978-79, cons., 1979— vis. prof. Tex. A&M U., 1984; mem. vis. staff Tex Accelerator Ctr., 1984; guest scientist Lawrence Berkeley Lab., 1985, 2002, cons., 1985—, Stanford Linear Accelerator Center, 1995. Fellow Am. Phys. Soc.; Mem. Am. Geophys. Union, AAAS, Am. Math. Soc. Mem. Christian Reformed Ch. Mem. Christian Reformed Ch. Achievements include research in theoretical physics and applied math. Office: U Md Dept Physics College Park MD 20742-0001 Business E-Mail: dragt@physics.umd.edu.

DRAGUSHANSKAYA, LYUDMILA, language educator, department chairman; b. Kishinev, Moldova, Russia, Aug. 26, 1954; arrived in US, 1992; d. Mikail Dragushanskiy and Riva Dragushanskaya; 1 child, Sandy Achmiz. MA in Linguistics, St. Petersburg Tchrs. U., Russia, 1976; PhD in Edn., Kennedy Western U., Wyo., 2002; MA in TESOL, Adelphia U., NY, 2003. ESL instr. SCS Bus. Inst., NYC, 1992—95; chairperson ESL Globe Inst. Tech., NYC, 1995—2001; chairperson asst. ASA Inst., Bklyn., 2001—. Mem.: TESOL. Avocations: movies, theater, sports, swimming. Personal E-mail: dragmil@gmail.com.

DRAHOS, SANDRA P., retired chemist; b. Chgo., Aug. 3, 1943; d. Berlyn and Elizabeth Anna Pierce; children: David Mark, Elizabeth Anne. BS, U. Wis., 1966. Chemist Ashland Chem., Willow Springs, Ill., 1983—93, Enviropur, McCook, Ill., 1993—95, Chempet, Inc., Addison, Ill., 1995—97, Henkel Adhesives, Eligin, Ill., 1997—2002. Leader, tng. chmn., instr. Boy Scouts of Am., Morris, Ill., 1979—89; leader Girl Scouts of Am., Joliet, Ill., 1983—86; mem. Wee Care, Scottsdale, Ariz., 2002—05, Landscaping Com. for Camello Vista, Scottsdale, 2004—05; vol. Rialto Theatre, Joliet, 1998—2005. Recipient Hobson award, 1999. Mem.: Soc. Tribiologists and Lubricating Engrs. (life; various offices). Achievements include patents for Adhesives for Shoes. Avocations: travel, piano, bridge, art, gardening. Personal E-mail: sdrahos1@hsn.com.

DRAIN, ALBERT STERLING, business management consultant; b. Decatur, Tex., July 5, 1925; s. Albert S. and Bessie (Burk) D.; m. Mauvaline Joyce Beam, Apr. 18, 1946; children: Ronald Dale, Deborah Kay Drain Crawford. Student, Bellville Jr. Coll., Ill., Tex. Christian U., Iowa U., Milsaps Coll., Pittsburg Coll., Kans. With Armour & Co., 1945-79, regional mgr. Pitts., 1966-67, mgr. pork div. Chgo., 1967-68, fresh meats div. mgr., 1968-69, corporate v.p., 1968-75, exec. v.p., 1971-73, group v.p. food marketing div., 1973-75; pres. Armour Foods, 1975-79; also dir.; exec. v.p. for Iowa Beef Processors Inc., Dakota City, Nebr., 1979-80; group v.p. Greyhound Corp., Phoenix, 1977—; pres. Sterling Mktg. Inc. (ind. bus. cons. to meat industry), Phoenix, 1980-91; pvt. practice mgmt. cons. meat packing Phoenix, 1991-94; pvt. practice Al Drain Mgmt. Cons., Phoenix, 1994—. Served with USNR, 1943-45. Mem. Am. Soc. Agrl. Cons., Masons, Shriners. Baptist. Home: 7550 N 16th St Apt 6128 Phoenix AZ 85020-7640 Fax: 602-266-4797. E-mail: AlDrainl@aol.com.

DRAIN, CECIL B., dean, nursing educator, retired military officer; b. Ft. Worth, Aug. 25, 1943; s. Harry Eugene and F. Colene (McDonald) D.; m. Cynthia M. Pfaff, Aug. 21, 1965; children: Timothy, Stephen, Kathryn. Diploma, St. Joseph Hosp. Sch. Nursing, Ft. Worth, 1967; BSN, U. Ariz., 1976, MS in Med.-Surg. Nursing, 1980, NS in Adult Pulmonary Nursing, 1980; PhD in Ednl. Curriculum and Instrn. in Higher Edn., Tex. A&M U., 1986. RN, Va., Tex.; cert. RN anesthetist. Staff nurse recovery room, head nurse psychiatry St. Joseph Hosp., 1967; commd. 2d lt. U.S. Army, 1968, advanced through grades to col.; chief nurse anesthetist 121st Evacuation Hosp., Seoul, Republic of Korea, 1972—73; staff nurse anesthetist, chief respiratory therapy U.S. Gen. Leonard Wood Army Community Hosp., Ft. Leonard Wood, Mo., 1973-74; staff nurse anesthetist Tucson Med. Ctr., 1974—76, Brooke Army Med. Ctr., Ft. Sam Houston, Tex., 1976—78, spl. project officer, 1986-89; asst. program dir. U.S. Army-SUNY-Buffalo anesthesiology for ANC officers course U.S. Army Acad. Health Sciences, Ft. Sam Houston, 1980-83; program dir. program in anesthesia nursing U.S. Army-Tex. U.S. Army/Tex. Wesleyan U./Acad. of Health Scis., Ft. Sam Houston, 1989-92; dir. program in anesthesia nursing U. Tex. Health Sci. Ctr. Houston/AMEDD Ctr. and Sch., Ft. Sam Houston, 1992-93; prof. clin. nursing U. Tex. Health Sci. Ctr., Houston, 1992-93; prof. Va. Commonwealth U., Med. Coll. Va. Campus, Richmond, 1993—; chmn. dept. nurse anesthesia Med. Coll. Va., Va. campus Commonwealth U., Richmond, 1993-96, interim dean Sch. Allied Health Professions, 1996-97, dean Sch. Allied Health Professions, 1997—. Teaching asst. U. Ariz., 1979-80; clin. instr. family medicine U. Okla., 1983; adj. prof. Tex. Wesleyan U., 1989-92; guest lectr. Tex. A&M U., 1986-93; numerous presentations in field; mem. long-term civilian profls. Schooling Selection Bd., Alexandria, Va., 1988; reviewer Clin. Rev. Series in Critical Care Nursing, 1988—. Author: Perianesthesia Nursing: A Critical Care Approach; mem. editl. bd.: Heart and Lung: Jour. Critical Care, 1977—92, Nurse Anesthesia, 1987—94, Am. Jour. Critical Care, 1992—, Jour. Am. Assn. Nurse Anesthetists, 1980—93, 1992—2000, Jour. Perianesthesia Nursing, 2002—; contbr. articles abstracts and book revs. to profl. jours., chpts. to books. Baseball commr., Ft. Sam Houston, 1980-81; bd. dirs. March of Dimes, San Antonio, 1981-83; umpire USTA, Bryan, Tex., 1985—; trustee Yankton Coll., 2003--. Decorated Legion of Merit, Meritorious Svc. medal with oak leaf cluster; named Alumni of Yr., Yankton Coll., 2003, Tex. A&M U., 2004 Fellow Am. Acad. Nursing, Assn. Schs. Allied Health Profls. (treas. 2002-04), Assn. Schs. Allied Health Professions (treas. 2002-04); mem. ANA, AACN (cert. of achievement 1980), Am. Assn. Nurse Anesthetists (jour. faculty 1982-83, bd. dirs. Ednl. and Rsch. Found. 1983-91, rsch. com. 2005—, cert. of profl. excellence 1976), Am. Soc. Post Anesthesia Nurses (rsch. com. 1986-87, Helen Lamb award 2007), Tex. Assn. Post Anesthesia Nurses (life), 38th Parallel Nurses Soc. (pres. 1971), So. Assn. Allied Health Deans of Acad. Med. Ctrs. (treas. 2002-04), Mil. Officers Assn. Am. (life), Ret. Officers Assn. (life), Ret. Army Nurse Corps Assn. (assoc.), Order of Mil. Med. Merit, Downtown Kiwanis, Sigma Theta Tau, Phi Delta Kappa, Sigma Epsilon Chi. Republican. Methodist. Home: 5511 W Bay Rd Midlothian VA 23112-2509 Office: Va Commonwealth U Med Coll Va Campus Sch Allied Health Profs Richmond VA 23298-0233 Office Phone: 804-828-7247. Personal E-mail: crnacol@aol.com. Business E-Mail: cbdrain@vcu.edu.

DRAINE, BRUCE THOMAS, astrophysicist, educator; b. Kolkata, India, Nov. 19, 1947; came to US, 1950; s. Thomas Paul and Dolly (Rieck) D.; m. Dina Gutkowicz-Krusin, Dec. 26, 1975; children: David G., Alexander K. BA, Swarthmore Coll., Pa., 1969; PhD, Cornell U., 1978. Vol. US Peace Corps, Ghana, 1969-71; fellow Ctr. Astrophysics, Cambridge, Mass., 1977-79; long-term mem. Inst. Advanced Study, Princeton, NJ, 1979-82; asst. prof. Princeton U., 1981-84, assoc. prof., 1984-90, prof., 1990—. Contbr. articles to profl. jours. Mem. Am. Astron. Soc. (Dannie Heineman prize in Astrophysics, 2004), NAS. Achievements include research in physics of interstellar matter and radiation, physical and optical properties of small particles and magnetohydrodynamic shock waves. Office: Dept Astrophysy Scis Princeton U 108 Peyton Hall Princeton NJ 08544-1001 Office Phone: 609-258-3810. E-mail: draine@astro.princeton.edu.*

DRAKE, ALBERT ESTERN, retired statistics educator, farming administrator; b. Stamping Ground, Ky., June 12, 1927; s. John L and Dullia Zena (Humphrey) D.; m. Katherine Ashby, June 22, 1952; children: Alan Sanford, Paul Steven, Jane, Philip David. Student, Georgetown Coll., 1946-47; BS, U. Ky., 1950, MS, 1951; PhD, U. Ill., 1958; postgrad., N.C. State U., 1959-63, U. Fla., 1960. Rsch. asst. U. Ill., 1953-55, rsch. assoc., 1955-59; assoc. prof., assoc. biometrician Auburn U., 1959-62, prof., biometrician, 1962-63; dir. computer ctr. W.Va. U., 1963-65, acting coord. stats., 1965-66; prof. stats. U. Ala., 1966-92, coord. quantitative methods, 1966-72, acting head stats and mgmt. sci., 1981, interim assoc. dean undergrad. programs Coll. of Commerce and Bus. Adminstrn., 1988-90, assoc. dean undergrad. programs Coll. of Commerce and Bus. Adminstrn., 1990-92; prof. emeritus, 1992—; part-time mgr. farming enterprise and rock quarry Georgetown, Ky., 1992—. Cons. in field. Contbr. articles to profl. jours., papers to profl. meetings. Bd. dirs. Little League, Auburn, 1961-63; active local council Boy Scouts Am., 1962-63, 66-67. Served with USMC, 1945-46. NSF grantee, 1959, 60, 63; Venture Fund grantee, 1975, 76, 81; inducted to Coll. Commerce & Bus. Adminstrn. U. Ala. Faculty Hall of Fame, 1998. Mem. Biometrics Soc., Am. Statis. Assn. (pres. Ala. chpt. 1972), Decision Scis. Inst. (sec. 1973-74, coun. 1969-72, 75-77, mem. editl. bd. 1969-72), Am. Agrl. Econs. Assn., Pi Kappa Alpha (Disting. Alumni award Omega chpt. 2001, hon. Ky. col. 2002). Republican. Home: 5533 E Desert Hills Dr Scottsdale AZ 85254 Home Phone: 502-863-0476; Office Phone: 480-664-0231.

DRAKE, ANN M., consumer products company executive; b. Sept. 4, 1947; d. James and Mary Lou McIlrath; m. John Drake, II; stepchildren: Joanna, Tracy. B in English, U. Iowa, 1969; MBA, Northwestern U., 1984. Founder, prin. Camwilde Interiors; mem. adv. bd. DSC Logistics, 1983—90, exec. v.p. DesPlaines, Ill., 1990—94, CEO, 1994—. Mem. bd. dirs. A.M. Castle & Co.; vice-chmn. Bus. Adv. Coun. (BAC), Northwestern U. Transp. Ctr.; co-chmn. Transp. Com. for the Met. Planning Coun.; mem. bd. governors The Com. of 200; mem. bd. dirs. Ctr. for Women's Bus. Rsch. Named one of Ten Outstanding Women Bu. Owners, Diversity Edge Mag., 2006, Chicago's Most Powerful Entrepreneurs, Today's Chicago Woman, 2006, 25 Women to Watch, Crain's Chgo. Bus., 2007. Mem.: Warehouse Edn. Rsch. Coun., The Coun. for Supply Chain Mgmt. (CSCMP), The Econ. Club of Chgo., Commercial Club of Chgo., Chgo. Network. Office: DSC Logistics 1750 S Wolf Rd Des Plaines IL 60018*

DRAKE, CHARLES WHITNEY, physicist; b. South Portland, Maine, Mar. 8, 1926; s. Charles Whitney and Katharine Gabrielle (O'Neill) D.; m. Ellen Tan, June 15, 1952; children— Judith Ellen, Robert Charles, Linda Ann. BS, U. Maine, 1950; MA, Conn. Wesleyan U., 1952; PhD, Yale U., 1958. Scientist Westinghouse Atomic Power Div., 1952-53; instr. Yale U., New Haven, 1957-60, asst. prof., 1960-66, rsch. assoc., 1966-69; assoc. prof. Oreg. State U., 1966-74, prof., 1974-93; prof. emeritus, 1993—; chmn. dept. physics, 1976-84. Vis. prof. Oxford U. Clarendon Lab. and St. Peter's Coll., 1972-73, U. Tuebingen (W.Ger.), 1982. Contbr. articles to profl. jours. Served with USN, 1944-46. Recipient various fellowships and grants. Fellow Am. Phys. Soc.; mem. Am. Assn. Physics Tchrs., Sigma Xi, Tau Beta Pi, Sigma Pi Sigma. Office: Oreg State U Dept Physics Corvallis OR 97331 Personal E-mail: drakec@onid.orst.edu.

DRAKE, DALLAS SUMNER, researcher; s. Wayne Canedy Drake and Miriam Ethel Mikkelsen-Drake; life ptnr. Joseph Ervin Shulka. Degree in sociology magna cum laude, U. Minn., Mpls., 2005. Cert. fire instr. 3 Minn. Fire Svc. Cert. Bd., apparatus operator 4 Minn. Fire Svc. Cert. Bd., firefighter 3 Minn. Fire Svc. Cert. Bd., EMT-ambulance Nat. Registry EMTs. Firefighter, fire motor operator Burnsville Fire Dept., Minn., 1982—2001; prin. rschr. Ctr. Homicide Rsch., Mpls., 1999—. Cmty. engagement rep. Mpls. Police Dept., 2002; program chair Homicide Rsch. Working Group, Orlando, Fla., 2004. Contbr. chapters to books, conf. papers to procs. books. Mem. neighborhood revitalization program steering com. Kingfield Neighborhood, Mpls., 1996; grand marshal Twin Cities Pride Festival, 2007; bd. dirs. Fire Instrs.' Assn. Minn., Minnetonka, 1981—84; sponsor Shulka-Drake scholarship award Philanthrofund Found., Mpls., 2000—. Recipient Best News Photo award, Neighborhood and Cmty. Press Assn., 1989, citation of merit, Burnsville Fire Dept., 1993, award of meritorious action, 2000, cert. of recognition, Colin Higgins Found., 2003. Mem.: World Soc. Victimology, Sociologists of Minn., Midwest Sociol. Soc., Am. Soc. Victimology (Founding Lifetime Mem. 2003), Internat. Homicide Investigators Assn., Homicide Rsch. Working Group, Am. Soc. Criminology. Achievements include first openly gay firefighter in Minnesota; co-founder of the Center for Homicide Research, the only homicide research center in the United States. Avocations: gardening, backroad travel, woodworking, bicycling. Office: Ctr for Homicide Rsch 3036 University Ave SE Ste E Minneapolis MN 55414-3316 Home Phone: 612-827-4658; Office Phone: 612-331-4820. E-mail: info@chronline.org.

DRAKE, DIANA ASHLEY, retired financial planner; b. Poughkeepsie, NY, Apr. 28, 1937; d. Albert Jackson and Jane Ashley (Ketchum) D.; m. José Akel Abizaid, Dec. 2, 1956 (div. Nov. 1979); children: Cynthia A. Rush, Allison J. Abizaid, Linda A. Wiener, Carol Lynn Abizaid, Amanda Jo Abizaid, Richard Alan Abizaid; m. Sherrill Cleland, Sept. 3, 1988; stepchildren: Ann Cleland Feldmeier, Douglas S. Cleland, Sarah Cleland Allen, Scott C. Cleland. Student, Cornell U., 1955-56, Am. U. of Beirut, Lebanon, 1956-57; BS in Psychology cum laude, Vassar Coll., 1980; CFP, Inst. Fin. Planners, Denver, 1986. CFP. Divorce mediator Fin. Planning Corp. of Va., McLean, 1983-86; investment advisor Cert. Fin. Svc., McLean, 1986; ptnr. Koelz Drake Advisors, Falls Church, Va., 1987-89; pres. Drake Fin. Svcs., Falls Church, 1986-98; bronze distbr. Nikken health and wellness products, prin. Magnetic Living, 1998—2003; ret., 2003. Sec., mem. Bd. Equalization, Falls Church, 1992-94. Contbr. articles to various mags. Elder Falls Church Presbyn. Ch., 1993-96, chair Christian Edn. Com., 1996, planned giving com. 1997-99, revision com. 1997; co-chmn. 100 yrs. aquatics YMCA, New Orleans, 1986. Recipient Disting. Svc. award for 25 Yrs. svcs. Nat. YMCA, 1986. Mem.: DAR, AAUW, Inst. CFPs, No. Va. Inst. Cert. Fin. Planners (sec. 1994—97, bd. dirs. facilities), Sarasota Camera Club, Cornell Club (Sarasota), Zonta (dir. Arlington club 1992—99, cmty. svc. coord.), Cornell Club of Washington (mem. investment and audit com. 1990—99), Meadows Chorus (Sarasota), Vassar Club (Sarasota, Fla.), Highland Oaks Cir. Assn. (bd. dirs., pres. 2003), Delta Gamma. Republican. Avocations: swimming, bridge, writing, photography, travel. Home and Office: 4489 Highland Oaks Cir Sarasota FL 34235 E-mail: dadcleland@yahoo.com.

DRAKE, DONALD CHARLES, journalist, playwright; b. NYC, Jan. 12, 1935; s. Albert E. and Gloria (Walters) D.; 1 child, Valerie; m. Molly Hindman; 1 step-child, Jennifer. Student, NYU, 1953-56. Copy boy New York Herald Tribune, 1954-55; reporter Patent Trader, Mt. Kisco, NY, 1956-57, New Haven Register, 1957-58, Newsday, Garden City, NY, 1958-65; med. writer Phila. Inquirer, 1966-93; narrative editor, 1993-2001. Author: Medical School, 1978, (plays) Words, Saintly Mother, Clear and Present Danger, Final Edition, Gorked!, The Last Appointment, Love Knot, The Passage, Aria, Tom, Dick and Harriet. Recipient Russell L. Cecil Writing award Arthritis Found., 1968, John S. Packard award Pa. Tb. and Health Soc., 1968, Howard W. Blakeslee awards Am. Heart Assn., 1969, 76, 81, Walter J. Donaldson awards Pa. Med. Soc., 1970, 71, Keystone Press awards, 1974-81, 83, 84, 87, 88, 90, 93, 2002, Claude Bernard award Nat. Soc. for Med. Research, 1978, AP Mng. Editors award Pa., 1978, 81, 84, 93, Robert F. Kennedy Journalism award, 1982, Morse award Am. Psychiat. Assn., 1982, Gen. Motors Cancer Rsch. Found. prize, 1990, others. Mem. Nat. Assn. Sci. Writers, Dramatists Guild, Phila. Dramatists Ctr. Office Phone: 215-726-5580. Personal E-mail: thedondrake@hotmail.com. *Journalism would serve a greater good if it sought the truth instead of just the facts, but that's a lot harder to do.*

DRAKE, ELISABETH MERTZ, chemical engineer, consultant; b. NYC, Dec. 20, 1936; d. John and Ruth (Johnson) Mertz; m. Alvin William Drake, July 31, 1957 (div. 1984); 1 child, Alan Lee. SB in Chem. Engring., MIT, 1958, ScD in Chem. Engring., 1966. Registered profl. engr., Mass. Staff engr. Arthur D. Little Inc., Cambridge, Mass., 1958-64, sr. staff, 1966-76, mgr. risk analysis, 1977-82, v.p. tech. risk mgmt., 1980-82, 86-89, cons., 1990-94; assoc. dir. new tech. MIT Energy Lab., 1990-2000, dir., 1994-95, cons., 2000—; lectr. U. Calif., Berkeley, 1971; vis. prof. MIT, Cambridge, 1973-74; chmn. chem. engring. dept. Northeastern U., Boston, 1982-86. Corp. mgr. MIT, 1981-86; mem. tech. pipeline safety stds. com. U.S. Dept. Transp., 1980-85; mem. mng. bd. AIChE, 1988-90; vice chair com. on rev. and evaluation on army chem. stockpile disposal program NRC, 1993-98, mem., 2002-2004, vice chair com. on chem. demil., 2004-07. Contbr. articles to profl. jours.; inventor fractionation method and apparatus, 1972. Fellow AIChE (bd. dirs. 1987-90); mem. AAAS, NAE, Am. Chem. Soc., Sigma Xi. Home: 80B Seminary Ave Apt 154 Auburndale MA 02466-2654 Business E-Mail: edrake@alum.mit.edu.

DRAKE, EVELYN DOWNIE, retired secondary school educator; b. Longmont, Colo., Aug. 23, 1940; d. Milford West and Colette Dorothy (Mraz) Downie; m. Sherman Hoffman Drake, May 18, 1963 (div. 1971); children: Marcella Colette Drake-Bettis, Sherman Downie Drake; m. Robert Dale Mager, July 14, 1975 (div. 1981). BS, U. Wyo., 1962; MA, U. No. Colo., 1980; postgrad., U. Edinburgh, Scotland, 1982, Cambridge U., Eng., 1986. Cert. tchr./vocat. tchr., Colo. Sec./receptionist Barnard Realty, Casper, Wyo., 1959-61, Pure Oil Co. (now UNOCAL), Casper, 1961; coord., tchr. St. Mark's Pre-Sch., Casper, 1965; reporter, feature writer Casper Star-Tribune, Casper, 1970-71; instr., tchr. Casper Coll., 1964-69; tchr. home econs. Kelly Walsh High Sch., 1971-72; tchg. asst. U. No. Colo., Greeley, 1979-80; tchr. of English, journalism, art, home econs. Jefferson County R-1 Schs., Golden, Colo., 1972—97, ret., 1997. Cons., tchr. Casper North Side Ctr., 1969-71. Artist: weaving exhibit, Pub. Libr., Casper, 1968, others. Ctrl. com. Jefferson County Democrats, Lakewood, Colo., 1989—; candidate bd. dirs. Green Mt. Townhouse Corp. #1 Lakewood, 1987; tchr. Lakewood Sister Cities Exch. Program to Miranda, New South Wales, Sutherlandshire, Australia, 1995. Nominated Colo. Tchr. of Yr., Evergreen (Colo.) Jr. High, 1989. Mem. Colo. Lang. Arts Soc., Nat. Coun. Tchrs. of English (planning com. nat. conf. 1989-90), NEA (faculty rep.), Colo. Educators Assn. (faculty rep.), JCEA Edn. Assn. (faculty rep.), Denver Press Club, Phi Delta Kappa (sec. 1995-2006), Delta Kappa Gamma. others. Avocations: art, writing, literature.

DRAKE, FRANCIS LEBARON, law librarian; b. Pitts., Aug. 17, 1944; s. Francis LeBaron Sarah Jane (Fultz) D. BA, Oberlin Coll., 1966; MMus, U. Tex., 1973, MLS, 1978. Info. specialist Telemedia, Inc., Chgo., 1979-83; dir. libr. svcs. Arnstein & Lehr LLP, Chgo., 1983—. Profl. mem. Chgo. Symphony Chorus, 1980—2004. Capt. USAF, 1967—71. Mem. Chgo. Assn. Law Librs. (sec. 1992-93, pres. 2000-01, chair nominations com. 2002-03, chair relations with Information Vendors Com. 1994-96, chair bylaws com. 2003—, chair corp. memory com. 2005—, Agnes and Harvey T. Reid award Outstanding Contbn. to Law Librarianship,2004-05), Am. Assn. Law Librs. (chair coun. of chpt. presidents, 2001-02) Office: Arnstein & Lehr LLP Ste 1200 120 S Riverside Plz Chicago IL 60606-3910 Office Phone: 312-876-7170. Business E-Mail: fldrake@arnstein.com.

DRAKE, GEORGE ALBERT, retired academic administrator, historian, educator; b. Springfield, Mo., Feb. 25, 1934; s. George Bryant and Alberta (Stimson) D.; m. Susan Martha Ratcliff, June 25, 1960; children: Christopher George, Cynthia May, Melanie Susan. AB, Grinnell Coll., 1956; Fulbright scholar, U. Paris, 1956-57; AB (Rhodes scholar), Oxford U., 1959, MA, 1963; BD, U. Chgo., 1962, MA, 1963, PhD (Rockefeller fellow), 1965; LLD (hon.), Colo. Coll., 1980, Ripon Coll., 1982; LHD (hon.), Ill. Coll., 1985, Ursinus Coll., 1988, Doane Coll., 1995, Morningside Coll., 1998. Instr. history Grinnell Coll., 1960-61, pres., 1979-91, prof., 1979—, prof. emeritus, 2004—, pres. emeritus, 2006—. Asst. prof., assoc. prof., prof. history Colo. Coll., Colorado Springs, 1964-79, acting dean of Coll., 1967-68, dean, 1969-73 Trustee Grinnell Coll., 1970-79, Penrose Hosp., 1976-84, Grinnell Gen. Hosp., 1980-86, Doane Coll., 1995—; bd. dirs. Iowa Peace Inst., 1994—2004, chair, 1996-99; vol. U.S. Peace Corps, Lesotho, 1991-93; commr. North Ctrl. Assn. Colls. and Schs., 1998-2001; bd. dirs. FINE Found., 1998—, chair 2003—. NEH fellow, 1974. Mem. Am. Hist. Assn., Am. Ch. History Soc., Nat. Coll. Athletic Assn. (pres. commn. 1984-89), Nat. Merit Scholarship Corp. Home Phone: 641-236-8243; Office Phone: 641-269-3720. Business E-Mail: drake@grinnell.edu.

DRAKE, HUDSON BILLINGS, aerospace and electronics executive; b. LA, Mar. 3, 1935; s. Hudson C. and Blossom (Billings) Drake; m. Joan M. Johnson, Feb. 9, 1957 (dec. 1997); children: Howard Billings, Paul Marvin; m. Mary H. Vaugier, Nov. 1, 2000. BA in Econs., UCLA, 1957, grad. Exec. Program, 1991; MBA, Pepperdine U., Malibu, Calif., 1976. Mgr. autonetics divsn. N.Am. Aviation, Rockwell Inc., Anaheim, Calif., 1958-68; exec. dir. Pres.'s Commn. White House Fellows, Washington, 1969-70; dep. under sec. U.S. Dept. Commerce, Washington, 1970-72; v.p., gen. mgr. Teledyne Ryan Electronics, San Diego, 1972-80, pres., 1980-84; pres., group exec. Teledyne Ryan Aero., San Diego, 1984-88; pres. aerospace and electronics Teledyne Inc., LA, 1988—97; ltd. ptnr. Carlisle Enterprises, La Jolla, Calif., 1997—. Mem. Def. Procurement Adv. Com. Trade, Washington, 1988—93; cons. unmanned aerial systems Evergreen Internat. Aviation, 2004—; bd. dirs. Compass Aerospace Corp. Contbr. articles to profl. jours. Bd. dirs. Johnson Cancer Ctr. Found., UCLA, 1998—2005; vestry St. James by Sea, La Jolla, Calif., 1998—2002; trustee Children's Hosp., San Diego, 1981—86, chmn. rsch. corp., 1983—86; pres.'s coun. San Diego State U., 1984—90; bd. overseers U. Calif., San Diego, 1985—88. With USNR, 1953—61. Named Silver Knight of Mgmt., Nat. Mgmt. Assn., 1975, Gold Knight of Mgmt., 1986; recipient Exec. of the Yr. award, 1995, San Diego Bd. Suprs. resolution, 1988; White House fellow, 1968—69. Mem.: AIAA, IEEE, San Diego C. of C. (bd. dirs.), Inst. Navigation, Navy League (life), La Jolla Beach and Tennis Club, La Jolla Country Club. Republican. Episcopalian. Avocations: golf, fly fishing. Home: 1707 Soledad Ave La Jolla CA 92037 Personal E-mail: hdrake1@san.rr.com.

DRAKE, JOHN WARREN, aviation consultant; b. Chgo., July 5, 1930; s. Robert Warren and Winifred Elizabeth (Bramhall) D.; m. Miriam Anna Engleman, Dec. 19, 1960 (div. Dec. 1985); 1 child, Robert Warren; m. Mary Pat O'Kelly, Sept. 24, 2000. BS, Rensselaer Poly. Inst., 1952; MBA, Harvard U., 1954, DBA, 1972. Rsch. assos. Aero. Rsch. Found., Cambridge, Mass., 1956-57; prin. United Rsch., Inc., Cambridge, 1957-61; v.p. Sys. Analysis and Rsch. Corp., 1961-69; prof. emeritus, air transp. area Sch. Aerospace and Astronautics Sch. Engring. Purdue U., 1972-92, mem. pres.'s coun., 1992—. Cons. in field; mem. Transp. Research Bd. NRC. Author: The Administration of Transportation Modeling Projects, 1973. Served with U.S. Army, 1954-56. Mem. Air Transp. Rsch. Internat. Forum (coun.), AIAA, Soc. Automotive Engrs. Home: 341 Riverview Dr Ann Arbor MI 48104-1847

DRAKE, KENNETH DAVID, geologist; b. Linton, Ind., Apr. 18, 1959; s. Kenneth Eugene and Marilyn Kay Drake; m. Kathleen Rose Smith, May 31, 1980. BS in Geology, Ind. U., 1984; MS in Urban Environ. Geology, U. Mo., 1999. Registered geologist Mo., profl. geologist Tenn. Geologist U.S. Army Corps Engrs., Kansas City, Mo., 1986—93; geologist, project mgr. U.S. EPA, Kansas City, Kans., 1993—. Contbr. articles to profl. jours. Pres. Lansing (Kans.) Lions Club, 1995. Recipient Bronze medal, U.S. EPA, 1999, Silver medal, 2001. Mem.: KC, Nat. Ground Water Assn., Assn. Engring. Geologists, Assn. Mo. Geologists, Geol. Soc. Am. Office: US EPA 901 N 5th St Kansas City KS 66101 Office Phone: 913-551-7626. Office Fax: 913-551-7063. E-mail: drake.dave@epa.gov.

DRAKE, MICHAEL V., academic administrator, ophthalmologist, educator; b. NYC; AB, Stanford U.; BS, MD, U. Calif., San Francisco. Resident U. Calif., San Francisco, asst. prof. ophthalmology, 1979—87, chief eye clinic, 1979—91, assoc. prof., dir. vision care and clin. rsch. unit, asst. dean student affairs, 1991—93, prof., 1993—98, Stephen P. Shearing prof., 1998—, vice chmn. dept. ophthalmology, assoc. dean admissions and student programs, sr. assoc. dean admissions and extramural academic programs, 1998—2000, v.p. health affairs, 2000—05, chancellor, 2005—. Author: (with D.O. Harrington) The Visual Fields: Text and Atlas of Clinical Perimetry, 1990. Recipient Herbert W. Nickens award, Assn. Am. Med. Colls., 2004. Fellow: Am. Acad. Arts & Scis. Office: U Calif The Chancellor's Office Irvine CA 92697-1900 Office Phone: 949-824-5111. Office Fax: 949-824-2087.*

DRAKE, MIRIAM ANNA, retired librarian, educator, writer, consultant; b. Boston, Dec. 20, 1936; d. Max Frederick and Beatrice Celia (Mitnick) Engleman; m. John Warren Drake, Dec. 19, 1960 (div. Dec. 1985); 1 child, Robert Warren. BS, Simmons Coll., Boston, 1958, MLS, 1971, DLS (hon.), 1997; postgrad., Harvard U., Cambridge, Mass., 1959—60; LHD (hon.), Ind. U., 1994. Assoc. United Rsch., Cambridge, Mass., 1958-61; with mktg. svcs. Kenyon & Eckhardt, Boston, 1963-65; cons. Boston, 1965-72; head rsch. unit libraries Purdue U., West Lafayette, Ind., 1972-76, asst. dir. libraries, prof. library sci., 1976-84; dean, dir. libraries, prof. Ga. Inst. Tech., Atlanta, 1984-2001, prof. emerita, 2001—; ret., 2001. Trustee Online Computer Libr. Ctr., Inc., 1978-84, chair, 1980-83; trustee Corp. for Rsch. and Edn. Networking, 1991-94, U.S. Depository Libr. Coun., 1991-94, Simmons Coll., 1999-2004; trustee, corporator adv. bd. Engring. Info., 1997-2001; trustee emerita Simmons Coll., 2004—; bd. dirs. Women's Commerce Club, 2005—. Author: User Fees: A Practical Perspective, 1981, Information Today, 2002; co-author: (with James Matarazzo) Information for Management, 1994; editor: Ency. Libr. Info. Sci., 2nd edit.; mem. editl. bd. Coll. and Rsch. Librs. Jour., 1985-90, Librs. and Microcomputers Jour., 1983-93, Sci. and Tech. Librs., 1989-98, Database, 1989-97; contbr. chpts. to books, articles to profl. jours. and trade mags. Recipient Alumni Achievement award Simmons Coll. Sch. Libr. and Info. Sci., 1985, Kent Meckler Media award U. Pitts., 1994. Fellow: Nat. Fedn. Advanced Info. Svs. (hon.); mem.: ALA (councilor at large 1985—89, Hugh Atkinson Meml. award 1992), Assn. Info. and Dissemination Ctrs. (pres. 2001—03), Spl. Librs. Assn. (pres.-elect 1992—93, pres. 1993—94, H.W. Wilson award 1983, John Cotton Dana award 2002), Am. Soc. Info. Sci., Am. Mgmt. Assn. Office Phone: 404-636-0154. Business E-Mail: mdrake@bellsouth.net.

DRAKE, PATTI LINN, retired consumer products company executive; b. Cin., June 25, 1925; d. John and Mildred Thyra Linn; m. Melvin Richard Drake, Sept. 15, 1953 (dec.); 1 child, Julie Ann Daniel. Student, U. Cin., 1946; degree, Art Acad. Cin., 1945; diploma, Cuisine Dieppe, France, 1973. Fashion copy writer Mables, Cin., 1938—45; jewelry design Wadsworth Co., Dayton, Ky., 1945—51; fashion art dir. H&S Pogue Co., Cin., 1951—55; art dir. classified Cin. Enquirer, 1955—60; v.p. fashion promotion Donenfelds, Dayton, Ohio, 1965—95; ret.; art seminar instr. Fairfield Glade, Tenn. Author poetry; mags. Mem.: Fairfield Guild (pres. 1998), Mensa, Oak Ridge Art Ctr. Republican. Episcopalian. E-mail: pldrake@frontiernet.net.

DRAKE, RICHARD BRYANT, retired history professor; b. Ames, Iowa, Aug. 5, 1925; s. G. Bryant and Alberta Stimson Drake; m. Julia Leland Angerine, Sept. 5, 1945; children: Anne D. Khoury, John B., Margaret D. Groves. AB, Doane Coll., Crete, Nebr., 1948; MA, U. Chgo., 1950; PhD, Emory U., Atlanta, 1957. Prof. history Piedmont Coll., Demorest, Ga., 1950—53; instr. history Agnes Scott Coll., Decatur, Ga., 1956; from instr. to full prof. history Berea Coll., Ky., 1956—92; ret., 1992. Vis. prof. Kobe Coll., Japan, 1982, 92. Author: A History of Appalachia, 2001, One in Spirit, 2003; contbr. articles to profl. jours. Ensign USN, 1943—46. Mem.: Appalachian Studies Assn. (founder 1976, pres. 1986), Am. Hist. Assn., So. Hist. Assn. Home: 110 Vanwinkle Grove Berea KY 40403

DRAKE, ROBERT, academic administrator, educator; s. Robert and Patricia Drake; m. Cheryl Tonneson, July 10, 2004; children: Thomas, Shannon. PhD, SUNY, Albany, 2003. Dir. Ctr. for Excellence in Tchg. Siena Coll., Loudonville, NY, 2002—. Home: 2628 County Rt 2 Grafton NY 12082 Office: Siena College 515 Loudon Rd Loudonville NY 12211 Home Phone: 518-279-1824; Office Phone: 518-782-6821.

DRAKE, RODMAN LELAND, investment company executive, consultant; b. Terre Haute, Ind., Feb. 2, 1943; s. Leland Rodman and Helen Virginia (Frederick) Drake; m. Lenir Leme-Lambert, July 26, 1975 (div. 1998); children: Stephan Rodman, Philip Lambert; m. Jacqueline B Weld, Dec. 18, 1998. BA, Yale U., 1965; MBA, Harvard U., 1969. Assoc. Cresap, McCormick & Paget, Inc., NYC, 1969-70, Monterrey, Mexico, 1971-72, mng. ptnr. São Paulo, Brazil, 1972-77, v.p., bd. dirs. NYC, 1977-81, mng. dir., CEO, 1981-90; pres. Mandrake Group, Inc., NYC, 1993-97; pres., dir. Continuation Investments Group Inc., NYC, 1997—2002; co-founder Baringo Capital LLC, 2002—. Chmn. Hyperion Strategic Mortgage Income Inc., Hyperion Total Return Fund Inc., Excelsior Funds; co-chmn. KMR Power Corp., 1993—96; lead dir. Crystal River Capital Inc.; bd. dirs. Jackson Hewitt Tax Svc. Inc., Parsons Brinckerhoff Inc., Celegene Corp., Student Loan Corp., Apex Silver Inc. Bd. dirs. Animal Med. Ctr., Lebanese Am. U., 1983—88. With US Army, 1965—67. Mem.: New Holland Soc., Waccabuc Club (NY), Banyan Golf Club (Fla.), River Club (NYC). E-mail: rdrake@cipmgmt.com.

DRAKE, SYLVIE (JURRAS), theater critic; b. Alexandria, Egypt, Dec. 18, 1930; arrived in U.S., 1949, naturalized, 1952; d. Robert and Simonette (Barda) Franco; m. Kenneth K. Drake, Apr. 29, 1952 (div. Dec. 1972); children: Jessica, Robert I.; m. Ty Jurras, June 16, 1973. M. Theater Arts, Pasadena Playhouse, 1969. Free-lance TV writer, 1962-68; theater critic Canyon Crier, LA, 1968-72; theater critic, columnist L.A. Times, 1971-91, chief theater critic, 1991-93, theatre critc emeritus, 1993—; lit. dir. Denver Ctr. Theatre Co., 1985; pres. L.A. Drama Critics Circle, 1979-81, free lance travel writer, translator, book reviewer. Mem. Pulitzer Prize Drama Jury, 1994; adv. bd. Nat. Arts Journalism Program, 1994-97. Dir. publs. Denver Ctr. for the Performing Arts, 1994—; artistic assoc. for spl. projects Denver Ctr. Theatre Co., 1994—. Mem.: Am. Theater Critics Assn. Office: Denver Ctr Performing Arts 1101 13th St Denver CO 80204-2100 Office Phone: 303-893-4000. Business E-Mail: sdrake@dcpa.org.

DRAKE, THELMA DAY, congresswoman; b. Elyria, Ohio, Nov. 20, 1949; m. Ted Drake; 2 children. Grad. high sch. Realtor RE/MAX Allegiance Realty, Hampton Roads, Va.; mem. Va. State Ho. Dels. from 87th dist., 1995—2004; chair Va. Housing Commn.; mem. Chesapeake Bay Commn., US Congress from 2nd Va. dist., 2005—, mem. edn. and the workforce com., mem. resources com., mem. armed svcs. com. Bd. mem. Va. Zool. Soc. Named Citizen of Yr., Va. Crime Prevention Assn., Legislator of Yr., YMCA, Commrs. of the Revenue, Va. Cable & Telecom. Assn.; named one of Outstanding Profl. Women of Hampton Roads; recipient John Marshall award, Va. Property Rights Coalition. Republican. United Church Of Christ. Office: US Ho Reps 1208 Longworth Ho Office Bldg Washington DC 20515-4602 Office Phone: 202-225-4215.*

DRAKE, VAUGHN PARIS, JR., electrical engineer; b. Winchester, Ky., Nov. 6, 1918; s. Vaughn Paris and Margaret Turney (Willis) D.; m. Lina Louise Wilson, May 5, 1946; 1 child, Samuel Willis. Student, U. Ky., Lexington, 1936—41. Registered profl. engr., Ky. From asst. engr. to gen. valuation and cost engr. Gen. Tel. Co. Ky., Lexington, 1945-81; ret., 1981. Author: (manual) Conduit Engineering for Telephone Engineers, 1958. Profl. adv. bd. Zoning Commn., Lexington and Fayette County, Ky., 1955-57. Comm. chief, combat engr. group AUS, 1941—45. Decorated Pearl Harbor Commemorative medal; recipient 10-Yr. Svc. award, Boy Scouts Am. Mem. IEEE (sr., chmn. Lexington sect. 1956-57), NSPE, Am. Mil. Engrs., Ky. Soc. Profl. Engrs. (pres. Bluegrass chpt. 1961-62, chmn. engrs. in industry sect. 1967-68, Outstanding Engr. in Industry award 1979), Ind. Tel. Pioneer Assn. (life), Ky. Hist. Soc., Pearl Harbor Survivors Assn. Home and Office: 633 Portland Dr Lexington KY 40503-2161

DRAKE, W. HOMER, JR., federal judge; b. 1932; AB, Mercer U., Macon, Ga., 1954, LLB, 1956. Law clk. to Hon. Lewis R. Morgan U.S. Dist. Ct. Ga., 1961-64; ptnr. Swift, Currie, McGhee & Hiers, 1976-79; judge US Bankruptcy Ct., 1964-76, chief judge, 1968-76; bankruptcy judge US Bankruptcy Ct. (no. dist.) Ga., 1979—. Adj. prof. U. Ga. Law Sch., 1971-72, Emory U. Law Sch., Atlanta, 1973-75. Author: Bankruptcy Practice for the General Practitioner, 3d edit., 1995; co-author: Chapter 13 Practice & Procedure, 1983, Chapter 11 Reorganizations, 2d edit., 1998. 1st lt. JAGC, US Army, 1956-59. Recipient David W. Pollard Achievement award Atlanta Bar Assn., 1994, Leadership award, 2007; Walter Homer Drake professorship of bankruptcy law established at Walter F. George Sch. Law at Mercer U., 1996, Outstanding Alumnus award Mercer U. Sch. Law, 2003, Dist. Svc. award for Lifetime Achievement Emory Bankruptcy Devel. Jour., 2007, Atlanta Bar Assn. Leadership award, 2007. Fellow: Am. Coll. Bankruptcy; mem.: Nat. Conf. Bankruptcy Judges (pres. 1972—73), Southeastern Bankruptcy Law Inst. (founder, advisor). Address: PO Box 1408 Newnan GA 30264-1408 Office: Lewis R Morgan Fed Bldg US Courthouse 18 Greenville St Newnan GA 30263-2602 Office Phone: 678-423-3080.

DRAKE, WILLIAM FRANK, JR., lawyer; b. St. Louis, Mar. 29, 1932; s. William Frank and Beatrice Drake; m. Martha Minohr Mockbee. BA, Principia Coll., 1954; LLB, Yale U., 1957. Bar: Pa. 1958. Pvt. practice, Phila., 1958—68, 1984—; mem. Montgomery, McCracken, Walker & Rhoads, 1958—68, of counsel, 1984—87, mem., 1987—96, of counsel, 1996—; sr. v.p., gen. counsel Alco Std. Corp., 1968—79, 1996—98, sr. v.p. adminstrn., 1979—83; chmn., CEO Alco Health Svcs. Corp., 1983—84, vice chmn., 1984—98, also bd. dirs.; vice chmn., gen. counsel Alco Std. Corp. (now Ikon Office Solutions Inc.), 1996—98. Hon. Trustee Peoples Light & Theatre Co., Malvern, Pa., 1982-2006. With US Army, 1957-58. Mem. ABA, Phila. Bar Assn., Union League (Phila.), Roaring Fork Club (Basalt, Colo.), First Troop, Phila. City Calvary. Office: Montgomery McCracken Walker & Rhoads 123 S Broad St Fl 24 Philadelphia PA 19109-1099

DRAKE-HAMILTON, LILLIE BELLE, retired secondary school educator; b. College Park, Ga., July 15, 1919; d. Charley Grady Drake and Lillie Vesta Gullatt; children: Cynthia Belle, Hilary Phyllis. BA, Agnes Scott Coll., 1940; MA, Middlebury Coll., Vt.; student, U. San Marcos, 1950. Cert. tchr. Fulton County Bd. Edn., 1940. Instr. Spanish Agnes Scott Coll., Decatur, Ga., 1948—51; tchr. Women's Tchr. Tng. Coll., Tripoli, Libya, 1951—53, Glen Burnie Sr. HS, Md., 1957—58, Waterloo Jr. HS, Elkridge, Md., 1958—59, Coll. Park HS, Ga., 1959—81; ret., 1981—. Co-dir. Pan-Am. Student Forum Atlanta (Ga.) Met. Area, 1946—48; mem. governing bd. Nat. Jr. Classical League, 1974; del. congress Am. Classical League, Madrid, 1974. Contbr. articles to profl. jours. Named to Ga. Tchrs. Hall Fame, 1981; recipient Ga. State Achievement award, Key Women Educators, 1996. Mem.: NEA, Spanish Hon. Soc., Fgn. Lang. Assn. Ga. (pres. 1973—75, Lifetime Achievement award for outstanding svc. & contributions to fgn. lang. edn. 2005), Women's Caucus Modern Langs., Vergilian Soc., Classical Assn. Mid. West and South (v.p. Ga.), Am. Classical League, Ga. Assn. Educators (recipient Exceptional Svc. plaque), Am. Assn. Tchrs. Spanish and Portuguese (life; v.p. Ga. chpt. 1960—62, sec., treas. Ga. chpt. 1964—70, pres. Ga. chpt. 1970—72). Democrat. Avocations: travel, gardening. Home: 6201 Roosevelt Hwy PO Box 362 Union City GA 30291

DRAKEMAN, DONALD LEE, venture capitalist; b. Camden, NJ, Oct. 21, 1953; s. Fred J. and Jean (Faucett) D.; m. Lisa Natale Drakeman, Aug. 23, 1975; children: Cynthia and Amy. BA magna cum laude, Dartmouth Coll., 1975; JD, Columbia U., 1979; MA, Princeton U., 1984, PhD, 1988. Bar: NJ 1979; US Dist. Ct. NJ 1979, NY 1980; US Supreme Ct. 1984. Assoc. Milbank, Tweed, Hadley and McCloy, NYC, 1979-82; gen. counsel Essex Chem. Corp., Clifton, NJ, 1982-89, v.p., 1987-89; pres. Essex Med. Products, Clifton, NJ, 1988-89; pres., CEO Medarex, Inc., Annandale, NJ, 1987—2006; venture capitalist Advent Venture Ptnrs., London, 2007—. Adj. prof. polit. sci. Montclair State Coll., NJ, 1984; rsch. cons. Lilly Found., Inc., 1989—90; lectr. politics dept. Princeton U., 1990—93, 1995—, co-chair adv. coun. religion dept.; chmn. adv. coun. James Madison Program in Am. Ideals and Instn., Princeton Univ., 2000—; mem. adv. coun. Index Ventures, Geneva, 2002—03; chmn. NJ Commn. Sci. and Tech., 2004—06. Author: Church and State Constitutional Issues, 1990; co-editor Church and State in Am. History, 2d edit., 1986, 3d edit., 2003; contbg. articles to profl. journals. Chmn. Montclair bd. adjustment, 1984; trustee, chair Biotech. Coun. NJ, 1996-98; trustee, U. Charleston, 1999-2003, Drew U., 2002—; adv. coun. Rutgers Bus. Sch., 2002—; trustee, Woodrow Wilson Nat. Fellowship Found., 2003-06. Harlan Fiske Stone Scholar, Columbia Univ., 1976-79; inducted NJ High Tech. Hall of Fame, 2000. Mem.: AAAS, ABA, John Maclean Soc., Assn. Bar City of NY, Yale Club, Princeton Club, Princeton Alumni Coun.

DRAKEMAN, LISA N., biotechnologist; b. Boston, Oct. 30, 1953; d. Paul and Josephine (Covino) Natale; m. Donald L. Drakeman, Aug. 23, 1975. BA, Mt. Holyoke Coll., South Hadley, Mass., 1975; MA, Rutgers U., New Brunswick, NJ, 1983, Princeton U., NJ, 1986, PhD, 1988. Chair, v. chair Monclair Redevelopment Agy., NJ, 1981-84; vis. scholar Dartmouth Coll., 1988-89; lectr. Princeton U., 1989-92; asst. dir. Alumni Coun. of Princeton U., 1991; dir. adminstrn. Medarex, Inc., Princeton, NJ, 1991-94, v.p. adminstrn., 1994-96, v.p., 1996-98, sr. v.p., head bus. devel., 1998-2000; CEO Genmab A/S, 1999—. Faculty fellow Grad. Coll. Princeton U., 1991-93, mem. adv. coun. dept. religion, 1996-; bd. dir. Medarex Europe, B.V., GenPharm. Internat., Inc., Biotech. Coun. NJ. Mem. biopharm. adv. coun. Tech. Coun. Greater Phila., 1993-96; mem. Gov.'s Biopharm. Task Force NJ Econ. Master Plan Commn., Trenton, 1994-95; mem.biotech. adv. com. The Franklin Inst., Phila., 1994-96; commr. Prosperity NJ, 1995-2000; mem. Cancer Inst. NJ Leadership Coun., 2004—06; bd. dirs., mem. exec. com. Biotechnology Coun. NJ, 2005—, sec., 2007—. Garden State grad. fellow State of NJ, 1981-85; named to NJ High Tech. Hall of Fame, 2000. Mem. Soc. Advancement of Women's Health Rsch. (steering com., corp. adv. coun. 1994-97), Biotech. Industry Orgn. (chair nat. capital formation task force 1995-98, Advocate of Yr. award 1995), Biotech. Coun. NJ (v.p. 1996-2000, sec., 2007—, Outstanding Industry Woman of Yr. 1996), European Fedn. Pharm. Industries and Assns. (bd. dir. emerging pharm. enterprises sect. 2004-06, v.p. 2006). Office: 457 N Harrison St Princeton NJ 08540 also: Genmab A/S Toldbodgade 33 DK 1253 Copenhagen Denmark

DRAMIS, FRANCIS (FRAN) A., JR., communications executive; m. Terri Dramis; children: Billy, Katelyn, Mollie, Jeni, Jimmy. BA, Rutgers U.; MS, Pace U. V.p., co-founder Am. Transtech; corp. exec. dir. data systems ops., exec. dir. MIS Bell Labs.; exec. dir. info. product mgmt. and automation AT&T; pres., COO TELIC Corp.; mng. dir. Salomon Bros. Inc., 1989-91; pres. Salomon Tech. Svcs., Inc.; pres., CEO Network Mgmt. Inc., Fairfax, Va., 1991-98; cons., transitional CIO CIO Strategy, Inc., Clifton, Va.; exec. v.p., CIO BellSouth Corp., Atlanta, 1998—, eCommerce & security officer. Dir., chmn. BellSouth Tech. Svcs., Inc.; bd. dir. BellSouth Solutions Group, Inc., Internet Policy Inst., BellSouth Found. Named one of Top 100 CIOs, CIO Mag., 1999, Top 100 Leaders for Next Millennium, 2000, Premier 100 IT Leaders, Computerworld mag., 2002. Avocations: golf, manages youth sports teams. Office: Bell South Corp 1155 Peachtree St NE Ste A Atlanta GA 30309-3610 Office Phone: 404-249-2000. Office Fax: 404-249-2071.

DRANCE, STEPHEN MICHAEL, ophthalmologist, educator; b. Bielsko, Poland, May 22, 1925; Can. citizen; MB,ChB, U. Edinburgh, Scotland, 1948, MD, 1949; Diploma in Ophthalmology, Royal Coll. Surgeons, London, 1953; LLD (hon.), Dalhousie U., Halifax, 1995; DSc (hon.), U. Oulu, Finland, 1998, U. B.C., Vancouver, 1998. Intern Western Gen. Hosp., Edinburgh, 1948-49; resident County Hosp., York, Eng., 1952-53, Edinburgh Royal Infirmary, 1953-55, Oxford Eye Hosp., Eng., 1955-57, Oxford U., 1955-57; asst. prof. and assoc. prof. medicine U. Sask., Saskatoon, Can., 1957-63; assoc. prof. ophthalmology U. B.C., Vancouver, Can., 1963-66, prof., 1966-90, dir. ophthalmologic research, 1967-73, head dept. ophthalmology, 1973-90. Cons., lectr. medicine; vis. prof., lectr. numerous univs. Author: (with H. Reed) The Essentials of Perimetry, 2d edit., 1971, (with A. Neufeld) Applied Pharmacology of Glaucoma, 1984, (with D.R. Anderson) Automatic Perimetry in Glaucoma, 1985, (with A. Neufeld, M. van Buskirk) Applied Pharmacology of Glaucoma, 1991; assoc. editor Am. Archives Ophthalmology, 1961-74; mem. editorial bd. Can. Jour. Ophthalmology, 1966; mng. editor Albrecht von Graefe's Archive for Clin. and Exptl. Ophthalmology, 1979-90; editl. bd. Am. Jour. Opthalmology, 1994-99; contbr. articles to profl. jours., chpts. to books Pres. Vancouver Summer Festivals Soc., 1997-2002. With RAF, 1949-51. Decorated officer Order of Can., 1987; recipient numerous awards and grants for excellence in medicine. Fellow Royal Australian Coll. Ophthalmologists U.K. (hon.), Coll. Ophthalmology U.K. (hon.), Royal Soc. Medicine, Royal Coll. Physicians and Surgeons Can. (sec. 1976-77), Royal Coll. Surgeons Eng.; mem. Can. Assn. Clin. Rsch., Assn. Ophthalmologic Rsch. (U.K.), Assn. for Rsch. in Vision and Ophthalmology, Can. Ophthalmol. Soc. (pres. 1974-75), B.C. Oto-Ophthalmol. Soc., Ophthal. Soc. U.K., Oxford Ophthalmol. Congress, Am. Acad. Ophthalmology (v.p. 1993), Can. Med. Assn., B.C. Med. Assn., Internat. Perimetric Soc. (pres. 1982-88), Glaucoma Soc. Internat. Congrss (pres. 1983-90), Pan-Am. Ophthalmol. Congress, Pan-Am. Glaucoma Soc., Pan-Am. Assn. Ophthalmology, Assn. N.Am. Glaucomatologists, N.Z. Ophthalmol. Soc. (hon.), Academia Ophthalmol. Internat., Internat. Congress Ophthalmology (pres. 1994), Concillium Ophthalmol. Univaersale (visual function com.) E-mail: smd@interchange.ubc.ca.

DRANGO, MARK A., mechanical services specialist; s. Joseph R. and Mary A. Drango; m. Lori Lipuma, June 18, 1977; children: Dawn M. Drango Hodges, Mark A. Jr. AAS, Washenaw CC, Ann Arbor, Mich., 2006. Refrigeration, HVAC mgr. Echo Real Estate Services and Devel. Inc., Pitts., 2002—06; dir. svc. ops. Fazio Mech. Svcs. Inc., Sharpsburg, Pa., 2006—. Mem.: ASHRAE, Refrigeration Svc. Engrs. Soc. (cert.). Office: Fazio Mechanical Services Inc 300 S Main St Sharpsburg PA 15215 Home Phone: 724-744-4928. Personal E-mail: moprk@hotmail.com.

DRANITZKE, RICHARD J., surgeon; b. L.I., NY, 1940; MD, Columbia U., 1966. Diplomate Am. Bd. Surgery, Am. Bd. Thoracic Surgery. Intern Columbia-Presbyn. Hosp., NYC, 1966-67; resident in surgery Bellevue Hosp. Ctr., NYC, 1969-73; resident in cardiothoracic surgery Albany (N.Y.) Med. Ctr., 1973—75; chief thoracic and vascular surgery St. Charles Hosp., Port Jefferson, NY, 1991—, St. Charles and J.T. Mather Meml. Hosp., 1985—; clin. instr. dept. surgery Stony Brook U. Hosp., 1994—; chief vascular surgery Mather Hosp., 1991—. Mem. ACP, ACS, AMA, Soc. Thoracic Surgeons, Eastern Vascular Soc., N.Y. Soc. for Cardiovasc. Surgery. Office: 635 Belle Terre Rd Port Jefferson NY 11777 also: 286 Sills Rd Patchogue NY 11772-8810 Office Phone: 631-473-1602.

DRANOVE, DAVID STUART, business educator, consultant, economist; b. NYC, July 25, 1956; s. Alfred and Dorothy Dranove; m. Deborah Salgo, Aug. 21, 1983; children: Daniel, Michael. BA, Cornell U., Ithaca, NY, 1977, MBA, 1979; PhD, Stanford U., Calif., 1983. Asst. prof. U. Chgo., 1983—91; Richard Paget disting. prof. strategy Northwestern U., Evanston, Ill., 1995—99, chmn. dept. mgmt. and strategy, 1996—2000, Walter McNerney disting. prof. health industry mgmt., 2000—, founder, dir. Ctr. Health Industry Market Econ., 2001—. Mem. adv. bd. Am. Assn. Nurse Anesthetists, 1993—95, Beecken Petty, 1997—99, Clean Air Engring., 1997—98, YellowBrick, 2006—, Huron Cons. Group, 2006—; bd. dirs. Pediat. Faculty Found., Chgo., 2001—05; cons. US FTC, Dept. of Justice, Ill. Atty. Gen. Author: How Hospitals Survived, 1999, Economic Evolution of American Health Care, 2001, Economics of Strategy 4th edit., 2006, What's Your Life Worth?, 2003, Kellogg on Strategy, 2005; contbr. articles to profl. jours., chapters to books. Mem. adv. bd. Highland Park Park Dist., 1994—95; trustee Roycemore Sch., 2005—06. Recipient John Thompson prize, Assn. Univ. Programs Health Adminstrn., 1993, Rsch. prizes, Nat. Inst. Health Care Mgmt., 1998, 2003, Assn. Health Svcs. Rsch., 1999, Amer. Acad. Med Admin., 1993, 1996, 1999, Levy Tchg. award, Kellogg, 2002, 2005, Reiter Rsch. prize, 2005. Mem.: Internat. Health Econ. Assn., Am. Econ. Assn., Beta Gamma Sigma (hon.). Achievements include research in breakthroughs in the study of competition in health care; development of bringing fundamental changes to business strategy education. Avocations: audiophile, sports enthusiast, fine dining enthusiast, bodybuilding. Office: Kellogg Sch Management 2001 Sheridan Rd Evanston IL 60208 Home: 857 Highland Pl Highland Park IL 60035 Office Phone: 847-491-8682. Business E-Mail: d-dranove@northwestern.edu.

DRANOVSKY, ALEX, psychiatrist, researcher; b. Moscow, Russia, Soviet Union, Mar. 23, 1970; s. Yefim and Sofia Dranovsky; m. Ting Wang, July 2, 2006. MD, PhD, SUNY, Stony Brook, 2000. Cert. psychiatry Am. Bd. Psychiatry and Neurology, 2006, lic. NY, 2002. Rsch. fellow Columbia U., NYC, 2004—06, asst. prof. clin. psychiatry, 2007—. Grantee Young Investigator Award, Nat. Alliance Rsch. Schizophrenia and Depression, 2006—, NIMH, 2007—. Office: NYSPI Columbia Univ Box 87 1051 Riverside Dr New York NY 10032 Home Phone: 917-902-5510.

DRAPALIK, BETTY R., volunteer, artist, educator; b. Cicero, Ill., July 4, 1932; d. Henry William and Jennie Margaret (Robbins) Degen; m. Joseph James Drapalik, Oct. 30, 1951; children: Betty Jennifer Drapalik Coryell, Joseph Henry. Grad., HS, Cicero. Sec., clk. Gt. Lakes (Ill.) Naval Base, until 1982; sect. to asst. dir. Arden Shore Boys' Home, Lake Bluff, Ill., 1984-87; sub. tchr. art Visual Art Ctr., Waukegan, Ill. One-woman shows include Jack Benny Ctr. Arts, 1995—2004, 2006, Wauconda Area Pub. Libr., 1999, 2002, Invitational First Lady Hearts and Flowers Art Exhbn., Ill., 2001—07 (First Lady award, 2004), GreenBelt Cultural Art Ctr., North Chgo., 2003, Pikes Peak Watercolor Soc. Internat. Watermedia XIII/ Fine Art Ctr., Colo. Springs, 2003, St. Charles Nat. Juried Art Exhbn. and Music Festival, 2005, Lake County Discovery Mus., 2005, exhibited in group shows at Layson Gallery, Waukegan, Ill., 1993, Cmty. Gallery Art, Coll. Lake County, Grayslake, Ill., 1993—99, 2000—06, Women's Works, Old Courthouse Art Ctr., Woodstock, Ill., 1994—2000, 2002, Anderson Art Ctr., Kenosha, Wis., 1994—2005, Hardy Gallery, Ephraim, Wis., 1996—2002 (Purchase award, 1998), North Point Marina, Winthrop Harbor, Ill., 1996—2003 (1st pl. watercolor, 1996, 1999, 2d pl. watercolor, 1997, 1998, Best of Show, 1996, 1997, award of Merit watercolor, 1998, award of Excellence, 1999, 3d pl., 2001, 3d pl. watercolor, 2002), Truman State U., Kirksville, Mo., 1997, Moorehead State U., Minn., 1997, Kenosha Art Assn. and Lake County Art League Combined Art Event, 1997 (Best of Show, 1997), David Adler Cultural Ctr., Libertyville, Ill., 1997—2002, Hawthorne Hollow Art Festival, Kenosha, 1997—98, Deer Path Art League Festival, Lake Forest, 1997, 1999, N.W. N.Mex Arts Coun., Farmington, 1997, Waukegan Visual Arts Ctr., 1998, Zion Chamber Orch. Concert and Art Contest, 1998 (Best of Show, 1st pl.), Kenosha Pub. Mus., 1998 (award of excellence), Spotlight Gallery, Kenosha, 1998—99, Monne's Gallery, 1998, Deilora A. Norris Cultural Ctr., St. Charles, Ill., 1998—2006, 1st ann. Art Discovery Festival, Lake County Discovery Mus. and Lake County Art League, Wauconda, 2006, Clausen Art Shop, Wilmette, Ill., 1999, Gull Lake Gallery, Richland, Mich., 1999—2002, Nippersink Gallery, Richmond, Ill., 1999—2001, Deer Path Gallery, Lake Forest, 1999—2003, Wauconda Pub. Libr., 1999, 2002, 2006—07, Kenosha Art Assn. and Lake County Art League Combined Art Event, 2000 (Best of Show, 2001), Kenosha Art Assn. Art Event, 2001—05 (3d pl., 2002), Green Belt Cultural Ctr., North Chgo., 2000, 2005, City of Zion, Ill., 2001—02, Centennial Days Fine Art Show, 2001, Harring Galleries, Racine, Wis., 2001—05, Guenzel Gallery, Fish Creek, Wis., 2001—02, Jack Benny Ctr. Arts, 2003—07, Colo. Fine Art Ctr., 2003, Cmty. Gallery Art, Coll. Lake County, 2001—05, Western Colo. Watercolor Soc. exhbn., 2004, William M. Scholl Coll. Pediat. Medicine, Rosalind Franklin U. Medicine and Sci., North Chicago, 2005—07 (2d pl., 2005), Art Wauk, Waukegan, Ill., 2005, 2006, St. Charles Nat. Art Exhbn. and Music Festival, 2005, Volo Bog Nature Ctr., 2006—07, N.W. Art Coun., Crystal Lake, Ill., 2007, Indian Festival, 2007, traveling exhbn., America the Beautiful, 2001—03; work published in Celebrating Door Country's Wild Places, 2001. Former leader, mem. pub. rels. com. Girl Scouts U.S.; visual arts cons. Green Belt Cultural Ctr. Lake County Forest Preserve Dist.; organizer meml. svc. and exhbn. Phil Austin's Life, Waukegan, 2004; leader art program Walkerville (Mich.) Schs., 2003; com. 2d Ann. Art Discovery Festival at Lake County Discovery Mus., 2007; mem. outreach and evangelism missions bd. First Presbyn. Ch. Waukegan, 2000—02. Recipient Purchase award, Coll. Lake County, Grayslake, 1994, numerous courtesy awards. Mem.: Nat. Mus. Women in the Arts (charter), Bloomin' Artists, N.W. Area Arts Coun., Kenosha Art Assn., Red River Watercolor Soc., Deerpath Art League, Lakes Region Watercolor Guild (past rec. sec., co-program chair, exhibit chair), Lake County Art League (resource person, past pres., various bd. positions, fine arts cons. Green Belt Cultural Ctr. Lake County Forest Preserve), Transparent Watercolor Soc. Am. (life), Internat. Starcraft Camper Club (Ill. chpt. sec./treas. 1975). Evangelical. Avocations: painting, photography, camping, gardening, hiking. Home: 2018 W Grove Ave Waukegan IL 60085-1607

DRAPEAU, MARK DAVID, defense contractor; b. Holyoke, Mass., Sept. 30, 1975; s. David A. and Simone B. Drapeau. BS, U. Rochester, NY, 1997; PhD, U. Calif., Irvine, 2003. Postdoctoral rsch. scientist NYU Ctr. for Devel. Genetics, NYC, 2003—06; def. contractor Quantum Leap Health Scis., Arlington, Va., 2006—. Cons. BioAtom, Inc., Newport Beach, Calif., 2007—. Contbr. articles to profl. jours. Recipient Leadership Amb. award, Hugh O'Brian Youth Found., 1992, Athlete-Scholar Meml. award, Am. Legion, 1993, USAR Nat. Scholar/Athlete Award medal, 1993, Harvard Book award, 1993; Trustees' scholar, U. Rochester, 1993—97, Sr. Rsch. scholar, 1996—97, DeKiewiet Summer Rsch. fellow, 1996, James J. Harvey Dissertation fellow, U. Calif., Irvine, 2002—03, Ruth R. Kirchenstein Postdoctoral Rsch. fellow, NIH, 2004—06, AAAS Sci. and Tech. Policy fellow in Nat. Def. and Global Security, 2006—07. Mem.: AAAS, Am. Inst. Biol. Scis. Independent. Roman Catholic. Achievements include consortium member Honeybee Genome Project; research in role of the major royal jelly proteins in honeybee social behavior; neurogenetic control of innate sexual behaviors; evolution and genetics of aging and immortality; animal speciation and sexual isolation and behavior. Avocations: running, squash, chess, wine, travel. Home: 711 D St NE Washington DC 20002 Office: US Dept Def Nat Def Univ Ctr Tech and Nat Security Policy Fort Lesley J McNair Bldg 20 Suite 3 Washington DC 20319 Office Phone: 202-685-2406. Personal E-mail: dr.mark.david.drapeau@gmail.com. Business E-Mail: drapeaum@ndu.edu.

DRAPER, DOROTHY E., middle school mathematics educator; b. Wilmington, Del., June 30, 1954; d. Michael and Mary L. (Kelley) Ferenc; m. Bruce L. Draper, Dec. 27, 1975; children: Alison, Bryn, Catherine. BS in Elem. Edn., U. Del., 1976; MA in Edn., U. N.Mex., 1986, PhD, 1991. Asst. coach women's volleyball Princeton U., NJ, 1976-78; math. instr. St. Mary's Sch., Albuquerque, 1978-80; math. instr., elem. tchr. Our Lady of Fatima Sch., Albuquerque, 1986-89; instr. U. N.Mex., Albuquerque, 1987-89; tchr. La Mesa Elem. Sch., Albuquerque, 1989-93; math. instr. Albuquerque Acad., 2000—. Family Math. coord. La Mesa Elem. Sch., Albuquerque, 1990-92; regional coord. N.Mex. Systemic Initiative in Math/Sci. Edn., 1993-98; Child Find coord. Ctrl. Region Endl. Cooperative, 1998-99; volleyball coach Albuquerque Acad., 2000—. Mem. Nat. Coun. Tchrs. Math., N.Mex. Coun. Tchr. Math. (v.p. 1989-91, pres. 2000-02), Todos, Math. For All, N.Mex. Symphony Guild, Phi Delta Kappa. Home: 8415 Guadalupe Trl NW Albuquerque NM 87114-1124 Office Phone: 505-828-3139. Business E-Mail: draper@aa.edu.

DRAPER, EDGAR, psychiatrist; b. St. Louis, Feb. 5, 1926; s. Neal McLain and Florence Mabel (Meyers) D.; m. Norma Jane Alexander, Mar. 16, 1949; children: Sue Draper Masteller, Anne Draper Klevay, Neal Edgar. AB, Washington U., 1946, Duke Div. Sch., 1948; BD, Garrett Biblical Inst., 1949; MD, Washington U. Med. Sch., 1953; grad., Inst. for Psychoanalysis, Chgo., 1966. Diplomate Am. Bd. Psychiatry and Neurology; ordained deacon, elder Meth. Ch., 1946. Asst. pastor Edenton St. Meth. Ch., Raleigh, 1947; pastor Garden Prarie, Ill., 1949; intern Washington U. Svc. City Hosp., St. Louis, 1953-54; resident in psychiatry U. Cin., 1954-55, 57-59; sr. asst. surgeon USPHS, Ft. Worth, 1955-57; from instr. to assoc. prof. U. Chgo., 1959-68; co-dir. psychiat. outpatient dept., prof. psychiatry U. Mich., Ann Arbor, 1968, dir. psychiat. resident edn., 1968-74, prof. postgrad edn., 1970-75; prof., chmn. dept. psychiatry U. Miss. Med. Ctr., Jackson, 1975-93; prof. psychiatry U. Miss., Jackson, 1993-94; prof. emeritus, 1994—. Cons. in field. Contbr. numerous articles to profl. jours. Bd. dirs. Friends Libr. Named Vis. scholar U. Chgo., 1987, Fellow Soc. for Sci. Study of Religion, 1987, Man of Month Pastoral Psychology, 1970; recipient Physicians Recognition award, 1982-85, Cert. Appreciation Mental Health Assn. Hinds County, 1983, Plaque of Commendation Chgo. Acad. Religion and Mental Health, 1966-67. Fellow Am. Psychiat. Assn. (disting. life fellow), Am. Coll. Psychiatry (life), Am. Soc. Psychoanalytic Physicians, Soc. for Sci. Study of Religion (life), Am. Coll. Psychoanalysts (life, program chmn., bd. regents), So. Psychiat. Assn. (parlimentarian 1980—), Soc. for Study of Psychiatry and Culture; mem. Miss. Psychiat. Assn. (past pres., Disting. Svc. award 2001), Miss. State Med. Soc., Mich. Psychiat. Soc., Washtenaw County Med. Soc., Mich. State Med. Soc., So. Psychiat. Assn., Mich. Psychoanalytic Soc., Mental Health Assn. (bd. dirs. Jackson, Spl. Svc. award, 2006, 07). Office Phone: 601-982-2176. E-mail: purpledoced@aol.com.

DRAPER, E(RNEST) LINN, JR., retired electric utility executive; b. Houston, Feb. 6, 1942; s. Ernest Linn and Marcia L. (Saylor) D.; m. Mary Deborah Doyle, June 9, 1962; children: Susan Elizabeth, Robert Linn, Barbara Ann, David Doyle. Student, Williams Coll., 1960-62; BAChemE, Rice U., 1964, BSChemE, 1965; PhD in Nuclear Engring., Cornell U., 1970. Asst. prof. nuclear engring. U. Tex., Austin, 1969-72, assoc. prof., 1972-79; tech. asst. to CEO Gulf States Utilities Co., Beaumont, Tex., 1979, v.p. nuclear tech., 1980-81, sr. v.p. engring, tech. services, 1981-82, sr. v.p. external affairs, 1982-84, sr. v.p. external affairs and prodn., 1984-85, exec. v.p. external affairs and prodn., 1985-86, vice chmn., 1985-87, COO, 1986, pres., CEO, 1986-92, chmn. bd. dirs., 1987-92; pres. AEPCo., Inc.; pres., COO Am. Electric Power Svc. Corp., Columbus, Ohio, 1992-93; chmn., pres., CEO Am. Electric Power Co. and Svc. Corp., Columbus, 1993—2004. Bd. dirs. Temple Inland Corp., Alpha Natural Resources, NorthWestern Corp., Alliance Data Sys., TransCan., Resources for the Future. Fellow NSF, 1965-66, AEC, 1967-68. Mem. NAE, Am. Nuclear Soc. (pres. 1984-85), Nuclear Energy Inst. (chmn. 1993-95), Edison Electric Inst. (chmn. 1996-97). E-mail: eldraper@aep.com.

DRAPER, GERALD LINDEN, retired lawyer; b. Oberlin, Ohio, July 14, 1941; s. Earl Linden and Mary Antoinette (Colloto) Draper; m. Barbara Jean Winter, Aug. 26, 1960; children: Melissa Leigh Price, Stephen Edward. BA, Muskingum Coll., 1963; JD, Northwestern U., 1966. Bar: Ohio 1966, US Dist Ct (so dist) Ohio 1966, US Ct Appeals (6th cir) 1975, US Supreme Ct 1980, US Dist Ct (no dist) Ohio 2000. Ptnr. Bricker & Eckler, Columbus, Ohio, 1966-88, Thompson, Hine & Flory, Columbus, 1989-95, Draper, Hollenbaugh, Briscoe, Yashko & Carmany, Columbus, 1996-99, Roetzel & Andress, Columbus, 1999—2004; ret. Trustee Ohio Bd. Bar Examiners, 1986—89; mem. Ohio Bd. Commn. on Unauthorized Practice of Law, 2002—, Ohio Med. Malpractice Commn., 2003—. Trustee, pres Wesley Glen Retirement Ctr, Columbus, Ohio, 1979—95; trustee Meth Elder Care Servs, Inc, 1995—, Muskingum Coll., New Concord, Ohio, 1988—92, Ohio, 1993—, vice chair, 1994—; trustee, pres Wesley Ridge Retirement Ctr, 1995—2000, treas, 2001—. Fellow: Am Bd Trial Advs (trustee Ohio chpt. 2001), Am Col Trial Lawyers; mem.: ABA (House Dels 1991—97, 1999—2001), Def Research Inst, Ohio Asn Hosp Attys, Ohio Continuing Legal Educ Inst (trustee 1992—98, chair 1997—98), Nat Conf Bar Found (trustee 1987—90, 1991—94), Columbus Bar Found (pres 1984—86), Columbus Bar Asn (pres 1982—83, Bar Serv Medal 1998), Ohio State Bar Found (trustee 1992—97), Ohio State Bar Asn (pres 1990—91). Avocations: travel, golf, photography.

DRAPER, JAMES DAVID, art museum curator; b. Lebanon, Mo., Mar. 6, 1943; s. John Hilton and Hazel (Berg) D. BA, U. Mo., 1965; MA, NYU, 1967, PhD, 1984. Curatorial asst. Met. Mus. Art, NYC, 1969, various positions, 1969-84, dept. curator, 1984—, Henry R. Kravis curator, 1995—. Fellow J. Paul Getty Mus., Malibu, Calif., 1987; exec. dir. The Isaacson-Draper Found., 1999. Author: Bertoldo di Giovanni, Sculptor of the Medici Household, 1992; co-author: (exhbn. catalogs) Augustin Pajou, Royal Sculptor, 1998, La giovinezza di Michelangelo, 1999, Playing With Fire: European Terracotta Models, 1740-1840, 2004; editor: (rev. critical edit.) The Italian Bronze Statuettes of the Renaissance (W. von Bode), 1980. Decorated chevalier Order of Arts and Letters (France). Episcopalian. Office: Met Mus Art 1000 5th Ave New York NY 10028-0113 Business E-Mail: james.draper@metmuseum.org.

DRAPER, NORMAN RICHARD, statistician, educator; b. Eng., Mar. 20, 1931; came to U.S., 1955; s. Norris and Helen (Draper). BA, Cambridge U., Eng., 1954, MA, 1958; PhD, U. NC, 1958. Tech. officer, statistician plastics div. Imperial Chem. Industries, 1958-60; mem. Math. Rsch. Ctr., U. Wis., Madison, 1960-61, mem. faculty, 1961—, prof. statistics, 1966-99, prof. emeritus, 1999—, chmn., 1967-73, 94-97. Vis. prof. Imperial Coll., London, fall 1967, 68. Author: (with H. Smith) Applied Regression Analysis, 1966, 3d edit., 1998, (with G.E.P. Box) Evolutionary Operation, 1969, (with W. E. Lawrence) Probability: An Introductory Course, 1970, (with G.E.P. Box) Response Surfaces, Mixtures, and Ridge Analyses, 2d edit., 2007. Recipient Max-Planck-Forschungs-Preis, Alexander von Humboldt-Stiftung, 1994. Fellow Royal Statis. Soc., Am. Statis. Assn., Inst. Math. Statistics, Am. Soc. Quality Control; mem. Internat. Statis. Inst. Address: U Wis Dept Statistics 1300 University Ave Madison WI 53706-1532

DRAPER, PAUL, winemaker; b. Ill., Mar. 10, 1936; m. Maureen Draper. PhB, Stanford U., 1958. CEO, profl. winemaker Ridge Vineyards, Cupertino, Calif. Translator military intelligence, Italy. Named Outstanding Wine and Spirits Profl., James Beard Found., 2007; recipient Lifetime Achievement award, Wein Gourmet, 2005. Office: Ridge Vineyards 17100 Monte Bello Rd Cupertino CA 95014 Office Phone: 408-868-1350.*

DRAPER, RONI JO, literature and language professor; d. Timothy Evan Minard and Marcia Lee James; m. Kyle Vincent Draper, Nov. 30, 1985; children: Evan Dale, Quinlan James. BS in Math., U. Nev., Reno, MS in Secondary Edn., PhD in Curriculum and Instrn.-Literacy Studies, 2000. Math. tchr. Washoe County Sch. Dist., Reno, 1993—97; prof. Brigham Young U., Provo, Utah, 2000—. Young scholar, Brigham Young U., 2006. Democrat. Church Of Jesus Christ Of Latter-Day Saints. Office: Brigham Young Univ 206-Q MCKB Teacher Education Provo UT 84664 Office Phone: 801-422-4960. Business E-Mail: roni_jo_draper@byu.edu.

DRAPER, SHARON M., writer, elementary school educator; married. BA summa cum laude, Pepperdine U., 1970; MA summa cum laude, Miami U., 1973. Cert. Nat. Bd. Profl. Tchg. Stds. Mem. faculty Walnut Hills (Ohio) H.S., 1978. Spkr., presenter in field; bd. dirs. Nat. Bd. Profl. Tchg. Stds. Author: Tears of a Tiger, 1994 (Best Book for Young Adults, King Genesis award ALA), Lost in the Tunnel of Time, Forged By Fire, 1997, Teaching from the Heart: Reflections, Encouragement and Inspiration, 1999, Darkness Before Dawn, 2001 (Young Adult Choice IRA 2003, Buckeye Book award 2005), Not Quite Burned Out But Crispy Around the Edges: Inspiration, Laughter and Encouragement for Teachers, 2001, Double Dutch, 2002 (Coretta Scott King Book 2004), Battle of Jericho, 2003, We Beat the Street, 2005, Cooper Sun, 2006 (Coretta Scott King Book award 2007), November Blues, 2007; Ziggy and the Black Dinosaurs Series; also short stories including One Small Torch (Ebony mag. 1st prize 1991); Romiette and Julio, 1999 (named a Notable Book for Global Soc. Internat. Reading Assn., 2000). Recipient Excellence in Tchg. award Nat. Coun. Negro Women, 1998, Gov.'s Ednl. Leadership award Gov. of Ohio, 1998, honors Miss. Coun. Tchrs., Cin. City Coun., Ohio State Ho. of Reps., Cin. Bd. Edn.; named Ohio Tchr. of the Yr., 1997, Nat. Tchr. of Yr., 1997. Mem. Am. Fedn. Tchrs., Ohio Fedn. Tchrs., Cin. Fedn. Tchrs., Nat. Coun. Tchrs. English, Internat. Reading Assn., Delta Kappa Gamma, Phi Delta Kappa. Mailing: PO Box 36551 Cincinnati OH 45236*

DRAPER, THOMAS B., lawyer; b. July 10, 1953; BA cum laude, Yale Univ., 1975; JD, Univ. Tex., 1979. Bar: Tex. 1979, Mass. 1980. Law clk. Judge Homer Thornberry, US Dist. Ct. 5th cir., 1979—80; assoc. Ropes & Gray, Boston, 1980—89, ptnr. corp. dept., 1989—, chmn. debt fin. practice group. Instr. Boston Univ. Sch. Law. Mem.: ABA, Boston Bar Assn. Office: Ropes & Gray 1 International Pl Boston MA 02110-2624 Office Phone: 617-951-7430. Office Fax: 617-951-7050. Business E-Mail: thomas.draper@ropesgray.com.

DRAPER, WILLIAM DAVID, systems engineer; b. Riverdale, Md., Dec. 1, 1949; s. Woodrow Wilson and Elsie (Cosden) D.; m. Deborah Kathrine Dunn, Feb. 7, 1950; children: Matthew Dunn, Owen William. BA, U. Md., 1971; postgrad., George Mason U., 1981. Computer specialist U.S. Social Security Adminstrn., Balt., 1971-74; computer programmer Computer Scis./Technicolor Assocs., Greenbelt, Md., 1974-75; systems engr. MCI Telecommunications Corp., Washington, 1975-77; sr. systems analyst Infodata Systems Inc., Falls Church, Va., 1977-86; systems engr. Hughes Aircraft Co., Arlington, Va., 1986; sys. adminstr. Infodata Systems Inc., Herndon, Va., 1986—2005, McDonald Bradley Inc., Herndon, 2005—. Mem. Baltimore County Aux. Police, 1972-76; cadet program officer group 3 Va. wing CAP, 1987-88, plans and programs officer, 1994-95; mem. cadet program staff Prince William County squadron Manassas, Va., 1984-87, 88-92, aero edn. officer, 1992-94; mem. AEO PWCS, 1995-99, leadership officer, 1999-2000, cadet program officer, 2000—; elder Presbyn. Ch. Recipient Grover Loening Aerospace award CAP, 1986, Paul A. Garber award, 1988, Exceptional Svc. award, 1993, Meritorious Unit Citation U.S. Govt., 1991. Republican. Avocations: woodworking, photography. Office: McDonald Bradley Inc 2250 Corporate Park DrSte 500 Herndon VA 20171

DRAPER, WILLIAM HENRY, III, venture capitalist; b. White Plains, NY, Jan. 1, 1928; s. William Henry and Katherine (Baum) Draper; m. Phyllis Culbertson, June 13, 1953; children: Rebecca, Polly, Timothy. BA, Yale U., 1950, MA (hon.), 1991; MBA, Harvard U., 1954; LLD (hon.), Southeastern U., 1985. With Inland Steel Co., Chgo., 1954-59, Draper, Gaither & Anderson, Palo Alto, Calif., 1959-62; pres. Draper & Johnson Investment Co., Palo Alto, 1962-65; founder, gen. ptnr. Sutter Hill Ventures, Palo Alto, 1965-81; pres., chmn. U.S. Export-Import Bank, Washington, 1981-86; adminstr., CEO, UN Devel. Programme, 1986-93; mng. dir. Draper Richards, San Francisco, 1994—, Draper Internat., San Francisco, 1994—. Bd. dirs. numerous cos. Nat. co-chmn. fin. com. George Bush for Pres., 1980; bd. dirs., former chmn. Rep. Alliance; chmn. bd. Am. Conservatory Theatre, 1980—81, bd. dirs., 1977—81; chmn. Internat. Inst. Edn. West, 1989—2000; vice chmn. Population Action Internat., 1993—; mem. adv. bd. Stanford Grad. Sch. Bus. Adminstrn., 1980—86; chmn. World Affairs Coun. No. Calif., 2000—02; trustee Yale U., 1991—98, George Bush Libr. Found., 1993—; bd. dirs. Population Crisis Com., 1976—81, Atlantic Coun., 1989—, World Rehab. Fund, 1988—92, Ctr. for Econ. Policy Rsch., Stanford U., 1988, Inst. Internat. Studies Stanford U., 1997—99, UN Assn.-USA, 2003—. With US Army, 1946—48, with US Army, 1951—52. Named one of U.S.'s 50 New Corp. Elite, Bus. Week mag., 1985; named to, Dow Jones Venture Capital Hall of Fame, 2005; recipient Alumni Achievement award, Harvard Bus. Sch., 1982, medal of Honor, Ellis Island, 1992, Citizen Diplomacy award, Internat. Diplomacy Coun., 1996, Woodrow Wilson award for pub. svc., 2002, Vision award, So. Forum, 2005. Mem.: Overseas Devel. Coun., Coun. Fgn. Rels., River Club, Chevy Chase Club, Met. Club, Bohemian Club, Pacific Union Club. Home: 91 Tallwood Ct Atherton CA 94027-6431 Office: Draper Richards 50 California St Ste 2925 San Francisco CA 94111-4726 Office Phone: 415-616-4050. E-mail: bill@draperrichards.com.

DRAPKIN, DENNIS B., lawyer; b. NYC, Feb. 17, 1948; s. Eli and Ruth Drapkin; m. Adrienne Miller, June 30, 1974; children: Benjamin, Jennifer, Rebecca. AB summa cum laude, Dartmouth Coll., 1968, BE, 1969; JD, Yale U., 1972; LLM, London Sch. Econs., 1973. Bar: NY 1975, DC 1978, Tex. 1985. Assoc. Paul, Weiss, Rifkind, Wharton & Garrison, NYC, 1974—77; atty.-adv. to Tax Legis. Counsel, spl. asst. to asst. sec. tax policy Office of Tax Policy, U.S. Treasury Dept., 1977—80; assoc., ptnr. Cohen & Uretz, Washington, 1980—83; ptnr. Jones Day, Dallas, 1984—. Former mem. alumni coun. Dartmouth Coll., Hanover, NH, former mem. nominating and alumni trustee search com., former mem. joint com. alumni governance and trustee nominations, former mem. com. trustees; mem. Exec. Com. Dartmouth Club of Dallas. Named one of the Top Tax Lawyers in US, Euromoney/Internat. Tax Rev., 1997—, Best Lawyers in Am., 1999—, Tex. Super Lawyers, 2003—. Mem.: ABA (former vice-chair profl. svcs., former rep. to Nat. Conf. of Lawyers and CPAs, former chmn. sect. of taxation, chair tax sect. task force patenting tax strategies), Am. Tax Policy Inst. (trustee), Am. Coll. Tax Counsel, Am. Law Inst. Office: Jones Day 2727 N Harwood St Dallas TX 75201-1515 Office Phone: 214-220-3939. Office Fax: 214-969-5100. Business E-Mail: dbdrapkin@jonesday.com.

DRAPKIN, DONALD G., venture capitalist; m. Ellen Drapkin (div.); 1 child, Matthew Adam; m. Bernice Drapkin; children: Dana Gabrielle, Nicole, Dustin, David, Amanda. Grad., Brandeis U., 1968; LLB, Columbia U., 1971. Atty. Cravath, Swaine & Moore; mergers ptnr. Skadden, Arps, Slate, Meagher & Flom; vice chmn., dir. MacAndrews & Forbes Holdings Inc., NYC, 1987—2007; vice chmn., chmn. investment com. Lazard Internat., 2007—. Bd. dirs. SIGA, 2001—, chmn., 2001—07; bd. dirs. Anthracite Capital, Inc., Playboy Enterprises, Inc., Revlon Consumer Products Corp., Revlon Inc., Nephros, Inc., 1997—, PharmaCore, Inc., TransTech Pharma, Inc. Bd. dirs. Brandeis U., Lincoln Ctr. Theatre, Phoenix House Found. Inc.; bd. visitors Columbia Law Sch. Office: Lazard 30 Rockefeller Plaza New York NY 10020 Office Phone: 212-632-6000.*

DRASLER, GREGORY JOHN, artist; b. Waukegan, Ill., June 7, 1952; s. John W. and Patricia A. Drasler; m. Nancy B. Davidson, June 15, 1985. BFA, U. Ill., 1980, MFA, 1983. Tchr. Williams Coll., 1994, Princeton U., 1999—. One person shows include Marianne Deson Gallery, Chgo., 1988, R. C. Erpf Gallery, N.Y., 1986, 87, 88, Shea & Beker Gallery, N.Y., 1990, Ctr. for Contemporary Art, Chgo., 1990, Queens Mus., Bulova Ctr., N.Y., 1994, Generous Miracles Gallery, N.Y., 2000, Eyre Moore Gallery, Seattle, Wash., 2000, Van Brunt Gallery, N.Y., 2004, Calif. State Coll., Fullerton, 2005; exhibited in group shows New Mus. Contemporary Art, N.Y.C., 1983, 87, 92, 95, Germans Van Eck Gallery, N.Y., 1984, John Berggruen Gallery, San Francisco, 1985, Jack Tilton Gallery, N.Y.C., 1986, Wellesley (Mass.) Coll. Mus., 1986, Robeson Ctr. Gallery, Rutgers U., Newark, 1987, Ben Shahn Galleries, William Patterson Coll., Wayne, N.J., 1988, Three Rivers Arts Festival, Carnegie Mus. Art, Pitts., 1989, U. Art Mus., SUNY, Binghamton, N.Y., 1989, Artist Space, N.Y.C., 1990, Flint (Mich.) Inst. Arts, Philharm. Ctr. for Arts, Knoxville Mus. Art, 1991-92, Flint Inst. Arts, 1993; represented in permanent collections Dow Jones Inc., N.Y.C., Krannert Art Mus., Champaign, Ill., Sammuel Lindenbaum, Fisher Bros., U. Ill., Champaign, John W. Heckenger, Barbara Toll, Emily Landau, Henry Luce III Found., Sawyer Miller Group, N.Y.C.; featured in Flint Inst. Arts Cat., Art Press, 1991, Chgo. Tribune, 1990, Art in Am. mag., 1987, 90, N.Y. Times newspaper, 1987, 88, 91, The Independent Press newspaper, 1991, Ben Shahn Gallery cat., 1988, SUNY Binghamton U. Art Mus. cat., Carnegie Mus. Art cat., Artist Space cat., 1990, Mary C. MacLellan fellow, 1980; MacDowell Colony Residence fellow, 1986; art fellow N.Y. Found of Arts, 1991; Nat. Endowment of Arts fellow, 1993; Djerassi Resident Artist Program fellow, 1996.

DRATCH, RACHEL, comedienne, actress; b. Lexington, Mass., Feb. 22, 1966; d. Paul and Elaine Dratch. BA in Psychology and Theater, Dartmouth Coll., 1988. Former cast mem. Second City, Chicago, 1992—99; cast mem. Saturday Night Live, 1999—. Actor: (films) Martin & Orloff, 2002, The Hebrew Hammer, 2003, Down with Love, 2003, After School Special, 2003, Dickie Roberts: Former Child Star, 2003, Home of Phobia, 2004, Looking for Kitty, 2004, Her Minor Thing, 2005, Winter Passing, 2005, Click, 2006; (TV series) Game Over, 2004, 30 Rock, 2006; guest appearances include (TV series) Third Watch, 2000, The King of Queens, 2002—04, Kim Possible, 2002, Monk, 2004, Frasier, 2004, O'Grady, 2005, writer, dir., actor (films) The Vagina Monologues Monologues, 2001, writer, actor (two-woman show with Tina Fey) Dratch & Fey, 2000. Office: Saturday Night Live NBC Studios 30 Rockefeller Plz New York NY 10112

DRAWBAUGH, DANIEL, information technology executive, biomedical engineer; BS in Biomedical and Elec. Engring., Temple Univ., Phila.; MBA, Duquesne Univ. Dir. biomedical engring. Shadyside Hosp., Pitts., 1983—90, chief info. officer, 1990—97, Univ. Pitts. Med. Ctr., Pitts., 1997—; and pres. BioTronics Inc. (subs. UPMC), Pitts. Office: Corporate Communications UPMC 200 Lothrop St Pittsburgh PA 15213-2582

DRAY, MARK STANLEY, lawyer; b. Alliance, Ohio, Feb. 8, 1943; s. Dwight Leroy and N. Pauline (Clark) Dray; m. Jonadell Pascoe, June 5, 1965; children: Melisa Louise, Justin Clark. BA, Mount Union Coll., Alliance, Ohio, 1965; JD, Coll. William and Mary, 1968, M in Law and Taxation, 1969. Bar: Va. 1968, U.S. Dist. Ct. (ea. dist.) Va. 1970, U.S. Tax Ct. 1971. Tax sr. Price Waterhouse, Washington, 1969—70; assoc. Hunton & Williams LLP, Richmond, Va., 1970—77, ptnr., 1977—. Mem. So. Employee Benefits Conf., 1974—; mem. adv. coun. William and Mary Tax Conf., 1980—88; trustee So. Fed. Tax Inst., 1989—, chair, 1997; spkr. in field. Contbr. articles to profl. jours. Fellow: Am. Bar Found., Va. Law Found., Am. Coll. Tax Counsel, Am. Coll. Employee Benefits Counsel (bd. govs. 2004—07, officer 2005—07, charter); mem.: ABA (com. employee benefits 1975—, mem. joint com. employee benefits 1989—91, chmn. 1989—90, 1990—91), Order of Coif, Richmond Bar Assn., Va. Bar Assn., Blue Key, Country Club Va. Episcopalian. Avocation: golf. Office: Hunton & Williams LLP Riverfront Plz East Tower 951 E Byrd St Richmond VA 23219-4074 Office Phone: 804-788-8408. Business E-Mail: mdray@hunton.com.

DRAY, WILLIAM HERBERT, philosophy educator; b. Montreal, June 23, 1921; s. William John and Florence Edith (Jones) D.; m. Doris Kathleen Best, Sept. 18, 1943; children: Christopher Reid, Jane Elizabeth. BA in History, U. Toronto, 1949; BA in Philosophy, Politics and Econs., Oxford U., 1951, MA, 1955, DPhil, 1956; LLD (hon.), Trent U., 1987. Lectr. U. Toronto, 1953-55, asst. prof., asso. prof., 1956-63, prof., 1963-68, Trent U., 1968-76, chmn. dept. philosophy, 1968-73; prof. philosophy U. Ottawa, Ont., 1976—85, prof. emeritus, 1986—. Author: Laws and Explanation in History, 1957, Philosophy of History, 1964, 2d edit., 1993, Perspectives on History, 1980, On History and Philosophers of History, 1989, History as Re-enactment, 1995; editor: Philosophical Analysis and History, 1966; co-editor: Substance and Form in History, 1981, Philosophie de l'histoire et la Pratique historienne d'aujourd'hui, 1982, The Principles of History, 1999. Served with RCAF, 1941-46, Active Res., 1956-66, wing comdr. ret. Am. Council Learned Socs. fellow, 1960-61; Can. Council fellow, 1971-72, 78-79; Killam research fellow, 1980-81; Nat. Humanities Ctr. fellow, 1983-84; recipient Can. Council Molson prize, 1986, Lifetime Achievement award Collingwood Soc., 2005. Fellow: Royal Soc. Can. Home: 818-32 Clarissa Dr Richmond Hill ON Canada L4C 9R7 Office: Dept Philosophy Univ of Ottawa Ottawa ON Canada K1N 6N5 Personal E-mail: whdray@aol.com.

DRAYER, BURTON PAUL, hospital administrator, neuroradiologist; b. N.Y.C., Mar. 19, 1946; s. Alexander and Marion Horowitz; m. Michaele Gerri Cohen, June 13, 1968; children: Aron Stuart, Alex Nathan. A.B., U. Pa., 1967; M.D., Chgo. Med. Sch., 1971. Diplomate Am. Bd. Psychiatry and Neurology, Am. Bd. Radiology. Intern, U. Vt. Med. Center, Burlington, 1971-72, resident in neurology, 1972-75; fellow, resident in radiology, U. Pitts. Health Center, 1975-78; asst. prof. neurology, U. Pitts., 1977-79, assoc. prof. radiology, 1978-79; dir. neuroradiology Children's Hosp. U. Pitts., 1978-79; assoc. prof. radiology and asst. prof. neurology, Duke U. Med. Center, Durham, N.C., 1979, chief sect. neuroradiology, 1981; dir. neuroradiol. rsch. Barrow Neurol. Inst.; Charles M. and Marilyn Newman Prof. and chmn. dept. radiology, Mt. Sinai Med. Sch., exec. v.p. hosp. and clinical affairs, Mt. Sinai Med. Ctr., pres., Mt. Sinai Hosp., 2004-. Past pres. Neuroradiology Edn. and Rsch. Found. Grantee, Squibb Research Inst., 1981-82, 82-83, Nat. Heart, Lung, and Blood Inst., 1983. Fellow Am. Acad. Neurology, Am. Coll. Radiology; mem. Am. Soc. Neuroradiology (past pres.), Soc. for Neuroscis., Am. Roentgen Ray Soc., Am. Heart Assn. (exec. com. stroke coun.), Radiol. Soc. N.Am. (bd. dirs. 2004—), Am. Acad. Neurology, Sigma Xi, Alpha Omega Alpha. Editor: Neuroimaging Clinics of N.Am.; mem. editl, bd. Neuroradiology; contbr. articles to books and jours. Office: Mt Sinai Med Ctr Dept Radiology One Gustave L Levy Pl Box 1234 New York NY 10029 Office Phone: 212-241-6403. Business E-Mail: Burton.Drayer@mountsinai.org.

DRAYTON, BILL (WILLIAM DRAYTON), social entrepreneur, lawyer, management consultant; b. NYC, June 15, 1943; s. William A. and Joan (Bergere) D. BA, Harvard U., Cambridge, Mass., 1965; MA, Oxford U., Eng., 1967; JD, Yale U., New Haven, 1970; LLD (hon.), Polytechnic U., 2006. Bar: NY 1971, DC 1976. Cons. McKinsey and Co., Inc., NYC, 1970-77, of counsel, 1981-87; vis. assoc. prof. law Stanford U., 1975-76; lectr. John F. Kennedy Sch. of Govt., Harvard U.; also dir. Harvard Regulatory and Mgmt. Group, 1976-77; cons. White House Domestic Policy Coun., 1977; asst. adminstr. for planning and mgmt. EPA, 1977-81; pres. Environ. Safety, Washington, 1981-89, chair, 1989—; pres., founder Ashoka: Innovators for the Pub., Arlington, Va., 1980-2001, chmn., CEO, 2001—. Nat. staff Hubert H. Humphrey Presdl. Campaign, Washington, 1968; dir. Corp. for Fiscal Policy, 1971-75; founder, chmn. Yale Legis. Svcs.; adv. coun. Carnegie Commn. Sci., Tech. and Govt., 1990-96. Contbr. articles to profl. jours. Pres. Ams. in India for McGovern, 1972; mem. Carter-Mondale Policy Planning, 1976, Carter-Mondale Govt. Reorgn. Transition Group, 1976-77; dep. dir. for issues Mondale-Ferraro campaign, 1984; energy and environment com. Dem. Nat. Com., 1982-86; bd. dirs. Oxfam Am., 1985-89, Appropriate Tech. Internat., 1988-97, chmn. bd. dirs., 1989-97; trustee Black Rock Forest (formerly Harvard Forest), NY; chmn. bd. dirs. Youth Venture, 1994—; founder, chair Get Am. Working!, 1997—; pres. Save EPA, Washington, 1981-83; chair Cmty. Greens, 2000—; founder, dir. Social Entrepreneur Assocs., 1998—. Recipient Entrepreneurial Excellence award Yale U. Sch. Mgmt., 1987, Nat. Pub. Svc. award Nat. Acad. Pub. Adminstrn. and Am. Soc. Pub. Adminstrn., 1995, Pub. Svc. Achievement award Common Cause, 1999, Vanguard Nonprofit Lawyers award ABA, 2002, Edward A. Smith award for excellence in nonprofit leadership, 2002, Fast Co. Fast 50 award, 2004, Nat. Conservation award Nat. Wildlife Fedn., 2005, Social Entrepreneur award Skoll Found., 2005, Merit award Yale Law Sch., 2005, others; named an Hon. fellow U. Pa. Sch. Law, 2007; named one of Am.'s Best Leaders US News and World Report and Harvard U., 2005; Henry fellow, 1965-67, MacArthur Prize fellow, 1984-89; Hon. fellow U. Pa. Law Sch., 2007. Mem. AAAS (com. on sci. pub. policy 1973-76), Assn. Bar City NY, Friends of India Soc. (chmn. 1974-75), Coun. Fgn. Rels., Pacific Coun. Internat. Policy, Nat. Acad. Pub. Adminstrn., Am. Acad. Arts and Scis., Asia Soc. (contemporary affairs com. 1987-2000), India Internat. Ctr. (New Delhi), Yale Law Sch. Assn. (exec. com. 2005—), Yale Club NY, Harvard Club NY, Phi Beta Kappa. Home: 1200 N Nash St Arlington VA 22209-3616 Office: 1700 N Moore St Ste 2000 Arlington VA 22209-1921

DRAZDOFF, NOLA GAY, psychologist; d. Michael John and LaJuana Joy Drazdoff. BS in Computer Sci. and Bus., U. Puget Sound, WA, 1986; MA in Psychology, Antioch U., Seattle, 1999; Ordained Interfaith Min., One Spirit Interfaith Sem., NY, 2005. Programmer, analyst Weyerhaeuser Real Estate Co., Federal Way, Wash., 1984—88; systems engr. Electronic Data Sys, Southfield, Mich., 1986—87; pres., founder Soundex Info. Sys., Inc., Federal Way, Wash., 1988—90; program mgr. Microsoft, Redmond, Wash., 1990—93; tour leader, counselor Self Employed, Issaquah, Wash., 1999—2000; pres., founder Inspired Path, Inc., Issaquah, Wash., 2001—. Precinct com. officer WA State Dem. Party, Olympia, Wash., 2004—05; bd. adv. Bustan L'Shalom, Jerusalem, 2004—05; bd. dirs. Compassionate Listening Project, Seattle, 2004—05; vol. Friend to Friend: Nursing Home Visitation, Seattle, 1996—2005; vol., fundraiser Child Care Resources, 2003—05. Recipient Proactive Peacemaker award, Season for Non-Violence, Oreg. Chpt., 2002. Mem.: ACA, APA (assoc.), Am. Mental Health Counseling Assn. Avocations: travel, exploring cultures and spiritual tradition, hiking, gardening. Office: Inspired Path Inc 4580 Klahanie Drive SE PMB 434 Issaquah WA 98024 Office Phone: 425-785-5389. Office Fax: 425-222-3543. E-mail: noladr@inspiredpath.com.

DRAZEN, JEFFREY MARK, medical educator; b. St. Louis, May 19, 1946; s. Yale and Sylvia (Wainer) D.; m. Erica Coburn Drazen, July 27, 1969; children: David, Daniel. BS, Tufts U., 1968; MD, Harvard U., 1972. Diplomate Am. Bd. Internal Medicine, Am. Bd. Pulmonary Medicine. Asst. prof. medicine Harvard U., Boston, 1977—81, assoc. prof. medicine, 1981—89, prof. medicine, 1989—90, Parker B. Francs prof. medicine, 1990—2000, prof. medicine, 2000—04, Disting. Parker B. Francis prof. medicine, 2004—; asst. prof. physiology Harvard Sch. Pub. Health, 1980—81, assoc. prof. physiology, 1981—91, prof. physiology, 1991—; chief pulmonary and critical care medicine divsn. Brigham & Women's Hosp., Boston, 1985-2000, sr. physician, 1989—; editor-in-chief New England Jour. of Medicine, 2000—. Mem. respiratory and applied physiology study sect. NIH, 1981-86, pulmonary disease adv. coun., 1988-92, lung bio. & pathology study sec., 1996-2000; Nat. Heart, Lung & Blood Inst. (NHLBI) adv. coun., 2000-2004. NIH grantee, 1972—. Mem. Am. Soc. Clin. Investigation, Am. Thoracic Soc., Am. Physiology Soc., Am. Fedn. Clin. Rsch., Am. Soc. Clin. Investigation, Am. Soc. Pharmacology and Exptl. Therapeutics, Assn. Am. Physicians, Inst. Medicine., Interurban Clin. Club. Office: Brigham & Women's Hosp 75 Francis St Boston MA 02115-6106 also: New England Journal Medicine 10 Shattuck St Boston MA 02115 Home Phone: 781-721-2333; Office Phone: 781-434-7870. E-mail: jdrazen@rics.bwh.harvard.edu, jdrazen@nejm.org.

DR. DRE, (ANDRE YOUNG), rapper, record producer; b. LA, Feb. 18, 1965; Co-founder Ruthless Records, 1987; founder Aftermath, 1996—. Albums include (with N.W.A.) Straight Outta Compton, 1989, 100 Miles and Runnin', 1990 (EP) Efil4zaggin, 1991, (solo) The Chronic, 1993 (Grammy award Best Pop Solo for "Let Me Ride" 1994), Concrete Roots, 1994, Back N Tha Day, 1994, First Round Knock Out, 1996, NWA Greatest Hits, 1996, Dr. Dre Presents the Aftermath, 1996, Dr. Dre 2001, 1999; prodr. Snoop Doggy Dog's album "Doggy Style", 1993, U Can't Cee Me and California Love singles, 1996; prodr. soundtrack albums Above the Rim, 1994, Murder Was the Case, 1994, Wild Wild West, 1999, The SLim SHady Lp, 1999, The Marshall Mathers LP, 2000, Death Row: Snoop Doggy Dogg at His Best, 2001, The Eminem Show, 2002; actor Who's The Man, 1993, Ride, 1998, Whiteboyz, 1999, The Wash, 2001, Training Day, 2001. Mailing: Aftermath Entertainment 10900 Wilshire Blvd Ste 1040 Los Angeles CA 90024-6501

DREBSKY, DENNIS JAY, lawyer; b. NYC, Sept. 28, 1946; s. Benjamin and Ronnie (Penso) D.; m. Norma Louise Linschitz, Aug. 16, 1970; children: Richard Michael, Joshua William Evan. BBA magna cum laude, CCNY, 1967; JD, Cornell U., 1970. Bar: N.Y. 1971, U.S. Dist. Ct. (so. dist.) N.Y. 1972, U.S. Ct. Appeals (2d cir.) 1971, U.S. Ct. Appeals (5th cir.) 1980, U.S. Ct. Appeals (9th cir.) 1982, U.S. Ct. Appeals (1st cir.) 1981, U.S. Ct. Appeals (10th cir.) 1984, U.S. Ct. Appeals (4th cir.) 1986, U.S. Ct. Appeals (D.C. cir.) 1998. Assoc. Skadden, Arps, Slate, Meagher & Flom, NYC, 1970-77, ptnr., 1978-91, Clifford, Chance, Rogers & Wells, 1991—2004, Nixon Peabody, LLP, 2004—. Trustee Community Law Offices, N.Y.C., 1980—. Mem. Assn. of Bar of City of N.Y. (mem. com. on corp. reorgn. 1985—). Jewish. Avocations: reading, jogging, theater.

Home: 7 Glen Hill Ct Dix Hills NY 11746-4819 Office: Nixon Peabody LLP 437 Madison Ave New York NY 10022-0800 Office Phone: 212-940-3091. Business E-Mail: ddrebsky@nixonpeabody.com.

DREBUS, JOHN RICHARD, computer consultant; b. Madison, Wis., Feb. 11, 1951; s. Richard William and Hazel Mae (Redford) D.; m. Pamela Kay Perfetto, Jan. 5, 1974; children: Bethea Lynn, Scott Bryan, Cynthia Ann. BA in Zoology, Ind. U., 1973; MS in Mgmt., Purdue U., 1983; Honor Grad., Command & Gen. Staff Coll., 1991. Commd. 2d lt. U.S. Army, 1973, armor officer Baumholder, Germany, 1973-77, armor officer, capt. Fort Knox, Ky., 1977-81; mfg. assoc. Am. Can Co., Hammond, Ind., 1983-84; project mgr. The System Works, Marietta, Ga., 1984-87; bus. rels. specialist Electronic Data Systems, Warren, Mich., 1988-91, supr. Ypsilanti, Mich., 1991-93, systems engr. Troy, Mich., 1993-98; prin. cons. Price Waterhouse Coopers LLP, Southfield, Mich., 1998—. Project officer Army Force Modernization Team, Fort Knox, 1979-80. Contbr. articles to profl. jours. Dir. sch. bd. Faith Luth. Sch., Marietta, Ga., 1986-88; treas. ann. fund drive St. John Luth. Sch., Rochester, 1992-95; bd. mem. Boy Scout Troop 188, Rochester Hills, Mich., 1993-95. Capt. USAR, 1981-87, maj., 1987-90, lt. col., 1995— Army Strategic and Advanced Computer Ctr., The Pentagon. Recipient Disting. Mil. Grad award U.S. Army, 1973, Army Commendation medal, 1977, Army Parachute Badge, 1973. Mem. Computer Soc. of IEEE, N.Y. Acad. Sci., U.S. Army Armor Assn., Assn. of U.S. Army, Mensa. Lutheran. Avocations: classical piano, kayaking, fencing, back packing, scuba diving. Home: 1631 Ridgecrest Rochester Hills MI 48306-3159 Office: Price Waterhouse Coopers LLP 40 Oak Hollow St Ste 155 Southfield MI 48034-7470

DRECHSEL, ROBERT EDWARD, journalism educator; b. Fergus Falls, Minn., Aug. 7, 1949; BA, U. Minn., 1971, MA, 1976, PhD, 1980. Reporter, city editor Daily Jour., Fergus Falls, 1971—74; instr. dept. journalism S.D. State U., Brookings, 1976—77; asst. prof. dept. tech. journalism Colo. State U., Ft. Collins, 1979—83; from asst. prof. to assoc. prof. Sch. Journalism and Mass Comm. U. Wis., Madison, 1983—91, prof., 1991—, dir., 1991—98; affiliated prof. law U. Wis., Madison, 2000—. Author: News Making in the Trial Courts, 1983; contbr. articles to profl. jours. Mem. Assn. Edn. Journalism and Mass Comm. (Krieghbaum Outstanding Achievement Rsch., Teaching & Pub. Svc. award 1989), Am. Judicature Soc., Wis. Freedom Info. Coun., Internat. Comm. Assn. Office: U Wis Sch Journalism & Mass Comm 821 University Ave Madison WI 53706-1412

DRECHSLER, BEATRICE KRAIN, lawyer; BA magna cum laude, Barnard U., 1984; JD cum laude, Harvard U., 1987. Bar: NY 1988, NY 1988. Ptnr. Real Estate Dept. Kaye Scholer LLP, NYC. Mem.: Internat. Coun. of Shopping Ctrs., Estate Women - NY, Inc., NY Women Execs. in Real Estate.

DREEBEN, MICHAEL R., federal agency administrator; b. 1954; BA, U. Wis., Madison; MA, U. Chgo.; JD, Duke U., 1981. Bar: 1982. Law clk. to Judge Jerre S. Williams US Ct. Appeals (5th cir.); asst. to solicitor gen. Office of Solicitor Gen., US Dept. Justice, Washington, DC, 1988—95, dep. solicitor gen., 1995—. Lectr. Duke Law Sch., Mich. Law Sch., U. Tex. Law Sch.; adj. prof. law Georgetown U. Recipient Atty Gen.'s Award for Disting. Svc., 1998. Office: US Dept Justice 950 Pennsylvania Ave, NW Washington DC 20530

DREHER, FRANK H., JR., retired optician; b. Phila., Sept. 21, 1923; s. Frank H. and Mary Catherine Dreher; m. Kathryn Marie Dreher, Aug. 27, 1955; children: Frank H. Dreher, III, George W. Modern Bus., Alexander Hamilton Inst., New York, New York, 1962; Optics and Math., Drexel Inst., Philadelphia, Pennsylvania, 1968. Real estate salesperson Craig J. Turnbull Atty., Camden, NJ, 1950—54; opthalmic dispenser Meserall Opticians, Haddonfield, NJ, 1969—77, hearing aid dispenser, 1974—77; opthalmic dispenser Cole Nat. Corp., Willingboro, NJ, 1977—87, Dr. David J. Mellish, O.D., Williamstown, NJ, 1987—98; ret., 1998. Creative writing tchr. Salem C.C., Carneys Point, NJ, 1996—97. Contbr. articles to profl. mags. Scout master Boy Scouts of Am., Erial, NJ, 1949—51; sunday sch. supt. Episcopal churches, Clementon and Chews Landing, NJ, 1952—79. T/4 US Armed Forces, 1943—46, New Guinea and Luzon. Mem.: The Internat. Order of St. Luke the Physician. Independent. Episcopal Methodist. Avocations: writing, classical music, travel, cooking. Home: 248 Route 40 Lot F5 Newfield NJ 08344 Personal E-mail: fhdreher@netscape.com.

DREHER, MELANIE CREAGAN, dean, nursing educator; BSN magna cum laude, L.I. U.; D in Anthropology, Columbia U. Mem. faculty Columbia U., NYC; dean Sch. Nursing, William Ryan disting. prof. U. Miami; dean Sch. Nursing, prof. U. Mass., 1988—97; Kelting dean, prof. U. Iowa Coll. Nursing, 1997—. Mem. Council on Public Relations for the National Institutes of Health, Washington, 1999—2001; adv. bd. mem. Pfizer Fellowship Prog. in Nursing Rsch., 2000—01; dir. Beverly Enterprises, Inc., 2004—. Mem. editl. bds. various profl. jours. Recipient May A. Brunson award, CASE award. Mem. Sigma Theta Tau (pres. Beta Zeta chpt. 1995). Office: U Iowa Coll Nursing 101 Nursing Bldg 50 Newton Rd Iowa City IA 52242-1121

DREICER, ROBERT, oncologist, director, medical educator; b. Brooklyn, NY, May 30, 1955; BS, Colo. State U., Fort Collins; MD, U. Tex., 1983. Intern, internal medicine Ind. U., Indpls., 1983—84, resident, oncology, 1984—86; fellow U. Wis., 1986—89; assoc. prof. medicine U. Iowa, Iowa City, 1989—99; dir. med. oncology Cleve. Clinic Found., 1999—. Fellow: Am. Coll. Physicians; mem.: Am. Soc. Clin. Oncology (chair membership com. 1997—2000). Office: Cleve Clinic Found Mail Code R35 9500 Euclid Cleveland OH 44195*

DREIER, DAVID TIMOTHY, congressman; b. Kansas City, Mo., July 5, 1952; s. H. Edward and Joyce (Yeomans) D. BA cum laude, Claremont McKenna Coll., 1975; MA in Am. Govt., Claremont Grad. Sch., 1976. Dir. corp. rels. Claremont McKenna Coll., 1975-78; dir. mktg. and govt. rels. Indsl. Hydro, San Dimas, Calif., 1978-80; mem. U.S. Congress from 26th (formerly 33rd) Calif. dist., 1981—; v.p. Dreier Devel. Co., Kansas City, Mo., 1985—. Vice chmn. rules of the house com., 1995-99, chmn. rules com., 1999—; bd. dirs. Internat. Rep. Inst.; mem. spkrs. steering com. Recipient Golden Bulldog award Watchdogs of the Treasury, 1981-99, Taxpayers Friends award Nat. Taxpayers Union, 1981-99, Clean Air Champion award Sierra Club, 1988. Republican. Office: US Ho Reps 233 Cannon Ho Office Bldg Washington DC 20515-0526*

DREIER, MARC S., lawyer; b. NYC, May 12, 1950; BA, Yale U., 1972; JD, Harvard U., 1975. Bar: NY 1976, Ariz., US Ct. Appeals (2nd, 3rd and 9th cirs.) 1976, US Dist. Ct. (so. and ea. dists.) NY 1976, US Dist. Ct. Dist. Ariz., US Supreme Ct. Ptnr. Rosenman & Colin LLP; head litig. dept. Fulbright & Jaworski LLP, NYC; mng. ptnr. Dreier LLP. Mem.: NY County Lawyers Assn., NY State Bar Assn. Office: Dreier LLP 499 Park Ave New York NY 10022 Office Phone: 212-328-6111. Office Fax: 212-328-6101. Business E-Mail: mdreier@dreierllp.com.

DREIER, R. CHAD, construction and mortgage company executive; BSBA, Loyola Marymount U., 1969. Exec. v.p. Golden West Holding Corp., LA, 1979-80; v.p., dir. devel. Daon Corp., 1980-85; exec. v.p., CFO Kaufman and Broad Home Corp., 1986; chmn. Kaufman & Broad Mortgage Corp.; pres., CEO The Ryland Group, Inc., Woodland Hills, Calif., 1993—, chmn., 1994—. Bd. Occidental Petroleum Corp.; chmn. bd. trustees Loyola Marymount U.; adv. bd. Joint Ctr. Housing Studies, Harvard U. 1st lt. USAF, 1969—72. Avocation: sports. Office: Ryland Group Suite 400 24025 Park Sorrento Calabasas CA 91302*

DREIFKE, GERALD EDMOND, electrical engineering educator; b. St. Louis, June 21, 1918; s. Herman A. and Anna Margaret (Hollenbeck) D.; m. Lorraine Ann Feldhaus, June 9, 1951; children: Mark A., Matthew G., Laura Maria, Anne Marie. BS, MS, Washington U., 1948, DSc (NSF fellow), 1961. Registered profl. engr., Mo. Layout man Curtiss-Wright Co., St. Louis, 1936-39, design engr., 1939-44; layout man Douglas Aircraft Co., 1939; instr. engring. St. Louis U., 1948-50, asst. prof., 1950-54, assoc. prof. elec. engring., dir. grad. program elec. engring., 1954-61, prof. elec. engring., 1961-71; mgr. r & d Union Electric Co., 1971-77; cons., 1977—; vis. prof. physics U. Mo.-St. Louis, 1979-94. Cons. Emerson Electric Co., 1951-71, Monsanto Co., 1961-71; mem. tech. staff Bell Telephone Labs. NJ, summer 1963 Editor-in-chief: ISA Transactions, 1966-89; contbr. articles profl. jours. Mem. St. Louis County Bd. Elec. Examiners, Gov.'s Sci. Adv. Com. Mo. Served with USNR, 1944-45. Recipient cert. of merit WPB, 1942; rsch. grants NSF, 1964; rsch. grants NASA, 1965; rsch. grants Monsanto Co., 1965-69; Nancy McNair-Ring Outstanding Faculty award St. Louis U. chpt. Gamma Pi Epsilon, 1965-66 Fellow ISA; mem. Am. Soc. Engring. Edn. (past sec., com. chmn.), IEEE (past chmn. St. Louis sect.), Mo. Soc. Profl. Engrs. (past pres. St. Louis chpt., Engr. of Yr. St. Louis chpt. 1977), St. Louis Elec. Bd. Trade, Sigma Xi, Tau Beta Pi, Eta Kappa Nu, Pi Mu Epsilon, Phi Eta Sigma. Home and Office: 6 Westmoreland Pl Saint Louis MO 63108-1228 Office Phone: 314-361-2321.

DREIFUS, CLAUDIA, journalist, educator; b. NYC, Nov. 24, 1944; Life ptnr. Andrew Hacker. BS in Dramatic Arts, NYU, 1966. Assoc. vis. prof. dept. journalism NYU, 1975, instr. mag. writing Sch. Continuing Edn., 1979; lectr. non-fiction writing YWCA N.Y., 1979-84; represented by Robin Strauss Lit. Agy.; vis. prof. grad. English creative writing program CCNY, 1994-98; sr. fellow World Policy Inst., New Sch. for Social Rsch., NY, 1997—; adj. prof. Columbia U. Sch. Internat. and Pub. Affairs, 2002—. Writer on politics of TV TV Guide, 1991—; lectr. in field. Editor: Seizing Our Bodies: The Politics of Women's Health, 1978; author: Interview, 1997, Scientific Conversations: Interviews on Science from The New York Times, 2001; contbr. chpts. to textbooks, anthologies; commentator health and sci. City Edition and Spl. Edition programs Sta. WNET-TV, 1979-80, guest host local issues Live Wire program, 1991; interviewer Sunday mag. L.I. Newsday, 1976-81, Books sect. N.Y. Post, 1990, Playboy Mag., 1981—; sci. interviewer N.Y. Times, Sci. Times; contbr. articles to popular publs. Recipient award of Merit for Svc. to Women, YWCA NY, 1976. Mem: PEN, Am. Soc. Journalists and Authors (Outstanding Article award 1987, Investigative Journalism award 2003, Lifetime Achievement award 2007), Sigma Xi (hon. mem.). Office: c/o NY Times 229 W 43rd St Fl 8 New York NY 10036-3913

DREILING, RICHARD W., retail executive; b. 1953; BA in Industrial Relations, Rockhurst U., Mo. Various mgmt. positions Safeway, Inc., 1969—97; pres. Vons (divsn. Safeway, Inc.), 1998—99; exec. v.p. mfg. and distbn. Safeway, Inc., 2000—03; chief operations officer, exec. v.p. Longs Drug Stores Corp., 2003—05, COO, 2005; pres., CEO Duane Reade Inc., NYC, 2005—. Office: Duane Reade Inc 440 9th Ave New York NY 10001*

DREIMANIS, ALEKSIS, emeritus geology educator; b. Valmiera, Latvia, Aug. 13, 1914; s. Peteris and Marta Eleonora (Leitis) D.; m. Anita Kana, Apr. 18, 1942; children: Mara Dreimanis Love, Aija Dreimanis Downing. Mag. rer. nat., U. Latvia, 1938; D.Sc. (hon.), U. Waterloo, Ont., Can., 1969, U. Western Ont., 1980; D Geography (hon.), U. Latvia, 1991, Habilitation, 1942. Asst. to pvt. docent U. Latvia, 1937-44; mil. geologist Latvian Legion, 1944-45; assoc. prof. geology Baltic U., Hamburg and Pinneberg, Germany, 1946-48; mem. faculty U. Western Ont., London, Can., 1948—, prof. geology, 1964-80, prof. emeritus, 1980—. Pres. Commn. on Genesis and Lithology of Quaternary Deposits, Internat. Union Quaternary Research, 1973-87; cons. in field. Assoc. editor Geosci. Can., 1976-78, Quaternary Sci. Revs., 1981-87, Tech. Rev. (in Latvian), 1978—, Latgeo (in Latvian), 1990-98, Geology Proc. Estonian Acad. Scis., 1991-97, Latvijas Geologijas Vestis, 2000—02; contbr. articles to profl. jours. Decorated officer Three Star Order of Latvia; recipient Centennial medal (Can.); Queen Elizabeth II 25th Anniversary medal; Centennial medal Geol. Survey of Finland, U. Helsinki medal; Albrecht Penck medal, teaching award Ont. Confedn. Univ. Faculty Assns., 1978. Fellow Royal Soc. Can. (Disting.), Geol. Assn. Can. (Logan medal 1978), Geol. Soc. Am. (Disting. Career award Quarternary geology and geomorphology divsn. 1987); mem. Swedish Geol. Soc. (hon. corr. mem.), Can. Quaternary Assn. (W.A. Johnston medal 1989), Am. Quarternary Assn. (pres. 1981-83), Assn. Advancement Baltic Studies, Internat. Union for Quaternary Rsch. (hon.), Latvian Nat. Fedn. Can. (chmn. coun. 1953-71, hon. mem.), Latvian Acad. Scis. (fgn. hon.), Latvian Cultural Found. (exec. com. 1973-77), London Latvian Soc. (pres. 1948—), Fraternity Lidums (pres. 1935-36, editor newsletter 1969—), Geol. Soc. Finland (hon. corr. mem.), Latvian Am. Assn. Univ. Profs. and Scientists (pres. 1983-85), Geog. Assn. Latvia (hon.), Assn. Latvian Geologists (hon.), Baltic Rsch. Inst. (hon. corr. mem.), Estonian Geol. Soc. (hon.). Home: 287 Neville Dr London ON Canada N6G 1C2 Office: U Western Ont Dept Earth Scis London ON Canada N6A 5B7 Personal E-mail: aija@csd.uwo.ca.

DREIMANN, LEONHARD, manufacturing executive; b. Riga, Latvia; D. in Mktg., Melbourne U., Australia. Pres. Salton Inc., a wholly-owned subs. SEVKO Inc., 1987—88; mng. dir. Salton Australia Pty. Ltd., 1988—93; founder Salton Inc., Lake Forest, Ill., 1988—, pres., 1988—98, CEO, 1988—, dir. Dir. Glacier Water Systems, 1987—93; officer, dir. Glacier Holdings Inc., 1988—93, Salton Time, 1989—93. Recipient Ernst & Young Entrepreneur Of The Year for Ill./North West Ind., 1999. Achievements include the successful mktg. of The George Foreman Grill, Breadman, Juiceman, Ingraham, Farberware and Toastmaster - growing the co. from $8 million to $1 billion in sales. Office: Salton Inc 1955 West Field Ct Lake Forest IL 60045

DREISBACH, JOHN GUSTAVE, investment banker; b. Paterson, NJ, Apr. 24, 1939; s. Gustave John and Rose Catherine (Koehler) D.; m. Janice Lynn Petitjean; children: John Gustave Jr., Christopher Erik. BA, NYU, 1963. With Dreyfus & Co., 1959-62, Shields & Co., Inc., 1965-68, Model, Roland & Co., Inc., NYC, 1968-72, F. Eberstadt & Co., Inc., NYC, 1972-74; asst. v.p., trust officer Bessemer Trust Co., 1974—76; pres. Cmty. Housing Capital, Inc., 1978-80; chmn., pres. John G. Dreisbach, Inc., Santa Fe, 1980—, JDG Housing Corp., 1982—, JGD Mgmt. Corp., 1996—. Gen. ptnr. numerous real estate ltd. partnerships; bd. dirs., pres. The Santa Fe Investment Conf., 1986—; assoc. Sta. KNME-TV. Mem. Santa Fe Cmty. Devel. Commn. With USAR, with USAFR, 1964. Mem. Internat. Assn. for Fin. Planning, Nat. Assn. Securities Dealers, Inc., NYU Alumni Assn., N.Mex. First, Friends of Vieilles Maisons Francaises Inc., Mensa, Santa Fe C. of C., Augustan Soc., St. Bartholomew's Cmty. Club, Essex Club, Hartford Club, Amigos del Alcalde Club. Avocations: travel, marathoning, architecture, classical music, shotokan karate (1st dan). Office: 369 Montezuma Ave No 215 Santa Fe NM 87501-2626 Home: 72 Gras Lawn Barrack Rd Exeter Devon EX2 4SZ England Personal E-mail: john@dreisbach.freeserve.co.uk.

DREISHPOON, DOUGLAS SCOTT, curator, art historian; b. NYC, Apr. 19, 1954; s. Irving and Georgene Simon Dreishpoon; m. Lisa Beth Rafalson, June 13, 1999; children: Maia, Mina Kean. BA, Skidmore Coll., Saratoga Springs, NY, 1976; MA, Tufts U., Medford, Mass., 1980; PhD, CUNY, NYC, 1993. Curator exhbns. and rsch. Hirschl & Adler Galleries, NYC, 1982—91; curator contemporary art Tampa Mus. Art, Fla., 1992—95; curator collections, adj. asst. prof. Weatherspoon Art Mus., Greensboro, NC, 1995—98, interim dir., 1997—98; curator 20th Century art Albright-Knox Art Gallery, Buffalo, 1998—2003, sr. curator, 2003—. Peer profl. Gen. Svcs. Adminstrns. Art in Arch. Program, Washington, 2004—06; peer panelist utilization of collections Nat. Endowment for the Arts, Washington, 1994; peer panelist museums NY State Coun. on the Arts, NYC, 2001—03. Author, editor: exbhn. catalogue Edwin Dickinson: Dreams & Realities, 2002, The Tumultuous Fifties: A View from the New York Times Photo Archives, 2002, Petah Coyne: Above and Beneath the Skin, 2005, author essays; contbr. articles to profl. jours. Bd. dirs. Mandelman-Ribak Found., Santa Fe, 2004—06. Grantee, Judith Rothschild Found., 2000, Henry Luce Found., 2000, 2006, NY State Coun. on the Arts, 2006. Mem.: Coll. Art Assn., Internat. Assn. Art Critics (bd. dirs. 1996—). Avocation: jazz drummer/percussionist. Office: Albright-Knox Art Gallery 1285 Elmwood Ave Buffalo NY 14222

DRELA, MARK, aeronautical engineer, educator; SB, SM, MIT, Cambridge, 1983, PhD, 1985. Asst. prof. MIT, Cambridge, 1986—91, Carl Richard Soderberg asst. prof., 1988—90, T. Wilson assoc. prof., 1991—92, assoc. prof., 1991—2000, prof., 2000—01, Terry J. Kohler prof. fluid dynamics Cambridge, 2001—. Contbr. articles to sci. jours. Recipient Presdl. Young Investigator award, 1987—91. Fellow: AIAA (Lawrence Sperry award 1991). Office: Dept Aeronautics and Astronautics 37-475 MIT 77 Massachusetts Ave Cambridge MA 02139 Office Phone: 617-253-0067. Office Fax: 617-258-5143. E-mail: drela@mit.edu.*

DRELL, PERSIS SYDNEY, physicist; B, Wellesley Coll.; PhD in Atomic Physics, U. Calif., Berkeley, 1983. Postdoctoral rsch. assoc. in high-energy physics Lawrence Berkeley Nat. Lab., 1983—88; asst. prof. physics Cornell U., 1988—97, prof. physics, 1997—, dep. dir., Lab. Nuclear Studies, chair, Synchrotron Radiation Com., Lab. Nuclear Studies; mem. program adv. com. Stanford Linear Accelerator Ctr. (SLAC), Menlo Park, Calif., 1993—95, assoc. dir., 2002—, current chair, scientific policy com. Leader of Cornell Group, Wilson Lab. CLEO (one of the world's most advanced particle detectors), 2000. Named One of the 50 Most Important Women in Science, Discover Mag., 2002. Fellow: Am. Acad. Arts & Scis. Office: Stanford Linear Accelerator Ctr 2575 Sand Hill Rd Menlo Park CA 94025 Address: Stanford Linear Accelerator Ctr PO Box 20450 Stanford CA 94309 Office Phone: 650-926-3300.*

DRELL, SIDNEY DAVID, physicist, arms control and national security specialist; b. Atlantic City, Sept. 13, 1926; s. Tulla and Rose (White) D.; m. Harriet Stainback, Mar. 22, 1952; children: Daniel White, Persis Sydney, Joanna Harriet. AB, Princeton U., 1946; MA, U. Ill., 1947, PhD, 1949, DSc (hon.), 1981, Tel Aviv U., 2001, Weizman Inst. Sci., 2001. Rsch. assoc. U. Ill., 1949-50; instr. physics Stanford U., 1950-52, assoc. prof., 1956-60, prof., 1960-63, Lewis M. Terman prof. and fellow, 1979-84; co-dir. Stanford U. Ctr. for Internat. Security and Arms Control, 1983-89; prof. Stanford Linear Accelerator Ctr., 1963-98, dep. dir., 1969-98, exec. head theoretical physics, 1969-86, prof. emeritus, 1998—. Rsch. assoc. MIT, 1952-53, asst. prof., 1953-56, adv. bd. Lincoln Lab., 1985-90; vis. scientist Guggenheim fellow CERN Lab., Switzerland, 1961, U. Rome, 1972; vis. prof., Loeb lectr. Harvard U., 1962, 70; vis. Schrodinger prof. theoretical physics U. Vienna, 1975; vis. fellow All Souls Coll., Oxford, 1979; I.I. Rabi vis. prof. Columbia U., 1984; adj. prof. engring., pub. policy Carnegie Mellon U., 1989-96; cons. Office Sci. and Tech., 1960-73, Office Sci. and Tech. Policy, 1977-82, ACDA, 1969-81; adviser NSC, 1973-81, Office Tech. Assessment US Congress, 1975-90, House Armed Svcs. Com., 1990-93, Senate Select Com. on Intelligence, 1990-93; original mem. JASON, 1960—; mem. high energy physics adv. panel Dept. Energy, 1973-86, chmn., 1974-82, energy rsch. adv. bd., 1978-80; mem. Carnegie Commn. on Sci., Tech. and Govt., 1988-93, Pres.'s Fgn. Intelligence Adv. Bd., 1993-2001; Richtmyer lectr. Am. Assn. Physics Tchrs., San Francisco, 1978; Danz lectr. U. Wash., 1983; Hans Bethe lectr. Cornell U., 1988; chmn. U.C. pres. coun. on nat. labs., 1992-99; chmn. internat. adv. bd. Inst. Global Conflict and Cooperation, U. Calif., 1990-93; mem. bd. dirs. Internat. Sci. Found., 1993-96; Brickwedded lectr. John Hopkins U., 1997; chair sr. rev. bd. Intelligence Tech. Innovation Ctr., 2001-02; mem. adv. com. Nat. Nuc. Secuirty Adminstrn., 2001-03; mem. sr. adv. group LANL, 2003—. Author: (books) Electromagnetic Structure of Nucleons, 1961, The Reagan Strategic Defense Initiative: a Technical, Political and Arms Control Assessment, 1985, In the Shadow of the bomb: Physics and Arms Control, 1993, The Gravest Danger: Nuclear Weapons, 2003; co-author (with Sergei P. Kapitza): Sakharov Remembered: A Tribute by Friends and Colleagues, 1991; co-author: (with J.D. Bjorken) Relitivistic Quantum Mechanics, 1964, Relitivistic Quantum Field, 1965; co-author: others; editor: (books) The New Terror: Facing the Threat of Biological and Chemical Weapons, 1999, The Gravest Danger. Trustee Inst. Advanced Study, Princeton, 1974-83; bd. govs. Weizmann Inst. Sci., Rehovoth, Israel, 1970—; bd. dirs. Ann. Revs., Inc., 1976-97; mem. Pres. Sci. Adv. Com., 1966-70. Recipient Ernest Orlando Lawrence Meml. award AEC, 1972, Alumni award U. Ill., 1973, Alumni Achievement award, 1988, Hilliard Roderick prize AAAS, 1993, Woodrow Wilson award Princeton U., 1994, Ettore Majorana-Erice Sci. for Peace prize, 1994, Gian Carlo Wick medal, 1996, Disting Assoc. award US Dept. Environ., 1997, I. Pomeranchuk prize, 1998, Linus Pauling medal Stanford U., 1999-2000, Enrico Fermi award, 2000, Presidential award, U. Calif., 2000, Heinz R. Pagels Human Rights of Scientists award, 2001, Nat. Intelligence Disting. Svc. medal, 2001, William O. Baker award Security Affairs Support Assn., 2001, Heinz award, 2005, others; MacArthur fellow, 1984-89, Sr. fellow Hoover Instn., 1998—. Fellow Am. Phys. Soc. (pres. 1986, Leo Szilard award 1980); mem. AAAS, NAS, Am. Acad. Arts and Scis., Am. Philos. Soc., Arms Control Assn. (bd. dirs. 1978-93), Coun. on Fgn. Rels., Aspen Strategy Group (emeritus 1991). Office: Stanford Linear Accelerator Ctr 2575 Sand Hill Rd MS 80 Menlo Park CA 94025-7015 Office Phone: 650-926-2664. Business E-Mail: drell@slac.stanford.edu.

DRENDEL, FRANK MATTHEW, cable company executive; b. Paxton, Ill., Jan. 16, 1945; s. Nora and Odell (Drendel); m. Marilyn Beste, 1968; 1 son. BS, No. Ill. U., 1970; postgrad., St. Louis U., 1973. Vice-pres., corp. mgr. Continental Transmission, St. Louis, 1969-72; v.p. ops. Cypress Communications, Los Angeles, 1972-73; CEO Commscope NC Gen. Instrument Corp., 1976—86, chmn., CEO CommScope NC, 1986—97; chmn., CEO CommScope, Hickory, NC, 1997—. Bd. dir. Sprint Nextel Comm., Nat. Cable Telecommunications Assn. Served with U.S. Army, 1968-74. Named to Cable TV Hall of Fame, 2002. Mem. Calif. Cable TV Assn. (past dir., asso. dir.), Nat. Cable TV Assn. (past dir.), C. of C. Clubs: Lake Hickory Country. Presbyterian. Office: CommScope 1100 CommScope Pl SE Hickory NC 28603*

DRENGLER, WILLIAM ALLAN JOHN, lawyer; b. Shawano, Wis., Nov. 18, 1949; s. William J. and Vera J. (Simmonds) D.; m. Kathleen A. Hintz, June 18, 1983; children: Ryan, Jeffrey, Brittany. BA, Am. U., 1972; JD, Marquette U., 1976. Bar: Wis. 1976, U.S. Dist. Ct. (ea. and we. dists.) Wis. 1976. Assoc. Herrling, Swain & Drengler, Appleton, Wis., 1976-78; dist. atty. Outagamie County, Appleton, 1979-81; corp. counsel Marathon County, Wausau, Wis., 1981-96, Drengler Law Firm, Wausau, Wis., 1997—. Vice chmn. Wis. Equal Rights Coun., 1978—83, Wis. Coun. Criminal Justice, Madison, 1983—87, Wis. State Pub. Defender Bd., 2006—. Nat. pres. Future Bus. Leaders Am., 1967—68; chmn. local Selective Svc. Bd., Wausau, 1982—89; mem. adv. bd. Wausau Salvation Army, 1986—, chair, 2006—; judge advocate officer Wis. Army NG, 1989—96; mem. Troop 453 com. Samoset coun. Boy Scouts Am., 2000—07; mem. nat. Dem. del., 1974—76; del. Wis. Dem., Madison State Conv., 1972—, conv. co-chair, 1980, conv. parliamentarian, 1986—; mem. adminstrv. com. Wis. Dems., Madison, 1977—81, 1986—88; bd. dirs.

Wausau Youth/Little League Baseball, 1988—, team mgr., 1994—2002. Mem.: KC, ABA (chair com. on govt. lawyers, sect. state and local govt. 1991—93, bylaws com. govt. and pub. sect. lawyers divsn. 1993—98), State Bar Wis. (govt. lawyers divsn., bd. dirs. 1982—86, sec. 1986—87, professionalism com. 1987—91, prse. 1989—91, professionalism com. 1992—2000, solo and small firm practice com. 2001—06, bench bar com. 2006—), Nat. Assn. Counties (bd. dirs. 1991—92, taxation and fin. steering com. 1991—93, justice and pub. safety steering com. 1993—94, deferred compensation adv. com. 1993—95), Nat. Assn. County Civil Attys. (dir. 1986—88, v.p. 1988—91, pres. 1991—92), Kiwanis Internat. Found. (Hixon Fellowship award 2001), Kiwanis (lt. gov. 1985—86, club pres. 1989—90, chair past lt. govs. coun. 1990—91), Wausau Elks (parliamentarian 2000—03, 2007—). Roman Catholic. Avocations: baseball, camping, fishing, tennis, golf. Office: 609 Scott St PO Box 5152 Wausau WI 54402-5152

DRENNAN, JOSEPH PETER, lawyer; b. Albany, NY, Apr. 15, 1956; s. Richard Peter and Ann Marie (Conlon) D.; m. Adriana Sonia Miramontes, Sept. 26, 1987; children: Patricia Solange, Monica Adriana, Michael Robert II. BA in Polit. Sci., U. Richmond, 1978; JD, Cath. U. of Am., Washington, 1981. Bar: DC 1981, US Dist. Ct. DC 1983, US Ct. Appeals (fed. cir.) 1983, Va. 1984, US Ct. Appeals (D.C. cir.) 1984, US Dist. Ct. (ea. dist.) Va. 1987, US Ct. Appeals (4th cir.) 1987, US Dist. Ct. Md. 1990, US Bankruptcy Ct. (ea. dist.) Va. 1991. Pvt. practice, Washington/Alexandria, Va., 1981—. Adj. faculty mem. Germanna C.C., Fredericksburg, Va., 1995-2000; adj. faculty mem. U. Balt., 2007-. Mem. Am. Assn. for Justice, Nat. Assn. Criminal Defense Attys., Nat. Legal Aid & Def. Assn., Bar Assn. DC, Am. Bankruptcy Inst., Alexandria Bar Assn., Va. Trial Lawyers Assn., Trial Lawyers Met. Washington. Democrat. Roman Catholic. Address: 218 N Lee St Fl 3 Alexandria VA 22314-2631 Home Phone: 540-786-6338; Office Phone: 703-519-3773. Personal E-mail: joseph@josephpeterdrennan.co.

DRENNAN, ROBERT D., archeology educator, researcher; b. Lexington, Ky., Oct. 15, 1947; s. Robert M. and Ruth (Dickerson) D.; m. Jeanne Ferrary, May 3, 1974; 1 child, Margaret. BA in Art and Archeology, Princeton U., 1969; MA in Anthropology, U. Mich., 1970, PhD in Anthropology, 1975. Curator R.S. Peabody Found. Archeology, Andover, Mass., 1974-77; asst. prof. dept. anthropology U. Pitts., 1977-81, assoc. prof. dept. anthropology, 1981-87, prof. dept. anthropology, 1987—2005, disting. prof. dept. anthropology, 2006—, chair dept. anthropology, 1996—99, 2000—03, faculty assoc. Ctr. Latin Am. Studies, 1977—, interim dir. Ctr. Latin Am. Studies, 1992-93, dir. Latin Am. Archeology Publs., 1988—. Assoc. rsch. scientist Mus. Anthropology U. Mich., Ann Arbor, 1976-80; adj. prof. dept. anthropology U. Nat. Colombia, Bogotá, 1988-89; vis. prof. dept. anthropology U. Los Andes, Bogotá, 1983—2000; rsch. assoc. sect. anthropology Carnegie Mus. Natural History, Pitts., 1978—; organizer, participant in archeol. meetings, confs.; presenter, rschr. in field. Author: Statistics for Archeologists: A Commonsense Approach, 1996, Las Sociedades Prehispanicas del Alto Magdalena, 2000; contbr. articles to profl. jours. Fellow AAAS; mem. NAS, Am. Anthropol. Assn. (exec. com. archeology sect., program editor 1986-88), Soc. Am. Archeology (editl. adv. com. Lat. Am. Antiquity 1989-93, mem. editl. bd. 1996—; chair task force Lat. Am. 1993-95; com. on Ams. 1997—, chair 1995-97). Office: U Pittsburgh Dept Anthropology Pittsburgh PA 15260 Business E-Mail: drennan@pitt.edu.

DRENNEN, WILLIAM MILLER, JR., cultural organization administrator, film producer, writer; b. Charleston, W.Va., Nov. 5, 1942; s. William Miller and Margaret (Morton) D.; m. Sarah Polk Wilson, Nov. 27, 1969; children: Zachary Polk, Samuel Boyd. BArch., Yale U., 1964; postgrad., George Washington U., 1977, U. Charleston, 1978, W.Va. Grad. Coll., 1989-92, MA in Humanities, 1993. Freelance writer, film maker, 1967-69; v.p. Communication Corps, Inc., Washington, 1969-79; pres. Briar Mountain Coal and Coke Co., Charleston, 1980-89; founder, pres. Max Media, Inc., Charleston, 1984-89; commr. W.Va. Culture and History Div., 1989—97; instr. history W.Va. State Coll., 1997—2001; freelance writer, prodr., cons., 2001—. Mng. gen. ptnr. C&D Enterprises, 1979—; pres. Cox Morton Co., 1980-89; past pres., founder W.Va. Internat. Film Festival, Charleston, 1986-89; owner, sec., real estate agt. Greg Didden Assocs., Shepherdstown, W.Va., 2003-. Author: One Kanawha Valley Bank, 2002, Red, White, Black, and Blue: A Dual Memoir of Race and Class in Appalachia, 2004; cameraman (film) Evolving Environment, 1972 (Cine Golden Eagle award); editor (film) River of Life, 1975 (U.S. Film Festival award); patentee computerized optical system. Founder, pres. W.Va. Youth Soccer Assn., 1979-84; bd. dirs. Sunrise Mus., Charleston, 1983-86, Renaissance Com., Charleston, 1984-89, Jefferson Co. Hist. Soc., 2002—. Contemporary Am. Theatre Festival, 2002—; mem. Pare Lorentz award panel Internat. Documentary Assn.; trustee U. Charleston, 1985-89; founder W.Va. Assn. Mus., 1990; v.p., sec. W.Va. History Film Project, Inc., 1991-97. Served in USN, 1964-67. Decorated Bronze Star; recipient 2 Cine Eagle awards, cert. Excellence for documentary film work, award Hist. Landmarks Commn. Kanawha County, Tele award, 1997. Mem. Film Arts Guild W.Va. (pres. 1981-87), Orgn. Am. Historians, Am. Hist. Assn., W.V. Hist. Soc., Shepherdstown Rotary, Cress Creek Golf and Country Club. Democrat. Episcopalian. Avocations: tennis, golf, mountain biking, jogging. Office Phone: 304-876-6400. Personal E-mail: bill@billdrennen.com. Business E-Mail: bill@gregdidden.com.

DRENTLICHER, DAVID, lawyer, educator, physician; b. Washington, May 2, 1955; s. Herman Israel and Jeanette Adah (Levin) O. BA in Economics, Brandeis U., 1977; MD, Harvard U., 1981, JD, 1986. Bar: D.C. 1988, Ill. 1993, Ind. 1999. Med. intern U. Mich. Med. Ctr., Ann Arbor, 1981-82; pvt. practice Detroit, 1982-83; law clk. U.S. Ct. Appeals, Baton Rouge, 1986-87; assoc. Sidley & Austin, Washington, 1987-89; ethics and health policy counsel AMA, Chgo., 1989-95; Samuel R. Rosen prof. law Ind. U. Sch. Law, Indpls., co-dir. Ctr. for Law and Health, 1995—. Lectr. in law U. Chgo. Law Sch., 1993-95; adj. asst. prof. medicine Northwestern U. Med. Sch., Chgo., 1992-95; vis. DeCamp prof. bioethics Princeton U., 1997-98; state rep. Ind. Gen. Assembly, 2002—. Contbr. articles to profl. jours. Mem. ABA, Am. Soc. Law, Medicine and Ethics. Avocations: cajun dancing, racquet sports. Office: Ind U Sch Law 530 W New York St Indianapolis IN 46202-3225 Office Phone: 317-274-4993. E-mail: dorentli@iupui.edu.

DREPAUL, LORIS OMESH, internist, infectious diseases physician; b. Georgetown, Guyana, Feb. 6, 1960; naturalized U.S. citizen; s. Frank Eric and Iris Ismay Etwaria (Masih-Das) D. BA in Philosophy with honors, CUNY, 1985, BS in Biology magna cum laude; MD, NYU, 1989. Lic. NYS, 1994. Intern in internal medicine St. Luke's Hosp.-Columbia U. Coll. Physicians and Surgeons, NYC, 1989-90, jr. resident in internal medicine, 1990—91; sr. resident in internal medicine Booth Meml. Med. Ctr.-NYU Sch. Medicine, Queens, 1991-92; fellow in infectious diseases Bronx VA Med. Ctr.-Mt. Sinai Sch. Medicine, NY, 1992-94, asst. coord. phys. diagnosis course, 1994; attending in infectious diseases Mary Immaculate Hosp. Queens, Cath. Med. Ctr.-Albert Einstein Coll. Medicine, Bronx, 1995-96; faculty, attending in infectious diseases Highland Hosp., Rochester, NY, 1997-98; pvt. practice Rochester, NY, 1997—98, 2007—. Founder HIV/AIDS Bilingual Primary Care Outreach Program, Bridge Plaza Rehab. Clinic, Queens, N.Y., 1995-96; med. dir. Cmty. Health Network, Inc., Rochester, 1997-98. Mem. AMA, ACP, Med. Soc. State N.Y., Med. Res. Corps N.Y.C., Phi Beta Kappa. Avocations: music, bridge, chess, soccer, computers. Home: 952 E 214th St Bronx NY 10469 Business E-Mail: drepaul@pol.net.

DRESANG, ELIZA T., library and information scientist; BA summa cum laude, Emory U., 1963; MLS with high distinction, UCLA, 1966; PhD, U. Wis.-Madison, 1981. Children's libr. LA Pub. Libr., Encino-Tarzana Br., 1966—67, Atlanta Pub. Libr., Ida Williams Br., 1967—68; sch. libr. media specialist Lapham Elementary Sch., Madison, Wis., 1974—78; lectr. U. Wis.-Madison, 1978—80, adj. asst. prof., 1981—88, adj. assoc. prof., 1989—96; dir. libr. media, tech. & communication Madison Met. Sch. Dist., Wis., 1980—96, asst. to supt. of schools, 1987—96; learning resource coord. Fla. State U. Sch. Info Studies, Tallahassee, 1996—98, assoc. prof., 1996—2002, prof., 2002—, Eliza Atkins Gleason prof., 2004—. Adv. bd. Voice of Youth Advocates, 1999—, Studies in Media & Info. Literacy Edn., 2000—, New Advocate, 2000—02, Sch. Libr. Media Rsch., 2000—; mem. adv. com. Laura Bush Found. for Am.'s Librs., 2002—; bd. dirs. Libr. Quarterly, 2003—. Author: The Land & People of Zambia, 1975 (Outstanding Trade Book in Social Sciences, Nat. Coun. Social Studies & Children's Book Coun., 1976), Radical Change: Books for Youth in a Digital Age, 1999 (Profl. Book of Yr., Voice of Youth Adv. Jour., 1999); co-author: School Censorship in the 21st Century: A Guide for Teachers & School Library Media Specialists, 2001; contbr. articles, chapters to books. Bd. trustees Freedom to Read Found., 2002—04; mem. Jane Addams Children's Book Award com. Women's Internat. League for Peace & Justice: Jane Addams Peace Assn., 2000—. Recipient Wis. Sch. Libr. of Yr. award, Wis. Libr. Assn., 1978, Humanitarian Svc. award, Madison Met. Sch. Dist., 1983, Disting. Svc. award, 1989, Judy A. Harris award, Madison Met. Sch. Dist. Bd. Edn., 1996, Alumna of Yr., U. Wis.-Madison Sch. Libr. & Info Studies, 2001, Outstanding Faculty Mem. of Yr., Fla. State U. Sch. Info. Studies, 2001; fellow, U. Wis.-Madison, 1978—80. Mem.: ALA (Accreditation com. 1988—89, councilor 1991—95, Status of Women in Librarianship com. 1996—98, councilor 1996—2000, Orgn. com. 1999—2001, Scholastic Libr. Pub. award 2007), Wis. Women Libr. Workers, Wis. Ednl. Media Assn., N.E. Modern Lang. Assn., Fla. Libr. Assn., Fla. Ednl. Media Assn., Am. Computing Machinery, US Book Bd. for Youth (chair Bridges to Understanding com. 1994—98), Assn. Libr. & Info. Sci. Edn. (Awards & Honors com. 1999—2001), Internat. Children's Literature Assn. (Article awards com. 2000—03), Young Adult Libr. Svcs. Assn. (Margaret A. Edwards award com. 2005—07), Am. Assn. Sch. Librs. (chair Nat. Sch. Libr. Media Program of Yr. award com. 1985—88, Awards com. 1988—90), Assn. Libr. Svc. to Children (chair Svc. to Children with Spl. Needs com. 1980—87, Newbery award com. 1982—83, Notable Children's Books Revisited com. 1984—86, bd. dirs. 1984—88, chair Batchelder award com. 1988—89, Caldecott award com. 1990—91, priority cons. 1990—96, bd. dirs. 1996—2000, exec. com. 1996—2000, bd. liason to Children & Tech. com. 1997—98, chair Pura Belpré Latino Literature award com. 2000—02, chair Newbery award com. 2003—04, chair R&D com. 2005—07), Beta Phi Mu, Phi Beta Kappa, Phi Eta Sigma. Office: Fla State U Sch Info Studies 101 Louis Shores Bldg Tallahassee FL 32306-2100 Office Phone: 850-644-5877. Office Fax: 850-644-9763. E-mail: edresang@ci.fsu.edu.

DRESCHER, DENNIS GEORGE, biochemist, researcher; s. George Gustave and Lillian Frances (Wendlandt) Drescher; m. Marian Jean Partridge, Feb. 1, 1969; children: David Alan, Andrew Jeremy. BS, U. Wis., 1963, MusM, 1964, PhD, 1971; postgrad studies, Harvard U., 1964—66. Rsch. assoc. Ctrl. Inst. for the Deaf, St. Louis, 1971-74; sr. staff fellow NIH, Bethesda, Md., 1974-78; prof. Wayne State U., Detroit, 1978—, dir. molecular rsch. Sch. Medicine, 1978—, chmn. Neurosci. Program. Mem. comm. disorders rev. com. NIH, Bethesda, 1987—90, hearing rsch. study sect., 1996—99, mem. ad hoc rev. coms., 2000—, mem. auditory study sect., 2006, 07; mem. grant rev. bd. New Zealand Health Rsch. Coun., 1993—. Author: (book) Auditory Biochemistry, 1985; mem. editl. bd.: Hearing Rsch. Jour., 1989—, mem. guest rev. bd.: Jour. Brain Rsch., 1990—. Recipient Senator Jacob K. Javits Neuroscience Investigator award, NIH, 1986—90, Claude Pepper award, Nat. Inst. on Deafness and Other Comm. Disorders, NIH, 1990—94, Intergovernmental Pers. Act award, NIH, 1990—91, Faculty Recognition award, Wayne State U. Bd. Govs., 1987; grantee Rsch. grant, NIH, 1980—; Internat. Symposium on Auditory Biochemistry Conf. grant, 1984—86. Mem.: Assn. Rsch. in Otolaryngology, Acoustical Soc. Am., Soc. Neurosci., Am. Soc. Neurochemistry, Am. Soc. Biol. Chemists. Achievements include first to purify an inner-ear enzyme; research in inner-ear calcium channels. Avocations: piano, music composition. Home: 461 University Pl Grosse Pointe MI 48230-1637 Office: Wayne State U Sch of Medicine 540 E Canfield St Detroit MI 48201-1928 Business E-Mail: ddresche@med.wayne.edu.

DRESCHER, FRAN, actress; b. Flushing, NY, Sept. 30, 1957; d. Mort and Sylvia D.; m. Peter Marc Jacobson, 1978. Co-creator, writer, prodr., actress in TV series The Nanny, 1993-99; appeared in feature films: Saturday Night Fever, 1977, American Hot Wax, 1978 (Five-Minute Oscar award Esquire mag.), Gorp, 1980, The Hollywood Knights, 1980, Ragtime, 1981, Young Lust, 1981, Dr. Detroit, 1983, This Is Spinal Tap, 1984, The Rosebud Beach Hotel, 1984, UHF, 1989, The Big Picture, 1989, It had to be You, 1989, Cadillac Man, 1990, Wedding Band, 1990, We're Talking Serious Money, 1992, Jack, 1996, Car 54, Where Are You:, 1996, The Beautician and the Beast, 1997 (also exec. prodr.), Picking Up the Pieces, 2000, Kid Quick, 2000; starred in TV series Charmed Lives, 1986, Princesses, 1991, Good Morning Miami, 2003-04; (TV film) Stranger in Our House, 1978, Rock 'n' Roll Mom, 1988, Love and Betrayal, 1989, What's Alan Watching?, 1989, Terror in the Towers, 1993, Beautiful Girl, 2003; actress, exec. prodr. (TV series) Living with Fran, 2005-; guest appearances on TV programs Civil Wars, Alf, Night Court, Nine to Five, Fame, The Tracy Ullman Show; Spokesperson: Old Navy; Author: Enter Whining, 1995, Cancer Schmancer, 2002; (theatre) Some Girl(s), 2006. Recipient Spirit of Life award, City of Hope Cancer Ctr., 2006. Office: Gersh Agy Inc 232 N Canon Dr Beverly Hills CA 90210-5302

DRESCHER, JOHN WEBB, lawyer; b. Norfolk, Va., May 13, 1948; s. Otto Charles and Anne Best (Webb) D. BA, Hampden-Sydney Coll., 1970; JD, U. Richmond, 1973. Bar: Va. 1973, US Supreme Ct. 1980, US Ct. Appeals (4th cir.) 1985, US Dist. Ct. (ea. dist.) Va. 1976. Assoc. Brydges, Hammers & Hudgins, Virginia Beach, 1973-74; asst. atty. Office of Commonwealth Atty., Virginia Beach, 1974-75; assoc. Pickett, Spain & Lyle, P.C., Virginia Beach, 1976-78; ptnr. Pickett, Lyle, Siegel, Drescher & Croshaw P.C., Virginia Beach, 1979-87, Breit, Drescher & Imprevento P.C., Norfolk, 1988—. Trustee Hampden-Sydney Coll., 2003—. Named one of Best Lawyers in Am., Naifch & Smith, 1995—, Top Ten Lawyers in Va., Super Lawyers, 2006. Fellow Am. Bd. Trial Advocates; mem. ATLA, Va. Trial Lawyers Assn. (bd. govs. 1990—), Am. Inns Ct., Norfolk-Portsmouth Bar Assn., Hampden-Sydney Coll. Alumni Assn. (pres. 1990), U. Richmond Law Sch. Alumni Assn., Virginia Beach Bar Assn. (pres. 1990). Democrat. Episcopalian. Avocations: physical fitness, golf. Office: Breit Drescher & Imprevento 1000 Dominion Twr 999 Waterside Dr Ste 1000 Norfolk VA 23510-3304 Office Phone: 757-622-6000. Business E-Mail: jdrescher@breitdrescher.com.

DRESCHER, JUDITH ALTMAN, library director; b. Greensburg, Pa., July 6, 1946; d. Joseph Grier and Sarah Margaret (Hewitt) Altman; m. Robert A. Drescher, Aug. 10, 1968 (div. 1980); m. David G. Lindstrom, Jan. 10, 1981. AB, Grove City Coll., 1968; MLS, U. Pitts., 1971. Tchr. Hempfield Sch. Dist., Greensburg, 1968—71; children's libr. Cin. Pub. Libr., 1971—72, br. mgr., 1972—74; dir. Rolling Meadows Pub. Libr., Ill., 1974—79, Champaign Pub. Libr., Ill., 1979—85; dir. librs. Memphis Pub. Libr. and Info. Ctr., 1985—. Tenn. del. White House Conf. on Librs. and Info. Svcs. Task Force, 1991-92; mem. Tenn. Sec. of State's Commn. on Tech. and Resource Sharing, 1991, 93, steering com. Tenn. Info. and Infrastructure, 1994-97, nat. adv. panel for assessment of role of sch. and pub. librs. US Dept. Edn., 1995-98. Commn. on 21st century Rhodes Coll., Memphis, 1986-88, presdl. adv. com., 1992-2000; active Leadership Memphis, 1987—, selection com., 1992-96; active Memphis Arts Coun., 1989-94; bd. dirs. Literacy Coun., 1986-91, Memphis NCCJ, 1989-93, Memphis Grants Info. Ctr., 1992-97, sec., 1993-95; bd. dirs. Memphis Literacy Found., 1988-92, v.p., 1989-90; bd. dirs. Goals for Memphis, 1988-93, chair edn. com., 1989-91, chair nominating com., 1992, leadership acad., 1999—; bd. dirs. U. Memphis Soc., 1998-2004; bd. mem. Cmty. Svcs. Agy., 2000-05, fin. com., 2002, bd. dirs., 2002-05, v.p., 2003-05; exec. adv. bd. Children's Mus., 1988-94, exec. adv. coun. U. Memphis, 1989-99; allocations subcommittee United Way, 1989-91, allocations com. Memphis Arts Coun., 100 for the Arts, 1989-91, Libr. Self-study Com. U. Memphis; pres. adv. coun. Lemoyne Coll.; search com. for dean librs. U. Memphis, 1999-2001; adv. com. Memphis Symphony Orch., 2003—; v.p. Tennshare, 2004-05, pres., 2005—; bd. mem., treas. Mid South Reads, 2004-06, mem. bd. govs., 2006—. Paul Harris fellow Rotary, Memphis, 2002; recipient Govt. Leader award U. Ill. YWCA, 1981, Communicator of Yr. award Pub. Rels. Soc. Am., 1992, Humanitarian award NCCJ, Memphis, 2003, Charlie Robinson award Pub. Libr. Assn., 2003; named Libr. Coun. Libr. of Yr., 2002. Mem.: ALA (chmn. intellectual freedom com. 1985—87, mem. coun. 1992—99, mem. nominating com. 2001—02), Assn. Pub. Adminstrs. (midsouth chpt., Adminstr. of Yr. 2002), Pub. Libr. Assn. (v.p., pres. 1994—95), Memphis Libr. Coun., Urban Librs. Coun., Tenn. Libr. Assn., Rotary (bd. dirs. 1992—94, sec. 1993—94, chair membership devel. com. 1994—95, bd. dirs. 2004—06), Beta Phi Mu. Office: Memphis Pub Libr & Info Ctr 3030 Poplar Ave Memphis TN 38111-3527 Office Phone: 901-415-2748.*

DRESCHER, SEYMOUR, historian, educator, writer; b. NYC, Feb. 20, 1934; s. Sidney and Eva Rita (Levine) D.; m. Ruth Lieberman, June 19, 1955; children: Michael, Jonathan, Karen. BA, CCNY, 1955; MS, U. Wis., 1956, PhD, 1960. Instr. history Harvard U., 1960—62; asst. prof. U. Pitts., 1962—65, assoc. prof., 1965—69, prof., 1969—86, Univ. prof., 1986—, chmn., 1980—83; acad. dean. semester-at-sea, 1998, 2002. Vis. disting. prof. CUNY, 1987; Roger T. Anstey Meml. lectr., Canterbury, Eng., 1984; bd. advisors Slavery and Abolition, 1985—; George A. Miller lectr., 1987, Pa. Commonwealth Speakers Program, 1989-91, rsch. fellow Univ. Ctr. Internat. Studies, Pitts., 1992, 2000, Elsa Goveia lectr., 2006, Embry-Riddle lectr., 2006; C-SPAN adv. com., Tocqueville. Author: Toqueville and England, 1964, Dilemmas of Democracy, 1968, Econocide, 1977, Capitalism and Antislavery, 1986, From Slavery to Freedom, 1999, The Mighty Experiment: Free Labor versus Slavery in British Emancipation, 2002 (Frederick Douglass Book prize 2004); co-author: The Abolition of Slavery and the Aftermath of Emancipation in Brazil, 1988; editor Jour. Contemporary History, 1991-99; editor: Tocqueville and Beaumont on Social Reform, 1968, Anti-Slavery, Religion and Reform, 1980, Political Symbolism in Modern Europe, 1982, The Meaning of Freedom, 1992, A Historical Guide to World Slavery, 1998, Slavery, 2001, Tocqueville's Memoir on Pauperism, 1997; contbr.: Fifty Years Later: Antislavery, Capitalism and Modernity in the Dutch Orbit, 1995, Is the Holocaust Unique?, 1996, Jews and the Expansion of Europe to the West, 2001, Freemasonry on both sides of the Atlantic, 2002, Slavery in the Development of the Americas, 2004, The Chattel Principle, 2004, The Cambridge Companion to Tocqueville, 2006, Profiles of Revolutionaries in Atlantic History, 2007, Women's Rights and Transatlantic Antislavery in the Era of Emancipation, 2007, The British Slave Trade: Abolition, Parliament and People, 2007; creator film: Confrontation, Paris, 1968, 70. Recipient Pres.'s Rsch. award U. Pitts., 1992; Fulbright scholar, 1957-58; NEH fellow, 1973-74, Guggenheim Found. fellow, 1977-78, Resident fellow Bellagio Ctr. for Scholars, 1980, 90, Woodrow Wilson fellow, 1983-84, sec. European program Wilson Ctr., 1984-85. Mem. Am. Hist. Assn., Hist. Soc., Soc. for French Hist. Studies (v.p. 1978-79), N.Am. Conf. on Brit. Studies, Dutch Royal Inst. Linguistics and Anthropology, Fulbright Assn., Commn. Tocqueville (France). Home: 5550 Pocusset St Pittsburgh PA 15217-1913 Office: U Pitts Dept History Pittsburgh PA 15260 Office Phone: 412-648-7451. E-mail: syd@pitt.edu.

DRESCHHOFF, GISELA AUGUSTE MARIE, physicist, researcher; b. Moenchengladbach, Germany, Sept. 13, 1938; came to U.S., 1967, naturalized, 1976; d. Gustav Julius and Hildegard Friederike (Krug) D. PhD, Tech. U. Braunschweig, Germany, 1972. Staff scientist Fed. Inst. Physics and Tech. Ger., 1965-67; rsch. assoc. Kans. Geol. Survey, Lawrence, 1971-72; vis. asst. prof. physics U. Kans., 1972-74; dep. dir. radiation physics lab. Space Tech. Ctr., 1972-78, assoc. dir., 1979-84, co-dir., 1984-86, dir., 1996—; sr. sci. geology U. Kans., 1991, adj. assoc. prof. physics and astronomy, 1992. Assoc. program mgr. NSF, Washington, 1978-79. Patentee identification markings for gemstones and method of making selective conductive regions in diamond layers. Named to Women's Hall of Fame, U. Kans., 1978; recipient Antarctic Service medal U.S.A., 1979; recipient NASA Group Achievement award, 1983; named mountain Dreschhoff Peak, Antarctica, 1997. Fellow Explorers Club; mem. AAAS, Am. Phys. Soc., Am. Geophys. Union, Am. Polar Soc. (pres. 2000-03), Antarctican Soc., Sigma Xi. Achievements include naming of Dreschhoff Peak, Antarctica by U.S. Board of Geographic Names, 1997. Home: 2908 W 19th St Lawrence KS 66047-2301 Office: U Kans Dept Physics & Astronomy Lawrence KS 66045-7541 Business E-Mail: giselad@ku.edu.

DRESDEN, JACOB A., headmaster; b. Netherlands; m. Patricia Markle BA in Polit. Sci., MA in Internat. Polit., U. Penn. Various teaching & administrative positions including asst. headmaster William Penn Charter Sch., Phila., 1969—91; various teaching & administrative positions Abington Friends Sch.; head of sch. Collegiate Sch., NYC, 1991—99, Concord Acad., Concord, Mass., 2000—. Former teacher Columbia's Klingenstein Ctr. for Independent Edu. Mem.: Nat. Assn. of Principals of Schools for Girls. Office: Concord Acad 166 Main St Concord MA 01742 Office Phone: 978-402-2200. Office Fax: 978-402-2210.*

DRESKIN, JEANET STECKLER, painter, medical artist, educator; b. New Orleans, Sept. 29, 1921; d. William Steckler and Beate Bertha (Burgas) Steckler Gureasko; m. E. Arthur Dreskin, May 9, 1943; children: Richard Burgas, Stephen Charles, Jeanet Dreskin Haig, Rena Dreskin Schoenberg. BFA, Newcomb Coll., 1942; grad. in med. art, Johns Hopkins U., Balt., 1943; MFA, Clemson U., SC, 1973; postgrad., Art Students League, NYC, 1946, Art Inst. Chgo., 1946. Cert. med. illustrator. Staff artist Am. Mus. Natural History, NYC, 1943—45, U. Chgo. Med. Sch., 1945—50; mem. faculty Mus. Sch. Art, Greenville, SC, 1950—, dir., 1968—75; adj. prof. art U. SC at Mus. Sch. Art, 1973—. Mem. faculty Gov.'s Sch. for Arts, Greenville, 1980—; condr. workshops, lectr. in art edn., 1970—2005; mem. arts adv. bd. S.C. State Mus., Columbia, 1984—90; bd. dirs. S.C. Arts Found., 1999—2002; workshop leader art dept. U. Ga., 1985; rep. by Hampton III, Taylors, SC. Exhibited in group shows at Butler Inst. Am. Art, Youngstown, Ohio, 1974, 1983, Chatauqua exhbn. Am. Art, NY, 1970, Nat. Mus. Illustrators, NYC, 1986, Represented in permanent collections Smithsonian Nat. Mus. Am. Art, Washington, DC, SC State Art Collection, Columbia, Ga. Mus. Art, Athens, Greenville County Mus., Guild Hall Mus., East Hampton, N.Y., Gibbes Mus., Charleston, SC, Columbia Mus. Art, Tex. Fine Art Assn., Sunrise Valley Mus., Charleston, W.Va., Beaufort Mus., SC, Kate Shipworth Mus. at U. Miss., McDonald Corp. Coll., Chgo., N.C. Nat. Bank Coll., Asheville Mus. Art, NC, Fed. Res. Bank, Richmond, Va., C & S Collection, Columbia, SC, U. Ala. Mus., Zimmerli Art Mus. (NAWA), Rutgers U., New Brunswick, N.J., Wachovia Bank, SC, NC, exhibitions include Nat. Print and Drawing, Clemson U., 1987—89, 1993, 9th Internat. Grand Prix, Cannes, France, 1973, Mid-Am. Arts Alliance, Emporia, Kans., 1989—91, 1993—94, Broome St. Gallery, NYC, 1995—96, 2000—05, Am. Contemporary Artists, 1994, S.C. State Mus., Columbia, 100 years, 100 artists invitational, 2000, Greenville County Mus. of Art, 2005, others; contbr. med. drawings Anatomy of the Gorilla, 1950, med. drawings Surgery of Repair, 1950, med. drawings Williams Obstetrics, 1959, med. drawings Surgical Anatomy, 1990. Mem. Cmty. Found. Greenville, 1968—84, chmn. project coms., 1968—76; historian, hon. mem. Rose Ball, Greenville, 1972—; mem. Commn. on Future Clemson U.; bd. dirs. Charity Ball, Greenville, 1971—, SC Arts Found. Recipient Kaplan award, Nat. Assn. Painters in Casein, 1969, 1971, Keenan award, Am. Contemporary Exhbn., Palm Beach, Fla., 1970, Merit award, Internat. Grand Prix, Cannes, 1973, Govs. award for the Arts, Lifetime Achievement, Verner, 2004. Mem.: So. Watercolor Soc. (Mabry award 1981, 1985, 1988, 1997, 2001, 2006), Greenville Artists Guild, Am. Contemporary Artists NYC, Nat. Assn. Med. Illustrators, Nat. Assn. Women Artists (S.C. membership chmn. 1970—), SC Watercolor Soc. (pres. 1983—84, bd. dirs. 1985—, awards 1976—2006), Guild SC Artists (pres. 1970—71, bd. dirs. 1981—86, pres. 1956—58, 1963, bd. dirs. 1954—83, numerous awards), So. Graphics Coun. (hon.; v.p. 1981 1983, treas. 1988—, invitational exhibits 1975—77, 1988). Avocation: sailing. Home: 60 Lake Forest Dr Greenville SC 29609-5038 Personal E-mail: jeanet@dreskin.net.

DRESKIN, STEPHEN CHARLES, immunologist, allergist; b. Chgo., Aug. 11, 1949; s. E. Arthur and Jeanet (Steckler) D.; m. June Inuzuka, May 8, 1982; children: Andrea T., Samuel M., Lauren F. BA, U. Pa., 1971; PhD, Emory U., 1975, MD, 1977. Diplomate allergy and clin. immunology and diagnostic lab. immunology Am. Bd. Internal Medicine. Intern U. Calif., Davis, 1977-78, resident, 1978-80; med. staff fellow NIH, Bethesda, Md., 1981-85, guest rschr., 1985-87, expert, 1987-88; asst. prof. dept. medicine U. Colo. Health Scis. Ctr., Denver, 1989—96, assoc. prof. dept. medicine, 1996—2004, prof. dept. medicine, 2004—. Contbr. articles to profl. jours. Recipient investigator award Arthritis Found., 1985-88, developing investigator award Bouroughs Wellcome Found., 1990-1994; rsch. grantee NIH, 1991-95, 2003—. Mem. AAAS, Am. Acad. Allergy and Immunology, Am. Fedn. Clin. Investigation, Western Soc. for Clin. Investigation, Clin. Immunology Soc. Avocations: tennis, bridge.

DRESNER, BYRON, lawyer; b. NYC, Nov. 13, 1927; s. Leo and Minnie (Plisner) Dresner; m. Irene Helen Dresner, Nov. 18, 1956; children: Lisa, Cheryl, Andrea. BS, City. Coll. N.Y., 1949; LLB, NYU, 1951. Bar: N.Y. 1952, U.S. Supreme Ct. 1961, U.S. Ct. Appeals (2d cir.), U.S. Dist. Ct. (no., so., ea. dists.), N.Y. Assoc. Alexander Rockmore, NYC, 1952—57; ptnr. Kronish, Dresner & Henle, NYC, 1957—66, Dresner & Henle, NYC, 1966—2004, Dresner & Dresner, NYC, 2005—. Spl. master N.Y. State Supreme Ct., 1977—. Chmn. Anti-Defamation League Young Adults, 1954—55; bd. dirs. YMHA-YWHA, Flushing, NY, 1979—91, v.p., 1990—91; treas. Maspeth Jewish Ctr., 1959—71; pres., co-pres. Flushing Jewish Ctr., 1971—2003; exec. v.p. Queens Jewish Cmty. Coun., 1981—84, pres., 1984—85, bd. trustees, 1985—; pres. Flushing Jewish Cmty. Coun., 1986—89, 1992—, v.p., 1991—92; co-pres. Flushing Fresh Meadows Jewish Ctr., 2003—. With AUS, 1946—47. Mem.: ABA, Comml. Law League Am., Brandeis Assn., N.Y. County Lawyers Assn., Bankruptcy Lawyers Bar Assn., B'nai B'rith, Camera. Home: 45-57 189th St Flushing NY 11358-3430 Office: 276 Fifth Ave # 1007 New York NY 10001 Home Phone: 718-445-2812; Office Phone: 212-679-6240. Personal E-mail: bdresner@nyc.rr.com. Business E-Mail: bdr@dresnerlaw.com.

DRESSEL, MARGARET JANE, artist, educator; b. Brookline, Mass., Aug. 25, 1949; d. Chauncey Lovett Megargle and Esther Laura Field; m. Richard Dressel; children: Bethany, Keith. Student, Moore Coll. Art, 1967—68, Nat. Acad. Art, 1985—86; Assoc. in Occupl. Studies, Pratt Inst., 1985. Owner, artist Peggy Dressel Studio, Oakland, NJ, 1990—; graphic designer Intra Design Inc., Ramsey, NJ, 1990—94; illustrator, asst. Jacqui Morgan Studio, NYC, 1986-90; painting instr. Ramsey Adult Sch., 1996—, Glen Rock (N.J.) Cmty. Sch., 1997—, Art Ctr. No. N.J., New Milford, 1999—2001, 2005—, Ridgewood Art Inst., 2002—. Founder Pastel Plus, N.J., pres., 1997—; mem. Blackwell St. Ctr. Arts; chmn. CAA Nat. Juried Exhbns., Ridgewood, N.J., 1993, 94, 95. One-woman show include St. Peter's Ch., N.Y.C., 1992, Blackwell St. Gallery , Dover, N.J., 1994, Lena DiGangi Gallery, West Paterson, N.J., 1994, Ringwood Manor W. Wing Gallery, N.J. State Pk., 1994, ADP, Inc. Gallery, Roseland, N.J., 1995, Dow Jones & Co., S. Brunswick, N.J., 1994, 96; N.Y. Theol. Sem., N.Y.C., 1998, The Interch. Ctr., N.Y.C., 1998, Kurth Coll. Ridgewood, N.J., 2002, Morristown Cmty. Theatre, 2005; represented in numerous juried exhbns. and pvt. collections; illustrator mags., children's books, brochures, ads, posters; featured artist poster and calendar N.J. Fine Artist Collection, 1998. Recording sec. Oakland Libr. Bd., 1979-80, pres., 1980-82. Recipient Purchase award Degas Pastel Soc., 1992, Merit award Degas Pastel Soc., 1992, Cynthia Goodgal Meml., Ridgewood Art Inst., Nat. Bergen Mus., 1997, others; named Best in Show, Inserria Corp., 1992, Bergen Mus. Music & Art Festival, 2002. Mem. Cmty. Arts Assn. (pres. 1994-96), Southea. Pastel Soc. (signature mem.), Oreg. Pastel Soc. (signature mem.), Am. Artist Profl. League, Degas Pastel Soc. Democrat. Methodist. Avocations: art, music, travel, gardening. Office: Peggy Dressel Studio 11 Rockaway Ave Oakland NJ 07436-2122 Office Phone: 201-337-2143. Personal E-mail: pegdartist@aol.com.

DRESSEL, MELANIE J., bank executive; m. Bob Dressel; children: Robb, Brent. BS in Polit. Sci., Univ. Wash. With Bank of Calif., 1974—78; dir. private banking Puget Sound Bank; sr. v.p., private banking Columbia Bank, Tacoma, 1993—97, exec. v.p. retail banking, 1997—2000, pres., 2000—; also CEO Columbia Banking System, Inc., Tacoma, 2003—. Chmn. Washington Bankers Assn. Bd. mem. Foss Waterway Devel.; chmn. Exec. Coun. Greater Tacoma; bd. mem. Washington Roundtable, Bellarmine Prep. Sch.; Mary Bridge Children's Found. Tacoma. Named one of 25 Most Powerful Women in Banking, US Banker, 2005, 2006. Office: Columbia Banking System Ste 800 1301 A St Tacoma WA 98402 Office Phone: 253-305-1900.*

DRESSELHAUS, MILDRED SPIEWAK, physics and engineering professor; b. Bklyn., Nov. 11, 1930; d. Meyer and Ethel (Teichteil) Spiewak; m. Gene F. Dresselhaus, Aug. 25, 1958; children: Marianne Dresselhaus Cooper, Carl Eric, Paul David, Eliot Michael. BA, Hunter Coll., 1951; DSc (hon.), CUNY, 1982, Hunter Coll., 1982; Fulbright fellow, Cambridge U., Eng., 1951—52; MA, Radcliffe Coll., 1953; PhD in Physics, U. Chgo., 1958; D Engring. (hon.), Worcester Poly. Inst., 1976; DSc (hon.), Smith Coll., 1980, Hunter Coll., 1982, N.J. Inst. Tech., 1984; DHC (hon.), U. Catholique de Louvain, 1988; DSc (hon.), Rutgers U., 1989, U. Conn., 1992, U. Mass., Boston, 1992, Princeton U., 1992; DEngring, Colo. Sch. Mines, 1993; D (hon.), Technion, Israel Inst. Tech., Haifa, 1994; DHC (hon.), Johannes Kepler U., Linz, Austria, 1993; DSc (hon.), Harvard U., 1995, Ohio State U., 1998; PhD (hon.), U. Paris, Sorbonne, 1999; DSc (hon.), Columbia U., 1999; DHC (hon.), Cath. U. Leuven, 2000; DSc (hon.), Northwestern U., 2003, Weizmann Inst., Rehovot, Israel, 2003, U. Mich., 2005, George Washington U., 2005, U. Pa., 2007, U. Ark., 2007. NSF postdoctoral fellow Cornell U., 1958—60; mem. staff Lincoln Lab., MIT, Lexington, 1960—67; prof. elec. engring. MIT, Cambridge, 1968—, assoc. dept. head elec. engring., 1972—74, Abby Rockefeller Mauze chair, 1973—85, dir. Ctr. for Materials Sci. and Engring., 1977—83, prof. physics, 1983—, Inst. prof., 1985—; dir. Office of Science, U.S. Dept. of Energy, Washington, 2000—01. Vis. prof. dept. physics U. Campinas, Brazil, 1971, Technion, Israel, 1972, 90, Nihon and Aoyama Gakuin Univs., Tokyo, 1973, IVIC, Caracas, Venezuela, 1977; vis. prof. dept. elec. engring. U. Calif., Berkeley, 1983; Graffin lectr. Am. Carbon Soc., 1982; chmn. steering com. on evaluation panels Nat. Bur. Stds., 1978—83; mem. Energy Rsch. Adv. Bd., 1984—90; bd. dirs. Rogers Corp. Contbr. articles to profl. jours. Mem. governing bd. NRC, 1984—87, 1989—90, 1992—96; trustee Calif. Inst. Tech., 1993—2000; overseer Harvard U., 1997—2000; chmn. bd. Am. Inst. Physics, 2003—; bd. govs. Argonne Nat. Lab., 1986—89, Weizmann Inst., Rehovot, Israel, 1999—2000, 2001—. Named to Hunter Coll. Hall of Fame, 1972, Women in Tech. Internat. Hall of Fame, 1998; recipient Alumnae medal, Radcliffe Coll., 1973, Killian Faculty Achievement award, 1986—87, Nat. medal of Sci., 1990, Sigri Great Lakes Carbon award, 1997, Profl. Achievement award, Hunter Coll., CUNY, 1998, Nicholson medal, 2000, Karl T. Compton medal, 2001, Weizmann Woman and Sci. Millennial Lifetime Achievement award, 2000, Nat. Materials Advancement award, Fedn. Materials Socs., 2000, Heinz Award for Tech., the Economy and Employment, 2005, Pender award, U. Pa., 2006, USA Laureate L'Oréal UNESCO For Women in Sci.-N.Am., 2007. Fellow: AAAS (bd. dirs. 1985—89, pres. 1997—98, chair bd. dirs. 1998—99), IEEE (Founders medal 2004), Am. Carbon Soc. (Achievement medal carbon sci. and tech. 2001), Am. Acad. Arts and Scis., Am. Phys. Soc. (pres. 1984); mem.: NAS (coun. 1987—90, chmn. engring. sect. 1987—90, chmn. class III 1990—93, coun. 1992—96, treas. 1992—96), Am. Philos. Soc., Brazilian Acad. Sci. (corr.), Ioffe Inst., Russian Acad. Scis. (hon.), Engring. Acad. Japan (fgn. assoc. 1993—), Soc. Women Engrs. (Achievement award 1977), Nat. Acad. Engring. (coun. 1981—87). Office: MIT 77 Massachusetts Ave Rm 13-3005 Dept Elec Engring Cambridge MA 02139

DRESSER, DAVID LELAND, municipal official; b. Balt., Nov. 4, 1938; s. James Leland and Elisabeth (Jenkins) Dresser; m. Judith Anderson Dresser, Aug. 16, 1997; 1 child, Sarah Catherine Meyers; m. Rohm (div.); children: Crescent Lynn, Cynthia Dawn, David Leland. BS in Sci. Edn., Cornell U., Ithaca, NY, 1960, MEd in Secondary Edn., 1966; PhD, Syracuse U., NY, 1971. Head resident Cornell U., Ithaca, 1960—61; tchr., coach Baldwinsville Acad., NY, 1964—67; asst. provost Syracuse U., 1970—73, asst. prof., 1970—73; v.p.; dean Eisenhower Coll., Seneca Falls, NY, 1973—79; dean, assoc. dean Rochester Inst. Tech., NY, 1979—83; assoc. dean, dean Ithaca Coll., 1984—2005; supr. Town Ovid, NY, 2005—. Author: (book) Eisenhower College: The Life and Death of a Living Memorial, 1995 (Legacy award, 2005). Lt. US Army, 1961—64, Vietnam. Decorated Air medal US Army, Vietnam; recipient Pres. award, Ithaca Coll., 1998. Mem.: Seneca County Bd. Suprs., Friends of Three Bears. Democrat. Presbyterian. Avocations: skiing, tennis, sailing, reading, gardening. Office: Town Ovid 7160 Main St Ovid NY 14521

DRESSER, JAMES VAN BENSCHOTEN, retired management consultant; b. NYC, Dec. 21, 1941; s. James van Benschoten and Elizabeth Jenks Dresser; m. Evan Crosby, Apr. 19, 1986. BA, Wesleyan U., Middletown, Conn., 1963; MA, Fletcher Sch. Law and Diplomacy, Medford, Mass., 1968; MBA, Harvard U., Cambridge, Mass., 1970. Chief adminstrv. officer, sr. v.p., cons. Boston Consulting Group, 1970—97. Bd. dirs. Merrimack Pharm., Cambridge, 1998—; chair Wesleyan U., 2005—. Selectman Town of Salisbury, Conn., 2005—. Capt. USAF, 1963—67, Japan and Vietnam. Avocations: reading, carpentry. Home: 1 E Main Box 286 Salisbury CT 06068

DRESSLER, ALAN MICHAEL, astronomer; b. Cin., Mar. 23, 1948; s. Charles and Gay (Stein) Dressler. BA in Physics, U. Calif., Berkeley, 1970; PhD in Astronomy, U. Calif., Santa Cruz, 1976. Carnegie Instn. of Washington fellow Hale Obs., Pasadena, Calif., 1976-78, Las Campanas fellow, 1978-81; sci. staff Carnegie Obs. (formerly Mt. Wilson and Las Campanas Obs., formerly Hale Obs.), Pasadena, 1981—, acting assoc. dir., 1988-89. Chair origins subcomS NASA, 2000—03. Contbr. to sci. jours. Recipient Pub. Svcs. medal NASA 1999. Fellow Am. Acad. Arts and Scis.; mem. NAS, Am. Astron. Soc. (councilor 1989-91, Pierce prize 1983), Internat. Astron. Union. Office: Carnegie Obs 813 Santa Barbara St Pasadena CA 91101-1232

DRESSLER, CHRISTY ANNA, elementary school educator; d. Glenn Thomas and Linda Carol (Hibbs) Dressler. BS in Edn., Shippensburg U. of Pa., 1993, MEd, 2002. Long term substitute tchr. grade 1 Juniata County School Dist., Mifflintown, Pa., 1994—95, long term substitute tchr. kindergarten, 1996, tchr. intermediate grades, 1996—. Mem.: NEA, Nat. Coun. Tchrs. English, Juniata County Edn. Assn., Pa. Edn. Assn.

DRESSLER, DAVID CHARLES, retired aerospace transportation executive; b. Cleve., June 21, 1928; s. Walter Carl and Beatrice (Albin) D.; m. Dorothea Walker, Dec. 22, 1950; children: David Charles, Bradley, Christopher. BA, Yale U., 1950; grad., Advanced Mgmt. Program, Harvard Bus. Sch., 1973. With Armstrong Cork Co., 1950-51; with Martin Marietta Corp., 1953-92, pres. Master Builders div., 1977-80, pres. Martin Marietta Chem. Co., 1979-81, corp. v.p., 1979-83, sr. corp. v.p., 1983-92; pres. Master Builders Co. Ltd., Toronto, 1977-81, Martin Marietta Aluminum, 1982-85; chmn. bd. Internat. Light Metals, 1985-91; pres. Martin Marietta Materials, Bethesda, Md., 1985-91. Chmn. bd. Martin Marietta Ordnance Sys., 1985—87; chmn. corp. com. Corcoran Mus. Art, 1992; bd. dirs. Bowles Fluidics; pres. Dressler Corp.; ethics judge Nat. Capital Bus. Awards, 2003—, chmn., 2007. Served to capt. USMCR, 1951-53. Mem.: Nat. Press Club, Harvard Bus. Sch. Club (pres. Washington club 1983, chmn. bd. dirs. 1984), Congl. Country Club (Washington) (bd. govs. 1990—96), Phi Beta Kappa. Episcopalian.

DRESSLER, ROBERT A., lawyer; b. Ft. Lauderdale, Fla., Aug. 20, 1945; s. R. Philip and Elisabeth Dressler; children: James Philip, Kathryn S. AB cum laude, Dartmouth Coll., 1967; JD cum laude, Harvard U., 1973. Bar: Mass. 1973, Fla. 1974, D.C. 1980, U.S. Dist. Ct. (so. dist.) Fla., U.S. Dist. Ct. Mass., U.S. Ct. Appeals (1st cir.), U.S. Ct. Appeals (5th cir.), U.S. Supreme Ct. Assoc. Goodwin, Proctor & Hoar, Boston, 1973-75; ptnr. Dressler & Dressler, Ft. Lauderdale, 1975-82; mayor City of Ft. Lauderdale, 1982-86; pvt. practice law Ft. Lauderdale, 1982—. Bd. regents State Univ. System, 1987-93; mem. Estate Planning Coun. Capt USMC, 1969-72. Named Person of Yr. Fla. Atlantic U., 1993. Mem. Greater Ft. Lauderdale C.of C. (bd. govs. 1982-89), Broward County Bar Assn., Fla. Bar Assn., Vietnam Vets. Am., Rotary Internat., Tower Forum (bd. govs. 1983-2005), Phi Beta Kappa. Presbyterian. Avocations: hiking, travel. Home: 1215 E Broward BlvdSuite 201 Fort Lauderdale FL 33301 Office: PO Box 2425 Fort Lauderdale FL 33303-2425 Office Phone: 954-523-9595. Business E-Mail: dresslerlaw@bellsouth.net.

DREW, BENJAMIN ALVIN, JR., astronaut; b. Washington, Nov. 5, 1962; s. Benjamin Drew, Sr. and Muriel Drew. BS in Astronautical Engring., US Air Force Acad., 1984, BS in Physics, 1984; Masters Degree in Aerospace Sci., Embry Riddle U., 1995; Masters Degree in Strategic Studies in Polit. Sci., US Air Force Air U., 2006. 2nd lt. US Air Force Acad., 1984; completed undergraduate pilot tng.-helicopter, earned wings Fort Rucker, Ala., 1985; flew combat missions in ops. JUST CAUSE, DESERT SHIELD/DESERT STORM and PROVIDE COMFORT Air Force Spl. Ops. Command, 1993; completed USAF Fixed-Wing Qualification, 1993; completed US Naval Test Pilot Sch., 1994; commanded two flight test units and served on Air Combat Command Staff; mission specialist, astronaut NASA, Houston, 2000—. Mission specialist STS-118 Mission (Endeavour) to Internat. Space Station, 2007. Mem.: Am. Helicopter Soc., Soc. Exptl. Test Pilots. Address: Astronaut Office Lyndon B Johnson Space Center Houston TX 77058*

DREW, CLIFFORD JAMES, dean, psychologist, educator; b. Eugene, Oregon, Mar. 9, 1943; s. Albert C. and Violet M. (Caskey) D. BS magna cum laude, Ea. Oreg. Coll., 1965; EdM, U.Ill., 1966; PhD (hon.), U. Oreg., 1968. Asst. prof. edn. Kent State U., Ohio, 1968-69; asst. prof. dir. rsch. and spl. edn. U. Tex., Austin, 1969-71; assoc. prof. spl. edn. U. Utah, Salt Lake City, 1971-76, prof., 1977—, asst. dean Grad. Sch. Edn., 1974-77, assoc. dean, 1977-79, 89-95, prof. spl. edn. , ednl. psychology, 1979—, coord. instrnl. tech., acad. v.p. office, 1995-97, assoc. acad. v.p., 1997—2004, assoc. dean Coll. Edn., 2004—. Cons. HEW, 1969-80; Bd. dir. Far West Lab. Ednl. Rsch. and Devel., San Francisco, 1974-80; mem. exec. bd. Salt Lake County Assn. Retarded Children, 1971-72; mem. adv. com. Mental Retardation Counseling Svc., Tex. Dept. Mental Health Mental Retardation, 1969-70. Author: Intro. to Designing Rsch. and Evaluation, 2d edit., 1976, Designing and Conducting Behavioral Rsch., 1985; co-author (with B. Wampold): Theory and Application of Stats., 1990; co-author: (with M. Hardman and A. Hart) Designing and Conducting Rsch.: Inquiry in Edn. and Social Sci., 1996; co-author: (with M. Hardman) Mental Retardation: A Life Cycle Approach, 2000, 8th edit., 2004; co-author: (with D. Gelfand) Understanding Child Behavior Disorders, 2003; co-author: (with M. Hardman) Mental Retardation: A Life Cycle Approach to People with Intellectual Disabilities, 8th edit., 2004, Intellectual Disabilities Across the Lifespan, 2006, 9th edit., 2007; co-author: (with M. Hardman and W. Egan) Human Exceptionality: School, Community, and Family, 2006; contbr. numerous articles to profl. jours. NDEA fellow, 1965-66; U.S. Office Edn. fellow, 1966-68. Fellow Am. Assn. Mental Retardation; mem. Am. Psychol. Assn., Am. Ednl. Rsch. Assn. Office: U Utah Dean's Office 1705 Campus Center Dr Rm 225 Salt Lake City UT 84112-9007 Home Phone: 435-783-2743. Business E-Mail: cliff.drew@utah.edu.

DREW, DONALD ALLEN, mathematical sciences educator; b. Margaretville, NY, Sept. 11, 1945; s. Howard Charles and Marjorie Belle (Liddle) D.; m. Margaret Esther Miller, June 4, 1966; children— Elizabeth Margaret, Stacey Lynn BS in Math., Rensselaer Poly. Inst., 1967, MS, 1969, PhD, 1970. Instr. MIT, Cambridge, 1970-71; asst. prof. NYU, 1971-73; from asst. prof. math. to prof. Rensselaer Poly. Inst., Troy, NY, 1973—95, Ricketts prof., 1995—, chmn. Dept. Math. Sci., 2002—. Cons. Battelle, Richland, Wash., 1975-77, Chevron, 1996; mathematician U.S. Army Rsch. Office, Research Triangle Park, N.C., 1980-81; vis. assoc. prof. U. Wis.-Madison, 1981; summer faculty Sandia Nat. Labs., Albuquerque, 1984; vis. prof. theoretical and applied mechanics Math. Scis. Inst., Cornell U., 1988-89; assoc. dir. Ctr. Multiphase Rsch., 1987-94, dir., 1994-96; vis. faculty Centro Atomico, Bariloche, Argentina, 1997, Southampton (Eng.) U., 1997; vis. scientist Los Alamos (N.Mex.) Nat. Labs., 1997. Contbr. articles to profl. jours. Pres. Faculty Senate, 1993-94. Mem. AAAS, Soc. Math. Biol., Soc. Indsl. and Applied Mathematics (edn. com. 1977-80), Soc. Engring. Sci., Soc. Natural Philosophy, Sigma Xi. Democrat. Home: 10 Eaton Rd Troy NY 12180-3603 Office: Rensselaer Poly Inst Dept Math Scis Troy NY 12180 Business E-Mail: drewd@rpi.edu.

DREW, FRASER BRAGG ROBERT, language educator; b. Randolph, Vt., June 23, 1913; s. George Albie and Hazel (Fraser) Drew. AB magna cum laude, U. Vt., 1933; MA, Duke U., 1935; PhD, U. Buffalo, 1952. Instr. Latin Green Mt. Coll., Poultney, Vt., 1936-39; grad. asst. English Syracuse U., 1939-41; instr. English Buffalo State Coll., 1945-47, asst. prof., 1947-52, prof., 1952-73, Disting. Tchg. prof., 1973-83. Author: (book) John Masefield's England, 1973; contbr. articles to profl. jours. Chmn. St. Patrick Scholarship Fund, Buffalo, 1969—79. Recipient Disting. Alumnus award, U. Vt., 1968, Irishman of the Yr. award, United Irish Socs. Western NY, 1970; grantee, SUNY Rsch. Found., 1960, 1967; St. Patrick scholar, 1967. Mem.: Robinson Jeffers Tor Ho. Found., Hemingway Soc., Boulder Soc., Wilbur Soc., Ira Allen Soc., John Masefield Soc., Housman Soc., Green Mountain Cir., Friends Duke U. Chapel, Duke U. Heritage Soc., Friends Bailey/Howe Libr., Friends Hemingway Collection John F. Kennedy Libr., Iron Dukes, Washington Duke Club, Phi Beta Kappa, Lambda Iota. Home: 33 Dante Ct Williamsville NY 14221

DREW, INA R., bank executive; BA, Johns Hopkins U., 1978; MA, Columbia U. Floor trader Bank of Tokyo, Manhattan, NY; with Chemical Bank, Springfield, NJ, 1982—96; mng. dir. Global Treasury Divsn. J.P. Morgan Chase & Co., NYC, 1996—. Mem. mgmt. com. J.P. Morgan Chase & Co., 1997—, mem. exec. com., 2003—. Named One of Most Powerful Women in Banking, U.S. Banker Mag., 2003. Office: JP Morgan Chase & Co 270 Park Ave New York NY 10017-2070

DREW, J.D., professional baseball player; b. Valdosta, Ga., Nov. 20, 1975; m. Sheigh Drew. Attended, Fla. State Univ. Outfielder St. Louis Cardinals, 1998—2003, Atlanta Braves, 2004, LA Dodgers, 2005—06, Boston Red Sox, 2006—. Recipient Golden Spikes award for Top Amateur Player, 1997. Office: Boston Red Sox 4 Yawkey Way Boston MA 02215-3496*

DREW, KATHERINE FISCHER, history professor; b. Houston, Sept. 24, 1923; d. Herbert Herman and Martha (Holloway) Fischer; m. Ronald Farinton Drew, July 27, 1951. BA, Rice Inst., 1944, MA, 1945; PhD, Cornell U., 1950. Asst. history Cornell U., 1948-50; instr. history Rice U., 1946-48, mem. faculty, 1950—, prof. history, 1964—, Harris Masterson, Jr. prof. history, 1983-85, Lynette S. Autrey prof. history, 1985-96, prof. emeritus, 1996—, chmn. dept. history, 1970-80; editor Rice U. (Rice U. Studies), 1967-81, acting dean humanities and social scis., 1973, acting chmn. dept. art and art history, 1996-98. Author: The Burgundian Code, 1949, Studies in Lombard Institutions, 1956, The Lombard Laws, 1973, Law and Society in Early Medieval Europe, 1988, The Laws of the Salian Franks, 1991, Magna Carta, 2004, also articles; editor: Perspectives in Medieval History, 1963, The Barbarian Invasions, 1970; mem. bd. editors Am. Hist. Assn. Guide to Hist. Lit., 1987-94, Am. Hist. Rev. 1982-1985; contbr.: Life and Thought in the Middle Ages, 1967. Guggenheim fellow, 1959, Fulbright scholar, 1965, NEH sr. fellow, 1974—75. Fellow Mediaeval Acad. Am. (coun. 1974-77, 2d v.p. to pres. 1985-87, del. to Am. Coun. Learned Socs. 1977-81); mem. Am. Hist. Assn. (coun. 1983-86), Am. Soc. Legal History, So. Hist. Assn. (vice chair, chair European sect. 1986-88, exec. com. 1989-91), Phi Beta Kappa. Home: 9333 Memorial Dr # 306 Houston TX 77024-5739 Office: Rice U Dept History MS 42 PO Box 1892 Houston TX 77251-1892 E-mail: kdrew@rice.edu.

DREW, PAUL S., entrepreneur; b. Detroit, Mar. 10, 1935; s. Harry and Elizabeth (Schneider) Schlachman; m. Dove Ann Austin, Sept. 9, 1961. BA, Wayne State U., Detroit, 1957. Disc jockey, Port Huron, Mich. and Atlanta, 1955-67; program dir. Sta. WQXI, Atlanta, 1966-67, Sta. CKLW, Detroit, 1967-68; program cons. Storer Broadcasting Co., Phila., 1968-69; program dir. RKO Radio stas. in, Detroit, San Francisco, Washington and L.A., 1970-73; v.p. programming RKO Radio stas., 1973-77; pres. Paul Drew Enterprises, LA, 1977—; dir. USIA-Radio Marti, 1984-85; pres. USA Japan Co., 1985—, The Mobotron Corp., Hollywood, Calif., 1988—, Fuzzmug Corp., 1991—, 2151 Corp., 1991—. Personal mgr. Pink Lady, outside Japan, 1978; ptnr. Teacup-Teaspoon Music Pub. Co., 1978; chmn. Billboard Internat. Programming Conf., 1976; commr. Calif. Motion Picture Coun., 1979-85. Del. Dem. Nat. Conv., 1976; mem. Dem. Nat. Com., Calif. Dem. Com., Dem. Nat. Fin. Council. Named DeeJay of Year Sixteen Mag., 1965; Program Dir. of Year Bill Gavin Report, 1967; recipient Superior Achievement award RKO Radio, 1973; also numerous gold records for contbs. toward million selling records. Mem. NARAS, Am. Advt. Fedn., Am. Film Inst., Hollywood Radio and TV Soc., L.A. World Affairs Coun., Town Hall Calif., Japan Am. Soc., Variety, Friars, Frat. of Friends, Music Ctr. Home and Office: 4155 Morningside Dr Cumming GA 30041-6609 E-mail: pauldrewla@gmail.com. *Don't make the same mistake once.*

DREW, PHILIP GARFIELD, retired engineering company executive, consultant; b. Dedham, Mass., Jan. 25, 1932; s. Garfield Albee and Katherine Marion (Dowling) D.; m. Anne Spengler, June 10, 1961 (div. 1972); children: Katherine, Philip Garfield; m. Patrice Anne Prall, May 20,

1978 (div. 1998); children: Evlyn Albee, Charles Prescott. BS, Carnegie-Mellon U., 1954; MS, Harvard U., 1959, PhD, 1964. Registered profl. engr., Mass. Staff Arthur D. Little, Inc., Cambridge, Mass., 1964-81; pres. Drew Cons., Inc., Carlisle, Mass., 1981—, Concord (Mass.) Cons. Group, 1996—97, 1999—2004, ret., 2004. Contbg. editor: Diagnostic Imaging, 1982—; assoc. sci. editor: Test and Measurement World, 1984-86; contbr. articles to profl. jours. Chmn. bd. overseers Bustins Island Village Corp., Freeport, Maine, 1981-84; pres. Savoyard Light Opera Co., 1988-90, Brown Bag Opera, 1993-2000. Served to 1st lt. AUS, 1954-58. Mem. IEEE, Soc. Photo-Optical Instrumentation Engrs., Soc. Computer Applications in Radiology (chmn. 1996), Harvard Club of Boston. Republican. Home and Office: 101 Bedford Rd Carlisle MA 01741-1817 Office Phone: 978-369-9276. Personal E-mail: pdrew@concordcg.com.

DREW, RICHARD ALLEN, retired electrical engineer; b. Milw., Jan. 10, 1941; s. Frank Emmons and Irene Louise Drew. BSEE, Milw. Sch. Engring., 1970. Registered profl. engr., Wis., 1974. Instrument engr. Nekoosa Papers Inc., Port Edwards, Wis., 1970—74, sr. instrument engr., 1974—85, Specialty Sys. Inc., Mosinee, Wis., 1985—87; chief elec. and instrument engr. Zimpro Environ. Inc., Rothschild, Wis., 1988—96, ret., 1997. With USAF, 1963—67. Recipient Outstanding Svc. award Pulp and Paper Industry divsn. Instrument Soc. Am., 1983, Outstanding Alumnus award Milw. Sch. Engring., 1985 Mem. Instrument Soc. Am. (sr., chpt. pres. 1974-75), Am. Radio Relay League (life), Milw. Sch. Engring. Alumni Orgn. (chpt. pres. 1991-95) Achievements include research in pulp and paper industrial control systems and waste treatment control systems. Home: 5625 Sandpiper Dr Apt 301 Stevens Point WI 54481

DREW, SHARON LEE, sociologist; b. LA, Aug. 11, 1946; d. Hal Bernard and Helen Elizabeth (Hammond) D.; children: Keith, Charmagne. BA, Calif. State U., Long Beach, 1983; postgrad., Calif. State U., Dominguez Hills, 1988—92. Clerical support Compton (Calif.) Unified Sch. Dist., 1967-78; case worker L.A. County Dept. Pub. Social Svcs., 1978—. Den mother Boy Scouts Am., Compton, 1971—72; employee vol. Dominguez Sr. H.S., Compton, 1972—73; project coord. Calif. Tomorrow's Parent Edn. Leadership Devel. Project, 1990; mem. L.A. Caregiver's Network, 1993—94; vol. Calif. State U., Dominguez Hills Older Adult Ctr., 1994, AIDS Project, Long Beach, Calif., 2003; lay min., lay reader St. Lukes Episcopal Ch., Long Beach, 1999—2005. Recipient cert. Calif. Tomorrow-Parent Edn. Leadership Devel. Project, 1990. Mem. Am. Statis. Assn. (So. Calif. chpt.), Internat. Soc. Exploration of Tchg. and Learning, Dominguez Hills Gerontology Assn. (chairperson 1990-91), Alpha Kappa Delta (Xi chpt. treas. 1992-95). Home: 927 N Chester Ave Compton CA 90221-2105 E-mail: msblakcelt@aol.com.

DREW, WALTER HARLOW, retired paper company executive; b. Chgo., Feb. 23, 1935; s. Ben Harlow and Marion Elizabeth (Heineman) D.; m. Gracia Ward McKenzie, June 27, 1959; children: Jeffrey, Martha. BS, U. Wis., 1957. With Kimberly-Clark Corp., 1959-88, exec. v.p., 1985-88; pres., CEO Menasha Corp., 1989-92. Bd. dirs. U. Wis. Found.; chmn. bd. visitors U. Wis. Bus. Sch., 1992—93. Lt. (jg.) USNR, 1957—63. Mem.: Ocean Club (Amelia Island, Fla.), North Shore Golf Club (Menasha, Wis.) (pres. 1983—85).

DREWAL, HENRY JOHN, art historian, educator; b. Brooklyn, Mar. 11, 1943; BA, Hamilton Coll., 1964; MA, Columbia U., 1968, PhD, 1973. Asst. prof. art hist. Cleve. State U., 1973—77, prof., chairperson art dept., 1982—85, prof. art dept., 1982—90; Evjue-Bascom Prof. Art Hist. U. Wis.-Madison, Dept. Art Hist., 1990—. Vis. prof. art hist. SUNY Purchase, 1986, U. Calif., Santa Barbara, 1988. Fellow Guggenheim Meml. Found., 2004. Mem.: Wis. Acad. of Scis., Arts, and Letters, Midwest Art Soc., Congress on Rsch. in Dance, Coll. Art Assn., African Studies Assn. Office: Chazen Mus Art U Wis Madison WI 53706 Office Phone: 608-263-9362, 608-263-2340. E-mail: hjdrewal@wisc.edu.

DREWES, ALFRED H., consumer products company executive; BSEE, U. Mass., 1978; MBA, Columbia U., 1982. Fin. analyst Pepsi Bottling Group, NJ, 1982; v.p. mfg. ops. Pepsi-Cola Internat., 1991, v.p. bus. planning and new bus. devel., 1994, v.p., CFO Europe and Sub-Saharan Africa Bus. Unit London, 1996, sr. v.p., CFO, The Pepsi Bottling Group, Inc., Somers, NY, 2001—. Bd. dirs. Meredith Corp. Office: The Pepsi Bottling Group Inc One Pepsi Way Somers NY 10589-2201 Office Phone: 914-767-6000. Office Fax: 914-767-7761.*

DREWES, MATTHEW A., lawyer; BA cum laude, Concordia Coll., Moorhead, Minn., 1998; JD cum laude, U. Minn. Law Sch., 2001. Bar: Minn. 2001, US Ct. Appeals (8th cir.) 2001, US Dist. Ct. (dist. Minn.) 2004. Assoc. litig. practice grp. Thomsen & Nybeck, P.A., Edina, Minn., 2003. Named a Rising Star, Minn. Super Lawyers mag., 2006. Mem.: Assn. Trial Lawyers of Am., ABA, Minn. State Bar Assn. Office: Thomsen & Nybeck PA 3300 Edinborough Way Ste 600 Edina MN 55435 Office Phone: 952-835-7000. E-mail: mdrewes@tn-law.com.*

DREWES, ROBERT W., communications systems company executive; B in Econs., Colby Coll., Waterville, Maine; M, Harvard Bus. Sch.; grad., Air Command and Staff Coll., Indsl. Coll. of Armed Forces. Retired with rank of maj. gen. USAF; v.p. productivity Raytheon Co.; sr. v.p., pres. Integrated Systems Group L-3 Comm. Holdings, Inc., 2001—. Author: The Air Force and the Great Engine War. Office: L-3 Comm Holdings Inc 600 Third Ave New York NY 10016 Office Phone: 212-697-1111. Office Fax: 212-805-5477.*

DREWRY, DON NEAL, fire protection engineer; b. Chgo., Oct. 6, 1949; s. Ruben Neal and Vlasta A. (Walleck) D.; m. Patricia Ann English, Mar. 8, 1975; children: Neal Thomas, Michelle Lynn. BA, Govs. State U., 1978; BS in Engring., U. Hartford, 1984; MS in Fire Protection Engring., Worcester Polytech. Inst., 1986. Mfg. engring./NC programmer Bloomer-Fisk, Chgo., 1974-75; inspector, supr. Hartford Steam Boiler, Chgo., 1975-78; asst. mgr. quality assurance svc. Hartford Steam Boiler Inspection and Ins. Co., 1978-80, project engr., 1980-81, rsch. engr., 1982-84, fire protection cons., 1984-87, regional mgmt. property engr. Basking Ridge, NJ, 1987-92, regional manage ins. engr., 1992-94; br. mgr., property program mgr. power generation HSB Profl. Loss Control, Basking Ridge, 1994-97, v.p. industry svcs., 1997-99, v.p. loss control svcs., 1999—. Com. fire protection task force Edison Elec. Inst., Washington, 1995. With USN, 1970-74. Mem. ASME, Soc. Fire Protection Engrs., Nat. Fire Protection Assn. (com. NFPA-850 1985—), Nat. Bd. of Boiler and Pressure Vessel Inspectors. Home: 1401 Sycamore Ave Easton PA 18040-8106 Office: HSB Profl Loss Control 188 Mount Airy Rd Basking Ridge NJ 07920-2021

DREWRY, MARCIA ANN, physician; b. St. Louis, Feb. 15, 1951; d. Owen and Annie Vernell (Smith) Palmer; m. Norman T. Drewry, Sept. 18, 1970 (dec. May 1978); 1 child, Tammy Robbins; m. David W. Worsdell Jr., Dec. 7, 1991. AS with honors, Forest Park Coll., 1989; DO, Kirksville Coll. Osteo. Med., 1993. Diplomate Nat. Bd. Osteo. Med. Examiners; bd. cert. family practice. Intern Riverside Hosp., Wichita, 1993-94; med. transcriptionist Malcolm Bliss Mental Health, St. Louis, 1970-78; asst. adminstr. radiology Incarnate Word Hosp., St. Louis, 1977-79; grant writer molecular virolgoy St. Louis (Mo.) U., 1977-79; med. transcriptionist Neurosurg. Assocs., Inc., St. Louis, 1979-87, Stat Transcription, St. Louis, 1987-88, PRN Transcription, St. Louis, 1988-90; physician Anthony (Kans.) Primary Care Ctr., 1994-96; chief of staff Harper County Hosp. Dist. #6, 1995-96; family practice physician Kiowa (Kans.) Hosp. and Clinic, 1997—2000; staff physician Cen. Fla. Family Health Ctr., Sanford, 2000—04; resident Fla. Hosp., East Orlando, 2002—04. Dir. credentials, emergency dept. and med. records Anthony (Kans.) Primary Care Ctr., 1995-96. Capt. Operation Safe St., St. Louis, 1985-89; choir mem. Dover Place Christian Ch., St. Louis, 1986-93; mem. Careers for Homemakers, St. Louis, 1987-89. Mem. Am. Coll. Osteo. Family Physicians, Am. Acad. Osteopathy, Am. Osteo. Assn., Fla. Osteopathic Med. Assn. (Sci. Rsch. award 2004), Kans. Assn. Osteo. Medicine, Bus. and Profl. Women, Beta Sigma Phi, Phi Theta Kappa (pres. 1988-89), Alpha Phi Omega (sec. 1990-91), Theta Psi (promotions asst. 1990-91). Avocations: travel, singing. Home: 2664 Shiprock Ct Deltona FL 32738-8803 Office: 2400 SR 415 Sanford FL 32771

DREWS, JÜRGEN, pharmaceutical researcher; b. Berlin, Aug. 16, 1933; came to U.S., 1991; s. Walter and Charlotte (Schneider) D.; m. Helga Eberlein, July 26, 1963; children: Ulrike, Karoline, Bettina. MD, Free U. Berlin, 1959; Professorship, U. Heidelberg, Fed. Republic of Germany, 1973. Head chemotherapy Sandoz Rsch. Inst., Vienna, 1976-79, head of inst., 1979-82; head internat. pharm. rsch. and devel. Sandoz, Ltd., Basel, Switzerland, 1982-85; dir. pharm. rsch. F. Hoffmann-La Roche Ltd., Basel, 1985-86, chmn. rsch. bd., mem. exec. com., 1986-90; pres. internat. rsch. and devel., mem. exec. com. Hoffmann-La Roche Inc., Basel, 1991-97, pres. global rsch., mem. exec. com. Nutley, NJ, 1996-97; chmn. Internat. Biomedicine Mgmt. Ptnrs., Basel, 1998—2000; mng. ptnr. Bear Stearns Health Innoventures, NYC, 2002—. Prof. medicine U. Heidelberg, 1973—; mem. sci. adv. bd. (jour.) Infection, München, Fed. Republic of Germany, 1973-95, Drug News & Perspectives, Barcelona, Spain, 1988—, Klinische Pharmakologie, München, 1989-2000; bd. dirs. Genentech, Inc., South San Francisco, 1990-97, Protein Design Labs., Mountain View, Calif., MorphoSys GmbH, Munich; bd. dirs., internat. bd. advisors Basel Inst. Immunology, 1986-97; mem. dean's coun. Yale U. Sch. Medicine, 1993-96, chmn. sci. panel inter-company collaboration for AIDS drug devel., 1993-96, chmn. bd. participants inter-company collaboration for AIDS drug devel., 1996-97; mem. adv. com. Mass. Gen. Hosp., Boston, 1994-98; chmn. steering com. Sr. Adv. Group Biotech., 1994-96; chmn. bd. mgmt. EuropaBio, 1997-98; bd. dirs. Human Genome Scis., Rockville, Md. Author: Chemotherapie: Grundlagen und Perspektiven, 1979, Immunpharmakologie, Grundlagen und Perspektiven, 1986, Immunopharmacology, Principles and Perspectives, 1990, In Quest of Tomorrow's Medicines, 1999; editor: (with others) Topics in Infectious Diseases, vol. 1, 1975, vol. 2, 1977; also over 250 articles. Personal E-mail: info@j_drews.de.

DREXEL, BARON JEROME, lawyer; b. Miami Beach, Fla., Sept. 3, 1954; s. Gustave L. and Dorris J. (Haas) D. AA, U. Fla., 1973; BA, U. Calif. Berkeley, 1979; MA in Econs., U. Miami, 1983, JD cum laude, 1985. Bar: Fla. 1985, Calif. 1987, U.S. Ct. Appeals (9th cir.) 1987, U.S. Ct. Appeals (11th cir.) 1989, U.S. dist. Ct. (no. dist.) Calif. 1986, U.S. Dist. Ct. (ctrl. dist.) Calif. 1987, U.S. Dist. Ct. (so. dist.) Calif. 1988. Survey crew mem. U.S. Forest Svc., Hayfork, Calif., 1979; sales rep. real estate Allen Morris Co., Miami, Fla., 1981-82; assoc. Shutts & Bowen, Miami, 1985-88, Lasky, Haas, Cohler & Munter, San Francisco, 1988-89, Aiken, Kramer & Cummings, Oakland, Calif., 1989-92, Bostwick & Tehin, San Francisco, 1992-95; pvt. practice Oakland, 1995—. Recipient J.B. Spence award U. Miami Law Rev. Mem. Order of Coif. Achievements include co-trial couns. for $15.4 million verdict. Office: Madison Square Professional Ctr 212 Ninth St Penthouse Suite 401 Oakland CA 94607 Home Phone: 925-736-8013; Office Phone: 510-444-3184. E-mail: drexlex@sbcglobal.net.

DREXLER, CLYDE, retired professional basketball player; b. New Orleans, June 22, 1962; Student, U. Houston, 1980-83. Basketball player Portland Trailblazers, 1983-94, Houston Rockets, 1994-98. Mem. U.S. Men's Olympic Basketball Team (The Dream Team), Barcelona, 1992. Performer: Dancing with the Stars, 2007. Mem. NBA All-Star Team, 1986, 1988-1994, 1996-1997; mem. all-NBA first team, 1992; mem. All-NBA second team, 1988, 91; mem. All-NBA third team, 1990. Achievements include mem. Gold medal U.S. Men's Basketball Team, Barcelona Olympic Games, 1992; mem. NBA Champion Houston Rockets, 1995.*

DREXLER, KENNETH, lawyer; b. Aug. 2, 1941; s. Fred and Martha Jane Drexler; m. Sarah Leach, Jan. 1, 1982; 1 child, Daniel Warren. BA, Stanford U., 1963; JD, UCLA, 1969. Bar: Calif. 1970. Assoc. David S. Smith, Beverly Hills, Calif., 1970, McCutchen, Doyle, Brown and Enersen, San Francisco, Calif., 1970-77, Chickering & Gregory, San Francisco, Calif., 1977-80, ptnr., 1980-82, Drexler & Leach, San Rafael, Calif., 1982—. Served with AUS, 1964-66. Mem. Calif. State Bar (resolutions com. conf. of dels. 1979-83, chmn. 1982-83, adminstrn. justice com. 1983-89, chmn. 1987-88, adv. mem. 1990-2000), Marin County Bar Assn. (bd. dirs. 1985-87), Bar Assn. San Francisco (bd. dirs. 1980-81), San Francisco Barristers Club (pres. 1976, dir. 1975-76), Marin Conservation League (bd. dirs. 1985-97, 98—, treas. 2001—). Office: 1330 Lincoln Ave Ste 300 San Rafael CA 94901-2143 Home Phone: 415-482-8284; Office Phone: 415-485-1330. E-mail: kdrexler@svn.net.

DREXLER, MICKEY (MILLARD STEVEN), retail executive; b. Bronx, NY, 1944; m. Peggy F. Drexler. BA, SUNY, Buffalo, 1966; MBA, Boston U., 1968. Pres., CEO Ann Taylor Co., NYC, 1980—83; exec. v.p. merchandising, pres. Gap Stores, San Bruno, Calif., 1983—87; pres. The Gap Inc., San Bruno, Calif., 1987—95, pres., CEO San Francisco, 1995—2002; chmn., CEO J. Crew Group, Inc., NYC, 2003—. Bd. dirs. Apple Computer, Inc., 1999—. Recipient Israel Fellows Prize, 2001. Office: J Crew Group Inc 770 Broadway New York NY 10003*

DREXLER, MILTON, medical association administrator; b. Bronx, NY, Apr. 3, 0914; s. Samuel and Ann Drexler; married, Oct. 1941; children: Andrew Jay, Sharon. MD, Berne Med. Sch., Switzerland, 1937. Pres. med. staff United Hosp., Port Chester, NY, 1969—71. Assoc. chief of staff Vets. Adminstrn. Hosp., Bronx. Capt. med. US Army. Decorated Silver Star US Army, League of Merit award, Bronze Star, Purple Heart, NY Army and Navy medal NY State, Asiatic and Pacific Theater medal US Army, Am. Campaign Victory medal. Mem.: Weschester Med. Soc. (pres. med. staff 1980). Home: 10101 Gov Warfield Pkwy Columbia MD 21044

DREXLER, RICHARD ALLAN, manufacturing executive; b. Chgo., May 14, 1947; s. Lloyd A. and Evelyn Violet (Kovaloff) D.; m. Clare F. Stunkel, Aug. 24, 1990; children by previous marriage: Dan Lloyd, Jason Ian. BS, Northwestern U., 1968, MBA, 1969. Staff v.p. Allied Products Corp., Chgo., 1971-75, sr. v.p. adminstrn., 1975-79, exec. v.p., COO, CFO, 1979-82, pres., COO, 1982-86, pres., CEO, 1986-93, chmn., pres., CEO, 1993—.

DREXLER, RUDY MATTHEW, JR., professional law enforcement dog trainer; b. Elkhart, Ind., Jan. 16, 1941; s. Rudy Matthew Sr. and Elaine Irene (Hardman) D.; m. Patricia Ann Overmyer, Apr. 4, 1981; children: Scott M., Tina S. Thode. Student, Purdue U., 1960-63. V.p. Custom Booth Mfg. Corp., Elkhart, Ind., 1962-80; pres. Orchard Kennels, Elkhart, Ind., 1964-79; pres., treas. Rudy Drexler's Sch. for Dogs, Inc., Elkhart, Ind., 1980—. Lectr. civic orgns.; instr. U. Del. Continuing Edn., Wilmington, 1978. Named to Honorable Order of Ky. Colonels, 1989; named hon. dep. Middlesex County Sheriff's Dept., New Brunswick, N.J., 1984, Daviess County Sheriff's Dept., Owensboro, Ky., 1988, Fairfield County Sheriff's Dept., Lancaster, Ohio, 1982. Mem. Midwest Police K-9 Assn. (founder 1984, tng. dir. 1984-87), Am. Soc. Law Enforcement Trainers (charter mem.), Internat. Narcotics Enforcement Officers Assn. (assoc. mem.), Can. Police K-9 Assn. (assoc. mem.), Nat. Police Res. Officers Assn. (hon. mem.), Moose. Office: Rudy Drexler's Sch for Dogs 50947 County Road 7 Elkhart IN 46514-8853 Office Phone: 574-264-7518. Business E-Mail: rudydrexler@aol.com.

DREY, LEO, environmentalist; b. St. Louis, Jan. 19, 1917; m. Kay Drey. Founder L-A-D Found., 1962. Coord. Pioneer Forest Project. Named one of top 60 US Philanthropists, Slate mag., 2005, 50 Most Generous Philanthropists, BusinessWeek, 2005. Office: L-A-D Found 721 Olive St Saint Louis MO 63101

DREYER, ALEC GILBERT, electric power industry executive; b. Murphysboro, Ill., Mar. 15, 1958; s. Gilbert Dean and Norma Mae (Cluster) D.; m. Sheri L. Snider, July 26, 1980; children: Hillary Christine, Ahren Grant. BA in Polit. Sci. and Acctg., U. Ill., 1980; MBA with honors, Washington U., 1987. CPA, Ill., Mo. Staff acct. Price Waterhouse, St. Louis, 1980-82, sr. acct., 1982-85, mgr., 1985-88, sr. mgr., 1988-92; contr. Ill. Power Co., Decatur, 1992-94, treas., contr., 1994-95, sr. v.p., 1999-2000; pres. Illinova Generating Co., Decatur, 1995-2000; sr. v.p. Illinova Corp., Decatur, 1999-2000; pres. Generation Dynegy, Inc., 2000—05; CEO Horizon Wind Energy LLC, Houston, 2005—. Asst. treas. Com. To Expand Cervantes Conv. Ctr., St. Louis, 1987-88; mem. Citizens Adv. Coun., Edwardsville, Ill., 1990-91; chmn. pers. svcs. divsn. United Way Macon County, Ill., 1994, bd. dirs., 1995-99, co-chmn. campaign drive, 1995, chmn. campaign drive, 1996, vice chmn. bd. dirs., 1997-98, chmn. bd. dirs., 1999; mem. Cmty. Leaders Coun. United Way Tex. Gulf Coast, 2001-03. Mem. AICPA, Ill. Soc. CPAs, Phi Beta Kappa, Beta Gamma Sigma. Republican. Baptist. Avocations: golf, computing, in-line skating, reading. Home: 2631 Tangley St Houston TX 77005-2456 E-mail: alec.dreyer@horizonwind.com.

DREYER, JEFFREY S., parochial school educator; b. Fort Knox, Ky., July 2, 1957; s. Jerry W. and Barbara A. Dreyer; m. Elizabeth A. Wilson, Mar. 26, 1983; children: Adam B., Jamie E. Decker, Ethan J. BA, Tenn. Temple U., Chattanooga, 1981; EdM in Math., Millersville U., Pa., 2001. Faculty mem. Centre County Christian Acad., Bellefonte, Pa., 1981—89, Lancaster Christian Sch., Pa., 1989—2001, Oak Hill Acad., Mouth of Wilson, Va., 2001—05, Christian Sch. York, Pa., 2005—. Choir dir. First Bapt. Ch., Bellefonte, 1987—88. Mem.: Nat. Coun. Tchrs. Math. Home Phone: 717-792-0972; Office Phone: 717-767-6842. Business E-Mail: jdreyer@csyonline.com.

DREYFOOS, ALEXANDER W., JR., investor, research scientist; b. 1932; m. Renate Dreyfoos; 1 child, Cathy; 1 child, Robert. BS, MIT, 1954; MBA, Harvard U., 1958; DSc (hon.), Lynn U., 1999. Chmn., chief rschr. The Dreyfoos Group, West Palm Beach, Fla., 1963—. Lifetime trustee MIT Corp.; chmn. Raymond F. Kravis Ctr. for Performing Arts; bd. trustees Scripps Rsch. Inst., 2004—; founding mem., former chmn., hon. mem. Econ. Coun. Palm Beach County; bd. dir. FPL Group, Inc., Juno Beach, Fla., 1997—. Recipient Marshall B. Dalton Award, MIT, 1997, Bronze Beaver Award, 1997, Henry Laurence Gantt medal, ASME, 2002. Fellow: Am. Acad. Arts and Scis.; mem.: Sailfish Club of Fla., Beach Club, Harvard Club of N.Y.C., N.Y. Yacht Club. Avocations: yachting, flying, photography, scuba diving, fishing. Office: FPL Group Inc PO Box 14000 North Palm Beach FL 33408-0420

DREYFUS, LEE SHERMAN, international speaker; b. Milw., June 20, 1926; s. Woods Orlow and Clare (Bluett) D.; m. Joyce Mae Unke, Apr. 5, 1947; children: Susan Dreyfus Fosdick, Lee S. Jr. BA, U. Wis., 1949, MA, 1952, PhD, 1957; LLD (hon.), Lakeland Coll., Wis., 1978; LHD (hon.), Blackbourne Coll., Ill., 1984; LCD (hon.), Marian Coll., Wis., 1985; LLD (hon.), Hangyang U., Seoul, Korea, 1982. Assoc. prof., gen. mgr. Radio WDET Wayne State U., Detroit, 1952-62; prof., gen. mgr. WHA-TV U. Wis., Madison, 1962-67, chancellor Stevens Point, 1967-79; gov. State of Wis., Madison, 1979-83; pres., COO Sentry Ins. Corp., Stevens Point, 1983-84; pres. L.S.D. Inc., Waukesha, Wis., 1985—2005; internat. spkr. Washington Spkrs. Bur., Alexandria, Va., 1988—. Interim state supt. pub. instrn., 1993; chief of mission U.S. AID, Vietnam, 1967-74; bd. dirs. Am.-Can. Great Lakes Commn., Washington, 1979-83, Marcus Corp., Assoc. Bank Corp., Nat. Telemedia, Inc.; del. Am. Assn. State Coll. and Univ., China, Taiwan, Poland, 1973-76. Radio child actor regular weekly drama broadcasts Sta. WISN Milw., 1933-44; creator world's 1st intercontinental video classroom, U.S. to France, 1965. Regent U. Wis., Madison, 1990-96; trustee Emerson Coll., Boston, 1988-91; co-chmn. Wis. Sesquicentennial, Madison, 1996-2000; presdl. del. to Benin, Africa, 1991; spl. del. State Dept. Acad. Mission to Cyprus, 1983; chmn. Wis. Cable TV Commn., Madison, 1972; mem. Wis. Land Stewardship Commn., 1998, Wis. Humanities Commn., 1998; spokesman Angelus Ret. Cmtys., 2003. With USNR, 1944-46; comdr.-in-chief Wis. N.G., 1979-83. Recipient Disting. Pub. Svc. medal Dept. Def., 1982, Pres.'s Gold medal U.S. Army, 1984, U. Wis. Sys. Pres.'s medal, 2001, Heritage Found. award, 2004, Friend Edn. award, 2004; named Man of the Yr., Kappa Sigma, 1980; named to Hall of Fame, DeMolay Internat., 1991, Milw. Washington H.S., 2001, Wis. Broadcasters Assn., 2006; named bldg. in his name Dreyfus Tower, Ellsworth, Wis., 1996, Dreyfus State Office, Waukesha, Wis., 2001, Dreyfus Student Ctr., Stevens Point, Wis., 2006. Mem. Nat. Inst. Former Govs. (sec. 1990-94), Am. Legion (life), VFW (life), Masons (33 deg.), Shriner. Republican. Episcopalian. Avocations: charitable fund raising, reading, civic projects, politics. Home: 3159 Madison St Waukesha WI 53188

DREYFUS, SUSAN KAHN, middle school educator; b. Atlanta, Dec. 8, 1946; d. Truman Frederick and Gloria Charlotte (Shefsky) Kahn; children: Diane, Wendy, David. BS, U. Memphis, Tenn., 1970; M in Adminstrn., Trevecca Nazarene Coll., Nashville, 1991. Tchr. Montrose Acad., Ark., 1976—77, Memphis City Schs., 1986—. Founder Circuit Playhouse, Inc., Memphis, 1969; leader The Creative Cir., Overland Park, Kans., 1982-84. V.p. Dem. Women of Memphis, 1993-94, exec. com., 1991-93; vol. Hadassah, Memphis, 1981—, Memphis Polit. Caucus, 1991—; treas. Memphis Women's Leadership Forum, 1998—; vol. Memphis Race for the Cure. Mem. NEA, Tenn. Edn. Assn., Memphis Edn. Assn., Nat. Reading Assn. Jewish. Avocations: stamp collecting/philately, fitness training, reading, travel. Office: Memphis City Schools Memphis TN

DREYFUSS, ERIC MARTIN, allergist; b. Bad Homburg, Germany, July 11, 1930; came to U.S., 1934; s. Walter and Hedwig (Herz) D.; m. Sandra Dale Gasul, June 16, 1957; children: Peter, Lisa. AB, Cornell U., 1953; MD, Chgo. Med. Sch., 1957. Diplomat Am. Bd. Allergy and Immunology. Intern Beth Israel Hosp., NYC, 1957-58; resident in pediats. SUNY, Syracuse, 1958-60; fellow in allergy Rochester, NY, 1962-64; allergist Allergy Assocs. Rochester, 1964—. Asst. clin. prof. U. Rochester Sch. Medicine and Dentistry, 1970—. Capt. U.S. Army, 1960-62. Fellow Am. Acad. Allergy and Immunology, Am. Coll. Allergists, Am. Acad. Pediatrics. Office: Allergy Assocs Rochester 300 Goodman St S Rochester NY 14607-3105

DREYFUSS, RICHARD STEPHAN, actor; b. NYC, Oct. 29, 1947; s. Norman and Gerry Dreyfuss; m. Jeramie Rain, 1983 (div. 1995), children: Emily, Benjamin, Harry; m. Janelle Lacey, May 30, 1999 (div.); m. Svetlana Erokhin, March 16, 2006 Student, San Fernando Valley State Coll., 1965-67. Actor (films): Valley of the Dolls, 1967, The Graduate, 1967, The Young Runaways, 1968, Hello Down There, 1969, American Graffiti, 1973, Dillinger, 1973, The Apprenticeship of Duddy Kravitz, 1974, The Second Coming of Suzanne, 1974, Jaws, 1975, Inserts, 1975, Close Encounters of the Third Kind, 1977, The Goodbye Girl (Golden Globe award for Best Actor, Acad. award for Best Actor), 1977, The Big Fix, 1978, Othello, 1979, The Competition, 1980, Whose Life Is It Anyway?, 1981, The Buddy System, 1984, Down and Out in Beverly Hills, 1986, Stand By Me, 1986, Tin Men, 1987, Stakeout, 1987, Nuts, 1987, Moon Over Parador, 1988, Let It Ride, 1989, Always, 1989, Postcards from the Edge 1990, What About Bob?, 1991, Rosencrantz and Guildenstern Are

Dead, 1991, Lost in Yonkers, 1993, Another Stakeout, 1993, Silent Fall, 1994, Mr. Holland's Opus, 1995 (Acad. award nominee for Best Actor 1996), The Last Word, 1995, The American President, 1995, Mad Dog Time, 1996, James and the Giant Peach (voice only), 1996, Night Falls on Manhattan, 1997, Krippendorf's Tribe, 1998, A Fine and Private Place, 1998, The Crew, 2000, The Old Man Who Read Love Stories, 2000, Who Is Cletis Tout?, 2001, Rudolph the Red-Nosed Reindeer and the Island of Misfit Toys (voice only), 2001, Silver City, 2004, Poseidon, 2006; actor, prodr. (films) The Big Fix, 1978, Once Around, 1991; actor (TV movies) Untold Damage, 1971, Two For The Money, 1972, Shadow of a Gunman, 1972, Catch-22, 1973, Victory at Entebbe, 1976, The Call of the Wild: Dog of the Yukon (voice only), 1997, Lansky, 1999, Fail Safe, 2000, The Day Reagan Was Shot, 2001, Coast to Coast, 2004; actor, prodr.(TV movies) Prisoner of Honor, 1991, Oliver Twist, 1997, Copshop, 2004; (TV appearances) Ben Casey, 1965, Gidget, 1966, Bewitched, 1966, The Big Valley, 1967, Occasional Wife, 1967, That Girl, 1967, Hey, Landlord, 1967, Please Don't Eat the Daisies, 1967, The Second Hundred Years, 1967, Judd for the Defense, 1968, Felony Squad, 1968, The Ghost & Mrs. Muir, 1969, The New People, 1969, The Bold Ones: The New Doctors, 1970, Room 222, 1970, The Young Lawyers, 1971, The Mod Squad, 1973, Gunsmoke, 1973, A Touch of Grace, 1973, The New Dick Van Dyke Show, 1973; host (TV series) The Class of the 20th Century, 1991; actor (TV series) Karen, 1964; actor, prodr. (TV series) The Education of Max Bickford, 2001-2002; theatrical appearances include: Julius Caesar, 1978, Othello, 1979, Total Abandon, 1983, Death and the Maiden, 1992exec. prodr. (films) Quiz Show, 1994; dir., writer (TV movies) Present Tense, Past Perfect, 1995 Participant civil rights marches, lobbying for amnesty bills. Served alt. mil. duty Los Angeles County Gen. Hosp., 1969-71. Mem. ACLU, Screen Actors Guild, Equity Assn., AFTRA, Motion Picture Acad. Arts and Scis.

DREZ, DAVID JACOB, JR., orthopedic surgeon, educator; b. Lake Charles, La., Aug. 21, 1938; s. David Jacob and Hester Adele (Bingham) D.; m. Judith Diane Wolfe, June 5, 1963; children: Susan, Catherine Ann Self, David Jacob III. BS, Tulane U., 1959, MD, 1963. Diplomate Am. Bd. Surgery, Am. Bd. Orthopaedic Surgery. Intern Charity Hosp., New Orleans, 1963-64, resident in gen. surgery, 1964-68, resident in orthopaedic surgery, 1968-71; resident Scottish Rite Hosp., Atlanta, 1969, USPHS Hosp., New Orleans, 1970; pvt. practice Orthopaedic Assocs., Lake Charles, 1971-82; pvt. practice Orthopaedic and Sports Injury Clinic Knee and Sports Medicine Ctr., Lake Charles, 1982-94; pvt. practice Ctr. for Orthopaedics, Lake Charles, 1994—. Staff Lake Charles Meml. Hosp., 1973—, bd. trustees, 1973, 80-82, sec.-treas., 1977, pres., 1981, chief surgery, 1984, 85; med. staff dept. orthopaedics Children's Hosp., New Orleans, 1988; La. state chmn. Orthopaedic Rsch. and Edn. Found., 1987, 90-92; network of orthopedic surgeons U.S. Gymnastics Fedn., 1988—; physician U.S. Soccer Assn., 1988—; examiner Am. Bd. Orthopaedic Surgery, 1989, 91, 92, bd. dirs.; vis. prof. numerous hosps. and univs.; speaker in field. Author: (with R. D'Ambrosia) Prevention and Treatment of Running Injuries, 1982, Prevention and Treatment of Running Injuries, 2d edit., 1989, (with D.W. Jackson) The Anterior Cruciate Deficient Knee-New Concepts in Ligament Repair, 1986, Orthopaedic Sports Medicine: Principles and Practice , 1994 (with Jesse DeLee); author 8 chpts. in books; editor Am. Jour. Sports Medicine, 1988—, Jour. Orthopaedic Techniques, 1993—; co-editor Operative Techniques in Sports Medicine jour., 1993—; mem. editl. bd. Orthopaedics, 1983—, Arthroscopy, 1984-89, Sports Medicine News, 1989—; author 5 video tapes, audio tape; adv. bd. Clin. Update, Sports Medicine, 1983—, Clin. Orthopaedics and Related Rsch., 1987-93; con. rev. bd. Jour. Bone and Joint Surgeons, 1989—; contbr. articles to profl. jours. Team orthopaedist athletic dept. McNeese State U., Lake Charles, 1974—, pres. 100 Club, 1979; co-dir. Runner's Clinic, La. State U. Sch. Medicine, New Orleans, 1978-81; chief physician NAAU Boxing Championship, Lake Charles, 1979; mem. Gov.'s Coun. on Phys. Fitness and Sports, 1981; bd. dirs. Lake Area Runners, 1989-92. Maj. La. N.G., 1963-71. Named to La. Athletic Trainers Assn. Hall of Fame, 1989, McNeese State U. Hall of Honors, 1990. Mem. Acad. Orthopaedic Soc., Am. Acad. Orthopaedic Surgeons, Am. Acad. Sports Physicians, Am. Coll. Sports Medicine, Am. Coll. Surgeons, Am. Orthopaedic Assn., Am. Orthopaedic Foot Soc., Am. Orthopaedic Foot and Ankle Soc., Am. Orthopaedic Soc. Sports Medicine, Arthroscopy Assn. N.Am., Assn. Bone and Joint Surgeons, Assn. Sports Medicine Fellowship Dirs., Mid. Am. Orthopaedic Assn., Assn. Arthritic Hip and Knee Surgery, Australian-Am. Orthopaedic Soc., Calcasieu Parish Med. Soc., Clin. Orthopaedic Soc., European Soc. Knee Surgery and Arthroscopy, Herodicus Sports Medicine Soc. (past sec., v.p., pres.), Internat. Arthroscopy Assn., Internat. Soc. Knee, La. Orthopaedic Assn. (pres. 1992), La. State Med. Assn., Oscar Creech Surg. Soc., Orthopaedic Rsch. Soc., Soc. Internat. Chirurgie Orthopedique Traumatologie, Soc. Internat. Recherche Orthopedique Tramatologie. Avocations: reading, jogging, travel. Office: Orthop Clinic SW La 2615 Enterprise Blvd Ste B Lake Charles LA 70601-8990 Office Phone: 337-480-8900. Business E-Mail: drezmd@pol.net.

DRIGGS, CHARLES MULFORD, lawyer; b. East Cleveland, Ohio, Jan. 26, 1924; s. Karl Holcomb and Lila Vandeveer (Wilson) D.; children: Ruth, Rachel, Carrie, Karl H., Charles M.; m. Ann Eileen Zargari, Oct. 25, 1991. BS, Yale U., 1947, JD, 1950. Bar: Ohio 1951. Assoc. Squire, Sanders & Dempsey, Cleve., 1950-64, ptnr., 1964-88, of counsel, 1988-91; pvt. practice civil law Cleve., 1991-95; prin. Driggs, Hogg & Fry Co., LPA, Willoughby Hills, Ohio, 1995. Pres. Bratenahl (Ohio) Sch. Bd., 1958—62; mem. adv. coun. Cleve. Ctr. for Theol. Edn., 1978—. Mem. ABA, Ohio Bar Assn., Lake County Bar Assn., Cleve. Bar Assn., Greater Cleve. Growth Assn., Cleve. Law Libr. Assn. (trustee 1977-91), Ct. Nisi Prius (judge 2000), Citizens League Greater Cleve., Geauga County Bar Assn., Phi Delta Phi, Tau Beta Pi, Phi Gamma Delta. Home: 8011 Eagle Rd Kirtland OH 44094 Office: 38500 Chardon Rd Willoughby OH 44094 Office Phone: 440-391-5100. E-mail: charles@driggslaw.com. *Any success I may have achieved I attribute to my continuing attempt to live and conduct my affairs in a manner that my family and friends may later reflect upon with pride.*

DRINKO, JOHN DEAVER, lawyer; b. St. Marys, W.Va., June 17, 1921; s. Emery J. and Hazel (White) D.; m. Elizabeth Gibson, May 14, 1946; children: Elizabeth Lee Sullivan, Diana Lynn Drinko, John Randall, Jay Deaver. AB, Marshall U., 1942; JD, Ohio State U., 1944; postgrad., U. Tex. Sch. Law, 1944; LLD (hon.), Marshall U., 1980, Ohio State U., 1986, John Carroll U., 1987, Capital U., 1988, Cleve. State U., 1990; DHL (hon.), David N. Myers Coll., 1990, U. N.H., 1992, Baldwin-Wallace Coll., 1993, Ursuline Coll., 1994, Notre Dame Coll., 1997, U. Rio Grande, 1999, Marietta Coll., 2001. Bar: Ohio 1945, D.C 1946, U.S. Dist. Ct. (no. dist.) Ohio 1958. Assoc. Baker & Hostetler, Cleve., 1945-55, ptnr., 1955-69, mng. ptnr., from 1969, sr. adviser to mng. com. Chmn. bd. Cleve. Inst. Electronics Inc., Double D Ranch Inc., Ohio, Orvis Co. Inc., Preformed Line Products Inc. Trustee Elizabeth G. and John D. Drinko Charitable Found., Orvis-Perkins Found., Mellen Found., The Cloyes-Myers Found., Marshall U. Found.; founder Consortium of Multiple Sclerosis Ctrs., Mellen Conf. on Acute and Critical Care Nursing, Case Western Res. U. Disting. fellow Cleve. Clinc Found., 1991; Ohio State Law Sch. Bldg. named in his honor, 1995, libr. at Marshall U. named in his honor, 1997; inducted into Bus. Hall of Fame, Marshall Univ., 1996. Mem. ABA, Am. Jud. Assn., Bar Assn. Greater Cleve., Greater Cleve. Growth Assn., Ohio State Bar Assn., Jud. Conf. 8th Jud. Dist. (life), Soc. Benchers, Case Western Res. U. Law Sch. Assn., Cleve. Play House, Cleve. Civil War Round-table, Mayfield Sand Ridge Country Club, Union Club, The Club at Soc. Ctr., O'Donnell Golf Club, Order of Coif, 33o Scottish Rite Mason, Knight Templar, York Rite, Euclid Blue Lodge No. 599 (Jesters, Shrine, Grotto). Republican. Presbyterian. Home: 4891 Middledale Rd Cleveland OH 44124-2522 also: 1245 Otono Dr Palm Springs CA 92264-8445 Office: Baker & Hostetler LLP 1900 E 9th St Ste 3200 Cleveland OH 44114-3485

DRINKWARD, CECIL, construction company executive; m. Sally Drinkward. BS in Engring., Calif. Tech. With Del E. Webb Corp., Phoenix; joined as exec. v.p., gen. mgr. Hoffman Corp., 1967; pres.; CEO Hoffman Corp., Portland, Oreg. Pres., mem. bd. trustees Oregon State U. Found.; mem. Oregon State U. Coun. Regents. Office: Hoffman Construction Co 805 SW Broadway Ste 2100 Portland OR 97205-3361

DRINKWATER, WILLIAM WAYNE, lawyer; b. Meridian, Miss., Feb. 20, 1949; s. William Wayne and Margaret (Dement) D.; m. Ouida C. Creekmore, June 3, 1972; children: Jennifer Dement, William Woods. BA, U. Miss., 1971, JD, 1974. Bar: Miss. 1974, U.S. Dist. Ct. (no. and so. dists.) Miss. 1974, U.S. Ct. Appeals (5th cir.) 1974, U.S. Supreme Ct. 1982. Law clk. to William C. Keady U.S. Dist. Ct. Miss., Greenville, 1974-76; law clk. to chief justice Warren Burger U.S. Supreme Ct., Washington, 1976-77; assoc. Lake, Tindall, Hunger & Thackston, Greenville, 1977, ptnr, 1977-87, Butler, Snow, O'Mara, Stevens & Cannada, Jackson, Miss., 1987-93, Lake Tindall, LLP, Jackson, Miss., 1993—2001, Bradley, Arant, Rose & White LLP, 2001—. Mem. adv. group Civil Justice Reform Act of 1990, 1990-93; mem. model civil jury instrn. com. Miss. Jud. Coll., Jackson, 1989-90; chmn. Gov.'s adv. com. on Yazoo Basin Project, Jackson, 1988-89; Gov.'s com. on Corrections, 1981. 1st lt. U.S. Army, 1971-76. Mem. Am. Law Inst., Am. Acad. Appellate Lawyers, Am. Coll. Trial Lawyers, Miss. Bar Assn. (pres. young lawyers sect. 1982-83), Supreme Ct. Hist. Soc. Office: 188 E Capitol St Ste 450 Jackson MS 39201-2127 Office Phone: 601-448-8000. Business E-Mail: wdrinkwater@bradleyarant.com.

DRINNON, JANIS BOLTON, artist, poet, volunteer; b. Pineville, Ky., July 28, 1922; d. Clyde Herman and Violet Ethiele (Hendrickson) Bolton; m. Kenneth Cleveland Drinnon, June 13, 1948; 1 child, Dena Daryl. Student, Lincoln Meml. U., Harrogate, Tenn., 1947-48, Newspaper Inst. Am.; comml. art cert., Art Instrn. Sch., Mpls., 1968. Author: (poems) In HIS Care: A Book of Inspirational Poetry, 1998. Organizer, prodr., dir. religious plays drama dept. Alice Bell Bapt. Ch., Knoxville, Tenn.; mem. New Hopewell Bapt. Ch., Knoxville. Named to Internat. Poetry Hall of Fame, 1996. Mem.: Internat. Soc. Poets (disting. mem.). Republican. Avocations: arts, crafts, painting, composing poetry. Home: 7342 Hodges Ferry Rd Knoxville TN 37920-9732 E-mail: kcdrinnon@aol.com.

DRINNON, RICHARD, retired historian; b. Portland, Oreg., Jan. 4, 1925; s. John Henry and Emma (Tweed) D.; m. Anna Maria Faulise, Oct. 20, 1945; children: Donna Elizabeth, Jon Tweed. BA summa cum laude, Willamette U., 1950; MA, U. Minn., 1951, PhD, 1957. Instr. humanities U. Minn., 1952-53, social sci., 1955-57; instr. Am. history U. Calif., 1957-58, asst. prof., 1958-61; Bruern fellow in Am. studies U. Leeds, 1961-63; faculty research fellow Social Sci. Research Council, 1963-64; asso. prof. history Hobart and William Smith Colls., 1964-66; chmn. dept. history Bucknell U., 1966-74, prof. history, 1974-87, prof. emeritus, 1987—. Vis. prof. U. Paris, 1975 Author: Rebel in Paradise: a Biography of Emma Goldman, 1961, White Savage: The Case of John Dunn Hunter, 1972, Facing West: The Metaphysics of Indian-Hating and Empire-Building, 1980, 90, 97, Keeper of Concentration Camps: Dillon S. Myer and American Racism, 1987; co-editor: Nowhere at Home: Letters from Exile of Emma Goldman and Alexander Berkman, 1974; contbr. articles and revs. to profl. jours. and mags. Served with USNR, 1942-46. NEH sr. fellow, 1980-81 Office: PO Box 1001 Port Orford OR 97465-1001

DRISCOLL, CHARLES FREDERICK, physicist, educator; b. Tucson, Feb. 28, 1950; s. John Raymond Gozzi and Barbara Jean (Hamilton) Driscoll; m. Suzan C. Bain, Dec. 30, 1972; children: Thomas A., Robert A. BA in Physics summa cum laude, Cornell U., 1969; MS, U. Calif. San Diego, La Jolla, 1972, PhD, 1976. Staff scientist Gen. Atomics, San Diego, 1969; rsch. asst. U. Calif. San Diego, La Jolla, 1971-76, rsch. physicist, sr. lectr., 1976-96, prof. physics, 1996—, assoc. dir. Inst. for Pure and Applied Scis., 1998—. Cons. Sci. Applications, Inc., 1980-81; staff physicist, cons. Molecular Biosystems, Inc., 1981-82. Editor: Non-Neutral Plasma Physics, 1988; contbr. numerous articles to sci. jours. Fellow NSF, 1969-71. Fellow Am. Phys. Soc. (Excellence in Plasma Physics Rsch. award 1991, Disting. Lectr. divsn. plasma physics 1999-2000); mem. AAAS, Math. Assn. Am., Phi Beta Kappa. Achievements include development of quantitative analysis of magnetic targeting of microspheres in capillaries, experiments and theory on magnetized electron plasmas, new camera-diagnosed electron plasma apparatus, new laser-diagnosed ion plasma apparatus for in-situ transport measurements; establishment of magnetic containment characteristics of unneutralized plasmas; measurement of collisional transport of heat and particles to thermal equilibrium; observation of new 2D fluid instability and relaxation of 2D turbulence to vortex crystal states. Office: U Calif San Diego Dept Physics 0319 9500 Gilman Dr Dept 0319 La Jolla CA 92093-5004 E-mail: fdriscoll@ucsd.edu.

DRISCOLL, CHARLES THURSTON, JR., civil and environmental engineering educator; b. Rochester, NH, Mar. 17, 1952; BS with distinction in Civil Engring., U. Maine, Orono, 1974; MS in Environ. Engring., Cornell U., Ithaca, NY, 1976, PhD in Environ. Engring., 1980. Asst. prof. civil engring. dept. Syracuse U., NY, 1979—83, assoc. prof., 1983—85, prof. dept. civil and environ. engring., 1985—93, prof. earth scis. (courtesy appointment), 1989—, prof. chemistry (courtesy appointment), 1993—, disting. prof. civil and environ. engring., 1993—2001, dir. Ctr. Environ. Engring. in L.C. Smith Coll. Engring. and Computer Sci., 1998—, prof. biology (courtesy appoitnement), 2001—, Univ. prof. environ. systems engring., 2001—. Bd. dirs. Upstate Freshwater Inst., 1981—; Onondaga Lake adv. com. Onondaga County, 1983—; vis. scientist dept. soil sci. and geology Agrl. U. Wageningen, Netherlands, 1983; dir. hydrogeology prog. Syracuse U., 1986—96, chair dept. civil and environ. engring., 2001—03; vis. scientist Inst. Ecosystem Studies, Millbrook, NY, 1987—88; mem. sci. adv. com. Hubbard Brook Ecosystem Study, 1987—; mem. long-term ecol. rsch. coordinating com. NSF, 1988—; sec. bd. dirs. Hubbard Brook Rsch. Found., 1993—. Contbr. articles to sci. jours.; co-author: Impacts of Acidic Deposition: Context and Case Studies of Forest Soils in the Southeastern US, 1989; editor: Experimental Watershed Liming Study, 1996. Recipient Presdl. Young Investigator award, 1984, Environ. Rsch. Prog. award, IBM Corp., 1993. Mem.: ASCE, Am. Geophys. Union, Soil Sci. Soc. Am., Assn. Environ. Engring. and Sci. Prof., Am. Chem. Soc., NAE, Sigma Xi (Rsch. award 1987). Office: Dept Civil and Environ Engring Syracuse U Syracuse NY 13244-1190 Office Phone: 315-443-3434. Office Fax: 315-443-1243. E-mail: ctdrisco@mailbox.syr.edu.*

DRISCOLL, CONSTANCE FITZGERALD, education educator, writer, consultant; b. Lawrence, Mass., Mar. 29, 1926; d. John James and Mary Anne (Leecock) Fitzgerald; m. Francis George Driscoll, Aug. 21, 1948; children: Frances Mary, Martha Anne, Sara Helene, Maribeth Lee. AB, Radcliffe Coll., 1946; postgrad., Harvard U., U. Hartford, U. Bridgeport, U. Mass. Secondary sch. tchr., North Andover, Mass., 1946-48; book reviewer N.Y.C. and Boston pubs., 1955-64; asst. conf. edn. dir. U. Hartford, 1964-68; lectr. Pace U., NYC, 1973-74; edn. commentary Radio WVOX, New Rochelle, N.Y., 1974-75; asst. ednl. adv. Nat. Girl Scouts, 1972-74; pres., owner, dir. Open Corridor Schs. Cons., Inc., Bronxville, N.Y., 1972-84; pres., dir. Open Corridor Schs., Inc., Oxford, Mass., 1984—, Worcester, Mass., 2000—, Sarasota, Jacksonville and Bradenton, Fla., 2003—. Dir. assoc. grad. edn. program with U. Hartford, Bronxville, N.Y., 1975-82; dir. grad. edn. program with U. Bridgeport, Greenwich, Conn., 1975-82; creator in svc. edn. programs pub. schs., Norwalk, Conn., 1983-88; assoc. Worcester State Coll., 1984-85, Fitchburg State Coll., 1986-87; dir. assoc. grad. edn. for tchrs. Anna Maria Coll., Paxton, Mass., 1990-94; assoc. grad. tchr. edn. courses Fitchburg State Coll., 1995-99; English instr. grades 9-12, Bais Chana HS for Girls, Worcester, Mass., 2000—, chair English dept., 2000—; provider long distance learning grad. edn. courses, Antigua and Anguilla, 1997—, U. Bridgeport, Conn., 1995—, assoc. agy. for grad. edn. courses for tchrs., 1995—; profl. devel. points provider Mass. State Dept. Edn., 1995—; tutor, cons. Worcester County Sch. Dists., 1989-95; CEU mgr. for Conn. Dept. Edn. O.C.S., Inc., Conn., 1989—; bi-lingual instr. for Indian and Vietnamese students in grades 5-12, 1988-91; dir. grad. edn. courses for tchrs. Mass. Coll. Liberal Arts, North Adams, 1999—; cons. coll./univ. and grad. sch. placement, admissions procedures, 2000—; adviser, cons. Radcliffe Coll. Admissions Coun., 1946-48; summer dir. swim program ARC, North Andover, Mass., 1942-47; cons. Girl Scouts U.S., health guide multicultural program Greater Lawrence, Mass., 1946-48, holiday radio program, Thanksgiving 1774, Antigua and Barbuda; lectr., series for Girl Guides, Antigua, W.I., 1974. Author numerous poems; contbr. articles to profl. jours., local newspapers. Recipient Educator award Nat. Coun. ARC, Washington, 1985, Edn. award Nipmuc Am. Indian Coun., Webster, Mass., 1985. Office: Open Corridor Schs Inc 212 Lakewood Dr Bradenton FL 34210 also: Open Corridor Schs Inc 1015 Atlantic Blvd Ste 273 Atlantic Beach FL 32233 Personal E-mail: opcorridor@aol.com.

DRISCOLL, DAVID P., school system administrator; m. Kathy Driscoll; 4 children. BA in Math, Boston Coll.; PhD in Ednl. Adminstrn., Boston Coll; MA in Ednl. Adminstrn., Salem State Coll. Math. tchr. Jr. HS, Somerville, Mass., Sr. HS, Melrose, Mass.; asst supt. Melrose, Mass., 1972—84; supt., 1984—93; dep. commr. edn. Mass. Dept. Edn., 1993—98, interim commr. edn., 1998—99, commr. edn., 1999—. Prin. investigator in Mass. NSF Math. and Sci. Program; co-developer five year master plan Mass. Dept. Edn., 1995; mem. oversight bds. School to Work Initiative, Mass.; chmn. Mass. Tchrs. Retirement Bd., 1998—; mem. Nat Assessment Governing Bd., 2006—. Mem.: Coun. Chief State Sch. Officers (pres.). Avocations: golf, writing. Office: Mass Dept Edn 350 Main St Malden MA 02148-5023 Mailing: Council of Chief State Sch Officers One Massachusetts Ave NW Ste 700 Washington DC 20001-1431 Office Phone: 202-336-7000. Office Fax: 202-408-8072.*

DRISCOLL, JOHN, publishing executive; Territory mgr. Oakley; sales, mktg. mgr. Deltran Corp.; we. advt. mgr., Cycle World Hachette Filapacchi Media US Inc., 1995—98, we. advt. mgr. to we. dir., auto group, 1998—2004, assoc. pub., Road & Track Mag. Ann Arbor, Mich., 2004—05, v.p., pub., Road & Track, 2005—. Office: Road & Track Hachette Filapacchi Media US Inc 2002 Hogback Rd Ann Arbor MI 48105 also: Hachette Filapacchi Media 1633 Broadway New York NY 10019*

DRISCOLL, KAREN, communications executive; b. 1970; Dir. mktg. KinderActive; v.p., Nickelodeon brand mktg. Nickelodeon, sr. v.p., mktg. and strategic planning, 2005—. Designer La Casa de Dora campaign (Cable & Telecom. Assn. for Mktg. award). Named one of 40 Executives Under 40, Multichannel News, 2006. Office: Nickelodeon Networks 1515 Broadway 42nd Fl New York NY 10036 Office Phone: 212-258-7500. Office Fax: 212-258-7705.

DRISCOLL, KIMBERLEE MARIE, lawyer; b. Binghamton, NY, July 17, 1961; d. Patrick Donald and Diane Cecile (Richmond) Lake; m. Matthew Victor Driscoll, Aug. 6, 1983; children: John Patrick, Bennett George. BA, Colgate U., 1983; JD, Union U., 1986. Bar: N.Y. 1987, Mass. 1988. Asst. gen. counsel Oxbow Corp., Dedham, Mass., 1987-90; corp. counsel, sec. Putnam, Hayes & Bartlett, Inc., Cambridge, Mass., 1990-92; v.p., gen. counsel Merrill Internat. Ltd., Cambridge, 1992—2000; gen. counsel Arthur D. Little, Inc., Cambridge, 2000—01; pres. Resolutions Mgmt. Ltd., Houston, 2001—. Mem. ABA (vice chair spl. com. internat. energy law 1993—), Mass. Bar Assn., N.Y. Bar Assn., Turnaround Mgmt. Assn. Office Phone: 781-929-6919. Business E-Mail: kmdriscoll@resolutionsmanagement.com.

DRISCOLL, LORI, neuroscientist, educator; b. Brush, Colo., Oct. 20, 1971; d. Larry and Ellen Larsen; m. Jonathan Driscoll. BA, Colo. Coll., Colorado Springs, 1994; PhD, Cornell U., Ithaca, NY, 2003. Asst. prof. Colo. Coll., 2003—. Spkr. in field. Mem.: AAAS, Neurobehavioral Teratology Soc., Assn. Women Sci., Soc. Neurosci., Alpha Lambda Delta, Psi Chi, Phi Beta Kappa. Office: The Colorado College 14 East Cache La Poudre Colorado Springs CO 80903 Office Phone: 719-227-8201. Business E-Mail: ldriscoll@coloradocollege.edu.

DRISCOLL, MEGAN, executive recruiter; m. Eric Greenstein, Aug. 26, 2000; 1 child, Madeline Greenstein. BA, Davidson Coll., NC, 1997. Exec. recruiter Fortune Pers. Cons., Peabody, Mass., 1998—2002; pres., founder PharmaLogics Recruiting, Braintree, Mass., 2002—. Spkr. in field. Mem.: Internat. Soc. Xenobiotics, Am. Chem. Soc., Am. Assn. Pharm. Scientists, Amercan Soc. Cell Biology, Am. Soc. Quality, Internat. Soc. Pharm. Engrs., Parenteral Drug Assn. Independent. Unitarian. Office: PharmaLogics Recruiting 220 Forbes Rd Braintree MA 02184 Home Phone: 617-827-0404; Office Phone: 781-848-5500. Business E-Mail: mdriscoll@pharmalogicsrecruiting.com.

DRISKELL, CLAUDE EVANS, college director, educator, dentist; b. Chgo., Jan. 13, 1926; s. James Ernest and Helen Elizabeth (Perry) D., Sr.; m. Naomi Roberts, Sept. 30, 1953; 1 child, Yvette Michele; stepchildren: Isaiah, Ruth, Reginald, Elaine. BS, Roosevelt U., 1950; BS in Dentistry, U. Ill., 1952, DDS, 1954. Practice dentistry, Chgo., 1954—; adj. prof. Chgo. State U., 1971—; dean's aide, adviser black students Coll. Dentistry U. Ill., 1972—. Dental cons., supervising dentist, dental hygienists supportive health services Bd. Edn., Chgo., 1974. Author: The Influence of the Halogen Elements Upon the Hydrocarbon, and their Effect on General Anesthesia, 1962; History of Chicago's Black Dental Professionals, 1850-1983; co-author (with Claude Driskell) Essays on Professor Dr. Earl Renfroe-A Man of Firsts, 2001; author, editor and publisher: Original Forty Club's 75th Anniversary Book (1920-1995); author, editor, archivist, historian Forty Club, 1993-2000; mem. editl. bd. Nat. Dental Assn. Quar. Jour., 1977—; contbr. articles to profl. jours. Vice pres. bd. dirs. Jackson Park Highlands Assn., 1971-73. Served with AUS, 1944-46; ETO. Fellow Internat. Biog. Assn., Royal Soc. Health (Gt. Britain), Acad. Gen. Dentistry; mem. Lincoln Dental Soc. (editor), Chgo. Dental Soc., ADA, Nat. Dental Assn. (editor pres.'s newsletter; dir. pub. relations, publicity; recipient pres.'s spl. achievement award 1969) dental assns., Am. Assn. Dental Editors, Acad. Gen. Dentistry, Soc. Med. Writers, Soc. Advancement Anesthesia in Dentistry, Omega Psi Phi. Home: 6727 S Bennett Ave Chicago IL 60649-1031 Office: 11139 S Halsted St Chicago IL 60628-3910 Office Phone: 773-233-0460.

DRISKELL, LUCILE G., artist; b. NYC, Dec. 20, 1924; d. Charles Albert and Clarice Dorothy (Jung) Gall; m. Richard O. Driskell, Sept. 4, 1946; children: Douglas G., Donald A., David O. AA, Finch Coll., 1945; student, La Jolla Art Ctr., Calif., 1956-63, Fratelli Da Prato Foundry, Pietra Santa, Italy, 1973-78, Art Students League, NYC, 1984-88. Artist, San Diego, 1950-63, Cin., 1963-67, Aspen, Colo., 1967-72, Greve in Chianti, Italy, 1972-79, Wellsboro, Pa., 1979—, Phila., 1985—. Represented by Environment Gallery, NYC, 1968—84, Rodger Lapelle Gallery, Phila., 1984—, Agora Gallery, NY, 1993—2002, Amsterdam Whitney Internat. Fine Arts, NYC, 2002—. Paintings, 1995—, sculptures, 1960—, wall reliefs, 1988—, prints, 1956—, Represented in permanent collections Woodmere Art Mus., Phila. Recipient Purchase award, Exxon, N.Y.C.,

1978, Wachovia Bank, Wilmington, Del., 1996, Macy's, Washington, 1989, SAS Inst., Inc., Cary, N.C., 2001. Mem.: Nas. Assn. Women Artists, Washington Sculpture Group, Internat. Sculpture Ctr., Art Students League (life). Avocations: hiking, photography, travel. Home: 389 Fischler St Ext Wellsboro PA 16901-8925 E-mail: drisk@epix.net.

DRISKILL, JAMES LAWRENCE, minister; b. Rustburg, Va., Aug. 18, 1920; s. Elijah Hudnall and Annie Pharr (Carwile) D.; m. Ethel Lillian Cassel, May 28, 1949 (dec. Aug. 2004); children: Edward Lawrence, Mary Lillian; m. Edina de Rosa, Apr. 18, 2007. BA, Pa. State U., 1946; BD, San Francisco Theol. Sem., 1949; ThM, Princeton Sem., 1957; S.T.D., San Francisco Theol. Sem., 1969. Ordained minister in Presbyn. Ch. 1949. Missionary Presbyn. Ch. USA, Japan, 1949-72; stated supply pastor Madison Square Presbyn. Ch., San Antonio, 1973; minister Highland Presbyn. Ch., Maryville, Tenn., 1973-82; supply pastor of Japanese-Am. chs. Presbyn. Ch. USA, Long Beach, Calif., Hollywood, Calif., Altadena, Calif., 1984-99. Vis. prof. religion dept. Trinity U., 1972-73. Author: Adventures in Senior Living, 1997, Christmas Stories from Around the World, 1997, Worldwide Mission Stories for Young People, 1996, Cross-Cultural Marriages and the Church, 1995, Mission Stories from Around the World, 1994, Japan Diary, 1993, Mission Adventures in Many Lands, 1992; contbr. articles to profl. jours. Trustee Osaka (Japan) Girls Sch., 1952-65, Seikyo Gakuen Christian Sch., Japan, 1953-92. With USN, 1943-46. Mem. Am. Acad. Religion, Presbyn. Writers Guild, Sierra Club. Democrat. Presbyterian. Home and Office: 3716 Grace Ave Baldwin Park CA 91706 *Experience has taught me that, ultimately, the meaning and value of a person's life is determined by the quality of one's personal relationships, especially by the quality of one's relationship to God.*

DRISKILL, THOMAS K., transportation executive; b. Feb. 20, 1948; Student, San Francisco City Coll., 1980. Transp. coord., San Francisco. Fellow: Mensa.

DRISKO, CONNIE LEE HASTINGS, dean, dental educator; Degree, Caruth Sch. Dentistry, Baylor Coll. Dentistry, 1961; BS, Baylor Coll. Dentistry, 1975; DDS, U. Mo., Kansas City, 1980. Cert. in periodontics Dept. Vet. Affairs Med. Ctr. Pvt. practice dental hygienist; prof. periodontics U. Louisville Sch. Dentistry, assoc. dean for academic planning, faculty devel., dir. clin. rsch.; dean, Merritt prof. of periodontics Sch. Dentistry, Med. Coll. Ga., 2003—. Bd. dirs. Young Innovations, Inc., 1998. Fellow: Exec. Leadership in Acad. Med. Program for Women, Am. Coll. Dentists. Office: Med Coll Ga Sch Dentistry 1120 15th St Augusta GA 30912

DRIVER, JOE LUTHER, state legislator, consultant, insurance agent; b. Rockwall, Tex., Sept. 29, 1946; s. Marshall Laguin and Alice Elizabeth (Patillo) D.; m. S. DeAnne Browning, Nov. 20, 1993; stepchildren: Eric Browning, Lynsey Browning. BBA, U. North Tex., 1971; grad., Garland Citizen's Police Acad., 1993. With Steak & Ale Restaurants, Dallas, 1971—73; instr. Garland (Tex.) Ind. Sch. Dist., 1972; mgr. Marshall Driver Ins., Garland, 1972-73; owner, agt. Joe Driver Ins.-State Farm, Garland, 1973—; mem. Tex. Ho. of Reps., 1993—. Chmn. law enforcement com. Tex. Ho. Reps., 2003—, mem. environ. regulations com., 2005—. Pres. Christian Singles Unltd., Garland, 1979; bd. dirs. First United Meth. Ch., Garland, 1979-81, Garland Econ. and Devel. Authority, 1986, Garland Crimestoppers, 1985-88, 93—, Am. Heart Assn., 1991-93; bd. dirs. New Beginning Family and Violence Prevention Ctr., 1988-91, v.p., 1990-91; chmn. SITE Found. of Garland, Inc., 1991-92; mem. bd. mgmt. Garland YMCA, 1983-85; fundraising chmn. YWCA, 1992; mem. long-range planning com. City of Garland, 1986-88; mem. devel. coun. Baylor Med. Ctr., Garland, 1991-2006; mem. Downtown Citizen Rev. Com., 1991-92; active Tex. Conservative Coalition, 1993—, Rep. Caucus Tex. Ho. of Reps., 1993—. Recipient Human Rels. award Dale Carnegie Cos., 1978. Mem. Nat. Assn. Life Underwriters (Nat. Quality award 1978-83, 86-92, 2002), Dallas Assn. Life Underwriters, Garland C. of C. (bd. dirs. 1983-87, chmn. 1986, corp. coun. 1988-90), Rowlett C. of C., Sachse C. of C., Tex. Dist. Exch. Clubs (dist. dir. 1984, Outstanding Dist. Dir. award 1985, Pres.'s award 1986), Noon Exch. Club Garland (bd. dirs. 1982-86, 90-91, pres. 1983, 90, Outstanding Svc. award 1986-87), Leadership Garland Alumni Assn. (bd. dirs. 1990-91), U. North Tex. Alumni Assn. (bd. dirs. 2001-), Lambda Chi Alpha (pres. 1971). Avocations: golf, weight training. Office: 201 S Glenbrook Dr Garland TX 75040-6227

DRIVER, MARTHA WESTCOTT, literature educator, researcher, writer; b. NYC, Oct. 24; d. Albert Westcott and Martha Louise (Miller) D.; m. Thomas Edward Earl Rhodes, Aug. 4, 2001. BA, Vassar Coll., 1974; MA, U. Pa., 1975, PhD, 1980. Lectr. English Vassar Coll., NYC, 1980-81; from asst. prof. to assoc. prof. Pace U., NYC, 1981-95, prof. English, 1995—2003, Disting. prof. English, 2003—, dir. honors program, 1998-2000. Cons. N.Y. Pub. Libr., 1984; seminar participant Folger Inst., Folger Shakespeare Libr., 1994. Editor: Jour. of the Early Book Soc., 1998—; guest editor: Film & History: The Middle Ages, 1998—99, Literary and Linguistic Computing, 1999; editor: The Medieval Hero on Screen, 2004; author: The Image in Print, 2004; contbr. articles to profl. jours; co-author (with Michael Orr): An Index of Images in English MSS, 2007. Mem., lectr. St. John the Divine , NYC, 1995. Recipient Dyson Achievement award, 2003; grantee Rsch. tools grantee, NEH, 1995, travel grantee, Am. Coun. Learned Socs., 1995, NSF, 2001—; Houghton Libr. Harvard U. fellow, 1996—97. Mem. Early Book Soc. (chair 1988—), Coll. Art Assn., Medieval Acad. Am., Modern Humanities Rsch. Assn. (U.K.), Medieval Club of N.Y. (conf. coord. 1989-94. pres. 1987-89), Internat. Ctr. Medieval Art, Internat. Arthurian Soc., Medieval Feminist Art History Project, New Chaucer Soc. Episcopalian. Avocations: dance, museums, theater, concerts. Office: Pace U English Dept 41 Park Row New York NY 10038-1508 Office Phone: 212-346-1672. Business E-Mail: mdriver@pace.edu.

DRIVER, MICHAEL J., lawyer; b. Highland Park, Ill., Dec. 4, 1944; BA, Amherst Coll., 1967; JD, Univ. Denver, 1974. Bar: Colo. 1974. Ptnr., Public Policy, Legis. Affairs, Environ. Health & Safety practices, mem. exec. com. Patton Boggs LLP, Denver. Mem. Clinton for Pres. Nat. Exec. Com., Clinton Nat. Fin. Com., Pres. Inaugural Com., Clinton Transition Team Nat. Resources sect. Mem. Native Am. Rights Fund Nat. Sponsorship Com., John F. Kennedy Ctr for Performing Arts Adv. Com. on the Arts. Mem.: ABA, Colo. Bar Assn., Denver Bar Assn. Office: Patton Boggs LLP Suite 1900 1660 Lincoln St Denver CO 80264-1901 Office Phone: 303-830-1776. Office Fax: 303-894-9239. Business E-Mail: mdriver@pattonboggs.com.

DRIVER, MINNIE, actress; b. London, Jan. 31, 1970; d. Ronnie and Gaynor Driver. Actress: (films) Circle of Friends, 1995, GoldenEye, 1995, Sleepers, 1996, Big Night, 1996, Grosse Pointe Blank, 1997, Mononoke Hime, 1997, Good Will Hunting, 1997, The Governess, 1998, At Sachem Farm, 1998, Hard Rain, 1998, Slow Burn, 1999, An Ideal Husband, 1999, Tarzan, 1999, South Park: Bigger, Longer and Uncut, 1999, Return to Me, 2000, Beautiful, 2000, High Heels and Low Lifes, 2001, Owning Mahowny, 2003, Hope Springs, 2003, Ella Enchanted, 2004, The Phantom of the Opera, 2004, Ripple Effect, 2006, The Virgin of Juarez, 2006, Delirious, 2006, Take, 2007; (TV series) The Riches, 2007-; (TV miniseries) Mr. Wroe's Virgins, 1993, The Politician's Wife, 1995; prodr. At Sachem Farm, 1998; TV appearances include Lovejoy, 1986, Casualty, 1986, God on the Rocks, 1990, Murder Most Horrid, 1991, Peak Practice, 1993, The Day Today, 1994, Knowing Me, Knowing You with Alan Partridge, 1994, That Sunday, 1994, Cruel Train, 1995, Will & Grace, 2003, 04; Musician (albums) Everything I've Got in My Pocket, 2004, Seastories, 2007. ShoWest Female Star of Tomorrow award, 1998. Office: Creative Artists Agy 9830 Wilshire Blvd Beverly Hills CA 90212 Fax: 310-205-0879.*

DRIVER, ROBERT BAYLOR, JR., opera company director; b. Sao Paolo, Brazil, Aug. 26, 1942; came to U.S., 1949, naturalized, 1960; s. Robert Baylor and Mary Louise (Riechman) D.; m. Monica B. Macrae, 1968; 1 child, Katharine. BA, U. Va., 1964; MA, Middlebury Coll., Vt., 1971; postgrad., Johns Hopkins U. Asst. stage dir. Die Bayerische Staatsoper, 1966-68; asst. dir. Ky. Opera Assn., 1968-71; assoc. dir. Kansas City Lyric Opera, 1974-75; artistic dir. Opera Theatre, Syracuse, N.Y., 1975-87, Indpls. Opera, 1981-91, Opera Co. Phila., 1991—, gen. dir. Sec. Opera Memphis, Tenn., 1984-91. Named Citizen of Yr., PENJERDEL Coun., 1993, Honoree of Yr., Chamounix Youth Hostel, Phila., 1995. Mem.: OPERA Am. (bd. dirs.). Office: Opera Co of Philadelphia 1420 Locust St Ste 210 Philadelphia PA 19102-3601*

DRIVER, TOM FAW, theologian, writer, advocate; b. Johnson City, Tenn., May 31, 1925; s. Leslie Rowles and Sarah (Broyles) D.; m. Anne L. Barstow, June 7, 1952; children: Katharine Anne, Paul Barstow, Susannah Ambrose. AB, Duke U., 1950; M.Div., Union Theol. Sem., 1953; PhD, Columbia U., 1957; DLitt, Denison U., 1970. Ordained to ministry United Meth. Ch., 1951. Dir. youth work Riverside Ch., NYC, 1955-56; faculty Union Theol. Sem., NYC, 1956-93, Paul J. Tillich prof. theology and culture, 1973-93, emeritus, 1993—. Drama critic Christian Century, 1956-62, Sta. WBAI-FM, 1960-61, The Reporter, 1963-64; vis. assoc. prof. English Columbia U., 1964-65; vis. assoc. prof. religion Barnard Coll., 1965-66, Fordham U., 1967; cons. humanities and arts Coll. Old Westbury (N.Y.), 1970; William Evans vis. prof. religion U. Otago, N.Z., 1976; vis. prof. religion Vassar Coll., 1978, Montclair State Coll., 1981; vis. prof. English lit. Doshisha U., Kyoto, Japan, 1983. Author: liberetto for oratorio The Invisible Fire, 1958; The Sense of History in Greek and Shakespearean Drama, 1960, Jean Genet, 1966, Romantic Quest and Modern Query: A History of The Modern Theater, 1970, Patterns of Grace: Human Experience as Word of God, 1977, Christ in a Changing World: Toward an Ethical Christology, 1981, The Magic of Ritual: Our Need for Liberating Rites that Transform Our Lives and Our Communities, 1991, Liberating Rites: Understanding the Transformative Power of Ritual, 1998, 2006; editor: (with Robert Pack) Poems of Doubt and Belief, 1964; prodr., photographer (video, with Anne Barstow): Colombia: The Next Vietnam?, 2001, Colombians Speak Out about Violence and U.S. Policy, 2003, also articles. Bd. dirs. dept. worship and arts Nat. Council Chs., 1958- 63, Found. Arts, Religion and Culture, 1963-67; affiliate mem. Presbyn. Ch., United Ch. of Christ, mem. Holston conf., United Meth. Ch. Served US Army, 1943—46. Kent fellow, 1953; Guggenheim fellow, 1962-63 Mem. ACLU, Am. Acad. Religion, New Haven Theol. Group, Presbyn. Peace Fellowship, Witherspoon Soc. (co-recipient Andrew Murray award 2006), Witness for Peace, Vets. for Peace, Soc. for Arts, Religion and Contemporary Culture, Phi Beta Kappa, Omicron Delta Kappa. Home: 501 W 123rd St Apt 14G New York NY 10027-5010 E-mail: tfd3@columbia.edu.

DRIVER, WALTER W., JR., lawyer; b. El Paso, Tex., Apr. 10, 1945; s. Walter Williamson and Carolyn Bonds (Mayfield) D.; m. Bettie Townsend Willerson, Dec. 27, 1970; children: Eleanor, Anna, Walter III. AB, Stanford U., 1967; JD, U. Tex., 1970. Bar: Ga. 1970. Assoc. King & Spalding, LLP, Atlanta, 1970—76, ptnr., 1976—, chmn. policy com., 1992-94, 98-99, mng. ptnr., chmn., 1999—2005. Bd. dir. Total Systems Services, Inc., Old Mutual Advisors Funds. Mem. exec. com. Children's Mus. Atlanta, 1990-95; bd. dirs. Ctrl. Atlanta Progress, 1993—; chair Celebration of Life Cancer Soc., 1993. Mem. ABA, State Bar Ga., U.S. Golf Assn. (gen. counsel 1997-99, mem. exec. com. 1999—, treas. 2000-01, v.p. 2001—), Ga. State Golf Assn. (gen. coun., exec. com. 1988-97), Atlanta C. of C. (exec. com., bd. dirs.), Piedmont Driving Club, Peachtree Golf Club (bd. dirs.). Office: King & Spalding LLP 191 Peachtree St Atlanta GA 30303-1763 Office Phone: 404-572-4799. Office Fax: 404-572-5103. Business E-Mail: wdriver@kslaw.com.

D'RIVERA, PAQUITO, clarinetist, saxophonist, conductor, composer; b. Marianao, Cuba, June 4, 1948; s. Francisco Lorenzo and Maura Rivera; m. Brenda Feliciano; 1 child, Franco. D honoris causa (hon.), Berklee Sch. Music, Boston, 2003. Recording musician Blowin' and Manhattan Burn, Celebration, CBS Record Co.; recording musician Portraits of Cuba Chesky Record Co., Ticotico; artist-in-residence NJ Performing Arts Ctr. Composer: Conversations with Cachao, Gran Danzon (Bel Air Concerto), Three Poems from the New World, Fiddle Dreams, Fantasias Messiaenicas, Aires Tropicales, Elegy to Eric Dolphy, Wabango, Music Minus Me, Vol. I, II, and III; mem. UN Orch., The Jazz Festival in Punta del Este, Uruguay; composer-in-residence Caramoor Ctr. for Music and the Arts, Katonah, NY. Author: My Sax Life, 1999, 2005; contbr. numerous articles to profl. jours. Bd. dirs. Chamber Music Am. Recipient Grammy awards Irakere, 1979, Portraits of Cuba, 1996, Tropicana Nights, 2000, Paquito D'Rivera, Live at the Blue Note, 2001, Historia del Soldado, 2003, Brazilian Dreams, 2003, Merengue, 2004, Riberas, 2005; Lifetime Achievement award The Carnegie Hall, Nat. Medal of Arts Nat. Endowment for the Arts, 2005, Fellowship award for music composition John Simon Guggenheim Found., 2007, Living Jazz Legend award The Kennedy Ctr., 2007; named Clarinet of Yr., Jazz Journalist Assn., 2004, 06. Mem. The NJ Chamber Soc. (artistic dir.). Avocation: collecting Volkswagen beetle paraphenalia. Office Phone: 201-295-3176. Business E-Mail: paquito1@aol.com.

DRIZIN, STEVEN A., lawyer, educator; BA, Haverford Coll., 1983; JD, Northwestern U., 1986. Law clk. to Hon. Ilana D. Rovner US Dist. Ct. (no. dist.) Ill., 1988—89; litig. assoc. Sachnoff & Weaver Ltd., Chgo., 1986—88, 1989—91; supervising atty. Children and Family Justice Ctr., 1993—; clin. prof. law Northwestern U. Sch. Law, 2001—, asst. dir. Bluhm Legal Clinic, 2001—, legal dir. Ctr. on Wrongful Convictions. Contbr. articles to profl. jours. Policy com. mem. Ill. Coun. for prevention of violence, 1996—. Recipient PASS Award, Nat. Coun. Crime & Delinquency, 1999, Juvenile Defender Leadership Award, Nat. Juvenile Defender Ctr., 2000. Mem.: Chgo. Bar Assn. Office: Northwestern U Sch Law 357 E Chicago Ave Chicago IL 60611 E-mail: s-drizin@law.northwestern.edu.

DRIZO, ALEKSANDRA, researcher, educator; b. Uzice, Serbia, Yugoslavia, Dec. 9, 1964; d. Aleksandar and Zorica Drizo; life ptnr. Hugo Picard. BS, U. Belgrade, Serbia and Montenegro, 1988; MS, U. Edinburgh, Eng., 1993, PhD, 1998. Rsch. scientist U. Edinburgh, 1994—98, rsch. asst., 1998—99; postdoctoral rsch. scientist Ecole Polytechnique Montreal, 1999—2002, rsch. assoc., 2003—04, U. Colo., Boulder, 2002; rsch. asst. prof. U. Vt., Burlington, 2004—. Constructed wetlands rsch. ctr. dir. U. Vt., Burlington, 2004—; R&D exec. PhosphoReduc Inc., Burlington, 2006—, Bedford, Quebec, Canada, 2006—. Co-author: (scientific book) American Water Works Association. Mem. Missisqui Bay Coun., Swanton, Vt., 2005. Mem.: Internat. Water Assn. Achievements include patents pending for non point source phoshorus removal system; research in phosphorus removal technologies for wastewater treatment; environmental science and technology, water science and technology. Avocations: travel, skiing, hiking. Home: 22 Rue Du Pont Bedford Quebec Canada J0J 1A0 Office: U Vt 105 Carrigan Dr Burlington VT 05405 Home Phone: 450-248-3803; Office Phone: 802-656-2717.

DRNEVICH, VINCENT PAUL, engineering educator; b. Wilkinsburg, Pa., Aug. 6, 1940; s. Louis B. and Mary (Kutcel) D.; m. Roxanne M. Hosier, Aug. 20, 1966; children: Paul, Julie, Jenny, Marisa. BSCE, U. Notre Dame, 1962, MSCE, 1964; PhD, U. Mich., 1967. Registered profl. engr., Ky., Ind. Asst. prof. civil engring. U. Ky., Lexington, 1967-73, assoc. prof., 1973-78, prof., 1978-91; chmn. civil engring., 1980-84; acting dean engring. U. Ky., Lexington, 1989-90; prof., head Sch. Civil Engring. Purdue U., West Lafayette, Ind., 1991-2000. Dir. joint hwy. rsch. project Purdue U., 1991-95; pres. Soil Dynamics, Instruments, Inc., West Lafayette, 1974—. Inventor in field. Fellow ASCE (chmn. dept. heads coun. exec. com. 1996-2000, vice chmn. com. on edn.-practitioner interface, 1994-98, Norman medal 1973, Huber Rsch. prize 1980), ASTM (exec. com., tech. editor Geotech. Testing Jour. 1985-89, C.A. Hogentogler award 1979, Merit award 1993, Woodland Shockley award 1996); mem. NSPE, Am. Soc. Engring. Edn. (sec./treas. civil engring. divsn. 1995-98, dir. 1999—, vice chair 2002-03, chair 2003—), Transp. Rsch. Bd., Earthquake Engring. Rsch. Inst., Ind. Soc. Profl. Engrs. (pres. A.A. Potter chpt.), Chi Epsilon (Harold T. Larson award 1985, James M. Robbins award 1989). Roman Catholic. Avocations: golf, fishing. Office: Purdue U 550 Stadium Mall Dr West Lafayette IN 47907-2051

DROBAC, NIKOLA (NICK), education educator, consultant; b. Rochester, Pa., Feb. 11, 1953; s. Stevan Sr. and Madeline Mildred (Resanovich) D. AS, C.C. of Beaver County, 1975; BS, U. Pitts., 1977; MS, U. So. Calif., 1986. Sr. loss control cons. Fireman's Fund Ins. Cos., Fairfax, Va., 1977-87; risk mgmt. coord. Carnegie-Mellon U., Pitts., 1988-89; ins. mgr. Gen. Nutrition, Inc., Pitts., 1989-90; pers. cons. Tricon Tech., Pitts., 1990-92; lectr. bus. dept. C.C. Beaver County, Monaca, Pa., 1992-93; intermittent intake interviewer unemployment compensation Commonwealth Pa. Dept. Labor and Industry Beaver County Job Ctr., 1992-96; instr. C.C. of Allegheny County, 1994-95; tchr. So. Garrett County H.S., Oakland, Md., 1995—2003; head golf coach So.Garrett County H.S., Oakland, Md., 1995-96; head tennis coach So. Garrett County H.S., Oakland, Md., 1997, asst. mock trial advisor, 2000; acctg. tchr. Ephrata Sr. H.S., Pa., 2003—06; tech. edn. tchr. Reading Sch. Dist., Pa., 2006—07, instrnl. supr., 2007—. Adj. instr. bus./computer applications Garrett C.C., McHenry, Md., 1996, 97. Del. Rep. Presdl. Conv., Washtenaw County, Mich., 1980; vol. basketball coach Carnegie-Mellon U., Pitts., 1988-89; vol. football coach and scout Aliquippa (Pa.) H.S., 1991-92; mem. choir St. Elijah Serbian Orthodox. Ch.; instrument player St. Lawrence Adult Tamburitzan Group, Steelton, Pa., Sveti Nikola Adult Tamburitzan Group, Ambridge, Pa. Mem. Masons (Monaca Ctr.), Am. Serbian Eastern Rite Brothers (3d v.p. 1997-99, 2d v.p. 1999-2001, 1st v.p. 2002—), Shriners. Serbian Orthodox. Avocations: computers, golf, photography, church choir. Home: 1616 Tyler St Aliquippa PA 15001-2036 Office Phone: 610-775-1913. E-mail: ahs15001@yahoo.com.

DROBENA, THOMAS JOHN, minister, educator; b. Chgo., Aug. 23, 1934; s. Thomas and Suzanne (Durec) D.; m. Wilma S. Kucharek, Dec. 27, 1980; children: Thomas Samuel, Joshua Michael. BA, Valparaiso U., 1964; ThB, Concordia Theol. Sem., 1961, MDiv, 1974; MA, Hebrew U., Jerusalem, 1968; PhD, Calif. Grad. Sch. Theology, 1975; STM, Luth. Theol. Sem., 1986; DSc (hon.), London U. Ordained to ministry Evang. Luth. Ch. in Am., 1962. English pastor Redeemer Luth. Ch., Jerusalem, 1967-68; prin. St. Mark's Luth. Ch., Bklyn., 1968-69; pastor Ascension Luth. Ch., Binghamton, 1969-78, Holy Emmanuel, Mahoney City, Pa., 1981-86, St. John, St. Clair, Pa., 1981-86, Nanticoke, Pa., 1981-86; co-pastor Holy Trinity Luth. Ch., Torrington, Conn., 1986—. Adj. prof. SUNY, Binghamton, 1975-77; chair Global Missions, Evang. Luth. Ch. in Am., Chgo., 1985—; rsch. scholar Slavic Heritage Inst., Torrington, 1964-, v.p., treas., 1965—. Co-author: Heritage of the Slavs, 1976; editor The Zion, 1995—, Slovo, 1998—; translator: Lutheran Churches in Slovakia; contbr. articles to profl. jours. Chaplain Civil Air Patrol USAFA, 1964—; bd. dirs. ARC, 1986-1999; pres. Crimestoppers, 1988—, New Eng. Hist. Soc., 1990—; chair internat. rels. com. ELCA-Slovak Zion Synod, 1995, adminstrv. asst. to the bishop, 2002-. Grantee U.S. State Dept., Jerusalem, 1967-68, U. Ill. Russian and East European Ctr., Urbana, 1980—. Fellow Istituto Slovacco; mem. Am. Assn. for the Advancement of Slavic Studies, Am. Assn. of Tchrs. of Slavic and East European Langs., Czechoslovak Soc. for the Arts and Scis., New Eng. Luth. Hist. Soc. (pres. 1990—, editor Jour. New Eng. Luth. Hist. Soc. 1995—). Office: Slavic Heritage Inst PO Box 1003 Torrington CT 06790-1003

DROEGE, MARCUS, medical educator, researcher; b. Luenen, Germany, Feb. 23, 1969; s. Franz Josef and Ute Droege; m. Wiebke Deckers, Oct. 11, 1996; children: Lennart Paul, Pauline Sophie, Ella Frances. BS, U. Muenster, 1995; PhD, MS, U. Minn., 2003. Lic. pharmacist. Asst. prof. NSU Coll. Pharmacy, Ft. Lauderdale, Fla., 2003—. Mng. ptnr. PharmaConcepts. Bd. dirs. Falls Maintenance Assn., Weston, Fla., 2006. Mem.: Rho Chi Soc. Office: NSU Coll Pharmacy 3200 S University Dr Fort Lauderdale FL 33328-2018 Home Phone: 954-349-3623; Office Phone: 954-262-1328. Office Fax: 954-262-2278. Business E-Mail: droege@nsu.nova.edu.

DROEGEMEIER, KELVIN K., meteorologist, educator; b. Ellsworth, Kans., Aug. 23, 1958; m. Lisa Roevekamp, Sept. 27, 1983. BS in meteorology with spl. distinction, U. Okla., 1980; MS in atmospheric sci., U. Ill., 1982, PhD in atmospheric sci., 1985. Meteorol. aide Nat. Severe Storms Lab., 1976—78, meteorol. technician, 1978—80; grad. rsch. asst. U. Ill., 1980—85; asst. prof., sch. meteorology U. Okla., 1985—91, co-founder, dep. dir. rsch. Ctr. Analysis and Prediction of Storms, 1989—92, dir. Ctr. Analysis and Predictions of Storms, 1989—, assoc. prof., sch. meteorology, 1991—98, prof., sch. meteorology, 1998—2001, regents' prof., sch. meteorology, 2001—, Roger and Sherry Teigen presdl. prof., 2004—; founder, dir. Environ. Computing Applications System Rsch. and Ednl. Superconducting Ctr., 1996—2001; dep. dir. Engring. Rsch. Ctr. Collaborative Adaptive Sensing Atmosphere, NSF, 2003—. Bd. dirs. NSF Nat. Sci. Bd., 2004—; cons. Sperry Comml. Flight Systems Group, Honeywell Corp., 1989—92, Climatol. Cons. Corp., 1997, Am. Airlines, 1997, 1999—, Nat. Transportation Safety Bd., 1997—98; chair SoM Undergraduate Studies Com. U. Okla., 2001—, mem. Williams Chair Search Com., 2001—; mem. bd. advisors Supercomputing Ctr. Edn. and Rsch., 2001—; mem. patent adv. com. U. Okla., 2003—; spkr. in field; fellow NOAA Cooperative Inst. Mesoscale Meteorol. Studies, 1987—. Contbr. articles to profl. jours., chapters to books. Bd. dirs. Norman, Okla. C. of C., 2003—; chmn. Weather and Climate Team, Okla. Econ. Devel. Generating Excellence (EDGE) Gov. Task Force, 2003; deacon Riverside Ch., Norman, 2003—. Recipient Pioneer award, NSF, 2001, Excellence in Aviation award, Fedn. Aviation Adminstrn., 2002. Fellow: Am. Meteorol. Soc.; mem.: Phi Kappa Phi. Office: U Okla Ctr Analysis and Prediction of Storms Sarkeys Energy Ctr Rm 1110 100 E Boyd Norman OK 73019 Office Phone: 405-325-0453. Business E-Mail: kdroege@tornado.gcn.uoknor.edu, kkd@ou.edu.

DROGA, DAVID, advertising executive; b. Australia, 1969; married; 3 children. Grad., Australian Writers & Art Dirs. Sch. Ptnr. & exec. creative dir. OMON Sydney, 1991—96; exec. creative dir. Saatchi Singapore, 1996—98; regional creative dir. Saatchi Asia, 1996—98; exec. creative dir. Saatchi & Saatchi, London, 1998—2003; worldwide chief creative officer Publicis Network, NYC, 2003—05; founder & chief creative officer Droga5, NYC, 2006—. Jury pres. Cannes Internat. Advt. Festival, 2006. Named World's Best Creative Dir., Advt. Age, Australian Creative Person of the Decade, Creative mag.; named one of 50 Most Influential Men in Am. Under 38, Details mag., 2003, 2004; named to Am. Advt. Fedn. Hall of Achievement, Media Mktg. Hall of Fame; recipient 48 Cannes Lion awards, Cannes Internat. Advt. Festival, 3 Grand prix, Lifetime Achievement award, Boards mag., Campaign Brief Asia; fellow, World Econ. Forum, 2006—07. Office: Droga5 5th Fl 444 Broadway New York NY 10013 Office Phone: 917-237-8888. Office Fax: 917-237-8889.*

DROHAN, DAVID F., medical products company executive; BS in Indsl. Rels., Manhattan Coll., NYC. With Baxter Healthcare Corp., 1965—, territory mgr. N.Y., various positions, v.p. sales parenteral divsn., 1983-87, pres. pharmacy divsn., 1987-96, pres. intravenous systems, corp. v.p., 1996—. Bd. trustees St. Louis Coll. of Pharmacy. Chmn. Wake County Econ. Devel. Bd., dir. Riverside Found, dir. Baxter Credit Union.

DROMM, DANIEL PATRICK, elementary school educator; b. Bklyn., Nov. 27, 1955; s. Warren William Dromm and Mary Audrey Gallagher. BA, Marist Coll., 1973—77; MS in edn., City Coll., 1978—81. Asst. dir. Grant Day Care Ctr., 1978—84; tchr. P.S. 199Q, LI, NY, 1984—. Mem. Jackson Hts. Beautification Group of Queens, 2002—; founder New Visions Dem. Club, 2002—; del. Dem. Nat. Conv., 2000; dist. leader Queens County Dem. Org., 2002—; founder Queens Lesbian and Gay Pride, 1992—; co-founder Lesbian and Gay Dem. Club, 1994—, Generation Q Youth Svcs. Program, Astoria, NY, 2000—. Recipient Puerto Rican Soc. of Queens Annual award, 1998, Aaron Weiss Humanitarian award, 1994, award, New Visions Dem. Club, 2004. Mem.: United Fedn. Tchrs. (union rep., Trachtenberg award 2000, Dist. 24 award 2006, Marsh-Raimo award 2006), Lesbian and Gay Tchrs. Assn. Office: PS 199Q 39-20 48th Ave Long Island City NY 11104 Office Phone: 718-784-3431. Personal E-mail: ddromm@aol.com.

DROMS, WILLIAM GEORGE, finance educator, investment advisor; b. Schenectady, Aug. 20, 1944; s. George William and Frances (Maguire) D.; m. JoAnn Gilberti, June 17, 1967; children: Courtney, Justin. AB, Brown U., 1966; MBA, George Washington U., 1971, DBA, 1975. Chartered financial analyst. Prof. Georgetown U., Washington, 1973—, John J. Powers Jr. Chair prof., 1990—, assoc. dean, faculty chair Sch. Bus., 1978-81, 87-89, 92-94, 98-99. Pres. Droms Strauss Advisors, Inc., 1994—. Author: Finance and Accounting for Nonfinancial Managers, 1979, 5th edit., 2003, Dow Jones-Irwin No-Load Mutual Funds, 1984, 85, 86; author: (with others) The Dow Jones Irwin Guide to Personal Financial Planning, 1982, 86, Personal Financial Management, 1982, 86, The Life Insurance Investment Advisor, 1988, Investment Fundamentals, 1994; editor: Asset Allocation for Individual Investors, 1987, Managing a Global Investment Program, 1991; contbr. articles to profl. jours. Lt. USN, 1966-70. Mem. Am. Fin. Assn., Chartered Fin. Analyst Inst., Fin. Mgmt. Assn., DC Soc. Investment Analysts, Cosmos Club. Republican. Roman Catholic. Avocations: tennis, golf. Office: Georgetown U Sch Bus Washington DC 20057-0001 Office Phone: 202-687-3820. Business E-Mail: dromsw@msb.edu.

DRONAMRAJU, KRISHNA RAO, geneticist; b. Pithapuram, India, Jan. 14, 1937; came to U.S., 1963; s. Bapiraju and Rajeswaramma (Vankayalapati) D.; m. Sheila Marion McHarg, Mar. 31, 1962 (div. 1978); 1 child, Raj Gopal. MSc, Agra U., India, 1957; PhD, Indian Statis. Inst., Calcutta, 1966. Cert. cancer cytogenetics Fox Chase Cancer Ctr., Phila. Rsch. fellow U. Alta., Edmonton, Canada, 1966-68; asst. prof. U. Sask., Saskatoon, Canada, 1968-69; chief geneticist Lancaster (Pa.) Cleft Palate Clinic, 1969-73; writer, lectr. Balt., 1973-77; pers. cons. City of Balt., 1978-79, job devel. advisor, 1979-81; sr. fellow U. Tex., Houston, 1982-85; pres., dir. Found. for Genetic Rsch., Houston, 1985—. Vis. prof. Hershey Med. Ctr., Pa. 1969-73, Osmania U., India, 1995, U. Turin, Italy, 2004, 2005-06, U. Hong kong Med. Ctr., 2005; mem. recombinant DNA adv. com. NIH, Bethesda, Md., 1992—; hon. rsch. fellow U. London, 1994; vis. prof. U. Paris, 1994, Jawaharlal Nehru U., New Delhi, 1994; hon. prof. Albert Schweitzer Internat. U., Geneva, 1996; advisor Tex. State Coun. on Biotech., 2000-; hon. prof. Andhra U., 2003; mem. adv. bd. to U.S. Sec. Agr., 2002-; chmn. internat. adv. bd. Chemtech Found., 2002-; del. Indian Sci. Congress, 2006, chmn. Frontier Techs., 2006; disting. centennial lecturer Tamil Nadu Agrl. U., 2006. Author: Cleft Lip and Palate: Aspects of Reproductive Biology, 1986, The Foundations of Human Genetics, 1989, If I am To Be Remembered, The Life and Work of Julian Huxley with Selected Correspondence, 1993; editor: Haldane and Modern Biology, 1968, Haldane, The Life and Work of J.B.S. Haldane with special reference to India, 1985, Foundations of Human Genetics, 1989, Selected Genetic Papers of JBS Haldane, 1990, The History and Development of Human Genetics: Progress in Different Countries, 1992, Haldane's Daedalus Revisited, 1995, Haldane in India, 1997, Science and Society, 1998, Biological and Social Issues in Biotechnology, 1998, Biological Wealth and Other Essays, 2002, Infectious Disease: Host-Pathogen Evolution, 2004, Malaria: Genetic and Evolutionary Aspects, 2006, Biotechnology and Sustaining Biodiversity, 2007; contbr. articles to profl. jours. Bd. dirs. Sickle Cell Assn., Houston, 1992—; mem. US Pres. del. India, 2000. Recipient Sr. Scientist award NIH, 1982-85, merit award History of Sci. Soc., 1989, Yellapragada Subbarow award for med. rsch., 1997, Y. Nayudamma award for sci. and tech., India, 1997, Welcome Trust Travel awards, 1995-00, Indian Sci. Congress award, 2006; Rockefeller U. Archives grantee, 2002, Chem. Heritage Found. grantee, 2003, 06, 07. Fellow N.Am. Acad. Arts and Scis.; mem. AAAS, Am. Soc. Human Genetics, Asia. Avocations: travel, walking. Office: Found for Genetic Rsch PO Box 27701 Houston TX 77227-7701 Home Phone: 713-816-3681. Office Fax: 713-667-5881. Personal E-mail: kdronamraj@aol.com.

DRONEY, CHRISTOPHER F., judge; b. June 22, 1954; m. Elizabeth Kelly, Oct. 13, 1979. BA, Coll. Holy Cross, 1976; JD, U. Conn., 1979. Ptnr. Reid & Riege, P.C., Hartford, Conn., 1983-93; U.S. atty. for dist. of Conn. U.S. Dept. Justice, New Haven, 1993-97; judge U.S. Dist. Ct., Conn., 1997—. Notes and comments editor Conn. Law Rev., 1978-79. Mem. U.S. atty. gen. adv. com., 1996-97. Office: 450 Main St Hartford CT 06103-3022 Office Phone: 860-240-2635.

DROOYAN, RICHARD E., lawyer; b. LA, 1950; BA summa cum laude, Claremont Men's Coll., 1972; JD cum laude, Harvard U., 1975. Bar: Calif. 1975. Assoc. Kadison, Pfaezler, Woodard, Quinn & Rossi, 1975; asst. atty. States Atty.'s Office, LA, 1978—84; cheif Criminal Complaints Unit, 1982, US State Office, 1982—84; chief asst. US Atty. Robert C. Bonner, 1984—88; mem. Skadden, Arps, Slate, Meagher & Flom, 1988—93; cheif US Atty.'s Office, LA, 1993—96; chief asst. US Atty. Nora Manella, 1997—99; ptnr. Munger, Tolles & Olson LLP, LA. Lectr. So. Calif. Law Ctr., Loyola Law Sch.; dep. gen. counsel Ind. Comm. LA Police Dept., 1991; gen. councel Rampart Ind. Rev. Panel., 2000. Mem. (bd. trustees) Camp Ronald McDonald Good Times; mem. Children's Law Ctr., LA. Mem. LA County Bar Assn.'s (bd. trustees) LACBA com., pres. LA Chpt. Fed. Bar Assn. Office: Munger Tolles & Olson LLP 355 S Grand Ave 35th Fl Los Angeles CA 90071-1560 Office Phone: 213-683-9136. Office Fax: 213-683-5136. Business E-Mail: richard.drooyan@mto.com.

DROSDICK, JOHN GIRARD, oil industry executive; b. Hazelton, Pa., Aug. 9, 1943; m. Gloria J. Shenosky, May 10, 1944; children: Scott E., Candice M., Courtney J., Brooke K. BSChemE, Villanova U., 1965; MSChemE, U. Mass., 1968. Crude oil coordinator Exxon USA, Houston, 1973—74, marine planning mgr., 1974—76, corp. analysis mgr., 1978—81, facilities devel. dept. head Baton Rouge, 1976—78, refinery ops mgr., 1981—83; v.p. refining Tosco Corp., Santa Monica, Calif., 1983—85, sr. v.p. refining, 1985—86, exec. v.p., 1986—87, pres., COO, 1987—89, also bd. dirs.; pres., CEO Tosco Refining Co., Santa Monica, Calif., 1989—92, Ultramar, Inc., Long Beach, 1992—96; pres., COO Sunoco, Inc., Phila., 1996—2000, chmn., pres., CEO, 2000—. Mem.: Am. Petroleum Petroleum Refiners Assn. (bd. dirs. 1985—87), Nat. Petroleum Refiners Assn. (bd. dirs. 1985—), Jonathan Wilshire. Roman Catholic. Avocations: running, skiing, tennis, golf. Office: Sunoco Inc 10 Penn Ctr 1801 Market St Philadelphia PA 19103-1699*

DROSKE, JOHN P., chemistry professor; s. Edward, Sr. and Mary Droske; m. Mary S. Droske; children: Timothy, Kathryn, Christopher. BS, DePaul U., Chgo., MS, 1978; PhD, Colo. State U., Fort Collins, 1982. Prof. chemistry U. Wis., Stevens Point, 1983—, dir. nat. info. ctr. polymer edn., 1990—. Mem. nat. air and space mus. materials adv. group Smithsonian Instn., Washington, 2002—; co-chair, dir. POLYED Edn. Com. Am. Chem. Soc. Polymer Divisions, 1989—; cons. in field. Pres. Intersociety Polymer Edn. Coun., 2001—03, dir., 1989—; founding mem. Pl. Peace, Stevens Point, 2000—06. Recipient POLY/PMSE Disting. Svc. award, Am. Chem. Soc. Polymer Divisions, 1995; scholar, U. Wis., 1987. Roman Catholic. Achievements include research in high use temperature composite resins. Avocation: music. Office: University of Wisconsin Dept of Chemistry 2001 Fourth Ave Stevens Point WI 54481 Office Phone: 715-346-3771. E-mail: jdroske@uwsp.edu.

DROSSMAN, DOUGLAS ARNOLD, medical investigator, educator, gastroenterologist; b. Bklyn., Mar. 20, 1946; s. Murray and Ruth (Cohen) D.; m. Deborah Risa Ducoff, June 3, 1970; children: David, Daniel. BA cum laude, Hofstra U., 1966; MD, Albert Einstein Coll., 1970. Diplomate Am. Bd. Internal Medicine, Gastroenterology. Intern, resident U. N.C., Chapel Hill, 1970-72; resident N.Y.U.-Bellevue Med. Ctr., NYC, 1972-73; fellow in psychosomatic medicine U. Rochester, N.Y., 1975-76; fellow in gastroenterology U. N.C., Chapel Hill, 1976-78, instr. in medicine, 1977-78, asst. prof. medicine and psychiatry, 1978-83, assoc. prof. medicine and psychiatry, 1983-90, prof. medicine and psychiatry, 1990—. Internship selection com. U. NC, 1977-84, housestaff-faculty com., 1980-84,; health promotion/disease prevention steering com., 1983, co-dir. med.-psychiat. liaison program faculty-resident study group in behavioral medicine, 1977-91; vis. prof. med. ctrs. and univs.; chair Functional Brain-Gut Rsch. Group, 1989-1993, co-dir. Ctr. Functional GI and Motility Disorders, 1993—, chmn. Rome Found., Rome I, II and III, 1990—, internat. sci. com., pres. Editor: The Functional Gastrointestinal Disorders, 1994, 3d edit., 2006, Functional Brain Gut Rsch. Group Newsletter, 1989—, Participate, 1997—, The Merck Manual, 15-17th edit., 2006; assoc. editor: Gastroenterology, 2001-06; mem. editl. bd.: Behavioral Medicine Abstracts, 1985-91, Stress Medicine, 1985-92, Current Concepts Gastroenterology, 1986-90, Jour. Clin. Gastroenterology, 1986—, Psychosomatic Medicine, 1998—; ad hoc reviewer over 30 profl. jours.; contbr. over 400 articles to profl. jours., chpts. to textbooks; prodr. 10 ednl. videotapes. Maj. Med. Corps, USAF, 1973-75. Grantee S.S. Zlinkoff Found., 1979, Smith, Kline, Beckman, 1982, NIH, 1983-86, 91-96, 2003—, Core Ctr. for Diarrheal Diseases, U. NC, 1986, Nat. Found. for Ileitis and Colitis, 1987-88. Master Am. Coll. Gastroenterology; mem. Am. Psychosomatic Soc. (councillor 1985-88, 90-92, 1986 program com. 1985-86, chmn. membership com. 1988-92, sec.-treas. 1992-96, pres. 1997-98), Am. Acad. on Phys. and Patient (charter fellow), Am. Fedn. for Clin. Rsch., Am. Gastroenterol. Assn. (program selection com. 1985-86, program selection chmn., coun. co-chair 2001-03, chair nerve-gut 2003-06), Am. Soc. for Gastrointestinal Endoscopy, So. Soc. for Clin. Investigation (Janssen award 1999, AGA Dist. Educator award 2004, AGA Educator award in clin. rsch. 2005, fellow 2006, Rsch. Mentor award 2007). Avocations: tennis, magic, jogging. Office: U NC Div Digestive Diseases # 7080 4150 Bioinformatics Bldg Chapel Hill NC 27599-7080 Office Phone: 919-966-0142. Business E-Mail: drossman@med.unc.edu.

DROST, MARIANNE, lawyer; b. Waterbury, Conn., Feb. 21, 1950; d. Albin Joseph and Henrietta Jean (Kremski) D. BA, Conn. Coll., 1972; JD, U. Conn., 1975. Bar: Conn. 1975. Assoc. Ritter, Tapper & Totten, Hartford, Conn., 1975-77; sr. atty. GTE Svc. Corp., Stamford, Conn., 1977-84, Chesebrough-Pond's Inc., Greenwich, Conn., 1984-85; corp. sec. GTE Corp., Stamford, Conn., 1985—91; v.p., assoc. gen. counsel fin. GTE Svc. Corp., Stamford, Conn., 1991-97, v.p., dep. gen. counsel, 1997-2000; sr. v.p., dep. gen. counsel, corp. sec. Verizon Comm. Inc., NYC, 2000—. Tutor Lit. Vols., Stamford, 1985-90, bd. dirs. Lit. Vols. Am., 1988-94. Mem. ABA, Am. Soc. Corp. Secs. (former pres., bd. dirs. Fairfield-Westchester chpt.).

DROUGHT, JAMES HENRY, healthcare business owner, exercise physiologist; b. Aurora, Ill., Mar. 29, 1957; s. James William and Lorna Beryl (Carlson) D.; m. Sarah Jacqueline Drought; 1 child, John Carlson. Student, U.S. Mil. Acad., 1975-77; BS in Phys. Edn., Rutgers U., 1980; MS in Clin. Exercise Physiology, Northeastern U., 1995. Comm. coord. Lake Placid Olympic Organizing Com., NY, 1980-81; dir. Rainmaker Prodns., Boston, 1982-85; health promotion mgr. City of Boston, 1986-87; owner Personal Trainers Strength & Conditioning Consulting, Boston, 1987—, Personal Trainers.com website, 1995—. Cons. City of Boston, 1988-89, State of Mass., Boston, 1988-89, Lotus Devel. Corp., Cambridge, Mass., 1990-91, Madison Town Employee Wellness Program, Conn., 2006—; mem. (C.O.R.P.S.) nat. bd. Reebok Internat., Ltd., Stoughton, Mass., 1992-96; articles cons. SHAPE mag., 1995—, Men's Health mag., 1998—. Exec. editor Conditioning Instr., 1991-93; contbr. chpt. to book, articles to profl. jours.; author Ask the Experts Column, Boston Globe, 1990-92; chpt. author: Essentials of Personal Training. Exec. com. Boston vs. Montreal Fitness Challenge, City of Boston, 1989; James Henry Drought collection donated to Howard Gotlieb Archival Rsch. Ctr., Mugar Meml. Libr., Boston U. Named one of 100 Best Trainers in Am., Men's Jour. mag., 2004. Mem. Am. Coll. Sports Medicine, Nat. Strength and Conditioning Assn. (Mass. state dir. 1992-98, nat. bd. dirs. 1998-2001, task analysis com. 1992—, nat. conf. com. 1993-95, chmn. personal trainer com. 1991, exam devel. com., 1994-98, exec. coun., state dirs. com. 1997-98, job analysis com., 2007, Challenge Scholarship 1993, State Dir.'s award 1995, Personal Trainer of Yr. award 2000, Cert. Commn. award 1993). Avocations: screenwriting, writing, weightlifting, running, tai chi, golf. Home and Office: PO Box 1058 Madison CT 06443 Office Phone: 203-245-1199. E-mail: drought@personaltrainers.com.

DROUILHET, PAUL RAYMOND, JR., retired science administrator, electrical engineer; b. San Pedro, Calif., Mar. 11, 1933; s. Paul R. and Elizabeth (Moffatt) D.; m. Betty Bratton; children: Ann, Stephen, Susan. BS, MS in Elec. Engring., MIT, 1955, EE, 1957. Various positions MIT Lincoln Lab., Lexington, 1959-81, div. head, 1981-85, asst. dir., 1985-93; fed. aviation adminstr. Chi Sci. for GPS/CNS, 1994-95, spl. asst. to dir. aviation rsch., 1996; cons. to dir. MIT Lincoln Lab., 1997—. Contbr. articles to profl. jours.; patentee in field. 1st lt. USAF, 1957-59. Fellow IEEE. Avocations: tennis, sailing, travel. Office: MIT Lincoln Lab 244 Wood St Lexington MA 02420-6426 E-mail: drouilhet@ll.mit.edu.

DROUIN, JOE, automotive executive; b. Memphis; B in Mgmt. Info. Sys., U. Memphis, 1990. With Electronic Data Sys. Corp. GM, Detroit; with Perot Sys. Corp.; IS dir. TRW Chassis Sys. Europe TRW, Germany, 1998—2002; v.p., CIO global info. sys. TRW Automotive, Livonia, Mich., 2002—. Bd. dirs. Automotive Industry Action Group; mem. Covisint Global Customer Adv. Coun. Office: TRW Automotive 12025 Tech Center Dr Livonia MI 48150

DROWOTA, FRANK F., III, retired state supreme court justice; b. Williamsburg, Ky., July 7, 1938; married; 2 children. BA, Vanderbilt U., 1960, JD, 1965. Bar: Tenn. 1965, U.S. Dist. Ct. Tenn. 1965. Pvt. practice, 1965-70; chancellor Tenn. Chancery Ct. Div. 7, 1970-74; judge Tenn. Ct. Appeals, Middle Tenn. Div., 1974-80; assoc. justice Tenn. Supreme Ct., Nashville, 1980-89, chief justice, 1989-93, 2001—05; assoc. justice Tenn. Supreme Ct., Nashville, 1993-2001; ret. Former pres. Nashville Am. Red Cross, Nashville Rotary Club; mem. exec. com. YMCA of Nashville and Middle Tenn., Cumberland Museum & Sci. Ctr., NCCJ, Bill Wilkerson Speech & Hearing Ctr. With USN, 1960—62. Mem.: Tenn. Bar Assn.*

DROZD, LESZEK STANISLAW, film producer, composer, musician; b. Warsaw, May 23, 1969; arrived in US, 1994; s. Hanna Eugenia Drozd. Student, Weryho-Radziwillowiczowej, Warsaw, 1991-93; grad., Sch. Music of Fryderyk Chopin. Music composer Sta. WPNA-AM, WSBS-AM, Chgo., 1995-97; music composer, performer STYOPA Productions, Calif., 1998; pres. Hanna's Employment Agy., Inc., 2001; prin., owner, CEO Story Tellers Prodns., Inc., 2005—. Soloist, mem. numerous symphonic orchs., bands, choirs; pres. Hannah's Employment Agy. Composer (and performer): (films) (soundtrack) The Innocents, 2000 (Film winner of 3 awards in Nat., Internat. film festivals.); composer: (documentary for Time Warner cable) Short Impression About Isolation, 2002; dir.: webTV channel, storytellersfilms.com; exec. prodr.: (various ednl. videos). Mem. Nat. Campaign for Tolerance, 2005; ednl. videos prodr., spl. edn. music composer for films. Personal E-mail: coposer@storytellersfilms.com.

DROZDZIEL, MARION JOHN, aeronautical engineer; b. Dunkirk, NY, Dec. 21, 1924; s. Steven and Veronica (Wilk) D.; m. Rita L. Korwek, Aug. 30, 1952; 1 child, Eric A. BS in Aero. Engring., Tri State U., 1947, BSME, 1948; postgrad., Ohio State U., 1948, Niagara U., 1949-51, U. Buffalo, 1951-52. Stress analyst Curtiss Wright Corp., Columbus, Ohio, 1948; project engr. weight analysis Bell Aerospace Textron, Buffalo, 1949-52, stress analyst, 1952-60, asst. supr. stress analysis, 1960-64, chief stress analysis propulsion, 1964-79, chief engr. stress and weights, 1979-84, staff scientist, 1984-85, cons. structures and fractures mechanics, 1985—. Del. Internat. Citizens Ambassador Program; active Buffalo Fine Arts Acad., N.Y. Acad. Scis.; mem. Tech. Socs. Coun. of the Niagara Frontier. With US Army, 1944—47. Recipient cert. of achievement NASA-Apollo, 1972, Wisdom award Wisdom Soc. for Advancement of Knowledge, Learning and Rsch. in Edn., 2000; cert. commendation U.K. NATO program, 1982; named to Wisdom Hall of Fame, Wisdom Soc. for Advancement of Knowledge, Learning and Rsch. in Edn., 2000. Mem. AAAS, AIAA (Mem. Chmn.'s award 1988-90, 92-93), Soc. Reliability Engrs. (bd. dir. 1998-2007), U.S. Naval Inst., Am. Space Found., Nat. Conservancy, Nat. Audubon Soc., Sierra Club, Am. Acad. Polit. and Social Sci., Acad. Polit. Sci., Union Concerned Scientists, Air Force Assn., Nat. Space Soc., Soc. Allied Weight Engrs., Planetary Soc., Am. Mgmt. Assn.,Bibl. Archeology Soc., Archeol. Inst. Am., Cousteau Soc., Smithsonian Assocs., Buffalo Audubon Soc., Bell Mgmt. Club, Natural History Mus., Internat. Hypersonic Rsch., Disabled Am. Vets, Kosciuszko Found., Polish Arts Club Buffalo, Exch. Club of Tonawandas (sec. 1996-98, bd. dir. 1999-2000), Nat. Exch. Club (Disting. Sec. award 1996-99). Republican. Roman Catholic. Achievements include development of criteria and methods of structural analysis extending analyses into the plastic and creep ranges for titanium and columbium rocket nozzle extensions; of criteria and methods of structural analysis for extendable rocket nozzle extensions, including rapid nozzle deployment involving plasticity; of methods of structural analysis for low strength, high ductility steels, aluminums, and teflons as positive expulsion devices for zero gravity application in propellant tanks including bellows, reversing heads, rolling diaphragms devices and collapsing or folding concepts; structural analysis on "X" series of aircraft, on Mercury, Gemini, and Apollo spacecraft reaction control and propulsion systems; structural and weight analysis of programs involving rocket engines, propulsion systems, aircraft, air cushion vehicles, surface-effect ships, laser systems avionics, airborne and ground antennae, Army tanks and fighting vehicles. Home and Office: 152 Linwood Ave Tonawanda NY 14150-4020 Office Phone: 716-693-6250.

DR. PHIL, (PHILLIP CALVIN MCGRAW), psychologist, television personality; b. Vinita, Okla., Sept. 1, 1950; s. Joseph and Jerri McGraw; m. Debbie Higgins, 1970 (div. 1973); m. Robin Jameson, 1976; children: Jay, Jordan. Student U. Tulsa; BA in Clin. Psychology, North Tex. State U., MA in Clin. Psychology, 1976, PhD in Clin. Psychology, 1979. Bd. cert. and licensed Clin. Psychologist 1978. Clin. psychologist, behavioral medicine practitioner; co-founder Courtroom Scis., Inc. (litigation consulting firm), Irving, Tex., 1989; regular commentator Oprah Winfrey Show, 1986—; host The Dr. Phil Show, 2001—, Dr. Phil's Prime Time Spl.-Escaping Addiction, 2006; monthly columnist O, the Oprah Magazine. Cons., MindFindBind with Dr. Phil match.com, 2006—; pub. spkr. in field. Author: Life Strategies: Doing What Works, Doing What Matters, 1999, Relationship Rescue: A Seven-Step Strategy for Reconnecting with Your Partner, 2000, Self Matters: Creating Your Life from the Inside Out, 2001, The Ultimate Weight Solution: The Seven Keys to Weight Loss Freedom, 2003, The Ultimate Weight Solution Food Guide, 2003, Family First: Your Step-by-Step Plan for Creating a Phenomenal Family, 2004 (Publishers Weekly Bestseller list, 2004), The Ultimate Weight Solution Cookbook: Recipes for Weight Loss Freedom, 2004; introduced themes to Dr. Phil Show such as: The Ultimate Weight Loss Challenge, Relationship Rescue Retreat Series, Brandon's Intervention; contbr. articles to profl. jours.; actor: (films) Scary Movie 4, 2006. Founder Dr. Phil Foundation, 2003—. Named one of Most Intriguing People of 2002, People mag., Ten Most Fascinating People, Barbara Walters TV special, 2002, 100 Most Powerful Celebrities, Forbes.com, 2007. Avocations: golf, tennis, scuba diving, coaching Little League baseball. Office: The Dr Phil Show 5482 Wilshire Blvd 1902 Los Angeles CA 90036*

DRU, JEAN-MARIE PAUL, advertising executive; b. Boulogne-Billancourt, France, Jan. 24, 1947; s. René Dru; m. Marie Virginie(Corre); children: Pierre Marie, François Marie, Noemie, Clemence, Matthieu. HEC, Bus. Sch., France, 1969. Acct. exec. Dupuy Compton, Paris, 1970—72, exec. creative dir., 1972—77; mng. dir. Young and Rubicam, Paris, 1977—81, CEO, 1981—83; co-founder BDDP, Boulogne-Billancourt, France, 1984—98; pres. Internat. TBWA Worldwide, Boulogne-Billancourt, France, 1998—2001; pres., CEO TBWA Worldwide, 2001—. Pres. Outdoor Advt. Grand Prix, 1987, 88, Cannes Advt. Film Festival Jury, 1993, 98. Author: The Creative Leap, 1984, Disruption: Overturning Conventions and Shaking Up the Marketplace, 1996, Beyond Disruption: Changing the Rules in the Marketplace, 2002. Mem.: European Advt. Assn., French Nat. Advt. Assn. (pres.). Office: TBWA Worldwide 488 Madison Ave New York NY 10022 Business E-Mail: jean-marie.dru@tbwaworld.com.*

DRUCKENMILLER, STANLEY F., investment company executive; m. Fiona Biggs; 3 children. BA in English, Bowdoin Coll., Maine, BA in Econs.; PhD student in Econs., U. Mich. Analyst to dir. investments Pitts. Nat. Bank, 1980; founder, head Duquesne Capital Mgmt., Pitts., 1981—; with Quantum Fund; mng. dir. Soros Fund Mgmt., 1988. Cons. Dreyfus, 1985; head Dreyfus Fund. Chair Harlem Children's Zone. Named one of 400 Richest Ams., Forbes mag., 2006. Office: Duquesne Capital Mgmt Co 2579 Washington Rd Ste 322 Pittsburgh PA 15241-2591

DRUCKER, ALAN STEVEN, mechanical engineer; b. Boston, Apr. 22, 1948; s. Eugene Elias and Corrine Ruth (Mintzer) D.; m. Patricia Ellen Sori, Aug. 10, 1974; children: Aaron, Zachary. BS, Cornell U., 1970. Jr. devel. engr. Carrier, Syracuse, N.Y., 1972-78, sr. devel. engr., 1978-82, program mgr., 1982-85, from staff engr. to prin. engr., 1985—2006, cons. engr., 2007—. Inventor, patentee in field. Democrat. Jewish. Avocations: diving, scuba, gardening, tennis. Home Phone: 315-446-9290; Office Phone: 315-432-6307. E-mail: al.drucker@carrier.utc.com.

DRUCKER, JACQUELIN F., lawyer, arbitrator, writer; b. Celina, Ohio, Oct. 15, 1954; d. Jack Burton and Dorothea (Eckenstein) Davis; m. John H. Drucker, Sept. 8, 1990. BA with distinction and honors, Ohio State U., 1977, JD with honors, 1981. Bar: Ohio 1981, N.Y. 1992, U.S. Supreme Ct. 1989. Legis. asst. Speaker of Ohio Ho. of Reps., Columbus, 1974-78; lobbyist United Auto Workers, Columbus, 1978-81; labor and employment atty. Porter, Wright, Morris & Arthur, Columbus, 1981—84; gen. counsel

Ohio Employment Rels. Bd., Columbus, 1984-86, exec. dir., 1986-88, vice chmn., 1988-90; pvt. practice arbitration of employment, labor and comml. cases nationwide and internat., 1990—; dir. labor mgmt. programs Cornell U. Sch. Indsl. and Labor Rels., Ithaca, NY, 1994—97, dir. programs for neutrals, 1997—2005, adj. faculty, 2005—; dir. ednl. svcs. Cornell Inst. Conflict Resolution, 1998—2005, adj. faculty, 2005—. Adj. faculty Inst. Conflict Resolution Cornell U., 2005-; cons. to W.J. Usery Ctr. Workplace, Ga. State U.; counsel to Gov.'s Task Force on Collective Bargaining, Columbus, 1983-84; adj. prof. labor law Franklin U., Columbus, 1988-89; mem. panel of arbitrators Fed. Mediation and Conciliation Svc., Am. Arbitration Assn., AAA Employment Roster of Neutrals, NY State Employment Rels. Bd.; mem. roster of neutrals NYC Office of Collective Bargaining; mem. panel V.I. Pub. Employment Rels. Bd., N.J. Pub. Employment Rels. Commn., NY Pub. Employment Rels. Bd., Port Authority Employment Rels. Panel; mem. permanent arbitration panel United Mine Workers and Bituminous Coal Operators Assn., Am. Postal Workers Union and US Postal Svc., Westchester County Health Care, Off-Track Betting Corp. and Local 32E, State of NY and Pub. Employees Fedn., State of NY and Civil Svc. Employees Assn., Consolidated Edison and Utility Workers Local 1-2, U. Cin. and Dist. 925, Beth Israel Med. Ctr. and 1199 Nat. Health and Human Svcs. Employees Union, Suffolk County and Suffolk PBA, Infineum and Teamsters Local 877, Orange County Sheriff and PBA; cons., lectr., spkr. in field. Author: Collective Bargaining Law in Ohio, 1993; editor L.I. Indsl. Rels. Quar., 1995-98; contbg. editor Pub. Sector Law and Employment Law supplement, 1995, Pub. Sector Labor and Employment Law, 2d edit.; assoc. editor Discipline and Discharge in Arbitration, 1998; editor in chief ADR in Employment Law; contbr. numerous articles to profl. jours. Fellow Coll. Labor and Employment Lawyers, Am. Bar Found.; mem. ABA (labor and employment law sect., neutral chmn. alternative dispute resolution in employment and labor law com. 2001-06, neutral chair regional CLE programs, co-chair tng. devel. sub-com. of ADR com., 1998-2001, liaison to Nat. Acad. Arbitrators 2004—), Nat. Acad. Arbitrators (chair ann. meeting 2006, mem. task force on employment arbitration, bd. govs. 2006-, vice chair region 2), Ohio State Bar Assn., Assn. Bar City NY, NY State Bar Assn. (labor and employment law sect., chmn. 2003-04, sec. 1997-98, co-chair ADR in employment com. 1998-2001, continuing legal edu. chair, 2001-2002), NY County Lawyers Assn. (employment law and labor rels. com., chmn. 2003-04), Nassau County Bar Assn., Suffolk County Bar Assn., Indsl. Rels. Rsch. Assn. (nat. bd. dir. 2007-), Soc. Fed. Labor Rels. Profls., Civil Svc. Employees Assn., Inc. Jewish. Office: 432 E 58th St Suite 2 New York NY 10022-2331 Office Phone: 212-688-3819. Business E-Mail: jd32@cornell.edu.

DRUCKER, JONATHAN, lawyer; BA, U. Pa., Phila.; JD, Stanford U., Calif. Assoc. Cadwalader, Wickersham & Taft, 1985—88, Rubin Baum Levin Constant and Friedman, 1988—96, ptnr., 1996—99; gen. counsel, mng. dir. Veronis Suhler Stevenson; sr. v.p, gen. counsel Polo Ralph Lauren Corp., NYC, 2005—. Office: Polo Ralph Lauren Corp 625 Madison Ave New York NY 10022

DRUCKER, MITCHELL DAVID, physician, educator; b. Apr. 23, 1955; BA, Cornell U., Ithaca, NY, 1977; MD, U. Fla., Gainesville, 1981. Diplomate Am. Bd. Ophthalmology, Am. Bd. Medical Examiners. Assoc. prof. ophthalmology and neurology U. South Fla. Coll. Medicine, Tampa, 1987—94, 1991—2006. Named to Best Drs. in Am., 1997—2006; recipient Clin. Tchg. award, dept. ophthalmology U. South Fla., 1992, 1993, 1996, 1997, 2002. Mem.: N.Am. Ophthalmology Soc., Am. Acad. Ophthalmology, Mensa.

DRUCKER, RICHARD ALLEN, lawyer; b. NYC, Mar. 30, 1952; s. Charles and Bette Drucker; m. Jeanmarie Hamilton, Sept. 30, 1989; children: Richard Allen Jr., Hamilton Charles. BA, U. Vt., 1974; JD, U. Va., 1977. Bar: N.Y. 1978. Law clk. to Hon. William H. Webster, U.S. Ct. Appeals for 8th Cir., St. Louis, 1977-78; ptnr. Davis Polk & Wardwell, NYC, 1978—. Contbr. articles to profl. jours. Mem. ABA, NY State Bar Assn., Assn. Bar City NY (Asian affairs com. 1998-99, securities regulation com. 2000-03, fin. reporting com. 2004—), Coun. Fgn. Rels. Avocations: golf, running, classical music. Office: Davis Polk & Wardwell 450 Lexington Ave Fl 31 New York NY 10017-3982 Office Phone: 212-450-4745. E-mail: drucker@dpw.com.

DRUCKMAN, DANIEL, social sciences educator, consultant, researcher; b. NYC, Dec. 14, 1939; s. Irving and Gladys (Marcus) D.; m. Marjorie Kahn, July 22, 1962; children: Kathy Lee Berggren, James N. BA with honors, Mich. State U., 1961; student, Duke U., 1961-62; MS, Northwestern U., 1965, PhD, 1966. Sr. rsch. scientist Inst. Juvenile Rsch., Chgo., 1966-72, program dir., 1972-75; sr. rsch. analyst Mathematica, Inc., Bethesda, Md., 1975-79, math. tech. scientist, 1979-82; sr. scientist, program mgr. Booz-Allen & Hamilton, Bethesda, 1982-85; prin. study dir. Nat. Acad. Scis., Washington, 1985-97; Vernon M. and Minnie I. Lynch prof. conflict resolution George Mason U., Fairfax, Va., 2001—04, dir. doctoral program, 1997—2002; prof. pub. and internat. affairs George Mason Sch. Polit. Sci. and Internat. Studies, U. Queensland, Brisbane, Australia, 2006—. Vis. faculty IIS Inst. Mgmt., Cochin, India, 1998—; vis. scientist Internat. Inst. Applied Sys. Analysis, Vienna, Austria, 1991-92; cons. Nat. Rsch. Coun., Washington, 1997-2000. Mem. editl. bd. Jour. Conflict Resolution, 1990—, Am. Behavioral Scientist, others; assoc. editor, Negotiation Jour., Simulation & Games, Group Decision and Negotiation, editor spl. issue Annals of Am. Acad. Polit. and Social Sci., 1995; author, editor 14 books; contbr. over 150 articles to sci. jours. Active Nat. Charity Campaigns, Tennis Profls. Tournament Wash. Tennis Patrons, 1990—; coach Montgomery Soccer, Inc., Md., 1979-87. Recipient award U.S. Inst. of Peace, Washington, 1992-93, 96-97, award for enhancing human performance U.S. Army Rsch. Inst., Alexandria, Va., 1986-97, Tchg. Excellence award, George Mason U., 1998. Fellow Soc. Psychol. Study of Social Issues (Otto Klineberg Intercultural and Internat. Rels. award 1995), Soc. Exptl. Social Psychology, Internat. Studies Assn., Internat. Assn. Conflict Mgmt. (Outstanding Article award 2001, Lifetime Achievement award 2003, Outstanding Book award 2004-05), Sigma Xi. Achievements include research in studies of negotiation and nationalism. Home: 10509 Gainsborough Rd Potomac MD 20854-4045

DRUDGE, MATT, journalist, celebrity blogger; b. Oct. 27, 1967; s. Bob Drudge. Gift shop mgr. CBS-TV, LA; founder, editor The Drudge Report website, 1995—; host TV show Drudge, 1998—99; host radio show ABC Network, 1999—2000, Premiere Radio Networks. Inc., 2001—. Author: Drudge Manifesto, 2000. Named one of 100 Most Influential People, Time Mag., 2006, Top 25 Web Celebs, Forbes mag., 2007. Achievements include the Webby Awards rated the 1998 Drudge Report news break of the Monica Lewinsky scandal as #2 on the top 10 web moments that changed the world. Office: Premiere Radio Networks Inc 15260 Ventura Blvd 5th Fl Sherman Oaks CA 91403 Office Phone: 818-377-5300. Office Fax: 818-377-5333.*

DRUE, KERRY ERICA, former attorney general; b. St. Thomas, VI, Mar. 15, 1966; d. Ive Arlington Swan and Gertrude Maria (Niles) Drue Swan. BA, Princeton U., 1988; JD, Harvard U., 1991. Bar: Fla. 1991, DC 1992, US Dist. Ct. (mid. dist.) Fla. 1992. Assoc. Steel, Hector & Davis, Miami, Fla., 1991-92; jud. clk. VI Territorial Ct., Saint Thomas, 1992-93; assoc. Steel, Hector & Davis, Miami, Fla., 1993; asst. atty. gen. VI, atty gen., 2005—07. Vol. lawyer Guardian Ad Litem Program, Miami, 1991. Mem. ABA, Fla. Assn. Women Lawyers, Black Lawyers Assn., Nat. Bar Assn., Harvard Club Miami, Japanese Cultural Soc. Avocations: travel, martial arts, politics. Office Phone: 340-774-5666.

DRUFFEL, ANN BERNICE, researcher, writer; b. Riverside, Calif., Aug. 12, 1926; d. William and Aileen (Walsh) McElroy; m. Charles K. Druffel, Jan. 24, 1953; children: Ellen, Diana, Carolyn, Charlotte, Allis Ann. BA in Sociology, Immaculate Heart Coll.; postgrad., Cath. U. RSW Calif. Family and child welfare worker Cath. Welfare Bur., L.A. and Long Beach, Calif., 1948-53; rschr. Nat. Investigations Com. Aerial Phenomena, Washington, 1957—73, Ctr. UFO Studies, Chgo., 1975—; investigator Mut. UFO Network, Bellvue, Colo., 1973—; rschr., cons. Mobius Soc., LA, 1986—. Spkr. in field. Author: How to Defend Yourself Against Alien Abductions, 1998, Firestorm!: Dr. James E. McDonald's Fight for UFO Science, 2003; co-author: (with D. Scott Rogo) The Tujunga Canyon Contracts, 1980, paperback expanded edit., 1989, The Psychic and the Detective, 1983, expanded edit., 1995; (with Armand Marcotte) Past Lives: Future Growth, 1986, 2d edit., 1994, (with Armand Marcotte) Standing in God's Light: In End Times, 2006; contbr. chpts. to books; contbr. articles to profl. jours.; cons. Flying Saucer Rev., London, 1980-2005; assoc. editor Mufon UFO Jour., 1978-84; author (filmscript) Dixie North; cons. (TV documentaries) Psychic Detectives, 1989, Report from Unknown, 1990. Named to Am. Libr. Directory, Skynet Libr. Achievements include research in Ireland for lost grave of Robert Emmet (patriot). Avocations: hiking, ocean swimming, snorkeling, exploring sacred sites, orchard gardening. Personal E-mail: ann@anndruffel.com.

DRUGAS, THEODORE GEORGE, retired surgeon; b. Chgo., Nov. 27, 1924; s. George Theodore Drugas and Georgia Demas; m. Joanna Stefanos, June 24, 1956 (dec. 1996); children: George, Peter, Diane. BS in Medicine, U. Ill. Med. Sch., Chgo., 1947, MD with honors, 1949. Diplomate Am. Bd. Surgery, Am. Bd. Abdominal Surgery. Fellow in surgery Lahey Clinic, Boston, 1957, Overholt Thoracic Clinic, Boston, 1958; mem. surgery staff Holy Cross Hosp., Chgo, 1960—95, Palos Cmty. Hosp., Palos Heights, Ill., 1972—95. Mem. U. Ill. Found., 1997; donor Drugas Family Found. Endowed Chair in Vasc. Surgery U. Ill. Med. Sch., Chgo., 1997. Lt. comdr. USNR, 1956—58. Fellow: ACS, Internat. Coll. Surgeons; mem.: AMA, Chgo. Med. Soc., Warren H. Cole Soc. (hon.), Alpha Omega Alpha. Greek Orthodox. Home: 8808 Berkeley Ct Orland Park IL 60462 Personal E-mail: tdrugas@webtv.net.

DRUKE, WILLIAM ERWIN, judge, lawyer; b. Phoenix, Dec. 5, 1938; s. Erwin J. and Mary Nell (Hadden) D.; m. Shirley Jean Robinson, Aug. 12, 1978 (div. 1990); children: John E., Michael C.; m. Barbara L. Ross, Mar. 4, 1995. BS, Ariz. State U., 1961; JD, U. Ariz., 1969. Bar: Ariz. 1969, U.S. Dist. Ct. Ariz. 1969. Law clk. Ct. of Appeals, Phoenix, 1969-70; prosecutor Pima County Atty., Tucson, 1970-72; magistrate Tucson City Ct., 1972-74; judge Pima County Superior Ct., Tucson, 1975-85, presiding judge, 1980-85; ptnr. Druke, Feulner & Cornelio P.C., Tucson, 1985-86; assoc. Fred R. Esser, P.C., Sedona, Ariz., 1986-88; pvt. practice Tucson, 1988-92; judge Ariz. Ct. Appeals, Tucson, 1992—2003, chief judge, 1994-99. Mem. Commn. on Jud. Conduct, 1992-96; mem. Ariz. Jud. Coun., 1993-99; mem. Ariz. Supreme Ct. Appellate Study Com., 1994-95; chair bench/bar ad hoc criminal com., 1994-95; chair Ariz. Supreme Ct. Ct. Reporters Com., 1995-97; dean Ariz. Jud. Coll., 1999-2001. Mem. Juvenile Pro Bon Task Force, Tucson, 1991-92; bd. dirs. The Haven, Am. Heart Assn., Tucson, 1984-85, Alcoholism Counsel of Tucson, 1980-83; mem. Ariz. Criminal Justice Commn., Phoenix, 1983-85; judge Teen Ct.; vol. U. Med. Ctr. Fellow Ariz. Bar Found.; mem. Ariz. Judges Assn. (pres. 1984), Pima County Bar Assn. (bd. dirs. 1981-85). Avocations: rollerblading, travel, reading, tap dancing. Mailing: PO Box 30602 Tucson AZ 85751-0602 E-mail: bdruke@comcast.net.

DRUKER, BRIAN JAY, medical educator, researcher; b. St. Paul, Apr. 30, 1955; s. Jean S. Druker. MD, U. Calif.-San Diego, La Jolla, 1981. Internship and residency in internal medicine Barnes Hosp., Washington Sch. of Medicine, St. Louis; trained in oncology Harvard's Dana-Farber Cancer Inst.; prof. medicine Oreg. Health & Sci. U., Portland, 1993—2001, JELD-WEN chair, dir., leukemia ctr. Recipient medal of honor, Am. Cancer Soc., 2001, AACR-Richard and Hinda Rosenthal award, 2001, Dameshak prize, Am. Soc. Hematology, 2001, Warren Alpert Found. award, Harvard Med. Sch., 2001, John J. Kenney award, Leukemia and Lymphoma Soc., 2000, Brupbacher Found. Cancer Rsch. award, 2001, Emil J. Freireich award for clin. rsch., MD Anderson Cancer Ctr., 2001, Charles F. Kettering prize, GM Cancer Rsch. Found., 2002, Pioneer Survivorship award, Lance Armstrong Found., 2002. Mem.: NAS, Inst. Medicine, 2004. Avocations: running, bicycling. Office: Oreg Health and Sci U 3181 SW Sam Jackson Park Rd Portland OR 97201

DRUKER, DAVID, medical association administrator; b. Marshalltown, Iowa, Aug. 16, 1941; s. Harry and Rose Druker; m. Karen Druker, Apr. 3, 1966; children: Daniel, Ellen. BA, Harvard U., Cambridge, Mass., 1963; MD, U. Iowa, Iowa City, 1968. Intern Good Samaritan Hosp., Dayton, Ohio, 1968—69; resident dermatology U. Oreg. Sch. Medicine, 1971—74; dermatologist Palo Alto Med. Found., Calif., 1975—2007, COO, 1994—99, pres., CEO, 1999—; exec. dir. Palo Alto Med. Clinic, 1989—94; regional exec. officer Sutter Health, Sacramento, 2003—. Chmn. Am. Med. Group Assn., DC, 1999—2000, Calif. Med. Group Assn., 2004—05. Capt. US Army, 1977—81. Mem.: Am. Acad. Dermatology. Avocations: golf, exercise. Home: 14190 Wild Plum Ln Los Altos Hills CA 94022 Office: Palo Alto Medical Found 795 El Camino Palo Alto CA 94301

DRUKS, HERBERT MICHAEL, history educator; b. Apr. 1, 1937; BA, CCNY, 1958; MA, Rutgers U., 1959; PhD, NYU, 1964. Asst. prof. Nassau CC, NY, 1960-64; mem. humanities faculty Sch. Visual Art, 1972—; prof. Bklyn. Coll., 1972—. Author: Harry S Truman and the Russians, 1967, 81, From Truman through Johnson, A Documentary, 1971, The U.S. and Israel, 1979, The Uncertain Friendship, The U.S. and Israel from F.D.R. to Kennedy, 2000, The U.S. and Israel from Kennedy to the Peace Process, 2001, John F. Kennedy of Israel, 2005. Home: 50 Hill Park Ave Great Neck NY 11021-3757 Office Phone: 718-951-5229. Personal E-mail: hdsmile36@yahoo.com.

DRUM, ALICE, academic administrator, educator; b. Gettysburg, Pa., June 22, 1935; d. David Wentz and Charlotte Rebecca (Kinzey) McDannell; m. D. Richard Guise, June 15, 1957 (div. Aug. 1975); children: Gregory, Brent, Richard, Robert, Clay; m. Ray Kenneth Drum, Mar. 2, 1979; 1 child, Trevor. BA magna cum laude, Wilson Coll., 1957; PhD, Am. U., 1976. Adj. prof. gen. studies Antioch U., Columbia, Md., 1976-78; adj. asst. prof. English Gettysburg Coll., 1977-80; lectr. gen. studies Georgetown U., Washington, 1980-81; lectr. gen. honors U. Md., College Park, 1980-83; asst. prof. English Hood Coll., Frederick, Md., 1981-85, coord. writing program, 1981-83, assoc. dean acad. affairs, 1983-85; dean freshmen Franklin and Marshall Coll., Lancaster, Pa., 1985-88, v.p., 1988-2001, prof., chair women's studies, 2001—. Team mem. Mid. States Accreditation Assn., 1989-2003; cons. in field. Co-author: Funding A College Education, 1996; contbr. chpts. to books, articles and book revs. to profl. jours. Chair Lancaster County DA Commn., Lancaster, 1990-91; mem. Lancaster County Commn. on Youth Violence, Lancaster, 1990-91; bd. trustees Wilson Coll., 1997—, YWCA, Lancaster. Mellon grantee, 1979; Davison Foreman fellow, 1975-76. Mem. MLA, N.E. MLA, Deans (pres. 1988-89), Coll. English Assn., Phi Beta Kappa (pres. chpt. 1990-91), Phi Kappa Phi. Democrat. Episcopalian. Avocations: hiking, reading, visiting art museums. Home Phone: 717-392-8747; Office Phone: 717-291-3980. Business E-Mail: alicedrum@fandm.edu.

DRUM, BRUCE ALAN, physicist; b. Wauseon, Ohio, May 18, 1947; s. Virgil and Clela Drum; m. Pamela Joy Neff, June 16, 1973; children: Rachel, Kevin, Erin. BSc, Ohio State U., Columbus, 1969; PhD, Ohio State U., 1973. Postdoctoral fellow Wilmer Eye Inst., Johns Hopkins U., Balt., 1973—74, asst. prof., 1984—91; rsch. faculty George Wash. U., Washington, 1975—84; physicist FDA, Rockville, Md., 1994—. Vision cons., Columbia, Md., 1985—. Contbr. articles to profl. jours., chapters to books; author: procs. to confs. Mem. Ctrl. Md. Chorale, Laurel, 2002—. Recipient Outstanding Svc. award, FDA, 2001, Clear Sci. Comm. award, 2003, Spl. Recognition awards, Ctr. for Devices and Radiol. Health, FDA, 1996, 1998, 2003, 2004; grantee, Nat. Eye Inst., NIH, 1975—82, 1981—84, 1985—89, 1988—91. Mem.: Fedn. of Am. Scientists, Internat. Perimetric Soc., Internat. Color Vision Soc. (sec.-treas. 1985—94), AAAS, Optical Soc. of Am., Assn. for Rsch. in Vision and Ophthalmology. Achievements include development of model of brightness perception; model of human color vision; research in normal and abnormal vision; premarket regulation of ophthalmic devices. Avocations: running, singing, playing classical piano, gardening, reading. Office: Food and Drug Administration 9200 Corporate Blvd (HFZ-460) Rockville MD 20850 Office Phone: 240-276-4244. Office Fax: 240-276-4234. E-mail: bruce.drum@fda.hhs.gov.

DRUM, SYDNEY MARIA, artist; b. Calgary, Alta., Can., Nov. 20, 1952; d. Ian Mondelet and Dorothy Mary (Weaver) D.; m. Frank DeSalvo, Nov. 7, 1987; 1 child, Christopher. BFA with distinction in art, U. Calgary, 1974; MFA, York U., 1976. Tchr. U. Ill., 1978-83, Govs. State U., 1983-84, Rutgers U., 1984-87. One-woman and 2 person exhibits include Art Gallery Ont., 1978, Condeso/Lawler Gallery, N.Y., 1981, Gallery Pascal, 1983, U. Pitts., 1984, Bau-Xi Gallery, Toronto, 1987, 90, 92, 95, 55 Mercer Gallery, N.Y., 1993, 96, 98, 2000, 02, 04, Mus. am Ostwall, Dortmund, Germany, 1994, Hart House-U. Toronto, 1995, Robert Birch Gallery, Toronto, 1999, 2002, Gallery Surge, Tokyo, 1999, Kunsturein Alle Fuerwache, Dresden, 2002, Optisches Mus., Jena, Germany, 2004, Birch Libralato Gallery, Toronto, 2005, Art Gallery of Peel, Ont., 2005; represented in pub. collections Can. Coun. Art Bank, U. Toronto, Toronto-Dominion Bank, Petro Can., Mus. Modern Art, N.Y., Phila. Mus. Art, Robert McLaughlin Gallery, Oshawa; commissions include Pope, Ballard, Shepard & Fowle, Chgo., 1983, Zimmerli Mus., Rutgers U., 1990; reviewer art exhibits New Art Examiner, Chgo., 1983-84. Can. Coun. grantee, 1978. Home: 138 W 120th St New York NY 10027-6401

DRUMHELLER, ANTHONY D. (ANDY), lawyer; b. Charlottesville, Va., Dec. 26, 1969; m. Barbara Drumheller; 3 children. BA, U. Tex., 1992; JD, Tex. Tech U., 1995. Bar: Tex. 1995, US Supreme Ct., US Dist. Ct. (so. dist. Tex.), cert.: Tex. Bd. Legal Specialization (criminal law). Asst. dist. atty. Harris County, Tex., 1995—98; assoc. Rusty Hardin & Assocs., P.C., Houston, 1998—. Named a Rising Star, Tex. Super Lawyers mag., 2006. Mem.: Houston Young Lawyers Assn., Houston Bar Assn. Avocations: reading, running. Office: Rusty Hardin & Assocs PC 1401 McKinney Ste 2250 Houston TX 77010 Office Phone: 713-652-9000. E-mail: adrumheller@rustyhardin.com.*

DRUMHELLER, LINDA BLOCHER, language educator; b. Carlisle, Pa., May 27, 1960; d. Richard Plank and Janice Lee Blocher; m. Tyler Scott Drumheller, June 20, 1981; 1 child, Livia Ann. BA in Sociology, George Mason U., Fairfax, Va., 2004; MA in Secondary Edn., George Wash. U., Washington, DC, 2006. Rsch. asst. CIA, Langley, Va., 1986—96; with Fairfax County Pub. Schs., Va., 1996—. Precinct capt., nat. affairs com. mem. Fairfax County Dem. Com., Vienna, Va., 2002—06; ESL tchr. English as a Second Language and Immigrant Ministries, Wesley Methodist Ch., Vienna, Va., 2004—06; coorespondence sec. SHARE Inc., McLean, Va., 2002—06. Mem.: Am. Women's Assn. (v.p. charity 1999—2001), Golden Key. Democrat-Npl. Methodist. Avocations: squash, running, flute. Home: 8122 Boss St Vienna VA 22182 Home Phone: 703-448-6702. Personal E-mail: drumheller5@cox.net.

DRUMMER, DONALD RAYMOND, diversified financial services company executive, educator; b. Binghamton, NY, Oct. 10, 1941; s. Donald Joseph and Louise Frances (Campbell) D.; m. Rita Kovac, May 22, 1965; children: Shelley Rita, Adam Donn. BS, U. Colo., 1972; MBA, Regis U., 1981. With Lincoln First Bank, Binghamton, 1962-69; asst. comptr. Adams & Horne, Denver, 1969; with Colo. State Bank, 1969-87, v.p., 1972-81, comptr., 1972-87, sr. v.p., 1981-87; sr. v.p., CFO Wyo. Nat. Bancorp. (formerly Affiliated Bank Corp. of Wyo.), Casper, 1987-91, Wyo. Nat. Bank, Casper, Cheyenne, 1987—91; v.p., contr. Crop Hail Mgmt., Kalispell, Mont., 1991—92; sr. v.p. fin. Am. Nat. Bank, Cheyenne, 1993—95; v.p. Cmty. First Bancorp, Inc., 1994—95, cons., 1995—2001; sr. v.p., CFO Citizens Bank Fla., 2001—06, exec. v.p., CFO, 2006—. Bd. dirs. Wyo. Nat. Bank, Lovell and Kemmerer, 1987-88; corp. sec. Wyo. Nat. Bancorp. (formerly Affiliated Bank Corp. of Wyo.), 1987-91; bd. dirs. Wheatland Ins. Agency, 1989-91; CFO, exec. com. Am. Bankers Assn., 1989-91; adj. faculty Regis U., mem. grad. edn. task force, 1986-87. Editor: Chronicle, 1980—81. Bd. dirs. Girls Club of Casper, 1988. Mem. Inst. Mgmt. Accts. (dir. 1975-79, v.p. 1977-79), Am. Acctg. Assn., Am. Taxation Assn., Denver Sertoma Club (past pres.), City Club (v.p., dir. 1979-83). Office: Citizens Bank Oviedo PO Box 620729 Oviedo FL 32762-0729 Office Phone: 407-365-6611. Business E-Mail: ddrummer@mycbfl.com.

DRUMMOND, ALEXANDER R., priest; b. Chambley, Lorraine, France, Oct. 20, 1957; BA in Philosophy, Schiller Internat. U., Strasbourg, France, 1980; MA in Internat. Rels., Schiller Internat. U., Paris, 1981; MDiv, St. Charles Borromeo Sem., 1993, MA in Theology, 1994. Ordained Diocese Arlington, Va., 1994. Legis. asst. U.S. Congress, Washington, 1981—85; various positions The Close Up Found., Arlington, Va., 1986—88; tchr. Children's House of Blacksburg, Va., 1988—89; assoc. pastor St. Timothy Cath. Ch., Chantilly, Va., 1994—98, St. Michael Cath. Ch., Amandale, Va., 1998—2002, Good Shepherd Cath. Ch., Mt. Vernon, Va., 2002—04; adminstr. St. Catherine of Siena Cath. Ch., Great Falls, Va., 2004—. Office: St Catherine of Siena Cath Ch 1020 Springvale Rd Great Falls VA 22066 Office Phone: 703-759-4350.

DRUMMOND, CAROL CRAMER, voice educator, lyricist, writer, artist; b. Indpls., Mar. 5, 1933; adopted d. Burr Ostin and L. Ruth Welch; m. Roscoe Drummond, 1978 (dec. 1983). Student, Butler U., 1951—53; studied voice with Todd Duncan, Frances Yeend, James Benner, Rosa Ponselle, Dr. Peter Herman Adler and John Bullock; studied drama with Adelaide Bishop, DC. Original performer Starlite Musicals, Indpls., 1951; singer Am. Light Opera Co., Washington, Seagle Opera Colony, Schroon Lake, NY, 1963, 64; soloist St. John's Episcopal Ch., Lafayette Sq., Washington, 5th Ch. of Christ, Scientist, Washington, 1963-78; performer Concerts in Schs. Program, Washington Performing Arts Soc., 1967—97; soloist with Luke AFB band ofcl. opening Boswell Meml. Hosp, Sun City, Ariz., 1970; painter, artist, 1980—; pvt. tchr. voice Ellsworth H.S., 1986—2006, Mt. Desert Island H.S., 1986—2006, McLean, Va., 2006—; voice tchr. McLean Sch. Music, 2006—, Flint Hill Sch., Oakton, Va., 2006—, Oakcrest Sch., McLean, 2006—. Soloist numerous oratorio socs.; appearances with symphony orchs. including Nat. Symphony Orch., Fairfax (Va.) Symphony Orch., Buffalo Philharm. Orch., Concerts in the Pk., Arlington Opera Co., Lake George Opera Co., Glens Falls, NY, The Nat. Cathedral, Washington, Noye's Flood, Lufkin, Tex., 1965, Washington Nat. Opera; voiceover radio and TV commls., 1965—84; U.S. Govt. host The Sounding Bd., Sta. WGTS-FM, Washington, 1972—78; dir. ensembles, music/voice cons. Summer Festival of the Arts, S.W. Harbor, Maine, 1992—95, mem. adv. bd., 1986—2006; dir. Amahl and the Night Visitors, 1992; vocal solo concert The Smithsonian Instn., 1980; pub. svc. announcements 4 Bangor Radio Stas., 2005. Former columnist: Animal Crackers, writer: newspaper and mag. articles and stories; one-woman shows include, Lemon Tree, Bangor, 1995—96, Grand Theater, Ellsworth, Maine, 1995, Southwest Harbor (Maine) Pub. Libr., 1997, U. Maine, 1999, Border's, Bangor, 2002, two-woman shows, Am. Art League, Washington,

1997, Cosmos Club, 1996, Arts Club, 1994—96; artist, owner Dream Come True Notecards, 1997—2006. Bd. dirs. Washington Sch. Ballet, 1978, Animal Rescue Found., Trenton, Maine, 2004—05; aux. bd. Bar Harbor Aux. Music Festival, 2004—07; life bd. dirs. Internat. Soundex Reunion Registry, Carson City, Nev. Recipient 1st pl. women's divsn. Internat. Printers Ink Contest, 1951. Mem.: Music Tchrs. Nat. Assn., Nat. League Am. Pen Women, Beta Sigma Phi, Kappa Kappa Gamma. Republican. Presbyterian. Avocations: pets, reading, travel.

DRUMMOND, DAVID C., information technology executive, lawyer; BA in History, Santa Clara U; JD, Stanford Law Sch., 1989. Former ptnr. corp. transactions group Wilson, Sonsini, Goodrich, & Rosati, 1998; exec. v.p. fin., CFO CBT Group PLC, 1999, SmartForce; v.p. corp. devel. Google Inc., Mountain View, Calif., 2002—, gen. counsel, 2002—06, sec., 2002—06, sr. v.p. corp. devel. Office: Google Inc 1600 Amphitheatre Pky Mountain View CA 94043 Office Phone: 650-623-4000. Office Fax: 650-618-1499.*

DRUMMOND, DIXIE DALE, retired adult education educator; b. Monterey, Calif., Sept. 9, 1943; d. Ray Dale and Norma Kathryn Drummond. BS, Okla. Coll. Liberal Arts, Chickasha, 1966; MA in Tchg., Western N.Mex. U., Silver City, 1973. Tchr. Lovington Schs., N.Mex., 1966—2001; prof. Coll. of the SW, Hobbs, N.Mex., 2001—06; ret., 2006. Part-time prof. N.Mex. Jr. Coll., Hobbs, 2002—.

DRUMMOND, DOROTHY WEITZ, geography education consultant, educator, author; b. San Diego, Dec. 19, 1928; d. Frederick W. and Dora (Weidenhofer) Weitz; m. Robert R. Drummond, Sept. 5, 1953 (dec. June 1982); children: Kathleen, Gael, Martha. AB, Valparaiso U., 1949; MA, Northwestern U., 1951. Cert. tchr., Ind. Tchr. social studies Woodrow Wilson Jr. H.S., Oxnard, Calif., 1949—50; editl. asst. Am. Geog. Soc., NYC, 1951—53; substitute tchr. Vigo County Sch. Corp., Terre Haute, Ind., 1960—67; tchr. social studies Ind. State U. Lab. Sch., Terre Haute, 1963—64. Geog. edn. cons., author, workshop presenter, Terre Haute, 1953—; adj. asst. prof. geography Saint Mary-of-the-Woods (Ind.) Coll., 1967-99, Ind. State U., Terre Haute, 1990-99; dir. project GEO, Ind. State U., 1992-96; cons. McGraw-Hill, Scott-Foresman, Agy. Instrnl. Tech., Hudson Inst.; grant developer GIS Twenty-First Century, Ind. State U., 1996-98. Author: People on Earth, 3d edit., 1988, Thinking Geographically: All Things Considered, 1990, 1998, Holy Land, Whose Land?: Modern Dilemma, Ancient Roots, 2002, 2d edit., 2004; co-author: The World Today, 3d edit., 1971, World Geography, 1989; contbr. numerous articles to profl. jours. Tour organizer, China, Australia, New Zealand, Peru, Ecuador, Turkey, India, 1986—; bd. dir. United Campus Ministries, Terre Haute, 1991—94, 2003—. Fulbright scholar, Burma, 1957-58; grantee Geography Educators Network Ind., 1988-96, Ind. Commn. Higher Edn., 1990, 92, 94, 96, NSF, 1993, 95, 96, 97, U.S. Dept. Edn., 1992-96. Mem.: soc. Women Geographers, Assn. Am. Geographers, Am. Geog. Soc., Ind. Coun. Social Studies, Geography Educators Network Ind., Nat. Coun. Geog. Edn. (pres. 1990), Nat. Coun. Social Studies. Business E-Mail: dd2@indstate.edu.

DRUMMOND, MALCOLM MCALLISTER, electronics engineer; b. London, Eng., Sept. 22, 1937; came to U.S., 1966, naturalized, 1977; s. George James and Winifred Ethel (Jaye) D.; m. Linda Jerome Banning, May 25, 1968; 1 child, Heather Lynn. BSEE with honors, City U., London. Registered profl. elec. engr. Engr. Brit. Fgn. Office, Cheltenham, England, 1964—66; sr. engr. Gen. Dynamics Corp., Rochester, NY, 1966—70; tech. rep. Tymshare Inc., Rochester, 1970—72; project engr. Sybron Corp., Taylor Instrument Co., Rochester, 1972—85, Hampshire Instruments Corp., 1985—93, User Friendly Operating Systems, Inc., 1993—2000, Eastman Kodak Co., Rochester, 2000, ENI/MKS, An Emerson Co., Rochester, 2000—. Dir. Care & Svc., Inc., 1982-90, pres. 1986-89. Christian Sci. min. for VA Hosp., 1974-80; chmn., bd. trustees Ch. of Christ Scientst, Rochester, 1993-94, 98-99. Mem. IEEE (life sr. mem., chmn. Rochester sect. 1979-80, past chmn. pension task force 1983-84, Region I PAC coord. 1980-82, Area D chmn. 1982-85, ASIC seminar chmn. 1987-88), Engrs. and Scientists Joint Com. on Pensions (vice chmn. 1983-84), N.Y. State Soc. Profl. Engrs., Engring. Mgmt. Soc. (chmn. 1990-2003), Computer Soc. (past pres.), Instrument Soc. Am., Rochester Engring. Soc. (emeritus; dir. 1979-83, IEEE rep. 1984-2004, treas. 1993-2003), Principle Found. Western N.Y. (treas. 1994—), Am. Mgmt. Assns., Inst. Elec. Engrs. Great Britain, Monroe County Bar Assn. (mem. ethics com. 1994-95). Home: 60 Marberth Dr Henrietta NY 14467-9014 Office: ENI/MKS Instruments 100 Highpower Rd Rochester NY 14623-3498 Business E-Mail: mdrummond@mksinst.com.

DRUMMOND, MARSHALL EDWARD (MARK), academic administrator; b. Stanford, Calif., Sept. 14, 1941; s. Kirk Isaac and Fern Venice (McDeritt) D.; 2 children. BS, San Jose State U., 1964, MBA, 1969; EdD, U. San Francisco, 1979. Adj. prof. bus. and edn. U. San Francisco, 1975-81; adj. prof. bus. and info. systems San Francisco State U., 1981-82; prof. MIS, Ea. Wash. U., Cheney, 1985—98, exec. dir. info. resources, 1988, assoc. v.p. adminstrv. svcs., chief info. officer, 1988-89, v.p. adminstrv. svcs., 1989-90, exec. v.p., 1990, pres., 1990-98; chancellor L.A. C.C. Dist., 1999—2004, Calif. C.C. sys., 2004—. Cons. Sch. Bus., Harvard Coll., U. Ariz. Contbg. editor Diebold Series; contbr. articles to profl. jours. Democrat. Avocations: horse breeding and traing, equestrian sports. Office: Calif Cmty Colls Chancellor's Office 1102 Q St Sacramento CA 95814-6511 Home Phone: 916-444-7538; Office Phone: 916-322-4005. Business E-Mail: mdrummond@cccco.edu.

DRUMMOND, NEIL HIDEN, retired secondary school educator; b. Newport News, Va., Sept. 6, 1940; s. Milton Dwight and Ethel Virginia (Hiden) D. BS, Coll. William and Mary, 1962, MA in Math., 1964. Cert. tchr., Va. Math. tchr. Warwick High Sch., Newport News, 1962-65, chmn. math. dept., 1966-91; ret., 1991. Treas., exec. bd. Newport News Edn. Assn., 1965-72; chmn. City Textbook Adoption Com., Newport News, 1965-91; mem. State Textbook Adoption Com., Richmond, VA., 1968; speaker State Math. Conf., Alexandria, Va., 1969; exec. bd. Newport News Retired Tchrs. Assn., 1993-96, pres. 1996-2003; com. chmn. 3 Cheers for Tchrs., 1996-2002. Sponsor Mu Alpha Theta, Newport News, 1965-91, Sr. Class Warwick HS, Newport News, 1966-67, Hi-Y and Jr. Hi-Y, Newport News, 1965-71; coord. Second Presbyn. Ch. Youth Club, Newport News, 1970's; mem. Nat. Honor Soc. Com., Newport News, 1976-91; fin. com. First United Meth. Ch., Newport News, 1987-91. Mem. NEA, Nat. Coun. Tchrs. Math., Am. Swedish Hist. Soc., Va. Edn. Assn., Evaluating Teams of HS in Va., Vasa Order of Am. Drott Lodge. Avocations: travel, collecting, attending broadway shows, reading, swimming. Home: 27 Nutmeg Quarter Pl Newport News VA 23606-3911 Personal E-mail: nhdsaint@aol.com.

DRUMMOND, SALLY HAZELET, artist; b. Evanston, Ill., June 4, 1924; d. Craig Potter and Frances (Gillam) Hazlet; m. F. Weichel Drummond, Mar. 25, 1961; 1 child, Craig Potter. Student, Rollins Coll., 1942-44; BS, Columbia U., 1946, postgrad., 1946-48, Inst. Design, Chgo., 1949-50; MA, U. Louisville, 1952. Instr. Skowhegan Sch. Art, 1973. Exhibited in solo shows at, Hadley Gallery, Louisville, 1952, Tanager Gallery, N.Y.C., 1955, 57, 60, Green Gallery, N.Y.C., 1962, Fischbach Gallery, N.Y.C., 1978, Aldrich Mus., Ridgefield, Conn., 1981, Merida Galleries, Louisville, 1982, Artists Space, N.Y.C., 1984, "Surface and Proportion", Margaret Roeder Gallery, N.Y. 1990, Cornell Fine Arts Ctr., Rollins Coll., Winter Park, Fla., 1989, Louisville Visual Arts Assn., 1990, Mitchell Algus Gallery, N.Y.C., 2003; exhibited in group shows at, Am. embassy, Rome, 1953, Fgn. Artists Invitational, Bordighiera, Italy, 1953, Am. Artists Ann., 1960, Whitney Mus., N.Y.C., 1958-59, 64, Green Gallery, 1961, Mus. Modern Art, N.Y.C., 1963, Am. Inst. Arts and Letters, N.Y.C., 1982, L.I. City, N.Y., 1987, Owensboro (Ky.) Mus. Art, 1987, Alexandre Gallery, N.Y.C., 2005; 2 person exhbn.: Springfield (Ohio) Art Ctr., 1988, Urban Callery, N.Y.C., 1989, Hunter Coll., N.Y.C., 2003; retrospective exhbn. at Corcoran Gallery, Washington, 1972; rep. permanent collections at, Mus. Modern Art, Whitney Mus., Met. Mus. Art, N.Y.C., Chase Manhattan Bank, N.Y.C., Ciba-Geigy Corp., Speed Mus., Louisville, U. Iowa Mus. Art, Iowa City, Hirshorn Mus. Art, Washington, Greenwich, Conn., Hudsons Dept. Store, Detroit, AVCO Corp., Citizens Fidelity Bank and Trust Co., Louisville. Recipient Fulbright grant to Venice, 1952-53, Guggenheim grant to France, 1967-68

DRUMMOND, WILLA HENDRICKS, neonatologist, educator, information technology executive; b. Harrisburg, Pa., Dec. 5, 1945; d. George Edson and Leah Clementine (Connelly) Hendricks; m. Thomas Weston Drummond, June 1966 (div. 1978). BA cum laude, Brown U., 1966; MD, U. Pa., 1970; MS in Med. Informatics, U. Utah, 1999. Resident in pediat. Children's Hosp. Phila., 1970-72, cardiology fellow, 1972-74; instr. pediat. U. Pa., Phila., 1973-74; rsch. fellow perinatology U. Oreg., Portland, 1974-75; staff pediatrician Kaiser-Permanente Clinics, Portland, 1975-76; instr. neonatology, fellow Cardiovasc. Rsch. Inst.-U. Calif., San Francisco, 1976-78; asst. prof. pediat. U. Fla., Gainesville, 1978-82, asst. prof. pediat. and physiology, 1981-82, assoc. prof. pediat. physiology and vet. med. scis., 1982-88, prof., 1988—. Cons. Baxter-Travenol Labs., Deerfield, Ill., 1986-88; co-chair Equine Neonatology Study Group, Gainesville, 1981-91; dir. Neonatology Fellowship Program U. Fla., Gainesville, 1981-85; cons., CIO, chief med. info. officer, ICU Data Sys., Inc., Gainesville, 2001-05, interim CEO, exec. v.p. med. affairs, 2004-06, founder, chief med. info. exec., 2006—; CCHIT commr. Child HC Exp. Panel, 2007-. Contbr. numerous rsch. papers and abstracts to profl. jours.; poet: Carousel of Progress, 1979. Named Best Dr. in USA, Best Doctors, Inc., 2005-; named one of Am.'s Top Pediatricians, 2007; rsch. grantee Am. Heart Assn., NIH, Dept. of Def., others, 1976—; sr. fellow Med. Informatics, 1997-99. Mem. Am. Physiologic Soc., Soc. Pediat. Rsch., Am. Pediat. Soc., Am. Acad. Pediat.(exec. steering com. Coun. Clin. Info. Tech. 2005-), Am. Med. Informatics Assn., Am. Heart Assn., So. Soc. Pediat. Rsch., Internat. Soc. Vet. Perinatology (bd. dirs., pres. 1995-97), Internat. Physicians Prevention of Nuc. War (collective Nobel Peace prize 1985), Union of Concerned Scientists, NOW, NRDC, Sierra Club, Greenpeace. Democrat. Office: U Fla Coll Medicine PO Box 100296 Gainesville FL 32610-0296 Home Phone: 352-337-0622; Office Phone: 352-392-4195. Business E-Mail: DrWilla@peds.ufl.edu.

DRUMMOND, WILLIAM KENNETH, small business owner, mechanical engineer, consultant; b. St. Louis, Oct. 31, 1927; s. William Foster and Irene Augusta (Ballenger) Drummond; m. Shirley Jean Stevens, May 28, 1948; children: Dana Lynn, Linda Susan, William Steven. BSChemE, Finlay Engring. Coll., Kansas City, Mo. Mech. engr. Ford Motor Co., Kansas City, 1952—54, Natin and Co., Kansas City, 1954—58, gen. mgr. Columbia, Mo., 1958—68; consulting engr. Drummond Mech. Contractors, Columbia, Mo., 1968—88, owner, pres., 1968—. Ptnr. N and D Engring. Svc., Columbia, Mo., 1964—78. Commr. Bd. Mech. Examiners, Columbia, Mo., 1992; bd. dirs. Centerre Bank, Columbia, 1984, Boatman's Bank, Columbia, 1986. With USN, 1951—53, Korea. Mem.: Country Club Mo. (bd. dirs. 1972—), Optimist Club, Shriners (32nd degree 1965—), Masons (3rd degree 1956—). Lutheran. Avocations: golf, poker, fishing. Home: 3444 Woodrail Ter Columbia MO 65203 Office: Drummond Mechanical Contractors 910 Dinwiddie Cir Columbia MO 65202

DRUMMOND BORG, LESLEY MARGARET, geneticist; b. Wellington, New Zealand, Oct. 26, 1948; arrived in U.S., 1986; d. Grant Allen and Yolanda Drummond; m. Kenneth Irvin Borg; children: Marc Borg, Kyle Borg. MBChB, Otago Med. Sch., New Zealand, 1971; MD, Otago Med. Sch., 1983; BSc, Auckland U., New Zealand, 1976. Diplomate Am. Bd. Pediat., Am. Bd. Med. Genetics, cert. clin. geneticist. Fellow clin. genetics U. Auckland Med. Sch., 1974—77, med. geneticist, 1977—79; resident pediat. Hosp. Sick Children, Toronto, Ont., Canada, 1980—82; gen. practitioner ARAMCO, Saudi Arabia, 1983—86; sr. fellow med. genetics U. Wash., Seattle, 1986—88; clin. geneticist Genetic Screening and Counseling Svc., Denton, Tex., 1988—95; dir. genetics divsn. Tex. Dept. Health, Austin, 1995—2004; mgr. health screening br. Tex. Dept. State Health Svcs., Austin, 2004—05, physician cons. health screening and case mgmt. unit, 2005—. Clin. asst. prof. Tex. A&M U., College Station, 1991—98; cons. staff Odessa Women's Children's Hosp., Tex., 1991—96, Cook/Ft. Worth Children's Med. Ctr., 1991—98. Contbr. articles to profl. jours. Fellow: Am. Coll. Med. Genetics (founder), Am. Acad. Pediat.; mem.: AMA, Am. Soc. Human Genetics. Avocations: jogging, swimming, hiking. Office: Dept State Health Svcs Health Screening Unit MC1918 1100 W 49th St Austin TX 78756-3160

DRURY, CHARLES LOUIS, JR., hotel executive; b. Cape Girardeau, Mo., Nov. 4, 1955; s. Charles Louis Sr. and Shirley Jean (Luebbers) D.; m. Michelle Marguerite Swenson, Apr. 28, 1979; children: Charles L. III, Thomas Michael. BSBA, St. John's U., Collegeville, Minn., 1978. Gen. mgr. Drury Inns, Inc., St. Louis, 1978-79, regional mgr., 1979-81, v.p. ops., 1981-85, pres., 1985—, chief exec. officer, 1988—, also bd. dirs. Bd. dirs. Drury Industries, Inc., Cape Girardeau, Drury Displays, Inc., St. Louis, Druco, Inc., St. Louis; mem. exec. bd. Enterprise Bank, St. Louis, 1989— Bd. dirs. Dismas House of St. Louis, 1987—, Cardinal Glennon Children's Hosp. Devel. Bd. Mem. Pres. Assn., Am. Mgmt. Assn. Roman Catholic. Office: 721 Emerson Rd #400 Saint Louis MO 63141-6770

DRURY, CHRIS, professional hockey player; b. Trumbull, Conn., Aug. 20, 1976; m. Rory Drury; children: Dylan, Luke. Grad., Boston U. Center Colo. Avalanche, 1998—2002, Calgary Flames, 2002—03, Buffalo Sabres, 2003—07, co-capt., 2004—07; center NY Rangers, 2007—. Mem. USA Olympic Hockey Team, Salt Lake City, 2002, Torino, Italy, 06, Team USA, World Cup of Hockey, 2004. Recipient Hober Baker Meml. Award, 1998, Calder Meml. Trophy, 1999. Achievements include being a member of Stanley Cup Champion Colo. Avalanche, 2001; being a member of silver medal winning USA Hockey Team, Salt Lake City Olympics, 2002. Office: NY Rangers 1 Pennsylvania Plaza New York NY 10121

DRURY, KENNETH CLAYTON, biologist; b. Madera, Calif., Mar. 27, 1945; s. Carma and Alice (Zollinger) Drury; m. Sandra Rosemary Hanlon, Apr. 28, 1972; children: Allison Hanlon, Vanessa Laura. BA, Westmont Coll., 1967; PhD, U. Geneva, Switzerland, 1979. Cert. in andrology and embryology high complexity lab dir. Am. Bd. Bioanalysts. NIH fellow U. Calif., Berkeley, 1979-82; rsch. scientist Codon Corp., South San Francisco, Calif., 1982-84; sr. scientist Microgenics Corp., Concord, Calif., 1984-86; dir. U. Louisville, 1986-92; dir. In Vitro Fertilization and Gamete Physiology Labs. U. Fla., Gainesville, 1992—. Editor: The Clinical Embryologist, 2006; contbr. articles to profl. jours. 1st lt. US Army, 1969—72, Vietnam. Mem.: Am. Soc. Reproductive Medicine, Am. Coll. Reproductive Biology, Am. Fertility Soc. Achievements include research in directly implicating phosphorylation in the mechanism of action for the maturation promoting factor; preimplantation genetic diagnosis to eliminate inherited genetic disease in pregnancy; obtaining a human live birth after ultra rapid freezing of embryos. Office: Univ Fla Dept Ob-Gyn Division Reproductive Endocrinology PO Box 100294 Gainesville FL 32610-0294 E-mail: druryk@obgyn.ufl.edu.

DRURY, LEONARD LEROY, retired oil company executive; b. Gillespie, Ill., Nov. 5, 1928; s. Roy August and Regina Loretta (Finnegan) D.; m. Myra Lee Klunk, June 30, 1951; 1 child, Marilyn Jo Drury Chandler. BS in Indsl. Mgmt., St. Louis U., 1950; MBA in Mgmt., U. Houston, 1957. Mgr. systems program info. and computer services Shell Oil Co., NYC, 1966-68, mgr. data processing info. and computer services Menlo Park, Calif., 1968, mgr. acctg. info. and computer services, 1968-69, mgr. MTM bus. systems div. info. and computer services NYC and Houston, 1969-71, mgr. planning Houston, 1971-73, mgr. planning and tech. info. and computer services, 1973-75, asst. treas. fin., 1975-77, gen. mgr. info. and computer services, 1977-80, liaison Shell Ctr. London, 1980-81, gen. mgr. products fin. Houston, 1981-83, v.p. purchasing and adminstrv. services, 1983-86, v.p. info. and computer services, 1986-89, ret., 1989. Mem. United Way, Houston, 1982-89; bd. dirs. South Main Ctr. Assn., Houston, 1986-89. Mem.: Am. Petroleum Inst., Fin. Execs. Inst., Houston Bus. Coun. (pres. 1985—86), West Houston Assn. (bd. dirs. 1984—88), The Houstonian Club, Sigma Iota Epsilon. Roman Catholic. Home: 11711 Flintwood Dr Houston TX 77024-5110 E-mail: lldhouston@aol.com.

DRUSHAL, MARY ELLEN, retired education educator; b. Peru, Ind., Oct. 24, 1945; d. Herrell Lee and Opal Marie (Boone) Waters; m. J. Michael Drushal, June 12, 1966; children: Lori, Jeff. B of Music Edn., Ashland Coll., 1969; MS, Peabody Coll., 1981; PhD, Vanderbilt U., 1986. Dir. music and spl. edn. projects Smithville (Ohio) Brethren Ch., 1969-74; tchr. music Orrville (Ohio) Pub. Schs., 1969—70; seminar leader Internat. Ctr. for Learning, Glendale, Calif., 1974-76; dir. Christian edn. First Presbyn. and Christ Presbyn. Ch., Nashville, 1976-84; assoc. prof. Ashland (Ohio) Theol. Sem., 1984-91, acad. dean, 1991-95; provost Ashland U., 1995—2001, prof. edn., 2001—05, prof. emeritus, 2006—. Cons. in strategic planning for not-for-profit orgns. Author: On Tablets of Human Hearts: Christian Education with Children, 1991; co-author: Spiritual Formation: A Personal Walk Toward Emmaus, 1990; contbr. articles to profl. jours. Trustee Brethren Care Found., Ashland, 1989-99, Ashland Symphony Orch., 1986-87; pres., fundraiser Habitat for Humanity, Ashland, 1990-94; bd. dirs. JOY Day Care Ctr., 1988-90. Grantee Lilly Endowment Inc., 1991, 93, Brethren Ch. Found., 1989, 90. Mem. Assn. Theol. Schs. (com. under-represented constituencies 1994-96), Am. Assn. for Higher Edn., Nat. Assn. Ch. Bus. Adminstrs., N.Am. Assn. Profs. of Christian Edn., Assn. Profs. and Rschrs. in Religious Edn., Nat. Assn. Evangelicals, Nat. Assn. Black Evangelical Assns., Epiphany Assn. (bd. dirs. 1994-98). Republican. Lutheran. Avocations: reading, needlepoint. Home: 20041 Sanibel View Cir 102 Fort Myers FL 33908-6991 Personal E-mail: drushal@comcast.net.

DRUSKIN, ROBERT A., diversified financial services company executive; b. 1947; BA, Rutgers U., 1969. With Shearson Hammill & Co., 1969—80, treas., 1980—84, CFO, 1984; CFO, mem. exec. com. Shearson Lehman Bros. Inc.; sr. exec. v.p., chief adminstrv. officer Smith Barney, 1991—96, vice chmn., 1993, head asset mgmt. and futures divsn., 1996—97, chief adminstrv. officer, 1997—2000; chief ops. & tech. officer Citigroup Inc., 2000—02, pres., COO global corp. and investment banking group NYC, 2002—03, pres., CEO, global corp. & investment banking group, 2003—06, mem. Office of Chmn., 2007—, COO, 2007—. Trustee, mem. dean's adv. com. Rutgers U.; mem. bd. overseers Rutgers U. Found. Office: Citigroup Inc 399 Park Ave New York NY 10043*

DRUSKOFF, BARBARA THERESE, elementary school educator; d. Edward Francis and Helen Sullivan; children: Jennifer Bernier, Mark. Student, Calif. State U., Long Beach, 1980, San Diego State U., 1986; BS in Edn., CUNY, 1966; MEd, Azusa Pacific U., Calif., 1994. Tchr. 1st grade Matawan Sch. Dist., NJ, 1966—67; tchr. elem. sch. Newston Sch. Dist., NJ, 1968—69, Bainbridge Unified Sch. Dist., NY, 1972—74, Lake Elsinore Unified Sch. Dist., Calif., 1987—. Co-chair visual and performing arts Luiseno Elem., Corona, Calif., 1992—, chair math field day, 1999—, provider beginning tchr. support and assessment, 2001—03. Author numerous poems. Mem. Habitat for Humanity, 2003—. Named Tchr. of Yr., Luiseno Elem. and Lake Elsinore Sch. Dist., 1994—95; recipient Best Actress award, North County Cmty. Theater, 1983—86; NY Regents scholar, 1961. Mem.: AAUW (past membership chair 1982—, Scholarship established in her name 1987), Art and Cultural Soc. Fallbrook, Nat. Assn. Educators Am., Nat. Women's History Mus., Mission Conservation Dist. Avocations: acting, the arts, antiques, reading, gardening. Office: Lake Elsinore Unified Sch Dist 545 Chanly st Lake Elsinore CA 92530 Office Phone: 951-674-0750.

DRUTCHAS, GREGORY G., lawyer; b. Detroit, June 2, 1949; s. Gilbert Henry and Elaine Marie D.; m. Cheryl Aline Fox D. June 9, 1973; children: Gillian, Gregory, Ethan, Allison. BA in Journalism, U. Mich., 1970; JD, Duke U., 1973. Bar: Mich. 1973, US Dist. Ct. (ea. dist.) Mich. 1974, US Dist. Ct. (we. dist.) Mich. 1983, US Ct. Appeals (6th cir.) 1978, US Supreme Ct. 1984. Assoc. Kitch Drutchas Wagner Valitutti & Sherbrook, Detroit, 1973-78, sr. prin., shareholder 1978—; mem. comml. panel arbitrators, Am. Arbitration Assn. East Providence, RI, 1980-; faculty mem. Lansing CC, 1994-2000; lectr., seminar presenter on med. profl. liability and ins.; contbr. articles to profl. publs. and chpts. to books. Commr., Bloomfield Hills Youth Soccer League, Mich., 1993-97; legal cons., Bloomfield Hills Soccer Club, 1999-2004; bd. dirs. Project Compassion Inc., South Lyon, Mich., 2003-. Served to capt., USAF, 1972-82. Disting. Mich. Supreme Ct. Brief award, Cooley Law Sch., Lansing, Mich., 1985. Mem. ABA (chair ins. law com., 1985-87), State Bar Mich. (mem. ins. law com., 1981-87, chairperson, 1984-87, coun. mem. health care law sect., 1995, treas., 1997-99, chair-elect, 2000-01, chair, 2001-02), Oakland County Bar Assn. (vice-chmn. ct. appeals com., 1978-79, chair, 1979-80, mem. med., legal com., 1981-83, 1992-96, vice-chmn., 1982-83), Am. Health Lawyers Assn., Mich. Health and Hosp. Assn. (mem. ad hoc subcommittee med. malpractice legis., 1983-84, mem. com. pub. policy and govt., 1983-84, legal cons. malpractice legis., 1985-87, mem. coun. sys. and networks, 1996-98, mem. legis. policy panel, 1994-96, 2004-), Healthcare Fin. Mgmt. Assn. (mem. tax and legal issues com., 1990-92, 94, co-chair health law com., 1996-2002, Folmer Bronze Svc. award 2003), Mich. Soc. Healthcare Attys. (bd. dirs., 2001-), Mich. Soc. Healthcare Risk Mgmt. (mem. edn. com., 1998-2000), Birmingham Country Club. Avocations: golf, youth soccer. Republican. Unitarian. Office: Kitch Drutchas Wagner Valitutti & Sherbrook One Woodward Ave 24th Fl Detroit MI 48226 Home Phone: 248-645-9468; Office Phone: 313-965-7930.

DRUTZ, DAVID JULES, venture capitalist; b. Knoxville, Tenn., Apr. 20, 1938; s. Abe Morris and Lillian (Billig) D.; m. Lydia Anne Hall, June 28, 1962; children: Gretchen, Adam, Gregory, Jonathan. BA, U. Louisville, 1958, MD, 1962. Cert. Am. Bd. Internal Medicine. Intern Louisville Gen. Hosp., 1962—63; resident Vanderbilt U. Hosp., 1963-65; infectious disease fellow Vanderbilt U. Med. Ctr., 1965-67; chief infectious diseases San Francisco Gen. Hosp., 1969—74; asst. prof. medicine U. Calif., San Francisco, 1969-74; chief infectious diseases U. Tex. Health Sci. Ctr., San Antonio, 1974-86, prof. medicine and microbiology, 1974-86, founder, dir. Ctr. for Cell Regulation, 1984-86; v.p. SmithKline & French Labs., King of Prussia, Pa., 1986-90; pres., CEO, dir. Sennes Drug Innovations, Inc., Houston, 1994-95, Inspire Pharms. Inc., Durham, NC, 1995-99; pres. Pacific Biopharma Assoc., Chapel Hill, NC, 1999—; gen. ptnr. Pacific Rim Ventures Co., Ltd., Tokyo, 1999—. Clin. prof. medicine Seton Hall U. Sch. Grad. Med. Edn., Newark, 1990-95, U. Pa. Sch. Medicine, Phila., 1986-90, adj. prof. medicine and microbiology Temple U. Med. Sch., Phila., 1986-90; adj. prof. microbiology Coll. Medicine Baylor U., Houston, 1995-99; bd. dirs. MethylGene Inc., Montreal, Synthelia, Inc., Rsch. Triangle Park, NC, Tranzyme Pharma Inc., Research Triangle Park. Editor: Systemic Fungal Infections, 1988-89; contbr. articles and abstracts to profl. jour.; assoc. editor Jour. Infectious Diseases, 1983-88, editorial bd., 1988-91; editorial bd. Am. Rev. Respiratory Diseases, 1979-84, Am. Jour. of the Med. Sci., 1983-91. Chmn. sci. adv. bd. Leonard Wood Meml., 1984-87. Lt. comdr. USNR, 1967-69, Taiwan, Vietnam. Rsch. grantee

NIAID, VA, NSF, 1970-86. Fellow ACP, Infectious Diseases Soc. Am. (councillor 1986-88); mem. AMA, Am. Soc. Clin. Investigation, Western Soc. Clin. Investigation, So. Soc. Clin. Rsch., Nat. Assn. Corp. Dirs., Am. Soc. Microbiology, Nat. Assn. Corp. Dirs., Alpha Omega Alpha. Avocations: swimming, skiing, biking. Office: Pacific Biopharma Assocs PO Box 3616 Chapel Hill NC 27515-3616

DRUTZ, JAN EDWIN, pediatrics educator; b. Louisville, Jan. 8, 1942; s. Abe Morris and Lillian (Billig) D.; m. Anne Edwina Sussman, June 7, 1965; children: Jeffrey Benjamin, Lisa Michele, Dana Nicole. BA, U. Louisville, 1964, MD, 1968. Pvt. practice, Houston, 1973-87; intern, then resident Baylor Coll. Medicine, Houston, 1968-71, from clin. asst. prof. to assoc. prof. pediat., 1973—2002, dir. pediat. continuity clinic, 1987—, prof. pediat., 2002—; pres. med. staff Tex. Children's Hosp., 1995, prof. pediats., 2002—. Maj. U.S. Army, 1971-73. Mem. AMA, Harris County Med. Soc., Tex. Pediat. Soc. (adv. com., mem. student preceptorship program 1995-96), Houston Pediat. Soc. (sec. 1984-85, pres. 1988-89), Ambulatory Pediat. Assn. (chmn. continuity clinic spl. interest group 1990-95, edn. com. 1993—). Office: Tex Children Hosp Clin Care Ctr Ste 1540-00 6701 Fannin St Houston TX 77030 Business E-Mail: jdrutz@bcm.tmc.edu.

DRUZDZEL, MAREK JOZEF, information systems educator, researcher; b. Radom, Poland, Oct. 7, 1957; s. Edward and Regina (Szymczak) Druzdzel; children: Marcin, Stefan, Roman, Julian. MS in Computer Sci. with distinction, Delft U. Tech., 1985, MSEE with distinction, 1987; PhD, Carnegie Mellon U., 1992. Vis. scientist Thomas J. Watson Rsch. Ctr. IBM, Yorktown Heights, NY, 1987—88; rsch. asst., adj. prof. Carnegie Mellon U., Pitts., 1988—91, rschr. assoc., 1993; rschr. Rockwell Internat. Sci. Ctr., Palo Alto, Calif., 1993; rsch. assoc. Inst. for Decision Sys. Rsch., Palo Alto, 1993; assoc. prof. intelligent sys. Sch. Info. Scis. U. Pitts., 1993—. Lectr. U. Pitts., Carnegie Mellon U., Imperial Cancer Rsch. Fund, London, U. Utrecht, The Netherlands, Delft U. of Tech., The Netherlands, Free U. of Amsterdam, Rockwell Internat., many others. Contbr. articles to profl. jours. Recipient Career award, NSF. Mem. IEEE, Am. Assn. for Artificial Intelligence, Inst. for Ops. Rsch. and Mgmt. Sci., Assn. for Uncertainty in Artificial Intelligence, European Assn. for Decision Making, Sigma Xi. Office: Univ Pitts Dept Info Sci Pittsburgh PA 15260 Business E-Mail: marek@sis.pitt.edu.

DRUZHNIKOV, YURI ILYA, literature educator, writer; b. Moscow, Apr. 17, 1933; m. Valerie Linetsky, June 3, 1983; children: Elena, Ilya. B in History, Latvian U., Riga, 1953; MD, Moscow Pedagogy U., 1955; PhD, History and Theory Edn. Inst., Moscow, 1960. Prof. U. Tex., Austin, 1987—88, U. Calif., Davis, 1988—. Author: Informer 001, 1996, Prisoner of Russia, 1999, Angels on the Head of a Pin, 2003, Passport to Yesterday, 2004, Madonna from Russia, 2005, The Life and Death of Pushkin: A Genius At Odds with Himself, 2006. Named Best Russian Writer of 1998, City of Moscow, 1998; named to the "Author of 10 Best Russian Novels of the XXC" List, U. Warsaw, 1998; recipient Dostoyevsky Prize, Writer's Union of Poland, 2001. Mem.: Internat. Pen Club (v.p. 1993—). Office: German & Russian Dept Univ Calif Davis CA 95616

DRVOTA, MOJMIR, retired cinema educator, author; b. Prague, Czechoslovakia, Jan. 13, 1923; came to U.S., 1958, naturalized, 1963; s. Jan and Zdenka (Krejcikova) D.; m. Jana Kratochvilova, May 18, 1957; 1 child, Monica. Student, Charles U., 1945-48; PhD, Palacky U., 1953; MS, Columbia U., 1961. Stage dir. state theaters, Czechoslovakia, 1952-56; libr. Bklyn. Pub. Libr., 1958-62; asst. prof. dramatic arts Columbia U., NYC, 1962-69; assoc. prof. cinema NYU, NYC, 1969-72; prof. cinema Ohio State U., Columbus, 1972-92, prof. emeritus, 1992—; ret., 1992. Script writer Czechoslovak State Film, Prague, 1948-52; author: Short Stories, 1946, Boarding House for Artists, 1947, Solitaire, 1974, Triptych, 1980, Solitaire, Triptych in Czech, 1993; The Constituents of Film Theory, 1973, in Czech, 1994, How Many ANgels Can Dance on the Tip of a Needle?, in Czech, 2002. Mem. Univ. Film Assn., AAUP, Phi Kappa Phi. Home: 3541 Prestwick Ct Columbus OH 43220-5097 *Everything I stood for was defeated, everything I longed for remained unfulfilled, everything I loved passed beyond reach. In the chasm thus rent I captured a glimpse of what is real and what only is, of what is an act of becoming and what is a mere activity. Henceforth, I made it my task to share in the linking effort of those individuals who communicate in the services of reality: the reality screened by objects into which we are situated.*

DRYCE, H. DAVID, accountant, consultant; b. Bronx, NY, Feb. 18, 1930; s. Theodore and Ruth Dryspiel; m. Norma Stein, June 12, 1955; children: Mimi, Arthur, Debra. BA, Yeshiva U., 1952; postgrad., Isaac Elchanan Theol. Sem., NYC, 1955; MBA, CUNY, 1959. CPA, N.Y. 1st lt. U.S. Army, 1955-57, capt., 1957-64; sr. acct. various firms, LI, NY, 1959-63; prin. H. David Dryce, CPA, Old Bethpage, NY, 1963—98; exec. officer CHB Inc., Buffalo, 1985-96. Instr. SUNY, Farmingdale, 1966-68; cons. Video Art Prodns. Inc., Palm Harbor, Fla., 1986—. Author: Inventory Verification-Extent of Observation and Acceptable Limitations, 1959; contbr. articles to profl. publs. V.p. United Coun. Civil Assns., Oyster Bay, N.Y., 1966-67, Old Bethpage Civic Assn., 1966-67; pres. Metro Region Men's Clubs, N.Y.C., 1970-71; treas. Reggie Lewis Found., 1993-2000. Mem. N.Y. State Soc. CPAs (chmn. mgmt. svcs. com. Nassau County chpt. 1967-69). Home and Office: 4692 Sweetmeadow Cir Sarasota FL 34238-4333 Home Phone: 941-927-4692. E-mail: nordavid@comcast.net.

DRYDEN, KEN, legislator, former sports team executive, retired professional hockey player; b. Hamilton, Ont., Can., Aug. 8, 1947; m. Lynda Dryden; children: Sarah, Michael. BA, Cornell U.; JD, McGill U.; LLD (hon.), U. Windsor, U. B.C., York U., Toronto. Goaltender Montreal Canadiens, 1971-79; pres., gen. mgr. Toronto Maple Leafs, 1997—2004; v.p. Maple Leaf Gardens Ltd., 1997—2004; mem. Ho. of Commons, min. social devel. Govt. Canada, Ottawa, Canada, 2004—. Colour commentator Winter Olympic Games ABC-TV, 1980, 84, 88. Author: The Game, Home Game, The Moved and the Shaken: The Story of One Man's Life, In School. Ont. youth commr., 1984—86; initiator Ken Dryden Scholarships. Recipient Conn Smythe Trophy, 1971, Calder Meml. Trophy, 1972, Vezina Trophy, 1973, 1976—79. Achievements include being a member of Stanley Cup Champion Montreal Canadiens, 1971, 1973, 1976-79; being inducted into the Hockey Hall of Fame, 1983; having his number, 29, retired by Montreal Canadiens, 2007. Office: House of Commons Minister Social Devel Parliament Buildings Ottawa ON Canada K1A 0L1*

DRYDEN, ROBERT EUGENE, lawyer; b. Chanute, Kans., Aug. 20, 1927; s. Calvin William and Mary Alfreda (Foley) D.; m. Jetta Rae Burger, Dec. 19, 1953; children: Lynn Marie, Thomas Calvin. AA, City Coll., San Francisco, 1947; BS, U. San Francisco, 1951, JD, 1954. Bar: Calif. 1955; diplomate Am. Bd. Trial Advocates (pres. San Francisco chpt. 1997). Assoc. Barfield, Dryden & Ruane (and predecessor firm), San Francisco, 1954-60, jr. ptnr., 1960-65, gen. ptnr., 1965-89; sr. ptnr. Dryden, Margoles, Schimaneck & Wertz, San Francisco, 1989—. Lectr. continuing edn. of the bar, 1971-77; evaluator U.S. Dist. Ct. (no. dist.) Calif. Early Neutral Evaluation Program; master atty. San Francisco Am. Inn of Ct. Mem. bd. counsellors U. San Francisco, 1993—. With USMCR, 1945-46. Fellow Am. Coll. Trial Lawyers, Am. Bar Found., Internat. Acad. Trial Lawyers; mem. ABA, San Francisco Bar Assn., Assn. Def. Counsel (bd. dirs. 1968-71), Def. Rsch. Inst., Internat. Assn. Ins. Counsel, Fedn. Ins. Counsel, U. San Francisco Law Soc. (mem. exec. com. 1970-72), U. San Francisco Alumni Assn. (mem. bd. govs. 1977), Phi Alpha Delta. Home: 1320 Lasuen Dr Millbrae CA 94030-2846 Office: Dryden Margoles Schimaneck & Wertz 101 California St Ste 2050 San Francisco CA 94111-5427

DRYDEN, STEPHEN DAVID, artist, product designer; b. London, Eng., May 3, 1955; s. David Gordon and Elsie May Dryden; m. Sandra Carole Denyer, July 3, 1976; children: Kimberley, Jack. BA, Hornsey Sch. Art, London, 1974. Freelance artist Nova Arts Ltd., London, 1971—85; owner, mgr. Composing Room Ltd., London, 1985—2001; CEO London Framer LLC, Bradenton, Fla., 2004—. Poster, Suncoast Wine Festival Inaugural, 2006 (Addy award, 2007). Recipient Promotional Monotype DA&D award, 1996. Mem.: Nat. Soc. Muralists, Profl. Picture Framing Assn. (dir. 2005—), Rotary. Avocations: painting, golf, reading, cooking. Office: The London Framer LLC 9122 Town Center Pkwy Bradenton FL 34202

DRYDEN, WOODSON E., lawyer; b. Anadarko, Okla., Dec. 21, 1924; s. Harry Ernest and Ruth Sally (Woodson) D.; divorced; children: Judith, Carol, Kim, Christine, Erich. BBA, Kans. U., 1948; LLB, Tex. U., 1951. Sole practice, Beaumont, Tex., 1951—. With USNR, 1942-46. Mem. Tex. Trial Lawyers Assn. (pres. 1972-73). Democrat. Episcopalian. Home: 6625 Windwood Ln Beaumont TX 77706-4239

DRYER, MURRAY, physicist, educator; b. Bridgeport, Conn., Nov. 4, 1925; s. Sol and Sarah (Shapiro) D.; m. Geraldine Gray Goodsell, May 12, 1955; children: Steven Michael, Lisa Dryer Travis. Student, U. Conn., 1943-44; BS, Stanford U., 1949, MS, 1950; PhD, Tel-Aviv U., 1971. Research asst. NACA-NASA Ames Research Ctr., Calif., 1949; aero. research scientist NACA-NASA Lewis Research Ctr., Cleve., 1950-59; assoc. research scientist Martin Marietta Corp., Denver, 1959-65; chief interplanetary physics Space Environ. Lab., NOAA Environ. Research Labs., Boulder, Colo., 1965-94, guest worker emeritus, 1994—; sr. scientist Coop. Inst. for Rsch. in Environ. Scis., U. Colo., Boulder, 1994-96; cons. Exploration Physics Internat., Inc., 1996—, Geophysical Inst. U., Fairbanks, Ala., 2001—. Lectr. dept. aerospace engring. scis. U. Colo., 1963-76, dept. astrogeophysics, 1978; vis. assoc. prof. dept. mech. engring. Colo. State U., 1966-67; mem. com. solar terrestrial rsch. NAS, 1976-80, 84-91, com. geophys. data NAS, 1987-93. Author: (with others) Solar-Terrestrial Physics in the 1980's, 1981; editor: (with others) Solar Observations and Predictions of Solar Activity, 1972, Exploration of the Outer Solar System, 1976, Solar and Interplanetary Dynamics, 1980, Advances in Solar Connection wirh Interplanetary Phenomena, 1998; spl. issue editor Space Sci. Revs., 1976; contbr. articles to profl. jours. With U.S. Navy, 1944-46. Mem. Am. Phys. Soc., Am. Geophys. Union, AAAS, Sci. Com. Solar-Terrestrial Physics, Internat. Astron. Union, Com. Space Research, AIAA (Space Sci. award 1975), Sigma Xi Office: Space Environment Ctr NOAA NCEP NWS Mail Code R-E-SE Boulder CO 80305-3328 Home Phone: 303-798-1440; Office Phone: 303-497-3978. Personal E-mail: murraydryer@msn.com. Business E-Mail: murray.dryer@noaa.gov.

DRYHURST, GLENN, retired chemistry professor; b. Birmingham, Eng., Sept. 15, 1939; came to U.S., 1965; s. Leonard Ernest and Ethel Mary (Willmot) D.; m. June Diane Floyd, Sept. 11, 1965 (div. 1982); children: Claire Louise, Victoria Anne, Gregory Peter; m. Monika Zofia Luszczewska, Mar. 9, 1984 BSc, U. Aston, Eng., 1962; PhD, U. Birmingham, Eng., 1965. Asst. prof., then assoc. prof. chemistry U. Okla., Norman, 1967-74, prof., 1974—2007, chmn. dept., 1981—2006, George Lynn Cross rsch. prof., 1983, Regents prof., 1998; ret., 2007. Author: Periodate Oxidation, 1969, Electrochemistry of Biological Molecules, 1977, Biological Electrochemistry, 1983, Redox Chemistry and Interfacial Behavior of Biological Molecules, 1988; mem. editl. adv. bd. Chem. Rsch. in Toxicology, 1997-2000, Neurotoxicity Rsch., 1998—; contbr. articles to profl. jours. Fulbright sr. prof. award Konstanz U., Fed. Republic Germany, 1987-88. Mem. Am. Chem. Soc. (Okla. Chemist award 1989), Electrochem. Soc. (Young Author prize 1969, editor organic and biol. divsn. 1984-92, chmn. divsn. organic and biol. electrochemistry 1989-91), Soc. Neurosci., Sigma Xi (rsch. award 1972), Phi Beta Kappa. Avocations: downhill skiing, horseback riding, fishing, reading, music. Home: 4230 Valley Vista St Norman OK 73072-3165 Home Phone: 405-364-0327. Personal E-mail: gdryhurst@ou.edu.

DRYMAN, AMY, epidemiologist; d. Sylvia and Irving Armin Dryman. BA, Yale U., New Haven, Conn., 1977—81; postgrad., Columbia U., NYC, 1981—82; DSc, Johns Hopkins U., Sch. of Hygiene and Pub. Health, Balt., 1982—87. Rsch. scientist, rsch. assoc. Johns Hopkins U. Sch. Hygiene and Pub. Health, Balt., 1987—88; cons. Pfizer, Inc., NYC, 1993, project leader, 1993—99, asst. dir., 1999—2001, mgr., 2001—04. Contbr. articles to profl. jours. Personal E-mail: amydryscd@aol.com.

DRZIK, JOHN P., management consulting firm executive; BSE summa cum laude, Princeton U. Joined Oliver, Wyman & Co., 1984, pres., 1995, chmn., 2000; pres. Mercer Oliver Wyman, 2003—, Mercer Specialty Cons., 2006—. Founder Oliver Wyman Inst.; spkr. in field. Adv. bd. mem. Fin. Engring. Program, Princeton U.; industry adv. bd. Wharton Fin. Institutions Ctr. Office: Mercer Specialty Cons 1166 Avenue of Americas New York NY 10036*

D'SOUZA, ROHIT, investment company executive; BA in Math. and Computer Sci., Bethany Coll., Lindsborg, Kans. With Barra, Investment Tech. Grp.; with prog. tng. grp. Morgan Stanley, 1996, head North Am. equity trading businesses; with Merrill Lynch, NYC, 2004—, head global equity market, sr. v.p., head global equities and Ams. global markets Global Markets & Investment Banking, 2006—. Office: Merrill Lynch 4 World Fin Ctr 250 Vesey St New York NY 10080

DU, CHUNGUANG CHARLES, biologist, educator; arrived in U.S., 1993; s. Lianzhong and Ronglan Du; m. Limei He; 1 child. Bo. BS in Agronomy, Henan Agrl. U., China, 1983; PhD, Tex. A&M U., Coll. Sta., 1997. Rsch. scientist N.C. State U., Raleigh, 1999—2002; dir. sci. informatics program Montclair State U., NJ, 2002—. Vis. investigator Rutgers U., Piscataway, NJ, 2004—. Editor: The Journal of Plant Genomics, 2006—. Recipient Outstanding Grad. Rsch. award, Tex. A&M U., 1997, Met. Area Biologist Assn., 2003; grantee, U.S. Dept. of Agr., 2005—, NSF, 2006—. Mem.: AAAS, Bioinformatics Orgn., Am. Soc. Crop Sci., China Soc. Genetics (hon.), Asia American Friendship Assn. (mgr. campaign 2005—06). Achievements include design of maize genomics database; discovery of LTR retrotransposons carry functional genes in maize genome which plays an very important role in maize genome evolution; research in cloned disease resistance gene analogs in cotton and wheat. Office: Montclair State Univ 1 Normal Ave Montclair NJ 07043 Home Phone: 908-561-2239; Office Phone: 973-655-4405. Office Fax: 973-655-7047. E-mail: duc@mail.montclair.edu.

DUA, SUMEET, computer scientist, educator; s. Virender Jit and Kanta Dua; m. Prerna Sethi, 2002. MS, La. State U., Baton Rouge, 2000, PhD, 2002. Upchurch asst. prof., coord. IT rsch. La. Tech U., Ruston, 2002—. Achievements include patents for business process, method and apparatus to determine geographical locations for IP addresses. Office: La Tech U 600 W Arizona Ave Ruston LA 71272 Home Phone: 318-513-1750; Office Phone: 318-257-2830. Office Fax: 318-257-4922; Home Fax: 318-257-4922. Business E-Mail: sdua@coes.latech.edu.

DUAN, LIAN, civil engineer; arrived in US, 1986; s. Pezhi Duan and Yuzhen Wan; m. Jenny Fu, Oct. 16, 1981; children: Furui, Gary Peng. MSCE, Taiyuan U. Tech., China, 1981; PhD, Purdue U., West Lafayette, Ind., 1990. Registered engr., Calif., 1993. Structural engr. China Northeast Power Design Inst., Changchun, Jilin, 1975—78; lectr. Taiyuan U. Tech., 1981—85; sr. bridge engr. Calif. Dept. Transp., Sacramento, 1991—. Co-editor: Bridge Engineering Handbook, 2000 (Choice Mag. Outstanding Academic Title award, 2001). Mem. steel com. Transp. Rsch. Bd., 2000—. Mem.: ASCE (Arthur M. Wellington prize 2000), Profl. Engrs. Calif. Govt. (sacramento, calif. 1991—2007). Office: Calif Dept Transp 1801 30th St Sacramento CA 95816 Office Phone: 916-227-8220. Business E-Mail: lian_duam@dot.ca.gov.

DUAN, QIANG, computer scientist, educator; b. Baoding, Hebei, China, June 11, 1970; arrived in US, 1999; s. Shuangyu Duan and Peizhen Dong; m. Wu Tong, Jan. 29, 1971; 1 child, Kevin Shizhuo. BS in Elec. and Computer Engring., North China Electric Power U., Baoding, 1992; MS in Telecomm. and Electronic Sys., Comm., Telemetry and Telecontrol Inst., Shijiazhuang, China, 1995; PhD in Elec. Engring., U. Miss., Oxford, 2003. Rsch. engr. Comm., Telemetry and Telecontrol Inst., Shijiazhuang, Hebei, 1995—97, rsch. group leader, 1998—99; grad. instr., rsch. asst. U. of Miss., Oxford, 1999—2003; vis. rsch. engr. TranSwitch Corp., Shelton, Conn., 1996, engring. intern, 2000; asst. prof. U. of Cen. Ark., Conway, 2003—. Author: (book chpt.) Quality of Service Provision in High-Speed Packet Switches, (book) ATM Technology; contbr. scientific papers to rsch. publs. (Best Paper award, 2005). Recipient Grad. fellowship, U. Miss., 1999—2002, Doctoral Dissertation fellowship, 2002—03, Faculty Rsch. grant for improving Internet performance, U. Ctrl. Ark., 2005—06, Summer Rsch. grant, 2006, Rsch. grant for enhancing Enterprise Grid Security, Acxiom Lab. for Applied Rsch., 2005—06. Mem.: IEEE. Achievements include development of ATM access switch supporting multi-service in the Internet; design of Network calculus-based model for supporing quality of services in buffered crossbar packet switches; research in Attack tree-based framework for distributed computing security evaluation. Office: U Cen Ark 201 Donaghey Ave Conway AR 72035 Home Phone: 501-513-9371; Office Phone: 501-450-3308. Office Fax: 501-450-5615. Business E-Mail: qduan@uca.edu.

DUAN, ZHENHAO, geochemist, educator, editor; s. Xiujiu Duan and Guiying Wang; m. Xia Cao, Nov. 18, 1987; 1 child, Peter Sheng. PhD, China U. Geosciences, Beijing, 1988. Postdoctoral rschr. U. Calif., San Diego, 1988—92, rsch. scientist, 1992—2004; rsch. prof. Inst. Geology and Geophysics Chinese Acad. Scis., Beijing, 2002—. Contbr. articles to profl. jours. Recipient Young scientist award, Energy Inst. Calif. U., 1993, Nat. Outstanding Young Scientist award, Nat. Sci. Found. China, 2002, Exellent One hundred Scientists project, Chinese Acad. Scis., 2005; fellow, 2002. Mem.: Overseas Chinese Earth Sci. and Tech. Assn. (v.p. 2000—), Chinese Assn. Sci. and Tech. (hon. pres. 2001—05), Geochemical Soc. USA (licentiate; assoc. editor 2006—), Am. Geophys. Union (assoc.). Achievements include development of accurate equations of state for natural fluids; a model widely used worldwide for CO2 sequestration; a model widely used worldwide for studying CH4 hydrate; research in prediction of the fluid properties up to 100000 atm and 2500K. Office: Inst Geology and Geophysics 19 Beituchengxi Rd Beijing 100029 China Home Phone: 8610 62007447; Office Phone: 8610-62007447.

DUARTE, PROSPERO VILLACIN, retired entrepreneur; arrived in U.S., 1973, naturalized, 1979; s. Rizalino Batiancila and Rebecca Villacin Duarte; m. Anita Tobes Duarte, June 23, 1973; children: Maria Theresa, Alyssa Ann. BSBA, U. Philippines, Diliman, Quezon City, 1963; postgrad., Wayne State U., Detroit, 1978. Data processing mgr. D. W. Hacker Co., Detroit, 1976—78; sr. programmer/analyst State of Mich., Detroit, 1978—85; systems engr. Electronic Data Sys. Corp., Troy, 1985—87; pres. Azpen Inc., Troy, Mich., 1986—. Contbr. poem (Editors Award, 1998); author: (poem) A Vision Is Born (Best Poems in Am. finalist, 2000); editor: (newsletter) Cosmo Kiwanis; contbr. articles to profl. mags. Pres. Kiwanis Club of Cosmopolitan Detroit, Southfield, Mich., 1999—2000; cmty. rep. Filipino Am. Cmty. Coun., Southfield, 1999—2001; mem. - bd. of directors Filipino Am. Polit. Assn. of Mich., Southfield, 1997—2001; mem. & bd. of directors U. Philippines Alumni Assn. of Mich., Troy, 1990—2001; mem. Toastmasters Club, Birmingham, Mich., 1999—2000. Grantee, Tidewater Oil Corp., 1960—61. Roman Catholic. Avocations: writing, singing, gardening, reading, fishing. Personal E-mail: aqz48083@yahoo.com.

DUAX, WILLIAM LEO, biologist, researcher; b. Chgo., Apr. 18, 1939; s. William Joseph and Alice B. (Joyce) Duax; m. Caroline Townsend Dowell, May 6, 1966; children: Julia, Sarah, William, Stephen. BA, St. Ambrose Coll., Davenport, Iowa, 1961; PhD, U. Iowa, Iowa City, 1967; DSc (hon.), U. Lodz, Poland, 1999. Postdoctoral research fellow Ohio U., Athens, 1967-68; rsch. assoc. Hauptman-Woodward Med. Rsch. Inst. (formerly Med. Found.), Buffalo, 1968-69; head crystallography dept. Med. Found. Buffalo, 1969-70, head molecular biophysics dept., 1970-88, assoc. dir. research, 1983-88, research dir., 1988-93, exec v.p. rsch., 1993-99, v.p., 1998-99, H.A. Hauptman Disting. Scientist, 2000—. Adj. assoc. prof. dept. medicinal chemistry SUNY, Buffalo, 1973—, assoc. rsch. prof. dept. biochemistry, 1981—, prof. dept. structural biology, 2001-; dir. distbn. Cambridge Database in US, Buffalo, 1983-99; lectr. various internat. confs. Editor: Atlas of Steroid Structure Vol. I, 1975, Vol. II, 1984, Molecular Structure and Biological Activity, 1982, Molecular Structure and Biological Activity of Steriods, 1992, Internat. Union of Crystallography Newsletter, 1993—. Mem. Am. Field Svc., Amherst, NY. Served with USAR, 1961-67. Fulbright scholar Coun. for Internat. Exchange, 1987; grantee NIH, 1971—; recipient Spl. Merit award Inst. Arthritis and Metabolic Diseases NIH, 1987—03, Disting. Alumni award, St. Ambrose Coll., 1983, Clin. Ligand Assay Soc. Disting. Scientist award, 1994. Mem. AAAS, Am. Crystallographic Assn. (v.p. 1985, pres. 1986, exec. officer 1988—, Am. Chem. Soc., Am. Cancer Soc., Biophys. Soc., Endocrine Soc., Peptide Soc., Protein Soc., Internat. Union Crystallography (charter mem., sec. com. on small molecules 1984-90, exec. com. 1999—, pres. 2002-05), Am. Inst. Physics (bd. govs. 1987-94, exec. com. 1992), Coun. Sci. Soc. Pres. (govt. and pub. affairs com. 1987), Saturn Club (Buffalo). Democrat. Office: Hauptman Woodward Med Rsch Inst Inc 700 Ellicott St Buffalo NY 14203-1102 Office Phone: 716-898-8600, 716-898-8616. Business E-Mail: duax@hwi.buffalo.edu.

DUBANEVICH, KEITH SCOTT, lawyer; b. Springfield, Vt., Nov. 19, 1957; S. Walter Joseph and Sylvia Beatrice (Ward) D. BS, Northeastern U., 1980; JD, Tulane U., 1983. Bar: Tex. 1983, Mass. 1988, Oreg. 1997, US Dist. Ct. (ea. and so. dists.) Tex. 1983, US Ct. Appeals (5th cir.) 1984, US Ct. Appeals (9th cir.) 2001, US Dist. Ct. (we. dist.) Wis. 1989, US Dist. Ct. Oreg. 1998, US Supreme Ct. 1997, US Ct. Appeals (2nd cir.) 2006. Assoc. Fulbright and Jaworski, Houston, 1983-87, jr. ptnr., 1987—91, ptnr., 1992-98; assoc. Hale and Dorr, Boston, 1988-89; exec. com. Garvey Schubert Barer, Portland, Oreg., 2003—06. Contbr. articles to profl. jours. Recipient La. Trial Lawyers award, 1983. Mem. ABA, Order of Barristers, Multnomah Bar Assn. (domestic violence project), Owen M. Panner Am. Inn of Ct., Oreg. State Bar (exec. com. bus. litig. sect., sec. 2005, treas. 2006, chair elect 2006), Mazamas Mountaineering Assn. (bd. dirs. 2004—, pres. 2006—). Avocations: skiing, mountain climbing, American history. Office: Garvey Schubert Barer 11th Fl 121 SW Morrison St Portland OR 97204-3117 Home: PO Box 10151 Portland OR 97296-0151 Office Phone: 503-228-3939. Business E-Mail: kdubanevich@gsblaw.com.

DUBBER, MARKUS DIRK, law educator; AB, Harvard Univ., 1988; JD, Stanford Univ., 1991. Law clk. U.S. Ct. Appeals Eleventh cir., Atlanta, 1991—92; lectr. Univ. Chgo. Law Sch., 1992—93; assoc. prof. SUNY Buffalo Sch. Law, 1993—99, prof., 1999—; dir. Buffalo Criminal Law Ctr., 1996—. Humboldt Rsch. Fellow Inst. Legal Phil., Ludwig Maximilians Universität, Munich, 2000—01; vis. prof. Univ. Mich. Law Sch., 2001. Editor: Buffalo Criminal Law Rev., 1996—; mem. bd. editors Law & History Rev., 2001—; contbr. articles to prof. jour. Mem.: Assn. Am. Law

Sch. (chmn., comparative law sec.), Am. Law Inst. Office: School of Law SUNY Buffalo 712 O'Brian Hall Buffalo NY 14260 Office Phone: 716-645-6213. Office Fax: 716-645-2064. Business E-Mail: dubber@buffalo.edu.*

DUBÉ, LAWRENCE EDWARD, JR., lawyer; b. Chgo., Sept. 25, 1948; s. Lawrence Edward and Rosemary Nora (Cooney) D.; m. Paula Ann Goodgal, Jan. 10, 1982; 1 child, Charles Bernard. BA in Polit. Sci. cum laude, Knox Coll., 1970; JD with distinction, U. Iowa, 1973. Bar: Ill. 1973, Md. 1982, Pa. 1982, D.C. 1983, U.S. Supreme Ct., 1987. Field atty. NLRB, Chgo., 1973—80, supr. atty., 1980—81; sole practice Balt., 1981—85; assoc. Grove, Jaskiewicz, Gilliam & Cobert, Washington, 1985—87; counsel Grove, Jaskiewicz and Cobert, Washington, 1987—. Author: Management on Trial-The Law of Wrongful Discharge, 1987, New Employment Issues: How to Shield your Business from Costly Lawsuits, 1988, Employment References and the Law, 1989; co-author: The Maryland Employer's Guide, 1984. Home: 622 W University Pky Baltimore MD 21210-2908

DUBE, MONTE L., lawyer; b. Jan. 20, 1956; AB, Boston U., 1977; JD, Benjamin N. Cardozo Sch. Law, 1981. Lic.: Ill. Supreme Ct., U.S. Dist. Ct. N. Dist. Ill., U.S. Ct. Appeals. Third Cir. Ptnr., chmn. firm health law dept. McDermott Will & Emery LLP, Chgo. Lectr. & Bigelow Teaching Fellow U. Chgo. Sch. Law, 1981—82. Mem.: ABA, Chgo. Bar Assn., Ill. Bar Assn., Ill. Supreme Ct. Office: McDermott Will & Emery LLP 227 W Monroe St Chicago IL 60606-5055 Office Phone: 312-984-7549. Office Fax: 312-984-7700. Business E-Mail: mdube@mwe.com.

DUBERSTEIN, JOEL LAWRENCE, internist, pulmonologist, educator; b. Bklyn., Jan. 8, 1937; m. Judith Schwartz; children: Laura, Amy. AB, Princeton U., 1957; MD, Columbia U., 1961. Diplomate Am. Bd. Internal Medicine, Am. Bd. Pulmonary Diseases. Intern Mt. Sinai Hosp., NYC, 1961-62, rsch. fellow in medicine, 1962, 65, asst. med. resident, 1963, chief med. resident, 1964, clin. asst., rsch. fellow, 1965-67; asst. chief medicine, chief pulmonary diseases Morrisania Hosp., Montefiore-Morrisania Affiliation, Bronx, N.Y., 1969-71; attending physician dept. medicine Overlook Hosp., Summit, N.J., 1971—, chmn. pulmonary sect., ICU com., med. dir. ICU, 1985-97, divsn. chief pulmonary disease dept. internal medicine; assoc. clin. prof. medicine Columbia U., 1998—. Assoc. vis. physician Morrisania City Hosp., Bronx, 1969-71; mem. staff Morristown Meml. Hosp., 1972—, med. co-dir. respiratory svcs., 1977-82; attending phsician dept. medicine St. Barnabas Med. Ctr., Livingston, N.J., 1971-89, past chmn. pulmonary sect.; mem. staff Newark Beth Israel Med. Ctr., 1971-82; spkr. in field; mem. Essex County Med. Soc. TB Control. Contbr. articles to profl. jours. Maj. U.S. Army, 1967-69. Recipient Recognition award Soc. N.J.'s Physicians. Fellow ACP, Am. Coll. Chest Physicians; mem. AMA (Physician's Recognition award), N.J. Med. Soc., Essex Thoracic Soc., N.J. Acad. Medicine. Address: 65 Troy Dr Short Hills NJ 07078 Office Phone: 973-467-2713.

DUBERSTEIN, KENNETH MARC, management consultant, former White House chief of staff; b. Bklyn., Apr. 21, 1944; s. Aaron D. and Julie C. (Falb) D.; m. Sydney M. Greenberg, Feb. 27, 1982; children: Jeffrey Ryan, Andrew Brian; 1 child from previous marriage, Jennifer Darie. AB in Govt., Franklin and Marshall Coll., 1965; MA in Am. Polit. Dynamics, Am. U., 1967. Research asst. to to Congressman Fred B. Rooney US Ho. Reps., 1965-66; research asst. to to Senator Jacob K. Javits US Senate, 1966-67, co-dir. campaign ops. NYC, 1968; adminstrv. asst. to pres. Franklin and Marshall Coll., Lancaster, Pa., 1967-70; congl. liaison officer GSA, Washington, 1970-71, dep. dir. for congl. liaison, 1971-72, dir. congl. affairs, 1972-76; dep. under sec. legis. affairs US Dept. Labor, Washington, 1976-77; v.p., dir. bus. and govt. relations Com. for Econ. Devel., Washington, 1977-81; dep. asst. to Pres. U.S. The White House, Washington, 1981-83, asst. to Pres. U.S. for legis. affairs, 1982-83, dep. chief of staff to Pres., 1987-88, chief of staff to Pres., 1988—89; v.p. Timmons and Co., Washington, 1983-87; chmn., CEO Duberstein Group, Washington, 1989—. Bd. dirs. Boeing Co., 1997—, Fannie Mae, 1998—2007, Conoco, 2000—02, ConocoPhillips, 2002—, St. Pail Travelers Cos. Trustee Franklin and Marshall Coll.; bd. dirs. Am. Cancer Soc., Am. Council for Capital Formation, nat. capitol regional Boy Scouts Am.; adv. bd. George Washington U.; exec.-legis. relations steering com. Ctr. Strategic and Internat. Studies Georgetown U., nat. adv. council Ctr. for Study of Presidency, Alexandria, Va. Office: Duberstein Group 2100 Pennsylvania Ave NW Washington DC 20037 Office Phone: 202-728-1100.

DUBIE, BRIAN E., lieutenant governor; b. Burlington, Vt., Mar. 9, 1959; m. Penny Bolio; 4 children. Student, USAF Acad., 1977—80; BS in Mech. Engring., U. Vt., 1982. Aerospace industry project mgr. B.F. Goodrich, Vergennes; capt. Am. Airlines, 1988; lt.gov. State of Vt., Montpelier, 2003—. Emergency preparedness officer Nat. Security Emergency Preparedness Agy.; bd. dirs. Vt. Sys., Inc. Active Essex Junction Sch. Bd., 1995—2000, chair, 1996—2000, sch. dist. moderator, 2000—; active Essex Junction Cmty. Drug Awareness Com., 1993—95; asst. coach Youth Football and Little League. Lt. col. Vt. Air Nat. Guard, col. USAF, 1998. Decorated Meritorious Svc. medal with oak leaf cluster. Republican. Office: Officer Lt Governor 115 State St Montpelier VT 05633-5401 Office Phone: 802-828-2226. Office Fax: 802-828-3198.

DUBIK, JAMES M., career military officer; b. Erie, Pa., Dec. 6, 1949; m. Sharon Basso; 2 children: Kerith, Katie. BS in Philosophy, Gannon U., 1971; MA in Philosophy, Johns Hopkins U., 1980; attended, US Marines Amphibious Warfare Sch., Quantinc, Va., 1978, Army Command Gen. Staff Coll., Ft. Leavenworth, Kans., 1981; MS in Mil. Arts and Scis., Army Sch. Advanced Mil. Study, 1992. Commd. 2d lt. US Army, 1971, advanced through grades to lt. gen., 2004, from platoon leader to brigade staff officer 82d Airborne Divsn. Ft. Bragg, NC, 1972-74, co. exec. officer 2d Ranger Bn., civil affairs officer, Ft. Lewis, Wash., 1974-78; assoc. prof. philosophy US Mil. Acad., West Point, NY, 1982—85; exec. officer 1st Ranger bn. Hunter Army Airfield US Army, Savannah, Ga., 1985-87, inspector gen., 25th Infantry Divsn. Schofield Barracks, 1987—88, comdr. 5th Bn., 14th Infantry, 1988—90; instr. Army's Sch. Advanced Mil. Studies, Ft. Leavenworth, Kans., 1990-92; spl. asst. to chief of staff US Army, 1992-94, comdr. 2d brigade, 10th Mountain Divsn. Ft. Drum, NY, 1994—96, exec. officer to chief of staff, 1996—97, dir. Army Tng. , Office Dep. Chief Staff Ops. & Plans, 1997-99, asst. divsn. comdr. 1st Cavalry Divsn. Ft. Hood, Tex., 1999—2000, comdr. 25th Infantry Divsn. (Light) Schofield Barracks, Hawaii, 2000—02, dir. Joint Experimentation J-9, US Joint Forces Command Norfolk, Va., 2002—04, commdg. gen. I Corps & Ft. Lewis Tacoma, 2004—07, comdr. Multinational Security Transition Commd. Iraq Baghdad, 2007—. Assoc. prof. philosophy U.S. Mil. Acad., West Pt., N.Y., 1982-85. Fellow MIT, 1992.*

DUBIN, ANNE, medical educator; b. NY; MD, U. Rochester, 1988. Assoc prof. pediat. Stanford U., Palo Alto, Calif., 1995—. Office: Packard Children's Hospital 750 Welch Rd Ste 305 Palo Alto CA 94304 Office Phone: 650-723-7913. Office Fax: 650-725-8343.

DUBIN, ARTHUR DETMERS, retired architect; b. Chgo., Mar. 14, 1923; s. Henry and Anne (Green) D.; m. Lois Amtman, Mar. 10, 1951 (dec. Sept. 1980); children: Peter Arthur, Polly Louise (Mrs. Scott Pollak); m. Phyllis Vollen Burman, Nov. 27, 1981; stepchildren: Garry Arthur, Jill Meredyth, David Yale, Eric Vollen. Student, Lake Forest Coll., 1943—44; B Arch., U. Mich., 1949. Architect, ptnr. Dubin & Dubin (architects and engrs.), Chgo., 1950—65, Dubin, Dubin & Black (architects and engrs.), 1965—66, Dubin, Dubin, Black & Moutoussamy, 1966—78, Dubin, Dubin & Moutoussamy, 1978—93; ret., 1994. V.p., dir. 7337 South Shore Dr. Corp., 1958—81, 7345 South Shore Dr. Corp., 1962—86; gen. ptnr. 340 Wellington Assocs., 1962—73; mem. adv. bd. Amtrak, 1972—95; v.p. DDBM, Inc., 1975—85; hon. rsch. assoc. Smithsonian Instn., 1975; tech. cons. Paramount Pictures, 1991, TV, 1998—2001; spkr. in field. Author: Some Classic Trains, 1964, More Classic Trains, 1974, Pullman Paint and Lettering Notebook, 1997; author: (editor for N.Am.) The Great Trains, 1973; contbr. articles to mags.; archtl. works include govt. bldgs., rail transit stas. and transp. facilities, mil. installations, banks, indsl. plants, schs. and colls., hosps., housing and urban renewal planning. Chmn. Civic Beautification Com., Highland Park, Ill., 1965—74; mem. Bicentennial Commn., Highland Park, 1974—76, Ill. Commn. on High Speed Rail Transit, 1966—68, Met. Housing and Planning Coun., Chgo., Nat. Coun. Archtl. Registration Bds., 1971—; trustee NORTRAN, Des Plaines, Ill., 1980—91; trustee emeritus George Krambles Transit Scholarship Fund, 1985—, John W. Barriger III Nat. R.R. Libr., St. Louis, 1989—; life mem., friend Art Inst. Chgo. With inf. US Army, 1943—46. Decorated Bronze Star with cluster, Purple Heart; recipient award Gen. Svcs. Adminstrn. for U.S. Custom House, Chgo., 1993. Mem.: AIA (emeritus), Am. Pub. Transit Assn., Rlwy. and Locomotive Hist. Soc. (bd. dirs. 1960—93, hon. life dir. 1993, Sr. Achievement award 2004, 2004), Train Collectors Assn., Steamship Hist. Soc. Am., Cliff Dwellers Club (bd. dirs. 1972—75, emeritus), Builders Club (pres. 1970—71, bd. dirs. 1970—80), Arts Club (Chgo.). Home: 229 Park Ave Highland Park IL 60035-2523

DUBIN, CHARLES LEONARD, lawyer; b. Harry and Ethel D.; m. Anne Ruth, 1951. BA, U. Toronto, Ont., 1941; LL.B., Osgoode Hall Law Sch., 1944. Bar: Ont. 1944, appointed Queen's Counsel 1952. Practiced in, Toronto, 1945-73; judge Ont. Supreme Ct. Appeal, Toronto, 1973—; chief justice Ont. Ct. Appeal, Toronto, 1990-96; counsel Torys LLP (formerly Tory Tory Des Lauriers & Binnington Barristers), Toronto, 1996—; dir. Can. Steamship Lines, 2003—05. Royal Commr. to inquire into air safety in Can., 1979; Head of Inquiry into the practices and procedures of Hosp.for Sick Children, 1983; Royal Commr. to inquire into use of drugs and banned practices in athletics, 1988; apptd. to Bd. of Canadian Centre for Ethics in Sport, 2000-03, hon. counsel, 2003; lectr. Osgoode Hall Law Sch., 1945-48. Mem. York Club, Toronto Hunt Club, Toronto Club. Home: 619 Avenue Rd Apt 1702 Toronto ON Canada M4V 2K6 Office: Torys Barristers Toronto Dominion Ctr PO Box 270 #3000 Toronto ON Canada M5K 1N2

DUBIN, DAVID MEYER, lawyer, educator; b. Denver, Oct. 19, 1956; s. Gene and June (Wolf) D. AB, Colgate U., 1978; JD, Tulane U., 1982. Bar: NY 1983, La. 1984, US Dist. Ct. (so. and ea. dists.) NY 1983, US Dist. Ct. (ea. and mid. dists.) La. 1985, US Ct. Appeals (2d cir.) 1984, US Ct. Appeals (5th cir.) 1985, US Supreme Ct. 1988. Assoc. Mudge Rose Guthrie Alexander & Ferdon, NYC, 1982-84, Jones Walker Waechter Poitevent Carrere & Denegre, New Orleans, 1984-88; ptnr. Twomey Latham Shea, Kelley, Dubin & Quartararo, LLP, Riverhead, NY, 1988—. Adj. prof. LI U., Southampton, NY, 1989-2005. Office Phone: 631-727-2180. Business E-Mail: ddubin@suffolklaw.com.

DUBIN, HOWARD VICTOR, dermatologist; b. NYC, Mar. 28, 1938; s. Meyer and Blanche D.; m. Patricia Sue Tucker, June 10, 1962; children—Douglas Scott, Kathryn Sue, David Andrew, Michael Stonier. AB, Columbia U., 1958, MD, 1962. Diplomate: Am. Bd. Dermatology, Am. Bd. Internal Medicine. Intern U. Mich., 1962-63, resident in internal medicine, 1963-64, resident in dermatology, 1968-70, asst. prof., 1970-72, asso. prof., 1972-75, clin. asso. prof., 1975-77, clin. prof., 1977—. Contbr. articles to profl. jours. Trustee Greenhills Sch., Ann Arbor, 1979-87, pres. bd. trustees, 1981-84. With U.S. Army, 1964-66. Fellow ACP; mem. Am. Acad. Dermatology, Am. Dermatol. Assn., Soc. Investigative Dermatology, Dermatology Found. (mem. exec. com. 1987-2001, sec.-treas. 1988-91, pres. 1991-98), Mich. Dermatol. Soc. (pres. 1985-87), AMA, Mich. Med. Soc., Washtenaw County Med. Soc., Rotary.

DUBIN, JAMES MICHAEL, lawyer; b. NYC, Aug. 20, 1946; s. Benjamin and Irene (Wasserman) D.; m. Susan Hope Schraub, Mar. 15, 1981; children: Alexander Philip, Elizabeth Joy. BA, U. Pa., Phila., 1968; JD, Columbia U., NYC, 1974. Bar: NY 1975, DC 1984, US Dist. Ct. (so. and ea. dist.s) NY 1975, US Ct. Appeals (2d cir.) 1975. Assoc. Paul, Weiss, Rifkind, Wharton & Garrison, LLP, NYC, 1974-82, ptnr., 1982—, chmn. corp. dept., 1995—2005. Bd. dirs. Conair Corp., Carnival Corp.; internat. bd. govs. Tel-Aviv U., 2001—; chmn. bd. govs. Tel-Aviv U. Law Sch., 2001—04. Mem. editl. bd.: Columbia Law Rev., 1973—74. Trustee Solomon Schechter Sch. Westchester, 1991—, vice chmn., 1997—2007; bd. dirs. Nat. Found. Advancement in Arts, 1991—, vice chmn., 1994—2006, treas., 2007—; bd. dirs. Jewish Guild for the Blind, 1989—, chmn., 1995—99, chmn. exec. com., 2000—; bd. dirs. YM-YWHA of Mid-Westchester, Scarsdale, NY, 1983—86; dir. Greater Boston Guild for the Blind, 2004—. With US Army, 1969—71. Mem.: ABA, Am. Arbitration Assn. (comml. panel arbitrators 1989—), Assn. Bar City NY, Univ. Club, Snowmass Club, The Dukes Golf Club, Indian Harbor Yacht Club, Sunningdale Country Club (bd. govs. 1989—2004, pres. 2000—04), Queenwood Golf Club, Colony Club, Drones Club, Phi Delta Phi. Office: Paul Weiss Rifkind Wharton & Garrison LLP 1285 Avenue Of The Americas New York NY 10019-6064 Office Phone: 212-373-3026. Business E-Mail: jdubin@paulweiss.com.

DUBIN, JOSEPH WILLIAM, federal mediator; b. Middletown, Conn., Apr. 7, 1948; s. Emanuel Saul and Hazel (Brenner) D.; m. Brenda Charlotte Ellen Clark, June 27, 1976; children: Brian Joseph Finnegan, Darren Clark Finnegan, Evan Jared. BA, U. Conn., 1970; postgrad., U. Mass., 1970—73. Rsch. asst. U. Conn. Health Ctr., Farmington, 1973-81; organizer Am. Fedn. Tchrs., Hartford, Conn., 1981-82; field rep. AFT-Conn., Rocky Hill, 1982—2000, interest arbitrator, 1990—2000; commr. Fed. Mediation and Conciliation Svc., 2000—. Vice-chmn. Fedn. Nurses and Health Profls. Nat. Steering Com., Washington, 1980-81; v.p. Greater Hartford Labor Coun., AFL-CIO, 1982-84, del., 1980-2000. Contbr. articles to profl. jours. Mem. Boy Scouts Am., 1979—, com. chmn. troop 355, Newington, Conn., 1980-95, mem. advancement com. Mark Twain dist., 1994—. Recipient Dist. award of Merit Long Rivers Coun. Boy Scouts Am., 1992, Spl. Recognition award Univ. Health Profls., 1990, George Meany award AFL-CIO, 1981. Mem. ACLU, Am. Chem. Soc. (student affiliate chmn. 1969-70), Labor Employment Rels. Assn. (Connecticut Valley chpt. steering com. 1994—, v.p. 2001—), U. Conn. Health Ctr. Profl. Employees Assn. (pres. 1980-81), Staff Union of Conn. (sec.-treas. 1982-87), Nat. Trust Hist. Preservation, Newington Hist. Soc. and Trust, Inc., Nat. Audubon Soc., Nat. Wildlife Fedn., World Wildlife Fedn., The Wilderness Soc., Friends of Lucy Robbins Welles Libr. Avocations: photography, cooking. Home: 57 Kirkham Pl Newington CT 06111-2408 Office: Fed Mediation Conciliation Svc 333 East River Dr Ste 507 East Hartford CT 06108 Home Phone: 860-666-3990. Office Fax: 860-528-3383. Business E-Mail: jdubin@fmcs.gov.

DUBIN, LEONARD, lawyer; b. Trenton, NJ, July 30, 1934; s. Isadore and Selma (Lotman) D.; m. Marlene B. Bronstein, July 12, 1962; children: Elisa K., David I., Michael B. BS, Temple U., 1956, LLB, 1961. Bar: Pa. 1962. Law clk. Ct. Common Pleas, Phila., 1961-62; assoc. Blank Rome Comisky & McCauley LLP, Phila., 1962-69; ptnr. Blank Rome LLP and predecessor cos., Phila., 1969—. Contbr. articles to profl. jours. Bd. dirs. Juvenile Diabetes Found., 1974-95. 1st lt. U.S. Army, 1956-58. Fellow Am. Bar Found., Pa. Bar Found., Am. Coll. Trial Lawyers, Am. Acad. Matrimonial Lawyers; mem. ABA (ho. of dels. 1988-96), Pa. Bar Assn. (house of dels. 1977— , bd. govs. 1981-84, v.p. 1987-88, pres.-elect 1988-89, pres. 1989-90, chair family law sect. 1991-92), Phila. Bar Assn. (bd. govs. 1975-77). Democrat. Jewish. Office: Blank Rome LLP One Logan Sq Philadelphia PA 19103 Office Phone: 215-569-5602. E-mail: dubin@blankrome.com.

DUBIN, MARK WILLIAM, neuroscientist, educator, academic administrator; b. NYC, Aug. 30, 1942; s. Sidney Stanley and Dorothy (Cirinsky) D.; m. Alma Hermine Heller, June 27, 1964; children: Lila Rachel, Miriam Rebecca AB in Biophysics, Amherst Coll., 1964; PhD in Biophysics, Johns Hopkins U., 1969. Research fellow Australian Nat. U., Canberra, 1969-71; asst. prof. dept. molecular, cellular and devel. biology U. Colo., Boulder, 1971-77, assoc. prof., 1977-82, prof., 1982—87, chmn. dept., 1983-87, assoc. chmn. dept., 2000—, assoc. vice chancellor for acad. affairs, 1988-97, chief info. officer, 1996-97, faculty fellow info. tech. svcs., 1997-98, dir. acad. devel. BP Ctr. for Visualization, 2003—05. Sci. cons. Wills Found., 1981-91; cons., mem. bd. sci. advisors Columbine Venture Fund, Denver, 1984-94, Photometrics, Tucson, 1987-89; founding ptnr. 3D Embodiment LLC; owner MWm Crafts, 1996—; co-founder 3D Embodiment, LLC, 2005—; mem. acad. adv. bd. higher edn. Apple Computing, 1997-98. Author: How the Brain Works; contbr. articles to profl. jours. Bd. dirs. Congregation Har Ha-Shem, Boulder, 1976-80, pres., 1978, 79, Cmty. Access TV of Boulder, 1996-97. Grantee NIH-Nat. Eye Inst., 1972-90, NSF, 1976-83, March of Dimes Found., 1982-83; Fight for Sight fellow Australian Nat. U., 1969-71 Mem. AAAS, AAUP, Soc. Neurosci., Sigma Xi. Democrat. Jewish. Avocation: woodworking. Home: 1010 Grape Ave Boulder CO 80304-2129 Office: Univ Colo Dept Molecular Cellular Biology PO Box 347 Boulder CO 80309-0347 Home Phone: 303-442-7818; Office Phone: 303-250-6668. Business E-Mail: dubin@colorado.edu.

DUBIN, MARTIN STEVEN, principal; b. Queens, NY, July 1, 1950; s. Herman and Fay Dubin; m. Ellen Marlene Kohn, Aug. 18, 1973; children: Rachel Fay, David Isaac. BA, Hofstra U., 1972, MS in Edn. with univ. honors, 1974; D of Edn., Vanderbilt U., 1981. Cert. nursery, kindergarten, grades 1-6, social studies 7-9, spl. classes for emotionally disturbed K-12, Va.; kindergarten, elem. 1-7, spl. edn. for emotional disturbance and learning disabilities, elem. prin., secondary prin. Tchr. emotionally disturbed Mt. Vernon Ctr., Alexandria, Va., 1974—76; head tchr. emotionally disturbed Riverside Elem., Alexandria, 1976—77; resource tchr. emotionally disturbed Franconia Ctr., Alexandria, 1977—81; dept. chmn. learning disabled Robinson Secondary, Fairfax, Va., 1981—83; LD/MMR secondary specialist Area IV, Fairfax, Va., 1983—88; prin. Armstrong Ctr., Reston, Va., 1988—90, Franconia Ctr., Alexandria, 1990—97, Crestwood Elem., Springfield, Va., 1997—98; adminstrv. prin. Hayfield Secondary, Alexandria, 1998—2005. Adj. prof. George Mason U., Fairfax, 1988-93, 2005—; learning disabilities/mild mental retardation specialist Area IV Adminstrv. Office, Fairfax, 1983-88; grant evaluator U.S. Office of Edn., Washington, spring 1991, 93, 95; adminstrv. liaison Office Design and Constrn. FCPS, Fairfax, Va., 2006—. Pres. Adat Reyim, Springfield, Va., 1997-99; mem. Springfield Coalition, 1997-98. U.S. Office of Edn. rsch. grantee, 1979. Mem. CEC, Nat. Assn. Elem. Sch. Prins., Phi Delta Kappa. Achievements include study in how attitudes of non-disabled students influence the integration and mainstreaming of emotionally disabled students. Office: Hayfield Secondary Sch 7630 Telegraph Rd Alexandria VA 22315-3898 Home Phone: 703-690-0318. Personal E-mail: 4dubins@verizon.net. Business E-Mail: martin.dubin@fcps.edu.

DUBIN, MORTON DONALD, II, lawyer; BA in Polit. Sci., Columbia U., 1993; JD cum laude, U. Mich. Law Sch., 1995. Bar: NY 1997, US Dist. Ct., NY (So. & Ea. Dist.) 1998. Law clerk to Judge Sidney Fitzwater US Dist. Ct., Tex. No. Dist., 1996—97; assoc. then ptnr., general commercial, products liability, mass tort and employment litigation Orrick, Herrington & Sutcliffe LLP, NYC, 1998—. Mem.: NY State Bar Assn. Office: Orrick, Herrington & Sutcliffe LLP 666 Fifth Ave New York NY 10103-0001 Office Phone: 212-506-5000. Office Fax: 212-506-5151. Business E-Mail: mdubin@orrick.com.

DUBIN, STEPHEN VICTOR, lawyer; b. Bklyn., June 17, 1938; s. Herman E. and Rhoda (Fogel) D.; m. Paula L. Dubin, June 28, 1959; children: Jeffrey D., Michelle L. BA, CUNY, 1961; JD, Boston U., 1961. Bar: N.Y. 1961, Ill. 1975, Pa. 1984, U.S. Dist. Ct. (so. and ea. dists.) N.Y. 1966, U.S. Dist. Ct. (no. dist.) Ill. 1975, U.S. Ct. Appeals (2d cir.) 1975, U.S. Supreme Ct. 1970, U.S. Dist. Ct. (ea. dist.) Pa. 1993, U.S. Ct. Appeals (3d cir.) 1993. Assoc. Kronish, Lieb, Weiner & Hellman, NYC, 1965-67; counsel corp. sec Seligman & Latz, NYC, 1967-72; gen. atty. Montgomery Ward & Co., Inc., NYC, 1972-75, regional counsel, asst. sec. Chgo., 1975-78; gen. counsel, exec. v.p., dir. CSS Industries, Inc., Phila., 1978—2005, dir. emeritus, 2005. Lectr. consumer law Am. Mgmt. Assn., 1974, 79, 81, Practicing Law Inst., 1982, 88. Nassau County Dem. committeeman, 1967-75, mem. county jud. screening com., 1972-75, del. Nat. Dem. Issues Conv., 1974; pres. Phila. chpt. Am. Jewish Com., 1995-97, chmn. 1997-99, nat bd. govs., 1997—, nat. v.p., 2002-05, nat. bd. trustees, 2006—; trustee Jewish Fedn. of Greater Phila., 2006—; bd. dirs. Phila. Jewish Family and Children's Svc., 2005—; mem. bd. visitors Boston U. Sch. Law, 2005—. Capt. JAGC USAR, 1961-65. Mem. ABA, N.Y. State Bar Assn., Pa. Bar Assn., Ill. Bar Assn., Chgo. Bar Assn., Phila. Bar Assn., Bar Assn. Nassau County, N.Y. County Lawyers Assn., Am. Soc. Corp. Secs., Masons (master 1982). Personal E-mail: stevedub@verizon.net.

DUBINA, JOEL FREDRICK, federal judge; b. Elkhart, Ind., Oct. 26, 1947; BS, U. Ala., 1970; JD, Cumberland Sch. Law, 1973. Pvt. practice law Jones, Murray, Stewart & Yarbrough, 1974—83; law clk. to Hon. Robert E. Varner US Dist. Ct. (mid. dist.) Ala., Montgomery, 1973—74, US magistrate, 1983—86, US Dist. judge, 1986—90; judge US Ct. Appeals (11th cir.), 1990—. Mem.: FBA (pres. Montgomery chpt. 1982—83), appellate ct. advisory com., US ct., Montgomery County Bar Assn. (chmn. Law Day com. 1975, constrn. and bylaws com. 1977—80, grievance com. 1981—83), 11th Cir. Hist. Soc., Ala. State Bar Assn., Supreme Ct. Hist. Soc., Fed. Judges Assn., Nat. Coun. US Magistrate Judges, Cumberland Sch. Law Alumni Assn., Am. Inn of Cts. (pres. Montgomery chpt. 1993—94), Lions, Phi Delta Phi. Office: US Cir Ct Appeals 11th Cir PO Box 867 Montgomery AL 36101-0867 also: US Courthouse Ste C5 1 Church St Montgomery AL 36104 Business E-Mail: jfd@call.uscourts.gov.*

DUBINSKY, DONNA L., information technology executive; b. Cleve., Ohio, July 4, 1955; m. Len Shustek, 2000; 1 adopted child. BA in History, Yale U., 1977; MBA, Harvard Bus. Sch. Mktg. and sale positions Apple, Inc., 1981—85; with Claris Corp., 1986—91; sabbatical France, 1991—92; co-founder Palm Computing (sold to US Robotics in 1995, in 1997 sold to 3Com Corp., now palmOne Inc.), 1992—98, Handspring, Inc. (merged with Palm Hardware Group to create new co. palmOne, Inc., 2003, now called Palm, Inc., 2005), 1998, CEO, 1998—2003; co-founder, CEO, bd. chair Numenta, Inc., Menlo Park, Calif., 2005—. Bd. dir. palmOne, Inc. (now called Palm, Inc., 2005); bd. trustee Computer History Mus., Yale U. Mem. univ. coun. Yale U. Named one of Digital 50 with Jeff Hawkins, Time Mag., 1999; named to Innovators Hall of Fame with Jeff Hawkins; Successor Fellow, Yale U., 2006. Numenta Inc. is creating a new pattern recognition software called Hierarchical Temporal Memory modeled on the human brain's neocortex. Office: Numenta Inc 1010 El Camino Real Ste 380 Menlo Park CA 94025*

DUBLON, DINA, former bank executive; b. Brazil, Aug. 1953; BA in Econs. and Math., Hebrew U.; MS, Carnegie Mellon U. Exec. v.p. corp. planning Chase Manhattan Corp., NYC, 1996—2000; CFO, exec. v.p. J.P.

Morgan Chase & Co., NYC, 2000—04. Bd. dirs. Accenture, PepsiCo, Inc., Microsoft, 2005—. Trustee Carnegie Mellon U., Global Fund for Women, The Women's Commn. for Refugee Women and Children, Worldlinks. Named Woman of the Year, The Fin. Women's Assn., 2004.

DUBNER, DANIEL WILLIAM, pediatrician; b. Newark, Apr. 18, 1947; s. Nathan M. and Sara K. (Kuskin) D.; m. Janet Lee, Oct. 5, 1975; children: Sarah, Jeffrey, Emily. BS, Rutgers U., 1969; MD, U. Pa., 1973. Intern, resident Childrens Hosp. Phila., 1973-76; pediatrician Med. Assoc., Chelmsford, Mass., 1978-88, Greater Lowell (Mass.) Pediatrics, 1988—. Author: The Pediatricians' Best Baby Planner for the First Year of Life, 1994. Behavioral Pediatrics fellow U. Wash., Seattle, 1976-77, genetic counseling and birth defect edn. fellow Tufts U., Boston, 1977-78. Fellow Am. Acad. Pediatrics; mem. Mass. Med. Soc. Avocations: running, biking, travel. Office: Greater Lowell Pediatrics 33 Bartlett St Ste 306 Lowell MA 01852-1318 also: 504 Groton Rd Westford MA 01886-1151 Office Phone: 978-392-2200.

DU BOFF, JILL BONNIE CANDISE, sound effects artist; b. Mamaroneck, NY, July 17, 1975; d. Michael Harold and Diane Gail Du Boff. B, New Sch., NYC, 1997. Sound designer Broadway, off-Broadway, Regional Theatre. Nominee Hewes award, Am. Theater Wing, 2005, Drama Desk award, 2005, 2005. Avocations: biking, rock climbing, music. Home: 459 W49th St #2W New York NY 10019 Home Phone: 212-246-3592. Personal E-mail: jill@jillduboff.com.

DU BOFF, MICHAEL H(AROLD), lawyer; b. NYC, June 27, 1945; s. Rubin Robert and Millicent Barbara Du B.; widowed; children: Jill Bonnie, Robert Evan. BBA, Pace U., 1967; JD, Bklyn. Law Sch., 1970. Bar: N.Y. 1971, U.S. Dist. Ct. (so. and ea. dists.) N.Y. 1972, U.S. Supreme Ct. 1974, U.S. Tax Ct. 1973, U.S. Ct. Internat. Trade 1973. Sr. trial asst. dist. atty. Bronx County, NYC, 1970—73; ptnr. Gainesburg, Gottlieb, Levitan & Cole, NYC, 1974—81; counsel Hahn & Hessen, NYC, 1981-84; ptnr. Salon, Marrow & Dyckman, NYC, 1985-97, Davidoff, Malito & Hutcher LLP, NYC, 1997—2005, Snow Becker Krauss PC, 2005—. Dir., cons. Harwell Group, Inc., N.Y.C., 1982—; mem. panel of arbitrators NASD, 1991--, N.Y. Stock Exch., 1991--; v.p. Classic Antique & Restored Spls., Ltd., N.Y.C., 1980—; bd. trustees, gen. coun. Soundview Preporatory Acad., 1993—; bd. trustees The Harvey Sch. 1997—. Contbr. article to Bklyn. Law Sch. Law Review, 1969, Patron Children's Art Workshop, Mamaroneck, N.Y., 1979—. Sponsor Children's Med. Ctr., Lake Success, N.Y., 1979—; mem. Westchester Coun. Arts., N.Y., 1980—; assoc. chmn. fin. industries divsn. Nat. Asthma Ctr., Denver, 1981. Recipient award for disting. svc. Bronx Dist. Atty., 1973. Mem. ABA, Am. Arbitration Assn. (panel of arbitrators 1979—, guest spkr. 1983), Assn. Bar City of N.Y. (com. uniform state laws 1972-81), Fed. Bar Coun., N.Y. State Bar Assn. (arbitration com.), Lawyers Assn. Textile and Apparel Industries (pres.), Alpha Phi Omega (v.p. N.Y.C. chpt. 1964-67). Office Phone: 212-455-0322. Personal E-mail: jbcdb@aol.com. Business E-Mail: mduboff@sbklaw.com.

DUBOIS, ARTHUR BROOKS, physiologist, educator; b. NYC, Nov. 21, 1923; s. Eugene Floyd and Rebeckah (Rutter) DuB.; m. Roberdeau Callery, June 21, 1950; children: Anne R., Brooks, James E.F. Student, Harvard U., 1941-43; MD, Cornell U., 1946. Intern in medicine NY Hosp., 1946-47; med. research fellow U. Rochester, 1949-51; asst. resident Peter Bent Brigham Hosp., Boston, 1951-52; asst. prof. to prof. physiology and medicine U. Pa., 1952-74; prof. epidemiology and physiology Yale U., 1974—2005, emeritus prof. epidemiology, 2006—. Fellow John B. Pierce Found. Lab., 1974-2005, dir., 1974-88, emeritus fellow, 2006. Author: The Lung, 3d ed. 1986, Body Plethysmography, 1969; contbr. articles to profl. jours. Served with USNR, 1947-49. Recipient Rsch. Career award NIH, 1963-74; Edward Livingston Trudeau medal Am. Lung Assn., 1989. Mem. Am. Physiol. Soc., Am. Soc. Clin. Investigation, Assn. Am. Physicians, Undersea Med. Soc. Clubs: Harvard, Cosmos. Democrat. Home: 370 Livingston St New Haven CT 06511-1336 Office: 290 Congress Ave New Haven CT 06519-1403 Home Phone: 203-777-8135; Office Phone: 203-562-9901. Business E-Mail: adubois@jbpierce.org.

DUBOIS, MICHEL, anesthesiologist; arrived in U.S., 1978; s. Yvon and Renee Dubois; m. Judith Ray Jamison-Dubois, June 25, 1976; children: Marie-Laure, Matthieu. MD, Paris Sch. Medicine, 1968. Diplomate Am. Bd. Anesthesiology, Am. Bd. Pain Medicine, French Nat. Bd. Anesthesiology, lic. practitioner Gen. Med. Coun., London. Staff anesthesiologist Hopital Henri Mondor, Creteil, France, 1972—74; lectr. in anaesthesia The London Hosp. Med. Sch., 1974—76, sr. lectr. in anaesthesia, 1976—78; instr. anesthesiology Georgetown U. Sch. Medicine, Washington, 1978—80, asst. prof. anesthesiology, 1980—85, assoc. prof. anesthesiology, 1985—92, prof. anesthesiology, 1992—94, NYU Sch. Medicine, 1996—; dir. NYU Pain Program, 1996—. Staff attending NYU Med. Ctr., 1996—; chmn. instl. rev. bd. Georgetown U. Sch. Medicine, 1990—94; dir. clin. investigation unit, dir. pain mgmt. svcs. dept. anesthesia Georgetown U. Hosp., 1988—93; hon. cons. The London Hosp., 1976—77. Editor: Ethics Forum. Mem.: Am. Bd. Pain Mgmt. (pres.-elect 2007), Ea. Pain Assn. (pres. 2001—02, chmn. nomination com. 2002—), France-USA Pain Assn. (pres., founder 1993—95), Am. Acad. Pain Medicine (chmn. ethics com. 1998—2003, chmn. by-laws com.), Am. Soc. Anesthesiolologists (pain therapy com. 1993—94). Avocations: reading, petanque. Office: NYU Pain Mgmt Ctr 317 E 34th St Ste 902 New York NY 10016 Office Phone: 212-201-1004. Personal E-mail: michel.dubois@med.nyu.edu.

DUBOIS, PHILIP LEON, academic administrator, political scientist, educator; b. Oakland, Calif., Oct. 17, 1950; s. Fernand Edmond and Germaine (Goodrich) D.; m. Lisa Lewis, Aug. 28, 1976; 3 children. AB in Polit. Sci. with highest honors, U. Calif., Davis, 1972; MA in Polit. Sci., U. Wis., 1974, PhD in Polit. Sci., 1978. Asst. prof. polit. sci. U. Calif., Davis, 1976—82, faculty asst. to vice chancellors, 1982—83, assoc. prof., 1982—87, assoc. vice chancellor, 1983—90, exec. assoc. dean letters and sci., 1990—91, prof., 1987—91; vice chancellor acad. affairs, provost U. NC, Charlotte, 1991—97, chancellor, 2005—; pres. U. Wyo., 1997—2005. Author (with Floyd Feeney): Lawmaking by Initiative, 1998; author: From Ballot to Bench: Judicial Elections and the Quest for Accountability, 1980; editor: The Analysis of Judicial Reform, 1982, The Politics of Judicial Reform, 1982; contbr. numerous articles, book revs. to law revs. and jours., other profl. pubs.; cons. (profl. jours., comml. book pubs.). Scholar, U. Wis., Madison; Ford Found. fellow, Jud. fellow, U.S. Supreme Ct., 1979—80. Mem.: Am. Assn. for Higher Edn., Am. Polit. Sci. Assn. (Edward S. Corwin award 1978), Phi Beta Kappa, Phi Kappa Phi. Democrat. Office: Univ NC Charlotte office Chancellor 9201 Univ City Blvd Charlotte NC 28223 Home Phone: 704-547-0527; Office Phone: 704-687-2201. Business E-Mail: pdubois@uncc.edu.

DUBOIS, RAYMOND FRANCIS, JR., civilian military employee, former marketing professional; b. Washington, June 5, 1947; married; 2 children. AB in Politics and Econs., Princeton U., 1972; postgrad., Columbia U., 1977-79. Rep. Smith, Barney and Co., NYC, 1972-73; staff asst. to Sec. of Def. US Dept. Def., Washington, 1973-75, dep. under sec. US Army, 1975-77; pvt. cons. NYC, 1978-80, Washington, 1984-85; management consultant Alexander Proudfoot Co. and Affiliates, 1980-84; prin. Carre, Orban and Ptnrs. Internat., Brussels, 1985-86; dir. govt. affairs, mng. dir. fed. systems divsn. Nat. Edn. Corp. and Applied Learning Internat., Washington, 1987-90; dir. strategic initiatives U.S. govt. systems group Digital Equipment Corp., Washington, 1990-91, dir. strategic plans and policies, 1991-93, dir. def. industries mktg., 1993-95; mng. ptnr. Flint Hill Comm., Washington, 1995—2002; dep. under sec. installations & environments US Dept. Def., Washigton, DC, 2001—05, dir. adminstrn. & mgmt., Office of Sec. Washingto, DC, 2001—05, spl. asst. to sec. US Army Washington, 2005—. Sr. counselor The Potomac Rsch. Group, Washington, 1995—. Mem. com. on internat. investment, tech. and devel. Dept. of State, Washington, 1982-88; rsch. asst. to chief economist U.S. C. of C., Washington, 1971. Sgt. U.S. Army, 1967-69. Kneller Found. grantee, 1970. Mem. Nat. Security Industry Assn., Assn. of U.S. Army, Armed Forces Comms. and Electroncis Assn., Mil. Order of Carabao (exec. com.). Office: US Army 102 Army Pentagon Washington DC 20310

DUBOIS, RAYMOND N., medical educator, researcher; BS in biochemistry, Tex. A&M U.; PhD in biochemistry, Tex. Southwestern Med. Sch.; MD, U. Tex. Health Sci. Ctr., San Antonio. Osler medicine intern, resident John Hopkins Hosp., Balt.; with Vanderbilt U. Med. Ctr., 1991—, head divsn. gastroenterology, hepatology, and nutrition Nashville, 1998—2003, Mina. C. Wallace prof. medicine and cell biology, 1998—2003, prof. medicine, cancer biology, cell and devel. biology, 2003—; dir. Vanderbilt Digestive Disease Rsch. Ctr., 1999—; Hortnse B. Ingram prof. molecular oncology Vanderbilt-Ingram Cancer Ctr., Vanderbilt U. Med. Ctr., 2004, dir. cancer prevention program, 2005—07. Scientific adv. bd. Nat. Colorectal Cancer Rsch. Alliance Found.; bd. scientific advisors Nat. Cancer Inst.; adv. bd. Nat. Inst. Diabetes and Digestive and Kidney Diseases, NIH; chmn. bd. dirs. Keystone Symposia on Molecular and Cellular Biology. Assoc. editor Gasteroenterology and Cancer Rsch.; contbr. articles to profl. jour. Recipient Outstanding Investigator award, AFMR, 2000, Disting. Achievement award, Am. Gastroenterological Assn., 2004. Fellow: AAAS; mem.: Am. Assn. Cancer Rsch. (pres.-elect 2007—, Dorothy P. Landon prize translational cancer rsch. 2004, Richard and Hinda Rosenthal award 2002), Am. Soc. Clin. Investigation, Am. Assn. Physicians, Royal Coll. Physicians. Achievements include first to report the link between cyclooxygenase-2 (COX-2) enzyme and colon cancer. Office: Vanderbilt U Med Ctr 694 Preston Rsch Bldg Nashville TN 37232-6838 Office Phone: 615-343-0527. Business E-Mail: raymond.dubois@vanderbilt.edu.*

DUBOIS, ROBERT BRADFORD, natural resources research scientist; b. Brighton, Mass., Sept. 4, 1953; s. Robert Paul and Malvina Pauline DuBois; m. Linda Lou Knutson, July 31, 1982; children: Sarah Carol, Danielle Clarice, Christina Noelle. AS, Tompkins-Cortland C.C., Dryden, New York, 1979; BS, Cornell U., 1981. Natural resources specialist - fisheries Wis. Dept. Natural Resources, Brule, 1983—87, natural resources rsch. scientist - advanced Superior, 1987—. Presenter in field. Author: (book) Damselflies of the North Woods, 2005; contbr. revs. to profl. publs., articles to profl. jours. Chess team coach Lakeview Christian Acad., Duluth, Minn., 2000—03. Recipient Disting. award, Tech. Publos. Competition, 1994; grantee, Nat. Marine Fisheries Svc., 1990—99. Mem.: Am. Fisheries Soc. (tech. com. chair 1998—2000), Wis. Entomol. Soc., Dragonfly Soc. Ams. Achievements include research in improved scientific knowledge of Odonata species distributions and taxonomy in Wisconsin; trout research led to improved management of trout fisheries and habitat in Wisconsin. Office: Wis Dept Natural Resource 1401 Tower Ave Superior WI 54880 Home Phone: 715-394-3192. Office Fax: 715-392-7993. Business E-Mail: robert.dubois@dnr.state.wi.us.

DUBOSE, CHARLES WILSON, lawyer; b. Sumter, SC, Mar. 2, 1949; s. Frank Elsivan and Fannie Louise (Wilson) DuB.; m. Patricia Holman Rayle, Dec. 5, 1987; children: Charles Wilson Jr., Margaret Louise Rayle, Frank Elsivan IV. AB magna cum laude, Harvard U., Cambridge, Mass., 1971; JD, U. Va., Charlottesville, 1974. Bar: Ga. 1974, SC 1992, US Dist. Ct. (no. dist.) Ga. 1974, US Ct. Appeals (5th cir.) 1976, US Ct. Appeals (4th cir.) 1978, US Supreme Ct. 1979, US Ct. Appeals (11th cir.) 1981, US Dist. Ct. (mid. dist.) Ga. 1982, US Dist. Ct. SC 2000. Assoc. Kutak, Rock & Huie and predecessor firms, Atlanta, 1974-79; ptnr. Kutak, Rock & Huie, Atlanta, 1979-84; of counsel Griffin, Cochrane & Marshall, PC, Atlanta, 1985-86, ptnr., 1986-89, mng. ptnr., 1989-92; ptnr. Schnader, Harrison, Segal & Lewis, Atlanta, 1992—2000, Atlanta mng. ptnr., 1995-2000; ptnr. Winkler & DuBose LLC, Atlanta and Madison, Ga., 2000—. Mem. Chief Justice's Commn. on Indigent Def., 2000—; chmn. Ga. Pub. Defender Stds. Coun., chmn., 2007-; mem. mediation and arbitration panels Closure Group ADR and Am. Arbitration Assn. Elder Peachtree Presbyn. Ch., Atlanta, Madison Presbyn. Ch.; mem. adv. bd. Atlanta's Table, 1991—2006, chmn., 1995; exec. vice chmn. Atlanta Billy Graham Crusade. Fellow Lawyers Found. Ga., Am. Bar Found.; mem. ABA (house of dels. 2000-2006), Am. Law Inst., State Bar Ga. (bd. govs. 1998—, chair ind. def. com. 1997—, exec. com. 2006-), Atlanta Bar Assn. (pres. 1995-96, bd. dir. 1992-97, 00—, sec. 1993-94, v.p., pres.-elect 1994-95, bd. dir. litig. sect. 1988-94, chmn. litig. sect. 1992-93), Lawyers Com. Civil Rights Under Law (Atlanta steering com.), Atlanta Bar Found. (fellow; bd. dir. 1995-96, 00-06), Atlanta Vol. Lawyers Found. (bd. dir. 1995-96), Inst. Continuing Legal Edn. in Ga. (bd. trustees 1995-96), Lawyers Club of Atlanta, World Trade Ctr. Atlanta. Avocations: photography, piano, architecture, historic preservation. Home: 1050 East Ave Madison GA 30650-1467 Office: 285 N Main St PO Box 192 Madison GA 30650 also: 260 Peachtree St NE Ste 2000 Atlanta GA 30308-3263 Office Phone: 706-342-7900. Business E-Mail: wdubose@winklerdubose.com.

DUBOSE, GAYLAN RAY, elementary school educator, musician, writer; b. Pearsall, Tex., Oct. 4, 1941; s. Austin Gay and Luning Inez (Hull) DuBose. BA, North Tex. State U., 1964; MA in Classics, U. Minn., 1970. Tchr. Grapevine HS, Tex., 1964—67, John Jay HS, San Antonio, 1967—69, 1971—73, Escobar Jr. HS, San Antonio, 1970, Travis HS, Austin, Tex., 1973—86, Westwood HS, Austin, 1986—97, Fulmore Mid. Sch., Austin, 1998—2000, St. Andrew Episcopal Sch., Austin, 2001—. Author: Farrago Latina, 1997; co-author: Excelability, 2003. Co-chair Tex. State Jr. Classical League, Austin, 1988—99, Dist. Adv. Com., Round Rock, Tex., 1996—97; acad. contest chair Nat. Jr. Classical League, Oxford, Ohio, 1996—2005; organist, 2d min. music St. Augustine's Orthodox Ch. and Procathedral, Pflugerville, Tex., 1998—. Named Tchr. of Yr., Travis H.S., 1979, 1983, Westwood H.S., 1996, Hon. Ky. Col., 2002. Office: St Andrew's Episcopal Sch 1112 West 31st St Austin TX 78705 Office Phone: 512-299-9895. Personal E-mail: gaylan1004@yahoo.com.

DUBOSE, GUY STEVEN, lawyer; b. Hollywood, Calif., June 12, 1954; s. Donald Thomas DuBose and Normalee Carol (Johnson) Farris. AB, U. So. Calif., 1976; JD, Whittier Coll., 1979; LLM, Cambridge U., Eng., 1981; cert., The Hague Acad. Internat. Law, The Netherlands, 1981. Bar: Calif. 1979, U.S. Dist. Ct. (cen. dist.) Calif. 1979. In house counsel Di-Line Corp., Orange, Calif., 1980-82; project contract adminstr. Rockwell Internat., Los Angeles, 1982-84; corp. counsel So. Calif. Savs., Beverly Hills, Calif., 1984-87; sr. v.p. gen. counsel Mercury Savs., Huntington Beach, Calif., 1987-91; COO, gen. counsel Guardian Fed., Huntington Beach, Calif., 1991-92; sr. v.p., gen. counsel Westcorp (Western Fin.), Irvine, Calif., 1992—. Mem. Orange County Bar Assn. Office: Westcorp 23 Pasteur Irvine CA 92618-3816 Office Phone: 949-727-1044.

DUBOSE, KATHRYN MICHAUD, secondary school educator; b. San Antonio, Tex., Sept. 6, 1954; d. Alfred L. and Mary Anne Michaud; m. Clarence D. Dubose, May 26, 2001; children: Gerald, Aaron Jones, Rebecca Caldera, Laura Jones, Rupert, Christopher. BS in Edn., English Lang. Arts Composite, The U. Tex., Austin, Tex., 1976, MEd, 1990. Cert. tchr. Tex. Edn. Agy., 1976. Tchr. English Tomball Jr. H.S., Tex., 1976—77, St. Austin Parish Sch., Austin, Tex., 1979—84, Mapp-Estima Migrant Attrition Program, Austin, 1985; tchr. lang. arts, journalism Dobie Mid. Sch., Austin, 1985—93; tchr. English Murchison Mid. Sch., Austin, 1993—. Mem. tchr. adv. bd. Holt, Rinehart, Austin, 2003—. Mem. choir St. Richard's Episc. Ch., Round Rock, Tex., 1985—2001. Named Tchr. of the Yr., U. Area Kiwanas Club, 1996, Murchison Mid. Sch. Tchr. of Yr., Austin Ind. Sch. Dist., 1996, Mid. Sch. Tchr. of Yr., 1997; recipient Lyndon Baines Johnson L'Dor V'Dor Tchg. Excellence award, Cmty. Rels. Coun. and Anti-Defamation League Austin, 2006; fellow, King Found. and Tex. A&M U., 1994; scholar, Tracor, Inc., 1995. Mem.: Tex. State Tchrs. Assn., Edn. Austin. Episcopalian. Avocations: reading, travel, crafts. Office: Murchison Middle School Austin ISD 3700 North Hills Drive Austin TX 78731 Home Phone: 512-251-5787. E-mail: krmd26@hotmail.com.

DUBOW, CRAIG A., publishing executive; b. Oct. 26, 1954; m. Denise Dubow; 3 children. BS in radio/TV/film, U. Tex., Austin, 1977. Various positions Gannett Co. Inc., 1981—, gen. sales mgr. KVUE-TV Austin, Tex., 1987—88, v.p. sta. mgr. KVUE-TV, 1988, v.p., gen. mgr. KVUE-TV, 1988—90, pres., gen. mgr. KVUE-TV, 1990—92, pres., gen. mgr. WXIA-TV Atlanta, 1992—2000, exec. v.p. Gannett TV, 1996—2000, pres. & CEO Gannett Broadcasting, 2000—05, bd. dir., 2005—, pres., CEO, 2005—06, chmn., pres., CEO, 2006—. Bd. dir. Nat. Assn. Broadcasters, Assn. Maximum Svc. TV Inc., BMI. Office: Gannett Co Inc 7950 Jones Branch Dr Mc Lean VA 22107*

DUBOWSKI, KURT MAX, toxicologist, educator, consultant; b. Berlin, Nov. 21, 1921; came to U.S., 1935; s. Jacques Dubowski and Gertrud (Baron) Steinberg. AB, NYU, 1946; MSc, Ohio State U., 1947, PhD, 1949; LLD (hon.), Capital U., 1984. Diplomate Am. Bd. Clin. Chemistry (pres. emeritus, sec.-treas. emeritus), Am. Bd. of Forensic Toxicology (founding pres., past pres.). Biochemist, asst. dir. labs. Norwalk (Conn.) Hosp., 1950-53; dir. chemistry Iowa Meth. Hosp., Des Moines, 1953-58; state criminalist State of Iowa Divsn. of Criminal Investigation, Des Moines, 1954-58; assoc. prof. clin. chemistry and toxicology U. Fla., Gainesville, 1958-61; George Lynn Cross disting. prof. medicine U. Okla., Oklahoma City, 1961-98, prof. surgery, prof. pathology, dir. toxicology labs., dir. forensic sci. labs. health scis. ctr., mem. clin. staff Univ. Hosps., 1961-2001, emeritus prof., 1998—; prin. rsch. scientist Civil Aerospace Med. Inst. FAA U.S. Dept. Trans., Oklahoma City, 2001—. Cons. clin. chemistry and toxicology Dept. Vets. Affairs Med. Ctr., Oklahoma City, 1962-2001; cons. lab. medicine Okla. Med. Rsch. Found., Oklahoma City, 1967-2001; state dir. tests for alcohol and drug influence, State of Okla., 1967-97, state dir. emeritus, 1997—; chmn. emeritus Bd. Tests for Alcohol and Drug Influence, State of Okla., 2000—; sci. dir. Okla. Dept. Pub. Safety; ret. criminalist Okla. Dept. Pub. Safety/Okla. Hwy. Patrol, Okla. State Bur. Investigation, Oklahoma City Police Dept.; mem. sci. adv. bd. Armed Forces Inst. Pathology, U.S. Dept. Def., 1991-97; mem. Internat. Coun. Alcohol, Drugs and Traffic Safety; mem. exec. bd., co-chair subcom. alcohol pharmacology, toxicology and tech. com. on alcohol and other drugs Nat. Safety Coun.; past advisor subcom. urine drug testing NCCLS; toxicologist advisor DEC program Nat. Hwy. Traffic Safety Adminstrn., U.S. Dept. Transp.; cons. in field; mem. various fed. adv. groups; vis. lectr. and prof. various colls. and univs.; expert witness in forensic sci. matters. Author numerous books; contbr. chpts. to books and articles to profl. jours.; mem. editl. bd. Jour. Forensic Scis., Therapeutic Drug Monitoring, Forensic Sci. Rev.; past mem. editl. bd. Am. Jour. Forensic Medicine and Pathology, Clin. Chemistry, Internat. Microform Jour. Legal Medicine, Jour. Analytical Toxicology. 1st lt. U.S. Army, 1942-55. Recipient Widmark award Internat. Coun. Alcohol, Drugs and Traffic Safety, 1980, CIIT award Chem. Industry Inst. Toxicology, 1983, Cert. of Merit Forensic Scis. Found., 1984, Robert F. Borkenstein award Nat. Safety Coun., 1992, Disting. Svc. to Safety award NSC, 1995, Outstanding Contbn. to Clin. Chemistry award Am. Assn. for Clin. Chemistry, 1996; Kurt M. Dubowski Award established by Internat. Assn. Chem. Testing, 2002; numerous others; named Disting. Alumnus Ohio State U., 1994, hon. Tex. Ranger, 2007; Nat. Rsch. Coun. fellow in phys. scis. Ohio State U., 1948-49. Fellow Am. Acad. Forensic Scis. (founding fellow, disting. fellow, past pres., editor procs., Award of Merit 1980, Rolla N. Harger award 1983), Am. Inst. Chemists (life), Assn. Clin. Scientists (emeritus), Am. Coll. Forensic Examiners (life, Golden Eagle award 1996); mem. AMA, Am. Chem. Soc. (sr., emeritus mem. com. clin. chemistry), Am. Assn. Clin. Chemistry (emeritus, past pres., chmn. com. constn. & bylaws, assn. parliamentarian, Outstanding Clin. Chemist award Tex. sect. 1981, Past Pres.'s award 1986, Presdl. citation 1992, award for outstanding contbn. to clin. chemistry 1996), Indian Acad. Forensic Scis. (hon. life), Southwestern Assn. Forensic Scientists (charter, emeritus), Internat. Assn. Forensic Toxicologists (founding mem.), Internat. Assn. of Chiefs of Police (life), Internat. Assn. Forensic Scis. (charter), Internat. Soc. Clin. Forensic Medicine (founding mem.), Acad. Clin. Lab. Physicians and Scientists (emeritus), Biomed. Engring. Soc. (founding mem./emeritus), Rsch. Soc. Alcoholism (emeritus), Soc. Forensic Toxicologists (charter, emeritus), Soc. Toxicology (emeritus), U. Okla. Univ. Club, Ind. Univ. Club, Phi Lambda Upsilon, Sigma Xi. Avocations: horology, photography, music, travel. Office: PO Box 7245 Oklahoma City OK 73153-1245 Office Phone: 405-799-6066. Business E-Mail: kurt-dubowski@ouhsc.edu.

DUBREUIL, FRANCIS W., lawyer; b. Westport, Mass., Sept. 15, 1948; m. Marcia Beall Dubreuil; children: Jessie Beall Dubrieul, Owen Beall Dubrieul, Ellen Beall Dubreuil. BA summa cum laude, Boston Coll., 1970; JD cum laude, Harvard U., 1974; MS, Stanford U., 1990. Bar: Mass. 1974, Calif. 1997, US Dist. Ct. Mass., US Dist. Ct. (no. dist.) Calif., US Ct. Appeals (1st cir.) 1974, US Ct. Appeals (9th cir.) 1997, US Tax Ct. 1997. Ptnr., chmn. estate planning dept., co-chmn. pvt. bus. grp., mem. exec. com. Goodwin Procter, LLP, Boston; ptnr., mem. estate planning and wealth mgmt. grp., chmn. tax svcs. grp. Wilson, Sonsini, Goodrich & Rosati, P.C., Palo Alto, Calif.; nat. mng. dir. Bernstein Global Wealth and Mgmt., San Francisco. Named one of Top 100 Attys., Worth mag., 2005—06. Fellow Am. Coll. Trust and Estate Counsel; mem. ABA (mem. corps., taxation, real property, probate, trust law sects.), Mass. Bar Assn., Boston Bar Assn., Calif. Bar Assn. Office: Bernstein Global Wealth Mgmt 555 California St Ste 4300 San Francisco CA 94104 Mailing: 2465 South Ct Palo Alto CA 94301-4239 Office Phone: 415-217-8072. Business E-Mail: francis.dubreuil@bernstein.com.

DUBRIN, ANDREW JOHN, management educator, writer, behavioral sciences educator, writer; b. NYC, Mar. 3, 1935; s. Albert Edward and Louise Theresa (Walsh) D.; m. Drew, Douglas, Melanie. AB, Hunter Coll., 1956; MS, Purdue U., 1957; PhD, Mich. State U., 1960. Diplomate: Am. Bd. Profl. Psychology; cert. psychologist N.Y. state. Psychologist Data Systems div. IBM, Kingston, NY, 1962-63; teaching asst., part-time instr. Purdue U., West Lafayette, Ind., 1956-57; psychol. cons. Clark, Cooper, Field & Wohl, NYC, 1963-64, Rohrer, Hibler & Replogle, NYC, 1964-70, ptnr., 1964-70; assoc. prof. Rochester (N.Y.) Inst. Tech., 1970-72, prof. behavioral sci., 1972—, dept. head mgmt., 1982-84, prof. mgmt., 1984—. Mem. N.Y. State Bd. Psychology, 1979-94; cons. lectr. in field Author: The Practice of Managerial Psychology, 1972, Women in Transition, 1972, The Singles Game, 1973, Fundamentals of Organization Behavior: An Applied Perspective, 1974, Survival in the Sexist Jungle, 1974, The New Husbands and How to Become One, 1976, Casebook of Organizational Behavior, 1979, Human Relations: A Job Oriented Approach, 1978, 8th edit., 2004, 9th edit., 2006, Fundamentals of Organizational Behavior: An Applied Perspective, 2d edit., 1978, Winning at Office Politics, 1979, Contemporary Applied Management, 1982, 4th edit., 1994, Essentials of Management, 1986, 7th edit., 2005, The Last Straw, 1987, Human Relations for Career and Personal Success, 3d edit., 1992, 8th edit., 2007, Management and Organization, 1989, 2d edit., 1992, Effective Business Psychology, 1980, 6th edit., 2004, Winning Office Politics: DuBrin's Guide for the '90s, 1990, Bouncing Back: How to Overcome Adversity in the Workplace, 1992, Your Own Worst Enemy: How to Prevent Career Self-Sabotage, 1992, Stand Out! 330 Ways to Gain the Edge with Superiors, Subordinates, Co-workers, and Customers, 1993, Getting It Done: The Transforming Power of Self-Discipline, 1995, The Reengineering Survival Guide, 1995, The Breakthrough Team Player, 1995, Leadership: Research Findings, Practice and Skill, 1995, 5th edit., 2007, Human Relations: Job-Oriented Interpersonal Skills, 2000, 2d edit., 2003, 3rd edit., 2006, Fundamentals of Organizational Behavior, 1998, 4th edit., 2007, The 10-Min. Guide to Effective Leadership, Personal Magnetism, 1997, Complete Idiot's Guide to Leadership, 1998, 2000, Looking Around Corners, 1999, The Active Manager, 2000. Capt. U.S. Army, 1960-62. Mem. Am. Psychol. Assn., Am. Mgmt. Assn., Acad. of Mgmt. Office: 192 Barclay Square Dr Rochester NY 14618 Office Phone: 585-442-0484. Personal E-mail: ajdubrin@frontiernet.net. Business E-Mail: ajdbbu@rit.edu.

DUBROFF, HENRY ALLEN, editor, journalist, entrepreneur; b. Neptune, NJ, Nov. 28, 1950; s. Sol and Gilda (Burdman) D.; married, 1980 (div. 1986). AB in History and Lit., Lafayette Coll., 1972; MS in Journalism, Columbia U., 1982. Program analyst Dept. Health and Human Svcs., Washington, 1972-73; tchr. English Holyoke St. Sch., Mass., 1974-78; employment & tng. program mgr. Knoxville-Knox CY Community Action, Tenn., 1978-81; bus. writer, columnist Springfield Newspapers, Mass., 1982-85, The Denver Post, Colo., 1985-88, bus. editor, 1988-95; editor Denver Bus. Jour., Colo., 1995-99; founder, editor, chmn. Pacific Coast Bus. Times, 1999—. Contbg. writer CFO Mag., Boston, 1985-90; guest lectr. U. Wis., Madison, Calif. State U., Channel Islands, U. Colo., Denver, U. Calif., Santa Barbara. Contbr. articles to N.Y. Times, 1982-89. Vol. Russian Resettlement Program Jewish Family & Children's Svcs., Denver, 1989—90; mem. bd. United Way, 2005—; chmn. Santa Barbara County United Way Campaign, 2004—05; bd. dirs. Ventura County Econ. Devel. Assn., U. Calif. Santa Barbara Econ. Forecast Project, Ptnrs. in Edn., Santa Barbara, Jewish Fedn. Santa Barbara. Recipient NY Fin. Writers Assn. scholarship, 1982, Morton Margolin prize U. Denver, 1988, Bus. Story of Yr. award AP, 1989, Gen. Excellence award Am. City Bus. Jour., 1996, 1997, Human Svc. award Am. Jewish Com., 1999, Small Bus. of the Yr. Calif. Legis. 38th Dist., Blue Ribbon Shield Bus. award US C. of C. 2007, S. Coast Bus. Tech. award, 2006; finalist Gerald Loeb award, 1997; semi-finalist Ernest & Young Entrepreneur of Yr. award, LA, 2006; named Small Bus. Journalist of Yr., LA dist. US SBA, 2004. Mem. Soc. Am. Bus. Editors and Writers (past pres., bd. govs., Best in Bus. award 1995, 96, 98, 2000, 06). Avocations: writing, golf, restoring 1975 Porsche. Office: 14 E Carrillo St Ste A Santa Barbara CA 93101 Home (Summer): 1125 Vine St Denver CO 80206 Office Phone: 805-560-6950 ext. 222. Personal E-mail: hadubroff@aol.com.

DUBROW, HEATHER, literature educator; b. San Antonio, Mar. 5, 1945; d. Hilliard and Helen (Volk) D.; m. Ian Ousby, June 21, 1969 (div. Dec. 1979). BA summa cum laude, Harvard/Radcliffe, 1966; PhD, Harvard U., 1972. Asst. prof. U. Mass., Boston, 1972-73; Leverhulme vis. fellowship U. Kent, Canterbury, Eng., 1973-74; lectr. U. Sussex, Brighton, Eng., 1974-75; from vis. asst. prof. to asst. prof. U. Md., College Park, 1975-80; from assoc. to prof. Carleton Coll., Northfield, Minn., 1980-90; from prof. to John Bascom prof. and Tighe-Evans prof. U. Wis., Madison, 1990—. External rev. team Oberlin Coll., Bryn Mawr Coll. Author: Genre, 1982, Captive Victors, 1987, A Happier Eden, 1990, Echoes of Desire, 1995, Transformation and Repetition, 1997, Shakespeare and Domestic Loss, 1999, Border Crossings, 2001; contbr. articles to profl. jours. Recipient Capt. Jonathan Fay award, Radcliffe Coll., 1966; sr. fellow Nat. Endowment for the Humanities, 1987—88, 2003—04, Guggenheim fellow, 2004. Mem. MLA (mem. editl. bd., exec. coun. 1996-2000), Milton Soc. of Am. (exec. com. 1997-99), Renaissance Soc. Am. (disciplinary rep. 2001-03), Spenser Soc., Phi Beta Kappa. Democrat. Avocations: architecture, art, cooking. Office: U Wis Dept of English 600 N Park St Madison WI 53706-1403 Office Phone: 608-263-2913. Business E-Mail: hdubrow@wisc.edu.

DUBROW, JOHN, artist; b. Salem, Mass., Oct. 14, 1958; s. Jerome David and Sally Ann (Grover) D.; m. Linda M. Morgenstern, July 6, 1986. BFA, San Francisco Art Inst., 1979-80, MFA, 1981-83. Prof. N.Y. Studio School of Drawing, Painting, and Sculpture. One man shows include Forum Gallery, N.Y.C., 1985, 87, 90; exhibited in group shows Am. Acad. Arts and Letters, Nat. Acad. Design, N.Y. Studio School, Hackett Freedman Gallery; represented in public collection Met. Mus. Art, N.Y.C.; permanent collections, Salander-O'Reilly Galleries. Recipient Pollock Krasner Found. award, 1986-87. Office: Lori Bookstein Fine Art 37 West 57th St 3rd Fl New York NY 10019 Office Phone: 212-750-0949.

DUBROW, MARSHA ANN, management consultant, musicologist; b. Newark, Dec. 27, 1948; d. Leo and Rose (Haberman) Dubrow; m. Daniel Leon Chaykin, Jan. 17, 1970 (div. 1985); 1 child, Alexander; m. David Lorin Rosenberg, July 3, 1988; 1 stepchild, Oliver. BA cum laude, U. Pa., Phila., 1970; MA, NYU, 1975; MFA, Princeton U., NJ, 1977, PhD, 2001; postgrad., Tufts U., Medford, Mass., 1987, Am. Women's Econ. Devel. Corp. Inst., 1987—88, Leadership Am., 1988, Leadership N.J., 1990, Leadership Inst. for Workforce Devel., 1993. Prodn. coord. Children's TV Workshop, NYC, 1970—73; instr. Princeton U., NJ, 1976—78; mgr. mktg. comm., ops., human resources AT and T Tech., Inc., Morristown, NJ, 1978—80; dir. mktg. and ops. Acadia Comm., NYC, 1980—83; dir. planning and mktg. Access Methods, Inc., NYC, 1984—85; mng. dir. Marsha Dubrow Assoc., Upper Montclair, NJ, 1981—; pres., CEO Technolog, Inc., Upper Montclair, 1985—2004, Dubrow Group, 2004—. Cantor Congregation B'nai Jacob, Jersey City, 2005—; adj. prof. NYU, 2006. Bd. dirs. Greater Newark (N.J.) Conservancy. Recipient Theodore Presser Award U. Pa., 1970; fellow Tisch Sch. Arts, 1993-94; named William C. Langley Fellow N.Y. Univ., 1974, Princeton U. fellow, 1976-78, Josephine de Karman Fellow Aerojet Gen. Corp., 1981, Composer's Fellow in Opera Musical Theatre N.J. State Coun. Arts, 1990, Folk Arts Fellow N.J. State Coun. Arts, 1996-98, 2003-05. Mem.: Leadership Found., N.J. Women's Forum (bd. dir., pres.), N.J. Bus. Higher Edn. Forum, Leadership Am. Assn., Dramatists Guild, Internat. Women's Forum (bd. dir.), Women Presidents Orgn., Princeton U. Alumni Coun. (exec. com.), Princeton U. Assn. Princeton Grad. Alumni (governing bd.). Home: 34 Marion Rd Montclair NJ 07043-1932 Office: The Dubrow Group PO Box 43427 Montclair NJ 07043 Personal E-mail: madubrow@comcast.net.

DUBRULLE, FRANÇOISE M., architect, painter, interior designer; b. Orleans, France, May 26, 1929; d. Robert Jean Marie Dubrulle and Madeleine Marie Coutout de Sery. BA in Arch. and arts, Sorbonne/Beaux Arts, Florence; MBA in fine arts and bus., Sorbonne/Beaux Arts, Rome; PhD in History of Arts and Urbanism, Sorbonne/Beaux Arts, Paris. Owner La Bastille Fine Art Gallery, 1972—. Represented in permanent collections in univs. and mus. in U.S. and abroad. Mem.: Art Guild (assoc.; founder). Home: 2748 SE Rood Bridge Dr Hillsboro OR 97123 Personal E-mail: franceusa@qwiknet.com.

DUBUC, CARROLL EDWARD, lawyer; b. Burlington, Vt., May 6, 1933; s. Jerome Joachim and Rose (Bessette) D.; m. Mary Jane Lowe, Aug. 3, 1963; children: Andrew, Steven, Matthew. BS in Acctg., Cornell U., 1955; LLB, Boston Coll., 1962; postgrad., NYU, 1963-64. Bar: NY 1963, DC 1972, Va. 1999; US Dist. Ct. (so. and ea. dists.) NY 1964, US Ct. Appeals (2d cir.) 1965, US Supreme Ct. 1970, DC 1972, US Ct. Appeals (DC cir.) 1972, US Dist. Ct. DC 1973, US Ct. Claims 1975, US Ct. Appeals (4th cir.) 1977, US Ct. Appeals (7th cir.) 1984, US Ct. Appeals (9th cir.) 1985, US Ct. Appeals (5th cir.) 1986, US Ct. Appeals (fed. cir.) 1988, US Ct. Internat. Trade 1988, US Ct. Appeals (6th cir.) 1989, Va. 1999; cert. ct. mediator 1998. Assoc. Haight, Gardner, Poor & Havens, NYC, 1962-70, ptnr., 1970—82; resident ptnr. Finley Kumble Wagner Heine Underberg Manley Myerson & Casey, Washington, 1983-87, Laxalt, Washington, Perito & Dubuc, Washington, 1988-90, Washington, Perito & Dubuc, 1990-91; ptnr. Graham & James, 1991-95, of counsel, 1996-98, Cohen Gettings & Dunham, 1998—2003, Dubuc & Assocs. PC, 2003—. Capt. AC USN, 1954-59, Res. 1959-79. Mem.: ABA (vice chmn. ins. com. 1982—84, chmn. aviation and space law com. 1985—86, subcom. aviation ins., subcom. internat. practice 1985—87, vice chmn. alternative resolution com., mktg. legal svcs. com. 1991—92), ATLA, Internat. Soc. Air Safety Investigators, Internat. Bar Assn., Def. Rsch. Inst. (past chair alternative dispute resolution com. 2003—05), Fed. Ins. and Corp. Counsel (past chmn. alternative dispute resolution sect. 1996—99, aviation transp. 1996—2001), Internat. Assn. Def. Counsel (past chmn. alternative dispute resolution com.), Maritime Law Assn. U.S., Fed. Bar Coun., Fed. Cir. Bar Assn., Assn. Bar of City of NY (aeroav. com.), Va. Bar Assn., DC Bar Assn., NY State Bar Assn. (past chmn. aviation law com.), Boston Coll. Law Sch. Alumni (pres. Washington chpt. 1992—96), Naval Aviation Command (past vice comdr.), Congrl. Country Club, Cornell Club, Sigma Chi. Office Phone: 703-573-0698. Personal E-mail: dubucpc@verizon.net.

DUBUC, NANCY, communications executive; b. 1969; m. Michael Dubuc; 1 child, Jackson. Grad., Boston U. Worked in World Monitor newsroom; prodr. WGBH, Boston, 1992—95; series prodr. Discover Mag., The Discovery Channel; dir., hist. programming Hist. Channel; v.p., non-fiction and alternative programming A&E Network, 2003—05, sr. v.p., non-fiction programming & new media content, 2005—06; exec. v.p., gen. mgr. The History Channel, 2006—. Named one of 40 Executives Under 40, Multichannel News, 2006, 40 Under 40, Advt. Age, 2007. Office: A&E Television Network 235 E 45th St New York NY 10017 Office Phone: 212-210-1400. Office Fax: 212-850-9370.*

DUBUISSON, BERNARD LOUIS, science educator, administrator; b. Brive, France, Oct. 12, 1945; s. René Dubuisson and Ginette (Dessus) Come; m. Francine Filleul, July 8, 1967; children: Marie-Pierre, Sophie, Severine. Engr., Nat. Inst. Applied Scis., Lyon, France, 1966; 3rd cycle degree, U. Lyon, 1968, Dr. Scis., 1971. Asst. prof. Nat. Inst. Applied Scis., 1969-73; prof. U. Compiegne UMR Nat. Ctr. Sci. Rsch., France, 1973-91, prof. classe exceptionnelle, 1991—; rsch. head U. Tech. Compiegne, 1998—. Dep. dir. Nat. Ctr. Sci. Rsch., Paris, 1992-01; head Heuristique et Diagnostic des Systemes Complexes (Heudiasyc) Lab. U. Compiegne, 1980-94; cons. Ministry of Edn., Paris, 1983-85, 02-03; head dept. nouvelles tech. Ministry Rsch., Paris, 2003-06; sci. dir. Del. Generale Armement, 2006-; bd. dirs. Cetim, Ensam. Author: Systems Diagnosis Using Pattern Recognition, 1990; editor European Jour. Automated Systems, 1991; coord. Ency. Computer Scis.; contbr. more than 100 articles to profl. jours. Decorated officer des Palmes Acad., chevalier Ordre du Merite, chevalier Ordre Legion d'Honneur. Mem. IEEE (sr.), Soc. Electriciens et Electroniciens (pres. 1998-2000). Avocations: history, reading. Home: 33 Rue Saint Hubert 60610 La Croix Saint Ouen France Office: U Compiegne UMR Nat Ctr Sci Rsch Heudiasyc BP 20529 60205 Compiegne Cedex France Home Phone: 33 344910295; Office Phone: 33 344234478. Business E-Mail: bernard.dubuisson@hds.utc.fr.

DU BUSKE, LAWRENCE MICHAEL, immunologist, rheumatologist; b. Jersey City, Oct. 16, 1954; BS, Northwestern U., 1976, MD, 1978; diploma (hon.), Polish Allergy Soc., 2001; diploma in medicine (hon.), Crimean Med. U., 2001; diploma (hon.); Belarussian Inst. Epidemiology and Microbiology, Minsk, Belarus, 2001, Ukrainian Med. U., Ukraine, 2001, Russian Fed. Inst. Immunology, Moscow, 2002. Diplomate Am. Bd. Allergy and Immunology, Am. Bd. Internal Medicine, Am. Bd. Rheumatology. Dir. Allergy and Arthritis Family Treatment Ctr., Gardner, Mass., 1984—, Immunology Rsch. Inst. New England, Gardner, 1990—; dir. immunology Ednl. Inst. New Eng., 1999—2003. Clin. instr. Harvard Med. Sch., Boston, 1984—; co-dir. allergy fellow tng. program Brigham and Women's Hosp., Boston, 1994—98; adv. bd. Hycor Biomedical, Garden Grove, Calif., 1995—97; hon. prof. Crimean Med. U., 2001, Inst. Immunology, Ministry of Health of Russia, Russia, 2002; cons. Schering Plough, Kenilworth, NJ, 1994—, Hoechst Marion Roussel Pharms., Kansas City, Kans., 1995—97, Hycor Biomedical, Garden Grove, 1995—97, Upjohn Pharms., Mich., 1997, Novartis Pharm., East Hanover, NJ, 2002, Aventis Pasteur Inc., Swiftwater, Pa., 2002—03, Genentech, San Francisco, 2002—, Allergy Theraputics, 2004—. Contbg. editor: Asthma and Allergy Procs., 1994—, Jour. Allergy and Clin. Immunology Supplement, 1996—97, Internat. Allergology Rev., 1997—, Internat. Jour. Immune Rehab., 1998—, Am. Jour. Respiratory Medicine, 2001—; mem. editl. bd. Balkan Allergy Jour., 2002—, Allergy, Hypersensitivity, Asthma; contbr. chapters to books, articles Exercise Induced Allergy Syndromes. Fellow: ACCP, ACAAI (bd. regents 2007—), ACP, ACR, Am. Acad. Asthma, Allergy and Immunology (chmn. practice and therapeutics com. 1996—2000, chmn. practice stds. coun. 1999—2000); mem.: Interasma (bd. dirs. 2004—, sec. gen. 2006—), Am. Assn. Cert. Allergists (pres. 2004—06), Alpha Omega Alipha (pres. northwestern chptr. 1977—78). Office: Immunology Rsch Inst New Eng 358 Elm St Gardner MA 01440-3926 E-mail: ldubuske@aol.com.

DUCANTO, JOSEPH NUNZIO, lawyer, educator; b. Utica, NY, Mar. 18, 1927; s. Joseph and Martha (Purchine) D'Acunto; m. Connie Davis (div. May 1990); children: Anthony D. DuCanto, James C. DuCanto; m. Patricia Naegle, 1995; children: 1 adopted child, William P. Heiman-DuCanto BA, Antioch Coll., 1952; JD, U. Chgo., 1955. Bar: Ill. 1955, U.S. Tax Ct. 1960, U.S. Ct. Mil. Appeals 1960, U.S. Supreme Ct. 1960. Rsch. asst. Law and Behavioral Sci. Rsch. Project U. Chgo., 1953—55; assoc. Cotton, Fruchtman & Watt, Chgo., 1955—61; ptnr. Bentley, Campbell, DuCanto & Silvestri, Chgo., 1961—81; prin. Schiller, DuCanto & Fleck, Ltd., Chgo., 1981—; chmn. bd. Securatex, 1982—. Adj. prof. family law Loyola U., Chgo., 1968—2005, vis. prof., 2003; lectr. on family law, taxation, fin. planning and estate planning in connection with divorce. Author: Tax Aspects of Litigation, 1979; contbr. articles to profl. jours.; editor, pub. Tax, Fin. and Estate Planning Devels. in Connection with Divorce and Family Law, 1970-85. Served with USMCR, 1944-47, PTO, Guam, Iwo Jima, China. Fellow Am. Acad. Matrimonial Lawyers (nat. pres. 1977-79, chmn.-dir. Inst. Matrimonial Law 1976-85); mem. Ill. State Bar Assn. (bd. govs. 1983-89, Laureate 2003), Scribes, Cliff Dwellers Club, Union League Club. Republican. Unitarian Universalist. Office: 200 N LaSalle St 30th Fl Chicago IL 60601-1089 Home Phone: 708-366-9289; Office Phone: 312-609-5505. Business E-Mail: jducanto@sdflaw.com.

DUCASSE, ALAIN, chef; b. Castelsarrazin, France, Sept. 13, 1956; Trained with Alain Chapel. Chef L'Amandier, Mougins, France, 1980—87; chef, owner Le Louis XV, Hôtel Paris, Monaco, 1987—, Alain Ducasse, Paris, 1997—, Spoon, Food & Wine, Paris, 1998—, Alain Ducasse at the Essex House, NYC, 2000—, MIX, Las Vegas, Beige, Tokyo, 2004—, tamaris, Beirut; chmn. Châteaux et Hôtels Indépendents, 1999; owner La Bastide de Moustiers, Provence, France, L'Hostellerie de l'Abbaye de la Celle, L'Andana, Tuscany, Italy, 2004—, Ostape, Basque Country, 2004—. Author: Spoon Cook Book, 2004. Achievements include induction into the James Beard Found. for Alain Ducasse at the Essex House, 2002. Office: Alain Ducasse 155 W 58th St New York NY 10019-1530

DUCATMAN, ALAN MARC, physician; b. Plainfield, NJ, July 19, 1950; s. Fred Paul and Shirley (Buchman) D.; m. Barbara Steinmetz, June 18, 1978; children: Joseph, David, Samuel. BA, Columbia U., NYC, 1972; MSc, CUNY, 1974; MD, Wayne State U., Detroit, 1978. Resident, fellow Mayo Clinic, Rochester, Minn., 1979-82; dir. occupational health Columbia Park Med., Mpls., 1982-83; dir. Environ. Med. Svcs. MIT, 1986-92; prof., dir. Inst. Occupational and Environ. Health W.Va. U., Morgantown, 1992-97, chair dept. cmty. medicine, 1996—. Adj. assoc. prof. Boston U. Sch. Medicine, 1990-92, U. Miss. Sch. Medicine, 1991—; adj. prof. medicine Med. U. S.C., 1994; trustee Am. Bd. Preventive Medicine, 1994—. Contbr. articles to profl. jours. Cmdr. USNR, 1983-86. Fellow ACP, Am. Coll. Occup. and Environ. Medicine (chmn. toxicology com. 1987-92, Adolph G. Kammer Merit Authorship award 1993, Harriet Hardy award 1997). Office: Inst Occupl & Environ Health WVa U/Sch Medicine Morgantown WV 26506-9190 Office Phone: 304-293-3693.

DUCE, ROBERT ARTHUR, atmospheric chemist, oceanographer, educator; b. Midland, Ont., Can., Apr. 9, 1935; s. Leonard Arthur and Irma Harriet (Gynn) Duce; m. Mary Elizabeth Untz, June 8, 1968; children: Patricia Jean, David Robert. BA cum laude, Baylor U., 1957; postgrad., U. Colo., 1954; PhD in Inorganic and Nuclear Chemistry, MIT, 1964. Teaching asst. dept. chemistry MIT, Cambridge, Mass., 1961-62, rsch. asst. in geochemistry, 1962-63, USPHS predoctoral fellow in air pollution, 1963-64, rsch. assoc. dept. geology and geophysics, 1964-65; from asst. prof. to assoc. prof. chemistry U. Hawaii, Honolulu, 1965-70; assoc. prof. oceanography U. R.I., Kingston, 1970-73, prof. oceanography, 1973-91, dir. Ctr. for Atmospheric Chemistry Studies, 1981-91, dean Grad. Sch. Oceanography, vice provost marine affairs, 1987-91; prof. oceanography and atmospheric scis. Tex. A&M U., College Station, 1991—2004, disting. prof. oceanography and atmospheric scis., 2004—, dean coll. geosciences and maritime studies, 1991-97. Participant disting. lecture series US-USSR Joint Working Group Effects Marine Pollution, 1974; vis. prof. Inst. Marine Scis., U. Tex., Ft. Aransas, 1975, U. East Anglia, Norwich, England, 1997—98, vis. prof. environ. scis., 1997—98; vis. scientist aeronomy lab. NOAA Environ. Rsch. Labs., Boulder, 1977; collaborateur entragner CFR/Nat. Ctr. Sci. Rsch., Gif-sur-Yvette, France, 1976—77; William Evans vis. prof. chemistry U. Otago, Dunedin, New Zealand, 1983; mem. bd. atmospheric scis. and climate NAS/NRC, 1982—86, 1989—93, mem. com. atomospheric chemistry, 1987—90, chmn. com. haze nat. pks. and wilderness areas, 1990—93, chair panel global tropospheric chemistry, 1982—85, mem. ocean studies bd., 2001—07, chair com. reviewing US Ocean Sci. Decadal Plan, 2006; sr. vis. fellow Nat. Environ. Rsch. Coun., England, 1984; mem. UN Group Experts Sci. Aspects Marin Environ. Protection, 1986—, chmn., 2000—03, vice chmn., 2003—; mem. sci. com. Internat. Geosphere-Biosphere; program bd. govs. Joint Oceanog. Insts., 1987—97, vice chair, 1990—91, Consortium Oceanog. Rsch. and Edn., 1994—97; trustee Univ. Corp. Atmospheric Rsch., 1986—93; mem. exec. com. Ocean Drilling Program, 1987—97, Nat. Assn. State Univs. and Land Grant Colls. Bd. Oceans and Atmospheres, 1993—97; mem. adv. com. geosciences NSF, 1994—97; pres. Internat. Assn. Meterology and Atmosphere Scis., 1995—99; mem. Nat. Sea Grant Rev. Panel, 2000—. Contbr. articles to profl. jours. Capt. USAF, 1957—61. Fellow: AAAS (chmn. sect. atmospheric and hydrospheric scis. 1987—88, mem. coun. 1990—93), Oceanography Soc. (pres. 1996—98), Am. Geophys. Union, Am. Meteorol. Soc. (mem. coun. 1988—91); mem.: ICSU (pres. sci. com. oceanic rsch. 2000—04, past pres. 2004—), Internat. Coun. Sci., Am. Geol. Inst., Geochem. Soc., Am. Chem. Soc. (chmn.-elect Hawaiian sect. 1969), Sigma Xi, Alpha Chi. Avocations: travel, collecting single malt scotch. Home: 4708 Scrimshaw Ln College Station TX 77845-9399 Office: Tex A&M U Dept Oceanography College Station TX 77843-3146 Home Phone: 979-690-6926; Office Phone: 979-845-5756. Business E-Mail: rduce@ocean.tamu.edu.

DUCH, STEPHEN, corporate financial executive; b. Rochester, NY, Aug. 26, 1952; s. Michal and Johanna (Langer) Duch; m. Kathleen Ann Haberer, June 21, 1980; children: Sarah, Eric. BS, Cornell U., 1974, MBA, 1975. Fin. analyst Chase Manhattan Bank, NYC, 1975-79, fin. mgr. Europe Inst., 1979-81, v.p., fin. mgr. Internat. Inst., 1981-84, v.p., fin. mgr. Global Electronic Banking, 1984-88, v.p., fin. contr. InfoServ Ops. and Sys., 1988-92, v.p., fin. contr. Retail Banking Tech. Svc. Ctr., 1992-93, v.p., product mgr. Bklyn., 1993-2000; product mgr. J.P.Morgan Chase, 2001—02; fin. mgr. Meml. Sloan Kettering Cancer Ctr., 2003—. Avocations: canoeing, nordic skiing, woodworking. Office: Meml SloanKettering Cancer Ctr 633 3d Ave New York NY 10017 Office Phone: 646-227-2234. Business E-Mail: stephen.duch@duchgroup.biz.

DUCHAN, JUDITH FELSON, retired speech pathology/audiology services professional; b. Cin., Jan. 25, 1939; d. Walter and Roslyn Marcus Felson; m. Alan Isaac Duchan, July 1, 1962. PhD, U. Ill., Champaign, 1973. Speech lang. pathologist Madison Pub. Sch., Wis., 1965—69; prof. Buffalo State Coll., 1973—78, SUNY, Buffalo, 1978—2000; ret., 2001. Speech pathologist Cleve. Pub. Sch, 1962—65. Author: (book) Supporting Language: Learning in Everyday Life, 1995, Assessing Children's Language in Naturalistic Contexts, 1993, Pragmatics: From Theory to Practice, 1994, Constructing (In)Competence, 1999, (books) Frame Work in Language and Literacy, 2004; editor: (book) Deixis in Narrative: A Cognitive Science Approach, 1995, Aphasia Inside Out, 2003, Challenging Aphasia Therapies, 2004, Diagnosis as Cultural Practice, 2005, Aphasia Therapy Files, 2005. Fellow: Am. Speech Lang. and Hearing Assn. (Inagural Cadre of Advisors in Childhood Lang. Disorders 2002, cert.); mem.: Internat. Assn. of Logopedics and Phoniatrics (assoc.). Home: 130 Jewett Pky Buffalo NY 14214 Home Phone: 716-836-1363. Business E-Mail: duchan@buffalo.edu.

DUCHARME, FRANCINE CAROLE, nursing educator, researcher; PhD; BSc in Nursing, U. Montréal, 1977, MSc in Nursing, 1982; PhD in Nursing, McGill U., 1990. RN. Full prof. faculty of nursing U. Montréal; sr. rschr. Inst. U. de gériatrie de Montréal. Postdoc psychosocial rsch. unit Douglas Hosp.; chair Rsch. in Nursing Care of Elderly & Their Families; sr. rschr. Ctr. Excellence for Women's Health. Grantee, MRC-NHRDP, 1995—2000, FRSQ, 2000—06. Office: Faculty Nursing U Montreal PO 6128 Sta Centre-ville Montreal PQ H3C 3J7 Canada

DUCHENE, TODD MICHAEL, lawyer; b. Akron, Ohio, June 19, 1963; s. Glenn Robert DuChene and Judith Ann (Dipnall) Kehoe; m. Jennifer Lee Belt, May 25, 1990; children: Elizabeth, Margaret, Emily. BA in polit. sci. with honors, Coll. Wooster, 1985; JD, U. Mich., 1988. Bar: Ohio 1988. Assoc. Baker & Hostetler, Cleve., 1985-93; v.p., gen. counsel, asst. sec. Office Max, Inc., Shaker Heights, Ohio, 1994—95, sr. v.p., gen. counsel, sec., 1995—96; v.p., gen. counsel, sec. Fisher Sci. Internat. Inc., Hampton, NH, 1996—2005; exec. v.p., gen. counsel, sec. Solectron, 2005—. Mem.: New England Law Found., Ohio State Bar Assn. Office: Solectron Corp 847 Gibraltar Dr Milpitas CA 95035*

DUCHESNE, CARLOS A., epidemiologist, military officer; b. San Juan, Mar. 18, 1963; s. Carlos A. Duchesne and Aida Duchesne-Jimenez; m. Laura E. Rivera, Feb. 10, 1965; 1 child, Cristina Isabel. MD, U. Ctrl. del Caribe, PR; degree in Infectious Diseases, U. Miami, 2000. Infectious Diseases Specialist U. of Miami Jackson Meml. Hosp., 2000. Chief med. residents U. Hosp. Ramon Ruiz Arnau, Bayamon, PR, 1993—94, clin. instr. medicine, 1994—96; clin. dir. FCI Three Rivers, Tex., 2000—04; sr. med. officer Krome Med. Referral Ctr., Miami, Fla., 2004—06; clin. dir. El Centro Fed. Med. Facility, Calif., 2006—. Cons. infectious diseases Fed. Bur. Prisons, 2000—04; mem. adv. com. infectious diseases Divsn. Immigration Health Svcs., Miami, 2004—. Comdr. USPHS US Army, 2000—. Decorated Hazardous Duty award USPHS, Achievement medal. Mem.: Assn. Mil. Surgeons U.S., Coll. Physicians and Surgeons P.R. Office: US Public Health Service 18201 SW 12th Street Miami FL 33194 Home: Po Box 1863 El Centro CA 92244-1863 Home Phone: 305-207-7509; Office Phone: 786-897-5130. Personal E-mail: duchesnec@adelphia.net.

DUCHIN, PETER OELRICHS, musician; b. NYC, July 28, 1937; s. Edwin Frank and Marjorie (Oelrichs) D.; m. Cheray Zauderer, June 22, 1964 (div. 1982); children: Jason Edwin, Courtnay Oelrichs, Colin Zauderer; m. Brooke Hayward, Dec. 24, 1985. BAU, Yale U., 1958; student polit. scis. and music conservatory, Paris, 1957. Pres. Peter Duchin Orchs.,

1963—. Bd. dirs. Chamber Music Soc., Lincoln Ctr., Ballet Theater Found., Citizens Com. for N.Y.C., Inc., N.Y. Found. for the Arts, World Policy Inst., Nat. Jazz Svc. Orgn.; mem. adv. bd. Congl. Arts Caucus Ednl. Program, Planned Parenthood, Musicians Emergency Fund. Mem. Am. Ctr. (bd. dirs.), N.Y. State Coun. on Arts. Clubs: Yale (N.Y.C.); Racquet and Tennis, Century Assn. Office: Peter Duchin Orchs Inc 305 Madison Ave Rm 755 New York NY 10165-0006 Office Phone: 212-972-2260. Personal E-mail: pdomessages@att.net.

DUCHOSSOIS, CRAIG J., manufacturing executive; m. Janet Duchossois; 2 children. BA, MBA, So. Meth. U., Dallas. Joined Duchossois Industries, 1971—, CEO, pres. Elmhurst, Ill. Vice chmn. bd. trustees Ill. Inst. Tech.; chmn. bd. dirs. Thrall Car Mfg. Co.; bd. dirs. Churchill Downs Inc., LaSalle Nat. Bank, Trinity Industries, Inc., 2002—. Trustee Culver Educational Found., Ill. Inst. Tech., Kellogg Grad. Sch. Mgmt., U. of Chicago. Officer USMC, 1968—71. Recipient Disting. Alumni, So. Meth. U., 2002. Office: Duchossois Industries 845 N Larch Ave Elmhurst IL 60126

DUCHOVNY, DAVID, actor; b. Aug. 7, 1960; s. Amram and Meg Duchovny; m. Tea Leoni, May 6, 1997; children: Madeline West, Kyd Miller. Student, Yale U.; grad., Princeton U. Actor: (TV series) Red Shoe Diaries, 1992, The X-Files, 1993—2002 (Golden Globe for best actor in drama series, 1996), Larry Sanders Show, 1996, Fraiser, The Simpsons, Dr. Katz, Professional Therapist, Californication, 2007—; (TV films) Baby Snatcher, 1992; (films) Working Girl, 1988, New Year's Day, 1989, Bad Influence, 1990, Julia Has Two Lovers, 1991, The Rapture, 1991, Don't Tell Mom the Babysitter's Dead, 1991, Venice/Venice, 1992, Ruby, 1992, Chaplin, 1992, Beethoven, 1992, Kalifornia, 1993, Playing God, 1997, The X-Files, 1998, Return to Me, 2000, Evolution, 2001, Full Frontal, 2002, Connie and Carla, 2004; actor, dir., writer: House of D, 2004; actor: (TV series, guest appearance) Twin Peaks, 1990, 1991, (voice) Eek! The Cat, 1995, Duckman, 1996; (TV series) Frasier, 1996; (TV series, guest appearance) Space: Above and Beyond, 1996, (voice) The Simpsons, 1997; (TV series) The Lone Gunmen, 2001, Life with Bonnie, 2002, Sex and the City, 2003. Office: Creative Artists Agy 9830 Wilshire Blvd Beverly Hills CA 90212*

DUCK, PATRICIA MARY, librarian; b. Bklyn., Jan. 22, 1951; d. Warren James and Virginia Susan (Noonan) Johnson; m. John Jacob Duck, Feb. 2, 1973; children: Michael, Jennifer, Matthew. BA, George Washington U., 1974; MLS, U. Pitts., 1980, PhD in Libr. Sci., 1992. Libr., serials cataloger U. Pitts., 1980-84, libr., coord., 1984-85, libr., project supr., 1985-86, dir. libr. Greensburg, Pa., 1986—2004, coord. regional univ. libr. sys. librs., 2004—. Facilitator region 10 Gov.'s Conf. Libr. and Info. Svcs., Pitts., 1990. Contbr. articles to profl. jours. Leader troop 47 Girl Scouts U.S., 1990-91; trustee Penn Area Libr., Level Green, Pa., 1989-91. Mem. ALA, Beta Phi Mu. E-mail: pmd1@pitt.edu Avocation: art. Office: U Pitts Greensburg Campus 1150 Mount Pleasant Rd Greensburg PA 15601-5860

DUCKER, BRUCE, writer, lawyer; b. NYC, Aug. 10, 1938; s. Allen and Lillian Ducker; m. Jaren Jones, Sept. 1, 1962; children: Foster, Penelope, John. AB, Dartmouth Coll., 1960; MA, Columbia U., 1963, LLB, 1964. Bar: Colo. 1964, U.S. Dist. Ct. Colo. 1964, U.S. Ct. Appeals (10th cir.) 1964. Gen. counsel Great Western United Corp., Denver, 1972-73; pres., chmn. bd. dirs. Great Western Cities Inc., Denver, 1974-75; pres. Ducker, Montgomery, Aronstein & Bess P.C., Denver, 1979—97, of counsel, 1998—. Author: (novels) Rule by Proxy, 1976, Failure at the Mission Trust, 1986, Bankroll, 1989, Marital Assets, 1993, Lead Us Not Into Penn Station, 1994, Bloodlines, 2000, Mooney in Flight, 2003; contbr. articles, poetry and short stories to lit. jours. Former trustee Legal Aid Found. of Colo., Denver Symphony Assn., Kent Denver Country Day Sch. Recipient Colo. Book award, Macallan Story Prize. Mem. ABA, PEN/America, Authors' Guild, Poetry Soc. Am., Denver Club, Cactus Club. Office: Ducker Montgomery et al 1560 Broadway Ste 1400 Denver CO 80202-5151 Office Phone: 303-861-2828. Business E-Mail: bducker@duckerlaw.com.

DUCKWORTH, ANGELA LEE, psychology professor; d. Ying Kao and Theresa Lee; m. Jason Matthew Duckworth, Mar. 14, 1998; children: Amanda Lee, Lucy Lee. BA, Harvard U., Cambridge, Mass., 1992; MSc, Oxford U., Eng., 1996; PhD, U. Pa., Phila., 2006. Dir., founder Summerbridge Cambridge, Calif., 1992—94; tchr. San Francisco Unified Sch. Dist., 1997—2000; COO GreatSchools.net, San Francisco, 2000—01; rsch. assoc. U. Pa., Phila., 2006—, asst. prof. Founding bd. mem. Caring For Carcinoid Found., Cambridge, Mass., 2004—; exec. com. Mastery Charter Sch., Phila., 2005—; bd. mem. Charter H.S. for Art and Design, 2001—02. Recipient Fay prize, Harvard, Radcliffe, 1992, Better Govt. award, Pioneer Found., 1994; Marshall scholar, Marshall Commn., 1994, Grad. fellow, NSF, 2003—. Achievements include discovery that self-discipline provides significant incremental predictive validity for academic achievement over and beyond IQ. Home Phone: 610-668-8844; Office Phone: 215-898-1339. E-mail: duckwort@psych.upenn.edu.

DUCKWORTH, JERRELL JAMES, electrical engineer; b. Ft. Payne, Ala., July 22, 1940; s. James K. and Maggie Lee (Hartline) D.; m. Yvonne Cheryl Jones, Nov. 2, 1974; one child, Shelby Elizabeth. AAS in Elec. Engring., DeVry Inst. Tech., 1963. Gen. engr. McDonnell Aircraft Corp., St. Louis, 1963-66; sr. assoc. engr. IBM Corp. Space Sys. Ctr., Huntsville, Ala., 1966-72; chief engr. Electric Sys. Inc., Chattanooga, 1972-80; dir. elec. engring. Chattanooga Corp., 1980-91; dir. engring. Chattanooga Group Inc., 1991-95; v.p. of engring. GoPro, Inc., Hendersonville, Tenn., 1995-2000; program mgr. ISC, Inc., Hendersonville, 2000—01; cons., 2001—. Served with US Army, 1958-61. Recipient Apollo 8 medallion NASA, 1968, Apollo 11 medallion, 1969, Apollo Achievement award, 1970. Mem. IEEE, Engring. Medicine Biology Soc., Assn. Advancement Med. Instrumentation, Instrument Soc. Am., US Space Found. Mem. Ch. of God. Achievements include development of the Recent History Storage Unit used to locate both hardware and software faults, AC and DC drive systems and a therapeutic ultrasound generator with a multiple-frequency transducer. Home and Office: 7916 Shallowmeade Ln Chattanooga TN 37421-1930 E-mail: jduckworth6@comcast.net.

DUCKWORTH, RUTH, sculptor; b. Hamburg, Germany, Apr. 10, 1919; arrived in US, 1964; d. Edgar Windmüller and Ellen Elise Strack. Student, Liverpool U., Eng., 1936—40, Hammersmith Sch. of Art, 1955, Ctrl. Sch. Arts & Crafts, London, 1956—58; D (hon.), DePaul U., 1982; D, Detroit Inst. Art, 2007. Tchr. Ctrl. Sch. Arts & Crafts, London, 1959—64, U. Chgo., 1964—66, 1968—77; vis. artist Corsham Sch. of Art, England, 1965. Tchr. various workshops and seminars, 1972—93; lectr. in field, 1994—. One-woman shows include Appolinaire Gallery, London, 1953, Primavera, 1960, 1962, 1967, Arnolfini, Bristol, Eng., 1964, U. Chgo., 1965, Craftsmen's Gallery, Chgo., 1965, Agra Gallery, Washington, 1965, The Chgo. Pub. Libr., 1966, Gallery Mid-North, Chgo., 1966, Matsuya Dept. Store, Tokyo, 1967, Jacques Barach Gallery, Chgo., 1972, Kunstkammer Ludger Koster, Monchen-Gladbach, Germany, 1973, Calvary Sch. of Art, Alta., Can., 1974, Mus. fur Kunst und Gewerbe, Hamburg, 1976, Exhibit A, Evanston, Ill., 1977, Chgo., 1980, 1982, 1984, Hadler Gallery, N.Y.C., 1978, Mus. Boymans-Van Beuningen, Rotterdam, The Netherlands, 1979, Lake Forest (Ill.) Coll., 1984, Helen Drutt Gallery, Phila., 1986, Contemporary Art Ctr., London, 1986, Soc. of Art in Crafts, Pitts., 1987, Dorothy Weiss Gallery, San Francisco, 1989, 1992, 1994, Garth Clark Gallery, N.Y.C., 1990, 1996, 1999, 2002, L.A., 1991, Bellas Artes Gallery, Santa Fe, 1991, 1993, 1996, 2000, Pewabic Gallery, Detroit, 1992, Keramik-Galerie Bowig, Hannover, Germany, 1993, Schleswig-Holsteinische Landesmuseum, Rendsburg, Germany, 1994, galerie b15, Munich, 2000, exhibited in group shows at Art Inst. Chgo., 1969, Victoria and Albert Mus., London, 1972, Mus. Contemporary Art, Chgo., 1976, 1984, 1996, Milw. Art Mus., 1984, Am. Craft Mus., N.Y.C., 1987, Internat. Acad. Ceramics, Saga, Japan, 1996, Met. Mus. of Art, N.Y.C., 1999, L.A. County Mus. of Art, 2000, numerous others, prin. works include St. Joseph's Ch., New Malden, Eng., 1959—60, Solel Synagogue, Highland Park, Ill., 1965, Lab. for Geophys. Sci. Bldg., U. Chgo., 1967—68, Purdue U., Lafayette, Ind., 1972, Dresdner Bank, Bd. of Trade (moved to Options Exch. Bldg.), Chgo., 1976, Hodag Chem. Co. (transferred to Lewis & Clark Coll., Godfrey, Ill.), Skokie, Ill., 1978, Rozansky & Kay Co., Bethesda, Md., 1981, Sonnenschein, Carlin, North and Rosenthal Offices, Chgo., 1981, Main Bank of Chgo., 1982, Perkins & Will Arch. Offices, Chgo., 1982, Congregation Beth Israel, Hammond, Ind., 1982—83, Amcore Bank, Rockford, Ill., 1983, Teradyne Ctrl., Deerfield, Ill., 1984, Dr. R. Lee Animal Care Ctr. (commd. by Chgo. Coun. on Fine Arts 1/2% for the Arts Program), 1984, State of Ill. Bldg., Capitol Devel. Bd., Springfield, 1984—85, Unisys Offices, N.Y.C., 1986, St. Mary's Ch., Walsingham, Eng., 1987, Stowell, Cook, Frolichstein, Inc., Clearwater, Fla., 1988, Palm Beach (Fla.) Airport Terminal, 1990, State of Ill. Bldg., State Commn., Rockford, 1992, Chgo. Children's Mus., 1995, State of Ill. Commn., Lewis and Clark Coll., Godfrey, Ill., 1997—98, City of Chgo., Dept. Cultural Affairs, 1999, First Nat. Bank Collection, Columbia, Mo., 1999, Represented in permanent collections Windsor Castle, Eng., Nat. Mus. Modern Art, Japan, Smithsonian Instn., Washington, Mus. Contemporary Art, Chgo., St. Louis Art Mus., Boston Mus. Fine Arts, Art Inst. of Chgo., Phila. Mus. of Art, Fine Arts Mus. of San Francisco, Am. Craft Mus., N.Y.C., L.A. County Art Mus., Nat. Mus. Scotland, Edinburgh, Met. Mus. of Art, N.Y.C., numerous others. Recipient Gold medal, Ceramic Art of the World, Calgary, Can., 1973, Gold medal in craft arts category, Ill. Acad. Fine Arts, 1992, Lifetime Achievement in the Craft Arts Gold medal, Nat. Mus. of Women in the Arts, Washington, 1993, Gold medal, Nat. Soc. Arts and Letters, Washington, 1996, The Madigan prize for best sculpture in State of Ill., Springfield, 1999, Master of the Medium Gold medal, Renwick Alliance, Renwick Gallery, Washington, 2001, 3 Art award, Disting. Artist of Yr., 2003, Arts in Edn. award, 2003, 3 Arts award, 3Arts Club Chgo., 2003, Visionary award, Mus. Arts and Design, NY, 2003, Beaux Arts Celebration award, Union League Club Chgo., 2003, Internat. Lifetime Achievement award, U. Wales, 2007. Fellow: Am. Craft Coun. (award 1993, Gold medal 1997); mem.: Internat. Acad. Ceramics, Arts Club. Office: Thea Burger Assocs Inc 651 North Rd PO Box 68 Barnard VT 05031-0068 E-mail: BurgerThea@aol.com.

DUCKWORTH, TARA ANN, insurance company executive; b. Seattle, June 7, 1956; d. Leonard Douglas and Audrey Lee (Limbeck) Hill; m. Mark L. Duckworth, May 16, 1981; children: Harrison Lee III, Andrew James, Kathryn Anne. AAS, Highline C.C., Seattle, 1976. From acctg. clk. to info. sys. supr. SAFECO Ins. Co., Seattle, 1977-90, rate sys. mgr., 1990-94; sys. mgr. SAFECO Mut. Funds, SAFECO Credit, PNMR, Seattle, 1994-97, mktg. comm. and incentives, quality assurance mgr., 1997-98, dir. comml. lines sys., 1998—2001, dir. quality assurance, 2001—03, dir. personal policy sys., 2003—06; application devel. mgr. Seattle City Light, 2007—. Mem. tech adv. com. for the computer info. svcs. program North Seattle Community Coll., 1984-96, chairperson tech. adv. com., 1988-90. Mem. Star Lake Improvement Club, 1988-94; mem. St. Lukes Luth. Ch., 1986—; mem. Boy Scouts Am., 1996-2003; vol. coord. Mike McGavick Senate Campaign, 2006. Mem. NAFE, Nat. Assn. for Ins. Women, Soc. for State Filers, Nat. PTA.

DUCKWORTH, WINSTON HOWARD, researcher; b. Greenfield, Ohio, Oct. 15, 1918; s. Benton Raymond and Carrie Lois (Schrock) D.; m. Clara Elizabeth Ayres, Dec. 15, 1941 (dec. July 1999); children— Winston (dec.), Christopher. BChemE, Ohio State U., 1940, MS, 1941. Registered profl. engr., Ohio. With Battelle Meml. Inst., Columbus, Ohio, 1946-94, research engr., 1946-48, asst. chief ceramic research, 1948-52, chief ceramic research, 1952-66, fellow, 1966—; dir. Battelle Meml. Inst. (Def. Ceramic Info. Center), 1967-71, mem. research council, 1979-85. Mem. Engrs. Joint Council, 1968-78, trustee, 1975-77 Co-author: Engineering Properties of Ceramics, 1966; contbr. over 100 articles to profl. jours. With AUS, 1941-46; lt. col. USAF; Ret. Fellow Am. Ceramic Soc. (Cramer award 1974, trustee 1968-74, v.p. 1976, disting. life mem. 1985); mem. Nat. Inst. Ceramic Engrs. (pres. 1964, trustee 1963-74, permanent sec. 1978-91, Greaves-Walker award 1987), Can. Ceramic Soc., AAAS, Ohio Acad. Sci., Keramos, Sigma Xi. Home: 63 Brevoort Rd Columbus OH 43214-3823 Office Phone: 614-267-6502.

DUCREST, JOHN P., state agency administrator; BSBA, U. La., Lafayette, 1984; grad., La. State U. Grad. Sch. Banking, 1994. CPA; cert. fraud examiner, exams. mgr. Fin. examiner La. Office Fin. Instns., Baton Rouge, 1984—94, dep. chief examiner, 1994, commr., 2004—. Mem.: Soc. Cert. Fraud Examiners, AICPA, La. Soc. CPA. Office: La Office Fin Instns PO Box 94095 Baton Rouge LA 70804-9095 Office Phone: 225-925-4660. Office Fax: 225-925-4548.

DUDA, MICHAEL, advertising executive; b. 1972; Grad., St. John Fisher Coll., Rochester, NY, 1993. Dir. bus. devel. & corp. initiatives Deutsch, Inc., NYC, 1998—2007, ptnr., 2005—, chief corp. strategy officer, 2007—. Named one of 40 Under 40, Crain's NY Bus., 2007. Mem.: Ad Club NY, Am. Assn. Advt. Agy. New Bus. Com. Office: Deutsch Inc 111 8th Ave New York NY 10011 Office Phone: 212-981-8104.*

DUDA, RICHARD FRANK, architect, engineering executive; b. New York, Sept. 23, 1923; s. Frank and Emma Louise Duda; m. Wynema Jane Bond, May 3, 1945 (dec. Jan. 2001); children: Wynema Jane, Richard Frank, Lesley June, Desiree Joan. Cert. in Meteorology, NYU, 1944; BS in Chem. Engring., Rensselaer Poly. Inst., 1948. Registered profl. engr., NY. Project engr. Kellex-Vitro Engring. Co., NYC, 1948-54; project mgr. Vitro Engring. Co., NYC, 1954-62, chief process engr., mgr. chem. programs, 1962-67; project mgr. Parsons-Jurden, NYC, 1967-68; project dir. Nuc. Materials and Equipment Co., Apollo, Pa., 1968-70; mgr. facilities design and constrn. nuc. fuel divsn. Westinghouse Power Sys., Monroeville, Pa., 1970-73, engring. mgr. Recycle Fuels Group, nuc. fuel divsn., 1973—79, mgr. fuel cycle planning Advanced Energy Sys. divsn., 1980-84; cons. Fuel Cycle Svc. Inc., Greensburg, Pa., 1984-85; project mgr. Ralph M. Parsons Co., Pasadena, Calif., 1985-90, v.p., 1990-94; cons. Westinghouse-Savannah River, Aiken, SC, 1994-99, SC&A Inc., McLean, Va., 1994-99. Liaison chmn. industry interface State Dept. and Arms Control Agy., 1983-84; nuclear industry expert US Internat. Nuclear Fuel Cycle Evaln. Asst. scoutmaster Boy Scouts Am., Paramus, NJ, 1960-62, cubmaster, 1960. 1st lt. USAF, 1943-46. Mem. ASTM, Am. Nuc. Soc. (com. for std. N287 criteria 1981-82, design of mixed oxide fuel plants com. 1982-83, mem. com. fuel cycle and waste mgmt. divsn. 1982-84, tech. reviewer Nuc. Tech. 1983-85), ASTM (chmn. std. E909-83 1983), Inst. Nuc. Materials Mgmt. (mem. exec. com. 1983-84, chmn. sub-com. govt. liason 1984). Republican. Presbyterian. Achievements include project engineering for 1st Pu reprocessing plant, for first nerve gas plant, for many first-of-a-kind plants. Avocations: gardening, reading. Home: 3822 Coconut Palm Cir Oviedo FL 32765 Personal E-mail: wynema211@aol.com.

DUDAS, JONATHAN W., federal agency administrator; b. 1968; married; 4 children. BS summa cum laude, U. Ill.; JD with honors, U. Chgo. Bar: Ill., U.S. Dist. Ct. Ill. (no. dist.). Atty. Neal Gerber & Eisenberg; counsel to subcommitte on Courts and Intellectual Property U.S. Ho. of Reps., Washington, dep. gen. counsel com. on judiciary, sr. floor asst. Office of Speaker; dep. under sec. for intellectual property US Dept. Commerce, Washington, 2002—04, under sec. for intellectual property, 2004—; dep. dir. US Patent & Trademark Office, Washington, 2002—04, dir., 2004—. Office: US Dept Commerce Crystal Park Bldg 2 2121 Crystal Dr Rm 906 Arlington VA 22202 Office Phone: 703-305-8600.

DUDDEN, ALEXIS, history professor; b. Bryn Mawr, Pa., May 26, 1969; d. Arthur Power and Adrianne Onderdonk Dudden; m. Robert Julian Gay, May 29, 2004; 1 child, Julian Onderdonk Gay. BA, Columbia U., 1991; MA, U. Chgo., 1993, PhD, 1998. Asst. prof. Conn. Coll., New London, Conn., 1998—2004, assoc. prof., 2004—07, U. Conn., Storrs, 2007—. Author: Japan's Colonization of Korea, 2004. Recipient Fulbright award, Seoul, 2002—03, Tokyo, 1995—96, ACLS award, 2001, Japan Found. award, 2001—02. Mem.: Assn. Asian Studies, Am. Hist. Assn. Democrat.

DUDDEN, ARTHUR POWER, historian, educator; b. Cleve., Oct. 26, 1921; s. Arthur Clifford and Kathleen (Bray) D.; m. Adrianne Churchill Onderdonk, June 5, 1965 (dec. Oct. 15, 2005); 1 child, Alexis Dudden; children by previous marriage: Kathleen Dudden Rowlands, Candace L. Dudden (Schweitzer). AB, Wayne State U., 1942; A.M., U. Mich., 1947, PhD, 1950. Faculty Bryn Mawr Coll., 1950—, prof. history, 1965-92, Fairbank prof. humanities, 1989-92, Katharine E. McBride prof. history, 1992-95, 98-99, prof. emeritus history and Fairbank prof. emeritus humanities, 1992—; rsch. prof., 2004—. Instr. CCNY, 1950; vis. asst. prof. Am. civilization U. Pa., 1953-54, ednl. coord. spl. program Am. civilization, 1956, faculty Inst. Humanistic Studies for Execs., 1953-59, vis. assoc. prof. history, 1958, 62-65, vis. prof. history, 1965-68; vis. assoc. prof. Princeton U., NJ, 1958-59, Haverford Coll., 1962-63; vis. prof. Trinity Coll., 1965; cons. Peace Corps, 1962-66; mem. Bicentennial Com. on Internat. Confs. of Americanists, 1973-76; founding pres. Fulbright Assn. of Alumni, 1976—, exec. dir., 1980-84; cons. Nat. Archives, 1993-95; adj. prof. history Lehigh U., 1993-95. Author: Teachers Manual to the American Republic, vols. I and II, 1959, 60, 70, Understanding the American Republic, vols. I and II, 1961, 70, Objective Tests, The American Republic, 1962, The Assault of Laughter, 1962, The United States of America: A Syllabus of American Studies, 2 vols, 1963, The Instructor's Guide to the United States, 3d edit, 1972, The Student's Guide to the United States, 2d edit, 1967, Joseph Fels and the Single Tax Movement, 1971, Pardon Us, Mr. President!, 1975, The Fulbright Experience, 1946-1986, 1987, American Humor, 1987, paperback edit., 1989, The American Pacific, 1992, paperback edit., 1993; editor: Woodrow Wilson and the World of Today, 1957, The Logbook of the Captain's Clerk, 1995; compiler: International Directory of Specialists in American Studies, 1975; contbr. Ency. Am. Social History, 1993, Ency. U.S. Fgn. Rels., 1997, American Empire in the Pacific, 2004. Served with USNR, 1942-45. Sr. Fulbright scholar Denmark, 1959-60 and West Europe, 1992. Mem. Fellows Am. Studies (sec.-treas. 1957-59, pres. 1960-61), Am. Studies Assn. (treas. 1968, 72, exec. sec. 1969-72, Bode-Pearson prize 1991), Am. Hist. Assn., Orgn. Am. Historians (local arrangements chmn. Phila. 1969), Harriton Assn. (bd. dirs. 1962-2007), Hist. Soc. of Pa. (trustee 1993-99). Home: 829 Old Gulph Rd Bryn Mawr PA 19010-2910 Home Phone: 610-525-6584; Office Phone: 610-525-6584. Personal E-mail: adudden@brynmawr.edu.

DUDDLESTEN, KEVIN M., lawyer; b. Hattiesburg, Miss. BA summa cum laude, U. Louisville, 1991; JD with honors, U. Tex., Austin, 1994. Bar: Mo. 1994, Tex. 1995, Ariz. 1998. Asst. gen. counsel labor and employment Brink's US; of counsel Fisher & Phillips, L.L.P., Dallas. Named a Rising Star, Tex. Super Lawyers mag., 2006. Office: Fisher & Phillips LLP 4343 Thanksgiving Tower 1601 Elm St Dallas TX 75201 Office Phone: 214-220-8303. E-mail: kduddlesten@laborlawyers.com.*

DUDEK, HENRY THOMAS, management consultant; b. Queens, NY, Dec. 29, 1929; s. Wojciech and Magdalena (Swiader) D.; m. Olga Waranitsky, June 14, 1953; children: Kathryn, Nancy, Linda, Andrew, Henryk. BBA, CCNY, 1955. Acctg. mgr. A.D.T. Co., NYC, 1948-54; asst. controller Dancer Fitzgerald Sample, Inc., NYC, 1955-60; chief fin. officer Wunderman Ricotta & Kline, Inc., NYC, 1961-69, Van Brunt & Co., NYC, 1970; controller, stockholder Compton Advt., Inc., NYC, 1971; pres., chief exec. officer Henry T. Dudek & Assocs., Inc., Floral Park, N.Y., 1972—. Frequent speaker on finance and advt. Mem. Advt. Agy. Fin. Mgmt. Assn. (bd. dirs.). Roman Catholic. Home: 90 Beech St Floral Park NY 11001-3103 Office: PO Box 478 Floral Park NY 11002-0478 Office Phone: 516-437-3006.

DUDEK, RICHARD ALBERT, engineering educator; b. Clarkson, Nebr., Sept. 3, 1926; s. Emil E. and Jennie (Indra) D.; m. Helen M. Staver, Dec. 19, 1954; children: Richard Emil, Rustin Max. BS in Mech. Engring., U. Nebr., 1950; MS in Indsl. Engring., U. Iowa, 1951, PhD, 1956. Plant indsl. engr. Fairmont Foods Co., Sioux City, Iowa, 1951-52, div. indsl. engr. Omaha, 1952-53; research asst. U. Iowa, 1953-54; asst. prof. mech. engring. U. Nebr., 1954-56; research assoc. Sch. of Health Professions, also asso. prof. indsl. engring. U. Pitts., 1956-58; prof., head dept. indsl. engring. Tex. Tech U., Lubbock, 1958-86; dir. Ctr. of Biotech. and Human Performance, 1969-74, P.W. Horn prof., 1970-92, P.W. Horn prof. emeritus, 1992—. Tech. cons. industry, instns., religious orgns., hosps., 1951—; instr. TV courses; dir. Found. Internat. Rsch. and Devel., Lubbock, 1960-65, MASET, Inc., Lubbock, 1974-85, Jay Bee Mfg. Inc., Tyler, Tex., 1984-86, Cellular Tech., Inc., Lubbock, 1984-88, Rowden Gas Inc., Lubbock, 1986-92, Sone Energy, Inc., Dallas, 1988-94. Mem. editl. bd. Engring. Costs and Prodn. Econs., 1980-94; contbr. articles to profl. jours. Bd. dirs. South Plains chpt. Muscular Dystrophy Assn. Am., 1966-76, campaign chmn., 1968. Recipient Faculty Recognition award, 1978, Disting. Scientist award Achievement Rewards for Coll. Scientists, 1984, award of Excellence Halliburton Edn. Found., 1987; named South Plains Engr. of Yr. Tex. Soc. Profl. Engrs., 1986. Fellow Am. Inst. Indsl. Engrs. (pres. Great Plains chpt. 1960-61, chmn. nat. student chpt. 1961-63, ECPD guidance rep. 1965-68, research com. 1967-69, regional v.p. 1969-71, Appreciation award 1970, spl. service award 1971); mem. Council Indsl. Engring. Acad. Dept. Heads (asst. sec. 1980, sec. 1981-82, vice chmn. 1982-83, chmn. 1983-84), Am. Soc. Engring. Edn. (editor indsl. engring. div. 1965-66, sec. indsl. engring. div. 1966-67, vice chmn. 1967-68, chmn. 1968-69, chmn. planning com. of council of tech. divs. 1970-71, sec. council 1972-73), Inst. Mgmt. Sci., ASME, Human Factors Soc., Tech. Assessment Soc., Sigma Xi (pres. Tex. Tech. chpt. 1971-72), Tex. Tech. Acad. Indsl. Engrs., Phi Kappa Phi (chpt. pres. 1967), Pi Mu Epsilon, Pi Tau Sigma, Alpha Pi Mu, Tau Beta Pi, Phi Beta Delta. Home: 3707 46th St Lubbock TX 79413-3446 E-mail: kgric@ttacs.ttu.edu, radudek@sbcglobal.net.

DUDERSTADT, JAMES JOHNSON, academic administrator, engineering educator; b. Ft. Madison, Iowa, Dec. 5, 1942; s. Mack Henry and Katharine Sydney (Johnson) D.; m. Anne Marie, June 24, 1964; children: Susan Kay, Katharine Anne. B in Engring. with highest honors, Yale U., 1964; MS in Engring. Sci, Calif. Inst. Tech., 1965, PhD in Engring. Sci. and Physics, 1967. From asst. prof. nuclear engring. to pres. U. Mich., 1969—88, pres. univ., 1988—96, pres. emeritus, prof. sci. engring., 1996—. Dir. Millennium Project, 1996—. Mem. Sec. of Edn.'s Commn. on Future of Edn., 2005. AEC fellow, 1964-68; recipient E. O. Lawrence award U.S. Dept. Energy, 1986, Nat. medal of Tech., 1991; named Nat. Engr. of Yr., NSPE, 1991. Fellow Am. Nuclear Soc. (Mark Mills award 1968, Arthur Holly Compton award 1985); mem. NAE (coun.), Am. Phys. Soc., Nat. Sci. Bd. (chair 1991-94), Am. Acad. Arts & Scis., Sigma Xi, Tau Beta Pi, Phi Beta Kappa. Office Phone: 734-647-7300. Business E-Mail: jjd@umich.edu.

DUDHIA, JIMY, atmospheric scientist; b. London, Sept. 20, 1957; s. Maneklal Laxmanbhai and Armi Sointu Haijele Dudhia. BSc with Honors, Imperial Coll., London U., 1979, MSc in Atmospheric Physics and

Dynamics, 1980, PhD, 1984. Rsch. asst. Imperial Coll., London, 1984—85; rsch. assoc. Pa. State U., State Coll., 1985—89; vis. scientist Nat. Ctr. for Atmospheric Rsch., Boulder, Colo., 1989—93, assoc. scientist, 1993, project scientist, 1993—. Fellow: Royal Meteorol. Soc.; mem.: Am. Meteorol. Soc. Achievements include development of high-resolution numerical weather prediction models. Office: Nat Ctr for Atmospheric Rsch PO Box 3000 Boulder CO 80307-3000 Home Phone: 303-499-8786. Personal E-mail: dudhia@msn.com. Business E-Mail: dudhia@ucar.edu.

DUDLEY, ANNA CAROL, singer, voice educator; b. Puunene, Hawaii, Jan. 20, 1931; d. Robert Wells and Anna Catherine (McCune) Kingdon; m. Richard Eldridge Dudley, June 16, 1956; children: Shannon Kingdon, David Raymond, Justin McAfee. BA, Oberlin Coll., 1952; MA, Oberlin Conservatory Music, 1956. Tchr. Lady Doak Coll. and OCPM Sch., Madurai, India, 1952—54; instr. Stanislaus State U., Turlock, Calif., 1974—77, San Francisco State U., 1976—94; faculty, dir. workshop San Francisco Early Music Soc., San Rafael, Calif., 1977—; opera dir. San Francisco Conservatory Music, 1999—2002; instr. U. Calif., Berkeley, 2000—. Judge music competitions throughout Calif. Music critic: San Francisco Classical Voice, 1998—; singer: Mills Coll. Performing Group, The Houle Consort, Young Audiences ensembles, Music Now, Tapestry, 1974—90, The Cazadero Baroque Players, 1981—83, Annadama Trio, 1982—84, Sounds New, 2002, (soloist) San Francisco Symphony, Bay Area Women's Philharmonic, Philharmonia Baroque, Cabrillo Music Festival, Basically Baroque Festival series, U. Calif., San Francisco City Chorus and Orch., Britt Festival, San Francisco Contemporary Music Players, Earplay, Composers Inc., Kronos Quartet, (recs.) CRI. Recipient Meritorious Performance and Profl. Promise award, San Francisco State U., 1989. Mem.: San Francisco Early Music Soc. (pres. 1980—82, bd. mem.), Jr. Bach Festival Assn. (music dir. 1993—96), Nat. Assn. Tchrs. Singing (pres. emerita San Francisco Bay chpt. 1985—88), Pi Kappa Lambda, Phi Beta Kappa. Congregational. Avocations: dance, travel, hiking. Home: 1745 Capistrano Ave Berkeley CA 94707

DUDLEY, ARTHUR, II, lawyer; b. Detroit, June 6, 1951; s. Arthur and Lethia Mae (Green) D.; m. Doreen Shepherd, June 24, 1972; children: A. Frederick, Alexander C. BA cum laude (hon.), Harvard Coll., 1973; MA, JD, Yale U., 1977. Bar: NY 1978, Mich. 1983. Assoc. Coudert Bros., NYC, 1977-83; shareholder Donovan, Hammond, Ziegelman, Roach & Sotiroff, P.C., Detroit, 1983-87; ptnr. Burnham, Connolly, Oesterle & Henry, Detroit, 1987-88; shareholder Butzel Long, P.C., Detroit, 1988—. Adj. prof. Coll. Bus. Adminstrn. U. Detroit Mercy, 1990—; mem. securities adv. com., corp. and securities bur. Mich. Dept. Commerce. Mem. minority econ. devel. com. New Detroit (chair & bd. dirs.) 1987-91, Mich. Minority Bus. Devel. Coun.(dir.), adv. bd. Black United Fund Mich.(chair of bd.), bd. dirs. Minority Tech. Coun. Mich., Ann Arbor, Detroit Urban League (dir. and vice chair of bd.) 1995-, Legal Aid and Defender Assn., Mich. Dept. of Consumer and Industry Svc. Recipient Nat. Merit Scholar. Mem. ABA, Mich. Bar Assn. (co-chmn. state regulation securities com. bus. law sect.), Detroit Bar Assn., Wolverine Bar Assn., Yale Assn. Internat. Law and Workshop (urban legal problems), One Stop Capital Shop (dir. and chair of bd.), Fin. and Ins. Svc. (adv com. of divsn of Securities). Editor Yale Studies in Pub. World Order. Office: Butzel Long PC 150 W Jefferson Ave Detroit MI 48226 Office Phone: 313-225-7070. Office Fax: 313-225-7080. Business E-Mail: dudleya@butzel.com.

DUDLEY, CRAIG, actor; b. Bklyn., Jan. 22, 1945; s. Wilbur Estes Dudley and Geraldine Veronica Boyton. Diploma in theatre, Am. Theatre Wing, NYC, 1964, Am. Acad. Dramatic Arts, 1966. Actor Bklyn. Acad. Music, Bklyn., 1966, Boston Herald Repertory, 1966; appeared in NY Misalliance, War and Peace, Trelawny of the Wells, Ursula's Permanent, Lion in Winter, Measure for Measure, Richard of Bordeaux, Macbeth, Othello, Zou (Blue Angel), The Miser. Theatre lectr. Farmingdale U., LI, 2005—06. Co-prodr. (documentaries) Brit. Actor Sir Derek Jacobi, (for TV documentaries) The 58th Ann. Theatre World Awards; actor: (plays) Richard II, 1979, Hamlet, 1980, Mary Stuart, 1981, A Tale of Two Cities, 1982, Dial M for Murder, 1984, The Hasty Heart, 1984, Milton, 1986, Crown of Kings, 1987, The Real Thing, 1989, Cyrano de Bergerac, 1990, Amadeus, 1992, An Inspector Calls, 1997, Racing Demon, 1998, various others. Office Phone: 212-560-2389.

DUDLEY, DURAND STOWELL, retired librarian; b. Cleve., Feb. 28, 1926; s. George Stowell and Corinne Elizabeth (Durand) Dudley; m. Dorothy Woolworth, July 3, 1954; children: Jane Elizabeth, Deborah Anne. BA, Oberlin Coll., Ohio, 1948; MLS, Case Western Res. U., Cleve., 1950. Ordained to ministry as deacon Presbyterian Ch. Libr. Marietta Coll. Libr., Ohio, 1953—55, Akron Pub. Libr., Ohio, 1955—60, Marathon Oil Co., Findlay, Ohio, 1960—74, sr. law libr., 1974—86; supr. tech. svcs. dept. Findlay-Hancock County Pub. Library, 1986—88; ret., 1988. Mem.: Spl. Libraries Assn. Presbyterian. Home: 807 Red Maple Ct Bluffton OH 45817-8551

DUDLEY, GARY EDWARD, psychologist; b. Columbus, Ohio, July 19, 1947; s. Ray Leonard and Mary Virginia (Russi) D.; m. Linda Jean Patterson, June 21, 1969; children: Michelle Denise, Karen Elizabeth. BS, Ohio State U., 1969; MS, U. Miami, 1972, PhD, 1975. Lic. psychologist, Ga., Fla. Tchr. Columbus Pub. Schs., 1969—70; intern in clin. psychology Mt. Zion Hosp. and Med. Ctr., San Francisco, 1972—73; clin. psychologist Met. Dade County Jail, Miami, Fla., 1974—76, Southeast Inst. Criminal Justice, Miami, 1974—76, Ga. So. U., Statesboro, 1976—80; pvt. practice Marietta, Ga., 1980—. Cons. Child Devel. Ctr., Ga. Psycho-Ednl. Network, Atlanta; bd. dirs. svcs. Atlanta Area Psychol. Assocs., PC; pres. Accurate Assessment Svcs. Atlanta. Contbr. articles to profl. jours. NIMH fellow, 1971, 73, VA fellow, 1971. Mem. APA, Nat. Acad. Neuropsychologists, Am. Bd. Med. Psychotherapists, Southeastern Psychol. Assn., Ga. Psychol. Assn., Nat. Honor Soc. Psychology, Sigma Xi. Office: Doctors Bldg/Windy Hill 2520 Windy Hill Rd Ste 203 Marietta GA 30067-8650 Office Phone: 770-953-6401. Personal E-mail: ged69@hotmail.com.

DUDLEY, GEORGE ELLSWORTH, lawyer; b. Earlington, Ky., July 14, 1922; s. Ralph Emerson and Camille (Lackey) D.; m. Barbara J. Muir, June 28, 1950 (dec. Feb. 1995); children: Bruce K., Camille Dudley McNutt, Nancy S., Elizabeth Dudley Stephens. BS in Commerce, U. Ky., 1947; JD, U. Mich., 1950. Bar: Ky. 1950, D.C. 1951, U.S. Dist. Ct. (we. dist.) Ky. 1962, U.S. Ct. Appeals (6th cir.) 1987. Assoc. Gordon, Gordon & Moore, Madisonville, Ky., 1950-51; pvt. practice law Louisville, 1952-59; ptnr. Brown, Ardery, Todd & Dudley, Louisville, 1959-72, Brown, Todd & Heyburn, Louisville, 1972-92, of counsel, 1992—, mem. mgmt. com., 1972-90, chmn., 1989-90. Pres. Ky. Easter Seal Soc., Louisville, 1971-72; treas. Ky. Dem. Party, Frankfort, 1971-74; bd. dirs. Alliant Adult Health Svcs., Louisville, 1976—; 1st v.p. Nat. Easter Seal Soc., Chgo., 1981. Capt. inf. U.S. Army, 1943-46, ETO; capt. JAGC, U.S. Army, 1951-52. Mem. ABA, Ky. Bar Assn., Louisville Bar Assn., U.S. 6th Cir. Jud. Conf. (life), Harmony Landing Country Club (pres. 1978-79), Barristers Soc., Omicron Delta Kappa. Presbyterian. Avocations: golf, tennis, travel, sports spectator. Home: 1905 Crossgate Ln Louisville KY 40222-6405 Office: Frost Brown Todd 3200 Aegon Ctr Louisville KY 40202

DUDLEY, JOHN HENRY, JR., lawyer; b. Lansing, Mich., June 22, 1941; s. John Henry and Elizabeth (Dean) D.; m. Elizabeth Merrill Casgrain, Dec. 27, 1975; 1 child, John. BA, Denison U., 1963; LLB, Stanford U., 1966; MA, U. Mich., 1968. Bar: Mich. 1968, U.S. Ct. Appeals (6th cir.) 1972, U.S. Ct. Appeals (2d cir.) 1987. Assoc. Devine & Devine, Ann Arbor, Mich., 1968-69; ptnr. Butzel Long, Detroit, 1969—. Adj. prof. law sch. U. Detroit, 1991. Chair, bd. dirs. Ann Arbor YMCA, 1997-99. Named Master of Bench U. Detroit-Mercy. Fellow Mich. State Bar Found.; mem. ABA (litig. sect.), Mich. State Bar Assn. (rep. assembly 1974-77), Detroit Bar Assn. (vol. lawyers com. 1989—), Washtenaw County Bar Assn., Am. Inn of Ct. Office: Butzel Long 150 W Jefferson Ave Fl 9th Detroit MI 48226-4430 Office Phone: 313-225-7012, 734-213-3609. Business E-Mail: dudleyj@butzel.com.

DUDLEY, PERRY, JR., retired electronics executive; b. New Haven, June 5, 1928; s. Perry and Ella (Leach) D.; m. June Ungar, Feb. 13, 1993; children: Bruce Lawrence, Virginia Barbara (from previous marriage). BSEE, Purdue U., 1952; MBA, Santa Clara U., 1966. Sales engr. Reliance Elec. Co., Cleve. and L.A., 1952-60, GTE Sylvania, Burlingame, Calif., 1960-65; sr. applications engr. Varian Assocs., Palo Alto, Calif., 1965-68; product mgr. Ampex Corp., Redwood City, Calif., 1968-70; program mgr. Genesys Sys., Inc., 1972-73; indsl. real estate broker, salesman, 1974-80; program mgr. Dalmo Victor Ops., Bell Aerospace Divsn., Textron, 1980-85; mktg. and program mgr. Loral Data Sys., San Diego, 1986-88; mgmt. cons. San Diego, 1989-94; real estate agent Prudential Atlanta Realty, 1995-96; program mgr. EMS Scis., Norcross, Ga., 1996-97; plan owner GTE Wireless, 1997-2000; financial svcs. rep. South Trust Bank, 2000—02, ret., 2002. Instr. mktg. and mgmt. San Francisco State U., 1982, West Coast U., 1990-94. Pres. Young Rep. Club, Pasadena, Calif., 1959; precinct capt. Menlo Park (Calif.) Rep. Com., 1961-72; elder Presbyn. Ch. With USN, 1946-48. Mem. Nat. Assn. of Mgmt., Assn. of Old Crows, North Fulton County Rep. Club, Purdue Alumni Club (pres. 1959), Mensa, Phi Gamma Delta. Avocations: sailing, cruising. Home: 8198 Natures Way Unit 15 Bradenton FL 34202-4128 E-mail: dudleypj@earthlink.net.

DUDLEY, RICHARD MANSFIELD, mathematician, educator; b. East Cleveland, Ohio, July 28, 1938; s. Winston Mansfield and Charlotte Mae (Wheaton) D.; m. Elizabeth Allen Martin, June 3, 1978. AB, Harvard U., 1959; PhD, Princeton U., 1962. Asst. prof. math. U. Calif., Berkeley, 1963-66; asso. prof. MIT, 1967-72, prof., 1972—. Author: Real Analysis and Probability, 1989, 2d edit., 2002, Uniform Central Limit Theorems, 1999; editor: White Mountain Guide, 1979, Annals of Probability, 1979—81. Alfred P. Sloan Found. fellow, 1966-68, Guggenheim Found. fellow, 1991. Fellow AAAS, Am. Statis. Assn., Inst. Math. Stats.; mem. APHA, Am. Math. Soc., Bernoulli Soc., Internat. Statis. Inst. Democrat. Home: 92 Lewis St Newton MA 02458-1840 Office: MIT 77 Massachusetts Ave Rm 2-245 Cambridge MA 02139-4307 Home Phone: 617-969-0590; Office Phone: 617-253-7567.

DUDLEY, RICK (RICHARD C. DUDLEY), professional sports team executive; b. Jan. 31, 1949; m. Ja-Hee Dudley. Player Am. Hockey League, Internat. Hockey League, World Hockey Assn., Cleve., Cin., 1969-79, Buffalo Sabres, 1972—81, Winnipeg Jets, 1981; head coach Carolina Thunderbirds, 1981—86, New Haven Nighthawks, 1988—89, Flint Spirits, 1986—88, Buffalo Sabres, 1989—92, San Diego Gulls, 1992—93, Phoenix Roadrunners, 1993—94; head coach, gen. mgr. Detroit Vipers, 1994—96; v.p., gen mgr Ottawa Senators, 1996-99; gen. mgr., v.p. Tampa Bay Lightning, 1999—2002; gen. mgr. Fla. Panthers, Sunrise, 2002—04, head coach, 2003—04; cons. hockey ops. Chgo. Blackhawks, 2004—06, asst. gen. mgr., 2006—. Office: Chgo Blackhawk Hockey Team 1901 W Madison St Chicago IL 60612

DUDLEY, THORA LOUISE, rehabilitation services professional; b. Ansley, Ala., June 12, 1927; d. Willie Gussie and Henry Dudley. BA, Talladega Coll., 1958; MA in Rehab. Tchg., Hunter Coll., 1959. Cert. Am. Braille Assn. Rehab. tchr. N.Y. Assn. for Blind, NYC, 1959—92; ret. Task force hiv/aids N.Y. Assn. for Blind, NYC, 1992. Singer: (record) My Heavenly Father Watches Over Me. Mem. Lighthouse Choral Group, NYC, 1965—89; performer Tuskegee U., Ala.; pres. chancel choir Butler Meml. United Meth. Ch., Bronx, NY, 1981, lay spkr., 2003, pres. united meth. women, 1986. Recipient Resident of Honor Ho., Talledega Coll., 1954—58, 1st pl., Legendary Apollo Theater, 1970; scholar, Vocat. Rehab. Group, 1958. Mem.: NAACP (life), Little Theater Group (assoc. Key Award 1958), Alpha Kappa Alpha (parliamentarian 1980, charter mem. Eta Omega Omega chpt.). Methodist. Achievements include first black, blind woman to graduate college and graduate school in the state of Alabama; One of the first blind members of Alpha Kappa Alpa. Avocations: singing, reading. Home Phone: 718-220-1223.

DUDLEY, WILLIAM C., economist; m. Ann E. Darby. BA, New Coll., Sarasota, Fla., 1974; PhD, U. Calif., Berkeley, 1982. Economist Fed. Reserve Bd., 1981—83; v.p. Morgan Guaranty Trust Co., 1983—86; sr. economist Goldman Sachs, 1986, chief US economist, 1995—2005, mng. dir., 1996—2006, advisory dir., 2006; exec. v.p., head markets group Fed. Reserve Bank NY, 2006—. Mem. econ. advisory com. Fed. Reserve Bank NY; tech. cons. group Congressional Budget Office, 1999—2005. Office: Fed Reserve Bank NY 33 Liberty St New York NY 10045*

DUDLEY, WILLIAM SHELDON, historian; b. Bklyn., July 14, 1936; s. William Henry and Dorothy (Lawson) D.; m. Julia Bartel, Aug. 21, 1965 (dec.); children: Jennifer Bee, Mary Megan; m. Donna Tully, Feb. 20, 2001 BA, Williams Coll., 1958; MA, Columbia U., 1966, PhD, 1972. History tchr. Poly. Prep. County Day Sch., Bklyn., 1963-66; asst. prof. History So. Meth. U., Dallas, 1970-77; supervisory historian Naval Hist. Ctr., Washington, 1977-82, head early history br., 1982-90, sr. historian, 1990-95, dir., sr. exec. svc., 1995—2004. Editor: Naval War of 1812, vol. 1, 1985, vol. 2, 1992, vol. 3, 2002; mem. editl. adv. bd. Sea History Mag., 2005—. Bd. dir. Naval Hist. Found., 2005—. Lt. USNR, 1959—63. Recipient Samuel Eliot Morison award USS Constitution Mus., 1993, Nat. Trust for Historic Preservation, Nat. Pres. awards U.S.S. Constn., 1997, H.L. Hunley Recovery, 2002, Navy Superior Civilian Svc. award, 2004, Spl. Recognition award Surface Navy Assn., 2005, K. Jack Bauer award Nasoh, 2005 Mem. Am. Revolution Roundtable (pres. 1987), Soc. History in the Fed. Govt. (pres. 1989-90, Thomas Jefferson prize 1993), Md. Hist. Soc. (maritime com. 1994—), N.Am. Soc. Oceanic History (pres. 1999—2003), Mass. Hist. Soc. (corr. mem.), Annapolis Maritime Mus. (dir.), Md. Adv. Com. Archeology. Avocations: sailing, gardening, writing. Home: 4420 Cobalt Dr Harwood MD 20776

DUDMAN, RICHARD BEEBE, journalist; b. Centerville, Iowa, May 3, 1918; s. Virgil Ernest and Wilma (Beebe) D.; m. Helen Sloane, Mar. 14, 1946; children: Iris Janet Sloane, Martha Tod. BA, Stanford U., 1940; LLD (hon.), U. Mo., St. Louis, 1979. Reporter, photographer Oroville (Calif.) Mercury-Register, 1937; reporter Denver Post, 1945-49, St. Louis Post-Dispatch, 1949-53, Washington corr., 1954-68, bur. chief, 1969-81; chmn. bd., treas. Dudman Communications Corp., Ellsworth, Maine, 1981-92, chmn. emeritus, 1992-99. Adv. com. Nieman Found. for Journalism, 1977-81; trustee South-North News Svc., 1985-95, pres., 1987-90, mng. editor, 1987-95; cons. to Washington Bur., St. Louis Post Dispatch, 1997; editl. writer Bangor (Maine) Daily News, 2000--; bd. dirs. Islesford Boatworks. Author: Men of the Far Right, 1962, 40 Days with the Enemy, 1971, also articles. Trustee Washington Journalism Ctr., 1974-92, Inst. Current World Affairs, 1983-89, 95-98; bd. dirs. Downeast Family YMCA, Ellsworth, 1987-91; pub. mem. Maine Lobster Promotion Coun., 1991-2000. With USNR, 1942-45. Recipient award Asia Overseas Press Club, 1972, Edward Weintal award, 1979, Mo. medal U. Mo., 1981, George Polk Career award, 1993; Nieman fellow Harvard U., 1953-54, Knight Internat. Press fellow, South Africa, 1994, 96. Mem. Nat. Assn. Broadcasters (First Amendment com. 1985-89). Clubs: Gridiron (Washington). Lodges: Rotary. Avocations: sailing, boat building. Home Phone: 207-667-9557. Personal E-mail: rdudman@gwi.net.

DUDRICK, STANLEY JOHN, surgeon, research scientist, educator; b. Nanticoke, Pa., Apr. 9, 1935; s. Stanley Francis and Stephania Mary (Jachimczak) Dudrick; m. Theresa M. Keen, June 14, 1958; children: Susan Marie, Paul Stanley, Carolyn Mary, Stanley Jonathan, Holly Anne, Anne Theresa. BS cum laude, Franklin and Marshall Coll., 1957; MD, U. Pa., 1961; MA (hon.), Yale U., 1999. Diplomate Am. Bd. Surgery. Intern Hosp. U. Pa., Phila., 1961—62, resident gen. surgery, 1962—67; acad. practice specializing in surgery Phila., 1967—72; prof. surgery U. Tex. Med. Sch., Houston, 1972—82, clin. prof. surgery, 1982—95; dir. Med. Edn. St. Mary's Hosp., Waterbury, 1995—2000; chmn. surgery dept., dir. surg. edn. Bridgeport Hosp.-Yale U. New Haven Health Sys., 2000—02; dir. Med. Edn. St. Mary's Hosp., Waterbury, 2002—. Acad. practice specializing in surgery, Houston, 1972—88, Houston, 1990—94, Phila., 1988—90, New Haven, 1994—2000, Waterbury, 2000—02, Bridgeport, 2002; cons. in surgery M. D. Anderson Hosp. and Tumor Inst., 1973—88, clin. prof. surgery, cons. to pres., 1982—88; chief. surg. svcs. Hermann Hosp., Houston, 1972—80; surgeon-in-chief, dir. Ctr. Cardiovasc. Disease, dir. nutritional support svcs. Nutritional Sci. Ctr., 1990—94; chmn. dept. surgery U. Tex. Med. Sch., Houston, 1972—80; sr. cons. surgery and medicine Tex. Inst. Rehab. and Rsch., 1974—88; mem. anat. bd. State of Tex., 1973—78; examiner Am. Bd. Surgery, 1974—78, bd. dirs., 1978—84, sr. mem., 1984—2002, mem. and chmn. various. com.s; chmn. sci. adv. com. Tex. Med. Ctr. Libr., 1974; mem. food and nutrition bd. NRC-Nat. Acad. Scis., 1973—75; mem. sci. adv. com. Nat. Found. Ileitis and Colitis; mem. surgery, anesthesia and trauma study sect. NIH, 1982—86; chmn. dept. surgery Pa. Hosp., Phila., 1988—90, surgeon-in-chief, 1988—91, hon. surgery staff, 1991—; clin. prof. surgery U. Pa., 1988—93, assoc. chmn. dept. surgery, 1994—2000, 2002—04, chmn. dept. surgery, 2004—, dir. surgery program, 1994—2000, 2002—; clin. prof. Yale U., New Haven, 1995—99, prof., 1999—; adj. prof. Quinnipiac U., 1996—. Editor: Manual of Surgical Nutrition, 1975, Manual of Preoperative and Postoperative Care, 1983, Current Strategies in Surgical Nutrition, 1991, Practical Handbook of Nutrition in Clinical Practice, 1994, Surgical Nutrition: Strategies in Critically Ill Patients, 1995; assoc. editor: Nutrition in Medicine, 1975—; mem. editl. bd. Annals of Surgery, 1975—, Infusion, 1978—, Nutrition and Cancer, 1980—2002, Nutrition Support Services, 1980—86, Jour. Clin. Surgery, 1980—83, Nutrition Rsch., 1981—, Intermed. Comm. Nursing Svcs., 1981—, Postgrad. Gen. Surgery, 1992—, others; contbr. chapters to books, articles to profl. jours. Bd. dirs. Found. Children, Houston, Harris County unit Am. Cancer Soc., Phila., 1988—90; founder Benjamin Rush Soc., 1987, hon. chmn., 1999—; trustee Franklin and Marshall Coll., 1985—, mem. student life, art collection and trusteeship coms., mem. exec. com., mem. overseers bd., 1986—2002, mem. alumni programs and devel. com., 1991—2002, pres. regional adv. coun., 1992—94, vice chmn., 1994—2002, John Marshall Soc., 1993—, campaign nat. chmn., 1995—2002, mem. bldgs. and grounds com., 2002—, acad. investments com., 2002—. Decorated knight Order St. John of Jerusalem Knights Hospitalier; named Stanley J. Dudrick MD Surg. Edn. and Rsch. Fund in his honor, St. Mary's Hosp., 2003, Disting. Alumnus, U. Pa. Med. Sch., 2007; recipient VA citation for Significant Contbn. to Med. Care, 1970, Mead Johnson award for Rsch. in Hosp. Pharmacy, 1972, Seale Harris medal, So. Med. Assn., 1973, AMA-Brookdale award in Medicine, 1975, Great Texan award, Nat. Found. Ileitis and Colitis, 1975, Modern Medicine award, 1977, Disting. Alumnus citation, Franklin and Marshall Coll., 1980, Alumni medal, 2002, Presdl. medal, 2007, WHO, Houston, 1980, Stinchfield award, Am. Acad. Orthopedic Surgery, 1981, Bernstein award, Med. Soc. State of NY, 1986, Alumni Svc. award, U. Pa. Med. Sch., 1996, Excellence in Surgery Tchg. award, St. Mary's Hosp., 1999, Roswell Park award, Buffalo Surgery Soc., 2000, Nos Magni Nominis Umbra Tchg. and Rsch. award, Yale Gen. Surgery Residents, 2000, Alumni medal, Franklin and Marshall Coll., 2002, Jacobson Innovation award, ACS, 2005, others. Fellow ACS (vice chmn. pre and post operative com. 1975, gov. 1979-85, com. med. motion pictures 1981-90, SESAP com. 1990-94, co-chmn. multiple choice com. 1993-94), Fellows Leadership Soc. (life, mem. Conn. chpt.), Philippine Coll. Surgeons (hon.), Coll. Medicine and Surgery Costa Rica (hon.), Am. Coll. Nutrition (Grace A. Goldsmith award 1982), Leadership Soc. (life), Phi Beta Kappa; mem. AMA (coun. food and nutrition 1971-76, exec. com. 1975-76, coun. sci. affairs 1976-81, Goldberger award clin. nutrition 1970), AAAS, AAUP, Am. Surg. Assn. (Flance-Karl award 1997), Am. Acad. Pediat. (hon., Ladd medal 1988), Am. Pediat. Surg. Assn. (hon.), Am. Soc. Nutritional Support Svcs. (bd. dirs. 1982-87, pres. 1984, Outstanding Humanitarian award 1984) Soc. Univ. Surgeons (exec. coun. 1974-78), Assn. for Acad. Surgery (founders group), Assn. Polish Surgeons (hon.), Internat. Soc. Surgeons, Internat. Fedn. Surg. Colls., Internat. Soc. Parenteral Nutrition (exec. coun. 1975-81, pres. 1978-81), Internat. Fedn. Surgery Soc., So. Med. Assn. (chmn. surgery sect. 1984-85), Houston Gastroent. Soc., Houston Surg. Soc., Tex. Surg. Soc., Tex. Med. Assn. (com. nutrition and food resources), Tex. Med. Found., Harris County Med. Soc., New Haven County Med. Soc., Conn. Soc. Am. Bd. Surgeons, New Eng. Surg. Soc., L.A. Surg. Soc. (hon.), Am. Radium Soc., Am. Soc. Clin. Oncology, Am. Soc. Parenteral and Enteral Nutrition (pres. 1977, bd. advs. 1978—, chmn. bd. advisers 1978, Vars award 1982, Rhoads lectr. 1985, 2005, Dudrick Rsch. Scholar award named in his honor), Pa. Nutritionists Soc. (pres. 1985), Am. Gastroent. Assn., Soc. Surg. Oncology, James Ewing Soc., Ravdin-Rhoads Surg. Assn., Excelsior Surg. Soc. (Edward D. Churchill lectr. 1981), Soc. Laparoendoscopic Surgery, Soc. Surg. Chairmen, So. Surg. Assn., Southwe. Surg. Congress, Southea. Surg. Congress, Surg. Biology Club II, Surg. Infection Soc. (chmn. membership com. 1987-90), We. Surg. Soc., Halsted Soc., Allen O. Whipple Surg. Soc., Am. Inst. Nutrition, Soc. Clin. Surgery, Am. Soc. Clin. Investigation, Soc. Surgery Alimentary Tract, Am. Trauma Soc. (founders group), Am. Assn. Surgery Trauma, Soc. Clin. Surgery, Am. Soc. Clin. Nutrition, Fedn. Am. Soc. Exptl. Biology, Am. Burn Assn., Assn. Program Dirs. Surgery (bd. dirs.), John Marshall Soc., Coll. Physicians Phila., Phila. Acad. Surgeons, George Hermann Soc., Polish Soc. Parenteral and Enteral Nutrition (hon.), Polish Soc. Surgery (hon.), Union League Phila., Med. Club Phila., Franklin Club Phila., Houston Doctors Club (gov. 1973-76), Nat. Alumni Coun. U. Pa. Med. Sch. (chmn. 1994-2001), Conn. United for Rsch. Excellence (bd. dirs. 1995-2001), Waterbury Symphony Orch. (bd. dirs., 1999-, chmn. endowment com. 2002-05), Cosmos Club, Athenaeum, The Penn Club (charter), Phi Beta Kappa Assocs., Sigma Xi, Alpha Omega Alpha. (sec.-treas. Houston chpt. 1982-83) Achievements include invention of new technique of intravenous feeding and anti-cholesterol therapy. Home: 40 Beecher St Naugatuck CT 06770-2721 Office: St Mary's Hosp 56 Franklin St Waterbury CT 06706 Office Phone: 203-709-6479. Business E-Mail: sdudrick@stmh.org.

DUDUIT, MICHAEL, editor, academic administrator; b. Sandwich, Ill., Aug. 18, 1954; s. James Loren and Sarah Lee (Baker) D.; m. Laura Ann Niemann, Aug. 10, 1959; 1 child, James Robert. BA in Speech, Stetson U., DeLand, Fla., 1975; MDiv, So. Bapt. Sem., 1979; PhD in Humanities, Fla. State U., Tallahassee, 1983. Ordained to ministry Bapt. Ch., 1977. Dir. news So. Bapt. Sem., Louisville, 1975—77; dir. pub. affairs Palm Beach Atlantic Coll., West Palm Beach, Fla., 1977—80; asst. to pres. Cuneo Advt., Tallahassee, 1980—81; assoc. pastor Immanuel Bapt. Ch., Tallahassee, 1981—84; dir. comm. So. Bapt. Sem., 1984—87; dir. devel. Samford U., Birmingham, Ala., 1987—93; exec. v.p. Union U., Jackson, Tenn., 1996—2001; pres., CEO Am. Ministry Resources LLC, Franklin, 2002—06; editor Preaching Mag., Franklin, 1985—; editor-in-chief Preaching Mag., Salem Comm., Nashville, 2006—. Author: Joy in Ministry, 1991, Preaching With Power, 2006; editor: Handbook of Contemporary Preaching, 1993, Abingdon Preaching Annual, 1995, 96, 97, 98, 99, Communicate with Power, 1996. Mem. Bapt. Communicators Assn. (pres. 1994-95), Acad. of Homiletics, Evang. Homiletics Soc.

DUDUKOVIC, MILORAD P., chemical engineering educator, consultant; b. Beograd, Yugoslavia, Mar. 25, 1944; arrived in U.S., 1968; s. Predrag R. and Melita Maria Dudukovic; m. Judith Ann Reiff, Dec. 27, 1969; children: Aleksandra Anne, Nicole Maria. BS in Engrng., U. Beograd, 1967; MS, Ill. Inst. Tech., 1970, PhD, 1972. Rsch. engr. Process Design Inst., Beograd, 1967-68; instr. Ill. Inst. Tech., Chgo., 1970-72; asst. prof. Ohio U., Athens, 1972-74; assoc. prof. Washington U., St. Louis, 1974-80, prof., dir., 1980—, Laura and William Jens prof. environ. engrng., 1993—, chmn. dept. chem. engrng., 1998—2006. Cons. in field. Assoc. editor: Indsl. and Engineering Chemistry Research, 1991—; contbr. articles to profl. jours. Recipient Burlington No. Found. Tchg. award, 1986, Nat. Catalyst award Chem. Mfrs. Assn., 1988, St. Louis award ACS, 1995, Malcolm E. Pruitt award Coun. Chem. Rsch., 1999; 2 NASA certs. of recognition and citations; Fulbright scholar Inst. for Higher Edn., 1968. Fellow AIChE (R.H. Wilhelm award 1994, Fuels & Petrochem. Divsn. award, 2005), St. Louis Acad. Scis.; mem. AAAS, Am. Chem. Soc., Am. Assn. Engrng. Edn., Yugoslav Acad. Engrng. (fgn. mem.), Sigma Xi, Century Club (St. Louis). Achievements include pioneering work on trickle bed reactors, bubble columns; research in Czochralski crystal growth, novel experimental techniques for multiphase reactors; environmentally benign processing. Office: Washington U Dept Chem Engrng Campus Box 1198 One Brookings Dr Saint Louis MO 63130-4899 Business E-Mail: dudu@wustl.edu.

DUDZIAK, DONALD JOHN, nuclear engineer, educator; b. Alden, NY, Jan. 6, 1935; s. Joseph and Josephine Mary (Ratajczak) Dudziak; m. Judith Ann Staib, Aug. 22, 1959; children: Alan Joseph, Matthew John, Karin Marie. BS in Marine Engrng., US Mcht. Marine Acad., 1956; MS in Radiation Biology/Radiol. Physics, U. Rochester, NY, 1957; PhD in Applied Math., U. Pitts., 1963. Registered profl. engr., Calif., USCG lic. engr. steam & diesel 1956-92. Commd. ensign USN, 1956, advanced through grades to capt.; sr. engr. Bettis Atomic Power Lab., Pitts., 1957-65; staff mem. U. Calif.-Los Alamos Nat. Lab., 1965-68, 69-74, assoc. and alt. group leader, 1974-78, group leader, 1978-82, theoretical divsn. tech. advisor, 1982, dep. group leader, sect. leader, 1983—88, lab. fellow, 1988—; ret. USN, 1995; prof., head dept. nuclear engrng. NC State U., Raleigh, 1990—2001; pres. Pinorealosa Corp, 1989-90. Vis. prof. U. Va., Charlottesville, 1968-69; adj. prof. U. N.Mex., 1966, Kans. State U., 1989-90; guest scientist Swiss Fed. Inst. Reactor Rsch., Wuerenlingen, 1981-82; mem. lab. microfusion facility steering com. US Dept. Energy, 1986-90, inertial confinement fusion adv. com., 1992-96; vice-chair accelerator prodn. of tritium rev. panel Los Alamos Nat. Lab., 1995-98; chmn. fusion tech. working group Neutronics, Brookhaven, NY, 1975; mem. Nat. Nuc. Accrediting Bd., Nat. Acad. Nuc. Tng., 1998-2004; cons. nuc. power schs. USN, 1962-65; cons. Oak Ridge Nat. Lab., 1993-96, TSI Rsch. Co., 1992-, US Nuc. Regulatory Commn., 1997, Am. Coun. on Edn., 1995-, Duke U., 1997-98. Editor: Reactor Principles, 1964, Radiation Shielding, 1964, Progress in Nuclear Energy, 1992—; contbr. editor Fusion Tech., 1987-2001; contbr. articles to profl. jours. Vice-chmn. Los Alamos County Planning and Zoning Commn., 1969-74. Fellow Am. Nuc. Soc. (divsn. chair 1972-73, 77-78, 92-93, gen. chair fusion energy divsn. nat. meeting 1994); mem. Am. Soc. Engrng. Edn., US Naval Inst., Los Alamos Sunrise Kiwanis (treas. 1987-89), Sigma Xi, Phi Kappa Phi. Libertarian. Avocations: hunting, hiking, skeet shooting, rifle shooting, pistol shooting. Office: Los Alamos Nat Lab Tech Assessment Group AET-2 MS F609 Los Alamos NM 87545 Business E-Mail: dudziak@lanl.gov.

DUDZIAK, MARY LOUISE, law educator; b. Oakland, Calif., June 15, 1956; d. Walter F. Dudziak and Barbara Ann Campbell; 1 child, Alicia. AB in Sociology with highest honors, U. Calif., Berkeley, 1978; JD, Yale Law Sch., 1984; MA, MPhil in Am. Studies, Yale U., 1986, PhD in Am. Studies, 1992. Adminstrv. asst. to dep. dir. Ctr. Ind. Living, Berkeley, 1978-80; law clk., nat. legal staff ACLU, NYC, 1983; law clk. Judge Sam J. Ervin, III Fourth Cir. Ct. Appeals, Morganton, N.C., 1984-85; assoc. prof. coll. law U. Iowa, Iowa City, 1986-90, prof. coll. law, 1990-98. Vis. prof. U. So. Calif., 1997-98, Harvard Law Sch., 2005-; prof. U. So. Calif., 1998-2002, Judge Edward J. and Ruey L. Guirado prof. law and history, 2002-; vis. scholar Kennedy Sch. Govt., Harvard U., 2006-; mem. faculty senate task force on faculty devel. U. Iowa, 1989-90, mem. faculty welfare com., 1990-92, mem. faculty senate task force on faculty spouses and ptnrs., 1991-92, mem. presdl. lecture com., 1992-95; v.p. rsch. adv. com. in social scis., 1992-94; fellow law and pub. affairs program Princeton U., 2002; presenter in field. Author: Cold War Civil Rights: Race and the Image of American Democracy, 2000; editor, co-author: September 11 in History: A Watershed Moment?, 2003; co-editor Legal Borderlands: Law and the Construction of American Borders, 2006, mem. bd. mng. editors Am. Quar., 2003—; contbr. articles to profl. jours. Bd. dirs. Iowa Civil Liberties Union, 1987-88; chairperson office svcs. for persons with disabilities program rev. com., U. Iowa, 1987-88, law sch. ombudsperson, 1991. Charlotte W. Newcombe Doctoral Dissertation fellow Woodrow Wilson Fellowship Found., 1985-86; Old Gold fellow U. Iowa, 1987, 88, 89, Moody Grant Lyndon Baines Johnson Fdn., 1998, Theodore C. Sorenson Fell., JFK Libr. Fdn., 1997, Orgn. Am. Historians-Japanese Assn. for Am. Studies fellow 2000; travel grantee Eisenhower World Affairs Inst., 1993; recipient Scholars Devel. award Harry S. Truman Libr. Inst., 1990. Fellow Am. Coun. on Learned Soc., 2006-, Mem. Am. Soc. Legal History (mem. com. on documentary preservation 1988-2000, mem. program com. for 1988 conf., mem. exec. com., bd. dirs. 1990-92, 95-97, chairperson program com. 1993, mem. nominating com. 1999-2001, chair nominating com. 2001), Am. Hist. Assn. (Littleton-Griswold rsch. grantee 1987), Am. Studies Assn. (mem. nominating com. 1999-2002, chair nominating com. 2002), Assn. Am. Law Schs. (sec.-treas. legal history sect. 1987, vice chair 1988, chair 1989), Law and Soc. Assn. (bd. trustees, 2005-, mem. com., 2004-06, mem. Hurst prize com. 1992), Orgn. Am. Historians, Soc. Am. Law Tchrs., Soc. for Historians Am. Fgn. Rels. Democrat. Office: U So Calif Law Sch Los Angeles CA 90089-0001

DUEL, WARD CALVIN, retired healthcare consultant; b. Fond du Lac, Wis., Mar. 13, 1924; s. Myrton M. and Matie Rose (Tidyman) D.; m. Madelyn Mae Kressin, Oct. 1, 1950; children: Ward Rick, Christine Selma, Roxanne Matie, Beth Dawn. BS, U. Wis., 1950; postgrad., Marquette U., 1955-57; MPH, U. Calif., Berkeley, 1959. Registered environ. health specialist, Calif., Nat. Environ. Health Assn. Sanitarian City of Kenosha (Wis.), 1951-59; br. office mgr. Lake County Health Dept., Waukegan, Ill., 1959-65; dir. health Skokie (Ill.) Dept. Health, 1965-68; dir. McHenry County Health Dept., Woodstock, Ill., 1968-70; asst. dir. pub. and environ. health AMA, Chgo., 1971-81; chief environ. health City of Chgo., 1981-82; dir. Mid-Ohio Valley Dept. Health, Parkersburg, W.Va., 1982-83; dir. environ. health, pub. and mental health Choctaw Indians, Philadelphia, Miss., 1984—2005; cons. on environ. health various jails, prisons, juv. detention ctrs., and secure mental hosps. in 44 states and D.C., 1995—2002; ret., 2002. Capt. US Pub. Health Svc. Commn. Corps Res., 1958—; cons. in field; lectr. in field. Co-editor: Clinical Implications of Air Pollution Research; author monographs: Physicians Guide to Solid Waste, 1975, Physicians Guide to Air Pollution, 1973-80, Flood Area Health Guide, 1961; contbr. articles to profl. jours. Served in U.S. Army, 1944-45. Decorated 3 Battle Stars and Bronze Star for heroism; recipient Theta award Defenders, 1969, Samuel J. Crumbine award Single Svc. Inst., 1963, Walter S. Mangold award Nat. Environ. Health Assn., 1978, Outstanding Citizen award Ill. Dept. Edn., 1984, Jour. Environ. Health Editors award, 1979, Pres. Vol. Svc. award, 2005. Fellow Am. Pub. Health Assn. (Disting. Svc. award 2002); mem. Nat. Environ. Health Assn. (pres. 1967-68), Wis. Environ. Health Assn. (pres. 1957-58), Ill. Environ. Health Assn. (pres. 1964-65), Am. Correctional Assn., Am. Jail Assn. (nat. stds. com. 1993—). Lutheran.

DUELFER, CHARLES ALFRED, aerospace transportation executive, weapons inspector, director; b. Stamford, Conn., Sept. 18, 1952; s. Charles A. and Grace H. Duelfer. BA, U. Conn., 1974; MS, MIT, 1977. Nat. security analyst Office of Mgmt. and Budget, Washington, 1977—82; polit.-mil. affairs officer US Dept. State, Washington, 1982—85, dir. Office of Internat. Security Policy, 1985—90, dep. to asst. sec. of state, 1990—93; dep. chmn. UN spl. commn. on Iraq-UN, NYC, 1993—2000; dir. CIA Iraq Survey Group, 2004—05; CEO T/Space Inc., 2005—. Polit.-mil. expert various TV and radio programs, 2000—; vis. scholar Ctr. for Strategic and Internat. Studies, Washington, 2000—03. Contbr. articles to profl. jours., 2000. Mem.: Coun. Fgn. Rels. Avocations: skydiving, ice hockey, painting. Business E-Mail: charles.duelfer@transformspace.com.

DUEMLING, ROBERT WERNER, diplomat, museum director; b. Ann Arbor, Mich., Feb. 8, 1929; s. Werner William and Anne (Lindemulder) D.; m. Louisa duPont Copeland, May 15, 1982. BA, Yale U., 1950, MA, 1953; student, Cambridge U., Eng., 1950-51. Joined fgn. service Dept. State, Washington, 1957, with, 1957-60, 66-70, Am. embassy, Rome, 1960-63, Kuala Lumpur, 1963-65, Tokyo, 1970-74; U.S. consul Kuching, Malaysia, 1965-66; exec. asst. to dep. sec. state Dept. State, Washington, 1974-76; dep. chief of mission with rank of minister Am. embassy, Ottawa, Ont., Canada, 1976-80; chief Fgn. Contingents, Multinat. Force and Observers, Sinai, 1981-82; U.S. ambassador to Suriname, to Paramaribo, 1982-84; dir. Nicaraguan Humanitarian Assistance Office, Dept. State, 1985-87; pres., dir. Nat. Bldg. Mus., Washington, 1987-94. Sr. fellow Washington Coll., 1983—. Trustee Cafritz Found., Washington Nat. Monument Assn., Nat. Gallery of Art, Soc. Archtl. Historians. Served in U.S. Navy, 1953-57. Henry fellow, 1950-51; decorated Order of the Palm (Suriname). Fellow Royal Soc. for Arts (U.K.); mem. Washington Inst. Fgn. Affairs, Met. Club (trustee), Century Assn., Alibi Club. Home: 2950 University Ter NW Washington DC 20016-3461

DUENAS, LAURENT FLORES, health and nursing consultant; b. Yigo, Guam, Jan. 9, 1947; d. Joaquin Garcia and Maria Acosta (Calvo) Flores; m. Jimmy J. Duenas, Jan. 9, 1971; children: James Richard, Sherry Marie, Kenneth Ray. ADN, U. Guam, 1968; BSN, Mont. State U., 1969; MPH, U. Hawaii, Manao, 1984. RN, Guam, 1968, Mont., 1969; CNA, NLN; cert. SMDP trng., Internat. Pub. Health. Staff nurse Dept. Pub. Health and Social Svc., Guam, 1969—70, nurse supr. I Guam, 1970—71, nurse supr. II Guam, 1972—78, asst. adminstr. Bur. Cmty. Health and Nursing Svc. Guam, 1978—89, detailed adminstr. Guam, 1986—88, adminstr. Guam, 1989—95, ret. Guam, 1995. Health and nursing cons. Guam Legislature and U. Guam, 1996—,"HLATTE" project dir. U. GU, 2003-; adj. faculty health adminstrn., 1999-, bd. dir., chair Pacific Basin Maternal Child Health Resource Ctr., Mangilao, Guam, 1984-96, Pacific Basin MCH coord., Honolulu, 1984-95; mem. State and Territorial Dir. Nursing, 1987-98; mem. Interagy. Leadership Consortium for Individual's with Spl. Needs, 1990-98; mem. Maternal Child Health Task Force, 1996-98, Governor's Vision, 2000; Health Task Force, 1996-2000; chair Nurse Leaders Com., 1995-98, mem., 1998-2000; preceptor nursing students U.Guam, 1995—; bd. dir. Pacific Island Primary Care Assn., 2003-, bd. dir. Pacific Assn. Clin. Tng., 2003-; affiliate mem. Pacific Island Health Officers APNLC, 2003-; presenter in field. Author: Caring for Young Children, modified version, 1998. Recipient Centennial Award Nat. League of Nursing, 1994, Governor's Chief Gadao Disting. Award, 1995. Mem. ANA, APHA, Y'netnon Famaloan Dem. Women Leaders, Am. Pacific Nursing Leaders (coun. pres. 2001-05, treas., 1986-92, vice mem. 1986—), Commn. on Licensure, Guam Bd. Nurses Examiners (bd. dir., chair 1981-90), Guam Nurses Assn. (bd. dir. 1992-94, Leadership Award 1988, Nursing Excellence Award 1990, Guam Nurse of Yr. 1993, Pub. Health Unit Award 1994, Guam Legis. Resolution 1995, 98, CDC Minority Health Champions Health Equity award, 2004), Orgn. Health and Med. Profl. Women (treas. 2003—), Pacific Island Health Officers Assn., Pacific Island Primary Care Assn. (bd. dirs., v.p., 2003), Pacific Assn. Clin. Tng. (bd. dirs., 2003-), Assn. Tchrs. Preventative Medicine. Democrat. Roman Catholic. Avocations: crocheting, collecting recipes, baking, campaign strategies, visiting sick. Home: 3 N Cupa Perez Acres Yigo GU 96929-0142 Office: Univ Guam HLATTE Project UOG Sta Mangilao GU 96923 Business E-Mail: hlatte05@gmail.com.

DUENSING, DOROTHY JEAN, music educator, vocalist; d. George Prescott Duensing I and Patricia Ann (dec.) Gasthoff-Duensing, Catherine Dew-Duensing (Stepmother); m. Michael William Miller, Nov. 9, 1997 (div. Nov. 18, 2004); m. Thomas Andrew Cormie, Oct. 10, 1987 (div. Oct. 3, 1996); 1 child, Mason Andrew Cormie. MusB, Ind. U., 1984; MusM, U. of Mich., 1990. Orff Schulwerk Music-Level I Madonna U., Livonia, Mich., 2001, Orff Schulwerk Music-Level II Madonna U., Livonia, Mich., 2002, Orff Schulwerk Music-Level III Madonna U., Livonia, Mich., 2003. Adj. prof. voice Wayne State U. Dept. Music, Detroit, 1999—; educator, primary music dir. Acad. Sacred Heart, Bloomfield Hills, Mich., 2000—03; dir. mid. sch. vocal music Sherman Mid. Sch., 2004—, Richter Intermediate Sch. Holly Area Schs., Holly, Mich., 2004—. Soprano soloist, sect. leader Christ Episcopal Ch., Dearborn, Mich., 1986—94; part-time voice faculty Ctr. for Creative Studies' Inst. of Music and Dance, Detroit, 1990—2000; alto soloist, sect. leader Temple Israel, West Bloomfield, Mich., 1991—97; artist-in-residence Toledo Opera Co., 1991—99; performing artist Omni Arts in Edn., Southfield, Mich., 1992—; full-time vocal music substitute U. Liggett Mid. and Upper Schools, Grosse Pointe Farms, Mich., 1996; part-time voice, piano faculty Ward Church's Christian Sch. of Fine and Performing Arts, Northville Twp., Mich., 1998—2002; adj. prof. voice William Tyndale Coll., Farmington Hills, Mich., 2001—02; alto soloist, sect. leader Met. United Meth. Ch., Detroit, 2001—02, First Presbyn. Ch., Royal Oak, Mich., 2002—. Choral music dir. Music Study Club, Detroit, 1995—96, Bel Canto Choral Group, Southfield, Mich., 1998—2001; deacon Faith Cmty. Presbyn. Ch., Novi, Mich., 1998—2000; teen choir dir. Faith Cmty. Presbyn., Novi, Mich., 1999—2000. Recipient Hazel Mueller Meml. award, Interlochen Ctr. for the Performing Arts, 1979, 1980, First Pl. Vocalist in the State of Mich., Mich. Schs. Vocal Music Assn., 1980, Dist. Finalist, Met. Opera Assn. (Midwest Dist.), 1991, Second Pl. Winner, Harold Haugh Light Opera Vocal Competition, Ann Arbor, MI, 2001; scholar Interlochen Alumnae Scholarship for Half Tuition at Nat. Music Camp, Interlochen Ctr. for the Performing Arts, 1979, Scholarship, Iota Epsilon Patroness Chpt., Bloomington, IN, 1983, Patricia Brinton-Becirovic Meml. Scholarship, Am. Inst. of Musical Studies, Austria, 1989. Mem.: Livonia Area Piano Tchrs. Forum, Mich. Music Tchrs. Assn., Music Tchrs. Nat. Assn., Detroit Orff Schulwerk Assn., Nat. Orff Schulwerk Assn., Nat. Assn. Tchrs. Singing, Nat. Fedn. Music Clubs' Tuesday Musicale Detroit, PEO Sisterhood, Chpt. FE, Novi, MI (life; chaplain 2001—02), Sigma Alpha Iota (life; Detroit Alumnae chptr. v.p. mem. 2002—). Office: Wayne State U Dept of Music 1321 Old Main Bldg Studio #2315 Detroit MI 48202 Mailing: PO Box 107 Novi MI 48376-0107 Personal E-mail: Divaduensing@aol.com.

DUERINCK, LOUIS T., retired rail transportation executive, lawyer; b. Chgo., Aug. 1, 1929; s. Aloys L. and Thais E. (De Backer) D.; m. Patricia A. Bird, June 27, 1953; children: Louis M., Kathleen M. Lutgen, Kevin F., Mark V., Lynn P. Dressel, Brian T., Paul S. Student, U. Notre Dame, 1947-48; JD, DePaul U., Chgo., 1952. Bar: Ill. 1952. Commerce atty. N.Y. Cen. R.R., Chgo., 1955-65; gen. atty. Nat. Ry. Labor Conf., Chgo., 1967-68; with C&NW Ry. Co., Chgo., 1965-67, 68-89; sr. v.p. law and real estate C&NW Transp. Co., 1979-83, sr. v.p. traffic, 1983-88, sr. v.p., 1988-89, also bd. dirs. With AUS, 1952—55. Mem. ABA, Assn. Transportation Law Profls., Ill. Bar Assn., Glen Oak Country Club, Wyndemere Country Club Roman Catholic. Home and Office: 718 Midwest Club Pky Oak Brook IL 60523-2531 Personal E-mail: duerlou@aol.com.

DUERKSEN, GEORGE LOUIS, music therapist, educator; b. St. Joseph, Mo., Oct. 29, 1934; s. George Herbert and Louise May (Dalke) D.; m. Patricia Gay Beers, June 3, 1961; children— Mark Jeffrey, Joseph Scott, Cynthia Elizabeth Student, Tabor Coll., 1951-52; BMusEdn, U. Kans., 1955, MMusEdn, 1956, PhD in Music Edn., 1967. Cert. music educator Kans., Mo., registered music therapist Nat. Assn. Music Therapy, 1975, bd. cert. music therapist Cert. Bd. Music Therapists, 1987. Tchr. music Tonganoxie HS, Kans., 1955-56, Stafford Jr. and Sr. HS, Kans., 1959-60, Labette County HS, Altamont, Kans., 1960-62, Shawnee Mission North HS, Kans., 1962-63; asst. prof., dir. psychology of music lab. Mich. State U., East Lansing, 1965-69; prof., chmn. dept. art and music edn. and music therapy U. Kans., Lawrence, 1969-93, dir. Singing Jayhawks, 1979-83, prof., dir. music edn. and music therapy divsn., 1993—2004, prof., interim chair dept. music and dance, 2000-01, prof., dir. grad. studies, music edn. and music therapy, dir. Ctr. for Rsch. on Music Behavior, 2001—; assoc. dir. Kans. North Ctrl. Assn. Colls. and Schs., 1992-2000. Cons., vis. prof. U. Hawaii, Honolulu, summer 1978; cons., vis. prof. U. Melbourne, Australia, summer 1981; cons., lectr. N.Z. Soc. for Music Therapy, Wellington, 1983, Ctr. for Contemporary Music Rsch., Athens, 1991, U. Thessaloniki, Greece, 1993, Korean Assn. for Music Therapy, 1994, 97, Sook Myung U., Seoul, 1997; cons. functional music applications, 1967—, Deakin U., Geelong, Victoria, Australia, 1990. Author: (monograph) Teaching Instrumental Music, 1973; Music for Exceptional Children, 1981; contbr. articles to profl. jours., chpts. to books. Fulbright scholar Inst. for Internat. Edn., Australia, 1956-57; U.Kans. fellow, Lawrence, 1963-64; U.S. Office Edn. grantee, 1966-67, 73-75, 78-81. Mem. AAAS, Music Educators Nat. Conf., Am. Music Therapy Assn.(award of merit, 2000), Music Edn. Rsch. Coun. (chmn. 1980-82), Brit. Soc. for Music Therapy, Coun. for Rsch. in Music Edn., Pi Kappa Lambda, Phi Mu Alpha, Phi Delta Kappa. Avocations: photography, boating, travel. Home Phone: 785-843-0418; Office Phone: 785-864-9632. E-mail: gduerksen@ku.edu.

DUERR, DAVID, civil engineer; b. Newark, July 4, 1953; s. Warren August and Dorothy (Lanzillo) D.; m. Roberta Kay Apolant, Oct. 12, 1991. B of Engring., Pratt Inst., 1975; MS, U. Houston, 1985. Registered profl. engr. Project engr. Hoffman Internat., Pt. Newark, N.J., 1974-76; chief engr. Williams Crane & Rigging, Richmond, Va., 1976-79; sr. structural engr. Hudson Engrng. Corp., Houston, 1980-86; pres. 2DM Assocs., Inc., Houston, 1986—. Frequent lectr. constrn. industry seminars. Contbr. tech. papers to profl. jours. Mem.: ASME (chair BTH stds. com. on below-the-hook lifting devices, mem. B30.1 subcom.), ASCE, Specialized Carriers and Rigging Assn., Soc. Naval Archs. and Marine Engrs., Soc. Automotive Engrs., Am. Coun. Engrng. Cos. Achievements include research in the design of pinned connections and development of standards for the design of telescopic hydraulic gantries. Office: 2DM Assocs Inc 9235 Katy Freeway Ste 350 Houston TX 77024-1526

DUERR, DIANNE MARIE, sports medicine consultant, educator; b. Buffalo, July 14, 1945; d. Robert John and Aileen Louise D. BS in Health and Phys. Edn., SUNY, Brockport, 1967; cert., SUNY, Oswego, 1982; postgrad., Canisius Coll., 1970-71. Cert. tchr. NY. Tchr. North Syracuse (NY) Sch. Dist., 1967—2004; project dir. dept. orthop. surgery SUNY Upstate Med. U., Syracuse, 1982—2003; creator Inst. for Human Performance SUNY Health Sci. Ctr., Syracuse, 1988. Coord. scholastic sports injury reporting system project SUNY, 1985-98; mem. com. on scholastic sports-related injuries NIH Inst. Arthritis, Musculoskeletal and Skin Diseases, 1993-96; project dir. dept. orthop. surgery North Syracuse Ctrl. Sch. Dist., 1967-2004. Author: SSIRS Pilot Study Report, 1987, SSIRS Fall Study Report, 1988, SHASIRS Report, 1991; creator Scholastic Sports Injury Reporting System, 1985, Scholastic Head and Spine Injury Reporting System, 1989. Co-chmn. sports medicine USA Amateur Athletic Union, Nat. Jr. Olympic Games, Syracuse, NY, 1987; vol. sports medicine NY State Sr. Games, 1990—95, sports medicine coord., 1990—95, US Roller Skating Nat. Championships, 1995, NY State Womens Lacrosse Championships, 1995, US Nat. Precision Ice Skating Championships, 1997, Youth Basketball of Am., Northeast Regional Tournament, 1999; co-chmn. healthcare, security Empire State Games, Syracuse, 2002; mem. com. sports injury surveillance Ctrs. for Disease Control, 1995; cons. NY Sci., Tech. and Soc. Edn. Project, 1995. Mem. AAUW, NY State AAHPERD (pres. exercise sci. and sports medicine sect., 1994-98), Am. Coll. Sports Medicine, United Univ. Profs., Women's Sports Fedn., Am. Fedn. Tchrs., NY United Tchrs., North Syracuse Tchrs. Assn., Phi Kappa Phi. Avocations: swimming, bicycling, ice skating, reading, photography. Office: 418 Buffington Rd Syracuse NY 13224-2208 Home Phone: 315-449-9509; Office Phone: 315-449-9509. Personal E-mail: dmduerr@twcny.rr.com.

DUERR, HERMAN GEORGE, retired publishing executive; b. Nagold, Germany, June 24, 1931; came to U.S., 1949, naturalized, 1975; s. Adolf Gustav and Wilhelmine Dorothea (Walz) Durr; m. Shirley Yvonne Jones, June 29, 1957; children: Suzanne, Steffan, Krista. B.F.A., Wayne State U., 1958. Pubs. designer Ceco Comm. Inc., Warren, Mich., 1958-60; art dir. Am. Youth mag., 1960-67, Friends mag., 1967-86, exec. editor, 1978-87; v.p. Ceco Comm., Inc., 1981-91; dir. mktg. prodn. Ceco Pub. Co., 1987-91. Adj. faculty Mid Mich. C.C., 1991—. Served with U.S. Army, 1952-55.

DUESENBERG, RICHARD WILLIAM, lawyer; b. St. Louis, Dec. 10, 1930; s. (John August) Hugo and Edna Marie (Warmann) D.; m. Phyllis Evelyn Buehner, Aug. 7, 1955; children: Karen, Daryl, Mark, David. BA, Valparaiso U., Ind., 1951, JD, 1953, LLD, 2001; LLM, Yale U., New Haven, Conn., 1956. Bar: Mo. 1953. Prof. law NYU, NYC, 1956-62, dir. law ctr. publs., 1960-62; sr. atty. Monsanto Co., St. Louis, 1963-70, asst. gen. counsel, asst. sec., 1975-77, sr. v.p., sec., gen. counsel, 1977-96. Dir. law Monsanto Textiles Co., St. Louis, 1971-75; corp. sec. Fisher Controls Co., Marshalltown, Iowa, 1969-71, Olympia Industries, Spartanburg, SC, 1974-75; vis. prof. law U. Mo., 1970-71; faculty Banking Sch. South, La. State U., 1967-83; vis. scholar Cambridge U., Eng., 1996; vis. prof. law St. Louis U., 1997-98. Author: (with Lawrence P. King) Sales and Bulk Transfers Under the Uniform Commercial Code, 2 vols, 1966, rev., 1984, New York Law of Contracts, 3 vols, 1964, Missouri Forms and Practice Under the Uniform Commercial Code, 2 vols, 1966; editor: Ann. Survey of Am. Law, NYU, 1961-62; mem. bd. contbg. editors and advisors: Corp. Law Rev, 1977-86; contbr. articles to law revs., jours. Mem. lawyers adv. coun. NAM, Washington, 1980, Adminstrv. Conf. U.S., 1980-86, legal adv. com. NY Stock Exch., 1983-87, corp. law dept. adv. coun. Practising Law Inst., 1982; bd. dirs. Bach Soc., St. Louis, 1985-86, pres., 1973-77; bd. dirs. Valparaiso U., 1977-2006, chmn. bd. visitors law sch., 1966-2005, Luth. Charities Assn., 1984-87, vice chmn., 1986-87; bd. dirs. Luth. Med. Ctr., St. Louis, 1973-82, vice chmn., 1975-80; bd. dirs. Nat. Jud. Coll., 1984-90, St. Louis Symphony, 1988-2002, Opera Theatre St. Louis, 1988—, Luth. Brotherhood, Mpls., 1992-2000, Liberty Fund, Inc., Indpls., 1997—. Served with US Army, 1953-55. Decorated officer's cross Order of Merit (Germany); named Disting. Alumnus, Valparaiso U., 1976. Fellow Am. Bar Found.; mem. ABA (chmn. com. uniform comml. code 1976-79, coun. sect. corp., banking and bus. law 1979-83, sec. 1983-84, chmn. 1986-87), Mo. Bar Assn., Am. Law Inst., Mont Pelerin Soc., Nat. Jud. Coll. (bd. dirs. 1984-90), Order of Coif, Bach Soc., Am. Soc. Corp. Sec. (bd. chmn. 1987-88), Assn. Gen. Coun., Am. Arbitration Assn., St. Louis Club. Republican. Lutheran. Home: 1 Indian Creek Ln Saint Louis MO 63131-3333 Home Phone: 314-993-1559. Personal E-mail: rwduesenberg@sbcglobal.net.

DUESENBERG, ROBERT H., retired lawyer; b. St. Louis, Dec. 10, 1930; s. Hugo John August and Edna Marie (Warmann) D.; m. Lorraine Freda Hall, July 23, 1938; children: Lynda Renee, Kirsten Lynn, John Robert. BA, Valparaiso U., Ind., 1951, LLB, 1953; LLM, Harvard U.,

1956. Bar: Mo. 1953, U.S. Supreme Ct. 1981, Va. 1993. Pvt. practice, St. Louis, 1956-58; atty. Wabash R.R. Co., St. Louis, 1958-65, Norfolk & Western Ry. Co., St. Louis, 1962-65; atty., assoc. gen. counsel Pet Inc., St. Louis, 1965-77, v.p., assoc. gen. counsel, 1977-80, v.p., gen. counsel, 1980-83, Gen. Dynamics Corp., Falls Church, Va., 1984-91, sr. v.p. and gen. counsel, 1991-93; ret., 1993. Bd. dirs. Valparaiso (Ind.) U., QuidTech Marine, Inc.; adv. bd. ELawForum, Inc., Washington. Contbr. numerous articles to profl. jours. Sec., treas., legal advisor Am. Kantorei, St. Louis, 1970-75; mem. Coun. on World Affairs, St. Louis, 1975—, Mo. Coordinating Bd. for Higher Edn., Jefferson City, 1976-83, chmn., 1978-81; mem. pres.'s coun. Valparaiso (Ind.) U., 1979—, bd. dirs., 1995—; bd. dirs. Higher Edn. Loan Authority, 1982-84; mem. adv. bd. Northwestern U. Corp. Counsel Ctr., 1988—, chmn. adv. bd., 1992; bd. dirs. Opera Theatre of St. Louis, 1988—; bd. dirs. Luther Inst., Washington, 1999—, chair, 2000-03; mem. adv. bd. ELawForum, Washington. Cpl. U.S. Army, 1953-55. Recipient Disting. Alumnus award Valparaiso U., 1982. Mem. ABA, Va. Bar Assn., Mo. Bar Assn., St. Louis Bar Assn. (chmn. antitrust com. 1971-73, v.p. bus. law sect. 1972-73, chmn. 1973-74), Am. Law Inst., Gen. Counsels Assn., Machine and Allied Products Inst. (legal counsel 1986—), Am. Corp. Counsel Assn., S.W. Legal Found. (adv. bd.), Aerospace Industry Assn. (legal com. 1981-88), Bach Soc. of St. Louis (bd. dirs.). Republican. Lutheran. Home: 10171 Castlewood Ln Oakton VA 22124-3027 Personal E-mail: rhduesenberg@earthlink.net.

DUFF, ERNEST ARTHUR, political scientist, educator; b. Charlottesville, Va., Dec. 27, 1929; s. Ernest Ragland and Emma Ruth (Bennett) D.; m. Barbara Ellen Jones, Aug. 30, 1955; children: Ernest A. Jr., Melanie Duff Badesch, Cameron John, Valerie Duff-Strautmann. BA, U. Va., 1952, MA, 1957, PhD, 1964. Fgn. svc. officer Dept. of State, Havana, Cuba, 1957-60, Washington, 1960-62, Bogota, Colombia, 1962-63; prof. Randolph-Macon Woman's Coll., Lynchburg, Va., 1964-97, Charles Dana prof., 1986, prof. emeritus, 1997—. Spl. field rep. Rockefeller Found., Cali, Colombia, 1966-67; vis. Fulbright prof. U. Mexico, Mexico City, 1979-80. Author: Agrarian Reform in Colombia, 1968, Violence and Repression in Latin America, 1974, Leader and Party in Latin America, 1984; reviewer Choice mag. Am. Libr. Assn. Polit. analyst WSET-TV, Lynchburg, Va., 1987—. Lt. USN, 1952-55, Korea. NROTC scholar USN and U. Va., 1948-52; Helen Wessell fellow, U. Va., 1963-64, NEH fellow, Brown U., Providence, 1990. Mem. Latin Am. Studies Assn., So. Polit. Sci. Assn., Southeastern Coun. Latin Am. Studies, Va. Polit. Sci. Assn. Baptist. Avocations: tennis, gardening. Home: 1633 Dogwood Ln Lynchburg VA 24503-1923 Personal E-mail: ebdu@earthlink.net.

DUFF, GILL, advertising executive; married; 4 children. BA, Univ. Tenn. Sr. acct. positions Young & Rubicam, D'Arcy, Leo Burnett, Foote Cone & Belding; worldwide sr. acct. dir. BBDO; pres., CEO Publicis NY, 2004—. Bd. dir. Advt. Week, 2005—. Office: Publicis NY 4 Herald Sq 950 Sixth Ave New York NY 10001 Office Phone: 212-279-5550. Office Fax: 212-279-5560.

DUFF, HILARY ANN, singer, actress; b. Houston, Sept. 28, 1987; d. Bob and Susan Duff. Released own product line Stuff by Hilary Duff. Actor: (TV films) True Women, 1997, Soul Collector, 1999; (TV series) Lizzie McGuire, 2001—03; (films) Human Nature, 2001, Cadet Kelly, 2002, Agent Cody Banks, 2003, The Lizzie McGuire Movie, 2003, Cheaper by the Dozen, 2003, A Cinderella Story, 2004, Raise Your Voice, 2004, The Perfect Man, 2005, Cheaper by the Dozen 2, 2005, Material Girls, 2006, (TV appearances) Chicago Hope, 2000, George Lopez, 2003, American Dreams, 2003, Frasier (voice), 2004; singer: (albums) Santa Claus Lane, 2002, Metamorphosis, 2003 (charted #2 on Billboard 200 first week of release), Hilary Duff, 2004, Most Wanted, 2005, Dignity, 2007, (soundtracks) Lizzie McGuire Television, 2001, The Lizzie McGuire Movie, 2003. Internat. spokesperson Kids With A Cause, 1999—. Recipient Nickelodeon Kids Choice Award for Favorite Female Singer, 2004. Office: Pmk Hbh Public Relations 161 Avenue Of The Americas Rm 10r New York NY 10013-1205

DUFF, JAMES C., lawyer; b. Hamilton, Ohio, July 8, 1953; Attended, U. Edinburgh; BA magna cum laude, U. Ky., 1975; JD, Georgetown U., 1981. Bar: U.S. Claims Ct., DC 1981. Adminstrv. asst. to Chief Justice William H. Rehnquist U.S. Supreme Ct., 1996—2000; mng. ptnr. Baker, Donelson, Bearman, Caldwell Berkowitz, Washington; dir. Administrv. Office U.S. Courts, 2006—. Exec. dir. Jud. Fellows Commn., 1996—2000; trustee Supreme Ct. Hist. Soc., 1996—; asst. to bd. regents Smithsonian Instn., 1996—; adj. faculty mem. Brookings Instn., 1997—99; adj. prof. constitutional law Georgetown U., 1998—; bd. dirs. Nat. Leadership Ctr., Coun. Court Excellence; sec. The Freedom Forum. Mem.: ABA, Bar Assn. DC. Office: Office Pub Affairs Adminstrv Office US Courts Washington DC 20544

DUFF, JAMES GEORGE, retired finance company and automotive executive; b. Pittsburg, Kans., Jan. 27, 1938; s. James George and Camilla Matilda (Vinardi) D.; m. Linda Louise Beeman, June 24, 1961 (div.); children: Michele, Mark, Melissa; m. Beverly L. Pool, Nov. 16, 1984. BS with distinction, U. Kans., 1960, MBA, 1961. With Ford Motor Co., Dearborn, Mich., 1962-97, various positions fin. staff, 1962-71; dir. product, profit, price, warranty Ford of Europe, 1972-74; controller Ford Div., 1974-76, controller car ops., 1976, controller car product devel., 1976-80; exec. v.p. Ford Motor Credit Co., 1980-88, bd. dirs.; pres., COO US Leasing Internat. Inc., San Francisco, 1988-89, pres., CEO, 1990-91; chmn., CEO USL Capital (formally US Leasing Internat. Inc.), San Francisco, 1991-97, also bd. dirs.; ret., 1999. Bd. dirs. Boulder Total Return Fund, 1997-99; mem. Conf. Bd., 1990-97. Mem. adv. bd. U. Kans. Sch. Bus., 1980-98; bd. dirs. Bay Area Coun., 1990-97; trustee San Francisco Mus. Modern Art, 1990-97; chmn. bus. devel. unit Detroit United Fund, 1980-85, chmn. edn. and local govt. unit Detroit United Fund, 1986-88. Sunray Mid-Continent scholar, Bankers scholar, to 1960. Mem. San Francisco C. of C. (bd. dirs. 1990-91). Home: 7200 S Dunns Farm Rd Maple City MI 49664-8718 also: 1 The Courtyard 65 Old Church St London SW3 5BS England Personal E-mail: onmyduff@msn.com.

DUFF, JAMES HENRY, museum director, environmental services administrator; b. Pitts., Oct. 11, 1943; s. James Sylvester and Virginia (Henry) D.; m. Sally Kathryn Tredwell, Sept. 14, 1963; children: Abigail Margaret, Jessica Lauren. BA, Washington and Jefferson Coll., 1965; MA, U. Mass., 1970; postgrad., Met. Mus. Art, 1971. Teaching asst. U. Mass., Amherst, 1965-66; dir. Mus. of Hudson Highlands, Cornwall-on-Hudson, NY, 1966-73, Brandywine River Mus., Chadds Ford, Pa., 1973—; exec. dir. Brandywine Conservancy, Chadds Ford, 1976—. Cons. N.Y. State Coun. on Arts, 1970-72; panel mem. Pa. Coun. on Arts, 1976-79, 83-85; mem. adv. coun. Nat. Mus. Act, 1982-85; mem. Nat. Mus. Svcs. Bd., 1986-95. Author: The Western World of N. C. Wyeth, 1980, Landscapes, Still Lifes and Portraits by N. C. Wyeth, 1982, An American Vision, 1987; contbr. articles on mus. programs to profl. jours. Trustee Wyeth Endowment for Am. Art, 1986-95, Am. Arts Alliance, 1995-96, Greater Phila. Cultural Alliance (trustee 2001-06). With U.S. Army, 1967-69. Mem. Mid-Atlantic Assn. Mus. (pres. 1983-85, The Katherine Coffey award 1992), Assn. Art Mus. Dirs. (trustee 1993-98, 2001—04, v.p. 1995-96, pres. 1996-97), Am. Assn. Mus. (trustee 1983-88). Home: PO Box 297 Chadds Ford PA 19317-0297 Office: Brandywine River Mus Brandywine Conservancy PO Box 141 Chadds Ford PA 19317-0141 Home Phone: 610-388-6889; Office Phone: 610-388-2700. Business E-Mail: jduff@brandywine.org.

DUFF, JOHN A., law educator; BS, Univ. Lowell; JD, Suffolk Univ.; LLM, Univ. Wash.; MA, Univ. Miss. Dir. Miss./Ala. Sea Grant Legal Prog., U. Miss., 1995—99; assoc. rsch. prof. U. Maine Sch. Law, 1999—, dir., Marine Law Inst. Vis. instr. Univ. Victoria, BC, Canada, 1998; mem. sci. team NOAA vessel Ron Brown, VENTS expdn., 1998; mem. United Nations Environment Programme, Nairobi, Kenya. Mem. Submerged Lands Adv. Bd., Maine, 2001. Mem.: Coastal Soc. (pres. 2003—). Office: Marine Law Inst U Maine Sch Law 246 Deering Ave Portland ME 04102 Business E-Mail: jduff@usm.maine.edu.*

DUFF, JOHN EWING, sculptor; b. Lafayette, Ind., Dec. 2, 1943; s. John Ewing and Ruth (Miller) Duff. B.F.A., San Francisco Art Inst., 1967. One man shows include: Margo Leavin Gallery, L.A., 1981, Blum-Helman Gallery, N.Y.C., 1985-90, L.A., 1987, 91, San Jose (Calif.) Mus. Art, 1991, Gallery 57, Madrid, 1992, Salama Caro Gallery, London, 1992, David McKee Gallery, 1995, Johnson County C.C. Gallery Art, 1995, Knoedler Gallery, N.Y.C., 1997, 2001, 04, Hill Gallery, Birmingham, Mich., 1999, Brantley Gallery, Scottsdale, Ariz., 1999, Ingred Rabb Gallery, Berlin, 1999, Manfred Baumgartner Gallery, N.Y.C. 2001 (recent work), Weatherspoon Art Mus., Greensboro, N.C., 2005, Rosenwald-Wolf Gallery, U. of Arts, Phila., 2006; two-person show at Hill Gallery, Birmingham, Mich., 1996; group exhbns. include Whitney Mus., N.Y.C., 1969, 81, David Whitney Gallery, N.Y.C., 1970, 71, Irving Blum Gallery, L.A., 1972, John Bernard Meyers Gallery, N.Y.C., 1972, 73, Willard Gallery, N.Y.C., 1975-78, Whitney Mus. Equitable Ctr., 1987, The Edward R. Broida Collection, Orlando Mus. of Art, 1998, Anderson Gallery, Va. Commonwealth U., 2000, Am. Acad. Invitational Exhbn. of Painting and Sculpture, 2002; represented in public collections Kaiser Wilhelm Mus., Krefeld, Fed. Republic Germany, Mus. Modern Art, N.Y.C., Walker Art Ctr., Mpls., Met. Mus. Art, N.Y.c., Solomon R. Guggenheim Mus., N.Y.C., L.A. Mus. Contemporary Art, Mus. Contemporary Art, Chgo. Recipient Theodoren award Guggenheim Mus., 1977, award Am. Acad. and Inst. Arts and Letters, 1981, John Simon Guggenheim fellowship, 1979-80, Brandeis U. Creative Arts award Citation in Sculpture, 1987. Home and Office: 7 Doyers St New York NY 10013-5112

DUFF, KEVIN, neuropsychologist, psychiatry professor; b. Worcester, Mass., Sept. 13, 1968; s. John Charles and Patricia Ann Duff; m. Ali Josephine Johnson, Nov. 26, 1969; children: Jack, Audrey. BA, U. of Mass., North Dartmouth, 1990; MA, U. of No. Colo., Greeley, 1993; PhD, SUNY, Albany, 2001. Lic. psychologist Iowa. Postdoctoral fellow U. Okla. Health Scis. Ctr., Oklahoma City, 2001—03; neuropsychologist, asst. prof. psychiatry U. Iowa, Iowa City, 2003—. Author: (research project) Predicting cognitive decline with lifetime affective burden; contbr. articles to rsch. publs. (NARSAD Young Investigators award, 2005). Grantee, NIH - Nat. Inst. of Aging, 2005—07. Mem.: APA, Internat. Neuropsychological Soc., Nat. Acad. of Neuropsychology. Achievements include research in Predicting cognitive decline with lifetime affective burden. Office: U of Iowa Psychiatry 1-308 MEB Iowa City IA 52242-1000 Office Phone: 319-335-6640. Business E-Mail: kevin-duff@uiowa.edu.

DUFF, MICHAEL A., lawyer, transportation executive; b. Balt., 1960; m. Diane Duff; children: Alex, Steven. BA, Johns Hopkins U., 1982; JD, U. Balt. Sch. Law, 1985. Bar: Md. 1985, Pa. 1992. Real estate assoc. Venable Baetjer & Howard, Balt.; sr. counsel Penske Truck Leasing Co, Reading, Pa., 1991, asst. gen. counsel, 1997—99, sr. v.p., gen. counsel, 2003—; named exec. v.p., gen. counsel, asst. sec. UnitedAuto Group, Inc., 1999. Office: Penske Truck Leasing Co Rte 10 Green Hills Reading PA 19607 Office Phone: 610-775-6000. Office Fax: 610-775-6432.

DUFF, PATRICIA, civic activist; b. LA, Apr. 12, 1954; d. Robert Orr and Mary Williamson; 1 child, Caleigh Sophia Perelman. Student, Internat. Sch. Brussels, 1971, Barnard Coll.; BS in Internat. Econs., Georgetown U., 1976. Spl. asst. to chief counsel house select com. on assassinations U.S. Ho. of Reps., Washington, 1976-78; prodr., writer, researcher John McLaughlin Show-NBC Radio, Washington, 1979-80; asst. rsch. dir. Dem. Nat. Com., Washington, 1980; v.p. Patrick Caddell and Assocs., Washington, 1980-82, Squier, Eskew Assoc., 1982-84; with Mondale for Pres., LA, 1984, Americans for Hart, LA, 1984; ind. producer Columbia Pictures, Burbank, Calif.; pres. Revlon Found., 1995-97. Assoc. producer Dem. Nat. Conv., Atlanta, 1988; mem. nat. media adv. bd. Hart for Pres., L.A., 1988 Contbg. editor Vogue Mag., 1989; editor at large Premier Mag., 1995-97; host Duff Talk, Plum TV, 2004—; guest co-host WABC-Radio, 2004-05 Founder Am. Spirit Awards, 1992; chair N.Y. Gov.'s Task Force on Teen Pregnancy, 1994—95, Women Vote Campaign of Emily's List, 1996, Saves Women's Leadership Coun., 1999—2004; mem. platform com. Dem. Nat. Conv., 1984, 1992; mem. Hollywood Women's Polit. Com., 1986; co-chair N.Y. fin. com. Clinton for Pres., 1996; bd. dirs. People for the Am. Way, 1996—2002; mem. bd. councilors Ascus sch. pub. policy and adminstrn. U. So. Calif.; founder, chair bd. dirs. Show Coalition The Common Good, LA, 1988—; mem. bd. visitors Sch. Fgn. Svc. Georgetown U., 1988—; mem. pvt. sector adv. bd. Inter Am. Devel. Bank; bd. trustees Save the Children, chmn., 2006; bd. dirs. L.A. Colors United, Summer of Svc., Nat. Svc., 1993, L.A. Commn. on Status of Women, 1994—96, Women in Film, 1990—, Lincoln Ctr. Film Soc., 1995—2000; trustee Nat. Pub. Radio, Am. Ballet Theatre, 1995—96; mem. Presdl. Commn. on Libr. of Congress Trust Fund, 1994—2000; founder Families for Justice, 2004. Named one of Rising Young Stars L.A. Times, 1989; named Dem. of Yr. L.A. County, 1989; recipient Women We Love award for polit. activism Esquire Mag., 1990, Women in Film award Women in Film, 1995, Citizen's Achievement award NDD, 1998. Office Phone: 212-722-6390. Personal E-mail: mspduff@aol.com, mspduff@yahoo.com.

DUFF, PHILIP, investment company executive; BA, Harvard Coll.; MBA, MIT. Pres., CEO Van Kampen Investments; CFO, mng. dir. Morgan Stanley Group Inc., NYC; mng. dir. Tiger Mgmt., NYC, COO; co-founder, CEO FrontPoint Ptnrs., Greenwich, Conn., 2000—06; founder, chmn., CEO Robson Ventures LLC, Greenwich, Conn., 2007—. Bd. dir. Black Diamond Equipment Ltd., RiskMetrics Group, Solar Power Corp., Managed Funds Assn.; past bd. dir. Fin. Acctg. Found. Chmn. bd. dir. Greenwich Acad. Office: Robson Ventures LLC 100 Field Point Rd Greenwich CT 06830*

DUFF, WILLIAM BRANDON, lawyer; s. Daniel Vincent and Priscilla (Booth) Duff; m. Terri Ann Sherman, June 16, 1985; children: Elizabeth, Madeleine. AB, Coll. of Holy Cross, 1971; JD, Georgetown U., 1975. Bar: DC 1975, U.S. Dist. Ct. DC 1975, U.S. Ct. Appeals (DC cir.) 1975, N.Y. 1983. Assoc. McChesney & Pyne, Washington, 1975—78, Carter, Ledyard & Milburn, NYC, 1980—84; pvt. practice NYC, 1984—86; ptnr., dept. head DeForest & Duer, NYC, 1986—96, Baer, Marks & Upham, NYC, 1996—2000, Jenkens & Gilchrist Parker Chapin LLP, NYC, 2000—02, Katten Muchin Rosenman LLP, NYC, 2002—. Instr. fed. employee benefit plans law Georgetown U. Sch. Continuing Edn., Washington, 1977, Washington, 78. Mem. legislature City of Greenwich, Conn., 1994—98. Office: Katten Muchin Rosenman LLP 575 Madison Ave New York NY 10022 Office Phone: 212-940-8532. Business E-Mail: william.duff@kattenlaw.com.

DUFF, WILLIAM GRIERSON, electrical engineer, educator; b. Alexandria, Va., Dec. 16, 1936; s. Johnnie Douglas and Annetta Osceola (Rind) D.; m. Sandra K. Via, June 25, 1983; children: Warren David, Valerie Lynn, Dawn Elizabeth, Deborah Arleen, Kelly Juanita. BEE, George Washington U., 1959, postgrad., 1959-72; MS, Syracuse U., 1969; DSc in Elec. Engring., Clayton U., 1977. Pres. SEMTAS, Fairfax, Va., 1959—. Asst. prof. Capitol Inst. Tech., Greenbelt, Md., 1972—; instr. Interference Control Technologies, Don White Cons., Inc., Gainesville, Va. Author: EMI Handbook, vol. 5, EMI Prediction and Analysis Techniques, 1972, Mobile Communications, 1976, Fundamentals of EMC, 1988, EMC in Telecommunications, 1988; contbr. articles to profl. jours. Counselor Meth. Sr. High Youth Group, 1965-73. Recipient Good Citizenship award DAR, 1955, Math. award George Washington H.S., Alexandria, 1955. Fellow IEEE (pres. EMC Soc., assoc. editor group newsletter 1970—); mem. AIEE (Best Paper award 1961), George Washington U. Engring. Alumni Assn. (pres. 1963-64, Engring. Alumni Svc. award 1980), Springfield Golf and Country Club, Occoquan Water Ski Club (pres. 1976), Sigma Tau, Theta Tau. Home: 7601 S Valley Dr Fairfax VA 22039-2965 Office: SEMTAS 7601 S Valley Dr Fairfax Station VA 22039 Personal E-mail: wmduff@cox.net.

DUFF, WILLIAM LEROY, JR., retired dean, finance educator; b. Oakland, Calif., Sept. 14, 1938; s. William Leroy and Edna Francis (Gunderson) D.; m. Arline M. Wight, Sept. 1, 1962; children— Susan M., William Leroy III. BA, Calif. State U.-, San Francisco, 1963, postgrad., 1963-64; MSSc., Nat. Econs. Inst., U. Stockholm, 1965; PhD, UCLA, 1969. Rsch assoc. C.F. Kettering Found., 1967-69; asst. JOBS program Nat. Alliance Businessmen, 1969-70; prof. U. No. Colo., Greeley, 1970—, Bur Bus. and Pub. Research, 1972-75, dean Coll. Bus. Adminstrn., 1984—, interim v.p. acad. affairs, 1987, chmn. faculty senate, 1981-82. On leave as UN adviser to Govt. of Swaziland, 1975-77; cons. in field. Contbr. articles to profl. jours. Mem. Greeley Planning Commn., 1972-75, chmn., 1974-75; trustee U. No. Colo., 1983; mem. Greeley Water and Sewer Bd., 1994-98, Greeley City Coun., 2000; bd. dirs. Centennial Svcs., 2003, United Way of Weld County, 2003, exec. bd. and investment com., UNC Found., 2003, treas., mem. exec. com., investment com.; bd. dirs. Greeley Philharm., U. NC Found. With U.S. Army, 1958-60. Mem. Greeley Rotary Club (bd. dirs.), Greeley Area C. of C. (bd. dirs.). Home: 1614 Lakeside Dr Greeley CO 80631-5343 Office: U No Colo Coll Bus Adminstrn Kepner Greeley CO 80639-0001

DUFFEY, JOSEPH DANIEL, academic administrator; b. Huntington, W.Va., July 1, 1932; s. Joseph I. and Ruth (Wilson) Duffey; m. Anne Wexler, 1974; children: Michael, David, Danny Wexler, David Wexler. BA, Marshall U., 1954; STM, Yale U., 1963; BD, Andover Newton Theol. Sch., 1958; PhD, Hartford Sem. Found., 1969; LHD, CUNY, 1978, U. Cin., 1978, U. Mass., 1991; LittD, Dickinson Coll., Pa., 1978, Centre Coll., Ky., 1977, Gonzaga U., Wash., 1980, Monmouth Coll., 1980, CCNY; LLD, Amherst Coll., Bethany Coll., Austin Coll., Ritsuimaneu U., Kyoto, Japan, 1993; LittD, Alderson-Broadus Coll., Adelphi U., Central Fla. Asst. prof. Hartford (Conn.) Sem., 1960—63; assoc. prof., dir. Ctr. Urban Studies, 1965—70; fellow Harvard U. Kennedy Sch. Govt., 1971; adj. prof. and fellow Calhoun Coll., Yale U., 1971—73; exec. officer AAUP, 1974—77; asst. sec. for edn. and cultural affairs Dept. State, 1977; chmn. NEH, 1978—81; chancellor U. Mass., Amherst, 1982—, pres., 1990—91, Am. U., Washington, 1991—93; dir. U.S. Info. Agy., Washington, 1993—98; sr. exec., chmn. internat. univ. project Sylvan Learning Sys., Washington, 1999—. Mem. U.S. dept. 20th and 21st gen. confs. UNESCO, 1978, 80; mem. exec. com. Nat. Coun. Competitiveness Govt. and Industry Univ. Panel Nat. Acad. Scis.; bd. dirs. Bay Bank, Springfield, Mass. Contbr. articles to profl. jours. Bd. dirs. Woodrow Wilson Internat. Ctr. Scholars, East-West Ctr., Western Mass. Area Devel. Corp., Jewish Theol. Sem. Libr., Springfield Symphony. Decorated Order of The Crown Belgium; recipient Tree of Life award, Nat. Jewish Fund, 1987; scholar, Rockefeller Found., 1966—68. Mem.: Century Assn., Coun. Fgn. Rels., Cosmos Club. Office: Laureate Learning Sys 2801 New Mexico Ave NW Apt 311 Washington DC 20007-3913 Home Phone: 202-965-1044. Personal E-mail: jduffey@earthlink.net.

DUFFEY, WILLIAM SIMON, JR., federal judge, former prosecutor; b. Phila., May 9, 1952; s. William Simon and Elinor (Daniluk) D.; m. Betsy Byars, Dec. 17, 1977; children: Charles, Scott. BA with honors in English, Drake U., Des Moines, Iowa, 1973; JD cum laude, U. SC, 1977. Bar: SC 1977, Ga. 1982, US Dist. Ct. (no., mid. and so. dists.) Ga. 1982, US Ct. Appeals (llth cir.) 1983, US Supreme Ct., 1992. Atty. Nexson, Pruet, Jacobs & Pollard, Columbia, SC, 1977-78; assoc. King & Spalding, LLP, Atlanta, 1981—87, ptnr., 1987—94, 1995—2001; dep. ind. counsel Office of the Ind. Counsel, Little Rock, 1994-95; U.S. Atty. (No. dist.) Ga. US Dept. Justice, Atlanta, 2002—04; judge U.S. Dist. Ct. (No. dist) Ga, 2004—. Adj. prof. U. S.C. Law Sch., 2000—01; mem. com. on civil justice Ga. Supreme Ct., 2006—. Articles editor S.C. Lawyer, 1990-94. Pres. Pine Hills Civic Assn., Atlanta, 1984-88; trustee Drake U.; Ga. Rep. Found., Leadership Atlanta; bd. dirs. Ga. Wilderness Inst., 1992-2001; mem. Peachtree Rd. Race Com., 1993—, chmn. Ga. Good Govt. Com., 1995-2001; chmn. bd. advisors Coverdell Leadership Inst., 1995-2002; bd. mem. North Ga. Walk to Emmaus, 1999-2001; founder New Century Forum. Asst. staff judge advocate USAF, 1978—81. Mem. Altanta Bar Assn. (chmn. alt. dispute resolution com. 1984-88), Lawyers Club, Atlanta Track Club (gen. counsel 1993-2001). Republican. Avocations: running, cooking, woodturning. Office: 1721 US Courthouse 75 Spring St SW Atlanta GA 30303-3361 Office Phone: 404-215-1480. Personal E-mail: billduffey@bellsouth.net.

DUFFIE, DARRELL, finance educator; m. Denise Savoie; 2 children. BS in Civil Engring., Univ. New Brunswick, 1975; M in Econ. Statistics, Univ. New England, Australia, 1980; PhD in Engring. Econ. Sys., Stanford Univ., 1984. Jr. engr., facilities Bell Telephone Co. Canada Ltd., 1975—76; lectr., civil engring. Univ. New Brunswick, 1978—79; engr., decision sys. Systems Control Technology Inc., Palo Alto, Calif., 1981—83; faculty, grad. sch. bus. Stanford Univ., 1984—, current Dean Witter disting. prof. fin. Named Fin. Engr. of Yr., Internat. Assn. Fin. Engring., 2003. Fellow: Am. Acad. Arts & Scis. Office: Grad Sch Business Stanford Univ 518 Memorial Way Stanford CA 94305-5015 Office Phone: 650-723-1976. Office Fax: 650-725-7979. Business E-Mail: duffie@stanford.edu.*

DUFFIE, L. TRAYWICK, lawyer; b. Augusta, Ga., Feb. 13, 1947; BA, Wofford Coll., 1969; JD, Univ. SC, 1972. Bar: SC 1972, Fla. 1975, Ga. 1977. Ptnr., co-head, labor, employment Hunton & Williams LLP, Atlanta. Mem. Magistrate Judge Merit Selection Panel, 1998—2000. Named a Top 100 Georgia Super Lawyer, Atlanta Mag., 2004; named an Employment Litig. Super Lawyer, Georgia Super Lawyers Mag., 2005; named one of Georgia's 2004 Legal Elite, Georgia Trend Mag., 2004. Mem.: Phi Delta Phi. Office: Hunton & Williams Bank of Am Plz Ste 4100 600 Peachtree St NE Atlanta GA 30308-2216 Office Phone: 404-888-4004. Office Fax: 404-888-4190. Business E-Mail: tduffie@hunton.com.

DUFFIÉ, MARY KATHARINE, anthropologist, educator; b. Phila., June 23, 1963; d. Claire Alfred Pelton III and Nikki Joan (Newcomb) D. BA, U. Ariz., 1985, MA, 1989; PhD, Wash. State U., Pullman, 1994. Asst. prof. Mont. State U., Bozeman, 1995-97; asst. prof. anthropology UCLA, 1997—. Prin. investigator UCLA/Calif. Dept. Health Svcs., 1997-98, CDC, Atlanta, 1996-97, Ariz. Humanities Coun., Tucson, 1989-90. Author: Heeni: A Tainui Elder Remembers, 1997, Through the Eye of the Needle: A Maori Elder Remembers, 2001. Chair So. Calif., Am. Indian Health Working Group, LA, 1997—; vol. Together, Inc., Glassboro, NJ, 1976-81, Hospice, Tucson, 1987-89. Recipient W.H.R. Rivers award Soc. for Med. Anthropology, 1993; book recognized among top 20 titles for 1997 Listener Women's Book Festival, Auckland, New Zealand, 1997; nominated Victor Turner award Am. Anthropology Assn., 2001. Democrat. Presbyterian. Avocations: reading, writing, horseback riding, hiking. Home: 8050 Lupine Ln Bozeman MT 59718 E-mail: mkduffie@aol.com.

DUFFIELD, DAVID A., application developer, former computer software company executive; b. Shaker Heights, OH, Sept. 21, 1940; m. Cheryl Duffield; 9 children. BS in Elec. Engring., Cornell U., 1962, MBA, 1964. Mktg. rep., sys. engr. IBM, 1964—69; co-founder Info. Assocs.; founder, chmn. Integral Systems Inc., Walnut Creek, Calif., 1972—87, PeopleSoft Inc., Pleasanton, Calif., 1987—2004, pres., 1987—99, CEO, 1987—99,

2004; co-founder Workday, Incline Village, Nev., 2005—. Co-founder Maddie's Fund, Alameda, Calif., 1999—. Named one of Forbes' Richest Americans, 2006. Office: Workday PO Box 5230 Incline Village NV 89450

DUFFNER, LEE R., ophthalmologist; b. June 3, 1936; m. Alvina Bross, Aug. 31, 1957; children: Fay, Rachel, Tamar. BS Engring., Purdue U., 1957; MS Physiology, Marquette U., Milw., 1961; MD, Med. Coll. Wis., 1962. Diplomate Am. Bd. Ophthalmology. Intern Stanford U., 1962—63; resident U. Miami, Fla., 1966—69; practice medicine specializing in ophthalmology Hollywood, Fla., 1969—; clin. prof. ophthalmology U. Miami Sch. Medicine, 1969—; dir. Am. Bd. Ophthalmology, 1995—2002, chmn., 2002. Pres. town coun. Town of Golden Beach, Fla., 1983—95. Capt. USAF, 1963—66. Fellow: ACS, Am. Acad. Ophthalmology; mem.: Miami Ophthal. Soc. (pres. 1983—84). Avocation: racewalking. Home: 185 Ocean Blvd Golden Beach FL 33160-2208 Office: 2740 Hollywood Blvd Hollywood FL 33020-4826 Office Phone: 954-925-2740.

DUFFY, ANN PATRICIA, retired elementary school educator; b. Chgo., June 12, 1947; d. Daniel Justin and Ruby Hearne Duffy. B in History, U. Chgo., Ill., 1972; MEd, No. Ill. U., DeKalb, 1976; M in History, Chgo. State U., 1978. Tchr. Sherman Elem., Chgo., 1970—81, Nixon Elem., Chgo., 1981—92, O.A. Thorpe, Chgo., 1992—94; tchr., asst. prin. Lincoln Elem., Chgo., 1994—2006; ret., 2006. Adv. bd. Chgo. Met. History Edn. Ctr. Recipient Olive Foster award, Ill. State Preservation Agy., 1993, Govs. award, 1995. Mem.: Nat. Coun. Social Studies, Orgn. Am. Historians. Avocation: baseball.

DUFFY, BILL, professional sports team executive; b. Ho-Ho-Kus, NJ, Feb. 28, 1956; m. Cathryn Duffy; children: Erin, Caitlin. Grad., Princeton U., NJ; M, NYU. CPA. Dir. fin. NFL Miami Dolphins and Sta. Properties, 1988; treas. Robbie Sta. Cos., 1990—93; dir. compliance NFL Mgmt. Coun., 1993—96; CFO, v.p. bus. ops. NFL San Francisco 49ers, 1996—99; v.p. adminstrn. NFL Buffalo Bills; with NHL Fla. Panthers; exec. v.p., CFO Atlanta Spirit, LLC (parent co. of NBA Atlanta Hawks, NHL Atlanta Thrashers and Philips Arena), 2004—. Bd. mem. Big Bros. Big Sisters Metro Atlanta, Ireland C. of C. US Atlanta Chpt.; mem. adv. bd. MBA in Sports Mgmt. Fla. Atlantic U. Office: Atlanta Spirit LLC 101 Marietta St NW Ste 1900 Atlanta GA 30303 Office Phone: 404-878-3800.*

DUFFY, DAN, computer company executive; BA, Ind. Kelley Sch. Bus.; MBA, Northwestern Kellogg Sch. Bus. Sr. exec. Ernst & Young LLP; CFO, chief devel. officer MachineWeb; CEO ePartners, 2000—.

DUFFY, DENNIS J., rail transportation executive; B in Acctg., U. Nebr., Omaha; grad. in mgmt. devel. program, Harvard U. Various positions in ops., fin., mktg. and sales Union Pacific Corp., Omaha, v.p. quality, sr. v.p. customer svc. planning and delivery, sr. v.p. safety assurance and compliance process, exec. v.p. ops., 1998—. Examiner Malcolm Baldrige Nat. Quality Award Bd. Examiners, 1994, sr. examiner, 95. Office: Union Pacific Corp 1400 Douglas St Omaha NE 68179 Office Phone: 402-544-5000.*

DUFFY, EARL GAVIN, hotel executive; b. Boston, Oct. 11, 1926; s. William Emmett and Mary Irene (Costello) D.; m. Bernice Rose MacMaster, Feb. 14, 1948; children— Earl Gavin, Joan Irene, Mark Charles, Neil William, Lynn Anne. Student public schs., Boston. In various hotel positions, Boston, 1941-52; sales mgr. Somerset Hotel, Boston, 1952-56; eastern sales mgr. Hotel Corp. Am., Boston, 1956-59, asst. nat. sales mgr., 1959-61, nat. sales mgr., 1961-64; v.p., gen. mgr. Hotel America, Houston, 1964-67, Hartford, Conn., 1967-69, Royal Sonesta Hotel, New Orleans, 1969-71, Soneta Beach Hotel, Key Biscayne, Fla., 1971-76, Boston Park Plaza Hotel, 1977-80; pres. Earl G. Duffy & Assos., 1981—. Guest lectr. Cornell U., 1961, U. Houston, 1965, Wash. State U., 1966, Fla. Internat. U., 1971-76; pres. Greater Hartford Conv. and Visitor's Bur., 1969 Chmn. div. bus. and industry Harris County (Tex.) March of Dimes, 1964-67; pres. New Orleans Jazz Festival, 1970-71. Served with USN, 1943-46. Recipient Golden Host award Wash. State U., 1964 Mem. Skal Club, Am. Hotel and Motel Assn., Hotel Sales Mgmt. Assn. Internat., Greater Boston Hotel and Motor Inn Assn., Mass. Hotel and Motel Assn., New Eng. Innkeepers Assn., Boston Exec. Club. Clubs: Rotary. Roman Catholic. Home and Office: 600 Three Islands Blvd 1503 Hallandale Beach FL 33009 *There is no question in my mind that anyone who wants to "make it" in America can do so.*

DUFFY, EDMUND CHARLES, lawyer; b. NYC, Jan. 16, 1942; s. Thomas and Helen (Fisher) D.; m. Terry L. Davis, Oct. 21, 1973; children: Elisabeth, Margot. AB in Eng., Boston Coll., 1963; LLB, Columbia U., 1966. Bar: N.Y. 1967. Assoc. Cravath, Swaine & Moore, NYC, 1968-77; from assoc. to ptnr. Skadden, Arps, Slate, Meagher & Flom, NYC, 1977—. Served to capt. U.S. Army, 1966-68, Vietnam. Mem. ABA, N.Y. State Bar Assn. Office: Skadden Arps Slate Meagher & Flom LLP 4 Times Sq New York NY 10036-6595 Office Phone: 212-735-3950. E-mail: eduffy@skadden.com.

DUFFY, JAMES EARL, JR., state supreme court justice; b. St. Paul, June 4, 1942; s. James Earl and Mary Elizabeth (Westbrook) Duffy; m. Jeanne Marie Ghiardi; children: Jennifer, Jessica. BA, Coll. St. Thomas, 1965; JD, Marquette U., 1968. Bar: Wis. 1968, Hawaii 1969. Assoc. Cobb & Gould, Honolulu, 1968—71, Chuck & Fujiyama, Honolulu, 1972—74; partner Fujiyama, Duffy & Fujiyama, Honolulu, 1975—2003; assoc. justice Hawaii Supreme Ct., 2003—. Mem. Am. Bd. Trial Advocates, med. ethical resources com. Kapiolani Children's Med. Ctr., 1984—. recipient Lifetime Achievement award, Consumer Lawyers of Hawaii, John S. Edmunds award for Civility & Vigorous Advocacy. mem. Hawaii Bar Found. (bd. dirs. 1984—), Hawaii Bar Assn. (pres. 1982, Lifetime Achievement award), Hawaii Trial Lawyers Assn. (pres. 1981), Hawaii Supreme Ct. Jud. Coun., Trial Lawyers Assn. Am. (bd. govs. 1982-85), Hawaii Acad. Plaintiff's Attys. (pres. 1986-93), Am. Inns of Court IV. Office: Ali'iolani Hale 417 S King St Honolulu HI 96813-2902*

DUFFY, JAMES FRANCIS, III, lawyer; b. Providence, Jan. 28, 1956; s. James Francis Jr. and Eileen (Barry) D.; m. Catherine Anne Barrett, Oct. 20, 2001; 1 child, Mary Margaret. BA, U. R.I., 1978; JD, Harvard U., 1981. Bar: Mass. 1981, U.S. Dist. Ct. Mass. 1982. Assoc. Peabody & Brown, Boston, 1981-89, ptnr., 1989-99, Nixon Peabody LLP, Boston, 1999—. Mem. ABA, Boston Bar Assn. (real estate steering com. 1991-93, chmn. equity fin. com. of real estate sect. 1991-93), Mass. Bar Assn. Home: 17 Jackson Rd Somerville MA 02145-2908 Office: Nixon Peabody LLP 100 Summer St Fl 24 Boston MA 02110-2131 Office Phone: 617-345-1129. E-mail: jduffy@nixonpeabody.com, james.f.duffy@verizon.net.

DUFFY, JAMES HENRY, writer, retired lawyer; b. Lowville, NY, Feb. 3, 1934; s. William Christopher and Phyllis Catherine (Rofinot) D.; m. Martha McDowell, May 25, 1968 (dec. 1997). AB, Princeton U., 1956; LLB, Harvard U., 1959. Bar: N.Y. 1960. Assoc. Cravath, Swaine & Moore, NYC, 1959-67, ptnr., 1968-88. Bd. dirs. Albanian-Am. Enterprise Fund. Author: Domestic Affairs: American Programs and Priorities, 1979, Dog Bites Man: City Shocked, 2001, (under pseudonym Haughton Murphy) Murder for Lunch, 1986, Murder Takes a Partner, 1987, Murders and Acquisitions, 1988, Murder Keeps a Secret, 1989, Murder Times Two, 1990, Murder Saves Face, 1991, A Very Venetian Murder, 1992. Mem. Mayor's Commn. Cultural Affairs, 1981-91; bd. dirs. Nat. Corp. Fund for Dance, Inc., 1981-88, Sch. Am. Ballet, Paul Taylor Dance Found., Baryshnikov Dance Found., Commonweal Mag., Alliance for the Arts, N.Y.C.; trustee N.Y.Pub. Libr. Mem. Assn. of Bar of City of N.Y., Coun. Fgn. Rels., Mystery Writers Am. (bd. dirs. 1986-92, treas. 1992), Authors Guild (mem. coun. 1993—), Crime Writers Assn. (U.K.), Century Assn. Democrat. Roman Catholic. Address: 116 E 68th St New York NY 10021-5955 Personal E-mail: jduffy@attglobal.net.

DUFFY, JAMES RAYMOND, lawyer; b. NYC, July 22, 1936; s. Terence Patrick and Roasleen (Layden) D.; m. Mary Ellen Powers, Aug. 29, 1959; children: Terence, James Jr., Sean, Michael, Mary Ellen. BBA, St. John's U., NYC, 1961; LLB, Bklyn. Coll. Law, 1965. Bar: N.Y. Ptnr. Kramer Dillof Tessel Duffy & Moore, NYC, 1971-2000; sr. ptnr. Duffy, Duffy & Burdo, Uniondale, NY, 2001—. Author: Who Killed JFK?, 1988, Lone Crazed Gunman?, 2004 Recipient Martin Luther King Legal Svcs. award Congress of Racial Equality, 1995. Mem. N.Y. State Acad. Trial Lawyers (founding. mem. 2004). Office: Duffy Duffy & Burdo Reckson Plz Uniondale NY 11556-1370 E-mail: xxexam@aol.com.

DUFFY, JOHN CHARLES, psychiatrist, educator, consultant; b. Cleve., June 19, 1934; s. John Joseph and Hannah (McIllwee) D.; m. Francoise C. Antonini; children: Charles, Robert, John. Grad., Boston Coll., 1956; MD, N.Y. Med. Coll., 1960. Intern Henry Ford Hosp., Detroit, 1960-61; resident Mayo Clinic, Rochester, Minn., 1963-67; exec. dir. Tucson Child Guidance Ctr., 1971-74; commd. med. officer USPHS, 1974; prof., assoc. chmn. Uniformed Svcs. U. Sch. Medicine, Bethesda, Md., 1974-81; assoc. commr. health affairs FDA, cons. Surgeon Gen., Rockville, Md., 1981-88; asst. surgeon gen. USPHS, 1983-92, chief physician officer, 1983-88; dir. C. Everett Koop Inst. Dartmouth Coll., Hanover, NH, 1992-94; prof. psychiatry Uniformed Svcs. U. Sch. Medicine, Bethesda, 1981-94, clin. prof., 1994—. Nat. and internat. surveyor Joint Commn. on Accreditation of Healthcare Orgns., 1998—; founder Integrative Healthcare Solutions; med. cons. Joint Comm. Internat. Author: Psychiatric Morbidity of Physicians, 1964, Psychiatric Issues in the Lives of Physicians, 1966, Child Psychiatry, 1972, 86, Psychiatric Reviews, 1976; founding editor-in-chief Child Psychiatry and Human Devel., 1970-83; editor: Ship's Medical Chest, 1984; mem. editl. bd. MD mag., 1976—. Recipient OutstandingSvc. medal Bd. Regents Uniformed Svcs. U., 1981, Surgeon Gen.'s medallion. Fellow Am. Psychiat. Assn. (life), Aerospace Med. Assn. (assoc.; Longacre medal); mem. Assn. Mil. Surgeons U.S., Sigma Xi. Catholic. Home: 3625 S Washington Ave Titusville FL 32780 Home Phone: 321-639-0515; Office Phone: 312-626-9373. E-mail: jcduffy34@hotmail.com.

DUFFY, JOHN FITZGERALD, lawyer, educator; b. Pittsfield, Mass., Nov. 22, 1963; s. Thomas Francis and Noreen (Brett) D.; m. Anne Sprightley Ryan, July 3, 1998; 1 child, Clara Trinity. AB in Physics cum laude, Harvard Coll., 1985; JD cum laude, U. Chgo., 1989. Bar: Pa. 1991, D.C. 1994, U.S. Patent and Trademark Office 1996. Law clk. to Hon. Stephen Williams U.S. Ct. Appeals (D.C. Cir.), Washington, 1989-90; atty. advisor Office of Legal Counsel, U.S. Dept. Justice, Washington, 1990-92; law clk. to Justice Antonin Scalia U.S. Supreme Ct., Washington, 1992-93; assoc. Covington & Burling, Washington, 1993-96; asst. prof. law Cardozo Law Sch., Yeshiva U., NYC, 1996-2000; assoc. prof. law William and Mary Sch. Law, Williamsburg, Va., 2000; prof. law George Washington U. Law Sch., 2003—; of counsel Fried, Frank, Harris, Shriver & Jacobson, Washington, 2006—. Avocation: distance running. Office: George Washington Law Sch 2000 H Street NW Washington DC 20052 E-mail: jfduffy@law.gwu.edu.

DUFFY, JOHN JOSEPH, retired academic administrator, historian, educator; b. Charleston, SC, Apr. 25, 1931; s. John Joseph and Mary (McMahon) D.; m. Marcia Fletcher Tinkham, Aug. 15, 1959; children: Katharine, John Joseph, Eleanor. BA in History, Coll. Charleston, 1952; MA in History, U. S.C., 1955, PhD in History, 1963. Dir. U. S.C., Beaufort, 1959-66, assoc. prof. history Columbia, 1964-98, acad. coord. Coll. Gen. Studies, 1966-67, asst. provost regional campuses, 1967-68, assoc. provost regional campuses, 1968-72, assoc. v.p. regional campuses, 1972-77, system v.p. univ. campuses and continuing edn., 1977-88, chancellor univ. campuses and continuing edn., 1988-91; vice provost for regional campuses and continuing edn., 1991-92; vice provost, exec. dean regional campuses/continuing edn. U. S.C., Columbia, 1992-98; ret., 1998. Author: (radio script) Secession Convention of 1860, 1960; (pamphlet) A Short History of Beaufort County, 1975, also articles. Dist. chmn. Midlands coun. Boy Scouts Am., 1969-71; sustaining mem. S.C. Dem. Party. Recipient Disting. Svc. award Garnet and Black of U. S.C., 1969, Outstanding Edn. Profl. award S.C. Assn. Higher Continuing Edn., 1983, Disting. Svc. award Ednl. Found. U. S.C., 1989; named Young Man of Yr. Jaycees, Beaufort County, S.C., 1964 Mem. So. History Assn., S.C. History Assn., Nat. Univ. Continuing Edn. Assn. (chair region III 1980-82), Nat. Assn. State Univs. and Land Grant Colls., Rotary, Phi Beta Kappa Roman Catholic. Avocations: reading, music.

DUFFY, JOHN LEWIS, retired Latin, English and reading educator; b. Whittemore, Iowa, Oct. 6, 1934; s. Lewis A. and Dorothy (Bestenlehner) D.; m. Anne O'Brien, July 19, 1958; children: Jane, Paul, Sarah, Steven. BA, Loras Coll., 1956; MS Edn., Creighton U., 1961; student, U. Minn., 1967. Tchr. jr. and sr. H.S., coach Presentation Acad., Whittemore, Iowa, 1957—58; H.S. tchr. Clear Lake Cmty. Schs., Iowa, 1958—61; tchg. asst. U. Iowa, Iowa City, 1961—62; tchr. Latin Larkin H.S., Elgin, Ill., 1962—96, students' coun. advisor, 1965—71, chmn. English and fgn. langs., 1969—77, chmn. English and reading divsn., 1977—96. Tchr. prep. courses for ACT, PSAT and SAT Elgin YWCA and Larkin H.S., Elgin, 1977-96. Summer chef's asst. The Frugal Gourmet, WTTW-TV, Chgo., 1983. Trustee Elgin C.C., 1975—, chmn. bd., 1980-81, 85-87, 97-99, vice-chmn., 1981-84, 94-95; bd. dirs. Elgin Area Cath. Social Svcs., 1981-90, pres., 1986-88; mem. St. Laurence Parish Bd., 1974-79, Edn. Commn., 1972-79, chmn. Edn. Commn., 1974-79; state advisor Iowa Jr. Classical League, 1960-61 Named Kane County Disting. Educator of Yr., 1982, Outstanding Young Men in Am., 1970; recipient Outstanding Young Educator award Elgin Jaycees, 1969. Mem.: Am. Assn. Cmty. and Jr. Colls., Ill. Coun. Tchrs. English, Nat. Coun. Tchrs. English, Ill. Classical League, Am. Classical League, Elgin Assn. Sch. Adminstrs., Elgin Tchrs. Assn. (welfare chmn. and chief negotiator 1963—65, pres. 1966—67), Ill. Edn. Assn. (legis., chmn. northeastern divsn. 1968—71, chmn. ad hoc com. on tchr. tenure 1972—73), Ill. C.C. Trustees Assn. (exec. com. 1981—84, chmn. west suburban region 1981—84, chmn. fed. rels. com. 1982—87, bd. rep. 1986—95, 1997—, exec. com. 1998—2000, chmn. west suburban region 1998—2000, exec. com. 2002—04, chmn. west suburban region 2002—04, Trustee of Yr. award 2002), Am. Assn. C.C. (bd. dirs. 1990—93), Assn. C.C. Trustees (chmn. ctrl. region nominating com. 1981—82, sgt.-at-arms ann. conv. 1982, mem. com. on internat. rels. 1983—84, bd. dirs. 1983—89, chmn. future directions com. 1984—86, fed. rels. commn. 1985—93, chmn. ctrl. region, vice-chmn. fed. rels. commn. 1987—88, chmn. fed. rels. commn. 1988—89, chmn. ctrl. region nominating com. 1992—93, select com. 2001—, Ctrl. Region Trustee of Yr. award 1991, 2002). Home (Winter): 4840 Heron Run Cir Leesburg FL 34748-7819 Home (Summer): 192 Kathleen Dr Elgin IL 60123-5914 Home Phone: 847-742-0134. Home Fax: 352-323-1827, 847-429-0408.

DUFFY, KEVIN, dean; b. Ireland; B in Food Svc. Mgmt., Johnson & Wales U., M in Teacher's Edn. Owner, operator gourmet shop, restaurant, Smithfield, RI; chef Ritz Carlton Hotel, Boston, Royal Bermuda Yacht Club, Hamilton, Bermuda, Skyline Hotel, London; chef instr. Coll. Culinary Arts, Johnson & Wales U., Providence, 1979—99, asst. dir. culinary edn., 1999, dean culinary edn. Mgr. Student Culinary Team. Recipient Escoffier award, Coll. Culinary Arts, Johnson & Wales U., 1998. Mem.: Am. Culinary Fedn. Avocation: golf. Office: Johnson & Wales U Coll Culinary Arts 8 Abbott Park Pl Providence RI 02903 Office Phone: 401-598-1760. Business E-Mail: kevin.duffy@jwu.edu.*

DUFFY, KEVIN THOMAS, federal judge; b. NYC, Jan. 10, 1933; s. Patrick John and Mary (McGarrell) D.; m. Irene Krumeich, Nov. 9, 1957; children: Kevin Thomas, Irene Moira, Gavin Edward, Patrick Giles. AB, Fordham Coll., 1954, LLB, 1958. Bar: N.Y. 1958. Clk. to chief circuit judge, NYC, 1955-58; asst. chief criminal div. U.S. Atty.'s Office, NYC, 1958-61; assoc. Whitman, Ransom & Coulson, NYC, 1961-66; ptnr. Gordon & Gordon, NYC, 1966-69; regional adminstr. SEC, NYC, 1969-72; judge U.S. Dist. Ct. (So. Dist.), NY, 1972—, sr. judge, 1997—. Adj. prof. securities law Bklyn. Law Sch., 1975-80; prof. trial advocacy NYU, 1982-84, Pace Law Sch., 1984-85, Fordham Law Sch., 1993—. Author: Cross-Examination of Witnesses: The Litigator's Puzzle, 1990, Impeachment of Witnesses, 1990. Recipient Achievement in Law award Fordham Coll. Alumni Assn., 1976, Alumni Gold medal Fordham Law Sch., 1984, Kupferman's award Laymen's Nat. Bible Assn., 1992, Disting. Pub. Svc. award N.Y. County Lawyers' Assn., Lifetime Achievement award SEC, 1995. Mem. ABA, Am. Bar Assn., N.Y. State County Bar Assn., Westchester County Bar Assn., Assn. of Bar of City of N.Y., Fed. Bar Council (trustee 1970-72), Fordham Law Sch. Alumni Assn. (trustee 1969—, v.p.). Clubs: Merchants (N.Y.C.). Office: US Dist Ct US Courthouse 500 Pearl St Rm 2540 New York NY 10007-1502

DUFFY, LAWRENCE KEVIN, biochemist, educator; b. Bklyn., Feb. 1, 1948; s. Michael and Anne (Browne) D.; m. Geraldine Antoinette Sheridan, Nov. 10, 1972; children: Anne Marie, Kevin Michael, Ryan Sheridan. BS, Fordham U., Bronx, NY, 1969; MS, U. Alaska, 1972, PhD, 1977. Tchg. asst. dept. chemistry U. Alaska, 1969-71, rsch. asst. Inst. Arctic Biology, 1974-77; postdoctoral fellow Boston U., 1977-78, Roche Inst. Molecular Biology, 1978-80; rsch. asst. prof. U. Tex. Med. Br., Galveston, 1980-82; asst. prof. neurology (biol. chemistry) Med. Sch. Harvard U., Boston, 1982-87, adv. biochemistry instr. Med. Sch., 1983-87; instr. gen. and organic chemistry Roxbury C.C., 1984-87; prof. chemistry and biochemistry U. Alaska, Fairbanks, 1992—, head dept. chemistry and biochemistry, 1994-99, assoc. dean for grad. studies and outreach Coll. Natural Sci. and Math., 2000—06, interim dean Grad. Sch., 2007—. Coord. program biochemistry and molecular biology for summer undergrad. rsch., 1987-96; dir. Alaska Basic Neurosci. Program, 2000-06; pres. U. Alaska Fairbanks Faculty Senate, 2000-01; curriculum adv. bd. North Star Sch. Sys., 2002-04, pollution control. commn., 2004-06. Mem. editl. bd. Sci. of Total Environment. Pres., bd. dirs. Alzheimer Disease Assn. of Alaska, 1994-95; mem. instnl. rev. bd. Fairbanks Meml. Hosp., 1990; sci. adv. bd. Am. Fedn. Aging Rsch, 1994-95. Lt. USNR, 1971-73. NSF trainee, 1971; J.W. McLaughlin fellow, 1981; W.F. Milton scholar, 1983; recipient Alzheimer's Disease and Related Disorders Assoc. Faculty Scholar award, 1987; Carol Fiest Outstanding Advisor award, 1994, 97, 2005, Nat. Inst. Deafness & Commn. Disorders, NIH mentoring cert. merit, 1996, North Star Bough Sch. Dist. Svc. award, 1998, Alumni Achievement award U. Alaska-Fairbanks, 1999, Usibelli profl. activity award, 2002, Sven Ebbesson neurosci. svc. award, 2007. Fellow: Arctic Inst. North Am., Am. Inst. Chemists (pres. 2006); mem.: AAAS (arctic divsn. exec. dir.), Am. Soc. Circumpolar Health (bd. dirs. 2003—06), Am. Chem. Soc. (Analytical Chemistry award 1969), N.Y. Acad. Scis., Am. Soc. Biol. Chemists, Am. Soc. Neurochemists, Sigma Xi (assoc. regional dir. 2000—02, pres. 1991 Alaska club, nominating com.), Phi Lambda Upsilon. Roman Catholic. Office: U Alaska Fairbanks Box 756160 Fairbanks AK 99775 Office Phone: 907-474-7525. Business E-Mail: fflkd@uaf.edu.

DUFFY, MARTIN EDWARD, management consultant, economist; b. Fall River, Mass., May 24, 1940; s. Arthur Louis and Edna Marie (Cunneen) D.; m. Irene Patricia Daley, Aug. 24, 1968 (div. Jan. 1980); 1 child, Kathryn; m. Priscilla Claire Stieff, May 14, 1988; 1 child, Brianna. BS in History, BSEE, Tufts U., 1963; MBA, U. Pa., 1967. Asst. dean U. Pa., 1967-71; asst. dir. Fels Ctr., U. Pa., 1971-73; v.p. Data Resources, Lexington, Mass., 1975-84; v.p., gen. mgr. MRCA Info. Svcs., Cambridge, 1984-86; pres. The Perseus Group/RCG, Boston, 1986—; co-founder AllSeasons Investments, 1999—. Planning com. White Ho. Conf. on Aging, Washington, 1981; cons. La in 2001, Baton Rouge, 1982; lectr. in field; adj. prof. mgmt. Emmanuel Coll., Suffolk U.; conf. leader Presdl. Summit for Am.'s Future, 1997, chmn. uplando adv. com., 2004—. Author: The Elderly in Future Economy, 1981. Lt. USN, 1963-65. Mem. Am. Econs. Assn., Nat. Assn. Forensic Economists, Cambridge Sports Union, Tufts U. Alumni Assn. (pres. 1985, exec. com. 1982-87, mem. coun. 1978—), Nat. Bus. Travelers Assn. (bd. dirs. edl. com. 1988-93). Roman Catholic. Avocations: running marathons, mountain climbing, biking. *A career is an unfolding process, like the gradual opening of an exotic design, demanding only our presence, attention and determination to do well.*

DUFFY, MARTIN PATRICK, lawyer; b. Louisville, Feb. 2, 1942; s. Martin Joseph and Elsie (Schrader) D.; m. Virginia Schoo, Mar. 20, 1970; children: Timothy Brian, Kathleen Kelly. AB in English, U. Notre Dame, 1964; JD, U. Louisville, 1975. Bar: Ky. 1975, U.S. Tax Ct. 1980. Ptnr. Olson, Baker, Henriksen & Duffy, Louisville, 1978-79, Wyatt, Tarrant & Combs, Louisville, 1979--. Bd. dirs. Bellarmine Coll. Overseers, Louisville, 1974-80; trustee St. Mary & Elizabeth Hosp., Louisville, 1980-86, chmn. bd. 1982-85. With U.S. Army, 1964-65, 68-69. Mem. ABA, Ky. Bar Assn., Louisville Bar Assn. Democrat. Roman Catholic. Avocations: running, golf. Office: Wyatt Tarrant & Combs 2700 Citizens Plz Louisville KY 40202 Office Phone: 502-562-7564. Office Fax: 502-589-0309. Business E-Mail: pduffy@wyattfirm.com.

DUFFY, MICHAEL, art educator; s. Thomas and Donna Duffy; m. Judith Goodman. BA, U. NH, Durham, 1973, MA in History, 1975; MA in Art History, Mich. State U., East Lansing, 1984; PhD, U. Ill., Urbana-Champaign, 1990. Instr. art dept. Western Ill. U., Macomb, 1989—90; instr. Sch. Art and Design, East Carolina U., Greenville, NC, 1990—94, asst. prof., 1994—99, assoc. prof., 1999—. Contbr. articles to profl. jours.; editor Southea. Coll. Art Conf. Rev., 2004—06; contbr. essays to exhbn. catalogs. Mem.: Southeastern Coll. Art Conf., 19th Century Historians of Art, Coll. Art Assn., Am. Soc. 18th Century Studies, 19th Century Studies Assn. (bd. dirs. 2005—07). Mailing: PO Box 7332 Greenville NC 27835

DUFFY, MICHAEL F., commissioner; BA, Catholic U. Am., 1971; JD, George Washington U., Nat. Law Ctr., 1976. Bar: Am., DC. Atty. Fed. Mine Safety Health Rev. Commn., 1977—79; sr. counsel Am. Mining Congress, 1979—87; counsel to chmn. Fed. Mine Safety Health Rev. Commn., 1987—93, commr., 2002—03, chmn., 2003—; dep. gen. counsel Nat. Mining Assn., 1993—2002. Author: Resolution of MSHA Disputes The Need for Change and Suggestions for a More Productive Approach, 1993, Safety and Health Beyond the Gates The Overlap of EPA and MSHA Standards on Explosives: A Case Study, 1994, Prometheus Re-Bound: How Adoption of the Kyoto Protocol on Climate Change Would Devastate the Western U.S. Coal Industry, 1999. Office: Fed Mine Safety Health Rev Commn 601 New Jersey Ave Washington DC 20001 Business E-Mail: mduffy@fmshrc.gov.

DUFFY, NANCY KEOGH, newscaster, broadcast executive; b. Washington, Nov. 24, 1947; d. William Francis and Gertrude K. (Keogh) D.; divorced; children: Peter Patrick, Matthew Michael. Student, St. Mary of the Woods Coll.; AB, Marywood Coll., 1967. News reporter Sta. WHEN TV and Radio, Syracuse, NY, 1967-70; press sec. City of Syracuse, 1970; news reporter Sta. WTVH, Syracuse, 1971-77; news anchorperson Sta. WIXT-TV, Syracuse, 1977—. Talk show host Syracuse New Channels, 1986-87; talk show host, producer Community Connections, 1987-89; instr. Syracuse U. Prodr. TV series Duffy's People, With Steve on Sunday. Founder Syracuse St. Patrick's Parade, 1983, pres., organizer, 1983-2001, hon. pres., 2002-; organizer Cooperstown 50th Ann. Baseball Hall of Fame

Parade, 1989, opening ceremonies Empire State Games, 1990; co-organizer Save Our Syracuse Symphony, 1984—; organizer Bark-Out Against Rabies Paws Parade, 1995-98, Artist Eagle Faces Exhibits, 1999-2003; bd. dirs. Syracuse Symphony, 1992-98, The Media Unit, 1977-97; active Project children, Syracuse, YMCA; telethon hostess Muscular Dystrophy Assn.; organizer poetry workshops for children, 1995—; mem. Onondaga County Traffic Safety Bd., 1977-2002, Le Moyne Coll. Pres. Assocs.; honorary chair, Civil War Weekend, Peterborough, NY.; bd. dirs. Native Am. Svc. Agy., 2002. Recipient Nat. Angel award Best Spl. Religion in Media, Post Std. Woman of Achievement award, 1st Downtown award for excellence, 1986, Mayor's Achievement award, 1985, Humanitarian award Project Children, 1993, N.Y. State Senate commendation, 1995; named Woman of Achievement N.Y. State Fair, 1994, YWCA Acad. Diversity Achievers, 2004. Mem. Am. Women in Radio and TV (nat. award 1973), Women in Comms. (Outstanding Communicator award 1985), Syracuse Press Club (bd. dirs. 1987—, v.p. 1990, 97, 98, pres. 1991-92, Bernard and Dorothy Newer Svc. award 1995, lifetime achievement award 2000), Syracuse Rotary (pub. rels. 1989-92), Am. Heart Assn. (hon. co-chair Ctrl. N.Y. 1997). Roman Catholic. Office: Sta WIXT-TV 5904 Bridge St East Syracuse NY 13057-2941 Office Phone: 315-446-9999.

DUFFY, NORMAN VINCENT, chemistry professor; b. Washington, Nov. 1, 1938; s. Norman Vincent and Glenn Mae (Drury) D.; m. Marianne Youdell, Oct. 13, 1962; children: Norman Vincent III, Mary Virginia, Joseph Leslie, Anne-Marie, Maureen Glenn. BS in Chemistry, Georgetown U., 1961, PhD in Chemistry, 1966. NATO postdoctoral fellow chemistry dept. Univ. Coll. London, 1965—66; vis. asst. prof. Kent State U., Ohio, 1966—67, asst. prof. chemistry, 1967—70, assoc. prof., 1970—80, asst. dean arts and scis., 1973—75, assoc. dean, 1975—76, prof. chemistry dept., 1980—96, chmn. dept. chemistry, 1981—86; prof. chemistry Wheeling Jesuit U., 1996—, chmn. dept. biology and chemistry, 1996—2000, chmn. dept. chemistry, 2000—02. Contbr. articles to encys.; prodr. ednl. films in field. Recipient US Prof. of Yr. award, Carnegie Found. for Advancement of Tchg. and Coun. for Advancement and Support of Edn., 2006. Mem. Am. Chem. Soc., The Chem. Soc., Sigma Xi. Roman Catholic. Office: Dept Chemistry Wheeling Jesuit U Wheeling WV 26003 Office Phone: 304-243-2261. E-mail: nduffy@wju.edu.

DUFFY, ROBERT ALOYSIUS, aeronautical engineer; b. Buck Run, Pa., Sept. 9, 1921; s. Joseph Albert and Jane Veronica (Archer) D.; m. Elizabeth Reed Orr, Aug. 19, 1945 (dec.); children: Michael Gordon, Barclay Robert (dec.), Marian Orr (dec.), Judith Elizabeth Parsons, Patricia Archer; m. Jenifer Williams Pickett, Nov. 28, 1992. BS in Aero. Engring., Ga. Inst. Tech., 1951. Commd. 2d lt. U.S. Army, 1942; commd. U.S. Air Force, advanced through grades to brig. gen., 1967; vice comdr. USAF Space and Missile Systems Orgn., LA, 1970-71; ret., 1971; v.p., dir. Draper Lab. div. MIT, Cambridge, Mass., 1971-73; pres., chief exec. officer Charles Stark Draper Lab., Inc., 1973-87, dir., 1973-91, dir. emeritus, 1991—. Contbr. articles to profl. jours. Decorated Disting. Svc. medal, Legion of Merit; recipient Thomas D. White award Nat. Geog. Soc., 1970; named to Ga. Tech. Engring. Hall of Fame, 1994. Fellow AIAA; mem. NAE, Internat. Acad. Astronautics, Inst. Navigation (Thurlow award 1964, pres. 1976-77), Air Force Assn., Tau Beta Pi. Home: 1001 Arbor Lake Dr #1108 Naples FL 34110 Office: Charles Stark Draper Lab 555 Technology Sq Cambridge MA 02139-3539 Personal E-mail: jenduff@comcast.net.

DUFFY, SEAMUS C., lawyer; b. Phila., 1961; BA, Villanova Univ., 1984, JD summa cum laude, 1987. Bar: Pa. 1988. Clerk US Dist Ct., Phila., 1987—88; joined Drinker Biddle & Reath LLP, Phila., 1988, ptnr., litig., and mem., mgmt. com. Bd. dir. Leadership, Inc. Lectr. in field. Office: Drinker Biddle & Reath LLP One Logan Sq 18th & Cherry Sts Philadelphia PA 19103-6996 Office Phone: 215-988-2440. Office Fax: 215-988-2757. Business E-Mail: seamus.duffy@dbr.com.

DUFFY, SIMON P., telecommunications industry executive; MA, Oxford U., Eng.; MBA, Harvard U. Dir. ops. United Distillers, Guinness plc, dir. corp. fin.; dep. chmn., group fin. dir. EMI Group; group fin. dir. THORN EMI EMI Group plc; dep. chmn., CEO World Online Internat. NV; CEO End2End, 2001; CFO Orange SA; COO NTL Europe, 2003; CEO NTL Inc., NYC, 2003—06, exec. vice chmn., 2006—. Office: NTL Europe Inc 22 Suffolk St London SW1Y 4HG England also: Ntl 909 3rd Ave Rm 2800 New York NY 10022-4790

DUFFY, TERRENCE A., mercantile exchange executive; b. 1958; BSBA, U. Wis., Whitewater, 1980. Pres. TDA Trading, Inc., 1981—; mem. Chgo. Merc. Exch. Inc., 1981—, bd. mem., 1995—, vice chmn., 1998—2002, chmn., 2002—07; vice. chmn. Chgo. Merc. Exch. Holdings Inc., 2001—02, chmn., 2002—07; exec. chmn. CME Group Inc. (formerly Chgo. Merc. Exch. Holdings Inc.), Chgo., 2007—. Mem. bd. World Bus. Chgo., Ill. Agrl. Leadership Found.; bd. regents Mercy Home for Boys and Girls; bd. trustees Saint Xavier Univ.; co-chair Mayo Clinic Greater Chgo. Leadership Coun. Named Top 100 Irish Bus. Leaders, Irish America Magazine, 2003, 2004, 2005. Mem.: Pres. Circle of the Chgo. Coun. on Foreign Rels., Exec. Club of Chgo., Econ. Club of Chgo. Achievements include apptd. by President Bush to Nat. Saver Summit on Retirement Savings, 2002, Fed. Retirement Thrift Investment Bd. (FRTIB), 2003. Office: CME Group Inc 20 S Wacker Dr Chicago IL 60606*

DUFFY, THOMAS M., transportation services executive, lawyer; b. 1961; BBA, JD, U. Ga. Bar: 1986. Assoc. Peterson Dillard Young Asselin & Powell LLP, 1986—94, ptnr., 1994—97, Troutman Sanders LLP, Atlanta, 1997—98; v.p. Allied Holdings, Inc., Decatur, Ga., 1998—2000, gen. counsel, 1998—, sec., 1998—, sr. v.p., 2000—04, exec. v.p., 2004—. Office: Allied Holdings Inc Ste 200 160 Clairemont Ave Decatur GA 30030 Office Phone: 404-373-4285. Office Fax: 404-370-4206.*

DUFFY, VIRGINIA, minister; b. Cleve., Apr. 10, 1939; d. Paul Daniel and Anna (Nagy) Szaniszlo; 1 child, Steven T. Eisentrout. BA, Elmhurst Coll., Ill., 1962; MA, Oberlin Coll., Ohio, 1965; MDiv, Oberlin Grad. Sch. Theology, Ohio, 1966; MA, Coll. Mount St. Joseph, Cin., 1982. Ordained Min. United Ch. Christ, 1966, cert. Secondary Tchr. Ohio, 1982. Assoc. min. First Congl. United Ch. Christ, Elyria, Ohio, 1965—71, United Ch. in Walpole, Mass., 1971—73; co-min. Mt. Zion St. Paul United Chs. of Christ, New Richmond, Ohio, 1976—83; tchr. West Clermont Local Sch. Dist., Amelia, Ohio, 1984—94; co-min. York St. Congl. United Ch. Christ, Newport, Ky., 1988—90; min., sr. min. Philippus United Ch. Christ, Cin., 1994—2004; interim min., cons. Southwest Ohio No. Ky. Assn., 2005—. Corp. bd. mem. United Ch. Christ, United States, 1996—99; bd. dirs. Religare Assembly Greater Cin. No. Ky., Cin., 1995—99; assoc. coun. Southwest Ch. No. Ky. Assn., Southwest, Ohio, 1977—83. Author of poems, (ednl. resource) The Healthy Life: A Biblical Approach, 1989; co-author: Called tobe Gifted and Giving, 1985. Bd. dirs., chair, vice chair United Ch. Homes, 2000—; bd. trustees IMPACT Over the Rhine, Cin., 1995—2004, Vol. Am., Cin., 1996—2000. Recipient Outstanding Young Women Am., 1971, Excellence Tchg., Cin. Gas and Elec., 1992. Mem.: Delta Kappa Gamma. United Church Of Christ. Avocations: music, reading. Home: 2921 Timberview Dr Cincinnati OH 45211

DUFFY, W. LESLIE, lawyer; b. NYC, Dec. 31, 1939; s. William L. and Edna (Torseillo) D.; 1 child, Alexander Durand. BA, U. Notre Dame, 1961; LLB, Columbia U., 1964; LLM, NYU, 1967. Assoc. Cahill, Gordon & Reindel, NYC, 1965-73, ptnr., 1973—. Bd. dirs. various pub. cos. Contbr. articles to profl. jours. Served to lt. USNR. Mem. ABA, N.Y. State Bar Assn. Office: Cahill Gordon & Reindel LLP 80 Pine St Fl 17 New York NY 10005-1790 Business E-Mail: wduffy@cahill.com.

DUFFY, WILLIAM J., lawyer; b. Allentown, Pa., Nov. 25, 1954; s. James Edward and Shirley Ritter Duffy; m. Teri S. Anderson, Aug. 30, 1986; children: Lucas James, Katherine Jeanne. BS, U. Del., 1976; MS, Pa. State U., 1983; JD, U. Denver, 1986. Bar: Colo. 1986, U.S. Dist. Ct. (D.C. dist.), U.S. Ct. Appeals (10th cir.). Assoc. Kelly Standsfield/O'Donnel, Denver, 1986-89; dir. Parcel Mauro Hultin & Spaanstra, Denver, 1989-98, Parcel Mauro, PC, Denver, 1998—; ptnr. Davis Graham & Stubbs, LLC, Denver, 1999—. Office: Davis Graham & Stubbs 1550 17th St Ste 500 Denver CO 80202-1500 E-mail: william.duffy@dgslaw.com.

DUFOUR, JACK EDWARD, small business owner, retired special education educator; b. Oakland, Calif., Feb. 5, 1942; s. George Pierre and Adele Marie Dufour; m. Marite Soriano de Luzuriaga, Aug. 30, 2003; children: Geraldine Soriano Ruiz de Luzuriaga, Henry Soriano Ruiz de Luzuriaga. AA in Edn., Cabrillo Coll., Aptos, Calif., 1966; BA in Psychology & Phys. Edn., Calif. State U., Chico, 1970; MEd, Calif. State U., Sacramento, 1975. Cert. secondary tchr. Calif. State U., 1969, learning handicapped credential Calif., 1972, adminstrn. svc. credential Calif., 1974, standard designated tchg. credential Calif., 1975, pupil personnel credential Calif., 1975, public safety and accident prevention credential Calif., 1975, cc instr. credential Calif., 1978, resource specialist credential Calif., 1981. Educationally handicapped tchr., psychology tchr., phys. edn. tchr. San Juan Unified Sch. Dist., Sacramento, 1970—78; learning disability tchr., resource specialist, spl. day class tchr., adaptive phys. edn. tchr., phys. edn. tchr. Santa Cruz City Schs., Calif., 1978—2002; athletic dir. Harbor HS, Santa Cruz, 1989—2002; owner Heavenly Cafe, Scotts Valley, Calif., 2003—06. Head boys and girls water polo and swim coach Casa Roble HS, Orangevale, Calif., 1972—78, founder, first coach boys and girls water polo swim swim team, 1973; head coach Citrus Heights, USA Swim Club, Calif., 1975—76; coach Founder First Girl's Water Polo Program, Sacramento, 1975—78, Santa Cruz, 1979—91; pres. San Juan Water Polo League, Sacramento, 1975—77, San Juan Swim League, Sacramento, 1975—78; head boys and girls water polo and swim coach Harbor HS, 1978—93; founder, pres., head coach Santa Cruz Water Polo Club, US Water Polo, 1978—93. Mem. Nat. Heritage Found., 2003—, Native Sons of Golden West, Santa Cruz, 2002—; comdr. Marine Corps League, Monterey Bay Detachment 711, Monterey Bay Area, Calif., 1999—; commandant Marine Corps League, 2007. Cpl. USMC, 1962—65, Vietnam Era. Decorated Nat. Def., Good Conduct, Armed Forces Expeditionary, Marine Corps Overseas Svc. Ribbon, Vietnam Vets USMC; recipient Water Polo Coach of theYear and Honor Coach, Ctrl. Coast Sect., 1989-90, Letter of Appreciation, People to People Program, USMC, Coach, Okinawan Little League, 1964/1965, Coach of the Yr., San Juan Unified Sch. Dist. and Santa Cruz City Sch. Dist., 1973 - 1993: 12 Awards. Mem.: Marine Corp. Assn., Am. Fedn. Of Teachers (assoc.), Calif. Teachers Assn. (assoc.), Am. Legion, VFW, Santa Cruz Paleontology (assoc.), Lambda Pi (life; alumni rep. 1999—). Avocations: paleontology, travel, physical fitness, Japanese language and culture. Home Phone: 831-335-3017.

DUFOUR, JEAN-MARIE, economist, statistician, educator; b. Montreal, Que., Can., Dec. 27, 1949; s. Jean-Marie Dessureault and Bella Dufour. BA, U. Montreal, 1969; BSc in Math. with hon., McGill U., Montreal, 1971; MSc in Stats., U. Montreal, 1973; MA in Econs., Concordia U., 1974, U. Chgo., 1978, PhD in Econs., 1979. Lectr. stats. U. Que., Trois-Rivières, 1972-73; prof. math. Coll. Édouard-Montpetit, Montreal, 1973-75; rsch. assoc. Inst. Applied Econ. Rsch. Concordia U., 1978-79; lectr. econs. U. Montreal, 1978-79, mem. rsch. staff ctr., 1979—85, sr. mem. rsch. staff, dir. rsch. program in econometrics and macroecons. ctr. de recherche et développement en économique, 1985-90, asst. prof., 1979-83, assoc. prof., 1983-88, prof., 1988—, dir. ctr. recherche et développment en économique, 1988—95, 1997—98, chmn. dept. econs., 1995—97, Can. rsch. chair in econometrics, 2001—. Vis. scholar MIT, 1980, Queen's U., 1986, CEPREMAP, Paris, 1986, U. Libre de Bruxelles, 1988, 89, 90, 91, 93, Ecole Nat. des Stats. et l'Adminstrn. Economique, Paris, 1990-91, 93, 95, 2000-01, 04, U. Scis. Sociales de Toulouse, France, 1992, 94, 2002, Humboldt U. Berlin, 1994, German Bundesbank, Frankfurt, 2001-04; cons. Econ. Coun. Can., 1981, Office de Planification et Devel. economique du Que., 1982, Royal Commn. Econ. Union and Devel. prospects for Can., 1983-84; invited prof. U. Toulouse I, 1983, 94, 2002, U. Pa., 1992, U. Lausanne, 1995; rsch. fellow Ctr. Ops. Rsch. and Econometrics U. Cath., Louvain, 1985-86; Benjamin Meaker chair, U. Bristol, 1993, 99; vis. prof. Stanford U., 1999, Tilburg U., 2000, Technische U. Dresden, 2000, U. Amsterdam, 2003-04, Inst. Fur Wirtschaftsforschung Halle, Germany, 2005-06. Assoc. editor Econometrica, 1996-2002, Jour. Econometrics, 1994—, Empirical Econs., 1994—, Econometric Theory, 1991-93, Econometric Reviews, 1991-96, 98—, Annales d'Économie et de Statistique, 1990—, Cahiers de Centre d'Études de Recherche Opérationnelle, 1989—95, Can. Jour. Econs., 1984-88; guest editor Jour. Econometrics, 1992-93, Empirical Econs., 1993—; contbr. 100 articles to profl. jours. Recipient award Social Scis. and Humanities Rsch. Coun. Can., 1980, Econ. Coun. Can., 1981, Govt. Que., 1982, Royal Commn. on Econ. Union and Devel. Prospects per Can., 1983-84, Natural Scis. and Engring. Rsch. Coun. Can., 1983—, Govt. Que. and Communauté française de Belgique, 1989-90, Govt. Que. and Govt. France, 1990-92, Can. Internat. Devel. Agy., 1991-93, Can. Network Ctrs. Excellence, 1998-, Can. Found. Innovation, 2001, Fonds quebecois de recherche sur la nature et les technogies, 2003-06, Fonds quebecois de rsch. sur la societe et la culture, 2003-, Inst. Fin. Math. Montreal, 2003-, Bank o Can., 2004-, Konrad Adenaver Rsch. award Alexander von Humboldt Found., 2005, Killam prize for social scis., 2006; rsch. grantee Ministry Edn. Que., 1979-82; fellow Can. Coun., 1975-78, Govt. Que., 1975-78, Social Scis. and Humanities Rsch. Coun. Can., 1985-86, Guggenheim Found., 2006-07; rsch. fellow Bank of Can., 2007; scholar U. Montreal, 1971-72. Mem.: Can. Econ. Assn., Soc. Can. Sci. Econ. (bd. dirs. 1984—87, pres. 1998—2001, Excellence in Rsch. award 1988, 2000, Marcel-Dagenais prize 2000), Inst. Math. Stats., Econometric Soc., Internat. Statis. Inst., Can. Econometric Study Group Bd. (dir. 2002—), Can. Econs. Assn., Am. Econ. Assn. (pres. 1999—2000), Ordre Nat. Du Québec (officer 2006). Achievements include research in statistical methodology in econometrics, exact distribution-free and parametric methods, time series analysis, casuality analysis, and statistical inference in weakly identified models; macroeconomics, finance, public finance, development. Avocations: philosophy, history, movies, art. Home: 1060 Ave Bernard Apt 5 Outremont PQ Canada H2V 1V2 Office Phone: 514-343-2400. Business E-Mail: jean.marie.dufour@umontreal.ca.

DUFRESNE, CRAIG ROGER, plastic surgeon, educator; b. Newport, RI, Sept. 20, 1951; s. Roger Joseph and Molly T. Dufresne; m. Katherine Ann Scrive, Aug. 11, 1978; children: Jacqueline Melissa, Elizabeth Ashley, Christopher Scrive. BA in Zoology summa cum laude, U. Vt., 1973; MD, Columbia U., 1977. Diplomate Am. Bd. Plastic Surgery. Intern Johns Hopkins Hosp., Balt., 1977-78, jr., then sr. resident in surgery, 1978-82; registrar in thoracic surgery Frenchay Hosp., Bristol, Eng., 1980-81; jr. res., then sr. resident in plastic surgery NYU Med. Ctr., NYC, 1982-84, fellow in microvascular surgery, 1984, fellow in craniofacial surgery, 1985; asst. prof., dir. Ctr. for Reconstructive Surgery, Johns Hopkins U., 1985-89, dir. Cleft Lip and Palate Clinic, 1985-89, clin. asst. prof. to clin. assoc. prof. Balt., 1989—; pvt. practice, Fairfax and Annandale, Va., 1989—, Chevy Chase, Md., 1989—; dir. craniofacial program Inova Fairfax Hosp. for Children. Clin. instr. George Washington U., Washington, 1990-93; clin. assoc. prof. Georgetown U., Washington, 1994—; numerous presentations in field; chief plastic surgery svc. Loch Raven VA Med. Ctr., 1985-89; clin. assoc. in plastic surgery U. Md. Hosps., 1985-89; attending physician Md. Inst. for Emergency Med. Svcs. Ctr., 1985-89; mem. exec. com., and med. adv. bd. Internat. Craniofacial Found., 1990-92; co-dir. Ctr. for Facial Rehab., Fairfax Hosp., 1989—; vis. prof. U. Rochester, N.Y., 1992, Ea. Va. Med. Coll., Norfolk, 1993; cons. plastic surgery svc. Bethesda Naval Hosp. Co-editor: Complex Craniofacial Problems: Guide to Analysis and Treatment, 1992; contbr. numerous articles to med. jours., chpts. to books. Asst. scoutmaster troop 1449 Boy Scouts Am., Washington, 1994-95. Named One of Best 150 Drs. in Balt., Balt. Mag., 1986; One of Best Regional Breast Surgeons, The Washingtonian, 1986, One Best Plastic Surgeons in Washington Area, 1993, 95, One of Best Doctors in DC Region, Washington Family mag., 2007, also others; grantee AO/ASIF, Howmedica, Inc., Nat. Inst. Dental Rsch., Bowles Fund, Children's Hosp., Storz, Inc. Fellow ACS; mem. AMA, Am. Soc. Aesthetic Plastic Surgery, Am. Soc. Plastic Surgeons, Am. Cleft Lip and Palate Assn., Am. Soc. Plastic and Reconstructive Surgeons (govt. rels. com. 1989—), Internat. Soc. Craniomaxillofacial Surgery, Am. Soc. Maxillofacial Surgeons (govt. rels. com. 1990—, best paper award com. 1993—), Plastic Surgery Rsch. Coun., John Staige David Soc., John M. Converse Soc., Northeastern Plastic Surgery Soc. (sci. program com. 1992-93), Southeastern Med. Soc., Pan-Pacific Plastic Surgery Assn., Fairfax Med. Soc., Nat. Capital Med. Soc., Montgomery Med. Soc., Johns Hopkins Med. and Surg. Assn. Avocations: tennis, golf, art and sculpture. Office: 5530 Wisconsin Ave #1235 Chevy Chase MD 20815 Address: 8501 Arlington Blvd #420 Fairfax VA 22031*

DUGAN, BRENDAN J., bank executive; b. Aug. 24, 1947; m. Barbara Dugan. BBA, St. Francis Coll., 1968. Sr., exec. mgmt. positions, pres. NatWest Bank USA; pres., COO European Am. Bank, NY, 1992—2001; COO Comml. Markets Group, Citibank, 2001—03; exec. v.p. Bus. Banking Divsn. Cmty. Bank, 2003—07; chmn., CEO Metro NY/NJ divsn. Sovereign Bancorp Inc., 2007—. Bd. dirs. Bklyn. Acad. of Music, Regional Plan Assn., Good Shepherd Svcs., Bklyn. St. Francis Coll., Futures in Edn. Found.; adv. bd. mem. Child Abuse Prevention Svcs., L.I., Neighborhood Housing Svcs. N.Y.C.; mem. Fin. Coun. of the Roman Catholic Diocese of Bklyn. Office: Sovereign Bancorp Inc 1500 Market St Philadelphia PA 19102*

DUGAN, CHARLES CLARK, retired physician, surgeon; b. Penn Yan, NY, Jan. 24, 1921; s. Charles Emanual and Wilhemia May (Clark) D.; m. Eugenie Alice Pounds, Aug. 12, 1944 (div. 1963); children: Charles Clark II, Douglas Craig, Timothy Gene; m. Ruth Louise Fugh, Dec. 3, 1965 (dec. 1983); adopted children: Dain Walters, Carl Jay. AA, Wentworth Mil. Jr. Coll., 1940; AB, Cornell U., 1942; MD, Jefferson Med. Coll., 1946; MPH, Naval Med. Sch. and Johns Hopkins U., 1956. Diplomate Am. Bd. Dermatology, Am. Bd. Allergy and Immunology, Spl. Bd. Dermatopathology, Am. Bd. Cosmetic Plastic Surgery, Am. Bd. Preventive Medicine, Aviation Medicine and Pub. Health, Nat. Bd. Med. Examiners. Resident in psychiatry Pa. Psychiat. Hosp., Phila., 1945-46; rotating intern extended in gen. surgery Harrisburg (Pa.) Gen. Hosp., 1946-47; resident in dermatology U. Colo. Med. Ctr., Denver, 1956-57; resident in dermatology and allergy Henry Ford Hosp., Detroit, 1957-59; pvt. practice dermatology, allergy, immunology, cosmetic plastic surgery West Palm Beach, Fla., 1959—2004; ret., 2004. Physician mem. bd. Palm Beach County Environ. Control Hearing Bd., West Palm Beach, 1981-94; active staff Palm Beach Gardens (Fla.) Cmty. Hosp., Good Samaritan Hosp., West Palm Beach, St. Mary's Hosp., West Palm Beach; mem. Wellington Regional Med. Ctr., West Palm Beach. Contbr. articles to profl. jours. Lt. col., pilot/flight surgeon USAF, 1947—56. Recipient Cert. of Svc., Am. Cancer Soc., West Palm Beach, 1961, numerous other awards; named Surgeon of Yr., Fla. Soc. Dematol. Surgeons, 1997. Fellow AMA, Fla. Med. Assn., Palm Beach County Med. Soc., Am. Acad. Dermatology, Am. Coll. Preventive Medicine, Am. Coll. Allergy, Asthma and Immunology, Am. Acad. Allergy, Asthma and Immunology, Internat. Acad. Cosmetic Surgery, Am. Acad. Facial Plastic and Reconstructive Surgery, Am. Acad. Cosmetic Surgery, Am. Soc. for Dermatol. Surgery (bd. dirs. 1980-83), Am. Soc. Dematopathology, Am. Soc. Cryosurgeons, Am. Soc. Cert. Allergists, Internat. Soc. Dematopathology, Fla. Soc. Dermatology (pres. 1973-74, Practitioner of Yr. award 1993), Am. Soc. Dermatol. Surgery (coun. 1980-83) Fla. Soc. Dermatol. Surgery (Lifetime Achievement award, 2005), numerous others; mem. Noah Worcester Dermatologic Soc. Republican. Presbyterian. Achievements include development of vaccine for herpes simplex and herpes immune virus; first person to describe correct pathophysiology of cerebral concussion correctly. Avocations: swimming, scuba diving, tennis, stamp collecting/philately, coin collecting/numismatics. Personal E-mail: ccdugan554@aol.com.

DUGAN, JOHN CUNNINGHAM, federal agency administrator, lawyer; b. Washington, June 3, 1955; m. Beth Dugan; children: Claire, Jack. BA in English Lit, with high distinction, U. Mich., 1977; JD cum laude, Harvard U., 1981. Bar: DC 1981. Minority gen. counsel US Senate Com. Banking, Housing & Urban Affairs, 1987—89; asst. sec. treasury domestic fin. to Pres. George HW Bush The White House, Washington; dep. asst. sec. Fin. Inst. Policy US Dept. Treasury, Washington, 1989—92, asst. sec. domestic fin., 1992—93, comptr. of the currency, 2005—; ptnr. Covington & Burling, Washington, 1993—2005, coord., Fin. Inst. Practice Group. Office: Comptr of the Currency Independence Sq 250 E St SW Mail Stop 9-1 Washington DC 20219-0001 Office Phone: 202-874-4900.*

DUGAN, JOHN F., lawyer; b. Phila., May 25, 1935; s. Albert C. and Helen Josephine (Pritchard) D.; m. Colette Gregory, Jan. 18, 1987. AB, U. Pa., 1956, LLD, 1960. Bar: Pa. 1961, U.S. Ct. Appeals (3d cir.) 1961, Va. 1966, U.S. Supreme Ct. 1967. Assoc. Obermayer Rebmann Maxwell & Hippel, Phila., 1960-66; of counsel Reynolds Metals Co., Richmond, Va., 1966-69, Pennwalt Corp., Phila., 1969-71; ptnr. Berkman Ruslander, Pitts., 1971-85, Kirkpatrick & Lockhart, Pitts., 1985—. Labor rels. law rep. mgmt., Kirkpatrick & Lockhart. Mem. Pitts. Field Club, Order of the Coif, Phi Beta Kappa. Office: Kirkpatrick & Lockhart 1500 Oliver Building Pittsburgh PA 15222-2312

DUGAN, JOHN LESLIE, JR., foundation executive; b. Phila., Nov. 6, 1921; s. John Leslie and Ellen May (Reid) D.; m. Barbara McClelland Day, Dec. 21, 1946; children: Barbara Nicholas, Geoffrey McClelland, Sara Ellen. BS, Swarthmore Coll., 1943; postgrad., Harvard U., 1947-48; MBA, U. Pa., 1950. Instr. Swarthmore Coll., 1946-47, U. Pa., 1948-50; cons. Booz, Allen and Hamilton, 1951-55; asst. to pres. Grace Nat. Bank, NYC, 1955-58; treas. Underwood Corp., NYC, 1958-60; v.p. fin. Chicopee div. Johnson & Johnson, New Brunswick, NJ, 1960-75; dir., adminstr. Robert Wood Johnson Found., Princeton, NJ, 1975-77; exec. v.p. Am. Diabetes Assn., Inc., NYC, 1977-80; exec. dir. Fin. Analysts Fedn., NYC, 1981-84; pres. The Greenwall Found., NYC, 1981-90; founder, pres. Buck Hill Conservation Found., 1992-97, trustee, 1992-99. Adj. prof. mgmt. St. Peter's Coll., 1975-81 Committeeman Millburn Twp., N.J., 1975-79, commr. fin. and welfare, 1976-79; vestryman, warden, lay reader Christ Ch. in Short Hills, N.J. Served to lt. comdr. USNR, 1942-61. Mem. Baltusrol Golf Club, Short Hills Club, Ozone Club, Buck Hill Golf Club, Sea Oaks Beach and Tennis Club, Tau Beta Pi. Republican. Home: 10 Blue Mill Rd PO Box 851 New Vernon NJ 07976-0851 Personal E-mail: jandbdugan@verizon.net.

DUGAN, KEVIN F., lawyer; b. Kingston, NY, Oct. 30, 1959; s. Owen F. and Helen A. (Frost) D.; m. Diane Tremaine, Dec. 30, 1988; children: Molly, Brighid, Owen. BS, Fla. State U., 1981; JD, Stetson Coll. Law, 1985. Bar: Fla. 1985, U.S. Dist. Ct. (mid. dist.), Fla., 1986, U.S. Ct. Appeals (11th cir.) 1987, N.H. 1991, U.S. Supreme Ct. 1991. Lawyer Woodworth & Dugan, St. Petersburg, Fla., 1985-90, Abramson, Brown & Dugan, Manchester, N.H., 1990—, Masterson, Rogers, Masterson &

Gustafson, St. Petersburg, 1998—. Mem. ATLA, N.H. Trial Lawyers Assn. (Bd. Govs. award 1997, bd. govs. 1995—, pres. 1999-2000, chair legis. com. 1999—), N.H. Bar Found., Inns of Ct. Democrat. Roman Catholic. Office: Abramson Brown & Dugan 1819 Elm St Manchester NH 03104-2910 E-mail: kdugan@arbd.com.

DUGAN, MARIELLEN, lawyer; BA summa cum laude, Montclair State U., 1988; JD magna cum laude, Seton Hall U., 1991. Law clk. to Hon. Dickinson R. Debevoise US Dist. Judge, Dist. of NJ; of counsel Kevin H. Marino PC, Newark, 1999—2003; chief staff, exec. asst. atty. gen. State of NJ, 2003—04, fist asst. atty. gen., 2004—05; v.p., gen. counsel NJ Resources Corp., Wall, 2005—. Office: NJ Resources Corp 1415 Wyckoff Rd Wall NJ 07719*

DUGAN, MAUREEN, biology educator, consultant; b. Boston; d. John and Catherine (Cahill) Dugan. BA, Framingham State Coll., Mass., 1971; MEd, Boston Coll., Chestnut Hill, Mass., 1980. Cert. Tchr. Commonwealth Mass., 1971, Nat. Bd. Certification AYA/Sci Nat. Bd. for Profl. Tchg. Stds., 1999. Tchr. sci. Nashoba Regional Sch. Dist., Bolton, Mass., 1971—2006. Cons. Coll. Bd., NYC, 2001—; adj. faculty Fitchburg State Coll., 1998—2000. Named Outstanding Biology Tchr. Mass., Nat. Assn. Biology Tchrs., 2002; recipient Who's Who Among America's Teachers, 1993. Mem.: Mass. Tchrs. Assn., Mass. Audubon Soc., Appalachian Mountain Club. Roman Catholic. Home: 87 Old County Rd Lancaster MA 01523 Home Phone: 508-331-9282.

DUGAN, MICHAEL JOSEPH, former career officer, health agency executive; b. Albany, NY, Feb. 22, 1937; s. D. Joseph and Dorothy M. (Krebs) D.; m. Grace A. Robinson, Aug. 9, 1958; children: Colleen, Erin, Mike, Sean, Kathleen, Kevin. BS, U.S. Mil. Acad., 1958; MBA, U.Colo., 1972. Commd. officer USAF, 1958, advanced through grades to gen.; comdr.-in-chief U.S. Air Forces Europe, 1989—90; comdr. Allied Air Forces Cen. Europe, 1989—90; chief of staff USAF, 1990, ret., 1991; lectr. in strategic studies Johns Hopkins U., Washington, 1991—92; pres., CEO Nat. Multiple Sclerosis Soc., NYC, 1992—2005; ret., 2005. Decorated three D.S.M., Silver Star, two Legion of Merit, D.F.C., Purple Heart; Knight's Cross (Germany). Home: 36 James Ct Dillon CO 80435 E-mail: mike@mikedugan.net.

DUGAN, PATRICK J., lawyer; b. Lima, Ohio, 1957; BSBA cum laude, Bowling Green State U., 1979; JD with honors, Ohio State U., 1981. Bar: Ohio 1982. Ptnr. Squire, Sanders & Dempsey LLP, Columbus & Cleve., co-chmn., Corp. Practice Group, 2002—05, chmn., Fin. Services Practice Group, 2005—. Bd. trustees Raymond E. Mason Found.; bd. dir. Ariel Corp.; mem. exec. com. Columbus Venture Network. Named an Ohio Super Lawyer mergers & acquisition, Law & Polit. Media, Inc., 2004, 2005; named one of 100 Leaders for New Millennium, Columbus Smart Bus. News, 2000, Columbus Power 100, 2002, 2003, 2004, 2005. Mem.: Beta Alpha Psi, Order of Coif. Office: Squire Sanders & Dempsey LLP 4900 Key Tower 127 Public Sq Cleveland OH 44114-1304 also: Squire Sanders & Dempsey LLP 1300 Huntington Ctr 41 South High St Columbus OH 43215-6197 Office Phone: 216-479-8500, 614-365-2709. Office Fax: 216-479-8780, 614-365-2499. Business E-Mail: pdugan@ssd.com.

DUGAN, PATRICK RAYMOND, microbiologist, educator, dean; b. Syracuse, NY, Dec. 14, 1931; s. Francis Patrick and Joan Irma (Clause) D.; m. Patricia Ann Murray, Sept. 22, 1956; children: Susan Eileen, Craig Patrick, Wendy Shawn, Carolyn Paige. BS, Syracuse U., 1956, MS, 1959, PhD, 1964. Assoc. rsch. scientist Syracuse U. Rsch. Corp., 1956-63; mem. faculty Ohio State U., Columbus, 1964—, asso. prof., 1968-70, prof., chmn. dept. microbiology, 1970-73; acting dean Ohio State U. (Coll. Biol. Scis.), 1978-79, dean, 1979-85; prin. scientist EG&G Idaho Nat. Lab., Idaho Falls, 1987-91, sci. and engring. fellow, 1991-94, dir. Ctr. for Bioprocessing Tech., 1987-94; ret., 1994—. Cons., 1994—. Author: Biochemical Ecology of Water Pollution, 1972. Trustee Columbus Zool. Assn. and Zoo, 1982—87. Fellow Am. Acad. Microbiology; mem. AAAS, Am. Soc. Microbiology (Ohio pres. 1968-70), Soc. Indsl. Microbiology, Am. Chem. Soc. Personal E-mail: pdugan001@columbus.rr.com.

DUGAS, DAVID ROY, prosecutor, lawyer; b. New Iberia, La., July 4, 1953; s. Claude Anthony and Gladys Marie (Hippler) D.; m. Dolores Ann Broussard, Mar. 22, 1974; children: Brandy Nicole, Kelly Ann, Mary Katherine. JD, La. State U., 1978. Bar: La. 1978, US Dist. Ct. (mid. dist.) La. 1978, US Dist. Ct. (we. dist.) 1980, US Ct. Appeals (5th cir.) 1981, US Dist. Ct. (ea. dist.) 1984. Assoc. Sanders, Downing, Kean & Cazedessus, Baton Rouge, 1978-80; from assoc. to ptnr. Caffery, Oubre, Dugas & Campbell, New Iberia, 1980—2000; US atty. (mid. dist.) La. US Dept. Justice, 2001—. Editor La. State U. Law Rev., 1977. Chmn. Iberia Parish Reps., 1984, Dist. H delegation to Rep. State Convention, 1984. Mem. ABA, La. Bar Assn., Iberia Parish Bar Assn., La. Assn. Def. Counsel (bd. dirs. 1985—), Order of Coif, Phi Kappa Phi, Omicron Delta Kappa. Lodges: Kiwanis. Republican. Roman Catholic. Avocations: golf, sailing. Office: US Attys Office 777 Florida St Ste 208 Baton Rouge LA 70801*

DUGAS, RICHARD J., JR., construction executive; b. 1965; m. Susan O. Dugas. BS, La. State U., 1986. Various positions in mktg., retail and customer svc. Exxon, 1986—89; various positions in process improvement and plant operational efficiency PepsiCo, 1990—94; with Pulte Homes Inc., Bloomfield Hills, Mich., 1994—, v.p. process improvement, city pres. and market mgr. for Atlanta divsn., coastal region pres., exec. v.p., COO, 2002—03, pres., CEO, 2003—. Office: Pulte Homes Inc 100 Bloomfield Hills Pky Bloomfield Hills MI 48304-2946*

DUGDA, MULUGETA TUJI, education educator; s. Tuji Dugda Badebo and Desbale Temesgen Turiye; m. Aster Desta Habtewold, Aug. 21, 2004. BSc in Elec. Engring., Addis Ababa U., Ethiopia, 1990; MSc in Elec. Engring., Addis Ababa U., 1998; MS in Seismology, Penn State U., 2003, PhD in Seismology, 2006. Asst. lectr. Alemaya U., Oromiya, Ethiopia, 1990—94; student lectr. Addis Ababa U., Ethiopia, 1994—98, lectr., 1998—2001; grad. asst. Penn State U., Pa., 2001—. Recipient Chancellor's List Honoree, Ednl. Comm. Inc., 2005, Academic Excellence award, Ethiopian Sci. Soc., 1996; grant, Internat. Centre for Theoretical Physics, 1999, GFZ and UNESCO, 2000, US NSF (NSF) MARGINS program, 2006, Travel grants, Dept. of Geosciences, Penn State U., 2005, Krynine Travel grant, 2004, DAAD scholarship, German Academic Exch., 1994—98, Travel grant, Internat. Ctr. for Theoretical Physics, 1999. Mem.: Am. Geophys. Union. Home: 901 S Allen St Apt B4 State College PA 16801 Office: Pennsylvania State U 410 Deike Bldg University Park PA 16802 Home Phone: 814-234-0914; Office Phone: 814-865-3622. E-mail: mulugeta@geosc.psu.edu.

DUGGAN, JAMES E., JR., state supreme court justice; b. 1942; Grad., Georgetown U., DC, Georgetown U. Law Ctr. Prof. Franklin Pierce Law Ctr., 1977—2001, interim dean, 1997—99; chief appellate defender State of NH, 1981—2001; assoc. justice NH Supreme Ct., 2001—. Chair N.H. Bd. of Claims. Supervises production Annual Survey N.H. Law. Named Merrimack County Lawyer of the Yr., 1991. Mem.: N.H. Bar Found., Am. Coll. Trial Lawyers Assn. (bar examiner, bd. mem.), Am. Acad. of Appellate Lawyers, N.H. Bar Assn. (mem. bd. govs.). Office: Supreme Ct Bldg One Noble Dr Concord NH 03301-6160*

DUGGAN, JAMES EDGAR, law librarian; b. Roanoke, Va., Mar. 24, 1961; s. Daniel David Sr. and Margaret Candler (Mallonee) D. BA, Va. Tech., 1983; JD, U. Miss., 1986; MLIS, La. State U., 1987. Bar: Miss. 1987, U.S. Dist. Ct. (so. dist.) Miss., U.S. Ct. Appeals (5th cir.). From asst. prof. to assoc. prof. So. Ill. U. Sch. Law, Carbondale, 1988-98, prof., 1998—. Ref. libr. So. Ill. U. Sch. Law, Carbondale, 1988—90, computer svcs. libr., 1990—98, dir. info. tech., 1998—2006, assoc. dir., 2006—; mem. faculty senate So. Ill. U., Carbondale, 2001—07, pres. faculty senate, 2004—05. Del. synergy The Ill. Libr. Leadership Initiative, 2005, del. leadership Carbondale class 2006, 2006; pres. bd. trustees Carbondale Pub. Libr., 2001—05, trustee, 1998—2007; trustees Shawnee Libr. Sys., 2001—04, pres. bd. trustees, 2002—03. Scholar West Pub. Co., 1987. Mem. Miss. State Bar Assn., Am. Assn. of Law Librs. (chair coun. chpt. pres. 1999, exec. bd. 2001-04, v.p./pres.-elect 2007—, grant 1987, grant New Orleans chpt. 1987, Call for Papers Competition award 1990), Mid-Am. Assn. of Law Librs. (pres. 1997-98), Phi Alpha Delta, Pi Kappa Delta, Beta Phi Mu. Roman Catholic. Home: PO Box 605 Carbondale IL 62903-0605 Office: So Ill U Law Sch Carbondale IL 62901 E-mail: duggan@siu.edu.

DUGGAN, JUANITA DONAGHEY, trade association administrator; b. Mobile, Ala., 1959; BS, Georgetown U., 1981. Spl. asst. to Pres. for pub. liaison The White House, dir. domestic policy divsn., 1987—88, exec. sec. domestic policy coun., 1989, spl. asst. to Pres. for cabinet affairs, 1989—90; exec. v.p. govt. affairs and comm. Nat. Food Processors Assn.; v.p. fed. rels. Philip Morris Corp., Inc., 1996—98; pres., CEO Wine & Spirits Wholesalers Am., Inc., Washington, 1998—2006, Am. Forest & Paper Assn., Washington, 2006—. Office: Am Forest & Paper Assn 1111 19th St NW Ste 800 Washington DC 20036 Office Phone: 202-463-2700. Office Fax: 202-463-2785.

DUGGAN, KEVIN, information technology professional; b. St. Louis, Feb. 29, 1944; s. Leo Patrick and Jean Claire (McHenry) D.; m. Lillian Carol Cook, Dec. 29, 1973. BA, U. S.C., 1977; MA, Webster U., 1988. With S.C. Nat. Bank, Columbia, 1970—79; mgr. tech. support, 1978—79; dir. info. sci. tech. Midlands Tech. Coll., Columbia, 1979—97; faculty mem. Info. Sys. Tech., 1998—. Cons. electronic data processing. Mem. Richland County Friends of Libr., Literacy Coun. S.C.; chmn. fin. com. Washington St. Meth. Ch., 1987-90, chmn. stewardship com., 1982-86, mem. evangelism and membership coms., 1982-86, mem. coun. on ministries, 1982-96, mem. exec. com., 1987-90, mem. adminstrv. bd., 1982-96, 99-2001, lay leader, 1992-96, mem. Missions, 1997-99, mem. ch. coun., 2005-, mem. fin. com., 2005-; del. to S.C. United Meth. Ch. ann. conf., 2005-. Served with USMC, 1963-67. Decorated Bronze Star (3). Mem. Assn. Sys. Mgr., IBM Users Group, Data Processing Mgmt. Assn., Palmetto Fencing Soc., Amateur Fencing League Am., Rotary. Methodist. Office: PO Box 2408 Columbia SC 29202-2408

DUGGAN, THOMAS PATRICK, management consultant; b. Hartford, Conn., Mar. 17, 1946; s. Edward O. and Mildred B. (Balf) Duggan; m. Marcia McCormack, Aug. 31, 1968 (div. 1978); children: Mary Christina, T. Patrick; m. Ann Hailey, Sept. 21, 1985; 1 child, Christopher T. AB, Providence Coll., 1968; postgrad. studies in Mgmt., We. N. Eng. Coll., 1969-71. Mgr. Travelers Mgmt. Svcs., Hartford, Conn., 1968—75; mgr. mgmt. cons. svcs. Coopers & Lybrand, NYC, 1975-79; prin., dir. ins. mgmt., cons. svcs. Hay Assocs., NYC, 1979-84; exec. v.p., nat. dir. bus. strategy cons. group Alexander & Alexander Mgmt. Cons. Svcs., NYC, 1984; pres. Duggan Cons. Assocs., New Albany, Ohio, 1984—. 1st lt. USAR, 1968-75. Mem. Human Resource Planning Soc., Am. Mgmt. Assn., Ins. Acctg. and Statis. Assn. (session chmn. 1975-79), New Albany Country Club. Home: 7531 Ehret Round New Albany OH 43054-8926 Personal E-mail: tpatrickduggan@insight.rr.com.

DUGGER, CELIA WILLIAMS, journalist; b. Austin, July 3, 1958; d. Ronnie Dugger; m. Barry Bearak; 2 children. BA magna cum laude, Harvard Coll., 1980. Intern Washington Post, 1979, 1980; reporter Atlanta Jour.-Constitution, 1980—84, Miami Herald, 1984—91; with NY Times, 1991—, met. news reporter NYC, 1991—98, co-chief South Asia bur. New Delhi, 1998—2002. Co-recipient Madeline Dane Ross award, Overseas Press Club Am., 2007, Grand prize, Robert F. Kennedy Journalism Awards, 2007; recipient George Polk award, 1983; fellow Edward R. Murrow fellow, Coun. Fgn. Rels., 2003. Office: NY Times 229 W 43rd St New York NY 10036*

DUGGER, DEBRA MARTIN, school counselor; b. Charles Town, W.Va., Oct. 22, 1954; d. Willard Blaine and Norma Jean Martin; m. Terry Gray Dugger, June 2, 1974; children: Kevin Gray, Aimee Renee. BS in Soc. Welfare, Shepherd U., 1976; MA in Counseling, W.Va. U., 1992. Nat. Cert. Counselor Nat. Bd. of Cert. Counselors, 1993, Lic. Profl. Counselor W.Va. Bd. of Examiners in Counseling, 1994, Permanent Counselor, Grades K-8 W.Va. Bd. of Edn., 1992. Substitute tchr. Jefferson County Schs., Charles Town, W.Va., 1990—90; sch. counselor Berkeley County Schs., Martinsburg, W.Va., 1990—. Supr. of counseling students W.Va. U., Morgantown, 2000—01. Angel tree coord. Westview Bapt. Ch., Martinsburg, W.Va., 2001—04, choir mem., 1984—2005, worship team mem. Recipient Character Educator Yr., Eagle Sch. Intermediate, 2004, PTA Hon. Life Membership, W.Va. Congress of Parents and Tchrs., Inc., 2004. Mem.: Valley View Elem. PTA (PTA Exec.Com. award), W.Va. Sch. Counselors' Assn., Phi Delta Kappa. Baptist. Avocations: travel, collecting cookbooks, swimming, singing, flute. Office: Berkeley County Schs 401 S Queen St Martinsburg WV 25401 Home: 113 Blanchard Ln Martinsburg WV 25403-5840 Home Phone: 304-263-0240; Office Phone: 304-263-0422. Office Fax: 304-263-6506. Personal E-mail: ddugger1@adelphia.net. Business E-Mail: ddugger@access.k12.wv.us.

DUGGER, MARGUERITE J., retired special education educator; b. Iron River, Mich., Oct. 14, 1916; d. August John Waffen and Ethel May James; m. Clifford Rayson (dec.); 1 child, Suzanne (dec.); m. James A. Dugger; stepchildren: James II, John, Elaine Shaw, Robert. BS, Ea. Mich. U., 1938; MA, Wayne State U., 1952, EdD, 1969. Tchr. physically handicapped Battle Creek Pub. Schs., 1938—51; spl. edn. tchr., summers Syracuse U., 1950—52; prin. Gorman Sch. for Physically Handicapped, Ohio, 1952—55; prin., spl. edn. dir. Kalamazoo Pub. Schs.; edn. dir. Pathway Sch., Phila., 1964; mem. spl. edn. faculty Wayne State U., Detroit, 1965—66; supr. ADHD San Francisco Unified, 1968—72; mem. faculty Western Mich. U., Kalamazoo; coord. spl. edn. Calif. State U., Hayward, 1972—81; ret., 1981. Camping and outdoor activities Battle Creek Pub. Schs., 1941—42. Author: Hands-On Learning in Science, 1982, Adventures and Exceptional Children 1934-1981, 2004. Vol. for homeless, San Francisco, 1992—93; sr. warden St. Andrews Ch., San Bruno, Calif., 1990—93. Recipient Nomads of East Sudan award, Am. Artists for Africa, award, Bd. Edn., Burlingame, Calif.; grantee, Glide Meml. Ch., San Francisco. Mem.: Hamilton Home Owners Assn. (bd. dirs. 1997—99). Democrat. Episcopalian. Home: 555 Byron #102 Palo Alto CA 94301 E-mail: margdugger@aol.com.

DUGGER, ROY WESLEY, academic administrator, retired military officer; b. Waxahachie, Tex., Jan. 22, 1925; s. William Warren and Arra Mae (Davis) Dugger; m. Margaret Dugger, May 28, 1976; children: Linda Talley, Alane Allen, Paul, Don, David. BS, Tex. A&M U., College Station, 1948, MS, 1950; EdD, PhD, Okla. State U., Stillwater, 1956; LittD (hon.), Paul Quinn Coll., Waco, Tex., 1972. Head agrl. sci. dept. Hearne H.S., Tex., 1948—53; asst. prof. Tex. A&M U., College Station, 1949—54, v.p., 1965—69; assoc. prof. Okla. State U., Stillwater, 1955—62; asst. commr. vocat. edn. US Office Edn., Washington, 1962—65; pres., chancellor Tex. State Tech. Coll. Sys., Waco, Harlingen, Sweetwater, 1969—76, founding pres., chancellor emeritus, 1976—. V.p. Tech. Edn. Rsch. Ctr., Cambridge, Mass., 1966—76; dir. Computer Tutors, Inc., NYC; founder Okla. Tech. Soc., Tex. Tech. Soc. Life mem. Shriner Crippled Children Hosp. Adm. USN, 1941—. Mem.: Okla. Acad. Scis. (life; dir.), Am. Vocat. Tech. Assn. (life). Home: 1750 Sunnybrook New Braunfels TX 78130-3017

DUGONI, ARTHUR A., retired dean, orthodontics educator; b. San Francisco, June 29, 1925; s. Arthur B. and Lina Maria (Bianco) D.; m. Katherine Agnes Groo, Feb. 5, 1949; children: Steven, Michael, Russell, Mary, Diane, Arthur, James. DDS, Coll. Physicians and Surgeons, San Francisco, 1948; MSD, U. Wash., 1963; BS, Gonzaga U., 1986; DHL honoris causa, U. Detroit, 1997. Diplomate Am. Bd. Orthodontics (bd. dirs., pres. 1979-86). Clin. instr. operative dentistry Coll. Physicians and Surgeons, San Francisco, 1951-55, asst. clin. prof. operative dentistry, 1955-60, asst. clin. prof. orthodontics, 1963-64, chair dept. orthodontics, 1963-67; assoc. prof. orthodontics U. Pacific, San Francisco, 1966-77, prof., 1977—, dean Sch. Dentistry, 1978—2006, dean emeritus, 2006. Chair coun. deans Am. Assn. Dental Schs., 1985; active Pew Commn. for the Health Professions, 1993-96. Recipient Disting. Svc. award San Mateo County Dental Soc., 1971, 1990, Disting. Svc. award Pacific Coast Soc. Orthodontists, 1976, Merit award, 1976, 2001, Disting. Practitioner award Nat. Acads. Practice Press Club, 1987, Hinman medallion, 1989, medallion of distinction U. Pacific, 1989, Orthodontic Edn. and Rsch. Found. disting. merit award, 1993, Albert H. Ketcham award Am. Bd. Orthodontics, 1994, Chmn.'s award Am. Dental Trade Assn., 1994, Dr. Irving E. Gruber award, 1997, List of Honor of FDI World Dental Fedn., 1998; named Person of Yr., South San Francisco, 1960, Alumnus of Yr., U. Pacific Sch. Dentistry, 1983, U. Wash., 1984, U. San Francisco, 1988, Gonzaga U., 1992, Gold medal Pierre Fauchard Acad., 1996, Callahan Internat. award Ohio Dental Assn., 1999, William J. Gies award Am. Coll. Dentists, 2001, Excellence in Dentistry award 13th Dist.'s Internat. Coll. Dentists, 2002, Willard C. Fleming Meritorious Svc. award No. Calif. sect. Am. Coll. Dentists, 2003, Arthur A. Dugoni Lifetime Achievement award Alumni Assn. U. Pacific, Arthur A. Dugoni Sch. Dentistry, 2006; named Arthur A. Dugoni Sch. Dentistry in his honor U. Pacific, 2004. Fellow Pierre Fauchard Acad., Acad. Dentistry Internat. (Internat. Dentist of Yr. 2005), Acad. Gen. Dentistry (hon.); mem. ADA (trustee 1984-87, treas. 1987-88, pres. 1988-89, Found. pres., Pres.'s citation 1994, 99, Disting. Svc. award 1995), Fedn. Dentaire Internat. (councilor 1989-98, treas. 1992-98, List of Honour 1999), Am. Assn. Dental Schs. (pres. 1995, Disting. Svc. award 2000), Calif. Dental Assn. (pres. 1982-83, Dist. Svc. award, 1978, Dale F. Redig Dist. Svc. award, 2003), Am. Dental Assn. (found. pres. 2003-), Concordia-Argonaut Club, Peninsula Golf and Country Club, Phi Kappa Phi, Omicron Kappa Upsilon, Tau Kappa Omega, Xi Psi Phi. Republican. Roman Catholic. Avocation: golf. Office: U Pacific Arthur A Dugoni Sch Dentistry 2155 Webster St San Francisco CA 94115-2333 Office Phone: 415-929-6425. Office Fax: 415-929-6419. Business E-Mail: adugoni@pacific.edu.

DUGUNDJI, JOHN, aeronautical engineer; b. NYC, Oct. 25, 1925; s. Basile and Rosa (Finale) D.; m. Wraye Polkey, July 25, 1965; children: Elenna Rose, Elisa Anthe. BAE, NYU, 1944; MS in Aero. Engring, MIT, 1948, Sc.D. in Aero. Engring, 1951. Research engr. Grumman Aircraft Co., Bethpage, NY, 1948-49; dynamics engr. Republic Aviation Corp., Farmingdale, NY, 1951-56; research asso. M.I.T., 1956-57, asst. prof. aero. engring., 1957-62, asso. prof., 1962-70, prof., 1970-93, sr. lectr., 1993-2001. Served with USN, 1944-46. Mem. AIAA, Sigma Xi, Tau Beta Pi. Greek Orthodox. Home: 39 Albert Ave Belmont MA 02478-4203 Office: MIT Dept Aeros & Astronautics Cambridge MA 02139

DUHAIME, MICHAEL, political organization worker; b. May 14, 1973; s. Richard and Ann DuHaime. BA in Journalism and Polit. Sci., Rutgers U., 1995. Dep. campaign mgr. for Bob Franks Senate Campaign, 2000; founder DuHaime Comm., Inc., Hoboken, NJ, 2001—03; exec. dir. NJ State Rep. Party, 2002; northeast regional polit. dir. Bush-Cheney Campaign, 2004; polit. dir. Rep. Nat. Com., 2005—06; exec. dir. for Rudolph Giuliani Presdl. Exploratory Com., 2006—.*

DUHAIME, NINA LEE, energy and research and development company executive; Founder, exec. v.p., treas., dir. Atom, Inc., Santa Fe, 1967—81; owner-broker Sun Mountain Agy., Santa Fe, 1964—84; owner, rancher, farmer, operator Bar V Ranch, N.Mex.; tech. writer and journalist R.W. Byram Co., Austin, Tex., 1966—78; owner, broker Sun Mountain Real Estate Agy. Contbr. columns and articles to newspapers, trade, and profl. jours. Recipient U.S. Presdl. Fitness award, 1073. Mem.: NY Acad. Scis. Achievements include studies and participation in evaluating and helping to institute activities to aid developing countries. Address: Santa Fe NM Office Phone: 505-983-9395.

DUHAMEL, JOSH DAVID, actor; b. Minot, ND, Nov. 14, 1972; s. Larry and Bonny Duhamel. BS, Minot State U. Co-owner 10 North Main restaurant, Minot, ND, 2005—. Actor: (TV series) All My Children, 1999—2002 (Emmy for Outstanding Supporting Actor in a Drama Series, 2002), Las Vegas, 2003—, (guest appearance) Crossing Jordan, 2004, 2007,: (films) The Picture of Dorian Gray, 2004, Win a Date with Tad Hamilton!, 2004, Turistas, 2006, Transformers, 2007. Avocations: golf, skiing, football, basketball. Office: c/o Gersh Agency 232 N Canon Dr Beverly Hills CA 90210*

DUHAMEL, JUDITH REEDY OLSON, public information officer, former state senator; b. Mitchell, SD, June 24, 1939; d. John Marvin and Camille (Murphy) Reedy; m. Robert George Olson, Aug. 5, 1961; children: Jeffrey, Jennifer, Jon, Jaime, Jason, Jeremy; m. William F. Duhamel, Aug. 2, 2003. EdB, U. Ariz., Tucson, 1961; MEd, S.D. State U., 1984; postgrad., U. S.D., 1985—. Cert. secondary tchr., edn. adminstrn. Tchr. jr. high sch. Mpls. Pub. Schs., 1961-63; mem. State Bd. Edn., S.D., 1972-83, pres. S.D., 1975-78; dir. S.D. Edn. Policy Seminar, 1975-79; substitute tchr. Rapid City (S.D.) Schs., 1979-81, tchr. adult basic edn., 1979-81, supr. community relations, 1981-88, supr. community edn., pub. info., 1988—95; senator S.D. Legis. (dist. 33), Pierre, SD, 1989—93; edn. dir. Career Learning Center of the Black Hills. Speaker, cons. sch. bds., adminstrs., tchrs., sch. dists., pub. relations, various states, 1972—. Bd. dirs. Black Hills Symphony, 1987—; chair SD State Dem. Party, 1998-2006. Mem. AAUW (Women of Worth award), Rotary, PEO, Delta Kappa Gamma. Democrat. Roman Catholic. Avocations: reading, spectator sports. Home: 1106 Hyland Dr Rapid City SD 57701-4456

DUHE, JOHN MALCOLM, JR., federal judge; b. Iberia Parish, La., Apr. 7, 1933; s. J. Malcolm and Rita (Arnandez) D.; children: Kim Duhe Holleman, Jeanne Duhe Sinitier, Edward M., M. Bofill. Student Washington and Lee U., 1951-53, BBA, Tulane U., 1955, LLB, 1957. Atty. Helm, Simon, Caffery & Duhe, New Iberia, La., 1957-78; dist. judge State of La., New Iberia, 1979-84; judge US Dist. Ct. (we. dist.) La., Lafayette, 1984-88; judge, US Ct. Appeals (5th cir.), Lafayette, 1988-99, sr. judge, 1999—. Assoc. editor Tulane Law Rev., 1956, editor-in-chief, 1967. Mem. Order Coif, Omicron Delta Kappa, Kappa Delta Phi. Home: PO Box 3548 Lafayette LA 70502-3548*

DUHL, MICHAEL FOSTER, lawyer; b. Chgo., July 12, 1944; s. Samuel Harold and Gertrude (Crodgen) D.; m. Judith Ann Currie, Jan. 30, 1970; children: Emilie Ann, Benjamin Currie. BBA, U. Mich., 1966; JD magna cum laude, Harvard U., 1969. Bar: Ill. 1969; CPA, Ill. Law clk. to presiding justice Ill. Supreme Ct., Chgo., 1969-70; assoc. Hopkins & Sutter, Chgo., 1971-75, ptnr., 1976-96; prin. Deloitte & Touche, L.L.P., Chgo., 1997—. Bd. editors Harvard Law Rev., 1967-69. Treas. Winnetka (Ill.) Pub. Libr. Dist. Bd., 1980-85; bd. dirs. Winnetka Hist. Soc., 1990-94, Winnetka

Landmark Preservation Commn., 1992-96; bd. trustees Village of Winnetka, 1996-2000, pres., 2001—. Mem. ABA, Univ. Club Chgo. Jewish. Office: Deloitte & Touche LLP 2 Prudential Plz 180 N Stetson Ave Fl 19 Chicago IL 60601-6779

DUHL, OLGA ANNA, literature educator, researcher; arrived in U.S., 1984; d. Emeric and Olga Kiss; m. Joseph Samuel Duhl, Oct. 17, 1981; 1 child, Esther Annamaria. MA, U. Cluj-Napoca, Romania, 1979; PhD, Rutgers U., 1992. Instr. Barnard Coll., NYC, 1991; French lit. cons. Jane Voorhees Zimmerli Art Mus., New Brunswick, NJ, 1991; head tchg. asst. Rutgers U., New Brunswick, NJ, 1991; vis. prof. Eotvos Lorand U., Budapest, Hungary, 1998; adj. asst. prof. Columbia U., NYC, 1999; instr. Lafayette Coll., Easton, Pa., 1992—93, asst. prof., 1993—2000, assoc. prof., 2000—07, prof., 2000—. Mem. U. Burgundy Rsch. Ctr., 1998—. Author: Folie et Rhétorique Dans la Sottie, 1994, Sotise a huit personnaiges Le Nouveau Monde, 2005; editor: Le Théâtre Français Des Années 1450-1550, 2002, Quêtes spirituelles et actualités contemporaines dans le theâtre de Marguerite de Navarre, Renaissance and Reformation, Special Issue, 2002, John Pace in The New Dictionary of National Biography, 2004; editl. bd. (other) Revue d'Etudes Françaises, 1998—; contbr. articles to profl. jours. and the New Dictionary of Nat. Biography; reviewer: Renaissance and Reformation/Renaissance et Réforme. Grantee, The Renaissance Soc. Am., 2003. Mem.: MLA. Avocations: music, theater.

DUHME, CAROL MCCARTHY, civic worker; b. St. Louis, Apr. 13, 1917; d. Eugene Ross and Louise (Roblee) McCarthy; m. Sheldon Ware, June 12, 1941 (dec. 1944); 1 child, David; m. H. Richard Duhme, Jr., Apr. 9, 1947; children: Benton (dec.), Ann, Warren (dec.). AB, Vassar Coll., 1939; DHL (hon.), Eden Theol. Sem., 2002. Tchr. elem. sch., 1939-41, 42-44; moderator St. Louis Assn. Congl. Chs., 1959—62; trustee 1st Congl. Ch., 1964—66; mem. ch. coun. St. Louis Assn. Congl. Ch., 1974-75, 84-85, 87-89, bd. deaconesses, 1978-81, bd. deacons 1982-85, 92-95, chmn. bd. Christian Edn., 1987-88. Former bd. dirs. Cmty. Music Schs., St. Louis, Cmty. Sch., Ch. Women United, John Burroughs Sch., St. Louis Bicentennial Women's Com., St. Louis Jr. League; pres. St. Louis Vassar Club; pres., bd. dirs. YWCA, St. Louis, 1973-76, chmn. ann. fund, 1989-90; bd. dirs. North Side Team Ministry, 1968-84, Chautauqua (NY) Instn., 1971-79, mem. adv. coun. to bd., 1987—. Mem. adv. coun. Mo. Bapt. Hosp., 1973—89; mem. exec. com. bd. dirs. Eden Theol. Sem., 1981—95, presdl. search com., 1986—87, 1992—93, v.p., bd. dirs., 1991, chmn. 150th ann. com., 1996—2000; sec. bd. dirs. UN Assn., St. Louis, 1976—84, coun. advisors, 1993—, nat. coun., 1995—2001; mem. nat. coun. UN-USA, 1995—2001; pres. bd. dirs. Family and Children's Svc. Greater St. Louis, 1977—79; mem. chancellor's long range planning com. Wash. U., 1980—81, mem. Nat. Coun., Sch. Social Work, 1987—; chmn. Benton Roblee Duhme Scholar Fund; trustee Joseph H. and Florence A. Roblee Found., St. Louis, 1984—, pres., 1984—90; bd. dirs.; chmn. Chautaugua Bell Tower Scholar Fund, 1961—; bd. dirs. Nat. Inland Waterways Libr., St. Louis Merc Libr.; mem. corp. assembly Blue Cross Hosp. Svc. Mo., 1978—86; pres. Joseph H. and Florance A. Roblee Found., 2002. Recipient Mary Alice Messerley award for volunteerism Health and Welfare Coun. St. Louis, 1971, Vol. of Yr. award, YWCA, 1976, Woman of Achievement award St. Louis Globe Democrat, 1980, Outstanding Lay Women nomination Mo. United Ch. of Christ, 1991, Outstanding Alumna award John Burroughs Sch., 1992, Humanitarian award Planned Parenthood St. Louis, 2000. Home: 8 Edgewood Rd Saint Louis MO 63124-1817

DUJACK, STEPHEN RAYMOND, editor; b. NYC, Apr. 7, 1953; s. Raymond Leon and Inge (Wassermann) D. BA, Princeton U., 1976. Assoc. editor Princeton (N.J.) Alumni Weekly, 1976-80; graphic artist Forte, Inc., Alexandria, Va., 1980-81; editor Fgn. Svc. Jour., dir. comms. Am. Fgn. Svc. Assn., Washington, 1981-88; dir. comms. Worldwatch Inst., Washington, 1988-90. Lectr. George Washington U., Washington, 1983-88. Editor: The Environ. Forum, 1990—; contbr. articles on pub. policy to The Washington Post, The L.A. Times, The New Republic, The Christian Sci. Monitor, Gannett Syndicate, L.A. Times Syndicate. Recipient Allen Furniss award Daily Princetonian, Princeton, 1976; Best Feature Article, Soc. Nat. Assn. Publs., 1983, Best Spl Issue, 1983, Most Improved Mag., 1992, Best Ann. Report, 1994, 96, 98, 99, 1st pl. Master's Divsn., TriAtlantic Biathlon Series, 1994, 3d pl. 45-49 divsn., 1998, 1st pl., 2000. Office: Environ Law Inst 2000 L St NW Ste 620 Washington DC 20036 Personal E-mail: srdujack@earthlink.net. Business E-Mail: dujack@eli.org. *Honor is the central principle of a moral life.*

DUJARDIN, RICHARD CHARLES, journalist; b. Queens, NY, Dec. 20, 1944; s. Julien Camille and Veronica (Venesoen) D.; m. Rosemarie Catherine Levesque, Jan. 20, 1947; children: Julianne, Peter, Philip, Joelle, Jean-Paul, Jeffrey. BA in Comm. Arts, Fordham U., 1966. Reporter Providence Jour.-Bulletin, 1966-68, 71-75, bur. mgr., 1975-77, religion writer, 1977—. V.p. Action for Franco-Ams. in N.E., 1991-93, dir., 1986-94; dist. pres. Union St. Jean Baptiste, 1990-94. Lt. (j.g.) USN, 1968-71. Recipient Wilbur award Religious Pub. Rels. Coun., 1986, 91, 95. Mem. Religion Newswriters Assn. (treas. 1989-90, v.p. 1990-94, pres. 1994-96, Supple Meml. award 1986, Templeton Reporter of Yr. award 1991). Roman Catholic. Home: 129 Hillside Ave Providence RI 02906-2900 Office: Providence Journal Bull 75 Fountain St Providence RI 02902-0050 Office Phone: 401-277-7384. E-mail: rdujardi@projo.com, rcdujardin@cox.net.

DUKAKIS, OLYMPIA, actress; b. Lowell, Mass., June 20, 1931; d. Constantine S. and Alexandra (Christos) D.; m. Louis Zorich, Dec. 5, 1962; children: Christina, Peter, Stefan. BS, Boston U., 1952, MFA, 1957. Co-founder, artistic dir. Whole Theatre, Montclair, NJ, 1970-90; co-founder Charles Playhouse, Boston; master tchr. NYU, 1970-85. Appeared in over 125 prodns. for regional theatres, N.Y. Shakespeare Theatre, Circle Repertory Theatre, American Place Theatre and numerous Off-Broadway theatres; appearances on stage include A Mother, Mother Courage, The Rose Tattoo, The Cherry Orchard, Three Sisters, The Sea Gull, Long Day's Journey Into Night, Iphegenia in Aulis, Othello, Miss Julie, A Streetcar Named Desire, The Night of the Iguana, King of America, Social Security, Rose, 2005; appearances in film include Lilith, 1964, Twice a Man, 1964, John and Mary, 1969, Made for Each Other, 1971, Death Wish, 1974, Rich Kids, 1979, The Wanderers, 1979, The Idolmaker, 1980, National Lampoon Goes to the Movies, 1982, Flanagan, 1985, Moonstruck, 1988 (Golden Globe, Academy Award Suppporting Actress), Working Girl, 1988, Steel Magnolias, 1988, Look Who's Talking, 1988, Dad, 1989, In the Spirit, 1990, Look Who's Talking II, 1990, Over the Hill, 1992, Look Who's Talking Now, 1993, The Cemetery Club, 1993, I Love Trouble, 1994, Digger, 1994, Jeffrey, 1995, Mighty Aphrodite, 1995, Mr. Holland's Opus, 1996, Dead Badge, 1995, Picture Perfect, 1997, Never Too Late, 1997, Jane Austen's Mafia!, 1998, A Life for a Life, 1998, Better Living, 2000, Brooklyn Sonnet, 2000, The Intended, 2002, The Event, 2003, Charlie's War, 2003, Jesus, Mary and Joey, 2003, The Great New Wonderful, 2005, The Thing About My Folks, 2005, A Mother, A Daughter, And A Gun, 2005, 3 Needles, 2005, Whisky School, 2005, Jesus, Mary and Joey, 2006, Away from Her, 2006, Day on Fire, 2006, In the Land of Women, 2007; (TV films) Nicky's World, 1974, The Neighborhood, 1982, The Last Act is a Solo, 1990 (Ace award), Lucky Day, 1991, Fire in the Dark, 1991, Sinatra: The Mini-Series, 1992, Armistead Maupin's Tales of the City, 1994, A Century of Women, 1994, Young at Heart, 1995, A Match Made in Heaven, 1997, Scattering Dad, 1998, The Pentagon Wars, 1998, More Tales of the City (mini-series), 1998, Joan of Arc, 1999, Last of the Blonde Bombshells, 2000, And Never Let Her Go, 2001, Ladies and the Champ, 2001, Further Tales of the City (mini-series), 2001, My Beautiful Son, 2001, Guilty Hearts (mini-series), 2002, Mafia Doctor, 2003, Babycakes, 2003, The Librarian: Quest for the Spear, 2004, The Librarian: Return to King Solomon's Mines, 2006; (TV series) Center of the Universe, 2004. Del. Dem. Nat. Convention, 1988. Recipient 2 Obie awards, Los Angeles Film Critics award, 1988. Mem. Actor's Equity Assn., Screen Actors Guild, Am. Fedn. TV and Radio Artists. Office: William Morris Agy care Parseghian 1325 Avenue Of The Americas Fl 32 New York NY 10019-4702*

DUKE, ANTHONY DREXEL, retired sociologist, educator, philanthropist; b. NYC, July 28, 1918; s. Angier Buchanan and Cordelia (Biddle) D.; children by previous marriage: Anthony D. Jr., Nicholas R., Cordelia Duke Jung, Josephine Duke Brown, December Duke McSherry, John O., Douglas D.; m. Maria Luly de Lourdes Alcebo, Sept. 27, 1975; children: Lulita C., Washington A., James B. Student, Princeton U., 1941; DHL (hon.), Adelphi Coll., 1957, L.I. U., 1988, Drexel U., 1991. With Import Export Co., 1946-50; prin. A.D. Duke Realty, Inc., 1955-65. Chmn. bd. dirs., pres., founder Boys Harbor Inc., 1937—. Trustee Big Brother Movement, 1951-63; past trustee Henry St. Settlement, N.Y.C.; del. Internat. Conf. Pvt. Sector Initiatives, 1986; hon. commr. Manhattan Borough Projects, 1954-57, Civic Affairs and Pub. Events, N.Y.C.; mem. N.Y.C. Youth Bd., 1955-58; rep. Internat. Rescue Com., Vietnam War, Meriel refugee crisis Cuba, 1983; active Save the Children, Pomfret Sch., Duke U. Lt. comdr. USNR, 1941-46, PTO, ATO, ETO. Decorated Bronze Star. Recipient Town and Country Most Generous Am. award 1988, Save the Children award, 1977; Presdl. citation for pvt. sector commendation, 1986, Citation for Promotion of Human Welfare Commonwealth of Mass., 1987. Mem. Bodman and Achelis Found., Nat. Com. on Am. Fgn. Policy, Maidstone Club (former gov.), Piping Rock (former gov.), River Club, Racquet and Tennis Club, Beaver Dam Club. Office: Boys Harbor Inc PO Box 3000 New York NY 10029-0300

DUKE, BETSY (ELIZABETH A.), bank executive; b. July 1952; BFA U. NC, Chapel Hill; MBA, Old Dominion U., Norfolk, VA; grad., Stonier Grad. Sch. Banking, Am. Bankers Assn. Sch. of Bank Investments, Va. Bankers Assn. Sch. Bank Mgmt. Pres., CEO Bank of Tidewater, 1991—2001; sr. v.p. govt. rels. SouthTrust Corp., Va. Beach, Va., 2001—03, exec. v.p. cmty. bank devel., 2003—05; exec. v.p. Merger Project Team Wachovia Bank, Va. Beach, Va., 2005; sr. exec. v.p., COO Towne Bank, Portsmouth, Va., 2005—. Nat. adv. coun. Fannie Mae, 2004—. Named One of 25 Women to Watch, U.S. Banker Mag., 2003. Mem.: Am. Bankers Assn. (chmn.-elect 2003—04, chmn. 2004—05). Office: TowneBank 5716 High St Portsmouth VA 23703*

DUKE, CAROL MICHIELS, health products executive; b. Alexandria, La., Sept. 2, 1944; d. Leo A. and Elva L. Michiels; m. M. Carey Duke, Apr. 23, 1971; 1 child, Perrianne. Student, Nichols State U., 1974—77; grad., Dale Carnegie Inst., Realtors Inst. Office mgr. Bayou Constrn. Co., Houma, La., 1974—76; mgr. Glynn & Assoc., Houma, 1976—79; owner, broker Century 21 Real Estate One, Houma, 1979—81; v.p., mgmt. cons. Century 21 of Tex. and La., Houston, 1981—82; v.p., gen. mgr. Doyle Stuckey, Houston, 1982—83; broker/mgr. Gary Greene Realtors, Better Homes & Gardens, Houston, 1983—85; regional mgr. Better Homes & Gardens, Des Moines, 1985—95; regional mgr., hearing instrument spec. Miracle Ear, Austin, Tex., 1995—. Dist. mgr. Miracle Ear, Austin, Tex.; seminar condr.; chmn. conv. booth Realtors Nat. Home Builders, Houston, 1983. Editor: Training and Policy Manual, 1982. Chmn. Easter Seal Soc., Houma, 1979. Recipient Top Listing award, numerous Top Quarterly awards, La. Dist. of Century 21, 1980. Mem. Houston Bd. Realtors (edn. com. 1984-85), Tex. Assn. Realtors (realtor/builder, sec. 1983-), Nat. Assn. Realtors, Realtors Nat. Mktg. Inst., Jaycee Jaynes (state bd. dirs. 1976-77, sec. 1977-78). Democrat. Roman Catholic. Home: PO Box 90758 Austin TX 78709-0758 Personal E-mail: hearmeduke@aol.com.

DUKE, CHARLES BRYAN, electronics executive, physicist, educator; b. Richmond, Va., Mar. 13, 1938; s. Charles Joseph Jr. and Virginia (Welton) Duke; m. Ann Evans, July 1, 1961; children: Amy Dickerson, Emily Elizabeth. BS in Math., Duke U., 1959; PhD in Physics, Princeton U., 1963. Staff corp. rsch. GE, Schenectady, NY, 1963-69, cons., 1969-72; prof. physics U. Ill., Urbana, 1969-72; mgr., sr. fellow Xerox Corp., Webster, NY, 1972-88, sr. rsch. fellow, 1989-96, v.p., sr. rsch. fellow, 1996—2005; dep. dir., chief scientist Battelle Pacific Northwest Div., Richland, Wash., 1988-89; prof. physics U. Rochester, NY, 2006—. Bd. govs. Am. Inst. Physics, NYC, 1976—82, 1984—87; adj. prof. physics U. Rochester, NY, 1972—88; affiliate prof. physics U. Wash., Seattle, 1988—89; gen. chmn. Phys. Electronics Conf., 1997—2000. Author: Tunneling in Solids, 1969, Surface Science: The First Thirty Years, 1994, Color Systems Integration, 1998, Frontiers in Surface and Interface Science, 2002; editor-in-chief: Jour. Materials Rsch., 1985—86, Surface Sci., 1992—2001; contbr. articles to profl. jours. Named one of 1000 Most Cited Scientists, Inst. Sci. Info., 1981. Fellow: IEEE, Am. Phys. Soc. (councillor 1995—98, exec. bd. 1997—98, George E. Pake prize 2006), Am. Vacuum Soc. (hon.; bd. dirs. 1973—76, pres. 1979, trustee 2003—05, M.W. Welch award in vacuum sci. and tech. 1977); mem.: NAS, NAE, Materials Rsch. Soc. (councillor 1988—90, treas. 1991—92, councillor 1995—97). Office: U Rochester Dept Physics and Astronomy 500 Wilson Blvd PO Box 270171 Rochester NY 14627-171 Business E-Mail: aed22cbd@frontiernet.net.

DUKE, CHARLES RICHARD, dean; b. West Stewartstown, NH, July 6, 1940; s. George Tunicliffe and Evelyn Agnes (Murray) D.; m. Leona Ruth Hubbard, June 1, 1983. BE, Plymouth State Coll., NH, 1962; MA, Middlebury Coll., Vt., 1968; PhD, Duke U., Durham, NC, 1972. Tchr. English, head dept. Sunapee H.S., NH, 1962-68; prof. English Plymouth State Coll., 1968-78, Murray State U., Ky., 1978-84; prof., head dept. secondary edn. Utah State U., Logan, 1984-89; dean Coll. Edn. and Human Svcs. Clarion U., Pa., 1989-94; dean Coll. Edn. Appalachian State U., Boone, NC, 1995—. Dir. West Ky. Writing Project, 1980-84; co-dir. Utah Writing Project, 1984-89, Clarion U. Student Literacy Corps, 1990-94. Author: Creative Dramatics and English Teaching, 1974, Writing Through Sequence, 1983, Strategies for teaching, 1987; contbr. articles to profl. jours; editor: Exercise Exchange, 1979—2001, Poets Perspectives, 1992, American Overseas Education, 2000, Assessing Writing Across the Curriculum, 2001. Am. Studies fellow Coe Found., 1964; recipient Alumni Outstanding Svc. award Plymouth State Coll., 1977. Mem. ASCD, Internat. Reading Assn., Nat. Coun. Tchrs. English, Am. Assn. Colls. Tchr. Edn., Assn. Tchr. Educators, Phi Delta Kappa. Office: Appalachian State U 222 Duncan Hall PO Box 32038 Boone NC 28608-2038 Business E-Mail: dukecr@appstate.edu.

DUKE, DONALD NORMAN, publishing executive; b. LA, Apr. 1, 1929; s. Roger V. and Mabel (Weineger) D. BA in Ednl. Psychology, Colo. Coll., 0951. Comml. photographer, Colorado Springs, Colo., 1951-53; pub. rels. Gen. Petroleum, LA, 1954-55; agt. Gen. S.S. Corp., Ltd., 1956-57; asst. mgr. retail advt., sales promotion Mobil Oil Co., 1958-63; pub. Golden West Books, Alhambra, Calif., 1964—. Dir. Pacific R.R. Publs., Inc., Athletic Press; pub. rels. cons. Santa Fe Rlwy., 1960-70. Author: The Pacific Electric: A History of Southern California Railroading, 1958, Southern Pacific Steam Locomotives, 1962, Santa Fe.Steel Rails to California, 1963, Night Train, 1961, American Narrow Gauge, 1978, RDC: the Budd Rail Diesel Car, 1989, The Brown Derby, 1990, Camp Cajon, 1991, Fred Harvey: Civilizer of the American West, 1994, editor: Water Trails West, 1977, Branding Iron, 1988-91, Santa Fe.The Railroad Gateway to the American West, Vol. 1, 1995, Vol. 2, 1997, Incline Railways of Los Angeles and Southern California, 1998, Electric Railroads of San Francisco Bay, Vols. 1 and 2, 1999, Pacific Electric Railway (The No. Divsn.), vol. 1, 2001, Pacific Electric Railway (The Ea. Divsn.), vol. 2, 2002, Pacific Electric Railway (The So. Divsn.), vol. 3, 2003, Pacific Electric Railway (The We. Divsn.), vol. 4, 2004, The Union Pacific in Southern California, 2005, Pacific Coast Interurbans, vol. 1, 2007. Recipient Spur award for Trails of the Iron Horse Western Writers Am., 1975. Mem. Rlwy. and Locomotive Hist. Soc. (dir. 1944-98), Western History Assn., Newcomen Soc., Lexington Group of Transp. History, Western Writers Am., PEN Internat. (v.p. 1975-77), Authors Guild Am., Book Pubs. Assn. So. Calif. (dir. 1968-77), Calif. Writers Guild (dir. 1976-77), Calif. Book Pubs. Assn. (dir. 1976-77), Westerners Internat. (hon., editor Branding Iron 1971-80, 88-91), Hist. Soc. So. Calif. (dir. 1972-75), Henry E./Arabella Huntington Soc., Kappa Sigma (lit. editor Caduceus 1968-80). Home: PO Box 80250 San Marino CA 91118-8250 Office: Golden West Books 525 N Electric Ave Alhambra CA 91801-2032 Office Phone: 626-458-8148. Personal E-mail: trainbook@earthlink.net.

DUKE, EDWARD MARION, III, (MICKEY DUKE), health facility administrator, consultant; b. Yakima, Wash., Feb. 16, 1948; s. Edward M. Duke, Jr. and Margueritte M. (Young) Duke; m. Sharon Diane Page, June 21, 1968; children: Lisa S., Lain J., Crystal A., Amber J., Amy L. AB in Social Sci., San Diego State U., 1970; M in Urban Planning, U. Oreg., 1974. Exec. dir. Oreg. Dist. 4 Health Planning Coun., Corvallis, Oreg., 1972—76, Lane County Med. Soc., Eugene, Oreg., 1976—82; dep. dir., pub. affairs Oreg. Med. Assn., Portland, 1983; dir. med. delivery sys. Health Plan of Am., Emeryville, Calif., 1983—85; exec. dir. med. affairs Sierra Health Svcs., Las Vegas, 1985—94; sr. dir. managed care, we. region Universal Health Svcs., Las Vegas, 1994—2002; CEO Oasis Health System, LLC, Las Vegas, 2002—. Pres. E.M. Duke & Assocs., LLC, Henderson, Nev., 2002—; adj. faculty, guest lectr., healthcare adminstrn. program U. Nev., Las Vegas; guest spkr., workshop presenter various symposia. Author: National Managed Care Certification Study Guide, 2007; contbr. articles to profl. newsletters. Dist. com. commr. Boy Scouts of Am., Boulder Dam Coun., Las Vegas, 2002—05. Mem.: Healthcare Fin. Mgmt. Assn. (pres. Nev. chpt. 2005—06, lead author Nat. Managed Care Cert. Exam Study Guide 2007—08, Follmer Bronze award 2001, Reeves Silver award 2003, Muncie Gold award 2005). Avocations: bicycling, woodworking. Office: Oasis Health Sys LLC 4170 S Decatur Blvd # A-8 Las Vegas NV 89103 Office Phone: 702-493-0606. Personal E-mail: emduke@aol.com.

DUKE, ELIZABETH M., federal agency administrator; B in polit. sci., Rutgers U.; M in polit. sci., Northwestern U., M in African Studies; PhD in polit. sci., George Washington U. Founder, dir. Govt. Affairs Inst., Office of Exec. and Mgmt. Devel. US Office Pers. Mgmt., 1978—84, dep. asst. dir., dir. policy and systems, Office Training and Devel., 1984—86; prin. dep. sec. Office of Asst. Sec. for Mgmt. and Budget, HHS; dep. asst. sec. adminstrn. Adminstrn. for Children and Families, HHS, 1997—2001; acting adminstr. Health Resources and Services Adminstrn., HHS, 2001—02, adminstr., 2002—. Office: Health Resources and Services Adminstrn Parklawn Bld 5600 Fishers Ln Rockville MD 20857

DUKE, ELLEN (BEBE DUKE), bank executive; AB, Princeton Univ. Trading positions with Citibank, Lehman Bros., Smith Barney, 1982—95; head market risk mgmt. dept. Smith Barney; head, market risk Solomon Smith Barney; global head market risk mgmt., corp. & investment banking Citigroup Inc., NYC, 2000—03, mng. dir., co-head risk mgmt., mem. mgmt. com., 2003—. Office: Citigroup Inc 399 Park Ave New York NY 10043

DUKE, GEORGE, jazz keyboardist, composer; b. San Rafael, Calif., Jan. 12, 1946; Student, San Francisco Conservatory. Keyboardist, rec. artist, 1966—. Played with numerous musicians including Frank Zappa, Gerald Wilson, Dizzy Gillespie, Bobby Hutcherson, Don Ellis, Jean Luc-Ponty, Cannonball Adderley, Billy Cobham, Stanley Clarke, Flora Purim, Airto, Simone and Raul de Souza; albums include The Primal George Duke, The Inner Source, Feel, The Aura Will Prevail, 1976, From Me to You, 1977, Reach for It, 1977, Don't Let Go, 1978, Follow the Rainbow, 1979, Master of the Game, 1979, A Brazillian Love Affair, 1979, Clarke-Duke Project, Thief in the Night, 1988, Dream On, 1991, Snapshot, 1992, Muir Woods Suite, 1993, Rendezvous, 1995, Illusions, 1995, Is Love Enough?, 1997, After Hours, 1998, Cool, 2000, Face the Music, 2002, Duke, 2005, In a Mellow Tone, 2006.*

DUKE, J. RICHARD, lawyer; BSBA, Auburn U.; LLM in Taxation, U. Miami Sch. Law; JD, Samford U. Cumberland Sch. Law. Prin. Duke Law Firm, Birmingham, Ala. Mem. adv. bd. Am. Internat. Depository & Trust, Denver; adj. prof. law Samford U. Cumberland Sch. Law, 1983—99; prof. law Walter H. & Dorothy B. Diamond Grad. Internat. Tax Prog. Thomas Jefferson Sch. Law (formerly St. Thomas U. Sch. Law), Miami, Fla.; prof. law Aristotle U. Coll. Law. Co-author: Offshore Tax Strategies; contbg. editor: Tax Havens of the World; contbr. Named one of Top 100 Attys., Worth mag., 2005—06. Fellow: Royal Soc. Fellows; mem.: Ala. State Bar (tax sect.), Fla. Bar (internat. law sect., tax sect.), ABA (tax sect., real property, probate & trust law sect., internat. law and practice sect.), Inter-Am. Bar Assn., Internat. Bar Assn. (sect. on bus. law, com. on taxes), Soc. of Trust and Estate Practitioners, Internat. Tax Planning Assn. Office: Duke Law Firm PC 400 Vestavia Pky Ste 100 Birmingham AL 35216-3750 Office Phone: 205-823-3900. Office Fax: 205-823-2630. E-mail: richard@assetlaw.com.

DUKE, LAWRENCE KENNETH, banker; b. Lexington Park, Md., Mar. 7, 1956; s. Marvin Leonard and Judith Anne (Jackoway) D. BSMechE, MIT, 1978; BS in Polit. Sci., SUNY, 1982; MBA, Harvard Bus. Sch., 1984. Registered engr. in tng., Minn. Asst. mgr., treasury div. Citibank NA, Dubai, United Arab Emirates, 1984-86; chief dealer, treasury div. Midland Bank, London, 1986; dep. gen. mgr., treasury div. Nomura Bank Internat., London, 1986—; global head of new product devel. State Street Bank, London, 1990—. Vis. fellow in fin. Bus. Sch. City U., London, 1989—; bd. dirs. State St. Global Advisors U.K. Ltd., 1991—, U.K. Invest-in-Tng., 1991—. Recipient Cert. Recognition Gov. Guam, 1979, Navy Achievement medal, 1982. Mem. Forex Assn. (internat. mgr. 1984—), Internat. Soc. Fin. Analysts, Soc. Investment Analysts. Avocations: reading, music, travel, jogging. Home: 30 Prospect Pl Wapping Wall London E1 9TJ England also: 11F 8 Tung Teh St Pei Tou District Taipei ROC Taiwan Office: State St Bank 20 Birchin Ln London EC3V 9AQ England

DUKE, MARGARET JOYCE, sound recordist, broadcast engineer; b. Baton Rouge, La., Nov. 18, 1945; d. James Henry and Joyce Olga (Boyd) D.; children: Diane Alana, Julie Rene, Richard Mark. BFA, La. State U., 1980. Sound recordist (films) John Huston and the Dubliners, The Wild West, Comic Strip Live, Destined to Live, Diabetes Camp, Prisoners of Wedlock, It Was a Wonderful Life, Labours of Eve, Wise Women, Science, Math and Middleschool Girls, The Desert is No Lady, Far Out Man, Galaxies Are Colliding, Bang, Street Pirates, George Shdanoff and Hollywood, Your Children, The Thistle Hotel, Mortuary Acad., The Trouble With Dick; broadcast engr.: (TV) The View, General Hosp., Port Charles, Sledgehammer, Days of Our Lives, Acad. Awards, 2000-01, The Wild West, Comic Strip Live, Dan Rather Evening News, Street Pirates, Marilyn and Me, others. Mem. Women in Film, Cinewomen. Avocations: photography, gardening, art, antiques. Home: 756 S Ridgeley Dr Apt 209 Los Angeles CA 90036-3866

DUKE, MICHAEL T., retail executive; m. Susan Duke; 3 children. Bachelor's in Indsl. Engring., Ga. Tech. With Federated Dept. Stores, May Dept. Stores, Venture Stores; sr. v.p. logistics Wal-Mart Stores, Inc., 1995—2000, sr. v.p. distbn., exec. v.p. logistics, 2000, exec. v.p. adminstrn., 2000—03, exec. v.p., 2003—05, pres. Wal-Mart Stores div., 2003—05, vice chmn. Wal-Mart Stores Internat., 2005—. Mem. adv. bd. Ga. Tech; bd. dirs. Arvest-Bank of Bentonville. Mem.: Internat. Mass Retail Assn. (bd. dirs.). Office: Wal-Mart Stores Inc 702 SW Eighth St Bentonville AR 72716*

DUKE, PATTY (ANNA MARIE DUKE), actress; b. NYC, Dec. 14, 1946; d. John P. and Frances (McMahon) Duke; m. John Astin, 1973 (div. 1985); children: Sean, Mackenzie; m. Michael Pierce, March 15, 1986. Grad., Quintano's School for Young Profls. Pres. SAG, 1985-88, lectr. Am. Film Inst., 1988 TV appearances include Armstrong Circle Theatre, 1955, The SS Andrea Doria, The Prince and the Pauper, 1957, Wuthering Heights, 1958, U.S. Steel Hour, 1959, Meet Me in St. Louis, 1959, Swiss Family Robinson, 1958, The Power and the Glory, 1961, All's Fair, 1981-82; (series) The Brighter Day, 1957, Kitty Foyle, 1958, Patty Duke Show, 1963-66, It Takes Two, 1982-83, Hail to the Chief, 1985, Karen's Song, 1987; (TV films) The Big Heist, 1957, My Sweet Charlie, 1970 (Emmy award 1970), Two on a Bench, If Tomorrow Comes, 1971, She Waits, Deadly Harvest, 1972, Nightmare, 1972, Look What's Happened to Rosemary's Baby, 1976, Fire!, 1976, Rosetti and Ryan: Men Who Love Women, Curse of the Black Widow, Killer on Board, The Storyteller, 1977, Having Babies III, Captain and the Kings, 1977 (Emmy award 1977), A Family Upside Down, 1978, Women in White, Hanging by a Thread, Before and After, The Miracle Worker, 1979 (Emmy award 1980), The Women's Room, Mom, The Wolfman and Me, The Babysitter, 1980, Violation of Sarah McDavid, Please, Don't Hit Me Mom, 1981, Something So Right, 1982, September Gun, 1983, Best Dept Secrets, 1984, George Washington: The Forging of a Nation, 1984, A Time to Triumph, 1986, Fight for Life, 1987, Perry Mason: The Case of the Avenging Angel, Fatal Judgement, 1988, Everybody's Baby: The Rescue of Jessica McClure, Amityville: The Evil Escapes, 1989, Call Me Anna, 1990, Always Remember I Love You, 1990, Absolute Strangers, 1991, Last Wish, 1992, Grave Secrets: The Legacy of Hilltop Drive, 1992, A Killer Among Friends, 1992, A Family of Strangers, 1993, Cries From the Heart, 1994, One Woman's Courage, 1994, When the Vows Break, 1995, To Face Her Past, 1996, Race Against Time: The Search for Sarah, 1996, The Disappearing Act, 1997, A Christmas Memory, 1997, When He Didn't Come Home, 1998, A Season For Miracles, 1999, Love Lessons, 2000, Miracle on the Mountain, 2000, Love Lessons, 2000, Little John, 2002, Wrong Turn, 2003, Murder Without Conviction, 2004, Falling in Love with the Girl Next Door, 2006; (theatre) The Miracle Worker, 1959-61, Isle of Children, 1962, Oklahoma!, 2002, Golda's Balcony, 2005; (motion picture appearances) I'll Cry Tomorrow, 1955, The Goddess, 1958, Happy Anniversary, The 4-D Man, 1959, The Miracle Worker, 1962 (Acad. award as best supporting actress 1962), Billie, 1965, Valley of the Dolls, 1967, Me, Natalie, 1969 (Golden Globe award as best actress 1970), the Swarm, 1978, Something Special, 1987, Prelude to a Kiss, 1992, Kimberly, 1999, Bigger Than the Sky, 2005; guest appearances Police Story, 1975, Police Women, 1975, Marcus Welby M.D., 1975, Touched By an Angel, 2003, Judging Amy, 2004 and several others; co-author Surviving Sexual Assalt, 1983, Call Me Anna, 1987, A Brilliant Madness: Living With Manic-Depressive Illness, 1992. Nat. corp. council Muscular Dystrophy Assns. Am. Recipient Emmy Awards, 1964, 69, 76, 79 Mem. AFTRA. Office: William Morris Agy 151 S El Camino Dr Beverly Hills CA 90212-2775

DUKE, ROBERT DOMINICK, lawyer; b. Goshen, NY, Oct. 14, 1928; s. Robert DeWitt and Elma Christina (Dominick) D.; m. Jeannette Parham, Apr. 24, 1954; children: Katherine Campbell, Robert Dominick, Peter Benjamin DeWitt, Lois Christina. BA, Va. Mil. Inst., 1947; LL.B., Yale U., 1950; MBA, U. Pa., 1952. Bar: N.Y. 1950, Conn. 1989. With Cravath, Swaine & Moore, NYC, 1951-52, 54-64, Freeport-McMoRan Inc. and predecessors, NYC, 1964—84, gen. counsel, 1970—84, sr. v.p., 1973—80; sr. v.p., gen. counsel The Brink's Co. (formerly The Pittston Co.), Richmond, Va., 1984—93, sr. counsel, 1993—2002, also bd. dirs., 1991—93. Served as 1st lt. JAGC, U.S. Army, 1952-54. Mem.: ABA, Assn. Bar City NY, Silver Spring Golf Club, Yale Club (N.Y.C.). Presbyterian. Home: 67 Ridgefield Rd Wilton CT 06897-3006

DUKE, ROBIN CHANDLER TIPPETT, retired public relations executive, former ambassador; b. Balt., Oct. 13, 1923; d. Richard Edgar and Esther (Chandler) Tippett; m. Angier Biddle Duke, May 1962; children: Jeffrey R. Lynn, Letitia Lynn, Angier Biddle Jr. Fashion editor N.Y. Jour. Am., NYC, 1944-46; freelance writer NYC, 1946-50; rep. Orvis Bros., NYC, 1953-58; mem. pub. rels. staff Pepsi Cola Co., Internat., NYC, 1958-62; US amb. to UNESCO US Dept. State, Belgrade, 1980, US amb. to Norway Oslo, 2000—01. Bd. dirs. Am. Home Products, NYC, Internat. Flavors & Fragrances, NYC, East River Bank, New Rochelle, NY; dir. Rockwell Corp., 1977—95; dir. emeritus Inst. Internat. Edn. Co-chmn. Population Action Internat., N.Y.C., 1975-96; Met. Club Washington; bd. dirs. David Packard Found., U.S. Japan Found. Recipient Albert and Mary Lasker Social Svc. award, 1991, Margaret Sanger Woman of Yr. Valor award, 1995. Mem. Coun. on Fgn. Rels., Acad. Arts & Scis., World Affairs Coun. L.I. (co-chmn.), Colony Club, River Club. Democrat. Avocations: skiing, swimming.

DUKE, STEPHEN OSCAR, physiologist, research scientist, educator; b. Battle Creek, Mich., Oct. 9, 1944; s. Oscar and Azalee Rosa (Tallant) D.; m. Barbara Alice Rowe, June 2, 1967 (div. Dec. 1993); children: Gregory Ivan, Robin Anne. BS, Henderson State U., 1966; MS, U. Ark., 1969; PhD, Duke U., 1975. Plant physiologist So. Weed Sci. Lab., USDA, Stoneville, Miss., 1975-84, rsch. leader, 1984-87, lab. dir., 1987-96, rsch. leader Oxford, Miss., 1996—. Adj. prof. U. Miss., Oxford, 1996—. Co-author: Physiology of Herbicide Action, 1993; editor: Weed Physiology, 2 vols., 1985, Pest Control with Enhanced Environmental Safety, 1993, Porphyric Pesticides, 1994, Herbicide Resistant Crops, 1995, Natural Products for Pest Management, 2006; contbr. articles to profl. jours. Head referee Greenville Youth Soccer Assn. (Miss.), 1982-96; soccer coach Washington Sch., Greenville, 1986-88. Lt. US Army, 1968—70, Vietnam. Decorated Bronze Star; recipient Edminster award USDA, 1986, Disting. Alumnus award Henderson State U., 1989, CIBA-GEIGY/Weed Sci. Soc. Am. award CIBA-GEIGY Corp., 1990, Outstanding Sr. Scientist award USDA, Agr. Rsch. Svc., 2001, Extraordinary Prof. award U. Pretoria RSA, 2002-, Molisch award Internat. Allelopathy Soc.; elected Henderson State U. Acad., 2001. Fellow AAAS, Weed Sci. Soc. Am. (assoc. editor 1978-83, pres. 1996, Outstanding Young Scientist award 1984, Outstanding Article award 1984, Rsch. award 1990); mem. Am. Soc. Plant Physiology (chmn. so. sect. 1985-86), Coun. for Agrl. Sci. and Tech. (bd. dirs. 1993-94), Am. Chem. Soc.(Internat. Rsch. award agrochem. divsn. 2004), So. Weed Soc. (pres. 1995, disting. svc. award 1998), Internat. Weed Sci. Soc. (pres. 2000-04), Internat. Allelopathy Soc. (v.p. 2005—). Avocations: gardening, writing. Home: 9 Private Rd 3078 Oxford MS 38655 Mailing: PO Box 3964 University MS 38677 Business E-Mail: sduke@olemiss.edu.

DUKE, STEVEN BARRY, law educator; b. Mesa, Ariz., July 31, 1934; s. Alton and Elaine (Altman) D.; m. Janet Truax, 1956 (div. 1971); children: Glenn, Warren, Alison, Sally; m. Margaret Munson, 1984 (div. 1999); children: Jennifer, Lauren. BS, Ariz. State U., 1956; JD, U. Ariz., 1959; LL.M., Yale U., 1961. Bar: Ariz. 1959. Law clk. to Supreme Ct. Justice Douglas, 1959; grad. fellow Yale Law Sch., 1960, mem. faculty, 1961—, prof. law, 1966—81, 2003—, Law of Sci. and Tech. prof., 1982—2003. Vis. prof. U. Calif.-Berkeley, 1965, Hastings Coll. Law, 1981, Ariz. State U., 1986; bd. dirs. New Haven Legal Assistance Assn., 1968-70; cons. Commn. to Revise Fed. Criminal Code; mem. Conn. Commn. on Medicolegal Investigations, 1976—; bd. visitors Fordham U. Law Sch., 1986-1999. Author: (with A. Gross) America's Longest War: Rethinking Our Tragic Crusade Against Drugs, 1993; editor-in-chief Ariz. Law Rev.; contbr. articles to profl. jours. Mem. Woodbridge (Conn.) Bd. Edn., 1970-72; mem. Woodbridge Democratic Town Com., 1967-72. Mem. Nat. Assn. Criminal Def. Lawyers, Am. Trial Lawyers, ACLU, Phi Kappa Phi, Alpha Tau Omega. Home: 250 Grandview Ave Hamden CT 06514-3028 Office: Yale Law Sch PO Box 208215 New Haven CT 06520-8215

DUKE, WANDA K., artist; b. New Castle, Ind., Mar. 19, 1924; d. Raymond Emil and Flemmie (Toppin) Kepner; m. Robert Kerr Duke, Aug. 21, 1945 (div. July 1968); children: Sandra Toppin Hodge, Gregory Hamilton Kerr Duke. Student, So. Meth. U., 1942-43, Purdue U., 1943-44; postgrad., Ariz. State U., 1977. Various positions RCA; med. writer Modern Medicine Mag., Mpls., 1969-71; editl. asst., writer The Am. Philatelist, 1975-77; admintrv. asst. in ethnomusicology Ariz. State U. Instr. water media Pima C.C., Green Valley, Ariz., 1993, 95, Green Valley Recreation Assn., 1995, 96; pvt. instr., 1993-97. Exhbns. include N.C. Mus. of Art Exhbn., 1971, Nat. Aqueous, Tubac, Ariz., 1992, 95, 99, Western Fedn. of Water Color Socs., 1990, Nat. Acrylic Painters Assn., Gt. Britain, 1997, Marin Soc. Artists, Ross, Calif., San Francisco Women Artists, Peninsula Art Assn., San Mateo, Calif., Palo Alto Art Group, Calif., Art League, Houston, Walnut Creek Rental Gallery, Calif., Minn. Artists Assn., Mpls., Facet Gallery, Taos, N.Mex., N.C. Mus. of Art, Raleigh, So. Ariz. Water Color Guild, others; work collected in pvt. collections, including L. Boulton, Can., and Neil Armstrong. Active Red Cross Orgn. Recipient numerous painting awards including Best in Show Sonoran Br. Nat. League of Am. Pen Women, 1995, N.C. Mus. of Art Benefit Show, Raleigh, others. Mem. ARC (signature mem.), Nat. League of Am. Pen Women (pres., charter mem. Sonoran Desert Br., 1995), Nat. Acrylic Painters Assn. (signature mem.) So. Ariz. Water Color Guild (signature mem.), DAR, Kappa Alpha Theta (bd. dirs.), Tugac Ctr. Arts. Avocations: singing (Augusta Choral Soc., San Francisco Bach Choir), golf, tennis, skiing, table tennis. Home: Apt 28A 5801 Lowell St NE Albuquerque NM 87111-5959 Personal E-mail: juanda3@webtv.net.

DUKE, WILLIAM EDWARD, public affairs executive; b. Bklyn., July 18, 1932; m. Leilani Kamp Lattin. BS, Fordham U., 1954. City editor Middletown (N.Y.) Record, 1956—60; asst. state editor Washington Star, 1961—63; exec. asst. U.S. Sen. Jacob K. Javits, Washington, 1963—69; dir. pub. affairs Corp. Pub. Broadcasting, Washington, 1969—72; dir. fed. govt. rels. Atlantic Richfield Co., Washington, 1973—78, mgr. pub. affairs LA, 1978—91; mgr. external affairs We. States Petroleum Assn., 1993—95; pres. W.E. Duke and Co., 1996—. Lectr. U. So. Calif. Grad. Sch. Journalism, 1988—; cons. in field. Fellow: Pub. Rels. Soc. Am., Nat. Press Club. Office Phone: 310-454-3480.

DUKE DE LEONEDES OF SPAIN SICILY GREECE, HIS ROYAL HIGHNESS See SANCHEZ, LEONEDES

DUKKIPATI, RAO VENKATESWARA, engineering educator, researcher, scientist; b. Bhyravapatnam, India, Jan. 20, 1945; came to U.S., 1971; s. Nagabhushanam and Annapurnamma (Vallurupalli) D.; m. Sudha R. Tummala, May 28, 1969; 1 child, Ravi. BS in Mech. Engring., Sri Venkateswara U., Tirupathi, India, 1966; MS, Andhra U., Waltair, India, 1969; MScE, U. N.B., Can., 1971; PhD, Okla. State U., 1973. Registered profl. engr., Ont. Structures analyst Pratt & Whitney Aircraft, Montreal, 1973-78; sr. rsch. officer NRC, Ottawa, Ont., Can., 1978-95; sr. rsch. engr. U. Windsor, Ont., 1976; vis. prof. U. Toledo, Ohio, 1997—. Adj. prof. Concordia U., Montreal, 1978—, U. Western Ont., London, 1988-94. Co-author: Dynamics of Railway Vehicle Systems, 1984, Computer-Aided Simulation in Railway Dynamics, 1988, Mechanism and Machine Theory, 1992, Computer-Aided Analysis and Design, 1997. Recipient Disting. Engr. award TANA-N.Am., 1985, B. Roth award Applied Mechanisms and Robotics, 1997. Fellow ASME, Can. Soc. for Mech. Engrs.; mem. Soc. Automotive Engrs. Hindu. Avocations: swimming, philosophy, social service. Office: U Toledo Mime Dept Toledo OH 43606 Home: 35 Claudia Dr # 318 West Haven CT 06516 Office Phone: 203-254-4000 x3154. Personal E-mail: rdrvd@yahoo.com. Business E-Mail: rdukkipati@mail.fairfield.edu.

DUKMEJIAN, MICHAEL, publishing executive; Advt. mgr., mgr. bus. devel. Time Mag., 1980—93; dir. sales devel. Sports Illustrated, 1993—98; pub. Mut. Funds Mag., 1999—2002, Money Mag., NYC, 2002—06; co-pub. Bus. and Fin. Network (combination of Fortune, Money, Fortune Small Bus. and Bus. 2.0) Time Inc., 2006—. Office: Time Inc Bus and Fin Network Time & Life Bldg Rockefeller Ctr New York NY 10020 Office Phone: 212-522-2824. Office Fax: 212-467-1178.*

DUL, CARLA MARIE, music educator; d. Lazelle Cyrus and Grace Rosalie Aldrich; m. Ronald Joseph Dul, Dec. 18, 1998. MusB of Music Edn., U. Wis., Stevens Point, 1990, MusD of Music Edn., 1998. Cert. k-12 vocal music educator. Instr. voice Conservatory Creative Expression, 1987—89; dir. vocal music Mosinee H.S., 1990—. Asst. condr. Wausau Lyric Choir, Wis., 2002—. Cantor, musician St. Francis Xavier Parish, Knowlton, Wis., 2000—; dir. youth choir St. Mark's Cath. Ch., Rothschild, 1994—98. Named Tchr. of Yr., Mosinee Sch. Dist., 1994—95. Mem.: Wis. Choral Dirs. Assn., Nat. Assn. Tchrs. Singing, Wis. Music Educators Assn. (north ctrl. v.p. 1995—98). Roman Catholic. Avocations: theater, reading, fishing, singing, travel. Office: Mosinee HS 1000 High St Mosinee WI 54455 Office Phone: 715-693-3200 x 3405.

DUL, JOHN A., lawyer, electronics executive; b. 1961; BBA, U. Miami; JD, Northwestern U. Bar: Ill., 1986. Assoc. gen. counsel. Anixter Inc. (subsidiary of Anixter Internat.), 1990—96, sec., gen. counsel, 1996—; v.p., gen. counsel Anixter Internat., Skokie, Ill., 1998—, sec., 2002—. Office: Anixter Internat Inc 2301 Patriot Blvd Glenview IL 60025-8020 Office Phone: 224-521-8000.

DULAC, CATHERINE, biology professor, researcher; Grad., Ecole Normale Supérieure de la rue d'Ulm, Paris; PhD, U. Paris. Rschr. Institut d'Embryologie du Collège de France; postdoctoral fellow Columbia U.; asst. prof. molecular & cellular biology dept. Harvard U., 1996—2000; asst. investigator Howard Hughes Med. Inst., 1997—2002, investigator, 2002—; assoc. prof. molecular & cellular biology dept. Harvard U., Cambridge, Mass., 2000—01, prof. molecular & cellular biology, 2001—06, Higgins prof. molecular & cellular biology, 2006—. Mem. scientific advisory bd. Senomyx, Inc., Allen Brain Atlas, Max Planck Inst., Friedrich Miescher Inst. Contbr. articles to profl. jours. Recipient Richard Lounsbery award, NAS, 2006. Fellow: AAAS. Achievements include discovery of genes encoding families of pheromone receptors in mammals. Office: Harvard U Rm 4017 16 Divinity Ave Cambridge MA 02138 Office Phone: 617-495-7893. Business E-Mail: dulac@fas.harvard.edu.

DULAINE, PIERRE, ballroom dancer; Became ptnr. to Yvonne Marceau, 1976; founder Am. Ballroom Theatre, NYC, 1984—; faculty mem. Sch. of Am. Ballet, 1986—, The Juilliard School, 1992—. Guest tchr. Sch. Am. Ballet, NYC, The Juilliard Sch., NYC. Appearances include Smithsonian Inst., Washington, JFK Ctr. Performing Arts, Washington, White House, 1992, (Broadway and London show) Grand Hotel, 1989-92; toured with Yvonne Marceau and Am. Ballroom Theatre numerous internat. locations, dance cons. (films) Take the Lead, 2006. Recipient Brit. Theatrical Arts Championships 4 times, Spl. Astaire award, Dance Educator awards, Outstanding Achievement in Dance award Nat. Dance Coun. Am., 1992, Dance Mag. award, 1993, Dance Educators of Am. award, 1990, Edn. award, Americans for the Arts, 2005. Office: Pierre Dulaine Dance Club 25 W 31st St Fl 4 New York NY 10001-4413 Office Phone: 212-244-9442. Fax: 212-244-9299. E-mail: pdulaine@msn.com.

DULANEY, RICHARD ALVIN, lawyer; b. Charlottesville, Va., Oct. 18, 1948; s. Alvin Tandy and Susie Lucille (Sims) D. BA, Yale U., 1971; JD, Coll. William and Mary, 1977. Bar: Va. 1977, U.S. Dist. Ct. (ea. dist.) Va. 1978. V.p. Christian Ctr., Charlottesville, Va., 1972-73; rsch. asst. Marshall-Wythe Sch. Law, Williamsburg, Va., 1975; assoc. Niles & Chapman, Remington, Va., 1977-79; gen. ptnr. Niles, Dulaney & Parker, Culpeper, Va., 1980-92; of counsel Chandler, Franklin, and O'Bryan, Culpeper, Va., 1988—2004; ptnr. Niles Dulaney Parker and Lauer LLP, Culpeper, 1992-98, Dulaney, Parker, Lauer & Thomas LLP, Culpeper, 1999-2001, Dulaney, Lauer & Thomas LLP, Culpeper, 2001—; of counsel The Chandler Law Group, 2004—. Bd. dirs. Rappahanock Legal Svcs., Fredericksburg, Va., 1981-83. Bd. dirs. Christian Ctr., Syria, Va., 1974-89, U. Sci. and Philosophy Swannanoa, Waynesboro, Va., 1985-2002, The Quest Inst., Charlottesville, Va., 1986-87; mem. Bd. Zoning Appeals, Culpeper County, Culpeper, Va., 1983-90. Mem. Piedmont Bar Assn., Va. Bar Assn., Va. Trial Lawyers, Assn., Am. Trial Lawyers Assn., Culpeper Bar Assn. (pres. 1985-86), New Haven chpt. Pierson Fellowship, Omicron Delta Kappa. Home: PO Box 511 Culpeper VA 22701-0511 Office: Dulaney Lauer & Thomas LLP PO Box 190 Culpeper VA 22701-0190 E-mail: dulaneylaw@aol.com.

DULANY, ELIZABETH GJELSNESS, editor; b. Charleston, SC, Mar. 11, 1931; d. Rudolph Hjalmar and Ruth Elizabeth (Weaver) Gjelsness; m. Donelson Edwin Dulany, Mar. 19, 1955; 1 son, Christopher Daniel. BA, Bryn Mawr Coll., 1952. Editor, R.R. Bowker Co., 1948-52; med. editor U. Mich. Hosp., Ann Arbor, 1953-54; editorial asst. E.P. Dutton & Co., NYC, 1954-55, U. Ill. Press, Champaign, 1956-59, asst. editor, 1959-67, assoc. editor, 1967-72, mng. editor, 1972-90, asst. dir., 1983-90, assoc. dir., 1990—98, editor, 1998—. Democrat. Episcopalian. Home: 73 Greencroft Dr Champaign IL 61821-5112 Office: U Ill Press 1325 S Oak St Champaign IL 61820-6903 Office Phone: 217-244-0158. Business E-Mail: edulany@uillinois.edu.

DULANY, WILLIAM BEVARD, lawyer; b. Sykesville, Md., Sept. 4, 1927; s. William Washington and Helen Marie (Bevard) D.; m. Anna Winifred Spencer, Aug. 16, 1952; children: William Bryant, Thomas Patrick, Anne French. AB, McDaniel Coll., 1950, LLD (hon.), 1989; postgrad., U. Mich., 1950—51; JD, U. Md., 1953. Bar: Md. 1953, U.S. Dist. Ct. Md. 1954, U.S. Tax Ct. 1979, U.S. Supreme Ct. 1990. Assoc. Baldwin, Jarman & Norris, Balt., 1953—59; sr. ptnr. Dulany, Leahy & Curtis, LLP, Westminster, Md., 1959—. Mem. character com. Md. Ct. Appeals, Annapolis, 1974—93. Mem. Md. Ho. of Dels., Annapolis, 1962-66, Md. Constl. Conv., Annapolis, 1967-68, Md. Regional Planning Coun., 1964-66; chmn. Md. Fair Campaign Practices Commn., 1975-78; chmn. adv. com. Carroll County C.C., 1976; trustee McDaniel Coll., Westminster, Md., 1976—, vice chair bd., 2007—; bd. dirs. nat. office Am. Heart Assn., Dallas, 1982-89, chmn., 1987-88; bd. dirs. Episcopal Ministries to Aging, Inc., Fairhaven, 1982-2005, chmn., 1986-2005; former commr. Md. Human Rels. Commn.; vice chmn. Md. Spl. Com. on Gen. Equality, 1989-91; mem. commn. on Racial and Ethnicity Fairness in Judicial Process, 2002-04; trustee Md. Hist. Soc., 1991-01; past pres. Hist. Soc. Carroll County; former mem. Vestry Ascension Episc. Ch. Named one of Outstanding Young Men of Am., Westminster chpt. Jaycees, 1961, Alumnus of Yr., McDaniel Coll., 1986; recipient Outstanding Citizen award Westminster chpt. Rotary, 1985, Trustee of Yr. award Am. Assn. Homes and Svcs. for the Aging, 2002. Fellow Md. Bar Found. (pres. 1986-88, bd. dirs.); mem. ABA, Md. Bar Assn. (v.p. 1970-71), Carroll County Bar Assn. (pres. 1966-67), Am. Judicature Soc., Am. Bar Found., Bachelor's Cotillon Club (Balt.), Phi Alpha Delta. Avocations: travel, volunteer work in non-profit organizations. Home: 1167 Old Taneytown Rd Westminster MD 21158-3605 Office: Dulany Leahy & Curtis LLP 127 E Main St Westminster MD 21157-5012 Home Phone: 410-876-2974; Office Phone: 410-876-2117. Business E-Mail: dulany@dulany.com.

DULAS, DEANNE L., lawyer; b. St. Paul, Aug. 29, 1970; BA, U. Minn., 1992; JD, U. Minn. Law Sch., 1995. Bar: Minn. 1995, US Dist. Ct. (dist. Minn.) 1996, US Ct. Appeals (8th cir.) 1996. Shareholder Strandemo, Sheridan & Dulas, P.A., Eagan, Minn. Named a Rising Star, Minn. Super Lawyers mag., 2006. Mem.: Collaborative Law Inst., Minn. Women Lawyers (co-chair jud. elections endorsement com.), Legal Assistance of Dakota County (bd. dirs., pres.), First Dist. Bar Assn., Minn. State Bar Assn. (mem. family law sect.), Dakota County Bar Assn. Office: Strandemo Sheridan & Dulas PA 1380 Corp Ctr Curve Ste 320 Eagan MN 55121 Office Phone: 651-686-8800. E-mail: ddulas@strandemoandsheridan.com.*

DULAUX, RUSSELL FREDERICK, lawyer; b. West New York, NJ, Dec. 30, 1918; s. Frederick and Theresa A. (Noble) L.; m. Ann deFriedberg, Aug. 22, 1962 (dec.); m. Eva DeLuca, Dec. 24, 1985. Student, Drake's Bus. Sch., 1937, Pace Inst., 1938-40, Fordham U., 1946-48; LLB summa cum laude, N.Y. Law Sch., 1950; postgrad., Pace Coll., 1951, Columbia U., 1955; DBA (hon.), Adam Smith U. Am., 2001. Bar: N.Y. 1951, U.S. Dist. (so. dist.) N.Y. 1951, U.S. Ct. Appeals (2d cir.) 1951, U.S. Ct. Claims 1952, U.S. Tax Ct. 1952, U.S. Dist. Ct. (ea. dist.) N.Y. 1953, U.S. Ct. Customs and Patent Appeals 1963, U.S. Ct. Mil. Appeals 1963, U.S. Supreme Ct. 1963. Mem. staff N.Y. State Dept. Law, Richmond County Investigations, 1951-54, N.Y. State Exec. Dept. Office of Commr. of Investigations, 1954-57; comptroller-counsel Odyssey Productions, Inc., 1957-59; ptnr. Ryan, Murray & Laux, NYC, 1951-61, Ryan & Laux, NYC, 1961; pvt. practice NYC, 1961—; prof. of bus. law and legal studies Adam Smith Univ., 2001. Served with AUS, 1940-46; capt. JAG, vet. corps. of arty. State of N.Y., 1975-92, maj., 1992—; spl. agt. counter intelligence corps and security intelligence corps; col. U.S. Army. Recipient Eloy Alfaro Grand Cross Republic of Panama, Cert. of World Leadership for Leadership and Achievement, 1987, Cert. of Merit for Disting Achievement, 1984, Cert. for Internt. Contemporary Achievement for Outstanding Contbr. to Soc., 1984, Disting. Leadership award for Contbns. to the Legal Profession, Award of Merit for Outstanding Profl. and Pub. Svc., Guglielono Marconi Bronze award, 1987, 1st Century award for achievements in bus. adminstrn. and law, 2001; inducted Hall of Fame for Contbn. to Legal Profession, recipient, Am. Medal of Honor, ABA, 2002, Outstanding People of 21st Century award, England Internat. Bar Assn., 2002. Mem.: NATAS, Bronx County Bar Assn. (Townsend Wandell Gold medal), Humanity Against Hatred, Am. Legion (past post comdr. admen's post 209), Asia Soc., China Inst. Am., Army and Navy Union USA, Mid Manhattan C. of C., English Speaking Union, Met. Opera Guild, Internat. Platform Assn, Am. Def. Preparedness Assn., Soc. Am. Wars, Heroes of '76, Navy League, St. Andrews Soc. N.Y., St. George Soc. N.Y., Soc. Friendly Sons St. Patrick, Sailors' and Airmen's Club, Soldiers' Club, Grand St. Boys' Club, Res. Officers Assn. U.S. (col.), Nat. Sojourners, Lambs Club, Sovereign Mil. Order of Knights of St. James of Spain (grand prior 2003), Sons Union Vets. Civil War, VFW (adjutant Floyd Gibbons Post 500, cert. of Recognition and Appreciation Polit. Action Com. 1990, cert. of svc. on Pres. Rehab. Com. Vets. sect.), Knights Hospitaller of St. John of Jerusalem, Sovereign Mil. Order of Temple of Jerusalem, Knights of Malta, Masons (past comdr. N.Y. Masonic War Vets,), Order Ea. Star, Order of Lafayette, Delta Theta Phi. Home: 3510 Brainbridge Ave Apt 2F Bronx NY 10467-1419

DULBECCO, RENATO, biologist, educator; b. Catanzaro, Italy, Feb. 22, 1914; arrived in U.S., 1947, naturalized, 1953; s. Leonardo and Maria (Virdia) D.; m. Gulseppina Salvo, June 1, 1940 (div. 1963); children: Peter Leonard (dec.) , Maria Vittoria; m. Maureen Rutherford Muir; 1 child, Fiona Linsey. MD, U. Torino, Italy, 1936; DSc (hon.), Yale U., 1968; LL.D., U. Glasgow, Scotland, 1970; DSc (hon.), Vrije Universiteit, Brussels, 1978, Ind. U., 1984, U. Bologna, 1988. Asst. U. Torino, 1940-47;

research asso. Ind. U., 1947-49; sr. research fellow Calif. Inst. Tech., 1949-52, asso. prof., then prof. biology, 1952-63; sr. fellow Salk Inst. Biol. Studies, San Diego, 1963-71; asst. dir. research Imperial Cancer Research Fund, London, 1971-74, dep. dir. research, 1974-77; disting. research prof. Salk Inst., La Jolla, Calif., 1977—, pres., 1989-92, pres. emeritus, 1993—; prof. pathology and medicine U. Calif. at San Diego Med. Sch., La Jolla, 1977-81, mem. Cancer Ctr.; with Nat. Rsch. Coun. Milan. Vis. prof. Royal Soc. G.B., 1963—64; Leeuwenhoek lectr., 1974; Clowes Meml. lectr. , Atlantic City, 61; Harvey lectr. Harvey Soc., 1967; Dunham lectr. Harvard U., 1972; 11th Marjory Stephenson Meml. lectr., London, 73; Harden lectr., Wye, England, 73; Am. Soc. for Microbiology lectr., LA, 79; mem. Calif. Cancr Adv. Coun., 1963—67; mem. vis. com. Case Western Res. Sch. Medicine; adv. bd. Roche Inst., 1968—71, Inst. Immunology, Basel, Switzerland; esperto Italian Nat. Rsch. Coun.; trustee Am.-Italian Fedn. for Cancer Rsch.; bd. dirs. Scientific Counselors Dept. Etiology NCI; cons. Nat. Rsch. Coun. ESPERTO, 1994—. Trustee La Jolla Country Day Sch., Am.-Italian Fedn. for Cancer Rsch.; bd. mem. sci. counselors dept. etiology Nat. Cancer Inst.; mem. commissionary CCB Cariplo Found., Milan. Decorated grand ufficiale Italian Republic; co-recipient (with David Baltimore and Howard Martin Temin) Nobel prize in medicine, 1975; named Man of Yr., London, 1975, Italian Am. of Yr., San Diego County, 1978, hon. citizen, City of Imperia (Italy), 1983, City of Arezzo, City of Sommariva Perno, City of Catanzaro, City of Torino, hon. founder, Hebrew U., 1981; recipient John Scott award City Phila., 1958, Kimball award Conf. Pub. Health Lab. Dirs., 1959, Albert and Mary Lasker Basic Med. Rsch. award, 1964, Howard Taylor Ricketts award, 1965, Paul Ehrlich-Ludwig Darmstaedter prize, 1967, Horwitz prize, Columbia U., 1973, Targa d'oro Villa San Giovanni, 1978, Mandel Gold medal, Czechoslovak Acad. Scis., 1982, Via de Condotti prize, 1990, Cavaliere di Gran Croce Italian Rep., 1991, Natale Di Roma prize, 1993, Columbus prize, 1993, S. Ambrogio medal, City of Milan, 1993, Spl. Oscar of Italian TV, 1999; fellow Guggenheim and Fulbright fellow, 1957—58. Mem.: NAS, Am. Acad. Arts and Scis., Fedn. Am. Scientists, Royal Soc. (fgn.), Academia Nazionale del Lincel (fgn.), Am. Philos. Assn., Internat. Physicians for Prevention Nuclear War, Am. Assn. Cancer Rsch., Comitato di Collaborazione Culturale (hon.), Academia Ligure di Scienze e Lettre (hon.), Alpha Omega Alpha. Office: Salk Inst PO Box 85800 San Diego CA 92186-5800 Office Phone: 858-453-4690.

DULCHINOS, PETER, retired lawyer; b. Chicopee Falls, Mass., Feb. 2, 1935; s. George and Angeline D.; children: Matthew George, Paul Constantine, Gregory Peter. BSEE, MIT, 1956, MSEE, 1957; MS in Engring. Mgmt., Northeastern U., 1965; JD, Suffolk U., 1984. Bar: Mass. 1984, US Dist. Ct. (Mass.) 1984, US Ct. Appeals (1st cir.) 1985, US Supreme Ct. 1988, US Patent and Trademark Office 1989, US Claims Ct. 1989. With Sylvania Co., Waltham, Mass., 1957-61, Needham, Mass., 1963-66, Tech Ops, Burlington, Mass., 1961, RCA, Burlington, 1962-63, Raytheon Co., Waltham, Mass., 1966—2006; ret. Computer ops. mgr. tactical software devel. facility Patriot Ground Computer System, 1977-86, intellectual property mgr., 1986-2006; lectr. Fitchburg State Coll., 1985-90; corporator Ctrl. Savs. Bank, Lowell, Mass., 1980-92; sec.-treas. U. Lowell Bldg. Authority, 1974-85; mem. statewide adv. coun. Dept. Mental Health, 1996—. Mem. statewide adv. coun. Dept. Mental Retardation, 1993-96; mem. human studies subcom. Bedford VA Hosp., 1987-90; pres. Chelmsford Rep. Club, 1964-70; chmn. Chelmsford Rep. Town Com., 1972-76, 80—, chmn., 2000-04; Rep. state committeeman, 2004—; assoc. town counsel Tyngsborough, Mass., 1985-87; mem., chmn. Chelmsford Bd. Health, 1972-87, 93—; mem. Nashoba Tech. High Sch. Com., 1970-71; trustee, chmn. Medfield State Hosp., 1993-2003; trustee Westborough State Hosp., 2003—, Northern Essex CC, 2006-; v.p. Greater Lowell Comprehensive Cmty. Support Systems Bd. Dept. Mental Health, 1994-99; mem. State Mental Health Planning Coun., 1999—; corporator Lowell Gen. Hosp., 2005—; trustee No. Essex C.C., 2006—. 2d lt. US Army, 1957-58. Mem. Mass. Bar Assn., Boston Patent Law Assn., Raytheon Employees Profl. Assn. (treas. 1998, pres. 1999). Republican. Greek Orthodox. Home and Office: 17 Spaulding Rd Chelmsford MA 01824-1021 Personal E-mail: pdulchinos@comcast.net.

DULIN, ERIC D., archivist; b. Nuremberg, Germany, Jan. 10, 1969; s. Cleo L. and Ynez D. Dulin. BA, Fayetteville State U., NC, 1991; MA, Temple U., Phila., 1994; MS in Libr. Sci., Clarion U., Pa., 2003. Cert. archivist Acad. Cert. Archivists, 2006. Archivist Cheyney U., Pa., 1996—2005, CIGNA, Phila., 2005—. Asst. treas. Ch. Christ, Phila., 2005—, historian, archivist, 1994—. Mem.: Del. Valley Archivists Group, Mid-Atlantic Regional Archives Conf., Soc. Am. Archivists. Avocations: reading, computers, exercise. Home Phone: 610-544-1264.

DULIN, MAURINE STUART, volunteer; b. Lonerock, Iowa, Feb. 16, 1919; d. Frank Meagher and Fern Adrienne (Wetzel) Stuart; m. William Carter Dulin, Oct. 5, 1940; children: Jacquelyn Dulin Wilson, Patricia F., Stuart M. AB in Polit. Sci./Econs., Coll. of William and Mary, 1939. Coll. cons. Woodward and Lothrop, Washington, 1939-40; adminstv. asst. Sightler and Cox, Washington, 1942-43; acctg. dept. asst. Am. U., Washington, 1964-69; corp. sec. Bittinger and Dulin, Arlington, Va., 1949-73; ptnr. 41 Ltd. Partnership, Bethesda, Md., 1979—, Montrose-270 Ltd. Partnership, Bethesda, 1979—. Mem. Rock Creek Womens Rep. Club, Bethesda, 1951-57; sgt.-at-arms Montgomery County Fed. of Rep. Women, Bethesda, 1952-53, State Fedn. of Womens Rep. Club, 1953-54; charter mem., com. chmn. Nat. Mus. of Women in the Arts; women's bd. Cathedral Choral Soc. 1975—, com. chmn., 1988-90; women's bd. George Washington U. Hosp., 1970—, Save Our Seminary at Forest Glen, Md., 1989—. Mem. The Town Club (pres. 1958-59), Pi Beta Phi (nat. com. chmn. 1971-75, province officer 1967-71). Episcopalian. Home: 9707 Old Georgetown Rd Apt 1416 Bethesda MD 20814

DULIN, THOMAS N., lawyer; b. Albany, NY, May 26, 1949; s. Joseph Paul and Mary Carol (Keane) D.; m. Pamela Lee Kendall, May 14, 1983; children: Chelsea K., Danielle Y. Boshea, Amanda L. Boshea, Thomas M. Boshea. BA, Siena Coll., 1972; JD, Western New England U., 1976. Bar: N.Y. 1977, U.S. Dist. Ct. (no. dist.) N.Y. 1977, U.S. Supreme Ct. 1984. Asst. dist. atty. Albany County, 1977-81; assoc. McCarthy & Evanick, Albany, 1981-83; sole practice Albany, 1983-88; sr. ptnr. Dulin, Harris & Bixby, Albany, 1988-92; ptnr. Gerstenzang, Weiner & Gerstenzang, Albany, 1992-93, The Dulin Law Firm, Albany, 1993—. Staff atty. Albany County Pub. Defender's Office, 1983—. Bd. dirs. Big Bros. and Sisters of Albany County, Inc., 1983-92, pres., bd. dirs. , 1988-90. Mem.: N.Y. State Trial Lawyers Assn., Assn. Trial Lawyers Am., Albany County Bar Assn., Capital Dist. Trial Lawyers Assn., N.Y. State Assn. Criminal Def. Lawyers, N.Y. State Bar Assn. Democrat. Avocations: skiing, golf, swimming. Office: 500 New Karner Rd Albany NY 12205-3822 Office Phone: 518-690-4411.

DULL, DAVID A., lawyer; b. 1949; BA in Am. Studies with honors, Yale U., 1971, JD, 1982. Staff mem. UN Assn. U.S.A.; ptnr. Irell & Manella LLP, Century City, Silcon Valley, Calif., 1985—98; v.p. bus. affairs, gen. counsel Broadcom Corp., Irvine, Calif., 1998—. Bd. dirs. Magfusion. Office: Broadcom Corp 16215 Alton Pkwy Irvine CA 92618 Office Phone: 949-450-8700. Office Fax: 949-450-8710.*

DULL, WILLIAM MARTIN, retired engineering executive; b. Buchanan, Mich., June 24, 1924; s. Curtis Frank and Daisy Julia (Sharp) D.; m. Margaret Ann McMillan, Apr. 10, 1976; children: Richard William, Beverly Ann, William McMillan. BSME, U. Mich., 1945. Registered profl. engr., Mich. Dir. tech. staff Detroit Edison, 1951-66, asst. gen. supt. cen. plants, 1966-70, gen. supt. underground lines, 1970-71, mgr. employee relations, 1971-74, mgr. orgn. planning and devel., 1974-89; pres. Charleston Engring. Cons., 1990-92; ret., 1992. Chmn. Charleston Engrs. Joint Coun., 1991—, chmn. 1993-94. Bd. dirs. World Med. Relief, Detroit, 1971-90, chmn., 1988-90; bd. dirs. Jr. Achivement, Southeastern Mich., 1971-90; trustee Detroit Sci. Ctr., Inc., 1979-85. Served to lt. (s.g.) USN, 1942-51, PTO. Recipient Gold Leadership award Jr. Achievement, 1985. Fellow Engring. Soc. Detroit (pres. 1970-71, Disting. Svc. 1980, life); mem. ASHRAE (pres. 1964-65, Outstanding Engr. award 1965, life), ASME (life), IEEE (chmn. nat. conf. 1971), NSPE (life), Architects, Engrs., Surveyors Registration Coun. (chmn. 1968-69), Mich. Soc. Profl. Engrs. (bd. dirs. 1973-75, Disting. Engr. 1980), S.C. Soc. Profl. Engrs. (bd. dirs. 1994-95), Charleston Engrs. Joint Coun. (chmn. 1993-94), U. Mich. Alumni Assn. (v.p., bd. dirs. 1964-71, Disting. Svc. award 1970), Charleston Navy League (v.p., bd. dirs. 1993—), Detroit Yacht Club. Republican. Methodist. Office Phone: 843-849-8213. Personal E-mail: mwmdull@aol.com.

DULLEA, KEIR, actor; b. Cleve., May 30, 1936; s. Robert and Margaret (Ruttan) D.; m. Margo Bennett, 1960 (div.1968); m. Susan Lessons, 1969 (div. 1970); m. Susie Fuller, 1972 (dec. Jan. 5, 1998); m. Mia. Dillon, 1999. Grad., Neighborhood Playhouse. Appeared in motion pictures: The Hoodlum Priest, 1961, David and Lisa, 1962 (best male performance San Francisco Film Festival 1962), Thin Red Line, 1964, The Naked Hours, Mail Order Bride, 1964, Bunny Lake is Missing, 1965, Madame X, 1966, The Fox, 1968, 2001: A Space Odyssey, 1968, De Sade, 1969, Paperback Hero, 1973, Devil in the Brain, 1972, Pope Joan, 1972, Paul and Michelle, 1974, Black Christmas, 1975, Silent Night, Evil Night, 1975, Welcome to Blood City, 1977, Full Circle, 1977, Leopard in the Snow, 1978, Brainwaves, 1983, Blind Date, 1983, 2010, 1984, Oh, What a Night, 1992, The Divine Inspiration, 2000, 3 Days of Rain, 2002, Alien Hunter, 2003, The Day My Towers Fell, 2006, The Good Shepherd, 2006; appeared on Broadway in Dr. Cook's Garden, 1967, Butterflies Are Free, 1969-70, Cat on a Hot Tin Roof, 1974, P.S. Your Cat is Dead, 1975, appeared on stage in Toronto in The Servant, 1990; TV shows include Law and Order, 1976, 2001-06, Legend of the Golden Gun, 1978, Brave New World, 1980, No Place to Hide, 1980; stage appearances include Mary Rose, 2007. Address: c/o Bret Adams Ltd 448 W 44th St New York NY 10036-5205*

DULLES, AVERY, cardinal, theologian; b. Auburn, NY, Aug. 24, 1918; s. John Foster and Janet Pomeroy (Avery) D. AB, Harvard U., 1940, postgrad. in law, 1940—41; PhL, Woodstock Coll., 1951, STL, 1957; STD, Pontifical Gregorian U., Rome, 1960; LLD (hon.), St. Joseph's Coll., Phila., 1969; LHD (hon.), Georgetown U., 1977; ThD (hon.), U. Detroit, 1978; LLD (hon.), Iona Coll., New Rochelle, NY, 1980; DD (hon.), St. Anselm Coll., Manchester, NH, 1981; LHD (hon.), Creighton U., 1983; DD (hon.), Jesuit Sch. Theology, Berkeley, Calif., 1984, Protestant Episcopal Theol. Sem., Alexandria, Va., 1986; LHD (hon.), Seton Hall U., 1989, Stonehill Coll., 1990, Loyola U., Chgo., 1990; STD (hon.), Providence Coll., 1991; DD (hon.), Carthage Coll., Kenosha, Wis., 1991; ThD (hon.), U. Dayton, 1992; LHD (hon.), Christ the King Seminary, East Aurora, NY, 1994; DD (hon.), Nashotah House, Wis., 1996; LittD (hon.), Fordham U., 1996; DD (hon.), John Carroll U., Cleveland, Ohio, 1997; LLD (hon.), U. Mass., Boston, 1998; LHD (hon.), St. Francis Coll., Bklyn., 1999; ThD (hon.), Theol. Faculty Paderborn, Germany, 2000; LLD (hon.), U. Notre Dame, 2001; LHD (hon.), LeMoyne Coll., Syracuse, NY, 2001, Univ. St Thomas, Miami, 2001, Seminary St. Charles Borromeo, Overbrook, Pa., 2002, Univ. St. Thomas, St. Paul, Minn., 2002; DD (hon.), Univ. Scranton, Pa., 2002; STD (hon.), Franciscan Univ., Steubenville, Ohio, 2002; LHD (hon.), St. Joseph's Coll., Renssalear, Ind., 2003, Christendom Coll. Front Royal, Va., 2003, Coll. of the Holy Cross, Worcester, Mass., 2003; STD (hon.), Siena Coll., Londonville, NY, 2003, Coll. New Rochelle, 2003, Bobolanum, Warsaw, Poland, 2003; DD (hon.), Heythrop Coll., London, 2003; LHD (hon.), Ohio State U., 2004; DHL (hon.), Wheeling Jesuit U., W.Va., 2006, Ave Maria U., Naples, Fla., 2006; DRE (hon.), Marquette U., Milw., 2006. Joined S.J., Roman Cath. Ch., 1946, ordained priest, Soc. of Jesus, 1956, created cardinal, 2001. Instr. philosophy Fordham U., 1951-53, vis. lectr., 1970, Laurence J. McGinley prof. religion and society, 1988—; mem. faculty Woodstock Coll., NYC, 1960-74, prof. theology, 1969-74, Cath. U. Am., Washington, 1974-88; Gasson prof. theology Boston Coll., Boston, 1981-82; prof. emeritus Cath. U. Am., Washington, 1988—. Vis. lectr. Weston Coll., 1971, Union Theol. Sem., 1971—74, Princeton Theol. Sem., 1972, Pontifical Gregorian U., 1973, 90, 93, Episcopal Theol. Sem., 1975, Luth. Sem. Pa., 1978; Martin C. D'Arcy lectr. Campion Hall, Oxford U., England, 1983; vis. John A. O'Brien prof. theology Notre Dame U., 1985; vis. prof. theology Cath. U. of Leuven, 1992; vis. prof. religious studies Yale U., New Haven, 1996; fellow Woodrow Wilson Internat. Ctr. for Scholars, 1977; scholar-in-residence St. Joseph's Sem., Dunwoodie, NY, 1996; mem. Commn. on Christian Unity, Archdiocese of Balt., 1962—70; mem. Cath. Bishops' Adv. Coun., 1969—75; consultor to Papal Secretariat for Dialogue with Non-Believers, 1966—73; mem. USA Luth.-Cath. Dialogue, 1972—92; cons. to Com. on Doctrine, Nat. Conf. Cath. Bishops, 1991—; mem. Internat. Theol. Com., 1992—97, Luth.-Roman Cath. Coord. Com., 1994—96. Author: Princeps Concordiae, 1941, A Testimonial to Grace, 1946, (with others) Introductory Metaphysics, 1955, Apologetics and the Biblical Christ, 1963, The Dimensions of the Church, 1967, Revelation and the Quest for Unity, 1968, Revelation Theology: A History, 1969, (with others) Spirit, Faith and Church, 1970, The Survival of Dogma, 1971 (Christopher award 1972), A History of Apologetics, 1971, 2d edit., 2005, Models of the Church, 1974, 3d rev. edit., 2002, Church Membership as a Catholic and Ecumenical Problem, 1974, The Resilient Church, 1977, A Church to Believe In, 1982, Models of Revelation, 1983, 2d rev. edit., 1992, (with Patrick Granfield) The Church: A Bibliography, 1985, The Reshaping of Catholicism, 1988, The Craft of Theology, 1992, expanded edit., 1995 (Best Book in Theology Cath. Press Assn. 1993), The Assurance of Things Hoped For, 1994, A Testimonial to Grace and Reflections on a Theological Journey, 1996, The Priestly Office, 1997, (with Patrick Granfield) The Theology of the Church: A Bibliography, 1999, The Splendor of Faith: The Theological Vision of Pope John Paul II, 1999, rev. edit., 2003, The New World of Faith, 2000, Newman, 2002; assoc. editor for ecumenism Concilium, 1963-70, adv. editl. bd., 1970-92; adv. editl. bd. Midstream: An Ecumenical Jour., 1974—; mem. editl. bd. Logos: A Jour. of Cath. Thought and Culture, 1997—; contbr. column to Theology for Today, America, 1967-68; contbg. editor New Oxford Rev., 1990-2001; cons. Theology Digest, 1985—; mem. adv. coun. Pro Ecclesia, 1991—; contbr. articles to theol. publ. Bd. dirs. Georgetown U., 1966-68, Woodstock Theol. Ctr., 1974-79; trustee Fordham U., 1969-72, St. Mary's Sem. and Univ., Balt., 1992-98; acad. coun. Irish Sch. Ecumenics, 1971-78. Served to lt. USNR, 1942-46. Decorated Croix de Guerre with silver star (France); named to Hall of Fame, NY Mil. ROTC, 2004, Order of St. Thomas, U. St. Thomas, Houston, 2006; recipient Cardinal Spellman award for disting. achievement in theology, 1970, Religious Edn. Forum award, Nat. Cath. Edn. Assn., 1988, Campion award, Cath. Book Club, NY, 1989, F. Sadlier Dinger award, 1994, Choate Alumni Seal prize, Choate Rosemary Hall, 1995, Christus Magister medal, U. Portland, 2001, James Cardinal Gibbons medal, Cath. U. Am., Washington, 2001, Gold Medal award, Nat. Inst. Social Sci., NYC, 2001, John Henry Newman award, Cardinal Newman Soc., 2001, John Carroll Soc. medal, Washington, 2002, John Paul II award, Inst. for Social Sci., Arlington, Va., 2002, Jerome award, Cath. Libr. Assn., 2002, Newman medal, Loyola Coll., Md., 2004, Marianist award, U. Dayton, Ohio, 2004, Saint Thomas Aquinas medallion, Saint Thomas Aquinas Coll., Santa Paula, Calif., 2005, St. Joseph's Sem. 7th Ann. Dinner award, 2005, Pres. medal, Canisius Coll., Buffalo, 2005, Loyola medal, Seattle U., 2006, Veritas medal, Aquinas Ctr. for Theol. Renewal, Ave Maria U., 2007, Cath. Chaplaincy award, Harvard U., 2007, Bene Merenti medal, Fordham U., 2007. Mem. Cath. Theol. Soc. Am. (bd. dir. 1970-72, 74-77, v.p. 1974-75, pres. 1975-76), Am. Theol. Soc. (v.p. 1977-78, pres. 1978-79), Cath. Commn. on Intellectual and Cultural Affairs (exec. com. 1991-94), Phi Beta Kappa. Roman Catholic. Office: Fordham U Faber 255 Bronx NY 10458 Office Phone: 718-817-4747. Business E-Mail: mcgchair@fordham.edu.

DULLES, JOHN WATSON FOSTER, history professor; b. Auburn, NY, May 20, 1913; s. John Foster and Janet Pomeroy (Avery) D.; m. Eleanor Foster Ritter, June 15, 1940; children: Edith, John, Ellen, Avery. AB, Princeton U., 1935; MBA, Harvard U., 1937; BS in Metall. Engring., U. Ariz., 1943, Metall. Engr., 1951. Clk. The Bank of NY, NYC, 1937-38; miner Callahan Zinc-Lead Co., Patagonia, Ariz., 1938-41; head ore dept., smelter operator Cia Minera de Peñoles, S.A., Monterrey, Mex., 1943-49, head comml. divsn., 1949-51, asst. gen. mgr., 1951-59, exec. v.p., 1959; v.p. Cia Mineração Novalimense, Belo Horizonte, Brazil, 1959-62; prof. history U. Ariz., Tucson, 1966-91; univ. prof. L.Am. studies U. Tex., Austin, 1962—. Advisor to US delegation to OAS Conf., Vina Del Mar, Chile, 1967; cons. US Dept. State, Bur. Intelligence and Rsch., 1968-72. Author: Yesterday in Mexico, 1961, Vargas of Brazil, 1967, Unrest in Brazil, 1970, Anarchists and Communists in Brazil, 1973, Castello Branco: The Making of a Brazilian President, 1978, President Castello Branco, 1980, Brazilian Communism, 1935-1945, 1983, The São Paulo Law School, 1986, Carlos Lacerda: Brazilian crusader, Vol. 1, 1991, Vol. 2, 1996 (Brazilian Union Writers and Carioca Acad. Leters prize 2000), Sobral Pinto: The Conscience of Brazil, 2002, Resisting Brazil's Military Regime, 2007. Pres. exec. bd. Union Ch. Monterrey, Mexico, 1948—49, elder, 1957—59. Recipient Achievement medal, U. Ariz., 1960, Ptnrs. of the Alliance Medal, Brazilian Govt., 1966. Fellow Calif. Inst. Internat. Studies; mem. The Am. Soc. of the Most Venerable Order of the Hosp. of St. John of Jerusalem (knight), Am. Hist. Assn., Tex. Inst. of Letters, Theta Tau (Alumni Hall of Fame), Inst. History and Geography Brasil. Avocation: tennis. Office: U Texas PO Box 7934 Austin TX 78713-7934 Home Phone: 210-657-2765; Office Phone: 512-505-2705. Office Fax: 512-505-2725. Business E-Mail: dulles@mail.utexas.edu.

DUMA, RICHARD JOSEPH, epidemiologist, microbiologist, educator, pathologist, researcher, physician; b. Bethlehem, Pa., Apr. 2, 1933; s. Joseph Anthony and Helen Veronica (Bartek) D.; m. Mary Alyce Fridley, Apr. 18, 1957; 1 child, Scott. BA, Va. Poly. Inst., 1955; MD, U. Va., 1959; PhD, Va. Commonwealth U.-Med. Coll. Va., 1978. Diplomate Am. Bd. Internal Medicine; lic. physician, Fla., Va.; lic. pvt. pilot. Intern, then resident in medicine U. Ala. Med. Center, Birmingham, 1959-60, 62-65; research fellow Harvard U. Med. Sch.-Mass. Gen. Hosp., 1965-67; mem. faculty Med. Coll. Va., Richmond, 1967-91, chmn. div. infectious diseases, 1974-92, prof. medicine and pathology, 1975-92, prof. microbiology, 1977-92. Mem. U. S. Pharmacopeia Adv. Panel on Hosp. Practices, 1971-82, chmn. subcom. rsch., 1976-82, clin. prof. medicine and infectious diseases Med. Coll. Richmond, 1992—; exec. dir. Nat. Found. for Infectious Diseases, 1991-94, v.p. bd. dirs., 1973-75, pres., 1975-91, trustee, 1994-2003, bd. dirs., 2004—; chmn. Nat. Coalition for Adult Immunization, 1988-94; didr. infectious diseases Halifax Med. Ctr., Daytona Beach, Fla., 1995—. Mem. bd. visitors Embry-Riddle Aero. U., 1999—. Served with M.C., USNR, 1960-62. Fellow ACP, Infectious Disease Soc. Am., Royal Soc. Tropical Medicine and Hygiene, Am. Soc. Tropical Medicine and Hygiene, Am. Soc. Rickettsiology, Fla. Infectious Disease Soc. (pres. 1997-99, bd. dirs. 1997-); mem. AAAS, Am. Fedn. Clin. Rsch., Am. Soc. Microbiology, Va. Soc. Microbiology, Am. Soc. Internal Medicine, Va. Soc. Internal Medicine, Richmond Soc. Internal Medicine, So. Soc. Clin. Investigation, Am. Thoracic Soc., Royal Soc. Medicine, Med. Soc. Va., Richmond Acad. Medicine, Acad. of Medicine, Washington, Med. Assn. Fla., Volusia Med. Soc., Sigma Xi, Tau Beta Pi. Home: 1 Capri Ct Palm Coast FL 32137- Office: Halifax Medical Ctr 303 N Clyde Morris Blvd Daytona Beach FL 32114-2700 Office Phone: 386-258-4871.

DUMANOSKI, DIANNE, journalist, writer; b. 1944; BA, Vassar Coll.; MA, Yale U. Prodr. WGBH-TV, Boston; staff writer The Boston Phoenix; with Boston Globe, 1979—, environ. journalist, 1983—93; now freelance sci. writer. Lectr. in field; bd. dirs. Environ. Media Svcs.; mem. Ted Scripps Fellowships adv. bd. Author (with Theo Colborn and Pete Myers): (book) Our Stolen Future: How Man-Made Chemicals are Threatening Our Fertility, Intelligence and Survival, 1996. Fellow Ctr. Environ. Journalism, U. Colo., Knight Fellow in Sci. Journalism, 1983—84. E-mail: ddumanoski@earthlink.net.

DUMARS, JOE, III, professional sports team executive, retired professional basketball player; b. Shreveport, La., May 24, 1963; m. Debbie Nelson, 1989; children: Jordan, Aren. Grad. in Bus. Mgmt., McNeese State U., 1985. Player Detroit Pistons, 1985—99, v.p. player pers., 1999—2000, pres. basketball ops., 2000—. Mem. US Men's Nat. Basketball Team (Dream Team II), 1994; mem. exec. com. US Tennis Assn., 1999. Named MVP, NBA Finals, 1989, NBA Exec. of Yr., Sporting News, 2003; named to NCAA All-Am. 2nd team, 1985, NBA All-Rookie team, 1986, NBA All-Defensive 1st team, 1989—90, 1992—93, All-NBA 3rd team, 1990—91, NBA All-Star team, 1990—93, 1995, 1997, NBA All-Defensive 2nd team, 1991, All-NBA 2nd team, 1993, Mich. Sports Hall of Fame, 2003, La. Sports Hall of Fame, 2003, Naismith Meml. Basketball Hall of Fame, 2006; recipient Citizenship award, 1994, NBA Sportsmanship award (now named Joe Dumars Trophy), 1996. Achievements include winning NBA Championships as a member of the Pistons, 1989, 90. Office: Detroit Pistons 5 Championship Dr Auburn Hills MI 48326-1753*

DUMAS, LAWRENCE B., academic administrator; BA in Biochemistry with high honors, Mich. State U., 1963; MA in Biochemistry, U. Wis., 1965, PhD in Biochemistry, 1968. Faculty mem. Northwestern U., Evanston, Ill., 1970—, assoc. prof., 1975—80, prof. biochemistry, molecular biology and cell biology, 1980—95, provost, 1996—. Recipient Career Devel. award, USPHS, 1974—79, John Boezi award for outstanding molecular biology rsch., Mich. State U., 1987; USPHS Predoctoral fellowship at Wis., 1964—67, Postdoctoral Fellowship, Calif. Inst. Tech., 1968—70. Mem.: AAAS, Am. Soc. for Microbiology, Am. Soc. Biol. Chemists. Office: Office of the Provost Northwestern Univ 2-143 Crown Evanston Campus 633 Clark St Evanston IL 60208 Office Phone: 847-491-5117. Office Fax: 847-467-1630. Business E-Mail: nu-provost@northwestern.edu.*

DUMAS, MICHAEL GODFREY JOSEPH, artist; b. Whitney, Ont., Can., Sept. 20, 1950; s. Alphyr Adrian and Caroline Anna (Cenzura) D.; m. Ellen Kocsis, July 19, 1975; 1 child, Shae Shannon-Mae. Student, Art Instrn. Sch., Mpls., 1968, Humber Coll., 1970, postgrad., 1971, Cornell U., 1984. Apprentice to his painter Lewis Parker Lazare & Parker Studios, 1971-72. Mem. adv. bd. Art Impressions mag., 1993—97. Major exhibits include Nat. Mus. Nat. Sci., Ottawa, Ont., 1977, Theodore Roosevelt Inaugural Nat. Hist. Site, Buffalo, 1977, McMichael Can. Coll., Kleinburg, Ont., 1981, Royal Bot. Gardens, Hamilton, 1985, R.O.M., 1987-88, Yamanaakako-Takamura Mus. Art, 1991-2001, Mitsukoshi Galleries, Tokyo, 1994-2003, Algonquin Gallery, Algonquin Park, Ont., 1995-2002, Suntory Mus. Art, Osaka, 1995, Suntory Mus. Art, Tokyo, 1996, Matsuya Gallery, Tokyo, 1997, Sogo Gallery, Osaka, 1997, Yumehodaka Mus., Nagano, 1997, Spanierman Gallery, NY, 1998, Mitsukoshi Gallery, Sendai, 1999-2004, Arai Gallery, Tokyo, 2002-04, Cedar Ridge Creative Ctr., Scarborough, 1999, Fukuyu Gallery, Hiroshima, Japan, Buckingham Gallery, Uxbridge, Ont., Can., 2003-04, Algonquin Art Ctr., 2005-07, Lindsay Pub. Gallery, Ont., 2006-07; represented in permanent collections including Internat. Mus. Art Inspired By Nature, Gloucester, Eng., Yamanakako-Takamura Mus. Art, Japan, Imaoka Collection, Japan, Ont. Provincial Collection, Queen's Park, Ont. Binghamton U. Art Mus.; major conservation events include The Spirit of the Wild fundraiser and exhibit, 1982, Kenya Wild Elephant fundraiser, Toronto, 1987, 91, Bird Preservation fundraiser, Osaka, Japan, 1990, Save the Rhino Trust, Namibia, 1998; commd. to design four coins for Royal Can. Mint, 1994, commd. to design Can. commemorative postage stamps; author: Nature in Art, 1991; columnist Angler & Hunter, 1976-83; contbr. articles to mags. Recipient Waterfowl Art award Ducks Unltd., 1983-84, Carling-O'Keefe Profl. Conservation award, 1986, Wildlife Conservation award Ont. Min. Natural Resources, 1987, Bronze Teal Conservation award Ducks Unltd., 1989; named Artist of the Yr., Can. Collector's Clubs, 1987, first winner by competion Wildlife Habitat Can., 1990, Internat. Flyway Artist, Ducks Unltd., Inc., 1992, Artist of the Yr., Ont. Fedn. Anglers and Hunters, 1993-2004, Outdoor Card Program award Ont. Ministry of Natural Resources, 1998, Peterborough Pathway to Fame award, 2004, Master Palette award Masterworks in Miniature, Gallery One, 2005. Mem. Soc. Animal Artists, Soc. Wildlife Art of the Nations (charter). Avocations: travel, photography, camping. Address: PO Box 8314 RR 1 Peterborough ON Canada K9J 6X2 E-mail: natures.studio.inc@sympatico.ca.

DUMAS, SANDRA LEE, medical technician, microbiologist; b. Amsterdam, NY, Nov. 15, 1949; d. Richard Carl and Eunice Yetive Teschka; children: Stacey Ann Warner, Joseph William Hodlin; m. C. Clifford Jr. A in Clin. Lab. Sci., Empire State Coll., Saratoga Springs, NY, 1987, BS in Biology, 1991. Cert. clin. lab. scientist Nat. Cert. Agy. for Med. Lab. Pers.; lic. lab. tech., NY. Med. tech. Johnstown (N.Y.) Hosp., 1968-70, Nathan Littauer Hosp., Gloversville, N.Y., 1967-68, med. tech. in microbiology, 1975—. Avocations: painting, golf, boating, photography.

DUMAS, SARA LEE, psychologist; b. Boston, Apr. 21, 1949; d. Herbert Michael and Joyce (Chaban) Marcus; m. Steven Silber, June 21, 1968 (div. Feb. 1989); children: Rachel, Victoria, Adam; m. John R. Dumas, Apr. 26, 1991. BA, U. Tex., 1977; MS, Va. Poly. Inst., 1979, PhD, 1982. Lic. psychologist, Tex. Staff psychologist Southwestern State Hosp., Marion, Va., 1980-81; intern Austin (Tex.) State Hosp., 1981-82, cons. cmty. programs, 1982-84; counseling specialist Travis County Jail, Austin, 1982-83; pvt. practice clin. psychology Austin, 1983—. Mental health cons. Head Start Program, Bastrop County, Tex., 1984-90, Ctr. for Battered Women, Austin, 1986—; cons. Nat. Multiple Sclerosis Soc., Austin, 1986-91. Vol. Capital Area Mental Health, Austin, 1983-85; del. Dem. Party State Conv., Ft. Worth, 1994, Travis County Dem. Conv., Austin, 1994; coord. Mother Earth's Festival, Austin, 1996. Avocations: gardening, theater, travel. Home: 10601 Little Thicket Rd Austin TX 78736-7436 Office: 3755 CapTX Hwy So Ste 180 Austin TX 78704 Office Phone: 512-441-6789. Personal E-mail: saradumas@austin.rr.com.

DUMERER, LORRAINE JOANNE LORI, secondary school educator, consultant; b. Providence, July 10, 1946; d. John and Edith (Flippin) Florio; m. James Edward Dumerer, Nov. 23, 1966; children: James, Marc, Jennifer, Matthew, Paul. Student, Seton Hill Coll., Greensburg, Pa., 1964-66, St. Louis U., 1966; AB, U. Ill., Champaign-Urbana, 1969, MAT, 1972; postgrad., Tex. Women's U., Denton, 1987—88, U. Tex., Dallas, 1993, So. Meth. U., 1999-2001. Cert. social studies tchr. talented and gifted Tex., coll. bd. endorsed Advanced Placement cons. Tchr. Dayton Pub. Schs., Ohio, 1970—71, St. Benedicts Sch., San Antonio, 1979—80, Incarnate World H.S., San Antonio, 1980—81, Diocese of Dallas, 1981—88, Dallas Ind. Sch. Dist., 1988—97; tchr., chmn. social studies dept., dean of faculty Long Trail Sch., Dorset, Vt., 1997—98; tchr. advanced placement govt. and politics, advanced placement macro and microecons., law studies econ. in free enterprise sys. Carrollton-Farmers Branch Ind. Sch. Dist., 1998—, dist. lead social studies tchr. advanced placement govt. and politics, 2006—; owner LJD Edn. Connection. Coord. nat. history day Diocese of Dallas, 1985-87, Jane Goodall CHIMP project, 1991; clinician Acad. Clin. Svc., Dallas, 1985—; chmn. dept. social studies, student coun. advisor North Dallas HS, 1993-97; coach Fed Challenge econs. competition, 1998-2001, North Dallas HS CIS-site based team, 1996-97, model UN teams, 2000, Texas Citizen Bee, 2007; mem. R.L. Turner H.S. CIC-site based team, 1999-04, 2006-08; reader Coll. Bd. Am. Govt., 2001-07, Found. Tchg. Econs., Dallas, 2002, Key Briscayne, Fla., 2004, St. Charles, Il. 2007, Fed. Res. Bank, Global Inst. Econs., San Antonio, 2007; instr. selected for Tng. of Writers Project, Nat. Coun. Econ. Edn., US Depts. of State and Edn., Bucharest, Romania, 2003, Nat. Constitution Ctr. Annenberg Tchr. Superior Inst., Phila., 2007, Liberty Found. Seminar, Indpls. 2007, Found. Tchg. Econs. Seminar, Fairfax, Va. 2007; curriculum writer Dallas Pub. Schs., 1995-1997, Carrollton Farmers Br. Ind. Sch. Dist., 2002-07, econs., 2004-07; advanced placement instr. Summer Inst. US Govt., U. Ark., Fayetteville, 2005, U. Tex.-Pan Am., Edinburg, 2006, U. Tex. Tyler, 2007; presenter TCSS, NCSS, NCEE and APNC; reviewer in field; cons. in field. Author: (essays) The Dilemma of Ethical Citizenship and the Political Outsider, 1995, numerous poems; contbr. chapters to books. Referee coord. N.E. Youth Soccer Assn., 1979-80, coach, 1979-80; coach, referee Mesquite Soccer Assn., 1981-86, referee liaison, 1981-82, sec., 1982-83, commr. of coaches, 1982-83; coach Tex. Citizen's Bee, 2007. Mellon grantee, 1994; named Tchr. of Yr. Dallas Coun. for Social Studies, 1996, Outstanding HS Social Studies Tchr. of Yr., Tex. Coun. for Social Studies, 2002; named one of 50 Elite Tchrs., Nat. Coun. Econ. Edn. Tex. Coun. Econ. Edn., 2001. Mem. Nat. Coun. Social Studies, Tex. Coun. for Social Studies (sec. Peter's Colony Coun. for social studies 1998-99, v.p. 2000, pres. 2001-03, programs chair 2004-05), Global Assn. for Tchrs. of Econs., North Tex. Women's Soccer Assn. (capt. 1989-95), Ctr. for Applied Linguistics (cons. World Culture Project 1996) Avocations: writing, soccer, travel. Home: 3535 Misty Meadow Dr Dallas TX 75287-6027 Office Phone: 972-968-5400. Personal E-mail: dumererl@earthlink.net. Business E-Mail: dumererl@cfbisd.edu.

DUMEZ, STEVE, architect; Student, U. London Bartlett Coll.; BArch with honors, La. State U., Baton Rouge, 1982; MArch with honors, Yale U., New Haven, 1989. With Perez Assocs., New Orleans, Eskew Vogt Salvado & Filson, New Orleans, Cesar Pelli & Assocs., New Haven, Urban Innovations Group, LA; owner, design dir., v.p. Eskew+Dumez+Ripple, New Orleans. Prin. works include Shell River Rd. Mus., 1997, Keating Magee Advt. Offices, 2000, Kate and Laurance Eustis Chapel, 2002 (Gulf States AIA Honor award, 2002, Citation, Wood Design awards, 2004), St. Martha Cath. Ch., 2003, Ochsner Health Svcs. Pediatric Facility, 2004, Whitney Nat. Bank, Carrollton br., 2004, Acadiana Ctr. for Arts, 2004, Key West Weather Forecast Office, 2005, Rivercamps at Crooked Creek, 2005, So. Living Idea House, 2006, La. State Mus. (Chgo. Athenaeum Am. Architecture award, 2006, Gulf States AIA Honor award, 2006), Paul and Lulu Hilliard Univ. Art Mus. (Gulf States AIA Honor award, 2004, Inst. Honor award for Interior Architecture, 2005, Chgo. Athenaeum Am. Architecture award, 2006). Chmn. percent for art com. Art Coun. New Orleans, 2003—; bd. mem. Preservation Resource Ctr. New Orleans, 2004—, La. Hurricane Katrina Meml. Commn., 2006. Fellow: AIA (pres. AIA La. 2004, bd. dirs. AIA La. 2001—05). Office: Eskew+Dumez+Ripple One Canal Pl 365 Canal St Ste 3150 New Orleans LA 70130 Office Phone: 504-561-8686. Office Fax: 504-522-2253. E-mail: sdumez@studioedr.com.*

DUMINUCO, VINCENT JOSEPH, academic administrator, educator; b. Bronx, NY, Jan. 13, 1934; s. Joseph S. Duminuco and Mary Dora Morreale. BA, Fordham U., 1957; degree in Sacred Theology, Woodstock Coll., 1965; MA, Stanford U., 1966, PhD, 1969. Headmaster Xavier H.S., NYC, 1969—74; dir. rsch. U.S. Jesuit Conf., Washington, 1974—77; pres. Jesuit Secondary Edn. Assn., Washington, 1977—86; sec. edn. Soc. Jesus, Rome, 1987—97; rector Jesuit Cmty. Fordham U., Bronx, 2001—07. Bd. adv. H.K. Internat. Inst. Ednl. Leadership, Hong Kong, 1998—2007; dir. worldwide Internat. Jesuit Leadership Program, Rome, 1996—; dir. Joseph O'Hare Jesuit Tchr. Leadership Program, NYC, 2003—; bd. dirs. St. Barnabus Hosp., Bronx; bd. trustees Fordham U., Loyola U., New Orleans, 1976—92; mem. pontifical coun. interreligious dialogue, Rome, 1990—96; bd. trustees St. Peters Coll., LeMoyne Coll. Author: Ignatian Pedagogy: A Practical Approach, 1993; editor: The Jesuit Ratio Studiorum, 2000; co-author: Catholic Education: Inside Out, Outside In, 1999. Recipient The Guerra award, Nat. Cath. Edn. Assn., 2003; fellow, Stanford U., 1967—69, 1969. Mem.: Nat. Cath. Ednl. Assn. (pres. secondary sch. dept. 1983—86), N.Y. Botanical Gardens. Independent. Roman Catholic. Avocations: bonsai, fishing, gardening, swimming. Office Phone: 212-636-7874.

DUMITRESCU, DOMNITA, Spanish language educator, researcher; b. Bucharest, Romania; came to US, 1984; d. Ion and Angela (Barzotescu) D. Diploma, U. Bucharest, 1966; MA, U. So. Calif., 1987, PhD, 1990. Asst. prof. U. Bucharest, 1966-74, assoc. prof., 1974-84; asst. prof. Spanish Calif. State U., LA, 1987-90, assoc. prof., 1990-94, prof., 1995—. Author: Gramatica Limbii Spaniole, 1976, Indreptar Pentru Traducerea Din Limba Romana in Limba Spaniola, 1980, (with Dan Munteanu)Limba Spaniola, 2005; translator from Spanish to Romanian; assoc. editor: Hispania, 1996-2000, S.W. Jour. Linguistics, 2000-05; contbr. articles to profl. jours. Recipient Outstanding Prof. award Calif. State U., LA, 2003-04, Pres.' Disting. Prof. award, 2007; Fulbright scholar, 1993—. Mem. MLA, Linguistic Soc. Am., Internat. Assn. Hispanists, Linguistic Assn. S.W. (pres. 2005, Am. Assn. Tchrs. Spanish and Portuguese (past pres. So. Calif. chpt., Tchr. of Yr. award 2000), Sigma Delta Pi (v.p. West 1996—). Office: Calif State U 5151 State University Dr Los Angeles CA 90032-4226 Business E-Mail: ddumitr@exchange.calstatela.edu.

DUMITRU, DANIEL, physiatrist; b. Massillon, Ohio; MD, U. Cin., 1980. Diplomate Am. Bd. Phys. Medicine and Rehab. Resident phys. medicine and rehab. VA Hosp., San Antonio, 1980—83; prof. U. Tex. Health Sci. Ctr., San Antonio, 1983—. Attending physician Audie Murphy Vets. Hosp., San Antonio. Mem.: Am. Assn. Neuromuscular and Electrodiagnostic Medicine, Am. Acad. Phys. Medicine and Rehab. (pres. 2002—03). Office: U Tex Health Sci Ctr Dept RM/PMR 7703 Floyd Curl Dr San Antonio TX 78229-3900

DUMKE, MELVIN PHILIP, dentist; b. Sleepy Eye, Minn., Jan. 23, 1920; s. Herman Gustav and Else Ida (Battig) D.; m. Phyllis Lorraine Steuck, June 25, 1950; children: Pamela, Bruce, Shari. DDS, U. Minn., 1943. Practice dentistry, Sleepy Eye, 1946-50, Morgan, Minn., 1950-66, Mankato, Minn., 1966—2003; ret., 2003. Lectr. dental assts. Mankato State Coll., 1967-69. Mem. Town Coun., Morgan, 1960-65; bd. control Martin Luther Acad., New Ulm, Minn., 1965-79; bd. dirs. The Luth. Home, Belle Plaine, Minn., 1981-96; sr. bd. dirs. Orgn. Wis. Luth. Svcs., 1996-2000; pres. Luth. Congregation, 1970, 86-87. Served to capt., Dental Corps, AUS, 1943-46. Fellow Royal Soc. Health, Internat. Coll. Dentists, Am. Coll. Dentists, Pierre Fouchard Acad.; mem. ADA (ho. of dels. 1977-87), Minn. Dental Assn. (chmn. peer rev. com. 1973-79, mem. ho. of del. 1978-89, pres. 1983-84, guest of honor 1993), So. Dist. Dental Soc. (exec. coun., trustee 1988-89, guest of honor 1986), South Cen. Dental Study Club (pres. 1970), Fedn. Dentaire Internationale, U. Minn. Alumni Assn., VFW (Disting. Svc. award 1966, comdr. 1965), Am. Legion, Lions (pres. 1965, 74, zone chmn. 1975, Melvin Jones fellow 1999), Mankato Golf Club, St. Paul U. Club, U. Minn. Sch. Dentistry Century Club, Psi Omega. Home: 364 Carol Ct Mankato MN 56003-3300 Office: 430 S Broad St Mankato MN 56001-3703 Personal E-mail: dumkes@hickorytech.net.

DUMMETT, CLIFTON ORRIN, dentist, educator; b. Georgetown, British Guiana, May 20, 1919; s. Alexander Adolphus and Eglantine Annabella (Johnson) Dummett; m. Lois Maxine Doyle, Mar. 6, 1943; 1 child, Clifton Orrin Jr. BS in Psychology, Roosevelt U., Chgo., 1941; DDS, Northwestern U., 1941, MScD, 1942, DSc (hon.), 1976; MPH, U. Mich., 1947; ScD (hon.), U. Pa., 1978; DSc (hon.), Meharry Med. Coll., 2004. Diplomate Am. Bd. Periodontology, Am. Bd. Oral Medicine. Dean, prof. periodontology Meharry Med. Coll., Nashville, 1945-49; chief dental service VA Hosp., Tuskegee, Ala., 1949-65, assoc. chief staff for rsch. and edn., 1958-65, chief dental service Chgo., 1965-66; dental dir., dir. ctr. Watts Health Ctr., LA, 1966-69; assoc. dean, chmn. dept. cmty. dentistry U. So. Calif. Sch. Dentistry, LA, 1969-75, prof., 1969-89, prof. emeritus, 1989-96, disting. emeritus prof., 1997—. Adj. prof. Northwestern U. Dental Sch., 1989; vis. prof., cons. Sch. Vet. Medicine Tuskegee Inst., 1962—65; vis. prof. Meharry Med. Coll., 1989—; trustee Am. Fund Dental Health, Chgo., 1968—78; chem. devel. component rev. panel Calif. Regional Med. Programs, LA, 1975—77; mem. Pres.'s Com. Nat. Health Ins., 1977; sr. reviewer US Surgeon Gen. Report Oral Health, 2000. Author: Community Dentistry, 1974, Afro-Americans in Dentistry: Sequence and Consequence of Events, 1977, Charles Edwin Bentley, 1982, Dental Education at Meharry Medical College: Origin and Odyssey, 1992, Culture and Education in Dentistry at Northwestern University, 1993, NDA.II The Story of America's Second National Dental Association, 2000, (editl.) Nor Yet the Last, 1962 (W.J. Gies award, 1963), The Hillenbrand Era, 1986; editor: Nat. Dental Assn., 1953—75; contbr. chapters to books, more than 300 articles to profl. jours. Chmn. adv. bd. Econ. and Youth Opportunity Agy. Project Head Start, Tuskegee, Ala., 1964—65; mem. spl. health adv. com. Calif. Bd. Edn., LA, 1972—74; mem. L.A. regional hearing planning coun. Pres.'s Com. on Health Edn., LA, 1973—74. Lt. col. USAF, 1955—58. Named to, U. So. Calif. Dental Hall of Fame, 1997; recipient Alumni Merit award, Northwestern U., 1971, Fones Gold medal, Conn. Dental Assn., 1976, Pierre Fauchard Gold medal, Pierre Fauchard Acad., 1980, Lifetime Achievement award, U. Md., 2000, John R. Callahan award, Ohio Dental Assn., 2003. Fellow: AAAS (chmn. dental sect. 1975—76, 1987—88), APHA (v.p. for U.S. 1995—96, John W. Knutson Disting. Svc. award 1992), Am. Acad. History of Dentistry (pres. 1982—83, Hayden and Harris award 1987), Internat. Coll. Dentists; mem.: ADA (hon.), Am. Dental Edn. Assn. (Presdl. citation 2003), Inst. Medicine of NAS (sr. mem.), Nat. Acads. Practice (Disting. Practitioner 1987), Am. Assn. Dental Editors (editor 1963—72, pres. 1974—75, Disting. Svc. medal 1976), Assn. Mil. Surgeons (life), Internat. Assn. Dental Rsch. (pres. 1969—70), Am. Coll. Dentists (Wm. J. Gies award 1992, Salute of Coll. 1988), Sigma Xi, Omicron Kappa Upsilon (pres., founder Nashville chpt. 1947—49), Delta Omega, Alpha Phi Alpha, Sigma Pi Phi. Democrat. Episcopalian. Avocations: music, politics, track. Home: 5344 Highlight Pl Los Angeles CA 90016-5119 Office: U So Calif Sch Dentistry PO Box 77006 Los Angeles CA 90007-0006

DUMONT, ALLAN ELIOT, retired physician, educator; b. NYC, Oct. 8, 1924; m. Joan Auerbach, Oct. 1, 1949; children: Mark E., James A., David H. BA, Hobart Coll., 1945; MD, NYU, 1948. Diplomate Am. Bd. Surgery. Intern Bellevue Hosp., NYC, 1948-49, resident, 1949-51, 53-54, chief resident, 1954-55; instr. surgery NYU, 1955-59, asst. attending surgeon Univ. Hosp., asst. vis. surgeon 3d and 4th surg. divs. Bellevue, 1955-60, asst. prof. surgery, 1959-62, assoc. vis. surgeon 3d and 4th surg. div. Bellvue, 1961-65; attending surgeon Manhattan VA Hosp., NYC, 1958-67, cons. surgeon, 1967-90; assoc. attending surgeon Univ. Hosp. NYU, 1961-68, attending surgeon, 1968-90, assoc. prof. surgery, 1962-68, prof. surgery, 1968-73, Jules Leonard Whitehill prof. surgery, 1973-90, prof. emeritus, 1990—; clin. prof. surgery U. Conn. Sch. Medicine, 1991. Career scientist N.Y.C. Health Research Council, 1959-62; univ. senate NYU, 1966-69; vis. surgeon Bellevue Hosp., 1965-90, assoc. dir. surg. service, 1975-90, Hartford, 1990—. Editor: Lymphology. 1974-84. Served to lt (j.g.) USN, 1951-53. Recipient Research Career Devel. award USPHS, 1961-71, Purkinje medal, Czechoslovakia, 1977. Mem. Am. Coll. Surgeons, New Eng. Surg. Soc., Harvey Soc., N.Y. Surg. Soc. (pres. 1987-88), Am. Physiol. Soc., Soc. Univ. Surgeons, Soc. for Surgery Alimentary Tract, Internat. Soc. Lymphology (pres. 1979-83), Am. Surg. Assn.

DUMONT, JAMES KELTON, JR., actor, theater producer; b. Chgo., Aug. 12, 1965; s. James Kelton and Judith Katherine (Johnson) DuMont; m. Wendell Faith Hall, Dec. 14, 1968; children: Sinclair Marie, Kelton Hall. Student, Boston U., 1983-85. Field recruiter Nat. Rsch. Group, Hollywood, Calif., 1993-2000; pres., CEO DuMont Entertainment Group, Hollywood, 1994—; v.p. sales and mktg. PACE Am., Hollywood, 2000—04, website, 2005—. Mem. Ensemble Studio Theatre, NYC, 1989—, co-artistic dir. L.A. Project, 1996. Actor: (Broadway plays) Six Degrees of Separation, 1990—93, (off-Broadway play) Tony & Tina's Wedding, 1989—90; (films) Speed, 1993, Combination Platter, 1993, Bombshell, 1996, The Peacemaker, 1996, Primary Colors, 1996, Erasable You, 1997, In Quiet Night, 1997, Bellyfruit, 1998, Love & Basketball, 1999, Catch Me if You Can, 2002, S.W.A.T., 2003, Seabiscuit, 2003, Along Came Polly, 2003, Miss Congeniality 2, 2004, Dating Games People Play, 2004, War of the Worlds, 2005, The Sound, 2005, Statistics, 2006, Oceans 13, 2006; (TV series) NYPD Blue, 1995, Lois & Clark, 1996, Chgo. Sons, 1996, Tracy Takes on, 1995, Fallen Angels, 1995, The Client, 1995, Sweet Justice, 1995, Can't Hurry Love, 1995, Arliss, 1998, Then Came You, 1999, The West Wing, 2000, Becker, 2000, Titus, 2001, That's Life, 2001, That Was Then, 2002, Cold Case, 2003, C.S.I., 2003, ER, 2004, Joan of Arcadia, 2005, Close to Home, 2005, House, 2006; (TV films) Pentagon Wars, 1998, Winchell, 1999, Gotta Kick It Up, 2001, Pandemic (Part 1), 2006; prodr.: Satistics, 2006; prodr., actor: (films) The Confession, 1996; co-exec. prodr.: (TV films) The Sound, 2005. Democrat. Buddhist. Avocation: writing prose and short stories, plays and screenplays. Office: 5225 Wilshire Blvd # 410 Los Angeles CA 90036 E-mail: dumontentgrp@earthlink.net.

DUMONT, MARY, chef; b. Hampton Falls, NH; Chef Jardiniere, San Francisco, Campton Place, San Francisco, Elisabeth Daniel, San Francisco, Blackbird, Chgo.; exec. chef Sonoma Saveurs, The Dunaway Restaurant, Portsmouth, NH, 2005—. Dir. cheese prog. Campton Place, San Francisco. Recipient America's Best New Chef award, Food and Wine Mag., 2006. Office: The Dunaway Restaurant 66 Marcy St Portsmouth NH 03801 Office Phone: 603-373-6112.

DU MONT, NICOLAS, psychiatrist, educator; b. San Juan, Dec. 22, 1954; s. Joseph Henri and Isabel (Solano) Du M. Postgrad. adult psychiatry, Columbia U., 1990; MD, U. P.R., 1986; postgrad. child, adolescent psychiatry, Columbia U., 1992, postgrad. pub. cmty. psychiatry, 1993. Assoc. prof. Polytech. U., San Juan, 1984-88, InterAm. U., San Juan, P.R., 1986-87; med. dir. Holistic Med. Ctr., NYC, 1993-94; asst. prof. Albert Einstein Coll. of Medicine, NYC, 1991-96, Mt. Sinai Sch. of Medicine, NYC, 1993-96, Columbia Physicians and Surgeons Coll. Medicine, NYC, 1997—; asst. attending physician Elmhurst Med. Ctr., NYC, 1993-94; asst. physician Mt. Sinai Med. Ctr., NYC, 1993-96; v.p., CEO Engring. Med. Support, Inc., NYC, 1992—; asst. prof. Columbia Physicians and Surgeons Coll. Medicine, NYC, 1997—. Attending physician Westchester Jewish Med. Svcs., Hartsdale, N.Y., 1990-95, Montefiore Med. Ctr., N.Y.C., 1991-96, Albert Einstein Coll. Medicine, 1991-96, Puerto Rican Family Inst., 1994—; asst. attending physician and med. dir. Tavares Hispanic Mental Health Clin. at Columbia Presbyn. Med. Ctr., 1997—. Mem. editl. bd.: Jour. Pagan Studies, NY edit., 1990—. Vis. fellow N.Y. State Psychiat. Inst., 1992-93. Mem. Assn. Hispanic Mental Health Profls. (exec. bd. dirs. 1999-2003, sr. advisor, 2003—, treas.). Office: Engring Med Support Inc 200 W 70th St Ste 8F New York NY 10023-4326 Home Phone: 212-721-5374; Office Phone: 212-787-8168. Business E-Mail: info@dumont.org.

DUMOUCHELLE, ERNEST J., art appraiser; s. Joseph N. DuMouchelle and Charlotte D.; m. Lucy DuMouchelle. BA, Univ. Detroit Coll.; student, Wayne State Univ., Gemological Inst. Cert. appraiser. V.p. DuMouchelle Art Gallery Co., Detroit. Appraiser Antiques Roadshow, WGBH-PBS. Mem.: Am. Gemological Inst., Am. Soc. Appraisers. Office: DuMouchelle Gallery 409 E Jefferson Detroit MI 48226 Office Phone: 313-963-6255. Office Fax: 313-963-8199. Business E-Mail: bobdumo@dumouchelle.com.

DUMOUCHELLE, LAWRENCE F., art appraiser; s. Joseph N. DuMouchelle and Charlotte D.; married. CEO DuMouchelle Art Galleries, Detroit, 1957—. Past. pres. Founders' Soc., Jr. Coun., Detroit Inst. for Arts; past pres. Detroit & Canada Tunnel Corp.; appraiser Antiques Roadshow, WGBH-PBS. Past pres. St. Paul's Parish Coun. Mem.: Internat. Soc. Appraisers, Nat. Auctioneers Assn., Mich. Auctioneers Assn., Am. Soc. Appraisers, Appraiser's Assn. Am., Meadowbrook Arts Commn. Office: DuMouchelle Gallery 409 E Jefferson Ave Detroit MI 48226 Office Phone: 313-963-6255. Office Fax: 313-963-8199. Business E-Mail: bobdumo@dumouchelles.com.

DUMVILLE, JOHN P., historic site director; b. Hanover, NH, Feb. 17, 1950; BA, U. Vt., 1972, MA, 1976. Tchr. Turnbridge (Vt.) Sch. Sys., 1974-75; arch. historian State of Vt., 1976-79; dir. Vt. State Historic Sites, Montpelier, 1979—. Trustee Vt. Hist. Soc., 1976-82, 86-92, Royalton Meml. Libr., 1969-97; selectboard Town of Royalton, Vt., 1994—. Office: Historic Preservation Nat Life Bldg Drawer 20 Montpelier VT 05620-0001 Office Phone: 802-828-3051. Business E-Mail: John.Dumville@state.vt.us.

DUNAGIN, WILLIAM G., dermatologist; b. Topeka, Oct. 2, 1950; s. Jack Allison and Muriel Elaine (Henry) Dunagin. MD, U. Kans., Kansas City, 1975. Diplomate Am. Bd. Dermatology, 1979. From asst. to assoc. prof. medicine U. Mo., Columbia, 1979—85; chief dermatology VA Hosp., Columbia, 1979—85; pvt. practice Franklin, Pa., 1985—. Summerfield scholar, U. Kans., 1968—72. Fellow: Pa. Acad. Dermatology, Am. Acad. Dermatology; mem.: AMA, Am. Conifer Soc., Phi Beta Kappa, Alpha Omega Alpha. Achievements include research in DNCB immunotherapy of verruca resistant to common treatment modalities. Office Phone: 814-437-2122.

DUNAIF, ANDREA ELIZABETH, endocrinologist; b. NYC, Feb. 26, 1952; d. Samuel Lewis and Nancy Marie (Peters) D. BA, Sarah Lawrence Coll., 1973; MD, Columbia U., 1977. Diplomate Am. Bd. Internal Medicine, Am. Bd. Endocrinology, Diabetes and Metabolism. Intern, resident in medicine Presbyn. Hosp., NYC, 1977-80; clin. and rsch. fellow in endocrinology Mass. Gen. Hosp., Boston, 1980-81, clin. and rsch. fellow in medicine and gynecology, 1981-82; instr. in ob-gyn., reproductive sci. and medicine Mt. Sinai Sch. Medicine, NYC, 1982-88, asst. prof. medicine, ob-gyn., reproductive sci., 1985-88, assoc. program dir. clin. rsch. ctr., assoc. prof. medicine, 1988-91, assoc. prof. ob-gyn. and reproductive scis., 1989-91; prof. medicine and cellular and molecular physiology Pa. State Coll., Hershey, 1991-96, program dir. gen. clin. rsch. ctr., 1995-96, dean's lectr., 1995; assoc. dir. Nat. Ctr. for Infertility Rsch. Brigham and Women's Hosp., Boston, 1996—, dir. and chief medicine and ob-gyn divsn. women's health, 1997-2001, sr. physician, 1997—; dir. Nat. Ctr. Excellence in Women's Health Harvard Med. Sch., 1998-2001; chief divsn. of endocrinology metabolism/molecular medicine, Charles F. Kettering prof. medicine Northwestern U. Med. Sch., Chgo., 2001—. Asst, attending physician Mt. Sinai Hosp., N.Y.C., 1982-88, assoc. attending physician, 1988-91; attending physician medicine Hershey (Pa.) Med. Ctr., 1992-96; sr. dir. Diabetes, Med. and Sci. Affairs, Parke-Davis, Morris Plains, N.J., 1996-97. Editor (with others, book) The Polycystic Ovary Syndrome, 1992; assoc. editor Jour. Clin. Endocrinology and Metabolism, 1993-2000; contbr. numerous articles to profl. jours, also abstracts and revs.; mem. editl. bd. Molecular and Cellular Endocrinology. Named Kelly West lectr., U. Okla., Okla. City, 1995; recipient Sinsheimer Scholar award, 1986—89, Pennsylvanians of Vision award, Tri-County chpt. Am. Diabetes Assn., Pa. affil., 1995, Citation for alumnae achievement, Sarah Lawrence Coll., 1996, Woman of Achievement award, Big Sister Assn. Greater Boston, 1999; fellow Charles H. Revson fellow, 1983—85; grantee NIH, 1985—2002, others. Mem.: Assn. Am. Physicians, Am. Soc. Clin. Investigation, Am. Fedn. Med. Rsch. (future directions com. 1997), Endocrine Soc. (mem. clin. initiatives com. 1992—94, steering com. recent progress in hormone meeting 1995—97, mem. coun. 1998—2001), Am. Diabetes Assn. (chair 1992—93, liason com. with endocrine soc.), Women in Endocrinology (chair program com. 1990—94). Avocation: opera. Office: Northwestern U Med Sch Tarry 15-709 303 E Chicago Ave Chicago IL 60611-3008 E-mail: a-dunaif@northwestern.edu.

DUNATHAN, HARMON CRAIG, college dean; b. Celina, Ohio, July 25, 1932; s. Harry V. and Mildred B. (Greek) D.; m. Katy Mary Dragati, Mar. 15, 1956 (div. July 1990); children: Christine, Susan, Amy, Andrea; m. Mary Frances Pitts, Sept. 29, 1990. BA, Ohio Wesleyan U., 1954; MS, Yale U., 1956, PhD, 1958. Mem. faculty Haverford Coll., Pa., 1957-75, assoc. prof. chemistry, 1964-70, prof., 1970-75; provost, dean faculty Hobart and William Smith Colls., Geneva, NY, 1975-84, acting pres., 1978-79; dean faculty Hampshire Coll., 1984-87; dean acad. affairs Rhodes Coll., Memphis, 1987-93; prof. chemistry, dir. rsch. and sponsored programs LeMoyne-Owen Coll., Memphis, 1993-95, prof. chemistry, interim v.p. instl. advancement, 1996-97, 00-01, prof. chemistry, dir. instl. rsch. and planning, 1997—2006. Home: 2014 Hallwood Dr Memphis TN 38107-4703

DUNAWAY, CAMMIE, marketing executive; b. 1962; m. Lendy Dunaway; 1 child, Davis. BS, U. Richmond, 1984; MBA, Harvard U., 1990. Mktg. analyst Martin Agency, Richmond, Va.; account exec. Howard Merrell and Ptnrs., NC; asst. brand mgr. Frito-Lay, Dallas, product mgr., v.p. sales for No. Calif., Wash., Ore., Alaska and Hawaii, head nat. sales force, v.p. for kids and teens mktg., 2001—03; chief mktg. officer Yahoo, Inc., Sunnyvale, Calif., 2003—. Co-founder TravelingChefs; bd. dirs. Brunswick Corp., 2006—. Vol. San Jose Tech Mus.; bd. mem. Jr. Achievement of Silicon Valley. Named one of 100 Top Marketers, Advt. Age Mag. Mem.: Am. Mktg. Assn. Office: Yahoo! Inc 701 First Ave Sunnyvale CA 94089 Office Phone: 408-349-3300. Office Fax: 408-349-3301.

DUNAWAY, CAROLYN BENNETT, retired sociology professor; b. Atlanta, Mar. 3, 1943; d. Clarence Rhodes and Gay (McKenzie) Bennett; m. William Preston Dunaway, Aug. 26, 1967; 1 child, Robert Bennett Dunaway. BA in Social Scis., Auburn U., 1966, EdD, 1983; MA in Sociology, U. Ala., Tuscaloosa, 1967. Instr. sociology Jefferson State CC, Birmingham, Ala., 1967-69; prof. Auburn U., Montgomery, Ala., 1970-71; prof. sociology and gerontology dept. Jacksonville State U., Ala., 1971-95; prof. emeritus, 1999—. Student counselor Jacksonville State U., Ala., 1971—. Contbd. articles to profl. jours. Cons., trainer Calhoun County Hospice Anniston, Ala., 1983—; presenter Calhoun County Gerontology, Anniston, 1985—; officer Nat. Alliance Mentally Ill, Jacksonville, Ala., 2007; elder, tchr. First Presbyn. Ch., Jacksonville, 1993. Recipient 100 Most Outstanding Women Alumna award Auburn U., 1991, U. Rsch. award Jacksonville State U., 1989. Mem. Ala.-Miss. Sociol. Assn. (v.p. 1975-76, Sociology Club, Inter-Se Study Club, Ala. Fedn. Womens Club (dist. sect.), Phi Kappa Phi, Kappa Delta Pi, Delta Delta Delta, Phi Delta Kappa. Democrat. Presbyn. Avocations: flower arranging, gardening, reading, swimming. Home: 902 11th St NE Jacksonville AL 36265-1230 Office Phone: 256-435-3231.

DUNAWAY, FAYE (DOROTHY DUNAWAY), actress; b. Bascom, Fla., Jan. 14, 1941; d. John and Grace D.; m. Peter Wolf, Aug. 7, 1974 (div. 1979); m. Terrence O'Neill, 1983 (div. 1987); 1 child, O'Neill. Student, U. Fla., Boston U. Appearances include as original mem. Lincoln Ctr. Repertory Co., N.Y.C., off-Broadway in Hogan's Goat; also in (play) Curse of the Aching Heart, 1982; motion picture appearances include Bonnie and Clyde, 1967, Hurry Sundown, 1967, Puzzle of a Downfall Child, The Happening, 1967, The Thomas Crown Affair, 1968, A Place For Lovers, 1969, The Arrangement, 1969, The Extraordinary Seaman, 1969, Little Big Man, 1970, The Puzzle of a Downfall Child, 1970, Doc, 1971, La Maison Sous les Arbres, 1971, Oklahoma Crude, 1973, The Three Musketeers, 1973, Chinatown, 1974, The Towering Inferno, 1974, The Four Musketeers, 1975, Three Days of the Condor, 1975, Network, 1976 (Acad. award for Best Actress), The Voyage of the Damned, 1976, The Eyes of Laura Mars, 1978, The Champ, 1979, The First Deadly Sin, 1980, Mommie Dearest, 1981, The Wicked Lady, 1982, Ordeal by Innocence, 1984, Supergirl, 1984, Barfly, 1987, Burning Secret, 1988, La Partita, 1988, Midnight Crossing, 1988, The Gamble, 1989, On a Moonlit Night, 1989, Wait Until Spring, Bandini, 1989, The Handmaid's Tale, 1990, Three Weeks in Jerusalem, 1990, Scorchers, 1990, Arrowtooth Waltz, 1991, Double Edge, 1992, Arizona Dream, 1993, The Temp, 1993, Even Cowgirls Get the Blues, 1994, Don Juan DeMarco, 1995, En brazos de la mujer madura, 1996, The Chamber, 1996, Albino Alligator, 1996, Dunston Checks In, 1996, Twilight of the Golds, 1997, Drunks, 1997, Fanny Hill, 1998 Love Lies Bleeding, 1999, The Messenger: The Story of Joan of Arc, 1999, The Thomas Crown Affair, 1999, The Yards, 2000, Stanley's Gig, 2000, Changing Hearts, 2002, The Rules of Attraction, 2002, Mid-Century, 2002, The Calling, 2002, Blind Horizon, 2004, The Last Goodbye, 2004, El Padrino, 2004, Jennifer's Shadow, 2004, Ghosts Never Sleep, 2004, Love Hollywood Style, 2005; TV movies: Hogan's Goat, 1971, The Woman I Love, 1972, After the Fall, 1974, The Disappearance of Aimee, 1976, Evita Peron, 1981, The Country Girl, 1982, 13 at Dinner, 1985, Beverly Hills Madame, 1986, Raspberry Ripple, 1986, Casanova, 1987, Cold Sassy Tree, (co-exec. prodr.), 1989, Silhouette, 1990 (co-exec. prodr.), Columbo: It's All in the Game (Emmy award for Guest Actress in Drama 1994), Mother Love, 1995, A Family Divided, 1995, The People Next Door, 1996, Rebecca, 1997, Twilight of the Golds, 1997, Gia, 1998, A Will of Their Own, 1998, Running Mates, 2000, The Biographer, 2002, Anonymous Rex, 2004, Back When We Were Grownups, 2004; TV appearances: Seaway, 1965, The Trials of O'Brien, 1966, Road to Avonlea, 1995, Touched By An Angel, 2001, Soul Food, 2002, Alias, 2002, 03; TV miniseries: Ellis Island, 1984, Christopher Columbus, 1985; TV series: It Had To Be You, 1993, A Will of Their Own, 1998, Starlet, 2005-; Acted, dir, prodr. (films): The Yellow Bird, 2001; Author: Looking for Gatsby: My Life, 1995. Recipient Most Promising Newcomer Award Brit. Film Acad., 1968

DUNAWAY, FRANK ROSSER, III, emergency physician; b. Albuquerque, Sept. 2, 1953; s. Frank Rosser and Constance (Durham) D.; m. Marcia Lee Moore, May 24, 1975 (div. 1990); children: Melissa Sommer, Amanda Durham, Vanessa Lee; m. Amy Jane Rutledge, Apr, 7, 1990; children: Kiera Elizabeth Eirwyn, Reagan Kailean Maira. BS, Duke U., 1975; MD, U. Ill., 1988. Diplomate Nat. Bd. Med. Examiners, Am. Bd. Emergency Medicine, 1993. Resident inspector nuclear engr. U.S. Nuclear Regulatory Commn., Glen Ellyn, Ill., 1982-84; resident emergency physician St. Francis Med. Ctr., Peoria, Ill., 1988-91; attending emergency physician Qualified Emergency Specialists Inc., Cin., 1991-93; med. dir. emergency svcs., chmn. dept. emergency medicine Proctor Hosp, Peoria, 1993—; attending emergency physician Proctor Hosp., Peoria, 1993—, assoc. chmn. interventional dept., 1997—99; v.p. Proctor Emergency Physicians, P.C., Peoria, 1995-97, pres., 1997—; consulting physician Hyperbaric Medicine, Peoria, 1996—2000; med.-legal cons. in emergency medicine, 1998—. Mem. faculty Ill. Coll. Emergency Physicians Oral Bd. Rev. Course, 1995—, AHA, 1985—; chmn. dept. emergency medicine Proctor Hosp., 1993—; assoc. project med. dir. Peoria Area Emergency Med. Svcs., 1994—. Contbr. articles to profl. jours. Bishop's warden St. Paul's Episc. Cathedral, 2006—. Lt. USN, 1975—82, capt. USNR, 1982—2002. Fellow: Am. Coll. Emergency Physicians; mem.: SAR, Shriners, Masons. Republican. Anglican. Avocations: skiing, sailing, scuba, backcountry canoeing. Office Phone: 309-691-1069.

DUNAWAY, MARSHA LANDRUM, special education educator; b. Roanoke, Va., Feb. 24, 1951; d. John Edward Landrum, Jr. and Diana Smith Landrum; m. Thomas Larry Dunaway, Mar. 17, 1973; children: Larry Scott, Shawn Michael. BS, East Tenn. State U., Johnson, 1973; MS, Radford U., Va., 1982. Postgrad. profl. lic. Va., 1973, cert. swim ofcl. and trainer Va. Swimming Inc., 1990, YMCA Nat., 1982, swim ofcl. Nat. Collegiate Swim Ofcls. Assn., 1990. Spl. edn. tchr. Radford City Schs., 1990—. Dir. Hensel Eckman YMCA, Pulaksi; pres. SW Aquatic Team, Radford. Mem.: NEA (life), Radford Edn. Assn. (treas. 1998—2002, pres. 2002—06), Va. Edn. Assn. (pres. New River Uniserv Dist. 3 2005—06, chair PAC New River Uniserv Dist. 3), Phi Kappa Phi. Office: Radford City Schools 12th St Radford VA 24141 Home Phone: 540-674-4228. Personal E-mail: mdunaway@rcps.org.

DUNAWAY, WILLIAM PRESTON, retired school system administrator; b. Lineville, Ala., June 30, 1936; s. Robert Johnson and Zylpha Mae (Preston) D.; m. Carolyn Bennett, Mar. 3, 1943; 1 child, Robert Bennett. BS, Jacksonville State U., Ala., 1959; MEd, Auburn U., Ala., 1966; AA, U. Ala., Tuscaloosa, 1972; EdD, U. Miss., University, 1974. Tchr. math. Clay County High Sch., Ashland, Ala., 1960-61, Benjamin Russell High Sch., Alexander City, Ala., 1961-65; asst. supt. Alexander City Bd. Edn., 1965-67; asst. prin. Erwin High Sch., Birmingham, Ala., 1967-70; headmaster St. James Sch., Montgomery, Ala., 1970-71; prin. Anniston (Ala.) High Sch., 1971-73; prof. Sch. Adminstrn. Jacksonville (Ala.) State U., 1974-91, prof. emeritus, 1993—. Cons. in field; computer edn. dir. Jacksonville State U., 1983-91. Contbr. articles to profl. jours. Boy scout and cub scout master, bd. dirs. coun. Boy Scouts Am., Anniston, contbr. Handicapped Scouting Manual 1980; officer, tchr., First Presbyn. Ch., Jacksonville, 1975—; mem. Jacksonville Housing Authority Commn., 1992—, vice chair, 1993—; founding mem. Nat. Campaign for Tolerance, Wall of Tolerance. Capt. U.S. Army Res. and N.G., 1954-68. Recipient Jacksonville State U. Research award, 1988, Citizen of Yr. award, 1984; grantee Ala. Commn. on Higher Edn., 1986, ROTC Alumni Civilian Excellence award, 2004. Mem. Nat. Assn. Secondary Sch. Prins., Am. Assn. Sch. Adminstrs., Coun. for Computer Edn., Assn. Pub. Housing and Devel., Kiwanis, Sierra Club, Kappa Delta Pi, Phi Delta Kappa. Democrat. Avocations: computers, gardening, church activities. Home and Office: 902 11th St NE Jacksonville AL 36265-1230

DUNBAR, DIANA (DIANE) L., educator, dancer, artist, writer, storyteller; b. Troy, Ala., Mar. 2, 1954; d. Donal Steuben and Sara Lee Dunbar. Attended, Model Agy. Sch., DC, 1974—75; BA in Fine Arts & Theater, Coll. Charleston, 1979, postgrad., 1979—81; MA in Creative Arts, NYU, 1990, studied dance and dance history with Lavinia Williams, 1981—89, studied classical East Indian Dance with Indrani Rahman, Vija Vetra, Uttara Coorlawala; studied modern dance, choreography, pre-classic dance with Mary Anthony, studied with Anna Sokolow, studied with Daniel Maloney. Cert. English tchr. 7-12 grades 1993, spl. edn. tchr. NY, 1994, permanent cert. spl. edn. NY, 1995. Elem. HS tchr. K-12 NYC Pub. Sch. 106, 1991—2001, NYC Pub. Sch. 94, 2001—02, Hosp. Schs., 2002—; elem. HS tchr. K-12 dept. edn. NYU Med. Ctr. Tisch, 2005—. Co-pres. Eric & Co. Video, NYC, 1983—2006; tchr., video cons. Youth Can, NYC, Troy, Ala., 1997—98; dancer, choreographer modern, classical E. Indian, Afro-Haitian, ballroom, hip-hop, world folk dance, jazz, reggae, tap, musical comedy beg. ballet Children's Dance; tchr. cons. with Eric Miller U. Pa. and India, 2004. Actress Hernando DeSoto Conquistador Spain, Hot Springs, Ark., 1979, singer, actress, dancer (musicals) Bound To Rise, NYC, 1999, Shakespeare and Porter, Medicine Show Theatre, 2001; dancer Classical East Indian Dances, 1986—, Classical East Indian Dance, La Mama Art Galleria, 1989—90; author, storyteller, dancer Lavinia Williams: The Dancer, NYC, 1989 (Writer's Series Performance award Medicine Show Theater, 1989). Founding sponsor Martin Luther King Jr. Natl. Meml., 2006—; active Nat. Arbor Day Found., United Fedn. Tchrs.; vol. tchg. asst. Classical East Indian Dance adj. prof. Indrani Rahman, NYU, NYC, 1988—91; leadership coun. So. Poverty Law Ctr., East Village, NY, 2003—; legis. intern Capitol Hill, 1974; worked to save and preserve cmty. gardens and parks NYC, 1997—; mem. Albert's Garden, NYC, 1997—99, 2006—. Named Outstanding Freshman Girl award, Troy State U., 1972, Outstanding Dancer/Performer Yancey Dance Theatre, NY Times, 1992; named to Wall of Tolerance in Montgomery, Ala., So. Poverty Law Ctr., 2003; recipient Sangam award, Classical East Indian Dance, 1990, Tchr. award, Children's Creative Writing Fund, 2000. Mem.: LWV, United Fedn. Tchrs., Nat. Ocean Conservatory, Sacred Dance Guild, Medicine Show Theatre, Smithsonian, GreenGuerillas, Audubon Club, Alpha Gamma Delta Sorority (life Highest GPA Award at Troy State U. for 1972, '73). Achievements include research in mainstream and holistic methods of treating asthma. Avocations: environmental activism, animal rescues, writing, dance, music composition, lyricist.

DUNBAR, JEFFREY, lawyer; b. Wanatchee, Wash., Nov. 19, 1968; BA, Univ. Wash., 1992; JD magna cum laude, Seattle Univ. Sch. Law, 1996. Bar: Wash. 1996. Atty. Ogden Murphy Wallace PLLC, Seattle. Contbr. articles to numerous profl. jours. Named Wash. Rising Star, SuperLawyer Mag., 2006. Mem.: ABA, Wash. State Bar Assn., King Co. Bar Assn. Office: Ogden Murphy Wallace PLLC Ste 2100 1601 Fifth Ave Seattle WA 98101-1686

DUNBAR, LESLIE WALLACE, writer, consultant; b. Lewisburg, W.Va., Jan. 27, 1921; s. Marion Leslie and Minnie (Crickenberger) Lee; m. Peggy Rawls, July 5, 1942; 1 foster child, Nha Van children: Linda Dunbar Knox, Anthony Paul. MA, Cornell U., 1946, PhD, 1948. Asst. prof. polit. sci. Emory U., Atlanta, 1948-51; chief community affairs Savannah River plant AEC, Aiken, SC, 1951-54; asst. prof. polit. sci. Mt. Holyoke Coll., 1955-58; dir. research So. Regional Council, Atlanta, 1958-61, exec. dir., 1961-65; exec. dir., sec. Field Found., NYC, 1965-80; vis. prof. polit. sci. U. Ariz., 1981. Cons. Fund for Peace, Nat. Urban League, 1981-84; sr. project assoc. social welfare policy, 1985-87, Ford Found.; guardian ad litem State of N.C., 1993-2001. Author: A Republic of Equals, 1966, The Common Interest, 1988, Reclaiming Liberalism, 1990, The Shame of Southern Politics, 2002; co-author: Where We Stand, 2004; co-author, editor: Minority Report, 1984; book rev. editor So. Changes, 1989-93. Deacon Watts St. Bapt. Ch., Durham, 1998—2001; bd. dirs. Nation Inst., 1980—86, pres., 1980—84; bd. dirs. Village of Pelham Libr. Bd., 1980—84, pres., 1982—84; bd. dirs. Children's Found., 1980—86, pres., 1982—84, Franklin and Eleanor Roosevelt Inst., 1987—2001, v.p., 1987—92; bd. dirs. Eleanor Roosevelt Inst., 1976—87, Field Found., 1978—80, Minority Rights Group, NYC, 1980—85, Ctr. Nat. Security Studies, 1980—87, Amnesty Internat./U.S.A., 1984—86, Winston Found. for World Peace, 1985—89, Voter Edn. Project, 1987—90, N.C. Coun. Chs., 1991—93, Southeastern Efforts Developing Sustainable Spaces, Inc., 1998—2001, Ruth Mott Fund, 1988—99, chair, 1992—94; bd. dirs., mem. selection com. Windcall Resident Program, 1990—94. Guggenheim fellow, 1954-55; United Negro Coll. Fund scholar-at-large, 1984-85. Fellow So. Regional Coun. (life). Home: 3050 Military Rd NW Washington DC 20015 E-mail: lesdunbar@earthlink.net.

DUNBAR, MARY ASMUNDSON, communications executive, public information officer, consultant, investor; b. Sacramento, Calif., Feb. 6, 1942; d. Vigfus Samundur and Aline Mary (McGrath) Asmundson; m. Robert Copeland Dunbar, June 21, 1969; children: Geoffrey Townsend, William Asmundson. BA in English Lit., Smith Coll., 1964; MA in Mass Comm., Stanford U., 1967; MBA in Fin., Case Western Res. U., 1985. Cert. pub. rels. profl. Tchr. Peace Corps, Cameroun, Africa, 1964-66; writer, editor Ednl. Devel. Corp., Palo Alto, Calif., 1967-68, Addison-Wesley, Menlo Park, Calif., 1969-70; freelance writer, editor various cos., Cleve., 1970-85; account exec. Edward Howard & Co., Cleve., 1985-87, Dix & Eaton, Inc., Cleve., 1987-89, sr. account exec., 1990-92, v.p., 1992-96, sr. v.p., 1997—. Author publs. in field. Trustee Cleve. Coun. World Affairs, 1994—99. Smith Coll. scholar, Northampton, Mass., 1960-64; fellow Stanford U., Palo Alto, Calif., 1967; recipient Internat. Assn. Bus. Comm. award, 1987, Women in Comm. award, 1987, Arthur Page award, 1990. Mem.: CFA Soc. Cleve., Nat. Investor Rels. Inst. (past pres. Cleve.-No. Ohio chpt., nat. bd. dirs. 2002—07, chmn. bd. 2005—06), Pub. Rels. Soc. Am. (Silver Anvil award 1997), Smith Coll. Club Cleve. Republican. Episcopalian. Avocations: yoga, music. Home: 2880 Fairfax Rd Cleveland OH 44118-4014 Office: Dix & Eaton Inc 200 Public Square Ste 1400 Cleveland OH 44114-2316 Office Phone: 216-241-4601. Business E-Mail: mdunbar@dix-eaton.com.

DUNBAR, MAURICE VICTOR, language educator; b. Banner, Okla., May 24, 1928; s. Moyer Haywood and Louise Edna (Curry) D.; m. Carol Ann Cline, July 28, 1948 (div. 1963); children: Kurt, Karl, Karla, Karen, Kristen. AA, Compton Jr. Coll., 1948; BA, U. Calif., Berkeley, 1952; MA, Calif. State U., Sacramento, 1965. Elem. tchr. Lone Tree Sch., Beale AFB, Calif., 1962-64; tchr. Anna McKenney Jr. H.S., Marysville, Calif., 1964-66, Yuba City (Calif.) H.S., 1966-67; instr. Foothill Coll. Jr. Coll., Los Altos Hills, Calif., 1967-82; prof. English, De Anza Coll., Cupertino, Calif., 1982-98; ret., 1998. Author: Fundamentals of Book Collecting, 1976, Books and Collectors, 1980, Collecting Steinbeck, 1983, Hooked on Books, 1997; contbr. articles to profl. jours. With U.S. Army, 1948-58, PTO. Mem.: B'nai B'rith, Scottish Rite (orator, libr., 33d degree), Masons. Avocations: book collecting, reading, travel, visiting university campuses.

DUNBAR, ROBERT EVERETT, writer, educator; b. Quincy, Mass., Nov. 24, 1926; s. Charles Wheeler Dunbar and Eva Emma Duquette; m. Thelma Rose Arseneault, June 26, 1954 (div. Apr. 1986); children: Yvette Maria Dunbar Orsini, Jesse Robert. BA, Marietta Coll., 1951; MS, Northwestern U., 1954. Asst. editor publs. Continental Assurance Co., Chgo., 1954—57; dir. comm. Jr. Achievement, Chgo., 1957—58; editor Nat. Sporting Goods Assn., Chgo., 1958—67; dir. comm. Am. Soc. Anesthesiologists, Park Ridge, Ill., 1967—70; dir. pub. info. divsn. Am. Fund for Dental Health, Chgo., 1970—74; owner Dunbar Edit., Nobleboro and Gardiner, Maine, 1974—; internet bookseller Christiesplus, Gardiner, Maine, 2004—. Instr. U. Health Sci., Chgo. Med. Sch., 1973—74, adj. asst. prof., 1974—75; judge HS debate tournaments, 1992—2003; judge nat. tournament Cath. Forensic League, 1995. Columnist: Maine Life Mag., 1981—86; author: Learning How to Cope with Arthritis, Rheumatism, and Gout, 1973 (Beth Fonda award for Excellence, Chgo. area chpt., Am. Med. Writers Assn., 1974), How to Debate, 1987, (15 books including) Homosexuality, 1996 (named one of the Notable Books of 1996, Nat. Coun. Social Studies and Children's Books Coun., 1996), (books for musicals) Vaudeville Gold, 1987, Friends and Lovers, 1988, Folk and Fancy, 1991; co-author: (stage adaptation) It's A Wonderful Life, 1986; actor, singer (plays and musicals) various cmty. theatres, 1984—; singer ann. concerts. A founder, first elected pres. Saint Andrew's Soc. Maine, 1980—81; vol. Maine State Music Theater, 1995—, Portland Stage Co., 1998—; first selectman Nobleboro, Maine, 1977—78. With USN, 1944—45. Fellow: Am. Med. Writers Assn. (pres. Chgo. area chpt. 1970—71, gen. chmn. ann. meeting 1971, nat. co-chmn. edn. com. 1971—75, founder, chmn. organizing com. New Eng. chpt. 1975—76, treas. New Eng. chpt. 1976—77, Judith Linn mem. award com. 2001—, judge nat. book awards, judge Will Solermine awards New Eng. chpt.); mem.: Thoreau Soc., Authors Guild, New Eng. Sci. Writers, Nobleboro Hist. Soc. (pres. 1978—79, applefest publicity 2006—, oral history project 2006—), Gaslight Theater. Republican. Roman Catholic. Achievements include design of two courses in scientific writing, one basic, one advanced, for The School of Related Health Sciences and The University of Health Sciences/Chicago Medical School. Avocations: singing, acting. Home and Office: 552 Water St Gardiner ME 04345 Office Phone: 207-588-2065. Business E-Mail: dunbarroberte@yahoo.com.

DUNBAR, W. ROY, finance company executive; b. Jamaica; Grad. in pharmacy, Manchester Univ., England, 1982; MBA, Manchester Univ. Mgmt. positions Eli Lilly, 1990—99, v.p. information tech. & CIO, 1999—2003, pres. intercontinental region, 2003—04; pres. global tech. & ops. MasterCard Worldwide, Purchase, NY, 2004—. Bd. dir. Humana Inc., EDS Corp. Bd. mem. Exec. Leadership Council Found. Named CIO of the Yr., Information Week mag., 2003. Office: MasterCard Worldwide 2000 Purchase St Purchase NY 10577*

DUNCAN, A. BAKER, investment banker; b. Waco, Tex., Dec. 29, 1927; s. A. Baker and Frances (Higginbotham) Duncan; m. Sally P Witt, Jan. 31, 1953; children: Addison Baker III, Richard Witt, Andrew Prescott. Grad., Woodberry Forest Sch., Va., 1945; BA, Yale U., 1949; MA, U. Tex., 1952. Master Hill Sch., Pottstown, Pa., 1949-51; ptnr. Rotan Mosle & Co. (investment bankers), Houston, 1953—61; headmaster Woodberry Forest Sch., 1962-70; sr. v.p., dir. Rotan Mosle Inc., 1970-78; chmn. Duncan-Smith Co., 1978—. Bd dirs SW Research Inst; gov emeritus Trinity U.; chmn. devel. com. Episcopal Diocese W. Tex. Mem.: Chi Psi. Democrat. Episcopalian. Home: 610 Garraty Rd San Antonio TX 78209-6149 Office: 711 Navarro Ste 740 San Antonio TX 78205-1786 Office Phone: 210-223-9807. E-mail: mvaaler@duncansmith.com.

DUNCAN, ALLYSON K., federal judge; b. Durham, NC, Sept. 5, 1951; BA, Hampton U., 1972; JD, Duke U., 1975. Bar: NC 1975, DC 1977. Assoc. editor Lawyers Coop. Publ. Co., 1976—77; law clk. to Hon. Julia Cooper Mack DC Ct. Appeals, Washington, 1977—78; appellate atty., asst. to dep. gen. counsel, asst. to chmn. EEOC, 1978—86; assoc. prof. NC Ctrl. U. Sch. Law, 1986—90; assoc. judge NC Ct. Appeals, 1990; commr. NC Utilities Commn., 1991—98; ptnr. Kilpatrick Stockton LLP, Raleigh, NC, 1998—2003; judge US Ct. Appeals (4th cir.), 2003—. Mem.: Wake County Bar Assn. (pres. 2002—03), NC Bar Assn. (pres.-elect 2002).*

DUNCAN, ARNE, school system administrator; JD (hon.), Lake Forest Coll., 2003; M in Sociology magna cum laude, Harvard U., 1987. Profl. basketball player, Australia, 1987—91; dir. Ariel Edn. Initiative, Chgo., 1992—98; deputy chief of staff for CEO Chgo. Pub. Sch., 1999—2001, CEO, 2001—. Bd. mem. Ariel Edn. Initiative, Bold Chgo., Chgo. Cares, The Children's Ctr., The Golden Apple Found., Ill. Coun. Against Handgun Violence, Jr. Achievement, The Nat. Assoc. Basketball Coaches' Found. Scholarship Chgo. and South Side YMCA; co-chmn. Mayor Daley's Reading Adv. Coun.; vis. com. U. Chgo. Sch. Social Svc. Admin. Fellow: Leadership Greater Chgo's Class of 1995; mem.: Aspen Inst. Henry Crown Fellowship Program. Office: Chgo Pub Sch 125 S Clark St 5th Fl Chicago IL 60603*

DUNCAN, BRUCE W., hotel and retired real estate company executive; b. Aug. 15, 1951; BS in Econ., Kenyon Coll., 1973; MBA, U. Chgo., 1975. Various positions JMB Instl. Realty Corp., Chgo., 1978—92, pres., co-CEO, 1992—94; chmn., pres., CEO Cadillac Fairview Corp., Toronto, Canada, 1995—2000; pres. Equity Residential, Chgo., 2002—03, pres., CEO, 2003—06; chmn. Starwood Hotels & Resorts Worldwide, Inc., White Plains, NY, 2005—, interim CEO, 2007—. Bd. trustees Amresco Capital Trust, Equity Residential, Chgo., 2002—; bd. dirs. Starwood Hotels & Resorts Worldwide, Inc., 1999; mem., partnership com. Rubenstein Co. LP, 2001—. Office: Starwood Hotels & Resorts Worldwide Inc 1111 Westchester Ave White Plains NY 10604*

DUNCAN, CHARLES WILLIAM, JR., investor, retired federal official; b. Houston, Sept. 9, 1926; s. Charles William and Mary Lillian (House) D.; m. Thetis Anne Smith, June 10, 1957; children: Charles William III, Mary

Anne. BSChemE, Rice U., 1947; postgrad. mgmt., U. Tex., 1948-49. Roustabout, chem. engr. Humble Oil & Refining Co., 1947; with Duncan Foods Co., Houston, 1948-64, adminstrv. v.p., 1957-58, pres., chmn. adv. bd., 1958-64; pres. Coca-Cola Co. Food Div., Houston, 1964-67; chmn. Coca-Cola Europe, 1967-70; exec. v.p. Coca-Cola Co., Atlanta, 1970-71, pres., 1971-74; chmn. bd., dir. Rotan Mosle Fin. Corp., Houston, 1974-77; dep. sec. Dept. Def., Washington, 1977-79; sec. Dept. Energy, Washington, 1979-81. Trustee emeritus, past chmn. Rice U.; lifetime bd. dirs., past treas. The Meth. Hosp. With USAAF, 1944—46. Mem. Coun. Fgn. Rels., Houston Country Club, River Oaks Country Club, Allegro Club, Sigma Alpha Epsilon, Sigma Iota Epsilon. Methodist. Home: 2 Briarwood Ct Houston TX 77019-5801 Office: 600 Travis St Ste 6100 Houston TX 77002-3007

DUNCAN, CONSTANCE CATHARINE, psychologist, educator, researcher; b. Watertown, Wis., Nov. 2, 1948; d. Howard Burton and Mary Elizabeth (Fagan) Duncan; m. R.E. Johnson, Jr., 1974 (div. 1984); m. Allan Franklin Mirsky, July 4, 1986. BA, Northwestern U., 1970; AM, U. Ill., 1973, PhD, 1978. Sr. rsch. analyst Adolf Meyer Mental Health Ctr., Decatur, Ill., 1971-73; asst. in rsch. and tchg. dept. psychology U. Ill., Champaign, 1974-78; NIMH postdoc. fellow in neurosciences Stanford U. Sch. Medicine, Palo Alto, Calif., 1978—81; rsch. psychologist VA Med. Ctr., Palo Alto, 1978-81; sr. staff fellow Lab. Psychology and Psychopathology, NIMH, 1981-88; chief unit on psychophysiology NIMH, Bethesda, Md., 1982-89, rsch. psychologist, 1988-89, rsch. specialist, 1989-93; pvt. practice Bethesda, Md., 1981—. Adj. assoc. prof. Johns Hopkins Sch. Hygiene and Pub. Health, Balt., 1987—; guest rschr. Lab. Psychology and Psychopathology NIMH, 1993—97, Sect. on Clin. and Exptl. Neuropsychology NIMH, 1997—2007; rsch. assoc. prof. Uniformed Svc. Univ. Health Sci., 1993—. Assoc. editor Psychophysiology, 1987-91; mem. editl. bd. Internat. Jour. Psychophysiology, 2002—, editor-in-chief, 2007—; cons. editor numerous sci. jour.; contbr. articles to profl. jour., chpt. to books. Found. assoc. Nat. Women's Econ. Alliance; mem. NIMH/NINCDS Assembly of Sci. Coun., 1982-84. Recipient Nat. Rsch. Svc. award, NIMH, 1978-81, Golden Anniversary Scholarship award, AAUW, 1974; NIMH fellow, 1970-74. Fellow: APA (mem. awards com. 2001—05), Internat. Orgn. Psychophysiology (mem. world congress com. 2004—, mem. working com. learning disabilities and attentional disorders 2005—), Am. Psychol. Soc.; mem.: EEG and Clin. Neurosci. Soc., Am. Psychopathol. Assn., Internat.Neuropsychol. Soc., Soc. for Neurosci., Soc. for Rsch. in Psychopathology (bd. dir. 1986—88, membership com. 1987—88), Soc. for Psychophysiol. Rsch. (program com. 1979, 1980, nominating com. 1981, chmn. early career award com. 1981—84, program com. 1982, bd. dir. 1982—85, nominating com. 1983, chmn. conv. com. 1983—87, program com. 1986, chmn. program com. 1987, program com. 1988, nominating com. 1989, Blue Ribbon Panel on state of soc. in Yr. 2000 1990—93, chmn. enhancement com. 1992—93, chmn. early career award com. 1994—96, conv. com., sec.-treas. 1996—99, com. governance and ops. 2000—01, program com. 2001, sr. award com. 2001—04, chair sr. award com. 2002—03, pres. 2002—03, chair student award com. 2003—04, chair coun. on women in sci. edn. 2005—, chair nominating com. 2004—05, Early Career Contbn. award 1980), Phi Beta Kappa, Pi Mu Epsilon, Alpha Lambda Delta, Phi Kappa Phi, Sigma Xi, Shi-Ai, Mortar Bd. Achievements include electrophysiological and neuropsychological research on normal and disordered attn. and cognition. Office: Uniformed Svcs U Health Sci Dept Psychiatry Clin Psychophysiology & Psychopharm Lab 5502 Spruce Tree Ave Bethesda MD 20814-1623 Office Phone: 301-295-2192. Business E-Mail: cduncan@usuhs.mil.

DUNCAN, DAN L., energy executive; b. Jan. 2, 1933; s. James Duncan and Maggie Ray. Grad., Massey Bus. Coll.; student, South Tex. Coll. With Wanda Petroleum, 1957—69; prin. EPCO Inc., Houston, 1969—70, pres., 1970—79, CEO, 1970—95, chmn., 1979—; chmn., dir. Enterprise Products GP, Houston, 1998—, Enterprise GP Holdings LP, Houston, 2005—. Bd. trustees Baylor Med. Coll. With US Army. Named one of Forbes Richest Ams., 2005—, World's Richest People, Forbes Mag., 2005—; recipient World Hunting Award Ring, Safari Club Internat., 1997, Internat. Hunting award, 1998, Weatherby Hunting and Conservation award, 1999, Conklin award, 2005. Office: Enterprise GP Holdings LP PO Box 4323 Houston TX 77210-4323 Office Phone: 713-381-6500.*

DUNCAN, DAVID EWING, editor, writer; Contbg. editor, writer Harper's, Atlantic Monthly, Smithsonian, Outside, NY Times, San Francisco Chronicle, Wired, Discover. Founder, editl. dir. BioAgenda; commentator Morning Edit. Nat. Pub. Radio; tchr. in field. Author: (book) Pedaling the Ends of the Earth, 1985, Calendar: Humanity's Epic Struggle to Determine a True and Accurate Year, 1998, Hernando de Soto: A Savage Quest in the Americas, 1996, Residents: The Perils and Promise of Educating Young Doctors, 1996, The Geneticist Who Played Hoops With My DNA, 2005; dir.: Grotto Nights; spl. corr., prodr. (television) Nightline ABC, 20/20; prodr.: (television) Discovery TV; corr., writer (television) ScienceNow PBS Nova sci. mag. program, founder, editl. dir. BioAgenda. Office Phone: 415-861-3795. E-mail: deduncan@literati.net.

DUNCAN, DIANNE WALKER, elementary school educator; b. Altavista, Va., Nov. 15, 1954; d. Robert and Catherine Forte. BS in History and Govt., Longwood Coll., 1977; MEd in Curriculum and Instrn., Va. Commonwealth U., 1993. Cert. tchr. social studies. Social studies tchr. Stonewall Jackson Mid. Sch., Mechanicsville, Va., 1977—98; civics tchr. John Witherspoon Mid. Sch., Princeton, NJ. Cmty. svc. coach John Witherspoon Mid. Sch. Do Something, NYC; mem. Character Edn. Partnership, Washington, DC; character edn., citizenship presenter N.J. Edn. Assn. Conf., Atlantic City, 2001; mentor jr. level presvc. tchrs. Rider U., Lawrenceville, NJ, Princeton U., NJ. Mem. So. Poverty Law Ctr., Mont., Ala., 2001—; sponsor, coord. of food dr. John Witherspoon and Crisis Ministry Trenton and Princeton, 1999—2003; sponsor, supervise mid. sch. tutors Princeton Young Achievers After Sch. Programs, Princeton, 2000—03; mem. People to People Amb. Programs' Social Studies Edn. Del. to South Africa, 2004. Recipient John Marshall award for excellence in tchg. the Constn., Va. Ctrl. Region, 1995, Best Practices award in citizenship, character edn., N.J., 2000. Mem.: N.J. Edn. Assn., N.J. Coun. Social Studies, Nat. Coun. Social Studies, Assn. Supervision and Curriculum Devel. D-Liberal. Avocations: gardening, reading. Office: Princeton Regional Schs 217 Walnut Ln Princeton NJ 08540 Office Phone: 609-806-4270. Business E-Mail: dianne_duncan@monet.prs.k12.nj.us.

DUNCAN, DONALD WILLIAM, lawyer; b. Baldwin, Md., May 18, 1932; s. William Rush and Mary Alice (MacBlane); children: David (dec.), Lisa; m. Auria Adorno Duncan; 1 child, Roberto Millan. AA, U. Balt., 1956, JD, 1960. Bar: Md. 1960, Fla. 1992. Asso. Haynie & McFerrin, C.P.A., Balt., 1956-61; controller H.C. Weiskettel Co., Balt., 1961-62; v.p., counsel, sec., Balt. Aircoil Co., Inc., 1962-87; pvt. practice Palm Coast, Fla., 1987—. Mem. Md. Bar Assn., Fla. Bar. Republican. Presbyterian. Office: B-110 21 Old Kings Rd N Palm Coast FL 32137 Office Phone: 386-445-0500. Personal E-mail: dwduncan@bellsouth.net.

DUNCAN, DORIS GOTTSCHALK, information systems educator; b. Seattle, Nov. 19, 1944; d. Raymond Robert and Marian (Onstad) D.; m. Robert George Gottschalk, Sept. 12, 1971 (div. Dec. 1983). BA, U. Wash., Seattle, 1967, MBA, 1968; PhD, Golden Gate U., 1978. Cert. data processor, systems profl., computer profl., data educator. Comm. cons. Pacific N.W. Bell Tel. Co., Seattle, 1968-71; mktg. supr. AT&T, San Francisco, 1971-73; sr. cons., project leader Quantum Sci. Corp., Palo Alto, Calif., 1973-75; dir. co. analysis program Input Inc., Palo Alto, 1975-76; lectr. acctg. and info. systems Calif. State U., East Bay Hayward, Calif., 1976-78, grad. advisor program Computer Info. Sys., E-Bus. programs, 1999—, grad. advisor MSBA-CIS, quantitative bus. methods, 2005—, dir. MBA programs, 2006—, assoc. prof. Hayward, 1978-85, prof., 1985—, coord. computer info. sys., 1994-97; dir. info. sci. dept. Golden Gate U., San Francisco, 1982-83, mem. info. systems adv. bd., 1983-85. Vis. prof. U. Wash., Seattle, 1997-98; spkr., cons. in field. Author: Computers and Remote Computing Services, 1983; mem. editl. bd. Jour. Info. Sys. Edn., 1992-97, Jur. Info. Tech. Edn., Jour. Informatics Edn. Rsch., 2000-02, assoc. editor, 2003—; contbr. over 70 articles to profl. jours. and conf. procs. Loaned exec. United Good Neighbors, Seattle, 1969; nat. com. woman bd. dirs. Young Reps., Wash., 1970-71; advisor Jr. Achievement, San Francisco, 1971-72; nat. bd. Inst. for Certification of Computer Profls. Edn. Found., 1990-93; bd. dirs. Computer Repair Svcs., 1992-94, adv. bd. Ximnet Corp., 2000-02 Recipient Disting. Rsch. award Allied Acads., 1999; named Computer Educator of Yr., Internat. Assn. Computer Info. Systems, 1997. Mem. Data Processing Mgmt. Assn. (Meritorious Svc. award, Bronze award 1984, Silver award 1986, Gold award 1988, Emerald award 1992, Diamond award 1994, Double Diamond award 1999, Triple Diamond award 2001, Nat. grantee, 1984, dir. edn. chmn. San Francisco chpt. 1984-85, sec. and v.p. 1985, pres. 1986, assn. dir. 1987, by-laws chmn. 1987, chair awards com. 1992-95, nat. bd. dirs. spl. interest group in edn. 1985-87), Am. Inst. Decision Scis., Western Assn. Schs. and Colls. (accreditation evaluation team 1984-85), Assn. Computing Machinery, Assn. Info. Sys., Computer Hist. Mus. (vol. docent, 2003-), Jr. Club Seattle (Beautiful Home award Foster City 1994, 95, winner Tournament of Christmas Lights 1996, 2003), Bus. Honor Soc., Beta Gamma Sigma. Achievements include development of info. systems (info. science), curriculum development, professional certification, industry standards, computer literacy and user education, system analysis and design, design of databases and data banks, electronic commerce. Office: Calif State U East Bay Coll Bus and Econs Hayward CA 94542

DUNCAN, ED EUGENE, lawyer; b. Gary, Ind., Dec. 10, 1948; s. Attwood and Freddie Leon (Ballard) D.; m. Patricia Louise Revado, Sept. 8, 1973 (div.); children: Kristin, Anika, Gregory. BA, Oberlin Coll., 1970; JD, Northwestern U., 1974. Bar: Ohio 1974, U.S. Dist. Ct. (no. dist.) Ohio 1977, U.S. Supreme Ct. 1977. Assoc. Arter & Hadden, Cleve., 1974-82, ptnr., 1982—2003, Tucker Ellis & West, Cleve., 2003—. Bd. dirs. Glenville br. YMCA, Cleve., 1979—95, Ohio Bd. of Bldg. Standards, Columbus, 1986-89; trustee Legal Aid Soc., Cleve., 1990-91. Mem.: Cleve. Bar Assn., Ohio Bar Assn. Avocations: writing, reading. Home: 935 Roland Rd Cleveland OH 44124-1033 Office: Tucker Ellis & West 925 Euclid Ave Ste 1150 Cleveland OH 44115-1475 Home Phone: 440-449-0758; Office Phone: 216-696-2862. Business E-Mail: EDuncan@TuckerEllis.com.

DUNCAN, FRANCES MURPHY, retired special education educator; b. Utica, NY, June 23, 1920; d. Edward Simon and Elizabeth Myers (Stack) Murphy; m. Lee C. Duncan, June 23, 1947 (div. June 1969); children: Lee C., Edward M., Paul H., Elizabeth B., Nancy R., Frances B.(dec.) , Richard L.(dec.). BA, Columbia U., 1942; MEd, Auburn U., 1963, EdD, 1969. Head sci. dept. Arnold Jr. H.S., Columbus, Ga., 1960-63; tchr. physiology, Spanish Jordan H.S., Columbus, Ga., 1963-64; tchr. spl. edn. mentally retarded Muscogee County Sch. Sys., Columbus, Ga., 1964-65; instr. spl. edn. Auburn (Ala.) U., 1966-69; assoc. dir. Douglas Sch. for Learning Disabilities, Columbus, 1969-70; prof. edn. and spl. edn. Columbus Coll., 1970-85, ret., 1985. Past dir. Columbus Devel. Ctr.; past sec. exec. bd. Muscular Dystrophy Assn., 1968-70; 73-74; mem. Gov.'s Commn. on Disabled Georgians; past trustee Listening Eyes Sch. for Deaf; past mem. Mayor's Com. on Handicapped; mem. team for evaluation and placement of exceptional children Columbus Pub. Schs.; past pres., Aux., Columbus Med. Ctr. Vol. Med. Ctr. Columbus Regional Healthcare Sys., Ga. Fellow Am. Assn. Mental Retardation; mem. AAUP, AAUW (pres. 1973-75, divsn. rec. sec. 1975—), Coun. Exceptional Children (legis. chmn. 1973-74), Psi Chi, Phi Delta Kappa. Roman Catholic. Home: 100 Spring Harbor Dr #655 Columbus GA 31904 Personal E-mail: duncanf@knology.net.

DUNCAN, JACK G., lawyer; b. Horry, SC, Dec. 8, 1939; s. Jack and Theresa (McKenzie) D. BA, Furman U., Greenville, SC, 1960; JD, U. S.C., Columbia, 1963. Atty. U.S. Dept. State, Washington, 1964-65, U.S. Dept. HEW, Washington, 1965-68; counsel and staff dir. Subcom. on Select Edn., Edn. and Labor Com., U.S. Ho. Reps., Washington, 1968-79; owner Duncan & Assocs., Washington, 1979—. Counsel State Humanities Coun., Assn. Ind. Colls. of Art and Design, Coalition Orgns. Representing the Deaf and Hard of Hearing, Dole Found., Scholastic Writers and Artists Found.; spl. counsel Am. Coun. Arts, 1979—, pres. 1996-97; gen. counsel Coun. State Adminstrs. of Vocat. Rehab., Washington, 1990—; bd. dir. Nat. Coun. Disabilities; mem. exec. com. Presdl. Com. Employment/Persons with Disability. Editor Update Arts newsletter, 1979—. Mem. Pres.'s Coun. on Disabilities. Recipient Pres. award, Am. Acad. Phys. Medicine, 1979, Nat. Rehab. Assn., 1979. Mem. ABA, Fed. Bar Assn., SC Bar Assn., DC Bar Assn. Office: 1320 Linthicum Rd Dickerson MD 20842-8719

DUNCAN, JEAN MARIE, language educator; d. Ambrose William and Margaret Jane Naughton; 1 child from previous marriage, Lindsey Nicole. BS in Edn., Truman State U., Kirksville, Mo., 1979; MS in Edn., N.E. Mo. State U., Maryville, 1982. Reading specialist endorsement Harding U., 2006. Spl. edn. tchr. Jefferson C-123 Schs., Conception Junction, Mo., 1979—87, prin., 1982—87; tchr. Decatur Pub. Schs., Ark., 1987—2003, literacy specialist, 2003—. Mem.: Ark. Edn. Assn. Avocations: reading, counted cross stitch, movies. Home: PO Box 432 Gravette AR 72736

DUNCAN, JOHN ALEXANDER, lawyer; b. Seattle, May 5, 1937; s. John A. Sr. and Elizabeth M. Duncan. BA in Econs., U. Wash., 1960; JD, U. Calif., San Francisco, 1963. Bar: Calif. 1964. Sole practice, Santa Ana, Calif., 1968-76, Newport Beach, Calif., 1976-93, Orange, Calif., 1993—. Lectr. estate and trust litigation Calif. Continuing Edn. of Bar, 1986—. Contbg. author: Estate and Trust Litigation, 2005, 2006. Fellow Am. Coll. Trust and Estate Counsel; mem. Orange County Bar Assn., Orange County Estate Planning Coun. (chair probate trust law sect. 1996). Office: 333 City Blvd W Ste 1420 Orange CA 92868-2992

DUNCAN, JOHN J., JR., congressman; b. Lebanon, Tenn., July 21, 1947; m. Lynn Hawkins; children: Tara, Whitney, John J. III, Zane. BS in Journalism, U. Tenn., 1969; JD, George Washington U. Nat. Law Ctr., 1973. Bar: Tenn. 1973. Lawyer pvt. practice, Knoxville, Tenn., 1973-81; state trial judge, 1981-88; mem. US Congress from 2nd Tenn. dist., 1989—, mem. transp. and infrastructure com., chmn. water resources and environment subcommittee, mem. resources com., mem. govt. reform com. Bd. dirs. or past bd. dirs. ARC, YWCA, Sunshine Ctr. for Mentally Retarded, Beck Black Heritage Ctr., Knoxville Union Rescue Mission, St. Citizens Home Aid Svc., Knoxville Girls Club, others; active elder Eastminster Presbyn. Ch. Positions up to capt. N.G. and Res. US Army, 1970—87. Named One of Top 5 Most Fiscally Conservative Mems. of Ho. and Senate, Nat. Taxpayers Union; recipient Super Hero award Citizens Against Govt. Waste, Golden Bulldog award Watchdogs of Treasury, Inc., Hartranft award Airline Operators and Pilots Assn., 1998; honored by Ams. for Tax Reform, Nat. Fedn. Ind. Bus., Concord Coalition, US C. of C., Citizens for Sound Economy. Mem. Am. Legion, Elks, Sertoma Club, 40&8, Masons, Shriners. Republican. Office: US Ho Reps 2267 Rayburn Ho Office Bldg Washington DC 20515-4202 Office Phone: 202-225-5435.*

DUNCAN, JOHN PATRICK CAVANAUGH, lawyer; b. Kalamazoo, Jan. 25, 1949; s. James H. and Colleen Patricia (Cloney) D.; children: Sarah Ellen, James Patrick Cloney; m. Anita M. Sarafa, Dec. 3, 2005; stepchildren: Hayden Williams, Madeleine Williams. BA cum laude, Yale U., 1971; JD, U. Chgo., 1974. Bar: Ill. 1974, U.S. Dist. Ct. (no. dist.) Ill. 1974, U.S. Ct. Appeals (7th cir.) 1975, U.S. Supreme Ct. 1979, trial bar U.S. Dist. Ct. Assoc. firm Holleb & Coff, Chgo., 1974-79; mem., 1979-87; ptnr. Jones Day, Chgo., 1987-99; leader banking and investment practice area Jones, Day, Reavis & Pogue, Chgo., 1996-99; prin. Duncan Assocs., 2000—; founder Pvt. Trust Assn., 2000. Adj. prof. IIT Chgo.-Kent Coll. Law Fin. Svcs. LLM Program, 1988—; mem. Fulbright Vis. Scholar Adv. Bd., 1995—98; mem. Chgo. com. Chgo. Coun. on Fgn. Rels., 1998—2000; author fed. and state trust co. laws. Contbr. articles to profl. jours. Fellow NSF, 1970. Fellow: Ill. Bar Found.; mem.: ABA (chmn. securities activities banks subcom. 1995—98, privacy task force 1998—2001, banking com.), Ill. Bankers Assn. (legal affairs com. 1986—87), Chgo. Bar Assn. (chmn. fin. insts. com. 1985—86), Yale Club (Chgo., N.Y.). Office: Duncan Associates Attorneys And Couns Pc 180 N La Salle St Ste 3850 Chicago IL 60601-2759 Office Phone: 312-580-4949. Business E-Mail: jpcd@duncancounsel.com.

DUNCAN, JOHNNY LEE, historian; b. York, Ala., Dec. 31, 1952; s. John Rancher and Annie Mae Duncan-Cyprian; m. Patricia Nell Perryman, Sept. 15, 1982. BA, La. State U., Baton Rouge, 1973, MA, 1974; DD, Prog. Universal Life Ch. Sch., Sacramento, 2001; PhD, Prog. Universal Life Ch. Sch., Sacremento, 2001. Prof. history Ala. State U., Montgomery, Ala., 1975—76; chair history polit. sci. dept. Stillman Coll., Tuscaloosa, Ala., 1976—77; prof. english City Coll. Chgo., Weisbaden, Germany, 1985—86; commd. officer US Army, Ft. Benning, Ga., 1981—2003; case mgmt. specialist Colo. Dept. Corrections, Delta, Colo., 1989—92; pub. The Black History Calendar, Colorado Springs, 1987—2007. Cons. NAACP/SCLC, Eutaw, Ala., 1979—81. Author: The Black History Calendar, You Might Be A N-R!; contbr. poetry anthology (Editor's Choice award, 2005). Ordained min. Prog. Universal Life Ch., 2000. Capt. US Army, 1988—2003, Ft. Carson. Mem.: NAACP (life; pres., sec. 2004—06, Lifetime Achievement 2005). Independent. Achievements include renamed Blacks, African American with 1987 poem I CAN; first to lead desegregation movement in Amite Louisiana 1971-1975; intergrated La. State U. 1972-1974; southern individual drill meet champion; first to Coach Alabama State first black female tennis champ, Debra Hunter (1976). Avocations: tennis, baseball, softball, martial arts, writing. Home: 309 S Third St Amite LA 70422 Home Phone: 985-748-4956. Personal E-mail: johnnyduncan@aol.com.

DUNCAN, LINDA B., social sciences educator; d. Richard Edward and Marguerite Aldine Tucker; children: Elizabeth Ann, Brien Ray. MA in History, Ea. Ill. U., Charleston, 1976. Cert. tchr. Ill., 1970. Tchr. social studies Bethany CUSD, Ill., 1971—89; tchr. social sci./history Lovington CUSD 303, Ill., 1989—. Supt. edn. First Christian Ch., Lovington, 2005—. Mem.: NEA, Ill. Edn. Assn. Office: Lovington HS 445 E Church St Lovington IL 61937 Home Phone: 217-873-7191; Office Phone: 217-873-4316.

DUNCAN, LINDSAY, actress; b. Edinburgh, Nov. 7, 1950; m. Hilton McRae; 1 child, Cal. Attended, Ctrl. Sch. Speech and Drama, London. Actor: (films) Loose Connections, 1983, Prick Up Your Ears, 1987, Manifesto, 1988, Body Parts, 1991, The Reflecting Skin, 1991, A Midsummer Night's Dream, 1996, City Hall, 1996, An Ideal Husband, 1999, Mansfield Park, 1999, Star Wars: Episode 1 - The Phantom Menace, 1999, Under the Tuscan Sun, 2003, Afterlife, 2004 (Best Actress award Bratislava Film Festival, Best Actress Bowmore Scottish Screen awards), Starter for Ten, 2006; (TV series) Just William, 1977—78, Reilly Ace of Spies, 1983, Dead Head, 1986, Traffik, 1989 (FIPA Golden award Cannes Internat. Film Festival, 1990), Jake's Progress, 1995, Spooks, 2005, Poirot: The Mystery of the Blue Train, 2005; (TV miniseries) G.B.H., 1991, A Year in Provence, 1993, The Rectors Wife, 1994, The History of Tom Jones, 1997, Oliver Twist, 1999, Shooting the Past, Perfect Strangers, Rome, 2005, Rome 2, 2006; (TV films) Longford, 2006, Frankenstein, 2007; (Broadway plays) Les Liaisons Dangereuses (Tony award nomination, 1987, Theatre World award, 1987), Top Girls (Obie award, 1982), A Midsummer Night's Dream, Ashes to Ashes, Celebration, The Room, Private Lives (winner Tony award Best Performance Leading Actress in a Play, 2002, Drama Desk Best Actress award, 2002). Office: ICM Oxford House 76 Oxford St London W1D 1B5 England

DUNCAN, MARGARET CAROLINE, physician; b. Salt Lake City, June 9, 1930; d. Donald and Margaret Aileen (Eberts) D.; m. N. Paul Arceneaux, Dec. 26, 1958; children: David Paul, Eleanor Anne, Stephen Louis, Andre. BA, U. Tex., 1952, MD, 1955. Intern Kings County Hosp., Seattle, 1955-56; resident in pediat. John Sealy Hosp., Galveston, Tex., 1956-58; resident in neurology Charity Hosp., New Orleans, 1958-60; fellow child neurology Johns Hopkins Hosp., Balt., 1960-61; mem. faculty La. State U. Med. Ctr., New Orleans, 1961—, prof. neurology and pediat., 1973-2000, prof. neurology emeritus, 2000—. Chmn. La. Com. Epilespy and Cerebral Palsy, 1976-79. Fellow Am. Acad. Neurology, Am. Acad. Pediat.; mem. Child Neurology Soc., Profs. Child Neurology, Alpha Omega Alpha. Episcopalian. Office: Children's Hosp 200 Henry Clay New Orleans LA 70118

DUNCAN, MARK, prosecutor; b. Philadelphia, Miss. m. Joni Duncan; 1 child, Ben. BA in Banking and Finance, U. Miss., 1981; JD. Solo practice, Philadelphia, Miss., 1983; part time public defender, 1984—88; asst. dist. atty., 1988—2004; dist. atty. 8th Judicial Dist., 2004—. Achievements include prosecuted (with Atty. Gen. Jim Hood) Edgar Ray Killen for the 1964 triple murders of civil rights workers Andrew Goodman, James Chaney and Michael Schwerner, June 2005. Avocations: gourmet cooking, golf. Office: P O Box 603 Philadelphia MS 39350 Office Phone: 601-656-1991. Office Fax: 601-656-2287.

DUNCAN, MICHAEL CLARKE, actor; b. Chgo., Dec. 10, 1957; Attended, Alcorn State U., Kankakee CC. Actor: (TV series) The Bold and the Beautiful, 1992—94, Skwids, 1996; (films) Friday, 1995, Back in Business, 1997, Caught Up, 1998, The Players Club, 1998, Bulworth, 1998, Armageddon, 1998, A Night at the Roxbury, 1998, Breakfast of Champions, 1999, The Green Mile, 1999, The Underground Comedy Movie, 1999, The Whole Nine Yards, 2000, Wrestlemania 2000, 2000, Soldier of Fortune, 2000, See Spot Run, 2001, The Immigrant Garden, 2001, Cats & Dogs, 2001, Planet of the Apes, 2001, They Call Me Sirr, 2001, Hollywood Digital Diaries, 2001, The Scorpion King, 2002, Daredevil, 2003, George and the Dragon, 2004, Pursued, 2004, (voice) Dinotopia: Curse of the Ruby Sunstone, 2004, Racing Stripes, 2005, American Crude, 2005, The Island, 2005, Sin City, 2005, Talladega Nights: The Ballad of Ricky Bobby, 2006, School for Scoundrels, 2006, The Last Mimzy, 2007, One Way, 2007, Slipstream, 2007, numerous TV guest appearances. Office: Dolores Robinson Ent 9250 Wilshire Blvd Ste 220 Beverly Hills CA 90212-3344*

DUNCAN, MIKE (ROBERT MICHAEL), political organization administrator, lawyer; b. Oneida, Tenn., Apr. 14, 1951; s. Robert C. and Barbara (Taylor) D.; m. Joanne Kirk, June 3, 1972; children: Robert Michael. BA, Cumberland Coll., 1971; JD, U. Ky., 1974; postgrad., U. Wis., 1977-80; LLD (hon.), Cumberland Coll., 1990; D.Pub. Svc. (hon.), Coll. of Ozarks, 1992. Cert. lener-bus. banking, 1994. V.p. Inez Deposit Bank, 1974—77, exec. v.p., 1977—81, chmn., 1981—, Cmty. Holding Co., Inez, 1983—; with First Nat. Bank (now Inez Deposit Bank FSB), Louisa, Ky., 1984—; treas. Rep. Nat. Com., 2001—02, gen. counsel, 2002—07, chmn., 2007—. Del. Rep. Nat. Conv., 1972, 76, 92, 96, 2000, 2004, chair contest com. 2000 conv.; nat. committeeman for Ky., 1992-, Rep. Nat. Com., vice chmn. so. region, 1992-2001, exec. com., 1996; chmn. Ky. Rep. Com., 1995; active Govt. Rels. Coun., White House Conf. on Small Bus., 1995; chmn. Govs. Scholars, 1995—, bd. dirs. 1996—; chmn. Bunning for U.S. Senate campaign, 1998; midwest regional chmn. Bush Presdl. campaign, 1999; chmn. Morehead State U., 1985-86; trustee, chmn. Alice Lloyd Coll., Pippa

Passes, Ky., 1978—, acting pres., 1993-94; mem. class XX Pres.'s Commn. on Exec. Exch. assigned to White House Office Pub. Liaison as asst. dir.; dir. Christian Appalachian Project, 1995—; mem. Pres.'s Commn. on White House Fellows, 2001-06; polit. commentator WYMT-TV, 1999—; chmn.transition team Gov.-elect Fletcher, State of Ky., 2003-04; acting sec. revenue; trustee Highlands Regional Med. Ctr., 1977—, sec., 1994 chmn. East Ky. Corp., 1996, vice chmn. Ctr. Econ. Devel. bd. dirs. Cin. Br. of Cleve. Fed. Res. Bank, 1987-90, Tenn. Valley Authority, 2006- Named Cumberland Coll. Outstanding Alumnus, 1976, Outstanding Young Man, Ky. Jaycees, 1982; U. Ky. fellow, 1978, White House fellow finalist, 1989; recipient Cmty. Leadership award McConnell Scholars U. Louisville, Cmty. Leadership award, 1999, Vic Hellard award Pub. Svc., 2003; named to U. Ky. Coll. of Law Hall of Fame, 2002. Mem. Am. Bankers Assn., Ky. Bankers Assn. (pres. 1985-86, dir.), Ky. Bar Assn., Ky. C. of C. (dir.), Kiwanis (lt. gov. 1983-84). Baptist. Office: Rep Nat Com 310 First St SE Washington DC 20003

DUNCAN, PATRICIA, lawyer, broadcast executive; b. LA; m. Winston Peters; children: Collin, Shannon. BA, Pomona Coll., 1979; JD, U. Calif. Berkeley, 1984. Bar: Calif. 1984, U.S. Dist. Ct. (ctrl. dist.) Calif. Assoc. Lillick, McHose & Charles, LA, 1984—86, Dewey Ballantine, LA, 1986—88, Leopold, Petrich & Smith, LA, 1988—92, ptnr., 1992—94; sr. counsel intellectual property and legal affairs Nat. Broadcasting Co., Inc., Burbank, 1994—2000; with NBC-TV, Burbank; assoc. counsel Home Box Office, 2000—02, v.p., sr. counsel west coast programming, 2002—. Mem. Calif. Law Rev., 1982—84. Office: c/o Time Warner Inc One Time Warner Ctr New York NY 10019-8016

DUNCAN, PEARL ROSE, writer; AB, Bryn Mawr Coll., Pa., 1969; MPhil, Newton Coll., Mass., 1972. Writer non-fiction books, novels and short stories. Spkr. in field. Author: Water Dancing; author: (contbg.) Essence Mag., NY Mag. Recipient Coat of Arms and Letters Patent Nobles in Noblesse Scotland, Ct. of Lord Lyon, 2005. Mem.: Am. Program Bureau Spkrs. Home: 40 Harrison St 36H New York NY 10013 Business E-Mail: pearlduncan@att.net.

DUNCAN, RICHARD FREDRICK, JR., retired secondary school educator, consultant; b. Millry, Ala., July 12, 1947; s. Richard F. and Claire Louise (Wood) D.; m. Rebecca Susan Davis, July 14, 1973. AA, Okaloosa-Walton Jr. Coll., 1967; BS, Fla. State U., 1969, MS, 1971; postgrad., Ore. State U., 1981-82. Tchr. Gadsden County Sch. Bd., Quincy, Fla., 1970-71, Leon County Sch. Bd., Tallahassee, 1972-73, Beaverton (Oreg.) Sch. Dist. No. 48, 1973—2006, tchr. emeritus, 2006—. Microbiologist Washington County, Hillsboro, Ore., 1971-72; cons. on sci. edn. Northwest Regional Ednl. Lab., Portland, Ore., 1978-79; cons. on marine edn. Ore. Dept. Edn., Salem, 1980-81; adj. prof. Portland State U., 1981-2006. Recipient award for excellence in sci. teaching Ore. Mus. Sci. and Industry, Portland, 1984, Psdl. award, 1984. Mem. Assn. Presdl. Awardees in Sci. Teaching (nat. pres. 1987-88), Nat. Assn.Biology Tchrs. (Ore. Biology Tchr. of Year award 1981), Nat. Sci. Tchrs. Assn. (Presdl. award for excellence in sci. teaching, 1983, Sheldon award 1993, Nat. Disting. Svc. to Sci. award 2001), Oreg. Sci. Tchrs. Assn. (pres. 1980-81, Oreg. Jr. High Tchr. of Yr. award 1982), North Assn. Marine Educators (state dir. 1978-80), Masons, Shriners, Pi Lambda Theta. Democrat. Avocations: sports, photography, sailing, scuba diving, camping. Office: Beaverton Sch Dist # 48 PO Box 200 Beaverton OR 97075-0200 Home: 1035 Northshore Pl Lake Oswego OR 97034-3722 Office Phone: 503-744-0794. Personal E-mail: r2duncan@comcast.net.

DUNCAN, ROBERT BANNERMAN, dean, strategy and organizations educator; b. Milw., July 4, 1942; s. Robert Lynn and Irene (Hoenig) D.; m. Susan Jean Phillips, June 12, 1965; children: Stephanie Olcott, Christopher Robert. BA, Ind. U., 1964, MA, 1966; PhD, Yale U., 1971. From asst. prof. to prof. Kellogg Grad. Sch. Mgmt. Northwestern U., Evanston, Ill., 1970—96, prof. leadership orgnl. change, 1996—2002, provost, 1987—91; Eli and Edythe L. Broad dean Eli Broad Coll. Bus. Mich. State U., East Lansing, 2002—. Co-author: Innovations and Organizations, 1973, Strategies for Planned Change, 1977; also numerous articles in profl. jours. Fellow Acad. Mgmt. (chair nat. program 1980-81, pres. 1983-84). Avocation: sailing. Office Phone: 517-355-8377.

DUNCAN, ROBERT D., real estate company executive; m. Marcy Duncan; 6 children. BBA, MBA, LLB, U. Tex., Austin. With Trammell Crow Co., Dallas; founder, chmn. Transwestern Comml. Svcs., Inc., Houston, 1978—. Founding mem. adv. coun. U. Tex. Real Estate Ctr.; dir. Greater Houston Cmty. Found., Greater Houston YMCA. Mem.: Urban Land Inst., World Pres. Orgn. Office: Transwestern Comml Svcs Ste 1300 1900 W Loop S Houston TX 77027*

DUNCAN, SAM K., retail executive; b. Blytheville, Ark. Joined as courtesy clerk Albertson's Inc., 1969, numerous mgmt. positions, 1969—91; dir. operations Albertson's, 1991—92; v.p. grocery dept. Fred Meyer, Inc., 1992—97, exec. v.p. food divsn., 1997—98, pres., 2001—02, Ralph's Supermarkets, 1998—2001; pres., CEO ShopKo Stores Inc., 2002—05; pres., CEO, chmn. OfficeMax Inc., Itasca, Ill., 2005—. Office: OfficeMax Inc 150 E Pierce Rd Itasca IL 60143*

DUNCAN, STEPHEN ROBERT, elementary school educator; b. Lancaster, Pa., June 23, 1950; s. Robert L. Duncan and Joan L. (McLaughlin) Turns; m. Deborah R. Jakubik, June 30, 1973; children: Rhiannon Alissa, Teague Stephen BS Edn., California U. Pa., 1972; MEd, Coll. N.J., 1977, postgrad. Cert. elem. tchr., sch. program specialist, Pa. Tchr. 5th grade Council Rock Sch. Dist., Richboro, Pa., 1972—83, 1985—90, tchr. 2d grade, 1983—85, math./tech. integration specialist, 1990—, instr. staff computer, 1982—, bldg. lead tchr., 2001—, dist. staff math. resource, 1995—. Presenter in field. Chmn. Newtown Twp. Youth Aid Panel, Pa., 1987—97. Recipient Outstanding Svc. award Bucks County Juvenile Cts., 1991; Council Rock Found. tech. grantee, 1998. Mem. NEA, Nat. Coun. Tchrs. Math. (presenter Nat. Conv. Anaheim, Calif. 2005, St. Louis 2006, Atlanta 2007), Pa. State Edn. Assn., Council Rock Edn. Assn. (bldg. rep. 2002-2006). Avocations: golf, tennis, computers. Office: Newtown Elem Sch 1 Wrights Rd Newtown PA 18940-1336 Office Phone: 215-944-2200. E-mail: sduncan@crsd.org.

DUNCAN, TIM, professional basketball player; b. Apr. 25, 1976; m. Amy Duncan, 2001. BA in Psych., Wake Forest, 1997. Center San Antonio Spurs, 1997—. Mem. US Olympic Basketball Team, Athens, 2004. Founder, exec. v.p. Tim Duncan Found. Named MVP, NBA Finals, 1999, 2003, 2005, NBA, 2002, 2003, Co-MVP, NBA All-star game, 2000; named to Western Conf. All-Star Game, NBA, 1997, 1998, 2000—07, All-NBA First Team, 1998—2005, 2007, NBA All-Defensive First Team, 1999—2003, 2005, 2007, USA Basketball Men's Sr. Nat. team, 2003; recipient Naismith award, 1996, Rookie of Yr., 1998. Achievements include being a member of NBA Champion San Antonio Spurs, 1999, 2003, 2005. Mailing: San Antonio Spurs 1 AT&T Ctr San Antonio TX 78219*

DUNCOMBE, PATRICIA WARBURTON, retired social worker; b. London, Jan. 30, 1925; came to U.S., 1940. d. P.G. Eliot and Mary Louise (Thompson) Warburton; m. David S. Duncombe, July 11, 1947 (dec. Apr. 1976); children: Elizabeth, Mari, Edward, David, Peter. BA, Barnard Coll., 1944; MS in Social Work, Columbia U., 1947. Cert. social worker. Social worker YWCA, Chgo., Evanston, Ill., 1947-50, B.I.A., Elko, Nev., 1966-67, Nev. State Welfare Div., Elko, Nev., 1967-69; dir. St. Michael's Youth Residence, Ethete, Wyo., 1970-76; asst. prof. U. Wyo., Laramie, 1976-83; program dir. St. Jude's Ranch, Boulder City, Nev., 1983-85; med. social worker home health agys., Las Vegas, Nev., 1985-95; retired. Author: Within the Circle, 1981, Parish the Thought, 1994, (with Ann Titus) When Death Comes Suddenly, 2000. Mem. Wyo. Commn. for Women, 1971-83, chmn., 1975-77; bd. dirs. SE Wyo. Mental Health, 1980-83; founder Lend-A-Hand Program, Boulder City, 1989 (awarded 700th Point of Light, 1992). Recipient Gov.'s award, 2000. Mem. NASW (chpt. pres. 1979, 81, commn. on women 1977-79, exec. dir. Nev. chpt. 1985-90, Social Work of Yr. award Wyo. chpt. 1980, Nev. chpt. 1989, lifetime achievement award 1992), AAUW (nat. bd. dirs. 1983-85), Mesquite Club (Las Vegas, pres. 1998-99), Phi Theta Kappa. Democrat. Episcopalian. Avocations: gardening, travel, reading, art. Home: 3890 N Buffalo Dr Unit 264 Las Vegas NV 89129-8818

DUNCOMBE, RAYNOR BAILEY, lawyer; b. Washington, July 17, 1942; s. Raynor Lockwood and Avis Ethel (Bailey) D.; m. Janice Assunta Rini, Apr. 12, 1969; children: Christina Luccioni, Raynor Luccioni. AB, Franklin and Marshall Coll., Lancaster, Pa., 1965; JD, Syracuse U., NY, 1968. Bar: NY 1972, US Dist. Ct. (no. dist.) NY 1972. Staff atty. State of NY, Albany, 1968-70; mgmt. trainee State Bank Albany, 1970-72; staff atty. Vibbard, Donaghy & Wright, Schoharie, NY, 1972-73, F. Walter Bliss, Esq., Schoharie, 1973-74; pvt. practice Schoharie, 1974—; agent Old Republic Nat. Title Insurance Co., 1986—. Chmn. bd. dirs. Fulmont Mut. Ins. Co., Mohawk Minden Ins. Co.; town atty. eight towns, one village, one sewer and one water dist. in Schoharie County, 1975—; adminstr. Assigned Counsel Program, 1975—; sch. atty. Middleburgh Schs., NY, 1981—85, NY, 1997—; atty. Schoharie County, 1982—87, 1990—91, Schoharie County Hist. Soc., 1975—; mem. tax cons. tech. adv. group Catskill Watershed Corp., 1998—2005. Dist. commr. Boy Scouts Am., 1987—92, asst. scoutmaster, 1988—91, Explorer advisor, 1991—99, dist. chmn., 1992—95, asst. coun. commr., 1995—96, coun. commr., 1996—99, coun. pres., 1999—2002, cub master, 2004—06, adventuring adv., 2006—; mem. Area 3 commn., 2002—03; Rep. committeeman Schoharie county, 1984—92; chmn. Middleburgh Rep. Town Com., 1995—2000; elder Presbyn. Ch., 1992—98, 2001—; mem. pers. com. Albany Presbytery of Presbyn. Ch., 1998—2001. Mem. ABA, NY State Bar Assn., Schoharie County Bar Assn. (sec.-treas. 1975—), Rotary (past pres.), Masons (past master), Lions. Avocations: camping, cross country skiing, collecting stamps. Home: 190 Main St Middleburgh NY 12122-9415 Office: PO Box 490 283 Main St Schoharie NY 12157 Office Phone: 518-295-7515.

DUNCOMBE, RAYNOR LOCKWOOD, astronomer; b. Bronxville, NY, Mar. 3, 1917; s. Frederic Howe and Mabel Louise (Taylor) D.; m. Julena Theodora Steinheider, Jan. 29, 1948; 1 son, Raynor B. BA, Wesleyan U., Middletown, Conn., 1940; MA, U. Iowa, 1941; PhD, Yale U., 1956. Astronomer U.S. Naval Obs., Washington, 1942-62; dir. Nautical Almanac Office, 1963-75; prof. aerospace sci. U. Tex., Austin, 1976—. Research assoc. Yale U. Obs., 1948-49; lectr. dynamical astronomy U. Md., 1963, Yale Summer Inst., 1959-70, Office Naval Research Summer Inst. in Orbital Mechanics, 1971, NATO Advanced Study Inst., 1972; cons. orbital mechanics Projects Vanguard, Mercury, Gemini, Apollo, USN Space Surveillance System; mem. NASA space scis. steering com., NASA research adv. panel in applied math., 1967; adviser Internat. Com. on Weights and Measures, Internat. Radio Consultative Com., Internat. Telecommunications Union; mem. NAS-NRC astronomy survey com., 1970-72, Hubble Space Telescope Astrometry Team, 1976—. Author: Motion of Venus, 1958, Coordinates of Ceres, Pallas, Juno and Vesta, 1969; editor: (with V.G. Szebehely) Methods in Celestial Mechanics, 1966, Dynamics of the Solar System, 1979; (with D. Dvorak and P.J. Message) The Stability of Planetary Systems, 1984; assoc. editor: Fundamentals of Cosmic Physics, 1971; exec. editor: Celestial Mechanics, 1977-85; contbr. articles to profl. jours. Fellow Royal Astron. Soc., AAAS (sect. chmn.); assoc. fellow AIAA; mem. Internat. Astron. Union (pres. com. on ephemerides), Minor Planet 3368 named Duncombe, 1988), Am. Astron. Soc. (chmn. div. dynamical astronomy 1970), Inst. Navigation (councillor 1960-64, v.p. 1964-66, pres. 1966-67, Superior Achievement award 1967, Hays award 1975), ASME (sponsor applied mechanics div. 1968-70), Internat. Assn. Insts. Nav. (v.p.), Assn. Computing Machinery, Sigma Xi. Home: 1804 Vance Cir Austin TX 78701-1035 Office: U Tex Dept Aerospace Engring Austin TX 78712 Business E-Mail: duncombe@csr.utexas.edu.

DUNDON, MARGO ELAINE, museum director; b. Cleve., July 3, 1950; d. Elmer Edward and Ruth Ann (Dreger) Buckeye. BS in Comm. cum laude, Ohio U., 1972; postgrad. in Mus. Studies, U. Okla, 1987. Mem. gen. staff Grout Mus. History and Sci., Waterloo, Iowa, 1974—75, coord. edn., 1976—78, co-dir., 1979—87, dir., 1988—90; exec. dir. Mus. Sci. and History, Jacksonville, Fla., 1990—99, pres., 1999—. Apptd. grievance com. Fla. Bar 4th Jud. Cir., 2002—05. Chair Waterloo Hist. Preservation Commn., 1987—88; cultural com. Visitors and Conv. Bur., Waterloo, 1988—90, My Waterloo Days, 1982—83; active Jacksonville Women's Network, Non-Profit Execs. Round Table, 1990—95; appointee Fla. Hist. Commn., Fla., 2006—; bd. dirs. Resource Plus, Waterloo-Cedar Falls, Iowa, 1986—88, CJI, Girls Inc. of Jacksonville, 1994—95, Ritz Theater & LaVilla Mus., 1998—2000, Jacksonville and the Beaches Conv. and Vis. Bur., 2001—, pres., chmn. bd. dirs., 2004—05. Am. Law Inst.-ABA scholar, 1979, 86; recipient Mayor's Vol. Performance award, Waterloo, 1983, Vol. award Gov. of Iowa, 1990. Mem.: Fla. Hist. Commn., Iowa Mus. Assn. (pres. 1984—86), Fla. Attractions Assn. (bd. dirs. 1997—98), Fla. Assn. Mus. (pres. 1995—96, Lifetime Achievement award 2006), Southeast Mus. Conf., Midwest Mus. Conf. (pres. 1988—90), Am. Assn. Mus. (site surveyor mus. assessment program 1982—, site examiner mus. accreditation commn. 1987—, regional councilor 1988—90, Peer Reviewer award 2000), Jacksonville C. of C., Quota Club (pres. 1982), Rotary. Avocations: snorkeling, scuba diving, travel, gardening. Office: Mus Sci & History 1025 Museum Cir Jacksonville FL 32207-9053 Home Phone: 904-538-9265; Office Phone: 904-396-7062. E-mail: director@themosh.com. *Share your life with a cat. When life is cold and hard edged, a cat is warm and soft. Cats do not fawn over our successes or judge us lacking for our failures. Cats remind us of the importance of life's simple gifts: a good meal, a warm nap, a relaxing bath, and an interesting bird at the window. For balance, there is nothing like living with a cat.*

DUNE, STEVE CHARLES, retired lawyer; b. Vithkuqi, Korca, Albania, June 15, 1931; s. Constantine Pappas and Evanthia (Vangel) D.; m. Irene Duff Boudreau, Sept. 4, 1955; children: Michelle Dune Gesky, Christopher Michael. AB, Clark U., 1953; JD, NYU, 1956. Bar: N.Y. 1957. Law clk. U.S. Ct. Appeals 1st Cir., 1956-57; from assoc. to ptnr. Cadwalader, Wickersham & Taft, NYC, 1957-95; counsel Albanian-Am. Enterpise Fund, 1995-96. Trustee Clark U., Worcester, Mass., 1974-86, 93-97, hon. trustee, 1997-2001, vice-chmn. bd. dirs., 1980-84, chmn. bd. dirs., 1984-86, chmn. presdl. search com., 1983-84, mem. pres.'s coun., 1987-90; dir. Albanian Children Fund, 1998-2002, chmn. Albanian-Am. C. of C., 1995-96. Recipient Disting. Svc. award, Clark U. Alumni Assn., 2003; Root-Tilden scholar, NYU Law, 1953—56. Mem.: ABA (divsn. sr. lawyers), Assn. Bar City NY, NY State Bar Assn. (com. on Ea. European affairs 1992—95, admiralty com. 1976—79, 1987—90), India House, Phi Beta Kappa. *Commitment, determination and perseverance are a person's best allies in solving any problem, meeting any challenge and realizing upon any opportunity of life.*

DUNEA, GEORGE, nephrologist, educator; b. Craiova, Rumania, June 1, 1933; came to U.S., 1964; s. Charles L. and Gerda (Low) D.; 1 dau., Melanie. MD, U. Sydney, Australia, 1957. Diplomate Am. Bd. Internal Medicine, Am. Bd. Nephrology. Intern Royal North Shore Hosp., Sydney, 1958—59; resident internal medicine Australia, 1959—63, England, 1959—63; fellow in nephrology Cleve. Clinic, Presbyn.-St. Luke's Hosp., Chgo., 1964—66; practice internal medicine specializing in nephrology Chgo., 1972—; attending physician Cook County Hosp., Chgo., 1966—, dir. dept. nephrology-hypertension, 1969—; prof. medicine U. Ill., Chgo., 1986—; pres., CEO Hektoen Inst. of Med. Rsch., Chgo., 1991—. Vis. prof. medicine Rush Med. Sch., Chgo., 1976—. Contbr. chpts. to books, articles to profl. publs. Fellow A.C.P., Royal Coll. Physicians (London, Edinburgh); mem. AMA, Am. Soc. Nephrology, Brit. Med. Assn., Soc. Med. History. Home: 222 E Chestnut St Chicago IL 60611-2360 Office: 1835 W Harrison St Chicago IL 60612-3701 Office Phone: 312-948-2510. Personal E-mail: gdu222@yahoo.com.

DUNFEE, THOMAS WYLIE, law educator; b. Huntington, W.Va., Nov. 15, 1941; s. Wylie Ray and Chloe Edith (Wylie) D.; m. Dorothy Jane Taylor, Aug. 26, 1967; children: John Wylie, Jennifer Sue, Shannon Elizabeth. AB, Marshall U., 1963; JD, NYU, 1966, LLM, 1969. Instr. N.Y. Inst. Tech., 1965-68; asst. prof. Ill. State U., Normal, 1968-70, Ohio State U., Columbus, 1970-72, assoc. prof., 1972-74; assoc. prof. legal studies Wharton Sch., U. Pa., Phila., 1974-79, prof., 1979—, Kolodny prof. social responsiblity, 1982—, chmn. dept. legal studies and bus. ethics, 1980—84, 1987—91, 2005—, dir. Wharton ethics program, 1995-96, dir. Zicklin Ctr. for Bus. Ethics Rsch., 1997—2000, vice dean, 2000—03. Vis. prof. U. Fla., 1989, U. Newcastle, Australia, 1981, 85, Georgetown U., 1994, U. Mich., 2000; cons. United Way of Am., McGraw-Hill, Ind. Stds. Bd., Citibank, GM, Honda, GlaxoSmithKline, AT&T. Author: Business and Its Legal Environment, 1992, Modern Business Law, 1996; co-editor: Business Ethics: Japan and the Global Economy, 1993; co-author: (with Thomas Donaldson) Ethics in Business and Economics, 2 vols., 1997, Ties That Bind: A Social Contracts Approach to Business Ethics, 1999; editor-in-chief Am. Bus. Law Jour., 1976-79; contbr. articles to profl. jours. Grantee Exxon Found., 1985-86, Kemper Found., 1993. Mem. Acad. Legal Studies in Bus. (pres. 1989-90, Disting. Sr. Faculty award for Excellence 1991), Soc. Bus. Ethics (pres. 1995-96). Office Phone: 215-898-7691. Business E-Mail: dunfeet@wharton.upenn.edu.

DUNFORD, JAMES CHRISTOPHER, entomologist, educator; s. James Dunford and Karen Schwind. BA, U. Wis., Milwaukee, 1996; MS, U. Wis., Madison, 2000; PhD, U. Fla., Gainesville, 2007. Lepidoptera inventory specialist Nature Conservancy, Madison, 1997—2000; curator Milw. Pub. Mus., 2000—01; tchg. asst. U. Fla., Gainesville, 2001—; lab. technician Fla. State Collection Arthropods, Gainesville, 2001—03; rsch. asst. Fla. Mus. Natural History, Gainesville, 2005—. Contbr. articles to profl. jours. Officer candidate USN, 2004—. Named Jack L. Fry Tchr. of Yr., U. Fla., 2005; recipient Tchg. Excellance award, North Am. Colls. and Tchrs. Agr., 2005; Med. Officer Healthcare scholar, USN, 2004—, Rsch. scholar, Fla. Entomol. Soc., 2005, Theodore Roosevelt Meml. grantee, Am. Mus. Natural History, NY, 2002, 2003. Mem.: Nat. Mil. Fish and Wildlife Assn., Coleopterists Soc., Willi Hennig Soc., Lepidopterists' Soc., Entomol. Soc. Am. Achievements include development of protocols to examine insect DNA. Avocations: hiking, camping, flag football, golf, softball. Office: U Fla SW 34th St and Hull Rd Gainesville FL 32611 Office Phone: 352-846-2000. Business E-Mail: dunford@ufl.edu.

DUNGAN, JOHN RUSSELL, JR., (12TH VISCOUNT DUNGAN OF CLANE, HEREDITARY PRINCE OF FERMOY AND ARRA), anesthesiologist, health facility administrator; b. Boston, Dec. 12, 1953; s. John Russell and Nancy Pauline (Beaton) Dungan; m. Nancy Elizabeth Perkins, July 12, 1986 (div. 1997); children: Elizabeth Adelaide, Thayer Warren, Eleanor Grace Appleton. AB magna cum laude, Harvard U., 1977, EdM, 1978; DDS, Baylor U., 1984; MD cum laude, Creighton U., 1989. Diplomate Nat. Bd. Anesthesiology (dir. 1989-92, 97-, v.p. 1997-), Am. Acad. Pain Mgmt. Instr. anesthesiology Boston U. Sch. Medicine, 1987—88; attending staff anesthesiologist, residency instr. Boston City Hosp., 1986-89; anesthesiologist, chief Tobey Hosp., Wareham, Mass., 1990—91; chief anesthesia Mary Lanning Hosp., Hastings, Nebr., 1991—, chief surgery, 1995, 2001; pres. Hastings Anesthesiology Assocs., 1992—; med. dir. Hastings Surg. Ctr., 2006—. Author: The Kings of the Picts and Dál Riads, 1976, The Beatons, 1976, Angus MacDonald, 1977; contbr. articles to profl. jours. Rschr. nat. trust Restoration of Celbridge Chapel and Cemetery, Kildare, Ireland, 1995. Named to, Honorable Order Ky. Cols.; 13th head and comdr., Mil. Order Knights of Leinster (estab. 1645), John Eliot scholar, 1966, Nat. Merit scholar, 1971, Harvard Coll. scholar, 1976, John Harvard scholar, 1975, 1977. Mem.: Soc. Interventional Pain Physicians (pres. 2003—), Adams County Med. Soc. (pres. 2001—), Nebr. Soc. Anesthesiologists, Am. Soc. Anesthesiologists, Cum Laude Soc. (Tabor chpt.), United Empire Loyalists Assn. (Can.), New Eng. Hist. Geneal. Soc., N.Y. Irish History Roundtable, English-Speaking Union U.S. (Internat. fellow 1971—72), N.Y. Biog. and Geneal. Soc., Harvard Club Nebr., Clan Dungan (clan chief, pres. 1998—), Wild Geese, Old Tonbridgian Soc., Hasty Pudding Inst. 1770, Phi Beta Kappa. Republican. Episcopalian. Avocation: history. Home: Heartwell Park 923 N Elm Ave Hastings NE 68901-4021 Office: Hastings Anesthesiology Ste 101 420 W 5th St Hastings NE 68901-7551 Office Phone: 402-463-9841. Business E-Mail: jdungan@inebraska.com.

DUNGAN, WILLIAM JOSEPH, JR., insurance agent, educator, economist; b. New London, Conn., Mar. 19, 1956; s. William Joseph and Alpha (Combs) D.; m. Janet Dudek, May 28, 1983. BS in Biology, Old Dominion U., 1978, postgrad. in Econs., 1978-80; postgrad., U. Pa., 1984-85, Coll. for Fin. Planners, 1983-84; MS in Fin. Svcs., Am. Coll., 1988, MS in Mgmt., 1990. CLU; chartered fin. cons., cert. fund. specialist. Rep. Prudential Ins. Co., Norfolk, Va., 1979-80; assoc. Russ Gills and Assocs., Virginia Beach, Va., 1980-88; instr. Tidewater C.C., Virginia Beach, Va., 1979-86; v.p. life and employee benefits Henderson & Phillips Inc., Norfolk, Va., 1988—; founding prin. First Fin. Resources, 1987—; sr. v.p. USI Ins., 2003—. Instr. employee benefits and econs. Inst. Mgmt., Old Dominion U., 1988—, chmn. cert. employee benefit specialists adv. bd.; instr. employee benefits U. Va., 2000—; instr. CEBS program U. Va., 2000—. Bd. dirs. Epilepsy Assn. Va.; trustee Old Dominion U. Ednl. Found., 1991-99; v.p. Epilepsy Assn. Va.; treas. Hampton Roads Youth Hockey Assn., 1999—; profl. adv. bd. United Way Hampton Roads, 2004—. Mem. Internat. Assn. Fin. Planning (pres. Hampton Rds. chpt.), Nat. Assn. Life Underwriters, Assn. for Advanced Life Underwriting, Inst. Cert. Fin. Planners, Inst. Cert. Employee Benefits Specialists, Am. Soc. CLUs, Norfolk Assn. Life Underwriters (bd. dirs.), Monarch Bus. Soc., Old Dominion Univ.'s Ins. and Fin. Svcs. Ctr., Epilepsy Assn. Va. (bd. dirs.), Million Dollar Round Table. Republican. Avocations: tennis, travel, reading. Home: 4201 Mercedes Ct Virginia Beach VA 23455-5649 Office: Henderson & Phillips Inc 235 E Plume St Norfolk VA 23510-1755 Office Phone: 757-640-5474. Personal E-mail: dubwjd@aol.com.

DUNGY, GWENDOLYN JORDAN, educational association administrator; BS, MS, Ea. Ill. U.; MA, Drew U., NJ; PhD, Washington U., St. Louis. Faculty mem. St. Louis Cmty. Coll.; sr. adminstr. Catonsville Cmty. Coll., Md., Montgomery Coll., Md., County Coll. Morris, NJ; assoc. dir. Curriculum and Faculty Devel. Network, coord. Nat. Diversity Network Assn. Am. Colls. & Univs.; exec. dir. Nat. Assn. Student Pers. Adminstrs., Washington, 1995—. Cons. Ctr. Higher Edn. Transformation, South Africa. Contbr. articles to profl. publs. Office: Nat Assn Student Pers Adminstrs 1875 Connecticut Ave NW Ste 418 Washington DC 20009 Office Phone: 202-265-7500. Office Fax: 202-797-1157.*

DUNGY, KATHRYN R., humanities educator; b. Stanford, Calif., Sept. 21, 1969; d. Claibourne I. and Madgetta Thornton Dungy; life ptnr. Timothy Voigt. BA magna cum laude, Spelman Coll., Atla., 1997; MA, Duke U., 1993, PhD, 2000. Vis. lectr. U. Vt., Burlington, 1999—2000, asst.

prof. Latin Am. and Caribbean history, 2000—04, New Coll., Sarasota, Fla., 2004—. Contbr. articles to profl. jours., chapters to books. Co-chair Pres.'s Coun. on Racial Equality, 2000—02. Internat. Student Identity Card scholar, CIEE, 1989—90, Fgn. Study scholar, Spelman Coll./Charles A. Merrill Found., 1989—90, Minority fellow, Dana Found., 1989—91, Ford Found. Predoctoral fellow for Minorities, 1991—94, Tinker Found. Summer Rsch. grantee, Duke U., 1993, Latin Am. Studies fellow, 1994—96, George Washington Henderson fellow, U. Vt., 1998—99, Travel grantee, Women's Studies Program, U. Vt., 2001. Mem.: Am. Hist. Assn., Caribbean Studies Assn., Assn. Caribbean Historians, Mortar Bd., Sigma Delta Epsilon (v.p. chpt. 1990—91), Phi Alpha Theta (pres. chpt. 1990—91), Delta Sigma Theta. Avocations: photography, travel. Office: New Coll 5800 Bay Shore Dr Sarasota FL 34243 Office Phone: 941-487-4699. Business E-Mail: kdungy@ncf.edu.

DUNGY, TONY, professional football coach; b. Jackson, Mich., Oct. 6, 1955; s. Wilbur and Cleomane Dungy; m. Lauren Harris; 5 children. BA in Bus. Adminstrn., U. Minn., 1977. Profl. football player Pitts. Steelers, 1977—78, defensive asst., 1981-83, defensive back coach, 1982-83, defensive coord., 1984-88, Minn. Vikings, 1992-95; profl. football player San Francisco 49ers, 1979, NY Giants, 1980; defensive backs coach U. Minn., 1980, Kans. City Chiefs, 1989-91; head coach Tampa Bay Buccaneers, Fla., 1996—2001, Indpls. Colts, 2002—. Author: Quiet Strength: The Principles, Practices, & Priorities of a Winning Life, 2007 (reached number 1 on the NY Times bestseller list). Founder Mentors for Life, Tampa Bay. Mem. Super Bowl Championship Team, 1978; Recipient Fatherhood award, Nat. Fatherhood Initiative, 2002, Espy award, Best Coach-Mgr., 2007; named one of The World's Most Influential People, TIME mag., 2007 Achievements include becoming one of two first African-Am. coaches in Super Bowl, 2007; first African-Am. coach to win a Super Bowl, Feb. 4, 2007. Office: Indianapolis Colts 7001 West 56th Street Indianapolis IN 46254*

DUNHAM, ARCHIE WALLACE, petroleum company and chemicals executive; b. 1938; m. Linda Dunham; 3 children. BS, MBA, U. Okla. Assoc. engr. Conoco Inc., 1966—73, mgr. gas prodn., 1978—81, v.p. logistics and downstream planning, 1981—83, v.p. transp. natural gas, gas products, 1983—85, exec. v.p. div., 1985, pres., CEO Houston, 1996—, chmn., 1999—; exec. v.p. Douglas Oil Co., 1976—79, pres., 1979; group v.p. chems. and pigments E.I. du Pont de Nemours & Co., Wilmington, Del., 1987—96; v.p. Exploration Products, Houston, 1992—96. Bd. dirs. LA Pacific Corp., Phelps Dodge Corp., Union Pacific Corp., API, Energy Inst. Ams., Meml. Hermann Healthcare System; served on Commn. Nat. Energy Policy, Nat. Infrastructure Advisory Coun.; chmn. NAM; past chmn. US Energy Assn., Nat. Petroleum Coun.; exec. com. and bd. dirs. US-Russia Bus. Coun.; mem. Bus. Round Table, Bus. Coun.; mem. exec. com. and bd. dirs. Greater Houston Partnership; bd. gov. Houston Forum. Bd. dirs. Smithsonian Inst.; trustee George Bush Presdl. Libr. Found.; mem. Marine Corps Heritage Found., Bretton Woods Com., Beta Gamma Sigma Dir. Table, 2003—; trustee Houston Symphony, United Way Tex. Gulf Coast; bd. dirs. Horatio Alger Assn. Disting. Am.; sr. mem. bd. visitors M.D. Anderson Cancer Ctr.; sr. chmn. Houston Grand Opera, past pres. Capt. USMC, 1960—64. Recipient Father Yr., Houston, 1998, inducted into Okla. Hall of Fame, 1998, CEO Yr. for Global Vision in Energy, 2000, Internat. Achievement award, 2000, Horatio Alger award, 2001, Ellis Island Medal Honor, 2001, Legend of the Industry, A&D Summit, 2002, Houston's Internat. Citizen Yr., World Affairs Coun. Office: ConocoPhillips 600 N Dairy Ashford St Houston TX 77079-1175

DUNHAM, BENJAMIN STARR, editor, art association administrator; b. NYC, Sept. 19, 1944; s. George Roscoe and Portia Elizabeth (Playfair) Dunham; m. Wendy H. Rolfe, Apr. 12, 1986; 1 child, Samuel Edward Rolfe; m. Mimi Cox, Sept. 9, 1978 (div.). BA, Harvard U., 1966; postgrad., Boston U., 1970, Cath. U., 1971-73. Asst. editor Music Educators Jour., Washington, 1967-70; editor Symphony News, Vienna, 1971-78; dir. spl. projects Chamber Music Soc. Lincoln Ctr., NYC, 1982; exec. dir. Chamber Music Am., NYC, 1978-82, Am. Symphony Orch., NYC, 1982-84; exec. v.p. Nat. Music Coun., NYC, 1984-90; editor Am. Recorder, 1990—2002, Early Music Am. Mag., 2002—. Cons. to TV, fundraising and mktg. in chamber music, pubs. and rsch.; pvt. tchr. recorder, 1971—78; mem. music faculty Trinity Coll., Washington, 1973—75; pvt. tchr. recorder MusiCoop, Wareham, Mass., 1986—92, Cranberry Concerts, 1993—; cons. on period instrument orch. program Andrew W. Mellon Found., 1989—91; lectr. in field. Contbr. articles to profl. jours.; prin. recorder performer: Handel Festival Orch., 1977—78. Mem. Wareham Arts and Humanities Coun., 1986—90, 1992—94; Hist. Dist. Commn. Wareham, 1986—97; bd. dirs. Marion Art Ctr., 1996—99; Sippican Elem. Sch. Coun., 1998—2001. Named Arts Adminstr. of the Yr., Arts Mgmt. Mag., N.Y.C., 1981. Mem.: Am. Recorder Soc. (bd. dirs. 1984—89), Nat. Guild Cmty. Schs. Art (trustee 1982—87), Early Music Am. (bd. dirs. 1988—92, 1993—99, 2000—02, treas. 1993—95). E-mail: dunhamb@post.harvard.edu.

DUNHAM, CHRISTOPHER COOPER, lawyer; b. NYC, Jan. 29, 1937; s. Robert Secrest and Elizabeth Walls (Cooper) D.; m. Marjorie Jean Corliss, June 14, 1958; children: Douglas Webber, William Sigler, Anne Corliss. BA, Wesleyan U., 1958; JD, Columbia U., 1961. Bar: N.Y. 1961, U.S. Dist. Cts. (so. and ea. dists.) N.Y. 1963, U.S. Patent and Trademark Office 1964, U.S. Ct. Appeals (2d cir.) 1964. Assoc. Cooper, Dunham, Dearborn & Henninger, NYC, 1961-68; ptnr. Cooper & Dunham LLP and predecessor firms, NYC, 1968—. Chmn. Westport Democratic Town Com., Conn., 1965-66, 67-70, 80-86; mem. Conn. Dem. Ctrl. Com., 1978-80; del. Conn. Dem. Conv., Conn., 1966, 68, 74, 80, 82, 84, 90, 98; alt. Westport Planning and Zoning Com., 1965; mem. Westport Bd. Fin., 1975, Conn. Safety Commn., 1977-78, Westport Rep. Town Meeting, 1986-93. Mem. N.Y. Intellectual Property Law Assn., Gamma Psi, Phi Beta Kappa. Congregationalist. Home: 277 Compo Rd S Westport CT 06880-6513 Home Phone: 203-227-5880; Office Phone: 212-278-0419. E-mail: cdunham@cooperdunham.com.

DUNHAM, ELIZABETH GRACE, librarian; d. Edward Willson and Jean Reynolds Dunham. BA in History, Pomona Coll., 2002; MA in History, U. Tenn., 2005, postgrad., 2005—. Libr. and archives intern Lowell Obs., Flagstaff, Ariz., 2001—02; tchg. asst. U. Tenn., Knoxville, 2002—03; student libr. asst. U. Tenn. Spl. Collections Libr., Knoxville, 2003—04; para-professional libr. Spl. Collections Libr. U. Tenn., Knoxville, 2004—. Contbr. articles to profl. jours. Recipient award, Woodmen of the World, 1996; Bixby scholar, Pomona Coll., 2001, Vannier scholar, 2001. Mem.: Soc. fMil. History, Soc. Am. Archivists. Democrat. Roman Catholic. Avocations: ballroom dancing, reading, singing, embroidery. Home Phone: 865-560-0337.

DUNHAM, J. ANDREW, bank executive; B in Math. and Econs., Ohio Wesleyan U., Delaware; grad. student, U. Akron, Ohio. Asst. v.p., future and options trader Nat. City Corp., 1987, v.p., domestic funding mgr., 1989, sr. v.p., asst. dept. mgr. investment and funding divsn., 1994, mgr. investment and funding divsn., sr. v.p., 1997—. Office: Nat City Corp Nat City Ctr 1900 E Ninth St Cleveland OH 44114-3484 Office Phone: 216-222-2000.*

DUNHAM, JOAN ROBERTS, administrative assistant; b. Dayton, Ohio, Jan. 25, 1933; d. Harold Hathaway and Lydia Roberts Dunham. BA, U. Colo., Bulder, 1954; postgrad., U. Pa., Phila., 1959—65, U. Chgo., 1971—72. Office clk. Daniels & Fisher Stores, Denver, 1954-56; clk., stenographer Dept. of State, Madras, India, 1957-59; clk. admissions office Temple Buell Coll., Denver, 1969—71; typist, adminstrv. clk. State of Colo., Denver, 1987-99; ret., 1999. Fgn. lang. fellow U.S. Dept. Health, Edn. and Welfare, U. Pa., 1961-62. Republican. Christian Scientist. Home: 1350 Josephine St Unit 210 Denver CO 80206-2243

DUNHAM, RICHARD E., III, lighting designer, consultant, set designer, educator; b. Lancaster, Pa., June 15, 1957; s. Richard E. Dunham, Jr. and Lois O. Dunham; m. Joelle Ré Arp, Aug. 18, 1990; children: Chelsea, Richard IV. BA, Millersville U. Pa., 1979; MFA, Ohio State U., Columbus, 1987. Cert. lighting cert. Nat. Coun. on Qualifications for the Lighting Profession. Freelance lighting/scenic designer Dunham Design Assocs., Athens, Ga., 1979—; instr., designer Stephens Coll., Columbia, Mo., 1987—89; asst. prof. lighting design SUNY, Stony Brook, 1989—96; designer, instr. Vanderbilt U., Nashville, 1996—98; asst. prof., designer U. Ctrl. Fla., Orlando, 1998—2000; assoc. prof. U. Ga., Athens, 2000—. Off Broadway lighting designer Cocteau Repertory Theater, NYC, 2005—06; designer Regional NY Theater. Contbr. articles to profl. jours. Chair student affairs com. U. Ga., Athens, 2005—06; elder Presbyn. Ch. USA, Smithtown, NY, 1993—96, Ovieto, Fla., 1999—2000, Central Presbyn. Ch., Athens, 2002—05. Recipient Harold award, L.I. Press, 1993, 1999. Mem.: Illumination Engring. Soc. N.Am., US Inst. for Theater Tech. (bd. dirs., lighting commr. 1998—2006, Herb Gregs award 2001, 2004), Internat. Assn. Lighting Designers (assoc.). Home: 160 Snapfinger Ln Athens GA 30605 Office: Univ Ga Dept Theatre and Film Studies Fine Arts Bldg Athens GA 30602 Business E-Mail: rdunham@uga.edu.

DUNHAM, SCOTT H., lawyer; b. Seattle, May 7, 1950; BA with highest honors, Wash. State U., 1972; JD, U. Wash., 1975. Bar: Calif. 1975, U.S. Dist. Ct. (ctrl. dist.) Calif. 1976, U.S. Supreme Ct. 1977. Mem. O'Melveny & Myers, LLP, LA, chair labor and employment law group. Author: Avoiding and Defending Wrongful Discharge Claims, 1987, Designing an Effective Fair Hiring and Termination Compliance Program, 1992; contbr. chpts. to books; editor-in-chief Wash. Law Rev., 1974-75. Fellow Coll. Labor and Employment Lawyers; mem. ABA (mem. and co-chair com. occupational safety and health labor and employment law sect.), LA County Bar Assn. (tchr., lectr. Calif. Bus. Law Inst., ABA nat. Inst., Pers. and Indsl. Rels. Assn., Japan Bus. Assn., Inst. Applied Mgmt. and Law, Inc., Calif. Continuing Edn. Bar and various other employer assns.), Order of Coif, Phi Beta Kappa, Phi Kappa Phi, Omicron Delta Kappa, Phi Delta Phi (magister Ballinger inn chpt. 1974). Office: O'Melveny & Myers LLP 400 S Hope St Los Angeles CA 90071-2899

DUNHAM, WOLCOTT BALESTIER, JR., lawyer; b. NYC, Sept. 14, 1943; s. Wolcott Balestier and Isabel Caroline (Bosworth) D.; m. Joan Scott Findlay, Jan. 26, 1974; children: Mary Findlay, James Wolcott. AB magna cum laude, Harvard U., 1965, LLB cum laude, 1968. Bar: NY 1969. Vol. VISTA, 1968—69; assoc. Debevoise & Plimpton LLP and predecessor Debevoise, Plimpton, Lyons & Gates, NYC, 1969-76, ptnr., 1977—. Spkr. in field. Co-author: Insurance M&A, 1997—; contbr. articles to profl. jours.; gen. editor and chpt. author, New York Insurance Law, 1991, and ann. supplements. Treas., trustee Fund for Astrophys. Rsch., NYC, 1970—, sec., 1970—84, pres., 1984—; exec. dir. NY State Exec. Adv. Commn. on Ins. Industry Regulatory Reform, 1982; mem. NY State Commn. to Modernize the Regulation of Fin. Svcs., 2007—; vestry mem. St. James Ch., NYC, 1987—93, clk., 1988—93, jr. warden, 1993—94, sr. warden, 1994—95, chancellor, 1994—; bd. dirs. UN Assn., NYC, 1973—79, vice chmn., 1975—79, adv. coun., 1992—2000; bd. dirs. Neighborhood Coalition for Shelter, Inc., 1983—, Dutchess Land Conservancy, 1996—; pres., bd. dirs. East Side Cmty. Ctr., Inc., 1988—; bd. mgrs. Shekomeko Valley Farm Assn., LLC, 1996—2003; bd. dirs. Episcopal Charities of Diocese of NY, 2005—. Fellow Am. Coll. Investment Counsel; mem. ABA (chmn. com. on ins. sect. adminstrv. law 1979-83), Assn. Bar City N.Y. (com. on ins. 1981-87, chmn. com. 1984-87), Assn. Life Ins. Counsel, Union Internationale des Avocats, Am. Soc. Internat. Law, Harvard Law Sch. Assn. N.Y.C. (dir. 1978-81). Episcopalian. Office: Debevoise & Plimpton LLP 919 Third Ave New York NY 10022-3902

DUNHILL, ROBERT, advertising executive; b. LA, Sept. 28, 1929; s. Herbert G. and Irma (Meyer) Odza; m. Joan Scheer, Dec. 19, 1952; children: Andrew, Candy, Cindy. BS, Adelphi Coll., 1952; MBA, NYU, 1954. Prin. Dunhill Internat. List Co., Inc., NYC, 1952—, pres., chmn., 1975—. With USNR, 1955-57. Mem. Chgo. Assn. of Direct Mktg., Widener U. Alumni Assn., Direct Mktg. Assn., Fla. Direct Mktg. Assn. (chmn.). Republican. Office: 621 NW 53rd St Ste 200 Boca Raton FL 33487-8239 Home: 11272 Westland Cir Boynton Beach FL 33437 Business E-Mail: robert@dunhills.com.

DUNIPACE, IAN DOUGLAS, lawyer; b. Tucson, Dec. 18, 1939; s. William Smith and Esther Morvyth (McGeorge) D.; m. Janet Mae Dailey, June 9, 1963; children: Kenneth Mark, Leslie Amanda. BA magna cum laude, U. Ariz., 1961, JD cum laude, 1966. Bar: Ariz. 1966, U.S. Supreme Ct. 1972, Nev. 1994, Colo. 1996. Reporter, critic Long Branch (N.J.) Daily Record, 1963; assoc. firm Jennings, Strouss, Salmon & Trask, Phoenix, 1966-69; assoc. Jennings, Strouss & Salmon, PLC, Phoenix, 1969-70, ptnr., 1971-93, mem., 1993—2003, chmn. comml. practice dept., 1998—2001; mem. I. Douglas Dunipace, PLC, Phoenix, 2004—. Comments editor Ariz. Law Rev., 1965-66. Reporter Phoenix Forward Edn. Com., 1969-70; mem. Phoenix Arts Commn., 1990-93, chmn., 1992-93; bd. mgmt. Downtown Phoenix YMCA, 1973-80, chmn. 1977-78; bd. dirs. Phoenix Met. YMCA, 1976-87, 1988-2005, chmn. 1984-85; bd. mgmt. Paradise Valley YMCA, 1979-82, chmn. 1980-81; bd. mgmt. Scottsdale/Paradise Valley YMCA, 1983, legal affairs com. Pacific Region YMCA, 1978-81; chmn. YMCA Ariz. State Youth and Govt. Com., 1989-95, cmty. resource bd., 2005—; bd. dirs. Schoolhouse Found. 1990-96, pres. 1990-94, Kids Voting, 1990-94, Beaver Valley Improvement Assn. 1977-79, Pi Kappa Alpha Holding Corp., 1968-72, Heard Mus. 1993-94, Ariz. Bar Found., 1996-2003, pres., 2001-02, Phoenix Kiwanis Charitable Found., 2001-06, pres., 2005-06, Phoenix Ctr. Cmty. Devel., 2002-04; trustee Paradise Valley Unified Dist. Employee Benefit Trust, 1980-93, chmn. 1987-93, Sch. Theology, Claremont, Calif. 1994-2006, chmn., 2004-06; bd. mgrs. Desert Schs. Fin. Svcs., 2003—; trustee First Meth. Found. Phoenix, 1984-93, 99—, pres., 2002-04; active Greater Paradise Valley Cmty. Coun., 1985-87; bd. dirs. Heard Mus. Coun., 1990-95, pres. 1993-94; mem. Ariz. Venture Capital Conf. Planning Com., 1994-2003, exec. com. 1997-2003, chmn., 2000; mem. Assn. for Corp. Growth, 1995-96, Ariz. Bus. Leadership Assn., 1996-2005, bd. dirs., 2001-04, sec.-treas., 2002-04, Ariz. Town Hall, 2003—; bd. vis. U. Ariz. Law Coll., 1996-2003; mem. met. Phoenix commn., Meth. Ch., 1968-71, lay leader, 1975-78, trustee, 1979-81, pres., 1981; mem. Pacific S.W. ann. Meth. Conf., 1969-79, lawyer commn., 1980-85, chancellor Desert S.W. ann. conf. 1985-2005. Capt. AUS, 1961-63. Mem. State Bar Ariz. (securities regulation sect. 1970-2004, chmn. 1991-92, mem. com. unauthorized practice of law 1972-84, chmn. 1975-83, mem. bus. law sect. 1981—, chmn. 1984-85), State Bar Nev., State Bar Colo., Am., Fed. (pres. Ariz. chpt. 1980-81), Maricopa County Bar Assns. (bd. dirs. Corp. Coun. divsn. 1996-99), U. Ariz. Law Coll. Assn. (bd. dirs. 1983-90, pres. 1985-86), U. Ariz. Alumni Assn. (bd. dirs. 1985-86), Masons, Kiwanis (pres. Phoenix 1984-85, disting. lt. gov. 1986-87, S.W. dist. cmty. svc. chmn. 1987-88, dist. activity com. coord. 1988-89, dist. laws and regulation chmn. 1989-90, 92-93, 95-96, 2002—, asst. to dist. gov. for club svcs. 1990-91, field dir. 1991-92, dist. conv. chmn. 1993-94, pub. rels. chmn. 1996-98, mem. internat. com. on Project 39, 1988-89, internat. com. On to Anaheim 1990-91, internat. com. on leadership tng. and devel. 1991-92, 93-94, trustee SW dist. found. 1987-92, 1st v.p. 1990-92), Orange Tree Club, Phi Beta Kappa, Phi Kappa Phi, Phi Delta Phi, Phi Alpha Theta, Sigma Delta Pi, Phi Eta Sigma, Pi Kappa Alpha (nat. counsel 1968-72). Democrat. Methodist. Home: 2527 E Vogel Ave Phoenix AZ 85028-4729 Office: I Douglas Dunipace PLC 3116 E Shea Blvd # 251 Phoenix AZ 85028 Office Phone: 602-370-6895. Personal E-mail: dunipaceplc@cox.net.

DUNIPHAN, J. P., state legislator, small business owner; b. Aug. 31, 1946; Mem. SD Ho. of Reps., Pierre, 1995—2002, mem. commerce com., judiciary com., chair local govt. com., 1995—2002; mem. SD State Senate, Dist. 33, 2002—. Ptnr. Elks II, 1993—, Quad Investments, 1993—. Republican. Fax: 605-342-6399.

DUNKELMAN, LORETTA, artist; b. Paterson, NJ, June 29, 1937; d. Samuel and Rae (Gutkind) Dunkelman. BA, Rutgers U., 1958; MA, Hunter Coll., 1966. Lectr. Hunter Coll., NYC, 1966-67; vis. artist U. Cin., 1974; asst. prof. U. R.I., Kingston, 1974-75, Cornell U., Ithaca, NY, 1977-80; vis. artist Ohio State U., Columbus, 1984; asst. prof. Va. Commonwealth Univ., Richmond, 1986-88; vis. artist The Sch. of the Art Inst. of Chgo., 1990; vis. prof. art U. Calif., Berkeley, 1993-94. One woman shows include A.I.R. Gallery, NY, 1973-74, 78, 81, 83, 87, Douglass Coll., New Brunswick, 1973, U. Cin., 1974, U. RI, Kingston, 1975, 1708 E. Main Gallery, Richmond, 1987; exhibited in group shows at Whitney Mus. Am. Art, NY, 1973, NY Cultural Ctr., NY, 1973, Newark Mus., 1973, Cranbrook Acad. Art Mus., Bloomfield Hills, Mich., 1974, Grand Rapids (Mich.) Art Mus., 1974, Johnson Mus., Cornell U., Ithaca, NY, 1977, Inst. Art and Urban Resources, Pub. Sch. 1, NYC, 1978, McIntosh/Drysdale Gallery, Washington, 1980, Douglass Coll., Rutgers U., New Brunswick, NJ, 1981, Kulturhuset, Stockholm and Lunds Konsthall, Sweden, 1981-82, Picker Art Gallery, Colgate U., Hamilton, NY, 1983, Hopkins Hall Gallery, Ohio State U., 1984, Kenkeleba Gallery, NY, 1985, A.I.R. Gallery, NYC, 1985, 91, 97, Bernice Steinbaum Gallery, NY, 1986, Anderson Gallery, Va. Commonwealth U., Richmond, Va., 1987, Rabbet Gallery, New Brunswick, NJ, 1989, Michael Walls Gallery, 1989, 148 Duane St., NYC, 1992, Contemporary Art Inst., NYC, 1994, Mason Gross Sch. of the Arts Galleries, Rutgers U., New Brunswick, NJ, 1996, Kingsborough CC, Bklyn., 1998, Yaddo Centennial Arts Festival, NYC, 2000, Mabel Smith Douglass Libr., Rutgers U., New Brunswick, 2005, Andre Zarre Gallery, NYC, 2007; represented in permanent collections Bellevue Med. Ctr., NYC, Chase Manhattan Bank, NYC, City U. Grad. Ctr., NYC, Picker Art Gallery, Dana Art Ctr., Colgate U., Hamilton, NY, U. Cin., Gene Swenson Collection at U. Kansas Art Mus., Lawrence, Bristol-Myers, Squibb, Lawrenceville, NJ, Hunter Coll., NYC, Spencer Mus. Art, Lawrence, Smithsonian Mus., Washington. CAPS fellow N.Y. State Coun. Arts, 1975; Visual artist fellow Nat. Endowment for the Arts, 1975, 82, 93, AAUW fellow, 1976-77, Artist fellow N.Y. Found. for the Arts, 1991; grantee Adolph & Esther Gottlieb Found., 1991. Home and Office: 151 Canal St New York NY 10002-5033

DUNKLAU, RUPERT LOUIS, financial planner, consultant; b. Arlington, Nebr., May 19, 1927; s. Louis Z. and Amelia S. (Gnuse) Dunklau; m. Ruth Eggert, June 4, 1950 (dec. Nov. 1998); children: Paul, Janet; m. Ruth King, Sept. 3, 2000. BS, U. Nebr., 1950; LittD (hon.), Concordia Coll., St. Paul, 1982; LLD (hon.), Midland Luth. Coll., Fremont, Nebr., 1985, Valparaiso U., 2005. Exec. v.p. Valmont Industries, Inc., Valley, Nebr., 1950-73; dir. Fremont Nat. Bank, Nebr., 1968-2000. Bd. dirs. Midland Luth. Coll., Cmty. Chest Fremont; bd. dirs. Concordia Pub. House Valparaiso (Ind.) U.; chmn. bd. dirs. Meml. Hosp. Dodge County; bd. dirs. Luth. Ch.-Mo. Synod, St. Louis. With USNR, 1945. Mem.: Rotary Club. Republican. Home: 2948 Deer Run Fremont NE 68025 Office: PO Box 1558 Fremont NE 68026-1558 Office Phone: 402-721-6046.

DUNLAP, BENJAMIN BERNARD, academic administrator; b. Columbia, SC; m. Anne Dunlap, 1963; children: Boykin Dunlap Bell, Susannah, Ben. Grad. summa cum laude, U. South, 1959; BA with honors, Oxford U., Eng., 1962, MA, 1966; PhD in English Lang. and Lit., Harvard U., 1967. Mem. faculty Harvard U.; Carolina rsch. prof., prof. English, adj. prof. anthropology U. S.C., SC, 1968—93; Chapman Family prof. humanities Wofford Coll., Spartanburg, SC, 1993—2000, pres., 2000—. Moderator Exec. and CEO Seminars Aspen (Colo.) Inst.; lectr. in field. Writer, prodr. (over 200 programs for pub. television). Named Sr. Fulbright lectr., Chulalongkorn U., Bangkok, Chiang Mai U., Thailand; Rhodes scholar, Oxford U., 1959—62, U.S.-Japan Leadership fellow, Japan Soc. N.Y. and Tokyo, 1984—85. Office: Wofford Coll 429 N Church St Spartanburg SC 29303 Office Phone: 864-597-4010. Office Fax: 864-597-4018. E-mail: dunlapbb@wofford.edu.*

DUNLAP, CATHERINE MARY, clergywoman; b. Toronto, Ohio, Oct. 28, 1927; d. Michael Nicholas and Lena (Conti) Reale; children: Charles E., Linda Catherine Dunlap Molinaro, Thomas Michael; m. William Freese (dec. Jan. 1980). AS in Bus., Steubenville Bus. Coll., 1946; MA in Christian Edn., Meth. Theol. Sem., Delaware, Ohio, 1983. Ordained diaconal minister United Meth. Ch., 1983. Dir. fin. assistance and ch. rels. Meth. Theol. Sem., 1983-89; diaconal min. Kent United Meth. Ch., Ohio, 1989—2002. Vice pres. bd. diaconal ministry East Ohio Conf., United Meth. Ch., Canton, 1989-92, v.p. NC jurisdictional program com., Detroit, 1988-92, NC jurisdictional bd. ministry, Chgo., 1988-92; pres. East Ohio Conf. United Meth. Women, 1975-79; v.p. bd. publ. United Meth. Ch., 1972-84, mem. bd. higher edn. and ministry, 1984-89. Trustee Ohio No. U., Ada, 1979-89. Recipient Community Svc. award B'nai B'rith, 1967, nat. award United Meth. Women, 1983. Mem. Ch. Women United (pres. 1969-73), Order Ea. Star (chaplain 1969). Avocations: travel, crewel embroidery, reading, walking. Home: 3740 St Andrews Dr Youngstown OH 44505-1670

DUNLAP, CHARLES J., JR., judge advocate, military officer; BA, St. Joseph's U., Phila., 1972; JD, Villanova U. Sch. Law, Pa., 1975; grad., Squadron Officer Sch., Maxwell AFB, Ala., 1979, Armed Forces Staff Coll., Norfolk, Va., 1984, Air War Coll., 1989; disting. grad., Nat. War Coll., Ft. Lesley J. McNair, Washington, 1992; grad. in Nat. Security Prog., Syracuse U. Maxwell Sch. Citizenship and Pub. Affairs, NY, 1996. Bar: Supreme Ct. Commonwealth of Pa. 1975. Commd. 2d lt. USAF, 1972—75; asst. staff judge adv. 2nd Combat Grp. Barksdale AFB, La., 1976—77; asst. staff judge adv. 51st Combat Grp. Osan Air Base, Republic of Korea, 1977—78; chief civil law divsn. 20th Combat Grp. RAF, Upper Heyford, England, 1978, chief mil. justice divsn. 20th Tactical Fighter Wing, 1978—80; faculty mem. Air Force JAG Sch., Maxwell AFB, Ala., 1980—83, chief mil. justice divsn., 1983—84; staff judge adv. 97th Bombardment Wing Blytheville AFB, Ark., 1984—87; cir. mil. judge Air Force Legal Svcs. Agy., Bolling AFB, DC, 1987—89; chief pers. action law br. Gen. Law Divsn. USAF, Washington, 1989—91; dep. staff judge adv. US Ctrl. Command MacDill AFB, Fla., 1992—95; staff judge adv. US Strategic Command, Offutt AFB, Nebr., 1995—98; staff judge adv. 9th Air Force Shaw AFB, SC, 1998—2000; staff judge adv. Hdqs. Air Edn. and Tng. Command, Randolph AFB, Tex., 2000—02, Hdqs. Air Combat Command, Langley AFB, Va., 2002—06; advanced through ranks to maj. gen. USAF, 2006—, dep. JAG Washington, 2006—. Contbr. articles to profl. publs. Decorated Def. Superior Svc. Medal with oak leaf cluster, Legion of Merit with two oak leaf clusters, Meritorious Svc. Medal with four oak leaf clusters, Air Force Commendation medal, Armed Forces Expeditionary medal, S.W. Asia Svc. Medal with two bronze stars, Humanitarian Svc. medal, Air Force Overseas Ribbon, short, Air Force Overseas Ribbon, long, Small Arms Expert Marksmanship Ribbon; named Outstanding Judge Adv. of Yr., Strategic Air Command, 1984, USAF Outstanding Career Armed Svcs. Atty., 1992; recipient Thomas P. Keenan award for internat. and ops. law, 1996. Office: HQ USAF/JA 1420 Air Force Pentagon Rm 4E112 Washington DC 20330 Office Phone: 703-614-5732.

DUNLAP, CONNIE, librarian; b. Lansing, Mich., Sept. 9, 1924; d. Frederick Arthur and Laura May (Robinson) Robson; m. Robert Bruce Dunlap, Aug. 9, 1947. AB, U. Mich., 1946, AM in Libr. Sci., 1952. Head acquisitions dept., then head grad. library U. Mich. Libr., 1961-75, dep. assoc. dir., 1972-75; univ. libr. Duke U., 1975-80; cons., 1981—. Contbr. articles to publs. in field, chpts. in books. Forewoman Grand Jury U.S. Dist. Ct. 13th Dist. Mich., 1967-68; bd. dirs. U. Mich. Libr. Friends, v.p., 1997-2000, officer at large, 2000-02, bd. dirs. A.B. Bach, 1999—, v.p., 2002, chair, 2003—; treas. Ann Arbor Hist. Found., 1998—. Recipient Disting. Alumnus award U. Mich. Sch Libr. Sci., 1977 Mem. ALA (mem. coun. 1974-83, mem. exec. bd. 1978-83, pres. resources and tech. svcs. divsn. 1972-73), AAUP, Assn. Coll. and Rsch. Librs. (bd. dirs. 1975-78, pres. 1976-77), Assn. Rsch. Librs. (bd. dirs. 1976-80, pres. 1979-80). Address: 1570 Westfield Ave Ann Arbor MI 48103-5740

DUNLAP, ELLEN S., library administrator; b. Nashville, Oct. 12, 1951; d. Arthur Wallace and Elizabeth (Majors) Smith; m. Arthur H. Dunlap, Jr., Dec. 27, 1972 (dec. 1977); m. Frank Armstrong, May 11, 1979; 1 child, Libbie Sarah. BA, U. Tex., Austin, 1972, MLS, 1974. Rsch. assoc. Humanities Rsch. Ctr. U. Tex., Austin, 1973-76, rsch. libr., 1976-83; exec. dir. Rosenbach Mus. and Library, Phila., 1983-92; pres. Am. Antiquarian Soc., Worcester, Mass., 1992—. Dir. 18th Century Short Title Catalogue/N.Am., 1992—. Dir. Worcester Mcpl. Rsch. Bur., 1993—; mem. fin. com. Town of West Boylston, Mass., 1997—, chmn., 2001—05; bd. dir. Greater Worcester Cmty. Found., Mass., 2004—, clerk, 2005—; bd. dir. Mass. Found. for Humanities, 1996—2004, pres., 2002—04; bd. dir. Rare Books Sch. U. Va., 1994—. Mem. Am. Antiquarian Soc., Mass. Hist. Soc., Colonial Soc. Mass., Grolier Club (N.Y.C.), Worcester Club. Office: Am Antiquarian Soc 185 Salisbury St Worcester MA 01609-1636

DUNLAP, F. THOMAS, JR., lawyer, retired electronics executive; b. Pitts., Feb. 7, 1951; s. Francis Thomas and Margaret (Hubert) D.; m. Kathy Dunlap; children: Bridgette, Katie. BSE.E., U. Cin., 1974; JD, U. Santa Clara, Calif., 1979. Bar: Calif., 1979, U.S. Dist. Ct. (no. dist.) Calif. 1979. Mgr. engring. Intel Corp., Santa Clara, Calif., 1974-78, adminstr. tech. exchange, 1978-80, European counsel, 1980-81, sr. atty., 1981-83, gen. counsel, sec., 1983-87, v.p., gen. counsel, sec., 1987—2001, sr. v.p., gen. counsel, 2001—04. Drafter, lobbyist Semiconductor Chip Protection Act, 1984 Republican. Roman Catholic. Avocation: jogging.*

DUNLAP, JOHN B., lawyer, educator; b. Elkton, Md., Jan. 14, 1978; s. J. Barry and Ruth Ellen Dunlap. BA, Gettysburg Coll., Pa., 2000; JD, Syracuse U., NY, 2003. Bar: Md. 2003, Pa. 2004. Law clk. US Atty.'s Office Dist. Md., Balt., 2001, Balt. City State's Atty.'s Office, 2002, Dist. Ct. Frederick County, Md., 2003—04; asst. state's atty. Wash. County State's Atty.'s Office, Hagerstown, Md., 2004—. Law clk. US Attorney's Office for the Dist. of Md., Baltimore, Md., 2001—01; adj. prof. Hagerstown C.C., Md., 2005. Mem. Wash. County Rep. Ctrl. Com., Hagerstown, Md., 2004—06, chmn., 2006—07. Recipient William Paca award, State of Md., 1996, Citizenship award, Am. Legion Post 194, 1996. Conservative. Methodist. Home: 901 Woodland Way Hagerstown MD 21742 Office: Washington County States Attys Office 33 W Washington St Hagerstown MD 21740 Home Phone: 240-291-2242; Office Phone: 240-313-2009. Personal E-mail: jbdunlap08@yahoo.com. Business E-Mail: jdunlap@washco-md.net.

DUNLAP, LOREN EDWARD, painter, educator; s. Langley Theodore and Luva Maire Dunlap; m. Nancy Ann Martori, 1992. BFA, John Herron Art Sch., Indpls., 1956; MFA, Tulane U., New Orleans, 1958. Instr. Herron Sch. Art, 1959—62; lectr. U. Calif., Santa Barbara, 1963—65; art designer Self-Employed, NYC, 1966—. Bd. trustees Hampton Day Sch., Bridgehampton, Ky. Exhibitions include paintings.

DUNLAP, MATTHEW GORDON, state official, former state legislator; b. Ellsworth, Maine, Nov. 26, 1964; s. Robert Gordon and Susan Perkins Dunlap; m. Michelle Ann Dunphy, Dec. 22, 1996; 1 child, Emily Charlotte. BA in Roman History, U. Maine, 1987, MA in English Lit., 1994; postgrad., Harvard U., 2000. Finish sewer Dunlap Weavers, Bar Harbor, Maine, 1974—89; cook, bartender various, Orono, Bangor, Maine, 1986—2003; asst. editor Nat. Poetry Found., Orono, 1987—89; mem. Maine Ho. Reps., Augusta, 1996—2004, chair fish and wildlife com., 1998—2004, mem. ho. elections com., 2002—03, chair govt. oversight com., 2003; sec. state State of Maine, Augusta, 2005—. Columnist: Northwoods Sporting Jour., 1999—, assessing editor: Jour. Mind and Behavior, 1997—; contbr. articles to profl. jours. Chair Maine Citizens Commn. on Wildlife, Augusta, 1999—2001, Old Town (Maine) Dem. Com., 1998—, Marsh Island Deer Com., Old Town, 2002—; bd. mem. Grad. M-Club, Orono, 1995—; bd. mem., founder Maine Youth Fish and Game, 2001—. Recipient Govt. Svc. award, Maine Merchants Assn., 2003; fellow, Flemming Fellows/Ctr. for Policy Alts., 1997; grantee, Am. Coun. Young Polit. Leaders, Russia, 2002. Mem.: Maine Profl. Guides Assn., Friends Maine Track (v.p. 1994—98), Old Town Grange. Democrat. Episcopalian. Avocations: hunting, fishing, writing, chess, books and antiquities. Office: Office Sec State Nash School Bldg 148 State House Station Augusta ME 04333*

DUNLAP, MICHAEL S., student loan company executive; b. 1963; BS in Fin. and Acctg., U. Nebr., 1986, JD, 1988. Chmn., CEO Nelnet. Non-exec. chmn. Union Bank and Trust Co.; dir., pres. Farmers & Mchts. Investment, Inc.; bd. mem. Capital Casualty Co., BankFirst of Norfolk. Mem. Lincoln Group 2015; mem. Pres.'s Cmty. Coun. Union Coll.; bd. dirs. U. Nebr. Found. Mem.: Nebr. State Bar Assn. Office: Nelnet Inc 121 S 13th St Ste 201 Lincoln NE 68508 Office Phone: 402-458-2370.*

DUNLAP, PATRICIA C., state legislator; b. Rochester, NH, Nov. 6, 1926; Grad. h.s. Mem. N.H. Ho. of Reps., mem. comm., small bus., consumer affairs, econ. devel. coms., also mem. com. environment and agr. Ward clk., Rochester, NH, 1991—92; supr. checklist, 1992; bank customer rels. rep., 90. Treas. Gafney Home for Aged Mgmt. Bd., 1992—; asst. treas. 1st Ch. Congl., 1992-95, fin. sec., 1996—. Mem. DAR (asst. treas. Mary Torr chpt. 1992-94), OWLS (treas. 2001—).

DUNLAP, RILEY EUGENE, sociologist; b. Wynne, Ark., Oct. 25, 1943; s. Riley W. Dunlap Jr. and F. Eugenia (Jones) Anderson; m. Lonnie Jean Brown, Aug. 20, 1966 (div. 2002); children: Sara Jean, Christopher Eugene. MS, U. Oreg., 1969, PhD, 1973. From asst. prof. to prof. sociology Wash. State U., Pullman, 1972—96, Boeing Disting. prof. environ. sociology, 1997—2002; Donner prof. Abo Akademi U., Finland, 2002—04; prof. sociology U. Ctrl. Fla., Orlando, 2005, Okla. State U., Stillwater, Okla., 2006—07, regents prof. sociology, 2007—. Mem. socio-economic peer review panel Office of Exploratory Rsch., U.S. EPA, 1991; mem. panel on aesthetic attributes in water resources planning NRC/Nat. Acad. Scis., 1982. Editor: (jour. symposium) Am. Behavioral Scientist, 1980, Internat. Sociology, 1988, American Environmentalism: The U.S. Environmental Movement, 1970—90, 1992, Pub. Reactions to Nuclear Waste, 1993, Handbook of Environmental Sociology, 2002, Sociological Theory and the Environment, 2002. Gallup scholar in environment Gallup Orgn., 1999—. Fellow AAAS (rural sociol. soc. rep. to sect. K 1986-89); mem. Internat. Sociol. Assn. (pres., rsch. com. on environ. and soc. 1994-98), Am. Sociol. Assn. (chmn. sect. on environ. sociology 1981-83, disting. contbn. award 1986), Rural Sociol. Soc. (chmn. natural resources rsch. group 1978-79, award of merit 1985, Excellence in Rsch. award 2002), Soc. for Study of Social Problems (chmn. environ. problems divsn. 1973-75). Achievements include being credited as co-founder of field of environmental sociology. Office: Dept Sociology Okla State Univ Stillwater OK 74078 Home: 2010 E Matthews St Stillwater OK 74075 Office Phone: 405-744-6108. Office Fax: 405-744-5780. E-mail: rdunlap@okstate.edu.

DUNLAP, WILLIAM, artist, educator, art critic, educator; MFA, U. Miss. Prof. Appalachian State U., NC, 1970—79, Memphis State U., 1979—80; art commentator, "Around Town" WETA-TV, Arlington, Va. Spkr. in field; lectr. on art related subjects at colleges, universities, institutions and profl. confs. Represented in permanent collections, Met. Mus. Art, Corcoran Gallery Art, Lauren Rogers Mus., Mobil Corp., Riggs Bank, IBM Corp., Fed. Express, Equitable Collection, Ark. Art Ctr., U.S. State Dept., U.S. Embassies throughout the world, Rogers Ogden Collection, one-man shows include, Corcoran Gallery Art, Nat. Acad. Sci., Aspen Mus. Art, Southeastern Ctr. Contemporary Art, Mus. Western Va., Albany Mus. Art, Cheekwood Fine Arts Ctr., Mint Mus. Art, Miss. Mus. Art, Contemporary Art Ctr., New Orleans, exhibitions include Reconstructed Recollections, Inaugural Exhibition: Story of South, Ogden Mus. Southern Art, New Orleans, 2003—04, What Boys Draw & Other Works, Soren Christensen Gallery, New Orleans, 2004, Panorama Am. Landscape, Gibbes Mus. Art, Charleston, S. C., 2004—05, In Spirit of the Land; co-curator (exhibitions) Winding River: Contemporary Painting from Vietnam, Meridian Internat. Ctr., Washington D.C., 1997—98, Outward Bound: Am. Art Brink of 21st Century, writer Art & Antiques, Washingtonian, Arts Review. Office: WETA TV 2775 South Quincy St Arlington VA 22206 Office Phone: 703-998-2600. Office Fax: 703-998-3401. E-mail: bill@williamdunlap.com.

DUNLAP, WILLIAM CRAWFORD, physicist; b. Denver, July 21, 1918; s. William Crawford and Helen (Kiester) D.; m. Ellen Hebrew, Mar. 22, 1940; 1 dau., Nancy. BS, U. N.M., 1938; PhD, U. Calif., Berkeley, 1943. Asst. physicist Dept. Agr., 1942-45; research asso., research lab. Gen. Electric Co., 1945-55, cons. physicist electronics lab., 1955-56; supr. solid state research, research lab. Bendix Corp., 1956-58; dir. solid state electronic research Raytheon Co., 1958-64; asst. dir. electronic components research Electronics Research Center, NASA, Cambridge, Mass., 1964-68, dir. research, 1968-70; sci. adviser to dir. U.S. Transp. Systems Center, Cambridge, 1970-75; pres. W.C. Dunlap & Co., 1975—. Author: An Introduction to Semiconductors, 1957; founding editor, editor-in-chief Solid State Electronics, 1959-94. Fellow IEEE (dir. 1966-68, dir. region I 1966-68), Am. Phys. Soc., AIAA (assoc.). Achievements include special research transistor production techniques in alloying, diffusion, epitaxy. Home and Office: 126 Prince St Newton MA 02465-2604 E-mail: crawdunlap@aol.com.

DUNLAP, WILLIAM DEWAYNE, JR., advertising agency executive; b. Austin, Minn., Apr. 8, 1938; s. William D. and Evelyn (Hummel) D.; m. Lois Mary Apple, Sept. 23, 1961; children: Kristin, Leslie, Brenda. BA, Carleton Coll., 1960. Brand mgr. soap Procter & Gamble, Cin., 1960-69; asst. postmaster gen. U.S. Postal Svc., Washington, 1970-75, chmn. postmaster gen.'s customer coun., 1971-75, chmn. stamp adv. coun., 1972-75; pres. MCA Advt., Westport, Conn., 1976-81, Campbell-Mithun Esty, Mpls., 1981—2003, CEO, 1983—2003, chmn., 1994—2003, Petters Consumer Brands, Mpls., 2004—. Bd. dirs. Operation Smile Internat. Lutheran. Office: Petters Consumer Brands 4400 Baker Rd Hopkins MN 55343-8684 Office Phone: 952-934-9918.

DUNLAY, CATHERINE TELLES, lawyer; b. Cin., Apr. 5, 1958; d. Paul Albert and Donna Mae Telles; m. Thomas Vincent Dunlay, July 10, 1981; children: Christine Jennifer, Thomas Paul, Brian Patrick. Student, Ind. U., 1976-78; BA in English Lit. summa cum laude, U. Cin., 1981; JD summa cum laude, Ohio State U., 1984. Bar: Ohio 1984. Teaching asst., legal rsch. and writing Ohio State U. Coll. of Law, Columbus, 1982; law clk. Brownfield, Bowen & Bally, Columbus, 1983; assoc. Schottenstein, Zox & Dunn, LPA, Columbus, 1984-91, atty., principal, 1991—. Mng. editor Ohio State Law Jour., 1983-84; co-author Health Span, 1993, Akron Law Rev., Fall 1993; co-editor Health Law Jour. of Ohio, 1994-95. Grad. Columbus Leadership Program, 1991; admissions/inclusiveness com. United Way of Franklin County, Columbus, 1991-94, 96; bd. dirs. Ctrl. Ohio chpt. Arthritis Found., 2003—. Recipient C. Simeral Bunch award Ohio State U., 1984, Law Jour. Past Editors award, 1984. Mem. ABA, Ohio State Bar Assn. (chair healthcare law com. 2000-02), Columbus Bar Assn., Ohio Women's Bar Assn., Women Lawyers of Franklin County (trustee, treas. 1990-93, 91-92), Am. Health Lawyers Assn., Soc. of Ohio Hosp. Attys., Order of the Coif. Roman Catholic. Avocations: cooking, hiking, camping, reading. Office: Schottenstein Zox & Dunn 250 West St Columbus OH 43215 Office Phone: 614-462-2236. Business E-Mail: cdunlay@szd.com.

DUNLEAVY, MICHAEL JOSEPH, SR., professional basketball coach; b. Bklyn., Mar. 21, 1954; m. Emily Dunleavy; children: Michael, Jr., William Baker, James. Grad., U. SC, 1976. Player Phila. 76ers, 1976-77, Houston Rockets, 1977—82, San Antonio Spurs, 1982—83, Milw. Bucks, 1983—85, 1988—90, asst. coach, 1986—90, head coach, 1992—96, v.p. basketball ops., 1993-96, gen. mgr., 1993—97; player-coach All-Am. Basketball Alliance Carolina Lightning; head coach LA Lakers, 1990-92, Portland Trail Blazers, Oreg., 1997—2001, LA Clippers, 2003—. Named NBA Coach of Yr., 1989, 1999. Office: LA Clippers Staples Ctr 1111 S Figueroa St Ste 1100 Los Angeles CA 90015*

DUNLEAVY, WILLA GILL, music educator, director; b. Benton, Ill., Feb. 12, 1937; d. Joseph Edward McGovern and Celia Belle Gill/McGovern; m. Kevin Joseph Dunleavy, Mar. 17, 1999; 5 children. AA, William Rainey Harper Coll., 1972; MusM in Edn., MusB in Edn., U. North Tex., 1980, postgrad., 1982. Cert. pub. sch. adminstr. Tex., all level tchr., choral, gen. music K-12 Tex. Organist, choir dir. Presbyn. Synod, Chgo., 1956—73; pvt. tchr. piano, organ; choral dir. Ft. Worth Ind. Sch. Dist., 1974—87, program dir., choral and gen. music k-12, 1987—2002; cons. Macmillan/McGraw Hill, NYC, 2002—; arts edn. cons. Ft. Worth, 2002—. Pres. Youth Orch. Greater Ft. Worth, 2004—; chair, artistic com. Ft. Worth Acad. Fine Arts, 2004—; founding mem. Ft. Worth Arts Edn. Ptnrs., 2002—; past nat. chair and founding mem. Urban Music Leadership Conf., Detroit, 1995—; sec. Nat. Supervisors Music Edn. (Music Educator's Nat. Conf.), Reston, Va., 2001—02; pres. Ft. Worth Administrator's Assn., 1998—99; presenter in field. Author: (music education textbook) Spotlight on Music. Coord. music activities Sister Cities of Ft. Worth, 1987—2002; pres. Palos Twp. Rep. Women, Palos Park, Ill., 1964—67; organist, choir dir. Hickory Hills Presbyn. Ch., 1956—67; pres., founding mem. Urban Music Leadership Conf., Detroit, 1995—2005; sec. Nat. Coun. Supervisors Music Edn., Reston; pres. Youth Orch. Greater Ft. Worth, 1990—2005; chair, artistic com. bd. of directors Ft. Worth Acad. Fine Arts, 2004—; founder, mem. Ft. Worth Arts Edn. Ptnrs., 2002—05; music edn. liaison Imagination Celebration (Kennedy Ctr.), 1986—2002. Mem.: Urban Music Leadership Conf. (assoc.; pres. 1999—2002), Am. Orff Schulwerk Assn. (assoc. Service award), Tex. Choral Dirs. Assn. (assoc.), Tex. Music Educators Assn. (assoc.), Am. Choral Dirs. Assn. (assoc.), Music Educators Nat. Conf. (assoc.), The Ft. Worth Club (assoc.). Conservative. Presbyterian. Avocations: music, writing, travel, reading, theater. Home and Office: 3920 Dawn Dr Fort Worth TX 76116 Home Phone: 817-560-0334. Home Fax: 817-560-4616. Personal E-mail: willab@swbell.net.

DUNLEVIE, STEVEN S., lawyer; b. Atlanta, Apr. 24, 1948; BA, U. NC, Chapel Hill, 1970; JD, Emory U., 1973. Bar: Ga. 1973, admitted to practice: All Ga. Trial and Appellate Cts., US Dist. Ct. (No. Dist. Ga.). Atty. Office of Judge Advocate, US Navy, Charleston, SC, 1973; assoc. atty. Hule, Stern, Brown & Ide (formerly known as Ware & Sterne), Atlanta, 1973—77; ptnr. Ware, Hopkins, Dunlevie & McNairy, Atlanta, 1977—80, Parker, Johnson, Cook & Dunlevie, Atlanta, 1981—96; mem. mgmt. com. Womble Carlyle Sandridge & Rice, PLLC, Atlanta, 1996—, mng. mem. Lt. USNR, 1970—73. Mem.: Ga. State Bar, Internat. Assn. of Attys. and Execs. in Corp. Real Estate, Ga. Bankers Assn. (mem. bank counsel sect.), Am. Judicature Soc., ABA (mem. real property, probate & trust law sect., mem. brokers & brokerage and conveyancing Committees), Atlanta Bar Assn. (mem. corp., banking & real property law sect.). Office: Womble Carlyle Snadridge & Rice PLLC One Atlantic Ctr Ste 3500 1201 West Peachtree St Atlanta GA 30339 Office Phone: 404-888-7401. Office Fax: 404-870-4828. Business E-Mail: sdunlevie@wcsr.com.

DUNLOP, DAVID JOHN, geophysics educator, researcher; b. Toronto, Ont., Can., Jan. 30, 1941; s. Harry John Ewart and Mary Scott Dunlop; children: Lisa Karen, Jennifer Michelle; m. Özden Özdemir, June 2, 1987. BASc, U. Toronto, 1963, MA, 1964, PhD, 1968. Postdoctoral studies U. Tokyo, 1968-69; rsch. fellow Université de Paris VI, 1969-70; asst. prof. U. Toronto, 1970-73, assoc. prof., 1973-78, prof., 1978—. Vis. scientist NASA Johnson Space Ctr., Houston, 1972; sr. vis. scientist CSIRO, Sydney, Australia, 1992; assoc. prof. U. Montpellier, France, 1997; vis. prof. U. Paris VII, 2004. Editor: Origin of Thermomagnetism, 1977; assoc. editor Can. Jour. Earth Scis., 1983-94; co-author: Rock Magnetism Fundamentals and Frontiers, 1997, 2d edit., 2001. Killam Found. fellow, Can. Coun., 1983-85, USSR Acad. Scis. fellow, 1988, Sr. Rsch. fellow Tokyo Inst. Tech., 1988-89, DAAD Rsch. fellow Munich, 1990, Sr. Rsch. fellow Kyoto (Japan) U., 1997, 03; recipient Louis Néel medal European Geophys. Soc., 1999, Achievement in Physics medal Can. Assn. Physicists, 2007. Fellow Royal Soc. Can. (Bancroft award 2006), Am. Geophys. Union (sect. pres. 1992-94), Geol. Assn. Can. (councillor 1985-87); mem. Can. Geophys. Union (pres. 1985-87, Tuzo Wilson medal 1999). Avocations: canoeing, hiking, lepidoptera, photography, restoring old houses. Office: U Toronto Dept Physics Toronto ON Canada M5S 1A7

DUNLOP, EDWARD ARTHUR, computer company executive; b. Wilmington, Del., 1951; BS, U. Del., 1978, postgrad., 1978-79. Rsch. asst., cons. U. Del., Newark, 1972-78; pres. Technology Logistics, Newark, 1978-85, West Chester, Pa., 1989—; asst. to v.p. Continental Ins. Co. NY, Neptune, NJ, 1985—88; sr. project mgr., asst. to vice chmn. Roy F. Weston Inc., West Chester, 1988-89. Voting mem. Nat. Stds. Com. on Local and Metro. Area Networks, 1994—; advisor Nat. Computer Security Ctr., Nat. Security Agy., Nat. Inst. Stds. and Tech., U.S. Govt., 1985-2001. Mem. Coun. on Environ Control State of Del., 1975-81. Univ. fellow bus. and govt. ethics U. Del., 1983-85. Mem. IEEE, IEEE Computer Soc., IEEE Comms. Soc., IEEE Engring. Mgmt. Soc. (chair Phila. sect. 2004—), IEEE Soc. on Social Implications of Tech. (chair Phila. chpt. 2004—), Assn. for Computing Machinery. Office: Technology Logistics 1265 Estate Dr West Chester PA 19380-1258 E-mail: ed@computer.org.

DUNLOP, FRED HURSTON, lawyer; b. Clarksville, Tenn., May 3, 1946; s. William Barrett and Nelle Major (Hurston) D.; m. Jacqueline Rae Thompson, Aug. 17, 1968; children: Holt McKinney, Lindsay Barrett. BA, Vanderbilt U., 1968, JD, 1971. Bar: Tenn. 1971, Tex. 1972; comml. mediator, arbitration cert. Internat. Ctrs. Arbitration. Assoc. Baker Botts LLP, Houston, 1972—78, ptnr., 1979—. 1st lt. U.S. Army, 1971-72. Named Best Lawyer in Real Estate, Inside Houston Mag., 2003, Texas Super Lawyer, Texas Monthly, 2003—, Law & Politics, 2003—. Fellow Tex. Bar Found.; mem. ABA, Am. Coll. Real Estate Lawyers, State Bar Tex., Houston Bar Assn., Houston Real Estate Lawyers Coun., Coll. of State Bar of Tex. Avocations: golf, hunting, skiing. Home: 5609 Tupper Lake Dr Houston TX 77056-1628 Office: Baker Botts LLP 1 Shell Pla 910 Louisiana St Ste 3100 Houston TX 77002-4916 E-mail: fred.dunlop@bakerbotts.com.

DUNLOP, MARIANNE, retired language educator; b. Niobrara, Nebr., Mar. 14, 1933; d. Harvey Wesley LaBranche and Karen Sanna Arneson; m. Richard Campbell Dunlop, Apr. 26, 1959; 1 child, Christopher Campbell. BA, Vt. Coll., Bennington, 1985, MA, 1989. Bd. dir. and bd. mem. The Sargent House Mus., Gloucester, Mass., 1992—96; ESL educator Penasquitos Laubach Literacy Ctr., San Diego, 1999—2002; ret., 2002. Author: (book) Judith Sargent Murray: Champion of Social Justice, 1993; editor: (book) Judith Sargent Murray: Her First 100 Letters, 1995; writer, contbr.: (book) Standing Before Us: Unitarian Universalist Women and Social Reform 1776-1936, 1999; spkr., contbr. (documentary) Judith Sargent Murray: 18th Century Feminist. Officer, bd. dirs. Sargent House Mus., Gloucester, Mass., 1992—96, mem. adv. bd., 1996—; ESL educator Penasquitos Laubach Literacy Ctr., San Diego, 1999—2002; mem. Sargent House Mus. Mem. Virginia Woolf's Outsider Soc. Unitarian Universalist. Avocation: honoring otherness. Home: 11032 Ipai Ct San Diego CA 92127-1382

DUNLOP, NEIL, computer scientist, department chairman; s. Leslie and Julie Dunlop. BA, U. Wis., Madison, 1970; MBA, John F. Kennedy U., Orinda, Calif., 1981. Cis dept. chair Berkeley (Calif.) City Coll., 1984—; cons. Neil H. Dunlop & Assocs., Berkeley, 1984—. Faculty senate co-pres. Berkeley City Coll., 1991—2002. Author: dBASE for Professionals, 1990, Bridging dBASE and Clipper 5, 1992. Mem.: Commonwealth Club Calif. Office: Berkeley City Coll 2050 Center St Berkeley CA 94704 Home Phone: 510-234-1436; Office Phone: 510-981-2906. Personal E-mail: professor_94704@yahoo.com. Business E-Mail: ndunlop@peralta.edu.

DUNN, ADAM, professional baseball player; b. Houston, Tex., Nov. 9, 1979; Outfielder Cin. Reds, 2001—. Named to NL All-Star Team, 2002. Office: Great American Ballpark 100 Main St Cincinnati OH 45202

DUNN, ALBERT EDGAR, electrical engineer; s. Albert E. Dunn and Pearline Striplin Dunn Thompson; m. Captola Spiller Dunn; 1 child, Joseph Malcolm. Degree, Mich. Tech. Inst., Detroit, 1957. Foreman, supr. air-conditioning missiles and airfraft C.G. Hokanson Co., LA, 1956—64; elec. mech. supr. Dept. Water and Power, LA, 1964—88. Home: 5322 E 94th St N Sperry OK 74073 Office Phone: 918-288-2007.

DUNN, ANNE EWALD NEFFLEN, retired elementary school educator; b. Elkins, W.Va., Feb. 9, 1935; d. Edgar Lantz and May (Bradley) Nefflen; m. Delma Douglas Dunn, July 20, 1961; children: Susan Bradley Dunn, Robert Cameron, Richard Tullos. BS in Home Econs., U. Md., 1956; student, U. Miami, 1953-54, San Diego State Coll., 1958-60; MEd, U. Ark., 1985. Cert. elem. tchr., reading specialist, gifted and talented, Ark. Tchr. 2d grade San Diego City Schs., 1958-61, Oak Harbor (Wash.) Schs., 1961-63; tchr. 2d and 3d grades Albuquerque Pub. Schs., 1963-65; tchr. 3d grade Prairie Grove (Ark.) Sch. Dist., 1978-85, tchr. gifted and talented, coord., 1985-88, tchr. remedial reading and math., 1988-92, tchr., coord. At-Risk Alternative Edn. 1st grade, 1992-94, chpt. I reading specialist, reading tchr., 1994—2003; ret. Interviewer Navy Relief Soc., Whidbey Island, Wash., 1961-63. Leader 4-H Horse Club, Whidbey Island, 1961-63, 4-H Club, Prairie Grove, 1979-81; leader, trainer Girl Scouts U.S., Prairie Grove, 1975-78; mem. Prairie Grove Libr. Bd., 1980-82; show sec. Nat. Arabian Horse Assn. Show, Albuquerque, 1965. Mem. Phi Delta Kappa. Presbyterian. Avocations: sewing, reading, horseback riding. Home: 22530 Cove Crk S Prairie Grove AR 72753-9230 Office: Prairie Grove Elem Sch 824 N Mock St Prairie Grove AR 72753-2610

DUNN, ARNOLD SAMUEL, biochemistry educator; b. Rochester, NY, Jan. 31, 1929; s. Alexander and Dora (Cohen) D.; m. Doris Ruth Frankel, Sept. 14, 1952; children: Jonathan Alexander, David Hillel. BS, George Washington U., 1950; PhD, U. Pa., 1955; LHD (hon.), Hebrew Union

Coll., 1995. Research assoc. Michael Reese Hosp. Research Inst., Chgo., 1955-56; asst. prof. NYU Sch. Medicine, NYC, 1956-62; vis. prof. Weizmann Inst. Sci., Rehovot, Israel, 1972-73, 83-84, Hebrew U., Jerusalem, 1972-73; prof. molecular biology U. So. Calif., Los Angeles, 1962—, dir. molecular biology LA, 1982-90, assoc. dean, 1990-92; vis. fellow history sci. Princeton U., 1993. Contbr. articles to profl. jours.; mem. editorial bd.: Am. Jour. Physiology, 1979-, Analytical Biochemistry, 1980-. UPSHS fellow, 1972, 83; Meyerhoff fellow Weizmann Inst. Sci., 1983. MEm. Am. Physiol. Soc., Am. Soc. Biol. Chemists, Endocrine Soc., Phi Beta Kappa, Sigma Xi, Phi Kappa Phi, Golden Key. Home Phone: 310-454-9661. Business E-Mail: arnolddu@usc.edu.

DUNN, BARBARA ANN, language educator; b. Chgo., Oct. 23, 1952; d. Joseph W. and Helen Elizabeth Wenckus; m. Edward George Dunn, July 1975; children: Matthew, Patrick. BA, No. Ill. U., DeKalb, 1974, MS in Edn., 1984; MA, Roosevelt U., Chgo., 1990. Cert. secondary counselor Ill. Spanish tchr. Immaculate Heart of Mary HS, Westchester, Ill., 1974—81, Riverside-Brookfield HS, Riverside, Ill., 1981—. Presenter in field. Recipient Tech. award, West Cook, Ill., 2000. Mem.: Ill. Fgn. Lang. Tchrs. Assn., Am. Assn. Tchrs. Spanish and Portuguese, Delta Kappa Gamma (2d v.p. 1985—86). Avocations: photography, travel, sewing. Office: Riverside Brookfield HS 160 Ridgewood Riverside IL 60546

DUNN, BERNARD DANIEL, former naval officer, consultant; b. Providence, Feb. 10, 1934; s. Alexander Gerard and Mary Alice (Fitzpatrick) D.; m. Hilda Hughes Tunney, Jan. 4, 1958; children: Bernard Daniel Jr., Brian Lindsay, Mary Catherine, J. Alexander. BS in Econs., Villanova U., Pa., 1956; MBA in Transp., Mich. State U., East Lansing, 1971. Commd. ensign USN, 1956, advanced through grades to capt.; asst. supply and disbursing officer USS Rushmore, Little Creek, Va., 1957-58; asst. material divsn. officer, stock control divsn. officer Sub Base New London, Groton, Conn., 1958-61; material and fiscal divsn. supt. Ship Repair Facility, Guam, 1961-63; nuclear weapons material divsn. officer Naval Supply Ctr., Oakland, Calif., 1963-64; supply ops. officer Nuc. Weapons Supply Annex, Oakland, Calif., 1964-65; commn. supply officer USS Fox, 1965-68; project officer Naval Supply Sys. Command, Washington, 1968-70; asst. for sea transp. Office Chief Naval Ops., Washington, 1971-73; sr. mem. Mobile Tng. Team to Colombian Navy, Bogota, Colombia, 1973; dir. warehousing, chief transp. office Def. Depot, Tracy, Calif., 1973-76; dep. project mgr., Navy rep. Joint Container Steering Group Office of Sec. of Def., Washington, 1976-77; dir. transp. field ops. divsn. Naval Supply Sys. Command, Washington, 1977-78; head transp. mgmt. and policy br. Office Chief Naval Ops., Washington, 1978-83; comptr./dir. supply Naval Edn. and Tng. Command, Newport, R.I., 1983-85; A-76 program officer Mil. Sealift Command, Washington, 1985; acting dir./chief staff commn. on Merchant Marine and Def., Alexandria, Va., 1985-88; bd. dirs., corp. sec. Greenwich Ctr., Inc., East Greenwich, RI, 1988—2002. Cons., Alexandria, Va., 1988-91; chief program analyst Resource Cons., Inc., Vienna, Va., 1991-94, sr. supply specialist, 97-98. Life mem. East Greenwich (R.I.) Vol. Fire Dept., 1953—. Decorated Def. Meritorious Svc. medal, Meritorious Svc. medal, Joint Svc. Commendation medal with oak leaf cluster, Navy Meritorious Unit commendation, Air Force Outstanding Unit award, Humanitarian medal, Nat. Def. Svc. medal, Vietnam Svc. medal with one bronze star, Rep. of Vietnam Campaign medal. Mem. U.S. Naval Inst., Nat. Def. Transp. Assn. (pres. San Joaquin chpt. 1974-75), USCG Acad. Found., East Greenwich Vets. firemen Assn., Mil. Officers Assn., Washington Area Navy Supply Corps Assn., Naval Submarine League, USS Rushmore Assn. (founder and charter mem., assoc. treas.1995-2001, 1st v.p. 2003-05). Roman Catholic. Avocations: stamp collecting/philately, ice hockey, running, golf. Home: 5817 Shalott Ct Alexandria VA 22310-1427 E-mail: bddunn3@verizon.net.

DUNN, BRIAN J., retail executive; m. Sue Dunn; 3 children. Sales assoc. Best Buy Co., Richfield, Minn., 1985—89, store mgr., 1989—90, dist. mgr., 1990—96, regional mgr., 1996—98, regional v.p. northeastern region, 1998—2000, sr. v.p. div. 3 retail sales, 2000—02, exec. v.p. U.S. retail, 2002—04, pres. No. Am. retail, 2004—06, pres., COO, 2006—. Office: Best Buy Co 7601 Penn Ave S Minneapolis MN 55423 Mailing: Best Buy Co PO Box 9312 Minneapolis MN 55440-9312*

DUNN, BRUCE SIDNEY, materials scientist, educator; m. Wendy Joan Rader, 1970; 1 child. BS in Ceramic Engring., Rutgers U., 1970; MS in Materials Sci., UCLA, 1972, PhD in Materials Sci., 1974. Staff scientist GE, Schenectady, NY, 1976-80; assoc. prof. materials sci. UCLA, 1981-85, prof., 1985—, Nippon Sheet Glass chair materials sci., 2003. Invited prof. U. Paris, 1986, 91-93, 98, U. Bordeaux, 2000; cons. in field Contbr. articles to profl. jours. Fulbright fellow, 1985-86. Fellow Am. Ceramic Soc.; mem. Electrochem. Soc., Materials Rsch. Soc. Achievements include patents in field. Office: UCLA Dept Materials Scis & Engring 6532 Boelter Hl Los Angeles CA 90095-0001

DUNN, CHARLES DEWITT, academic administrator; b. Magnolia, Ark., Dec. 2, 1945; s. Charles Edward and Nora Lucille (Bailey) D.; m. Donna Jane Parsons, Apr. 9, 1966; children: Aimee, James, Joseph, Mary Elizabeth. BA, So. Ark. U., 1967; MA, North Tex. State U., 1970; PhD, So. Ill. U., 1973; cert. inst. ednl. mgmt., Harvard U., 1991. Instr. polit. sci. U. Ark., Monticello, 1969-72, asst. prof., 1972-75; assoc. prof. U. Ctrl. Ark., Conway, 1975-80, prof., 1980—, chmn. dept. polit. sci., 1976-82, dir. govt. rels., 1982-86; pres. Henderson State U., Arkadelphia, Ark., 1986—. Chmn. Commn. Ark.'s Future, 1989-93; chmn. Ark. Higher Edn. Coun., 1992-96; chmn. fin. com. Ark. Cmty. Found. Bd. Dirs., v.p., 2000-02, pres., 2002-03; active Blue Ribbon Commn. Pub. Edn., 2001-02, Ark. Commn. Coordination Edn., 2004-; bd. dirs. Meth. Children's Home, 2003-06. Mem. Am. Assn. State Coll. and Univs., NCAA (pres.'s commn. 1996-97, pres.' coun. 1997-2001, pres. Gulf South conf. 1998-2000), Ark. Polit. Sci. Assn. (pres. 1976-77), Conway C. of C. (bd. dirs. 1984-85, v.p. 1985-86), Arkadelphia C. of C. (bd. dirs. 1987-91), Rotary. Methodist. Office: Henderson State U 1100 Henderson St PO Box 7532 Arkadelphia AR 71999-0001 Home Phone: 870-246-3099; Office Phone: 870-230-5091. Business E-Mail: cddunn@hsu.edu.

DUNN, CRAIG ANDREW, entertainer, conductor, writer, composer, educator; b. Point Pleasant, NJ, Nov. 11, 1947; s. Andrew Robert and Ruth Agnes (Schott) D.; m. Crystal Lynn Kesler, May 26, 1970. MusB, U. Cin., 1972; MusM, Ohio U., 1973; EdD, Nova Southeastern U., 1996. Cert. tchr., Fla. Dir. bands Greenville Sr. HS, SC, 1973-74, Bayonne HS, NJ, 1974-75; studio instr. Buddy Rogers Music Studios, Inc., Cin., 1975-78; music specialist, music dir. Diocese of St. Petersburg, Fla., 1979-88; music specialist Sch. Dist. of Hillsborough County, Tampa, Fla., 1988—; performing artist, entertainer, 1972—; mem. faculty music St. Petersburg Coll., Fla., 2001—; entertainer on world class cruise ships, 2006—. Mem. adv. bd. Am. Youth Symphony Band and Chorus, Pitts., 1980-85, artistic advisor, coach, 1980, 83, 85; dir. sch. dance and choral ensembles Fla. State Fair, 1992—. Composer: The Devil's Jester, 1971, Come to Me, 1971, Fishers of Men, 1976, The One-Hundred Fiftieth Psalm, 1976, A Mass for the Feast of the Triumph of the Cross, 1981; contbr. articles to profl. jours. Mem. Music Educators Nat. Conf., Fla. Music Educators Assn., Nat. Acad. Songwriters (pub. composer, author). Avocations: orchestrating, writing, reading. Home: 11800 4th St E Isle of Capri Treasure Island FL 33706

DUNN, DANA-LORI, counselor; b. Covina, Calif., Aug. 6, 1957; d. Lowell Roland and Dorothy Jane Butterfield; m. Mark Philip Dunn, Nov. 3, 1979; children: Ian Roland, Brittany Jane. Cert. Program land devel. cmty. planning, U. Calif., Irvine, 1991; PhD in Metaphysics, U. Metaphysics, Studio City, Calif., 1996. Ordained Metaphys. min. Internat. Metaphys. Ministry, 1995; bd. cert. pastoral counselor; cert. hypnotherapist Am. Bd. Hypnotherapy. Sec. Garrett Airesearch, Torrance, Calif., 1975-78; adminstrv. asst. Panel-Air Corp., Costa Mesa, Calif., 1979-81; exec. sec. Rockwell Internat., Newport Beach, Calif., 1984-86; adminstrv. asst. Las Flores Group, Inc., Dana Point, Calif., 1990-92, Cymbolic Scis. Internat., Aliso Viejo, Calif., 1992-93; acctg. asst. Quigley Ins. Svcs., Mission Viejo, Calif., 1993-95; pvt. practice Aliso Viejo, 1995—. Author: A Leap of Faith: Back to the Garden, 1998, The Power and the Glory of the RAYS, 1998. Active Nat. Campaign for Tolerance. Recipient Bus. award Bank of Am., 1975, Meritorious Achievement award IBC, 2000. Mem. Lucis Trust, United Lodge of Theosophists, Planetary Soc. Republican. Avocations: pianist, composer, hiking, skiing. Home: 23572 El Rio Aliso Viejo CA 92656-1110

DUNN, DAVID, federal agency administrator; m. Renee Dunn. BA in Polit. Sci., Baylor U.; MA in Govt., U. Tex., Austin. Edn. and fiscal policy analysis State of Tex.; assoc. exec. dir. Tex. Assn. Sch. Boards; staff, Domestic Policy Coun. The White House, Washington, 2002—05, spl. asst. to the pres., domestic policy; chief of staff US Dept. Edn., Washington, 2005—. Office: Chief of Staff 400 Maryland Ave SW Washington DC 20202*

DUNN, DAVID B., ambassador; b. Great Falls, Mont. s. Elmer and Marjory Dunn; m. Maria-Elena Dubourt; two children: Tom, Brian. AB, Occidental Coll.; MA, Am. U.; MS, Nat. War Coll. Entered U.S. Fgn. Svc., 1979, dir. for East African Affairs, U.S. State Dept. African Bur.; US consul gen. US Consulate, Johannesburg, 2002—05; US amb. to Zambia US Dept. State, Lusaka, 1999—2002, US amb. to Togo Lome, 2006—. Office: US Dept State 2300 Lome Pl Washington DC 20521-2300 Office Phone: 228-221-2991.

DUNN, DAVID JOSEPH, investment company executive; b. Bklyn., July 30, 1930; s. David Joseph and Rose Marie (McLaughlon) Dunn; m. Marilyn Percaccia, June 1955 (div.); children: Susan, Steven, Linda; m. Marilyn Bell, Apr. 1994. BS, US Naval Acad., 1955; MBA, Harvard U., Cambridge, Mass., 1961. Investment banker G.H. Walker & Co., NYC, 1961-62; ptnr. J.H. Whitney & Co., NYC, 1962-70; mng. ptnr. Idanta Ptnrs., San Diego, 1971—. Chmn. bd. dirs. Munchkin, Inc.; bd. dirs. Engineous Software, NanoNexus. With USMC, 1950—51, with USMC, 1955—59. Mem.: Glenwild Country Club, Del Mar Country Club, Vintage Club, Univ. Club (NYC). Office: Idanta Ptnrs 12526 High Bluff Dr Ste 160 San Diego CA 92130

DUNN, DEBRA L., computer company executive; B in Comparative Econs., Brown U., Providence; M in Bus., Harvard U. Exec. devel. mgr. corp. tng. divsn. Hewlett-Packard Co., Palo Alto, Calif., 1983—86, various devel. and mfg. mgmt. positions, 1986—92, mfg. mgr., 1992—93, mktg. mgr., 1993—96, gen. mgr. video comm. divsn., 1996—98, gen. mgr. exec. com., 1998, v.p., 1999—2000, v.p. strategy and corp. ops., 2000—02, sr. v.p. corp. affairs, 2002—. Mem. UN Info. and Comm. Tech. Task Force; bd. dirs. Opportunities Industrialization Ctr. West, BayCat. Office: Hewlett Packard Co 3000 Hanover St Palo Alto CA 94304

DUNN, DELMER DELANO, political science professor; b. Sentinel, Okla., Oct. 31, 1941; s. Robert Patrick and Mildred Marion D.; m. Ann Gregg Swinford, May 15, 1971; children: John Swinford, Kielly McKee BA, Okla. State U., 1963; MS, U. Wis., 1964, PhD, 1967. Asst. prof. polit. sci. U. Ga., Athens, 1967-71, assoc. prof., 1971-77, dir. Inst. Govt., 1973-82, prof., 1977-82, Regents prof., 1982—2006; rsch. assoc. The Brookings Instn., Washington, 1969-70; acting head dept. polit. sci. U. Ga., Athens, 1987-88, assoc. v.p. acad. affairs, 1988-91, dir. Inst. Higher Edn., 2001—02, v.p. instrn., 2002—06; ret; prof. emeritus U. Ga., Athens, 2006—. Vis. fellow dept. polit. sci. faculty of arts Australian Nat. U., Canberra, 1992. Author: Public Officials and the Press, 1969, Financing Presidential Campaigns, 1972, Politics and Adminstration at the Top: Lessons from Down Under, 1997 (Charles Levine Book award 1998); mem. editl. bd. Social Sci. quar., 1988-94; contbr. articles to profl. jours. Trustee Leadership Ga., 1976-82; pres. Clarke/Oconee unit Am. Cancer Soc., 1981-82, chmn., 1982-83. Mem. Am. Polit. Sci. Assn. (Congl. fellow, 1968-69), Nat. Assn. Schs. of Pub. Affairs and Adminstrn. (pres. 1987-88), Pi Alpha Alpha (nat. pres. 1983-85). Presbyterian. Office: Univ Ga Sch Pub and Internat Affairs Athens GA 30602 Business E-Mail: ddunn@uga.edu.

DUNN, DONALD GLENN, electrical engineer, consultant; b. Houston, Oct. 11, 1962; s. Jon W. and Kay O. Dunn; m. Lisa K. Nichols, July 9, 1983; children: Zachery A., Nicholas P., Elyssabeth L. BSEE, Prairie View A&M, Tex., 1991. Mgr. Kroger Stores, Houston, 1985—91; sr. IEA & controls engr. Diamond Shamrock, Mont Belvieu, Tex., 1991—98; prin. IEA & controls engr. Lyondell Chem. Co., Channelview, Tex., 1998—2006; consulting engr. Aramco Svcs. Co., Houston, 2006—. Cons. Dorchester-Hugoton, Ltd., Hooker, Okla., 1994—95, Liberal, Kans., 1995—96. Author: conf. papers and articles in tech. publs. Mem. Goose Creek Consolidated Jr. Sch. Redistricting Com., Baytown, Tex., 2003, Goose Creek Consol. Sch. Dist. Visions Com., 2004; jr. sch. subcommittee facilitator Goose Creek Consol. Sch. Dist. Facility Planning Com., 2004; vice chmn. Goose Creek Consol. Sch. Dist. Citizens Bond Adv. Bd., 2005; chair presentation com. Friends of Goose Creek Sch. Polit. Action Com., Baytown, 2005; mem. bd. Little League, Highlands, Tex., 2001, 2003; den leader pack Troop 107 Boy Scouts of Am., Highlands, Tex., 1997—2002, troop com. mem. Troop 107, 2002—, troop com. treas. troop 107, 2003. Recipient Operational Excellence award, Reliability East Utilities Chiller Team, Lyondell Chem. Co., 2002, Operational Excellence award, Environ., Environ. Improvement Team, 2005. Mem.: Industry Applications Soc., Internat. Soc. for Measurement and Ctrl., Power Engring. Soc., Ctrl. Sys. Soc., IEEE (treas. Houston sect. 1999, sec. Houston sect. 2000, vice chmn. Houston sect. 2000, chmn. Industry Application Soc. PCIC Chem. subcom. 2005—, chmn. Houston sect. 2006—, mem. admission and advancement com. 2006—, mem. edn. activties bd. 2006—, numerous other com. memberships, Third Millennium medal, Houston sect. 2000). Achievements include development of Alkyation Unit Optimization Using Coriolis Mass Flow Meters; Hydrocarbon Interface Detection Using Coriolis Technology; Unique Applications Utilizing Coriolis Technology. Avocations: golf, travel. Home: 514 Aberdeen Way Highlands TX 77562 Office: Lyondell Chemicals 2502 Sheldon Rd Channelview TX 77530 Office Phone: 713-432-8588. Personal E-mail: donald.dunn@ieee.org. Business E-Mail: donald.dunn@aramcoservices.com.

DUNN, DONALD JACK, law librarian, educator, dean; b. Tyler, Tex., Nov. 9, 1945; s. Loren Jack and Clara Inez (Milam) Dunn; m. Cheryl Jean Sims, Nov. 24, 1967; 1 child, Kevin. BA., U. Tex.-Austin, 1969, MLS, 1972; JD, Western New Eng. Coll., 1983. Asst. to law libr. U. Tex., 1969-72, supervising libr. Criminal Justice Reference Libr., 1972-73; law libr., prof. law Western New Eng. Coll., Springfield, Mass., 1973-96, interim dean, 1996-98, dean, 1998—2001, assoc. dean for libr. and info. resources, prof. law, 2002—03; dean, prof. law U. La Verne Coll. Law, Ontario, Calif., 2003—. Editor (with Flynn): Immigration and Nationality Law Rev., vols. 3-7, 1979—84; editor: (with Mersky) Fundamentals of Legal Research, 8th edit., 2002. Bd. dirs. Pioneer Valley chpt. ARC. Fellow: Am. Bar Found.; mem.: ABA (chair law librs. com. 1988—92), ALA, Am. Law Inst., Law Librs. New Eng. (pres. 1982—83), Spl. Libr. Assn., Am. Assn. Law Librs. (chair acad. law librs. spl. interest sect. 1989—90), Scribes. Democrat. Episcopalian. Office: U La Verne Coll Law 320 East D St Ontario CA 91764 Office Phone: 909-460-2020. Business E-Mail: dunnd@ulv.edu.

DUNN, DONNA R., public health service officer; d. Jack Smith and Hermine Luise Russell; m. Jerry Vann Dunn, Oct. 27, 1990; children: Heather Olinger, Carla Bundrick, Tiffany. BS in Pre-Vet. Medicine, Auburn U., Ala., 1982. Environ. health supr. Cullman County Health Dept., Ala., 1983—. Office: Cullman County Health Dept 260 County Rd 1397 Falkville AL 35622-3583

DUNN, EDWIN RYDELL, lawyer; b. Boston, July 24, 1942; s. Richard Joseph and Clara Hudson (Rydell) Dunn; m. Kathleen Lynch, July 23, 1966; children: Jeanne, Kathleen, Anne, Daniel. BA, U. Notre Dame, Ind., 1964; JD cum laude, Northwestern U., Chgo., 1967. Bar: Ill. 1967. Assoc. Baker & McKenzie, Chgo., 1967—73, ptnr., 1973—. Mem. law bd. Northwestern U. Law Sch., 1996—, chmn., 2004—06; bd. dirs. Nr. West Side Cmty. Devel. Corp., 1991—. Mem. bd. advisors Cath. Charities, Chgo., 1999—. Mem.: ABA, Ill. Bar Assn., Chgo. Bar Assn. Office: Baker & McKenzie 1 Prudential Pla 130 E Randolph Dr Ste 3900 Chicago IL 60601-6342 Home Phone: 847-446-0176; Office Phone: 312-861-2864. Business E-Mail: edwin.r.dunn@bakernet.com.

DUNN, FLOYD, biophysics and biomedical engineering professor; b. Kansas City, Mo., Apr. 14, 1924; s. Louis and Ida (Leibtag) Dunn; m. Elsa Tanya Levine, June 11, 1950; children: Andrea Susan, Louis Brook. Student, Kans. City Jr. Coll., 1941-42, Tex. A&M U., College Station, 1943; BS, U. Ill., Urbana, 1949, MS, 1951, PhD, 1956. Rsch. assoc. elec. engrng. U. Ill., Urbana, 1954-57, rsch. asst. prof. elec. engring., 1957-61, assoc. prof. elec. engring. and biophysics, 1961-65, prof., 1965—95, prof. elec. engring., biophysics and bioengring., 1972-95, faculty mem. Beckman Inst. Advanced Sci. and Tech., prof. emeritus, 1995—, dir. bioacoustics rsch. lab., 1976-95, chmn. bioengring. faculty, 1978-82. Vis. prof. U. Coll., Cardiff, Wales, 1968—69, Inst. Chest Diseases and Cancer, Tohoku U., Sendai, Japan, 1989—90, U. Nanjing, China, 1983; mem. bioengring., radiation and diagnostic radiology study sects. NIH, 1970—81; steering com. workshop interaction ultrasound and biol. tissues NSF, 1971—72; vis. sr. scientist Inst. Cancer Rsch., Sutton, Surrey, England, 1975—76, Sutton, 1982—83, Sutton, 1990; chmn. working group health aspects exposure to ultrasound radiation WHO, London, 1976; mem. tech.-elec. products radiation stds. com. FDA, 1974—76; vis. prof. radiation oncology U. Ariz., Tucson, 1996—; mem. Nat. Coun. Radiation Protection and Measurement, 1980—2003, fellow, 2003—; treas. Interscience Rsch. Inst., Champaign, Ill., 1957—58; mem. sci. adv. bd. Resonant Med. Inc., Montreal, 2005—. Mem. editl. bd. Jour. Acoustical Soc. Am., 1968—, Ultrasound Medicine and Biology, 1981—, Ultrasonics, 1981—2003, Encyclopedia of Acoustics, 1981—97, Encyclopedia of Applied Physics, 1981—, Am. Inst. Physics Series Modern Acoustics and Signal Processing, 1990—97; contbr. articles to profl. jours. Trustee Hensley Twp., Ill., 1980—81. With AUS, 1943—46. Recipient Spl. Merit medal, Acoustical Soc. Japan, 1988, History Med. Ultrasound Pioneer award, AIUM/WFUMB, 1988; Spl. Rsch. fellow, NIH, 1968—69, Eleanor Roosevelt-Internat. Cancer fellow, Am. Cancer Soc., 1975—76, 1982—83, Fulbright fellow, 1982—83, Japan Soc. Promotion Sci. fellow, 1982, 1996, Fogarty Internat. fellow, 1990. Fellow: AAAS, IEEE (life), Inst. Acoustics (U.K.), Am. Inst. Ultrasound in Medicine (William J. Fry meml. award 1984, Joseph H. Holmes Basic Sci. Pioneer award 1990), Acoustical Soc. Am. (assoc. editor Jour. 1968-, exec. coun. 1977-80, v.p. 1980-81, pres. 1985-86, chmn. pub. policy com. 1994-, Silver medal 1989, Gold medal 1998), Am. Inst. Med. Biol. Engring. (IEEE Engring. Medicine and Biology Soc. Career Achievement award 1995, Edison medal 1996), Internat. Acad. Med. Biol. Engring.; mem.: NAE, NAS, Biophys. Soc., Rochester Soc. Biomed. Ultrasound (hon.), Japan Soc. Ultrasound in Medicine (hon.), Am. Inst. Physics (mem. editl. bd. series in modern acoustics and signal processing 1990—97, publs. policy com. 1992—2000), NCRP Alumni Assn., NIH Alumni Assn., Sigma Xi, Phi Sigma Phi, Phi Sigma, Pi Mu Epsilon, Tau Beta Pi, Eta Kappa Nu, Sigma Tau. Home: 13500 N Rancho Vistoso Blvd # 143 Tucson AZ 85755-5956 Personal E-mail: floyd@ece.arizona.edu. *Excellent, dedicated and understanding teachers, bright and energetic students, and a single-mindedness to see a problem to solution are the ingredients for a modest success.*

DUNN, H. STEWART, JR., lawyer; b. Pitts., July 9, 1929; s. H. Stewart and Marie (Galvin) D.; m. Martha J. Hoovler (dec. Sept. 1975); children—Christopher T., Anthony S., Timothy P.; m. Loti Kennedy, Aug. 3, 1978. AB, Yale U., 1951; LL.B. magna cum laude, Harvard U., 1954. Bar: D.C. 1954, U.S. Supreme Ct. 1960. Assoc. firm Ivins, Phillips & Barker, Washington, 1957-61, ptnr., 1962—. Adj. prof. Georgetown U. Law Ctr., 1996; mem. U.S. Com. Selection Jud. Officers, 1977-79, chmn., 1979-81; lectr. Harvard Law Sch., 1987. Bd. editors: Harvard Law Rev, 1953-54. Fellow Am. Bar Found., Am. Coll. Trust and Estate Counsel; mem. ABA (vice chmn. sect. taxation 1970-73), Coll. Tax Counsel, Am. Law Inst. Office: 1700 Pennsylvania Ave NW Washington DC 20006-4704 Office Phone: 702-393-7600.

DUNN, HELEN ELIZABETH, retired secondary school educator; b. Peoria, Ill., July 14, 1930; d. Albert Edward and Corinne Ada (Rudel) Joos; m. Harry Christie Dunn, Feb. 4, 1951; children: Pamela Elizabeth Dunn Baumann, Patricia Louise Dunn Workley. BS in Edn., Bradley U., 1951, MA in Guidance/Counseling, 1969. Tchr. Pub. Schs. of Hawaii, Lanai City, 1951-54, Ulupalakua, 1954-56, Pub. Schs. of Peoria, 1956-69; English LaSalle (Ill.)-Peru H.S., 1970-71; counselor, tchr. Peru (Ill.) Pub. Schs., 1971-89; ret., 1989. Author: This Life I Love, 2005, numerous poems. Presenter programs on Hawaii, Peoria; project upward tutor Literacy Vols. Am., Inc., 2004—06; bd. govs. Common Pl. Cmty. Svc. Orgn., Peoria, 2004—. Mem.: PEO, LWV (bd. dirs. 1973—89, treas. 1982—89), NEA (del. 1951—56, rep. 1957—69), Ret. Tchrs. Assn. (legis. com. 1991—98), Peoria Area Ret. Tchrs. Assn. (sec. 2001—02, archives and history chair 2003—), Peoria Women's Club Chorus, Peoria Women's Club (corr. sec. 2000—), Phi Lambda Theta, Sigma Kappa (alumni chpt., pres. 1962, 1991), Delta Kappa Gamma (pres. 1968—70, 1978—80, 1992—94). Methodist. Avocations: poetry, tennis, dance, reading, singing. Home Phone: 309-692-2838.

DUNN, HORTON, JR., organic chemist; b. Coleman, Tex., Sept. 3, 1929; s. Horton and Lora Dean (Bryant) D. BA summa cum laude, Hardin-Simmons U., 1951; MS, Case Western Res. U., 1975, PhD, 1979. Instr. chemistry Hardin-Simmons U., 1951; ONR fellow Ohio State U., Columbus, 1951-52; teaching fellow in chemistry Purdue U., Lafayette, Ind., 1952-53; rsch. chemist Lubrizol Corp., Cleve., 1953-70, dir. tech. info. ctr., 1970-79, supr. rsch. divsn., 1980-98; pvt. practice Cleve., 1998—. Chmn. bd., bus. mgr. Isotopics, Cleve., 1964-67, editor, 1961-63, supr. rsch. divsn., 1989-97, cons. in field Contbr. articles to profl. jours.; patentee in field. Treas. Cleve. Cir. Decorative Arts Trust, 1990-91, 93—, v.p., 1992-93; bd. mgrs. One Bratenahl Place, 2001—; active Cleve. Art Assn., Rock and Roll Hall of Fame, Mus. Founders Club.; mem., vol. Great Lakes Sci. Ctr., Cleve. Mus. Natural History; mem. Cleve. Bot. Garden, Condr.'s Cir. of Cleve. Orch. Fellow Am. Inst. Chemists; mem. AAAS, SAR (life), Am. Chem. Soc. (treas. Cleve. chpt. 1968-70, chmn. 1987, bd. dirs. 1990—), Am. Soc. for Info. Sci. (chpt. pres. 1973-74), Royal Soc. Chemistry (life), Soc. Tribologists and Lubrication Engrs., Nat. Coun. Met. Opera, Royal Oak Soc. (life), Cleve. Tech. Soc. Coun. (treas. 1987), Cleve. Art Assn., Univ. Club, Cleve. Club, Cleve. Play House Club, Rock and Roll Hall of Fame Mus. Founders Club (charter), English Speaking Union (bd. dirs. Cleve. br. 2005—), Trideca Soc. of Cleve. Mus. Art, Cleve. Skating Club. Home and Office: 1 Bratenahl Pl Apt 103 Bratenahl OH 44108-1152

DUNN, JACK NEWTON, urologist; s. Isaac Newton and Geraldine K. Dunn; m. Helen F. Snelling; children: Diane, Jack Jr., Sharon. BA, The Citadel, Charleston, SC, 1951, BS, 1955; MD, Med. Coll. SC, Charleston,

1960. Intern Charity Hosp., New Orleans; urology resident Tulane U., 1963—67; urologist Western Carolina Urology, Hendersonville, SC, 1967—91. With US Pub. Health Svcs., Alaska, 1961—63. Col. USAR. Fellow: Internat. Coll. Surgeons, AMA; mem.: Am. Urol. Assn. (southeastern sect.), Western Carolina African Med. Mission, NC Med. Soc. Avocations: flying, genealogy, photography, travel. Personal E-mail: dramadoc_dink@bellsouth.net.

DUNN, JAMES MILTON, retired religious organization administrator; b. Ft. Worth, June 17, 1932; s. William Thomas and Edith (Campbell) Dunn; m. Marilyn McNeely, Dec. 19, 1958. BA, Tex. Wesleyan Coll., 1953; BD, Southwestern Bapt. Theol. Sem., 1957, ThD, 1966, PhD, 1978; LLD, Alderson-Broaddus Coll., William Jewell Coll.; DHL, Linfield Coll.; DD, Ctrl. Bapt. Theol. Sem., Furman U.; DD (hon.), Franklin Coll., 2004. Ordained to ministry So. Bapt. Conv. and Am. Bapt. Ch. in U.S.A., 1955. Assoc. pastor First Bapt. Ch., Weatherford, Tex., 1955-57; pastor Emmanuel Bapt. Ch., Weatherford, 1957-61; religion instr., campus minister W. Tex. State U., Canyon, 1961-66; dir. christian life commn. Bapt. Gen. Conv. Tex., Dallas, 1967-80; exec. dir. Bapt. Joint Com. on Pub. Affairs, Washington, 1981-99, pres. endowment, 1999—; prof. Christianity and pub. policy Wake Forest U. Div. Sch., 1999—. Sec. bd. Ams. United for Separation of Ch. and State, 1978-88; bd. dirs. Bread for the World, Washington, pres., 1987; chmn. ethics commn. Bapt. World Alliance, McLean, Va., 1975-80; chmn. adv. bd. ProVision Asia, 1985—; bd. dirs. Ch.'s Ctr. for Theology and Pub. Policy, Washington, 1993—02; vis. prof. Wake Forest Div. Sch., 1999—. Editor, co-author: Politics a Guidebook for Christians, 1970, Endangered Species, 1976; co-author: An Approach to Christian Ethics, 1979, Teacher Renewal, 1987; author: (with others) Equal Separation, 1990, The Fundamentalist Phenomenon, 1990, Defining Baptist Convictions, 1996, Proclaiming the Baptist Vision, Religious Liberty, 1997, Why I Am a Baptist, 1999, Baptists in the Balance, 1997, Soul Freedom: Baptist Battle Cry, 2000. Sec. Anti-Crime Coun. Tex., Dallas, 1968-80; founding mem. Dallas Dem. Forum, 1976-80, People for the Am. Way; mem. Fair Campaign Practices Com., Dallas, 1972-76, Gov.'s Juvenile Justice Coun., State of Tex., Austin, 1976-77; pres. Whitsitt Hist. Soc., 2003-04. Recipient Disting. Svc. award Christian Life Commn. of So. Bapt. Conv., 1979, Moore-Bowman Award of Excellence, Tex. Coun. on Family Relations, 1979, Disting. Svc. award Chs. Ctr. for Theology and Pub. Policy, 1993, T.B. Maston Christian Ethics award, 1995, Abner V. McCall Religious Liberty award Baylor U., 1998, Disting. Svc. award Christian Life Commn. Bapt. Gen. Conv. Tex., 1998, Madison-Jefferson award Americans United, 1999, Disting. Svc. medal Colgate Rochester Div. Sch., 2000. Mem. Soc. for the Sci. Study of Religion, Hymn Soc. US. and Can., Alumni Assn. London Sch. Econs. and Polit. Sci. (life), Roger Williams Fellowship (life). Baptist. Avocation: music. Office: Baptist Joint Com 200 Maryland Ave NE Ste 302 Washington DC 20002-5797 Office Phone: 336-758-4409. Business E-Mail: dunnj@wfu.edu. *All freedom is rooted in our being made in the image of God and is one aspect of the two-sided coin of freedom and responsibility. The two go together inextricably.*

DUNN, JAMES W., communications systems company executive; Various systems engring. and mgmt. positions Kearfott Divsn. Singer Co., 1966—78; engring. dir. ALR56C Radar Warning Receiver program Loral Corp., 1978, sr. v.p. engring. to sr. v.p. program mgmt., pres. Fairchild Systems, 1990; pres. Def. Systems Group and Fairchild Systems Lockheed Martin, pres. NESS Eagan, Akron and Archibald divsns., pres. Tactical Def. Systems; pres. Link Simulation & Tng. divsn. L-3 Comm. Holdings, Inc., NYC, 2000, sr. v.p., pres. Sensors & Simulation Group. Office: L-3 Comm Holdings Inc 600 Third Ave New York NY 10016 Office Phone: 212-697-1111. Office Fax: 212-805-5477.*

DUNN, JEFFREY A., lawyer; b. East Orange, NJ, July 26, 1951; BA cum laude, U. Kansas, 1973; JD, Georgetown U., 1976. Bar: Mo. 1976, Md. 1984, DC 1984, US Dist. Ct., DC & Md., US Supreme Ct. Ptnr., intellectual property litigation, commercial litigation, public contract law Venable LLP, Balt. Mem.: ABA, Md. Assn. of Defense Trial Counsel, Md. State Bar Assn., Balt. Bar Assn., DC Bar Assn. Avocation: flying. Office: Venable LLP 2 Hopkins Plaza 1800 Mercantile Bank & Trust Bldg Baltimore MD 21201 Office Phone: 410-244-7400. Office Fax: 410-244-7742. Business E-Mail: jadunn@venable.com.

DUNN, JEFFREY EDWARD, neurologist; b. Shaker Heights, Ohio, Nov. 27, 1960; s. John Kenneth and Mary Margaret (O'Neill) D.; m. Sandra Lee Judy, Feb. 3, 1990; children: Caitlin Irene, Bronwyn Leigh, Colin John Donald. BA in French Lit., Haverford Coll., Pa., 1983; MD, Temple U., 1989. Diplomate Am. Bd. Psychiatry and Neurology. Molecular immunologist Fox Chase Cancer Ctr., Phila., 1984-85; intern Ea. Va. Grad. Sch., Norfolk, 1989-90; resident in neurology U. Wash., Seattle, 1990-93, clin. prof. neurology, 1993—2004; attending physician Neurol. Assocs. Wash., Bellevue, 1993—2004; founder, med. dir. Overlake Multiple Sclerosis Ctr., Bellevue, Wash., 1996—2006; pres., chief med. officer MS Hub Med Group, Seattle, 2004—06; clinician, rschr. in clin. neuroimmunology Evergreen Neurosci. Inst., Kirkland, Wash., 2006—. Gen. mgr. Coventry Prodns., LLC, Redmond, Wash., 2005—. Guest physician TV: MS Update, Denver, 1994, ALS Update, Seattle, 1995, MS Ctr. Vision, Seattle, 2001, PBS Documentary on MS, 2005. Recipient Cert. of Excellence in MS Rx, Prodigy Online Com., 1995; named to Outstanding Young Men of Am., 1996. Fellow Royal Soc. Medicine; mem. Am. Acad. Neurology, Am. Neurol. Assn., World Congress Neurology, North Pacific Soc. of Psychiatry and Neurology, Pacific N.W. Alliance of MS Ctrs. Avocations: golf, skiing, camping, outdoor recreation. Office: Evergreen Neurosci Inst MS Ctr 12333 NE 130th Ln # 225 Kirkland WA 98034 E-mail: jedunn@evergreenhealthcare.org.

DUNN, JENNIFER BLACKBURN, former congresswoman; b. Seattle, July 29, 1941; d. John Charles and Helen (Gorton) Blackburn; div.; children: Bryant, Reagan. Student, U. Wash., 1960-62; BA in English Lit., Stanford U., 1963. Sys. engr. IBM, 1964-69; with King County Dept. of Assessments, 1979-80; former chmn. Rep. Party State of Wash., 1981-92; mem. U.S. Congress from 8th Wash. dist., Washington, 1993—2005. Bd. dirs. Nat. Endowment Democracy; mem. ways and means com., homeland sec. com., econ. com.; mem. adv. bd. Internat. Rep. Inst.; participant Preparatory Commn. World Conf. Status of Women, Nairobi, 1985, World Econ. Forum, Davos, Switzerland, 2000. Del. Rep. Nat. Conv., 1980, 84, 88; presdl. apptd. adv. coun. Historic Preservation, adv. coun. volunteerism SBA; apptd. presdl. commn. on debates; N.W. Regional Dir. Met. Operal Regional Auditions; mem. Jr. League of Seattle Named one of 25 Smartest Women in Am., Mirabella mag., one of 10 Most Powerful Women in Wash., Washington Law and Politics mag. Mem. Internat. Women's Forum (Wash. chpt.), Gamma Phi Beta. Republican.

DUNN, JOHN FRANCIS, lawyer, state representative; b. Logansport, Ind., Dec. 24, 1936; s. John Francis and Bertha (Newman) D.; m. Barbara Burke, Feb. 10, 1962; children: John F. III, Robert E., William M., Nancy L. BS in Chem. Engring., U. Notre Dame, 1958, JD, 1961. Bar: Ill. 1961, Ind. 1961, U.S. Dist. Ct. (so. dist.) Ill. 1961, U.S. Ct. Appeals (4th cir.) 1962. Atty. Standard Oil Ind. (now Amoco), Chgo., 1961-64; assoc. Morey and Dunn, Attys., Decatur, Ill., 1964-74; ptnr. Dunn and Fichter, Attys., Decatur, Ill., 1975-85; pvt. practice Decatur, Ill., 1986—. State rep. Ill. Gen. Assembly, Springfield, 1974-94, asst. majority leader; city councilman City of Decatur, 1971-74. Democrat. Roman Catholic. Avocations: bicycling, jogging. Office: 301 Millikin Ct Decatur IL 62523-1399

DUNN, JOHN RAYMOND, JR., stockbroker; b. Pittsfield, Mass., Aug. 24, 1937; s. John Raymond and Margaret Mary (Coyne) D.; 1 child, John Raymond III. AB, Boston Coll., 1960. Ins. agt. John Hancock Ins. Co., Boston, 1964-67; dist. mgr. Nat. Life Ins. Co., Montpelier, Vt., 1967-74; gen. agt. United Life & Accident Ins. Co., Concord, NH, 1974—; stockbroker, regional mgr. Cornerstone Fin. Svcs., Inc., Boston, 1974-80; stockbroker, br. mgr. Weinrich, Zitzman, Whitehead Fin. Svcs., Inc., St. Louis, 1980—; pres. Dunn Assocs., Amherst, Mass., 1965—; br. mgr. Jefferson Pilot Securities Corp., 1998—. Field adv. mem. Pres. Adv. Coun. CFS-Div. Weinrich, Zitzman, Whitehead, Inc., 1982—; named to gen. agts. adv. com. Chubb Life Am./Chubb Securities Corp., 1988-89; dist. mgr. Chubb Securities Leaders' Club; lectr. in field. Author seminar: Let's Make Money; freelance writer Investment Dealer Digest, 1980; film prodr. Ernest Hemingway documentary. Dir. Parents and Tchrs. for Social Responsibility, Moretown, Vt., 1982-85. Mem. White Mountain Club (Club award 1984-92), Summit Club, Life U.S.A. Club, Chmns. Club., Pres. Club. Roman Catholic. Fax: 413-253-9356.

DUNN, JON MICHAEL, logician, dean; b. Ft. Wayne, Ind., June 19, 1941; s. Jon Hardin and Philomena Elizabeth (Lauer) D.; m. Sarah Jane Hutchison, Aug. 8, 1964; children— Jon William, Jennifer Anne AB, Oberlin Coll., 1963; PhD, U. Pitts., 1966. Asst. prof. philosophy Wayne State U., Detroit, 1966-69; vis. asst. prof. philosophy Yale U., New Haven, 1968-69; assoc. prof. philosophy Ind. U., Bloomington, 1969-76, prof., 1976—, Oscar Ewing prof. philosophy, 1989—2007, chmn. dept. philosophy, 1980-84, 94-97, adj. prof. computer sci., 1987-89, prof., 1989—2007, assoc. dean Coll. Arts and Scis., 1988-91, exec. assoc. dean, 1991-93, dean. Sch. Informatics, 2000—07, prof. informatics, 2002—07, prof. emeritus, 2007—. Vis. fellow Inst. Advanced Studies, Australian Nat. U., Canberra, 1975-76; sr. visitor Math. Inst., U. Oxford, Eng., 1978; faculties vis. scholar U. Melbourne, Australia, 1983; fellow Ind. U. Inst. for Advanced Study, 1984; sr. visitor Ctr. for Philosophy of Sci., U. Pitts., Nov. 1984; adj. prof. U. Mass., Amherst, spring 1985; NSF prin. investigator, 1969-74. Author: (with G. Hardegree) Algebraic Methods in Philosophical Logic, 2001; contbg. author: Entailment, Vol. I, 1975, co-author Vol. II, 1992; editor: (with A. Gupta) Truth or Consequences: Essays in Honor of Nuel Belnap, 1990, (with G. Epstein) Modern Uses of Multiple-Valued Logic, 1975, (with G. Hardegree) Algebraic Methods in Philosophical Logic, 2001; editor Jour. Symbolic Logic, 1982-87; chief editor Jour. Philos. Logic, 1987-95; N.Am. editor Bull. Logic Sect., Polish Acad. Scis.; mem. editl. bds. Jour. Philos. Logic, 1979-87, Nous, 1968—, Studia Logica, 1978-2000, Jour. Non-Classical Logic, 1985-91, Annals of Math., Computing and Teleinformatics, Logic and Logical Philosophy, 1993—. Recipient Ind. U. Provost's medal, 2007, Sagamore Wabash award, 2007; Am. Council Learned Socs. fellow, 1984-85; Fulbright-Hays rsch. sr. scholar, 1975-76. Mem. Assn. Symbolic Logic (exec. com. 1978-81, coun. 1982—), Soc. Exact Philosophy (treas. 1982-84, v.p. 1986-88, pres. 1988-90), Am. Philos. Assn. (com. rsch. and publs. 1985-88), Computing Rsch. Assn. (vice chair IT deans group 2004-06). Office: Ind U Sch Informatics 901 E 10th St Bloomington IN 47408

DUNN, KENNETH B., dean; b. Ohio, Nov. 2, 1951; m. Pamela Dunn; children: Brett, Amy. BBA, Ohio State U., 1974, MBA, 1976; PhD in Indsl. Adminstrn., Purdue U., 1979. Asst. prof. indsl. adminstrn. Carnegie Mellon U., 1979, prof. fin. and economics, 1987—89; dean Carnegie Mellon Kepper Sch. Bus., 2002—, also prof. fin. economics; Leslie Wong disting. prof. U. British Columbia, 1986; joined Miller Anderson & Sherrerd, 1987, named ptnr., 1989; (Miller Anderson & Sherrerd acquired by Morgan Stanley 1996); mng. dir. Morgan Stanley Investment Mgmt.; co-dir. US Core Fixed Income Team and Morgan Stanley's Mortgage Team. Assoc. editor: Jour. Fixed Income. Trustee Friends' Ctrl. Sch., Phila., chair investment com.; trustee Ardmore United Meth. Ch., Pa. Office: Dean's Office Carnegie Mellon Univ Tepper Sch Bus 5000 Forbes Ave Pittsburgh PA 15213-3890 Office Phone: 412-268-2265. Office Fax: 412-268-8163. Business E-Mail: kbdunn@andrew.cmu.edu.*

DUNN, LEO JAMES, obstetrician, gynecologist, educator; b. Trenton, NJ, May 23, 1931; s. Augustine Leo and Molly (McDaid) Dunn; m. Betty Beatrice Buchanan, Aug. 28, 1954; children: Laurie, Cary. AB, Hofstra U., 1952; MD, Columbia U., 1956. Diplomate Am. Bd. Ob-Gyn., Am. Bd. Gyn. Oncology. Intern Cin. Gen. Hosp., 1956—57; resident Sloane Hosp for Women, Columbia-Presbyn. Med. Ctr., 1957—62; asst. prof. ob-gyn U. Iowa Coll. Medicine, Iowa City, 1962—65, assoc. prof. ob-gyn, 1965—67; prof., former chmn. dept. Med. Coll. Va., Richmond, 1967—, interim dean, chmn. of dept. Ob-Gyn., 1983—85, prof. emeritus; pres. Am. Bd. Med. Specialties, 1998—2000. Bd. dirs. Am. Bd. Ob-Gyn, 1975—, pres., 1982—; mem. Nat. Bd. Med. Examiners, 1979—83. Recipient Silver medal as disting. alumnus, Columbia U. Coll. Physicians and Surgeons, 1967; scholar Markle, 1963. Fellow: ACOG (dist. v.p. 1976—78); mem.: Va. Ob-Gyn. Soc. (pres. 1981—82), Am. Assn. Ob-Gyn. (coun. 1975—79, pres. found. 1980—82, trustee 1975—82), Soc. Gynecol. Oncology (chmn. program com., v.p.), Phi Beta Kappa. Office: Med Coll Va MCV Station PO Box 980034 Richmond VA 23298-0034

DUNN, LINDA BAUGH, middle school educator; b. Richmond, Va., Feb. 18, 1949; d. Haywood Ambrose and Dorothy Johnson Baugh; children: Melinda Dunn Lawson, Rhonda Dunn White, Ashlee Monique Easter, Alyssa Lenee' Easter, Brandon Jamil Easter. Student, John Tyler C.C., Chester, Va., 1968—70; BA in English, Va. Commonwealth U., Richmond, Va., 1993, M in Tchg., 1993. Cert. tchr. Va., 1993. Tutor John Tyler CC, Chester, Va., 1969—70; substitute tchr. Richmond Pub. Schs., 1970—72, 1976—78; unit clerk Med. Coll. Va., 1972—75, med. rsch. asst., 1975—76; photocopy technician Va. Employment Commn., Richmond, 1978—90; rsch. asst. Va. Commonwealth U., Richmond, 1992—93; tchr. Richmond Pub. Schs., 1993—. Tchr. asst. Garfield F. Childs Meml. Fund Afternoon Tutorial, 1991; writer English curriculum Richmond Pub. Schs., 1996, coord. 21st Century Afternoon Tutorial, 2004—06, English dept. chair, 2004—; Elkhardt Sch. coord. Johns Hopkins U.'s Ctr. for Talented Youth, 2000; coord. 21st Century Summer and Afternoon Tutorial, 2004—06; presenter in field. Contbr. articles to profl. jours. Nominee Elkhardt Mid. Sch. Tchr. of Yr., Colleagues Elkhardt Mid. Sch., 1995, Ttchr. of Yr., Disney, 1996. Mem.: NEA, Assn. for Supervision of Curriculum Devel., Internat. Reading Assn., Nat. Mid. Sch. Assn. Avocations: travel, reading, collecting trinket boxes. Office: Richmond Public Schools Elkhardt Middle 6300 Hull Street Road Richmond VA 23224 Office Phone: 804-745-3600. Office Fax: 804-674-5518. Personal E-mail: ldunn@richmond.k12.va.us.

DUNN, LINDA KAY, retired physician; b. Grand Rapids, Mich., Jan. 11, 1947; d. Roger John and Mary Kathryn (Bouwer) Kloote; m. Jeffrey Marc Dunn, June 3, 1972; children: David Alan, Kathryn Ann. AB in Chemistry, Hope Coll., 1968; MD, U. Mich., 1972. Diplomate Am. Bd. Ob-Gyn, Am. Bd. Maternal-Fetal Medicine, Am. Bd. Med. Genetics. Resident in ob-gyn. U. Mich., Ann Arbor, 1972-75, fellow in maternal-fetal medicine, 1975-77; hon. rsch. registrar St. Mary's Hosp., London, 1977-78; dir. of perinatology Temple U. Sch. Medicine, Phila., 1978-79, assoc. prof. ob-gyn, 1991-97; dir. subsect. on genetics Pa. Hosp., Phila., 1980-90; pres Medigen, Inc., Phila., 1987-90; dir. maternal-fetal medicine and genetics Abington (Pa.) Meml. Hosp., 1991-97; dir. maternal-fetal medicine, chair dept. ob-gyn. Allegheny U., 1997—99; pres., CEO Allegheny U. Hosp. at City Av.; chair dept. ob-gyn. Chestnut Hill Hosp., Phila., 1999—2007; ret., 2007. Med. dir. Comprehensive Maternal and Infant Svcs., Phila., 1987-90; pres. Abington Perinatal Assocs., P.C., 1993-97. Fellow Am. Coll. Ob-Gyn.; mem. AMA, Soc. Maternal Fetal Medicine, Am. Soc. Human Genetics, Am. Coll. Med. Genetics, Pa. State Med. Soc., Phila. Obstet. Soc., U. Mich. Med. Ctr. Alumni Soc. (chair 1996), Norman Miller Gynecologic Soc. (pres. 1996). Mem. Soc. Of Friends. Avocations: travel, piano.

DUNN, MARTIN, editor-in-chief; b. England, Jan. 26, 1955; Journalist Dudley Herald, England, 1974—77, Evening Mail, Birmingham, England, 1977, Birmingham Post, England, 1978, Daily Mail, London, 1978—79, News of the World, London, 1979—83; NY corr. Sun, London, 1984—88, dep. editor, 1989—91; editor Today, London, 1991—93, Boston Herald, 1993; editor-in-chief NY Daily News, 1993—96; editor in chief Assoc. New Media, London, 1996—2000; pres. Front of Mind, London, 2000; editl. dir., dep. pub. NY Daily News, 2003—, editor-in-chief, dep. pub., 2006—. Cons. Assoc. Newspapers. Office: NY Daily News 450 W 33rd St New York NY 10001-2681*

DUNN, MARVIN IRVIN, physician; b. Topeka, Dec. 21, 1927; s. Louis and Ida (Leibtag) D.; m. Maureen Cohen, Mar. 10, 1956 (dec. Nov. 1988); children: Jonathan Louis, Marilyn Paulette. BA, U. Kans., 1950, MD, 1954. Intern USPHS, San Francisco, 1954-55; resident U. Kans., 1955-58, fellow, 1958-59, instr. medicine, 1958-60, assoc. in medicine, 1960-62, asst. prof. medicine, 1962-65, assoc. prof., 1965-70, prof., 1970-2000, prof. emeritus, 2001—, Franklin E. Murphy Disting. prof., 1978-2000, dir. Cardiovascular Lab., head sect. Cardiovascular Disease Med. Center, 1963-92, dean Sch. of Medicine, 1979-84. Cons. USAF, 1971—95; spl. cons. to fed. air surgeon of FAA, 1990—; spl. ednl. cons. to Kansas City Mo. Met. Coll. Author: Home Study Course: Difficult EKG Diagnosis, 1969, Translator Deductive and Polyparametric Electrocardiography, 1970; (with others) Clinical Vectorcardiography and Electrocardiography, 2d edit., 1977, Clinical Electrocardiography, 8th edit., 1989; editor in chief Cardiovascular Perspectives, 1985-89; mem. editl. bd. Am. Jour. Cardiology, 1970-75, Catheterization and Cardiovascular Diagnosis, 1980-87, AMA Archives Internal Medicine, 1984-94, Jour. Am. Coll. Cardiology, 1983-89, Biomedicine and Pharmacotherapy, 1985-90, Am. Jour. Noninvasive Cardiology, 1985-89, Chest, 1984-89, 94-98, Practical Cardiology, 1980-88, Heart and Lung, 1986-88, Bd.-Advanced in Therapy, 1992, Slovak Jour. Noninvasive Cardiology, 1993, Griffith Resource Libr., 1980-90, Am. Heart Jour., Jour. Acoustical Soc.; mem. internat. sci. bd. Italian Heart Jour., 2005—. Bd. dirs. Hebrew Acad. Jewish Geriatric and Convalescent Center, Beth Shalom Synagogue. Served with AUS, 1946-47. Recipient Alumnus of Yr. award U. Kansas Sch. Medicine, 1987, silver medal U. Socrates, Thessaloniki, Greece, 1992. Master Am. Coll. Chest Physicians (mem. bd. regents, pres. 1988-89, gov. State of Kans.); fellow ACP (Laureate award 1990), Am. Coll. Cardiology (trustee), Am. Heart Assn., Royal Acad. Medicine (Ireland), Royal Coll. Physicians (Valencia, Spain); mem. Am. Physicians Fellowship (dir.), Univ. Cardiologists, Alpha Omega Alpha, Phi Chi (cited Best Doctors in Am., 1998). Home: 3205 Tomahawk Rd Shawnee Mission KS 66208-1861 Office: U Kans Hosp 3901 Rainbow Blvd Kansas City KS 66160-0001 *My small modicum of success was achieved by hard work, dedication to a single goal, and an application of total energy in achieving this goal. Open-mindedness, imaginativeness, and fair play have helped to make the road easier.*

DUNN, MARY MAPLES, academic administrator; b. Sturgeon Bay, Wis., Apr. 6, 1931; d. Frederic Arthur and Eva (Moore) Maples; m. Richard S. Dunn, Sept. 3, 1960; children— Rebecca Cofrin, Cecilia Elizabeth. BA, Coll. William and Mary, 1954, LHD (hon.), 1989; MA, Bryn Mawr Coll., 1956, PhD, 1959; LLD (hon.), Marietta Coll., 1987, Amherst Coll., 1987, Brown U., 1989; LittD (hon.), Lafayette Coll., 1988, Haverford Coll., 1991; LHD (hon.), Transylvania U., 1991, U. Pa., 1995, Mt. Holyok Coll., 1996, Smith Coll., 1998, U. Mass., 1998, U. South, 1999. Faculty Bryn Mawr Coll., 1958-85, prof. history, 1974-85; acting dean Undergrad. Coll. Bryn Mawr (Pa.) Coll., 1978-79, dean, 1980-85; pres. Smith Coll., Northampton, Mass., 1985-95; Carl and Lily Pforzheimer Found. dir. Arthur and Elizabeth Libr. Radcliffe Coll., 1995-99; acting pres., acting dean radcliffe Coll., Inst. for Advanced Study, Harvard U., 1999—2000. Author: William Penn: Politics and Conscience, 1967; editor: Political Essay on the Kingdom of New Spain (Alexander von Humboldt), 1972, rev., 1988, (with Richard S. Dunn) Papers of William Penn, vols. I-IV, 1979-87. Trustee The Clark Sch. for the Deaf, 1988-95, Acad. Mus., 1985-95, Hist. Deerfield, Inc., 1986—, Bingham Fund for Teaching Excellence at Transylvania U., 1987—, John Carter Brown Libr., 1994-99, NOW/Legal Def. and Edn. Fund., 1996—, Marlboro Music, 1996—. Recipient Disting. Tchg. award Lindbeck Found., 1969, Radcliffe medal Radcliffe Assn., 2001; fellow Inst. Advanced Study Princeton U., 1974. Mem. Berkshire Conf. Women Historians (pres. 1973-75), Coordinating Com. Women Hist. Profession (pres. 1975-77), Am. Hist. Assn., Am. Philos. Soc. (co-exec. officer 2002—), Inst. Early Am. History and Culture (chmn. adv. council 1977-80), Mass. Hist. Soc., Phi Beta Kappa. Office: American Philosophical Society Exec Office 104 S Fifth St Philadelphia PA 19106-3287

DUNN, MELVIN EDWARD, retired judge; b. Chgo., Oct. 31, 1933; s. Raymond E. and Josephine (Fitzgerald) D.; m. Judith Wilkinson, Oct. 28, 1972; children: Lori Dunn, Richard A. Vester Jr., Jonathan T. Vester, Geoffrey A. Vester, Andrea Lynn Dunn. JD, Ill. Inst. Tech., 1971. Bar: Ill. 1971. Owner Melvin E. Dunn, Ltd., Elburn, Ill., 1972-82; assoc. judge 16th Jud. Cir., Kane County, Ill., 1982-86; cir. judge, 1986-98; presiding judge family divsn., 1988-89; presiding judge chancery/probate divsn., 1993-98; presiding judge felony divsn., 1990—92. Served with USCG, 1952-56. Mem. Am. Acad. Matrimonial Lawyers (bd. mgrs. Ill. chpt.), Ill. Bar Assn. (chmn. family law sect. coun.). Lutheran. Personal E-mail: pelicanonmarco@cs.com.

DUNN, MICHAEL J., dean; m. Patricia O'Reilly; 5 children. MD, Med. Coll. of Wisconsin, 1962. Intern Johns Hopkins Hosp, Baltimore, 1962—63, resident, 1963—65; asst. prof. & co-dir., nephrology unit U. Vermont Coll. Medicine, 1969—77; various pos. Case Western Reserve, 1977—95; dean, prof. of med. and exec v.p. Med. Coll. Wis., Milw., 1995—. Grantee Fogarty Senior International Fellow. Mem.: Am. Soc. Nephrology (pres. 1989—90). Office: Med Coll Wis Office of the Dean 8701 W Watertown Plank Rd Milwaukee WI 53226-3548

DUNN, MICHAEL M., military association executive, retired military officer; b. 1950; BS in Astrodynamics, USAF Acad., 1972; grad., Squadron Officer Sch., 1976; MS in Sys. Mgmt., U. So. Calif., 1981; grad., Air Command & Staff Coll., 1983; nat. security mgmt. course, 1984; grad., Air War Coll., 1986. Commd. 2d lt. USAF, 1972, advanced through grades to lt. gen., 2003; student pilot training Moody AFB, Ga., 1972—73; student F-106 Tyndall AFB, Fla., 1973—74; instr. pilot, standardization & evaluating officer & weapons officer 84th Fighter Interceptor Squad, 1974—78; action officer Air Staff tng. program, sec. Air Force legis. liaison, Washington, 1978-79; instr. pilot, chief of tactics, R&D Interceptor Weapons Sch., Tyndall AFB, Fla., 1979-82; F-15 pilot, chief plans, programs, spl. projects 18th Tactical Fighter Wing, Kadena Air Base, Japan, 1983-85; F-15 pilot, dir. fighter ops. Hdqs. 5th Air Force, Yokota Air Base, Japan, 1985—88; div. chief Pacific East divsn., dir. plans, dep. chief staff Hdqs. USAF, Washington, 1989-90, dep. asst. dir. Joint Nat. Security Coun. Matters, 1991, exec. asst. to dep. chief of staff, plans and ops., 1991-92; comdr. 1st Ops. Group 1st Fighter Wing, Langley AFB, Va., 1992-93; divsn. chief strategy, resources, legis. affairs divsn. U.S. European Command, Stuttgart, Germany, 1993-94, exec. officer to dep. comdr. in chief, 1994-95; sr. mil. fellow Coun. on Fgn. Rels., NYC, 1995-96; sr. mil. asst. to dep. sec. US Dept. Def., Washington, 1996-97; dir. plans and programs Hdqs. Pacific Air Forces, Hickam AFB, Hawaii, 1997-99; dep. chief staff UN Command and Forces Korea Youngsan Army Garrison, Seoul, Republic of Korea, 1999—2001; vice dir. strategic plans & policy, The Joint Staff The Pentagon, Washington, 2001—03; pres. Nat. Def. U., Washington, 2003—06; pres., CEO Air Force Assn., Arlington, Va., 2007—. Decorated Def. Disting. Svc. medal with oak leaf cluster, Def.

Superior Svc. medal, Legion of Merit, Meritorious Svc. medal with 3 oak leaf clusters, Air Force Commendation medal with two oak leaf clusters. Office: Air Force Assn 1501 Lee Highway Arlington VA 22209*

DUNN, MICHAEL V., commissioner; m. Brook Dunn; 2 children. Acting under sec. rural econ. and comty. devel. USDA, Washington, 1994-95, asst. sec. agr. for mktg. and regulatory programs, 1995-98, undersec. for mktg. and regulation program, 1998—2001; mem. bd. Farm Credit Assn., 2001, dir., 2002—04; commr. Commodity Futures Trading Commn., 2004—. Housing dir., adminstr. City of Keokuk, Iowa; chair Iowa State's City Devel. Bd.; former commr. Iowa Devel. Commn.; staff specialist farm credit and rural devel. Senate Com. Agriculture, Nutrition and Forestry; v.p. Nat. Farmers Union, Washington; Midwest dir. Farmers Home Adminstrn., 1977-81, adminstr., 1993-94. Office: Commodity Futures Trading Commn Three Lafayette Ctr 1155 21st St NW Washington DC 20581

DUNN, M(ORRIS) DOUGLAS, lawyer; b. Ionia, Mich., Nov. 1, 1944; s. Morris Frederick and Lola Adella (Gee) D.; m. Jill Lynn Fasbender, July 22, 1967; children: Brooks, Gillian, Joshua. BSME, U. Mich., 1967; JD, Vanderbilt U., 1970. Bar: NY 1970, US Dist. Ct. (so. dist.) NY 1972, US Ct. Appeals (2d cir.) 1973, US Supreme Ct. 1978. Assoc. Winthrop Stimson, Putnam & Roberts, NYC, 1970-78, ptnr., 1978-84; sr. v.p., mng. dir. Shearson Lehman Bros., Inc., NYC, 1984-85; ptnr. Milbank, Tweed, Hadley & McCloy, NYC, 1985—. Mem. nat. coun. law sch. Vanderbilt U., 2006—; bd. trustees bus. rsch. inst. CBR Inst. Biomed. Rsch., 2006—. Contbr. articles to profl. jours. Fellow: Am. Bar Found.; mem.: ABA (fed. regulation of securities com. bus. law sect. 1981—, chair pub. utility, comms. and transp. law sect. 1997—98, bd.govs. 1998—2001), Internat. Bar Assn. (com. chmn. 1990—94), Assn. Bar City NY, Grey Oaks Country Club, Canoe Brook Country Club, Down Town Assn. Office: Milbank Tweed Hadley & McCloy LLP 1 Chase Manhattan Plz Fl 47 New York NY 10005-1413 Home Phone: 973-644-2680; Office Phone: 212-530-5062. Business E-Mail: mdunn@milbank.com.

DUNN, PHILIP J., retail executive; Asst. controller Circuit City, 1984—90, treas., 1990—92, v.p., treas., 1992—96, v.p., treas., contr., 1996—99, sr. v.p., treas., controller Richmond, Va., 1999—. Office: Circuit City 9950 Mayland Dr Richmond VA 23233-1464*

DUNN, RANDALL LAWSON, judge; b. Gary, Ind., May 28, 1950; s. Jack Harold Wheeler and Doris Marjorie (Rose) D.; m. Laurie Marie Loomis, Sept. 17, 1954; children: Jonathan Loomis, Andrew Jack. BA with honors, Northwestern U., Evanston, Ill., 1972; JD, Stanford U., 1975. Bar: Oreg., Wash., U.S. Dist.Ct. Oreg., U.S. Dist. Ct. Utah, U.S. Ct. Appeals (9th and 10th cirs.), U.S. Dist. Ct. (ea. and we. dists.) Wash. Law clk. Hon. James J. Richards Chief Judge Superior Ct. Lake County, Hammond, Ind., 1973-74; assoc. Berman & Giauque, Salt Lake City, 1975-76; assoc., ptnr. to mng. ptnr. Copeland, Landye, Bennett & Wolf, Portland, Oreg., 1977—98; apptd. bankruptcy judge US Dist. Ct. Oreg., 1998—. Articles editor Stanford Law Rev., 1974-75; editor-in-chief Bankruptcy Briefs, 1991-95; cons. editor Fed. Bar News and Jour., 1994; editor-in-chief, author Oreg. Debtor Creditor Newsletter, 1988-95. Pres., treas., bd. dirs. Beaverton (Oreg.) Arts. Commn., 1986-92; pres., bd. dirs. Portland Festival Symphony, 1985—98; chmn. West Sylvan Mid. Sch. Funding Com., Portland, 1993. Mem. ABA (sects. on antitrust, corp. banking and bus. law), Oreg. State Bar Assn. (sects. on antitrust, debtor/creditor, treas. exec. com.), Fed. Bar Assn. (chmn. exec. com. bankruptcy sect. 1994-95), Wash. State Bar Assn. (sects. on creditor, debtor, corp., bus. and banking law), Am. Fedn. Musicians. Avocations: playing the clarinet, weightlifting, reading, gardening. Office: 1001 SW 5th Ave Ste 700 Portland OR 97204-1141 Office Phone: 503-326-1538.

DUNN, RANDY EDWIN, lawyer; b. Hutchinson, Kans., Oct. 8, 1954; s. Roy Edwin and Joan Irene (Farney) D.; m. Michelle Renee Sandwith, Dec. 18, 1976 (div. Aug. 1979); 1 child, Brandi Dawn Sandwith; m. Rosalind O'Nita Heiman, Dec. 22, 1990. BA magna cum laude, Wichita State U., 1977; JD, U. Colo., 1983. Bar: Colo. 1983, U.S. Dist. Ct. Colo. 1986. Store and sales mgr. Pop Shoppe, Inc., Wichita, Kans., 1976-77; sales rep. Lifesavers, Inc., Wichita, 1977-80; asst. mgr. Quik Trip, Inc., Wichita, 1980; assoc. McIntyre & Varallo, P.C., Greeley, Colo., 1983-85; pvt. practice law Denver, 1985-87; ptnr. Dean & Dunn, P.C., Denver, 1987-89; assoc. Lau & Choi, P.C., Denver, 1989-90, Baker & Hostetler, Denver, 1991, Hopper & Kanouff, P.C., Denver, 1991-95; pvt. practice law Denver, 1995—; assoc. Clanahan, Tanner, Downing, and Knowlton P.C., 1997—2002, Ireland, Stapleton, Pryor, & Pascoe, P.C., 2002—04, Sage & Vargo, P.C., Lakewood, Colo., 2004—05, Dean, Dunn & Phillips LLC, Denver, 2005—. Mem. ABA, Colo. Bar Assn., Denver Bar Assn., Masons. Democrat. Office: Ste 703 4155 E Jewell Ave Denver CO 80222 Office Phone: 303-756-6744. E-mail: randy@lawatddp.com.

DUNN, RANDY J., academic administrator; b. Aledo, Ill., July 5, 1958; s. Charles A. and Shirley A. (Forrest) D.; m. Laurie R. Waltrip, Dec. 17, 1977; children: Lindsey S., Erin L. BS in Edn., Ill. State U., 1980, MS in Edn., 1983; EdD, U. Ill., 1991. Tchr. Gibson City Schs., Ill., 1980-83; prin. Lee Ctr. Schs., Paw Paw, Ill., 1983-84, Roanoke Benson Schs., Ill., 1984-89; supt. Argenta Oreana Schs., Ill., 1989-91, Chester Pub. Schs., Ill., 1991; chair Dept. of Ednl. Adminstrn. and Higher Edn. So. Ill. U., Carbondale, 1995—2004; interim supt. edn. State of Ill., 2004—05, supt. edn., 2005—07; pres. Murray State U., Ky., 2007—. Cons. Ednl. Svc., Ottawa, Ill., 1991—; trainer Ctr. #9 Administrs.' Acad. Contbr. articles to profl. jours. Chair United Way, Decatur, Ill., 1989; active Argenta Civic Club, 1989-91, Macon County Rural Leaders, Decatur, 1990-91, Chester Mcpl. Band, Chester, 1992—. Rsch. grantee Ill. Assn. Sch. Bds., Springfield, 1991. Mem. ASCD, Am. Assn. Sch. Adminstrs., Ill. Assn. Sch. Adminstrs., Univ. Ill. Ednl. Adminstrn. Alumni Assn. Avocations: travel, reading. Office: Office of Pres 218 Wells Hall Murray State U Murray KY 42071 Office Phone: 270-809-3763. Office Fax: 270-809-3413. E-mail: randy.dunn@murraystate.edu.*

DUNN, RICHARD JOSEPH, retired investment advisor; b. Chgo., Apr. 5, 1924; s. Richard Joseph and Margaret Mary (Jennett) Dunn; m. Marygrace Calhoun, Oct. 13, 1951 (dec. May 2000); children: Richard, Robert(dec.) , Marianne, Anthony, Gregory, Noelle. AB, Yale U., New Haven, Conn., 1948; JD, Harvard U., Cambridge, Mass., 1951; MBA, Stanford U., Calif., 1956. Bar: Tex. 1952. Mem. Carrington, Gowan, Johnson & Walker, Dallas, 1951-54; investment counselor Scudder, Stevens & Clark, San Francisco, 1956-84, gen. ptnr., 1974-84, ret., 1984. Mem. Sovereign Coun., Rome, 1999—2004. With AUS US Army, 1943—46. Decorated Combat Inf. badge, Purple Heart, Bronze Star, Bailiff Grand Cross of Honor and Devotion Obedience of the Sovereign Mil. Hospitaller Order St. John of Jersusalem Rhodes and Malta, knight comdr. with star Papal Order St. Gregory. Roman Catholic.

DUNN, RICHARD M., lawyer; b. Coral Gables, Fla., Sept. 3, 1945; s. Raymond Melvin and Mary Louise Dunn; children: Megan, Emily. BBA, U. Notre Dame, 1967; JD, U. Miami, 1970. Bar: (so. dist.) Fla. (US Dist. Ct.) 1971, (mid. dist.) Fla. 1978, (no. dist.) Fla. 1979, US Ct. Appeals: (5th cir.) 1971, (11th cir.) 1981, US Supreme Court: 1976. Capt. US Army, 1967—77. Mem.: ABA (chair torts and ins. practices aviation and space law com.), Internat. Assoc. Def. Coun. Avocation: tennis. Home: 125 Sans Souci Coral Gables FL 33133 Office: Cozen O'Connor 200 S Biscayne Blvd Ste 4410 Miami FL 33131-2303 Home Phone: 305-667-5338; Office Phone: 305-704-5940. Office Fax: 305-704-5955. Business E-Mail: rdunn@cozen.com.

DUNN, ROBERT LAWRENCE, lawyer; b. Westerly, RI, Jan. 2, 1938; m. Sammie Louise Sanford (dec. Sept. 1999); children: Christopher Jon, Geoffrey Robert; m. Linda Elizabeth Barry, 2003. BA, Cornell U., 1958; JD magna cum laude, Harvard U., 1962. Bar: N.Y. 1962, Calif. 1966, U.S. Dist. Ct. (no. dist.) Calif. 1966, U.S. Ct. Appeals (9th cir.) 1966, U.S. Dist. Ct. (ea. dist.) Calif. 1970, U.S. Supreme Ct. 1984, U.S. Dist. Ct. (cen. dist.) Calif. 1987. Law clk. to cir. judge U.S. Cir. Ct., Hartford, Conn., 1962-63; assoc. Paul, Weiss, Rifkind, Wharton & Garrison, NYC, 1963-65, Bancroft, Avery & McAlister, San Francisco, 1965-71; ptnr. Bancroft & McAlister, San Francisco, 1971-93, Cooper, White & Cooper, San Francisco, 1993-99; corp. counsel Real Restaurants, Sausalito, Calif., 1999—. Author: Recovery of Damages for Lost Profits, 1978, rev. edit., 2005, Recovery of Damages for Fraud, rev. edit., 2004, Expert Witnesses: Law and Practice, 1996, Winning with Expert Witnesses in Commercial Litigation, 2003; contbr. articles to profl. jours. Planning commn. Town of Corte Madera, Calif. 1974-78, town coun., 1978-84, mayor, 1979, 82; bd. dirs. Merola Opera Program, 1995—, Philharmonia Baroque Orch., San Francisco, 1991-94. 1st lt. U.S. Army, 1958-59. Mem.: Ferrari Club Am. (bd. dirs. pacific region 2007—). Avocations: travel, opera, literature. E-mail: attydunn@comcast.net.

DUNN, RONNIE GENE, musician; b. Coleman, Tex., June 1, 1953; div.; children: Whitney, Jesse Wayne; m. Janine Dunn. With Brooks & Dunn, 1988—; recording artist Artista, 1991—. Singer: (albums) (with Kix Brooks) Brand New Man, 1991 (Acad. Country Music award Album of Yr., 1992), Hard Workin' Man, 1993 (Grammy award Best Country Vocal Performance by Duo or Group for "Hard Workin' Man", 1993), Waitin' on Sundown, 1994, Borderline, 1996 (Grammy award Best Country Vocal Performance by Duo or Group for "My Maria", 1996), Greatest Hits Collection, 1997, If You See Her, 1998, Tight Rope, 1999, Super Hits, 1999, Steers and Stripes, 2001, It Won't Be Christmas Without You, 2002, Red Dirt Road, 2003, Greatest Hits Collection: Volume II, 2004, Hillbilly Deluxe, 2005 (Single of Yr., Song of Yr. & Music Video of Yr. for Believe, Country Music Assn. Awards, 2006, Song of Yr. for Believe, Acad. Country Music, 2006), (singles) Boot Scootin' Boogie, 1992, We'll Burn That Bridge, 1993, Rock My World (Little Country Girl), 1993, (songs) (8 Seconds soundtrack) Ride 'Em High, Ride 'Em Low, 1994, (with Hank Thompson) Hooked on Honky Tonk, 1997, (with Reba McEntire) If You See Him, If You See Her, 1998; background vocals, chorus: albums T-r-o-u-b-l-e (Travis Tritt), 1992, appears on: albums Common Thread: The Songs of the Eagles, 1994 (Country Music Assn. Album of Yr., 1994). Co-recipient Top New Vocal Duo or Group award, Acad. Country Music, 1991, Entertainer of Yr. award, 1995, 1996, 2001, Top Vocal Duo award, 1991—97, 2000—03, 2005—07, Vocal Event of Yr. award, 2007, Home Depot Humanitarian award, 2007, Vocal Duo Yr. award, Country Music Assn., 1992—99, 2001—06, Entertainer of Yr. award, 1994, Favorite Country Group award, Am. Music Awards, 2004, 2005. Office: Brooks and Dunn PO Box 120669 Nashville TN 37212-0669

DUNN, TERRENCE P., manufacturing executive; b. Oct. 14, 1949; BA, Rockhurst Coll.; MBA, U. Miss. With Dunn Indus. (formerly J.E. Dunn Construction Co.), 1974—; pres., CEO Dunn Indus., Kansas City, Mo. Office: Dunn Industries 929 Holmes St Kansas City MO 64106-2639

DUNN, THOMAS E., lawyer; b. Salem, Oreg., June 17, 1966; BA, Coll. William & Mary, 1987; JD, Duke Univ., 1992. Bar: NY 1993. Assoc. Cravath Swaine & Moore LLP, NYC, 1992—2000, ptnr., corp., 2000—. Mem.: ABA, Assn. of Bar of City of NY. Office: Cravath Swaine & Moore LLP Worldwide Plz 825 Eighth Ave New York NY 10019-7475 Office Phone: 212-474-1108. Office Fax: 212-474-3700. Business E-Mail: tdunn@cravath.com.

DUNN, VIRGINIA, artist; b. Long Island, NY, Dec. 11, 1951; d. James Joseph and Margaret Virginia Dunn. Student, Marymount Coll., Boca Raton, Fla., Lynn U., 1970—71, SUNY, Purchase, 1972-75, Propersie Sch. of Art, Conn., 1975—76, Silvermine Art Ctr. Nurse's aide St. Joseph's Hosp., Stamford, Conn., 1967-70; with advt. dept. Cuisinart, Greenwich, Conn., 1977-89; tchr. oriental painting Newton Studios. One-woman shows include Greenwich Hosp., 2002, Garden Cafe, Greenwich, 2002, Nathaniel Witheral, exhibitions include Hurlbutt Gallery, Greenwich Libr., various yrs., Conn., Gertrude White Gallery, Greenwich, 1998—2002, Greenwich Garden Ctr., Cos Cob, Conn., 1989—2002 (honorable mention, 2002, 2d place, 2 honorable mentions), Ferguson Libr., Stamford, Conn., 1993—2002 (Koi Fish Chinese Hon Mention, 3d Pl. award, 2001, 2002, 2002, 2003), Hammond Mus. & Japanese Stroll Garden, North Salem, NY, 1993—2006, Whitby Sch., Greenwich, 1994, Rush-Holley House, Cos Cob, 1994, Wilton Libr., Conn., 1995—96, E.C. Potter Gallery, Greenwich, 1996—2002, The Coffee Shoppe, Greenwich Hosp., 1997, Stamford Art Assn., 1999 (3d Pl. award, 2000), Greenwichart, Stamford, 1999, Art Soc. Old Greenwich Sidewalk Shows, 1999—2003, Stamford Art Assn., 2001, Westfield Ct., 2001, Greenwich Libr., Flinn Gallery, 2001, 2002, Landson Park, Katona, NY, 2001—04, Flynn Gallery, Greenwich Libr., 2001—02, Landson Park, Katona, NY, 2002, St. Raphael's Hosp., New Haven, 2002, Hammond Mus., 2002, Circe d'Art Gallery, Rowayton Art Ctr., Hammond Mus., 2002—03, Greenwich Libr., 2003, Riversville Art Show, Gaylordsville, Conn., 2006, Dr. Vincent Carlesi Pain Mgmt., Danbury, Conn. Donator paintings to people and places around the world. Recipient Honorable Mention award Greenwich Art Soc., 1999, other awards for art. Mem. Oriental Brush Artist Guild (mailing com. 1993-2002), Eastern Arts Connection, The Greenwich Art Soc. (mailing com. 1988-89, Second Place award 2000), The Art Soc. of Old Greenwich (hostess 1988-89, 2d place award 2002, numerous honorable mentions), Conn. Graphic Art Ctr., Greenwich Arts Coun., The Stamford Art Assn., The Hammond Mus., Women in the Arts, Rowayton Art Assn. Avocations: music, travel, cats, Bluegrass banjo. Home: 12 Newton Rd Gaylordsville CT 06755

DUNN, WALTER SCOTT, JR., writer, museum director, consultant; b. Detroit, Mich., Apr. 5, 1928; s. Walter Scott and Minnie (Van Lahr) D.; m. Jean Wendeberg, July 11, 1959. BA, U. Durham, Eng., 1951; MA, Wayne State U., 1953; PhD, U. Wis., 1971. Curator indsl. history Detroit Hist. Mus., 1952-56; chief curator State Hist. Soc. Wis., Madison, 1956-63; mus. cons., 1962—; dir. Buffalo and Erie County Hist. Soc., 1963-78, Des Moines Ctr. Sci. and Industry, 1978-84, Nat. Mus. Transport, St. Louis, 1984-86, Dog Mus., St. Louis, 1987-89. Author: Western Commerce, 1760-1774, 1971, Second Front Now, 1943, 80, Hitler's Nemesis: The Red Army, 1994, The Soviet Economy and the Red Army 1930-1945, 1995, Kursk: Hitler's Gamble, 1943, 1997, Frontier Profit and Loss, 1760-1764, 1998, Views of America: Walworth County, 1998, Soviet Blitzkrieg, 2000, The New Imperial Economy, 2000, Opening New Markets, 2002, Heroes or Traitors, 2003, People on the Frontier, 2005, Stalin's Keys to Victory, 2006, Choosing Sides, 2007; host several Pub. TV series on mil. history, Madison, Wis. and Buffalo, 1959-78. Served with AUS, 1946—47. Mem. Walworth County Hist. Soc. (pres. 1996). Home: N6539 Peck Station Rd Elkhorn WI 53121-3246 Office Phone: 262-642-9771. E-mail: peterjolly@elknet.net. *Human progress can be achieved only through constant questioning of the past and innovative action to solve the problems of the future.*

DUNN, WILLIAM BRADLEY, lawyer; b. Newark, Dec. 2, 1939; s. Ernest William and Ruth Harriet (Bradley) D.; m. Judy Ann Shepherd, Aug. 2, 1988; children: John, Peter, Brian, Kelly. AB, Muskingum Coll., 1961; JD, U. Mich., 1964. Bar: Mich. 1964. Mem. Clark Hill PLC (formerly Clark, Klein & Beaumont), Detroit, 1964—. Lectr. in field. Contbr. articles to legal jours. Mem.: ABA (chair sect. real property, probate and trust law 1989—90, mem. ho. dels. 1990—98, mem. standing com. on professionalism 1993—96, mem. standing com. on ethics and profl. responsibility 1998—2001, spl. adv. standing com. on ethics and profl. responsibility 2001—02, mem. standing com. on ethics and profl. responsibility 2003—06, chmn. standing com. ethics and profl. responsibility 2005—06), State Bar Mich. (mem. com. profl. ethics 2002—07, chmn. com. profl. ethics 2007—), Internat. Assn. Attys. and Exec. Corp. Real Estate, Am. Coll. Real Estate Lawyers (pres. 1983—84). Episcopalian. Home: 6398 Catalpa Ct Troy MI 48098-2231 Office: Clark Hill PLC 500 Woodward Ave Ste 3500 Detroit MI 48226-3435 Office Phone: 313-965-8511. Business E-Mail: wdunn@clarkhill.com.

DUNN, WILLIAM BRUNA, III, journalist; b. Streator, Ill., Jan. 26, 1947; s. William Bruna and Mary Elizabeth (Allgaier) D.; m. Sandra Lee Ann Klein, Aug. 23, 1969; 1 child, William IV. BS in Journalism, U. Fla., 1969. Reporter Orlando (Fla.) Sentinel, 1967-69, mag. editor, 1970-80, dep. mng. editor, 1979-81, mng. editor, 1981-91, assoc. mng. editor, photos, graphics and design, 1991-2001; design editor Orlando (Fla.) Sentinel , 2001—02. Author: Kidding Around, 1973; editor: SHAQ! That Magical Rookie Season, 1993; editor: Martin Andersen: Editor, Publisher, Galley Boy, 1996. Recipient Silver Gavel award ABA, 1974; Gold and Silver medals Soc. News Design, 1984. Mem. Nat. Press Photographers Assn., Soc. Profl. Journalists (past pres. Cen. Fla. chpt.), Soc. of News Design. Roman Catholic. Home: 4 E Vanderbilt St Orlando FL 32804-5925 Personal E-mail: willbdunn@aol.com.

DUNNE, DIANE C., marketing professional; b. Milw. d. Francis and Ruth Cantine; 1 child, Dana Philip. BS, Marquette U.; MBA, NYU. Mgr. advt. NBC, NYC, 1975-77; dir. mktg. CBS, NYC, 1977-80; dir. funding Bloomingdale's, NYC, 1980—; v.p. Corcoran Group; cons. Am. Express, DuPont de Nemours. Dir. Women's Econ. Round Table, 1988—, 750 Park Ave. Corp., NYC, 1999—. Author: Guidelines to Advertising All News Radio, 1976, Guidelines for Catalogue Copywriters, 1985; assoc. editor: Am. Cancer Soc., Gourmet Guide for Busy People by Famous People, 1985, International Directory of Distinguished Leadership, columnist: N.Y. Sun, writer: Art and Living Mag.; contbr. articles AM/NY Daily Newspaper, to profl. jours. Mem. Am. Cancer Soc., NYC, 1980—; chair Feed the Homeless com. St. James Ch., NYC, 1984—87; mem. pastoral and cmty. ministry com. St. James Altar Guild. Named to Corcoran Multi-Million Dollar Club; recipient Contribution honor, Oxford U. Mem.: NYU Exec. MBA Assn., Women's Econ. Roundtable (bd. dirs. 1988), Fashion Group (co-chair regional com.), Oxford U. Alumni Assn. NY (v.p. events, bd. dirs. 1993—, award), Corcoran's Multi-Million Dollar Club. Episcopalian. Avocations: opera, jogging, skiing, rollerblading. Home: 750 Park Ave New York NY 10021-4252 Office Phone: 212-893-1420.

DUNNE, DOMINICK, writer; b. Hartford, Conn., Oct. 29, 1925; s. Richard and Dorothy B. D.; m. Ellen Griffin, Apr. 24, 1954 (div.); children: Griffin, Alexander, Dominique (dec. Nov. 4, 1982). BA, Williams Coll., 1949. Stage mgr. Howdy Doody Show, NBC-TV; prodr. CBS Studio One, Dunne-Didion-Dunne, from 1970s; exec. prodr. 20th Century Fox; v.p. Four Star Co.; contributing editor Vanity Fair Mag., 1982—93, spl. corr., 1993—. Prodr.: (films) The Boys in the Band, 1970, Panic in Needle Park, 1971, Play It As It Lays, 1972, Ash Wednesday, 1973, (TV series) Adventures in Paradise, ABC-TV, 1959-62, (TV movie) The Users, ABC-TV, 1978; author (novels): The Winners: Part II of Joyce Haber's The Users, 1982, The Two Mrs. Grenvilles, 1985, People Like Us, 1988, An Inconvenient Woman, 1990, The Mansions of Limbo, 1991, A Season in Purgatory, 1993, Sins of the Sons, 1995, Another City Not My Own, 1997, (non-fiction) Fatal Charms and Other Tales of Today, 1986, The Way We Lived Then: Recollections of a Well-Known Name Dropper, 1999, Justice: Crimes, Trials, and Punishments, 2001; adaptations: The Two Mrs. Grenvilles, 1987, People Like Us, 1990; host (TV), Power Privilege & Justice, Court TV, 2003-. Served in US Army. Decorated Bronze Star, Battle of Bulge. Democrat. Roman Catholic. Address: c/o William Morris Agency 1350 Avenue Of The Americas New York NY 10019-4702 Mailing: Power Privilege & Justice Court TV 600 Third Ave New York NY 10016

DUNNE, FREDERICK R., JR., lawyer; b. Kearny, NJ, Mar. 27, 1944; s. Frederick R. and Agnes M. (Lynch) D.; m. Donna M. Polc, Nov. 17, 1973; children: Kelly Anne, Jaime Elizabeth, Frederick R. III. BA, Niagara U., 1966; JD, Seton Hall U., 1970. Bar: NJ 1972, US Dist. Ct. NJ 1972, NY 1984, US Dist. Ct. Colo. 1997, US Ct. Appeals (3rd cir.) 1998, US Dist. Ct. (so. and ea. dists.) NY 2000; cert. tchr. NJ. Tchr. St. Benedict's Prep. Sch., 1966-68, Essex Coll. Bus., 1968-69, East Orange HS, NJ, 1969-73; atty. NJ Office Pub. Defender, 1973; ptnr. Harrington & Dunne, Kearny, 1973-77; sole practice Kearny, 1977-81; owner Dunne & Waller, Kearny, 1981-86, Dunne & Thompson PC, Kearny, 1987—2004; atty. Kearney Fed. Savings & Loan, 1985—92, Arco Globus Internat. Co. Inc., 2001—; mng. mem. Dunne & Assocs. LLC, Kearny, 2004—. Examining atty. Chgo. Title Ins. Co., 1973—2007, Chelsea Title and Guaranty Co., 1973-93; atty. Kearny Bd. Edn., 1978-95; pub. defender Borough of North Arlington, 1984-2003, spl. prosecutor ABC violations, 1985-2003; atty. Alice Holdings LLC, 2004-; alpine ofcl. USSA Ski Racing, 1994—. V.p. Immaculate Heart of Mary Sch. Bd., Wayne, NJ, 1981-82; bd. trustees Pioneer Boys Am., 1976-78; chmn. St. Benedict's Alumni Fund, 1978-92. Recipient Svc. and Citizenship award, Pioneer Boys Am., 1978, Outstanding Performance Resolution, Kearny Bd. Edn., 1980, Cert. of Appreciation, Supreme Ct. NJ, 1985, 1986, 1989, 1990, 1991, 1992, 1999, 2000, 2001, 2002, 2003, 2004, 2005, 2006, 2007. Mem.: West Hudson Bar Assn. (Hudson County matrimonial early settlement panel 1978—, pres. 2004—, matrimonial blue ribbon panel 2006—, Niagara U. alumni co-chair 2006). Home: 81 Hemlock Ter Wayne NJ 07470-4341 Office: 683 Kearny Ave Kearny NJ 07032-3004 Office Phone: 201-998-2727. Personal E-mail: attorneydunne@verizon.net.

DUNNE, KEVIN JOSEPH, lawyer; b. Pitts., Sept. 22, 1941; s. Matthew S. and Marjorie (Whelan) D.; m. Heather Wright Dunne, Sept. 27, 1963; children: Erin, Kevin Jr., Patrick, Sean. BA, U. Conn., 1963; JD, Georgetown U., 1966. Bar: Calif. 1967, U.S. Dist. Ct. (no. dist.) Calif., 1967, U.S. Dist. Ct. (ea. dist.) Calif. 1969, U.S. Dist. Ct. (ctrl. dist.) Calif. 1971, U.S. Ct. Appeals (9th cir.) 1971. Assoc. Sedgwick, Detert, Moran & Arnold, San Francisco, 1968-75, ptnr., 1975—, chmn., 2001—. Adj. prof. U. San Francisco Sch. Law, 1980-86; bd. editorial advisors Bender's Drug Product Liability Reporter, 1988-92. Author: Dunne on Depositions, 1995; contbr. articles to profl. jours. Capt. U.S. Army, 1966-68, Vietnam. Recipient Bronze Star, Army Commendation medal; recipient Exceptional Performance award Def. Rsch. Inst., 1988. Fellow: Am. Coll. Trial Lawyers, Internat. Acad. Trial Lawyers; mem.: Lawyers for Civil Justice (pres. 1998—2000), Am. Bd. Trial Advocates, Internat. Assn. Def. Counsel (pres. 1994—95), No. Calif. Assn. Def. Counsel (pres. 1987—88). Roman Catholic. Avocation: golf. Office: Sedgwick Detert Moran & Arnold Stewart Tower 8th Fl One Market Plz San Francisco CA 94105 Office Phone: 415-627-1475.

DUNNE, MYRA SCHLEY, nurse, consultant; b. Stamford, Conn., June 10, 1950; d. Charles Henry and Myra Catherine Schley; m. Frank Edward Dunne, May 23, 1981 (div. Sept. 23, 1997); children: Elizabeth Anne, Michael Edward. BSN, Sacred Heart U., 1972, MBA, 1989. Cert. case mgr. Commn. for Case Mgr. Cert., Rolling Meadows, Ill., 1997, legal nurse cons. Am. Legal Nurse Cert. Bd., Chgo., 2001. Nurse case mgr. CNA Ins., Quincy, Mass., 1996—2000; med. cons. Encompass Ins., Quincy, 2000—05; with Blue Cross Blue Shield Mass., Rockland, 2005—. Trainer Encompass Ins., Quincy, 2003—. Vol. Boston Rescue Mission, 2004—. Mem.: Am. Assn. Legal Nurse Cons. (assoc.). Democrat. Roman Catholic. Avocations: walking, yoga, weightlifting, ballroom dancing. Home: 23

Smith Rd Hingham MA 02043 Office: Blue Cross Blue Shield 1030 Hingham St Rockland MA 02370 Home Phone: 781-749-1080; Office Phone: 617-246-5822. Business E-Mail: myra.dunne@bcbsma.com.

DUNNE, NANCY ANNE, retired social services administrator; b. Ionia, Mich., Aug. 5, 1929; d. Warner Kingsley and Hazel Fern (Alliason) McSween; m. James Robert, Oct. 28, 1952; children: James Robert Jr., Stephen Michael. BA, Albion Coll., Mich., 1951. Tchr. Oakdale Elem., Grand Rapids, Mich., 1951-53, Lakeside Sch., East Grand Rapids, Mich., 1953; clk. Office of Naval Rsch., Washington, 1954-55; dir. pub. rels. Diocesan Office Health and Social Svcs., Albany, NY, 1971-74; dir. vol. action dept. Coun. of Human Resources, Schenectady, NY, 1974-76; pers. asst. Am. Soc. Assn. Execs., Washington, 1977-78; adminstrv. asst. N.Y. Soc. Cons. Engrs., NYC, 1978-79, Assessment Designs, Inc., Orlando, Fla., 1980-82, Catholic Social Svcs., Orlando, Fla., 1982-84, ret., 1984. Active NY State Comm. Cultural Resources, Albany, 1970-73, Anna Maria Island Cmty. Ctr., 2000-01; bd. dirs. Coalition for the Homeless, Orlando, 1983-87; tutor Anna Maria Island Elem. Sch., Fla.; vol. Blake Hosp., Bradenton, Fla., 1999-2003, Imagine Manatee Task Force, Bradenton, 2003; 1st v.p. Performing arts Downtown Manatee County, Inc., 2003; tutor Anna Maria Island Elem. Sch. Mem. AAUW (pres. Manatee County br. 2001-03), Jr. League of Schenectady (Vol. of Yr. award 1965-66), Schenectady Symphony Orch. (pres. 1969-70), Ladies of Charity (pres. Albany chpt. 1970-72, pres. Orlando chpt. 1984-86, nat. pres. 1990-94, nat. bd. dirs. 2001-02, v.p. internat. 1990-94, bd. dirs. 1994-2000), Women's Club Anna Maria Island (1st v.p. 2004—, pres. 2005-06, rotary club fellowship award, 2003). Roman Catholic. Avocations: reading, travel, golf, bridge, entertaining friends. Home: 6400 Flotilla Dr Apt 31 Holmes Beach FL 34217-1425

DUNNE, PATRICK W., federal agency administrator, retired military officer; BS, U.S. Naval Acad., Annapolis, 1972; MS, Naval Postgraduate Sch., 1973. Commd. ensign USN, advanced through grades to rear adm., 2001, ret., 2006; served at sea USS Nathanael Greene (SSBN 636), USS Batfish (SSN 681), USS Baton Rouge (SSN 689); comdr. USS Baltimore (SSN 704), USS Frank Cable (AS40); material officer Submarine Squadron Eight; naval aide to Pres. Ronald Reagan; spl. asst. to CNO for Joint Chiefs of Staff Matters; congl. liaison officer for submarine programs; dir. naval programs; dep. chief legis. affairs; comdr. US Naval Forces Marianas, 2001—03; pres. Naval Postgraduate Sch. USN, Monterey, Calif., 2003—06; asst. sec. for policy, planning & preparedness US Dept. Vets Affairs, Washington, 2006—. Decorated Def. Superior Svc. medal (2 awards), Legion of Merit (4 awards), Meritorious Svc. award (2 awards), Navy Commendation medal (5 awards), Navy Achievement medal (2 awards), Humanitarian Svc. medal. Office: US Dept Vets Affairs 810 Vermont Ave NW Rm 300 Washington DC 20420

DUNNE, THOMAS, geology educator; b. Prestbury, U.K., Apr. 21, 1943; arrived in U.S., 1964; s. Thomas and Monica Mary (Whitter) D. BA with honors, Cambridge U., Eng., 1964; PhD, Johns Hopkins U., 1969. Rsch. assoc. USDA-Agrl. Rsch. Svc., Danville, Vt., 1966—68; rsch. hydrologist U.S. Geol. Survey, Washington, 1969; asst. prof. McGill U., Montreal, Que., Canada, 1969—73; from asst. prof. to prof. U. Wash., Seattle, 1973—95, chmn. dept., 1984—89; prof. Sch. Environ. Scis. & Mgmt. U. Calif., Santa Barbara, 1995—. Vis. prof. U. Nairobi, Kenya, 1969—71; cons. in field, 1970—. Author (with L.B. Leopold) Water in Environmental Planning; (with L.M. Reid) Rapid Evaluation of Sediment Budgets, 1996. Fulbright scholar 1984; grantee NSF, NASA, Rockefeller Found., 1969—; Guggenheim fellow, 1989-90. Fellow AAAS, Am. Acad. Arts and Scis., Am. Geophys. Union (Robert E. Horton award 1987, Langbein lectr. 2003), Calif. Acad. Scis.; mem. NAS (G.K. Warren prize in Fluviatile Geology 1998), Geol. Soc. Am. (Easterbrook Disting. Scientist award 2003), Sigma Xi. Office: U Calif Donald Bren Sch Environ Scis & Mgmt 3510 Bren Hall Santa Barbara CA 93106 Office Phone: 805-893-7557. Business E-Mail: tdunne@bren.ucsb.edu.

DUNNER, DAVID LOUIS, medical educator; b. Bklyn., May 27, 1940; s. Edward and Reichel (Connor) D.; m. Peggy Jane Zolbert, Dec. 27, 1964; children: Laura Louise, Jonathan Michael. AA, George Washington U., 1960; MD, Washington U., St. Louis, 1965. Diplomate Am. Bd. Psychiatry and Neurology. Intern Phila. Gen. Hosp., 1965-66; resident in psychiatry Barnes Renard Hosp. of Washington U., St. Louis, 1966-69; research psychiatrist N.Y. State Psychiat. Inst., NYC, 1971-79; from asst. prof. to assoc. prof. clin. psychiatry Columbia U., NYC, 1972-79; chief psychiatry Harborview Med. Ctr., Seattle, 1979-89, dir. outpatient psychiatry, 1989-97; prof. psychiatry and behavioral scis. U. Wash., Seattle, 1979—2006, prof. emeritus, 2006—, vice chmn. clin. svcs., 1989-97; dir. Ctr. for Anxiety & Depression, 1997—; pvt. practice psychiatry, 2006—. Cons. Found. for Depression and Manic Depression, N.Y.C., 1974—. Editor-in-chief Comprehensive Psychiatry, 1997—; contbr. articles to profl. jours. Served to lt. comdr. USPHS, 1969-71. Fellow Am. Psychiat. Assn., Am. Psychopathol. Assn. (pres. 1986), Am. Coll. Neuropsychopharmacology, West Coast Coll. Biol. Psychiatry (charter, pres. 1987); mem. Psychiat. Research Soc. (pres. 1984). Office: Ctr for Anxiety & Depression 7525 SE 24th St Ste 400 Mercer Island WA 98040 Office Phone: 206-230-0330. Personal E-mail: dldunner@comcast.net.

DUNNER, DONALD ROBERT, lawyer; b. Bklyn., 1931; s. Edward Dunner and Mollie Friedman; m. Jenny Sue Dailey, 1957; children: Jennifer D. Weaver, Lisa A. BSChemE, Purdue U., 1953; JD, Georgetown U., 1958. Bar: D.C. 1958, U.S. Supreme Ct. 1963, U.S. Ct. Appeals (fed. cir.) 1982. Patent examiner U.S. Patent & Trademark Office, Washington, 1955-56; law clk. U.S. Ct. Customs and Patent Appeals, Washington, 1956-58; assoc. Strauch, Nolan & Neale, Washington, 1958-60; assoc., ptnr. Diggins & Le Blanc, Washington, 1960-62; ptnr. Lane, Aitken, Dunner & Ziems, Washington, 1962-78; of counsel Finnegan, Henderson, Farabow & Garrett, Washington, 1978-79; ptnr. Finnegan, Henderson, Farabow, Garrett & Dunner, Washington, 1979—. Mem. Pres. Adv. Com. on Indsl. Innovation, 1978-79; professorial lectr. in law George Washington Law Ctr., 1969-82; adj. prof. Washington Coll. of Law, Am. U., 1992-99. Co-author: Patent Law Perspectives, 1970-89, Court Review of Patent Office Decisions: CCPA, 1973, Court of Appeals for the Federal Circuit: Practice and Procedure, 1985. Chmn. Fed. Cir. Adv. Com., 1982-92; mem. adv. commn. on Patent Law Reform, 1991-92. With U.S. Army, 1953-55. Recipient Best Article of Yr. award Patent Office Soc., 1980, award Patent Resources Group, 1980, named one of 100 most influential lawyers, Nat. Law Jour., 2000, named one of best lawyers in intellectual property law, Best Lawyers in Am., 2005. Fellow Am. Coll. Trial Lawyers; mem. ABA (chair intellectual property law sect. 1995-96, ho. of dels. 2002—), Am. Intellectual Property Law Assn. (pres. 1979-80), D.C. Bar Assn. (chmn. patent, trademark and copyright law sect. 1964-65), D.C. Bar (chair patent, trademark and copyright law sect. 1976-77), Fed. Cir. Bar Assn. (bd. dirs. 1999-2002), Am. Inn of Ct. (pres. Giles S. Rich Inn 1994-95), Cosmos Club. Avocations: tennis, skiing, sailing. Office: Finnegan Henderson Farabow Garrett & Dunner LLP 901 New York Ave NW Washington DC 20001-3315 E-mail: dunnerd@finnegan.com.

DUNNETT, DENNIS GEORGE, retired state official; b. Auburn, Calif., Aug. 5, 1939; s. George DeHaven and Elizabeth Grace (Sullivan) D. AA in Elec. Engring., Sierra Coll., 1959; AB in Econs., Sacramento State Coll., 1966. Engring. technician State of Calif., Marysville, 1961-62, data processing technician Sacramento, 1962-67, EDP programmer and analyst, 1967-74, staff services mgr. and contract adminstr., 1974-76, hardware acquisition mgr., 1976-86, support services br. mgr., information security officer, 1986-90, chief Office Security and Operational Recovery, 1990-92, spl. projects mgr., 1992-93, customer support ctr. mgr., 1994, procurement mgr., 1994-97, chief bur. adminstrn., 1997-2000, ret., 2000—. Patron San Francisco Opera, TV Sta. KVIE. Mem. AARP, IEEE, ACLU, IEEE Computer Soc., Fine Arts Mus. of San Francisco, Crocker Art Mus., Sons in Retirement, Calif. State U.-Sacramento Alumni Assn. (life). Home: 729 Blackmer Cir Sacramento CA 95825-4704 Personal E-mail: dpdennis39@comcast.net.

DUNNIGAN, BRIAN LEIGH, historian, curator; b. Detroit, July 11, 1949; s. James Patrick and Dorothy Jane (McKay) D.; m. Carol Lynn Fredriksen, Sept. 21, 1974 (div. Oct. 1988); m. Candice Maria Cain, Apr. 22, 1989; children: James Cain, Claire Beausom. BA in History, U. Mich., 1971, MA in History, 1973; MA in History and Museum Studies, Cooperstown Grad. Programs, 1979. Curator Mackinac Island (Mich.) State Park Commn., 1971-74; mng. dir. Historic Fort Wayne, Ind., 1974-79; exec. dir. Old Fort Niagara Assn., Youngstown, NY, 1979-96; curator of maps William L. Clements Libr. U. Mich., Ann Arbor, 1996—. Author: History and Guide to Old Fort Niagara, 1985, Siege-1759, 1986, rev. edit., 1996, Glorious Old Relic, 1987, Forts Within A Fort, 1989, Old Fort Niagara in Four Centuries, 1991; editor: Pouchot's Memoirs on the Late War in North America, 1994, Niagara, 1796, 1996, Frontier Metropolis, 2001. Fellow Co. Mil. Historians. Home: 4531 Maute Rd Grass Lake MI 49240 Office: William L Clements Libr 909 S University Ave Ann Arbor MI 48109-1190 Home Phone: 517-522-6797; Office Phone: 734-764-2347. Business E-Mail: briand@umich.edu.

DUNNIGAN, JOHN H., federal agency administrator; m. Linda Dunnigan; 3 children. BA, Calif. State U.; JD, LLM, U. Wash. With Nat. Oceanic and Atmospheric Adminstrn., 1972—, dir. office sustainable fisheries, dir. ecosystem goal team, staff atty. gen., regional counsel, asst. adminstr. Nat. Ocean Svc., 2006—. Exec. dir. Atlantic States Marine Fisheries Commn. Mem.: Wash. State Bar Assn., DC Bar Assn. Office: Nat Ocean Svc SSMC Bldg 4 1305 East West Highway Silver Spring MD 20910

DUNNIGAN, T. KEVIN, retired electrical and electronics manufacturing company executive; b. Montreal, Que., Can., Jan. 31, 1938; s. John George and Olive Mary (Brophy) D.; m. Beverley Alice Laramee, Apr. 11, 1960 (div. June 1980); children: David, Kathleen; m. Leah Anne Merlo. BA in Commerce, Loyola U., 1971. With Can. Elec. Distbg. Co., prior to 1962; salesman No. Telecom, Montreal, 1956-60; purchasing agt. Black-MacDonald, Montreal, 1960-62; salesman Thomas & Betts Corp., Iberville, Que., 1962-67, v.p. sales, 1967-70, pres., 1970-73, pres., N.Am. Elec. Divsn. Bridgewater, NJ, 1974—80, v.p., gen. mgr., N.Am. Elec. Divsn., 1974—83, corp. exec. v.p. electronics Bridgewater, NJ, 1978-80, pres., 1980—96, chief oper. officer, 1980-85, chief exec. officer, 1985—96, pres., CEO, 2000—04, chmn. bd. Memphis, 1992—96, 2000—05, ret. chmn. Memphis, 2005. Bd. dirs. C.R. Bard Inc.,1994-, Deere & Co.,2000-, Imagistics Inc., Pro-Mach, Inc. Office: Thomas & Betts Corp 8155 T&B Blvd Memphis TN 38125

DUNNING, HERBERT NEAL, government agency administrator, chemist; b. Hazard, Nebr., June 2, 1923; s. Herbert P. and Maude Lillian (Welsh) D.; m. Margaret Stovall (div. 1973); 1 child, Margaret Diane Aulik; m. Raquel Reichmann, Oct. 10, 1974; 1 child, Denise Raquel. BS, Kearney State Coll., 1944; MS, U. Nebr., 1948, PhD, 1950; postdoctoral studies, U. Minn., 1964-66. Dir. surface chemistry lab. Dept. Interior, Bartlesville, Okla., 1951-60; rsch. dir. Gen. Mills Inc., Mpls., 1961-70, Delmark Foods and Pharm., Mpls., 1970-71; dir. divsn. foods rsch. FDA, Washington, 1972-74; dir. office mfg. assistance FDA, Medical Devices, Rockville, Md., 1979—90; pres. NDA, Inc., Rockville, 1991—. Dir. divsn. oil and gas, U.S. ERDA, Washington, 1974-78; leader US-USSR exchange on natural gas tech., 1976-78; Donald E. Fox Meml. lectr. Kearney State Coll., 1983. Contbr. articles to profl. jours., publs. and books; patentee in field. Lt. USNR, 1944-46. Recipient Superior Performance award U.S. Bur. Mines, 1958, Meritorious Svc. award Dept. Interior, 1959, Merit award FDA, 1985, Outstanding Alumnus award Kearney State Coll., 1989, Disting. Svc. award Dental Mfrs. Am., 1993. Fellow AAAS; mem. Am. Chem. Soc., AIChE, Am. Soc. Quality Control (Svc. award 1985), Explorers Club. Avocations: painting, water-skiing, golf. Home and Office: 26420 Summer Greens Dr Bonita Springs FL 34135 Office Phone: 239-498-9153. E-mail: nealdunning@att.net.

DUNNING, JEAN, artist; b. Granby, Conn., 1960; MFA, Sch. Art Inst. Chgo., 1985. One-woman shows include, Feature, Chgo., 1987, 1988, Hirshhorn Mus., Washington, 1994, Mus. Contemporary Art, Chgo., 1994, Richard Telles Fine Art, LA, 1995, Galerie Massimo de Carlo, Milan, 1995, Feigen Inc., Chgo., 1996, Feigen Contemporary, 1997, Galleria Massimo de Carlo, Milan, 1998, Malmö Konstmuseum, Sweden, 1999, James Harris Gallery, Seattle, 2000, Bodybuilder & Sportsman Gallery, Chgo., 2001, exhibited in group shows at Changing Views, Feigen Inc., Chgo., 1994, Traces: Body in Contemporary Photog., Bronx Mus. Art, NYC, 1995, Wallflower, Randolph St. Gallery, Chgo., 1995, Up Close & Personal, Phila. Mus. Art, 1996, Slad, Apex Art, NYC, 1997, New Photog. 14, Mus. Modern Art, NYC, 1998, Rapture, MassArt, Boston, 2000, Wanderings of the Mind's Eye: Photographs by Ill. Artists, Mus. Contemporary Art, Chgo., 2004. Grantee, Louis Comfort Tiffany Found., 1993; Individual Artist Fellowship, Ill. Arts Coun., 1992, 1991, Cmty. Arts Assistance Grant, Chgo. Office Fine Arts, 1989, Spl. Assistance Grant, Ill. Art Coun., 1987. Mailing: c/o Museum Contemporary Art 220 East Chicago Ave Chicago IL 60611

DUNNING, JENNIFER, dance critic, reporter; Dance critic, reporter NY Times, NYC. Author: Alvin Ailey: A Life in Dance, 1998, Geoffrey Holder: A Life in Theater, Dance and Art, 2001; co-author: Great Performances: A Celebration, 1997. Office: NY Times 229 W 43rd St New York NY 10036 Office Phone: 212-556-1591. Office Fax: 212-556-1516. E-mail: dunning@nytimes.com.

DUNNING, JEREMY DAVID, application developer, dean, educator; b. Washington, Feb. 15, 1951; s. John Laurance and Jacquelin (Creamer) D.; m. Deborah Humeler, June 3, 1972; children: Katherine, Nicholas, Abigail. BA in Geology with honors, Colgate U., 1973; MS, Rutgers U., 1975; PhD, U. N.C., 1978. Asst. prof. Oreg. State U., Corvallis, 1978-79, Ind. U., Bloomington, 1979-84, assoc. prof., 1984—94, full prof., 1994—, assoc. dean Bloomington, 1985—, dir. indsl. rsch. liaison program, 1986—. Hearst disting. lectr. U. Calif., Berekely, 1986; advisor Nat. Acad. Sci.; pres. ArJung Multimedia; cons. in field. Contbr. articles to profl. jours. Mem. bd. advisors NASA/USRA, nationwide, 1987—; mem. nat. adv. bd. Gov.'s Tech. Assessment, Ind., 1989-90; mem. Gov.'s Modernization Bd., Ind., 1990; dir. Ind. Univ. Res. Park, 1993-96; dean Sch. of Continued Studies, 1996-2003. Recipient Sloan C. Effective Practices award, 2003, Best Paper award, EISTA, 2003, Gold Medal, ICI, 2003, Novel Use of Technology award, ACHE, 2004. Mem. Am. Geophys. Union, Econ. Devel. Assn., NAMTAC. Office: Ind U Dept Geology Rm 121 Bloomington IN 47401 Business E-Mail: dunning@indiana.edu.

DUNNING, JOHN HARRY, economics educator; b. Eng., June 26, 1927; s. John Murray and Anne Florence (Baker) D.; m. Christine Mary Brown, Aug. 4, 1975; 1 son by previous marriage, Philip. BSc in Econs., U. London, 1952; PhD, Southampton U., 1957; PhD (hon.), U. Uppsala, Sweden, 1975, U. Autonoma Madrid, 1991; PhD (hon.), U. Antwerp, 1997, Chinese Culture U., Taiwan, 2007, U. Lund, Sweden, 2007. Lectr. U. Southampton, 1952-64; mem. faculty U. Reading, Eng., 1964-92, found. prof. econs., 1964-74, Esmee Fairbairn prof. internat. investment and bus. studies, 1975-87, chmn. dept. econs., 1964-87, ICI rsch. prof. internat. bus., 1987-92, 94—. Vis. prof. U. Western Ont., London, Can., 1968-69, U. Calif. Berkeley, 1976; vis. prof. internat. mgmt. U. Boston, 1976; prof. internat. bus. Rutgers U., N.J., 1989-2002; chmn. Economists Adv. Group Ltd., 1985-2000; mem. chems. econ. devel. com. Royal Econ. Soc., 1970-77; mem. S.E. Econ. Planning Coun., 1965-69; mem. coms. econ. and social rsch. coun. OECD, European Commn., UN; hon. prof. U. Beijing, 1995; lectr. in field. Author: Explaining International Production, 1988, Multinational Enterprises, Technology and Competitiveness, 1988, Multinational Enterprises and the Global Economy, 1993, rev. edit., 2007, The Globalization of Business, 1993, Alliance Capitalism and Global Business, 1997, Globalization at Bay, 2000, (with R. Narula) Multinationals and Industrial Comptetitiveness, 2004; editor: The Multinational Enterprise, 1971, International Investment, 1972, Economic Analysis and Multinational Enterprise, 1974, Structural Change in the World Economy, 1990, The Theory of Transnational Corporations, 1992, The New Globalism and Developing Countries, 1997, Governments, Globalization and International Business, 1997, Regions, Globalization and the Knowledge Based Economy, 2001, Making Globalization Good, 2003; contbr. articles to acad. and profl. jours. Home: Holly Dell Satwell Close Rotherfield Greys Henley-on-Thames Oxon RG 9 4QT England Office: U Reading Whiteknights Pk Reading Berkshire England Fax: 001 44 1491 628902. E-mail: j.mturner@virgin.net.

DUNNING, JOHN WILSON, II, music educator, vocalist; s. Robert L. and Norma J. Dunning, Jr. BA in Vocal Music, Culver-Stockton Coll., 1998, BSc in Vocal Music Edn., 1999; MusM, Kans. State U., 2002. Vocal music tchr. Houston, Mo. Pub. Schs., 2000; grad. tchg. asst., dept. music Kans. State U., Manhattan, Kans., 2000—02; choir dir. Immanuel Luth. Ch., Junction City, Kans., 2001—02; vocal tchr., vocal music coord. Ariz. Sch. Arts, Phoenix, 2002—03; dir. traditional music First United Meth. Ch., Glendale, Ariz., 2002—04; substitute tchr. Glendale Union HS, 2003—04, Phoenix Union HS, 2003—04, Peoria Unified Sch. Dist., Ariz., 2003—04; dir. music and programming First United Meth. Ch., Center, Tex., 2004—06; music educator Topeka Pub. Schs., 2006—. Pvt. voice tchr., Manhattan, Kans., 2000—02, Phoenix, 2002—04, Center, Tex., 2004—06; baritone Manhattan Cmty. Chorus, Kans., 2000—02, Ariz. State Univ. Choral Union, Phoenix, 2003—04. Leader of singles ministry First United Meth. Ch., Center, 2004—06; treas., interfraternity coun. Culver-Stockton Coll., Canton, Mo., 1995—96; treas. grad. student coun. Kans. State U., Manhattan, 2001—02. Recipient Mable E. McCray Endowed Music award, Dept. Music, Culver-Stockton Coll., 1996, J. Leslie Pierce Music award, 1998, award, US Achievement Acad., 2000, Appreciation award, First United Meth. Ch., 2004. Mem.: Kans. Music Educators Assn., Am. Guild English Handbell Ringers, Nat. Assn. Ch. Musicians, Am. Choral Dirs. Assn., Music Educators Nat. Conf., Tri-M Music Honor Soc. (pres. 1992—93), Pi Kappa Lambda, Sigma Phi Zeta (pres. 1995—98), Delta Upsilon (chpt. treas. 1994—97, alumni pres. 1999—2000). Home: Apt 5 6105 SW 27th St Topeka KS 66614 Personal E-mail: jdunning74@hotmail.com.

DUNPHY, EDWARD JAMES, science educator, crop extension specialist; b. Frederick, Md., Nov. 14, 1940; s. Edward John and Marie W. (Barlow) D.; m. Judith Kay Mitchell, Aug. 18, 1962; children: Kevin James, Brian Patrick, Cory Edward. MS, U. Ill., 1964; PhD, Iowa State U., 1972. Rsch. asst. U. Ill., Urbana, 1962-64; agronomist Dunphy's Feed & Fertilizer, Sullivan, Ill., 1964-66; rsch. asst. Iowa State U., Ames, 1969-72, crop prodn. specialist Des Moines, 1972-75; extension specialist soybeans N.C. State U., Raleigh, 1975—, prof. crop sci., 1986—. Instr. soybean prodn. N.C., 1975—; mem. N.C. Land Use Value Adv. Bd., Raleigh, 1987—. Author 4 computer programs; contbr. numerous articles to profl. jours. Cubmaster Boy Scouts Am., Raleigh, 1976-81, troop com. chair, 1979-98; officer Athens Dr. Band Boosters, Raleigh, 1983-90. Sgt. U.S. Army, 1966-69. Recipient Meritorious Svc. award N.C. Soybean Producers. Fellow Am. Soc. Agronomy (bd. mem., com. chair, Agronomic Extension Edn. award); mem.Crop and Soil Sci. Socs. Am., Am. Soybean Assn. (Ext. Edn. award, mem. S.Am. soybean mission), Coun. Agrl. Sci. and Tech., Internat. Cert. Crop Advisers (bd. mem., com. chair), Alpha Zeta, Epsilon Sigma Phi, Gamma Sigma Delta, Phi Eta Sigma, Phi Kappa Phi, Sigma Xi. Achievements include research on soybean varieties, production, management and econ. Home: 3708 Swift Dr Raleigh NC 27606-2572 Office: NC State U Box 7620 Raleigh NC 27695-7620 Office Phone: 919-515-5813. E-mail: jim_dunphy@ncsu.edu.

DUNPHY, FRAN, men's college basketball coach; m. Ree Dunphy; 1 child, J.P. BS in Mktg., La Salle, 1970; Master's Counseling and Human Relations, Villanova. Head basketball coach U. Penn., 1989—2006, Temple U., Phila. Nat. chair, coaches vs. cancer classic Am. Cancer Soc., 2003. Mem. bd. dir. Big Brothers/Big Sisters, Phila.; corp. com. Nat. Adoption Ctr. Recipient Coach Yr., Nat. Coaches Vs. Cancer, 2002. Achievements include winner eight Ivy League titles, seven trips to post-season NCAA Tournament. Office: Temple Athletics 4th Fl Vivacqua Hall Philadelphia PA 19122

DUNSAY, CHARLES WILLIAM, elementary school educator; b. Buffalo, Nov. 11, 1943; s. Solomon Herzel and Elizabeth Lillian Dunsay; m. Bernadette (Carima) Rosemarie Curcio, Jan. 16, 1970; 1 child, Emily Mae. BS Secondary Edn., SUNY, New Paltz, NY, 1965. Cert. Instrnl. Tech. Proficiency Framingham State Coll., Mass., 2002. Grade 4 tchr. Webatuck Ctrl. Sch. Dist., Amenia, NY, 1965—66, New Rochelle Pub. Sch. Dist., New Rochelle, NY, 1966—74; grade 2-3 tchr. So. Berkshire Regional Sch. Dist.Sheffield, Mass., 1974—, k-5 math tchr. leader Mass., 2003—. Tchr. instrnl. tech. ednl. website, 2003—. Contbr. conf. presentor (3 person team). Office: New Marlborough Ctrl Schl 44 Hartsville Mill River Rd Mill River MA 01244 Home Phone: 413-229-3139; Office Phone: 413-229-8867.

DUNSHEE, MELANIE J., law librarian, educator; BA, U. Minn.; JD, AMLS, U. Mich. Law firm libr., Detroit; reference libr. Duke U. Sch. Law Libr., Durham, NC, 1994, head reference svcs., 2001—04, dep. dir., sr. lecturing fellow, dir. legal rsch. instruction. Contbr. articles to profl. jours. Mem.: Am. Assn. Law Librs. Office: Duke U Sch Law Libr Rm 3046 Box 90361 Durham NC 27708-0361 Office Phone: 919-613-7119. E-mail: Dunshee@law.duke.edu.

DUNSIRE, DEBORAH, pharmaceutical executive; arrived in US, 1994; MD, U. Witwatersrand, South Africa. Gen. practitioner, South Africa; clinical rschr. Sandoz (now Novartis), 1988, head mktg. and sales of specialty brands, Basel, Switzerland, 1991; head N.Am. oncology ops. Novartis Pharmaceuticals Corp., US pharm. exec. com.; pres., CEO Millennium Pharmaceuticals, Inc., 2005—. Bd. dirs. Allergan Inc., 2006—. Recipient Rising Star award, Health Care Business Women's Assn., 2000, Excalibur Award, Am. Cancer Soc., 2001. Office: Millennium Pharm 40 Landsdowne St Cambridge MA 02139

DUNSIRE, P(ETER) KENNETH, insurance company executive; b. Spearhill, Man., Can., Mar. 1, 1932; came to U.S., 1969; s. Robert Anderson and Margaret (Kinnear) D.; m. Lily Martha Bell (div. Nov. 1971); children: Robert K., Barbara L. Dunsire Belanger; m. Stephanie Alice Mooradian. Student, U. B.C., Can., 1949-50, U. Alta., 1955-56. V.p. Avco Fin. Services, Newport Beach, Calif., 1961-71; exec. v.p. Carte Blanche, Los Angeles, 1971-74, pres., 1974-78; chmn. Am. Benefit Plan Adminstrn., Los Angeles, 1978-80; exec. v.p. Paul Revere Life Ins. Co., Worcester, Mass., 1980-84, Lincoln Nat. Life Ins. Co., Ft. Wayne, Ind., 1984-86, also bd. dirs.; exec. v.p. Lincoln Nat. Corp., Ft. Wayne, Ind., 1986-95, ret., 1995. Bd. dirs. Ft. Wayne Med. Soc. Found., Ft. Wayne C. of C. Found., Nat. Auto & Truck Mus.; chmn. Cannon Lincoln Plc., London, 1984-90, chmn. bd., 1992-95. Chmn. bd. Sta. WFWA-TV, Ft. Wayne,

1985-91, Auburn Cord Duesenberg Mus., Ind., 1986-2001, Ft. Wayne Civic Theater, 1985-86. Mem. Ft. Wayne C. of C. (vice-chmn. 1989-91, chmn. 1991-92). Republican. Avocation: automobile collecting. Home: 8140 Auburn Rd Fort Wayne IN 46825-3016 E-mail: pkdunsire@aol.com.

DUNSKER, STEWART B., neurosurgeon; b. Cin. s. Shiel and Tillie Dunsker; m. Ellen Lothian Treiman, July 2, 1966. BA, Harvard U., 1956; MD, U. Cin., 1960. Diplomate Am. Bd. Neurol. Surgery (pres.). Intern U. Ill., Chgo., 1960-61; resident in internal medicine U. Cin., 1961-62, resident in gen. surgery, 1964-65; resident in neurol. surgery Washington U., St. Louis, 1965-69; prof. clin. neurosurgery U. Cin.; treas. Mayfield Clinic, Cin. Capt. U.S. Army, 1962-64. Fellow: ACS; mem.: Am. Bd. Neurol. Surgeons (vice chair), Am. Acad. Neurol. Surgeons (v.p.), Am. Assn. Neurol. Surgeons (pres., Harvey Cushing medal 2003), Ohio State Neurosurg. Soc. (pres.), Soc. Univ. Neurosurgeons (pres.), Ohio State Med. Assn. (pres., Ohio Neurosurgeon of Yr. 1992, Evans award 1998). Office: Mayfield Clinic 2123 Auburn Ave # 441 Cincinnati OH 45219-2906

DUNSON, WILLIAM ALBERT, biology professor, ecological consultant; b. Cedartown, Ga., Dec. 17, 1941; s. James Blake and Eleanor (Adams) D.; m. Margaret E. Kvashay, Aug. 19, 1963; children: Mary Elizabeth, William Albert, David Brian. BS in Zoology with honors, Yale U., 1962; MS, U. Mich., 1964, PhD, 1965. Teaching fellow U. Mich., Ann Arbor, 1962-63; mem. faculty Pa. State U., University Park, 1965—, prof. biology, 1974-97, prof. emeritus, 1997—; environ. scientist Seminole Tribe Fla., 1997—2002. Adj. prof. biology U. Miami, Old Dominion U., Fla., Atlantic U. (now Atlantic Coll.); chief scientist various internat. oceanographic expdns.; collaborator Everglades Nat. Park. Author: The Biology of Sea Snakes, 1975; contbr. over 140 articles to profl. jours. Queens marine sci. fellow, 1972, hon. Fulbright fellow, 1972; grantee NSF, U.S. Dept. Interior, U.S. Geol. Survey, U.S. EPA. Mem. Soc. for Study Amphibians and Reptiles (jour. edit. bd.). Achievements include study of ecotoxicology, physiological ecology and wetlands ecology. Office: 577 State Shd Ln Galax VA 24333 Business E-Mail: wad4@psu.edu.

DUNST, KIRSTEN, actress; b. Point Pleasant, NJ, Apr. 30, 1982; d. Klaus and Inez Dunst. Appeared in films Bonfire of the Vanities, 1990, High Strung, 1991, Greedy, 1994, Interview with the Vampire, 1994 (Recipient Golden Globe Award nomination for best supporting actress, 1995, Boston Soc. of Film Critics Award for best supporting actress, 1994, Chicago Film Critics Assn. Award for most promising actress, 1994, Best Breakthrough Performance MTV Movie Awards, 1995), Little Women, 1994, Jumanji, 1995, Wag the Dog, 1997, (voice) Anastasia, 1997, Drop Dead Gorgeous, 1999, Dick, 1999, The Virgin Suicides, 1999, Bring It On, 2000, Crazy/Beautiful, 2001, The Cat's Meow, 2001, Spider-Man, 2002 (Best Kiss, Best Female Performance, MTV Movie Awards, 2003), Levity, 2003, Mona Lisa Smile, 2003, Eternal Sunshine of the Spotless Mind, 2004, Spider-Man 2, 2004, Wimbledon, 2004, Elizabethtown, 2005, Marie Antoinette, 2006, Spider-Man 3, 2007; TV appearances include ER, 1996, 97, The Outer Limits, 1997.*

DUNST, LAURENCE DAVID, advertising executive; b. NYC, Feb. 21, 1941; s. Philip R. and Mae (Fruchthendler) D.; m. Diane Gordon, Dec. 22, 1962; children: Lee Gordon, Melissa Susan. BA, Syracuse U., 1961. Advt. copywriter R.H. Macy & Co., 1961-63; with Daniel & Charles, NYC, from 1963; pres. Laurence, Charles, Free & Lawson, Inc., NYC, 1969-86, chmn., 1986-91, pres., CEO, 1991-95; chmn, CEO Gotham Inc., NYC, 1995—. Mem. Young Pres.'s Orgn., The Met. Club. Office: Gotham Inc 100 Fifth Ave Fl 16 New York NY 10011-6996 Home: 41 Hunting Ln East Hampton NY 11937

DUNSTON-COLEMAN, AINGRED GHISLAYNE, history professor; b. Atlantic City, June 14, 1943; parents Alfred Gilbert Dunston, Jr. and Permilla Flack Dunston; m. Raymond Lee Coleman, Jan. 22, 1988. AB, Livingstone Coll., Salisbury, NC, 1965; MA in Edn., U. NC, Charlotte, 1971; PhD in History, Duke U., Durham, NC, 1981. History instr. Barber-Scotia Coll., Concord, NC, 1974—77; asst. prof. history NC Ctrl. U., Durham, 1978—81, So. Ill. U., Carbondale, 1981—82, U. Ky., Lexington, 1981—89; assoc. prof. history Ea. Ky. U., Richmond, 1989—. Coord. veterans & continuing edn. programs Barber-Scotia Coll., Concord, 1974—77; dir. student tchg. in history & social sci. NC Ctrl. U., 1979—81. Contbr. articles to profl. jours. Assoc. missionary supr. AME Zion Ch., St. Thomas, 1964—94, assoc. missionary St. Croix, 1964—94; adv. bd. Ky. Civil Rights Project, Frankfort, 1989—99, Ky. Black History Commn., Frankfort, 1990—2000, Ky. Commn. on Women, Frankfort, 1992—98. Grantee Rsch. grant, Mid. Sch. Academic Achievement Program, Ea. Ky. U., 2002—03, Tchg. & Learning Ctr., Ea. Ky. U., 2004, Distance Learning Acad., Ea. Ky. U., 2005—06. Avocations: travel, aerobics. Office: Ea Ky Univ Lancaster Ave Richmond KY 40505 Office Fax: 859-622-1357. Business E-Mail: a.dunston@eku.edu.

DUNTON, GARY C., insurance company executive; Attended, Northeastern U.; MBA, Harvard Grad. Sch. Bus. Adminstrn. Cert. Fin. Analyst, Chartered Property Casualty Underwriter. In sr. positions Aetna Life & Casualty Co., 1980s; mgmt. positions USF&G, 1992—95, pres. family & bus. ins. group, 1995—97; with MBIA Inc., Armonk, NY, 1998—, pres., dir., 1999—, COO, 2000—04, CEO, 2004—, chmn., 2007—. Office: MBIA Ins Inc 113 King St Armonk NY 10504-1610

DUNTON, JAMES RAYNOR, publisher; b. Wilmington, Del., June 17, 1955; s. Guthrie Raynor III and Jane (Hill) D. BA, U. Va., 1977; MBA, Boston U., 1981. Editor Quorum Books, Westport, Conn., 1984-87; sr. editor Praeger Pubs., NYC, 1987-91, editor-in-chief, 1991-94; pub. acad. and trade Greenwood Pub. Group, Westport, 1994-96; dir. publs. Ctr. for Strategic and Internat. Studies, Washington, 1996—; consulting editor Praeger Pubs., Washington, 1996—, Brassey's, Inc., Washington, 2003—. Mem.: Washington Book Pubs., Soc. for Scholarly Pub., English-Speaking Union, Va. Club of N.Y. Home: 1520 16th St NW Apt 704 Washington DC 20036-1448 Office: Ctr for Strategic and Internat Studies 1800 K St NW Washington DC 20006-2202 Office Phone: 202-775-3160. Business E-Mail: jdunton@csis.org.

DUNWODY, EUGENE COX, architect; b. Macon, Ga., July 19, 1933; s. William Elliott and Mary Bennet (Cox) D.; m. Susan Howe Foxworth, June 15, 1957; children: Susan, Eugene Jr., George, Mary Bennet. BS, Ga. Inst. Tech., 1955, BArch, 1956. Registered architect, Ga., Fla. V.p., treas. W. Elliott Dunwody Jr., Macon, 1959-69; pres. Dunwody and Co., Macon, 1969-81, Dunwody, Beeland and Henderson Architects Inc., Macon, 1981-97, Dunwody, Beeland, Azar, Walsh, and Matthews, Architects Inc., Macon, 1997-2000, Dunwody/Beeland, Archs., 2000—. Pres. Rotary, Macon, 1974, City Coun., Macon, 1975-87, C. of C., Macon, 1977; dir. Ga. Mcpl. Assn., Atlanta, 1982-83, Nat. League Cities, Washington, 1985-87; chmn. Macon-Bibb County Indsl. Authority, 1992-93, 99, 2000, Macon Econ. Devel. Commn., 1992-2007, chmn., 1992, 93, 99; pres. Macon Symphony Orch., 2000-02; deacon Presbyn. Ch. Named Community leader of Yr. Robins Air Logistics Ctr., Warner Robins, Ga., 1987; recipient Motie Wiggins award for Outstanding elected ofcl. Ga. Mcpl. Assn., Atlanta, 1987, Ga. Tech.'s Dean Griffin Cmty. Svc. award, 2000, Macon Arts Alliance Cultural award, 2002. Fellow AIA; mem. Middle Ga. chpt. AIA (pres. 1993), Ga. Assn. AIA (dir. 1992-93). Democrat. Presbyterian. Avocations: golf, piano, choir. Office: Dunwody/Beeland 300 Mulberry St Ste 604 Macon GA 31201-7922 Personal E-mail: ecd@dbdgn.com.

DUNYE, CHERYL, artist, filmmaker; b. Phila. BA, Temple U.; MFA, Rutgers U. Part-time instr. dept. media studies Pitzer Coll., Calif. Film maker (short film films) Greetings from Africa, 1994, (video films) The Potluck and the Passion, creator (films) The Watermelon Woman, contbr. articles to profl. jours. Recipient Major Artists award, MARMAF Pa., 1993; fellow, Rutgers U., 1990, 1991, Art Matters, Inc., 1992, grantee, Astrea Found., 1992, Frameline, 1992, NEA, 1995. Office: c/o Media Studies Pitzer Coll Scott Hall Basement 1050 N Mills Ave Claremont CA 91711-3908

DUONG, ANH, artist, actress; b. Talence, Gironde, France, Oct. 25; came to U.S., 1988; d. Loi and Esther (Tejedor) D. BA, Lycee Evariste Galois, Yvelines, France, 1978; student, Ballet Sch. Acad. Nora Kiss, Paris, 1978-82, U. Beaux Arts, 1979. Ballet dancer various cos., France, 1978-82. Dir. documentary film: El Cuartel Del Carmen, 1988; appeared in films I Shot Andy Warhol, 30, Scent of a Woman, The Mambo Kings, High Art, A Vendre; paintings exhibited in one person shows at Sperone Westwater, N.Y., 1990, Fukuoka, Japan, 1995, Mus. Modern Art PMMK, Belgium, 1997, Gallery Jerome de Noirmont, Paris, 1999, 2001, 2003, Tony Shafrazi Gallery, N.Y., 2000, in group shows at Annina Nosei, N.Y., 1991, Daniel Blau, Munich, 1993; model for numerous mags. including Vogue, Harper's Bazaar, N.Y. Times Mag., Mirabella, Harpers and Queens, Glamour, Donna, Elle, also for numerous runways shows and campaigns for designers, including Donna Karan, Calvin Klein, The Gap, Banana Republic, Christian LaCroix, John Galliano, Isaac Mizrahi, others.

DUPIES, DONALD ALBERT, retired civil engineer; b. Waukegan, Ill., Apr. 17, 1934; s. Renie Bernard and Catherine Marie (Dowe) D.; m. Margaret T. McKibbin, Sept. 29, 1962; children: Mark, Patrick, Peggy, Colleen. BCE, Marquette U., 1957. With Howard, Needles, Tammen & Bergendoff, Milw., 1959—, office engr., 1969-71, engr. in charge, 1971-74, assoc., 1974-79, cons. engr., ptnr., 1980-95. Pres. Great Lakes divsn. HNTB Corp., ret., 1995. Bd. dirs. Centurions of St. Joseph Hosp., Milw., 1971-76; cubmaster Milw. County coun. Boy Scouts Am., 1973-75; mem. Bd. Appeals, Town of Delafield, Wis., 1996-2002. Served with C.E. U.S. Army, 1957-59. Mem. ASCE (nat. dir. 1982-85), Internat. Inst. of Transportation Engrs., Marquette Club of Milwaukee, Marquette U. Engring. Alumni Assn. (dir. Milw. 1976-83pres. 1981-82), Tau Beta Pi, Chi Epsilon. Roman Catholic. Home: 1637 Jardin Ct The Villages FL 32162 Personal E-mail: dadupies@yahoo.com.

DUPLECHIN, D. JAMES, lawyer; b. Rayne, La., Aug. 1, 1967; s. Kermit Joseph and Neva (Boudreaux) D.; m. Deborah Lynn McEachern, Oct. 13, 1990; children: Ryan James, Andrew David. BS, Troy State U., 1990, MPA, 1991; JD, Birmingham U. Sch. Law, 1996. Bar: Ala. 1997, U.S. Dist. Ct. (mid. dist.) Ala. 1997, U.S. Dist. Ct. (so. dist.) Ala. 2001. Case mgr. Norris & Assocs., Birmingham, 1991-95; intern McCallum & Assocs., Birmingham, 1996; from law clk. to assoc. Powell, Powell & Powell, Crestview, Fla., 1996—2002; atty. D. James Duplechin LLC, Florala, Ala., 2002—. Adv. coun. USAF Tactical Air Warfare Ctr., Eglin AFB, Fla., 1988-91, 8th Tactical Fighter Wing, Kunsan Air Base, South Korea, 1987-88. Mem. ABA, Ala. State Bar Assn., ATLA, Acad. Fla. Trial Lawyers. Roman Catholic. Office: 24147 Fifth Ave Florala AL 36442 Office Phone: 334-858-5858.

DUPLESSIS, AUDREY JOSEPH, school system administrator; b. New Orleans, June 23, 1920; d. Louis Joseph and Sidonie Josephine (DeLaRose) Boyer; m. Norwood Jerome Duplessis, Sr., June 27, 1984. B in Vocat. Edn., So. U., Baton Rouge, 1942; BA, Calif. State U., 1959, MA, 1966. Tchr., dir. Tri State Coll., New Orleans, 1948-50; from elem. tchr. to dir. Magnet Sch. L.A. Unified Schs., 1954—2002, dir. Magnet Sch., 2002—. Playground L.A. Unified Schs., 1956-59, reading resource tchr., 1965-70, curriculum coord., 1972-78, dir. L.A. Unified Magnet Sch., 1978-02; reading tchr. Calif. Lutheran Coll., Thousand Oaks, 1968-70. Mem. United Tchrs. PAC, L.A., 1980-88. Recipient svc. award Congress of Parents, L.A., 1988, spl. recognition U.S. Congress, 1988. Mem. Internat. Assn. Childhood Edn. (state pres. 1987-89, appreciation award 1989), St. Brigid Edn. Com., Delta Sigma Theta. Democrat. Roman Catholic. Avocations: reading, sewing, travel, opera, music.

DUPLESSY, JEAN CLAUDE, research scientist; b. Paris, Oct. 3, 1942; s. Andre and Lucette (Fauvet) D.; m. Sylwia Kowalska, Sept. 21, 1968; children: Jacques-Eric, Catherine. Agrégation Physics, Ecole Normale Sup., Paris, 1967; D. Geology, U. Paris, 1967, D. Scis./Physics, 1972; D. (hon.), Univ. Kiel, 2003. Rsch. intern Ctr. Natl. de la Recherche Scientifique, Gif Sur Yvette, France, 1967-68, rsch. attaché, 1968-73, rsch. asst., 1973-76, rsch. master, 1976-84, dir. rsch., 1984-91, dir. rsch.-exceptional class, 1991—. Dir. Ctr. des Faibles Radioactivites, Gif Sur Yvette, 1985-96. Co-Author: Gros Temps Sur la Planete, 1990; co-editor: (2 book series) Nato, 1989-94. Recipient prix Aime Berthe, French Acad. Sci., 1987, Milankovitch medal European Geophys. Soc., 1995, prix Dolomieu, French Acad. Scis., 2004, prix. Louis D. Inst. France, 2005. Mem. Acad. Europaea. Office: Lab des Scis Climat et L'environnement Parc Du CNRS 91198 Gif-sur-Yvette France Office Phone: 33169823526. Business E-Mail: jean.claude.duplessy@lsce.cnrs-gif.fr.

DUPONT, ANTOINETTE LOIACONO, judge; b. NYC, Jan. 10, 1929; d. Albert J. Loiacono and Helen Utano; m. Albert W. Cretella Jr., Aug. 24, 1990; children: Ellen, Antonia, William. AB, Brown U., 1950; JD, Harvard U., 1954; LLD (hon.), Conn. Coll., 1998. Judge Hartford (Conn.) Superior Trial Ct., 1977-83; chief judge Appellate Ct. of Conn., Hartford, 1984-98, sr. judge, 1998—. Office: Appellate Ct of Conn 95 Washington St Hartford CT 06106-4431

DUPONT, AUGUSTUS IRÉNÉE, lawyer; b. NYC, Oct. 18, 1951; s. Francis I. and Rosamont S. (Lee) duP.; m. Jill Greenwood, June 23, 1979; children: Jessie G., John W., Hilary G. AB, Stanford U., 1975; JD, U. Chgo., 1978. Bar: Mass. 1978, N.Y. 1980. Assoc. Skadden, Arps, Slate, Meagher & Flom, NYC, 1978-84; assoc. counsel The Penn Cen. Corp., Greenwich, Conn., 1984-86, asst. gen. counsel, 1986-87; v.p., gen. counsel, sec. Sprague Techs., Inc., Stamford, Conn., 1987—93; v.p., gen. counsel Reeves Industries, Inc., 1994—95; v.p., sec., gen. counsel Crane Co., Stamford, Conn., 1996—. Mem. ABA, Am. Corp. Counsel Assn. Home: 346 North St Greenwich CT 06830-3930 Office: Crane Co 100 First Stamford Pl Stamford CT 06902 Office Phone: 203-363-7223. Office Fax: 203-363-7295. E-mail: adupont@craneco.com.*

DUPONT, HERBERT LANCASHIRE, medical educator, researcher; b. Toledo, Nov. 12, 1938; s. Robert L. and Martha (Lancashire) DuPont; m. Margaret Wright, June 9, 1963; children: Denise Lorraine, Andrew Wright BA, Ohio Wesleyan U., 1961; MD, Emory U., 1965; doctorate (hon.), U. Zurich, 2004. Diplomate Am. Bd. Internal Medicine. Resident U. Minn. Med. Ctr., Mpls., 1965-67; officer epidemic intelligence svc. CDC Atlanta, infectious disease fellow U. Md. Sch. Medicine, Balt., 1967-69; faculty, prof., dir. Infectious Diseases Program & Clin. Microbiology U. Tex., Houston, 1973—88; dir. Ctr. for Infectious Diseases U. Tex. Sch. Pub. Health, Houston, 1989—95; dir. Ctr. for Infectious Diseases, Sch. Pub. Health U. Tex., Houston, 2000—, prof. epidemiology, Sch. Pub. Health, 1975—, Mary W. Kelsey chair med. sci., 1988—, interim chmn. dept. internal medicine, 1977—78, 1987—89; chief internal medicine svc. St. Luke's Episcopal Hosp., Houston, 1995—; clin. prof. dept. medicine Baylor Coll. Medicine, Houston, 1995—, vice chmn. dept. medicine, H. Irving Schweppe chair, 1995—; prof. grad. sch. biomed. sci. U. Tex., 2002, Baylor Coll. Medicine, 2004—. Vaccines and related biologic products adv. com. US FDA, 1989—93, cons., 1989—; sci. adv. com. Inst. Medicine, NAS, 1989—94; bd. sci. counselors Nat. Ctr. for Infectious Diseases, CDC, 1992—96; bd. Kelsey Rsch. Found., 2001—. Author various med. books; assoc. editor: Am. Jour. Epidemiology, 1978—81, Jour. Infectious Diseases, 1983—88; mem. editl. bd. Clin. Infectious Diseases, 1990—95, Infectious Diseases in Clin. Practice, 1992—, Jour. of Infection, 1997—, dep. editor Jour. of Travel Medicine, 2003—; contbr. articles to profl. jours. Lt. comdr. USAF, 1967—69. Recipient John P. McGovern Outstanding Tchr., U. Tex.-Houston Med. Sch., 1991, Bronze medal of honor, government of France, 1993, Benjy Brooks award, U. Tex.-Houston, 1997, Disting. Achievement citation, Ohio Wesleyan U., 2006, Maxwell Finland award for Scientific Achievement, Nat. Found. Infectious Diseases, Washington, 2007; Rsch. grant NIH, 1975-97. Fellow ACP; mem. Am. Soc. Clin. Investigation, Infectious Diseases Soc. Am. (counselor 1978-81, sec. 1982-87, pres. 1989-90), Nat. Found. Infectious Diseases (bd. dirs. 1981-2002, v.p. 1994-97, pres. 1997-99), Am. Clin. and Climatol. Assn. (recorder 2000-05, coun. mem. 2000-, pres.-elect. 2005-06, pres. 2006-07), Am. Epidemiology Soc., Assn. Am. Physicians, U.S. Mex. Found. Sci. and Tech. (com. chair health 1994-99), Tex. Acad. Internal Medicine (bd. dirs. 2003-07), Internat. Soc. Travel Medicine (pres. 1991-93), Am. Coll. Physicians (gov. S. Tex. bd. govs. 2003-07), Alpha Omega Alpha. Republican. Methodist. Office: St Luke's Episcopal Hosp # MC 1-164 6720 Bertner St Houston TX 77030-2697

DUPONT, RALPH PAUL, lawyer, educator; b. Fall River, Mass., May 21, 1929; s. Michael William and Gertrude (Murphy) Dupont; m. Barbara Joan Dupont; children: Ellen O'Neill, Antonia Chafee, William Albert, Christien Paul. AB in Am. Civilization cum laude with highest honors, Brown U., 1951; JD cum laude, Harvard U., 1956. Bar: Conn. 1956, U.S. Supreme Ct. 1967, diplomate: Nat. Bd. Trial Advocacy, cert.: Conn. (civil trial specialist). Assoc. Davies, Hardy & Schenck, NYC, 1956-57; ptnr. Copp & Dupont, New London, Conn., 1957-60; mem. Suisman, Shapiro & Wool, New London, 1961-63; ptnr. Dupont & Dupont (and successor firms), New London, 1963-91; of counsel Durant, Nichols, Houston, Mitchell & Sheahan, Bridgeport, Conn., 1992-97; ptnr. Dupont and Radlauer LLP, New London, Stamford, 1997—2005; of counsel The Dupont Law Firm, Stamford, Conn. Instr. Am. history and bus. law Mitchell Coll., New London, 1955, New London, 1957—58, trustee, 1991—94; vis. prof. Northeastern U. Sch. Law, 1977—78; lectr.-on-law U. Conn. Sch. Law, 1980—86; mem. adv. coun. Conn. Legal Svcs., 1980—82; trustee Anne S. K. Brown Mil. Collection Brown U., 1988—92, presiding trustee, 1990—92; vis. prof. law Bridgeport Law Sch. Quinnipiac Coll., 1991—92; vis. prof. We. New Eng. Coll. Law, 1992—94; mem. exec. bd., adj. prof. Sch. Law Quinnipiac U., Hamden, Conn., 1994—96; instr. bus. law U. New Haven, 1998. Author: (book) Litigation in 1 Attorney's Desk Library, 1994, Dupont on Connecticut Civil Practice, 2003. Mem. New London Bd. Edn., 1959—61; Dem. candidate Conn. Senate, 1960; trustee U.S. Atlantic Tuna Tournament, 1984—93, pres., 1988—90, chmn., 1991—92. Lt. (j.g.) USNR, 1951—53. Named Outstanding Young Man of the Yr., Conn. Jr. C. of C., 1960; recipient Disting. Svc. award, Greater New London Jr. C. of C., 1960. Fellow: Am. Coll. Trust and Estate Coun.; mem.: ABA, Internat. Acad. Estate and Trust Law, Conn. Bar Found. (bd. dirs. 1975—79), Conn. Bar Assn., Harvard U. Law Sch. Assn., Pacific Club, Harvard Club, Kappa Sigma, Delta Sigma Rho. Roman Catholic. Home: 6770 Hawaii Kai Dr apt PH 9 Honolulu HI 96825 Office Phone: 203-321-2176. Personal E-mail: radlaw2001@aol.com.

DUPONT, ROBERT LOUIS, psychiatrist, physician; b. Toledo, Mar. 25, 1936; s. Robert Louis and Martha Ireton (Lancashire) DuP.; m. Helen Gayden Spink, July 14, 1962; children: Elizabeth, Caroline. BA, Emory U., 1958; MD, Harvard U., 1963. Diplomate in psychiatry and addiction psychiatry Am. Bd. Psychiatry and Neurology; cert. med. rev. officer. Intern Western Res. U., 1963-64; resident in psychiatry Harvard Med. Sch., 1964-66; clin. assoc. NIH, 1966-68; research psychiatrist, acting assoc. dir. for community services D.C. Dept. Corrections, Washington, 1968-70; practice medicine specializing in psychiatry, 1968—. Adminstr. Narcotics Treatment Adminstrn., D.C. Dept. Human Resources, 1970—73; acting adminstr. Alcohol, Drug Abuse and Mental Health Adminstrn., HEW, Rockville, Md., 1974; dir. Nat. Inst. on Drug Abuse, HEW, Rockville, 1973—78, Spl. Action Office for Drug Abuse Prevention, Exec. Office Pres., Washington, 1973—75; pres. Inst. for Behavior and Health Inc., 1978—, Am. Coun. Drug Edn., 1980—85; U.S. del. UN Commn. on Narcotic Drugs, 1973—78; mem. Coordinating Coun. on Juvenile Justice and Delinquency Prevention, Dept. Justice, 1974—76; assoc. clin. prof. psychiatry and behavioral scis. George Washington Med. Sch., 1972—80; clin. prof. psychiatry Georgetown U. Med. Sch., 1980—; vis. assoc. clin. prof. psychiatry Harvard U. Med. Sch., 1978—84; chmn. Ctr. Behavioral Medicine, 1978—89; v.p. Bensinger, DuPont Assocs., Inc., 1982—; chair Prescription Drug Rsch. Ctr., 2004—. Author: The Selfish Brain, 2000, The Anxiety Cure, 2003, The Anxiety Cure for Kids, 2003, Drug Testing in Treatment Settings, 2005, Drug Testing in Schools, 2005, Drug Testing in Correctional Settings, 2005; contbr. articles in fields of drug abuse, criminology and mental health to profl. jours.; appeared on Good Morning Am., ABC-TV, 1978—80. Bd. dirs. Washington Soc. for Performing Arts, 1972-76; mem. adv. com. Washington Jr. League, 1972-76. Served to surgeon (maj.) USPHS, 1966-68. Fellow: Am. Soc. Addiction Medicine (life; diplomate), Am. Psychiat. Assn. (life); mem.: Anxiety Disorders Assn. Am. (pres. 1982—85), Washington Psychiat. Soc. Home: 8708 Susanna Ln Chevy Chase MD 20815-4714 Office: 6191 Executive Blvd Rockville MD 20852-3901 Home Phone: 301-657-8194; Office Phone: 301-231-9010. Personal E-mail: bobdupont@aol.com. *As a practicing physician dealing with addiction and anxiety disorders, I have seen first-hand the intense suffering experienced by those afflicted and by those who love them. As a public health practitioner, I have seen the immense cost of these disorders. The miracle of recovery has been the inspiration of my career.*

DUPONT, WILLIAM DUDLEY, biostatistician, educator; b. Montreal, Que., Can., Nov. 6, 1946; came to U.S., 1971; s. Charles Thomas and Jean (White) Dupont; m. Susan Miller McChesney, July 20, 1974; children: Charles Thomas, Peter William. BSc, McGill U., 1969, MSc, 1971; PhD, Johns Hopkins U., 1976. Lectr. U. Md., Balt., 1976-77; asst. prof. biostats. Vanderbilt U. Sch. Medicine, Nashville, 1977-85, assoc. prof., 1986-92, prof., 1992—, dir. divsn. biostats., 1989—2003. Nat. Cancer Inst. grantee, 1980—. Mem. AAAS, Am. Statis. Assn., Biometric Soc., Soc. Clin. Trials, Soc. Epidemiol. Rsch. Office: Vanderbilt U Sch Medicine Dept Biostats 1161 21st Ave S S-2323 MCN Nashville TN 37232-2158 Home Phone: 615-343-4100; Office Phone: 615-322-2001. E-mail: william.dupont@vanderbilt.edu.

DUPPSTADT, WILLIAM HOMER, retired botanist, educator, lay worker; b. Buffalo Mills, Pa., May 18, 1919; s. William Oren and Stella Duppstadt; m. Esther Irene Ringler, Apr. 20, 1946; children: Joyce Elaine, Carol Ann, Paul Luther, David Allen. BS in Sci., Shippensburg U., Pa., 1941; post grad. in Biology, U. Hawaii, Honolulu, 1945; post grad. in Christian Edn., Luth. Theol. Sem., Gettysburg, Pa., 1946—47, post grad. in Christian Edn., 1949—50; post grad. in Edn., U. Pitts., Johnstown, Pa., 1957—58; EdM, Pa. State U., State Coll., 1960; MA, W.Va. U., Morgantown, 1966; cultural doctorate in Botany (hon.), World U., Benson, Ariz., 1983. Lay minister Bedford County Luth. Chs., Pa., 1947—; farmer Buffalo Mills, Pa., 1950—88; farm cons., 1988—; tchr. Chestnut Ridge H.S., Fishertown, 1955—73; plant taxonomist - herbarium asst. W. Va. U., Morgantown, 1974—92; botanist W.Va. Dept. Natural Resources, Charleston, 1977—82; grad. rsch. asst. in systematic botany W.Va. U., Morgantown, 1978—79; plant taxonomist and vegetation analyst Academic Assoc., Inc., Morgantown, 1979—82; sr. lectr. plant taxonomy Frostburg State U., Md., 1989, 1990. Participant Rare Plant Survey of W.Va.,

1979—81; pres. Chestnut Ridge Edn. Assn., 1967—69; charter mem. Bedford Farm Coop. Co-author (with Earl L. Core): Spring Wildflowers of Central Pennsylvania, 1978; co-author: (with R.B. Clarkson and R.L. Guthrie) Forest Wildlife Plants of Monongahela National Forest, 1980; contbr. scientific papers, articles to profl. jours. Project leader Bedford County 4-H, Pa., 1974—89; mem. Mt. Olive Luth. Ch., 1973—. Sgt. Signal Corps US Army, 1942—46. Recipient Century Farms award, Pa. Dept. Agr., 1987. Mem.: AAA, W.Va. Acad. Sci. (life), Nat. Assn. Biology Tchrs. (life), Am. Soc. Plant Taxonomists (life), WWII Meml. Soc. (charter mem.), Scotland Sch. Veterans Children (life), Pa. State Coll. Edn. Alumni Assn. (life), Nat. Ret. Tchrs. Assn. (life), Pa. State Alumni Assn. (life), W.Va. U. Alumni Assn. (life), Am. Legion (life), Phi Epsilon Phi, Phi Delta Kappa. Republican. Lutheran. Achievements include research in flora of southwestern Pennsylvania and northern West Virginia. Avocations: botanical field trips, blacksmithing, gardening. Home: 551 Greenbrier Ln Buffalo Mills PA 15534

DUPRÉ, LOUIS, retired philosopher, educator; b. Veerle, Belgium; arrived in U.S., 1958, naturalized, 1966; s. Clement and Francisca (Verlinden) D. PhD, U. Louvain, Belgium; PhD (hon.), Loyola Coll., Balt., 1989, Sacred Heart U., Fairfield Conn., 1992, Georgetown U., Washington, 1996, Siena Coll., Loudenville, NY, 1997, Regis Coll. U. Toronto, Can., 1998, St. Michael's Coll., 2002, Marquette U., Milw., 2007. From asst. prof. to prof. philosophy Georgetown U., Washington, 1959-73; T. Lawrason Riggs prof. philosophy of religion Yale U., New Haven, 1973-98. Author: Kierkegaard as Theologian (also in Dutch), 1963, The Philosophical Foundations of Marxism, 1966, Dutch edit., 1970, Korean edit., 1982, The Other Dimension, 1972, French edit., 1977, Chinese edit., 1986, 2006, Polish edit., 1990, Dutch edit., 1991, Korean edit., 1995, Spanish edit., 1999, Transcendent Selfhood, 1976, Dutch edit., 1981, A Dubious Heritage, 1979, The Deeper Life, 1981, Polish edit., 1994, German edit., 2002, Marx's Social Critique of Culture, 1983, The Common Life, 1984, Polish edit., 1994, German edit., 2003, Passage to Modernity, 1993, Metaphysics and Culture, 1994, Religious Mystery and Rational Reflection, 1997, Symbols of the Sacred, 2000, German edit., 2007, The Enlightenment and the Intellectual Foundations of Modern Culture, 2004; editor: Faith and Reflection, 1968; co-editor: Light from Light, 1987, 2d edit., 2001; contbr. articles to profl. jours. Recipient Phi Beta Kappa medal as Tchr. of Yr. at Yale U., 1996, Aquinas medal, Am. Cath. Philos. Assn., 1997. Mem. Am. Cath. Philos. Assn. (pres. 1971), Hegel Soc. Am. (pres. 1972-73), Am. Acad. Arts and Scis., Belgian Acad. Letters, Arts, & Scis. Roman Catholic. Home: 67 N Racebrook Rd Woodbridge CT 06525-1407 Business E-Mail: louis.dupre@yale.edu.

DUPREE, CANDICE, professional basketball player; b. Aug. 16, 1984; Student, Temple U., Phila. Forward Chgo. Sky, 2006—. Mem. USA Women's Sr. Nat. Team. Named MVP, Atlantic 10 Tournament, 2004, 2005, Atlantic 10 Defensive Player of Yr., 2005, Atlantic 10 and Phila. Big Five Player of Yr., 2005; named to Atlantic 10 All-Rookie Team, 2003, Atlantic 10 Second Team, 2004, Atlantic 10 All-Defensive Team, 2004, 2005, Big Five First Team, 2004, 2005, Atlantic 10 First Team, 2005, E. Conf. All-Star Team, WNBA, 2006—07. Mailing: Chgo Sky 20 W Kinzie St Ste 1010 Chicago IL 60610*

DUPREE, CLIFFORD H. R., lawyer; b. Phila., Sept. 11, 1950; s. Frederick Douglass and Dorothy Olivia (Rylander) DuP. AB, Princeton U., 1972; JD, Harvard U., 1975. Bar: N.Y. 1976. V.p., assoc. gen. counsel and sec. Terra Industries Inc.; assoc. Chadbourne, Parke et al, NYC, 1976-83; v.p., assoc. gen. counsel, sec. Inspiration Resources Corp., NYC, 1983-92; assoc. gen. counsel, asst. sec. Reader's Digest Assn., Pleasantville, N.Y., 1992-97, v.p., assoc. gen. counsel, sec., 1997, corp. sec., 1998—. Mem. ABA, N.Y. Bar Assn., Am. Soc. Corp. Secs. Office: Readers Digest Assn Inc Readers Digest Rd Pleasantville NY 10570 Office Phone: 914-238-1000. Office Fax: 914-241-5644.

DU PREZ, JOHN, composer; b. Sheffield, England, Dec. 14, 1946; Composer: (films) The Pantomime Dance, 1982, Monty Python's The Meaning of Live, 1983, The Crimson Permanent Assurance, 1983, Bullshot, 1983, She'll Be Wearing Pink Pyjamas, 1984, Oxford Blues, 1984, A Private Function, 1984, Once Bitten, 1985, Personal Services, 1987, Number 27, 1988, A Chorus of Disapproval, 1988, A Fish Called Wanda, 1988 (ASCAP award, 1989), UHF, 1989, Teenage Mutant Ninja Turtles, 1990 (BMI Film Music award, 1991), Bullseye!, 1990, Teenage Mutant Ninja Turtles II: The Secret of the Ooze, 1991 (BMI Film Music award, 1992), Mystery Date, 1991, Carry On Columbus, 1992, Teenage Mutant Ninja Turtles III, 1993, A Good Man in Africa, 1994, The Wind in the Willows, 1996, Fascination, 2004, (TV films) Love with the Perfect Stranger, 1986, Sweet as You Are, 1987, The Kremlin, Farewell, 1990, (TV series) Sunday Premiere: Claws, 1987, Captain Star, 1997, (Broadway plays) Spamalot, 2005 (Tony award for Best Musical, 2005, Drama Desk award, Outstanding New Musical, 2005, Grammy award, Best Musical Show Album, 2006); musical dir. Eric Idle Exploits Monty Python, 2000, The Greedy Bastard Tour, 2003, co-author The Fairly Incomplete & Rather Badly Illustrated Monty Python Song Book. Mem.: Royal Coll. Music. Office: Decca Broadway 19th Fl 825 8th Ave New York NY 10019

DUPRI, JERMAINE, recording industry executive, music producer; b. Asheville, NC, Sept. 23, 1973; s. Michael and Tina Mauldin; 1 child, Shaniah. Record prodr., 1987—; founder, CEO So So Def Prodns., Atlanta, 1989—; solo artist, 1998—; sr. v.p. Arista Records, 2003—05; pres. Virgin Records Urban Music, 2005—06, Island Records Urban Music divsn., NYC, 2007—. Singer, songwriter (albums) Jermaine Dupri Presents: Life in 1472, 1998, Jermaine Dupri Presents: 12 Soulful Nights, 1998, Instructions, 2001, Green Light, 2004, prodr. for artists including Aaliyah, Destiny's Child, Da Brat, Warren G, Aretha Franklin, Dru Hill, Jay-Z, Alicia Keys, Lil' Kim, Elton John, Kris Kross, Run DMC, Whodini, Usher, Funkmaster Flex, Johnny Gill, Murphy Lee, Ludacris, MC Lyte, Master P., Monica, Chante' Moore, Nelly, New Edition, TLC, Tamia, Tyrese, Lil' Bow Wow, Mariah Carey and others; actor: (films) In Too Deep, 1999, The New Guy, 2002; (TV films) Carmen: A Hip Hopera, 2001, (TV appearances) A Different World, 1992, Moesha, 1996; host (TV series) Cuttin' Up, 2004—; co-prodr.: (films) Like Mike, 2002. Co-recipient Best R&B Song for We Belong Together, Grammy Awards, 2006; named Songwriter of Yr., ASCAP, 1999; recipient Prodr. of Yr., Black Entertainment TV (BET) Hip-Hop Awards, 2006. Achievements include making it to #1 on Top R&B/Hip Hop Chart and #3 on the Billboard 200 for "Jermaine Dupri Presents: Life in 1472" in 1998. Office: Island Records 825 Eighth Ave New York NY 10019 also: So So Def Recordings Inc NW #750 1350 Spring St Atlanta GA 30309-2870*

DUPRIEST, DOUGLAS MILLHOLLEN, lawyer; b. Ft. Riley, Kans., Dec. 28, 1951; s. Robert White and Barbara Nadine (Millhollen) DuP. AB in Philosophy with high honors, Oberlin Coll., 1974; JD, U. Oreg., 1977. Bar: Oreg. 1977, U.S. Dist. Ct. Oreg. 1977, U.S. Ct. Appeals (9th cir.) 1977. Assoc. Coons & Anderson and predecessors, Eugene, Oreg., 1977—81, Hutchinson, Harrell et al 1981; ptnr. Hutchinson, Cox, Coons, DuPriest , Orr, and Sherlock and predecessors, 1982—. Adj. prof. sch. law U. Oreg., 1986; mem. task forces Wetlands Mgmt., 1988-89, 92-93. Author: (with others) Land Use, 1982, 2000, Administrative Law, 1985; contbg. editor Real Estate & Land Use Digest, 1983-86; articles editor, mng. bd. mem. U. Oreg. Law Rev., 1976-77. Bd. dirs. Home Health Agy., Eugene, 1977-79, pres., 1978-79; bd. dirs. Oreg. Environ. Coun., Portland, 1979-84, pres., 1980-81, McKenzie River Trust, 1998—; chair voters pamphlet com. Eugene City Club, 1993. Recipient Disting. Svc. award Oreg. Environ. Coun., 1988. Mem. Oreg. Bar Assn. (exec. com. real estate and land use sect. 1978-81). Office: Hutchinson Cox Coons DuPriest Orr & Sherlock 777 High St Ste 200 Eugene OR 97401-2750 Office Phone: 541-686-9160. Business E-Mail: dupriest@engene-law.com.

DUPUIS, ROBERT SIMEON, sales executive; b. Palmer, Mass., Aug. 31, 1941; s. Bertrand Leonard and Hanora Theresa (Crean) D.; m. Dianne Cecile Gibouleau, Aug. 20, 1960; children: Kathleen, Corinne, Lynn, Robert. Student, Springfield Tech. C.C. Laborer Springfield (Mass.) Foundry, 1959-60; warehouse forklift operator Ludlow (Mass.) Industries, 1960-62; machinists, mechanic Tambrands, Inc., Palmer, Mass., 1962-64; apprentice toolmaker Pratt & Whitney Aircraft, East Hartford, Conn., 1964-66; toolmaker Target Tool Co., Three Rivers, Mass., 1966-68; tool and die maker Brookfield Machine Corp., West Brookfield, Mass., 1968-75, Prodn. Tool & Die, Springfield, 1975-77; tool and die engr. Vogform Tool & Die, West Springfield, 1977-85; regional mgr. Dayton (Ohio) Progress Corp., 1985—. Cons., speaker Worcester (Mass.) Poly. Inst., 1991—. Chmn., vice chair Palmer (Mass.) Sch. Com., 1977—; sec. Three River Prudential Fire Dept. Com., 1978-80; chmn., subcom. Palmer Fin. Com., 1971-77; mem. Palmer Libr. Com., 1988-90. Mem. SME (sr., speaker), Precision Metal Forming Assn. (tech. cons., speaker 1985—), Three Rivers C. of C. Roman Catholic. Avocations: deep sea fishing, scuba diving, hiking, biking, golf, boating. Home and Office: Dayton Progress Corp 322 Flynt St Palmer MA 01069-1657 Office Phone: 413-531-9696. Home Fax: 413-283-5521. Business E-Mail: bdupuis@daytonprogress.com.

DUPUIS, RUSSELL DEAN, electrical engineer, researcher; 1 child. BSEE, U. Ill., 1970, MSEE, 1971, PhD in Elec. Engring., 1973. Lic. profl. engr., Tex., 2001. Mem. tech. staff Tex. Instruments Corp., Dallas, 1973—75, Rockwell Internat. Corp., Anaheim, Calif., 1975-79, AT&T Bell Labs., Murray Hill, NJ, 1979-85, disting. tech. staff mem., 1985-89; prof., Judson S. Swearingen Regents Chair in Engring. Dept. Elec. and Computer Engring U. Tex., Austin, 1989—2003; prof., Steven W. Chaddick endowed chair in electro-optics Ga. Inst. Tech., Atlanta, 2003—. Contbr. articles to profl. jours. Recipient Disting. MTS award AT&T-Bell Labs., 1985, Nat. Acad. Engring, 1989, Young Scientist award GaAs Symposium, 1986, Disting. Alumnus award U. Ill., 1987, Nat. Medal Tech., US Dept. Commerce, 2002, John Bardeen award, Minerals and Metals Soc., 2004. Fellow IEEE (Morris Liebmann award 1985, Edison medal, 2007), Optical Soc. Am.; mem. NAE, Lasers and Electro-Optics Soc. of IEEE (bd. govs. 1989, tech. achievement award 1995), Am. Phys. Soc., Electrochem. Soc., Electronics Materials Com. Achievements include first to use Metalorganic Chemical Vapor Deposition (MOCVD) to grow high quality thin films and devices; demonstrate room temperature continuous wave operation of AlGaAs-GaAs quantum well injection lasers establishing that these lasers were reliable enough for practical use. Avocation: genealogy.*

DUPUIS, VICTOR LIONEL, retired curriculum and instruction educator; b. Chgo., Oct. 30, 1934; s. Edward G. and LaVerne Ann (Brown) D.; m. Mary Jean Miles, Aug. 11, 1956; children: Mary Catherine, Victor Edward, Elizabeth Ann. BS, Northwestern U., Evanston, Ill., 1956; MA, Am. U., DC, 1961; PhD, Purdue U., West Lafayette, Ind., 1965. Tchr. jr. high sch., Arlington, Va., 1956-61; tchr. Klondike Sch. Dist., West Lafayette, Ind., 1961-63, curriculum dir., 1962-63; grad. instr. Purdue U., West Lafayette, 1963—65; asst. prof. Pa. State U., University Park, 1967—70, assoc. prof. curriculum, 1970—74, prof., chmn. curriculum and supervision, 1974—91, prof. edn. curriculum and instrn., 1989-91, Waterbury prof. secondary edn., 1990-92, chmn. curriculum and suprvision, 1991, prof. emeritus curriculum and instrn., 1992—; CEO Dupuis Assocs., 1985—. Cons. to various pvt. and public schs., state depts. edn. Native Am. programs. Author: Resource Booklet and Overhead Transparency Masters for Foundation of American Education, 1966, (textbooks) Introductory Readings in the Foundation of American Education, 1966, An Introduction to the Foundations of American Education, 1969, 14th edit., 2008; author: (with others) Introduction to the Foundations of American Education, 1966; author: Foundation of American Education: Readings, 1969, 1985, Issues in Education, 1991, Resource Booklet: Foundations of American Education, 2002, video collection of articles in profl. jours. Chmn. Patton Twp. (Pa.) Park Bd., 1969-70, Patton Twp. Planning Commn., 1971-73; Democratic precinct committeeman Patton Twp., 1971-76, chmn., twp. supr., 1973-92. Served to 2d lt. inf. U.S. Army, 1957-59. Recipient Waterbury Chair honoree, Pa. State U., 1989—91. Mem. ASCD, Am. Ednl. Rsch. Assn., Nat. Staff Devel. Coun., Pa. Assn. Supervision and Curriculum Devel., Phi Delta Kappa. Home: 205 Presidents Dr State College PA 16803 E-mail: vdupuis@aol.com.

DUPUY, BOB (ROBERT A. DUPUY), major league baseball executive; AB, Dartmouth Coll., 1968; JD, Cornell U., 1973. With Foley and Lardner, 1973—89, ptnr., 1980—89; legal counsel Major League Baseball, NYC, 1989—92, prin. outside counsel to commr. and exec. coun., 1992—98, exec. v.p. adminstrn., chief legal officer, 1998—2002, pres., COO, 2002—. Lectr. Northwestern U., U. Wis., Marquette U.; facutly mem. Nat. Inst. Trial Advocacy; pres., coord. World Baseball Classic, 2006. With US Army, 1968—70, served with 504th Military Police Battalion. Decorated Army Commendation Medal. Mem.: State Bar Wis. (past chmn.). Office: Major League Baseball 245 Park Ave New York NY 10167*

DUPUY, CHRISTOPHER MICHAEL, lawyer; b. Houston, Tex., Aug. 26, 1971; m. Adrienne Dupuy, Sept. 28, 2001; children: Benjamin Thomas, Chloe Michele. BSME, So. Meth. U., Dallas, Tex., 1996; JD, U. Houston, Tex. Litig. atty. Howrey Simon Arnold White, Houston; ptnr. Dupuy & Assocs., P.C., League City, Tex., 2006—. Mem.: ABA, Houston Maritime Arbitrators Assn., Houston Bar Assn., Houston Assn. Realtors, Gulf Coast Mariners Assn., Galveston Bar Assn., Southeastern Admiralty Law Inst., US Counsel Internat. Bus., League City Mayor's Leadership Coun., League City C. of C., Waterford Yacht Club, Mensa, Sigma Chi. Office: Dupuy & Assocs PC 2600 South Shore Blvd Ste 300 League City TX 77573 Office Phone: 281-668-9121. Office Fax: 281-668-9123. Business E-Mail: cdupuy@southshorelegal.com.

DUQUES, RIC (HENRY C. DUQUES), information technology company executive; b. 1943; m. Dawn Duques. BA in Acctg., Washington Univ., St. Louis, 1965, MBA, 1969. Group pres.-fin. svcs. Automatic Data Processing, 1973—87; pres., CEO Data Based Svcs. Group (div. of AmEx Co.), 1987—89; CEO First Data Corp., Atlanta, 1992—2002, 2005—, chmn., 1992—2003, 2005—. Bd. dir. Unisys Corp. 1998-, non-exec. chmn. 2006-; bd. dir. No. Trust Fla.; mem. planning and policy com. Am. Express, 1987-93. Bd. trustees George Washington Univ. Office: First Data Corp 6200 S Quebec St Greenwood Village CO 80111*

DUQUETTE, DANIEL F., professional baseball team executive; V.p. of player personnel, gen. mgr. Montreal Expos, 1991-94; exec. v.p., gen. mgr. Boston Red Sox, 1994—2001; dir. Duquette Internat. Baseball Acad., 2002—; dir. player devel. Israel Baseball League, 2004—. Office: Israel Baseball League Ste 317 119 Braintree St Boston MA 02134

DUQUETTE, DIANE RHEA, library director; b. Springfield, Mass., Dec. 15, 1951; d. Gerard Lawrence and Helen Yvette (St. Marie) Morneau; m. Thomas Frederick Duquette Jr., Mar. 17, 1973. BS in Sociology, Springfield Coll., 1975; MLS, Simmons Coll., 1978. Libr. asst. Springfield City Libr., 1975—78; reference libr. U. Mass., Amherst, 1978—81; head libr. Hopkins Acad., Hadley, Mass., 1980; instr. Colo. Mountain Coll., Steamboat Springs, 1981—83; dir. East Routt Libr. Dist., Steamboat Springs, 1981—84; agy. head Solono County Libr., Vallejo, Calif., 1984; dir. libr. svcs. Shasta County Libr., Redding, Calif., 1984—87; dir. librs. Kern County Libr., Bakersfield, Calif., 1987—. Chmn. San Joaquin Valley Libr. Sys., 1988. Contbr. articles to profl. jours. Active San Joaquin Valley Libr. Assn., Calif., 1987—. Recipient John Cotton Dana Spl. Pub. Rels. award, H.W. Wilson and ALA, 1989, 2nd ann. Pub. Libr. Mgmt. award of excellence, Urban Librs. Coun./Libr. Systems and Svcs., 2002. Mem. ALA, Calif. Libr. Assn. (mem. coun. 1987—), Calif. County Librs. Assn. (pres. 1990). Democrat. Roman Catholic. Achievements include serving as director of Kern County Library when it was awarded the John Cotton Dana award for Public Relations. Avocations: golf, skiing, bicycling, reading, gardening. Office: Kern County Libr 701 Truxtun Ave Bakersfield CA 93301-4800 Office Phone: 661-868-0789. Office Fax: 661-868-0799. Business E-Mail: duquette@kerncountylibrary.org.

DUQUETTE, DONALD NORMAN, law educator; b. Manistique, Mich., Apr. 3, 1947; s. Donald Francis and Martha Adeline (Rice) D.; m. Kathy Jo Loudenbeck, June 17, 1967; 1 child, Gail Jean. BA, Mich. State U., 1969; JD, U. Mich., 1974. Bar: Mich. 1975. Children's caseworker Mich. Dept. Social Svcs., Muskegon, 1969-72; asst. prof. pediatrics and human devel. Mich. State U. Coll. Human Medicine, East Lansing, 1975-76; clin. prof., dir. child advocacy law clinic U. Mich., Ann Arbor, 1976—, co-dir. interdisciplinary project on child abuse and neglect, 1979-89, dir. permanency planning legal svcs., 1984—90, dir. interdisciplinary grad. edn. in child abuse-neglect, 1986-92, dir. Kellogg child welfare law program, 1995-98, clin. prof., dir. child advocacy law clinic, 1976—, dir. mediation clinic, 2004—. Bd. visitors U. Ariz. Sch. of Law, 1995—99; legal cons. U.S. Children's Bur., Pres. Clinton's Initiative on Adoption and Foster Care, 1997—98; bd. dirs. Nat. Assn. Counsel for Children, 1999—. Author: (non-fiction) Advocating for the Child, 1990, Michigan Child Welfare Law, 1990, Michigan Child Welfare Law, rev. edit., 2000; editor (mem. editl. bd.): (jour.) Child Abuse and Neglect Internat. Jour., 1985—90; editor: Child Welfare Law and Practice: Representing Children, Parents, and State Agencies in Abuse, Neglect, and Dependency Cases, 2005; contbr.: articles to profl. jours. Mem. Washtenaw County Bd. Commrs., 1981-88; bd. dirs. Children's Trust Fund for Prevention of Child Abuse, 1983-85; mem. Permanency Planning Com. Mich. Supreme Ct., 1982-85, Probate Ct. Task Force, 1986-87, Govs. Task Force on Children's Justice, 1992—; trustee Bay Vierw Assn., 1998--. Named Citizen of Yr. Huron Valley NASW, Ann Arbor, 1985; recipient Rsch. in Advocacy award Nat. Ct. Apptd. Spl. Advocate Assn., Seattle, 1985, Outstanding Legal Advocacy award Nat. Assn. of Counsel for Children, 1996, Hicks Child Welfare Leadership award Mich. Fedn. Children's Agys., 1998. Mem.: Mich. State Bar (co-chair Children's Task Force 1993—95), Am. Profl. Soc. on Abuse of Children. Democrat. Unitarian Universalist. Avocations: piano, sailing. Home: 1510 Linwood Ave Ann Arbor MI 48103-3659 Office: U Mich Sch Law Child Advocacy Law Clinic 625 S State St Ann Arbor MI 48109-1215 Office Phone: 734-763-5000. Business E-Mail: duquette@umich.edu.

DUQUETTE, JIM, professional sports team executive; m. Pam Duquette; children: Lauren, Lindsey, Matthew. Grad., Williams Coll., 1988. Asst. Mets Minor League and Scouting Dept. N.Y. Mets, 1991—96; dir. player devel. Houston Astros, 1996—97; dir. player pers. N.Y. Mets, Flushing, 1997—98, asst. gen. mgr., 1998—2000, sr. asst. gen. mgr., 2000—03, gen. mgr., 2003—04, sr. v.p., baseball operations, 2004—05; v.p. baseball ops. Balt. Orioles, 2005—. Office: Baltimore Orioles 333 W Camden St Baltimore MD 21201

DUR, PHILIP ALPHONSE, retired shipbuilding executive, military officer; b. Bethesda, Md., June 22, 1944; s. Philip Francis and Elena (Delgado) D.; children: Courtney Morris, Philip Ralston. BA, U. Notre Dame, 1965, AM, 1966; MPA, Harvard U., 1973, PhD, 1976. Commd. ensign USN, 1965, advanced through grades to rear adm., 1991, strategic planner Office of the Chief Naval Ops. Washington, 1977-79, mil. asst. Office of Sec. Def., 1979-80, dir. polit. mil. affairs Nat. Sec. Coun., 1982-84, exec. asst. Chief Naval Ops. plans, policy, ops., 1984-86, exec. asst. sec. of navy, 1988-89, comdg. officer USS Comte De Grasse Norfolk, Va., 1980-82, comdg. officer USS Yorktown, 1986-88, 91-93; U.S. def. attache Am. embassy Paris, 1989—91; comdr. Cruiser Destroyer Group Eight, 1991-93; dir. strategy and policy Office of the Chief Naval Ops., Washington, 1993—94, dep. asst. CNO plans, policy and ops., 1994—95; retired USN, 1995; v.p. Tenneco Inc., Houston, 1995-96; exec. v.p. Walker-Gillet Europe, Edenkoben, Germany, 1996-97; v.p. worldwide bus. devel. & strategy Tenneco, Inc., Lake Forest, Ill., 1997-2000; v.p. program ops. Northrop Grumman, Balt., 2000—01; pres. Northrop Grumman Ship Sys., 2001—05. Scoutmaster Boy Scouts Am., Gaeta, Italy, 1967, exec. v.p. Pine Burr area coun. Decorated Def. Disting. Svc. medal, Navy Disting. Svc. medal, Def. Superior Svc. medal, Legion of Merit; comdr. Ordre Nat. du Merite (France); named one of 50 Most Important Hispanics in Tech. & Bus., Hispanic Engr. & Info. Tech. mag., 2005. Mem. U.S. Naval Inst. Found., Coun. on Fgn. Rels., Cercle de l'Union Interalliee, Surface Navy Assn., Marine Acad. (France), Nat. Eagle Scouts Assn., Notre Dame Alumni Club, Army-Navy Club, Harvard Club. Avocations: history, golf, foreign languages. Office Phone: 228-712-2090. Personal E-mail: philnd65@cableone.net.

DURAN, GEORGE, chef; b. Venezuela; Grad. in Comm. Studies, NYU; attended, Ecole Superieure de Cuisine Francaise Group Ferrandi, Paris. Host (radio shows) HYE Time, WNYU, comedy segments, WPLJ-FM, NY, prodr., host WABC, 1999; prodr.: (TV series) House of Style, 2000; host (TV series) Top 21 Videos of 2001, HTV, Pachanga!, Miami, Pop Cuisine, Cuisine TV, France, writer (culinary articles) FHM mag. Office: TV Food Network GP 1180 Ave of Americas 11th Fl New York NY 10036

DURAN, KARIN JEANINE, librarian; b. Burbank, Calif., Aug. 31, 1948; d. Jose Antonio and Sophia (Cortez) D.; m. Richard Mark Nupoll, Sept. 5, 1971. AA, L.A. Pierce Coll., Woodland Hills, Calif., 1968; BA, Calif. State U., 1970; MLS, U. So. Calif., 1972, PhD, 1986. Libr. Calif. State U., Northridge, 1972—. Lectr. Calif. State U., Northridge, 1977—. Mem. Comision Femenil San Fernando Valley, Calif., 1987-2006. Named Woman of Year Calif. Women Higher Edn., Northridge, 1989, Bicentennial Woman, L.A. Human Rels. Com., 1976; recipient Northridge Extraordinary Svc. Facility award, CSU, 2006, Svc. to Soc. Recognition, 2003. Mem. ALA, Nat. Assn. Chicano Studies, Calif. Libr. Assn., Calif. Acad. Rsch. Librs., REFORMA, Phi Kappa Phi. Avocations: travel, theater, reading. Office: Calif State U Northridge Libr 18111 Nordhoff St Northridge CA 91330-8327 Business E-Mail: karin.duran@csun.edu.

DURAN, MATIAS MARTIN, retired adult education educator; b. Valladolid, Yucatan, Mexico, Feb. 24, 1922; s. Marcelo Duran, Aureliana Martin; m. Faasoa Togiaso Duran, Nov. 15, 1980; children: Mary F., Martin T., Marcelo, Matthias. Aa, Riverside City Coll., Calif., 1970; BA, U. Calif., Riverside, 1974; MA, U. Dominguez Hills, Long Beach, Calif., 1988; postgrad., Charles Sturt U., 2006—. Psychiat. technician Met. State Hosp., Norwalk, Calif., 1965; correctional officer Calif. Rehab. Ctr., Norco, 1966—72; probation officer Riverside County Probation, Blythe, Calif., 1975—77; ESL tchr./bilingual crosscultural instr. Compton Unified Sch. Dist., Calif., 1977—93, ret., 1993. Vol. Help Hospitalized Vets.; commissionary Missionary Oblates, 2005. Named A Good Samaritan of Yr., Help Hospitalized Vets., 2005. Mem.: K.C. (warden of coun. 1999—). Home: 140 W Barclay St Long Beach CA 90805-2108 Office Phone: 310-639-1958. Personal E-mail: mmduran1922@aol.com.

DURAN, ROBERTO, retired boxer; b. El Chorrillo, Panama, June 16, 1951; Profl. boxer, 1968—2001; lightweight champion World Boxing Assn., 1972, jr. middleweight champion, 1983; welterweight champion World Boxing Coun., 1980, middleweight champion, 1989; co-founder, exec. dir. pub. rels. DRL Promotions, LLC. Named to World Boxing Hall of Fame, 2006, Internat. Boxing Hall of Fame, 2007. Office: DRL Promotions LLC Ste 204 8700 E Vista Bonita Scottsdale AZ 85255 Office Phone: 480-575-8100.*

DURAND, JORGE, anthropologist; Prof. social anthropology & geography U. Guadalajara; co-dir. Mexican Migration Project. Co-author: Return to Aztlan, Miracles on the Border; co-author: (with Nolan J. Malone and Douglas S. Massey) Beyond Smoke and Mirrors: Mexican Immigration in an Era of Economic Integration, 2002; co-author: (with Douglas S. Massey) Crossing the Border, 2004. Mem.: NAS (assoc.). Achievements include becoming an expert on Mexican migration to the US. Office: U Guadalajara Ave de los Maestros y Alcalde Puerta 1 CP 44260 Jalisco Guadalajara Mexico

DURANG, CHRISTOPHER, actor, playwright; b. Montclair, NJ, Jan. 2, 1949; s. Francis Ferdinand and Patricia Durang. BA, Harvard U., 1971; MFA, Yale U., 1974. Playwright: The Nature and Purpose of the Universe, 1971, 75, 'dentity Crisis, 1971, 75, Better Dead than Sorry, 1972, 75 (with Albert Innaurato) I Don't Generally Like Poetry but Have You Read 'Trees'?, 1972, 73, The Life Story of Mitzi Gaynor, or Gyp, 1973, The Marriage of Bette and Boo, 1973, revised 1979, 85, (with Albert Innaurato) The Idiots Karamazov, 1974, Titanic, 1974, 76, Death Comes to Us All, Mary Agnes, 1975, (with Wendy Wasserstein) When Dinah Shore Ruled the Earth, 1975, Das Lusitania Songspiel, 1976, 80, Sex and Longing, The Vietnamization of New Jersey, 1977, 78, Sister Mary Ignatius Explains it All For You, 1982 (Obie award 1984), The Actor's Nightmare, 1982, Beyond Therapy, 1982, 83, Baby with the Bath Water, 1983-84, Adrift in Macao, Mrs. Bob Cratchit's Wild Christmas Binge, 2004, Miss Witherspoon, 2005; actor: (stage prodns.) Hotel Play, 1981, The Birthday Present, 1983, Putting It Together, 1993, Laughing Wild, 1987, 2005. Recipient Kenyon Festival Playwriting award, 1983; CBS fellow, 1975, Guggenheim playwriting fellow, 1979; Rockefeller grantee, 1976; named to Playwrights Sidewalk, Lucille Lortel Theatre, 2007. Mem. Dramatists Guild, Writers Guild, Actors' Equity Assn., ASCAP. Office: care Helen Merrill Helen Merrill Agy 337 W 22nd St New York NY 10011-2607 also: Creative Artists Agy 9830 Wilshire Blvd Beverly Hills CA 90212-1804*

DURANT, JOHN RIDGEWAY, retired oncologist, health facility administrator, consultant; b. Ann Arbor, Mich., July 29, 1930; s. Thomas Morton and Jean Margaret (deVries) D.; m. Mary Sue Avery Dillon, Jan. 13, 1990; children by previous marriage: Christine Joy, Thomas Arthur (dec.), Michele Grace, Jennifer Margaret. BA, Swarthmore Coll., Pa., 1952; MD, Temple U., Phila., 1956; degree (hon.), U. Ala., 1993. Diplomate: Am. Bd. Internal Medicine. Intern, then jr. asst. resident in medicine Hartford (Conn.) Hosp., 1956-58; resident in medicine Temple U. Med. Center, 1960-62; spl. fellow med. neoplasia Meml. Hosp. for Cancer and Allied Diseases, NYC, 1962-63; Am. Cancer Soc. advanced clin. fellow Temple U. Health Scis. Center, 1964-67, instr., then asst. prof. medicine, 1963-67; clin. assoc. chemotherapy Moss Rehab. Hosp., Phila., 1964-67; research assoc. Fels Research Inst., Phila., 1965-67; mem. faculty U. Ala. Med. Center, Birmingham, 1968-82, prof. medicine, dir. comprehensive cancer center, 1970-82, prof. radiation oncology, 1978-82, chmn. Southeastern coop. cancer study group at univ., 1975-82, Disting. faculty lectr., 1980; pres. Fox Chase Cancer Ctr., Phila., 1982-88; sr. v.p. health affairs and dir. med. ctr. U. Ala., Birmingham, 1988-95; exec. v.p. Am. Soc. Clin. Oncology, Alexandria, Va., 1995-2000; cons. med. dir. Walther Cancer Inst., Indpls., 2000—; cons. Baptist Health Sys., Birmingham, Ala., 2000—. Chmn. coop. group exec. com. Nat. Cancer Inst., NIH, 1977-82, chmn. coop. group chairmen, 1979-82; cons. VA Hosp., Tuskegee, Ala., 1970-82; exec. com. Birmingham chpt. ARC, 1972-77; mem. Nat. Cancer Adv. Bd., 1986-92. Mem. editorial bd. Cancer Clin. Trials, 1979-82, assoc. editor, 1982—; editorial bd. Med. and Pediatric Oncology News, 1975-90; assoc. editor Cancer, 1984-92; contbr. numerous articles to med. jours. Mem. adv. coun. for sci. Notre Dame U., 2002—. Served as officer M.C. USNR, 1958-60. Recipient Oncologist of Yr. award So. Oncology Assn., 1999; named Temple U. Med. Sch. Alumnus Yr., 1982, Cancer Fighter of Yr., Cancer Fighter Awards Trust, 2000. Fellow ACP, Coll. Physicians Phila.; mem. Am. Cancer Soc. (vice chmn. advanced clin. fellowship com. 1974-76, 85-87, mem. instl. rsch. grant com. 1979-82, pres. Ala. divsn. 1973-75, 77-79, mem. blue ribbon com. to rev. nat. rsch. program 1994-95), Am. Assn. Cancer Rsch., Am. Radium Soc. (pres. 1984), Am. Bd. Int. Med. Oncology (subcom. 1979-85, chmn. 1983-85), Assn. Am. Cancer Insts. (dir. 1978—, pres. 1982-83), Assn. Cmty. Cancer Ctrs. (dir. 1979-81), Am. Soc. Clin. Oncology (chmn. pub. rels. com. 1976-79, bd. dirs. 1979-82, 84-87, pres. 1985-86, Spl. Recognition award 1999), others. Baptist.

DURANT, KEVIN WAYNE, professional basketball player; b. Washington, Sept. 29, 1988; s. Wayne and Wanda Pratt. Student, U. Tex., Austin, 2006—07. Draft pick Seattle SuperSonics, 2007. Mem. USA Basketball Men's Sr. Nat. Team, 2007—. Named a McDonald's All-Am., 2006; named co-MVP, McDonald's All-Am. game, 2006, MVP, Jordan All-Am. Classic, 2006, ESPN All-Am., 2007, ESPN Player of Yr., 2007, Divsn. 1 Player of Yr., Nat. Assn. Basketball Coaches, 2007, AP Player of Yr., 2007; named to AP All-Am. First Team, 2007; recipient Oscar Robertson Trophy, US Basketball Writers Assn., 2007, Adolph Rupp Trophy, 2007, Naismith Coll. Player of Yr. award, Atlanta Tipoff Club, 2007, John R. Wooden award, 2007. Achievements include being picked second in the 2007 NBA draft. Office: Seattle SuperSonics 351 Elliott Ave W Ste 500 Seattle WA 98119*

DURANT, MARC, lawyer; b. NYC, Jan. 17, 1947; s. Sidney Irwin and Estelle (Haas) D.; m. Karen Rose Baker, June 9, 1968 (div. 1975); children: Lauren, Elyssa; m. Rita Mary Tatar, Dec. 31, 1979; children: David, Alexander. BS, Cornell U., 1968; JD, Harvard U., 1968-71. Bar: Pa. 1972, U.S. Dist. Ct. (ea. dist.) Pa. 1972, U.S. Supreme Ct. 1980, U.S. Ct. Appeals (3d cir.) 1981, N.Y. 1991. Law clk. U.S. Dist. Ct., Wilmington, Del., 1971-72; assoc. Schnader, Harrison, Segal & Lewis, Phila., 1972-75; asst. U.S. Atty. U.S. Dept. Justice, Phila., 1975-77; dep. chief criminal divsn.v. U.S. Atty.'s Office, Phila., 1977-81; ptnr. Durant and Durant, Phila., 1981—. Mem.: ABA, Phila. Bar Assn., Pa. Bar Assn., Nat. Assn. Criminal Def. Lawyers, Fed. Bar Assn. Office: Durant & Durant 325 Chestnut St Philadelphia PA 19106-2614 E-mail: mdurant@durantlaw.com.

DURBIN, DEAN D., marketing executive; Acctg. supr. McGraw-Hill Cos., v.p., group controller constrn. info. group; v.p., chief fin. officer Thomson Profl. Pub.; sr. v.p., chief fin. officer TC Advt. (not Vertis), 1997—2000; chief fin. officer Vertis Inc., Balt., 2000—04, pres., 2004—, COO, 2005—06, CEO, 2006—, bd. dir., 2006—. Bd. dir. Balt. Mus. Industry. Office: Vertis 250 W Pratt St Baltimore MD 21201 Office Phone: 410-361-8367. Business E-Mail: ddurbin@vertisine.com.

DURBIN, DICK (RICHARD JOSEPH DURBIN), senator; b. East St. Louis, Ill., Nov. 21, 1944; s. William and Ann D.; m. Loretta Schaefer, June 24, 1967; children: Christine, Paul, Jennifer. BS in Economics, Georgetown U., 1966, JD, 1969. Bar: Ill. 1969. Chief legal counsel to Lt. Gov. Paul Simon State of Ill., 1969—72; parliamentarian Ill. Senate, 1969-77, mem. staff minority leader, 1972-77; assoc. prof. med. humanities So. Ill. U., 1978—; ptnr. Durbin & Lestikow, Springfield, Ill., 1979—82; mem. US Congress from 20th Dist. Ill., 1983-97; US Senator from Ill., 1997—; minority whip, 2004—07; majority whip, 2007—. Mem. appropriations com. US Senate, judiciary com., com. on rules and adminstrn.; asst. Dem. fl. leader; co-chmn. Democratic Nat. Convention Platform Com., 2000, Democratic Nat. Com., 2004. Campaign worker Sen. Paul Douglas of Ill., 1966; staff Office Ill. Dept. Bus. and Econ. Devel., Washington; candidate for Ill. Lt. Gov., 1978; staff alt. Pres.'s State Planning Council, 1980; advisor Am. Council Young Polit. Leaders, 1981; mem. YMCA Ann. Membership Roundup, YMCA Bldg. Drive, Pony World Series; bd. dirs. Cath. Charities, United Way of Springfield, Old Capitol Art Fair, Springfield Youth Soccer; mem. Sch. Dist. 1986 Referendum Com. Recipient Lifetime Achievement award, Am. Lung Assn., Friend of Agr., Ill. Farm Bur., 2000, Excellence in Immunization award, Nat. Partnership for Immunization, 2001, Ground Water Protector award, Nat. Ground Water Assn., 2005, Leadership award, Nat. Orgn. Fetal Alcohol Syndrome, 2005, Public Svc. award, Am. Chem. Soc., 2005. Mem.: Trial Lawyers Assn., NAACP Springfield, Ill., Sangamon County Bar Assn., Ill. Bar Assn. Democrat. Roman Catholic. Office: US Senate 332 Dirksen Sen Office Bldg Washington DC 20510-0001 Mailing: District Office 525 S Eighth St Springfield IL 62703-1606 Office Phone: 202-224-2152, 217-492-4062. Office Fax: 202-228-0400, 217-492-4382.*

DURBIN, RICHARD LOUIS, SR., health facility administrator, consultant; b. Millersport, Ohio, Aug. 28, 1928; s. Clark Babe and Mabel (Bushee) Durbin; children: Richard Louis, Margot Jane, Melissa Bushee. BA, Ohio State U., 1949; MBA, U. Chgo., 1956; MPA, U. Ariz., 1969; postgrad., Pace Coll., 1973; MPH, U. Tex. Sch. Pub. Health, 1992, postgrad, 1999—. Cert. govt. fin. mgr., Assn. Govt. Accts.; profl. sanitarian. Research chemist Battelle Meml. Inst., Columbus, Ohio, 1949—50; sales rep. Am. Cyanamid Co., NYC, 1953—54; adminstrv. asst. Lancaster (Ohio)-Fairfield Hosp., 1954; with Bus. Devel. Outreach Helath, Austin, 1995—; asst. adminstr. City of Memphis Hosps., 1956—58, assoc. adminstr., 1958—60; dir. outpatient and profl. services Presbyn.-St. Luke's Hosp., Chgo., 1960—61; assoc. dir. grad. program in hosp. adminstrn., faculty U. Chgo. Grad. Sch. Bus., 1961—62; exec. sec. Am. Assn. Univ. Programs in Hosp. Adminstrn., 1960—62; assoc. prof. bus. adminstrn. Temple U., 1967—69, prof. mgmt., 1969—70; exec. dir. Lubbock (Tex.) County Dist. Hosp., 1970—71; v.p. Coll. Medicine and Dentistry N.J., 1971—75; also v.p. Acad. Health Center; asst. prof. N.J. Med. Sch., 1973—75; pres., CEO Harris County Hosp. Dist., Houston, 1975—89; asst. regional dir. region #6 Tex. State Dept. Health, 1989—92; adminstr. Tex. Alcoholic Beverage Commn., Austin, 1992—93; pres., CEO Durbin Internat., San Marcos, Tex., 1993—; health dir. Cameron County Health Dept., San Benito, Tex., 1995—; CEO/dir. Maverick County Hosp. Dist., Eagle Pass, Tex.; dir. Maverick County Health Dist., Eagle Pass; pres. Health Edn. Found. for Deserving Students, Eagle Pass; CEO, Montgomery County Hosp. Dist.; pres. Vineyard Inc., Houston, 2003—. Founder, dir. grad. program in health care adminstrn., 1967—70; exec. dir., 1966—70; cons. in field; pres. D&H Enterprises, Durbin Internat., CIA, 1967—71; project dirl., chief planner, exec. dir. Newark Comprehensive Health Plan, 1974; cons. divsn. hosp. and med. facilities HEW, 1967—; design adv. group, nat. rev. com., cons. exptl. health systems, 1971—73; cons. Nat. Commn. on Productivity, U.S. Bur. Prisons, 1968—; mem. Hosp. Devel., Inc. N.J. Gov.'s Correctional Health Svc. Investigations Com.; mem. adv. bd. Comprenetics, Inc., 1967—; steering com. Tucson Hosp. and Health Planning Commn., 1962—, Assoc. Hosp. Svcs. Ariz., 1963—64; treas. Ariz. League Nursing, 1963—64; adj. assoc. prof. Tex. Woman's U.; mem. coordinating coun. Tex. Health and Human Svcs., 1986—; appraisal rev. bd. Travis Ctrl. Appraisal Dist., 1994—; dir. bus. devel. Outreach Health Svcs., 1995—; adj. assoc. prof. U. Tex. Sch. Pub. Health, 1996—2003; med. adv. com. Tex. Workman's Compensation Commn.; lectr. informal classes U. Tex., Mexico, 1994—. Author: A Statistical Methodology of Evaluating a Medical Staff, 1961, New Ideas and Concepts in Outpatient Management, 1963; author: (with others) Ivory Tower to Workshop, 1964; author: Ambulatory Care Development, 1966; author: (with W.H. Springall) Organization and Administration of Health Care, 1974; author: (with Springall, P. High) Manual for Hospital Program and Performance Budgeting at the Operating Level, 1968; author: (with G. Connor) Design of a City-Wide HMO, 1974; author: Border Issues, 2000; cons. editor Hosp. Topics, editor The Forum, What's Going On: Hospital Topics, mem. editl. bd. Physician Weekly; contbr. articles to profl. jours. Mem. Phila. Crime Commn., 1967—, Tex. Indigent Care Task Force; chmn. Harris County Jail com., 1987—88, Health Svcs. com. AIDS panel; ch. deacon; bd. dirs. Ariz. Blue Cross, Mexic-Arte Mus., 1994—. Lt. USNR, 1945—46, lt. USNR, 1950—53. Recipient Editl. award, Hosp. Mgmt. mag., 1961, 1963, 1965, cert. of merit, Gov. Ariz., 1967, 1968, Silver medal (DeBakey) award, Baylor Coll. of Medicine, 1986. Fellow: Am. Coll. Hosp. Adminstrs. (cert.); mem.: AAUP, Tex. Pub. Health Assn., Am. Coll. Managed Care Adminstrs., Am. Coll. Healthcare Assn. (chmn. book award com. 1983, membership com. 1986), Am. Mgmt. Assn. (Excellence award 1968), Internat. Hosp. Fedn., Am. Inst. Mgmt., Am. Soc. Pub. Adminstrn., Am. Criminology Soc., So. Ariz. Hosp. Coun. (pres. 1963), Tex. Hosp. Assn. (bd. dirs., mem. exec. com. 1987—88), Pa. Hosp. Assn., Am. Hosp. Assn. (coun. pub. hosps.), Nat. Assn. Clinic Mgrs., Am. Chem. Soc., Nat. Assn. Pub. Hosps. (dir., founder), U. Tex. Littlefield Soc., Blanton Art Mus., Texans Standing Tall, U. Tex. Recreational Sports (life), Tucson Press Club (life), U. Tex. Faculty Ctr., Quadrangle Club (U. Chgo.), Midway Club (Chgo.), Buckeye Lake Yacht Club, Columbian Yacht Club (Chgo.), Pa. Soc. Club, Army-Navy Capitol Hill Club (Washington), Houston Yacht Club, Headliners Club (Austin, Tex.), Hillcrest Country Club, Rotary, Houston C. of C. (health com.), Sigma Xi, Sigma Alpha Epsilon. Presbyterian. Home and Office: 505 W 7th St Apt 319 Austin TX 78701-2836 Office Phone: 512-477-1147. Personal E-mail: durbin_dick@yahoo.com.

DURBURG, JACK E., real estate company executive; b. Evanston, Ill. Grad., Indiana U.; MBA, DePaul U. With William Kritt & Co., Sherman & Sons, Inc.; v.p., regional leasing dir. Jones Lang LaSalle, Inc., 1995—2001; mng. dir. CB Richard Ellis, Chgo., 2001—03, sr. mng. dir., 2003—. Mem.: Nat. Assn. Indsl. and Office Properties. Office: CB Richard Ellis 311 S Wacker Dr Ste 400 Chicago IL 60606 Office Phone: 312-935-1400. Office Fax: 312-935-1880. E-mail: jack.durburg@cbre.com.

DURCHSLAG, STEPHEN P., lawyer; b. Chgo., May 20, 1940; s. Milton Lewis and Elizabeth (Potovsky) D.; m. Ruth Florence Mayer, Nov. 21, 1976; children: Rachel Beth, Danielle Leah. BS, U. Wis., 1963; LLB, Harvard U., 1966. Bar: Ill. 1966. Assoc. Sidley & Austin, Chgo., 1966-72, ptnr., 1972-89, Winston & Strawn, Chgo., 1989—. Contbr. articles to profl. jours. Trustee Nathan Cummings Found., 1996—, Anshe Emet, Chgo., 1983—, pres., 2000—02. Mem. ABA (AAF legal com.), Promotion Mktg. Assn. (bd. dirs.), Am. Standard Club, East Bank Club. Jewish. Avocations: skiing, running, tennis, rare books. Office: Winston & Strawn 35 W Wacker Dr Ste 3600 Chicago IL 60601-1695 Office Phone: 312-558-5288. Business E-Mail: sdurchsl@winston.com.

DURDEN, ROME L., aircraft manufacturing company executive; b. LA, Apr. 5, 1935; s. Rome and Hortense (Anderson) D.; m. Priscilla Louise Bibby, Oct. 27, 1962; children: Suzette, Steven. B of Laws, La Salle Extension U., 1971; DD (hon.), Universal Life, Modesto, Calif., 1980. Tech. writer Hughes Aircraft Co., Culver City, Calif., 1962-72, sr. tech. editor, 1972-79, sr. mgmt. systems specialist, 1979-89. Author: (Manuals) Guide for Drafting Procedure, 1981, Simplified Drawing Substitutions, 1984. Treas. Marysville United Meth. Ch., 1997-99; mem. Lake Stevens Governance Coun., 1999, 2000. Recipient Presentation gavel Ramona Park Adv. Coun., Long Beach, Calif., 1971. Mem. Harmony Woods Homeowners Assn. (bd. dirs., treas. 1996-99, v.p. 2000-02). Home: PO Box 1322 Lake Stevens WA 98258-1322

DURDEN, WILLIAM G., academic administrator; Grad., Dickinson Coll., 1971; MA in German Lit. and Lang., PhD in German Lit. and Lang., Johns Hopkins U.; postgrad., U. Freiburg, Germany, U. Münster, U. Basle, Switzerland. Exec. dir. Inst. for the Acad. Advancement of Youth; faculty mem. German dept. Johns Hopkins U.; pres. Sylvan Acad., Sylvan Learning Sys. Inc., Dickinson Coll., Carlisle, Pa., 1999—. Sr. edn. cons. US Dept. State, chair adv. com. exceptional children and youths; mem., adv. bd. Ctr. for Internat. Exchange of Scholars, Fulbright Scholar Program. Actor: (books); contbr. articles to profl. jours. Recipient Klingenstein award, Tchrs. Coll., Columbua U.; fellow Klingenstein fellow, Wis. Policy Rsch. Inst.; grantee, Am. Coun. Learned Socs., Volkswagen Found., German Soc. Md.; scholar, Fulbright. Office: Dickinson Coll PO Box 1773 Carlisle PA 17013-2896 Fax: 717-245-1457.*

DURDIK, PAUL A., lawyer; b. Cleve., Apr. 9, 1962; s. Paul Albert and Evelyn Josephine Durdik; m. Yukari Goto, June 13, 2002. BSEE and Applied Physics, Case Western Res. U., Cleve., 1984; MBA, St. Edwards U., Austin, Tex., 1991; JD, Boston U., 1993. Bar: US Patent and Trademark Office 1993, NY 1995, Calif. 1997. Sr. assoc. engr. IBM Corp., Austin, 1984—90, sr. assoc. programmer Endicott, NY, 1991—97; patent atty. Townsend and Townsend and Crew LLP, Palo Alto, Calif., 1997—2000; fgn. legal advisor Squire Sanders and Dempsey LLP, Tokyo, 2001—03; patent atty. Hickman Palermo Truong and Becker LLP, San Jose, Calif., 2003—04, Fliesler Meyer LLP, San Francisco, 2004—06; dir. intellectual property. sr. corp. counsel Salesforce.com, Inc., San Francisco, 2006—. Contbr. articles to profl. jours. Vol. Goodwill, San Mateo, Calif., 2006. Mem.: Am. Intellectual Property Assn. (assoc.), City Club San Francisco (assoc.). Achievements include patents in field. Avocations: flying, gemology. Office: Salesforcecom Inc The Landmark at One Market St San Francisco CA 94105 Home Phone: 650-525-9659; Office Phone: 415-536-4656.

DUREK, DOROTHY MARY, retired language educator; b. Pitts., Jan. 23, 1926; d. Joseph Adam and Helen Barbara (Ondich) D. BS in Edn., Youngstown State U., 1962; MS in Edn., Westminster Coll., 1969. Cert. English tchr., Ohio, comprehensive English cert., Pa. Tchr. English Brookfield (Ohio) Schs., 1962-64, Sharon (Pa.) City Schs., 1964-88. Mem., pres. Coll. Club Sharon, 1993-94. Charter mem., bd. dirs. LWV Mercer County, Pa., 1993—97; docent Butler Inst. Am. Art, Youngstown, 1988—2004, LWV, Montgomery County, Md., 2005—; mem. Shenango Valley Women's Interfaith Coun., Jewish-Christian Dialogue Group, Sharon; charter mem. Mus. Women's Art, Washington, Nat. Mus. of the Am. Indian, Washington; mem., bd. dirs. Christian Assocs. Shenango Valley. Mem.: AAUW (Bethseda-Chevy Chase br.), NEA, Read and Discuss Group, Sharon Lifelong Learning Coun. (bd. dirs. 1995), Sharon Tchrs. Assn., Pa. State Educators Assn., Prospect Heights Lit. Club. Roman Catholic. Personal E-mail: dorothy_durek@yahoo.com.

DUREK, THOMAS ANDREW, computer company executive; b. Sharpsville, Pa., July 1, 1929; s. Joseph Adam and Helen Barbara (Ondish) D.; m. Phyllis H. Norris, Aug. 1, 1987 (dec. June 2005). BA, Pa. State U., University Park, 1953; MA, Baylor U., Waco, Tex., 1957; MS, Stanford U., Calif., 1959. Mgmt. scientist USAF, Pentagon, Washington, 1959-65; project engr. North Am. Rockwell Corp., Washington, 1965-68; systems engr. TRW, Inc., Washington, 1968-81, facility mgr. Patuxant, Md., 1981-82, project mgr. Washington, 1982-86; project mgr., prin. mem. tech. staff Software Productivity Consortium, Herndon, Va., 1986-89; sr. tech. staff, software technologist Systems Integration Group TRW, Inc., Fairfax, Va., 1989-92; founder, prin. TAD Assocs., Bethesda, Md., 1992—. Personal investment software developer; professorial lectr. George Washington U., 1960-66, George Mason U., 1991; chair software reusability conf. Nat. Inst. for Software Quality and Productivity, 1989-91, mem. adv. bd., 1991-96, chair info. systems engring. for downsizing conf., 1993; speaker in field of software reuse and productivity. Contbr. articles to profl. jours. Mem. parish coun. Ch. of St. Stephen Martyr, Washington, 1970-78, pres. 1975-78, liturgical min., 1973-87, mem. pastoral coun. Shrine Most Blessed Sacrament, Washington, mem. continuing edn. com., 1993-96; established religious edn. audio-cassette libr., 1995-2001; leader Action in Montgomery, 2000—; mem. sr. vital living steering com. Montgomery County, Md., 2000—; pres. Archdiocese Washington Post Cana, 2006—. With USAF, 1953-65; to col. USAFR, ret., 1984. Decorated Meritorious Svc. medal, 1984. Mem.: Riverhill Home Owners Assn. (bd. dirs. 2005—, v.p.). Roman Catholic. Home and Office: 7915 Quarry Ridge Way Bethesda MD 20817-6956 Office Phone: 301-469-7916. Personal E-mail: tadurek@aol.com.

DURELL, JACK, psychiatrist; b. NYC, July 5, 1928; s. Sam and Helen (Schwartzman) D.; m. Viviane M. diGioja, May 19, 1955. BA summa cum laude, Harvard U., 1949; MD cum laude, Yale U., 1953. Rsch. biochemist NIMH, Bethesda, Md., 1954-57, chief, sect. of psychiatry, 1963-67; v.p. med. affairs, clin. dir. The Psychiat. Inst., Washington, 1967-72, pres., med. dir., 1972-78; assoc. dir. sci. Nat. Inst. Drug Abuse, Rockville, Md., 1979-86; med. dir. clin. affairs div. Ea. Va. Med. Authority, Norfolk, 1986-87; chmn. dept. psychiatry Mercy Cath. Med. Ctr., Phila., 1987-92; prof. psychiatry U. Pa., Phila., 1987—. Exec. dir. Treatment Rsch. Inst., 1992—; pres. Delta Metrics, 1994—; pres. The Psychiat. Inst. Found., Washington, 1973-78; trustee Phila. Mental Health Care Connection, 1987-89. Editor: The Changing Clinical Picture of Schizophrenia, 1977; asst. editor-in-chief Jour. Psychiat. Rsch., 1966-82, mem. editorial bd., 1982—; contbr. to numerous med. publs. With USPHS, 1953-86. Fellow Am. Psychiat. Assn.; mem. Am. Acad. Psychiatrists in Alcoholism and Addictions (sec.-treas. 1985-93), Am. Psychopathological Assn., Am. Coll. Neuropsychopharmacology. Personal E-mail: jadurell@aol.com. Business E-Mail: jdurell@deltametrics.com.

DURELL, VIVIANE G., psychologist, small business owner; b. Paris, Mar. 22, 1926; d. Andre Di Gioja and Francoise Martinez; m. Jack Durell, May 19, 1955. BSFS, Georgetown U., 1955; MA, George Wash. U., 1958. Cert. Bd. Psychologist, Washington, 1976. Statician IBRD, Washington, 1951—55; rsch. psychologist Gesell Inst. Child Devel., New Haven, 1958—59; psychologist Montgomery Count Bd. Edn., Rockville, Md., 1961—77; cons. psychologist Psychiat. Inst., Washington, 1967—77; group therapist Cmty. Psychiat. Clinic, Bethesda, Md., 1968—73; instr. Montgomery Coll., Takoma Park, 1971—73; pres. Vivianna Inc., McLean, Va., 2002—. Co-author: (book) When Schools Care, Family Therapy Techniques for Problem Behavior of Children and Teenagers. Friends of first ladies Smithsonian Mus. Am. History, 1990—92; pres. bd. trustees Samaritans of Washington, 1980—96; bd. assocs. mem. Nat. Rehab. Hosp., 1995—. Recipient Lifetime Dedication award, Samaritans of Washington, 1984, Blanch Keith Samaritan of the Yr. award, 1986. Mem.: APA, The Hist. Georgetown Club, Sulgrave Club, Capital Speakers Club (life), Psi Chi (life). Avocations: public speaking, music, travel, languages, cooking. Home Phone: 703-525-6641; Office Phone: 703-525-6641. Personal E-mail: viviannainc@aol.com.

DURGLISHVILI, NANA Z., psychologist, language educator; b. Tbilisi, Rep. of Georgia, Aug. 23, 1963; arrived in US, 1997; d. Zurab Vladimir Durglishvili and Rusudan Noe Tsnobiladzo; m. Jimmy Givi Mukhuradze (div.); 1 child, Zurab J. MA, Ibilisi State U., 1985; BA, Inst. Foreign Lang., 1986; PhD, U. Saarbrucken, 1992. French tchr., asst. prin. Secondary Sch. 91, Tbilisi, Georgia; prof. psychology Tbilisi State U., Tbilisi, Georgia, 1995—97; apt. mgr. MaxMaron, NYC, 1998—2001; asst. psychology Meridian Health Care, Belleville, NJ, 2001—03; French tchr. Matawan Pre-Sch., Matawan, NJ, 2003—04. Pres. France-Georgian Assn., Tbilisi, Georgia, 1992—95; project. mgr. Euro Unions, Tbilisi, Georgia, 1994—97. Author: Defiant Teens, 1993, Personality Disorders in Children, 1999. Avocation: tennis. Home: 55 E 208 St 1H Bronx NY 10467 Personal E-mail: ndurglishv@aol.com.

DURHAM, CHRISTINE MEADERS, state supreme court chief justice; b. LA, Aug. 3, 1945; d. William Anderson and Louise (Christensen)

Meaders; m. George Homer Durham II, Dec. 29, 1966; children: Jennifer, Meghan, Troy, Melinda, Isaac. AB, Wellesley Coll., 1967; JD, Duke U., 1971. Bar: N.C. 1971, Utah 1974. Sole practice law, Durham, N.C., 1971-73; instr. legal medicine Duke U., Durham, 1971-73; adj. prof. law Brigham Young U., Provo, Utah, 1973-78; ptnr. Johnson, Durham & Moxley, Salt Lake City, 1974-78; judge Utah Dist. Ct., 1978-82; assoc. justice Utah Supreme Ct., 1982—2002, chief justice, 2002—. Pres. Women Judges Fund for Justice, 1987-88. Fellow Am. Bar Found.; mem. ABA (edn. com. appellate judges' conf.), Nat. Assn. Women Judges (pres. 1986-87), Utah Bar Assn., Am. Law Inst. (coun. mem.), Nat. Ctr. State Courts (bd. dirs.), Am. Inns of Ct. Found. (trustee). Office: Utah Supreme Ct PO Box 140210 Salt Lake City UT 84114-0210*

DURHAM, HARRY BLAINE, III, lawyer; b. Denver, Sept. 16, 1946; s. Harry Blaine and Mary Frances (Oliver) Durham; m. Lynda L. Durham, Aug. 4, 1973; children: Christopher B., Laurel A. BA cum laude, Colo. Coll., 1969; JD, U. Colo., 1973. Bar: Wyo. 1973, U.S. Tax Ct. 1974, U.S. Ct. Appeals (10th cir.) 1976. Assoc. Brown, Drew, Apostolos, Massey & Sulllivan, Casper, Wyo., 1973-77; ptnr. Brown & Drew, Casper, 1977-98, Brown, Drew & Massey, LLP, Casper, 1998—. Articles editor: U. Colo. Law Rev., 1972—73. Bd. dirs. Natrona County United Way, 1974—76, pres., 1975—76; mem. City of Casper Pks. and Recreation Commn., 1985—94, vice chmn., 1987—94; Rep. precinct committeeman, 1999—2002; bd. dirs. Casper Symphony Assn., 1974—88, vice chmn., 1979—82, pres., 1983—87. Named Permanent Class Pres., Class of 1969, Colo. Coll., Mem. Nat. Alumni Coun.; recipient State Heroes award, Sporting Goods Mfg. Assn., 1997. Mem.: Nat. Assn. R.R. Trial Counsel, Natrona County Bar Assn., Wyo. Bar Assn. (Wyo. editor fifty state constrn. lien and bond law), Wyo. Amateur Hockey Assn. (bd. dirs., sec. 1974—85, pres. 1985—88), Casper Amateur Hockey Club (bd. dirs. 1970—77, sec. 1974—77), Phi Beta Kappa. Home: 3101 Hawthorne Ave Casper WY 82604-4975 Office: 159 N Wolcott St Ste 200 Casper WY 82601-7009 Office Phone: 307-234-1000.

DURHAM, HARVEY RALPH, retired academic administrator; BS, Wake Forest U., 1959; MA, U. Ga., 1962, PhD in Math., 1965. Asst. prof. math. Appalachian State U., Boone, NC, 1965-67, assoc. prof., chair dept. math., 1967-71, prof. math., 1971-74, assoc. dean faculty, 1971-74, assoc. vice chancellor for acad. affairs, 1974-79, acting vice chancellor for acad. affairs, 1979-80, vice chancellor for acad. affairs, 1980-89, provost, exec. vice chancellor, 1989—2003, interim chancellor, 2003—04, ret., 2004. Office: 474 Industrial Park Rd Boone NC 28607-3937 E-mail: durhamhr@appstate.edu.

DURHAM, IAN THOMAS, physicist, educator; s. Thomas Fisher and Patricia Ann Durham; m. Alyson Suzanne Brod, May 25, 1997; children: Nathaniel Ross, Sarah Hathaway. BSME, U. Buffalo, 1997; MS in Applied Physics, Johns Hopkins U., Balt., 2001; PhD in Math., U. St. Andrews, Scotland, 2005. Lectr. dept. physics Simmons Coll., Boston, 2001—04; asst. prof. dept. physics St. Anselm Coll., Manchester, NH, 2004—. Contbr. articles to profl. jours. Historian First Parish Unitarian Universalist Ch., Kennebunk, Maine, 2006. Rsch. grant, NSF, 2000. Fellow: Royal Astron. Soc.; mem.: Brit. Soc. for the Philosophy Sci., Am. Phys. Soc., Astron. Soc. No. New Eng. (bd. dirs. 2004—06). Independent. Unitarian Universalist. Achievements include research in history and philosophy of quantum mechanics and cosmology; quantum information science. Avocations: writing, reading, music, canoeing, astronomy. Home: Kennebunk ME 04043 Office: Saint Anselm Coll Dept Physics 100 Saint Anselm Dr Box 1759 Manchester NH 03102 Office Phone: 603-222-4073.

DURHAM, JAMES W., lawyer; b. Nov. 18, 1937; m. Kathleen B. Wollman; children: Linda, Cynthia, Andrea. BSBA, Pa. State U., 1959; MBA in Bus. Adminstrn., U. Portland, 1962; JD, Pa. State U., 1965. Bar: Oreg. 1965, U.S. Dist. Ct. Oreg., U.S. Ct. Appeals (9th cir.), U.S. Supreme Ct. Assoc. Davies, Biggs, Strayer, Stoel & Boley, Portland, Oreg., 1965—68; ptnr. Durham, Smith, Todd & Ball, Portland, 1968—70; atty. Oreg. Dept. Justice, Salem, Oreg., 1970—78; sr. v.p., gen. counsel, sec. Portland Gen. Electric Co., 1978—87; sr. v.p., gen. counsel Phila. Electric Co. (now Exelon Corp.), Phila., 1988—2001, mediator, arbitrator, 2001—. Chmn. bd. dir. Oreg. Pub. Broadcasting Found., 1984—88; chmn. Oreg. Pub. Defender Com., 1984—85. Chmn., bd. dir. Columbia-Willamette YMCA; bd. dir., trustee Franklin Inst., 1991—2001; bd. dir. Del. Valley Citizens Crime Commn., vice chmn., 2000—02, chmn., 2002—04; mem. legal adv. com. Rep. Com. Oreg., 1984—86. Fellow: Coll. Comml. Arbitrators; mem.: ABA, Nat. Coun. on Pa. State Philanthropy, Phila. Bar Found. (trustee 1991—94), Del. Valley Corp. Counsel Assn. (bd. dir. 1989—, pres. 1998), Phila. Bar Assn., Pa. Electric Assn. (chmn. 1993—94), Pa. Bar Assn., Oreg. Law Found. (bd. dir. 1986—88, pres. 1988), Oreg. State Bar (bd. govs. 1983—86, pres. 1985—86), Rotary, Tau Kappa Epsilon (fraternity alumnus of yr. 1987). Office: 2620 N Providence Rd Media PA 19063 Office Phone: 610-566-6608. Personal E-mail: durhamjw@aol.com.

DURHAM, JEANETTE RANDALL, artist, educator; b. Plainfield, NJ, June 17, 1945; d. F. Gilbert and Alice (Petricek) Randall; m. Ormonde G. Durham III, June 26, 1971; 1 child, O. Ethan. BA in Fine Arts, Montclair State U., 1967; postgrad., Art Students League, 1970, 71, 72, Westchester Art Workshop, 1980-81; MS in Edn., SUNY, Oneonta, 1991. Cert. art tchr. N.Y., N.J., reading tchr. N.Y. Art instr. Mohawk Valley Ctr. Arts, Little Falls, N.Y., 1983, Owen D. Young Cen. Sch., Van Hornesville, N.Y., 1987-92; adj. humanities instr. Herkimer County C.C., 1998—. Mem. decentralization grants panel Ctrl. NY Cmty. Arts Coun., Utica, 1999—2001, mem. exhbn. coms., 2001—04; mem. exhbn. com. Mohawk Valley Ctr. for the Arts, 1995—. One-woman shows include Gallery 57, Cambridge (Mass.) Arts Coun., 1984, Gannett Gallery, SUNY Tech., Utica, NY, 1988, South Shore Arts, Little Falls, NY, 1991, Pleiades Gallery, NYC, 1993, Mohawk Valley Ctr. for the Arts, Little Falls, 1994, 2004, Rensselaer Poly. Inst., Troy, 1997, Herkimer County C.C., 1997, Arts Ctr. Old Forge, NY, 1998, 2-person shows, Cazenovia (NY) Coll., 2001, exhibited in group shows at Art of NE USA, Silvermine, New Canaan, Conn., 1996, 1998 (award), 2006, NY State Mus., Albany, 1988, Cooperstown Art Assn., 1991, 1994, 1997, 1999, Butler Inst. Am. Art, 1992, Albany Inst. History and Art, 1993, 1996 (award), Arts Coun. Ctrl. NY, Utica, 1994, 2001, Pleiades Gallery, 1991—2004, Schweinfurth Art Ctr., 1998, Albany Ctr. Galleries, 1999, Gallery 210, Syracuse, 1999, South Shore Art Gallery, Little Falls, 1987—2001, Tex. A&M, College Station, 2004. SOS grantee N.Y. Found. for Arts, 1997. Mem. Nat. Assn. Women Artists (William Meyerowitz Meml. award 1991, Florence Anderson award 1998), Coll. Art Assn. Home: 111 Hoke Rd Jordanville NY 13361-2017 Office: Herkimer County CC Reservoir Rd Herkimer NY 13350 Business E-Mail: durhamjr@ntcnet.com.

DURHAM, JIMMIE, artist, poet; b. Ark., 1940; BFA in Sculpture, Ecole des Beaux-Arts, Geneva, 1972. Founder, exec. dir. Internat. Indian Treaty Coun., UN; writer, editor Art and Artists Newspaper, 1982—86; exec. dir. Found. Cmty. Artists, NYC. Exhibitions include Souvenirs of Site-Seeing: Travel and Tourism in Contemporary Art, Whitney Mus. Am. Art, 1991, Land, Spirit, Power, Nat. Gallery Can., Ottawa, 1992, Crossings, 1998, On taking a normal situation and retranslating it into overlapping and multiple readings of conditions past and present, Antwerp Cultural Capital of Europe, 1993, A certain lack of coherence, Palais des Beaux-Arts, Brussels, 1993—94, Original Re-runs, Inst. Contemporary Art, London, 1993—94, 100 Artists See God, 2004, Cocida y Crudo, Nat. Ctr. Art Mus. Reina Sofia, Madrid, 1994, Transformers, Illingworth Kerr Gallery, Alberta Coll. Art and Design, 1996, Interruptions, Nat. Mus. Contemporary Art, Lisbon, 1999, Venice Biennial, 1999, 2001, 2003, 2005, Stoneheart, Ctr. Contemporary Art, Kitakyushu, 2000, Gallery Nordenhake, Stockholm, 2000, Internat. Triennial Contemporary Art, Tokyo, 2001, Through a Sequence of Space, Gallery Nordenhake, Berlin, 2002, Sydney Biennial, 2004, Off Grid, Ottawa Art Gallery, 2005, Ordering the Ordinary, Timothy Taylor Gallery, London, 2005, Tirana Biennial, 2005, Guangzhou Triennial, 2005, Carnets du Sous-Sol, Galerie Michel Rein, Paris, 2006, Day for Night, Whitney Biennial, 2006, Designing Truth, Stiftung Wilhelm Lehmbruck Mus., Duisburg, 2006, Saudades, Crac Alsace, Altkirch, 2006, Represented in permanent collections Volpinum Kunstsammlung, Vienna, MuHKA, Antwerp, Stedelijk Mus. voor Actuele Kunst, Belgium, Irish Mus. Modern Art, Dublin, Zerynthia Roma, Mus. het Domein, Netherlands, representing galleries, Christine König Gallery, Vienna, Barbara Wien Gallery, Berlin, Galleria Francosoffiantino Artcontemporanea, Turin, Lumen Travo, Amsterdam, Centro Difusor de Arte, Lisbon, Galerie Nordenhake, Stockholm, Exit Art, NYC.*

DURHAM, JO ANN FANNING, artist; b. Sulphur Springs, Tex., May 31, 1935; d. William Jeffress and Merle Jo (Barrett) Fanning; m. William E. Durham (dec.); children: William, John Lee (dec.). BS, Tex. A&M U., College Station, 1956; postgrad., U. Tex., Austin, 1953-55, Tex. Woman's U., Denton, Tex., 1953-55; docteur honoris causa in arts, 1994. Exhibited in group shows at Galerie Jean Lammelin, Paris, 1991, Salon D'Automne Grand Palais, 1992—93, Vanderbilt Mus., L.I. VIU, N.Y., 1995, Lever House, VIU, 1995, Pen and Brush Club, 1995, 1996, VIU, N.Y., 1996, Templeton, Ft. Worth Artists and Co., Ft. Worth, 1996, Sumner Art Mus., Washington, 1996, 2004, Belgium Grand Prix, De Paadestallen Van Het Park Van Enghien, Belgium, 1996, Soc. Internat. Des Beaux Arts, Paris, 1996—97, Southwestern Watercolor Soc., D-Art, Dallas, 1996—97, Anthology Art Gallery, Lebanon, 1997, Longboat Key Art Ctr., N. Tex. Health Sci. Ctr., 1997, Atrium Gallery, Ft. Worth, 1998, Laura Knott Gallery, Bradford Coll., Mass., 1998, Lee Scarfone Gallery, U. Tampa, Fla., 1998, Fort Mason, San Francisco, 1998, Yale Med. Sch. Libr., 2000, La Chapelle des Penitents, Gordes, France, 2000, Artist's Mag., 2001, Nautilus Fellowship, Internat. Soc. Exptl. Artists, 2001, Chgo., 2003, Encaustic Works Biennial, 2001, Dennos Mus., Traverse City, 2001, Minetrista Cultural Ctr., Muncie, 2002, Salmagundi Club, N.Y.C., 2002—03, 2005, Columbia U., 2000, Huntsville Mus. Art, Ala., 2001, Beverly Arts Ctr., Chgo., 2003, WALES, Aberdare, 2003—04, Splash 8, 2004, Lee County Alliance of the Arts, Ft. Meyers, Fla., 2004 (Best of Show), The Art Inst., Houston, Tex., 2004, St. David's Hall, Cardiff, Wales, 2005, Salmagund Club, NYC, 2006, Represented in permanent collections 15 paintings Tex. A&M, Tarleton, Ft. Worth Pub. Libr. Downtown, Sulphur Springs Pub. Libr., Ft. Worth Woman's Club. Recipient Gold medal Belgium Grand Prix, 1993, Best of Show, Internat. Soc. of Experimental Artists, 2003, Samuel Leifman Meml. award, Salmagundi Club, 2006, Nautiulus fellowship, 2000. Mem. Soc. Watercolor Artists (signature), Internat. Soc. Exptl. Artists (signature; pres. 1999, Nautilus fellow 2000), Soc. Layerists in Multimedia (signature), Allied Artists, Tex. Fine Arts Assn. (past pres., regional dir., exec. bd.), D Art, Dallas Women's Caucus for the Arts, Dallas Artists Rsch. and Exhbn., Southwestern Watercolor Soc. (signature), Tex. Visual Artists Assn., Fort Worth Woman's Club Art Dept., Templeton Art Ctr., Nat. League of Am. Pen Women, Contemporary Art Ctr., Christians in the Visual Arts, Nat. Coll. Soc., Salmagundi Club (Samuel Leitman Meml. award). Home: 4300 Plantation Dr Fort Worth TX 76116-7607 Office Phone: 817-244-3807. Home Fax: 817-737-6520.

DURHAM, J(OSEPH) PORTER, JR., lawyer, educator; b. Nashville, May 11, 1961; AB in Polit. Sci. and History cum laude, Duke U., 1982, JD, 1985. Bar: Tenn. 1985, Md. 1988, NC 2005. Ptnr. Miller & Martin, Chattanooga, 1990-96, Baker, Donelson, Bearman & Caldwell, Chattanooga, 1997—2003, chmn. corp. dept., 1998—2003; dir. edn. divsn., gen. counsel Duke Endowment, 2003—07; COO, gen. counsel Global Endowment Mgmt. LP, 2007—. Adj. prof. dept. acctg. and fin. U. Tenn., Chattanooga, 1992-98; participant Russian tax code adv. group, 1999; mem. grievance com. NC Bar. Editor Duke Law Mag., 1984-85; contbr. articles to profl. jours. Mem. Balt. Citizens Planning and Housing Assn., 1988-90; career edn. spkr. Explorer Scout program Boy Scouts Am., 1985, 88, 90-92; mem., v.p. bd. dirs., chmn. fin. com. Waxter Ctr. Found., 1989-91; mem., sec. bd. dirs. Assn. for Visual Artists, 1993-96; trustee Good Shepherd Sch., 1992-93, Good Shepherd Endowment, 2003-04; chmn. spl. mgmt. com. Nashville Rehab. Hosp., 1995; trail maintenance vol. U.S. Pk. Svc., 1993-95; mem. adv. com. Chattanooga State Tech. C.C.; bd. dirs. Sr. Neighbors, Inc., 2001-03; mem. investment com. Trinity Epsicopal Sch., 2005—; mem. bd. visitors Davidson Coll., 2006—, Johnson C. Smith U., 2006—. Recipient Outstanding Svc. award Waxter Ctr. Found., 1991. Mem. ABA, Tenn. Bar Assn., Md. Bar Assn., N.C. Bar Assn., Duke U. Law Sch. Alumni Assn. (bd. dirs. 1994-97), Duke U. Gen. Alumni Assn. (bd. dirs. 1986-92, exec. com. 1989-92). Office: The Duke Endowment 100 N Tryon St Ste 3500 Charlotte NC 28202-4012 Office Phone: 704-376-0291. Business E-Mail: pdurham@globalendowment.com.

DURHAM, MICHAEL JONATHAN, investment professional; b. NYC, Jan. 19, 1951; s. Walter Alan and Joyce D. (Packham) D.; m. Marilyn James Marr, May 19, 1984; children: Michael Allen, Elizabeth Marr. BA in Econs., U. Rochester, 1973; MBA in Fin., Cornell U., 1977. Asst. v.p. Bank Julius Bar & Co., NYC, 1978-79; sr. analyst fin. planning Am. Airlines, Ft. Worth, 1979-80, mgr. corp. fin., 1980-82, dir. corp. fin., 1982-84, asst. treas. corp. fin., 1984-85, v.p. corp. devel., 1985-87, v.p. fin. and planning, 1987-89, CFO, 1989-95, sr. v.p. fin., CFO, 1989-95; pres., CEO Sabre Inc., Dallas, 1995-99, Cognizant Assocs., Dallas, 2000—; Non-exec. chmn. Asbury Automotive Group, 2003—. Bd. dir. Bombardier, AGL Resources, Acxiom Corp., Culligan Internat., Northwest Airlines, Hertz Global Holdings, SCI Solutions. Bd. dirs. Zale Lipshy U. Hosp., 1991—, Dallas Opera, 1992—; trustees coun. U. Rochester, 1992—. Mem. Brookhollow Golf Club. Republican. Episcopalian. Avocations: bridge, tennis, golf. Address: 3416 Caruth Blvd Dallas TX 75225-4823*

DURHAM, ROBERT DONALD, JR., state supreme court justice; b. Lynwood, Calif., May 10, 1947; s. Robert Donald Durham and Rosemary Constance (Brennan) McKelvey; m. Linda Jo Rollins, Aug. 29, 1970; children: Melissa Brennan, Amy Elizabeth. BA, Whittier Coll., 1969; JD, U. Santa Clara, 1972; LLM in the Jud. Process, U. Va., 1998. Bar: Oreg. 1972, Calif. 1973, U.S. Dist. Ct. Oreg. 1974, U.S. Ct. Appeals (9th cir.) 1980, U.S. Supreme Ct. 1987. Law clk. Oreg. Supreme Ct., Salem, 1972-74; ptnr. Bennett & Durham, Portland, Oreg., 1974-91; assoc. judge Oreg. Ct. Appeals, Salem, 1991-94; assoc. justice Oreg. Supreme Ct., Salem, 1994—. Adv. com. Joint Interim Judiciary Com., 1984-86; chmn. Oreg. Commn. on Adminstrv. Hearings, 1988-89; faculty Nat. Jud. Coll., Reno, Nev., 1992; mem. Case Disposition Benchmarks Com., 1992-93, Coun. on Ct. Procedures, 1992-93, 95—; mem. Oreg. Rules of Appellate Procedure Com., 1998-2002; bd. dirs. Oreg. Law Inst.; chmn. commn. on jud. rule 4 Oreg. Supreme Ct., 1995-97, 2002-05. Mem. ACLU Lawyer's Com., Eugene and Portland, Oreg., 1978-91. Recipient award for civil rights litig. ACLU of Oreg., 1988, Ed Elliott Human Rights award Oreg. Edn. Assn., Portland, 1990. Mem. Am. Acad. Appellate Lawyers (ninth cir. screening com. 1991—, rules com. 1994, co-chair appellate cts. liaison com. 1994), Oreg. Appellate Judges Assn. (pres. 1996-97), Oreg. State Bar (chair labor law sect. 1983-84, adminstrv. law com. govt. law sect. 1986), Willamette Valley Inns of Ct. (master of bench, team leader 1994—). Office: Oreg Supreme Ct 1163 State St Salem OR 97301-2563 Home Phone: 503-274-2766; Office Phone: 503-986-5725. Business E-Mail: robert.d.durham@ojd.state.or.us.

DURHAM, WALTER THOMAS, historian, researcher; b. Nashville, Oct. 7, 1924; s. George Franklin and Celeste McAlister Durham; m. Anna Armstrong Coile, Apr. 23, 1949; children: Anna Durham Windrow, Robert, James F., Elizabeth Durham Lindsey. BA, Vanderbilt U., 1948, MA, 1953. Mng. ptnr. Durham Mfg. Co., Gallatin, Tenn., 1948—63, chmn., prin. owner, 1972—98; sec. Gallatin Aluminum Products Co., 1958—63, pres., CEO, 1963—72; pres., prin. owner Wholesale Plumbing and Electric, Gallatin, 1975—93; chmn. bd. First and People's Nat. Bank, Gallatin, 1976—87; state historian State of Tenn., Nashville, 2001—. Mem. bd., v.p. Tenn. Bldg. Material Soc., Nashville, 1948—64; mem. bd., treas. Archtl. Alumni Mfg. Assn., Chgo., 1966—72; mem. adv. bd., chair AmSouth Bank, Gallatin, 1995—2001. Author: The Great Leap Westward, 1969, Old Sumner, 1972, A College for this Community, 1974, Daniel Smith, Frontier Statesman, 1976, James Winchester, Tennessee Pioneer, 1979, Rebellion Revisited, 1982, Nashville The Occupied City, 1985, Reluctant Partners, Nashville and the Union, 1987; author: (with James W. Thomas) A Pictorial History of Sumner County, Tennessee, 1796-1986, 1986; author: Before Tennessee: The Southwest Territory, 1990, Wynnewood, Bledsoe's Lick, Castalian Springs, Tennessee, 1994; author: (with James W. Thomas and John F. Creasy) A Celebration of Houses Built Before 1900 in Sumner County, Tennessee, 1995; author: Volunteer Forty-Niners: Tennesseans and the California Gold Rush, 1997, The Life of William Trousdale, Soldier, Statesman, Diplomat, 2001; author: (with Glenda Milliken) Gallatin 200, A Time Line History Celebrating the Bicentennial of Gallatin, Tennessee, 2002; author: Josephus Conn Guild and Rosemont: Politics and Plantation in Nineteenth Century Tennessee, 2002, Balie Peyton of Tennessee: Nineteenth Century Politics and Thoroughbreds, 2004; contbr. essays to ency., articles to profl. jours., chapters to books; consulting editor, mem. editl. com., contbr. Tennessee Encyclopedia of History and Culture, 1998. Sgt. Army Air Force, 1943—46, Italy, Africa. Mem.: Tenn. Hist. Soc. (mem. bd., past pres. 1973), Fairview Plantation, Lions Internat. (various local positions, Melvin Jones fellow 1949—2003). Democrat. Methodist. Avocations: watching spectator sports, travel, music, reading. Office: Office State Historian State Tenn 1010 Durham Dr Gallatin TN 37066 Office Phone: 615-452-3201. Office Fax: 615-452-3251.

DURIE, DARALYN J., lawyer; b. 1967; Degree, Stanford U., 1988; M, U. Calif. Berkeley, 1989; grad., Boalt Hall Sch. Law, U. Calif. Berkeley, 1992. Clerk US Ct. Appeals, DC Cir.; assoc. Keker & Van Nest, San Francisco, ptnr., 1999—. Co-chair Lawyer Representatives to Ninth Cir. Jud. Conf.; tchr. Nat. Inst. Trial Adv. Bd. dirs. Berkeley Montessori Sch. Named one of Best Intellectual Property Lawyers in Calif., Chambers & Partners, Top 75 Women Litigators in Calif., Daily Jour., Litigation's Rising Stars, The Am. Lawyer, 2007; named to Best Lawyers in Am. Mem.: Northern Calif. Assn. Bus. Trial Lawyers, Assn. Bus. Trial Lawyers, ABA. Office: Keker & Van Nest LLP 710 Sansome St San Francisco CA 94111 Office Phone: 415-391-5400. Office Fax: 415-397-7188.*

DURINGER, DAVID ROBERT, lawyer; b. Coronado, Calif., June 28, 1964; 1 child, Ayn. BA in Econs., U. Calif., San Diego, 1986; JD, U. Calif., San Francisco, 1989; LLM in Taxation, Chapman U. Sch. Law, Orange, Calif., 2005. Bar: Calif. 1989, Wash. 1997; lic. real estate broker, Calif. Sole practice, Orange County, Calif., 1989-95; owner, broker Adv. Realty Mgmt., Vancouver, Wash., 1995-97; gen. counsel Genisys Fin. Corp., San Diego, 1997—2001; atty., pres. Law News.TV, P.C., Carlsbad, Calif., 1999—2006; atty. Duringer Law Office, 2006—. Mem. Calif. Bar Assn. (estate planning, trust and probate sect.), Wash. State Bar Assn., Nat. Eagle Scout Assn., NRA, Calif. Rifle and Pistol Assn. (NRA pistol instr.). Independent. Office Phone: 949-757-4148.

DURIO, WILLIAM HENRY, lawyer; b. Crowley, La., May 15, 1947; s. Lennard Edwin and Helen Hazel (Miller) D.; m. Rita Jane Putch, June 6, 1971; children: Matthew, Caroline. BS, U. La., Lafayette, 1970; JD, La. State U., 1975. Pvt. practice, Lafayette, La., 1976-78, 83-89; ptnr. Hughes Durio & Grant, Lafayette, 1978-83; gen. counsel Global Industries Ltd., Maurice, La., 1990-91; pvt. practice. Lafayette, 1991—. Adj. prof. mineral law U. La., Lafayette, 1983-84. With US Army, 1970—72. Mem. La. Bar Assn., Lafayette Town House Club, Order of Troubadours. Avocations: running, fishing, scuba diving, hunting, travel. Personal E-mail: w.durio@att.net.

DURITZ, ADAM, musician; b. Aug. 1, 1964; s. Gilbert and Linda D. Student, U. Calif., Berkeley. Founder, lead singer Counting Crows, 1991—; founder E Pluribus Unum record label (bought by Geffen Records, 2000), 1997, Tyrannosaurus Records, 2007. Singer: (albums) August and Everything After, 1993, Recovering the Satellites, 1996, Across a Wire: Live in New York, 1998, This Desert Life, 1999, Hard Candy, 2002, Films About Ghosts: The Best Of, 2004, New Amsterdam: Live at Heineken Music Hall, 2006, (songs) Accidentally in Love, 2004. Office: c/o DGC/Geffen Records 9130 W Sunset Blvd Los Angeles CA 90069-3110

DURKEE, WILLIAM ROBERT, retired internist; b. Kansas City, Mo., Apr. 12, 1923; s. Dwight and Bessie Deane (Williams) D.; m. Billie Maxine Schreiner, Sept. 19, 1946; m. Jeanne Elizabeth Wells, June 7, 1975; children— Bruce William, Ellen Jeanne AA, Kansas City Jr. Coll., 1941; student, U. Chgo., 1941-42; MD, U. Kans., 1945. Diplomate Am. Bd. Internal Medicine. Intern U. Kans. Med. Ctr., Kansas City, 1945-46, resident, 1948-51; practice medicine specializing in internal medicine Manhattan, Kans., 1951-91; ptnr. Ball Meml. Clinic, 1951-76, Drs. Durkee and Boese, 1976-91; med. dir. Kans. Farm Bur. Life Ins. Co., Manhattan, 1963-91; ret., 1991. Mem. staff Mercy Health Ctr.; trustee Meml. Hosp., Manhattan, Kans., 1994-03, chmn. 2001-03. Bd. dirs. Friends of McCain, 1988-95, Sunset Zoo Wildlife Conservation Trust, Manhattan, 1995-2002, pres., 1998; mem. adv. bd. Friends of Libr., Kans. State U., 1993-2002. Capt. U.S. Army, 1943-48. Fellow ACP, Am. Coll. Cardiology (assoc.); mem. AMA, Riley County Med. Soc., Kans. Med. Soc., Am. Soc. Internal Medicine, Manhattan C. of C., Pres.'s Club Kans. State U., Manhattan Country Club, Rotary. Republican. Methodist. Home: 2121 Meadowlark Rd Apt 238 Manhattan KS 66502

DURKIN, DOROTHY ANGELA, university official; b. Glen Cove, NY, June 23, 1945; d. Frank Vincent and Rose Marie Durkin; 1 child, David Francis. BA, SUNY, Stony Brook, 1968; MA, NYU, 1974. Adminstrv. asst. SUNY, Stony Brook, 1965-67; prodn. editor Holt, Rhinehart & Winston, Inc., Stony Brook, 1967-69; editor Hill & Wang Pub., Inc., NYC, 1969-70; asst. dir. pub. info. NYU Sch. Continuing Edn., 1970-72; assoc. dean pub. affairs and student svc. NYU Sch. Continuing and Profl. Studies, 1983—2002, assoc. dean strategic devel., 2002—, co-acting dean, 2005—06. Cons. NYC Ctr. for Lifelong Learning, 1974; prodr. TV series Continuum, Sta. WNYC, 1974; mem. UCEA Commn. on Futures and Markets, 2003-06. Editor: NSF student mag., 1961. Recipient Merit award Andy Advt., 1972, Art Dirs. Club, 1980, Soc. Illustrators, 1980, Big Apple award NY Radio Broadcasters Assn., 1985, Admissions Mktg. Report awards, 1987-88, 98-2001, Catalog Age awards, 1988, 93, Silver and Bronze award in Print Advt., 2004, Gold and Silver award in Print Pub., 2004, Walton S. Bittner citation for outstanding svc., UCEA, 2007. Mem. Univ. Continuing Edn. Assn. (chair info. svc. 1980-81, nat. award chair, chair mktg. adv. com. 1989-98, group leader Learn From Success series 1989-90, bd. dir. 1991-93, membership com. 1994-95, mktg. conf. planning com. 1993-00, presenter, Bronze, Silver and Gold awards 1978, 81-2002, Internat. Leadership in Continuing Edn. award 1999, Gold award in publications, 2002, Gold and Bronze award in Electronic Marketing Communications, 2002, Silver award in Mixed Media: Publications, Advertising, PR and Web, chair commn. on Futures and Markets, 2001-03, mem. commn. on futures and markets 2003-05, chair strategic mktg. com. 2005-2007.) Am. Coll. Pub. Rels. Assn. (nat. award 1973), Coun. for

Advancement and Support of Edn. (awards 1982-83, 85-87, 89-90, 92-94), Women in Comms. (job chair), Pub. Rels. Soc. Am. (Am. demographics adv. bd. 1989-90), Direct Mktg. Assn. (Echo Leadership award 1987, 88), Internat. Direct Mktg. Assn., SUNY Alumni Assn. (bd. dir.), The College Bd. (speaker, cons.), Learning Resources Network. Office: NYU Sch Continuing Edn and Profl Studies 244 Greene St Rm 204 New York NY 10003 Business E-Mail: dorothy.durkin@nyu.edu.

DURKIN, G. MICHAEL, food products executive; BS in Mktg. Fin., U. RI; MBA, Pace U. Fin. oper. PepsiCo, Inc., 1981; v.p., customer devel. PepsiCo Inc., Heartland Bus. Unit (acquired by Whitman 1999); sr. v.p., gen. mgr. Whitman Corp., Eastern Group (prior to merger with PepsiAmericas); sr. v.p., CFO PepsiAmericas, Mpls., 2002—. Office: PepsiAmericas 4000 Dain Rauscher Plz 60 S Sixth St Minneapolis MN 55402

DURKIN, KEITH FRANCIS, sociologist, researcher; b. Kearney, NJ, July 24, 1967; s. Frank James and Joan Durkin; m. Amy Michele Pendrak, June 29, 1996; children: Elizabeth Erin, Christopher Keith. BA magna cum laude, Marywood Coll., Scranton, Pa., 1990; MS, Va. Poly. Inst. and State U., Blacksburg, 1992; PhD, Va. Polytechnic Inst. and State U., 1996. Asst. prof. of sociology McNeese State U., Lake Charles, La., Ohio No. U., Ada, 1999—2002, assoc. prof. of sociology, 2002—, chair, dept. of psychology and sociology, 2004—, dir., inst. for social rsch., 2001—. Assoc. editor Sociol. Spectrum, Sociol. Inquiry, Deviant Behavior: An Interdisciplinary Jour.; editor MSSA Forum. Author: (book) How Chiropractors Think and Practice; contbr. encyclopedia entries (4), articles to profl. jours., chapters to books. V.p., campaign chair United Way, Ada-Liberty, Ohio, 2002—03, bd. dirs. Hardin County, Ohio, 2003—06. Recipient Irene Casteel Chair in Edn., Profl., and Social Sci., Ohio No. U., 2004—05, Recent Grad. award, Marywood U. Alumni Assn., 2002; fellow Shearman Rsch. fellow, McNeese State U., 1998—99. Mem.: Am. Soc. Criminology, Mid-South Sociol. Assn. (chair com. on the profession 2001—04, v.p. 2005—06, pres.-elect 2006—07), Delta Epsilon Sigma, Pi Gamma Mu, Mortar Bd., Alpha Kappa Delta. Roman Catholic. Achievements include research in chiropractor's attitudes; Internet crime and deviance; binge drinking and drunk driving by college students. Home: 210 Willeke Ave Ada OH 45810 Office: Ohio Northern University Department of Psychology and Sociology Ada OH 45810 Home Phone: 419-634-2393; Office Phone: 419-772-2138. Office Fax: 419-772-2746. Business E-Mail: k-durkin@onu.edu.

DURKIN, KEVIN P., lawyer; b. Chgo., July 22, 1955; BS, U. Ill., 1977; JD, DePaul U., 1980. Bar: Ill. 1980, US Dist. Ct. (no. & ctrl. dists. Ill.) 1983, US Ct. Appeals (7th cir.) 1995, US Dist. Ct. (we. dist. Mich.) 2000. Asst. state atty. Cook County, Ill., 1980—88; ptnr. Clifford Law Offices, Chgo., 1988—. Adj. prof. DePaul U. Mem.: ABA (mem. sect. Litig. 1992—, mem. sect. Tort & Ins. Practice 1992—, mem. Aviation Litig. comm. 1992—, mem. Aviation & Space Law comm. 1992—, co-chair, Aviation Litig. com. 2000—), Chgo. Bar Assn. (chmn. Hearing divsn. 1995—97, chmn. Jud. Evaluation com. 1995—97, gen. chmn. 1997—98, bd. mgr. 1998—2000, treas. 2002—), Ill. Trial Lawyers Assn. (bd. advocates 1993—2001, bd. mgrs. 2001—), Assn. Trial Lawyers Am., Nat. Coll. Dist. Attys. Assn., Trial Lawyers Club Chgo., Chgo. Bar Found. Achievements include obtained the largest personal verdict of the year involving a motor vehicle accident, 2004. Office: Clifford Law Offices 31st Fl 120 N LaSalle St Chicago IL 60602 Office Phone: 312-899-9090. Office Fax: 312-251-1160. E-mail: kpd@cliffordlaw.com.*

DURNEY, MICHAEL CAVALIER, lawyer; b. Piedmont, Calif., May 20, 1943; s. James Joseph and Camille (Cavalier) D.; m. Ann E. Belanger, Nov. 27, 1971 (dec. Oct. 2001); 1 child, Christine Cavalier; m. Carla Voetsch, June 6, 2002; 1 child, James McIvor. BA, U. Calif., Berkeley, 1965; JD, U. Calif.-Hastings Coll. of Law, 1968. Bar: Calif. 1969, DC 1972, admitted to practice: US Supreme Ct. 1972. Trial atty. Tax div. Dept. Justice, Washington, 1968-72, dep. asst. atty. gen. Tax div., acting asst. atty. gen., 1986-88; assoc. Hamel and Park, Washington, 1972-78, ptnr., 1978-86, Myerson, Kuhn & Sterrett, Washington, 1988-89, Law Offices of Michael C. Durney, Washington, 1990—. Chmn. bd. trustees St. Patrick's Episcopal Day Sch., Washington, 1989—92. Named one of 75 Best Lawyers in Washington, Washingtonian mag., 2002. Mem. ABA (tax and litigation sects.), Fed. Bar Assn. (chmn. tax sect. 1982-84), Calif. Bar Assn., D.C. Bar Assn. Clubs: Metropolitan (Washington), Burning Tree. Republican. Episcopalian. Avocation: golf. Office: 1072 Thomas Jefferson St NW Washington DC 20007-3832 Home: 832 Mackall Ave Mc Lean VA 22101 Office Phone: 202-965-7744. Business E-Mail: mcd@mdurney.com.

DURNING, STEVEN JAMES, internist, educator; b. Neptune, nj, Aug. 31, 1968; s. James Charles Durning and Judy Davis; m. Kristen L. Durning, June 8, 1991; children: Andrew Steven, Daniel Richard. BS, Pa. State U., 1991; MD, U. Pitts., Sch. of Medicine, 1995. Resident, 1995—98; clerkship dir., staff internist Wright Patterson Med. Ctr., Dayton, 1998—2002; course dir., staff internist Uniformed Svcs U., Bethesda, Md., 2002—. Reviewer Intersite Consistency As A Measurement of Programmatic Evaluation (New Investigator Award, Rsch. In Med. Edn. Meeting, 2004). Bd. govs. Soc. of Air Force Physicians, San Antonio, 2002—; chair, med. student com. Am. Coll. Physicians, Washington, 2003—. Maj. USAF, 2002—, Uniformed Svcs. U. Decorated Meritorious Svc. medal USAF, Joint Svc. Commondation medal; recipient William P. Clements award, Excellence in Edn., Uniformed Svcs U., 2001, Inaugeral Waxman award, Nat. Am. Coll. Physicians. Fellow: Am. Coll. Physicians (bd. gov. DC chpt.). Home: 19800 Fawn Vista Way Montgomery Village MD 20886 Home Phone: 301-947-9840.

DU ROCHER, JAMES HOWARD, lawyer; b. Racine, Wis., Aug. 4, 1945; s. Howard James and Frances Ann (Rasmussen) Du R.; m. Rosalyn Ann, Sept. 2, 1972; children: Jessica Lynn, James Howard, Emily Rosalyn. Student, U.S. Mil. Acad., 1963-65, Ripon Coll., Wis., 1965-66; JD, U. Wis., 1969. Bar: Wis. Assoc. Stewart, Peyton, Crawford & Josten, Racine, 1972—78; pres. Du Rocher, Murphy, Murphy & Schroeder, S.C., Racine, 1978-96, Du Rocher Law Offices, S.C., 1996—. Bd. dirs., Careers Industries, Inc., pres., 1988-89. Bd. dirs. Racine Area United Way, 1973-79, v.p., 1977-79; chmn. Park Trails Dist. Boy Scouts Am., 1979-82; bd. dirs. Careers for Retarded Adults, Inc., 1982, pres., 1983, 90; bd. dirs. A-Center of Racine, Inc., 1978-85, pres., 1985; bd. dirs. Careers Industries Support Found., Inc., 1993-2000, Rotary Found. Racine-West, Inc., organizer, 1974, sec., 1999—; deacon Atonement Luth. Ch., Racine, 1978-81; mem. adv. bd. Children's Svc. Soc. Wis.; treas. Faith Cmty. Ch., Racine, 2002-04. Capt. JAGC, U.S. Army, 1969-72. Decorated Bronze Star. Mem. State Bar Wis., Rotary (pres. Racine-West club 1998-99, trustee 1999-). Home: 5531 Whirlaway Ln Racine WI 53402-1865 Office: 827 Main St Racine WI 53403 Office Phone: 262-634-9899. Personal E-mail: durlaw@sbcglobal.net.

DUROCHER, VERNLE C. (SKIP), JR., lawyer; b. Menominee, Mich., Aug. 9, 1961; s. Vernle Charles and Judith Ann (Stodola) D.; m. Ann M. Novacheck, Sept. 13, 1986; children: Tyler, Justin, Kelsey. BA in Polit. sci., Marquette U., Milw., 1983; JD, U. Wis., 1986. Law clk. U.S. Dist. Ct. (no. dist.) Tex., Dallas, 1986-87; assoc. Kirkland & Ellis, Chgo., 1987-90, Dorsey & Whitney, Mpls., 1990-95, ptnr., trial dept., chmn., ins. law, 1995—. Adj. prof. Hamline U., St. Paul, 1992-96. Note and Comment editor U. Wis., 1986. Mem. Minn. State Bar Assn. (investigator Hennepin County ethics panel 1992—), Order of the Coif. Avocations: basketball, fishing, skiing. Office: Dorsey & Whitney Ste 1500 50 S 6th St Minneapolis MN 55402-1498 Office Phone: 612-390-7855. Office Fax: 612-340-2868. Business E-Mail: durocher.skip@dorsey.com.

DURON, ROBERT J., school system administrator; BS, Ea. Tex. State Univ., 1981, MEd, 1993; D edn. adminstrn., Baylor Univ. Tchr., elem. sch. prin., middle sch. asst. prin., Tex.; asst. supt. Clear Creek Ind. Sch. Dist., 1997—2003; adj. prof. Univ. Houston, Clear Lake; supt. Socorro Ind. Sch. Dist., El Paso, 2003—06, San Antonio Ind. Sch. Dist., 2006—. Office: San Antonio Ind Sch Dist 141 Lavaca St San Antonio TX 78210 Office Phone: 210-299-5500.

DUROSE, STANLEY CHARLES, JR., retired insurance company executive; b. Joliet, MT, Oct. 26, 1923; s. Stanley Charles and Wilhelmena Amelia (Zwicky) DuR.; m. Lorraine Homan, May 27, 1977. BS, U. Wis., 1948. Various positions Wis. Dept. Ins., Madison, 1948-65; dep. commr. ins. State of Wis., Madison, 1965-69, commr. ins., 1969-75; v.p. govt. rels. Cuna Mut. Ins., Madison, 1976-80; sr. v.p. adminstrn. Cumis Ins. Soc., 1980-86, sr. v.p. reinsurance, 1986-88; dep. commr. of ins. State of Wis., 1989-91; ret., 1991. Contbr. articles to profl. publs. With USAF, 1943-45, 51-52. Mem. Casualty Actuarial Soc., Am. Acad. Actuaries. Home: 201 Durose Ter Madison WI 53705-3322

DURR, ROBERT JOSEPH, construction executive, mechanical engineer; b. NYC, June 25, 1932; s. Otto and Veronica U. (Quinlan) D.; m. Julia Loretta, Apr. 16, 1955; children— Kathryn A., Robert J. Jr., Kenneth A., Jennifer L. BBA, Iona Coll., 1954; Cert. in Mech. Engring., NYU, 1957. Mem. staff Courter & Co., Inc., NYC, 1955-60, mgr., 1960-71, v.p., 1971-81, pres. Secaucus, NJ, 1981-85, Durr Mech. Constrn., Inc., NYC, 1986-98, chmn., 1998—. Chmn. Nat. Joint Steamfitter Apprenticeship Com., Washington, 1980-84; trustees Nat. Cert. Pipe Welding Bur., Washington, 1983—. Recipient Recognition award Nat. Cert. Pipe Welding Bur., 1980 Mem. Subcontractors Trade Assn., Mech. Contractors Assn. Am. (bd. dirs. 1989—, mem. exec. bd. 1993, pres. 1996), Mech. Contractors Assn. N.Y. (bd. dirs., pres. 1976-82, Appreciation award 1982), N.Y. Bldg. Congress (bd. govs. 1978-84), Bldg. Trade Employers Assn. N.Y. (Greater N.y. welding chpt. 1975-88, chmn. 1979-88), Upper Montclair (N.J.) Country Club. Roman Catholic. Avocations: golf, swimming, sailing. Business E-Mail: rdurrsr@durrmech.com.

DURRANI, SAJJAD HAIDAR, retired aerospace and communications engineer; b. Pakistan, Aug. 27, 1928; came to U.S., 1959, naturalized, 1966; s. Inayat Ullah and Hameedah Khanum D.; m. Brita Katarina Yasmin Portin, May 21, 1959; children: Zarina, Amina, Arif. BA, Govt. Coll., Lahore, Pakistan, 1946; BSc in Elec. Engring. with honors, Engring. Coll. Lahore, 1949; MScTech, Coll. Tech., Manchester, Eng., 1953; ScD, U. N.Mex., 1962. Lectr., asst. prof. Engring. Coll., Lahore, 1949-59; instr., research assoc. U. N.Mex., Albuquerque, 1959-62; sr. engr. Gen. Electric Co., Lynchburg, Va., 1962-64; prof., chmn. dept. elec. engring. Engring. U. Lahore, 1964-65; assoc. prof. Kans. State U., Manhattan, 1965-66; sr. engr. RCA Space Center, Hightstown, NJ, 1966-68; staff scientist, br. mgr. COMSAT Labs., Clarksburg, Md., 1968-73; sr. scientist Ops. Research, Inc., Silver Spring, Md., 1973-74; sr. engr. NASA-Goddard Space Flight Center, Greenbelt, Md., 1974-79; chief communications scientist NASA Hdqrs., Washington, 1979-81; mgr. for system planning, tracking and data relay satellite system NASA-GSFC, 1981-84; mgr. research and planning NASA Communications Div., 1984-88; program mgr., Advanced Systems Office NASA Hdqrs., Washington, 1988-92; consulting engr. Computer Scis. Corp., Beltsville and Seabrook, Md., 1992-98; ret., 1998. Vis. prof. U. Md., 1972, adj. prof. Univ. Coll., 1997-2004; adj. prof. George Washington U., 1980-82, 86-87, rsch. prof., 1993-97; mem. Engring. Manpower Commn., Am. Assn. Engring. Socs., 1981; exec. fellow, tech. advisor Fed. Comm. Commn., 2000-01, fellow, tech. advisor State Dept., 2004-05. Mem. editorial bd.: COMSAT Tech. Rev., 1972, IEEE Spectrum, 1975-78, IEEE Procs., 1988-92. Pres. Muslim Cmty. Ctr., Silver Spring, Md., 1976-82, trustee, 1989-94, 95-2000, chmn., 1998-2000. Recipient spl. achievement award NASA, 1977, 78, 90, Amb. award Computer Scis. Corp., 1996. Fellow: IEEE (bd. govs. aerospace and electronic sys. soc. 1977—93, pres. 1982—83, dir. Divsn. IX 1984, 1985, publs. bd. 1986, 1987, 1991, bd. dirs. nat. telesys. conf. 1991—94, publs. bd. 1992, bd. govs. aerospace and electronic sys. soc. 1997—2003, Citation of Honor U.S. Activties Bd. 1980, Outstanding Mem. Region 2 1982, Meritorious Achievement in Continuing Edn. award 1994, Millennium medal 2000, Profl. Activities award 2001, Centennial medal 1984), AIAA (assoc.), Wash. Acad. Scis. (v.p. adminstrn. 2001—04); mem.: DC Coun. Engring. Archtl. Socs. (v.p. 2005—06, pres. 2006—07). Personal E-mail: s.durrani@ieee.org.

DURRANT, GEOFFREY HUGH, retired language educator; b. Pilsley, Eng., July 27, 1913; s. John and Charlotte (Atkinson) D.; m. Barbara Joan Altson, June 2, 1942; children: John Guy, Catherine Jane. BA, Cambridge U., Eng., 1932-35; diploma in edn., London U., 1935-36; student, Tuebingen U., West Germany, 1937-39. Prof., English U. Natal, South Africa, 1945-60, head dept. English; prof. U. Man., Winnipeg, Canada, 1961-66; now prof. emeritus U. BC, Vancouver, Canada, master tchr., 1973. Author: William Wordsworth, 1969, Wordsworth and the Great System, 1970. Served with South African Armed Forces, 1940-44. Carnegie fellow, 1960; Killam sr. fellow, 1976 Fellow Royal Soc. Can.; mem. Assn. Can. Univ. Tchrs. English. Anglican. Home: 10-4388 Moncton St Richmond BC Canada V7E 6R9 Personal E-mail: ghdurrant@shaw.ca.

DURRANT, M. PATRICIA, diplomat; BA, U. W.I., Diploma in Internat. Rels.; Diploma in Overseas Devel. Studies, U. Cambridge, Eng. With Jamaica Fgn. Svc., 1971—, minister, dep. permanent rep. to UN, 1983—87, amb. to Germany, 1987—92, non-resident amb. to Israel, the Netherlands, Switzerland and the Holy See, 1987—92; dir.-gen. Min. of Fgn. Affairs and Fgn. Trade, 1992—95, permanent rep. of Jamaica to UN NYC, 1995—, rep. for Jamaica on Security Coun. UN, 2000—01, vice chair Open-Ended Working Group on the Reform of UN Security Coun.; ombudsman United Nations, NYC. Chair consultative com. UN Devel. Fund for Women; pres. High Level Com. on Tech. Coop. Among Developing Countries, 1999—2001; vice chair preparatory com. spl. session on population and devel. UN Gen. Assembly, 1999. Named Disting. Grad., U. W.I., 1998; recipient Order of Distinction in the rank of Comdr., 1992, Order of Jamaica, 2000, Disting. Achievement award, World Assn. of Former UN Interns and Fellows. Office: Permanent Mission of Jamaica to UN 767 Third Ave 9th Flr New York NY 10017

DURRANT, MATTHEW B., state supreme court justice; JD, Harvard U., 1984. Adj. prof. Brigham Young U., Salt Lake City; law clerk U.S. Supreme Ct. Appeals (10th cir.), Salt Lake City; shareholder Parr, Waddoups, Brown & Gee, Salt Lake City; judge Third Dist. Ct., Salt Lake City, 1997-2000; justice Utah Supreme Ct., 2000—. Founding chair Supreme Ct. Professionalism Com.; former chair Judicial Council Technology Com. Office: Utah Supreme Ct PO Box 140210 Salt Lake City UT 84114-0210*

DURRETT, JAMES FRAZER, JR., retired lawyer; b. Atlanta, Mar. 23, 1931; s. James Frazer and Cora Frazer (Morton) D.; m. Lucretia McPherson, June 9, 1956; children: James Frazer III, William McPherson, Lucretia Heston Miller, Thomas Ratcliffe. AB, Emory U., 1952; postgrad., Princeton U., 1952-53; LLB cum laude, Harvard U., 1956. Bar: Ga. 1955. Ptnr. Alston & Bird (and predecessor firm), Atlanta, 1956-97, retired, 1997. Adj. prof. Emory U. Law Sch., 1961—77. Trustee emeritus Student Aid Found., The Howard Sch. Mem. Am. Law Inst. (life, adv. estate and gift tax project, restatement, second, property, Fed. Income Tax project), Capital City Club, Harvard Club (Atlanta). Presbyterian. Home: 2734 Peachtree Rd NW C 302 Atlanta GA 30305-2944 Office: Alston & Bird 1 Atlantic Ctr Atlanta GA 30309-3400

DURRETT, RICHARD T., mathematics professor; PhD, Stanford U., 1976. Prof. Dept. Math., Stanford U., Ithica. Author: (novels) The Essentials of Probability (Statistics), 1993, Stochastic Calculus: A Practical Introduction (Probability and Stochastics Series), 1996, Mutual Invadability Implies Coexistence in Spatial Models, 2002, Probability: Theory and Examples, 2004, The Annals of Applied Probability: Vol. 1-9, 1999; contbr. articles to profl jour. Mem.: NAS. Office: Cornell Univ 524 Malott Hall Ithaca NY 14853 Office Phone: 607-255-8282. Office Fax: 607-255-7149. E-mail: rtd1@cornell.edu.*

DURST, RICHARD WAYNE, academic administrator; b. Scotts Bluff, Nebr., Aug. 31, 1945; s. Wayne E. Durst and Pearle (Jenson) Hubka; m. Karen Lee Grubb, June 28, 1974; children: Amanda, Derek. BA, Mo. Western State Coll., 1971; MFA, U. Okla., 1973. Designer Jim Halsey TV Prodns., LA, 1971, Black Hills Playhouse, Custer, SD, 1976-78; designer, mng. dir. Minn. Repertory Theatre, Duluth, 1983-89; head dept. theatre U. Minn., Duluth, 1977-89, dean Sch. Fine arts, 1989—96; dean Coll. Fine and Performing Arts U. Nebr.-Lincoln, Lincoln, 1996—2000, spl. asst. to chancellor, 1997—2000; dean, exec. dir. Coll. arts and Architecture Pa. State U., 2000—06; pres. Baldwin-Wallace Coll., Berea, Ohio, 2006—. Designer numerous live theatre prodns., 1972—. With USN, 1965-69, Vietnam. Mem. Internat. Orgn. Theatre Designers, Archs. and Technicians (pres. 1997-2000), US Inst. for Theatre Tech. (pres. 1994-96, exec. com., bd. dirs. 1985-2000), Internat. Coun. Fine Arts Deans (exec. dir. 2000-06), Assn. Theatre in Higher Edn. Avocations: raising arabian horses, golf. Office: Baldwin-Wallace Coll Office of Pres 275 Eastland Rd Berea OH 44017-2088

DURST, ROBERT JOSEPH, II, lawyer; b. Pitts., Jan. 23, 1943; s. Robert J. and Catherine (Thomas) D.; m. Sandra A. Cattani; children: Thomas Sandberg, Eric Francis. BA, Gettysburg Coll., 1964; JD, Villanova U., 1967. Bar: Pa. 1967, N.J. 1968, U.S. Dist. Ct. (we. dist.) Pa. 1967, U.S. Dist. Ct. (N.J.) 1968, U.S. Supreme Ct. 1973. Corp. staff atty. Alcoa, Pitts., 1967; assoc. Herr & Fisher, Flemington, N.J., 1967-76; ptnr. Bernhard, Durst & Dilts, Flemington, 1976-89, Stark & Stark, Princeton, N.J., 1989—. Board cert. matrimonial atty. N.J. Supreme Ct., 1982—; lectr., author on divorce and family law. With USMC, 1960—64. Fellow Am. Acad. Matrimonial Lawyers (pres. N.J. chpt. 1998-99); mem. ABA, Am. Trial Lawyers Assn., N.J. Bar Assn. (mem. exec. com. family law sect., Saul Tiscu;er award Lifetime Contbn. Family Law 2003), Hunterdon County Bar Assn., Mercer County Bar Assns., Am. Coll. Family Trial Lawyers (diplomate). Home: 28 Marvin Ct Lawrenceville NJ 08648-2112 Office: Stark & Stark PO Box 5315 Princeton NJ 08543-5315

DURYEA, ELIAS J., education educator; s. Robert Duryea and Dorothy Woods; m. Karen Marie ReHill, Jan. 26, 1957; children: Danielle, Maxwell. BS, U. San Diego, 1977; MS, U. Utah, Salt Lake City, 1979; PhD in Psychol. and Cultural Studies, U. Nebr., Lincoln, 1982. Prof. Coll. Edn., U. N.Mex, Albuquerque, 1990—, assoc. dean rsch., 2001—05. Sci. rev. panelist Ctrs. for Disease Control, Atlanta, 1990—. Contbr. scientific papers to profl. jours. Cons. Dist. Atty.'s Office, Salem, Mass., 2001—07. Fellow, Teachers Coll. Columbia U., 1982—83. Mem.: Am. Acad. Health Behavior. Independent. Roman Catholic. Achievements include research in alcohol abuse prevention program for schools. Avocations: swimming, running, bicycling, travel. Home: 19 Rattlesnake Ridge Tijeras NM 87059 Office: Univ NMex 112 Johnson Center UNM Albuquerque NM 87131 Home Phone: 505-277-8187; Office Phone: 505-277-8173.

DURYEE, DAVID ANTHONY, management consultant; b. Tacoma, July 29, 1938; s. Schuyler L. and Edna R. (Muzzy) Duryee; m. Anne Getchell Peterson, Nov. 26, 1966; children: Tracy Anne, Tricia Marie. BA in Bus., U. Wash., 1961, MBA, 1969; diploma, Pacific Coast Banking Schs., Seattle, 1973. Lending officer Seattle 1st Nat. Bank, 1964-68, v.p., trust officer, 1970-80; cons., chmn. Mgmt. Adv. Svcs., Inc., Seattle, 1980-93; mng. prin. Moss Adams Adv. Svcs., Moss Adams LLP, 1994—2001; dir. Horizon Mgmt. Svcs. LLC, 2002—. Lectr. in field; expert witness, Wash., NY, Md., Calif., Mass., Ind., Fla.; bd. dirs. Lafromboise Newspapers, Inc. Author: The Business Owners Guide to Achieving Financial Success, 1994; contbr. articles to profl. jours. Capt. US Army, 1962—64. Mem.: Northwest Family Bus. Advisors, Estate Planning Coun. Seattle, Seattle Tennis Club. Avocations: tennis, golf. Home and Office: 3301 E John St Seattle WA 98112-4938 Home Phone: 206-329-6403; Office Phone: 206-329-4911. Personal E-mail: dduryee@comcast.net.

DURYEE, HAROLD TAYLOR, insurance consultant; b. Willoughby, Ohio, Feb. 11, 1930; s. Gerald Fancher and Margaret Grace (Taylor) D.; m. Phyllis Annette Painter, June 18, 1966. AB, Kenyon Coll., 1951. Field rep. Mahoning Valley Coun., Boy Scouts Am., Youngstown, Ohio, 1951-56; mgr. claims svcs. Nationwide Ins. Cos., Canton, 1956-65; legis. and field dir. Ohio Rep. Party, Columbus, 1965-70, exec. dir., 1970-77, cons., 1980-81; dep. adminstr. Ohio Bur. Workers' Compensation, Columbus, 1977-84; exec. dep. adminstr. Fed. Ins. Adminstrn., Washington, 1984-86; adminstr. fed. ins. Fed. Emergency Mgmt. Agy., Washington, 1986-90; dir. Ohio Dept. Ins., 1991-99; sr. advisor Internat. Ins. Found., 1999—. Trustee, exec. com. Griffith Found. for Ins. Edn.; mem. Ohio Elections Commn., 1980-84. Vice chmn. North Canton City Planning Commn., 1958-67; precinct committeeman Stark County Cen. Com., 1958-72; organizer North Canton Rep. Com., 1958, chmn., 1960-72; sec. North Canton Area Devel. Com., 1959-64; chmn. North Canton City Charter Commn., 1960; campaign mgr. U.S. Rep. Frank T. Bow, 1962, Oliver P. Bolton for U.S. Congress, 1964, Clarence J. Brown, Jr. for U.S. Congress, 1965; state chmn. Ohio League Young Rep. Clubs, 1962-63; nat. vice chmn. Young Rep. Nat. Fedn., 1963-65; former chmn. bd. trustees Nat. Assn. Ins. Commrs. Edn. and Rsch. Found.; former trustee ASFPM Edn. and Rsch. Found. Recipient Disting. Svc. award Jaycees, 1961, Civic Affairs award Rotary, 1964, Meritorious Svc. award Fed. Emergency Mgmt. Agy., 1989, Disting. Civilian Svc. medal, Fed. Emergency Mgmt. Agy., 1990. Mem. Acad. Polit. Sci. Episcopalian. Avocation: genealogy. Home: 925 City Park Ave Columbus OH 43206-2511 Office Phone: 614-443-8285. Personal E-mail: hduryee@columbus.rr.com.

DUSANSKY, RICHARD, economist, educator; b. Bklyn., Dec. 23, 1942; m. Abigail November, July 3, 1965; children: Eric, Deborah. BA cum laude, Bklyn. Coll., 1964; PhD in Econs., Brown U., 1969. Asst. prof. econs. SUNY, Stony Brook, 1968-72, assoc. prof, 1972-74, prof., 1974-84, dir. Econ. Rsch. Bur., 1977-82; prof., head dept. econs. U. Ga., 1984-89; Powell Centennial prof. dept. econs. U. Tex., Austin, 1989-91, Richard Gonzalez Regents Chair prof. econs., 1991—, chmn., 1989-97,98-2000, dir. Ctr. for Applied Rsch. in Econs., 1999—2004. Contbr. articles on econs. to profl. jours. Ford Found. fellow, 1967-68. Mem. Am. Econs. Assn., Econometric Soc. Office: U Tex Dept Econ Austin TX 78712 Office Phone: 512-471-3664. Business E-Mail: dusansky@eco.utexas.edu.

DUSCHA, JULIUS CARL, journalist; b. St. Paul, Nov. 4, 1924; s. Julius William and Anna (Perlowski) D.; m. Priscilla Ann McBride, Aug. 17, 1946 (dec. Sept. 1992); children: Fred C., Steve D., Suzanne, Sally Jean; m. Suzanne Van Den Heurk, June 21, 1997. Student, U. Minn., 1943—47; AB, Am. U., 1951; postgrad., Harvard Coll., 1955—56. Reporter St. Paul Pioneer Press, 1943-47, Congl. Quar., 1947—48; publicist Dem. Nat. Com., 1948, 52; writer Labor's League for Polit. Edn., AFL, 1949-52, Internat. Assn. Machinist, 1952-53; editl. writer Lindsay-Schaub Newspapers, Ill., 1954-58; nat. affairs reporter Washington Post, 1958-66; assoc. dir. profl. journalism fellowships program Stanford (Calif.) U., 1966-68; dir. Washington Journalism Ctr., 1968-90; columnist, freelance journalist, West Coast corr. Presstime mag., San Francisco, 1990-99; sr. corr. News Inc., San Francisco, 1998—. Mem. Commn. on Presdl. Press Confs., U.

Va., 1981. Author: Taxpayer's Hayride: The Farm Problem from the New Deal to the Billie Sol Estes Case, 1964, Arms, Money and Politics, 1965, The Campus Press, 1973, From Pea Soup to Politics - A Memoir, 2005; editor: Defense Conversion Advisory; contbr. articles to mags., including Washingtonian, N.Y. Times Mag., Changing Times, Harper's, Reporter, Progressive, New Leader. Recipient award for Disting. Washington corr. Sigma Delta Chi, 1961 Mem.: Cosmos Club (Washington), Kappa Sigma. Home: 2200 Pacific Ave Apt 7D San Francisco CA 94115-1412 Personal E-mail: duschaduscha@sbcglobal.net.

DUSENBERY, WALTER CONDIT, sculptor; b. Alameda, Calif., Sept. 21, 1939; s. Walter A. and Allegra V. (McIlrath) D.; m. Irene McManus, Jan. 25, 1986. Student, San Francisco Art Inst., 1961; M.F.A., Calif. Coll. Arts and Crafts, Oakland, 1969. Instr. U. Calif. Extension-San Francisco, 1967-69; vis. sculptor Grad. Sch. Design-Harvard U., Cambridge, Mass., 1979—; dir. Stone divsn. Johnson Atelier, 1996—2003; chmn. bd. Digital Stone Project, Mercerville, NJ, 2003—. Exhibitor one-man shows, Laumeir Internat. Sculpture Park, St. Louis, 1983, Va. Commonwealth U., Richmond, 1983, Harvard U. Grad. Sch. Design, 1982, Nassau County Mus. Fine Art, Roslyn, N.Y., 1981, Hamilton Gallery Contemporary Art, N.Y.C., 1978, 80, Fendrick Gallery, Washington, 1986, 88; represented in permanent collections, Carnegie Inst., Pitts., Columbus (Ohio) Mus. Art, Commune of Glostrup, Denmark, Solomon R. Guggenheim Mus., N.Y.C., Huntington (W. Va.) Galleries, Met. Mus. Art, N.Y.C., San Francisco Mus. Modern Art, U. N.Mex. Mus., Albuquerque, Jerusalem Found, Israel, City of Portland Oreg., U. No. Iowa, Cedar Falls, Rainier Bank, Seattle; author: The Story of the Bed, 1970. Recipient Meml. prize Augustus St. Gaudens Found.; fellow Creative Artists Program Svc., N.Y.C., 1980, Nat. Endowment for Arts, 1980. Home: PO Box 144 Fly Creek NY 13337 Office Phone: 607-547-8431. E-mail: wdusenbery@stny.rr.com.

DUSENBURY, RUTH ELLEN COLE, business owner; b. Balt., June 19, 1929; Social worker Balt. City Welfare Dept., 1950-51; civil rights desk clk. FBI, 1951; asst. buyer, br. store sect. mgr., rsch. supr. Hutzler Bros. Dept. Store, Balt., 1951-58, pub. rels. rep., 1969-72; real estate rep. Robert Knatz Agy., 1969-70; sec., treas., officer mgr., co-owner Speer Cushion Co., Holyoke, Colo., 1974—99; ret., 1999. Active Bus. and Profl. Women's Orgn., 1976—87, Colo. Workforce Devel. Coun., 1999—2001, Rep. Party, 1968—; del. White House Conf. on Small Bus., Washington, 1995; apptd. Congressman Bob Schafer's Bus. Adv. Com., 1998; bd. dirs. Holyoke Cmty. Arts Coun., 1976—2002; charter mem. bd. Colo. Arts. Consortium, chmn., hon. bd. dirs.; pres. Colo. Arts. Coalition; mem. leadership coun. Colo. Nat. Fedn. Ind. Bus., 2002—. Office Phone: 970-854-2204. E-mail: wadusenbury@petelcom.coop.

DUSHENSKY, JACQUELINE AMELIA, banker, educator; b. Albany, NY, Jan. 22, 1950; d. Andrew John and Ida Regina; children: George Leon, Andrew John. BS in Med. Tech., Albany Coll. Pharmacy, NYC, 1972. Registered med. technologist Am. Soc. Clin. Pathologists, 1972. Supr. tchg. St. Peter's Sch. Med. Tech. St. Peter's Hosp. Albany Coll. Pharmacy, 1972—81, adj. instr. microbiology, 1993—2003; adj. instr. Hudson Valley C.C., Troy, NY, 1983—; mgr. Trustco Bank, Rensselaer, NY, 2003—. Author: Microbiology Lab Manual. Tchr. St. Clare's Ch., Albany. Named Tulip Queen, Albany, 1974; recipient Outstanding Young Women award, 1974, Outstanding Performance award, Trustco Bank, 2005. Mem.: Am. Soc. Clin. Pathology (licentiate). Home: 37 Sunset Blvd Albany NY 12205 Home Phone: 518-869-7892; Office Phone: 518-479-7233. Personal E-mail: jdushensky@hotmail.com.

DUSICK, RYAN MICHAEL, musician; b. Los Angeles, Calif., Sept. 19, 1977; Band mem. Kara's Flowers (name changed to Maroon 5, 2001), LA, 1994—; signed to Reprise Records, 1997—99, Octone Records, 2001—. Musician (as Kara's Flowers): (albums) Fourth World, 1997; musician: (as Maroon 5) Songs About Jane, 2002, 1.22.03.Acoustic, 2004, Live Friday the 13th, 2005, It Won't Be Soon Before Long, 2007, (songs) Harder to Breathe, 2003, This Love, 2004 (MTV Video Music award for Best New Artist, 2004, Grammy award for Best Group Pop Performance, 2006), She Will Be Loved, 2004, Shiver, 2005, contbr. to Spider-Man 2 soundtrack, 2004. Recipient World Music award for Best New Group, 2004, MTV Europe award for Best New Act, 2004, Grammy award for Best New Artist (with Maroon 5), 2005. Address: Maroon 5 PO Box 884564 San Francisco CA 94188 Office: Octone Records Rm 500 560 Broadway New York NY 10012 Office Phone: 646-613-0200. E-mail: maroon5@maroon5.com.

DUSKIN, J. ERIC, history professor; s. Elizabeth Duskin. BA, Wesleyan U., Middletown, Conn., 1981; MA, U. Mich., Ann Arbor, 1988, PhD, 1993. Asst. prof. history Christopher Newport U., Newport News, Va., 2002—06, assoc. prof., 2006—. Lectr. in field. Author: Stalinist Reconstruction and the Making of a New Elite, 2001. Socialist. Office: Christopher Newport Univ 1 University Pl Newport News VA 23606 Office Phone: 757-594-7121. Office Fax: 757-594-8771. Business E-Mail: eduskin@cnu.edu.

DUSOLD, LAURENCE RICHARD, chemist, computer specialist; b. Chgo., Nov. 15, 1944; s. Henry E. and Colette M. Dusold; m. Karen A. Marsh, Aug. 29, 1970; children: Amy, Lauren, Patricia, Amanda. BS in Chemistry, Purdue U., 1966; MS, U. N.C., 1969; postgrad., Wayne State U., 1969-71. Rsch. chemist, residue analysis and methods investigation br. Bur. Foods FDA, Washington, 1971—75, chemist, computer specialist, div. chemistry and physics, 1975—81, sr. chemist, computer specialist, div. of chemistry and physics, 1981—86, chief telecomms. and sci. computer support, 1986—2003, dep. info. tech. dir. sci. computing, 2004—06, info. tech. dir. sci. computing, 2006—. Faculty, evening divsn. U. Md., 1973-2000; fed. engrng. planning group Dept. HHS, 1990-95. Mem. editl. bd. Sci. Computing and Automation, 1990-2003; contbr. articles to profl. jours., chpts. to books. Mem. AAUP, Am. Chem. Soc., Internet Soc., IEEE, IEEE Computer Soc., Assn. Computing Machinery (chmn. SIGAPL, D.C. chpt. 1978-91, vice chmn. Potomac chpt. 1993-96), Greater Washington Fed. Agy. APL Users Group (co-chmn. 1977-87), Alpha Chi Sigma, Phi Lambda Upsilon. Republican. Roman Catholic. Office: FDA 5100 Paint Branch Pky College Park MD 20740-3835 Home Phone: 410-719-1047; Office Phone: 301-436-1481. Business E-Mail: laurence.dusold@fda.hhs.gov.

DUSSAN V. ELIZABETH B., scientific adviser; Assoc. prof. chem. engrng. U. Pa.; scientific advisor Schlumberger-Doll Rsch., Ridgefield, Conn. Adv. bd. Dept. Chem. Engrng., U. RI, 2004. Guggenheim Fellowship, 1984. Mem.: NAE. Office: Schlumberger-Doll Rsch 36 Old Quarry Rd Ridgefield CT 06877

DUSTER, TROY, sociology educator; b. Chgo., July 11, 1936; s. Benjamin Cecil and Alfred Margarita (Barnett) D.; m. Ellen Marie Johansson, May 16, 1964 (div. 1974) BS, Northwestern U., 1957, PhD, 1962; MA, UCLA, 1959; DSc (hon.), Northwestern U., 2005. Asst. prof. sociology U. Calif., Riverside, 1963-65, asst. research sociologist Berkeley, 1965-69, assoc. prof. sociology, 1970-78, prof. to Chancellor's prof., 1979—, chmn. dept., 1986—. Dir. Inst. for Study of Social Change, U. Calif., 1976—; Bernhard prof. anthropology and sociology Williams Coll., 1985; mem., chair adv. com. ethical, legal and social issues in human genome project NIH/DOE, 1996-98; dir. Am. Cultures Ctr. U. Calif., Berkeley, 2000-02; mem. adv. bd. Social Sci. Rsch. Coun., 2003-07; chmn. bd. dirs. Assn. Am. Colls. and Univs., 2003-04; Silver prof. sociology, dir. Inst. for the History of the Prodn. of Knowledge, NYU, 2005—. Author: Legislation of Morality, 1970, (monograph) Aims and Control of the Universities, 1972, Backdoor to Eugenics, 1990; co-editor: Cultural Perspectives on Biological Knowledge, 1984. Mem. assembly of behavioral and social scis. Nat. Acad. Scis., Washington, 1973-78; mem. research panel Pres.'s Commn. on Mental Health, Washington, 1977-78; cons., advisor Pres.'s Commn. for Study of Ethical Problems in Medicine, Washington, 1980; mem. bio-tech. adv. council State of Calif.; chmn. Ethical, Legal, and Social Issues Commn. Nat. Ctr. Human Genome Rsch., Washington, 1996—, Nat. Panel of the Am. Commitments Initiative Assn. Am. Colls. and Univs., Washington, 1993—, Com. Social and Ethical Impact of Advances in Biomedicine Inst. of Medicine, Nat. Acad. Scis., Washington, 1991-94, Spl. Commn. Meeting the Challenge of Diversity in an Acad. Democracy Assn. Am. Law Schs., Washington, 1991-95, Subcom. Protection of Human Subjects, Health and Environ. Rsch. Adv. Com. Dept. Energy, 1994; adv. bd. Ctr. for Study of Race, Crime, and Social Policy Swedish Govt. fellow Uppsala U., 1962-63; Guggenheim Found. fellow London Sch. Econs., 1971-72; Ford Found. fellow, 1978-79 Mem. Am. Sociol. Assn. (mem. exec. office of the budget coun. 1991-94, pres. 2004-05). Avocations: ceramics; photography; tennis; chess. Home: 3031 Benvenue Ave Berkeley CA 94705-2509 Office: U Calif-Berkeley Dept Sociology Berkeley CA 94720-0001 Business E-Mail: troy.duster@nyu.edu.

DUSTMAN, PATRICIA (JO) ALLEN, elementary school educator, consultant; b. Salem, Ohio, Mar. 22, 1947; d. Alton Davis Allen and Mary Evaline Allen (Iler); m. George Bird Dustman, June 10, 1972; 1 child, Mary Elizabeth Wastchak. BS, Kent State U., 1967—69, MA, 1970—71; EdD, Ariz. State U., 1998. Cert. Teacher AZ. Tchr. Ashtabula City, Ravenna City, N. Ridgeville City Sch. Districts, Ohio, 1969—75; prin. North Ridgeville City Schools, Ohio, 1975—80; asst. supt. Madison Local Schools, Ohio, 1980—82; supt. of schools St. Clairsville-Richland City Schools, Ohio, 1982—85; dist. and bldg. adminstr. Scottsdale Pub. Schools, Ariz., 1985—94; supt. of schools Queen Creek Unified Sch. Dist., Ariz., 1994—98; rschr., cons. SW Interdisciplinary Rsch. Consortium, Ariz. State U., Tempe, Ariz., 1999—; ednl. cons. The Dustman Group, Scottsdale, Ariz., 1999—. Mem. Bel-Tech Adv. Bd., St. Clairsville, Ohio, 1982—85; academic standards design team mem. Ariz. Dept. of Edn., Phoenix, 1996—98; mem. East Valley Think Tank, Mesa, Ariz., 1994—98, Mesa C.C. Adv. Bd., Ariz., 1997—98; mentor SPR-Early Career Preventionist Network, Washington, 2003—; mem., cmty. adv. bd. for student services Osborn Elem. Sch. Dist., Phoenix, 2000—; mem., acad. profls. Sch. of Social Work, Ariz. State U., 2003—. Contbr. articles to profl. jours. Mem. C. of C., St. Clairsville, Ohio, 1982—85; founding mem. and chair Scottsdale Prevention Inst., Ariz., 1985—87; mem. Scottsdale Ednl. Enrichment Services, Ariz., 1985—2003; donor Kent State U. Alumni Assn., The Wilson Conf. of the Coll. of Edn., The Bowman Fellowship Fund, Ariz. State U. Alumni Assn. Founders' Day, 1990—2003. Recipient Key to the City, Mayor and City Coun. of St. Clairsville Ohio, 1985; grantee Key Pers.: Devel. and Implementation Dir.: SW Interdisciplinary Rsch. Consortium, NIH/NIDA, 2002—; Tech. grant, Olin Charitable Trust, 1995—98, Saturday Sch., Rural Metro Corp., 1998, Summer Acad. scholarships, MGC Pure Chemicals Am., 1997—98, grant, Key Pers.: Drug Resistance Strategies Project, NIH/NIDA, 1999—. Mem.: Belmont- Harrison Superintendents' Assn. (chair 1983—85), Soc. for Prevention Rsch., Ariz. Sch. Administrators (life), Phi Delta Kappa (program chair 1978—80). Avocations: reading, writing, travel, skiing. Office: Southwest Interdisciplinary Research Con P O Box 873711 Tempe AZ 85287-3711 Business E-Mail: dustmangroup@yahoo.com, patricia.dustman@asu.edu.

DUTCHER, JANICE JEAN PHILLIPS, oncologist; b. Bend, Oreg., Nov. 10, 1950; d. Charles Glen and MayBelle (Fluit) Phillips; m. John Dutcher, Sept. 8, 1971 (div. 1980). BA with honors, U. Utah, 1971; MD, U. Calif., Davis, 1975. Diplomate Am. Bd. Internal Medicine, Am. Bd. Med. Oncology. Intern Rush-Presbyn. St. Luke's Hosp., Chgo., 1975-76, resident, 1976-78; clin. assoc. Balt. Cancer Rsch., Nat. Cancer Inst., 1978-81, sr. investigator, 1981-82; asst. prof. U. Md., Balt., 1982, Albert Einstein Coll. Medicine, NYC, 1983-86, assoc. prof., 1986-92, prof., 1992-98, course co-dir. Advances in Cancer Treatment Rsch. Manhattan, 1984-96; prof. medicine N.Y. Med. Coll., 1998—; assoc. dir. for clin. affairs Comprehensive Cancer Ctr., Our Lady of Mercy Med. Ctr., 1998—. Chmn. biol. response mod. com. Ea. Coop. Oncology Group, Madison, Wis., 1989-95, mem. exec. com., 1995-97, chair renal subcom., 1998—; mem. data safety com. Nat. Heart Lung Blood Inst., Bethesda, Md., 1990-95; mem. biologic response modifier study sect. Nat. Cancer Inst., Bethesda, 1988, 90, 94, 96; mem. NIH Consensus Panel on Early Melanoma, 1992; mem. FDA Oncology Drug Adv. Bd., 1995-99, chair FDA-ODAC, 1996-99, NCI subcom. D for program project rev., 1995-98, mem. subsplty. med. oncology bd. Am. Bd. Internal Medicine, 1997-2003; mem. NCI subcom. A for Cancer Ctrs., 1998-2002; mem. faculty AACR/ASCO Workshop on Clin. Trials Devel., 1996-2002, NIH Progress Rev. Group on Kidney Cancer, 2001. Editor: Handbook of Hematology/Oncology Emergencies, 1987, Modern Transfusion Therapy, 1990; sect. editor: Neoplastic Diseases of the Blood, 3d edit., 1996, 4th edit., 2003; mem. editl. bd. Jour. Immunotherapy, Med. Oncology, Jour. Clin. Oncology, Jour. Clin. Pharm., Ann. Intern. Med.; sect. editor Current Treatment Options in Oncology, 2000-06, Chronic Leukemia, 2000-06; contbr. articles to Blood, Leukemia, Jour. Clin. Oncology, Jour. Immunotherapy, Clin. Cancer Rsch., Soc. Am. Cancer Jour. Recipient Beecham award in Hematology So. Blood Club, 1983, Henry C. Moses Clin. Rsch. award Montefiore Med. Ctr., 1989, Outstanding Alumnus award U. Calif., Davis, 1989; named Outstanding Young Investigator Ea. Coop. Oncology Group, 1993; recipient numerous grants. Mem.: Am. Assn. of Blood Banks, Am. Radium Soc., Am. Soc. Hematology, Am. Assn. for Cancer Rsch., Am. Soc. Hematology, Am. Soc. Clin. Oncology, Internat. Soc. Biol. Therapy, Alpha Omega Alpha, Phi Kappa Phi, Phi Beta Kappa. Achievements include findings related to management of alloimmunization to platelet transfusions, intensive maintenance of patients with acute leukemia, studies of new biologic response modifiers as antitumor drugs, management of renal cell cancer, melanoma and breast cancer, study and treatment with biologic antitumor agents, study and treatment of targeted therapies in renal cell cancer and melanoma. Address: Our Lady of Mercy Med Ctr Comprehensive Cancer Ctr 600 E 233rd St Bronx NY 10466-2604 Office Phone: 718-304-7200. Personal E-mail: jpd4401@aol.com.

DUTCHER, JOANA, elementary school educator, singer; b. Bklyn., July 15, 1975; d. Joseph and Lois Duffy; m. Dustin Dutcher, Sept. 27, 2002; 1 child, Matthew. BS in Music, SUNY, Oneonta, 1998, BS in Elem. Edn., 2000; M, AIU U., 2005. Cert. tchr. NY, 2005. ILC head tchr. RJK Mid. Sch., Monticello, NY, 2003, reading, English, math. AIS tchr., 2001—03. Singer solo cabaret performances, Monticello Rotary Star Search, 2006 (First prize). Mem.: UFT. Home: PO Box 224 Monticello NY 12701 Office: RJK Middle School 45 Breakey Ave Monticello NY 12701 Home Phone: 914-799-0755. Personal E-mail: dutcherjl@yahoo.com.

DUTEIL, HERVÉ PIERRE, bank executive; b. Paris, Aug. 6, 1968; m. Marilys Duteil, June 17, 2000. BS in Math. and Physics, U. Paris, 1987; M in Computer Sci., U. Cambridge, Eng., 1990; MS in Gen. Engrng., Ecole Centrale, France, 1990; diploma in Harmony, Counterpoint and Fugue, The Juilliard Sch., NY, 2000; MBA with distinction, Harvard Bus. Sch., Cambridge, 2004. Cert. Uniform Securities Agent N.Am. Securities Adminstrs. Assn., 2004, Gen. Securities Rep., Series 7 Nat. Assn. of Securities Dealers (NASD), 2004, Mcpl. Securities Prin., Series 53 Nat. Assn. Securities Dealers, 2005. Mng. dir. BNP Paribas, NYC, 1990—. Artist in residence NYU, 1997—2002; dir. music, organist St. Patrick's Old Cathedral, 1995—97, Our Lady the Presentation, Brighton, Mass., 2003—04. Musician: (concert organist, jury mem.) Paris UFAM Internat. Competition (First prize, 1999); composer: (sacred art) The Mystery of Christmas. Night vol. Mother Theresa's Gift Love, NYC, 1998—99; counselor Pregnancy Help, NYC, 2000—02; US coord. Emmanuel Cmty., NYC, 2006—. Achievements include first to several financial derivative transactions on specific commodity indices; invention of numerous organ improvisations during recitals and liturgical accompaniments.

DUTILE, FERNAND NEVILLE, law educator; b. Lewiston, Maine, Feb. 15, 1940; s. Wilfred Joseph and Lauretta Blanche (Cote) D.; m. Brigid Dooley, Apr. 4, 1964; children: Daniel, Patricia. AB, Assumption Coll., 1962; JD, U. Notre Dame, 1965. Bar: Maine 1965. Atty. U.S. Dept. Justice, Washington, 1965-66; prof. law Cath. U. Am., Washington, 1966-71, U. Notre Dame Law Sch., Ind., 1971—. Bd. dirs. Ind. Lawyers Commn., Indpls., 1975-85, Legal Svcs. No. Ind., South Bend, 1975-83; dir. South Bend Work Release Ctr., 1973-75, Ind. Criminal Law Study Commn., 1991-99. Editor: Legal Education and Lawyer Competency, 1981; author: Sex, Schools and the Law, 1986; co-editor: Early Childhood Intervention and Juvenile Delinquency, 1982, The Prediction of Criminal Violence, 1987; co-author: State and Campus, 1984. Mem.: Athletics Reps. Assn. (exec. com. 2004—06). Democrat. Roman Catholic.

DUTILE, ROBERT ARTHUR, executive management consultant; b. Stoneham, Mass., Dec. 26, 1959; s. Robert Arthur and Mary-Helene (Revane) D.; m. Ellen R. Ahearn, June 9, 1995. BS, Boston Coll., 1981. Cons. Monchik-Weber, Boston, 1981—83, Gately, Glew & Co., Wellesley, Mass., 1983—84; dir. MIS Reebok Internat., Ltd., Stoughton, Mass., 1984—91; sr. cons. Grant Thornton, LLP, Boston, 1992, mgr., 1992—95, sr. mgr., 1995—97, prin., 1997—99, Value Edge, Solon, Ohio, 2005—; exec. v.p. Key Corp., Cleve., 1999—2005; pres. Sharp End Enterprises LLC, 2005—; cons. US Tech. Resources, 2005—. Author: The Benchmarking Course, 1993. Mem. Am. Soc. Quality Control, Am. Mgmt. Assn., Am. Prodn. & Inventory Control Soc., Am. Mountain Guides Assn., Am. Alpine Club (life), Two/Ten Found, (life.). Avocations: writing, rock climbing, mountain climbing, golf. Home: 55 Brook Rd Amherst NH 03031 Office: Sharp End Enterprises LLC 120 Vantis Aliso Viejo CA 92656 Office Phone: 216-410-0359. Business E-Mail: robert_dutile@valueedge.net, dutile@ameritech.net.

DUTILLE, JESSICA ANNIE ORF, social services administrator, educator; b. Amityville, NY, Oct. 15, 1980; d. Robert A. and Darlene J. Orf; m. Bryan J. Dutille, Aug. 2, 2003; 1 child, Noah B. BS in Mktg., Plymouth State U., NH, 2003, MBA, 2004. Asst. dir., counselor Lebanon Recreation Dept., NH, 2000—03; tutor Plymouth State U., 2000—03, adj. faculty, 2006—; staff mem. Pemi Bridge Ho. Homeless Shelter, Plymouth, 2003—04; tchr. Holy Trinity Sch., Laconia, NH, 2004—05; exec. dir. Pemi Youth Ctr., Plymouth, 2005—; co-pres., co-founder The Faith, Hope & Love Found., NH, 2006—. Vol. Habitat for Humanity, SC, Ga., 2001, 2002, Ronal Mc Donald Ho., Tex., 2003. Named Outstanding Bus. Student, Plymouth State U., 2000, 2002, Most Outstanding Female Student, 2003; named one of 40 Under 40, Union Leader of NH, 2007. Mem.: Delta Mu Delta. Roman Catholic. Office: Pemi Youth Ctr 111 Main St Plymouth NH 03264 Office Phone: 603-536-7264. Personal E-mail: jdutille@hotmail.com.

DUTKO, MICHAEL EDWARD, lawyer; b. Memphis, Jan. 18, 1954; s. Edward James and Norma Dean (Sparks) D.; m. Bettie Ballowe, Mar. 14, 1981; children: Michael, Christina, Ashley. BA, Biscayne Coll., 1978; JD, Nova U., 1984. Police officer, detective Ft. Lauderdale (Fla.) Police Dept., 1976-81; pros., asst. state atty. Broward State Atty.'s Office, Ft. Lauderdale, 1984-86; assoc. Kay & Bogenschutz, P.A., Ft. Lauderdale, 1986-90; ptnr. Kay, Bogenschutz & Dutko, Ft. Lauderdale, 1990-92, Bogenschutz Dutko & Kroll, P.A., Ft. Lauderdale, 1992—. Mem. Broward Assn. Criminal Def. Lawyers, Fla. Assn. Criminal Def. Lawyers, Nat. Assn. Criminal Def. Lawyers, St. Thomas More Soc. South Fla. (bd. govs.), Canon Law Soc. Am. (assoc.). Democrat. Roman Catholic. Avocations: golf, boxing, motorcycles. Office: Bogenschutz Dutko & KrollPA 600 S Andrews Ave Ste 500 Fort Lauderdale FL 33301-2851

DUTKOWSKY, ROBERT M., computer company executive; b. Jan. 2, 1955; BS in Indsl. Engrng. & Labor Rels., Cornell U., 1977. Mgmt. positions through v.p. distbn. Asia Pacific & v.p. sales & mktg. RS/6000 IBM, 1977—97; exec. v.p. sales & mktg. EMC Corp., 1997—2000; chmn., pres., CEO GenRad Inc., 2000—02; pres. assembly test div. Teradyne Inc., 2001—02; chmn., pres., CEO J.D. Edwards Inc., 2002—03, Egenera Inc., Marlboro, Mass., 2004—06, chmn., 2006; CEO Tech Data Corp., Clearwater, Fla., 2006—. Bd. dir. McAfee Inc., SEPATON Inc. Recipient Ellis Island Medal of Honor, 2000. Office: Tech Data Corp 5350 Tech Data Dr Clearwater FL 33760*

DUTRO, JOHN THOMAS, JR., geologist, paleontologist; b. Columbus, Ohio, May 20, 1923; s. John Thomas and Dorothy Durstine (Smith) D.; m. Nancy Ann Pence, Jan. 2, 1948; children: Sarah Dutro Cormier, Christopher, Susan Dutro Hultman. BA, Oberlin Coll., 1948; MS, Yale U., 1950, PhD, 1953; DSc, Denison U., 1993. Geologist, U.S. Geol. Survey, 1948-94, chief paleontology and stratigraphy br., 1962-68, mem. geologic names com., 1962-83; ret., 1994; emeritus vol. U.S. Geol. Survey, 1994—; rsch. assoc. Smithsonian Instn., 1962—. Vis. lectr. Am. U., 1957-59, George Washington U., 1962-63; mem. geology panel Bd. Civil Svc. Examiners, 1958-65; dir., field trip chmn. 9th Internat. Carboniferous Congress, 1979. Active area PTA, 1959-69, Boy Scouts Am., 1963-66, Fairlington Players, 1965-75. With Army Air Corps, 1943-46. Recipient Meritorious Svc. award U.S. Dept. Interior, 1983, Disting. Svc. award, 1996; Sterling fellow, 1949. Fellow AAAS (sec. sect. E 1981-85, Pacific divsn. pres. 1996-97), Arctic Inst. N.Am., Geol. Soc. London, Geol. Soc. Am. (assoc. editor 1974-82); mem. Am. Geol. Inst. (vis. geoscientist 1961-67, bd. dirs., sec.-treas. 1965-71), Paleontol. Soc. (tech. editor 1991), Palaeontol. Assn., Paleontol. Rsch. Inst. (trustee 1986—, v.p. 1990-91, pres. 1992-94), Internat. Paleontol. Assn., Paleontol. Soc. Washington (pres. 1955-56, 2003-04), Geol. Soc. Washington (sec. 1959-60, pres. 1978), Assn. Earth Sci. Editors (pres. 1989-90), Am. Polar Soc., Alaska Geol. Soc., Sigma Xi, Pick and Hammer Club, Cosmos Club, Yale Club (Washington). Democrat. Achievements include research in brachiopoda, Paleozoic biostratigraphy and biogeography of Arctic regions and western hemisphere, biostratigraphy of East Asia, and history of paleontology. Home: 5173 Fulton St NW Washington DC 20016-3448 Office: US Nat Mus Natural History Washington DC 20560-0137 Office Phone: 202-633-1322. Office Fax: 202-786-2832. Business E-Mail: dutrot@si.edu.

DUTSON, THAYNE R., dean; b. Idaho Falls, Oct. 3, 1942; s. Rollo and Thelma (Fugal) D.; m. Joyce Cook, Dec. 19, 1962 (div. 1980); 1 child, Bradley; m. Margaret McCallum, June 23, 1989; children: Taylor, Alexandra. BS, Utah State U., 1966; MS, Mich. State U., 1969, PhD, 1971. Postdoctoral fellow U. Nottingham, Sutton Bonnington, Eng., 1971-72; prof. Tex. A&M U., College Station, 1972-83; dept. head Mich. State U., East Lansing, Mich., 1983-87; dir. agrl. exptl. sta. Oreg. State U., Corvallis, 1987-93, dean, dir. Coll. Agrl. Sci., 1993—. Editor: Advances in Meat Research (11 vols.) 1985-97; contbr. articles to profl. jours. Scoutmaster Boy Scouts Am., Mich., 1966-71. Fellow Inst. Food Technologists; mem. Am. Meat Sci. Assn. (bd. dirs. 1979-81, Disting. Rsch. award 1985), Am. Soc. Animal Sci. (Meat Rsch. award 1981), Coun. for Agr. Sci. and Tech. (pres. 1988), Phi Kappa Phi, Sigma Xi. Avocations: skiing, running, exercise, golf.

DUTT, KAMLA, medical educator; b. Lahore, Punjab, India; came to U.S., 1969; d. Gulzari Lal and Raj Bansi Dutt. BS with honors, Panjab U., Chandigarh, India, 1961, MS in Zoology with honors, 1962, PhD, 1970. Rsch. assoc. Harvard Med. Sch. Sidney Farber Cancer Ctr., Boston, 1972-76; rsch. assoc. Eye Inst. Retinal Fedn., Boston, 1977-80; sr. rsch.

assoc. Yale Med. Ctr., New Haven, 1980-81, Emory U., Atlanta, 1981-82; asst. prof. Morehouse Sch. Medicine, Atlanta, 1983-89, assoc. prof., 1989—2001, prof., 2001—. Sci. adv. bd. Fernbank Sci. Ctr., Atlanta. Contbr. numerous articles to sci. jours.; author short stories (in Hindi); prodr., actor 3 maj. plays, Atlanta; actor 11 maj. plays, India. Bd. dirs. VSEI (vol. fundraising orgn. for edn. in India), 1973-78; v.p. Indian Am. Cultural Assn., 1985; podium spkr., participant King Week, 1990, 91, 93; spkr. Gandhi Day Celebration, 1984, 85; key participant Intercultural Conf., 1990; main participant joint document Women's Perspective; active human rights issues; stake holder Vision 20/20 Collaborative State of Ga., diversity and edn. coms., 1995. Hindu. Achievements include establishment of human ocular cell lines by gene transfection, used as model for study of eye diseases and tissue engineering. Office: Morehouse Sch Medicine 720 Westview Dr Atlanta GA 30310-1458 Office Phone: 404-752-1769. Business E-Mail: kdutt@msm.edu.

DUTT, VARUN, systems and software engineer; b. Lucknow, Uttar Pradesh, India, Aug. 30, 1982; arrived in US, 2005; s. Vijay Kumar and Poonam Dutt. BE in Computer Sci. and Engring., Thapar Inst. of Engring. and Tech., Patiala, India, 2004; M in Info. Tech. and Software Engring., Carnegie Mellon U., Pitts., 2006. Software engr. Tata Consultancy Svcs., New Delhi, Delhi, 2005—; rschr. Carnegie Mellon U., 5000 Forbes Avenue, Pittsburgh, Pa., 2006—. Rschr., cons. Carnegie Mellon U., Pitts., 2006—. Author, rschr.: rsch. publ. The Concept of Classification in Data Mining using Neural Networks (Best Paper and Poster Presentation award, 2005); contbr. articles to profl. jours. Rep. of software engring. dept.grad. student assembly Carnegie Mellon U., Pitts., 2005—06. Recipient 1st Prize for Rsch. Paper, Nat. Conf. on Bio Informatics and Computing at Thapar Inst. of Engring. and Tech., 2005. Mem.: IEEE (founding exec. mem. Gold chpt. 2004—06). Brahmin, Hindu. Achievements include research in Communication Protocols between Software Elements (runtime objects) in Software Architectures. Avocations: travel, cricket, reading books and management journals. Home: Apt #1 315 North Neville St Pittsburgh PA 15213-1653 Office: Carnegie Mellon Univ 5000 Forbes Ave Pittsburgh PA 15213 Home Phone: 412-628-1379; Office Phone: 412-268-9078. Personal E-mail: varundutt@ieee.org.

DUTTA, MITRA, engineer, educator; m. Michael A. Stroscio; 1 child, Gautam Dutta Stroscio. BS, Delhi U., India, MSc, 1973; PhD, U. Cin., 1981. Lectr. Coll. Arts, Sci. and Tech., Kingston, Jamaica, 1973-76, U. West Indies, Kingston, 1973-76; rsch. assoc. Purdue U., West Lafayette, Ind., 1981-83; sr. rsch. assoc. CCNY, NYC, 1983-86; rsch. engr. Systematic Gen. Corp., Eatontown, NJ, 1986-88; rsch. physicist and leader optoelectronics team Army Rsch. Lab. Electronics and Power Sources Directorate, Ft. Monmouth, NJ, 1988—94; dir., phys. scis. directorate Army Rsch. Lab, 1994—96, assoc. dir., electronics div., 1996—99; dir., rsch. and tech. integration directorate Army Rsch. Office, 1999—2001, disting. prof. and head, elec. and computer engring. dept., 2001—. Contbr. approximately 400 papers and proceedings; 31 US and Can. patents; co-author: 1 book; editor: 5 books. Nat. Merit scholar Govt. of India, 1968-71, Univ. Grants scholar Univ. Grants Commn., Delhi, India, 1971-73, R & D Achievement award, U.S. Army, 1990, 92, 94, ETDL Harold Jacobs award, 1991, Paul A. Siple Meml. award, 1993, Nat. Achievement award, Soc. for Women Engrs., 2003. Fellow IEEE (Harry Diamond award 2000), AAAS, Optical Soc. Am., Army Rsch. Lab (emeritus). Office: U Ill at Chgo 851 S Morgan M/C 154 Chicago IL 60607 Office Phone: 312-355-2131. E-mail: dutta@ece.uic.edu.

DUTTA, RAJIV, Internet company executive; BA in Econs. with honors, Delhi U., India; MBA, Claremont U., Calif. With Bio-Rad Labs., Inc., 1988—98; controller worldwide sales KLA-Tencor, 1998; fin. dir. eBay Inc., San Jose, Calif., 1998—99, v.p. fin., investor rels., 1999—2001, sr. v.p., CFO, 2001—06; pres. Skype Technologies S.A. (subsidiary of eBay, Inc.), Luxembourg and London, 2006, PayPal, Inc. (subsidiary of eBay, Inc.), San Jose, Calif., 2006—. Bd. dir. Jamadat Mobile Inc. Office: Pay Pal Inc 2211 N First St San Jose CA 95131*

DUTTA, SANJEEV, surgeon; b. Lucknow, India, Jan. 14, 1972; arrived in US, 2004; s. Basu Dev and Bhakti Leena Dutta; m. Trenna Lee Sutcliffe, Aug. 20, 2005. MD, U. Calgary, Can., 1996; MA in Surg. Edn., U. Ill., Springfield, 1999. Intern surgery Dalhousie U., Halifax, 1996—97, resident gen. surgery, 1997—2001; fellow pediatric surgery Hosp. for Sick Children, Toronto, Canada, 2002—04; instr. surgery Stanford U., Calif., 2005—06, asst. prof. surgery and pediat., 2006—. Assoc. dir. dept. surgery Goodman Simulation Ctr. Stanford U., 2006—, co-director surg. skills curriculum dept. surgery, 2006—; surg. dir. intestinal rehab. program Lucile Packard Children's Hosp., Stanford, 2006—; surg. dir. and prin. investigator Stanford/SRI Internat. Multidisciplinary Initiative for Surg. Tech. Rsch., Stanford and Menlo Park, 2006—. Fellow, McMaster U., Hamilton, Can., 2002. Fellow: Royal Coll. Physicians and Surgeons Can.; mem.: Soc. Am. Gastrointestinal and Endoscopic Surgeons, Internat. Pediatric Endosurgery Group (new technologies com., edn. com.), Am. Acad. Pediat.

DUTTON, DIANA CHERYL, lawyer; b. Sherman, Tex., June 27, 1944; d. Roy G. and Monett Dutton; m. Anthony R. Grindl, July 8, 1974. BS, Georgetown U., DC, 1967; JD, U. Tex., 1971. Bar: Tex. 1971. Regional counsel U.S. EPA, Dallas, 1975—79, dir. enforcement divsn., 1979—81; ptnr., head firm-wide environ. practice, mem. Dallas practice com. Akin, Gump, Strauss, Hauer & Feld, L.L.P., 1981—. Chair Greater Dallas Chamber Environ. com., 2001; bd. dirs. Girls Inc., 2004—, bd. chair, 2006—; bd. dirs. Mental Health Assn. Dallas, 2005—. Named a Tex. Super Lawyer, Tex. Monthly Mag., 2003—05; named one of Best Lawyers in Am., 1995—, Best Lawyers in Dallas, D Mag., 2001—05, Ams. Leading Bus. Lawyers, Chambers USA, 2003—07, Top 50 Tex. Women Attys., Tex. Monthly Mag., 2003—06. Mem.: ABA, Dallas Bar Found., Dallas Bar Assn. (chmn. environ. law sect. 1984), Tex. Bar Assn. (chmn. environ. and natural resources law sect. 1985—86). Episcopalian. Office: Akin Gump Strauss Hauer and Feld LLP 1700 Pacific Ave Ste 4100 Dallas TX 75201-4675 Office Phone: 214-969-2855. Office Fax: 214-969-4343. E-mail: ddutton@akingump.com.

DUTTON, FRANK ELROY, data processing executive, writer; b. Warren, Ohio, Nov. 16, 1946; s. Robert Wade and Ann Victoria (Sessions) D.; m. Nancy June Gephart, Nov. 6, 1965 (div. 1981); children: Cynthia, Frank, Robert; m. Margaret Elizabeth Sessions, Dec. 16, 1981 (div. Dec. 1987); m. Paula Kay Gately, Feb. 14, 1992 (div. Sept. 1994). With sales dept. Zylco Cutlery Rena Ware Distrs., Warren, 1964—68; advt. salesman Directory Dept. Ohio Bell Telephone Co., Cuyahoga Falls, 1968—69; pvt. practice residential constrn. Warren and Hammond (La.), 1970—74; technician J. Ray McDermott & Co., New Orleans, 1974—83, McDermott Internat., Antwerp, Belgium, 1975, McDermott SE Asia, Singapore, 1981—83; owner Computer Time, Inc., Hammond, 1983—85; mgr. tech. services Industry Programs, Inc., Houston, 1985—86; owner Affordable Automation, Houston, 1987—89; program, analyst The Phillips Group, Stafford, Tex., 1989—92; owner software and hardware integrator IHMS Software Support, Many, La., 1992—; owner computer software, internet web site design hosting Fred Software, Many, 1998—. Cons. in computer comm. Southmark Industries, Houston, 1986-87, Crown Broadcasting, Hammond, La., 1987-89, Bee-Line Delivery Svc., Houston, 1986-89. Author, designer computer games, utility software programs, computer software for radio stas., computer software for retail furniture stores, Turbo Pascal Toolbox, 1988 (award of disting. tech. communication 1989, award of excellence Internat. Soc. Tech. Communication 1989), French transl., 1988, Portuguese trans., 1990, French trans., 1990; contbr. articles to profl. jours. With USAR, 1966—72. Recipient semi-finalist award, Global Info. Infrastructure, 1999. Mem.: Am. Mensa Soc. Avocation: photography. Home and Office: 80 Anna St Many LA 71449

DUTTON, JOHN ALTNOW, meteorologist, educator; b. Detroit, Sept. 11, 1936; s. Carl Evans and Velma (Altnow) D.; m. Frances Elizabeth (Andrews), Jan. 13, 1962; children: Christopher Evan, John Andrews, Jan Frederik. BS, U. Wis., 1958; MS, 1959, PhD, 1962. Mem. faculty Pa. State U., Univ. Pk., 1965—2002, assoc. prof. meteorology, 1968—71, prof., 1971—2002, head dept. meteorology, 1981—86, dean Coll. Earth and Mineral Sci., 1986—2002; chmn. Weather Ventures Ltd., 2000—, pres., 2005—. Expert aero. sys. div. USAF, 1965-71; vis. scientist Riso Rsch. Establishment, Roskilde, Denmark, 1971-72, summer 1975, 78-79; vis. prof. Tech. U., Denmark, 1978-79; v.p. UCAR Found., 1986-87, pres., 1987-95, chmn. bd. dirs., 1995-2001; trustee Mt. Nittany Med. Ctr., 1996—, mem. exec. com., 1999—. Author: The Ceaseless Wind: An Intro. to the Theory of Atmospheric Motion, 1976, 2d edit., 1986 (reprinted as Dynamics of Atmospheric Motion, 1995); (with H.A. Panofsky) Atmospheric Turbulence: Models and Methods for Engring. Applications, 1984; assoc. editor: Meteorol. Monographs, 1973-79, editor, 1979-84; contbg. articles to profl. journals. Trustee Univ. Corp. for Atmospheric Rsch., 1974-81, sec., 1977, treas., 1978-79, vice-chmn., 1980-84, chmn. unidata steering com., 1982-86, chmn. unidata policy com., 1986-88; chmn. long range planning com. NSF, Univ. Corp. for Atmospheric Rsch., 1986-87; mem. bd. atmospheric sci. and climate NRC, 1982-83, 88-97, chmn. bd., 1989-97, mem. internat. space yr. planning com., 1986-89, panel of experts on earth sci. and tech. Internat. Space Yr. 1992, 1989-92, space sci. bd. com. on earth sci., 1987-89, mem. space studies bd., 1989-93, chmn. task group priorities space rsch. of space studies bd., 1989-94, mem. nat. weather svc. modernization com., 1989-95; mem. Nat. Aviation Weather Svc. Com., 1994-95; mem. com. long term retention sci. and tech. records of fed. govt., 1993-95; ex-officio mem. Com. on Global Change Rsch., 1995-97, chmn. com. on aeronautics rsch. and tech. for environ. compatibility, 2000-02, mem. com. on the impact of high-end computing on four illustigive fields, 2006-07; mem. space and earth sci. adv. com. NASA, 1982-86, earth system sci. com., 1983-87, ctr. sci. assessment team, 1986-88. 1st lt. USAF, 1962-65. Fellow AAAS (sect. atmospheric and hydrospheric sci.), fellow, Am. Meteorol. Soc. (councillor 1986-88, chmn. publ. commn. 1984-85); mem. Math. Assn. Am., Soc. Indsl. and Applied Math., Sigma Xi, Phi Kappa Phi, Theta Delta Chi. Home: 240 Mt Pleasant Dr Boalsburg PA 16827-1810 Office: Pa State U 508 Walker Bldg University Park PA 16802-2710

DUTTON, MARK ANTHONY, lawyer; b. Moulton, Ala., Jan. 24, 1964; s. William B. and Judith C. (Barrett) D. BA, Huntingdon Coll., Montgomery, Ala., 1987; JD, Samford U., 1990. Bar: Ala. 1991, U.S. Dist. Ct. (no. dist.) Ala. 1991, U.S. Ct. Appeals (11th cir.) 1991. Pvt. practice, Moulton, Ala., 1991—. Exec. committeeman Dem. Party, Lawrence County, Ala., 1993-, former pres. of Lawrence Continental, Al. Bar Assn. Mem. Ala. Bar Assn., Ala. Trial Lawyers Assn., Masons, The Players Club (N.Y.C.). Democrat. Baptist. Avocations: racquetball, politics, reading. Home: 14220 Market St Moulton AL 35650-1442 Office: 714 East St Moulton AL 35650-1668

DUTTON, PAULINE MAE, fine arts and reference librarian; b. Detroit; d. Thoralf Andreas and Esther Ruth (Clyde) Tandberg; m. Richard Hawkins Dutton, June 21, 1969; 1 child, Nancy Katherine. BA in Art, Calif. State U., Fullerton, 1967; MLS, U. So. Calif., LA, 1971. Elem. tchr., Anaheim, Calif., 1967-68, Corona, Calif., 1968-69; fine arts libr. Pasadena Pub. Libr., Calif., 1971-80; art cons., rschr., theatrical performer, 1981—85; mgr. adult svcs. Altadena Libr. Dist., adult svcs. coord., 1985—, acting dist. dir., 2004, adult svcs. prin. libr., 2005—, principal libr. Ref. chair Met. Coop. Libr. Sys., 1998-99. Author When Daughters Fly 2006; contbr. Poetry and Cookies 2003-07, Out of Alhambra 2006, Out of Pasadena 2007; one woman show Ch. 56 Charter Cable 2006. Mem. Am. Film Inst., Am. Entrepreneurs Assn., NAFE, Am. Libr. Assn., Calif. Libr. Assn., Calif. Soc. Librs., Art Librs. N.Am., Pasadena Librs. Assn. (sec. 1978, treas. 1979-80), Telling Tales Theatre, Gilbert and Sullivan Soc., Emerging Urban Poets, Toastmistress, Alpha Sigma Phi. Office: Altadena Libr Dist 600 E Mariposa St Altadena CA 91001-2211

DUTTON, P(ETER) LESLIE, biochemist, educator; b. Ashton-Under-Lyne, Lancashire, U.K., Mar. 12, 1941; came to U.S., 1968; s. Arthur Bramwell and Mary (Drake) D.; mn. Julia R. Dwyer, July 19, 1965; children: Michael, Sara, Simon. BSc in Chemistry with honors, U. Wales, 1963, PhD in Biochemistry, 1967. Postdoctoral fellow with W. Charles Evans U. Wales, U.K., 1967; postdoctoral fellow Johnson Rsch. Found., U. Pa., Phila., 1968, asst. prof., 1971-75; assoc. prof. dept. biochemistry and biophysics U. Pa., Phila., 1976-80, Eldridge Reeves Johnson prof. dept. biochemistry and biophysics, 1981—, acting chmn. dept., 1993-94, chmn. dept., 1994—, dir. Johnson Rsch. Found., 1991—, Inst. on Aging fellow. Vis. prof. Imperial Coll., London, 1994, Univ. Coll., London, 1995. Author: Frontiers of Biological Energetics: From Electrons to Tissues, 1978, Protein Structure: Molecular and Electronic Reactivity, 1987; patentee in field; mem. editorial bd. Archives of Biochemistry, 1976-79; editor FEBS Letters, 1981-89; mng. editor Bioenergetics Revs. Sect. Biochimica et Biophysica Acta, 1981-96, Biochimica et Biophysica Acta, 1989-96. Mem. NIH adv. com. Molecular and Cellular Biophysics Study Sect., 1986-90; reserve mem. NIH Adv. Coms., 1990-94. Fellow Royal Soc. London. Office: Johnson Rsch Found 1005 Stellar Chance Labs 422 Curie Blvd Philadelphia PA 19104-6059

DUTTON, STEPHEN JAMES, lawyer; b. Chgo., Sept. 20, 1942; S. James H. and Marjorie C. (Smith) D.; m. Ellen W. Lee; children: Patrick, Mark. BS, Ill. Inst. Tech., 1965; JD, Ind. U., 1969. Bar: Ind. 1969, U.S. Dist. Ct. (so. dist.) Ind. 1969, U.S. Ct. Appeals (7th cir.) 1972, U.S. Ct. Appeals (D.C. cir.) 1980, U.S. Supreme Ct. 1978. With McHale, Cook & Welch, P.C., Indpls., 1969-86, Dutton & Overman, P.C., 1986-91, Dutton & Bailey, P.C., 1991-94, Locke, Reynolds, Boyd & Weisell, 1994-99, Leagre Chandler & Millard LLP, Indpls., 1999—2003, Barnes & Thorburg, Indpls., 2003—. Mem. Com. on Law of Cyberspace Bus. Law Sect.; chair TechPoint, Inc., 2005—. Mem. ABA. Office: 11 S Meridian St Indianapolis IN 46208 Office Phone: 317-231-7542. Business E-Mail: sdutton@btlaw.com.

DUUS, GORDON COCHRAN, lawyer; b. Ridley Park, Pa., Oct. 17, 1954; s. Frank Martin and Shirley (Cochran) D.; m. Mary Ellen Moses, Nov. 9, 1985; children: Alexander, Hannah, Julianne. BA in Aquatic Biology magna cum laude, U. Pa., 1977; JD with honors, George Washington U., 1981. Bar: D.C. 1981, N.J. 1982, Calif. 1987, U.S. Dist. Ct. N.J. 1982, U.S. Supreme Ct. 1989. Assoc. Previti, Todd, Gemmel, Fitzgerald & Nugent, Linwood, N.J., 1982-87; ptnr., chmn. environ. law dept. Margolis, Chase, Kosicki, Aboyoun & Hartman, Verona, N.J., 1987-90, Cole, Schotz, Meisel, Forman & Leonard, Hackensack, N.J., 1990—. Spkr. in field. Contbr. articles to profl. jours. Mem. ABA, N.J. Bar Assn., Bergen County Bar Assn. Office: Cole Schotz Meisel Forman & Leonard 25 Main St Hackensack NJ 07601-7015 Office Phone: 201-525-6245. Business E-Mail: gduus@coleschotz.com.

DUUS, PETER, retired historian; b. Wilmington, Del., Dec. 27, 1933; s. Hans Christian and Mary Anita (Pennypacker) D.; m. Masayo Umezawa, Nov. 25, 1964; 1 child, Erik. AB magna cum laude, Harvard U., 1955, PhD, 1965; MA, U. Mich., 1959. Asst. prof. history Washington U., St. Louis, 1964-66, Harvard U., Cambridge, Mass., 1966-70; assoc. prof. history Claremont (Calif.) Grad. Sch., 1970-73, Stanford (Calif.) U., 1973-78, prof., 1978—2003, ret., 2003. Author: Party Rivalry and Political Change in Taishō Japan, 1968, Feudalism in Japan, 1969, The Rise of Modern Japan, 1976, The Cambridge History of Japan, Vol. 6: The Twentieth Century, 1989, The Japanese Informal Empire in China, 1989, The Abacus and the Sword: The Japanese Penetration of Korea, 1995, The Japanese Discovery of America, 1996, Modern Japan, 1997. Exec. sec. Inter-Univ. for Japanese Lang. Studies, Tokyo, 1974-90; bd. dirs. Com. for Internat. Exch. of Scholars, Washington, 1987-91. Served with U.S. Army, 1955-57. NEH sr. fellow, 1972-73, Japan Found. postdoctoral fellow, 1976-77, Fulbright rsch. fellow, 1981-82, 94-95, Japan Found. rsch. fellow, 1986-87. Fellow AAAS, mem. Assn. for Asian Studies (bd. dirs. 1972-75, nominating com. 1983, v.p. 1999-2000, pres. 2000-01), Am. Hist. Assn. (bd. editors 1984-87). Home: 818 Esplanada Way Palo Alto CA 94305-1015 Office: Stanford U History Dept Stanford CA 94305 Business E-Mail: pduus@leland.stanford.edu.

DUVAL, CYNTHIA, art historian, museum administrator, consultant, curator; b. Port Talbot, South Wales, Oct. 6, 1932; came to U.S., 1972; d. Joseph and Esther (Goldberg) Armstrong; m. Marcel Duval, Aug. 26, 1973; 1 son, Jonathan Armstrong. Degree, Chelsea Sch. Art, London, 1953. Antiques buyer Harrod's, London, 1972-73; gen. appraiser Sotheby's, N.Y., 1973-77; lectr. Ringling Sch. Art, Sarasota, Fla., 1977-79; adminstr. Ringling program Tampa Ringling Mus. Art, Sarasota, 1979-80, sr. curator decorative arts, 1980-86; advisor State Div. of Culture, 1985-86; grants panelist for visual arts Fla., 1985; asst. dir./curator decorative arts Mus. Fine Arts, St. Petersburg, 1989-93; prof. art history St. Petersburg Jr. Coll., 1994—. Cons. curator Bouchelle Ctr. of Decorative Arts Mus. Arts and Scis., Daytona Beach, Fla, 1993-98, cons. to the dir. Wonders cultural program, City of Memphis; liaison to Gov.'s Mansion, Tallahassee, 1984-85; coord. mus. studies program St. Petersburg Coll.; curator Fla. Internat. Mus., 2003-07; chief curator Daytona Beach Mus. Arts and Scis., 2007—. Author: History of Lighting and Lamps, 1972; Toys of Long Ago, 1972; The Life of a Gentleman, 1972; Love and Marriage, 1972, (catalogs) 500 Years of the Decorative Arts, 1984, Medieval and Renaissance Armor, 1984, Jewelry Through the Ages, 1989, Figures from Life: Porcelain Sculpture from the Metropolitan Museum of Art, 1740-1780, 1992. Recipient Designers Image award Am. Assn. Interior Designers, 1983. Mem. Appraisers Assn. Am. (fine and decorative arts appraiser 1977), Am. Assn. Mus., Icom, (mem. curators com.). Avocation: study of social history. Home: 28 Cormorant Cir Daytona Beach FL 32119 Office: Mus Arts and Scis Daytona Beach FL 32114 Office Phone: 386-255-0285. Business E-Mail: cduval@moas.org.

DUVAL, DANIEL WEBSTER, electronics executive; b. Cin., May 27, 1936; s. Harry A. and Wilda (Webster) V.; m. Sue Ann Howard, July 20, 1962; children: Laurie Ann, Paula Lee, Christopher Webster. BA, U. Cin., 1960. V.p. staff elec. products divsn. Midland-Ross, Cleve., 1976-78, group v.p., 1979-81, exec. v.p., 1981-83, pres., COO, 1983-86; pres., CEO Robbins & Myers Inc., Dayton, Ohio, 1986-98, vice chmn., 1999, pres., CEO, 2003—04; interim pres., CEO Arrow Electronics Inc., NYC, 2002—03. Bd. dirs. Gosiger, Inc., Dayton, The Manitowac Co., Wis., Arrow Electronics Inc., NYC, 1987—, chmn., 2002—06, lead dir., 2006—. Patentee container coupling mechanism. Trustee Wright State U., 1991-2000, Wright State U. Found.; pres. Civitan Found., Ariz., 1973-74, Dayton Ballet Assn., 1990-93; participant Leadership Cleve.; bd. dirs. US Air and Trade Show. Republican. Roman Catholic. Office: Arrow Electronics Inc 50 Marcus Dr Melville NY 11747-4210 Office Phone: 937-225-3340, 631-847-2000.*

DUVAL, DAVID ROBERT, professional golfer; b. Jacksonville, Fla., Nov. 9, 1971; Student, Ga. Inst. Tech. Profl. golfer PGA, 1993—. Mem. Walker Cup team, 1991, Presidents Cup team, 1996, 98, Ryder Cup Team, 1999. Winner Nike Wichita Open, 1993, Nike Tour Championship, 1993, Michelob Championship at Kingsmill, 1997, Walt Disney World/Oldsmobile Classic, 1997, The Tour Championship, 1997, Tucson Chrysler Classic, 1998, Shell Houston Open, 1998, NEC World Series of Golf, 1998, Michelob Championship at Kingsmill, 1998, Mercedes Championship, 1999, Bob Hope Chrysler Classic, 1999, The Players Championship, 1999, Bell South Classic, 1999, Ryder Cup, 1999; recipient Dave Williams award, 1993, Jasper award, Jacksonville, 1996; named Collegiate Player of Yr., 1993. Avocations: reading, fly fishing, surfing, skiing, baseball. Office: PGA of Am Box 109601 100 Ave of Champions Palm Beach Gardens FL 33410

DUVAL, OLIVIA BLACKMON, music educator; b. Louisville, Nov. 6, 1970; d. Albert Blackmon and Barbara Jean Trotter-Hayes, adopted d. Robert and Connie Fraction. MusB, Oberlin Coll. Conservatory, 1993; MusM, U. Louisville, 2001. Singing tchr. Gov.'s Sch. Arts, Louisville, 2003—. Finalist and 1st Pl. winner, Met. Opera Nat. Coun. Auditions, 1999; recipient 3d Pl. Philip Glass award, Orpheus Nat. Vocal Competition, 1999, Merola Opera program award, San Francisco Opera Ctr., 2001; Career grantee, 2001—02, U. Mich. Sch. Music fellow, 2004—. Mem.: Coll. Music Soc., Nat. Assn. Tchrs. Singing. Home Phone: 734-973-2056. Personal E-mail: oduval11@sbcglobal.net.

DUVAL, STANWOOD RICHARDSON, JR., judge; b. New Orleans, Feb. 8, 1942; BA, La. State U., 1964, JD, 1966. Ptnr. Duval, Arceneaux & Lewis, Houma, La., 1966-94, Duval, Funderburk, Sundberry & Lovell, L.L.P., 1966-94; asst. city atty. Terrebonne Parish Consol. Govt., 1970-72, parish atty., 1988-92; dist. judge US Dist. Ct. (ea. dist.), New Orleans, 1994—. Mem. Indigent Def. Bd., 1976-82; elected La. Constnl. Conv., 1973, mem. exec. br. com., Com. to Write Rules of Procedure. Mem. Terrebone Parish; bd. dirs. Covenant House, New Orleans, 2001-. Mem. ABA (adv. com. appellate rules 1997-2003), La. Law Inst. (coun. 1996-2000), Tulane Inns Ct. (pres. 2001-04). Avocations: travel, scuba diving, fishing, performing arts. Office: US Dist Ct Ea Dist 500 Poydras St New Orleans LA 70130

DUVALL, CHARLES PATTON, internist, retired oncologist; b. Evanston, Ill., June 16, 1936; s. Charles Fleming and Edith (Osgood) Duvall; m. Nancy Ash, June 21, 1958; children: Lawrence Charles, Stephen Rogers, Douglas Patton, Lauren Duvall Meacham. AB, Cornell U., Ithaca, NY, 1958; MD, U. Rochester, NY, 1962. Diplomate Am. Bd. Internal Medicine, Am. Bd. Med. Oncology. Intern Yale New Haven Med. Ctr., 1962—63; resident internal medicine U. Rochester, 1963—64; clin. assoc. Nat. Cancer Inst., NIH, Bethesda, Md., 1964—66; resident medicine Georgetown U. Hosp., Washington, 1966—67, USPHS spl. fellow hematology, 1967—68; physician Foxhall Internists, Washington, 1968—2000. Clin. prof. medicine Georgetown U. Hosp., Washington, 1968—2000; chmn. dept. medicine Sibley Hosp., Washington, 1989—90, Washington, 1990—91; mem. emeritus staff Washington Hosp. Ctr., 1988—. Contbr. articles to profl. jours. Chmn. bd. dirs. Blue Cross Blue Shield Nat. Capital area, Washington, 1986—94; vice chmn., trustee Vols. Medicine Inst., Hilton Head Island, 1998—2002; elder Bradley Hills Presbyn. Ch., Bethesda, Md., 2003—05; elder, deacon, Stephen min. 1st Presbyn. Ch., Hilton Head Island, SC, 2003—05, pres. Men of the Ch., 2005; bd. dirs. VIM Clinic, 2007—. Lt. comdr. USPHS, 1964—66. Named Mem. of Yr., Bradley Hills. Presbyn. Ch., 2007, Man of Yr., Men of the Ch., 1st Presbyn. Ch., 2007; recipient 5 Yr. Svc. award, Am. Cancer Soc., 1978, President Emeritus hon. designation, ACP, 2005. Master: ACP (Outpatient Tchg. award 1998, Laureate award 2000); mem.: AMA (del. 1988—93, coun. legis. 1991—2000, coun. legis. chmn. 1996—97), Clin. Pathologic Soc. (pres. 1995—96), Osler Soc. DC (pres. 1978—79), Sect. Coun. Internal Medicine AMA (chmn. 1987—88), Spltys. and Svcs. Soc. AMA (pres. 1990—91, sect. coun. IM), Am. Soc. Internal Medicine (pres. DC chpt. 1977, pres. rsch. found. 1987—88, pres.-elect 1988—89, pres. 1989—90, chmn. federated coun. internal medicine 1989—90, spkr. ho. of dels. 1991—95, Spl. Recognition award 1979), Bear Creek Club (pres. SC), Congl. Country Club, Sigma Chi, Alpha Omega Alpha. Republican. Presbyterian. Avocations: golf, skiing, photography, painting. Home: 316 Seabrook Dr Hilton Head Island SC 29926-1979 Personal E-mail: cduvall636@aol.com.

DUVALL, DEBRA, school system administrator; Asst. supt. elem. edn. Mesa Pub. Sch., Ariz., 1987—95, asst. supt. curriculum and instrn., 1987—95, acting assoc. supt., 1995—2000, supt., 2000—. Chair Mesa Cmty. Coll. Commn. on Excellence in Edn., 2001—03. Recipient Disting. Adminstr. award (Supt. Divsn.), Ariz. Sch. Adminstrs. Assn., 2003. Office: Mesa Pub Sch #101 63 E Main St Mesa AZ 85201-7400 Office Phone: 480-472-0000. E-mail: dlduvall@mpsaz.org.

DUVALL, HOLLIE JEAN, music educator; b. Greensburg, Pa., Dec. 8, 1953; d. William Gilbert Smail and Betty Jane Rygiel; m. Charles Timothy Duvall, Feb. 18, 1977; children: Charles Timothy, Renee Jean. B in Music Edn., Seton Hill Coll., 1995; MA, Ind. U. of Pa., 1997. Pa. instrnl. cert. in music edn. Music dir. Ch. of God (Holiness), Greensburg, Pa., 1970—; wedding and fashion show cons. Greensburg, 1982-98; interior designer, 1982—; freelance pianist, 1985—; instr. piano and voice Pvt. Studio, Greensburg, 1985—; prof. music Westmoreland County CC, Youngwood, Pa., 1996—, music coord., 1998—; prof. music CC of Allegheny County, West Mifflin, Pa., 1999—, Pa. State U., Fayette, Pa., 2002—. Judge-fine arts Keystone Christian Edn. Assn., Pa., 1989—, Ea. Nazarene Regional Div., Greensburg, Pa., 1990, Am. Fedn. Women's Clubs, Greensburg, 1995-97; choral clinician Pa. State Cooperative Ext., 2004. Reviewer in field. Sunday sch. tchr. Ch. of God (Holiness), Greensburg, 1975—. Scholar, AAUW, 1993, PEO Sisterhood, 1994. Mem. Profl. Music Educator's Assn., Armbrust Recreation Assn. (pres. 2006), Alpha Sigma Lambda (Scholarship award 1992). Republican. Avocations: reading, floral arranging, decorating. Office: Pa STate/Fayette One University Dr Uniontown PA 15401 Office Phone: 724-430-4140. Personal E-mail: hollie_duvall@yahoo.com. Business E-Mail: hjd11@psu.edu.

DUVALL, RICHARD OSGOOD, lawyer; b. Washington, Sept. 25, 1942; s. Charles F. and Edith (Osgood) D.; m. Donna Morris; children: Julianne T., Tyler D., Nicholas C., Jacqueline L. AB in Liberal Arts and Sciences ((hon.)) and with distinction in Polit. sci., U. Ill., 1964; JD, U. Va. Sch. Law, 1967. Bar: Md. 1967, D.C. 1970, Va. 1999, U.S. Ct. Fed. Claims, 1971, U.S. Ct. Appeals for the Fed. Cir., U.S. Supreme Ct., U.S. Ct. Appeals (4th Cir.), U.S. Ct. Appeals (D.C. Cir.), U.S. Dist. Ct. (Dist. Md.), U.S. Dist. Ct. (Ea. Dist. Va.), U.S. Dist. Ct. (No. Dist. Calif.), U.S. Dist. Ct. (D.C.), Md. Ct. Appeals, Va. Supreme Ct., D.C. Ct. Appeals. Assoc. Pierson, Ball & Dowd, Washington, 1970-73; founding mem. Dunnells & Duvall, 1974—93, assoc., 1973-94, mng. ptnr., 1980-84, mem. exec. com., 1987—93; with Holland & Knight LLP, 1993—, mem. dirs. com., 1994—2002, chair litig. practice group Washington, 1994—95, chair litigation dept., 2003—; sec. litig. sect., 2002; chair, nat. govt. contracts practice team Holland & Knight LLP, 1994—2002, exec. ptnr. McLean, Va., 1998—2003, ptnr. Washington. Chair govt. contracts nat. practice group H & K Cons., Washington, 1997—2001. Mem. editl. bd. Va. Law Review, 1965—66, assoc. editor Public Contracts Law Jour., 1991, 1992. Gen. counsel Fairfax County C. of C., 2000-2002, mem. exec. com., 2000-04, bd. dirs. 2000-04, chair bd. dirs., 2004-05; bd. dirs. No. Va. Cmty. Found., 1999—, bd. dirs. VA. C. of C., 2003-; Lt. U.S Navy, JAGC, 1968-70. Fellow Am. Bar Assn. Found.; mem. Bar Assn. D.C. (bd. dirs. 1988-89), Bd. Contract Appeals Bar Assn. (bd. dirs. 1999-2001), FBA (mem. bid protest com.), Va. State Bar, D.C. Bar, Bar Assn. DC (bd. dir. 1990-93, Md. and ABA. Office: Holland & Knight LLP 1600 Tysons Blvd Ste 700 Mc Lean VA 22102-4867 Address: Holland & Knight LLP 2099 Pennsylvania Ave NW Ste 100 Washington DC 20006-6801 Office Phone: 703-720-8620, 202-457-7120. E-mail: richard.duvall@hklaw.com.

DUVALL, ROBERT (ROBERT SELDEN DUVALL), actor; b. San Diego, Calif., Jan. 5, 1931; s. William Howard Duvall; m. Barbara Benjamin, 1964 (div. 1975); m. Gail Youngs, Aug. 1982 (div. 1986); m. Sharon Brophy, May 1, 1991 (div. 1996). Grad., Principia Coll., Ill.; student, Neighborhood Playhouse, NYC. Film appearances include To Kill a Mockingbird, 1963, Captain Newman, M.D., 1964, The Chase, 1965, Countdown, 1968, The Detective, 1968, Bullitt, 1968, True Grit, 1969, The Rain People, 1969, M*A*S*H, 1970, The Revolutionary, 1970, THX-1138, 1971, Lawman, 1971, The Godfather, 1972 (N.Y. Film Critics award for best supporting actor 1972, Acad. award nominee for best supporting actor), Tomorrow, 1972, The Great Northfield, Minnesota Raid, 1972, Joe Kidd, 1972, Lady Ice, 1973, Badge 373, 1973, The Outfit, 1974, The Conversation, 1974, The Godfather Part II, 1974, Breakout, 1975, The Killer Elite, 1975, Network, 1976, The Seven Per Cent Solution, 1976, The Eagle Has Landed, 1977, The Greatest, 1977, The Betsy, 1978, Apocalypse Now, 1979 (Acad. award nominee for best supporting actor), The Great Santini, 1980 (Acad. award nominee for best actor 1981), True Confessions, 1981, The Pursuit of D.B. Cooper, 1981, Tender Mercies, 1983 (Acad. award for best actor 1984), The Stone Boy, 1984, The Natural, 1984, The Lightship, 1986, Let's Get Harry, 1986, Belizaire the Cajun, 1986, Colors, 1988, Convicts, Roots in a Parched Ground, The Handmaid's Tale, 1990, A Show of Force, 1990, Days of Thunder, 1990, Rambling Rose, 1991, Newsies, 1992, Falling Down, 1993, Geronimo, 1993, Wrestling Ernest Hemingway, 1993, The Paper, 1994, The Stars Fell on Henrietta, 1995, The Scarlet Letter, 1995, Sling Blade, 1996, Phenomenon, 1996, A Family Thing, 1996, Gingerbread Man, 1997, The Apostle, 1997 (also prodr., dir., writer) (nominated Oscar for best actor), Deep Impact, 1998, A Civil Action, 1999, Gone in Sixty Seconds, 2000, A Shot at Glory, 2000, Thank You For Smoking, 2005; (also prodr.), The Sixth Day, 2000, John Q, 2002, Assassination Tango, 2002 (also prodr., dir., writer), Gods and Generals, 2003, Open Range, 2003, Secondhand Lions, 2003, Kicking & Screaming, 2005, Lucky You, 2007; TV movies include Fame is the Name of the Game, 1966, The Terry Fox Story, 1983, Stalin, 1992 (Emmy nomination, Lead actor-Miniseries, 1993), The Man Who Captured Eichmann, 1996; plays including A View From the Bridge, 1965 (Obie award), Wait Until Dark, 1966, American Buffalo, 1977; TV miniseries include Ike, 1979, Lonesome Dove, 1989; dir.: film We're Not the Jet Set; actor, dir. film: Angelo My Love, 1983; rec. artist: Triad Records. With US Army, 1953—54. Recipient Golden Globe award, Brit. Acad. award, Nat. Assn. Theatre Owners award, Nat. Medal of Arts Nat. Endowment for the Arts, 2005; named to Hollywood Walk of Fame, 2003; decorated Nat. Def. Svc. Medal.*

DUVALL, TYLER DAVIS, federal agency administrator; b. 1973; m. Andrea Duvall; children: Olivia, Julia. BA, Washington and Lee U.; JD, U. Va. Bar: 1998. Bus. and fin. assoc. Hogan & Hartson LLP, 1998—2002; spl. asst. to asst. sec. transp. policy U.S. Dept. Transp., 2002—03, acting asst. sec. transp. policy, dep. asst. sec. transp. policy, asst. sec. transp. policy, 2006—. Office: US Dept Transp 400 Seventh St SW Rm 10228 Washington DC 20590 Office Phone: 202-366-4540. Office Fax: 202-366-0089.

DUVA-MIKHAIL, DONNA MARIE, financial executive; b. Paterson, NJ, June 28, 1956; d. Alfred Dominick and Frances P. (D'Andrea) D. AAS, Bergen Community Coll., 1976; BS in Acctg., Ramapo Coll., 1985. Bookkeeper Passaic County Treas. Office, Paterson, 1973-77; acctg. tutor Bergen Community Coll., Paramus, N.J., 1974-76; full charge bookkeeper Weisz Supermarket, Inc., Clifton, N.J., 1977-79; acct. Beechman, Inc., Clifton, 1980-85; CFO, contr. Al Duva Enterprises, Inc., Paterson, 1976—98, Power Battery Corp., Paterson, 1986-96, Atlantic Battery Corp., 1986-96, Power Auto & Truck Parts of Fla., 1986-96, Power Battery & Truck Parts of Vt., 1986-96; pvt. practice, 1997—2002; CFO Consolidated Mortgage, Las Vegas, 2003—. Author newspaper editorials Paterson Evening News, 1976. Mem. Ramapo Coll. Alumni Assn., Bergen Community Coll. Alumni Assn., Nat. Assn. Female Execs. Democrat. Roman Catholic. Avocations: games of chance, bowling, tennis, travel. Home: 8284 Orange Vale Ave Las Vegas NV 89131 Office Phone: 702-739-9090. E-mail: dmikhail@cmclv.com.

DUVERNAY, JENNIFER, librarian; BA summa cum laude, Carroll Coll., 1991; MLS, U. NC, Chapel Hill, 1996. Reference libr. Ariz. State U. Librs., Tempe, 2000—, coord. instruction, outreach & mktg. Named one of the Movers & Shakers, Libr. Jour., 2005; recipient Innovator of Month award, Tutor.com, 2004, NY Times Libr. award, 2006. Office: University Libraries Ariz State U PO Box 871006 Tempe AZ 85287 Office Phone: 480-727-7636. E-mail: jennie.duvernay@asu.edu.

DUVIN, ROBERT PHILLIP, lawyer; b. Evansville, Ind., May 18, 1937; s. Louis and Henrietta (Hamburg) D.; m. Darlene Chmiel, Aug. 23, 1961; children: Scott A., Marc A., Louis A. BA with honors, Ind. U., 1958, JD with highest honors, 1961; LLM with highest honors, Columbia U., 1963. Bar: Ohio 1964. Since practiced in, Cleve.; pres. Duvin, Cahn & Hutton, 1972—. Lectr. law schs.; labor adviser corps., cities and hosps. Contbr. to books and legal jours.; bd. editors: Ind. Law Jour., 1961, Columbia Law Rev., 1963. Served with AUS, 1961-62. Mem. ABA, FBA, Ohio Bar Assn., Cleve. Bar Assn., Cleve. Racquet Club, Beechmont Country Club, Soc. Club, Canterbury Golf Club, Sanctuary Golf Club. Jewish. Home: 2775 S Park Blvd Cleveland OH 44120-1669 Office: Littler Mendelson 1100 Superior Ave Cleveland OH 44114 Business E-Mail: rduvin@littler.com.

DUVIVIER, KATHARINE KEYES, lawyer, educator; b. Alton, Ill., Jan. 1, 1953; d. Edward Keyes and Marjorie (Attebery) DuVivier; m. James Wesley Perl, Mar. 30, 1985 (dec. Feb. 2002); children: Alice Katharine, Emmett Edward Perl; m. Lance Wright, Aug. 28, 2006. BA in Geology and English cum laude, Williams Coll., 1975; JD, U. Denver, 1982. Bar: Colo. 1982, U.S. Dist. Ct. Colo. 1982, U.S. Ct. Appeals (10th cir.) 1982. Intern-curator Hudson River Mus., Yonkers, N.Y., 1975; geologist French Am. Metals Corp., Lakewood, Colo., 1976-79; assoc. Sherman & Howard, Denver, 1982-84, Arnold & Porter, Denver, 1984-87; atty. Office of City Atty., Denver, 1987-90; sr. instr. sch. law Univ. Colo., 1990-00; reporter of decisions Colo. Ct. of Appeals, Denver, 2000; asst. prof., dir. lawyering process program U. Denver Coll. Law, 2000—06; assoc. prof., dir. lawyering process program U. Denver Coll. Sturm Coll. Law, 2006—. Vice-chmn. Appellate Practice Subcom., 1996—98, 2000—04, chair, 1998—2000, 2004—06. Contbr. articles to profl. jours. Mem. Denver Botanic Gardens, 1981—88, Denver Mus. Nature and Sci., 1982—; vol. Outdoor Colo., Denver, 1985—87, 1998—2005. Mem.: ABA (vice chmn. subcom. 1985—91), Order of St. Ives, Legal Writing Inst., Assn. Legal Writing Dirs., Am. Law Inst., Boulder Women's Bar Assn. (pres. 1991—93), Colo. Bar Assn., Alliance Profl. Women (bd. dirs. 1985—90, pres. 1988—89), St. Ives, William Coll. Alumni Assn. (co-pres. Colo. chpt. 1984—86), Work and Family Consortium (bd. dirs. 1988—90), Phi Beta Kappa. Avocations: geology, skiing, swimming, dance, yoga. Office: D U Coll Law 2255 E Evans Ave Denver CO 80208 Home: 1960 S Gilpin St Denver CO 80210 Office Phone: 303-871-6281. Business E-Mail: kkduvivier@law.du.edu.

DUXBURY, THOMAS CARL, planetary scientist; b. Fort Wayne, Ind. s. John and Justine D.; m. Natalia D.; children: Brett Harding, Katerina. BSEE, Purdue U., 1965, MSEE, 1966. Planetary scientist Jet Propulsion Lab., Pasadena, Calif., 1966—; mem. NASA Mariner mission sci. investigation of Mars, Venus and Mercury, 1969—74; mem. NASA Viking mission sci. team, Mars, Phobos and Deimos investigations, 1974—81; mem. NASA Voyage mission sci. teams, Jupiter and Saturn investigation, 1977—82; project sci. NASA Sci. Internat., 1984—86; mem. US-Russia Joint Working Group for Mars Exploration, 1987—97; mem. Soviet PHOBOS mission, interdisciplinary sci., 1988—89; mem. Dept. Defense Clementon mission sci. team for lunar exploration, 1992—94; mem. Russian Mars mission interdisciplinary sci., 1990—96; project mgr. NASA Stardust mission, 1999—2007; NASA Mars Global Surveyor mission sci. team, 1996—2007; mem. European Space Agy. MarsExpress mission interdisciplinary sci., 1999—; sci. definition team dep. leader, Dod Clementine II, 1997—98; cartography chair NASA Mars Program, 2002—; scientist Mars Odyssey THEMIS, 2006—; mem. sci. team Mars Reconnaissance Orbiter, 2007—. Co-author: Television Investigations of Phobos, 1994. Recipient Sci. Achievement medal NASA, Washington, 1972, Burka award Inst. of Navigation, 1973, Achievement awards NASA, 1978-82, Space Mission Svc. medal, Russian Lavochkin Assn., The Hague, Netherlands, 1991, Innovation award, Popular Mechanics 2006 , Program Excellence award, Aviation Week, 2006 , Nelson P. Jackson award, Nat. Space Club, 2007, Laureate award, Aviation award, 2007, Stellar award, Rotary Space Achievement, 2007. Mem. Am. Geophysical Union, Am. Astronomical Soc., Russian Assn. for Space Sci. & Tech. Achievements include production of first map of another planet's moon; discovery of the Groove Network on Phobos (Mars moon); co-discovery of the Rings of Jupiter, co-discoverer of the Jupiter Lightning; produced the most precise cartographic maps of Mars landing sites for Viking, Pathfinder, Mars Polar Lander, Beagle 2 and MER Spirit and Opportunity; led the nation's first planetary mission to return cometary samples to Earth. Office: Jet Propulsion Lab 4800 Oak Grove Dr # 264-379 Pasadena CA 91109-8099 Office Phone: 818-354-4301. Business E-Mail: tduxbury@jpl.nasa.gov.

DUYCK, KATHLEEN MARIE, poet, musician, retired social worker; b. Portland, Oreg., July 21, 1933; d. Anthony Joseph Dwyer and Edna Elisabeth Hayes; m. Robert Duyck, Feb. 3, 1962; children: Mary Kay Boeyen, Robert Patrick, Anthony Joseph. BS, Oreg. State U., 1954; MSW, U. Wash., 1956. Cert. NASW, Oreg. Adoption worker Cath. Svcs., Portland, 1956-61, Cath. Welfare, San Antonio, 1962; musician Tucson Symphony, 1963-65; prin. cellist Phoenix (Ariz.) Coll. Orch., 1968-78, Scottsdale (Ariz.) Symphony, 1974-80; poet, 1993—. Author: (poetry cassettes) Visions, 1993 (Contemporary Series Poet 1993), Visions II, 1996 (Contemporary Series Poet 1996); author numerous poems. Rep. worker Maricopa County Reps., Phoenix, 1974; mem. Scottsdale Cultural Coun.; NASW bd. Cath. Charities Rep., Portland, 1959-61. Recipient Golden Poet award, World of Poetry, 1991-92, Sec. gift, Phoenix Exec. Bd., 1976, Recognition award, Archbishop Howard, 1961, 5-Yr. Kathleen Duyck award, Cello Congress V, 1996. Mem. Internat. Poetry Hall Fame, Ariz. Cello Soc., Nat. Libr. Poetry (Editor's Choice awards, 1993-2003), Internat. Soc. Poets (Internat. Poet of Merit award, 2003, Outstanding Achievement in Poetry award, 2005, 06), Phoenix Symphony Guild (exec. bd. 1970-80), Women in Arts, World War I Mus., St. Mary's Alumni Assn., Phoenix Art Mus., Oreg. State U. Alumni Assn., U. Wash. Alumni Assn., Mental Health Guild, Friends Family Svc. Republican. Roman Catholic. Avocations: piano, photography, poetry, music. Home and Office: 4545 E Palomino Rd Phoenix AZ 85018-1719

DUZEY, ROBERT LINDSEY, lawyer; b. Long Beach, Calif., Nov. 15, 1960; s. Donald Bohdan and Noreen (Rosen) D.; m. Susan Misook Yoon, Mar. 14, 1987; children: Dylan Grey, Zenon Drake. BA, U. Calif., Irvine, 1984; JD, Western State U., Fullerton, Calif., 1994. Bar: Calif. 1994., U.S. Dist. Ct. (so., ctrl., ea. and no. dists.) Calif., U.S. Ct. Appeals (9th cir.), U.S. Supreme Ct. Claims rep., mgr. Farmers Ins. Group, Santa Ana, Calif., 1985-89; risk mgr. Dollar Rent A Car, Irvine, 1989-93; law clk. Callahan, McCune & Willis, Tustin, Calif., 1994-96; atty. Madigan, Evans & Boyer, Costa Mesa, Calif., 1996-98, Law Offices of Robert Lindsey Duzey, Santa Ana, Calif., 1998—. Intern Cummins and White LLP, 1994. Recipient Am. Jurisprudence award. Mem. ATLA, ABA, Orange County Bar Assn., Fed. Bar Assn., Orange County Barristers, L.A. County Bar Assn., Delta Theta Phi. Avocations: bicycling, badminton, home decorating. Office: 1439 W Chapman Ave Ste 350 Orange CA 92868 Office Phone: 714-744-2700. Office Fax: 714-744-2705. Personal E-mail: robertduzey@yahoo.com.

DVORAK, ALLEN DALE, radiologist; b. Dodge, Nebr., Mar. 13, 1943; s. Rudolph Charles and Mildred B. (Misek) D.; m. Carol Ann Cockson, July 22, 1967; children: Kristin Ann, Andrea Marie, Ryan Allen. Grad., Creighton U., 1964, MD, 1969. Intern Creighton Meml. St. Joseph Hosp., Omaha, 1969-70; resident Ind. U. Med. Ctr., Indpls., 1970-73, chief resident, 1972—73; asst. prof. radiology Creighton U. Sch. Medicine, Omaha, 1973-83; diagnostic radiologist Nebr.-Iowa Radiology Cons., Papillion, Nebr., 1983—, mng. ptnr., 1987—, pres., cons. ptnr., 2004—. Staff radiologist Alegent Midlands Cmty. Hosp., Papillion, 1983—, med. staff exec. bd., 1996—, pres. med. staff, 2001-02; mem. Nebr. Bd. Health, 1995-2000; bd. dirs. Blue Cross Blue Shield Nebr., 2000—, PRIME Therapeutics, Inc., 2002-04. Contbr. chpt. to book, articles to profl. jours. Chmn. Midlands Area Health Adv. Coun., State of Nebr., 1982-86; trustee Duchesne Acad., 1988-91, Boys Town Nat. Coun. Friends, 1989—; bd. dirs. Safety and health Coun. of Greater Omaha, 1990-91; mem. Gov.'s Blue Ribbon Coalition to Study Health Care in Nebr., 1991-98; mem. Creighton Med. Sch. Alumni Adv. Bd., 1993—, pres., 1998-2000; trustee Western Conf. Prepaid Med. Svc. Plans, 2004—, pres.-elect, 2006. Fellow Am. Coll. Radiology; mem. AMA (alt. del. 1992-98, del. 1999-2000), Nebr. Radiol. Soc. (pres. 1980-81), Omaha Midwest Clin. Soc. (pres. 1982), Nebr. Assn. Nuclear Physicians (pres. 1976-78, del. 1984-94), Met. Omaha Med. Soc. (exec. com. 1980-2000, pres. 1990), Nebr. Med. Assn. (del. 1986—, pres. 1997-98), Regency Lake and Tennis Club (bd. dirs. 1981-85, chmn. bd. 1983-85), Happy Hollow Country Club. Avocations: golf, gardening. Home: 9733 Brentwood Rd Omaha NE 68114-4970 Office: Nebr-Iowa Radiology Cons 401 E Gold Coast Rd Ste 102 Papillion NE 68046-4194 Office Phone: 402-339-8991.

DVORAK, DAVID C., medical products executive, lawyer; BS in Fin., Miami U., Ohio; JD magna cum laude, Case Western Reserve U., 1991. Sr. v.p., gen. counsel, corp. sec. STERIS Corp., mem. exec. com.; sr. v.p. corp. affairs, gen. counsel Zimmer Holdings, Inc., Warsaw, Ind., 2001—03, exec. v.p. corp. svcs., chief counsel, sec., 2003—05, group pres. global bus., chief legal officer, 2005—07, pres., CEO, 2007—. Office: Zimmer Holdings Inc 345 E Main St Warsaw IN 46580*

DVORAK, DELYLE DENNIS, music and early childhood educator, consultant; b. Olivet, SD, Nov. 13, 1941; s. Alvin John and Frieda K. (Rembold) Dvorak; m. Patricia Ann Dunlap, May 11, 1979; children: Lori Michele, Debra Jean Baker, Jeff Michael. BS, U. S.D., Springfield, 1959—62; MusM, U. S.D., Vermillion, 1963—65; EdD, Ariz. State U., Tempe, 1969—73. Dir., bands & choral music Delmont Pub. Schs., SD, 1961—62, Armour Pub. Schs., SD, 1962—64; dir., bands Chamberlain HS, SD, 1964—66; asst. dir., bands Minot State Coll., ND, 1966—67; dir., bands Palo Verde Unified Sch. Dist., Blythe, Calif., 1967—69; grad. tchg. asst. Ariz. State U., Tempe, 1969—72; dir., bands, acting dept. chmn. William Penn Coll., Oskaloosa, Iowa, 1972—75; asst. prof., music Southwestern Okla. State U., Weatherford, 1975—76; dir., bands Mt. San Jacinto CC, Calif., 1976—81; music dept. program leader, dir. bands Jefferson Sch. Performing Arts, Portland, Oreg., 1982—85; french horn instr. Colo. State U., Fort Collins, 1988—90; owner Dvorak Assocs., Loveland, Colo., 1988—92, Dvorak Enterprises, Las Vegas, 1992—; educator CCSD, Las Vegas, Nev., 1995—. Asst. musical condr. Douglas County Bi-Centennial, Corsica, SD, 1961—61; dir., bands Minot State Coll. Model Sch., Minot, ND, 1966—67; dean, students Internat. Peace Garden Music Camp, Dunseith, ND, 1967, guest band condr., 76; state chmn. Nat. Band Assn., Ariz., 1970—72, Iowa, 1972—74. Contbr. articles to profl. jours. Ch. organist & vocal soloist St. John's Luth. Ch., Kaylor, SD, 1953—59; choir dir. Redeemer Luth. Ch., Armour, SD, 1962—64; choir dir. & organist Zion Luth. Ch., Chamberlain, SD, 1964—66; organist, confirmation tchr. Zion Luth., Blythe, Calif., 1967—69; choir dir. Luth. Ch., Knoxville, Iowa, 1973—74; Ariz. State U. rsch. rep. Music Educator's Nat. Conf., Atlanta, 1970. Recipient Outstanding Educator of Am., 1974—75. Mem.: Music Educator's Conf. (life). Conservative. Lutheran. Avocations: photography, travel, computers, golf. Home: 4917 Pounding Surf Ave Las Vegas NV 89131 Office: CCSD 400 Sky Rd Indian Springs NV 89018 Home Phone: 702-656-9480; Office Phone: 702-799-0932. Personal E-mail: drddd@cox.net, drddd1@yahoo.com.

DVORAK, GEORGE J., mechanics and materials engineering educator; came to U.S., 1964; Degree in Civil Engring., Czech Technol. U., Prague, 1956, DSc (hon.), 1997; C.Sc., Czechoslovak Acad. Sci., Prague, 1964; PhD, Brown U., 1968. Rsch. assoc. divsn. engring. Brown U., 1964-67; with civil engring. and biomedical engring. dept. Duke U., Durham, NC, 1967-79; prof., chmn. civil engring., prof. materials sci. U. Utah, Salt Lake City, 1979-84; prof., chmn. dept. civil and environ. engring. Rensselaer Poly. Inst., Troy, NY, 1984—95, prof. mech. engring., aero. engring. and mechanics, chmn. civil and environ. engring., William Howard Hart prof. mechanics, 1995—. Sr. vis. fellow Brit. sci. rsch. coun. Cambridge U., Eng.; vis. fellow Clare Hall, Cambridge, 1975-76; vis. prof. Politecnico di Milano, Milan, Italy; with inst. ctr. composite materials and structures Rensselaer Poly. Inst., dir. univ. rsch. initiative Dept. Def. Assoc. editor Internat. Jour. Plasticity, 1984-2001, Mech. Composite Mater Structures, 1993—, Jour. Applied Mechanics, 1989-95, Applied Mechanics Revs., 1989-95, Jour. Composite Materials, 2000—. Recipient Citations for Accomplishment of Spl. Merit, Army Rsch. Office, 1977, 79; Fulbright fellow Tech. U. Denmark, 1995, Brown Engring. Alumni medal Brown U., 1999. Fellow ASME (founding chmn. com. composite materials applied mechanics divsn., Arpard L. Nadai award 1992, Daniel C. Drucker medal 2002), ASCE (Theodore von Karman medal 2006), Am. Acad. Mechanics, Soc. Engring. Sci. (William Prager medal in mechanics of solids 1994), Nat. Acad. Engring. Achievements include research in mechanics, physics of solids, micromechanics of heterogeneous media, mechanical behavior of composite materials. Office: Dept Mech & Aero Engring and Mechanics Jonsson Engring Ctr 5003 Rensselaer Polytech Inst Troy NY 12180 Business E-Mail: dvorak@rpi.edu.

DVORAK, HAROLD FISHER, retired pathologist; b. Milw., June 20, 1937; s. Harold J. and Laura (Fisher) D.; m. Ann Marie Tompkins, June 13, 1962; children: John, Laura, Jane. AB, Princeton U., 1958; MD, Harvard U., 1963. Diplomate: Am. Bd. Pathology. Practice medicine specializing in pathology, Boston; asst. prof. pathology Harvard Med. Sch., Boston, assoc. prof., prof., Mallinckrodt prof. pathology, 1979—; mem. staff Mass. Gen. Hosp., asst. pathologist, 1969-75, assoc. pathologist, 1975-78, head immunopathology unit, 1976-80; chief dept. pathology Beth Israel Hosp., Boston, 1979-96, Beth Israel Deaconess Med. Ctr., Boston, 1996—2005; ret., 2005. Mem. study sect. pathology B NIH, 1978-82, Am. Cancer Soc., N.Y.C., 1982-86; chmn. merit rev. bd. immunology VA, Washington, 1982-84. Served to lt. comdr. USPHS, 1965-67. Recipient Albert Szent-Gyorgyi prize for Progress in Cancer Rsch., 2006. Mem. Am. Assn. Immunologists, Am. Soc. Investigative Pathology (v.p. 1996, pres.-elect), Internat. Acad. Pathology, Pluto Club, Collegium Internat. Allergologicum, Phi Beta Kappa, Sigma Xi, Alpha Omega Alpha Office: Beth Israel Deaconess Med Ctr 330 Brookline Ave Boston MA 02215-5400 Business E-Mail: hdvorak@bidmc.harvard.edu.

DVORSON, NATALYA, lawyer; d. Vladimir Mendel Dvorson and Evgenia Vladislavovna Ravdonikas; m. Alexius George Klimantov, Mar. 29, 2000. BA in Govt. and Politics, U. Md., College Park, 2000; BS in Computer Sci., U. Md., 2000; JD, George Mason Sch. of Law, Arlington,

Va., 2003. Bar: DC 2003, Va. 2003, NJ 2003. Atty. at law Sughrue Mion, PLLC, Washington, 2002—. Mem.: ABA, Am. Intellectual Property Law Assn. Home Phone: 301-294-2423. Personal E-mail: ndvorson@gmail.com.

DWAN, DENNIS EDWIN, broadcast executive, photographer; b. St. Joseph, Mich., Oct. 6, 1958; s. Edwin O. and Elizabeth L. (Miller) D.; m. Tami L. Nixon, Oct. 13, 1984; children: Megan, Kaitlyn. BA, Mich. State U., 1981. Photographer Sta. WJIM-TV, Lansing, Mich., 1981-83, Sta. KAYU, Spokane, Wash., 1984-86, Sta. KREM-TV, Spokane, 1984-87; ops. mgr. Sta. KOMO-TV, Seattle, 1987—. Mem. Nat. Press Photographers Assn. E-mail: DennisD@Komotv.com.

DWEK, CYRIL S., bank executive; b. Kobe, Japan, Nov. 9, 1936; s. Nessim S. and Alice (Stambouli) Dwek; children: Nevil, Alicia. BS, U. Pa., 1958. With Trade Devel. Bank, Geneva, 1962-65; with Republic Nat. Bank of NY, 1966-99, dir., 1967—, exec. v.p., 1973—, vice chmn., 1983-99; dir. Republic NY Corp., 1974—, vice chmn., 1983-99; chmn. HSBC Republic Adv. Bd., NYC, 2000—04; sr. cons. HSBC Pvt. Bank divsn. HSBC Bank USA, Monaco, 2005—. Bd. dir., chmn. HSBC Republic, France, dir., vice chmn., chmn., Monaco, 2000—05. Mem.: Racing Club de France (Paris). Office: HSBC USA 452 5th Ave New York NY 10018-2706 Business E-Mail: cyril.s.dwek@hsbcpb.com.

DWIGHT, DONALD RATHBUN, publishing executive, corporate communications specialist; b. Holyoke, Mass., Mar. 26, 1931; s. William and Dorothy Elizabeth (Rathbun) D.; m. Susan Newton Russell, Aug. 9, 1952 (div. Aug. 1982); children: Dorothy Campbell, Laura Newton, Eleanor Addison, Arthur Ryan, Stuart Russell.; m. Nancy John Sinnott, Dec. 18, 1982; children: Christopher Sinnott, Helen Rathbun. AB, Princeton U., 1953; DSc (hon.), U. Mass., Lowell, 1974. Reporter, asst. to pub. Holyoke (Mass.) Transcript-Telegram, 1955-63, assoc. pub., 1966-69; assoc. commr. Mass. Dept. Pub. Works, Boston, 1963-66; commr. adminstrn. Commonwealth Mass., Boston, 1969-70, lt. gov., 1971-75; assoc. pub., v.p. Mpls. Star and Tribune, 1975-76, pub., sr. v.p., 1976-81; pres., pub. Star & Tribune Newspapers, Mpls., 1981-82; exec. v.p., dir. Cowles Media Co., 1981-82; chmn. Newspapers of New Eng., Inc., 1982-98, chmn. emeritus, 1999—; assoc. The Prospect Group, NYC, 1983-88; chmn., mng. ptnr. Clark, Dwight & Assocs., Inc., 1988-90; pres. Dwight Ptnrs., Inc., Lyme, NH, 1988—. V.p. Wood River Capital Corp., 1984—88; exec. v.p. Entretech Inc., 1988—90; trustee Eaton Vance Mut. Funds, Boston, 1986—2003, The Royce Funds, NYC, 1998—. Mem. Town Meeting, South Hadley, Mass., 1957—69; trustee Twin Cities Pub. TV, 1976—82; chmn. bd. Guthrie Theater Found., 1978—81; v.p., dir. Nat. Corp. Theatre Fund, 1985—88; dir. Joint Action in Cmty. Svc., Washington, 1989—92, Lyme (NH) Found., Inc., 1994—98; trustee Trust Funds, Lyme, 1987—2000; mem. Planning Bd., Lyme, 2005—; mem. vestry St. Thomas Episcopal Ch., Hanover, NH, 1998—2001; bd. dirs. Mpls. Soc. Fine Arts, 1979—82, Upper Valley Land Trust, Hanover, The Josiah Bartlett Ctr. Pub. Policy, Concord, NH. 1st lt. USMCR, 1953—55. Mem. Newspaper Assn. Am., Knickerbocker Club, Round Hill Club, Somerset Club, Hillsboro Club, Country Club. Republican. Episcopalian. Home and Office: 92 Shoestrap Rd Lyme NH 03768-3301 Home Phone: 603-795-4995; Office Phone: 603-795-2800. Business E-Mail: dondwight@mac.com.

DWIGHT, REGINALD KENNETH See SIR JOHN, ELTON

DWIVEDI, YOGESH, science educator; b. Gorakhpur, India, Apr. 22, 1965; PhD, CDNI, India, 1992. Asst. prof. U. Ill., Chgo., 2003—. Treas. UP Assn., Chgo., 1998—99. Recipient Young Investigator award, Am. Found. Suicide Prevention, 2002—04, Internat. Congress Biol. Psychiatry, 2003, Nat. Inst. Mental Health, 2004—; CNIP fellowship, Collegium Internationale Neuropsychopharmacology, 2000. Office: Univ Illinois 1601 W Taylor St Chicago IL 60612 Home Phone: 312-637-8209. Office Fax: 312-355-3857. Business E-Mail: ydwivedi@psych.uic.edu.

DWORETZKY, JOSEPH ANTHONY, lawyer, city manager; b. NYC, Sept. 17, 1951; s. Lawrence H. and Grace W. (Jackson) D.; m. Amy L. Banse; children: Lydia Light, Adam Eliot, Alex John, Anna Grace. BA with distinction, Purdue U., 1972; JD summa cum laude, Villanova U., 1977. Bar: Pa. 1977, D.C. 1978. Law clk. to judge U.S. Ct. Appeals 2d Cir., NYC, 1977-78; assoc. Drinker Biddle & Reath, Phila., 1978-84, ptnr., 1984-93, mng. ptnr., 1992-93; chmn. corp. group law dept. City of Phila., 1993, city solicitor, 1994-96; shareholder Hangley Aronchick Segal & Pudlin, 1997—, exec. com., 1998—. Adj. prof. Rutgers U. Sch. Law, Camden, 1986-93, Temple U. Sch. Law, 2005—06; vice chair Third Cir. Lawyers Adv. Com., 2006-. V.p., bd. dirs. Phila. Vol. Lawyers for Arts, 1981-84, Phila. Bd. Pensions, 1994-96, Phila. Indsl. Devel. Corp., 1994-96, Phila. Theatre Co., 1998-2000, William Penn Found., 2001-05, Moore Coll. Art and Design, 2003—06, Pa. Energy Devel. Authority, 2004—, Pky. Coun. Found., 2005—; sec.-treas., bd. dirs. Consumer Bankruptcy Assistance Project, 1992—, Acad. for Law, Pub. Adminstrn. and Criminal Justice, 1995-98; chair East Dist. Pa. Bankruptcy Conf., 2001; bd. dirs. Pkwy. Coun. Found., 2005—. Fellow Am. Coll. Bankruptcy (3d cir. regent); mem. ABA, Pa. Bar Assn., Phila. Bar Assn., Order of Coif, Phi Beta Kappa. Home: 7801 Huron St Philadelphia PA 19118-4218 Office Phone: 215-496-7014. Business E-Mail: jad@hangley.com.

DWORETZKY, MURRAY, retired physician, educator; b. NYC, Aug. 18, 1917; s. Samuel and Frieda (Newhoff) D.; m. Barbara Ratner, June 11, 1943; children: Thomas Alan, Joan Mara. BA, U. Pa., 1938; MD, SUNY, Coll. Medicine, NYC, 1942; MS in Medicine, U. Minn., 1950. Diplomate: Am. Bd. Internal Medicine (examiner allergy subbd. 1967-71), Am. Bd. Allergy and Immunology (founding mem., dir. 1971-74), Pan Am. Med. Assn. Intern City Hosp., NYC, 1942-43, asst. resident pathology, 1943, fellow in pathology, 1946-47; resident pathology U. Chgo., 1947-48; fellow in medicine Mayo Found., Rochester, Minn., 1948-50; practice medicine, specializing in internal medicine, allergy and clin. immunology NYC, 1951—2005; asst. physician NY Hosp., 1951; physician NY Hosp. (now NY Presbyn. Hosp.), 1951-56, asst. attending physician, 1956-61, assoc. attending, 1961-66, attending physician, 1966—2005, physician-in-charge Allergy Clinic, 1961-88; asst. in medicine Cornell U. Med. Coll., 1951-52, instr. medicine, 1952-56, clin. asst. prof., 1956-61, clin. asst. prof. pub. health, 1957-62, clin. assoc. prof. medicine, 1961-66, dir. tng. program div. allergy and immunology, 1961-88, clin. prof. medicine, 1966—2005, clin. emeritus prof. medicine, 2005—; attending physician Manhattan Eye, Ear and Throat Hosp., 1953-62; ret., 2005. Med. dir.-at-large Asthma-Allergy Found. Am., 1963-64, bd. dirs., 1964-78, mem. exec. com., 1964-77; founding mem. bd. dirs. Am. Bd. Allergy and Immunology, 1971-74; examiner sub-bd. allergy Am. Bd. Internal Medicine, 1967-71. Co-editor Allergy Archives, Jour. Allergy and Clin. Immunology, 2001-04; contbr. articles to profl. jours. Served to capt., M.C. AUS, 1943-46. Recipient Frank L. Babbott M.D. Meml. award Alumni Assn. Coll. Med. SUNY, 1992. Fellow: ACP, N.Y. Acad. Medicine, Am. Acad. Allergy and Immunology (past pres. 1968, Disting. Svc. award 1989, Spl. Achievement award 2002); mem.: AMA (chmn. allergy sect. coun. 1974—77, residency rev. com. for allergy and immunology 1980—85), Am. Assn. Immunologists, Am. Fedn. Clin. Rsch., Harvey Soc., Soc. Exptl. Biology and Medicine, N.Y. Allergy Soc. (past pres., exec. com. 1958—94, tchg. day dedicated in his honor 1995), N.Y. County Med. Soc., Sigma Xi. Home: 21 E 87th St New York NY 10128-0506 Home Phone: 212-876-1810. Personal E-mail: mbjdwor@aol.com.

DWORK, DEBÓRAH, history professor; d. Bernard and Shirley Dwork; m. Kenneth Marek, June 16, 1974; children: Miriam Marek, Hannah Marek. BA, Princeton U., NJ, 1975; MPH, Yale U., New Haven, 1978; PhD, U. Coll., London, 1984. Rose prof. Holocaust history Clark U., Worcester, Mass., 1996—, dir. Strassler Ctr. Holocaust and Genicide Studies, 1996—. Bd.d irs. Jewish Cultural Heritage Found., Stockholm; adv. bd. mem. Facing History and Ourselves, Brookline, Mass.; adv. bd. mem. Internat. Inst. on Jewish Women Brandeis U., Waltham, Mass.; postdoctoral fellow Smithsonian Instn., 1984. Author: War is Good for Babies and other Young Children, 1987, Children With A Star: Jewish Youth in Nazi Europe, 1991, Voices and Views: A History of the Holocaust, 2002; co-author: Auschwitz, 1270 to Present, 1996 (Nat. Jewish Book Award, Nat. Book Critics list - Germany, Spiro Kostoff Award), Holocaust: A History, 2002, author monographs in field. Trustee, vice chmn. Jewish Found. for Righteous, NYC, 1995—; mem. anti-semitism task force Am. Jewish Com., NYC. Fellow, Wellcome Trust, 1979—83, 1985, Am. Coun. Learned Socs., 1988, Woodrow Wilson Internat. Ctr. Scholars, 1989, Guggenheim Found., 1993—94; grantee, Am. Philos. Soc., 1987, Lustman Fund, 1991—94, NEH, 1992; Rackham Faculty rsch. grantee, U. Mich., 1988, Tapper Rsch. grantee, Tapper Charitable Found., 2003—05. Mem.: Am. Hist. Assn. Office: Clark U 950 Main St Worcester MA 01610 Office Phone: 508-793-8897.

DWORKIN, AARON P., violinist, educator; b. 1970; BM, U. Mich., 1997, MM, 1998. Founder, pres. Sphinx Orgn., 1996—. Advisor to various edn. and music orgns.; spkr. in field; organizer of various music outreach and edn. programs to attract minorities to careers in classical music. Named Michiganian of Yr., Detroit News, 2003, MacArthur fellow, John D. and Catherine T. MacArthur Found., 2005; named one of 40 Under 40, Crain's Detroit Bus., 2006; recipient SBC Ameritech Excellence award, 5 Under 10 award, U. Mich. African-Am. Alumni Coun., 2002, Mich. Governor's award for Arts & Culture, 2003, Nat. Governor's award, 2005, Newsweek Giving Back award, 2006. Office: Sphinx Orgn 400 Renaissance Ctr Ste 2120 Detroit MI 48243 Office Phone: 313-877-9100. Office Fax: 313-887-0164.*

DWORKIN, GARY STEVEN, insurance company executive; b. NYC, July 7, 1947; s. Irving Milton and Grace Wilhelmina (Korn) D.; student Hofstra U., 1965-68, NYU, 1969-71; m. Linda Lee Fuchs, Aug. 28, 1970; children: Robert Benjamin, Alexandra Tenille. Sales mgr. Chatham Blankets, NYC, 1968-70; ins. agt. Travelers Ins. Co., Hartford, Conn., 1970-74; broker Dworkin Assos., Rochester, NH, 1974-76; pres. Dworkin Assos., Inc. (DAI), Rochester, 1976—. Registered health underwriter; chartered life underwriter. Mem. Nat. Assn. Ins. Fin. Advisors, Life, Inc., Lifemark Ptnrs. Inc., Home Office Life Underwriters Assn., NH NAIFA, New Eng. Forum, Nat. Assn. Health Underwriters, Am. Risk and Ins. Assn., Risk Appraisal Forum, Nat. Assn. Ind. Life Brokerage Agys. (charter, bd. dirs.), Soc. Fin. Svcs. Profls. Republican Office: PO Box 2000 Rochester NH 03866-2000 Office Phone: 800-777-0061. E-mail: gsd@dworkin.com.

DWORKIN, HOWARD JERRY, retired nuclear medicine physician, educator; b. Bklyn., Oct. 29, 1932; s. Joseph Henry and Mollie M. (Hodas) Dworkin; m. Gina Gora; children: Rhonda Fran, Steven Irving, Paul J., Edward Joshua, Joseph Jacob. BSChemE, Worcester Poly. Inst., 1955; MD, Albany Med. Coll., 1959; MS in Radiation Biology, U. Mich., 1965. Diplomate Am. Bd. Internal Medicine, Am. Bd. Nuclear Medicine. Intern Albany Hosp., NY, 1959-60; resident Rochester (N.Y.) Gen. Hosp., 1960-62, U. Mich. Hosps., 1962-65, asst. coord. nuclear medicine unit, 1963-66, instr., 1965-66; asst. prof. medicine U. Toronto, Ont., Canada, 1966, assoc. prof. Ont., 1967; head dept. nuc. medicine Princess Margaret Hosp., Toronto, 1967; head nuc. medicine sect. radiology Nat. Naval Med. Ctr., Bethesda, Md., 1967-69; dir. sch. nuc. medicine tech. William Beaumont Hosp., Royal Oak, Mich., 1969—, chief dept. nuc. medicine, 1969—2002, dir. nuc. medicine resident tng. program, 1970—2006, chmn. CME com., 1993—2006; ret., 2006. Clin. asst. prof. dept. medicine Wayne State U. Med. Sch., Detroit, 1970—; clin. assoc. prof. dept. radiology Mich. State U., East Lansing, 1976—; clin. prof. med. physics Ctr. Health Scis. Oakland U., Rochester, Mich., 1977—; adj. prof. radiology U. Mich., 2003—. Author (with N. Aspin and R. G. Baker): (book) Use of Isotopes in the Physics of Radiology, 1969, Part Two, Clinical Procedures in Radioisotope Laboratory Procedures, 1969; contbr. articles and chpts. to med. jours. and texts. With USN, 1967—69. Mem.: AMA, Mich. State Med. Soc. (chmn. continuing med. edn. com. 1999—), Am. Coll. Nuc. Physicians (sec. 1974—75, pres. 1978—79), Endocrine Soc., Am. Thyroid Assn., Soc. Nuc. Medicine (trustee 1973—81, v.p. 1982, pres. 1986—87), Am. Bd. Nuc. Medicine (treas. 1982—84), Accrediation Coun. Continuing Med. Edn. (chmn. 1998). Achievements include patents for radioactive labeled protein material process and apparatus. Office: William Beaumont Hosp Dept Nuclear Medicine Royal Oak MI 48073 Home Phone: 248-673-6168; Office Phone: 248-898-4100. E-mail: hdworkin@beaumont.edu.

DWORKIN, MARTIN, microbiologist, educator; b. NYC, Dec. 3, 1927; s. Hyman Bernard and Pauline (Herstein) D.; m. Nomi Rees Buda, Feb. 2, 1957; children: Jessica Sarah, Hanna Beth. BA, Ind. U., 1951; PhD (NSF predoctoral fellow), U. Tex., Austin, 1955. NIH research fellow U. Calif., Berkeley, 1955-57, vis. prof., summers 1958-60; asst. prof. microbiology Ind. U. Med. Sch., 1957-61, assoc. prof., 1961-62; from assoc. prof. to prof. emeritus U. Minn., 1962—2004, prof. emeritus, 2004—. Vis. prof. U. Wash., 1965, Stanford U., 1978-79; vis. scholar Oxford (Eng.) U., 1970-71; Found. for Microbiology lectr., 1973-74, 76-77, 81-82; Sackler scholar Tel Aviv U., 1992. Author: Developmental Biology of the Bacteria, 1985, Microbial Cell-Cell Interactions, 1991; contbr. numerous articles, revs. to profl. publs.; mem. editorial bd. Jour. Bacteriology, 1967-74, 86-88, Ann. Revs. Microbiology, 1975-79, The Prokaryotes, 2d edit., editor-in-chief 3d edit. Alt. del. Democratic Nat. Conv., 1968; mem. Minn. Dem. Farm Labor Central Com., 1969-70. Served with U.S. Army, 1946-48. Recipient Career Devel. award NIH, 1963-73; John Simon Guggenheim fellow, 1978-79 Fellow Am. Acad. Arts and Scis. (chmn. Midwest ctr., v.p., 2002), Am. Soc. Microbiology (vice chmn. div. gen. microbiology 1977-78, chmn. 1978-79, div. councillor 1980-82); mem. Soc. Gen. Microbiology (Eng.). Home: 2123 Hoyt Ave W Saint Paul MN 55108-1314 Office: U Minn Dept Microbiology Minneapolis MN 55455 Office Phone: 612-624-5634. Business E-Mail: martin@lenti.med.umn.edu.

DWORKIN, MICHAEL LEONARD, lawyer; b. Bridgeport, Conn., Oct. 10, 1947; s. Samuel and Frances (Stein) D.; m. Christina Lyn Hildreth, Sept. 25, 1977; children: Jennifer Hildreth, Amanda Hildreth. BA in Govt. with honors, Clark U., 1969; JD with honors, George Washington U., 1973. Bar: D.C. 1973, Calif. 1975, U.S. Supreme Ct. 1978, U.S. Ct. Appeals (9th cir.) 1982, U.S. Claims Ct. 1983. Atty. FAA, Washington, L.A., 1973-77, United Airlines, San Francisco, 1977-81; pvt. practice San Francisco, 1981-95, San Mateo, Calif., 1995—. Instr. Embry Riddle Aeronautical U., San Francisco, 1980-81; dir. Poplar Ctr., San Mateo, Calif., 1979-86. Jonas Clark scholar Clark U., 1966-69. Mem. ABA, State Bar Calif., DC Bar Assn., Bar Assn. San Francisco, Lawyer Pilots Bar Assn., Nat. Transp. Safety Bd. Bar Assn. (regional v.p. 1986-87, 90-99, chmn. rules com. 1985-99, pres. 2000-02), Aircraft Owners and Pilots Assn., Internat. Soc. Air Safety Investigators (bd. dir. San Francisco regional chpt. 1988-89), Nat. Bus. Craft Assn., Aero Club No. Calif. Jewish. Office: 465 California St Ste 210 San Francisco CA 94104 Home Phone: 650-573-9607; Office Phone: 415-421-2500. Business E-Mail: law@avialex.com.

DWORKIN, PAUL HOWARD, pediatrician; b. Paterson, NJ, Oct. 22, 1947; s. Bernard and Ruth (Steinhauer) D.; m. Sheila Ann Maher, Oct. 7, 1979; children: Molly Maher, Eamon Timothy. AB, Rutgers U., 1969; MD, Johns Hopkins U., 1973. Diplomate Am. Bd. Pediatrics, 2006. Pediatric registrar Paddington Green Children's Hosp./St. Mary's Med. Sch., London, 1976; resident in pediatrics Children's Hosp., Boston, 1973-75, fellow in ambulatory pediatrics, 1976-78; asst. prof. pediatrics W.Va. U. Sch. Medicine, Morgantown, 1978-81; prof./asso. chair pediats., head div. gen. peds., asst. dean U. Conn. Sch. Medicine, Farmington, 1981-98, prof./chair pediats., 1998—. Dir., chair pediats. St. Francis Hosp. and Med. Ctr., Hartford, Conn., 1992-03; physician-in-chief Conn. Children's Med. Ctr., Hartford, 1998—. Author: Learning and Behavior Problems of Schoolchildren, 1985; editor: Pediatrics: National Medical Series for Independent Study, 1987, 4th edit., 2000, Developmental-Behavioral Pediatrics: Evidence and Practice, 2007; editor Jour. Devel. & Behavioral Pediats., 1996-2002; mem. editl. bd. Pediats., 1991-98, Ambulatory Child Health, Current Pediatrics, 1991—. Vol. Salvation Army Shelter Pediat. Clinic, Hartford, 1991—. Fellow: Am. Acad. Pediats. (chair com. on sci. mtgs. 1994—96); mem.: Soc. Devel. and Behavioral Pediats. (pres. 2005—06), Ambulatory Pediat. Assn. Office: Conn Children's Med Ctr 282 Washington St Hartford CT 06106-3322 Business E-Mail: pdworki@ccmckids.org.

DWORKIN, RONALD MYLES, law educator; b. Worcester, Mass., Dec. 11, 1931; s. David and Madeline (Taber) D.; m. Betsy Ross, July 18, 1958; children: Anthony Ross, Jennifer. BA, Harvard U., 1953, LLB, 1957; BA, Oxford U., 1955; MA; LLB (hon.), Yale U., 1965. Bar: N.Y. 1959. Law clk. to Judge Learned Hand, 1957-58; assoc. firm Sullivan & Cromwell, 1958-62; faculty Yale Law Sch., 1962-69, master Trumbull Coll., 1966-69, Hohfeld prof. jurisprudence, 1968-69, Oxford, England, 1969-98; Quain prof. jurisprudence Univ. Coll., London, 1998—2004, Bentham prof. juris prudence, 2004—; prof. law NYU, 1975—. Prof.-at-large Cornell U., 1976—; vis. prof. philosophy Princeton (N.J.) U., 1963, 74-75, Gauss seminarian, 1966; vis. prof. law Stanford U., 1967; vis. prof. law and philosophy Harvard U., Cambridge, Mass., 1977, vis. prof. philosophy, 1979; acad. freedom lectr. U. Witwatersrand, 1976. Author: Taking Rights Seriously, 1977, A Matter of Principle, 1985, Law's Empire, 1986, A Bill of Rights for Britain, 1990, Life's Domain, 1993, Freedom's Law, 1996, Sovereign Virtue, 2000, Justice in Robes, 2006, Is Democracy Possible Here, 2006; editor: Philosophy of Law, 1977, A Badly Flawed Election, 2002; contbr. articles to profl. jours. Chmn. Dems. Abroad, 1972-74; del. Dem. Nat. Conv., 1972, 76; mem. Dem. Charter Commn., 1974. Fellow Brit. Acad., Am. Acad. Arts and Scis. Office: NYU Law Sch 40 Washington Sq S New York NY 10012-1099

DWORS, ROBERT F., retail executive; BA, Bowling Green State U., Ohio; MBA, Ohio State U., 1967. Sr. v.p. corp. real estate svcs. AutoNation, Inc., Ft. Lauderdale, Fla., 1996—. Office: AutoNation Inc 110 SE 6th St Fort Lauderdale FL 33301

DWORSKY, DANIEL LEONARD, architect, educator; b. Mpls., Oct. 4, 1927; s. Lewis and Ida (Fineberg) D.; m. Sylvia Ann Taylor, Aug. 10, 1957; children: Douglas, Laurie, Nancy. BArch, U. Mich., 1950. Practice architecture as Dworsky Assocs., LA, 1953-2000, Cannon Dworsky, LA, 2000—03; design critic, lectr. architecture U. So. Calif., 1983—84, U. Mich., 1983—84, UCLA, 1983—84. Chmn. archtl. rev. panel Fed. Res. Bank. Recipient Design citation Progressive Arch. mag. 1967, Gov. Calif. award 1966, 3 LA Grand Prix awards So. Calif. AIA and City of LA 1967; prin. works include Angelus Plz. Elderly Housing, LA, 1981, Ontario (Calif.) City Hall, 1980, CBS Exec. Office Bldg., North Hollywood, Calif., 1970, UCLA Stadium, 1969, Fed. Res. Bank Bldg., LA, 1987, U. Mich. Crisler Arena at Ann Arbor, 1966, Dominguez Hills State U. Theatre, 1977, Ventura County Govt. Ctr., 1979, Northrop Electronics Hdqrs., LA, 1983, Hewlett-Packard Region Office, North Hollywood, 1984, LA County Mcpl. Cts. Bldg., 1985, Tom Bradley Internat. Terminal LA Airport, 1984, City Tower, Orange, Calif., 1988, Fed. Office Bldg., Long Beach, Calif., 1992, Las Vegas Fed. Cts. Bldg., 2000. Disting. Alumnus award Coll. Architecture, U. Mich., 2005. Fellow AIA (more than 100 awards including 24 awards Calif. chpts., Nat. Honor award 1974, 68-69, Firm award Calif. chpt. 1985, L.A. Gold Medal award 1994, State of Calif. Lifetime Achievement award 2004). Home: 9225 Nightingale Dr Los Angeles CA 90069-1117 Home Phone: 310-271-2106; Office Phone: 310-271-2106. Business E-Mail: dandworsky@mac.com.

DWORZAN, HELENE LIBERMAN, novelist, poet, playwright; b. Paris, France, Mar. 13, 1925; d. Ansjel and Rebecca Liberman; came to U.S., 1950, naturalized, 1952; student Lycee Victor Hugo, Paris, 1937-42, New Sch. for Social Research, 1952-53; BA, CUNY, 1974; m. George R. Dworzan; 1 son, Patrice Olivier; m. 2d, Donald H. Reiman, 1975. Translator, Robin Internat./Cinerama, N.Y.C., 1954-59; freelance translator NBC, 1962-72; assoc. editor Chelsea, lit. rev., 1970-81; tchr. French, Lang. Inst., N.Y.C., 1970-73, Riverdale Country Sch., N.Y.C., 1973-86; founder, dir. Continuum, poetry and fiction readings, 1970-76. Recipient novel grant Material Jewish Claims against Germany, 1961, Short Story award Dial Press, 1953; Prairie Schooner prize for fiction, 1978. Mem. Authors League Am., Dramatists Guild. Author: (novel) Le Temps de la Chrysalide, 1957; editor: (with Donald H. Reiman) Shelley's Last Notebook, 1990; also short stories and poems in various publs.

DWYER, CARRIE ELIZABETH, lawyer, investment company executive; b. San Mateo, Calif., Dec. 19, 1950; d. Robert Harold and Alice Marian (Daley) Dwyer; m. Richard M. Konecky, Feb. 12, 1977; children: Rachel Anne, Philip. BA in English, U. Santa Clara, 1973, JD, 1976. Bar: Calif., NY. Staff atty. Am. Stock Exchange, NYC, 1977-79, exec. asst. to exec. v.p. legal and regulatory affairs, 1979—81, asst. v.p., exec. asst. to pres., 1981—83, v.p., exec. asst. to pres., 1983—85, v.p., assoc. gen. counsel, 1985—87, sr. v.p., gen. counsel, 1987—89; contract lawyer Milbank, Tweed, Hadley & McCoy, NYC; sr. counsel to chmn. Arthur Levitt SEC, 1993—96; exec. v.p. corp. oversight The Charles Schwab Corp., San Francisco, 1996—, gen. counsel, 1998—. Named one of Bay Area's 100 Most Influential Women, San Francisco Bus. Women, 2007. Mem. ABA, The Assn. of Bar of City of NY, NY State Bar Assn., Investment Assn. Office: The Charles Schwab Corp 101 Montgomery St San Francisco CA 94104*

DWYER, DARRELL JAMES, finance company executive; b. Vermillion, SD, Nov. 27, 1946; s. Michael Leroy and Faye Awilda (Hansen) Dwyer; m. Helen K. Howard, 1989; 1 child, Sean Patrick. BS, Minn. State U., 1977; MBA, U. Calif., Berkeley, 1978. CPA, cert. mgmt. acct., internal auditor; data processor. Acct. Touche Ross & Co., Salem, Oreg., 1978-79; cons. Arthur, Persons Co., Salem, 1980-82; v.p. fin. Evergreen Internat. Airlines Inc, McMinnville, Oreg., 1982-87; CFO Erickson Group Ltd., Medford, Oreg., 1987-89; sr. v.p., corp. sec. Evergreen Internat. Aviation, Inc., McMinnville, 1989-90; pres., CEO Dwyer Co., Rocklin, Calif., 1990—. Capt. US Army, 1967—71. Recipient award of merit, Evergreen Internat. Aviation, McMinnville, 1984; Calif. State scholar. Mem.: Inst. Cert. Mgmt. Accts., Calif. Soc. CPA. Republican. Episcopalian. Avocations: skiing, tennis, travel. Office: Dwyer Co 3111 Sunset Blvd Rocklin CA 95677 Home Phone: 530-886-8694. Personal E-mail: djdwyer@pacbell.net.

DWYER, DENNIS D., information technology executive; b. Oak Park, Ill., July 19, 1943; s. John J. and Jessie M. Dwyer; m. Carolyn R. Schultz, Apr. 29, 1967; children: David, Julianne. Various positions Harris Bank, Chgo., 1967-83, mgr. info. tech. planning, 1983-86, v.p. tech. facilitation, 1986—. Resolutions chmn. Cooperating Users of Burroughs Equipment, Detroit, 1978-82; mem. computer sci. adv. bd. Northeastern Ill. U., 2001—; cons. Unisys mainframe computers. Pres. Hunting Ridge Homeowners Assn., 1983-85; mem. Palatine Plan Commn., 1984—, chmn., 1989—. Recipient Tom Grier award for Excellence Unisys Users Group, 1988. Home: 1032 Raven Ln Palatine IL 60067-6649 Office: Harris Bank PO

Box 755 Chicago IL 60690-0755 Home Phone: 847-359-6998; Office Phone: 312-461-6941. Business E-Mail: dennis.dwyer@harrisbank.com. E-mail: dennis-carolyn@ravenlane.com.

DWYER, GERALD PAUL, JR., economist, bank executive; b. Pittsfield, Mass., July 9, 1947; s. Gerald Paul and Mary Frances (Weir) Dwyer; m. Katherine Marie Lepiane, Jan. 15, 1966; children: Tamara K., Gerald P. III, Angela M., Michael J. L., Terence F. BBA, U. Wash., 1969; MA in Econs., U. Tenn., 1973; PhD in Econs., U. Chgo., 1979. Economist Fed. Res. Bank, St. Louis, 1972-74, Chgo., 1976-77, asst. v.p. Atlanta, 1997-98, v.p., 1998—; asst. prof. Tex. A&M U., College Station, 1977-81, Emory U., Atlanta, 1981-84, sr. rsch. assoc. Law and Econ. Ctr., 1982-84; assoc. prof. U. Houston, 1984-89; prof. Clemson (S.C.) U., 1989-99, acting head dept. econ., 1992-93. Cons. Arthur Bros., Corpus Christi, Tex., 1980—81, FTC, Washington, 1983—84, Amerigas, Houston, 1985, We. Container Corp., 1987, Metrica, Inc., Bryan, Tex., 1989—93; vis. scholar Fed. Res. Bank, Atlanta, 1982—84, St. Louis, 1987—89, Atlanta, 1994—97, Mpls., 1995; vis. fin. economist Commodity Futures Trading Commn., Washington, 1990; vis. faculty Ga. State U., 1997, U. Ga., 1999—2000, 2003, U. Rome, 2000—04, U. Carlos III, Madrid, 2005—. Contbr. articles to profl. jours. Fellow, Earhart Found., 1975—77; vis. scholar, Inst. for INternat. Integration Studies, Trinity Coll., 2005, Cambridge Endowment for Rsch. in Fin., Cambridge U., 2006, Ctr. Fin. Analysis and Policy, Cambridge U., 2007; Weaver fellow, Intercollegiate Studies Inst., 1974—75, Rsch. grantee, Earhart Found., NSF. Mem.: Western Econ. Assn. (exec. com. 2005—), Assn. of Pvt. Enterprise Edn. (exec. com. 2002—), Soc. Nonlinear Dynamics and Econometrics (treas. 1997—2003, exec. com. 1997—2006, pres. 2003—05), Am. Fin. Assn., Am. Econ. Assn., Italian Assn. Banking and Fin. (mem. internat. adv. bd. 2006—), Phi Kappa Phi, Beta Gamma Sigma. Avocation: sailing. E-mail: gdwyer@dwyerecon.com.

DWYER, JIM, reporter, columnist; b. NYC, 1957; s. Philip and Mary (Molloy) Dwyer; m. Catherine Muir; children: Maura, Catherine. BS, Fordham Coll., 1979; MS, Columbia U., 1980. Reporter Hudson Dispatch, Union City, NJ, 1980—82, Elizabeth Jour., NJ, 1982, Bergen Record, Hackensack, NJ, 1983—84; reporter, columnist NY Newsday, NYC, 1984—95; columnist NY Daily News, 1995; gen.assignment reporter, Metro Desk NY Times, 2001—, reporter, Objects series, 2001. Author (with others): (songs) (book) Journalism Collection of Best Newspaper Writing, 1991, Two Seconds Under the World, 1994, Actual Innocence, 2000; author: Subway Lives, 1990; co-author: 102 Minutes, 2005. Co-recipient Pulitzer Prize (part of New York Newsday team), 1992; recipient Outstanding Column award, Nat. Headliners Soc., 1987, 1988, Meyer Berger prize, Columbia U., 1988, Writing award for commentary, Am. Soc. Newspaper Editors, 1991, Pulitzer Prize for commentary, 1995. Roman Catholic. Office: NY Times 229 West 43rd St New York NY 10036 E-mail: dwyer@nytimes.com.

DWYER, JOHANNA TODD, nutritionist, educator; b. Syracuse, NY, Oct. 20, 1938; d. M. Harold and Frances (Markey) D. BS with distinction, Cornell U., 1960; MSc, U. Wis., 1962; MS, Harvard Sch. Pub. Health, Boston, 1965, DSc, 1969. Asst. prof. Harvard Sch. Pub. Health, 1969-73; home economist Procter & Gamble, Cin., 1962-64; rsch. asst. U. Wis., Madison, 1960-62; assoc. prof. Tufts Med. Sch., 1974, prof. medicine and nutrition, 1984—; sr. scientist human nutrition rsch. USDA, Boston, 1988—, asst. adminstr. for human nutrition Agrl. Rsch. Svc. Washington, 2001—02; sr. nutrition rsch. scientist Office of Dietary Supplements, NIH, 2003—. Dir. Frances Stern Nutrition Ctr., New Eng. Med. Ctr., Boston, 1974—; adj. prof. Harvard Sch. Pub. Health, 1988—. Author 3 books, 1979, 83; editor Nutrition Today, 1995—; contbr. over 450 articles to profl. jours. Mem. Mass. Nutrition Bd., Boston, 1980-2004; cons. Exec. Office of Pres., Washington, 1976; mem. bd. sci. counselors Nat. Cancer Inst., 1985-89; com. mem. and nuitrition work study Am. Cancer Soc., 1990-94; sec. ADA Found., 2004 Robert Wood Johnson Health Policy fellow, 1980-81, John Stalker award Am. Sch. Food Svc. Assn., 1990, Alumni Merit award Harvand Sch. Pub. Health, 2004. Fellow: Am. Soc. Nutrition Scis. (Conrad Elvejhem award for pub. policy 2005), Am. Inst. Nutrition (pres. 1994—95, bd. dirs.), Am. Soc. Clin. Nutrition (sec. 1990—93), Soc. for Nutrition Edn. (bd. dirs. 1975—77, pres. 1976, J. Harvey Wiley award 1983); mem.: APHA (program devel. bd. 1990—92), Dannon Inst. (sci. adv. bd. 2003—06), Internat. Life Scis. Inst. (bd. dirs. 1999—, exec. com. 2005—), Food and Drug Law Inst. (bd. dirs. 1980—95), Am. Inst. Food and Wine (bd. dirs. 1991—95), Nutrition Screening Initiative (tech. and sci. rev. com. 1990—2004), Inst. Medicine of NAS (food and nutrition bd. 1990—2000, councilor 2001—03, mil. nutrition com. mem. 2004—, report renew com. 2005—), Am. Dietetic Assn. (legis. and pub. policy com. 1998—2004, sec. found. 2005, lectr., bd. mem. ADA Found., Lenna Frances Cooper award 1980, Medallion award 2002), Am. Soc. Parenteral and Enteral Nutrition (adv. bd. 1978—). Office: Tufts New Eng Med Ctr 750 Washington St PO Box 783 Boston MA 02102-0783 Office Phone: 617-636-5273. Personal E-mail: toddyd@msn.com. Business E-Mail: jdwyer1@tufts.nemc.org.

DWYER, JOHN CHARLES, lawyer; b. San Francisco, Mar. 26, 1962; s. Richard Thomas and Dorothy (Blake) D. BS in Bus. Adminstrn. summa cum laude, U. Calif., Berkeley, 1984; JD magna cum laude, Harvard U., 1988. Bar: Calif. 1988, US Dist. Ct. (no. dist.) Calif. 1988, US Ct. of Appeals (9th cir.) 1988, US Supreme Ct. 1996, DC. Assoc. Jackson, Tufts, Cole & Black, San Francisco, 1989-93; dep. assoc. atty. gen. U.S. Dept. Justice, Washington, 1993-96, acting assoc. atty. gen., 1997; ptnr. Cooley Godward LLP, Palo Alto, Calif., 1998—. Auditor Arthur Andersen & Co. Recipient Calif. Lawyer of the Yr., Calif. Lawyer mag., 2005. Mem.: US Supreme Ct., ABA, Phi Beta Kappa. Democrat. Roman Catholic. Office: Cooley Godward LLP PA Square Bldg 5 Palo Alto Sq 3000 El Camino Real Palo Alto CA 94306-2155 Office Fax: 650-857-0663. Business E-Mail: dwyerjc@cooley.com.

DWYER, JOHN M., mathematician, statistician, computer scientist; b. Ann Arbor, Mich., June 8, 1937; s. Paul Sumner and Florence Baylis (Brown) D.; children: Anne Louise, Laura Beth. BA, U. Mich., 1959, MS, 1965; PhD, Tex A&M U., 1971. Asst. prof. stats. U. Wyo., Laramie, 1962-66; asst. prof. math. U. Detroit, 1969-73, assoc. prof. math., 1974—, chair, 1974-77, interim chair, 1989-91. Vis. assoc. prof. dept. mgmt. and mktg. Northern Mich. U., Marquette, 1983-84; dir. rsch. Detroit Inst. Abuse Rsch. and Tng., 1973-74; cons. Detroit Tax Assessor's Office, 1971; expert witness Focus: HOPE, Detroit, 1981-86; panelist "Ask the Professor" radio show U. Detroit, 1977-83. Mem.: AAAS, Computer Profls. for Social Responsibility (co-founder Mich. chpt. 1997, chair 1998—2001, nat. bd. dirs. 2002—06, nat. treas. 2002—06, bd. dirs. 2001—06), Assn. Computing Machinery, Union of Concerned Scientists, Math. Assn. Am. Office: U Detroit Mercy Dept Math and Computer Sci 4001 W McNichols Detroit MI 48221 Business E-Mail: dwyerjm@udmercy.edu.

DWYER, JOHN P., law educator; b. 1951; BA DePauw U.; PhD, Calif. Inst. Tech., 1978; JD, U. Calif., Berkeley, 1980. Bar: D.C. 1981, Calif. 1982. Law clk. to Hon. Harry T. Edwards U.S. Ct. Appeals (D.C. cir.), Washington, 1980-81; law clk. to Hon. Sandra O'Connor U.S. Supreme Ct., Washington, 1981-82; staff atty. D.C. Pub. Defender Svc., 1982-84; prof. U. Calif. Berkeley, 1984—2002, dean, 2000—02, John H. Boalt Prof. Law, Emeritus, 2002—. Visiting prof. Harvard Law Sch., Vrije Universiteit, Amsterdam.

DWYER, MAUREEN ELLEN, lawyer; BA, Smith Coll., Northampton, Mass., 1973; JD, Cath. U. Am. Columbus Sch. Law, 1978. Bar: DC 1979, US Dist. Ct. (DC), US Ct. Appeals (DC cir.), US Supreme Ct. Shareholder Wilkes Artis, Washington; ptnr. real estate grp. Pillsbury Winthrop Shaw Pittman, Washington, mng. ptnr. DC office. Chmn. adv. bd. Salvation Army; past chmn. Eugene & Agnes Meyer Found. Named one of 100 Most Powerful Women in Washington, Washingtonian mag., 2001. Mem.: Comml. Real Estate Women (pres. 1989—91), Fed. City Coun., DC C. of C., Urban Land Inst., Greater Washington Bd. Trade, DC Bldg. Industry Assn., Econ. Club. Office: Pillsbury Winthrop Shaw Pittman 2300 N St NW Washington DC 20037-1128 Office Phone: 202-663-8834. Office Fax: 202-663-8007. Business E-Mail: maureen.dwyer@pillsburylaw.com.*

DWYER, STACEY H., construction executive; BS in Acctg., Southeastern Okla. State U., Durant; MS in Acctg., U. Tex., Arlington. CPA. Auditor Ernst and Young, Ft. Worth, 1989—91; acctg. mgr. D.R. Horton, Inc., Ft. Worth, 1991, with investments divsn., 1996, asst. sec., asst. v.p., 1998—2000, exec. v.p. investor rels., 2000—, treas., 2003—. Office: DR Horton Inc DR Horton Tower 301 Commerce St Ste 500 Fort Worth TX 76102 Office Phone: 817-390-8200.*

DWYER, WILLIAM H., real estate company executive; b. Milw., Sept. 6, 1950; s. Thomas H. and Eileen M. Dwyer; m. Sue D., Sept. 6, 1980; 2 children. BS, U. We. Wis., 1973. Cert. property mgr.; accredited resident mgr. Real estate broker Dwyer/Kloce Realtor, 1972—80; pres. Premier Real Estate Mgmt., LLC (formerly Calvin Akin), Brookfield, Wis., 1990—2003; v.p. Bartlein & Co., Inc., 1980—90. Mem.: Notary.

DWYER, WILLIAM MICHAEL, health care company advisor; b. Sparta, Wis., Sept. 7, 1952; s. William Ambrose and Beatrice Helen (Kopenhafer) D.; m. Ruth Elaine Heitzman, Feb. 21, 1976; children: Meghan Ruth, Gretchen Mary, William Theodore, Michelle Elizabeth. BA in adolescent psychology, U. Minn., Mpls., 1974; MBA in marketing, health svs. mgmt., gen. mgmt., Northwestern U., Evanston, Ill., 1989. Psychiat. technician Mounds Park Hosp., St. Paul, 1974-77; hosp. sales rep. Abbott Labs., Rochester, Minn., 1977-81, profl. sales specialist Houston, 1981-83, sr. market rsch. analyst Abbott Park, Ill., 1983—85, mgr. major market planning, 1985-88, dir. major market planning, 1988-90, dir. corp. account devel., 1990-94, sr. dir. strategic mtkg., 1994—2000; divisional v.p. Abbott Labs. Strategic Mktg., Abbott Park, 2000—04; sr. v.p. Cerner Corp., Kansas City, Mo., 2004—07, exec. advisor, 2007—. Mem. payment adv. bd. Health Industry Mfrs. Assn., Washington, 1994-1997; mem. Patient Safety Task Force, chmn., 2000-03; bd. dirs. Nat. Com. Quality Health Care, Washington, chmn., 1996; mem. Nat. Ctr. for Healthcare Leadership, Health Rsch. and Ednl. Trust, 1997-2004; mem. planning com. of bd. Advocate HealthCare, Banner Health Systems; mentor, preceptor J.L. Kellogg Program Health Adminstrn., Evanston, Ill., 1995-96; mem. coun. Nat. Quiality Forum. Contbg. author: Reinventing Health Care: Revolution At Hand, 1992, Total Quality Management: Health Care Pioneers, 1992, Medical Group Practices Face Uncertain Future, 1995, Enhancing Physician Performance, 2000, Careers in Healthcare Management, 2002, Hospital of the Future: A Leaders' Perspective, 2003. Pres. Tullamore Home Assn., Mundelein, Ill., 1990; deacon Calvary Bapt. Ch., Mundelein, 1992-94; state del. Rep. Party, State of Minn., 1972 Stout Meml. Found. scholar, 1970; recipient A.B. Dick Trustee Forum award Lake Forest (Ill.) Hosp., 1991, Laura G. Jackson Disting. Alumnus award Health Svcs. Mgmt., J.L. Kellogg Grad. Sch. Mgmt., Northwestern U., 1998, Marshall A. Faulk, M.D. Disting. Lectureship Finch U. Health Scis., 2001, Edward John Noble Lecture Greenwich Hosp., 2003, Disting. Svc. award Ohio State U., 2003. Mem. Am. Hosp. Assn./Soc. Hosp. Plan and Mktg., Am. Coll. Healthcare Execs. (mem. leadership adv. bd. 1994-97), Beta Gamma Sigma. Avocations: skiing, fly fishing, wilderness canoeing. Office: 2800 Rockcreek Pkwy Kansas City MO 64117-2551 Home: 4315 N Hickory Ln Kansas City MO 64116

DWYER SOUTHERN, KATHY, museum administrator; m. Hugh Southern; 1 child. BA in Mktg., U. Wis., 1968, MA in Arts Adminstrn., 1972. Exec. dir. Nat. Cultural Alliance, 1990—94, Montpelier, Va., 1994—96; pres., CEO Port Discovery, Balt., 1996—2001, Capital Children's Mus., 2001—. Arts mgmt. prof. Am. U., Va. Commonwealth U., Shenandoah Conservatory Music; bd. dirs. Am. Assn. Mus. Named to Centennial Honor Roll, Am. Assn. Museums, 2006; recipient Disting. Bus. Alumni award, U. Wis. Sch. Bus., 2000. Office: National Children's Museum Ste 5100 955 L'Enfant Plaza North SW Washington DC 20024-2103 Home Phone: 703-465-7607; Office Phone: 202-675-4120.*

DWYRE, WILLIAM PATRICK, journalist; b. Sheboygan, Wis., Apr. 7, 1944; s. George Leo and Mary Veronica (O'Brien) D.; m. Jill Ethlyn Jarvis, July 30, 1966; children— Amy, Patrick BA, U. Notre Dame, Ind. Sports copy editor Des Moines Register, 1966-68; sports writer, asst. sports editor, sports editor Milw. Jour., 1968-81; asst. sports editor, sports editor LA Times, 1981—2006, columnist sports, 2006—. Columnist Referee Mag., 1977-02; voting mem., bd. dir. Amateur Athletic Found. Nat. Sports Hall of Fame, 1981—. Bd. dir. Honda-Brockerick Cup Women's Collegiate Athlete of Yr.; bd. dir. Casa Colina Hosp. Rehab., Pomona. Named Sportswriter of Yr., Wis. Nat. Sportscasters and Sportswriters Assn., 1980; Nat. Editor of Yr., Nat. Press Found., 1985; recipient award Sustained Excellence by Individual, L.A. Times, 1985, Red Smith award AP sports Editors, 1996, Acad Literary award, 2004, Los Angeles Sports and Entertainment Commn. Ambassador award, 2005, Good Guy award, Calif. Golf Writers Assn., 2007. Mem. Nat. Sportscasters and Sportswriters Assn. (bd. dirs., Powerade Sport Story of Yr. award 1999), Assoc. Press Sports Editors (pres. 1989), LA Sports and Entertainment Commn. Amb. award, 2005, Subiaco (Ark.). Avocations: tennis, golf. Office: Los Angeles Times Times Mirror Sq Los Angeles CA 90012 E-mail: bill.dwyre@latimes.com.

DYAR, KATHRYN WILKIN, pediatrician; b. Colquitt, Ga., Feb. 20, 1945; d. Patrick McWhorter and Virginia (Wilkin) Dyar; m. James Ansley Patten, Jan. 1, 1985. BS in Biology, Emory U., Decatur, Ga., 1966; MD, Med. Coll. Ga., Augusta, 1970. Resident in pediatrics Eugene Talmadge Meml. Hosp., Augusta, Ga., 1970-72, Georgetown U. Hosp., Washington, 1972-73; pediatrician Children's Clinic, Tifton, Ga., 1973-74, Children and Youth Project, Norfolk, Va., 1974-83, 90-95, dir., 1990-94; pediatrician Hampton (Va.) Health Dept., 1983-90. Fellow: Am. Acad. Pediatrics.

DYBEK, STUART, language educator, writer; b. Chgo., Apr. 10, 1942; s. Stanley and Adeline (Sala) S.; m. Caren Bassett, Feb. 7, 1967; children: Anne, Nicholas. BS, Loyola U., Chgo., 1964, MA, 1967; MFA, U. Iowa, 1973. Tchr. US V.I. Sch., St. Thomas, 1968-70, U. Iowa, Iowa City, 1970-73; prof. English Western Mich. U., Kalamazoo, 1973—, adj. prof. Vis. prof. creative writing Princeton U., NJ, 1991, U. Calif., Irvine, 1995, U. Iowa, 1998, Northwestern U., 2001; disting. writer-in-residence Northwestern U., 2006-. Author: (poetry) Brass Knuckles, 1979, Streets In Their Own Ink, 2004; (fiction) Childhood and Other Neighborhoods, 1980, The Coast of Chicago, 1990, I Sailed With Magellan, 2003. Recipient Whiting Writers award, 1985, O. Henry first prize, 1985, Acad. award in fiction Am. Acad. Arts and Letters, 1994, PEN/Malamud award, 1995, Lannan Lit. prize, 1998, Mark Twain award, 2007; Guggenheim fellow, 1982. Mem. PEN. Home: 320 Monroe St Kalamazoo MI 49006-4436 Office: Western Michigan U Dept English Kalamazoo MI 49008 also: care Amanda Urban Intl Creative Mgt 40 W 57th St New York NY 10019-4001 Personal E-mail: sdybek@earthlink.net.

DYBNER, RUBEN, urologist; b. Buenos Aires, Oct. 1, 1937; s. Pedro and Mania Dybner; m. Ana Berlaute Dybner, Jan. 17, 1965; children: Karen, Ariel, Alan. BS, Buenos Aires U., 1962. Surg. resident U. Hosp., Buenos Aires, 1962—65; intern Elmmurst Neural, NY, 1965—66; surg. resident VA Hosp., NYC, 1966—67; urology resident Beth Israel Med. Ctr., NYC, 1967—70; pediat. urology fellow Columbia U., NYC, 1970—71; pvt. practice Forest Hills, NY, 1971—. Co-chair urology Pkwy. Hosp., Forest Hills, NY. Mem.: Am. Urol. Assn.

DYBOWSKI, CECIL, chemistry educator; b. Sept. 23, 1946; s. Hermin Romana Dybowski and Ruth Joyce Geffert; m. Mary A. Kaiser, May 12, 1979; 1 child, Marta Marie. BS, U. Tex., 1969, PhD, 1973. Rsch. fellow Calif. Inst. Tech., 1973—76; prof. U. Delware, 1976—. Mem. gov. bd. Eastern Analytical Symposium, 1985—; dir. Del. Acad. Chem. Sci., 2003—. Co-author: (book) Transient Technique in the NMR of Solids, 1985; assoc. editor Applied Spectroscopy, sect. editor Encyclopedia of Analytical Chemistry. Named Disting. Vis. Prof., Jagiellonian U., Cracow, Poland. Fellow: AAAS; mem.: Materials Rsch. Soc., Soc. Applied Spectroscopy, Am. Phys. Soc., Am. Chem. Soc. Avocation: music. Office: U Del Dept Chemistry and Biochemistry Newark DE 19716

DYBUL, MARK RICHARD, ambassador; b. Sept. 23, 1963; AB, Georgetown U., 1985, MD, 1992. Resident internal medicine U. Chgo. Hospitals, 1992—95; fellow Nat. Inst. Allergy and Infectious Diseases, 1998; capt. U.S. Pub. Health Svc. Commissioned Corps; staff clinician lab. immunoregulation Nat. Inst. Allergy and Infectious Diseases/NIH; asst. dir. medical affairs Nat. Inst. Allergy and Infectious Diseases NIH; co-exec. sec. HIV therapy guidelines US Dept. Health & Human Services, head internat. prevention mother and child HIV initiative, mem. emergency plan planning task force; dep. global AIDS coord. US Dept. State, acting global AIDS coord., global AIDS coord., 2006—. Office: Office of Global AIDS Coord SA-29 2d Floor 2201 C St NW Washington DC 20522-2920

DYBVIG, MARY MCILVAINE, educational consultant, psychologist; b. Chgo., Feb. 23, 1936; d. John Harmon and Mildred Petrina McIlvaine; m. Noel Tyl, June 13, 1958 (div. Apr. 1976); 1 child, Kimberly Tyl; m. Paul Dybvig, Mar. 21, 1978 (div. Feb. 1999); m. Melvin Leonard Sward, Apr. 7, 2002; stepchildren: Alyssa Quanbeck, Mary Eide, Mark Sward, Paul Sward, Natalie Nutting, Carole Sward. BA cum laude, Radcliffe/Harvard U., 1958; MA in Ednl. Psychology, NYU, 1968; PhD in Ednl. Adminstrn., U. Minn., 1992. Tchr. Kinkaid Sch., Houston, 1958—60, Dalton Sch., NYC, 1960—63, Packer Collegiate Inst., Brooklyn, NY, 1963—68, Am. Army Sch., Munich, 1968—69, Düsseldorf (Germany) Internat. Sch., 1969—72, Heinrich-Heine Gymnasium, 1972—73, St. Paul Acad., 1973—77; sch. psychologist St. Paul (Minn.) Schs., 1977—94, prin., 1994—2001; pvt. practice cons./sch. psychologist St. Paul/Mpls., 2001—. Instr. St. Thomas U., St. Paul, 1990—94; cons. in field; presenter in field. Active St. Luke Luth. Ch., St. Paul, 1996—. Mem.: Minn. Assn. Sch. Psychologists, Nat. Assn. Sch. Psychologists, Alpha Delta Kappa. Avocations: travel, golf, cooking. Home: 1640 Mackubin St Saint Paul MN 55117

DYCHE, DAVID BENNETT, JR., management consultant; b. Port Chester, NY, July 23, 1932; s. David B. and Julia H. D.; m. Mary J. Moorman, Apr. 28, 1956; children— David B. III, Williard H. AB, Dartmouth Coll., 1954; MBA, U. Pa., 1958. Chartered fin. analyst. With J.P. Morgan & Co., and Morgan Guaranty Trust Co., NYC, 1958-81; dir. fin. industries Arthur D. Little, Inc., 1981-98; cons. Tiax LLC, 1999—2004; mgr. North Creek Cons. LLC, 2005—. Chmn., commr. Boca Grande Fire Control Dist., 2000-04. With U.S. Army, 1954-56. Mem. Assn. Investment Mgmt. Rsch., N.Y. Soc. Security Analysts. Home: 61 Bayhead Ln Osprey FL 34229-8992

DYCHE, JANE WINKLER, lawyer; Bar: Ky. 1995. Atty. Tooms & House; solo pvt. practice London, Ky. Bd. mem. Lawyers Mutual Insurance of Ky. Mem.: Ky. Bar Assn. (prse.-elect 2006—07). Office: PO Box 5156 London KY 40745 also: Lawyers Mutual Insurance of Ky Waterfront Plaza 323 W Main St, Ste 600 Louisville KY 40202 Office Phone: 606-877-2991. Office Fax: 606-877-9973.

DYCK, MARTIN, literary theorist, mathematics historian; b. Grünfeld, Ukraine, Jan. 16, 1927; came to U.S., 1956; s. Martin and Helene (Peters) Sommer D.; m. Marie Wiens, June 12, 1949 (div. 1983); children: Vernon, Victor, Martin Christopher Columbus and Ingrid Rose Marie (twins). BA German and Pure Math. (double hons.), U. Manitoba, Can., 1953, MA in German and Math., 1954; PhD in German Lit., U. Cin., 1956. Grad. asst. math. U. Manitoba, 1952-53, sessional lectr. in Germn, 1953-54; Taft Meml. fellow U. Cin., 1954-56; asst. prof. German and Russian MIT, Cambridge, 1956-58, prof. German and humanities, 1965-87, prof. emeritus, 1987—; from asst. to prof. German U. Mich., Ann Arbor, 1958-65. Author: Goethe und die Mathematik, 1954, Novalis and Mathematics, 1960, 70, Die Gedichte Schillers, 1967; mem. editorial bd. Historia Mathematica, 1972-76; contbr. articles to profl. jours. and book chpts. Fellow Guggenheim, 1961-62, Am. Coun. Learned Socs., 1961-62; grantee Am. Philos. Soc., 1969. Mem. MLA (del. assembly 1979-81), Modern Humanities Rsch. Assn., Assn. Lit. Scholars and Critics, History of Sci. Soc., Lessing Soc., Am. Soc. for Eighteenth Century Studies, Am. Assn. Tchrs. German, German Studies, Assn., N.E. MLA. Avocations: mountain climbing, walking, reading. Home: PO Box 1179 Lincoln NH 03251-1179 Office: MIT Rm E38-277 6th Fl 77 Massachusetts Ave Cambridge MA 02139-4307 *I have striven to test and taste the poetry, comedy, and mathematics of man against matter and nothingness.*

DYCK, WALTER PETER, gastroenterologist, educator, academic administrator; b. Winkler, Man., Can., 1935; MD, U. Kans., 1961. Diplomate Am. Bd. Internal Medicine, Am. Bd. Gastroenterology. Intern Henry Ford Hosp., Detroit, 1961—62, resident in internal medicine, 1962-63, 65-66; rsch. fellow gastroenterology U. Zurich, Switzerland, 1963—64; fellow enzymology rsch. U. Toronto, Ont., Canada, 1964—65; fellow gastroenterology Mt. Sinai Sch. Medicine, NYC, 1966—68; mem. sr. staff Scott and White Clinic, Temple, Tex., 1968—2006, chmn. dept. rsch., 1969—72, dir. divsn. gastroenterology, 1972—96; prof. medicine, dir. divsn. gastroenterology Tex. A&M Coll. Medicine, 1978—96, sr. assoc. dean, 1996—2003, exec. assoc. dean, 2003—06, prof. emeritus, 2006—; adminstr. dir. rsch. and edn. divsn., chief acad. officer Scott and White Meml. Hosp., Temple, 1996—2006; sr. advisor Temple Health and Biosci. Econ. Devel. Corp., 2006—. Mem. gen. medicine study sect. A NIH, 1973-77. Fellow ACP, Am. Coll. Gastroenterology; mem. AMA, Am. Fedn. Clin. Rsch., Am. Gastroenterology Assn., Am. Physiol. Soc., So. Soc. Clin. Investigation, Soc. for Exptl. Biology and Medicine, Am. Pancreatic Assn., N.Y. Acad. Scis. E-mail: wdyck@swmail.sw.org.

DYCKMAN, THOMAS RICHARD, accountant, educator; b. Detroit, Feb. 25, 1932; s. Clovis E. and Wildarene A. (Andrus) Dyckman; m. Alice Ann Pletta, Nov. 4, 1955; children: Daniel, James, Linda, David. BA, U. Mich., 1954, MBA, 1955, PhD, 1961. Asst. prof. acctg. U. Calif., Berkeley, 1961-64; assoc. prof. Cornell U., Ithaca, NY, 1964-68, prof., 1968—, Ann Whitney Olin prof. bus., 1978—, assoc. dean Johnson Grad. Sch. Mgmt., 1985-95, acting dean, 1996-97, acting v.p. for info. tech., 1998-99. Cons. IBM, GTE, SNET, Fin. Acctg. Stds. Bd., mem. adv. com., 1984—88; chair audit com. bd. dirs. Galaxy Nutritional Foods, 2002—. Author: (book) Topics in Cost Accounting and Decisions, 1963, Statistical Decision Theory, 1968, Algebra and Calculus for Business, 1975, Managerial Cost Accounting, 1971, 2d edit., 1976, Fundamental Statistics for Business and Economics, 1977, Efficient Capital Markets, 1975, 2d edit., 1986, Cases in Financial Accounting, 1987, 3d edit., 1989, Cost Accounting: Concepts and Managerial Applications, 1990, 2d edit., 1994, Intermediate Accounting, rev. edit., 1992, 5th edit., 2001, Financial Accounting, 2006, 2007. Mem. adv. com. Fin. Acctg. Found., 1990—93. With USNR, 1955—58. Recipient

Gold medal award, AICPA, 1968, 1976. Mem.: Am. Acctg. Assn. (pres. 1981—82, dir. rsch. 1976—78, Outstanding Acctg. Educator award 1987). Office: Cornell U Sage Hall Ithaca NY 14853 Office Phone: 607-255-3491. Business E-Mail: trd2@cornell.edu.

DYCUS, ELIZABETH RASMUSSEN, academic administrator; d. John Juergen Rasmussen and Elise Louise Leinhardt; m. J. Stephen Dycus, Sept. 21, 1968; children: Jamie Stephen, Anne Lee Dycus Shapiro. BA, So. Meth. U., 1962. Staff asst. Congressman Speedy O. Long, Washington, 1966—68; itinerary sec. Senator Elect Lloyd Bentsen, Houston, 1970; asst. to chair Three Mile Island Commn., Hanover, Washington, 1979; asst. to the pres. Dartmouth Coll., Hanover, NH, 1980—83; dir. external rels. CLIPP, Dartmouth Coll., Hanover, NH, 1988—95; asst. dir. for recruitment IDE, Dartmouth Coll., Hanover, NH, 1999—2003; sr. cons. Korn Ferry Internat., Strafford, Vt., 2003—. Mem. Vt. State Bd. Health, Burlington, 1988—, chair, 1988—; mem. exec. com. Vt. State Dem. Party, 1985—91. Democrat. Congregationalist.

DYCUS, STEPHEN, law educator; b. Dallas, Nov. 13, 1941; m. Elizabeth Rasmussen, Sept. 21, 1968; children: Jamie S., Anne Lee. BA, So. Meth. U., 1963, LLB, 1965; LLM, Harvard U., Cambridge, Mass., 1976. Bar: Tex. 1965, Vt. 1980. Trust officer, 1965—72; asst. dean Law Sch. So. Meth. U., Dallas, 1972—75; prof. Vt. Law Sch., South Royalton, 1976—. Vis. scholar Law Sch., U. Calif., Berkeley, 1983-84, Nat. Resources Def. Coun., Washington, 1991; vis. prof. U.S. Mil. Acad., West Point, N.Y., 1991-92; mem. Vt. Water Resources Bd., Montpelier, 1993-97. Co-author: National Security Law, 1990, 4th edit., 2006, Counterterrorism Law, 2007; author: National Defense and the Environment, 1996; co-editor: Jour. Nat. Security Law and Policy, 2004—. Mem. Am. Law Inst. Democrat. Congregationalist. Home: 215 Justin Morrill Mem Hwy Strafford VT 05072-7703 Office: Vt Law Sch South Royalton VT 05068 Business E-Mail: sdycus@vermontlaw.edu.

DYE, GLORIA A., education educator; d. Walter T. and Rita C. Rydzak; m. Larry A. Dye, July 5, 1986. MA, U. N.Mex, Albuquerque, 1988, EdS, 1990, PhD, 1994. Tchr. mid. sch. lang. arts St. Mary Mid. Sch., Warren, Ohio, 1982—84; tchr. spl. edn. Albuquerque Pub. Schs., 1984—90, clin. supr., 1990—91; instr. U. N.Mex, Albuquerque, 1991—93; asst. prof. Washburn U., Topeka, 1994—2000, co-chair edn. dept., 2001—02, assoc. prof., 2000—07. Coord. Albuquerque Pub. Sch./U. N.Mex Tchr. Exch. Program, 1991—93. Mem. profl. adv. bd. Kans. Learning Disabilities Assn. Am., Topeka, 1998—2007. Recipient Ned N. Fleming award Excellence Tchg., Washburn U., 2004. Office: Washburn U 1700 SW Coll Ave Topeka KS 66621 Office Phone: 785-670-1432. E-mail: gloria.dye@washburn.edu.

DYE, JAMES LOUIS, retired chemistry professor; b. Soudan, Minn., July 18, 1927; s. Ray Ashley and Hildur Ameda Dye; m. Angeline Rosalie Medure, June 10, 1948; children: Roberta Rae, Thomas Anthony, Brenda Lee. AA, Virginia Jr. Coll., Minn., 1948; BA, Gustavus Adolphus Coll., 1949; PhD, Iowa State U., Ames, 1953; DSc (hon.), No. Mich. U., Marquette, 1992. Rsch. assoc. Iowa State U., Ames, 1953; asst. prof. chemistry Mich. State U., East Lansing, 1953-60, assoc. prof., 1960-63, prof., 1963-94, chmn. dept. chemistry, 1986-90, prof. emeritus, 1994—. Vis. scientist Ohio State U., Columbus, 1968-69; cons. AT&T Bell Labs., Murray Hill, N.J., 1982-83. Author: Thermodynamics and Equilibrium, 1978; contbr. more than 220 articles to profl. jours. With U.S. Army, 1945-46. NSF fellow, 1961-62, Guggenheim fellow, 1975-76, 90-91, Fulbright scholar, 1975-76; recipient Disting. Alumni award Gustavus Adolphus Coll., 1969. Fellow AAAS; mem. NAS, Am. Acad. Arts and Scis., Am. Chem. Soc. (Inorganic Chemistry award 1997), Am. Inst. Chemists (Chem. Pioneer award 1990), Am. Phys. Soc., Materials Rsch. Soc., Phi Kappa Phi, Sigma Xi (rsch. awards 1968, 87), Golden Key (teaching award 1986). Lutheran. Avocations: fishing, golf. Home: 2698 Roseland Ave East Lansing MI 48823-3847 Office: Mich State Univ Dept Of Chemistry East Lansing MI 48824 Office Phone: 517-355-9715 ext. 288. Business E-Mail: dye@msu.edu.

DYE, JERMAINE, professional baseball player; b. Overland, Kans., Jan. 28, 1974; Student, Cosumnes River C.C. Player Atlanta Braves, 1996-97, Kansas City Royals, 1997—2001, Oakland A's, 2001—04, Chicago White Sox, 2004—. Named to Am. League All-Star Team, MLB, 2000; recipient World Series MVP, 2005, AL Outstanding Player, Players Choice awards, 2006. Office: Chicago White Sox 333 W 35th St Chicago IL 60616

DYE, NANCY SCHROM, historian, educator, former academic administrator; b. Columbia, Mo., Mar. 11, 1947; d. Ned Stuart and Andrea Elizabeth (Ahrens) Schrom; m. Griffith R. Dye, Aug. 21, 1972; children: Molly, Michael. AB, Vassar Coll., 1969; MA, U. Wis., 1971, PhD, 1974; LittD (hon.), Obirin U., 2005. Asst. prof. U. Ky., Lexington, 1974—80, assoc. prof., 1980—88, prof., 1988, assoc. dean arts and scis., 1984—88; dean faculty Vassar Coll., Poughkeepsie, NY, 1988—92, acting pres., 1992—94; pres. Oberlin Coll., Oberlin, Ohio, 1994—2007. Author: As Equals And As Sisters, 1981; contbr. articles to profl. jours. Bd. mem. Pomona Coll. Mem.: Coun. Colls. of Art and Scis. (bd. dirs. 1980—91). Office Phone: 440-775-8400. Fax: 440-775-8937.*

DYE, ROBERT HARRIS, retired manufacturing company executive; b. NYC, Feb. 22, 1918; s. Abatha Agusta and Julia (Harris) D.; m. Tereseua Vergine, May 13, 1950; 1 child, Leslie Julie. BSEE, Purdue U., 1942. Engr. GE, Schenectady, 1942—43, 1946—47, mgr. field engr. test group Key West, Fla., 1947—49, prog. mgr. Schenectady, 1949—53; divsn. chief guidance and control Dept. of Navy, Newport, RI, 1953—56; sect. mgr. Gen. Precision Co., Little Falls, NJ, 1956—60; prog. mgr. missile Gen. Precision Co./Singer, Little Falls, 1960—87; ret., 1987. Author: Post-WWII Com Sub Pac Training Doctrine. Lt. USNR, 1942—46. Mem.: NRA, IEEE, Submarine Vet. WWII, Am. Legion. Republican. Achievements include development of procedures for mine field penetration by submarine.

DYE, STUART SELLEY, lawyer; b. Ogden, Utah, 1939; BS cum laude with honors, U. Utah, 1961; LLB, U.Va., 1967. Bar: Va. 1967, D.C. 1967. Sec. Navy staff Deep Submergence Sys. Rev. Group, Office Legis. Affairs, 1963-64; spl. asst. Law of the Sea matters internat. law divsn. Office Judge Adv. Gen., 1965-66; ptnr. Holland & Knight, Washington. Adv. bd. Latin Am. Law and Bus. Report, 1994—. Mem. editl. bd. Va. Jour. Internat. Law, 1966-67; contbg. editor Oil and Gas Regulations Analyst, 1976-82. Mem. nat. adv. coun. U. Utah, 2001--. Lt. comdr. USNR. Mem. ABA (natural resources law sect., adminstrv. law sect.), Maritime Law Assn. US (exec. com.), Maritime Adminstrv. Bar Assn., US-Mex. C. of C. (chmn., bd. dirs. 1998-04, chmn. transp. task force), Caribbean-Ctrl. Am. Action (bd. trustees, sec. 2003-), Phi Alpha Delta. Office: Holland & Knight LLP 2099 Pennsylvania Ave NW Washington DC 20006-6801 Home Phone: 301-229-7410; Office Phone: 202-457-7074. Business E-Mail: stuart.dye@hklaw.com.

DYE, THOMAS ROY, political science professor; b. Pitts., Dec. 16, 1935; s. James Clair and Marguerite Ann (Dewan) D.; m. Joan Grace Wohleber, June 29, 1957; children: Roy Thomas, Cheryl Price. BA, Pa. State U., 1957, MA, 1959; PhD, U. Pa., 1961. Asst. prof. polit. sci. U. Wis., Madison, 1962-63; asso. prof., head dept. polit. sci. U. Ga., Athens, 1963-68; prof., chmn. dept. govt. Fla. State U., Tallahassee, 1968-72, dir. policy scis., 1978-91, McKenzie prof. govt., 1991—98, prof. emeritus of polit. sci., 1998—. Vis. prof. polit. studies Bar Ilan U., Israel, 1972, U. Ariz., 1976 *Thomas R. Dye is emeritus professor of political science at Florida State University. His books have been translated into many languages, including Russian and Chinese, and published abroad. He is the recipient of the Harold Lasswell Award for career contributions to the study public policy and the Donald C. Stone Award for career contribution to the study of of American Federalism. He received the Outstanding Alumni Award in 2001 from Penn State's College of Liberal Arts. He is a frequent consultant to government agencies, private foundations, "think tanks," law firms, and other organizations in the public sector.* Author: Politics, Economics and the Public, 1966, Politics in States and Communities, 1969, 13th edit., 2007, The Irony of Democracy, 1970, 13th edit., 2005, The Politics of Equality, 1971, Understanding Public Policy, 1972, 12th edit., 2007, Power and Society, 1975, 10th edit., 2005, Who's Running America, 1976, Policy Analysis, 1976, Who's Running America-The Carter Years, 1979, Determinants of Public Policy, 1980, Who's Running America-The Reagan Years, 1983, Politics in the Media Age, 1983, Who's Running America-The Conservative Years, 1986, Power Elites and Organizations, 1987, Who's Running America-The Bush Era, 1990, American Federalism: Competition Among Governments, 1990, Politics in America, 1994, 7th edit., 2007, Who's Running America-The Clinton Years, 1994, Politics in Florida, 1998, Top Down Policymaking, 2000, Who's Running America: The Bush Restoration, 2002. 1st lt. USAF, 1961—62. Mem. Am. Polit. Sci. Assn. (sec. 1969-72), So. Polit. Sci. Assn. (v.p. 1974-75, pres. 1976-77), Phi Beta Kappa, Omicron Delta Kappa. Home: 1448 Estuary Trl Delray Beach FL 33483 Office Phone: 561-302-9233. Personal E-mail: tomrdye@aol.com.

DYEN, ISIDORE, linguistic scientist, educator; b. Phila., Aug. 16, 1913; s. Jacob and Dena (Bryzell) D.; m. Edith Brenner, June 11, 1939 (dec. 1976); children— Doris Jane, Mark Ross. BA, U. Pa., 1933, MA, 1934, PhD in Indo-European Linguistics, 1939; postgrad. Slavic, Columbia, 1938-39, Yale, 1939-40. Faculty Yale U., 1942-84, prof. Malayan langs., 1957-58, prof. Malayopolynesian and comparative linguistics, 1958-73, prof. comparative linguistics and Austronesian langs., 1973-84, prof. emeritus, 1984—, dir. grad. studies Indic and Far Eastern langs. and lit., 1960-62, Indic and Southeast Asia, 1960-66, dir. grad. studies linguistics, 1966-68; adj. prof. linguistics U. Hawaii, 1985-89; linguist Coordinated Investigation Micronesian Anthropology, Truk, 1947, Sci. Investigation Micronesia, Yap, 1949. Vis. prof. U. Padjadjaran, Bandung, 1960-61, U. Auckland, summer 1969, Australian Nat. U., fall 1971, U. Philippines, spring 1972, Inst. Study of Langs. and Cultures of Asia and Africa, Tokyo U. for Fgn. Langs., 1982-83; coordinator linguistics sect. 10th Pacific Sci. Congress, Honolulu, 1961; asso. prof. U. Chgo. and Linguistic Soc. Am. Summer Inst., 1955; prof. U. Mich. and Linguistic Soc. Am. Summer Inst., 1957; dir. SE Asia Linguistics Program, 28th Internat. Congress Orientalists, Canberra, 1971; organizing com. Conf. Genetic Lexicostatistics, New Haven, 1971; organizer 1st Eastern Conf. Austronesian Linguistics, New Haven, 1973; adv. com. 1st Internat. Conf. Comparative Austronesian Linguistics, Honolulu, 1974; mem. adv. bd. Oceanic Linguistics. Author: Spoken Malay, 2 vols., 1945, The Proto-Malayo-Polynesian Laryngeals, 1953, A Lexicostatistical Classification of the Austronesian Languages, 1965, A Sketch of Trukese Grammar, 1965, A Descriptive Indonesian Grammar, 1967, Beginning Indonesian, 4 vols., 1967, Lexicostatistics in Genetic Linguistics: Proc. of Yale Conf., 1973, (with David Aberle) Lexical Reconstruction: The Case of the Athapaskan Kinship System, 1974, Linguistic Subgrouping and Lexicostatistics, 1975, (with Guy Jucquois) Lexicostatistics in Genetic Linguistics II, 1976, (with Joseph B. Kruskal and Paul Black) An Indoeuropean Classification: A Lexicostatistical Experiment, 1992. Research fellow Slavic Am. Council Learned Socs., 1938-40; Guggenheim fellow, 1949, 64; Tri-Instl. Pacific Program grantee, 1956-57; NSF grantee, 1960-77 Mem. Linguistic Soc. Am., Am. Oriental Soc. (v.p. 1965-66), Am. Anthrop. Assn., Current Anthropology, Société de Linguistique de Paris, Koninklijk Instituut voor Taal-, Land-, en Volkenkunde, New Haven Oriental Club (pres. 1963-64, 74-76) Office: Univ Hawaii Manoa Dept Linguistics Honolulu HI 96822 also: Yale U Dept Linguistics Hall Grad Studies New Haven CT 06520 *My aim has been to further linguistic science, particularly in comparative linguistics, by research in both Austronesian and Indoeuropean languages. In large part my work has been devoted to combining traditional and mathematico-statistical methods to improve subgrouping procedures. The different interlocking roles of theory, hypothesis, and methodology have been kept to the fore throughout. I hope my research will develop strong evidence regarding the Austronesian homeland.*

DYER, BARBARA F., retired accountant, writer; b. Rockland, Maine, May 19, 1924; d. Milton Earl and Elizabeth Ayoube Dyer. Grad., LaSalle Ext. U., 1967; student, U. Maine, Thomaston, 2001. Office mgr., acct. Camden Shipbuilding Co., 1942—86; tchr. Adult Edn. Sch. Adminstrv. Dist. #28, Camden, 1987—93; freelance writer Camden, 1984—. Hist. lectr., 1984, 2004—; writer Village Soup.com, Village Soup Times, 1999—. Author: (books) Grog Ho, 1984, Vintage Views, 1987, History 1st Congregational Church, 1991, Images Camden-Rockport, 1995, Home Sweet Home, 1996, More Memories of Camden, 1997, Vessels of Camden, 1998, Streets Are Paved With Gold, 2005; contbr. articles to publs. Bd. selectmen Town Camden, Maine, 1992—95, budget com., 2003—; ind. commr. Camden Pub. Libr., Maine, 1998—2002; mem. Camden War Meml. Com., 2003—; bd. mem. Camden Area History Ctr., 2005, mem. book com., 2005, mem. oral history com., 2005; deacon First Congl. Ch., Camden, 1970—74, historian, 1985—2002, 2003—05, 200th ann. com., 2003—05. Named Paul Harris fellow, Rotary Internat., Camden, 1995, Townsperson of Yr., Camden, Lincolnville, Rockport C. of C., Camden, 1996; recipient Disting. Personal Enrichment award, Maine Adult Edn. Assn., 1993, first place/weekly award, Maine Press Assn., 1993. Mem.: Camden H.S. Alumni Assn. (com.), Camden Women's Club (charter, past pres.), Phi Theta Kappa. Republican. Avocations: knitting, crocheting, painting, swimming, dancing. Home: 11 Highland Ave Camden ME 04843-2119

DYER, CAROLYN PRICE, artist, writer; b. Seattle, Dec. 19, 1931; d. Herbert Frederick and Evelyn Ida (Nelson) Price; m. M. Clark Dyer, Sept. 7, 1954; children: Philip Nelson, Paul Clark, Andrew Mark Price. Student, U. Wash., 1949-50; BA, Mills Coll., Oakland, Calif., 1953; MA, Mills Coll., 1955. Coll. level teaching credential, Calif. Owner Stone Ct. Gallery Contemporary Art, Yakima, Wash., 1958-65, Carolyn Price Dyer Gallery, Tacoma, 1994—2006; prin. Carolyn Dyer Textiles, Pasadena, Calif., 1965-93, Tacoma, 1993—; mem. faculty LA CC, 1970-78, Pasadena Art Mus. Art Workshops, 1971-73. Freelance writer art and travel publs., 1976—; juror N.W. Craftsmen's Exhbn., Seattle, 1964, Fiber Structure Nat., Downey, Calif., 1983; curator So. Calif. Galleries, 1974, Blue Heron Ctr. Arts, Vashon, Wash., 1991, Larson Gallery, Yakima, Wash., 2007. One-woman shows include Kennedy-Douglass Ctr. Arts, Florence, Ala., 1992, Commencement Gallery, Tacoma, 1995, 01, Two Walls Gallery, Vashon, Wash., 2007; group exhbns. include multiple West Coast galleries/mus., 1985-2005, Meadows Gallery, Denton, Tex., 2006-07, Nordic Heritage Mus., Seattle, 2006-07, Hallie Ford Mus. Art, Silverton, Oreg., 2006-07, Northwind Arts Ctr., Wash., 2006-07; represented in numerous pvt. and corp. collections; contbg. editor: Fiberarts mag., 1978-93; editor: (newsletter) Lineup, 1978-89. Bd. dirs. Pasadena Art Alliance, 1981-87, Pasadena Arts Coun., 1977-79. Recipient Gold Crown award Pasadena Arts Coun., 1982; Trustee scholar Mills Coll., 1950-53, Grad. fellow, 1953-55. Mem. Am. Craft Coun., Northwest Designer Craftsmen, Tapestry Artists of Puget Sound, Calif. Fibers, Textile Soc. Am., Am. Tapestry Alliance, Tacoma Art Mus., Sigma Kappa. Achievements include research in textiles, carpets, antique and contemporary. Office: PO Box 13013 Burton WA 98013-0013 E-mail: cpricedyer@msn.com.

DYER, CHARLES ARNOLD, lawyer; b. Blairstown, Mo., Aug. 29, 1940; s. Arnold and Mary Charlotte (West) D.; children: Kristine, Erin, Kathleen, Kerry. BJ, U. Mo., 1962; JD, U. Calif., 1970. Bar: Calif. 1971, U.S. Supreme Ct. 1976. Ptnr. Dyer & White, Menlo Park, Calif.; judge Pro Tem Mcpl. and Superior Ct., San Mateo County, Calif., Pro Tem Superior Ct., Santa Clara County, Calif., arbitrator, mediator. Lectr. in field. Bd. dirs. Boys Club of San Mateo, 1971-83, pres., 1975; mem. exec. coun. Boys Clubs of Bay Area, 1977-83; mem. Dem. Nat. Fin. Com., 1978. Served to capt. USNR, 1963-93, ret. Mem. State Bar Calif., San Mateo County Bar Assn., Santa Clara County Bar Assn., Palo Alto Bar Assn., Consumer Attys. Calif., Consumer Attys. San Mateo County, Assn. Atty. Mediators, Trial Lawyers Pub. Justice, Am. Bd. Trial Advs., Nat. Bd. Trial Advocacy. Roman Catholic. Office: Dyer & White 800 Oak Grove Ave Menlo Park CA 94025-4477 Office Phone: 650-325-7000.

DYER, CHARLES RICHARD, law library director, educator; b. Richmond Heights, Mo., Aug. 20, 1947; s. Helmuth Kinner and Sue Anne (Stone) D.; m. Cecelia Ann Duncan, Dec. 20, 1969 (div. June 1982); m. Roberta Sharlyn Monroe, June 2, 1984; 1 child, Christina L. Floyd. BA, U. Tex., 1969, JD, 1974, MLS, 1975; MA, Northwestern U., 1971. Bar: Tex. 1974. Assoc. law libr., asst. prof. law St. Louis U., 1975-77; law libr., assoc. prof. U. Mo., Kansas City, 1977-87; dir. librs. San Diego County Pub. Law Libr., 1987—. Cons. in field. Editor Law Libr. Jour., 1972-74. Centre City adv. com. City of San Diego, 2000—02; chair relocation appeal bd. City of San Diego Redevel. Agy., 2001—05. Mem. Am. Assn. Law Librs., Mid-Am. Assn. Law Librs (sec.-treas. 1976-78), Southwestern Assn. Law Librs. (v.p. 1981-82, pres. 1982-83), So. Calif. Assn. Law Librs. (mem. exec. bd. 1991-93), Coun. Calif. County Law Librs. (pres. 1998-2000). Democrat. Unitarian Universalist. Office: San Diego County Pub Law Libr 1105 Front St San Diego CA 92101-3904 Home: 808 E Maple St Bellingham WA 98225-5225 Office Phone: 619-531-3904. Business E-Mail: cdyer@sdcpll.org.

DYER, COLIN, real estate services executive; BSc in Mech. Engring., Imperial Coll., London; MBA, INSEAD, Fontainebleau, France. Client mgr. McKinsey & Co., Amsterdam, 1978—82; mng. dir. GDL Cortaulds Textiles plc, 1982, CEO, 1996—2000; founding CEO WorldWide Retail Exch., 2000—04; pres., CEO, bd. dirs., chmn. global exec. com. Jones Lang LaSalle, 2004—. Non-exec. dir., chmn. audit com. No. Foods plc. Office: Jones Lang LaSalle 200 E Randolph Dr Chicago IL 60601 Office Phone: 312-228-2430. Office Fax: 312-228-0980.*

DYER, CROMWELL ADAIR, JR., lawyer, legal association administrator; b. St. Louis, Sept. 9, 1932; (parents Am. citizens); s. Adair and Tompie Leora (Giles) Dyer; m. Margaret Copeland Peickert, June 12, 1958 (div. Aug. 1976); children: Gretchen, Jack, Julie, Stephen; m. Susan Aynesworth, Aug. 20, 1977; stepchildren: Carol Godso, Amanda McDonough, Donnella Railsback. BA, U. Tex., 1954; JD, 1961; LLM, Harvard U., 1971. Bar: Tex. 1961, U.S. Dist. Ct. (no. dist.) Tex. 1965, U.S. Ct. Appeals (5th cir.) 1965, U.S. Dist. Ct. (ea. dist.) Tex. 1966, U.S. Ct. Appeals (11th cir.) 1982, U.S. Ct. Appeals (9th cir.) 1999, U.S. Dist. Ct. (we. dist.) Tex. 2003. Law clk. FTC, Washington, 1960; assoc. Branscomb, Gary, Thomasson & Hall, Corpus Christi, Tex., 1961-62; staff atty. So. Union Gas Co., Dallas, 1962-64; assoc. Dedman & May, Dallas, 1964-65, White, McElroy & White, Dallas, 1965-67; pvt. practice, 1967-73, Tex., 1997—; sec. Hague (The Netherlands) Conf. Pvt. Internat. Law, 1973-78, 1st sec., 1978-93, dep. sec. gen., 1993-97; observer, cons. to intergovtl. orgns., 1976-97. Lectr. Asser Coll. Europe, 1992—96, Sch. Law U. Calif., Davis, Brigitte M. Bodenheimer Meml. Lecture Family, 1996; moderator Common Law Jud. Conf. Internat. Child Custody, Washington, 2000; mem. US dels. Spl. Commn. on Internat. Child Abduction, 2001, 06; condr. seminars. Honoree of symposium Globalization of Child Law The Role of the Hague Conventions, 1999; co-author: Report on Trusts and Analogous Institutions, 1982; contbr. articles to profl. jours. Mem. adv. com., faculty internat. kidnapping program Nat. Jud. Coll., Reno, 2003; faculty mem. Internat. Parental Abduction Course, Reno, 2004; juror award diploma in internat. law Hague Acad., 1980, 1984—87, 1991, 1994—96, dir. studies, 1985, instr. unfair competition in pvt. internat. law, 1988. Ensign USN, 1954, lt. (j.g.) USNR, 1957. Named hon. mem., Mexican Acad. Pvt. Internat. and Comparative Law; recipient Leonard J. Theberge award. Mem.: ABA (chair com. on internat. family law 2002—03, co-chair 2003—04, law sect. internat. law and practice 2000—, Leonard J. Theberge award for pvt. internat. law), Internat. Law Assn. (Am. br.), Inter-Am. Bar Assn., Internat. Bar Assn., Assn. Louis Chatin pour la Def. des Droits de l'Enfant (Paris), Internat. Soc. Family Law, Dallas Bar Assn., Austin Bar Assn., Am. Fgn. Law Assn., Acad. Mexicana de Derecho Internacional Privado y Comparado (hon.), Club du jeudi (The Hague) (pres. 1983—85). Office: PO Box 30020 Austin TX 78755-3020 Office Phone: 512-343-7899. Personal E-mail: adairdyer@austin.rr.com.

DYER, CYNTHIA MYERS, college librarian, archivist; b. Camp Lejeune, NC, June 26, 1955; d. Louis B. and Shirley (Shimon) Myers; m. Grant E. Dyer, Nov. 24, 1984; children: Katherine Elizabeth, Sarah Caroline BA, U. Iowa, Iowa City, 1977, MLS, 1978. Tech. svcs. libr. Simpson Coll., Indianola, Iowa, 1978-83, coll. libr., 1983—, prof., 2001—. Program co-chmn. Iowa Gov.'s Pre-White House Conf. on Librs., 1990-91. Pres. Simpson Guild, Indianola, 1995-96, mem. exec. bd., 1998-2000; Big Brothers Big Sisters, Warren County; spkr. on AIDS, 1992—; chmn. various libr. adv. coms., 1986—, Women's History Month, 1990-91, 96; tri-chmn. Campus Capital Campaign, 1990; v.p. Indianola Music Boosters, 2002; mem. Indianola Sch. Bd., 2001—, v.p. 2005-06, pres. 2006-; exchange officer, Rotary Youth; elder Presbyn. Ch. Recipient Indianola/Simpson Cmty. Svc. award, Indianola C. of C., 1998, Better Boardsmanship award of achievement, IASB, 2003. Mem. ALA, Iowa Libr. Assn. (acad. and rsch. librs. conf. planner 1979, 82, 95, exec. bd. dirs. 1984-86, 88-90, pres. 1989, nominating com. 1991-93, strategic planning com. 1993, chmn. strategic planning 2003-05, editl. com. mem.), Iowa Libr. Assn. Found. (v.p. 1990-92, pres. 1993-94, chair continuity com. 1995, LEAD campaign 1997), Iowa Pvt. Acad. Librs. (chmn. 1986, panelist 1993, cmty. adv. bd. chair 1996-98), PEO (spkr. state projects 2002), Warren County Leadership Inst., Phi Beta Kappa, Phi Beta Mu, Epsilon Sigma, Delta Gamma. Democrat. Presbyterian. Office: Simpson Coll Dunn Libr 508 N C St Indianola IA 50125 Home Phone: 515-961-2104; Office Phone: 515-961-1519. Business E-Mail: cyd.dyer@simpson.edu.

DYER, DAVID F., apparel company executive; B in Engring., Vanderbilt U. Various Burdines, Miami, 1972-89; from mng. dir. coming home catalog to v. chmn. merchandising Lands' End, Inc., Dodgeville, Wis., 1989-93, v. chmn. merchandising and sales, 1993-94, pres., CEO, 1998—2002; pres., COO Home Shopping Network, 1994-97; catalog/retail cons. Tex. Pacific Group, San Francisco, 1997—98, J. Crew Group, NYC, 1997; CEO Lands' End, 1998—2003; pres., CEO Tommy Hilfiger Corp., 2003—. Dir. ADVO, Inc.; bd. dirs. Lands' End. Office: Tommy Hilfiger Corp 9 F Novel Industrial Bldg 850-870 Lai Chi Kok Rd Cheung Sha Wan Hong Kong Address: Tommy Hilfiger Corp 25 W 39th St New York NY 10018 Office Phone: 212-840-8888, 852 2216 0668.

DYER, EDWARD JAMES, public utilities commissioner; b. St. Joseph, Mo., Dec. 9, 1937; m. Shari Dyer; children: Jim, Andy, Matt. BA in English, Benedictine Coll., 1959; BA in Career Counseling, Fort Lewis Coll., 1986. Commd. ensign USN, 1959; transfer to USMC, 1964, advanced through grades to Lt. Col., 1975, served in Vietnam 3yrs Vietnam, commd. field artillery battery and battalion, 1979, ret.; sales mgr. Power Motive Corp., 1979—86; rep. Colo. House Rep., 1986—98; Colo. Senate, 1999—2001; commr. Colo. Dept. Regulatory Agys., Denver, 2001—. Mem. various coms. Colo. House Rep.; chmn. Senate Agrl.

Natural Resources Com. Coach Youth Soccer, Youth Baseball; active local campaigns. Decorated 3 Bronze Stars with V USMC, Soldier's medal; Toll fellow, 1988. Avocations: reading, walking, crossword puzzles. Office: Colo Dept Regulatory Agencies PUC 1580 Logan St OL2 Denver CO 80203

DYER, HUGH NELSON, III, management company owner; b. Troy, NY, Dec. 8, 1942; s. Hugh Nelson Dyer, Jr. and Jean Foster Dyer; m. Kathleen Johnston Dyer, Aug. 29, 1970; children: Hugh Nelson IV, William Robert, Kathleen Caird. BS, U. Vt., Burlington, 1964; MS, U. So. Calif., LA, 1971. Sect. mgr. Avon Products, Inc., Monrovia, Calif., 1970—74; fin. mgr. subcontracts Hughes Helicopters, Culver City, Calif., 1974—79; mgr. program planning & control Princeton Plasma Physics Lab., NJ, 1979—89; owner Am. Mgmt. Co., Belle Mead, NJ, 1989—. Dir. RPM Sys., Inc., Poulsbo, Wash. Co-chair Vets. Meml. Com., Montgomery Twp., NJ, 1985—. Lt. USN, 1965—70. Mem.: Beverly Yacht Club. Republican. Presbyterian. Avocations: antique automobiles, sailing. Home and Office: American Management Co 15 Bunker Dr Belle Mead NJ 08502

DYER, IRA, ocean engineering educator, consultant; b. NYC, June 14, 1925; s. Charles and Frieda (Griffman) D.; m. Betty Ruth Schanberg, Sept. 4, 1949; children: Samuel S., Debora J. SB, MIT, 1949, SM, 1951, PhD, 1954. V.p. Bolt Beranek & Newwman Inc., Cambridge, Mass., 1951-70; prof. ocean engring. MIT, Cambridge, 1971-89, Weber Shaughness prof., 1989-96, head dept., 1971-81, dir. MIT Sea Grant program, 1973-75, Robert Bruce Wallace lectr., 1982-83, emeritus prof., 1996—. Vis. fellow Cambridge (Eng.) U., 1979-80; cons. Oasis Inc., Lexington, Mass., 1988—; advisor U.S. Dept. Def., Washington, 1988—, Am. Inst. Physics, N.Y.C., 1988-91 Contbr. over 100 articles to sci. jours. With USAAF, 1944-45. Recipient Meritorious Pub. Svc. award USCG, 1979. Fellow AAAS, IEEE (disting. tech. award 1982), ASME (Per Bruel gold medal 2002), Acoustical Soc. Am. (pres. 1986-87, Lindsay award 1960, gold medal 1996); mem. NAE, Marblehead Yacht Club Avocation: sailing.

DYER, JAMES HAROLD, JR., language educator; b. Christiansburg, Va., Mar. 23, 1946; s. James Harold and Dorothy Louise (Bennett) Dyer. BA in English, Augusta Coll., 1970; MEd in English Edn., Ga. State U., 1975, EdS in English Edn., 1978; PhD in Brit. Lit., U. S.C., 1992. Cert. secondary sch. tchr. S.C. English tchr. Aiken (S.C.) HS, 1975-79; prof. English Ga. Mil. Coll., Ft. Gordon, 1979—2000; prof. grad. English, grad. English MEd program coord. Troy U., Augusta, Ga., 2002—. Grad. tchg. asst. U. S.C., Columbia, 1982—83. Mem.: MLA, Acad. Am. Poets, Children's Lit. Assn., Dickens Fellowship, Lambda Iota Tau (Saul Bellow hon. pres.). Avocations: book collecting, chess, golf. Office: Troy U Dept Grad English 2743 Perimeter Pky Ste 201 Augusta GA 30909 Office Phone: 866-557-8617. Personal E-mail: jimdyer2@netzero.net.

DYER, JAMES MASON, JR., investment company executive; b. Corsicana, Tex., Sept. 22, 1928; s. James Mason Sr. and Tabby (Jackson) D.; m. Lorelle Wright, Dec. 29, 1954; children: James Mason IV, Diane Dyer Campbell. BBA, U. Tex., 1950. V.p. J. M. Dyer Co., Corsicana, 1954-77, pres., 1977—87; nmg. ptnr. J.M. Dyer Co., Corsicana, 1987—; pres. The Piccolo Co., Corsicana, 1988—. 1st lt. US Army, 1952—54, ETO. Episcopalian. Office: JM Dyer Co PO Box 620 Corsicana TX 75151-0620 Office Phone: 903-874-4735.

DYER, JOSEPH WENDELL, retired naval officer; b. Murphy, NC, Mar. 2, 1947; s. Joseph Wendell Sr. and Margaret (Kale) D. BSChemE, N.C. State U., Raleigh, 1969; MS in Fin. Mgmt., Naval Post Grad. Sch., Monterey, Calif., 1981. Commd. ensign USN, 1969, advanced through grades to vice admiral, 2000; test pilot USN Naval Air Test Ctr, Patuxent River, Md., 1976-80; sys. integrator USN, China Lake, Calif., 1982-84, Commanding Officer Plant Rep. Office Melbourne, Australia, 1984-87, dep. program mgr. F/A-18 program Washington, 1988-90, AX airplane chief engr., 1990-91, exec. asst. to comdr. naval air sys. command, 1991-92, navy's chief test pilot Patuxent, Md., 1992-93, mgr. F/A 18 program Washington, 1993-97; comdr. Naval Air Warfare Ctr., Aircraft Divsn., 1997—2000; asst. comdr. for rsch. and engring. Naval Air Sys. Command, 1997-2000, comdr. naval air sys. command, 2000—03; ret. USN, 2003; gen. mgr., exec. v.p. govt. and indsl. divsn. iRobot Corp., Burlington, Mass., 2003—06, pres. govt. and indsl. divsn., 2006—. Chair aeroispace safety adv. panel NASA. Contbr. articles to profl. jours. Decorated DSM USN; recipient Acquisition Excellence award, US Dept. Def., J.H. Doolittle award, 2001. Fellow Soc. Exptl. Test Pilots, Nat. Acad. Pub. Adminstrn. Achievements include leading DOD's first counter stealth, tactical data-fusion effort. Avocation: sailing. Office: iRobot 63 South Ave Burlington MA 01803 Personal E-mail: dyerjoseph2@aol.com. Business E-Mail: jdyer@irobot.com.

DYER, RAYMOND B., diagnostic radiology physician; MD, U. Va., 1977. Diplomate Diagnostic Radiology Am. Bd. Radiology, Ariz., 1981. Prof. radiology and urology Wake Forest U. Sch. Medicine, Winston-Salem, NC, 1991—. Contbr. articles to sci. jours. Fellow: Soc. Uroradiology, Am. Coll. Radiology. Office: Wake Forest U Sch Med Medical Center Blvd Winston Salem NC 27157 Home Phone: 336-716-2471; Office Phone: 336-716-2471. Office Fax: 336-716-0555. Business E-Mail: rdyer@wfubmc.edu.

DYER, SUSAN KRISTINE, editor, librarian; b. Coos Bay, Oreg. d. Stanley Keith and Betty Loray (Jameson) Dyer; m. Michael E. Gehringer. BA, U. Oreg., 1967, MLS, 1968; MBA, Golden Gate U., 1983. Libr. Morrison & Foerster, San Francisco, 1968-75, info. and gen. svcs. mgr., 1975-80; law libr., records mgr. Thelen, Marrin, Johnson & Bridges, San Francisco, 1980-83; libr. World Bank Sectoral Libr., Washington, 1984-89; ops. mgr. Faxon Co. Fed. Divsn., Herndon, Va., 1989-90, dir., 1990-92, nat. sales mgr. fed., 1992-94; fed. ops. mgr. EBSCO Industries, Springfield, Va., 1994-95, gen. mgr., 1995—2000; sr. editor Am. Assn. of U. Women, Washington, 2000—07. Author: Manual of Procedures for Private Law Libraries Supplement, 1984, Friends of Torpedo Factory Ann. Report, 2001. Bd. dirs. Miriam's Kitchen, Washington, 1986—88, Friends of the Torpedo Factory art Ctr., 2000—02. Mem.: ALA, DC Libr. Assn., Spl. Librs. Assn., N.Am. Serials Interest Group, Am. Assn. Law Librs. (editor Recruitment Checklist 1974, newsletter editor 1976—79, pres. Western Pacific chpt. 1977—79, exec. bd. 1979—82).

DYER, WAYNE WALTER, psychologist, writer, radio and television personality; b. Detroit, May 10, 1940; s. Melvin L. and Hazel I. (Vollick) D.; m. Marcelene Louise Dyer; children: Tracy, Stephanie, Skye, Sommer, Serena, Sands Jay, Saje Eykis. BS, Wayne State U., 1965, MS in Counseling and Ednl. Psychology, 1966, EdD in Counseling and Psychology, 1970. Tchr. and counselor Pershing H.S., Detroit, 1965-67; instr. counselor edn. Wayne State U., Detroit, summer, 1970, 71, 72, 73; dir. guidance and counseling Mercy H.S., Farmington, Mich., 1967-71; staff cons. and trainer guidance and sch. psychol. personnel Half Hollow Sch. Dist., Huntington, N.Y., 1973-75; staff cons. Drug Info. and Svc. Ctr., N.Y., 1972-74, Herman Kiefer Hosp., Detroit, 1974-75; mem. tchg. faculty North Shore U. Hosp. divsn. Cornell U. Med. Coll., Manhasset, N.Y., 1974-75; pvt. practice counseling and psychotherapy Huntington, N.Y., 1973—; asst. prof. counselor edn. St. John's U., Jamaica, N.Y., 1971-74; assoc. prof., 1974-77. Over 4000 appearances on TV and radio shows and programs including Phil Donohue Show, Tonight Show, Dinah Shore Show, Merv Griffin Show, Mike Douglas Show, Good Morning America, Canada A.M., Oprah Winfrey Show, numerous other talk shows in every state; radio host for: Kathryn Crosby Show, San Francisco, At Your Service program, Sta. KMOX, St. Louis.; Author: (with John Vriend) Counseling Effectively in Groups, 1973, Counseling Techniques That Work, 1974, 2d edit., 1977, Group Counseling for Personal Mastery, 1980, Your Erroneous Zones, 1976 (Literary Guild selection, Psychology Today Book Club selection, also 4 others), Pulling Your Own Strings, 1977, 1978 (Lit. Guild main selection, also 6 others), The Sky's the Limit, 1980 (Lit. Guild selection); novel Gifts from Eykis, 1983, What Do You Really Want for Your Children?, 1985, Happy Holidays, 1986, You'll See It When You Believe It, 1988, Real Magic, 1992, Everyday Wisdom, 1994, Your Sacred Self, 1995, Staying on the Path, 1995, A Promise is a Promise, 1996, Manifest Your Destiny, 1997, Wisdom of the Ages, There's A Spiritual Solution To Every Problem, 2000, The Power of Intention: Learning to Co-create Your World Your Way, 2004, Change Your Thoughts - Change Your Life, 2007; cassette tape series The Wit & Wisdom of Dr. Wayne W. Dyer, 1977, How To Be a No-Limit Person, 1981, Secrets of the Universe, Choosing Your Own Greatness, What Do You Really Want for Your Children?, Transformation: You'll See It When You Believe It, The Awakened Life, others; contbr. chpts. on counseling to books on psychology, numerous articles on psychology to popular mags. and articles on counseling to profl. jours.; producer tape recordings on counseling techniques; audio cassette program Secrets of the Universe. Served with USN, 1958-62. Named Disting. Alumni of Yr., Wayne State U., 1980; recipient Golden Gavel award Internat. Toastmasters, 1987.*

DYER, WILLIAM EARL, JR., retired newspaper editor; b. Kearney, Nebr., May 15, 1927; s. William Earl and Hazel Maud (Hosfelt) D.; m. Betty M. Meisinger, June 26, 1967; children: Lee Michael, Scott William. BA, U. Nebr., 1949. Reporter Nebr. City Daily News Press, 1943-44; reporter, copy editor The Lincoln Star, Nebr., 1948-50, city editor, 1951-60, exec. editor, 1960-92. Pres. Nebr. AP Editors, 1964. Author: Headline: Starkweather, 1993. Pres. Lincoln Unitarian Ch., 1962-63; state chmn. Nebr. We Shake Hands Indian Project, 1958-60; mem. Nebr. Adv. Com. on Indian Law Enforcement, 1960-62; mem. State Adv. Com. to Welfare Dept., 1970-73, 80-84. With AUS, 1945-46. Named hon. mem. Omaha Indian Tribe. Mem. Open Forum Club, Phi Beta Kappa, Sigma Delta Chi. Democrat. Home: 247 N 56th St West Lincoln NE 68504 Office: Jour-Star Printing Co PO Box 81609 926 P St Lincoln NE 68508-3615 E-mail: dyers@inebraska.com.

DYER-RAFFLER, JOY ANN, retired special education diagnostician, educator; b. Stiltner, W.Va., Aug. 10, 1935; d. Ralph William and Hazel (Terry) Dyer; m. John William Raffler, Sr., Jan. 1, 1993; 1 child from a previous marriage, Keith Brian DeArmond. BA, U. N.C., Chapel Hill, 1969; MEd in Secondary Edn., U. Ariz., Tucson, 1974, MEd in Spl. Edn., 1976. Cert. spl. edn.-learning disabilities, art edn., spl. edn.-emotionally handicapped. Art educator Tucson Unified Sch. Dist., Tucson, 1970-75, tchr. spl. edn., 1975-89, diagnostician spl. edn., 1989—2003, tchr. exceptional edn., 2003—05; ret., 2005. Den mother Cub Scouts Am., Raleigh, N.C., 1968-69. Recipient grant Tucson Unified Sch. Dist., 1977. Mem.: Ariz. Edn. Assn. Avocations: painting, skiing, birdwatching, weightlifting, jogging. Home: 1781 S Desert Vista Dr Tucson AZ 85748

DYESS, BOBBY DALE, lawyer; b. Waxahachie, Tex., Jan. 27, 1935; s. Robert Olin and Rubie Lee (Odom) D.; m. Janet Lee Hassell, Jan. 30, 1960 (dec. 1973); children: Robert Dale, Jonathan David, Julianna Whitfield; m. Sharon Erwin Saylor, June 6, 1974. BA, U. N. Tex., Denton, 1956; JD, So. Meth. U., Dallas, 1959. Bar: Tex. 1959. Ptnr. Elliott, Churchill, Hansen, Dyess & Maxfield, 1965-82, DeHay & Blanchard, 1983-92, Payne & Blanchard, Dallas, 1992—. Chmn. bd. Rainbow Sound, Inc., 1975-85; dir. edn. found. Waxahachie Ind. Sch. Dist., 2004—, vice chair, 2006—. Editor: Bests, Life and Health Ins. Edit., 1973-85. Mem. bd. mgmt. East Dallas YMCA, 1970, 1976, campaign chmn., 1976, chmn. bd. mgmt., 1977—79; chief Indian Guides, 1971; chmn. Cub Scout pack com. Boy Scouts Am., 1970; vice chair Baylor Med. Ctr., Waxahachie, Tex., 2004—05, chmn. bd. trustees, 2005—; bd. dirs. Waxahachie Found., 1999—2003. Mem.: Am. Counsel Assn. (membership chmn. 1976, pres. 1979—80, sec.-treas. 1984—87, membership chmn. 1996—98), Coll. State Bar Tex. (dir. 1996—, chmn. 1999—2001), Scribes (bd. dirs. 1976), Am. Soc. Legal Writers, Dallas Bar Found. (charter), Tex. Bar Assn. Presbyterian. Home: 110 Magnolia Dr Waxahachie TX 75165 Office: Payne and Blanchard 500 N Tower Plz of America Dallas TX 75201 Office Phone: 972-938-1181. Personal E-mail: bdyess@247365.com.

DYK, TIMOTHY BELCHER, federal judge; b. Boston, Feb. 14, 1937; s. Walter and Ruth (Belcher) Dyk; m. Inga Shirer, June 18, 1960 (div. 1970); children: Deirdre, Caitlin; m. Sally Katzen, Oct. 31, 1981; 1 child, Abraham Benjamin. AB, Harvard U., 1958, LLB magna cum laude, 1961. Bar: DC, NY. Law clk. to Justices Reed and Burton US Supreme Ct., Washington, 1961—62, law clk. to Chief Justice Earl Warren, 1962—63; spl. asst. to asst. atty. gen. US Dept. Justice, Washington, 1963—64; assoc. Wilmer Cutler & Pickering, Washington, 1964—69, ptnr., 1969—90, Jones, Day, Reavis and Pogue, Washington, 1990—2000; judge US Ct. Appeals (Fed. cir.), 2000—. Adj. prof. Georgetown U. Law Ctr., Washington, 1983, Washington, 86, Washington, 89, Washington, 91, U. Va. Law Sch., Charlottesville, 1984—85, Charlottesville, 1987—88, Yale U. Law Sch., 1986—87, 1989; pres. The Edward Coke Appellate Inn of Ct., 2000—02. Mem.: Harvard Law Rev., 1959—61; contbr. articles to profl. jours. Office: US Court Appeals Fed Cir 717 Madison Pl NW Ste 915 Washington DC 20439 Office Phone: 202-633-8200.*

DYKAS, MATTHEW J., psychologist; b. Stoughton, Mass., Mar. 5, 1978; s. Michael and Donna Dykas; m. Annalise Dykas, Aug. 10, 2001; children: Craig, Brett, Leah. BA, Fairfield U., Conn., 2000; MA, U. Md., College Park, 2003, PhD, 2006. Asst. project dir. Adrienne Kirby Family Literacy Project, Bridgeport, Conn., 1999—2000; rsch. assoc. Md. Child and Family Devel. Lab., U. Md., 2000—06; rsch. fellow Family Rsch. Lab., U. NH, Durham, 2006—07; asst. prof. psychology SUNY, Oswego, 2007—. Posdoctoral Rsch. fellows in family violence, NIMH, 2006—07. Mem.: APA, Soc. Rsch. Child Devel., Alpha Sigma Nu, Sigma Xi, Phi Beta Kappa.

DYKE, CHARLES WILLIAM, retired army officer; b. Covington, Ga., July 28, 1935; s. John William and Chessie Belle (Burke) D.; m. Hedwig Friederike Adam, Dec. 1958 (div. 1979); children: Michael Alexander, Eva Joyce, Charles Martin, Robert William; m. Nancy Jeanne Bearg, June 22, 1980 (div. 2002); children: Sarah Claire, Rachel Anne; m. Ann Stouffer Bisconti, Oct. 13, 2002. BA in History, U. So. Miss., 1963; MMil Arts and Sci., U.S. Army Command and Gen. Staff Coll., 1967; MA in Internat. Rels., George Washington U., 1968; postgrad., U.S. Army War Coll., 1970—71; postgrad. in polit. sci., Shippensburg State Coll., 1970—71. Enlisted U.S. Army, 1954-55, commd. 2d lt., 1955, advanced through grades to lt. gen., 1985, exec. officer 1st Brigade, 101st Airborne Divsn. Vietnam, 1968, comdr. 2d Bn., 327th Inf., 1968-69, G1, later G3, 101st Airborne Divsn., 1969-70, exec. asst. Ops. Directorate J3 Orgn. Joint Chiefs of Staff Washington, 1971-72, asst. sec. of gen. staff Office Chief of Staff, 1972-73, mil. asst., later exec. to sec. of army the Pentagon, 1973-75, comdr. 1st Brigade, 101st Airborne Divsn. Ft. Campbell, Ky., 1975-76, asst. divsn. comdr. 3d Inf. Divsn. Germany, 1976, exec. to supreme allied comdr. Europe Belgium, 1977-78, dir. internat. standardization for NATO Hdqs. Dept Army Washington, 1978-79, vice dir. J3, later vice dir. joint staff Orgn. Joint Chiefs of Staff, the Pentagon, 1979-82, dep. chief staff for ops. Europe, 1982-83, comdg. gen. 8th Inf. Divsn. (Mech), 1983-85, comdr. Japan/IX Corps, 1985-88, ret., 1988; exec. advisor Aerospace divsn. Mitsubishi Corp., Tokyo, 1988—; chmn., CEO Internat. Tech. and Trade Assocs. Inc., Washington, 1989—. Mem. NATO Indsl. adv. group, 1999—2004, vice chmn., 2001—04. Decorated D.S.M. with oak leaf cluster, Silver Star with oak leaf cluster, Def. Superior Svc. medal, Legion of Merit with 3 oak leaf clusters, Soldiers medal, Bronze Star with V device and 2 oak leaf clusters, Joint Svc. Commendation medal, Army Commendation medal with 4 oak leaf clusters, Air medal (19), Purple Heart, U.S. Presdl. Unit citation, Joint Chiefs of Staff and Army Gen. Staff indentification badges, Combat Infantry Badge, others, also various fgn. decorations including Japanese Order of Rising Sun (2d class) with gold and silver stars. Mem. Assn. U.S. Army, 101st Airborne Divsn. Assn., Army Aviation Assn., Nat. Def. Indsl. Assn., USAF Assn., Armed Forces Comm. and Electronics Assn., Pen and Sword Assn., Nat. Beta Club, Pi Gamma Mu, Phi Alpha Theta. Office: Internat Tech and Trade Assocs Inc 2120 L St NW Ste 400 Washington DC 20037-1527 Office Phone: 202-828-2614 ext. 601. Business E-Mail: cdyke@itta.com.

DYKEMAN, ALICE MARIE, public relations executive; b. Fremont, Nebr., May 18; d. Cecil Victor and Dorothy Lillian (Sillik) Jansen; divorced; children: David Clair, Cinda Cecille Dykeman Nordgren. Pub. relations dir. Meth. Hosp., Dallas, 1961-72; regional pub. info. officer Small Bus. Adminstrn., Dallas, 1972-74; owner Dykeman Assocs. Inc., Dallas, 1974—. Adj. prof. U. Dallas Grad. Sch. Mgmt., Irving, Tex. 1972-78; guest lectr. numerous Univs., and seminars; mem. pub. rels. com. Dallas/Ft. Worth Fed. Exec. Bd., 1973, mem. minority bus. opportunity com., 1974; mem. Gov.'s Coun. on Small Bus., Tex., 1980-81, 500, Inc., 1982-90; chmn. export coun. pub. affairs task force U.S. Dept. Commerce, 1980-83. Contbr. articles to bus., health care and pub. rels. jours. Mem. fgn. visitors com. Dallas Coun. on World Affairs, 1992-98, Dallas Pub. Health Bd., 1972-74, Dallas Urban Rehab. Stds. Bd., 1981-83, Econ. Devel. Adv. Bd., City of Dallas, 1983-86; pres. Concerned Citizens for Cedar Springs, 1982-2006; bd. dirs. Oak Lawn Forum, 1983-92; mem. exec. com. Oak Lawn Com., 1983-95. Recipient Matrix award Women in Comm., Dallas, 1968, 88, Lifetime Achievement award Religion Communicators Coun., 2004. Fellow Pub. Rels. Soc. Am. (accredited, chmn. S.W. dist. 1971-72, bd. dirs. North Tex. chpt. 1966-72, pres. 1969, assembly del. 1970-73, 91, Norm Teich award for contbns. to pub. rels. 2004); mem. North Dallas Fin. Forum (pres. 1991), Nat. Assn. Women Bus. Owners, North Dallas C. of C. (bd. dirs. 1980-82, chmn. networking skills workshop 1990—), co-founder Breakfast Dallas 1994—), Press Club Dallas (bd. dirs. 1981-83, headliner 4 times), SMU Mustang Club (bd. dirs. 1996-99). United Methodist. Office: Dykeman Assocs Inc 4115 Rawlins St Dallas TX 75219-3661 Office Phone: 214-528-2991. Business E-Mail: adykeman@airmail.net.

DYKEN, MARK LEWIS, JR., neurologist, educator; b. Laramie, Wyo., Aug. 26, 1928; s. Mark L. and Thelma Violet (Achenbach) D.; m. Beverly All, June 8, 1951; children: Betsy Lynn, Mark Eric, Julie Suzanne, Amy Luise, Andrew Christopher, Gregory Allen. BS in Anatomy and Physiology, Ind. U., 1951, MD, 1954. Diplomate Am. Bd. Psychiatry and Neurology. Intern Indpls. Gen. Hosp., 1954-55; resident in neurology Ind. U. Med. Ctr., 1955-58; clin. dir., dir. rsch. New Castle (Ind.) State Hosp., 1958-61; asst. dept. neurology Ind. U., 1958-61, assoc. prof. neurology, 1964-69, prof., 1969—, chmn. dept. neurology, 1971-94, prof. emeritus, 1994—. Chmn. profl. adv. coun. Nat. Easter Seal Soc., 1974-82; cons., chmn. panel on rev. neurol. devices subcom. FDA, 1979-83; bd. dirs. Am. Bd. Psychiatry and Neurology, 1988-96, pres., 1995. Editor-in-chief Stroke, 1992-2000; contbr. numerous articles on topics including cerebral vascular disease, blood flow, epilepsy, electroencephalography, muscle disease, to profl. jours. With U.S. Army, 1946-48. Recipient numerous grants in cerebrovascular disease. Fellow ACP; mem. AMA, Am. Assn. Univ. Profs. Neurology (pres. 1986-88), Epilepsy Found. Am., Am. Heart Assn (chmn. stroke coun. 1984-86, v.p. for sci. couns. 1988-89), Ind. Neurol. Assn. (charter pres. 1966-68), Am. Acad. Neurology, Am. Neurol. Assn., Sigma Xi, Alpha Omega Alpha. Home: 7406 W 92nd St Zionsville IN 46077-9103 Office: Ind U Med Ctr Neurol Dept 545 Barnhill Dr EM124 Indianapolis IN 46202 Home Phone: 317-873-4211; Office Phone: 317-278-2340. E-mail: mdyken@aol.com.

DYKES, ARCHIE REECE, finance company executive; b. Rogersville, Tenn., Jan. 20, 1931; s. Claude Reed and Rose (Quillen) Dykes; m. Nancy Jane Haun, May 29, 1953; children: John Reece, Thomas Mack. BS cum laude, East Tenn. State U., 1952, MA, 1956; EdD, U. Tenn., 1959. Prin., Church Hill (Tenn.) HS, 1955-58; supt. Greeneville (Tenn.) Schs., 1959-62; prof. edn., dir. Ctr. Advanced Grad. Study Edn. U. Tenn., 1962-66, chancellor Martin, 1967-71, Knoxville, 1971-73, U. Kans., 1973-80; chmn., pres., CEO Security Benefit Group Cos., Topeka, 1980-88; chmn. Capital City Holdings Inc., 1988—. Chmn. bd., CEO, Fleming Cos., Inc., Dallas; chmn. bd. dirs. Pepsi Amns., Inc.; bd. dirs. Raytech Corp., Midas, Inc., Arbor Realty Trust, Inc.; trustee Keene Industries Trust, NYC, Kans. U. Endowment Assn., Raytech Corp. Trust, NYC. Author: School Board and Superintendent, 1965, Faculty Participation in Academic Decision Making, 1968. Vice chmn. Commn. Operation U.S. Senate, 1975—76; mem. Nat. Adv. Coun. Edn. Professions Devel., 1975—76; trustee Truman Libr. Inst., 1973—80, Nelson Art Gallery, 1973—80, Menninger Found., 1982—88, Dole Found., William Allen White Found.; mem. bd. regents State of Kans., 1982—86; mem. adv. commn. U.S. Army Command and Gen. Staff Coll., 1974—79, chmn., 1978—79; chmn. bd. trustees U. Mid.-Am., 1978—79; mem. consultative bd. regents U. Qatar, 1979—80. Named Outstanding Alumnus, E. Tenn. State U., 1970; Ford Found. fellow, 1957—59, Am. Coun. Edn. Postdoctoral fellow, U. Ill., 1966—67. Mem.: Kans. Assn. Commerce and Industry (bd. dirs. 1975—82), Nat. Assn. State Univs. and Land Grant Colls. (coun. pres. 1971—80), Am. Coun. Life Ins. (bd. dirs. 1981—86), Tenn. Coll. Assn. (pres. 1969—70), Newcomen Soc. N.Am., Phi Kappa Phi. Home: 2102 W 116TH St Leawood KS 66211-2953

DYKES, OSBORNE JEFFERSON, III, lawyer; b. LA, Dec. 3, 1944; s. Osborne J. Jr. and Frances (Fox) D.; m. Ann Dennis, Dec. 29, 1973; children: Barbara Nell, Osborne J. IV. BA, Stanford U., 1966, MA, 1968; JD, U. Tex., 1972. Bar: Tex. 1973, U.S. Supreme Ct. 1977, U.S. Ct. Appeals (5th cir.) 1973, U.S. Ct. Appeals (11th cir.) 1981, U.S. Dist. Ct. (so. dist.) Tex. 1975, U.S. Dist. Ct. (ea. dist.) Tex. 1976, U.S. Dist. Ct. (no. dist.) Tex. 1994. Law clk. to Hon. Homer Thornberry U.S. Ct. Appeals 5th Cir., Austin, Tex., 1972-73; ptnr. Fulbright & Jaworski, Houston, 1973—. Contbr. articles to profl. publs. With U.S. Army, 1969-71. Fellow Am. Bar Found., Tex. Bar Found. (life), Houston Bar Found. (life); mem. ABA (chmn. property ins. law com. 1983-84, tort and ins. practice sect.), Fed. Bar Assn. (v.p. South Tex. chpt. 2005), Energy Bar Assn., Bar Assn. of Fifth Fed. Cir., Am. Bd. Trial Advs., Tex. Assn. Civil and Appellate Trial Specialists (pres. 2002-2003). Republican. Episcopalian. Avocation: bicycling. Home: 5135 Holly Terrace Dr Houston TX 77056-2125 Office: Fulbright & Jaworski 1301 Mckinney St Houston TX 77010-3031 Office Phone: 713-651-5545. Personal E-mail: jdykes@fulbright.com.

DYKES, RONALD MITCHELL, retired telecommunications industry executive; BSEE, Auburn U., 1969; MBA, Emory U., 1981; MS in Mgmt., Stanford U., 1986. With Southern Bell, Atlanta, 1971-83; dir. fin. mgmt. BellSouth Corp., Atlanta, 1983-85; asst. to the pres., dir. bus. and fin. planning BellSouth Ent., Atlanta, 1986-88, v.p. fin., 1988-93; v.p., contr. BellSouth Corp., Atlanta, 1993-95, CFO, 1995—2005; dir. Cingular Wireless. Trustee St. Joseph's Health Sys. With Signal Corps. US Army, 1969—71. Sloan fellow Stanford U., 1985-86 Office: Bellsouth Corp 1155 Peachtree St NE Ste 2008 Atlanta GA 30309-3610 E-mail: ron.dykes@bellsouth.com.

DYKEWICZ, MARK STEVEN, physician; b. Flint, Mich., May 21, 1955; s. Richard Alfred and Evelyn Ellen Dykewicz; m. Lenora-Marya Anop. BS, U. Mich., 1977; MD, St. Louis U., 1981. Resident medicine Northwestern U. Med. Sch., Chgo., 1981-84, fellow allergy-immunology, 1984-86, asst. prof. medicine, 1986-90; asst. prof. internal medicine St. Louis U. Med. Sch., 1990—94, assoc. prof., 1994—2002, prof., 2002—, dir. allergy immunology postgrad. tng. program. Mem. pulmonary allergy drug adv. com. FDA, 1999—2003, chmn., 2001—03; bd. dirs. Am. Bd. Allergy and Immunology, 2004—. Lead editor: Joint Task Force Practice Parameters on Rhinitis, 1998—. Recipient Disting. Svc. award, Am. Coll. Allergy, Asthma and Immunology, 1999. Fellow ACP, Am. Coll. Chest Physicians, Am. Acad. Allergy-Immunology; mem. Am. Thoracic Soc., Am. Acad. Allergy, Asthma and Imunology (chmn. com. on occupl. lung disease 1998-2000, chmn. com. on adverse reactions to drugs and biols. 2001-03, chmn. com. on rhinitis 2004-05, Spl. Recognition award 1999) Office: St Louis U Med Sch 1402 S Grand Blvd #R209 Saint Louis MO 63104-1004 Business E-Mail: dykewicz@slu.edu.

DYKSTRA, DAVID ALLEN, real estate broker; b. Kalamazoo, Feb. 5, 1938; s. Alle and Elizabeth (VanderHorst) D. m. Kathryn Ann DeNio, Aug. 4, 1962 (div. Nov. 1985); children: Brian Thayer, Kristen Lee, Holly Beth. BBA, Western Mich. U., 1966. Pres. Dyco Corp., Portage, Mich., 1970—; realtor Crossroads Real Estate, Kalamazoo, 1994-96, Callander Woollam & Britigan Comml. Realtors, Portage, Mich., 1996-2000, Exit Gulder Real Estate, Naples, Fla., 2000—02, VR Bus. Brokers, Naples, 2002—. Cons. Waste Industry, Mich., 1976-82; owner Dairy World Yogurt Shops. Bd. dirs. Portage C. of C., 1980-83, econ. devel. com.; alt. del. Rep. Conv., Mich., 1984; adv. bd. Naples Christian Chamber, 89.5FM; exec. bd. dirs. Parkinson Assn. SW Fla. Mem.: Beacon Club, Safari Club Internat. (bd. dirs. Ft. Myers/Naples chpt.). Republican. Avocations: hunting, golf. Home: 2068 Crestview Way Naples FL 34119-3306 Office: VR Bus Brokers 5311 Strand Blvd Naples FL 34110 Home Phone: 239-596-7396; Office Phone: 239-207-1151. Home Fax: 239-596-7622. Personal E-mail: ddykstra@swfla.rr.com.

DYKSTRA, DAVID CHARLES, management executive, consultant, accountant, author, educator; b. Des Moines, July 10, 1941; s. Orville Linden and Ermina (Dunn) Dykstra; m. Susan Ogden, Aug. 18, 2001; children from previous marriage: Suzanne, Karin, David S. BSChemE, U. Calif., Berkeley, 1963; MBA, Harvard U., 1966. CPA, Calif. Corp. controller Recreation Environs., Newport Beach, Calif., 1970-71, Hydro Conduit Corp., Newport Beach, 1971-78; v.p. fin. and adminstrn. Tree-Sweet Products, Santa Ana, Calif., 1978-80; pres., owner Dykstra Cons., Irvine, Calif., 1980-88, Marcer Island, Wash., 1998—. Pres. Easy Data Corp., 1981-88; pub. Easy Data Computer Comparisons, 1982-87; sr. mgr. Deloitte & Touche, Costa Mesa, Calif., 1988-90; prof. mgmt. info. sys. Nat. U., Irvine, 1984-90; pub. Dykstra's Computer Digest, 1984-90; pres., owner Golden West Pers., Long Beach, Wash., 1992-93; exec. v.p. Tegris Corp., Bellevue, Wash., 1994-98. Author: Manager's Guide to Business Computer Terms, 1981, Computers for Profit, 1983; contbr. articles to profl. jours. Chmn. 40th Congl. Dist. Tax Reform Immediately, 1977-80; mem. nat. com. Rep. Com.; vice-chmn. Orange County Calif. Rep. Assembly, 1979-80; bd. dirs. Corona Del Mar Rep. Assembly, 1980-94, v.p., 1980-87, pres., 1987-89; mem. Mercer Island Presbyn. Ch., 1998—. Mem. AICPA, Am. Mgmt. Assn., Calif. Soc. CPAs, Data Processing Mgmt. Assn., Am. Prodn. and Inventory Control Soc., Ind. Computer Cons. Assn., Internat. Platform Assn., Data Processing Mgmt. Assn., Orange County C. of C., Newport Beach C. of C., Harvard U. Bus. Sch. Assn. Orange County (bd. dirs. 1984-90, v.p. 1984-86, 87-88, pres. 1986-87, 91-92, chmn. 1993-94), Harvard U. Bus. Sch. Assn. So. Calif. (bd. dirs. 1986-87, 91-92, v.p. 1992-93), Harvard U. Bus. Sch. Assn. Puget Sound, Town Hall, Mercer Island Presbyn. Ch., Mercer Island Country Club, John Wayne Tennis Club, S. Cowichan Lawn Tennis Club, Lido Sailing Club, Columbia Tower Club, Rotary (bd. dirs. 1984-86). Home and Office: 3465 W Mercer Way Mercer Island WA 98040-3355

DYKSTRA, DENNIS DALE, physiatrist; b. Lakewood, Ohio, Feb. 21, 1950; s. Gerald and Grace Maire (Thomas) D.; m. Mary Louise Kerker, May 16, 1992; children: Dorothy, Perry, Caitlin, Patrick. AB in Zoology summa cum laude, Ohio U., 1972; MD, U. Cin., 1976; PhD, U. Minn., 1988, M in Health Adminstrn., 1999. Diplomate Am. Bd. Pediatrics, Am. Bd. Phys. Medicine and Rehab. Intern/resident Cin. Children's Hosp., 1976-81; instr. U. Minn., Mpls., 1981-88, asst. prof., 1988-92, assoc. prof. phys. medicine/rehab./pediatrics/urol. surgery, 1992—, head dept. phys. medicine/rehab., 1992—; assoc. chief staff for rehab. VA Med. Ctr., Mpls., 1994-97. Author: Krusen's Handbook of Phys. Medicine and Rehabilitation, 1991; contbr. articles to profl. jours. Med. advisor Minn. Spasmodic Torticolits Soc., Duluth, Minn., 1991—. Recipient Phys. Med. and Rehab. Investigator award Phys. Med. and Rehab. Rsch. Found., 1984, 85; Spinal Cord Soc. grantee, 1990. Fellow Am. Acad. Phys. Med. and Rehab. (chair edn. com. 1996—), Am. Acad. Pediatrics, Am. Assn. Electrodiagnostic Medicine. Achievements include 2 patents on method of apparatus for mechanical stimulation of nerves, method and device for pharmacological control of spascticity. Office: Univ Minn 420 Delaware St SE Box 297 Mayor Bldg Minneapolis MN 55455 Office Phone: 612-626-5399.

DYKSTRA, GRETCHEN, not-for-profit developer; b. SI, NY, Aug. 22, 1948; d. Franz and Jean Dykstra; m. Nathan Leventhal, Feb. 12, 1993. BA, U. Wis.; MEd, PhD, Bank St. Coll. Edn. Founding pres. Times Square Bus. Improvement Dist., NYC, 1992—98; with Rockefeller Found., Edna McConnell Clark Found.; commr. NYC Dept. Consumer Affairs, 2002—05; pres., CEO World Trade Ctr. Meml. Found., 2005—06. Bd. dirs. Save the Children.

DYKSTRA, PAUL HOPKINS, lawyer; b. Chgo., July 13, 1943; s. Paul C. and Frances Marie (Hopkins) D. Student, Exeter Coll. Oxford U., Eng., 1964; AB, Princeton U., 1965; LLB, Yale U., 1968. Bar: Ill. 1968, D.C. 1977. Assoc. Gardner, Carton & Douglas, Chgo., 1968-74, ptnr., 1975—2003, ptnr. Washington office, 1977-79, fin. ptnr., 1985-89, chmn., 1989-95; mem. Bell, Boyd & Lloyd LLC, Chgo., 2003—. Adj. prof. law Northwestern U. Sch. Law, 2001—. Contbr. articles to profl. jours. Trustee Chgo. Theatre Group, Inc. (Goodman Theatre), 1975—, pres., 1983-85, vice chmn., 1988-92, pres., 1992-97; mem. aux. bd. Art Inst. Chgo., 1973-77, 79-88, exec. com., 1976-77, 82-87, 2000—; chmn. Orange and Black Club of Princeton Club of Chgo., 1987-90; chmn. maj. gifts Princeton U. Class of 1965, 1982-85; mem. cultural affairs adv. bd. City of Chgo., 1990-2003, Blue Skies for Kids, Chgo. Cmty. Trust, Chgo. Pub. Libr. Bd., 1991-97, chmn. adminstrn. and fin. com., 1996—; trustee Chgo. Pub. Libr. Found., 1999—. Mem. ABA (fed. and regulation of securities com.), Chgo. Bar Assn. (sec. 1976-77), Chgo. Hist. Soc. (trustee 1999—, mem. Making History awards com. 1994—, chmn. 2000-2002), Econ. Club of Chgo. (reception com. 1982-85), Legal Club of Chgo., Law Club Chgo., Racquet Club of Chgo. (bd. govs., vice chmn. membership com. 1980-83), Chgo. Club (bd. dirs., sec. 1996-2000), Shoreacres, Chgo. Commonwealth Club, The Comml. Club of Chgo. (sec., mem. exec. com. 2001-03), Chgo. Coun. Fgn. Rels. (Chgo. com.). Episcopalian. Avocations: travel, golf, bicycling. Office: Gardner Carton Douglas 191 N Wacker Dr Chicago IL 60606-1698 Office Phone: 312-781-6029. E-mail: pdykstra@bellboyd.com.

DYKSTRA, ROBERT, retired education educator; b. Vesper, Wis., Feb. 26, 1930; s. John and Anna (Holstein) D.; m. Lou Ann Conselman, Oct. 6, 1956; children: S. Kim, Paul, Randall. BS in Elem. Edn., U. Wis., River Falls, 1957; MA in Ednl. Psychology, U. Minn., 1959, PhD in Ednl. Psychology, 1962. Cert. elem. edn. Elem. tchr. Cedar Grove (Wis.) Pub. Sch., 1954-55; asst. prof. U. Minn., Mpls., 1962-64, assoc. prof., 1965-69, prof., 1970-73, chair dept. curriculum and instrn., 1974-85, prof., 1986-93, ret., 1993. Co-author: Teaching Reading, 1974, Language Arts: Teaching and Learning Effective Use of Language, 1988; contbr. articles to profl. jours. With US Army, 1952—54. Recipient Disting. Alumnus award U. Wis./River Falls, 1998; elected to Reading Hall of Fame, 1996; U.S. Office Edn. rsch. grantee, 1963, 65. Mem. Nat. Coun. Tchrs. of English (mem. exec. com. 1969-71), Nat. Conf. on Rsch. in English (pres. 1984-85), Twin City Area Reading Coun. (pres. 1990-91), Internat. Reading Assn. (mem. pub. com. 1975-77), Nat. Reading Conf. (mem. pub. com. 1978-80). Lutheran. Avocations: barbershop quartet singing, reading, golf. Home: 1998 16th St NW Saint Paul MN 55112-5555 Personal E-mail: bolo19@netzero.com.

DYKSTRA, WILLIAM DWIGHT, management executive, consultant; b. Grand Rapids, Mich., June 15, 1927; s. John Albert and Irene (Staplekamp) D.; m. Ann McGuiness, Nov. 2, 1957 (dec. 1988); children: William Hugh, Mary Irene. AB, Hope Coll., 1949; MBA, Ind. U., 1951. Asst. mgr. Ply-Curves, Inc., 1950; originator magnesium metal furniture, 1951; pres. Dwignt Corp., 1952-56, W.D. Dykstra Group, Grand Rapids, 1956—. Pres. Burton L. Norton Co., 1990, Tie Life Care, Inc.; bd. dirs. Sheldon Co., Orchard Machine Co. Author: Management and the 4th Estate, New Profits for Management. George F. Baker Scholar selector; elder Dutch Ref. Ch. Recipient Outstanding Furniture Merit award, 1955, Vehicle Color Design award, 1967, P.I.A. Graphic award, 1971, Am. Advt. Fedn. award, 1971, 73, 76, Disting. Entrepreneur Alumnus award Ind. U., 1983. Mem. Am. Econs. Assn., Am. Inst. Graphic Arts (Packaging award 1965, 67), Acad. Polit. Sci., Am. Mktg. Assn. (Mktg. Man of Yr. 1981), Engring. Soc. of Detroit, Soc. Packaging and Handling Engrs., Rotary, Phi Kappa Psi, Pi Kappa Delta. Home: 1145 Edison Ave NW Grand Rapids MI 49504-3919 Office: Old Tallmadge Grange Hall 01845 Leonard St NW Grand Rapids MI 49534-9510

DYKSTRA LYNCH, MARY ELIZABETH, library and information scientist, educator; b. Phila., May 21, 1939; arrived in Canada, 1964; d. Edward and Marietta R. (Kuiper) Heerema: m. Michael F. Lynch, Aug. 12, 1995; children from previous marriage: Mark Edward, Jeffrey Garth. BA, Calvin Coll., 1960; MLS, Dalhousie U., 1970; PhD, Sheffield U., 1986. Head cataloguer Dalhousie U. Libr., Halifax, Nova Scotia, Canada, 1970—74; asst. prof. Sch. Libr. Svc. Dalhousie U., 1974—78, assoc. prof., 1978—82, assoc. prof. Sch. Libr. and Info. Studies, 1983—86, dir. Sch. Libr. and Info. Studies, 1986—95, prof., 1987—97, prof. emeritus, 1997—. Sr. audiovisual libr. Nat. Film Bd. of Can., Montreal, 1982-83l mem. adv. bd. Sch. Health Records Sci., Halifax Infirmary, 1984-97, Libr. Technician Programme, Kings Regional Vocat. Sch., N.S., 1987-90; mem. Can. Commn. on Cataloguing, 1986-94; mem. working group on stds. for subject access Nat. Archives of Can., 1987-93; mem. Can. Adv. Com. for Internat. Orgn. for Standardization, Tech. Commn., Info. and Documentation, 1991—; mem. nat. info. highway adv. coun. of Can., 1994-95, 96-97; rsch. officer U. Sheffield (Eng.), 1996-97; cons. in field Author: Access to Film Information, 1977, Precis: A Primer, 1985; editor 2 books, several film catalogues; editl. bd. Film Canadiana, 1982-84, Cataloging and Classification Quar., 1980-86, Expert Sys. for Info. Mgmt., 1990-93, Libr. and Info. Sci. Rsch., 1992-96; series editor, occasional papers Sch. Libr. and Info. Studies Dalhousie U., 1986-94; contbr. articles to profl. jours. Pres. Citadel North Neighbourhood Assn., Halifax, 1988; bd. dirs. CANARIE (Canadian Network for Advancement of Rsch., Industry & Edn.), 1996-98, internat. consultants com. World Info. and Comm. Report, UNESCO, Paris, 1998-99, Biblioteca nazionale centrale, Florence, Italy, 2001. Rsch. grantee Dalhousie U., 1976, 80, 90, 96, Social Scis. and Humanities Rsch. Coun., Ottawa, 1987-90. Mem. Can. Libr. Assn. (rep. Can. com. on cataloguing 1986-94), Nova Knowledge, Internat. Soc. for Knowledge Orgn. Office Phone: 902-494-3656. E-mail: m.lynch@sheffield.ac.uk.

DYLAN, BOB (ROBERT ALLEN ZIMMERMAN), singer, musician; b. Duluth, Minn., May 24, 1941; s. Abe Zimmerman and Beatrice Rutman; m. Sara Rowndes, Nov. 22, 1965 (div. June 19, 1977); children: Jakob, Jesse, Samuel, Anna, Maria; m. Carolyn Y. Dennis, June 4, 1986 (div. Oct. 1992); 1 child, Desiree Gabrielle. Self-taught on guitar, piano, autoharp, harmonica; student, U. Minn., 1960; Mus D (hon.), Princeton U., 1970. Musician: (albums) Bob Dylan, 1962, The Freewheelin' Bob Dylan, 1963, The Times They Are A-Changin', 1964, Another Side of Bob Dylan, 1964, Bringing It All Back Home, 1965, Highway 61 Revisited, 1965, Blonde on Blonde, 1966, John Wesley Harding, 1967, Bob Dylan's Greatest Hits, 1967, Nashville Skyline, 1969, Self Portrait, 1970, New Morning, 1970, Bob Dylan's Greatest Hits, Vol. 2, 1971, Dylan, 1973, Planet Waves, 1974, Blood on Tracks, 1975, Desire, 1976, Hard Rain, 1976, Street Legal, 1978, Masterpieces, 1978, Slow Train Coming, 1979 (Grammy award for Best Male Rock Vocal Performance for "Gotta Serve Somebody", 1980), Bob Dylan At Budokan, 1979, Saved, 1980, Shot of Love, 1981, Infidels, 1983, Real Live, 1984, Empire Burlesque, 1985, Biograph, 1985, Knocked Out Loaded, 1986, Down In The Groove, 1988, Oh Mercy, 1989, Under the Red Sky, 1990, The Bootleg Series, Vols. 1-3: (Rare and Unreleased 1961-1991), 1991, Good as I Been to You, 1992, World Gone Wrong, 1993 (Grammy Award for Best Traditional Folk Album, 1994), Bob Dylan's Greatest Hits, Vol. 3, 1994, MTV Unplugged, 1995, Time Out of Mind, 1997 (Grammy Award for Album of Yr., 1998, Grammy Award for Best Contemporary Folk Album, 1998, Grammy Award for Best Male Rock Vocal Performance for "Cold Irons Bound", 1998), The Best of Bob Dylan, 1997, The Bootleg Series, Vol 4: The Royal Albert Hall Concert, 1998, Essential Bob Dylan, 2000, The Best of Bob Dylan, Vol. 2, 2000, The Very Best of Bob Dylan, 2000, Love and Theft, 2001 (Grammy Award for Best Contemporary Folk Album, 2002), The Bootleg Series, Vol. 5, Live 1975, The Rolling Thunder Revue, 2002, The Bootleg Series, Vol. 6: Live 1964, 2004, The Bootleg Series, Vol. 7: No Direction Home: The Soundtrack, 2005, Live at the Gaslight 1962, 2005, Modern Times, 2006 (Grammy award for Best Contemporary Folk Album, Best Solo Rock Vocal Performance, 2007); musician: (with various artists) The Concert for Bangladesh, 1971 (Grammy Award for Album of Yr., 1973), Bob Dylan 30th Anniversary Concert Celebration, 1993; musician: (with The Band) Before the Flood, 1974, The Basement Tapes, 1976; musician: (with Grateful Dead) Dylan and the Dead, 1988; musician: (with Traveling Wilburys) Traveling Wilburys Vol. 1, 1988 (Grammy Award for Best Rock Performance by a Duo or Group with Vocal, 1990), Traveling Wilburys Vol. 3, 1990; musician: (soundtracks) Pat Garrett and Billy the Kid, 1973, The Last Waltz, 1976, Wonder Boys, 2000 (Acad. Award for Best Original Song for "Things Have Changed", 2001), Masked and Anonymous, 2003; composer: (songs) Like a Rolling Stone; dir., editor (films) Eat the Document, 1972; appeared in: (documentaries) Don't Look Back, 1967; No Direction Home, 2005; actor: (films) Pat Garret and Billy the Kid, 1973, Hearts of Fire, 1987; actor, composer, dir., editor, writer (films) Renaldo and Clara, 1978, actor, composer, writer Masked and Anonymous, 2003; actor: (TV films) The Madhouse on Castle Street, 1963; author: Tarantula, 1971, Writings and Drawings, 1973, Tarantula: Poems, 1994, (book of sketches) Drawn Blank, 1994, (memoirs) Chronicles, Vol. 1, 2004 (Quills award-biography/memoir, 2005). Named to Rock and Roll Hall of Fame, 1988; recipient Lifetime Achievement Award, Grammy Awards, 1991, Prince of Asturias Arts award, Prince of Asturias Found., 2007. Achievements include devising and popularizing folk-rock. Office: Columbia Records 550 Madison Ave New York NY 10022-3211*

DYLESKI-NAJJAR, DEBRA, lawyer; BA summa cum laude, Wellesley Coll., 1980; JD summa cum laude, Boston U., 1983. Bar: Mass. 1983, NH 1989, US Dist. Ct. (Mass.) 1984, US Dist. Ct. (NH) 1989, US Ct. Appeals (1st cir.) 1984, US Supreme Ct. 2000. Assoc. Peabody & Brown, Boston, 1983—84, Choate, Hall & Steward, Boston, 1984—89; ptnr. Wiggin & Nourie, PA, Manchester, NH, 1989—96, Hinckley, Allen & Snyder, Boston, 1997—2005; of counsel Friedman & Atherton, Boston, 1996—97; ptnr. The Wagner Law Group, P.C., Boston, 2005—. Chmn. labor and employment group Wiggin & Nourie, PA, NH, 1989—96; bd. mem. Zoning Bd. Appeals City of Lawrence, 1998—2000, sec., 1999—2000; lectr. Lorman Bus. Enterprises, Nat. Bus. Inst., Coun. Edn. Mgmt. Contbr. articles to profl. jours. Mem. Austin Prep. Adv. Coun., 2001—04; bd. dirs. Women's Bus. Ctr., Inc., 2005—07, vice chair, 2005—07; bd. dirs. Hospice Care Inc., 2005—; alumnae com. Leadership NH, 2004—. Named one of N.H. Leading Employment Law Attys., N.H. Edits., 1994, N.H. Emerging Leaders, Leadership N.H., 2004—05, Top 10 Women Attys. Mass., Women's Bus. Mag., 2005, Am.'s Leading Lawyers, Chambers U.S. Guide, 2005, Mass. Super Lawyers, 2006; Charles A. Rome scholar, 1983. Fellow: Coll. Labor and Employment Lawyers; mem.: ABA, ATLA (assoc.), Soc. Human Resources Mgmt., Nat. Assn. Coll. and U. Attys., N.H. Bus. and Industry Assn. (human resource com. 1989—2005), N.H. Bar Assn. (chmn. labor and employment sect. 1993—94, continuing legal edn. com. 2001—, liaison, moderator ann. labor and employment update program 2001—), Mass. Bar Assn., Labor and Employment Sect., Merrimack Valley C. of C., Phi Beta Kappa. Office: The Wagner Law Group PC 99 Summer St Boston MA 02111 Office Phone: 617-357-5200. Office Fax: 617-357-5250.

DY-LIACCO, GABRIEL S., psychotherapist, social sciences educator; AB in Psychology, Ateneo de Manila U., Quezon City, Philippines, 1993; MS in Pastoral Counseling, Loyola Coll., 1999, PhD in Pastoral Counseling, 2006. Cert. Nat. Bd. Cert. Counselors Md., lic. clin. profl. counselor 2002, Va. lic. profl. counselor, 2006. Adult and adolescent psychotherapist Key Point Health Svcs., Inc., Catonsville, Md., 1999—2004; doctral rsch. fellow dept. pastoral counseling Loyola Coll., Columbia, Md., 2002—03, tchg. asst. dept. pastoral counseling, 2003—04, rsch. asst. dept. psychology, 2004—05, asst. prof. dept. pastoral counseling, 2007—; asst. prof. Sch. Psychology and Counseling Regent U. Grad. Ctr., Alexandria, Va., 2005—07; therapist Pastoral Counseling and Consultation Ctr. Greater Washington, Washington, Saint Luke Inst. Patient care monitor Key Point Health Svcs., Inc., Catonsville, Md., 2003—04, clin. peer trainer, 2003—04, clin. internship supr., 2002—03; individual clin. supr. Pastoral Counseling Dept., Loyola Coll. in Md., Columbia, Md., 2002—03; mem. editl. adv. bd. Scientific Jours. Internat. Contbr. articles and revs. to profl. jours.; translator: (Tagalog version) Spiritual Transcendence Scale. Vol. Parish Pastoral Coun. for Responsible Voting, Quezon City, Philippines, 1992, SJ Prison Ministry, Muntinlupa, Metro Manila, Philippines, 1989—90; mem. Arvisu Ho. SJ Prenovitiate, Quezon City, Philippines, 1989—91. Recipient William James award, Coun. on Spiritual Practices, 2005. Mem.: APA (exec. com. divsn. 36 2006—07), Am. Counseling Assn., Am. Mental Health Counselors Assn. (clin. mem.), Profl. Assn. Diving Instrs. (life; dive master (inactive) 1989—), Chi Sigma Iota (founding chpt. faculty advisor U. Washington), Alpha Sigma Nu. Avocations: scuba diving, travel. Office Phone: 410-617-7620, 443-538-4987. Business E-Mail: gdyliacco@loyola.edu.

DYLLA, H. FREDERICK, science administrator, physicist; b. 1949; BS in Physics, MS in Physics, MIT, 1971, PhD in Physics, 1975. Mem. rsch. staff surface physics br./PLT and PDX projects Princeton U. Plasma Physics Lab., 1975—78, mem. rsch. staff I, 1975—77, mem. rsch. staff II, 1977—80, supr. vacuum preparation lab./PLT and PDX projects, 1978—81, rsch. physicist, 1980—85, head vacuum ops. sect./TFTR project, 1981—86, prin. rsch. physicist, 1985—90, head physics ops. br./TFTR project, 1986—90; mgr. Free Electron Laser prog., mgr. tech. devel. and transfer Thomas Jefferson Nat. Accelerator Facility, US Dept. Energy, Newport News, Va., 1990—2007, head superconducting RF tech. dept., 1991—94; exec. dir., CEO Am. Inst. Physics, College Park, Md., 2007—. Adj. prof. physics and applied sci. Coll. William and Mary, 1990—; mem. governing bd. Am. Inst. Physics, 2004—, mem. corp. assocs. adv. com., mem. com. on pub. policy, chair Physics Today adv. com. Contbr. articles to sci. jours. Fellow: Am. Phys. Soc., Am. Vacuum Soc.; mem.: Optical Soc. Am., Materials Rsch. Soc. Office: Am Inst Physics One Physics Ellipse College Park MD 20740-3843 Office Phone: 301-209-3131.*

DYM, CLIVE LIONEL, engineering educator; b. Leeds, Eng., July 15, 1942; came to U.S., 1949, naturalized, 1954; s. Isaac and Anna (Hochmann) D.; children: Jordana, Miriam; m. Joan Dym, June 28, 1998. BCE, Cooper Union, 1962; MS, Poly. Inst. Bklyn., 1964; PhD, Stanford U., 1967. Asst. prof. SUNY, Buffalo, 1966-69; assoc. professorial lectr. George Washington U., Washington, 1969; research staff Inst. Def. Analyses, Arlington, Va., 1969-70; assoc. prof. Carnegie Mellon U., Pitts., 1970—74; vis. assoc. prof. TECHNION, Israel, 1971; sr. scientist Bolt Beranek and Newman, Inc., Cambridge, Mass., 1974-77; prof. U. Mass., Amherst, 1977-91, head dept. civil engring., 1977-85; Fletcher Jones prof. engring. design Harvey Mudd Coll., Claremont, Calif., 1991—, dir. Ctr. Design Edn., 1995—, chair dept. engring., 1999—2002. Vis. sr. rsch. fellow Inst. Sound and Vibration Rsch., U. Southampton, Eng., 1973; vis. scientist Xerox PARC, 1983-84; vis. prof. civil engring. Stanford U., 1983-84, Carnegie Mellon U., 1990; Eshbach vis. prof. Northwestern U., 1997-98, U. So. Calif., 2004; cons. Bell Aerospace Co., 1967-69, Dravo Corp., 1970-71, Salem Corp., 1972, Gen. Analytics Inc., 1972, ORI, Inc., 1979, BBN Inc., 1979, Avco, 1981-83, 85-86, TASC, 1985-86, D.H. Brown Assocs., 1991, Johnson Controls, 1996; vice chmn. adv. bd. Amerinex Artificial Intelligence, 1986-88. Author: (with I.H. Shames) Solid Mechanics: A Variational Approach, 1973, Introduction to the Theory of Shells, rev. edit. 1990, Stability Theory and Its Applications to Structural Mechanics, 1974, 2002, (with E.S. Ivey) Principles of Mathematical Modeling, 1980, (with I.H. Shames) Energy and Finite Element Methods in Structural Mechanics, 1985, (with R.E. Levitt) Knowledge-Based Systems in Engineering, 1990, Engineering Design: A Synthesis of Views, 1994, Structural Modeling and Analysis, 1997, (with P. Little) Engineering Design: A Project-Based Introduction, 1999, 2d edit., 2004, (with P.D. Cha and J.J. Rosenberg), Fundamentals of Modeling and Analyzing Engineering Systems, 2000, Principles of Mathematical Modeling, 2nd edit., 2004; editor: (with A. Kalnins) Vibration: Beams, Plates, and Shells, 1977, Applications of Knowledge-Based Systems to Engineering Analysis and Design, 1985, Computing Futures in Engineering Design, 1997, Designing Design Education for the 21st Century, 1999, (with L. Winner) Social Dimensions of Engineering Design, 2001, Designing Engineering Education, 2003, Artificial Intelligence for Engring. Design Analysis and Mfg., 1986-96; contbr. articles and tech. reports to profl. publs. NATO sr. fellow in sci., 1973; Boeing Outstanding Engring. Educator award (first-runnerup), 2001. Fellow Acoustical Soc. Am., ASME (Ruth and Joel Spira Outstanding Design Educator award 2004), ASCE (Walter L. Huber rsch. prize 1980), ASEE (Western Electric Fund award 1983, Fred Merryfield Design award 2002, Archie Higdon Disting. Educator award 2006). Jewish. Office: Harvey Mudd Coll Engring Dept 301 E 12th St Claremont CA 91711-5901 Office Phone: 909-621-8853.

DYMALLY, MERVYN MALCOLM, retired congressman; b. Cedros, Trinidad, W.I., May 12, 1926; s. Hamid A. and Andreid S. (Richardson) D.; m. Alice M. Gueno; children: Mark, Lynn. BA in Edn., Calif. State U., 1954; MA in Govt., Calif. State U., Sacramento, 1970; PhD in Human Behavior, U.S. Internat. U., 1978; LLD (hon.), U. W. L.A., 1970; JD (hon.), Lincoln U., Sacramento, 1975; LLD (hon.), Calif. Coll. Law, 1976; HLD (hon.), Shaw U., NC, 1981; PhD (hon.), Calif. Western. U., 1982; LLD (hon.), Lincoln U., San Francisco, 1984, Fla. Meml. Coll., 1987. Cert. elem., secondary and exceptional children tchr. Tchr. L.A. City Schs., 1955-61; coord. Calif. Disaster Office, 1961-62; mem. Calif. Assembly, 1962-66, 2002—, Calif. Senate, 1967-74; lt. gov. Calif., 1975-79; mem. 97th-102nd Congresses from 31st Calif. dist., 1981-92; pres. Dymally Internat. Group Inc., Inglewood, Calif., 1992—. Mem. Com. on Fgn. Affairs and its subcoms. on Internat. Ops., chmn. subcom. on Africa, 1989-92; mem. Com. on D.C. and chmn. subcom. on judiciary and edn., 1981-92; chmn. Congl. Task Force on Minority Set Asides, 1987-92; chmn. Senate Majority Caucus, Senate Select Com. on Children and Youth; chmn.

Senate coms. on mil. and vets. affairs, social welfare, elections and reapportionment, subcom. on med. edn. and health needs; chmn. joint coms. on legal equality for women, on revision of election code; chmn. assembly com. on indsl. rels.; current mem. Congl. Hispanic Caucus, Congl. Caucus Women's Issues, Congl. Human Rights Caucus, Congl. Black Caucus and chmn. of its task force on Caribbean; chmn. Caribbean Action Lobby, Caribbean Am. Rsch. Inst.; founder Congl. Inst. for Space, Sci. and Tech., chmn. adv. bd.; past chmn. Calif. Commn. Econ. Devel., Commn. of Califs. (U.S., Baja Calif., Calif. Sur, Mex.); past vice chmn., Nat. Conf. Lt. Govs.; former Gov.'s designee U.S. Border States Commn.; past mem. State Lands Commn., others; lectr. Claremont (Calif.) Grad. Sch., Golden Gate U., Sacramento, Pepperdine U., L.A., Pomona (Calif.) Coll., U. Calif., Davis, Irvine, Whittier (Calif.) Coll., Shaw U., Raleigh, N.C.; Disting. prof. Ctrl. State U.; mem. faculty Drew U. Medicine and Sci.; adj. prof. Compton Coll.; cons. to chancellor L.A. C.C. Author: The Black Politician-His Struggle for Power, 1971; co-auhtor: (with Dr. Jeffrey Elliot) Fidel Castro: Nothing Can Stop the Course of History, 1986, also articles; former editor:The Black Politician (quar.) Mem. L.A. County Water Appeals Bd.; advisor to Calif. Assembly Spkr. for Cmty. Congress; chmn. Calif. Black Leadership Roundtable, Caribbean Am. Coalition; chair select com. cmty. colls. Prof. Charles R. Drew U. Medicine Sci.; mem. Calif. Assembly, 2003—. Recipient numerous awards including Chaconia Gold medal Govt. Trinidad and Tobago, Adam Clayton Powell award Congl. Black Caucus, Dr. Solomon P. Fuller award Black Psychiatrists of Am., others from Golden State Med. Assn., United Tchrs. L.A., Bd. Suprs. L.A., L.A. City Coun., various univs., colls., orgns. Mem. AAUP, NAACP, Am. Acad. Polit. Sci., Am. Polit. Sci. Assn., Am. Acad. Polit. and Social Sci., ACLU, Urban League, Phi Kappa Phi, Kappa Alpha Psi Democrat. Office: Calif Assembly 322 W Compton Blvd # 100 Compton CA 90220 Home: 223 S Acacia Ave # 206 Compton CA 90220 Home Phone: 310-635-4641; Office Phone: 310-223-1201. Business E-Mail: mervyn.dymally@asm.ca.gov.

DYMOND, LEWIS WANDELL, lawyer, educator; b. Lansing, Mich., June 28, 1920; s. Lewis Wandell and Irene (Parker) D.; m. Betty Louise Blood, Sept. 6, 1942; children: Lewis W., Jean Ann; m. Joann Surrey, Sept. 3, 1966; 1 son, Steven Henry. JD cum laude, U. Miami, 1956. Bar: Fla. 1957; cert. ct. mediator, Fla. With Nat. Airlines, Inc., Miami, Fla., 1938-62, mechanic, agt., sta. mgr., flight dispatcher, ops. mgr., pilot, v.p. ops., maintenance and engring., 1955-62; pres., chief exec. officer, dir. Frontier Airlines, 1962-79. Adj. prof. Sch. Bus. U. Miami, Coral Gables, Fla. Mem. U. Miami Alumni Club, Union League, Surf Club, Masons, Shriners, Phi Kappa Phi, Phi Alpha Delta. Home and Office: 6 E Belleview Way Greenwood Village CO 80121-1408

DYNES, ROBERT C., academic administrator, physicist; b. London, Ont., Can., Nov. 8, 1942; m. Frances Dynes Hellman. BS of Math. & Physics, U. Western Ont., 1964; MS of Physics, McMaster U., 1965, PhD of Phys., 1968. Postdoctoral fellow AT&T Bell Labs, Murray Hill, NJ, 1968—70, mem., technical staff, 1970—74, dept. head, semiconductor & chem. physics rsch., 1974—81, dept. head, solid state & physics of materials rsch., 1981—83, dir., chem. physics rsch., 1983—90; physics prof. U. Calif., San Diego, 1991—; chair, dept. physics U. Calif, San Diego, 1994—95; sr. vice chancellor, acad. affairs U. Calif., 1995—96, chancellor, 1996—2003; pres. U. Calif. Sys., Oakland, 2003—. Founding mem. San Diego Sci. and Tech. Coun.; adv. bd. Tex. Ctr. Superconductivity U. Houston; spkr. in field. Contbr. articles to profl. jours. Dir. Calif. C. of C.; mem. Calif. Commn. Jobs and Econ. Growth. Recipient Fritz London award Low Temp. Physics, 1990. Fellow: Can. Inst. Advances Rsch., Am. Phys. Soc.; mem.: NAS, Am. Acad. Arts & Scis. Office: Office of Pres Univ Calif 1111 Franklin St Oakland CA 94607-5200*

DYREGROV, MICHAEL See BAKER, JOHN

DYRENFURTH, MICHAEL JOHN, education educator, academic administrator; b. Schlitz, Fed. Republic Germany, June 16, 1946; came to U.S., 1970; m. Mary Belle Gullekson, June, 1967; children: Walter John, Michelle Lee, Grant Michael. EdB, U. Alta., Can., 1968, MEd, 1970; PhD, Bowling Green State U., Ohio, 1973. Cert. tchr., Alta. Tchr. indsl. arts pub. schs., Alta., 1967—69; asst. prof., chmn. dept. indsl. edn. Valley City (N.D.) State Coll., ND, 1972—75; assoc. prof. indsl. edn. Montclair (N.J.) State Coll., 1975—78; prof. tech. and industry, practical arts, vocat. tech. edn. U. Mo., Columbia, 1978—98; prof., grad. coord. dept. indsl. edn. and tech. Iowa State U., Ames, 1998—2001; asst. dean, grad. & internat. Sch. Tech., Purdue U., 2001—. Pres. Applied Expertise Assocs.; chair World Coun. Assns. Tech. Edn. Contbr. articles to profl. jours. Mem. Internat. Tech. Edn. Assn. (Outstanding Young Leader award 1985), Internat. Vocat. Edn. and Tng. Assn., Am. Vocat. Assn. (Svc. award 1983, IAD Profl. Leadership award 1986), Coun. Tech. Tchr. Edn., Nat. Assn. Indsl. and Tech. Tchr. Edn. (pres.), Indsl. Tech. Edn. Assn. Mo., Mo. Vocat. Assn. (Outstanding Svc. award 1985), Phi Delta Kappa, Kappa Delta Phi, Epsilon Pi Tau (Disting. Svc. Laureate Citation 1996). Office: Purdue Univ Coll Tech Knoy 150 West Lafayette IN 47907-1410 Office Phone: 765-496-1203.

DYRO, FRANCES MARY AGNES, medical educator; b. Portland, Maine, Oct. 15, 1941; d. Sigmund Stanislaus and Mary Agnes (Dyro) D. SB, MIT, 1963; MD, U. Md., 1967. Diplomate Am. Bd. Psychiatry and Neurology. Intern Maine Med. Ctr., Portland, 1967-68; resident in neurology Johns Hopkins Hosp., Balt., 1968-69, N.Y. Med. Coll., NYC, 1969-71; fellow in neurophysiology Columbia-Presbyn. Hosp., NYC, 1972-73; pvt. practice Portland, 1973-77; asst. prof. Med. Sch. Temple U., Phila., 1977-78; asst. prof. Sch. of Medicine Harvard U., Boston, 1978-94. Dir. clin. neurophysiology VA Med. Ctr., West Roxbury, Mass., 1978-93; med. dir. DLA Zdrowia, Boston, 1993—; assoc. prof. neurology NY Med. Coll., Valhalla, 2001—. Author: EEG Handbook, 1989, (chpt.) Late Onset Neuromuscular Disorders, 1987, Electrophysiology of the Lower Urinary Tract, 1988, Stein's Textbook of Medicine, 1990, 2d edit., 1994. Fellow Am. Acad. Neurology; mem. Altrusa Internat. Russian Orthodox. Avocations: quilting, gourmet cooking, singing. Office: WDG Inc 300 Danforth St Portland ME 04102-3624 also: 19 Bradhurst Ave Ste 2800 Hawthorne NY 10532

DYSART, BENJAMIN CLAY, III, conservationist, consultant, engineer; b. Columbia, Tenn., Feb. 12, 1940; s. Benjamin Clay and Kathryne Virginia (Thompson) D.; m. Betty Blanche Walthall, June 7, 2005. BE, Vanderbilt U., 1961, MS in San. Engring., 1964; PhD in Civil Engring., Ga. Inst. Tech., 1969. Staff engr. Union Carbide Corp., 1961-62, 64-65; from asst. prof. to prof. Clemson U., 1968-90, McQueen Quattlebaum prof. engring., 1982-83, dir. S.C. Water Resources Rsch. Inst., 1968-75, dir. water resources engring. grad. program, 1972-75, adj. prof., 1990-93; facility devel. mgr. Chem. Waste Mgmt., Inc., Marietta, Ga., 1990-91, regional facility devel. mgr. Memphis, 1991; dir. project planning and integration Waste Mgmt., Inc., Washington, 1991-92; pres. Dysart & Assocs., Inc., Nashville, 1992—. Sci. advisor Office Sec. of Army, Washington, 1975-76; mem. EPA Sci. Adv. Bd., 1983-, Reinvention Cuitevia Com., NACEPT, US EPA, 1998-2000; sr. fellow The Conservation Found., 1985-90; mem. adv. coun. Electric Power Rsch. Inst., 1989-95; mem., chief of engrs. environ. adv. bd. U.S. Army Corps Engrs., 1988-92; mem. Glacier Nat. Park Sci. Coun., Nat. Park Svc., 1988-91; mem. S.C. Gov.'s Wetlands Forum, 1989-90; sec. appointee Outer Continental Shelf Adv. Bd. and OCS Sci. Com. Dept. Interior, 1979-82; mem. S.C. Environ. Quality Control Adv. Com., 1980-90, chmn., 1980-81; mem. Sci. Panel to Rev. Interagy. Rsch. on Impact of Oil Pollution NOAA, Dept. Commerce, 1980; mem. Nuclear Energy Ctr. Environ. Task Force Dept. Energy-So. States Energy Bd., 1978-81; mem. Nonpoint Source Pollutant Task Force EPA, 1979-80; mem. civil works adv. com. Office Sec. Army-Young Pres.'s Orgn., 1975-76; mem. S.C. Heritage Adv. Bd., 1974-76; mem. Pangue Project, ind. review panel, World Bank, 1996-97; chmn. Ga. Erosion & Sedimentation Control Tech. Study Com., 1996-2001; cons. on effective stakeholder engagement, value adding corp. social responsibility and pub. accountability matters to corp., internat. inst., & govt.; sr. assoc. Internat. Council Mining & Metals, London, 2001-02; leader Ind. Review on Compliance Advisor Ombudsman Ofice, World Bank, 2003. Editor: (with Marion Clawson) Managing Public Lands in the Public Interest, 1988, Public Interest in the Use of Private Lands, 1989; contbr. articles on math. modeling in water quality and environ. mgmt. and pub. involvement to profl. jours.; author numerous profl. papers, reports. Trustee Rene Dubos Ctr. for Human Environs., 1985-94, vice chmn., mem. exec. com., 1988-94; trustee Issue Mgmt. Coun., 1997-2003, 2005-; bd. visitors Kanuga Episcopal Conf. Ctr., 1988—. Recipient Tribute of Appreciation for Disting. Svc. EPA, 1981, 86, McQueen Quattlebaum Engring. Faculty Achievement award Clemson U., 1982, Order of Palmetto Gov. S.C., 1984; named Hon. Ky. Col., 1976. Mem. Trout Unltd. (trustee 1990-94), Nat. Wildlife Fedn. (bd. dirs. 1974-90, v.p. 1978-83, pres., chmn. bd. dirs. 1983-85), Assn. Environ. Engring. Profs. (bd. dirs. 1978-83, pres., chmn. bd. dirs. 1981-82), Water Environ. Fedn. (hon., bd. dirs. Rsch. Found. 1989-91), S.C. Wildlife Fedn. (bd. dirs. 1969—, pres., chmn. bd. dirs. 1973-74, S.C. Wildlife Conservationist Yr.), The Ga. Conservancy (bd. trustees 1994-97), Cosmos Club (Washington), Sigma Xi, Tau Beta Pi, Phi Kappa Phi, Chi Epsilon, Omega Rho, Sigma Nu. Episcopalian.

DYSHKANT, ALEXANDER SERGEEVICH, physicist, researcher; b. Kapitanovka, Ukraine, Sept. 13, 1946; arrived in U.S., 1998; s. Sergei Michailovich and Mariya Ivanovna (Balyuk) Dyshkant; m. Nina Panteleevna Dovgenko, Apr. 23, 1971. MS, Moscow Engring. and Physics Inst., 1971; PhD, Inst. High Energy Physics, Protvino, Russia, 1985. Rsch. scientist Inst. High Energy Physics, 1971—85, sr. rsch. scientist, 1986—99; rsch. assoc. U. Rochester, NY, 1999—2001; sr. rsch. scientist No. Ill. U., DeKalb, 2001—. Mem.: IEEE. Avocations: beekeeping, gardening, calligraphy. Home: 496 Bush Dekalb IL 60115 Office: No Ill Univ Physics Dept 1425 W Lincoln Hwy Dekalb IL 60115 Office Phone: 815-753-8351. E-mail: dyshkant@fnal.gov.

DYSINGER, PAUL WILLIAM, preventive medicine physician, educator; b. Burns, Tenn., May 24, 1927; s. Paul Clair and Mary Edith (Martin) D.; m. Yvonne Minchin, May 11, 1958; children: Edwin, Wayne, John, Janelle. BA, So. Missionary Coll., 1951; MD, Loma Linda U., 1955; M.P.H., Harvard, 1962. Diplomate Nat. Bd. Med. Examiners, Am. Bd. Preventive Medicine. Intern, Washington, 1955-56; sr. asst. surgeon USPHS; with Blackfeet Indians in Mont., Navajos of Ariz., 1956-58; physician, med. adviser Am. embassy, PhnomPenh, Cambodia, 1958-60; rsch. assoc. dept. preventive medicine Loma Linda (Calif.) U. (formerly Coll. Med. Evangelists), 1960-62, dir. field sta. Western Tanganyika, 1962-64, adminstrv. asst. div. pub. health, 1964-67, asst. to dean, chmn. dept. tropical health Sch. Pub. Health, 1967-69, asst. dean for acad. affairs and internat. health Sch. Pub. Health, 1969-71, assoc. dean for acad. affairs, 1971-79, assoc. dean emeritus, sch. public health, dir. preventive med. residency Sch. of Medicine, 1983-88, clin. prof. emeritus, preventive medicine; pres. Devel. Svc. Internat., Williamsport, Tenn., 1992—. Med. cons. dept. Vocat. Rehab., Riverside, Calif., 1964-88; mother and child health cons. Ministry of Health, Tanzania, 1978-80; med. dir. Village Health Program, Punjab, Pakistan, 1980-81, tchr., cons., S.Am. and Caribbean, 1981-83; chief preventive medicine Pettis Meml. VA Hosp., Loma Linda, 1986-88; sr. health advisor Adventist Devel. and Relief Agy., 1988-92; country dir. ADRA, Yemen, 1998-99. Contbr. articles to med. publs. WHO fellow, Somalia, Ethiopia, India, Nepal and Burma, 1969. Fellow Royal Soc. Tropical Medicine and Hygiene, Am. Pub. Health Assn., Am. Coll. Preventive Medicine, Internat. Health Soc. (pres.); mem. AMA, Global Health Coun., Adventist Internat. Med. Soc. (pres. 1983-84), Delta Omega (nat. pres. 1977-78). Adventist. Home and Office: 684 Dry Prong Rd Williamsport TN 38487-0210 Office Phone: 931-583-2792. Personal E-mail: pwdys@bellsouth.net.

DYSON, ALLAN JUDGE, retired librarian; b. Lawrence, Mass., Mar. 28, 1942; s. Raymond Magan and Hilda D.; m. Susan Cooper, 1987; 1 child, Brenna Ruth. BA in Govt., Harvard U., 1964; MSLS, Simmons Coll., 1968. Asst. to dir. Columbia U. Librs., NYC, 1968-71; head Moffitt Undergrad. Libr. U. Calif., Berkeley, 1971-79, univ. libr. Santa Cruz, 1979—2003, ret., 2003. Editor Coll. and Rsch. Librs. News, 1973-74; chmn. editl. bd. Choice mag., 1978-80, Am. Librs., 1986-89. CFO Cabrillo (Calif.) Music Festival, 1985-86; chmn. No. Calif. Regional Libr. Bd., 1986-88, 94-98, U. Calif. Librs. Group, 1998-2001. Lt. U.S. Army, 1964-66. Decorated Army Commendation medal; Coun. on Libr. Resources fellow, 1973-74. Mem. ALA, ACLU, Librs. Assn. U. Calif. (pres. 1976), Sierra Club.

DYSON, ANDRE, professional football player; b. Logan, Utah, May 25, 1979; Attended, Utah Univ. Cornerback Tenn. Titans, 2001—04, Seattle Seahawks, 2005—06, NY Jets, 2006—. Named to All-Western Athletic Conference, NCAA, 2000. Office: NY Jets 1000 Fulton Ave Hempstead NY 11550

DYSON, ESTHER, editor-in-chief; b. Zurich, Switzerland, July 14, 1951; d. Freeman John and Verena Esther (Huber) D. BA in economics, Harvard U., 1972. Reporter Forbes Mag., NYC, 1974-77, columnist, 1987—; v.p. New Ct. Securities, NYC, 1977-80, Oppenheimer & Co., NYC, 1980-82; editor Rosen Electronics Letter, 1982; founder, owner, chmn. EDventure Holdings, Inc. (acquired by CNET Networks 2004), 1983—2004; editor at large CNET Networks, 2004—. Founding chmn. ICANN, 1998—2000; bd. dirs. EverNote Corp., 2006—. Author: Release 2.0: A Design for Living in the Digital Age, 1997; columnist Release 3.0, N.Y. Times syndicate; moderator ann. Personal Computer Forum; contbr. articles to profl. jours. Trustee Glasses for Humanity, Nat. Endowment for Democracy. Mem. Women's Forum N.Y., Assn. Data Processing Svc. Orgns., Software Pubs. Assn., ICANN (mem. reform com., 2004). Avocation: swimming. E-mail: edyson@boxbe.com.

DYSON, FREEMAN JOHN, retired physics professor; b. Crowthorne, Eng., Dec. 15, 1923; s. George and Mildred Lucy (Atkey) D.; m. Verena Haefeli-Huber, Aug. 11, 1950 (div. 1958); children: Esther, George; m. Imme Jung, Nov. 21, 1958; children: Dorothy, Emily, Mia, Rebecca. BA, Cambridge U., 1945. Ops. rsch. RAF Bomber Command, 1943-45; fellow Trinity Coll., Cambridge U., Eng., 1946-49; Commonwealth fellow Cornell U., Princeton, 1947-49; prof. physics Cornell U., 1951-53; prof. Inst. Advanced Study, Princeton, 1953-94; prof. emeritus, 1994—. Author: Disturbing the Universe, 1979, Weapons and Hope, 1984, Origins of Life, 1986, Infinite in all Directions, 1988, From Eros to Gaia, 1992, Imagined Worlds, 1997, The Sun, the Genome and the Internet, 1999, The Scientist as Rebel, 2006, A Many-colored Glass, 2007. Recipient Wolf prize in physics, Wolf Found., Israel, 1981, Enrico Fermi award U.S. Dept. of Energy, 1995, Templeton prize for Progress in Religion, 2000. Fellow Royal Soc. London; mem. NAS, Am. Phys. Soc. Home: 105 Battle Road Cir Princeton NJ 08540-4904 Home Phone: 609-924-2152; Office Phone: 609-734-8055. Business E-Mail: dyson@ias.edu.

DYSON, SIR JAMES, manufacturing executive, inventor; b. Norfolk, Eng., May 2, 1947; Degree, Royal Coll. Art, 1966—70; LittD (hon.), Staffordshire U., 1996; DSc, Oxford Brookes U., 1997; DSc (hon.), Huddersfield U. Bus. Sch., 1997; DSc, Bradford U., 1998; DEng, West of England U., 1999; doctorate (hon.), U. Middlesex, U. Brunel, Bath Spa U., Royal Coll. Art, U. Bath. Designer new theatre for New Stratford East Theatre, 1967, auditorium and seats for the Roundhouse, London, 1967; co-designer with Conran Design Group Chrome seating and crèche furniture design for Terminal 1, Heathrow, Peter Dominic wine shops; designer, engr. Sea Truck for Jeremy Fry; joined Rotork, Bath, England, 1970—73, dir., 1973—74; developer Ballbarrow, 1974; designer Waterolla, a water-filled plastic garden roller, 1974; inventor Trolleyball, a boat launcher with ball wheels, 1978; discovers idea of bagless cleaner while renovating home in Cotswolds, 1978; developing the cleaner and builds 5,127 prototypes of the Dual Cyclone (tm) vacuum cleaner, 1979—84; produces first prototype vacuum cleaner, G-Force, 1983; travels throughout UK and Europe for someone to license the product, 1982—84; works with co. in Japan (sales start in G-Force in Japan in 1986), 1985; G-Force displayed at the British Design Exhbn. Vienna, 1987; G-Force included in and displayed in poster for the British Design: New Traditions Exhbn. Rotterdam, 1989; chmn. Bath Coll. Higher Edn., 1990—92; G-Force becomes status symbol, 1991; opens rsch. ctr. and factory Dyson Appliances, Chippenham, Wiltshire, England, 1993; launch of Dyson DC01 (best-selling vacuum cleaner in UK, 1995), 1993, Dyson Dual Cyclone(tm) DC02 (second highest selling cylinder model in UK, 1995), 1995; moves Dyson Appliances, Malmesbury, England, 1995; opens sales and service subsidiaries in Australia and France, 1996; launch of DC02 Absolute, first vacuum with both HEPA Filtration and bacteria-killing screen, 1996, Ltd. Edit. DC02 De Stiji, 1996; plans in progress for an edn. ctr. sponsored by Dyson at the Design Mus., 1997; establishes subsidiary office in Germany, 1998; establishes subsidiary office in Spain, 1998; launch of DC05, 1998; establishes subsidiary office in Japan, 1998; launch of DC04, 1999; DC06-Dual Cyclone (tm) robotic vacuum cleaner goes on home trial, 1999; launch of DC04 Zorbster, first Dual Cyclone (tm) integrated carpet cleaning sys., 2000, Contrarotator (tm), the world's first washing machine with 2 drums rotating in opposite directions, 2000; establishes subsidiary office in Austria, 2000; launch of New Root8 Cyclone technology vacuum cleaner: the Dyson DC07, more suction than Dual Cyclone vacuum cleaners and is the most powerful upright vacuum cleaner on the market, 2001. External examiner, indsl. design engring. faculty Royal Coll. Art, 1993—96; exhibits products Glasglow Internat. Festival of Design, 1996, 'Doing a Dyson' exhbn. opens at Design Mus., 1996, Sonsbeek Design and Art Mus. in Arnhem, Holland, 1997, 'Englishman at Home' exhbn. at Purves and Purves, 1998; patron The Roundhouse in Chalk Farm, London, 1998, Meningitis Rsch. Found., 2000, Nat. Assn. of Inspectors and Advisors in Design and Tech., 2000; mem. coun. Royal Coll. of Art, 1998; chmn. Design Mus., 1999; Dyson Demo opens in Paris: a space where Dyson displays its own specialty created exhbns. to explain design, engring. , manufacturing, and technology, 2000; products exhibited at San Francisco Mus. Modern Art, Grand Central Station, NY, Metropolitan Mus. Art (A Century of Design Exhbn.), NY, Sci. Mus., London, Victoria and Albert Mus., London, Pompidou Centre, Paris, Design Mus. Autobiography published Against the Odds, 1997. Named Philanthropist of Yr., 1997, Designer of Decade; recipient Indsl. Design Prize of Am., European Design prize, Ideal Home award-Best Filtration Upright, British Allergy Found. Seal of Approval, Design Coun. award for the Sea Truck, Duke of Edinburgh's Spl. prize for the Sea Truck, 1975, Bldg. Design Innovation award for the Ballbarrow, 1977, Internat. Design Fair prize for the G-Force, Japan, 1991, Gerald Frewer Meml. Trophy, Inst. Engring. Design, 1996, Grand Prix Trophy and the Consumer Product Design award, UK Design Coun. and Design in Bus. awrds (DBA), 1996, Prince Philip Designers prize, 1997, CBE in the New Year's Honours, 1998, Japan Super Good of Yr. 1999 Silver Prize for DC05, 2000, Etoiles de l'Observeur du Design for DC05, 2000, Etoiles de l'Observeur du Design 2001 in the Mobilite Category for DC06, 2000, Mingay 2000 award for DC04, Australia, 2000, Lord Lloyd of Kilgerran prize, 2000, Kitchens, Bathrooms and Bedrooms Review award for the Contrarotator (tm) for Appliance Innovation, 2000, Classic Design Reader's award for the Contrarotator (tm), Homes and Gardens mag., 2001; named Hon. Fellow of Liverpool john Moores U., 1998. Fellow: Chartered Soc. Engrs.; mem.: Inst. Engring. Designers (Hon. MEID 1997), Design Coun. Achievements include Dyson becomes the first British company to win European Design award in 1997; becomes trustee of the Design Mus., beside one other person he is the only person to hold this post, and be a member of the Design Coun; Dyson Center for Design Education and Training at the Design Museum open in 1997; Tony Blair announces that the DC02 is selected as one of the first Millennium Products in April, 1998. Office: Dyson Ltd Tetbury Hill Malmesbury Wiltshire SN16 0RP England Address: Dyson Inc 520 West Erie St Ste 410 Chicago IL 60610*

DYSON, JAMES DAVID, lawyer; BS, BA, La. Tech. U., 1968; JD, Emory U., 1973, LLM, 1980. Bar: Ga. 1974. Asst. atty. gen. State of Ga., 1974—79; sr. atty., asst. sec. Gold Kist Inc., Atlanta, 1980—98, v.p., gen. counsel, sec., 1998—. Office: Gold Kist Inc PO Box 2210 Atlanta GA 30301 Office Phone: 770-393-5000. E-mail: david.dyson@goldkist.com.

DYSON, MICHAEL ERIC, religious studies educator, writer; b. Detroit, Oct. 23, 1958; s. Everett and Addie D.; m. Marcia Louise Dyson, June 24, 1992; children: Michael, Maisha. BA magna cum laude, Carson-Newman Coll., 1982; MA, Princeton U., 1991; PhD, 1993. Min. various Baptist chs.; instr. to asst. prof. Chgo. Theol. Sem., 1989—92; asst. prof. Brown U., Providence, 1993—95, U. NC, Chapel Hill, 1995—97; vis. disting. prof. Columbia U., 1997—99; Ida B. Wells-Barnett U. prof. DePaul U., Chgo., 1999—2002; Avalon Found. prof. humanities Dept. Religious Studies, U. Pa., 2002—07; Univ. prof. English, theology and African-Am. studies Georgetown U., 2007—. Author: Reflecting Black: African American Cultural Criticism, 1993, Making Malcolm: The Myth and Meaning of Malcolm X, 1995, Between God and Gangsta Rap, 1996, I May Not Get There With You: The True Martin Luther King Jr., 2000, Holler If You Hear Me: Searching for Tupac Shakur, 2001, Open Mike: Reflections on Philosophy, Race, Sex, Culture and Religion, 2002, Why I Love Black Women, 2003, Is Bill Cosby Right? Or Has the Black Middle Class Lost Its Mind?, 2005 (NAACP Image award for outstanding lit. work--non-fiction, 2006), Pride: The Seven Deadly Sins, 2006, Come Hell or High Water: Hurricane Katrina and the Color of Disaster, 2006, Know What I Mean?, 2007, (essay collection) Race Rules: Navigating the Color Line, 1997; columnist Savoy Mag.; contbg. editor: Christian Century; contbr. articles Vibe Mag. Named to The Ebony Power 150, Ebony mag., 2007; recipient Nat. Mag. award, Nat. Assn. Black Journalists, 1992, Most Influential Black Ams., Ebony mag., 2006. Mem.: Dem. Socialist Soc. Am. Baptist. Office: Georgetown U 37th and O Streets, NW Washington DC 20057*

DYSON, TIM, public relations executive; Student, Loughborough U., Eng. CEO Next Fifteen Comm. Group plc, parent co. of Text 100, San Francisco. Bd. dir. Text 100; advisory bd. Biz360, Ketera. Mem. U.K. Inst. Dirs., Inst. Pub. Rels., Pub. Rels. Soc. Am., Washington Software Assn. and Digital Media Alliance, Seattle C. of C. Office: Next Fifteen plc Power Rd Studios 114a Power Rd London W4 5PY England Office Fax: +44(0)20 8996 1200.

DYSON, WILLIAM R., state legislator, educator; b. Waycross, Ga., July 12, 1940; s. Edward James Jr. and Lula Lorene (William) D.; m. Rebecca Johnson, 1964; children: Sonia, Wilfred, Erick, Michael. BA, Morris Coll., 1962; postgrad., NYU, 1963-66, Howard U., 1970; MA, So. Conn. State U., 1976, diploma, 1981. Alderman, New Haven, 1976; mem. Dist. 94 Conn. House of Reps., 1977—, asst. minority leader, mem. edn. com., mem. gov.'s child care study com.; tchr. Blackshear, Ga., 1967, Douglas, Ga., 1968-69, New Haven, 1970—. Mem. NEA, Conn. Edn. Assn., New Haven Edn. Assn., Masons. Home: PO Box 2064 New Haven CT 06521-2064

DYWAN, JEFFERY JOSEPH, judge; b. Hammond, Ind., Apr. 26, 1949; s. Joseph Michael and Florence Marie (Buda) D.; m. Jacque Ann Shulmistras, 1971; children: Dina, Abigail, Kathryn. BS in Indsl. Engring., Purdue U., 1971; JD, Valparaiso U., 1974; M in Judicial Studies, U. Nev., 2003. Bar: Ind. 1974, U.S. Dist. Ct. (no. and so. dists.) Ind. 1974, U.S. Ct. Appeals (7th cir.) 1975, Ill. 1984, U.S. Dist. Ct. (no. dist.) Ill. 1986. Assoc. Breclaw & Dywan, Griffith, Ind., 1974-77; sole practice Griffith, 1977-81; dep. prosecuting atty. Lake County, Crown Point, Ind., 1978-80, pub. defender, 1981-83; assoc. Chudom & Meyer, Schererville, Ind., 1981-89; ptnr. O'Drobinak, Dywan & Austgen, Crown Point, 1989-91; judge Lake Superior Ct., Crown Point, 1991—, chief judge, 1998-2000. Instr. Calumet Coll., Hammond, Ind., 1974-76, Ind. Vocat. and Tech. Coll., Gary, Ind., 1978-79. Contbr. articles to profl. jours. Mem. Ind. State Bar Assn., Lake County Bar Assn., Am. Judicature Soc., KC. Roman Catholic. Office: Lake Superior Ct 2293 N Main St Crown Point IN 46307 Office Phone: 219-648-6150.

DYYON, MARIO (LEROY FRAZIER), artist; b. Fort Myers, Fla., May 2, 1946; s. Sallie Frazier. Lectr., Westside Community Ctr., NYC, 1971, Case Western Res. U., 1983. Group exhbns. include Cleve. Top Artists, Intown Club, Cleve., 1969, Art Inst. Akron, 1969-70, Mus. Modern Art, N.Y.C., 1970, Whitney Mus. Ann., 1972, Mus. Contemporary Hispanic Art, 1985; one-man show at Case Western Res. U., 1983; represented in permanent collections Mus. Modern Art, N.Y.C., Whitney Mus. Am. Art, N.Y.C., Case Western Res. U., Larry Aldrich Mus., Conn., various pvt. collections. Printmaker's Workshop scholar, 1982. Roman Catholic. Address: 155 W 73rd St New York NY 10023-2921 Office Phone: 212-595-1324. *Success is a love for your work. This may be too broad. Let me put a fine point on it. How to be successful really? In all your deeds, and in your dreams, try to make God smile. So, throw your vanity out the window and get to work. Be as the commen tern, on the move.*

DZAPO, KYLE JEAN, musician, educator; b. Warren, Ohio; d. Carl Joseph and Marjorie Dugan Dzapo. B in Music Edn., U. Mich., 1983; MusM with distinction in performance, New Eng. Conservatory, 1987; MusD, Northwestern U., 1996. Music instr. Wausau (Wis.) Conservatory Music, 1991—93; prof. Bradley U., Peoria, Ill., 1993—; prin. flutist Peoria Symphony Orch., 1993—. Author: Joachim Andersen: A Bio-Bibliography, 1999; editor: Fünf Leichtere Stücke, Op 56, 2005. Recipient Slane Coll. Faculty Achievement award for excellence in scholarship, Bradley U., 1998, Caterpillar Inc. New Faculty Tchg. award, 1998. Mem.: Nat. Flute Assn. (sec. 2002—03, conv. program chair 2005). Home Phone: 309-497-0126; Office Phone: 309-677-2596. Business E-Mail: kdzapo@bradley.edu.

DZAU, VICTOR JOSEPH, cardiologist, director, researcher; b. Shanghai, Oct. 23, 1946; MD, McGill U., 1972. Cert. in internal medicine, subspecialty in cardiovasc. disease. Intern N.Y. Hosp., 1972-73; resident in medicine Peter Bent Brigham Hosp., Boston, 1974-76, chief resident, 1976-78; fellow in rsch. Mass. Gen. Hosp., Boston, 1976-78, fellow in cardiology, 1979-80; chief divsn. vascular medicine and atherosclerosis Brigham & Women's Hosp., 1984-90; chief divsn. cardiovasc. medicine Stanford U. Sch. Medicine, 1990-96, dir. cardiovasc. rsch. ctr., assoc. chmn. dept. medicine, 1993-96, chmn. dept. medicine, 1995-96; dir. Am. Heart Assn.-Bugher Found. Ctr. for Molecular Biology, 1991-96; chmn. dept. med., dir. rsch. Brigham & Women's Hosp., 1996—2004; chancellor Duke U., 2004—; pres., CEO Duke U. Health Sys., 2004—. From asst. prof. medicine to assoc. prof. medicine Harvard Med. Sch., 1980—90, Hersey prof. theory and practice of medicine, 1996—2004; William G. Irvin prof. medicine Stanford U. Sch. Medicine, 1990—96, Arthur L. Bloomfield prof., chmn. medicine, 1995—96; James B. Duke prof. medicine Duke U., 2004—. Office: Duke U Med Ctr 1 Davison Blvd Box 3701 Durham NC 27710 Office Phone: 919-684-2255. Business E-Mail: victor.dzau@duke.edu.

DZHANDZHULYAN, LEV, business analyst, consultant; b. St.Petersburg, Russia, Jan. 6, 1965; s. Eduard and Larisa Dzhandzhulyan. Diploma with honours in Applied Math., Yerevan State U., Armenia, 1986; PhD in Math., Inst. for Problems of Informatics and Automation, NAS, Yerevan, 1992; MBA in Internat. Bus., Ctrl. Conn. State U., New Britain, 1999. Cert. personal software process Carnegie Mellon U., Software Engring. Inst., 2006; actuarial exam Series 100 Soc. Actuaries, 1999; registered gen. securities prin. Series 24 Nat. Assn. Securities Dealers, 2002, limited rep. - equity trader Series 55 Nat. Assn. Securities Dealers, 2000, gen. securities rep. Series 7 Nat. Assn. Securities Dealers, 1999, registered continuing edn. Series 101 Nat. Assn. Securities Dealers, 2001, cert. investment cons. FOREX Global Index Consulting Svcs. (Singapore), St. Petersburg, 1997. Rsch. scientist Inst. for Problems of Informatics & Automation, Dept. Artificial Intelligence, NAS, Yerevan, 1990—93; chief acct. GNT Ltd., Mgmt. Consulting, Moscow, 1993—94; cons. Jepsail A/S, Finnish-Am. Internat. Mgmt. Consulting Co., St. Petersburg, 1994—97, Helsinki, Finland, 1994—97; trader/analyst Worldco LLC., Wall St., NYC, 1999—2003; bus. analyst CQG Inc., Yerevan, 2005—, Denver, 2005—. Dir. Young Mathematicians' Sch., Yerevan State U., 1984—86; ind. cons. Investment Mgmt. Co. of a Def. Industry Group, St. Petersburg, 2004, Yerevan Commodities Exch., 2005. Best Student scholar, Yerevan State U., Dept. Applied Math., 1984—86. Achievements include patents for new fundamental instrument for financial markets. Avocations: swimming, checkers, Aikido. Personal E-mail: lev_djan@hotmail.com.

DZIAK, JACK, telecommunications industry executive; BS cum laude, Va. Polytechic Inst.; MBA, Univ. Chgo., 1988. Cert. fin. analyst. Sr. mgr., info. & comm. strategy cons. practice Coopers & Lybrand; ptnr., comm. & high tech. cons. practice Accenture, 1995—2003; sr. v.p. corp. strategy & bus. develop. MCI Communications, 2003—06; sr. v.p. services & distbn. Mobile Satellite Ventures LP, 2006—07; sr. v.p. strategy Sprint Nextel, Reston, Va., 2007—. Office: Sprint Nextel 2001 Edmund Halley Dr Reston VA 20191*

DZIEWANOWSKA, ZOFIA ELIZABETH, pharmaceutical executive; b. Warsaw, Nov. 17, 1939; came to U.S., 1972; d. Stanislaw Kazimierz Dziewanowski and Zofia Danuta (Mieczkowska) Rudowska; m. Krzysztof A. Kunert, Sept. 1, 1961 (div. 1971); 1 child, Martin. MD, U. Warsaw, 1963; PhD, Polish Acad. Sci., 1970. MD recert. U.K., 1972, U.S., 1973. Asst. prof. psychiatry U. Warsaw Med. Sch., 1969—71; sr. house officer St. George's Hosp., U. London, 1971—72; assoc. dir. Merck Sharp & Dohme, Rahway, NJ, 1972—76; vis. assoc. physician Rockefeller U. Hosp., NYC, 1975—76; adj. asst. prof. psychiatry Cornell U. Med. Ctr., NYC, 1978—; v.p., global med. dir. Hoffmann-La Roche, Inc., Nutley, NJ, 1976—94; sr. v.p., dir. global med. affairs Genta Inc., San Diego, 1994—97; sr. v.p. drug devel. and regulatory Cypros Pharms. Corp., Carlsbad, Calif., 1997—99; pres., med. dir. New Drug Assocs., La Jolla, Calif., 1999—; sr. v.p. clin. and regulatory Maxia Pharms, San Diego, 2001—02; v.p. clin. rsch. Ligand Pharm, Inc., San Diego, 2002—. Lectr. in field. Contbr. articles to profl. publs. Bd. dirs Royal Soc. Medicine Found.; mem. alumni coun. Cornell U. Med. Ctr. Recipient TWIN Honoree award for Outstanding Women in Mgmt., Ridgewood (N.J.) YWCA, 1984. Mem. AMA, AAAS, Am. Soc. Pharmacology and Therapeutics, Am. Coll. Neuropsychopharmacology, N.Y. Acad. Scis., PhRMA. (vice chmn. steering com. med. sect., chmn. internat. med. affairs com., head biotech. working group), Royal Soc. Medicine (U.K.), Drug Info. Assn. (Woman of Yr. award 1994), Am. Assn. Pharm. Physicians. Roman Catholic. Achievements include original research on the role of the nervous system in the regulation of respiratory functions, research and development and therapeutic uses of many new drugs, pharmaceutical medicine and biotechnology; molecular biology derived as well as conventional products including antisense, interferon efficacy in cancer, virology and AIDS and drugs useful in cardiovascular, immunological, neuropsychiatric, infectious diseases, and others; impact of different cultures on medical practices and clinical research; drug evaluation and development management strategies of pharmaceutical industries; treatments against cardiac and brain ischemia, cytoprotection.

DZIEZAK, JUDIE D., lawyer; d. Martin and Martha Dziezak; BS in Chemistry and Biology, Marian Coll., 1977; MS, Purdue U., 1980; JD, Loyola U., 1994. Bar: Ill. 1994, U.S. Dist. Ct. (no. dist.) Ill. 1994, U.S. Patent and Trademark Office 1997, Can. Patent Office 2004, DuPage County (Cert. Arbitrator, 18th jud. cir.) 1997. Lab. technician, endocrinology dept. Ind. U. Sch. Medicine, Indpls., 1976—77; chemist Morton Chem. Co., Woodstock, Ill., 1981; assoc. scientist The Quaker Oats Co., Barrington, Ill., 1981—85; assoc. editor, Food Tech. Inst. of Food Technologists, Chgo., 1985—91; rsch. asst. Loyola U. Sch. of Law, Chgo., 1993—94, contract atty., 1993—94; assoc. atty. Kostow & Daar, P.C., Chgo., 1995—96, Knight, Hoppe, Fanning & Knight, Des Plaines, Ill., 1996—98, Ryndak & Lyerla, Chgo., 1998—2000, Wildman Harrold Allen & Dixon, Chgo., 2000—01; sr. assoc. atty. Wallenstein & Wagner, Chgo., 2001—02; pvt. practice Hoffman Estates, Ill., 2003—. Cons. to food and chem. industries, Hoffman Estates, 1991—92, 1994—95. Faculty (seminar) Mining Patent Portfolios; contbr. over 80 articles to profl. pubs.; speaker (Chgo. Section meeting of Inst. of Food Technologists), (12th World Congress, Food Sci. & Tech.), (symposium, Soc. Cosmetic Chemists) Overview of Patents, Trademarks and Copyrights, (seminar on agricultural biotechnology) Ag-Biotech Food Forum, (presentation) Chicago Section meeting of American Chemical Society, Meeting of the American Association of Confectionary Technologists, author (article on food labeling) Prepared Foods. Clin. assoc. Crisis and Suicide Intervention Svc., Indianapolis, Ind., 1974—77; vol. classroom asst. - worked with children with autism and down's syndrome Noble I Ctr. for Retarded Children, Indianapolis, Ind., 1973—77; chair, legislative com. AAUW, Schaumburg, Ill., 1984—85. Recipient Three awards for excellence in writing - one from Society's nat. competition, two from the Chgo. Chpt.'s regional competitions, Am. Soc. Bus. Press Editors, 1989—90, Am. Jurisprudence Awards for Moot Ct., Legal Writing, and Advanced Legal Bibliography, Loyola U. Sch. of Law, 1992—94, Leadership and Svc. Award, 1993; fellow, NIH, 1977; Newman Scholarship, Marian Coll., 1973—77, Sixth Armored Divsn. Scholarship, 1973—77, Williams Fellowship, Loyola U. Sch. of Law, 1993. Mem.: ABA, Licensing Executives Soc., Inst. Food Technologists, Chgo. Bar Assn., Am. Intellectual Property Law Assn., Am. Chem. Soc., Kappa Gamma Pi, Pi Tau Sigma, Iota Sigma Pi. Avocations: running, gourmet cooking, landscape architecture and gardening, writing. Office: 2300 N Barrington Rd Hoffman Estates IL 60169 Office Phone: 847-490-5370.

DZOMBAK, DAVID ADAM, environmental engineering educator; b. Latrobe, Pa., Apr. 17, 1957; s. William Charles and Agnes Marie (Reiter) D.; m. Carolyn Jane Menard, Oct. 6, 1984; children: Daniel Charles, William Gerard, Rachel Victoria. BA in Math., St. Vincent Coll., Latrobe, 1979; BSCE, Carnegie Mellon U., 1979, MS in Civil-Environ. Engring., 1981; PhD in Civil-Environ. Engring., MIT, 1986. Registered profl. engr., Pa.; diplomate Am. Acad. Environ. Engrs. Rsch. asst. Carnegie Mellon U., Pitts., 1979-81, MIT, Cambridge, 1981-86; sr. staff cons. Paul C. Rizzo Assocs., Monroeville, Pa., 1986-88; asst. prof. environ. engring. Carnegie Mellon U., Pitts., 1989-93, assoc. prof., 1994-97, prof., 1998—, assoc. dean for grad. and faculty affairs Coll. Engring., 2006—, chair faculty senate, 2006—07; dir. Steinbrenner Inst. Environ., Edn. and Rsch., 2007—, Walter J. Blenko, Sr. prof. environ. engring., 2007—. Mem. sci. adv. bd. EPA, 2002—, mem. nat. adv. coun. on environ. policy and tech., 2004—; chair com. Miss. River and Clean Water Act NRC. Author: (with others) Surface Complexation Modeling: Hydrous Ferric Oxide, 1990, Cyanide in Water and Soil: Chemistry, Risk, and Management, 2006; contbr. articles to profl. jours. Recipient Presdl. Young Investigator award, NSF, 1991; Aldo Leopold Leadership Program fellow, Packard Found., 2000. Fellow ASCE (Walter L. Huber Civil Engring. Rsch. prize 1997, chmn. EWRI/EMMC awards com. 1999-02); mem. Am. Acad. Environ. Engrs. (chmn. publs. com. 2000-04), Am. Chem. Soc. (assoc. editor Environ. Sci. and Tech. 2005-; ES&T Excellence in Rev. award 2003), Am. Geophys. Union, Am. Soc. Engring. Edn., Am. Water Works Assn., Nat. Ground Water Assn. (mem. editl. bd. jour. 1990-93), Assn. Environ. Engring. and Sci. Profs. (bd. dirs. 1996-99, Doctoral Thesis award 1987, Dist. Svc. award 1999, chmn. strategic planning com. 2001-03), Soc. Environ. Toxicology and Chemistry, Water Environ. Fedn. (chmn. ground water com. 1993-96, mem. editl. bd. jour. 1993-98, H.P. Eddy medal 1993, J.E. McKee medal 2000, WEA of Pa. Profl. Rsch. award 2002). Home: 6929 Rosewood St Pittsburgh PA 15208-2638 Office: Carnegie Mellon Univ Dept Civil/Environ Engring Pittsburgh PA 15213-3890 Office Phone: 412-268-2946. Business E-Mail: dzombak@cmu.edu.

DZYALOSHINSKII, IGOR EKHIELIEVICH, physicist; b. Moscow, Feb. 1, 1931; s. Ekhiel Moiseevich and Maria Semionovna (Aseeva) D.; m. Elena Aronovna Lebedeva, Dec. 2, 1960; 1 child, Elena. MA in Physics, Moscow State U., 1953; PhD in Physics, Inst. for Phys. Problems, Moscow, 1957, DSc in Physics, 1962. Sr. rschr. Inst. for Phys. Problems, Moscow, 1957—65; head dept. magnetism Landau Inst. for Theoretical Physics, Moscow, 1965—91; prof. physics U. Calif., Irvine, 1992—2004, prof. emeritus, 2004—. Author: Methods of Quantum Field, Theory in Statistical Physics (in Russian, English, Japanese and Chinese), 1962, 3d edit., 1975, 2d Russian edit., 1998. Decorated Order of Red Banner of Labour, Order of Honor, Medal of Vet. of Labour, Govt. of Russia; recipient State prize Govt. USSR, 1984. Fellow AAAS, Am. Phys. Soc.; mem. Russian Acad. Scis. (Lomonosov prize 1962, Landau prize 1989), Am. Acad. Art and Scis. (hon. fgn. mem.). Achievements include research in theory of weak ferromagnetism; theory of van der Waals forces in condensed media; theory of one-dimensional metals. Office: Univ Calif Dept Physics Irvine CA 92697-0001

EACHEMPATI, SOUMITRA R., surgeon; b. Hyderabad, India, Jan. 2, 1966; s. Rama and Uma Eachempati. MD, Northwestern U., Chgo., 1991. Residency Wayne State U.; assoc. prof. surgery and pub. health Weill Med. Coll. of Cornell U., NYC, 2002—. Fellowship, Duke U. Fellow: Am. Coll. Surgeons; mem.: Soc. of Univ. of Surgeons. Office Phone: 212-746-5312.

EADE, GEORGE JAMES, retired military officer, researcher; b. Lockney, Tex., Oct. 27, 1921; s. George William and Isabel Theresa (Barnd) E.; m. Colette Eliane Cachelin, May 18, 1946 (dec. 1994); children: George Walter, Helen Marie-Louise (Mrs. Jean Oesch), Anne Catherine Eade Berry, Christine Colette, Dominique Frances. Commd. 2d lt. USAAF, 1942; advanced through grades to gen. USAF; pilot 37 combat missions in Europe World War II, 1942-46; pilot, squadron comdr., B-52 wing comdr.; airborne emergency action officer, sr. staff officer Strategic Air Command, Nat. Strategic Target Planning Staff, 1947-70; dep. chief of staff plans and ops. Hdqrs. USAF, Washington, 1971—72; dep. comdr.-in-chief U.S. Forces Europe, 1972-75; ret., 1975. Pres. Cath. Edn. Assn., Omaha, 1968—70. Decorated DSM with two oak leaf clusters, Legion of Merit, DFC, Air medal with five oak leaf clusters, Air Force Commendation medal with two oak leaf clusters; Order of Merit (France). Home: 1131 Sunnyside Dr Healdsburg CA 95448-3536 *Establish some general goals and lay plans to reach them. Neither be capricious nor struggle doggedly toward a goal no longer of interest. Above all follow your own plan, not what someone plans for you. The ultimate objective is to make a contribution to mankind and be happy in the process of so doing. Putting the two together is to discover the art of living and the meaning of life.*

EADENS, ETHAN ENNIS, minister, writer; b. Bowling Green, Ky., Mar. 12, 1967; s. David Mack Eadens and Nova Dell Milam; m. Lori Ann Abshire, May 15, 2004; 1 child, Travis Phillip. Sgt. US Army, 1985—92; min. Dry Fork Ch. of Christ, Ky., 1993—97, Helen Street Ch. of Christ, Fayetteville, NC, 1997—99, Scottsville Ch. of Christ, Ky., 1999—2002, Cody Ch. of Christ, Wyo., 2002—04, Minot Ch. of Christ, ND, 2004—. Author: Traveler, 2006, A Guided Tour of Heaven, 2006. Recipient Expert Infantry Badge, US Army, 1987, Army Achievement medal, 1987—88, Army Commendation medal, 1988. Mem.: NRA, VFW, Legion of Vets. (pres. 1992—93). Avocations: hunting, chess, writing songs and poetry, travel. Office: Minot Ch of Christ 1315 1st St NE Minot ND 58703 Office Phone: 701-839-6202. Personal E-mail: lori.eadens@min.midco.net.

EADIE, JOHN WILLIAM, historian, educator; b. Ft. Smith, Ark., Dec. 18, 1935; s. William Robert and Helen (Montgomery) B.; m. Joan Holt, Aug. 18, 1957; children: Robin, Christopher. BA with honors, U. Ark., 1957; MA, U. Chgo., 1959; PhD, Univ. Coll., London, 1962. Asst. prof. Ripon Coll., Wis., 1962-63; asst. prof. history U. Mich., Ann Arbor, 1963-67, assoc. prof., 1967-73, prof., 1973-86, assoc. chmn. dept. history, 1970-71, humanities-arts advisor Office V.p. for Research, 1974-86, assoc. dean Rackham Sch. Grad. Studies, 1984-86; prof. history, dean Coll. Arts and Letters Mich. State U., East Lansing, 1996—97, sr. advisor to provost, 1997—2000, prof. and dean emeritus, 2002—. Dir. Consortium for Inter-Instnl. Collaboration in African and L.Am. Studies, 1989-2000, chmn. liberal arts and scis. dean Consortium for Instnl. Collaboration, 1991-94, bd. mem. Santa Fe Coun. Internat. Rels. Author: The Breviarium of Festus: A critical-Edition with Historical Commentary, 1967, The Conversion of Constantine, 1971, (with others) Western Civilization, 1975; editor: Classical traditions in Early America, 1976; co-editor The Craft of the Ancient Historian, 1985, Urban Centers and Rural Contexts in Late Antiquity, 2001. Chmn. Mich. Council for Humanities, E. Lansing, Mich., 1977-80, Mich. Alliance for Conservation Cultural Heritage, 1988-90. Marshall scholar Brit. Marshall Commn. Univ. Coll., London, 1960-62; recipient Disting. Service award Mich. Council Humanities, 1980, Ralph Smucker award for advancing internat. programs, 2001. Mem.: Archaeol Inst. Am. Democrat. Presbyterian. E-mail: jweadie@msu.edu.

EADS, GEORGE CURTIS, economic consultant; b. Clarkesville, Tex., Aug. 20, 1942; s. Delbert Curtis and Eliza Mae (Hicks) E.; m. Margaret Helen Hall, Nov. 17, 1973; children: Geoffrey Thomas, Katherine Elizabeth. BA, U. Colo., 1964; MA, Yale U., 1965, MPhil, 1967, PhD, 1968. Asst. prof. econs. Harvard U., Cambridge, Mass., 1968-69, Princeton (NJ) U., 1969-71; spl. asst. antitrust divsn. Dept. Justice, Washington, 1971-72; assoc. prof. George Washington U., Washington, 1972-74; asst. dir. Coun. Wage and Price Stability, Washington, 1974-75; exec. dir. Nat. Commn. Supplies and Shortages, Washington, 1975-77; economist, rsch. program dir. Rand Corp., Santa Monica, Calif., 1977-79, 81; mem. Pres.'s Coun. Advisors, Washington, 1979-81; prof. Sch. Pub. Affairs, U. Md., College Park, 1981-85, dean Sch. Pub. Affairs, 1985-86; v.p., chief economist GM, 1986-95; v.p. Charles River Assocs., Washington, 1995—. Mem. com. on consequences on uninsurance Inst. Medicine, 2000—04; lead cons. sustainable mobility project World Bus. Coun. Sustainable Devel., 2002—04. Author: The Local Service Airline Experiment, 1972, Relief or Reform? Reagan's Regulatory Strategies, 1984. Mem. Am. Econ. Assn. Democrat. Home: 3718 Harrison St NW Washington DC 20015-1816 Office: Charles River Assoc Ste 700 1201 F St SW Washington DC 20004-1204 E-mail: geads@crai.com.

EADS, JOHN A., accountant; b. Dallas, Feb. 6, 1939; s. Arver A. and Nettie Mae Eads; m. Joanna Y. Eads, Aug. 12, 1967; children: Leslie, Ashley, John Jr. BBA, U. Tex., 1966. CPA, Tex. Staff acct., 1966—74; pvt. CPA practice, 1974-81; pres., mng. shareholder Eads, Hunter & Co., P.C., Dallas, 1981-98; tax shareholder Jackson & Rhodes, P.C., Dallas, 1998—2002; ptnr. Smith, Jackson, Boyer & Bovard, PLLC, Dallas, 2002—. Pres. Practice Mgmt. Group, Dallas, 1981, 2002; sec. Haemachem Rsch. Assocs., Inc., Dallas, 1983—; pres., chmn. bd. dirs. United Investment Corp. Tex., 2000—. Author: Practice Continuation Agreements, 1992. Vice chmn. bd. trustees Charlton Meth. Hosp., Dallas, 1988-2004; pres., chmn. bd. dirs. Citizens Devel. Ctr., Dallas, 1990-95; adv. coun. Dallas Meth. Hosp. Found., 1991-98, Cmtys. Found. of Tex., 1988—, Dallas Found., 1998—; treas., bd. dirs., exec. com. DeSoto Ind. Sch. Dist. Found., 2000-. Served with USAF, 1960-66. Recipient Disting. Pub. Svc. Award for CPA, White House Office of Pvt. Sector Initiatives, 1987. Mem. AICPA (mem. coun. governing body 1995-2001, Pub. Svc. award 1995), Tex. Soc. CPAs (bd. dirs., treas. 1991, pres. 1996-97, Outstanding Chpt. Pres. award, CPA of Yr. 1988, 2005, Meritorious Svc. Acctg. in Tex. 2001), Dallas CPA Soc. (pres. 1989, Past Leader Yr. award 2004-05), Dallas Estate Planning Coun. (mem. bd. govs.), Internat. Assn. Lions Clubs (gov. 1985-86, state coun. chmn. 1986-87, chmn. Tex. Lions Camp endowment com. 1999-2003, 07-, bd. dirs. 1984-86), Past Dist. Gov. Assn. Tex. (pres. 1993-94). Republican. Methodist. Avocations: golf, bird hunting. Office: 9400 NCX Ste 910 9400 N Central Expy Dallas TX 75231

EADS, ORA WILBERT, clergyman, church administrator; b. Mill Spring, Mo., Jan. 2, 1914; s. John Harrison and Effie Ellen (Borders) E.; m. Mary Ivaree Cochran, Mar. 25, 1944; children— Ora Wilbert, Wayne B., Carol Vernice, Janet Karen and Janice Inez (twins). JD, John Marshall Law Sch., Atlanta, 1940, LL.M., 1941; postgrad., Sch. Theology, St. Lawrence U., Canton, NY, 1947-48. Bar: Ga. bar 1940. Practiced in, Atlanta, 1940-46; ordained to ministry Christian Congregation, Inc., 1946; parish minister Sampson County, N.C., 1948-52; evangelist Charlotte, N.C., 1952-61; gen. supt. Christian Congregation, Inc., 1961—. Author numerous books of poetry, 1967—. Mem. Christian Congregation Ch. Home and Office: Christian Congregation Inc 812 W Hemlock St La Follette TN 37766 *A high school teacher asked her class, "What is our purpose on earth? Why are we here?" We students didn't know the answer. I now believe, some 70 years later, that the highest responsibility of any individual is to achieve his best potential.*

EADS, PAUL BRYAN, production designer; b. Belfonte, Pa., Jan. 2, 1952; s. Robert Howard and Carlene Rosboro Eads; m. Mindy Roffman, June 26, 1986; children: James Robin, Sean Jackson. BA, Kalamazoo Coll., Mich., 1973, Yale Drams Sch., New Haven, 1990. Prodn. designer, art dir.: (films) The Fan, 1980; Arthur, 1981; So Fine, 1982; Tempest, 1983; Jaws 3-D, 1984; Muppets Take Manhatten, 1984; Turk 182, 1984; Wise Guys, 1985; Brighton Beach Memoirs, 1985; Wanted Dead or Alive, 1986; Poltergeist 3, 1987; The End of Innocence, 1988; Frequency, 1999; Save the Last Dance, 2000; Fracture, 2006; (TV series) Nick Knight, 1989; Equal Justice, 1989—90; WIOU, 1990; Civil Wars, 1991—93; Middle Ages, 1992; NYPD Blue, 1993—95 (Emmy award, 1994); Brooklyn South, 1997—98; Boston Public (Emmy award, 2001); Philly, 2001; Girls Club, 2002; Blind Justice, 2004—05; Close To Home, 2005. Recipient Prodn. Design award, Art Dirs. Guild, 1997, Emmy award for Murder One, Acad. TV Arts and Scis., 1996. Mem.: Dirs. Guild Am., Art Dirs. Guild, United Scenic Artists.

EAGAN, CLAIRE VERONICA, chief district court judge; b. Bronx, NY, Oct. 9, 1950; d. Joseph Thomas and Margaret (Lynch) E.; m. M. Stephen Barrett, Aug. 25, 1978 (div. 1984); m. Anthony J. Loretti, Jr., Feb. 13, 1988. Student, U. Fribourg, Switzerland, 1970-71; BA, Trinity Coll., Washington, 1972; postgrad., U. Paris, 1972-73; JD, Fordham U., 1976. Bar: N.Y. 1977, Okla. 1977, U.S. Dist. Ct. (no. dist.) Okla. 1977, U.S. Ct. Appeals (10th cir.) 1978, U.S. Supreme Ct. 1980, U.S. Dist. Ct. (we. dist.) Okla. 1981, U.S. Ct. Appeals (5th cir.) 1982, U.S. Dist. Ct. (ea. dist.) Okla. 1988, U.S. Ct. Appeals (Fed. cir.) 1990. Mem. Hall, Estill, Hardwick, Gable, Golden & Nelson, Tulsa, 1978-98, shareholder, 1981-98; magistrate judge U.S. Dist. Ct. (no. dist.) Okla., Tulsa, 1998—2001, dist. judge, 2001—, chief judge, 2005—. Mem. Jud. Conf. Com. on Defender Svcs., 2002—, chair budget subcom., 2004—. Editor: Fordham Law Rev., 1975—76. Bd. dirs. Okla. Med. Rsch. Found., 2003—, Cath. Charities, Tulsa, 1983-98, Cystic Fibrosis Found., Tulsa, 1982-84; bd. trustees St. Francis Assisi Tuition Assistance Trust, 2006—; mem. Jr. League Tulsa, Inc., 1983—; trustee Gannon U., Erie, Pa., 1995-98; bd. dirs. Okla. Sinfonia, Tulsa, 1982-86; adj. settlement judge, Tulsa County, 1990-97. Fellow Am. Bar Found.; mem. Tulsa County Bar Assn., Tulsa Women Lawyers Assn. (pres. 2000-02), 10th Cir. Jud. Conf., Am. Inns of Ct. (master; chpt. pres. 1999-2000, mem. exec. com.). Republican. Roman Catholic. Office: US Dist Ct No Dist Okla 333 W 4th St Ste 411 Tulsa OK 74103-3819 Office Phone: 918-699-4795.

EAGAN, SHERMAN G., producer, communications executive; b. Peoria, Ill., Feb. 12, 1942; s. Joseph K. and Gracia (Sherman) E.; m. Paige Mannelly, Aug. 13, 1966; children: S. Joseph, Shannon Colleen. BA, U. N.Mex., 1968; postgrad., Northwestern U., 1967-68. Mgr. sales adminstrn. NBC-TV, Chgo., 1967-68; copywriter, producer D'Arcy Advt., St. Louis, 1968-69, Ad Com div. Quaker Oats, Chgo., 1969-71; writer CBS TV, Chgo., 1971-75; producer CBS News, NYC, 1975-79; producer, dir. CBS Sports, NYC, 1979-84; pres. Conn. Yankee Internat., Darien, 1984—. Cons. Tokyo Broadcasting Co., 1976-84. Producer, dir. U.S. Open Tennis, 1980-90, Daytona: Drama, Danger, Dedication, 1991; producer, dir. Daytona 500, 1992, producer, 1994; dir., writer Battle of the NASCAR Legends, CBS, 1991; dir. Internat. Emmy Presentation, 1989, supervising producer The Winners, 1991; exec. producer IBM TV, 1993, 94; producer NFL Sunday, Fox Sports, 1995-98; editor: (book) Aerodynamic Trading, 1995. Recipient Emmy award NATAS, 1984, 86, Telly award, 1995, 96, 97, 98, Exec. Prodr. and Dir. Entrepreneur of Yr. awards CNBC, 1996, 97, field producer Fox Superbowl Sunday, 1997; 1st Classic Telly award for Best Bus. Video of Last 20 Yrs.; named one of Am.'s Top 100 Prodrs., Prodr. mag., 2000, 2001. Mem. Dirs. Guild Am. Office: Conn Yankee Internat Inc 3 Valley Vieal Rd #20 Norwalk CT 06851 E-mail: rlmotto@aol.com.

EAGAN, WILLIAM LEON, lawyer; b. Tampa, Fla., Feb. 10, 1928; s. John Robert and Margaret (Williams) Eagan; m. Marjorie Young, Mar. 6, 1949; children: Barbara Anne, Rebecca Elizabeth, Laurel Lea. Student, U. Tampa, 1959; LLB, JD with honors, U. Fla., 1961. Bar: Fla. 1961, U.S. Dist. Ct. (mid. dist.) Fla. 1959, U.S. Dist. Ct. (so. dist.) Fla. 1962, U.S. Ct. Appeals (5th cir.) 1972; bd. cert. civil trial lawyer, Fla., 1984. Assoc. Dexter, Conlee & Bissell, Sarasota, Fla., 1961-62; ptnr., v.p. Arnold, Matheny & Eagan, P.A., Orlando, 1962—2004, of counsel, 2004—. Mem. Fla. Bar Ninth Circuit Grievance Com., 1982-84; mediator Family Law Mediation Program. Articles editor U. Fla. Law Rev., 1961. Chmn. bd. trustees First Bapt. Ch., Winter Park, Fla., 1970-72, chmn. bd. deacons, 1967-69; active Indsl. Devel. Commn. Mid-Fla., Orlando, 1979-84. Served to seaman 2d class USN, 1945-46. Mem. Atty.'s Title Ins. Fund Inc., Orange County Bar Assn. (exec. coun.), Univ. Club, Order of Coif, Phi Alpha Delta, Phi Kappa Phi. Republican. Baptist and Methodist. Office: Arnold Matheny & Eagan PA 605 E Robinson St Ste 730 Orlando FL 32801 Office Phone: 407-841-1550. Business E-Mail: Weagan@ameorl.com.

EAGAR, THOMAS WADDY, metallurgist, educator; b. Chattanooga, Jan. 9, 1950; s. Harry Douglas Sr. and Emily Clarkson (Thompson) E.; m. Pamela Dozier Garrett, Apr. 17, 1973; children: Matthew, Rebekah, Linda, Karen, James, Anna, Thomas. BS in Metallurgy, MIT, 1972, ScD in Metallurgy, 1975, postgrad., 1988, Lehigh U., 1975-76. Registered profl. engr., Mass. Rsch. engr. Homer Rsch. Labs. Bethlehem (Pa.) Steel Corp., 1974-76; asst. prof. materials engring. MIT, Cambridge, 1976-80, assoc. prof., 1980-87, prof., 1987—, acting dept. head, 1989, Richard P. Simmons prof. materials engring., 1990-93, Posco prof. materials engring., 1993-99, Thomas Lord prof. engring. systems, 2001—05, dir. Materials Processing Ctr., 1990-93, dir. mfg. program, 1993-95, dept. head, 1995—2000. Liaison Scientist U.S. Office Naval Rsch., Tokyo, 1984-85; dir. metall. engring. Simpson, Gumpertz and Heger, Inc., 1994; adv. bd. Edison Welding Inst., Columbus, Ohio, 1989-95; unit mfg. process rsch. com. Nat. Rsch. Coun., Washington, 1990-94, nat. materials adv. bd., 1998-2003, mfg. and engring. design bd., 2003—; tech. rev. bd. U.S. Army Rsch. Labs., 1993-95; cons., presenter and lectr. in field. Mem. adv. and tech. rev. bds. Materials Tech.; key reader Welding Jour.; contbr. over 200 articles to tech. publs.; patentee method of resistance welding, non-hygroscopic welding flux binders, large diameter stud and method and apparatus for welding same, laser instrument, age-hardenable sterling silver, emissivity independent multi-wavelength pyrometry, silver alloys of exceptional and reversilbe hardness; wear-resistant bond for abrasive tools, abrasive tool containing coated abrasive grain. Named Internat. Jr. Civitan of Yr., 1968; Dennison K. Bullens scholar, 1969-71, Foundry Edn. Fund scholar, 1970-71; grad. fellow NSF, 1972-74, Creativity Ext. award, 1988-90. Fellow AAAS, Am. Soc. Metals (Henry Marion Howe medal 1992), Am. Welding Soc. (hon. mem. Adams membership award 1979-83, Warren F. Savage award 1990, 96, Williams Sparagen award 1991, 94, Comfort A. Adams lectr., 1992, Charles H. Jennings Meml. medal 1983, 91, 2003, William Irrgang award 1993, Silver Quill award 2002); mem. AIME (metallurgy and metals prize Boston sect. 1972, Champion H. Mathewson Gold medal 1987, Henry Krumb lectr. 1987), Nat. Acad. Engring., ASTM, ASME, Am. Ceramic Soc., Materials Rsch. Soc., Soc. Automotive Engrs., Soc. Mfg. Engrs., Welding Rsch. Coun. Internat. Inst. Welding (Am. coun. Houdremont lectr. 1990), Tau Beta Pi (bd. dirs. New England dist. 1977-80, chief advisor MIT chpt., disting. svc. award 1980), Phi Lambda Epsilon. Mem. Lds Ch. Office: MIT Rm 4-136 77 Massachusetts Ave Cambridge MA 02139-4307

EAGER, GEORGE SIDNEY, JR., electrical engineer, engineering executive; b. Balt., Sept. 5, 1915; s. George S. and Ada Elizabeth (Heinz) E.; m. Ruth Duff, Oct. 13, 1945; children: Robert W., John W., George S. III. BEE, Johns Hopkins U., 1936, PhD in Engring., 1941. Rsch. supr., asst. dir., assoc. dir. to dir. rsch. Gen. Cable Corp., Highland Heights, Ky., 1945-80; pres. Barr Duff Corp., Upper Montclair, NJ, 1998—. Contbr. numerous articles to profl. jours. Author 35 patents elec. wires and cables. Lt. col. Signal Corps, U.S. Army, 1941-45, ETO. Fellow IEEE, Montclair Golf Club. Republican. Congregationalist. Home: 14 Bellegrove Dr Montclair NJ 07043-2527 E-mail: geager@earthlink.net.

EAGLEBURGER, LAWRENCE SIDNEY, former secretary of state; b. Milw., Aug. 1, 1930; s. Leon Sidney and Helen (Van Ornum) E.; m. Marlene Ann Heinemann, Apr. 23, 1966; 1 son by previous marriage, Lawrence Scott; children: Lawrence Andrew, Lawrence Jason. Student, Cen. State Coll., Stevens Point, Wis., 1948-50; BS, U. Wis., 1952, MS, 1957; LLD (hon.), U. S.C., 1985, George Washington U., 1986. Teaching asst. U. Wis., 1956-57; joined U.S. Fgn. Service, 1957, 3d sec. Tegucigalpa, Honduras, 1957-59; assigned US Dept. State, 1959-62, 65-66; 2d sec. Belgrade, Yugoslavia, 1962-65; mem. staff NSC, 1966-67; spl. asst. to under sec. US Dept. State, 1967-69; exec. asst. to asst. to Pres. for nat. security affairs The White House, 1969; polit. adv., counselor for polit. affairs U.S. Mission to NATO, Brussels, 1969-71; dep. asst. sec. US Dept. Def., 1971-73, dep. asst. to Pres. for nat. security ops., 1973, exec. asst. to sec., 1973-75; dep. under sec. for mgmt., exec. asst. to sec. US Dept. State, 1975-77, US amb. to Yugoslavia Belgrade, 1977-81, asst. sec. for European affairs, 1981-82, undersec. for polit. affairs, 1982-84, dep. sec., 1989—92, acting sec., 1992, sec., 1992-93; pres. Kissinger Assocs., Inc., NYC, 1984—89; sr. pub. policy adv. Baker, Donelson, Bearman & Caldwell, Washington, 1993—. Bd. dirs. ITT Corp., Josephson Internat., Inc., Phillips Petroleum Co., Halliburton Co., Universal Corp.; trustee Mutual of N.Y.; mem. Iraq Study Group, 2006 Vice chmn. 7th Dist. Young Republicans Wis., 1950-51; mem. Wis. Young Rep. Exec. Com., 1949-51. Served to 1st lt. AUS, 1952-54. Recipient Disting. Civilian Service medal US Dept. Def., 1973; Pres. award for Disting. Fed. Civilian Svc., 1977, William J. Carr award, US Dept. State, 1984, Presdl. Citizen's medal by Pres., 1991, Disting. Svc. award, US Dept. State, 1992; awarded honorary knighthood by Britain, 1995; named ARC internat. amb.-at-large. Mem. Alpha Sigma Phi. Republican. Lutheran. Mailing: Baker Donelson Bearman & Caldwell 555 11th St NW Washington DC 20004 E-mail: leagleburger@bakerdonelson.com.*

EAGLEEYE-LORD, AMY, writer, editor; d. Jack W. and Lynn C. Eagleeye; m. William N. Lord; 1 child, Daisy R. Lord. BA, U. Toledo, 1988—93. Tech. editor Am. Prep. Inst., Killeen, Tex., 1998—2000; medical editor Pro ED Comm., Inc., Beachwood, Ohio, 2001; assoc. writer, editor Am. Greetings Corp., Cleve., 2005—. Independent. Office: American Greetings Corp One American Rd Cleveland OH 44144 Home Phone: 216-227-1692.

EAGLES, SIDNEY SMITH, JR., retired judge; b. Asheville, NC, Aug. 5, 1939; s. Sidney Smith Sr. and Mildred Truman (Brite) E.; m. Rachel Phillips, May 22, 1965; children: Virginia Brite, Margaret Phillips. BA, Wake Forest U., 1961, JD, 1964. Bar: N.C. 1964. Revisor Gen. Statutes Commn., Raleigh, NC, 1967-70; asst. atty. gen. legis. drafting service Office Atty. Gen. N.C., Raleigh, 1970-74, dep. atty. gen. spl. prosecution divsn., 1974-76; counsel to speaker N.C. State Legislature, Raleigh, 1976-80; ptnr. Eagles Hafer & Hall, Raleigh, 1977-82; judge N.C. Ct. Appeals, Raleigh, 1983—2004, chief judge, 1998—2004; of counsel Smith Moore LLP, 2004—. Adj. prof. Campbell U. Sch. Law, 1977—; chmn. N.C. Jud. Stds. Commn., 1994—96; mem. faculty Appellate Judges Sch. Law Sch. NYU, NYC, 1993—99; mem. Uniform Laws Conf., 1968—83, 1992—, life mem., 2000. Co-author: North Carolina Criminal Procedure Forms, 1975, 3d edit., 1989; contbr. articles to profl. jours. V.p. Raleigh Jaycees, 1972-73; mem. Senatorial Dist. Dem. Com., 1979-81; bd. dirs. Wake County (N.C.) Symphony Soc., 1980-81, Women's Aid of Wake County, 1978—, Carolinas Dist. Kiwanis Found, 2004-2005.; bd. elders, bd. deacons, trustee, tchr. Sunday sch. Hillyer Meml. Christian Ch., 1980—, chmn bd., 1989; bd. visitors Wake Forest U. Sch. Law; vice chair bd. trustees Barton Coll., 1999, chair, 2002—. Served to capt. USAF, 1964-67; col., ret. 1991. Named Disting. Law Alumnus, Wake Forest U., 1981; N.C. Justice Found. fellow, 1972. Mem. ABA (chmn. appellate judges conf. 1993-94, mem. appellate jud. edn. com. 1994-98, ho. of dels. 1992-, mem. legal edn. 2002—), Am. Law Inst. (life), N.C. Bar Assn. (v.p. 1989-90), Wake County Bar Assn. (chmn. exec. com. 1975, pres. 2006—), N.C. State Bar, Execs. Club (pres. 1985), Kiwanis (disting. pres. Raleigh 1986-87, disting. lt. gov. 1995, Kiwanian of Yr. award 1989), Phi Delta Phi, Phi Alpha Delta (James Iredell award 1990). Avocations: politics, reading. Office: Smith Moore LLP PO Box 27525 Raleigh NC 27611 Office Phone: 919-755-8771. Business E-Mail: sid.eagles@smithmoorelaw.com.

EAGLES, STUART ERNEST, real estate company officer; b. Saint John, NB, Can., July 29, 1929; s. Ernest Lyle and Evelyn Gertrude (Feltmate) E.; m. Margaret Anne Gulliver, Sept. 30, 1952; children: James Stuart, Patricia Anne, Mark Edward. BS, Acadia U., 1949, DCL (hon.), 1992. Pres. Aegean Devel. Inc., Toronto, 1988—. Bd. dirs. Hardit Corp., OPB Realty Inc.; past trustee, dir. Internat. Coun. Shopping Ctrs.; past pres. and dir. Can. Inst. Pub. Real Estate Cos. Gov. Jr. Achievement Can. Mem. Nat. Club (past pres.), Can. Club, Empire Club. Home: 24 Garfield Ave Toronto ON Canada M4T 1E7 Home Phone: 416-485-1971; Office Phone: 416-601-3925. Business E-Mail: stuart.eagles@opb.ca.

EAGLESON, PETER STURGES, civil and environmental engineer, educator; b. Phila., Feb. 27, 1928; s. William Boal and Helen (Sturges) E.; m. Marguerite Anne Partridge, May 28, 1949 (div.); children: Helen Marie, Peter Sturges, Jeffrey Partridge; m. Beverly Grossmann Rich, Dec. 27, 1974. BS in Civil Engring, Lehigh U., 1949, MS, 1952; Sc.D., MIT, 1956; D of Engring. (hon.), Lehigh U., 1998. Jr. engr. George B. Mebus (cons. engr.), Glenside, Pa., 1950-51; teaching asst. Lehigh U., 1951-52; research asst. Mass. Inst. Tech., 1952-54; mem. faculty MIT, 1954-93, prof. civil engring., 1965-93, head dept. civil engring., 1970-75, emeritus prof. civil and environ. engring., 1993—. Vis. asso. Calif. Inst. Tech., 1975-76; Fulbright sr. research scholar Commonwealth Sci. and Indsl. Research Orgn., Canberra, Australia, 1966-67 Author: (with others) Estuary and Coastline Hydrodynamics, 1966, Dynamic Hydrology, 1970, Ecohydrology, 2002. Served to 2d lt. C.E. AUS, 1949-50. Recipient Desmond Fitzgerald medal, 1959, Clemens Herschel prize, 1965 both Boston Soc. Civil Engrs., rsch. prize ASCE, 1963, William Bowie medal Am. Geophysical Union, 1994, Stockholm Water prize Stockholm Water Found., 1997. Fellow AAAS, Am. Meteorol. Soc. (hon.), Am. Geophys. Union (Robert E. Horton award 1979, Robert E. Horton medal 1988, pres. 1986-88, William Bowie medal 1994), Internat. Assn. Hydrological Scis. (Internat. Hydrology prize 1991); mem. NAE, European Geophys. Soc. (John Dalton medal 1999). Office: MIT Dept Civil & Environ Engring Room 48-325 Cambridge MA 02139 Home Phone: 617-232-6530; Office Phone: 617-253-2725.

EAGLESON, WILLIAM BOAL, JR., banker; b. Phila., Dec. 10, 1925; s. William Boal and Helen (Sturges) E.; m. Catherine West McLean, May 28, 1960; children: Elizabeth E. Mackie, John McLean. BS, Lehigh U., 1949, LLD, 1983; MBA, U. Pa., 1951. With Fed. Res. Bank Phila., 1949-51; investment officer Girard Bank, Phila., 1951-61, v.p., 1961, exec. v.p., 1967; pres., dir. Girard Co., Girard Bank, 1970-80, chmn. bd., 1974-85, Mellon Bank Corp., 1983-85, chmn. emeritus, 1985—. Chmn. bd. Grant St Nat. Bank, 1988-95; trustee The Gen. Theol. Sem.; former mem. adv. bd. Yamaichi Internat. Am.; bd. dirs., chmn. exec. com. Gen. Accident Ins. Co.; advisor Tokai Bank Ltd.; hon. consul gen. Japan in Phila., 1991-99. Mem. Phila. City Planning Commn., 1970-74; mem. U.S. Treas. Govt. Borrowing Com., 1976-80, Fed. Adv. Council, 1978-80; bd. dirs. Nat. Alliance of Bus.; chmn. Gov.'s State Job Tng. Council, 1983-84; chmn. Pvt. Industry Council Phila., 1978-83; trustee Acad. Natural Scis., Phila., 1967-75; former trustee, chmn. fin. com. Lehigh U.; bd. dirs. Phila. Orch. Assn.; vice chmn. World Affairs Council of Phila.; mem. adv. council East Asian studies Princeton U. With USNR, 1944-46. Decorated Govt. Japan Order of Sacred Treasure with gold rays. Mem. Am. Philos. Soc. (chmn. fin. com., treas.), Phila. Club, Gulph Mills Golf Club, Rolling Rock Club, Phi Beta Kappa. Episcopalian. Home: 1241 Denbigh Ln Radnor PA 19087-4646 Personal E-mail: weagleson@att.net.

EAGLET, ROBERT DANTON, electrical engineer, aerospace scientist, consultant, retired military officer; b. Cleve., Mar. 2, 1934; s. Albert Rudy and Dorothy Margaret (Beamer) E.; m. Sally Perry; children: Suzanne Carolyn, Allison Leigh, Kevin Robert. BSEE, U. Ariz., 1962; MSEE, U. So. Calif., 1968, PhD in Elec. Engring. and Physics, 1970. Commd. 2d lt. USAF, 1956, advanced through grades to maj. gen., 1986, forward air contr. in Vietnam, 1965-66, chief, classified program, space div. LA, 1966-68, chief strategic def. div. hdqrs. Washington, 1970-74, mil. asst. to dep. undersec. def., 1974-75; dep. gen. mgr. NATO airborne early warning program Brussels, 1975-79; dep. chief of staff devel. planning, sys. command USAF, Andrews AFB, Md., 1979-84, dep. comdr. armament divsn. Eglin AFB, Fla., 1984-86, dir. F-16 multinat. fighter program Wright Patterson AFB, Ohio, 1986-89; dep. asst. sec. of Air Force Pentagon, Washington, 1989-91; ret. USAF, 1991; pres. Eaglet Internat. Assocs., McLean, Va., 1992—. Decorated Disting. Svc. medal with oak leaf cluster, Legion of Merit with oak leaf cluster, Silver star, Disting. Flying Cross with oak leaf cluster, Bronze star with Valor device, Air medal with 24 oak leaf clusters, Purple Heart; named Outstanding Alumnus U. So. Calif. Mem. Air Force Assn., Nat. Defense Indsl. Assn., Assn. U.S. Army, Navy League, Belgian-Am. Assn. (bd. dirs.). Republican. Avocation: wind surfing. Business E-Mail: eaglet@compuserve.com.

EAGLETON, EDWARD JOHN, lawyer; b. Tulsa, Jan. 22, 1932; s. William L. and Pauline (Dellinger) E.; m. Norma Lee, Oct. 6, 1956; children: Courtney Jean, Richard John. BA, U. Okla., Norman, 1954, JD, 1956. Bar: Okla. 1955, US Dist. Ct. (ea., we. and no. dists.) Okla. 1956, US Tax Ct. 1958, US Supreme Ct. 1964; CPA, Tex., Okla. Acct. Peat Marwick Mitchell, Dallas, 1956-58; with IRS, Dallas and New Orleans, 1958-62; assoc. Houston & Klein, Tulsa, 1962-65; ptnr. Kothe & Eagleton, Tulsa, 1965-74, Houston & Klein Inc., Tulsa, 1974-94, Eagleton Eagleton & Harrison Inc., Tulsa, 1994—. Served with US Army, 1956. Named one of Best Tax Lawyers in Am., Bar Register of Preeminent Lawyers, 1983—2006. Republican. Unitarian Universalist. Home: 3210 E 65th St Tulsa OK 74136-1225 Office: Eagleton, Eagleton & Harrison Inc 320 S Boston Ave Ste 1700 Tulsa OK 74103-4706 Home Phone: 918-494-3016; Office Phone: 918-584-0462. Personal E-mail: eaglelaw@swbell.net.

EAKELEY, DOUGLAS SCOTT, lawyer; b. Morristown, NJ, Mar. 2, 1946; m. Priscilla Van Tassel, June 2, 1973. BA, Yale U., 1968, JD, 1972; BA in Jurisprudence, MA in Jurisprudence, Oxford U., Eng., 1970. Bar: NY 1973, US Ct. Appeals (2nd cir.) 1974, NJ 1978, US Ct. Appeals (3rd cir.) 1980, US Supreme Ct. 1981. Law clk. judge Harold R. Tyler, Jr. US Dist. Ct. (so. dist.) NY, NYC, 1972-73; assoc. Debevoise, Plimpton, NYC, 1973-80; ptnr. Riker, Danzig, Scherer, Hyland & Perretti, Newark, Morristown, NJ, 1980-90, 91-94; first asst. atty. gen. State NJ, 1990-91; ptnr. Lowenstein Sandler, PC, Roseland, NJ, 1994—. Chmn. Legal Svcs. NJ, North Brunswick, 1981-90, Legal Svcs. Corp., Washington, 1993-2003; pres. Legal Svc. Found. Essex County, Newark, 1981-90; chmn. NJ Sentencing Policy Study Commn., 1992-93; trustee Practising Law Inst., NYC, 1994—; trustee Boys Girls Clubs Newark, 1993-2003. Chmn. bd. editors NJ Law Jour., 1984-90. Trustee NJ Network Found., 1994—, NJ Inst. Social Justice, 1996—; pres. NJ Shakespeare Festival, Madison, 1982-86. Rhodes scholar Oxford U., 1968. Fellow Am. Bar Found.; mem. ABA (John Minor Wisdom award, litigation sect. 1997), NJ Bar Assn., Essex County Bar Assn., Fed. Bar Assn. NJ (v.p. 1983-90), Urban League Essex County (trustee 1987-88), Assn. Am. Rhodes Scholars (bd. dirs. 1995-2002), Phi Beta Kappa. Democrat. Office: Lowenstein Sandler PC 65 Livingston Ave Roseland NJ 07068-1791 Office Phone: 973-597-2348. Business E-Mail: deakeley@lowenstein.com.

EAKER, CHARLES WILLIAM, chemistry professor; b. St. Louis, May 25, 1949; s. Charles Mayfield and Mildred Catherine (Staples) E.; m. Mary Alice Eisenmann, July 6, 1974; children: Stephanie Eisenmann Eaker, Sara Marie. BS, Mich. State U., 1971; PhD, U. Chgo., 1974. Instr. U. Dallas, Irving, Tex., 1976-78, asst. prof., 1978-81, assoc. prof., 1981-89, prof., 1989—; dean Constantin Coll., 2005—. Contbr. articles to profl. jours. Rsch. grantee Robert A. Welch Found., 1984, faculty devel. grantee Arthur Vining Davis, 1980, NSF equipment grantee 1997; recipient Presdl. award U. Dallas, 1987, 91, 95, 96, 98. Mem. Am. Chem. Soc. (rsch. grantee 1978, 88), Sigma Xi. Office: U Dallas 1845 E Northgate Dr Irving TX 75062-4736 Office Phone: 972-721-5391. E-mail: eaker@udallas.edu.

EAKER, SETH A., financial consultant; BA, U. of the South, Sewanee, Tenn., 1995; MBA, Drexel U. LeBow Coll. Bus., 2004. Founder & owner Black Marble Consulting, LLC, Phila., Oceanus Life Mgmt., LLC, Phila. Spkr. in field. Founding mem. Holy Trinity Comty. Ch., Nashville; active in SADD; student trustee Bacchus & Gamma Peer Edn. Network, 1994—95; active in Nashville CARES, Blue Ball, Phila., 1998—; founding mem. Sapphire Fund, Phila., 2002—, chair fin. devel., 2006—. Recipient Student of Yr., SADD, 1991, 40 Under 40 award, Phila. Bus. Jour., 2006. Office: Black Marble Consulting/Oceanus Life Mgmt Ste 131 1315 Spruce St Philadelphia PA 19107 Office Phone: 215-869-4471, 215-416-2199. E-mail: info@oceanuspartners.com, info@blackmarbleconsulting.com.

EAKER, SHERRY ELLEN, editor; b. NYC, Nov. 30, 1949; d. Ira and Lee (Eisenberg) Eaker. BA, Queens Coll., 1971, MS, 1976. Tchr. art, English N.Y.C. Bd. Edn., 1971-76; editor-in-chief Back Stage, The Actor's Resource, NYC, 1977—2006, editor-at-large, 2006—. Editor, compiler Handbook for Performing Artists: The How-to and Who-to-Contact Reference for Actors, Singers, Dancers, 1989, rev. edit., 1991, 1995, 2004, The Cabaret Artist's Handbook-Creating Your Own Act in Today's Liveliest Theatre Setting, 2000. Mem. Drama Desk (sec. 1984-87, v.p. 1987-91), Am. Theatre Critics Assn. (exec. com.), Nat. Music Theater Network (bd. dirs.), Nat. Theatre Conf., League Profl. Theatre Women, NY Coalition Profl. Women in Arts and Media (spl. adv.), Inst. Outdoor Drama (adv. coun.), Manhattan Assn. Cabarets, NY Women in Film and TV. Avocations: theater, cabaret. Office: Back Stage 770 Broadway New York NY 10003-9595

EAKIN, J. MICHAEL, state supreme court justice; b. Mechanicsburg, Pa., Nov. 18, 1948; m. Heidi Eakin; children: Michael, Zachary, Chase. BA in Govt., Franklin & Marshall Coll., 1970; JD, Pa. State U., 1975; LLD (hon.), Widener U., 2005. Asst. dist. atty. Cumberland County, 1975—83, dist. atty., 1984—95; pvt. practice, 1980—83; judge Pa. Superior Ct., 1995—2001; justice Pa. Supreme Ct., 2001—. Lectr. Nat. Coll. Dist. Attys. Contbr. articles to profl. jours. With Pa. Army N.G., 1971—77. Recipient Sweetheart of the Yr. award, MADD, 1988, Best Catch award, Mid-Penn Anglers, 1991, Career Achievement award, Dickinson Sch. Law, 2000. Mem.: ABA, Pa. Dist. Atty.'s Inst. (bd. dirs. 1987—95, pres. 1994—95), Pa. Dist. Atty.'s Assn. (mem. exec. com., chmn. edn. 1987—95, pres. 1992—93), Pa. Bar Inst. (faculty, mem. criminal law sympsoium planning com.), Am. Inns Ct., Cumberland County Bar Assn., Dauphin County Bar Assn., Lancaster County Bar Assn., Pa. Bar Assn. (mem. plain English com.), Am. Judges Assn., Brehon Soc. Office: Pa State Supreme Ct 4720 Old Gettysburg Rd #405 Mechanicsburg PA 17055

EAKIN, RICHARD RONALD, academic administrator, mathematics educator; b. New Castle, Pa., Aug. 6, 1938; s. Everett Glenn and Mildred May (Hammerschmidt) E.; m. Jo Ann McGeehan, Aug. 23, 1960; children: Matthew Glenn, Maridy Lynn. AB in Math., Geneva Coll., Beaver Falls, Pa., 1960; MA in Math., Washington State U., 1962, PhD in Math., 1964. Asst. prof. math. Bowling Green (Ohio) State U., 1964-68, assoc. prof. math., 1968-87, asst. dean grad. sch., 1969-72, vice-provost student affairs, 1972-80, vice-provost instl. planning, 1979-80, exec. vice-provost budgeting and planning, 1980-83, v.p. budgeting and planning, 1983-87; chancellor, prof. math. East Carolina U., Greenville, 1987—2001, prof. ednl. leadership, 2001—06; ednl. cons., 2007—. Editor revs. and evaluations sect. (jour.) The Math. Tchr., 1968-70. V.p. and mem. bd. dirs. Nat. Hemophilia Found., N.Y.C., 1983-84, chmn. bd., v.p. adminstrn. and fin., 1984-87; mem. bd. dirs. Ednl. Commn. for Fgn. Med. Grads., 2002—. NDEA fellow Wash. State U., Pullman, 1960-63, NSF fellow, 1963-64. Mem. Math. Assn. Am., So. Assn. Colls. and Schs. (commn. on colls.), Phi Kappa Phi, Omicron Delta Kappa. Office: East Carolina U Ragsdale Bldg Rm 217 Greenville NC 27858 Home Phone: 252-551-3846. E-mail: eakinr@mail.ecu.edu.

EAKIN, THOMAS CAPPER, sports promotion executive; b. New Castle, Pa., Dec. 16, 1933; s. Frederick William and Beatrice (Capper) E.; m. Brenda Lee Andrews, Oct. 21, 1961; children: Thomas Andrews, Scott Frederick. BA in History, Denison U., 1956. Life ins. cons. Northwestern Mut. Life Ins. Co., Cleve., 1959-67; dist. mgr. Putman Pub. Co., Cleve., 1968-69; regional bus. mgr. Chilton Pub. Co., Cleve., 1969-70; dist. mgr. Hitchcock Pub. Co., Cleve., 1970-72; founder, pres. Golf Internat. 100

Club, Shaker Heights, Ohio, 1970—; pres. TCE Enterprises, Shaker Heights, 1973—; founder, pres. Ohio Baseball Assocs., 2005—. Founder, pres. Ohio Humanitarian Hall of Fame, 2000—, Internat. Humanitarian Hall of Fame, 2004—, US Humanitarian Hall of Fame, 2004—, Ohio Pacesetters Hall of Fame, 2004—, Ohio Baseball Hall of Fame and Mus., 1976, Ohio Youth Sports Hall of Fame, 1996—, Tuscarawas County Sports Promotions Enterprises, 1987—, Ohio Sports Promotions Co., 1989, Ohio Sports Hall of Fame Promotional Enterprises, 1990—, Summit County Sports Promotion Enterprises, 1990—, Geauga County Hist. and Sports Traditions Enterprises, 1990—, Licking County Sports Stars Enterprises, 1990—, Lake County Cmty. Promotions Enterprises, 1990—, Trumbull County Sports Stars Publs., 1990—, Portage County Hist. and Sports Publs., 1990—, Cuyahoga County Promotion Co., 1990—, Ashtabula County Hist. and Sports Publs., 1990—, Ohio Pride in Cmty. Publs., 1990—, Mahoning County Sports Headlines Publs., 1990—, Ohio Fire Dept. Promotional Publs., 1990—, Ohio Law Enforcement Cmty. Publs., 1990—, Erie County Excellence in H.S. Sports Publs., 1990—, Ohio Sports Logo Creations, 1991—, Ohio Sports Stars Enterprises, 1991—, Ohio Sports Licensing Enterprise, 1991—, Huron County Sports Pub., 1995, Lucas County Baseball Pub., 1995, Winners of Wood County Pub., 1995, Harrison County Baseball Digest, 1998—, Belmont County Baseball League, 1998—, Ohio Promotions For Sports, 2000—, Ohio Baseball Digest Harrison County, 1998—, Ohio Baseball Assoc., 2005—; founder, chmn. Twinsburg (Ohio) Cmty. Heritage Publs., Garrettsville (Ohio) Cmty. Svc. Publ., lectr. series Catch The Spirit, 2000—; founder, pub. Touching All the Bases, 1991; bd. dirs. New Hope Records, Hit and Run Records, Red Hour Records, Nat. William "Dummy" Hoy Baseball Com., 1995—; founder, dir. Cy Young Mus., 1975; adv. bd. Sportsbeat, 1985—, sch. Calendar Co., Inc., 1984, 89, D & D Sports Prodn. and Mktg. Creations, 1990—, Damascus Steel Casting Co., 1987—, Advantage Sports Co., 1989—, Base Sports Co., 1989, M & M Publs., 1987— Founder, pres., dir. Cy Young Mus., 1975-80; founder, pres. Ohio Sports Hall of Fame, 1985—, Shaker Hts Sports Hall of Fame, 1989—, Ohio Sports Legends Found., 1991—, Moses Fleetwood Walker Baseball Meml. award, 1991—, Toledo Baseball Bluecoats, 1984—, Tuscarawas County Sports Hall of Fame, 1980—, Tuscarawas County Am. Revolution Bicentennial Commn., exec. com. 1974-1976, Tuscarawas Valley Tourist Assn., 1979-81, Buckeye Baseball Lecture Series, 1989—, Cleve. Baseball Old Timers Assn., Ohio Sports Celebrity Golf Invitational, 1991—, Midwest Sports Coun., Chesterland (Ohio) Hist. Found. Enhancement Fund, 1989—, Berea (Ohio) Hist. and Sports Fund, 1984—, Windham (Ohio) Cmty. Svc. Found., 1990—, Jefferson Hist. and Sports Found., 1986—, Ohio Sports Ednl. Coun., 1991—, Youth in Cmty. Svc. and Vols. are Winners Lecture Series, 1991—, Ohio Minor League Baseball Hall of Fame Assn., 1992—, U.S. Sports Hall of Fame, 1989—, Ohio Founders League, 1990—, Ohio Negro Baseball Hall of Fame Vets. Coun., 1991—, Ohio Women's Baseball Hall of Fame, 1998—, Alta Weiss Meml. award, 1998—, Ohio Baseball History Mus, 2002—; founder, nat. chmn. Cy Young Centennial, 1967, Cy Young Golf Invitational; founder, chmn. Streetsboro (Ohio) Athletic Found., 1989—, Wickliffe (Ohio) Cmty. and Sports Fund, Madison (Ohio) Fund, Middlefield (Ohio) Fire Dept. Cmty. Promotions Fund, Burton Athletic Enhancement Fund, Fairview Pk. (Ohio) Cmty. Svc. Fund, Bath-Richfield Ohio Cmty. Fund, Independence Freedom Fund, 1988—, Aurora Hist. Preservation Fund, 1988—, Conneaut (Ohio) Cmty. Promotional Fund, 1991—; founder, dir. Target/Reach Youth, 1971—; trustee Hiram House, 1989—, Nat. Jr. Tennis League, 1985—; hon. bd. dirs. Chautaugua Sports Hall of Fame, 1982—; bd. dirs. Greater Toledo Sports Hall of Fame; exec. sponsor, Ohio chmn. World Golf Hall of Fame, Pinehurst, NC, 1979—; founder Famous Ohioans in Print Hall of Fame, 1994; adv. bd. Portage County Sports Hall of Fame, 1983—, Cuyahoga Hills Boys Sch., Warrensville Hts., Ohio, 1971—, Camp Hope, Warrensville Hts., 1973—, Cleve. Sports Legend Found., 1988—, Great Ohioans Hall of Fame, 1988—, Solon Cmty. Promotional Fund, 1989—; disting. citizens adv. bd. Am. Police Hall of Fame and Mus., 1987—; career adv. bd. Denison U., 1990—; nom. com. Ohio Profl. and Amateur Athlete of Yr. Awards, 1990—; active Geauga County Hist. Soc., Summit County Sports Hall of Fame, Dunham Tavern Mus.; founder, chmn. Shaker Hts. Youth Hall of Fame, 1996; chmn. Ray Chapman Meml. com., 2000, others; assoc. Merrick Art Gallery; trustee Great Expectations Ltd., 2004—; adv. bd. Cleve. Coun. on Corrections, 2005—; founder, chmn. Scott F. Eakin Meml. Music Fund, 2007. Served in AUS, 1956-58. Named to Order of Long Leaf Pine, NC State Senate, 1984, Sch. Calendar Co. Hall of Fame, 1985, Hon. Order of Ky. Cols., 1986, Venerable Order Michael the Archangel, Am. Police Hall of Fame, 1989; named Hon. Citizen, City of Memphis, 1986, City of Little Rock, 1986, Ohio Baseball Man of Yr., 1991; named to Chautauqua Sports Hall of Fame, 1983, Ohio Baseball Hall of Fame, World Biog. Hall of Fame, 1984, Ohio Record Holders Hall of Fame, 1989, City of Cleve. Vol. Hall of Fame, 1991, Am. Athletic Assn. of Deaf Hall of Fame, 1992, Cy Young Tuscarawas County Old Timers Baseball Assn. Hall of Fame, 1993, Greater Akron Baseball Hall of Fame, 1993, Greater Stark County Baseball Hall of Fame, 1994, Ohio Sr. Citizens Hall of Fame, 1995, Ohio Vets Hall of Fame, 1995, Old Time Ball Players Assn. Wis. Hall of Fame, 1998, Wis. Baseball Hall of Fame, 1998; recipient Disting. Svc. award Hubbard, Ohio, 1986, Vermilion Kiwanis, 1996, Internat Friendship award Premier Ont., Can., 1985, Commr.'s award Trumbull County, 1985, Gov.'s citation State of Md., 1987, Hon. West Virginian award, 1987, J. Edgar Hoover award Am. Police Hall of Fame, 1991, Humanitarian award City of Cleve., 1991, Mayor's Volunteerism award, 1991, Vol. of Yr. award No. Ohio Live, 1991, Ohio Govs. award, 1978, Ohio Govs. award Cmty. Action, 1974, Sports Achievement award Dapper Dan Club of Upper Ohio Valley, 1993, Sports Hero award Am. Athletic Assn. of Deaf, Inc., 1992, Ohio Profl. and Athlete of Yr. award, 1995, Lifetime Achievement award, 1995, 20th Century award Achievement Nat. Assn. Chiefs Police, 1998, A Spl. Friend award Blair County Spl. Olympics, 1998, Lifetime Achievement award Lake County Hist. Soc., 1998, Disting. Svc. award Rotary, Twinsburg, Ohio, 1998, Solon, Ohio, 1999, Nordonia Hills, 2005, Cmty. Svc. award Ohio Dr. Martin Luther King, Jr. Holiday Commn., 1999, Newbury Kiwanis, 2005, Cmty. Builders award Flushing Ohio Masonic Lodge No. 298, 1998, Disting. Cmty. Svc. award Lorain County Assn. Township Trustees and Clks., 2001; commendation State of NC Senate, 1984, State of Pa. Senate, 1984, State of La., State of Ohio Senate and Reps.; Columbus (Ohio) City Coun., 1985, Cleve. City Coun., 1989; Thomas C. Eakin Day declared City of Cleve., 1974, N.Mex., 1987, others; world record holder Guinness Book of World Records, 1991; Sports Hero award, 1992, Rufus Putnam Disting. Svc. award Ohio Masons, 1999, medal of Honor DAR, 2000, Trumbull County Baseball Commendation Mahoning Valley Profl. Baseball Assn., 2000; named Trustee of Yr. Nat. Jr. Tennis League, Cleve., 1996, Paul Harris fellow Rotary Internat., 1999, Ohio's Outstanding Sr. Vol. Med. Mutual Ohio, 2006, Outstanding Citizen Portage County Ohio Commisioners, 2007; Honor award Ravenna Kiwanis, 2001, Munroe Falls Kiwanis, 2001, Commendation award Mahoning Valley Profl. Baseball Assn., 2002, Ellis Island Medal of Honor, 2002, Am. Spirit award, 2002, U.S. Marine Corps. Commendation, 2002, Cmty. Svc. award Middlefield Fire Dept., 1999, Copley Ohio Hist. Soc., 2002, Wellington Kiwanis Club, 2003, Outstanding Spkr. award Stow-Munroe Falls Ohio C. of C., 2002, Golden Legion of Phi Delta Theta, 2003, Baseball Achievement award, Greater Youngstown Old Timers Assn., 2003, Liberty Bell Hist. award Independence Hist. Soc., 2004, Svc. award N.W. Summit Country Rotary, 2004, Hist. Merit award Aurora Hist. Soc., 2004, Svc. award Oberlin Exch. Club, 2005, Cmty. Svc. award Avon Hist. Soc., 2006, Svc. Above Self award Aurora Rotary Club, Bedford Hist. Soc., 2006, Cmty. Svc. award Fairview West Park Rotary Club, Northampton Rotary Club, 2006, FairThe Spirit of 76 award Bedford Hist. Soc., 2006, Ruritan Cmty. Svc. award Grand Valley Ruritan Club, 2006; named Ohio's Outstanding Sr. Vol., Med. Mut. Ohio, 2006, Outstanding Citizen Portage County, Portage County Commrs., 2007, others. Mem. Internat. Hist. Preservation Assn. (founder, pres. 2007), White House Hist. Assn. (charter), U.S. Assn. Sports Halls of Fame, U.S. Hist. Soc., Soc. Am. Baseball Rsch., Nat. Trust Hist. Preservation, Ohio Hist. Soc., Ohio Hist. Preservation Assn. (founder, pres. 2007), Ohio Sports Halls of Fame, Ohio Baseball Roundtable (founder, pres. 1991—), Ohio Assn. Old Time Baseball Players (founder, pres. 1990—), Ohio Racquetball Assn. (adv. bd. 1981-82), Old Time Ball Players Assn. Wis., Western Pa. Sports Hall of Fame, North Ohio Old Time Baseball Players Club (adv. bd. 1978—), Tuscarawas County Old Timers Baseball Assn. (hon. dir. 1972—, pres. 1985—, commendation 1970), Tuscarawas County Hist. Soc. (trustee 1978-81), Lawrence County Hist. Soc., Greater Youngstown Old Timers Baseball Assn. (Ohio Baseball Man of Yr. award 1991, Hall of Fame 1994, King of the Realm award 2004), Maple Heights Hist. Soc. (Hist. Honor award 2007), Madison Hist. Soc., Middlefield Hist. Soc. (adv. bd. 1986—), Clinton Hist. Soc. (hon. trustee 1987—), Windsor Hist. Soc. (adv. bd. 1987—), Solon Hist. Soc., Newcomerstown Hist. Soc., Shaker Hist. Soc. (trustee 1980-82), Bainbridge Twp. Hist. Soc. (Hist. Preservation award 2007), Greater Canton Amateur Sports Hall of Fame Assn. (commendation 1994), Barberton Sports Hall of Fame (founder, chmn. publs. 1989—), Holloway Old Timers Baseball Club (adv. bd. 1990—), Temperance House Mus., Negro Leagues Baseball Mus., Internat. Platform Assn., English Speaking Union (trustee 1994—), Internat. Spkrs. Century Assn. (founder, pres. 2005—), Am. Spkrs. Century Assn. (founder, pres. 2005—), Denison U. Cleve. Men's Club, Gustave Courbet Soc., Western Res. Hist. Soc., Interact Club (adv. bd. Twinsburg chpt. 1981—, founder, dir. Shaker Heights chpt. 1971—), Exec. Club (Woodmere, Ohio chpt., Hall of Fame 1990), Univ. Sch. Tennis Club, Grandview Golf Club, PGA Nat. Golf Club (internat. mem.), Legend Lake Golf Club, Beachwood Athletic Club, Rotary (Svc. Above Self award Wickliffe chpt. 1991, Disting. Svc. award Swanton chpt. 1991, Outstanding Sports and Civic Svc. award Bellevue chpt. 1990, Spirit of Twinsburg award Twinsburg chpt. 1991, pres. Shaker Heights chpt. 1970-71), The Order of St. George (named Knight Comdr., 1994), Phi Delta Theta (exec. com. nat. Lou Gehrig award com. 1975—, charter mem. trustees roundtable 2003, charter inductee Ohio Iota Hall of Fame 1989, Outstanding Alumnus award 1989, Cleve. pres. 1970, Hall of Fame 1975, Disting. Alumnus award 1997, Internat. Fraternity Hall of Fame 1997, Mr. Ohio Iota award 2004, Golden Legion 2003), Ray Chapman Meml. Com. (chmn. 2000), Merrick Art Gallery (assoc.), Ohio Patriots Assn. (founder, pres. 2004), Masons, Brunswick Rotary (County Svc. award 2005), VFW (Post 5047, Outstanding Vet. award 2007). Address: 245 Sandover Dr Aurora OH 44202 Office Phone: 330-995-4468.

EAKINS, WILLIAM SHANNON, lawyer; b. Glen Cove, NY, July 22, 1951; s. William Shannon and Jean (Pickup) E.; 1 child, Amelia Moore. BA, Yale U., 1974; JD, Cornell U., 1977. In-house lawyer, trust adminstr., portfolio mgr. J.P. Morgan Bank, NYC, 1977-81; counsel com. on taxation, investigations & govt. ops. NY State Senate, Albany, 1981-84; assoc. Gelberg & Abrams, NYC, 1981-84, Phillips, Nizer, Benjamin, Krim & Ballon, NYC, 1984-88, ptnr., 1989-92; ptnr., chmn. dept. trusts and estates Olshan, Grundman, Frome & Rosenzweig, NYC, 1993—98, Patton, Eakins, Lipsett, Holbrook & Savage (formerly Forsythe, Patton, Ellis, Lipsett & Savage), NYC, 1998—. Bd. dir. Asphalt Green Inc.; mem. estate planning com. Arthritis Found. Contbr. articles to profl. jours. Vice-chmn. N.Y. Rep. County Com., N.Y.C., 1985-89, exec. com., 1979-87, dist. leader, 1979-87; dir. Knickerbocker Republican Club, 1979-87; pres. Ivy Republican Club, 1980-82; vice-chmn. Manhattan Cmty. Bd. 8, NYC, 1980-84, 93-97; Rep., Ind. Neighbors and Conservative candidate NY State Assembly, 1992; bd. dir. Homecrest Cmty. Svcs., Inc., 1999-05, NY Found. Sr. Citizens, 1981-93, 06-; sec. Hellgate Hill-Highgate Cmty. Assn.; elder, mem. session Brick Presbyn. Ch., 2003-06, v.p. bd. trustees, 2006-; mem. NY Presbyn.-Jewish Dialogue Steering Com., Am. Jewish Com. and Auburn Theolog. Sem. Com. on Jewish-Presbyn. Rels., 2005-; overture adv. NYC Presbytery Presbyn. Ch. USA Gen. Assembly, Birmingham, Ala., 2006; mem. steering com. Auburn Theol Sem. Faith to Faith-Face to Face program, 2006-; bd. dirs. NY Theol. Sem., 2007-. Mem. NY State Bar Assn., Assn. Bar City NY (com. on estate and gift taxation, com. on NY state legis.), Yale Club, St. Andrews Soc. State of NY (bd. mgrs. 2003-04). Republican. Presbyterian. Office: Patton Eakins Lipsett Holbrook & Savage 420 Lexington Ave New York NY 10170-0002 E-mail: wmeakins@rcn.com.

EAKLE, ARLENE HASLAM, genealogist; b. Salt Lake City, July 19, 1936; d. Thomas E. and Margaret Haslam; m. Alma D. Eakle, Jr., Feb. 8, 1957; children: JoAnn, Richard, Linda, John. ADN, Weber State U.; MA in English history, U. Utah, PhD of English history. Author: (with Linda Brinkerhoff) Genealogy in Land Records, 1998, Migration Patterns of American Families, 1999, Family History for Fun and Profit-The Genealogy Research Process, 30th anniversary edit., 2003, Naming Patterns of American Families, 2007, Genealogy in Scotland: Jurisdictional Approach, 2007; (with Johni Cerny) The Source: A Guidebook for American Genealogy, 1984, Ancestry's Guide to Research, 1985; editor: Research News, Immigration Digest; editor: Virginia Notebooks, N.Y. Rsch. Fellow Utah Geneal. Assn., 1987; recipient Award of Merit Fedn. Geneal. Soc., 1984, Julian Bickersteth medal Inst. Heraldic and Geneal. Studies, Eng., 1988, Gold and VIP awards Kennedy Inner Cir., 2002-07. Mem. Am. Family Records Assn. (bd. dirs. 1990-2004, founding dir.), Assn. Profl. Genealogists (pres. 1980-82, founding dir., Grahame Thomas Smallwood Jr. Award of Merit 1984), Md. Geneal. Soc., West Fla. Geneal. Soc. Office: Genealogical Inst 56 W Main St PO Box 129 Tremonton UT 84337-0129 Office Phone: 800-377-6058. E-mail: genealogy@utahlinx.com.

EALY, CYNTHIA PIKE, artist, real estate agent; b. Eveleth, Minn., Apr. 13, 1932; d. Robert Sheldon Pike and Lila Mary Saari; m. Donald Rae Ealy, Dec. 14, 1952; children: Elizabeth, Dennis, Jonathan, Richard. Student, Coll. of Ams., Mexico City, 1950-52, U. So. Calif., 1952-53. Actress, Mexico City, 1950-52; owner Woodland World Travel, Tarzana, Calif., 1965-70; decorator Ridgewood, NJ, 1970-71; artist, 1972—; realtor, 1987—. Bd. dirs., pres. Rep. Women's club, Woodland Hills, Calif., 1964-69; active Internat. Sch. of Brussels, 1975-80; co-chmn. Reps. Abroad, Europe, 1978-82. Recipient Outstanding Svc. award Am. Women's Club of Brussels, 1984. Mem. North Tahoe Arts, Niguel Art Assn. of Orange County. Avocation: instructing french language and cuisine. Home: 27142 Paseo Del Este San Juan Capistrano CA 92675-4927

EALY, JONATHAN BRUCE, lawyer; b. LA, Apr. 20, 1960; s. Donald Rae and Cynthia Howland (Pike) E. AB cum laude, Harvard U., 1982; JD, Duke U., 1985. Bar: Alaska 1986, U.S. Ct. Appeals (9th cir.) 1986. Clk. judge Karen Hunt Alaska Superior Ct., Anchorage, 1985-86; assoc. Taylor & Hintz, Anchorage, 1986-89, Heller, Ehrman, White & McAuliffe, Anchorage, 1989-93; gen. counsel Borisovich Internat., Inc., Anchorage, 1993—; of counsel Partnow, Sharrock & Tindall, Anchorage, 1995-2000; spl. counsel Heller Ehrman White and McAuliffe, Anchorage, 2000—03, Tindall Bennett & Shoup, Anchorage, 2003—. Bd. dirs. Borealis Brewing Co.; prin. Na'au, Inc., 1998—. Author: Third Story, 1998, What, If Anything, Is an E-mail, 2002. Pres. Anchorage Youth Ct., 1993-94, legal advisor, 1989-92; bd. dirs. Kids Voting Alaska, Anchorage, 1993, Alzheimer's Disease Resource Agy. of Alaska, 2003—, v.p., 2004-06, pres., 2006—. Mem. Anchorage Bar Assn. (pres. 1994, v.p. 1993, pres. young lawyers sect. 1988-90). Office: 508 W 2d Ave 3d Fl Anchorage AK 99501

EARENFIGHT, THERESA MARIE, education educator; b. Mpls., Minn., Feb. 25, 1954; d. John Tobin and Norma Arline (Singsaas) Earenfight. BA, U. Minn., 1981; MA, Fordham U., 1989, PhD, 1997. Rsch. asst. U. Minn., 1977—81; art sales C.G. Rein Gallery, Mpls, 1981—84, Pace Gallery, NYC, 1984—87; vis. asst. prof. Queensborough Cmty. Coll., 1997—98; asst. prof. Seattle U., 1998—2004, assoc. prof., 2004—. Bd. dirs. Fulbright Assn., Seattle, 2000—, Soc. of Medieval Feminist Scholarship, Eugene, Oreg., 2004—. Author (and editor): Queenship and Political Power in Medieval and Early Modern Spain. Fulbright fellowship, Fulbright Commn., 1993—94, grant, Nat. Endowment for the Humanities, 2003. Mem.: Renaissance Soc., Medieval Acad. Am. Office Phone: 206-296-5477.

EARHART, EILEEN MAGIE, retired elementary school and child and family life educator; b. Hamilton, Ohio, Oct. 21, 1928; d. Andrew J. and Martha (Waldorf) Magie; m. Paul G. Earhart; children: Anthony G., Bruce P., Daniel T. BS, Miami U., Oxford, Ohio, 1950; MA in Adminstrn. and Ednl. Services, Mich. State U., 1962, PhD in Edn., 1969; H.H.D. (hon.), Miami U., Oxford, Ohio, 1980. Tchr. home econs. W. Alexandria (Ohio) Schs., 1950-51; elementary tchr. Waterford Twp. Schs., Pontiac, Mich., 1958-65, reading specialist, 1965-67; prof., chmn. family and child ecology dept. Mich. State U., East Lansing, 1968-84; prof., head dept. home and family life Fla. State U., Tallahassee, 1984-89; ret., 1989. Author: Attention and Classification Training Curriculum; co-editor spl. issue of Family Relations, 1984; contbr. chpts. to profl. jours., books. Mem. adv. bd. Lansing Com. on Children's TV, Family/Sch./Cmty. Partnership Project, Tallahassee; bd. dirs. Women's Resource Ctr., Grand Rapids, Mich., Wesley Found., Fla. State U., 1989-99; mem. campus ministries bd. Fla. A&M U., 1995-98; Sunday sch. tchr. Haines City United Meth. Ch., 2001-06; mem. Mich. Gov.'s Task Force on Youth. Mem. Nat. Coun. Family Rels. (pres. Assn. of Couns. 1987-88, bd. dirs. 1986-88, chair nat. meeting local arrangements 1992), Fla. Coun. Family Rels. (pres. elect 1985-86, pres. 1986-87), Nat. Assn. Edn. Young Children, Assn. Childhood Edn. Internat., Am. Home Econs. Assn. (named AHEA leader at 75th Ann. of Assn. 1984), Internat. Fedn. Home Econs., Mich. Home Econs. Assn. (pres. 1980-82), Fla. Home Econs. Assn. (chmn. scholarship com. 1986-88, dist. chmn. 1990-91, chmn. nominating com. 1991-92, co-chair ann. meeting 1995), Ednl. Rsch. Assn., Killearn United Meth. Ch., United Meth. Women (cir. chair 1993-97, pres. 1994), Phi Kappa Phi (pres. Fla State U. chpt. 1988-89), Delta Kappa Gamma, Omicron Nu, others. Home (Summer): 22 Oak Tree Ct Franklin NC 28734 Home: 23 Ivywood Sq Oxford OH 45056 E-mail: emearhart@aol.com.

EARL, ANTHONY SCULLY, retired governor, lawyer; b. Lansing, Mich., Apr. 12, 1936; s. Russell K. and Ethlynne Julia (Scully) E.; children: Julia, Anne, Mary, Catherine. BS, Mich. State U.; JD, U. Chgo. Bar: Wis., Minn. Asst. dist. atty. Marathon County, Wausau, Wis., 1965-66; city atty. City of Wausau, 1966-69; mem. Wis. Assembly, Madison, 1969-74; mem. firm Crooks, Low & Earl, 1969-74; sec. Wis. Dept. Adminstrn., Madison, 1974-75, Dept. Nat. Resources, Madison, 1975-80; v.p. firm Foley & Lardner, Madison, 1980-82; gov. State of Wis., Madison, 1983-87; ptnr. Quarles and Brady, Madison, 1987—. Served as lt. USN, 1962-65. Democrat. Roman Catholic. Office: Quarles & Brady 1 S Pinckney St PO Box 2113 Madison WI 53701-2113 also: 360 W Washington Ave Unit 1007 Madison WI 53703-2766 Office Phone: 608-283-2471. Business E-Mail: ase@quarles.com.

EARL, ARCHIE WILLIAM, SR., mathematician, educator; b. Suffolk, Va., Nov. 28, 1946; s. Edward and Thelma Virginia Earl; m. Doristine Gause; children: Karen LaVera Maynor, Keisha Archelle, Archie William Jr. BS, Norfolk State U., Va., 1971; MA, Hampton U., Va., 1976; degree, EdD, Coll. William and Mary, 1986. Lic. tchr/ State Bd. Edn., Va. Prof. math. Tidewater C.C., Portsmouth, Va., 1978, Old Dominion U., Norfolk, Va., 1978—79, Fla. C.C., Jacksonville, Fla., 1979—80; prof. stats. Hampton (Va.) U., 1983; prof. math. City Colls. Chgo., 1986, Royal Saudi Naval Forces Tech. Inst. Naval Studies, Dammam, Saudi Arabia, 1986—87, Christopher Newport U., Newport News, Va., 1987—90, Norfolk (Va.) State U., 1991—. Tchr. math. Norfolk (Va.) Cath. H.S., 1971—73, Newport News (Va.) Pub. Schs., 1973—77; tchr. math. Rehabilitative Sch. Authority St. Brides Correctional Ctr., Chesapeake, Vt., 1977; tchr. math. Suffolk (Va.) City Pub. Schs., 1977—78, Williamsburg-James City County Pub. Schs., Williamsburg, Va., 1980—82; rsch. fellow Elizabeth City (N.C.) State U., 1996, Naval Med. Rsch. Ctr., Silver Springs, Md., 2002, U. Ala., Tuscaloosa, Ala., 2005; rsch. fellow Dept. Def. Army Pentagon, Washington, 1999; cons. in field; spkr. in field. Author: What Every Prospective College Student Should Know, 1995, What Every Prospective Grad Student Should Know, 1995, Business Statistics With Computer Applications, 1995, University Services and Auxiliary Enterprises, 1995, High Tech Higher Education, 1995, Probability and Statistics for the Sciences with Computer Applications, 1995, Probability and Statistics for Educators and Social Scientists with Computer Applications, 1995, Calculus Based Probability and Statistics for Y2K and Beyond wiht Computer Applications: A Book of Practice Tests and Answers, 2000, Differential Equations: A Quick Reference of Select Topics, Techniques, Procedures, and Examples, 2003, The Inside Scoop on American Colleges and Universities, 2004; editor: Increasing America's Knowledge of Aviation Through the Mathematics Curriculum: A Book of Lesson Plans, 1997; author: (films) Linear Algebra Series: Gaussian Elimination Method II, 2003, Algebra and Functions Lecture Series: Rational Functions (Rules for Vertical and Horizontal Asymptotes), 2003, Linear Algebra Lecture Series: Eigen Value Problems, 2006; contbr. articles to profl. jours. Deacon Union Missionary Bapt. Ch., Suffolk, Va., Mt. Pleasant Bapt. Ch., Williamsburg, Va., treas. With USAR, 1967. Nominee One of 2000 Intellectuals Twenieth Century, Internat. Biog. Ctr., 1999; recipient Sabbatical Leave award, Norfolk (Va.) State U., 2002; fellow, U.S. Dept. Def., 1999, NSF, 1972—74; grantee, Shodor Found., 2004—05, Coll. William and Mary, 1982—86. Mem.: NAACP, Am. Statis. Assn., Nat. Assn. Mathematicians, Math. Assn. Am., Assn. Study Higher Edn. (assoc.), Soc. Indsl. and Applied Math. (assoc.), Am. Soc. Engring. Edn. (assoc. fellow 2002). Home: 4728 Barn Swallow Dr Chesapeake VA 23321 Office: Norfolk State University 700 Park Avenue Norfolk VA 23504 Home Phone: 757-488-5104; Office Phone: 757-823-9564. Office Fax: 757-823-8427; Home Fax: 757-823-8427. Business E-Mail: awearl@nsu.edu.

EARL, CHRISTOPHER D., health products executive; BA in Biology, U. Pa.; PhD in Cellular and Developmental Biology, Harvard U. Gen. ptnr. Plant Resources Venture Funds; pres., CEO Avitech Diagnostics, Inc.; mng. dir. Perseus-Soros Biopharm. Fund, LP; chmn. bd. GeneFormatics, Inc. Mem. Com. for Econ. Devel.; trustee The Nutre Conservancy of Pa. Address: Perseus-Soros Biopharm Fund 29th Fl 888 7th Ave New York NY 10106

EARL, LEWIS HAROLD, economist, consultant, lawyer; b. Guthrie, Tex., Dec. 17, 1918; s. Henry W. and Ruth (O'Neal) E.; m. Patricia Miller, Mar. 5, 1943 (dec. 1973); children: William Lee, Patricia Lewise, Robert Charles, James Michael; m. Meade Randolph Loomis, July 1, 1977 (div. 1979); m. Maxine Durrett Marks, Jan. 31, 1981. BA, Tex. Technol. Coll., 1939; student, U. Tex., 1939-40, Am. U., Washington, DC, 1941-42, George Washington U., 1942-62; JD, Georgetown U., Washington, DC, 1950. Bar: DC 1950, US Supreme Ct. 1972, Tex. 1983. With Bur. Labor Stats., Dept. Labor, 1940-42, 46-51; industry, commodity economist NPA Dept. Commerce, 1951-53; productivity specialist, economist, program analyst, asst. program officer US Tech. Cooperation Program, Brazil, 1953—57; program officer US Ops. Missions, Brazil, 1957—58, Argentina, 1957—59, El Salvador, 1959—61; internat. rels. officer US AID, Washington, 1961-63; chief internat. rsch. Office of Manpower Automation and Tng., US Dept. Labor, 1963—65; chief fgn. manpower program staff Office Manpower Policy, Evaluation and Rsch. Dept. Labor, 1965—70; US del. 8th meeting Am. mem. states ILO, Ottawa, Canada, 1966, US del. to chem. industries com. Geneva, 1969; tech. dir. Seminar Ministry Labor Tng. Coordinators OAS, Mexico City, 1970; asst. dir. for program devel. Ctr. for Human Resources U. Houston, 1970-75; manpower planning officer Gulf Coast CAMPS Secretariat, Mayor's Office, City of Houston,

1970-74; cons. Tex. Gov.'s Office Policy Coordination, Austin, 1974; asso. dir. human resources program, instr. econs. U. Mo.-Columbia, 1975-78; expert cons. Human Resources Devel., Bur. Internat. Labor Affairs, U.S. Dept. Labor and UN Devel. Program for Egypt, 1978-80; staff adv. Am. Productivity Center, Houston, 1980. Expert cons. UN Indsl. Devel. Orgn., Cairo, Egypt, 1981; lectr. Coll. Bus. Adminstrn. Tex. Tech U., 1982-83; mgr. Post C. of C., 1984-87. Sec.-treas. Post Econ. Devel. Corp., 1984-90; bd. dirs. Common Cause, Tex., 1987—, legis. liaison, 1991, 93-; mem. Lubbock-Garza County Pvt. Industry Coun., 1986-92, Friends of the Libr., Tex. Tech. U., Tex. Indsl. Devel. Coun.; chmn. Garza County Dem. Com., 1986-87, 91—; bd. dirs. Tex. Alliance for Edn. and the Arts, 1991-97, Maxine Durrett Earl Charitable Found., 1994—; founder Lewis and Maxine Earl Survey Rsch. Lab., Tex. Tech U., 2001; del. Dem. Nat. Conv., Chgo., 1996. Lt. comdr. active USNR, 1942—46. Mem. ASTD, VFW, South Plain Assn. Govt. (vol. ombudsman), Am. Statis. Assn., Am. Acad. Polit. and Social Ssis., Acad. Polit. Sci., Tex. Hist. Assn., Houston Pers. Assn., South Plains Cmty. Action Assn., Soc. Internat. Devel., Nat. Planning Assn., Indsl. Rels. Rsch. Assn., Nat. Economist Club, Caprock Fin. (capital fin. com.), Garza County Trail Blazers (pres. 1994-97), Rotary, Lions (pres. 1996-97, 2001-02), Alpha Chi, Omicron Delta Epsilon, Pi Sigma Alpha, Sigma Iota Epsilon. Methodist. Home: 1929 Stoney Brook Houston TX 77063-1809 Office: PO Box 580 Post TX 79356-0580 Personal E-mail: 1hearl@arn.net. *I believe that individuals will make the right decisions if they have full and adequate information and facts, and therefore, I have sought to find the truth that will make men free.*

EARL, MARCIA HUNT, music educator, director; d. George Cornelius Hunt and Frieda Overa Allen; m. Robert Gary Earl, July 9, 1994; children: Joshua Allen, Timothy Hunt Finley; m. Mark Timothy Finley, Mar. 15, 1980 (dec. Sept. 6, 1985). BA, Concordia U., Wis., 1997, MusM, 2005. Music instr. Hunt Piano Studio, Cape Girardeau, Mo., 1973—88; model Christian LaCroix Parfums, Dallas, 1988—89; account coord. Revlon Cosmetics, Dallas, 1989—91; music instr. Earl Piano Studio, Colgate, Wis., 1991—; music dir. Zion United Meth. Ch., Colgate, Wis., 1994—; accompanist Menomonee Falls (Wis.) Sch. Dist., 1998—. Mem. Tripoli Women's Aux. to the Shriner's Hosp. For Children, Minpls., 2004; chmn. music tchrs. jr. club Miwaukee Music Tchrs. Assn., Milw., 2003—06. Mem.: Nat. Guild Piano Tchrs. (assoc.), Daughters of the Nile, Order of Ea. Star (worthy matron 2003—04, trustee 2005—, Grand Organist (Wis.) 2002, 2004). Democrat. United Methodist. Avocations: music, reading, travel. Home: 3942 Wooded Ridge Trail Colgate WI 53017 Home Phone: 262-628-1337; Office Phone: 262-628-2521.

EARL, SISTER PATRICIA HELENE, religious studies educator, director; b. Cleve. d. Warren and Helen McLaughlin Earl. BA, Dunbarton Coll. of Holy Cross, DC, 1970; MA, Villanova Univ., Villanova, Pa., 1980; PhD, George Mason Univ., Fairfax, Va., 2003. Cert. Advanced Catechist Diocese of Arlington, basic in Catehetics Notre Dame Inst., Arlington, Va.; lic. Supr. Commonwealth of Va., profl. elem. prin., sec. prin., elem. grades pk-8, English7-12 Commonwealth of Va., Instrl. II Pa. Mem. religious cmty. Sisters, Servants of the Immaculate Heart of Mary, Immaculata, Pa., 1974—; dir. religious edn. Our Lady of Lourdes Parish, Arlington, Va., 1983—85; elem. religion, English tchr. Archdiocese of Phila., Diocese of Arlington, Va., asst. supt. of schs., 1990—2003; elem. religion, English tchr. Diocese of Allentown, Pa.; asst. prof., dir. Cath. sch. leadership program Marymount U., Arlington, 2003—. Mem. prin. search com. Diocese of Arlington, 1990—2003; mem. Arlington Diocesan Sch. Bd., 1990—2003, Notre Dame Acad. Sch. Bd., Middleburg, Va., 1990—2003; dir. Cath. Diocesan partnership adv. bd. Marymount Univ., Arlington, 2004—; mem. vis. team-rep. of Va. dept Edn. Mary Washington Coll., Fredericksburg, Va., 2005; speaker in field. Author: Building the Builders: Faith Foundation in Virtue, 2007. Reader for the Prin. of the Yr. award Pvt. Sch. Divsn., Washington Metropolitan area, 1999, 2002. Mem.: Nat. Cath. Edn. Assn., Assn. for Supervision and Curriculm Devel., Nat. Assn. of Secondary Sch. Prin., Nat. Assn. of Elem. Sch. Prin. Roman Catholic. Avocations: piano, guitar, reading, writing. Home: 101 N Spring St Falls Church VA 22046 Office: Marymount Univ 2807 N Globe Rd Arlington VA 22207 Office Phone: 703-284-1517. Office Fax: 703-284-1631. Business E-Mail: patricia.earl@marymount.edu.

EARLE, CLIFFORD JOHN, JR., mathematician; b. Racine, Wis., Nov. 3, 1935; s. Clifford John and Anne Elizabeth (Griffith) E.; m. Elizabeth Joan Deutsch, Dec. 27, 1960; children— Rebecca Ann, Susan Deborah. BA, Swarthmore Coll., 1957; MA, Harvard U., 1958, PhD, 1962. Instr. Harvard U., 1962-63, vis. lectr., 1968-69; mem. Inst. for Advanced Study, Princeton, NJ, 1963-65, 81; asst. prof. Cornell U., Ithaca, NY, 1965-66, assoc. prof., 1966-69, prof., 1969—2004, prof. emeritus, 2005—, chmn. dept. math., 1976-79; vis. prof. U. Warwick, 1967; vis. lectr. Inst. Mittag-Leffler, 1972. Mem. geometric function theory program, Math. Scis. Rsch. Inst., Berkeley, Calif., 1986; hon. prof. U. Warwick, 1999—. Assoc. editor Duke Math. Jour., 1973-79; contbr. articles to math. rsch. jours. John Simon Guggenheim Meml. fellow, 1974-75 Mem. Am. Math. Soc. (editor Proc. 1989-97, mng. editor 1997-2001). Home: 314 Elmwood Ave Ithaca NY 14850-4812 Office: Cornell U Dept Math Ithaca NY 14853-4201 Business E-Mail: cliff@math.cornell.edu.

EARLE, JEAN BUIST, finance executive; b. Newton, NJ, Oct. 5, 1951; d. Richardson and Jean (Mackerly) Buist; m. Terry Dean Earle, Mar. 4, 1989; children: Morgan, Abigail. AB, Cornell U., 1973; MEd, Coll. William and Mary, 1974; MBA, U. Pa., 1987. Mgr. The Korman Corp., Jenkintown, Pa., 1975-77; v.p. ops. Community Assn. Mgmt. Co., Havertown, Pa., 1977-78; adminstrv. asst. Albert Einstein Med. Ctr., Phila., 1978-83; assoc. adminstr. Meml. Hosp. Burlington County, Mt. Holly, NJ, 1983-87; v.p. Overlook Hosp., Summit, NJ, 1987-95; exec. dir. Summit (N.J.) Child Care Ctrs., Inc., 1995-96; owner, ptnr. Elrae, LLP, Chatham, NJ, 1996—; CFO ECLC of N.J., Chatham, 1998—. Past pres. Family Link of Union and Essex Counties, 1994—96; chmn. Kirby Ctr. YMCA Family Coun., 1996—98. Recipient Diana Cuthbertsen award in health, NJ Statewide Parent Advocacy Network, 2003. Fellow Am. Coll. Healthcare Execs; mem. AICPA, Am. Hosp. Assn., U. Pa. Wharton Sch. Alumni Assn., Cornell Club, Ctr. for Enabling Tech. (trustee 1997-2004, treas. 1999-2004), Chatham Assn. for Support in Edn. (founding mem.) Home: 37 Rose Ter Chatham NJ 07928-1826 Office: ECLC NJ 21 Lum Ave Chatham NJ 07928 Home Phone: 973-635-4734; Office Phone: 973-635-1705. E-mail: jbearle@hotmail.com.

EARLE, JONATHAN HALPERIN, history professor; b. Ann Arbor, Mich., June 16, 1968; s. Richard Alan and Janice Milgrim Earle; m. Leslie Renee Tuttle, Oct. 29, 1994. PhD, Princeton U., NJ, 1996. Prof. U. Kans., Lawrence, 1997—; assoc. dir. Robert J. Dole Inst. Politics, Lawrence, 2003—. Author: (book) Jacksonian Antislavery and the Politics of Free Soil (Soc. Historians Early Am. Repubilc Book prize, 2005). Office: U Kans 1445 Jayhawk Blvd Lawrence KS 66045 Home Phone: 323-259-2635; Office Phone: 785-864-3569.

EARLE, SYLVIA ALICE, research biologist, oceanographer; b. Gibbstown, NJ, Aug. 30, 1935; d. Lewis Reade and Alice Freas (Richie) E. BS, Fla. State U., Tallahassee, 1955; MA, Duke U., Durham, NC, 1956, PhD, 1966, PhD (hon.), 1993, Monterey Inst. Internat. Studies, 1990, Ball State U., Muncie, Ind., 1991, George Wash. U., Washington, DC, 1992; grad., U. RI, Kingston, 1996, Plymouth State Coll., 1996; DSc (hon.), Ripon Coll., Wis., 1994, U. Conn., Storrs, 1994. Resident dir. Cape Haze Marine Lab., Sarasota, Fla., 1966-67; rsch. scholar Radcliffe Inst., 1967-69; rsch. fellow Farlow Herbarium, Harvard U., 1967-75, rschr., 1975—; rsch. assoc. in botany Natural History Mus. Los Angeles County, 1970-75; rsch. biologist, curator Calif. Acad. Scis., San Francisco, from 1976; rsch. assoc. U. Calif., Berkeley, 1969-75; fellow in botany Natural History Mus., 1989—; chief scientist U.S. NOAA, Washington, 1990-92, advisor to the adminstr., 1992-93; founder, pres., CEO, bd. dirs. Deep Ocean Engrs., Inc., Oakland, Calif., 1981-90; founder, chmn., CEO Deep Ocean Exploration and Rsch., Oakland, 1992—, bd. dirs., 1992—; advisor SeaWeb, 1996—2000. Bd. dirs. Dresser Industries, Oryx Energy, Inc.; explorer-in-residence Nat. Geog., 1998-; dir., Natl. Geographic Suatainable Seas Expedition, 1998—; chair, adv. coun. Harte Rsch. Inst., Tex. A&M U., Corpus Christi. Author: Exploring the Deep Frontier, 1980, Sea Change, 1995; editor: Scientific Results of the Tektite II Project, 1972-75; contbr. 150 articles to profl. jours. Trustee World Wildlife Fund US, 1976-82, mem. coun., 1984-90; trustee World Wildlife Fund Internat., 1979-81, mem. coun., 1981-95; trustee Charles A. Lindbergh Fund, pres., 1990-95; trustee Ctr. Marine Conservation, 1992-2000, Perry Found., chmn., 1993-95; mem. coun. Internat. Union for Conservation of Nature, 1979-81; corp. mem. Woods Hole Oceanographic Inst., trustee, 1996—; mem. Nat. Adv. Com. on Oceans and Atmosphere, 1980-94. Recipient Conservation Svc. award US Dept. Interior, 1970, Boston Sea Rovers award, 1972, 79, Nogi award Underwater Soc. Am., 1976, Conservation Svc. award Calif. Acad. Sci., 1979, Order of Golden Ark Prince Netherlands, 1980, David B. Stone medal New Eng. Aquarium, 1989, Gold medal Soc. Women Geographers, medal Radcliffe Coll., 1990, Pacon Internat. award, 1992, Dirs. award Natural Resources Coun. Am., 1992, Washburn award Boston Mus. Sci., 1995, Charles A. and Ann Morrow Lindbergh award, 1996, Julius Stratton Leadership award, 1997, Kilby award, 1997, Bal de la Mar Found. Sea Keeper award, 1997, Sea Space Environment award, 1997; Environmental Global 500 award, 1998; US Environmental award, 1998; named Woman of Yr. LA Times, 1970, Scientist of Yr., Calif. Mus. Sci. and Industry, 1981. National Women's Hall of Fame, 2000. Fellow AAAS, Marine Tech. Soc. (Compass award 1997), Calif. Acad. Scis., Calif. Acad. Sci., Explorers Club (hon., bd. dirs. 1989-, Lowell Thomas award 1980, Explorers medal 1996); mem. Internat. Phycological Soc. (sec. 1974-80), Phycological Soc. Am., Am. Soc. Ichthyologists and Herpetologists, Am. Inst. Biol. Scis., Brit. Phycological Soc., Ecol. Soc. Am., Internat. Soc. Plant Taxonomists. Planted a flag in the seafloor off Hawaii to mark the first solo dive to 1,250 feet without a support vessel, wearing hardened diving suit "JIM"; Set and still holds the depth record for women's solo dive:3,300 feet; lived for two weeks underwater with an all-female crew to test the effects of prolonged subsea habitation. Office: DOER 1827 Clement St Alameda CA 94501 Personal E-mail: saearle@aol.com.

EARLE, TIMOTHY KEESE, anthropology educator; b. New Bedford, Mass., Aug. 10, 1946; s. Osborne and Eleanor (Clark) E.; m. Eliza Howe, June 14, 1969; children: Caroline, Hester. BA summa cum laude, Harvard U., 1969; MA, U. Mich., 1971, PhD, 1973. Rsch. archaeologist Bishop Mus., Honolulu, 1971-72; prof. anthropology UCLA, 1973-95, dir. Inst. of Archaeology, 1987-92; prof. anthropology Northwestern U., Evanston, Ill., 1995—, chair dept., 1995-2000. Author: Bronze Age Economics, 2002, How Chiefs Come to Power, 1997; co-author: Evolution of Human Society, 1987, 2nd edit., 2000; editor: Exchange Systems in Prehistory, 1977, Contexts for Prehistoric Exchange, 1982, Chiefdoms, 1991. Mem.: Soc. Econ. Anthrop., Soc. Am. Archaeology, Am. Anthrop. Assn. (pres. archaeology divsn. 1995—97, exec. bd. 1999—2002), Phi Beta Kappa. E-mail: tke299@northwestern.edu.

EARLE, VICTOR MONTAGNE, III, lawyer; b. NYC, June 13, 1933; s. Victor Montagne and Marian Jeanette (Litonius) E.; m. Lois MacKennan, Dec. 28, 1955 (div. Jan. 1980); children: Jane Stewart, Susan Elizabeth, Anne McCallum; m. Karen Peterson Howard, Aug. 24, 1985. AB, Williams Coll., 1954; LLB, Columbia U., 1959. Bar: NY 1960, US Supreme Ct. 1963. Law clk. to Hon. Leonard Moore, US Ct. Appeals (2nd cir.), 1959-60; assoc. Cravath, Swaine & Moore, NYC, 1960-68; gen. counsel KPMG, NYC, 1968-86, Peat, Marwick Internat., 1978-86; ptnr. Cahill, Gordon & Reindel, NYC, 1986-89; sr. v.p., gen. counsel Minet, NYC, 1989-93; gen. counsel KWELM Co. and KWELM Holdings, London, 1993—98, KWELM Co. and KWELM Holdings Ltd., NYC, 1993-98, sr. counsel, 1998-2000; of counsel O'Melveny & Myers, NYC, 2000—. Lectr. constl. and corp. law issues, U.S. and abroad. Contbr. articles to profl. jour. and popular mag. With US Army, 1954-56. Recipient Constitutional Law prize Columbia U. Mem.: Fund for Modern Ct. (bd. dirs. 1974—2005), Legal Aid Soc. (bd. dirs. 1980—86), Assn. Bar of City of NY (judiciary com. 1983—86), Am. Law Inst. (life), Columbia U. Alumni Assn. (bd. dirs. 1982—87). Office: O'Melveny & Myers Times Sq Tower 7 Times Sq New York NY 10036 E-mail: vearle@omm.com.

EARLEY, ANTHONY FRANCIS, JR., utilities company executive, lawyer; b. Jamaica, NY, July 29, 1949; s. Anthony Francis and Jean Ann (Draffen) E.; m. Sarah Margaret Belanger, Oct. 14, 1972; children: Michael Patrick, Anthony Matthew, Daniel Cartwright, Matthew Sean. BS in Physics, U. Notre Dame, 1971, MS in Engring., 1979, JD, 1979. Bar: Va. 1980, N.Y. 1985, U.S. Ct. Appeals (6th cir.) 1981. Assoc. Hunton & Williams, Richmond, Va., 1979-85, ptnr., 1985; gen. counsel L.I. Lighting Co., Hicksville, N.Y., 1985-89, exec. v.p., 1988-89, pres., COO, 1989-94, The Detroit Edison Co., Mich., 1994—98; chmn., CEO DTE Energy Co., Detroit, 1998—. Dir., past chmn. Nuclear Energy Inst.; mem. elec. adv. bd. U.S. Dept. Energy; bd. dir. Comerica Inc., Masco Corp. Contbr. articles to profl. jours. Chmn. United Way SE Mich.; mem. listed mem. adv. bd. NYSE; bd. dir. Detroit Renaissance, Detroit Zoological Soc., Cornerstone Schools; mem. adv. bd. Coll. Engring., Univ. Notre Dame. Served to lt., qualified as chief engr. officer nuclear submarine prog. USN, 1971—76. Mem.: ABA. Roman Catholic. Avocations: skiing, tennis, furniture restoration. Office: DTE Energy Co 2000 2nd Ave Detroit MI 48226-1279*

EARLEY, DEBORAH LORAINE, education educator, researcher; b. Orlando, Fla., Apr. 12, 1970; d. Claris M and Don D Deily (Stepfather), LaVerne M Earley. BA, Fla. Atlantic U., 1990—92, Med, 1994—96, EdD, 1999—2002. Professional Teaching License Fla. Dept. of Edn., 1992. Tchr. Sch. Bd. of St. Lucie County, Ft. Pierce, Fla., 1992—99; adj. faculty Indian River C.C., Ft. Pierce, Fla., 1997—2000; adj. faculty and u. supr. Fla. Atlantic U., 1999—2002, dir., intensive tchr. edn. and devel., 2002—03, dir. of assessment & program evaluation, coll. of edn., 2003—. Program evaluator Fla. Dept. of Edn., 2003—. Contbr. articles to profl. jours. Altar server and lector St. Mark the Evangelist Cath. Ch., 1996—2005. Nominee Disting. Paper, Fla. Edn. Rsch. Assn., 2002, 2003, 2004; grant, Fla. Dept. of Edn., 2004. Mem.: Fla. Assn. of Tchr. Educators, Assn. for Supervision & Curriculum Devel., Internat. Reading Assn. Conservative-R. Catholic. Avocations: golf, boating. Office: Florida Atlantic Univ 500 NW California Blvd CO 116 Port Saint Lucie FL 34986 Home Phone: 772-489-4174; Office Phone: 772-873-3351. E-mail: dearley@fau.edu.

EARLEY, LAURENCE ELLIOTT, retired medical educator; b. Ahoskie, NC, Jan. 23, 1931; s. Frank Claxton and Eleanor (Dilday) Earley; m. Joanne Frances Sinclair, Sept. 5, 1953; children: Laurence Elliott Earley Jr., Peter Hunter Earley. BS, U. N.C., 1953, MD, 1956; MA (hon.), U. Pa., 1978. Diplomate Am. Bd. Internal Medicine. Asst. prof. Harvard Med. Sch., Boston, 1967—68; assoc. prof. U. Calif. Sch. Medicine, San Francisco, 1968—69, prof., 1969—73, chief of nephrology, 1968—73; prof., chmn. dept. medicine U. Tex. Health Sci. Ctr., San Antonio, 1973—77; chmn. dept. medicine, Frank Wister Thomas Prof. U. Pa., Phila., 1977—90, chmn. dept. phys. medicine & rehab., 1987—90, Francis C. Wood prof., 1983—95, sr. assoc. dean., 1992—95; clin. prof. medicine U. N.C., Chapel Hill, 1995—2000; ret., 2001. Study sect. NIH, Bethesda, Md., 1969—77; chmn. Am. Bd. Internal Medicine , 1987—88. Editor: Diseases of The Kidney; contbr. articles to profl. jours. Chmn. sci. adv. bd. Nat. Kidney Found., NYC, 1973—74. Sr. asst. surgeon USPHS, 1959—61. Recipient Kaiser award, U. Calif., 1972, Disting. Svc. award, U. N.C., 1976. Master: ACP; mem.: Phila. Coll. Physicians, Assn. Am. Physicians (pres. 1988—89), Inst. Medicine, Am. Soc. Nephrology (pres. 1977—78), Am. Soc. for Clin. Investigation (pres. 1975—76), Assn. Profs. Medicine (pres. 1983—84), Alpha Omega Alpha, Phi Beta Kappa. Achievements include research in kidney disease, physiology. Avocations: photography, woodwork. Home: 10 Gevrey Arbordeau Devon PA 19333 Personal E-mail: jselee@verizon.net. E-mail: jseleech@aol.com.

EARLING, DEBRA MAGPIE, writer, educator; Student, Spokane Falls Cmty. Coll., Univ. Calif., Berkeley; BA, Univ. Washington; MFA in Creative Writing, Cornell Univ., 1991. Assoc. prof., creative writing, Native Am. studies Univ. Mont., Missoula. Author: (novels) Perma Red, 2002 (Am. Book award, 2003, WILLA award, Spur award, Mountains and Plains Bestsellers Assn. award); contbr. chapters to books The Last Best Place: A Montana Anthology, Circle of Women: Anthology of Western Women Writers, Wild Women: Anthology of Women Writers, short stories to Talking Leaves: Contemporary Native American Short Stories. Mem. Confederated Salish and Kootenai Tribes of Mont. Address: Author Mail c/o Penguin USA Publicity 375 Hudson St New York NY 10014 Office Phone: 406-243-4963.

EARLL, JERRY MILLER, internist, educator, endocrinologist; b. Hawarden, Iowa, Aug. 15, 1928; s. Harry Ezra and Magdalene Anna (Miller) E.; m. Faith Anne Allbaugh, Sept. 14, 1956; children: Leslie Anne, Nikki Lee, Holly Magdalene. BS, U. Nebr., 1950; MD, U. Iowa, 1958; postgrad., U. Calif., 1965-66. Diplomate Am. Bd. Internal Medicine, Am. Bd. Endocrinology, Am. Bd. Nuc. Medicine, Am. Bd. Geriat. Commd. 2d lt. U.S. Army, 1951, advanced through grades to col., 1972; intern Letterman Gen. Hosp., San Francisco, 1958, resident in internal medicine, 1959-62; chief endocrinology and metabolism William Beaumont Gen. Hosp., El Paso, 1963-65, Tripler Gen. Hosp., Honolulu, 1965-69, Walter Reed Army Inst. Rsch. and Walter Reed Army Hosp., Washington, 1969-76; chief dept. medicine Walter Reed Army Hosp., 1976-79; cons. endocrinology Office Surgeon Gen.; assoc. prof. medicine U. Hawaii, 1967—69; clin. prof. medicine Georgetown U., Washington, 1976—79, prof., 1979—, chief divsn. internal medicine, 1979—94, dir. geriatrics svc. dept. medicine, 1993—2000; prof. medicine, vice chmn. dept. medicine Uniformed Svcs. U. Health Scis., Washington, 1977-79; med. dir. to v.p. med. affairs Washington Home, 1996, 97—. Decorated Legion of Merit, Army Commendation medal, Meritorious Service medal. Fellow ACP (regional laureate); mem. Am. Med. Dirs. Assn., Endocrine Soc., Am. Geriatric Soc. (Clinician of Yr. 2002, 03), Assn. Mil. Surgeons, Acad. Medicine of Washington, Physicians for Nat. Health Program (spkr.). Achievements include research and publs. on pituitary and thyroid physiology. Home: 313 6200 Oregon Ave Washington DC 20015 Office: Georgetown U Hosp 3800 Reservoir Rd NW Washington DC 20007-2113 Office Phone: 202-895-0122. Business E-Mail: jearll@thewashingtonhome.org.

EARLY, ALEXANDER RIEMAN, III, judge; b. Phila., Sept. 22, 1917; s. A.R. Jr. and Elizabeth Frances (Dence) Early; m. Mary Celeste Worland, Aug. 15, 1959; children: A.R. IV, Lucia C. Stroh, Elizabeth V., John Drennan, V. BA, Cornell U., 1938; LLB, Harvard U., 1941. Bar: Calif. 1946. Pvt. law practice, LA, 1946—50; sr. atty. Divsn. of Hwys., State of Calif., 1950-55; asst. U.S. atty. Lands divsn. U.S. Dept. Justice, LA, 1955-57; asst. county counsel Los Angeles County, Calif., 1957-72; judge Superior Ct., LA, 1972-87, chmn. Exec. Com., Rules Com., BAJI Com.; judge by assignment, 1987—; ret., 1987. Adj. prof. Southwestern Law Sch., L.A., 1970-79. Contbr. articles to profl. jours. Mgr. internat. fedn. rels. boxing venue 1984 Olympics. Comdr. USNR, 1941-46. Served U.S. Navy in Destroyers, Pacific (earned nine battle stars); dir. sinking I.J.N. sub. RO-38, 1943. Decorated comdr. Order Polonia Restituta (Poland); knight grand cross Order of Holy Sepulchre (Vatican), Law Enforcement medal SAR, 1981. Fellow: Samuel Victor Constant Soc.; mem.: Nat. Conf. State Tax Judges, Am. Bd. Trial Adv., Navy League, Aztec Club, U.S. Naval Inst. (hon. mem. crew USS Canberra), Md. Hist. Soc., Soc. Cincinnati, Soc. War of 1812 (v.p. gen., Disting. Svc. award), Calif. Soc. Colonial Wars (dep. gov. gen., Disting. Svc. medal), Calif. Soc. Sons of Revolution (pres., Disting. Svc. award). Roman Catholic. Avocations: American history, genealogy, camellia seedlings. Home: 3017 Kirkham Dr Glendale CA 91206-1127

EARLY, BERT HYLTON, retired lawyer, consultant; b. Kimball, W.Va., July 17, 1922; s. Robert Terry and Sue Keister (Hylton) E.; m. Elizabeth Henry, June 24, 1950; children— Bert Hylton, Robert Christian, Mark Randolph, Philip Henry, Peter St. Clair Student, Marshall U., 1940-42; AB, Duke U., 1946; JD, Harvard U., 1949. Bar: W.Va. 1949, Ill. 1963, Fla. 1981. Assoc. Fitzpatrick, Marshall, Huddleston & Bolen, Huntington, W.Va., 1949-57; asst. counsel Island Creek Coal Co., Huntington, W.Va., 1957-60, assoc. gen. counsel, 1960-62; dep. exec. dir. ABA, Chgo., 1962-64, exec. dir., 1964-81; sr. v.p. Wells Internat., Chgo., 1981-83, pres., 1983-85, Bert H. Early Assocs. Inc., Chgo., 1985-94, Early Cochran & Olson, Chgo., 1994-98, of counsel, 1999—2004; ret., 2005. Dir. Am. Bar Found., Chgo., 1993-95; instr. Marshall U., Huntington, W.Va., 1950-53; legal search cons. and lectr. in field. Bd. dirs. Morris Meml. Hosp. for Crippled Children, 1954-60, Huntington Pub. Libr., 1951-60, W.Va. Tax Inst., 1961-62, Huntington Mus. Art, 1961-62; mem. W.Va. Jud. Coun., 1960-62, Huntington City Coun., 1961-62; bd. dirs. Cmty. Renewal Soc., Chgo., 1965-76, United Charities Chgo., 1972-80, Hinsdale (Ill.) Hosp. Found., 1987-93, Internat. Bar Assn. Found., 1987-89; bd. dirs. Am. Bar Endowment, 1983-95, sec., 1987-89, treas., 1989-91, v.p., 1991-93, pres., 1993-95, dir. emeritus, 1995-2000; mem. vis. com. U. Chgo. Law Sch., 1975-78; trustee Davis and Elkins Coll., 1960-63; mem. Hinsdale Plan Commn., 1982-85. 1st lt. AC, U.S. Army, 1943-45. Fellow Am. Bar Found., Ill. Bar Found. (charter); mem. ABA (ho. of dels. 1958-59, 84-93, chmn. young lawyers divsn. 1957-58, Disting. Svc. award young lawyers divsn. 1983), Am. Law Inst. (life), Internat. Bar Assn. (asst. sec. gen. 1967-82), Nat. Legal Aid and Defender Assn., Am. Judicature Soc. (bd. dirs. 1981-84), Fla. Bar, W.Va. Bar Assn. Presbyterian. Personal E-mail: earlybandb@aol.com.

EARLY, DELOREESE PATRICIA See REESE, DELLA

EARLY, JACK JONES, foundation executive; b. Corbin, Ky., Apr. 12, 1925; s. Joseph M. and Lela (Jones) E.; m. Nancye Bruce Whaley, June 1, 1952; children: Lela Katherine, Judith Ann, Laura Hattie. AB, Union Coll., Barbourville, Ky., 1948; MA, U. Ky., 1953, Ed.D. (So. scholar 1955-56), 1956; B.D., Coll. of Bible, Lexington, Ky., 1956; D.D., Wesley Coll., Grand Forks, ND, 1961; LL.D., Parsons Coll., 1962, Iowa Wesleyan Coll., 1972; Litt.D., Dakota Wesleyan U., 1969; L.H.D., Union Coll., Barbourville, Ky., 1979; D.Adminstrn., Cumberland Coll., 1981. Ordained to ministry Methodist Ch., 1954; pastor Rockhold Circuit, Ky., 1943-44, Craig's Chapel and Laurel Circuit, London, Ky., 1944-47, Trinity Ch., Oak Ridge, summer 1945, Hindman Ch., Ky., 1947-52; dean of men Hindman Settlement Sch., 1948-51; assoc. pastor Park Ch., Lexington, Ky., 1952-54; asst. to pres., dean Athens Coll., Ala., 1954- 55; v.p., dean of coll. Iowa Wesleyan Coll., Mount Pleasant, 1956-58; pres. Dakota Wesleyan U., 1958-69, Pfeiffer Coll., Misenheimer, NC, 1969-71; exec. dir. Am. Bankers Assn., Washington, 1971-73; pres. Limestone Coll., Gaffney, SC, 1973-79; exec. dir. edn. Combined Ins. Co. Am., Chgo., 1979-82, v.p., exec. dir. edn. and communications, 1982-84; pres. Ky. Ind. Coll. Fund, Louisville, 1984-93, pres. emeritus, 1993—; dir. edn., con. Napoleon Hill Found., Northbrook, Ill., 1997—. Pres. W. Clement Stone PMA Communications, Inc., Chgo., 1987—. Active Boy Scouts Am.; mem. pres. adv. coun. North Pk. Coll.; mem. Felician adv. bd. Felician Coll.; mem. Ky. Ho. of Reps., 1952-54; bd. dirs. S.D. Found. Pvt. Colls., S.D. Meth. Found., Nat. Coun. on Youth Leadership, Ctr. for Citizenship Edn., YMCA, Motivational Inst.,

Mid-Am. chpt. ARC, 1980—, W. Clement and Jessie V. Stone Found., Northbrook Symphony Orch., Ky. Mountain Laurel Festival, 1990—, Internat. Coun. on Edn. for Teaching, 1990—; chmn. bd. Religious Heritage Am., 1989-92, Internat. Leadership Network, 1991—; Rep. nominee for Metro Mayor, Louisville, 2002. Recipient Spoke award Mitchell Jr. C. of C., 1959, Disting. Svc. award, 1960, Disting. Svc. award S.D. Jr. C. of C., 1960, Gaffney Jaycees, 1979, Chief Iron Eyes Cody medal of Peace, 1987, Outstanding Kentuckian award O'Tucks, 1990; named Outstanding Former Kentuckian, 1963; hon. fellow Wroxton Coll., Oxfordshire, Eng.; named to Disting. Alumni Hall of Fame, U. Ky., 1965, Union Coll. Hall of Fame, 2000, U. Ky. Coll. Edn. Hall of Fame, 2006. Mem. Am. Soc. Assn. Execs., Louisville C. of C., Blue Key, Masons (33d degree, chaplain Valley of Louisville chpt. 1990—, Viceroy and Sovereign Red Cross Constantine), Rotary (pres. Louisville 1992-93, dist. 6710 gov. 1996—), First Families Ky. (dep. gov. gen., gov. gen. 2007—), Ky. Soc. SAR (pres. 1998—), Order of Founders and Patriots of Am. (gov. Ky. chpt. 2003-, dep. chaplain gen., chaplain gen.), Soc. War of 1812 in the Commonwealth of Ky. (pres. 1997—), Huguenot Soc. Ky. (pres. 1999—), Huguenot Soc.-Soc. of Manakin (Ky. br. pres. 1999—), Nat. Soc. Sons and Daus. of Pilgrims (gov. Ky. br. 2000—), Gen. for Pub. Rels.-Gen. Soc. of the War of 1812 (v.p. 1998—), Del. State Soc. of Cin., Gen. Soc. Sons of Revolution (gen. chaplain), Ky. Soc. Colonial Wars (dep. gov.), Nat. Sojourners Camp #134, Heroes of '76 (E.B. Jones Camp), Jamestowne Soc., Ky. Co. (chaplain), First FAmilies of Ga., First Families of Tenn., Presdl. Families Am., Kappa Delta Pi, Phi Delta Kappa (bd. dirs. Northwestern U. chpt. 1980—), Kappa Phi Kappa, Alpha Psi Omega, Theta Phi, Pi Tau Chi, Sigma Beta Delta. Republican. Home: 9002 Hurstwood Ct Louisville KY 40222-5716 Home Phone: 502-426-6078; Office Phone: 502-426-6078.

EARLY, JAMES H., JR., lawyer; b. Henderson, NC, May 6, 1939; s. James Howard and Nettie Anna (Hicks) E.; children from previous marriage: James H. III, Anna Elizabeth, Mary Elizabeth. AA, Mars Hill Coll., 1960; BA, Wake Forest U., 1962, LLB, 1964, JD, 1970. Bar: NC 1964, US Dist. Ct. (mid. dist.) NC 1970, US Ct. Appeals (4th cir.) 1995; cert. mediator Superior Cts. of NC, 1992. Pvt. practice, Winston-Salem, 1964—; mediator Adminstrv. Office of the Cts. of NC, 1992—. Mediator Am. Arbitration Assn., 1992—. Author: The Best Tar Heel Barbecue Manteo to Murphy, 2000, Jim Early's Reflections The Memories and Recipes of a Southern Cook, 2005; contbr. articles pub. to profl. jours. With US Army, 1957. Chmn. fundraising Cub Scouts/Boy Scouts Am., Little League, Pop Warner, Indian Guides, March of Dimes, others. Mem. ABA, ATLA, NC Bar Assn. (chmn. continuing legal edn. subcom., mem. effectiveness and quality of life com., moderator skills course com.), , Forsyth County Bar Assn. (sec. 1970-71), NC Acad. Trial Lawyers, Phi Alpha Delta (alumni advisor 1969-84, Outstanding Alumnus award 1967), Kiwanis (pres. 1989-90, 91-92), Masons. Baptist. Avocations: hunting, fishing, walking horses, bird dogs, racing. Home: 144 Sterling Pt Ct Winston Salem NC 27104 Office: 1320 Westgate Center Dr Winston Salem NC 27103-2933 Home Phone: 336-794-3208; Office Phone: 336-768-2546. E-mail: jim@jimearly.com.

EARLY, S. ALLEN, III, lawyer; b. Waco, Tex., Oct. 27, 1946; BA, Olivet Coll., 1968; JD, Yale U., 1971. Bar: Mich. 1971, DC 1972, Calif. 1978, US Dist. Ct. (ea.dist.) Mich., US Ct. of Appeals (6th cir.), US Supreme Ct. 1989. Law clk. to Hon. Harold R. Tyler, Jr. U.S. Dist. Ct. (so. dist.) N.Y., 1971-72; asst. U.S. atty. criminal divsn. Washington, 1972-75; mem. Miller, Canfield, Paddock and Stone, Detroit; pvt. practice Detroit. Mem. ABA, DC Bar, State Bar Calif., State Bar Mich. Office: 660 Woodward Ave Ste 1480 Detroit MI 48226 Office Phone: 313-962-2320. Office Fax: 313-962-2341.

EARLY, TERI WILSON (DENISE WILSON), elementary school educator, educator; b. Jacksonville, Ill., Sept. 3, 1952; d. Arthur Amos and LaVada Inez (Norton) Wilson (dec.); 1 child, Bill Duane (dec.). BS, No. Ill. U., 1973, MS, 1974. Tng. and tech. grad. asst. Head Start/No. Ill. U., DeKalb, 1973-74; tchr. 2d grade North Chicago (Ill.) Dist. 64, 1974-75; Head Start site adminstr. Archdiocese Bd. Edn., Chgo., 1975-76; Head Start tchr. Denver Pub. Schs., 1976-77; tchr., dir. day care lab. Met. State Coll., Denver, 1977; instr. Cmty. Coll., Denver, 1980; toddler day-care dir. Denver Pub. Schs., 1977-80, tchr. 4th grade, 1980-81, kindergarten tchr., 1981-85; fin. rep. Equitable Fin. Svcs., 1985-86; kindergarten tchr. San Diego Unified Sch. Dist., 1986-89, resource CRISD tchr., 1989-90, race and human rels. facilitator, 1991-92; project resource tchr. Keiller Mid. Sch., 1992-93; v.p. Garfield H.S., 1993-95, Freese Elem. Sch., 1997—99; prin. Birney Elem. Sch., 1999—2002; resource tchr. Valencia Park Elem., San Diego, 2002—, tchr. computer lab., 2005—06. V.p. spl. assignment Sch. Cmty. Safety Network, grant coord. Race Human Rels. and Guidance Program, 1995-96; pres. African Am. Educators, 1997-98; del. People-to-People, China, 2001. Gov.'s subcom. on infants and toddlers State of Colo., 1979-80; bd. dirs. Big Sisters League, San Diego, 1994-96. Fellow San Diego Area Writing Project, 1987, Sci. Tchrs. Inst. U. Calif.-San Diego, 1988-90, Future Adminstrs. Academy-San Diego County; mem. Nat. Sci. Tchrs. Assn., Nat. Assn. Edn. Young Children, African Am. Educators, Nat. Coun. Negro Women, Assn. Calif. Sch. Adminstrs., ASCD, Alpha Kappa Alpha, Pi Lamba Theta, Phi Delta Kappa. Mem. African Methodist Episcopalian Ch. Home: 4937 Brighton Ave San Diego CA 92107-2519 Office: Valencia Park Elem 5880 Skyline Drive San Diego CA 92114 Personal E-mail: teridenet@yahoo.com.

EARNER, WILLIAM ANTHONY, JR., naval officer; b. Pitts., Nov. 2, 1941; s. William Anthony and Marie Veronica (Ward) E.; m. Jennifer Elizabeth Laurence, Dec. 11, 1971; children: William Andrew, John Laurence. BS, U.S. Naval Acad., 1963; MS, U.S. Naval Postgrad. Sch., 1969; DBA, Harvard U., 1973. Commd. ensign USN, 1963, advanced through grades to vice adm., 1994, 1st lt. USS Blue Yokosuka, Japan, 1963-65, weapons officer USS Black San Diego, 1965-67, ops. officer River Sect. 534 Vietnam, 1967-68, weapons officer USS Dale Mayport, Fla., 1973-75, exec. officer USS Luce, 1975-77, prof. Naval War Coll. Newport, RI, 1977-78, fellow strategic studies group, 1987-88, with Office Chief Naval Ops. Washington, 1978-81, comdg. officer USS Deyo, 1981-83, mil. asst. to dir. NET assessment Office of Sec. Def. Washington, 1983-85, comptr. naval air systems, 1988-90, comdr. Destroyer Squadron Four Charleston, SC, 1985-87, comdr. naval Surface Group Mid-Pacific Pearl Harbor, Hawaii, 1990-92; budget officer Dept. Navy, 1992-94, dep. chief naval ops. (logistics), 1994—96, exec. v.p. Navy Fed. Credit Union Merrifield, Va., 1996—97, sr. exec. v.p. Navy Fed. Credit Union, 1998—2003, COO, Navy Fed. Credit Union, 2003—. Instr. Harvard Grad. Sch. Edn., Cambridge, Mass., 1972-73; adj. prof. Bryant Coll., Smithfield, R.I., 1977-78; COO Navy Fed. Credit Union, 1998—; bd. dirs. Service Source, Inc. Chmn. George Mason dist. Boy Scouts Am., 2000—02; mem. supervisory com. Wescorp Fed. Credit Union, 2004—. Decorated D.S.M., Legion of Merit, Bronze Star with V device. Mem. U.S. Naval Inst., Am. Soc. Mil. Comptrs., Credit Union Exec. Soc., U.S. Naval Acad. Alumni Assn., CUNA Govt. Affairs Com. Avocations: running, gardening. Office: Navy Fed Credit Union PO Box 3000 Merrifield VA 22119-3000 Business E-Mail: william_earner@navyfederal.org.

EARNEST, CRAIG HOPKINS, psychologist, consultant; s. George Sites Earnest and Lucia Elizabeth Hopkins. BS, Colo. State U., 1969; MA, U. Chgo., 1973; PhD, Northwestern U., 1991. Swimming instr. San Diego County Red Cross, 1969; psychiat. social worker Ill. Dept. Mental Health, Hines, 1969—71; clin. therapist Chgo. Dept. Health, 1973—94; psychology cons. Associated Behavioral Consultants, Inc., Lincolnwood, Ill., 1994—. Mem. adv. bd. Mental Health Coun., Chgo., 1980—82. Mem.: Soc. Personality Assessment. Presbyterian. Avocation: scuba diving. Office: Associated Behavioral Consultants Inc 6600 N Lincoln Ave Ste 412 Lincolnwood IL 60645 Office Fax: 847-568-1675.

EARNEST, MELISSA WEBB, education educator; d. John Richard and Janet French Webb; m. John Walter Earnest, June 20, 1981; 1 child, Amanda Jo. BS, Austin Peay State U., 1982, MA in Edn., 1994. Adj. prof. Hopkinsville C.C., Ky., 1993—; tchr. Caldwell County H.S., Princeton, Ky., 1998—; STI coord., webmaster Caldwell County Schs., 2006—. Mem. coun. Caldwell County H.S. Sch.-Based Decision Making Coun., Princeton, 2002—06. Musician: (organist) First Christian Church (Disciples of Christ); mem. editl. adv. bd. N.Y. Times Upfront, 2001—05. Leader Girl Scouts USA, Princeton, Ky., 1983—2005; mem. com. Caldwell County HS Tech. Com., Princeton, Ky., 1998—2006; deacon First Christian Ch. (Disciples of Christ), Dawson Springs, Ky., 1997—2004, elder, 2005—. Mem.: NEA, ASCD (assoc.), Caldwell County Edn. Assn. (v.p. 2004—06), Ky. Edn. Assn., Family, Career & Cmty. Leaders Am. (hon.), Kappa Delta Pi, Tri-M Music Honor Soc. (life). Mem. Ch. Disciples Of Christ. Avocations: music, movies, counted cross stitch. Office: Caldwell County Bd Edn 612 W Washington St PO Box 229 Princeton KY 42445-0229 Home Phone: 270-365-6273; Office Phone: 270-365-8000. Personal E-mail: melissa.earnest@caldwell.kyschools.us.

EARNEST, OLA MAY, curator; b. Montrose, Mo., Apr. 5, 1934; d. Marion Leslie Callahan and Vianna Elizabeth Wallace; m. Jesse E. Earnest, Dec. 6, 1950; children: Jesse L., Linda K., Billy J., Rodney G., Diana L. Attended in genealogy, Ft. Scott Cmty. Coll., 1974, Pitts. State U., Kans., 1974. V.p. Linn Co. Genealogical Soc., Pleasanton, Kans., 1975—78, pres., 1978—79; pres., curator Linn Co. Hist. Soc. Mus. and Libr., Pleasanton, 1980—. Author: 100 Cemetaries - Linn County, Kansas, 1987; editor (designer): (brochure) Bleeding Kansas, 2003. Mem. Linn Co. Rep. Women, Linn Co., Kans.; treas. Potosi Twp., Linn Co., Kans., 1992—; mem. South East Kans. Tourism, Kans., 1990—. Named Woman of Yr., Iota Phi Sorority, 1985; recipient Cmty. Svc. award, Beta Pi Sorority, 1989, Commitment to History award, Kans., 2005. Mem.: Kans. State Hist. Soc., Territorial Kans. Heritage Alliance, Nat. Soc. Daughters Am. Revolution, Nat. Soc. Wash. Family Descendants. Republican. Meth. Avocations: genealogy, gardening, reenactments. Home: 7535 White Rd Pleasanton KS 66075 Office: Linn County Hist Soc 307 E Park St Pleasanton KS 66075 Office Phone: 913-352-8739. Office Fax: 913-352-8739. E-mail: linncohist-gen@ckt.net.

EARNHARDT, DALE, JR., race car driver; b. Concord, NC, Oct. 10, 1974; s. Dale Earnhardt. NASCAR Nextel Cup Series driver (formerly Winston Cup Series) No. 8 Budweiser Chevrolet Dale Earnhardt Inc., 1998—; co-owner, driver Chance 2 Motorsports (subs. Dale Earnhardt Inc.), 2002—; owner JR Motorsports, 2002—. Guest appearance (TV) 60 Minutes, 2004, The Tonight Show with Jay Leno, MTV Diary, VH1 Driven, 2003, (films) Talladega Nights: The Ballad of Ricky Bobby, 2006; actor(voice): (films) Cars, 2006; author: Driver #8, 2002; exec. prodr., host: (radio shows) Dale Jr. Unrestricted, 2006—; (TV series) Back in the Day with Dale Jr., 2006—. Recipient Espy Award for Best Driver, 2004. Achievements include becoming the only third-generation NASCAR champion with Busch Series Championship, 1998, 1999; winner, Daytona 500, 2004; sponsors include Budweiser, Remington, Drakkar Noir, Enterprise Rent-a-car, Napa Auto Parts, Ritz, Gillette, Wrangler, Polaris; 22 Busch Series victories; 17 NASCAR Nextel Cup victories. Avocations: water sports, computers. Office: Dale Earnhardt Inc 1675 Coddle Creek Hwy Mooresville NC 28115-8245*

EARNHARDT, TERESA, race team owner; b. Hickory, NC; d. Hal Houston; m. Dale Earnhardt, 1982 (dec. Feb. 18, 2001); 1 child, Taylor Nicole stepchildren: Kerry, Kelley, Dale Jr. CEO, team owner Dale Earnhardt Inc., Mooresville, NC, 1982—. Named Outstanding Mother of Yr., Nat. Mother's Day Com., 2002. Achievements include car owner for four Busch Series championships in 1998, 1999, 2004 and 2005; Car owner for two Craftsman Truck Series championships in 1996 and 1997. Office: Dale Earnhardt Inc 1675 Coddle Creek Hwy Mooresville NC 28115-8245*

EARNS, LANE ROBERT, academic administrator, historian, educator; b. Flint, Mich., May 8, 1951; s. Robert Lewis Earns and Shirley M. Earns (nee Martin). BA, Mich. State U., 1973; MA, U. Hawaii, 1977, PhD, 1987. Lectr. Kwassui Women's Jr. Coll., Nagasaki, Japan, 1977—79, 1984—86; asst. prof. U. Wis., Oshkosh, 1987—93, assoc. prof. history, 1993—97, prof. history, 1997—, John M. Rosebush prof., 2000, assoc. vice chancellor, 2002—05, interim provost, vice chancellor, 2004—05, provost, 2005—, vice chancellor, 2005—. Co-founder., editor, writer Nagasaki Harbor Light, Nagasaki, 1985. Author: Nagasaki Kyoryuchi no seiyojin, 2002; co-author: Across the Gulf of Time: The International Cemeteries of Nagasaki; co-editor: Crossroads: A Jour. of Nagasaki History and Culture, 1993—98. Fellow, Fulbright Found., 1974—75; grantee, Japan Found., 1983, NE Asian Coun. Assn. Asian Studies, 1989, NEH, 1990—91. Mem.: Midwest Conf. Asian Affairs (program chair 1992), Midwest Japan Sem. (exec. bd. mem. 1989—92, chair 1992—94). Home: 1219 Merritt Ave Oshkosh WI 54901 Office: University of Wisconsin Oshkosh 800 Algoma Blvd Oshkosh WI 54901 E-mail: earns@uwosh.edu.

EARP, NAOMI CHURCHILL, federal official, lawyer; b. Newport News, Va., Feb. 15, 1950; d. Robert Henry and Naomi (Johnson) Davis; m. Samuel E. Earp, July 19, 1987. BA, Norfolk State U., 1972; MA, Ind. U., 1977; JD, Cath. U., 1982. Bar: Pa. 1985. Social worker City of Norfolk Dept. Welfare, Va., 1972-73, City of Indpls. Employment and Tng., 1973-76; civil rights specialist US Dept. Commerce, Chgo., 1976-79; investigator US Dept. Labor, Washington, 1981-83; pvt. practice as cons. Washington, 1983-85; civil rights specialist Dept. of Navy, US Dept. Def., Washington, 1985-86; adminstr. equal opportunity programs USDA, Washington, 1987; atty. US Equal Employment Opportunity Commn., Washington, 1986-87, vice chmn., 2003—06, chair, 2006—. Active Forum Blacks in Agriculture, Washington, 1988, Womens' Action Task Force, Washington, 1988, Nat. Black Rep. Coun. Recipient Am. Jurisprudence award Property Am. Jurisprudence, 1980. Mem. ABA, Supreme Ct. Bar, Pa. Bar Assn., Coun. 100. Republican. Avocations: jogging, biking, dance. Office: US Equal Employment Opportunity Commn 1801 L St NW Washington DC 20507*

EASLEY, CHARLES D., JR., state supreme court justice; 3 children. BBA, U. Miss., 1972; MBA, Miss. State U., 1976; JD, U. Miss., 1979; attended, Nat. Dist. Attorneys Coll., 1980; grad., Am. Acad. Jud. Ed. Asst. dist. atty. 3d Jud. Cir. Ct. Dist., 1980—83; pvt. practice Columbus, Miss., 1983—2000; prosecutor Caledonia, 1999, judge, 2000; assoc. justice Miss. Supreme Ct., 2001—. Mem. security com., library com., salary policy com. Miss. Supreme Ct., chmn. continuing judicial ed. com. Bd. dirs. Big Brothers & Big Sisters of Miss., Am. Cancer Soc., Miss. Prosecutor's Assn. Mem.: AARP, NRA, ABA, Am. Judges Assn., Lowndes County Bar Assn., Shriners, Masons (life). Office: Miss Supreme Ct Gartin Justice Bldg 450 High St Jackson MS 39201 also: PO Box 249 Jackson MS 39205 Office Phone: 601-359-3697.*

EASLEY, DAVID, economics professor; b. Lexington, Ky., Nov. 3, 1952; s. Alan Eugene and Jean (Ogden) E.; m. Maureen O'Hara, July 13, 1977; children: Megan, Casey. BA, U. Ky., 1974; PhD, Northwestern U., 1979. Asst. prof. econs. Cornell U., Ithaca, NY, 1979-84, assoc. prof., 1984-88, prof., 1988—, chmn. econs. dept., 1988-93, Henry Scarborough prof. econs., 1996—. Vis. prof. Calif. Inst. Tech., Pasadena, 1985-86; Overseas fellow Churchill Coll., Cambridge U., 1993-94. Contbr. articles to profl. jours. Recipient numerous grants NSF. Fellow Econometric Soc. Office: Cornell U Dept Econ Uris Hall Ithaca NY 14853 Office Phone: 607-255-6283. E-mail: dae3@cornell.edu.

EASLEY, JUNE ELLEN PRICE, genealogist; b. Chgo., June 7, 1924; d. Fred E. and Bernadette (Mailloux) Price; m. Raymond Dale Easley, Dec. 24, 1945. Student, McCormack Sch. Commerce, Chgo., 1942—43, Englewood Jr. Coll., 1943—45. Lic. genealogist Assn. Profl. Genealogists. Statis. clk. Arthur Andersen & Co., Chgo., 1968-74; corr. sec. ICG R.R., Chgo., 1974-86; self-employed genealogist-computers Arlington Heights, Ill., 1986-94, Mountain Home, Ark., 1994—2001, Springfield, Mo., 2001—. Editor, typist geneal. books, 1996—. Contbr. religion articles to Daily Herald, 1991; editor romance stories, 1990—, genealogy books, 1996—. Sec. Citizens for Clean Water, Mountain Home, Ark., 1996-98. Mem. AARP (sec. 1997-98), DAR (auditor-treas. Chgo. chpt. 1981-82, rec. sec. Chgo. chpt. 1982-88, Mountain Home ROTC 1995-97, publicity chmn. 1996-97), Huguenot Soc., Nat. Soc. R.R. Bus. Women (newsletter editor 1991-2002), Northwest Suburban Coun. Genealogists (pres. 1988-90, corr. sec. 1990-94), Daus. of War 1812, Daus. of Union Vets. (Civil War), Civil War Roundtable, Springfield Writers Guild (treas. IOOF Rebeka chpt. 2006-07). Republican. Avocations: genealogy, writing, antiques, computers, travel. Home and Office: 2315 E Lark St Springfield MO 65804 Home Phone: 417-823-3835; Office Phone: 417-823-3835. Personal E-mail: juneeasley@sbcglobal.net.

EASLEY, MICHAEL F., governor; b. Rocky Mount, NC, Mar. 23, 1950; m. Mary Pipines; 1 child, Michael F., Jr. BA in Polit. Sci. cum laude, U. N.C., 1972; JD cum laude, N.C. Ctrl. U. Dist. atty. 13th Dist., N.C., 1982-91; pvt. practice Southport, N.C., 1991-93; atty. gen. N.C., 1993-2000; gov. State of N.C., 2000—. Contbr. numerous articles in field. Recipient Pub. Svc. award U.S. Dept. Justice, 1984. Pres. N.C. Conf. Dist. Attys.; mem. N.C. Dist. Attys. Assn. (past pres., legis. chmn.). Democrat. Avocations: hunting, sailing, woodworking. Office: Office of the Gov 20301 Mail Service Ctr Raleigh NC 27699-0303 Office Phone: 919-733-4240, 919-733-5811. Office Fax: 919-733-2120. E-mail: governor.office@ncmail.net.*

EASLEY, ROBERT J., retail executive; BBA, Tex. A&M Univ.; MBA, Univ. Tex. Mgmt. positions through sr. v.p., chief mktg. officer & head of pharmacy H.E. Butt Grocery Co., 1991—2007; COO Rite Aid Corp., Camp Hill, Pa., 2007—. Office: Rite Aid Corp 30 Hunter Ln Camp Hill PA 17011-2410*

EASSON, WILLIAM MCALPINE, psychiatrist, educator; b. Evanston, Ill., July 3, 1931; s. Alexander and Anne Meldrum (Watson) E.; m. Gwendolyn Bowen, May 31, 1958; children: Anne, Jane, David, Michael. M.B., Ch.B., U. Aberdeen, Scotland, 1954, MD, 1967. Fellow in medicine and psychiatry Mayo Clinic, Rochester, Minn., 1956-59; resident in psychiatry U. Sask., 1959-60, instr. psychiatry, 1959-61; fellow in child psychiatry Menninger Clinic, Topeka, 1961-63, staff child psychiatrist, 1963-67; prof. psychiatry, chmn. dept. Med. Coll. Ohio, Toledo, 1967-72; prof., dir. div. child and adolescent psychiatry U. Minn. Med. Sch., Mpls., 1972-74; prof. psychiatry La. State U. Med. Ctr., New Orleans, 1974-96, head dept. psychiatry, 1974-82, prof. emeritus, 1996—. Vis. prof. psychiatry U. Garyounis Med. Sch., Benghazi, Libya, 1979; prof. grad. studies U. Riyadh, Saudi Arabia; U.S.-USSR health scientist, Moscow and Leningrad. Author: The Severely Disturbed Adolescent, 1969, The Dying Child, 2d edit., 1981, Psychiatry Exam. Rev., 5th edit., 1994, Psychiatry Patient Mgmt. Rev., 1977, (with N. Rock) Psychiatry Splty. Bd. Rev., 1991, The Management of the Severely Disturbed Adolscent, 1996; editor: Jour. Clin. Psychiatry, 1977-80. Carnegie fellow, 1956-58; Anderson fellow, 1956-58; WHO fellow, 1976 Fellow Am. Psychiat. Assn. (life). Home: 5218 Saint Charles Ave New Orleans LA 70115-4943

EAST, JOHN, computer company executive; married. BSEE, MBA, U. Calif. Berkeley. Various mktg., engring. and mgmt. positions Fairchild Semiconductor; sr. v.p. AMD; joined Actel Corp., 1988, pres., CEO Sunnyvale, Calif. Bd. dirs. Adaptec Corp. Office: 2061 Stierlin CT Mountain View CA 94043-4698

EASTAUGH, ROBERT L., state supreme court justice; b. Seattle, Nov. 12, 1943; BA in English Literature, Yale U., 1965; JD, U. Mich., 1968. Bar: Alaska 1968. Asst. atty. gen. State of Alaska, 1968—69, asst. dist. atty., 1969—72; lawyer Delaney, Wiles, Hayes, Reitman & Brubaker, Inc., 1972—94; assoc. justice Alaska Supreme Ct., 1994—. Charter mem. Advisory Com. on Rules of Practice & Internal Operating Procedures, Alaska Ninth Circuit Ct., 1983—92; mem. Alaska Supreme Ct. Appellate Rules Com., 1985—; co-chair Alaska Supreme Ct. Fairness & Access Implementation Com., 1998—. Mem.: Alaska Bar Assoc. (bar examiner). Office: Alaska Supreme Ct 303 K St Anchorage AK 99501-2048 Office Phone: 907-264-0624.*

EASTBURN, CHRISTOPHER AMERS, composer, choral director; b. Doylestown, Pa., May 19, 1969; s. William Henry and Constance Allen Eastburn; m. Jane Hammer, June 29, 2002; children: Quinn Edward, Adrian Rigopulos, Simon Rigopulos. BA, Conn. Coll., New London, 1991; MusM, Boston U., 1997. Composer: I'm Going to Spangola (winner Internat. Composer's Competition, 2000), Castles in the Air, Call Across the Generations, (ballet score) Consent to Gravity. Trustee PALS Children's Chorus, Brookline, Mass., 2000—. Fellowship Composer fellow, Bowdoin Summer Music Festival, 1993. Home: 15 Philemon St Arlington MA 02474 Home Phone: 781-648-2575. Personal E-mail: eastburnmusic@rcn.com.

EASTER, STEPHEN SHERMAN, JR., biology professor; b. New Orleans, Feb. 12, 1938; s. Stephen Sherman and Myrtle Olivia (Bekkedahl) E.; m. Janine Eliane Piot, June 4, 1963; children: Michele, Kim BS, Yale U., 1960; postgrad., Harvard U., 1961; PhD, Johns Hopkins U., 1966. Postdoctoral fellow Cambridge U., Eng., 1967; postdoctoral U. Calif., Berkeley, 1968-69; asst. prof. biology U. Mich., Ann Arbor, 1970-74, assoc. prof., 1974-78, prof., 1978—2004, assoc. chmn., 1992-93, mem. Coll. Lit., Sci. and the Arts exec. com., 1993-96, dir. neurosci. program, 1984-88, Mathew Alpern Collegiate prof., 1998—2004, prof. emeritus, 2004—. Vis. prof. U. Murcia, Spain, 1997, Ecole Normale Supérieure, Paris, 1997. Editor Vision Rsch., 1978-85, Jour. Neurosci., 1989-95, Visual Neurosci., 1990-92, Investigative Ophthalmology and Visual Sci., 1992-97, Jour. Comparative Neurology, 1994-99. Recipient Sokol award, 1998. Mem. Soc. Neurosci., Assn. Rsch. in Vision and Ophthalmology, Internat. Brain Rsch. Orgn., Soc. for Devel. Biology. Office: U Mich Dept Biology 3113 Natural Sci Bldg Ann Arbor MI 48109-1048 E-mail: sseaster@umich.edu.

EASTER, WILLIE, JR., artist, writer; b. York, SC, Oct. 27, 1963; Author: (book) Dawn of a New Age (Copyright award, 1998), Dawn of a New Age II: The Dragon People (Copyright award, 1999), Combinations, 2005, (animated film) Dawn of a New Age: Conflict, Dawn of a New Age: Wasteland, 2006. Active connectional Lay Coun. Trinity A.M.E. Zion Ch., Gastonia, NC, 1991—92. Recipient Cert. Enrollment, Attendance, and Cooperation, Vocat. Bible Sch. Trinity A.M.E. Zion Ch., 1990, Outstand Achievement in Poetry award, Internat. Libr. Poetry, 2007. Address: 310 S Broad St Gastonia NC 28054 Office Phone: 980-329-2056. Personal E-mail: easterone77@yahoo.com.

EASTERBROOK, FRANK HOOVER, federal judge; b. Buffalo, Sept. 3, 1948; s. George Edmund and Vimy (Hoover) E. BA, Swarthmore Coll., 1970; JD, U. Chgo., 1973. Bar: D.C. Law clk. to Hon. Levin H. Campbell US Ct. Appeals (1st cir.), Boston, 1973-74; asst. to solicitor gen. US Dept. Justice, Washington, 1974-77, dep. solicitor gen., 1978-79; asst. prof. law U. Chgo., 1978-81, prof. law, 1981—85, Lee & Brena Freeman prof., 1984-85; prin. employee Lexecon Inc., Chgo., 1980-85; sr. lectr. U. Chgo., 1985—; judge US Ct. Appeals (7th cir.), Chgo., 1985—, chief judge, 2006—. Mem. adv. com. on tender offers SEC, Washington, 1983 Author: (with Richard A. Posner) Antitrust, 1981, (with Daniel R. Fischel) The Economic Structure of Corporate Law, 1991; editor Jour. Law and Econs., Chgo., 1982-91; contbr. articles to profl. jours. Trustee James Madison Meml. Fellowship Found., 1988—. Recipient Prize for Disting. scholarship Emory U., Atlanta, 1981 Mem. AAAS, Am. Law Inst., Mont Pelerin Soc., Order of Coif, Phi Beta Kappa. Office: US Ct Appeals Everett McKinley Dirksen Fed Bldg 219 S Dearborn St Ste 2746 Chicago IL 60604-1803*

EASTERBROOK, GREGG EDMUND, writer; b. Buffalo, Mar. 2, 1953; s. George Edmund and Vimy Roslyn (Hoover) Easterbrook; m. Nan Terese Kennelly, Jan. 1, 1988; 3 children. BA, Colo. Coll., 1976; MSJ, Northwestern U., 1977; LittD (hon.), Colo. Coll., 1992. Former contbg. editor Newsweek, Washington, US News & World Report; contbg. editor The Washington Monthly, Washington, The Atlantic Monthly, Boston, 1980—; sr. editor The New Republic, 1998—, BeliefNet.com. Visiting fellow, economic studies Brookings Instn., 2000—; contr. Tuesday Morning Quarterback column Slate, 2000—02, ESPN.com's Page 2, 2002—03, 2006—, NFL.com, 2004—06; commentator NFL Total Access, 2004—. Author: This Magic Moment, 1986, Surgeon Koop, 1991, A Moment on the Earth, 1995, Beside Still Waters, 1998, Tuesday Morning Quarterback, 2001, The Here and Now, 2002, The Progress Paradox, 2003. Recipient Investigative Reporters and Editors award (with Thomas Bethell), 1980, Investigative Reporters and Editors award, 1982, Livingston award, 1986; disting. fellow, Fullbright Found., 1996. Fellow: Fulbright Found. Democrat. Office: The New Republic 1331 H St NW Ste 700 Washington DC 20005 Office Phone: 202-508-4444.*

EASTERDAY, BERNARD CARLYLE, veterinary medicine educator; b. Hillsdale, Mich., Sept. 16, 1929; s. Harley B. and Alberta M. Easterday D.V.M., Mich. State U., 1952; MS, U. Wis., 1958, PhD, 1961. Diplomate Am. Coll. Veterinary Microbiologists. Pvt. practice veterinary medicine, Hillsdale, Mich., 1952; veterinarian U.S. Dept. Def., Frederick, Md., 1955-61; assoc. prof., then prof. veterinary sci. U. Wis., Madison, 1961-94, prof. emeritus, 1994—, dean Sch. Vet. Medicine, 1979-94, dean emeritus, prof emeritus Sch. Vet. Medicine, 1994—. Mem., chmn. com. animal health Nat. Acad. Sci.-NRC, Washington, 1980-83, mem. com. on sci. basis meat and poultry inspection program, 1984-85; mem. tech. adv. com. Binat. Agrl. Research and Devel., Bet-Degan, Israel, 1982-84; mem. expert adv. panel on zoonoses WHO, Geneva, 1978-94; mem. tech. adv. com. on avian influenza USDA, 1983-85; mem. sec. USDA adv. com. on fgn. animal and poultry diseases, 1991-96. 1st lt. V.C., U.S. Army, 1952-54. Recipient Disting. Alumnus award Coll. Vet. Medicine, Mich. State U., 1975, Disting. Alumni award Mich. State U., 1999, Disting. Alumni award U. Wis., Madison, 2003; named Wis. Veterinarian of Yr., Wis. Vet. Med. Assn., 1979. Mem. AVMA, Am. Assn. Vet. Med. Colls. (pres. 1975), Am. Assn. Avian Pathologists Office: U Wisconsin-Madison Sch Vet Medicine 2015 Linden Dr W Madison WI 53706-1100

EASTERSON, SAM, artist; b. Hartford, Jan. 24, 1972; BFA, Cooper Union Sch., 1994; MS, U. Minn., 1999. Exhibited in group shows at Whitney Mus. Am. Art, N.Y.C., 1997, Walker Art Ctr., Mpls., 1998, New Mus., N.Y.C., 1998, Williams Coll. Mus. Art, 2001, Palm Beach Inst. Contemporary Art, 2001, Mass. Mus. Contemporary Art, North Adams, Tang Mus., Saratoga Springs, NY, Natural History Mus., LA, U. So. Calif., Exporatorium, San Francisco, exhibitions include Internat. Ctr. Photography, NY. Recipient Louis Comfort Tiffany prize, 1999; Creative Capital grantee, 2001. Home: 4286 Tujunga Ave Studio City CA 91604-2746 also: PO Box 470845 San Francisco CA 94147 Office Phone: 818-415-0955. Personal E-mail: anivegvideo@hotmail.com, sam@aniveguideo.com.

EASTHAM, ALAN WALTER, JR., foreign service officer, lawyer; b. Dumas, Ark., Oct. 16, 1951; s. Alan Walter and Ruth E. (Clayton) E.; m. Carolyn Laux, Aug. 2, 1974; children: Mark A., Michael S.G. BA, Hendrix Coll., Ark., 1973; JD cum laude, Georgetown U., 1982. Bar: D.C. 1982. Mgr. KDDA-AM Radio, Dumas, Ark., 1973-74; vice consul Am. Embassy, Kathmandu, Nepal, 1975-78; info. officer Dept. State, Washington, 1978-80, staff mem. office for combatting terrorism, 1980-82, desk officer Sri Lanka and Maldives, 1982-83, polit. officer for India, 1983-84; prin. officer Am. consulate, Peshawar, Pakistan, 1984-87; spl. asst. to under sec. polit. affairs Dept. State, 1987-89; counselor Am. Embassy, Nairobi, Kenya, 1989-92, Kinshasa, Zaire, 1992-94; consul gen. Bordeaux, France, 1994-95; counselor Am. Embassy, New Delhi, 1995-97, dep. chief of mission Islamabad, Pakistan, 1997-99; dep. asst. sec. of state for South Asian affairs Dept. of State, Washington, 1999—2001, spl. negotiator for conflict diamonds, 2001—02, dir. Cen. African affairs, 2002—05, U.S. amb. to Republic of Malawi, 2005—. Methodist. Office: Am Embassy Lilongwe Malawi Office Phone: 265-1-773166. E-mail: easthamaw@state.gov.

EASTHAM, JOHN D., marketing executive; Profl. Degree, Burnley Sch., Seattle, 1967. Mng. ptnr. EMB Ptnrs., Seattle, 1994—2002, Eastham Hinton & Simpson LLC, 2002—. Recipient Clio awards, 1986, Effie, Am. Mktg. Assn., 1991, Totem awards Pub. Rels. Soc. Am., 1982. Office: Eastham Hinton & Simpson LLC 87 Wall St #2 Seattle WA 98121-1330

EASTHAM, THOMAS, retired foundation administrator; b. Attelboro, Mass., Aug. 21, 1923; s. John M. and Margaret (Marsden) Eastham; m. Berenice J. Hirsch, Oct. 12, 1946; children: Scott Thomas, Todd Robert. Student English, Northwestern U., 1946-52. With Chgo. American, 1945-56, asst. Sunday editor, 1953-54, feature writer, 1954-56; news editor San Francisco Call Bull., 1956-62, exec. editor, 1962-65; exec. editor, then D.C. bur. chief San Francisco Examiner, 1965-82; dir. pub. info, press sec. to mayor of San Francisco, 1982-88; v.p., western dir. William Randolph Hearst Founds., 1988—2005; ret., 2005. Active Nat. Trust Hist. Preservation; mem. Amnesty Internat.; mem. Pres.'s roundtable U. San Francisco. Finalist Pulitzer prize, 1955; recipient Disting. Achievement in Journalism award, Assn. Schs. Journalism and Mass Comm., 1994. Mem.: ACLU, San Francisco Planning and Urban Rsch. Assn., Coun. Founds., Ind. Sector, Nat. Press Club, White House Corrs. Assn., Am. Internat. Press Insts., Inter-Am. Press Assn., Am. Soc. Newspaper Editors, Peninsula Tennis Club, Commonwealth Club, Marine Meml. Club, Sigma Delta Chi. Home: 1473 Bernal Ave Burlingame CA 94010-5559 Office: Hearst Found 90 New Montgomery St Ste 1212 San Francisco CA 94105-4596 Personal E-mail: t.eastham@comcast.com. Business E-Mail: teastham@hearstfdn.com.

EASTIN, DELAINE ANDREE, education educator; b. San Diego, Aug. 20, 1947; d. Daniel Howard and Dorothy Barbara Eastin. BA in Polit. Sci., U. Calif., Davis, 1969; MA in Polit. Sci., U. Calif., Santa Barbara, 1971. Instr. Calif. Community Colls., various locations, 1971-79; acctg. mgr. Pacific Bell, San Francisco, 1979-84; corp. planner Pacific Telesis Group, San Francisco, 1984-86; assemblywoman Calif. State Legis., Sacramento, 1986-95; supt. of public instruction Calif. Edn. Dept., Sacramento, 1995—2003; exec. dir. Nat. Inst. Sch. Leadership, 2003—04; disting. prof. ednl. leadership Mills Coll., Oakland, Calif. Ex officio mem. bd. regents U. Calif., 1995—2003; ex officio mem. bd. trustees Calif. State U., 1995—2003. Bd. dirs. CEWAER, Sacramento, 1988-2003, Pence Gallery, 2003—, Internat. Assn. Fgn. Students Found., 2003—; commr. Commn. on Status of Women, Sacramento, 1990-2003; mem. coun. City of Union City, Calif., 1980-86; chair Alameda County Libr. Commn., Hayward, Calif., 1981-86; planning commr. City of Union City, 1976-80; mem., pres. Alameda County Solid Waste Mgmt. Authority, Oakland, Calif., 1980-86. Named Outstanding Pub. Ofcl. Calif. Tchrs. Assn., 1988, Cert. of Appreciation Calif. Assn. for Edn. of Young Children, 1988-92, Legislator of the Yr. Calif. Media Libr. Educators, 1991, Calif. Sch. Bd. Assn., 1991, 94, Ednl. Excellence award Calif. Assn. Counseling and Devel., 1992. Mem.: Am. Bus. Women's Assn. (Outstanding Bus. Woman 1988), The Internat. Alliance (21st Century award 1990), World Affairs Coun., Commonwealth Club. Democrat. Avocations: photography, hiking, reading, theater, travel. Home: 4228 Dogwood Pl Davis CA 95616-6066 Office Phone: 510-430-2365.

EASTIN, KEITH E., civilian military employee, lawyer; b. Lorain, Ohio, Jan. 16, 1940; s. Keith Ernest and Jane E. (Heimer) E. AB, U. Cin., 1963, MBA, 1964; JD, U. Chgo., 1967. Bar: Ill. 1967, Tex. 1974, Calif. 1975, U.S. Supreme Ct. 1975, D.C. 1983. Atty. Vedder, Price, Kaufman & Kammholz, Chgo., 1967-73; v.p., sec., gen. counsel Nat. Convenience Stores, Inc., Houston, 1973-79; ptnr. Payne, Eastin & Widmer, Houston, 1977-83; dep. under sec. US Dept. Interior, 1983-86; prin. dep. asst. sec., Dept. of Navy US Dept. Def., 1986-88; ptnr. Hopkins & Sutter, Washington, 1989-91; sr. v.p. Guy F. Atkinson Co., San Francisco, 1991-92; dir. environ. svcs. Deloitte & Touche, Washington, 1992-98, Pricewaterhouse-Coopers, 1998—2000; v.p., gen. counsel The Customer Co., 2000—03; sr. adv. Ministry of Environment, Baghdad, Iraq, 2004—05; asst. sec. for installations & environment, Dept. Army US Dept. Def., Washington, 2005—. Bd. dirs. Theatre Under the Stars, Houston, Statue of Liberty-Ellis Island Found.; mem. exec. com. Harris County Republican Party, 1976-83. Mem. ABA, Ill. Bar Assn., Tex. Bar Assn., D.C. Bar Assn., State Bar Calif., Knights Templar, Met. Club (Washignton, Capitol Hill Club (Washington), Beta Gamma Sigma, Phi Delta Phi, Beta Theta Pi. Office: Dept Army 110 Army Pentagon Rm 3E464 Washington DC 20310

EASTMAN, DEAN ERIC, physicist, researcher; b. Oxford, Wis., Jan. 20, 1940; m. Ella Mae Staley. BSEE, MIT, 1962, MSEE, 1963, PhDEE, 1965. Rsch. staff IBM T.J. Watson Rsch. Ctr., Yorktown Heights, NY, 1963-71, mgr. photoemission and surface physics group, 1971-81, mgr. lithography packaging and compound semicondr. tech., 1981-82, dir. Advanced Packaging Tech. Lab., 1983-85, rsch. v.p. system tech. and sci., 1986-94; dir. product devel. IBM Systems Tech. Div., Danbury, Conn., 1985-86; dir. hardware devel. reengring. IBM Corp., Armonk, NY, 1994-96; dir. Argonne Nat. Lab., 1996-98; prof. physics U. Chgo., 1998—. Prof. physics U. Chgo., 1998—. Contbr. over 180 articles to profl. jours. Recipient Oliver E. Buckley prize, 1980; IBM Corp. fellow, 1974. Fellow Am. Phys. Soc.; mem. NAS, NAE, Am. Acad. Arts and Scis. Office: University of Chicago JFI Box 15 Rl 231 5640 S Ellis Ave Chicago IL 60637-1433

EASTMAN, DONNA KELLY, composer; b. Denver, Sept. 26, 1945; d. Donald Lewis and Frances Marie (Smith) Kelly; m. John Bernard Eastman, July 1, 1973; children: Jonathan Kelly, James Alan; stepchildren: Barbara Kathleen, Sally Toye. B in Music Edn., U. Colo., 1967; MA, U. Md., 1973, D in Mus. Arts, 1992. Pvt. studio tchr., coach, 1960—; choral dir. Dept. Def. Overseas Sch., Okinawa, Japan, 1970—72; dir. Choraleers Choral Ensemble, Stuttgart, Germany, 1974—76, Bangkok Music Soc. Ensemble and Madrigal Singers, 1982—84; instr. in music No. Va. C.C., Alexandria, 1986—89. Creator, pianist, vocalist Am. Music Programs for U.S. Mission, Thailand, 1981-84; vis. asst. prof. Ill. Wesleyan U., Bloomington, 1994; vis. composer Sweet Briar (Va.) Coll., 1998, Grinnell (Iowa) Coll., 1999. Composer choral, orchestral, opera, vocal/instrumental solo and chamber, and electronic works; recs. include Capstone Records-Soc. of Composers, Inc. Series CPS 8632, 1996, and New Music for Flute and Piano, CPS 8664, 1999; Living Artist Recs.-Music from the Setting Century Series, Vol. 2, 1996; New Ariel Recordings-Contemporary American Eclectic Music for the Piano Series, AE002, 1996; Columbine Chorale Recs.-European Tour, 1999, Blue House Productions-Alone Into the Crowd, 2002; contbr. to jours. Recipient 6 Internat. Composition awards, Composer Guild, 1991—, Internat. Piano Composition award, Roodeport Internat. Eisteddfod, South Africa, 1991, Glad-Robinson-Youse Composition award, Nat. Fedn. Music Clubs, 1992, Internat. Choral Composition award, Florilège Vocal Tours, France, 1995, Keyboard award, Delius Composition Competition, 1997, Margaret Fairbank Jory Copying Assistance award, Am. Music Ctr., 1999, Nat. Music Composition Competition award, Nat. League of Am. Pen Women, 2000, Miriam Gideon prize for New Music, 2002; fellow, Charles Ives Ctr. for Am. Music, 1990; grantee, 1993, Ragdale Found., 1991, Va. Ctr. for Creative Arts, 1991—2002. Mem. Soc. for Electro-Acoustic Music in the U.S., Internat. Alliance for Women in Music, Soc. of Composers, Inc. (life), Nat. Mus. Women in Arts (charter), Broadcast Music, Inc., Am. Composers Forum, Southeastern Composers League (past. pres.), Phi Kappa Phi, Pi Kappa Lambda, Sigma Alpha Iota. Avocations: travel, art glass work, photography. Home: 15253 W Morningtree Dr Surprise AZ 85374-4619 Personal E-mail: dkeastman@cox.net.

EASTMAN, FRANCESCA MARLENE, volunteer, art historian; b. Jamaica Plain, Mass., Jan. 26, 1952; d. Therald Carlton and Martha Jane (Welch) E.; m. Edward Charles Goodstein, Aug. 27, 1989. AB in Art History, Manhattanville Coll., 1972; MA in Art History, Clark Art Inst./Williams Coll., 1974; postgrad., Stanford U., 1976-80. Intern Mus. of Fine Arts, Boston, summers 1971-73; lectr. in art Regis Coll., Weston, Mass., 1974-76; sr. house assoc. Stanford (Calif.) U., 1977-80, tchg. fellow, 1978-79; Stanford student svcs. intern Menlo Coll., Atherton, Calif., 1980-81; now freelance editor. Bd. sec. Trinity Episcopal Sch., Menlo Park, Calif., 1992—96, bd. chair, 1996—98; adv. bd., chair Trinity Sch., 1998; trustee David B. and Edward C. Goodstein Found., LA, 1995—; vol. scholarship com. Peninsula Cmty. Found., San Mateo, Calif., 1995—; grad. Leadership Redwood City, Calif., 1995—; arts commr., chair Town of Atherton Arts Com., Calif., 1996—, 75th ann. com. leadership coun. Calif., 1998, chair Calif., 1999—; mem. steering com., chair edn. com., founding trustee Episcopal Sch. of the Peninsula, Foster City, Calif., Calif., 1996—; mem. steering com. Arts Coun. San Mateo County Cultural Planning; mem. Menlo Sch. Bd. Fine Arts Com., Atherton, Calif. Mem. Cornell Club (N.Y.C.), Williams Club (N.Y.C.), Pacific Athletic Club. Democrat. Roman Catholic. Avocations: herb gardening, piano.

EASTMAN, JOHN ROBERT, education educator; b. San Diego, June 30, 1945; s. John Henry and Theresa (Wimberger) E. BA, Va. Poly. Inst. and State U., 1968; PhD, Julius-Maximilians U., Wuerzburg, 1985. Cert. tchr., Va. Tchr. So. H.S., Harwood, Md., 1968-69; restoration worker Blersch-Lenz, Munich, 1971—75; instr. for English Dolmetscher Inst., Wuerzburg, 1976-83; bilingual tourist guide Arbeitsamt, Wuerzburg, 1976-85; summer sch. tchr. Archbishop Spalding H.S., Severn, Md., 1992; substitute tchr. Ft. Meade High Sch., 1990, Old Mill H.S., 1992, Anne Arundel Co., Md., 1987-97, Hampton (Va.) City Schs., 2001—04; tchr. Peninsula Cath. H.S., Newport News, Va., 1997—2001; asst. prof. German Old Dominion U., Norfolk, Va., 2002—03; tchr. Walsingham Acad., Williamsburg, Va., 2003—05; adj. faculty history Christopher Newport U., Newport News, 2005. Tutor Huntington Learning Ctr., Newport News, 2006. Author: Papal Abdication in Later Medieval Thought, 1990; editor: Aegidius Romanus, De Renunciatione Pape, 1992; contbr. Internat. Medieval Bibliography, 1995—; contbr. articles to profl. jours. Mem. Am. Hist. Assn., Southeastern Medieval Assn., Nat. Coalition Ind. Scholars, Capital Area Ind. Scholars (sec.-treas. 1992-94, newsletter editor 1994-96), Am. Philol. Assn., Am. Cath. Hist. Assn., Am. Assn. Tchrs. German. Avocation: genealogy. Home: 11311 Winston Pl Apt 8 Newport News VA 23601-2238

EASTMAN, LESTER FUESS, electrical engineer, educator; b. Utica, NY, May 21, 1928; s. Howard Socrates and Mayme Lois (Fuess) E.; m. Anne Marie Gardner, Dec. 22, 1948; children: David Joel, Daniel Gardner, Laurie Suzanne. BEE, Cornell U., 1953, MS, 1955, PhD, 1957. Instr. Cornell U., Ithaca, NY, 1954-56, asst. prof., 1957-60, assoc. prof., 1960-66, prof. elec. engring., 1966-84; John L. Given Found. Chair prof. elec. engring., 1985—; founder, dir. joint services electronics program and research lab., 1977-87. Founding mem. Nat. Rsch. and Resource Facility for Submicron Structures, 1977—; laborator Chalmers Tech. U., Gothenburg, Sweden, 1960—61; mem. tech. staff RCA Rsch. Lab., 1964—65; founder, pres. Cayuga Assoc., Ithaca, 1971—72; mem. tech. staff MIT, Lincoln Lab., Lexington, Mass., 1978—79; dir. Cornell Rsch. Found., 1974—86; mem. U.S. Adv. Group Election Devices, 1978—85, 1986—88; vis. scientist IBM Watson Rsch. Lab., 1985—86; founder, chmn. bd. dirs. N.E. Semicondr., Inc., 1987—93; chmn. sci. adv. bd. Nova Crystals, 1998—2003; mem. kuratorium, sr. advisory bd. Fraunhofer Applied Physics Inst., 1994—2000; cons. to industry. Guest editor IEEE transactions, 1967, 78; Contbr. articles to profl. jours.; patentee in field. Served with USN, 1946-48. Recipient Welker medal and award Internat. Symposium Gallium Arsenide and Related Compounds, 1991, Aldert Van Der Ziel award, 1995, Prof. William Gould Dow Lectureship award U. Mich., 2002, Microwave Theory and Technique Soc. Disting. Educator award, IEEE, 2003; Sperry Gyroscope fellow, 1953-54, GE fellow, 1956-57, Humboldt Sr. fellow, 1994—. Fellow IEEE (Grad. Educator award 1999, Third Millenium Medal, 2000, J.J. Ebers award 2002, Lester F. Eastman Biennial conf., 2002—), Am. Phys. Soc.; mem. NAE, Electromagnetics Acad., Sigma Xi, Eta Kappa Nu, Tau Beta Pi, Phi Kappa Phi. Presbyterian. Home: 418 Savage Farm Dr Ithaca NY 14850 Office: Cornell U 425 Phillips Hall Ithaca NY 14853-5401 Office Phone: 607-255-4369. *As a professor, I believe that my life contribution is through giving many students the opportunity to reach their full potential in the highest technology available.*

EASTMAN, W. DEAN, secondary school educator; b. Lawrence, Mass., Feb. 22, 1948; s. Weston D. and Harriett R. Eastman. BS in Social Sci. Edn., Drake U., 1970; MS in Edn., Springfield Coll., Mass., 1976, cert. advanced grad. adminstrn. studies, 1977; M in Liberal Arts, Harvard U., 2000. Coach track and field Springfield Coll. and U. Mass., Lowell, 1970-81; tchr. social sci. Beverly (Mass.) H.S., 1970—. Vis. prof. edn. Drake U., 1994—95. Contbr. biography on Nathan Dane to Yale Biographical Dictionary of American Law, 2004; featured in I Am a Teacher, 1990, (mags.) Tchg. Tolerance, Boston Mag.; featured for work with homeless students Today Show, NBC-TV, 1991; host 10-part series on immigration Mass. Ednl. TV, 1992; features include (PBS series) Only a Teacher, 2001; contestant ABC's Who Wants to be a Millionarie?, 2005; contbr. articles to profl. jours. and mags. Mem. ednl. steering com. Mass. Civil Liberties Union, Boston, 1990—; mem. PBS Tchg Adv. Bd., 2004—; mem. Com. for Adminstrn. of Adams Family Papers, 2005—. Christa McAuliffe fellow Mass. Dept. Edn., 1989, resident fellow Mass. Hist. Soc., 2001; recipient Outstanding Tchr. award John F. Kennedy Presdl. Libr., 1989, Am. Tchr. award Disney Channel, 1991, Alumni Achievement award Drake U., 1991, Derek Bok prize Harvard U., 2000, Prince Saunders award for contbns. in African-Am. hist. rsch. Nat. Pk. Svc., 2005; named one of Outstanding Young Men of Am., 1982, Preserve Am. Mass. History Tchr. of the Yr., 2004. Mem. Nat. Assn. Scholars. Avocations: surf casting, poetry, football. Office: Beverly HS 100 Sohier Rd Beverly MA 01915-5533 Business E-Mail: wdeastman@post.harvard.edu.

EASTMENT, THOMAS JAMES, lawyer; b. NYC, Mar. 3, 1950; s. George Thomas and Grace Anne Eastment. BChemE, Manhattan Coll., 1972; JD, U. Mich., 1975. Bar: NY 1976, DC 1977. Assoc. Morton, Bernard, Brown, Washington, 1975-77, Baker Botts LLP, Washington, 1977-84, ptnr., 1985—. Named Leading Lawyer in Energy, Legal Times, 2005. Mem. DC Bar Assn., Fed. Energy Bar Assn. Office: Baker Botts LLP The Warner 1299 Pennsylvania Ave NW Washington DC 20004-2400 Office Phone: 202-639-7717. Business E-Mail: Tom.Eastment@BakerBotts.com.

EASTMOND-ROBINSON, JUNE PATRICIA, nursing educator; b. NYC, June 21, 1938; d. Claude T. Eastmond and Olivia G. DeBello; m. Maroa W. Gikuuri, 1968 (div. 1978); children: Maroa L., Nyahiri Gikuuri-Bandele; m. Arthur L. Robinson, May 16, 1981; 1 stepchild, Randall. RN, Kings County Hosp. Sch. Nursing, Bklyn., 1958; BSN, NYU, 1964; MS Cmty. Health, L.I. U., Bklyn., 1974; EdD, Fla. Atlantic U., 1999. RN Fla. Bd. Nursing, 1978; cert. healing touch IIB Fla. Ctr. for Healing Touch. Staff nurse Kings County Hosp., Bklyn., 1958—59, dir. patient rels., 1974—78; pub. health nurse Dept. Health, Bklyn., 1961—63; pub. health nurse for pregnant teens Project Teen Aid, Bklyn., 1968—72; in svc. edn. coord. Medgar Evers Coll., Bklyn., 1972—74; dir. nursing Fla. Cmty. Health Ctrs., West Palm Beach, 1978—80; assoc. prof. nursing Indian River C.C., Fort Pierce, Fla., 1980—2001, ret., 2001. Co-chair State of Fla. Sci. Taskforce, 1980—86; test cons. Nat. Coun. State Bds. Nursing, Atlanta, 1994, Atlanta, 97. Co-author: (textbook) Nursing Assistant Fundamentals, 1998. Active, past pres., publicity chair African-Am. Cultural Exposition for the Arts, Fort Pierce, Fla., 1983—2002; treas., actor Faces and Voices of St. Lucie County Inc., 2001—03; mem. The Links Inc. Orlando chpt., 1996—; v.p. region III Fla. Spl. Needs Assn., 1986—89; bd. dirs. Big Bros. Big Sisters, Fort Pierce, Fla., 2001—03. Recipient cert. of appreciation, Nat. Coun. State Bd. Nursing, 1997, cert. acad. excellence award, Fla. Atlantic U., 1997. Mem.: NAACP, Ctrl. Fla. Black Nurses Assn. (sec. 2005—07), Nurses Assn., Inc. (sec. 2005—), Fla. Nurse Assn. (treas. 2000—03, dist. 8 bd. dirs. 2003—07), Caribbean Nurses Assn. (bd. dirs. 1999—2003, gratitude award 2000), Assn. Practical Nurse Educators (pres., treas., bd. dirs. 1991—2000). Avocations: reading, exercise, organizing community activities, acting. Home: 14556 Lycastle Cir Orlando FL 32826-4212

EASTON, CHARLES CLEMENT, JR., corporate financial executive; b. Allentown, Pa., July 14, 1930; s. Charles Clement and Harriet Ida (Williamson) E.; m. Priscilla Emma Herbert, Dec. 26, 1954; children: Joanne, Charles III, June, Jennifer. BS in Econs., Wharton Sch., 1952; MBA, Harvard U., 1956. CFP. Asst. to treas. Inmont Corp., NYC, 1956-62, asst. treas., 1962-67, treas., 1967-80, Inmont Div./United Technologies, Clifton, NJ, 1980-84; dir. fin. planning Coatings and Inks Div./BASF Corp., Clifton, 1984-88; sr. rep. Excel Comms., Inc., 1995—2004; mem. adv. bd. Cmty. Agys. Corp., Newark, 2005—. Co-dir. Clem Easton Super Seniors, 1999-; trustee, bd. dirs. Comm. Agys. Corp., Newark, NJ, 1989-2004. 1st lt. USAF, 1952-54, Korea. Mem. Soc. Mayflower Descendants in State of NJ, Wyo. Club of Millburn, NJ, Racquets Club of Boca Raton, Alpha Chi Rho. Republican. Congregationalist. Avocations: tennis, bridge. Personal E-mail: ceastonjr74@yahoo.com.

EASTON, GLENN HANSON, JR., management consultant, federal official, military officer; b. NYC, Mar. 11; s. Glenn Herman and Cornelia Blanchard (Hanson) E.; m. Jeanne Milhall, June 15, 1944; children: Jeanne, Glenn Hanson III, Michelle, Carol. Assoc. in Bus. Adminstrn., U. Pa., 1949, BA in Econs., 1950; MBA, PhD candidate, NYU, 1959. USCG lic. 3d asst. engr. steam vessels of any horsepower, 3d mate of steam and motor vessels of any gross tons upon the waters of oceans, Panamanian master; CLU. Various positions to asst. traffic mgr. Keystone Shipping Co., Phila., 1940—54, Phila. Jr. C. of C., 1946-54; various positions to mgr. transp. econs. div. Standard-Vacuum Oil Co., White Plains, NY, 1954-59; various positions to cons. to pres. S.R. Guggenheim Found., NYC, 1959-84; pres. Glenn Easton & Assocs. (mgmt. and ins. cons.), Port Chester, NY, 1970—; emeritus spl. agent Northwestern Mutual Life Ins. Co., 1974—; polit. appointee U.S. Dept. Labor, Washington, 1982-88; emeritus spl. agt. Northwestern Mut. Life Ins. Co., 1974—. Assoc. prof. mgmt. LI U.,

Brookville, NY, 1971—72. Rep. candidate for congressman, N.Y., 1972, 74, 80; pres. local Rep. Club, 1973-74; mem. Westchester County Rep. Com., 1972-83; Rep., Conservative and Ind. candidate for supr. Town of Rye, N.Y., 1973, 75, 79, 81, Rep. Candidate for councilman, 1977; vice chmn. Ind. Conservative Caucus, Westchester, 1977-83; exec. v.p. bd. trustees N.Y.-Phoenix Schs. Design, 1968-74; Eagle Scout with 4 Silver Palms. With Maine N.G., 1936-38; served to comdr. USN, 1938-40, 43-46, 50-54, 70, PTO, ret., 1979. Mem. Soc. Naval Archs. and Marine Engrs. (life, Golden award), Navy Athletic Assn., Sr. Execs. Assn., Fed. Exec. Inst., Ret. Officers' Assn., C. of C., Am. Mgmt. Assn., Naval Res. Assn. (life, v.p. Westchester chpt.), Militia Assn. N.Y. (life), Westchester Organ Soc. (v.p.), Met. Organ Soc. Va., No. Va. Ragtime Soc., Am. Theatre Organ Soc., Washington Piano Accordian Soc., U.S. Capitol Hist. Soc., The Conservative Network (life), Am. Legion, Kiwanis, Elks, Masons (32 deg.), Shriners, Pi Gamma Mu, Sigma Kappa Phi, Phi Delta Theta (Golden Legionnaire). Avocations: swimming, reading, music, archery, coin collecting/numismatics. Home: 1385 Old Quincy Ln Reston VA 20194-1309 Office: 1537 Inlet Ct Reston VA 20190-4423 Office Phone: 703-437-1666. *Much hard work, a desire for knowledge, great integrity, persistence, enthusiasm, determination, and some vision are essential ingredients in the success formula. In addition, successful leaders must never shrink from responsibility! While it helps to be lucky, to have friends in the right places, or to be in the right place at the right time, it is more important in a man's quest for success to deal honestly and fairly with one's fellowman in order that when material success is achieved peace of mind and happiness come with it.*

EASTON, JAMES L., International Olympic Committee Member, sports equipment company executive; b. LA, July 26, 1935; m. Phyllis Faasse; 2 stepchildren; 2 children from previous marriage. Grad., UCLA Sch. Engring. Chmn. internat. diversified sports equipment company. Pres. Internat. Archery Fedn., 1989—2005; organizer World Outdoor Target Championships, LA, 1983; bd. dirs. Nat. Archery Assn. Found. Prodr.: (films) Fédération Internationale de Tir à l'Arc tech. film at 5 different Olympics. Commr. archery, mayor Athletes' Olympic Village UCLA, Games of XXIII Olympiad, LA, 1984; mem., commn. press Internat. Olympic Com., 1995—96, mem., eligibility, 1996, mem. as IF rep. sports and environ. commn., 1996—99, mem., marketing, 1998—99, 2000—, mem., fin., 1999—2000, mem., nominations, 2000—, v.p., 2002—06, exec. bd. mem., 2002—06; bd. mem. Amateur Athletic Found., LA.

EASTON, J(OHN) DONALD, neurologist, educator; b. Saskatoon, Sask., Can., Apr. 1, 1938; s. John and Winnifred J. (Small) E.; m. Carol Anne May, 1959 (div. 1984); children: Erin, John, Murray; m. K. Von Gunten, May 19, 1985; children: Andrew, Alexander. BS in Zoology, Wash. State U., 1960; MD, U. Wash., 1964. Cert. Am. Bd. Psychiatry and Neurology (examiner, dir. 1984-92). From asst. to assoc. prof. U. Calif., San Diego, 1970-73; from assoc. prof. to prof. So. Ill. U. Sch. Medicine, Springfield, 1974-77; prof., chair neurology dept. U. Mo. Sch. Medicine, Columbia, 1977-82, U. Tex. Health Sci. Ctr., San Antonio, 1982-86, Brown U. Sch. Medicine, Providence, 1986—. Pres. Neurology Found., Inc., Providence, 1990—. Author med. books; editor med. jours. Fellow Am. Heart Assn. Stroke Coun., 1971—, chmn., 1991-93, vol., Providence, 1986—. With USN, 1968-70. Fellow Am. Acad. Neurology; mem. Am. Neurol. Assn., Alpha Omega Alpha, Phi Beta Kappa. Presbyterian. Avocations: travel, computers, sports. Home: 7 Seaview Ave Jamestown RI 02835-1644 Office: RI Hosp Brown U 110 Lockwood St Providence RI 02903-4801 Office Phone: 401-444-8795. Business E-Mail: j_easton@brown.edu.

EASTON, JOHN JAY, JR., lawyer; b. San Francisco, June 16, 1943; s. John Jay and Julia (Crawford) Easton; m. Donna Cecilia Ringger Startzel, May 4, 1996. BS, U. Colo., 1964; JD, Georgetown U., 1970. Bar: Va. 1970, Vt. 1971. Mktg. rep. Gen. Dynamics Corp., Washington, 1968-70; assoc. Paterson, Gibson, Noble & Brownell, Montpelier, Vt., 1970-72; ptnr. Davison & Easton, Stowe, Vt., 1972-75; asst. atty. gen., chief consumer protection Office Vt. Atty. Gen., 1975-78; dir. div. rate setting Vt. Agy. Human Svcs., 1978-80; atty. gen. State of Vt., 1981-85; pvt. practice Burlington, Vt., 1985-86; v.p. Syn-Cronamics, Inc., Englewood Cliffs, NJ, 1986-87, Miller, Eggleston & Rosenberg, Ltd., 1987-89; asst. sec. Internat. Affairs and Energy Emergencies Dept. Energy, Washington, 1989-91, gen. counsel, 1991-92, asst. sec. Domestic and Internat. Energy Policy, 1992-93; pvt. practice, 1993-94; v.p. internat. programs Edison Elec. Inst., Washington, 1994—. Product safety adv. coun. U.S. Consumer Product Safety Com., 1977—79; industry sector adv. com. energy for trade policy matters, 1997—. Mem. Vt. Natural Resources Coun., 1976—89; Rep. nominee for gov. Vt., 1984. Served to capt. USAF, 1964—68. Mem.: VFW, ABA (ho. dels. 1979—84), Vt. Bar Assn. (del. 1980—84, chmn. coms. 1974—78, bd. mgrs. 1973—75), Am. Legion. Roman Catholic. Office: Edison Elec Inst 701 Pennsylvania Ave NW Washington DC 20004-2696 Home Phone: 410-252-1001; Office Phone: 202-508-5633. Business E-Mail: jeaston@eei.org.

EASTON, KENNETH GLENN, retired utilities executive; b. Mattoon, Ill., Jan. 7, 1923; s. Omer Otis Easton and Inza Burrage Reagin; m. Hazel Florence Duncan, Aug. 25, 1946. Diploma, Franklin Credit Sch., Va., 1949. Apprenticeship Local 489 I.B.E.W., 1955. Announcer Radio Sta. WLBH, Mattoon, Ill., 1948—51; owner Music Studio, Mattoon, Ill., 1948—60; pres. Local 489, Mattoon, Ill., 1961—73; gen. foreman Decatur Indsl. Electric, Decatur, Ill., 1961—71; br. mgr. Maron Electric Co., Chicago, Ill., 1971—74, maintenance br. office Mattoon, Ill.; supr. Comstock Electric, Chicago, Ill., 1975—88. Organist Matteson Lodge #175 A.F. & A.M., Joliet, Ill., 1990—2005. Author (editor): Richard Easton, Descendents and Allied Families. Constable Mattoon Twp., Coles County, Mattoon, Ill., 1948—56; republic precinct com. Mattoon, Ill., 1948—56. Technician 5th grade US Army, 1942—46. Decorated knight York Cross of Honor Joliet Commandery, Joliet, IL, Coronated a 33rd Degree Mason Ancient Accepted Scottish Rite, knight comdr. Holy Royal Arch knight Templar Priests, Order of the Purple Cross York Rite Sovereign Coll. N.Am., Eminent Comdr. commandery. Mem.: Ancient Accepted Scottish Rite (mem. spkrs. bur. Valley Danville and Chgo.), York Rite Masons (Royal Arch chpt. 27, high priest Royal Arch chpt. 27), Rose Croix (most wise master 1983), Scottish Rite (32 degree), Grand Lodge (grand lectr. 1978), Royal and Select Masters (illustrious master coun.), Masons Ill., Mattoon Lodge (sublime degree) (master mason A.F. and A.M. 1962, worshipful master A.F. and A.M. 260 1970), East Ctrl. York Rite Coll. Am., Ansar Shrine Temple, Ill. Grand Lodge Rsch. (corr.; chmn. edn. 1992—96), Peotone Lodge (hon.), Elwood Lodge (hon.), Braidwood Lodge (hon.), Mt. Joliet Lodge (hon.), Matteson Lodge (hon.). Avocations: genealogy, history. Home: 1012 John St Joliet IL 60435 Personal E-mail: easton8@juno.com.

EASTON, ROGER L., former operations research specialist, consultant; b. Apr. 1921; m. Barbara Easton. With US Naval Rsch. Lab., Washington, 1964—95; cons., owner RoBarCo Inc., Canaan, NH. State rep. Grafton County, Dist. 11; Rep. gubernatorial cand., NH, 1986. Recipient Magellanic Premium award, Am. Philosophical Soc., 1998, 2004 Nat. Medal Tech., 2005. Fellow: Inst. Navigation. Achievements include being recognized for pioneering achivements in spacecraft tracking, navigation and timing technology, which led to the development of the NAVSTAR-Global Positioning System; patents in field.

EASTON, STEPHEN DOUGLAS, lawyer, educator; b. Pasco, Wash., May 11, 1958; s. T. Alex and Zona Gayle (Walker) E.; m. Marivern Slaveck, July 12, 1986. AA, Northland Community Coll., Thief River Falls, Minn., 1978; BBA in Acctg., Dickinson State U., ND, 1980; JD, Stanford U., 1983. Bar: N.D. 1983, U.S. Dist. Ct. N.D. 1984, U.S. Ct. Appeals (8th cir.) 1990, Mont. 1994, Mo. 1998. Aide Sen. Wendell R. Anderson, Washington, 1978; acct. Eide, Helmeke & Co., CPAs, Dickinson, 1980; law clk. N.D. Atty. Gen., Bismarck, 1981, U.S. Ct. Appeals (9th cir.), San Francisco, 1983-84; assoc. Pearce & Durick, Bismarck, ND, 1984-88, 93-94, ptnr., 1988—90, 1995—98; U.S. atty. Dist. of N.D., 1990-93; assoc. prof. Sch. Law U. Mo.-Columbia, 1998—2006, C.A. Leedy prof., 2006—. Pres. Stanford Law Forum, 1981-82. Author: How To Win Jury Trials: Building Credibility with Judges and Jurors, 1998; co-author: Problems, Cases and Materials in Professional Responsibility, 3d edit., 2004; assoc. mng. editor Stanford Law Rev., 1982-83; contbr. articles, columns to profl. publs. Del. N.D. State Republican Conv., 1980, 86, 88, 94, 96, Rep. Nat. Conv., 1996; Rep. nat. committeeman for N.D., 1996-98; chmn. N.D. Rep. Victory Club, Bismarck, 1986-90; candidate for state treas., N.D., 1988. Recipient 1st ann. Warren E. Burger prize, Am. Inns of Ct., 2004, Richard S. Jacobson award for excellence in tchg. trial advocacy The Pound Civil Justice Inst., 2006. Mem. The Mo. Bar, State Bar Mont., State Bar Assn. N.D., AICPA, N.D. Soc. CPAs. Roman Catholic. Avocations: golf, writing, bicycling. Office: Hulston Hall Sch Law U Mo-Columbia Columbia MO 65211 E-mail: eastons@missouri.edu.

EASTON, SUSAN DAWN, biochemist, educator; b. Harvey, Ill., Oct. 8, 1959; d. Dee Charles and Barbara Louise Shaffer. BS in Biol. Scis., Ill. State U., Normal, 1981. Med. rsch. technician Washington U. Sch. Medicine, St. Louis, 1981-83; biol. lab. technician VA Med. Ctr., Indpls., 1983-86; rsch. technician Ind. U., Bloomington, 1987-88, rsch. assoc., 1988-92; chemistry, microbiology, validation, document control, quality assurance mgr. Cook Imaging Corp., Bloomington, 1993-96, regulatory affairs mgr., 1996-99, tech. svcs., 1999—2001; tech. svcs. mgr. Baxter Pharm. Solutions, LLC, Bloomington, 2001—05, dir. tech. svcs., 2005—, mem. emergency response team, 2001—. Mem. emergency response team Cook Imaging Corp., Bloomington, 1995-2001; lectr. Ctr. Profl. Advancement, East Brunswick, NJ, 1996—, Internat. Soc. Pharm. Engrs., 2001—; lectr. Internat. Soc. for Pharm. Engrs., 2001. Author: Protein Expression and Purification, 1993. Named one of Outstanding Young Women of Am., 1983. Mem. Internat. Soc. Pharm. Engrs., Parenteral Drug Assn., Phi Sigma. Office: Baxter Pharm Solutions LLC 927 S Curry Pike Bloomington IN 47403 Home: 3702 Stoney Brook Blvd Bloomington IN 47404 Business E-Mail: susan_easton@baxter.com.

EASTTOM, CHUCK, computer scientist, educator; b. Bangkok, Oct. 5, 1968; m. Misty Dawn Baker, Oct. 15, 1994; 1 child, Andrew Jay (AJ). BA, Southeastern Okla. State U., 1997, MEd, 2000; MS, Mt. State U. Cert. Microsoft Certified Database Adminr. Microsoft, 2001, Microsoft Certified Systems Adminr. Microsoft, 2002, A+ Certified PC Technician CompTIA, 1998, Network+ CompTIA, 1999, Server + CompTia, 1999, I-Net+ CompTia, 2000, Linux+ CompTIA, 2001, A+ CompTIA, MCDBA Microsoft, 2002. Contract programmer/analyst Boeing Aerospace Ops., Midwest City, Okla., 1995—96; sr. software engr. Alegis Corp. Systems Group, N. Richland Hills, Tex., 1996—98; dir. ednl. tech. Southeastern Okla. State U., Durant, 1998—99; sr. software engr. DSSI, Richardson, 1999—2000; dept. chair for software info. systems dept Remington Coll. - Dallas Campus, Garland, Tex., 2000—03; sys. dir. Great Am. Ins., Profl. Liability Divsn., Richardson, Tex., 2003—05; independent cons., 2005—. Adj. instr. Collin County C.C., Plano, Tex., 2003—; subject matter cons., devel. or revision of four cert. exams CompTIA. Author: (computer programming book) Learn Java Script, 2000;: Learn VB.Net, 2001, EJB Programming with JBuilder 7.0, 2002, Learn EJB with JBuilder 7.0, 2002, Computer Programming with C+;: Fundamentals of C+ Programming, 2003, Learn VB.Net, Learn JavaScript, JFC Programming with JBuilder;: Learn VB-.Net, 2001, (book) JFC and Jbuilder, 2002, (computer programming book) Learn EJB with JBuilder 7.0. With US Army, 1987—91. Achievements include worked as a subject matter expert for the computer technology industry association in the development of their Server+ Certification test; worked as a subject matter expert for the computer technology industry association in the development of their Linux+ Certification test; worked as a subject matter expert for the computer technology industry association in the development of their Security+ Certification test. Home: 3605 Willow Creek Trail Mc Kinney TX 75071 Office: Great American Ins Ste 505 1755 N Collins Richardson TX 75080 Personal E-mail: chuckeasttom@yahoo.com.

EASTWOOD, CLINT (CLINTON EASTWOOD JR.), actor, film director and producer; b. San Francisco, May 31, 1930; s. Clinton and Ruth Eastwood; m. Maggie Johnson, Dec. 19, 1953 (div.); children: Kyle Johnson, Alison Johnson; m. Dina Ruiz, Mar. 31, 1996; children: Morgan Ruiz, Kimber Lynn Ruiz, Scott Ruiz, Kathryn Ruiz, Francesca Ruth Ruiz. Grad., Oakland Tech. High Sch., 1948; attended, LA City Coll.; DFA (hon.), Wesleyan U., 2000. Worked as lumberjack in Oreg. before being drafted into the Army. Owner Malpaso Records Co., Mission Ranch Resort, Carmel, Calif., Tehama Golf Club, Carmel, Calif; co-founder, ptnr. Tehama Inc.; co-owner Pebble Beach Co. Actor (films) Revenge of the Creature, 1955, Francis in the Navy, 1955, Lady Godiva, 1955, Tarantula, 1955, Never Say Goodbye, 1956, The First Travelling Saleslady, 1956, Star in the Dust, 1956, Away All Boats, 1956, Escapade in Japan, 1957, Ambush at the Cimmaron Pass, 1958, Lafayette Escadrille, 1958, Ambush at Cimarron Pass, 1958, A Fistful of Dollars, 1964, For a Few Dollars More, 1965, The Good, the Bad and the Ugly, 1966, The Witches, 1967, Hang 'Em High, 1968, Coogan's Bluff, 1968, Where Eagles Dare, 1968, Paint Your Wagon, 1969, Two Mules for Sister Sara, 1970, Kelly's Heroes, 1970, The Beguiled, 1971, Dirty Harry, 1971, Joe Kidd, 1972, Magnum Force, 1973, Thunderbolt and Lightfoot, 1974, The Enforcer, 1976, Every Which Way But Loose, 1978, Escape from Alcatraz, 1979, Any Which Way You Can, 1980, City Heat, 1984, The Dead Pool, 1988, Pink Cadillac, 1989, In the Line of Fire, 1993; actor, dir., prodr. (films) Firefox, 1982, Honkeytonk Man, 1982, Sudden Impact, 1983, Pale Rider, 1985, Heartbreak Ridge, 1986, White Hunter Black Heart, 1990, Unforgiven, 1992 (Academy Award for Best Director & Best Picture, 1992, Golden Globe award for best director, 1993), A Perfect World, 1993, The Bridges of Madison County, 1995, Absolute Power, 1997, True Crime, 1999, Space Cowboys, 2000, Blood Work, 2002, Million Dollar Baby, 2004 (Golden Globe award for best director, 2005, Director's Guild award for best feature, 2005, Acad. award for Best Director & Best Picture, 2005); (actor, dir.) Play Misty For Me, 1971, High Plains Drifter, 1973, The Eiger Sanction, 1975, The Outlaw Josey Wales, 1976, The Gauntlet, 1977, Bronco Billy, 1980, The Rookie, 1990; (actor, prodr.) Tightrope, 1984; (dir., prodr.) Bird, 1988, Midnight in the Garden of Good and Evil, 1997, Mystic River, 2003, Flags of Our Fathers, 2006 (Runner-up, Dir. of Yr., LA Film Critics Assn., 2006), Letter from Imo Jima, 2006 (Best Picture of Yr., LA Film Critics Assn., 2006 & Runner-up, Dir. of Yr., 2006, Best Fgn. Film, Golden Globe award, Hollywood Fgn. Press Assn., 2007); dir. (films) Breezy, 1973; prodr. (films) The Stars Fell on Henrietta, 1995; exec. prodr. (films) Thelonious Monk-Straight, No Chaser, 1989; actor (TV series) Rawhide, 1959-1966; dir. (TV series) Amazing Stories - episode Vanessa in the Garden, 1985; dir. (TV miniseries) The Blues - episode Piano Blues, 2003. Singer (singles) Unknown Girl, 1981, Rowdy, For You, For Me, For Evermore, Cowboy in a Three Piece Suit, 1981, (albums) Rawhide's Clint Eastwood Sings Cowboy Favorites, 1962, (appeared on soundtracks) Kelly's Heroes, Bronco Billy, Any Which Way you Can, Midnight in the Garden of Good and Evil, (appeared on country recordings) Make My Day with TG Sheppard, Smokin' the Hive with Randy Travis. Mem. Nat. Coun. Arts, 1972-78; mem. bd. Monterey Jazz Festival; chmn. Monterey Peninsula Found.; hon. bd. governors Entertainment Industry Found.; mayor City of Carmel, Calif., 1986-88; Calif. State Parks commr. for Carmel, 2002-; vice-chair Calif. State Parks & Recreation Commn.; nat. spokesman Take Pride in Am., 2005-. Named one of Time Mag. Most Influential People, 2005; recipient Golden Globe award for world film favorite, Hollywood Fgn. Press. Assn., 1971, Cecil B. DeMille Award, 1988, Irving G. Thalberg Meml. award, Acad. Motion Picture Arts & Sciences, 1995, Life Achievement award, Film Soc. at Lincoln Ctr., 1996, Am. Film Inst., 1996, Kennedy Ctr. Honors, John F. Kennedy Ctr. Performing Arts, 2000, Lifetime Career Achievement award, NY Nat. Bd. Review, 2000, Hank award, Henry Mancini Inst., 2003, Lifetime Achievement Award, Screen Actors Guild, 2003, Milestone award, Producers Guild Am., 2006, Lifetime Achievement Award, Directors Guild Am., 2006, Stanley Kubrick Britannia award for Excellence in Film, British Acad. Film & Television Arts/LA, 2006, Golden Boot award, Motion Picture & Television Fund, 2006, Jack Valenti Humanitarian Award, Motion Picture Assn. Am., 2007, Legion d'Honneur order, Govt. of France, 2007. Office: c/o Leonard Hirshan 1680 Clearview Dr Beverly Hills CA 90210*

EASTWOOD, GREGORY LINDSAY, former academic administrator; b. Detroit, July 28, 1940; s. William Inwood and Kathryn (Bradley) E.; m. Lynn Marshall, June 19, 1964; children: Kristen, Lauren, Kara. AB, Albion Coll., 1962; MD, Case Western Res. U., 1966. Diplomate: Am. Bd. Internal Medicine, Am. Bd. Gastroenterology. Resident in internal medicine Hosp. U. Pa., 1966—70; asst. prof. medicine Harvard U., Boston, 1974-77; assoc. prof. medicine U. Mass., Worcester, 1977-82, prof., 1982—89, dir. gastroenterology, 1977-89; dean Sch. Medicine Med. Coll. Ga., Augusta, 1989—92; pres. SUNY Upstate Med. U., Syracuse, 1993—2006; trustee Case Western Reserve U., Cleve., 2003—06, interim pres., 2006—07. Coun., past chair bd. dirs. Assn. Acad. Health Ctrs. Editor: Core Textbook in Gastroenterology, 1984, Manual of Gastroenterology: Diagnosis and Therapy, 1988, Premalignant Conditions of the Gastrointestinal Tract, 1990; contbr. articles to profl. jours. Fellow: ACP; mem.: AMA, Assn. Am. Med. Colls., An. Hosp. Assn., Am. Gastroenterological Assn., Am. Clin. and Climotological Assn. Office: Case Western Reserve U 10900 Euclid Ave Cleveland OH 44106-7001 Office Phone: 216-368-5094. Office Fax: 216-368-4325. E-mail: gregory.eastwood@case.edu.*

EATMAN, LOUIS PERKINS, lawyer; b. Montgomery, Ala., Nov. 16, 1948; s. Jack Bernard and Margaret Worthington (Perkins) E. BS in Fgn. Svc., Georgetown U., 1970; MBA, JD, Stanford U., 1974. Bar: Calif. 1974. Ptnr. Loeb and Loeb, LA, 1974—94, Mayer, Brown, Rowe & Maw LLP, LA, 1994—, co-adminstr., nat. real estate practice group, 1994—96, ptnr.-in-charge, LA office, 1996—2007, co-leader global real estate practice group, 2002—04; pres. Constitutional Rights Found., 2004—06. Mem. Los Angeles County Bar Assn., Internat. Coun. Shopping Ctrs., Riviera Country Club, City Club on Bunker Hill. Phi Beta Kappa. Avocations: golf, fly fishing. Office: Mayer Brown Rowe & Maw LLP 25th Fl 350 S Grand Ave Los Angeles CA 90071-1503 Office Phone: 213-229-5144. Business E-Mail: leatman@mayerbrownrowe.com.

EATON, ALVIN RALPH, JR., aeronautical engineer, applied physics executive, systems engineer; b. Toledo, Ohio, Mar. 13, 1920; s. Alvin Ralph and Katherine (Hasel) E., m. Kathleen Steiner, Aug. 15, 1942 (div.); children: Eric Lloyd, Alan Ralph; m. Ellen Griffiths Phillips, Oct. 3, 1970. AB in Physics, Oberlin Coll., 1941; MS in Aero. Engring., Calif. Inst. Tech., 1943. Rsch. asst. Calif. Inst. Tech., 1941-44; engr. So. Calif. Co-op Wind Tunnel, Pasadena, 1944-45; with The Johns Hopkins U. Applied Physics Lab., Silver Spring, Md., 1945-75, Laurel, Md., 1975—, mem. prin. profl. staff, 1950—, supr. aerodynamics, dynamics and guidance analysis groups, 1949-54, program supr. supersonic missile and weapon sys. programs, 1954-64, supr. missile sys. divsn., 1964-73, faculty evening coll. grad. sch., 1973-75, supr. fleet sys. dept., 1973-83, asst. dir. for tactical sys. Applied Physics Lab., 1973-79, asst. dir., 1979-86, assoc. dir., 1986-89, dir. spl. programs, 1989-2000, sr. fellow, 1989—. Mem. Johns Hopkins U. adv. bd. for Applied Physics Lab., 1963, 69-70, 73-89; chmn. Def. Sci. Bd. Task Force on Patriot Air Def. Sys., 1977-78, mem. task forces, 1979-83; cons. to under sec. def. for rsch. and engring., 1977-83, chmn. and mem. spl. NATO and U.S. task forces, 1977-92, mem. under sec. def. high energy laser rev. group, 1981-83, mem. under sec. def. durability of electronic countermeasures rev. group, 1983-86; mem. Navy planning and steering adv. Group for Surface Ship Security, 1979-82, chmn. and mem. subgroups, 1979-82; cons. to Asst. Sec. of Army for rsch., devel., and acquisition, 1969-74, 80-86, 2005, chmn., Asst. Sec. of Army ind. rev. panel for Patriot air def. sys., 1980-86; mem. Army Sci. Bd., 1980-86, 89-95; chmn. panel on adv. sys. test, 1980-81; dep. chmn. summer studies on sci. and engring. pers. and future devel. goals, 1982-83, mem. subgroup on ballistic missile def., 1984-86, 89; chmn. atmospheric scis. lab. effectiveness rev., 1985, chmn. panel on electromagnetic/electrothermal gun tech. devel., 1989-92; chmn. subgroup on Army tactical space sys., 1991-92; mem. rsch. and new initiatives issue group, 1991-95; mem. ad hoc study group on space sys. and airland ops., 1992; mem. summer study on future army missile programs, 1993; mem. ad hoc study group missile tech. shelf life, 1994; cons. army sci. bd., 2002-04, mem.summer studies on future Army combat systems, 2002, 2003; chmn., asst. sec. army rsch., devel. and acquisition ind. rev. panel for anti-tactical missile programs, 1986-2002; chmn. high altitude theater missile def. sensor panel Army Strategic Def. Command, 1992-93; dep. chmn., exec. bd. Air Armaments Sys. Divsn. of Am. Def. Preparedness Assn., 1984-90 (life mem.). Mem. editl. bd. Jour. Def. Rsch., 1988-92, Johns Hopkins APL Tech. Digest, 1995—; inventor in field; contbr. articles to profl. jours. Trustee Howard County (Md.) Gen. Hosp., 1977-85, chmn. fin. com., treas., 1979-81, vice-chmn., 1981-83, chmn., 1983-85, chmn. Cmty. Rels. Coun., 1988-94. Recipient Meritorious Pub. Svc. award USN, 1957, Disting. Pub. Svc. award, 1975, Gov. Md. citation for leadership of Howard County (Md.) Gen. Hosp. Cmty. Rels. Coun., 1994, Patriotic Civilian Svc. award U.S. Army, 1995, 2005, Disting. Alumni award Morrison R. Waite H.S., Toledo, Ohio, 1995. Fellow Explorers Club; mem. Balt. Coun. on Fgn. Affairs, Rotary, Cosmos Club (Washington), Country Club of Hilton Head, Sons of Am. Revolution (Hilton Head Island Chapter), Sigma Xi, Phi Beta Kappa. Methodist. Office: Johns Hopkins U Applied Physics Lab 11100 Johns Hopkins Rd Laurel MD 20723-6099 Home Phone: 301-596-9638; Office Phone: 240-228-5058. Business E-Mail: alvin.eaton@jhuapl.edu.

EATON, CURTIS HOWARTH, banker, lawyer; b. Twin Falls, Idaho, Sept. 3, 1945; s. Curtis Turner and Wilma (Howarth)E.; m. Mardo Ohisson, Aug. 2, 1969; 1 child, Dylan Alexander. BA, Stanford U., 1969; MPA, Johns Hopkins U., 1971; JD, U. Idaho, 1974. Bar: Idaho 1974. Atty. Idaho Atty. Gen.'s Office, Boise, 1974-76; ptnr. Stephan, Slavin, Eaton, Twin Falls, 1975-82; exec. v.p. Twin Falls Bank & Trust, 1982-84, area pres., from 1984, also bd. dirs., from 1984; former v.p., bd. dirs. 1st Security Bank at Idaho, Twin Falls, pres., 1992—; exec. dir. CSI Foundation (planning & devel.), Twin Falls, Idaho. Bd. dirs. San Francisco Fed. Res. Bank, Salt Lake City. Bd. dirs. United Way Magic Falley, 1978—, Sr. Citizens, 1978-82; mem. Idaho Bd. Edn., 1993—, now pres.; trustee YFCA, 1981—; pres. Coll. So. Idaho Found., 1986-88. Mem. ATLA, Idaho Bar Assn. Office: Coll So Idaho P O Box 1238 315 Falls Ave Twin Falls ID 83303-1238 Office Phone: 208-732-6242 6242. Business E-Mail: ceaton@csi.edu.*

EATON, DORLA DEAN See KEMPER, DORLA

EATON, GARETH RICHARD, chemistry professor, dean; b. Lockport, NY, Nov. 3, 1940; s. Mark Dutcher and Ruth Emma (Ruston) E.; m. Sandra Shaw, Mar. 29, 1969. BA, Harvard U., 1962; PhD, MIT, 1972. Asst. prof. chemistry U. Denver, 1972-76, assoc. prof., 1976-80, prof., 1980-97, dean natural scis., 1984-88, vice provost for rsch., 1988-89, John Evans prof., 1997—. Organizer Internat. Electron-Paramagnetic Resonance Symposium. Author, editor: 7 books, mem. editl. bd.: 4 jours.; contbr. articles to profl. jours. Lt. USN, 1962-67. Mem. AAAS, Am. Chem. Soc., Royal Soc.

Chemistry (London), Internat. Soc. Magnetic Resonance, Soc. Applied Spectroscopy, Am. Phys. Soc., Internat. Electron Paramagnetic Resonance Soc. Office: U Denver Dept Chem/Biochem Denver CO 80208 Home Phone: 303-759-1932; Office Phone: 303-871-2980. Business E-Mail: geaton@du.edu.

EATON, GORDON PRYOR, geologist, consultant; b. Dayton, Ohio, Mar. 9, 1929; s. Colman and Dorothy (Pryor) E.; m. Virginia Anne Gregory, June 12, 1951; children: Gretchen Maria, Gregory Mathieu. BA, Wesleyan U., 1951, Doctorate (hon.), 1995; MS, Calif. Inst. Tech., 1953, PhD, 1957; Doctorate (hon.), Colo. Sch. Mines, 2001. From instr. geology to asst. prof. Wesleyan U., Middletown, Conn., 1955-59; from asst. prof. to assoc. prof. U. Calif., Riverside, 1959-67, chmn. dept. geol. sci., 1965-67; with U.S. Geol. Survey, 1963-65, 67-81, 94-97; dep. chief Office Geochemistry and Geophysics, Washington, 1972-74; project chief geothermal geophysics Office Geochemistry Geophysics, Denver, 1974-76; scientist-in-charge Hawaiian Volcano Obs., 1976-78; assoc. chief geologist Reston, Va., 1978-81; dean Tex. A&M U. Coll. Geoscis., 1981-83; provost, v.p. acad. affairs Tex. A&M U., 1983-86, prof. emeritus, 2003—; pres. Iowa State U., Ames, 1986-90; dir. Lamont-Doherty Earth Obs. Columbia U., Palisades, NY, 1990-94, U.S. Geol. Survey, Reston, 1994-97. Former mem. Com. on Internat. Edn., Am. Coun. Edn.; bd. earth scis. and resources; ocean studies bd., com. on formation of nat. biol. survey NRC, geophysics study com.; bd. dirs. Midwest Resources, Inc., Bankers Trust; mem., chair adv. com. U.S. Army Command and Gen. Staff Coll.; adv. bd. Sandia Nat. Lab. Geoscis. & Environ. Ctr., Ohio State U. Ctr. Mapping. Mem. editl. bd. Jour. Volcanology and Geothermal Rsch., 1976-78; contbr. articles to profl. jours. Trustee Wesleyan U., 1995-98, Geol. Soc. Am. Found., 1999-2003; pres., bd. dirs. Iowa 4-H Found., 1986-90; mem. adv. bd. Sch. Earth Sci. Stanford (Calif.) U., 1995-2000; mem. U.S. del. sci. and tech. com. Gore-Chernomyrdin Commn., 1996-97; mem. vis. com. Colo. Sch. Mines, 2002-04; mem. water res. adv. com. Island Co., 2001-03. Named Gordon P. Eaton Hall in his honor, Iowa State U., 2003; grantee, NSF, 1955—59; Standard Oil fellow, Calif. Inst. Tech., 1953. Fellow: AAAS, Geol. Soc. Am.; mem.: Am. Geophysical Union. Home: 201 Pershing Ave College Station TX 77840 Office: Tex A&M U Dept Geology & Geophysics College Station TX 77844 Personal E-mail: gordon.eaton@verizon.net.

EATON, HARVILL CARLTON, academic administrator; b. Nashville, May 16, 1948; s. Robert Caldwell and Margaret Elizabeth (Stewart) E.; m. Lois Jean Acuff, June 28, 1969; children: Christopher Carlton, Mary Elizabeth. BS, Tenn. Tech. U., 1970, MS, 1972; PhD, Vanderbilt U., 1976. Asst. prof. of engring. sci. La. State U., Baton Rouge, 1976-78, assoc. prof., 1981-87, assoc. dean. engring., 1986-88, prof., 1988—97, vice chancellor for rsch., 1989—91; vice chancellor for rsch. and econ. devel., 1991; vice chancellor for corp. initiatives and pub. svc. La. State U., Baton Rouge, La.; asst. prof. Tenn. Tech. U., Cookeville, 1978-80; provost and sr. v.p. for acad. affairs Drexel U., Phila., 1997—2003; pres. Cumberland U., Lebanon, Tenn., 2004—. Bd. dirs. Baton Rouge Bank, La. Rsch. Pk. Corp.; tech. cons. La. Rsch. Pk. Corp. Contbr. articles to profl. jours. Bd. dirs. Boys and Girls Club, Baton Rouge, La. Arts and Sci. Ctr., Baton Rouge, Baton Rouge Urban League. Numerous rsch. grants 1976-92. Mem. Am. Soc. for Mechanical Engrs., Am. Ceramic Soc., Sigma Xi, Theta Tau (Hall of Fame 1992). Office: Cumberland U One Cumberland Sq Lebanon TN 37087-3408 Home Phone: 615-444-3248; Office Phone: 615-547-1223. E-mail: eaton@cumberland.edu.

EATON, JOE OSCAR, federal judge; b. Monticello, Fla., Apr. 2, 1920; s. Robert Lewis and Mamie (Gireadeau) E. AB, Presbyn. Coll., 1941, LLD (hon.), 1979; LLB, U. Fla., 1948. Pvt. practice law, Miami, Fla., 1948-51, 55-59; asst. state atty. Dade County, Fla., 1953; circuit judge Miami, 1954-55, 59-67; mem. Fla. Senate, 1956-59; mem. law firm Eaton & Achor, Miami, 1955-58, Sams, Anderson, Eaton & Alper, Miami, 1958-59; judge U.S. Dist. Ct. (so. dist.) Fla., 1967-83, chief judge, 1983-85, sr. judge, 1985—. Instr. law U. Miami Coll. Law, 1954-56 Served with USAAF, 1941-45; Served with USAF, 1951-52. Decorated D.F.C., Air medal. Mem.: Kiwanian. Methodist.

EATON, JOEL DOUGLAS, lawyer; b. Miami, Fla., Oct. 31, 1943; s. Joe Oscar and Patricia (MacVicar) E.; m. Mary Benson, June 24, 1967; children: Douglas, Darryl, David. BA, Yale U., 1965; JD, Harvard U., 1975. Bar: Fla. 1975, U.S. Dist. Ct. (so. dist.) Fla. 1976, U.S. Ct. Appeals (5th cir.) 1976, U.S. Supreme Ct. 1978, U.S. Ct. Appeals (11th cir.) 1981, U.S. Ct. Appeals (Fed. cir.) 1996. Ptnr. Podhurst Orseck, P.A. and predecessors, Miami, 1975—. With USN, 1965-71. Decorated Air medal with Bronze Star and numeral 14, Navy Commendation medal with 2 gold stars, Cross of Gallantry (Viet Nam). Mem. ABA, ATLA, Am. Law Inst., Acad. Fla. Trial Lawyers, Fla. Bar Assn. (appellate rules com. 1981-2002, chmn. 1989-90, jud. evaluation com. 1995-98, Fla. std. jury instn. com. 1998-2004), Am. Acad. Appellate Lawyers. Democrat. Office: Podhurst Orseck PA 25 W Flagler St Ste 800 Miami FL 33130-1720 Office Phone: 305-358-2800. Business E-Mail: jeaton@podhurst.com.

EATON, JOSEPH W., sociology educator; b. Nuremburg, Germany, Sept. 28, 1919; s. Jacob and Flora (Wechsler) E.; m. Helen Goodman, June 8, 1947; children: David, Seth, Debra, Jonathan. BS, Cornell U., 1940; PhD, Columbia U., 1948. Faculty Wayne State U., Detroit, 1947—56; lectr., then vis. prof. Sch. Social Welfare, UCLA, 1956—60; prof. social work rsch. U. Pitts., 1960—70, dir. advanced program, 1966—69, prof. sociology in pub. health and social work rsch., 1970—73, Sch. Pub. and Internat. Affairs, 1974—, prof., later dir. program in econ. and social devel.; co-dir. U.S. Comparative Mgmt. Survey Title Ins., 1999—. Russell Sage Found. vis. prof. We. Res. U. (Med. Sch.), 1958-59; project dir. Conf. on Social Welfare Consequences of Migration and Residential Movement, 1969; dir. instn. bldg. program Interuniv. Rsch. Consortium, 1966-71; curriculum cons., later dir. social work and social adminstrn. program U. Haifa, Israel, 1970-74 USIA cons., lectr., Africa, 1979, Sweden, Fed. Republic Germany, 1982, 86, Romania, 1982, Abu Dhabi, Pakistan, Egypt, Sudan, Israel, 1986, Nepal, Pakistan, Egypt, Ethiopia, Iraq, 1988, Yugoslavia, USSR, 1989; Fulbright lectr. and cons., 1979, NAS. guest scholar in Poland and German Dem. Republic, 1980; co-dir. Jordan River Basin Water Resources Devel., U.S. Inst. Peace, 1992—; co-investigator search for inherited causes of schizophrenia in a genetically isolated cmty., 1997—. Author: (with Saul M. Katz) Research Guide on Cooperative Group Farming, 1942, Exploring Tomorrow's Agriculture, 1943, (with Albert Mayer) Man's Capacity to Reproduce, 1954, (with Robert J. Weil) Culture and Mental Disorders, 1955, (with Kenneth Polk) Measuring Delinquency, 1961, Stone Walls Not a Prison Make: The Anatomy of Planned Adminstrative Change, 1962, Prisons in Israel, 1964, (with Michael Chen) Influencing the Youth Culture: A Study of Youth Organization in Israel, 1970, The Rurban Village, 1980, Can Business Save South Africa, 1980, Card Carrying Americans: Security, Privacy and the National ID Card Controversy, 1986, (with Yuri Lvov) Capitalist Communism, 1991, The Privacy Card: A Low Cost Strategy to Combat Terrorism, 2003, The American Title Insurance Industry: How a Cartel Fleeces the American Consumer, 2007, (with David Eaton) The American Title Insurance Industry, 2007; also contbr. chpts. to books, articles to profl. jours.; editor: Institution Building and Development, 1972. Mem. cable svc. adv. com. City of Pitts. City Coun., 1994—, chmn., mem. cable comm. adv. com., 1996—. With AUS, 1941-46. Faculty Rsch. fellow, Social Sci. Rsch. Coun., 1962. Mem. NASW (chmn. rsch. coun. 1968-71), Internat. Assn. Social Psychiatry (coun. 1969-72). Home: 1008 Summerset Dr Pittsburgh PA 15217-2535 Office Phone: 412-421-5868.

EATON, JUDITH SHEILA, educational association administrator; b. Trenton, NJ, June 6, 1942; BA in Philos., U. Mich., 1964, MA in Hist., 1966; PhD in Edn., Wayne State U., 1975; PhD (hon.), Drexel U., 1988; A (hon.), Phila. CC, 1990. Claims investigator Mich. Civil Rights Commn., 1967—68; instr., asst. prof. natural sci. Wayne State U., Detroit, 1968—70; instr., asst. prof. hist Orchard Ridge Campus Oakland CC, 1970—74, admissions counselor Orchard Ridge Campus, 1974—75, dean adminstrv. svcs. Highland Lakes Campus, 1975—76; academic v.p. Johnson County CC, 1976—79; pres. CC So. Nevada, 1979—83, CC Phila., 1983—89; v.p. Am. Coun. Edn., Washington, 1989—92; pres. Coun. for Aid to Edn., NYC, 1992; chancellor Minn. State Colls. and Univs.; pres. Coun. Higher Edn. Accreditation, Washington, 1997—. Project com. mem. on Good Practice in Gen. Edn., 1988—; external adv. bd. Ctr. Tchg. Excellence, Ohio State U., Columbus, 1991—; bd. dirs. Coun. for Aid to Edn., 1991—; adv. bd. mem. Corp. Philanthropy Report, 1992—; mem. Commn. on Govt. Rels., Am. Coun. Edn., 1993—; bd. dirs. Allegheny Health, Edn. and Rsch. Found., 1993—. Editor: Women in Community Colleges, 1981, Colleges of Choice: The Enabling Impact of the Community College, 1988, Financing Nontraditional Students: A Seminar Report, 1992, Faculty and Transfer: Academic Partnerships At Work, 1992; author: The Unfinished Agenda: Higher Education and the 1980s, 1991, Strengthening Collegiate Education in Community Colleges, 1994; contbr. numerous articles to profl. jours. Mem. nat. adv. com. Black Higher Edn. and Black Colls. and Univs., 1979-82; mem. pres.'s adv. com. Assn. CC Trustees, 1980-83; bd. dirs. CC Polit. Action Com., 1987-89; presdl. com. on info. literacy ALA, 1987-89; nat. adv. bd. U. Mich. CC Consortium, 1987—; bd. trustees Univ. of the Arts, 1988-91; mem. Pa. State Bd. Edn., 1987-94. Recipient Outstanding Young Women of Am. award, 1976, Thomas J. Peters Nat. Leadership award, 1989. Mem. Am. Coun. Edn. (chair, bd. dirs. 1988), Am. Assn. Cmty. and Jr. Colls. (chair, bd. dirs. 1984-85), League for the Humanities (chair, bd. dirs. 1980—), Pa. Assn. Colls. and Univs. (chair 1987-88), Pa. Commn. for Cmty. Colls. (chair 1986-87). Office: Coun Higher Edn Accreditation One Dupont Cir Ste 510 Washington DC 20036-1135*

EATON, KATHERINE GIRTON, retired library educator; b. St. Paul, Mar. 9, 1924; d. John Frances and Mary Ahleen (Peck) Girton; m. Burt Elliott Eaton, Oct. 18, 1947; children: John Girton, Marilee Eaton Warkentin, David Elliott. BA in Journalism, U. Minn., Mpls., 1944; MS in Journalism, U. Oreg., Eugene, 1952, MLS, 1968. Reporter Bakersfield Calif., 1945-46; women's editor Rochester Post Bulletin, Minn., 1946-47; legal sec. Broady Law Offices, St. Paul, 1949-51; editor Oreg. State System Higher Edn., Eugene, 1952-53; cons. Oreg. State Libr., Salem, 1968-70; head pub. affairs libr. U. Oreg., Eugene, 1970-85, assoc. prof. emerita, 1985—. Contbr. articles to profl. jours. Chmn. Lane County Mental Health Bd., Eugene, 1964-88, Lane County Libr. Bd., 1981-85, Eugene City Budget Com., 1986-92, Citizens for Lane County Librs., 1980—, Human Resources Planning Project, Lane County, 1986-89; planning and mgmt. coun. Oreg. Mental Health Svcs., 1988-2005, chair, 1996-99, co-chair adv. com., 2005-; founding bd. dirs. Passages, Lane County substance abuse residential program for offenders, 1990-2001; pres. Wilani coun. Camp Fire Inc., 1967-68, nat. bd. dirs., 1966-70, N.W. regional chmn. 1966-70; adv. bd. Oreg. State Mental Health, 1989-2003, chmn. 1999-2003; elections team LWV, Hungary, 1993; mem. U.S. State Dept. Bosnia Elections Supr., 1997, 2000; coord., convener Oreg. Women's Summit, 1996—; Oreg. steering com. Help Am. Vote Act, 2002—. Named Outstanding Young Woman, Eugene Jaycettes, 1956, Outstanding Women of Yr., Lane County Orgns., 1974, Ln. County Vol. Yr., 1989; recipient Gulick, Seaton, Hiitina awards Camp Fire, Inc., 1959, 66, 71, Outstanding Lib. Pub. award The Wilson Co., 1993, U. Oreg. Disting. Svc. award, 1997, Soroptimist Internat. Women of Distinction award, 1998, OASIS Sr. Role Model award, 1998, Adult Vol. of Yr. award J.C. Penney/United Way, 2000. Mem. AAUP (bd. dirs. U. Oreg. 1976-85, pres. 1977-78), ALA (coun. 1976-80), AAUW (del. NGO women's forum Kenya 1985, China 1995), Oreg. Libr. Assn. (hon. life, pres. 1973-74), Nat. Coun. Planning Librs. (pres. 1978-79, 88-89, Disting. Svc. award 1994), Pacific N.W. Libr. Assn. (editor, quar 1985-96, hon. life), Internat. Fedn. Univ. Women (coun. mem. 1983-85), Assn. Oreg. Faculties (state bd. dirs. 1981-89, v.p. 1983-85), AAUW (pres. Oreg. 1975-77, pres. nat. legal adv. fund 1981-85, nat. exec. v.p. 1981-85, Eugene-Lane br. pres. 1962-63, pub. policy com. 1971—), LWV Oreg. (1st v.p. 1989-91, pres. 1991-93, governance coord. 1999-, disting. svc. award 1995), LWV Lane County (pres. 1963-65, 97-99), Oreg. Women's Rights Coalition (pres. 1994-2001, v.p. 2002—), Virginia Gildersleeve Internat. Fund (archival historian, bd. dirs. 1995—, 1st v.p. 1999-2002), Social Order of Beaucean (pres. 1993, 96), Sigma Kappa. Democrat. Presbyterian. Avocations: mystery reading, lobbying, research, editing, reader's theater.

EATON, LARRY RALPH, lawyer; b. Quincy, Ill., Aug. 18, 1944; s. Roscoe Ralph and Velma Marie (Beckett) E.; m. Janet Claire Rosen, Oct. 28, 1978; child Justin Ross Eaton. BA, Western Ill. U., 1965; JD, U. Mich., 1968. Bar: Ill. 1968, , NY 1997, US Dist. Ct. (no. dist.) Ill. 1978, US Dist. Ct., US Dist. Ct. (central dist.) Ill. 2001, US Dist Ct. (eastern dist.) Wis. 2001, US District Ct. (no. dist.) Ind. 2002, US Dist. Ct. (so. dist.) Ill. 2005, US Ct. Appeals (DC cir.) 1984, US Ct. Appeals (7th cir.) 1989US Ct. Appeals (3rd cir.) 1994. Vol., instr. law U. Liberia Sch. Law, U.S. Peace Corps, Monrovia, 1968-70; lawyer Forest Park Found., Peoria Heights, Ill., 1970-71; asst. atty. gen. State of Ill., Springfield, 1971-75; ptnr. Peterson & Ross and predecessors, Chgo., 1975-94; founder Blatt, Hammesfahr & Eaton, Chgo., 1994-2000; sr. mem. Cozen O'Connor, Chgo., 2000—. Instr. environ. law Quincy Coll., Ill., 1973—75; contbg. writer Chgo. Daily Law Bull., 1975—77; field editor. Pollution Engring., 1976. Bd. dirs. Edgewater Cmty. Coun., Chgo., 2000—; pres. Lakewood Balmoral Residents' Coun., Chgo., 2000—02; bd. dirs. Near North Montessori Sch., 1989—95, vice chmn., 1992—95; bd. dirs. Edgewater Devel. Corp., 2000—, v.p., 2002—. Recipient Ill. Super Lawyer, 2005. Fellow: Ill. Bar Found. (charter); mem.: ABA (environ. ins. litig. task force 1990), Bar Assn. for 7th Jud. Cir., Chgo. Bar Assn., Ill. Bar Assn. (editor sect. newsletter 1972—77, coun. 1973—77, chmn. environ. control law sect. 1976—77, assembly 1980—86, 1989—92, coun. 1990—94, coun. jud. evaluation Cook County 2000—), Atticus Finch Inn of Ct., Lawyers Club Chgo. Office Phone: 312-382-3100. Business E-Mail: leaton@cozen.com.

EATON, LEONARD KIMBALL, retired architecture educator; b. Mpls., Feb. 3, 1922; s. Leo Kimball and Elizabeth (Barber) E.; m. Ann Valentine White, Dec. 24, 1979; children— Mark. R., Elisabeth K. BA, Williams Coll., 1943; MA, Harvard U., 1948, PhD, 1951. Mem. faculty U. Mich., Ann Arbor, 1950-89, prof. architecture, 1963-89. Author: New England Hospitals, 1790-1833, 1957, Landscape Artist in America, 1964, Two Chicago Architects and Their Clients, 1969, American Architecture Comes of Age, 1972, Gateway Cities and Other Essays, 1989, Hardy Cross: American Engineer, 2006; book rev. editor Jour. Soc. Archtl. Historians, 1967-69; contbr. articles to profl. jours. Democratic candidate for coun., City of Ann Arbor, 1957. With AUS, World War II, MTO. Decorated Bronze Star; recipient Finlandia award Finlandia Soc. Met. N.Y., 1965; Ford Found. faculty fellow, 1954-55 Mem. Soc. Archtl. Historians (bd. dirs. 1957-58), Phi Beta Kappa Clubs: Army-Navy (Washington). Home: PO Box 102 Depoe Bay OR 97341

EATON, MAJA CAMPBELL, lawyer; b. 1955; BA, U. Iowa, 1977, JD, 1984. Bar: Ill. 1984, U.S. Dist. Ct. (no. dist.) Ill. 1984, U.S. Dist. Ct. (no. dist.) Calif. 1993. With Sidley Austin Brown & Wood, Chgo., ptnr., 1993—. Former adj. prof. law Chgo.-Kent Coll. Law. Mem.: Def. Rsch. Inst. Office: Sidley Austin Brown & Wood Ste 900 1 S Dearborn St Chicago IL 60603-2010

EATON, MICHAEL WILLIAM, lawyer, educator; b. Dallas, July 28, 1958; s. Charles H. and Helen Gilbough (Miller) E. BS in Polit. Sci., So. Meth. U., 1980, JD, 1984; postgrad., U. Tex., Dallas, 1997—. Bar: Tex. 1984, U.S. Dist. Ct. (no. dist.) Tex. 1985, U.S. Ct. Appeals (5th cir.) 1986, U.S. Supreme Ct. 1988. Asst. gen. counsel Kirby Oil Co., Inc., Dallas, 1984-85; ptnr. Leonard & Eaton, Dallas, 1985-86; assoc. Page & Addison, P.C., Dallas, 1986-87; pvt. practice Dallas, 1987; pres. San Jacinto Investments Group, 1992—2000; founding ptnr. Eaton, Deaguero & Bishop, LLP, Dallas, 2002—. Lectr. in econs. El Centro (Tex.) Coll., 1995—; lectr. in constl. law U. Tex., Dallas, 1996—; founder, dir. Tex. Jury Rsch. Inst., 1996—; founding ptnr. Affordable Housing Solutions, 1998—. Co-author: Expert Witnesses in The Courtroom, 1996; reviewer Am. Jour. of Polit. Sci., 1994—. Vol. Texans for Bush/Quayle, Dallas, 1988; del. John Connolly for Pres. Campaign, Dallas, New Orleans, 1980; north Tex. youth coord. William P. Clements for Gov. Campaign, Dallas, Ft. Worth, Denton, 1978; So. Meth. U. re-election chmn. John Tower for U.S. Senate Campaign, Dallas, 1978. Mem. Nat. Audubon Soc., Nature Conservancy, State Bar Tex., Assn. Trial Lawyers Am., Lawyers Concerned for Lawyers (officer Dallas Lawyers Concerned Lawyers 1996-97, 1997—), Smithsonian Instn. Nat. Arbor Day Found., Phi Alpha Delta, Ancient Order of Hibernians (pres. 1998-2000). Republican. Avocations: golf, gourmet cooking, travel. Office: Eaton Deaguero & Bishop LLP 1111 W Mockingbird Ste 1150 Dallas TX 75247

EATON, NANCY RUTH LINTON, librarian, dean; b. Berkeley, Calif., May 2, 1943; d. Don Thomas and Lena Ruth (McClellan) Linton; m. Edward Arthur Eaton III, June 19, 1965 (div. 1980) AB, Stanford U., 1965; MLS, U. Tex., 1968, postgrad., 1969. From cataloger to asst. to dir. U. Tex. Libr., Austin, 1968-74; automation libr. SUNY, Stony Brook, 1974-76; head tech. svcs. Atlanta Pub. Libr., 1976-82; dir. libr. U. Vt., Burlington, 1982-89; dean libr. svcs. Iowa State U., Ames, 1989-97; dean univ. librs. Pa. State U., University Park, Pa., 1997—. Bd. dir. Ctr. for Rsch. Libr., 1988-92, chair, 1989-90; del. users coun., mem. exec. com. Online Computer Libr. Ctr., Inc., Dublin, Ohio, 1980-82, 86-88, trustee, 1987-02, chair bd. trustees 1992-96; mgr. Nat. Agrl. Text Digitalizing Project, 1986-92; bd. dir. New Eng. Libr. Network, 1987-89; chair steering com. Digital Libr. Fedn., 2000-02; mem. adv. bd. Nat. Digital Info. Infrastructure and Preservation Program, 2001-02; bd. dir. Rsch. Librs. Group, 2004-06; co-prin. investigation Mellon Found., 2004—. Co-author: Optical Information Systems: Implementation Issues for Libraries, 1988.; co-editor: A Cataloging Sampler, 1971, Book Selection Policies in American Libraries, 1972; contbr. articles to profl. jours. U.S. Office of Edn. post-master's fellow, 1969; Dept. Edn. Title II-C grantee, 1985, 87-88, Title II-D grantee, 1992-96, Mellon Found. grant. Mem. ALA, Libr. and Info. Tech. Assn. (pres. 1984-85, bd. dir. 1980-86), Assn. Rsch. Librs. (bd. dir. 1994-97), Digital Libr. Fedn. (exec. com. 1997-2003), Coalition Networked Info. (steering com. 1999-2005), Rsch. Librs Group (bd. dir. 2004-2006). Democrat. Avocations: tennis, walking. Home: 441 Homan Ave State College PA 16801-6337 Office: Pa State Univ 510 Paterno Library University Park PA 16802-1812 Office Phone: 814-865-0401. E-mail: neaton@psu.edu.

EATON, PHILIP W., academic administrator; m. sharon Eaton; children: Mark, Michael, Todd. BA, Whitworth Coll.; MA, PhD, Ariz. State Univ. Interim pres. Whitworth Coll., Spokane, Wash., 1992—93; v.p. acad. affairs Seattle Pacific Univ., Wash., 1993—95, provost Wash., 1995—96, pres. Wash., 1996—. Bd. dir. Independent Coll. Wash. Named one of 100 Most Influential People in Washington State, Washington CEO Mag., 2002, 50 US Coll. and U. Character-Bldg. Presidents, John Templeton Found., 2002. Avocations: golf, reading, sports. Office: Seattle Pacific Univ President's Office 3307 3d Ave W Seattle WA 98119-1997*

EATON, RICHARD GILLETTE, retired surgeon, educator; b. Forty Fort, Pa., Dec. 3, 1929; s. Walter L. and Ruth (Shaw) E.; BA, Franklin and Marshall Coll., 1951; MD, U. Pa., 1955; m. Du Ree Hunter, June 13, 1954; children: Bradford (dec.), Holly, Hillary. Intern, U. Pa. Grad. Hosp., 1956; gen. surg. resident Peter Bent Brigham Hosp., Boston, 1957; orthop. resident Children's Hosp. Med. Center, Mass. Gen. Hosp. and Peter Bent Brigham Hosp., Boston, 1959-62; hand surgery fellow J.W. Littler, Roosevelt Hosp., NYC, 1962, orthop. surgery and reconstrn., chief hand surgery service, ret. 2002; prof. emeritus clin. orthop. surgery Columbia Coll. Physicians and Surgeons, NYC Ruling elder Huguenot Presbyn. Ch., Pelham, NY Capt., M.C., U.S. Army, 1957-59. NIH fellow, 1963-64. Diplomate Am. Bd. Orthop. Surgeons. Mem. Am. Acad. Orthop. Surgery, Am. Orthop. Assn., Am. Soc. Surgery Hand, ACS, Interurban Orthop. Club, NY Acad. Medicine, J.W. Littler Soc., NY Soc. Surgery Hand. Author: Joint Injuries of the Hand, 1971; contbr. articles to profl. jours. Home: 6 Greens Way New Rochelle NY 10805 Office Phone: 914-738-5498. Personal E-mail: rgehand@aol.com.

EATON, RICHARD KENYON, federal judge; b. Walton, NY, Aug. 22, 1948; s. Paul Francis and Frances Emmaretta E.; m. Susan Henshaw Jones, Sept. 26, 1981; children; Alice, Elizabeth. BA, Ithaca Coll., 1970; JD, Albany Law Sch., NYC, 1974. Bar: N.Y. 1975. Chief of staff Senator Daniel Patrick Moynihan, Washington, 1983, 1991—93; assoc. Mudge Rose Guthrie Alexander & Ferdon, 1983—91, ptnr., 1993—95, Stroock & Stroock & Lavan, 1995—2000; judge U.S. Ct. Internat. Trade, NYC, 2000—. Office: US Ct of Internat Trade 1 Federal Plaza New York NY 10278-0001*

EATON, SABRINA CATHERINE ELIZABETH, journalist; b. NYC, Mar. 5, 1965; d. Barton Denis and Anne Elizabeth (Schaeffer) Eaton; life ptnr. Wendy Ann Rodgers; children: Isaac Nicholas, Gillian Elizabeth Rodgers Eaton. BA, U. Pa., 1985. Correspondent The Record, Hackensack, N.J., 1985-87; reporter Daily Record, Morristown, N.J., 1987-88; Washington correspondent States News Svc., Washington, 1988-90; metro reporter The Plain Dealer, Cleve., 1990-94, Washington correspondent Washington, 1994—. Mem. DAR, Nat. Press Club, Nat. Lesbian and Gay Journalists Assn., Investigative Reporters and Editors. Episcopalian. Office: The Plain Dealer Wash Bur 930 National Press Building Washington DC 20045-1928 Home Phone: 301-588-7882.

EATON, SHIRLEY M., medical/surgical nurse; d. Benjamin W. Randall Sr. and Rena B. Randall; children: Everett Kennedy, Eran Margret Eaton Parker. MPH, So. Conn. U., 1997. RN Conn. Nursing positions, SC and Conn., 1960—; mem. staff ombudsman program Norwalk (Conn.) Social Svcs., 1996—. Mem. adv. coun. Area of Nursing, Norwalk, 1997—. Author: Handbook for Caregivers to the Elderly, 1998. Deaconess First Presbyn. Ch. of Stamford, Conn. Presbyterian. Avocations: singing, sewing, writing, travel, designing.

EATON, THOMAS R., state legislator; b. Keene, NH, Nov. 23, 1949; children: Kristin, Tom Jr. Grad., New Eng. Inst. Anatomy. Pres., treas. Fletcher Funeral Home, Keene; mem. N.H. Senate from 10th Dist., Concord, 2000—, dep. majority leader, chmn. trans. com., 2001—02, pres., 2002—05, mem. fin., ways and means, environment coms., 2000—, mem. wildlife and recreation coms., 2000—. Bd. trustees Cheshire Med. Ctr., Cedarcrest, the Home Health & Cmty. Svcs. Bd., Cheshire County chpt. ARC, Cheshire County Crimestoppers; active Keene Family YMCA. Mem. Greater Keene C. of C., Lions, Elks, Masons, Shriner, Old Homestead Garden Club. Republican. E-mail: senate10Ajuno.com. Office: State House 107 N Main St Rm 124 Concord NH 03301

EATON, WILLIAM A., ambassador, former federal agency administrator; BA magna cum laude, U. Va., 1978. Polit. and consular officer U.S. Dept. State, Georgetown, Guyana, 1979—81, gen. svcs. officer Moscow, 1982—84, spl. asst. to asst. sec. adminstrn., 1984, spl. asst. to asst. sec. for diplomatic security, 1985—86, spl. asst. to under sec. state for mgmt., 1986—87, adminstrv. officer Istanbul, Turkey, 1988—89, coord. in office of dep. sec. state, 1992—94, adminstrv. officer Milan, 1993—94, adminstrv. counselor Ankara, Turkey, 1994—98, exec. dir. of bus. European affairs, 1998—2000, sr. adviser to under sec. for mgmt., 2001, asst. sec. state for adminstrn. Washington, 2001—05, U.S. amb. to Panama Panama City, 2005—. Dir. internat. ops. Young Pres. Orgn., 1989—90, exec. dir., 1991—92; former reporter, news editor Shenandoah Valley Herald, Woodstock, Va. Recipient Va. Press Assn. award. Office: US Embassy Panama 9100 Panama City Washington DC 20521-9100

EATON, WILLIAM A., biomedical researcher; BA, U. Pa., Philadelphia, 1959; student, Free U., Berlin, 1960; MD, U. Pa., 1964, PhD, 1967. Chief lab. chem. physics NIH Nat. Inst. Diabetes and Digestive and Kidney Diseases, Bethesda, Md. Adj. prof. depts. chemistry and biochemistry and biophysics U. Pa.; vis. prof. Harvard U.; mem. US Nat. Com. for Internat. Union of Pure and Applied Biophysics; mem. nat. sci. steering com. Inst. Complex Adaptive Matter, 2004. Contbr. articles to sci. jours. Fellow: Am. Phys. Soc., Am. Acad. Arts Scis., Biophysical Soc. (Founders award 2006); mem.: Am. Chem. Soc. (vice chair biophysical subdivision of divsn. physical chemistry 1998—99), Assn. Am. Physicians, NAS. Achievements include landmark discoveries on the dynamics and function of proteins. Office: Nat Inst Diabetes Digestive and Kidney Diseases NIH Bldg 5 Rm 104 Bethesda MD 20892-0520

EAVES, ALLEN CHARLES EDWARD, hematologist, health facility administrator; b. Ottawa, Ont., Can., Feb. 19, 1941; s. Charles and Margaret E.; m. Connie Jean Halperin, July 1, 1975; children: Neil, Rene, David, Sara. BSc, Acadia U., Wolfville, NS, Can., 1962; MSc, Dalhousie U., Halifax, NS, 1964, MD, 1969; PhD, U. Toronto, Ont., Can., 1974. Intern Dalhousie U., Halifax, N.S., Canada, 1968-69; resident in internal medicine Sunnybrook Hosp., Toronto, 1974-75, Vancouver Gen. Hosp., 1975-79; dir. Terry Fox Lab., Cancer Control Agy. B.C., Vancouver, Canada, 1980—; asst. prof. medicine U. B.C., 1979-83, assoc. prof., 1983-88, head div. hematology, 1985—2003, prof., 1988—; pres. StemCell Technologies Inc., Vancouver, 1993—, Malachite Mgmt. Inc., 1996—, StemSoft Software Inc., 2000—. Treas. Found. for Accreditation of Hematopoetic Cell Therapy, 1995-2002. Fellow Royal Coll. Physicians (Can.), ACP; mem. Internat. Soc. Hematotherapy and Graft Engring. (pres. 1995-97), Am. Soc. Blood and Marrow Transplantation (pres. elect 1998-99, pres. 1999-2000). Office: Terry Fox Lab 675 W 10th Ave Vancouver BC Canada V5Z 1L3 Office Phone: 604-675-8125. E-mail: aeaves@bccrc.ca.

EAVES, GEORGE NEWTON, health facility administrator, educator; b. Athens, Tenn., Mar. 12, 1935; s. Felmont Farrell and Margaret Isabel (Dobson) E. BA, U. Chattanooga, 1957; MS, U. Tenn., 1959; PhD, Wayne State U. Sch. Medicine, 1962. Postdoctoral fellow Bryn Mawr Coll., Pa., 1963-65; postdoctoral fellow, guest investigator The Rockefeller U., NYC, 1970-71; exec. sec. molecular biology study sect. NIH, Bethesda, Md., 1967-73; exec. sect. Nat. Heart and Lung Adv. Coun., NIH, Bethesda, 1973-74; assoc. staff dir. Pres.'s Biomed. Rsch. Panel, Washington, 1974-76; dep. dir. Divsn. Blood Diseases and Resources, NIH, Bethesda, 1976-83, dep. dir. Divsn. of Stroke and Trauma, 1983-94. Lectr. on tech. writing, grant applications and peer rev.; bd. dirs. Cyclotec Med. Industries, Inc.; asst. prof. Washington and Jefferson Coll., 1962-63. Cons. editor Procs. NAS, 1973-76; mem. editl. bd. Grants Mag., 1978-81, Nonprofit Mgmt. and Fin., 1981—; contbr. articles to tech. jours. and chpts. to sci. books. Mem. adv. coun. Park and Tree Commn., City of Savannah, 1994—. Recipient Citation for Profl. Achievement, McDonnell Douglas Corp., 1968, NIH Dir.'s award, 1976, 86, Sustained High Quality Performance award NIH, 1970, 74, 79, Spl. Achievement award HHS, 1989, Spl. Recognition award Pub. Health Svc., 1990. Mem. Sigma Xi. Republican. Anglican. Avocation: church organist. Home: 110 W Gordon St Savannah GA 31401-4909 Personal E-mail: georgeeaves@bellsouth.net.

EAVES, MARIA PERRY, realtor; b. Cluj, Romania; d. Nicholas Brudan and Ema (Filipescu) Perry; m. John Eaves, June 16, 1951; children: Bryan Perry, Susan Eaves Clark. BA, MA, UCLA, 1945; postgrad., Columbia U., 1947-51, U. London, 1953-54. Lic. realtor, Md., Va.; rev. appraiser. Advt. and market analyst Foote, Cone & Belding, NYC, 1948-49; fgn. affairs officer U.S. Dept. State, NYC, 1950-53; dir. rsch. Radio Free Europe Press, NYC, 1955-56; info. officer, media reaction analyst USIA, Washington, 1956-58, rsch. cons., 1958-61; market and pub. opinion cons., Washington, 1969-72; realtor Colquitt Carruthers Inc., Bethesda, Md., 1972-81, Long & Foster Real Estate Inc., Potomac, Md., 1982—. One-woman paintings show at Nicosia, Cyprus; group shows include New Delhi (India), White Plains, NY, Bethesda, Md.; also pvt. collections. Vol. Gov. Nelson Rockefeller's Com. to Welcome UN Diplomats, NYC, 1968, 69; mem. World Affairs Coun. Washington, Woodrow Wilson Info. Ctr. for Scholars, Washington, Nat. Parks Conservation Assn.; charter mem. Nat. Mus. Women in the Arts, Washington, Nat. Mus. Am. Indian, Nat. Women's History Mus. Mem. NAFE, LWV, AAUW, NARFE, FIAPCI, Internat. Fedn. Realtors, Internat. Real Estate Inst. (registered), Nat. Assn. Realtors, Nat. Assn. Rev. Appraisers and Mortgage Underwriters, Md. Assn. Realtors, Greater Capital Area Assn. Realtors, UCLA Alumni Assn. (life), Meridian Internat. Ctr., Woman's Nat. Dem. Club (Washington), Tournament Players Club (Potomac, Md.), Diplomatic and Officers Club Ret., Columbia U. Club (Wash.), Mil. Dist. of Washington Club. Democrat. Episcopalian. Avocations: bridge, painting, classical music, reading, computers. Office: Long & Foster Realtors 9812 Falls Rd Potomac MD 20854-3996 Home Phone: 301-541-5083. Personal E-mail: mariaeaves@erols.com. Business E-Mail: maria.eaves@longandfoster.com.

EAVES, STEPHEN DOUGLAS, high school and vocational administrator, educator, consultant; b. Honolulu, Aug. 30, 1944; s. Alfred Aldee and Phyllis Clarissa (Esty) E.; m. Sally Ann Winslow, Apr. 27, 1974; children: Trevor Bernard, Lindsay Douglas, Christian Francis. BA in Polit. Sci., U. Hawaii, 1967; MS in Bus. Mgmt., U. Ark., 1974; PhD in Edn. Adminstrn., Colo. State U., 1997. Cert. secondary tchr., prin., vocat. dir., post secondary bus. tchr., Colo. Commd. 2d lt. USAF, 1967, advanced through grades to lt. col., ret., 1989; aerospace sci. tchr. Adams County Sch. Dist. 50, Westminster, Colo., 1989-94, vocat. dir./prin., 1994—2003; asst. prin. Westminster HS, 2003—. Cons. Dept. of Edn., Colo., 1993—. Eucharistic min. Spirit of Christ Cath. Ch., Arvada, Colo., 1989—. Decorated Silver Star, DFC, Air medals, Commendation medals, Air Force Achievement medal; named Outstanding Tchr. Focus on Excellence Program, 1992, Outstanding Nat. Aerospace Sci. Tchr., 1994. Mem. Colo. Assn. Sch. Execs., Am. Nat. Rose Soc., Royal Nat. Rose Soc., Lions (sec. Adams Centennial chpt. 1991-92, Lion of Yr. 1992), Elks, Phi Delta Kappa, Omicron Tau Delta. Avocations: skiing, rose gardening. Home: 8708 Independence Way Arvada CO 80005-1247 Office: Westminster High Sch Westminster CO 80030

EBB, PETER L., lawyer; BA, Harvard Univ., 1984; JD, Boston Univ., 1990. Bar: Mass. 1990, US Dist. Ct. (Mass.). Law clk. Justice Herbert P. Wilkins, Supreme Judicial Ct. Mass.; rsch. dir. Mass. Legislature Joint Com. on Pub. Svc.; ptnr. labor & employment dept. Ropes & Gray, Boston. Trustee Urban Coll., Boston. Mem.: ABA. Office: Ropes & Gray 1 International Pl Boston MA 02110-2624 Office Phone: 617-951-7457. Office Fax: 617-951-7050. Business E-Mail: peter.ebb@ropesgray.com.

EBBERS, LARRY HAROLD, education educator; b. Rockwell, Iowa, June 17, 1941; s. Harold Theodore and Gertrude Eleanor (Robeoltmann) E.; m. Barbara Ellen Smith, June 17, 1962; children: Lori Ann, Kimberly Jo. BS, Iowa State U., 1962, MS, 1968, PhD, 1971. Vocat. agrl. instr. Iowa Falls (Iowa) Sch., 1962-63, Spencer (Iowa) Schs., 1963-65; asst. dir. residences Iowa State U., Ames, 1965-72, asst. prof., 1972-75, assoc. prof., 1975-80, prof. edn., 1981—, disting. Univ. prof., 2004—, dept. chair, prof. studies in edn., 1983-93, asst. to dean Coll. Edn., 1972-76, asst. dean Coll. Edn., 1976-83, assoc. dean, 1996-2000, prof., 2004—. Contbr. articles to profl. jours. Bd. dirs. Ames Parks and Recreation Commn., 1983-86, Iowa State U. Meml. Union, 1989-94; pres. Ctrl. Iowa Regional Substance Abuse Ctr., Ames, 1984-85, Meeker Sch. PTO, Ames, 1975-76; mem. task force on campus ministry Am. Luth. Ch., Des Moines, 1979-84; bd. regents Waldorf Coll., Iowa, 1999—, vice chair, 2005—. Recipient Outstanding Young Alumnus award, 1976, Outstanding Acad. Adv. award, 1977, Human Rels. award Human Rels. Commn., 1984, Human rels. award Student Affairs Divsn., 1985, Outstanding Faculty Citation award, 1991, Cardinal Key Leadership Hon., 1995, Golden Key Honor Soc., 1996, Pres.'s Disting. Svc. award, 1999, Regents award for faculty excellence, 2001, Thomas B. Thielen award, 2007 all received from Iowa State U., Disting. Svc. award Coun. for Study of C.C., 2006; Rotary Found. fellow, Brazil, 1977; Fulbright scholar, Germany, 2000. Mem. AACC (coun. for study of cmty. coll.), Nat. Assn. Student Pers. Adminstrs. (dir. rsch. and program devel. 1979-81, chmn. Am. Coun. on Edn. Inst. 1984-86, editor jour. 1981-84, pres. 1987-88, v.p. Found. 1989-92, Disting. Svc. award 1990, Fred Turner award 1991, nat. conf. program chair 1992, chair Acad. Leadership and Exec. Effectivness, dir. acad. leadership and exec. effectiveness, 2002-04, Robert Shaffer award for acad. excellence as a grad. faculty mem. 1996), Kiwanis (Ames pres. 1977-78), Phi Delta Kappa, Phi Kappa Phi (pres. 1977-79, centennial medalist 1997). Lutheran. Avocations: sports, jogging, farming. Home: 220 24th St Ames IA 50010-4832 Office: Iowa State U N226 N Lagomarcino Hl Ames IA 50011-0001 Home Phone: 515-232-0073. Business E-Mail: lebbers@iastate.edu.

EBBS, GEORGE HEBERLING, JR., university executive; b. Sewickley, Pa., Sept. 20, 1942; s. George Heberling and Mae Isabelle (Miller) E.; m. Agnes Rak, 1989; children: Stacey Kirsten, Cynthia Lynn, George Heberling III, Alexandra Christine. BS in Engring., Purdue U., 1964; MBA, U. Wash., 1966; PhD in Bus., Columbia U., 1970. Sr. engr. Boeing Co., Seattle, 1966; assoc. Booz Allen & Hamilton, NYC, 1969—72, sr. v.p., 1974—86; v.p. Fry Cons., 1973; chmn. and pres. The Canaan Group, Park City, Utah, 1986—98; pres. Embry-Riddle Aeronautical U., Daytona Beach, Fla., 1998—2005; pres., CEO Dubai Aerospace U., United Arab Emirates, 2006—. Bd. dir. Pinnacle Bank, 3Plains Corp., Ngrain Corp., Aerospace Edn. Adv. Bd.; chmn. bd. dir. Southeast SATS Lab Consortium. Named Iron Key, 1963, Purdue Old Master, 1980; fellow, Royal Aeronautical Soc., 1995; Bronfman fellow, 1967. Mem.: AIAA, Air Force Assn., Nat. Bus. Aviation Assn. (assoc. mem. adv. coun.), Wings Club, Aero. Club Washington, Emirates Golf Club, Oceanside Country Club, Beta Gamma Sigma, Omicron Delta Kappa. Presbyterian.

EBEID, RUSSELL JOSEPH, glass manufacturing executive; b. Detroit, Feb. 9, 1940; s. Joseph Zahour and Theresa (Salamie) E.; m. Carolee M. Cram, Feb. 11, 1961; children: Kevin, Evon, Carrie, Scott. BEE, Kettering U., 1963; MS in Indsl. Engring., Wayne State U., 1969. Registered profl. engr., Mich. Sr. mech. engr. Gen. Motors Corp., Detroit, 1968-70; maintenance supt. Guardian Industries Corp., Carleton, Mich., 1970-71, plant engr., 1971-73, prodn. mgr., 1974-76, plant mgr. Kingsburg, Calif., 1977-80, group v.p., 1981-84, pres. glass div., dir., 1985—. Bd. dirs. Del Claux Cia S.A., Bilbao, Spain, Vidrierias de Llodio S.A., Llodio, Alava, Spain, Guardian Industries, Auburn Hills, Mich., Knight Industries, Toledo, Consol. Glass and Mirror, Galax, Va., Guardian Japan Ltd., Lift GmBH, Germany, Guardian de Venezuela, Monagas, Gulf Guard, Jubail, Saudi Arabia; chmn., mng. dir. Guardian Europe S.A., Luxembourg, Industries Cover Inc., Quebec City, Gujarat Guardian Ltd., India, Siam Guardian Glass Co. Ltd., Bangkok, Thailand; dir. Guardian Africa, Johannesburg, Guardian Flachglass Gmbh, Thalheim, Guardian Brazil, Resende, Egyptian Glass Co., 10th of Ramadan City, Egypt. Author: Instrumentation of Welding, 1963. Bd. dirs. Arab Am. Nat. Mus., 2005. Decorated knight Order of Merit, Luxembourg, Fed. Cross of Merit, Germany; recipient Employee of Yr. for Corp. award Guardian Industries Corp., 1979; named Nat. Arab Am. Businessman of Yr., Am. Arab C. of C., 2003; named to Hall of Fame Coll. Engring., Wayne State U., 2006. Roman Catholic. Office: Guardian Industries Corp 2300 Harmon Rd Auburn Hills MI 48326-1714

EBEL, DAVID M., federal judge; b. 1940; BA, Northwestern U., 1962; JD, U. Mich., 1965. Law clk. to Justice Byron White US Supreme Ct., Washington, 1965—66; pvt. practice Davis, Graham & Stubbs, Denver, 1966—88; judge US Ct. Appeals (10th cir.), Denver, 1988—2006, sr. judge, 2006—. Adj. prof. law U. Denver Law Sch., 1987—89; sr. lectr. fellow Duke U. Law Sch., 1992—94. Mem.: Jud. Conf. U.S. (com. on codes of conduct 1991—98, co-chair 10th cir. gender bias task force 1994—99), Colo. Bar Assn. (v.p. 1982), Am. Coll. Trial Lawyers. Office: US Ct Appeals 1823 Stout St Rm 109L Denver CO 80257-1823 E-mail: david_m_ebel@ca10.uscourts.gov.*

EBELING, VICKI, marriage and family therapist, writer; b. Detroit, Nov. 18, 1948; d. Paul F. and Constance Jean Ebeling; m. James Robert Marchese, 1983; 1 child, Drew Ebeling Marchese. BA, Mich. State U., 1969; M of Sci., Marriage, Family & Child Counseling, Calif. State U., Dominguez Hills, 1990; PhD in Human Behavior, Newport U., 1999. Diplomate Am. Psychotherapy Assn.; cert. youth effectiveness tng. instr.; bd. cert. ednl. therapist., Assn. Ednl. Therapists. With various TV and radio prodn. cos., Detroit, Lansing, Mich., 1969-74; TV and film prodn. cos. LA, 1974-90; psychotherapist/marriage, family and child therapist Torrance, Calif., 1990—; ednl. therapist, 1994—. Pub. Pier Avenue Pub., 2006—. Author: The Winners Group, 2007, The Winners Group, 2007. Counselor South Bay Rape Crisis Ctr., 1988-92; mem. orientation team St. Peter's by Sea Presbyn. Ch., Palos Verdes Estates, Calif., 1993-95; vol. cons. 1736 Family Crisis Ctr., 1988, Calif. Spl. Olympics, 1990-91, pediat. ward UCLA-Harbor Hosp., 1991-92, Child Shelter Care, Los Angeles County Children's Ct., 1992-93, ARC Disaster Svc., 1995—. Named Adult Amateur Horsemanship Champion, Los Serranos Award Circuit, Rolling Hills, Calif., 1993. Mem. Calif. Assn. Marriage and Family Therapists (South Bay newsletter editor 1992-94), Assn. Ednl. Therapists. Office: Vicki Ebeling Phd LMFT BCET 3138 Pacific Coast Hwy Torrance CA 90505-6708

EBERBACH, STEVEN JOHN, retired electronics company executive; b. Ann Arbor, Mich., Apr. 30, 1943; s. Robert Ottmar and Marie (Eichelberger) E.; m. Mary Jean Head, Oct. 15, 1983; children: Amy Elizabeth, Michael James, Amanda Claire, Kathryn Louise. BSEE, MIT, 1965; MBA, U. Mich., Ann Arbor, 1967. Engr. U. Mich. Space Physics Rsch. Lab., Ann Arbor, 1967-73; founder, owner, engr., pres. and chmn. DCM Corp., Ann Arbor, 1974-99; ret., 1999. Inventor loudspeaker design. Mem. IEEE, IEEE Consumer Elect. Soc., IEEE Signal Processing Soc., Audio Engring. Soc., Foresight Inst. (sr. assoc.). Avocations: sailing, photography, computers. Home: 4455 E Loch Alpine Dr Ann Arbor MI 48103-9422 Personal E-mail: seberbach@aol.com.

EBERHARD, MARTIN, automotive executive, electronics engineer; m. Carolyn Eberhard; 2 children. B in computer engring, U. Ill., Urbana-Campaign, MEE. V.p. electronics Belfort Memory Internat.; co-founder & chief engr. Network Computing Devices; co-founder & CEO NuvoMedia, Mountain View, Calif., 1997—2000, Tesla Motors, San Carlos, Calif., 2003—. Named one of 50 Who Matter Now, Business 2.0, 2007. Achievements include development of the Tesla Roadster, a battery-powered sports car. Office: Tesla Motors 1050 Bing St San Carlos CA 94070 Office Phone: 650-413-4000.*

EBERHARD, WILLIAM THOMAS, architect; b. St. Louis, Apr. 11, 1952; s. George Walter and Bettie Alma (Seilkop) E.; m. Cynthia Ann Hardy, Aug. 20, 1977 (div. 1981); m. Linda W. Bayer, Dec. 5, 1986; children: Elena Lynn, Alysse Marie. BArch, U. Cin., 1976; postgrad., Archtl. Assn., London, 1974. Registered arch. Ohio, Mich., Pa., Fla., D.C., Ill., Mo. V.p. Visnapuu & Assocs., Inc., Cleve., 1972-82; prin.-in-charge Oliver Design Group, Cleve., 1983—. V.p., prin.-in-charge Grubb & Ellis, Cleve., Detroit, Pitts., 1989-90, Grubb & Ellis Nat. Accounts Team, 1987-90. Author: Public Interiors, 1986, 2d edit., 1996, Professional Office Design, 1988, Docket, 1988, Facility Design & Management, 1990, 91, Interior Design, 1992, Contract Design, 1995, Architecture Record Lighting, 1996, Facility Management Journal, 1996; contbr. articles to profl. jours. Profl. team leader Inst. Urban Design, Cleve., 1983; mem. evangelism com. First Bapt. Ch. of Greater Cleve., 1990—. Recipient Best Comml. Interior Design Project award NAIOP, 1991-96, 2000, Best Office Interior Design Project award, 1992, Best Renovation Project, 1995, Design award Nat. Inst. Bus., 1992, 93, Best Comml. Space, 1993, NAIOP Design award Best Pub. Space, 1993, Best Comml. Interior Design, 1994, 95, 96, 97, 2000, Best Renovation Project, 1995, 1st Pl. award Build Ohio Competition, 1992. Mem. AIA (chpt. sec. 1982-84, 1st Pl. award 1993, Cleve. Chpt. Design award 1993, 94, 99, 2004, Ohio Area Design award 1994-95, 2005, Internat. Int. Design award 1992, 94, 95, Best of Show, First Place Large Corp. Category, Details Category award 1993, 1994, 99, 2005), Internat. Facility Mgrs. Assn., Cleve. Art Assn., Nat. Trust for Hist. Preservation, Inst. Urban Design, Am. Soc. Interior Designers (assoc.), Seminotic Soc. Am. (founding), Design Forum of Cleve. (founding 1990—, pres. 1991—), Club Soc. Ctr. (founding), Cleve. Design Task Force (founding pres. 1996—), Shaker Heights Country Club (house com., design com.), Union Club of Cleve, IIDA/IESNA (Regional Design award, 2002, 03, 04, 05, Regional Merit Retail Category Design Program award 1998, 2002, 03, 04), Leadership Cleve. Class of 2006. Avocations: drawing, photography, tennis, snowmobiling, golf. Home: 2867 Torrington Rd Shaker Heights OH 44122-2555 Office: Oliver Design Group 1301 E 9th St Ste 2900 Cleveland OH 44114-1835 Business E-Mail: wte@oliver-design.com.

EBERHARD-NEVEAUX, CHRISTINE, aviation executive, dispute resolution executive; b. Fremont, Ohio, Jan. 12, 1951; d. Richard Lesley and Elva Lucille (Ransom) Eberhard; m. Michael Lee Neveaux, May 24, 1997; stepchildren: Jamie, Stephen, Sarah, Spencer. Student, U. Am., Cholula, Mex., 1972-73; BA in Internat. Studies, Ohio State U., 1973; postgrad., Pepperdine U., 1999. Cert. in dispute resolution; lic. helicopter pilot. Account exec. News-Times Pub. Co., Anaheim, Calif., 1975-77; asst. dir. pub. rels. and devel. Hawthorne Cmty. Hosp., 1977-80; dir. pub. rels. Presbyn. Intercmty. Hosp., Whittier, Calif., 1980-82; pres. CommuniQuest, Simi Valley, Calif., 1982—. Mem. mediation panel Ventura County Superior Ct., Los Angeles County Superior Ct.; contracts with numerous airports and FAA including a contract to teach cmty. involvement course to FAA mgmt. Bd. dirs. L.A. South Bay-Harbor Industry Edn. Coun., 1978-81. Served with USAR, 1975-93. Mem. Res. Officers Assn. (Calif. Outstanding Jr. Officer 1983), Profl. Helicopter Pilots Assn. (past bd. dirs.), L.A. County Commn. on Local Govt. Svcs. (chair air svcs. com. 1994-99), Helicopter Assn. Internat. (past chair heliport promotion and devel. com., chair pub. rels. adv. coun., spl. advisor to bd. dirs. 1991-98), Am. Assn. Airport Execs. (S.W. chpt. bd. dirs. 2002-06, Corp. award Excellence 2001, Pres. award 2006), Internat. Assn. Pub. Participation Practitioners, Whirly-girl Number 766, So. Calif Mediation Assn., Ventura County Dispute Settlement Mediation Panel (mediator). Office: CommuniQuest 2728 Bitternut Cir Simi Valley CA 93065-1315

EBERHARDT, DANIEL HUGO, lawyer; b. Milw., Feb. 19, 1938; s. Erwin M. and Hazel M. (Daley) E.; m. Josephine E. Jeka, Sept. 10, 1960; children: Daniel Hugo Jr., Mark John. BS, Colo. State U., 1962; JD, Marquette U., 1968. Bar: Wis. 1968, U.S. Dist. Ct. (ea. dist.) Wis. 1968. Assoc. Morrissy, Morrissy, Sweet & Race, Elkhorn, Wis., 1968-70; ptnr. Sweet & Eberhardt, Elkhorn, 1970-76; pvt. practice Elkhorn, 1976. Commr. Walworth County Cir. Cts., 1975—2004. Served to 1st lt. US Army, 1962—65. Mem. Wis. Bar Assn., Walworth County Bar Assn. (sec., treas. 1983-85, v.p. 1985-86, pres. 1986-87), VFW (comdr. 1980-81). Lodges: Rotary (pres. 1980-81). Republican. Roman Catholic. Home and Office: N6601 Peck Station Rd Elkhorn WI 53121-3247 Office Phone: 262-642-7560.

EBERHART, ROBERT CLYDE, biomedical engineering educator, researcher; b. Oakland, Calif., Apr. 17, 1937; s. George Perrin and Roberta Eberhart; m. Carol Eberhart, Aug. 4, 1960; 3 children. AB in Applied Physics, Harvard U., 1958; MS in Mech. Engring., U. Calif., Berkeley, 1960, PhD, 1965. Staff scientist Inst. Med. Scis., San Francisco, 1964—70, sr. scientist, 1970—75; assoc. prof. mech. engring. U. Tex., Austin, Tex., 1975—76; assoc. prof. surgery U. Tex. So. Med. Ctr., Dallas, 1976—86; chmn. biomed. engring. U. Tex. So. Med. Ctr. and U. Tex.-Arlington, 1983—2001; prof. engring. in surgery U. Tex. So. Med. Ctr. and U. Tex., Arlington, 1984—2005; adj. prof. surgery U. Tex. So. Med. Ctr., Dallas, 2006—; prof. bioengring. and mech. engring. U. Tex., Arlington, 2006—. Pres. Tex. Stent Tech., 2005—; bd. sci. advisors Andev, Inc.; cons. in field. Editor: Heat Transfer in Medicine and Biology, 1985; co-editor: Biomaterials-Living Sys. Interactions, 1993—98; mem. editl. bd.: Jour. Applied Biomaterials, Jour. Biomaterials Sci.; contbr. articles to profl. jours., chpts. in books. Recipient C.W. Hall Rsch. award So. Biomed. Engring. Conf., 1987, Career Achievement award Houston Symposium for Biomed. Engring., 1996. Fellow: ASME (Engr. of Yr. 2007, North Tex. divsn. Engr. of Yr. 2007), Biomed. Engring. Soc. (Inaugural fellow 2005), Am. Inst. Med. and Biol. Engring. (founding fellow 1993—); mem.: Biomaterials Soc., Soc. Critical Care Medicine (editl. bd. 1973—75), Am. Soc. Artificial Internal Organs (pres. 1994—95), Harvard Club. Achievements include patentee nonthrombogenic treatment for med. polymers 1985; patents for expandable biodegradable polymeric stents for combined mechanical support and pharmacological or radiation therapy. Office: U Tex So Med Ctr Dept Surgery 5323 Harry Hines Blvd Dallas TX 75390-9130 Office Phone: 214-648-2052. Business E-Mail: robert.eberhart@utsouthwestern.edu.

EBERHART, STEVEN WESLEY, psychologist; b. St. Louis, Oct. 12, 1952; s. Carl A. and Cora H. (Kruckeberg) E. BA in Psychology, So. Ill. U., 1974; MS in Psychology, Western Ill. U., 1980; EdS in Sch. Psychology, U. Iowa, 1984, PhD in Sch. Psychology, 1986. Lic. cons. psychologist, Minn.; cert. sch. psychologist Minn., Ill., Iowa, nat. cert. sch. psychologist. Mental health technician Anna (Ill.) State Hosp., 1974-78; clin. psychologist Barren River Comprehensive Care, Bowling Green, Ky., 1980-82; sch. psychologist Meeker and Wright Spl. Edn. Co-op, Cokato, Minn., 1985-92; clin. pvt. practice St. Joseph, Minn., 1990-92; with Ministry of Edn. Govt. of Bermuda, 1992-96; psychologist Tri-County Spl. Edn. Coop., Murphysboro, Ill., 1996—. Adj. faculty mem. Southern Ill. U., 1998—. Contbr. article to profl. jours. Ill. State scholar. Mem. APA, Nat. Assn. Sch. Psychologists, Ill. Sch. Psychologist Assn. (governing bd. mem). Avocations: race walking, karate (4th degree black belt), travel, juggling, scuba diving. Personal E-mail: eberpsy@verizon.net.

EBERLE, CHARLES EDWARD, paper and consumer products executive; b. St. Louis, Mar. 20, 1928; s. Charles Edward and Hazel (Williams) Eberle; m. Nancy Ellen Paddock, Aug. 1, 1953 (div. June 1995); children: Charles Edward, Richard Clay, Julia Lee; m. Denise S. Jackson, Apr. 12,

1997 (dec. Nov. 2002); m. Bonnie M. Shaub, Sept. 28, 2003. BS in Chem. Engring., Washington U., St. Louis, 1949. Prodn. mgr. Procter & Gamble, St. Louis, 1949-55, plant mgr. Lexington, Ky., 1955-57, St. Louis, 1957-60, Sacramento, 1960-64, mgr. mfg. Cin., 1964-79, v.p. mfg., 1979-84, v.p. engring., 1984-85; pres. CEE Enterprises, Cin., 1985-88, Thomas & Eberle Assocs., Inc., Cin., 1986-88; v.p., James River Europe James River Corp., 1988-90, sr. v.p., group exec., 1990, exec. v.p. consumer products bus., 1990-91; pres. CEE Enterprises, Richmond, 1992—; chmn. exec. com. Richmond area TEC, Midlothian, Va., 1997-98; v.p. corp. devel. Lloyd Assocs., Inc., Richmond, 1999-2001. Mem. mfg. studies bd. NRC/NAS, 1984-89. Vice pres. bd. trustees Children's Hosp. Med. Ctr., Cin., 1975-78; mem. Cin. Council on World Affairs, 1979-89; v.p. Dan Beard coun. Boy Scouts Am., 1982-85. With U.S. Army, 1951-52. Recipient Engring. Alumni Achievement award Washington U., 1977 Mem. Commonwealth Club. Home and Office: 1756 Old Powhatan Est Powhatan VA 23139-7622 E-mail: ceeberle@verizon.net.

EBERLE, WILLIAM DENMAN, international management consultant; b. Boise, Idaho, June 5, 1923; s. Julius Louis and Clare (Holcomb) E.; m. Jean Cilista Quick, Sept. 20, 1947; children— Jeffrey Louis, William David, Francis Quick, Cilista Clare. BA, Stanford U., 1945; MBA, Harvard U., 1947, JD, 1949; LLB (hon.), Gonzagua U., 1976. Bar: Idaho 1950. Ptnr. firm Richards, Haga & Eberle, Boise, 1950—57; mem. Idaho Ho. of Reps. from Ada County, 1953-61, majority leader, 1957, minority leader, 1959; dir., v.p. Boise Cascade Corp., 1959—70; speaker Idaho Ho. of Reps. from Ada County, 1961; chmn. Tertiary, Inc., Boise, 1965—66; pres., chmn., dir. Am. Standard, Inc., NYC, 1965—71; U.S. trade rep., amb. Washington, 1971-75; exec. dir. Cabinet Council on Internat. Econ. Policy, 1974-75; mem. Pres.'s Econ. Policy Bd., 1974-75; pres., chief exec. officer Motor Vehicle Mfrs. Assn., 1975-77; chmn. Manchester Assocs. Ltd., Washington, 1977—. Bd. dirs. Ampco-Pitts. Corp., Am. Svc. Group; of counsel Kaye, Scholer, LLP, N.Y.C., Mid-States Plc. Chmn. Idaho Rep. Fin. Com., 1961-66; mem. nat. Rep. Fin. Com., 1968-80; trustee Stanford U., 1970-80. Com. for Econ. Devel., 1966-. Lt. USNR, 1942-46. Mem. ABA, Idaho Bar Assn., Coun. Fgn. Rels., Univ. Club (N.Y.C.), Met. Club (Washington). Episcopalian. Office: Manchester Assoc PO Box 1425 13 Garland Rd Concord MA 01742-2214 Home Phone: 978-371-2594; Office Phone: 978-287-1470. E-mail: wd.eberle@tertiaryinc.com, wdeberle@verizon.com.

EBERLEIN, TIMOTHY J., surgeon; b. New Kensington, Pa., 1951; BS, U. Pitts., 1973, MD, 1977; MA (hon.), Harvard U., 1996. Cert. gen. surgery. Surgical intern, resident Peter Bent Brigham Hosp., Boston, 1977—79; rsch. fellow, surgery br. Nat. Cancer Inst., Bethesda, Md., 1979—82; surgical resident to chief resident surgery Brigham & Women's Hosp., Boston, 1982—84, chief surgical oncology div., vice chmn. rsch., dept. surgery; Richard E. Wilson prof. surgery Harvard Med. Sch., Boston; Spencer T. & Ann W. Olin disting. prof. Washington U. Sch. Med, St. Louis, 1998—; Bixby prof. surgery Washington U. Sch. Med., St. Louis, 1998—, chmn. surgery, 1998—, dir. Alvin J. Siteman Cancer Ctr., 1998—; surgeon-in-chief Barnes-Jewish Hosp., St. Louis. Bd. dirs. Barnes-Jewish Hosp.; mem. adv. bd. Nat. Cancer Inst. Editor-in-chief Jour. Am. Coll. Surgeons, 2004—, assoc. editor Yearbook in Surgery, mem. editorial bd. Surgical Oncology, Annals of Surgical Oncology, Annals of Surgery, Current Opinion in Gen. Surgery, Jour. Surgical Oncology, Seminars in Surgical Oncology, The Oncologist, Surgery. Fellow: Am. Coll. Surgeons (mem. surgical rsch. & ed. com. 1994—, vice chair surgical rsch. & ed. com. 1998—2000, chair surgical rsch. & ed. com. 2000—02, mem. Corp. Rsch. Roundtable 1994—2002); mem.: Inst. Medicine, Alpha Omega Alpha, Phi Beta Alpha. Office: Washington U Sch Med Dept Surgery Campus Box 8109 660 S Euclid Ave Saint Louis MO 63110 Office Phone: 314-362-8020. Office Fax: 314-454-1898. E-mail: everleint@wustl.edu.

EBERLEY, HELEN-KAY, opera singer, recording industry executive, poet; b. Sterling, Ill., Aug. 3, 1947; d. William Elliott and P. (Conneely) E. MusB, Northwestern U., 1970, MusM, 1971. Chmn., pres., artistic coord. Eberley Inc., Evanston, Ill., 1973-92; founder H.K.E. Enterprises, 1993—, pres., 1993—; circulation libr. Evanston Pub. Libr., 1995-98; prin., adminstr. The Kidusche Eberley Trust. Founder EB-SKO Prodns., 1976-92, tchr., coach, 1976—; exec. dir., performance cons. E-S Mgmt., 1985-92; featured artist Honors Concert, Northwestern U., 1970, Alumni Concert, 1999, Master Class and guest lectr. various colls. and univs.; host Poetry in Process monthly seminar Barnes & Noble; music lectr. rep. Harvard Club, Chgo.; numerous TV and radio talk show appearances and interviews. Operatic debut in Peter Grimes, Lyric Opera, Chgo., 1974; starred in: Der Rosenkovalier, Cosi Fan Tutte, Le Nozze Di Figaro, Dido and Aeneas, La Boheme, Faust, Tosca, La Traviata, Falstaff, Don Giovanni, Brigadoon, others; jazz appearances with Duke Ellington, Dave Brubeck and Robert Shaw; performing artist Oglebay Opera Inst., Wheeling, W.Va., 1968, WTTW TV/PBS, Chgo., 1968; solo star in: Continental Bank Concerts, 1981-89, United Airlines-Schubert, Schumann, Brahms, Mendelssohn, Faure, Mozart, Duparc/Wolf, Supersta. WFMT Radio, Chgo., 1982-90; featured artist with North Shore Concert Band, 1989; starring artist South Bend Symphony, 1990, Mo. Symphony Soc., 1990, Milw. Symphony, 1990; spl. guest artist New Studios Gala Sta. WFMT, 1995, West Valley Fine Arts Concert Series, Phoenix, 1999; prodr.-annotator Gentlemen Gypsy, 1978, Strauss and Szymanowski, 1979, One Sonata Each: Franck and Szymanowski, 1982; starring artist-exec. prodr. Separate But Equal, 1976, All Brahms, 1977, Opera Lady, 1978, Eberley Sings Strauss, 1980, Helen-Kay Eberley: American Girl, 1983, Helen-Kay Eberley: Opera Lady II, 1984; performed Am. and Can. nat. anthems for Chgo. Cubs Baseball Team, 1977-83, Chgo. Bears Football, 1977; also starred in numerous concert recital and symphony appearances, Europe, Can., U.S.; author: Angel's Song, 1994, The Magdaleva Poems, 1995, ChapelHeart, 1996, Desert Dancing, 1997, Canyon Ridge, 2000, Rivervoice, 2002, The Chichester Psalms, 2006. Docent, new mem. tour guide Art Inst. Chgo.; spl. events hotline vol. Art Inst. Chgo., Chgo. Christian Indsl. League, St. Joseph's Table of St. Peter's in the Loop, Chgo.; vol., facilitator City Yr. Chgo.-Urban Peace Corps; Chgo. Humanities Festival VIII of Ill. Humanities Coun., Evanston Shelter for Battered Women, Rape Victim Adv., Habitat for Humanity; Midwest Vol. Facilitator 1st Indsl. Realty Trust; mem. Mayor's founding com. Evanston Arts Coun., 1974-75; judge Ice-Skating Competition, Wilmette (Ill.) Park Dist., 1974-77, bd. dirs., 1973-77; bd. dirs. Ctr. for Voice, Chgo., 1994-96; vol. Saints-Usher Corps of Chgo., 1998-99; chmn. fin. Chgo. (Ill.) Youth Symphony. Recipient Creative and Performing Arts award Ind. Jr. Miss. and South Bend Jr. Miss, 1965, Milton J. Cross award Met. Opera Guild, 1968; prize winner Met. Opera. Nat. Auditions, 1968, 1st pl. prize for The Pond, Chicagoland Poetry Contest, 1997, 1st pl. prize and Best of the Best award for The Rose Garden, 1999; F.K. Weyerhauser scholar Met. Opera, 1967. Mem. People for Ethical Treatment of Animals, Am. Soc. for Prevention of Cruelty to Animals, Assisi Animal Found., Am. Guild Mus. Artists, Internat. Platform Assn., Whale Adoption Project, Amnesty Internat., Environ. Def. Fund, Doris Day Animal Found., Poets and Patrons, Humane Soc., Greenpeace, Physicians Com. for Responsible Medicine, Notre Dame Alumni Club, St. Mary's Acad. Alumnae Assn., Save the Chimps, Delta Gamma. Office: HKE Enterprises 1726 Sherman Ave Evanston IL 60201-5619 Home Phone: 847-869-8231.

EBERLY, CHARLES, counseling and student development educator; b. McComb, Ohio, Sept. 8, 1941; s. George and Herma Elizabeth (Sower) Eberly; m. Sharon Rosalee Newcomer, June 21, 1964; children: Mary Barbara, Judith Elizabeth, Michael Charles. BS in Chemistry, Bowling Green State U., 1963; MS in Edn., Syracuse U., 1966; PhD in Higher Edn., Mich. State U., 1970. Acting asst. dean students Wilmington Coll., Ohio, 1964; instr. student pers. U. Wis., Oshkosh, 1966—69; asst. prof. evaluation svcs. Mich. State U., East Lansing, 1970—74, assoc. prof. undergrad. univ. divsn., 1974—87, asst. to dir. admissions, 1981—87; asst. prof. ednl. psychology, coord. grad. program coll. pers. work Ea. Ill. U., Charleston, 1987—, assoc. prof. counseling and student devel., 1990—, prof., 1994—. Vis. instr. Mie U., Tsu, Japan, 1977—78; mem. nat. adv. bd. Chronicle Guidance Publs., Moravia, NY, 1987—; bd. dirs. Ea. Ill. U., Stockman Inst., 1990—93. Author: Building and Maintaining the Chapter Library, 1970; mem. editl. bd.: Jour. Coll. Student Retention, 1999—, Oracle: The Rsch. Jour. Fraternity Advisors, 2005—. Mem. zoning bd., Mason, Mich., 1970—71; bd. dirs. Ctr. Study of Coll. Fraternities, 1999—, pres., 2000—05. Named to Hall of Fame, Midwest Meeting Grad. Students in Student Personnel, 2002, Order of the Golden Heart, 2003; recipient Carter Ashton Jenkens award, Sigma Phi Epsilon, 1964, Disting. Alumnus award, 1995, Spirit of Greek award, Bowling Green U., 2002, Dr. Charles G. & Mrs. Sharon Eberly Essence Fraternity Values award, Interfraternity Coun., 2003. Mem.: ACA (human rights commn. 1991—94), AACD, Ea. Instl. Rev. Bd. (alt.), Ea. Ill. U. (faculty senate 1994—95, 1996—2001, sec. 2000—01), Ill. Counseling Assn. (senator 1990—91, jour. editl. bd. 1995, 2001—06, conv. program com.), Ill. Assn. Assessment in Counseling (Disting. Svc. award), Assn. Interdisciplinary Initiatives in Higher Edn., Assn. Fraternity Advisors (mem. perspectives editl. bd. 1993—95, Oracle editl. bd. 2005—, Robert H. Schafer award 2003), Am. Assn. Collegiate Registrars and Admissions Officers, Ill. Assn. Measurement and Evaluation on Counseling and Devel. (pres. 1991—92, past pres. 1992—93), Ill. Coll. Pers. Assn. (Dennis Trueblood award 2002), Mich. Coll. Pers. Assn. (mem.-at-large exec. com. 1986—87), Nat. Assn. Student Pers. Adminstrs. (Dissertation of Yr. award com. 1989—2002, bd. dirs. men and masculinities com. 2005—, regional adv. bd. 2005—, Greek summit com.), Am. Coll. Pers. Assn. (dir. Commn. IX 1969—72, co-founder Commn. XVI 1979, mem. profl. stds. com. 1980—83, chmn. conv. evaluation com. 1991, mem. transition team 1991—92), Mich. Assn. Counseling and Devel. (chmn. adminstrv. asst. evaluation com. 1984—85, editor jour. 1985—87), Mich. Assn. Measurement and Evaluation in Guidance (pres. 1984—85, Outstanding Profl. Svc. award 1985—86), Mich. ACT Coun. (exec. coun. 1981—86), Assn. Measurement and Evaluation in Counseling and Devel. (newsletter editor 1979—84, treas. 1984—88, pres.-elect 1988—89, pres. 1989—90, past pres. 1990—91), Rotary, Order of Omega, Omicron Delta Kappa, Phi Kappa Phi, Alpha Phi Omega, Sigma Phi Epsilon (chpt. counselor Ill. No. U. 1991—, mem. residential learning cmty. com. 2005—, Fraternity Advisor award 1992, Individual Initiative award 1994, Fraternity Advisor award 1996, 2001), Phi Delta Kappa (Ea. Ill. U. Chpt. Rsch. award 1994). Republican. Methodist. Avocations: bicycling, woodworking, music, early American pattern glass. Home: 2609 6th Street Cir Charleston IL 61920-4113 Office: Ea Ill U Dept Counseling and Student Devel Buzzard Hall Charleston IL 61920-3099 Office Phone: 217-581-7235. Business E-Mail: cgeberly@eiu.edu.

EBERLY, HARRY LANDIS, retired communications company executive; b. Lancaster, Pa., Nov. 1, 1924; s. Chester Landis and Nola Marie (Clark) E.; m. Marion Ruth Royer, May 26, 1951; children: Jenny Ellen Eberly Holmes, Susan Lynn Eberly Patrick. BS in Chem. Engring., Pa. State U., 1945; postgrad., Lehigh U., 1947-48, Franklin and Marshall Coll., 1949. Engr. We. Electric, NYC, 1945-49; mfg. engr. RCA, Lancaster, Pa., 1949-51, product devel. Harrison, NJ, 1951-64, mgr. mfg. Somerville, NJ, 1964-66, plant mgr. Palm Beach Garden, Fla., 1996-68, mgr. purchasing Palm Beach Gardens, Fla., 1968-72; v.p. Telex Computer Products, Inc., Tulsa, 1972-76, sr. v.p., 1976-77, pres. Communication Products div. Raleigh, NC, 1977-83, exec. v.p., 1983-88, mem. exec. com. Tulsa, 1984-88, dir., 1982-84; exec. v.p. Memorex Telex Corp., 1988-90; COO, Novatel Comm., Ltd., Calgary, Canada, 1991-92. Mem. bd. assocs. Meridith Coll., Raleigh, 1981—98, presdl. adv. coun., 1999—2002; mem. bd. assocs. Barton Coll. Global Focus Program, 1988—97; bd. dirs. Wake Tech. Cmty. Coll. Found., Raleigh, 1982—97, chmn., 1990—94; mem. N.C. State U. Engring. Found., Raleigh, 1984—87; exec. com. Edn. and Psychology Found., 1990—95; vice-chmn. Triangle East N.C., 1986—90, chmn., 1990—92; regional maj., gifts chmn. Campaign for Pa. State, 1986—90; chair Pa. State Grand Destiny Campaign Coll. of Edn., 1999—2003; mem. presdl. adv. bd. Pa. State U.; bd. dirs., exec. com. Occoneechee Coun. Boy Scouts Am., 1989—95; bd. dirs. Raleigh Little Theatre, 1989—92, 1995—2003, Raleigh Housing Authority Scholarship Fund, 1993—98; bd. dirs., 1988 campaign chmn. United Way Wake County, 1980—89. Mem. IEEE (life), Wake County Edn. Found. (bd. dirs. 1990-92), Greater Raleigh C. of C. (bd. dirs. 1979-87), North Ridge Country Club, Masons, Shriners, Delta Gamma Delta. Methodist. Home: 7003 N Ridge Dr Raleigh NC 27615-7036

EBERLY, JOSEPH HENRY, physics professor, consultant, quantum optics scientist; b. Carlisle, Pa, Oct. 19, 1935; s. Norman McKinley and Mary Weigle (Keeny) E.; m. Shirley Warren Smith; children: Rebecca Leas, Virginia Westcott, Lynn Elizabeth. BS, Pa. State U., 1957; PhD, Stanford U., 1962. Prof. physics U. Rochester, NY, 1976-79, prof. physics and optics NY, 1979—; Andrew Carnegie prof. physics, 1996—; dir. Rochester Theory Ctr. for Optical Sci. and Engring., 1995—. Vis. fellow Joint Inst. for Lab. Astrophysics and Nat. Bur. Std., Boulder, Colo., 1977-78, sci. and engring. rsch. coun. physics dept. London Imperial Coll., 1983; vis. mem. Max-Planck Inst. Quantum Optics, Munich, 1985, 89, 95; adv. editor for physics John Wiley Publ., NYC, 1975—; cons. US Dept. Energy, 1974—, Battelle Labs., Durham, NC, 1974-84, Inst. Def. Analyses, 1986-94; mem. physics adv. com. Lawrence Livermore Nat. Lab., 1995-97; mem. adv. bd. Inst. Theoretical Physics, U. Calif. Santa Barbara, 2001-03; guest prof. Peking U., 2004—. Author: Lasers, 1988, Optical Resonance and Two-Level Atoms, 1975, Contemporary Physics, Laser Physics; editor: Multiphoton Bibliography, 1970—, Multiphoton Processes, 1978, Optics Express, 1996-2001. Recipient Alexander von Humboldt award, 1984, Marian Smoluchowski medal, 1987, Charles H. Townes award Optical Soc. Am., 1994, Disting. Alumni award Pa. State Coll. Sci., 1998. Fellow Optical Soc. Am. (bd. dirs., chair bd. editors, 2002-04, v.p. 2005, pres. 2007), Am. Phys. Soc. (chair divsn. laser sci. 1996-97, mem. coun. 2003-05); mem. C.V. Tummer Soc. (founding mem.), Acad. Sci. Poland (fgn. mem.), Inst. Theoretical Atomic, Molecular and Optical Physics Harvard-Smithsonian Obs. (mem. adv. bd. 2004-), Am. Inst. Physics (governing bd. 2003-04, investment adv. com. 2004-).

EBERSOL, DICK (DUNCAN DICKIE EBERSOL), television broadcasting executive; b. Torrington, Conn., July 28, 1947; s. Charles Ebersol; m. Susan Saint James; children: Charles Duncan, William James, Edward Bright(dec.) stepchildren: Sunshine, Harmony. Student, Yale U. Rschr. Grenoble Olympics, 1968; exec. asst. to Roone Arledge ABC Sports, 1974; sports prodr. ABC Wide World of Sports, 1974; dir. weekend late night programming NBC, NYC, 1974-75, v.p. late night programming, 1976-77, v.p. comedy, variety and event programming, 1977-81; co-creator Saturday Night Live, NYC, 1975, exec. prodr., 1981-85; founder No Sleep Prodns., 1983—; pres. NBC Sports, 1989-98; sr. v.p. NBC News, 1989; chmn. NBC Sports & NBC Olympics, 1998—2004, NBC Universal Sports & Olympics, 2004—. Creator: NBC's Friday Night Videos, 1983, Saturday Night's Main Event, 1985, Later with Bob Costas, 1988. Named Most Powerful Person in Sports, The Sporting News, 1996; named one of the 100 Most Powerful Sports Figures; named to US Olympic Hall of Fame, 2005; recipient Olympic Order, Internat. Olympic Com., 1992, Corp. Leadership award, March of Dimes, 2000, Dick Schaap Lifetime Achievement award in Sports, Michael S. Modell Awards Dinner, 2003, Trustees award, Nat. Acad. TV Arts and Scis., 2006. Office: NBC Sports 30 Rockefeller Plz New York NY 10112-0036

EBERSOLE, CHRISTINE, actress; b. Chgo., Feb. 21, 1953; m. Peter Bergman (div.). Student, McMurray Coll., Am. Acad. Dramatic Arts. Actress: (stage prodns.) Angel Street, 1976, Green Pond, 1978, On the Twentieth Century, 1978, Oklahoma!, 1979, Camelot, 1980, The Three Sisters, 1982, Geniuses, 1983, Harrigan 'n Hart, 1985, Getting Away with Murder, 1996, Gore Vidal's The Best Man, 2000, 42nd Street, 2001 (Tony award, best actress in a musical, 2001), Dinner at Eight, 2002, Steel Magnolias, 2005, Grey Gardens, 2005 (Outer Critics' Cir. award outstanding actress in a musical 2006, OBIE award Village Voice 2006, Drama Desk award outstanding actress in a musical 2006, Tony award best performance by a leading actress in a musical, 2007) (feature films) Tootsie, 1982, Amadeus, 1984, Thief of Hearts, 1984, Mac and Me, 1988, (TV movies) The Doll Maker, 1984, Acceptable Risks, 1986, (TV series) The Cavanaughs, 1986; cast mem. Saturday Night Live. Co-recipient Nightlife award for outstanding cabaret duo in a major engagement, 2007.*

EBERSOLE, J. GLENN, JR., engineering, marketing, management, public relations and strategic planning executive; b. Lancaster, Pa., Feb. 8, 1947; s. J. Glenn and Marie Christine (Stoner) E.; m. Helen Walton, July 11, 1970. Student, Ohio No. U., Ada, 1965-67; BSCE, Pa. State U., 1970, M of Engring. Sci., 1973. Registered profl. engr., Pa. Vt., Md., Del., NJ. Rsch. tech. Pa. State U., University Park, 1968-70; civil engring. intern Pa. Dept. Transp., Harrisburg, 1970-71, asst. dist. design liaison engr., 1971, head rsch. & spl. studies Bur. Traffic Engring., 1971-76; asst. chief engr.-traffic Pa. Turnpike Commn., Harrisburg, 1976-78; chief transp. engr. Huth Engrs., Inc., Lancaster, 1978-81; exec. engr. GSGSB, Clarks Summit, Pa., 1981-82; founder, CEO J.G. Ebersole Asocs., Lancaster, Pa., 1982—; TAB cert. facilitator The Alternative Bd., 2001—04; founder, CEO The Renaissance Group TM, Lancaster, Pa., 1983—; assoc. Ctr. Simplified Strategic Planning, 2006—. Part-time lectr. Pa. State U.; bus. agt. former NFL players; profl. mgr. and publicist artists and authors. Author: Glenn's Guiding Lines-Thoughts from your Strategic Thinking Business Coach, 2004; contbr. articles to profl. jours. Past chmn. Rapho Twp. Planning Commn.; mem. regional devel. coun. Pa. State U.; active Pa. State legis. liaison program; mem. bd. and co-chair Hall of Achievment Dinner Ctrl. Pa. Jr. Achievement; mem. leadership coun. Pa. chpt. Nat. Multiple Sclerosis Soc., mem. Multiple Sclerosis Leadership Class, 2004; past ch. sch. tchr., lector, past chmn. brochure com. Ch. of the Apostles, past chmn. faith promise campaign, past mem. ch. coun., ch. steering com. for long range planning, past chmn. cable TV com.; bd. dirs. and past pres. bd. trustees Actors Co. Pa.; past co-chmn. Le Cabaret Moulin Rouge Gala; past co-chmn. devel. com. Great Gatsby Gala; past chmn. fundraising campaign restoration project Mill Mus.; past trustee, past treas. bd. trustees Lancaster Found. Ednl. Enrichment; asst. sec., bd. dirs. Lancaster Indsl. Devel. Authority; past bd. dirs. Ctrl. Pa. Friends Jazz, Lancaster Family YMCA; planning commn., econ. devel. task force, urban issues subcom. Lancaster County; bd. advisor Pa. State Harrisburg-The Capitol Coll.; chmn. bd. dirs. The First Tee Susquehanna Valley; past bd. mem. Ctrl. Pa. Jr. Achievement; mem. Disting. Citizen Award Dinner Com.; bd. dirs., mem. exec. com., chair strategic planning com. Modern Transit Partnership. Mem. Am. Mktg. Assn. (dir., past Ctrl. Pa. chpt. pres.), Inst. Transp. Engrs., Lancaster C. of C. (govt. affairs com., chmn. golf com. 1985-87, long range transp. task force, local affairs com., mem. mktg./comm. coun., mem. transp. com., mem. mktg. coun., mem. bus. & mcpl. coop. task force), Pa. Soc. Profl. Engrs., Pa. Soc., Pa. State Alumni Assn. (regional devel. coun.), Pa. State of Lancaster County (past pres., bd. dir.), Pa. State Civil & Environ. Engring. Soc. (past pres., bd. dir.), Pa. State Engring. Soc. (past bd. dir.), Lancaster Country Club (mem. membership devel. com.), Shriners, Masons (past master Mt. Joy, Pa. club, Royal Order of Jesters, Allentown, Ct.), Phi Eta Sigma, Alpha Sigma Phi. Home and Office: 1305 Wheatland Ave Lancaster PA 17603-4720 Office Phone: 717-393-9350. Personal E-mail: jgeprman@aol.com. Business E-Mail: glenn@renaissanceman4u.com.

EBERSOLE, MARK CHESTER, emeritus college president; b. Hershey, Pa., Nov. 3, 1921; s. Benjamin W.S. and Mary (Patrick) E.; m. Dorothy Baugher, June 26, 1943; children— Philip B., Stephen B. BS, Elizabethtown Coll., Pa., 1943, LL.D., 1969; MDiv, Crozer Theol. Sem., 1946; MA, U. Pa., 1948; PhD, Columbia, 1952. UNRRA relief adminstr., Europe, 1946-47; asst. prof. religion and philosophy Elmira Coll., 1952-53; faculty Bucknell U., 1953-69, prof. religion, chmn. dept., chaplain of univ., 1958-61, asst. dean univ., 1961; dean Coll. Arts and Scis., 1961-62, v.p. acad. affairs, 1961-68, univ. provost, 1968-69; project specialist, spl. projects in edn. Ford Found., 1967-69, program adviser, 1969-71; dean Grad. Sch.; assoc. v.p. for acad. affairs Temple U., 1971-77; pres. Elizabethtown (Pa.) Coll., 1977-85, pres. emeritus, 1985—. Bd. dirs. Educators Mutual Life Ins. Co.; interim pres. Maryville Coll., 1992-93; ednl. cons., 1987—. Author: Christian Faith and Man's Religion, 1961; editor: Hail to Thee, Okoboji U. A Humor Anthology on Higher Education, 1992; contbr. articles to profl. jours. Trustee Linden Hall Sch., 1992—. J.P. Crozer Found. fellow, 1949-51 Mem. Pa. Soc., Cliosophic Soc. Home: 3001 Lititz Pike PO Box 5093 Lancaster PA 17606-5093 Office Phone: 717-391-9770.

EBERSOLE, W. DANIEL, state official; Dir. Ga. Office Treasury and Fiscal Svcs. Exec. bd. Savings Plans Network; commnr. Ga. Merit Sys., 1997. Mem.: Nat. Assn. State Treas. (sr. v.p., pres. 2001—02). Office: Ga Office Treas Ste 1202 West Tower 200 Piedmont Ave Atlanta GA 30334 Office Phone: 404-656-2168. Office Fax: 404-656-9048. Business E-Mail: debersole@otfs.ga.gov.*

EBERSTEIN, ARTHUR, former biomedical engineering educator, researcher; b. Chgo., Apr. 23, 1928; s. Nathan and Sara (Estes) E.; m. Marion Apfel, Aug. 1, 1961; children— Sharon, Laura BS, Ill. Inst. Tech., 1950; MS, U. Ill., 1951; PhD, Ohio State U., 1957. Asst. mem. Inst. for Muscle Disease, NYC, 1959-61; sr. scientist Am. Bosch Arma Corp., 1961-63; dir. biomed. engring. Lundy Electronics, Inc., Glen Head, NY, 1963-64; prof., dir. research dept. rehab. medicine NYU Med. Ctr, NYC, 1964-96; rsch. coord. dept. rehab. medicine Kingsbrook Jewish Med. Ctr., Bklyn., 1997—2003. Co-author: Electrodiagnosis of Neuromuscular Disease, 1983 Served with U.S. Army, 1955-57 Fellow NSF, 1958, NIH, 1959 Mem. Am. Physiol. Soc., Biophys. Soc., Biomed. Engring. Soc. Am. Assn. Electrodiagnostic Medicine, Sigma Pi Sigma. Avocations: skiing, tennis.

EBERT, LAWRENCE BURTON, lawyer; b. Bronxville, NY, Jan. 14, 1949; s. Burton Eidell and Mildred Elizabeth (Hearting) E.; m. Rebecca Ann Vares, Aug. 3, 1997. BS, U. Chgo., 1971, JD, 1993; PhD, Stanford U., 1975. Bar: N.Y. 1994, U.S. Dist. Ct. (ea. and so. dists.) N.Y. 1995, Fed. Cir. Ct. 1995, N.J. 2001. Staff scientist Exxon Corp. Rsch., Annandale, NJ, 1975—90; assoc. Pennie & Edmonds LLP, NYC, 1993—98, Kenyon & Kenyon, NYC, 1998—2000, Reed Smith LLP, Princeton, NJ, 2000—03, IPAnalytics/IPBiz/ipABC, Hamilton, NJ, 2004—. Contbr. articles to profl. jours. Fannie and John Hertz Found. fellow, 1971-75. Mem. ABA, Am. Phys. Soc., Am. Chem. Soc. Home: 390 Garretson Rd Bridgewater NJ 08807-1967 Office: IPAnalytics/IPBiz/ipABC 1850 Greenwood Ave Hamilton NJ 08609-2332 Office Phone: 609-588-0660. Business E-Mail: ebertip@yahoo.com.

EBERT, LESLIE, artist; b. Oregon City, Oreg., Sept. 20, 1962; d. Larry Dwayne Ebert and Carol Kay Bino; m. Paul Ian Boundy, May 2, 1988. BArch, U. Oreg., 1987. Archtl. intern, Portland, Oreg., 1986; studio apprentice Debra Olsen, Portland, 1990—91; owner Leslie Ebert Studio, Portland, 1994—. Exhbn. artist Celebration of Am. Paper Arts, Crane Mus. Papermaking, Mass., 2003, Landmarks in Paper, Friends of Dard Hunter, St. Paul, 2003, Crossing Boundaries, Internat. Symposium of Print Arts, Portland, 2000. Contbr. artwork to book The Artful Greeting, 2003, artwork to mag. Somerset Studio, 2000, artwork Am. Mus. Papermaking, 2003;

one-man shows include Wene Gallery, Portland, Ore., 2006, Represented in permanent collections Crane Papermaking Mus., exhibitions include Washington State U. Gallery, 2005, Nat. Coll. Soc. Small Works Exhibit, Cork Gallery, NYC, 2004, SLMM Nat. Exhbn., 2004, Peninsula Fine Arts Ctr., Newport News, Va., 2005, Coos Art Mus., Oreg., 2006, solo exhbns., Wené Gallery, Portland, 2006; curator (exhibitions) Washington State U., 2006, contbg. artist The Art of Layering: Making Connections, 2004. Founding bd. dirs. Art in the Pearl, Portland; mem. curatorial adv. bd. Am. Inst. Archs., Portland, 1992; publicity chair Waterstone Gallery, Portland, 1994; N.W. regional coord. Soc. Layerists in Multi-Media, 2004—. Mem.: Nat. Oil and Acrylic Painters, Internat. Soc. Exptl. Artists, Nat. Coll. Soc., Internat. Assn. Papermakers, Friends of Dard Hunter, N.W. Print Coun., Soc. Layerists in Multimedia (mem. com. 2006, juror for mem. com. 2007). Avocations: travel, photography, gardening, reading. Office: Leslie Ebert Studio PO Box 68604 Portland OR 97268 E-mail: leslie@leslieebert.com.

EBERT, LORETTA CAREN, librarian; BA, SUNY Binghamton; MA, Colgate U.; MLS, SUNY Geneseo. Past libr. positions U. Rochester, Syracuse U., Mich. State U.; dir. rsch. libraries Rensselaer Poly. Inst., 1994—2006; dir. rsch. libr. NY State Libr., Albany, NY, 2006—. Bd. trustees Troy Pub. Libr., NY. Office: Dir Rsch Libr NY State Libr Cultural Edn Ctr Empire State Plz Albany NY 12230 Office Phone: 518-474-5355.*

EBERT, ROBERT PETER, German language professor; b. Mt. Vernon, NY, Aug. 5, 1944; s. Robert Frederick and Verna Marion (Lashier) E.; m. Martha Ann Epp, June 9, 1969; children: Peter, Margaret. AB, Union Coll., 1966; MA, U. Wis., 1968, PhD, 1972. Asst. prof. U. Chgo., 1972-79; assoc. prof. Princeton Univ., 1979-87, prof. German dept., 1987—. Vis. asst. prof. U. Calif., Berkeley, 1977-78. Author: Infinitival Complement Constructions in Early New High German, 1976. Mem. Phi Beta Kappa. Avocation: musician.

EBERT, ROBERT T., lawyer; BBA magna cum laude, U. Notre Dame, 1984; JD cum laude, U. Mo., 1987. Bar: Mo. 1987. Ptnr., mem. oper. group Bryan Cave LLP, St Louis. Mailing: One Metropolitan Square 211 N Broadway, Ste 3600 Saint Louis MO 63102 Office Phone: 314-259-2633. E-mail: rtebert@bryancave.com.

EBERT, ROGER JOSEPH, film critic; b. Urbana, Ill., June 18, 1942; s. Walter H. and Annabel (Stumm) E.; m. Chaz Hammelsmith, July 18, 1992. BS, U. Ill., 1964; postgrad., U. Cape Town, South Africa, 1965, U. Chgo., 1966-67; LHD (hon.), U. Colo., 1993; degree (hon.), Am. Film Inst., Sch. of the Art Inst. Chgo. Editor Daily Illini, 1963-64; pres. U.S. Student Press Assn., 1963-64; staff writer News-Gazette, Champaign-Urbana, Ill., 1958-66; film critic Chgo. Sun-Times, 1967—, US mag., 1978-79, NBC-TV News, Chgo., 1980-83, ABC-TV News, Chgo., 1984—, N.Y. Post, NYC, 1986-88, N.Y. Daily News, 1988-92, Compu Serve, 1991—; pres. Ebert Co., Ltd., 1981—; Microsoft Cinemania, 1994-97; columnist Yahoo Internet Life mag., 1997—. Instr. English Chgo. City Coll., 1967-68; lectr. film criticism, fine arts program U. Chgo., 1969-; Kluge fellow U. Va., 1995-96, adj. prof. U. Ill., 2000—; lectr. film Columbia Coll., Chgo., 1973-74, 77-80; cons. Nat. Endowments for Arts and Humanities, 1972-77; juror film festivals. Co-host (TV shows) Sneak Previews, PBS, 1976-82, At the Movies, syndicated, 1982-86, Siskel & Ebert (now Ebert & Roeper), syndicated, 1986—; broadcaster: Movie News, ABC Radio, 1982-85; author: An Illini Century, 1967, (screenplay) Beyond the Valley of the Dolls, 1970, Beyond Narrative: The Future of the Feature Film, 1978, A Kiss Is Still a Kiss, 1984, Roger Ebert's Movie Home Companion, 1986-93, Roger Ebert's Video Companion, 1994-98, (with Daniel Curley) The Perfect London Walk, 1986, Two Weeks in the Midday Sun, 1987, The Future of the Movies, 1991, Behind the Phantom's Mask, 1993, Ebert's Little Movie Glossary, 1994, Roger Ebert's Book of Film, 1996, Questions for the Movie Answer Man, 1997, Roger Ebert's Movie Yearbook, 1998, The Little Book of Hollywood Cliches, The Bigger Little Book of Hollywood Cliches, 1999, Ebert's Bigger Little Movie Glossary, 1999, I Hated, Hated, Hated This Movie, 2000, Great Movies I, 2002, Great Movies II, 2005; co-author: The Future of the Movies, The Computer Insectiary, 1994. Recipient Overseas Press club, 1963, award Chgo. Headline Club, 1963, award Chgo. Newspaper Guild, 1973, Pulitzer prize, 1975, Emmy award, 1979, Peter Lisagor award, 1998, Online Film Critics Soc. Best Movie Website award, 1999; inducted into Chgo. Journalism Hall of Fame, 1997; Rotary fellow, 1965, Kluge fellow in film studies U. Va., 1995-96; received star on Hollywood Walk fo Fame, 2005. Mem. Newspaper Guild, Writers Guild Am. West, Nat. Soc. Film Critics, Acad. TV Arts and Scis., Arts Club of Chgo., Cliff Dwellers, Acad. Club (London), Sigma Delta Chi, Phi Delta Theta. Avocations: drawing, painting, art collecting. Office: Chicago Sun Times 350 N Orleans St Ste 1270 Chicago IL 60654-2148

EBESU, DUANE KEN, human services administrator; b. LA, Aug. 11, 1962; s. Kenneth Hayato and Eiko Ebesu; m. Ming Kew Ng; children: Abbey May-Yun, Molly May-Yi. BA, Calif. State U., Long Beach, 1986; MBA, Calif. State U., Dominguez Hills, 1988; MS, NYU, NY, 1992; MPhil., Columbia U., NY, 2002. Mng. dir. EBESU Cons., NY, 1990—96; sr. v.p, Housing Works, NY, 1997—, chief info. officer, 1997—. Statistician Exploring the Metropolis, NY, 1996—98. Bd. dirs. United Way NYC Tech News, 2003—; adv. bd. Bailey Ho. Cmty., NY, 1999—2002. Named one of 25 Most Influential CTOs, InfoWorld Mag., 2002; fellow, The Johns Hopkins U., 1989; scholar, NYU, 1990, U. So. Calif., 1990, Columbia U., 1993. Mem.: Columbia U. Club NY, Mensa (life). Achievements include patents for Triple Pet Dish. Office: Housing Works 57 Willoughby St Brooklyn NY 11201 Home Phone: 917-734-4028; Office Phone: 347-473-7425. Office Fax: 347-287-6788; Home Fax: 347-287-6788. Personal E-mail: ebesu@optonline.net. Business E-Mail: ebesu@housingworks.org.

EBIE, WILLIAM D., retired museum director; s. William P. and Mary Louise (Karam) E.; m. Gwyn Anne Schumacher, Apr. 11, 1968 (div. Jan. 1988); children: Jason William, Alexandra Anne; m. Mary Teresa Hayes, June 10, 1989. BFA, Akron Art Inst., 1964; MFA, Calif. Coll. of Arts and Crafts, 1968. Graphic artist Alameda County Health Dept., Oakland, Calif., 1967-68; instr. painting Fla. A&M U., Tallahassee, 1968-69; instr. photography Lawrence (Kans.) Adult Edn. Program, 1969-70; asst. dir. Roswell (N.Mex.) Mus. & Art Ctr., 1971-87, dir., 1987-98, Millicent Rogers Mus., Taos, N.Mex., 1998—2002. Juror various art exhbns., 1971—; panelist N.Mex. Arts Divsn., Santa Fe, 1983-87; field reviewer Inst. for Mus. Svcs., 1988-90; mem. State Capitol Renovation Art Selection Com., Santa Fe, 1991-92; bd. dirs. Capitol Art Found., Santa Fe, 1992-2002, 2006-. Bd. dirs. Helene Wurlitzer Found., Taos, N.Mex., 1999—. Mem. Am. Assn. of Mus., Mountain Plains Mus. Assn., N.Mex. Assn. of Mus. Democrat. Avocations: photography, carpentry. Personal E-mail: billebie@earthlink.net.

EBIN, DAVID GREGORY, mathematician, researcher, educator; b. LA, Oct. 24, 1942; s. Norman and Elizabeth (Nimiec) E.; m. Barbara J. Burkhard, June 6, 1971; children: Hannah Rebekah Hamermesh, Jacob Benjamin, Zachary Israel, Abigail Cilia. AB, Harvard Coll., 1964; PhD, MIT, 1967. Lectr. U. Calif., Berkeley, 1967-69; assoc. prof. math. SUNY, Stony Brook, 1969-78, prof. math., 1978--, adj. prof. applied math., 1989—94; editor Am. Math. Soc. Procs., Transurg. Inc., 1998—2000; chmn. math. dept. SUNY, Stony Brook, 2004—. Editor Am. Math. Soc. Proceedings, Providence, R.I., 1983-88; cons. Biosense, Inc., 1997-98, Transurgical, Inc., 1998—. Co-author: (with J. Cheeger) Comparison Theorems in Riemannian Geometry, 1975; contbr. numerous articles to Annals of Mathematics, Communications on Pure and Applied Mathematics, Communications in Partial Differential Equations. Postdoctoral fellow, NSF, 1967—68, rsch. grantee, 1967—89, 1993—97. Office: SUNY Math Dept Stony Brook NY 11794-3651 Office Phone: 631-632-8290. Business E-Mail: ebin@math.sunysb.edu.

EBINER, ROBERT MAURICE, lawyer; b. LA, Sept. 2, 1927; s. Maurice and Virginia (Grand) E.; m. Paula H. Van Sluyters, June 16, 1951; children: John, Lawrence, Marie, Michael, Christopher, Joseph, Francis, Matthew, Therese, Kathleen, Eileen, Brian, Patricia, Elizabeth, Ann. JD, Loyola U., LA, 1953. Bar: Calif. 1954, U.S. Dist. Ct. (cen. dist.) Calif. 1954. Pvt. practice, West Covina, Calif., 1954—. Judge pro tem L.A. Superior Ct., 1964-66, 90—, arbitrator, 1979—; arbitrator San Bernardino Superior Ct., 1990—; judge pro tem Citrus Mcpl. Ct., 1966-70, 1990—, El Monte Mcpl. Ct., 1998—, Whittier Mcpl. Ct., 2001—, mediator, 2000-; mem. disciplinary hearing panel Calif. State Bar, 1968-75. Bd. dirs. West Covina United Fund, 1958-61, chmn. budget com., 1960-61; organizer Joint United Funds East San Gabriel Valley, 1962, bd. dirs., 1961-68; bd. dirs. San Gabriel Valley Cath. Social Svcs., 1969—, pres., 1969-72; bd. dirs. Region II Cath. Social Svc., 1970—, pres., 1970-74; trustee LA Cath. Welfare Bur. (now Cath. Charities), 1978—; charter bd. dirs. East San Gabriel Valley Hot Line, 1969-74, sec., 1969-72; charter bd. dirs. N.E. LA County unit Am. Cancer Soc., 1973-78, chmn. by-laws com., 1973-78; bd. dirs. Queen of the Valley Hosp. Found., 1983-89; organizer West Covina Hist. Soc., 1982—; active Calif. State Dem. Cen. Com., 1963-68; mng. meet dir. Greater La Puente Valley Spl. Olympics, 1985-88, Bishop Amat Relays, 1981-96; mem. MSAC Relays Com., 1978—99; campaign mgr. Congressman Ronald B. Cameron, 1964; bd. dirs. Cal-Nev-Ha Found. 1986-98, pres. 1994-96. With U.S. Army, 1945-47. Recipient L.A. County Human Rels. Commn. Disting. Svc. award, 1978, Thomas A. Kiefer Humanitarian award, 1993; named West Covina Citizen of Yr., 1986, San Gabriel Valley Daily Tribune's Father of Yr., 1986. Mem. ABA, Calif. Bar Assn., L.A. County Bar Assn. (arbitrator 1975—), Fed. Ct. So. Dist. Calif. Assn., Consumer Attys. LA, Ea. Bar Assn. L.A. County (pres. Pomona Valley 1965-66), West Covina C. of C. (pres. 1960), Am. Arbitration Assn. (arbitrator 1965-98), KC, Bishop Amat H.S. Booster Club (bd. dirs. 1973-96, pres. 1978-80), Kiwanis (charter West Covina, pres. 1976-77, 2002-04, lt. gov. divsn. 35 1980-81, Kiwanian of Yr. 1978, 82, Disting. Lt. Gov. 1980-81, Disting. Pres., 2003-04) Avocation: collector western U.S. historical olympic and political memorabilia. Office: 100 N Citrus St Ste 520 West Covina CA 91791-1694 Office Phone: 626-918-9000.

EBITZ, DAVID MACKINNON, art historian, educator, museum director; b. Hyannis, Mass., Oct. 5, 1947; s. Robert White Creeley and Ann (MacKinnon) Kucera; m. Mary Ann Stankiewicz, Jan. 1, 1983; children: Rebecca Aemilia, Cecilia Charlotte. BA, Williams Coll., 1969; AM, Harvard U., 1973, PhD, 1979. Teaching fellow, then head teaching fellow dept. fine arts Harvard U., Cambridge, Mass., 1975-78; asst. prof., then assoc. prof. dept. art U. Maine, Orono, 1978-87, interim dir. galleries, curator univ. art collection, 1986-87; head dept. edn. and acad. affairs J. Paul Getty Mus., Santa Monica, Calif., 1987-92; dir. John and Mable Ringling Mus. Art, Sarasota, Fla., 1992-2000; assoc. prof. art and art edn. Pa. State U., University Park, 2000—. Vis. faculty Bangor (Maine) Theol. Sem., 1981; lectr. in field; presenter workshops. Author exbhn. revs., book revs.; contbr. articles to arts publs., exhbn. catalogues. Heritage Found. fellow, 1968. Mem. Coll. Art Assn., Nat. Art Edn. Assn., Am. Assn. Museums (mus. edn. com.), Mus. Edn. Roundtable, Internat. Ctr. Medieval Art, Phi Beta Kappa. Office: Pa State U 212 Arts Cottage University Park PA 16802 Home Phone: 814-235-6973; Office Phone: 814-863-1004. Business E-Mail: dme12@psu.edu.

EBNETER, STEWART DWIGHT, utility industry management consultant; b. Ledgewood, NJ, Oct. 10, 1933; s. William and Emily Ann (Burd) E.; m. Evadna Grace Custer, Dec. 28, 1957; children: Stewart D. Jr., Steven D., Scott D. BSEE, Tri-State U., 1959; MBA, Athens State Coll., 1971. Registered profl. engr., Calif. System engr. Boeing Co., Seattle, 1959-61; reliability dept. head Spaco, Inc., Huntsville, Ala., 1961-70, v.p. engring., 1971-73; div. dir. br. chief U.S. Nuclear Regulatory Commn., Atlanta, King of Prussia, Pa., 1973-87, dir. office spl. projects Washington, 1987-88, dir. div. radiation safety, regional adminstr. Atlanta, 1989-97; mgmt. cons. to utility industry, 1997—. Mem. allocation com. United Way, Huntsville, 1970-73; scout leader Boy Scouts Am., Huntsville, 1970-73. Sgt. USAF, 1953-57. Mem. Am. Soc. for Quality Control (sr.), Am. Nuclear Soc., Nat. Nuclear Accrediting Bd. Home and Office: 107 Whitfield Run Peachtree City GA 30269-3313 E-mail: s.ebneter@comcast.net.

EBOZUE, BENSON OBIAN, financial analyst; b. Onitsha, Anambra, Nigeria, Nov. 14, 1960; came to U.S., 1984; s. Benjamen A. Ebozue and Regina A. Abanafo; m. Comfort N. Ndubisi, Feb. 16, 1994; children: Benson Onyeka Jr., Jesse Mezue Nna. Diploma in acctg., Sch. of Accountancy & Mgmt., Aba, Imo, Nigeria, 1982; BBA, Dallas Bapt. U., 1991; cert., U. Tex., Arlington, 1992. CPA, Tex.; cert. adminstrv. acct., U.K. Tutor Sch. of Commerce, Onitsha, 1980—81; sr. acctg. asst. Ekwenibe & Sons Trading Co., Onitsha, 1982—84; accounts payable asst. Makai Bros., Orlando, Fla., 1984—88, CompUsa, Dallas, 1989; loan auditor Mortgage Bankers Cons., Dallas, 1991—92; acctg. analyst Sunbelt Nat. Mortgage, Dallas, 1992—; default auditor FTB Mortgage Svcs., Dallas, 1992—97; pres., CFO, Home Health Care Response, Dallas, 1997—98; mgr., owner Diamond Shamrock (BCE Mart), Dallas, 1998—99; sr acct. Fed. Mgmt. System, Inc., Washington, 2000—; owner Benson O. Ebozue CPA, Cedar Hill, Tex., 2001—. Staff auditor Logan & Assocs., CPA, Cedar Hill, Tex., 1999—. Tutor Dallas Ind. Sch. Dist., 1991-92; vol. Boys Brigade, Onitsha, 1971-76. Mem. AICPA, Tex. Soc. CPAs (cert.). Avocations: soccer, ping pong/table tennis. Home and Office: PO Box 4238 Cedar Hill TX 75106-4238 Mailing: 2504 Lost Mesa Grand Prairie TX 75052 Office Phone: 972-641-0699.

EBRAHEIM, NABIL ANWAR, orthopedist, surgeon; MD, Cairo U., 1975. Lic. NY, 1981, Md., 1983, Ind., 1985, Ohio, 1985, Mich., 1998, diplomate Am. Bd. Orthop. Surgery, 1987, re-cert. 1998, 2004. Intern Ministry Pub. Health, Cairo, 1975—76, surg. resident, 1976—77, St. Clare's Hosp., NYC, 1978—80; orthop. resident Kings County Hosp. Ctr., Bklyn., 1980—83; orthop. trauma fellowship U. Md., Balt., 1983—84; pelvic and acetabular trauma fellowship Sunny Brook Hosp., Toronto, Canada, 1984; spine and acetabular trauma fellowship Pitie Salpetriere, Paris, 1984—85; AO fellowship Kantonsspital Chur, Switzerland, 1985, Hanover Trauma Ctr., Germany, 1985, Divisione Orthropadia E. Traumatologia, Lecco, Italy, 1989; vice chmn. dept. orthop. surgery Med. U. Ohio, Toledo, 1985—97, acting chmn., 1997—98, prof., chmn. dept. orthop. surgery, 1998—. Instr. Internat. Fixation Technique, Toronto, Canada, 1986, 88; orthop. residency program dir. Med. U. Ohio, dir. orthop. trauma fellowship program, chief divsn. orthop. trauma, dir. Office Orthop. for Practicing Physicians, 1995; dir., chmn., moderator numerous seminars in field. Contbr. articles to profl. jours. Recipient Foot and Ankle Rsch. award, 1999. Office: Med Univ Ohio 3065 Arlington Ave Toledo OH 43614 Office Phone: 419-383-4020. E-mail: nebraheim@meduohio.edu.

EBRAHIM, ARBIN, electrical engineer, researcher; b. Alappuzha, Kerala, India, May 27, 1977; s. Hashim Sait and Shamim Ebrahim. B in Engring., B.M.S Coll. Engring., Bangalore, 1989; MSEE, Wayne State U., Detroit, 2003; PhD in Electrical Engring., U. Ala., Tuscaloosa, 2007. Software engr. Datamate Software Consultancy, Thiruvananthapuram, Kerala, India, 1999—2001; rsch. asst./tchg. asst. U. Ala., Tuscaloosa, 2004—. Mem.: IEEE. Achievements include design of novel adaptive controllers for induction motor control. Home Phone: 313-443-6739. Personal E-mail: arbinsait@hotmail.com. Business E-Mail: ebrah001@ua.edu.

EBRECHT, RONALD, musician; Diplome des etudes superieures, Schola Cantorum, Paris, 1979. Editor: (biography) Maurice Durufle: 1902-1986 The Last Impressionist. Bd. mem. Arts Coun. Greater New Haven, 1991—99; mem. New Haven Symphony Orch.; dean Am. Guild Organists, Waterbury Chpt. Office: Wesleyan U High St Middletown CT 06459 Home Phone: 203-776-7339; Office Phone: 860-685-2282. Personal E-mail: rebrecht@wesleyan.edu.

EBRIGHT, RICHARD HIGH, molecular biologist; b. Reading, Pa., June 11, 1959; s. Richard Jerome and Jacqueline Katherine (Muth) Ebright; m. Yon Won, Dec. 39, 1985; children: Richard Yon, Katherine Yon. BA in Biology summa cum laude, Harvard U., 1981, PhD in Microbiology, Molecular Genetics, 1987. Jr. fellow Harvard U., Cambridge, 1984-87; asst. prof. dept. chemistry Rutgers U., New Brunswick, N.J., 1987-92, assoc. prof. dept. chemistry, 1992-95, prof. dept. chemistry, 1995—. Investigator Howard Hughes Med. Inst., Chevy Chase, Md., 1997—. Editor: Jour. Molecular Biology, 1997—; contbr. articles to scientific jours.; mem. editl. bd. Jour. Bacteriology, 1995-98; patentee in field (2). Searle scholar Searle Found., 1989; recipient Walter J. Johnson prize Acad. Press, 1995. Fellow Am. Acad. Microbiology, AAAS,; mem. Am. Soc. Biochem. Molecular Biology (Schering-Plough Sci. Achievement award 1995), Am. Chem. Soc., Am. Soc. Microbiology, Biophys. Soc. Lutheran. Address: HHMI/Waksman Inst Rm B201 190 Frelinghuysen Rd Piscataway NJ 08854-8020 Office Phone: 732-445-5179. Office Fax: 732-445-5735. Business E-Mail: ebright@waksman.rutgers.edu.

EBSWORTH, BARNEY A., retired travel company executive; m. Pamela Ebsworth. Founder, chmn., pres., CEO INTRAV, 1959—99, Royal Cruise Line, 1972—86, Clipper Cruise Line, 1981—97; founder, chmn., CEO Windsor Inc., St. Louis, 1979—. Commr. Am. Art Mus., Smithsonian Inst.; dir. Build-A-Bear Workshop Inc., 2000—06, dir. emeritus, 2006—; trustee St. Louis Art Mus., Seattle Art Mus.; mem. trustee coun. Nat. Gallery, Washington, co-chmn. collectors com., 1996—. Stationed in Paris during Korean War. Named one of Top 200 Collectors, ARTnews Mag., 2004. Avocation: collector of Am. modern & contemporary art. Home: 4053 Hunts Point Rd Hunts Point WA 98004-1109

EBY, MICHAEL JOHN, marketing research and technology consultant; b. South Bend, Ind., Aug. 3, 1949; s. Robert T. and Eileen Patricia (Holmes) Eby; m. Judith Alyson Gaskell, May 17, 1980; children: Elizabeth, Katherine. Student, Harvey Mudd Coll., 1969-70; BS in Biochemistry with high honors, U. Md., 1972, MS in Chemistry, 1977; postgrad., IMEDE, Lausanne, Switzerland, 1984. Product mgr. LKB Instruments Inc., Rockville, Md., 1976-79; mktg. mgr. LKB-Produkter AB, Bromma, Sweden, 1979-87; strategic planning mgr. Pharmacia LKB Biotech. AB, Bromma, 1987-88; dir. mktg. Am. Bionetics, Hayward, Calif., 1988-89; pres. PhorTech Internat., San Carlos, Calif., 1989—. Author: The Electrophoresis Explosion, 1988, Electrophoresis in the Nineties, 1990, DNA Amplification, 1993, Blotting and Hybridization, 1993, Capillary Electrophoresis, 1993, Densitometers and Image Analysis, 1995, Visualization Reagents, 1995, U.S. Laboratory Product Usage, 1996, Cell Biology Reagent Systems, 1996, Centrifugation, 1996, Molecular Biology Reagent Systems, 1997, DNA Diagnostics, 1997, DNA Amplification in Europe, 1998, Recombinant Protein Expression Systems, 1998, DNA Sequencing in Europe, 1998, Molecular Biology Reagent Systems in the Far East, 1998, HPLC in the Life Sciences, 1998;: Cytokines and Growth Factors, 1998, Cell and Tissue Culture, 1998, Monoclonal Antibodies, 1999, Microplate Instrumentation in Europe, 1999, DNA Sequencing, 1999, 2000, Global Laboratory Product Usage, 2000, DNA Amplification, 2000, Electrophoretic Equipment and Reagents, 2001, Densitometers and Image Analysis in Europe, 2001, DNA Sequencing in the Far East, 2001, DNA Amplification Instrumentation, 2002, DNA Amplification Regents and Methodology, 2002, Microplate Readers and Equipment, 2002, Global Laboratory Product Usage, 2002, Proteomics Research, Vols. 1-2, 2003, Protein Expression Systems, 2003, Molecular Biology Reagent Systems, 2003, HPLC Columns in the Life Science, 2004, Electrophoresis Instruments & Reagents, 2004, Worldwide Directory of Life Science Distributors, 2005, Microarrays, Arrayers & Scanners in Europe, 2005, DNA Sequencing, 2005, North American Laboratory Product Usage, 2006, Amplification Instrumentation, 2006, others; contbr. articles to profl. jours. Mem.: AAAS, Am. Soc. Cell Biology, Am. Chem. Soc., Am. Philat. Soc., U. Md. Alumni Assn., Calif. Separation Sci. Soc., Am. Mensa. Episcopalian. Avocations: astronomy, cheese-making, photography, travel. Office: PhorTech Internat 238 Crestview Dr San Carlos CA 94070-1503 E-mail: mikeby@phortech.com.

ECHOHAWK, JOHN ERNEST, lawyer; b. Albuquerque, Aug. 11, 1945; s. Ernest V. and Emma Jane (Conrad) E.; m. Kathryn Suzanne Martin, Oct. 23, 1965; children: Christopher, Sarah. BA, U. N.Mex., 1967, JD, 1970. Bar: Colo. 1972, US Dist. Ct. Colo. 1972, US Appeals (8th Cir.) 1976, US Ct. Appeals (9th Cir.) 1980. Research assoc. Calif. Indian Legal Services, Escondido, 1970, Native Am. Rights Fund, Berkeley Calif. and Boulder, Colo., 1970-72, dep. dir. Boulder, 1972-73, 1975-77, exec. dir., 1973-75, 1977—. Mem. task force Am. Indian Policy Rev. Commn., US Senate, Washington, 1976-77; bd. dirs. Am. Indian Lawyer Tng. Program, Oakland, Calif., 1975—; bd. dirs. Assn. Am. Indian Affairs, 1980—, Nat. Com. Responsive Philanthropy, Washington, 1981-2000; mem. Clinton Adminstrn. Transition Team for Interior Dept., 1992-93. Presdl. appointee Western Water Policy Rev. Adv. Commn., 1995-97; Ind. Sector, Washington, 1986-92; mem. Natural Resources Def. Coun., NYC, 1988—; bd. dirs. Nat. Ctr. Enterprise Devel., 1988—, Keystone Ctr., 1993-99. Environ. and Energy Study Inst., 1994—. Recipient Disting. Service award Ams. For Indian Opportunity, 1982, Pres. Indian Service award Nat. Congress Am. Indians, 1984, Annual Indian Achievement award Indian Council Fire, 1987; named one of most influential attys. Nat. Law Jour., 1988, 91, 94, 97, 2000. Mem. Native Am. Bar Assn., Colo. Indian Bar Assn. Democrat. Avocations: fishing, skiing. Office: Native Am Rights Fund 1506 Broadway St Boulder CO 80302-6217 Office Phone: 303-447-8760. Office Fax: 303-443-7776.

ECHOLS, MARY EVELYN, training services executive, writer; b. LaSalle, Ill., Apr. 5, 1915; d. Francis Ira and Mary Irene (Coleman) Bassett; m. David H. Echols, Aug. 31, 1951 (dec.); children: Susan Echols O'Donnell, William. Grad. St. Mary's Nursing Hosp., Chgo. Founder Internat. Travel Tng. Courses, Inc., Chgo., 1962—; pres. Evelyn Echols Cons. Ltd., 1998, Echols Comms. Ltd., 2004—. Author: Saying Yes to Life. Cons. Harold Washington Coll.'s Hospitality Courses; bd. dirs. Chgo. Conv. and Tourism Bur., Am. Cancer Soc., Gus Giordiano Jazz Dance Chgo., Little Sisters of the Poor; past pres. Pres. Reagan's Adv. Com. for Women's Bus. Ownership; v.p. United Cerebral Palsy Assn.; nat. spokesperson Prevent Blindness in Am.; mem. Women's Internat. Forum. Named Entrepreneur of Yr. Women Bus. Owners N.Y., 1985, Bus. Woman of Yr. Nat. Assn. Women Bus. Owners, 1985, Crain's Chgo. Bus., 1993; named to Chgo.'s Entrepreneurial Hall of Fame, 1992. Mem.: Soc. Am. Travel Agts., Acad. TV Arts and Scis., Chgo. Execs. Club. Office Phone: 773-348-1553. E-mail: evelyn@evelynechols.com.

ECHOLS, ROBERT L., federal judge; b. 1941; BA, Rhodes Coll., 1962; JD, U. Tenn., 1964. Law clk. to Hon. Marion S. Boyd US Dist. Ct. (we. dist.) Tenn., Memphis, 1965—66; legis. asst. Congressman Dan Kuykendall, 1967-69; ptnr. Baily, Ewing, Dale & Conner, Nashville, 1969-72, Dearborn & Ewing, Nashville, 1972-92; fed. judge US Dist. Ct. (mid. dist.) Tenn., Nashville, 1992—, chief judge, 1998—2005; civilian aide at-large Sec. of Army, 2007. Mem. Jud. Br. Com. US Jud. Conf.; mem. libr. com. 6th Cir. Ct. Appeals, ann. conf. planning com. 6th Cir.; mem. exec. com. Fed. Judges Assoc., Tenn. State-Fed. Jud. Ct. With US Army, 1966; brig.

gen. Tenn. Army N.G., 1969-2001, ret. Mem. ABA, Am. Bar Found., Tenn. Bar Found., Tenn. Bar Assn., Nashville Bar Assn., Nashville Bar Found., Rhodes Sports Hall of Fame, Harry Phillips Am. Inn of Ct., NG Assocs. Tenn. and US. Office: US Dist Ct 801 Broadway Ste 824 Nashville TN 37203-3868 Office Phone: 615-736-2774.

ECHOLS, ROBERT L., emergency physician; b. Selma, Ala., July 11, 1948; MD, U. Ala., 1974. Diplomate Am. Bd. Emergency Medicine. Intern Lloyd Noland Hosp., fairfield, 1974-75, resident in surgery, 1975-76; resident in urology U. Hosp., Birmingham, 1976-77; dir. emergency medicine Cullman Regional Med. Ctr., Cullman; clin. instr. U. Hosp., Birmingham, 1986-95. Mem. AMA, ACEP.

ECHOLS, VERNA K., volunteer; b. Mar. 7, 1929; AB in Edn., Fla. Atlantic U. Author: (children's book) Story of T.W. and O., 2004. Active Planned Parenthood, Nat. Resource Def. Coun.; Fla. rep. Nat. Coalition Against Legalized Gambling; Clinton rep. Dem. Nat. Conv., Chgo., NYC; vol. Dem. Exec. Com. Home: 621 Osceola Ave E Lake Wales FL 33853-3346

ECK, GAIL ANN, elementary school educator; b. Jacksonville, Ill., May 29, 1948; d. Charles Joseph and Gloria Ann (Bentley) Standley; m. George E. Eck, June 21, 1969. BA, Ill. Coll., 1971; MS in Edn., Western Ill. U., 1981. Cert. elem. tchr., Ill. Asst. phys. therapist Norris Hosp., Jacksonville, 1966-70; tchr. 1st, 2d grades, chpt. I Franklin (Ill.) Cmty. Schs., 1971-90; Reading Recover tchr. leader Springfield (Ill.) Pub. Schs., 1990—. Summer sch. coord., summer libr. program dir., jr. high softball coach Franklin Cmty. Schs.; adj. prof. U. Ill., 1991-97; adj. prof. Nat.-Louis U., 1997—. Mem. NEA, ASCD, Internat. Reading Assn., Nat. Coun. Tchrs. Math., Ill. Edn. Assn., Ill. Reading Coun., Cen. Ill. Reading Coun. (past pres., treas., v.p.), Ill. Assn. Supervision and Curriculum Devel., Ill. Coun. Math. Tchrs., Ill. Assn. Chpt. I Dirs., Franklin/Alexander Classroom Tchrs. (past pres., sec., v.p., mem. negotiations team), Springfield Edn. Assn, Reading Recovery Coun. N.Am. (charter mem.). Roman Catholic. Avocations: genealogy, reading, calligraphy, swimming, canoeing, travel. Home: RR 1 Box 18 Alexander IL 62601-9801

ECK, GEORGE GREGORY, lawyer; b. Evanston, Ill., Sept. 3, 1950; s. George F. and Dorothy E. (Frake) E.; m. Margaret K. Gorman, Sept. 1, 1973; children: Jessica Elizabeth, Michelle Margaret. BS, No. Ill. U., 1972; JD cum laude, U. Minn., 1977. Bar: Minn. 1977, U.S. Dist. Ct. Minn. 1977, U.S. Ct. Appeals (8th cir.) 1977. Assoc. Dorsey & Whitney, Mpls., 1977-83, ptnr., 1983—. Mem. editorial bd. U. Minn. Law Rev., 1977. With US Army, 1972—74. Home: 6413 Mendelssohn Ln Hopkins MN 55343-8424 Office: Dorsey & Whitney LLC 50 S 6th St Ste 1500 Minneapolis MN 55402-1498 Home Phone: 952-938-0362; Office Phone: 612-340-2772. E-mail: eck.george@dorsey.com.

ECK, KENNETH JAMES, agronomist; BS, Purdue U., West Lafayette, Ind., 1989, MS, 1991. Lic. pesticide applicator Office Ind. State Chemist, 1989. Asst. farm mgr. Eck Farms, Inc., Otwell, Ind., 1980—88; greenhouses & tours tech. specialist Land Pavilion, Walt Disney World, Lake Buena Vista, Fla., 1988—89; tchg. & rsch. grad. asst. Purdue U. Agronomy Dept., 1989—91, soil & water conservation specialist Jasper, Ind., 1992—2004; clean water ind. program specialist Ind. Dept. Natural Resources, Jasper, 2004—06; dist. support specialist Ind. State Dept. Agr., Jasper, 2006—. Contbr. articles to profl. jours. Sec., deacon St. John's Luth. Ch. Coun., Otwell, Ind., 1993—97; mem. SWCD Found., Indpls., 1997—2002, Lemmons Cmty. Found., Jasper, 1993—2007. Recipient Team Performance award, IDNR, 1999. Mem.: Ind. Assn. Profl. Soil Classifiers, Ind. Soc. Paleontology, Soil & Water Conservation Soc. Am., Crop Sci. Soc. Am., Soil Sci. Soc. Am., Am. Soc. of Agronomy (young professionals com.), Alpha Zeta (advisor), Gamma Sigma Delta, Epsilon Sigma Phi. Avocation: reading. Office: Ind State Dept Agrl 1486 Executive Blvd Ste A Jasper IN 47546-9300 Office Phone: 812-482-1171 ext. 3. Office Fax: 812-482-9427. Business E-Mail: keck@isda.in.gov.

ECK, ROBERT EDWIN, retired physicist; b. Ames, Iowa, Nov. 28, 1938; s. John Clifford and Helen (Behrendt) E.; m. Carolyn Jennie Vodicka, May 11, 1974; children: David Michael, Elizabeth Claire. BA in Physics, Rutgers U., 1960; MS in Physics, U. Pa., 1962, PhD in Physics, 1966; MA in Econs., U. Calif., Santa Barbara, 1973. Sr. rsch. scientist Ford Motor Co., Newport Beach, Calif., 1966-69; project engr. Santa Barbara Rsch. Ctr., Goleta, Calif., 1969-73, asst. mgr. infrared components, 1974-81, mgr. major program, 1982-84, dir. tech., 1985-88, dir./mgr. engring., 1989-95; new bus. devel. mgr. R.G. Hansen & Assocs., Santa Barbara, Calif., 1995-96; program mgr. Optoelectronics-Textron, Petaluma, 1996-2000; adminstrv. dir. Enhancement Inst., Houston, 2002—03. Bd. dirs. Goleta Edn. Found. Mem. Goleta Noontime Rotary Club (pres. 1989-90). Achievements include patents on superconductors, infrared detector testing and magnetoresistor sensors.

ECKAUS, RICHARD SAMUEL, economist, educator; b. Kansas City, Mo., Apr. 30, 1926; s. Julius and Bessie (Finklestein) E.; m. Patricia L. Meaney; 1 child, Susan L. BS, Iowa State Coll., 1946; MA, Washington U., St. Louis, 1948; PhD, MIT, 1954. Instr., asst. prof., assoc. prof. Brandeis U., 1951-62; rsch. assoc. Ctr. Internat. Studies MIT, Cambridge, 1954-61, from assoc. prof. to prof., 1962—96, Ford internat. prof., 1977-96, head dept. econs., 1987-90, emeritus prof., 1996—. Vis. scholar Roxbury C.C., 1996—2002; nat. adv. coun. for environ. and tech. policy EPA, 2002—04; joint program sci. and policy climate change; mem. Bd. Econ. Advisors to Gov. Mass., 1963—65; cons. ADB, OECD, AID, World Bank, govts. of Jamaica, Portugal, Egypt, Sri Lanka, Chile, China, Mexico. Author: (with K. Parikh) Planning for Growth, 1968; editor: (with J. Bhagwati) Foreign Aid, 1970, Development and Planning, 1973, Basic Economics, 1972, Estimating the Returns to Education, 1973, Appropriate Technologies for Developing Countries, 1976; contbr. articles to profl. jours. Served with USNR, 1944-46. Decorated gt. cross Order of Prince Henry (Portugal); Guggenheim and Social Sci. Rsch. Coun.fellow, 1962; Ford Found. Faculty fellow, 1965. Mem. Am. Econ. Assn. Home: 131 Sewall Ave Apt 72 Brookline MA 02446-5336 Office: MIT Dept Econs 50 Memorial Dr Cambridge MA 02142-1347 Office Phone: 617-253-3367. Business E-Mail: eckaus@mit.edu.

ECKEL, JAMES ROBERT, JR., financial planner; b. Morley, Tenn., Nov. 3, 1927; s. James Robert and Jane Scott (Seymour) E. BS magna cum laude, U. Tenn., 1953, MS, 1957; JD, U. West L.A., 1974. CFP; enrolled agt.; registered patent agt. Instr. elec. engring. U. Tenn., 1953-57, U. Wis., 1957-62; sr. engr. Northrop Corp., LA, 1962-66; staff engr. TRW Systems, LA, 1966-69; sr. project engr. Hughes Aircraft Co., Culver City, Calif., 1969-89; fin. planner Culver City, 1989—. Real estate broker, Calif. With USN, 1946-49. Mem. IEEE, Am. Inst. Aeros. and Astronautics, Am. Soc. for Engring. Edn., Sigma Xi, Kappa Sigma, Omicron Delta Kappa, Phi Kappa Phi, Tau Beta Pi, Eta Kappa Nu, Phi Eta Sigma. Episcopalian. Home and Office: 5104 Copperfield Ln Culver City CA 90230-7501

ECKELMAN, RICHARD JOEL, engineering specialist; b. Bklyn., Mar. 25, 1951; s. Leon and Muriel (Brietbart) E.; m. Janet Louise Fenton, Mar. 21, 1978; children: Christie, Melanie, Erin Leigh, Alexandra. Student, Ariz. State U., 1988—. Sr. engr., group leader nondestructive testing Engring. Fluor Corp., Irvine, Calif., 1979-83; sr. engr. nondestructive testing McDonnell Douglas Helicopter Co., Mesa, Ariz., 1983-91; engring. specialist Convair div. Gen. Dynamics, San Diego, 1991-94; sr. tech. specialist McDonnell Douglas Techs., Inc., San Diego, 1994-96; scientist, engr. The Boeing Co., Mesa, Ariz., 1996-99, prin. engr., scientist Huntington Beach, Calif., 1999—. Mem. Am. Soc. Nondestructive Testing (nat. aerospace com. 1987—, sec. Ariz. chpt. 1987-88, treas. 1988—, sect. chmn. 1989—, sect. bd. dirs. 1990-91), Am. Soc. Quality Control, Soc. Mfg. Engrs., Lindbergh Yacht Club, Porsche Club Am. Avocations: racquetball, sailing. Home: 3342 Hillrose Dr Los Alamitos CA 90720-4802

ECKENHOFF, EDWARD ALVIN, health facility administrator, educator; b. Durham, NC, Mar. 4, 1943; s. James Edward and Bonnie Lee E.; m. Judi G. Vicich, May 27, 1978 BA, Transylvania U., 1966, PhD (hon.), 2000; MA, U. Ky., 1968; MHA, Washington U., 1974. V.p., adminstr. Rehab. Inst. Chgo., 1976-82; pres., chief exec. officer Nat. Rehab. Hosp., Washington, 1982—; asst. prof. dept. community and family practice Med. Sch., Georgetown U., Washington, 1983-94; v.p. Medlantic Healthcare Group, 1987-99. V.p. Medlantic Healthcare Group, 1987-98; pres. Nat. Rehab. Services Corp., 1987-92; chmn. bd. NASCOTT, IBIS; instr. Med. Sch., Northwestern U., preceptor Grad. Sch. Bus.; mem. Ill. Commn. on Health Assistance Programs; mem. Ill. adv. com., chmn. exec. com. Internat. Yr. of Disabled; surveyor Commn. on Accreditation of Rehab. Facilities; com. on accreditation and edn. Am. Phys. Therapy Assn.; mem. Healthcare Rsch. Devel. Inst Contbr. articles to profl. jours. Bd. dirs. Am. Occupl. Therapy Found., Easter Seal Soc., Boy Scouts Am., Chgo. Area coun., Nat. Area, 1987-87, Operation ABLE Chgo., Access Living of Met. Chgo., Am. Chamber Symphony, Chgo., Nat. Assn. Rehab. Facilities, 1982-83, Am. Med. Rehab. Provider Assn., chmn. bd. dirs., 2000-01 Named Washingtonian of the Yr., Washingtonian Mag., 1989; recipient Citation for Disting. Svc., AMA, 1990, Ann. Healthcare Leader award B'nai B'rith, 2003. Fellow Inst. Medicine Chgo., Am. Coll. Hosp. Execs.; mem. Am. Hosp. Assn. (chmn. governing coun. for rehab. hosps. 1985, trustee 1991-93, chmn. policy com. 1993, exec. com. 1993, Honor award 2007), Am. Congress Rehab. Medicine (chmn. policy and devel. com.), Chgo. Hosp. Coun. (chmn. com. rehab. 1978-82, exec. com. 1983), Healthcare Devel. and Rsch. Inst. (bd. dirs. 2005—), Am. Med. Rehab. Providers Assn. (chmn. bd. dirs. 2000-01), Nat. Orgn. on Disability (medicare coverage adv. commn. 1999-2002, presdl. appointment commr. commn. on care for Ams. wounded warriors, 2007), DC Hosp. Assn. (bd. dirs. 2003—). Episcopalian. Office: Nat Rehab Hosp 102 Irving St NW Washington DC 20010-2949

ECKER, HOWARD, lawyer; b. NYC, June 10, 1946; s. David and Sylvia (Goldstein) E.; children: David, Ashley. BA, U. Mich., 1967; JD, NYU, 1971. Bar: Nev. 1973, U.S. Dist. Ct. Nev. 1974, U.S. Ct. Appeals (9th cir.) 1976, U.S. Supreme Ct. 1976. Pub. defender Clark County Pub. Defender's Office, Nev., 1973-77; ptnr. Ecker & Standish, Chtd., Clark County, Nev., 1977—. Guest lectr. in field. Mem. Nev. Employee Mgmt. Rels. Bd., Las Vegas, 1990-94. Mem.: Am. Acad. Matrimonial Lawyers, Am. Inns of Ct. (barrister 1990—93, master 1993—), Nev. Trial Lawyers Assn. (bd. govs. 1977—89, pres. 1985—86), Clark County Bar Assn., State Bar Nev. (bd. govs. 1984—90). Avocations: travel, golf, reading. Office: Ecker & Standish Chtd 300 S 4th St Ste 901 Las Vegas NV 89101-6025 Office Phone: 702-384-1700.

ECKER, JOSEPH R., plant molecular and cellular biologist; BA in Biology and Chemistry, Coll. NJ, Ewing; PhD in Microbiol., Pa. State U. Coll. Medicine. Postdoctoral fellow Stanford U. Sch. Medicine, Calif.; faculty mem. U. Pa., 1987—2000; prof. plant biology lab. Salk Inst. Biol. Studies, La Jolla, 2000—, dir. genome analysis lab., 2000—. Contbr. articles to sci. jours.; editl. bd.: Pub. Libr. of Sci. Genetics. Recipient Kumho Sci. Internat. award in plant molecular biology and biotechnology, 2001, Disting. Rsch. award, Internat. Plant Growth Substances Assn., 2004, Martin Gibbs medal, Am. Soc. Plant Biologists, 2005. Mem.: NAS (John J. Carty award for the Advancement of Sci. 2007), Internat. Soc. Plant Molecular Biology (pres.). Achievements include the sequencing of the common mustard seed Arabidopsis and the discovery of a method to identify its functional genes; being named a rsch. leader in agr. Sci. Am. 50, 2004. Office: Salk Inst for Biol Studies PO Box 85800 San Diego CA 92186-5800*

ECKER, ROBERT DONIGER, neurosurgeon; b. Boston, Apr. 6, 1972; s. Howard Malcolm and Wendy Lee Ecker; m. Lissa Diaz, Apr. 29, 2001; children: Emily Doniger, Alexander Diaz. AB, Harvard U., 1995; MD, Med. Coll. Va., 1999. Resident in neurol. surgery Mayo Clinic, Rochester, Minn., 1999—; endovascular fellow U. Buffalo, 2004—. Contbr. articles to profl. jours. Intern Office of Senator Albert Gore, Jr., Washington, 1990—91. Lt. comdr. USN, 1999—. U.S. Health Profl. scholar., USN, 1999—. Mem.: AMA (assoc.), Am. Assn. Neurol. Surgeons (assoc.), Congress Neurol. Surgeons (assoc.), Phi Kappa Phi, Alpha Omega Alpha. Avocations: scuba diving, triathalons. Home: PSC 482 Box 2695 FPO AP 96362 Home Phone: 716-836-1563; Office Phone: 716-200-8494.

ECKER, SIDNEY WOLF, urologist, consultant; s. Morris and Rose Ecker; m. Karen Garber, Mar. 1, 1964; children: Felice Ecker-Ramaikas, Erica. BS, U. Scranton, 1962; MD, Albert Einstein Coll. Medicine, Bronx, NY, 1966. Diplomate Am. Bd. Urology, Diplomate Nat. Bd. Med. Examiners. Surg. intern Georgetown U. Med. Sch., Washington, 1966—67, urology resident, 1967—71; pvt. practice Urol. Assn., 1973—96; chmn. surgery sect. Shady Grove Adventist Hosp., Rockville, Md., 1996—97, chmn. surg. rev., 1991—95; mem. regular affiliate staff Walter Reed Army Med. Ctr., Washington, 1998—; chief of urology Wash. VA Med. Ctr., Washington, 2001—03, surg. cons., 2005—; clin. prof. of urology Georgetown U. Med. Sch., Washington, 2004—. Guest worker surgery br. NIH, Bethesda, Md., 1968—69; urol. surgeon to Belize Found. for Global Health, Washington, 1975; vis. urologist to China People to People Med. Ambs., Spokane, 2002. Contbr. scientific papers to profl. publs. Maj. USAF, 1971—73. Recipient Residents Sci. Presentation 1st prize, Wash. Urol. Soc., 1969. Fellow: ACS (life); mem.: Wash. Urological Soc. (pres. 1991—92), Med-chi Md. (life), Am. Urol. Assn. (life), Cosmos Club Wash. Avocations: Apple and Mac computers, photography, travel and travel lecturing, international cooking. Home: 132 Silvertail Ln New Hope PA 18938

ECKERT, ALLAN WESLEY, writer; b. Buffalo, Jan. 30, 1931; s. Edward Russell and Ruth Rose (Roth) E.; m. Joan Dowling, 1955 (div. 1975); children: Joseph Matthew, Julie Anne; m. Gail Greene, 1977 (div. 1978); m. Nancy Dent, 1978 (div. 2007). Student, U. Dayton, 1951-52, Ohio State U., 1953-54; PhD (hon.), Bowling Green State U., 1985, Wright State U., 1998. Assoc. editor Nat. Cash Register Co. News, Dayton, Ohio, 1955-58; reporter, columnist Dayton Jour. Herald, Dayton, Ohio, 1958-60; free-lance writer, 1960—. Cons. LaSalle Extension U., Chgo. Writer over 200 TV scripts for NBC's Wild Kingdom; created courses article and short story writing Writer's Digest; author: The Great Auk, 1963, A Time of Terror, 1965, The Silent Sky, 1965, Wild Season, 1967, The Frontiersmen, 1967, Bayou Backwaters, 1967, The Dreaming Tree, 1967, The Crossbreed, 1968, Blue Jacket, 1968, The King Snake, 1968, Wilderness Empire, 1968, In Search of a Whale, 1969, The Conquerors, 1970, Incident at Hawk's Hill, 1971, The Court-Martial of Daniel Boone, 1973, The Owls of North America, 1973, The HAB Theory, 1976, The Wilderness War, 1978, The Wading Birds of North America, 1979, Savage Journey, 1979, Song of the Wild, 1980, Whattizzit?, 1981, Gateway to Empire, 1982, Johnny Logan: Shawnee Spy, 1982, The Dark Green Tunnel, 1983, The Wand, 1984, The Scarlet Mansion, 1985, Earth Treasures, 4 vols., 1987, Twilight of Empire, 1988, A Sorrow in Our Heart: The Life of Tecumseh, 1991, That Dark and Bloody River: Chronicles of the Ohio River Valley, 1995, The World of Opals, 1997, Return to Hawk's Hill, 1998, Territory!, 2006, The Goldseekers, 2007,(outdoor drama) Tecumseh!, 1971, (screenplays) Kentucky Pioneers, 1969, The Legend of Koo-Tan, 1971, (playscript) Tecumseh!, 1974; editor: A Treasury of Tips for Writers, 1966; contbr. articles to popular and profl. publs. Trustee Dayton Museum Natural History, 1963-65; Founder, chmn. bd. Lemon Bay Conservancy, Englewood, Fla. Served with USAF, 1948-52; honorably discharged from rank as staff sgt. Recipient Ohioana Book award, 1968, Best Book award Friends of Am. Writers, 1968, Emmy award outstanding program achievement Nat. Acad. TV Arts and Scis., 1968-69, Newbury-Caldecott Honor Book award, 1972, George G. Stone/Claremont Colls. Recognition of Merit, 1974, Austrian Juvenile Book of Yr. award, 1976, Americanism award The Daniel Boone Found., 2d Ann. Silver Arrow Humanitarian award Scioto Soc., 1987, Internat. Readers Assn. Tchrs. Choice award, 1999; commd. Ky. Col. by Gov. State of Ky., 1987; finalist Spur award Western Writers Am., 1995; named Writer of Yr., Am. Culture Assn., 1997; nominated 7 times for Pulitzer prize; Allan W. Eckert Collection established at Howard Gotlieb Meml. Libr., Boston U., 1965, at the Filson Club Hist. Soc., Louisville, 1993, named by Citizens of Ohio as favorite Ohio writer of all time, Ohioana Libr. Assn., 1999; Allan W. Eckert Nature Trail, Scioto County Commrs., Riverside Park, 2001. Mem. Dayton Soc. Natural History (life), Am. Soc. of Gem Cutters, Mazon Creek Project (life). Avocations: history, archaeology. Office: care Russell Galen Scoville Chichak and Galen 381 Park Ave S Rm 1020 New York NY 10016-8806 Office Fax: 212-679-6710. Personal E-mail: allaneckt@earthlink.net.

ECKERT, CHARLES ALAN, chemical engineering educator; b. St. Louis, Dec. 13, 1938; s. Clarence Theodore and Mildred Hortense (Potlitzer) E.; children: Carolyn Helen, Theodore James; m. Susan Schneider, 1997. SB, MIT, 1960, SM, 1961; PhD, U. Calif., Berkeley, 1964. Postdoctoral fellow Nat. Ctr. Sci. Rsch., Paris, 1964-65; asst. prof. U. Ill., Urbana, 1965-69, assoc. prof., 1969-73, prof., 1973-89, head dept. chem. engring., 1980-86; J. Erskine Love, Jr. inst. chair, prof. chem. engring. and chemistry Ga. Inst. Tech., Atlanta, 1989—. Dir. Splty. Separations Ctr., 1991—; cons. numerous cos. Author: several books, instructional computer progs.; contbr. articles to sci. jours. Co-recipient Presdl. Green Chemistry Challenge award, 2004; grantee NATO fellowship, 1964, Guggenheim Found. fellowship, 1971. Fellow AIChE (Alan P. Colburn award 1973, William H. Walker award 1999, Clarence Gerhold award, 2006); mem. NAE, Internat. Soc. for Advancement of Supercritical Fluids (v.p.), Am. Chem. Soc. (Ipatieff prize 1977, Murphree award 1995), Am. Soc. Engring. Edn. Office: Ga Inst Tech Environ Sci and Tech 311 Ferst Dr NW Atlanta GA 30332-0100 E-mail: cae@gatech.edu.

ECKERT, JEAN PATRICIA, elementary school educator; b. Pitts., July 22, 1935; d. Homer Mitchel and Berdena Leona (Kessler) Canel; m. William L. Eckert, June 13, 1959; 1 child, Suzanne Mary. BS, Indiana U. Pa., 1957; postgrad., U. Pitts., 1958-59, U. San Diego, 1981. Cert. pub. instrn., Pa. Elem. tchr. Pine-Richland Sch. Dist., Gibsonia, Pa., 1957—60, substitute tchr., 1963—65; elem. tchr. Shaler Twp. Sch. Dist., Glenshaw, Pa., 1965—66, St. Scholastica Sch., Diocese of Pitts., Aspinwall, Pa., 1966—91, substitute tchr., 1991—, tutor, 1991—. Judge election 4th dist. Rep. Party, Aspinwall, 1962-65, 91-98. Mem.: AAUW, Nat. Cath. Edn. Assn., Literacy Vols. Am., Ind. U. (Pa.) Alumni Assn., Delta Zeta (sec. 1955, pres. 1956). Roman Catholic. Avocations: travel, literature. Home: 210 12th St Pittsburgh PA 15215-1600

ECKERT, ROBERT A., consumer products company executive; m. Kathie Eckert; 4 children. BSBA, U. Ariz., 1976; MBA in Mktg. and Fin., Northwestern U., 1977. Various mktg. positions Kraft Foods, 1977-87, v.p. strategy and devel. grocery products divsn., 1987-89, v.p. mktg. refrigerated products, 1989-90, v.p., gen. mgr. cheese divsn., 1990-97, pres., CEO, 1997-2000; chmn. bd., CEO Mattel, Inc., 2000—. Bd. dirs. McDonalds Corp., 2003—; com. mem. Trilateral Commn. Active adv. bd. J.L. Kellogg Grad. Sch. Mgmt., Northwestern U.; bd. visitors, Anderson Sch., UCLA; bd. dirs., mem. exec. com. Met. Family Svcs.; trustee Ravinia Festival Assn., Art Inst. Chgo.; nat. trustee Lake Forest Coll. Bd. dirs., chmn. govt. affairs coun. Grocery Mfrs. Am.; bd. dirs. L.A. World Affairs Coun., Bus. Coun., Wash. D.C.; mem. Asia Society, Young Presidents' Org., L.A., Town Hall L.A. Office: Mattel Inc 333 Continental Blvd El Segundo CA 90245-5012 Fax: 310-252-2179.*

ECKHARDT, CRAIG JON, chemistry professor; b. Rapid City, SD, June 26, 1940; s. Reuben H and Hilda W. (Craig) E. BA magna cum laude, U. Colo., 1962; MS, Yale U., 1964, PhD, 1967. Asst. prof. chemistry U. Nebr., Lincoln, 1967-72, assoc. prof., 1972-78, prof., 1978—, interim chmn. dept. chemistry, 1986-87, prof. physics, 1988—. Cons., mem. adv. panel, condensed matter scis. div. materials research NSF, 1976-79 NIH predoctoral fellow, 1964-67; Yale predoctoral fellow, 1967; John Simon Guggenheim fellow, 1979-80; German Acad. Exchange fellow; Fulbright Sr. fellow, 2006; grantee NSF, 1974-84, Dept. Energy, 1979-82, Petroleum Rsch. Fund-Am. Chem. Soc., 1968-72, Rsch. Corp., 1971-74, 3M Corp., 1983-89, Army Rsch. Office, 1989-97, Office Naval Rsch., 2000—. Mem. Am. Phys. Soc., Am. Assn. Physics Tchrs., Optical Soc. Am., Am. Chem. Soc., Royal Chemistry Soc., Phi Beta Kappa, Sigma Xi. Office: U Nebr Dept Chemistry Lincoln NE 68588 Office Phone: 402-472-2734. Business E-Mail: eckhardt@undserve.und.edu.

ECKHARDT, LAUREL ANN, biologist, researcher, educator; b. Palo Alto, Calif., Sept. 4, 1951; d. Joseph Carl Augustus Eckhardt and Ada Jane Williams Smith; m. Michael Warren Young, Dec. 27, 1978; children: Natalie Alice Eckhardt Young, Arissa Caroline Eckhardt Young. BA summa cum laude, U. Tex., 1974; PhD in Genetics, Stanford U., Calif., 1980. Damon Runyon-Walter Winchell postdoctoral fellow Albert Einstein Coll. Medicine, Bronx, 1980-83; asst. prof. Dept. Biol. Sci., Columbia U., NYC, 1984-88, assoc. prof., 1989-92; prof. Dept. Biol. Sci., Hunter Coll. of CUNY, 1992—, Marie Hesselbach prof. biology, 1999—. Reviewer immunobiology study sect. Dept. Rsch. Grants, NIH, Bethesda, Md., 1993-96; reviewer grand rev. com. Am. Heart Assn., N.Y.C., 1990-93, sci. rev. Immunological Sciences peer rev. com., Dept. of Def. Breast Cancer Rsch. Program, 1998, 2000, 03, rev. panelist for rsch. tng. fellowships for med. students, Howard Huges Med. Student, Howard Hughes Med. Inst., 2002-04. Assoc. editor Jour. Immunology, 1997-2001; contbr. articles to profl. jours. Rsch. grantee NIH-Inst. Allergy and Infectious Diseases, 1984-90, 90—, Am. Cancer Soc., 1990-95, NIH-Nat. Cancer Inst., 1994-99. Mem. Am. Assn. Immunologists (program com. mem. 1995-99), N.Y. Acad. Scis., Harvey Soc. Democrat. Avocations: tennis, gardening, dance. Office: Hunter College of CUNY Dept Biol Sci 695 Park Ave New York NY 10021-5085

ECKHARDT, WILLIAM RUDOLF, III, lawyer; b. Houston, Dec. 14, 1915; s. William Rudolf and Ura (Link) E.; m. Elra Hodges, Oct. 11, 1940; 1 son, Donald Kent. BA, Rice Inst., 1937; LL.B., U. Tex., 1940. Bar: Tex. 1940. Asst. U.S. atty. Dept. Justice, So. Dist. Tex., 1940-44, 46-52; assoc. McGregor & Sewell, Houston, 1952-56, Vinson & Elkins, Houston, 1956—91. Served to lt. (j.g.) USN, 1944-46. Fellow Am. Coll. Trial Lawyers; mem. ABA, Tex. Bar Assn., Maritime Law Assn., Tex. Def. Attys. Assn., Chancellors, Order of Coif, Phi Delta Phi, Chi Phi. Republican. Baptist. Home: 25 Robinlake Ln Houston TX 77024-7121 Office: Ste 111 7880 San Felipe Houston TX 77063 Office Phone: 713-977-8772.

ECKHART, AARON, actor; b. Calif., Mar. 12, 1968; BA, Brigham Young U., 1994. Actor: (films) Slaughter of the Innocents, 1994, In the Company of Men, 1997 (Ind. Spirit award for Best Debut Performance, 1998, Satellite Spl. Achievement award for Outstanding New Talent, 1998), Your Friends & Neighbors, 1998, Thursday, 1998, Molly, 1999, Any Given Sunday, 1999, Tumble, 2000, Erin Brockovich, 2000, Nurse Betty, 2000, The Pledge, 2001, Possession, 2002, The Core, 2003, The Missing, 2003, Paycheck, 2003, Suspect Zero, 2004, Conversations with Other Women, 2005, Thank You for Smoking, 2006, The Black Dahlia, 2006, The Wicker

Man, 2006, No Reservations, 2007; actor, co-prodr. (films) Neverwas, 2005; actor: (TV films) Double Jeopardy, 1992; (TV miniseries) Ancient Secrets of the Bible, Part II, 1993; (TV series) Aliens in the Family, 1996. Office: c/o Barry Hirsch and David Matlof 23rd Fl 10100 Santa Monica Blvd Los Angeles CA 90067 also: Creative Artists Agy 9830 Wilshire Blvd Beverly Hills CA 90212-1825

ECKHART, MARYLOUISE CHRISTINE SANTILLI, pre-school educator; d. Richard William and Louise May Santilli; m. Jeffery Gene Eckhart, Sept. 4, 1983; children: Andrew William, Kyle Gene, Matthew Russell. BEd, U. Toledo, 1982; MEd, Ashland U., Ohio, 1994. Cert. tchr. Ohio Dept. of Edn., 1982. Spl. edn. tchr. Anthony Wayne Local Schs., Ohio, 1982—85; from spl. edn. tchr. to early childhood intervention specialist Canton (Ohio) City Schs., 1985—2000, early childhood resource specialist, 2000—. Adj. instr. Ashland U., Massillon, Ohio, 2001—05. Contbr. chpt. to book. Mem.: ASCD, Canton Area Assn. Edn. Young Children, Nat. Assn. Edn. Young Children. Avocations: travel, camping, reading, exercise, spending time with my family. Home: 6589 Dale St NW Massillon OH 44646 Home Phone: 330-837-4860. Business E-Mail: eckhart_m@ccsdistrict.org.

ECKHART, WALTER, molecular biologist, educator; b. Yonkers, NY, May 22, 1938; s. Walter and Jean E. BS, Yale U., 1960; postgrad., Cambridge U., Eng., 1960-61; PhD, U. Calif.-Berkeley, 1965. Postdoctoral fellow Salk Inst., San Diego, 1965-69, mem., 1970-73, assoc. prof. molecular biology, 1973-79, prof., 1979—, cancer ctr. dir., 1976—. Adj. prof. U. Calif.-San Diego, 1973-2003. Contbr. articles on molecular biology and virology to profl. jours. NIH research grantee, 1967—. Mem. AAAS, Am. Soc. Microbiology. Home: 951 Skylark Dr La Jolla CA 92037-7731 Office: Salk Inst PO Box 85800 San Diego CA 92186-5800 Home Phone: 858-454-6566; Office Phone: 858-453-4100 1386. Business E-Mail: eckhart@salk.edu.

ECKL, WILLIAM WRAY, lawyer; b. Florence, Ala., Dec. 2, 1936; s. Louis Arnold and Patricia Barclift (Dowd) E.; m. Mary Lynn McGough, June 29, 1963; children: Eric Dowd, Lynn Lacey. BA, U. Notre Dame, 1959; LLB, U. Va., 1962. Bar: Va. 1962, Ala. 1962, Ga. 1964. Law clk. Supreme Ct. of Ala., 1962; ptnr. Gambrell, Harlan, Russell & Moye, Atlanta, 1965-68, Swift, Currie, McGhee & Hiers, Atlanta, 1968-82, Drew, Eckl & Farnham, Atlanta, 1983—. Served to capt. JAGC USAR, 1962—65. Mem. Am. Bd. Trial Advocates, Trial Attys. Am., Lawyers Club of Atlanta, Brookwood Hills Club. Roman Catholic. Home: 348 Camden Rd NE Atlanta GA 30309-1513 Office: Drew Eckl & Farnham 880 W Peachtree St PO Box 7600 Atlanta GA 30357-0600 Office Phone: 404-885-6327. Business E-Mail: weckl@deflaw.com.

ECKLAND, WILLIAM S, lawyer; b. 1954; BA, Univ. Md., 1976; JD with honors, George Washington Unv, 1979. Bar: DC 1979, NY 1989. Ptnr. fed. regulatory issues Sidley Austin Brown & Wood LLP, Washington, and mem. exec. com. Mem. George Washington Univ. Law Rev., 1979. Mem.: ABA, Order of Coif. Office: Sidley Austin Brown & Wood LLP 1501 K St NW Washington DC 20005 Office Phone: 202-736-8267. Office Fax: 202-736-8711. Business E-Mail: weckland@sidley.com.

ECKLEY, WILTON EARL, JR., humanities educator; b. Alliance, Ohio, June 25, 1929; s. Wilton Earl and Louise (Bert) E.; m. Grace Ester Williamson, Sept. 12, 1954; children: Douglas, Stephen, Timothy. BA, Mt. Union Coll., 1952; MA, Pa. State U., 1955; PhD, Case Western Reserve U., 1965; John Hay fellow, Yale U., 1961-62. Chmn. English Euclid (Ohio) Sr. High Sch., 1955-63; dir. tchr. tng. Hollins Coll., 1963-65; prof. English Drake U., 1965-84, chmn. dept. English, 1965-80; head dept. humanities and social scis. Colo. Sch. Mines, 1984-93, dir. honors program, 1989-92; prof. humanities Drake U., 1984—; prof. humanities and internat. studies Colo. Sch. Mines, 1994-99, prof. emeritus, 1999—. Fulbright prof. Am. lit. U., Ljubljana, Yugoslavia, 1972-73, U. Veliko, Turnovo, Bulgaria, 1981-82; vis. prof. Bilkent U., Ankara, Turkey, 1993-94. Chmn. bd. dirs. Colo. Endowment for the Humanities, 1989-91. Coe fellow Am. Studies, 1957—. Mem. MLA, Circus Hist. Soc., AAUP, Phi Kappa Tau. Home: 636 Ridgeside Dr Golden CO 80401-5757

ECKMAN, FERN MARJA, journalist; b. NYC, Aug. 27; d. Isidor Peter and Zara Nettie (Sloate) Friedman; m. Irving Eckman, June 21, 1957. BA, N.Y. U., 1957. Reporter N.Y. Post, 1944-78; assigned to UN, 1945-49, 60-65. Author: The Furious Passage of James Baldwin, 1967; contbg. editor Working Mother, 1981-91; feature writer for nat. publs., 1965-90. Recipient George Polk Meml. award for distinguished met. reporting, 1951, 55; Page One award for community service N.Y. Newspaper Guild, 1955, for best feature reporting, 1961; citation for community service Council Puerto Rican and Spanish-Am. Orgns., 1955; Lasker award for med. journalism, 1960; Front Page award for distinguished feature writing, News Women's Club N.Y., 1949, 51, 56, 64; for distinguished series (co-recipient), 1970; Cultural News award Newspaper Reporters Assn., N.Y.C., 1967; Empire State award for excellence in med. reporting, 1968 Home: 749 W End Ave New York NY 10025-6224

ECKMANN, RORY ALBERT, telecommunications industry executive; s. Donald George Eckmann and Anita Sue Farley; m. Lisa Caron Hedgepath, Aug. 10, 1985; children: Joshua David, Sarah Katlyn, Thomas Michael, Zachary David. Diploma, Wauconda HS., Ill., 1983. With USN, 1983—93; submarine sonar technician USS Von Steuben Ship Submersible Ballistic Nuc. 632, Charleston, SC, 1986—90; testing specialist US Navy, Chgo. Mil. Entrence Processing Sta., DesPlaines, Ill., 1990—92; bench repair technician Calif. Microwave, Bloomingdale, Ill., 1993—97; telecomm. specialist Ameritech, Chgo., 1997—2001, AT&T, Palatine, Ill., 2001—. Mem. Friends of Libr., Wauconda, 2003—; leader Stockade Boys Christian Svc. Brigade, Wauconda, 1996—; bd. dirs. Evang. Free Ch., Wauconda. Decorated Submarine Dolphins FBM Patrol pin with 6 stars, 2 Good conduct medals US Navy. Mem.: Telecom Pioneers (assoc.), Vets. of AT&T. Republican. Avocations: camping, swimming, coaching wrestling, softball. Home Phone: 847-487-8132; Office Phone: 847-358-9930.

ECKNER, SHANNON F., lawyer; BA in English Lit., U. Cin., 2000, JD, 2003. Bar: Ohio 2003. Law clerk Phyllis G. Bossin Co., L.P.A., Cin., assoc. Mem. Big Sister. Named one of Ohio's Rising Stars, Super Lawyers, 2006. Mem.: ABA, Ohio State Bar Assn. (Family Law Com.), Cin. Bar Assn. (mem, Domestic Rels. Com.), Order of Coif, Phi Beta Kappa. Office: Phyllis G Bossin Co LPA Ste 1210 36 E Fourth St Cincinnati OH 45202 Office Phone: 513-421-4420. Office Fax: 513-421-0691.

ECKSTEIN, DAVID MARK, professional baseball player; b. Sanford, Fla., Jan. 20, 1975; s. Whitey and Patricia Eckstein; m. Ashley Drane, Nov. 26, 2005. Attended Univ. Fla. Shortstop Anaheim Angels, 2001—04, St. Louis Cardinals, 2005—. Named World Series MVP, 2006; named to Nat. League All-Star Team, 2005, 2006; recipient Babe Ruth award, 2002. Office: St Louis Cardinals 250 Stadium Plz Saint Louis MO 63102

ECKSTEIN, JENS W., venture capitalist, biotechnologist; b. Friedrichshafen, Germany, Sept. 4, 1963; s. Werner Georg Erich Eckstein and Ute Kramer; m. Gabrielle Strobel, Apr. 25, 1992; children: Jakob Wolfgang Strobel Eckstein, Leonora Strobel Eckstein, Benedikt Peter Strobel Eckstein. D, U. Konstanz, Germany, 1991. Group leader, scientist Mitotix, Inc., Cambridge, Mass., 1993—99; rsch. dir. Enanta Pharms., Inc., Watertown, 1998—2003; founder, pres. Akikoa Pharms., Inc., Dover, 2003—; prin. TVM Capital, Boston, 2004—07, ptnr., 2007—. Advisor Sirtris Pharms., Inc., Cambridge, 2004—07; sr. advisor Magen Bioscis. Inc., Cambridge, 2006—; mem. adv. coun. Cure Dystonia Initiative. Mng. editor Frontiers in Bioscience - Current Topics in Lead Discovery, editl. advisor IDrugs; mem. editl. bd.: Gene Therapy, Molecular Biology. Fellow, U. Calif., San Francisco, 1991—93, Ctr. Venture Edn./Kauffman Found., 2005—07; grantee, European Union, 1991; scholar, Harvard U., DAAD, 1988—89; Kauffman fellow, 2005—. Mem.: NVCA. Achievements include patents in field. Office: TVM Capital 101 Arch St Boston MA 02110 Office Phone: 617-345-9320. Office Fax: 617-345-9377. Business E-Mail: eckstein@tvm-capital.com.

ECKSTEIN, JEROME, philosopher, retired educator; b. NYC, June 28, 1925; s. Marcus and Blanche (Wohlberg) E.; m. Kathleen Sharon Hoisington; 1 stepchild, Mari O'Donnell Midurski; children: Esther Schwartz, Sandra Bellehsen, Michael. Student, Rabbi Isaac Elchanan Theol. Sem., 1943-45; BA, Bklyn. Coll., 1949; postgrad., New Sch. Social Research, 1949-50; PhD, Columbia U., 1961. Buyer antique silverware Blanche Eckstein Silverware, Bklyn., 1945-53; dir. edn. and youth activities, various Hebrew congregations, 1950-61; lectr. philosophy CCNY, 1955-56, Bklyn. Coll., 1955-60; instr. contemporary civilization and philosophy Columbia U., NYC, 1960-63; asst. prof., then assoc. prof. philosophy, coordinator div. humanities Adelphi Suffolk Coll., Adelphi U., 1963-66; prof. philosophy of edn. SUNY-Albany, 1966-70, also first chmn. Judaic studies, 1970-74, prof. Judaic studies, 1970-97, prof. religious studies, 1990-97, prof. emeritus, 1997—. Participant Internat. Philosophy Yr., Brockport, N.Y., 1967, Conf. on Gerontology, U. Minn., 1978; vis. prof. philosophy Bar-Ilan U., Israel, 1978-79 Author: The Platonic Method: An Interpretation of the Dramatic-Philosophic Aspects of the Meno, 1968; The Deathday of Socrates, 1981, Metaphysical Drift: Love and Judaism, 1991, On Meanings or Life: Their Nature and Origin, 2002; contbr. articles to profl. jours. Fellow in logic CCNY, 1955-56; vis. scholar Va. Commonwealth U., Richmond, 1975; Am. Council Learned Socs. sr. fellow, 1973 Mem. Phi Beta Kappa

ECKSTEIN, JOHN WILLIAM, internist, educator, retired dean; b. Central City, Iowa, Nov. 23, 1923; s. John William and Alice (Ellsworth) Eckstein; m. Imogene O'Brien, June 16, 1947; children: John Alan, Charles William, Margaret Ann, Thomas Cody, Steven Gregory. BS, Loras Coll., 1946; MD, U. Iowa, 1950; DSc (hon.), Ind. U., 1995. Asst. prof. internal medicine U. Iowa, Iowa City, 1956—60, assoc. prof., 1960—65, prof., 1965—92, prof. emeritus, 1993; assoc. dean VA Hosp. affairs, 1969—70, dean coll. medicine, 1970-91, dean emeritus, 1993. Chmn. cardiovasc. study sect. NIH, 1970—72, Nat. Heart, Lung and Blood Adv. Coun., 1974—78; mem. adv. com. to dir. NIH, 1990—95. Author papers and abstracts. Mem. VA Manpower Study Group, 1988—92. With USAF, 1943—45, with U.S. Army Med. Corps., 1950—51. Named established investigator, Am. Heart Assn., 1958—63, in his honor, Eckstein Med. Rsch. Bldg., U. Iowa, 1988; recipient Rsch. Career award, USPHS, 1963—70, Dist. Alumni Svc. award, U. Iowa, 1994, Disting. Physicians, Dept. Vets. Affairs, 1995—98; fellow postdoctoral, Rockefeller Found., 1953—54, Am. Heart Assn. Rsch., 1954—55, spl. rsch., Nat. Heart Inst., 1955—56. Mem.: Assn. Acad. Health Ctrs. (mem. sci. policy study group 1988—93), Inst. Medicine, Assn. Am. Med. Colls. (exec. coun. 1981—82, adminstrv. bd. 1980—82, 1985—86), Assn. Am. Physicians, Am. Clin. and Climatol. Assn., Am. Soc. Clin. Investigation, Ctrl. Soc. Clin. Rsch. (sec.-treas. 1965—70, pres. 1973—74), Am. Fedn. Clin. Rsch. (chmn. Midwestern sect. 1965), AMA (mem. health policy agenda panel 1982—86, mem. study sect. faculty and rsh. 1985—86, governing. coun. sect. on med. schs. 1985—95, alt. del. Ho. of Dels. 1986—90, del. 1990—92, Disting. Svc. award 1992), Am. Heart Assn. (v.p. 1969, chmn. coun. on circulation 1969—71, pres. 1978—79). Home: 1415 William White Blvd Iowa City IA 52245-4443 Office: U Iowa Hosps & Clinics Iowa City IA 52242-1101 E-mail: john-eckstein@uiowa.edu.

ECO, UMBERTO, semiotics educator, author; b. Alessandria, Italy, Jan. 5, 1932; s. Giulio and Giovanna (Bisio) Eco; m. Renate Ramge, Sept. 24, 1962; children: Stefano, Carlotta. PhD, U. Turin, 1954; degrees (hon.). Lectr. aesthetics U. Turin, Milan Poly., 1961—64; assoc. prof. visual comm. U. Florence, 1966—69; assoc. prof. semiotics Milan Poly., 1969—71, U. Bologna, 1971—75, prof. semiotics, 1975—. Dir. Instituto di Discipline della Communicazione e dello Spettacolo U. Bologna, 1976—77, 1980—83, dir. Instituto di Discipline della Communicazione, 1983—88, dir. semiotics PhD program, 1986, 2002, pres. Scuola Superiore di Studi Umanistici, 1999—; mem. exec. sci. com. U. San Marino, 1989—95, pres. Internat. Ctr. Semiotics & Cognitive Studies, 1989—; pres. Inst. Italiano di Scienze Umane, 2002—; vis. prof. NYU, 1969—70, 1976, Northwestern U., 1972, U. Calif. San Diego, 1975, Yale U., 1977, 80, 81, Columbia U., 1978, 84, Collège de France, Paris, 1992—93, École Normale Superiore, Paris, 1996; vis. Fellow, Italian Acad. Columbia U., 1996; Tanner lectr. Cambridge U., 1990; Norton lectr. Harvard U., 1992, 93; Goggio lectr. U. Toronto, 2002; Weidenfeld lectr. Oxford U., 2002; chair, Corso di Laurea, Scienze della Communicazione U. Bologna, 1993—98. Editor cultural programs RAI Italian Radio-TV, Milan, 1954—59, sr. non-fiction editor Bompiani Pub. House, 1959—75, columnist Il giorno, La stampa, Corriere della Sera, La Repubblica, L'Espresso, Il Manifesto, 1962—, co-founder Marcatré rev., 1961, Quindici rev., 1967; editor: Versus, 1971—; mem. editorial bd. Semiotica, Poetics Today, Degrès, Structuralist Rev., Text, Communication, Problemi dell'informazione, Word & Images, Alfabeta; author: (fiction works include) The Name of the Rose, 1983 (Premio Strega, 1981, Premio Anghiari, 1981, Prix Medicis best fgn. novel, 1982, LA Times fiction prize nom., 1983), Foucault's Pendulum, 1989, The Island of the Day Before, 1995, Baudolino, 2002, The Mysterious Flame of Queen Loana, 2005, (non-fiction works include) A Theory of Semiotics, 1977, The Role of the Reader, 1979, Postscript to The Name of the Rose, 1984, Semiotics & the Philosophy of Language, 1984, Art & Beauty in the Middle Ages, 1985, Travels in Hyperreality, 1986, The Aesthetics of Thomas Aquinas, 1988, The Open Work, 1989, The Middle Ages of James Joyce, 1989, The Limits of Interpretation, 1990, Interpretation & Overinterpretation, 1992, Misreadings, 1993, Apocalypse Postponed, 1994, How to Travel with a Salmon, 1994, Six Walks in the Fictional Woods, 1994, The Search for the Perfect Language, 1995, Talking of Joyce, 1998, Serendipities: Language & Lunacy, 1999, Belief or Nonbelief?, 2000, Kant & the Platypus, 2000, Experiences in Translation, 2000, Five Moral Pieces, 2001, Mouse or Rat?: Translation as Negotiation, 2003; editor: History of Beauty, 2004; co-editor: The Picture History of Inventions, 1963, Il caso Bond (The Bond Affair), 1965, A Portrait of Italy, 1967, A Semiotic Landscape, 1979, The Sign of Three: Pierce, Holmes, Dupin, 1983, Carnival!, 1984, Meaning & Mental Representations, 1988, On the Medieval Theory of Signs, 1989, Conversations About the End of Time, 1999. Named Commandeur de l'Ordre des Arts et des Lettres, France, 1985, Chevalier de la Legion d'Honneur, 2003, Cavaliere di Gran Croce al Merito, Italy, 1996; recipient Prix Medicis Etranger, France, 1892, Columbus award, Rotary Club, Florence, 1983, Marshall McLuhan award, Unesco Canada & Teleglobe, 1985, Golden Cross of the Dodecannese, Greece, 1995, Orden pour le Merite für Wissenschaften und Künst, Germany, 1999, Crystal award, World Economic Forum, 1999, Austrian State award for European Literature, 2002, Prix Mediterranée Etranger, France, 2002. Fellow: St. Anne's Coll., Oxford (hon.), Kellogg Coll., Oxford (hon.); mem.: Internat. Acad. Philosophy & Art, Coun. Advisors Bibliotheca Alexandrina, Acad. Europea de Yuste, Acad. Sci. Bologna, Acad. Sci. Bologna, Acad. Universelle des Cultures, Internat. Assoc. Semiotic Studies (sec. gen. 1972—79, vice pres. 1979—83, hon. pres. 1994—), James Joyce Assoc. (hon.), Am. Acad. Arts & Letters (hon.). Office: Scuola Superiore di Studi Umanistici Via Marsala 26 Bologna Italy Office Phone: 051.2917111. E-mail: simona@dsc.unibo.it.

ECONOMAKI, CHRIS CONSTANTINE (CHRISTOPHER), publishing executive; b. Bklyn., Oct. 15, 1920; s. Christopher C. and Gladys Toomey (Burt) E.; m. Alvera H. Tomljanovic, May 29, 1946; children: Christine, Corinne. Student, Drake U. Sales rep. Divco Corp., 1946-49; editor, pub. emeritus Nat. Speed Sport News newspaper; pres. Kay Pub. Co., Harrisburg, N.C., 1949—; Color commentator Wide World of Sports ABC-TV, 1961-83, CBS-TV Sports, 1984-93. Served with AUS, 1942-46, ETO. Recipient Tom Marchese award for dedication to automobile racing, 1972, Henry McLemore award for excellence in broadcast journalism, 1973, Ken Purdy award Internat. Motor Press Assn., 1978, Ray Marquette Meml. award, 1981, Patrick Jacquemart award for service to motorsports, 1983, Dave Fritzlen Meml. award Outstanding Service to Chgo. Lathrop Boys Club, 1984, Walt Ader Meml. award, 1985, 1st Hugh Deery Meml. award for long service to automobile racing, 1985, Excellence award Nat. Assn. for Stock Car Auto Racing, 1990, Presdl. award U.S. Auto Club, 1992, Appreciation award svc. auto racing Charlotte, N.C. Motor Speedway, 1990, Chevy Proud award to Dean Am. Motorsports Journalism, 1990, Achievement award svc. racing Ford Motor Co., 1990, Dean Batchelor award Lifetime Achievement, 1996, Lifetime Media award NASCAR/ESPN, 1998; Economaki Award named in his honor Driver of Yr. Panel, 1991; Amb. Motorsports Time, Cleve., 1992; Lifetime Achievement award named in his honor; named to Stock Car Hall of Fame, Oceanside (Fla.) Rotary Club, 1993, Nat. Sprint Car Hall of Fame, Knoxville, Iowa, 1993, Motorsports Hall of Fame, 1994, Nebr. Auto Racing Hall of Fame, 1999,Indpls. Motor Speedway Hall of Fame, 2005; NASCAR's Buddy Shuman award for svc. to auto racing, 2000, Speedvision Lifetime Achievement award for motorsports journalism, 2000; recipient 12th ann. Good Scout award Great Sauk Trail Coun., Boy Scouts Am., 2002, Lifetime Achievement award Ea. Motorsports Press Assn., 2003; Mayor Indpls. pronounces May 2, 2002 Chris Economaki Day; Gov. Jeb Bush declares Sunday, February 20, 2005 Chris Economaki Day in Fla. Mem. Am. Assn. Auto Racing Writers and Broadcasters (pres. 1969-71, Angelo Angelopolous Meml. award 2000), Nat. Motorsports Press Assn., Ea. Motorsports Press Assn., Oceanside Rotary, Order of Long Leaf Pine. Home: Apt 314 The Kentshire 187 Paterson Ave Midland Park NJ 07432 Office: PO Box 1210 Harrisburg NC 28075-1210

ECONOMON, PAUL DAVID, lawyer, management consultant; b. Silver Spring, Md., Oct. 18, 1967; m. Kimberley Ann Kubas, Apr. 10, 1998; children: Sophia Eva, Paul David Jr., Harry Daniel. BS, U. So. Calif., 1990; JD, MBA, George Washington U., 1994. Gen. counsel OneSoft Corp., McLean, Va., 1998—2001; ptnr. Koltun & King, PC, Washington, 2001—05; gen. counsel Ineo Mktg., Inc., Herndon, Va., 2005—. Soccer coach. Mem.: Bus. Alliance George Mason (bd. dirs. 2003), Assn. Corp. Growth. Greek Orthodox. Avocations: travel, soccer, scuba diving. Home: 7526 Evans Ford Rd Clifton VA 20124 Office: Ineo Mktg Inc 12801 Worldgate Dr Ste 505 Herndon VA 20170 Home Phone: 703-830-8883; Office Phone: 703-453-9120. Personal E-mail: paul@economon.com.

ECONOMOS, CORA MATHENY, librarian; b. Camden, Ark., July 15, 1921; d. Walter Stanton and Cora Smith Matheny. BS in Edn. summa cum laude, Centenary Coll. La., 1963; MS in LS, U. Miss., 1965, PhD, 1972; postgrad., U. Okla., 1973. Tchr. pub. schs., Shreveport, La., 1963—64; dir. Pine Bluff and Jefferson County Pub. Libr., Pine Bluff, Ark., 1965—86, mem. bd. trustees, 1991—97, libr. emerita, cons., 1987—. Bd. dirs. Pine Bluff Cmty. Art Ctr., 1966—67; steering com. Pine Bluff-Jefferson County Am. Revolution Bicentennial Celebration, 1975—76. Mem.: Alpha Chi, Phi Delta Kappa, Kappa Delta Pi. Episcopalian. Home: Westminster Village 500 Spanish Fort Blvd Apt 27 Spanish Fort AL 36527

ECONOMOU, GREG, professional sports team executive; m. Betsy Economou; children: Rip, Luke, A.J. Grad. in Comm. and Hist., U. Conn., 1988. Profl. basketball player Europe; prin., COO, chief mktg. officer SME Power Branding; sr. v.p. SFX sports grp. SFX Entertainment; mng. dir., CEO Brandthink; sr. v.p. mktg. and comm. NBA, 2006; exec. v.p., chief mktg. officer Bobcats Sports & Entertainment (parent co. of NBA Charlotte Bobcats), 2006. Avocation: golf. Office: Bobcats Sports & Entertainment 333 E Trade St Charlotte NC 28202*

ECTON, DONNA R., business executive; b. Kansas City, Mo., May 10, 1947; d. Allen Howard and Marguerite (Page) E.; m. Victor H. Maragni, June 16, 1986; children: Mark, Gregory. BA (Durant Scholar), Wellesley Coll., 1969; MBA, Harvard U., 1971. V.p. Chem. Bank, NYC, 1972-79, Citibank, N.A., NYC, 1979-81; pres. MBA Resources, Inc., NYC, 1981-83; v.p. adminstrn., officer Campbell Soup Co., Camden, NJ, 1983-89; chmn. Triangle Mfg. Corp. subs. Campbell Soup Co., Raleigh, NC, 1984-87; sr. v.p., officer Nutri/System, Inc., Willow Grove, Pa., 1989-91; pres., CEO Van Houten N.Am., Delavan, Wis., 1991-94, Andes Candies Inc., Delavan, 1991-94; chmn., pres., CEO Bus. Mail Express, Inc., Malvern, Pa., 1995-96; bd. dirs. PETsMART, Inc., Phoenix, 1994—98, COO, 1996-98; chmn., pres., CEO EEI Inc., Paradise Valley, 1998—. Bd. dirs. H&R Block, Kansas City, Mo., 1993—, Johns Hopkins' JHPIEGO, Balt., 2004—; commencement spkr. Pa. State U., 1987. Bd. overseers Harvard U., 1984-90; mem. Coun. Fgn. Rels., NYC, 1987—; trustee Inst. for Advancement of Health, 1988-92. Named one of 80 Women to Watch in the 80's, Ms. mag., 1980, one of All Time Top 10 of Last Decade, Glamour mag., 1984, one of 50 Women to Watch, Bus. Week mag., 1987, one of 100 Women to Watch, Bus. Month mag., 1989; recipient Wellesley Alumnae Achievement award, 1987; Fred Sheldon Fund fellow Harvard U., 1971-72; Margaret Rudkin scholar Harvard U., 1969-71. Mem. Harvard Bus. Sch. Assn. (pres. exec. council 1983-84), Harvard Bus. Sch. Club Greater N.Y. (pres. 1979-80, lifetime bd. dir.), Wellesley Coll. Nat. Alumnae Assn. (bd. dirs., 1st v.p. 1977-80). Avocations: public speaking, art, gardening, reading, bicycling.

EDDEY, GARY ERWIN, physician, administrator, educator; b. Englewood, NJ, Dec. 10, 1951; s. Erwin Carnes and Emma (Bogart) E.; m. Ilene N. Eddey, July 31, 1976 (div.); children: John, AnnMichele, Emily. BS, U. Md., 1976; ScM, U. Pitts., 1978; MD, Cornell U., 1983. Diplomate Am. Bd. Pediats. Intern U. NC, Chapel Hill, 1983-84; resident NY Hosp.-Cornell U., NYC, 1984, chief resident in pediats., 1984; asst. prof. pediats. Cornell Med. Coll., 1986-88; clin. asst. prof. pediats. Columbia U., NYC, 1986-88; from clin. assoc. prof. to assoc. prof. pediats. NJ Med. Sch., Newark, 1997—; assoc. med. dir. Matheny Hosp., Peapack, NJ, 1990—, dir. comprehensive continuum of care, 2001, med. dir., 2005—; assoc. med. dir. Matheny Ctr. Medicine and Dentistry, Peapack, 2002—05; med. dir. Matheny Med. and Ednl. Ctr. (formerly Matheny Hosp.), Peapack, 2005—. Bd. dirs. Lesch-Nyhan Coun., Matheny. Contbr. articles to profl. jours. Recipient Outstanding Pediatrician award Morris County Office Hispanic Affairs, 1993. Mem. Am. Acad. Pediats., Am. Acad. Devel. Medicine, Internat. Soc. for the Study of Behavioural Phenotypes. Unitarian Universalist/Methodist. Achievements include research in culture of disability and medical education. Avocations: genealogy, history, creative writing, jazz, recording arts. Office: Matheny Hosp Main St Peapack NJ 07977 Home: 83 Skyline Dr Morristown NJ 07960 Home Phone: 973-993-8774; Office Phone: 908-234-0011. Business E-Mail: GaryEddey@matheny.org.

EDDLEMAN, FLOYD EUGENE, retired language educator; b. Mena, Ark., Dec. 3, 1930; s. Floyd Newton and Ruby Kate (Cannon) E. BSE, U. Cen. Ark., 1951; MA, U. Ark., 1955, PhD, 1961. Teaching asst. U. Ark., Fayetteville, 1953-55, 56-58; instr. U. Colo., Boulder, 1955-56; instr. English, Tex. Tech U., Lubbock, 1958-62, asst. prof., 1962-65, assoc. prof., 1965-75, prof., 1975-90, prof. emeritus, 1991—. Author: American Drama Criticism, 1976, 79, 84, 89, 92; co-editor: Almayer's Folly in the Cambridge Edit. of the Works of Joseph Conrad, 1994; contbr. articles to profl. jours. Sgt. US Army, 1951—53. Democrat. Mem. Christian Ch. (Disciples Of Christ). Avocations: travel, collecting bison art objects. Home: 1309 Cole Ave Mena AR 71953-3722

EDDLESTON, KIMBERLY ANN, management educator; b. Fall River, Mass., May 8, 1970; d. John George and Gloria Jean Rego; m. Robert Matthew Eddleston, Sept. 6, 1997; children: Evan Jay, Heidi Jeanne. BS, Bryant Coll., Smithfield, RI, 1988—92; cert. in Hotel Mgmt., Swiss Internat. Tng. Ctr., Neuchatel, 1989—90; MBA, Cornell U., Ithaca, NY, 1993—95; PhD, U. Conn., Storrs, 1996—2001. Instr. U. Conn., Storrs, 1999—2001; asst. prof. Northeastern U., Boston, 2001—. Asst. dir., Wolff family program in entrepreneurship U. Conn., Storrs, 1996—2001. Contbr. articles to profl. jours. Editl. bd. Group & Orgn. Mgmt., 2001—04. Mem.: Cornell Soc. Hotelmen, Acad. Mgmt. Achievements include research in the studies on managerial & entrepreneurial careers. Office: Northeastern Univ 319 Hayden Hall Boston MA 02115-5000 Office Phone: 617-373-4014. Business E-Mail: k.eddleston@neu.edu.

EDDY, CARL F., engineering educator; b. July 19, 1944; AAS in Electronics, Luzerne County Coll., Nanticoke, Pa., 1973; BS in Electronics, Edison State Coll., Trenton, NJ, 1985; attended, Millersville U., Pa., 1991—93. Cert. telecomm. engr., Austin, Tex., 1988. Sr. technician Bendix Corp., Mountaintop, Pa., 1967—72; instr. West Side Tech., Pringle, Pa., 1973—85; prof. Luzerne County CC, Nanticoke, Pa., 1988—. Mem.: Mensa, Nat. Assn. Radio Telecomm. Engr. (sr.). Office: 1333 S Prospect St Nanticoke PA 18634

EDDY, CHARLES ALAN, chiropractor; b. Kansas City, Mo., Feb. 20, 1948; s. Sam Albert and Ella Louise (Gani) E.; m. Donna Darlene Perry, Oct. 23, 1971. Student, U. Mo., Kansas City, 1967; D in Chiropractic, Cleveland Chiropractic, Kansas City, 1970. Diplomate Nat. Bd. Chiropractic Examiners. Pvt. practice, Kansas City, 1970—. Peer rev. bd. Blue Cross and Blue Shield, Kansas City, 1972; pres. hon. bd. govs. Bapt. Hosp., Kansas City, 1993-94; cons. Quality Corp., Overland Park, Kans., 1988. Res. officer Kansas City Police Dept., 1970—77, sgt., 1977—82, capt., 1982—94; vice chmn. Citizens Assn., 1995—98; mem. pub. improvement adv. com. City of Kansas City, 1997—98; city councilperson 6th Dist., 1999—2007; chmn. bd. Mid. Am. Reg. Coun., Kansas City, 2003—05, 1st v.p., 2001—02; bd. dirs. Econ. Devel. Coun., 1999—2007, 1st v.p., 2001—03; chmn. Mo. Total Transp. Com., 2003—07; candidate for City Coun. Kansas City, 1995; candidate for mayor, 2007; leader, profl. musician Chuck Eddy Band, Kansas City, 1964—. Mem. Am. Chiropractic Assn., Mo. State Chriopractic Assn., Mo. Dist. II Chiropractic Assn. (bd. dirs., v.p. 1998-2003), Cleve. Chiropractic Coll. (trustee 1990, vice chmn. 1992-03, chmn. 2003—), Cleve. Chiropractic Alumni Assn. (v.p. 1995-97, pres. 1997-99, bd. dirs. 1990—, amb.'s soc. 1983—, chmn. 1990-96, 2001-03, bd. dirs. Truman Med. Ctr.), Optimist Club of Landing (pres. 1980, lt. gov. Mo. dist. 1982), South Kansas City C. of C. (Sml. Bus. of Yr. award 1998), Am. Lebanon Syrian Men's Club (pres. 1988-91, chmn. bd. 1992), St. Andrews Soc. (drummer in pipe band), DeMolay Legion Hon. (sec. 1988, treas. 1990, vice-dean 1991, dean 1992), Pipes and Drums of Ararat (treas. 1977-90, pres. 1985, dir. 1989, 90), Elks, Shriners (Potentate of Ararat shrine temple 1999, publicity chmn. 1991-92), Royal Order Jesters, Order Quetzalcoatl, Rotary Club (Paul Harris fellow). Episcopalian. Avocations: photography, guns, stereo and video entertainment. Home: 406 W 109th St Kansas City MO 64114-4910 Office: 8301 State Line Rd Ste 108 Kansas City MO 64114-2019 Office Phone: 816-363-5311. Personal E-mail: dr.eddy@juno.com.

EDDY, DARLENE MATHIS, poet, educator; b. Elkhart, Ind., Mar. 19, 1937; d. William Eugene and Fern (Paulmer) Mathis; m. Spencer Livingston Eddy, Jr., May 23, 1964 (dec. May 1971). BA, Goshen Coll., Ind., 1959; MA, Rutgers U., New Brunswick. NJ, 1961, PhD, 1967. Instr., lectr. Douglass Coll. and Rutgers U., 1962-64, 66-67; asst. prof. English Ball State U., Muncie, Ind., 1967-70, assoc. prof., 1971-75, prof., 1975-99, poet-in-residence, 1989-93, prof. emerita, 1999. Whitinger lectr. Honors Coll., 1998-99; adj. prof. core program and coll. seminar program U. Notre Dame, 2001-; adj. prof. Eng. Goshen Coll., 2002-; cons., presenter in field. Author: The Worlds of King Lear, 1968, Leaf Threads, Wind Rhymes, 1985, Weathering, 1991, Portraits, 1992; poetry editor Forum, 1985-89; contbg. editor Snowy Egret, 1988-89; cons. editor Blue Unicorn, 1995—; founding editor The Hedge Row Press, 1995; contbr. articles to English Lang. Notes, Am. Lit., others; author numerous poems. Mem. commn. on the status of women in the profession, Nat. Coun. of Teachers of English, 1976-79; coord. Women's Studies program, 1976-82. Woodrow Wilson Nat. fellow, 1959-62, Notable Woodrow Wilson fellow, 1991, Rutgers U. grad. honors fellow, 1964-65; recipient numerous rsch., creative teaching and creative arts grants. Mem. AAUW, DAR, Soc. Mayflower Descs., Nat. League Am. Pen Women, League Women Voters. Home: 1840 Cobblestone Blvd Elkhart IN 46514

EDDY, DAVID MAXON, health policy and management advisor; BA, Stanford U., Calif., 1964, PhD with great distinction, 1978; MD, U. Va., 1968. Gen. surg. intern Stanford U. Med. Ctr., 1968-69, resident, postdoct. fellow cardiovascular surgery, 1969-71, acting asst. prof., 1976-78; asst. prof. dept. engrng.-econ. sys. Stanford U., 1978-80, prof., 1980-81; J. Alexander McMahon prof. health policy and mgmt. Duke U., 1986-90, prof. health policy and mgmt., 1980—95; dir. WHO Collaborating Ctr. for Rsch. in Cancer Policy, 1984-95. Sr. advisor health policy, mgmt. Kaiser Permanente So. Calif. Region, 1991—; columnist Jour. of the AMA, 1990—; spl. govt. employee Hillary Rodham Clinton's Health Care Task Force, 1993; expert adv. panel on cancer WHO, 1981-96; founder, dir. Archimedes, Inc., San Francisco, Calif.; cons. numerous cos., orgns. and assns. Author: A Manual for Assessing Health Practices and Designing Practice Policies, 1992, FAST*PRO: Software for Meta-Analysis by the Confidence Profile Method, 1992, The Synthesis of Statistical Evidence: meta-Analysis by the Confidence Profile Method, 1992, Common Screening Tests, 1991, Screening for Cancer: Theory, Analysis and Design, 1980, (Lanchester Prize, 1981), Clinical Decision Making: From Theory to Practice, 1996; contbr. articles to profl. jours. Recipient Sci. and Technol. Achievement award EPA, 1993, FHP Prize Internat. Soc. of Tech. Assessment in Health Care, 1991, USQA Quality Algorithm award, 1995, Novartis Outcomes Leadership award, 1997, Founders award Am. Coll. Med. Quality, 1998, Disting. Achievement award, CDC, 2005. Mem. Inst. of Medicine, Nat. Acad. Scis.

EDDY, DON, artist; b. Long Beach, Calif., Nov. 4, 1944; s. Myron and Ruth (Chase) Eddy King; m. Nancy Walker, June 12, 1967 (div. 1976); 1 child, Sarah. B.F.A., U. Hawaii, 1967, M.F.A., 1969. Artist, NYC. Subject of monographs: Don Eddy: The Resonance of Realism in the Art of Post War America, Virginia Anne Bonita, Internet Publ.; Conversations with Don Eddy, interviewer Lela Cempollin, Pub. Cleup Scarl, Padua, Italy; Don Eddy: The Art of Paradox, Donald Kuspit, 2002. One-man shows include Galerie Petit, Paris, 1973, Nancy Hoffman Gallery, NYC, 1974, 1976, 1979, 1983, 1986, 1990, 1992—94, 1996, 1998, 2000, 2002, 2005, 2006, Mitch Shaheen Gallery, Cleve., 1994, Molly Barnes Gallery, LA, 1970, 1971, French & Co., NYC, 1971, Huntington (W.Va.) Mus., 1996, Duke U. Mus. Art, 2000, Boca Raton Mus. Art, 2000, New Orleans Contemporary Art Ctr., 2000; exhibited in group shows U.S. and Europe; Represented in permanent collections Akron Art Inst., Cleve. Mus. Art, Fogg Art Mus., Harvard U., Utrecht Mus. Belgium, Whitney Mus. Am. Art, Met. Mus. Art, NYC, others. E-mail: artdoneddy@yahoo.com.

EDDY, DONALD DAVIS, language educator; b. Norfolk, Va., Apr. 19, 1929; s. Clarence Ford and Rebekah (Proctor Davis) E.; m. Edith Ann Quattlebaum, Dec. 20, 1954; children: Edith Evelyn, Elizabeth Nelson. BA, Dartmouth Coll., 1951; MA, PhD, U. Chgo.; MA (Munby fellow), Cambridge U., Eng., 1978. Prof. English Cornell U., Ithaca, NY, 1961-96, head dept. rare books univ. libr., 1968-89, prof. emeritus, 1996—. Works include A Bibliography of John Brown, 1971, Samuel Johnson: Book Reviewer in the Literary Magazine, 1979, Samuel Johnson, LL.D., 1983, Bibliography of Richard Hurd, 1999; editor John Brown, Essays on the Characteristics, 1969, Samuel Johnson and Periodical Literature, 16 vols., 1978-79, Sale Catalogues of the Librs. of Samuel Johnson, Hester Lynch Thrale (Mrs. Piozzi) and James Boswell, 1993. Served with USN, 1952-55. Mem. MLA, Bibliog. Soc., Oxford Bibliog. Soc., Cambridge Bibliog. Soc., Bibliog. Soc. Am., Bibliog. Soc. U. Va. Clubs: Grolier; Athenaeum (London); The Johnsonians. Episcopalian. Home: 240 Renwick Dr Ithaca NY 14850-2142 E-mail: dde2@cornell.edu.

EDDY, GLADYS LOUISE, retired educational administrator; b. Castle Rock, Colo., Dec. 25, 1915; d. William Adam and Jessie Louise (Cozens) Shellabarger; m. Willard Oscar Eddy, Aug. 21, 1938; children: Sandra Carol, William Radford. BSBA, U. Denver, 1937. Asst. Colo. State U., Ft. Collins, 1937—42, sect. to pres., 1945—46, instr., 1957—62, 1967—69, asst. prof. bus., 1979—84, asst. to dean, Coll. Bus., 1984—2007; instr. U.S. Army Air Force, Ft. Collins, 1942—43; tchr. Poudre R-1 Sch. Dist., Ft. Collins, Colo., 1957—62; ret., 2007. Cons. in field; pres., bd. dirs. Colo. Assn. Sch. Bds., Denver, 1973-83; mem. Nat. Adv. Coun. on Vocat. Edn., Washington, 1982-84. Mem. Poudre R-1 Bd. Edn., Ft. Collins, 1971-83, Colo. State Bd. Edn., Denver, 1987-90; bd. dirs. Colo. Parks and Recreation Found., 1984-90; mem. scholar com. Griffin Found., 1996—. Mem. PEO, Mortar Bd. (nat. program dir. 1982), Ft. Collins Country Club, Order Eastern Star, Delta Kappa Gamma, Sigma Kappa. Republican. Episcopalian. Avocation: travel. Home: 509 Remington St Fort Collins CO 80524-3022

EDDY, JOHN JOSEPH, diplomat; b. Lakewood, Ohio, Jan. 8, 1933; s. John Ezekiel and Pauline Edna (Ryan) E.; m. Armonia Badenes, Feb. 14, 1967; children— John Louis, Christopher Robert, William Francis, Isabel Ann (dec.) AB, Boston Coll., 1960; MA, Fletcher Sch. of Law and Diplomacy, 1961; student, Nat. Def. U., 1979-80. Joined Fgn. Service, Dept. State, 1966; asst. comml. attache Am. Embassy, Caracas, Venezuela, 1966-69, comml. attache San Salvador, El Salvador, 1970-71, first sec., comml. attache Bogota, Colombia, 1971-74, counselor for econ. and comml. affairs Nairobi, Kenya, 1974-77, dep. chief of mission Bridgetown, Barbados, 1977-79; dir. Office Regional Econ. Policy, Bur. Inter-Am. Affairs, Dept. State, 1980-81; consul gen. Am. consulate gen., Dhahran, Saudi Arabia, 1983-87, Am. Consulate Gen., Bombay, 1987-90; sr. spl. asst. to dir. gen. Fgn. Svc., Dept. State, Washington, 1991-92; sr. insp. Dept. State, 1992-94, ret., 1994, cons., 1994—. Served with USAF, 1952-56, Korea. Roman Catholic. Office: Dept State OIG ISP Rm 930 (SA-39) 1700 N Moore St Arlington VA 22209 Home: 252 Forest Ln Rochester VT 05767

EDDY, KELLY J., history educator; b. Lansing, Mich., Aug. 2, 1973; d. Garry J. and Judith K. Eddy. BA, Western Mich. U., 1996; MA, Marygrove Coll., 2001. Cert. tchr. Mich. Tchr. Livonia (Mich.) Pub. Schs., 1997—. Recipient Founders Night honoree, Livonia PTSA, 2006; Medallion scholar, Western Mich. U., 1992—96, Landmarks in Am. History grantee, NEH, 2005—07. Mem.: Nat. Coun. Social Studies (assoc.). Democrat. Avocations: reading, writing, travel. Home Phone: 734-254-0371. Personal E-mail: keddy@comcast.net. Business E-Mail: keddy@livonia.k12.mi.us.

EDDY-JOHNSON, DEANNA M., home health care advocate; b. Bklyn., Aug. 26, 1950; d. Charles Jess and Virginia Fern (Hoelscher) Deck; m. Dennis R. Eddy (div.); children: Denny R. Eddy, Ginger Deann Spillers. Degree in computer programming, Parkland Jr. Coll., Champaign, Ill., 1983; degree in real estate, Parkland Jr. Coll., 1985, nursing cert., 1990. CEO Jenn Swing Co., Urbana, Ill., 1993—97; ptnr. PDC Entertainment Ptnrs., 2006—. Inventor Jenn Swing, 1st full body accessible swing, 1996, The Cubby, toddler swing, 2004; author: Idea to Financial Success, 2003, Patty Panda Joins the Circus, 2005; lyricist I Want to Rock with you Jesus, 2005. Recipient Sec. award, Ambucs Assn., Urbana, 1996. Republican. Baptist. Avocations: walking, bicycling, concerts, plays. Home: 306 Dodson Dr E Urbana IL 61802 E-mail: djohns1105@mchsi.com.

EDELCUP, NORMAN SCOTT, management and financial consultant; b. Chgo., May 8, 1935; s. Irving L. and Pauline (Bolz) Edelcup. BS in Bus. Adminstrn, Northwestern U., 1957. CPA Fla., Ill. Sr. accountant Arthur Andersen & Co., Chgo., 1957-62; sec.-treas. Acme Printing Ink Co., Chgo., 1962-65; accountant, asst. to chmn. Commonwealth Edison Co., Chgo., 1965-68; sr. v.p., vice-chmn. bd. Keller Industries, Miami, Fla., 1968-76; v.p., treas. Avatar Holdings (formerly GAC Corp.), 1976-80, exec. v.p., treas., chief fin. officer, dir., mem. exec. com., 1980-83; pres., treas., dir. Avatar Properties Inc. (formerly GAC Properties, Inc.), 1976-83, Avatar Properties Credit (formerly GAC Properties Credit, Inc.), 1976-83; vice chmn., chief operating officer Nat. Banking Corp. Fla., Miami, 1983-84; chmn. treas. Scroll Casual Inc., 1983-84; chmn. Fla. Powder Coatings, Inc., Confidata Corp., 1983-87; chmn., treas. First United Leasing Corp., 1983-86; ptnr. E&H Assocs., 1983-91; chmn. Item Processing Am. Inc., Miami, 1987-98. Sr. v.p., dir. Fla. Savs. Bancorp, Pinecrest, Fla., 2001—; bd. dirs. Valhi Inc., Baron Asset Fund. Mayor City of Sunny Isles Beach, Fla., 2003; bd. dirs. Mt. Sinai Med. Ctr. Found., 2003. With AUS, 1958—60. Mem. Am. Inst. CPA's, Fla. Inst. CPA's, Ill. Inst. CPA's, Greater Miami C. of C. (trustee 1979-83). Lodges: Kiwanis. Home: 244 Atlantic Isle Sunny Isles Beach FL 33160 Office: Sunny Isles Beach City Hall 18070 N Collins Ave Sunny Isles Beach FL 33160 Office Phone: 305-947-0606. Personal E-mail: nsedelcup@aol.com.

EDELHEIT, LEWIS S., research physicist; b. Chgo., Aug. 24, 1942; m. Susan Wershkoff, 1965; children: David, Dena. BS in Engrng. and Physics, U. Ill., 1964, MS in Physics, 1965, PhD in Physics, 1969. Physicist GE R&D Ctr., Schenectady, NY, 1969—76; mgr. Applied Sci. & Diagnostic Imaging Lab. GE Med. Sys., Milw., 1976—80; mgr. computed tomography prodn. engrng. GE Corp. R&D, Schenectady, 1980—82, gen. mgr. dept. engrng., 1982—83, gen. mgr. dept. computed tomography programs, 1983—86; pres., CEO Quantum Med. Sys., 1986—91; mgr. electronics sys. rsch. ctr. GE Corp. R&D, Schenectady, 1991—92, sr. v.p., 1992—2001; ret., 2001. Bd. dir. Silicon Graphics, Inc., Mountain View, Calif., 2002—, Sonic Innovations, Inc., Pacific Northwest Nat. Lab. Bd. trustees Rensselaer Polytechnic Inst., Troy, NY, 1995—2002; adv. bd. OVP Venture Partners. Fellow: Am. Physics Soc. (George E. Pake prize 2001); mem.: NAE, Indsl. Rsch. Inst. (named as the Medalist 2003), Sigma Xi. Achievements include research in medical imaging systems, computerized imaging systems. Office: GE Corp R&D Ctr Bldg K1 Rm 5A1 One Rsch Cir Niskayuna NY 12309

EDELMAN, ALAN IRWIN, lawyer; b. Poughkeepsie, NY, June 14, 1958; s. Edwyn Herman and Shirley Frances (Kandel) E.; m. Erica Joy Schwartz, Aug. 16, 1981; children: Leah Hanit, Avram Natan, Samuel Aaron. BA, Cornell U., 1980; JD, Boston U., 1983. Bar: D.C. 1983, U.S. Dist. Ct. D.C. 1985, U.S. Supreme Ct. 1991. Atty. enforcement div. SEC, Washington, 1983-86, atty. Office of Gen. Counsel, 1986-87; counsel U.S. Senate Permanent Subcom. on Investigations, Washington, 1987-97, U.S. Senate Com. on Govtl. Affairs, 1997-99; trial atty. divsn. enforcement Commodity Futures Trading Commn., Washington, 1999—. Edward F. Hennessy scholar Boston U., 1983. Mem. ABA, Fed. Bar Assn. Office: Commodity Futures Trading Commn Three Lafayette Centre 1155 21st St NW Washington DC 20581-0001

EDELMAN, DANIEL JOSEPH, public relations executive; b. NYC, July 3, 1920; s. Selig and Selma (Pfeiffer) Edelman; m. Ruth Rozumoff, Sept. 3, 1953; children: Richard, Renee, John. Grad., Columbia U., 1940; MS, 1941. Reporter Poughkeepsie (N.Y.) newspapers, UPI, 1941—42; news writer CBS, 1946—47; staff mem. Edward Gottlieb & Assocs., 1947; pub. rels. dir. Toni Co., Chgo., 1948—52; founder, chmn. 45 offices Daniel J. Edelman, Inc. (Edelman, Zeno, Blue Advt., Strategy One Rsch., Edelman Interactive Svcs.), Chgo., 1952—. Chmn. vis. com. U. Chgo. Libr., 1976; chmn. sustaining fellows individual campaign Chgo. Art Inst., 1982; bd. dirs. Lyric Opera, Chgo., 1995—2003; dir. Comm. for Econ. Growth of Israel, The Chgo. Project for Violence Prevention. With US Army, 1942—46. Named Pub. Rels. Profl. of Yr., Pub. Rels. News, 1993; named to Chgo. Bus. Hall of Fame, Jr. Achievement, 1998, Entrepeneurship Hall of Fame, U. Ill., Chgo., 2001; recipient Disting. Alumnus award, Columbia U., 1988, John Jay award, 1990, Agy. of Yr., Inside PR Mag., 1993, Lifetime Achievement All-Star award, 1998, Tom Mosser award, St. Bonaventure U., 1998, First award, China Pub. Rels. Assn., 1999, First Lifetime Achievement award, Publicity Club Chgo., 2003, Atlas award for Internat. Pub. Rels., Pub. Res. Soc. Am., 2003, Agy. of the Yr. award, Holmes Report, 2003, 1st Annual Dean's Pub. Svc. award, Columbia U. Grad. Sch. Journalism, 2005. Fellow: Pub. Rels. Soc. Am. (past chmn., counselor sect., Top Gun Career Achievement award 1998, Gold Anvil award for outstanding contbns. to pub. rels. profession 1999, 35 Silver Anvil awards); mem.: Pub. Rels. Seminar, Arthur Page Soc. (Hall of Fame 1997), Chief Execs. Orgn., Young Pres. Orgn. (chmn. Chgo. chpt. 1963), Casino Club, Chgo. Club, Mid-Am. Club, Harmonie Club, Std. Club, Phi Beta Kappa (dir., Living Treasure award Chgo. area chpt. 2004). Jewish. Home: 1301 N Astor St Chicago IL 60610 Office: Edelman Aon Ctr 200 E Randolph Dr Chicago IL 60601-6436 Home Phone: 312-943-4278; Office Phone: 312-240-2600. Business E-Mail: dan.edelman@edelman.com.

EDELMAN, ERIC STEVEN, federal agency administrator, former ambassador; m. Patricia Davis; children: Alexander, Stephanie, Terrence, Robert. BA in History and Govt., Cornell U., 1972; PhD in U.S. Diplomatic History, Yale U., 1981. With U.S. Fgn. Svc., U.S. Middle East Delegation to West Bank/Gaza Autonomy Talks, 1980-81, watch officer State Dept. Ops. Ctr., 1981-82, staff officer Secretariat Staff, 1982, spl. asst. to Sec. of State George P. Shultz, 1982-84; mem. Office of Soviet Affairs US Dept. State, Moscow, 1984-86, head external polit. sect., 1987-89, spl. asst. to under sec. for polit. affairs, 1989-90; asst. dep. under sec. for Soviet/East European Affairs US Dept. Def., 1990-93; dep. to spl. advisor to sec US Dept. State, 1993, dep. chief of mission Prague, Czech Republic, 1994-96, exec. asst. to dep. sec. Washington, 1996-98, US amb. to Finland Helsinki, 1998—2001, US amb. to Turkey Ankara, 2003—05; prin. dep. asst. to v.p. for nat. security affairs The White House, Washington, 2001—03; under sec. for policy US Dept. Def., Washington, 2005—. Recipient Sec. of Def. award for disting. Civilian Svc., 1993, Superior Honor award State Dept., 1989, 90, 95. Office: US Dept Def 2000 Def Pentagon Rm 3E634 Washington DC 20301

EDELMAN, GERALD MAURICE, biochemist, neuroscientist, educator; b. NYC, July 1, 1929; s. Edward and Anna (Freedman) Edelman; m. Maxine Morrison, June 11, 1950; children: Eric, David, Judith. BS, Ursinus Coll., 1950, ScD, 1974; MD, U. Pa., 1954, DSc, 1973; PhD, Rockefeller U., 1960; MD (hon.), U. Siena, Italy, 1974; DSc (hon.), Gustavus Adolphus Coll., 1975, Williams Coll., 1976, U. Paris, 1989; LSc (hon.), U. Cagliari, 1989; DSc (hon.), Georgetown U., 1989, U. degli Studi di Napoli, 1990, Tulane U., 1991, U. Miami, 1995, Adelphi U., 1995, U. Bologna, 1998, U. Minn., 2000; MD (hon.), U de A Coruña, Spain, 2000. Med. house officer Mass. Gen. Hosp., 1954—55; asst. physician hosp. of Rockefeller U., 1957—60, mem. faculty, 1960—92, assoc. dean grad. studies, 1963—66, prof., 1966—74, Vincent Astor disting. prof., 1974—92; mem. faculty and chmn. dept. neurobiology Scripps Rsch. Inst., La Jolla, Calif., 1992—. Mem. biophysics and biophys. chemistry study sect. NIH, 1964—67; mem. Sci. Council Ctr. for Theoretical Studies, 1970—72, assoc., sci. chmn. Neurosciences Research Program, 1980—, dir. Neuroscis. Inst., 1981—; mem. adv. bd. Basel Inst. Immunology, 1970—77, chmn., 1975—77; non-resident fellow, trustee Salk Inst., 1973—85; bd. overseers Faculty Arts and Scis. U. Pa., 1976—83; trustee, mem. adv. com. Carnegie Inst., Washington, 1980—87; bd. govs. Weizman Inst. Sci., 1971—87, mem. emeritus; researcher structure of antibodies, molecular and devel. biology. Author: The Mindful Brain, 1978, Neural Darwinism, 1987, Topobiology, 1988, The Remembered Present, 1989, Bright Air, Brilliant Fire, 1992, A Universe of Consciousness: How Matter Becomes Imagination, 2000, Wider than the Sky: The Phenomenal Gift of Consciousness, 2004, Second Nature: Brain Science and Human Knowledge, 2006. Trustee Rockefeller Bros. Found., 1972—82. Capt. M.C. US Army, 1955—57. Recipient Spencer Morris award U. Pa., U. Pa., 1954, Ann. Alumni award, Ursinus Coll., 1969, Nobel prize for physiology or medicine, 1972, Albert Einstein Commemorative award, Yeshiva U., 1974, Buchman Meml. award, Calif. Inst. Tech., 1975, Rabbi Shai Shacknai meml. prize, Hebrew U.-Hadassah Med. Sch., Jerusalem, 1977, Regents medal Excellence, N.Y. State, 1984, Hans Neurath prize, U. Wash., 1986, Sesquicentennial Commemorative award, Nat. Libr. Medicine, 1986, Cécile and Oskar Vogt award, U. Dusseldorf, 1988, Disting. Grad. award, U. Pa., 1990, Personnalité de l'année, Paris, 1990, Warren Triennial Prize award, Mass. Gen. Hosp., 1992, C.V. Ariens-Kappers medal, 1999, medal of the Presidency of the Italian Republic, 1999, medaille de la Ville de Paris, 2002, Cátedra Santiago Grisolia prize, Spain, 2003, Caianiello Internat. award, INNS, 2003, Calabria award, Italy, 2003. Fellow: AAAS, N.Y. Acad. Medicine, N.Y. Acad. Scis.; mem.: NAS, Am. Chem. Soc. (Eli Lilly award biol. chemistry 1965), Century Assn., Coun. Fgn. Rels., Soc. Developmental Biology, Acad. Scis. of Inst. France (fgn.), Am. Soc. Cell Biology, Japanese Biochem. Soc. (hon.), Pharm. Soc. Japan (hon.), Am. Acad. Arts and Scis., Harvey Soc. (pres. 1976—77), Genetics Soc. Am., Am. Assn. Immunologists, Am. Soc. Biol. Chemists, Am. Philos. Soc., Cosmos Club, Alpha Omega Alpha, Sigma Xi, Phi Beta Kappa. Office: Scripps Rsch Inst Dept Neurobiol SBR-14 10550 N Torrey Pines Rd La Jolla CA 92037-1000

EDELMAN, HENDRIK, library and information science professor; b. Wageningen, Netherlands, Nov. 27, 1937; came to U.S., 1967; s. Cornelis Hendrik and Johanna (van Werkhoven) E.; m. Antoinette M. Kania; children: Stijn Willem, Mark Bastiaan, Kees Maarten. MLS, George Peabody Coll., 1969. With Martinus Nijhoff (Pubs. & Booksellers), Netherlands, 1958-65, D. Reidel Pub. Co., Netherlands, 1965-67; bibliographer Vanderbilt U., 1967-70; asst. dir. Cornell U. Libraries, Ithaca, NY, 1970-78; libr. Rutgers-State U. N.J., New Brunswick, 1979-85, prof. libr. and info. sci., 1985—2000. Adj. prof. Palmer Sch. Libr. and Info. Sci., L.I. U., 2002—07; chmn. bd. Ctr. Book Rsch., U. Scranton, 1983-88; chmn. bd. Rsch. Libr. Group, Inc., 1982-83; bd. dirs. Book Industry Study Group, 1977-84; USIA/ALA Libr./Book fellow, U. Surinam, 1992-93; editl. mktg. cons. Am. European pubs. (booksellers); acad. libr. cons.; chmn. edn. com. Netherland Am. Found., 1993-2002; chmn. adv. bd. Rutgers Inst. Jazz Studies, 2001—. Author: The Dutch Language Press in America, 1986, Libraries and Information Science in the Electronic Age, 1986, A History of Religious Publishing and Bookselling in the United States and Canada, 1640-1985, 1987, Marketing to Libraries for the New Millennium, 2002, The Netherland Club of New York, An Illustrated History, 2003; contbr. articles, revs. to profl. jours. Mem. ALA, Bibliog. Soc. Am., Am. Antiquarian Soc., Grolier Club, Beta Phi Mu. Home: 126 Elm St Milton NH 03851 Personal E-mail: edelmanh@earthlink.net.

EDELMAN, JANICE, artist, educator; b. Phila., Apr. 13, 1933; d. Samuel and Anna (Finkelstein) Fishman; 1 child, Susan Helfrich. Degree, Art Inst. Phila., 1956; studied with, Henry Hensche, Provincetown, Mass., 1957, Boris Blai, Phila., 1979—80; BA, Thomas Edison State U., NJ, 2006. Cert.

art tchr., Pa. Advt. illustrator John Wanamaker, Phila., 1954-66; advt. art dir. Strawbridge & Clothier, Phila., 1967-76; comml. art instr. Hussian Sch. of Art, Phila., 1976-77; head of art dept. Montgomery County Vocat. Sch., Upper Moreland, Pa., 1978-79; watercolor instr. Woodmere Art Mus., Phila., 1991—. Docent Woodmere Art Mus., 1989-91; judge juror Glassboro State Coll., NJ, 1992, Norristown Art League, 1999; bd. dirs. Friends of Moore Coll. of Art, Phila., 1977; workshop leader Pa. Acad. Fine Arts; watercolor instr. Louwer Moreland high Sch., 2003—, Penny Pack Trust, 2003—; lectr. in field. Exhibited in group shows at Fashion Group of Phila., 1955 (Fine Arts Gala award, 1955, 1st prize, 1957), 1957, Phila. Club Advt. Women 12th Ann., 1966, 1967 (1st prize for layout, 1966, for art-layout, 1967), 13thAnn., 1974 (1st prize for art-layout, 1974, 1975), Artist Guild of Delaware Valley 25th Ann., 1975 (Bronze award, 1975), Art Dirs. Club of Phila. 39th Ann., 1979 (2 awards for excellence, layout design, 1979), Am. Coll., 1985, Phila. Water Color Club 67th Ann., 1985, 70th Ann., 1988, 71st Ann., 1989, 74th Ann., 1992, 75th Ann., 1993 (award of excellence, 1988, show chmn., 1992), Watercolor Soc. Ala. 45th Ann., 1986, Oreland Art Ctr. Ann., 1986 (1st prize in watercolor, 1986), Artilleries Gallery, 1987, Perkiomen Valley Retirement Cmty., 1987, Charlotte Watercolor Soc., 1987, Woodmere Art Mus. 47th Ann., 1987, 48th Ann., 1988, 49th Ann., 1989, 52d Ann., 1992, 56th Ann., 1996, Abington Art Ctr. Ann., 1988, Pa. Watercolor Soc. 10th Ann., 1988, 11th Ann., 1989 (Grumbacher award, 1988), 20th Ann., 1999, Salmagundi Club 11th Ann., NY, 1988, 16th Ann., 1993 (Merit award, 1988), Yellow Spring Art Show, 1989, Art Inst. Phila., 1989, Phila. Art Show, 1989, 1990, Balt. Watercolor Soc., 1990, Susquehanna Art Soc. 84th Biennial, 1990, Barn Studio Gallery, 1990, Greater Harrisburg Arts Coun., Pa., 1993, Springfield Art League 74th Nat., 1993, Artist Guild Nat., Scottbluff, Nebr., 1993, Batavia Soc. Artists 9th Nat., NY, 1993, Watercolor Art Soc., Houston, 1994, W.Va. Water Color Soc., 1994, Watercolor West XXVI Ann., Brea, Calif., 1994, Main Line Arts Festival, Haverford, Pa., 1994, Nat. Watercolor Soc., Calif., 1995, Pitts. Watercolor Soc. Ann., 1995, Bald Eagle Art League Nat., 1995, N.W. N.Mex. Arts Coun., 1997 (award), Woodmere Art Mus., 2003, San Diego Watercolor Soc., 2007, one-woman shows include Woodmere Art Mus., Phila., 1997, Phila. Water Color Club 98th juried exhbn., 1998, Pa. Watercolor Soc. Ann., 1999, Atlantic City Art Mus., 1999, Krasdale Gallery, NY, 1999—2003, Beth Or Congregation, Springhouse, Pa., 2003, Represented in permanent collections Woodmere Art Mus., Two Watercolors, Woodmere Art Must. Chmn. art study group, exec. sec. Ret. Execs. and Profls., Cheltenham, Pa., 1999—; juror Norristown Art League, 1999, art lectr., 1999—2003; mem. mus. com. Keneseth Israel Congregation. Mem. Am. Watercolor Soc. (assoc.), Nat. Watercolor Soc. (assoc.), Pa. Watercolor Soc., Phila. Watercolor Soc., Art Dirs. Club Phila. (pres. 1978-80), Phila. Water Color Club (v.p. 1993-94, lectr. and slide presenter on art and artists, 2000-2007), Art Goes Sch. (lower Moreland chpt.). Jewish. Avocations: painting, travel, reading, creative cooking. Home: 3505 Hale Rd Huntingdon Valley PA 19006-3230 Personal E-mail: jan.e1@verizon.net.

EDELMAN, JOEL, health facility administrator; b. Chgo., Mar. 24, 1931; s. Maurice B. and Ethel J. (Newman) E.; m. Beth L. Sommers, July 31, 1955; children: Peter J., Ann Elizabeth, Deborah S. BA in Spl. Edn., U. Mich., 1952; JD, DePaul U., 1960. Bar: Ill. 1961. Program dir. Chgo. Heart Assn., 1955-61; staff atty. Michael Reese Hosp. and Med. Center, Chgo., 1961-70, exec. v.p., 1971-73; dir. Ill. Dept. Pub. Aid, 1973-74; exec. dir. Ill. Legis. Adv. Com. on Pub. Aid, 1974-77; pres. Rose Med. Ctr., Denver, 1979-95; prin., sr. v.p. Frontier Holdings, Inc., Englewood, Colo., 1995—. Asst. prof. dept. preventive medicine U. Colo.; U.; dir. office legal affairs Am. Hosp. Assn., 1970 Contbr. articles to profl. jours. Served with AUS, 1955. Mem. Soc. Hosp. Attys. (charter) Home: 3156 S Hills Ct Denver CO 80210-6830

EDELMAN, JUDITH H., architect; b. Bklyn., Sept. 16, 1923; d. Abraham and Frances (Israel) Hochberg; m. Harold Edelman, Dec. 26, 1947; children: Marc, Joshua. Student, Conn. Coll., 1940—41, NYU, 1941—42; BArch, Columbia U., 1946. Designer, drafter Huson Jackson, NYC, 1948-58; Schermerhorn traveling fellow, 1950; pvt. practice, 1958-60; ptnr. Edelman & Salzman, NYC, 1960-79, Edelman Partnership (Archs.), NYC, 1979—2002, Edelman, Sultan, Knox, Wood /Archs. LLP, NYC, 2002—. Adj. prof. Sch. Architecture CUNY, 1972-76, vis. lectr. grad. program in environ. psychology, 1977, 77; vis. lectr. Washington U., St. Louis, 1974, U. Oreg., 1974, MIT, 1975, Pa. State U., 1977, Rensselaer Poly. Inst., 1977, Columbia U., 1979; First Claire Watson Forrest Meml. lectr. U. Oreg., U. Calif., Berkeley, U. So. Calif., 1982. Prin. works include Restoration of St. Mark's Ch. in the Bowery, N.Y.C., 1970-82, Two Bridges Urban Renewal Area Housing, 1970-96, Jennings Hall Sr. Citizens Housing, Bklyn., 1980, Goddard Riverside Elderly Housing and Cmty. Ctr., N.Y.C., 1983, Columbus Green Apartments, N.Y.C., 1987, Chung Pak Bldg., N.Y.C., 1992, Child Care Ctr., Queens, N.Y., 1999. Recipient Bard 1st honor award City Club N.Y., 1969, Bard award of merit, 1975, 82, award for design excellence HUD, 1970, 1st prize Nat. Trust for Hist. Preservation, 1983, award of merit Mcpl. Art Soc. N.Y., 1983, Pub. Svc. award Settlement Housing Fund, 1983, Women of Vision award NOW, 1989, 1st prize for design excellence C. of C., Borough of Queens, N.Y., 1989, Best in Srs.' Housing award Nat. Assn. Home Builders, 1993, Hamilton-Madison House Cmty. Svc. award, 1997. Fellow AIA (dir. N.Y. chpt., chmn. commn. on archtl. edn. 1971-73, chmn. nat. task force on women in architecture 1974-75, v.p. N.Y. chpt. 1975-77, chmn. ethics com. 1975-77, Residential Design award 1969, Pioneer in Housing award 1990, N.Y. State Assn. Archs.-AIA Honor award 1975, Design Merit award N.Y. chpt. 2005); mem. Alliance of Women in Architecture (founding, mem. steering com. 1972-74), Archs. for Social Responsibility (mem. exec. com. 1982-85), Columbia Archtl. Alumni Assn. (bd. dirs. 1968-71). Home: 37 W 12th St New York NY 10011-8502 Office: Edelman Sultan Knox Wood 100 Lafayette St Ste 204 New York NY 10013 Office Phone: 212-431-4901. Personal E-mail: judithedelman@mac.com. Business E-Mail: jedelman@edelmansultan.com.

EDELMAN, LAUREN B., sociologist, law educator; d. Murray J. and Bacia Edelman. JD, Boalt Hall, 1986; PhD, Stanford U., 1986. Asst. to assoc. prof. U. Wis., Madison, 1986—96; Agnes Roddy Robb prof. law and prof. sociology U. Calif., Berkeley, 1996—. Fellow, Guggenheim Found., 2000, Ctr. for Advanced Study in the Behavioral Scis., 2003—04, 2005—06. Mem.: Am. Sociol. Assn. (chair, sociology of law sect. 1993—94, Dist. Scholarship award 1995), Law and Soc. Assn. (pres. 2002—03). Achievements include research in analyses of relationship between employment law and organizational governance. Office: JSP Program/ UC Berkeley 2240 Piedmont Ave Berkeley CA 94720-2150 Home Phone: 510-558-0923; Office Phone: 510-642-4038. Office Fax: 510-642-2951. Business E-Mail: ledelman@law.berkeley.edu.

EDELMAN, MARIAN WRIGHT, not-for-profit developer, lawyer; b. Bennettsville, SC, June 6, 1939; d. Arthur J. and Maggie (Bowen) Wright; m. Peter B. Edelman, July 14, 1968; children: Joshua, Jonah, Ezra. Merrill scholar, Univs. Paris, Geneva, 1958-59; BA, Spelman Coll., 1960; LLB, Yale U., 1963, LLD (hon.), Smith Coll., 1969, Lowell Tech. U., 1975, Williams Coll., 1978, Columbia U., U. Pa., Amherst Coll., St. Joseph's Coll.; DHL (hon.), Lesley Coll., 1975, Trinity Coll., Washington, Russell Sage Coll., 1978, Syracuse U., Coll. New Rochelle, 1979, Swarthmore Coll., 1980, SUNY Old Westbury, Northeastern U., 1981, Bard Coll., 1982, U. Mass., 1983, Hunter Coll., U. So. Maine, SUNY, Albany, 1984, Bates Coll., Maryville Coll., Bank St., 1986, Claremont Grad Sch., Lincoln U., Georgetown U., Chgo. Theol. Coll., 1987, Wheaton Coll., Tulane U., Grinnell Coll. Brandeis U., Wheelock Coll., Dartmouth Coll., U. S.C., U. N.C., Grad. Ctr. CUNY, U. Wis. Milw., 1988, Interdenom. Theol. Ctr., Hofstra U., Tufts U., Borough Manhattan Community Coll., Wesleyan U., Calif. State U. L.A., Dillard U., U. Md., U. Miami, 1989, Howard U., Beloit Coll., Queens Coll., Am. U., New Sch. of Social Rsch., Coll. of Notre Dame, DePaul U., 1990, Beaver Coll., Fordham U., Simmons Coll., Hamline U., Clark U., Harvard U., Union Coll., 1991, Tuskegee U., Washington U. St. Louis, Hood Coll., Duke U., Mercy Coll., 1992, Princeton U., U. Ill., Calif. State U. San Francisco, Wittenberg Coll., Shaw U., So. Meth. U., 1993, Brown U., U. Balt., Ea. Conn. State U., U. Notre Dame, 1994. Bar: D.C., Miss., Mass. Staff atty. NAACP Legal Def. and Ednl. Fund, Inc., NYC, 1963-64, dir. Jackson, Miss., 1964-68; Congl. and fed. liaison Poor People's Campaign, summer 1968; partner Washington Research Project of So. Center for Pub. Policy, 1968-73; dir. Harvard U. Center for Law and Edn., 1971-73; pres., founder Children's Def. Fund, 1973—. Author: The Measure of Our Success: A Letter To My Children and Yours, 1992, Families in Peril, 1987. Mem. exec. com. Student Non-Violent Coordinating Com., 1961-63; mem. adv. coun. Martin Luther King Jr. Meml. Libr.; mem. adv. bd. Hampshire Coll.; mem. Presdl. Commn. on Missing in Action, 1977, Presdl. Commn. on Internat. Yr. of Child, 1979, Presdl. Commn. on Agenda for 80's, 1980; bd. dirs. NAACP Legal Def. and Ednl. Fund; trustee Spelman Coll., Carnegie Coun. on Children, 1972-77, Martin Luther King Jr. Meml. Ctr.; mem. Yale U. Corp., 1971-77, Aetna Found., Nat. Commn. on Children, 1989—; bd. dirs. Aetna Life Casualty Found., Citizens for Constitutional Concerns, US. com. UNICEF, Robin Hood Found., Aaron Diamond Found., Nat. Alliance Business, City Lights, Leadership Conf. Civil Rights, Skadden Fellowship Found., Parents as Tchrs. Nat. Ctr., Inc.; U.S. rep. UNICEF; active U.S. Olympic Com. Named one of Outstanding Young Women of Am., 1966, 100 Most Influential Black Americans, Ebony mag., 2006; recipient Mademoiselle mag. award, 1965, Louise Waterman Wise award, 1970, Washington of Yr. award, 1979, Whitney M. Young award, 1979, Profl. of Yr. award Black Ent., 1979, Leadership award Nat. Women's Polit. Caucus, 1980, Black Womens Forum award, 1980, medal Columbia Tchrs. Coll., Barnard Coll., 1984, Eliot award Am. Pub. Health Assn., John W. Gardner Leadership award of Ind. Sector, Pub. Svc. Achievement award Common Cause, Compostela award Cathedral St. James, 1987, MacArthur prize fellow, 1985, Albert Schweitzer Humanitarian prize Johns Hopkins U., 1987. Philip Hauge Ahelson award AAAS, 1988, Hubert Humphrey Civil Rights award, AFL-CIO award, 1989, Radcliffe Coll. medal, 1989, Fordham Stein prize, 1989, Gandhi Peace award, 1990, M. Carey Thomas award, Robie award for humanitarianism, Essence award, numerous others; hon. fellow U. Pa. Law Sch. Mem. Phi Beta Kappa (hon.), Inst. Medicine. Office: Children's Def Fund 25 E St NW Washington DC 20001-1522

EDELMAN, NORMAN HERMAN, dean, medical educator, academic administrator; b. NYC, May 21, 1937; s. Irving H. and Pearl Ruth (Solomon) E.; m. Ida Nadel, June 1959; children: David, Ruth, Deborah. AB, Bklyn. Coll., 1957; MD, NYU, 1961. Diplomate Am. Bd. Internal Medicine, Am. Bd. Pulmonary Diseases. Intern NYU Med. Sch., NYC, 1961-62, resident, 1962-63; rsch. fellow NIH, Balt., 1963-65; vis. fellow Columbia U., Presbyn. Med. Ctr., Balt., 1965-67; rsch. assoc. Michael Reese Med. Ctr., Chgo., 1967-69; asst. prof. medicine U. Pa. Sch. Medicine, Phila., 1969-72; prof. medicine, chief pulmonary medicine Robert Wood Johnson Med. Sch., U. Medicine and Dentistry of NJ, New Brunswick, NJ, 1972-95, dean, 1988-95; prof. preventive medicine and physiology and biophysics SUNY, Stony Brook, 1996—, dean Sch. Medicine, 1996—2005, v.p. Health Sci. Ctr., 1996—2006. Cons. for sci. Am. Lung Assn., NYC, 1984—; mem. pulmonary disease adv. com. NIH, 1984-88. Contbr. articles, abstracts to profl. jours., chpts. to med. textbooks; mem. editorial bd. Jour. Applied Physiol., Am. Rev. Respiratory Diseases. Served as surgeon USPHS, 1963-65. Fellow AAAS; mem. Assn. Am. Physicians, Am. Soc. Clin. Investigation, Am. Thoracic Soc., Am. Physiol. Soc. Home Phone: 631-941-3836; Office Phone: 631-444-3484. Personal E-mail: edelmannorman@optonline.net. Business E-Mail: norman.edelman@stonybrook.edu.

EDELMAN, PAUL STERLING, lawyer; b. Bklyn., Jan. 2, 1926; s. Joseph E. and Rose (Kaminsky) Edelman; m. Rosemary Jacobs, June 15, 1951; children: Peter, Jeffrey. AB, Harvard U., 1946, JD, 1950. Bar: NY 1951, US Dist. Ct. (so. and ea. dists.) NY 1954, US Ct. Appeals (2d cir.) 1963, US Supreme Ct. 1967. Ptnr. Kreindler & Kreindler, NYC, 1953-95, counsel, 1996—. Legal advisor Andrea Doria TV show, 1984, QE2 TV show, 1995; legal advisor, internat. treaty cruise line liability US State Dept., 2006; cons. Slave Ship TV Program, April, 2001. Author: Maritime Injury and Death, 1960, Maritime Personal Injuries, 2007; co-author: Maritime Personal Injury and Death Tort Law, 2007; editor: Maritime Law Reporter, 1987-99, Marine Laws, 1993, 94; columnist: NY Law Jour.; contbr. 17 Causes of Action 2d on Personal Injury of Maritime Pers. With US Army, 1944—46. Fellow NY Bar Found.; mem. ABA (past chmn. admiralty com., toxic hazardous substances litigation com., mem. long range planning com. 1982-84, mem. TIPS coun. 1984-88, Soviet-Am. lawyers conf. Moscow 1987, 94, TIPS lawyer conf. Russia 1993), ATLA (past chmn. admiralty coms.), Maritime Law Assn. (rep. law sea seminar Moscow 1994), NY State Bar Assn. (TICL award 1980, 90, 93, 2005, chmn. INCL sect. 1982-83, editor Ins. Jour. 1973—), Maritime Law Assn. (acting chair maritime pers. com.), Hastings Hist. Soc., Oliver Wendell Holmes Soc. Harvard Law Sch., Supreme Ct. Hist. Soc., World Peace Through Law Ctr., Hudson Valley Tennis Club, Hastings Hudson (past chmn., planning bd.), Supreme Ct. Hist. Soc., Hastings Hist. Soc. Democrat. Jewish. Home: 57 Buena Vista Dr Hastings On Hudson NY 10706-1103 Office Phone: 212-687-8181. Business E-Mail: pedelman@kreindler.com.

EDELMAN, PETER BENJAMIN, lawyer, educator; b. Mpls., Jan. 9, 1938; s. Hyman and Miriam Hazel (Lieberman) E.; m. Marian Elizabeth Wright, July 14, 1968; children: Joshua, Jonah, Ezra. AB, Harvard U., 1958, LL.B., 1961. Bar: N.Y. 1962, D.C. 1979. Law clk. Judge Henry J. Friendly, NYC, 1961-62, Justice Arthur J. Goldberg, Washington, 1962-63; spl. asst. to asst. atty. gen. John Douglas Dept. Justice, Washington, 1963-64; legis. asst. to Sen. Robert F. Kennedy, Washington, 1964-68; asso. dir. Robert F. Kennedy Meml., Washington, 1969-70; staff dir. Pres.'s Com. on the Future of U. Mass., Boston, 1971; v.p. univ. policy U. Mass., 1972-75; dir. N.Y. State Div. Youth, Albany, 1975-79; ptnr. Foley, Lardner, Hollabaugh & Jacobs, Washington, 1979-82; prof. law Georgetown U. Law Ctr., Washington, 1982-93, 96—, assoc. dean, 1989-92; counselor Sec. of Health and Human Svcs., Washington, 1993-95; asst. sec. for planning and evaluation Dept. of Health and Human Svcs., Washington, 1995-96. Lectr. MIT, 1972-75; issues dir. presdl. campaign Senator Edward M. Kennedy, 1980; co-dir. Justice Dept. Transition, 1992-93. Chmn. bd. New World Found., 1982-87; vice chmn. bd. Ctr. for Cmty. Change, 1983-87, chmn., 1987-93, bd. dirs., 1996—; mem. exec. com. Washington Lawyers Com. for Civil Rights Under Law, 1981-93, 97—; bd. dirs. Ctr. for Nat. Policy, 1981-93; trustee U. D.C., 1984-90; bd. dirs. Food Rsch. and Action Ctr., 1988-93, Pub. Voice, 1988-93; mem. nat. gov. bd. Common Cause, 1989-93; chmn. bd. Fair Employment Coun. Greater Washington, 1990-93; co-chmn. Americans for Peace Now, 1990-93, bd. dirs., 1997—; bd. dirs. Pub. Welfare Found., 1994-95, 96—, New Israel Fund, 1997—, bd. pres. 2002—, Ctr. for Law and Social Policy, 1997—, Juvenile Law Ctr., 1997—, Nat. Ctr. for Youth Law, 1997—, bd. chair, 2004—, Chapin Hall Ctr. for Children, 1997-2005; chmn. Comn. Access to Justice, Washington, D.C., 2005—. With Air N.G., 1963. Ford Found. travel-study grantee, 1968; U.S.-Japan leadership program fellow, 1985; J. Skelly Wright Meml. fellow Yale Law Sch., 1991. Democrat. Jewish. Home: 3208 Newark St NW Washington DC 20008-3345 Office: Georgetown U Law Ctr Washington DC 20001 Office Phone: 202-662-9074. Business E-Mail: edelman@law.georgetown.edu.

EDELMAN, RIC, investment advisor; Grad., Rowan Univ., 1980, HHD (hon.), 1999. Founder, head Edelman Fin. Services LLC, Fairfax, Va. Mem. NASD Bd. Arbitrators. Contbr. columns in newspapers; fin. commentator Ric Edelman Show, ABC radio prog. (AIR award for best talk show host, 1993); author: Ordinary People, Extraordinary Wealth: The New Rules of Money, Discover the Wealth Within You, What You Need to Do Now, The Truth About Money, The Lies About Money, 2007. Past chmn. United Way Capital Area; bd. mem. Boys & Girls Clubs Greater Washington; ptnr. Am. Savings Edn. Council. Named #1 Fin. Advisor, Research Mag., 2004; named one of Top 100 Fin. Advisors, Barron's Mag., 2004—07, Top 50 Advisors, Registered Rep mag., 2004; named to Fin. Advisor Hall of Fame, 2004; recipient Blue Chip Enterprise award, U.S. C. of C., Washington Entrepreneur of the Yr. award, Ernst & Young. Office: Edelman Fin Services 9th Fl 4000 Legato Rd Fairfax VA 22033*

EDELMAN, SCOTT A., lawyer; b. Flushing, NY, 1963; BA summa cum laude, Yale Univ., 1985, MA, 1985; JD magna cum laude, Harvard Univ., 1988. Bar: N.Y. 1989. Assoc. Wachtell Lipton Rosen & Katz, NYC; asst. US atty. So. Dist. NY, US Dept. Justice; assoc. Milbank Tweed Hadley & McCloy, NYC, 1994—95, ptnr. Litigation Dept. & mem. global exec. com., 1995—. John Olin Fellow. Mem.: Phi Beta Kappa. Office: Milbank Tweed Hadley & McCloy 1 Chase Manhattan Plz New York NY 10005-1413 Office Phone: 212-530-5149. Office Fax: 212-530-5219. Business E-Mail: sedelman@milbank.com.

EDELMAN, SCOTT ALAN, lawyer; b. Mar. 25, 1959; BA with distinction, Stanford U., 1981; JD, U. Calif., 1984. Bar: Calif. 1984. Law clk. to Hon. Jesse W. Curtis US Dist. Ct. (ctrl. dist.) Calif., 1984—85; co-chair Media and Entertainment Practice Group Gibson, Dunn & Crutcher LLP, LA, ptnr. Litigation Dept. and Intellectual Property Group, Nat. Pro Bono coord. Contbr. chapters to books. Chmn. bd. dir. KCET Pub. TV, exec. com.; bd. dir. Bet Tzedek Legal Svcs., past pres. Named one of LA Super Lawyers, LA Mag., Best Lawyers in Am., Am. Lawyer Media, Am. Leading Lawyers for Bus., Chambers USA, 2006, Hollywood's Top Litigators, Daily Variety, 2007. Office: Gibson Dunn & Crutcher LLP 2029 Century Park E Los Angeles CA 90067-3026 Office Phone: 310-557-8061. Office Fax: 310-552-7041. Business E-Mail: sedelman@gibsondunn.com.

EDELMAN, STUART EDWARD, psychiatrist; b. NYC, Mar. 14, 1947; s. Norman David and Mollie (Wollruch) E.; children: Joseph Jake, Kimberly Jean. BS cum laude, Trinity Coll., Hartford, Conn., 1968; MD, Columbia U., 1972. Diplomate Am. Bd. Psychiatry and Neurology. Resident psychiatry Harvard U. Med. Sch., Boston, 1972—75, clin. instr. psychiatry, 1975—2002; pvt. practice Wayland, Mass., 1975—; asst. clin. prof. psychiatry Sch. Medicine Boston U., 1993—. Staff psychiatrist Trinity Mental Health Ctr., Framingham, Mass., 1975-80; chief dept. psychiatry, med. dir. Eliot Cmty. Mental Health Ctr., Concord, Mass., 1980-90; supr. Erikson Ctr., Harvard U., Cambridge, Mass., 1982-90. Contbr. articles to med. jours. Mem. Am. Psychiat. Assn., Mass. Psychiat. Assn., New Eng. Soc. for Adolescent Psychiatry (v.p.), Phi Beta Kappa. Avocations: tennis, squash, skiing, painting, golf. Office: 58 Glezen Ln Wayland MA 01778-1604

EDELSBERG, SALLY COMINS, retired physical therapist, educator; b. Rowno, Poland, Aug. 6, 1939; came to U.S., 1949; d. Joseph Luria and Chana (Bebczuk) Comins; m. Warde C. Pierson, Oct. 8, 1968 (div. 1978); m. Paul Edelsberg, Feb. 2, 1979; 1 child, Tema. BS in Phys. Medicine, U. Wis., Madison, 1963; MS, Northwestern U., Evanston, Ill., 1972. Lic. phys. therapist. Staff and supervisory phys. therapist Hines VA Hosp., Maywood, Ill., 1963-67; program dir. Health Careers Council of Ill., Chgo., 1967-70; instr., clin. edn. coord. Programs in Phys. Therapy, Northwestern U. Med. Sch., Chgo., 1970—72, dir., assoc. prof., 1972—99, dir. devel. and alumni rels., 1999—2003. Pres. Phys. Therapy Ltd., Chgo., 1986-95; v.p. World Confedn. Phys. Therapy, 1995-99, exec. com., 1991-95. Mem.: Am. Phys. Therapy Assn. (bd. dirs. 1975—78, 1979—82, Ill. pres. 1972—76, Catherine Worthingham fellow 1999). Personal E-mail: sce1323@sbcglobal.net. E-mail: s-edelsberg@northwestern.edu.

EDELSBRUNNER, HERBERT, computer scientist, educator, mathematician; b. Graz, Styria, Austria, Mar. 14, 1958; s. Herbert and Berta Edelsbrunner; m. Ping Fu, Nov. 14, 1991; children: Daniel, Xixi. MS in Tech. Math., Graz U. Tech., 1980, PhD in Tech. Math., 1982, doctorate (hon.), 2006. Mem. faculty Graz U. Tech., 1981-85, Universitätsassistent Inst. Informationsverarbeitung, 1984-85; asst. prof. dept. computer sci. U. Ill., Urbana-Champaign, 1985-87, assoc. prof. dept. computer sci., 1987-90, prof. dept. computer sci., 1990-99; arts and scis. prof. computer sci. and math. Duke U., Durham, NC, 1999—. Founder, dir. Raindrop Geomagic, 1996—. Author: Algorithms in Combinatorial Geometry, 1987, Geometry and Topology for Grid Generation, 2001. Recipient Alan T. Waterman award NSF, 1991. Mem.: AAAS. Achievements include research in data structures and algorithms, computational geometry, discrete geometry, combinatorial topology, computational biology, scientific computation. Office: Duke U Dept Computer Sci Durham NC 27708 Business E-Mail: edels@cs.duke.edu.

EDELSON, DAVID BICK, diversified holding company executive; s. Kenneth J. and Jill Edelson; m. Cynthia Ellen Frank, May 6, 1989; 3 children. AB magna cum laude, Dartmouth Coll., Hanover, NH; MBA, Stanford U., Calif. Assoc. mergers & acquisitions Goldman, Sachs & Co., v.p. mergers & acquisitions, 1989; positions up including corp. treas. JPMorgan Chase & Co., 1997—2005; sr. v.p. Loews Corp., 2005—. Trustee Ctrl. Synagogue, NYC, Jewish Bd. of Family & Children's Svcs. Office: Loews Corp 667 Madison Ave New York NY 10021 Office Phone: 212-521-2000.*

EDELSON, GILBERT SEYMOUR, lawyer; b. NYC, Sept. 15, 1928; s. Saul and Sarah (Sunshine) E.; m. Jane Barbara Levin, Sept. 6, 1953; children: Martha Jane, Paula Topal, Dorothy Rachel. BS, NYU, 1948; LLB, Columbia U., 1955. Bar: N.Y. 1955, U.S. Dist. Ct. (so. dist.) N.Y. 1959, U.S. Ct. Appeals (2nd cir.) 1959, U.S. Dist. Ct. (ea. dist.) N.Y. 1960, U.S. Ct. Appeals (9th cir.) 1995. Assoc. Rosenman Goldmark Colin & Kaye, NYC, 1955-63; ptnr. Rosenman & Colin, NYC, 1963-97, counsel, 1997—2002, Katten Muchin Rosenman, NYC, 2002—. Adminstrv. v.p., counsel Art Dealers Assn. Am., N.Y.C., 1985—. Editor Columbia Law Rev., 1955. Bd. dirs. Coll. Art Assn. Am., N.Y.C., 1969-88, High Five Tickets for the Arts, N.Y.C., 1999-2001; sec., trustee Am. Fedn. Arts, N.Y.C., 1984-94; trustee Internat. Found. for Art Rsch., 1986-99, N.Y. Studio Sch., 1989—, Archives Am. Art, N.Y.C., 1989—. With U.S. Army, 1950-52, JLC. Mem. ABA, N.Y. Bar Assn., Assn. Bar of N.Y.C. (chmn. com. on art law 1992-95), Columbia U. Law Sch. Alumni Assn. (bd. dirs. 1981-84), Century Assn. Jewish. Avocation: collecting art. Home: 580 W End Ave New York NY 10024-1723 Office: Katten Muchin Rosenman 575 Madison Ave New York NY 10022-2585 Home Phone: 212-362-0472; Office Phone: 212-940-7070. E-mail: gilbert.edelson@kattenlaw.com.

EDELSON, IRA J., venture capitalist; b. Chgo., Dec. 30, 1946; s. Alvin L. and Naomi Edelson; m. Starr Gramaila, Feb. 11, 1973; children: Jason Avrum, Megan Anne. BS, DePaul U., 1968. Spl. advisor to chmn. Chgo. Housing Authority, 1983; acting dir. revenue City of Chgo., 1984; ptnr.-in-charge bus. svcs. dept. Deloitte, Haskins & Sells, Chgo., 1979-87; ptnr.-in-charge corp. fin. Deloitte & Touche-U.S. Partnership, Chgo., 1987-91; pres. Transcap Trade Fin. LLC, Northbrook, Ill., 1991—. Fin. and policy advisor to mayor City of Chgo., 1984—85; former instr. Northwestern Grad. Sch. Bus.; cons., spkr. in field. Co-chmn. Chgo. Sports Stadium Commn., 1985. Mem.: AICPA, Fgn. Trade Assn., Turn Around Mgmt.

Assn., Nat. Contract Mgmt. Assn., Comml. Fin. Assn., Ill. Soc. CPAs. Office: Transcap Assocs Inc 900 Skokie Blvd Ste 210 Northbrook IL 60062-4031 Office Phone: 847-753-9600.

EDELSON, MARY BETH, artist, educator; b. East Chgo. d. Albert Melvin and Mary Lou (Young) Johnson; children: Lynn Switzman, Nick. BA, DePauw U., Greencastle, Ind., 1955, DFA (hon.), 1993; MA, NYU, 1959. Atty. Art Inst. Chgo.; instr. Corcoran Sch. Art, Washington, 1970-75; artist in residence U. Ill., Chgo., 1982, 88, U. Tenn., Knoxville, 1983, Ohio U., Columbus, 1984, Md. Inst. Art, Balt., 1985, Kansas City Art Inst., Mo., 1986, Cleve. Art Inst., 1991, U. Colo., 1993, Clemson U., 1994, McMullen Mus. of Art, Boston Coll., 1997, Danish Royal Acad., Copenhagen, 2000—02, Art and Film Sch., Kabelvag, 2004, Yaddo, 2005, U. So. Ind., 2006—, Internat. Artists Studio Program, Sweden, 2006. Lectr. at various art gatherings. Solo exhbns. include Nicole Klagsburn Gallery, NYC, 1993, A/C Project Rm., NYC, 1993, Creative Time, NYC, 1994, Nicolai Wallner, Copenhagen, Denmark, 1996, Halle für Kunst, Berlin, 1997, Agency Gallery, London, 1998, Malmö Mus., Sweden, 2000, traveling solo exhbn. to 8 sites in US, 2000-02, 30 yr. survey of Edelson's work with 200 page book, full color book, The Art of Mary Beth Edelson, Utopianna, New Harmony Art Gallery, Ind., 2006, Retrospective Malmö Konstmuseum, Sweden, 2006; group exhbns. include Feministische Kunst, Stichting de Appel, Amsterdam, The Netherlands, 1980, Mendel Gallery, Mus. du Que., Phillips Gallery, Can., 1986-88, Corcoran Gallery Art, Washington, 1989, Mus. Modern Art, NYC, 1988-89, Walker Art Ctr., Mpls., 1989, W.P.A., Washington, 1989, A.C. Project Room, NYC, 1991-97, Phillippe Rizzo, Paris, 1992, P.P.O.W., NYC, 1992, Fawbush Gallery, NYC, 1992, Amy Lipton Gallery, NYC, 1992, David Zwirner Gallery, NYC, 1993, Turner/Krail Galleries, LA, 1993, Mercer Union, Toronto, 1996, The Agency, London, 1995, Lombard/Freid, NYC, 1995, Linda Kirkland Gallery, NYC, 1996, Boston Mus. Art, McMullen, 1997, Magasin Ctr. National D'Art Contemporain, Grenoble, France, 1997, Dorfman Projects, NYC, 1998, Internat. Ctr. Photography, NYC, 1997, Neubergher Mus., Purchase, NY, 1999, Nicolai Wallner, Copenhagen, 1996, 99, Postmasters, NYC, 1999, New Mus., NYC, 2000, 01, Tate Mus., London, 2001, Gallerie LeLong, NYC, 2002, Guild Hall, East Hampton, 2002; Chelsea Mus., NYC, 2003, ShedHalle Space, Zurick, 2003, Mumok Museum, Vienna, 2003, Internat. Art Festival, Lofoten, Norway, 2004, Tina Kim Fine Arts, NYC, 2005, Remy Toledo Gallery, NYC, 2005, Mason Gross Arts Galleries, Rutgers, NJ, 2006, Rutgers U. Traveling Exhbn. to 5 Sites, 2006, Migros Mus., Zurich, 2006, MOCA, LA, 2007, Gender Battle, Centro Galego de Arte Contemprânea, Santago de Compostela, Spain; represented in permanent collections: Walker Art Ctr., Nat. Mus. Am. Art, Washington, Nat. Collection, Washington, Nat. Mus. Women in the Arts, Fine Arts Mus. Santa Fe, Seattle Art Mus., Guggenheim Mus. Art, NYC, Mus. Contemporary Art, Chgo., MOMA, NYC, Malmo Mus., Sweden, and others; Survey of Edelson's Work Rescripting the Story, various locations, 2000-02, travelling exhibit 2007-, Women's Mus., DC, NY; author: Seven Cycles: Public Rituals, 1981, To Dance: Painting with Performance in Mind, 1985, Seven Sites, 1988-90, Shape Shifter: Seven Mediums, 1990; author/photographer: Firsthand, 1993, The Art of Mary Beth Edelson, 2002; contbr. articles to profl. jours.; included in books including The Power of Feminist Art, 1994, Lone Visions, Crowded Frames, 1994, The Pink Glass Swan, 1995, Art and Propaganda, 1997, Saffrages and She-Devils, 1997, Where is Ana Mendiata, 1999, Picturing the Modern Amazon, 2000, Feminist Art-Theory; An Anthology, 1968-00, Art and Feminism, 2001, The Artists Body, 2000, Sex Politik, 2001, Century City: Art and Culture in the Modern Met., Tate Mus, London, 2001, Alternative Art NY, 2002, The Art of Mary Beth Edelson, 2002, The End of Art, 2004, Women's Culture in a New Era, 2005, A Well lived Life, 2006, Radical Gestures, 2006, Wack! Art and the Feminist Revolution, 2007. Recipient Visual Arts grant NEA, 1981, 2000, Creative Artists Pub. Svc. grant State of NY, 1982, Andy Warhol Found. grant NEA, Pollack/Krasner Found., Florsheim Found., 2000, Yaddo Residency, 2005, IASPIS Residency in Sweden, 2006. Mem. Conf. Women in Visual Arts (founding mem.), Women's Action Coalition, Heresies Mag. Collective (founding mem.).

EDELSON, ZELDA SARAH TOLL, retired editor, artist; b. Phila., Oct. 18, 1929; d. Louis David and Rose (Eisenstein) Toll; m. Marshall Edelson, Dec. 27, 1952 (dec. Jan. 16, 2005); children: Jonathan Toll Edelson, Rebecca Jo Edelson, David Edelson Tolchinsky. BA, U. Chgo., 1949, postgrad., 1949-52. Editor-writer Consol. Book Pubs., Chgo., 1953-56; social worker Balt. City Dept. Pub. Welfare, 1956-57; pub. rels. writer Md. Dept. Employment Security, Balt., 1958-59; mus. editor Yale Peabody Mus., New Haven, 1970-76, head publs., 1976-95, editor mus.'s Discovery mag., 1983-95; lectr. in sci. writing Yale U., 1983—84. Author (and illustrator): Apologies for a Nightingale: Images of Turkey, 1997; editor: numerous publs. including The Great Dinosaur Mural at Yale: The Age of Reptiles, 1990. U. Chgo. scholar, 1947-51. Personal E-mail: zeldaedelson@yahoo.com.

EDELSTEIN, BARBARA A., radiologist; b. NYC, 1952; MD, NY Med. Coll., 1977. Cert. diagnostic radiology 1983. Intern Lenox Hill Hosp., NYC, 1977—78; resident Montefiore Hosp., NYC, 1979—82; radiologist Women's Radiology, NYC, 1983—. Office: Womens Radiology 1045 Park Ave New York NY 10028-1030 Office Phone: 212-860-7700. Personal E-mail: b99xray@aol.com. Business E-Mail: barbara@women'sradiology.com.

EDELSTEIN, DAVID ROBERT, medical educator; s. Alan M. and D. Sybil Edelstein; m. Eve Lesser; children: Jennifer F., Hilary M., Matthew S. MD, Boston U., 1976—80. Lic. dr. Am. Bd. Otolaryngology, 1985. Clin. prof. otorhinolaryngology Weill Med. Coll., Cornell U., NYC, 1996—; chmn. otolaryngology Manhattan Eye, Ear & Throat Hosp., NYC, 1998—. Bd. mem. Manhattan Eye, Ear & Throat Hosp., 1999—, pres. bd. surgeon dir., 2004—. Author: (textbook) Revision Surgery in Otolaryngology. Recipient Chmn. award & Otolaryngology Tchg. award, Manhattan Eye, Ear & Throat Hosp., 1999, Disting. Svc. award, Helen Keller Manhattan League, 2001. Fellow: Am. Acad. Otolaryngology Head & Neck Surgery (licentiate; bd. govs. 2002, award 1996). Achievements include research in aging of the nose and sinuses. Office: Manhattan Otolaryngology 1421 Third Ave 4th Fl New York NY 10028 Home Phone: 212-439-7784. Office Fax: 212-472-3086. Personal E-mail: entdre@aol.com.

EDELSTEIN, ROBERT A., urologist; b. Chgo., June 8, 1963; BS, U. Calif., Davis, 1984; MD, Oreg. Health Sciences U., Portland, 1988. Diplomate Nat. Bd. Med. Examiners, 1989, Am. Bd. Urology, 1997. Attending urologist Boston Med. Ctr., 1995—98; urologist Merrimack Urology Assocs., Chelmsford, Mass., 1998—. Asst. prof. surgery Boston U. Sch. Medicine, 1995—2007; pres. Boston Urol. Soc., Boston, 2000—01; bd. mem. Tufts Health Plan, Boston, 2000—03, Mass. Assn. Practicing Urologists, Waltham, 2002—06. Editor: Manual of Urology; contbr. articles to profl. jours. Recipient Pfizer Scholars in Urology award, Pfizer Pharmaceuticals, 1996; fellow Neurourology and Female Urology, Boston U., 1995; grantee, Am. Cancer Soc., 1995. Fellow: ACS; mem.: AMA, Am. Assn. Clin. Urologists, Am. Urol. Assn., Guild Am. Luthiers. Achievements include patents for anastomosis suturing device. Avocation: crafting wooden musical instruments. Office: Merrimack Urology Associates PC 31 Village Square Chelmsford MA 01824 Home Phone: 781-860-9009; Office Phone: 978-256-9507. Office Fax: 978-256-6955.

EDELSTEIN, ROSEMARIE (HUBLOU), medical, surgical and geriatric nurse, educator; b. Drake, ND, Mar. 3, 1935; d. Francis Jerome and Myrtle Josephine (Merbach); m. Harry George Edelstein, June 22, 1957 (div.); children: Julie, Lori, Lynn, Toni Anne. BSN, St. Teresa of Avila Coll., Winona, Minn., 1956; MA in Edn., Holy Names Coll., Oakland, Calif., 1977; EdD, U. San Francisco, 1982, postgrad., 1987, U. Ariz., 1985—; cert. pub. health nurse, U. Calif., Berkeley, 1972. Dir., clin. supr. San Francisco Sch. for Health Professions, 1971-74, Rancho Arroyo Sch. of Vocat. Nursing, Sacramento, 1974-75; intensive care nurse Kaiser-Permanente Hosp., San Rafael, 1976-77; dir. insvc. edn. Ross Hosp., 1977-78; dir. nursing edn. St. Francis Meml. Hosp., San Francisco, 1978-85; med.-surg. staff nurse met. hosps., San Francisco, 1985-90; med.-legal nursing cons., med.-surg. staff nurse St. Luke's Hosp., Duluth, Minn., 1990-91, St. Charles Hosp., New Orleans, 1992, U. Tex. Med. Br., Galveston, Tex., 1992—94; staff nurse St. Anthony of Padua Hosp., Oklahoma City, 1994—95, med.-surg. nurse, 1994-95; nurse Northgate Conv. Hosp., San Rafael, Calif., 1995—, Idaho Falls Care Ctr., 2003—04, Minidoka Mem. Hosp. Extended Care Facility, Idaho, 2004—05, Minidoka Meml. Hosp., 2004—; nurse, charge nurse Ashton (Idaho) Living Ctr., 2005—. Night charge nurse Creekside Conv. Hosp., Santa Rosa, Calif., 1996; charge nurse medications, treatment and Alzheimer's Unit Fallon Conv. Ctr., Nev., 1996; charge nurse Medicare unit White Pine Conv. Ctr., Ely, Nev., 1997; emergency rm., ICU nurse Battle Mt. Gen. Hosp., Nev., 1997; nurse supr. Medicare-Med. Seaview Care Ctr. Sun Corp., Eureka, Calif., 1997—98; mem. staff Walker Post Manor Oxford, NE Lantis Corp., 1998, The Lincoln Ambassador, 1999, Rapid City (S.D.) Care Ctr. Beverly Enterprises, 2000—01, Houghton County Med. Care Facility, Hancock, Mich., 2000—, Norlite Nursing Ctr., Marquette, Mich., 2001—02; mem. staff Medicare unit Everett (Wash.) Rehab. and Care Ctr., 2001—02; mem. staff Whidbey Island Manor, Oak Harbor, Wash.; staff medicare unit St. Joseph Care Ctr., Spokane, 2003; invited mem. people to people nursing edn. and adminstrn. delegation to Japan, Hong Kong, and China Eisenhower Found. Wayne State U., 1985. Author: The Influence of Motivator and Hygiene Factors in Job Changes by Graduate Registered Nurses, 1977; Effects of Two Educational Methods Upon Retention of Knowledge in Pharmacology, 1981; co-author: (with Jane F. Lee) Acupunture Atlas, 1974. Candidate U.S. Senate Inner Circle, 1988, 89. Lt. col. USAR Med. Res. Mem. Am. Heart Assn., Calif. Nurses Assn., Sigma Theta Tau. Roman Catholic.

EDELSTEIN, TERI J., art educator, director, consultant; b. Johnstown, Pa., June 23, 1951; d. Robert Morten and Hulda Lois (Friedhoff) E. BA, U. Pa., 1972, MA, 1977, PhD, 1979; cert., NYU, 1984. Lectr. U. Guelph, Ont., 1977-79; asst. dir. for acad. programs Yale Ctr. Brit. Art, New Haven, 1979-83; dir. Mt. Holyoke Coll. Art Mus., South Hadley, Mass., 1983-90, Skinner Mus., 1983-90, mem. faculty dept. art., 1983-90; dir. Smart Mus. Art U. Chgo., 1990-92, sr. lectr. dept. art, 1990-2000; prin., owner Teri J. Edelstein Assocs., Chgo., 1999—. Dep. dir. Art Inst. Chgo., 1992—99; pres. Teri J. Edelstein Assocs. Museum Strategies, 1999—; mem. adv. bd. Sculpture Chgo., 1991—96, Mus. Loan Network, Knight and Pew Founds., 1994—96. Office: 1648 E 50th St # 6B Chicago IL 60615-3207 Office Phone: 773-241-9991. Fax: 773-241-9992. Business E-Mail: tedelstein@tedelstein.com.

EDELSTEIN, TILDEN GERALD, academic administrator, historian, educator; b. NYC, June 11, 1931; s. Theodore and Nettie (Strusser) Edelstein; m. Marjorie Sukoff, June 17, 1955 (div. July 1970); m. Rose Ann Stargardter, Nov. 1, 1970; children: Jordan, Russell. BS, U. Wis., 1953; PhD, Johns Hopkins U., 1961. From instr. to assoc. prof. Simmons Coll., Boston, 1957-67; from adj. assoc. prof. to prof. history Rutgers U., New Brunswick, NJ, 1967-89, chmn. history dept., grad. dir., 1974-81, assoc. dean social sci. and humanities, faculty personnel, 1981-84, dean faculty arts and scis., 1984-89; prof. history, provost, acad. v.p. SUNY, Stony Brook, 1989-93, prof. history, provost, exec. v.p. for academic affairs, 1992-94; v.p. for acad. affairs Wayne State U., Detroit, 1995-98, prof. history, 1998—2003. Hist. cons. Columbia Pictures, Hollywood, Calif., 1978-80, NBC, N.Y.C., 1980-89; chair Sponsors Bd. The Thomas A. Edison Papers Project, 1980-89. Author: Strange Enthusiasm, 1968, 2d edit., 1970; co-editor: The Black Americans, 1975. Commr. Housing Authority, Highland Park, N.J., 1977-89; Einstein Archives Adv. Com. Hebrew U., 1993-94; mem. adv. bd. Cohen/Haddow Ctr. for Jewish Studies, Mich. Civil War Regimental Round Table. Mem.: Prismatic Club Detroit. Office: Wayne State U Coll Liberal Arts & Scis Dept of History Detroit MI 48202 E-mail: aa1768@wayne.edu.

EDEN, ALVIN NOAM, pediatrician, writer; b. Bklyn., Mar. 21, 1926; s. Emanuel M. and Rae (Taran) Edelstein; m. Elaine R. Jaffe, Nov. 20, 1952; children: Robert, Elizabeth. BA, Columbia Coll., 1948; MD, Boston U., 1952. Intern Bellevue Hosp., NYC, 1952-53; resident in pediat. Univ. Hosp., NYC, 1953-55; pvt. practice specializing in pediat. Forest Hills, NY, 1955—. Assoc. clin. prof. pediat. NYU Sch. Medicine, 1960-84; chmn., dir. dept. pediat. Wyckoff Heights Med. Ctr., Bklyn., 1959—; lectr. SUNY-Downstate Med. Ctr., Bklyn., 1984-86, assoc. clin. prof. pediat., 1986-90; assoc. clin. prof. pediat. Cornell Med. Coll., 1990-99, clin. prof., 1999—. Author: Growing Up Thin, 1975, Handbook for New Parents, 1978, Positive Parenting, 1980, Dr. Eden's Healthy Kids, 1987, Positive Parenting, 2007; contbr. articles to profl. jours.; author text and reference materials. Mem. med. adv. com. YMCA of U.S., 1987—2003. With USMC, 1944-46. Mem. N.Y. Pediatric Soc. (pres. 1980-81), Queens Pediatric Soc. (pres. 1972-73), N.Y. Acad. Medicine (chmn. pediatric sect. 1985-89), Am. Acad. Pediatrics (chmn. nutrition com. chpt. 2 1985-89). Avocation: tennis. Home: 710 Park Ave New York NY 10021-4944 Office: 10721 Queens Blvd Forest Hills NY 11375-4451 Home Phone: 212-628-4475; Office Phone: 718-261-8989. Personal E-mail: babydoceden@hotmail.com.

EDEN, BARBARA JANIECE, commercial and residential interior designer; b. Inpls., Oct. 14, 1951; d. Justin January and Marjorie May (Miller) E.; m. Stephen A. Bowman, Oct. 25, 1975; children: Christopher Eden Bowman, Jessica Eden Bowman. BA, Purdue U., 1973. Interior design dir. Bohlen, Meyer, Gibson & Assoc., Indpls., 1973-78; interior designer, sole propr. Barbara Eden Design, Indpls., 1978-85; pres., prin. designer Eden Design Assocs., Inc., Carmel, Ind., 1985-97, Carson Design Assocs. Design/Project Mgmt./ Mktg., Carmel, Ind., 1997—. Past mem. accreditation team Found. for Interior Design Edn. Rsch. (FIDER); past mem. adv. bd. Purdue U. Interior Design Dept.; bd. dirs. Hamilton County Intercultural Svcs. Prin. projects include wheelchair accessible bathroom Kohler (Wis.) Design Ctr., United Airlines, Indpls. Maintenance Ctr., N.Am. hdqrs. Brightpoint, Inc., Plainfield, Ind., Peabody Retirement Ctr., North Manchester, Ind., Oakwood Inn, Syracuse, Ind., Resort Condominiums, Internat., Carmel, Ind., Merchants' Pointe, Carmel, restaurant, retail & office devel., arch., interior design; also corp., healthcare, schs., univs., librs., sr. living and residential interior design, space planning and project mgmt. Mem. Internat. Facility Mgrs. Assn., Internat. Interior Design Assn., Illuminating Engring. Soc., Carmel Clay C. of C. (mem. exec. bd., chair edn. com., Small Bus. Person of Yr. 1993). Avocations: hiking, horseback riding, travel. Office: Carson Design Assocs 2325 Pointe Pkwy 200 Carmel IN 46032-3283 E-mail: edenbj@carsondesign.com.

EDEN, F. BROWN, artist; b. Jericho Center, Vt., Oct. 10, 1916; d. Arthur Castle and Eva Merita (Lowrey) Brown; m. Edwin Winfield Eden, Sept. 4, 1937 (dec. 1990); children: Donna Jean, Sandra Elizabeth, Kathy Lynn; m. Allan L. Day, July 11, 1994 (dec.). Student, U. Fla. Extension, 1955—59, U. Mich., 1963. Art instr. Ann Arbor (Mich.) City Club, 1962-63; tchr., oil painting, printmaking Jacksonville (Fla.) Art Mus., 1963-68. One-woman shows include The Fox Galleries, Atlanta, 1986, Harmon Galleries, Sarasota, 1987, 1989—90, 1992—93, Gallery Contemporanea, Jacksonville, Artist Assocs. Gallery, Atlanta, 1965—90, Hodgell Gallery, Sarasota, 1997—, The Center, Ponte Vedra, Fla., 1998, Kent Campus Gallery, Fla. C.C., Jacksonville, 1999, Represented in permanent collections Fed. Res. Bank Atlanta, Bank Am., Coca-Cola, So. Bell, Sheraton Corp., AT&T, Trust Co. Ga., Shell Oil Co., Touche Ross, Cooper and Lybrand, Delta Airlines Crown Rm., 5th Dist. Ct. Appeals Bldg., Daytona Beach, Fla., Edwin and Ruth Kennedy Mus. Am. Art, U. Ohio, Athens, exhibited in group shows at Ala. Nat. Watercolors, exhibitions include Am. Painters in Paris, 1975—76, Painters in Casein and Acrylics, N.Y.C. Chmn. area VI Fla. Artist Group, Jacksonville Mus. Art, 1979—89. Recipient Painting of Yr. award, Mead Co., 1962—63, First award, Fla. Artist Group, 1971, 1979, Fla. Artists, 1969, The Painting award, Maj. Fla. Artists, 1979, others. Mem.: Fla. Crown Treasures, Fla. Artists Jacksonville, Jackson Coalition of Visual Artists, Ala. Watercolor Soc., Ga. Watercolor Soc., Fla. Watercolor Soc. (Signature artist), So. Watercolor Soc., Nat. Mus. of Women in Arts (charter), Am. Women Artists. Avocation: playing organ. Home: 5375 Sanders Rd Jacksonville FL 32277-1333 Office Phone: 904-744-1203.

EDEN, JAMES GARY, electrical engineer, physicist, educator, researcher; b. Washington, Oct. 11, 1950; s. Robert Otis and Joyce (West) Eden; m. Carolyn Sue Thomas, June 10, 1972; children: Robert Douglas, Laura Ann, Katherine Joy. BS, U. Md., 1972; MS, U. Ill., 1973, PhD, 1976. Rsch. asst. U. Ill., Urbana, 1972—75, asst. prof. elec. engring. dept., 1979—81, assoc. prof., 1981—83, prof. Dept. Elec. Engring., rsch. prof. Coordinated Sci. Lab., 1983—, rsch. prof. Micro and Nanotech. Lab., 2000—, dir. Lab. for Optical Physics and Engring., 1995—, assoc. vice-chancellor rsch., 2000—03, affiliate faculty materials sci. and engring., 2004—, asst. dean Coll. Engring., 1992—93, assoc. dean. Grad. Coll., 1994—96, Gilmore family prof. elect. and computer engring., 2007—; postdoctoral rsch. assoc. NRC, Washington, 1975—76; rsch. physicist US Naval Rsch. Lab., Washington, 1976—79. Mem. tech. adv. bd. Anvik Corp., Hawthorne, NY, Caviton, Inc., Urbana; mem. exec. adv. bd. U. So. Fla., Dept. Physics, Tampa; assoc. mem. Ctr. Advanced Study U. Ill., 1987—88; mem. adv. bd. Chem. Vapor Deposition, 1995—2003, CRC Handbook Series Laser Sci. and Tech., 1996—; Fulbright-Israel Disting. chair Natural Scis. and Engring., 2007—; cons. in field. Author: Photochemical Vapor Deposition, 1992, Gas Laser Technology, 2000; editor: IEEE Jour. Quantum Elecs., 1996—2002; editor-in-chief Progress in Quantum Electronics, 2007—; assoc. editor: Photonics Tech. Letters, 1988—94; contbr. chapters to books, more than 220 articles to profl. jours. Recipient Rsch. Publ. award, Naval Rsch. Lab., 1978, Beckman Rsch. award, U. Ill., 1988, IBM Rsch. award, 1994, Faculty Outstanding Tchg. award, Dept. Elec. and Computer Engring., U. Ill., 2000; James F. Towey Univ. scholar, U. Ill., 1996—99. Fellow: IEEE (active various coms., numerous confs., 3d Millennium medal 2000), Am. Phys. Soc., Optical Soc. Am. (C.E.K. Mees medal 2007); mem.: IEEE Lasers and Electro-Optics Soc. (bd. govs. 1991—93, v.p. tech. affairs 1993—95, pres. 1998, Disting. Svc. award 1996, Disting. Lectr. 2003—05, Aron Kressel award 2005), Phi Kappa Phi, Eta Kappa Nu, Tau Beta Pi, Sigma Xi. Achievements include patents for 24 inventions. Home: 914 Waters Edge Rd Champaign IL 61822 Office: U Ill Everitt Lab 1406 W Green St Urbana IL 61801-2918 Office Phone: 217-333-4157. Business E-Mail: jgeden@uiuc.edu.

EDEN, KATREINA, lawyer; b. Price, Utah, Dec. 18, 1975; d. W. Kent and Kristena E. Eden. JD, Southwestern U., LA, 2005. Bar: Calif. 2005; Notary Public Calif., 2007. Law clk. Mental Health Advocacy Svcs., LA, 2003; rsch. asst. Southwestern U. Sch. Law, LA, 2004—05; intern Internat. Bus. Legal Assocs., Amman, Jordan, 2005; assoc. atty. Law Offices of L. Scott Spears, Santa Rosa, Calif., 2006—07. Contbr. articles to profl. jours. Gardner Luther Burbank Home & Gardens, Santa Rosa, 2006—07; tutor Sonoma County Adult Literacy Program, Santa Rosa, 2006—07; missionary LDS Ch., Cabanatuan, Philippines, 1997—98. Scholar, Ricks Coll., 1994—96. Mem.: Women in Law, Bus. Network Internat. Avocations: travel, dance, reading, piano. Home Phone: 707-391-4806.

EDEN, MARIO RICHARD, engineering educator; b. Aabenraa, Denmark, Apr. 10, 1973; s. Richard and Asta Eden. MSc in Chem. Engring., Tech. U. Denmark, Kongens Lyngby, 1992—99, PhD in Chem. Engring., 1999—2003. Rsch. assoc. Tech. U. Denmark, 1999—99; vis. lectr. Auburn U., Ala., 2002—03, asst. prof., chem. engring., 2004—. Recipient Jr. Rsch. award, Auburn Engring. Alumni Coun., 2006; Process Integration PhD fellow, Nordic Energy Rsch. Program, 2000—03, Faculty Early Career Devel. grantee, NSF, 2006—. Mem.: AIChE, Danish Soc. Chem. Engrs., Danish Soc. Processing Tech., Soc. Danish Engrs., Am. Soc. Engring. Edn., Am. Chem. Soc. Home: 1731 VFW Rd Auburn AL 36832 Office: Auburn Univ Dept Chem Engring Auburn University AL 36849-5127 Home Phone: 334-329-8958; Office Phone: 334-844-2064. Office Fax: 334-844-2063. Business E-Mail: edenmar@auburn.edu.

EDENFIELD, BERRY AVANT, federal judge; b. Bulloch County, Ga., Aug. 2, 1934; s. Perry and Vera E.; m. Vida Melvis Bryant, Aug. 3, 1963. BBA U. Ga, 1956, LL.B., 1958. Bar: Ga. 1958. Partner firm Allen, Edenfield, Brown & Wright (and predecessors), Statesboro, Ga., 1958-78; judge U.S. Dist. Ct. (so. dist.) Ga., Savannah, 1978-90, chief judge, 1990-97, judge, 1997—2006, sr. judge, 2006—. Mem. Ga. Senate, 1965-66. Office: US Dist Ct PO Box 9865 Savannah GA 31412-0065 Office Phone: 912-650-4080.

EDENFIELD, GERALD M., lawyer; b. Guyton, Ga., July 6, 1945; s. Perry and Vera (Berry) E.; m. Sharon Carter; children: Shari, Kristie, Gerald Malcolm. AB in Polit. Sci. and Philosophy, U. Ga., 1967; JD, Mercer U., 1970. Ptnr. Heyman & Sizemore, Atlanta, 1970-78, Pye, Groover, Edenfield & Dailey, Atlanta, 1978-79, Allen, Brown & Edenfield, Statesboro, Ga., 1979-88, Edenfield, Stone & Cox, Statesboro, Ga., 1988—, Edenfield, Cox, Bruce & Classens, PC, Statesboro, Ga. Active Cancer Soc., United Way, Day for So., Bulloch 2000. Mem. ABA, State Bar Ga. (sec. 2004-06, pres.-elect 2007), Atlanta Bar Assn., Am. Trial Lawyers Assn., Ga. Industrial Devel. Assn., Ga. Sch. Bd. Attorneys Assn., Ga. Assn. Trial Lawyers, Ga. Assn. Criminal Defense Lawyers, Atlanta Lawyers Club, Statesboro Bulloch County C. of C. (bd. dirs. 1985-86, v.p. 1987-89), Rotary (sgt. arms 1986-87), Forest Heights Country Club, Chatham Club. Democrat. Baptist. Office: Edenfield Cox Bruce & Classens PC 115 Savannah Ave Statesboro GA 30459 also: Edenfield Cox Bruce & Classens PC PO Box 1700 Statesboro GA 30459-1700 Office Phone: 912-764-8600. Office Fax: 912-764-8862. E-mail: gerald@ecbcpc.com.

EDENS, BETTY JOYCE, reading recovery educator; b. Hillsboro, Tex., Oct. 20, 1944; d. Edward Alton and Mary Alma (Pendley) Harbin; m. Eugene Cliett Edens, May 29, 1964; children: Michael Eugene, Anne-Marie DeWitt, Kristen Babovec. BEd, Ind. U., 1985; MS, Tex. A&M of Commerce, 1995. Cert. elem. tchr., reading tchr., Tex. 1st grade tchr. Monday Primary, Kaufman, Tex., 1986-93, Franklin Elem., Hillsboro, Tex., 1993-96, reading recovery tchr., 1994-98, 99-00, 2nd grade tchr., 1998-99; reading recovery tchr. Hillsboro Elem. Sch., 1999—2005, reading specialist 2d and 3d grades, 2005—. Mem. early literacy com. TSRA, 1998, Susan G. Komen Found. Mem. Reading Recovery Coun. of N.Am., Internat. Reading Assn., Tex. Reading Assn., Heritage League hillsboro. Republican. Mem. Ch. of Christ. Avocations: recreational reading, walking, computers. E-mail: edens@hillsboro.net.

EDENS, FRANK WESLEY, physiologist; b. Big Stone Gap, Va., Dec. 18, 1946; s. Frank Ervin and Erma Marie (Daughertry) E.; m. Mary Elizabeth Ayers, June 17, 1977; 1 child, Wesley Aaron. BS, Va. Poly. Inst. and State U., 1969, MS, 1971; PhD, U. Ga., 1974. Asst. prof. N.C. State U., Raleigh, 1973-78, assoc. prof., 1978-84, prof., 1984—. Cons. Embrex Inc., Research Triangle Park, N.C., 1984—; sci. adv. bd. United EGG Producers, Decatur, Ga., 1987—; pres., owner Edenco Cons.-Sales, Raleigh, 1988—. Contbr. over 600 articles to profl. jours. Deacon Trinity Bapt. Ch., Raleigh,

1990—. Grantee Sterling Drug/Eastman Kodak, 1987-89, S.E. Poultry and Egg Assn., 1981, 84, 89, 91, 93, 94, 2000, 06, Schering-Plough, 1985-86, Zoecon, 1988, 89, N.C. Biotech. Ctr., 1989, N.C. Poultry Fedn., 1991, 93, Tex. Gulf, 1993, U.S. Agy. Internat. Devel., 1993, Alltech, Inc., 1994-2007. Mem. AAAS, Am. Physiol. Soc., Poultry Sci. Assn., Am. Assn. Avian Pathologists, So. Poultry Sci. Soc. (2d v.p. 1992, 1st v.p. 1993, pres. 1994), World Poultry Sci. Assn. Republican. Achievements include patent on inducing birds to molt. Home: 326 Northclift Dr Raleigh NC 27609-3723 Office: NC State U Dept Poultry Sci Raleigh NC 27695-0001 Home Phone: 919-847-4190; Office Phone: 919-515-2649. Personal E-mail: fwedens@mindspring.com.

EDENS, GARY DENTON, broadcast executive; b. Asheville, NC, Jan. 6, 1942; s. James Edwin and Pauline Amanda (New) E.; m. Hannah Suellen Walter, Aug. 21, 1965; children: Ashley Elizabeth, Emily Blair. BS, U. N.C., 1964. Account exec. PAMS Prodns., Dallas, 1965-67, Sta. WKIX, Raleigh, NC, 1967-69; gen. mgr. Sta. KOY, Phoenix, 1970-81; sr. v.p. Harte-Hanks Raido, Inc., Phoenix, 1978-81, pres., CEO, 1981-84; chmn., CEO Edens Broadcasting, Inc., 1984-95. Dir. Citibank Ariz., 1986—, Inter-Tel, Inc., 1994—; chmn. The Hanover Cos., Inc., 1995—; chair fin. seminar Chief Execs. Orgn./World Pres. Orgn., N.Y.C., 1998. Bd. dirs. Valley Big Bros., 1972-80, Ariz. State U. Found., 1979—, COMPAS, 1979—, Men's Arts Coun., 1975-78. Named one of Three Outstanding Young Men, Phoenix Jaycees, 1973; entrepreneurial fellow U. Ariz., 1989; inducted into Ariz. Broadcasters Assn. Hall of Fame, 2000. Mem. Phoenix Execs. Club (pres. 1976), Nat. Radio Broadcasters Assn. (dir. 1981-86), Radio Advt. Bur. (dir. 1981—), Young Pres. Orgn. (chmn. Ariz. chpt. 1989-90), Chief Execs. Orgn., Ariz. Pres. Orgn. Republican. Methodist. Office: 5112 N 40th St Ste 102 Phoenix AZ 85018-2142 E-mail: ge@garyedens.com.

EDGAR, HAROLD SIMMONS HULL, legal educator; b. 1942; AB, Harvard U., 1964; LLB, Columbia U., 1967. Bar: N.Y. 1968. Law clk. to judge U.S. Ct. Appeals (D.C. cir.), 1967—68; asst. prof. Columbia U., NYC, 1968—73; Julius Silver prof. law, sci. and tech. Columbia U. Sch. Law, NYC, dir. program in law, sci. and tech., 1985—. Rapporteur UNESCO Internat. Com. on Bioethics, 1992—96; chmn. bd. The Hastings Ctr., 2004—; comdr. Nat. Order Merit, France, 2004. Office: Columbia U Law Sch 435 W 116th St New York NY 10027-7201 Office Phone: 212-854-5059. Business E-Mail: hedgar@law.columbia.edu.

EDGAR, JAMES MACMILLAN, JR., management consultant; b. NYC, Nov. 7, 1936; s. James Macmillan Edgar and Lilyan (McCann) E.; m. Judith Frances Storey, June 28, 1958; children: Suzanne Lynn Randolph, James Macmillan III, Gordon Stuart. B in Chem. Engring., Cornell U., 1959, MBA with distinction, 1960. CPA; cert. mgmt. cons. New product rep. E.I. duPont Nemours, Wilmington, Del., 1960-63, mktg. svcs. rep., 1963-64; with Touche Ross & Co., 1964-78, mgr. Detroit, 1966-68, ptnr. in charge, mgt. svcs. ops. for No. Calif. and Hawaii San Francisco, 1971-78, ptnr. Western regional mgmt. svcs., 1978; sr. ptnr. Edgar, Dunn & Co., San Francisco, 1978-2000; ind. mgmt. cons., 2000—. Bd. dirs. Assoc. Oreg. Industries Svcs. Corp.; ptnr. Global Brand Positioning LLC, 2001—; owner Western Sport Shop, San Rafael, Calif., Santa Rosa, Calif. Patentee nonwoven fabrice. Active San Francisco Mayor's Fin. Adv. Com., 1976-2001, exec. com., 1978-2001, Blue Ribbon com. for Bus., 1987-88, Alumnae Resources adv. bd., 1986-94, San Francisco Planning and Urban Rsch. Bd., 1986-89, adv. bd., 1989-93; alumni exec. coun. Johnson Grad. Sch. Mgmt. Cornell U., Cornell Coun., 1970-73; steering com. Bay Area Coun., 1989-95, program adv. com., 1996-2001, bd. dirs., 1999-2001; chmn. San Francisco Libr. Found., 1989-96; bd. dirs. Rosenberg Found., 1996-2004, chmn. bd. dirs., 2001-02; bd. dirs. Harding Lawson Assoc. Group, 1996-2000, Golden Gate U., 1997-99; mem. San Francisco Com. on Jobs, 1994-2000. Recipient Merit award for outstanding pub. svc. City and County of San Francisco, 1978, Honor award for outstanding contbns. to profl. mgmt. Johnson Grad. Sch. Mgmt., Cornell U., 1978. Mem. AICPA, Assn. Corp. Growth (v.p. membership San Francisco chpt. 1979-81, v.p. programs 1981-82, pres. 1982-83, nat. bd. dirs. 1983-86), Calif. Soc. CPAs, Inst. Mgmt. Cons. (regional v.p. 1973-80, bd. dirs. 1975-77, v.p. 1977-80), San Francisco C. of C. (bd. dirs. 1987-89, 1991-2003, mem. exec. com. 1988-89, 91-95, chmn. mktg. San Francisco program 1991-92, membership devel. 1993, chmn. bd. dirs. 1994, dir. emeritus 1995-2003), Pacific Union Club, Marin Rod and Gun Club, Tau Beta Pi. Home: 10 Buckeye Way San Rafael CA 94904-2602 Office: James Edgar Mgmt Cons 10 Buckeye Way Kentfield CA 94904-2602 Office Phone: 415-279-4107. Personal E-mail: jedgarconsulting@aol.com, jedgar7777@aol.com.

EDGAR, JIM, former governor; b. Vinita, Okla., July 22, 1946; m. Brenda Smith; children: Brad, Elizabeth. Grad., Eastern Ill. U., 1968; postgrad., U. Ill., Sangamon State U., 1971-74. Legis. intern pres. pro tem Ill. Senate, 1968; key asst. to speaker ho. Ill. Ho. of Reps., 1972-73; aide to pres. Ill. Senate, 1974, to Ho. minority leader, 1976; mem. Ill. Ho. of Reps., 1977-79; dir. legis. affairs Ill. Gov., 1979-80; sec. state State of Ill., 1981-91; gov. State of Ill., 1991-98; disting. fellow Inst. Govt. and Publs. U. Ill., Urbana, 1999—. Co-lead gov. Nat. Gov.'s Assn. Transp. Com., 1995-96; chair Edn. Commn. of States, 1993-94; chair Nat. Gov.'s Assn. Com. on Econ. Devel. and Commerce, 1992-93; pres. Coun. State Govts., 1992-93; chair Gov.'s Ethanol Coalition, 1992-93; chair Nat. Gov.'s Assn. Com. on Econ. Devel. and Tech. Innovation, 1991-92. Precinct committeeman, treas. Coles County Rep. Com., 1974; dir. state svc. Nat. Conf. State Legislatures, 1975, 76; mem. campaign com. Ill. Ho. of Reps.; pres. Nat. Assn. Secs. of State, 1988; exec. com. Coun. State Govts., 1988, v.p. exec. com., 1991, pres., 1992-93; bd. dirs. Nat. Commn. Against Drunk Driving, 1989; chmn. Ill. Literacy Coun., 1989; chmn. Edn. Commn. of the States, 1993-94; chmn. Gov.'s Ethanol Coalition, 1992-93; pres. Bd. Coun. State Govts. Mem. Nat. Govs. Assn. (chmn. econ. devel. and commerce com. 1992-93, strategic planning rev. task force 1991—, past chmn. task force on edn., mem. edn. goals panel, chair com. econ. devel. and technol. innovation 1991-92, edn. commn. of states 1993-94, co-lead gov. transp. com. 1995-96), Coles County Hist. Soc. (pres. 1976-79). Baptist. Office: U Ill Inst Govt and Pub Affairs 1007 W Nevada St # MC-037 Urbana IL 61801-3812

EDGAR, R(OBERT) ALLAN, federal judge; b. Munising, Mich., Oct. 6, 1940; s. Robert Richard and Jean Lillian (Hansen) E.; m. Frances Gail Martin, Mar. 30, 1968; children: Amy Elizabeth, Laura Anne. BA, Davidson Coll., 1962; LLB, Duke U., 1965. Bar: Tenn. 1965. From assoc. to ptnr. Miller & Martin, Chattanooga, 1967-85; judge US Dist. Ct. (ea. dist.) Tenn., Chattanooga, 1985—, chief judge, 1998—2005. Mem. Tenn. Ho. of Reps., Nashville, 1970-72, Tenn. Wildlife Resources Commn., Nashville, 1979-85. Served to capt. U.S. Army, 1966-67, Vietnam. Decorated Bronze Star, 1967. Mem. Fed. Bar Assn., Chattanooga Bar Assn. Episcopalian. Office: US Dist Ct PO Box 1748 960 Georgia Ave Chattanooga TN 37402-2220

EDGAR, ROBERT S., biology professor; BS, McGill U.; PhD in Biology, U. of Rochester. Founding provost UC Santa Cruz, Kresge Coll., 1970. Founder, Contr. (articles) The Worm Breeder's Gazette, 1975—. Mem.: Sigma Xi: The Sci. Rsch. Soc., John Simon Guggenheim Meml. Found., NAS, Am Soc. Arts & Sci.

EDGAR, THOMAS FLYNN, chemical engineering professor; b. Bartlesville, Okla., Apr. 17, 1945; s. Maurice Russell and Natalie (Flynn) E.; m. Donna Jean Proffitt, July 15, 1967; children: Rebecca, Jeffrey. BS in Chem. Engring., U. Kans., 1967; PhD in Chem. Engring., Princeton U., 1971. Registered profl. engr., Tex. Process engr. Conoco, Balt., 1968-69; prof. chem. engring. U. Tex., Austin, 1971—, chmn. dept., 1985-93, Abell chair, 1991—, assoc. dean engring., 1993-96, assoc v.p. acad. computing, 1996-2001; prof. chem. engring. U. Calif., Berkeley, 1978. Pres. CACHE Corp., Austin, Tex., 1981-84, exec. officer, 2000-; pres. Am. Automatic Control Coun., Chgo., 1990-91; chair Coun. for Chem. Rsch., Washington, 1992-93. Author: Coal Processing and Pollution Control, 1983; co-author: Real Time Computing, 1982, Optimization of Chemical Processes, 1988, 2d edit., 2001, Process Dynamics and Control, 1989, 2d edit., 2004; editor: Chemical Process Control, 1981, In Situ (Marcel Dekker), 1977-89; also jours. Recipient Edn. award Am. Automatic Control Coun., 1992, IFAC Control Engring. prize, 2005. Fellow AIChE (editl. bd. jour. 1983-85, 03-, chmn. cast divsn. 1986, bd. dirs. 1989-92, v.p. 1996, pres. 1997, chair bd. dirs. Found. 2000—, Outstanding Counselor award 1975, Colburn award 1980, Computing in Chem. Engring. award 1995, Lewis award 2005), Am. Soc. Engring. Edn. (Westinghouse award 1988, Meriam-Wiley Disting. Author 1990, Chem. Engring. Divsn. Leadership award 1996); mem. Instrument Soc. Am. (Eckman Edn. award 1993, Process Automation Hall of Fame 2007), Am. Chem. Soc., Tau Beta Pi, Phi Lambda Upsilon, Omicron Delta Kappa, Phi Kappa Phi (Joe King award U. Tex. 1989, U. Kans. Disting. Engring. Svc. award 1990). Democrat. Methodist.

EDGAR, WALTER BELLINGRATH, historian, educator; b. Mobile, Ala., Dec. 10, 1943; s. Ernest, Jr. and Amelia E.; m. Elizabeth Giles, Aug. 6, 1966; children: Eliza, Amelia; m. Cornelia Danforth, Feb. 3, 2007. AB, Davidson Coll., NC, 1965; MA, U. S.C., 1967, PhD, 1969; LLD (hon.), Coker Coll., 1999; HLD (hon.), Coastal Carolina U., 2001; LLD (hon.), Davidson Coll., 2003, Newberry Coll., 2005, The Citadel, 2007. From asst. prof. to prof. history U. S.C., Columbia, 1974—, dir. Inst. So. Studies, 1980—, Neuffer prof. so. studies, 1995—, George Washington Disting. prof. history, 1999—. Author: History of Santee Cooper, 1984, South Carolina in the Modern Age, 1992, South Carolina: A History, 1998, Partisans and Redcoats, 2001; editor: The Letterbook of Robert Pringle, 1972, A Southern Renascence Man: Views of Robert Penn Warren, 1984, The South Carolina Encyclopedia, 2006; host Walter Edgar's Jour., S.C. Pub. Radio. Served to capt. U.S. Army, 1969-71; col. Res. Decorated Bronze Star, Legion of Merit. Mem. Hist. Soc., So. Hist. Assn., Royal Soc. Arts, SC Hist. Assn. (pres. 1982-83), SC Hist. Soc. (bd. mgrs. 2000—, pres. 2005-), South Caroliniana Soc. (pres. 1984-87), Blue Key, Omicron Delta Kappa, Phi Alpha Theta. Home: 1731 Hollywood Dr Columbia SC 29205-3215 Office: U SC Inst So Studies Columbia SC 29208-0001 Office Phone: 803-777-2340. E-mail: edgar@gwm.sc.edu.

EDGE, JAMES EDWARD, health care administrator; b. Anacortes, Wash., Apr. 29, 1948; s. Edward and Carol Marie (Lian) E.; m. Nellie Ruth Horton, Mar. 21, 1970; children: Elissa Marie, Gina Dawn. BS in Pharmacy, U. Wash., 1971; MPH, U. Hawaii, 1979. Registered pharmacist. Commd. USPHS, 1969-2000, advanced through grades to capt.; staff pharmacist USPHS Indian Hosp., Albuquerque, 1971-73; chief pharmacy, lab/x-ray S.W. Indian Poly. Inst., Albuquerque, 1972-73, Neah Bay Indian Health Ctr., Wash., 1973-75; svc. unit dir. Neah Bay Svc. Unit, Indian Health Svc., 1975-78, Western Oreg. Service Unit, Indian Health Svc., Salem, 1980-2000; mgr. policy unit Office of Med. Assistance Programs, State of Oreg., Salem, 2000—02; dep. state Medicaid dir. State of Oreg., 2003—. Cons. in field. Active Combined Fed. Campaign, Salem, 1985-2000. John Quick Pharmacy scholar, U. Wash., 1967, Health Professions scholar, 1969. Mem. APHA, Am. Coll. Healthcare Adminstrs., Am. Acad. Med. Adminstrs., Assn. Mil. Surgeons U.S., Mensa, Res. Officers Assn., Commd. Officer USPHS, Wash. Pharm. Assn., nat. Coun. Svc. Unit Dirs. (chmn. 1986-88). Avocations: running, sculling. Office: PO Box 932 Salem OR 97308 Personal E-mail: jeedge@aol.com.

EDGE, JOE D., lawyer; b. Birmingham, Ala., 1948; BSEE, Auburn Univ., 1970; JD, Univ. Ala., 1973; LLM, George Washington Univ., 1976. Bar: Ala. 1973, DC 1975. Trial atty. FCC, 1974—75; gen. counsel General Communication, Inc., Alaska, 1985—88; ptnr., bus., fin. dept. Drinker Biddle & Reath LLP, Washington, and head, comm. law practice group. Mem.: Am. Econ. Assn., IEEE. Office: Drinker Biddle & Reath LLP Ste 1100 1500 K St NW Washington DC 20005-1209 Office Phone: 202-842-8809. Office Fax: 202-842-8465. Business E-Mail: joe.edge@dbr.com.

EDGE, RONALD DOVASTON, physics professor; b. Bolton, Eng., Feb. 3, 1929; arrived in U.S., 1958, naturalized, 1968; s. James and Mildred (Davies) E.; m. Margaret Skulina, Aug. 14, 1956 (div. 1989); children: Christopher James, Michael Dovaston; m. Gertrude Hansen, Dec. 31, 1992. BA, Cambridge U., 1950, MA, 1952, PhD, 1956. Rsch. fellow Australian Nat. U., Canberra, 1954-58; asst. then assoc. prof. physics U. S.C., Columbia, 1958-63, prof., 1964-94, disting. prof. emeritus, 1994—. Rsch. assoc. Yale U., New Haven, 1963-64; vis. prof. Stanford U., Calif. Tech. Inst., U. Munich, U. Sussex, U. Witwatersrand, U. Aarhus, Oak Ridge Nat. Lab., Los Alamos Nat. Lab.; leader 1st Am. team Internat. Physics Olympiad, 1986; judge Internat. Young Physicists Tournament, 1999, 2001. Author: Physics in the Arts, 1973, String and Sticky Tape Experiments, 1978; contbr. articles to profl. jours. Recipient Russell award U. S.C., Guy And Rebecca Forman award tchg. Physics, Vanderbilt U., 1998. Fellow Am. Phys. Soc. (James B. Pegram award 1979), Am. Assn. Physics Tchrs. (apparatus award 1973, v.p. 1995, pres. elect 1996, pres. 1997). Unitarian (past pres. Columbia fellowship) Home: 220 Jadetree Dr Hopkins SC 29061-9347 Office: U SC Physics Dept Columbia SC 29208-0001 Personal E-mail: redge@sc.rr.com.

EDGERLEY, SUSAN, editor; BA in English and Journalism, cum laude, Kans. State U., 1976. Reporter Ark. City Traveler; reporter & editor Wichita Eagle, Kans., 1979—85; asst. mng. editor Phila. Daily News, 1985—89; copy editor NY Times, 1989—97; exec. editor NY Times News Svc., 1997—99; dep. met. editor NY Times, 1999—2003, met. editor, 2003—06, asst. mng. editor career develop., 2006—. Office: NY Times 229 West 43rd St New York NY 10036 Office Phone: 212-556-1533. Office Fax: 212-556-3690. E-mail: suedge@nytimes.com.

EDGERLY, WILLIAM SKELTON, banker; b. Lewiston, Maine, Feb. 18, 1927; s. Stuart and Florence (Skelton) E.; m. Lois Stiles, June 12, 1948; children: Leonard Stuart, Stephanie Lois. BS in Econs. and Engring., MIT, 1949; MBA, Harvard U., 1955. With Eastman Kodak Co., 1949-50; with Cabot Corp., Boston, 1952-75, fin. v.p., 1969-75, also dir.; chief exec. officer State St. Corp., 1975-91, chmn., 1992, chmn. emeritus, 1993—. Bd. dirs., former chmn. Met. Boston Housing Partnership, Fed. Res. Bank Boston, Depository Trust Co., N.Y.C., Arkwright-Boston Ins. Co.; life mem. emeritus MIT Corp. Bd. fellows Harvard Med. Sch.; bd. dirs. Jobs for Mass., former pres.; dir. Boston Pvt. Industry Coun., former chmn.; bd. dirs. Inst. for Fgn. Policy Analysis and Pioneer Inst.; trustee Com. Econ. Devel., The Gen. Hosp. Corp.; former mem. fed. adv. coun. Fed. Res. Bd., Washington. With USNR, 1945-46, 50-52. Fellow Am. Acad. Arts and Scis.; mem. MIT Alumni Assn. (pres. 1973-74), Harvard Bus. Sch. Assn., Assn. Res. City Bankers, Boston Econ. Club, Somerset Club, Cambridge Boat Club. Office: 124 Mount Auburn St Cambridge MA 02138-5758

EDGERTON, BRADFORD WHEATLY, plastic surgeon; b. Phila., May 8, 1947; s. Milton Thomas and Patricia Jane (Jones) E.; children: Bradford Wheatly Jr., Lauren Harrington; m. Louise Dungan Edgerton; stepchildren: Catherine Kelleher, Robert Kelleher. BA in Chemistry, Vanderbilt U., 1969, MD, 1973. Diplomate Am. Bd. Plastic Surgery, Am. Bd. Hand Surgery. Intern U. Calif., San Francisco, 1973-74; resident U. Va., Charlottesville, 1974-78; resident in plastic surgery Columbia-Presbyn., NY, 1979-81; fellow in hand surgery NYU, 1981-82, clin. instr. plastic surgery, 1981-89; ptnr. So. Calif. Permanente Med. Group, LA, 1989—; assoc. prof. clin. plastic surgery U. So. Calif., LA, 1989—. Mem. Pacific Coun. Internat. Policy. Trustee Harvard-Westlake Sch., L.A., 2001—; pres. Edgerton Found., Beverly Hills, Calif, 2001-. Mem. Am. Assn. Hand Surgery, Am. Soc. Plastic and Reconstructive Surgery, Am. Soc. Surgery of Hand, L.A. (Calif.) Tennis Club, L.A. (Calif.) Country Club Episcopal. Home: 494 S Spalding Dr Beverly Hills CA 90212-4104 Office: 6041 Cadillac Ave Los Angeles CA 90034-1702

EDGETT, WILLIAM MALOY, lawyer, arbitrator; b. Balt., Feb. 26, 1927; s. Eugene Albert and Priscilla Ruff (Streett) E.; m. Bronwen Winifred Reese, Nov. 25, 1950. AA, Towson State Coll., 1949; BA, U. Md., 1951, JD, 1959; LL.M., Georgetown U., 1970. Bar: Md. bar 1959. Asst. personnel mgr. Am. Sugar Refining Co., Balt., 1951-55; supr. indsl. relations Westinghouse Electric Co., Balt., 1955-61; sr. labor relations specialist Martin Co., Balt., 1961-64; asst. mgr. indsl. relations Md. Shipbuilding and Drydock Co., Balt., 1964-67; pvt. practice law, 1967—. Asst. prof. Towson State U., 1971-72 Mem. Md. Commn. Nursing, 1974-76; chmn. pub. law bds. Nat. Mediation Bd., 1971—; neutral mem. Nat. R.R. Adjustment Bd., 1971—. Served to staff st. USAAC, 1944-46. Mem. ABA. Nat. Acad. Arbitrators, Am. Arbitration Assn., Am., Roster Arbitrators Fed. Mediation and Conciliation Service.

EDGINGTON, BOBBIE GEORGE, communications engineer, consultant; b. Everton, Mo., Oct. 6, 1943; s. John Dodson Edgington and Betty Lou Larsh; m. Sandra Faye Wagner, May 17, 1963; 1 child, Anne Elizabeth. BSEE, U. Mo., 1969; MSEE, U.S. Naval Postgrad. Sch., Monterey, CA, 1978. Registered profl. engr., Va. Ops. officer USS Desoto County (LST 1171), Norfolk, 1971—72; dep. dir., SHF SATCOM U.S. Naval Electronic Systems Command, Washington; radar program officer US Naval Ship Engring. Ctr., Norfolk, 1972—74; prodn. officer ship repair dept. U.S. Naval Sta., Guantanamo Bay, Cuba, 1974—76; electronics engr. sys. devel. Def. Comm. Engring. Ctr., Reston, Va., 1978—80; dep. dir. SHF SATCOM Naval Electronic Systems Command, Washington, 1980—82; dir. ctrl. office engring. and digital applications Am. Satellite Co., Rockville, Md., 1980—82; consulting engr. satellite comm. systems Quality Systems, Inc., Fairfax, Va., 1984—85; freelance consulting engr. satellite comm. systems Herndon, Va., 1985—. Consulting engr. Continental Tel. Co., Vienna, 1984—86. Author: Engineer's Handbook for Earth Station Design and Implementation, 1994. Elder Trinity Presbyn. Ch., Herndon, 1982—85. Lt. comdr. USN, 1961—82. Scholar USN, 1965—69. Mem.: IEEE, Tau Beta Pi. Republican. Achievements include design of digital circuits, receivers and computer hardware for a satelllite signal analyzer. Avocations: flying, amateur radio, fishing, hunting. Home and Office: 4370 N Rte E Columbia MO 65202 E-mail: edgingtb@earthlink.net.

EDGINGTON, THOMAS S., pathologist, molecular and vascular biologist, educator; b. LA, Feb. 10, 1932; BA in Biol. Scis., Stanford U., 1953, MD, 1957. Diplomate Am. Bd. Pathology, spl. cert. immunopathology. Intern Hosp. Univ. Pa., Phila., 1957—58; resident Ctr. Health Scis. UCLA, 1958—60; sr. postdoctoral fellow immunology Scripps Clinic & Rsch. Found., La Jolla, Calif., 1965—68, assoc. mem. dept. exptl. pathology, 1968—71; founder, head dept. anatomic pathology and lab. medicine Scripps Clinic and Rsch. Found., La Jolla, 1968—74, prof. depts. immunology and vascular biology, 1971—; asst. prof., surg. pathologist dept. pathology UCLA Sch. Medicine, 1962—65; assoc. adj. prof. pathology U. Calif., San Diego, La Jolla, 1968—75, adj. prof., 1975—. Cons. Centocor, 1993—95, Eli Lilly, 1982—85, Becton-Dickinson, 1977—80; founder, bd. dirs. Corvas Internat., NuVas. Contbr. numerous articles to profl. jours. Recipient Coll. de France medal, 1981, John A. Lynch Molecular Biology award, U. Notre Dame, 1992, Rous-Whipple prize, Am. Soc. Investigative Pathology, 1995, Disting. Career award, Internat. Soc. Thrombosis and Hemostatis, 1995. Fellow: AAAS; mem.: Inst. of Medicine of NAS, Thrombosis Inst. (bd. sci. govs. 1995—), Internat. Soc. Thrombosis and Hemostatis, Fedn. Am. Socs. Exptl. Biology (pres. 1990—91, chmn. bd. 1990—91). Office: The Scripps Rsch Inst C-204 10550 N Torrey Pines Rd # C204 La Jolla CA 92037-1000 E-mail: tsedgington@hotmail.com.

EDGINTON, JOHN ARTHUR, lawyer; b. Kingsburg, Calif., July 23, 1935; s. Arthur George and Pochantas Clementina (Ball) E.; m. Jane Ann Simmons, June 25, 1960. AA, U. Calif., Berkeley, 1955, AB in Econs., 1957, JD, 1963. Bar: Calif. 1964, No. Marianas 1969, US Ct. Claims 1969, US Ct. Appeals (9th cir.) 1969, US Supreme Ct. 1969. Assoc. Graham & James, San Francisco, 1964-71, ptnr., 1971-94, Dezurick Edginton & Harrington LLP, Emeryville, Calif., 1994-98, Booth Banning LLP, San Francisco, 1999-2000; pvt. practice Point Richmond, Calif., 2000—. Author: Maritime Bankruptcy, 1989, Benedict on Admiralty, vol. 3B and 3C; editor-in-chief Maritime Practice and Procedure, vol. 29 Moore's Federal Practice, 1997, Benedict's Maritime Bull., 2003; editor Maritime Desk Reference, Benedict on Admiralty, vol. 8, 2001; contbr. articles to profl. jours. Bd. dirs. Richmond Conv. and Visitors Bur., 2004—, pres., 2005—06. With USN, 1957—60. Mem.: Richmond Conv. and Vis. Bur. (dir. 1994—, pres. 2005—), East Bay Model Engrs. Soc. (bd. dirs. 1996—2002, pres. 2000—02), Swedish-Am. C. of C. (bd. dirs. 1971—, pres. Western Nat. 1988—90, nat. vice chmn. 1988—90, pres. Western Nat. 1998—2000, bd. dirs. 1998—2003, CFO 1999—2000, corp. sec. 2000—03), Maritime Law Assn. (chmn. practice and procedure com. 1991—95, bd. dirs. 1993—96), Golden State Model R.R. Mus. (corp. sec., bd. dirs. 1995—), Sierra Club (nat. outing com. 1964—, chmn. ins. com. 1991—, internat. trips 1992—95, outing governance com. 1992—2006), U. Calif. Alumni Order Golden Bear. (permanent class pres. 1957—). Democrat. Methodist. Avocations: mountain climbing, hiking, photography, model railroads. Office: Law Office of John A Edginton 124 Washington Ave Ste A-1 Point Richmond CA 94801-3979 Home Phone: 510-843-6966; Office Phone: 510-232-7180. Office Fax: 510-232-7181. Business E-Mail: jedginton@edg-law.com.

EDGREN, GRETCHEN GRONDAHL, magazine editor; b. Portland, Oreg., Mar. 17, 1931; d. Jack W. and Alice Belle (Wells) Grondahl; m. James McNeese, Oct. 22, 1955 (div. Nov. 1974); children: Amy, Terence James; m. Alvin H. Edgren, Dec. 14, 1984. BJ, U. Oreg., 1952. Staff writer The Oregonian, Portland, 1952-61; editor Sunday mag. The San Juan (P.R.) Star, 1963-65; inventory and info. specialist USAF and U.S. Army Recruiting Command, San Antonio and Chgo., 1965-67; assoc. editor VIP mag. Playboy Clubs, Chgo., 1967-69, mng. editor, 1969-70; assoc. editor Playboy mag., Chgo., 1970-74, sr. editor, 1974-92, contbg. editor, 1992—. Author: The Playboy Book: 40 Years, 1994, The Playboy Book: 50 Years, 2005, The Playmate Book: Five Decades of Centerfolds, 1996, Inside the Playboy Mansion, 1998, The Playmate Book: Six Decades of Centerfolds, 2005; editor: New Credit Rights for Women, 1976; contbr. articles to mags. Adv. bd. Old Oreg. Alumni mag. U. Oreg., Eugene, 1988-96; bd. dirs. Civic Arts Coun., Oak Park, Ill., 1976-84, pres., 1979-80, Village Players, Oak Park-River Forest (Ill.) Symphony Assn., Oak Park Concert chorale, 1975-91, All Island Denominations, 2004—; mem. Oak Park Cable TV Commn., 1984-86; active Anna Maria Island (Fla.) Cmty. Chorus, 1992—, Anna Maria Island Turtle Watch, 1992—. Mem. Confrerie des Vignerons de St. Vincent Mâcon (maitresse du chpt. 1988-92, bd. all-island denom. 2004—), Webfoot Soc. U. Oreg., Phi Beta Kappa, Delta Delta Delta. Episcopalian. Avocations: singing, travel, loggerhead turtle rescue, wines. E-mail: aedgren@tampabay.rr.com.

EDIDIN, PETER, editor; Sr. editor Psychology Today, 1989—90; co-founder, editor in chief Lingua Franca, 1990—92; editor New Republic Books, 1992—96; gen. editor Worth, 1996—2000; Week in Review editor NY Times, 2000—. Office: NY Times 229 W 43rd St New York NY 10036 Office Phone: 212-556-1748. Office Fax: 212-556-3738. E-mail: edidin@nytimes.com.

EDIGER, MARLOW, retired education educator; b. Inman, Kans., Oct. 10, 1927; BS in Edn., Kans. State Tchrs. Coll., 1958, MS in Edn., 1960; EdD, U. Denver, 1963. Tchr. Sandcreek Sch., rural Newton, Kans., 1951-52; English tchr. Mennonite Sch., Jericho, 1952-53; tchr. English and geography Friends Boys Sch., Ramallah, Jordan, 1953-54; tchr. Countryside Sch., Lehigh, Kans., 1955-57; tchr., prin. Lincolnville Grade Sch., Kans., 1957-61; prof. edn. Truman State U., Kirksville, Mo., 1962—92, prof. emeritus, 1992. PhD thesis evaluator Annamalia U., St. Xavier Coll. Edn., Alagappa U., India, Mother Theresa U., U. Madras, 2007; v.p. NMSU-AAUP, 1974—75, pres., 1975—76; spkr. state and nat. convs. Author: 3rd edit., 2004, The Elem. Curriculum, A Handbook, 1977, Social Studies Curriculum in the Elem. Sch., 5th edit., 2000, Lang. Arts Curriculum in the Elem. Sch., 1983;: 2d edit., 1988, rev. edit., 1994, The Modern Elem. Sch., 1997, Tchg. Math in the Elem. Sch., 1997, Improving the Tchg. of Elem. Sch. Math., 1999, The Holy Land, 1998, Tchg. Sci. in the Elem. Sch., 2nd edit., 2000; co-author: Tchg. Reading Successfully, 2000, Tchg. Sci. Successfully, 2001, Tchg. Social Studies Successfully, 2001, Tchg. Math. Successfully, 2000, Lang. Arts Curriculum, 2003, Improving Sch. Admin., 2003, Elem. Curriculum, 2003;: Philosophy and the Curriculum, 2003, Organizing Schools, 2004, Issues in School Education, 2005, Quality in Schol Education, 2005, Successful School Education, 2006, Issues in the Curriculum, 2006; co-editor: Successful School Administration, 2006, Community College, 2006, Curriculum of School Subjects, 2007, Reading Curriculum and Instruction, 2007, Administration of Schools, 2007; mem. editl. bd.: The Edn. Rev.; author: Relevancy in the Elem. Curriculum, 1975; mem. editl. bd.: The Math Tchr., also Edn., Jour. Rsch. in Edn., Jour. Kamataka Sate Edn. Fedn., Experiments in Edn. Jour., Progress of Edn. in India, Edutracks, Reading Improvement, Edn., Jour. English Lang. Tchg. in India, Edutraks, Jour. Cmty. Guidance and Rsch. Treas. Marion County Kans. Tchrs. Assn., 1958-59, pres., 1959-60; mem. adv. coun. Himalayan Jour. Ednl. R&D, India; mem. nat. coun. social studies com. Religion in the Schs.; chmn. Marion County Curriculum Com., 1960-61tchr. Sunday sch., 1950-52, 54-58, 64-99. Mem. ASCD, NSTA (com. tchr. edn.), NEA (life, Mo. chpt., core competencies and key skills com., higher edn. com., com. on pub. rels. 2000-01), Internat. Reading Assn. (sub com. evaluating literacy standards, com. mem.), Nat. Coun. Social Studies (adv. coun. rural schs. and social studies, ethics com., pub. rels. curriculum com., archives com., com. on acad. freedom, tenure and ethics), Nat. Coun. Tchrs. English (vice chmn., chmn. rural lang. arts com., lang. and learning across the curriculum com., tracking in the pub. schs. com.), Mo. Coun. Social Studies (bd. control), Sci. Tchrs. Mo. (bd. dirs.), Mo. Geog. Alliance, Critical Perspectives in Reading, Phi Delta Kappa. Office: 201 W 22nd St North Newton KS 67117 Office Phone: 316-283-6283. Personal E-mail: mediger2@cox.net.

EDINGER, STANLEY EVAN, clinical chemist; b. Bklyn., Aug. 9, 1943; s. Louis and Lenore (Danenberg) E. BS in Chemistry cum laude, CUNY, 1964; MS in Phys. Chemistry, NYU, 1969, PhD in Phys. Chemistry, 1970. Lic. clin. chemistry lab. dir. N.Y.C., N.Y. State; cert. chemist, Nat. Cert. Commn. for Chemists and Chem. Engrs. From tchg. fellow to asst. rsch. N.Y.U., 1964-70; translator, editor NYC, 1970-71; clin. chemist Mt. Sinai Med. Ctr., NYC, 1971-76; sr. scientist bur. quality assurance USPHS, 1976-78; sr. scientist health standard and quality bureau U.S. Health Care Fin. Adminstrn., Balt., 1978-86, scientist dir., asst. to dir. OSC, 1986-87; scientist dir. Nat. Inst. on Drug Abuse, Pres. Initiative on Drug Testing in Work Place, Rockville, Md.; scientist dir. Office Program Assessment and Info. U.S. Health Care Fin. Adminstrn., Rockville, Md., 1988; USPHS rep. to com. on energy and commerce, Congl. fellow U.S. Ho. of Reps., Washington, 1989; sr. health policy analyst Agy. for Health Care Policy and rsch. office of forum for quality and effectiveness in health care USPHS, Rockville, 1990-93; spl. asst., chmn. subcom. on oversight and investigation U.S. Ho. of Reps. Com. on Energy & Commerce, Washington, 1991-94; sr. legis., adv., adminstr. Agy. for Healthcare Policy and Rsch., 1993-94, sr. sci. advisor Ctr. Info. Tech., 1994-98, sr. sci. advisor Ctr. Quality Measurement and Improvement, 1998-99; sr. sci. advisor Agy. for Health Care Rsch. and Quality Ctr. for Quality Improvement and Patient Safety, 2000—05; health scientist adminstr. Ctr. for Primary Care, Prevention, and Partnerships, 2005—06. Sr. legis. advisor Office of Surgeon Gen., 1995—96; project office HHS, Washington, 1977—80; sr. scientist bur. com. health svcs. and delivery systems, 1989—90; mem. U.S. Surgeon Gen.'s Scientist Profl. Adv. Com., Rockville, 1986—90, adv. com., 1984—87; commr. Nat. Cert. Commn. Chemistry and Chem. Engring., Bethesda, Md., 1987—; mem. U.S. Health Care Fin. Adminstrn. AIDS Task Force, Washington, 1986—90, Profl. Exam. Svc., Inc., NYC, 1974—76, Nat. Com. Clin. Lab. Stds. subcom. on cost acctg. and wellness testing and com. on quality of care, materials coms. on computer record sys., med. records and clin. lab. data sys.; chief staffer for quality work group Nat. Ctr. for Vital Health Stats., 1999—2003, mem. staff for quality workgroup and populations subcom., 2003—07; mem. mentor program NYU; mem. Nat. Cert. Commn. in Chemistry and Chem. Engring., 1986—; lead staff for health U.S. Quality Interagy. Com., 2004—06. Author: The Chemistry of Gypsum and its Dehydration Products, 1975, Infection Control As Health Care Facilities, 1977, Statistics for Laboratory Surveyors; co-author: The Federal Regulation of Clinical Laboratories Quality Assurance Standards and Technological Change, 1986; contbr. articles to profl. jours. Sr. scientist USPHS, 1976-77, comdr., 1976-86, capt., 1986—. N.Y. State Regents scholar, 1960-64, N.Y. State Scholar Incentive award, 1964-68. Fellow Am. Inst. Chemists (chmn. membership com. N.Y. sect. 1974-76, chmn. nat. coun. for health lab. svcs., 1988-92, govt. affairs com. 1993—, bd. dirs. 1996-98, 2000—), D.C. Inst. Chemistry (pres. 2004—), Royal Inst. Health, Washington Acad. Scis., Australian Chem. Soc.; mem. ASTM (com. computer records sys., med. records, clin. lab. data), Am. Assn. for Clin. Chemists (legis. com. 1989, advisor to legis. com. 1990—), Am. Chem. Soc., N.Y. Acad. Scis., Assn. Mil. Surgeons U.S., Soc. Armed Forces Mil. Lab. Scientists, Commd. Officers Assn. U.S., APHA (lab. sect. legis. com., chmn. membership com., planning com., action bd. 1984-96, joint policy com. 1993-96), U.S. Naval Sailing Assn., Annapolis Naval Acad. Sailing Assn., Bklyn. Coll. Chemistry Alumni (dir. 1970-86), Bklyn. Coll. Alumni Assn., NYU Alumni Assn., Washington Ski Club, Sigma Xi. Democrat. Jewish. Achievements include development of legislation and regulations to assure quality of clinical laboratory and drug abuse testing, oversight legislative initiatives to improve quality, access and financing of American health care system; medical informatics, bioterrorism and preparedness. Home: 5801 Nicholson Ln Apt 1016 North Bethesda MD 20852 Office: Am Inst Chemists 5801 Nicholson Ln Ste 1016 North Bethesda MD 20852 E-mail: stanedinger@earthlink.net.

EDIRISOORIYA, GUNAPALA, finance educator; s. Sadiris A. P. Edirisooriya and Abanchihamy K. Hennedige; m. Ariyamala W. Edirisooriya, Sept. 13, 1948; children: Milinda C. P., Sithari P. BCom, U. of Ceylon, Peradeniya, Sri Lanka, 1967; MLitt, U. of Glasgow, 1974; MA, U. Del., Newark, 1988, PhD, 1990. Asst. lectr., dept. of economics U. of Colombo, Colombo, Western, Sri Lanka, 1968—77, lectr., dept. of econs., 1977—80, sr. lectr., dept. of econs., 1980—81; inaugural chair, dept. of econs. and commerce Ruhuna U., Matara, Sri Lanka, 1978—79; grade one lectr. U. of Nigeria, Enugu, Anambra, Nigeria, 1981—84; rsch. asst. / temp. lectr. / merit grad. fellow / tchg. asst. U. of Del., Newark, 1984—90; rsch. and evaluation specialist Balt. City Pub. Schools, 1990—94; prof. East Tenn. State U., Johnson City, 1995—2002, assoc. dean, coll. of edn., 1998—2002; prof. Youngstown State U., Youngstown, Ohio, 2002—. Cons. ednl. restructuring project Ministry of Edn., Govt. of Sri Lanka, Colombo, Sri Lanka, 1999; del. Oxford Round Table, England, 2006. Cons. reviewer (manuscript reviewer) Ednl. Rschr. jour., mem. editl. bd. Edn. Policy Analysis Archives, 2006—. Maj. benefactor / founding chair Edirisooriya Found., Tangalle, Sri Lanka, 2001—05. Recipient British Coun. Overseas Students award, U. Glasgow, 1973—74; scholar, U. Colombo, 1970—73. Mem.: Am. Ednl. Rsch. Assn. (co-chair, best paper award comm.; judge, nominating comm. 1992—2005, web mgr. SIG-SRE chair 1997—2002, chair SIG on survey rsch. in edn. 1999—2002, web mgr. SIG-SRE chair 2004—05), Phi Kappa Phi. Achievements include research in evolution of the American higher education sector; doctoral research that laid the groundwork for Delaware Cost Study (estimation of institutional cost in higher education); complexity of state-university relationship; Attitude formation as the basis for attitude measurement: A new approach; development of SAS programming for graphical presentation of survey data. Avocations: jogging, travel. Office: Youngstown State Univ EARF BCOE One University Plz Youngstown OH 44555-0001 Home Phone: 330-270-3645; Office Phone: 330-941-1571. Office Fax: 330-941-3034. E-mail: gedirisooriya@ysu.edu.

EDIS, GLORIA TOBY, pediatrician; b. NYC, Dec. 6, 1939; d. Murray Alvin and Anna G. (Goldstein) E.; m. Myron Royal Schoenfeld, June 14, 1959; children: Bradley, Glenn, Dawn, Melody. BA, Cornell U., 1960; MD, NYU, 1963. Intern Montefiore Hosp., NYC, 1963-64; pediatric resident Columbia Presbyn. Med. Ctr., NYC, 1966-68; pediatrician Scarsdale (N.Y.) Pediatric Assocs., 1977—; pediatric attending Albert Einstein Med. Coll., Bronx, 1968-70; pediatrician Barsky Med. Group, NYC, 1970-80. Fellow Am. Acad. Pediatrics; mem. AMA, Westchester County Med. Soc., Cornell Alumni Assn. Avocations: hiking, bicycling, reading, weight training, theater. Office: Scarsdale Pediatric Assn 2 Overhill Rd Scarsdale NY 10583-5323 Home Phone: 914-428-5358; Office Phone: 914-725-0800.

EDISEN, CLAYTON BYRON, physician; b. Chgo. s. Byron Parker and Elsie Elinor (Mielkie) E.; m. Adele Uskali, 1948 (div. 1968); children: Laura, Glenn, Lynn; m. Barbara S., Dec. 1968 (dec. 2000). PhB, U. Chgo., 1949, MD, 1953. Diplomate Am. Bd. Neurology and Psychiatry. Various positions in field to psychiatrist The Monroe (La.) Area Guidance Ctr., 1956-58, med. dir., psychiatrist, 1957-58; instr. psychiatry Tulane U. Sch. Medicine, New Orleans, 1956-57; staff cons. Children's Bur., New Orleans, 1958-60; staff psychiatrist The Guidance Ctr., New Orleans, 1957-59; staff cons. Crippled Children's Divsn./La. State Dept. Health, 1959; with New Orleans Psychoanalytic Tng. Ctr., 1958-61; pvt. practice New Orleans, 1957—; apptd. in psychiatry De Paul Hosp., New Orleans, 1957—. Adj. full prof. exptl. comms. design, Tulane U., New Orleans, 1973-74; courtesy staff Coliseum Med. Ctr., New Orleans, 1974—; fellow Scientific Coun. of the Internat. Coll. of Angiology, 1972; del. Internat. Congress on Drug Edn., Montreux, Switzerland/World Psychiat. Assn., 1973, others; vis. faculty lectr. Sch. of Social Work, Tulane U., 1958-60; asst. vis. physician Charity Hosp. of La., New Orleans, 1954-56; vis. staff psychiatrist Touro Infirmary, New Orleans, 1958-72; temporary dir. De Paul Hosp., New Orleans, 1960; lectr. to Annual Life Inst., Jewish Fedn. New Orleans, 1961, others; panelist/lectr. in field. Contbr. numerous articles to profl. jours. and publs. Sgt. U.S. Army, 1945-47, ETO. Fellow Am. Geriatric Soc., Interam. Coll. Physicians and Surgeons, Royal Soc. Health/London; mem. AMA (Physicians Recognition awards), Am. Group Psychotherapy Assn., La. Group Psychotherapy Soc. and Inst., La. State Med. Soc. (numerous offices), Orleans Parish Med. Soc., Am. Psychiat. Assn., So. Med. Assn., New Orleans Psychiat. Forum, 2nd Dist. Med. Soc., La. Dist. Br. APA, New Orleans Area Psychiat. Soc., La. Psychiat. Assn., Pan Am. Med. Assn., World Psychiatric Assn., Assn. Am. Physcians and Surgeons, Am. Heart Assn., N.Y. Acad. Scis., Sigma Xi, others. Republican. Avocations: golf, bridge. Office: 2900 Hessmer Ave Metairie LA 70002-5820 Personal E-mail: cedisenmd@aol.com.

EDISON, ALLEN RAY, electrical engineer, educator; b. Plainview, Nebr., Sept. 21, 1926; s. Arthur and Lela (Johnson) E.; m. Betty Jean Broer, Dec. 27, 1949; children— Karl Arthur, Kathryn Johannah. BS, U. Nebr., 1950, MS, 1957; D.Sc., U. N.M., 1962. Engr. Silas Mason Co., Burlington, Iowa, 1950-53; instr. U. Nebr., Lincoln, 1953-57, prof. elec. engring., 1957-89, prof. emeritus, 1989—, chmn. dept. elec. engring., 1964-70. Served with USNR, 1944-46. Mem. I.E.E.E. (past sect. chmn.), Sigma Xi, Sigma Tau, Eta Kappa Nu. Home: 3747 N 58th St Lincoln NE 68507-1658

EDISON, BERNARD ALAN, retired apparel executive; b. Atlanta, 1928; s. Irving and Beatrice (Chanin) Edison; m. Marilyn S Wewers, Apr. 26, 1975. BA, Harvard U., 1949, MBA, 1951. With Edison Bros. Stores Inc., St. Louis, 1951—, asst. v.p., 1957-58, v.p. leased depts., 1958-67, v.p., asst. treas., 1967-68, pres., 1968-87, chmn. fin. com., 1987-89, dir. emeritus, 1989-96. Office: Edison Foundations 220 N Fourth St Ste A Saint Louis MO 63102

EDLAVITCH, SUSAN T., lawyer; b. Washington, Sept. 29, 1948; BS, Washington U., 1970; JD, Indiana U., 1976; LLM in Taxation with high honors, George Washington U., 1990. Bar: Indiana 1976, DC 1991, Md. 1991, US Tax Ct., US Ct. of Appeals, Fourth Circuit, US Supreme Ct. Law clerk to Judge V. Sue Shields and Judge Patrick D. Sullivan Indiana Ct. of Appeals, 1976—79; atty. Office of Gen. Counsel, FCC, 1980—88, Office of Chief Counsel, IRS, 1988—96; assoc. Venable LLP, Washington, ptnr., federal taxation law, 2000—. Mem. Thompson West Tax Advisory Bd. Author: Tax Management Memorandum, Journal of Real Estate Taxation. Mem.: ABA (mem. tax section, mem. corp. tax and partnership tax com.), DC Women's Bar Assn., Md. State Bar Assn., DC Bar Assn. (mem. corp. tax com.). Office: Venable LLP 575 7th St NW Washington DC 20004 Office Phone: 202-344-4000. Office Fax: 202-344-8300. Business E-Mail: stedlavitch@venable.com.

EDLES, GARY JOEL, lawyer, educator; b. NYC, Feb. 27, 1941; s. Allen Irving and Helen (Hurowitz) E.; m. Nadine Cohen, Feb. 15, 1973. BA, Queens Coll., 1962; JD, NYU, 1965; LLM, George Washington U., 1966, DJuridical Sci., 1975. Bar: N.Y. 1966, U.S. Ct. Appeals (D.C. cir.) 1970. Staff atty. Civil Aeronautics Bd., Washington, 1967-75, assoc. gen. coun., 1975-77, dep. gen. coun., 1977-80; dir. office of procs. Interstate Commerce Commn., Washington, 1980-81; adminstrv. appeals judge Nuclear Regulatory Commn., Washington, 1981-87; gen. coun. Administrv. Conf. U.S., Washington, 1987-95; fellow Am. U. Law Sch., 1995—. Faculty dept. justice Legal Edn. Inst., 1982-97; vis. prof. U. Sheffield, Eng., 1994, U. Hull, Eng., 1997—. Co-author: Federal Regulatory Process, 2d edit., 1989, An Interpretive Guide to the Government in the Sunshine Act, 2d edit., 2005; contbr. articles to profl. jours. Mem. ABA. Home: 10 Keldgate Beverley HU17 8HY England Home Phone: 011 44 1482 873566; Office Phone: 202-274-4186. E-mail: g.j.edles@hull.ac.uk, gedles@wcl.american.edu.

EDLEY, CHRISTOPHER F., JR., dean, law educator; b. 1953; m. Maria Echaveste. BA, Swarthmore Coll., 1973; JD, MPP, Harvard U., 1978. Bar: DC 1980. Asst. dir. White House Domestic Policy Staff, D.C., 1978-79; spl. asst. sec. Dept. Health Edn. and Welfare, Washington, 1979-80; assoc. asst. to the Pres. White House Office of the Chief of Staff, Washington, 1980; asst. prof. Harvard U. Law Sch., Cambridge, Mass., 1981-87, prof., 1987—; assoc. dir. Office of Mgmt. & Budget, Washington, 1993—95; dean, prof. law U. Calif., Boalt Hall Law Sch., Berkeley, 2004—. Mem. U.S. Civil Rights Commn., 1999—2005, Nat. Commn. on Fed. Election Reform. Editor and officer Harvard Law Review; author: Not All Black and White: Affirmative Action, Race and American Values, Administrative Law: Rethinking Judicial Control of Bureaucracy. Nat. issues dir. Dukakis for Pres. Campaign, Boston, 1987-88; co-founder, Civil Rights Project, 1996-; spl. consultant to Pres. Clinton on Race Initiative, 1997-99. Named one of 100 Most Influential Lawyers, Nat. Law Jour., 2006. Fellow: Am. Acad. Arts & Scis.; mem.: Divsn. on Behavioral and Social Scis. and Edn. Nat. Academies Scis. (adv. bd. exec. com.), Coun. on Fgn. Relations, Nat. Acad. of Pub. Adminstrn. Office: The Civil Rights Project 125 Mt Auburn St 3rd Fl Cambridge MA 02138 also: U Calif 215 Boalt Hall Berkeley CA 94720-7200 Office Phone: 510-642-6483. E-mail: edley@law.berkeley.edu.*

EDLICH, RICHARD FRENCH, biomedical engineer, educator; b. NYC, Jan. 19, 1939; MD, NYU, 1962; PhD, U. Minn., 1973. From instr. to assoc. prof. U. Va. Sch. Medicine, Charlottesville, 1971-76, prof. plastic surgery and biomed. engring., dist. prof. emergency medicine, 1976-82, disting. prof. plastic and maxillofacial surgery and biomed. engring., 1983-96, Raymoon F. Morgan prof. plastic surgery and disting. prof. biomed. engring., 1996—2001; dir. Trauma Prevention, Rsch. and Edn. Trauma Specialist LLP of Legacy Emanuel Hosp., Portland, 2004—. Founder dept. emergency medicine U. Va., 1973, DeCamp Burn and wound Healing Ctr., 1974—85, Pegasus Air Med. Transp. Sys., 1984; physician tech. adviser Bur. Emergency Svc., HEW, 1974—79; cons. Divsn. Health Manpower and Nat. Ctr. Health Svc. Rsch., 1977—79; founder North Fork Rsch. Pk., Charlottesville, Va., 1991. Editor-in-chief: Jour. Long-Term Effects Med. Implants, 2000—06. Named Richard Edlich rsch. prof. plastic surgery, U. Va. Health Sys., 1984—, 5th Ann. David Boyd Lectr. in Emergency Medicine, 2001, Inventor of Yr., U. Va. Patent Found., 2002—; recipient Disting. Pub. Svc. award for Contbns. to Emergency Medicine, USPHS, 1979, Outstanding Tchg. award, U. Va., 1989, Thomas Jefferson award, 1991, Outstanding Faculty award, Commonwealth of Va. Coun. Higher Edn., 1989, Disting. Alumni award, U. Minn. Med. Alumni Assn., 2005, The Lawn Soc., U. Va., 2006. Mem.: ACS, Am. Surg. Assn., Am. Coll. Emergency Physicians, Soc. Acad. Emergency Medicine, Am. Soc. Plastic and Reconstructive Surgeons, Univ. Assn. Emergency Medicine, Am. Burn Assn. (Harvey Stuart Allen award 2000), Am. Assn. Surg. Trauma, Soc. Univ. Surgeons, U. Va. Lawn Soc., Alpha Omega Alpha. Achievements include research in biology of wound repair and infection, systems approach to emergency medical and trauma care; development of Edlich gastric lavage; reinforced steri-strip; CSM gram stain procedure; Shur-Clens; stabilized topical pharmaceutical preperations. Home and Office: 22500 NE 128th Cir Brush Prairie WA 98606 Home Phone: 360-944-7641; Office Phone: 360-944-7641. Office Fax: 360-944-7612. Personal E-mail: richardedlichmd@gmail.com.

EDLIN, RICHARD A., lawyer; b. Rantoul, Ill., July 21, 1960; BA magna cum laude, Tufts Univ., 1982; JD, Columbia Univ., 1985. Bar: NJ 1985, NY 1986, US Supreme Ct., US Ct. of Appeal (2nd, 3rd, 7th, fed. cir.), US Tax Ct. Law clk. Hon. Lee P. Gagliardi US Dist. Ct. (so. dist.) NY, 1985—86; shareholder corp. and securities litig., co-chair nat. life sciences practice Greenberg Traurig LLP, NYC. Bd. dir. Firebrand Fin. Group. Bd. dir. Youth Edn. Through Sports Inc; adv. bd. mem. Entrepreneurship Inst.; bd. govs. Hackensack U. Med. Ctr.; mem. judiciary com. Fedn. Internationale du Sport Universitaire. Mem.: Bar Assn. NYC, Internat. Bar Assn. Office: Greenberg Traurig LLP MetLife Bldg 200 Park Ave New York NY 10166-1400 Office Phone: 212-801-6528. Office Fax: 212-805-5528. Business E-Mail: edlinr@gtlaw.com.

EDLIS, STEFAN T., plastics company executive; m. H. Gael Neeson. Pres. Apollo Plastics Corp., Chgo. Trustee Mus. Modern Art, NYC. Named one of Top 200 Collectors, ARTnews Mag., 2004. Mem.: Whitney Mus. Am. Art (nat. com.). Avocation: collector of contemporary art. Office: Apollo Plastics 5333 N Elston Ave Chicago IL 60630

EDLOW, KENNETH LEWIS, security firm executive; b. Washington, July 27, 1941; s. Ellis and Leonora (Kraft) Edlow; m. Mary Glanzrock, Dec. 19, 1970; children: E. Fielding, Brian. BS in Econ., U. Pa., 1963. Stockbroker Ferris & Co., Washington, 1963-69; various positions Bear, Stearns & Co., Inc., NYC, 1969—; corp. sec. Bear Stearns Cos. Inc., 1987—. Pres Monterey Fund Inc; vpres, secy Edlow Family Fund, Inc. Mem.: Am Numismatic Soc (trustee 1993—). Avocation: fishing. Home: 35 E 85th St New York NY 10028-0954 Office: Bear Stearns & Co Inc 320 Park Ave New York NY 10022 Home Phone: 212-861-8632; Office Phone: 212-272-4394. Business E-Mail: kedlow@bear.com.

EDMISTON, MARK MORTON, publishing company executive; b. Yonkers, NY, July 9, 1943; s. Marcus Morton and Josephine (Brown) E.; m. Lisa Mary Pustorino, Aug. 28, 1965; children: Ann Kathleen, Laura Mary. BA, Wesleyan U., 1966. Circulation mgr. Life mag., NYC, until 1969, circulation and mktg. dir. Tokyo, 1969-70; circulation dir. Saturday Rev., Inc., 1971-73; circulation dir. internat. edits. Newsweek, Inc., 1973-76, pub., 1976-78, pres., 1978-79, corp. exec. v.p., 1979-81, chmn. and pres., 1981-86; pres. TVSM Inc., NYC, 1987-91; exec. v.p. Times Mirror Mag., NYC, 1991-92; co-chmn. The Jordan Edmiston Group Inc., NYC, 1992—99; mng. dir. Admedia Ptnrs., Inc., NYC, 1998—. Bd. dirs., mem. governing bd. for pub. Am. Chem. Soc., Washington. Founder Civilization: The Mag. of the Libr. of Congress, Univ. Bus. Mag. Trustee emeritus Wesleyan U.; trustee Children's Aid Soc. of N.Y., Cmty. Svc. Soc. N.Y. Office: Admedia Ptnrs 444 Madison Ave New York NY 10022-6903 Business E-Mail: medmiston@admediapartners.com.

EDMISTON, SCOTT, academic administrator, educator; Artistic assoc. Huntington Theatre Co., Boston; asst. prof. - dramatic lit. Boston U. Coll. Fine Arts, chmn. MFA Directing Program; dir. office of arts Brandeis U., 2003—. Dir.: (plays) Harold Pinter's Betrayal, 2003 (Elliot Norton Award Outstanding Production, 2003), Brian Friel's Molly Sweeney, 1998 (Elliot Norton Award Outstanding Dir.), Jacques Brel is Alive & Well & Living in Paris, 2003. Named one of region's ten best theatre dir., Boston Herald. Mem.: Alliance Boston Theatre Artists & Producers (pres. bd., StageSource 1998—). Office: Dir Office of Arts Brandeis University MS 051 Waltham MA 02454 Office Phone: 781-736-2027. E-mail: scotted@brandeis.edu.

EDMO, JEAN UMIOKALANI, artist, poet; b. LA, Apr. 12, 1942; d. Lemuel Kanekikawaiola Cutter and Nancy James Watson; m. Edward McCleary Edmo, Mar. 17, 1984 (dec. Mar. 1996); 8 stepchildren. Grad., Comml. Art Sch., San Francisco, 1963. Author: (poetry) Songs of Life and Love, 2000, rev. edit., 2002, (short stories) Some Passions Never Die, 2002; one-woman shows include nine oil, acrylic and mixed media landscapes., Photographs in One Woman Shows, Chile, 1962; Nat. Photo Book. Nominee Poet of Yr., Internat. Poetry Guild, 2001; recipient Editors award, 2002, Outstanding Achievment cup, Internat. Soc. Poets, Merit Award medal. Green Party. Episcopalian. Avocation: walking, gardening, making craft wreaths, birdwatching.

EDMOND, JOHN, engineering company executive; b. NY; m. Rita Edmond. BS, Alfred Univ.; PhD in Materials Sci., Engring., NC State Univ. Co-founder Cree LED tech., Durham, NC, 1987—, rsch., devel. chief. Named one of One of 50 Who Matter Now, Business 2.0, 2007. Office: Cree Inc 4600 Silicon Dr Durham NC 27703 Office Phone: 919-313-5300. Office Fax: 919-313-5558.*

EDMONDS, ALBERT J., career officer; b. Columbus, Ga., Jan. 17, 1942; m. Jacquelyn Y. McDaniel; children: Gia, Sheri, Alicia. BS Chemistry, Morris Brown Coll., 1964; MA Counseling Psychology, Hampton U., 1969; grad., Air War Coll., 1980; completed, Harvard U. Nat. Security Program; DSc (hon.), Morris Brown Coll., 1990. Entered Air Force, 1964; data systems officer, tactical comm. area Keesler AFB, Miss., 1966; inspection team chief, dir. emergency mission support Pacific Comm. Area Hickam AFB, Hawaii, 1969; chief ops. 2083rd Comm. Squadron, Takhli Royal Thai AFB, Thailand, 1969-72; action officer Directorate Command, Control and Comm. Hdqs. USAF, Washington, 1973; head Commercial Comm. Policy Office Defense Comm. Agy., Washington, 1975; dir. comm.

electronics Strategic Air Command's 3rd Air divsn., commander 27th comm. squadron Andersen AFB (Guam), 1977; chief joint matters group, Directorate Command, Control, Telecom., Office Dep. Chief Staff Plans and Ops. Hdqs. USAF, Washington, 1980-83, dir. plans and prgrams for asst. chief info. systems, 1983; asst. dep. chief staff comm. and electronics, vice commander Tactical Comm. divsn. Hdqs. Tactical Air Command Langley AFB, 1983-84; dep. chief staff comm.-computer systems, commander Tactical Comm. divsn. AF Comm. Command Langley AFB, 1985-88; dir. Command and Control, Comm. and Computer Systems Directorate, US Ctrl. Command MacDill AFB, Fla., 1988—89; asst. chief staff, systems for command, control, comm. and computers AF Hdqs., Washington, 1989-90, dep. chief staff, command, control, comm. and computers, 1990-91, vice dir. command, control, comm. and computer systems directorate, dep. dir. Defense-Wide C4 support, 1991; lt. gen., dir. command, control, comm., computer systems directorate Joint Staff Dept. Defense, Washington, 1993; dir. Def. Information Sys. Agy., 1994—97; mgr. Nat. Comm. Sys., Arlington, Va.; dir. President's Nat. Security Telecommunications Adv. Com.; pres. TRI-COR Industries; v.p., COO Electronic Data Systems Federal, 1998—99; v.p. global sales and client solutions, US Gov. Electronic Data Systems, Plano, Tex., pres. US Gov. accounts, Information Solutions, 2001; sr. advisor, technology Dimensions Internat., Inc., Va., 2004—. Dir. comm.-electronics Strategic Air Command Third Air Divsn., comdr., 27th Comm. Squadron; mem. Nat. Infrastructure Adv. Coun., 2002. Recipient Disting. Svc. medal, Defense Superior Svc. medal, Legion of Merit, Meritorious Svc. medal with two oak leaf clusters, AF Commendation medal with three oak leaf clusters. Life Mem. Kappa Alpha Psi, Kappa Delta Pi, Armed Forces Comm. and Electronics Assn. (chmn.). Office: Dimension Internat Inc 2800 Eisenhower Ave Ste 300 Alexandria VA 22314 Office Phone: 703-998-0098. Office Fax: 703-379-1695.

EDMONDS, ANNE CAREY, librarian; b. Penang, Malaysia, Dec. 19, 1924; d. William John and Neil (Carey) E. Student, U. Reading, England, 1942-44; BA, Barnard Coll., 1948; MSLS, Columbia U., 1950; MA, Johns Hopkins U., 1959; postgrad., Western Res. U., 1960-61; LHD, Mount Holyoke Coll., 1994. With War Damage Commn., London, 1944-46; children's asst. Enoch Pratt Free Libr., Balt., 1948-49; reference libr. Sch. Bus. Adminstrn., CCNY, 1950-51; reference libr. then asst. libr. readers' svcs. Goucher Coll., Balt., 1951-60; exchange reference libr. European svcs. libr. BBC, London, 1955; instr. Sch. L.S., Syracuse U., summer 1960; libr. Douglass Coll., Rutgers U., New Brunswick, NJ, 1961-64, instr., summer 1962, fall 1963; libr. Mt. Holyoke Coll., 1964-94. Vis. libr. U. North, Turfloop, South Africa, 1976-77; mem. libr. vis. com. Wheaton Coll., Norton, Mass., 1978-92; mem. local systems adv. group Online Computer Libr. Ctr., Inc., 1984-87, mem. adv. com. on coll. and univ. librs., 1988-89. Author: A Memory Book: Mount Holyoke College, 1834-1987, 1988 (with Gai Carpenter and others) Computing Strategies in Liberal Arts Colleges, 1992. Mem. South Hadley (Mass.) Bicentennial Com., 1975—76; mem. accreditation teams Middle State Assn. Colls. and Secondary Schs., 1963—94, New Eng. Assn. Schs. and Colls., 1986—94; exec. com. New Eng. Libr. Info. Network, 1974—76, 1979—85, chmn., 1982—84; mem. Adv. Commn. Historic Deerfield, 1975—81, 1986—94; trustee Ctr. for Maine Contemporary Art, Rockport, Maine, 2001—; bd. dirs. U.S. Book Exch., 1973—76, 1980—83, Maine Grand Opera, Camden, Conservancy for Camden Harbor Park and Amphitheatre. Mem. AAUW (bd. dirs. main chpt. 1998—), ALA, Assn. Coll. Rsch. Librs. (pres. 1970-71, chmn. constn. and bylaws com. New Eng. chpt. 1975-76, pres. New Eng. chpt. 1983-84). E-mail: ACE13@midcoast.com.

EDMONDS, BETH, state legislator; m. Dan Nickerson. BA, Clark U., 1972; MA, Goddard Coll., 1974. Children's libr. Freeport Cmty. Libr., 1988—; mem. Maine Senate from 23d Dist., Augusta, 2001—, chair labor com., 2001—, mem. marine resources com., 2001—; pres. Maine State Senate, Augusta, 2004—. Mem. Freeport Housing Trust, 1987-95, chair, 1991-95; chair Freeport Mcpl. Employee Labor Com., 1996-97. Democrat. Home: 122 Hunter Rd Freeport ME 04032 Office: State House 3 State House Sta Augusta ME 04333 Office Phone: 207-287-1500. Office Fax: (207) 287-1585. E-mail: edmonds@gwi.net.

EDMONDS, CRYSTAL D., language educator, distance learning coordinator; d. James and Delores Quick; m. Derek Edmonds, Sept. 6, 1990, children: Daniel, Jewell, Elizabeth. BA, U. NC, Pembroke, 1988, MA, 1997. Admissions counselor U. NC, 1989—99; instr. English Robeson CC, Lumberton, 2000—, coord. distance learning, 2004—. Recipient Tchr. Yr., Robeson C.C., 2005. Mem.: NC CC Assn. Distance Learning, NC Conf. English Instrs., Robeson CC Assn. (assoc.; sec. 2004—05), Robeson CC Faculty Assn. (assoc.; pres. 2005—06). Office Phone: 910-272-3700.

EDMONDS, DEAN STOCKETT, JR., physicist, educator, director; b. NYC, Dec. 24, 1924; s. Dean Stockett and Mary Watkins (Arms) Edmonds; m. Mary Louise Wilson, July 28, 1951 (dec. May 1978); children: Dean Stockett III, Louis Round Wilson, Ann Helene Edmonds Mahoney, Elizabeth V. Casey; m. Wendy Nickerson Adams, Nov. 7, 1993. BS, MIT, 1950, PhD, 1958; MA, Princeton U., 1952. Co-founder, v.p., dir. Nuclide Corp., 1958—65; asst. prof. physics Coll. Liberal Arts Boston U., 1961—67, assoc. prof. physics, 1967—83, prof. physics, 1983—91, prof. emeritus, 1991—; co-founder, pres., chmn. Tachisto Laser Sys., Inc., 1971—85; dir., chief sci. adv. bd. Gen. Ionex Inc., 1974—85; regional v.p., dir. Nat. Aeronautic Assn., 1988—. Vis prof physics Univ Western Ont. London, 1972—74; research fellow Harvard Univ, Cambridge, Mass., 1959—61; guest physics dept MIT, Cambridge, Mass., 1959—61. Author: (book) Novel Experiments in Physics II, 1975; author: (with B. Cioffari) Experiments in College Physics, 6th ed, 1978, 7th edit., 1983, 9th edit., 1993, 10th edit., 1997; co-editor: Experiments in Physics for General Physics Courses Without Calculus, 1968, Experiments in Physics for General Physics Courses With Calculus, 1968; contbr. articles to profl jours. Master sgt US Army, 1943—47, ETO, PTO. Mem.: IEEE, Am. Assn. Physics Tchrs. (Spec Merit Award), Am Phys. Soc. Achievements include research in molecular beams leading to cesium atomic clock, the present internat. time standard; development of the racetrack microtron accelerator for cancer therapy. Avocations: amateur radio, restoring antique aircraft and sports cars, sport flying, opera, building high fidelity systems. Home: 1019 Spyglass Ln Naples FL 34102-7734 Office: Boston U Dept Physics 590 Commonwealth Ave Boston MA 02215-2521 Office Phone: 617-353-2612

EDMONDS, EDMUND P., law librarian, educator, dean; b. Mar. 3, 1951; m. Brigid Edmonds; children: Paul, Anne, Katherine. BA, U. Notre Dame, 1973; MLS, U. Md., College Park, 1974; JD, U. Toledo, 1978. Bar: Ohio 1978, Va. 1982. Head circulation dept. U. Toledo Coll. Law, 1974—78; assoc. law libr., asst. prof. Marshall-Wythe Sch. Law, Coll. William and Mary, 1978—82, acting law libr., 1982—83, law libr., assoc. prof. law, 1983—88; law libr., prof. law Loyola U. New Orleans Coll. Law, 1988—92, dir. law libr., prof. law, 1992—2000, assoc. dean academic affairs, 1992—93, asst. dean info. resources, 1994—97, stats. coord., 1997—2000; dir. Schoenecker Law Libr., prof. law U. St. Thomas Sch. Law, Minn., 2001—06; assoc. dean libr. and info. tech., dir. Kresge Law Libr., prof. law U. Notre Dame Law Sch., Ind., 2006—. Contbr. articles to profl. jours. Mem.: New Orleans Assn. Law Librs., Am. Assn. Law Librs. Office: Notre Dame Law Sch U Notre Dame PO Box 535 Notre Dame IN 46556-0535 Home: 53254 Bracken Fern Dr South Bend IN 46637 Office Phone: 574-631-5916. Personal E-mail: ebedmonds@comcast.net. E-mail: edmonds.7@nd.edu.*

EDMONDS, IVY GORDON, retired writer; b. Frost, Tex., Feb. 15, 1917; s. Ivy Gordon and Delia Louella (Shumate) E.; m. Reiko Mimura, July 12, 1956; 1 dau., Annette. Student pub. schs. Pub. rels. mgr. Northrop Corp., Anaheim, Calif., 1968-79, indsl. editor, Hawthorne, Calif., 1979-86. Freelance writer; author books including: Solomon In Kimono, 1957, Ooka the Wise, 1961, The Bounty's Boy, 1963, Hollywood RIP, 1963, Joel of the Hanging Gardens, 1966, Trickster Tales, 1966, Taiwan-the Other China, 1971, The Possible Impossibles of Ikkyo The Wise, 1971, The Magic Man, 1972, Mao's Long March, 1973, Motorcycling for Beginners, 1973, China's Red Rebel: Mao Tse-Tung, 1973, Micronesia, 1974, Pakistan, Land of Mystery, Tragedy and Courage, 1974, Automotive Tuneups for Beginners, 1974, Ethiopia, 1975, The Magic Makers, 1976, The Shah of Iran, 1976, Allah's Oil: Mid-East Petroleum, 1976, Second Sight, 1977, Motorcycle Racing for Beginners, 1977, Islam, 1977, The Mysteries of Troy, 1977, Big U Universal in the Silent Days, Buddhism, 1978, D.D. Home, 1978, Bicycle Motocross, 1979, Hinduism, 1979, Girls Who Talked to Ghosts, 1979, The Magic Brothers, 1979, (with William H. Gebhardt) Broadcasting for Beginners, 1980, (with Reiko Mimura) The Oscar Directors, 1980, The Mysteries of Homer's Greeks, 1981, The Kings of Black Magic, 1981, Funny Car Racing for Beginners, 1982, The Magic Dog, 1982; author textbooks: (with Ronald Gonzales) Understanding Your Car, 1975, Introduction to Welding, 1975; also author pulp and soft cover fiction and nonfiction under names of Gene Cross and Gary Gordon and publishers house names. With USAAF, 1940-45, USAF, 1946-63. Decorated D.F.C., Air medals, Bronze Star. Home: 5801 Shirl St Cypress CA 90630-3326

EDMONDS, JAMES PATRICK (JIM EDMONDS), professional baseball player; b. Fullerton, Calif., June 27, 1970; Grad., H.S., Calif. Outfielder Calif. Angels (now Anaheim Angels), 1993—99, St. Louis Cardinals, 2000—. Named to All-Star Team, Am. League, 1995, Nat. League All-Star Team, 2000, 2003, Nat. League All-Star Game, 2005; recipient Am. League Gold Glove Award, 1997, 1998, Nat. League Gold Glove Award, 2000—05. Office: St Louis Cardinals 250 Stadium Plz Saint Louis MO 63102-1722

EDMONDS, NICK, sculptor; b. 1937; Student, Ogunquit Sch. Painting and Sculpture, 1953—56; grad. with honors, Boston Mus. Sch., 1961. Prof. sculpture Mus. Sch. of Milton Acad., 1962—65, Boston U., 1965—2003, prof. emeritus, 2003—. Exhibitions include, Sullivan Goss, 808 Gallery, Saint Gaudens Historic Site, New Britain Museum of Am. Art, U. Art Gallery, NorthEastern U., Copley Soc. of Boston, Represented in permanent collections, NAD, New Britain Museum of Am. Art, Tufts U., Wiggen Gallery, St. Anselm Coll., SUNY Coll. at Cortland. Recipient Blanche E. Colman award, 1973, first prize for sculpture, 171st Ann. Exhbn. NAD, 1996, Orville Lance Prize for sculpture, 176th Ann. Exhbn. NAD, 2001; Fulbright grantee, Japan, 1975—76, Mass. Coun. for the Arts and Humanities grantee, 1977, Saint Gaudens fellow, 1981, Artist fellow, Berkshire Taconic Found., 2004. Mem.: NAD (Harry Watroos prize and medal 2005). Office: PO Box 86 Sharon MA 02067 Office Phone: 781-784-4531.

EDMONDS, SCOTT A., apparel executive; Positions up to pres. Ft. Myers, Fla. divsn. Ferguson Enterprises, Inc., 1980—93; ops. mgr. Chico's FAS, Inc., Ft. Myers, Fla., 1993—94, v.p. ops., 1994—95, sr. v.p. ops., 1996—2000, COO, 2000—01, pres., 2001—, CEO, 2003—, bd. dirs., 2004—. Office: Chicos FAS Inc 11215 Metro Pky Fort Myers FL 33966-1206 Office Phone: 239-277-6200. Office Fax: 239-277-5237.*

EDMONDS, THOMAS ANDREW, legal association administrator; b. Jackson, Miss., July 5, 1938; BA, Miss. Coll., 1962; LL.B., Duke U., 1965. Bar: Fla. 1965, Va. 1981. Pvt. practice law, Orlando, Fla., 1965-66; assoc. prof. law U. Miss., Oxford, 1966-70; assoc. prof.law Fla. State U., Tallahassee, 1970-74, prof., 1974-77; dean Sch. Law, U. Richmond (Va.), 1977-87, U. Miss. Sch. Law, University, 1987-89; exec. dir. Va. State Bar, Richmond, 1989—. Vis. assoc. prof. Duke U., 1968-69; vis. prof. McGeorge Sch. Law of the Univ. of the Pacific, 1975-76. Served with USMC, 1957-60. Office: VA State Bar 707 E Main St Ste 1500 Richmond VA 23219-2800

EDMONDS, THOMAS LEON, lawyer, management consultant; b. Borger, Tex., May 10, 1932; s. Cline Azel and Flora (Love) E.; m. Virginia Marguerite Leon, June 20, 1960; 1 child, Stephanie Lynn. BSChemE, Tex. Tech. U., 1953, JD, 1973. Bar: Tex. 1974, US Tax Ct. 1975, US Ct. Appeals (5th cir.) 1975, US Dist. Ct. (no. dist.) Tex. 1976, US Supreme Ct. 1996; registered profl. engr., Tex. Engr. computers-exec. dept. Phillips Petroleum, Bartlesville, Okla., 1953-67; mktg. specialist Control Data, Dallas, 1967-68; exec. v.p. CUI, Austin, Tex., 1968-70; mgmt. cons. Mcauto, St. Louis, 1970-71; sr. ptnr. Edmonds & Assocs., Borger, 1973—. City atty. City of Borger, 1991—; treas., dir. Ram Biochems., Inc. Mem. chancellor's coun. Tex. Tech. U.; bd. dirs. Can. River Mcpl. Water Authority, Hutchinson County Tex. Hist. Commn., chmn. 1992-00. Mem. 5th Cir. Bar Assn. (charter), Borger Bar Assn. (pres. 1998-2002). Home: 210 Broadmoor St Borger TX 79007-8210 Office: PO Box 985 Borger TX 79008-0985 Office Phone: 806-273-2828.

EDMONDS, TRACEY E., film company executive; b. LA, Feb. 18, 1967; m. Kenneth "Babyface" Edmonds, Sept. 5, 1994 (separated); children: Brandon, Dylan. Attended, Standford U. Pres., CEO Edmonds Entertainment Group, 1996—2006; pres., COO Our Stories Films, 2006—; pres. Yab Yum Entertainment. Actor, exec. prodr.: (films) Hav Plenty, 1997; prodr.: Soul Food, 1997, Light It Up, 1999, Punks, 2000, Josie and the Pussycats, 2001; exec. prodr.: (TV films) Maniac Magee, 2003; actor: (TV series) Soul Food, 2000, College Hill, 2004; exec. prodr.: Lil Kim: Countdown to Lockdown, 2006; featured in Ebony mag., 2007. Named one of 100 Most Powerful Women in Entertainment, Hollywood Reporter, 2006. Office: Yab Yum Entertainment 1635 N Cahuenga Blvd 6th Fl Los Angeles CA 90028*

EDMONDS, VELMA MCINNIS, nursing educator; b. NYC, Feb. 17, 1940; d. Walter Lee and Eva Doris (Grant) McInnis; children: Stephen Clay, Michelle Louise. Diploma, Charity Hosp. Sch. Nursing, New Orleans, 1961; BSN, Med. Coll. Ga., 1968; MSN, U. Ala., Birmingham, 1980; D of Nursing Sci., La. State U., 2001. Staff nurse Ochsner Found. Hosp., New Orleans, 1961—63, 1987—2002, clin. educator, 1987-89; staff nurse Suburban Hosp., Bethesda, Md., 1963-65; asst. DON svc., dir. staff devel. Providence Hosp., Mobile, Ala., 1967-70; staff nurse MICU U. So. Ala. Med. Ctr., Mobile, 1980-82, clin. nurse specialist, nutrition/metabolic support, 1982-84; instr., coord., BSN completion program Northwestern State U. Coll. Nursing, Pineville, La., 1984-86; head nurse So. Bapt. Hosp., New Orleans, 1986-87; instr. nursing La. State U. Health Sci. Ctr., New Orleans, 1989-91, asst. prof. nursing, 1991—2002; clin. coord. Transitional Hosp. Corp., 1994-95; cons., vis. prof. U. Guam Coll. Nursing and Health Scis., 2002—03; prin. investigator, vis. rsch. scholar U. Pa. Rsch. Inst., 2005—06. Gov.-apptd. mem. La. Bd. Examiners in Dietetics and Nutrition, 1990—98, sec.-treas., 1996—97; cons., faculty U. Guam, 2002—03; co-prin. investigator, project dir. The Recruitment and Retention of Hispanic Nursing Students, U. Tex. El Paso; rschr. with recently immigrated Honduran women; rschr. with recently immigrated Mex. women, 2004; presenter in field; reviewer pubs. and grants; cons. in field. Author: publs. in field. Advisor Hispanic C. of C., New Orleans; adv. bd. Cmty. Vietnamese Outreach Program, Meth. Hosp., New Orleans; chmn. Silent Auction, New Orleans Dollars for Scholars Found., 2000; founding bd. dirs., edn. coord. Orgn. Health and Med. Profession Women, Guam and Western Pacific; mem. ARC Disaster Team. Recipient Nursing Excellence group award Ochsner Fedn. Hosp., New Orleans, 1987, Merit cert. Tb Assn. Greater New Orleans, 1961; fellow USDA, 2004, Rsch. Inst. U. Pa., 2005-07. Mem. ANA, Nat. Soc. Nutrition Edn., La. State Nurses' Assn. (dist. 7), Tex. Nurses Assn., Am. Soc. Parenteral and Enteral Nutrition, La. State Soc. Parenteral and Enteral Nutrition (program and edn. coms.), Mobile Area Nonvolitional Nutrition Support Assn. (past pres.), Transcultural Nursing Soc., Soc. Nutrition Edn., Orgn. Health and Med. Profl. Women (Guam and We. Pacific region founding bd. dirs., edn. coord.), Am. Red Cross Disaster Team, Tex. Nurses Assn., Sigma Theta Tau. Office: U Tex at El Paso Sch Nursing 1100 N Campbell St El Paso TX 79902 Office Phone: 915-747-7261. Personal E-mail: vmedmonds@hotmail.com. Business E-mail: vedmonds@utep.edu.

EDMONDSON, DREW (WILLIAM ANDREW EDMONDSON), state attorney general; b. Washington, Oct. 12, 1946; m. Linda Larason; children: Mary Elizabeth, Robert Andrew. BA in Speech Edn., Northeastern State U., Tahlequah, Okla., 1968; JD, U. Tulsa, 1978. Mem. Okla. Legislature, 1974—76; intern Office Dist. Atty., Muskogee, Okla., 1978—, asst. dist. atty., 1979, chief prosecutor, 1982—, dist. atty., 1982—92; pvt. practice atty. Muskogee, 1979—82, Green & Edmondson, 1992—94; atty. gen. State of Okla., 1994—. With USN, 1968—72. Named Outstanding Dist. Atty., State of Okla., 1985. Mem.: Nat. Assn. Attys. Gen. (pres. 2002—03), Okla. Dist. Attys. Assn. (pres. 1983—85), Okla. Bar Assn. Democrat. Office: Office Atty Gen 2300 N Lincoln Blvd Rm 112 Oklahoma City OK 73105-4894 Office Phone: 405-521-3921.

EDMONDSON, FRANK KELLEY, retired astronomer; b. Milw., Aug. 1, 1912; s. Clarence Edward and Marie (Kelley) E.; m. Margaret Russell, Nov. 24, 1934 (dec. Jan. 1999); children: Margaret Jean Olson, Frank K. Jr. AB, Ind. U., 1933, A.M., 1934; PhD, Harvard U., 1937. Lawrence fellow Lowell Obs., 1933-34, research asst., 1934-35; Agassiz fellow Harvard Obs., 1935-36, asst., 1936-37; instr. astronomy Ind. U., Bloomington, 1937-4O, asst. prof., 1940-45, assoc. prof., 1945-48, prof., 1949-83, prof. emeritus, 1983—, dir. Kirkwood Obs., 1945-78; dir. Goethe Link Obs., 1948-78, chmn. astronomy dept., 1944-78; research asso. McDonald Obs., 1944-83. Observations of asteroids in cooperation with Internat. Astron. Union's Minor Planet Ctr.; statistical adviser to Prof. Alfred Kinsey for gall wasp and human sex behaviour rsch., 1939-56; program dir. for astronomy NSF, 1956-57; acting dir. Cerro Tololo Inter-Am. Obs., 1966; lectr. astron. socs.; mem. adv. bd. Lowell Obs., 1988-2000. Author: AURA and its US National Observatories, 1997; contbr. numerous papers to Am., Brit., German astron. jours. Decorated Order of Merit Chile, 1964; recipient Meritorious Pub. Svc. award NSF, 1983, Disting. Alumni Svc. award Ind. U., 1997; honored with Daniel Kirkwood (1814-95) in Ho. Resolution No. 58 adopted by Ind. 109th Gen. Assembly, First Session, 1995. Fellow AAAS (chmn. sect. D, v.p. 1962); mem. Assn. Univs. Rsch. in Astronomy (v.p. 1957-61, pres. 1962-65, dir. 1957-83, cons./historian 1983—2003, historian emeritus 2003—), Can. Astron. Soc., Am. Astron. Soc. (treas. 1954-75, 70 yr. attendence award 2001), Astron. Soc. Pacific, Internat. Astron. Union (chmn. U.S. nat. com. 1963-64, v.p. commn. minor planets, comets and satellites 1967-70, pres. 1970-73), Ind. Acad. Sci. (named Disting. Scholar 2004), Am. Mus. Natural History (corr. mem.), Friends of Ctr. for History of Physics (exec. com. 2001—), Explorers Club, Phi Beta Kappa, Sigma Xi. Home: 716 S Woodlawn Ave Bloomington IN 47401-4936 Office: Ind U Dept Astronomy 319 Swain Hall West 727 E 3rd St Bloomington IN 47405-7105 Business E-Mail: clirot@indiana.edu. *President Calvin Coolidge was right when he said: "Nothing in the world can take the place of persistence.".*

EDMONDSON, FRANK KELLEY, JR., lawyer, legal administrator; b. Newport, RI, Aug. 27, 1936; s. Frank Kelley Sr. and Margaret (Russell) E.; m. Christiane Semirot, Mar. 5, 1959 (div. Sept. 1969); children: Mylene Anne, Yvonne Marie, Catherine May; m. Elaine Sueko Kaneshiro, Aug. 17, 1970 (div. June 1992); m. Karen Louise Bishop, Feb. 27, 1993 (div. Feb. 1996). BBA, Ind. U., 1958; MBA, So. Ill. U., 1978; JD, U. Puget Sound, 1982. Bar: Wash. 1982, U.S. Dist. Ct. (we. dist.) Wash. 1983. Commd. 2d lt. USAF, 1959, advanced through grades to maj., 1969, ret., 1979; contracts specialist Wash. State Lottery, Olympia, 1982-85, asst. contracts adminstr., 1985-87; contracts officer 1989 Washington Centennial Commn., 1987-90; fin. svc. officer Office of the Adminstr. for the Cts., 1990-92; contracts officer, office of adminstr. for the cts. State of Wash. Supreme Ct., Olympia, 1992-99. Mem. scholarship com. Wash. State Employees Credit Union, 1995-2001. Bd. dirs. Friends of Chambers Creek, Tacoma, 1981-90; mem. pro bono panel Puget Sound Legal Assistance Found., Olympia, 1985-90; mock trial program com. Youth and Govt. YMCA, 1994-96. Mem. Wash. State Bar Assn. (spl. dist. counsel 1993-95), Thurston County Bar Assn., Ind. U. Soc. Advanced Study, Govt. Lawyers Bar Assn. (sec. 1985-86, 1st v.p. 1986-87, pres. 1987-89, liaison to Wash. State Bar Assn. 1989-93), Coll. Club, Seattle U. Sch. Law Alumni Soc. (nat. coun. 1997-2003), Beta Gamma Sigma. Home: 6600 Miner Dr SW Tumwater WA 98512-7282 E-mail: fkedmon@aol.com.

EDMONDSON, JAMES E., state supreme court justice; b. Kansas City, Mo., 1945; m. Suzanne Edmondson; 2 children. BA, Northeastern State U., Tahlequah, 1967; JD, Georgetown Law Sch., 1973. Asst. dist. atty. Muskogee County, Okla., 1976—78; asst. U.S. atty., 1978—80; acting U.S. atty., 1980—81; prtnr. Edmondson Law Office, 1981—83; judge Okla. Dist. Ct., 1983—2003; justice Okla. Supreme Ct., 2003—. Served in USN, 1967—69. Mem.: Okla. Bar Assn. Office: Okla Supreme Ct Rm 202 State Capitol Bldg Oklahoma City OK 73105*

EDMONDSON, JAMES HOWARD, investor, former insurance executive; b. Topeka, Kans. s. Frazor T. and Sally Ann (Anderson) E.; m. Janice Sue Elliott, July 1969 (div. Jan. 1993); children: Frazor T., James H., Robert. BA, Va. Mil. Inst., 1955. Ins. exec. Jim Edmondson & Assocs., Dallas, 1958-91; now in investments. Presbyterian. Avocations: tennis, reading. Home: 7704 Glenshannon Cir Dallas TX 75225-2054 E-mail: vml55jim@cs.com.

EDMONDSON, J.L. (JAMES LARRY EDMONDSON), federal judge; b. Jasper, Ga., July 14, 1947; s. James George and Betty Ruth (Holcomb) Edmondson; m. Eugenia Dettelbach (div. 1992); children: Kelley Eugenia, Alexandra Lisa. BA, Emory U., 1968; JD, U. Ga., 1971; LLM in Jud. Process, U. Va., 1990. Bar: Ga. 1971. Law clk. to Hon. Sidney O. Smith US Dist. Ct. (no. dist.), Gainesville, Ga., 1971—73; assoc. Webb, Fowler, Tanner & Edmondson, Lawrenceville, Ga., 1973—76, ptnr., 1976—81; mem. Tennant, Davidson & Edmondson, PC, Lawrenceville, 1982—86; judge US Ct. Appeals (11th cir.), Atlanta, 1986—2002, chief judge, 2002—. Instr. U. Ga. Sch. Law, 1975—84. Contbr. articles to profl. jours. Trustee Inst. Continuing Legal Edn., 1980—84. Mem.: Lawyers Club Am., ABA, Fellows Ga. Bar Found. (charter), Gwinnett County Bar Assn. (pres. 1980—81), State Bar Ga. (bd. govs. 1982—86), Old War Horse Lawyers Club, Order of Barristers, Pi Sigma Alpha. Episcopalian. Office: US Ct Appeals 11th Circuit 56 Forsyth St NW Rm 416 Atlanta GA 30303-2205*

EDMONDSON, RUBY JOHNSON, psychologist; d. Carl M. and Annie Bell Johnson. BS, Barton Coll., Wilson, NC, 1966; MA, Appalachian State U., Boone, NC, 1969; EdD, Nova U., Ft. Lauderdale, Fla., 1976. Cert. sch. psychologist, counselor, tchr., adminstr. NC. Dept. head, tchr., coord. Rowan-Cabarrus CC, Salisbury, NC, 1969—74; counselor Concord City Schs., NC, 1974—79; sch. psychologist Charlotte-Mecklenburg Schs., Charlotte, NC, 1979—81, 2004—05, Gaston County Schs., Gastonia, NC, 1988—90, Kershaw County Schs., Camden, SC, 1992—93, Northampton County Schs., Jackson, NC, 1993—94, Union County Schs., Monroe, NC, 1994—97; owner, cons. Edmondson Assocs., Charlotte, 1981—88, 1998—2004. Contbr. articles to profl. jours. Mem.: NC Sch. Psychologist Assn., Nat. Assn. Sch. Psychologists. Avocations: gardening, travel, cooking, antiques. Home: 2809 Greenbriar Rd Charlotte NC 28209

EDMONDSON, WILLIAM BROCKWAY, retired foreign service officer; b. St. Joseph, Mo., Feb. 6, 1927; s. Harold and Anna Laura (Sherman) E.; m. Donna Elizabeth Kiechel, Oct. 6, 1951; children: Barbara Elizabeth Edmondson Schneider, Paul William. AB with high distinction, U. Nebr., 1950; MA, Fletcher Sch. Law and Diplomacy, 1951; student African area studies, Northwestern U., 1957-58. Joined U.S. Fgn. Service, 1952; fgn. affairs officer Bur. UN Affairs, State Dept., 1951-52; adviser U.S. delegation 11th session UN Trusteeship Council, 1952; vice consul Dar es Salaam, Tanganyika, 1952-55; 3d sec., then 2d sec. embassy Bern, Switzerland, 1955-57; research analyst, then acting chief W. Africa div. Office Research and Analysis for Africa, State Dept., 1958-61; 2d sec., then 1st sec. and consul, polit. sect. chief Am. embassy, Accra, Ghana, 1961-64; officer charge Ghanaian affairs Bur. African Affairs, State Dept., 1964-65; counselor of embassy, dep. chief of mission Lusaka, Zambia, 1965-68; chargé d'affaires ad interim, 1968-69; assigned Nat. War Coll., 1969-70; dep. dir. African programs Bur. Ednl. and Cultural Affairs, Dept. State, 1970, dir. Office African Programs, 1971-74; minister-counselor, dep. chief mission Am. embassy, Pretoria, South Africa, 1974-76; dep. asst. sec. for African affairs State Dept., 1976-78; ambassador to South Africa Pretoria, 1978-81; sr. fgn. service insp., 1981-82; dep. insp. gen., 1982-86. Served to 1st lt. AUS, 1944-48. Mem. Am. Fgn. Svc. Assn. Diplomatic and Consular Officers Ret. (past pres., hon. life gov.), DACOR Bacon House Found. (past pres., trustee), Phi Beta Kappa. Address: 4900 28th St N Arlington VA 22207-2712 Personal E-mail: wbedmondson@aol.com. *Persistent hard work, sincerity, broad intellectual curiosity and a strong touch of idealism in striving for a better world are qualities I admire and try to emulate.*

EDMONSON, PHYLLIS DENTY, artist; b. Hope, Ark., Feb. 27, 1935; d. Nathaniel Wynne and Dell (McRae) Denty; m. Frank Alonzo Edmonson, Jan. 29, 1956; children: Frank Jr., Kathryn Dell BS in Edn., Henderson State U., 1956. Exhibitions include Mid-Southern Watercolorists Ann. Exhbn., 1999, 2001, 2005, Houston Ann. Internat. Exhbn. Watercolor Art Soc., 2001, Hilton Head Art League An. Nat. Exhbn., 2001, Fort Smith (Ark.) 51st Ann. Art Competition, 2001, North East Watercolor Soc. 25th Ann. Internat. Exhbn., 2001, Audubon Artist, Inc. 59th Ann. Exhbn. Salamagundi Club, N.Y.C., 2001, Southwestern Watercolor Soc. 39th Ann. Exhbn., 2002, 2004, Internat. Soc. Exptl. Artists Ann. Exhbn., 2000, 2002, Nat. Watercolor Okla. Ann. Exhbn., 2000, 2002, 2003, Tom Peyton Meml. Arts Festival, Alexandria, La., 2003, 2004, 2005, Art Ctr. of the Ozarks, Springdale, Ark., 2002, Ga. Ann. Nat. Exhbn., 2002, 2003, Watercolor, Houston, 2003, Western Fedn. 27th Ann. Watercolor Soc., 2002, 2003—04, We. Colo. Watercoloer Soc., 2004, Soc. Watercolor Arists 23d Ann. Exhbn., Ft. Worth, 2004, Tex. and Neighbors Annual Exhibn., 2004, Adirondacks Nat. Exhbn. Am. Watercolors, 2004, San Diego Internat. Ann. Exhbn., 2004, 2005, Ala. Watercolor Soc. Ann. Nat. Exhbn., 2005, one-woman shows include Southwestern Elec. Power Co. Bldg., Texarkana, 1992, Cantrell Art Gallery, Little Rock, 1994, 1998, 2002, Texarkana Regional Arts and Humanities Coun. Mus., 1999, exhibited in group shows at Cantrell Art Gallery, Little Rock, 1996, Little Rock, Ark., 2000, Sen. Blanche Lincoln's Little Rock Offices, 2003—, others, Mo. Watercolor Soc. Ann. Nat. Exhbn., 2005, Represented in permanent collections Ark. Arts Ctr., Little Rock, Southeast Ark. Arts and Sci. Ctr., Pine Bluff. Recipient 2d pl. award Texarkana Regional Arts and Humanities Coun. Ann. Exhbn., 1995, Purchase award, Ark. Arts. Coun., 1996, Corp. Purchase award, Henderson State U., 1996, First Place Mid-So. Watercolorists, Little Rock, 1997, Finalist The Artist's Mag. Art Competition, 1999, Merit award Tom Peyton Meml. Arts Festival, 2001, 02, 04, Neiman Marcus award Ga. Watersolor Soc. XXIII Exhbn., 2002, Merchandise award, Nat. Watercolor Okla. 28th Ann. Exhbn., 2002. Mem.: Ala. Watercolor Soc., Little River Arts Coun., Mo. Watercolor Soc., Nat. Collage Soc., Audubon Artist, Inc., Southwestern Watercolor Soc. (signature mem. 2004), Ark. Arts Ctr., Internat. Soc. Exptl. Artists, Nat. Mus. Women in the Arts, Texarkana Regional Arts and Humanities Coun., Mid-So. Watercolorists, PEO Internat. Sisterhood (treas. 1980—82, v.p. 1982—83, chaplain 1988—90, corr. sec. 1996—98). Baptist. Avocation: photography. Home: 210 Highway 32 West Ashdown AR 71822-8792 Office: The Carousel Studio 410 W Main St Ashdown AR 71822-2752

EDMONSTON, WILLIAM EDWARD, JR., retired publishing executive, writer, psychology professor; b. Balt., Nov. 20, 1931; s. William Edward and Helen (Mallonee) E.; m. Nellie Jane Kerley, Aug. 3, 1957; children: Kathryn Nell, Rebecca Jane, Owen William. BA, Johns Hopkins U., 1952; MA, U. Ala., 1956; PhD, U. Ky., 1960. Diplomate: Am. Bd. Psychol. Hypnosis. Instr., asst. prof. Washington U., St. Louis, 1960-64; mem. faculty Colgate U., Hamilton, NY, 1964-93, dir. neurosci. program, 1972-93, chmn. dept. psychology, 1971-81, prof. psychology, 1973-93, prof. emeritus, 1993—. Guest prof. U. Erlangen, Nürnberg, Germany, 1982. Author: Hypnosis and Relaxation: Modern Verification of an Old Equation, 1981, The Induction of Hypnosis, 1986, Unfurl the Flags: Remembrances of the American Civil War, 1989, The Strange Case of Mr. Nobody, 2000, The Case of the Hidden Dentures, 2007; editor: Am. Jour. Clin. Hypnosis, 1968-76; contbr. articles to profl. jours. Served with U.S. Army, 1952-54. Sloan Found. fellow, 1967, 69, Fulbright Found. fellow, 1982, U. Wash. sr. fellow, 1971; recipient Bernard E. Gorton award, 1961, grant USPHS, 1964-65, Prof. of Yr. award CASE N.Y. State, 1988. Mem. Sigma Xi. Home: 1841 Preston Hill Rd Hamilton NY 13346-9522 *By being born to intelligent parents, I started with the genetic potential for success and was reared in a social atmosphere in which hard work, honesty, thrift and accomplishment were highly regarded. I later recognized perseverance, even in the face of apparent failure, and a compulsive attention to (but not an obsession with) details as fundamental to accomplishment. Perseverance is by far the most regnant, for without tenacity one's genetic potential and early social learnings will lie fallow. There is a time for action and a time for reflection. Choosing the appropriate time for each is the secret of happiness and success.*

EDMUND, NORMAN WILSON, educational researcher; b. Feb. 27, 1916; Cert., U. Pa., 1939. Founder, pres. Edmund Sci. Co., Barrington, NJ, 1942-75; ednl. rschr. Ft. Lauderdale, Fla., 1989—. Author: The General Pattern of the Scientific Method, 1994, The Scientific Method Today, 2000, End the Biggest Educational and Intellectual Blunder in History, 2005. Office: 407 NE 3rd Ave Fort Lauderdale FL 33301-3233 E-mail: nwe@scientificmethod.com.

EDMUNDS, DARRYL B., mathematics professor; s. Glen B. and Gweneth P. Edmunds; m. Leslie Ann Kelly, Aug. 22, 1986. BA, Brigham Young U., Provo, 1986. Cert. tchg. Washington State, 1990. Substitute tchr. Lake Washington Sch. Dist., Redmond, 1991—96; tchr. Highline High Sch., Burien, Wash., 1997—. Math team coach Highline High Sch., Burien, 1999—2007, math. dept. head, 2006—. Mem.: Wash. State Math. Coun., Nat. Coun. Tchrs. Math., MENSA. Avocation: golf. Business E-Mail: dedmunds@hsd401.org.

EDMUNDS, JEFFREY GARTH, librarian; b. Scottsbluff, Nebr., Sept. 11, 1953; s. Lafe Rees and June LaFawn (Law) E.; m. Rachel Jeanette Hughes, July 17, 1982; children: Jeffrey Garth Jr., Gavin Nathaniel. BA, U. Va., 1975; MLS, Fla. State U., 1976; JD, George Mason U., 1986. Bar: Va. 1986, U.S. Ct. Appeals (4th cir.) 1986. Reference librarian J. Sargeant Reynolds Community Coll., Richmond, Va., 1976-78; spl. instr. U.S. Navy Program for Afloat Coll. Edn., Naples, Italy, 1978-79; devel. rsch. assoc. Georgetown U., Washington, 1979-84; law clk. U.S. Atty.'s Office for Ea. Dist. Va., Alexandria, 1985, U.S. Dept. Labor, Washington, 1985-86; asst. Commonwealth's atty. Pulaski County, Va., 1986-87, City of Petersburg, Va., 1988-89, City of Fredericksburg, Va., 1989-96; atty. pvt. practice, Fredericksburg, 1996—99; reference libr. Ctrl. Rappahannock Regional Libr., Fredericksburg, Va., 1999—. Sec., dir. FIMC & 3d Virginia Regiment, Inc., Fredericksburg, Va., 2000—04; v.p., dir. Fredericksburg Masonic Mus. Found., 2003—07. Mem. editorial bd., bus. mgr. Essays in History mag., 1973-75. Vestryman, St. George's Episcopal Ch., 1990-92, St. Luke's Anglican Cath. Ch., 2005-06; bd. dirs. Legal Aid Soc. New River Valley, Christiansburg, Va., 1986-87. Mem. Welsh Soc. Fredericksburg (pres. 1990-92), Delta Theta Phi. Home: 3524 Waverly Dr Fredericksburg VA 22407-6849 Office: 1201 Caroline St Fredericksburg VA 22401 Personal E-mail: jedmunds@crrl.org.

EDMUNDS, NANCY GARLOCK, federal judge; b. Detroit, July 10, 1947; m. William C. Edmunds, 1977. BA cum laude, Cornell U., 1969; MA in Teaching, U. Chgo., 1971; JD summa cum laude, Wayne U., 1976. Bar: Mich. 1976. With Plymouth Canton Public Schools, 1971-73; law clk. Barris, Sott, Denn & Driker, 1973-75; law clk. to Hon. Ralph Freeman U.S. Dist. Ct. (ea. dist.) Mich., 1976-78; with Dykema Gossett, Detroit, 1978-84, ptnr. litigation sect., 1984-92; apptd. judge U.S. Dist. Ct. (ea. dist.) Mich., 1992—. Commr. 21st Century Commn. on Cts., 1990; mem. faculty, bd. mem. Fed. Advocacy Inst., 1983-91. Editor in chief Wayne Law Review. Mem. com. of visitors Wayne Law Sch., Detroit; bd. dirs. Mich. Mems. of Stratford Festival; bd. trustees Stratford Shakespearean Festival of Am., Temple Beth El, 1990-97, Hist. Soc. U.S. Dist. Ct. (ea. dist.) Mich., 1993-98. Mem. ABA, FBA (exec. bd. dirs. 1989-92), Am. Judicature Soc., Fed. Judges Assn., State Bar Mich. (chair U.S. cts. com. 1990-91). Avocation: reading. Office: US Dist Ct US Courthouse #211 231 W Lafayette Blvd Detroit MI 48226-2700 E-mail: karen_hillebrand@mied.uscourts.gov.

EDMUNDS, ROBERT HOLT, JR., state supreme court justice; b. Danville, Va., Apr. 17, 1949; s. Robert Holt and Mary (Rucker) Edmunds; m. Linda M. Edmunds; 2 children. Student, Williams Coll., Williamstown, Mass., 1967—69; BA in English, Vassar Coll., 1971; JD, U. NC, Chapel Hill, 1975; LLM, U. Va., 2004. Bar: NC 1975, Va. 1977. Asst. dist. atty. 18th Judicial Dist., Guilford County, NC, 1978—82; asst. U.S. atty. Mid. Dist. N.C. U.S. Dept. Justice, Greensboro, 1982—86, US atty. Mid. Dist. NC, 1986—93; ptnr. Stern & Klepfer, 1993—98; assoc. judge NC Ct. Appeals, 1999—2001; assoc. justice Supreme Ct. NC, 2001—. Mem. Atty. Gen. Advisory Subcom. on Guideline Sentencing, 1987—93, chair, 1991—93; mem. Atty. Gen. Subcom. on Controlled Substances, 1987—93. Contbr. articles to profl. jours. Served in USN, 1975—77. Mem.: Greensboro Criminal Defense Lawyers Assn., Guilford Inn of Ct., Nat. Assn. of Former US Attorneys, Greensboro Bar Assn. Office: Supreme Ct NC PO Box 1841 Raleigh NC 27602

EDSALL, THOMAS BYRNE, reporter; b. Cambridge, Mass., Aug. 22, 1941; s. Richard Linn and Katharine (Byrne) E.; m. Mary Deutsch, Aug. 22, 1965; 1 child, Alexandra Tileston Victor Edsall. BA, Boston U., 1966. Reporter Providence Jour., 1965; vol. VISTA, Balt., 1966-67; reporter Balt. Sun, 1967-81, Washington Post, 1981—2007, ret., 2006; prof. Columbia U., 2006—; polit. editor Huffington Post, 2007—. Regents lectr. U. Calif., San Diego, 1991; lectr. Nuffield Coll. Oxford U., 1995; prof. Columbia Grad. Sch. Journalism, Joseph Pulitzer II & Edith Pulitzer Moore chair; guest op-ed columnist NY Times, 2006; corr. The New Republic, 2006—, The Nat. Jour., 2006—; guest columnist NY Times, 2006. Author: The New Politics of Inequality, 1984, Power and Money, 1988, (with Mary D. Edsall) Chain Reaction: The Impact of Race, Rights and Taxes on American Politics, 1991, Building Red America: The New Conservative Coalition & the Drive for Permanent Power, 2006; co-editor: The Reagan Legacy, 1988; contbr. articles to NY Rev. of Books, Atlantic, Am. Prospect, popular jour. Chmn. Standing Com. of Corr. US Congress, 1982. Recipient Front Page award, Bill Pryor Meml. award Washington-Balt. Newspaper Guild, 1981, Carey McWilliams award Am. Polit. Sci. Assn., 1994; finalist Pulitzer prize for general non-fiction, 1992; Woodrow Wilson found. fellow, 1996-97, Hoover Instn. media fellow, Stanford U., 1997, 2001, 03, 05. Home: 19 2nd St NE Washington DC 20002-7301 Office: Columbia U Grad Sch Journalism 2950 Broadway Rm 803 New York NY 10027 Home Phone: 202-494-5550; Office Phone: 212-854-6042. Business E-Mail: te2154@columbia.edu.

EDSFORTH, MAUREEN MCGILL, instructional technology specialist; d. James J. and Marie McGill; m. Wayne H. Edsforth, July 14, 1973; children: Brian P., David J. BS in Elem. Edn., U. Dayton, 1972; MA in Ednl. Tech., Pepperdine U., 2002. Cert. permanent elem. edn. NY, 2002. Sci. tchr. Broward County Pub. Sch., Ft. Lauderdale, Fla., 1972—73; med. libr. Am. Cyanamid, Wayne, NJ, 1973—74; sci., math tchr. Ctrl. Sch., Montville, NJ, 1974—81; math tchr. Kinnelon (NJ) Sch. Dist., 1983—84, St. Mary Sch., Pompton Lakes, NJ, 1986—90; propr. Greenwich (NY) Hardware Antiques, 1991—94; enrichment program coord., tchr. Greenwich Ctrl. Sch. Dist., 1992—94, computer instr., 1994—2002, instrnl. tech. specialist, 2002—. Site mgr. North Hudson Electronic Edn. Empowerment Project, Hudson Falls, NY, 1998—2002; liaison WSWHE BOCES Model Sch., Saratoga Springs, NY, 2002—. Mem., treas. Greenwich Women's Svc. Club, 1990—96; pres. Greater Greenwich C. of C., 1996—97, dir., 1992—2001, 2005—. Mem.: Assn. Supervision and Curriculum and Devel., Internat. Soc. for Tech. in Edn., NY State Assn. Computers and Tech. in Edn. Office: Greenwich Ctrl Sch Dist 10 Gray Ave Greenwich NY 12834 Home Phone: 518-692-9139; Office Phone: 518-692-9542. E-mail: medsforth@greenwichcsd.org.

EDSON, ANDREW STEPHEN, public relations executive; b. NYC, Jan. 8, 1946; s. Herbert and Frances (Bauling) E.; m. Marilyn Borer, July 22, 1972; children: Garrett Matthew, Gregory Todd. BA, Fairleigh Dickinson U., 1967; MA, Memphis State U., 1969. Staff writer Memphis Press-Scimitar, 1968-69; account exec. Harshe-Rotman & Druck, Inc., Memphis, 1969-70, Ruder & Finn, Inc., NYC, 1970-73; asst. dir. corp. pub. relations Anaconda Co., NYC, 1973-74; pub. affairs mgr. Citicorp, NYC, 1974-78; sr. account exec. Padilla & Speer Inc., NYC, 1978-79, v.p., 1979-86, sr. v.p., 1986, Padilla Speer Beardsley Inc., NYC, 1986-94; pres., COO Anreder and Co., NYC, 1994-96; pres. Andrew Edson & Assocs., Inc., NYC, 1996—; sr. counselor, corp. and fin. rels. Manning, Selvage & Lee, Inc., NYC, 1996-2001. Adj. asst. prof. NYU, 1983-87; sec., bd. dirs. The Worldcom. Group, Inc., NY, 1988-96; pres. bd. dirs. Finch Apt Corp., NYC Mem.: LI Capital Alliance, Nat. Investor Rels. Inst., Jericho Pub. Libr. (trustee 1998—99). Republican. Avocations: tennis, bicycling, golf. Address: Andrew Edson and Assoc 89 Bounty Ln Jericho NY 11753-2209 Office Phone: 516-850-3195. Business E-Mail: andrew@edsonpr.com.

EDSON, CHARLES LOUIS, lawyer; b. St. Louis, Dec. 14, 1934; s. Harry G. and Mildred (Solomon) E.; m. Susan Kramer, Mar. 29, 1959; children: Richard, Nancy, Margaret. AB, Harvard U., 1956, LLB, 1959. Bar: Mo. 1959, U.S. Supreme Ct. 1966, D.C. 1967. Assoc. Lewis, Rice, Tucker, Allen & Chubb, St. Louis, 1959-65; chief ops. officer Legal Svc. Program, OEO, Washington, 1966-67; gen. counsel Pres.'s Commn. on Postal Orgn., Washington, 1967-68; chief pub. housing sect. Officer of Gen. Counsel, HUD, Washington, 1968-70; ptnr. Lane and Edson, P.C., Washington, 1970-89, Kelley, Drye & Warren, Washington, 1989-93, Peabody & Brown, Washington, 1993-99, Nixon Peabody LLP, Washington, 1999—, ptnr., sr. counsel, 2002—. Adj. prof. law Georgetown U. Law Sch., Washington, 1970-76, 2000—; HUD coord. Pres. Carter's Transition Staff, 1976-77. Co-author: A Practical Guide to Low and Moderate Income Housing, 1972, A Leased Housing Primer, 1975, A Section 8 Deskbook, 1976, Guide to Federal Housing Programs, 1982, Secondary Mortgage Market Guide, 1985, HDR Affordable Seniors Housing Handbook, 2005. Councilman Town of Somerset, Md., 1976-78; trustee Md. Hist. Trust, 1995—, vice chair, 2000—. With USNR, 1953-61. Alt. White House fellow, 1965. Mem. ABA (chmn. forum com. on affordable housing and comm. devel. 1991-93, chmn. spl. housing and urban devel. 1987-90), Harvard U. Law Sch. Assn. D.C. (pres. 1972-73), Cosmos Club (Washington). Home: 5802 Surrey St Chevy Chase MD 20815-5419 Office: 401 9th St NW Ste 900 Washington DC 20004-2134 E-mail: cedson@nixonpeabody.com, granchuck@aol.com.

EDSON, HERBERT ROBBINS, retired foundation and hospital executive, military officer; b. Upper Darby, Pa., Dec. 26, 1931; s. Merritt Austin and Ethel Winifred (Robbins) E.; m. Constance Anne Lowell, May 20, 1961 (div. Nov. 8, 1967); m. Rose Anne McGowan, July 25, 1970; children: Patricia Anne, David William, Merritt Austin III, Herbert Robbins Jr. BA, Tufts U., 1955; MBA, U. Pa., 1972. Commd. 2d lt. USMC, 1955, advanced through grades to major, 1967, adminstr., mgr., supr. various orgns., 1955-72, asst. chief of staff and comptr. III Marine Amphibious Force and 3d Marine Div. Camp Butler, Japan, 1972—73, head stores investment analysis br., office of the comptroller Marine Corps Supply Activity Phila., 1973-75, ret., 1975; cons. acctg. Ardmore, Pa., 1975-77; CFO Mercy Meml. Hosp. Corp., Monroe, Mich., 1977-92, Mercy Meml. Hosp. Found., Monroe, 1986-92, Monroe Health Ventures Inc., 1986-92, Monroe Cmty. Health Svcs., 1989-92, Byerly Hosp., Hartsville, SC, 1992-95, Byerly Found., Hartsville, 1995-97; ret., 1997. Assoc. Quorum Health Resources, Inc., Brentwood, Tenn., 1992-95. Co-pres. Custer Elem. Sch. Parent Tchr. Orgn., Monroe, 1985—87; treas., chmn. Taylor Endowment Fund com. St. Paul's Evang. Luth. Ch., Ardmore, Pa., 1974—76, trustee, chmn. property com., 1976; v.p., trustee Christ Evang. Luth. Ch., Monroe, 1981—86; mem. endowment fund com. Faith Luth. Ch., Parrish, 2006—; bd. dirs. Monroe County C. of C., 1982—84; bd. dirs., treas. Foxchase Subdivsn. Homowners' Assn., Inc., Parrish, Fla., 2003—06; hon. bd. dirs. Wis. Naval Ship Assn., Inc., Greendale, 2007—. Decorated Purple Heart, Navy Commendation medal, Combat Action ribbon. Mem. NRA (life), U.S. Naval Inst. (life), Marine Corps Assn. (life), 1st Marine Divsn. Assn. (life), Edson's Raiders Assn. (hon. life 1st Marine Raider Bn.), Mil. Officers Assn. Am. (life), Am. Assn. Ret. Persons, Nat. Geog. Soc., Edson Geneal. Assn. Democrat. Lutheran. Home: PO Box 569 Ellenton FL 34222-0569

EDSON, WILLIAM ALDEN, retired electrical engineer, researcher; b. Burchard, Nebr., Oct. 30, 1912; s. William Henry and Pearl (Montgomery) E.; m. Saralou Peterson, Aug. 23, 1942; children: Judith Lynne, Margaret Jane, Carolyn Louise. BS (Summerfield scholar), U. Kans., 1934, MS, 1935; D.Sc. (Gordon McKay scholar), Harvard U., 1937. Mem. tech. staff Bell Telephone Labs., Inc., NYC, 1937-41, supr., 1943-45; asst. prof. elec. engring. Ill. Inst. Tech., Chgo., 1941-43; prof. physics Ga. Inst. Tech., Atlanta, 1945-46, prof. elec. engring., 1946-51, dir. sch. elec. engring., 1951-52; vis. prof., research assoc. Stanford U., 1952-56, cons. prof., 1956; mgr. Klystron sub-sect. Gen. Electric Microwave Lab., Palo Alto, Calif., 1956-61; v.p., dir. research Electromagnetic Tech. Corp., Palo Alto, 1961-62, pres., 1962-70; sr. scientist Vidar Corp., Mountain View, Calif., 1970— 71; from staff mem. to sr. staff scientist, assoc. dir. Radio Physics Lab of SRI Interat., Menlo Park, Calif., 1971—2004. Cons. high frequency sect. Nat. Bur. Standards, 1951-64; dir. Western Electronic Show and Conv., 1975-79 Author: (with Robert I. Sarbacher) Hyper and Ultra-High Frequency Engineering, 1943, Vacuum-Tube Oscillators, 1953. Life fellow IEEE (chmn. San Francisco sect. 1963-64, com. standards piezoelectricity 1950-67); mem. Am. Phys. Soc., Sigma Xi, Tau Beta Pi, Sigma Tau, Phi Kappa Phi, Eta Kappa Nu, Pi Mu Epsilon. Home: 2350 E Estates Dr #106 Fairfield CA 94533

EDSPARR, PATRIK L., diversified financial services company executive; Global head rates and structured products J.P. Morgan Chase & Co. Office: JP Morgan Chase & Co 270 Park Ave New York NY 10017-2070

EDUALINO, EMILIO QUIAL, school educator; b. Agutaya, Palawan, Philippines, May 13, 1917; s. Telesforo Saldiva and Agapita (Quial) Edualino. Elem. tchr. cert., Philippine Normal Sch., Manila, 1935; BS in Edn., Far Ea. U., Manila, 1948; MA, U. Mich., 1956, PhD, 1958. Tchr., then elem. sch. adminstr. various schs., Philippines, 1935—46; curriculum writer Dept. Edn., Manila, 1946—48; instr. edn. Philippine Normal Coll., Manila, 1948, master tchr., 1949—53, supr. student tchg., 1953—55, dir. field units, prof. edn., 1957—64; primary edn. expert UNESCO, Guyana, S. Am., 1964—66; tchr. edn. expert Afghanistan, 1969—74; chief tech. adviser Sierra Leone, 1974—79; prof. edn., chmn. dept. elem. edn. U. of the East, Manila, 1966—69; tchr. St. Mary's Elem. Sch., LA, 1979—85. Cons.; mem. selection com. U.S. Edn. Found., Manila. Author (with others): Integration as Practiced in the Philippine Normal College, 1952; author: children's songs and reading materials; contbr. articles to profl. jours. Grantee, U.S. Edn. Found., 1955—57; travel fellow, Philippine Govt., 1948—49. Mem.: Assn. Supervision and Curriculum Devel., Nat. Soc. Study of Edn., Childhood Edn. Internat., NEA, Mich. Alumni Club (Ann Arbor), Mich. Club (San Gabriel, Calif.), Lions Internat. Club, Phi Delta Kappa. Roman Catholic. Home: 8236 Golden Cypress Ave Las Vegas NV 89117-9138

EDWARD, JEFFREY N., diversified financial services company executive; BS in Physics, Haverford Coll.; MBA, Harvard U. Investment banking assoc. Merrill Lynch, London, NYC, 1987—91, several positions, Equity Capital Markets NYC, 1991—2000, co-head, Global Equity Capital Markets, 2000—03, head, Global Capital Markets, Fin., 2003—04, head, Investment Banking, Am. region, 2004—05, sr. v.p., CFO, 2005—. Bd. dirs. Nasdaq Stock Market Inc., 2004—. Office: Merrill Lynch 4 World Fin Ctr 250 Vesey St New York NY 10080 Office Phone: 212-449-1000.*

EDWARDS, ADRIEN, business executive; b. Nice, France, Dec. 3, 1983; (parents Am. citizens); s. Allister and Tatine Edwards. Student, U. Tampa, Fla., 2002—06. Head adminstr. Army Command, Fayetteville, NC, 1999—2000; cook McDonalds, Fayetteville, 2000—01; bagger Mil. Commissary, Fayetteville, 2001—02, cashier, 2003; personal asst. The Riddles, Fayetteville, 2001—03; sales rep. Vector Co., Fayetteville, 2003; founder, pres. Wishing Well/Edwards Corp. Gifts, Fayetteville, 2003—04; sales rep. Sears & Roebuck Co., Tampa, 2005; intern Hertel Group LLC Real Estate Investments, Tampa, 2005; pres., owner Tee2Greens.com, Tampa, 2005—. Student juror Youth Ct., Fayetteville, 2002. Named MVP Basketball, Cornerstone Christian Acad. Sports, 2000—01; recipient Global Student Entrepreneur Regional award, 2006. Master: Young Bus. Owners Club (mediator 2006—07). Personal E-mail: adrientedwards@aol.com.

EDWARDS, ANNMARIE MONICA, language educator, career coach, entrepreneur; b. Kingston, Jamaica, Jan. 26, 1962; arrived in U.S., 1989; d. Avell George Edwards and Stephanie H. Turner. AA, Fiorello H. LaGuardia C.C., 1991; BS, St. John's U., 1994; MA, Adelphi U., 1996. Cert. RI, 2001, N.E. regional tchg. credential 1996, cert. pub. sch. tchr. NY, 1995, provisional tchg. Mass., 1998. Student tchr. St. John's U., NYC, 1993; tchr. Blanche Cmty. Progress Day Care, Inc. No 2, NYC, 1993—95, Jamaica NAACP Day Care Ctr., NYC, 1995—96; substitute tchr. Portland (Maine) Pub. Sch., 1996, Westbrook (Maine) Sch. Dept., 1996—97, Falmouth (Maine) Sch. Dept., 1996—97, South Portland Pub. Sch., 1996—98; ESL spl. edn. tchr. Judge Rotenburgh Edn. Ctr., Canton, Mass., 1998—98; grade 6 ESL tchr. Providence Pub. Schs., 1998—; CEO, career coach Aria Career Devel. Pres. Rising Star Enterprises, Portland, 1997—98; career cons., workshop presenter Aria Career Devel. Svcs.; cmty. activist Aria Cmty. Devel. Designer (booklets) 50 Ways to Maximize Your Potential, 50 Ways to Maximize Your Job Hunting, 110 Tips for First Time Home Buyers, 50 Tips to Energize Your Workforce, 2006, 50 Proven Strategies to Maximize Your Job Search, 2006, Intuitive Creative Journal, 2006. Tutor Providence Pub. Sch., 2000; transp. coord. Am. Cancer Soc., Portland, 1996—98. Scholar, Carver Fed. Bank, 1991; Howard Meml. scholar, Howard Meml. Fund, 1990—95, Mayor's scholar, City of NY,

1991. Mem.: NAFE, Am. Fedn. Tchrs., Providence Tchrs. Union. Avocations: travel, writing, research, cooking, entertaining. Office Phone: 828-278-0632. Personal E-mail: aria4@charter.net.

EDWARDS, ANTHONY, actor; b. Santa Barbara, CA, July 19, 1962; m. Jeanine Lobell, Sept. 5, 1994; children: Bailey, Esme, Wallis, Poppy. Student, Royal Acad. of Dramatic Art, London, 1980; BA, U. So. Calif., 1988. Owner prodn. co. Aviator Films. Actor: (films) Fast Times at Ridgemont High, 1982, Heart Like a Wheel, 1982, Revenge of the Nerds, 1984, The Sure Thing, 1985, Gotcha!, 1985, Top Gun, 1985, Summer Heat, 1987, Revenge of the Nerds II: Nerds in Paradise, 1987, Mr. North, 1988, Miracle Mile, 1989, How I Got Into College, 1989, Hawks, 1989, Downtown, 1990, Pet Sematary II, 1992, Sexual Healing, 1993, The Client, 1994, Playing by Heart, 1998, Don't Go Breaking My Heart (also prodr.), 1998, Northfork, 2003, Thunderbirds, 2004, The Forgotten, 2004, Jackpot, 2001, Northfork, 2003, Zodiac, 2007; (TV films) The Killing of Randy Webster, 1981, High School U.S.A., 1983, Going for the Gold: The Bill Johnson Story, 1985, El Diablo, 1990, Hometown Boy Makes Good, 1990, In Cold Blood, 1996; (TV series) It Takes Two, 1982-83, Northern Exposure, 1992-93, ER, 1994-2002, Rock Story, 2000; dir.: (TV series) ER, 1996, 98, Charlies Ghose Story, 1994; prodr.: Us Begins with You, 1998, Die, Mommie, Die, 2003, (TV films) Border Line, 1999, N.Y.H.C., 1999, My Louisiana Sky, 2001; guest appearance Monday Nigh Clive, 1999, Strangers, 1996. Mem. Bd. of Cure For Autism Now Found. Recipient SAG award, 1996, 98, 99, Golden Globe, 1998.*

EDWARDS, ARDIS LAVONNE QUAM, retired elementary education educator; b. Sioux Falls, SD, July 30, 1930; d. Norman and Dorothy (Cade) Quam; m. Paul Edwards, Apr. 18, 1953 (dec. Sept. 1988); children: Kevin (dec. 1980), Kendall, Erin, Sally, Kristin, Keely. Tchg. credentials, Augustana Luth. Coll., Sioux Falls, 1949; provisional tchg. credentials, San Jose State Coll., 1953, student, 1953-57. Lic. pvt. pilot, FAA, 1984. Mgr. The Cottage Restaurant, Sioux Falls, 1943-50; one-room sch. tchr. Whaley Sch., Colman, S.D., 1949-50; one-room sch. tchr. 8 grades East Sioux Sch., Sioux Falls, 1950-51; recreation dir. City of Albany, Calif., 1951-52; first grade tchr. Decoto (Calif.) Sch. Dist., 1952-58; ret., 1958. Author: Health Instruction Unit Study Packet for Teachers, 1954. Treas. PTA, Hayward, Calif., 1959; chmn. Our Savior Luth. Ch. Blood Bank, 1968—; officer Healthy Cmtys., Healthy Youth; mem. Am. Heart Assn., March of Dimes, Am. Cancer Soc., Arthritis Found.; rm. mother Chadbourne Grammar Sch.; team mother Fremont Little League; Brownie leader, den mother; bible sch. tchr., Sunday sch. tchr. East Side Luth. Ch., Sioux Falls, SD, 1945—51; charter mem. Our Savior Luth. Ch., Fremont, Calif., 1964—, mem. choir, transition task force, Christian Week Day Sch. tchr., 1970, 1987, ch. historian, 1986—; other offices; pres. Luth. Women's Missionary League, 1976; edn. officer, fraternal communicator, respecteen officer Luth. Brotherhood; youth dir. Thrivent Fin. for Luth. Recipient Spl. Svc. award Girl Scouts U.S., 1971, Arthritis Found., Fremont, 1974-75, Spl. Commendation March Fong Eu, 1954. Mem. NAFE, AARP, Republic Airlines Ret. Pilots Assn., Ret. Airline Pilots Assn., N.W. Airlines Ret. Pilots Assn., Aircraft Owners and Pilots Assn., S.W. Airways Pilots Wives Assn., Concerned Women for Am., World Affairs Coun., Philomathian Lit. Soc., Tri-Cities Assn. Evangelicals, Union City Hist. Mus., Washington Twp. Hist. Soc., Mission Highlands Swim Club. Republican. Avocations: bible study, flying, history, antiques. *My greatest sense of fulfillment is in being a Christian, wife, mother, teacher and writer in that order.*

EDWARDS, AURA C., political organization worker, volunteer; b. Williams, Calif., Aug. 30, 1923; d. Clark Samuel and Madge Rosa Chatfield; m. Frederick R. Edwards, June 7, 1945 (dec.); 1 child, Thomas C. Student, U. Calif., Berkeley, 1941—43. Sec., product writer Cutter Labs., Berkeley, Calif., 1945—46; tchr. Aura Edwards Dream Seminars, Lafayette, Calif., 1970—. Lectr. in field; dir. Hermco Inc., Real Estate Investments, San Francisco and Hillsborough, 2003—; profl. theatre organist. Author: (workbook) Dreams, A Guide to Interpretation, 1978. Charter mem Nat. Women's History Mus., Washington, 2002—; mem. Contra Costa County Grand Jury, Martinez, Calif., 1981—82; life mem. Contra Costa Juvenile Hall Aux., Martinez; founder, pres., minister Ctr. of the Seven Gifts, 1984—. Scholar Regents scholar, U. Calif.-Berkeley, 1941—43. Mem.: State of Calif. Grant Jurors' Assn. Republican. Avocations: bridge, tasseography, sailing, writing. Home: 6 Cricket Hill Rd Lafayette CA 94549-2403

EDWARDS, BERT TVEDT, accountant; b. Washington, Aug. 23, 1937; s. Archie Campbell and Geniana (Rasmussen) Edwards; m. Susan Elizabeth Dye, July 18, 1964; children: Christopher Andrew, Stacey E. Leonard. BA, Wesleyan U., 1959; MBA, Stanford U., 1961. CPA D.C. With Arthur Andersen LLP, Washington, 1961-69, 70-94, mgr., 1965-69, 70-71, ptnr., 1971-94, cons., 1994—98, 2001, ret. ptnr., 1994—; fin. v.p. Leisure Time Industries, Inc., 1969-70; CFO, asst. sec. U.S. Dept. State, 1998-2001; exec. dir. office hist. trust acctg. U.S. Dept. Interior, 2001—. Mem. U.S. Comptr. Gen. Auditing Stds. Adv. Coun., 1985—88, 1999—2002; chmn. audit com. U.S. Dept. Air Force, 2004—. Mem. spl. adv. commn. for indsl. and comml. devel. D.C. City Coun., 1972—74; mem. D.C. Mayor's Commn. Budget and Fiscal Priorities, 1989—91, 1993—95, D.C. Tax Rev. Commn., 1996—98; bd. dirs. Children's Nat. Med. Ctr. Rsch. Inst., 2002—06; trustee Population Reference Bur., 1975—98, 2001—07, vice chmn., 1993—94, chmn. audit com., 2005—; bd. dirs. Com. Capital City, 1995—98, 2001—02; trustee Barker Found., 1968—78, 1994—96, treas., 1968—71, 1st v.p., 1971—72, pres., 1972—75; bd. dirs. Jr. Achievement Met. Washington, Inc., 1973—87, treas., 1973—74, 2d v.p., 1974—75, 1st v.p., 1975—77, pres., 1977—78, chmn., 1978—80; bd. dirs., treas. Heritage Walk Homes Corp., 1975—80; chmn. JA Nat. Bus. Leadership Conf., 1978, Boys & Girls Clubs Greater Washington Ann. Congl. Dinner, 1993, dinner com. mem., 1992—98, found. bd., treas., 1995—; mem. Nat. Com. Pub. Employees Pension Sys., 1993—98, treas., 1995—98; bd. dirs., treas. Bethany West Recreation Assn., 1994—98; bd. dirs. D.C. Appleseed Found. Ctr. Law and Justice, 1995—98, 2001—, treas., 1998; mem. cmty. rels. bd. Sta. WAMU, 1994—97, CFO coun., chmn. stds. com., 1998—2001. Mem.: AICPA (govt. acctg. and auditing com. 1981—84, fed. govt. audit subcom. 1981—84, ad hoc task force univ. audit 1985—87, govt. acctg. and auditing com. 1985—88, author single audit course 1985—96, task force on quality of govt. audits 1986—87, govt. acctg. and auditing com. 1989—92, task force on quality of fed. program audits 1991—94), Govt. Fin. Officers Assn. Met. Washington (co-founder, bd. dirs. 1984—91, Outstanding Svc. award 1993), Assn. Govt. Accts. (Andy Barr Lifetime Achievement award 1993, Frank Greathouse award 2004), Md. Govt. Fin. Officers Assn. (bd. dirs. 1992—94), Orgn. Am. States (chmn. bd. external auditors 2000—02), Govt. Fin. Officers Assn. (co-chmn. ann. conf. 1987), Am. Acctg. Assn. (vice chair govt. nonprofit sect. 1993—94), Inst. Mgmt. Accts., Va. Soc. CPAs, Assn. Govt. Accts. Edn. and Rsch. Found. (chmn. bd. dirs. 1993—95), Greater Washington Soc. CPAs (chmn. membership com. 1973—74, chmn. SEC com. 1974—75, chmn. govt. acctg. com. 1979—81, chmn. rels. with D.C. govt. com. 1995—98, bd. govs. 2002—05, Lifetime Pub. Svc. award 1997), Hist. Soc. Washington (bd. dirs. 2002—, chmn. fin. com. 2003—, treas. 2003—), Univ. Club (mem. bd. admissions 1976—82, chmn. 1980—82, bd. govs. 1982—85), Wesleyan U. Alumni Club Washington (pres. 1969—71). Methodist. Home: 309 Casey Ln Rockville MD 20850-4733 Office Phone: 202-327-5312. Personal E-mail: bert_tedwards@ids.doi.gov.

EDWARDS, BLAINE DOUGLASS, lawyer; b. Borger, Tex., Sept. 30, 1961; s. Charles Afton and Harriett (Hauser) E.; m. Jill Summers Hendrickson, Sept. 1, 1984; children: Audrey Summers, Cole Douglass. BBA in Acctg. and Fin., Tex. A&M U., 1984; JD magna cum laude, St. Mary's U., 1990. Bar: Tex. 1990, U.S. Dist. Ct. (so., no., and ea. dists.) Tex. 1991, 96, U.S. Ct. Appeals (5th and 11th cirs.). Oil and gas/real estate lending officer InterFirst Bank, San Antonio, 1984-87; participating assoc. Fulbright & Jaworski, LLP, Houston, 1990-95; ptnr. Shook, Hardy & Bacon, LLP, Houston, 1995—. Adj. prof. law South Tex. Coll. Law , Houston. Co-author: Texas Environmental Law Handbook, 1990, 92; editor St. Mary's Law Jour., 1989-90; contbr. articles to profl. jours. Mem. Phi Delta Phi. Avocations: reading, skiing, golf.

EDWARDS, BLAKE, film director; b. Tulsa, July 26, 1922; m. Julie Andrews. Writer, prodr., actor: Panhandle, 1947; writer, producer Stampede, 1948, Soldier in the Rain, 1963, The Pink Panther, 1963; writer: Sound Off, 1952, Rainbow 'Round My Shoulder, 1952, All Ashore, 1953, Cruisin' Down the River, 1953, Drive a Cooked Road, 1954, My Sister Eileen, 1955, Operation Mad Ball, 1957, The Notorious Landlady, 1962; writer radio shows Line-Up; writer-creator radio show Richard Diamond; creator TV show Mr. Lucky; writer, dir. Bring Your Smile Along, 1955, He Laughed Last, 1955, Mr. Cory, 1956, This Happy Feeling, 1958, The Perfect Furlough, 1958, The Great Race, 1964, The Tamarind Seed, 1973, A Fine Mess, 1985, That's Life, 1985, Sunset, 1987, Justin Case, 1988, Skin Deep, 1989, Peter Gunn, 1989, Switch, 1991, Son of the Pink Panther, 1993; writer, prodr., dir.: A Shot in the Dark, 1964, What Did You Do in the War, Daddy?, 1966, Gunn, 1967, The Party, 1968, Darling Lili, 1969, Wild Rovers, 1971, The Return of the Pink Panther, 1975, The Pink Panther Strikes Again, 1976, Revenge of the Pink Panther, 1978, 10, 1979, S.O.B., 1980, Victor/Victoria, 1981, Trail of the Pink Panther, 1982, Curse of the Pink Panther, 1982, The Man Who Loved Women, 1983; dir.: Operation Petticoat, 1959, High Time, 1960, Breakfast at Tiffany's, 1961, Days of Wine and Roses, 1962, The Carey Treatment, 1972, Micki and Maude, 1984, Blind Date, 1986; prodr.: Waterhole No. Three, 1967; writer, prodr., dir. (Broadway) Victor/Victoria, 1995. Served with USCGR, World War II. also: Creative Artists Agy 9830 Wilshire Blvd Beverly Hills CA 90212-1804 Office: 11948 Saltair Ter Los Angeles CA 90049-4137

EDWARDS, BOB (ROBERT ALAN EDWARDS), radio news anchor; b. Louisville, May 16, 1947; s. Joseph Richard and Loretta Bernardine (Fuchs) E.; m. Sharon Ann Kelly, May 14, 1979; children: Brean, Susannah, Eleanor. BS in Commerce, U. Louisville, 1969; MA in Communication, Am. U., 1972; D.Pub. Svc. (hon.), U. Louisville, 1985; LHD (hon.), Grinnell Coll., 1991, Spalding U., 1998, Albertson Coll., 2001, Willamette U., 2005. News dir., program dir. Sta. WHEL-AM, New Albany, Ind., 1968-69; news anchor Sta. WTOP-AM, Washington, 1972; corr., night editor Mut. Broadcasting Sys., Washington, 1972-73; assoc. producer Nat. Pub. Radio, Washington, 1974, co-host All Things Considered, 1974-79, host Morning Edit., 1979—2004; host Bob Edwards Show XM Satellite Radio, 2004—, PRI, 2006—. Author: Fridays with Red, 1993, Edward R. Murrow and the Birth of Broadcast Journalism, 2004. Served in U.S. Army, 1969-71, Korea. Named to Esquire Register, Esquire mag., 1986, Ky. Journalism Hall of Fame, 2003, Nat. Radio Hall of Fame, 2004; recipient Oral Comm. award, L.I.U., 1980, Unity award in media, Lincoln U., Jefferson City, Mo., 1983, Edward R. Murrow award, Corp. for Pub. Broadcasting, 1984, Fleur-de-Lis award, Louisville Forum, 1985, Gabriel award, Cath. Acad. Comm. Arts Profls., 1987, 1990, 2006, Oak award, Ky. Advs. for Higher Edn., 1991, Alumni Recognition award, Am. U., 1991, Alumni fellow, U. Louisville, 1994, duPont Columbia award, Silver Baton, 1995, George Foster Peabody award, Coll. Journalism and Mass Comm. U. Ga., 1999, Alumni Achievement award, Am. U., 2001, Douglas Edwards award, St. Bonaventure U., 2002, Robert L. Kozik award, Nat. Press Club, 2007. Mem. AFTRA (nat. v.p. 1988—), Radio-TV Corrs. Assn., Soc. Profl. Journalists, U. Louisville Alumni Assn., St. Xavier HS Alumni Assn. Avocations: softball, genealogy, tennis. Office: XM Radio 1500 Eckington Pl NE Washington DC 20002 Home Phone: 703-533-8332; Office Phone: 202-380-4800. E-mail: bob@xmradio.com.

EDWARDS, C. KAREN, consultant company executive; b. Washington, Dec. 2, 1949; d. Charles Frederick and Christine (Oakley) Edwards; m. James Walker Pearce, Apr. 5, 1980; children: Ryan Christopher, Loren McKenzie. BA, U. Tenn., 1970; postgrad., George Washington U., 1971-72. Russian linguist Dept. of Def., Washington, 1971-74; pers. specialist AEC, Oak Ridge, Tenn., 1975-78; labor rels. specialist Dept. Energy, Oak Ridge, 1978-82, supervisory pers. mgr., 1982-91, directives/stds. mgr., 1991-96; pres. Pegasus Cons. Corp., Lenoir City, Tenn., 1996—. Cons. Dept. Energy and Dept. Energy contractors, Oak Ridge and Washington, 1996—. Author: A Practical Guide to Work Smart Standards, 1997. Bd. dirs. Oak Ridge Civic Music Assn., 1976-80; pres. bd. dirs. Knox Arabian Horse Club, Knoxville, 1982-87; vol. Spanish tchr. Woodland Elem. Sch., Oak Ridge, 1996-97. Recipient Hammer award, Vice Pres. Gore, Washington, 1996. Mem. Internat. Arabian Horse Assn., Arabian Horse Registry, Soc. Fed. Labor Rels. Profls., Beefmaster Breeders Universal, Phi Beta Kappa. Avocations: horses, farming, art, creative writing, reading. Office: Pegasus Consulting Corp 254 Babbs Rd Lenoir City TN 37771-3616 E-mail: edwardskc@pegasustech.com, webmaster@sss-mag.com.

EDWARDS, CARL, race car driver; b. Joplin, Mo., Aug. 15, 1979; NASCAR Driver Roush Racing, 2002—. Recipient Rookie Yr., NASCAR, 2003. Achievements include winning, Ky. 225, 2003, Power Stroke Diesel 200, 2003, Federated Autoparts 200, 2003; winner, Golden Corral 500, 2005, Pocono 500, 2005, NASCAR NEXTEL Cup Series at Michigan, 2007; winner Sharpie Mini 300, 2007, Pepsi 300, 2007, Dover 200, 2007, Federated Auto Parts 300, 2007. Office: c/o Roush Racing 122 Knob Hill Rd Mooresville NC 28115*

EDWARDS, CARL NORMAN, lawyer; b. Norwood, Mass., Jan. 22, 1943; s. Wilfred Carl and Cecile Marie-Anne (Pepin) E.; m. Mary Louise Buyse, Jan. 22, 1982. MEd, Suffolk U., 1969; postgrad., Harvard U.; PhD, U. So. Calif., 1997; JD, Boston Coll., 1998. Cons. dept. social rels. Harvard U., Cambridge, Mass., 1966-69, rsch. fellow, 1969-71, lectr. social rels., 1971-72; cons. rsch. psychologist Cambridge Computer Assocs., 1966—; rsch. social psychologist Tufts-New Eng. Med. Ctr., 1969—; assoc. clin. prof. psychiatry Tufts U. Sch. Medicine, 1971—. Dir. Four Oaks Rsch. Inst., Norfolk, Mass., 1974—; sr. assoc. for policy planning and rsch. Justice Resource Inst., 1971—; field faculty grad. program Goddard Coll., Plainfield, Vt., 1972-82; chmn. bd. dirs. MEDx Systems, Ltd., Dover, Mass., 1985—; chmn. bd. trustees Ctr. for Birth Defects Info. Svcs., Inc., Dover, 1984—; tchr. seminars; cons. to major corps., govt. agys. and pub. instns. in human dynamics and pub. policy; lectr., thesis adviser, program devel. cons. schs., colls., insts. Author: Responsibilities and Dispensations: Behavior, Science and American Justice, 2001; contbr. articles to profl. jours., monographs, revs. Mem. USNG, 1963-64. Mem. ABA, APA, Mass. Psychol. Assn. (bd. dirs.), Am. Acad. Forensic Scis., Nat. Trust for Hist. Preservation, Harvard Club, Appalachian Mt. Club, Norfolk Hunt Club, Blue Ridge Hunt Club. Home: Four Oaks PO Box 1776 Dover MA 02030-0279 Office Phone: 774-200-0201. Personal E-mail: cedwards@socialaw.com.

EDWARDS, CARLA E., psychology professor; b. Manhattan, Kans., Nov. 14, 1955; d. Carl Emery and Frances Ann Edwards; m. Terry Lee Hall, July 28, 1999; children: Cari De Stammler, Aaron Z. Lokie, Benjamin J. Lokie, Robert C. Duke. BA in Psychology, Park U., Parkville, Mo., 1989; PhD in Counseling Psychology, U. Mo., Kansas City, 1997. Lic. psychologist Mo. Instr. Park U., Parkville, Mo., 1989—97; assoc. prof. Northwest Mo. State U., Maryville, 1997—. Pvt. practice psychologist, Maryville, Mo., 1997—; cons. psychologist Conception Abbey, 2002—, Clyde Monastery, 2004—. Recipient Mo. State Gov.'s award Excellence in Tchg., 2005. Mem.: AAUW (co-pres. (Maryville br.) 2005—), APA, Greater Kansas City Psychol. Assn. Home: 25831 Timothy Rd Maryville MO 64468 Office: NW Mo State U 800 Univ Dr Maryville MO 64468 Business E-Mail: edwards@nwmissouri.edu.

EDWARDS, CARYN LOUISE, educational consultant, special education educator; d. Carl Alvar Erickson and Louise Lempe Loven Erickson; m. James Phelps Edwards, Sept. 1, 1966; children: James E., Nicole Anne. BS in Spl. Edn., Wayne State U., 1968; student in Learning Disabilities, Mich. State U., 1969—71. Spl. edn. tchr. Detroit Pub. Sch.; tchr. Okemos Pub. Sch., Mich.; dir., owner Erickson Learning Ctrs., Okemos, adminstr. Jackson, Mich., Lansing, Mich. Presenter in field. Author: Erickson Reader, 2000, Erickson Workbooks, 2000. Mem.: Erickson Learning Found. (exec. cir.), Learning Disabilites Assn. (bd. dirs. 1989—2004, nat. bd. dirs. 1996—2003, 2005—). Office: Erickson Learning Ctrs 2043 Hamilton Rd Okemos MI 48864 Office Phone: 517-347-0122. Personal E-mail: carynjpe@aol.com.

EDWARDS, CHARLES, neuroscientist, educator; b. Washington, Sept. 22, 1925; s. James Moses and Lola (Rosenthal) Edlavitch; m. Lois Bender, Aug. 12, 1951; children: Jan, James, Sally, David. AB, Johns Hopkins U., 1945, MA, 1948, PhD, 1953. Found. Infantile Paralysis postdoctoral fellow, asst. lectr. Univ. Coll., London, 1953-55; instr., asst. prof. physiol. optics Johns Hopkins U., Balt., 1955-58; asst. prof. physiology U. Utah, Salt Lake City, 1958-60; assoc. prof. physiology U. Minn., Mpls., 1960-65, prof., 1965-67; prof. biol. scis., dir. neurobiology rsch. ctr. SUNY, Albany, 1967-84, prof. emeritus biol. sci., 1986—; spl. asst. to sci. dir. Nat. Inst. Diabetes and Digestive and Kidney Diseases, NIH, 1984-88; prof. physiology, assoc. dean rsch. and grad. affairs U. South Fla. Coll. Medicine, Tampa, 1988-91. Grass lectr. CIEA del IPN, Mexico City, 1966; vis. prof. Karolinska Inst., 1975, 79, 84; mem. physiology study sect. NIH, 1971-75. Mem. editorial bd. Am. Jour. Physiology, 1967-73, Gen. Physiology Biophysics, 1983-95, Neurosci., 1979-92, Neurosci. Rsch., 1984-94. Mem. ACLU, Md. chpt., 1956-58, Utah chpt., 1959-60; mem. citizen adv. com. Sarasota Bay Nat. Estuary Program, 1994—. Lalor fellow, 1957, Lederle fellow, 1959-60; Nat. Acad. Scis. Czechoslovak Acad. Sci. Exchange fellow, 1980, 82, 84, 87, Japan Soc. Promotion of Sci. fellow, 1981, Naito Found.fellow, 1985; named to Johns Hopkins Univ. Soc. Scholars, 1987. Fellow AAAS; mem. AAUP (mem. coun. 1972-75), Am. Physiol. Soc., Marine Biol. Lab., Biophys. Soc., Physiol. Soc. Japan (hon.), Soc. Gen. Physiology (sec. 1971-73), Neurosci. Soc.

EDWARDS, CHARLES ARCHIBALD, lawyer; b. Lumberton, NC, Sept. 19, 1945; s. Charles Edwin and Elizabeth Gertrude (Gooden) E.; m. Judy Carol Griffin, Aug. 14, 1966; children: Lee McNeill, Caroline Averitt Clark. AB, Davidson Coll., 1967; JD, U. N.C., 1970. Bar: Ga. 1970, U.S. Supreme Ct. 1974, D.C. 1981, N.C. 1987. Assoc. Connerat, Dunn, Hunter, Houlihan, Maclean & Exley, Savannah, Ga., 1970-71, ptnr., 1972-76, Constangy, Brooks & Smith, Atlanta, 1976-82, Greene, Buckley, Derieux & Jones, Atlanta, 1982-86, Graham & James, Raleigh, NC, 1986-94, Womble Carlyle Sandridge & Rice, PLLC, Raleigh, Winston-Salem, 1994—, labor & employment practice group leader. Author: Georgia Employment Law, 1983; contbr. articles to profl. publs. Mem. Warrenton Town Coun., 2001—05. Mem. ABA, N.C. Bar Assn., State Bar Ga., Atlanta Bar Assn. (chmn. labor law sect. 1983-84). Republican. Episcopalian. Office: Womble Carlyle Sandridge & Rice One W Fourth St Winston Salem NC 27101 Office Phone: 336-721-3795.

EDWARDS, CHARLES CORNELL, surgeon, medical association administrator; b. Overton, Nebr., Sept. 16, 1923; s. Charles Busby and Lillian Margaret (Arendt) Edwards; m. Sue Cowles Kruidenier, June 24, 1945; children: Timothy, Charles Cornell, Nancy, David. Student, Princeton U., 1941—43; BA, U. Colo., 1945, MD, 1948; MS, U. Minn., 1956; LLD (hon.), Phila. Coll. Pharmacy and Sci.; LHD (hon.), Pa. Coll. Podiatry; LHD (hon.), U. Colo., 1993. Diplomate Am. Bd. Surgery. Intern St. Mary's Hosp., Mpls., 1948—49; resident surgery Mayo Found., 1950—56; pvt. practice medicine specializing in surgery Des Moines, 1956—61; mem. surg. staff Georgetown U., Washington, 1961—62; also cons. USPHS; dir. div. socio-econ. activities AMA, Chgo., 1963—67; v.p., mng. officer health and sci. affairs Booz, Allen & Hamilton, 1967—69; commr. FDA, Washington, 1969—73; asst. sec. for health HEW, Washington, 1973—75; sr. v.p., dir. Becton, Dickinson & Co., 1975—77; pres. Scripps Clinic and Research Found., La Jolla, Calif., 1977—91; pres., CEO Scripps Insts. Medicine and Sci., La Jolla, 1991—93. Bd. dirs. Bergen Brunswig Corp., No. Trust Bank, IDEC Pharms., Materia, Inc., Scripps Health Sys. Bd. regents Nat. Libr. Medicine, 1981—85; mem. Nat. Leadership Commn. on Health Care, 1986—; bd. govs. Hosp. Corp. Am., 1986—89; trustee Scripps Insts. Medicine & Sci., Scripps Found.; Scripps Rsch. Inst.; chmn. bd. dirs., trustee San Diego Hospice; trustee San Diego, YMCA. Lt. M.C. USNR, 1942—46. Recipient Disting. Svc. award, HEW, Disting. Alumnus award, Mayo Found., 1986, Humanity award, Nat. Conf., 1994, Lifetime Achievement in Corp. Governancy award, Corp. Dirs. Forum, 2001. Mem.: Nat. Acad. Scis., Inst. Medicine, Am. Hosp. Assn. (hon.), La Jolla Beach and Tennis Club, La Jolla Country Club, Princeton Club. Office: Scripps Rsch Inst 10666 N Torrey Pines Rd La Jolla CA 92037-1027 Business E-Mail: c.edward@ix.netcom.com.

EDWARDS, CHARLES LLOYD, lawyer; b. Chgo., July 2, 1940; s. Ed and Anita (Sopkin) E.; m. Lois S. Levine, Apr. 5, 1970; children: Laura, Karen. BBA with highest honors, U. Wis., 1962; JD, U. Chgo., 1965. Bar: Ill. 1965. Assoc. Aaron, Aaron, Schimberg & Hess, Chgo., 1965-67; ptnr., sr. counsel, Real Estate Practice DLA Piper Rudnick Gray Cary, Chgo., 1968—. Adj. prof. John Marshall Law Sch., 1997—98; lectr. law U. Chgo. Law Sch., 2005—06. Mem. ABA, Ill. State Bar Assn., Chgo. Bar Assn. (chmn. subcom. real property fin. 1986-88, vice chmn. real property continuing legal edn. 1989-91, vice chmn. real property 1991-92, chmn. real property 1992-93), Lawyers Club Chgo., Am. Coll. Mortgage Attorneys, Am. Coll. Real Estate Lawyers, Phi Beta Kappa, Beta Gamma Sigma. Avocations: classic music, collecting art, fishing, driving. Office: DLA Piper Rudnick Gray Cary Suite 1900 203 N La Salle St Chicago IL 60601-1293 Office Phone: 312-368-4010. Office Fax: 312-630-5314. Business E-Mail: charles.edwards@dlapiper.com.

EDWARDS, CHARLES M., medical educator; b. Louisville, Aug. 20, 1965; m. Denise Edwards, Jan. 18, 2003; children: Andrew, William. MD, U. S.Fla., Tampa, 1994—98. Lic. dr. State Fla. Bd. Medicine, 1998. Physician Bay Area Hospitalists, Tampa, 2001—04; asst. prof. U. S.Fla. Coll. Medicine, 2004—. Assoc. program dir. dept. Internal Medicine U. S.Fla., 2004—06. Office: Univ S Fla 4 Columbia Dr Ste 630 Tampa FL 33606

EDWARDS, CHARLES MUNDY, III, financial consultant; b. NYC, Jan. 30, 1935; s. Charles Mundy Jr. and Nancy Blow (Rawls) E.; m. Janice Elaine Petty, Oct. 22, 1966; children: Melanie LeMoyne, Meghan Elizabeth Adams. AB, Princeton U., 1957; postgrad., NYU, 1959-63. With Shearson Lehman Bros., Inc., NYC, 1959-85, assoc., asst. v.p., v.p., sr. v.p.; prin. Grumman Hill Assocs., Inc., Westport, Conn., 1985—. Cons. Lynch & Mayer, Inc., N.Y.C., 1994; bd. dirs. EOMG, Inc., Virginia Beach, Va. Treas. fund for Ednl. Advancement, Newark, 1985-87, pres., 1988-90, v.p., 1990-97, trustee, 1985-2005; trustee Family Svc. Assn. of Summit, 1987-91; pres., adminstrv. bd. United Meth. Ch., Summit, 1987-94, trustee, 1990-94; mem. City Planning Bd., Summit, 1989-91; mem. adminstrv. bd. Mt. Bethel United Meth. Ch., Marietta, Ga., 1995—, mem. fin. com., 1995-2004, chmn. endowment com., 1997—; bd. advisors Thurston Arthritis Rsch. Ctr., Chapel Hill, N.C., 1999-2002. 1st lt. USMCR, 1957-59. Mem. Princeton Quadrangle Club, Beacon Hill Club (pres.

1987-88, v.p. 1986-87, treas. 1985-86), Chattahoochee Plantation Tennis Club. Republican. Methodist. Home: 495 Atlanta Country Club Dr Marietta GA 30067-4684 Personal E-mail: charlieandjanice@bellsouth.net.

EDWARDS, CHARLES RICHARD, entomology and pest management educator; b. Lubbock, Tex., Jan. 22, 1945; s. Troy B. and Jeanette E. E.; m. Claudia Frances Henderson, Dec. 21, 1966; children: Cecily Elizabeth, Celeste Elaine. BS, Tex. Tech. U., 1968; MS, Iowa State U., 1970, PhD, 1972. Bd. cert. entomoloist. Prof. entomology Purdue U., West Lafayette, Ind., 1972—, now emeritus. Cons. Consortium for Internat. Crop Protection, Corvallis, Oreg., 1985—, Food and Agr. Orgn. UN, 1995-2000; USAID Integrated Pest Mgmt. Collaborative Rsch. Support Program, 1993—2003; adj. prof. St. István U., Gödöllo, Hungary. Contbr. articles to profl. jours. Mem. Entomol. Soc. Am. (Ext. Achievement award 1984, award of merit 1985), Royal Entomol. Soc. London, Sigma Xi, Alpha Zeta, Gamma Sigma Delta. Avocations: running, woodworking. Office: Purdue U 901 W State St West Lafayette IN 47907-2089 Home Phone: 765-463-9480. Business E-Mail: edwards@purdue.edu.

EDWARDS, CHET (THOMAS CHESTER EDWARDS), congressman; b. Corpus Christi, Tex., Nov. 24, 1951; m. Lea Ann Wood; 2 children. BA, Tex. A&M U., 1974; MBA, Harvard Bus. Sch., 1981. Legis. and dist. aide Staff of US Rep. Olin E. "Tiger" Teague, 1974—77; exec. Trammell Crow Co., 1981—85; pres. Edwards Comm. Corp.; mem. Tex. State Senate, 1983—89; chmn. Tex. Sunset Commn.; mem. US Congress from 17th Tex. dist., 1991—, mem. budget com., mem. appropriations com., ranking mem. mil. quality of life and vets. affairs subcommittee, co-chair Army Caucus, Dem. chief dep. whip. Named one of 10 Outstanding Legislators, Tex. Monthly mag.; recipient Legislator of Yr. award, Assn. of the US Army, 2003, Inspirational Leadership award, Mil. Order of the Purple Heart, 2005, Deficit Hawk award, Concord Coalition, Spirit of Enterprise award, US C. of C., 2006, Walter Cronkite award, Interfaith Alliance. Democrat. Baptist. Office: US Ho Reps 2264 Rayburn Ho Office Bldg Washington DC 20515-4311 Office Phone: 202-225-6105.*

EDWARDS, CHRISTINE ANNETTE, lawyer; b. Ft. Monmouth, NJ, Aug. 30, 1952; d. Harry W. Jr. and Elizabeth Power; m. John H. Edwards, Aug. 24, 1974; children: Lindsey, John. BA, U. Md., College Park, 1974; JD with honors, U. Md., Balt., 1983. Bar: Md. 1983, D.C. 1984, Ill 1990. With Sears, Roebuck and Co., Md., 1971-81, sr. paralegal, staff asst. Washington, 1981-83, atty. govt. affairs, 1983-87; asst. v.p., dir. govt. affairs Dean Witter Fin. Svcs. Group, Washington, 1987-88, v.p., gen. counsel Lincolnshire, Ill., 1988-89, sr. v.p., 1989-91, exec. v.p., sec., chief legal officer NYC, 1991-97; exec. v.p., chief legal officer, corp. sec. Morgan Stanley Dean Witter & Co. (merger Dean Witter Discover & Co. with Morgan Stanley & Co. Inc.), NYC, 1997—99; legal dept. ABN AMRO, 1999—2000; v.p., gen. counsel Bank One Corp., 2000—03; ptnr. Winston & Strawn LP, Chgo., 2003—. Mem. bd. Fin. Svcs. Coun., Washington, 1990—; bd. trustees Nat. Found. for Consumer Credit Counseling Svcs., Silver Spring, Md., 1990-92; mem. Women in Housing and Fin., Washington, 1982—, SAI Letigation Com., 1995—, N.Y. Stock Exchange Legal Adv. Com., 1992-95; bd. dirs. Chgo. Bd. of Options Exchange, SPS Transaction Svcs. Inc.; exec. v.p., chief legal officer, corp. sec. CLO Roundtable, 1995—. Recipient Disting. Mem. award Women in Housing and Fin., Washington, 1988; named 1 of 50 Top Women Lawyers Nat. Law Journal, 1998. Mem. ABA, Securities Industry Assn. (mem. fed. regulation com. 1990—). Home: 70 Sequoia Ct Lake Forest IL 60045-2827 Office: Winston & Strawn LP 35 W Wacker Dr Chicago IL 60601-9703

EDWARDS, CHRISTOPHER LEVON, medical association administrator; PhD, U. Ky., 1997. Dir. Duke U. Med. Ctr., Chronic Pain Mgmt. Program, Durham, NC, 2001—03. Dir. Duke U. Med. Ctr., Neurobehavioral Cognitive Assessment Lab., 2001—. Orgnl. devel. Bridges Point Found., Inc., Durham, 2000—03. Grantee Fin., Nat. Alliance for Rsch. on Schizophrenia and Depression, 1. Mem.: APA (assoc.), Soc. of Behavioral Medicine. Achievements include research in race and pain; race and diabetes; prostate cancer and african am. men; Alzheimer's Disease and african ams; genetics and Alzheimer's Disease. Office: Duke U Med Ctr 932 Morreene Rd Rm 170 Durham NC 27705 Office Phone: 919-684-6908. Business E-Mail: christopher.edwards@duke.edu.

EDWARDS, CLIFFORD HENRY COAD, law educator; b. Jamalpur, Bihar, India, Nov. 8, 1924; s. George Henry Probyn and Constance Ivy (Coad) E.; m. Kathleen Mary Faber, Jan. 6, 1951; children: Jeanette Marie, John Philip, Michael Hugh, Margaret Susan. LLB with 1st class honors, U. London, 1945. Sr. lectr. Kumasi Coll., Chana, 1956-58; assoc. prof. law U. Man., Winnipeg, 1958-64, prof., dean Sch. Law, 1964-79; pres. Man. Law Reform Commn., 1979—2006; dean emeritus U. Man., Winnipeg, 1986—. Queen's coun., 1980. Recipient Stanton Tchg. Award for Excellence, U. Man., 1994. Mem. Soc. Internat. Ministries (chmn. 1984-90), Man. Bar Assn. (Disting. Svc. award 1995), Order of Can. Mem. Anglican Ch. Office: Univ of Manitoba Fort Garry Campus Robson Hall Winnipeg MB Canada R3T 2N2 Office Phone: 204-474-6138.

EDWARDS, CYNTHIA G., archivist; b. Piggott, Ark., July 27, 1959; d. Doilas E. Edwards and Patsy A. Hollis; m. Kevin Kelly, Apr. 24, 1987. BA in History, Politics and Philosophy with honors, Cornell Coll., Mt. Vernon, Iowa, 1981; JD, U. Mo., Columbia, 1984, MLS, 1999. Bar: Mo. 1984, Kans. 1993. Law clk. to Honr. Douglas W. Greene III, Mo. Ct. Appeals, We. Dist., Springfield, 1984—85; assoc. atty. Law Offices of William H. Perry III, Joplin, Mo., 1985—87; law clk. to Chief Judge Dennis J. Stewart US Bankruptcy Ct., We. Dist. Mo., Kansas City, 1987—88; atty. advisor US Dept. Justice, Office US Trustee, Kansas City, 1988—96; assoc. Kevin Kelly, P.C., Kansas City, 1997—99; archives technician Harry S. Truman Libr. Inst., Independence, Mo., 2000—03; archivist U. Mo., Kansas City, 2003—05, Fed. Res. Bank Kansas City, Mo., 2005—. Mem.: Greater Kans. City Heritage League, Am. Assn. State and Local History, Kans. City Area Archivists, Midwest Archives Conf., Soc. Am. Archivists. Office: Federal Res Bank Kansas City One Memorial Dr Kansas City MO 64198 Home Phone: 816-356-5612; Office Phone: 816-881-4763.

EDWARDS, D. M., retail, wholesale distribution and real estate company executive; b. Tyler, Tex., Apr. 12, 1953; s. Welby Clell and Davida (Mount) E.; m. Susan Alicia Pappas, 1984 (div. 1986). AA cum laude, Tyler Jr. Coll., 1974; BBA, Baylor U., 1976. Ordained deacon Bapt. Ch. Corp. coord. Dillard Dept. Stores, Inc., Ft. Worth, 1976-77; exec. v.p. W.C. Supply Co., Tyler, 1977-83; pres., owner Walker Auto Spring, Inc., Shreveport, La., 1978-88, Edwards & Assocs., Inc., 1984—96; v.p. W.C. Square, Inc., 1976-92; CEO, chmn. bd. dirs. Pruitt Co. Inc., Houston, 1988—; chmn. bd., CEO Odessa Spring Brake & Axle, Inc., 1991—; pres., owner Shreveport Spring, Brake & Axle, Inc., 1998—; v.p. CountryMedic, Inc., Ft. Worth, 2001—03. Comml. real estate investor, Shreveport, La., Houston, Odessa, and Tyler, Tex.; gen. ptnr. ESE Properties, Tyler, 1991—; mng. gen. ptnr. Heritage Dr. Plz. Office Stes., 1992-95. Mem. planning com. Tyler Heritage Tour, 1982-83; originator Designer Show-Case, Tyler, 1983; founder, chmn. Rose Garden Trust Fund, 1981-87; bd. dirs. Carnegie History Ctr., 1984-85; chmn. merger com. Smith County Hist. Soc. and Carnegie History Ctr. merger, 1993-94; pres. Smith County Youth Found., 1986-87, mem., bd. dirs., 1984-91; pres. East Tex. State Fair, 1991-94; bd. assocs. East Tex. Bapt. U., Marshall, 1988—, v.p. bd. assocs., 1990-91, pres. bd. assocs., 1991-93; mem. exec. com. bd. trustees, vice chmn. bd. trustees, 2001-2003, chair bd. trustees, 2003-2005; mem. bd. trustees East Tex. Baptist U., 1995-2005, 2007-; mem. exec. com. East Tex. State Fair, 1990—; v.p. Camp Fannin Assoc., 1992-97, Tyler, 1992—; trustee Timberline Bapt. Camp and Conf. Ctr., 1987-90, 2001-04,2006-, treas., 1989-90, 2007; mem. Smith County Hist. Commn., 1984-85, 1991-94; chmn. stewardship com. First Bapt. Ch., Tyler, 1995-96, mem. fin. com., 1997-2001, mem. long range planning com., 1999-2007; v.p. Camp Fannin Assn., 2001—; treas. Timberline Bapt. Camp and Conf. Ctr., 2002-03. Mem. Tyler Area C. of C., Smith County Hist. Soc. (chmn. bd. govs. 1984-85, 87-88, pres. 1984-85, bd. govs. 1991-94), Hist. Tyler, Inc., Tyler Jaycees (v.p. 1982-83, bd. dirs. 1982-85), Nat Trust for Hist. Preservation, SCV (treas. camp 124, 1979-83), Rotary Club of Tyler (bd. dirs. 1998—, pres. found. 2002-2005), Rotary Internat. (Paul Harris fellow 1998), Willow Brook Country Club (stockholder), Hollytree Country Club, East Tex. Baylor Club (chair scholarship com. 1997—, pres. 2001-05), Camp Ford Hist. Assn. (bd. dirs. 1999—, v.p. 2000, pres. 2005-2007). Baptist. Home: 3600 Jill Cir Tyler TX 75701-8619 Office: PO Box 929 Tyler TX 75710-0929 also: Mountwood Ranch 7596 CR 1143 Tyler TX 75704-9817

EDWARDS, DANIEL PAUL, lawyer; educator; b. Enid, Okla., Apr. 15, 1940; s. Daniel Paul and Joye Virginia (van Horn) E.; m. Virginia Lee Kidd, Mar. 27, 1976; children: Austin Daniel, David Paul, Anne Marie. BA, U. Okla., 1962; JD, Harvard Law Sch., 1965. Bar: Colo. 1965, Hawaii, 1987, Ariz. 1988. Ptnr. Beltz, Edwards & Sabo, Colorado Springs; lectr. law Colo. Coll., 1976-87. Pres. Springs Area Beautiful Assn., 1978. Mem. ABA, Colo., Ariz. and Hawaii Bar Assn., Harvard Law Sch. Assn. Colo. (pres. 1986-87), El Paso Club, Broadmoor Golf Club, Cheyenne Mt. Club, Garden of the Gods Club, Kapalua Tennis Club, Phi Beta Kappa, Phi Delta Theta. Republican. Presbyterian. E-mail: dpedwards@bestlawllp.com.

EDWARDS, DANIEL WALDEN, prosecutor, lawyer; b. Vancouver, Wash., Aug. 7, 1950; s. Chester W. Edwards and Marilyn E. Russell; m. Joan S. Heller, Oct. 18, 1987; children: Nathaniel, Matthew, Stephen, Alexander. BA in Psychology magna cum laude, Met. State Coll., Denver, 1973, BA in Philosophy, 1974; JD, U. Colo., 1976. Bar: Colo. 1977, U.S. Dist. Ct. Colo. 1977. Dep. pub. defender State of Colo., Denver, 1977-79, Littleton, 1979-81, Pueblo, 1981-86, head office pub. defender Brighton, 1987-89, mem. jud. faculty, 1988-91; magistrate Denver Juvenile Ct., 1993-99; pvt. practice Denver, 1991-93; sole practitioner, 1999—2004; chief dep. dist. atty. State of Colo. 14th Jud. Ct., Hot Sulphur Springs, Colo., 2004—. Instr. sch. of law U. Denver, 1988-91, adj. prof., 1991—, coach appellate advocacy team, 1991-99; adv. coun. Colo. Legal Svcs., 1989—; adj. mem. Colo. Supreme Ct. Grievance Com., 1991-95. Author: Basic Trial Practice: An Introduction to Persuasive Trial Techniques, 1995, Principles of Persuasion: Basic Appellate Advocacy Techniques, 1999. Mem. visual arts com. City Arts III, 1989-90, com. chmn., mem. adv. coun., 1991; bd. dirs. Metropolitan State Coll., Alumni Assn., 1991-92; vol. lectr. CSE Thursday Night Bar Pro Se Divorce Clinic, 1991-95. Named Pub. Defender of Yr. Colo. State Pub. Defender's Office, 1985, Outstanding Colo. Criminal Def. Atty., 1989. Mem. ABA, Assn. Trial Lawyers Am., Colo. Bar Assn., Adams County Bar Asss., Denver Bar Assn., Met. State Coll. Alumni Assn. (bd. dirs. 1991-94). Home: 2335 Clermont St Denver CO 80207-3134 Office: State of Colo 14th Jud Dist PO Box 168 416 Byers Ave Hot Sulphur Springs CO 80451 E-mail: dedwards@co.grand.co.us.

EDWARDS, DARREL, psychologist, researcher; b. San Francisco, July 9, 1943; s. Darrus and Rose Pearl (Sannar) E.; children: Alexander Hugh, Peter David, James Royce. BS in Psychology, Philosophy and Religion, Brigham Young U., Provo, Utah, 1965, MS in Psychology, Philosophy and Religion, 1967, PhD in Clin. Psychology, Philosophy and Religion, 1968. Diplomate Am. Bd. Profl. Psychology. Postdoctoral fellow in psycholinguistics Pa. State U., 1969; commd. lt. (j.g.) USN, 1970, advanced through grades to lt. comdr., 1978; dir. psychologist Tri Community Svc. Systems, San Diego, 1973-78; prof. Calif. Sch. Profl. Psychology, San Diego, 1971-78; dir. Grid Rsch., San Diego, 1978-83; pres. The Edwards Assoc., San Diego, 1983—. CEO Strategic Vision, 1989—; founder Inst. for Value-Centered Life, 1999; adv. bd. Marriott Sch. Bus., Brigham Young U., 2002—; cons. in field. Co-inventor in field; author The Secret to (Almost) Everything-A Guide to A Successful Value Centered Life, 2005; contbr. articles to profl. jours. Mem. adv. bd. Marriott Sch. Bus., Brigham Young U. Decorated Vietnam Svc. medal USN; fellow, NASA. Fellow: Inst. Gen. Psychology, Am. Acad. Clin. Psychology; mem.: APA, Am. Soc. Quality (sr.; chmn. pres.'s bus. adv. bd. So. Calif. chpt.). Conservative. Mem. Lds Ch. Achievements include devel. of total quality measures for the automotive industry; development: Infinite Learning: a computer program fpr academic success.; inventor of Shadows: a value centered game for life. Office: Edwards Assocs 10725 Tierrasanta Blvd San Diego CA 92124 Office Phone: 858-576-7141. Personal E-mail: drdarreledwards@aol.com. Business E-Mail: darrel.edwards@strategicvision.com.

EDWARDS, DONALD MERVIN, systems engineer, educator, dean; b. Tracy, Minn., Apr. 16, 1938; s. Mervin B. and Helen L. (Halstenrud) E.; m. Judith Lee Wilson, Aug. 8, 1964; children: John, Joel, Jeffrey, Mary. BS, S.D. State U., 1960, MS, 1961; PhD in Agrl. Engring, Purdue U., 1966. Registered profl. engr. With soil conservation svc. U.S. Dept. Agr., Marshall, Minn., 1957-62; teaching, rsch. asst. S.D. State U. and Purdue U., 1960-66; assoc. prof. agrl. engring. U. Nebr., Lincoln, 1966-71, prof., 1971-80, asst. dean Coll. Engring and Architecture, 1970-73, assoc. dean, dir. Engring Rsch. Ctr., Coll. Engring and Tech., 1973-80, dir. Energy Rsch and Devel. Ctr., 1976-80; prof. and chmn. dept. agrl. engring Mich. State U., East Lansing, 1980-89; prof. biol. systems engring., dean Coll. Agrl. Scis. and Natural Resources U. Nebr., Lincoln, 1989-00, spl. projects, 2000-01, emeritus prof. biol. sys. engring., 2001—, emeritus dean Coll. Agrl. Scis. and Natural Resources, 2001—. Mem. Engring. Accreditation Bd. Engring. and Tech.; collaborator, cons. to numerous industries and agys., 1966—. Contbr. numerous articles on irrigation, water pollution, remote sensing, energy, agrl., natural resources and engring. edn. to profl. jours. Past bd. dirs. Nat. Safety Coun.; past chmn. bd. dirs. Lincoln Transp. System. Recipient Massey-Furguson award Am. Soc of Agriculture Engineers, 1994, Outstanding Tchr. award U. Nebr. Fellow Am. Soc. Engring. Edn., Am. Soc. Agrl. Engrs., NSPE (past nat. bd. dirs., nat. v.p.); mem. Profl. Engrs. Nebr., Farmhouse Fraternity, Sigma Xi, Alpha Gamma Rho, Triangle. Home: 11420 Wenzel Dr Lincoln NE 68527-9484 E-mail: dedwards1@unl.edu.

EDWARDS, EDITH MARTHA, lawyer; b. Great Neck, NY, Mar. 7, 1945; d. Paul Walter and Alice Matilda (Hansen) Steen; m. Thomas Murray Edwards Sr., Dec. 27, 1966; children: Janice Audrey, Thomas Murray Jr. BS, Coker Coll., 1967; JD, Olgethorpe U., 1981. Bar: Ga. 1982, U.S. Dist. Ct. (no. dist.) Ga. 1983, U.S. Supreme Ct. 1986. Atty. Ga. Legal Svcs., Nashville, 1983—84; asst. dist. atty. Alapaha Cir., Ga., 1984—86; asst. dist. Cherokee Jud. Cir., Ga., 1987; atty. pvt. practice, Ga., 1988—. Republican. Episcopalian. Avocation: art. Home: S-8 Ocean Walk 850 Mallery St Saint Simons Island GA 31522 Office Phone: 912-634-5075. Personal E-mail: emelegalart@hotmail.com.

EDWARDS, (MARY) ELIZABETH, lawyer, writer; b. Jacksonville, Fla., July 3, 1949; m. John Edwards, July 30, 1977; children: Catharine, Lucius Wade(dec.), Emma Claire, Jack Atticus. BS in English Lit., U. NC, 1971, JD, 1977. Law clk. to Hon. Calvitt Clark, Jr. U.S. Dist. Ct., Norfolk, Va.; assoc. Harwell Barr Martin & Sloan, 1978—81; staff mem., Office of Atty. Gen. State of NC, 1981—84; atty. Merriman, Nicholls, and Crampton, 1984—96. Adj. instr. U. NC, 1981—83, mem. bd. visitors; bd. dirs. Books for Kids; co-founder Wade Edwards Found., 1996—. Author: Saving Graces: Finding Solace and Strength from Friends and Strangers, 2006. Named one of The World's Most Influential People, TIME mag., 2007; one of the first pub. fellow, Coll. Arts & Sciences, U. NC. Address: c/o Wade Edwards Found 714 St Marys St Raleigh NC 27605

EDWARDS, FRANKLIN RICHARD, economist, educator, consultant; b. Palmerton, Pa., May 5, 1937; s. Franklin Richard and Mary Edytha (Morgan) E.; m. Linda Nasif, June 9, 1968; children— Rebecca, Jarett BA in Econs., Bucknell U., 1958, MA in Econs., 1960; PhD in Econs., Harvard U., 1964; JD, NYU, 1968. Economist Bankers Trust Co., NYC, 1961; economist Fed. Res. Bd., Washington, 1962, 63-64; sr. economist Office of Comptroller of Currency, Washington, 1964-66; asst. prof. Bus. Sch. Columbia U., NYC, 1966-68, assoc. prof. Bus. Sch., 1968-74, prof. Bus. Sch., 1974—, vice dean acad. affairs, 1979-81, dir., prof. Columbia Futures Ctr., 1980—. Vis. scholar Am. Enterprise Inst., Washington, 1994-95; vis. prof. Inst. des Sci. Economique, Ctr. Rsch. Interdisciplinaires Droit-Economie, U. Cath., Louvain, Belgium, 1969-70. Assoc. editor Jour. of Futures Markets; editor Jour. Fin. Svcs.; contbr. articles to profl. jours. Mem. adv. bd. Futures Industry Assn. Bd., 1981-88; nominating com. Am. Stock Exchange, 1988-90; mem. bus. conduct com. N.Y. Merc. Exchange, 1989-92. Mem. Am. Econ. Assn., Am. Fin. Assn., Soc. Royale D'Economie Politique Belgique (hon.), Shadow Fin. Regulations Com., Fin. Economists Roundtable. Office: Columbia U Dept Fin Uris Hall 625 3022 Broadway New York NY 10027-6945

EDWARDS, GENE, energy executive; BS in Chem. Engring., Tulane U.; MBA, U. Tex., San Antonio. Process engr. CITGO; cons. refinery econs. Pace Consultants; mem. staff to sr. v.p. product supply and trading and wholesale mktg. Valero Energy Corp., San Antonio, 1982—2005, exec. v.p. corp. devel. and strategic planning, 2006—. Office: Valero Energy Corpn 1 Valero Way San Antonio TX 78292-0500

EDWARDS, GEOFFREY HARTLEY, newspaper publisher; b. Liverpool, Eng., Mar. 28, 1936; s. James S. and Edith (Ellison) E.; m. Pamela Duncan, Oct. 9, 1965; children: Robert James, Alistair Duncan HNC Mech. Engring., Merseyside Tech. Coll., Birkenhead. Plant mgr. Inverest Paper Group, Derbyshire, Eng., 1962-65; gen. mgr. Liverpool Web Offset Ltd., 1965-68; asst. gen. mgr. Liverpool Daily Post & Echo, 1968-71, dir., gen. mgr., 1971-77; pub. Jour. Newspapers, Inc., Washington, 1977-91, Army Times, Washington, 1991-93; pub., CEO Current Newspapers, Washington, 1993-94; v.p. Washington Times, 1994—. Bd. dirs. Greter Washington Bd. Trade, Cultural Alliance Greater Washington, pres., 1984-86; mem. kennedy Ctr. Cmty. & Friend Bd., 1987—; campaign chmn. United Way of Nat. Capital Area, 1989 Mem. Brit. Newspaper Soc. (coun. 1974-77), Indsl. Rels. Newspaper Soc. (vice chmn. 1974-77)

EDWARDS, GEORGE CHARLES, III, political science professor, writer; b. Rochester, NY, Jan. 3, 1947; s. George Charles Jr. and Mary Elizabeth (Laing) E.; m. Carmella Rose Pierce, May 22, 1981; 1 child, Jeffrey Allan. BA, Stetson U., 1969; MA, U. Wis., 1970, PhD, 1973. Asst. prof. polit. sci. Tulane U., New Orleans, 1973-78; assoc. prof. polit. sci. Tex. A&M U., College Station, 1978-81, prof., 1981-90, disting. prof., 1990—, Jordan prof. in liberal arts, 1991—, dir. Ctr. for Presdl. Studies, 1991—2001. Vis. asst. prof. U. Wis.-Madison, 1976; vis. prof. U.S. Mil. Acad., West Point, N.Y., 1985-88, Peking U., Beijing, 1993, Hebrew U., Jerusalem, 1997; clin. prof. Oxford U., 2005-06; John Adams fellow U. London, 2003; pres. Presidency Rsch. Group, 1984-85; lectr. U.S. Info. Svc., Europe, 1985, 89, U.S., 1988, 92, Brazil, 1988; cons. NSF, Washington, 1977—, Internat. Rep. Inst., Moscow, 1994, Ctr. for Strategic and Internat. Studies, Washington, 1990-91, Nat. Acad. Pub. Adminstrn., Washington, 1987-88; bd. dirs. Roper Ctr. Pub. Opinion Rsch.; bd. advisors Stetson U., Transition to Governing Project; bd. acad. advisers Ctr. for Congl. and Presdl. Studies; exec. com. White House Interview Program; mem. Coun. on Fgn. Rels., 2002—. Author: The Public Presidency, 1983, Presidential Leadership, 1985, 90, 94, 97, 99, 2001, Government in America, 1989, 91, 94, 96, 97, 98, 99, 2000, 01, Presidential Influence in Congress, 1980, Implementing Public Policy, 1980, The Policy Predicament, 1978, At the Margins, 1989, On Deaf Ears, 2003, Presidential Approval, 1990, Why The Electoral College Is Bad for America, 2004, Governing by Campaigning, 2006, 07; editor: Perspectives on Public Policy-Making, 1975, Studying the Presidency, 1983, Public Policy Implementation, 1984, The Presidency and Public Policy Making, 1985, National Security and the U.S. Constitution, 1988, Researching the Presidency, 1993, New Challenges for the American Presidency, 2004, Presidential Politics, 2005, The Polarized Presidency of George W. Bush, 2007, Presdl. Studies Quar.; mem. editl. bd. Am. Jour. Polit. Sci., 1985-87, 94—, Jour. Politics, 1997—, Am. Politics Quar., 1981-87, Presdl. Studies Quar., 1978-98, Congress and the Presidency, 1981—, Policy Studies Jour., 1981-83, Am. Rev. Politics, 1994—; contbr. articles to profl. jours. Pres. Greenfield Plaza Condominium Assn., Bryan, Tex., 1980-81; mem. East Tex. 2000 Commn., 1980. Capt. USAR, 1971-79. Decorated for Disting. Civilian Svc. U.S. Army, 1960; Woodrow Wilson fellow, 1969-70, Ford fellow, 1970-73, John Adams fellow U. London, 2003. Mem.: Coun. on Fgn. Rels., Ctr. Study of Presidency (bd. dirs. 1978—), Policy Studies Assn., Midwest Polit. Sci. Assn., So. Polit. Sci. Assn. (Pi Sigma Alpha award 2001), Am. Assn. Pub. Opinion Rsch., Am. Polit. Sci. Assn. (sect. pres. 1984—85), Phi Beta Kappa, Phi Kappa Phi, Phi Alpha Alpha, Phi Alpha Theta, Pi Sigma Alpha. Avocations: collecting art, skiing, tennis, scuba diving, sailing. Home: 2910 Coronado Dr College Station TX 77845-7716 Office: Texas A&M Univ Dept of Polit Sci 4348 TAMU College Station TX 77843 Office Phone: 979-845-9764. Business E-Mail: gedwards@tamu.edu.

EDWARDS, GREGORY LAWRENCE, lawyer; b. Cocoa Beach, Fla., Sept. 13, 1967; s. Lawrence Wayne and Joyce (Humphries) Edwards; m. Donna Marie Hendricks, Aug. 4, 2001. AA, Brevard CC, Cocoa, 1989; BA, U. Ctrl. Fla., Orlando, 1994; MAT, U. W. Ala., Livingston, 1999; JD cum laude, U. Fla., Gainesville, 2005. Bar: Fla. 2006. Tchr. Brewton City Schs., Ala., 2000—01; summer assoc. McLin and Burnsed, Leesburg, Fla., 2004; cert. legal intern 8th Cir. State Atty.'s Office, Gainesville, Fla., 2005, legal trainee Maclenny, Fla., 2006, asst. state atty., 2006—; extern N. Dist. Fla. US Atty.'s Office, Gainesville, 2005—06. Actor: (plays) Ft. Harrod Drama Prodns., 1994—95, Snow Camp Hist. Drama Assn., 1996, Looney's Tavern Prodns., 1998—99. Named Defensive Player of the Game, M.I. HS Alumni Football Game, 1996. Mem.: ABA, Mensa, Phi Delta Phi. Republican. Ch. Of Christ. Avocations: surfing, football, tennis, walking, skiing. Office: 8th Cir State Attys Office 339 E Macclenny Ave Ste 126 Macclenny FL 32063

EDWARDS, GREY HOLT, JR., academic administrator, adult education educator; b. Camp Rucker, Ala., Aug. 17, 1945; s. Grey Holt and Margaret Maddox Edwards. BA, Frederick Coll., 1967; MS, Longwood Coll., 1970; CAGS, Boston U., 1974; EdD, Nova Southeastern U., 1992. Cert. counselor Nat. Bd. Cert. Counselors, 1984. Tchr. Va. Beach (Va.) Pub. Schs.; prin. Charlotte (S.C.) County Pub. Schs., 1970—72; regional adminstr. Ctrl. Tex. Coll., Frankfurt, Germany, 1972—78; officer edn. svcs. U.S. Army Continuing Edn., Hanau, Germany, 1978—94; mgr. edn. U.S. Army Edn., Ft Hood, 1994—96; dir. edn. Dept. Army Edn., Giessen, Germany, 1996—. Pres. Commn. Mil. Edn., Alexandria, Va., 2001—05; bd. dirs. Assn. of Adult Edn., Washington. Prodr.: (films) Pride of Broken Arrow, 2003; contbr. articles to profl. jours. Avocations: travel, attending olympics, baseball, hiking. Home: 3 Unter Den Linden Obbornhofen 35410 Germany Address: PO Box 620412 Fort Rucker AL 36362-0412 Home Phone: 334-255-9966, 334-393-0542; Office Phone: 334-255-9966. Fax: 49-641-402-6875. Personal E-mail: grey_edwards@hotmail.com. E-mail: grey.edwards@us.army.mil.

EDWARDS, HAROLD MORTIMER, mathematics professor; b. Champaign, Ill., Aug. 6, 1936; s. Harold Mortimer and Marian Bell (Scarlett) E.; m. Betty Rollin, Jan. 21, 1979. BA, U. Wis., 1956; MA, Columbia U., 1957; PhD, Harvard U., 1961. Instr. Harvard U., 1961-62; rsch. assoc.

Columbia U., 1962-63, asst. prof., 1963-66, N.Y. U., NYC, 1966-69, assoc. prof., 1969-79, prof. math., 1979—2002, prof. emeritus, 2002—. Vis. sr. lectr. Australian Nat. U., 1971. Author: Advanced Calculus, 1969, Riemann's Zeta Function, 1974, Fermat's Last Theorem, 1977, Galois Theory, 1984, Divisor Theory, 1990, Linear Algebra, 1995, Essays in Constructive Mathematics, 2005. Guggenheim fellow, 1981-82 Mem. Am. Math. Soc. (Steele prize 1980, Albert Leon Whiteman Meml. prize 2005), Math. Assn. Am., N.Y. Acad. Scis. Home: 67 Park Ave New York NY 10016-2557 Office: 251 Mercer St New York NY 10012-1110 Office Phone: 212-998-3168. Business E-Mail: edwards@cims.nyu.edu.

EDWARDS, HARRY LAFOY, lawyer; b. Greenville, SC, July 29, 1936; s. George Belton and Mary Olive (Jones) E.; m. Suzanne Copeland, June 16, 1956; 1 child, Margaret Peden. *Third Great Grandfather, Judge Thomas Edwards, Revolutionary War soldier with Washington at Yorktown, Probate, County and District Judge and member of South Carolina Legislature from Greenville County, married Mary Ann McClanahan, niece of Mary Marshall, aunt of Chief Justice John Marshall. Great Great Grandfather, Francis Edwards, War of 1812 soldier, married Laodicea, daughter of Captain Daniel Bailey, Revolutionary War soldier at Kings Mountain and Cowpens. Great Grandfather, Thomas Edwards, was with Lee at Appomattox. Grandfather William Francis Edwards was a farmer. Father was President of the family real estate company. Mother was a descendant of the Aiken and Peden families.* LLB, U. S.C., 1963, JD, 1970. Bar: SC 1963, US Dist. Ct. SC 1975, US Ct. Appeals (4th cir.) 1974. Assoc. Edwards and Edmunds, Greenville, 1963; v.p., sec., dir. Edwards Co., Inc., Greenville, 1963-65; atty. investment legal dept. Liberty Life Ins. Co., Greenville, 1965-67, asst. sec., asst. v.p., head investment legal dept., 1967-70; asst. sec. Liberty Corp., 1970-75; asst. v.p. Liberty Life Ins. Co., 1970-75; sec. Bent Tree Corp., CEL, Inc., 1970-75; sec., dir. Westchester Mall, Inc., 1970-75; asst. sect. Libco, Inc., Liberty Properties, Inc., 1970-75; pvt. practice, Greenville, 1975—. Editor U. SC Law Rev., 1963. Com. mem. Hipp Fund Spl. Edn., Greenville County Sch. Sys.; mem. Boyd C. Hipp II Scholarship Com., Wofford Coll. Spartanburg, SC; scholarship com. Liberty Scholars, U. SC, 1984, 1986-2007; pres. Greenville County Hist. Soc., 2006—. With USAFR, 1957—63. Mem.: ABA, Greenville County Hist. Soc. (pres. 2006—), Greenville Lawyers, Greenville County Bar Assn., S.C. Bar Assn., Soc. Descs. of Knights of the Garter/Windsor Castle, Magna Charta Barons (Somerset chpt.), Poinsett Club (Greenville), Phi Delta Phi. Baptist. Home: 106 Ridgeland Dr Greenville SC 29601-3017 Office: PO Box 10350 Greenville SC 29603-0350 E-mail: harryedwards106@bellsouth.net.

EDWARDS, HARRY THOMAS, federal judge; b. NYC, Nov. 3, 1940; s. George H. Edwards and Arline Ross Lyle; m. Pamela Carrington; children: Brent, Michelle. BS, Cornell U., 1962; JD, U. Mich., 1965. Assoc. firm Seyfarth, Shaw, Fairweather & Geraldson, Chgo., 1965—70; prof. law U. Mich., 1970—75; vis. prof. Free U. Brussels, 1974; vis. prof. law Harvard U., 1975—76, prof., 1976—77; prof. law U. Mich., 1977—80; dir. AMTRAK, 1977—80, chmn. bd., 1979—80; judge US Ct. Appeals (DC cir.), Washington, 1980—2005, chief judge, 1994—2001, sr. judge, 2005—; disting. lectr. law Duke U., 1983—89; lectr. law Georgetown Law Ctr., 1985—86. Neutral arbitrator, 1970—80; mem. Adminstrv. Conf. of U.S., 1976—80; faculty mem. Inst. for Ednl. Mgmt., Harvard U., 1976—82; lectr. in law Pa. Law Sch., 1981—82; lectr. Harvard Law Sch., 1982—88, Mich. Law Sch., 1988—89; vis. prof. law NYU Law Sch., 1989—; mem. Judicial Conf. of the US, 1994—2001; vis. prof. Cornell Sch. Indsl. & Labor Relations, 2002. Co-author: Labor Relations Law in the Public Sector, 1974, 1979, 1985, Lawyer as a Negotiator, 1977, Collective Bargaining and Labor Arbitration, 1979, Higher Education and the Law, 1979; editl. and adv. bds. West Publishing Co., 1978—80. Chmn. Ann Arbor Model Cities Legal Svcs. Ctr., Inc., 1971—72; mentor Unique Learning Ctr., Washington. Mem.: ABA (sec. sect. labor law 1976—77), Supreme Court Hist. Soc., Fed. Judges Assn., Assn. Am. Law Sch., Am. Soc. Internat. Law, Am. Judicature Soc., Am. Bar Found., Am. Law Inst., Am. Arbitration Assn. (dir. 1979—80), Am. Acad. Arts and Scis., Nat. Acad. Arbitrators (dir. 1975—80, v.p. 1978—80), Order of Coif. Office: US Ct Appeals 333 Constitution Ave NW Washington DC 20001-2805*

EDWARDS, HELEN THOM, physicist; b. Detroit, May 27, 1936; d. Edgar Robertson and Mary (Milner) Thom; m. Donald A. Edwards. BS in Physics, Cornell U., 1957, MA in Physics, 1963, PhD in Physics, 1966. Rsch. assoc. Cornell U., Ithaca, NY, 1966-70; assoc. head booster Fermi Nat. Accelerator Lab., Batavia, Ill., 1970-71, staff physicist, M.R., 1971-75, head switchyard extraction group, 1975-78, leader tevatron design group, 1978-79, dep. head saver div., 1980-81, dep. head accelerator div., 1981-86, head accelerator div., 1987-88, guest scientist, 1992—; head accelerator constrn. div. SSC/URA, Dallas, 1989-90, tech. dir., 1990—92. Recipient Achievement in Accelerator Physics and Tech. U.S. Summer Sch. on Particle Accelerator Prize, 1985, Ernest O. Lawrence award Dept. of Energy, 1986, Nat. Medal Tech., 1989; MacArthur Found. Chgo. fellow, 1988. Fellow Am. Phys. Soc.; mem. NAE.

EDWARDS, HERMAN, professional football coach; b. Monmouth, NJ, Apr. 27, 1954; m. Lia Edwards; children: Marcus, Gabrielle Lee. Student, U. Calif., 1972, student, 1974, Monterrey Peninsula J.C., 1973; BA in Criminial Justice, San Diego State, 1976. Profl. football player Phila. Eagles, 1977—85, L.A. Rams, 1986, Atlanta Falcons, 1986; defensive backs coach San Jose State, 1987—89; scout, asst. coach Kans. City Chiefs, 1990—95, defensive backs coach, 1992—94; asst. head coach, defensive backs coach Tampa Bay Buccaneers, 1996—2000; head coach N.Y. Jets, 2001—06, Kans. City Chiefs, 2006—. Co-author (with Shelly Smith): You Play to Win the Game: Lessons for Success On and Off the Field, 2004. Office: Kans City Chiefs One Arrowhead Dr Kansas City MO 64129

EDWARDS, HOWARD LEE, retired oil and gas industry executive, lawyer; b. Baker City, Oreg., June 10, 1931; s. Elmer L. and Bernice (Stringham) E.; m. Carolyn Bagley, Mar. 19, 1954; children: Bryant B., H. McKay, Mitchell L., Paul S. BS, Brigham Young U., 1955; postgrad., Stanford U., 1955-56, U. Utah, 1956-57; JD, George Washington U., 1959. Bar: Utah 1959, Colo. 1981, Alaska 1982, Calif. 1987. Legal asst., atty. US Dept. Interior, Washington and Salt Lake City, 1957-61; ptnr. Van Cott, Bagley, Cornwall & McCarthy, Salt Lake City, 1961-68; asst. gen. counsel Anaconda Co., NYC, 1968, asst. to chmn. bd., 1969, v.p., sec., 1970-77; gen. atty. Denver, 1977-82, Anchorage, 1982-83; corp. sec. Atlantic Richfield Co., LA, 1984-95; ret., 1995. Bd. dirs. Dynatronics Corp., 1996—. Trustee Rocky Mountain Mineral Law Found., 1968-87, Utah Valley State Coll. Found., Orem, Utah, 2005—; mem. nat. adv. coun. Brigham Young U. Sch. Mgmt., 1972-85; mem. nat. adv. coun. Dixie State Coll., St. George, Utah, 1987—, chmn., 1994-95; bd. visitors J. Reuben Clark Law Sch., 1980-83; bd. dir. L.A. region NCCJ, 1987-94, Ettie Lee Homes Youth, 1989-96, Kostopoulos Dream Found., 1997-2002, Deseret Found.; chmn. cmty. adv. coun. Heart and Lung Rsch. Found., 1995-2002; mem. exec. bd. Verdugo Hills coun. Boy Scouts Am., 1992-95, Verdugo Hills Hosp. Found., 1992-95; honorary bd. Utah Symphony and Opera, 2002—. Recipient Disting. Citizen award, Dixie State Coll., St. George, Utah, 2000. Mem. Am. Mining Congress (chmn. pub. lands com. 1970-84, Disting. Svc. award 1983), Coun. Fgn. Rels., Pacific Coun. Internat. Policy, Brigham Young U. Alumni Assn. (bd. dir. 1974-83, pres. 1980-81), Econ. Round Table, Rotary. Republican. Mem. Lds Ch. Home: PO Box 680934 Park City UT 84068-0934 Personal E-mail: howardledwards@hotmail.com.

EDWARDS, IRENE ELIZABETH (LIBBY), dermatologist, educator, medical researcher; b. Winston-Salem, NC, Mar. 17, 1950; d. Robert Dixon Edwards and Irene Octavia (Temple) Fisher; m. Clayton Samuel Owens, Apr. 19, 1985; 1 child, Sarah Tay. BS magna cum laude, Wake Forest U., 1972; MD, Bowman Gray Sch. Medicine, 1976; postgrad., N.C. Bapt. Hosp., 1979, U. Ariz., 1981-84. Diplomate Nat. Bd. Med. Examiners, Am. Bd. Internal Medicine, Am. Bd. Pediatrics, Am. Bd. Dermatology. Intern N.C. Bapt. Hosp., Winston-Salem, 1976-78, resident in pediatrics, 1978-79; resident in internal medicine U. Ariz. Health Scis. Ctr., Tucson, 1979-81, resident in dermatology, 1982-84; instr. dermatology U. Ariz. Coll. Medicine, Tucson, 1984-85, asst. prof. dermatology, 1985-90; clin. rschr., chief sect. dermatology Tucson VA Med. Ctr., 1984-90; chief dermatology Carolinas Med. Ctr., Charlotte, NC, 1990—; clin. assoc. prof. dermatology, clin. rschr. Wake Forest U., Winston-Salem, 1993—, U. N.C., Chapel Hill, 1993—. Nat. lectr. in field. Author: Dermatology in Emergency Care, 1997; co-author: Genital Dermatology, 1994; editor: Genital Dermatology Atlas, 2004; contbr. chpts. to books, numerous articles to profl. jours. Reynolds scholar, 1969-72. Fellow Am. Acad. Dermatology, Am. Acad. Pediatrics; mem. Soc. Pediatric Dermatology, Internat. Soc. Tropical Dermatology, Women's Dermatologic Soc., Internat. Soc. Study Vulvovaginal Disease (pres.), Charlotte Dermatol. Soc., Phi Beta Kappa, Alpha Epsilon Delta. Home: 2409 Cuthbertson Rd Waxhaw NC 28173-8110 Office Phone: 704-367-9777.

EDWARDS, JACK, congressman, lawyer; b. Birmingham, Ala., Sept. 20, 1928; s. William Jackson and Sue (Fuhrman) E.; m. Jolane Vander Sys, Jan. 30, 1954; children: Mrs. Richard Weavil, Richard Arnold. BS in Commerce and Bus. Adminstrn., U. Ala., 1952, LLB, 1954. Bar: Ala. 1954, D.C. 1983. Practice, Mobile, 1954-64; mem. 89th-98th Congresses from 1st Dist. Ala., 1965-85; mem. com. appropriations; mem. def. and transp. subcom.; vice chmn. Ho. Rep. Conf.; with Hand Arendall L.L.C., Mobile, Ala., 1985—. Bd. dirs. ret. The Southern Co., Holnam Inc., Northrop Grumman Corp., Aerospace Corp., Dravo Corp., QMS, Inc. Trustee U. Ala. Served with USMC, 1946-48, 50-51. Mem. ABA, Ala. Bar Assn., Mobile Bar Assn. (sec. 1956), Mobile Jr. Bar Assn. (pres. 1957), D.C. Bar Assn., Mobile Area C. of C. (chmn. bd. 1986), Kappa Alpha (pres. 1951-53), Omicron Delta Kappa. Presbyterian. (elder). Office: Am South Bank Bldg 107 Saint Francis St Ste 3000 Mobile AL 36602-3330 Home Phone: 251-928-1013; Office Phone: 251-694-6234. Business E-Mail: jedwards@handarendall.com.

EDWARDS, JAMES ALFRED, lawyer; b. Orlando, Fla., Feb. 18, 1954; BA in Psychology with high honors, Auburn U., 1976; JD with high honors, U. Fla., 1979. Bar: Fla. 1979, US Dist. Ct. (mid. dist.) Fla. 1979, US Dist. Ct. (no. and so. dists.) Fla. 1981, US Ct. Appeals (11th cir.) 1982, US Supreme Ct. 1984; bd. cert. civil trial lawyer Fla. Bar Assn.; cert. mediator cir., dist. and ct. of appeals. Ptnr. Rumberger Kirk & Caldwell of Profl. Assocs., Orlando, Fla., 2001—. Mem. Fla. Bar Assn. (cert. civil trial lawyer, mem. trial lawyers, appellate practice sects., com. on professionalism), Orange County Bar Assn. (mem. jud. rels. com.), Coastal Conservation Assn. Avocations: fishing, water-skiing, skiing. Office: Rumberger Kirk & Caldwell PA 300 S Orange Ave Ste 1400 Orlando FL 32801 Office Phone: 407-872-7300. Office Fax: 407-841-2133.

EDWARDS, JAMES BENJAMIN, accountant, educator; b. Atlanta, Apr. 27, 1935; s. James T. and Frances L. (McEachern) E.; m. Virginia Ann Reagin, Feb. 21, 1958; children: James Benjamin II, Chad Reagin, Calli Ann, Judy Clair. BBA in Fin., U. Ga., 1958, MBA, 1962, PhD in Bus. Adminstrn., 1971. CPA Tenn., Ga., S.C.; cert. mgmt. acct.; cert. internal auditor; cert. in data processing; cert. cost analyst. Contbr. Better Maid Dairy Products, Inc., Athens, Ga., 1958-62; staff acct. Max M. Cuba & Co., Atlanta, 1962-63; mng. ptnr. Wilson, Edwards and Swang, accts., Nashville, 1964-66; ptnr. Q.F. Lester & Co., Athens, 1967-68; v.p., chmn. bd. dirs. Gen. Data Svc. Inc., Athens, Ga., 1970-71; internal cons. J.W. Hunt and Co., CPAs, Columbia, 1983-84; v.p. Integrated Cost Mgmt. Systems Inc., Arlington, Tex., 1990-91; instr. David Lipscomb Coll., Nashville, 1963-66; instr. Nashville Ctr. U. Tenn., 1964-66; instr. acctg. U. Ga., Athens, 1966-71; asst. prof. U. S.C., Columbia, S.C., 1971-73, assoc. prof., 1973-77, prof., 1977—, fellow Bus. Partnership Found., 1977-90, William W. Bruner Disting. Faculty fellow, 1990—. Instr. staff tng. program local C.P.A. firms, Nashville, 1963-66 Editor: (ann. publs. Warren, Gorham & Lamont, Inc.) Emerging Practices in Cost Management and, Activity-Based Mnagment, Handbook of Cost Management for Service Industries, 1997—; contbr. articles on mgmt. acctg. to profl. publs. Coach Little League Baseball, Columbia, 1972-76; bd. dirs. Atlanta Bible Camp, Inc.; bd. dirs. Ga. Christian Found., Inc., pres., 1968-69; bd. dirs. Spring Valley Edn. Found., 1983-93, v.p., 1983-85, treas., 1985-93. Recipient 8 nat. awards for contbns. to acctg. lit. Mem. Am. Acctg. Assn., Am. Inst. CPAs, Inst. Internal Auditors, Planning Execs. Isnt. (asst. editor nat. mag. 1971-77), Am. Inst. Decision Scis. (v.p. Southeastern sect. 1975-76), Inst. Mgmt. Accts. (pres. Columbia chpt. 1973-74, nat. rsch. com. 1974-75, nat. edn. com. 1977-80, 95—, nat. dir. 1975-77, pres. Carolinas coun. 1976, nat. v.p. 1980-81), S.C. Soc. CPAs, S.C. Assn. Acctg. Instrs. (founding pres. 1972-73), Omicron Delta Epsilon, Beta Alpha Psi, Delta Sigma Pi, Sigma Chi. Mem. Ch. of Christ. Clubs: Five Points Optimist of Athens, Spring Valley Band Boosters. Office: c/o U SC Sch Acctg Darla Moore Sch 1705 College St Columbia SC 29208-0001

EDWARDS, JAMES D., accounting company executive; b. Cleve., Nov. 4, 1943; s. James D. and Elizabeth (Reynolds) E.; m. Sharon E. Bordelon, May 2, 1968; 1 child, David. BS in Acctg., Bob Jones U., 1964. CPA, Ga. From staff acct. to ptnr. Arthur Andersen & Co., Atlanta, 1964-73, mng. ptnr. Atlanta office, 1979-87, mng. ptnr. Americas NYC, 1987—. Bd. dirs., exec. com. Atlanta C. of C., 1982-85, Woodruff Arts Ctr., Atlanta, 1986-87; chmn. Cen. Atlanta Progress, 1986-87. Mem. Board Room (N.Y.C.),d The Stanwich Club (Greenwich, Ct.) Atlanta Country Club.

EDWARDS, JAMES DALLAS, III, management consultant; b. Harriman, Tenn., Aug. 9, 1937; s. James Dallas, Jr. and Helen Louise (Milburn) Edwards; m. Louisa Diane Fultz, July 15, 1961. BBA, U. Tenn., 1959. Customer svc. supr. Aluminum Co. Am., Alcoa, Tenn., 1964-67, staff product planner Pitts., 1967-70, traffic mgr., 1970-74; plant mgr. Soundesign Corp., Santa Claus, Ind., 1974-78; v.p., gen. mgr. Thermwood Corp., Dale, Ind., 1978-81; pres., CEO Spencer Plastic Products Corp. (name now Spencer Industries), Dale, 1981-92, also bd. dirs.; pres. Edwards & Assocs., Santa Claus, Ind., 1992—. Chmn. bd. dirs. So. Ind. Rehab. Svcs., Boonville, 1977—82; bd. dirs. S.W. Ind. Pvt. Industry Coun., 1989—, Ind. Small Bus. Coun.; mem. Santa Claus Indsl. Pk. Bd., 1978—; pres. Licolnland Econ. Devel. Corp. Named Ind. Small Bus. Person of the Yr., 1989, Ind. Entrepreneur of the Yr., 1989; recipient Ind. Global Competitiveness award, 1989. Mem.: SBA (mem. Ind. adv. coun. 1989—), Soc. Mfg. Engrs., Soc. Plastic Engrs., Am. Prodn. and Inventory Control Soc. (bd. dirs. 1970—72), Dales C. of C., Ind. C. of C. (bd. dirs.), Naval Res. Assn. (pres. 1967—71), Res. Officers Assn., Rolling Hills Country Club, Optimist, Elks, Kiwanis. Presbyterian. Avocations: golf, reading. Home: 826 Balthazar Dr Santa Claus IN 47579 Office: PO Box 372 Santa Claus IN 47579-0372 Home Phone: 812-544-2276; Office Phone: 812-544-2276. Business E-Mail: jdedwards@psci.net.

EDWARDS, JAMES ROBERT, minister, educator; b. Colorado Springs, Oct. 28, 1945; s. Robert Emery and Mary Eleanor (Callison) E.; m. Mary Jane Pryor, June 22, 1968; children: Corrie, Mark. BA in History, cum laude, Whitworth U., Spokane, Wash., 1963; MDiv, Princeton Sem., 1970; PhD, Fuller Sem., Pasadena, Calif., 1978. Youth min. First Presbyn. Ch., Colorado Springs, 1971-78; prof. religion Jamestown (N.D.) Coll., 1978—97, Whitworth Coll., Spokane, Wash., 1997—. Mem. spkrs. bur. N.D. Humanities Coun., 1983-84; rsch. scholar U. Tuebingen, Germany, 1988, Tyndale House, Cambridge, England, 2000; mem. Ctr. for Theol. Inquiry, Princeton, NJ, 2007; spkr. in field. Author: (with others) The Layman's Overview of the Bible, 1987, Commentary on Romans, 1992, The Divine Intruder, 2000, Commentary on Gospel of Mark, 2002, Is Jesus the Only Savior?, 2005 (named Book of Yr., Christianity Today 2006); contbg. editor Christianity Today, 1993—, Scottish Jour. Theology, 2006—; contbr. articles to profl. jours. Recipient several tchg. awards; Templeton grantee in sci. and religion, 1996; scholar German Acad. Exch., 1993 Mem. Soc. Bibl. Lit. Office: Whitworth Univ Dept Theology Spokane WA 99251 Business E-Mail: jedwards@whitworth.edu.

EDWARDS, JASON RAY, music educator, musician; s. Dale Leroy and Peggy Jane Edwards. BS in Edn., Mo. Western State U., 1984; MA, Truman State U., 1988; MusD, Ind. U., 2004. Instr. of oboe and bassoon Truman State U., Kirksville, Mo., 1982—86; instr. of single and double reeds No. Mich. U., Marquette, 1992—95; instr. of oboe and bassoon Luther Coll., Decorah, Iowa, 1998—99; vis. asst. prof. of woodwinds U. of Nebr.-Kearney, Kearney, 2001—03; asst. prof. of bassoon and music history U. of Minn., Duluth, 2004—05; assoc. prof. of woodwinds and music theory Iowa Wesleyan Coll., Mt. Pleasant, 2005—. Prin. oboist Kearney Area Symphony Orch., 2001—03; prin. bassoonist Hastings (Nebr.) Symphony Orch., 2002—03; bassoonist S.E. Iowa Symphony Orch., Mt. Pleasant, Iowa, 2005—; English hornist LaCrosse (Wis.) Symphony Orch., 1998—99; adjudicator collegiate divsn. Nebr. Music Tchr. Assn. State Festival, Kearney, 2002—04; adjudicator collegiate divsn. collegiate divsn. Minn. Music Tchr. Assn. State Festival, Duluth, 2005. Contbr. articles to profl. jours. Mem.: Coll. Music Soc., Internat. Double Reed Soc., Nat. Assn. of Coll. Wind and Percussion Instructors, Music Educators Nat. Conf., Phi Mu Alpha. Avocation: antique phonographs and records. Office: Iowa Wesleyan Coll 601 N Main Mount Pleasant IA 52641 Home Phone: 319-986-6291; Office Phone: 319-285-6442. E-mail: jedwards@iwc.edu.

EDWARDS, JEFFREY N., investment company executive; BS in Physics, Haverford Coll., 1982; MBA, Harvard U. Assoc. investment banking Merrill Lynch & Co., Inc., 1987, with equity capital markets, 1991, co-head global equity capital markets, 2000, co-head global equity markets NYC, 2001—03, head global capital markets financing, 2003—04, head investment banking Ams. region, sr. v.p., CFO, 2005—. Bd. mem. Nasdaq Stock Market, Inc., 2004—. Office: Merrill Lynch & Co Inc 4 World Fin Ctr 250 Vesey St New York NY 10080*

EDWARDS, JENNIFER LYNN, adult education educator, researcher; b. International Falls, Minn., Aug. 10, 1960; d. Bernard M. and Doris G. Hanson; m. Jeffrey E. Edwards (div.); children: Joshua T., Autumn C., Trevor J. BS, Bemidji State U., Minn., 1996, MA, 1997; PhD, U. Iowa, Iowa City, 2002. Lab. technicians Bemidji State U., Minn., 1994—96, rsch. technician dept. biology, 1996—97, grad. asst. dept. biology, 1996—97; rsch. technician NASA Biol. Rsch. Projects Brookhaven Nat. Lab., NY, 1996; grad. rsch. asst. dept. microbiology U. Iowa, Iowa City, 1997—2002, post doctoral fellow dept. microbiology, 2002—04; asst. prof., prin. investigator Children's Rsch. Inst., Ohio State U., Columbus, 2004—. Contbr. chapters to books, articles to profl. jours. Participant Girls are Great Girl Scouts Am., Columbus, Ohio, 2005—06; judge Future Physician Scientist Award Ohio State U. Coll. Medicine, Columbus, 2005—06. Nominee D. C. Spriestersbach Dissertation prize, U. Iowa Dept. Microbiology, 2001—03; recipient Biology Departmental Merit award, Bemidji State U., 1994—96, First Pl. award Poster Competition, U. Iowa, Grad. Sch. Student Forum, 2001, U. Iowa, Coll. Medicine, 2001, Deans' Disting. Dissertation award, U. Iowa, 2003, Igor Stojiljkovic/Raoul Rosenthal Meml. award, Internat. Pathogenic Neisseria Conf. Com., 2004; Alliss Ednl. Found. scholar, Bemidji State U., 1994—96, Fishing for Fun scholar, Bemidji State U. Dept. Biology, 1995—96, Rachel Mason Travel grantee, U. Iowa Dept. Microbiology, 2000, NIH Pre-doctoral fellow, U. Iowa Dept. Internal Medicine, 2000—02, NIH Post-doctoral fellow, U. Iowa Divsn. Infectious Diseases, 2002—03, U. Iowa Dept. Internal Medicine, 2003—04. Mem.: Iowa Microscopy Soc. (First Pl. award Poster Competition 2000), Am. Soc. for Microbiology (Richard and Mary Finkelstein Student Travel grantee 2001). Achievements include patents pending for vaccine and compositions for the prevention and treatment of Neisserial infections; demonstration of the direct participation of secreted gonococcus proteins in cervical cell signal transduction events; identification of novel human cellular receptors used by the gonococcus to initiate infection; first to demonstrate the ability of gonococci to form biofilms on human epithelial cells; research in analysis of the cyclic, hormonal, modulation of Neisseria gonorrhoeae infection in women, first demonstration that progesterone augments gonococcal survival; analysis of the oxidative response generated by primary, human, cervical epithelial cells during gonococcal infection; first demonstration that nitric oxide, spatially, augments gonococcal infection; analysis of complement production by cervical epithelial cells; first demonstration of the production of full alternative and terminal pathway complement components by these cells; analysis of N. gonorrhoeae proteins released with infection of cervical epithelia; identification of novel gonococcal proteins; elucidation of the interaction of the gonococcus with complement receptor type 3; first demonstration of the direct adherence of a microorganism to the I-domain of this receptor; elucidation of the opsonic interaction of the gonococcus with complement components; first demonstration that lipid A serves as an acceptor molecule for complement protein C3. Office: Childrens Research Institute 700 Childrens Dr W510 Columbus OH 43205 Office Phone: 614-722-2915. Office Fax: 614-722-2818. Business E-Mail: edwardsj@ccri.net.

EDWARDS, JESSE EFREM, pathologist, educator; b. Hyde Park, Mass., July 14, 1911; s. Max and Nellie (Gordon) E.; m. Marjorie Helen Brooks, Nov. 12, 1952; children— Ellen Ann Villa, Brooks Sayre. BS, Tufts Coll., 1932, MD, 1935; DSc (hon.), Georgetown U., 1990. Diplomate Am. Bd. Med. Examiners, Am. Bd. Pathology. Resident Mallory Inst. Pathology, Boston, 1935-36, asst., 1937-40; intern Albany (N.Y.) Hosp., 1936-37; instr. pathology Boston U., 1938; instr. pathology, bacteriology, surgery Tufts Med. Coll., 1939-40; research fellow Nat. Cancer Inst. USPHS, 1940-42; cons. sect. pathologic anatomy Mayo Clinic, 1946-60; asst. prof. grad. sch. U. Minn., Mpls., 1946-51, asso. prof., 1951-54, prof. pathologic anatomy 1954-60, clin. prof. med. sch., prof. pathology grad. sch., 1960—96; chief pathologist United Hosp. (formerly Chas. T. Miller Hosp.), St. Paul, 1960-80; cons. pathologist Hennepin County Hosp., Mpls., 1964—; cons. dept. pathology Mpls. Vets. Hosp., 1966—90; cons. pathologist St. Paul Ramsey Hosp., 1967-80; dir. registry of cardiovascular disease United Hosp., St. Paul, 1980-87, sr. cons. registry of cardiovascular disease, 1987—, also sr. cons. Jesse E. Edwards Registry of Cardiovascular Disease, 1987—. Pres. World Congress Pediatric Cardiology, 1980; mem. pathology study sect. USPHS, 1957-62; civilian cons. surgeon gen. AUS, 1947-69 Author: Atlas Acquired Diseases of Heart and Great Vessels, 1961, (with T.J. Dry and others) Congenital Anomalies of the Heart and Great Vessels, 1948, (with others) An Atlas of Congenital Anomalies of the Heart and Great Vessels, 1954, (with R.S. Fontana) Congenital Cardiac Disease, 1962, (with J.R. Stewart, O. Kincaid) An Atlas of Vascular Rings and Related Malformations of the Aortic System, 1963, (with C.A. Wagenvoort, D. Heath) Pathology of Pulmonary Vasculature, 1963, (with others) Correlation of Pathologic Anatomy and Angiocardiography, 1965, Coronary Arterial Variations in the Normal Heart and in Congenital Heart Disease, 1975, Coronary Heart Disease, 1976, (with Brooks S. Edwards) Jesse E. Edwards Synopsis of Congenital Heart Disease, 2000, Pathology of Sudden Cardiac Death, 2006; Editor: (with others) Circulation; contbr. articles to profl. jours. Served from capt. to lt. col. M.C. AUS, 1942-46. Recipient Distinguished Tchr. award Minn. Med. Found., 1974; Gold Heart award Am. Heart Assn., 1970; Gifted Tchr. award Am. Coll. Cardiology, 1977 Mem. AMA, Minn. Med. Assn., Soc. Exptl. Biology and Medicine, Am. Heart Assn. (pres. 1967-68), Minn. Heart Assn. (pres. 1962-63), Internat. Acad. Pathology (pres. 1955-56), Am. Assn. Pathologists and Bacteriologists, World Congress Pediat. Cardiology, Coll. Am. Pathologists, Am. Soc. Exptl. Pathology, Sigma Xi, Alpha Omega Alpha. Office: United Hosp Saint Paul MN 55102 Home: 211 2d St NW Rochester MN 55901 E-mail: doctorjee@aol.com.

EDWARDS, JOANN LOUISE, human resources executive; b. Lebanon, Pa., June 15, 1955; d. Harold Eugene and Kathryn Faye Edwards. AA in Human Svcs. with honors, Harrisburg Area C.C., 1975; BS with honors, Pa. State U., 1981; MA in Indsl. Rels./Human Resources Mgmt., St. Francis Coll., 1994. Cert. sr. profl. mgmt. Residential program worker Pan Am. Corp., Hershey, Pa., 1975-80, residential program supr., 1981-82, intensive behavior shaping supr., 1982-83; program mgr. Devel. Resources, Inc., Harrisburg, Pa., 1983-85, dir. minimum supervision, 1985-86, dir. human resources, 1986-96, Northwestern Human Svcs., Inc. of Ctrl./Western Region, 1966—; corp. v.p. human resources NHS Human Svcs., Inc., 2002—. Mem. New Directions for Progress Pers. Com., Harrisburg, 1988-96; instr. Mt. Aloyusius Coll., 2000—; adj. prof. human resources mgmt. St. Francis U., 2001. Mem. Christian Chs. United Pers. Com., Harrisburg, 1989-90. Mem. Harrisburg Area SHRM (past pres.), Soc. Human Resource Mgmt. Avocations: theater, classical music, antiques. Office: NHS Human Svcs 620 Germantown Pike Lafayette Hill PA 19444 Office Phone: 610-260-4631.

EDWARDS, JOHN ALLEN, physician, director; m. Karen Fahs Edwards. BS in Biochemistry, Seattle U., 1988—92; MD, Uniformed Serviced U., Bethesda, Md., 1992—96; MPH, U. Wash., Seattle, 2002—04. Diplomate Am. Bd. Family Medicine, 2000. Squadron surgeon Hdqs. 8-10 Cav., Baghdad, Iraq, 2005—06; assoc. residency dir. dept. family medicine Madigan Army Med. Ctr., Tacoma, 2006—. Maj. US Army, 1992—2006, Ft. Lewis, Wash. Fellow: Am. Acad. Family Medicine. Home Phone: 360-893-2887. Office Fax: 253-968-2608. Business E-Mail: john.a.edwards@us.army.mil.

EDWARDS, JOHN CARVER, retired archivist; b. Charleston, SC, Dec. 8, 1939; s. John Pelham and Elizabeth Carver Edwards; m. Judith Brina Task, Jan. 29, 2002; children: Leigh Carver, John Spann, Liam Morgan Quinlan, Kelly Harris Quinlan. BA with honors, Wofford Coll., 1964; MA, U. Ga., 1966, PhD, 1975. Head, manuscripts divsn. Ga. Dept. of Archives and History, Atlanta, 1970—72; records officer U. Ga., Athens, 1972—77, archivist, 1977—93, spl. projects archivist, 1993—2000, emeritus, 2000—. Program co-director, exhibit preparator conf. and exhibit Deliver Them From Evil: A Commemoration of America's Role in the Global War Against Fascism, 1941-1945, 1994; regular history and biography book reviewer Libr. Jour., NYC, 1996—. Author: (books) Patriots In Pinstripe: Men Of The National Security League, 1982, Berlin Calling: American Broadcasters in Service to the Third Reich, 1991, Airmen Without Portfolio: U.S. Mercenaries In Civil War Spain, 1997, Flying For Orville: Howard Rinehart's Life of Adventure, 2004, Orville's Eaglets: Notable Alumni of the Wright Flying School, 1910-1916, 2007; contbr. 3 essays Encyclopedia Of World War I, two one hour radio broadcasts Berlin Calling, Nat. Pub. Radio (Best Documentary award Soc. of Profl. Journalists, The Pub. Radio News Directors Inc., Ga. Assn. of Broadcasters, 1994), Flyers Of Fortune, Nat. Pub. Radio (Hon. Mention award, 1999), articles to profl. publs. Active various polit. campaigns, Cleveland, Ga., 2002—03. Mem.: Acad. Cert. Archivists (cert., charter mem.), Soc. Am. Archivists, Delta Tau Kappa (assoc.), Pi Gamma Mu (assoc.), Phi Alpha Theta (assoc.), Phi Kappa Phi (assoc.). Independent. Episcopalian. Avocations: military modeling, reading, walking, baseball, fishing. Home: 1475 Highway 255 South Cleveland GA 30528 Business E-Mail: jedwards@uga.edu.

EDWARDS, JOHN FREDERICK, federal official; b. Washington, June 10, 1960; s. Frederick Lewis and Norma Jean (Timmons) E. BA in Econs., U. Va., 1982; JD with distinction, George Mason U., 1987. Bar: Va. 1987, US Claims Ct. 1989, DC 1990. Law clk. to justice US Claims Ct., Washington, 1987-90, chief of staff, 1990-91; trial atty. comml. litig. br. US Dept. Justice, Washington, 1990; spl. master US Ct. Fed. Claims, Washington, 1991—. Office: US Ct Fed Claims Office of Spl Masters 717 Madison Pl NW Washington DC 20005*

EDWARDS, JOHN RALPH, retired chemist, educator; b. Streator, Ill., Feb. 27, 1937; s. Ralph E. and Ruth M. Edwards; m. Margaret E. Smith, July 15, 1961; children: Peter J., Sharon E., Susan D. BS, Ill. Wesleyan U., 1959; PhD, U. Ill., 1964. NIH postdoctoral fellow Tufts U., Boston, 1964-66; asst. prof. chemistry Villanova (Pa.) U., 1966-73, assoc. prof., 1973-80, prof., 1980—, chmn. dept. chemistry, 1980-90, asst. chmn., 1996—2002, ret., 2002. Contbr. articles to profl. jours. Grantee, NIH, 1970—76. Mem. Am. Soc. Biochemistry and Molecular Biology, Am. Chem. Soc., U.S. Orienteering Fedn., Sigma Xi, Phi Kappa Phi Office: Villanova U Dept Chemistry Villanova PA 19085 Business E-Mail: John.Edwards@Villanova.edu.

EDWARDS, JOHN WESLEY, II, lawyer; b. Williamsport, Pa., Nov. 29, 1948; s. Robert Wesley Edwards and Jean Eleanor (Seitzer) Leprohon; m. Lee Ellen Berliner, May 22, 1971; children: Wesley David, Katherine Lee, Meredith Jean. BA cum laude in English, Colgate U., 1970; JD, Duke U., 1974. Bar: Ohio 1974, Calif. 2001, US Dist. Ct. (no. dist.) Ohio 1974, US Dist. Ct. (no. dist.) Calif. 2001, US Ct. Appeals (6th cir.) 1974, US Ct. Appeals (9th cir.) 2001. Assoc. Jones, Day, Reavis & Pogue, Cleve., 1974-82; ptnr. Jones, Day, Reavis & Pogue (now Jones Day), 1982—. Served to cpl. USMCR, 1970-76. Mem. Ohio State Bar Assn., Bar Assn. San Francisco, Assn. Bus. Trial Lawyers, Order of Coif, Phi Beta Kappa. Clubs: Mayfield Country (Lyndhurst, Ohio). Republican. Presbyterian. Office: Jones Day 2882 Sand Hill Rd Ste 240 Menlo Park CA 94025 E-mail: jwedwards@jonesday.com.

EDWARDS, KENNETH NEIL, chemical engineering executive; b. Hollywood, Calif., June 8, 1932; s. Arthur Carl and Ann Vera (Gomez) E.; children: Neil James, Peter Graham, John Evan. BA in Chemistry, Occidental Coll., 1954; MS in Chem. and Metall. Engring., U. Mich., 1955. Prin. chemist Battelle Meml. Inst., Columbus, Ohio, 1955-58; dir. new products rsch. and devel. Dunn-Edwards Corp., LA, 1958-72; sr. lectr. organic coatings and pigments dept. chem. engring. U. So. Calif., LA, 1976-80; CEO Dunn-Edwards Corp., 2001—. Bd. dirs. Dunn-Edwards Corp., LA; co-chair indsl. adv. coun., mem. pres.'s cir. Calif. Poly. U., San Luis Obispo. Contbr. articles to sci. jours. Recipient Judo Masters belt (6th dan), Korean Judo Assn., 2000, 38th Western Regional Indsl. Innovations award, 2003. Mem. Am. Chem. Soc. (chmn. divisional activities 1988-89, exec. com. divsn. polymeric materials sci. and engring. 1963—, chair divsn. 1970, mem. devel. adv. com. 1996-99, Disting. Svc. award 1996, chair Disting. Svc. award selection 1997—, chair So. Calif. local sect. 1999), Alpha Chi Sigma (chmn. L.A. profl. chpt. 1962, counselor Pacific dist. 1967-70, grand profl. alchemist nat. v.p. 1970-76, grand master alchemist nat. pres. 1976-78, nat. adv. com. 1978—). Achievements include patents for air-dried polyester coatings and application, for process and apparatus for dispensing liquid colorants into a paint can, fluidic fillers, and for mechanical mixers. Home: Bottle Bay Rd Sagle ID 83860 also: 2926 Graceland Way Glendale CA 91206-1331 Office: Dunn Edwards Corp 136 W Walnut Ave Monrovia CA 91016-3444 Personal E-mail: kneatde@aol.com.

EDWARDS, LACY LEE, JR., real estate agent; b. Roanoke, Va., Aug. 8, 1941; m. Carol Morris; 2 children. BS, Va. Poly. Inst. & State U., 1964, MS, 1966; grad., U. Va., 1971, Rutgers U., 1974. With Dominion Bank, NA subs. Dominion Bankshares Corp., 1966—; sr. v.p., dir. human resources Dominion Bankshares Corp., Roanoke, Va., 1983—93; real estate agent MKB Realtors, Roanoke, Va., 1994—. Bd. dirs., advisor FNEB-sponsored co. Jr. Achievement Roanoke Valley; treas. Roanoke Valley Health Care Coalition; bd. dirs. Soc. for Crippled S.W. Va., Inc.; campaign chmn. United Way; mem. 2d Presbyn. Ch., Roanoke. Named an Outstanding Young Man, Roanoke Jaycees, 1976; recipient Diamond award producer, Roanoke Valley Assn. Realtors, 1996—2004. Mem. Am. Bankers Assn. (trustee, fund for edn. in econs.), Va. Bankers Assn. (ins./pension trustees), Va. BankPac Trustees (contbns. com.), Nat. Assn. Realtors, 1994-, Roanoke Valley C. of C. (bd. dirs., pres. 1981, pres.-emeritus Backbone Club, past treas. Roanoke Valley Beautiful Found., Inc.), Omicron Delta Kappa. Office: MKB Real Estate 3801 Electric Road SW Roanoke VA 24018 Office Phone: 540-989-4555. Office Fax: 540-774-6396.*

EDWARDS, LARRY DAVID, internist, educator, dean; b. Macomb, Ill., June 20, 1937; s. Richard Marshall and Anna Louise (Hare) Edwards; m. Ann Leanor Will, Mar. 31, 1959; children: Elliott, Sharon, Beth. Pre-Med, U. Ill., 1961, MD, 1965. Diplomate Am. Bd. Internal Medicine, Am. Bd. Infectious Disease, Nat. Bd. Med. Examiners, Am. Bd. Med. Mgmt., Am. Coll. Healthcare Execs; cert. physician exec., healthcare exec. Rotating intern USPHS Hosp., Staten Island, NY, 1965-66, resident in internal medicine, 1966-68; fellow in infectious diseases Rush-Presbyn.-St. Luke's Med. Ctr., Chgo., 1968-70; instr. dept. internal medicine U. Ill. Coll. Medicine, Chgo., 1968-70; asst. prof. depts. internal medicine, preventive medicine, microbiology Rush Med. Coll., Chgo., 1972-74; assoc. prof. internal medicine U. Ill. Coll. Medicine, Rockford, 1974-80, prof., 1980-81; prof. internal medicine Oral Roberts U. Sch. Medicine, Tulsa, 1981-90; dir. div. infectious diseases Rockford Sch. Medicine, 1974-81, dep. head dept. biomed. scis., 1980-81; prof. internal medicine U. Va., Charlottesville, 1991-92; chief of staff VA Med. Ctr., Salem, Va., 1990-92; assoc. dean for acad. affairs VA, U. Va., Charlottesville, 1991-92. Adj. assoc. prof. epidemiology U. Ill. Sch. Pub. Health, 1977—81; affiliate dept. medicine Abraham Lincoln Sch. Medicine, U. Ill., Chgo., 1977—81; dir. divsn. infectious diseases Oral Roberts U., 1981—84; assoc. dean clin. affairs Oral Roberts Sch. Medicine, 1981, 84, vice chmn. dept. internal medicine, 1981—83, chmn., 1983—86, chmn. preventive and internat. medicine, 1987—88, dean, 1984—90, v.p. for health affairs, 1987—90; COO City of Faith Med. & Rsch. Ctr., 1989—90; med. dir. Cen. Bapt. Home for Aged, Norridge, Ill., 1968—74, Columbia County Homes, Wyocena, Wis., 1974—80; asst. dir. infectious diseases, hosp. epidemiologist, dir. infectious disease research Rush-Presbyn.-St. Luke's Hosp., Chgo., 1972—74, asst. sci. dept. microbiology, 1970—74; asst. med. dir. Mcpl. Contagious Disease Hosp., Chgo., 1970—74; cons. infectious diseases numerous other hosps. and med. ctrs.; med. dir. City of Faith Hosp., Tulsa, 1984—87, chmn. bd., 1989—90; bd. dirs. City of Faith Clinic, Tulsa, 1985—87; pres. Infectious Diseases Cons. Svcs., Inc., Barnhart, Mo., 1993—2001. Contbr. numerous articles to med. jours. Advisor resource com. Sch. Health Coalition of N.W. Ill., 1979-81; med. adv. com. State of Ill. Refugee Health Services Program, 1980-81; Ill. health svcs. task force State Ill. Dept. Pub. Health, 1980-81; infectious disease adv. com. Tulsa City-County Health Dept., 1981-88; physician manpower adv. com. Okla. Bd. Regents, 1984-88; Titan scholarship bd. Oral Roberts U., 1985-87; v.p. World-Wide Med. Missions, Oral Roberts Evangelistic Assn., 1986-88, pres. 1989-90; active Leadership Roanoke Valley, 1991-92; dir. Strategic Tchg. and Reaping; med. dir. Bible Basics Internat., 2002-05; Bible tchr., missionary in Russia, Dominican Republic, Chile, Honduras. With U.S. Army, 1955-58, with USPHS, 1965-70, lt. col. USAR, 1985, col. 1990-97, ret., 1997. Smith, Kline and French fellow for study in Ethiopia, 1964; named Outstanding Faculty Mem. of Yr. Oral Roberts U. Sch. Medicine, 1982-83. Fellow: ACP, Am. Coll. Healthcare Execs. (ret.), Infectious Diseases Soc. Am. (emeritus), Am. Coll. Physician Execs. (life). Avocations: reading, writing. Personal E-mail: ldealesk@earthlink.net.

EDWARDS, MARK U., JR., academic administrator, history professor, writer; b. Oakland, Calif., June 2, 1946; s. Mark U. and Margaret Edwards; m. Linda Johnson, Mar. 1968; 1 child, Teon. BA in Psychology, Stanford U., Calif., 1968, MA in History, 1969, PhD in History, 1974. Jr. fellow U. Mich., 1971-74; asst. prof. history Wellesley Coll., Mass., 1974-80; asst. prof. Purdue U., West Lafayette, Ind., 1980-83, assoc. prof., 1983-86, prof. history, 1986-87; prof. christianity Harvard U., Cambridge, Mass., 1987-94; pres. St. Olaf Coll., Northfield, Minn., 1994—2000; assoc. dean academic adminstrn. Harvard Div. Sch., 2003—. Founder, v.p. ELK Software Devel. Corp., 1985—; pres. Sixteenth Century Studies Conf., 1987-88; chair continuing com. Internat. Congress for Luther Rsch., 1988-94; bd. dirs. Wittenberg U., 1985—. Author: Luther and the False Brethren, 1975, Luther's Last Battles, 1983, Printing, Propaganda and Martin Luther, 1994; co-author: Luther, A Reformer for Churches, 1983, Religion on Our Campuses: A Professor's Guide to Communities, Conflicts and Promising Conversations; mem. editl. bd. The Ency. of the Reformation, 1989—. Bd. dirs. Holden Village, 1993-94, 96-98. Mem. Am. Norwegian Hist. Assn.

EDWARDS, MARTIN, real estate company executive; Degree, Memphis State U. Cert. comml. investment mem. Nat. Assn. Realtors. Realtor, 1965; ptnr., broker Colliers Wilkinson & Snowden, 1999—; prin., owner Edwards Mgmt. Inc. Mem. nat. adv. bd. dirs. Fed. Nat. Mortgage; mem. Pres. George W. Bush Transition Team on Housing and HUD Policy; trustee Memphis (Tenn.) State U. Edn. Found.; assoc. prof. Continuing Edn. Dept. Memphis (Tenn.) State U.; sr. instr. Comml. Investment Inst. Named Realtor of Yr., Tenn., 1989; recipient Cert. Recognition Outstanding Cmty. Svc., City of Memphis, 1990, 1994, Excellencein Real Estate Edn. award, Tenn. Real Estate Commn., 1999. Mem.: Memphis (Tenn.) Area Assn. Realtors, Nat. Assn. Realtors (pres. 2002, treas., CFO 1996—97). Office: Colliers Wilkinson & Snowden 3644 Winchester Rd Ste 101 Memphis TN 38118

EDWARDS, MARVIN RAYMOND, investment counselor, economical consultant; b. NYC, June 29, 1921; s. Albert H. and Blanche (Gans) Edwards; m. Helene C. Sirota, Mar. 20, 1955; children: Jeffrey Randall, Douglas Lee, Carolyn Beth. BS, NYU, 1947. Pres. White Star Sales Corp., Jacksonville, Fla., 1947-58; pres. Edwards & Edwards, Inc., Jacksonville, 1958—. Interviews on investments and the economy have appeared in numerous publs. including Bus. Week, Scrap Age, Miami Herald, Tampa Tribune, The Market Chronicle, Fla. Trend Mag., others; polit. columnist Folio Weekly, 1996—; subject of interview ABC World News Tonight, 1993, 94, 2002. Exec. v.p., bd. dirs. Greater Jacksonville Taxpayers Assn., 1965-71; pres., bd. dirs. Better Schs. Citizens Com, Jacksonville, 1959-65, Community Service Planning Council, Jacksonville, 1955-58; v.p., b.d dirs. Jacksonville Humane Soc., 1953-56, Jacksonville Safety Council, 1948-50; bd. dirs. North East Fla. Kidney Found., Jacksonville, 1971-73; mem. Office Strategic Svcs. Lt. USAAF, 1943—46. Decorated Air medal; recipient Outspoken Citizen's award Jacksonville Southside Bus. Men's Club, 1993, Cert. of Appreciation for Disting. Svc. and Dedication, Econ. Roundtable Jacksonville, 2005. Mem. CFA Jacksonville (pres., bd. dirs. 1977-78, 87-88), Econ. Roundtable Jacksonville (founder, pres., bd. dirs. 1975-77, 90-91, 95—), CFA Inst., Nat. Assn. Bus. Economists, Nat. Economists Club, Soc. Profl. Journalists, Nat. Press Club of Washington, The O.S.S. Soc., Inc., Mosquito Aircrew Assn. Eng., Smithsonian Nat. Air and Space Mus., Am. Mus. Natural History, Nat. Space Soc., Planetary Soc., Nat. Ctr. for Sci. Edn., Nat. Fedn. Press Women Office: Edwards & Edwards Inc 1345 Riverbirch Ln Jacksonville FL 32207-7540 Personal E-mail: eandeinc@earthlink.net.

EDWARDS, MICHAEL DONALD, artistic director, drama educator; b. Ararat, Victoria, Australia, Aug. 6, 1949; came to U.S., 1978; s. Donald Bernard and Norma Eileen (Clearson) E. BA (hons.), Monash U., Melbourne, Australia, 1970; Diploma in Edn., Monash U., 1971; MFA, UCLA, 1980. Drama lectr. State Coll. Victoria, 1974-75; freelance theater dir., 1976—; dir., mgr. Mitchell Coll. Theater, Bathurst, Australia, 1977; prof. U. Calif., Santa Cruz, 1982—98; artistic dir. Shakespeare Santa Cruz, 1986—92; producing artistic dir. Ind. Repertory Theater, 1994—2006, Oreg. Shakespeare Festival, 2000—04, San Jose Repertory, 2002, Geva Theater, 2004, Asolo Repertory Theater, Winter's Tale; artistic dir. Syracuse Stage, 2001—06; producing dir. Asolo Theater, Sarasota, Fla., 2006—. Dir. City Stage, L.A., 1980-82, Va. Opera, Norfolk, 1986-87, Met. Opera, N.Y.C., 1988-90, 90-91, The Magic Theatre, San Francisco, 1990. Dir. (plays) including Henry IV Part I, Julius Caesar, Anthony and Cleopatra, Henry V, Richard II, Hamlet, Merry Wives of Windsor, Romeo and Juliet, The Crucible, A Life in the Theater, West Side Story, Vampire, Runaways, Working, Moonchildren, Deathtrap, Transgressor, The Barber of Seville, Amadeus, The Normal Heart, Vampire Dreams, The Devils, Aida, Measure for Measure. Mem. Human Rights Campaign Fund. Mem. SAG, Am. Guild of Musical Artists, SSDC. Office: Asolo Theatre 5555 North Tamiami Trail Sarasota FL 34234 Office Fax: 941-351-5796. Business E-Mail: michael_edwards@asolo.org.

EDWARDS, OTIS CARL, JR., theology studies educator; b. Bienville, La., June 15, 1928; s. Otis Carl and Margaret Lee (Hutchinson) E.; m. Jane Hanna Trufant, Feb. 19, 1957; children: Carl Lee, Samuel Adams Trufant, Louise Reynes BA, Centenary Coll., 1949; postgrad., Duke U., 1949-51; STB, Gen. Theol. Sem., 1952; postgrad., Westcott House, Cambridge, Eng., 1952-53; STM, So. Meth. U., 1962; MA, U. Chgo., 1963, PhD, 1971; DD, Nashotah House, 1976, U. South, Sewanee, Tenn., 2006. Ordained priest Episcopal Ch., 1954. Curate Episcopal Ch., Baton Rouge, 1953-54, vicar Abbeville, La., 1954-57, Waxahachie, Tex., 1960-61, rector Morgan City, La., 1957-60, priest in charge Chgo., 1961-63; instr. Wabash Coll., 1963-64; asst. prof. Nashotah House, Wis., 1964-69, assoc. prof., 1969-72, prof., 1972-74, sub-dean, 1973-74, acting dean, 1973-74; dean Seabury-Western Theol. Sem., Evanston, Ill., 1974-83, prof., 1983-93, prof. emeritus, 1996; chaplain, scholar in residence Coll. Preachers. Chmn. Coun. for Devel. of Ministry, Episcopal Ch., Coun. Sem. Deans; mem. Bd. for Theol. Edn.; mem. Gen. Bd. Examining Chaplains; vis. prof. Notre Dame, 1986—, Duke U., 1996; rsch. assoc. The Newberry Libr.; interim priest Episcopal Ch., Asheville, NC Author: How It All Began, 1973, The Living and Active Word, 1975, (with Robert Bennett) The Bible for Today's Church, 1979, Luke's Story of Jesus, 1981, (with John Westerhoff) A Faithful Church: Issues in the History of Catechesis, 1981, Elements of Homiletic, 1982, How Holy Writ Was Written, 1989, A History of Preaching, 2004; book rev. editor Anglican Theol. Rev., 1971-76, v.p. of corp., 1975-85; chair editl. bd. Sewanee Theol. Rev., 2002-; contbr. articles and book revs. to various jours. and mags. Chmn. campus affairs com.; trustee Kendall Coll.; sec., co-chair Commn. on Faith and Order Nat. Coun. Chs.; bd. dirs., Native Am. Theol. Assn., U. NC at Asheville Found.; exec. com., Nat. Coun. Chs. in the USA; v.p. bd. dirs. Coll. for Srs./U. NC, Asheville; program com. Kanuga Confs., Inc., Friends of St. Benedict. Recipient Spl. award Mystery Writers Am., 1965; grantee The Conant Fund, Pew Foun., St. Paul's Ministry and Mission Found., Indpls. Mem. Soc. Bibl. Lit., Cath. Bibl. Assn., Am. Acad. Religion, Chgo. Soc. Bibl. Rsch., Acad. Homiletics, (pres.), Societas Homiletica (exec. coun., treas.), Coll. of Preachers (long-range planning com.), Mystery Writers of Am. Democrat. Home: 115 Murphy Hill Rd Weaverville NC 28787-8630 Personal E-mail: ocejr@verizon.net.

EDWARDS, PATRICK ROSS, retail executive, lawyer, management consultant; b. Montreal, Que., Can., Mar. 17, 1940; came to U.S., 1952; s. Claude Victor and Edith May Peace (Wyatt) E.; m. Gracelyn Regina LaSala, July 2, 1961; children— Pamela Lynn, Jennifer Anne BA, Kenyon Coll., 1962; JD, Columbia U., 1965. Bar: N.Y. 1967. Staff atty. Allied Stores Corp., NYC, 1965-69, asst. to pres., 1970-74, v.p. adminstrn., 1974-83, sr. v.p. ops. and adminstrn., 1983-85; pres., chief operating officer Genovese Drug Stores, Inc., Melville, NY, 1985-86; exec. v.p., chief operating officer Am. Trim Products, Inc., 1987-88, pres., chief exec. officer, 1988-89; prin. The Rosse Co., 1990—. Sr. v.p. sys. svcs. North Shore--L.I. Jewish Health Sys., 1996-2000. Trustee Northshore U. Hosp., Manhasset, N.Y., 1984-93, spl. asst. to pres., 1993-96; mem. exec. coun. Inner City Scholarship Fund, N.Y.C., 1983-93; mem. deans adv. coun. SUNY Sch. Bus., Albany, 1984-86; mem. Ea. regional panel Pres.'s Commn. on White House Fellowships, N.Y.C., 1984-86. Mem. Kenyon Coll. Alumni Assn. Clubs: Strathmore Vanderbilt Country (Manhasset). Roman Catholic.

EDWARDS, PAUL BEVERLY, retired science and engineering educator; b. Ridge Spring, SC, Nov. 12, 1915; s. Paul Bee and Chloe Agnes (Watson) E.; m. Sarah Dee Barnes, Apr. 10, 1943 (dec. July 1999); 1 child, Susan Dee Edwards Von Suskil. BS, U. Tampa, 1937; EdM, Harvard U., 1958; EdD, George Washington U., 1972. Owner, operator Edwards' Hobbies, Tampa, Fla., 1938—54; tchr. math. Hillsborough HS, Tampa, 1955—60; head dept. math. King HS, Tampa, 1960—63; coord. Grad. Ctr., supr. edn. and tng. Johns Hopkins U. and Applied Physics Lab., Balt. and Laurel, Md., 1963—75, dir. Grad. Ctr., supr. edn. and tng., 1975—81. Contbr. articles to profl. jours. Mem. Sun City Ctr. Voters League, 1989—, Cmty. Assn., Sun City Ctr., 1987—; mem. Greenbriar Property Owners Assn., Sun City Ctr., 1987—. Lt. comdr. USNR, 1942-46 Named Meritorious Tchr., State Fla., 1962; recipient various fellowships Mem. Ret. Officers Assn., Naval Res. Assn., Golf and Racquet Club. Avocations: swimming, computers, photography, flying. Home: 1843 Wolf Laurel Dr Sun City Center FL 33573-6422 Personal E-mail: pedwards@tampabay.rr.com.

EDWARDS, PHILLIP MILTON, retired import/export company executive; b. Borger, Tex., Feb. 24, 1933; s. Aaron Moses and Ada Elsie (Feist) E.; m. Mildred M. L. Weber, Aug. 18, 1956 (dec. Sept. 2001); m. Arlene Irvine Davis, Jan. 4, 2002. BA, Okla. U., 1958. Polit. officer U.S. Embassy, Jedda, Saudi Arabia, 1961-64; vice consul U.S. Consulate Gen., Dhahran, Saudi Arabia, 1965-67; sr. advisor Dept. of Army, Vinh Long, Vietnam, 1968-70; publs. mgr. DOT Systems, Incorp., Vienna, Va., 1971-77; v.p. Transcontinental Trade Corp., Washington, 1978-81; sr. writer, editor Sci. Applications Internat. Corp., McLean, Va., 1981-87; v.p. Security Support Svcs., Washington, 1981-92; mem. profl. staff Alderson Reporting Co., Washington, 1992-97; ret., 1997. Freelance writer, editor, 1997—. Contbr. articles to profl. jours. Recipient Silver medal SAR, 1979. Presbyterian. Avocations: flying, photography, mountain climbing, tennis. Home: 1917 Aubrey Place Ct Vienna VA 22182-1976 E-mail: pedwa666@aol.com.

EDWARDS, PRISCILLA ANN, small business owner; b. Orlando, Fla., Sept. 28, 1947; d. William Granville and Bernice Royster; m. Charles R. King, Apr. 4, 1981. Paralegal cert., U. Calif., Berkeley, 1994. Paralegal Charles R. Garry Esquire, San Francisco, 1989-90; owner, mgr. Fed. Legal Resources, San Francisco, 1991—2004; prin., owner SunWest Pub. Co., LLC, San Francisco, 2003—. Speaker Sonoma State U., Santa Rosa, Calif., 1993. Publisher: (book) Zero Weather, 1981; author (as Una King): Tiny Tug's Adventures On San Francisco Bay, 2003. Recipient Wiley W. Manuel award for pro bono legal svcs. Bd. Govs. State Bar of Calif., 1994, 95, 96, 97, 98. Episcopalian. Avocations: horseback riding, mountain biking.

EDWARDS, RALPH M., librarian; b. Shelley, Idaho, Apr. 17, 1933; s. Edward William and Maude Estella (Munsee) E.; m. Winifred Wylie, Dec. 25, 1969; children: Dylan, Nathan, Stephen. BA, U. Wash., 1957, MLS, 1960; DLS, U. Calif.-Berkeley, 1971. Libr. NY Pub. Libr., NYC, 1960-61; catalog libr. U. Ill. Libr., Urbana, 1961-62; br. libr. Multnomah County Libr., Portland, Oreg., 1964-67; asst. prof. Western Mich. U., Kalamazoo, 1970-74; chief Ctl. Libr. Dallas Pub. Libr., 1975-81; city libr. Phoenix Pub. Libr., 1981-95, ret., 1996—. Author: Role of the Beginning Librarian in University Libraries, 1975. U. Calif. doctoral fellow, 1967-70; library mgmt. internship Council on Library Resources, 1974-75 Mem. ALA, Pub. Library Assn. Democrat. Home: 2884 Spring Blvd Eugene OR 97403-1662 E-mail: wedwards@efn.org.

EDWARDS, RANDALL, state official; b. Eugene, Oreg., Aug. 13, 1961; m. Jill Brim-Edwards; 3 children. BA in Econs., Colo. Coll., 1983; MBA, George Washington Univ., 1990. Legis. aide US Senate, 1983—87; internat. trade analyst US Dept. Commerce, 1987—91; sr. adv. Oreg. State Treasury, 1992—96; mng. ptnr. EDJE Cons., 1996—2000; state treas. State of Oreg., 2000—. Rep. Oreg. Ho. Reps., 1996—2000. Mem.: Nat. Assn. State Treas. (pres. 2006). Democrat. Office: State Treas 350 Winter St NE Salem OR 97301-3896 also: 159 State Capitol 900 Court St NE Salem OR 97301-4043 Office Phone: 503-378-4329. Office Fax: 503-378-2870. Business E-Mail: oregon.treasurer@state.or.us.

EDWARDS, RICHARD ALAN, retired lawyer; b. Portland, Oreg., June 28, 1938; s. Howard A. and Kay E. (Sheldon) E.; m. Renee Rosier, June 18, 1960; children: Teri Edwards Obye, Lisa Edwards Smith, Steve. BS, Oreg. State U., 1960; JD summa cum laude, Willamette U., 1968. Bar: Oreg. 1968, U.S. Dist. Ct. Oreg. 1968, U.S. Ct. Appeals (9th cir.) 1969. Various positions 1st Interstate Bank of Oreg., Portland, 1960-65; assoc. Miller, Nash, Wiener, Hager & Carlsen, Portland, 1968-74, ptnr., 1974—99, mng. ptnr., 1991-96. Editor Willamette Law Jour., 1967-68. Mem. ABA (litig. sect. 1972), Oreg. State Bar (chairperson debtor-creditor sect. 1981-82, mem. various coms.). Republican. Presbyterian. Personal E-mail: richardaedwards@verizon.net.

EDWARDS, RICHARD LANSING, lawyer; b. Wilmington, Del., Apr. 16, 1944; s. Robert Wilson Jr. and Eleanor (Inscho) E.; m. Betsey Ann Barney, Aug. 24, 1980; children: Beth, Melissa, Jeffrey, Jason, Karen. BS in Indsl. Engring., Lehigh U., 1966; JD, Northeastern U., 1980. Bar: Mass. 1980, U.S. Dist. Ct. Mass. 1981, U.S. Ct. Appeals (1st cir.) 1983, U.S. Supreme Ct. 1985, U.S. Dist. Ct. Conn. 1998. Lawyer Craig & Macauley, Boston, 1980-83; lawyer, shareholder Campbell, Campbell, Edwards & Conroy P.C., Boston, 1983—. Faculty Internat. Assn. Def. Counsel Trial Acad., 1994, ABA TIPS Nat. Trial Acad., 2000. Contbr. articles to profl. jours. Capt. USAF, 1966—70. Decorated Bronze Star. Mem. ABA (tort and ins. practice and litigation sect. 1984—, faculty torts and ins. sect. Nat. Trial Acad. 2000), Mass. Bar Assn. (civil litigation sect. 1983—), Def. Rsch. Inst. (bd. dirs. 1999-2002, products liability com., chmn. 1997-99, chmn. duty to warn and labeling subcom. 1985-88, steering com. 1988-2003), Internat. Assn. of Def. Counsel (chmn. advocacy practice and procedure com. 1993-95, faculty Trial Acad. 1994), Mass. Def. Lawyers Assn., Product Liability Adv. Coun., Boston Bar Assn, Nat. Found. for Jud.Excellence (meme. program planning com. 2005-). Office: Campbell Campbell Edwards & Conroy PC One Constitution Plaza Boston MA 02129 Office Phone: 617-241-3000. Business E-Mail: redwards@campbell-trial-lawyers.com.

EDWARDS, RICHARD LEROY, dean, social sciences educator, management consultant; b. Rahway, NJ, Aug. 9, 1943; s. Richard Lorraine and Norma (Higley) E.; children: Jeffrey, Julia, Jennifer. BA, Augustana Coll., Rock Island, Ill., 1965; MA, U. Chgo., 1967; PhD with distinction, SUNY, Albany, 1986. Social worker Ill. State Psychiat. Inst., Chgo., 1967-70; asst. prof. Augustana Coll., 1970-74; staff assoc. Nat. Assn. Social Workers, Washington, 1974-78; assoc. dir. continuing social work edn. U. Tenn., Knoxville, 1978-80; assoc. prof., assoc. dean SUNY, Albany, 1980-88; prof., dean Mandel Sch. Applied Social Scis. Case Western Res. U., Cleve., 1988-92; dean sch. social work U. N.C., Chapel Hill, 1992—2000, interim provost, 2000—01, alumni disting. prof., 2001—. Editor: Skills for Effective Human Services Management, 1991, Skills for Effective Managementof non-Profit Organizations, 1996; editor-in-chief Ency. of Social Work, 1995; contbr. numerous articles to profl. jours.; chpts. to book. Elected mem. Bd. Edn., Davenport, Iowa, 1972-74; trustee numerous non-profit agy. bds. Recipient Achievement in Edn. award No. Ohio Live Mag., 1991. Mem. Acad. Cert. Social Workers, Nat. Assn. Social Workers (Social Worker of Yr. award N.Y. chpt. 1987, pres. 1989-91), Coun. on Social Work Edn. Avocation: golf. Office: U NC Sch of Social Work 301 Pittsboro St Chapel Hill NC 27599-3550 Home: 117 Walnut Ct Highland Park NJ 08904-1927

EDWARDS, ROBERT HAZARD, retired college president; b. London, May 26, 1935; s. Arthur Robinson and Marjorie Hazard (Mayes) E. (father Am. citizen); m. Blythe Morton Bickel, Nov. 5, 1988; children from previous marriage: Elizabeth, Daphne, Nicholas. AB, Princeton U., NJ, 1957; BA, Cambridge U., Eng., 1959, MA with honors, 1977; LLB, Harvard U., Cambridge, Mass., 1961; LHD (hon.), Carleton Coll., 1986, Bowdoin Coll., Colby Coll., 2001, U. Maine, 2007. Bar: Fed. 1961. Fellow Ford Found, 1961—63; with UN polit. affairs Dept. State, 1963—65, Ford Found., 1965—77; rep. for Pakistan, 1968—72; head Middle East and Africa, 1973—77; pres. Carleton Coll., Northfield, Minn., 1977—86; head social welfare dept. Secretariat of the Aga Khan, Paris, 1986—90; pres. Bowdoin Coll., Brunswick, Maine, 1990—2001. Mem. bd. visitors U. Maine; trustee Aga Khan U. Mem. Coun. on Fgn. Rels., Am. Acad. Arts and Sci.

EDWARDS, ROBERT L., corporate financial executive; BA, MBA, Brigham Young U. Various exec. positions Santa Fe Pacific Corp.; sr. v.p., CFO, chief adminstrv. officer Imation Corp., 1998—2003; exec. v.p., CFO Maxtor, Milipitas, Calif., 2003—04, Safeway Inc., 2004—. Office: Safeway Inc 5918 Stoneridge Mall Rd Pleasanton CA 94588*

EDWARDS, ROBIN MORSE, lawyer; b. Glens Falls, NY, Dec. 9, 1947; d. Daniel and Harriet Morse; m. Richard Charles Edwards, Aug. 30, 1970; children: Michael Alan, Jonathan Philip. BA, Mt. Holyoke Coll., 1969; JD, U. Calif., Berkeley, 1972. Bar: Calif. 1972. Assoc. Donahue, Gallagher, Thomas & Woods, Oakland, Calif., 1972—77, ptnr., 1977—89, Sonnenschein, Nath & Rosenthal, San Francisco, 1989—, mgmt. com., 1998—. Bd. dirs. Temple Sinai, 1997-2002. Mem. ABA, Calif. Bar Assn., Alameda County Bar Assn. (bd. dirs. 1978-84, v.p. 1982, pres. 1983), Alameda County Bar Found. (bd. dirs. 1998-2000). Jewish. Avocations: skiing, cooking. Office: Sonnenschein Nath Rosenthal 525 Market St 26th Fl San Francisco CA 94105-2708 Office Phone: 415-882-5019. Business E-Mail: redwards@sonnenschein.com.

EDWARDS, S. EUGENE, energy executive; BS in Chem. Engring., Tulane U.; MBA, U. Tex., San Antonio. Process engr. CITGO; cons., refinery econs. Pace Consultants; various managerial pos. in planning and econs., refinery ops., bus. devel., and mktg. Valero Energy Corp., San Antonio, v.p., 1998—2001, sr. v.p. product supply and trading, 2001—05, exec. v.p. corp. develop. & strategic planning, 2005—. Office: Valero PO Box 696000 San Antonio TX 78269-6000*

EDWARDS, SIR SAMUEL FREDERICK, physicist, researcher; b. Swansea, Wales, Feb. 1, 1928; m. Merriell Bland, 1953; 4 children. Student, Cambridge U., Harvard U.; DSc (hon.), U. Bath, U. Edinburgh, U. Loughborough, U. Salford, U. Birmingham, 1976, U. Strasbourg, 1986, U. Wales, 1987, U. Sheffield, 1989, U. Dublin, 1991, U. Leeds, U. Swansea, 1994, East Anglia, 1995, U. Cambridge, Eng., 2001, U. Mainz, 2002, Tel Aviv U., 2006. Mem. Inst. Advanced Study, Princeton, NJ; rsch. fellow U. Birmingham; prof. U. Manchester; emeritus Cavendish prof. physics Cavendish Lab.; pro vice chancellor Cambridge U., 1992-95; fellow, pres. Gonville and Caius Coll. Vis. prof. U. Calif., San Diego, 1980-81; dir. Lucas Industries, 1981-93; chmn. Sci. Rsch. Coun. U.K., 1973-77, Def. Sci. Adv. Coun., 1977-80; chief sci. advisor U.K. Dept. Energy, 1983-88; program dir. ITP U. Calif., Santa Barbara, 1997; hon. prof. chemistry Beijing U., Peking U. Contbr. articles to profl. jours. Recipient Sci. pour l'Art prize Louis Vuitton Moet Hennessy, 1993, Boltzmann medal Internat. Union Pure and Applied Physics, 1995, Dirac medal Abdus Salam Internat. Ctr. for Theoretical Physics, Trieste, 2005. Fellow Royal Soc. (Davy medal 1985, Royal medal 2001), Inst. Physics (Maxwell medal, Guthrie medal, Keller Meml. Polymer medal 2001), Royal Soc. Chemistry, Inst. Math. (Gold medal 1986), Am. Phys. Soc. (High Polymer Physics prize), Brit. Assn. Advancement of Sci. (chmn. 1977-82, pres. 1988-89), Brit. Soc. Rheology (Gold medal 1991), French Acad. Scis. (assoc.), NAS (fgn. assoc.), French Phys. Soc. (hon.), European Phys. Soc. (hon.), Russian Acad. Scis. (fgn. assoc.); mem. Athenaeum Club. Home: 7 Penarth Pl Cambridge CB3 9LU England Office: Cavendish Lab Cambridge CB3 OHE England Office Phone: (44)1223337259. Business E-Mail: sfe11@phy.cam.ac.uk.

EDWARDS, SAMUEL LAWRENCE, II, information technology executive, writer; b. Greenwood, Miss., Jan. 15, 1937; s. Samuel Lawrence and Marvella (Blanks) Edwards; m. Margaret Elizabeth Bishop, 1954; children: Michael, Lawrence, Marvella, Ronald, Phyllis, Gregory, Kenya, Michelle. Owner, CEO C-O Danyaic Industries., Newark, 1965—. Achievements include patents for rocket driven vehicle transmission, aircraft with vertical take off and landing capability. Home and Office: 1 Court St Newark NJ 07102 Home Phone: 973-675-4037, 973-373-7365; Office Phone: 973-752-9761.

EDWARDS, SAMUEL ROGER, retired internist; b. Santa Barbara, Calif., Aug. 11, 1937; s. Harold S. and Margaret (Spaulding) E.; m. Marcia Elizabeth Dutton, June 17, 1961; children: Harold S. II, Charles Dutton. BA, Harvard U., 1960; MD, U. So. Calif., 1964. Intern Presbyn. Hosp., Phila., 1964-65; resident in internal medicine U Calif., San Francisco, 1968-70; fellow in cardiology Pacific Presbyn. Med. Ctr., San Francisco, 1970; pvt. practice specializing in internal medicine Santa Paula, Calif., 1971-94; med. dir. Santa Paula Convalescent, Twin Pines Convalescent Hosps., 1974-95; pres. med. staff Ventura (Calif.) County Med. Ctr., 1979-80, med. dir., 1983-95, hosp. adminstr., 1995—2002; ret., 2002. Chief dept. medicine Ventura County Gen. Hosp., 1975; chief med. staff Santa Paula Meml. Hosp., 1977; mem. clin. faculty sch. medicine UCLA, 1980—95; chmn. Citizens State Bank of Santa Paula, 1994—97; bd. dir. Santa Barbara Bank and Trust, 1998—2006; chmn. Limoneira Co., 2003—04, bd. dirs. Lt. comdr. USNR, 1966-68. Recipient Disting. Svc. award Ventura County Heart Assn., 1974. Fellow: ACP; mem.: AMA, Am. Coll. Hosp. Execs. Episcopalian. Home: 19789 E Telegraph Rd Santa Paula CA 93060-9693

EDWARDS, SARAH ANNE, social worker, psychologist; b. Tulsa, Jan. 7, 1943; d. Clyde Elton and Virginia Elizabeth Glandon; m. Paul Robert Edwards, Apr. 24, 1965; 1 son, Jon Scott. BA with distinction, U. Mo., Kansas City, 1965; MSW, U. Kans., 1974; PhD in Applied Ecopsychology, Akamai U., Hilo, Hawaii, 2006. LCSW Calif.; cert. ecopsychologist Inst. Global Edn., 2005. Cmty. rep. OEO, Kans. City Regional Office, 1966-68; social svc./parent involvement and resource specialist Office of Child Devel., HEW, Kansas City, Mo., 1968-73; dir. tng. social svcs. dept., children's rehab. unit U. Affiliated Facility, U. Kans. Med. Ctr., Kansas City, 1975-76; co-dir. Cathexis Inst. S., Glendale, Calif., 1976-77; pvt. practice psychotherapy, tng. and cons. personal and interpersonal, orgnl. behavior, Sierra Madre, Calif., 1973-80; sys. operator CompuServe Info. Svc., 1983-98; faculty mem. grad. dept. applied ecopsychology Inst. Global Edn., 2005—; NGO cons. UNESCO, 2005—. Prodr., co-host radio show Working From Home, on Bus. Talk Radio, 1988-01; co-host radio show Entrepeneur's Home Business Edition, 2003— co-host cable show Working from Home Scripp's Howard Home and Garden Cable TV Network, 1995-97; commentator CNBC, 1996-99, NPR Marketplace, 1996-97; co-host Entrepreneurs Home Bus. Show, WS Radio, 2000—. Columnist for Home Office Computing Mag., 1988-97, Your Home Office, L.A. Times Syndicate, 1997-99, Entrepreneur's Home Office, 1998—, Price CostCo Connection, 1994—, Inc-Com., 2000—; co-author: How to Make Money with Your Personal Computer, 1997, Getting Business to Come to You, 1998, Working From Home, rev. edit., 1999, Secrets of Self-Employment, 1996, Finding Your Perfect Work, 1996, Teaming Up, 1997, Home Businesses You Can Buy, 1997, Cool Careers for Dummies, 1998, Making Money in Cyberspace, 1998, Best Home Business for the 21st Century, 1999, Working From Home, 1999, The Practical Dreamer's Handbook, 2000, Home-Based Business for Dummies, 2000, Changing Directions without Losing Your Way, 2001, Entrepreneurial Parent, 2002, Sitting with the Enemy, A Novel, 2002, Why Aren't You Your Own Boss?, 2003, Best Home Business for People 50+, 2004; mem. editl. bd. Jour. Applied Ecopsychology, 2005—. Dir. nature-guided career counseling and continuing edn. programs Pine Mtn. Inst., 2001—05, Post-Corp. Career Inst., 2006. Address: Box 6775 2624 Teakwood Ct Frazier Park CA 93222 Business E-Mail: sedwards@frazmtn.com.

EDWARDS, STEPHEN ALLEN, lawyer; b. Battle Creek, Mich., July 12, 1953; s. Louis Ward and Elizabeth Yvonne (Stahl) E.; m. Alice Veronica; children: Amelia Hatfield, Nathaniel Gordon. BA with high honors, U. Mich., 1975, JD cum laude, 1978. Bar: Wis. 1978, U.S. Dist. Ct. (ea. and we. dists.) Wis. 1978, Mich. 1980, Pa. 1980, Ga. 1999. Assoc. Godfrey & Kahn S.C., Milw., 1978-80, Pepper, Hamilton & Scheetz, Phila., 1980-82, Morgan, Lewis & Bockius, Phila., 1982-87, ptnr., 1987-98, Kilpatrick Stockton LLP, Altanta, 1998—. Author: Arbitrage, 1990; exec. editor: The Issuer's Guide to Tax-Exempt Finance, 1994, Municipal Leasing, 2002. Mem. ABA (tax sect.), Wis. Bar Assn., Mich. Bar Assn., Ga. Bar Assn., Phila. Bar Assn., Pa. Bar Assn., Nat. Assn. Bond Lawyers (chmn. arbitrage seminar 1990, edn. com. 1990-91, bd. dirs. 1991-94, treas. 1994-95), Bond Attys. Workshop (panelist 1984-95, steering com., chmn. arbitrage 1986-87), Pa. Soc. SR (bd. dirs. 1991-94), Phila. Club. Episcopalian. Avocation: bicycling. Home: 360 Cannady Ct Atlanta GA 30350-5622 Office Phone: 404-815-6278. Business E-Mail: sedwards@kilpatrickstockton.com.

EDWARDS, SYLVIA ANN, artist; b. Boston, Jan. 30, 1937; d. Junius Griffiths and Sylvia Emma (Mailloux) E.; m. Sadredin M. Golestaneh (div.); children: Shirin, Nader, Leila. Diploma, Mass. Coll. Art, Boston, 1957, Boston Mus. Fine Arts, 1958; postgrad., Modern Art Studies, London, 1980—81. One-woman shows include Grosvenor Gallery, London, 2003, CCA Gallery, Oxford, Eng., 1996, Munson Gallery, Chatham, Mass., 1992, Jaeshke Gallery, Braunschweig, Germany, 1991, Natalie Knight Gallery, Johannesburg, South Africa, 1991, Bankamura, Tokyo, 1991, Gallery K. Hyazaki Perfecture, 1991, The Berkeley Sq. Gallery, London, 1991; exhibited in group shows at Cadogan Contemporary Art, 1996, Berkeley Sq. Gallery, Korea Art Expo, Seoul, 1996, 2002, NY Art Expo, NYC, 1994, Lond Internat. Contemporary Art Fair, 1989, The Bath Arts Festival, Eng., 1988, Paris Art Salon, 1986, 1987, 1988, Sarasota Visual Art Ctr., State of Art Gallery, Sarasota, Fla., 2007, Represented in permanent collections Nat. Mus. for Women in the Arts, Washington, Boston U. Spl. Collections, Cape Mus Fine Arts, Dennis, Mass, Mus. Fine Arts, Alexandria, Egypt, Governorate of Alexandria, Mass. Gen. Hosp., Boston, Chelsea Westminster Hosp., London, Midwest Mus. Am. Art, Elkhart, Ind., Tate Gallery, London, publs., Valley of Sils, Lithograph, 1982, N.Mex. Watch, lithograph, 1982, covers, Arts Rev., 1982, 1985, others, numerous, UNICEF cards, Greenpeace publs., World Wildlife/U.K., book covers, reference and art books, others, monographs. Mem. U.K. UNICEF Com. Mem. London Royal Acad., World Watercolor Soc., Chelsea Arts Club/London. Avocations: writing, theater, travel, swimming, reading. Studio: 14 Cadogan Square Flat B London SW1X 0JU England

EDWARDS, TREVOR, apparel executive; b. London; With Colgate-Palmolive; joined Nike, Inc., Beaverton, Oreg., 1992, v.p. brand mgmt. Europe, Middle East and Africa, dir. mktg. Ams., v.p, US brand mgmt., corp. v.p. global brand and category mgmt., chief mktg. officer, 2002—. Office: Nike One Bowerman Dr Beaverton OR 97005-6453*

EDWARDS, VICTOR HENRY, chemical engineer; b. Galveston, Tex., Oct. 17, 1940; s. Philip Lacey and Margaret Ruth (Hopkins) E.; m. Mary Margaret Litzmann, June 10, 1963; children: Henry L., Mary E. BA, Rice U., 1962; PhD in Chem. Engring., U. Calif., Berkeley, 1967. Registered profl. engr., Tex. Asst. prof. chem. engring. Cornell U., Ithaca, NY, 1967-73; mgr. adv. tech. U.S. Nat. Sci. Found., Washington, 1971-72; rsch. fellow Merck, Sharp, Dohme Rsch., Rahway, NJ, 1973-76; supr. rsch. engring. United Energy Resources, Houston, 1976-79; vis. prof. environ. engring. Rice U., Houston, 1979-80; sr. process engr. Fluor Engrs. and Constructors, Houston, 1980-82; southwest editor Plant Services mag., Chgo., 1982-85; project engr. Allstates/BE&K, Inc., Houston, 1984-90, lead process engr., 1990-93, process engring. mgr., 1993-94, prin. engr. process and environ., 1994-95; process dir. Aker Kvaerner, Houston, 1995—2007, dir. process safety, 2007—. Tech. adv. com. Mary Kay O'Connor Process Safety Ctr., Tex. A&M U., 1995—, chmn., 2005—. Mem. editl. bd. Chem. Processing mag., 2003-; contbr. articles to profl. jours. Organizing com. Woodlands (Tex.) Harvest Festival, 1979-86; chmn. industry adv. coun. dept. chem. engring. Prairie View A&M U., 1991-94. Recipient Shield of Irenee award E.I. duPont de Nemours & Co., 1994, 98, 2001, Environ. Excellence award, 1994, Safety, Health, and Environ. Excellence award, 1996, Svc. award Mary Kay O'Connor Process Safety Ctr., 2002. Fellow: AIChE (chmn. Process Plant Safety Symposium 1992, exec. position 1 1993, program co-chmn. 1994, chmn. 1995, South Tex. sect. chmn. 2nd internat. plant ops. and design conf. 1997, Disting. Svc. award 1991, Disting. Svc. award Prairie View A&M U. student chpt. 1992, 1994); mem.: Nat. Fire Protection Assn., NSPE, AAAS, Engrs. Coun. Houston (councilor 1987—92), Rice U. Alumni Assn. (class of '62 reunion com. 1982, 1987, 1992, 1997, 2002, co-chmn. fundraising drive 1998, class of '62 reunion com. 2007, co-chmn. fundraising drive 2007), Am. Chem. Soc. (chmn. Ithaca sect. 1969, councilor divsn. biochem. and microbial tech. 1970—77), N.Y. Acad. Scis. (life). Methodist. Avocations: reading, tennis, sailing, golf. Office Phone: 713-270-2817. Business E-Mail: vic.edwards@akerkvaerner.com.

EDWARDS, WALLACE WINFIELD, retired automotive executive; b. Pontiac, Mich., May 9, 1922; s. David W. and Ruby M. (Nutting) E.; m. Jean Austin Wolfe, Aug. 24, 1944; children: Ronald W., Gary R., Ann E. BS in Mech. Engring, Gen. Motors Inst., 1949; MBA, Mich. State U., 1966. With GMC Truck & Coach div. Gen. Motors Corp., Pontiac, Mich., 1940-78, truck service mgr., 1961-62, head engine design, 1962-64, dir. reliability, 1964-66, dir. prodn. control and purchasing, 1966-70, dir. engring., 1970-78; dir. Worldwide Truck Project Center, Warren, Mich., 1978-80; gen. dir. Worldwide Truck and Transp. Sys. Center, 1980-81; v.p. G.M.O.D.C., 1980-81; group mgr. small and light truck and van ops. Truck and Bus. Group, Gen. Motors Corp., 1981-82, mgr. internat. staff, 1982-84, gen. dir. mil. vehicle ops. Power Products and Def. Group, 1984-86. Bd. dirs. Crystal Mountain Resort, Thompsonville, Mich., 1991-2003. Past pres., mem. exec. com. Clinton Valley coun. Boy Scouts Am.; dir. Grand Traverse Regional Land Conservancy, 1991-2003, chmn. 1996-98; regent Nat. Eagle Scout Assn. (life). Served with USNR, 1944-46. Mem. Soc. Automotive Engrs., U.S. Navy League, Tau Beta Pi, Beta Gamma Sigma. Office: 5089 Crystal Dr Beulah MI 49617-9617

EDWARDS, WILLIAM BENNETT, firearms industry consultant, gun dealer; b. Auburn, NY, Nov. 10, 1927; s. John Bowen and Virginia Hampton (Bean) E.; m. Virginia Jane Davis, Jan. 12, 1954. Fed. firearms dealer, U.S.A. Pvt. practice, Afton, Va., 1963—; prin., owner Benet Arms Co., various, 1947—; tech. dir. Mars-Centennial Arms Co., Chgo., 1955—62; prin., owner Gold Rush Gun Shop, various, 1964—; artistic creator Pastimes LTD, Staunton, Va., 1985—92. Cons. Saddam Hussein, 1990-91, Pres. Clinton, 1993, Pres. Reagan, Pres. Ford and with King Faisel II of Iraq Middle East problems. Author: The Story of Colt's Revolver, 1953, Civil War Guns, 1962, 2d edit., 1997; editor Conspiracy Press, 1994—; editor, founder GUNS Mag., 1955; inventor. With USNG, 1949-51. Mem. NRA, Sons of Confederate Veterans, Va. Arms Collectors Assn. Republican. Unitarian Universalist. Avocation: observation of Jesuit plans. Home and Office: PO Box 87 Waynesboro VA 22980 Office Phone: 540-943-0091. Office Fax: 540-943-5192.

EDWARDSON, JOHN ALBERT, information technology executive; b. Terre Haute, Ind., July 23, 1949; s. John Albert and Mildred Ruth (Anderson) E.; m. Catharine Orr, June 11, 1971; children: Laura, Anne, Shelley. BS in Indsl. Engring., Purdue U., 1971; MBA in Fin. and Internat. Bus., U. Chgo., 1972. Comml. banking officer First Bank-St. Paul, 1972-77; v.p., treas. Ferrell Cos. Inc., Kansas City, Mo., 1977-83, sr. v.p. fin. services group, 1983-85; exec. v.p., fin., chief fin. officer Northwest Airlines Inc. and NWA Inc., St. Paul, 1985-88; exec. v.p., chief fin. and adminstrv. officer Internat. Minerals and Chems. Corp., Northbrook, Ill., 1988-90; chief fin. officer United Airlines Employees Acquisition Corp., Chgo., 1990; exec. v.p., chief fin. officer Ameritech, Chgo., 1991-94; pres., COO UAL Corp., Elk Grove Village, Ill., 1994—; chmn., pres. & CEO Burns Internat. Svcs Corp, Chgo., 1999—2000; chmn., CEO CDW Corp., Vernon Hills, Ill., 2001—. Trustee, pres. Ravina Festival Assn., Highland Park, Ill., bd. trustees Art Inst. Chgo. Recipient Disting. Engring. Alumnus award Purdue U., 1988. Presbyterian. Avocations: sailing, hiking, bicycling. Office: CDW 200 N Milwaukee Ave Vernon Hills IL 60061*

EDWARDSON, SANDRA, dean, nursing educator; BSN, St. Olaf Coll., Minn., 1963; MN in Maternal and Child Nursing, U. of Wash., 1964; PhD, U. of Minn., 1980. Dean Sch. Nursing, U. Minn., Mpls. Office: U Minn Twin Cities Sch Nursing 6-101 Weaver-Densford Hall 308 Harvard St SE Minneapolis MN 55455-0353

EDWEEN, JULIE, plastic surgeon; BS, Andrews U.; DO magna cum laude, Kansas City U. Medicine & Biosciences, 1995. Cert. Am. Osteopathic Bd. Otolaryngology, Head & Neck Surgery & Facial Plastic Surgery, Am. Bd. Cosmetic Surgery, Nat. Bd. Osteopathic Med. Examiners. Resident otorhinolaryngology/facial plastic surgery Michigan State U., Botsford Hosp., 2000, chief resident, 2000; pvt. practice LA. Featured in (TV series) Plastic Surgery Beverly Hills, Discovery Channel, Bodywork, The Learning Channel. Co-founder Eunice Wavomba Found. Fellow, Am. Acad. Cosmetic Surgery, Culver City, Calif., 2001. Mem.: Calif. Coll. Osteopathic Physicians & Surgeons, Am. Osteopathic Assn., Am. Soc. Cosmetic Breast Surgery, Am. Acad. Cosmetic Surgery, Am. Acad. Facial Plastic & Reconstructive Surgery, Am. Osteopathic Acad. Otolaryngology Head & Neck Surgery. Office: 9201 Sunset Blvd Ground Level Los Angeles CA 90069 Office Phone: 310-859-8885.*

EDWIN, ROBERT, voice educator; b. Bklyn., June 18, 1946; s. Edwin Robert Steinfort and Helena Wilhelmina Monbo; m. Faith Marie Sanderson Steinfort, July 26, 1969; children: Kurt Steinfort, Matthew Steinfort. BA,

Thomas Edison State Coll., Trenton, NJ, 1983. Staff Camden County Coll., NJ, 1984—. Pvt. tchr. Robert Edwin Studio, Cinnaminson, NJ, 1975—; adj. music faculty Burlington County Coll., Pemberton, NJ, 1993—2003; adj. prof. music U. Mich., Ann Arbor, Mich., 2002—03; faculty Voice Found., Phila., 1995—; master tchr. Nats Intern Program, Rochester, NY, 2005; clinician Internat. Congress of Voice Tchrs., Vancouver, Canada, 2005; mem. adv. com. music theater Westminster Choir Coll., 2005—. Singer: Avant Garde Records, 1967, Fortress Records, 1970; assoc. editor: Nat. Assn. Tchrs. Jour. of Singing, 2002—; contbr. articles to profl. jours. Concert organizer Rainbow of Hope, Maple Shade, NJ, 1999—; umpire, referee Cinnaminson Twp. Pal, 1980—90; bd. trustees Silver Bay Assn., NY, 1998—2004. Mem.: Am. Acad. Tchrs. Singing, Nat. Assn. Tchrs. Singing (sec., treas. 2002), Phi Mu Alpha Sinfonia. Lutheran. Avocations: golf, boating, hiking, reading. Office: Robert Edwin Studio 1509 Glenview Dr Cinnaminson NJ 08077 Business E-Mail: robert@robertedwinstudio.com.

EELLS, WILLIAM HASTINGS, retired automobile company executive; b. Princeton, Mar. 30, 1924; s. Hastings and Amy (Titus) E.; 1 child, Jonathan William. BA, Ohio Wesleyan U., 1946; MA, Ohio State U., 1950; DHL (hon.), Kent State U., 1983; D of Pub. Svc., Bowling Green State U., 1983; D of Cmty. Leadership (hon.), Franklin U., 2005. Asst. to dir. Inst. Practical Politics Ohio Wesleyan U., 1948-50, dir., 1953-57, instr. dept. polit. sci., 1952-59; instr. polit. sci. Mt. Union Coll., 1950-51; mem. Ohio Gov.'s Cabinet, 1957-59; coord. Atomic Devel. Activities State of Ohio, 1957-59; Midwest regional mgr. civic and govtl. affairs Ford Motor Co., Columbus, 1959-87. Author: Your Ohio Government, 1953 (6 edits.); contbr. articles to profl. jours Mem. Nat. Coun. on Arts, NEA, 1976-82; chmn. bd. Blue Cross of Northeast Ohio, 1963-72, Blossom Music Ctr., Cleve., 1968—; chmn. bd. govs. Gov.'s Coun. on Rehab., 1966-68; mem. exec. com. Met. Opera's Nat. Coun., 1967-81; pres. Nat. Coun. High Blood Pressure Rsch., 1974-79; chmn. Ohio Pub. Expenditure Coun., 1981-84, Gov.'s Task Force on State Ops., 1984-85; vice chmn. Ohio Northwest Bicentennial Com., 1986-87; bd. dirs. Am. Heart Assn., 1974-79, Columbus Mus. Art, 1982-88, Opera/Columbus, 1984-86, Columbus Ballet, 1985-86, Nat. Coun. French Am. Scholarship Found., 1985-87; trustee Cleve. Orch., 1964—, Hist. Morven Found., Princeton, N.J., 1988-96, Ednl. TV, Cleve., 1965-75, Cleve. Playhouse, 1965-82, Cleve. Ballet, Cleve. Zoo, 1965-76, Ohio Arts Coun., Columbus Symphony, Cleve. Luth. Hosp., 1966-76, Mt. Union Coll., 1984—, Ohio Wesleyan U., 1988—; trustee Franklin U., 1987—, Columbus Assn. Performing Arts, 1978—, Ohio Found. Ind. Colls., 1986—, Grady Meml. Hosp., 1987-94, Riverside Hosp. Found., 1990-96; hon. chmn. Del. Arts Ctr., 1989—; life trustee Fairview Health Cleve., 1980—; trustee, v.p. Oak Grove Cemetery, 1983—; chmn. Ohio Commn. for Son of Heaven Imperial Arts of China, 1988; mem. Ohio Humanities Coun., 1993-95; patron Morgan Libr., N.Y.C., 1995—; trustee Del. County Dist. Libr. Bd., 1994—; mem. Ohio Bicentennial Commn., 1997-2002; trustee Columbus Zoo Assn., 1998—; mem. Friends Princeton U. Libr., 1997- Recipient USCG Disting. award, 1965, Silver medal Royal Life Saving Soc., Ohio State U. Devel. award, 1967, award for disting. svc. Am. Heart Assn., 1979, Ohio Arts Coun. award, 1979, Ohio Theatre Alliance award, 1981, Gov. award, 1985, Alumni Achievement award Ohio State U., 1987, Silver medal Japanese Red Cross Soc Mem.: Rock & Roll Hall of Fame (charter mem. 1995—), Blossom Bd. Overseers (life). Republican. Presbyterian (elder). Home: Honeystone 54 Elmwood Dr Delaware OH 43015-1617 *Parents, teachers and friends can do just so much, you have to do the rest. God helps those who help themselves, and being in the right place at the right time does help.*

EERKENS, JEFF W., nuclear scientist, educator, laser engineer; b. Djakarta, Indonesia, June 11, 1931; came to U.S., 1950; s. Josephus Wilhelmus and Elisabeth Maria (Zijderveld) E.; m. Martha Laura Stone, June 1, 1959 (div. May 1964); 1 child, Laura Elisabeth; m. Else Gertrude DeKock, Aug. 19, 1968; children: Jelmer Willem, Mieke Karen, Boukje Elisabeth. BS in Engring. Physics, U. Calif., Berkeley, 1954, MS in Nuclear Engring., 1957, PhD in Engring. Sci., 1960. Registered profl. engr., Calif. Nuclear engr. Aerojet-Gen.-Nucleonics, San Ramon, Calif., 1957-60; staff scientist Aerospace Corp., El Segundo, Calif., 1960-63; laser sys. br. chief Northrop Space Labs., Hawthorne, Calif., 1963-67; chief scientist Sci. and Tech. Assocs., West Los Angeles, Calif., 1967-71; program mgr. AiRsch. divsn. Garrett Corp., Torrance, Calif., 1971-77; pres. LISCHEM Corp., Lawndale, Calif., 1977-85, Isotope Tech., Pacific Palisades, Calif., 1990-93, Columbia, Mo., 1993—; rsch. prof. nuclear engring. U. Mo., Columbia, 1993—. Author: Rocket Radiation Handbook, 3 vols., 1973, 74, The Nuclear Imperative-A Critical Look at the Approaching Energy Crisis, 2006; editor, author: Laser Isotope Separation, 1995, The Nuclear Imperative, 2007. Recipient Best New Product award Lasers and Applications, 1985. Mem. Am. Nuclear Soc., Optical Soc. Am., Internat. Isotope Soc., Am. Chem. Soc. Achievements include 11 patents in fields of molecular laser isotope separation, laser design, nuclear pumped lasers and grasers, fuel cells.

EERNISSE, SUSAN FREEMAN, music educator; b. Anderson, SC, Feb. 18, 1957; d. Alvin and Florence Gantt Freeman; m. Glenn Phillip Eernisse, Aug. 26, 1976; children: Melody Eernisse Rouse, Jessica Lea. A in Fine Arts, Anderson U., 1977; MusB, Berry Coll., Rome, Ga., 1979, EdM, 1989. Cert. tchr. Ga. Tchr. Westside Elem., Cedartown, Ga., 1988—96; music tchr. Sally Meadows Elem., Vidalia, Ga., 1996—2005, Robert Toombs Christian Acad., Lyons, Ga., 2005—. Adj. prof. Brewton-Parker Coll., Mt. Vernon, Ga., 1997—; curriculum writer Lifeway Pub., Nashville, 2001—; presenter in field. Writer: music curriculums. Vol. choir dir. various chs., 1977—; camp counselor, faculty Ga. Bapt. Music Camps, 1999—; children's choir dir. The Oaks Bapt. Ch., Lyons, 2002—; choir mem., soloist Brewton-Parker Choral Soc., Mt. Vernon, Ga., 1996—. Named Tchr. of Yr., Sally Meadows Elem., 2000. Mem.: Ga. Music Educators Assn., Music Educators Nat. Conf. Avocations: singing, writing, reading, travel. Home: 1520 Lakewood Dr Vidalia GA 30474 Office: Robert Toombs Christian Acad Lyons GA

EFAW, CARY ROSS, manufacturing executive; b. Waynesburg, Pa., Dec. 26, 1949; s. William C. and Julia M. (Whitfield) Efaw; m. Kathleen E. Dunkle, July 21, 1973; children: Dawn, Heather, Nathan. BS in Acctg./Econs., Waynesburg Coll., 1975; MBA, Youngstown State U., 1989. CPA Pa., cert. mgmt. acct.; fin. mgmt., bus. mgmt. Sr. acct. Ernst & Young LLP, Pitts., 1975-79; staff acct. Equitable Resources, Pitts., 1979-81; sr. fin. analyst Joy Mfg. Co., Pitts., 1981-82; owner, cons. Efaw Enterprise, Pitts., 1982—; mgr. gen. and cost acctg. Cooper Energy Svcs., Grove City, Pa., 1987-98; ptnr. Ruddy & Assocs. CPAs, Wexford, Pa., 1999-2000; divsn. contr. GenSystems, Inc., Callery, Pa., 2000—; ind. contractr/cons., 2000—; contr. Chelsea Bldg. Products, 2001—04; assoc. Resources Global Profls., 2005—06, Urish Popech & Co. CPAs, 2006—07. Cons. Hodor Assocs., Eighty-Four, Pa., 1979—85, Lindley Enterprise, Washington, 1981—85, Zelienople, 2000—; advisor 84 Electronics, Houston, 1980—87; ind. cons., 2007. Contbr. articles to profl. jours. V.p. S.V. Track Boosters; chmn. bd. dirs. Grove City Area Fed. Credit Union, 1999—; advisor state rep., Upper St. Clair, Pa., 1981—84; Sunday sch. tchr. Westminster Ch., Upper St. Clair, 1982—85; elder, chmn. long range planning com., co-chmn. bldg. fund campaign Calvin Ch., Zelienople. With USMC, 1969—71, Vietnam. Named Competent Toastmaster, 1980. Mem.: VFW, AICPA, DAV (life), Marine Corps League, Marine Corps Assn., Assn. Profls. Bus. Mgmt., Nat. Assn. Accts. (assoc. dir. 1977—78), Assn. MBA Execs., Assn. Inst. Mgmt. Accts. (bd. dirs. Pitts. chpt. 1999—2001, pres., regional dir. 2001—02, pres. coun. 2002—), Pa. Inst. CPAs (contrs. conf. com.), Battalion Assn. (life; 1st recon), Steel Town Corvettes Club (treas. 1977—80), Masons, Am. Legion, Alpha Kappa Psi. Presbyterian. Avocations: auto racing, golf, softball, running, weightlifting. Home: 1 Zelie Dr Zelienople PA 16063-9707 Personal E-mail: efaw@zoominternet.net.

EFENDI, RIAD, biochemist; s. Emin Efendiev and Tamara Abbasova; m. Elena Gaidouk, Mar. 14, 1975; 1 child, Elias Jordan. PhD, Moscow Inst. Physics & Tech., 1996. Rsch. asst. prof. U. Houston, Coll. Pharmacy, 1997—. Mem.: Am. Heart Assn. (assoc.), Am. Soc. Nephrology (assoc.), Houston-Baku Sister City Assn. (it dir. 2005—). Achievements include research in hormonal regulation of sodium reabsorption in the kidney; discovery of intracellular sodium switch mechanism in the interplay of hormonal affects on sodium reabsorption in the kidney. Office: Univ of Houston College of Pharmacy 4800 Calhoun Houston TX 77204 Office Phone: 713-743-1228.

EFFEL, LAURA, lawyer; b. Dallas, May 9, 1945; d. Louis E. and Fay (Lee) Ray; m. Marc J. Patterson, Sept. 19, 1992 (dec. July 30, 2002); 1 child, Stephen Patterson; m. Robert A. Miltner, Aug. 26, 2006;. BA, U. Calif., Berkeley, 1971; JD, U. Md., 1975. Bar: NY 1976, US Dist. Ct. (so. and ea. dists.) NY 1976, US Ct. Appeals (2d cir.) 1980, US Supreme Ct. 1980, DC 1993, NC 1998, Va. 2001; cert. mediator Judicial Coun. Va., 2004. Assoc. Burns Jackson Miller Summit & Jacoby, NYC, 1975-78, Pincus Munzer Bizar & D'Alessandro, NYC, 1978-80; v.p., sr. assoc. counsel Chase Manhattan Bank, N.A., NYC, 1980-96; counsel Baker & McKenzie, NYC, 1996-99; gen. counsel Garban Cos., 1999-2000; counsel LeClair Ryan Flippin Densmore, Roanoke, Va., 2000—02, ptnr., 2002—06, ind. neutral, 2006—07; of counsel Jackson Lewis, LLP, San Francisco, 2007—. Mem. nat. roster of neutrals Am. Arbitration Assn. Meml. editl. bd.: Alternatives to the High Cost of Litigation. Mem. Workforce Devel. Com., New Century Tech. Coun., 2001-06; bd. dirs. Bklyn. Legal Svcs. Corp. A, 1992-2000, Blue Ridge Pub. TV, 2001-06. Named one of Best Lawyers in Am., 2005—06, Va. Legal Elite, 2006. Mem.: ABA, DC Bar Assn., NC Bar Assn. Office: Jackson Lewis LLP 199 Fremont St 10th Fl San Francisco CA 94105 Home Phone: 415-924-7229; Office Phone: 415-394-9400.

EFFREN, GARY ROSS, financial executive; b. Jersey City, Feb. 27, 1956; s. Ronald Lewis and Ethel Frances (Ross) E.; m. Francine Oberfest, May 24, 1980; children: Jessica Leigh, Jenna Ashlee. BS summa cum laude, Rider Coll., 1978; postgrad., U. Miami, Coral Gables, Fla., 1984-89. CPA, Fla. Sr. auditor Peat, Marwick, Mitchell & Co., Miami, 1978—80; sr. fin. acct. Knight-Ridder, Inc., Miami, Fla., 1980—82, mgr. fin. reporting, 1982—84, dir. corp. acctg., 1986—88, asst. to v.p./finance, 1988—95; bus. mgr. Viewdata Corp. Am., Miami Beach, Fla., 1984—86; v.p., contr. Knight Ridder, Inc., San Jose, Calif., 1995—2001, sr. v.p. fin., CFO, 2001—04, v.p. fin., 2004—. Mem. Am. Inst. CPA's, Fla. Inst. CPA's. Jewish. Avocations: guitar playing, racquetball. Office: Knight-Ridder Inc 50 W San Fernando St San Jose CA 95113-2413 E-mail: geffren@knightridder.com.

EFFRON, ANDREW S., federal judge; b. Stamford, Conn., Sept. 18, 1948; children: Robin, Michael. BA, Harvard U., 1970, JD, 1975; student, JAG's Sch. US Army, 1976, student, 1984. Intermittent legis. aide to Rep. William A. Steiger US Ho. Reps., Washington, 1970-76; with Office of staff Judge Adv., Ft. McClellan, Ala., 1976-77; atty.-advisor Office of Gen. Counsel US Dept. Def., Washington, 1977-87; counsel Senate Armed Svcs. Com., Washington, 1987—88, gen. counsel, 1988—95, minority counsel, 1995—96; judge US Ct. Appeals for the Armed Forces, Washington, 1996—. Office: US Ct Appeals Armed Forces 405 E St NW Washington DC 20442-0001

EFFRON, BLAIR WAYNE, investment advisor; b. June 19, 1962; BA, Princeton U., 1984; MBA, Columbia U., 1987. With UBS Investment Bank, NYC, 1987—2006, vice chair, 2004—06; co-founder, ptnr. Centerview Ptnrs., NYC, 2006—. Bd. dir. Nat. Archives Found., Lincoln Ctr., NYC, Bklyn. Mus. Art, Ctr. for Arts Edn. Inc. Named a Top Dealmaker, Dealmaker mag., 2006. Mem.: Coun. on Fgn. Rels. Democrat. Office: Centerview Partners 640 Fifth Ave 19th Fl New York NY 10019 Office Phone: 212-380-2650. Office Fax: 212-380-2651.*

EFFRON, DAVID LOUIS, conductor, performing company executive; b. Cin., July 28, 1938; s. Sigmund and Babette Jane (Holstein) E.; children: Michael, Daniel. MusB, U. Mich., 1960; MusM, Ind. U., 1962; Doctorate (hon.), NC State U., 2006. Asst. condr., condr. N.Y.C. Opera, 1964-82; asst. condr. Nat. Ballet, Washington, 1969-70; music dir. Central City (Colo.) Opera, 1972-76; condr. Curtis Inst. Music, Phila., 1970-77; music dir. Eastman Philharm., Eastman Sch., Rochester, NY, 1977-98, Youngstown (Ohio) Symphony Orch., 1987-96, Heidelberg (Fed. Republic Germany) Castle Festival, 1980-92, Chautaugua Instn. Music Sch. Festival Orch., 1990-96; artistic dir., prin. condr. Brevard (N.C.) Music Ctr., 1996—2007; prof. instrumental conducting Ind. U., Bloomington, 1998—, chmn. dept., 2006—. Guest condr. numerous assignments Europe, Far East, US, Mex., Can. Condr. recs. Schwantner Aftertones, 1983, Schuman Judith, 1984, Benita Valente, 1986, Mahler & Berlioz with Jan deGaetani, 1989. Recipient Grammy award, 1984, Best Contemporary Rec. award Ovation Mag., 1988, Musician of Yr. award Nat. Fedn. Music Clubs, 2003. Office: Indiana U Sch Music Bloomington IN 47405 Home Phone: 812-323-0790; Office Phone: 812-855-4752. Business E-Mail: deffron@indiana.edu.

EFFRON, SETH ALAN, editor, journalist; b. July 23, 1952; m. Nancy G. Thomas; children: Rebecca, Eve. BA in Polit. Sci. with honors, U. N.C., 1974. Asst. to editor Fayetteville (N.C.) Times (now Fayetteville Observer), 1974—75, reporter, 1975—77, Tallahassee Dem., 1977—80, Wichita (Kans.) Eagle-Beacon (now Wichita Eagle), 1980—82, 1983—85, coord. legis. coverage, 1982; state govt. and polit. reporter Greensboro (N.C.) News & Record, 1985—93; editor, founder the insider, N.C. State Govt. News Svc., Raleigh, 1993—96; exec. editor on-line content Nando Media, Nando Times, Raleigh, 1996—99; account exec. Capital Strategies, Raleigh, 2000—01; dep. curator Nieman Found. for Journalism, 2001—02, spl. projects dir., 2002—04; exec. editor State Govt. Radio, Curtis Media Group, Raleigh, 2004—. NEH summer fellow Williams Coll., 1979; lectr. Freedom Forum Media Studies Ctr. Columbia U., NYC, 1995; lectr. Annenberg Washington program Northwest U., 1995; lectr. Ctr. for Pub. TV U. N.C., fellow, 1993; lect. Inst. for Polit. Leadership, 1994; lectr. Salzburg (Austria) Seminar, 1994, Human Svcs. Automation Conf., 1994. Author: 100 Proof Pure Old Jess: Jesse Helms Quoted, 1993, Coachspeak: Triangle ACC Men's Basketball Coaches Quoted, 1995, North Carolina Almanac of Government and Politics, 1995—96; contbr. articles contributed articles to popular publs., including LA Herald-Examiner, Des Moines Register, Christian Science Monitor, 1995. Mem. adv. panel Z. Smith Reynolds Found., 1988—91; mem. area edn. adv. bd. Broughton HS, 1996—2001; v.p. Fred A. Olds Elem. Sch. PTA, 1994—95, pres., 1995—96; bd. dirs. Edenton St. United Meth. Ch. Child Devel. Ctr., 1986—88, 1993—94. Recipient Nieman fellow, Harvard U., 1991—92, Cert. of Merit, Am. Acad. Trial Lawyers, 1975, Pub. Svc. award, N.C. Press Assn., 1976, News Enterprise award, William Allen White Found., 1985, 2nd Pl. awards, N.C. Press Assn., 1987, 1989, 3rd Pl. awards, 1990. Home: 3613 Eden Ct Raleigh NC 27612 Office: State Govt Radio 3012 Highwoods Blvd Raleigh NC 27604 Office Phone: 919-882-3782. Business E-Mail: seffron@curtismedia.com.

EFIMOV, VALEREY GRIGORIJEVICH, physicist, researcher; b. Kopeisk, Russia, July 17, 1953; s. Gregorey Rudolfovich Bodamer and Anna Ivanovna Efimova; m. Efimova Lubove, Jan. 4, 1975; children: Elena, Alexey. B in Tech., Tomsk U., Russia, 1989, PhD in Physics, 2006. Engr. Fed. Reactor and Prodn. Ctr., Biysk, Russia, 1976—92; dept. dir. Conveyer Co. Ltd., Biysk, Russia, 1992—95; docent Bcysk Technol. Inst., Biysk, Russia, 1995—2002; sci. sec. Inst. Problem Chemistry/Energetic Technol., Biysk, Russia, 2002—04; rschr. Tomsk State U., Russia, 2004—. Docent Humanitarian U., Biysk, 1999—2002. Contbr. articles to profl. jours. Recipient Lenen Komsomol prize, 1983. Achievements include patentee in field. Avocations: reading, Beatles. Home: Decabristov 6 app 39 659302 Biysk Russia Office: Inst Problem Chemistry Socialistichoskaya 1 659322 Biysk Russia Office Phone: 340562. Business E-Mail: evg@bti.secna.zu.

EFIRD, FRANK KIMBALL, JR., archivist; b. Roanoke, Va., July 11, 1949; s. Frank Kimball Sr. and Sybil Trexler Efird. BA, Carthage Coll., Kenosha, Wis., 1971; MSc in Libr. Sci., U. Wis., Madison, 1972. Records archivist Ill. State Archives, Springfield, Ill., 1972—. Mem.: Midwest Archives Conf., Am. Assn. State Local History, Soc. Am. Archivists, Acad. Cert. Archivists, Spanish-Am. Club (dir., v.p.). Democrat. Lutheran. Avocations: travel, reading, bicycling, walking, dance.

EFIRD, JIMMY THOMAS, statistician; BA, UCLA, Los Angeles, CA, 1979; MSC, Calif. State U., Hayward, 1985; PhD, Stanford Sch. of Medicine, Palo Alto, CA, 2003. Pres. Applied Stats. Corp., Palo Alto, Calif., 1986—2002; dir. Biostats. and Data Mgmt. Facility John A. Burns Sch. Medicine, Honolulu, 2004—. Mem.: Am. Statis. Assn., Bay Area SAS Users Group (chmn.), Disting. Statistician Filming Com. Personal E-mail: jimmy.efird@stanfordalumni.org.

EFRON, BRADLEY, statistician, educator; b. St. Paul, May 24, 1938; s. Miles Jack and Esther (Kaufman) Efron; m. Gael Guerin, July 1969 (div.); 1 child, Miles James; m. Nancy Troup, June 1986 (div.). BS in Math., Calif. Inst. Tech., 1960; PhD, Stanford U., 1964; DSc (hon.), U. Chgo., 1995; D (hon.), U. Carlos III de Madrid, 1998; DSc (hon.), U. Oslo, 2002. Asst. and assoc. prof. stats. Stanford U., Calif., 1965-72, chmn. dept. stats. Calif., 1976-79, 1991-1994, chmn. math. scis. Calif., 1981—, prof. stats. and of health rsch. and policy Calif., 1974—, assoc. dean humanities and scis. Calif., 1987-90, endowed chair Max H. Stein prof. humanities and scis. Calif., 1991-94. Statis. cons. Alza Corp., 1971—, Rand Corp., 1962—. Author: Bootstrap Methods, 1979, Biostatistics Casebook, 1980. MacArthur Found. fellow, 1983; named Outstanding Statistician of Yr. Chgo. Statis. Assn., 1981; Wald and Rietz Lectr. Inst. Math. Stats., 1977, 81; recipient Fisher award, Chgo., 1996, Parzen prize for statis. innovation, 1998, Rao prize, 2003, Noether prize, 2006, 2005 Nat. Medal Sci., NSF, 2005. Fellow Inst. Math. Stats. (pres. 1987), Am. Statis. Assn. (pres. 2004, Wilks medal 1990, Noether prize); mem. NAS, Am. Acad. Arts and Scis., Internat. Statis. Assn. Achievements include invention of the bootstrap method. Office: Stanford U Dept Stats Sequoia Hall 390 Serra Mall Stanford CA 94305-4065

EFRON, ZAC, actor, singer; b. San Luis Obispo, Calif., Oct. 18, 1987; s. David and Starla Efron. Actor: (TV films) The Big Wide World of Carl Laemke, 2003, Triple Play, 2004, Miracle Run, 2004, If You Lived Here, You'd Be Home Now, 2006, High School Musical (Choice Breakout Star award & Choice Chemistry award, Teen Choice Awards, 2006), High School Musical 2, 2007; (TV series) Summerland, 2004—05; (films) The Derby Stallion, 2005, Hairspray, 2007 (Young Hollywood "One to Watch" award, 2007, Ensemble of Yr. award, Hollywood Film Festival, 2007); singer: (albums) High School Musical, 2006, Hairspray, 2007, High School Musical 2, 2007. Office: c/o Jason Barett Alchemy Entertainment 9229 Sunset Blvd Ste 720 Los Angeles CA 90069 also: Creative Artists Agency 2000 Ave of the Stars Los Angeles CA 90067 Office Phone: 424-288-2000, 310-278-8889.*

EFROS, ELLEN ANN, lawyer; b. NYC, Jan. 18, 1950; d. Edwin David and Judith (Breitman) E.; m. Fritz R. Kahn, June 26, 1983. BA, Case Western Res. U., 1971; MA, St. John's U., 1973; JD, Hofstra U., 1978. Bar: D.C. 1978, N.Y. 1979, Md. 1990, U.S. Ct. Appeals (5th cir.) 1978, U.S. Ct. Appeals (2d, 7th and D.C. cirs.) 1979, U.S. Ct. Appeals (Fed. cir.) 1993, U.S. Dist. Ct. D.C. 1981, U.S. Ct. Claims 1986, U.S. Supreme Ct. 1989. Trial atty. ICC Gen. Counsel, Washington, 1978-79; assoc. Verner & Liipfert, Washington, 1979-81; ptnr. Vorys, Sater, Seymour & Pease, Washington, 1981-97; hearing officer, office dispute resolution NASD Regulation, Inc., Washington, 1997-2000; ptnr. Rader, Fishman & Grauer, Washington, 2000—05; chief equity I, Office of Atty. Gen. Dist. of Columbia, Washington, 2005—. Asst. editor Antitrust Law Jour., 1987-90. Mem. ABA (sects. intellectual property and litigation), D.C. Bar Assn., N.Y. Bar Assn., Md. Bar Assn. Office: Office Atty Gen DC 441 4th St NW Flr 6S Washington DC 20001 Office Phone: 202-442-9886. Business E-Mail: ellen.efros@dc.gov.

EFSTATHIOU, JASON ALEXANDER, oncologist, radiologist; s. Aristide John and Ingrid Efstathiou; BSc, Yale U., New Haven, 1995; DPhil, U. Oxford, Eng., 1998; MD, Harvard Med. Sch., Boston, 2003. Lic. medicine Mass., 2006. Med. intern Brigham & Women's Hosp., Boston, 2003—04; radiation oncologist Harvard Radiation Oncology Program, 2004—. Recipient Stirling Boyd prize, Trinity Coll. U. Oxford, 1998, Merit award, Am. Soc. Clin. Oncology Found., 2006; fellow Yale Alumni Cmty. Svc. Fellowship, Yale U., 1994; grantee, Imperial Cancer Rsch. Fund, 1997—98; scholar, The Wellcome Trust, 1996; McKeown scholar, U. of Oxford, 1995—97, Andrus fellow, Harvard Med. Sch., 2000—03, Grunebaum scholar, 2000—03. Mem.: Mass. Med. Soc., Am. Soc. Therapeutic Radiology and Oncology. Achievements include research in use of prostate-specific antigen-based serial screening to decrease prostate cancer-specific mortality. Home: 18 Claremont Pk Boston MA 02118 Home Phone: 617-320-7859; Office Phone: 617-726-2000.

EFTEKHARI, NASSER, physiatrist; b. Aug. 15, 1940; MD, U. Tehran, 1965. Diplomate AM. Bd. Phys. Medicine and Rehab. Intern Greater Balt. Med. Ctr., 1967-68; resident in phys. medicine and rehab. Temple U. Sch. Med., Phila., 1968-70, Hahneman Med. U., Phila., 1970-71; rsch. fellow SUNY, Bklyn., 1971-72; chief dept. phys. medicine and rehab. Shafa Rehab. Hosp., Tehran, Iran, 1973-75; dean Coll. of Rehab. Scis., Tehran, 1973-79; phys. med. and rehab. cons. Golestan Clinic, Mehr Hosp., Tehran, 1980-84; staff physician VA Hosp., Miami, Fla., 1985—2005, Mercy Hosp., 1989—, Cedars Med. Ctr., 1989—, Bapt. Health Sys. Hosp. South Fla., Miami, 1996—; chief phys. med. and rehab. svc. VA Hosp., Miami, 1997—2005. Clin. assoc. prof. rehab. medicine U. Miami Sch. Medicine, 2003—. Fellow: Am. Assn. Electrodiagnostic Medicine; mem.: Am. Acad. Phys. Medicine and Rehab., Fla. Soc. Phys. Medicine and Rehab. Office: 8600 SW 92 St Ste 201 Miami FL 33156 Office Phone: 305-206-4726.

EFTHIMIOU, COSTAS JOHN, physicist, educator, researcher; s. John and Maria Efthimiou; BSc, U. Athens; MSc, PhD, Cornell U. Vis. scientist Cornell/Columbia U., Ithaca, NY, NYC, Harvard U., Cambridge, Mass.; rsch. assoc. Tel Aviv U.; lectr. Cornell U., Ithaca, NY; asst. prof. U. Ctrl. Fla. Editor (with B. Greene): Fields, Strings and Dualities, 1997. Mem.: Campus Freethought Alliance, U. Ctrl. Fla., Soc. Physics Students U. Ctrl. Fla., Am. Phys. Soc., Math. Assn. Am., Am. Assn. Physics Tchrs., Soc. Physics Students, Sigma Pi Sigma. Office: Dept Physics Univ Ctrl Fla Orlando FL 32816

EFTIMOFF, ANITA KENDALL, retired educational consultant; b. Granite City, Ill., May 3, 1927; d. David Harlow and Ollie Lorena (Galloway) Kendall; m. Vasil Eftimoff, June 14, 1959; 1 child, James Kendall. BA, Washington U., St. Louis, 1949; MA, So. Ill. U., Edwardsville, 1978, EdD, 1983. Cert. in multiple gen. edn., spl. edn., Ill. Spl. edn.

instr. Community Unit 9, Granite City, 1968-83; ednl. cons. Efti Enterprises, Granite City, 1982—95; program dir. At-Risk Presch. Grant, Granite City, 1986—95, ret., 1995. Del. NDEA Conf. Ea. Mich. U., Ypsilanti, 1968, Gifted Edn. Conf. Ill. Office of Edn., Springfield, 1975-77; adminstrv. intern Ill. State Bd. Edn., Springfield, 1981. Editor: Symphony Youth Orch. Newsletter, 1991—, Symphony Vol. Key Notes Newsletter, 1991-93. Bd. dirs. Ill. Gov.'s Adv. Coun. on Women's Affairs, Springfield, Rape Crisis and Sexual Abuse Ctr., So. Ill. U., 1978—, Family Resource Ctr.; chmn. adopt-a-friend St. Louis Ambs., 1982-84, co-chmn. Vets. Day, 1984-86; chmn. St. Louis Symphony Youth Orch., 1985—, St. Louis Symphony Young Artists Competitions, 1993—; mem. aux. St. Louis Children's Hosp., 1980; v.p. mus. activities St. Louis Symphony Vol. Assn.; bd. pres. Ill. Ctr. for Autism, 1993. At-risk presch. grantee Ill. Bd. Edn., 1986—. Mem. AAUW, LWV (co-pres. No. Nev. chpt. 2006-07), World Coun. for Gifted and Talented Children, Nat. Assn. for Gifted Children, Assn. for the Gifted, Ill. Coun. for the Gifted, Asthma and Allergy Found. Southeastern Mo., Am. Lung Assn. St. Louis, Women's Assn. (bd. dirs. 1961—, pres. 1989-91), No. Nev. League Women Voters (co-pres. 2006-07), St. Louis Symphony Women's Assn., St. Louis Art Access (bd. dirs. 2003-04), St. Louis Artist Guild, Nev. Women's Lobby, Progression Leadership Alliance Nev., Washoe County Alliance, Daus. of Nile, Carson Tahoe Regional Hosp. Auxilliary, Reno 20th Century Club (chaplin 2007—), Rotary-Anns, Delta Kappa Gamma, Phi Delta Kappa. Avocations: performing arts, classical music. Home and Office: 205 E Coyote Dr Carson City NV 89704 Office Phone: 775-849-0567.

EGAN, CHARLES JOSEPH, JR., lawyer, consumer products company executive; b. Cambridge, Mass., Aug. 11, 1932; s. Charles Joseph and Alice Claire (Ball) E.; m. Mary Bowersox, Aug. 6, 1955; children: Timothy, Sean, Peter, James. AB, Harvard U., 1954; LLB, Columbia U., 1959. Bar: N.Y. 1960, Mo. 1973. Assoc. Donovan, Leisure, Newton & Irvine, NYC, 1959-62; ptnr. Hall, McNicol, Marett & Hamilton, NYC, 1962-68; v.p., gen. counsel Thomson & McKinnon Securities, NYC, 1969-70, Hallmark Cards, Inc., Kansas City, Mo., 1972—2004. Bd. dirs. Am. Multi Cinema, Inc., Kansas City, Mo., 1996-2004. Trustee Notre Dame de Sion Sch., Kansas City, 1973-77, Pembroke Country Day Sch., Kansas City, 1976-82, Kansas City Art Inst., 1995—; bd. dirs. Kansas City YMCA, 1976-80; mem. dean's coun. Columbia Law Sch., 1991—; vice chmn. Harvard Coll. Fund, 1994-99, co-chmn., 2000-03; co-trustee Stanley H. Durwood Found. Served to 1st lt. USMC, 1954-56. Mem. Mo. Bar Assn., Kansas City Lawyers Assn., Harvard Alumni Assn. (pres. 1989-90, exec. com. 1987-2003), Century Assn., Somerset Club, Harvard Club of N.Y., Harvard Club of Kansas City (pres. 1985-87). Roman Catholic. Office: Hallmark Cards Inc 2501 Mcgee St Kansas City MO 64108-2600 Home Phone: 816-531-0424; Office Phone: 816-274-4687.

EGAN, CYNTHIA L., investment company executive; BA in English Lit., Boston Coll., 1978. Sr. operations analyst, bd. of gov. Fed. Reserve Sys., Washington, 1980—84; mgr. fin. svc. consulting KPMG Peat Marwick, 1984—88; v.p. large plan defined contribution svc. Bankers Trust Co., 1988—89; exec. v.p. Fidelity Institutional Tax-Exempt Svc. Co., 1989—92; pres. Fidelity Charitable Gift Fund, 1992—95; exec. v.p. mgmt. trust Fidelity Investments, 1996—98; pres. retirement plan services T. Rowe Price, 2007—. Mem. Boston Coll. President's Circle Exec. Com., Task Force on Women and Boston Coll. Office: T Rowe Price Group 100 E Pratt St Baltimore MD 21202*

EGAN, EDWARD MICHAEL CARDINAL, archbishop, cardinal; b. Oak Park, Ill., Apr. 2, 1932; s. Thomas J. and Genevieve (Costello) Egan. PhB, St. Mary of Lake, 1954; STL, Gregorian U., 1958, JCD, 1963; PhD (hon.), St. John's U., Thomas More Coll., Western Conn. State U., Fordham U., Manhattan Coll., U. Lublin; PhD Cardinal Wyszynski U. (hon.), Warsaw; PhD (hon.), Coll. of New Rochelle, Iona Coll., N.Y. Med. Coll. Ordained priest Roman Catholic Ch., 1957. Sec. to Albert Cardinal Meyer Archdiocese of Chgo., 1958—60, sec. to John Cardinal Cody, 1966—68, co-chancellor, 1969—72; faculty Pontifical N.Am. Coll., Vatican City, 1960—65; judge Sacred Roman Rota, Vatican City, 1972—85; aux. bishop, vicar for edn. Archdiocese of N.Y., NYC, 1985—88; bishop of Bridgeport Conn., 1988—2000; archbishop of N.Y. NYC, 2000—; cardinal Roman Cath. Ch., 2001—. Chmn. bd. Bishop Curtis Homes, Fairfield County, Conn., 1988—2000, St. Joseph Seminary, Yonkers, NY, 2000—; adminstrv. bd. U.S. Cath. Conf., 1991—94, 1996—99; chmn. bd. govs. Pontifical N.Am. Coll., Vatican City, 1991—95; mem. bd. Nat. Shrine Immaculate Conception, Washington, 2000—; mem. Pontifical Coun. for the Family and Pontifical Coun. for Fin. and Adminstrv. Affairs of the Holy See, 2000—; mem. bd. Bur. Black and Indian Missions, Washington, 2000—; mem. Supreme Tribunal of the Apostolic Signatura, 2002—, Prefecture of the Econ. Affairs of the Holy See, 2002—, Pontifical Commn. for the Cultural Goods of the Ch., 2002—; chmn. com. sci. and human values Nat. Conf. Cath. Bishops, mem. com. Canonical Affairs, com. nat. collections, com. edn., com. nominations. Trustee Cath. U. Am., Washington, 2000—; bd. trustees Ratisbonne Inst., Jerusalem, 2000—, Thomas More Coll., Merrimack, NH, 1995—, Nat. Shrine Immaculate Conception, Washington, Cath. U. Am., Washington, Ave Maria Sch. Law, Ann Arbor, Mich.; chmn. bd. trustees St. Joseph Med. Ctr., Stamford, Conn., 1988—96; chmn. Inner-City Found. for Edn. and Charity, Fairfield County, Conn., 1992—2000; chmn. bd. trustees Sacred Heart U., Fairfield, Conn. 1988—2000, bd. trustees; chmn. Inner City Scholarship Fund of NY, Cath. Charities of NY. Named one of New York's Influentials, New York Mag. 2006. Mem.: Cath. Neareast Welfare Assn. (chmn. 2000—). Roman Catholic.

EGAN, JOHN FREDERICK, retired electronics executive; b. Council Bluffs, Iowa, Feb. 25, 1935; s. Frederick Emerson and Ruth Pauline (Russell) E.; m. Anne B. Patterson, June 14, 1958; children: John Jr., James Michael. BA in Physics with honors, Grinnell Coll., 1957; MSEE, Northwestern U., 1958, PhD in Elec. Engring., 1961. Tech. dir. computer systems, Electronics Systems div. USAF, Bedford, Mass., 1964-67; sr. staff specialist intelligence Office Dir. Def., Research and Engring., Washington, 1967-71; chief scientist command support Office Chief Naval Ops., Washington, 1971-73; group dir. fed. systems Sanders Assocs., Inc., Nashua, NH, 1973-77; v.p. Sanders Assoc., Inc., Nashua, NH, 1977-87, group v.p. Lockheed Corp., 1987-93; corp. v.p. corp. devel. Lockheed Martin Corp., Bethesda, Md., 1993-98. Mem. exec. panel Chief Naval Ops., Washington, 1971—; mem. naval studies bd. NRC, 1990-98, 2004, chair 2005-. Trustee Grinnell Coll., 2002—, Hunt Cmty., 2002—, Daniel Webster Coll., 1998—, chair 2003-. Officer USAF, 1961—64. Mem.: AAAS, AIAA, IEEE, Rotary Internat., Sigma Xi. Home: 7 Beverlee Dr Nashua NH 03064-1674 E-mail: ergwatt@hotmail.com.

EGAN, KENNETH J., dermatologist; b. NYC, Feb. 2, 1956; m. Marcia Beth Robins, May 23, 1982; children: Heather, Daniel, Brian. BA, Franklin and Marshall Coll., 1978; MD, N.Y. Med. Coll., 1982. Bd. cert. Am. Acad. Dermatology. Resident internal medicine North Shore Univ. Hosp./Meml. Sloan-Kettering Hosp., Manhasset, NY, 1982-85; resident dermatology Albert Einsten Coll. Medicine, NYC, 1985-88; pvt. practice Ridgefield, Conn., 1988—. Fellow Am. Acad. Dermatology; mem. AMA, Am. Soc. for Laser Medicine, Fairfield County Med. Assn. Avocation: golf. Office: 38B Grove St Ridgefield CT 06877-4667 Office Phone: 203-438-4111.

EGAN, KEVIN JAMES, lawyer; b. Chgo., June 24, 1950; s. Raymond Basil and Harriet Olene (Landbo) E.; children: Ryan, Daniel. BA, U. Ill., 1972; JD, Northwestern U., 1975. Bar: Ill. 1975, U.S. Dist. Ct. (no. dist.) Ill. 1975, U.S. Ct. Appeals (7th cir.) 1976, U.S. Ct. of Customs and Patent Appeals 1978. Law clk. to judge U.S. Dist. Ct. (no. dist.) Ill., Chgo., 1975-77; assoc. Pattishall, McAuliffe & Hofstetter, Chgo., 1977-78; asst. U.S. atty. No. Dist. of Ill., 1978-82; assoc. Winston & Strawn, Chgo., 1982-84, ptnr., 1984-93, Sonnenschein, Nath & Rosenthal, Chgo., 1993-98, Foley & Lardner, Chgo., 1998—. Article editor Jour. Criminal Law and Criminology, 1974-75. Bd. trustees Village of Frankfort, 1991—. Mem. ABA, Chgo. Bar Assn. (com. mem.), Bar Assn. of 7th Cir., Prestwick Country Club (Frankfort, Ill.). Episcopalian. Avocation: hockey. Home: 904 Huntsmoor Dr Frankfort IL 60423-8747 Office: Foley & Lardner 321 N Clark St Ste 2800 Chicago IL 60610 Home Phone: 815-469-1571; Office Phone: 312-832-4500. Business E-Mail: kegan@foley.com.

EGAN, KRISTIN, otolaryngologist; b. NYC, Feb. 18, 1977; d. Frank and Karin Egan. BA, Princeton U., NJ, 1999; MD, Albert Einstein Coll. Medicine, Bronx, NY, 2003. Intern U. Calif., San Francisco, 2003—04, resident, 2004—, head & neck surgeon dept. otolaryngology, 2003—. Recipient Best Clin. Rsch. award, Bay Area Resident Rsch. Symposium, 2006, Resident Rsch. Travel Award, Triologic Meeting of the Western Sect., 2005. Mem.: Am. Acad. Otolaryngic Allergy, Calif. Soc. Facial Plastic Surgery, Am. Laryngological, Rhinological and Otological Soc., Am. Acad. Otolaryngology Head and Neck Surgery, Am. Assn. Facial Plastic Surgery, Alpha Omega Alpha. Office: Univ Calif San Francisco 400 Parnassus Ave Ste A730 San Francisco CA 94143 Home Phone: 415-566-6728; Office Phone: 415-476-4952.

EGAN, MICHAEL JOSEPH, retired lawyer, state legislator; b. Savannah, Ga., Aug. 8, 1926; s. Michael Joseph and Elise (Robider) E.; m. Donna Cole, Apr. 14, 1951; children: Moira Elizabeth, Michael Joseph, Donna, Cole, Roby, John Patrick. BA, Yale U., 1950; LL.B., Harvard U., 1955. Bar: Ga., D.C. Assoc. Sutherland, Asbill & Brennan, Atlanta, 1955-61, ptnr., 1961-77, 79-97, ret. ptnr., 1998; mem. Ga. Ho. of Reps., 1966-77, minority leader, 1971-77; assoc. atty. gen. U.S. Dept. Justice, Washington, 1977-79; mem. Ga. Senate, 1989-2001. Served with U.S. Army, 1945-47, 50-52. Mem. ABA, Atlanta Bar Assn., State Bar Ga., Am. Law Inst. Republican. Roman Catholic. Home: 3145 Argonne Dr NW Atlanta GA 30305-1949 Office: Sutherland Asbill & Brennan 999 Peachtree St NE Atlanta GA 30309-3915 also: 1275 Pennsylvania Ave NW Washington DC 20004-2404 Office Phone: 404-853-8056.

EGAN, PATRICIA JANE, foundation administrator, retired director; b. San Francisco, Aug. 7, 1951; 1 child, Kathryn Michele. AB, U. Calif., Berkeley, 1978; postgrad., N.J. Inst. Tech., 1996—. Cert. fund raising exec. Grants officer Mus. Modern Art, NYC, 1979—81; assoc. devel. officer grants Whitney Mus. Am. Art, NYC, 1981—84; assoc. dir. devel. Columbia Bus. Sch., Columbia U., NYC, 1984—86; mgr. major gifts New York Bot. Garden, NYC, 1987—88; dir. devel. N.Y.C. Partnership, 1989—91; dir. devel. Cal Performances U. Calif., Berkeley, 1991—92, instr. bus. and engring. ext. svcs., 2004—. Cons. various cultural and environ. orgns., NY; co-prodr. distance learning course proposal writing N.J. Inst. Tech., 1997—. Prodr., program host Terpischore, Sta. KUSF-FM, 1978—79. Bd. dirs. Universala Esperanto Asocio, NY, 1980—83, Dance Perspectives Found., NYC, 1985—2002, Shakespeare for Kids, 2005—; treas. Dance Perspectives Found., NYC, 1987—91, found. officer, treas.; trustee Riverside Ch., NYC, 1986—87. Fellow, Nat. Endowment Arts, 1977. Mem.: Women in Tech. Internat., Am. Soc. Info. Sci. and Tech., Coun. on Programs Tech. and Sci. Comm., Assn. Tchrs. Tech. Writing, Internat. Assn. Bus. Communicators, Women in Comm., Soc. Tech. Comm. (Bernard J. Goodman Meml. award N.Y. Metro chpt. 1998), Mensa, Jr. League San Francisco, Esperanto League N.Am., Soc. Dance History Scholars, Churchill Club, Alpha Epsilon Lambda. Avocations: art, ballet, dance, martial arts. Office: PO Box 194391 San Francisco CA 94119-4391

EGAN, RICHARD JOHN, retired information technology executive, former ambassador; b. Boston, Feb. 28, 1936; s. Kenneth Joseph and Constance Bianca E.; m. Maureen E. Fitzgerald; children: John R., Michael J., Maureen E. Petracca, Christopher, Catherine. BEE, Northeastern U., 1961; postgrad., MIT, 1963-64; LLD (hon.), Northeastern U., 1995; DSc (hon.), New England Inst. Tech., 1999. V.p. mktg. Cambridge Memories (now Cambex Corp.), Waltham, Mass., 1968-75; gen. mgr. comml. systems div. Intel Corp., Santa Clara, Calif., 1975-77; co-founder, dir. EMC Corp., Hopkinton, Mass., 1979—, pres., CEO, 1979-88, chmn., CEO, 1988—92, founder, chmn. emeritus, 2001—; US amb. to Ireland, 2001—02. Bd. dirs. Tech. Fin. Svcs., Westford, Mass.; steering com. chair George W. Bush Info. Tech. Nat. Steering Coun.; mem. Transition Adv. Group, US Dept. Commerce; dir. Mass. High Tech. Coun., Cognition Corp. and NetScout Sys. Inc. Supporter Boston Symphony Orch; dir., founder Hopkinton Tech. for Edn. Found.; trustee Cath. Schs. Found., Northeastern U., Inner City Scholarship Fund. Named one of Forbes Richest Americans, 2006. Mem.: Mass. Bus. Roundtable, Semper Fidelis Soc. Republican. Roman Catholic. Avocations: fishing, reading, music.

EGAN, RON, corporate financial executive; BA in Acctg. and Mgmt. first in class, U. Utah, Salt Lake City, MBA in Fin. and IT magna cum laude. CPA. Staff acct. Arthur Andersen, Salt Lake City, 1980—82; sr. fin. analyst Am. Express Corp., NYC, 1982—85; mgr. fin. and acctg. Kenway Eaton Corp., Salt Lake City, 1985—94, mgr. strategic and fin. planning Cutler Hammer Pitts., 1994—97, group contr. Oxford Automotive Ontario, Canada and Troy, Mich., 1997—99; v.p. global fin. and corp. contr. Eagle Ottawa Automotive/Woodbridge, Rochester Hills, 1999—. Bd. dir. Voyager Fin. Co.; course instr. U. Utah, Salt Lake City; instr. and trainer Internat. Divsn. Contr.; instr. ISO 9000 audit stds. Quality Inst. Mem. Boy Scouts Am.; tchr. and cons. applied econ. Jr. Achievement. Named Outstanding Exec. Advisor, Jr. Achievement Assn., QS 9000 Quality Sys. Internal Audit Champion. Mem.: Fin. Execs. Internat., Phi Kappa Phi Address: 13887 Woodsett Ct Utica MI 48315

EGAN, SHIRLEY ANNE, retired nursing educator; b. Haverill, Mass. d. Rush B. and Beatrice (Bengle) Willard. Diploma, St. Joseph's Hosp. Sch. Nursing, Nashua, NH, 1945; BS in Nursing Edn., Boston U., 1949, MS, 1954. Instr. sci. Sturdy Meml. Hosp. Sch. Nursing, Attleboro, Mass., 1949-51, Peter Bent Brigham Hosp. Sch. Nursing, Boston, 1951-53, ednl. dir., 1953-55, assoc. dir. Sch. Nursing, 1955-59, med. surg. coord., 1971-73, assoc. dir. Sch. Nursing, 1973-79, dir., 1979-85; cons. North Country Hosp., Newport, Vt., 1985-86; infection control practitioner, 1986-87; contract instr. Natchitoches Area Tech. Inst., 1988—90, Sabine Valley Tech Inst., 1990-91; coord. quality assurance Evangeline Health Care Ctr., 1991-92, asst. dir. nursing, 1992-93, coord. quality assurance Natchitoches, La., 1994-96, retired, 1996. Nurse edn. adviser AID (formerly JCA), Karachi, Pakistan, 1959-67; prin. Coll. Nursing, Karachi, 1959-67; dir. Vis. Nurse Service, Nashua, N.H., 1967-70; cons. nursing edn. Pakistan Ministry of Health, Labour and Social Welfare, 1959-67, adviser to editor Pakistan Nursing and Health Rev., 1959-67; exec. bd. Nat. Health Edn. Com., Pakistan; WHO short-term cons. U. W.I., Jamaica, 1970-71; mem. Greater Nashua Health Planning Council. Contbr. articles to profl. publs. Bd. dirs. Matthew Thornton health Ctr., Nashua, Nashua Child Care Ctr.; vol. ombudsman N.H. Council on Aging; mem. Nashua Service League. Served as 1st lt., Army Nurse Corps., 1945-47. Mem. Trained Nurses Assn. Pakistan, Nat. League for Nursing, Assn. for Preservation Hist. Natchitoches, St. Joseph's Sch. Nursing Alumnae Assn., Boston U. Alumnae Assn., Brit. Soc. Health Edn., Cath. Daus. Am. (vice regent ct. Bishop Malloy), Statis. Study Grads. Karachi Coll. Nursing, Sigma Theta Tau. Home: 729 Royal St Natchitoches LA 71457-5716

EGAN, SUSAN CHAN, securities analyst, writer; b. Manila, Feb. 11, 1946; came to U.S., 1969; d. Mariano Sui Ming and Rita Patricia (Quejong) Chan; m. Ronald Christopher Egan, Mar. 22, 1971; 1 child, Louisa. BA in Chinese Lang. and Lit., U. Wash., 1970; MBA, Boston U., 1981; MA in Comparative Lit., U. Wash., 1971. Chartered Fin. Analyst. Bus. counselor Local Devel. Corp. of South End, Boston, 1973-74; cons. Boston, 1974-76; dir. edn. and tng. Mass. Dept. Commerce and Devel., Boston, 1976-79, program devel. cons., 1979-81; trust investment officer State St. Bank and Trust Co., Boston, 1981-83, sr. trust investment officer, 1983-86, v.p., 1986-87, Scudder, Stevens & Clark, LA, 1987-98; pres. Pacific Trade Winds Co., Santa Barbara, Calif., 1998—. Author: Coping With Utility Bills and Other Enegry Costs, 1971, How to Do Business with the State, 1980, New Business, 1981, A Latterday Confucian, 1987, Hong Ye Zhuan, 1992, An Introduction to Securities Markets, 1997, A Pragmatist and His Free Spirit, 2007. Mem. Assn. for Investment Mgmt. and Rsch. Home: 921 W Campus Pt Santa Barbara CA 93117-4341 Personal E-mail: susanchangegan@yahoo.com.

EGAN, TERRENCE, foundation administrator; BS, No. Ill. U., DeKalb, 1993. Cert. fund raising exec. CFRE Internat., 2002. Dir. Fabricators & Manufacturers Assn. Found., Rockford, Ill., 2003—. Bd. dirs. Assn. Luth. Devel. Exe., Madison, 2002—06; pres. Oregon Sch. Found., Ill., 2004—. Bd. mem. Assn. Luth. Devel. Exec., Madison, 2002—06; pres. Oregon Sch. Found., 2004—07. Grant to Swim Alcatraz, Balance Bar Co., 2005. Mem.: Assn. Fundraising Profls., Assn. Luth. Devel. Exe., US Masters Swimming. Avocations: open water swimming, coach youth sports. Office: FMA Found 833 Featherstone Rd Rockford IL 61107 Home Phone: 815-732-6832; Office Phone: 815-381-1337.

EGAN, TIMOTHY K., writer, journalist; b. Seattle; m. Joni Balter; 2 children. BA in Journalism, U. Washington; LHD (hon.), Whitman Coll., 2000. Reporter Seattle Post-Intelligencer; pacific northwest corr. NY Times, nat. enterprise reporter. Commentator Letters from America series BBC. Author: (novels) The Good Rain: Across Time and Terrain in the Pacific Northwest, 1991 (Pacific Northwest Booksellers award, Washington State Book award, 1991), Lasso The Wind: Away to the New West, 1998 (Mountains and Plains Booksellers award, Gov. Writing award, 1999, Notable Book of Yr. NY Times Sunday Book Rev., 1999, Washington State Book award, 1999), The Winemaker's Daughter, The Worst Hard Time: The Untold Story of Those Who Survived the Great American Dust Bowl, 2006 (Nat. Book award nonfiction, 2006, Washington State Book award, 2006); co-author: How Race is Lived in America, 2001 (Pulitzer prize, 2001).*

EGAN, WESLEY WILLIAM, former ambassador; b. Madison, Wis., Jan. 21, 1946; s. Wesley William and Ruth (Skeuse) E.; m. Virginia Warren, Aug. 15, 1967; children: Wesley Matthew, Kimberly Katherine. BA with honors, U. N.C., 1968. Vice consul Am. Consulate Gen., Durban, South Africa, 1972-74; spl. asst. to sec. state Dept. State Washington, 1974-77; 1st sec. Am. embassy, Portugal, 1977-79, dep. chief mission Republic Zambia, 1979-82; ambassador to Republic of Guinea-Bissau, 1983-85, Chief of Staff to Dep. Sec. of State, 1985-87; Dep. Chief of Mission Am. Embassy, Lisbon, Portugal, 1987-90, Cairo, 1990-93; ambassador to Hashemite Kingdom of Jordan, 1994-98; dep. insp. gen. Dept. of State, Washington, 1998-2000. Chmn. bd., pres. Petra Nat. Found. (USA), Washington, 2003—. Mem.: Assn. for Diplomatic Studies and Tng. (bd. dirs.), Middle East Inst., Washington Inst. Fgn. Affairs (bd. dirs.). Episcopalian.

EGAS, ERIC, artist; b. NYC, July 27, 1944; s. Camilo Egas and Alice Lindsay; m. Edith Smith Egas, Sept. 1, 1966 (div. Oct. 1968); 1 child, Emile; m. Carolyn Marie Parry, Feb. 15, 1974; 1 child, Ean. Student, Pratt Inst., 1961—65, New Sch. for Social Rsch., 1965, Kunstfacskolan, Stockholm, Sweden, 1966. Asst. film maker Arnold Eagle Prodns., NYC, 1965—66; supr. film and media N.Y. State Mus., Albany, 1967—78; artist Cairo, NY, 1978—80; exec. dir. Greene County Coun. on Arts, Catskill, NY, 1980—82; artist Greenville, NY, 1982—90; dir., CEO Advanced Graphics Rsch. Inc., Greenville, 1990—99; artist Viegues, PR, 1999—, NY, 1999—. Bd. dirs. Art Awareness Inc., Lexington, NY, 1986—90; visual arts panelist N.Y. State Coun. on Arts, NYC, 1983—86. Grantee Creative Artist Pub. Svc. grantee, N.Y. Found. for Art, 1979; Media grantee, Haleakela Found., 1980—82, Sponsored Project grantee, N.Y. state Coun. on Arts, 1984. Atheist. Achievements include one of the earliest developers of Raster to vector conversion software; development of unique methodology for making anaglyphic (3D) photographs using the dye transfer process. Avocations: solar energy, architecture.

EGBERT, EMERSON CHARLES, retired publisher; b. Los Angeles, Nov. 30, 1924; s. Charles Barnes and Ethel Annette (Feader) E.; m. Kathryn Eleanor Tressel, Apr. 6, 1947; children— Susan Ann, John Charles, James Emerson, Michael Warren, Patricia Ann. Student, Pasadena Jr. Coll., Woodbury Bus. Coll. Distbn. mgr. Newsstand Distbrs., 1947-49, dist. sales mgr. So. Calif., Pocket Books, Inc., 1949-59, sales mgr. Eastern div., 1959-61, v.p., circulation dir., 1961-71; pres. Pocket Books Distbn. Corp., NYC, 1971-81; sr. v.p. Silhouette Books div. Simon & Schuster, 1981-85, sr. v.p. trade pub. group, 1985-89; ret., 1989; pres. B/K Book Cons. Svcs. Inc., Rockville Ctr., N.Y., 1990-93, Madison, Conn., 1993-97, ret., 1997. Past dist. commr. Boy Scouts Am.; bd. dirs. 25 Yr. Club; bd. dirs. YMCA, Westbrook, Conn.; mem. vestry com. St. Andrew's Episcopal Ch., Madison. With USNR, 1942-45. Decorated D.F.C., Air Medal with 4 oak leaf clusters. Mem. Ind. Newsstand Circulation Execs. Assn. (past chmn.), Internat. Periodical Distbrs. Am. (chmn.), Bur. Ind. Pubs. and Distbrs. (past chmn. book com.), Anti-Defamation League. Republican. Home: 87 Legend Hill Rd Madison CT 06443-1864

EGBERT, PETER ROY, ophthalmologist, educator; b. Indpls., Dec. 6, 1941; BA magna cum laude, DePauw U., Greencastle, Ind., 1963; MD, Yale U., 1967. Diplomate Nat. Bd. Med. Examiners, Am. Bd. Ophthalmology. Intern Cleve. Met. Gen. Hosp., 1967—68; resident in ophthalmology Yale U., New Haven, 1968—69; acting asst. prof. surgery (ophthalmology) Stanford (Calif.) U., 1973—74, dir. Ophthalmic Pathology Lab., 1973—, asst. prof. surgery, 1974—81; acting head divsn. ophthalmology Stanford U. Med. Ctr., 1980—82, assoc. prof. surgery, 1981—88, prof. ophthalmology, 1988—, chmn. dept. ophthalmology, 1992—97; resident in ophthalmology Yale U., New Haven, 1971—73. Recipient Bordon prize, DePauw U., 1960. Mem.: Verhoeff Ophthalmic Pathology Soc., Peninsula Eye Soc., Michael Hogan Eye Pathology Soc., Am. Intra-Ocular Implant Soc., Am. Assn. Ophthalmic Pathologists, Am. Acad. Ophthalmology (Outstanding Humanitarian Svc. award 2004), Phi Beta Kappa, Alpha Omega Alpha. Office: Stanford U Sch Medicine 300 Pasteur Dr Stanford CA 94305-5308

EGBERT, RICHARD MICHAEL, lawyer; b. Newton, Mass., Feb. 13, 1947; s. Marcus Manuel and Annette Honey (Segal) E.; children: Shea N., Danielle F., Manuel R. BBA, U. Mass., 1969; JD, Northeastern U., 1972. Bar: Mass. 1972, US Dist. Ct. Mass. 1973, US Ct. Appeals (1st cir.) 1974, US Supreme Ct. 1980. Founder Law Offices of Richard M. Egbert, Boston, 1972—. Lectr. Mass. CLE. Dir. Nat. Coun. Northeastern U., Boston, 1996—; mem. Chancellors Coun., U. Mass., Amherst, 1993—. Named one of top Boston lawyers, Boston Mag., 2004; named to Best Lawyers in Am., Mass. Super Lawyers. Fellow Internat. Acad. Trial Lawyers; mem. ABA, Boston Bar Assn., Mass. Bar Assn., Nat. Assn. Criminal Def. Lawyers, Mass. Assn. Criminal Def. Lawyers (pres. 1999-2000), Mass. Acad. Trial Lawyers. Office: 99 Summer St Ste 1800 Boston MA 02110-1213 Office Phone: 617-737-8222. Office Fax: 617-737-8223.

EGDAHL, RICHARD HARRISON, surgeon, educator, health science association administrator; b. Eau Claire, Wis., Dec. 13, 1926; s. Harry I. and Rebecca (Ball) Egdahl; m. Cynthia Taft, Apr. 1983; children from previous marriage: Scott, David, Bruce, Julie. MD, Harvard U., 1950; PhD, U. Minn., 1957. Intern U. Minn. Hosp., 1950—51, resident, 1956—57;

prof. surgery Med. Coll. Va., 1957—64; prof., chmn. surgery Boston U. Med. Ctr., 1964—73, dir., 1973—96, Health Policy Inst., Boston U.; Alexander Graham Bell prof. health care entrepreneurship Boston U. Trustee Pioneer Family of Mut. Funds. Past mem. editl. bd.: Am. Jour. Surgery, New Eng. Jour. Medicine. Trustee Boston Med. Ctr. Lt. USNR, 1952—55. Mem.: ACS, Am. Soc. for Clin. Investigation, Internat. Assn. Endocrine Surgeons (pres. 1981—83), Inst. Medicine NAS, Endocrine Soc. (CIBA award 1961), Soc. Med. Adminstrs., Boston Surg. Soc. (pres. 1977), Am. Surg. Assn. (1st v.p. 1980), Soc. Univ. Surgeons (pres. 1970—71), The Registry Resort, Badminton and Tennis Club, Algonquin Club, Brookline Country Club, Comml. Club, Alpha Omega Alpha, Phi Beta Kappa. Office: Boston U Healthcare Entrepreneurship program 53 Bay State Rd Boston MA 02215-2101 Office Phone: 617-353-4525. Business E-Mail: regdahl@bu.edu.

EGELSON, PAULINE C., director; b. Geneva, Ill., June 27, 1953; d. Donald and Pauline Wiese Ericson; m. Robert Louis Egelson, Sept. 1, 1979; children: Daniel, Benjamin. BA in Child Devel., Rockford Coll., 1975; MA in Reading Edn., Western Carolina U., 1982; EdD in Ednl. Leadership, U. NC, Greensboro, 1993. Cert. tchr. NC, prin. K-12 superintendency NC. Cmty. organizer United Meth. Ch., Asheville, NC, 1975—77; tchr. K-8 Diocese of Charlotte, Asheville, 1977—81; sales staff Dancer's Place, Asheville, 1981—84; reading clinician Western Carolina U., Oteen, NC, 1982—84; tchr. reading Buncombe County Schs., Asheville, 1983—90; ednl. rschr. South Eastern Regional Vision for Edn., Greensboro, NC, 1991—2005, program dir., 2002—05; dir. Ctr. for Partnership to Improve Edn. Coll. Charleston, Sch. Edn., NC, 2006—. Co-author: Formative Teacher Evaluation: Models and Current Findings, 1998, How Class Size Makes a Difference, 2002, Life at Draper Elementary: Taking Small Classes One Step Further, 2002, A Compedium of Senior Project Research, 2003—05, Preliminary Findings: Professional Learning Teams in Elementary Schools, 2004, Intensive Technical Assistance to Rural Low Performing School Districts: Implications for the Field, 2006; co-devel. (video) The Senior Project: Student Work for the Real World, 1999. Named Blue Ribbon Schs. panelist, U.S. Dept. Edn., 2000, 2002; Dropout Prevention grantee, NEA/NFIE, 1989. Mem.: Internat. Reading Assn., Am. Ednl. Rsch. Assn., Jt. Com. Stds. for Evaluation (exec. com. 2001—). Avocations: photography, travel. Office: Ctr for Partnership to Improve Edn Coll Charleston Sch Edn 66 George St Charleston SC 29424 Office Phone: 843-953-7629. Business E-Mail: egelsonp@cofc.edu.

EGEN, MAUREEN MAHON, publishing executive; BA, Trinity Coll., 1964. Editl. trainee and numerous other positions Doubleday & Co., Inc., 1964; mng. dir. Doubleday Book Clubs, 1979, pub., editl. dir., 1981; editor-in-cheif Warner Hardcover Books Time Warner Book Group, 1990—98, pres., chief oper. officer NYC, 1998—. Co-chair ann. book fair Goddard Riverside Cmty. Ctr.; mem. diversity steering com. Time Warner Book Group. Bd. dirs. The Ctr. Ind. of Disabled, NYC. Mem.: Assn. Am. Pubs. (mem. freedom to read com.), Women's Media Group. Office: Time Warner Book Group 1271 Ave of Americas New York NY 10020

EGENOLF, ROBERT F., lawyer; b. San Francisco, Jan. 23, 1946; s. John D. and Virginia (Kirkland) Butler; m. Judy Wish, Jan. 23, 1970; children: Cristi Michelle, Jonah Wish. BA, U.S. Internat. U., San Diego, 1970; JD, Calif. Western U., San Diego, 1973; LLM, U. Miami, Fla., 1974. Bar: Calif. 1973, U.S. Tax Ct. 1974. Assoc. Blum & Blum, Oakland, Calif., 1974-75; ptnr. Westwick & Collison, Santa Barbara, Calif., 1976-80, Egenolf & Moore, Santa Barbara, 1980-94. Pres., founder Calif. Exchange Corp., Santa Barbara, 1984-90, Santa Barbara Exch. Corp., 1984-90, 97—, First Exch. Corp., Santa Barbara, 1988-90, Amherst Exch. Corp., Santa Barbara, 1989—; instr., lectr. Santa Barbara City Coll., 1987—; lectr. in real estate exch. seminars Lawyers Throughout the U.S., 1987—. Bd. dirs. Tri Counties Devel. Disabilities Bd., Santa Barbara, 1977-78, Child Abuse Listening Mediation, Santa Barbara, 1979-80, Ensemble Theatre Project, Santa Barbara, 1981-83, Santa Barbara City Coll. Theatre Group, 1983-84; dir., Anti-Defamation League, Santa Barbara, 2000-04; trustee Laguna Blanca Sch., 1997-2003; dir. Am. Inst. Food and Wine, 1991-93, Santa Barbara Wine Auction, 1993-94, Semana Nautica Masters Volleyball Tournament, 1993-97; mem. polit. action com. Planned Parenthood, 1995; mem. fin. devel. steering com. Santa Barbara Contemporary Arts Forum, 1995-96; dir. Santa Barbara Bd. ACLU, 2002—04; dir. found. Santa Barbara City Coll., 2005—. With USN, 1963-69. Recipient Disting. Cmty. Svc. award, Anti-Defamation League, 2002. Mem. Calif. Bar Assn. (co-chair joint tax subsect. 1990-95), Santa Barbara Bar Assn. (bd. dirs. 1978, 95-2001, pres. 2000), Barristers Santa Barbara (pres. 1976-77). Avocations: pilot, volleyball, sailing. Office: Egenolf Assocs LLP 130 E Carrillo St Santa Barbara CA 93101-2111 Office Phone: 805-963-8906. Business E-Mail: egenolf@egenolf.com.

EGER, JOSEPH, conductor; b. Hartford, Conn., July 9, 1925; s. Abraham and Clara (Ellovich) E. Grad., Curtis Inst., Berkshire Music Ctr.; studied with, Monteux, Stokowski, Steinberg, Lert, Rudolf, Kahne. Faculty Aspen (Colo.) Music Festival, 1952-57; mem. faculty Peabody Conservatory, 1962-65, New Sch., 1971-72; condr. Greater Hollywood Philharm., 2001—03; lectr. Fla. Atlantic U., 2003, U. NC, Asheville, 2004—. Creator Harlem Music Project (pub. by Schirmer's, Consol. Music Pubs.); condr. seminar Smithsonian Instn., 1979; faculty, dir. internat. concert/seminar Salzburg Seminars, 1980; lectr. Nova Southeastern U, nationwide tours. First horn N.Y. Philharm., L.A. Philharm., Israel Philharm., other major orchs.; solo rec. artist: RCA Victor, (albums) Joseph Eger Retrospective Series, 1978, also for motion picture, TV and radio; French horn soloist world concert tours, 1956; lectr., music dir. Eger Players; founder, condr. Camera Concerti Chamber Orch., 1958, Westside Symphony Orch., 1961, N.Y. Orch. Soc., 1963-73; condr. Midland (Mich.) Symphony, 1962-64, Town Hall series, 1962-63, Carnegie Hall, 1964-71, Philharm. Hall, 1965-72, Athens Festival, young people and teenage concerts, (concert series) UN, 1980, N. Miami Beach Symphony, 1997; guest condr. Royal Philharm., London Philharm., Moscow State Symphony, Lithuania State Symphony, New Philharmonia, Sinfonia of London, Pitts. Symphony Orch., Dallas Symphony, Cin. Symphony Orch., Balt. Symphony Orch., Am. Symphony Orch., Vienna Radio Orch., Dessoff Choir, Haifa, Nat. Symphony Costa Rica, Symphony Philharm. Orch., Nat. Symphony Cuba, Nat. Symphony South Africa, Bucharest Philharm. Orch., 1997, Romanian Orch., 1997, others; assoc. condr. to Leopold Stokowski, 1967-70; composer: (recs.) Life mag., 1966, Westminster Record Co., 1967; (film score) Carolina, 1970, Hidden Fears; music dir. Indian Hill, 1967, N.Y. Symphony Premiere Performance, 1968, N.Y. Concertante, Symphony for UN, 1975—, UN Singers, 1975, Bklyn. Heights Symphony, 1978-82, S.W. Fla. Symphony, 1986-90, Champlain Islands Symphony, 1988—; founder, music dir. Symphony of N.Y., Aware, N.Y., 1971-74, Internat. Yoga Symphony, Can. and N.Y., 1973; founder Crossover; apptd. prin. guest condr. Ctrl. Symphony, Beijing, People's Republic of China; contbg. author: UNESCO Cultures; author: (guest editls.) Newsweek mag., 1980, Christian Sci. Monitor, 1981, N.Y. Times, 1982; editor: Citibank AWARE Playbill; exec. prodr.: (TV film/music video) Ode to Joy, 1988; author: Einstein's Violin: A Conductor's Notes on Music, Physics and Social Change, 2005. Chmn. UN Coord. Com. for Nongovtl. Orgns., 1990—; elected chmn. cultural com. City of Pompano Beach, 1999. Served to staff sgt. USAAF. Recipient Eleanor Roosevelt Man of Vision award, 1994, N.Y.C. Mayor's award, 1975, Internat. Music Therapist award, 1993; Maestro Joseph Eger Day named in his honor, Pompano Beach, 1999. Mem. Nat. Assn. Am. Condrs. and Composers (program chmn. 1965-67), Acad. Ind. Scholars. Home Phone: 954-782-9703. Personal E-mail: suneger@bellsouth.net.

EGGAN, KEVIN C., molecular and cellular biology professor, researcher; BS with Distinction in Molecular Biology, U. Ill., Urbana-Champaign, 1996; PhD in Biology, MIT, 2003. Postdoctoral fellow Whitehead Inst. for Biomedical Rsch., 2002—03; pre-doctoral fellow Nat. Inst. Child Health and Human Develop., Bethesda, Md.; junior fellow, dept. molecular and cellular biology Harvard Soc. Fellow, 2003; asst. prof., dept. molecular and cellular biology Harvard U., 2005. Spkr. in field; asst. investigator Stowers Med. Inst., 2006—. Contbr. articles to profl. jours. Named one of Brilliant 10, Popular Sci. mag., 2005; Basil O'Connor Scholar, March of Dimes, MacArthur Fellow, John D. and Catherine T. MacArthur Found., 2006. Avocation: French cooking. Office: Harvard U 437 Fairchild 7 Divinity Ave Cambridge MA 02138 Office Phone: 617-496-5611. Office Fax: 617-496-8116. Business E-Mail: eggan@mcb.harvard.edu.

EGGENBERGER, ANDREW JON, federal agency administrator; b. Harlowton, Mont., May 8, 1938; s. Andrew D. and Gladys E. Eggenberger. BS, Carnegie Mellon U., 1961, PhD, 1967; MS, Ohio State U., 1963. Prof. U. S.C., Columbia, 1967-72; project mgr. D'Appolonia Cons. Engrs., Pitts., 1972-84; program dir. NSF, Washington, 1984-89; chmn. Def. Nuclear Facilities Safety Bd., Washington, 1989—. Fellow Marshall Space Flight Ctr., Huntsville, Ala., 1969, Lewis Rsch. Ctr., Cleve., 1967, 68; rsch. engr. Boeing Co., Seattle, 1961-63. Recipient Ralph R. Teetor award Soc. Automotive Engrs., 1968. Mem. AIAA, Am. Nuclear Soc., Earthquake Engring. Rsch. Inst., Sigma Alpha Epsilon. Lutheran. Avocations: auto racing, flying. Office: Def Nuclear Facilities Safety Bd 625 Indiana Ave NW Ste 700 Washington DC 20004-2901

EGGER, ERICK, veterinarian; BS, Colo. State U., 1973; DVM, Colo. Stete U., 1975. Diplomate Am. Coll. Veterinary Surgeons. Intern, small animals Purdue U.; resident, small animal surgery U. Mo.; asst. prof. veterinary clin. sci. Iowa State U., 1975—82; assoc. prof. Colo. State U., 1982—97, affiliate prof., dept. clin. scis. and dept. mechanical engring., 1997—, assoc. prof., small animal orthop. surgery, dept. clin. scis., 2004—. Sabbatical work Orthop. Biomechanics Lab., Mayo Clinic, 1990; worked with Surgical Referral Svcs., Loveland; owner Veterinary Orthop. Consulting. Contbr. articles to profl. jours. Mem.: Orthop. Rsch. Soc., Am. Animal Hosp. Assn., Calif. Veterinary Med. Assn., AVMA. Achievements include outfitting a dog named Sally, stray from Kuwait, with a prosthetic leg that is implanted in her bone, rather than attached externally to the leg stump. Office: Dept Clin Scis Coll Veterinary Medicine & Biomedical Scis Colorado State University Fort Collins CO 80523-1678 Office Phone: 970-297-1274. Office Fax: 970-297-1275.*

EGGER, TERRANCE C.Z., publishing executive; b. Rock Island, Ill. m. Renuka Egger; children: Anthony, Ali, Danny. B., Augustana Coll., Sioux Falls, SD; M. in Speech Communication, San Diego State U. V.p. adv. Tucson Newspapers, 1992—96; gen. mgr. Post-Dispatch, 1996—2006; pub. St. Louis Post-Dispatch, LLC, 1999—2006, pres., 2000—06; pres., pub. & CEO Cleveland (Ohio) Plain Dealer, 2006—. Holder mktg. positions, adv. positions Copley Newspapers; tchr. coll. comm. courses, Calif. Office: Cleveland Plain Dealer 1801 Superior Ave NE Cleveland OH 44114-2198 Office Phone: 216-999-4216. Office Fax: 216-999-6354. E-mail: tegger@plaind.com.*

EGGERS, DAVE, fiction writer, magazine editor; b. Chgo., Mar. 12, 1970; m. Vandela Vida; 1 child, October Adelaide Eggers Vida. BA, U. Ill., Urbana Champaign. Former writer, editor Salon.com; founder, editor, contbr. McSweeney's Internet Tendency (now McSweeney's Publishing House); co-founder, tchr. 826 Valencia Sch., San Francisco, 2002—; creator The Believer, Wholphin. Contbr. articles to numerous publ. incl. New Yorker, Salon.com, New York Times, New York Mag., The Paris Review; author: A Heartbreaking Work of Staggering Genius, 2000 (NY Times Book Review Editor's Choice, 2000, Pulitzer Prize finalist, 2001, Book Yr., LA Times, San Francisco Chronicle, Wash. Post, Time Mag., 2000), What's The What, 2006, You Shall Know our Velocity!, 2002 (Independent Book award, 2003), (short story collection) How We are Hungry, 2004, (nonfiction) Surviving Justice: America's Wrongfully Convicted and Exonerated, 2005; co-author (with Scott Turow): Teachers Have it Easy: The Big Sacrifices and Small Salaries of America's Teachers, 2005; author: (sports book) The Thinking Fan's Guide to the World Cup, 2006; editor: Best American Non-required Reading Series, 2007; author: (humor books) Giraffes? Giraffes!, Your Disgusting Head, 2004, Animals in the Ocean, In Particular the Giant Squid, 2006, (short stories) Zoetrope: All-Story, 2003. Recipient Addison Metcalfe award, AAAL, 2001, Fiction award, Nat. Mag. Awards, Am. Soc. Mag. Editors, 2007. Home: c/o 826 Valencia 826 Valencia St San Francisco CA 94110 Office Phone: 416-642-5905.*

EGGERS, GEORGE WILLIAM NORDHOLTZ, JR., anesthesiologist, educator; b. Galveston, Tex., Feb. 22, 1929; s. George William Nordholtz and Edith (Sykes) E.; m. Mary Futrell, Dec. 30, 1955; children: Carol Ann, George William. BA, Rice U., Tex., 1949; MD, U. Tex., Galveston, Tex., 1953. Diplomate Am. Bd. Anesthesiology. Instr. dept. anesthesiology, U. Tex., Galveston, Tex., 1956-59; asst. prof. dept. anesthesiology, U. Tex., Galveston, Tex., 1959-61; assoc. prof. dept. anesthesiology, U. Mo., 1961-67; prof. dept anesthesiology U. Mo., 1967—94, acting chmn. dept. anesthesiology, 1969, chmn. dept. anesthesiology, 1970-94, prof. emeritus, 1994—2001. Vis. instr. USAF Hosp., Lackland AFB, San Antonio, 1956-61; vis. rsch. prof. dept. anesthesiology Northwestern U. Med. Sch., Chgo., 1968-69; rsch. assoc. Space Sci. Rsch. Ctr., U. Mo., 1965-66. Contbr. over 50 articles to profl. jours. Recipient Ashbel Smith Disting. Alumnus Award U. Tex., 1993. Mem. Am. Soc. Anesthesiology (bd. dirs. 1979-86, v.p. 1986-89, 1st v.p. 1990, pres. elect 1991, pres. 1992), Am. Coll. Anesthesiology (bd. govs., 1965-74, chmn. bd. govs., 1973), Soc. Acad. Anesthesiology Chmn. (pres. 1971), Assn. Am. Med. Colls. (adminstrv. bd. coun. acad. socs. 1976-79), Mo. Soc. Anesthesiologists (pres. 1970, Disting. Svc. Award 2001), Tex. Gulf Coast Anesthesiology Soc. (v.p. 1960), Boone County Med. Soc. (pres. 1988), Am. Bd. Anesthesiology (assoc. examiner 1968, joint coun. with Am. Soc. Anesthesiology on in-tng. exams.), Acad. Anesthesiology (pres. 1995, Citation of Merit 1997), Accreditation Coun. Grad. Med. Edn. (mem. residency rev. com. for anesthesiology 1989-94), Anesthesia Found. (trustee 1993-2003), Jefferson Club of U. Mo., Alpha Omega Alpha, Mu Delta, Sigma Xi. Republican. Roman Catholic. Avocations: hunting, astronomy, magic, photography, shooting. Home: 1509 Woodrail Ave Columbia MO 65203-0931 Office: U Mo Dept Anesthesiology 1 Hospital Dr Dept Columbia MO 65201-5276 E-mail: nordholtz@aol.com.

EGGERS, JAMES WESLEY, executive search consultant; b. Des Moines, Feb. 7, 1925; s. Paul William and Opal Imo (Cardiff) E.; m. Marjorie Mardell Freel, Aug. 2, 1947; children: James S., Barbara Bucher, Mark D. Grad., Knoxville High Sch., 1943. Farmer, Knoxville, Iowa, 1948-55; sales rep. Iowa Power & Light Co., Des Moines, 1953-60, Cedar Rapids, Iowa, 1960-62; sales exec. Thomas D. Murphy Co., Red Oak, Iowa, 1962-67; pres., owner Eggers Cos., Omaha, 1967—. Bd. dirs. Nebr. State Bank, Omaha; owner, mgr. Exec. Realty and Mgmt. Co., Omaha, 1979—. Bd. dirs. local Meth. Ch., Nebr. Meth. Hosp. Found.; chmn. local dist. George Bush for Pres. campaign, Nebr., 1988; chmn. State of Nebr. Merit Coun., Lincoln, 1979-83; mem. nat. adv. cabinet Guideposts, Pawling, N.Y.; chmn. and mem. various civic bds. Mem. Nebr. Assn. Pers. Cons. (pres. 1974-75), Nat. Assn. Pers. Cons. (mem. nat. com. 1979-83, cert.), Omaha C. of C. (bd. dirs. 1980-83), Rotary (bd. dirs. Omaha chpt. 1983—, sgt.-at-arms 1986-90), Masons, Shriners. Republican. Avocations: reading, travel, religious study, walking. Office: Eggers Cons Co Inc Eggers Plz 11272 Elm St Omaha NE 68144-4788 Home Phone: 402-330-5234; Office Phone: 402-333-3480. Business E-Mail: jamese@eggersconsulting.com.

EGGERS, SUSAN J., computer science educator; BA in Econs., Conn. Coll., 1965; PhD in Computer Sci., U. Calif., Berkeley, 1989. Computer scientist dept. computer sci. and math. Lawrence Berkeley Lab., 1979-83; rsch. asst. U. Calif, Berkeley, 1984-89; asst. prof. Dept. Computer Sci. and Engring. U. Wash., 1989-94, assoc. prof., 1994—99, prof., 1999—, Microsoft prof. computer sci. and engring. Lab. policy com. U. Wash., 1990-93, CSE/CE curriculum revision, 1991-92, quals evaluation com., 1992-93, computer sci. and engring. exec. com., 1993-94, grad. student evaluation com., 1993-95, grad. student recruiting, 1994-96, affiliate program chair, 1994-96, 97. Recipient Presdl. Young Investigator award NSF, 1990-95, Faculty Devel. award IBM, 1989-91, grad. fellowship, 1986-88; fellowship David and Lucile Packard Found., 1991, NSF Presdl. Faculty fellowship, 1993; numerous grants. Mem.: NAE. Office: U Wash PO Box 352350 Seattle WA 98195-2350

EGGERS, WILLIAM D., retired lawyer; b. Ft. Wayne, Ind., Apr. 9, 1944; BA, Yale U., 1966; JD, U. Pa., 1969. Bar: N.Y. 1970. Ptnr. Nixon Hargrave Devans & Doyle LLP, Rochester, NY, 1971-97; v.p., dep. gen. counsel Corning Inc., NY, 1997—98, sr. v.p., gen. counsel NY, 1998—2007. Mem. bd. dirs. Chemung Canal Trust Co., Chemung Financial Corp. Mem.: ABA.*

EGGERT, RUSSELL RAYMOND, lawyer; b. Chgo., July 28, 1948; s. Ralph A. and Alice M. (Nischwitz) E.; m. Patricia Anne Alegre, 1998. AB, U. Ill., 1970, JD, 1973; postgrad., Hague Acad. Internat. Law, The Netherlands, 1972. Bar: Ill. 1973, U.S. Supreme Ct. 1979. Assoc. U. Ill., Champaign, 1973-74; asst. atty. gen. State of Ill., Chgo., 1974-79; assoc. O'Conor, Karaganis & Gail, Chgo., 1979-83; legal counsel to Ill. atty. gen., Chgo., 1983-87; ptnr. Mayer, Brown, Rowe & Maw, LLP, Chgo., 1987—. Contbr. articles to profl. jours. Mem. ABA. Democrat. Office: Mayer Brown Rowe & Maw LLP 71 S Wacker Dr Chicago IL 60606 Office Phone: 312-701-7350. Business E-Mail: reggert@mayerbrownrowe.com.

EGGERTSEN, JOHN HALE, lawyer; b. Ann Arbor, Mich., Jan. 7, 1947; s. Claude Andrew and Nita (Wakefield) E.; m. Claire Chenoweth, July 19, 1969 (div. 1987); children: Melissa Anne, Helen Emma; m. Sharon Ingram, June 13, 1987 (div. 1994); children: Alexandria, Andrea; m. Robin Rich, Sept. 23, 1995; 1 child, Brendon Hale. BA, U. Mich., 1968; JD cum laude, U. Toledo, 1974; LLM in Taxation, NYU, 1975. Bar: Ohio 1974, Mich. 1975. Instr. Highland Park (Mich.) Sch. Dist., 1968; claims adjuster State Farm Mutual Ins. Co., Ann Arbor, Mich., 1968-70; ptnr. Honigman Miller Schwartz and Cohn, Detroit, 1975-2000; pvt. practice Ypsilanti, Mich., 2000—. Adj. prof. Wayne State U. Law Sch., Detroit, 1980-94; active Mich. Employee Benefits Conf., Detroit, 1980—. Contbr. articles to profl. jours. Bd. dirs. Neighborhood Svcs. Orgn., Detroit, 1992-2000, pres., 1994-97. Rsch. grantee NYU, 1974-75; Gerald Wallace scholar NYU, 1974-75. Mem. ABA (taxation sect., employee benefits com.), State Bar Ohio, State Bar Mich. Democrat. Mem. Lds Ch. Avocations: softball, bowling, reading. Office: 6270 Munger Rd Ypsilanti MI 48197-9026 Office Phone: 734-794-7100. Business E-Mail: john@jhelaw.com.

EGGINTON, EVERETT, educational administrator; b. NYC, Apr. 6, 1943; s. Hersey Benner and Mary Florence (Twining) Egginton; m. Wynn Meagher, Sept. 27, 1986; 1 child from previous marriage, William Everett. BA in Econs., Colgate U., 1965, MA in Social Sci. Edn., 1968; MS in Comparative Edn., Syracuse U., 1971, PhD in Edn. Founds., 1974; EdD (hon.), U. Francisco Gavidia, San Salvador, El Salvador, 1990. Asst. prof. U. Louisville, 1974-78, acting dir. Internat. Ctr., 1978-79, assoc. prof., 1978-84, prof. edn., 1984—2002, dir. L.Am. Edn. Ctr., 1986—2002, chair ednl. founds., 1989-2000, dir. Internat. Ctr., 1996—2002; dean Internat. and Border Programs N.Mex. State U., Las Cruces, N.Mex., 2003—. Sr. policy analyst U.S. Dept. Health and Human Svcs., Washington, 1980—81; pres. Consortium Ctrl. Am. Univs., 1990—96, sec.-gen., 1991—98; cons. Ministry of Edn. El Salvador and Honduras; cons. World Bank, US AID, 1992—; mem. exec. com. Commn. on Internat. Programs Nat. Assn. State Univs. and Land Grant Colls., 2000—; mem. bd. dirs., pres. elect NAFSA: Assn. Internat. Edcuators, 2007. Contbg. editor: U.S. Libr. of Congress, 1980—88, Handbook of Latin Am. Studies; contbr. revs. and articles to profl. publs. and encys. Recipient Fulbright Rsch./Lectr. award, El Salvador, 1999—2000; Fulbright/Hays fellow, 1973—74, Fulbright/Stanford fellow, U. Santiago Compostela Spain, 1977, HEW fellow, 1979—80. Mem.: Assn. Internat. Educators (pres. elect 2007—, bd. dirs. 2007—). Home: 5371 Redman Rd Las Cruces NM 88011 Office: New Mexico State Univ MSC 3567 PO Box 30001 Las Cruces NM 88003-8001 Office Phone: 505-646-7506. Business E-Mail: egginton@nmsu.edu.

EGGLESTON, W. NEIL, lawyer; b. July 5, 1953; BA, Duke U., 1975; JD, Northwestern U., 1978. Bar: Va. 1979, NY 1987, DC 1987. Law clk. to Hon. James Hunter III US Ct. Appeals (3rd Cir.), 1978—79; law clerk to Chief Justice Waren E. Burger US Supreme Ct., 1979—80; asst. US atty. (so. dist.) NY US Dept. Justice, 1981—87, chief appellate atty., 1986—87; assoc. counsel to Pres. The White House, Washington, 1993—94; ptnr. Howrey Simon Arnold & White, Washington, Debevoise & Plimpton LLP, Washington. Dep. chief counsel US House Rep. Select Com. Investigate Covert Arms Transactions Iran, Washington, 1987—88. Named one of 75 Best Lawyers in Washington, Washingtonian mag., 2002. Fellow: Am. Coll. Trial Lawyers; mem.: ABA (mem, white collar crimes com., criminal sect.), NY State Bar Assn., Va. State Bar Assn., DC Bar Assn. Office: Deveboise & Plimpton LLP 555 13 St NW Washington DC 20004 Business E-Mail: wneggleston@debevoise.com.*

EGIDIO, MARTHA L., real estate broker and salesman; b. Managua, Nicaragua, Feb. 16, 1970; arrived in U.S., 1988; d. Armando Detrinidad and Martha Mendoza; m. John R. Egidio, Feb. 12, 1999; children: Jennifer, Arum, Emily. Studied, So. Nev. Sch. Real Estate, 1997. Real estate agt. Coldwell Banker, Las Vegas, 1997—98, Tailored Mktg., Las Vegas, 1997—98, Properties Plus, Las Vegas, 1998—99, Am. Realty, Las Vegas, 1999—. Office: Am Realty 7331 W Charleston #160 Las Vegas NV 89117 Office Phone: 702-236-7070. Personal E-mail: pastaandbeans@aol.com.

EGIEBOR, NOSA O., engineering educator, consultant; s. Robert O. and Oteki M. Egiebor; m. Esohe E. Aloba, Dec. 26, 1999; children: Nosa S., Kyne E., Osarume W., Enina A. BS in Indsl. Chemistry, U. Benin, Nigeria, 1979; MS in Metall. Engring., U. Manchester, Eng., 1981; PhD in Metall. Engring., Queen's U., Kingston, Canada, 1985. Registered prof. engr., Assn. Profl. Engrs., Geologists and Geophysicists Alberta, 1990. Assoc. prof. U. Alta., Edmonton, Canada, 1988—93, prof., 1993—96; prof. environ. engring, Tuskegee U., Ala., 1996. Cons. MacMillan Bloedel, Pine Springs, Ala. Recipient Massie Chair of Excellence in Environ. Engring. award, US Dept. Energy, 1996, Outstanding Accomplishment in Environ. Engring. award, 1999, Outstanding Faculty Performance in Rsch. award, Tuskegee U., 2000; Alexander von Humboldt Sr. fellowship, Humboldt Found., Germany, 1994—95. Mem.: AIChE (life), Nat. Assn. Corrosion Engrs., Assn. Environ. Engring. and Sci. Profs., Am. Acad. Environ. Engrs. Achievements include patents for desulfurization of carbonaceous fuels. Avocations: travel, squash, exercise. Office: Tuskegee Univ 334 Lester H Foster Hall Tuskegee AL 36117 Business E-Mail: egiebor@tuskegee.edu.

EGIELSKI, RICHARD, illustrator; b. NYC, July 16, 1952; s. Joseph and Caroline (Rzepny) Egielski; m. Denise Saldutti, May 8, 1977. Student, Pratt Inst., Bklyn., 1970—71, Parsons Sch. Design, NYC, 1971—74. Illustrator (children's books) Moonguitars, 1974, The Porcelain Pagoda, 1976, The Letter, the Witch and the Ring, 1976, I Should Worry, I Should Care, 1979, Finders Weepers, 1980, Louis the Fish, 1980, Getting Even, 1982, It Happened in Pinsk, 1983 (Plaque award, 1985), Lower! Higher! You're a Liar!, 1984, The Little Father, 1985, Amy's Eyes, 1985, Hey, Al, 1986 (Caldecott medal, 1987), Friends Forever, 1988, Bravo Minski, 1988, The Tub People, 1989, Oh, Brother, 1989, A Telling of Tales: Five Stories, 1990, Christmas in July, 1991, The Lost Sailor, 1992, Ugh, 1992, The Tub Grandfather, 1993, Fire! Fire! Said Mrs. McGuire, 1995, Call Me Ahnighito, 1995, Buz, 1995 (Best Illustrated Book of 1995 by N.Y. Times), The Gingerbread Boy, 1997. Recipient Cert. of Merit, Soc. of Illustrators, N.Y.C., 1978, 1981, 1984, 1985. Avocation: playing the mandolin. Office: care Farrar Straus & Giroux 19 Union Sq W New York NY 10003-3304

EGINTON, WARREN WILLIAM, federal judge; b. Bklyn., Feb. 16, 1924; AB, Princeton U., 1948; LLB, Yale U., 1951. Bar: N.Y. 1952, Conn. 1954. Assoc. Davis Polk & Wardwell, NYC, 1951-53; ptnr. Cummings & Lockwood, Stamford, Conn., 1954-79; judge U.S. Dist. Ct., Bridgeport, Conn., 1979—. Editor-in-chief Products Liability Law Jour., 1988-93. Mem. ABA, Am. Judicature Soc., Am. Bar Found., Am. Law Inst., Conn. Bar Assn., Fed. Bar Coun., Fed. Bar Assn., Ins. Jud. Adminstrn., Jud. Leadership Devel. Coun., Internat. Jud. Acad., Fgn. Policy Assn., Raymond E. Baldwin Am. Inn of Ct. (founder, pres.). Office: US Dist Ct 915 Lafayette Blvd Ste 335 Bridgeport CT 06604-4765 Home Phone: 203-579-5819; Office Phone: 203-579-5819.

EGLAND, KATHERINE TATUM, educational consultant, director; b. Hattiesburg, Miss., Sept. 3, 1951; d. Felder Tatum and Ardessie Tatum-Eatman; m. William David Egland, Nov. 9, 1979; children: Antonio Karlos Edwards, Yolanda Makeva Egland Wilson, Yolanda Antoniette Edwards, Blanche Nekita Egland Young. Bachelor's, William Carey Coll., Hattiesburg, Miss., 1967, Master's in Edn. and Psychology, 1976. Cert. family life therapy Am. Guidance Coun., 1989. Spl. contbn. fund trustee NAACP, Balt., 1987—, nat. bd. dirs., 1997—. Cons. SPACE, Inc., Gulfport, Miss., 1986—. Author: (play book) SPACE Play for Creative Kids. Civil rights activist NAACP, Balt., 1996. Named to Wall of Tolerance, So. Poverty Law Ctr., 2004. Mem.: AAUW. Catholic. Achievements include development of early childhood education cirriculum. Avocations: travel, reading, art. Home: 605 Rosemary Dr Gulfport MS 39507 Office: SPACE Inc 49 Hardy Ct #116 Gulfport MS 39507 Home Phone: 228-896-5848; Office Phone: 228-617-0891.

EGLEE, CHARLES HAMILTON, scriptwriter, film and television producer; b. Boston, Nov. 27, 1951; s. Donald Read and Nancy (Hamilton) E.; m. Madeline Dalton, Feb. 29, 1984; children: Blythe Dalton, Eli Hamilton. BA in English, Yale U., 1974. Teaching asst. Yale U., New Haven, 1976; producer, writer for film Deadly Eyes Warner Bros., LA, 1982; story editor for TV series St. Elsewhere MTM Prodns., Studio City, Calif., 1984-86; exec. story cons. for TV series Moonlighting ABC Circle Films, LA, 1986-87, prodr. for TV series Moonlighting, 1987-89; prodr. 20th Century Fox TV, 1989-91; writer, co-exec. producer "Civil Wars" Steven Bochco Prodns., 1991-93; writer L.A. Law, 1992; co-creator, exec. producer The Byrds of Paradise (Steven Bochco Prodns.), 1993-94; co-exec. producer N.Y.P.D. Blue (Steven Bochco Prodns.), 1994-95; co-creator, exec. prodr. Murder One (Steven Bochco Prodns.), 1995-97, Total Security (Steven Bochco Prodns.), 1997-98; co-creator, exec. prodr. TV series Dark Angel Cameron-Eglee Prodns., 1999—2002; writer, exec. prodr. The Shield, FX, 2003—. Story editor (St. Elsewhere episode) Bye George, 1985 (Humanitas prize); co-writer (St. Elsewhere episode) Haunted, 1986 (Emmy nomination, Salute to Excellence Award nominee NAACP 1986), (Moonlighting episode) I Am Curious, Maddie, 1987 (Emmy nomination), N.Y.P.D. Blue, 1994 (Emmy award for best drama), Murder One, 1996 (People's Choice award for best new drama, Emmy nomination, best writing in one hour drama, pilot episode 1996, Golden Globe nomination 1996, best fgn. drama Brit. Acad. Film and TV, 1996, nominee Best Drama award Writers Guild Am., 1996), Dark Angel, 2001 (People's Choice award for best new drama 2001), The Shield (Peabody award 2005). Mem. Acad. TV Arts and Scis., Writers Guild Am., Yale U. Alumni Fund, Mory's Assn. (New Haven). Democrat. Avocations: sailing, skiing, pottery, gardening, dance.

EGLY, SHARON KAY, speech pathology/audiology services professional, director; b. Decatur, Ind., May 28, 1954; d. Dale E. and Lorena Mankey; m. Carl C. Egly, June 17, 1972; children: Katrina Renee Jones, Keith Allan. LPN, Ft. Wayne Cmty. Sch. Practical Nursing, Ind., 1979; BS, Ind. U. Purdue U., Fort Wayne, 1990; MA in Tchg., Ind. U., Bloomington, 1992. Continuing lectr., dir. speech and hearing clinic Ind. U. Purdue U., Ft. Wayne, 2002—. Office: Indiana UnivPurdue Univ 2102 E Coliseum Blvd Fort Wayne IN 46805 Home Phone: 260-493-7012; Office Phone: 260-481-6952. Business E-Mail: eglys@ipfw.edu.

EGNACZAK, RAYMOND CHARLES, design educator, graphics designer; b. Olean, NY, Aug. 11, 1951; s. Raymond Keith Egnaczak and Evelyn Unger. BS in Graphic Design, SUNY, Buffalo, 1976; MFA, La. Tech. U., Ruston, 1984. Asst. prof. Northwestern State U., Natchitoches, La., 1984—86; asst. prof. art U. Wyo., Laramie, 2003—, Black Hills State U., Spearfish, SD, 1991—94; art dir. Wild Hare Studio, Kansas City, Mo., 1994—96; creative dir. Banik Creative, Great Falls, Mont., 1996—97; sr. art dir. Wood Comms., Madison, Wis., 1997—2002. Cons., designer Wyo. State Prison Assn., Laramie, 2003—. Exhibitions include Off the Sq., Madison, 2000, Ctr. Visual Arts, Wausau, Wis., 2001, 2002, Foundry Art Show, St. Charles, Mo., 2005, Limner Gallery, NYC, 2005, Plano Art Assn., Tex., 2005. Mem. com. Wyo. Territorial Hist. Assn., Laramie, 2006—; bd. dirs. Eppson Sr. Ctr., Laramie, 2006—. Named Outstanding Instr. of Yr., Northwestern State U., 1986; recipient Addy award, Am. Advt. Fedn., 1997, 1998, 2005; grantee, US Dept. Commerce, 1996. Mem.: AAUP, Coll. Art Asns. Avocations: digital art, illustrating, raising free-range livestock.

EGOLF, PETER WILLIAM, physicist; b. Zurich, Switzerland, Aug. 26, 1953; s. Willi Arnold and Eileen Jean (Pickford) E.; m. Hildegard Klara Zett, Sept. 9, 1983; children: Seraina Patricia, Aaron Peter. Ing. Höhere Tech. Lehranstalt, Lucerne State Coll. Engring., Switzerland, 1977; diploma in Physics Eidgenössische Tech. Hochschule, Swiss Fed. Inst. Tech., Zurich, 1984, D Natural Scis., 1990. Cert. engr., physics. Apprentice Sulzer AG, Aarau, Switzerland, 1969-73, heating designer, 1973-74, rsch. fellow Winterthur, Switzerland, 1985-87; head lab. Hesco PG, Rüti, Switzerland, 1977-78; asst. Swiss Fed. Inst. Tech., Zurich, 1984-85, 87-90; rsch. fellow Swiss Fed. Labs. Materials Testing and Rsch., Dubendorf, Switzerland, 1990-2000; leader numerics divsn. Inst. Génie Thermique, U. Applied Scis. of Western Switzerland, Yverdon-les-Bains, 2000—. Inventor difference-quotient turbulence model, 1994, (with H. Manz) new melting/freezing model, 1994, (with H. Manz) translucent solar glass storage wall, 1992, new law of near-wall turbulence, 2000, (with G. Courret) condensing unit for air conditioning, 2002, (with A. Kitanovsky) Magnetocaloric Refrigerator and Heat Pump, Magnetocaloric Electricity Generator, 2005 With Swiss Army, 1973. Recipient Rsch. and Innovation Exhbn. award Swiss Fed. Inst. Tech., Zurich, 1988, Swiss Tech. award, Solothurn, 1996, Spl. prize Swiss Bank Soc., Zurich, 1996, Asea Brown Boveri Ltd., 2006, Swiss Fed. Office of Energy, 2006, Swiss Tech. award, 2006 Mem. Internat. Inst. Refrigeration (pres. working party on "magnetic refrigeration"), Swiss Phys. Soc., Swiss Soc. Refrigeration, Internat. Inst. Refrigeration (com. B2 mem). Avocations: fistball, drawing, philosophy, reading, travel. Home: Alte Wildeggerstrasse 5 5702 Niederlenz (Aargau) Switzerland Office: U Applied Scis Western Switzerland 1401 Yverdon-les-Bains Switzerland Fax: 41 24 557 75 79. E-mail: peter.egolf@heig-vd.ch, peter.egolf@freesurf.ch.

EGOYAN, ATOM, film director; b. Cairo, July 19, 1960; arrived in Can., 1962; s. Joseph and Shushan (Devletian) E.; m. Arsinee Khanjian; 1 child, Arshile. BA in Internat. Rels. with honours, U. Toronto, 1982; PhD (hon.), Trinity Coll., U. Toronto, U. Victoria. Dir. Ego Film Arts, Toronto, 1982—. Films shown at internat. film festivals of Sydney, Birmingham, Melbourne, Valladolid, Picadilly, Cleve., Berlin, Hong Kong, Locarno, Melbourne, Jerusalem, London, LA, Miami, Turin, Cairo, Antwerp, Montreal, Uppsala, Ghent, Chgo., Sao Paulo, NYC, Edinburgh, San Francisco, Rotterdam, Retrospective at Pompidou Ctr., Paris, 2007, others. Writer, dir., prodr. (feature films) Next of Kin, 1984 (Gold Ducat award Mannheim Internat. Film Week 1984), Family Viewing, 1987 (Internat. Critics award 1988, Best Feature Film award Uppsala, Priz Alcan, Festival du Nouveau Cinema, Montreal), Speaking Parts, 1989 (best screenplay prize Vancouver Internat. Film Festival), The Adjuster, 1991 (spl. prize of jury Moscow Film Festival, Golden Spike award Valladolid Film Festival), Calendar, 1993 (prix Berlin Internat. Film Festival), Exotica, 1994 (Internat. Film Critics award Cannes Film Festival 1994, Prix de la Critique award for best fgn. film 1994, Acad. award nominee), Salome Canadian Opera Co., 1996, 2002, Houston Grand Opera, 1997, The Sweet Hereafter, 1997 (Grand Prix, Internat. Critics prize Cannes Film Festival 1997, Acad. award nominee), Elsewhereless, 1998, Dr. Ox's Experiment, 1998, Felicia's Journey, 1999, Ararat, 2002 (Special Recognition for freedom expression, Nat. Bd. Rev., 2002, Genie for Best Motion Picture, Acad. Can. Cinema and TV, 2002, Golden Apricot Grand Prix 2004), Samuel Beckett's Krapp's Last Tape, 2000, Where the Truth Lies, 2005, Die Walkure/Wagner's Der Ring des Nibelungen, Can. Opera Co., 2004, Remount, 2006, EH JOE, interpretation of Samuel Beckett's teleplay for the stage, Dublin and London, 2006 (Best Dir. award Irish Times 2007). Recipient Officer Order Can., other numerous awards and nominations for awards. Avocation: classical guitar. Office: Ego Film Arts 80 Niagara St Toronto ON Canada M5V 1C5 E-mail: questions@egofilmarts.com.

EGUCHI, MIHARU, chemist, researcher; b. Tokyo, Apr. 25, 1978; PhD, Tokyo Met. U., 2006. Rsch. scientist Tokyo Met. U., 2004—06, Pa. State U., University Park, 2006—. Recipient Poster prize, Internat. Conf. Photochemistry, 2005, Oral Presentation prize, Chem. Soc. Japan, 2005.

EGUCHI, YASU, artist; b. Japan, Nov. 30, 1938; came to U.S., 1967; s. Chihaku and Kiku (Koga) E.; m. Anita Phillips, Feb. 24, 1968. Student, Horie Art Acad., Japan, 1958-65. Exhibited exhbns., Tokyo Mus. Art, 1963, 66, Santa Barbara Mus. Art, Calif., 1972-74, 85, Everson Mus. Art, Syracuse, N.Y., 1980, Nat. Acad. Art, N.Y.C., 1980—; one-man shows include Austin Gallery, Scottsdale, Ariz., 1968-87, Joy Tash Gallery, Scottsdale, 1989-99, Greystone Galleries, Cambria, Calif., 1969, 70, 72, Copenhagen Galleries, Calif., 1970-78, Charles and Emma Frye Art Mus., Seattle, 1974, 84, 98, Hammer Galleries, N.Y.C., 1977, 79, 81, 93, 2001, 2002, City of Heidenheim, Germany, 1980, Artique Ltd., Anchorage, 1981—, Heidenheim Mus. Art, 2000; pub. and pvt. collections, Voith Gmbh, Germany, City of Giengen and City of Heidenheim, Germany, represented, Deer Valley, Utah, Hunter Resources, Santa Barbara, Am. Embassy, Paris, Charles and Emma Frye Art Mus., Seattle, Nat. Acad. Art; author: Der Brenz Entlang, 1980; author: Yasu Eguchi, Kunstmuseum Heidenheim, 2000; contbr. to jours in field. Active Guide Dogs for the Blind, San Raphael, Calif., 1976, City of Santa Barbara Arts Coun., 1979, The Eye Bank for Sight Restoration, NY, 1981, Anchorage Arts Coun., 1981, Santa Barbara Mus. Natural History, 1989, Kinder & Kunst Artist Projecti, Heidenheim, Forest Lawn Mus., 2006. Recipient Selective Artist award Yokohama Citizen Gallery, 1965; recipient Artist of Yr. award Santa Barbara Arts Council, 1979, Hon. Citizen award City of Heidenheim, 1980, The Adolph and Clara Obrig prize NAD, 1983, Cert. of Merit NAD, 1985, 87. Home: PO Box 30206 Santa Barbara CA 93130-0206

EHIGIE, BENJAMIN ODION, radiographer, technologist; b. Benin-City, Edo, Nigeria, June 14, 1959; arrived in US, 1987; s. John E. and Amen E. Egharevba; m. Colett D. Burnett, Mar. 23, 1991; m. Ivie Ehigie, Dec. 29, 1993; m. Benny Ehigie, May 3, 2000. Nat. Edn. Cert., U. Abraka, Nigeria, 1984; AAS, Malcolm X Coll., Chgo., 1996. Radiographer Chgo. Agy., 1997—2000; spl. procedures technologist Provident Hosp. Chgo., 2000—. Mem. Akugbe-Ortin Club, Chgo., 2003—04. Avocations: photography, travel, sports.

EHLE, JENNIFER, actress; b. Winston-Salem, NC, Dec. 29, 1969; d. John Ehle and Rosemary Harris; m. Michael Ryan; 1 child, George. Actress (Broadway plays) The Real Thing, 2000 (Theatre World award, 2000, Tony award best actress in a play, 2000, Variety Club Showbusiness award best stage actress, 2000), Design for Living, 2001, The Coast of Utopia, 2007 (Tony award best featured actress in a play, 2007), (films) Backbeat, 1994, Paradise Road, 1997, Wilde, 1997, Bedrooms and Hallways, 1998, The Adventures of Young Indiana Jones: Adventures in the Secret Service, 1999, This Year's Love, 1999, Sunshine, 1999 (Golden Satellite award, 2001), Possession, 2002, The River King, 2005, Alpha Male, 2006, Before the Rains, 2007, (TV films) Micky Love, 1993, The Maitlands, 1993, Self Catering, 1994, Pleasure, 1994, La Recreation, 1994, Beyond Reason, 1995, (TV miniseries) The Camomile Lawn, 1992 (Radio Times award best newcomer, 1992), Pride and Prejudice, 1995, Melissa, 1997.*

EHLE, JOHN MARSDEN, JR., writer; b. Asheville, NC, Dec. 13, 1925; s. John M. and Gladys (Starnes) E.; m. Gail Oliver, Aug. 30, 1952 (div. Apr. 1967); m. Rosemary Harris, Oct. 22, 1967; 1 child, Jennifer Anne. BA, U. NC, 1949; DFA (hon.), NC Sch. Arts, 1981; LHD (hon.), Berea Coll., Ky., 1986, U. NC, Asheville, 1987; DLitt (hon.), U. NC, Chapel Hill, 1990. Faculty U. NC, Chapel Hill, 1951—63; spl. asst. to Gov. Terry Sanford, Raleigh, NC, 1963—64; program officer Ford Found., NYC, 1964—65. Spl. cons. Duke U., 1976-80; co-founder NC Gov.'s Sch., NC Sch. Arts, NC Sch. Sci. and Maths. Author: (novels) Move Over, Mountain, 1957, Kingstree Island, 1959, Lion on the Hearth, 1961, The Land Breakers, 1964, The Road, 1967, Time of Drums, 1970, The Journey of August King, 1971, The Changing of the Guard, 1975, The Winter People, 1981, Last One Home, 1983, The Widows Trial, 1989, (biographies) The Free Men, 1965 (Mayflower Soc. cup), The Survivor, 1968, Shepherd of the Streets, 1960, Dr. Frank, Living with Frank Porter Graham, 1993, (non-fiction) The Cheeses and Wines of England and France, with Notes on Irish Whiskey, 1972, Trail of Tears: The Rise and Fall of the Cherokee Nation, 1988; pub. also in several fgn. countries; (screenplay) The Journey of August King, 1996. Apptd. by Pres. Johnson to White House Group for Domestic Affairs, 1964-66, Nat. Coun. Humanities, 1966-70; exec. com. Nat. Book Com., NYC, 1972-75, NC Sch. Arts Found., Winston-Salem, 1970-75; awards commn. State of NC, 1982-93, Mary Reynolds Babcock Found., Winston-Salem, 1985-89; pres. Anne C. Stouffer Found., 1970-80; pres. Awards Com. Edn., 1980-90. With AUS, 1944-46. Recipient Walter Raleigh prize for fiction NC Dept. Cultural Affairs, 1964, 67, 70, 75, 84, State of NC award for lit., 1972, Gov.'s award for Disting. Meritorious Svc., 1978, Lillian Smith prize Southern Regional Coun., 1982, Disting. Alumnus award U. NC, Chapel Hill, 1984, Thomas Wolfe Meml. award Western NC Hist. Assn., 1984, W.D. Weatherford award Berea Coll., 1985, Caldwell award NC Humanities Coun., 1995; named to NC Lit. Hall of Fame, 1997 Mem. PEN, Authors League, Century Club (NYC). Democrat. Methodist. Home: 125 Westview Dr NW Winston Salem NC 27104

EHLERS, KATHRYN HAWES (MRS. JAMES D. GABLER), physician; b. Richmond Hill, NY, Aug. 22, 1931; d. Albert and Edna (Hawes) E.; m. James D. Gabler, Dec. 5, 1959; children— Jennifer K., Emily E. AB, Bryn Mawr Coll., 1953; MD, Cornell U.; MD (Hannah E. Longshore Meml. Med. scholar 1953-57, Elsie Strang L'Esperance scholar 1956-57), 1957. Diplomate: Am. Bd. Pediatrics, Am. Bd. Pediatric Cardiology. Intern N.Y. Hosp., 1957-58, asst. resident pediatrics, 1958-60; fellow in pediatric cardiology Cornell U. Med. Coll., NYC, 1960-64, instr. pediatrics, 1964-66, asst. prof., 1966-70, asso. prof. pediatrics, 1970-75, prof., 1975-96, prof. emeritus, 1996—, vice-chmn. pediat., 1988-96; practice medicine specializing in pediat. cardiology NYC, 1958-96. Contbr. articles to profl. jours. Research trainee N.Y. Heart Assn., 1960-62, Am. Heart Assn., 1962-64. Fellow Am. Coll. Cardiology; mem. N.Y. Heart Assn., Am. Heart Assn., Harvey Soc., Am. Pediatric Soc., Am. Acad. Pediatrics, Alpha Omega Alpha.

EHLERS, VERNON JAMES, congressman; b. Pipestone, Minn., Feb. 6, 1934; m. Johanna Meulink, 1958; children: Heidi, Brian, Marla, Todd. Student, Calvin Coll.; AB in Physics, U. Calif., Berkeley, 1956, PhD in Physics, 1960. Tchg. asst. U. Calif., Berkeley, 1956-57, rsch. asst., 1957-60, lectr. in physics, 1960-66; prof. physics Calvin Coll., 1966-83; mem. Mich. State Ho. of Reps., 1983-85, Mich. State Senate, 1985-94, pres. pro tem, 1991-94; mem. U.S. Congress from 3d Mich. dist., 1994—; chmn. Joint Com. Libr. Congress; mem. transp. and infrastructure com., sci. com., edn. and workforce com., house adminstrn. com. Mem. Gov. Milliken's Task Force on Environ. Problems, 1977, Kent County Rep. Exec. Com., Kent County Bd. Commrs., 1975-83, chmn., 1979-82, Mich. Toxic Substance Control Commn., 1982; asst. floor leader Mich. State Ho. of Reps., 1983-85 Contbr. NATO Rsch. fellow U. Heidelberg, Germany, 1961-62, Sci. Faculty fellow NSF, Joint Insts. for Lab. Astrophysics, U. Colo. 1971-72, fellow Calvin Coll. Ctr. for Christian Scholar, 1977-78; recipient Disting. Svc. award Assn. Independent Colleges and Universities, 1986, Outstanding Public Svc. award Mich. Paralyzed Veterans of Am., 1988, Presidential award Mich. Recreation and Park Assn., 1989, Mich. Environ. Legis. of Yr. Mich. Enviorn. Defense, 1990, Outstanding Public Svc. award Mich. Public Health Assn., 1991, Outstanding Citizen award Lake County Riverside Property Assn., 1992, Legis. Leadership aawrd Triangle Coalition Sci. and Tech. Edn., 2004, Leadership award Nat. Marine Sanctuary Found., 2005. Mem.: Am. Assn. Phys. Tchrs., Am. Phys. Soc., AAAS. Republican. Christian Reformed Ch. Home: 1848 Morningside Dr SE Grand Rapids MI 49506-5121 Office: US Congress 1714 Longworth House Ofc Bldg Washington DC 20515-2203 also: Gerald R Ford Federal Bdlg Rm 166 110 Michigan St Grand Rapids MI 49503-2313 Office Phone: 202-225-3831, 616-451-8383. Office Fax: 202-225-5144, 616-454-5630.*

EHLING, ELIZABETH SULLIVAN, psychotherapist, marriage and family therapist; b. Hornell, NY, Dec. 9, 1926; d. Henry Bissell and Florence Clarra Masterman Sullivan; m. Ernest Henry Ehling, Feb. 5, 1956; children: Deborah Elizabeth, Ernest Henry Jr. BA, U. Rochester, NY, 1948; MDiv, Union Theol. Sem., NYC, 1952; cert., William Aladsa White Inst., NYC, 1957, Blanton Peale Grad. Inst., 1957. Lic. marriage and family therapist NJ, 70. Parish assoc. Presbyn. Ch. Mission Field, Mt. Sterling, Ill., 1949; min. of edn. Ch. of the Master, Halem, NY, 1952—56; supr. pastoral counselors Inst. Religion and Health, NYC, 1957—59; pastoral psychotherapist Creative Living Counseling, Allendale, NJ, 1960—2005, assoc. dir., 1960—99, dir. grad. program, 1976—2002. Pvt. practice, Franklin Lakes, NJ, 1973—2007. Mem. Presbytery of Palisados, 1958—; mem. adv. bd. After Breast Cancer, 1957—. Recipient Dist. Alumnae award, Blanton-Peale Grad. Inst., NYC, 1988, Dist. Contbn. award, Creative Living Counseling Ctr. Fellow: Am. Assn. Marriage and Family Therapists; mem.: Am. Assn. Pastoral Counselors (chair cert. com. ea. region 1958—97, Dist. Contbn. award). Presbyterian. Avocations: swimming, sailing. Home: 1 Quiney Ct Freehold NJ 07728

EHLINGER, RALPH JEROME, lawyer; b. Oconto, Wis., Mar. 22, 1941; s. Jerome Nicholas and Margaret Ann (Otradovec) E.; m. Nancy L. McKinley, Dec. 26, 1966 (div. Oct. 1986); children: Nicholas Joseph, Martha Johanna; m. Mary Verstegen, Sept. 25, 1987; children: Autumn V., Andrea V., Jessa V., Jenna V. BA in Philosophy, St. Paul Sem., 1963; JD, Georgetown U., Washington, DC, 1968. Bar: Wis. 1968, DC 1988, US Dist. Ct. (ea. dist.) Wis. 1969, US Dist. Ct. (we. dist.) Wis. 1977, US Ct. Appeals (7th cir.) 1983, US Supreme Ct. 1986, US Ct. Appeals (4th cir.) 1988. Ptnr. Meissner, Tierney, Ehlinger & Whipp, Milw., 1968-86; pvt. practice Milw., 1986-87; counsel Casson, Harkins & LaPallo, Washington, 1987-88; pres. Ehlinger & Krill, SC, Milw., 1988-99, Ehlinger Law Office, Milw., 2000—; adj. prof. law Marquette U. Law Sch., 1999—. Articles editor: The Georgetown Law Jour., 1967-68 (Outstanding Editor 1968); editor-in-chief: The Milwaukee Lawyer, 1982-84. Trustee Wis. Sch. Profl. Psychology, Milw., 1990-93; bd. pres. Grand Ave Club, Milw., 1990-92, Mental Health Assn., Milw., 1992-93; dir. Centro Legal Por Derechos Humanos, 1996-2001; mem. planning commn. Town of Richfield, 2002-05, chmn. 2004-05. Mem. ABA, Milw. Bar Assn. Found. (pres. 1994-97), Nordic Ski Club (life), Milw. Bar Assn. (bd. dirs. 1990-93, Lawyer of Yr. award 1997), Washington County Bar Assn. Roman Catholic. Avocations: instrumental and vocal music, cross country skiing, backpacking, canoeing, poetry. Office: Ehlinger Law Office W175 N 11117 Stonewood Dr Germantown WI 53022 Office Phone: 262-255-5060. Business E-Mail: ehlinger@execpc.com.

EHMANN, ANTHONY VALENTINE, lawyer; b. Chgo., Sept. 5, 1935; s. Anthony E. and Frances (Verweil) E.; m. Alice A. Avina, Nov. 27, 1959; children: Ann, Thomas, Jerome, Gregory, Rose, Robert. BS, Ariz. State U., 1957; JD, U. Ariz., 1960. Bar: Ariz. 1960, U.S. Tax Ct. 1960, U.S. Supreme Ct. 1968; CPA, Ariz.; cert. tax specialist, trusts and estates specialist. Spl. asst. atty. gen., 1961-68; mem. Ehmann and Hiller, Phoenix, 1969—2004, Fennemore Craig, Phoenix, 2004—. Rep. dist. chmn. Ariz., 1964; pres. Grand Canyon coun. Boy Scouts Am., 1987-89, mem. exec. com., 1981—, v.p. western region, 1991-99; bd. dirs. Nat. Cath. Com. on Scouting, 1995—. Recipient Silver Beaver award Boy Scouts Am., 1982, Bronze Pelican award Cath. Com. on Scouting, 1981, Silver Antelope award Boy Scouts Am., 1994. Fellow Am. Coll. Trusts and Estate Counsel; mem. State Bar Ariz. (chmn. tax sect. 1968, 69), Ctrl. Ariz. Estate Planning Coun. (pres. 1968, 69), Rotary Club, KC (grand knight Glendale, Ariz. 1964, 65), Serra Internat. (pres. Phoenix 1992-93, dist. gov. 1993-95), Knight of Holy Sepulchre, Knight of Malta, Legatus. Republican. Roman Catholic. Office: Fennemore Craig 3003 N Central Ste 2600 Phoenix AZ 85012 Office Phone: 602-916-5416. Business E-Mail: ehmann@fclaw.com.

EHMANN, WILLIAM DONALD, chemistry professor; b. Madison, Wis., Feb. 7, 1931; s. William F. and Victoria V. (Koperski) E.; m. Nancy M. Gallagher, July 16, 1955; children: William J., John M., James T., Kathleen E. BS, U. Wis., 1952, MS, 1954; PhD, Carnegie Inst. Tech., 1957. NRC-NSF rsch. assoc. Argonne Nat. Lab., Ill., 1957-58; mem. faculty U. Ky., Lexington, 1958—, asst. prof., 1958-63, assoc. prof. chemistry, 1963-66, prof., 1966-95, chmn. dept., dir. grad. studies, 1972-76, Coll. Arts and Scis. Disting. prof., 1968-69, univ. rsch. prof., 1977-78, assoc. dean for rsch. Grad. Sch., 1980-84, prof. emeritus, 1995—. Vis. prof. Ariz. State U., Tempe, 1969, Fla. State U., Tallahassee, 1972; cons. Argonne Nat. Lab., 1958-67; rsch. dir. project AEC, 1960-71, Agr. Dept., 1968-70, NASA, 1968-77, NIH, 1977-80, 84-98, DOE, 1983-85, NSF EPSCOR, 1986-91, NIST, 1993-94 Author: Radiochemistry and Nuclear Methods of Analysis, 1991; contbr. articles to profl. jours. Hon. assoc. Sanders-Brown Ctr. on Aging, 1988-95; bd. dirs. U. Ky. Rsch. Found., 1991-93; bd. dirs., exec. com. Alzheimer's Disease Rsch. Ctr., U. Ky., 1990. Recipient William D. Ehmann award Am. Nuclear Soc., 1996, Sturgill award U. Ky., 1987; Fulbright scholar; hon. fellow Australian Nat. U. Inst. Advanced Studies, Canberra, 1964-65. Fellow AAAS, Meteoritical Soc.; mem. Am. Chem.

Soc. (chmn. Lexington sect. 1963-64, Herty medal for career achievements 1994, nat. award in nuclear chemistry 1996), Ky. Acad. Scis. (bd. dirs. 1964-67, Disting. Ky. Scientist award 1982), Sigma Xi, Phi Lambda Upsilon, Phi Eta Sigma, Phi Theta Kappa. Roman Catholic. Achievements include first analysis (with others) of Apollo Mission lunar samples; research on the chemistry of meteorites, lunar samples and trace elements involvement in neurological diseases; on the etiology of Alzheimer's Disease. Home: 769 Zandale Dr Lexington KY 40502-3371 Office: U Ky 312 Chem Physics Bldg Lexington KY 40506-0055 Personal E-mail: wdehmann@att.net.

EHNTHOLT, DANIEL JAMES, chemist; b. Manchester, NH, Sept. 19, 1945; s. Daniel James Dolores (Donohue) E.; m. Eileen Marie Dunne, Aug. 14, 1971; children: Kimberly, Amy, Christopher. BS, Fordham U., 1966; PhD, SUNY, Stony Brook, 1971. Postdoctoral fellow Brandeis U., Waltham, Mass., 1971-72; asst. prof. Boston U., 1972-77, Worcester (Mass.) State Coll., 1977-78; cons. Arthur D. Little, Inc., Cambridge, Mass., 1978-84, unit mgr., 1984-91, v.p., 1991—2002; dir. Nat. Security Programs, TIAX, LLC, Cambridge, Mass., 2002—. Contbr. articles to profl. jours. Commr. Conservation Commn., Hudson, Mass., 1974-79; mem. Bd. Health, Hudson, 1981-88, 91—, chmn. 1995-98, 2000-05, 06-07. N.Y. State Regents fellow, 1962-70, German Acad. Exchange fellow Max Planck Inst., Mülheim an der Ruhr, 1974. Mem. ACS (Petroleum Rsch. fellow 1970), Am. Inst. Chemists, Nat. Sci. Tchrs. Assn., Phi Lambda Upsilon. Roman Catholic. Office: TIAX LLC 15 Acorn Park Cambridge MA 02140-2301 Office Phone: 617-498-5057. Business E-Mail: ehntholt.d@tiaxllc.com.

EHREN, CHARLES ALEXANDER, JR., lawyer, educator; b. NYC, Dec. 13, 1932; s. Charles Alexander and Alma Elise (Holmstrom) E.; m. Joan Anne Bansemer, Sept. 4, 1954. AB, Columbia U., 1954, JD, 1956. Bar: N.Y. bar 1956. Asso. firm LeBoeuf, Lamb and Leiby, NYC, 1958-67; Reginald Heber Smith fellow U. Pa. Sch. Law at Legal Aid Soc. of Westchester County (N.Y.), White Plains, 1967-68, dir. soc., 1975-77; dir. curriculum Nat. Inst. Edn. in Law and Poverty, Northwestern U., 1968-70; asso. prof. law U. Denver, 1970-74, prof., 1974-75; dean, prof. Pace U. Sch. Law, 1975-76; vis. scholar Columbia U. Sch. Law, 1976-77; dean Valparaiso U. Sch. Law, 1977-82, prof., 1977-96, prof. emeritus, 1996—. Trustee Ind. Continuing Legal Edn. Found., Ind. Bar Found., 1977-82; dir. Westchester Legal Services, 1975-77 Author: (with others) Electricity and the Environment, The Reform of Legal Institutions, 1972. Served with U.S. Army, 1956-58. Mem. Ind. State Bar Assn. (ho. of dels. 1977-82), Assn. Bar City N.Y. (exec. dir. spl. com. on electric power and environment 1971-73), ABA, N.Y. State Bar Assn., Fed. Energy Bar Assn., Soc. Am. Law Tchrs. Democrat. Lutheran. Home: 16 High Point Rd East Hampton NY 11937-1059

EHRENBARD, ROBERT, lawyer; b. N.Y.C., Aug. 20, 1925; m. Lila T. Ehrenbard, Apr. 17, 1949; children— Richard, Dan. LL.B. cum laude, Harvard U., 1951. Bar: N.Y. 1951, U.S. Dist. Ct. (so. dist.) N.Y. 1952, U.S. Ct. Appeals (2d cir.) 1952, U.S. Ct. Appeals (3d cir.) 1971, U.S. Ct. Appeals (7th cir.) 1976, U.S. Ct. Appeals (D.C. cir.) 1982, U.S. Ct. Appeals (11th cir.) 1982, U.S. Ct. Appeals (9th cir.) 1984, U.S. Supreme Ct. 1969. Law clk. U.S. Dist. Ct. (so. dist.) N.Y. 1951-53, U.S. Dist. Ct. (so. dist.) N.Y. 1954; sr. litigation ptnr. Kelley Drye & Warren, N.Y.C., 1961—. Author: Interrogatories And Document Requests, 1983. Served to lt. (j.g.) USN, 1943-46; PTO. Mem. Lawyer's Com. for Civil Rights Under Law, ABA, N.Y. State Bar Assn., Assn. Bar City N.Y. Home: 239 Central Park W New York NY 10024-6038 Office: Kelley Drye & Warren 101 Park Ave Fl 30 New York NY 10178-0062

EHRENBERG, RONALD GORDON, economist, educator; b. NYC, Apr. 20, 1946; s. Seymour and Judith G. Ehrenberg; m. Randy Ann Birch, June 29, 1967; children: Eric L., Jason H. BA in Math., SUNY, Binghamton, 1966; MA, PhD, Northwestern U., Evanston, Ill., 1970. Instr. econs. Northwestern U., Evanston, Ill., 1970; asst. prof. econs. Loyola U., Chgo., 1970—71, U. Mass., Amherst, 1971—72, assoc. prof. econs., 1972—75; assoc. prof. econs. and labor econs. Cornell U., Ithaca, NY, 1975—77, chmn. dept. labor econs., 1976—81, prof. econs. and labor econs., 1977—85; dir. rsch. NY State Sch. Indsl. and Labor Rels., 1979—95; Irving M. Ives prof. indsl. and labor rels. and econs. Cornell U., 1985—, v.p. for acad. programs, planning and budgeting, 1995—98. Staff Coun. Econ. Advisors, 1970; rsch. assoc. Nat. Bur. Econ. Rsch., 1981—; dir. Cornell Inst. Labor Mktg. Policies, 1990—98, Cornell Higher Edn. Rsch. Inst., 1998—; cons. in field. Author: Fringe Benefits and Overtime Behavior: Theory and Econometric Analysis, 1971, The Demand for State and Local Government Employees: An Economic Analysis, 1975, The Regulatory Process and Labor Earnings, 1979; author: (with R. Smith) Modern Labor Economics: Theory and Public Policy, 1982, 9th edit., 2006; author: (with others) Economic Challenges in Higher Education, 1991, Labor Markets and Integrating National Economics, 1994, Contemporary Policy Issues in Education, 1995, The American University: National Treasure of Endangered Species, 1997, Gender and Family Issues in the Workplace, 1997, Tuition Rising: Why College Costs So Much, 2000, Governing Academia, 2004, What's Happening to Public Higher Education, 2006; contbr. articles to profl. jours.; with others: Science and the University, 2007. Trustee Cornell U., 2006—; endowment study advisors bd. Nat. Assn. Coll. and Univ. Bus. Officers, 2001—04, assoc. governing bds., rsch. adv. com., 2007—. Rsch. grantee, NSF, U.S. Dept. Labor, various pvt. founds., NDEA fellow, 1969, Dissertation Yr. fellow, Woodrow Wilson Nat. Fellowship Found., 1970. Fellow: TIAA-CREF Inst., Soc. Labor Economists; mem.: AAUP (chmn. com. econ. status of profession 2002—05), Nat. Acad. Soc. Ins., Nat. Acad. Edn., Nat. Acads. (assoc.), Am. Edn. Fin. Assn., Am. Econ. Assn. (mem. exec. com. 1996—98). Office: Cornell Higher Edn Rsch Inst 385A Ives Hall E Ithaca NY 14853-3901 Business E-Mail: rge2@cornell.edu.

EHRENFELD, DAVID WILLIAM, biology professor, writer; b. NYC, Jan. 15, 1938; s. Irving and Anne Ehrenfeld; m. Joan Gardner, June 28, 1970; children: Kate, Jane, Jonathan, Samuel. BA, Harvard Coll., 1959; MD, Harvard Med. Sch., 1963; PhD, U. Fla., 1966. From asst. prof. biology to assoc. prof. biology Barnard Coll. Columbia U., NYC, 1967-74; prof. biology Rutgers U., Sch. Environ. and Biological Scis., New Brunswick, NJ, 1974—96, prof. II, 1996—. Author: Biological Conservation, 1970, Conserving Life on Earth, 1972, The Arrogance of Humanism, 1978, Beginning Again: People and Nature in the New Millennium, 1993, 1995, Swimming Lessons: Keeping Afloat in the Age of Technology, 2002; co-author (with C.K. Mack): (novels) The Chameleon Variant, 1980; founder, editor Conservation Biology, 1987—93, consulting editor, 1994—, bd. editors Ecosys. Health, 1994—, mem. adv. bd. Conservation and Society, 2002—, mem. editl. adv. bd. Conservation in Practice, 1999—2005, contbg. editor Conservation, 2005, columnist (mag.) Orion, 1989—2002; contbg. editor: (mag.) Orion, 2003—; contbr. articles to profl. and popular publs. Trustee E.F. Schumacher Soc., Great Barrington, Mass., 1979-2002, bd. founders, 2003—; bd. trustees Caribbean Conservation Corp., Gainesville, Fla., 1980—, Ednl. Found. Am., Westport, Conn., 1987-93, 98-2002. Fellow AAAS; mem. Ecol. Soc. Am., Internat. Union for the Conservation of Nature, Marine Turtle Specialist Group. Jewish. Home: 44 N 7th Ave Highland Park NJ 08904-2931 Office: Rutgers Univ Sch Environ and Biological Scis New Brunswick NJ 08901-8551 Office Phone: 732-932-9553.

EHRENFELD, ELLIE (ELVERA EHRENFELD), biologist, researcher; b. Phila., Mar. 1, 1942; m. Donald F. Summers. BA cum laude, Brandeis U., 1962; PhD in Biochemistry, U. Fla., 1967; postdoctoral student, Albert Einstein Coll. Medicine, 1967—74. Asst. to assoc. prof. dept. cell biology Albert Einstein Coll. Med.; from assoc. prof.to prof. biochemistry and biology U. Utah, 1974—92; dean sch. biol. scis. U. Calif., Irvine, 1992—97; dir. Center for Scientific Review, NIH, Bethesda, Md., 1997—2003; chief picornavirus replication, Laboratory of Infectious Diseases NIH, Bethesda, Md., 1997—. Mem. various coms. including rsch. adv. panel Walter Reed Army Inst. Rsch., exptl. virology study sect. NIH; mem. bd. sci. counselors Nat. Inst. Allergy and Infectious Diseases; cons. immunopathology lab. Scripps Inst. Med. Rsch. Recipient Bill Joklik Lectureship award, Am. Soc. Virology; scholar Nat. Sci., Brandeis U. Office: NIAID MSC 6612 6610 Rockledge Dr Bethesda MD 20892-6612

EHRENFELD, JOHN ROOS, environmental policy educator; b. Chgo., May 16, 1931; s. Louis and Alice (Roos) E.; m. Myrna A. Goodman (div.); children: Elizabeth, Thomas; m. Ruth M. Rahn Budd. SB in Chem. Engring., MIT, 1953, SCD in Chem. Engring., 1957. Dir. applied rsch. GCA Corp., Bedford, Mass., 1962-67; pres. Walden Rsch. Corp., Cambridge, Mass., 1967-75; v.p. Energy Resources Co., Cambridge, 1975-78; chmn. New Eng. River Basin Commn., Boston, 1978-81; sr. cons. Arthur D. Little, Inc., Cambridge, 1981-85, Abt Assocs., Inc., Cambridge, 1985-86; sr. rsch. assoc. MIT, Cambridge, 1987—2001; exec. dir. Internat. Soc. Indsl. Ecology, 2000—. Prin. John Ehrenfeld & Assocs., Lexington, Mass., 1986—. Co-editor Jour. Indsl. Ecology, 1996—, mem. editl. adv. bd. Environ. Sci. and Tech., 1996—2002, mem. editl. bd. Jour. Sustainable Design, 1997—2001; contbr. articles to profl. publs. Chmn. Town Dem. Com., Acton, Mass., 1960-67, Lincoln, Mass., 1968-72. 1st lt. U.S. Army, 1957-59. Recipient Lifetime Achievement award, World Resources Inst., 1999; Fulbright scholar, 1999. Mem. AIChE (Gary Leach award 1995), Am. Chem. Soc. (chmn. divsn.), Air and Wast Mgmt. Assn. Avocation: fly fishing.

EHRENHAFT, PETER DAVID, lawyer; b. Vienna, Aug. 16, 1933; came to U.S., 1940, naturalized, 1945; s. Bruno B. and Ann J. (Polacek) E.; m. Charlotte Kennedy, May 4, 1958; children: Elizabeth Ann, James Bruno, Daniel Parker. AB with honors, Columbia Coll., 1954; LLB, M Internat. Affairs with honors, Columbia U., 1957. Bar: (N.Y.) 1958, (D.C.) 1961. Motions law clk. to U.S. Ct. Appeals (D.C. cir.), 1957—58; sr. law clk. to Chief Justice U.S. Supreme Ct., 1961—62; assoc. Cox, Langford & Brown, Washington, 1962—66, ptnr., 1966—68, Fried, Frank, Harris, Shriver & Kampelman, Washington, 1968—77; dep. asst. sec., spl. counsel tariff affairs U.S. Dept. Treasury, Washington, 1977—79; ptnr. Hughes Hubbard & Reed, Washington, 1980—83, Bryan Cave, Washington, 1984—95; mem. Ablondi, Foster, Sobin & Davidow, P.C., Washington, 1995—2001, Miller & Chevalier, Chartered, Washington, 2001—03, of counsel, 2004—06; sr. counsel Harkins Cunningham LLP, Washington, 2007—. Professorial lectr. law George Washington U., 1965-72, U. Pa., 1980-85; disting. practitioner-in-residence Am. U. Law Sch., 2006; mem. faculty Salzburg (Austria) Seminar in Am. Studies Law Session, 1973; mem. Fed. Jud. Ctr. Study Group on Workload of Supreme Ct., 1971-74; mem. adv. com. U.S. Ct. Appeals (fed. cir.), 1992-96; mem. industry trade adv. com. on svcs. Dept. Commerce and U.S. Trade Rep., 1999—. Contbr. articles and revs., primarily on internat. trade, to law jours.; mem. adv. bd. Georgetown Internat. Law Jour., 1967—, Patent, Trademark and Copyright Jour., 1970—; mem. editl. bd. Internat. Legal Materials, 1977-87. Pres. bd. trustees Nat. Child Rsch. Ctr., Washington, 1976-77; mem. adv. coun. George Washington U. Med. Ctr., 1990-96. With USAF, 1958-61, USAFR, 1962-88; judge Ct. Mil. Rev., 1987-88. Mem.: ABA (mem. coun. internat. law sect. 1983—85, 1989—97, chmn. task force on legal svcs. in Japan 1991—98, liaison to Gen. Agreement on Tariffs and Trade 1992—94, vice chair 1993—94, internat. legal scholar 1994—97, vice chair transnat. practice com. 1998—2005, commn. on multijurisdictional practice 2000—02, chair transnat. practice com. 2006—, liaison internat. legal svcs. task force 2004), Am. Arbitration Assn. (panel internat. arbitrators 1994—), Washington Fgn. Law Soc. (bd. govs. 1982—92, pres. 1986—87), Am. Soc. Internat. Law, Am. Law Inst. (mem. various cons. coms.). Home: 2510 Virginia Ave NW Washington DC 20037-1904 Office: Harkins Cunningham LLP 1700 K St NW Washington DC 20006 Office Phone: 202-973-7609. Business E-Mail: pde@harkinscunningham.com.

EHRENKRANTZ, DAN, rabbi; BA magna cum laude in Religion, Tufts U.; MA in Hebrew Letters, Reconstructionist Rabbinical Coll. Ordained Rabbi Reconstructionist Rabbinical Coll. Rabbi Congregation Bnai Keshet, Montclair, NJ; pres. Reconstructionist Rabbinical Coll., 2002—, Aaron and Marjorie Ziegelman Presidential Professor. Named one of The Top 50 Rabbis in America, Newsweek Mag., 2007. Mem.: Reconstructionist Rabbinical Assn. (past pres.). Office: Reconstructionist Rabbinical Coll 1299 Church Rd Wyncote PA 19095 Fax: 215-567-6143.

EHRENKRANZ, JOEL S., lawyer; b. Newark, Mar. 25, 1935; s. George J. and Hilda (Schreiber) Ehrenkranz; m. Anne B. Bick, June 9, 1963; children: Alissa, John, Jeanne. BS in Econs., U. Pa., 1956, MBA, 1957; LLB, NYU, 1961, LLM in Taxation, 1964. CPA NY; bar: NY 1961. Acct. Peat, Marwick, Mitchell & Co., NYC, 1957-62; sr. ptnr. Ehrenkranz & Ehrenkranz, NYC, 1962—. Trustee, treas. Blythedale Children's Hosp., 1966—74; trustee, distbn. com. Fedn. Jewish Philanthropies, NYC, 1979—83, United Jewish Appeal/Fedn. Jewish Philanthropies, NYC, 1982—92; trustee Archives Am. Art, 1973—92, pres., 1984—86; trustee Whitney Mus. Am. Art, 1973—, v.p., 1973—2002, pres., 1998—2002; trustee NYU Law Sch., 1992—, chmn. investment com., 2003—05; grad. bd. Wharton Sch. U. Pa., 1985—2004; trustee, vice chmn., mem. exec. com. Mt. Sinai Med. Ctr., NYC, 1987—; trustee NYU, 1998—2001, 2003—, chmn. capital campaign, 2004—; bd. overseers Calif. Inst. Arts, 2001—05; trustee Lincoln Ctr. for the Performing Arts, 2004. Mem.: Coun. on Fgn. Rels., Century Club (White Plains, NY). Office: 375 Park Ave New York NY 10152-0002 also: Keeler Ln North Salem NY 10560 also: Mayfly Dr Wilson WY 83014

EHRENKRANZ, RICHARD ALLAN, pediatrician; b. Newark, July 28, 1946; s. Robert and Miriam (Wiskind) Ehrenkranz; married, 2000. BS in Life Scis., MIT, 1968; MD cum laude, SUNY Downstate Med. Ctr., 1972. Diplomate Nat. Bd. Med. Examiners, Am. Bd. Pediatrics. Intern in pediatrics Yale-New Haven Med. Ctr., 1972-73, resident in pediatrics, 1973-74; rsch. assoc. pregnancy rsch. br. Nat. Inst. Child Health and Human Devel., NIH, Bethesda, Md., 1974-76; fellow in neonatology divsn. perinatal medicine Yale U. Sch. Medicine, New Haven, 1976-78, asst. prof. pediatrics, 1978-82, asst. prof. ob-gyn, 1979-82, assoc. prof. pediatrics and ob-gyn, 1982-88, prof. pediatrics and ob-gyn, 1988—; attending physician pediatrics Yale-New Haven Hosp., 1978—, clin. dir. newborn spl. care unit, 1982—2005, med. dir. newborn spl. care unit, 2005—. Mem. NIH pulmonary SCOR grant site visit, dept. pediatrics Vanderbilt U. Sch. Medicine, Nashville, 1981; mem. adv. com. perinatal medicine seminars Ross Labs., 1985-89; mem. ad hoc study sect. multictr. trial of cryotherapy for retinopathy of prematurity NEI, 1985, mem. ad hoc rev. group planning grants for retinopathy of prematurity trials, 1989; mem. adv. com. perinatal and devel. medicine symposium Mead Johnson, 1995-2000; prin. investigator NICHD Neonatal Rsch. Network, 1991—, mem. initial review group, pediatrics review subcom., 2003-05. Author book chpts., articles, abstracts, procs. in field. Lt. comdr. USPHS, 1974-76. Fellow: Am. Coll. Nutrition; mem.: AAAS, New Eng. Perinatal Soc., Am. Acad. Pediat., Am. Soc. Clin. Nutrition, Am. Pediatric Soc., Soc. for Pediatric Rsch., Alpha Omega Alpha, Sigma Xi. Office: Yale U Sch Medicine 333 Cedar St PO Box 208064 New Haven CT 06520-8064 Home: 25 Kildeer Rd Hamden CT 06517 Home Phone: 203-787-4381; Office Phone: 203-688-2320. Personal E-mail: richard.ehrenkranz@yale.edu.

EHRENPREIS, ELI DANIEL, physician, educator, biomedical researcher; b. NYC, Jan. 22, 1958; s. Seymour and Bella Ruth Ehrenpreis; m. Ana Esther Epelbaum, June 17, 1984; children: Benjamin, Jamie, Joseph. BS in Biology, Northeastern Ill. U., 1981; MD, Chgo. Med. Sch., 1985. Diplomate Am. Bd. Internal Medicine. Intern Univ. Ill., 1985-86, resident, 1986-88; fellow gastroenterology and clin. pharmacology Northwestern U., Chgo., 1988-91; staff physician Cleve. Clinic Fla., Ft. Lauderdale, 1991-96; asst. prof. clin. medicine U. Chgo., 1996-2001, assoc. prof. clin. medicine, 2001—. Tng. program dir. gastroenterology U. Chgo., 1997—2003; asst. prof. medicine Rush Med. Sch., 2003—. Author: A Clinician's Guide to Prescription Drugs, 2001, The Prescription and Over-the-Counter Drug Guide for Seniors, 2003, Anal and Rectal Diseases Explained, 2003. Grantee NIH, Washington, 2000. Mem. Am. Coll. Gastroenterology, Am. Gastroenterologic Assn. Jewish. Avocations: cello, gardening, outdoor activities. Office: Adult Care Specialists 1538 Arlington Heights Rd Arlington Heights IL 60004 Office Phone: 847-253-6464. E-mail: ehrenpreis@gipharm.net.

EHRENREICH, BARBARA, writer; b. Butte, Mont., Aug. 26, 1941; d. Ben Howes and Isabelle (Oxley) Alexander; m. John H. Ehrenreich, Aug. 6, 1966; children: Rosa, Benjamin; m. Gary Stevenson, Dec. 10, 1983 BA in Chem. Physics, Reed Coll., 1963; PhD in Biology, Rockefeller U., 1968; D (hon.), Reed College, SUNY, Old Westbury, College of Wooster, Ohio, John Jay College, UMass-Lowell, La Trobe University, Melbourne, Australia. Editor Health Policy Adv. Ctr., NYC, 1969-70; asst. prof. SUNY-Old Westbury, 1971-74; free-lance writer, lectr.; fellow NY Inst. Humanities, NYC, 1980, Inst. Policy Studios, Washington, 1982—; editor Seven Days mag., 1974; columnist Mother Jones mag., 1986-89; essayist Time mag., 1991—97; columnist The Guardian, United Kingdom, 1992—. Author: For Her Own Good: 150 Years of the Experts' Advice to Women, 1978, (with Deirdre English) The American Health Empire, 1970, (with John Ehrenreich) Witches, Midwives and Nurses: A History of Women Healers, 1972, (with D. English) Complaints and Disorders: The Sexual Politics of Sickness, 1973, The Hearts of Men: American Dreams and the Flight from Commitment, (with E. Hess & G. Jacobs) Re-Making Love: The Feminization of Sex, 1986, (with others) The Mean Season: The Attack on the Welfare State, 1987, Fear of Falling: The Inner Life of the Middle Class, 1989, The Worst Years of Our Lives: Irreverent Notes From An Age of Greed, 1990, Kipper's Game, 1993, Blood Rites: Origins and History of the Passions of War, 1997, Nickeled and Dimed: On (Not) Getting by in America, 2001 (Christoper award, 2002, LA Times Book award, 2002, NY Times Bestseller list), Bait and Switch: The (Futile) Pursuit of the American Dream, 2005; contbg. editor: Ms mag., 1981—, Mother Jones mag., 1988—, Leavs mag., 1988—. Recipient Nat. Mag. award, 1980, Ford Found. award for Humanistic Perspectives on Contemporary Issues, 1981; Guggenheim fellow, 1987, Sydney Hillman award for Journalism.

EHRENWERTH, DAVID HARRY, lawyer; b. Pitts., Apr. 22, 1947; s. Ben and Beatrice Lee (Schwartz) E.; m. Judith B. Ehrenwerth; children: Justin Reid, Lindsey Royce. BA, U. Pitts., 1969; JD, Harvard U., 1972. Bar: Pa. 1972, U.S. Dist. Ct. (we. dist.) Pa. 1972, U.S. Ct. Appeals (3d cir.) 1976. Asst. atty. gen. Commonwealth of Pa., Pitts., 1972-74; assoc. Kirkpatrick & Lockhart LLP, Pitts., 1974-79, ptnr., 1979—; adminstrv. ptnr., mem. mgmt. com. Kirkpatrick & Lockhart Preston Gates Ellis LLP, Pitts., 1988—. Pres. Pitts. chpt. Am. Jewish Com., 1988—90, nat. bd. govs., 1991—95, 2001—06, chmn. Pitts. chpt., 1996—98; mem. nat. adv. coun. Fed. Nat. Mortgage Assn., 1984—85; bd. dirs. Pa. Bd. Vocat. Rehab., Harrisburg, 1983—88, United Jewish Fedn., Pitts., 1991—93, Presbyn. U. Hosp., Pitts., 1993—94, Riverview Ctr. Jewish Srs., 1991—93, U. Pitts. Cancer Inst., 1995—99, Pitts. Symphony, 2001—, Montefiore Hosp., Pitts., 1985—93, treas., 1989, vice chmn., 1990—92, chmn., 1992—93; bd. mem. Am. Israel Pub. Affairs Com., 1995—99, 2001—04, 2007—; bd. govs. Pa. Econ. League, Western Region, 1999—. Recipient Human Rels. award Am. Jewish Com., 1999, Bonds award State Israel, 2004; named Pittsburgher to Watch Pitts. Mag., 1980, Pa. Super Lawyer, 2004, 05, 06. Mem. Pa. Bar Assn. (chmn. real estate fin. com. 1985-87), Allegheny County Bar Assn. (Bar fellow, 2000—, chmn. real property sect. 1989), Harvard U. Law Alumni Assn. Western Pa. (pres. 1986-87), Concordia Club, Westmoreland Country Club, Heinz Fifty-Seven Club (chmn. 1974-91), Duquesne Club, Phi Beta Kappa. Jewish. Home: 413 Windmere Dr Pittsburgh PA 15238-2440 Office: Kirkpatrick & Lockhart et al 535 Smithfield St Pittsburgh PA 15222-2312 Home Phone: 412-967-9225; Office Phone: 412-355-6532. Office Fax: 412-355-6501. Business E-Mail: david.ehrenwerth@klgates.com.

EHRET, JOSEPHINE MARY, microbiologist, researcher; b. Roswell, N.Mex., Feb. 26, 1934; d. Edward and Glenna (Memmer) E. BS, U. N.Mex., 1955. Med. technologist U. Colo. Health Scis. Ctr., Denver, 1956-75, rsch. microbiologist, 1956—, Denver Dept. Health and Hosps., 1980—2004; instr. Sch. Medicine, U. Colo., 1985—. Contbr. articles to profl. publs. Mem. Am. Soc. for Microbiology, Am. Soc. Med. Technologists (cert.), Am. Venereal Disease Assn., Calif. Assn. Continuing Med. Lab. Edn. Democrat. Avocations: reading, birding. Home: 1344 S Eudora St Denver CO 80222-3526 Office: U Colo Sch Medicine Div Inf Dis B168 Dept Medicine 4200 E 9th Ave Denver CO 80262 E-mail: JsphnEhret@aol.com.

EHRET, MEGAN J., pharmacist, educator; d. Robert Louis and Paula Jo Ehret; m. Kevin Michael Evringham, Nov. 4, 2006. BS in Pharmacy Sci., U. Toledo, Ohio, 2001, PharmD, 2003. Registered pharmacist Ohio, 2003, Fla., 2004, Conn., 2006. Resident psychiat. pharmacy practice Louis Stokes VA Med. Ctr., Cleve., 2003—04; fellow pharmacogenomics and clin. psychopharmacology Nova Southeastern U., Ft. Lauderdale, Fla., 2004—06; asst. prof. U. Conn., Storrs, 2006—. Pharmacist CVS, Hartford, Conn., 2003—; clin. pharmacist Inst. Living, Hartford, 2006—. Contbr. chapters to books, articles to profl. jours. Recipient Rsch. Abstract award, Ohio Coll. Clin. Pharmacy, 2003, New Investigator award, NIMH, 2006; grantee, Nova Southeastern U., 2004, 2006. Mem.: Am. Soc. Health-Sys. Pharmacists (mem. new practitioners forum 2004), Am. Coll. Clin. Pharmacists, Coll. Psychiat. and Neurologic Pharmacists (mem. membership com. 2005). Achievements include research in in vitro mechanism of a drug-drug interaction. Home Phone: 330-268-7355; Office Phone: 860-545-7470.

EHRHART, JOSEPH EDWARD, retired broadcast technician; b. Monterey Park, Calif., Dec. 27, 1933; s. Theophile George and Catherine Louise (Spaulding) E.; m. Mary Frances Bos, Nov. 30, 1957; children: James Edward and Teresa Louise. AA in Electronics, Pasadena City Coll., 1954. 1st class lic. radiotelephone, FCC. Child actor MGM, RKO, United Artists, Republic, Warner Bros., 20th Century Fox, Universal, Hollywood, Calif., 1939-54; TV broadcast engr. Sta. KOAT-TV, Albuquerque, 1957, Sta. KOB-TV, Albuquerque, 1958, Sta. KHJ-TV, Hollywood, Calif., 1959, ABC, Hollywood, 1960-93; videotape supr. Sta. KABC-TV, Hollywood, 1987-93, ret., 1993. Scoutmaster Boy Scouts of Am., Montrose, Calif., 1970-72; choir dir., Holy Redeemer Cath. Ch., Montrose, 1967-75, mem. Am. Assn. of Variable Star Observers, 1973-78; inspector County of San Diego Registrar of Voters, 1998—. Served in USNR, 1954-56. Mem.: KC, Pacific Pioneer Broadcasters, Cath. Press Coun., Soc. Motion Picture and TV Engrs., L.A. Astron. Soc., Mensa, Soc. Preservation and Encouragement of Barber Shop Quartet Singing in Am., Serra Club, Am. Legion, Order Alhambra (Illustrious Supreme Vizier 2003—05). Avocations: singing, music. Home: Apt 333 1255 N Broadway Escondido CA 92026-2865

EHRHORN, RICHARD WILLIAM, electronics executive; b. Marshalltown, Iowa, Jan. 21, 1934; s. Theodore Raymond and Zelda Elizabeth (Axtell) E.; m. Marilyn Patrick, Aug. 1, 1959; children: Scott Patrick,

Kimberlee Dawn. BSEE, U. Minn., 1955; MSEE, Calif. Inst. Tech., 1958. Sr. engr. Gen. Dynamics Corp., Pomona, Calif., 1956-60; sr. rsch. engr. Calif. Inst. Tech. Jet Propulsion Lab., Pasedena, 1960-63; mgr. advanced devel. lab. Electronic Communications Inc., St. Petersburg, Fla., 1963-68; gen. mgr. Signal/One div., 1968-70; chmn., CEO Ehrhorn Tech. Ops., Inc., Colorado Springs, Colo., 1970-95; vice chmn. ASTeX/ETO, Inc., Colorado Springs, 1996-99; regent Liberty U., 1995—; chmn., CEO Alpha/Power, Inc., Longmont, Colo., 1996-2000; ptnr. Alpha Radio Products, LLC, Boulder, Colo., 2005—. Author: (with others) Principles of Electronic Warfare, 1959; patentee in field. Mem.: IEEE (sr. life), Am. Radio Relay League (life). Home and Office: 11261 Forest Rd Forest VA 24551

EHRLICH, ALAN MARSHALL, lawyer, educator; b. Buffalo, Sept. 6, 1940; s. Melville and Sylvia (Kaplan) E.; m. Narda Wasley, Aug. 22, 1964 (div. Apr. 1979); 1 child, Gary; life ptnr. Barbara Brouse Polin; children: Nancy, Joanne. BA cum laude, SUNY, Buffalo, 1963; SM, MIT, 1965, PhD, 1968; MBA, Ga. State U., 1972; JD, George Washington U., 1991. Bar: Md. 1991, D.C. 1994; U.S. Dist. Ct. Md. 1992, U.S. Supreme Ct., 2006; registered with Patent and Trademark Office 1994. Spl. products group leader New England Nuclear Corp., Boston, 1967-69; sr. rsch. chemist The Coca-Cola Co., Atlanta, 1969-73; phys. scientist U.S. Consumer Product Safety Commn., Bethesda, Md., 1973-80; environ. scientist U.S. EPA, Washington, 1980-91, atty., 1991-94, patent atty., 1994-95, acting patent counsel, 1995-99, patent counsel, 1999—2004; of counsel Weiss & Moy, PC, 2005—, Rabin & Berdo PC. Assoc. profl. lectr. law George Washington U., Washington, 1992-97; presenter and lectr. in field. Author: (newsletter column) Environmental Voice, 1987-91; contbr. more than 90 articles to profl. publs. Bd. dirs. Hebrew Free Loan Assn. D.C., 1992-99, Young Concert Artists Washington, 1982-03; mem. B'nai B'rith Svc. Orgn., Atlanta and Washington, 1971—. Mem. ABA, NARAS, Am. Chem. Soc. (com. patents and related matters 1993—, chair 2000-02, divsn. chemistry and law, 1992—, chair regulatory affairs 1997-99, divsn. chair 2000, councilor 2002-, com. constn. and by laws 2004-, Md. Bar Assn., DC Bar Assn., Govt. Intellectual Property Law Assn. (pres. 1999-00), Am. Intellectual Property Law Assn., Choral Arts Soc. Washington, Phi Eta Sigma, Beta Gamma Sigma. Democrat. Jewish. Avocation: performing classical and liturgical choral music. Office: Weiss & Moy PC 1101 14th St NW Washington DC 20005 also: Rabin & Berdo PC 1101 14th ST NW Washington DC 20005 Personal E-mail: ehrlichpolin@comcast.net. Business E-Mail: aehrlich@weissmoy.com. E-mail: firm@rabinberdo.com.

EHRLICH, AVA, broadcast executive; b. St. Louis, Aug. 14, 1950; d. Norman and Lillian (Gellman) Ehrlich; m. Barry K. Freedman, Mar. 31, 1979; children: Alexander Zev, Maxwell Samuel. BJ, Northwestern U., 1972, MJ, 1973; MA, Occidental Coll., 1976. Reporter, asst. mng. editor Lerner Newspapers, Chgo., 1974-75; reporter, news editor Sta. KMOX, St. Louis, 1976-79; producer Sta. WXYZ, Detroit, 1979-85; exec. producer Sta. KSDK-TV, St. Louis, 1985—. Guest editor Mademoiselle mag., N.Y.C., 1971; freelance writer, coll. prof. Detroit, Chgo., St. Louis, 1987; adj. faculty mem. Washington U., St. Louis, 1994—. Trustee CORO Found., St. Louis, 1976-77, 1986—99, St. Louis Jewish Light, 1999—, Crown Ctr., 2000; bd. dirs. Nat. Kidney Found., St. Louis, 1987, Crown Ctr., 2000—, Hillel Found. of Washington U, 2005—; com. chairperson Crayton H.S. PTO, 2005—. Named Outstanding Woman in Broadcasting, Am. Women in Radio & TV, 1983, Among 18 Most Influential Women in the Region St. Louis Dispatch, 2000; recipient Journalism award Am. Chiropractic Assn., 1989, AP award Ill. UPI, 1989, Illuminator award AMC Cancer Rsch., 1994, Women in Comms. Nat. award, 1988, Emmy award, 1995, Virginia Betts award for Contbns. in Journalism, 1999; CORO Found. fellow in pub. affairs, 1975-76. Mem. NATAS (com. mem. 1986—, bd. dirs. 1994—, 18 local Emmy awards 1986—), Women in Comms., Inc. (sec. 1978-79, Clarion award 1989, Best in Midwest Feature award 1989), Soc. Profl. Journalists. Democrat. Jewish. Home: 8002 Walinca Ter Saint Louis MO 63105-2565 Office: Sta KSDK-TV 1000 Market St Saint Louis MO 63101-2011 Office Phone: 314-444-5120. Business E-Mail: aehrlich@ksdk.gannett.com.

EHRLICH, BERNARD HERBERT, lawyer, trade association administrator; b. Washington, Apr. 3, 1927; s. Samuel Zachary and Elsie (Klein) Ehrlich; m. Edna Kraft, June 17, 1951 (div.); children: Vivian Rose, Beverly Denise, Brenda Susan, Lisa Jean. AB, George Washington U., 1946, LLB, 1949, MA, JD, 1950. Pvt. practice, Washington; gen. counsel numerous corps., industries, 1947-89; mgr., gen. counsel Inst. Indsl. Launderers, Washington, 1947-89; counsel KEX Nat. Assn., 1960-94. Counsel Nat. Home Study Coun., 1947—89, Nat. Assn. Cosmetology Schs., 1967—83; gen. counsel KEX Nat. Assn., 1960—95, Accrediting Bur. Health Edn. Schs., 1965—92, Commn. Accredited Truck Driving Schs., 1968—86; mem. adv. panel employee recruitment and job devel. U.S. C. of C., 1967—84; mem. Pres.'s Com. Employing Handicapped, 1975—. Bd. dirs. Washington B'nai B'rith Hillel Found., 1997—2000; trustee Temple Emanu-el, Sarasota, Fla., 2005—. With USN, 1943—45. Recipient Svc. plaque, Am. Inst. Launderers, 1966, Nat. Assn. Trade and Tech. Schs., 1967, Nat. Home Study Coun., 1970, Accrediting Bur. Health Edn. Schs., 1992, Commn. Accredited Truck Driving Schs., 1992, N. F. Cimaglia award, Melody Pub. Co., 1985. Mem.: ABA, Am. Polit. Sci. Assn., Soc. Am. Travel Writers, Am. Soc. Assn. Execs., Am. Hist. Assn., Am. Soc. Internat. Law, Bar Assn. DC, Inst. Indsl. Launderers (hon.), KEX Nat. Assn. (hon.), Nat. Assn. Trade and Tech. Schs. (hon.), Am. Forestry Assn. (life), Phi Beta Kappa, Phi Delta Pi, Nu Beta Epsilon. Jewish. Home and Office: 4907 Lakescene Pl Sarasota FL 34243 Office Phone: 941-351-8341.

EHRLICH, BOB (ROBERT LEROY EHRLICH JR.), lawyer, former governor, congressman; b. Arbutus, Md., Nov. 25, 1957; s. Bob and Nancy Ehrlich; m. Kendel Sibiski, 1993; children: Drew Robert, Joshua Taylor. B, Princeton U., 1979; JD, Wake Forest U. Law Sch., 1982. Law clk. to H. Russell Smouse, 1981; assoc. Ober, Kaler, Grimes, and Shriver, 1982-92, of counsel, 1992-94; mem. Md. Ho. of Dels., 1987-94, mem. Ho. Jud. Com., Joint Legis. Ethics Com., Gov.'s Coun. Child Abuse & Neglect, Gov.'s Adv. Panel for Justice Adminstrn., mem. Gov.'s Select Panel on Drug-Addicted Newborns, Gov.'s Select Panel on the Hickey Sch., co-chmn. Joint Com. on Md.'s Procurement Laws; mem. US Congress from 2nd Dist. Md., Washington, 1995—2003; mem. commerce com., subcom. finance & hazardous waste, energy & power, telecomm., trade & consumer protection Washington; mem. budget com., banking & fin. services com., subcoms. fin. inst. & comml. credit, housing & fin. services, spl. adv. com. on corrections; asst. majority whip, nat. security working group, Ho. commerce com.; gov. State of Md., Annapolis, 2003—07; ptnr. Womble Carlyle Sandridge & Rice, PLLC, Balt., 2007—. Named Guardian of Small Bus. Nat. Fedn. Ind. Bus., 1987-90, Legislator of Yr. Md. State's Attys. Assn., 1989, Fraternal Order of Police Md. State Lodge, 1994, Nat. Conf. for Prevention of Child Abuse, 1994, Outstanding Young Marylander Md. Jaycees, 1995, Outstanding Rep. Male Md. Rep. State Ctrl. Com., 1995, Disting. Svc. award German Soc. Md., 1997, Legislator of Yr. Nat. Assn. Mortgage Brokers, 1997; recipient Spirit of Enterprise award U.S. C. of C., 1996, 97, Thomas Jefferson award Food Distbrs. Internat., 1996, Congl. Tax Fighter award Nat. Tax Limitation Com., 1996, Taxpayer Hero award Citizens Against Govt. Waste, 1997. Republican. Office: Womble Carlyle Sandridge & Rice PLLC 1302 Concourse Dr Linthicum MD 21090*

EHRLICH, BRUCE JAY, media consultant, psychologist, writer; b. Bklyn., Feb. 26, 1948; s. Samuel and Irene Ehrlich. MA, U. Calif., Santa Barbara, 1981. Owner Mind Media, Las Vegas, Nev., 1988—. Pres. Island Found., Las Vegas, 1997—2007. Author: (book) Ecstasy: The MDMA Story. Office: Mind Media 9360 W Flamingo Ave #110-524 Las Vegas NV 89147 Home Phone: 702-597-9291; Office Phone: 702-597-9291. Business E-Mail: bruceehrlich@lvcm.com.

EHRLICH, CHARLES DAVID, physicist; b. Miami, Fla., Sept. 10, 1951; s. Maurice Lee and Bena Zeva (Shechtman) E.; m. Susan Rae Morris, June 2, 1974; children: Rebecca, Gabriel. BS, U. Miami, 1973; PhD, U. Pa., 1979. Physicist R&D Varian Assocs. Extrion Div., Gloucester, Mass., 1979-83, mgr. batch process product devel., 1984; staff physicist Nat. Bureau of Standards, Gaithersburg, Md., 1984-87; group leader, pressure group Nat. Inst. Standards & Tech., Gaithersburg, Md., 1987-94, program analyst, 1994-95, sr. program analyst, 1995-96, dep. chief, tech. stds. activities program, 1996-99, nat. measurement and stds. needs assessment coord., 1999-2000, chief tech. stds. activities program, 2000—01, leader Internat. Legal Metrology Group, 2002—. U.S. rep. Internat. Orgn. Legal Metrology, 2000—; workshop organizer Nat. Inst. Stds. and Tech., 1987-89; instr. 1990-94; co-chmn. to Internat. Sts. Orgn. Tech. Adv. Group 4 on Metrology; invited conf. procs. author Proceedings of 4th Italy-U.S. Bilateral Seminar, 1992. Contbr. articles to profl. jours. Boy scout asst. patrol leader Boy Scouts Am., Gaithersburg, 1991-94, cub scout den leader Cub Scouts Am., Gaithersburg, 1989-91. Recipient Bronze Medal award U.S. Dept. Commerce, 1992, Best Paper award Nat. Conf. Stds. Labs., 1997, 2006, Andrew J. Woodington award for Professionalism in Metrology Measurement Sci. Conf., 1999, Outstanding Svc. Mem.: Am. Nat. Stds. Inst. Exec. Stds. Coun., Internat. Joint Com. Guides for Metrology, Intrinsic Derived Sts. Com., Nat. Conf. Stds. Labs. (chmn. 1989—98, William A. Wildhack award 2007), Internat. Bur. Weights and Measures, Am. Vacuum Soc., Am. Soc. Testing & Materials (vice chmn 1986—90), Internat. Orgn. Legal Metrology (U.S. rep.), Sigma Xi (NIST chpt. pres.-elect 2002—03, pres. 2003—04, Outstanding Svc. Nat. Inst. Sci. and Tech. chpt. 2007). Achievements include invited keynote speaker IMEKO World Congress, Turin, Italy, 1994; invited speaker Shanghai and Beijing, China, 1994, 2007, Bratislava, Slovakia, 1991 explained measured equilibration time constants in helium permeation leaks. Milestones in Metrology Congress, Maastricht, The Netherlands, 2003. Home: 9804 Darcy Forest Dr Silver Spring MD 20910-1176 Office Phone: 301-975-4834. E-mail: charles.ehrlich@nist.gov.

EHRLICH, CHARLES GORDON, insurance company executive, lawyer; b. London, Apr. 3, 1949; came to U.S., 1953; s. Josef and Lotte (Engel) E.; m. Ann Curry, Dec. 16, 1978; children: Lisa, Jennifer. AB, U. Calif., Berkeley, 1970, JD, 1973. Bar: Calif. 1973, Ill. 1995. Assoc. Lawler, Felix & Hall, LA, 1974-79, Pettit & Martin, San Francisco, 1979-80, ptnr., 1981-94; v.p., dep. gen. counsel Internat. Ins. Co., Chgo., 1994-96, acting gen. counsel, 1996-97, sr. v.p., 1997—2002, also bd. dirs.; sr. v.p., gen. counsel, sec. TIG Ins. Group Inc.; TIG Ins. Holdings, Manchester, NH, 2002—. Editl. cons. Calif. Forms of Jury Instruction, Matthew Bender, 1985, Proof in Competitive Bus. Practices Litigation, Calif. Continuing Edn. of Bar, 1993; bd. dirs. Resolution Group, Inc., TIG Ins. Co., RiverStone Ins. UK, River Stone Ins. UK; arbitrator San Francisco Superior Ct., 1987-94, US Dist. Ct. No. Dist. Calif., San Francisco, 1989-94; gen. counsel, sr. v.p. Fairmont Premier Ins. Co., 2006-, Fairmont Ins. Co., 2006-, Fairmont Splty. Ins. Co., 2006-, Fairmont Splty. Ins. Fin. Co., 2006-, Fairmont Splty. Mgrs. Corp., 2006-; sec., gen. counsel Fairmont Splty. Group, Inc., 2006-. Contbr. articles to profl. jours., local newspapers. Founder, bd. dirs. Legal Cmty. Against Violence, San Francisco, 1993-95; mem. bd. trustees Palace Theater Trust, 2006-. Recipient award of merit Bar Assn. San Francisco, 1993. Mem. ABA (co-chmn. sect. ligitation, corp. counsel com. regional workshop programs 1993—, vice chmn. sect. on tort and ins. practice 1995—, program chmn. sect. on litigation 1997), State Bar Calif. (com. on adminstrn. of justice 1992-94). Avocations: sports car racing, travel. Office: RiverStone Resources 250 Commercial St Manchester NH 03101 Home Phone: 603-249-9340; Office Phone: 603-656-2456. Business E-Mail: charles_ehrlich@trg.com.

EHRLICH, DAVID GORDON, film director, educator; b. Elizabeth, NJ, Oct. 14, 1941; s. Max and Jeannette (Gordon) E.; m. Marcela Josepha Rydlova, July 17, 1975. BA in Govt., Cornell U., 1963; sculpture cert., Madras Sch. Fine Arts, India, 1964; MA in Dramatic Art, U. Calif., Berkeley, 1966; MFA in Film, Columbia U., 1975. Artist-in-residence Vt. Coun. on Arts, Montpelier, Vt., 1978—, N.H. Coun. on Arts, Concord, NH, 1986—; vis. prof. film studies Dartmouth Coll., Hanover, NH, 1993—; vis. prof. animation Beijing Film Acad., 2007—. Lectr. art U. Vt., 1977-82; adj. asst. prof. interdisciplinary arts SUNY, Purchase, 1971-75; instr. animation summer session U. Calif., Berkeley, yearly 1988-93, summer session U. Hawaii, Honolulu, yearly 1991-98, Mongolia Coll. Art, Ulan, Baatar, Mongolia, CAS Sch., Karachi, Pakistan, 1993; mem. adv. bd. ADA Animation Inst., Shanghai, 1988—; vis. prof. film MRDH Coll., Volda, Norway, 1990-91; art therapy cons. Manhattan State Hosp., 1975-76; hon. pres. Ottawa Internat. Animation Festival, 2002; presenter various internat. confs. and festivals, spkr. in field. Author: The Bowel Book, 1981, chpts. to Chinese, Mongolian and Japanese animation Animation in Asia and the Pacific, 2001; dir., animator: (animated short films) Metamorphosis, 1975, Album Leaf, 1976, Vermont Etude, 1977, Robot, 1977, Vermont Etude, No. 2, 1979, Robot Two, 1979, Precious Metal, 1980, Fantasies: Animation of Vermont Schoolchildren, 1981, Dissipative Dialogues, 1982, Precious Metal Variations, 1983, Point, 1984, Dissipative Fantasies, 1986, Pixel, 1987, Dryads, 1988, Academy Leader Variations, 1987, Animated Self-Portraits, 1989, A Child's Dream, 1990, Dance of Nature, 1991, Genghiz Khan, 1993, Etude, 1994, Interstitial Wavescapes, 1995, Robot Rerun, 1996, Asifa Variations, 1997, Radiant Flux, 1999, Color Run, 2001, Taking Color for a Walk, 2001, Current Events, 2002, Line Dance, 2007; mem. editl. bd. Animation Jour., 1991—, Cartoons, 2005—; contbr. articles to profl. jours.; films in collections at MOMA, Pacific Film Archive, Berlin ASIFA Animation Archive, Tokyo Internat. Animation Libr., Montreal Cinematheque Quebecoise, Moscow Film Archive; film retrospectives include Kecskemet Animation Festival, Hungary, 2007, Taiwan Internat. Animation Festival, 2007, Hangzhou Animation Festival, China, 2007, Ottawa Internat. Animation Festival, 2002, Ballargues Animation Festival, France, 1998, Balt. Film Forum, Cinanima Animation Festival, Portugal, 1990, N.W. Film & Video Study Ctr., 1989, Pacific Film Archives, Shanghai Animation Festival, 1988, Mus. Modern Art, Varna World Animation Festival, Bulgaria, Belgrade Film Inst., Yugoslavia, 1987, Sinking Creek Film Celebration, Vienna Art Acad., 1986, Mus. Moving Image, 1985, Turin (Italy) City Hall, Cakovec Cultural Ctr., Yugoslavia, 1984, SUNY at Plattsburgh, Bradford Coll., 1982, Animators Gallery, N.Y.C., 1982, BVAU Gallery, Boston, Umwelt Galerie, Stuttgart, Germany, 1979; subject of book David Ehrlich: Citizen of the World, 2002. Recipient awards Cannes Film Festival, Chg. Film Festival, San Francisco Film Festival, Am. Film Festival, Krakow Film Festival, Cinanima Film Festival, Houston Film Festival, WorldFest, Charleston Film Festival, Roshd Film Festival, Iran, Murcia Film Festival, Spain, ASIFA-East Animation Festival, Sinking Creek Film Celebration, Black Maria Film Festival, NY Filmakers' Expo, Athens Film Festival, New Eng. Film Festival, ASIFA Spl. award, 2002; Travel grantee Arts Internat., NYC, 1992-93, Am. Film Inst. grantee, 1988, Holographic Film Found grantee, 1978, 83, 84, US Spkr. and Specialist grantee US State Dept. multi-ethnic animation workshop, Serbia, 2006; Fulbright fellow, 1963-64. Mem. Nat. Expressive Therapy Assn. (cert. expressive therapist), Internat. Animation Assn. (exec. bd. 1988-2000, v.p. 1991-97), Soc. Animation Studies (mem. steering com. 1999-2000), Asian Cinema Studies Soc., Vt. Coun. on Arts (filmmaking grantee 1978, 79, 84, 86, 89, 90, 91), Mongolia Soc., Miagmar Animation Workshop (bd. dirs. 1992—). Avocations: composing music, painting, sculpture, dance, travel. Office: Dartmouth Coll Film Studies Wilson Hall Hanover NH 03755

EHRLICH, GARTH DAVID, molecular biologist; b. Plattsburgh, NY, July 9, 1956; s. Robert Elias and Evelyn Gertrude (Talvitie) E.; children: Ian S.G., Nathan E.G. BA, Alfred U., 1977; PhD, Syracuse U., 1987. Rsch. microbiologist Bethesda Rsch. Labs., Md., 1980-81; rsch. specialist Syracuse U., NY, 1981-83; rsch. scientist C indsl. divsn. Bristol Meyers, 1981-83, rsch. scientist B, 1983-84; tech. specialist I SUNY Health Sci. Ctr., Syracuse, NY, 1984-86, rsch. instr., 1988-89, rsch. asst. prof., 1989-90; tech. specialist II SUNY Rsch. Found., Syracuse, NY, 1986-88; asst. to assoc. prof., dir. PCR facility U. Pitts., Pa., 1990-97; chief microbiology, virology and infectious diseases sect. molecular diogostics divsn. U. Pitts. Med. Ctr., Pa., assoc. prof. Pa., 1995-97; vis. prof. Cleve. Clin., 1992; founder, exec. dir. Ctr. Genomic Sci. Allegheny Singer Rsch. Inst., 1997—, governmental and regional affairs liason officer, 2001—; prof. microbiology, immunology Drexel Coll. Medicine, 1997—, prof., vice-chmn, dept human genetics, 1998—, prof., dir. rsch. dept. otolaryngology, 1997—. Cons. Teltech, Inc., 1990—, Kodak, Rochester, NY, 1991-95, Oncogenetics, Phoenix, 1993-95; Visible Genetics, 1997-99, CL Sci., 1997-99, Quest Diagnostics, 1998-99, Isis-Ibis, 2006-; invited participant NCI Symposia, 1989, NMMS Symposia, 1989, NIAID Symposia, 1991, NIDCA Coun., 1995, NILC Symposiun, 2000; adj. mem. Ctrl. Blood Bank Pitts., 1992—; lectr. Heritage Found. Cross Cancer Ctr., Edmonton, Can.; Feinstein lectr. Alfred U., 1995; invited participant Internat. Chromosome 10 Workshop, Crete, Greece; invited guest spkr. Mexican Infection Disease Soc. Ann. Meeting, 1995; exec. dir. Ctr. for Genomic Sci., Allegheny Singer Rsch. Inst., 1997—; prof. microbiology, immunology, otolaryngology and human genetics Drexel Univ. Coll. of Med., vice-chmn. dept. human genetics, 1998—; hon. prof. med. genetics West China U. of Med. Sci., Chengdu, Sichuan, 1999—; over 100 invited speaking engagements including World Congress of Pediat. Infectious Disease, Acapulco, Mex., 1996, Bicor Conf. on Antiinfective Agents, Leipzig, Germany, 1996, Case Western Res. U., 1997, Bacterial Genome Conf., 2005, USC Biofilms Symposia, 2005, Functional Genotics of Infectious Diseases, Giessen, Germany, 2006, Biofilms in Orthopedics, Naples, Italy, 2006; La Spienza, U. Rome, Italy, 2006, Weill Med. Coll., Cornelll U., 2007, others; lectr. Kaiyuon Bioengring., Xian, China, 1997, Chinese U. Hong Kong, 1999; hon. lectr. West China U. Med. Sci., 1999; vis. prof. Shantou U. Med. Coll., China, 2001; guest prof. Shantou U., 2003; mem. adv. com. Med. Biofilms, Tokyo, 2002, Extraordinary Meeting on Otitis Media, Amsterdam, 2005, MaxPlancx Inst. Marine Biology, Bremen, Germany, 2005, Nat. Inst. Microbiology, Chineses Acad. Sci., China, 2005; organizer symposia in field, 1995-1997, 2000, 2003, ASM Divisn. Symposium Conv., 2006; mem. numerous NIH grant rev. coms.; bd. dirs. Pitts. Tissue Engring. Initiative, 2005-; panel mem. Stryker (Infectious Diseases), 2007, Medtronics Biolfim, 2007. Author, editor: PCR-Based Diagnostics in Infectious Disease, 1994; contbr. 200 articles to profl. jours., chpts. to books, editls. to med. jours. Mem. gifted edn. adv. bd. Syracuse City Sch. Dist., 1989-90; lectr. on AIDS to secondary sch. children, sci. to elem. sch. children, 1989—. Recipient Disting. Alumni citation Alfred U., 1995, Feinstein Lectureship Alfred U., 1995, 4 NIH grants, 2000; named hon. prof. in med. genetics, West China U. of Med. Sci., 1999, keynote spkr. Indian Assn. Med. Microbiology, 2001; finalist Healthcare Hero award, Rsch. and Innovation, Pitts. Bus. Times, 2005. Mem. Soc. for Leukocyte Biology, Assn. for Rsch. in Otolaryngology, Assn. Med. Lab. Immunologists, Acad. Clin. Lab. Physicians and Scientists, Am. Soc. for Microbiology, Assn. Molecular Pathology (co-chair infectious diseases sect.), Sigma Xi, Phi Kappa Phi. Democrat. Avocations: sports car racing, skiing, scuba diving. Address: Allegheny Singer Rsch Inst Ctr Genomic Sci 320 E North Ave Pittsburgh PA 15212-4756 Office Phone: 412-359-4228. Business E-Mail: gehrlich@wpahs.org.

EHRLICH, GEORGE EDWARD, rheumatologist, consultant; b. Vienna, July 18, 1928; came to US, 1938, naturalized, 1944; s. Edward and Irene (Elling) E.; m. Gail S. Abrams, Mar. 30, 1968; children: Charles Edward, Steven L. Abrams, Rebecca Sayles. AB cum laude, Harvard U., Cambridge, Mass., 1948; MB, MD, Chgo. Med. Sch., 1952. Intern Michael Reese Hosp., Chgo., 1952; resident Francis Delafield Hosp., NYC, 1955, Beth Israel Hosp., Boston, 1956, New Eng. Center Hosp., Boston, 1957; fellow rheumatology NIH, Bethesda, Md., 1958, Hosp. for Spl. Surgery, NYC, 1959-61, asst. attending physician, 1960-64; spl. fellow Sloan Kettering Inst., 1960-61; instr. medicine Cornell U., 1960-64; dir. Arthritis Center, chief rheumatology Albert Einstein Med. Center and Moss Rehab. Hosp., Phila., 1964-80; asst. prof. medicine Temple U., 1964-67, asso. prof. medicine, 1967-72, prof. medicine, 1972-80, asso. prof. rehab. medicine, 1964-74, prof., 1974-80; vis. lectr. U. Pa., 1964-80; prof. medicine, dir. div. rheumatology Hahnemann U., Phila., 1980-83; v.p. Anti-Inflammatory/Endocrine CIBA-Geigy Pharmaceuticals, Summit, NJ, 1983-86; head med. affairs CIBA-Geigy Ltd., Switzerland, 1987-88; pres. George E. Ehrlich Assocs., pharmaceutical cons. Adj. prof. clin. medicine NYU Med. Ctr., 1984—; lectr. medicine U. Pa., 1989-91, adj. prof. medicine, 1992—; expert advisor, cons. Diabetes and Other Noncommunicable Diseases unit WHO, 1990-98, Chronic Disease Mgmt., 1998—; chmn. Internat. Low Back Pain Initiative; rep. of pres. Internat. League Assns. Rheumatology for Soft Tissue Rheumatisms, 1993-97, exec. com.; liaison to WHO, 1997—; mem. arthritis adv. com. FDA, 1993-96, chmn., 1993-96; expert, FDA, 1997-99; mem. coun. Chairs, FDA, 1996—; chmn. sci. adv. bd. Hochrheininstitut (Rheumatic Disease and Rehab. Rsch. Inst. of Upper Rhine in Germany, France and Switzerland for Treatment, Tchg., and Rsch.), 1993—; bd. dirs. Greenwich Inst. Am. Edn.; chmn., U.S. mem. Expert Adv. Panel on Chronic Degenerative Diseases, WHO, 1996—. Author: Differential Diagnosis of Rheumatoid Arthritis, 1972, Oculocutaneous Manifestations of Rheumatic Diseases, 1973; editor: Total Management of the Arthritic Patient, 1973, Rehabilitation Management of Rheumatic Conditions, 1980, 2d edit., 1986; editor: (with J. Fries) Prognosis, 1981; editor: (with H.E. Paulus) Controversies in the Clinical Evaluation of Analgesic-Anti-Inflammatory-Antirheumatic Drugs, 1981; editor: (with P. Utsinger, N. Zvaifler) Rheumatoid Arthritis, 1985; editor: (with W. Simon) Medicolegal Consequences of Trauma, 1992; editor: (with N. Khaltaev) Low Back Pain, 2000; editor: (with W. Simon A. Sadwin) Conquering Chronic Pain After Injury, 2002; editor: Jour. Albert Einstein Med. Ctr., 1966—71, Arthritis and Rheumatic Diseases Abstracts, 1968—71; mem. editl. bd.: Inflammation, 1974—88, Psychosomatics, 1977—83, Sexual Medicine Today, 1977—84, Jour. Rheumatology, 1982—, Internat. Jour. Immunotherapy, 1984—, Immunopharmacology, 1985—, Med. Problems Performing Artists, 1985—92, Brazilian Jour. Rheumatology, 1992, 1996—99, Italian Jour. Rheumatic Diseases, 1999—; contbr. articles to profl. jours. Pres. Ea. Pa. chpt. Arthritis Found., 1970-72; mem. Phila. Mayor's Sci. and Tech. Adv. Coun., 1972-81; chmn. ad hoc adv. com. Bur. Drugs, FDA, 1971; subcom. on redefinition of disability Social Security Adminstrn., 1982-86. Served to comdr. M.C. USNR, 1953-55; Res. to 1975, ret. Decorated Cavaliere Order of Star of Italian Solidarity; recipient citations, City Phila., 1969, 1974, Distinguished Alumnus award, Chgo. Med. Sch., 1969, Dr. Joseph Lee Hollander award, Ea. Pa. chpt., Arthritis Found., 2004. Fellow ACP, Royal Coll. Physicians Edinburgh, Phila. Coll. Physicians, Am. Coll. Rheumatology (elected master, 1994; com. for publ. Arthritis and Rheumatism, 1977-79, mem. editl. bd. 1980-83), Rheumatism Socs. Ecuador, India (hon.); mem. AMA (editl. bd. Jour. 1972-82), Am. Soc. Clin. Pharmacology and Therapeutics, Assn. Mil. Surgeons (Philip Hench award 1971), Brit. Assn. Rheumatology and Rehab. (overseas mem., editl. bd. 1979-82), Internat. Soc. for Behcet's Disease (hon. life pres.), Harvard Club (Boston, NYC), Alpha Omega Alpha. Office: 1 Independence Pl Ste 1101 241 S Sixth St Philadelphia PA 19106-3731 Personal E-mail: ge2@mindspring.com. *Respect for the ideas of others, but ultimately responsible for my own ideas, thus, a liberal philosophy in a conservative setting. Like Brecht's Galileo, I should like to be remembered as a lover of old wines and new ideas.*

EHRLICH, GERALDINE ELIZABETH, management consultant; d. Joseph Vincent and Agnes Barbara (Campbell) McKenna; m. S. Paul Ehrlich, Jr.; children: Susan Patricia, Paula Jeanne, Jill Marie. BS, Drexel Inst. Tech. Nutrition cons. hypertension rsch. team U. Calif. Micronesia, 1970; regional sales mgr. Marriott Corp., Bethesda, Md., 1976-78; dir. sales and profl. svcs. Coll. and Health Care divsn. Macke Co., Cheverly, Md., 1978-79, v.p. ops. divsn., 1979-80, pres. Health Care divsn., 1980-81; regional v.p. Custom Mgmt. Corp., Alexandria, Va., 1981-83, v.p. mktg., 1983-87; v.p. mktg. and healthcare sales Morrison's Custom Mgmt., Mobile, Ala., 1987-88; v.p. sales ARA Svcs., Phila., 1988-93; v.p. bus. devel. ARAMARK, Phila., 1993-95; exec. dir. The Resource Group, Phila., 1995—2001; healthcare mktg. cons., 2001—. Cons. mktg. The Green House, Tokyo, 1987-88; chmn. bd. Mktg. Matrix, Falls Church, Va., 1984—. Mem. Health Systems Agy. No. Va., 1976-77; chmn. Health Care Adv. Bd., Fairfax County, Va., 1973-77; vice chmn. Fairfax County Cmty. Action Com., 1973-77; treas. Fairfax County Dem. Com., 1969-73; trustee Fairfax Hosp., 1973-77; bd. dirs. Tennis Patrons, Washington, 1984-88, Phila. Singers, 1993-98, Physicians for Peace, 1993-98; mem. adv. bd. Nat. Mus. Women in the Arts, 2000—, mem. bd. Fla. State Com., 2005—. Mem. NAFE, AAUW, Internat. Women's Assn., Am. Mgmt. Assn., Soc. Mktg. Profls., Gulfstream Club, Rotary Club. Home: 1132 Seaspray Ave Delray Beach FL 33483 Office Phone: 561-573-2492. E-mail: gehrlich@profserve.com.

EHRLICH, GERT, science educator, researcher; b. Vienna, June 22, 1926; arrived in US, 1939; s. Leopold and Paula Maria (Kucera) Ehrlich; m. Anne Vogdes Alger, Apr. 27, 1957. AB in Chemistry with honors, Columbia U., NYC, 1948; AM, Harvard U., Cambridge, Mass., 1950, PhD, 1952. NIH postdoctoral fellow Harvard U., Cambridge, Mass., 1951—52; rsch. assoc. dept. physics U. Mich., Ann Arbor, 1952—53; rsch. staff GE Rsch. Lab., Schenectady, NY, 1953—68; prof. materials sci. Coordinated Sci. Lab. U. Ill., Urbana-Champaign, 1968—. Former mem. editl. adv. bd. Chem. Physics Letters, Jour. Chem. Physics, Jour. Vacuum Sci. & Tech., Surface & Colloid Sci., Progress in Surface & Membrance Sci.; contbr. articles to profl. jours. With US Army, 1945—47, ETO. Guggenheim fellow, 1985. Fellow: Am. Vacuum Soc. (Medard W. Welch award 1979), NY Acad. Scis., Am. Phys. Soc.; mem.: Am. Chem. Soc. (Kendall award 1982), Nat. Acad. Scis., Alexander von Humboldt Found. (Humboldt-Preis 1992), Sigma Xi. Office: U Ill Materials Rsch Lab 104 S Goodwin Ave Urbana IL 61801-2985 Office Phone: 217-333-6448. Business E-Mail: ehrlich@mrl.uiuc.edu.

EHRLICH, HENRY LUTZ, biology professor; b. Stettin, Pommerania, Germany, Aug. 31, 1925; came to U.S., 1940; s. Max and Gerda (Tannenwald) E. BS cum laude, Harvard Coll., 1948; MS, U. Wis., 1949, PhD, 1951. From asst. prof. to prof. biology Rensselaer Poly. Inst., Troy, NY, 1951-94; prof. emeritus, 1994. Cons. in field. Author: Geomicrobiology, 1996, 3d edit., 1995, 4th edit., 2002; author, co-editor: Workshop on Biotechnology for the Mining, Metal Refining and Fossil Fuel Processing Industries, 1986; co-author, co-editor: Microbial Mineral Recovery, 1990; editor-in-chief Geomicrobiology Jour., 1983-95; mem. editl. bd. Applied and environ. Microbiology, Applied Microbiology and Biotech. Mem. interdisciplinary com. World Cultural Coun., Monterrey, Mex. Am. Acad. Microbiology fellow. Fellow AAAS; mem. Symposia for Environ. Biogeochemistry (former v.p., treas.), Am. Soc. Microbiology, Soc. Indsl. Microbiology, Am. Inst. Biol. Scis., Sigma Xi. Jewish. Achievements include research on microbial manganese oxidation and reduction; microbial chromate reduction; microbial bauxite weathering; bioleaching. Home: 2423 21st St 3 Troy NY 12180-1826 Office: Rensselaer Polytech Inst Biology Dept 110 8th St Troy NY 12180-3590 Home Phone: 518-273-7224; Office Phone: 518-276-8428. Business E-Mail: ehrlih@rpi.edu.

EHRLICH, IRA ROBERT, mechanical engineering consultant; b. Washington, Sept. 1, 1926; s. Abraham Moses and Anna (Garonzik) E.; m. Sheila Lenor Kaminsky, June 11, 1950; children: Richard Mark, Heather Maureen Ehrlich Reiser BS, U.S. Mil. Acad., 1950; MS, Purdue U., 1956; PhD, U. Mich., 1960; MS (hon.), Stevens Inst. Tech., 1982. Registered profl. engr., Mich., N.J. Supr. ITT, Paramus, NJ, 1960-62; mgr. transp. research group Stevens Inst. Tech., Hoboken, NJ, 1962-74, dean research, 1974-83, head dept. mech. engring., 1979-83, v.p. research, 1983-85, v.p. acad. affairs, 1984-85, prof. emeritus, 1988—; pres. I. Robert Ehrlich P.A., Teaneck, NJ, 1988—. Chmn. sci. adv. com. U.S. Army Tank-Automotive Rsch. and Devel. Command, 1970-77; cons. to industry; mem. N.J. Motor Vehicle Insp. Sta. Rev. Commn., chmn. safety com., 1977-80. Asso. editor Tire Sci. and Tech, 1972-80. Capt. US Army, 1950—60. Themis grantee, 1967-72 Fellow Soc. Automotive Engrs., Internat. Soc. Terrain-Vehicle Systems (gen. sec. 1967-78, v.p. 1978-81, pres. 1981-84); mem. ASME, NSPE, ASTM, Nat. Safety Coun., Nat. Assn. Profl. Accident Reconstructionists (bd. dirs. 1997-99), B'nai Brith (chpt. pres. 1967-68). Jewish. Home and Office: 859 Columbus Dr Teaneck NJ 07666-6612 Office Phone: 201-833-8316. Personal E-mail: irehrlich@verizon.net. *Make the most of your scraps of time.*

EHRLICH, KENNETH JAMES, television producer; b. Cleve., May 11; s. Arthur A. and Lucile Ehrlich; m. Harriet Stromberg, Feb. 19, 1967; children: Mathew, Dori. BS in Journalism, Ohio U., 1964. Pres. Comminique, Chgo., 1970-72; dir. devel. Sta. WTTW-TV, Chgo., 1972-76; pres. Ken Ehrlich Prodns., Los Angeles, 1976—. Exec. producer (series) Showtime Coast to Coast, numerous spls. with Paul Simon, Stevie Wonder, Phil Collins, Elton John, Eric Clapton, Shania Twain, Faith HIll, Celine Dion, Christina Aguilera, Ricky Martin, Ray Charles, Patti LaBelle others, intimate portrait (9 episodes), 1997-2001; exec. prodr. or producer Grammy Awards Show, 1980—, Blockbuster Awards, 1995-2001, Latin Grammys, Alma Awards, 2002, Primetime Emmy awards, 2005-; producer Soundstage (creator), writer, dir. 1974-83, Fame, 1983-85; producer Soundstage (creator), Nelson Mandela Freedom Fest, 1988. Recipient Golden Rose of Montreax (Switzerland) Montreax Film Fest, 1975, Golden Globe award Hollywood Fgn. Press Assn., Los Angeles, 1983, Emmy award Acad. of TV Arts and Scis., Los Angeles, 1984, Emmy award nominations, 1986, 88, Visionary award, Producers Guild of Am., 2007. Mem. Nat. Assn. Cable TV (bd. dirs.). Avocations: golf, music, writing. Office: Ken Ehrlich Prodns 17200 Oak View Dr Encino CA 91316-4014*

EHRLICH, MICHELLE, dermatologist; AB, Princeton U., 1995; MD, SUNY, 2000. Resident Cleve. CLinic, 2003—04; dermatologist SPA-MD, La Jolla, Calif., 2004—05, Palos Verdes Dermatology, 2005—, UCLA, LA, 2005—. Grantee, Am. Soc. Dermatology, 2003, 2005. Mem.: Am. Acad. Dermatology. Office: Palos Verdes Dermatology Assocs 550 Deep Valley Dr Ste 287 Rolling Hills CA 90274

EHRLICH, MORTON, marketing executive, management consultant; b. NYC, Dec. 1, 1944; s. Milton and Anne (Tannenbaum) E.; children: Bruce, Ellen, Wendy; m. Paula Ehrlich, Feb. 25, 1991. BBA cum laude, CCNY, 1960; PhD in Econs. (Ford Found. fellow), Brown U., 1965. Economist Fed. Res. Bank of N.Y., 1965-67, Nat. Indsl. Conf. Bd., NYC, 1967-68; v.p. Eastern Airlines, Miami, 1968-76, sr. v.p., 1976-85, bd. dirs., 1976—85; exec. v.p. Transworld Airlines, NY, 1985-88; also bd. dirs.; pres. LIFECO Svcs. Corp., 1988—91; chmn., CEO Integrated Mgmt. Corp., 1991—96; CEO A Privileged Lifestyle, Inc., 1996—. Trustee U. Miami; bd. dirs. Nat. Bur. Econ. Rsch., IBM/AFEC, AETNA Mut. Funds, Eastern Airlines, TWA. Author: Discretionary Income, 1967, A Weekly Index of Business Activity, 1967, U.S. Foreign Trade, 1968, Computer Application in the Allocation of Airline Resources, 1975, An Integrated System for Airline Planning and Management Information, 1977, An Integrated Strategic Plan for Network Marketing, 1996, Paradigm Shift Syndrome, 1997, rev. edit., 2007. With US Army, 1953—56. Mem. Am. Econ. Assn., Nat. Assn. Bus. Economists, U.S. C. of C. Office: A Privileged Lifestyle Inc 1000 Venetian Way Ste 1702 Miami FL 33139-1009 Office Phone: 305-530-8011. Personal E-mail: lifestyle2@bigplanet.com.

EHRLICH, PAUL RALPH, biology professor; b. Phila., May 29, 1932; s. William and Ruth (Rosenberg) E.; m. Anne Fitzhugh Howland, Dec. 18, 1954; 1 child, Lisa Marie. AB, U. Pa., 1953; AM, U. Kans., 1955, PhD, 1957. Research assoc. U. Kans., Lawrence, 1958—59; asst. prof. biol. scis. Stanford U., 1959—62, assoc. prof., 1962—66, prof., 1966—, Bing prof. population studies, 1976—, dir. grad. study dept. biol. scis., 1966—69, pres. Ctr. for Conservation Biology, 1988—, dir. grad. study dept. biol. scis., 1974—76. Cons. Behavioral Rsch. Labs., 1963—67; corr. NBC News, 1989—92. Author: How to Know the Butterflies, 1961, Process of Evolution, 1963, Principles of Modern Biology, 1968, Population Bomb, 1968, Population Bomb, 2d edit., 1971, Population, Resources, Environment: Issues in Human Ecology, 1970, Population, Resources, Environment: Issues in Human Ecology, 2d edit., 1972, How to Be a Survivor, 1971, Global Ecology: Readings Toward a Rational Strategy for Man, 1971, Man and the Ecosphere, 1971, Introductory Biology, 1973, Human Ecology: Problems and Solutions, 1973, Ark II: Social Response to Environmental Imperatives, 1974, The End of Affluence: A Blueprint for the Future, 1974, Biology and Society, 1976, Race Bomb, 1977, Ecoscience: Population, Resources, Environment, 1977, Insect Biology, 1978, The Golden Door: International Migration, Mexico, and the U.S., 1979, Extinction: The Causes and Consequences of the Disappearance of Species, 1981, The Machinery of Nature, 1986, Earth, 1987, The Science of Ecology, 1987, The Birder's Handbook, 1988, New World/New Mind, 1989, The Population Explosion, 1990, Healing the Planet, 1991, Birds in Jeopardy, 1992, The Birdwatchers Handbook, 1994, The Stork & the Plow, 1995, Betrayal of Science and Reason, 1996, World of Wounds, 1997, Human Natures, 2000, Wild Solutions, 2001, Butterflies: Ecology and Evolution Taking Flight, 2003, On the Wings of Checkerspots, 2004, One with Nineveh, 2004; contbr. articles to profl. jours. Co-recipient Crafoord prize in population biology and conservation biol. diversity, 1990; recipient World Wildlife Fedn. medal, 1987, Volvo Environ. prize, 1993, World Ecology medal, Internat. Ctr. Tropical Ecology, 1993, UN Sasakawa Environ. prize, 1994, Heinz prize for the environment, 1995, Tyler Environ. prize, 1998, Heineken prize for environ. sci., 1998, Blue Plant prize, 1999, Disting. Achievement award, Kansas U. Alumni, 2003; fellow MacArthur Prize fellow, 1990—95. Fellow: AAAS, Entomology Soc. Am., Am. Philos. Soc., Am. Acad. Arts and Scis., Calif. Acad. Scis. (Fellows medal 2003); mem.: NAS, Lepidopterists Soc., Am. Mus. Natural History (hon.), Am. Mus. Natural History (life), Brit. Ecol. Soc. (hon.), Am. Soc. Naturalists, Soc. Systematic Biology, Soc. for Study of Evolution, Ecol. Soc. Am. (Eminent Ecologist award 2001). Office: Stanford U Dept Biol Scis Stanford CA 94305

EHRLICH, PHILIP, philosophy educator; b. Bklyn., Aug. 2, 1949; s. Irving and Lena Ehrlich; m. Carmella Matzuba-Ehrlich, May 9, 1993; children: Tirosh Matzuba-Ehrlich, Adar Matzuba-Ehrlich. PhD, U. Ill., Chgo., 1979. Asst. prof. dept. philosophy Brown U., Providence, 1986—92; assoc. prof. Ohio U., Athens, 1993—2000, prof., 2000—. Contbr. articles to profl. jours. Recipient Assoc. award, Ctr. for Philosophy of Sci., U. Pitts., 1999—; fellow, 2002; grantee, NSF, 1993—95, 1996—99; Presdl. Rsch. scholar in Arts and Humanities, Ohio U., 2002—07. Mem.: Am. Philos. Assn., Assn. for Symbolic Logic, Philosophy of Sci. Assn. Achievements include research in theory of absolute continua; history of non-Archimedean Mathematics; Number Systems with Simplicity Hierarchies: A Generalization of Conway's Theory of Surreal Numbers. Office: Philosophy Dept Ohio Univ Ellis Hall RM 202 Univ Ter Athens OH 45701 Office Phone: 740-593-4595. Office Fax: 740-593-4597. Business E-Mail: ehrlich@ohio.edu.

EHRLICH, STEPHEN RICHARD, lawyer; b. Rockville Centre, NY, Dec. 28, 1949; s. Harry Simon and Ida G. (Lable) E. BA, U. Pa., 1971; JD, U. Denver, 1977. Bar: Colo. 1977, U.S. Dist. Ct. Colo. 1977. Pvt. practice, Denver, 1977—. Mem. Assn. Trial Lawyers Am., Colo. Bar Assn., Colo. Trial Lawyers Assn., Denver Bar Assn. Avocations: skiing, tennis, bicycling. Office Phone: 303-830-7666.

EHRLICH, STEVEN DAVID, architect; b. June 12, 1946; s. Samuel J. and Betty Ehrlich; m. Marlo Lani Ehrlich, Jan. 3, 1981; children: Vanessa, Sarah, Julia, Bebecca. BS, Rensselaer Poly. Inst., Troy, NY, 1968, BArch, 1969. Registered architect, Calif. Arch. Peace Corps., Morocco, 1969—71; tchr. Ahmadu Bello U., Nigeria, 1974—77; pvt. practice arch. Venice, Calif., 1978—. Tchr. U. So. Calif., LA, 1982—83, Sci.-Arch., Santa Monica, Calif., 1983, UCLA, 1985. Recipient Builders Choice Grand award, Builders Mag., 1983, 1985. Fellow: AIA (Design awards LA chpt. 1981, 1982, 1983, 1987, Design awards Calif. chpt. 1983—84, 1988, Design awards Sunset chpt. 1983). Office: Steven Ehrlich Archs 10865 Washington Blvd Culver City CA 90232 Office Phone: 310-838-9700. Office Fax: 310-838-9737.*

EHRLICH, THOMAS, law educator; b. Cambridge, Mass., Mar. 4, 1934; s. William and Evelyn (Seltzer) E.; m. Ellen (Rome), June 18, 1957; children, David, Elizabeth, Paul. AB, Harvard U., Cambridge, Mass., 1956, LLB, 1959; LLD (hon.), Villanova U., 1979, Notre Dame U., 1980, Pa. State U., 1987. Bar: Wis., 1959. Law clk. Judge Learned Hand U.S. Ct. Appeals 2d. Cir., 1959-60; spl. asst. to legal adviser U.S. State Dept., 1962-64, spl. asst. to under-sec., 1964-65; assoc. prof. law Stanford U., Stanford, Calif., 1965-68; prof. Stanford U., Stanford, Calif., 1968-75; dean Stanford U., Stanford, Calif., 1971-75, Richard E. Lang dean and prof., 1973-75; pres. Legal Services Corp., Washington, 1976-79; dir. Internat. Devel. Coop. Agy., Washington, 1979-81; provost, prof. law U. Penn., Phila., 1981-87; pres., prof. law Ind. U., Bloomington and Indpls., Ind., 1987-94; vis. prof. Duke U., Durham, NC, 1994; disting. Univ. scholar U. Calif., San Francisco, 1995-2000. Vis. prof. Stanford Law Sch., 1994-99; sr. scholar, Carnegie Found. for Advancement of Tchg., 1997—. Author: (with Abram Chayes and Andreas F. Lowenfeld) The Internat. Legal Process, 3 vols., 1968; (with Herbert L. Packer) New Directions in Legal Edn., 1972, Internat. Crises and the Role of Law, Cyprus, 1958-67, 1974; editor: (with Geoffrey C. Hazard Jr.) Going to Law School?, 1975; (with Mary Ellen O'Connell) Internat. Law and the Use of Force, 1993, The Courage to Inquire, 1995, Philanthropy and the Nonprofit Sector in a Changing Am., 1998, Civic Responsibility and Higher Edn., 2000; (with Jane V. Wellman) How the Student Hour Shapes Higher Education: The Tie that Binds, 2003; (with others) Educating Citizens: Preparing America's Undergraduates for Lives of Moral and Civic Responsibility, 2003, (with Ray Bacchetti) Reconnecting Education & Foundations: Turning Good Intentions Into Educational Capital, 2006, (with others) Educating for Democracy: Preparing Undergraduates for Responsible Political Engagement, 2007. Office: Carnegie Found Advancement Tchg 51 Vista Ln Stanford CA 94305-8703 Home Phone: 650-853-8608; Office Phone: 650-566-5137. E-mail: ehrlich@carnegiefoundation.org.

EHRMAN, LEE, geneticist, educator; b. NYC, May 25, 1935; m. Richard Erhman, 1955 (dec. Mar. 2007); children: Esther, Judith. BS, Queens Coll., Flushing, NY, 1956; MS, Columbia U., NYC, 1957, PhD in Genetics, 1959; DSc (hon.), CUNY, 1989. Mem. faculty Barnard Coll., 1956-58; postdoctoral fellow in genetics Columbia U., NYC, 1959-61, assoc. seminar on population biology, 1981—; mem. faculty SUNY-Purchase, 1970—, prof. div. natural scis., 1972—; Disting. prof. biology SUNY, Purchase, 1995—; mem. spl. study sect. NIH, NIMH, 1979-80. Vis. disting. prof. U. Miami, Coral Gables, Fla., 1981; vis. lectr. U. Puerto Rico, Rio Piedras, 1987; coord., panelist workshops, programs in field; mem. panels NIH, 2003—. Author: Behavior Genetics and Evolution, 2nd edit., 1981; assoc. editor Evolution; assoc. editor for genetics and cytology Am. Midland Naturalist; co-editor: Behavior Genetics; assoc. editor, exec. com. Soc. Am. Naturalists, 1977-85, pres.-elect 1990; contbr. more than 500 articles to profl. jours. Recipient Lit. Soc. Found. medal in German, 1956; Shirley Farr postdoctoral fellow, 1961-62; USPHS postdoctoral fellow, 1959-61; faculty exch. scholar, 1974—; NSF grantee, 1979-84; Sr. Scientist awardee Whitehall Found., 1987, 93; NIH gen. med. scis. grantee, 1987—; SUNY travel grantee, 1988, 93, 96; Merck rsch. support grantee, 2000—. Fellow AAAS (Rsch. Support award Merck/AAAS, 2001), Inst. Soc. Ethics and Life Scis; mem. AAUW (life), Am. Soc. Naturalists (pres. 1990), Behavior Genetics Assn. (pres. 1978, Dobzhansky award for lifetime resch. 1988), Soc. for Study of Evolution (exec. council 1986), Phi Beta Kappa, Sigma Xi Home: 2 Jennifer Ln Rye Brook NY 10573-1916 Office: SUNY Div Natural Scis Purchase NY 10577 Office Phone: 914-251-6671. Office Fax: 914-251-6635.

EHRMANN, SUSANNA, language educator, photographer, writer; b. Detroit, Oct. 17, 1944; d. Frederick Michael and Stephanie (Fiala) Ehrmann. Student, U. Laval, summer 1965; BA, Antioch Coll., Yellow Springs, Ohio, 1966; MAT, U. Chgo., 1968. Cert. tchr., Ill., Tex., Va. Tchr. fgn. lang. U. Chgo. Lab. Schs., 1967-74, Maimonides Sch., Brookline, Mass., 1975-76, North Shore Country Day Sch., Winnetka, Ill., 1977-78, Copenhagen Internat. Jr. Sch., 1978-79, Houston C.C., 1979-81, 84, Kinkaid Sch., Houston, 1980-82, Alief Ind. Sch. Dist., Houston, 1982-85, Houston Ind. Sch. Dist., 1990-91, Sch. of the Woods, Houston, 2006—07, Plum Grove Jr. High, Rolling Meadows, Ill., 2007—; pvt. instr., 1986—; freelance rschr., editor, 1986—; writer, photographer, 1993—. Mem. North Ctrl. evaluating teams, Chgo., Rockford, 1971; mem. MAT coordinating com. on Romance langs., U. Chgo., 1971-74. Creator German Grammar Game, 1982. Reader for the blind, Chgo., 1972-74. NDEA fellow, 1966-68; Goethe Inst. grantee, 1983. Mem. MLA, Am. Assn. Tchrs. of French, Am. Assn. Tchrs. of German. Home: 200 W Campbell St #706 Arlington Heights IL 60005-5802 Home Phone: 847-222-7153. Personal E-mail: sfiala2@sbcglobal.net.

EHRNSCHWENDER, ARTHUR ROBERT, former utility company executive; b. Cin., Oct. 3, 1922; s. Arthur Michael and Lydia Carol (Widmer) E.; m. Grace Scholl Popplewell, Oct. 19, 1950 (dec. Apr. 2004); children: Barry N., Scott A. ME, U. Cin., 1948, BS in Commerce, 1959; MBA, Xavier U., 1959; D in Tech. Letters (hon.), Cin. Tech. Coll., 1980. Registered profl. engr., Ohio, Ky. Field engr. SKF Bearing Co., Cin., 1948-49; Chevrolet field rep. GM, Cin., 1949-50; with Cin. Gas and Electric Co., 1952-84, former sr. v.p. Bd. dirs. Porter Precision Products, Cin.; vice chmn., bd. dirs. OKI Supply Co., Cin.; past chmn. The Hwy. Rental Co., Cin. Electric Co. Past pres. Goodwill Industries, Cin., 1961-85; trustee emeritus Cin. Assn. for Blind, 1965—, Deaconess Hosp., Cin., 1970—, Hamilton County YMCA, 1974—. Capt. U.S. Army, 1943-46, 1950-52. Decorated Bronze Star, 1952; named Disting. Alumnus U. Cin., 1974, Xavier U. Mem. Soc. Automotive Engrs. (sect. chmn.), Engring. Soc. Cin., Edison Electric Inst. (divsn. chmn.), Am. Gas Assn. (sect. chmn.), Univ. Club Cin., Cin. Country Club, The Club Pelican Bay, Naples Yacht Club, Stumps Boat Club, Masons (hon. 33d degree). Republican. Presbyterian. Home: 1201 Edgecliff Pl Apt 1083 Cincinnati OH 45206-2853

EHSANI, MEHRDAD (MARK), electrical engineering educator, consultant; naturalized, US, 1980; s. Heshmat and Didar (Ahmadi) Ehsani; m. Zohreh Khadem; children: Evan Mancil, Nathaniel William. MS, U. Tex., 1974; PhD, U. Wis., 1981. Registered profl. engr., Tex. Rsch. engr. Fusion Rsch. Ctr. U. Tex., Austin, 1974-77; rsch. engr. Argonne (Ill.) Nat. Lab., 1977-81; prof. elec. engring. Tex. A&M U., College Station, 1981, Halliburton prof. elec. engring., 1992, Dress Industries prof., 1994, dir. Tex. Applied Power Electronics Ctr., 1999, dir. advanced vehicle systems rsch. program, Dow Chem. fellow Coll. Engring., 2001—02, Robert M. Kennedy endowed chair prof. elec. engring., 2004—. Lectr. in field. Author: Converter Circuits for Superconductive Magnetic Energy Storage, 1988, Modern Electrical Drives, 2000; co-author: ANSI/IEEE Standards 936, 1987, Vehicular Power Systems: Land, Sea, Air and Space, 2004, Modern Electric, Hybrid Electric and Fuel Cell Vehicles: Fundamentals, Theory and Design, 2005; contbr. articles to profl. jours. Named Outstanding Young Engr., Tex. Soc. Profl. Engrs., 1984, Disting. Lectr., IEEE-Industry Applications Soc., Inds. Elecs. Soc., IEEE Vehicular Tech. Soc., Dow Chem. fellow, Coll. Engring., Tex. A&M U., 2001. Fellow: IEEE (mem. steering com. Vehicle Power and Propulsion Conf., Field award in Undergrad. Tchg. 2003), Soc. Automotive Engrs.; mem.: Vehicular Tech. Soc. of IEEE (bd. govs., bd. dirs., assoc. editor, James R. Evans Avant Garde award 2001), Industry Applications Soc. of IEEE (exec. coun. 1989—93, Disting. lectr.), Power Electronics Soc. IEEE (mem. adminstrv. com. 1990—96, 2005—). Baha'I. Achievements include patents in field. Office: Tex A&M U Dept Elec Engring College Station TX 77843-0001 Home Phone: 979-694-1919; Office Phone: 979-845-7582. Business E-Mail: ehsani@ee.tamu.edu.

EIBELER, PAUL G., former computer game company executive; b. July 26, 1955; BA, Loyola Coll., 1978. Exec. positions Impact Inc., 1991—98; exec. v.p., gen. mgr. Acclaim N.Am., 1998—99, pres., COO, 2003; pres. Take2 Interactive Software, Inc., NYC, 2000—03, 2004—, CEO, 2005—07, bd. dirs., 2000—03, 2004—07. Bd. dirs. Dwango No. Am. Corp.; cons. Microsoft, Corp. Xbox Launch Team.

EIBEN, ROBERT MICHAEL, pediatric neurologist, educator; b. Cleve., July 12, 1922; s. Michael Albert and Frances Carlysle (Gedeon) E.; m. Anne F. Eiben; children: Daniel F., Christopher J., Thomas M., Mary, Charles G., Elizabeth A. BS, Western Res. U., 1944, MD, 1946. Diplomate Am. Bd. Pediatrics. Intern medicine Univ. Hosp., Cleve., 1946-47; asst. resident pediatrics and contagious diseases City Hosp., Cleve., 1947; asst. resident pediatrics Babies and Children's Hosp., Cleve., 1948, clin. fellow pediatrics, 1948-49; clin. instr. pediatrics Western Res. U., 1949-50; asst. med. dir. div. contagious diseases City Hosp., 1949-50, visitant in pediatrics, 1949-50; practice medicine specializing in pediatrics Cleve., 1949-90; acting dir. dept. pediatrics and contagious diseases City Hosp., 1950-52; asst. dir. dept. pediatrics and contagious diseases Cleve. Met. Gen. Hosp., 1952-60; med. dir. Respiratory Care and Rehab. Center, 1954-60, pres. med. staff, 1958-60; USPHS fellow in neurology U. Wash., 1960-63; pediatric neurologist Cleve. (Ohio) Met. Gen. Hosp., 1963—90, acting med. dir. comprehensive care program, 1966-67, med. dir., 1968-73, mem. med. exec. com., 1974-76; acting chief, sect. on clin. investigations and therapeutics Developmental and Metabolic Neurology br. Nat. Inst. Neurol. and Communicative Disorders and Strokes, NIH, Bethesda, Md., 1976-77; acting dir. dept. pediatrics Metro Health Med. Ctr., 1979-80; from instr. pediatrics to prof. emeritus Western Res. U., 1950—91, prof. emeritus pediatric neurology, 1991—. Cons., project site visitor Nat. Found. Birth Defects Center Programs, 1961-66; mem. adv. com. on grants to train dentists to care for handicapped Robert Wood Johnson Found., 1975-80; emeritus faculty marshall Case Western Res. U., 1992-2007, mem. regional leadership coun., 2003-. Mem. coun. Bratenahl Village-County of Cuyahoga, 1982-98. Recipient Presdl. award Internat. Poliomyelitis Congress, Geneva, 1957, Clifford J. Vogt Alumni Svc. award Case Western Res. U., Cleve., 1985; established Annual Robert M. Eiben, M.D. vis. professorship in child neurology MetroHealth Med. Ctr. Dept. Pediat., 1991. Mem.: Child Neurology Soc. (chmn. tng. program com. 1976—77, sec.-treas. 1978—81, pres. 1983—85, Lifetime Career Achievement award 2005), Innominatum Soc., No. Ohio Pediat. Soc., Am. Epilepsy Soc., Am. Pediat. Soc., Am. Soc. Human Genetics, Am. Acad. Neurology (chmn. residence exam. com.

1989—93), Am. Acad. Pediat., Case Western Res. U. Med. Alumni Assn. (pres. 1979, bd. of trustees 2002—), Pasteur Club. Home: 2 Oakshore Dr Bratenahl OH 44108-1118 Office: MetroHealth Med Ctr 2500 Metrohealth Dr Cleveland OH 44109-1900

EIBER, CAROL SHATTUCK, language educator; d. George H. and Rosemary Shattuck; m. Gary S. Eiber, Dec. 29, 1969; children: Jeffrey, Theresa. BA in French, Mt. Union Coll., Alliance, Ohio, 1969; MEd in Higher Edn., Kent State U., Ohio, 1991. French tchr. Copley Jr. HS, Ohio, 1969—70; English tchr. Nido de Aguilas Internat. Sch., Santiago, 1972; French tchr. Hudson Montessori Sch., Ohio, 1983—84; Spanish tchr. Stow-Monroe Falls HS, Ohio, 1984—. Mem.: Stow-Munroe Falls Fgn. Lang. Dept. (dept. chairperson 2005—), Ohio Fgn. Lang. Assn. (Secondary Outstanding Tchr. 2003), Jr. League Akron Bd. (corr. sec. 1988—89). Avocations: travel, golf, reading. Office: Stow Munroe Falls HS 3227 E Graham Rd Stow OH 44224

EIBERGER, CARL FREDERICK, lawyer; b. Denver, Jan. 17, 1931; s. Carl Frederick and Madeleine Anastasia (Ries) E.; children: Eileen, Carl III, Mary, James. BS in Chemistry magna cum laude, U. Notre Dame, 1952, JD magna cum laude, 1954; MBA, Denver U., 1959. Sole practice, 1954-55; ptnr. Rovira, DeMuth & Eiberger, Denver, 1957—79, Eiberger, Stacy, Smith & Martin, Denver, 1979-96; prin. Carl F. Eiberger & Assocs., Denver, 1996—. Chmn. CBA/DBA/Econs. of Law Practice Coms.; co-founder CBA/Steering Com. Labor Law Com., Denver; arbitrator Am. Arbitration Assn.; asst. bar examiner, 1963-68; lectr. on continuing legal edn. Contbr. articles to legal jours. Bd. dirs. Colo. Assn. Commerce and Industry; pres. Prospect Recreation and Park Dist.; founder Applewood Athletic Club, Jefferson County; gen. counsel Denver Symphony Orch. Recipient merit award Jefferson County Commrs., merit cert. Jefferson County Homeowners, McCafferty Disting Svc. award U. Notre Dame Law Sch.; named Man of the Yr. Notre Dame Club of Denver, Vol. of Yr. Channel 9TV, Denver., Citizen of Yr., Lions Club Internat., Citizen Amb. of US, Silent Hero of Notre Dame, 2006; Prospect Dist. Pk. named in his honor. Mem. ABA, Colo. Bar Assn. (bd. govs.), Denver Bar Assn. (nominated pres.), Notre Dame Law Assn. (bd. dirs. 1965—, exec. com. 1998—), Gov. Adv. Coun. to Colo dept. of labor, Notre Dame Club (pres., bd. dirs.), Athletic Club (Denver). Roman Catholic. Home and Office: 14330 Fairview Ln Golden CO 80401-2050 Office Phone: 303-278-0707. Fax: 303-278-0113.

EIBERSON, JEFFREY LAWRENCE, psychologist, consultant; b. NYC, July 24, 1944; s. Harold and Rosalyn K. Eiberson; m. Carol Galin Eiberson (div.). BA, Queens Coll., 1966; MA, Goddard Coll., 1976; PhD, Union Inst., 1977. Lic. Psychologist 1979. Personnel mgmt. analysis Phila. Sch. Dist., 1967—75, coord. data mgmt., 1975—83; staff counselor Eromin Ctr. Inc., Phila., 1973—75; psychologist Pvt. Practice, Phila., 1979—. Co-chmn., bd. dirs. Eromin Ctr. Inc., Phila., 1982—85; cons. Safeguards Project, Phila., 2000—05; cons. affiliate Friends Hosp., Phila., 2003—. Author: (serialized book) Becoming Gay: The Psychology of Homsexual Develop., 1979, (tng. manual) Diagnostic Approach to Transactional Awareness, 1976. Mem. bd. dirs. Political Action Group, Phila., 1992—94; co-founder Eromin Ctr. Inc., Phila., 1973; charter mem. Gay Activist Alliance, Phila., 1971—74; mem. William Way Cmty. Ctr., Phila., 1999—; co-founder City of Brotherly Love Softball League, 1984. Named Hall of Fame, City of Brotherly Love Softball League, 2004; recipient Lifetime Achievement award, City of Brotherly Love, 2004. Mem.: Sys. Centered Tng. and Rsch. Inst., Assn. for Advancement of Psychology, Pa. Psychol. Assn., Am. Psychol. Assn. Democrat. Avocations: sports, theater, exercise. Home: 1326 Spruce St #1905 Philadelphia PA 19107 Office: Jeffrey L Eiberson 1326 Spruce St Ste 1905 Philadelphia PA 19107 Office Phone: 215-546-1767. Personal E-mail: jledoc@aol.com.

EICH, WILBUR FOSTER, III, retired pediatrician; b. June 26, 1938; s. Wilbur Foster Jr. and Lula Olivia (Dudley) Eich; m. Eugenia Glass Graves, May 31, 1963; children: Paul Foster, Mark Samuel, Donna Eugenia. BA, Huntington Coll., 1960; MD, Tulane U., 1964. Diplomate Am. Bd. Pediatrics; ordained priest Episcopal Ch., 1981. Intern Lloyd Noland Hosp., Fairfield, Ala., 1964—65; resident in pediatrics U.S. Naval Hosp., Portsmouth, Va., 1967—69; pediatrician Infant and Children's Hosp., Florence, Ala., 1971—2006; ret., 2006. Contbr. articles and book revs. to med. and church jours. Trustee Huntingdon Coll., Montgomery, Ala., 1977—2002; Vol. Project Hope, Brazil, 1973. With USN, 1965—71. Fellow: Am. Acad. Pediatrics; mem.: AMA, Lauderdale County Med. Assn., Med. Assn. Ala. Home: 120 Limerick Ct Muscle Shoals AL 35661 Office: 421 W College St Florence AL 35630-5520 Personal E-mail: wfeich@yahoo.com.

EICHBERG, RODOLFO DAVID, physiatrist, educator; b. Pforzheim, Germany, July 26, 1937; came to the U.S., 1965; s. Julio and Ilse (Schonfarber) E.; m. Yvette Salama, May 21, 1965; children: William Amadeo, Matias David. Baccalaureate, St. Andrews Scots Sch., Argentina, 1955; MD, U. Buenos Aires, 0963. Diplomate Am Bd Phys Medicine and Rejab, cert. ind. med. examiner Am. Acad. Disability Evaluating Physicians, ringside physician Am. Assn. Profl. Ringside Physicians. Intern, resident Grace Hosp. Wayne State U., Detroit, 1965-67; orthopedic surgeon Mar Del Plata, Argentina, 1968-73; resident physical medicine NYU, 1973-75; pvt. practice Rehab. and Electro Diagnosis Assocs., P.C., Tampa, 1975-96, 98—; asst. prof. U. So. Fla., Tampa, 1975-93, clin. assoc. prof., 1994—; chief spinal cord injury rehab. Tampa Gen. Hosp., 1984-96; chief phys. medicine & rehab. VA Med. Ctr., New Orleans, 1997-98; med. dir. Meml. Hosp. Ctr. for Comprehensive Rehab., 1998—2004. Mem. state adv. coun. Head Spinal Cord Injuries, Tallahassee, 1976-96; clin. assoc. prof. La. State U. Sch. Medicine, 1997-98; physician advisor State of Fla. Athletic Commn., 1998-99; mem. advisor State of Fla. Agy. for Healthcare Adminstrn., 2001—; cons. MetLife Ins. Co., 2003-. Contbr. articles to profl. jours. Bd. trustees Congregation Schaaraizedek, Tampa, 1980-82. Recipient Honors award City of La Paz, Bolivia, 1994, Physician of Yr. award Tampa Bay Latin Am. Med. Soc., 1997. Mem. AMA, Am. Acad. Phys. Medicine and Rehab. (health policy legis. com. 1990-95), Am. Spinal Injury Assn. (internat. rels. rep. S.C. 1990-95), Assn. Med. Latino Americana de Rehab., Colombian Phys. Medicine Rehab. Soc. (corr.), Argentine Soc. Rehab. Medicine (corr.), Fla. Med. Assn., Fla. Soc. Phys. Medicine Rehab. (pres. 1994-96), Hillsborough County Med. Assn. (exec. coun. 2001-03), So. Soc. Phys. Medicine and Rehab. (pres. 1999-2000). Jewish. Avocations: boating, travel, aerobics. Office: Rehab and Electro Diag Assocs PA 2914 N Boulevard Tampa FL 33602-1208 Office Phone: 813-228-7696. Personal E-mail: eichberg@tampabay.rr.com.

EICHELBERGER, CHARLES BELL, retired career officer; b. LaGrange, Ga., Nov. 19, 1934; s. Charlie Wirt and Sybil Peavy (Johnson) E.; m. Jaqueline Ann Wood, July 17, 1955; children: Susan Christie Eichelberger Benator, Terrie Lynn Eichelberger Safranca. Cert. in Liberal Arts, Ga. Mil. Coll., 1955; BS in Law Enforcement, U. Nebr., 1971; MEd, Pepperdine U., 1977. Commd. 2d lt. U.S. Army, 1957, advanced through grades to lt. gen., 1989; comdr. U.S. Army Field Station, Berlin, 1978-80; div. chief Reconnaissance, Intelligence, Surveillance and Electronic Warfare Div., dep. chief of staff for ops. and plans, Dept. of Army, Washington, 1980-82; dep. comdt. U.S. Army Intelligence Ctr. and Sch., Ft. Huachuca, Ariz., 1982-84; dir. of intelligence (J-2) U.S. Cen. Command, MacDill AFB, Fla., 1984-86; dep. chief of staff for intelligence U.S. Army Europe, Heidelberg, Fed. Republic Germany, 1986-88, Dept. of Army, Washington, 1988-91; ret., 1991. Contbr. articles to profl. jours. Decorated D.S.M. with oak leaf cluster, Nat. Intelligence D.S.M. (CIA), Master Parachutist badge. Mem. Assn. Old Crows, Assn. U.S. Army, Ret. Officers' Assn. Home: 7121 Bailey Rd Sachse TX 75048-2542 E-mail: gen.ike@verizon.net.

EICHEN, JEFFREY L., lawyer; b. Rochester, NY; BSE cum laude, U. Penn., Wharton Sch. of Bus., 1987; JD cum laude, Georgetown U., 1990. Bar: NJ 1990, NY 1991, Fla. 1991, Pa. 1992, US Ct. of Appeals, Second, Third & Ninth Circuits, US Dist. Ct., NJ, NY (Ea. & So. Dist.), Pa. (Ea. Dist.), US Patent and Trademark Office. Ptnr. Schnader, Harrison, Segal & Lewis, Phila.; ptnr., intellectual property litigation Venable LLP, Washington, 2004—. Adjunct prof., intellectual property law Peirce Coll., Phila. Mem.: ABA, Bucks County Bar Assn., Pa. Bar Assn., NYC Bar Assn., AIPLA. Office: Venable LLP 575 7th St NW Washington DC 20004 Office Phone: 202-344-4985. Office Fax: 202-344-5775. Business E-Mail: jeichen@venable.com.

EICHENBERG, PETER THOMPSON, retired criminal investigator; s. Paul Lawrence Eichenberg and Patricia Ann Thompson; married, June 2, 1982; children: Cory Franklyn, Pete L. AS, BS, U. Albuquerque, 1986. Juvenile probation officer 2d Jud. Dist. Ct., 1974—75; security officer Fed. Protection Svc., 1975—76; fraud investigator, owner Albuquerque Investigation Svc., 1977—91; patrol operator, owner Peter Thompson & Assoc., 1978—80; recreation aide KAFB Youth Ctr., N.Mex., 1980—82, asst. dir. N.Mex., 1982—84; spl. dep. Sandoval County Sheriff's Dept., 1983—84; investigator litigation unit City Atty.'s Office, 1985—86; fraud investigator N.Mex. Workers' Compensation Adminstrn., 1991—2000; cons. Peter Eichenberg & Assocs., 2000—02; gaming auditor N.Mex. Gaming Control Bd., N.Mex., 2002—04. Instr., coach Youth Sports Assn., 1981—; dir. N.Mex. Respite Assn., Inc., 2001—04. Contbr. articles to profl. jours. Driver Catholic Charities of N.Mex.; sponsor Christian Found. for Children and Aging, Kansas City, Kans. With US Army, 1965—71. John Robert Meml. scholar, 1986. Mem.: VFW, Nat. Notary Assn., Nat. Police and Firefighters Assn., Delta Epsilon Sigma. Democrat. Roman Catholic. Avocations: reading, fishing, softball, running. Mailing: PO Box 11671 Albuquerque NM 87192 Office: News in NMex Albuquerque NM 87192

EICHENBERGER GILMORE, JULIE MAE, research scientist; b. New Hampton, Iowa, Aug. 12, 1956; d. Phillip Mathias Eichenberger and Harriette Elizabeth Porter; m. James Cecil Gilmore, Nov. 8, 1986; 1 child, Hallie Jean Gilmore. PhD, U. Iowa, Iowa City, 1998—2001. Registered Dietitian Am. Dietetic Assn., 1987. Dir., food and nutrition U. Iowa Hosps. and Clinics, Iowa City, 1992—96; rsch. scientist U. Iowa Coll. of Dentistry, Iowa City, 1997—. Mem.: Iowa Dietetic Assn. (assoc.; pres. 1998—99, Medallion award 2002), Am. Dietetic Assn. (assoc. Mary P. Huddleson award 2006). Office: Coll of Dentistry Univ of Iowa Iowa City IA 52242 Office Phone: 319-353-5476.

EICHENWALD, HEINZ FELIX, physician; b. Switzerland, Mar. 3, 1926; came to U.S., 1936, naturalized, 1945; s. Ernst M. and Stella E.; m. Linda E. Moragné, July 20, 1995; children: Kathryn S., Eric C., Kurt A., Michael M. BA in Biochem. Scis. magna cum laude, Harvard U., 1946; MD, Cornell U., 1950. Intern, sr. asst. resident, sr. resident pediatrician N.Y. Hosp., 1950-51; asst. in pediat. Cornell U. Med. Sch., 1951-53, instr., then asst. prof., 1955-58, assoc. prof., then prof. pediat., 1958-64; USPHS instr. pediat. Emory U. Med. Sch., 1953-55; also vis. physician Grady and Crawford Long hosps., Atlanta; mem. staff N.Y. Hosp., 1958-65, attending pediatrician, 1963-65; vis. asst. prof. Albert Einstein Med. Sch., 1956-58; cons. Hosp. Spl. Surgery, NYC, 1956-64, Patterson (N.J.) Gen. Hosp., 1958-64; prof. pediat., chmn. dept. U. Tex. Southwestern Med. Sch., Dallas, 1964-83; chief-of-staff Children's Med. Ctr., Dallas, 1964—83; chief pediat. Parkland Meml. Hosp., Dallas, 1964—83, prof. emeritus, 2006. Cons. St. Paul, Irving Cmty., Presbyn. Hosps., Dallas; chief hepatitis investigation unit, epidemiology br. USPHS, 1954-55; Richard Bruce Miller lectr. Harvard U. Med. Sch., 1960; lectr. Columbia U. Tchrs. Coll., 1960-64; chmn. Internat. Rsch. Confs. Mental Retardation, 1965-66; chmn. panel anti-infectives NAS-NRC, 1966-69; vis. prof. U. Saigon Med. Sch., 1968-72; Vanuxem lectr. Princeton U., 1970; bd. dirs. Dallas Free Clinic, 1970-74, Children's Devel. Ctr., Dallas, 1974—; mem. bd. maternal and child health NIH, 1974-78; cons. in field, mem. numerous profl. coms. Assoc. editor Pediatric Therapy, 1974; editor Practical Pediatric Therapy, 1985, Current Therapy in Pediatrics, 1989, Pediatric Therapy, 1993; mem. editorial bd. profl. jours.; contbr. numerous articles in profl. pubs. Bd. dirs., chmn. exec. com. Lamplighter Sch., Dallas, 1971—1980; bd. dirs. Winston Sch., 1974. Recipient Career Rsch. award NIH, 1963-65, Alexander von Humboldt prize Govt. of Germany (then Fed. Republic Germany), 1979, Weinstein-Goldeson award United Cerebral Palsy Found., 1980; Markle scholar med. sci., 1953. Mem. Harvey Soc., Soc. Pediatric Rsch., Am. Pediatric Soc., Infectious Disease Soc. Am., N.Y. Acad. Scis., Tex. Pediatric Soc., Phi Beta Kappa, Sigma Xi, Alpha Omega Alpha. Personal E-mail: echo18@swbell.net.

EICHENWALD, KURT, writer; b. NYC, June 28, 1961; married; 3 children. BA in Polit. Sci., with distinction, Swarthmore, 1983. Speechwriter Walter Mondale presidential campaign; writer, rschr. Election and Survey Unit CBS News, 1984—85; news clk. for Hedrick Smith NY Times, 1985, rsch. asst. to Hedrick Smith, 1985—86, news clk. for nat. desk NYC, 1986—88, bus. writer NYC & Dallas, 1987—2006, fin. reporter, sr. writer, investigative reporter, 1988—2006; assoc. editor Nat. Jour., Washington, 1986; sr. writer & investigative reporter Condé Nast Portfolio, NYC, 2006—. Author: (non-fiction) Serpent on the Rock, 1995, The Informant, 2000 (Business Week bestseller), Conspiracy of Fools, 2005 (NY Times bestseller, Publishers Weekly bestseller). Finalist Pulitzer Prize, 2000; recipient George Polk award, 1996, 1998, Payne award for Ethics in Journalism, U. Oreg. Sch. Journalism & Communication, 2006. Office: Condé Nast Publications Inc 4 Times Sq New York NY 10036 Office Phone: 212-556-1474. Office Fax: 212-556-1448. E-mail: kewald@nytimes.com.

EICHHOLZ, MARK JOSEPH (MICK), lawyer; b. St. Louis, Nov. 7, 1957; s. Bernard Joseph and Nancy Lee (Wolf) E.; children: Neil Andrew, Drew Charles. BA, Benedictine Coll., 1980; MBA, U. Kans., Lawrence, 1985; JD, U. Mo., Columbia, 1988. Bar: Mo. 1988, Kans. 1989. Economist/fin. bank analyst Fed. Reserve Bank of Kans. City, Kansas City, Mo., 1981-85; lawyer Armstrong, Teasdale Law Firm (successor to Dietrich Davis), Kansas City, 1988-91, Witt & Hicklin, P.C., Platte City, Mo., 1991-92, Hackler, Hinkle & Hackler, Olathe, Kans., 1993-98; with Hinkle & Eichholz, Chartered, 1998—. Contbr. articles to profl. jours. Bd. dirs. Olathe Babe Ruth Baseball; chmn. Olathe Citizens Police Adv. Bd., Salvation Army Olathe Corp.; chmn. Olathe Police Found. Recipient Wall St. Jour. award Benedictine Coll., Atchison, 1980. Mem. Kans. Bar Assn. (family law sect.), Mo. Bar Assn., Johnson County Bar Assn., Kans. Assn. Criminal Def. Attys. Republican. Roman Catholic. Avocations: baseball coach, soccer coach, weightlifting coach. Office: Hinkle & Eichholz Chartered 130 N Cherry St Ste 101 Olathe KS 66061-3460 Office Phone: 913-764-8000. Personal E-mail: mickeichholz@msn.com.

EICHHORN, GUNTHER LOUIS, chemist, researcher; b. Frankfurt am Main, Germany, Feb. 8, 1927; s. Fritz David and Else Regina (Weiss) E.; m. Lotti Neuhaus, June 25, 1964; children: David Mark, Sharon Julie. AB in Chemistry, U. Louisville, 1947; MS, U. Ill., 1948, PhD, 1950. From asst. prof. to assoc. prof. chemistry La. State U., 1950-57; commd. officer USPHS, 1954-57; assoc. prof. chemistry Georgetown U., 1957-58; guest scientist Naval Med. Rsch. Inst., 1957-58; chief sect. molecular biology Gerontology Rsch., NIH, Balt., 1958-78, chief lab. cellular and molecular biology and head sect. inorganic biochemistry, 1978-94; scientist emeritus NIH, 1994—. Counsellor La. State U. Hillel Found., 1952—54; pres. Nat. Inst. Child Health and Human Devel. Assembly of Scientists, 1972—73; disting. lectr. Mich. State U., 1972; lectr. Internat. Conf. Biology and the Future of Mankind, Paris, 1974, Internat. Conf. on Coordination Chemistry, São Paulo, Brazil, 1977, Internat. Symposium Biomolecular Structure, Bangalore, India, 1984, Internat. Conf. Molecular Mechanisms Metal Toxicity and Carcinogenicity, Urbino, Italy, 1988, G.L. Eichhorn Symposium on Metals, Nucleic Acids, Transcription and Aging, Balt., 1995; Watkins vis. prof. Wichita State U., 1983; acting sci. dir. Nat. Inst. Aging, 1988; Henry Lardy lectr. SD U., 1988; lectr. in field worldwide. Editor: Inorganic Biochemistry, 1973; co-editor: Advances in Inorganic Biochemistry, 1978—; contbr. numerous articles to profl. jours. Gen. Aniline and Film Co. grantee, 1949; Ohio State U. fellow, summers 1951-52; recipient Woodcock medal U. Louisville, 1947, Md. Chemist of Yr. award, 1978, NIH Dir.'s award, 1979, Sr. Exec. Svc. bonus award, 1982, 88. Fellow AAAS, Am. Inst. Chemists, Gerontol. Soc. (fin. com. 1980-82, research and edn. com. 1982-83); mem. Am. Chem. Soc. (organizer symposium NY 1961, 76, Pitts. 1966, Chgo. 1973, Washington 1983), NY Acad. Scis., Am. Soc. Biochemistry and Molecular Biology, Biophys. Soc. Achievements include reseach in metal-ion induced stabilization and destabilization of DNA double helix, mechanism of RNA degradation by metal ions, nucleic acid conformational changes induced by metal ions; structural basis by which RNA polymerase produces fidelity in transcription (of DNA to RNA), catalysis of double bond cleavage by metal ions, discovery of Schiff base tautomers in vitamin B6-metal complexes; molecular age changes involving metal ions, proteins and nucleic acids. Home: 10500 Rockville Pike Rockville MD 20852-3350 Office: NIH NIA Gerontology Rsch Ctr 5600 Nathan Shock Dr Baltimore MD 21224-6825 Personal E-mail: eichhorngl@juno.com.

EICHINGER, MARILYNNE KATZEN, museum administrator; children: Ryan, Kara, Julia, Jessica, Talik. BA in Anthropology and Sociology magna cum laude, Boston U., 1965; MA, Mich. State U., 1971. With emergency and outpatient staff Ingham County Mental Health Ctr., 1972; founder, pres., exec. dir. Impression 5 Sci. and Art Mus., Lansing, Mich., 1973-85; pres. Oreg. Mus. Sci. and Industry, Portland, 1985-95; bd. dirs. Portland Visitors Assn., 1985-95; pres. Informal Edn. Products Ltd., 1995—, Portland, 1995—. Bd. dirs. N.W. Regional Edn. Labs., 1991-97; instr. Lansing (Mich.) C.C., 1978; ptnr. Eyrie Studio, 1982-85; condr. numerous workshops in interactive exhibit design, adminstrn. and fund devel. for schs., orgns., profl. socs. Author: (with Jane Mack) Lexington Montessori School Survey, 1969, Manual on the Five Senses, 1974; pub. Mich. edit. Boing mag. Founder Cambridge Montessori Sch., 1964; bd. dirs. Lexington Montessori Sch., 1969, Mid-Mich. South Health Sys. Agy., 1978-81, Cmty. Referral Ctr., 1981-85, Sta. WKAR, 1981-85; active Lansing "Riverfest" Lighted Boat Parade, 1980; mem. state Health Coordinating Coun., 1980-82; mem. pres.'s adv. coun. Portland State U., 1986—90, mem. pres.' adv. bd., 1987-91; bd. dirs. Portland Visitors Assn., 1994-97, Friends of Tryon Creek State Pk., 2001-06. Recipient Diana Cert. Leadership, YWCA, 1976-77, Woman of Achievement award, 1991, Cmty. Svc. award Portland State U., 1992, Cataloguer of Yr. award Catalog Success, 2005. Mem. Am. Assn. Mus., Oreg. Mus. Assn., Assn. Sci. and Tech. Ctrs. (bd. dirs. 1980-84, 88-93), Mus. Store Assn., Direct Mktg. Assn., Zonta Lodge (founder, bd. dirs. East Lansing club 1978), Internat. Women's Forum, Woman Pres. Orgn., Portland C. of C. Office: Informal Edn Products Ltd 2517 SE Mailwell Dr Milwaukie OR 97222 Home Phone: 503-224-6374. Business E-Mail: sales@museumtour.com.

EICHLER, BURTON LAWRENCE, lawyer; b. Newark, Mar. 1, 1933; s. Philip and Anna (Kessler) E.; children: Betsy, Peter, Thomas. BS, Ohio State U., 1954; LLB, Rutgers U., 1957. Bar: NJ 1958, N.Y. 1983, U.S. Dist. Ct. NJ 1958, U.S. Ct. Appeals (3d cir.) 1981. Assoc., ptnr. Zucker, Brach & Eichler and predecessor, Newark, 1958-59, ptnr., 1959-67; ptnr. Eichler, Rosenberg & Silver, Newark, 1967-69, Brach, Eichler, Rosenberg, Silver, Newark, 1969-72, Brach, Eichler, Rosenberg, Silver, Bernstein & Hammer PA, East Orange, NJ, 1972-81, Brach, Eichler, Rosenberg, Silver, Bernstein, Hammer & Gladstone PC, Roseland, NJ, 1981-2003, Wolf Block Brach Eichler, Roseland, NJ, 2003—; chmn. dist. fee arbitration com. for Essex County, Dist. V-C, NJ Sup. Ct., 1983-86. Pres., chmn. bd. United Cerebral Palsy, East Oarnge, 1967-69; mem. South Orange/Maplewood Bd. Edn., 1979-83, v.p., 1981-83; bd. dirs. YM-YWHA Met. NJ, West Orange, 1970-74, 99-2002; former trustee Congregation B'nai Jeshurun, Short Hills; bd. dirs. Newark Beth Israel Med. Ctr. Recipient J.H. Cohn Outstanding Young Leadership award Jewish Cmty. Fedn. Met. NJ, East Orange, 1961; named Outstanding Citizen, NJ Acad. Medicine, 1998, one of Best Lawyers in NJ, NJ Monthly, Best Lawyers in Am. Mem. Eseex County Bar Assn. (chmn. med.-legal affairs com. 1985-86), NJ Bar Assn., ABA, Am. Health Lawyers Assn. Office: Wolf Block Brach Eichler 101 Eisenhower Pkwy Roseland NJ 07068 Office Phone: 973-228-5700. Business E-Mail: beichler@wolfblock.com.

EICHLER, HANS JOACHIM, physics professor; b. Berlin, Nov. 9, 1940; s. Hans and Lydia (Wagner) E.; m. Renate Bubel, Dec. 26, 1966; children: Stephanie, Katharina. Diploma in engring., Tech. U. Berlin, D Physics. Asst. Tech. U. Berlin, 1965—69, assoc. prof., 1967—72, prof. physics, 1972—, vice dean, spkr. dept. physics, 1972—. Dir. Optical Inst., Berlin, 1980—; founding bd. U. Paderborn, Germany, 1972, U. Potsdam, Germany, 1993; chmn. EU-Cost Action Optical Data Storage; spkr., Photonics Rsch. Ctr., Tech. U. Berlin, 2001-04; scientific dir., LMTB Inc., 2003—; guest prof. Zheijang U., China. Author: Laser-Induced Dynamic Gratings, 1985, Laser Grundlagen, Systeme, Anwendungen, 1990, 6th edit., 2006, Laser-Hitech mit Licht, 1995, Phys. Grundpraktikum, 2000, 2d edit., 2005; editor spl. issue Jour. Photonic Switching, 1987; assoc. editor IEEE Jour. Quantum Electronics, Jour. Nonlinear Optical Physics, Optical Materials; contbr. over 500 articles to sci. jours. Mem. Physikalische Gesellschaft, Arbeitsgemeinschaft Quantenoptik (chmn. 1980-84), Deutsche Gesellschaft Angewandte Optik, European Phys. Soc. Avocations: tennis, running, skiing, sailing. Office: Technische Univ Hardenbergstrasse 32 10623 Berlin Germany Office Phone: 0049 30 314 21699. Business E-Mail: eichler@physik.tu-berlin.de.

EICHLER, MARC, neurosurgeon; b. Kaisershetern, Germany, Feb. 23, 1966; s. Martin and Paula Eichler. BS, U. Mich., 1988; MD, Wash. U., Mo., 1999. Diplomate Am. Bd. Neurological Surgery. Instr. surgery Harvard Med. Sch., Boston, 1999; neurosurgeon Brigham and Women's Hosp., Boston, 1999, Boston's Children's Hosp., Boston, 1999. Contbr. articles various profl. jours., chapters to books. Fellow: ACS; mem.: AMA, Congress Neurological Surgeons, Am. Assn. Neurological Surgeons. Office: 831 Beacon St Ste 239 Newton Center MA 02459

EICHMAN, CHARLES MELVIN, counselor; b. Ft. Hays, Kans., June 16, 1950; s. Melvin Joseph and Barbara Ann (Bennett) E. BA, U. No. Colo., Greeley, 1972; MA, Fuller Theol. Sem., 1974; cert., U. Mo., 1991, Idaho State U., Pocatello, 2002. Cert. vocat. evaluator, career guidance specialist, sch. counselor, job devel. specialist, secondary sch. tchr, sch. admin. K-12, vocational admin. Coord. youth activity YMCA, Glendale, Calif., 1972—74; counselor U. Colo., Colorado Springs, 1975—76; resident hall advisor U. No. Colo., Greeley, 1976—77; secondary tchr., coach Jefferson County Dist. R-1, Lakewood, Colo., 1978—80; pres., owner Big Sky C.F.M. and Mgmt. Resources, Rock Springs, Wyo., 1980—85; secondary tchr. Boulder Valley Dist. RE-2, Colo., 1986—88; vocat. evaluator and dir. Vocat. Evaluation Ctr. Platte County Dist. RE-111, Platte City, Mo., 1988—92; pres., owner Career Assessment Svcs., Arvada, Colo., 1992—94; sch. counselor, head dist. elem. at-risk student program Albany Schs. Re-1, Laramie, Wyo., 1993—94; sch. counselor, dir. dist. model Kids at Risk program Franklin Jr. H.S. and New Horizons Alt. H.S., Pocatello, 1994—; developer counseling program New Horizons Alt. H.S., Pocatello, 1994—. Affiliate faculty and site supr. Idaho State U., 2001—. Contbr. articles to profl. jours. Bd. dirs. YMCA, Pocatello, Idaho. Mem. ACA (one of 25 nat. legis. inst. participants 2000), NEA, Am. Vocat. Assn., Nat. Assn. Vocat. Edn. Spl. Needs Pers. (region III com. chair 1989-90, cert. of recognition 1990), Am. Sch. Counselors Assn., Am. Assn. Marriage and Family Therapy, Vocat. Evaluation and Work Adjustment Assn. (Wyo. rep. 1993-94, conf. presenter 1991), Mo. Vocat. Spl. Needs Assn. (exec. v.p. 1990-92, spkr. 1989-92, Outstanding Achievement award 1990-91, certs. of appreciation 1988-91), Mo. Sch. Counselors Assn. (spkr. 1989-91), Mo. Vocat. Assn. (spkr. 1992), Idaho Edn. Assn. (assembly del. 2001-03, state legis. del. 2002-05), Idaho Sch. Counseling Assn., Idaho Counseling Assn. (chair pub. policy and legis. com. 1999-2002, conf. presentor, exec. bd. dirs. legis. bill writing), Idaho Assn. Marriage and Family Therapy, Idaho Vocat. Guidance Assn. (com. chair 1997), Idaho Assn. Career Devel., Kiwanis. Avocations: handball, skiing, outdoor adventure, creative arts, swimming. Mailing: PO Box 4931 Pocatello ID 83205-4931 E-mail: CMEichman@aol.com.

EICHMAN, JOHN C., lawyer; b. Atlanta, Aug. 14, 1957; AB magna cum laude, Georgetown U., 1979; JD, U. Chgo., 1982. Bar: Tex. 1982, US Ct. Appeals 5th Cir., US Ct. Appeals 9th Cir., US Dist. Ct. No., Ea., We. & So. Districts Tex. Shareholder, litig. practice group Jenkens & Gilchrist, P.C., Dallas, firm v.p. bd. dirs. Mem.: ABA, Tex. Bar Found., Dallas Bar Assn. Office: Jenkens & Gilchrist PC Ste 3200 1445 Ross Ave Dallas TX 75202-2799 Office Phone: 214-855-4372. Office Fax: 214-855-4300. Business E-Mail: jeichman@jenkens.com.

EICHORN, DANIEL J., lawyer; b. Lewiston, Maine, July 27, 1969; s. Charles R. and Dale L. Eichorn; m. Mary Beth Hayes, Oct. 11, 1997; children: Rosemary D., Victoria E. AB, Vassar Coll., Poughkeepsie, NY, 1991; JD, U. Maine, Portland, 1998. Bar: Maine 1999, US Dist. Ct. Maine 2002. Assoc. Kline Law Office, Portland, 1999, David Q. Whittlier, PA, 2002—05; comm. cons. Anthem Blue Cross Blue Shield, 1999—2002; ptnr. Whittier Glynn Martin & Eichorn, P.A., South Paris, Maine, 2005—06; owner Eichorn Law Offices, P.A., South Paris, 2006—. Mem. Planning Bd., Hebron, Maine, 2005—. Mem.: Oxford County Trial Lawyers Assn. (treas. 2005—07), Kiwanis (v.p. Norway-Paris chpt. 2005—06). Office: Eichorn Law Offices PA PO Box 368 South Paris ME 04281 Office Phone: 207-739-2977. Office Fax: 207-739-2296. Business E-Mail: daniel@eichornlaw.com.

EICK-GAMM, KIMBERLY MARIE, social worker; b. Waterloo, Iowa, Sept. 20, 1959; d. Darrell Herbert and Mary Louise (Vela) Eick; m. David William Gamm, July 29, 1995; children: Buckley Alan Necker, Kaleen Christina Necker. AA in Animal Sci., Hawkeye C.C., Waterloo, Iowa, 1995; AA in Human Svc., Kirkwood C.C., Cedar Rapids, Iowa, 1986; BA in Social Work, U. No. Iowa, Cedar Falls, 1998; postgrad. in Counseling, Seton Hall U., South Orange, NJ, 1998—. Cert. substance abuse counselor, lic. social worker Iowa. Shift leader, in-home therapist Four Oaks, Independence and Oelwein, Iowa, 1999—2001; caseworker Tanager Place, Cedar Rapids, 2001—02; in-house therapist Luth. Social Svcs., 2002—03; counselor Substance Abuse Svc. Ctr., 2003—04; caseworker Luth. Svcs. Iowa, Waverly, 2004—. Mem.: ACA. Avocations: golf, horseback riding, walking. Office: Luth Svcs Iowa 106 16th St SW Waverly IA 50677 E-mail: gumbo1@netins.net.

EICKHOFF, THEODORE CARL, infectious disease physician, epidemiologist; b. Cleve., Sept. 13, 1931; s. Theodore Henry and Clara (Strasen) E.; m. Margaret Heinecke, Aug. 24, 1952; children: Stephen, Mark, Philip. BA, Valparaiso U., 1953; MD, Case Western Res. U., 1957. Diplomate Am. Bd. Internal Medicine. Intern, then resident Harvard Med. Svcs., Boston City Hosp., 1957-59; fellow in medicine Harvard Med. Sch.-Boston City Hosp., 1961-64; epidemiologist Ctr. for Disease Control, 1964-67; prof. medicine U. Colo. Med. Ctr., 1975—2003, prof. emeritus, 2003—, head divsn. infectious disease, 1967-80, vice chmn. dept. medicine, 1976-81; dir. medicine Denver Gen. Hosp., 1978-81; dir. internal medicine Presbyn./St. Luke's Med. Ctr., 1981-92. Cons. FDA, CDC, Am. Hosp. Assn.; mem. nat. commn. orphan diseases HHS, 1986-90, mem. vaccines adv. com., 1995-99. Contbr. over 150 articles to med. jours. Served with USPHS, 1959-67. Recipient Commr.'s Spl. Citation, FDA, 1990, Trustee's award Am. Hosp. Assn., 1993. Master ACP (Disting. Internist award Colo. chpt. 1995); mem. Am. Fedn. Clin. Rsch., Am. Soc. Clin. Investigation, Assn. Am. Physicians, Infectious Diseases Soc. Am. (sec. 1978-82, pres. 1983-84, Finland Lectureship award 1995), Am. Epidemiol. Soc. (pres. 1985-86). Home: 15 S Franklin Cir Greenwood Village CO 80121-1245 Office: Univ Colo Health Sci Ctr Div Infectious Disease B 168 Denver CO 80262-0001 Home Phone: 303-789-0194; Office Phone: 303-315-3052. Business E-Mail: theodore.eickhoff@uchsc.edu.

EICKHORST, KRISTIN MICHELE, research scientist; b. Bangor, Maine, Aug. 30, 1976; d. William Sigurd and Edith Ann Eickhorst. BS, Creighton U., 1998; MS, U. Maine, 2000. Rsch. asst. Creighton U., Omaha, 1995—98, tchg. asst., 1996—98; rsch. asst. U. Maine, Orono, 1999—2006, tchg. asst., 2000—03. Mem. program com. Internat. Conf. Digital Govt. Rsch., 2003—. Web adminstr. Newman Ctr., Orono, 1998—2006; svc. coord. Spring Break Svc. Trip Program, Omaha, 1996—98. Presdl. scholar, Creighton U., 1994—98, Sci. Rsch. scholar, Barry M. Goldwater Scholarship Found., 1996—98, Clare Booth Luce scholarship for Women in Sci., Henry Luce Found., 1996—97, Grad. Student fellow, Sea Grant Program, 1998—99, Grad. fellow, Maine Space Grant Consortium, 2003—05. Mem.: Am. Congress Surveying and Mapping (vol. coord. 2002—05), Am. Soc. Photogrammetry and Remote Sensing (vol. coord. 2004—05, Z/I Imaging scholar 2004, Ta Liang Meml. award 2001), Biology Club (v.p. 1997—98), Phi Sigma, Phi Kappa Phi, Omicron Delta Kappa (sec. 1997—98), Alpha Sigma Nu, Alpha Phi Omega (life; v.p. svc. 1996—97). Green Party. Roman Catholic. Achievements include research in comparing object movements and changes with spatiotemporal helixes. Avocations: travel, singing, running, hiking, environmental issues.

EID, ALLISON, state supreme court justice; b. Spokane, Wash. BA in Am. Studies with honors, Stanford U., 1987; JD, U. Chgo., 1991. Former special asst. and speechwriter U.S. Dept. of Ed.; former clerk to Judge Jerry E. Smith U.S. Ct. of Appeals for Fifth Circuit, Houston; former clerk to Justice Clarence Thomas U.S. Supreme Ct.; former atty. Arnold & Porter; assoc. prof. U. Colo.; former chief legal officer Colo. Atty. Gen.; former solicitor gen. State of Colo.; justice Colo. Supreme Ct., 2006—. Mem. Permanent Com. for Oliver Wendell Holmes Devise. Mem.: Am. Law Inst. Office: Colo Supreme Ct 2 E 14th Ave Fourth Fl Denver CO 80203 Office Phone: 303-837-3790.*

EID, TROY A., prosecutor; b. Chgo., Nov. 2, 1963; m. Allison Eid; 2 children. BA, Stanford U., 1986; JD, U. Chgo., 1991. Bar: Colo. 1991, US Ct. Appeals (5th Cir.), US Dist. Ct. Colo. Law clk. to Hon. Edith H. Jones US Ct. Appeals (5th cir.), 1991—92; assoc. Holme Roberts & Owen, LLP, Denver, 1992—94; COO, gen. counsel InfoTEST Internat., 1994—98; chief legal counsel to Gov. State of Colo., Denver, 1999—2001, sec. pers. & adminstrn., 2001—03; ptnr. Greenberg & Traurig LLP, Denver, 2003—06; US atty. Dist. Colo. US Dept. Justice, Denver, 2006—. Recipient Coloradan of the Yr. award, Colo. Jaycees, Outstanding Govt. Advocate of the Yr. award, US Hispanic C of C; grantee Am. Marshall Meml. Fellowship, German Marshall Fund US. Mem.: Navajo Nation Bar Assn., Am. Law Inst., Colo. Bar Found., Colo. Bar Assn. Office: US Attys Office 1225 17th St Ste 700 Denver CO 80202

EIDELMAN, SHARON (SHERRY) R., marriage and family therapist; b. Montreal, June 6, 1944; arrived in U.S., 1970; d. Hyman and Lilyan Lipsey; m. Aaron Joshua Eidelman, June 20, 1976; children: Dov, Ilana Eidelman Traube. BA, Coll. of New Rochelle, NYC, 1987; MA, Columbia U., NYC, 1989; EdM, Columbia U., 1991; MSW, NYU, 1997. LCSW N.Y. Marriage/family therapist Counterforce, Bklyn., 1991—2003, Haverstraw, NY, 2001—. Pet therapist Golden Outreach, Westchester, NY, 1992—95, New Rochelle Humane Soc., 2001—; counselor Y. L. Help Line, Bklyn., 1997—; mem. cmty. adv. bd. Group Home, New Rochelle, 1982—. Mem.: Am. Mental Health Counseling Assn., Kappa Delta Pi. Avocation: gardening. Home: 165 Bon Air Ave New Rochelle NY 10804 Office: 85 New Main St Haverstraw NY 10927 Office Phone: 845-429-6070.

EIDLEMAN, JOHN C., lawyer; BA, Pa. State U., 1966; JD, U. Md., 1969. Atty. Legal Aid Bur. Md., 1969—95; prog. counsel & dep. dir. Md. Legal Svcs. Corp., 1995—2002; v.p. compliance & adminstrn. Legal Svcs. Corp., Washington, 2002, sr. prog. counsel. Bd. mem. Peoples Pro Bono Action Ctr.; mem. adv. coun. Md. Legal Svcs. Corp.; co-founder & bd. chmn. Homeless Persons Representation Project. Recipient Disting. Svc. award, Md. Legal Svcs. Corp. Mem.: Md. State Bar Assn. (bd. gov., chmn. sect. counsel Delivery of Legal Svcs., chmn. subcommittee Law & Elderly, mem. spec. com. Lawyer Referrals, Pres. award). Office: Legal Services Corp 3rd Fl 3333 K St NW Washington DC 20007-3522*

EIFLER, KAREN ELIZABETH, language educator; b. Des Moines, Oct. 17, 1960; d. Clyde Andrew and Marilyn Elizabeth (Quinn) Perlenfein; m. Mark Eifler. BA magna cum laude in Study of Religion, UCLA, 1982; PhD in Adminstrn., Curriculum and Instrn., U. Nebr., Lincoln, 1997. Clear multiple subject tchg. credential Holy Names Coll., Calif., 1986. Tchr. Our Lady of Peace Sch., Sepulveda, Calif., 1983—86, St. Mary's Jr. HS, Walnut Creek, Calif., 1986—90, Sch. of the Madeleine Jr. HS, Berkeley, Calif., 1990—92; grad. lectr. U. Nebr., Kearney, 1993—98; asst. prof. edn. U. Portland, Oreg., 1998—2004, assoc. prof., 2004—. Writing cons. U. Calif., Berkeley, Diocese of Oakland, Calif., 1989-90; lectr. St. Mary's Coll., Moraga, Calif., 1990. Contbr. articles to profl. jours.; prodr. video presentation Magnificat Anima, 1990. Bd. dirs. Garaventa Ctr. Cath. Intellectual Life and Am. Culture, 2005—. Recipient Assn. Liberal Arts Colls. for Tchr. Edn. Scholar award, US Prof. of Yr. award, Carnegie Found. for Advancement of Tchg. and Coun. for Advancement and Support of Edn., 2006. Mem.: Assn. Liberal Arts Colls. for Tchr. Edn., Am. Assn. Colls. of Tchr. Edn., Assn. Supervision and Curriculum Devel., Am. Ednl. Rsch. Assn., Nat. Assn. Multicultural Edn., Kappa Delta Pi, Phi Beta Kappa. Roman Catholic. Avocations: reading, sewing, crafts, hiking. Office: Sch Edn U Portland 5000 N Willamette Blvd Portland OR 97203-5798 Office Phone: 503-943-8014. E-mail: eifler@up.edu.*

EIGEL, EDWIN GEORGE, JR., mathematics professor, retired university president; b. St. Louis, June 4, 1932; s. Edwin George and Catherine (Rohan) E.; m. Marcia Jeanne Duffy, May 30, 1959; children: Edwin George III, Mary Marcia. BS, MIT, 1954; postgrad., U. Marburg, Germany, 1954-55; PhD, St. Louis U., 1961; DHL (hon.), U. Bridgeport, 1999. Lectr. math. George Washington U., 1961; asst. prof. math. St. Louis U., 1961-64, assoc. prof., 1964-69, asst. to dean Grad. Sch., 1965-67, prof., 1969-79, dean Grad. Sch., 1967-71, assoc. acad. v.p., 1971-72, acad. v.p., 1972-79, exec. v.p., 1973; assoc. prof. math. U. Bridgeport, Conn., 1979—82, prof., 1982—, Univ. prof., 1995—, v.p. acad. affairs, 1979—91, provost, 1981—91, pres., 1991—95, pres. emeritus, 1995—. Mem. adv. com. on accreditation Conn. Dept. Higher Edn., 1989—92. Commr. McDonnell Planetarium, St. Louis, 1972-79; mem. Conn. Disting. Citizens Task Force on Quality Tchg., 1982-83; acting exec. dir. Bridgeport Area Consortium Colls. and Univs., 1989; bd. dirs. Bridgeport Pub. Edn. Fund, 1993-97, Bridgeport Regional Bus. Coun., 1994-95, United Way Ea. Fairfield County, 1994-98, Univ. Bridgeport, 1995—. Capt. US Army, 1959—61. Mem. Am. Math. Soc., Math. Assn. Am., Rotary (bd. dirs. Bridgeport 1994-97), Rotary Internat. (Paul Harris fellow), Phi Beta Kappa, Phi Beta Kappa Fellows, Sigma Xi, Pi Mu Epsilon, Phi Kappa Phi, Beta Gamma Sigma, Upsilon Pi Epsilon, Sigma Beta Delta. Achievements include: research in math. applications of computers. Home: 33 Pepperbush Ln Fairfield CT 06824-4036 Personal E-mail: egeorgee@optonline.net.

EIGEN, HOWARD, pediatrician, educator; b. NYC, Sept. 8, 1942; s. Jay and Libbie (Kantrowitz) E.; children: Sarah Elizabeth, Lauren Michelle. BS, Queens Coll., 1964; MD, Upstate N.Y. Med. Ctr., Syracuse, 1968. Diplomate Am. Bd. Pediatrics, Am. Bd. Pediatric Pulmonology, Am. Bd. Critical Care Medicine, Nat. Bd. Med. Examiners (mem. pediatric test com. 1986-90). Resident in pediatrics Upstate Med. Ctr., Syracuse, 1968-71; fellow in pediatric pulmonology Tulane U., New Orleans, 1973-76; asst. prof. pediatrics Ind. U., Indpls., 1976-84, prof., 1984-96, Billie Lou Wood Prof. pediatrics, 1996—. Assoc. chmn. of Pediatrics for Clin. Affairs, dir. pediatric intensive care, pulmonology sect. Riley Hosp. for Children, med. dir. ambulatory care, 1989— Co-editor: Respiratory Disease in Children: Diagnosis and Management; assoc. editor Pediatric Pulmonology, 1984-91; contbr. articles to profl. jours. Served to maj. U.S. Army, 1971-73. Fellow Am. Acad. Pediatrics (pres. chest sect. 1983-85, pulmonology 1986—), Am. Thoracic Soc., Am. Bd. Pediatrics, Am. Lung Assn. (pres. Ind. 1984-85). Avocation: tennis. Office: Ind U Dept Pediatrics 702 Barnhill Dr Rm 2750 Indianapolis IN 46202-5128

EIGER, RICHARD WILLIAM, retired publisher; b. NYC, May 11, 1933; s. William and Helen M. (Fetten) E.; m. Ruth B. Engelke; 1 child, Keith R. BFA, Pratt Inst., 1955; MBA, NYU, 1960. With Western Pub. Co., NYC, 1958-80, pub. dir., 1968-74, v.p. pub., 1975-80; pres. Macmillan Ednl. Co., NYC, 1980-91; sr. v.p. Macmillan Pub. Co., NYC, 1980-91; v.p. K-III Reference Corp. (now PRIMEDIA Reference Corp.), Mahwah, NJ, 1991-93; pub. The World Almanac, 1993-98; ret., 1998. Cons. Langenscheidt Pub. Co., 2002—, VirtuelEd., Inc., 2000—; prof. Pratt Inst. Sch. Info. and Libr. Sci., NYC, 2004—; advisor Bearport Pub. Co., 2003—. Bd. dirs. alumni bd. Pratt Inst., NYC, 1986—, trustee, 1992—, exec. com., 1995—, sec. 1996—, chmn. devel. com., 1997—; pub. com. Brandeis U., Waltham, Mass., 1993-2000; trustee Katharine Gibbs Sch., Montclair, NJ, 1995-2001, Piscataway, NJ, 1996-2001, Hist. Soc. Princeton, NJ, 2002—, Del. Coll. Art and Design, Wilmington, 2004—. Lt. U.S. Army, 1956-57. Home: 6 Otter Creek Rd Skillman NJ 08558-2364 E-mail: dickeiger@aol.com.

EIGNER, RICHARD MARTIN, lawyer; b. Swampscott, Mass., July 7, 1929; s. Israel and Bessie (Polansky) E.; m. Beverly Israel, Dec. 26, 1964; children: David, Danielle. AB, Dartmouth Coll., 1951; LLB, Harvard U., 1954. Bar: Calif. 1955, Mass. 1956. Ptnr. Pillsbury Winthrop, San Francisco, 1965—. Cons. Internat. Tax Project, Am. Law Inst., 1981-86. Mem. Internat. Fiscal Assn., Phi Beta Kappa. Jewish. Home: 2955 Piedmont Ave Berkeley CA 94705-2342 Office: Pillsbury Winthrop 50 Fremont St Fl 9 San Francisco CA 94105 Office Phone: 415-983-1354. Personal E-mail: reigner@comcast.net. Business E-Mail: richard.eigner@pillsburylaw.com.

EIGNER, WILLIAM WHITLING, lawyer; b. Dover, Ohio, Feb. 4, 1959; s. Stanley Spencer and Jeraldine (Lippy) E.; m. Jeanne Beach, May 24, 1987. BA, Stanford U., 1981; JD, U. Va., 1986. Bar: Calif. 1986, U.S. Dist. Ct. (so. dist.) Calif. 1986. Jud. intern U.S. Supreme Ct., Washington, 1981; assoc. Higgs, Fletcher & Mack, San Diego, 1986-89, Procopio, Cory, Hargreaves & Savitch, LLP, San Diego, 1989-95, ptnr., 1995—. Bd. dirs. Concerto Networks, Inc., Mundoval Fund, CommNexus San Diego; bd. advisors QuantumThink Group, Inc., Bioelectric Med. Solutions, Inc., Am. Eco-Energy, Mobile DataComm, Pineapplehut.com; mem. San Diego Venture Group. Contbr. articles to profl. jours. Trustee, La Jolla (Calif.) Town Coun., 1988-92, chmn. land use com., 1988-90; trustee La Jolla Country Day Sch. Recipient spl. commendation San Diego City Coun., Vol. Advocate of Yr., San Diego Regional C. of C., 2004. Mem. ABA, State Bar Calif., San Diego County Bar Assn. (bus. sect.), San Diego Regional C. of C. (bd. dirs. 1998-2001, 03-06, chmn. bus. recognition and awards com. 1989-98, chmn. emerging bus. com. 1998-00, pub. policy com.). Republican. Jewish. Avocations: tennis, Civil War history. Office: Procopio Cory Hargreaves & Savitch LLP 530 B St Ste 2100 San Diego CA 92101-4496 Office Phone: 619-515-3210. Business E-Mail: wwe@procopio.com.

EIGSTI, ROGER HARRY, retired insurance company executive; b. Vancouver, Wash., Apr. 17, 1942; s. Harry A. and Alice E. (Huber) E.; m. Mary Lou Nelson, June 8, 1963; children: Gregory, Ann. BS, Linfield Coll., 1964. CPA, Oreg., Wash. Staff CPA Touche Ross and Co., Portland, Oreg., 1964-72; asst. to controller Safeco Corp., Seattle, 1972-78, controller, 1980, Safeco Life Ins. Co., Seattle, 1978-80; pres. Safeco Credit Co., Seattle, 1980-81, Safeco Life Ins. Co., Seattle, 1981-85; exec. v.p., CFO Safeco Corp., Seattle, 1985, CEO, chmn., 1985-2001. Bd. dirs. Ind. Colls. of Wash., Seattle, 1981-87, bus. dir. Seattle Repertory Theatre, 1981—, bd. dirs. 1981—. Mem. Am. Inst. CPA's, Life Office Mgmt. Assn. (bd. dirs. 1983—), Seattle C. of C. (chmn. metro budget rev. com. 1984—). Clubs: Mercer Island (Wash.) Country (treas., bd. dirs. 1981-84); Central Park Tennis. Republican. Home: 1503 Parkside Dr E Seattle WA 98112-3719

EIKENBERG, JOHN ROBERT, retired electronics executive; b. Balt., Jan. 2, 1931; s. George Charles Eikenberg and Julia Irene Franzoni; m. Mildred Patricia Hiltz, Oct. 1, 1955; children: Patricia, Steve, Julie, Sue, Jeanne, Jim. BS in Mgmt., Rutgers U., New Brunswick, NJ, 1963; MS in Fin. Mgmt., George Washington U., 1968. Logistics coord. Martin-Marietta Co., Balt., 1955—60; logistics specialist RCA Corp., Moorestown, NJ, 1960—63; mgr. field ops. support Westinghouse Elec. Corp., Balt., 1963—92, ret., 1992. Cons. Harford CC, Bel Air, Md., 1987. State rep., mem. ad-hoc com. Nat. Sr. Games Adminstrn.; v.p. PTA Holy Family Elem., Randallstown, Md., 1969, Randallstown Sr. HS, 1973; v.p. Forest Lake Civic Assn., Shrewsbury, Pa., 2002; vol. Southern York County Libr., Shrewsbury, 2005—; chmn. Md. Sr. Olympics, 2002—. Sgt. USAF, 1951—55, Korea. Named to Hall of Fame, Md. Sr. Olympics, 2006; recipient Pres. Quality Achievement award, Westinghouse. Mem.: IEEE, Soc. Logistic Engrs., Mensa. Democrat. Roman Catholic. Home: 15800 Magnolia Dr New Freedom PA 17349

EIKLEBERRY, LOIS SCHILLIE, physician; b. Novinger, Mo., July 19, 1927; d. Frank Carl and Sarah Louise (Gashwiler) Schillie; m. William Francis Eikleberry, June 14, 1952; children: Carol, Linda, Bill Jr.(dec.) , Beatrice. BA, William Jewell Coll., Liberty, Mo., 1949; BS in Medicine, Mo. U., Columbia, 1951; MD, State U. Iowa, Iowa City, 1953. Diplomate Am. Bd. Family Practice, 1975. Intern Mercy Hosp., Iowa City, 1954; pvt. practice West Branch, Iowa, 1954—56; physician William Beaumont Army Hosp., El Paso, Tex., 1957—58; pvt. practice Castle Rock, Wash., 1959—61; physician 6th Army Hdqrs., San Francisco, 1962—63; adminstr. Wash. State Dept. Pub. Assistance, Longview, 1963—69; pvt. practice Longview, 1969; with Tri County Health, Denver and Adams County, Colo., 1970—71; pvt. practice Lakewood, Colo., 1972—88; ret., 1988. Author: (biography) A Folk History of Charlie and Nettie Schillie, 1992, A Folk History of J.S. and Maude Gashwiler, 1993. Leader Girl Scouts, 1968. Recipient Citiation of Achievement, William Jewell Coll., 1982. Mem.: P.E.O. Sisterhood (recording sec. 1992—94, treas. 1996—98, pres. 2004—). Avocations: reading, hiking, genealogy, antiques, natural history. Home: 8544 W Iliff Ave Lakewood CO 80227-3030

EILAND, GARY WAYNE, lawyer; b. Houston, Apr. 25, 1951; s. William N. and Louise A. (Foltin) E.; m. Sandra K. Streetman, Aug. 4, 1973; children; Trina L. Wuensche, Peter T. BBA, U. Tex., 1973, JD, 1976. Bar: Tex. 1976, U.S. Ct. Claims 1977, U.S. Ct. Appeals (5th cir.) 1978, U.S. Ct. Appeals (11th cir.) 1981, U.S. Supreme Ct. 1989. Assoc. Wood, Lucksinger & Epstein, Houston, 1976-81, ptnr., 1981-91, Vinson & Elkins L.L.P., Houston, 1991—; sect. head designee health industry group, 1996—2006. Lectr. Aspen Health Care Industry seminars, Aspen Pubs., Inc., Rockville, Md., 1978-89, HLO Health Care seminars, 1990-91; charter mem. health law exam. commn. Tex. State Bd. Legal Specialization, 2002-05. Mem. Tex. Bar Assn. (chmn. health law sect. 1991-92), Am. Acad. Healthcare Attys. (bd. dirs. 1991-97, pres. 1996-97), Am. Health Lawyers Assn. (past pres., exec. com. 1997-98 Greenburg Svc. award 2005), Healthcare Fin. Mgmt. Assn. (pres. Tex. Gulf Coast chpt. 1992-93, Region 9 chpt. liaison rep. 1994-95, compliance officers forum adv. coun. 2000-02, Founders medal of honor 1999), Assn. Am. Med. Colls., Houston Ctr. Club, Bentwater Yacht and Country Club. Home: 23319 Holly Hollow Tomball TX 77377-3684 Office: Vinson & Elkins LLP First City Tower 1001 Fannin St Ste 2500 Houston TX 77002-6760 Home Phone: 281-351-6017; Office Phone: 713-758-3474. Business E-Mail: geiland@velaw.com.

EILEN, HOWARD SCOTT, lawyer, mediator; b. NYC, Mar. 28, 1954; m. Sharon R. Kornbluth, Oct. 21, 1979; children: Michael, Jeffrey. BA summa cum laude, CUNY, 1975, MA, 1975; JD, St. John's U., 1979. Bar: NY 1980, U.S. Tax Ct. 1980, U.S. Dist. Ct. (so., ea. dists.) NY 1980, U.S. Dist. Ct. (ea. dist.) Mich. 1982. Assoc. Bloom & Tese, NYC, 1980-83; ptnr. Bloom & Eilen, NYC, 1983-86, 87-94; of counsel Spengler, Carlson, Gubar, Brodsky & Frischling, NYC, 1986-87; ptnr. Lehman & Eilen, LLP, Uniondale, NY, 1994—. Arbitrator Nat. Assn. Securities Dealers, Inc., Nat. Futures Assn., Am. Arbitration Assn., U.S. Arbitration and Mediation, Inc., NY Stock Exch., Inc.; mediator Nat. Assn. Securities Dealers, Inc.; spl. master NY Supreme Ct.; mem. faculty securities arbitration program Practising Law Inst.; lectr. in field; presenter in field. Contbg. editor Futures Tribune Mag., Japan, Securities Arbitration, Practicing Law Inst., 1993-2006. Mem. NY County Lawyers Assn. (com. on securities and exchs. 1983—, chmn. subcom. on commodities regulation, com. on arbitration and conciliation 1990—), Nassau County Bar Assn. (securities law com., conciliation com.). Office: Lehman & Eilen LLP Ste 505 50 Charles Lindbergh Blvd Uniondale NY 11553-3612 Home Phone: 516-445-0621; Office Phone: 516-222-0888. Business E-Mail: heilen@lehmaneilen.com.

EIMER, NATHAN PHILIP, lawyer; b. Chgo., June 26, 1949; s. Irving A. and Charlotte Eimer; m. Lisa S. Eimer; children: Micah Jacob, Noah Joseph, Daniel Jordan, Anna Beatrice, Claire Elizabeth. AB magna cum laude in Econs., U. Ill., 1970; JD cum laude, Northwestern U., 1973. Bar: Ill. 1973, US Supreme Ct. 1978, NY 1985, Tex. 1998. Assoc. Sidley & Austin, Chgo., 1973—80, ptnr., 1980—2000, mem. exec. com., 1999—2000; founding ptnr. Eimer, Stahl, Klevorn & Solberg, LLP, Chgo., 2000—. Adj. prof. Law Sch., Northwestern U., Chgo., 1989-96. Note and comment editor Northwestern U. Law Rev., 1972-73. Bd. dirs. Chgo. Lawyers Com. Civil Rights, 1991—, pres., 1993-94; bd. dirs. UNICEF, 1992-93, Infant Welfare Soc., Chgo., exec. v.p., 1992-96, pres., 1996-98; mem. adv. bd. Children & Family Justice Ctr., Northwestern U. Legal Clinic, 1996—. Mem. ABA, Univ. Club. Office: Eimer Stahl Klevorn & Solberg LLP Ste 1100 224 S Michigan Ave Chicago IL 60604 Office Phone: 312-660-7601. E-mail: neimer@eimerstahl.com.

EIMERS, JERI ANNE, retired counselor; b. Berkeley, Calif., Jan. 20, 1951; d. Alfred D. Wallace and Marjorie E. (Nordheim) Stevens; m. Roy A. Neiman, June 12, 1969 (div. Aug. 1977); children: Lorien, Arwen; m. Richard A. Eimers, Mar. 2, 1996. AA, Palomar Jr. Coll., San Marcos, Calif., 1977; BA in Psychology with distinction, Calif. State U., Long Beach, 1979, MA in Psychology with distinction, 1981; postgrad. Human Sexuality Program, UCLA, 1991-92. Lic. marriage, family, child therapist, Calif.; cert. community coll. instr., counselor; cert. sex therapist. Rsch. asst. Calif. State U., 1978-82; tchr. Artesia (Calif.)-Bellflower-Cerritos Unified Sch. Dist., 1982-83; dir. Am. Learning Corp., Huntington Beach, Calif., 1983-85; social worker Los Angeles County Children's Protective Svcs., Long Beach, 1986-88; sr. social worker Orange County Social Svc. Agy., Orange, Calif., 1988-90; therapist Cypress Mental Health, Cypress, Calif.,

1988—, cons., 1990—. Cons., 1990—; group chair, leader Adults Abused as Children, Los Altos Hosp., Long Beach, 1991—, Coll. Hosp., Cerritos, 1993—; speaker, presenter in field. Mem. Child's Sexual Abuse Network, Orange, 1988—; mem. legis. com. Child Abuse Coun. of Orange County, 1988. Women's League scholar, 1980-81. Mem. AAUW, Am. Assn. Marriage, Family Therapists, Calif. Assn. Marriage, Family Therapists, Am. Profl. Soc. for Abused Children, Calif. Profl. Assn. for Abused Children, Phi Kappa Phi, Psi Chi. Republican. Methodist. Avocations: writing, theater, classical and jazz music, swimming. Personal E-mail: eimers@roadrunner.com.

EIN, DANIEL, allergist; b. Liege, Belgium, Nov. 26, 1938; arrived in U.S., 1941; s. Max Motel and Sabine (Toeman) E.; m. Marion Hess, June 25, 1961 (div. 1978); children: Mark David, Jon Spencer; m. Marina Wallach, Apr. 10, 1988; stepchildren: Jacqueline A. Newmyer, Tory Newmyer. AB, Columbia U., 1959; MD, Albert Einstein Coll. Medicine, 1964. Diplomate Am. Bd. Internal Medicine, Am. Bd. Allergy and Immunology. Intern Bronx Mcpl. Hosp., NYC, 1964—65; staff assoc. Nat. Cancer Inst., Washington, 1965—67, clin. assoc., 1967—68; asst. resident Mass. Gen. Hosp., Boston, 1968—69; sr. investigator Nat. Cancer Inst., Washington, 1969—71; pvt. practice Washington, 1971—2005. Clin. prof. medicine George Washington U., Washington, 1984—, dir. divsn. allergy, 2005—; founder, pres. Capital Physicians Network, 1994-99. Contbr. articles to profl. jours. and newspapers. Fellow ACP, Am. Acad. Allergy (AMA del. 1994), Am. Coll. Allergy (bd. dirs. 2000-03, v.p. 2004, pres. 2006); mem. Joint Coun. Allergy (pres. 1998-2000), Med. Soc. D.C. (pres. 1991), Greater Washington Allergy Soc. (pres. 1979), Cosmos Club. Jewish. Achievements include discovery of OZ factors on human immunoglobulin light chains. Home: 4636 Kenmore Dr NW Washington DC 20007-1924 Office Phone: 202-785-0668, 202-741-2770. Personal E-mail: dein@washingtonallergy.com.

EINAT, HAIM, social sciences educator; B of Med. Sci., Hebrew U. Jerusalem, 1985; BS, Tel-Aviv U., Israel, 1989, MS, 1991, McMaster U., Hamilton, Ont., Can., 1995; PhD, Ben Gurion U. Negev, Beersheba, Israel, 2000. Asst. prof. U. Minn., Duluth, 2004—. Recipient Young Investigator award, Brit. Assn. Pharmacology, 2001, FARE award, NIH, 2003, Young Investigators award, NARSAD, 2005; fellow, NIMH, Bethesda, Md., 2001—04; grantee, U. Minn., Acad. Health Ctr., 2005, Stanley Rsch. Inst., 2006. Mem.: Israeli Soc. Biol. Psychiatry, Internat. Behavioral Neurosci. Soc. (com. chair 2006), Soc. Biol. Psychiatry. Office: U Minn 379 Kirby Plz 1208 Kirby Dr Duluth MN 55812 Office Phone: 218-726-6029. Office Fax: 218-726-6500. E-mail: heinat@d.umn.edu.

EINBOND, LINDA SAXE, biologist, researcher; d. Harold and Rose Chayt Saxe; m. Bernard Einbond, Feb. 20, 1977; children: Aaron Michael, Julia. PhD, MIT, Cambridge, Mass., 1973. Vis. scientist CUNY, NYC, 2000—01; fellow Ctr. Complementary and Alternative Medicine, Columbia U., NYC, 2001—04, assoc. rsch. scientist, 2001—. Contbr. articles to profl. jours. Grantee, Susan G. Komen Breast Cancer Found., 2004—07; NIH Mentored Rsch. Scientist Devel. grantee, NIH, 2005—. Office: Columbia U 701 W 168th St New York NY 10032 Home Phone: 914-779-4564; Office Phone: 212-305-6924. Personal E-mail: l.einbond@gmail.com. Business E-Mail: le2012@columbia.edu.

EINENKEL, ROBERT HERBERT, theater educator, actor, director; b. NY, Feb. 23, 1944; s. Herbert Sherman and Virginia Grace Einenkel; m. Francie Fried Einenkel, Sept. 17, 1966; children: Walter Fried, Robert Nicholas, Timothy Leonard. BA in English-Speech, Queens Coll., Flushing, NY, 1965; MA in Speech, U. Mich., Ann Arbor, 1966; MFA in Directing, Yale U., New Haven, Conn., 1969. Actor Long Wharf Theatre, New Haven, 1969—70, N.Y. Shakespeare Festival, NYC, 1970, Chelsea Theater Ctr., New York, NY, 1970—73, Pub. TV WNET, NYC, 1970; from iinstr. to adj. asst. prof. Queens Coll., Flushing, NY, 1970—97; dir. Theatre Yale Drama Alumni, NYC, 1999—2001; from instr. to prof. Nassau C.C., Garden City, NY, 1986—2006, prof., 2006—. Supr. faculty summer theatre Queens Coll., 1981—97; guest artist, 1998. Dir.: (plays) Nassau C.C. Theatre; contbr. articles to profl. jours. Leader theatre workshop L.I. Theatre Educators Assn., Westbury, NY, 1995. Fellow, U. Mich., Yale U. Mem.: Phi Beta Kappa. Avocations: swimming, cooking, jazz, music. Office: Nassau Community College One Education Drive Garden City NY 11530 Home Phone: 914-965-9004; Office Phone: 516-572-7509. Business E-Mail: einenkr@ncc.edu.

EINHORN, DAVID ALLEN, lawyer; b. Bklyn., Dec. 11, 1961; s. Harold and Jane Ellen (Wiener) Einhorn. BA in Computer Sci. magna cum laude, Columbia U., 1983, JD, 1986. Bar: N.Y. 1987, DC 1988, U.S. Dist. Ct. (so. and ea. dists.) N.Y. 1989, U.S. Ct. Appeal (fed. cir.) 1992, U.S. Dist. Ct. (no. dist.) Calif. 1994, U.S. Dist. Ct. Conn. 2003. Assoc. Kaye, Scholer, Fierman, Hays & Handler, NYC, 1986-89; ptnr. Anderson Kill & Olick, PC, NYC, 1989—. Lectr. Am. Conf. Inst.; arbitrator Nat. Arbitration Forum, 2002—. Co-author: (2-vol. treatise) Patent Licensing Transactions; editor-in-chief: Intellectual Property for the New Millenium, 1997—; contbr. articles to profl. jours. Lt. col. JAGC, Army Divsn. N.Y. Guard, 1987—. Named to Order of Merit, Les Amis du Vin, 1982; recipient Nat. prize, Nathan Burkan Copyright Essay Competition, 1985, Off Off Broadway Rev. award for producing Ionesco Fest., Encore Bus. Vol. of Yr. award, Arts and Bus. Coun., 2004; Harlan Fiske Stone scholar, Columbia U., 1985. Mem.: ABA (chmn. software patent subcom. 1988—91, software licensing subcom. 1991—95, software copyright subcom. 1995—96, chmn. broadcasting, sound recordings, and performing artists com. 2000—02, chmn. com. online trademark issues 2002—, chmn. com. online copyright issues 2004—), Licensing Execs. Soc. (lectr.), DC Bar Assn. (computer law sect.), Internat. Trademark Assn., NY Intellectual Property Law Assn. (chmn. copyright com.), Am. Intellectual Property Law Assn. (chmn. software copyright subcom. 1999—), Intellectual Property Owners Assn. (vice chmn. cybersquatting com. 2003—), Untitled Theater Co. 61, Ltd. (chmn. bd. dirs., producing dir., treas. 1994—), Tasters Guild (v.p., bd. dirs. 1997—), NY Soc. Mil. and Naval Officers (v.p. 1995—). Democrat. Jewish. Avocations: tennis, wine tasting, theater. Office: Anderson Kill & Olick PC 1251 Ave of the Americas New York NY 10020-1182 Home: 36 Sutton Pl S Apt 7-A New York NY 10022 Office Phone: 212-278-1359. Business E-Mail: deinhorn@andersonkill.com.

EINHORN, JERZY, internist, endocrinologist, consultant; b. Sosnowiec, Poland, Mar. 17, 1919; s. Oskar Einhorn and Karola (Birman) Mazurkiewicz; m. Jadwiga Piaskowski, Mar. 17, 1946 (div. Apr. 1968); children: Janusz Richard, Robert Krzysztof (dec.), Ewa Krystyna; m. Ruth Mary Gregor, May 23, 1968; 1 child, Edward William. MD, Poznan Med. Acad., 1951; PhD, Silesia Med. Acad., 1963. Dir. State Endocrinology Consulting Ctr., Katowice, 1954—66; assoc. prof. 3d Dept. Internal Medicine, Katowice, 1962—66; endocrine rschr. Royal Postgrad. Med. Sch., London, 1965; assoc. prof. U. Pitts. Med. Sch., 1971—94; dir. Hazelwood & Greenfield Cmty. Health Ctrs., Pitts., 1971—84; dir. thyroid screening program U. Pitts. Med. Sch., 1976—93; endocrine rschr. Royal Postgrad. Med. Sch., London, 1967. Author: Recollections of the End of an Era, 2000; contbr. over 35 rsch. articles to profl. jours. Lt. to capt. Polish Light Horse Army, 1939, lt. to capt. Polish Underground Army, 1940—44, lt. to capt. Warsaw Uprising, 1944. Recipient Silver Cross of Merit, 1957, Endocrine rsch. awards Polish Endocrine Soc., 1962, 63, 1st Class prize Min. Health, 1967; recipient mil. awards Virtuti Militari, 1939, Cross of Valour, 1944, Cross of the Warsaw Uprising, 1944; named maj. Polish Ministry of Def., 2002. Avocations: woodworking, photography, horseback riding. Home: 415 Summit Dr Pittsburgh PA 15228-2617 Business E-Mail: jerzy.einhorn@verizon.net.

EINHORN, LAWRENCE HENRY, oncologist, medical educator; b. Dayton, Ohio, 1942; BS, Ind. U., 1965; MD, U. Iowa, 1968. Diplomate Am. Bd. Internal Medicine, Am. Bd. Oncology. Med. intern Ind. U. Hosp., Indpls., 1967—68; resident in medicine Ind. U., 1968—69, fellow, hematology and oncology, 1971—72, assoc. prof. medicine, clin. oncology and hematology, 1973—87, Disting. prof. medicine Indpls., 1987—, Lance Armstrong Found. prof., oncology, 2006—; fellow, oncology M.D. Anderson Hosp. and Tumor Inst., Houston, 1972—73. Contbr. several articles to profl jours. Capt. Med. Corps USAF, 1969—72. Recipient Richard and Hilda Rosenthal Found. award for Cancer Rsch., Am. Assn. Cancer Rsch. Mtg., Disting. Clinician award, Milken Found., 1989, ACCC Clinical Oncology award, 1991, Charles F. Kettering prize, GM Cancer Rsch. Found., 1992, Glenn Irwin Experience Excellence award, 1996, Herman B. Wells Visionary award, 2001. Mem.: Am. Philos. Soc., NAS. Achievements include developed a chemotherapy regimen to treat testicular cancer that improved the survival rate from 5% to 95%; led the medical team treating champion cyclist and testicular cancer survivor Lance Armstrong. Office: Ind U Sch Med Indiana Cancer Pavillion Rm 473 535 Barnhill Dr Indianapolis IN 46202-5289 Office Phone: 317-274-3515. Office Fax: 317-274-3646.*

EINHORN, MARTIN B., physicist, educator; b. Dayton, Ohio, Aug. 14, 1942; s. Aaron Howard and Rosalind (Rosen) E.; m. Vibeke Gjøe Geleff, Feb. 18, 1967; children: Michael, Linda. BS (hons.), Calif. Inst. Tech., 1965; PhD, Princeton U., 1968. Post-doctoral fellow Stanford (Calif.) Linear Accelerator Ctr., 1968-70, Lawrence Berkeley (Calif.) Nat. Lab., 1970-72, Fermi Nat. Accelerator Lab., Batavia, Ill., 1972-73, staff physicist, 1973-76; assoc. rsch. scientist U. Mich., Ann Arbor, 1976-79, assoc. prof., 1979-83, prof. physics, 1983—2004, prof. emeritus, 2004—; dep. dir. Kavli Inst. Theoretical Physics U. Calif., Santa Barbara, 2004—. Chair adv. bd. Theoretical Advanced Study Inst., Boulder, Colo., 1984-91, dep. dir. Inst. for Theoretical Physics, U. Calif., Santa Barbara, 1990-92. Contbr. 90 articles to profl. jours. Mem. high energy physics adv. panel Dept. of Energy, Washington, 1983-87, program dir. theoretical physics Nat. Sci. Fedn., 2000. John Simon Guggenheim Meml. Found. fellow, 2003—04. Fellow Am. Phys. Soc.; mem. AAAS. Office Phone: 805-893-6309.

EINIGER, CAROL BLUM, investment company executive; b. Nov. 30, 1949; d. Bernard Michael and Bella (Karff) Blum; m. Roger William Einiger, Dec. 21, 1969; 1 child. BA, U. Pa., 1970; MBA, Columbia U., 1973. With Conde Nast Publs., NYC, 1970-71, Goldman, Sachs & Co., NYC, 1971-72, 1st Boston Corp., NYC, 1973-88, mng. dir., 1982-88, head short-term fin. dept., 1983-88, head capital markets dept., 1985-88; vis. prof., exec.-in-residence Columbia U. Bus. Sch., NYC, 1988-89; mng. dir. Wasserstein Perella & Co. Inc., NYC, 1989-92; CFO, acting pres. Edna McConnell Clark Found., NYC, 1992—96; chief investment officer Rockefeller U., NYC, 1996—2005. Trustee Horace Mann Sch., 1988-94, U. Pa., 1989-99, mem. audit, budget and fin., investment, external affairs, and student life coms.; bd. overseers Columbia U. Bus. Sch., 1988-, nominating com.; investment com. Mus. Modern Art, 1994-2007; mem. adv. bd. Blackstone Alternative Asset Mgmt., 1999-; bd. dirs. Credit Suisse First Boston (U.S.A.), Inc., 2001-02, Boston Properties, Inc., 2004-, NYstem Cell Found., 2007—. Office: Post Rock Advisors LLC 610 Fifth Ave 7th Fl New York NY 10020

EINODER, CAMILLE ELIZABETH, retired secondary school educator; b. Chgo., June 15, 1937; d. Isadore and Elizabeth T. (Czerwinski) Popowski; m. Joseph X. Einoder, Aug. 5, 1978; children: Carl Frank, Mark Frank, Vivian Einoder, Joe Einoder, Tim Einoder, Sheila Einoder, Jude Einoder. Student, Fox Bus. Coll., 1954; BEd in Biology, Chgo. Tchrs. Coll., 1964; MA in Analytical Chemistry, Gov.'s State U., 1977; MA in Adminstrn. and Supervision, Roosevelt U., 1986; postgrad., 1992—. Sec., Chgo., 1955-64; tchr. biology Chgo. Bd. Edn., 1964-1975, tchr. biology and agr., 1975-81, tchr. biology, agr. and chemistry, 1981-2000, ret., 2000. Human rels. coord. Morgan Park High Sch., Chgo., 1980—, tchr. biology Internat. Studies Sch., 1983—, adv. bd., 1989—; owner Einoder Masonry, 1997—, Einoder Antiques, 1996—; career devel. cons. for agr. related curriculum; internat. baccalaureate tchr., Chgo. pub. schs. consulting tchr., 1997; edn. cons. Neighborhood Coun., 1974; rep. Chgo. Tchrs. Union, 1969; exec. bd. dir. The Lira Ensemble, 1996—; mem. Renaissance Circle, DePaul U.; edn. com. Polish-Am. Initiative of Chgo. Cmty. Trust, 1999—; owner Einoder Masonry, 1986—; antique dealer, 1995—. Bd. dirs., founding mem., author constn. Cmty. Coun., 1970—; bd. dirs., edn. cons. Neighborhood Coun., 1974; rep. Chgo. Tchrs. Union, 1969; exec. bd. dirs. The Lira Ensemble, 1996—; mem. Chums Giving Club Com.; charter mem. Humanists Cir. Chgo. Humanities Festival, 2003—. Mem. AAAS, NSTA, Polish Inst. for Arts and Sci., Am. Chem. Soc., Am. Biology Tchrs. Assn., Nat. Assn. Women Bus. Owners, Found. Women Contractors, Copernicus Found., Kosciuszko Soc., Polish Arts Club, Phi Delta Kappa, Iota Sigma Pi.

EINS, STEFAN, artist, curator, science researcher, writer; b. Prague, Czech Republic; arrived in US, 1967, permanent resident, 1972; s. Stefan and Daisy (Ganghofer) Schmid. MA in Theology, U. Vienna, 1965; BA in Sculpture, Akad. Bildenen Künste, Vienna, 1967. Founder, exec. dir., curator 3 Mercer St, NYC, 1972-79, Fashion Moda, NYC, 1978-84, 88-93. Exhibitions include 112 Greene St., NYC, 1971,1972, 3 Mercer, NYC, 1973, 1974, 1975,1976, PS 1, 1976, Documenta 6, 1977, FASHION MODA 1978. 1981, 1985, 1991, 1992, ABC Times Square Show, NYC, 1980, New Museum, NYC, 1980, 1981, documenta 7, 1982, NoRio, NYC, 1986,1989, Now Gal., NYC, 1987, 1988, Gal. Ariadne, Vienna, 1987, National Gallery, Vienna, 1991, Gal. X, NYC, 2000, Pfaffmen Gal., NYC, 2001, Grey Art Gal. NYC, 2006, Haven Gal., NYC, 2006, PS1/Museum of Modern Art, NYC, 2007, Kyrgyz National Fine Arts Museum, Bishkek, Kyrgyz Republic, 2007; Installations include Liquid Steel/Life, NYC, 1972, Freedom,Centennial, Statue of Liberty, 1986, Ave Juno, Thaon, Normandy, France, 1987, St. Ruprecht, St. Stefan, Vienna, 1992, Project Vertebrae, Gresten, Austria, 1994, Gravity Needless, NYC, 1996, Trees, NYC, 1998-, President Clinton Spot, NYC, 2003-, LUST/PAIN-PAIN/LUST, NYC, 2004-, PORTRAIT/SELF, NYC, 2007-, Modernist, Istanbul, 2006-; Curator: (exhbns.) Geoffrey Hendricks, 1976, Sherrie Levine, 1977, Fashion Moda Inaugural, 1978, Robert Cooney, 1978, End of Modernism, 1978, Art/Fashion Inter Mix, 1978, Mulitculturalism, 1978, Jenny Holzer, 1979, John Ahearn, 1979, David Wells, 1979, Christy Rupp, 1979, David Reed, 1980, Jane Dickson, 1980, Wally Edwards, 1980, Haim Steinbach, 1980, Marianne Edwards, 1980, Elizabeth Clark, 1980, Ilona Granet, 1980, Paulette Nenner, 1980, Calif. Billboards, NYC, 1980, Graffiti and the Arts/Graffiti Art Success Am., 1980, Sophie Calle, 1980, Rebecca Howland, 1980, Haim Steinbach, 1980, Justen Ladda 1980, Keith Haring 1981, Paul Koenigsberg, 1980, Dona McAdams, 1982, Tom Warren, 1982, Judy Glantzman, 1983, David Finn, 1983, Joy Walker, 1983, Dragan Ilic, 1983, Alyson Pou, 1983, Paolo Buggiani, 1984, Nancy Drew, 1986, Barbara Smith, 1988, Norbert Brunner, 1993, others; co-curator: (with Joe Lewis) Fashion Moda, New Mus., NYC, 1980, 81, (with Jenny Holzer) FASHION MODA, documenta 7, 1982. Co-founder chpt. The Audubon Soc., N.Y.C., 1979. Grantee, NEA, 1980, 1987, NY Found. for the Arts, 2002, Adolph and Esther Gottlieb Found., 2004. Mem. Collaborative Projects, Inc. (pres. 1988-89, 2001—). Achievements include research on liquids formation; discovery of formation process of vertebrae, 1985; uncovered stone age artifacts in Austria, 1987-94; conditions inherent in the sun necessarily creating life other than life on earth, 2004. Home: PO Box 33 New York NY 10013-0033 Home Phone: 917-605-0974; Office Phone: 212-987-9749. Personal E-mail: einsoneuno@aol.com.

EINSEL, NAIAD JUNE, illustrator, graphics designer; b. Phila., June 6, 1927; d. Samuel and Esther Giblan; m. Walter John Einsel, June 20, 1955; children: Leslie Chase, Hilary Newsby. BA, Pratt Inst., Bklyn., 1947. Asst. dir. art Seventeen Mag., NYC, 1947—48, Weintraub Agy., NYC, 1948—50, CBS Radio, NYC, 1950—53; freelance illustrator Westport, Conn., 1947—. Author: Art From the Heart, 2007. Mem.: Westport Hist. Soc., Westport Arts Ctr., Soc. Illustrators. Avocations: guitar, songwriting, gardening.

EINSPRUCH, BURTON CYRIL, psychiatrist; b. NYC, June 27, 1935; s. Adolph and Mala (Goldblatt) E.; m. Barbara Standen Traeger, Oct. 9, 1960; children: Julia E. Lewis, Alexander Louis, Robert Sands. BA, So. Meth. U., 1956, ScB, 1958; MD, Southwestern Med. Sch., Dallas, 1960. Diplomate Am. Bd. Psychiatry and Neurology (examiner 1974—). Intern Montefiore Hosp., NYC, 1960-61; resident Nat. Hosp. Inst. Neurology, London, 1962; resident, fellow U. Tex., Dallas, 1961—64; chief resident Parkland Meml. Hosp., Dallas, 1964; instr. psychiatry U. Pa., 1964-66; pvt. practice psychiatry Dallas, 1966—. Staff Presbyn. and Parkland Hosps.; clin. asst. prof. U. Tex., Health Sci. Center, Dallas, 1966-70, dir. Southwestern Adult Psychiat. Clinic, Dallas, 1966-74; dir. psychiat. service Dallas Geriatric Research Inst., 1974-80; adj. prof. sociology U. North Tex., Denton, 1975-82; cons. staff Baylor U. Hosp., Golden Acres Hosp.; clin. assoc. prof. psychiatry U. Tex. Health Scis. Ctr., Dallas, 1971—; prof. psychiatry U. Tex. Southwestern Med. Ctr., Dallas, 1971—; bd. dirs., founder Dallas Nat. Bank; clin. assoc. prof. psychiatry NYU Med. Ctr., N.Y.C., 1990; adj. prof. Dept. Occupl. and Environ. Med. U. Tex. Med. Ctr., Tyler, Tex., cognitive and neuroscience, U. Tex., Dallas; chmn. bd. dirs. Planned Behavioral Health Care, Inc., Dallas; affiliate Tex. Inst. Rsch. and Edn. on Aging, Health Sci. Ctr. Fort Worth; bd. dirs. Am. Svc. Group. Contbr. articles to profl. jours.; mem. editl. bd.: Tex. Medicine Bd., 1991—2002. Trustee Evans Fedn., N.Y.C., 1986-94, U. Tex., Dallas, 1987—, St. Mark's Sch. Tex., 1987-94, chmn. holocaust studies program bd., 1998—; mem. exec. bd. libr. So. Meth. U., 1992-97; adv. dir. Leonhardt Fedn., N.Y.C., 1990, Children of Alcoholics Fedn., 1991, 1995; arbitrator, N.Y. and Am. Exchs., N.Y.C., 1984; bd. dirs. Wyndham Internat., 1997-2000; dir. Dallas Mus. Natural History, Dallas, Tex. Lt. comdr. M.C., USNR, 1964-66. Fellow Am. Psychiat. Assn. (disting. life, Am. Coll. Psychiatrists, Am. Soc. Adolescent Psychiatry, N. Tex. Soc. Adolescent Psychiatry (past pres.); mem. Royal Coll. Psychiatry London, AMA, Tex. Med. Assn. Home: 3505 Lindenwood Ave Dallas TX 75205-3229 Office: 8330 Meadow Rd Ste 117 Dallas TX 75231-3750 Office Phone: 214-369-1636. Personal E-mail: einspruch@charter.net.

EINSPRUCH, NORMAN GERALD, physicist, engineering educator; b. NYC, June 27, 1932; s. Adolph and Mala (Goldblatt) E.; m. Edith Melnick, Dec. 20, 1953; children: Eric, Andrew, Franklin. BA in Physics, Rice U., 1953; MS in Physics, U. Colo., 1955; PhD in Applied Math, Brown U., 1959. Mem. tech. staff, central research labs. Tex. Instruments, Inc., Dallas, 1959-62, mgr. electron transport physics br., central research labs., 1962-68, dir. advanced tech. lab., central research labs., 1968-69, dir. tech., chem. materials div., 1969-72, dir. central research labs., 1972-75, asst. v.p., 1975-77, mgr. corp. devel., 1975-76, mgr. tech. and planning consumer products, 1976-77; prof. dept. elec. and computer engrng. Coll. Engrng. U. Miami, Coral Gables, Fla., 1977—, dean Coll. Engrng., 1977-90, sr. fellow in sci. and tech., 1990—, chmn. dept. indsl. engrng., 1994-99. Vis. prof. Rensselaer Poly. Inst., 2001-02; chmn. panel on thin film microstructure sci. and tech. NRC, 1978-79, mem. panel on impact of DoD very high speed integrated circuits program, 1980-81, panel on edn. and utilization of the engr., 1981-82; bd. dirs. Zinc Matrix Power, Inc.; advisor RF Saw, Inc. Author: Electronic Genie: The Tangled History of Silicon, 1998 editor: (series) VLSI Electronics: Microstructure Science, 24 vols., VLSI Handbook, 1985; contbr. articles to profl. jours. Recipient George Washington Honor medal Freedoms Found. Valley Forge. Fellow Am. Phys. Soc., Acoustical Soc. Am., IEEE, AAAS; mem. Golden Key, Iron Arrow, Sigma Xi, Omicron Delta Kappa, Tau Beta Pi, Eta Kappa Nu, Phi Kappa Phi, Alpha Pi Mu, Tau Sigma Delta. Home: 1415 Trillo Ave Miami FL 33146-2312 Office: U Miami Coll Engring PO Box 248581 Coral Gables FL 33124-8581 Office Phone: 305-284-3812. Business E-Mail: neinspruch@miami.edu.

EINSTEIN, CLIFFORD JAY, advertising executive; b. LA, May 4, 1939; s. Harry and Thelma (Bernstein) E.; m. Madeline Mandel, Jan. 28, 1962; children: Harold Jay, Karen Holly. BA in English, UCLA, 1961; PhD, DFA, Otis Coll. Art and Design, 2002. Writer Norman, Craig and Kummel, NYC, 1961-62, Foote, Cone and Belding, LA, 1962-64; ptnr. Silverman and Einstein, LA, 1965-67; pres., creative dir. Dailey and Assos., LA, 1968-93, chmn., 1994—, also bd dirs. Dir. Campaign '80, advt. agy. Reagan for Pres., 1980; lectr. various colls.; founder First Coastal Bank; bd. dirs. The Jewish Cmty. Found. Contbr. articles to Advertising Age; prodr.: (play) Whatever Happened to Georgie Tapps, L.A. and San Francisco, 1980; film appearances include Real Life, Modern Romance, Defending Your Life, Face/Off, 1997; T.V. appearance in Bizarre, Super Dave Show. Bd. dirs. Discovery Fund for Eye Rsch.; chmn. bd. Mus. Contemporary Art, L.A.; trustee Otis Coll Art & Design. With U.S. Army, 1957. Recipient Am. Advt. award, 1968, 73, 79, Clio award, 1973, Internat. Broadcast Pub. Svc. award, 1970, 85, Nat. Addy award, 1979, Gov.'s award, 1987; named Creative Dir. of the West, Adweek Poll, 1982, Exec. of West, 1986, Western States Assn. Advt. Agys. Leader of Yr., 1992, Leader of the West, Am. Advt. Fedn., 2002. Mem. AFTRA, ASCAP, SAG, Dirs. Guild Am., Hillcrest Country Club, Calif. Club. Office: Dailey & Assocs 8687 Melrose Ave West Hollywood CA 90069-5701

EINSTEIN, STEPHEN JAN, rabbi; b. LA, Nov. 15, 1945; s. Syd C. and Selma (Rothenberg) E.; m. Robin Susan Kessler, Sept. 9, 1967; children: Rebecca Yael, Jennifer Melissa, Heath Isaac, Zachary Shane. AB, UCLA, 1967; BHL, Hebrew Union Coll., LA, 1968, DHL, 1995, DD (hon.), 1996; MAHL, Hebrew Union Coll., Cin., 1971. Ordained rabbi. Rabbi Temple Beth Am, Parsippany, NJ, 1971-74, Temple Beth David, Westminster, Calif., 1974-76, Congregation B'nai Tzedek, Fountain Valley, Calif., 1976—. Lectr. Calif. State U., Fullerton. Co-author: Every Person's Guide to Judaism, 1989; co-editor: Introduction to Judaism, 1983. Pres., trustee Fountain Valley (Calif.) Sch. Bd., 1984—90; chmn. pers. commn. Fountain Valley Sch. Dist., 1991—; pres. Retinoblatoma Internat., 2000—01; chaplain Fountain Valley Police Dept.; pres. Greater Huntington Beach Inter-Faith Coun., 2001—02; active Anti Defamation League, Am. Jewish Com.; co-chmn. Commn. on Outreach and Synagogue Cmty., 1999—; regional bd. dirs. Nat. Conf. Cmty. and Justice, 2001—06; co-chair, cmty. adv. bd. KOCE-TV. Recipient Micah Award for Interfaith Activities, Am. Jewish Com., 1988. Mem.: Inst. for Character Edn. (exec. adv. bd.), Clergy for Choice, Orange County Bur. Jewish Edn. (v.p. 1982—84, 1992—94, pres. 1994—97, honored for Maj. Contbns. to Jewish Learning 1986), Jewish Educators Assn. Orange County (pres. 1979—81), Orange County Bd. Rabbis (pres. 1976—79, 1997—98), Pacific Assn. Reform Rabbis (exec. bd. 1987—91, 1998—2002, pres. 2002—03), Ctrl. Conf. Am. Rabbis (exec. bd. 1989—91, ethics com. 1993—98, 2006, chair 2007—), Alzheimers Assn. (religious adv. com.), Am. Cancer Soc. (v.p. West Orange County dist. 1994—98), Phi Beta Kappa. Democrat. Office: Congregation Bnai Tzedek 9669 Talbert Ave Fountain Valley CA 92708 Home Phone: 714-963-0285; Office Phone: 714-963-4611. Personal E-mail: rebgiraffe@aol.com.

EINSTEIN, STEVEN HENRY, lawyer, investment banker; b. NYC, Aug. 14, 1954; s. Ralph Gunther and Beatrice (Katz) E.; children: Theodore Aaron, Peter Raymond, Hannah Louise. BS, Lehigh U., 1976; JD, Seton Hall U., 1979; LLM in Taxation, NYU, 1985. Lic. CPA, N.Y., N.J.; Bar: N.J. 1979, N.Y. 1985, U.S. Dist. Ct. N.J. 1979, U.S. Tax Ct. 1982, U.S. Ct.

Appeals (3d cir.) 1983, U.S. Supreme Ct. 1985. Judicial law clk. to presiding justice Superior Ct., Hackensack, NJ, 1979—80; assoc. Wacks, Hirsch, Ramsey & Berman Esqs., Morristown, NJ, 1980—81; sr. tax mgr. Touche Ross & Co., Newark, 1981—86; v.p., investment banking, mergers & acquisitions dept. PaineWebber Capital Mkts., NYC, 1986—88; v.p., merchant banking/pvt. equity Kluge, Subotnick, Perkowski & Co., NYC, 1988—90; mng. dir. Price WaterhouseCoopers Corp. Fin. Group, NYC, 1991—98; ptnr. & mng. dir. PricewaterhouseCoopers Securities LLP, NYC, 1998—99, ptnr., chmn.'s office, global leader, corp. devel., 1999—, ptnr. transaction svcs. group, 2006—. Mem. editl. bd. Corp. Taxation Mag.; contbr. articles to profl. jours. Mem. ABA, AICPAs, N.J. State Bar Assn., N.Y. State Bar Assn., Essex County Bar Assn. (taxation divsn.), N.J. Soc. CPAs, Beta Gamma Sigma, Phi Eta Sigma. Jewish. Home: 203 Park St New Canaan CT 06840-5705 Office: PricewaterhouseCoopers LLP 300 Madison Ave New York NY 10017 Business E-Mail: steven.einstein@us.pwc.com.

EIRE, CARLOS, historian, educator, writer; b. Havana, Cuba; BA, Loyola U., 1973; MA, Yale U., 1974, MPhil, 1976, PhD, 1979. Lectr. Albertus Magnus Coll., New Haven, 1978; asst. prof. St. John's U., Collegeville, Minn., 1979—81, U. Va., Dept. Religious Studies, 1981—87, assoc. prof., 1987—94, U. Va. , Dept. Hist., 1989—94; prof. U. Va., Dept. Hist. and Religious Studies, 1994—96, Yale U., Dept. History and Religious Studies, 1996—2000; seminar leader Folger Inst., Folger Shakespeare Libr., 2000; chair Yale U., Dept. Religious Studies, 1999—2002; T. Lawrason Riggs prof. of hist. and religious studies Yale U., 2000—. Mem. Sch. of Hist. Studies, Inst. for Advanced Studies, Princeton, NJ, 1986—87; vis. Sch. of Hist. Studies, Inst. for Advanced Study, Princeton, NJ, 1992—93; mem. Ctr. for Advanced Studies, U. Va., 1992—93. Author: (book) War Against the Idols: The Reformation of Worship from Erasmus to Calvin, 1986, From Madrid to Purgatory: The Art and Craft of Dying in Sixteenth Century Spain, 1995; author: (with J. Corrigan, M. Jaffee, F. Denny) Jews, Christians, Muslims: A Comparative Introduction to Monotheistic Religions, 1997; author: Waiting for Snow in Havana: Confessions of a Cuban Boy, 2003 (Nat. Book award, 2003). Recipient U. Va. Alumni Bd. Trustees Tchg. award, 1990; Fulbright Program Fellowship for Rsch. in Spain, 1984, Exxon Edn. Found. Fellowship, Ctr. for Renaissance Studies. Office Phone: 203-432-1357.

EIRIKSSON, CHARLES EINAR, cardiologist; b. Milw., Wis, Sept. 27, 1947; MD, U. Wash., Seattle, 1973. Cert. Internal Medicine, Pediatric Critical Care Medicine, Cardiovascular Disease, Interventional Cardiology. Intern, cardiology U. Utah, Salt Lake City, 1973—74, resident, 1974—76; fellow, cardiology U. Calif. Davis Sch. Medicine, Martinez VA Hosp., Martinez, Calif., 1976—78; hosp. appointment St. Alphonsus Regional Med. Ctr., Boise, Idaho, 1982—, St. Luke's Regional Med. Ctr., Boise, Idaho, 1982—, St. Luke's Wood River, Idaho, West Valley Med. Ctr., McCall Meml. Hosp.; assoc. clin. prof. U. Wash.; co-founder, cardiologist Idaho Cardiology Associates, PA, 1994—. Fellow: Am. Coll. Cardiology. Office: Idaho Cardiology Associates PA 300 E Jefferson Ste 101 Boise ID 83712 Office Phone: 208-336-4141.*

EISCHEN, DONALD F., psychologist, educator, writer; s. Joseph Francis Eischen and Emily Elizabeth White-Eischen; m. Jennie Capriola (dec. Aug. 1999); children: Donna-Marie, Emily A. Kamansky. BA, Calif. State U., Fresno, 1949; MA, Columbia U., 1951; PhD, Stanford U., 2002, Madison U., 2004. Psychologist, Santa Cruz, Calif. Camp counselor Calif. State U., Trinity, 1959—60, prof. English, Fresno, 1959—62, supr., master tchr., 1960—85. Author: Mirror Up to Nature, 2002, Love Against Hate: As it Relates to Gays, Lesbians, Bisexuals, and Transgenders in the 21st Century, 2006. Vol. Cmty. Bridges, Santa Cruz, 1991—2006; flutist St. Joseph Ch., Capitola, Calif., 1993—2006. Recipient Outstanding Tchr., Fresno, 1988. Fellow: Elks (greeter, treas. 1994—2005); mem.: Sons of Italy (treas. 1991—95), Italian Cath. Fedn. (sec., orator 1975—2005), German Am. Club (sec. 2003—04), KC (faithful navigator 1980—82, Grand knight 1976—80, Sir knight 1980—82). Roman Catholic. Avocations: antiques, swimming, dance, walking, travel. Office Phone: 831-458-5122. Personal E-mail: dr_deischen@sbcglobal.net.

EISCHEN, MICHELLE ROBIN, art educator; b. Chgo., Feb. 8, 1972; d. Robert Charles Heinz and Sadie Alice Husko; m. James Patrick Eischen, June 2, 2000. BFA, Sch. Art U. Chgo., Chgo., 1999; MFA, U. S.D., Vermillion, SD, 2004. Vis. prof. S.D. State U., Brookings, SD, 2004—. One-woman shows include Wash. Pavilion Visual Art Mus., 2005, exhibitions include Ritz Gallery, 2006. Mem.: Coll. Art Assn. Democrat. Office: SD State U Visual Arts Dept 106F Grove Hall Brookings SD Business E-Mail: michelle.eischen@sdstate.edu.

EISDORFER, CARL, psychiatrist, health facility administrator; b. Bronx, NY, June 20, 1930; BA, NYU, 1951, MA, 1953, PhD, 1959; MD, Duke U., 1964; postgrad. in health systems mgmt., Harvard U., 1981. Lectr. in psychology Duke U. Med. Ctr., Durham, NC, 1959-72, intern in medicine, 1964-65, psychiat. trainee, 1964-67, dir. tng., research coordinator Ctr. for Study Aging and Human Devel., 1965-70, prof. psychiatry and med. psychology, 1968-72, dir. med. studies behavioral scis. program, 1970-72, head div. med. psychology dept. psychiatry, 1970-72, dir. Ctr. for Study Aging and Human Devel., 1970-72; founding dir. Inst. on Aging, U. Wash., Seattle, 1977-79, prof., chmn. dept. psychiatry and behavioral scis. Sch. of Medicine, adj. prof. psychology, 1972-81; sr. scholar in residence Inst. Medicine, Nat. Acad. Scis., Washington, 1979-80; prof. psychiatry and neurosci. Albert Einstein Coll. Medicine, NYC, 1981-85; chief exec. officer Montefiore Med. Ctr., NYC, 1981-85; prof., chmn. dept. psychiatry U. Miami, Fla., 1986—2005, dir. Ctr. on Aging Fla., 1986—, Knight profl, spl. asst. to pres. Fla., 2004—; chief div. mental health Jackson Meml. Med. Ctr., 1986—2003. Coordinator Community Mental Health Services, Halifax County N.C., 1969-70; vis. prof. architeture U. Calif.-Berkeley, 1969-70; H.T. Dozer vis. prof. geriatrics and psychiatry Ben Gurion U., Negev, Israel, 1980; cons. NIH, Bethesda, Md., Robert Wood Johnson Found., numerous others; del. White Ho. Conf. on Aging at Large, 2005; chair Group on Geriatrics and Biology of Aging, IOM, 2005; mem. Nat. Adv. Coun., NIA, 2006. Editor in chief Ann. Rev. Gerontology and Geriatrics, 1978; mem. editl. bd. Alzheimers Disease and Related Disorders-Internat. Jour., Aging and Human Devel., Western Jour. Medicine, Neurobiology of Aging: Exptl. and Clin. Rsch.; contbr. articles to profl. jours and books. With US Army, 1954—56. Recipient Kesten award Ethel Percy Andrus Gerontology Ctr., U. So. Calif., 1976, Potamkin prize, 1982, Disting. Alumnus award Duke U. Sch. of Medicine, 1985, Allid Signal award, 1991. Fellow Soc. Behavioral Medicine, N.Y. Acad. Medicine, Am. Psychol. Assn. (chmn. div. adult devel. and aging 1970-71, task force on aging 1971-73, award for disting. contbns. 1981, award for contbns. on aging research 1985), Gerontol. Soc. Am. (pres. 1971-72, Robert W. Kleemeier award 1969, Donald P. Kent award, 2002, Joseph Freeman award div. clin. medicine 1979), Am. Geriatrics Soc. (Edward B. Allen award 1974, Edward Henderson Meml. award 1988), Am. Psychiat. Assn. (Jack Weinberg Meml. award 1984), Am. Coll. Psychiatrists, Am. Coll. Physicians (Menninger award 1990), AAAS; mem. Am. Soc. Aging (pres. 1980-82), Am. Fed. Aging Res. (pres. 1986-88), Sigma Xi, Alpha Omega Alpha, Phi Beta Kappa. Office: U Miami Sch Medicine Dept Psychiatry D-28 PO Box 16960 Miami FL 33101-6960 Office Phone: 305-355-9040. E-mail: ceisdorf@med.miami.edu.

EISELE, CHARLES R., rail transportation executive; B in Civil Engring., Mich. State U., M in Transp.; grad. in Advanced Mgmt. Program, Harvard Bus. Sch. With Mich. Dept. Transp., CONSAD Rsch. Corp.; sr. analyst strategic planning Union Pacific Corp., 1978, various positions in fin., acctg., planning and analysis, mgmt. systems and exec. dept., v.p. supply, v.p. human resources, sr. v.p. strategic planning & adminstrn., 2001—. Office: Union Pacific Corp 1400 Douglas St Omaha NE 68179 Office Phone: 402-544-5000.*

EISELSTEIN, WILLIAM P. (BILLY EISELSTEIN), lawyer; b. Chatanooga, 1970; BA, Emory Univ., Atlanta, Ga., 1992; JD cum laude, Univ. Tenn., 1995. Bar: Ga. 1995. Assoc. atty., vice-chmn., litig. dept. Miller & Martin PLLC, Atlanta. Spkr. in field. Contbr. articles to numerous profl. jours. Alumni advisory coun. Univ. Tenn. Law Sch. Named Ga. Rising Star, SuperLawyer Mag., 2006. Mem.: ABA, State Bar Assn. Ga. Office: Miller & Martin Ste 800 1170 Peachtree St NE Atlanta GA 30309-7649

EISEN, GLENN PHILIP, management consultant, educator; b. Chgo., Feb. 8, 1940; s. Sol Eisen and Lorraine (Winsberg) Lukinsky; m. Devera Arne Chiz, May 7, 1961 (div. 1974); children: Julia, Steven; m. Barbara Baxter McNear, June 7, 1987. BS in Indsl. Mgmt., Ill. Inst. Tech., 1971. Cert. mgmt. cons.; registered EMT, Conn., Calif. Prodn. supr. Intercraft Industries, Chgo., 1961-64; sr. buyer Simoniz Co., Chgo., 1964-65; purchasing/packaging mgr. Paper Mate div. Gillette, La Grange Park, Ill., 1965-69; assoc. The Packaging House Inc., Chgo., 1969-73; cons. Israel Inst. of Packaging, Tel Aviv, 1973-74; prin. The Emerson Cons., NYC, 1975-80, Arthur Andersen & Co., Chgo., 1980-87; chief exec. officer The Eisen Group, Wilton, Conn., 1987-96; prin. The Omega Cons., LLC, 1996-2000. Internat. comml. arbitrator Am. Arbitration Assn., NYC, 1985-03; bd. fin. Wilton, Conn., 2001-02; lectr., mgr. mfg. industry edn. Arthur Andersen Ctr. for Profl. Edn., 1980-83; lectr., seminar leader Am. Mgmt. Assn., 1967-99; clin. instr. UCLA Ctr. Prehospital Care, 2003—; counselor Svc. Corps. Ret. Execs., 2003—; hazardous materials decontamination technician and supply mgmt. officer Nat. Disaster Med. Sys. and US Dept. Health and Human Svcs., 2003-; instr. driver safety program Am. Assn. Ret. Persons, 2006-. Author: Purchasing Negotiations, 1983, Group Buying in Health Care, 1985, Supply Market Management, 1989, Maximizing Your Value When Using Management Consultants, 1992, Ethical Practices and Conflicts of Interest Benchmark Study, 1994, Procurement Best Practices, 1997, Maintenance Planning and Management Best Practices, 1998; mem. editl. bd.: In Bound Logistics Mag., 1990. Active Westport Emergency Med. Svc. 2000-02; disaster med. assistance team LA County, 2002—; CPR and 1st aid instr. ARC, 1999—, Am. Heart Assn.; mem. FEMA US Dept. Homeland Security, 2003-2007; with Dept. Health and Human Svcs. 2007-. With US Army, 1958-61. Mem. Kiwanis Internat., Disabled Veterans. Jewish. Home and Office: 1860 Homewood Dr Altadena CA 91001-2848

EISEN, HERMAN NATHANIEL, immunology researcher, medical educator; b. Bklyn., Oct. 15, 1918; m. Natalie Aronson, 1948; 5 children. AB, NYU, 1939, MD, 1943; ScD (hon.), Washington U., St. Louis, 2003. Asst. in pathology Coll. Physicians and Surgeons, Columbia U., NYC, 1944—46; NIH fellow Coll. Medicine, NYU, 1947—48, fellow in chemistry, 1948—49, asst. prof. indsl. medicine, 1949—53, assoc. prof., 1953—55; prof. medicine Sch. Medicine, Washington U., St. Louis, 1955—61; dermatologist-in-chief Barnes Hosp., St. Louis, 1955—61; prof. microbiology, head dept. Sch. Medicine Washington U., St. Louis, 1961—73; prof. MIT, Cambridge, 1973—82, Whitehead Inst. prof. immunology, 1982—89; prof. emeritus, 1989—. Mem. adv. bd. Mass. Gen Hosp., Yale Med. Sch., Harvard Sch. Pub. Health, Children's Hosp., Boston, Merck, Sharpe, Dohme Rsch. Labs., Roche Inst. for Molecular Biology, Howard Hughes Med. Inst.; chmn. Nat. Inst. Health Study, 1962—66; bd. of sci. counselors Nat. Inst. of Arthritis and Metabolic Dis., 1971—75; chmn. World Health Orgn. Sci. Group on Regulation of Immune Responses, 1969; lectr. Harvey Soc., NYC, 1964; Phillips lectr. Haverford Coll., 1971; Burroughs & Wellcome vis. lectr. Med. Coll. So. Carolina, 1979; Culpepper Found. lectr. State Univ. of N.Y., Stonybrook, 1981; Lowry lectr. Washington Univ., St. Louis, 1989. Recipient Med. Sci. Achievement award, NYU, 1978, Outstanding Investigator award, Nat. Cancer Inst., NIH, 1986—93, Dupont award, Clin. Ligand Soc., 1987, Behring-Heidelberger award, 1993. Mem.: Am. Soc. for Clin. Investigation (v.p. 1965), Am. Assn. Immunologists (pres. 1968, Lifetime Svc./Achievement award 1997), Am. Acad. Arts and Scis., Inst. Medicine, Am. Assn. Physicians, Nat. Acad. Sci. (editl. bd. Procs. of the NAS 1994—2004). Office: MIT Ctr Cancer Rsch E17-128 77 Massachusetts Ave Cambridge MA 02139-4307 Business E-Mail: hneisen@mit.edu.

EISEN, HOWARD JOEL, internist, researcher; b. Forest Hills, NY, May 25, 1956; s. Ezra Michael and Gertrude Margaret (Schmidt) Eisen; m. Judith Ellen Wolf, June 26, 1983; children: Jonathan Ezra, Miriam Sarah. BA in Biology, Cornell U., 1977; MD, U. Pa., 1981. Diplomate Am. Bd. Med. Examiners, Am. Bd Internal Medicine, Am. Bd. Cardiovascular Diseases. Med. intern Hosp. U. Pa., Phila., 1981—82, resident in medicine, 1982—84; fellow in cardiology Washington U. Sch. Medicine-Barnes Hosp., St. Louis, 1984—87; asst. prof. medicine U. Pa., Phila., 1990—93; assoc. prof. medicine and physiology Temple U., Phila., 1993—97, prof. medicine and physiology, 1997—2004, dir. heart failure care unit, 1993—99, med. dir. cardiac transplant program, 1999—2004, assoc. dir. Gen. Clin. Rsch. Ctr., 1995—2002, med. dir. Cardiomyopathy and Transplant Ctr., 1999—2002, med. dir. advanced heart failure and transplant program, 1999—2002, dir. Advanced Heart Failure Ctr., 2002—04; Thomas J. Vischer prof. medicine Drexel U. Coll. Medicine, Phila., 2004—, dir., Ctr. Advanced Heart Failure Care at Hahnemann, dir. Ctr. Cardiovasc. Disorders; chief divsn. cardiology Drexel U. Coll. Medicine and Hahnemann U. Hosp. Mem. cryptosporidiosis adv. com. Dept. Pub. Health, Phila., 1995—2000. Fellow: Am. Heart Assn. (clin. coun. 1995—, rsch. com. 1995—, established investigatorship award 1996—2001, chmn. peer-review com. 1996—), Am. Coll. Cardiology, ACP; mem.: Am. Soc. Transplantation (chair thoracic com.), Southeastern Pa. Am. Heart Assn. Affiliate (pres. 2003—05), Internat. Soc. Heart and Lung Transportation, Am. Fedn. Clin. Rsch (mem. nat. coun. 1992—95, H. Christian award 1993), Phi Beta Kappa, Alpha Omega Alpha. Avocations: reading, rowing, classical music, running. Home: 507 Shortridge Dr Wynnewood PA 19096-1609 Office: Drexel Univ Coll Medicine Mail Stop 1012 245 N 15th St Philadelphia PA 19102 Office Phone: 215-762-3829. Business E-Mail: heisen@drexelmed.edu.

EISEN, LIZABETHANN R., lawyer; b. Portland, Oreg., June 14, 1972; m. Scott G. Eisen, Sept. 6, 1998. BA magna cum laude, Cornell Univ., 1994; JD, Univ. Pa., 1997. Bar: NY 1998. Assoc. Cravath Swaine & Moore LLP, NYC, 1997—2005, ptnr., corp., 2005—. Contbr. articles to profl. jours. Mem. coun. The Fresh Air Fund. Mem.: ABA, Assn. Bar City N.Y., Woodmont Country Club, Multnomah Athletic Club. Office: Cravath Swaine & Moore LLP Worldwide Plz 825 Eighth Ave New York NY 10019-7475 Office Phone: 212-474-1930. Office Fax: 212-474-3700. Business E-Mail: leisen@cravath.com.

EISEN, ROBERT L., lawyer; b. Bklyn., Mar. 26, 1947; BA, Queens Coll., 1967; JD, NYU, 1970. Asst. chief counsel NY Customs, 1970—80; ptnr. Global TAx, Customs and Internat. Trade practice Baker and McKenzie, NYC. Contbr. articles to profl. jours. Mem. adv. bd. Fashion Inst. of Tech., NYC. Mem.: ABA, NY State Bar Assn., Am. Assn. Exporters & Importers (bd. mem.), Customs & Internat. Trade Bar Assn. Office: Baker & McKenzie LLP 1114 Ave of the Americas New York NY 10036 Office Phone: 212-626-4492. Office Fax: 212-310-1622. Business E-Mail: robert.l.eisen@bakernet.com.

EISENBERG, ADI, chemist; b. Breslau, Germany, Feb. 18, 1935; emigrated to U.S., 1951; s. Oscar and Helene E.; m. Sandra M. Kloner, June 9, 1957 (div. 1985); 1 son, Elliot; m. Katia Chantal Wegliszewski, Sept. 1, 2002; 3 children by previous marriage. BSc, Worcester Poly. Inst., 1957; MA, Princeton U., 1959, PhD, 1960. Postdoctoral fellow U. Basel, Switzerland, 1961-62; asst. prof. chemistry UCLA, 1962-67; assoc. prof. chemistry McGill U., Montreal, Que., Canada, 1967-74, prof., 1975—; dir. Polymer McGill, 1991-99, Otto Maass Prof. Chemistry, 1993—. Cons. in field. Author 7 books in field; contbr. articles to profl. jours. NATO fellow, 1961-62; Killam Research fellow, 1987-88; recipient E.W.R. Steacie award, 1998, Prix Urgel Archambault, 2004. Fellow Royal Soc. Can:, Am. Phys. Soc. (chmn. div. high polymer physics 1975-76), Chem. Inst. Can. (Macromolecular Sci. and Engring.-Dunlop award 1988, E.W.R. Steacie award 1998); mem. Am. Chem. Soc. Achievements include patents in field. Office: McGill University 801 Sherbrooke St W Montreal PQ Canada H3A 2K6 Business E-Mail: adi.eisenberg@mcgill.ca.

EISENBERG, ALAN, retired professional society administrator; b. NYC, Apr. 15, 1935; s. Arthur and Mollie (Novak) E.; m. Claire Copley, May 23, 1982; children: Mollie Copley, Emma Copley. AB, U. Mich., 1956; LLB, NYU, 1959. Bar: N.Y., Va., D.C. Assoc. Booth. Lipton & Lipton, NYC, 1960, Hirson & Bertini, NYC, 1960-64; atty. NLRB, Washington and Chgo., 1964-68; assoc. Seligman & Seligman, NYC, 1968-72; ptnr. Eisenberg & Paul, Arlington, Va., 1972-81; exec. dir. Actors' Equity Assn., NYC, 1981—2006. Vis. prof. theatre adminstrn. Yale U. Sch. Drama, New Haven, 1982—; lectr. theatre dept. U. Mich., 2003—, NYU Sch. Law, 2004-06, theatre dept. Bklyn. Coll. , 2003-06. Gen. v.p. dept. profl. employees AFL-CIO; dir. Actors's Equity Found., Non Traditional Casting Project, Inc., Career Transition for Dancers, Times Square Bus. Improvement Dist.; trustee Equity League Pension and Health Funds, Actors' Found. Am.; trustee, v.p. Broadway Cares, Equity Fights AIDS. Office Phone: 212-869-8530. Personal E-mail: zeus205@earthlink.net. Business E-Mail: aeisenberg@actorsequity.org.

EISENBERG, BARBARA ANNE K., lawyer; b. NYC, Oct. 7, 1945; d. Jerome Comet and Joy Klein; m. Edward Eisenberg, Oct. 20, 1974; 1 child. BA with distinction, Barnard Coll., 1967; JD cum laude, Columbia U., 1970. Bar: NY. Assoc. Kaye, Scholer, Fierman, Hays & Handler, 1970—75; v.p., gen. counsel, corp. sec. Pantasote Inc., Greenwich, Conn., 1978—86; asst. gen. counsel Burlington Industries, Inc., NYC, 1986-88, v.p., assoc. gen. counsel, asst. sec., 1988-93, v.p., assoc. gen. counsel, corp. sec., 1993—98; sr. v.p., gen. counsel, corp. sec. J. Crew Group, Inc., 1998—2001; sr. v.p., gen. counsel, sec. Ann Taylor Stores Corp., NYC, 2001—05, exec. v.p., gen. counsel, corp. sec., 2005—. Pres. Columbia Law Sch. Assn., 2000—02; mem. bd. visitors Columbia Law Sch., 2002—, bd. dirs., Maidenform Brands, 2005—; first v.p. Columbia Law Sch. Assn., 1998—2000; mem. Info. Tech. Law Commn., 2000—01. Mem. ABA, Assn. of Bar of City of N.Y., Corp. Bar Assn. (bd. dirs. 1986-88, vice chmn. SEC-fin. com. 1984-85, chmn. 1985-86), Am. Soc. Corr. Secs. Office: Ann Taylor Stores Corp 7 Times Sq New York NY 10036 Office Phone: 212-536-4229. Office Fax: 212-536-4412. Business E-Mail: barbara_eisenberg@anntaylor.com.

EISENBERG, CAROLA, psychiatrist, educator; b. Buenos Aires, Sept. 15, 1917; came to U.S., 1945; d. Bernardo and Teodora (Kahan) Blitzman; m. Manfred Guttmacher, Oct. 11, 1946 (dec. 1966); m. Leon Eisenberg, Aug. 31, 1967; children: Laurence, Alan. M of Social Work, Liceo de Senoritas; MD, U. Buenos Aires, 1945. Resident in psychiatry U. Md., 1946-48; fellow in child psychiatry Johns Hopkins Hosp., 1948-50, asst. prof. psychiatry and pediatrics Balt., 1960-67; psychiatrist MIT, Boston, 1967-72, dean of students, 1972-78; dean student affairs Harvard Med. Sch., Boston, 1978-90, dir. internat. programs for students, 1990-92, lectr. psychiatry, 1970-92, lectr. social medicine, 1992—; hon. psychiatrist Mass. Gen. Hosp., Boston, 2005. Co-chmn. women in biomed. careers workshop Office on Women's Health, NIH, 1992, mem. adv. com. on rsch. and women's health, 1995-98; mem. com. on human rights ACP; mem. com. on women in sci. and engring. NAS, 1992-95. V.p. Physicians for Human Rights, Boston, 1987-. Recipient Morani Renaissance Woman award, Found. for History of Women in Medicine, 2003. Fellow Am. Psychiat. Assn. (Disting. life fellow 2003, mem. Coun. Internat. Affairs, com. on human rights, Human Rights award 2005), Am. Orthopsychiat. Assn. (life); mem. AAUP. Avocations: travel, music, reading. Home Phone: 617-868-0112.

EISENBERG, DANIEL, filmmaker; Instr. in film Collective For Living Cinema, NY, 1978, Boston Film/Video Found., 1979; asst. prof. film Mass. Coll. Art, Boston, 1979—82, 1993—94, instr. video, 1987; spl. instr. in film and photography U. R.I., Kingston, 1984; vis. artist in film San Francisco Art Inst., 1993; asst. prof. film, chair dept. filmmaking Sch. Art Inst. Chgo., 1994—97, assoc. prof. film, chair dept. filmmaking, 1998—2000, prof. film, video, new media, 2001. Editor various works WGBH, Boston, 1981—90; presenter in field. One-man shows include Collective for Living Cinema, NYC, 1981, 1989, MIT, Cambridge, 1984, Sch. Mus. Fine Arts, Boston, 1986, Boston Film/Video Found., 1987, Montserrat Sch. Art, Beverly, Mass., 1987, Brattle Theatre, Cambridge, 1988, Art Cinema, Binghamton, N.Y., 1988, Mass. Coll. Art, Boston, 1988, San Francisco Cinematheque, San Francisco, 1988, Pacific Film Archive, Berkeley, 1988, Kino Arsenal, Berlin, 1988, 1991, Am. Mus. Moving Image, NY, 1988, Inst. Contemporary Arts, Boston, 1989, Mus. Modern Art, Cineprobe, NY, 1989, 1998, Harvard U., Grad. Sch. Design, 1990, Boston Film/Video Found., 1991, London Filmmakers Coop, 1991, Hochschule der Kunst, Berlin, 1991, Braunschweig, 1991, Musée du Cinema, Brussels, 1991, Kommunales Kino, Hannover, 1991, Kiel, 1991, De Unie, Rotterdam, 1992, 't Hoogt, Utrecht, 1992, Filmmuseum, Frankfurt, 1992, Munich, 1992, Musee Nat. d'Art Moderne, 1992, Calif. Coll. Arts and Crafts, Oakland, 1993, Davis Mus., 1994, U. Iowa, Iowa City, 1996, L.A. Film Forum, 1997, Pacific Film Archive, Berkeley, Calif., 1997, Rocky Mountain Film Ctr., Boulder, Colo., 1998, Boston U., 1998, Harvard Film Archive, Cambridge, 1998, exhibited in group shows at Viper, Lucerne, Switzerland, 1995, Sydney Internat. Film Festival, 1997, Vue Sur Les Docs Festival, Marseilles, 1998, Goethe Inst., Chgo., 1999, numerous others; filmmaker: Matrice, 1975; Design and Debris, 1979; Mexican Sketch, 1980; Displaced Person, 1981; Native Shore, 1983; To A Brother In Asia, 1983; Motion Studies, 1979—90; Cooperation of Parts, 1987; Persistance, 1997; Something More Than Night, 2003. Named Berlin artist-in-residence, Deutscher Akademischer Austauschdienst, 1991, 1997; recipient Outstanding Film award, New Eng. Film Festival, 1981, CEBA awards for excellence, 1988, Hon. Mention, New Eng. Film Festival, 1988, Grand prize, Black Maria Film and Video Festival, 1988—89; fellow in film, Mass. Artists Found., 1982; grantee Mass. Prodns. grantee, Mass. Coun. on Arts, 1986—88, Sch. Art Inst. Faculty Enrichment, 1995, 1997; New Eng. Regional fellow, Nat. Endowment Arts, 1982, Media Arts grantee, 1989—92, artist fellow, The MacDowell Colony, 1990, fellow in film, Mass. Artists Found., 1991, John Simon Guggenheim Meml. Found. fellow, 1999—2000, Ill. Coun. Arts Fellowship, 2001. Home: 1411 W Edgewater Ave Chicago IL 60660-4208 E-mail: deisen@artic.edu.

EISENBERG, DOROTHY, federal judge; b. 1929; LLB, Bklyn. Law Sch., 1950. Bar: N.Y. 1951, U.S. Dist. Ct. (ea. and so. dists.) N.Y., U.S. Ct. Appeals (2nd cir.), U.S. Supreme Ct. Assoc. Otterbourg, Stiendler, Houston & Rosen, NYC, 1950-51, Goldman, Horowitz & Cherno, Mineola, NY, 1970-80; pvt. practice Garden City, NY, 1981; ptnr. Shaw, Licitra, Eisenberg, Esernio & Schwartz, P.C., Garden City, 1981-89; bankruptcy judge ea. dist. U.S. Bankruptcy Ct., NY, 1989—. Mem. Com. on Character and Fitness, Appellate divsn., 2nd Dept., 1983-89; panel trustee U.S. Bankruptcy Ct. (so. dist.) N.Y., 1979-89, U.S. Bankruptcy Ct. (ea. dist.) N.Y., 1975-89; mem. adv. group for NY State-Fed. Jud. Coun. Fellow: Am. Bar Found.; mem.: ABA, Fed. Bar Coun. (mem. adv. coun. 2nd cir.), Nassau Suffolk Women's Bar Assn. (former pres.), Bar Assn. Nassau

County, Am. Bankruptcy Inst., N.Y. State Women's Bar Assn. (Nassau County chpt.), Nat. Assn. Women Judges. Office: LI Fed Courthouse 290 Federal Plz PO Box 9013 Central Islip NY 11722-4437

EISENBERG, HERBERT, lawyer; b. Bklyn., Sept. 10, 1958; BA, SUNY Binghampton, 1979; JD, SUNY Buffalo, 1983. Bar: NY, US Dist Ct. (so. & ea. dists.) NY, US Ct. Appeals (2nd cir.) 1984. Mem. Eisenberg & Schnell LLP, NYC. Mem.: NY County Lawyers Assn. (co-chair Labor & Employment com. 1999—2001), Nat. Employment Lawyers Assn. (pres. NY ch. 2002—05, exec. bd. 2004—). Office: Eisenberg & Schnell LLP 9th Fl 377 Broadway New York NY 10013 Office Phone: 212-966-8900. Office Fax: 212-966-2505. E-mail: heisenberg@eisenbergschnell.com.*

EISENBERG, HOWARD MICHAEL, neurosurgeon; b. NYC, May 4, 1939; s. Monroe L. and Regina (Fish) Eisenberg; children: Nancy M. Hoy, John A. BA, Syracuse U., 1960; MD, SUNY, NYC, 1964. Diplomate Am. Bd. Neurol. Surgery. Intern NY Hosp., 1964-65; resident, fellow Cornell U. Med. Sch., 1964-66; resident neurosurgery Peter Bent Brigham Hosp., Boston, 1966-70; surgery instr. Harvard U., 1972-75; assoc. prof. U. Tex. Med. Br., Galveston, 1975-80, prof., chief neurosurgery, 1980-92; head divsn. neurosurgery U. Md., Balt., 1992-96, dir. med. svcs. Shock Trauma Ctr., 1992-96, prof. chair dept. neurosurgery, 1996—, R.K. Thompson prof., 2000—. Chmn. neurology A study sect. NIH, Bethesda, Md., 1980—87; numerous vis. professorships and guest lectureships. Mem. editl. bd. Jour. Neurosurgery, 1989—99, chair, 1997—99; editor: (book) The Cerebral Microvasulature, 1980, Neurobehavioral Recovery from Head Injury, 1987, Mild Head Injury, 1989, Neurosurgery Clinics of North America-Mangement of Head Injury, 1991, The Frontal Lobes, 1991; contbr. articles to profl. jours. Mem. devel. bd. Houston Grand Opera, 1989—92. Lt. comdr. USN, 1970—72. Recipient William Cavernes award, Nat. Head Injury Found., 1994, Wakeman award, 1990; numerous grants in field. Mem.: ACGME (mem. residency rev. com. neurosurgery 2001—02, v.p.), ACS (chair neurosurgical adv. coun.), Am. Surg. Assn., Acad. Neurol. Surgeons (v.p.), Soc. Neurol. Surgeons (v.p., pres.-elect, pres.), Am. Bd. Neurol. Surgery (bd. dirs., sec.-treas., bd. dirs. 1990—95, chmn. 1995—96), NY Yacht Club (mem. seamanship com.), Cruising Club Am., Annapolis Yacht. Club, Cosmos Club. Office: U Md Med Systems Dept Neurosurgery 22 S Greene St Ste S12D Baltimore MD 21201-1544 Office Phone: 410-328-3514. Business E-Mail: heisenberg@smail.umaryland.edu.

EISENBERG, JAY LYNN, marketing research professional; b. Mpls., Mar. 28, 1943; s. Benjamin Gene and Blanche (Goldfetter) E.; m. Gabriela Hubert, Aug. 17, 1975. BA, U. Minn., 1966, MA, 1970. Jr. project dir. Gen. Mills Inc., Mpls., 1968-70; mktg. rsch. analyst Green Giant Co., Bloomington, Minn., 1970-72; project mgr. Am. Guidance Svc., Circle Pines, Minn., 1973-80; mgr. mkt. rsch. Nash Finch Co., Mpls., 1981—, sr. market rsch. mgr., 1999—2005; ret. Co-author: Peabody Picture Vocabulary Test-Revised Technical Supplement, 1981; contbr. articles to profl. and popular publs. Co-coord. family coun. Sholom West Nursing Home, St. Louis Park, Minn., 1993-97. Grantee U. Minn. Computer Ctr., 1968; recipient Bronze award 40th Pacific Internat. Philatelic Exhb., 1980, others. Mem. Am. Mktg. Assn. (emeritus), Am. Topical Assn., Classic Corvettes Minn., Chesstamp Rev. (charter). Achievements include development of Store Insight Assessment Model.

EISENBERG, LEE B., writer; b. Phila., July 22, 1946; s. George M. and Eve (Blonsky) E.; m. Linda Reville, June 7, 1986; children: Edmund George, Katherine Eve. AB, U. Pa., 1968; MA, Annenberg Sch. Communications, 1970. Assoc. editor Esquire Mag., NYC, 1970-72, sr. editor, 1972-74, mng. editor, 1974-75, editor, 1976-77, v.p. devel., 1980-84, editor-in-chief, 1987-90; founding editor-in-chief Esquire, U.K., London, 1990-91; founding ptnr. The Edison Project, Knoxville, Tenn., 1992-95; editor creative devel. Time Mag., NYC, 1995-99; exec. v.p., creative dir. Lands' End, Dodgeville, Wis., 1999—2003, chief creative, adminstrv. officer, 2003—04. Cons. N.Y. Times Co., 1977-78, Warner Bros., Los Angeles, 1978-79; founder Eisenberg, McCall & Okrent, N.Y.C., 1978-81. Author: Sneaky Feats, 1974, Atlantic City, 1978, Ultimate Fishing Book, 1981, Breaking Eighty, 1997, The Number: A Completely Different Way to Think About the Rest of Your life, 2006 Founder Rotisserie League Baseball, N.Y.C., 1980—. Recipient One Show award Art Dirs. Club, 1976, Gold Cindy award Assn. Visual Comms., 1984, various nat. mag. awards, 1984-90. Mailing: care Nicole Kalian Simon & Schuster 1230 Ave Of Americas New York NY 10020 E-mail: LeeEisenberg@TheNumberBook.com.

EISENBERG, LEON, psychiatrist, educator; b. Phila., Aug. 8, 1922; s. Morris and and Elizabeth (Sabreen) E.; m. Ruth Harriet Bleier, June 11, 1948 (div. 1967); children: Mark Philip, Kathy Bleier; m. Carola Blitzman Guttmacher, Aug. 31, 1967; children: Laurence, Alan. AB, U. Pa., 1944, MD, 1946; MA (hon.), Harvard U., 1967; DSc (hon.), U. Manchester, Eng., 1973, U. Mass., 1991. Diplomate: in child psychiatry and psychiatry Am. Bd. Psychiatry and Neurology. Intern Mt. Sinai Hosp., NYC, 1946—47; instr. physiology U. Pa., 1947-48; resident psychiatry Sheppard-Pratt Hosp., Towson, Md., 1950-52; with Johns Hopkins, 1952-67, prof. child psychiatry Med. Sch., 1961-67; psychiatrist-in-charge children's psychiat. service Harriet Lane Home, 1958-67; prof. psychiatry Harvard U. Med. Sch., Boston, 1967—93, prof. psychiatry emeritus, 1993—, prof. of social medicine emeritus, 1993—, Maude and Lillian Presley prof. psychiatry, 1975-80, Maude and Lillian Presley prof. social medicine, 1980-93, chmn. exec. com. dept. psychiatry, 1973-80, chmn. dept., 1980-91; psychiatrist-in-chief Mass. Gen. Hosp., 1967-74, mem. bd. consultation, 1974—; sr. assoc. in psychiatry Children's Hosp., Boston, 1974—. Paley lectr. Cornell U., 1983; Schilder lectr. NYU, 1984; Eli Robins lectr. Washington U., St. Louis, 1985; plenary session lectr. Internat. Pediat. Assn., Amsterdam, 1998; lectr. Italian Psychiat. Soc., Bologna, 1998; Alpha Omega Alpha lectr. U. Rochester , 1999; plenary lectr. World Psychiat. Assn., Athens, 1999; vis. lectr. Yale U., 1987, John Peters lectr., 2002; R.W. Johnson vis. prof. U. Rochester, 1987; Carolyn Voorsanger lectr. Stanford U. Med. Sch., 1989; Willard Sears Simpkins lectr. Johns Hopkins U., 1989; William Potter lectr. Thomas Jefferson U., 1992; vis. prof. McMaster U., Canada, 1991, Charles U., Prague; psychiat. cons. Crownsville (Md.) State Hosp., 1954—58, Rosewood State Tng. Sch., Owings Mills, Md., 1957—60, Balt. City Hosp., 1959—62, Children's Guild, Balt., 1954—61; cons. Sinai Hosp., Balt., 1963—67; Mapother-Lewis ann. lectr. Maudsley Hosp., London, 1977; Baan Meml. lectr. Netherlands Psychiat. Soc., Amsterdam, 1978; Royal Soc. Medicine vis. prof., London, 83; mem. subcom. psychiat. nomenclature com. vital stats. USPHS; chmn. WHO Conf. Devel. Regulation, 1964—67; mem. Joint Commn. Mental Health of Children; cons. divsn. mental health WHO, 1974—, chmn. sci. group on evaluation of psychiat. treatment, 1989; mem. adv. com. to dir. NIH, 1977—80; lectr. Can. Royal Coll. Psychiatry, 1993, Italian Soc. for Biol. Psychiatry, Cagliari, Sardinia, 1994; Richard Goldbloom lectr. Dalhousie U., Halifax, N.S., Canada, 1995; Wolfe Adler lectr. Sheppard-Pratt Hosp. Sys., Balt., 1995; spl. lectr. Health of the Child of the Eve of the Yr. 2000, Bologna, Italy, 1995; plenary lectr. Royal Australian & New Zealand Coll. Psychiatry, 1999, World Congress of Psychiatry, Hamburg, 1999, XII World Congress of Psychiatry, Yokohama, Japan, 2002. Editor Am. Jour. Orthopsychiatry, 1963-73; mem. editl. bd.: Culture, Medicine and Psychiatry, Am. Jour. Psychiatry, 2004—, Psychol. Medicine, Jour. Psychiat. Research, 2005. Capt. M.C., U.S. Army, 1948-50. Recipient Theobald Smith award Albany Med. Coll., 1979, Orton award Orton Soc., 1980, Disting. Alumnus award U. Pa., 1992, Presdl. Commendation Am. Psychiat. Assn., 1992, Agnes Purchell McGavin award, 1994, Camille Cosby World of Children award Judge Baker Children's Ctr., 1994, Salmon medal N.Y. Acad. Medicine, 1995, Mumford award and lecture, 1996, Walshe McDermott Medal, Inst. of Medicine, 2003, Ruane prize for child and adolescent psychiatry rsch. Nat. Alliance for Rsch. on Schizophrenic and Affective Disorder, 2003, Child Psychiatry Rsch. award, Nat. Assn. Rsch. in Schizophrenia and Affective Disorder, 2005. Fellow: AAAS, Royal Soc. Medicine, Soc. Rsch. Child Devel. (Pub. Policy award 2003), Am. Orthopsychiat. Assn. (Ittleson Meml. award 1996), Am. Psychiat. Assn. (life; trustee 1973—76, Disting. Svc. award 2003, Human Rights award 2005), Royal Coll. Psychiatrists (hon.; Eli Lilly lectr. 1986); mem.: I.O.M. (chair com. on planned childbearing 1993—95, chair com. bridging the brain, behavioral and clin. scis. 1999—2000), AAUP (past pres. Johns Hopkins chpt.), Mass. Med. Soc., Soc. Neurosci., Psychiat. Rsch. Soc. (past pres.), Am. Acad. Arts and Scis. (comm. sec. 1995—2002), Md. Psychiat. Soc. (past pres.), Greek Soc. Neurology and Psychiatry (hon.), Ecuadorean Soc. Neurosci. (hon.), Am. Psychopath. Assn., Assn. Rsch. Nervous and Mental Disease, Can. Pediat. Soc. (Queen Elizabeth II lectr. 1986), Am. Pediat. Soc., Am. Acad. Pediat. (Dale Richmond lectr. 1989, Aldrich award 1980), Inst. Medicine NAS (coun. 1975—77, program and membership coms. 1979—82, bd. on health sci. policy 1989—91, Rhoda and Bernard Samat prize in mental health 1996), Johns Hopkins Soc. Scholars, Alpha Omega Alpha (lectr. Jefferson Med. Coll. 1994), Sigma Xi, Phi Beta Kappa (chpt. pres. 1958, vis. scholar 1994—95). Office: Harvard U Med Sch Dept Soc Med Boston MA 02115 Home: 130 Mt Aubrun St #311 Cambridge MA 02138 Business E-Mail: leon_eisenberg@hms.harvard.edu.

EISENBERG, MARVIN JULIUS, retired art history educator; b. Phila., Aug. 19, 1922; s. Frank and Rosalie (Julius) E. BA, U. Pa., 1943; M.F.A., Princeton, 1949, PhD, 1954; D.Litt. (hon.), St Andrews, 2003. Mem. faculty U. Mich., Ann Arbor, 1949-89, prof. art history, chmn. dept., 1960-69, Collegiate prof., 1974-75, prof. emeritus, 1989—; mem. Inst. for Advanced Study, Princeton, NJ, 1970. Vis. com. Freer Gallery Art, Washington, 1970-96; mem. dept. fine arts Harvard U., 1975-81, Commn. on Preservation and Access, Washington, 1991-94, Ga. Mus. Art, 1997—; vis. prof. Stanford U., 1973, Mt. Holyoke Coll., 1995; disting. Berg prof. Colo. Coll., 1990, 93, 95, 97, 2000, 02; Hooker disting. vis. prof. McMaster U., 1993; Robert Lehman lectr. Bowdoin Coll., 1985; Saunders lectr. St Andrews U., 1998; lectr. U. Dayton, 2002; adv. com. Center for Advanced Study in Visual Arts, Nat. Gallery, Washington, 1981-84. Author: Lorenzo Monaco, 1989; co-author: The Confraternity Altarpiece by Mariotto di Nardo, 1998; contbr. articles to profl. jours. Served with AUS, 1943-46. Recipient Star of Solidarity II Italy, 1966; Coll. Art Assn. Disting. Teaching of Art History award, 1987; Guggenheim fellow, 1959. Fellow Japan Soc. for Promotion of Sci.; mem. Coll. Art Assn. Am. (dir. 1965-70, v.p. 1966-67, pres. 1968-69), Royal Soc. Arts (Benjamin Franklin fellow 1969), Phi Beta Kappa, Phi Kappa Phi, Pi Gamma Mu. Home: 2200 Fuller Ct Apt 1002 Ann Arbor MI 48105-2307

EISENBERG, MELVIN A., law educator; b. NY, Dec. 3, 1934; s. Max and Laura (Wallance) E.; m. Helen Garlitz, Feb. 5, 1956; children: Bronwyn, David Abram (dec. 1997). AB, SCL, Columbia U., 1956; LLB, SCL, Harvard U., 1959, Faye Diploma in Law, 1959; LLD (hon.), U. Milan, 1998; LLD (hon.), U. Cologne, 2004. Bar: N.Y. 1960. Assoc. Kaye Scholer Fierman Hays & Handler, 1959-63, 64-66; corp. counsel City of N.Y., 1966; acting prof. U. Calif.-Berkeley, 1966-69, prof. law, 1969-83, Koret prof. law, 1983—. Vis. prof. Harvard U., 1969-70; vis. prof. law Columbia U., 1998—, Stephen and Barbara Friedman vis. prof. law, 2005—; asst. counsel Pres. Commn. on Assassination Pres. Kennedy, Warren Commn., 1964; counsel mayor's task force on reorgn N.Y.C. govt., 1966; mem. mayor's task force on N.Y.C. transp. reorgn., 1966; mem. mayors' task force on mcpl. collective bargaining, 1966; reporter Am. Law Inst., principles of corporate governance: analysis and recommendations, 1980-84, chief reporter, 1984-94, Ammi Cutter chair, 1991-93; adviser, restatement 3d of agy. 1996-2005; adviser, restatement 3d of restitution, 1998—; prof.-in-residence, Cologne U., 1984, U. Milan, 1992; mem. and cons. ABA com. on corp. laws, 1992—; U. Iowa Inaugural lectr., 1987, Roy R. Ray lectr. So. Meth. U., 1993, Robert L. Levine Distg. lectr., Fordham U., 1993; Pillegi lectr. Weidener U., 2004; chmn. AALS contracts sect., 1989, AALS contracts workshop, 1986; chmn. AALS bus. assns. sect., 1998; visitor-in-residence U. Murdoch, U. Western Australia, 1992, McGill U., 1981; Sobeloff lectr. U. Md., 1994; Freehill, Hollingsdale and Page vis. fellow U. New South Wales, Australia, 1994. Author: The Structure of the Corporation, 1977 (Coif Triennial Book award honorable mention 1980), The Nature of the Common Law, 1988, Cases and Materials on Corporations and Other Business Organization, 2005, (with L. Fuller) Basic Contract Law, 2006; also numerous articles. Pres. Queen's Child Guidance Ctr., 1963-66. Guggenheim fellow, 1971-72, Canterbury vis. fellow U. Canterbury, New Zealand, 1988, Kimber fellow York U., Toronto, 1989, Rabin fellow Yale Sch. Law, vis. fellow Doshisha U., Kyoto, Japan, 2003—; Fulbright Sr. scholar, Australia, 1987, Disting. Mellon scholar U. Pitts., 1989, Manuel F. Cohen vis. scholar George Washington U. Sch. Law; Cooley lectr. U. Mich., 1985; Baron de Hirsch Meyer lectr. U. Miami Sch. Law, 1983, Wythe lectr. William and Mary Law Sch., 1999, TePoel lectr. Creighton U. Sch. Law, 1982; recipient Faye Diploma Harvard U. Law Sch., Rutter Outstanding Tchg. award Boalt Hall Law Sch., 2002, Disting. Tchg. award U. Calif., Berkeley, 1990. Fellow AAAS; mem. Am. Law Inst., Am. Assn. Law Schs. (chair contracts sect. 1989, chair bus. assns. sect. 1999), Phi Beta Kappa. Office: U Calif Sch Law 331 Boalt Hl Berkeley CA 94720-0001 also: Columbia U Law Sch 435 W 116th St New York NY 10027-7201 Home: 1197 Keeler Ave Berkeley CA 94708-1753 Office Phone: 510-642-1799. Business E-Mail: eisenberg@law.berkeley.edu.

EISENBERG, MEYER, lawyer; b. Bklyn., Dec. 15, 1931; BA, Bklyn. Coll., 1953; LLB, Columbia U., 1958. Bar: N.Y. 1960, D.C. 1970, U.S. Supreme Ct. 1963. Law clk. to Chief Justice William McAllister Supreme Ct. Oreg., Salem, 1958-59; atty. SEC, Washington, 1959-70, counsel spl. study securities markets, 1962-64, asst. gen. counsel, 1966-68, exec. asst. to chmn., 1968-69, assoc. gen. counsel, 1969-70; with firm Lawler, Kent & Eisenberg, Washington, 1970-79, Rosenman, Colin, Freund, Lewis & Cohen, Washington, 1980-87, Ballard, Spahr, Andrews & Ingersoll, Washington, 1987-93, Kramer, Levin, Naftalis & Frankel, Washington, 1994-98; dep. gen. coun. sec. SEC, Washington, 1998—. Adj. prof. law George Washington U., 1972-75, Georgetown U. Law Sch., 1988-90; vis. prof. law U. Calif., Berkeley; dir. Nat. Ctr. Fin. Svcs., 1985-86; mem. adv. com. Calif. Securities Regulation Inst.; cons. in field. Contbr. articles to profl. publs. Mem. internat. bd. govs. B'nai B'rith, 1978-92; mem. nat. exec. com. Anti-Defamation League, 1980—, nat. vice chmn., 1994—, chmn. Nat. Civil Rights Com., 1992-94, Nat. Legal Affairs Com., 1980-92. Mem. ABA (chmn. com. on devels. in investment svcs. 1981-86, chmn. com. on long-range issues affecting bus. law practice 1986-90, coun. sect. bus. law 1990-94, chmn. com. on internat. tech. assistance 1994—, sec. bus. law), Fed. Bar Assn. (chmn. securities law com. 1984-85). Home: 8216 Lakenheath Way Potomac MD 20854-2740 Office: SEC Office of Gen Counsel 450 5th St NW Washington DC 20549-0001 E-mail: eisenbergm@sec.gov.

EISENBERG, MICHAEL BRUCE, library and information scientist, educator; b. Bklyn., Oct. 4, 1949; s. Leonard and Lenore (Zasuly) E.; m. Carol Ann Guptill, June 6, 1971; children: Brian, Laura. BA, SUNY, Albany, 1971, MLS, 1973; cert. advanced studies in info. studies, Syracuse U., 1981, PhD in Info. Studies, 1986. Libr. media specialist Eagle Hill Jr. HS, Manlius, NY, 1974; head libr. media specialist Fayetteville-Manlius Sr. HS, 1974-81; adj. instr. Sch. Info. Studies, Syracuse U., NY, 1977-82, asst. prof. NY, 1982-89, assoc. prof. NY, 1989-93, prof. info. studies NY, 1993—98, coord. sch. media and field work programs NY, 1979-82, assoc. dir. Ednl. Resouces Info. Ctr. Clearinghouse on Info. and Tech. NY, 1985-90; dir. Info. Inst. Syracuse, 1990—98, assoc. dir., 1998—2000; dean. & prof. U. Wash. Info. Sch., Seattle, 1998—2005, dean. emeritus & prof., 2006—. Co-dir. Big6 Skills Approach to Info. and Tech. Skills Instrn.; cons. NY State Edn. Dept., 1986-87, Internat. Inst. for Mgmt. Devel., Lausanne, Switzerland, 1991-92; cons. pub. svc. tng. program State of NY, 1986-91; chmn. ERIC exec. com. US Dept. Edn., Washington, 1991-93, project dir., 1992-98; co-founder, co-coord. LM_NET, 1992-98; founder, dir. ASKERIC Internet Svcs. Project, 1993-98; cons. numerous sch. dists. SD Edn. Dept., Conn. Edn. Dept., Utah Edn. Dept; keynote spkr. nat. and internat. edn. and libr. confs. Author: (with Robert Berkowitz) Resource Companion to Curriculum Initiative: An Agenda and Strategy for School Library Media Programs, 1988, Curriculum Initiative: An Agenda and Strategy for School Library Media Programs, 1988, Information Problem-Solving: The Big Six Skills Approach to Library and Information Skills Instruction, 1990, Helping with Homework: A Parent's Guide to Information Problem-Solving, 1996, (with Carrie Lowe & Kathy Spitzer) Information Literacy: Essential Skills for the Information Age, 2004; contbr. articles to profl. jours; referee profl. jours. in field. Trustee, v.p. Sullivan (NY) Free Libr., 1992-95; bd. dirs. Consortium on Sch. Networking, 1995-99, vice chair, 1998-99; mem. Nat. Forum on Info. Literacy. Recipient Disting. Alumni award SUNY Sch. Info. Sci. and Policy, 1990, Prof. of Yr. award, Syracuse U., 1992, Best WWW Site award, 1994, Best of Net award, Global News Network, 1995, Pioneer award, EdNet, 1999, LISTSERV Choice award, 2004. Mem. ALA, Am. Soc. for Info. Sci. (grantee 1986, Dissertation of Yr. award), Assn. Libr. & Info. Sci. Edn. (grantee 1986, Dissertation of Yr. award, chmn. resource com.), Am. Assn. Sch. Librs. (bd. dirs. 1994—, Disting. Svc. award, 2006), NY Libr. Assn. (Presdl. award for profl. achievement Sch. Libr. Media sect. 1994), Cen. NY Media Specialists, Wash. Libr. Media Assn. (Pres.'s award, 2002, 03) Achievements include development of KidsConnect, AskLN. Avocations: guitar, sailing, skiing. Office: U Wash Info Sch 4th Fl Roosevelt Commons Bldg 4311 11th Ave NE Seattle WA 98105 Office Phone: 206-616-1152. E-mail: mbe@u.washington.edu.

EISENBERG, MICHAEL JAMES, music educator; s. Charles and Marilyn Elaine Eisenberg. MusB in Piano Performance, Queens Coll., Flushing, NY, 1989; MusM in Piano Performance, Mannes Coll. Music, NY, 1992, MA in History Performance in Harpsichord, 1994; postgrad in Musicology & Medieval & Renaissance, CUNY, 2007—. Cert. in French Faculté Lettres Reims, 1986, in accompaniment studies Am. Inst. Musical Studies, 1989, tchr. NY, 2005. Lecture recitalist Carnegie Hall Edn., NYC, 1996—2004; tchg. artist Arts Connection, NYC, 1997—. Musician: (recording) Forbidden Dance; contbr. articles to profl. jours. Grantee, Bibliog. Soc. London, 2006, Eugene K. Wolf Award for European Rsch. grant, Am. Musicological Soc., 2007; Delmas fellow, Delmas Found., 2005—06, Ctr. Reformation & Renaissance Studies Vis. fellow, U. Toronto, 2006, Mellon fellow, Inst. Hist. Rsch., 2006, Newberry Short-Term fellow, Newberry Libr., 2007, fellowship, Bibliog. Soc. Am., 2007—. Mem.: Am. Coll. Musicians, Am. Musicological Soc. Avocations: languages, travel, skiing. Home: 161 Derby St Valley Stream NY 11581 Personal E-mail: mjeisenberg@gmail.com.

EISENBERG, PABLO SAMUEL, non-profit organization executive; b. Paris, July 1, 1932; came to U.S. 1939; s. Maurice and Paula (Halpert) E.; m. Helen Leone Cierniak, June 5, 1960; 1 child, Marina. BA, Princeton U., 1954; BLitt, Oxford U., Eng., 1957; LLD (hon.), Princeton U., 2004. Fgn. svc. officer USIA, 1960-63; program dir. Operation Crossroads Africa, NYC, 1963-65; coord. Pa. Office Econ. Opportunity, 1965-67; dep. dir. Rsch. and Demonstration Office, Office of Econ. Opportunity, Washington, 1967-68; asst. dir. Nat. Urban Coalition, Washington, 1968-73; ind. cons. Washington, 1973-75; pres. Ctr. for Cmty. Change, Washington, 1975-98; sr. fellow, cons. Georgetown Pub. Policy Inst., Washington, 1998—. Author: The Courage to Change, 2004; contbr. articles to profl. jours., chpts. to book; columnist Chronicle of Philanthropy. Mem. exec. com. Nat. Com. for Responsive Philanthropy, Washington, 1976—; pres. Friends of VISTA, Washington, 1976-98, 1980—; bd. dirs. Youth Today, Coll. Pub. Svc. and Citizenship, Tufts U., 1993-00, Milton Eisenhower Found., Citizens Funds. Recipient John Gardner Leadership award, 1998; German Marshall Fund of U.S. travelling fellow, 1988. Democrat. Jewish. Avocations: tennis, antique books, movies, sports. Home: 3729 Massachusetts Ave NW Washington DC 20016-5004 Office: Pub Policy Inst Georgetown U 3240 Prospect St NW Washington DC 20007-3214 Office Phone: 202-244-7885. E-mail: pseisenberg@erols.com.

EISENBERG, PAUL RICHARD, cardiologist, consultant, educator; b. Rome, Mar. 9, 1955; came to US, 1956; s. David Marvin and Sonia Maria (Benedetti) Eisenberg; m. Patricia Lynn Goodman, Apr. 25, 1982; 1 child, Jamie. BS, Tulane U., New Orleans, 1975, MPH, 1980; MD, NY Med. Coll., Valhalla, 1980. Diplomate Am. Bd. Internal Medicine, Am. Bd. Cardiology. Intern in internal medicine Barnes Hosp., St. Louis, 1980-83, fellow in cardiology, pulmonary medicine, 1983-85, asst. dir. CCU, 1986-91, dir. CCU, 1991-98; asst. prof. Washington U., St. Louis, 1985-91, assoc. prof., 1991-97, prof., 1997-98; med. dir. cardiovasc. therapeutics Eli Lilly & Co., Indpls., 1998-2000, exec. dir. cardiovasc. discovery, 2000—01, v.p. med., 2001—02, v.p. global drug safety, 2003—05; v.p. Amgen Global Safety, Thousand Oaks, Calif., 2005—06, v.p. global regulatory affairs and safety, 2007—. Asst. editor: Medical Management of Heart Disease; contbr. over 100 articles to profl. jours. Fellow Am. Heart Assn. (clin. cardiology), Am. Coll. Chest Physicians, Am. Coll. Cardiology; mem. Am. Fedn. Clin. Rsch., Internat. Soc. Thrombosis and Haemostasis. Office: Amgen 1 Amgen Ctr Dr Thousand Oaks CA 91320 Home Phone: 805-670-1944; Office Phone: 805-447-6453. Personal E-mail: piesenberg@attglobal.net.

EISENBERG, R. NEAL, restoration company executive; b. Newark, July 15, 1936; s. William C. and Elsie G. (Greenfield) E.; m. Barbara J. Mayer, Dec. 18, 1966; children: Michael S., Elissa P. Student, Stevens Inst. Tech., 1954-55; postgrad. Coll. Engring., NYU, 1955-57, BS in Acctg., 1960. Sr. acct. Puder & Puder (now Deloitte Touche), Newark, 1958-60, J.H. Cohn & Co., Roseland, NJ, 1960-63; ptnr. Universal Engring. Waterpoofing Svc., Newark, 1963-69; pres. Universal Restoration Waterproofing Svc., Inc., West Orange, NJ, 1970—; v.p. Universal Restoration, Inc., Washington, 1967-69, pres., CEO, 1993-96; v.p. Restoration Svcs., Inc., Washington, 1967-69; pres. Vitrifix N.Am., Inc., Washington, 1986-87; chmn. Universal Family Group, West Orange, 1987—; pres. Universal Waterproofing Svc., Inc., West Orange, 1969—. Cons. in field. Co-inventor Dekosit/Permo-Bond Restoration Method. Recipient Second Biennial Design award Gen. Svcs. Administrn., 1967. Mem. Constrn. Specifications Inst., Nat. Assn. Waterproofing Contractors, Nat. Trust Hist. Preservation, NJ Bus. Industry Assn., Masons. Office: Universal Waterproofing Svc 623 Eagle Rock Ave Ste 377 West Orange NJ 07052-2948

EISENBERG, RICHARD R., dermatologist; s. Abraham and Ida Eisenberg; m. Katherine Rozanski, Sept. 4, 1983; children: David, Alissa, Jennifer. BA summa cum laude in Biochemistry, U. Pa., Phila., 1977; MD, Cornell U., Ithaca, NY, 1982. Diplomate Am. Bd. Internal Medicine, 1985. Intern Bellevue Hosp. NYU Med. Ctr., 1982; resident in internal medicine NY Hosp. Meml. Sloan Kettering, 1983—85; resident in dermatology NY Hosp. Meml. Sloan Kettering Cancer Ctr. and Rockefeller U., 1986—89; pvt. practice Richard R. Eisenberg, MD, Watchung, NJ, 1989—. Med. dir. Consumer Products Testing Co., Fairfield, NJ, 1998; sect. chief dermatology Overlook Hosp., Summit, NJ, 2004; cons. pharm. cos., NJ. Contbr. articles to profl. jours. Mem. bd. Jewish Cmty. Ctr., Scotch Plains, NJ, 1994—96; mem. Somerset County Cancer Coalition, NJ, 2005—06. Recipient Rsch. prize, Deans, 1981, Rsch. award, Dean William Mecklenderg, 1982. Fellow: Am. Acad. Dermatology (assoc.); mem.: Nat. Psoriasis

Found. (assoc.), Med. Soc. State NJ (assoc.), Union County Med. Soc. (assoc.), Phi Beta Kappa. Avocations: tennis, running, travel, cooking. Office: Richard R Eisenberg MD 40 Stirling Rd Ste 203 Watchung NJ 07069 Office Fax: 908-753-3743; Home Fax: 908-753-3743.

EISENBERG, RICHARD S., chemistry professor; b. NYC, Feb. 12, 1943; s. Paul and Norma (Frommer) E.; m. Marcia Landau, Aug. 6, 1966; children: Alan, Robert. AB, Columbia U., 1963, MA, 1964, PhD, 1967. Asst. prof. chemistry Brown U., Providence, 1967-71, assoc. prof., 1971-73; assoc. prof. chemistry U. Rochester (N.Y.), 1973-76, prof., 1976-96, chair, 1991-94, univ. mentor, 1986-87, assoc. dean Coll. Arts and Scis., 1989-91, Tracy H. Harris prof., 1996—. Vis. scientist Calif. Inst. Tech., 1977-78; vis. scholar Cambridge (Eng.) U., 1978; vis. prof. Columbia U., 1985; vice chmn. Gordon Conf. on Organometallic Chemistry, 1987, chmn., 1988; cons. SOHIO, Cleve., 1982-83, Eastman Kodak, Rochester, 1982; mem. adv. bd. Petroleum Rsch. Fund, 1988-91; Closs lectr. U. Chgo., 1994; vis. prof. Chemistry Rsch. Promotion Ctr., Republic of China, 1994; Coates lectr. U. Wyo., 1966; Varon vis. prof. Weizmann Inst., 1997; Miller vis. prof. U. Calif., Berkeley, 2005; Lady Davis fellow Hebrew U., 1997 Editor (jour.) Inorganic Chemistry, 2001—; contbr. numerous articles on chemistry to profl. jours.; mem. editorial adv. bd.: Jour. Am. Chem. Soc., 1982-84, Inorganic Chemistry, 1997-98, Organometallics, 1998-2000. NSF fellow, 1964-66, George B. Pegram Hon. fellow, 1964-65, Alfred P. Sloan fellow, 1972-74, Guggenheim fellow, 1977-78 Mem. AAAS, Am. Chem. Soc. (chmn. organometallic subdiv. inorganic div. 1982, alt. councilor inorganic div. 1985-87, editorial adv. bd. jour. 1982-84, councilor inorganic div. 1988-90, chmn.-elect 1992, chmn. 1993, sci. com. 2003-05, Rochester Sect. award 2003, Disting. Svc. award 2003, Morley medal 2007), Chem. Soc. Achievements include rsch. interests in homogeneous catalysts, organometallic compounds of platinum group elements, binuclear complexes, inorganic photochemistry; bond activiation and oxidative addition, parahydrogen induced polarization, metal hydrides, structure-function relationships in catalytically active systems. Home: 175 Parkwood Ave Rochester NY 14620-3403 Office: U Rochester River Campus Dept Chemistry Rochester NY 14627 Office Phone: 585-275-5573. E-mail: eisenberg@chem.rochester.edu.

EISENBERG, SONJA MIRIAM, artist; b. Berlin, June 10, 1926; arrived in U.S., 1938, naturalized, 1947; d. Adolf and Meta Cecilie (Bettauer) Weinberger; m. Jack Eisenberg, Mar. 31, 1946; children: Ralph, Lynn, Lauren. Student, Queens Coll., Flushing, 1943—46, Middlebury Coll., Vt., 1945, NYU, 1952—54, BA, 1954; postgrad., Nat. Acad. Sch. Fine Arts, 1961. Artist-in-residence Cathedral of St. John the Divine, NYC; apptd. art dir. Hermes Media B.V., Amsterdam, 1992. One-woman shows include Bodley Gallery, NYC, 1970, 1973, 1975, 1980, Galerie Art du Monde, Paris, 1972, Buyways Gallery, Sarasota, Fla., 1973—75, 1978, Galerie de Sfinx, Amsterdam, Netherlands, 1974, Huntsville Mus. Art, Ala., 1974, Anglo-Am. Art Mus., Baton Rouge, 1974, Comara Gallery, L., 1974, Palm Spring Desert Mus., Calif., 1975, Fordham U., NY, 1976, Omega Inst., New Lebanon, NY, 1979, Am. Mus., Hayden Planetarium, NYC, 1980, Avila Graphics, Ltd., 1982, YWCA, NYC, 1981, Cathedral of St. John the Divine, 1983, 1985, The Millbrook Gallery, NY, 1989, 1994, Christopher Leonard Gallery, NYC, 1993, Park Hotel Gallery, Vitznau, Switzerland, 1994, Burgenstock, Switzerland, 1995, Wainscott Gallery, NY, 1997, Dussmann Kulturhaus, Berlin, 1998, Horton Gallery, Phila., 2001, exhibited in group shows at Mus. Fine Arts, St. Petersburg, Fla., 1973, Am. Watercolor Soc., 1974—75, Galerie Frederic Gollong, St. Paul de Vence, France, 1978, Betty Parson's Gallery, NYC, 1981, Foster Harmon Galleries of Am. Art, Sarasota, Fla., 1988, Tokyo Met. Art Mus., 1989, Galerie Herbert Leidel, Munich, 1991, Park Ave. Armory, NYC, 1996, Akim-USA, 1996, Represented in permanent collections Archives Am. Art, Smithsonian Inst., Jewish Mus., NYC, Fordham U. Mus., Palm Springs Desert Mus., Omega Inst., Cathedral of St. John the Divine; designer WFUNA cachet for UN Water Power Conf., 1977, UN Internat. Yr. of Disabled Persons, 1981, commd. commemorative painting Die Kristallnacht, Telecom Telefon Karte, Munich, 1993; author: Regent Cathedral of St. John the Devine, 1990, Poems and Paintings, 2001, The Red Painted House, 2002, Seeing the Gospel According to John, 2003, There Will Be No War, 2004, On Its Way (based on the I Ching), 2005, Poems and Paintings Nr. II, 2006. Regent Cathedral of St. John the Divine, 1990. Recipient Gold medal for artistic merit, Internat. Parliament for Safety and Peace, 1983, Palma D'Oro Europe, 1986. Mem.: Accademia Italia delle Arti e del Lavoro (Gold medal 1981). Home and Office: 1020 Park Ave New York NY 10028-0913 Personal E-mail: sonjaeisenberg@aol.com. *When you focus your mind, you may break through the Known with its borders of words and ideas, and get a glimpse of the "nothing" that is so creative.*

EISENBERG, TED STEVEN, plastic and reconstructive surgeon; b. Phila., June 21, 1952; s. Martin John and Mitzi Eisenberg; m. Joyce Janet Kirschner, Sept. 1, 1973; children: Ben, Samantha. BS, Pa. State U., 1972; DO, Phila. Coll. Osteo. Medicine, 1976. Diplomate Nat. Bd. Examiners for Osteo. Physicians and Surgeons; Bd. cert. in Osteo. Plastic Surgery, Laser Surgery, Gen. Surgery; lic. physician, N.Y., Pa. Intern North Miami Beach Osteo. Gen. Hosp., 1976-77; resident in gen. surgery Met. Hosp., Phila., 1977-81; resident in hand surgery Hand Rehab. Ctr./Jefferson U., Phila., 1981; preceptee in plastic surgery Rolling Hill and Albert Einstein Med. Ctrs., Phila., 1983-85; practice plastic and reconstructive surgery Phila. area, 1985—; assoc. prof. Phila. Coll. Osteo. Medicine, 1991—. Attending staff physician Grad. Hosp., John F. Kennedy Hosp., Northeastern Hosp., Suburban Genl. Hosp., others; cons. staff physician Delaware Valley Med. Ctr., Springfield Hosp.; lectr. in field. Contbr. numerous articles to profl. jours. Recipient numerous awards for sci. exhibits and publs. Fellow Am. Coll. Osteo. Surgeons; mem. Am. Acad. Aesthetic and Restorative Surgery (charter), Am. Osteo. Assn., Jefferson Hand Club (charter), Pa. Osteo. Med. Assn., Philadelphia County Osteo. Soc., Phila. Coll. Osteo. Medicine Alumni Assn. (life), Lambda Omicron Gamma (v.p. 1993-94). Office: Ste 102 2375 Woodward St Philadelphia PA 19115

EISENBERG, THEODORE, law educator; b. Bklyn., Oct. 26, 1947; s. Abraham Louis and Esther (Waldman) E.; m. Lisa Wright, Nov. 27, 1971; children: Katherine Wright, Ann Marie, Thomas Peter. BA, Swarthmore Coll., 1969; JD, U. Pa., 1972. Bar: Pa. 1972, N.Y. 1974, U.S. Ct. Appeals (2d cir.) 1974, Calif. 1977. Law clk. U.S. Ct. Appeals, D.C. Cir., 1972-73; law clk. to U.S. Supreme Ct. Justice Earl Warren, 1973; assoc. Debevoise & Plimpton, NYC, 1974-77; prof. law UCLA Law Sch., 1977-81, Cornell U. Law Sch., Ithaca, N.Y., 1981-96, Henry Allen Mark prof. law, 1996—. Vis. prof. law Harvard U. Law Sch., 1984-85, 2004; vis. prof. Law, Stanford U. Law Sch., 1987. Author: Civil Rights Legislation, 1981, 5th edit., 2004, Bankruptcy and Debtor-Creditor Law, 1984, 3d edit., 2004; editor Jour. Empirical Legal Studies; mem. adv. bd. Law and Soc. Rev., Am. Law and Econ. Rev.; contbr. articles to profl. jours. Am. Bar Found grantee, NSF grantee. Fellow Royal Statis. Soc.; mem. ABA, Assn. Bar City N.Y., Law and Soc. Assn., Am. Law and Econ. Assn., Am. Bankruptcy Inst. Office: Cornell U Law Sch Myron Taylor Hall Ithaca NY 14853 E-mail: te13@cornell.edu.

EISENBERG, WARREN, retail executive; Former employee Arlan's; co-founder, dir. Bed, Bath & Beyond, Union, NJ, 1971—, co-CEO, 1971—2003, chmn., 1992—99, co-chmn., 1999—. Office: Bed Bath & Beyond 650 Liberty Ave Union NJ 07083*

EISENBUD, DAVID, mathematics professor; b. NYC, Apr. 8, 1947; s. Leonard and Ruth-Jean (Rubinstein) E.; m. Monika Margarte Schwabe, June 3, 1970; children: Daniel, Alina. BS, U. Chgo., 1966, MS, 1967, PhD, 1970. Lectr. Brandeis U., Waltham, Mass., 1970-72, asst. prof., 1972—73, assoc. prof., 1976-80, prof., 1980—97, chmn. dept. of math., 1982-84, 1992—94; prof. math. U. Calif., Berkeley, 1997—. Vis. scholar, Harvard U., 1973-74; vis. prof. U. Bonn, Fed. Republic of Germany, 1979-80, Math. Sciences Rsch. Inst. (MSRI), Berkeley, 1986-87, Harvard U., 1987-88, 1994; Chercheur Associ'e a l'Institut Henri Poincar'e, Centre Nat. de la Recherche Scientifique, Paris, 1995; mem. adv. panel in maths. NSF, 1978-81; dir. Math. Sciences Rsch. Inst.(MSRI), Berkeley, 1997-2007; mem. bd. math. sci. and applications NRC, 2001-03. Editor: Procs. of Am. Math. Soc., 1978-82, Asterisque, 1983-88, (book series) Wadsworth Advanced, 1985-92, Jour. Algebraic Geometry, 1990—, Annals of Math, 2001-2004, Springer Algorithms and Computation in Math.; serves on several editl. boards; contbr. numerous books and articles to profl. jours. Alfred P. Sloan Found. fellow, 1973-75, Institut des Hautes Etudes Scientifiques (IHES-Bures-Sur-Yvette), 1974-75; NSF grantee, 1970—. Mem. Am. Math. Soc. (coun., pres. 2003-05, editor Bull. 1996-98, Bull. Sci. Math. 2000—), Soc. Indsl. and Applied Math., Assn. for Women in Math., Math. Assn. Am.; fellow Am. Acad. Arts & Sciences Avocations: flute, vocalist, juggling, hiking, music. Office: MSRI 17 Gauss Way Berkeley CA 94720 Office Phone: 510-642-0143. Office Fax: 510-642-8609. Business E-Mail: de@msri.org.*

EISENDRATH, CHARLES RICE, journalism educator, farmer, consultant; b. Chgo., Oct. 9, 1940; s. William Nathan and Erna Sarah (Rice) E.; m. Julia Cardozo, Jan. 28, 1967; children: Benjamin Cardozo, Mark William. BA, Yale U., 1962; MA, U. Mich., 1965. Reporter Post-Dispatch, St. Louis, 1962, 64, Evening Sun, Balt., 1966-68; corr. Time Mag., Washington, London, Paris, bur. chief Buenos Aires, 1968-73; prof. U. Mich., Ann Arbor, 1975—. Propr. Overlook Farm, East Jordan, Mich., 1972—; chmn. Grillworks, Inc., Ann Arbor, 1978—; cons. Midland Bank of London, Pfizer, W.K. Kellogg Found.; mem. Pulitzer Prize Jury, 2002—03. Contbr. articles to profl. jours.; inventor in field. Dir. Knight-Wallace Journalism Fellows, 1986—; founding dir. Livingston Awards, Ann Arbor, 1980—, Judge Soc. Pubs. in Asia Awards, 2005; judge nat. barbecue contest, 1994—; pres. task force journalism Columbia U., 2002-03. NEH Mich. Journalism fellow, 1974-75. Mem. Coun. Fgn. Rels., Century Assn. (NYC), Soc. Profl. Journalists, Com. of Concerned Journalists (founding), Project on the State of the Am. Newspaper (founding bd. dirs. 1998-00), Internat. Press Inst. (chair Am. com. 2006—), Landsdowne Club (London), Phi Kappa Phi. Jewish. Office: Wallace House 620 Oxford Rd Ann Arbor MI 48104-2623 E-mail: drath@umich.edu.

EISENHOWER, JOHN SHELDON DOUD, former ambassador, writer; b. Denver, Aug. 3, 1922; s. Dwight David (34th Pres. of U.S.) and Mamie (Doud) E.; m. Barbara Jean Thompson, June 10, 1947 (div. 1986); children: Dwight David II, Barbara Anne, Susan Elaine, Mary Jean; m. Joanne Thompson, Apr. 9, 1990. BS, U.S. Mil. Acad., 1944; MA in English Lit., Columbia, 1950; LHD (hon.), Northwood Inst., 1970. Commd. 2d lt. U.S. Army, 1944, advanced through grades to lt. col., 1963; assigned 1st Army, Europe, 1945, Army of Occupation, Europe, 1945-47, Korean War, 1952-53, Army Gen. Staff, 1957-58, White House Staff, 1958-61; resigned, 1963; brig. gen. USAR, 1974; engaged in writing, 1965-69; U.S. amb. to Belgium, Am. Embassy, Brussels, 1969-71. Cons. to the Pres.; also chmn. Interagency Classification Review Com., 1972-73; chmn. bd. Acad. Life Ins. Co., Atlanta; mem. adv. council Nat. Archives, 1974-77; chmn. President's Adv. Com. on Refugees, 1975; mil. editor Algonguin Books of Chapel Hill. Author: The Bitter Woods, 1969, Strictly Personal, 1974; editor: Letters to Mamie, 1978, Allies, 1982, So Far From God, 1989, Intervention!, 1993, Agent of Destiny, 1997, Yanks, 2001, General Ike, 2003. Mem. diplomatic coun., bd. govs. USO, 1983-85; trustee Alumni Fedn. Columbia U., 1976-80. Decorated Legion of Merit, Bronze Star, Combat Inf. badge, grand cross Order of Crown Belgium, Chungmu Disting. Service medal (Korea); recipient Grad. Faculties Alumni award for excellence Columbia U., 1970. Mem. Diplomatic and Consular Officers Ret., Capitol Hill Club.

EISENHOWER, SUSAN, business and political consultant; b. Dec. 31, 1951; d. John Sheldon Doud Eisenhower and Barbara Jean Thompson. Attended, Am. U., Paris. Former writer Saturday Evening Post, London; former columnist Wolfe Newspapers; sr. dir. Stonebridge Internat., Washington; founder Eisenhower World Affairs Inst., 1983; pres. Eisenhower Group, Inc., 2000—; chmn. emeritus, former pres. Eisenhower Inst. Mem. standing com. on internat. security and arms control Nat. Acad. of Sci.; mem. NASA Advisory Council, 1999—2001, Baker-Cutler Commn., U.S. Dept. of Energy, 2000, Internat. Space Station Mgmt. and Cost Eval. Task Force, 2001—, Task Force on Nuclear Energy, U.S. Dept of Energy; acad. fellow Internat. Peace and Security program, Carnegie Corp. of NY; dir. Carnegie Endowment for Internat. Peace and Nuclear Threat Initiative; analyst CNN Internat., MSNBC, Nightline, World News Tonight, FOX News. Co-editor: (books) Islam and Central Asia: An Enduring Legacy or an Evolving Threat?; author: Breaking Free: A Memoir of Love and Rebellion, 1995, Mrs. Ike: Memories and Reflections on the Life of Mamie Eisenhower, 1996, (articles appearing in) Washington Post, LA Times, USA Today, London Spectator. Bd. mem. Nitze Sch. of Advanced Internat. Studies, Atlantic Council. Office: Eisenhower Inst 915 15th St NW Washington DC 20005*

EISENHUTH, EDWARD GEORGE, social studies educator; b. Pottsville, Pa. s. George William and Mary Jane Eisenhuth; m. Nanette Marie Litwin, July 5, 1980; 1 child, Kent. B of Social Sci., Pa. State U., Harrisburg, 1974; M in Am. History, Kutztown U., Pa., 1978. Tchr. Minersville Area Sch. Dist., Pa., 1974—. Mem.: NEA, Nat. Coun. Social Studies, Pa. Coun. Social Studies (award 2000, 2004), Pa. Edn. Assn., Schuykill Lodge. Avocations: wrestling, travel. Home: 250 Margaret Ave Orwigsburg PA 17961 Office: Minersville Area High Sch PO Box 787 Minersville PA 17954

EISENMAN, PETER DAVID, architect, educator; b. Newark, Aug. 11, 1932; s. Herschel I. and Sylvia H. (Heller) E.; m. Elizabeth Henderson, 1963 (div. 1990); children: Julia, Nicholas; m. Cynthia Davidson, 1990; 1 child, Samuel Chapin. BArch, Cornell U., 1955; MS in Architecture, Columbia U., NYC, 1960; MA, U. Cambridge, Eng., 1962, PhD, 1963; DFA (hon.), U. Ill., Chgo., 1988, Pratt Inst., 1997; DArch (hon.), U. La Sapienza, Rome, 2003. Prin. Eisenman/Robertson Archs., NYC, 1980-88, Eisenman Archs., NYC, 1988—. Founder Inst. Architecture and Urban Studies, NYC, 1967, dir., 1967-82; mem. faculty Cambridge U., 1960-63, Princeton U., 1965-67; faculty Cooper Union, 1970—, adj. prof., 1975-86, Irwin Chanin Disting. prof. 1986—; arch.-in-residence Am. Acad. Rome, 1976; Kea prof. U. Md., 1978; Charlotte Davenport prof. Yale U., 1980, Louis I. Kahn prof. arch., 2001—; Arthur Rotch prof. Harvard U., 1982-85, Eliot Noyes vis. critic, 1993; Louis H. Sullivan rsch. prof. architecture U. Ill., Chgo., 1987-93; vis. prof. Ohio State U., 1991-93; John Williams prof. architecture U. Ark., 1997. Author: Diagram Diaries, Choral Works, (with Jacques Derrida) Blurred Zones, Giuseppe Terragni: Transformations, Decompositions, Critiques, 2003, Eisenman: Inside Out, Selected Writings 1963-1988, 2004; editor: Oppositions Books, House X Rizzoli, Houses of Cards; prin. works include pvt. residences Princeton, NJ, Hardwick, Vt., Lakeville and Cornwall, Conn., 1968-76; others Housing Koch-Friedrichstrasse, Berlin, 1980-86, Wexner Ctr. for Visual Arts, Columbus, Ohio, 1983-89, U. Cin. Coll. Design, Art, Architecture and Planning, 1988-96, Columbus Conv. Ctr., Ohio, 1988-93, Koizumi Sangyo Bldg., Tokyo, 1989-90, Nunotani Office Bldg., 1990-92, Emory U. Art Ctr., 1991-95, Rebstock Pk., Frankfurt, Germany, 1991-95, US Pavilion, Venice Biennale, 1991, Max Reinhardt Haus, Berlin, 1992, Haus Immendorff, Dusseldorf, Germany, 1993-94, Staten Island Inst. Arts and Scis., 1997-2001, Multi-Purpose Stadium, Glendale, Ariz., 1997—, Holocaust Meml., Berlin, Germany, 1998—, City of Culture, Santiago de Compostela, Spain, 1999—, Meml. to the Murdered Jews of Europe, Berlin, Germany, 2005. Served in US Army, 1955—57. Fellow Graham Found., 1966; Guggenheim Found., 1976; grantee Princeton U., 1964, 66; recipient Arnold W. Brunner Meml. prize in architecture Am. Acad. and Inst. Arts and Letters, 1984, medal of honor NYC AIA, 2001, Cooper-Hewitt Nat. Design award for architecture Smithsonian Instn., 2001, Premio Internacional de Artes Plásticas de la Fundación Cristóbal Gabarrón, Spain, 2003. Fellow AIA; mem. AAAL, Am. Acad. Arts and Scis., Archtl. League NY (v.p. 1970), Conf. Archs. Study Environ. (co-founder 1964) Clubs: Century Assn. (NYC). Office: Eisenman Architects 41 W 25th St New York NY 10010-2021 Office Phone: 212-645-1400. Office Fax: 212-645-0726. E-mail: info@eisenmanarchitects.com.*

EISENMANN-KLEIN, MARITA, plastic surgeon; b. Gars/Inn, Bavaria, Germany, Sept. 5, 1947; d. Johann B. and Therese (Thaler) Eisenmann; m. Helmfried Klein, Mar. 12, 1977; children: Julian, Silvan, Konstantin. MD, Ludwig-Maximilians U., Munich, Germany, 1974; diploma in quality mgmt. Bd. cert. gen. surgeon, plastic surgeon, hand surgeon. Surg. intern Hosp. Muenchen-Schwabing, Munich, 1974; med. and ob-gyn. intern Ludwig-Maximilians U. Hosp., Munich, 1975; intern, resident Maimonides Med. Ctr., NYC, 1975-76; resident in surgery City Hosp., Muenchen-Schwabing, 1976-83, gen. surgeon Munich, 1983-84, fellow in plastic surgery Muenchen-Bogenhausen, 1984-87, plastic surgeon, 1987-88; dir. surgery and plastic surgery Kreiskrankenhaus, Nittenau, Germany, 1988-93; dir. dept. plastic surgery Caritas Krankenhaus St. Josef, Regensburg, Germany, 1994—; internat. cons. plastic surgeon Oil Sector Svc. Co., Kuwait, 2006—. Pres. European Com. on Quality Assurance and Med. Devices, 1992-99, mem. Libyan Bd. Med. Specialties, 2007-. Author: Qualitaetsmanagement in der Medizin, 1997, Qualitaetsmanagement im Gesundheitswesen, 1999, Breast Implants: the Past, the Present, the Future, European Plastic Surgery Rev., 1999; editor: Innovations in Plastic and Aestheic Surgery, 2007; mem. editl. bd.: Aesthetic Plastic Surgery, 2002—. Pres. Red Cross Kreisverband, Regensburg, Germany, 2001—05, dep. chair, 2005—. Recipient Travel award Bavarian Assn. Surgeons, 1983. Mem. German Soc. Plastic, Reconstructive and Aesthetic Surgeons (bd. dirs. 1990-92, 02-03, 07—, v.p. 2004, pres. 2005-07), Internat. Confedn. Plastic, Reconstructive and Aesthetic Surgery (dep. gen. sec. 2003-06, gen. sec. 2006-), Internat. Soc. Aesthetic Plastic Surgery, European Soc. Mastology, Internat. Assn. Univ. Plastic Surgeons, Am. Soc. Plastic Surgery (Pres. award 2006). Roman Catholic. Avocations: contemporary art, jazz dance, windsurfing, skiing, golf. Office: Caritas Krankenhaus St Josef Landshuter Str 65 93053 Regensburg Germany Office Phone: 49 941 7823110. Business E-Mail: plastische.chirurgie@caritasstjosef.de.

EISENSTADT, G. MICHAEL, diplomat, writer, educator, researcher; b. Free City of Danzig (now Gdansk, Poland), Nov. 16, 1928; s. Isidor and Edith (Lange) E.; 1 child, Judith Luzann. BA, Queens Coll., 1951; MS, U. Wis., 1952; postgrad., Russian Inst. Columbia U., 1954—56, Fgn. Svc. Inst., 1982—83. Instr. history Queens Coll., Flushing, NY, 1955-60; jr. officer Am. Embassy, Belgrade, Yugoslavia, 1960-61; cultural officer Am. Consulate Gen., Guayaquil, Ecuador, 1962-63; asst. cultural affairs officer Am. Embassy, Belgrade, Yugoslavia, 1963-67, cultural attaché Warsaw, 1968-71, br. pub. affairs officer Bonn, Fed. Republic of Germany, 1973-76, counselor for pub. affairs Budapest, Hungary, 1977-80, dep. counselor for pub. affairs Bonn, 1983-84, counselor for pub. affairs Belgrade, 1984-88; dep. policy officer Voice of Am., Washington, 1971-73; dir. Office Internat. Visitors USIA, Washington, 1980-82; mem. sr. seminar State Dept., Washington, 1982-83; dir. Office European Affairs USIA, Washington, 1988-89; diplomat-in-residence NYU, 1989-90; dir. N.Y. Reception Ctr. USIA, 1990-92; sr. rsch. scholar Inst. East Ctrl. Europe Columbia U., 1992-94. Cons. on the Balkans, Ea. and Ctrl. Europe, countries of the former Soviet Union; chmn. coordinating com., chmn. drafting com. Conf. on Peace and Tolerance, Berne, Switzerland, 1992, Istanbul, 94; chmn. coordinating com. Conflict Resolution Conf., Vienna, 1995; election observer OSCE in Serbia, 1997; coord. Peace and Tolerance Conf. on Kosovo, Vienna, 1999; election observer Appeal of Conscience Found. in Russia, 1999; coord. Peace and Tolerance Conf. II, Istanbul, Turkey, 2005; lectr. in field. Sec. Appeal of Conscience Del. to Switzerland, 1997; dir. internat. programs Appeal Conscience Found. With U.S. Army, 1952-54. Home: 880 5th Ave Apt Phe New York NY 10021-4951 E-mail: gme1@earthlink.net.

EISENSTADT, PAULINE DOREEN BAUMAN, state legislator; b. NYC, Dec. 31, 1938; d. Morris and Anne (Lautenberg) Bauman; m. Melvin M. Eisenstadt, Nov. 20, 1960; children: Todd Alan, Keith Mark. BA, U. Fla., 1960; MS, U. Ariz., 1965; postgrad., U. N.Mex. Tchr., Ariz., 1961—65, PR, 1972—73; adminstrv. asst. Inst. Social Rsch. U. N.Mex., 1973—74; founder, 1st exec. dir. Energy Consumers N.Mex., 1977—81; chmn. consumer affairs adv. com. Dept. Energy, 1979—80; v.p. tech. bd. Nat. Ctr. Appropriate Tech., 1980—; pres. Eisenstadt Enterprises, investments, 1983—; mem. N.Mex. House of Reps., 1985—92, chairwoman majority caucus, chair rules com., 1987—, chair sub. com. on children and youth, 1987; mem. N.Mex. State Senate, 1996—2000, mem. senate fin. com., com. higher edn., com. econ. devel., sci. & tech., water & natural resources, electric deregulation com., chair conservation co, mem. senate fin. com., com. higher edn., com. econ. devel., sci. & tech., water & natural resources, electric deregulation com., chair conservation com. Mem. exec. com., vice chair pvt. coun. Nat. Conf. State Legislators, 1987; vice chmn. Sandoval County (N.Mex.) Dem. Party, 1981—; mem. N.Mex. Dem. State Ctrl. Com., 1981—; N.Mex. del. Dem. Nat. Platform Com., 1984, Dem. Nat. Conv., 1984; mem. cmty. adv. bd. Intel Corp., 2004. Dir., host (TV program) Consumer Viewpoint, 1980—82, host N.Mex. Today and Tomorrow, 1992—, exec. prodr., host Tech Talks, 2001—; author: Corrales, Portrait of a Changing Village, 1980; painter (gallery and art show), 2005. Pres. Anti Defamation League, N.Mex., 1994—95; mem. N.Mex. First; pres. Sandoval County Dem. Women's Assn., 1979—81; vice chmn. N.Mex. Dem. Platform Com., 1984—; mem. Sandoval County Redistricting Task Force, 1983—84, Rio Rancho Ednl. Study Com., 1984—. Named Outstanding Senator, N.Mex. Tech. Showcase, 2000; named to Miami Beach Sr. HS Hall of Fame, 2000; recipient Gov.'s award Outstanding N. Mex. Women, Commn. on the Status of Women and Gov. Bruce King, 1992; grantee, NSF, 1965. Mem.: Rio Rancho Rotary Club (pres. 1995—, Rotarian of Yr. 1995), Kiwanis (1st woman mem. local club). Home: PO Box 658 Corrales NM 87048-0658 E-mail: peisenstadt@aol.com.

EISENSTAT, THEODORE ELLIS, colon and rectal surgeon, educator; b. NYC, Sept. 24, 1942; m. Sharon Diane Leonard, July, 1966; children: Maren Elise, Loren Aline. BA, Vanderbilt U., 1964; MD, N.Y. Med. Coll., 1968. Diplomate Am. Bd. Surgery, Am. Bd. Colon and Rectal Surgery, Nat. Bd. Med. Examiners. Rotating intern St. Vincent's Hosp., Worcester, Mass., 1968-69; resident in surgery Thomas Jefferson U. Hosp., Phila., 1969-71; chief resident in surgery Pa. Hosp., Phila., 1971-73; fellow in colon and rectal surgery Muhlenberg Hosp.-Robert Wood Johnson Sch. Medicine, NJ, 1977-78; dir. surg. endoscopy U. Md., 1975-80, dir. colon & rectal svc., 1976-80; asst. prof. surgery U. Md. Sch. Medicine, 1975-80; sr. attending surgeon Muhlenberg Regional Med. Ctr., Plainfield, NJ, 1979—, John F. Kennedy Med. Ctr., Edison, 1979—; clin. assoc. prof. surgery U. Medicine and Dentistry of N.J., Newark, 1981—, clin. prof. surgery Robert Wood Johnson Med. Sch. New Brunswick, 1979-91, clin. prof. surgery, 1991—, dir. colon and rectal residency program, 1993—2005; dir. colon and rectal surgery Robert Wood Johnson U. Hosp. Cons. surgeon Lock Raven VA Hosp., Balt., 1975-80, U.S. Army, Kimbrough Army Hosp., Ft. Meade, Md., 1975-80; bd. dirs., ACS rep. Am. Bd. Colon and Rectal Surgery, 1990-96, pres., 1995-96; attending surgeon Robert Wood Johnson U. Hosp., New Brunswick, N.J., 1984—; exhibitor and presenter in field; vis. prof. U. Md. Sch. Medicine, 1983, Abington (Pa.) Meml. Hosp., 1985, York (Pa.) Hosp., 1990, Pa. Hosp., Phila., 1990, others. Contbr. articles to profl. jours. Maj. U.S. Army, 1973-75. Fellow ACS (adv. coun. colon and rectal surgery), Am. Soc. Colon and Rectal Surgeons (Walter A. Fansler award 1977, Purdue Frederick fellow 1977, 1st prize sci. exhibit 1979); mem. AMA, Soc. for Surgery of Alimentary Tract, Assn. for Acad. Surgery, Soc. Am. Gastrointestinal Endoscopic Surgeons (founder 1981, bd. govs. 1986-89), Am. Soc. Gastrointestinal Endoscopy, N.Y. Soc. Colon and Rectal Surgeons (mem. coun. 1983-85, sec.-treas. 1986-87, v.p. 1988-89, pres. 1990-92, 1st prize film 1978), Pa. Soc. Colon. and Rectal Surgeons, N.J. Soc. Colon and Rectal Surgeons (sec.-treas. 1983-85, pres. 1989-90), N.J. Soc. Gastroenterology, N.J. Soc. Gastrointestinal Endoscopy, Assn. Mil. Surgeons U.S., Soc. Surgeons N.J., Crohn's and Colitis Found. Am.

EISENSTEIN, EDWARD MILTON, psychologist, physiologist, radiologist, educator; b. LA, July 29, 1932; s. Phillip and Yetta Eisenstein; m. Doris Loretta Woolfe, June 21, 1953; 1 child, Jeremy. BA in Psychology, UCLA, 1956, MA in Psychology, 1959, PhD in Psychology and Physiology, 1962; MD, Mich. State U., East Lansing, 1978. Lic. physician Mich., 1982, NY, 1984. Postdoctoral fellow dept. biology Calif. Inst. Tech., 1961—63, U. Oreg., Eugene, 1963—64; lectr. psychology UCLA, 1963; asst. prof psychology SUNY, NY, 1964—67, assoc. prof. psychology, 1967—68, rsch. asst. prof., dept. radiology, 1985—97, asst. prof., dept. neurology, 1985—97, adj. prof., dept. psychology, 1987—97; rsch. assoc. Brookhaven Nat. Labs., Upton, NY, 1966—67, 1994—97; assoc. prof. biophysics Mich. State U., 1968—70, prof. biophysics, 1970—82, prof., mem. grad. faculty interdisciplinary neuroscience program, 1973—82, adj. prof., Coll. Natural Sci., 1982—85, chmn., biophysics dept., 1969—73, program dir., NIH tng. grant, dept. biophysics, 1969—73; intern, family practice Mich. State U., St. Lawrence Hosps., Lansing, 1980; resident in radiology Wayne State U., Harper-Grace Hosps., Detroit, 1982—85, chief resident, radiology, 1984—85; clin. prof. neurology Sch. Medicine, Wayne State U., 1983—85; radiologist, rschr. VA Med. Ctr., Northport, NY, 1985—97, chief, radiology svc., 1996—97; prin. rschr. West LA VA Med. Ctr., 1998—. Mem. neurobiology study panel NSF, 1971—73; chmn. com. VA Med. Ctr., 2003—, mem. R&D com., 2003—. Editor: (book) Aneural Organisms in Neurobiology, 1975; assoc. editor: The Physiology Tchr., 1979—82; contbr. articles to profl. jours. and book chpts. in field. Recipient Ann. Pavlovian Investigator award, 1997. Fellow: Internat. Behavioral Neuroscience Soc.; mem.: AMA, AAAS, APA, Am. Physiol. Soc., Internat. Soc. Magnetic Resonance in Medicine, Pavlovian Soc. N.Am. (Ann. Pavlovian Investigator award 1997), Soc. Neuroscience. Achievements include research in biological basis of learning and memory. Avocations: piano, nature walks, reading. Office: VA Greater LA Healthcare Sys 11301 Wilshire Blvd Los Angeles CA 90073 Office Phone: 310-268-3498. Business E-Mail: edward.eisenstein@med.va.gov.

EISENSTEIN, ELIZABETH LEWISOHN, historian, educator; b. NYC, Oct. 11, 1923; d. Sam A. and Margaret V. (Seligman) Lewisohn; m. Julian Calvert Eisenstein, May 30, 1948; children: Margaret, John (dec.), Edward. AB, Vassar Coll., 1944; MA, Radcliffe Coll., 1947, PhD, 1953; LittD (hon.), Mt. Holyoke Coll., 1979; LHD (hon.), U. Mich., 2004. From lectr. to adj. prof history Am. U., Washington, 1959-74; Alice Freeman Palmer prof. history U. Mich., Ann Arbor, 1975-88, prof. emerita, 1988—. Scholar-in-residence Rockefeller Found. Ctr., Bellagio, Italy, June 1977; mem. vis. com. dept. history Harvard U., 1975-81, vice-chmn., 1979-81; dir. Ecole des Hautes Etudes en Sciences Sociales, Paris, 1982; guest spkr., participant confs. and seminars; I. Beam vis. prof. U. Iowa, 1980; Mead-Swing lectr. Oberlin Coll., 1980; Stone lectr. U. Glasgow, 1984; Van Leer lectr. Van Leer Fedn., Jerusalem, 1984; Hanes lectr. U. N.C., Chapel Hill, 1985 first resident cons. Ctr. for the Book, Libr. of Congress, Washington, 1979; mem. Coun. Scholars, 1980-88; pres.'s disting. visitor Vassar Coll., 1988; Pforzheimer lectr. N.Y. Pub. Libr., 1989, Lyell lectr. Bodleian Libr., Oxford, 1990, Merle Curti lectr. U. Wis., Madison, 1992, Jantz lectr. Oberlin Coll., 1995, Clifford lectr. Austin, Tex., 1996; vis. fellow Wolfson Coll., Oxford, 1990; sem. dir. Folger Inst., 1999. Author: The First Professional Revolutionist: F. M. Buonarroti, 1959, The Printing Press as an Agent of Change, 1979 , 2 vols. paperback edit., 1980 (Phi Beta Kappa Ralph Waldo Emerson prize 1980), The Printing Revolution in Early Modern Europe, 1983 (reissued as Canto Book, 1993), 2d edit., 2005, Grub Street Abroad, 1992; mem. editorial bd. Jour. Modern History, 1973-76, 83-86, Revs. in European History, 1973-86, Jour. Library History, 1979-82, Eighteenth Century Studies, 1981-84; contbr. articles to profl. jours., chpts. to books. Bd. dirs. Folger Shakespeare Libr., 2000—. Belle Skinner fellow Vassar Coll., NEH fellow, 1977, Guggenheim fellow, 1982, fellow Ctr. Advanced Studies in Behavioral Scis., 1982-83, 92-93, Humanities Rsch. Ctr. fellow Australian Nat. U., 1988. Fellow Am. Acad. Arts and Scis., Royal Hist. Soc.; mem. Soc. French Hist. Studies (v.p. 1970, program com. 1974), Am. Soc. 18th Century Studies (nominating com. 1971), Soc. 16th Century Studies, Am. Hist. Assn. (com. on coms. 1970-72, chmn. Modern European sect. 1981, coun. 1982-85, Scholarly Distinction award 2003), Renaissance Soc. Am. (coun. 1973-76, pres. 1986), Am. Antiquarian Soc. (exec. com., adv. bd. 1984-87), Phi Beta Kappa. Office: U Mich Dept History Ann Arbor MI 48109 E-mail: eisenst@mindspring.com.

EISENSTEIN, JAMES P., physicist, educator; AB, Oberlin Coll., 1974; PhD, U. Calif., 1980. Prof. physics Calif. Inst. Tech., 1996—2004, Roshek prof., 2004—05, Roshek prof. physics and applied physics, 2005—. Bd. dirs. Boulder Sch. Condensed Matter and Materials Physics. Recipient Oliver E. Buckley Condensed Matter prize, Am. Phys. Soc., 2007. Mem.: NAS. Office: Condensed Matter Physics 114-36 Calif Inst Tech Pasadena CA 91125 Office Phone: 626-395-4649. E-mail: jpe@caltech.edu.

EISENSTEIN, TOBY K., microbiology professor; b. Phila., Sept. 15, 1942; d. Edward and Sylvia (Mandel) Karet; m. Bruce A. Eisenstein, Sept. 8, 1963; children: Eric, Andrew, Ilana. BA, Wellesley Coll., 1964; PhD, Bryn Mawr Coll., 1969. Instr. Med. Sch. Temple U., Phila., 1969-71, asst. prof., 1971-79, assoc. prof. microbiology and immunology Med. Sch., 1979-84, prof., 1984—, acting chair, 1990-92, co-dir. Ctr. Substance Abuse Rsch., 1992—. Mem. bacteriology and mycology study sect. NIH, 1976—80, 1988—92, mem. drugs abuse and AIDS study sect., 1994—2004. Contbr. articles to profl. jours. Recipient Lindback award, Temple U., 1986, Rsch. prize, 2003; NIH fellow, 1965—69, USPHS grantee, 1971—. Fellow: Am. Acad. Microbiology; mem.: AAAS, Coll. Problems Drug Dependence (bd. dirs. 2005—), Psychoneuroimmunology Rsch. Soc., Soc. Neuroimmune Pharmacology (Joseph Wybran award), Internat. Endotoxin and Innate Immunity Soc., Soc. Leukocyte Biology (sec. 1998—2000), Am. Assn. Immunologists, Am. Soc. Microbiology (pres. eastern Pa. br. 1983—86, mem. coun. policy com. 1993—96, chair membership bd. 2003—), Sigma Xi (pres. Temple U. chpt. 1981—83). Office: Temple U Sch Medicine Dept Microbiology and Immunology 3400 N Broad St Philadelphia PA 19140-5104 Office Phone: 215-707-3585. Business E-Mail: tke@temple.edu.

EISER, ARNOLD ROBERT, physician executive, bioethicist, nephrologist, internist; b. Newark, NY, Jan. 2, 1949; s. Harold H. and Anne Eiser; m. Barbara Joyce Andrews, June 15, 1975; 1 child, Arielle Veronica. BA magna cum laude, U. Pa., 1970; MD, Northwestern U., 1974. Intern Pa. Hosp., 1974-75; resident Med. Coll. Pa., 1975-77; fellow Hahnemann U., 1977-79; nephrologist Elmhurst (N.Y.) Hosp. Ctr., 1979-95, assoc. chief nephrology, 1993-95, dir. ambulatory care, 1995-97, dir. med. residency program, 1996-97; chief sect. gen. internal medicine U. Ill., Chgo., 1997—2001, prof. medicine, 1997—2003; v.p. Med. Edn. Mercy Health Sys., Darby, Pa., 2003—. Assoc. prof. medicine Mt. Sinai Sch. Medicine, NYC, 1986-97; adj. assoc. Hastings Ctr., Briarcliff Manor, NY, 1994-98; prof. medicine Drexel U., 2003—. Contbg. author: The Kidney in Collagen Vascular Diseases, 1993, Violence Against Women: Philosophical Perspective, 1998; contbr. articles to profl. jours. Fellow: ACP, Coll. Physicians Phila. (sec. history sect. 2006—), Inst. Medicine Chgo. (pres. Chgo. clin. ethics program 2001—03); mem.: Am. Coll. Physician Execs. Avocations: travel, fitness, cross-training. Office: 1500 Lansdowne Ave Darby PA 19023 Business E-Mail: aeiser@drexel.edu. E-mail: aeiser@mercyhealth.org.

EISERER, LEONARD ALBERT CARL, publishing executive; b. Polar, Wis., June 3, 1916; s. Herman Frederick and Anna Elizabeth (Schneider) E.; m. Lorraine Elizabeth Hickey, June 28, 1941; children: Carol Jean, Elaine Roberta, Leonard Arnold, Beverly Arlene. BA, Roosevelt U., Chgo., 1937; MS in Journalism, Northwestern U., 1939. Editor Am. Aviation Publs., Inc., Washington, 1939—42, v.p., gen. mgr., 1946—57, exec. v.p., sec., 1958-62; pres., pub. Sports Age, Inc., Washington, 1962-63; chmn., CEO Bus. Pubs., Inc., Silver Spring, Md., 1963—. Chmn. Carol Jean Cancer Found., Inc.; bd. dirs. U. N.C. at Greensboro Excellence Found.; pres., dir. Eiserer-Hickey Found., Inc.; dir. Univ. Club of Washington Found. Lt. USN, 1942-46. Named to Hall of Fame Newsletter Pubs. Found., 1994, Man of Yr. Univ. Club of Washington, 1995; inductee Hall of Achievement, Northwestern U. Medill Sch. Journalism, 1997. Mem.: Air and Waste Mgmt. Assn., Water Environ. Fedn., Soc. Profl. Journalists, Newsletter Pubs. Assn., Nat. Press Club, Univ. Club. Home: 9101 Sligo Creek Pky Silver Spring MD 20901-3360 Office: Bus Pubs Inc 8737 Colesville Rd Silver Spring MD 20910-4400

EISERT, EDWARD GAVER, lawyer; b. NYC, May 26, 1948; s. Israel Jay and Bess (Gaver) E.; div.; children: Carolyn B., Stephen J. AB, Cornell U., 1969; JD, NYU, 1973. Bar: N.Y. 1974. Law clk. to Judge Charles L. Brieant U.S. Dist. Ct. (so. dist.) N.Y., NYC, 1973-74; assoc. Simpson Thacher & Bartlett, NYC, 1974-76, Schulte Roth & Zabel, NYC, 1976-80, ptnr., 1981—2002; sr. v.p., gen. corp. counsel Fiduciary Trust Co. Internat., NYC, 2002—. Bd. dirs. N.Y. Small Bus. Venture Fund LLC., 1998—2004. Note and comment editor NYU Law Rev., 1972-73. Mem. ABA (com. on fed. regulation of securities 1983—, subcom. on ann. rev. fed. regulation of securities 1983-89, subcom. on mcpl. and govtl. obligations 1984-92, subcom. on investment cos. and investment advisors 1992—), Internat. Bar Assn., N.Y. Stat Bar Assn., Assn. Bar City N.Y., Univ. Club N.Y.C. Office: Kirkpatrick & Lockhart Preston Gates Ellis LLP 599 Lexington Ave New York NY 10022

EISLER, EDITH, violinist, educator; b. Vienna, Feb. 14, 1925; arrived in US, 1945; Diploma, Julliard Sch., 1950; Licentiate, Royal Acad. Music, England, 1940. Mem. Busch Little Symphony, NYC, 1945—46, Buffalo Philharmonic, 1946—47; tchr. Rudolf Steiner Sch., NYC, Mt. Kisco Music Sch., Horace Mann Sch., Turtle Bay Music Sch. Reviewer Amazon website. Contbr. articles to mags. Mem.: Chamber Music Am. Home: 300 Riverside Dr New York NY 10025 Office Phone: 212-865-9288. Personal E-mail: eewerther@aol.com.

EISLER, SUSAN KRAWETZ, advertising executive; b. NYC, Aug. 18, 1946; d. Aaron and Bertha (Platt) Krawetz; m. Howard Irwin Eisler, June 8, 1980; 1 stepchild, Robin Joy; 1 adopted child, Joseph. BA, U. Pitts., 1967; MA, New Sch. for Social Rsch., 1971. Analyst Marplan, Inc., NYC, 1968-69; project dir. Market Facts, Inc., NYC, 1969-70; assoc. rsch. mgr. Gen. Foods, Inc., White Plains, NY, 1970-75, product mgr., 1975-80; rsch. dir. Elizabeth Arden, NYC, 1980-81; v.p., assoc. rsch. dir. Lintas: N.Y. (formerly SSC&B: Lintas Worldwide), NYC, 1981-87, sr. v.p., assoc. rsch. dir., 1987-92, exec. v.p., dir. strategic planning and rsch., 1992-94, Gotham, Inc., 1995—, mng. ptnr., dir. rsch. and info. svcs. Named Woman of Yr., YWCA Acad. Women Achievers, 1989. Mem.: Advt. Rsch. Found. (copy rsch. coun.), Am. Mktg. Assn. Office: Gotham Inc 100 5th Ave Fl 16 New York NY 10011-6996

EISMANN, DANIEL T., state supreme court justice; b. Eugene, Oreg. m. Sheila Wood, 1982; 1 child, Matthew stepchildren: Catherine Richardson, Christine Putz. Grad. cum laude, U. Idaho, 1976. Former law clerk to justice Donaldson Idaho State Supreme Ct., Boise; magistrate judge Owyheee County, 1986—95; dist. judge Fourth Jud. Dist., 1995—98, adminstrv. dist. judge, 1998—2000; justice Idaho Supreme Ct., Boise, 2001—, chief justice, 2007—. Chair Idaho State Supreme Ct. Civil Rules Com., Idaho State Supreme Ct. Criminal Jury Instructions Com., Idaho State Supreme Ct. Drug Court Coordinating Com. Mem. Ada County Domestic Violence Task Force, Region III Coun. for Children and Youth; judge Ada County Drug Ct. With USAR. Decorated 2 Purple Hearts. Mem.: Inns of Ct. (Boise Chpt.), Idaho Bar Assn. (mem. Bar Exam Preparation Com.). Office: Idaho Supreme Ct PO Box 83720 Boise ID 83720*

EISNER, DIANA, pediatrician; b. Houston, May 7, 1951; d. Elmer and Edith (Dubow) E. BA in Biology cum laude, Brandeis U., 1973; MD, Southwestern Med. Sch., 1977. Diplomate Am. Bd. Pediat. Intern, resident Baylor Coll. Medicine, Houston, 1977-80; pvt. practice Houston, 1981—. Chmn. dept. pediat. Meml. N.W. Hosp., Houston, 1990. Recipient Commendation award Children's Protection Com. Tex. Children's Hosp., 1978, Physician's Recognition award AMA, 1983. Mem. Am. Acad. Pediatrics, Tex. Med. Assn., Tex. Pediatric Soc., Houston Pediatric Soc. (treas. 2001-02, sec. 2002-), Harris County Med. Soc. Avocations: ballet, swimming, walking. Office: 2030 North Loop W Ste 125 Houston TX 77018-8132 Office Phone: 713-688-8393. Personal E-mail: dr.diana@sbcglobal.net.

EISNER, ELLIOT W., education educator; MA in Art and Edn., Roosevelt U., 1954; MS in Art Edn., Ill. Inst. Tech., 1955; MA in Edn., U. Chgo., 1958, PhD in Edn., 1962. HS art tchr., Chgo., 1956—58; art tchr. U. Chgo., 1958—60, instr. edn., 1961—62, asst. prof. edn., 1962—65; instr., art edn. Ohio State U., 1960—61; assoc. prof. edn. & art Stanford U., 1965—70, edn. & art prof., 1970—. Consulting editor Curriculum Perspectives, 1981—; mem. editl. bd. Kappan, 1995—2000; mem. editl. advisory bd. Just & Caring Edn., 1995—2000; mem. editl. bd. Critical Inquiry into Curriculum & Instruction, 1998—. Contbr. articles various profl. jours.; co-author (with David W. Ecker): Readings in Art Education, 1966; co-author: (with Alan Peshkin) Qualitative Inquiry in Education: The Continuing Debate, 1990; co-author: (with Elizabeth Vallance) Conflicting Conceptions of Curriculum series on Contemporary Educational Issues, 1974; author: Confronting Curriculum Reform, 1971, Educating Artistic Vision, 1972, The Arts, Human Development, and Education, 1976, The Education Imagination: On the Design and Evaluation of School Programs, 1979, The Art of Educational Evaluation: A Personal View, 1985, The Role of Discipline-Based Art Education in America's Schools, 1988, The Enlightened Eye: Qualitative Inquiry and the Enhancement of Educational Practice, 1991, Cognition and Curriculum Reconsidered, 1994, Evaluating and Assessing the Visual Arts in Education: International Perspectives, 1996, The Kind of Schools We Need: Personal Essays, 1998, The Arts and the Creation of the Mind, 2002 (The Grawemeyer award for Edn., U. Louisville, 2005). Recipient Harold McGraw Jr. prize in Edn., Nat. Art Edn. Assn., 1998. Mem.: Nat. Acad. of Edn., John Dewey Soc. (pres. 1998—2000), J. Paul Getty Ctr. for Edn. in the Arts. Achievements include research in the rold of artistic thinking in the conduct of social sci. rsch., programs to further arts edn. in Am. schs., the role of artistry in ednl. theory and practice. Office: Stanford U Sch of Edn 485 Lasuen Mall Stanford CA 94305-3096 E-mail: eisner@stanford.edu.

EISNER, HOWARD, engineering executive, educator; b. NYC, Aug. 8, 1935; s. Samuel Eisner and Mary Wegodner; m. Joan Arlene Knopfer, Feb. 9, 1957(div. 1994); children: Seth Eric, Susan Rachel, Oren David; m. June B. Linowitz, Nov. 8, 1995. BEE, CCNY, 1957; MS, Columbia U., NYC, 1958; DSc, George Wash. U., Washington, DC, 1966. Teaching asst. Columbia U., 1957; lectr. dept. physics Bklyn. Coll., 1957-59; lectr., asst. professorial lectr. George Washington U., 1961-67; prof. U. Maryland, 1987-89; various engring. positions ORI, Inc., Rockville, Md., 1959-68, v.p., 1968-71, exec. v.p., 1971-84, corp. exec. v.p., 1984-85, also dir.; pres. Intercon Systems Corp. subs. ORI, Group, Inc., Rockville, 1985-89, Atlantic Research Services Corp., Alexandria, Va., 1987-89; Disting. rsch. prof. George Washington U., Washington, 1989—. Author: Advanced Algebra, 1960, Computer-Aided Systems Engineering, 1988, Essentials of Project and Systems Engineering Management, 1997, 2d edit., 2002, Reengineering Yourself and Your Company: From Engineer to Manager to Leader, 2000, Managing Complex Systems: Thinking Outside the Box, 2005; contbr. articles to profl. jours. Fellow (life) IEEE, Internat. Coun. Sys. Engring., NY Acad. Scis.; mem. AIAA, INFORMS, Sigma Xi, Tau Beta Pi, Eta Kappa Nu, Omega Rho. Avocations: tennis, choral singing, writing. Office: George Washington U Rm 157 SEAS-EMSE 1776 G St NW Washington DC 20052 Office Phone: 202-994-0584. Business E-Mail: heisner@gwu.edu.

EISNER, JONATHAN DAVID, lawyer; b. Silver Spring, Md., Apr. 13, 1967; BS, Drexel Univ., 1990; JD with honors, Univ. Md., 1993. Bar: Md. 1993. Law clk. Chief Judge Robert C. Murphy Ct. of Appeals, Md.; ptnr., chmn. Trusts & Estates practice group DLA Piper LLP, Balt. Assoc. editor Md. Law Rev. Asst. sec. South Atlantic divsn. Am. Cancer Soc.; profl. adv. counsel, mem. steering com. Balt. Cmty. Found.; bd. dirs. Hittman Family Found.; bd. dirs., mem. exec. com. Md. Sci. Ctr.; bd. mem. Balt. Sch. Arts. Recipient Judge Morton P. Fisher Meml. prize for best work in estate and gift taxation, U. Md., 1993, Edward H. Curlander prize for best work in estate planning, 1993. Mem.: Md. Sci. Ctr. (bd. mem.). Office: DLA Piper LLP 6225 Smith Ave Baltimore MD 21209-3600 Office Phone: 410-580-4142. Office Fax: 410-580-3001. Business E-Mail: jonathan.eisner@dlapiper.com.

EISNER, MICHAEL DAMMANN, investment and former entertainment company executive; b. Mt. Kisco, NY, Mar. 7, 1942; s. Lester and Margaret (Dammann) E.; m. Jane Breckenridge, 1967; children: Breck, Eric, Anders. BA, Denison U., 1964. Began career in programming dept. CBS; asst. to nat. programming dir. ABC, 1966-68, mgr. spls. and talent, dir. program devel.-East Coast, 1968-71, dir. program devel. East Coast, 1968-71, dir. feature films and program devel., 1969, v.p. daytime programming, 1971-75, v.p. program planning and devel., 1975-76, sr. v.p. prime time prodn. and devel., 1976; pres., COO Paramount Pictures Corp., 1976-84; chmn. Walt Disney Co., Burbank, Calif., 1984—2004, CEO, 1984—2005; founder The Tornante Co., LLC, Beverly Hills, Calif., 2005—; host, Conversations with Michael Eisner CNBC, 2006—. Bd. dirs. The Walt Disney Co., 1984-2005, Veoh Networks, Inc., 2006-; gov. Mighty Ducks of Anaheim, 1993; mem. bus. steering com. Global Business Dialogue on Electronic Commerce; founder, The Eisner Found., 1996-; lectr. in field Author (with Tony Schwartz): Work in Progress: Risking Failure, Surviving Success, 1998; author: Camp, 2005. Trustee Denison U., Calif. Inst. Arts; bd. dirs. Am. Hosp. of Paris Found., UCLA Exec. Bd. for Med. Sci. Office: The Tornante Co LLC 233 Beverly Dr S Beverly Hills CA 90212 also: The Eisner Found 9401 Wilshire Found Ste 760 Beverly Hills CA 90212*

EISNER, PETER NORMAN, journalist, writer; b. Jersey City, Aug. 27, 1950; s. Bernard and Lorraine (Gropper) Eisner; m. Musha Salinas, Aug. 27, 1981; children: Isabel, Marina. BA, Rutgers U., 1972. Reporter Hudson (N.Y.) Register-Star, 1974-75, Poughkeepsie (N.Y.) Jour., 1975-76; newsman AP, Columbus, NYC, 1978-1979, Brazil corr. Brasilia, 1979-81, Venezuela bur. chief. Caracas, 1982, news editor, Mex., Cen. Am. Mex. City, 1982-83; dep. fgn. editor Newsday, NYC, 1984-85, sr. editor fgn. news, 1985-89, sr. corr., 1989-94; mng. dir. NewsCom, Coral Gables, Fla., 1994-98, Ctr. for Pub. Integrity, Washington, 1999—2001; dep. fgn. editor Washington Post, 2003. Scholar in residence Am. U., Washington, 2006. Author editor, translator: Death Beat, 1994, America's Prisoner, 1997; author: The Freedom Line, 2004. Mem bd advisors Ctrl. Am Jounalists Program, 1989—93. Recipient Christopher award, 2005. Mem.: Inter-american Press Asn (freedom of press comt 1988—94, bd dirs 1988—94). Personal E-mail: peisner@gmail.com.

EISNER, THOMAS, biologist, educator; b. Berlin, June 25, 1929; s. Hans Edouard and Margarete (Heil) E.; m. Maria Lobell, June 10, 1952; children: Yvonne, Vivian, Christina. BA, Harvard U., 1951, PhD, 1955; DSc (hon.), U. Wüzburg, Germany, 1982, U. Zürich, Switzerland, 1983, U. Göteborg, Sweden, 1989, Drexel U., 1992. Postdoctoral fellow Harvard U., 1955—57; asst. prof. biology Cornell U., Ithaca, NY, 1957—62, assoc. prof., 1962—66, prof., 1966—76, Jacob Gould Schurman prof. chem. ecology, 1976—. Vis. scientist dept. entomology Sch. Agr., Wageningen, The Netherlands, 1964—65; vis. scientist Smithsonian Tropical Rsch. Lab., Barro Colorado Island, C.Z., 1968; sr. vis. scientist Max Planck Inst. fur Verhaltensphysiologie, Seewiesen, Germany, 1971, Divsn. Entomology, CSIRO, Canberra, Australia, 1972—73; Rand fellow Marine Biol. Labs., Woods Hole, Mass., 1974; vis. rsch. prof. U. Fla., Gainesville, 1977—78; disting. vis. fellow NY Inst. Humanities, NYU; chief scientist Biodiversity IMAX Film, 1996—2001; mem. internat. adv. bd. INBio, 1997—98, FUNDAQUIM U. de la Republica, Uruguay, 1997—, Butterfly Discovery Pk., 1997—2001; rsch. assoc. Archbold Biol. Sta., 1973—; vis. prof. Stanford U., 1979—80, U. Zürich, 1980—81. Co-author: Animal Adaptation, 1964, Life on Earth, 1973, For Love of Insects, 2003, Secret Weapons, 2005, and 7 other books; mem. editl. bd.: Sci., 1970—71, Am. Naturalist, 1970—71, Jour. Comparative Physiology, 1974—80, Jour. Chem. Ecology, 1974—, Behavioral Ecology and Sociobiology, 1976—97, Sci. Yr. World Books, 1979—82, Human Ecology Forum, 1981—85, Living Bird Quar., 1982—88, Experientia, 1982—96, Quar. Rev. Biology, 1983—87, Chemoecology, 1997—, Zoology, 1993—, Chemistry and Biodiversity, 2004—; co-editor: Explorations in Chemical Ecology Series, 1987—; contbr. articles to profl. jours. Recipient Archie F. Carr medal, 1983, Procter prize, Sigma Xi, 1986, Karl Ritter von Frisch medal, 1988, Centennial medal, Harvard U., 1989, Tyler Environ. Achievement prize, U. So. Calif., 1990, Esselen award, 1991, Silver medal, Internat. Soc. Chem. Ecology, 1991, Nat. medal sci., 1994, NWF Nat. Conservation Achievement award, 1997, Green Globe award, 1997, John Wiley Jones award, 1999, Iscol Disting. Environ. Lectr. award, 2000, Lewis Thomas award, 2005, Grand prix, Fondation de la Maison de la Chimie, 2006; Guggenheim fellow, 1964—65, 1972—73. Fellow: AAAS (chmn. biology sect. 1980—81, com. on sci. freedom and responsibility 1980—87, chmn. subcom. sci. and human rights 1981—87), Entomol. Soc. Am., Animal Behavior Soc., Royal Soc. Arts, Am. Acad. Arts and Scis.; mem.: NAS (rsch. opportunity in biology com. 1985, film com. 1986—96, com. on human rights 1987—90), Ency. of Biodiversity (internat. adv. bd. 1997—2000), Ctr. of Biodiversity Conservation Am. Mus. Natl. History (adv. com. 1995—2000), Nat. Mus. Natural History (adv. com. 1996—2001), Xerces Soc. (sci. adv. com. 1990—, pres. 1992—), Union Concerned Scientists (bd. dirs. 1993—), Com. Concerned Scientists (nat. sponsor 1988—), World Resources Inst. (adv. coun. 1988—95), Monell Chem. Senses Ctr. (adv. coun. 1988—95), Am. Soc. Naturalists (pres. 1989—90), Mo. Bot. Garden Ctr. Plant Conservation (adv. bd. econ. potential rare and threatened plants 1992), Am. Inst. Biol. Sci. (task force for 90s 1990—), Ctr. on Consequences Nuclear War (steering com. 1983—90), Fedn. Am. Scientists (coun. mem. 1977—81), Nat. Audubon Soc. (bd. dirs. 1970—75), Zero Population Growth (bd. dirs. 1969—70), World Wildlife Fund (sci. adv. coun. 1983—91), Nature Conservancy (nat. sci. adv. coun. 1969—74), Deutsche Acad. Naturforscher Leopoldina. Office: Cornell U W347 Seeley Mudd Hall Dept Neurobiology & Behavior Ithaca NY 14853 *I am a naturalist,* *interested primarily in field exploration and discovery. My research deals with the behavior and chemical ecology of insects, and with the photographic and cinematographic documentation of little-known aspects of the life of these animals. My chief goal in life is to relate my findings to the cause of wildlife and wilderness preservation.*

EISOLD, JOHN FRANCIS, physician; b. Balt., Oct. 21, 1946; Bachelor's degree, Dartmouth Coll., 1968, MD, 1976. Bd. cert. Internal Medicine 1980. Advanced through grades to admiral USN, nuc. submarine officer, 1968—72; chmn. internal medicine Nat. Naval Med. Ctr., Bethesda, Md., 1993—95; chief attending physician Office of the Attending Physician, Washington, 1995—, prof. medicine, Uniformed Svcs. U. Health Scis. Spkr. in field.*

EISSENSTAT, EVERETT H., lawyer; b. 1963; BS, Okla. State Univ., 1985; MA, Univ. Tex., 1988; JD cum laude, Univ. Okla., 1993. Bar: Tex. 1993. Legislative dir. U.S. Rep. Jim Kolbe, Washington; spl. asst. Office of U.S. Trade Rep., Washington; assoc. Dixon & Dixon; chief internat. trade counsel Fin. Com., U.S. Senate, 2003—. Office: Committee on Finance Room 219 Senate Dirksen Office Building Washington DC 20510-6200

EISSMANN, WALTER JAMES, consulting company executive; b. Newark, Apr. 20, 1939; s. Walter Curt Eissmann and Alice Delice (Irving) Clark; m. Dorothea Ann Donaldson, June 1, 1963; children: Patricia Helene Ridenhour, Walter William. BS in Indsl. Engring., Rutgers U., 1962. Account mgr. Gen. Electric, Engelwood Cliffs, N.J., 1962-67; regional sales mgr. Tymshare, Engelwood Cliffs, 1968-71, Buffalo, N.Y., 1971-73, v.p. mktg. svc. divsn. Cupertino, Calif., 1974-79, divsn. v.p., 1980-84; sr. v.p. McDonnell Douglas Corp., Cupertino, 1984-86; gen. ptnr. Archer Assocs., Cupertino, 1985-92; pres., chmn. bd. Walter J. Eissmann Inc., Napa, Calif., 1989—. Bd. dirs. NSF Corp., Nutri/system Franchisee Corp.; chmn. bd. BusinessWise Inc., 1992-93; mng. gen. ptnr. Grand Tyme Partnership, 1992-98. Lead singer: Barbershop Harmony Soc., 2001—, Men of Note, 2005—, Harmony 4 U, 2006—; exec. prodr.: (TV shows) Barbershop Harmony Soc., 2006—. Bd. dirs. Saratoga Little League, Calif., 1976-81, Saratoga Boosters, 1981-84, Reno Ct. Home Owners Assn., 2006—; active Vienna Theatre Players, Va., 1973; mem. Ch. Men's Choir, Saratoga, 1980-82; v.p. devel. Barbershop Harmony Soc., 2005—; v.p. devel. NAPA chpt. BHS, 2005—. Named to President's club Tymshare, Golden Circle, Nutri/system Master of the Keys. Mem. Pi Tau Sigma. Republican. Home and Office: 27 Reno Ct Napa CA 94558

EISWERTH, BARRY NEIL, architect, educator; b. Williamsport, Pa., Sept. 16, 1942; s. Eugene Lewis and Mary Jane (Winters) E.; m. Anne Caroline Essl, Apr. 8, 1967; children: Jason Andreas, Brendan Eugene. BArch., Pa. State U.-University Park, 1965. Registered architect, Pa. Assoc. H2L2 Architects/Planners, Phila., 1967-77, ptnr., 1977-88, sr. ptnr., 1988—; pres. H2L2 Design Co., Phila., 1980—; asst. prof. archtl. design Drexel U., 1975-81; mem. faculty, thesis advisor Phila. Coll. Art. Archtl. works include Children's Hosp., Phila., bldgs. Phila. '76 Bicentennial, Phila. Bourse Bldg., Cypress Sq. Townhouse Complex Phila. (recipient Design award Old Phila. Devel. Corp., Preservation Alliance award for Design Offices and Montgomery McCracken Warker & Rhodes), Constitutional Pavillion for We The People 200, Master Plan and New Classroom Adminstrn. Bldg. Cairo Am. Coll., Engring. and Computer Sci. Campus-Am. U. Cairo, Master Plan Am. Internat. Sch., Tel Aviv, Master Plan and New Classroom Bldgs. Am. Embassy Sch., New Delhi, Master Plan and Design new campus Am. Sch. of Warsaw, Brit. Internat. Sch., Cairo, Mobinil HQ, Cairo; Master Plan and Expansion Am. Sch. Paris; design Arab Bank HQ, Cairo. Trustee curator Phila. City Inst.; bd. dirs. Marymount Internat. Sch., Paris; bd. mem. World Affairs Coun., Penjer Del Coun. Recipient awards for archtl. designs, Alumni Achievement award Pa. State U., 2000. Mem. AIA, Pa. Soc. Architects, Nat. Acad. Design, Pen-Jer-Del Coun., Phila. Club. Democrat. Roman Catholic. Office: H2L2 Architects/Planners 714 Market St 6th Fl Philadelphia PA 19106-2372 Business E-Mail: eiswerth@hzlz.com.

EITEL, MITCHELL SCOTT, lawyer; b. NYC, Aug. 21, 1962; AB, Columbia U., 1984, JD, 1987. Bar: NY 1988. Assoc. Sullivan & Cromwell, NYC, 1987—96, ptnr., 1996—. Named a Dealmaker of Yr., Am. Lawyer mag., 2007. Fellow: ABA. Office: Sullivan & Cromwell 125 Broad St Fl 28 New York NY 10004-2489 Office Phone: 212-558-4000. Office Fax: 212-558-3588. E-mail: eitelm@sullcrom.com.*

EITNER, JAMES WILLIAM, physician, medical consultant, administrator; b. Phoenix, Mar. 12, 1957; s. Henry C. Jr. and Patty Ann (Lee) E. BS in Biology, BA in Chemistry, Ariz. State U., 1979, BA in Secondary Edn., 1980, MEd, 1982; DO, Coll. Osteo. Medicine Pacific, 1987. Lic. osteo. physician and surgeon, Ariz.; cert. Am. Coll. Osteo. Family Practitioners. Gen. mgr. Cave Creek Rd. Rentals, Phoenix, 1971—79; substitute tchr., 1979—81, 1986—87; student tchr. biology, advanced biology, microbiology Moon Valley HS, Phoenix, 1980; instr. chemistry and gen. sci. Shadow Mountain H.S., Phoenix, 1981—83; adj. instr. Ariz. State U. Portal Sch. Program, Tempe, 1983—84; intern then resident Phoenix Gen. Hosp., 1987—89; with Bell Rd. Med., Phoenix, 1989—90; osteopath Jay Bernstein, D.O., P.C., Phoenix, 1990—93; med. cons. Phoenix, 1994—; med. dir. Cmty. Hospice, Phoenix, 1996, Integra Hospice and Home Health, Phoenix, 1996; dir. clin. svcs. preventive med. svcs. Maricopa County Dept. Pub. Health, 1998—2001; prin. investigator MDS Pharma Svcs., Phoenix, 2002—03, Concertra, Phoenix, 2003—; med. dir. Concentra-Midtown, 2004—. Bd. dirs. Ariz. Sch. Health Assn., 1981-83, treas., 1988-95 (Outstanding Svc. award); asst. team physician Paradise Valley H.S., 1987-89, team physician, 1989-90; chmn. teen pregnancy, sexuality, and sexually transmitted disease com. Ariz. Adolescent Health Coalition, 1991—; preceptor nurse practitioner program Ariz. State U., 1993—; assoc. prof. family practice U. Osteo. Medicine and Health Scis., 1989—; team physician North HS, 1992-. Counselor, camp physician, health and safety com., Camp Geronimo chmn. Boy Scouts Am., 1975-94; chmn. health and edn. subcom. Gov's Adv. Com. on Tobacco Free Ariz., 1989-90; bd. dirs. Lakeside HOA, Gilbert, Ariz., 1994-96, Valvista Lakes C.A., Gilbert, 1995—; vol. Spl. Olympics, 1984—; mem. Phoenix Gen. Hosp. and Ctr. for Sports Medicine and Orthopedics Sports Medicine Clinics, 1979-95, Team of Physicians for Sports Clinics, 1996-; team physician North HS, Phoenix, 1992—; host KKLT/KTAR radio show on Ariz. youth and tobacco, 1990. Home: 1841 E Bay Tree Cir Gilbert AZ 85234-4935 Office Phone: 602-261-7888. E-mail: aquadoc@pol.net.

EITNER, LORENZ EDWIN ALFRED, art historian, educator; b. Brunn, Czechoslovakia, Aug. 27, 1919; came to U.S., 1935, naturalized, 1943; s. Wilhelm and Katherina (Thonet) E.; m. Trudi von Kathrein, Oct. 26, 1946; children: Christy, Kathy, Claudia. AB, Duke U., 1940; MFA, Princeton U., 1948, PhD, 1952. Research unit head Nuremberg War Crimes Trial, 1946-47; from instr. to prof. art U. Minn., Mpls., 1949-63; chmn. dept. art, dir. mus. Stanford U., Calif., 1963-89. Organizer exhbn. works of Gericault for museums of Los Angeles, Detroit and Phila., 1971-72 Author: The Flabellum of Tournus, 1944, Gericault Sketchbooks in the Chicago Art Institute, 1960, Introduction to Art, 1951, Neo-Classicism and Romanticism, 1969, Gericault's Raft of the Medusa, 1972, Gericault, His Life and Work, 1983 (Mitchell prize 1984, C.R. Morey award 1985), An Outline of 19th Century European Painting from David through Cezanne, 1987, Nat. Gallery, Washington, French Nineteenth Century Paintings, 2000; (with others) The Arts in Higher Education, 1963, Stanford Mus. Art, The Drawing Collection, 1993; contbr. articles to profl. jours. Mem. Regional Area Arts Coun. San Francisco Bay Area. Officer OSS, AUS, 1943-46; sect. head ministries divsn. Nuremberg War Crimes Trial, 1946-47. Fulbright grantee, Belgium, 1952-53; Guggenheim fellow, Munich, Federal Republic Germany, 1956-57; recipient Gold Medal for Meritorious Service to Austrian Republic, 1990. Mem. AAAS, Am. Acad. Arts and Scis., Coll. Art Assn. Am. (bd. dirs., past v.p.), Phi Beta Kappa Home: 684 Mirada Ave Stanford CA 94305-8475

EITTREIM, RICHARD MACNUTT, lawyer; b. Neptune, NJ, Feb. 10, 1945; s. Wilbur Lawrence and Leta Blanch (MacNutt) E.; m. Margaret Anne Nolan, June 11, 1967; children: Theodore Scott, Elisabeth Marie, Samantha Leta. AB, Yale U., 1967; JD, U. Va., 1973. Bar: N.J. 1973, U.S. Dist. Ct. N.J. 1973, U.S. Ct. Appeals (3d cir.) 1984, (11th cir.) 1996, U.S. Supreme Ct. 1998. Assoc. McCarter & English, Newark, 1973-80, ptnr., 1980—. Trustee Children's Psychiat. Ctr., Eatontown, N.J., 1977-87, Riverview Hosp. Found., Red Bank, N.J., 1988-93. Mem. ABA, N.J. State Bar Assn., Essex County Bar Assn., Phi Alpha Delta, Sea Bright Lawn Tennis and Cricket Club (pres. 2000-06, bd. govs. 1994-2006), Monmouth Boat Club (treas. 1983-86), Essex Club, Yale Club (pres. 1986-87). Democrat. Presbyterian. Office: McCarter & English 4 Gateway Ctr 100 Mulberry St Newark NJ 07102-4004 Home: 50 Bayside Dr Atlantic Highlands NJ 07716 Office Phone: 973-622-4444. Business E-Mail: reittreim@mccarter.com.

EITZEN, DAVID STANLEY, sociologist, educator; b. Glendale, Calif., Aug. 4, 1934; s. David Donald and Amanda Emma (Heidebrecht) E.; m. Florine Kay Voran, May 29, 1956; children: Keith, Michael, Kelly. AB in History, Bethel Coll., 1956; MS, Emporia State U., 1962; MA in Sociology, U. Kans., 1966, PhD in Sociology, 1968. Recreational therapist Menninger Found., Topeka, Kans., 1956-58; tchr. Galva (Kans.) High Sch., 1958-60, Turner (Kans.) High Sch., 1960-65; asst. prof. sociology U. Kans., 1968-72, asso. prof., 1972-74; prof. sociology Colo. State U., Ft. Collins, 1974-95, prof. emeritus, 1995—. Author: Social Structure and Social Problems, 1974, Sociology of American Sport, 1978, In Conflict and Order: Understanding Society, 1978, Sport in Contemporary Society, 1979, Social Problems, 1980, Elite Deviance, 1981, Criminology, Crime and Criminal Justice, 1985, Diversity in American Families, 1987, Society's Problems: Sources and Consequences, 1989, Crime in the Streets and Crime in the Suites: Perspectives on Crime and Criminal Justice, 1989, The Reshaping of America: Social Consequences of the Changing Economy, 1989, Paths to Homelessness, 1994, Solutions to Social Problems: Lessons from Other Societies, 1997, Fair and Foul: Beyond the Myths and Paradoxes of Sport, 1999, Experiencing Poverty: Voices from the Bottom, 2003, Globalization: The Transformation of Social Worlds, 2005, Solutions to Social Problems from the Top Down, 2007, Solutions to Social Problems from the Bottom Up, 2007, Inequality: Social Class and Its Consequences, 2007; editor Social Sci. Jour., 1978—84; contbr. articles to profl. jours. NDEA fellow, 1965-67 Mem. Internat. Sociol. Assn., Am. Sociol. Assn., Midwest Sociol. Soc., Soc. Study Social Problems, Western Social Sci. Assn., Southwestern Social Sci. Assn., Internat. Com. for Sociology Sport., N.Am. Soc. for Sociology of Sport (pres. 1986-87). Democrat. Mennonite. Home: 303 Lakewood North Newton KS 67117 Personal E-mail: seitzen2@cox.net.

EIZENSTAT, STUART ELLIOT, lawyer, former federal agency administrator; b. Chgo., Jan. 15, 1943; m. Fran Eizenstat; children: Jay, Brian. AB cum laude, U. N.C., 1964, LLD (hon.), 2000; LLB, Harvard U., 1967; LLD (hon.), Yeshiva U., 1998, Weizmann Inst. Sci., 1999, Jewish Theol. Sem., 2000, Hebrew Coll., 2000, Brandeis U., 2001, Fla. Atlantic U., 2002. Bar: Ga. 1967, D.C. 1981. Staff mem. The White House, 1967-68; mem. nat. campaign staff Hubert H. Humphrey, 1968; law clk. U.S. Dist. Ct. (no. dist.) Ga., 1968-70; ptnr. Powell, Goldstein, Frazer & Murphy, Washington, 1970-77, vice chmn., 1981-93; asst. to Pres. for domestic affairs & policy The White House, Washington, 1977—81, exec. dir. domestic policy staff, 1977—81; US amb. to European Union US Dept. State, Brussels, 1993-96, spl. envoy Dept. State Property Claims in Ctrl. Europe, 1995-2001; undersec. for internat. trade US Dept. Commerce, Washington, 1996-97; presdl. envoy for Promotion of Democracy in Cuba The White House, 1996-97; undersec. of state for econ., bus. and agrl. affairs US Dept. State, Washington, 1997-99; alt. gov. The World Bank, 1998-99, Regional Devel. Banks, 1998-99; dep. sec. US Dept. Treasury, Washington, 1999-2001; ptnr., Internat. Trade Practice Group & Trade Regulation Practice Group Covington & Burling, Washington, 2001—; sr. advisor APCO Worldwide, Washington, 2001—. Spl. rep. of Pres. and Sec. of State on Holocaust Issues, 1999-2001; adj. lectr. J.F. Kennedy Sch. Govt., Harvard U., 1981-92; guest scholar Brookings Inst., Washington, 1981; mem. Energy Coord. Coun., Econ. Policy Group, 1977-81, Pres. Bush task force on U.S. Internat. Broadcasting, 1991; head U.S. del. CSCE Econ. Forum, 1994; lectr. coll., bus. and civic groups; bd. dirs. Mirant Corp., Black Rock Funds; mem. internat. adv. bd. Coca-Cola, 2001-; chmn. internat. bd. govs. Weizmann Inst. Sci., 2002—. Author: Imperfect Justice: Slave Labor, Looted Assets and the Unfinished Business of World War II, 2003, paperback edit., 2004; co-author: Andrew Young: The Path to History, 1973, Environmental Auditing Handbook, 1984; co-editor: The American Agenda: Report to the 41st President of the United States, 1988, reprint, 1989; contbr. articles to profl. jours. and newspapers. V.p. Jewish Publ. Soc., 1981-85; chmn. Inst. U.S. Jewish-Israeli Rels., 1982-86; bd. dirs. Woodrow Wilson Ctr. for Internat. Scholars, 1978-87, Jerusalem Found., 1992-93, Eurasia Found., 1993; pres. Greater Washington Jewish Cmty. Ctr., 1989-91; mem. exec. com. Ctr. for Dem. Policy, 1982-93; bd. visitors U. N.C., Chapel Hill, 1987-90, bd. trustees Ctr. for Jewish Studies; co-dir. The Am. Agenda (with Pres. Ford and Pres. Carter), 1991; trustee Jerusalem Inst. Mgmt., 1987-93; mem. coun. Harvard Law Sch. Assn., 1988-92, Gov.'s Commn. on Fed. Funding, Commonwealth of Va., 1986, Com. on Federalism and Nat. Purpose, 1984-85; chmn. Econ. and Budget Strategy Com., Montgomery County Coun., 1986; v.p., bd. dirs. Am. Assocs., Ben-Gurion U. of the Negev, N.Y.C., 1981-89; trustee Washington Inst. for Jewish Leadership and Values, 1988—, Brandeis U., 1991—; commr. Commn. on Jewish Edn. in N.Am., 1988-90; v.p. Atlanta Bur. Jewish Edn., 1973-76; mem. exec. com. Atlanta Jewish Cmty. Ctr., 1970-76; mem. B'nai Brith Youth Commn., Washington, 1981-82; bd. dirs. United Synagogues Am., 1981-84.; internat. bd. dirs. Weizmann Inst., 1989-93, chmn. bd. govs., 2002—; active in Dem. party and polit. campaigns. Decorated Legion of Honor (France); pub. policy scholar Woodrow Wilson Ctr. Internat. Scholars, 2001; recipient Man of Yr. award Nat. Capital Assn., State Dept. award for Pub. Svcs., 1996, 99, B'nai B'rith Lodges, 1982, Outstanding Svc. to Summer Youth Program U.S. Dept. Labor, 1980, Outstanding Svc. award Hebrew Aid Immigration Soc., 1980, Outstanding Svc. award Opportunities Industrialization Ctrs., 1979, award Washington Internat. Bus. Coun., 1978, award Nat. Coalition Involved People, 1977, Young Man of Yr. award Am. Assn. Jewish Edn., 1973-74, Leadership award Acad. Jewish Religion, 1989, Tree of Life award Hadassah, Boston, 1989, Myrtle Wreath award Fla. Atlantic Region Hadassah, 1991, Benjamin Cardozo Professionalism award Atlanta Jewish Fedn., 1992, Export Fin. award Coalition for Employment Through Exports, 1993, award for pub. svc. Sec. of State, 1996, Moral Statesman award Anti-Defamation League, 1997, Phillip Klutznick B'nai B'rith award for Outstanding Pub. Svc., 1996, award for transatlantic svc. European Inst., 1997, Myrtle Wreath award Hadassah, 1997, 98, Transatlantic Svc. award European Inst., 1997, award for courage and conscience Israeli Knesset, 1998, Leadership award Sec. of State, 1999, B'nai B'rith Leadership award, 2000, Auschwitz Holocaust Ctr. award, 2000, Washington Inst. Jewish Leadership and Values, 2001, award for leadership Sec. of State, 1999, Alexander Hamilton award Sec. of Treasury, 2001, Humanitarian award Inst. Leadership and Values, 2001, knight comdr.'s cross Fed. Rep. Germany, 2002, Leadership award United Jewish Cmtys., 2002, Great Negotiator award Harvard Negotiation Group, 2003, medal of honor Czech Coun. Victims of Nazism, 2005. Fellow Nat. Acad. Pub. Adminstn., Ctr. for Excellence in Govt.; mem. ABA (spl. com. on lawyers in govt., mem. com. govt. stds. 1992-93), Atlanta Bar Assn., D.C. Bar Assn., Ga. Bar Assn., U.S. C. of C. (internat. policy com. 1982-89), Nat. Fgn. Trade Coun. (internat. trade com.), Washington Policy Coun. (Internat. Mgmt. and Devel. Inst.), Phi Beta Kappa, Phi Eta Sigma. Democrat. Jewish. Office: Covington & Burding 1201 Pennsylvania Ave NW Washington DC 20004-2401 Office Phone: 202-662-5745. Office Fax: 202-662-6291. Business E-Mail: seizenstat@cov.com.

EK, ALAN RYAN, forester, educator; b. Mpls., Sept. 5, 1942; BS in Forestry, U. Minn., St. Paul, 1964, MS, 1965; PhD, Oreg. State U., Corvallis, 1969. Rsch. officer Can. Dept. Forestry and Rural Devel., Sault Ste Marie, Ont., Canada, 1966-69; from asst. prof. to assoc. prof. forestry U. Wis., Madison, 1969-77; from assoc. prof. to prof. U. Minn., St. Paul, 1977—, head dept. forest resources, 1984—. Mem. forestry rsch. adv. coun. USDA, 1994—96, 1998—99, chair, 1998—99; cons. in field. Contbr. chapters to books, articles to profl. jours. Fulbright scholar, Finland, 1997. Fellow: Soc. Am. Foresters (various coms., chmn. forest sci. and tech. bd. 1989—90); mem.: AAAS, Am. Soc. Photogrammetry and Remote Sensing, Am. Statis. Assn., Nat. Assn. Profl. Forestry Schs. and Colls. (chmn. rsch. com. 1993—95, 1999—2002), Sigma Xi, Gamma Sigma Delta, Xi Sigma Pi. Avocations: reading, sports. Home: 4744 Kevin Ln Saint Paul MN 55126-5849 Office: U Minn Dept Forest Resources Saint Paul MN 55108 Office Phone: 612-624-3400. Business E-Mail: aek@umn.edu.

EKANGER, LAURIE, retired state official, consultant; b. Salt Lake City, Mar. 4, 1949; d. Bernard and Mary (Dearth) E.; m. William J. Shupe, Nov. 6, 1973; children: Ben, Robert. BA in English, U. Oreg., 1973. Various pos. Mont. State Employment & Tng. Divsn., Helena, 1975-80, dep. adminstr., 1980-82; adminstr. Mont. State Purchasing Divsn., Helena, 1982-85, Mont. State Personnel Divsn., Helena, 1985-93; labor commr. Mont. Dept. Labor and Ind., Helena, 1993-97; dir. Mont. Dept. Pub. Health and Human Svcs., 1997-2000; rsch. , analysis and pers. mgmt. projects, 2000—. Council chair State Employee Group Benefits Coun., 1985-93; bd. dirs. Pub. Employee Retirement Bd., 1988; mem. various state adv. couns. health and human svcs. Home: 80 Pinecrest Rd Clancy MT 59634-9505 Personal E-mail: ekanger@bresnan.net.

EKBATANI, GLAYOL, language educator, director, writer; b. Tehran, Iran; d. Saed and Parvin (Sohai) E. PhD, U. Ill., 1981. Dir., prof. English 2d lang. program U. Maine, Orano, 1987-90; dir. English 2d lang., bilingual programs C.C. Phila., 1990-92; dir., prof. English 2d lang. programs St. John's U., Jamaica, N.Y., 1992—. Rschr. Georgetown U., Washington, 1986-87. Author: Learner Directed Assessment, 1999; contbr. articles to profl. jours. Mem. Nat. Assn. Fgn. Students Washington, Tchrs. English to Spkrs. of Other Langs. (pres. 1991-92). Home: 301 E 79th St Apt 16 New York NY 10021-0951 Office: St John's U 8000 Utopia Pkwy Rm 377 Jamaica NY 11432-1343 Office Phone: 718-990-6097.

EKDAHL, JON NELS, lawyer; b. Topeka, Nov. 15, 1942; s. Oscar S. and Dorothy O. (Ekdahl) M.; m. Marcia Opp, May 24, 1975; children: Kirsten, Erika, Kristofer. AB magna cum laude, Harvard U., 1964, LLB, 1968; MS in Econs., London Sch. Econs., 1965. Bar: Ill. 1969, U.S. Ct. Appeals (7th cir.) 1981, U.S. Supreme Ct. 1981. Assoc. Sidley & Austin, Chgo., 1968—73, ptnr., 1973—75; mng. ptnr., gen. counsel Andersen Worldwide SC, Chgo., 1975—2000; sr. v.p., gen. counsel AMA, Chgo., 2001—. With USAR, 1968-74. Mem. ABA, Chgo. Bar Assn., Mid-Am. Club, Chgo. Club. Office: Am Med Assn 515 N State St Chicago IL 60610 Business E-Mail: jon.ekdahl@ama-assn.org.

EKICI, KIVANC, aerospace engineer, researcher; s. Enver and Mualla Ekici; m. Ebru Sahin Ekici; children: Defne, Arda Defne. BSc, Mid. East Tech. U., Ankara, Turkey, 1994, MSc, 1997; PhD, Purdue U., West Lafayette, Ind., 2001. Rsch., tchg. asst. Mid. East Tech. U., 1994—97; rsch. asst. Purdue U., 1997—2000, tchg. asst., 2000—01; rsch. assoc. Duke U., Durham, NC, 2001—. Contbr. articles to profl. jours. Recipient A. H. Ismail Interdisciplinary Program Doctoral Rsch. award, Purdue U., 2000, Magoon Excellence in Tchg. award, 2001; fellow, NATO, 1997—98. Mem.: ASME (mem. structures and dynamics com. mem. 2006—07), AIAA, Sigma Gamma Tau, Sigma Xi. Achievements include first to implementation of the harmonic balance technique to a multistage turbomachinery CFD code; development of a time-linearized CFD code for flutter analysis of multistage turbomachinery; new algorithms for efficient parallelization of Rotorcraft CFD codes. Office: Duke Univ 144 Hudson Hall Box 90300 Durham NC 27708-0300 Home Phone: 919-493-7161; Office Phone: 919-660-5348. Office Fax: 919-660-8963. Business E-Mail: ekici@duke.edu.

EKMAN, RICHARD H., educational association administrator; b. NYC, Oct. 1, 1945; s. Sheldon Victor and Judith (Saturen) E.; m. Caroline Read, June 15, 1975; children: Nathaniel Paul, Peter Sheldon Read. AB magna cum laude, Harvard U., 1966, AM, 1967, PhD, 1972. Asst. to provost U. Mass., Boston, 1971—73; dep. dir. divsn. edn. progs. NEH, Washington, 1973—78, dir. divsn. edn. progs., 1982—85, dir. divsn. rsch. progs., 1985—91; v.p., dean Hiram Coll., Ohio, 1978—82; sec. Andrew W. Mellon Found., NYC, 1991—99; v.p. progs. Atlantic Philanthropies, 1999—2000; pres. Coun. Ind. Colls., 2000—. Mem. nat. adv. com. Yale-New Haven Tchrs. Inst., 1984—, Johns Hopkins U. Press. Mem. Harvard Grad. Sch. Alumni Coun., 1997—. Mem. Harvard Club NYC, Cosmos Club. Office: Coun Ind Colls One Dupont Cir Ste 320 Washington DC 20036 Office Phone: 202-466-7230. E-mail: rekman@cic.nche.edu.*

EKSIOGLU, BURAK, engineering educator; b. Kadirli, Osmaniye, Turkey, Feb. 14, 1972; s. Galip and Inceser Eksioglu; m. Sandra Duni Eksioglu, Aug. 14, 1999; children: Deniz, Erol. BS, Bogazici U., 1994; MS, U. Warwick, 1996; PhD, U. Fla., Gainesville, 2002. Orgn. devel. specialist Marsa KJS, Adana, Turkey, 1995—96; rsch. asst. U. of Fla., Gainesville, 1997—2002; vis. asst. prof. Cleve. State U., 2002—03; asst. prof. Miss. State U., Mississippi State, 2003—. Grantee, Dept. Homeland Security, 2005, Dept. Agr., 2005, Dept. Transp., 2005. Mem.: The Am. Soc. Engring. Edn., Inst. Indsl. Engrs., Inst. Ops. Rsch. and Mgmt. Sci., Tau Beta Pi. Avocations: running, travel. Office: Mississippi State Univ 260 McCain Hall PO Box 9542 Mississippi State MS 39762 Home Phone: 662-320-2130; Office Phone: 662-325-7625. Office Fax: 662-325-7618.

EKSIOGLU, SANDRA DUNI, industrial engineering educator; b. Tirana, Albania, Sept. 10, 1972; d. Perikli and Leonora Duni; m. Burak Eksioglu, Aug. 14, 1999; children: Deniz, Erol. PhD, U. Fla., Gainesville, 2002. Asst. prof. mgmt. U. Evansville, Ind., 2003—04; asst. prof. Miss. State U., Starkville, 2005—. Office: Mississippi State U PO Box 9542 Starkville MS 39759 Office Phone: 662-325-9220. Business E-Mail: sde47@ise.msstate.edu.

EL-AASSER, MOHAMED S., engineering educator, academic administrator; b. Egypt, Feb. 10, 1943; naturalized, US; married; 2 children. BS, Alexandria U., Egypt, 1962, MS, 1966; PhD, McGill U., Montreal, Can., 1972. Post-doctoral fellow Ctr. for Surface and Coatings Rsch. Lehigh U., 1972—74, asst. prof. dept. chem. engring., 1974—78, assoc. prof., 1978—82, prof., 1982—, co-dir. Emulsion Polymers Institute, 1978—89, dir., 1989—, dir. Ctr. for Polymer Sci. and Engring., 1988—2001, dir. Polymer Interfaces Ctr., 1991—96, Iacocca Endowed Chair of Engring. and Applied Sci., 1992—2001, chmn. dept. chem. engring., 1996—2001, dean P.C. Rossin Coll. of Engring. and Applied Sci., 2001—04, provost, v.p. acad. affairs, 2004—. With Centre National de Recherche Scientifique Laboratoire Materiaux Organique, Vernaison, France, 1983—84; bd. mem. Pa. Infrastructure Tech. Alliance, 2001—; bd. dirs. Discovery Ctr., 2004—.

Author: over 300 papers. Co-recipient NASA Inventor of Yr. Award, 1985; recipient Kuwait Award, 1983, Best Paper Award, Tech. Transfer Workshop, Coun. Chem. Rsch., 1987, Eleanor and Joseph Libsch Rsch. Award, Lehigh U., 1988, O. Hugo Schuck Best Paper Award, Am. Automatic Control Coun., 1998, R.R. and E.C. Hillman Award, Lehigh U., 1999, Roy W. Tess Award in Coatings, Am. Chem. Soc. Divsn. of Polymeric Materials Sci. and Engring., 2002. Mem.: Assn. Engring. Colls. Pa. (chair 2003—04), Am. Chem. Soc. (divsn. polymeric materials sci. and engring. 2007), Am. Soc. Engring. Edn. (Engring. Dean's Coun. 2001—), Am. Inst. Chem. Engineers, AAAS, Coun. Chem. Rsch., Sigma Xi, Phi Beta Delta (Beta Pi Chpt., Faculty Award 1998). Achievements include 12 patents in field. Office: Lehigh U Provost Office 27 Memorial Dr W Bethlehem PA 18015 Business E-Mail: mse0@lehigh.edu.

ELACHI, CHARLES, aerospace engineer; b. Beirut, Apr. 18, 1947; m. Valerie Gifford; 2 children. BS, U. Grenoble, France, 1968; MS, Calif. Inst. Tech., 1969, PhD in Elec. Sci., 1971; MBA, U. So. Calif., 1978; MS, UCLA, 1983. Rsch. fellow Calif. Inst. Tech., Pasadena, 1971-74, leader Radar Remote Sensing Team, 1974-80, asst. lab. dir. space and sci. instruments, 1987-95, prof. elec. engring., 1982—2000, dir. & v.p., 2001—; sr. rsch. scientist CIT Jet Propulsion Lab., Pasadena, 1981—87, dir. space and earth sci. programs, 1995—2000, dir., 2000—. Prin. investigator NASA, 1973-87, mem. Solar Sys. Exploration Com. Coun., 1988—, Astrophysics Coun., 1988—; mem. Electromagnetic Acad., 1990-95; participant in archeological expeditions; spkr. in field. Contbr. over 200 articles to profl. jours.; mem. editl. adv. bd. Scientific American Chmn. JPL United Way Campaign. Recipient Prof. R.W.P. King award for outstanding contbrn. in field of electromagnetics, 1973, Nev. Medal Outstanding Achievement in Sci. and Engring., Desert Rsch. Inst., 1995, Wernher Von Braun award, 2000, Takeda award, 2002, Mem. AIAA (Dryden Lecturship in Rsch., 2000), NAE(councillor 2007-), IEEE (Geosensing and Remote Sensing Disting. Achievement award 1987, Engring. Excellence medal 1992), Am. Astronautical Soc., Electromagnetic Soc., Am. Geophys. Union, Planetary Soc., Internat. Acad. Astronautics, Sigma Xi. Achievements include development of a series of imaging radar systems for the Space Shuttle that allowed scientists to study the earth and other planets of the solar system; patents in field. Avocations: skiing, woodworking, travel, history. Office: Jet Propulsion Lab MS 180-704 4800 Oak Grove Dr Pasadena CA 91109-8001 also: M/C JPL 180-904 Pasadena CA 91109 E-mail: charles.elachi@jpl.nasa.gov.*

ELAM, FRED ELDON, retired military officer; b. Seminole, Okla., July 10, 1937; s. Jack Eldon Elam and Maye (Gaskill) E.; m. Judy Teller, Feb. 21, 1959; children: Jacqueline Marie Elam Kabat, Justin Eldon. BS, U. Ark., 1960; MBA, Mich. State U., 1964; grad. strategy mgmt. and naval ops., Naval War Coll., 1977; grad., Harvard Grad. Sch. Bus. Admin., 1998. Commd. 2d lt. U.S. Army, 1960, advanced through grades to maj. gen., 1986, with Div. G-4, 101st Airborne (Air Assault) Fort Campbell, Ky., 1976-77, comdr. Materiel Support Ctr. Waegwan, Republic of Korea, 1977-79, dir. programs and evaluation Army Materiel Command Alexandria, Va., 1979-82; comdg. gen. 19th Support Command, Taegu, Republic of Korea, 1982-84; dir. mgmt. Hdqrs. Dept. Army, Washington, 1984-85; chief U.S. Army Transp., Hdqrs. Transp. Ctr. Fort Eustis, Va., 1985-88; comdr. Joint U.S. Mil. Mission for Aid to Turkey Ankara, 1988-90; asst. dep. chief of staff for logistics, Dept. Army Washington, 1990—2003; v.p. profl. tech. svcs. Advancia Corp., Arlington, Va., 1993—2002; pres. Elam Consulting, 2003—. Mem. lifetime staff and faculty Army Logistics Mgmt. Ctr., Fort Lee, Va., 1971—, Va. Mil. Commn., 1986-88; disting. mem. Transp. Corps Rgt., U.S. Army; counselor Sr. Corps. Ret. Exec. Decorated D.S.M., Def. Superior Svc. medal, Legion of Merit, Bronze Star with two oak leaf clusters, Meritorious Svc. medal with two oak leaf clusters, Air medal, Army Commendation medal with three oak leaf clusters, Armed Forces expeditionary medal, Vietnam Svc. medal with four oak leaf clusters, Overseas Svc. ribbon with "4" device, Republic of Vietnam campaign medal, Republic of Korea Svc. medal, Medal of Merit of Turkish Armed Forces, Meritorious Svc. medal; named to US Army Transp. Corps Hall of Fame, 2005. Mem. Assn. US Army, Soc. of 173d Airborne Brigade, Res. Officers Assn. (pres.), Transp. Corps Regimental Assn. (hon. col.), Beta Gamma Sigma. Avocations: running, reading, military history. Office Phone: 703-644-0753. Personal E-mail: elamjf@msn.com.

ELAM, MATTHEW, industrial engineer, educator; BS in Math., U. Tex., Tyler, 1991, MS in Math., 1994; PhD, Okla. State U., 2001. Asst. prof. indsl. engring., mem. grad. faculty applied stats. U. Ala., Tuscaloosa, 2001—07; assoc. prof. dept. indsl. engring., tech. Tex. A&M U., Commerce, 2007—. Contbr. numerous articles to profl. jours. and conf. proceedings. Recipient Inst. for Ops. Rsch. and Mgmt. Scis. award for outstanding Tchg. Asst., Okla. State U., 1999, 2001; grantee, George C. Marshall Space Flight Ctr., NASA, 2003—04, Am. Cast Iron Pipe Co., 2004—05, Univ. Transp. Ctr. Ala., 2006, Coun. Cmty.-Based Partnerships, 2007; Eugene L. and Doris L. Miller Disting. Grad. fellow, Okla. State U., 1998—2001. Mem.: Am. Soc. Quality (cert. quality engr.), Alpha Chi Nat., Alpha Pi Mu, Tau Beta Pi.

ELANAYAR, SUNIL K., research and development engineer; arrived in U.S., 1986; s. Sivadasan Arangott and Komalam Sivadasan; m. Seema S. Nair, Dec. 27, 1996; 1 child, Adira Nair. BS in Tech., ITT, Delhi, India, 1986; MS, U. Ala., Tuscaloosa, 1988; PhD, Purdue U., West Lafayette, Ind., 1993. Rsch. fellow Purdue U., 1993—94; sr. engr. Computervision, Pune, India, 1994—96; dir. Gentech Corp., Tokyo, 1996—98; sr. rsch. engr. Caice Corp., Tampa, Fla., 1998—2000; sr. engr. Knowledge Tech., Lexington, Mass., 2000—. Fellow David Ross Found., West Lafayette, 1991—93. Contbr. articles to sci. jours. Achievements include research in neural networks in manufacturing process monitoring knowledge based engineering. Avocations: travel, tennis, photography. Home: 9301 Avondale Rd NE # B1009 Redmond WA 98052 Office: Dassault Systems 10330 David Taylor Dr Charlotte NC 28262

ELANDER, RICHARD PAUL, microbiologist, consultant; b. Worcester, Mass., Sept. 17, 1932; s. Arthur Waldemar and Edith Alma Louise (Engstrand) E.; m. Barbara Ann Sudz, Feb. 8, 1958; children: Tracy, Richard, Ronald BS with honors, U. Detroit, 1955, MS, 1956; PhD, U. Wis., 1960; postgrad., U. Minn., 1965—66. Rsch. scientist Eli Lilly and Co., Indpls., 1960-67; assoc. dir. Wyeth Labs., West Chester, Pa., 1967-72, Smith Kline and French, Phila., 1972-75; dir. fermentation devel. Bristol-Myers Squibb Co., Syracuse, NY, 1975-80, sr. dir. biotech. and rsch. devel., 1980-83, v.p. biotech., 1983-97; cons. to biotech./pharm. industry, 1997—; sci. adv. Nereus Pharm. Inc., 1999—2005. Lectr. Butler U., Indpls., 1965-66, Rensselaer Poly. Inst., 1983-88; rsch. prof. Syracuse U., 1983-97; biotech. adv. bd., Dartmouth, MIT, Cornell; mem. adv. bd., Engring. and Sci., Detroit Mercy Univ., 1997—, Coll. Agr. and Life Scis., Cornell U., 1998 Mem. editl. bd. Biotech. Letters, 1985-97, Jour. Indsl. Microbiology, 1985-94, Applied and Environ. Microbiology, 1974-83; contbr. articles to profl. jours., also chpts. to books in field; patentee in field Fellow Am. Acad. Microbiology, Am. Inst. Chemists, Soc. Indsl. Microbiology (sec. 1968, pres. 1974, Charles Thom award 1984); mem. AAAS, Am. Soc. Microbiology (chmn. divsn. 1977), Am. Chem. Soc., Lions (bd. dirs. 1970-73), N.Y. Acad. Sci., Sigma Xi (v.p. Syracuse chpt. 1991, pres. Syracuse chpt. 1992) Avocations: music, skiing, gardening, writing. Home and Office: 318 Gravilla St La Jolla CA 92037-6006 Office Phone: 858-551-4146. Personal E-mail: relander1@san.rr.com.

ELARABY, NABIL A., former judge, former diplomat; b. Cairo, Mar. 15, 1935; m. Nadia Teymour; children: May, Marwan, Hisham. Licencie en Droit, Cairo U., Egypt; LLM in Internat. Law, NYU, U.S.A., JSD. Legal advisor to Egyptian del. UN Mid. East Peace Conf., Ministry of Fgn. Affairs, Geneva, 1973-75; counsellor to mission from Egypt UN, Geneva, 1974-76, amb., dep. permanent rep. of Egypt NYC, 1978-81, 91-99, amb. extraordinary and plenipotentiary, permanent rep. of Egypt Geneva, 1987-91, permanent rep. NYC, 1991—99; legal advisor, dir. legal and treaties dept. Ministry of Fgn. Affairs, Geneva, 1976-78, 83-87; Egyptian amb. India, 1981-83; arbitrator (Suez Canal dispute) ICC Internat. Ct. of Arbitration, Paris, 1989—92; judge Jud. Tribunal Orgn. Arb Petroleum, 1990; commr. UN Compensation Commn., 1999—2001; mem. Internat. Ct. Justice, The Hague, Netherlands, 2001—06. Ptnr. Zaki Hashem & Ptnrs., Attys. at Law; mem. bd. Internat. Coun. Arbitration for Sport, Stockholm Internat. Peace Rsch. Inst.; mem. governing coun. UNIDROIT; rep. Egypt in UN orgns. including The Gen. Assembly, Security Coun., Econ. and Social Coun., Human Rights Commn., 1966—; head Egyptian Del. UN Conf. on Disarmament, 1987—91; leader Egyptian Delegation to Egyptian-Israeli Arbitration Tribunal Taba Talks, 1986—89; former chair numerous UN coms. and working groups; pres. Security Coun., 1996; lectr. The Hague acad. of Internat. Law, Columbia U., NYU, Duke U., Yale U., The Egyptian Soc. Internat. Law, Am. Soc. Internat. Law, many others. Contbr. to profl. jours. and internat. law publs. Adlai Stevenson fellow UN Inst. for Tgn. and Rsch., 1968, Spl. fellow, 1973. Mem. Egyptian Soc. Internat. Law (bd. dirs.). Address: 23 Kasr El Nil St Cairo 11211 Egypt

ELASMAR, MICHAEL, director, educator; m. Kathleen Sim, July 11, 1998. PhD, Mich. State U., East Lansing, 1993. Asst. prof. Boston U., 1993—99, dir. Comms. Rsch. Ctr., 1994—, assoc. prof., 1999—. Pres. U. Rsch. Consultants, Waltham, Mass., 1993—99. Editor: (scholarly book) The Impact of International Television; founding editor: Am. Jour. Media Psychology; contbr. articles to scholarly jours., chapters to books. Mem.: Assn. for Edn. in Journalism and Mass Comm. (chair of internat. comm. divsn. 1998—99). Achievements include development of Theoretical Model of Susceptibility to Imported Media. Avocations: fishing, swimming, travel. Office: Boston Univ Com Rsch Ctr 640 Commonwealth Ave Boston MA 02215 Office Phone: 617-358-1299. Business E-Mail: elasmar@bu.edu.

ELBAUM, CHARLES, physicist, educator, researcher; b. May 15, 1926; married; 3 children. MASc, U. Toronto, 1952, PhD in Applied Sci., 1954; MA (hon.), Brown U., 1961. Rsch. fellow in metal physics U. Toronto, 1954-57, Harvard U., 1957-59; asst. prof. applied physics Brown U., Providence, 1959-61; assoc. prof. physics, 1961-63, prof. physics, 1963—, chmn. dept. physics, 1980-86, also Hazard prof. physics, 1991—. Cons. to industry. Fellow Am. Phys. Soc.; mem. AIME, AAAS, Soc. Neurosci. Office: Brown U Dept Physics PO Box 1843 Providence RI 02912-1843 Business E-Mail: elbaum@physics.brown.edu.

ELBAZ, ALBER, apparel designer; b. Casablaca, Morocco, 1961; Grad., Shenkar Coll. Engring. & Design, Tel Aviv, 1986. Asst. Geoffrey Beene, 1989—97; head prêt-à-porter design Guy Laroche, 1997—98; women's prêt-à-porter design Yves Saint Laurent, 1998—99; designer Krizia Top, Milan, 1999—2001; creative dir. Jeanne Lanvin SA, Paris, 2001—02, head designer, 2002—. Served with Israeli Def. Forces. Named knight Legion d'Honneur, Pres. French Republic, 2006; named one of The World's Most Influential People, TIME mag., 2007; recipient Internat. award, Coun. of Fashion Designers of Am., 2005. Office: Jeanne Lanvin SA 15 rue de Faubourg Saint-Honoré 75008 Paris France Office Phone: 003144713121.*

EL-BAZ, FAROUK, science administrator, educator; b. Zagazig, Egypt, Jan. 1, 1938; came to U.S., 1967, naturalized, 1970; s. El-Sayed Mohammed and Zahia Abul-Ata (Hammouda) El-B.; m. Catherine Patricia O'Leary, 1963; children: Monira, Soraya, Karima, Fairouz. BSc, Ain Shams U., 1958; MS, U. Mo., 1961; PhD, U. Mo. and MIT, 1964; DSc (hon.), New England Coll., 1989; PhD (hon.), Mansoura U., 2004, Am. U., Cairo, 2004. Demonstrator geology dept. Assiut U., Egypt, 1958-60; lectr. Mineralogy-Petrography Inst., U. Heidelberg, Germany, 1964-65; geologist exploration dept. Pan Am.-UAR Oil Co., Egypt, 1966; supr. lunar exploration Bellcomm and Bell Tel. Labs., Washington, 1967-72; rsch. dir. Center for Earth and Planetary Studies, Nat. Air and Space Mus., Smithsonian Instn., Washington, 1973-82; v.p. sci. and tech. Itek Optical Sys., Litton Industries, Lexington, Mass., 1982-86; cons. geology, prof. geology and geophysics U. Utah, 1975-77; prof. geology Ain Shams U., Egypt, 1976-81, 95—; sci. adviser Pres. Anwar Sadat of Egypt, 1978-81; sr. advisor Nat. Rsch. Inst. for Astronomy and Geophysics, Helwan, Egypt, 1996—; dir. Ctr. for Remote Sensing Boston U., 1986—. Author: Say It in Arabic, 1968, Astronaut Observations from the Apollo-Soyuz Mission, 1977, Egypt as Seen by Landsat, 1979, The Geology of Egypt: An Annotated Bibliography, 1984; co-author: Coprolites: An Annotated Bibliography, 1968, Glossory of Mining Geology, 1970, The Moon as Viewed by Lunar Orbiter, 1970, Apollo Over the Moon: A View from Orbit, 1978; co-editor: Apollo-Soyuz Test Project Summary Science Report: Earth Observations and Photography, 1979, Desert Landforms of Southwest Egypt: A Basis for Comparison with Mars, 1982, Physics of Desertification, 1986, Remote Sensing and Resource Exploration, 1989, Sand Transport and Desertification in Arid Lands, 1990, The Gulf War and the Environment, 1994, Atlas of State of Kuwait from Satellite Images, 2000, Wadis of Oman, 2002, Sultanate of Oman, Satellite Image Atlas, 2004; editor: Deserts and Arid Lands, 1984; contbr. articles to profl. jours. Decorated Order of Merit 1st class Egypt; recipient certificate merit U.S. Bur. Mines, 1961, Exceptional Sci. Achievement medal NASA, 1971, Alumni Achievement award U. Mo., 1972, Honor citation Assn. Arab-Am. U. Grads., 1973, Outstanding Contbns. to Sci. and Space Tech. award Am.-Arab Anti-Discrimination Com., 1995, Achievement award Egyptian-Am. Profl. Soc., 1995, Human Needs award Am. Assn. Petroleum Geologists, 1996. Fellow: AAAS (Pub. Understanding of Sci. and Tech. award 1992), Geol. Soc. Am. (cert. commendation 1973), Royal Astron.; mem.: Desert Rsch. Inst. (Nev. medal 2003), Nat. Acad. Engring., Internat. Inst. of Boston (Golden Door award 1992), World Aerospace Edn. Orgn. (Cert. of Merit 1973), Explorers Club, Sigma Xi. Office: Boston U Ctr Remote Sensing 725 Commonwealth Ave Boston MA 02215-1401 E-mail: farouk@bu.edu.

ELBERGER, RONALD EDWARD, lawyer; b. Newark, Mar. 13, 1945; s. Morris and Clara (Denes) Elberger; m. Rena Ann Brodey, Feb. 15, 1975; children: Seth, Rebecca. AA, George Washington U., 1964, BA, 1966; JD, Am. U., 1969. Bar: Md. 1969, D.C. 1970, Ind. 1971, U.S. Ct. Appeals (7th cir.) 1971, U.S. Supreme Ct. 1973. Atty. Balt. Legal Aid Bur., 1969—70; chief counsel Legal Svcs. Orgn., Indpls., 1970—72; ptnr. Elberger & Stanton, Indpls., 1974—76; assoc. Bose, McKinney & Evans, LLP, Indpls., 1972—74, 1976—80, ptnr., 1980—; asst. sec. Chip Ganassi Racing Teams, Inc., 1998—, gen. counsel, 2005—. V.p. Worldwide Slacks, Inc., 1984—92, Cardboard Shoe Prodns., Inc., 1989—93; v.p., gen. counsel Emmis Comm. Corp., 1986—98, asst. sec., v.p., litig. counsel, 1998—2002. Mem., v.p. Med. Licensing Bd., Ind., 1982—98; pres., chmn. bd. dirs. Ind. Civil Liberties Union, Indpls., 1972—77, bd. dirs., 1980—82; mem. nat. coun. media and pub. affairs George Washington U., 2000—; bd. dirs. Jewish Cmty. Rels. Coun., 1997—2000, ACLU, NYC, 1972—77; trustee Children's Mus. Indpls., 1994—2003, Disting. advisor, 2003—; bd. dirs. Flanner Ho. Indpls., Inc., 1999—2007. Fellow Reginald Heber Smith, U. Pa., 1969—71. Fellow: Ind. Bar Found., Indpls. Bar Found.; mem.: ABA, DC Bar, Bar Assn. 7th Cir., Ind. Bar Assn. Democrat. Jewish. Avocations: fishing, music, gardening. Office: Bose McKinney & Evans LLP 2700 First Indiana Pla 135 N Pennsylvania St Indianapolis IN 46204-2400 Home Phone: 317-251-0289; Office Phone: 317-684-5195. Business E-Mail: relberger@boselaw.com.

ELBLE, JOSEPH M., computer scientist, researcher; s. Rodger Jacob and Suzanne Elble; m. Leslie Thoreen Elble, Aug. 7, 2004. BS with honors in Computer Sci., U. Ill., Urbana-Champaign, 2002, MS in Computer Sci., 2007, MS in Indsl. Engring., 2007. Rsch. asst. Nat. Ctr. Supercomputing Applications, Champaign, Ill., 2001—02; database engr. FactSet Rsch. Sys., Inc., Stamford, Conn., 2002—03, product engr., 2004—04, investment banking software engring. intern NY, 2006; rsch. asst. U. Ill., Urbana, 2004—. Grantee, Coll. of Engring., U. Ill., Urbana-Champaign, 2006; Edmund J. James scholar, 2002. Mem.: Int. for Ops. Rsch. and Mgmt. Scis., Tau Beta Pi. Roman Catholic. Home Phone: 217-418-9239.

ELCANO, MARY S., lawyer; BA cum laude, Lynchburg Coll., 1971; JD, Cath. U., Washington, 1976. Litigation atty. Balt. Legal Aide Bur., 1976; staff atty. Office Solicitor Dept. Labor, 1979; gen. trial and appellate atty. Office Labor Law U.S. Postal Svc., 1982, exec. dir. Office EEO, 1984, regional dir. human resources N.E. region, 1987, sr. v.p., gen. counsel, 1992-99, exec. v.p., gen. counsel, 1999-2000; ptnr. Sidley Austin Brown & Wood LLP, Washington, 2000—03; gen. counsel, corp. sec. ARC, Washington, 2003—. Office: ARC 430 17th St NW Washington DC 20006 Office Phone: 202-303-5422. Business E-Mail: ElcanoM@usa.redcross.org.

ELCIK, ELIZABETH MABIE, fashion illustrator; b. Bklyn., Sept. 16, 1933; d. Cornelius Peter and Anna Julia (Cunningham) Mabie; m. John Joseph Elcik, Apr. 20, 1963. Grad., Jamesine Franklin Sch. Profl. Arts, NYC, 1954; student in painting, NYU; student life class, Art Students League, NYC, Alliance of Queens Artists, 2003. Fashion illustrator Vogue patterns Conde Nast Publs., 1954-59; freelance illustrator various clients, NYC, 1960-74; fashion illustrator Butterick Fashion Mktg. Co., NYC, 1974-82, McCall Pattern Co., NYC, 1982—2001. Monitor profl. sketch classes, NYC, 1962—79. Exhibitions include Cedar House Gallery, 2004, Alliance Queens Artists, 2005, Weill-Cornell Med. Libr., 2007. Scholar NYC Art, 1951, Jamesine Franklin Sch., 1952. Mem.: Women's Studio Ctr. Inc., Nat. Mus. Women in Arts. Roman Catholic. Avocation: travel.

ELDARD, RON (RONALD J. ELDARD), actor; b. NYC, Feb. 20, 1965; Actor: (films) True Love, 1989, Drop Dead Fred, 1991, Scent of a Woman, 1992, Sex & the Other Man, 1995, The Last Supper, 1995, Sleepers, 1996, Delivered, 1998, Deep Impact, 1998, The Runner, 1999, Mystery, Alaska, 1999, Black Hawk Down, 2001, Just a Kiss, 2002, Ghost Ship, 2002, House of Sand and Fog, 2003, Freedomland, 2006; (TV films) When Trumpets Fade, 1998, Bash: Latter-Day Plays, 2000, Death of a Salesman, 2000, Fathers and Sons, 2005, One Life to Live, 1989, Arresting Behavior, 1992, Bakersfield, PD, 1993, ER, 1996, Men Behaving Badly, 1996—97, Blind Justice, 2005, (Broadway) On the Waterfront, 1995, Death of a Salesman, 1999, Doubt, 2006, (off-Broadway) Aven'U Boys, Servy 'n' Bernice 4Ever; guest appearances Tonight Show with Jay Leno, 1996, Rosie O'Donnell Show, 1998, Late Show with David Letterman, 1998, Politically Incorrect, 1998, The Sharon Osbourne Show, 2003, Dinner for Five, 2004, The View, 2005, The Tony Danza Show, 2005, Jimmy Kimmel Live, 2005. Achievements include Winner Golden Gloves amateur boxing competition.

ELDEN, GARY MICHAEL, lawyer; b. Chgo., Dec. 11, 1944; s. E. Harold and Sylvia Arlene (Diamond) E.; m. Phyllis Deborah Mandler, Apr. 20, 1975. BA, U. Ill., 1966; JD, Harvard U., 1969. Bar: Ill. 1969, US Dist. Ct. (no. dist.) Ill. 1969, US Ct. Appeals (7th cir.) 1973, US Supreme Ct. 1973, US Dist. Ct. (ea. dist.) Mich. 1985, US Ct. Appeals (8th cir.) 1988, US Ct. Appeals (6th and 10th cirs.) 1990, US Dist. Ct. (ea. dist.) Wis. 1992, US Ct. Appeals (4th cir.), 2007. Ptnr. Kirkland & Ellis, Chgo., 1969-78, Reuben & Proctor, Chgo., 1978-86, Isham, Lincoln & Beale, Chgo., 1986-88, Grippo & Elden, Chgo., 1988—. Contbr. articles to profl. jours. Fellow Am. Coll. Trial Lawyers, Am. Bar Found.; mem. ABA, Chgo. Bar Assn. (sec. com. appellate procedures 1975-77), Chgo. Coun. Lawyers, Appellate Lawyers Assn. (bd. dirs. 1975-77). Home: 3750 N Lake Shore Dr Chicago IL 60613-4238 Office: Grippo & Elden LLC 111 S Wacker Ste 5100 Chicago IL 60606 Home Phone: 773-281-2909; Office Phone: 312-704-7700. Business E-Mail: gelden@grippoelden.com.

ELDER, DEE A., literature and language educator; b. Wichita, Kans., Mar. 21, 1964; d. Glenna C. Lawson and Larry D. Hager; m. Gevin W. Elder, Jan. 11, 1997; children: Roxann N., Bryce A. BA in German, U. Mo., St. Louis, 2000, BS in Secondary Edn., 2000. Cert. tchr. K-12 Mo., 2000. German tchr. St. John Vianney H.S., St. Louis, 2000—. Tchr, moderator Amnesty Internat. Student Action Group, St. Louis, 2001—. Mem.: Am. Assn. Tchrs. German. Roman Catholic. Avocation: travel. Office: St John Vianney HS 1311 S Kirkwood Rd Saint Louis MO 63101 Home Phone: 636-447-7389; Office Phone: 314-965-4853. Business E-Mail: frauelder@yahoo.com.

ELDER, IRMA, retail executive; b. Xicotencalt, Mex., 1934; m. James Elder, 1963 (dec.); 3 children. Owner, CEO Elder Automotive Group, 1983—. Mem. VIP panel 36th Annual Northwood U. Internat. Auto Show; founder Woman's Automotive Assn. Internat. Bd. dirs. Northwood U., Coll. Creative Studies, Oakland Family Svcs., Econ. Club Detroit. Named Woman Yr., Woman's Automotive Assn. Internat., 2001; named one of 100 Most Influential Women, Crain's Detroit Bus., 100 Leading Women, Automotive News, 2000; recipient Automotive Hall Fame Svc. Citation award, 2000, Pres. award, Ford Motor Co., 2000, 2001, Pride of Jaguar award, 1999, 2000. Achievements include frequently honored for many charitable assn; first woman to own Ford dealership in metropolitan Detroit market; successfully expanded co. from one dealership to eight after death of husband, founder of Elder Automotive; number one Saab dealership in US in volume of automobile sales (Saab of Troy); number one Jaguar dealership in N. Am. in volume of automobile sales (Jaguar of Troy); Elder Automotive consistently ranks top ten of Hispanic Bus. mag. top 500 Hispanic owned co. Office: 777 John R Rd Troy MI 48083 Office Fax: 248-583-0815.

ELDER, JACK S., urologist, educator; s. Stanley Gordon and Alma Westfall Elder; m. Judith Rose Lenobel, June 16, 1973; children: Samuel Isaac, Benjamin Daniel, Kathryn Rachel, Allison Miriam, Abigail Paula. MD with Distinction, U. Okla., Oklahoma City, 1976. Diplomate Am. Bd. Urology, 1984. Chief pediat. urology Rainbow Babies and Children's Hosp., Cleve., 1986—2007; Carter Kissell prof. urology Case Sch. Medicine, Cleve., 2003—07, vice chmn. dept. urology, 2004—07; chmn., dept. urology Henry Ford Hosp. Sys., Detroit, 2007—. Pediatric urology editor Jour. Urology, Balt., 1998—; physician Perlman Music Program China Trip, NYC, 2002; cons. H. H. Sheikh Zayed, Abu Dhabi, United Arab Emirates, 1992. Contbr. articles to profl. jours., chpts. to books;, author 5 books and monographs in field. Named one of Best Doctors in Am., Castle Connolly, 1996, 1998, 2000, 2002, 2004, 2006. Fellow: ACS, Am. Acad. Pediat.; mem.: Am. Urol. Assn. (chmn. panel on reflux guidelines 1990—97, 1st prize lab. rsch. 1981), Soc. Pediat. Urology (pres. 2006—), Am. Assn. Genitourinary Surgeons, Alpha Omega Alpha (1st v.p. okla. chpt. 1975—76). Achievements include first to Development of sedation protocol for children undergoing urinary bladder diagnostic testing; research in cryptorchidism, androgenic regulation of the gubernaculum testis. Office: Vattikuti Urology Inst 2799 W Grand Blvd K-9 Detroit MI 48202-2689 Home Phone: 2216-470-5640; Office Phone: 313-916-2066. Office Fax: 313-916-2088. Personal E-mail: jack.s.elder@gmail.com.

ELDER, JANET, editor; b. 1956; Writer NY Times, 1984—2005, editor of news surveys & election analysis, 2005—. Office: NY Times 229 W 43rd St New York NY 10036 Office Phone: 212-556-5817. E-mail: jaelde@nytimes.com.

ELDER, MARY LOUISE, retired librarian; b. Ann Arbor, Mich., Sept. 7, 1937; d. John Dyer and Elsie (Phelps) Elder. BA, St. Louis U., 1959; MA, U. Chgo., 1962; postgrad., U. Calif., Berkeley, 1965-69. Libr. U. Chgo., 1961-63; rare book cataloger U. Kans., Lawrence, 1963-65; rare books libr. St. Louis Pub. Libr., 1969-74; rare book cataloger Duke U., Durham, NC, 1979-84, Smithsonian Inst., Washington, 1984-91, Libr. Congress, Washington, 1991—2002; ret., 2002. Mem. ALA, Am. Printing History Assn., Bibliog. Soc., Bibliog. Soc. Am., Cath. Libr. Assn., Soc. History Authorship, Reading and Publishing, Alpha Sigma Nu. Personal E-mail: lelder@verizon.net.

ELDER, RICHARD BRUCE, artist, writer; b. Hawkesbury, Ont., Can., June 12, 1947; s. David Murdoch and Edrie Maud (Campbell) E.; m. Kathryn LeRoy, Sept. 4, 1970. Student, McMaster U., 1969; MA, U. Toronto, 1970; B of Applied Arts in Media Studies, Ryerson Poly. Inst., 1976. Curator film programs for Can. Coun., 1982, Can. Images, 1982, 83, Festival of Festivals, 1984, Art Gallery Ont., 1986, 89, Internat. Exptl. Film Congress, 1989; rsch. chair Ryerson U. Prodr. (films) The Book of All the Dead, 1975-94. The Book of Praise, 1997—; works exhibited at Mus. Modern Art, Millennium, N.Y.C., San Francisco Cinematheque, Hood Mus., Atlanta, Kino Arsenal, Berlin, Festival of Festivals, Ctr. Georges Pompidou, George Eastman House, Albright-Knox Gallery, Munich Stadtmuseum, Cineteca, Bologna, Italy, Le Fresnoy, France, Cinema: Nouvelles Ecritures, Paris; retrospectives of film work Art Gallery Ont., 1985, Cinémathèque Québecoise, 1986, Anthology Film Archives, 1988, 95, Senzatitolo, Treno, Italy, 1996, Images '97, Toronto, The Antechamber, Regina, Can., 2000, Festival des Toutes les Cinema, Paris, Festival des Cinemas Differents, Paris; author: Image and Identity: Reflections on Canadian Film and Culture, 1989, The Body in Film, 1989, Stan Brakhage: A Retrospective, 1977-95, 1995, A Body of Vision, 1997; author: The Films of Stan Brakhage in the American Tradition of Ezra Pound, Gertrude Stein, and Charles Olson, 1998; contbr. articles to profl. jours. Recipient Can. Film award best exptl. film, 1976, LA Film Critics Circle award best ind. exptl. film, 1980, Auswortiges Amt. F.G.R. study tour award, 1986, Gov. Gen.'s award in media arts, 2007; Sarwan Sahoto Disting. scholar Ryerson U. Rsch., 2000; Creation in Fine Arts grantee Social Scis. and Humanities Rsch. Coun. Can. in rsch., New Media Initiative grantee CC/Nat. Security Engring. Rsch. Coun., Can. Coun. grantee, Ont. Arts Coun. grantee, Ryerson U. Rsch. Chair grantee. Address: Unit 5 692 St Clarens Ave Toronto ON Canada M6H 3X1 E-mail: elderb@acm.org.

ELDERFIELD, JOHN, art historian, museum curator; b. Yorkshire, Eng., Apr. 25, 1943; s. Henry and Rhoda May (Risbrough) E.; m. Joyce Davey, Jan. 9, 1965; children: Matthew, Jonathan; m. Jill Elizabeth Moser, Jan. 8, 1989 (div. 1995). Attended, U. Manchester, 1961-62; BA with honors, U. Leeds, 1966, MPhil with distinction; PhD, U. London, 1975. Lectr. art history Winchester Sch. Art, 1966-70; Harkness fellow Yale U., 1970-72; lectr. art history U. Leeds, 1973-75; curator painting and sculpture Mus. Modern Art, NYC, 1975-93, dir. dept. drawings, 1979-93, chief curator at large, 1993—. Author: Hugo Ball: The Flight Out of Time, 1975, Fauvism and Its Affinities, 1976, European Master Paintings, 1976, Matisse, 1978, The Cut-outs of Henri Matisse, 1978, The Masterworks of Edvard Munch, 1979, New Work on Paper, 1981, The Modern Drawing, 1983, The Drawings of Henri Matisse, 1984, Kurt Schwitters, 1985, Morris Louis, 1986, Drawings of Richard Diebenkorn, 1988, Helen Frankenthaler, 1988, (co-author) Matisse in Morocco, 1990, Matisse: A Retrospective, 1992. Recipient Mitchell prize, 1986, chevalier des Arts et Lettres, 1989; Guggenheim fellow, 1972-73; Named one of Time Mag. 100 Most Influential People, 2005. Fellow Royal Soc. Arts; mem. Internat. Assn. Art Critics, Century Assn. Office: Mus Modern Art 11 W 53rd St New York NY 10019-5498

ELDERKIN, CHARLES EDWIN, retired meteorologist; b. Seattle, Aug. 6, 1930; s. Andrew Charles and Hilda Olena E.; m. Mary DuPriest, May 28, 1959; 1 child, Christopher Charles. BS, U. Wash., 1953, PhD, 1966. Meteorologist Gen. Electric Co., 1959-65; mgr. atmospheric physics sect. Battelle Pacific N.W. Lab., Battelle Meml. Inst., Richland, Wash., 1965-72, assoc. mgr. atmospheric scis. dept., 1972-79, program mgr. wind characteristics program element of fed. wind energy program, 1976-79, mgr. atmospheric scis. dept., 1979-82, assoc. mgr. geoscis. research and engring. dept., 1982-84, mgr. Hanford environ. oversight office, 1984-85, assoc. mgr. earth scis. dept., 1985-86, sr. program mgr. earth and environment scis. ctr., 1986-92. Sci. dir. multi-lab. rsch. program Atmospheric Studies in Complex Terrain, Dept. Energy, 1989-92. Served with USAF, 1954-55. Recipient E.O. Lawrence award U.S. Energy Rsch. and Devel. Adminstrn., 1975. Mem.: Sigma Xi. Home: 531 Holly St Richland WA 99354-1822

ELDERS, JOYCELYN (MINNIE JOCELYN ELDERS, MINNIE JOYCELYN LEE), public health service officer, endocrinologist, former Surgeon General of the United States; b. Schaal, Ark., Aug. 13, 1933; d. Curtis and Haller Jones; m. Oliver B. Elders, Feb. 14, 1960; children: Eric D., Kevin M. BA in Biol., Philander Smith Coll., 1952; MD, U. Ark. Med. Sch., 1960; MS in Biochemistry, U. Ark., 1967. Pediatric intern U. Minn. Hosp., Mpls., 1960-61; pediatric resident U. Ark. Med. Ctr., Little Rock, 1961-63, chief pediatric resident, 1963-64, pediatric rsch. fellow, 1964-67, asst. prof. of pediatrics, 1967-71, assoc. prof. of pediatrics, 1971-76, prof. of pediatrics, 1976-87; dir. Ark. Dept. of Health, Little Rock, 1987-93; pres. Assn. of State & Territorial Health Officers, 1992; surgeon gen. US Dept. Health & Human Services, 1993-94; prof. pediatrics Univ. Ark. Med. Ctr., Little Rock, 1994—98, prof. emeritus, pediatric endocrinology, 1998—; medical dir. Apothecus Pharmaceutical Corp., 2006—. Bd. dirs. Nat. Bank of Ark., North Little Rock, 1979-89. Editorial bd. Jour. Pediatrics, 1981—; contbr. articles on pediatrics to profl. jours. Bd. dirs. Northside YMCA, Little Rock, 1973—; vol. vols. in pub. schs., Little Rock, 1973—. 1st lt. U.S. Army, 1953-56. Recipient NIH Career Devel. award, Worthen Bank's Ark. Profl. Woman of Distinction award, 1987; named one of 100 Women of Ark., 1980, Ark. Dem. Woman of Yr. statewide newspaper, 1988, Presdl. award, Ark. Sociological and Anthropological Assn., 1993. Mem. So. Soc. Pediatrics (rsch. pres. 1979-80), Lawson Wilkins Endocrine Soc. (com. chair 1976), Ark. Sci. and Tech. Commn. (sec. 1975-89), Little Rock C. of C. (bd. dirs. 1980—), Endocrine Soc., Acad. Pediatrics, Am. Pediatric Soc. First African Am. US Surgeon General. Office: U Ark Med Ctr 4301 W Markham # 820 Little Rock AR 72205

ELDRED, GERALD MARCUS, performing company executive; b. Cambridge, Ont., Can., Oct. 5, 1934; s. Albert Harold and Ethel Emily Hope (Bardwell) E.; m. Marjorie Christine Kidd, Aug. 4, 1956; 1 child, Peter Marcus (dec.). Diploma, Nat. Theatre Sch., Montreal, 1965. Adminstr. Nat. Ballet Can., Toronto, 1972-79; adminstrv. dir., acad. prin. Nat. Ballet Sch., Toronto, 1979-82; exec. dir. Stratford Festival, (Ont.), 1982-86; dir. fin. and ops. Harbourfront Corp., 1987-97. Cons. in field; mem. arts adv. com. The Laidlaw Found., 1980-90. Stage producer, dir., adminstr. Canadian Players, Toronto, 1965-66, Man. Theatre Centre, Winnipeg, 1966-72, Shaw Festival, Niagara-on-the-Lake., Ont., 1967, Expo '67, Montreal, 1967, Rainbow Stage, Winnipeg, 1968, Kawartha Summer Festival, Lindsay, Ont., 1966, producer commd. opera for Nat. Arts Centre, Ottawa, 1969—. Mem. adv. com. program in art York U., 1982-90; mem., officer, bd. dirs. The Theatre Mus. Corp., 1988-2001, The Pleiades Theatre, Toronto, 1996-2006. Named to Stairway of Excellence, Galt Collegiate Inst., 2003. Mem. Can. Actors Equity Assn., Assn. Cultural Execs., Can. Coun. (adv. arts panel 1970-72, adv. bd. touring office 1983-85), Nat. Theatre Sch. Can. Alumni Assn. (mem. bd. 2003-06), Region Waterloo Arts Fund (mem. bd. dirs.). Home: 5-260 Deer Ridge Dr Kitchener ON Canada N2P 2M3 E-mail: gm.eldred@sympatico.ca.

ELDRED, KENNETH MCKECHNIE, acoustician, consultant; b. Springfield, Mass., Nov. 25, 1929; s. Robert Moseley and Jean McKechnie (Ashton) E.; m. Helene Barbara Koerting Fischer, May 31, 1957; 1 dau., Heidi Jean. BS, MIT, 1950, postgrad., 1951-53, UCLA, 1960-63. Engr. in charge vibration and sound lab. Boston Naval Shipyard, 1951-54; supervisory physicist, chief phys. acoustics sect. U.S. Air Force, Wright Field, Ohio, 1956-57; v.p., cons. acoustics Western Electro-Acoustics Labs., Los Angeles, 1957-63; v.p., tech. dir. sci. services and systems group Wyle Labs., El Segundo, Calif., 1963-73; v.p., dir. div. environ. and noise control tech. Bolt Beranek and Newman Inc., Cambridge, Mass., 1973-77, prin. cons., 1977-81. Dir. Ken Eldred Engring.; mem. exec. stds. coun. Am. Nat. Stds. Inst., 1979-89, vice-chmn., 1981-83, chmn., 1985-87, bd. dirs., 1983-87; bd. dirs., Ince Found.; mem., past chmn. Acoustical Stds. Bd.; mem. com. hearing, bioacoustics and biomechanics NRC, 1963-88; chmn. Internat. Stds. Orgn. Tech. Com. TC108 Mechanical Shock and Vibration, 1994-99; bd. dirs., treas. Earcraft Tech. Inc., 1999-2003. 1st lt. USAF, 1954-56. Fellow Acoustical Soc. Am. (stds. dir. 1987-93, past chmn. coordinating com. environ. acoustics, Silver Medal in Noise 1994); mem. NAE, Inst. Noise Control Engring. (pres. 1976, bd. dirs. 1987-91), Down East Yacht Club. Home: Meadow Cove East Boothbay ME 04544 Office: PO Box 501 East Boothbay ME 04544-0501 Home Phone: 207-633-5991; Office Phone: 207-633-5991. Personal E-mail: keldred@alum.mit.edu.

ELDREDGE, CHARLES CHILD, III, art history educator; b. Boston, Apr. 12, 1944; s. Henry and Priscilla Marion (Bateson) Eldredge; m. Jane Allen MacDougal, June 11, 1966; children: Henry Gifford, Janann Bateson. BA in Am. Studies, Amherst Coll., 1966; PhD in Art History, U. Minn., 1971. Curator asst. Minn. Hist. Soc., St. Paul, 1966-68; mem. edn. dept. Mpls. Inst. Arts, 1967-69; tchg. assoc. art history U. Minn., 1968-70; curator collections Spencer Mus. Art U. Kans., Lawrence, 1970—71, dir., 1971—82, asst. prof. art history, 1970—71, assoc. prof., 1974—80, prof., 1980—82, Hall Disting. Prof. Am. Art and Culture, 1988—; dir. Nat. Mus. Am. Art, Washington, 1982-88. C.H. Hynson vis. prof. U. Tex., Austin, 1985; trustee Watkins Cmty. Mus., Lawrence, 1972-76, Assn. Art Mus. Dirs., 1982, 87, Reynolda House Mus. Am. Art, 1986-88, Amherst Coll., 1987-93, trustee Georgia O'Keeffe Found., 1989-95, Amon Carter Mus., 2003-06, Terra Found. Am. Art, 2007-; rsch. assoc. Smithsonian Instn., 1988—; founder Smithsonian Studies in Am. Art, 1987. Author: Marsden Hartley: Lithographs and Related Works, 1972, Ward Lockwood, 1894-1963, 1974, American Imagination and Symbolist Painting, 1979, Charles Walter Stetson, Color and Fantasy, 1982, Pacific Parallels: Artists and the Landscape in New Zealand, 1991, Georgia O'Keeffe, 1991, Georgia O'Keeffe: American and Modern, 1992, The College on the Hill, 1996, Reflections on Nature: Small Paintings by Arthur Dove, 1997, The Floor of the Sky: Artists and the North American Prairie, 2000, Tales from the Easel: American Narrative Paintings, 2004, John Steuart Curry's Hoover and the Flood, 2007; co-author: The Arcadian Landscape: 19th Century American Painters in Italy, 1972, Art in New Mexico, 1900-1945, 1986, Georgia O'Keeffe and The Calla Lily in American Art, 2002; gen. editor: The Register of Mus. Art, 1971—82; mem. editl. bd. Am. Studies, 1974—77, Am. Art, 1996—2006. Fulbright scholar N.Z., 1983; Smithsonian Instn. fellow Nat. Collection Fine Arts, 1979, Found. Visitor fellow U. Auckland, 1993, W.T. Kemper fellow for tchg. excellence, 2003; recipient Outstanding Alumnus award U. Minn., 1986. Mem. Coll. Art Assn. Am., Am. Studies Assn., Am. Assn. Mus., Assn. Art Mus. Dirs. (hon.), Phi Beta Kappa (hon.). Office: U Kans Dept Art History 209 Spencer Mus Art 1301 Mississippi St Lawrence KS 66045-0001 Office Phone: 785-864-4713. Business E-Mail: cce@ku.edu.

ELDREDGE, JONATHAN DEFOREST, medical librarian, educator, social informaticist; s. LeRoy Lincoln Jr. and Elizabeth Belding Eldredge; m. Regina Leslie Wolfe, Nov. 19, 1994; children: Nicolas-Etienne, Gabriela Regina. BA cum laude, Beloit Coll., 1976; MLS, U. Mich., 1978; PhD, U. NMex., 1993. Cert. Acad. Health Info. Profls. Med. Libr. Assn., 1989. Libr. dir. Ea. N.Mex U., Clovis, 1981—83; asst. prof., chief Collections and Info. Resources Devel. U. N.Mex, Albuquerque, 1986—2000, assoc. prof., acad. and clin. svcs. coord., 2001—. Oversight com. Nat. Libr. Medicine, Bethesda, Md., 2001—. Assoc. editor: Biomed. Digital Librs., 2003—, jour. rev. editor: Jour. AMA, 1994—2000, mem. adv. bd.: New Eng. Jour. Medicine, 2001—04; contbr. articles to profl. jours. Sec., bd. mem. Friends Librs., N.Mex., Albuquerque, 1995—2003. Mem.: ALA (life), Med. Libr. Assn. (Louise Darling medal for disting. achievement in collection devel. in health scis. 1999). Unitarian Universalist/Buddhist. Achievements include one of the main founders of the international Evidence-Based Librarianship movement. Avocations: skiing, surfing, bicycling, hiking, travel. Office: Univ NMex Health Sci Lib and Informatics Ctr Albuquerque NM 87131-5686 Business E-Mail: jeldridge@salud.unm.edu.

ELDREDGE, NILES, curator, paleontologist; b. Bklyn., Aug. 25, 1943; s. Robert L. and Eleanor R. Eldredge; m. Michelle J. Wycoff, June 6, 1964; children: Douglas R., Gregory C. AB summa cum laude, Columbia U., 1965, PhD in Geology, 1969. Adj. asst. prof. dept. geology Columbia U., 1969—74, adj. assoc. prof., 1974—81; paleontologist Am. Mus. Nat. Hist., NYC, 1969—, asst. curator dept. invertebrate paleontology, 1969—74, assoc. curator dept. invertebrates, 1974—79, curator, 1979—, chmn., 1984—91; adj. prof. biology CUNY, 1972—. Trustee Biodiversity Found. Africa. Author: several books, including Time Frames, 1985, Life Pulse, 1987, Macroevolutionary Dynamics, 1989, Miner's Canary, 1991, Life in the Balance, 1998, The Pattern of Evolution, 1999, The Triumph of Evolution.And The Failure of Creationism, 2000, Why We Do It, 2004, Darwin: Discovering the Tree of Life, 2005. Recipient Lappe award, The Hastings Ctr., 1997, Pres.'s Citation award, Am. Inst. Biol. Scis., 2007. Mem. AAAS, Paleontol. Soc. (councilor 1977-79, Schuchert award 1979), Paleontol. Assn., Soc. Systematic Zoology, Soc. for Study of Evolution. Achievements include development of the evolutionary theory of punctuated equilibrium with Stephen Jay Gould in 1972. Avocations: trumpet playing and collecting, birdwatching. Office: Divsn Paleontology Am Mus Natural Hist Central Park W At 79th St New York NY 10024 Office Phone: 212-769-5723. Office Fax: 212-769-5783.*

ELDRIDGE, DAVID CARLTON, art and antique appraiser; b. Lansing, Mich., July 15, 1949; s. Carlton Brady and Blythe (Axford) E.; m. Suzanne Hamrick, Dec. 12, 1970; 1 child, Morgan Worth B.F.A., Ill. Wesleyan U., 1971; postgrad., U. Denver, 1972-73; M.F.A., So. Ill. U., 1974. Accredited sr. appraiser Am. Soc. Appraisers. Curator exhibits Nature Sci. Park, Winston Salem, NC, 1974; curator exhibits Tenn. State Mus., Nashville, 1974-80; exec. dir. Mus. Arts and Scis., Macon, Ga., 1980-82; dir. Eldridge Appraisals, Naples, Fla., 1982—. Mem. Am. Soc. Appraisers (sr.), Appraisers Assn. Am. Office: 1839 Imperial Golf Course Blvd Naples FL 34110-8140 Office Phone: 239-598-2225. Personal E-mail: dceldrid@comcast.net.

ELDRIDGE, J. CHARLES, endocrinologist, educator, researcher; b. Chgo., June 7, 1942; s. John Godfrey Eldridge, Carol Boedeker Eldridge; m. Pat Hudler. BA in Biology, North Cen. Coll., Naperville, Ill., 1965; MS in Physiology, No. Ill. U., 1967; PhD in Endocrinology, Med. Coll. Ga., 1971. Instr. biology Orange County C.C., Middletown, NY, 1967—68; rsch. assoc. I.N.S.E.R.M., Bordeaux, France, 1971-72, Med. Coll. Ga., Augusta, 1973; asst. prof. lab. medicine Med. U. S.C., Charleston, 1974-79; asst. prof. physiology and pharmacology Wake Forest U. Sch. Medicine, Winston-Salem, NC, 1979—87, assoc. prof. physiology and pharmacology, 1987—99, prof. physiology and pharmacology, 1999—. Grant reviewer Nat. Inst. Aging, NIH, Bethesda, Md., 1990—93; rsch. cons. EPA, Washington, 1999—, mem. endocrine disruptors methods validation com., 2001—; cons. Internat. Life Scis. Inst., Washington, 1992—94; med. edn. cons. various schs., 1988—; faculty Harvard Macy Inst. Med. Educators, 2001—. Mng. editor: Basic Sci. Educator, 1999—2002, mem. editl. bd.: Biology of Reproduction, 2000—, Jour. Internat. Assn. Med. Sci. Educators, 2002—; contbr. articles to profl. jours. Coord. United Way, Winston-Salem, 1986—98; elder, deacon, other positions Reynolda Presby. Ch., 1992—. Recipient Disting. Alumni award, Med. Coll. Ga., 2002; grantee, NIH, 1976—97, Nat. Inst. Drug Abuse, 1990—98; Macy fellow in edn., Harvard Med. Sch., 2001. Mem.: Soc. for Study of Reproduction, Internat. Assn. for Med. Sci. Educators, Soc. Neurosci., Endocrine Soc., Shriners (bd. dirs. 1988—91), Masons. Presbyterian. Avocations: music, travel, cuisine. Office: Wake Forest U Sch Medicine Dept Physiology and Pharmacology Winston Salem NC 27157-1083 Office Phone: 336-716-8570.

ELDRIDGE, JAMES FRANCIS, lawyer, insurance company executive; b. Appleton, Wis., Nov. 6, 1946; s. C.H. and Florence M. (Dorschel) E.; m. Mary E. Evenson; children: Stacy M., Thomas J., Michael P., Kevin J. BA, Dartmouth Coll., 1968; JD, Marquette U., 1971. Bar: Wis. Assoc. counsel Kivett and Kasdorf, Milw., 1971-74; claim counsel Am. Family Mut. Ins. Co., Milw., 1974-81, regional claim counsel Madison, Wis., 1981-84, regional claim mgr., 1984-85, v.p. claims, 1985-90, chief legal officer, sec., 1990—. Mem. Civil Trial Counsel Wis., Wis. Acad. Trial Lawyers, Dane County Bar Assn., Am. Arbitration Assn., Nat. Assn. Ind. Insurers (laws com.). Republican. Roman Catholic. Avocations: golf, tennis, racquetball, softball, tropical fish. Office: Am Family Ins Group 6000 American Pky Madison WI 53783-0001 Office Phone: 608-249-2111. Business E-Mail: jeldridg@amfam.com.*

ELDRIDGE, TRUMAN KERMIT, JR., lawyer; b. Kansas City, Mo., July 27, 1944; s. Truman Kermit and Nell Marie (Dennis) E.; m. Joan Ellen Jurgeson, Feb. 9, 1965; children: Christina Joanne, Gregory Truman. AB, Rockhurst Coll., 1966; JD, U. Mo., Kansas City, 1969. Bar: Mo. 1969, U.S. Dist. Ct. (we. dist.) Mo. 1969, U.S. Ct. Appeals (8th cir.) 1977, (10th cir.) 1995, U.S. S. Ct., 1992, U.S. Dist. Ct. Kans. 1998. Assoc. Morris, Foust, Moudy & Beckett, Kansas City, 1969-70, Dietrich, Davis, Dicus, Rowlands & Schmitt, Kansas City, 1971-74, ptnr., 1975, Armstrong, Teasdale, LLP, Kansas City, 1989-2000; sr. counsel Schlee, Huber McMullen & Krause, 2001—. Author: (with othrs) Missouri Environmental Law Handbook, 1990, 2d edit., 1993, 3d edit., 1997; contbr. articles to profl. jours. Chmn. bd. dirs. Loretto Sch., Kansas City, 1981-83; mem. Energy and Environ. Commn. City of Kansas City, 1990-91, 1994, bd. dirs. Sheffield Place, 1997-2003, 2005—, vice-chair, 1998-99, chair, 1999-2000. Master Ross T. Roberts Inn of Ct.; mem. ABA, Mo. Bar Assn., Kansas City Met. Bar Assn. (fed. ct. com., vice chair 1989-90, chair 1990-91), Am. Arbitration Assn. (arbitrator), Nat. Arbitration Forum (arbitrator), Kansas City Club (athletic com. 1990-2001, chair 199-2001, house com. 1993-96, 98-99, long range planning com. 1993-97, fin. com. 2004—, bd. dirs. 1997-2001). Roman Catholic. Avocations: sailing, reading, photography, raquetball. Office: PO Box 32430 4050 Pennsylvania Ste 300 Kansas City MO 64171-5430 Home Phone: 816-363-6724; Office Phone: 816-360-2522. Personal E-mail: truman_eldridge@hotmail.com. Business E-Mail: teldridge@schleehuber.com.

ELECTRA, CARMEN (TARA LEIGH PATRICK), actress; b. Sharonville, Ohio, Apr. 20, 1972; m. Dennis Rodman, Nov. 14, 1998 (div. Apr. 6, 1999); m. David Navarro, Nov. 22, 2003 (div. Feb. 20, 2007). Co-host (TV series) Singled Out, 1997; actor: (TV series) Baywatch, 1997—98, Hyperion Bay, 1999, BattleBots, 2002, Livin Large, 2002—03, 2003—04, Manhunt, 2004, Tripping the Rift, 2005—; celebrity judge (TV series) Dance Fever, 2003, host Automotive Showcase, 2003, VH1's 100 Greatest Artists of Hard Rock; actor: (TV films) Christmas in Malibu, 1999, Baywatch Hawaiian Wedding, 2003, Lolo's Cafe, 2006; (films) An American Vampire Story, 1997, Starstruck, 1998, The Mating Habits of the Earthbound Human, 1999, Scary Movie, 2000, The Great White Dope, 2000, Sol Goode, 2000, Perfume, 2001, Get Over It, 2001, Whacked!, 2002, Rent Control, 2002, Uptown Girls, 2003, My Boss' Daughter, 2003, Starsky & Hutch, 2004, Max Havoc: Curse of the Dragon, 2004, Dirty Love, 2005, Searching for Bobby D, 2005, Getting Played, 2005, Cheaper by the Dozen 2, 2005, Date Movie, 2006, Scary Movie 4, 2006, Hot Tamale, 2006, Epic Movie, 2007; voice (TV series) The Simpsons, 2002, King of the Hill, 2003, (video) Lil' Pimp, 2005, American Dad!, 2005, appears in music video for Moby, "We Are All Made of Stars", guest appearance MADtv, 1997, 2000, Just Shoot Me!, 1997, The Drew Carey Show, 2000, The Osbourne Family Christmas Special, 2003, Punk'd, 2004, Monk, 2004, Hope & Faith, 2005, Summerland, 2005, House, M.D., 2005, Stacked, 2005, and several others; co-author (with Sheryl Berk): How to Be Sexy, 2007.*

ELEFANTE, MICHAEL BARRETT, lawyer; b. Ft. Wayne, Ind., Feb. 15, 1944; s. Michael Alfred and Jean Lytton (Harris) E.; m. Louise Sawyer; children: Mark Barrett, Amy Lytton, Peter Sawyer, Jeffrey Parsons. AB, Syracuse U., 1965; postgrad., Harvard U., 1965-66, JD, 1969. Bar: Mass. bar 1969. Law clk. Hon. Raymond S. Wilkins, Chief Justice Supreme Judicial Ct., Mass., 1969-70; ptnr. firm Hemenway and Barnes, Boston, 1976—, mng. ptnr., 1993—99. Bd. dirs. Greater Boston Legal Services, Inc., 1972—, v.p., 1987, pres., 1990—95; bd. dirs. Civil Liberties Union Mass., 1978—81, Dow Jones & Co., 2005—. Mem. Am. Law Inst., Boston Bar Assn., Mass. Bar Assn. Episcopalian. Office: Hemmenway 60 State St Boston MA 02109-7940

ELEQUIN, CLETO, JR., retired physician; b. Antique, Philippines, Oct. 18, 1933; s. Cleto and Enriqueta (Tengonciang) E.; m. Nancy Johnson, May 14, 1958; children: Tracy, Thomas Kyle, Stuart Scott MD, Far Eastern U., Philippines, 1957. Rotating intern Good Samaritan Hosp., Lexington, Ky., 1957-58; gen. practice resident Central Bapt. Hosp., Lexington, 1958-59; psychiat. resident State Hosp., Danville, Pa., 1959-60, 61-62, psychiat. resident with child psychiatry New Castle, Del., 1962-63; staff physician Eastern State Hosp., Lexington, 1960-61, dir. Fayette County Project, dir. intensive treatment service, 1964-67, supt., 1969-71; dep. commr. Dept. Mental Health, State Ky., 1967-69; pvt. practice specializing in family practice and psychiatry Pecos, Tex., 1971-72; practice medicine, specializing in family practice Austin, Tex., 1974-89; ret. Cons. psychiatrist Texas Youth Commn., Peyote, Tex., Permian Basin Cmty. Mental Health-Mental Retardation, Odessa, Tex., Prude Ranch for Emotionally Disturbed Children and Adolescents, Ft. Davis, Tex., Dept. Mental Health-Mental Retardation State of Tex.; vis. lectr. in medicine and psychiatry Am. U. of the Caribbean, Plymouth, Montserrat; asst. dep. commr. Tex. Dept. Mental Health and Mental Retardation, Austin, 1973-74, dep. commr. mental health, 1974; pvt. practice family medicine and psychiatry, Austin, 1974-85; mem. attending staff Brackenridge Hosp., St. David Med. Ctr., Seton Med. Ctr., Shoal Creek Hosp.; med. dir. Mary Lee Sch. and Found., 1974-80, bd. trustees, 1980-85; attending psychiatrist U. Ky. Med. Ctr., 1964-71, Good Samaritan Hosp., 1969-71, Ctrl. Bapt. Hosp., 1966-71; cons. psychiatrist U. Ky. Student Health Svc., 1965-71, Peace Corps, 1966-68, Bur. Rehab. State Ky., 1965-71, Blue Grass Cmty. Care Ctr., 1967-71, Covington (Ky.) Cmty. Care Ctr., 1969-71, Hazard Cmty. Care Ctr., 1969-71, Danville (Ky.) Cmty. Ctr., 1969-71, Maysville (Ky.) Cmty. Care Ctr., 1969-71; clin. instr., asst. clin. prof. dept. psychiatry U. Ky. Med. Ctr., 1964-69, assoc. clin. prof., 1969-71; cons. psychiatrist Tex. Youth Commn. Tex. Dept. of MH-MR, State of Tex.; pvt. practice in psychiatry, Austin, 1974-85; attending staff Brackenridge Hosp., St. David Med. Ctr.,

Seton Med. Ctr., Shoal Creek Hosp.; med. dir. Mary Lee Sch. and Found., 1974-80, bd. trustees, 1980-85. Profl. adv. coun. Cmty. Mental Health-Retardation Ctr., Lexington, 1967-71; active Lexington Hosp. Coun., 1969-71. Mem. AMA, Am. Psychiat. Assn., Am. Acad. Family Physicians (life), Assn. Med. Supts. Mental Hosps., Tex. Med. Assn., Travis County Med. Soc., Austin Psychiat. Soc. Home: 10101 Jupiter Hills Dr Austin TX 78747-1322 Office Phone: 512-280-9508. Personal E-mail: cinelequin@aol.com.

EL-ERIAN, MOHAMED A., investment manager; b. NYC, Aug. 19, 1958; BA, Cambridge U.; MA, Oxford U., PhD in Econs., 1983. Dep. dir. IMF, 1983—97, mem. Capital Markets Consultative Group; mng. dir. econ. rsch. Salomon Smith Barney, London, 1997—99; mng. dir., sr. mem. portfolio mgmt. and investment strategy group Pacific Investment Mgmt. Co. LLC (PIMCO), 1999—; CEO Harvard Mgmt. Co., Boston, 2005—. Mem.: Emerging Markets Creditors Assn., Emerging Market Traders Assn. Office: Harvard Mgmt Co 600 Atlantic Ave Ste 1500 Boston MA 02210-2203 also: PIMCO 1345 Ave of the Americas New York NY 10105-4800 E-mail: el-erian@pimco.com.*

ELEWSKI, BONI ELIZABETH, dermatologist, educator; b. Cleve., Aug. 7, 1953; d. John Stanley and Alberta (Gulish) E.; married. BA summa cum laude, Miami U., Oxford, Ohio, 1975; MD cum laude, Ohio State U., 1978. Intern U. N.C., Chapel Hill, 1978-79, resident, 1979-82; staff dermatologist Akron (Ohio) Clinic, 1982-88; prof. dermatology Univ. Hosps. of Cleve., Case Western Res. U., 1988-99; prof. U. Ala., 1999—, vice-chair dept. dermatology Birmingham, 2005, residency program dir., 2006. Author: (textbook) Differential Diagrams in Dermatology, 2005; editor: Cutaneous Fungal Infections, 1992, 2d edit., 1998; contbr. chpts. to books, articles to profl. jours. Trustee Annenberg Cir., 2006. Fellow Cleve. Dermatology Soc. (sec. bd. dirs., chair skin cancer screening program 1988—, pres. 1994), Am. Acad. Dermatology (bd. dirs. 1996-2000, v.p. elect, 2000, v.p. 2001, pres.-elect 2003-04, pres. 2004); mem. Am. Dermatol. Assn., Women's Dermatology Soc. (sec.-treas., pres.-elect 1999, pres. 2000), Dermatology Found. (trustee 1987-91). Roman Catholic. Home: PO Box 430037 Birmingham AL 35243 Office: U Alabama Birmingham Dept Derm 700 18th St S Birmingham AL 35233-1856 E-mail: BEElewski@aol.com.

ELEY, HUNTER R., lawyer; b. Williamsburg, Va. BA, Univ. Va., 1995; JD, Coll. William & Mary, 2000. Bar: Va. 2000, Calif. 2003. Judicial extern Justice Lawrence L. Koontz, Va. Supreme Ct.; law clk. Judge James C. Turk, US Dist. Ct. We. Va.; atty. Gibson Dunn & Crutcher LLP, LA, Browne Woods & George LLP, Beverly Hills, Calif.; ptnr., bus. & entertainment litigation Doll Amir & Eley LLP, LA. Named a Rising Star, So. Calif. Super Lawyers, 2006. Office: Doll Amir & Eley LLP Ste 1106 1888 Century Park E Los Angeles CA 90067 Office Phone: 310-557-9100. Office Fax: 310-557-9101. Business E-Mail: heley@dollamir.com.

ELEY, LYNN W., political science professor, retired mayor; b. Zearing, Iowa, Oct. 23, 1925; s. Wilbur Charles and Myrtle (Wolford) E.; m. Elizabeth Sherwood Hill, Aug. 25, 1950 (div. 1970); children— Thomas Wendell, David Matthew, Mary Sherwood; m. Janet Burdy, Aug. 26, 1971; children— Benjamin Charles, Margaret Burdy. BA, Harvard U., 1949; MA, U. Iowa, 1951; PhD, 1952. Orgn. and methods analyst Dept. Agr., Washington, 1952-55; research assoc., supr. Lansing Office, Inst. Pub. Adminstrn., 1955-58; assoc. dir. Extension Service; assoc. prof. polit. sci. U. Mich., 1959-64; dean Sch. Continuing Edn., and Summer Sch.; assoc. prof. polit. sci. Washington U., St. Louis, 1964-68; asst. chancellor U. Wis., Milw., 1968-72, prof. dept. govtl. affairs, 1972-91, prof. emeritus govtl. affairs, 1991—, chmn. dept., 1985-91. Editorial asst. com. on appropriations U.S. Ho. of Reps., 1953; instr. U.S. Dept. Agr. Grad. Sch., 1954-55; mayor City of Mequon, Wis., 1980-86 Author: The Executive Reorganization Plan: A Survey of State Experience, 1967, The Regionalization of Business Services in the Agricultural Research Service, 1967, Local Ombudsmen in America, 1973, An Ombudsman for Milwaukee? 1974; with others Representation of the Poor in Milwaukee's War on Poverty, 1977, A Guide to Citizen Participation in Government: Administrative Rule Making, 1979, 80; Sr. editor: with others The Politics of Fair-Housing Legislation: State and Local Case Studies, 1968, Wisconsin Government and Politics, 4th edit., 1987; mem. editorial bd.: Pub. Adminstrn. Rev, 1969-72. Sec. Gov.'s Adv. Com. Reorgn. State Govt. Mich., 1958-62; city councilman Ann Arbor, Mich., 1961-63; mem. Milw. Model Cities Policy Commn., 1970-75; bd. dirs. Wis. Congress on Aging, 1979-82, N.W. Gen. Hosp., Milw., 1990-94; exec. dir. Mid-Moraine Mcpl. Assn., 1986-95; pres. Riveredge Nature Ctr., Newburg, Wis., 1993-95; mem. planning and zoning commn. City of Bisbee, Ariz., 1998-99; pres. Unitarian-Universalist Ch., Sierra Vista, Ariz., 1999-2000. With USNR, 1944-46. Ellis L. Phillips Found. Postdoctoral intern in acad. adminstrn., 1963—64. Personal E-mail: eleyjanet@yahoo.com.

EL FATTAH, YOUSRI M., computer scientist; arrived in U.S., 1984; BSc in Aero. Engring., Cairo U., Egypt, 1967, PhD, 1972, U. Calif., Irvine, 1993. Bd. cert. control sys. engr., Calif. Owner Artificial Intelligence Tng., Tustin, Calif., 1986—91; lectr. Nat. U., Irvine, Calif., 1986—92, U. Calif. Irvine U. Ext., 1988—93, Calif. State U., Long Beach, 1988—93; vis. rschr. U. Vienna, 1994—95; rsch. scientist U. Calif., Irvine, 1995—96, Rockwell Sci., Thousand Oaks, Calif., 1996—99, sr. scientist, 1999—. Cons. UN McDonnel Douglas. Mem.: Am. Assn. Artificial Intelligence. Avocations: painting, writing, hiking, martial arts, travel. Home: 824 4th St 102 Santa Monica CA 90403 Office: Teledyne Sci 1049 Camino dos Rios Thousand Oaks CA 91360 Personal E-mail: yelfattah@teledyne.com.

ELFIN, MEL, magazine editor; b. Bklyn., July 18, 1929; s. Joseph and Bess (Margolis) E.; m. Margery Lesser, June 21, 1953; children: David, Dana. AB, Syracuse U., 1951; MA, Harvard U., 1952; postgrad., New Sch. Social Research, 1955-58; LHD, Ill. Wesleyan U., 1997. Copywriter Marvin and Leonard, Boston, advt. staff, 1953-54; successively reporter, travel editor, asst. city editor L.I. Daily Press, Jamaica, NY, 1954-58; mem. staff Newsweek mag., 1958—, gen. editor, 1964-65; chief Washington bur., 1965-85, sr. editor, 1985-86; editor spl. projects U.S. News and World Report, 1986-97; editor emeritus U.S. News Coll. Guides, 1997—. TV panelist; cons. Ednl. Facilities Lab., N.Y.C. Author: (with others) Bricks and Mortarboards, 1963; editor America's Best Colleges, 1987-97, Guide to America's Best Graduate Schools, 1987-97, Triumph Without Victory, 1992; contbr. articles to various publs. Served as officer SAC, USAF, 1952-53. Recipient George Polk Meml. award reporting, 1957, N.Y. Newspaper Guild Page One award, 1957; award Edn. Writers Assn., 1966 Mem. Phi Beta Kappa Home: 4515 30th St NW Washington DC 20008-2126 Personal E-mail: melfin@aol.com.

EL-FISHAWY, SAAD SAMUEL, lawyer; b. Tanta, Egypt, Feb. 20, 1924; arrived in U.S., 1957; s. Samuel Athanasious Bistawrous and Regina Youssef Ekdawy; m. Mona Youssef Milad, Sept. 15, 1960; children: Sani, Karim, Paul. Degree in law with honors, U. Cairo, 1944, MA in Civil Law with honors, 1949, MA in Econs. with honors, 1950; LLD, U. Chgo., 1959. Bar: Egypt, U.S. Ct. Appeals (D.C. cir.). Dist. atty. Minisry of Justice, Luxor, Egypt, 1945; ptnr. Saba Habashy Law Firm, Cairo, 1946-53, Maksoud El-Fishawy Law Firm, Cairo, 1953-57; atty. World Bank, Washington, 1959-63; gen. counsel Kuwait Fund for Arab Econ. Devel., 1963-66; sr. counsel legal dept. World Bank, Washington, 1966-74, sr. adviser fin. sect., 1974—, spl. adviser to pres., 1976-87. Adj. prof. Mid. Eastern Legal Instit. and Islamic Law, Columbia Law Sch., 1979-81, George Town Legal Ctr, 1982-92; counsel Arent Fox Law Firm, Washington, 1987-92, G. William Miller & Co.-Merchant Banking, Washington, 1987—. Author: Freedom of Belief in Egypt, 1954. Mem. supreme com. Nat. Party, Egypt, 1946-57. Named First Foreign Lawyer Accredited by D.C. Ct. Appeals, 1987; recipient Distinction prize, Islamic Law, 1944. Mem. Egyptian Bar Assn., D.C. Bar Assn., Cosmos Club. Avocations: swimming, tennis, chess. Home: 4155 27th St N Arlington VA 22207-5211 Office: G William Miller & Co 1100 Connecticut Ave Washington DC 20036-2401 Personal E-mail: saadel@gmail.com.

ELFMAN, DANNY, composer; b. Amarillo, Tex., May 29, 1953; m. Bridget Fonda, Nov. 29, 2003; 3 children. Lead singer, songwriter (band) Oingo Boingo, 1979—. Albums (with Oingo Boingo): Oingo Boingo, 1980, Only a Lad, 1981, Nothing to Fear, 1982, Good for Your Soul, 1984, Dead Man's Party, 1986, Boi-ngo, 1987, Boingo Alive, 1988, Skeletons in the Closet, 1988, Dark at the End of the Tunnel, 1990, Best O' Boingo, 1991, Boingo, 1994; composer: (film scores) Forbidden Zone, 1980, Back to School, 1985, Pee-wee's Big Adventure, 1985, Wisdom, 1987, Summer School, 1987, Beetlejuice, 1988, Hot to Trot, 1988, Midnight Run, 1988, Scrooged, 1988, Batman 1989 (Grammy award), Dick Tracy, 1990, Darkman, 1990, Edward Scissorhands, 1990, Nightbreed, 1990, Pure Luck, 1991, Article 99, 1992, Batman Returns, 1992, Somersby, 1993, March of the Dead Theme (Army of Darkness), 1993, The Nightmare Before Christmas, 1993, Black Beauty, 1994, Dolores Claiborne, 1995, Mission Impossible, 1996, The Frighteners, 1996, Bordello of Blood, 1996, Extreme Measures, 1996, Mars Attacks!, 1996, Men in Black, 1997 (Oscar nomination), Flubber, 1997, Good Will Hunting, 1997 (Oscar nomination), A Civil Action, 1998, Instinct, 1999, Sleepy Hollow, 1999, Proof of Life, 2000, The Family Man, 2000, Spy Kids, 2001, Planet of the Apes, 2001, Novocaine, 2001, Spiderman, 2002, Men in Black II, 2002, Red Dragon, 2002, Chicago, 2002, Hulk, 2003, Big Fish, 2003, Spider-Man 2, 2004, Charlie and the Chocolate Factory, 2005, Corpse Bride, 2005, Nacho Libre, 2006, Charlotte's Web, 2006, Meet the Ronsinsons, 2007, The Kingdom, 2007; (TV series score, Grammy nomination) The Simpsons (Emmy nomination), (TV) Tales of the Crypt, Pee-wee's Playhouse, 1986, Amazing Stories (2), Alfred Hitchcock Presents (1), Fast Times, 1986, Sledgehammer, 1986, Beetlejuice (animated), 1989, The Flash, 1990, Family Dog, 1992, Batman, 1992, Weird Science, 1994, Perversions of Science, 1997, Dilbert, 1999, Desperate Housewives, 2004; (albums) So-lo, 1984, Music for a Darkened Theatre, 1990. Office: The Kraft-Engel Management 15233 Ventura Blvd Ste 200 Sherman Oaks CA 91403*

ELFMAN, JENNA (JENNIFER MARY BUTALA), actress; b. LA, Sept. 30, 1971; m. Bodhi Rice Elfman, Feb. 18, 1995; 1 child, Story Elias Studied with Milton Katselas, LA. Actor: (films) Grosse Point Blank, 1997, Krippendorf's Tribe, Can't Hardly Wait, 1998, (voice only) Dr. Dolittle, 1998, EdTV, 1999, Keeping the Faith, 2000, (voice only) Cyber World, 2000, (voice only) The Tangerine Bear, 2000, Town & Country, 2001, Looney Tunes: Back In Action, 2003, (voice only) Clifford's Really Big Movie, 2004, (voice only) What's Hip, Doc?, 2005, Touched, 2005; TV films) Double Deception, 1993, Her Last Chance, 1996, Obsessed, 2002; (TV series) Townies, 1996, Dharma & Greg 1997-2002, Courting Alex, 2006-; TV appearances include Murder, She Wrote, 1992, Pointman, 1995, The Monroes, 1995, Roseanne, 1995, NYPD Blue, 1995, Murder One, 1995, Almost Perfect, 1996, The Single Guy, 1997, Two and a Half Men, 2004; starred in many music videos including Antrax video for Crossroads Films. Recipient TV Guide award, 1999, 2000, Spirit of the Cmty. award, Assn.for Better Living and Edn., 2005. Avocation: performing ballet. Mailing: c/o Creative Artists Agy 9830 Wilshire Blvd Beverly Hills CA 90212-1825

ELFNER, ALBERT HENRY, III, retired portfolio manager; b. Boston, Oct. 6, 1944; s. Albert Henry and Nellie May (Stewart) E.; m. Norma Elfner (div.); 1 child, Nicholas Stewart; m. Jane Colgrove, Oct. 10, 1980; 1 child, Kimberly Ann Stockwell. AB, Middlebury Coll., 1966; postgrad., Harvard U., 1993; D of Comml. Sci. (hon.), Merrimack Coll., 1999. CFA. Investment analyst Bank of Boston, 1966-69; portfolio mgr. Keystone Custodian Funds, Inc., Boston, 1969-81, pres., 1983-91; chmn. Keystone Investment Mgmt. Corp., Boston; pres. Keystone Group, Boston, 1990-95, pres., CEO, 1995—; CEO Keystone Investments, 1995; chmn., CEO Evergreen Investment Mgmt., 1996—99. Bd. dirs. NGM Ins., Jacksonville (Fla.) Unitil Corp., Hampton, N.H. Trustee Anatolia Coll., Middlesex Sch.; pres. Trustees of the Donations, Boston, Mass., 2004. Mem. Boston Soc. Security Analysts, Union Boat Club (bd. dirs., pres. 1983-86), Somerset Club, Boston Econs. Club, The Country Club (Brookline, Mass.), Ausable Club, Mt. Lake Colony Club. Republican. Episcopalian. Avocations: skiing, squash, golf, gardening. Home: 53 Chestnut St Boston MA 02108-3506 Home (Winter): Mountain Lake Lake Wales FL 33898-6626 E-mail: chipelfner@aol.com.

ELFVING, DON C., horticulturist, educator; b. Albany, Calif., June 20, 1941; BS in Botany, U. Calif., Davis, 1964, MS in Horticulture, 1966; PhD in Plant Physiology, U. Calif., Riverside, 1971. From asst. prof. to assoc. prof. pomology Cornell U., Ithaca, NY, 1972-79; rsch. scientist Hort. Rsch. Inst. Ontario, Simcoe, Canada, 1979-91, mgr. rsch. programs Vineland, Canada, 1991-93; supt. tree fruit rsch. and extension ctr. Wash. State U., Wenatchee, 1993-97, horticulturist, prof., 1997—. Cons. U.S. AID, 1977; cons. Internat. Agrl. Devel. Svc., Ark., 1981-82. Author: Training and Pruning of Apple and Pear Trees, 1992. Recipient U.P. Hedrick 1st Pl. award Am. Pomological Soc., 1992. Fellow Am. Soc. Hort. Sci.; mem. Am. Soc. for Hort. Sci. (bd. dirs. 1993-95, chair publs. com. 1993-95), Internat. Fruit Tree Assn. (R.F. Carlson Disting. lectr. 1993). Office: Tree Fruit Rsch & Ext Ctr 1100 N Western Ave Wenatchee WA 98801-1230 Business E-Mail: delfving@wsu.edu.

ELGAR, SHARON KAY, science educator; b. Geneseo, Ill., June 27, 1950; BA, Aurora U., Ill., 1972; M in Ednl. Leadership/Adminstrn., Benedictine U., 2006. Lic. EMT Waubonsee Coll.; cert. outdoor edn. and survival tng. courses U. Wis., death and dying, outdoor edn. issues, drugs and society, and gifted edn. courses No. Ill. U., tchr. Ill. Tchr. physics, chemistry, biology Aurora Cen. Cath. H.S., 2001—. Beauty cons. Mary Kay, Inc., Mich.; mem. adv. bd. Kane County Pre-Sch., Geneva; mem. homebound tutoring Kaneland Sch. Dist., Maple Park, Ill. Mem. Town & Country Libr. Dist., Elburn; counselor, aide for grief Conley Outreach Ctr., Elburn. Recipient Gold Ivy Leaf Scholar's honors, Aurora U., 1972. Mem.: Boy Scouts Am. Venture Crew, Am. Girl Scouts Assn., Rockford Cath. Diocese Tchrs. Assn., Ill. Tchrs. Assn. (sec. 1972—), Am. Chem. Soc., Nat. Sci. Tchrs. Assn., St. Peters Women Soc., Elburn Lion's Club, Elburn Legion Aux. Republican. Roman Catholic. Avocations: canoeing, hiking, swimming, exercise, reading. Home: 200 Oak Dr Elburn IL 60119 Office: Aurora Cen Cath H S 1255 N Edgelawn Dr Aurora IL 60506 Office Phone: 630-907-0095.

ELGART, EDWARD GUERRY, civilian military employee; AS, Brookdale CC, Lincroft, NJ, 1972, AA, 1979; BA, Kean U., Union, NJ, 1974; MBA, Fairleigh Dickinson U., Rutherford, NJ, 1979. Dir. contract mgmt. Def. Contract Mgmt. Agy., Chgo., 1987—89; dep. asst. sec. army (procurement) US Army Acquisition, Logistics and Tech., Washington, 1997—98, 1999—2001; dir. Acquisition Ctr. US Army COMM-ELEC Command, Ft. Monmouth, NJ, 1989—. Contbr. chapters to books. Recipient Presdl. Meritorious Exec. award, Pres. William J. Clinton, 1996, Pres. George W. Bush, 2002. Mem.: Nat. Contract Mgmt. Assn. (bd. advisor 2004—). Business E-Mail: edward.g.elgart@us.army.mil.

ELGART, LARRY JOSEPH, orchestra leader; b. New London, Conn., Mar. 20, 1922; s. Arthur M. and Bessie (Aisman) E.; m. Lynn Walzer, June 28, 1963; children by previous marriage: Brock, Brad. Altosaxophonist, formed Les and Larry Elgart Orch., 1947, rec. artist for Decca, RCA, Victor, MGM, Columbia labels. Recipient Billboard award, 1959, Downbeat Most Played Band award Disc Jockey poll, 1959, Downbeat, Cashbox and Billboards awards in popularity polls, Gold record album for Hooked on Swing, 1982, Platinum, 1984.

ELGART, MERVYN L., retired dermatologist, educator; b. Bklyn., Aug. 12, 1933; s. Jacob and Sally R. E.; m. Sheila Ruth Cliff, June 13, 1954; children— Brian, George, Paul, Adam, James. AB, Bklyn. Coll., 1953; MD, Cornell U., 1957. Intern Buffalo Gen. Hosp., 1957-58; resident in dermatology Walter Reed Gen. Hosp., Washington, 1960-63; chief dermatology Andrews AFB Hosp., Washington, 1964-66; mem. faculty George Washington U. Med. Sch., 1967-97, prof. dermatology, 1974-97, chmn. dept., 1975-97, prof. pediatrics, 1974-97, prof. medicine, 1974-97; clin. prof. dermatology, medicine and pediatrics Univ. Dermatology Assocs., Washington, 1997—2002, emeritus prof. dermatology, 2002—; ret., 2003. Mem. med. adv. com. Nat. Orgn. Rare Diseases, 2000—. Served as officer M.C. USAF, 1958—66. Fellow Am. Acad. Dermatology; mem. AMA, So. Med. Assn., Internat. Soc. Dermatology, Washington Dermatol. Soc., Am. Dermatol. Assn., Phi Beta Kappa, Alpha Omega Alpha. Roman Catholic. Personal E-mail: elgartm@aol.com.

ELGEE, NEIL JOHNSON, retired internist, endocrinologist, educator; b. Oxford, NS, Can., Apr. 3, 1926; arrived in U.S., 1946, naturalized, 1955; s. William Harris and Lucile (Nevers) Elgee; m. Leona Victoria Karlsson, Aug. 18, 1951; children: Joan, Susan, Laurie, Steven, Karen. BSc, U. N.B., Can., 1946; MD, U. Rochester, 1950. Intern Peter Bent Brigham Hosp., Boston, 1950—51; resident Strong Meml. Hosp., Rochester, NY, 1951—52; fellow in endocrinology U. Wash., 1952—54, co-chief resident in medicine Seattle, 1954—55, clin. prof. medicine, 1968—93, emeritus clin. prof. medicine, 1993—; practice medicine specializing in endocrinology Seattle, 1957—93; retired, 1993. Founder, pres. Ernest Becker Found., 1993—. Capt. USAF, 1955—57. Master: ACP (gov. for Wash. and Alaska 1965—71, regent 1974—78); mem.: Inst. Medicine, Endocrine Soc. Home: 3621 72nd Ave SE Mercer Island WA 98040-3330 Office Phone: 206-232-2994. Business E-Mail: nelgee@u.washington.edu.

ELGER, WILLIAM ROBERT, JR., accountant; b. Chgo., Mar. 20, 1950; s. William Robert and Grace G. (LaVaque) E.; m. Kathryn Michele Johnson, July 10, 1971; children: Kimberly, William, Kristin, Joseph. AS in Applied Sci., Coll. of DuPage, Glen Ellyn, Ill., 1970; BS magna cum laude, U. Ill.-Chgo., 1972. CPA, Ill. Staff acct. Ernst & Whinney, Chgo., 1973, in-charge acct., 1973-74, sr. acct., 1974-78, mgr., 1978-82, sr. mgr., 1982-88; chief fin. officer U. Ill. Eye and Ear Infirmary, 1988-89; CFO U. Mich. Med. Sch., Ann Arbor, 1989-99, exec. dir. adminstrn., CFO, 2000—. Chair fin. controls frame work task force U. Mich., 1999—2004, chmn. internal controls adv. group, 2005—; presenter various confs. in field. Author, developer: (tng. course) Auditing Third Party Reimbursement, 1986, 87; Author: Managing Resources in a Better Way: A New Financial Management Approach for the University of MIchigan Medical School, 2006. Active Union League Civic and Arts Found., Chgo., 1982-89, Union League Found. for Boys and Girls Clubs, Chgo., 1982-89; treas. Newport Assn., Carol Stream, Ill., 1982-83; coach Tri-City Soccer Assn., St. Charles, Ill., 1984, 87, Saline Soccer Assn., 1990, 91, 93, 94, 95, Saline H.S. Soccer Club, 1996, 97. Mem. AICPA, Healthcare Fin. Mgmt. Assn. (advanced mem., acctg. and reimbursement com. 1982-87, chpt. task force com. 1986, 87, auditing com. 1986, 87, Spl. Recognition award 1986, Follmer Bronze Merit award 1999), Ill. Soc. CPAs (mem. long term healthcare com. 1983, hosps. com. 1988-89), Nat. Coun. Univ. Rsch. Adminstrs., Med. Group Mgmt. Assn., Assn. Am. Med. Colls. (group on bus. affairs steering com. 2004, chair Midwest region 2004, profl. devel. com. 2004-, group on bus. affairs nat. chair 2006-2007). Methodist. Avocation: golf. Office: PO Box 624 1301 Catherine St Ann Arbor MI 48109-0624 Home Phone: 734-846-6799; Office Phone: 734-763-5202. Business E-Mail: welger@umich.edu.

ELGIN, RON ALAN, advertising executive; b. Milw., Sept. 15, 1941; s. Carl John and Vivian Elaine (Phillips) E.; m. Bonnie Kay Visintainer, Dec. 3, 1968; 1 child, Alison. BA in Advt., U. Wash., 1965. With Cole & Weber, Seattle, 1965-81; pres. Elgin Syferd, Seattle, 1981-89; chmn. Elgin Syferd/Drake, Boise, Idaho, 1987—; pres., CEO Elgin DDB, 1989-99; pres. DDB Needham Retail, Seattle, 2000—. Chmn. Hornall Anderson Design Works, Seattle, 1982-91; ptnr. Christiansen & Fritsch Direct, Seattle, 1988-96; bd. dirs. Hart Crowser; bd. dirs. Ctrl. Media, Inc., Knowledge Anywhere. Bd. dirs. Ronald McDonald House, Seattle, 1984—, Big Bros., Seattle, 1986—, Spl. Olympics, Seattle, 1987-90, Pacific N.W. Ballet, Seattle, 1988-98, Poncho, Seattle, 1991—, Odyssey, 1993-99, Swedish Hosp., 1995—; mem. adv. bd. U. Wash., Wash. State U. Lt. U.S. Army, 1965-69. Mem. Am. Assn. Advt. Agencies, Am. Mktg. Assn., Mktg. Comm. Execs. Internat. Office: DDB Seattle 1000 2nd Ave Seattle WA 98104-1004

ELGIN, SARAH CARLISLE ROBERTS, biology researcher and educator; b. Washington, July 16, 1945; d. Carlisle Bishop and Lorene (West) Roberts; m. Robert Lawrence Elgin, June 9, 1967; children: Benjamin Carlisle, Thomas James. BA in Chemistry, Pomona Coll., 1967; PhD in Biochemistry, Calif. Inst. Tech., 1971. Rsch. fellow Calif. Inst. Tech., Pasadena, 1971-73; asst. prof. biochemistry and molecular biology Harvard U., Cambridge, Mass., 1973-77, assoc. prof., 1977-81; assoc. prof. biology Washington U., St. Louis, 1981-84, prof., 1984—, prof. edn., 2001, prof. genetics, 2003, Viktor Hamburger prof. arts and scis., 2007; mem. Nat. Com. on Sci. Edn. Stds. and Assessment, NAS/NRC, 1992. Mem. editl. bd. Jour. Cell Biology, NYC, 1980-82, Jour. Biol. Chemistry, 1985-88, Molecular Cellular Biology, 1989-; exec. editor Nucleic Acids Rsch., 1983-88; assoc. editor Molecular Cell, 1998-, Bio Med Net; co-editor-in-chief Cell Biology Edn., 2002-05; contbr. articles to profl. jours. Mem. molecular biology study sect. NIH, 1986-89. Recipient Prof.'s award Howard Hughes Med. Inst., 2002, 2006; rsch. grantee NIH, 1987, 88, 91, 93, 98-99, 2003, 05, 07, NSF, 1986. Fellow AAAS (sect. on biol. scis. 1991—); mem. Am. Soc. Biol. Chemists (program com. 1984), Am. Soc. Cell Biology (coun. 1983-85, 92-94, publs. com. 1989-91, edn. com. 1992-2005), Genetics Soc. Am. Office: Washington Univ Biology Dept CB 1137 One Brookings Dr Saint Louis MO 63130-4899 Office Phone: 314-935-5348. Office Fax: 314-935-5125. Business E-Mail: selgin@biology.wustl.edu.

ELGISON, MARTIN J., lawyer; b. Miami, Fla., Feb. 22, 1951; s. Hyman and Rose (Lang) E.; m. Juli E. Elgison, June 2, 1984. BA, U. South Fla., 1972; JD, Miami U., Fla., 1981. Bar: Ga. 1981. From assoc. to ptnr. Alston & Bird LLP, Altanta, 1981—, founder, intellectual property practice. Contbr. articles to profl. jours. Avocations: golf, tennis. Office: Alston & Bird LLP 1 Atlantic Ctr 1201 W Peachtree St NW Ste 4200 Atlanta GA 30309-3424 Office Phone: 404-881-7167. Office Fax: 404-881-7777. Business E-Mail: melgison@alston.com.

EL-HADIDY, BAHAA, information scientist, educator, consultant; b. Cairo, June 21, 1931; arrived in U.S., 1961; s. Sadek Ayoub El-Hadidy and Tafida Mostafa Fahmy; m. Lily Ayad, Mar. 27, 1965. BSc, Cairo U., 1954; MLS, Rutgers U., New Brunswick, NJ, 1963; PhD, U. Pitts., 1974. Advanced cert. U. of Pitts., 1966. Sci. info. officer Nat. Rsch. Ctr., Cairo, 1955—61; info. analyst and chem. info. specialist U. Pitts., 1967—72, libr., 1972—74; asst. prof. Cath. U. Am., Washington, 1974—84; asst. sr. exec. and v.p. Islamic Internat. Bank, Cairo, 1984—87; assoc. prof. U. South Fla., Tampa, 1987—96; internat. cons. Tampa, 1996—. Cons. NSF, Washington, 1975, The Franklin Inst., Phila., 1977—78, African Regional Ctr. Tech., Dakar, Senegal, 1983—84, UN Indsl. Devel. Orgn., Vienna, 1989—95, Inst. Applied Sci. & Tech., Guyana, 1989, Acad. Sci. Ministry Sci. Rsch., Manila, 1990, Acad. Sci. Rsch. & Tech., Cairo, 1994—98; sr.

cons. Ga. Inst. Tech., Atlanta, 1979—84; prin. project investigator and cons. NASA Sci. Info. Facility, Balt., 1984; vis. prof. Cairo U., 1985—87; chmn. tng. Profl. Mgmt. Svcs. Ctr., Kuwait, 1987. Author: Approaches to the Economical Retrospective Machine-Searching of the Chemical Literature, in Computer-Based Chemical Information, 1973; editor: Infrastructure of an Information Society, 1982; contbr. chapters to books, articles and tech. reports to profl. jours. and orgns. Rep. friends group Bibliotheca Alexandrina, Egypt; bd. mem. U.S. Nat. Com. UNESCO Gen. Info. Program, Washington, 1981—84; chmn. U.S. interim com. Internat. Fedn. Documentation, Washington, 1982—84; bd. mem. Sertoma Club at U. South Fla., Tampa, 1997—99; v.p. north Tampa aux. The Children's Home of Tampa, 2000—03; chmn. bd. Am. Soc. Info. Sci./SIG Internat. Info. Issues, Washington, 2001—02; chmn. internat. rels. Am. Soc. Info. Sci., Washington, 1981—83, chmn. bd. (so. Fla. chpt.) Tampa, Fla., 1992—93. Recipient Oustanding Svc. Info. Sci. Profession, Info. Sci. and Tech. Coun., 1984; grantee, NSF, 1979—82, UN Indsl. Devel. Orgn., 1989. Mem.: AAUP, ALA (life), Suncoast Info. Specialists, Assn. Libr. and Info. Sci. Edn., Assn. Egyptian-Am. Scholars, Spl. Libraries Assn., Assn. Computing Machinery, Am. Soc. Info. Sci. and Tech. (certs. appreciation and recognition outstanding svcs. 1984—2004, SIG mem. of yr. award 2000), Tampa Palms Golf & Country Club (bd. mem. 2001—03), Beta Phi Mu (recognition guidance, tchg., and advising 1996). Achievements include development of economical system for searching large database in the 1970s; multifaceted approach for training information specialists from developing countries in the United States; information support systems for industrial projects in developing countries; research in bibliographic control among geoscience abstracting and indexing services; design of information support systems for industrial projects in developing countries. Avocations: classical music, travel, tennis. Home: 16104 Stowe Ct Tampa FL 33647-1147 Office Phone: 813-978-1551. Personal E-mail: elhadidy@cas.usf.edu.

ELHAUGE, EINER RICHARD, law educator; b. NYC, May 28, 1961; s. Einer Eduardo and Maria Ines (Robatto) Elhauge. AB, Harvard U., 1982, JD, 1986. Bar: Pa. 1986, US Ct. Appeals 9th Cir. 1987. Law clk. Office Solicitor Gen., Washington, 1986; law clk. to Judge William Norris US Ct. Appeals 9th Cir., LA, 1986-87; law clk. to Assoc. Justice William J. Brennan US Supreme Ct., Washington, 1987-88; assoc. prof. law U. Calif., Berkeley, 1988-92, prof., 1992-95; prof. law Harvard U., Cambridge, Mass., 1995—. Olin faculty fellow Yale U., 1993; vis. prof. law Harvard U., 1994, U. Chgo., 1995. Co-author: Antitrust Law, 1996. Office: Harvard Law Sch 1563 Massachusetts Ave Cambridge MA 02138 Office Phone: 617-496-0860. Office Fax: 617-496-0861. Business E-Mail: elhauge@law.harvard.edu.

EL-HILALI, OUSSAMA, application developer; b. Tetouan, Morocco; s. Zakia Soultan and M.A. El-Hilali; m. Cheryl M. Unterweger; children: Tarik, Alia. BA, Ripon Coll., Ripon, Wis., 2002; MS, U. St. Thomas, St. Paul, 2007. Sr. dir. Symantec, Roseville, Minn., 2001—. Author: Digital Data Integrity, 2007. Mem.: IEEE. Office: Symantec 2815 Cleveland Ave Roseville MN 55113

ELIA, MICHELE, mathematics educator; b. Berzano, Asti-Piemonte, Italy, Jan. 2, 1945; s. Luigi and Cristina (Fogliatti) E. Dr. engr., Politecnico di Torino, 1970. Rschr. FIAT, Torino, Italy, 1970-71, Politecnico di Torino, 1971-77, assoc. prof. math., 1977-90, prof., 1990—. Author: (with others) The Information Theory Approach to Communications, 1977; assoc. editor Math Jours.; contbr. articles to profl. jours. Mem. IEEE (sr.), Unione Matematica Italiana, Am. Math. Soc., Math. Assn. Am., Soc. Indsl. and Applied Math., NY Acad. Scis. Roman Catholic. Office: Politecnico di Torino Dipartimento Elettronica Corso Duca degli Abruzzi 24 10129 Turin Italy Office Phone: +39 0115644027. E-mail: michele.elia7@gmail.com.

ELIAS, ANTONIO L., aerospace transportation executive; b. Mar. 3, 1949; married, 1972; 4 children. BS, EAA, MIT, PhD Aeronautics, Astronautics. Rschr., staff mem. Space Guidance & Nav. Divsn., CS Draper Lab., 1972—80; asst. prof. aeronautics and astronautics MIT, 1980—86, sr. v.p. engring., 1986—93, sr. v.p. adv. project group, 1993—96; sr. v.p., chief tech. officer Orbital Sci. Corp., Dulles, Va., 1996—97, exec. v.p., gen mgr. advanced prog., 1997—. Contbr. numerous articles to sci. jours.; patentee in field. Recipient Nat. Medal Tech., 1991, Nat. Air & Space Mus. Trophy. Fellow: AIAA (Engineer of the Year 1991, Aircraft Design award), Am. Astron. Soc. (Brouwer award); mem.: Nat. Acad. Engring. Office: 21839 Atlantic Blvd Dulles VA 20166-6801 E-mail: ae@orbital.com.

ELIAS, KYRIAKIDES, electrical engineer, educator, researcher; b. Nicosia, Cyprus, Aug. 20, 1975; s. Kyriacos and Chrysavgi Elia. BSc, Ill. Inst. Tech., Chgo., 2000; MSc, Ariz. State U., Tempe, 2001, PhD, 2003. Rsch. assoc. Ariz. State U., Tempe, 2000—03, faculty rsch. assoc., 2003—04; lectr. U. Cyprus, Nicosia, 2004—. Contbr. articles to profl. jours. Recipient Presdl. award for the best overall performance among all graduating students at the Higher Tech. Inst., Republic of Cyprus, 1996, Alumni assn. award for the best overall performance among all graduating students, Ill. Inst. Tech., 2000, Palais Outstanding Doctoral Student award, Ariz. State U., 2004, Mentorship Appreciation cert., Preparing Future Faculty Program, Ariz. State U., 2004; Grad. Academic scholar, Ariz. State U., 2001—03, Academic scholar, Cyprus State Scholarship Authority, 2001, 2002, Fulbright fellow, Fulbright Commn., 1998—2000. Mem.: IEEE, Internat. Network for Engring. Edn. and Rsch., Tech. Chamber Cyprus (vice chair rsch. com. 2006), Internat. Coun. on Large Electric Systems, Instn. Engring. and Tech., Tau Beta Pi. Achievements include patents pending for system and method of estimating synchronous generator parameters. Office: University of Cyprus 75 Kallipoleos St PO Box 20537 1678 Nicosia Cyprus Office Phone: +357-22892291. Office Fax: +357-22892260. Business E-Mail: elias@ucy.ac.cy.

ELIAS, LORI ANNE, music educator, journalist, photojournalist; b. Willoughby, Ohio, Sept. 4, 1969; d. M. J. and Judith Helen Elias. MusB magna cum laude, Bowling Green State U., 1991; MusM, Cleve. State U., 2005. Music educator Rossford Exempted Village Schs., Rossford, Ohio, 1993—94, Tipp City Exempted Village Schs., Ohio, 1994—97, Wickliffe H.S., Wickliffe, Ohio, 1997—2001, Willoughby-Eastlake City Schs., 2001—. Presenter in field. Contbr., website, e-zine, articles to profl. jours. Presser scholar, Bowling Green State U., 1990. Mem.: Soc. Ethnomusicology, Can. Soc. Traditional Music, Lake County Music Educators Assn. (pres. 2001—03, v.p. 2003—05), Ohio Music Educators Assn., Music Educators Nat. Conf., Kappa Delta Pi, Pi Kappa Lambda, Sigma Alpha Iota. Avocation: coaching tennis. E-mail: indian1723@aol.com.

ELIAS, MAURICE JESSE, psychology educator; b. Bronx, NY, Dec. 1, 1952; m. Ellen Sue Rosen, Aug. 7, 1976; children: Sara Elizabeth, Samara Alexandra. BA in Psychology summa cum laude, CUNY, 1974; MA in Clin. Psychology, U. Conn., 1977, PhD in Clin. Psychology, 1980. Psychotherapist mental health svc. U. Conn., Storrs, 1977-78; prevention planning cons. Conn. Dept. Children and Youth Svcs., 1978-79; asst. prof. psychology Rutgers U., New Brunswick, NJ, 1979-85, assoc. prof., 1985—94, prof., coord. internship program in applied-cmty. psychology, 1979—, field supr. psychol. clinic grad. sch., 1979—. Mem. co-adj. faculty dept. psychiatry U. Medicine and Dentistry N.J.-Robert Wood Johnson Med. Sch., 1985, Schwartzman family parenting program Am. Jerusalem Acad. for Contemporary Judaic Studies, 1987—; cons. to numerous pub. sch. dists., pvt. schs., community groups, presenter in field. Author: Social Problem Solving Interventions in the Schools, 1996, Promoting Social & Emotional Learnings: Guidelines for Educators, 1997, Emotionally Intelligent Parenting, 1999, Raising Emotionally Intelligent Teenagers, 2002, The Educator's Guide to Emotional Intelligence and Academic Achievement, 2006, Community Psychology: Linking Individuals and Communities, 2007; contbr. articles to profl. jours. Treas., trustee Middlesex County Resources for Menatlly Handicapped, Inc., 1981-83; bd. dirs. Nat. Orgns. Adv. Coun. Children, 1981-85, Prevention Coalition NJ, 1990-92; mem. Interagy. Youth Devel. Consortium, 1982-86, Nat. Coalition Against TV Violence, 1979—; pres. religious sch. bd. edn. Highland Park Conservative Temple and Ctr., 1992-2004, trustee, 1992-2004; trustee Assn. for Children NJ, 1992—; exec. com. Collaborative for Academic of Social and Emotional Learning, 1995. Grantee Rutgers U., 1979-83, 84-85, 85-87, William T. Grant Found., 1982-90, 99—, NIMH, 1982-85, 88, 99—, Middlesex County Mental Health Bd. and Bd. Chosen Freeholders, 1984-87, Schumann Found. NJ, 1987-89, 90-93, Fetzer Inst., 1995-99, John Templeton Found., 2002-07, NJ Dept. Edn., 2005-; Lilly Endowment grantee William T. Grant Found., 1991-94, 99-2002, Surdna Found., 1999-2000. Mem. ASCD, APA (Nat. Psychology award 1986, 88, Nat. Psychol. Cons. to Mgmt. award 1990, Disting. Contbn. to Practice award 1993, Ethnic Minority Mendoring award, 1998), Nat. Assn. Sch. Psychologists, Phi Beta Kappa. Home: 139 N 5th Ave Highland Park NJ 08904-2924 Office: Tillett Hall Livingston Campus Rutgers U Dept Psychol New Brunswick NJ 08903 Business E-Mail: rutgersmje@aol.com.

ELIAS, PATRIK, professional hockey player; b. Trebic, Czech Republic, Apr. 13, 1976; m. Petra Volakova. Left wing HC Kladno, 1993—95, Albany River Rats (AHL), 1995—97, NJ Devils, 1997—, capt., 2006—. Mem. Czech Nat. Hockey Team, Olympic Games, Salt Lake City, 2002, Torino, Italy, 06, Czech Nat. Hockey Team, World Cup of Hockey, 2004; player NHL All-Star Game, 2000, 02. Goodwill amb. UNICEF, 2006—. Co-recipient Bud Light Plus/Minus Award, 2001; named to All-Rookie Team, NHL, 1998, First All-Star Team, 2001. Achievements include being a member of Stanley Cup Champion NJ Devils, 2000, 2003; being a member of bronze medal winning Czech Republic Hockey Team, Torino Olympics, Italy, 2006. Office: c/o NJ Devils Nat Newark Bldg 744 Broad St, 33rd Fl Newark NJ 07102*

ELIAS, PAUL S., retired marketing executive; b. Chgo., July 5, 1926; s. Maurice I. and Ethel (Tieger) E.; m. Jennie Lee Feldschreiber, June 28, 1953; children— Eric David, Stephen Mark, Daniel Avrum. BS, Northwestern U. Sch. Bus., 1950; degree (hon.), NYU, 1972. Buyer Mandel Bros., Chgo., 1950-53; salesman Internat. Latex Corp., Chgo., 1953-56; v.p. Hy Zeiger & Co., Milw., 1957-59; exec. v.p. K-Promotions, Inc., Milw., 1960-78, pres., 1979-80; chief exec. officer, pres. consumer promotions Carlson Mktg. Group, Mpls., 1981-84, chief exec. officer promotions div. Milw., 1985-86; pres. K-Promotions Div. Carlson Promotion Group, 1987-88, Giftmaster Div. Carlson Promotion Group, 1989—2001, Elias Mktg., Inc., 1989—2001; ret. Officer, dir. Milw. Jewish Community Center; pres. regional bd. Anti-Defamation League; pres. Regional Bd. Jewish Nat. Fund, 1993-96. Served with USAAF, 1945-46. Mem. Am. Jewish. Achievements include developing inflight mail order mktg. programs for airlines. Home and Office: Elias Mktg Inc 10134 N Gettysburg Ct Mequon WI 53092 Office Phone: 262-242-5978.

ELIAS, SARAH DAVIS, retired English language educator; b. Chgo., Aug. 9, 1934; d. Calvin Paul and Julia Elizabeth (Bush) Davis; m. Antoine Jack Elias, Aug. 28, 1960. BA, Roosevelt U., 1957; MA, Morgan State U., 1973; MS, Johns Hopkins U., 1983. Cert. tchr., Ill., Calif., Md. Elem. tchr. Chgo. Pub. Schs., 1958-62, Palo Alto (Calif.) Unified Sch. Dist., 1969-70; tchr. Balt. City Schs., 1969—92, chmn. reading dept., 1978-81, English tchr., 1982-92; supervising tchr. Coppin State Coll., Balt., 1973-75; instr. history Morgan State U., Balt., 1992—93, advisor academic devel. ctr., 2004—. Resource coord., tutor Johns Hopkins Tutorial Projects, Balt., 1968; social studies text cons. Harcourt, Brace, Jovanovich Pub., Balt., 1972; lectr. English and reading, Morgan State U., 1999-2003; bd. dirs. Charms with Clubs Inc., 2000-03; instr. history Coppin State U., 1992-93. Author: An Account of the Longview: Texas Riot of July 11, 1919, 2004. Mem. Mayor's Task Force on Edn., Balt., 1967-69, Mayor's Bicentennial Com., 1974-76. Am. Fedn. Tchrs.-Cornell U. fellow, 1967. Mem. Balt. Tchrs. Union (contract negotiator 1967-69), Herbert M. Frisbey Hist. Soc., NAACP (life), Delta Sigma Theta (life), Clubs: Chums (bd. dirs. 1992-94). Democrat. Baptist. Home: 20 Olmstead Green Ct Baltimore MD 21210-1508 Office: Acad Devel Ctr 1700 E Coldspring Ln Baltimore MD 21251 Home Phone: 410-532-8232; Office Phone: 443-885-2055.

ELIAS, SHERMAN, obstetrician, gynecologist, clinical geneticist, educator; b. Rome, Mar. 21, 1947; MD, U. Ky., 1972. Diplomate Am. Bd. Med. Genetics, Am. Bd. Ob-gyn. Resident in ob/gyn U. Louisville, 1976; postdoc. fellow in med. genetics Yale U., New Haven, 1975, Northwestern U., 1978; prof. ob/gyn. genetics U. Tenn., Memphis; prof. ob/gyn., molecular and human genetics Baylor Coll. Medicine, 1994—98; prof., head dept. ob-gyn. U. Ill., Chgo., 1998—2003; chair ob-gyn. Prentice Women's Hosp., Northwestern Meml., Chgo., 2003—; John J. Sciarra prof., chair dept. ob-gyn. Feinberg Sch. Medicine, Northwestern U., Chgo., 2003—. Contbr. articles to profl. jours. Mem. AAAS, Am. Soc. Human Genetics, Soc. Gynecologic Investigation, Am. Gynec./Obstet. Soc. Office: Northwestern U Feinberg Sch Medicine 333 E Superior St # 490 Chicago IL 60611 E-mail: selias@nmh.org.

ELIAS, STEVEN, surgeon; b. Bklyn., Feb. 14, 1953; s. Hyman and Arlene Elias; m. Maria Casella, Nov. 2, 1997; children: Erika, Jeremy, Mia, Sam. BA, The Johns Hopkins U., 1975; MD, SUNY, Buffalo, 1979. Dir. ctr. vein diease Englewood Hosp. and Med. Ctr., NJ, 2000—06, dir., anticoagulation and thrombosis ctr., 2006—. Cons. Smith and Nephew Inc., Andover, Mass., 2000—, Diomed Inc., 2003—, U.S. Surg. Inc., Norwalk, Conn., 2002—, Luminetx Corp., 2005. Vascular fellowship, England Hosp., 1984. Fellow: ACS, Soc. Clin. Vascular Surgery, Am. Coll. Phlebology, Am. Venous Forum; mem.: NJ Vascular Soc., Internat. Soc. Vascular Surgery. Achievements include development of Minimally Invasive Vein Surgery. Avocation: triatlhlons. Office: Englewood Hospital and Med Ctr 350 Engle St Englewood NJ 07631 Home Phone: 201-385-2587; Office Phone: 201-894-3252. Personal E-mail: veininnovations@aol.com.

ELIAS, THOMAS SAM, botanist, author; b. Cairo, Ill., Dec. 30, 1942; s. George Sam (dec.) and Anna (Clanton) E.; m. Barbara Ana Boyd (dec.); children: Stephen, Brian; m. Hiromi Nakaoji, 2000. BA in Botany, So. Ill. U., 1964, MA in Botany, 1966; PhD in Biology, St. Louis U., 1969; PhD (hon.), Russian Acad. Scis., Moscow, 2003. Asst. curator Arnold Arboretum of Harvard U., Cambridge, Mass., 1969-71; adminstr., dendrologist Cary Arboretum, N.Y. Botanical Garden, Millbrook, 1971-73, asst. dir., 1973-84; dir., CEO Rancho Santa Ana Bot. Garden, Claremont, Calif., 1984-93; chmn., prof. dept. botany Claremont Grad. Sch., 1984-93; dir. U.S. Nat. Arboretum, Washington, 1993—. Lectr. in extension Harvard U., 1971; adj. prof. Coll. Environ. Science and Forestry, Syracuse, N.Y., 1977-80; coord. U.S.A/U.S.S.R. Botanical Exch., Program for U.S. Dept. of Interior, Washington, 1976—, U.S.A./China Botanical Exch., Program for U.S. Dept. of Interior, 1988-94; sr. exec. svc. USDA, 1993—. Editor: Extinction is Forever, 1977 (one of 100 Best Books in Sci. and Tech. ALA 1977), Conservation and Management of Rare and Endangered Plants, 1987; author: Complete Trees of North America, 1980 (one of 100 Best Books in Sci. and Tech. ALA 1980), Field Guide to Edible Wild Plants of North America (one of 100 Best Books in Sci. and Tech. ALA 1983). Recipient Cooley award, Am. Soc. Plant Taxonomists, 1970, Disting. Alumni award, So. Ill. U., 1989, Presdl. Rank award, 2000, Writer's Artist and Photographer's award, Bonsai Clubs International, 2001. Home: 6276 15th Rd N Arlington VA 22205 Office: US Nat Arboretum 3501 New York Ave NE Washington DC 20002-1958 Office Phone: 202-245-4539. E-mail: tselias@msn.com.

ELIASHBERG, YAKOV, mathematician, educator; arrived in U.S., 1988; Doctorate, Leningrad U., 1972. Assoc. prof. Syktyvkar U., Russia, 1972—75, chair dept. math., 1975—79; head computer software group Russia, 1981—87; with Math. Scis. Rsch. Inst., Berkeley, Calif., 1988—89; prof. Stanford U., Calif., 1989—, chair math. dept. Recipient Oswald Veblen prize, Am. Math. Soc., 2001; Guggenheim fellow, 1995. Mem.: NAS. Office: Dept Math Bldg 380 Stanford U Stanford CA 94305-2125

ELIASI, JENNIFER REBECCA, dietician, consultant; b. L.I., NY, July 21, 1975; d. Hooshang Henry and Mahin May Eliasi; m. Jonathan Teich, Nov. 23, 2003. BA, Queens Coll., CUNY, 1997; MSc, Tufts U., Medford, Mass., 1999; registered dietitian, Frances Stern Nutrition Ctr. at New Eng. Med. Ctr., 1999. Cert. Dietitian Nutritionist NY, 2002. Nutrition intern God's Love We Deliver, NYC, 1996—97; AIDS rsch. vol. New Eng. Med. Ctr., Boston, 1998—99; rsch. asst. Frances Stern Nutrition Ctr., Boston, 1997—99; nutrition counselor Bklyn. AIDS Task Force, 2001—02; dir. nutrition svcs. AIDS Treatment and Health Program Bklyn. Hosp., 1999—2005; nutrition cons. Millennium Biotechs., Bernardsville, NJ, 2001—; key account mgr. Serono, Inc., 2005—. Sec. Bklyn AIDS Task Force Treatment Adherence Com., NY, 1999—; team leader Bklyn Hosp. World AIDS Day Team, NY, 1999—; cons. MTI Biotech, Inc., Ame, Iowa, 2000—, Agouron-Pfizer Pharmaceuticals, NYC, 2000—. Contbr. articles to profl. jours. Recipient Campus Ministries award for Promoting Racial Harmony, Queens Coll., CUNY, 1997, Dietetics Svc. award, 1997, Recognized Young Dietitian of the Yr., Am. Dietetic Assn., 2003, Alumni award, Tufts U., 2005;, N.Y. State Dietetic Assn. scholar, 1998. Mem.: Am. Dietetic Assn. Nutrition Entrepreneurs, Am. Dietetic Assn. HIV/AIDS Dietetic Practice Group (quality mgmt. chair 2002—03, chair elect 2003—04, chair 2004—), Nutritionists In AIDS Care (co-chair 2000—). Independent. Jewish. Achievements include research in relationship of testosterone deficiency and side effects; effect of steroids, nutrition and exercise in HIV/AIDs. Avocations: walking, travel, writing. Office: Bklyn Hosp Ctr Programs for AIDS Treatment and Health 100 Parkside Ave 5th Fl Brooklyn NY 11226 Personal E-mail: jenneliasi@aol.com.

ELIASON, ARLENE F., mathematician, educator; b. Kanawha, Iowa, June 14, 1949; d. Harold C. Eliason and Berneice J. Lein. AA, Waldorf Coll., Forest City, Iowa, 1969; BA, Concordia Coll., Moorhead, Minn., 1970; MA in Tchg. of Math., Minot State U., ND, 1997. Cert. tchr. ND, 1973. Instr. Minot Pub. Schs., ND, 1970—2001, Rasmussen Coll., Eagan, Minn., 2001—05, Minn. Sch. Bus., Shakopee, 2005—. Recipient Instl. Svc. award, Rasmussen Coll., 2005. Mem.: Coll. Reading Learning Assn., Math. Assn. Am. Home: 17250 Barberry Circle Eden Prairie MN 55346 Office: Minnesota School of Business - Shakopee 1200 Town Square Shakopee MN 55379 Home Phone: 952-937-0394; Office Phone: 952-345-1200. E-mail: aeliason@msbcollege.edu.

ELIASON, BIRDELL, painter, educator; d. Herman A. Eliason and Stella Berenice Fenney; m. Howard A. Wendt (dec.); 1 child, Mary Birdell Tagge. Diploma, Portland Art Sch., Oreg., 1943; diploma in portrait painting, 1994; cert., Portrait Inst., NYC, 1987. Tchr. parochial sch., Chgo., 1967—69; artist-in-residence Mt. Prospect Hist. Soc., Ill., 1980—97; lectr. art, painting Mcpl. Art League, Chgo., 1990—. Art tchr. Zio Luth. Sch., Chgo., 1967—69; contbg. artist Troutdale Hist. Soc., 1996—2004. Mural, YSleta Mission, Anapra, Mex., 2000—06, Dr. Vanbucek Orthodontics office, Mt. Prospect, 1989, 5 murals, Anapara, Mex. Chs., 2000—05; artist, illustrator Story Community - Mt. Prospect, 1992; Represented in permanent collections Rand McNally Co. Tchr. stroke victims Am. Health Care Ctr., Arlington Heights, Ill., 1979—80; tchr. Mexican children Ysleta Mission St. Paul Luth. Ch., El Paso, Tex., 2000—06. Named to Ency. of Living Art, Nat. Women's Libr., Washington, 1997; recipient We the People 1st Pl. award, BiCentennial Com., Mt. Prospect, 1976, Gold medal for art, Nat. PTA, CHgo., 1989—90, Statue of Victory, Cremona, Italy, 1985. Lutheran. Avocations: gardening, sketching, writing, painting, teaching. Home: 12 N Owen St Mount Prospect IL 60056 Office Phone: 847-259-6166.

ELIASON, JON TATE, electrical engineer; b. Menominee, Mich., Mar. 23, 1938; s. Edwin Adolph and Irene Albertyn (Longlais) E.; m. Barbara Ann Love, July 2, 1960 (div. Dec. 1980); children: Ellen Artimese, Eric Alan, Eileen Amber; m. Kathleen Ann Vitell, May 25, 1996. BS in Sci. Engring., U. Mich., 1960; MS in Physics, Oreg. State U., 1966. Registered profl. engr., Ala., Ill. Engr. Vallecitos Nuclear Lab. GE, Pleasanton, Calif., 1964—66; sr. staff engr., engring. cons. Sperry Rand Corp., Huntsville, Ala., 1966—76; sr. staff engr. Martin Marietta Corp., Denver, 1976—84; master program engr., group engr. Sundstrand Corp., Rockford, Ill., 1984—92; engr. Insight Industries, Inc., Platteville, Wis., 1993—96, Insight Info. Inc., Platteville, Wis., 1996; project engr. electronic sys. Smiths Aerospace (formerly known as Barber-Colman Co.), Rockford, 1996—2003; founder Eliason Applied Engring., Rockford, 2003—. Recipient New Tech. award NASA, 1973, 75; Regents/Alumni scholar U. Mich., 1956-60. Mem. IEEE (life sr.), AIAA, Am. Phys. Soc., Sigma Pi Sigma, (chpt. pres. 1963-64). Achievements include patents in field. Avocations: amateur radio, flying. Office: PO Box 7231 Rockford IL 61126-7231 Office Phone: 815-394-3983. Personal E-mail: jteliason@sbcglobal.net.

ELIASON, NANCY CAROL, education consultant; b. Washington, Feb. 24, 1929; d. Lester Frank Kirchner and Nancy Lee (Rhea) Wiebe; m. William A. Eliason, Jan. 29, 1956 (div. June 1969)(rem. May 30, 1970); children: Charles Henry, William T., Leslie C. AB, Mary Baldwin Coll., 1950; MA, U. Md., 1953. Editor, writer Telenews, Inc., Washington, 1951-53; exec. dir. Blue Ridge Area Girl Scout Coun., Inc., Winchester, Va., 1954-55; asst. registrar Wheaton Coll., Norton, Mass., 1966-68; registrar and instr. Social Scis. Massasoit Community Coll., North Abingdon, Mass., 1968-70; assoc. prof. Social Scis. Lehigh Carbon C.C., Schnecksville, Pa., 1970-76; dir. devel. and spl. projects Am. Assn. of C.C., Washington, 1976-85; edn. policy analyst Nat. Govs. Assn., Washington, 1985-86; dir. devel. Close Up Found., Arlington, Va., 1986-88. Cons., evaluator Fund for Improvement of Post Sec. Edn., Title III and Vocat. Edn. Programs; sch. bd. Charlotte County, Fla., vice-chmn., 1992-94; mem. Fla. Com. on Lang. Arts Textbook Selection, 1994-98; pres. Learning in Retirement, 1997-2005; sec. New Operation Coop., Inc., 1997-2005 Contbr. articles and booklets to profl. mags. and jours. on various areas of small bus. Mem. Nat. Adv. Com. on Small Bus. Devel. Ctrs., 1985-89, Univ. Bus. Collaboration/Am. Assn. State Colls. and Univs., 1985-87, Nat. Ctr. for Rsch. in Vocat. Edn., 1978-80, Nat. Adv. Bd. Adult Learning, Coll. Bd., 1979-86, Office Adult Learning Svcs., 1983-87; mem. Nat. Evaluation Com. on Future Funds for Post-Secondary Edn., 1978-79; vice chair Charlotte County Sch. Bd., 1992-96; pres. Learning Ret. at Edison C.C., 1996-2005, grad. Williamsburg Ch. of Commerce Cmty. Leadership Svc., 2006. Named Vol. of Yr. for Ret. Educators of Charlotte County, 1990—91, Cmty. Svc. Person of Yr., Mary Baldwin Coll., 2005. Mem. Am. Assn. Cmty. Colls. (Woman of Yr. 1977, Nat. Coun Community Svc. and Continuing Edn. Person of Yr. 1983), Charlotte County LW (pres. 1990-92), Alpha Xi Delta, Delta Kappa Gamma. Home and Office: 6307 St Johns Wood Williamsburg VA 23188 Personal E-mail: beliason@earthlink.net.

ELIASON, RUSSELL ALLEN, judge; b. Mpls., Jan. 28, 1944; s. Walter Joseph and Hazel Agnes Pearl (Jensen) Eliason; m. Karen L. Stevens; children: Nathaniel, Heidi, Justine, Danielle. At, U. Minn., 1964—65, JD, 1970; BA, Yale U., 1967; at, Wake Forest Law Sch., 1967—68. Bar: Minn. 1970, Iowa 1971, Nebr. 1975, U.S. Dist. Ct. (no. dist.) Iowa 1971, U.S. Dist. Ct. (mid. dist.) N.C. 1974, U.S. Dist. Ct. Nebr. 1975, U.S. Ct. Appeals

(8th cir.) 1971, U.S. Ct. Appeals (4th cir.) 1976. Law clk. to judge U.S. Ct. Appeals (8th cir.), 1970—71; asst. U.S. atty. Dept. Justice, Sioux City, Iowa, 1971—72; law clk. to judge U.S. Dist. Ct. (mid. dist.) N.C., 1972—74; assoc. Ryan, Scoville & Uhlir, South Sioux City, Iowa, 1974—75; asst. U.S. atty. Dept. Justice, Greensboro, NC, 1975—76; U.S. magistrate judge U.S. Dist. Ct. (mid. dist.) N.C., Winston-Salem, NC, 1976—. Lectr. in field; active law sch. skills programs. Trumpeter Salem Band, Old Salem Band. Mem.: ABA, Nebr. Bar Assn., Minn. Bar Assn., Forsyth County Bar, N.C. Bar Assn., Sons of Norway, Phi Alpha Delta. Mem. Moravian Ch. Office: 224 Fed Bldg 251 N Main St Winston Salem NC 27101-3914 Office Phone: 336-734-2520.

ELIASSEN, JON ERIC, retired corporate financial and utilities executive; b. Omak, Wash., Mar. 10, 1947; s. Marvin George and Helen Grace (Meyer) E.; m. Valerie A. Foyle, Aug. 14, 1971; 1 child, Michael T. BA in Bus., Wash. State U., 1970. Staff acct. Wash. Water Power Co., Spokane, 1970-73, tax acct., 1973-76, fin. analyst, 1976-80, treas., 1980-86, v.p. fin., CFO, 1986-96; sr. v.p., CFO Avista Corp., Spokane, 1996—2003; ret., 2003. Bd. dirs. Itron Corp., Red Lion Hotels, Inc., IT Lifeline, Inc.; 2003pres., CEO 2005Spokane Area Econ. Devel. Coun. Trustee Wash. State U. Found., Pullman, 1987-99, N.W. Mus. Art and Culture, 1998-2003; treas. Wash. State U. Found., 1995-97; trustee Spokane Symphony, 1989-95, treas., 1990-95, mem. symphony endowment bd., pres. 2002-04; pres., trustee Spokane Intercollegiate Rsch. and Tech. Inst. Found., 1996-2000; bd. dirs. Western Energy Inst., chair, 2001-02; bd. dirs. Wash. Tech. Ctr., 2002—, Wash. State U. Rsch. Found., 2002—. Mem. Fin. Exec. Inst. (Seattle chpt. 1983—). Episcopalian. Avocations: skiing, travel, bicycling, photography. Office: Terrapin Capital Group LLC 827 W 1st St Ste 317 Spokane WA 99201

ELIBOL, TARIK, gastroenterologist, educator; b. Sept. 1, 1939; s. Ismail Cemal and Nuriye (Tutkun) E.; m. Eileen Elibol, Aug. 30, 1997; children: Kimberly, Lisa, David, Adam, John. MD, U. Istanbul, 1964. Resident in internal medicine E.J. Meyer Hosp. U. Buffalo, 1964-66; fellow in gastroenterology Cleve. Clinic, 1966-68; clin. asst. prof. medicine U. Buffalo, 1975—; practice medicine specializing in digestive diseases Buffalo, 1969—97; primary care practice in internal medicine, 2004—. Former chief of staff DeGraff Meml. Hosp. Fellow ACP, Am. Coll. Gastroenterology; mem. Am. Soc. Internal Medicine, Am. Soc. Gastrointestinal Endoscopy, NY State Med. Soc., Erie County Med. Soc., Western NY Soc. Gastrointestinal Endoscopy (past pres.), Western NY Gastrointestinal Liver Soc. (pres. 1980—), Western NY Physician Found. (pres. 1980—). Home: 55 Leicester Rd Buffalo NY 14217-2111 Office: 2949 Elmwood Ave Kenmore NY 14217-1356

ELICKER, GORDON LEONARD, retired lawyer; b. Cleve., May 27, 1940; BA in Math., U. Mich., 1962, JD, 1965; postdoctoral, U. Aix-Marseille, Aix-En Provence, France, 1965-66. Bar: Mich. 1967, N.Y. 1968, U.S. Dist. Ct. (so. dist.) N.Y. 1973. Stagiaire EEC, Brussels, 1966-67; assoc. Shearman & Sterling, NYC, 1967-77, ptnr., 1977-91, Nixon Peabody LLP (formerly Nixon, Hargrave, Devans & Doyle), NYC, 1991—2001; ret., 2001. Dir., sec. The World Affairs Forum, Stamford, Conn., 2001—; spkr. in field. Contbr. articles to profl. jours. Mem. legal com. U.S.-U.S.S.R. Trade and Econ. Coun., N.Y.C., 1978-91; chmn. legis. com. N.Y. Dist. Export Coun., N.Y.C., 1980-86; mem. Dem. Town Com., New Canaan, 1985-87; mem. bd. edn., New Canaan, Conn., 1986-90, chmn., 1989-90. Fulbright scholar, 1965. Democrat. E-mail: elicker@earthlink.net.

ELIE, JEAN ANDRÉ, investment banker; b. Montreal, Que., Can., Oct. 8, 1943; s. Jean-Paul and Violet (Trempe) E.; m. Josée Langevin. BA, Coll. Jean de Brébeuf, 1962; BCL, McGill U., 1965; MBA, U. Western Ont., 1968. Bar: Que. 1966. With Rolland Inc., Montreal, 1968-81, sec., 1974-81, counsel, 1974-81, v.p. administrn., 1978-81; dir. corp. services Burns Fry Ltd., Montreal, 1981-88; v.p., dir. corp. and govt. svcs. Burns Fry Lte., Montreal, 1988-94; fin. cons. Birinco Holdings Internat., Inc., Montreal, 1994—. Mem. adminstrv. coun. Coopers & Lybrand, 1996; mng. dir. Corp. and Investment Banking, Can., Soc. Genérale, 1998; bd. dirs. Mount Copperwind Power Energy Inc., Alimentation Couchetard, Inc., Cambior, Inc., Iamgold Corp.; pres. Jelinco Internat., 2003—. Bd. dirs. Montreal Symphony Orch., Inst. Internal Auditors; bd. dirs., v.p. Found. Hosp. U. Montreal. Mem. Can. Bar Assn., Que. Bar Assn., Investment Dealers Assn. Can. (exec. com., bd. dirs.), Mt. Royal Club, St. Denis Club. Roman Catholic. Home: 1929 Laird Blvd Mount Royal PQ Canada H3P 2V2 Home Phone: 514-738-4520. Business E-Mail: jeanelie@videotron.ca.

ELIEL, ERNEST LUDWIG, chemist, educator; b. Cologne, Germany, Dec. 28, 1921; came to US, 1946, naturalized, 1951; s. Oskar and Luise (Tietz) E.; m. Eva Schwarz, Dec. 23, 1949; children: Ruth Louise, Carol Susan. Student, U. Edinburgh, Scotland, 1939-40; degree in phys.-chem. sci., U. Havana, Cuba, 1946; PhD, U. Ill., 1948; DSc (hon.), Duke U., 1983, U. Notre Dame, 1990, Babes-Bolyai U., Cluj, Romania, 1993, U. Havana, Cuba, 2004. Mem. faculty U. Notre Dame, South Bend, Ind., 1948-72, prof. chemistry, 1960-72, head dept., 1964-66; W.R. Kenan Jr. prof. chemistry U. NC, Chapel Hill, 1972—93; prof. emeritus U. N.C., 1993—. Le Bel Centennial lectr., Paris, 1974, Geoffrey Coates lectr. U. Wyo., 1989, Smith, Kline and French lectr. U. Ill., 1990, Richard and Doris Arnold lectr. U. So. Ill., 1997, Fry lectr. U. Ark., 2005; Sir C.V. Raman vis. prof. U. Madras, India, 1981. Author: Stereochemistry of Carbon Compounds, 1962, Elements of Stereochemistry, 1969, From Cologne to Chapel Hill, 1990; co-author: Conformational Analysis, 1965, Stereochemistry of Organic Compounds, 1994, Basic Organic Stereochemistry, 2001; co-editor: Topics in Stereochemistry, vols. I-XXI, 1967-94. Pres. Internat. Rels. Coun., St. Joseph Valley, Ind., 1961-63; chmn. bd. U.S.-Mex. Found. for Sci., 1994-96. Recipient Coll. Chem. Tchrs. award Mfg. Chemists Assn., 1965, Laurent Lavoisier medal French Chem. Soc., 1968, Amoco Teaching award U. N.C., 1975, Thomas Jefferson award U. N.C., 1991, N.C. award in Sci., 1986, Chirality medal Internat. Symposium on Chiral Discrimination, 1996; NSF sr. rsch. fellow Harvard U., 1958, Calif. Inst. Tech., 1958-59, E.T.H. Zurich, Switzerland, 1967-68, Guggenheim fellow Stanford U., Princeton U., 1975-76, Duke U., 1983-84; named One of Top 75 Disting. Contbrs. to Chem. Enterprise, Chem. and Engring. News, 1998. Fellow AAAS (chmn. chemistry sect. 1991-92), Royal Soc. Chems.; mem. NAS (award for chemistry in svc. to society 1997), AAUP (chpt. pres. 1971-72, 78-79), Am. Acad. Arts and Scis., Am. Chem. Soc. (chmn. St. Joseph Valley sect. 1960, councillor 1965-73, 75—, chmn. com. publs. 1972, 76-78, dir. 1985-93, chmn. bd. dirs. 1987-89, pres. 1992, Morley medal Cleve. sect. 1965, Harry and Carol Mosher award Santa Clara Valley sect. 1982, Herty medal Ga. sect. 1991, So. Chemist award Memphis sect. 1991, Madison Marshall award North Ala. sect., 1993, George C. Pimentel award in Chem. Edn. 1995, Priestley medal 1996), Coun. Sci. Soc. Pres.'s (pres. 1996), Royal Spanish Chem. Soc. (hon.), Argentine Chem. Assn. (hon.), Peruvian Chem. Soc. (corr.), Mex. Chem. Soc. (hon.), Mex. Acad. Scis. (corr.), Chilean Chem. Soc. (hon.), Cuban Chem. Soc. (hon.), Sigma Xi (pres. U. Notre Dame chpt. 1968-69), Phi Lambda Upsilon, Phi Kappa Phi. Home: 345 Carolina Meadows Villa Chapel Hill NC 27517-7519 E-mail: eliel@mindspring.com.

ELIMELECH, MENACHEM, environmental and chemical engineering educator; b. July 19, 1955; married; 2 children. BSc summa cum laude, Hebrew U., Jerusalem, israel, 1983, MSc summa cum laude, 1985; PhD in Environ. Engring., Johns Hopkins U., 1989. Served to capt. Israeli Air Force, 1974-80; rsch. asst. Hebrew U., Jerusalem, 1982-85, Johns Hopkins U., Balt., 1986-89, acting instr. dept. geography and environ. engring., 1988; asst. prof. dept. civil and environ. engring. UCLA, 1989-94, assoc. prof., 1994-97, prof., 1997-98; Llewellyn Jones prof. environ. engring. Yale U., New Haven, 1998, Roberto C. Goizueta prof. environ. and chem. engring. Reviewer for scholarly jours.; author articles. Recipient Rsch. Initiation award NSF, 1990, Engring. Teaching Excellence award W.M. Keck Found., 1994, others. Mem. ASCE (Walter L. Huber Civil Engring. Rsch. prize 1996), NAE, Am. Chem. Soc., Am. Geophys. Union, Assn. Environ. Engring. Profs., Am. Water Works Assn., Internat. Assn. Colloid and Interface Scientists, N.Am. Membrane Soc. Office: Yale U Environ Engring Program 9 Hillhouse Ave New Haven CT 06511-6815 Office Fax: 203-432-2881. E-mail: menachem.elimelech@yale.edu.

ELIN, RONALD JOHN, pathologist, educator; b. Mpls., Apr. 14, 1939; s. John Matthew and Helen Sophia Elin; m. Susan May Krogh, June 14, 1969; children: Derek, Justin. BA, U. Minn., 1960, BS, 1962, MD, 1966, PhD, 1969. Diplomate Am. Bd. Pathology, Am. Bd. Clin. Chemistry. Intern U. Hosp. Calif., San Diego, 1969-70; commd. med. officer USPHS, 1970, advanced through grades to med. dir., 1975; staff assoc. Nat. Inst. Allergy and Infectious Diseases NIH, Bethesda, Md., 1970-73, resident clin. pathology dept., 1973-74, chief clin. pathology dept., 1975-97, chief chemistry svc., 1977-97; vice chmn. pathology U. Louisville, Ky., 1997—2001, chmn. dept. pathology and lab. medicine, 2002. Clin. prof. Uniformed Svcs. U. of Health Scis., Bethesda, 1978-97; initiator, first chmn. Gordon Rsch. Conf. on Magnesium in Biomed. Processes and Medicine, 1978. Contbr. more than 220 articles to profl. jours. Decorated Commendation medal USPHS, 1980, Meritorious Svc. medal USPHS, 1984. Fellow Am. Coll. Nutrition, Coll. Am. Pathologists, Am. Soc. Clin. Pathologists; mem. Am. Assn. Pathologists, Am. Assn. Clin. Chemistry (Outstanding Contbns. to Clin. Chemistry in a Selected Area of Rsch. award 1994), Acad. Clin. Lab. Physicians and Scientists (sec.-treas. 1985-87, pres. 1990-91, Gerald T. Evans award 1995). Lutheran. Achievements include research on magnesium metabolism, properties of endotoxin. Office: U Louisville Hosp Dept Pathology and Lab Medicine 512 S Hancock St Rm 203 Louisville KY 40202-1675 Home Phone: 502-500-0236; Office Phone: 502-852-4464. Business E-Mail: rjelin01@gwise.louisville.edu.

ELINSON, JACK, social sciences educator; b. NYC, June 30, 1917; s. Sam and Rebecca (Block) Elinson; m. May Gomberg, July 5, 1941; children: Richard, Elaine, Mitchell, Robert. BS, CCNY, 1937; MA, George Washington U., 1946, PhD, 1954. Social sci. analyst Dept. Def., Washington, 1942-51; sr. study dir. Nat. Opinion Research Center, 1951-56; asst. prof. sociology U. Chgo., 1954-56; assoc. prof. adminstrv. medicine Columbia U., NYC, 1956-64, prof. adminstrv. medicine, 1964-68, prof. sociomed. scis. and sociology, 1968-86, prof. emeritus, 1986—; Service fellow Nat. Center Health Stats., 1977-81; vis. prof. behavioral scis. U. Toronto, 1969-77; Disting. vis. prof. Inst. Health Care Policy, Rutgers U., 1986-89, Disting. sr. scholar, 1990—; vis. prof. Robert Wood Johnson Med. Sch. (formerly Rutgers Med. Sch.), Univ. Medicine and Dentistry of N.J., 1986—; dir. program evaluation dept. patient care Harlem Hosp. Ctr., 1966-71. Bd. dirs. Med. and Health Rsch. Assn., NYC, 1977—89, Bergen County N.J. Tb and Health Assn., 1960—65; mem. adminstrv. bd. Bur. Applied Social Rsch. Columbia U., 1970—75; co-dir. health care orgn. and adminstrn. track Program for Master's in Pub. Health Rutgers U.-U. Medicine and Dentistry of N.J., 1983—92. Co-author (with R.E. Trussell): Chronic Illness in a Rural Area, 1959; co-author: (with J.J. Williams and R.E. Trussell) Family Medical Care Under Three Types of Health Insurance, 1962; co-author: (with E. Padilla and M. Perkins) Public Image of Mental Health Services, 1967; editor (with A.E. Siegmann): Sociomedical Health Indicators, 1979; editor: (with A. Mooney and A. Siegmann) Health Goals and Health Indicators: Policy, Planning and Evaluation, 1977; editor: (with N.K. Wenger, M.E. Mattson and C.D. Furberg) Assessment of Quality of Life in Clinical Trials of Cardiovascular Therapies, 1984. Named Jack Elinson Sociomed. Scis. Libr., Columbia U. Sch. Pub. Health, 1998; recipient Nat. Merit award, Delta Omega Soc., 1982, Festschrift, spl. issue of Social Sci. and Medicine, 1989. Fellow: APHA (1st award Assn. Social Scis. in Health 1984), Am. Assn. Pub. Opinion Rsch. (pres. 1979—80, Exceptionally Disting. Achievement award 1993), Am. Sociol. Assn. (chmn. med. sociology, Leo G. Reeder award 1985), AAAS; mem.: Med. and Health Rsch. Assn. N.U.C. (bd. dirs.), N.J. Pub. Health Assn. (exec. bd., Dennis J. Sullivan award 1990), N.Y.C. Pub. Health Assn. (bd. dirs.), Inst. Medicine NAS. Office: Columbia U Sch Pub Health Dept Sociomed Scis 600 W 168th St New York NY 10032-3722 Office Phone: 212-305-4027. Personal E-mail: jelinson@juno.com. Business E-Mail: je7@columbia.edu.

ELIOT, ALEXANDER, writer; b. Cambridge, Mass., Apr. 28, 1919; s. Samuel Atkins, Jr. and Ethel (Cook) E.; m. Jane Winslow Knapp, May 3, 1952; children: May Rose, Jefferson, Winslow. Student, Black Mountain Coll., 1936-38, Boston Mus. Sch., 1938-39. Dir. Pinkney St. Artists Alliance, Boston, 1940-41; asst. to producer March of Time newsreel, 1941-42; asst. dir. films Office of War Info., 1942-43; editor films Office of Coord. Inter-Am. Affairs, 1943-45; art editor Time mag., 1945-60. Prof. emeritus program Hampshire Coll., 1977. Editor Parabola mag., 1995-96; contbg. editor Harvard mag., 1988-95; author: Proud Youth, 1953, Three Hundred Years of American Painting, 1957, Sight and Insight, 1959, Earth, Air, Fire and Water, 1962, Greece, 1963, Love Play, 1966, Creatures of Arcadia, 1967, Socrates, 1967, A Concise History of Greece, 1972, Myths, 1976, Zen Edge, 1979, (with Jane Winslow Eliot) Fisher's Guide to Greece, 1984, Abraham Lincoln, 1985, The Universal Myths, 1990, The Global Myths, 1993, The Timeless Myths, 1996; (film with Jane Winslow Eliot) The Secret of Michelangelo, Every Man's Dream, 1968. Guggenheim fellow, 1960; Japan Found. sr. fellow, 1975 Mem. Century Assn., Dutch Treat Club (N.Y.C.). Home: 105 Paloma Ave Venice CA 90291-2572 *The moon, the planets, pass around my heart. The sun shines into me, and in me as well. Yet what am I? A goose-pimpled crazy on a skewed glass bicycle, continually crashing into scribbled walls. And this moment, this being is the thing.*

ELIOT, CHARLES WILLIAM JOHN, former university president; b. Rawalpindi, Pakistan, Dec. 8, 1928; s. William Edmund and Ann Catherine (McDougall) E.; m. Mary Williamson, Sept. 2, 1954; children: Charles, Sophia (dec.), Nicholas, Johanna, Luke. BA, U. Toronto, 1949, MA, 1951, PhD, 1961; DCL, King's Coll., 1988; DLitt, St. Mary's, 1999. Lectr., asst. prof., assoc. prof., prof. U. B.C., Vancouver, Canada, 1957—71; prof. archaeology Am. Sch. Classical Studies, Athens, 1971—76; prof. classics Mount Allison U., Sackville, N.B., Canada, 1976—85, acad. v.p., 1981—83; pres. U. P.E.I., Charlottetown, Canada, 1985—95, pres. emeritus, 1996—. Mem. Acad. Panel of the Social Scis. and Humanities Rsch., 1978-82, chmn., 1980-81. Author: Coastal Demes of Attika, 1962, Campaign of the Falieri and Piraeus in the Year 1827; or a Journal of a Volunteer, 1992. Contbr. revs. and articles to profl. jours. Mem. Sch. Bd. Dist. 14 N.B., 1983-85 Mem. Order of Can., 1994; scholar Am. Sch. Classical Studies, 1952-54, Can. Coun., 1965-66, Dumbarton Oaks, 1980, Social Scis. and Humanities Rsch. Coun. Can., 1984-85. Mem. Classical Assn. Can. (pres. 1992-94). Anglican. Avocation: works of john galt. Personal E-mail: wmeliot@pei.sympatico.ca.

ELIOT, THEODORE LYMAN, JR., former ambassador, consultant; m. Patricia P. Peters. BA, Harvard U., 1948, M.P.A., 1956; LL.D., U. Nebr., Omaha, 1975. With U.S. Fgn. Svc., 1949-78; spl. asst. to under sec. of state; to sec. treasury; country dir. for Iran Dept. State; exec. sec. State Dept.; also spl. asst. to sec. of state Dept. State; ambassador to Afghanistan; insp. gen. Dept. State., Washington; dean Fletcher Sch. Law and Diplomacy, Tufts U., 1979-85; exec. dir. Ctr. for Asian Pacific Affairs Asia Found., San Francisco, 1985-87. Bd. dirs. Neurobiol. Tech. Trustee Asia Found. Mem. Am. Acad. Diplomacy.

ELISE, KIMBERLY (KIMBERLY ELISE TRAMMEL, KIMBERLY ELISE OLDHAM), actress; b. Mpls., Minn., Apr. 17, 1967; d. Marvin and Erma Trammel; m. Maurice Oldham; children: AjaBleu Oldham, Butterfly Oldham. BA, Univ. Minn.; studied, Am. Film Inst. Actor: (films) Set It Off, 1996, Beloved, 1998, Bait, 2000, John Q, 2002, Woman Thou Art Loosed, 2004, The Manchurian Candidate, 2004, Diary of a Mad Black Woman, 2005 (NAACP Image award Oustanding Actress in a Motion Picture, 2006), Pride, 2007; (TV series) In The House, 1995, The Sentinel, 1996, Twilight Zone, 2003, Girlfriends, 2003, Soul Food, 2002—03, Close to Home, 2005— (NAACP Image award Actress in a Drama Series, 2007); (TV films) The Ditchdigger's Daughters, 1997, The Loretta Claiborne Story, 2000, Bojangles, 2001.*

ELISHA, LARISA, musician, performer, educator; b. Baku, Russia, Jan. 12, 1963; d. Vladimir Chumakov and Mariya Chumakova; m. Steven Kenneth Elisha, May 19, 2002; 1 child, Patrick A. BA, A. Lunatcharsky Conservatory of Music, Minsk, Belarus, 1986, MMus, 1987—89; D in Violin performance, K. Lipinski Acad. Music, Wroclaw, Poland, 1996—97; cert. in chamber music, U. Wis., Milw., 1997—99. Prof., violin M. Glinka Coll. Music, Minsk, Belarus, 1985—89, A. Lunatcharsky Conservatory of Music, Minsk, Belarus, 1987—89, K. Szymanowski Coll. of Music, Wroclaw, Poland, 1989—97, K. Lipinski Acad. Music, Wroclaw, Poland, 1989—97, prof., strings methodology, 1996—97, Inst. U. Wis., Milw., 1997—99; prof., violin Wis. Conservatory of Music, Milw., 1998—99; violinist artist in residence Washburn U., Topeka, 1999—. Concertmaster State Witold Lutaslawski Philharm. Symphony Orch., Wroclaw, Poland, 1989—97, Topeka Symphony Orch., 1999—, Wichita Grand Opera, 2002—; prin. violin Chamber Orch. Leopoldinum, Wroclaw, Poland, 1990—93; first violinist, artistic dir. String Quartet Wratislavia of Philharm. Hall, Wroclaw, Poland, 1995—97; violinist, Piano Trio U. Wis. Inst. Chamber Music, Milw., 1997—99; assoc. concertmaster Green Bay Symphony Orch., Waukesha, Wis., 1997—99; co-founder, violinist Elaris Duo, 2000—, Chamber Music Series, Elaris String Academy, 2004—; lectr. Hawaii Internat. Conf. on Arts and Humanities, 2007. Author: The Russian Violin School's Traditions, 1986, Methodology of Teaching Violin Players, 1986; musician (violinist): (soloist) Musica Polonica Nova, 1989, Acad. Music Concert Hall, 1990, Chamber Music Festival, 1991, State Witold Lutoslawski Philharm. Symphony Orch., 1991, Koszalin Philharm. Orch., 1991, Leopoldinum, 1992, K. Lipinski Acad. Music Concert Hall, 1993, Gioventi Musicale d'Italia Festival, 1993, Wieniawski Festival, 1993, Theater Hall Acad. Music, 1997, Topeka Symphony, 1999—2000, 2003, 2005, Pittsburg State U., 2001—03, Lawrence Chamber Orch., 2005, Sunflower Chamber Orch., 2005, Elaris Duo and Friends, 2006, (recitals) Elaris Duo, Washburn U., 2000—04, Sunflower Music Festival, 2000—, Miss. Symphony Orch., 2003, Solo Music Festival, 2000—01, Bergen Internat. Festival, 2004 (Musician Yr., Kans. Fedn. Music Clubs (KFMC), 2003), Koncertgebouw Hall, Warsaw Nat. Philharmony Hall, World Famous Concert Halls, Karajan Hall, Creighton Inst., Omaha Conservatory, 2006—07, (CD) Elaris Duo, 2005—, (albums) Amore, 2007. Named to Kans. Touring Program. Mem.: Chamber Music Am., Am. String Tchrs. Assn., Coll. Music Soc., Northeast Kans. Music Tchrs. Assn., Music Tchrs. Nat. Assn. Office Phone: 785-670-1891. E-mail: elarisduo@cox.net.

ELIX, DOUGLAS THORNE, computer company executive; b. Adelaide, Australia, July 27, 1948; s. David Llewellyn and Margaret Thorne (Martin) E.; m. Robin Claire Wallace; children: Claire, Penelope, David, Sarah. Dir. banking region IBM Australia Ltd., 1987-89; dir. fin. industry IBM Asia Pacific, Tokyo, 1990-91; dir. of ops. IBM Australia Ltd., 1991-92, gen. mgr. fin. svcs., 1992-93, asst. mng. dir., CEO, 1993-96; pres., CEO Integrated Sys. Solution Corp., Somers, NY, 1996-97; gen. mgr. IBM Global Svcs., N.A., 1997-98, IBM Global Svcs. Ams., 1998-99; sr. v.p., group exec. IBM Global Svcs., 1999—2004, IBM Global Sales & Distbn., 2004—. Bd. dirs. Royal Bank of Can. Fellow Australian Inst. Mgmt.*

ELIZABETH, , II, (ELIZABETH ALEXANDRA MARY), By the Grace of God of the United Kingdom of Great Britain and Northern Ireland and of Her Other Realms and Territories Queen, Head of the Commonwealth, Defender of the Faith; b. London, Apr. 21, 1926; d. King George VI (formerly Duke of York) and Queen Elizabeth (formerly Duchess of York); m. Prince Philip Mountbatten, Duke of Edinburgh, Nov. 20, 1947; children: Charles Philip Arthur George (now The Prince of Wales), 1948, Anne Elizabeth Alice Louise (now The Princess Royal), 1950, Andrew Albert Christian Edward (now The Duke of York), 1960, Edward Antony Richard Louis (now The Earl of Wessex), 1964. Succeeded to throne following death of father, Feb. 6, 1952; crowned Queen, June 2, 1953. Named one of The World's Most Influential People, TIME mag., 2007. Achievements include fluent speaker of French. Avocations: photography, horseback riding. Address: Buckingham Palace London SW1A 1AA England*

ELIZONDO, HECTOR, actor; b. NYC, Dec. 22, 1936; s. Martin Echevarria and Carmen Medina (Reyes) E.; m. Carolee Campbell, Apr. 13, 1969; 1 son, Rodd. Student, CCNY, 1955-56, Ballet Arts Co. of Carnegie Hall. Appearances include (plays) The Price (Broadway), Drums in the Night, Steambath, 1970 (OBIE award), Prisoner of Second Avenue, 1974, The Great White Hope, 1977, Sly Fox (Dr. Desk-Nun award), Medal of Honor Rag, American Playhouse; (movies) Report to the Commissioner, 1975, The Taking of Pelham-1-2-3, 1975, Cuba, 1978, American Gigolo, 1979, The Fan, 1979, Young Doctors in Love, 1983, The Flamingo Kid, 1984, Nothing in Common, 1985, Leviathan, Pretty Woman, 1990 (Golden Globe nominee best supporting actor), Chains of Gold, Paydirt, Necessary Roughness, Frankie and Johnny, 1991, Being Human, 1992, Exit to Eden, 1993, Getting Even with Dad, 1993, Beverly Hills Cop III, 1993, Safe House, 1996, Turbulence, 1996, Dear God, 1996, Romy & Michelle, 1996, The Other Sister, 1998, Runaway Bride, 1998-99, The Princess Diaries, 2001, sequel, 2004, Celestine Prophecies, 2004, The Princess Diaries 2: The Royal Engagements, 2004, Love in the Time of Cholera 2006, The Music Within, 2006; (CBS series) Kate Brasher, 2001, Tortilla Soup, 2001, How High, 2001, Miracles, 2003, Without a Trace, 2003; (TV series) Popi, 1976, Freebie and the Bean, Foley Square, 1985, Great Performances, WCET, 1987, The Impatient Heart, All in the Family, Chicago Hope (Emmy award best supporting actor, 3 nominations), 1994-2000, The West Wing, 2002, Century City, 2003-2004; (TV films) Casablanca, 1983, Medal of Honor Rag, 1982, Mrs. Cage (Emmy nominee for best supporting actor), 1992, The Dain Curse, 1978, Courage, 1986, Honey Boy, 1982, Out of the Darkness, 1985, Natica Jackson, 1987, Addicted to His Love, 1988, Your Mother Wears Combat Boots, 1989, The Amnesty File, 1990, The Burden of Proof, (nomination Emmy best supporting actor), 1992, Borrowed Hearts, 1997, American Playhouse The American Experience Discovery, Cane, 2007. Recipient Lifetime Achievement Image award, 1997, ALMA award for best actor, 1998, Best Actor in Drama Series, 2000, Latin Legends award, N.Y.C., 2000, Lifetime Achievement IMPACT award, 2002. Mem. Amnesty Internat., The Creative Coalition. Roman Catholic.

ELKES, TERRENCE ALLEN, communications executive; b. NYC, Apr. 28, 1934; s. Sidney and Beatrice (Sachnin) E.; m. Ruth Jerkowsky, June 14, 1959; children: Steven Andrew, David Adam, Daniel Arthur. BA cum laude, CCNY, 1955; JD, U. Mich., 1958. Bar: N.Y. 1959. Atty. Prentice Hall, Inc., 1958-59; counsel internat. div. Norwich Pharmacal Co., 1959-65; corp. counsel, also v.p., sec. Parsons & Whittemore, Inc., 1965-72; corp. counsel Black Clawson Co., 1965-72; treas. Prince Albert Pulp Co. Ltd., 1966-72; v.p., sec., gen. counsel Viacom Internat., Inc., NYC, 1972-76, exec. v.p., 1976-78, pres., 1978-87, chief exec. officer, 1984-87; prin. Apollo Ptnrs., LLC-NY, NYC, Conn., 1987—. Bd. dirs. IDC Svcs. Corp., Tennis Channel, 2001—; mng. dir. Apollo Radio, Ltd., 1989-96; chmn. Compact Video Corp., 1991-93, Internat. Post Ltd., 1994-97, Video

Svcs. Corp., 1997-2000. Trustee U. Mich. Law Sch., 1992, mem. pres. adv. group U. Mich., 1992, mem. investment adv. group & tech. transfer group, 1992; pres. Jewish Outreach Inst., 1999; mem. bd. regents Ctr. Security Policy, 2003, bd. dirs., 2005, chmn. exec. com., 2006; mem. pres. adv. com. CCNY, INUST adv. com., 2007. Home: 12 Trails End Rye NY 10580-2227 Office: Apollo Ptnrs LLC 500 5th Ave New York NY 10110-0002

EL KHADEM, HASSAN SAAD, chemistry professor, researcher; b. Cairo, Mar. 24, 1923; naturalized, 1975; s. Saad S. and Nimet (Zulficar) El K.; m. Nadia M. Said, Sept. 6, 1951 (dec. 2002); children: Samiha, Saad. DSc Tech., ETH Zurich, Switzerland, 1950; PhD, Imperial Coll., London, 1952; DSc, U. London, 1967; BSc with honors, Cairo U., 1946; DSc, U. Alexandria, Egypt, 1963. Lectr. Alexandria U., 1952-58, asst. prof., 1958-64, prof. organic chemistry, 1964-71; prof. chemistry Mich. Tech. U., Houghton, 1971-74, head dept. chemistry and chem. engring., 1974-80, pres. prof. chemistry, 1980-84; Isbell prof. chemistry The Am. U., Washington, 1984-93, Isbell prof. chemistry emeritus, 1993—. Author: Synthetic Methods for Carbohydrates, 1976, Carbohydrate Chemistry: Monosaccharides and their Oligomers, 1988, Anthracycline Antibiotics, 1982, others; mem. editl. bd. Carbohydrate Rsch., 1966-92; contbr. over 170 articles on carbohydrates and medicinal chemistry to profl. jours.; patentee in field. Fulbright scholar U.S. Dept. State, Ohio State U., Columbus, 1963-64; recipient Phys. Sci. award Washington Acad. Sci., 1992. Mem. AAAS, Am. Chem. Soc. (chmn. carbonhydrate div. 1984-85, Melville L. Wolfrom award 1989), Sigma Xi. Achievements include discovery of a lost Greek manuscript by Zosimos (300 A.D.) translated to Arabic in a twelveth century Alchemy book (donated to the Libr. of Congress). Home: 4948 Sentinel Dr Apt 101 Bethesda MD 20816-3586 Office: Am U Dept Chemistry Beeghly Bldg 4400 Massachusetts Ave NW Washington DC 20016-8001 Personal E-mail: helk@erols.com. *One reason why many students stop asking questions in class is that they do not get satisfying answers.*

ELKIE, KIMBERLY K., medical editor; d. Orring G. Hibner and Velma J. Dowling; m. Steven J. Elkie, Oct. 3, 1963; 1 child, Sheldon J. Student, Alpena CC, Mich.; student in Bus. and Healthcare Mgmt., Northwood U., 2007—. Med. transcriptionist Alpena Regional Med. Ctr., Mich., 1986—2000; med. editor, quality auditor Spheris, Franklin, Tenn., 2001—. Pub. rels. rep. Parent/Tchr. Support Group Hillman Elem. Sch., Mich., 2003—06, mem. playground renovation com., 2006—, pres. Parent/Tchr. Support Group, 2007—; pianist Greely Bapt. Ch., Liberty Bapt. Ch., Lachine, Mich., 1979—2006; membership chairperson Alpena Coop. Preschool, Mich., 2002—03. Recipient Above & Beyond award, Spheris Inc., 2006. Mem.: Am. Assn. Med. Transcriptionists. Home Phone: 989-379-3084.

ELKIN, JUDITH, lawyer; b. NYC, Jan. 1, 1956; BA in Am. History with honors summa cum laude, SUNY, Binghamton, 1978; JD cum laude, U. Wis., 1981. Bar: Wis. 1981, Tex. 1982, NY 2004, admitted to practice: Tex. Supreme Ct., US Supreme Ct., US Ct. Appeals (5th Cir.), US Ct. Appeals (6th Cir.), US Ct. Appeals (10th Cir.), US Ct. Appeals (11th Cir.), US Dist. Ct. (No. Dist.) Tex., US Dist. Ct. (So. Dist.) Tex., US Dist. Ct. (Ea. Dist.) Tex., US Dist. Ct. (We. Dist.) Tex. Ptnr., Bus. Reorganization & Bankruptcy Practice Group Haynes and Boone LLP, Dallas, co-chair, Fin. Sect. Spkr. in field. Bd. dir., exec. bd., sec. Dallas Zoological Soc., 1998—2004. Mem.: Internat. Women's Insolvency and Restructuring Confederation (IWIRC) (sec./trea. 2002—06), COMBAR (Hon. N. Am. Mem., Comml. Bar Assn. United Kingdom), Am. Bankruptcy Inst., Internat. Bar Assn. (com. J, Internat. Insolvency), ABA (cohmn. bankruptcy and insolvency litig. com., Litig. Sect. 1997—2001, bus. bankruptcy com., Bus. Law Sect.), Phi Beta Kappa. Office: Haynes And Boone Attorneys 153 E 53rd St Rm 4900 New York NY 10022-4636 Office Phone: 212-659-4968. Office Fax: 212-884-8228. Business E-Mail: judith.elkin@haynesboone.com.

ELKIN, LOIS SHANMAN, business systems company executive; b. Cin., Oct. 31, 1937; d. Jerome David and Mildred Louise (Bloch) Shanman; m. Alan I. Elkin, May 6, 1962; children: Karen A., Jeffrey R. BA in Math., Goucher Coll., 1959. Sys. engr. ea. region IBM, Balt. and Columbia, S.C., 1959-61, mgr. Computer Test Ctr. ea. region, 1961-64; exec. v.p. Advance Bus. Sys., Balt., 1964—, A&L Real Estate, Balt., 1970—; pres. Our World Gallery, Inc., Balt., 1995—. Mentor for math. and bus. Goucher Coll., Balt., 1982—86; co-owner ATMS, Balt., 1994—2002; guest lectr. MBA program Loyola Coll. Md., Balt., 1993—94, Towson U., 1999; steering com. Loyola Ctr. Closely Held Cos., Balt., 1993—; conducted seminars Towson U. Leadership Group, 1999; bd. dirs. Hunt Valley Bus. Forum, Balt.; mng. dir. Enable Technologies, Balt., 2001—; bd. dirs. Soshana S. Cardin Jewish Cmty. H.S., 2005—; judge Md. Entrepreneur of Yr. Awards by Ernst Young, 2006—07. Vol. House of Ruth, Balt., 1990—, Image Recovery Ctr., Union Meml. Hosp., Balt., 1995—96; exec. bd. dirs. Pride of Balt. II, 1994—2000; co-chair Multiple Sclerosis Class of '98 fundraiser, 1998; exec. bd. Md. chpt. Nat. Multiple Sclerosis Soc., 2000—05; sponsor maj. fundraising event Johns Hopkins Children's Ctr., Balt., 2002; chair Gala, Balt. Zoomerang!, 2004; bd. dirs. Hearing and Speech Agy., Balt., 1996—2001. Named Md. Entrepreneur of Yr., Ernst & Young, 2001; named to, Circle of Excellence, 2004; recipient AAA Torch award for ethics in bus., 1997, Champion of Children award, Casey Cares Found., 2004, Bravo! Entrepreneur award, SmartWoman Mag., 2005, honoree, Chimes Ann. Hall of Fame Tribute, 2002. Mem.: Women's Bus. Club (founder 2002—), Nat. Assn. Women Bus. Owners (Woman of the Yr. award Balt. chpt. 1985). Avocation: collecting art. Office: Advance Bus Sys 10755 York Rd Cockeysville Hunt Valley MD 21030-2114

ELKIN, MICHAEL S., lawyer; b. Richmond, Va., May 18, 1957; Attended, L'Université de la Sorbonne, Paris, 1977, L'Université de Tours, 1978; AB, Rutgers U., 1979, MSW, 1981; JD, Bklyn. Law Sch., 1984. Bar: NY 1985, NJ 1985. Ptnr., comml. litig. dept. Thelen Reid & Priest LLP, NYC; ptnr. Winston & Strawn LLP, 2007—. Exec. comments editor Bklyn. Jour. of Internat. Law. Mem.: French-Am. C. of C., Assn. Bar City NY (sec. internat. trade com. 1988—90, arbitration & alternative dispute resolution com. 1992—95), Paris-Am. Club. Fluent in French. Office: Winston & Strawn LLP 200 Park Ave New York NY 10166 E-mail: melkin@winston.com.*

ELKIND, DAVID, psychology professor; b. Detroit, Mar. 11, 1931; s. Peter and Bessie (Nelson) E.; children: Paul Steven, Robert Edward, Eric Allen. BA, UCLA, 1952, PhD, 1955; DSc (hon.), R.I. Coll., 1987; DHL (hon.), Mitchell Coll., 2000. Diplomate: Am. Bd. Profl. Examiners in Psychology. Research asst. to David Rapaport, Austen Riggs Ctr., Stockbridge, Mass., 1956-57; staff psychologist Beth Israel Hosp., Boston, 1957-59; asst. prof. Wheaton Coll., Norton, Mass., 1959-61; asst. prof. med. psychology U. Calif. Med. Sch., LA, 1961-62; assoc. prof., dir. Child Study Ctr., U. Denver, 1962-66; prof., dir. grad. tng. in developmental psychology, dept. psychology U. Rochester, NYC, 1966-78; chmn. Eliot Pearson dept. child devel. Tufts U., Medford, Mass., 1978-83; prof. child devel. sr. resident scholar Lincoln Filene Ctr. Eliot Pearson dept. child study Tufts U., Medford, Mass.; research dir. World of Inquiry Evaluation-NSF, 1970; project dir. Tng. of Early Childhood Specialists, U.S. Office Edn., 1970; psychol. cons. VA, 1962-74, Rochester Mental Health Center, 1966-74, Rochester Family Ct., 1967-73; headmaster Mt. Hope Sch., Rochester, 1974-77. Seamus Heany lectr. U. Coll., Dublin, 2000; co-host Lifetime TV series "Kids These Days". Author: (with H.J. Flavell) Studies in Cognitive Development, 1969, Children and Adolescents, 1974, A Sympathetic Understanding of the Child, 1974, (with I. Weiner) Child Development: A Core Approach, 1972, (with others) Psychology: An Introduction, 1973, Child Development and Education, 1976, (with D. Hetzel) Readings in Human Development: Contemporary Perspectives, (with I. Weiner) Development of the Child, 1978, The Child's Reality: Three Developmental Themes, 1978, The Child and Society, 1979, The Hurried Child, 1981, All Grown Up and No Place to Go, 1984, Miseducation: Preschoolers at Risk, 1987, Grandparenting: Understanding Today's Children, 1988; editor: Perspectives in Early Childhood Education, 1991, Parenting Your Teenager in the Nineties, 1993, Images of the Young Child, 1993, Understanding Your Child, 1994, A Sympathetic Understanding of the Child Birth to Sixteen, 1994, Ties that Stress: The New Family Imbalance, 1994, Reinventing Childhood, 1998. Recipient Great Friends to Kids award Assn. Youth Mus., 2001, Dale Richmond award Child and Adolescent Divsn. Am. Acad. Pediat.; NSF Sr. Postdoctoral fellow Geneva, 1964-65. Fellow Am. Psychol. Assn. (recipient Nicholas Hobbs Award div. 26), AAAS, Nat. Assn. Edn. of Young Children (pres. 1986-88). Home: 7 Lloyd Ln East Sandwich MA 02537-1225 Office: Tufts U Dept Child Devel Medford MA 02155 E-mail: delkind@emerald.tufts.edu.

ELKIND, MORT WILLIAM, management consultant; b. NYC, Sept. 10, 1925; s. Samuel William and Leah Fannie (Meschen) E.; m. Mary Johanna Ruggiero, June 10, 1962; children: Lori Ann, Susan Marie, Edward William. BS in Chemistry summa cum laude, U. S.W. La., 1949; MS Analytical Chemistry, La. State U., 1951; postgrad., Georgetown U. Inst. Lang. & Linguistics, 1952, UCLA, 1954-55, Berkeley Coll., 1991-92. Intelligence officer CIA, Washington, 1952-53; head waiter Scaroon Manor Hotel, Schroon Lake, NY, 1956-57; copywriter J. B. Rundle; Sanders & Lowen; Cayton, Inc., NYC, 1959-65; dir. profl. rels. Kings County Rsch. Labs., Bklyn., 1965-67; copywriter L.W. Frohlich, NYC, 1967-74; sr. copywriter William Douglas McAdams, NYC, 1974-76; copy supr. Kallir, Philips, Ross, Inc., NYC, 1976-85; cons. Chestnut Ridge, NY, 1965—; co-founder Photocell Corp. of Am., 1965, Screen Features, Inc., 1966; founder, prin. MWE Assocs. Advt., 1970; co-founder Quadrisec, Inc., 1980, Modular Exports, Inc., 1988; v.p. mktg. Am. Investor Note Paper Corp., NYC, 1985-86; dir. mktg. Air Baby, Inc., Blauvelt, NY, 1990-91. Author: Internecine, 1957; editor: McNeil Psychiatric Calendar, 1978-83; writer, producer: (TV series) Billy Bang-Bang, 1966-68; creator: (film) The Internecine Project, 1974, (TV series) Bringing Up Kids, 1989. Polit. cons. NY State Senator, Rockland County and Albany, NY, 1978-80. Sgt. C.E., US Army, 1943-46, ETO. Named U. S.W. La. Athletic Hall Fame, 1978; recipient Andy award NY Advt. Club, 1979. Mem. Internat. Soc. Poets (Disting. mem.), Blue Key, Phi Kappa Phi, Phi Lambda Upsilon. Avocations: reading, writing, math problem solving. Personal E-mail: melkind@optonline.net.

ELKINS, ALFRED DAVID, insurance company executive; b. N.Y.C., Sept. 16, 1946; s. Nathaniel and Emily Elkins; m. Ethel Lehman, Sept. 24, 1978. AB, Herbert H. Lehman Coll., Bronx, 1969. Corp. proofreader Mut. of Am., NYC, 1985-96, documents file adminstr., 1996—. Poet laureate Mutual of Am. NY, NY. Recipient Golden Poet Trophy, World of Poetry, 1991, Editor's Choice award, Nat. Libr. Poetry, 1994, Internat. Libr. Poetry, 2004. Mem.: Poetry Soc. Am., Acad. Polit. Sci., Internat. Soc. Poets, Acad. Am. Poets, Am. Hist. Assn., Smithsonian Instn. Avocations: reading, writing, poetry, music. Home: 2145 Matthews Ave Bronx NY 10462-2028

ELKINS, BRAD S., ophthalmologist; b. LA, Jan. 6, 1965; BS summa cum laude, UCLA, 1987; MD, U. Calif., San Francisco, 1991. Cert. Am. Bd. Ophthalmology. Intern internal medicine UCLA San Fernando Valley Program, 1991—92; resident ophthalmology Jules Stein Eye Inst., LA, 1992—95; fellow cornea and refractive surgery U. Utah, 1995—96; ophthalmologist Ophthalmology Assocs. of the Valley, Encino, Calif., 1996—. Physician instr. for Lasik, ALK and RK Casebeer Eye Ctr., 1996; clin. instr. ophthalmology Jules Stein Eye Inst., LA, 1996—; lectr. in field. Contbr. articles to profl. jours. Named Ophthalmology Cons. of Yr., 1992—93, Star Surgeon, VISX, 1999, Alumni scholar, UCLA. Fellow: ACS; mem.: Alpha Omega Alpha, Phi Beta Kappa. Office: Ophthalmology Assocs of the Valley 1631 Ventura Blvd #750 Encino CA 91436

ELKINS, CAROLINE M., history professor, writer; b. NJ, 1969; m. Brent Elkins; children: Andy, Jake. BA in African History, Princeton U., 1991; AM, Harvard U., 1996, PhD, 2001; Fellow, Radcliffe Inst., 2003—04. Asst. prof. history Harvard U., Hugo K. Foster assoc. prof. African studies. Author: Imperial Reckoning: The Untold Story of Britain's Gulag in Kenya, 2005 (Pulitzer Prize for nonfiction, 2006); co-editor (with Susan Pedersen): Settler Colonialism in the Twentieth Century, 2005. Conversant in Swahili, Kikuyu; subject of 2002 BBC documentary, Kenya: White Terror. Office: Harvard U CGIS S Bldg Rm S432 University Hall Cambridge MA 02138 Office Phone: 617-495-2568. Business E-Mail: elkins@fas.harvard.edu.

ELKINS, ELIZABETH A., library director; BA, Hartwick Coll., 1968; MLS, SUNY, Geneseo, 1970. Dir. F. Franklin Moon Libr. SUNY Coll. Environ. Sci. and Forestry, Syracuse. Treas. Ctrl. NY Libr. Resources Coun.; spkr. in field. Office: F Franklin Moon Libr SUNY Coll of Environ Sci and Forestry 1 Forestry Dr Syracuse NY 13214 Office Phone: 315-470-6715. E-mail: eaelkins@esf.edu.*

ELKINS, FRANCIS CLARK, historian, educator, director; b. Scranton, Ark., Feb. 24, 1923; s. Frank and Auby (Moore) E.; m. Norma Trice, Aug. 18, 1946; 1 dau., Annette. BA, U. Cen. Ark., 1943; MA, U. Ark., 1947; PhD, Syracuse U., 1953; postdoctoral, U. Minn., 1956. From instr. to prof., chmn. div. social sci. Henderson State U., Arkadelphia, Ark., 1946-61; pres. Chadron (Nebr.) State Coll., 1961-67, N.E. Mo. State Coll., Kirksville, 1967-69; coordinator Univ. Coll., Ark State U., 1969-70, v.p. instrn., 1970-78, v.p. univ. rels., 1979-80; v.p. univ. rels. and devel. No. Ariz. U., Flagstaff, 1980—88, prof. history, 1980-88, president's coord. univ. rels., 1983-88. Edn. cons., 1988—; mem. exec. com. Rocky Mountain Edn. Lab., 1965-67; examiner North Cen. Assn. Colls. and Schs.; examiner, cons. Nat. Council Accreditation Tchr. Edn., chmn. visitation and appraisal com., 1963-68; mem. Nebr. Ednl. TV Council Higher Edn., 1966-67, Ark. Council Econ. Edn., 1970-81. Mem. adv. coun. Mo. 4-H Found., 1968-69; mem. Ark Adv. Coun. on Career Edn.; bd. dirs. United Way, 1980-88. Served with USAAF, 1943-45. Decorated D.F.C., Air medal with four oak leaf clusters, Unit citation with 1 star; recipient John Vaughn Excellence in Edn. award, North Ctrl. Assn. Colls. and Schs. Commn. on Schs., 1988, Disting. Svc. award, Chadron (Nebr.) State Coll., 1989. Mem. NEA (life), Am. Assn. Colls. for Tchr. Edn. (dir. 1968-71, state liaison rep. 1974-77), Assn. Orgns. Tchr. Edn. (adv. coun.), Ark. Hist. Assn., Ark. Edn. Assn. (life), Ark. Assn. Colls. for Tchr. Edn. (charter pres. 1973-75), Flagstaff C. of C. (dir. 1980-88), Craighead County Hist. Assn. (life), Elks, Rotary Internat. (Paul Harris fellow), Phi Delta Kappa, Kappa Delta Pi, Phi Alpha Theta, Alpha Chi, Phi Kappa Phi, Sigma Tau Gamma, Sigma Nu. Methodist. Home and Office: 3004 Hillridge Cv Jonesboro AR 72401-5937 Home Phone: 870-932-5651; Office Phone: 870-932-5651.

ELKINS, GARY J., lawyer; b. Homer, La., Mar. 4, 1952; s. Joel C. and Beverly T. Elkins; m. Kate S. Sevier, May 24, 1975; children: Kathryn S. McLeod, Nicholas T., Elizabeth M., Geoffrey C. JD, La. State U., Baton Rouge, 1976; LLM, Georgetown U., Washington, 1979. Bar: La. 1976, US Tax Ct. Commd. ensign USN, 1973, advanced thru grades to lt. comdr., 1984; atty. USN JAG Corps, Washington, 1976—79; atty., ptnr. Barham & Churchill, New Orleans, 1979—88, Gelpi, Sullivan, New Orleans, 1988—89, Elkins, PLC, New Orleans, 1989—. Elder St. Charles Ave. Presbyn. Ch., New Orleans, 1985—2007. Decorated Navy Achievement medal Sec. of the Navy. Home: 1716 Gen Pershing St New Orleans LA 70115 Office: Elkins PLC 201 St Charles Ave Ste 4400 New Orleans LA 70170 Home Phone: 504-895-3957; Office Phone: 504-529-3600. Office Fax: 504-529-7163. Business E-Mail: gelkins@elkinsplc.com.

ELKINS, GLEN RAY, retired diversified management services company executive; b. Winnsboro, La., May 23, 1933; s. Ceicel Herbert and Edna Mae (Lewallen) E.; m. Irene Kay Hildebrand, Aug. 25, 1951 (div. 1990); children: Steven Breen, Douglas Charles, Karen Anne, Michael Glen; m. Diane Hodgson, Mar. 2, 1992. AA in Indsl. Mgmt., Coll. San Mateo, 1958. Successively mgr. prodn. control, mgr. logistics, plant mgr., asst. v.p. ops. Aircraft Engring. and Maintenance Co., 1957-64; from mgr. field ops. to pres. Internat. Atlas Svc. Co., Princeton, NJ, 1964-85; sr. v.p. Atlas Corp., Princeton, NJ; chmn., CEO, dir. Global Assoc., 1973-85; pres. Global Assoc. Internat. Ltd., 1975-84; pres., CEO Triad Am. Svc. Corp., 1985-2000; pres. Pacific Mgmt. Svc. Corp., TASC Enterprises Inc., dba. Gottschall Engraving Co., 1993-2000; ret., 2000. Area chmn. Easter Seals drive, 1974; bd. dirs. Utah Children's Mus. With USN, 1950—54. Mem. Nat. Mgmt. Assn., Electronic Industries Assn., Lakeview Club, Willow Creek Country Club (past pres.). Home: 1445 Harvard Ave Salt Lake City UT 84105-1917 Personal E-mail: grelkinsut@msn.com.

ELKINS, JAMES ANDERSON, III, financial consultant; b. Houston, May 21, 1952; s. James Anderson Jr. and Margaret K. (Wiess) E.; m. Mary Virginia Arnold, Dec. 8, 1984; children: Margaret Wiess, James Anderson IV, Buck Arnold, John Caldwell, Harry Carothers, Samuel Hill, Lucy Gray. BA, Princeton U., 1974; MBA, U. Tex., 1976. Asst. treas. Morgan Guaranty Trust Co., NYC, 1976-79; exec. v.p. First City Tex., Houston, 1979-93; chmn. Houston Trust Co., 1994—. Bd. govs. Rice U., Houston, 1982-06; chmn. Tex. Children's Hosp., Houston, 1997-04, trustee, 1989—; trustee Children's Mus., Houston, 1988—, Houston Mus. Natural Sci., 1993—, Houston Zoo Inc., 1993—, Baylor Coll. Medicine, 2001—, The Meth. Hosp., Houston, Tex., 2003—, Houston Police Found., 2005, Ctr. for Houston's Future, 2006; bd. advisors U. Tex. Health Sci. Ctr., Houston, 1990; vice chmn. Salvation Army, 1990—; chmn. Houston Pks. Bd. Mem. Am. Bankers Assn. (exec. bd. corp. council), Houston Club, Tex. Bankers Assn., Forum Club. Methodist. Office: Houston Trust Co 1001 Fannin St Ste 700 Houston TX 77002-6707

ELKINS, STANLEY MAURICE, historian, educator; b. Boston, Apr. 27, 1925; s. Frank and Frances (Reiner) E.; m. Dorothy Adele Lamken, June 22, 1947; children: Susan Roselyn, Robert Joel, Barbara Marion, Sara Ann. AB, Harvard, 1949; MA, Columbia, 1951, PhD, 1959. Tchr. Fieldston Sch., NYC, 1951-54; asst. prof. history U. Chgo., 1955-60; faculty Smith Coll., Northampton, Mass., 1960—, prof. history, 1964-69, Sydenham Clark Parsons prof. history, 1969—94; fellow Inst. for Advanced Study, 1970-71, 76-77. Author: Slavery: A Problem in American Institutional and Intellectual Life, 1959, The Age of Federalism, 1993 (Bancroft prize Soc. Cin. Book Prize 1995). Served with AUS, 1943-46. Social Sci. Research Council fellow, 1963-64; Rockefeller fellow, 1954-55; Guggenheim fellow, 1976-77 Mem. Orgn. Am. Historians, Am. Hist. Assn., Soc. of Am. Historians. Home: 126 Vernon St Northampton MA 01060-2905 E-mail: s-elkins@mediaone.net.

ELKINS-ELLIOTT, KAY, law educator; b. Dallas, Nov. 21, 1938; d. William Hardin and Maxidine (Sadler) E.; m. Michael Gail Hodgson, July 7, 1960 (div. Dec. 1974); children: Michael Brett, Ashley Kim, Samantha; m. Frank Wallace Elliott, Aug. 15, 1983. AA with honors, Stephens Coll., 1958; JD, U. Okla., 1964; LLM, So. Meth. U., 1984; MA, U. Tex., Dallas, 1990. Bar: Okla. 1964, Tex. 1982, U.S. Dist. Ct. (no. dist.) Tex. 1982, U.S. Supreme Ct. 1984, U.S. Dist. Ct. (we. dist.) Okla. 1989. Assoc. Ben Hatcher and Assocs., Oklahoma City, 1964-65; dir., gen. counsel Take-A-Tour Swaziland, Mbabane, Swaziland, 1966-74; atty. Dept. Health and Human Svcs., Dallas, 1975-80; hearing officer EEOC, Dallas, 1980-84; atty. pvt. practice, Dallas, 1984-92; vis. assoc. prof. Tex. Wesleyan U. Sch. Law, Dallas, 1992-95; arbitrator State Farm Ins., Dallas, 1991-96; assoc. Dale O'Neal Civil Mediators, Ft. Worth. Adj. prof. Wesleyan U. Sch. Law, 1995—, coach nat. ABA champion negotiation team, 1998; mediator pvt. practice, Dallas, Ft. Worth, Granbury, 1991—; coord. cert. in conflict resolution program Tex. Woman's U., 1996—; coach internat. champion online dispute resolution competition, 2002; cons. in field. Author: (with others) West Texas Practice, 1995; (with Frank Elliott) State Bar of Texas ADR Handbook, 2003. Dir. diversity tng. State Bar Tex. 9/11 project; founder, dir. and pres. Ala. Legal Reform Found., 2005—; registered lobbyist Ala., 2005—. Mem. ABA (negotiation and tng. coms., alternative dispute resolution sect.), Tex. Bar Assn. (ADR sect. coun. mem. 1998-2001, chair publs. com.), Tex. Bar Found., Tex. Initiatives for Mediation in Edn. (founder, planning com. 1993-95), Assn. for Conflict Resolution (pres. Dallas region 1995-97), Tex. Mediator Credentialing Assn. (bd. dir., disting. mediator), Tex. Assn. Mediators, Dallas Bar Assn. (coun. mem. 1993-94), Inst. for Responsible Dispute Resolution (charter), Toastmasters (v.p. 1993-94, pres. 1996-97). Avocations: singing, public speaking. Home: 1609 Sunset Terrace Fort Worth TX 76102 Office Phone: 214-546-3338. Personal E-mail: k4mede8@swbell.net.

ELKUS, RICHARD J., JR., electronics company executive; b. San Francisco, Feb. 25, 1935; s. Richard J. and Ruth (Kahn) E.; m. Helen Morrison, Aug. 17, 1956; children: Miriam Lyster, Richard M., Kevin J. BA, Stanford U., 1957; MBA, Dartmouth Coll., 1959. Prodn. control mgr. Ampex Corp., Redwood City, Calif., 1959-64, asst. to pres., 1968-71, mem. ops. bd., 1969-71, gen. mgr. ednl. and indsl. products divsn., 1969-72; pres., CEO, dir. Eyrle Co., Santa Clara, Calif., 1964-67; gen. mgr. Gould Med. systems, Santa Clara, Calif., 1973-74; exec. v.p., gen. mgr. Geometrics, Inc., Sunnyvale, Calif., 1974-80. Bd. dirs., chmn. bd. Integrated Systems, Inc., Santa Clara, 1985-92; bd. dirs. KLA-Tencor, San Jose, Calif., now vice-chmn. bd. Tencor Corp., 1994-, Lam Rsch., Fremont, Calif., SOPRA, Paris, Virage Logic, Fremont, Calif.; CEO Voyan Tech., Santa Clara. Mem. coun. on competitiveness, chmn. panel High Defination products and systems, NSF; mem. adv. bd. Ctr. Strategic and Internat. Studies Inst., 1990-96, Sch. Engring., Ga. Inst. Tech., 1996-98. Capt. USAR, 1957-65; bd. dirs. Nat. Sci. and Tech. Medals Found.; turstee Palo Alto Med. Found., Scripps Rsch. Ints.; pres. bd. sci. and innovation U. Calif. Mem. Am. Mgmt. Assn. (pres.'s coun.), Am. Electronics Assn. (bd. dirs., co-chmn. task force high resolutin systems), Electronics Assn. Calif. (vice chmn. nat. medal tech. nomination evaluation com. 1992-94, chmn. 1994-97), Econ. Strategy Inst. (adv. bd.), Foothills Tennis and Swim Club (Palo Alto, Calif.), Menlo Circus Club (Atherton, Calif.). Office: Voyan Tech 2700 Augustine Dr # 145 Santa Clara CA 95054

ELKWOOD, ANDREW IRA, plastic surgeon; b. NYC, Feb. 9, 1985; BS, Union Coll., Schenectady, NY; grad. degree in fin. and economics, Columbia U., NYC; MD, Albany Med. Coll., Union U., 1988. Cert. Am. Bd. Surgery, Am. Bd. Plastic Surgery (Gen. and Plastic Surgery). Intern, surgery NYU Med. Ctr., NYC, 1989, resident, plastic reconstructive surgery, 1989—94, fellow, 1994—96; attending Manhattan Eye Ear Throat Hosp., NYC, 1996, Riverview Med. Ctr., Red Bank, NJ, 1996, Monmouth Med. Ctr., Long Branch, NJ, 1996, chief, divsn. plastic surgery; private practice The Plastic Surgery Ctr. (NJ/NY); owner Smoothmed, NYC, 2007—. Tchg. appt. Robert Wood Johnson Med. Sch.; lectr. in field. Contbr. articles to profl. jours.; featured on TV programs CBS News, The Learning Channel, The Discovery Channel, 20/20, Rikki Lake Show & Ali and Jack Show, written about in newspapers and magazines Forbes, Asbury Park Press and The Star-Ledger; author: The Elkwood Advantage: A Physician's Holistic Guide to Looking Your Best. Named one of Best Surgeons in Am., Consumer Guide to Top Doctors. Fellow: Am. Soc. Aesthetic Plastic Surgery, Am. Coll. Surgery. Office: The Plastic Surgery

Ctr 535 Sycamore Ave Shrewsbury NJ 07702 Address: The Plastic Surgery Ctr 308 E 79th St New York NY 10021 Office Phone: 732-741-0970, 212-421-6725. Office Fax: 732-741-2606.*

ELLEDGE, STEPHEN JOSEPH, medical educator; b. Paris, Ill., Aug. 7, 1956; s. Joseph and Sarah (Greco) E.; m. Mitzi Kuroda. BS in Chemistry, U. Ill., 1978; PhD in Biology, MIT, 1983. Asst. prof. Baylor Coll. of Medicine, Houston, 1989-93, assoc. prof., 1993-96, asst. investigator, 1993-96, Howard Hughes investigator, 1996—, prof., 1995—. Recipient GHA Clowes Meml. award, Am. Assn. Cancer Rsch., Paul Marks prize for cancer rsch., Meml. Sloan-Kettering Cancer Ctr., John B. Carter Jr. Tech. Innovation award, Breast Cancer Innovator award, Genetics Soc. Am. medal. Mem.: Am. Acad. Arts and Sciences, NAS (Award in Molecular Biology 2002). Office Phone: 713-798-1655. Office Fax: 713-798-8884. Business E-Mail: relledge@bcm.tmc.edu.

ELLEK, ANTONIO, management consultant; s. Aldo and Edith Ellek. BS, U. Va., Charlottesville, 1991; MBA, Harvard U., Cambridge, Mass., 1996. CEO PASHA'S, Miami, Fla., 2000—, also bd. dirs. Dir. Rythm Found., Miami, 2006—07. Mem.: Harvard Bus. Sch. Club South Fla. (bd. dirs. 2000—). Office: PASHA'S 3801 N Miami Ave Miami FL 33127 Office Phone: 305-572-1150.

ELLEMAN, BARBARA, editor; b. Coloma, Wis., Oct. 20, 1934; d. Donald and Evelyn (Kissinger) Koplein; m. Don W. Elleman, Nov. 14, 1970. BS in Edn., Wis. State U., 1956; MA in Librarianship, U. Denver, 1964. Sch. libr. media specialist Port Washington (Wis.) High Sch., 1956-59, Homestead High Sch., Thiensville-Mequon, Wis., 1959-64; children's libr. Denver Pub. Libr., 1964-65; sch. libr. media specialist Cherry Creek Schs., Denver, 1965-70, Henry Clay Sch., Whitefish Bay, Wis., 1971-75; children's reviewer ALA, Chgo., 1975-82, children's editor, 1982-90, editor Book Links, 1990-96. Vis. lectr. U. Wis., 1974-75, 81-82, U. Ill., Circle Campus, 1983-85; Disting. scholar children's lit., Marquette U., 1996—; cons. H.W. Wilson Co., 1969-75; mem. Libr. Congress Adv. Com. on selection for children's books for blind and physically handicapped, 1980-88, Caldecott Calendar Com., 1986; judge The Am. Book Awards, 1982, Golden Kite, 1987, Boston Globe/Horn Book, 1990; mem. faculty Highlights for Children Writers Conf., 1985-90; mem. orgn. com. MidWest Conf. Soc. Children's Books Writers, 1974-76; chair Hans Christian Andersen Com., 1987-88; advisor Reading Rainbow, 1986-96, Ind. R.E.A.P. project, 1987-93; jury mem. VI Catalonia Premi Children's Book Exbhn., Barcelona, Spain, 1994; adv. bd. Parent's Choice, Cobblestone Publ., Georgia Pub. TV's 2000, The New Advocate mag., 20th Century Children's Writers, Encyclopedia of Children's Literature, Cooperative Children's Book Ctr., U. Wis., Madison, Riverbank Rev., 1998—, Ency. of Children's Lit., 1998—; lang. arts com. NCTE Notable Books, 1997—; spkr. in field. Author: Reading in a Media Age, 1975, 20th Century Children's Writers, 1979, rev. edit., 1984, What Else Can You Do With a Library Degree?, 1980, Popular Reading for Children, 1981, Popular Reading II, 1986, Children's Books of International Interest, 1984, Tomie dePaola, His Art and His Stories, 1999, Holiday House: It's First 65 Years, 2000, Virginia Lee Burton: A Life in Art, 2002; contbr. articles to profl. jours. Publicity chair Internat. Bd. Books for Young People Congress, Williamsburg, Va., 1990; bd. trustees Eric Carle Mus. Picture Book Art, 2004-. Recipient Jeremiah Ludington award Ednl. Paperback Assn., 1996, Hope S. Dean award Found. Children's Lit., 1996. Mem. ALA (2000 Caldecott Com. 1999—), Soc. Children's Book Writers (mem. orgn. com. MidWest Conf. 1974-76), Internat. Bd. Books for Young People (U.S. assoc. editor Bookbird 1978-86, chair nominating com., 1985, bd. dirs. 1990-92), Children's Reading Round Table Chgo. (award 1987), Nat. Coun. Tchrs. English (bd. dirs. children's lit. assembly 1986-88, mem. editl. adv. bd. CLA bull. 1989-91, mem. using nonfiction in classroom com. 1990-96, 2000 Caldecott com., Laura I. Wilder com. 2001--). Address: 20 Bayon Dr Apt 5 South Hadley MA 01075

ELLENBERGER, JACK STUART, law librarian; b. Lamar, Colo., Sept. 5, 1930; s. Emmert C. and Ruby F. (Overstreet) E. BS, Georgetown U., 1957; MLS, Columbia U., 1959. Law libr. HEW, 1957; libr. Carter, Ledyard & Milburn, NYC, 1957-60, Jones, Day, Reavis & Pogue (and predecessor firm), Cleve., 1960, Bar Assn. of DC, Washington, 1961-63, Covington & Burling, Washington, 1963-78, Shearman & Sterling, NYC, 1978-93, law libr. emeritus, 1994-95; ret., 1995. Editor: (with Mahar) Legislative History of the Securities Act of 1933 and the Securities Exchange Act of 1934, 1973. Served with USAF, 1951-54. Mem. Am. Assn. Law Libraries (pres. 1976-77, M.G. Gallagher Disting. Svc. award 1994), Spl. Libraries Assn.

ELLENBERGER, LON KARL, singer, music educator; s. Karol (Johnson) and Fred Ellenberger. BA, Beloit Coll., 1986; MA, Northeastern Ill. U., Chgo., 1993; DMus, Northwestern U., Evanston, Ill., 2007. Cert. Zeugnis Zentrale Mittelstufenprüfung Goethe-Institut Chgo., 1993. Voice tchr. Ctr. For Voice, Chgo., 1994—; soloist Rockefeller Meml. Chapel, 2006—. Singer: (operas) Dido and Aeneas, Johanespassion. Recipient Creative award, Anna Sosenko Charitable Trust, 2003—05; Scholarship award, Burstein Family Found., 1999-2001. Personal E-mail: lonellenberger@mindspring.com.

ELLENBOGEN, GEORGE, poet, educator; b. Montreal, Que., Can., Nov. 19, 1934; came to U.S., 1966; s. Moses and Jenny (Borenstein) E.; m. Karia Doris Feinzig, Dec. 18, 1960 (div. 1984); children: Sara Rachel, Adam. BA, McGill U., Montreal, 1955; MA, U. Montreal, 1962; PhD, Tufts U., 1969. Mem. faculty Bentley Coll., Waltham, Mass., 1965—, prof. English, 1980—, chmn. dept., 1980-85, dir. Forum for Creative Writing, 1987—2004; poetry editor Boston Today, 1978-81. Vis. prof., writer-in-residence U. Siegen, Germany, 1996. Author: Winds of Unreason, 1957, The Night Unstones, 1971, Along the Road from Eden, 1989, The Rhinogate Poems, 1996, La Porte aux rhinos et autres poemes (bilingual edit.), 1997; Winterfischer, 2002, Morning Gothic: New and Selected Poems, 2007; subject of German documentary film A Canadian Poet in America; author numerous poems. Recipient award Karolyi Meml. Found., 1986, Va. Ctr. for Creative Arts, 1987, 92, 93, 2000, 02, 03, 04, 05, Montalvo Assn., 1987, Whiting Found., 1994; grantee Can. Internat. Cultural Rels., 1997, Gesellschaft for Kanada Studies, 1998, Can. Dept. Fgn. Affairs, 2003, Ledig-Rowohlt Found., 2004. Mem. AAUP, MLA, Coll. English Assn., Nat. Council Tchrs. of English Home: 21 Wren St West Roxbury MA 02132-2625 Business E-Mail: gellenbogen@bentley.edu.

ELLENBOGEN, LEON, nutritionist, biochemist, retired pharmaceutical executive; b. NYC, May 3, 1927; s. Martin and Bella (Zalesnick) E.; m. Roslyn Barban, June 30, 1951; children: Kenneth Alan, Richard Glen, Cheryl Sue. BS, CCNY, 1949; MS, NYU, 1951; PhD, Ind. U., 1954. Technician and med. corpsman USN, 1945-47; rsch. technician Columbia U., NYC, 1949-51; teaching asst. gen. chemistry and biochemistry Ind. U., Bloomington, 1951-53; rsch. biochemist Lederle Labs., Am. Cyanamid Co., Pearl River, NY, 1953-59, sr. rsch. biochemist, group leader, 1959-77, chief nutritional sci., sr. assoc. dir. med. pharm. devel., 1977-95; asst. v.p. nutritional scis. Lederle Consumer Health divsn. Whitehall Robins Health Care, Am. Home Products, Madison, NJ, 1995-97; ret., 1997. Adj. prof. nutrition in medicine Cornell U. Med. Coll., 1978—2003; adj. prof. nutrition N.Y. Med. Coll., 1981—; adj. prof., adv. com. intrinsic factor Nat. Formulatory Com.; mem. sci. affairs com. Proprietary Assn., 1980-89. Contbr. numerous articles to profl. jours., tech. books; author, presenter abstracts and papers profl. meetings; editor Contemporary Issues in Clin. Nutrition, 1980—, guest editor vols. 2 and 12; editor Drug Nutrient Interactions, 1982-91; cons. editor Biochemistry, Jour. AMA, Am. Jour. Clin. Nutrition, Sci., The Med. Letter, Nutrition Reports Internat., Thrombosis Rsch., Jour. Medicinal Chemistry, Archives Biochem. and Biophys., Annals Internal Medicine, Jour. Biol. Chemistry, Biochem. Pharmacology. Pharmacists mate USN, 1945-47. Recipient Steuben apple for contbns. to sci. rsch. Coun. for Responsible Nutrition. Fellow Am. Soc. Nutritional Scis., N.Y. Acad. Scis. (steering com. biochem. pharmacology discussion group 1973-77); mem. Am. Heart Assn., Am. Soc. Hematology, Am. Inst. Nutrition (nomenclature com.), Am. Soc. Clin. Nutrition, Am. Soc. Biol. Chemists, Am. Soc. Pharmacology and Exptl. Therapeutics, Am. Chem. Soc. (chmn. biochem. discussion group N.Y. sect. 1959, counselor divsn. biol. labs. 1977-79), Soc. Exptl. Biology and Medicine (editor proc. 1961-62), U.S. Pharmacopeia (com. on revision 1990-95, subcom. for nonprescription drugs and nutritional supplements 1995-2000, U.S. Pharmacopia Nutrition and Electrolytes Expert Com., expert com. on bioavailabilty and nutrient absorption of U.S. pharmacopia 2000-05), Sigma Xi, Phi Lambda Upsilon. Avocation: sports. Home: 16 Morris Dr New City NY 10956-4652 Office: Wyeth Consumer Healthcare Madison NJ 07940-0871 Office Phone: 973-660-5767. Personal E-mail: ellenbl@wyeth.com, ellenblr@aol.com.

ELLENBOGEN, PAUL H., radiologist; b. Port Chester, NY, Apr. 8, 1947; s. Andrew A. and Lillian M. Ellenbogen; m. Maxine Platt Ellenbogen, June 24, 1972; children: Jeffrey, Marc. ScB, Brown U., Providence, 1969; MD, SUNY, NYC, 1973. Diplomate Am. Bd. Radiology. Radiologist SW Imaging and Interventional Specialists, Dallas, 1978—. Pres. Tex. Radiol. Soc., 2001. Fellow: Am. Inst. Ultrasound in Medicine, Am. Coll. Radiology (spkr. ACR Coun. 2002—04, treas. 2006—). Office: Presbyn Hosp Dallas 8200 Walnut Hill Ln Dallas TX 75231

ELLENBOGEN, RICHARD, plastic surgeon; b. Port Jervis, NY, 1944; married; 3 children. AA with honors, U. Fla., 1963; attended rsch. med. sch., Prenatal Determination of Fetal Sex Using Matenal Blood Through Chromosome Analysis, 1966; MD, U. Miami Sch. Medicine, 1968. Diplomate Nat. Bd. Med. Examiners, Am. Bd. Plastic and Reconstructive Surgery, 1978, lic. Calif. Surgical intern Albert Einstein Coll. Medicine, Bronx, NY, 1968—68, general surgery resident, 1968—69, Beth Israel Med. Ctr., Divsn. Mt. Sinai Sch. Medicine of CCNY, 1970—72; fellow, plastic surgery Red Cross Hosp., The Hague, Netherlands Plastic Surgery, 1972—73; hand surgery fellowship Hosp. for Joint Diseases Mt. Sinai Sch. Medicine, NYC, 1973; plastic and reconstructive surgery resident Nassau County Med. Ctr. of SUNY, 1973—75; dir., private practice, owner Beverly Hills Body, LA, 1976—. Hospital affiliations include Midway Hosp.; clin. instructor, divsn. plastic surgery U. So. Calif., LA; vis. prof. South African Plastic Surgical Conf., Sun City, 2001; cons. on chest-regarding silicone lung disease Official Publication of the Am. Coll. Chest Physicians; presenter in field. Featured on Dr. 90210, CNN Showbiz Today, Geraldo, Marilu Donahue, Hard Copy, 48 Hours, American Journal, A Current Affair, Montel Williams, quoted in Time, Newsweek, USA Today, Wall Street Journal, Cosmopolitan, Harper's Bazaar, GQ, LA Times Mag., Ladies Home Jour., Money, LA Med. Soc. Jour., Shape, West World, Sea Breeze, NOW, Life Extension, American Health Report, Movieline, American Salon, and Human Sexuality, guest appearances Oprah Winfrey, Donahue, Hour Mag., P.M. Mag., People Are Talking, Closer Look, A.M. Los Angeles, Frankly Female, Merv Griffin, Current Affair, NBC Medical News, ABC News, Trail Watch, CBS Medical News, Regis Philbin, & Hard Copy; contbr. articles to profl. jours. Active in helping raise funding and support for the Hosp. de la Fe in San Miguel de Allende, Mexico and Project Happy Face. Named one of Best Plastic Surgeons in Am., Town & Country mag. Fellow: Internat. Coll. Surgeons (Best Presentation award 2002—03), ACS; mem.: Am. Soc. Plastic and Reconstructive Surgeons, Am. Soc. for Aesthetic Plastic Surgery (Best Plastic Surgery jour. article on rhinoplasty in the world 2003), Am. Soc. for Laser Medicine and Surgery, Lipoplasty Soc. N.Am., LA Assn. Plastic Surgeons, Calif. Med. Assn. (Physician Recognition award (recipient twice)), LA County Med. Assn., AMA (AMA Physician Recognition award, Physician Recognition award (three time recipient)). Achievements include being one of the most published and innovative plastic surgeons; only plastic surgeon to be featured in National Geographic. Avocation: avid collector of art nouveau antiques. Office: Beverly Hills Body 9201 Sunset Blvd Ste 202 Los Angeles CA 90069 Office Phone: 310-276-3183.*

ELLENHORN, DAVID N., lawyer; b. NYC, Sept. 28, 1936; s. Henry L. and Laura Ellenhorn; 1 child, Adam. BA, Brown U., Providence, 1958; LLB, Yale U., New Haven, Conn., 1961. Bar: NY 1962. Asst. US Atty., Washington, 1963—68; atty. Kronish Lieb Weiner & Hellman, NYC, 1968—73; chief counsel NY Commn. on Investigations, NYC, 1979—81. Lectr. Yale Law Sch., New Haven, NYU Law Sch. Bd. govs. Am. Jewish Com., 1998—2004. Mem.: Fed. Bar Coun., Am. Law Inst., NYC Bar (chair sr. lawyers com.), Phi Beta Kappa. Jewish. Avocations: golf, reading, music, films, travel. Home: 7 W 81st St New York NY 10024 Office: Proskauer Rose 1585 Broadway New York NY 10036

ELLENS, J(AY) HAROLD, philosopher, educator, psychotherapist, minister; b. McBain, Mich., July 16, 1932; s. John S. and Grace (Kortmann) E.; m. Mary Jo Lewis, Sept. 7, 1954; children: Deborah, Jackie, Dan, Beckie, Rocky, Brenda, Brett. AB, Calvin Coll., 1953; BD, Calvin Sem., 1956, MDiv, 1986; ThM, Princeton Sem., 1965; PhD, Wayne State U., 1970; MA, U. Mich., 2000. Ordained to ministry Christian Reformed Ch., 1956; ordained theologian and pastor Presbyn. Ch., 1978. Pastor Newton Christian Reformed Ch., NJ, 1961-65, North Hills Ch., Troy, Mich., 1965-68; pvt. practice psychotherapy Farmington Hills, Mich., 1967—; pastor Univ. Hills Ch., Farmington Hills, Mich., 1968-78, Westminster Presbyn. Ch., 1980-84, Erin Presbyn. Ch., 1986-88, Cherry Hill Presbyn. Ch., 1994-96, White Lake Presbyn. Ch., 1998-2000, Troy Presbyn. Ch., 2000—01, 2004—, Mt. Clemens 1st Presbyn. Ch., 2001—02, Peoples Presbyn. Ch., Milan, Mich., 2003—04. Religious broadcaster TV, weekly, 1970-74, periodically to date; lectr. humanities and classics Wayne State U., John Wesley Coll., Oakland U., 1970-90, Wayne C.C., Oakland C.C., Calvin Sem.; vis. lectr. Princeton Theol. Sem., 1977-79; with Inst. for Antiquity and Christianity, Claremont U.; lectr. U.S. and abroad. Author: Program Format in Religious Television, 1970, Models of Religious Broadcasting, 1974, Chaplain (Major General) Gerhart W. Hyatt: An Oral History, 1977, (with others) Internat. Standard Bible Encyclopedia, 1979-89, Eternal Vigilance, 1980, God's Grace and Human Health, 1982, Life and Laughter, 1983, Psychology in Worship, 1984, (with others) Baker's Encyclopedia of Psychology, 1984, 1995, Psychotheology: Key Issues, 1986, (with others) Psychotherapy in Christian Perspective, 1987, (with others) Christian Counseling and Psychotherapy, 1987, Love, Life and Laughter, 1988, (with others) Psychology and Religion, 1988, (with others) The Church and Pastoral Care, 1988, (with others) Moral Obligation and the Military, 1988, (with others) God se genade is genoeg, 1989, (with others) Counseling and the Human Predicament, 1989, (with others) Turning Points in Pastoral Care, (with others) Christian Perspectives on Human Development, 1992, The Ancient Library of Alexandria and Early Christian Theological Development, 1993, 95, Alexander The Great and Hellenistic Culture, 1997, Human Disfunction, 1998, (with others) Humanistic Psychology, 1998, (with others) Dictionary of Pastoral Care and Counseling, 1990, (with others) The Interpretation of the Bible, 1998, Jesus as Son of Man, 2003, (with others) The Destructive Power of Religion (4 vols.), 2004, 05, (with others) God's Word for Our World, 2004, (with others) Psychology and the Bible (4 vols.), 2004, 05, (with others) Jesus as Son of Man, The Literary Character, A Progression of Images, 2004, (with others) Just War and Jihad, 2005, Sex in the Bible, 2006, three books in Portuguese and one in Spanish; editor: CAPS Internat. Directory vols. II-V, 1976-87, Ethical Reflections, 1977, The Beauty of Holiness, 2d edit., 1985, God's Grace in Free Verse, 1987, (with others) Eerdmans Dictionary of the Bible, 2000; editor in chief Jour. Psychology and Christianity, 1975-88; contbr. more than 165 articles to profl. jours. Served to col. AUS, 1956-61, ret., 1992. Created knight, Queen Juliana, The Netherlands, 1974. Mem. 23 profl. socs. including Christian Assn. Psychol. Studies (now exec. dir. emeritus), Soc. Bibl. Lit., Mil. Chaplain Assn., Ret. Officers Assn., Archeol. Inst. Am., Mil. Order World Wars. Home and Office: 26705 Farmington Rd Farmington MI 48334-4329 Office Phone: 248-231-4433. Personal E-mail: jharoldellens@juno.com. *Secular and religious communities alike tend continually to shift their focus toward some orthodoxy or other, usually in the form of according ultimate authority to an aspect of the community's traditional thought or behavior, thus imposing constraints upon the quest for growth and for truth which are not responsive to reality or authenticity or relevant and wholesome freedom. Orthodoxy is always, therefore, a form of idolatry; it is a psychological phenomenon; it is the posture of arrogance in those who see themselves as "the chosen" or the elect; it is a lunge for security vs. growth; it is designed to guard against the destablizing effect of change; it is, therefore inherently imperialistic, arbitrary, propagandist, and abusive.*

ELLENSON, DAVID, college president; PhD, Columbia U., NYC, 1981. Ordained Rabbi 1977. I.H. and Anna Grancell Prof. Jewish Religious Thought Hebrew Union Coll. - Jewish Inst. Religion, pres. Fell. Shalom Hartman Institute of Jerusalem; fell., lectr. Inst. of Advanced Studies at Hebrew U., Jerusalem. Author: Tradition in Transition: Orthodoxy, Halakhah and the Boundaries of Modern Jewish History, 1989, Rabbi Esriel Hildesheimer and the Creation of a Modern Jewish Orthodoxy, 1990 (nominated Outstading Book on Jewish History, National Jewish Book Coun., 1991), Between Tradition and Culture: The Dialectics of Jewish Religion and Identity in the Modern World, 1994, After Emancipation: Jewish Religious Responses to Modernity, 2004. Named one of The Top 50 Rabbis in America, Newsweek Mag., 2007. Office: HUC-JIR One West 4th St New York NY 10012*

ELLER, MARLIN, security firm executive; BA in Math. and Physics magna cum laude, U. Wash., 1979. Mgr. software devel. Microsoft Corp., 1982—95; founder, CEO, pres. Sunhawk.com, Seattle, 1995—. Vis. instr. in computer sci. Williams Coll., 1980—82; bd. dir. Fire Donations, Gig Harbor, Wash. Co-author: Barbarians Led by Bill Gates, 1998. Office: Sunhawk.com Corp 1463 E Republican St Seattle WA 98112-4517

ELLER, TIMOTHY R., construction and real estate company executive; b. 1948; BS in Constrn. Mgmt., U. Nebr., 1972. With Centex Homes, Ill., 1973, project mgr. Ill., 1975, v.p. Minn., 1977—81, divsn. pres. Minn., 1981—85, pres., CEO, 1991, chmn., 1998—2003; exec. v.p. Centex Real Estate Corp./Centex Homes, Dallas, 1985—90, pres., COO, 1990—96; CEO Centex Real Estate Corp., Dallas, 1991—2002, 2006—, chmn. Dallas, 1998—2003; exec. v.p. Centex Corp., Dallas, 1998—2002, pres. , COO, 2002—, bd. dirs., 2002—, chmn., CEO, 2004—. Bd. chmn. High Prodn. Home Builders Coun. Nat. Assn. Home Builders; life trustee Nat. Housing Endowment. Chmn. policy adv. bd. Harvard U. Joint Ctr. Housing Studies, 2002; bd. trustees Nature Conservancy Tex. Office: Centex Corp PO Box 199000 Dallas TX 75219-9000*

ELLERBEE, LINDA (LINDA JANE SMITH), reporter; b. Bryan, Tex., Aug. 15, 1944; m. Mac Smith, 1964 (div. 1966), m. Van Veselka, 1968 (div. 1971), children: Vanessa, Joshua, m. Tom Ellerbee, 1973 (div. 1974). Student, Vanderbilt U., Nashville, 1962—64. Newscaster, disc jockey Sta. WVON, Chgo., 1964-67; program dir. Sta. KSJO, San Francisco, 1967-68; reporter Sta. KJNO and AP, Juneau, Alaska, 1969-72; news writer AP, Dallas, 1972; TV reporter KHOU, Houston, 1972—73; gen. assignment reporter Sta. WCBS-TV, NYC, 1973-76; Washington corr. NBC News, 1976—78; co-anchor Weekend, NBC News, NBC-TV, 1978—79; corr. NBC Nightly News, 1979—82; co-anchor NBC News Overnight, 1982-84, Summer Sunday, 1984; corr., reporter Today Show, NBC-TV, 1984—86; reporter Good Morning America, 1986; writer, anchor Our World, ABC-TV, 1986—87; prodr., writer, host Nick News, Nickelodeon Network, 1993—; founder, pres. Lucky Duck Prodns., NYC, 1987—; commentator Cable News Network, 1989; writer, host On the Record, Microsoft online, 1996—. Author: And So It Goes: Adventures in Television, 1986, Move On: Adventures in the Real World, 1991, Take Big Bites: Adventures Around the World and Across the Table, 2005; exec. prod. (TV spls.) A Conversation with Magic (Cable ACE award 1992), It's Only Television (Peabody award 1992); exec. prod., writer, host (news/mag. program) Nick News (Columbia duPont award 1993, Parents' Choice Found. Gold TV award); writer, anchor, Our World (Emmy for best writing 1986); weekly syndicated columnist King Features, N.Y.; (narrator) Baby Boom, 1987, Addicted, 1997 (also exec. prodr., writer, filmography prodr.); filmography prodr. (miniseries) Oh What a Time It Was, 1999; exec. prodr. (TV) several Intimate Portraits 1998-2003, Feeding the Beast: The 24-Hour News Revolution, 2004; prodr. (TV mini series) Oh What a Time It Was, 1999; exec. prodr. (TV series) When I Was a Girl, 2001; prodr. Inside TV Land: Primetime Politics, 2004 (also writer), Inside TV Land: Tickled Pink, 2005; guest appearances Murphy Brown, 1989, 1993, Ellen, 1998, The Fight to be Fit, Nick News, 2005. Office: Lucky Duck Prodns 96 Morton St Fl 4 New York NY 10014-3326

ELLERBROOK, NIEL COCHRAN, gas industry executive; b. Rensselaer, Ind., Dec. 26, 1948; s. James Harry and Margaret (Cochran) E.; children: Jennifer, Jeffrey, Jayma. BS, Ball State U., 1970. CPA, Ind. Staff acct. audit Arthur Andersen & Co., Indpls., 1970-72, audit sr., 1972-75, audit mgr., 1975-80; asst. to sr. v.p. adminstrn. and fin. Ind. Gas Co., Inc., Indpls., 1980-81, v.p. fin., 1981-84, v.p. fin., chief fin. officer, 1984-87, sr. v.p., CFO, 1987; v.p., treas., CFO Ind. Energy, Inc., 1986—97, exec. v.p., treas., CFO, 1997, pres., COO, 1997—99, pres., CEO, 1999—2000; chmn., CEO Vectren Corp., Evansville, Ind., 2000—03, chmn, pres., CEO, 2003—. Bd. dirs. Ind. Gas Co., Ind. Energy, Inc. 5th 3d Bank of Ctrl. Ind Bd. dirs. Crossroads of Am. Coun. Boy Scouts Am., Indpls. Civic Theatre. Mem. AICPA, Ind. CPA Soc. (bd. dirs. Indpls. chpt., past pres. 1977-83, state bd. dirs. 1984-87), Fin. Exec. Inst., Ind. Fiscal Policy Inst. (bd. dirs. 1985—, vice chmn. 1988-91, chmn. 1991-94), Ind. C. of C. (taxation com. 1982-94, chmn. 1987-94), Ind. Gas Assn. (treas., asst. sec. 1988—). Office: Vectren PO Box 209 Evansville IN 47702-0209*

ELLERMAN, PAIGE L., lawyer; b. Covington, Ky., May 11, 1974; BA, U. Ky., 1995; JD, Salmon P. Chase Coll. Law, 1999. Bar: Ohio 1999, Ky. 2000, Ind. 2001, US Dist. Ct. Southern Dist. Ohio, US Dist. Ct. Eastern Dist. Ky., US Dist. Ct. Western Dist. Ky., US Supreme Ct. Assoc. Taft, Stettinius & Hollister LLP, Cin. Mem. Profl. Women's Resource Grp. Pres. The Yearlings, Inc.; mem., Ann. Support Com. Elizabeth Med. Ctr. Found., chair, Benefactor Drive, 2006—. Named one of Ohio's Rising Stars, Super Lawyers, 2005, 2006. Mem.: Salmon P. Chase Coll. Law Alumni Assn. (pres., Bd. Govenors), FBA, Cin. Bar Assn. Office: Taft Stettinius & Hollister LLP 425 Walnut St Ste 1800 Cincinnati OH 45202-3957 Office Phone: 513-381-2838. Office Fax: 513-381-0205.

ELLETT, ALAN SIDNEY, real estate developer; b. Seven Kings, Essex, Eng., Jan. 6, 1930; came to U.S., 1974, permanent resident, 1974; s. Sidney Walter and May (Fowler) E.; children: Denise, Michelle, Wayne. BSc in Bldg. Constrn., 1951, MBA. Mng. dir. Gilbert Ash Structures, 1960-68; dir., gen. mgr. Lyon Group (real estate), 1968-70; mng. dir. (pres.) Gilbert Ash Ltd., 1970-72; dir. Bovis Ltd.; chief exec. Bovis Property divsn. Audley Properties Ltd., 1972-74; chmn. bd. Forest City Dillon, Inc., 1974-88; exec. v.p., dir. Forest City Enterprises, Inc., Cleve., 1974-89; chmn. Forest City Rental Properties, 1982-89; chmn., pres. Forest City Comml. Constrn. Co., Inc., 1987-89; exec. v.p., COO Am. Malls Internat.,

Washington, 1997—2000; prin., owner Intercontinental Devel. and Investment Corp., Pembroke Pines, Fla., 1997—. Contbr. articles to profl. jours. Fellow Inst. Builders, Inst. Dirs Mem. Conservative Party. Mem. Church of England. (London).

ELLETT, JOHN SPEARS, II, retired taxation educator, accountant, lawyer; b. Richmond, Va., Sept. 17, 1923; s. Henry Guerrant and Elizabeth Firmstone (Maxwell) E.; m. Mary Ball Ruffin, Apr. 15, 1950; children: John, Mary Ball, Elizabeth, Martha, Henry. BA, U. Va., 1948, JD, 1957, MA, 1961; PhD, U. N.C., 1969. CPA, Va., La.; bar: Va. 1957. Lab. instr. U. Va., Charlottesville, 1953-58; instr. Washington and Lee U., 1958-60; asst. prof. U. Fla., 1967-71; assoc. prof. U. New Orleans, 1971-76, prof. taxation, 1976-94, prof. emeritus, 1994—. Trainee Va. Carolina Hardware Co., Richmond, 1948-51; acct. Equitable Life Assurance Soc., Richmond, 1951-52; staff acct. Musselman & Drysdale, Charlottesville, 1952-54; staff acct. R.M. Musselman, Charlottesville, 1957-58; mem. U. New Orleans Oil and Gas Acctg. Conf., 1973-92; bd. dirs., publicity chmn. U. New Orleans Energy Acctg. and Tax Conf., 1993-94, bd. dirs. publicity com.; pres. Maxwelton Farm and Timber Corp., 1994—; treas. U. New Orleans Estate Planning Seminar, 1975-78, lectr. continuing edn.; CPCU instr. New Orleans Ins. Inst., 1975-78. Author books; contbr. articles to profl. jours. Served with AUS, 1943-46. Mem. AICPA (40 yr. hon. mem. 2000—), Am. Acctg. Assn., Am. Assn. Atty.-CPAs (chmn. ptnrship. taxation continuing edn. com. 1989, ptnrship. taxation com. 1990, organized La. chpt., v.p. 1991-93), Va. Soc. CPAs, Soc. La. CPAs, Va. Bar Assn. (40 yr. hon. mem. 2000—). Democrat. Episcopalian. Home: 177 Maxwelton Rd Charlottesville VA 22903-7859

ELLETT, TED (E. TAZEWELL ELLETT), lawyer; b. Richmond, Va., June 9, 1952; s. Tazewell III and Marguerite (Rucker) E.; m. Alice Lee Withers, June 11, 1977; children: Elizabeth Pender, E. Tazewell Jr., Dabney McGuire. BA, Davidson Coll., NC, 1974; JD, U. Va., 1977. Bar: Va. 1977, D.C. 1978, U.S. Dist. Ct. (D.C. dist.) 1979, U.S. Ct. Appeals (D.C. cir.) 1979. Law clk. D.C. Ct. Appeals, 1977-78; assoc. Hogan & Hartson, Washington, 1978-82; spl. asst. to mem. Nat. Transp. Safety Bd., Washington, 1982-84; spl. counsel to adminstr. FAA, Washington, 1984-85, chief counsel, 1985-88; ptnr. Hogan & Hartson, Washington, 1988—. Mem. aviation adv. bd. U. So. Calif., L.A., 1988—. Mem. editorial adv. bd. Aviation Noise Report, 1990—, editl. bd. Va. Law Rev. 1976-77; contbr. articles to profl. jours. Bd. mem. Big Bros. of Nat. Capital Area, Washington, 1980-83; past pres. No. Va. Coun. Big Brothers; vestry mem. Christ Ch. Alexandria, Va., 1985-88. Mem. ABA (mem. forum com. air and space law 1983-, aviation law com. tort and ins. law sect. 1986-), Fed. Bar Assn. (mem. air and space law com. 1983-, adv. bd. transp. law sect. 1987, vice chmn. 1991-92, chmn. 1992-93, chmn. steering com. transp. law sect. 1988-90), Nat. Transp. Safety Bd. Bar Assn., Internat. Bar Assn., Lawyer-Pilots Bar Assn., Va. Bar Assn. (mem. bus. law sect. 1981-, mem. transp. law sect. 1993-, chmn., 1993-95, mem. exec. com. 2000-02, chmn. bd. govs. 2002, pres.-elect 2003, pres. 2004-05), Bar Assn. D.C., Aero Club of Washington (trustee 1986—), City Club of Washington, Assawoman Fishing Unltd. Club. Republican. Episcopalian. Avocations: running, fishing, hiking, camping, canoeing. Office: Hogan & Hartson LLP Ste 800E 555 13th St NW Washington DC 20004-1109 Office Phone: 202-637-8644. Office Fax: 202-637-5910. Business E-Mail: etellett@hhlaw.com.*

ELLICKSON, BRYAN CARL, economics professor; b. Bklyn., Feb. 12, 1941; s. Raymond Thorwald and Loene (Gibson) E.; m. Phyllis Lynn Rutter, June 19, 1965; 1 child, Paul Bryan. BA, U. Oreg., 1963; PhD, MIT, 1970. From asst. prof. to assoc. prof. UCLA, 1968-83, prof., 1983—, chair econs. dept., 1996-99. Cons. Rand, Santa Monica, Calif., 1970—. Author: Competitive Equilibrium, 1993; contbr. articles to profl. jours. Rsch. grantee HUD, 1979-81, NSF, 1982-87. Mem. Am. Econ. Assn., Econometric Soc. Avocation: scuba diving. Home: 18409 Wakecrest Dr Malibu CA 90265-5620 Office: UCLA Dept Econs 405 Hilgard Ave Los Angeles CA 90095-1477 Home Phone: 310-459-6798; Office Phone: 310-825-4556. Business E-Mail: ellickson@econ.ucla.edu.

ELLICKSON, DONALD LIEN, retired economist, county official; b. Madison, Wis., Mar. 30, 1929; s. Bernie and Ella Ellickson; m. Marion Smith, Dec. 19, 1954; children: Brian, Anne Swanson, Amy, Kent. BA, Luther Coll., 1950; MA, U. Wis., 1951, PhD, 1966. Mem. econs. and bus. faculty Heidelberg Coll., Tiffin, Ohio, 1952—58; mem. faculty dept. econs. U. Wis., Eau Claire, 1958—94, head dept. econs., 1967—90; mem. Eau Claire County Bd. of Supervisors, 1994—. Mem., sec. Chippewa Valley Innovation Ctr., Eau Claire. Mem.: Nat. Tax Assn. (mem. various coms.). Home Phone: 715-834-1558.

ELLICKSON, JEAN, anthropology educator; b. Cleve., Sept. 7, 1935; d. Curtis Arthur and Laura Mina (Koepke) E.; m. Muhammad Bazlul Karim, July 26, 1975. BA, Ohio State U., 1956; MLS, U. Mich., 1959; MA in Anthropology, Mich. State U., 1970, PhD in Anthropolgy, 1972. Asst. prof. anthropology Mich. Tech. U., Houghton, 1970-71; social sci. analyst Agy. for Internat. Devel., Washington, 1981-82; asst. prof. Western Ill. U., Macomb, 1971-74, assoc. prof., 1975-87, prof., 1987—, assoc. dir. honors program, 1988-90, chairperson dept. sociology, anthropology and social work, 1991—. Cons. anthropologist Rajshahi (Bangladesh) U., 1974-75. Contbr. articles to profl. jours. Fellow Am. Anthropol. Assn., Soc. for Applied Anthropology; mem. Assn. for Asian Studies (Bangladesh com. 1974-75), Am. Ethnol. Assn., Assn. for Women in Devel., Soc. for Internat. Devel., Women in Devel. (treas. Washington chpt. 1981-82), Bengal Studies Assn. (charter). Democrat. Avocations: cats, cooking. Home: 916 S Taylor Ave Oak Park IL 60304-1628 Office: Western Ill U Dept Sociol Anthropology And Socia Walk Macomb IL 61455

ELLICKSON, PHYLLIS LYNN, political scientist; b. Springfield, Mass., Apr. 22, 1942; d. Frank Walter Rutter and Winifred Annette Grayston; m. Bryan Carl Ellickson, June 19, 1965; 1 child, Paul Bryan. BA, Mount Holyoke Coll., 1963; PhD, MIT, 1973. Rschr. Arthur D. Little Inc., Cambridge, Mass., 1964—66; asst. prof. UCLA, 1973—74; social scientist Rand, Santa Monica, Calif., 1974—85, sr. behavioral scientist, 1985—. Mem. ednl. adv. bd. The Best Found., LA, 1994—; mem. nat. adv. bd. Monitoring the Future, Ann Arbor, Mich., 1998—; expert panel mem. Dept. Edn., Washington, 1998—2000. Contbr. articles to profl. jours. Adv. bd. Partnership for a Drug Free Am., NYC, 2002—. Mem.: Soc. for Prevention Rsch., Phi Beta Kappa. Achievements include development of award-winning drug prevention program Project ALERT. Avocations: travel, opera. Home: 18409 Wakecrest Dr Malibu CA 90265 Office: Rand 1776 Main St Santa Monica CA 90407 Business E-Mail: phyllis_ellickson@rand.org.

ELLICKSON, ROBERT CHESTER, law educator; b. Washington, Aug. 4, 1941; s. John Chester and Katherine Heilprin (Pollak) Ellickson; m. Lynn Hammer; children: Jenny, Owen. AB, Oberlin Coll., 1963; LLB, Yale U., 1966. Bar: D.C. 1967, Calif. 1971. Atty. adviser Pres.'s Com. Urban Housing, Washington, 1967-68; mgr. urban affairs Levitt & Sons Inc., Lake Success, NY, 1968-70; prof. law U. So. Calif., LA, 1970-81; prof. Stanford U., Calif., 1981-85, Robert E. Paradise prof. natural resources law, 1985-88; Walter E. Meyer prof. property and urban law Yale U., New Haven, 1988—, dep. dean, 1991-92. Author: Order Without Law, 1991 (Triennial award Order of the Coif), (with Rose & Ackerman) Perspectives on Property Law, 3d edit., 2002, (with Been) Land Use Controls, 3rd edit., 2005. Mem. Am. Acad. Arts and Scis., Am. Law and Econs. Assn. (pres. 2000-01), Am. Law Inst. Office: Yale U Law Sch PO Box 208215 New Haven CT 06520-8215 E-mail: robert.ellickson@yale.edu.

ELLICOTT, JOHN LEMOYNE, lawyer; b. Balt., May 26, 1929; s. Valcoulon LeMoyne and Mary Purnell (Gould) Ellicott; m. Mary Lou Ulery, June 19, 1954 (dec. Jan. 1995); children: Valcoulon, Ann; m. Beatrice Berle Meyerson, Sept. 14, 1996. AB summa cum laude, Princeton U., 1951; LLB cum laude, Harvard U., 1954. Bar: DC 1957, US Supreme Ct. 1959. Assoc. Covington & Burling, Washington, 1958-65, ptnr., 1965-98, chmn. mgmt. com., 1986-90, sr. counsel, 1998—. Pres. Fairfax County Fedn. Citizens Assn., Va., 1964; mem. governing bd. Nat. Cathedral Sch., Washington, 1973—80, 1989—90, chmn., 1978—79; trustee Landon Sch., Bethesda, Md., 1972—76; bd. dirs. Protestant Episc. Cathedral Found., Washington, 1980—88. Mem.: ABA (sect. internat. law and practice), Washington Inst. Fgn. Affairs, Am. Bar Found. (life), Phi Beta Kappa. Democrat. Home: 5117 Macomb St NW Washington DC 20016-2611 Office: Covington & Burling 1201 Pennsylvania Ave NW Washington DC 20004

ELLIFF, J(OHN) ERIC, lawyer; b. Sterling, Colo., Dec. 28, 1961; s. John Edgar and Gladys Vera (Cline) E. BS, Washington U., 1984; JD, U. Colo., 1987. Bar: Colo. 1987, U.S. Dist. Ct. Colo. 1987, U.S. Ct. Appeals (10th cir.), 1987, N.Y. 2004. Assoc. Morrison & Foerster LLP, Denver, 1987, ptnr. Instr. legal writing U. Colo., Boulder, 1986. Bd. dirs. Scenic Am. Recipient Am. Jurisprudence award, 1987. Mem. ABA, ASCE, Colo. Bar Assn., Denver Bar Assn., N.Y. State Bar Assn., Order of Coif. Democrat. Avocations: skiing, antique automobiles. Office: Morrison & Foerster LLP 5200 Republic Plz 370 Seventeenth St Denver CO 80202-5638 Office Phone: 303-592-2240. Office Fax: 303-592-1510. Business E-Mail: jelliff@mofo.com.

ELLIG, BRUCE ROBERT, retired personnel director; b. Manitowoc, Wis., Oct. 15, 1936; s. Robert Louis and Lucille Marie (Westphal) Ellig; m. Janice Reals; 1 child from previous marriage, Brett Robert. BBA, U. Wis., 1959, MBA, 1960. With Pfizer, Inc., NYC, 1960-96, mgr. compensation and pers. rsch., 1968-70, corp. dir. compensation and benefits, 1970-78, v.p. compensation and benefits, 1978-83, v.p. employee rels., 1983-85, v.p. pers., 1985-95, v.p. employee resources; ret., 1996. Spkr. in field; mem. standing coms. Pfizer, 1985—96; corp. edn. Employee Compensation and Mgmt. Devel., Retirement Plan, Retirement Plan Assets, Savs. and Investment, Corp. Adv. Coun., 1996—2001; cons. Orgn. Resources Counselors Inc., 1996—2001; mem. adv. panel, wave adv. bd. Career Ctrl., 2001—03. Author: Compensation and Benefits: Analytical Strategies, 1978, Executive Compensation: A Total Pay Perspective, 1982, Compensation and Benefits: Design and Analysis, 1985, Future Focus: Human Resources in the 21st Century, 1998, The Complete Guide to Executive Compensation, 2002, 2nd edit., 2007, The Evolution of Employee Pay in the United States, 2005; contbg. author: Encyclopedia of Professional Management, 1978, Handbook of Business Administration, 1984, Tomorrow's Human Resources Management, 1997; contbg. author The Future of Human Resource Management, 2005; cons. editor: Compensation and Benefits Rev., 1984—96, mem. adv. bd.: Jour. Compensation and Benefits, 1984—96, adv. bd.: Executive Compensation Reports, 1999—2002; contbr. more than 90 articles to profl. jours. Mem. Mayor's Adv. Pay Commn., NYC, 1977—78, chmn., 1980; mem. Presdl. Quadrennial Pay Commn., 1976; mem. merit pay task force U.S. Civil Svc. Commn., 1979; mem. sector staff Coun. Wage and Price Stability, 1979—80; mem. Ctr. Advanced Human Resource Studies Cornell U., 1985—95; adv. bd. Ky. Ednl. TV, 1987—90, Global Remuneration Orgn.; mem. dean's adv. bd. Sch. Bus. U. Wis., 2004—. Named Person of the Yr., U. Wis. Alumni Club NY, 1995, Human Resources Exec. of the Yr., Human Resource Exec. Mag., 1995; recipient Am. Compensation's Keystone award, 1999, Disting. Bus. Alumnus award, U. Wis. Sch. Bus., 2007; fellow Aresty, Wharton Bus. Sch. Fellow; Wharton's Aresty Inst., Employer Benefits Rsch. Inst., Nat. Acad. Human Resources (life); mem.: Sr. Execs. Forum, Human Resources Roundtable Group, Bus. Roundtable Conf. Bd. (adv. coun. human resource mgmt.), Soc. Human Resource Mgmt. (life; chmn. bd. dirs. 1996, faculty staff 1996—, Lifetime Achievement award 1999), Am. Compensation Assn. (life; cert. program developer 1996—2005), Pers. Round Table (life), NE Sr. Human Resources Exec. Mtg. Group, NY Pers. Mgmt. Assn. (past pres.), Am. Mgmt. Assn., NY Assn. Compensation Adminstrs. (charter pres.), U. Wis. Bus. Sch. Alumni (bd. dirs. emeritus), Wharton/Spencer Stuart Dir. Inst., NY C. of C., Wall of Fame, Ind. C. of C. (human resource com.), U. Ill. Ctr. Human Resource Mgmt. (past ptnr.), U. So. Calif. Ctr. Effective Orgns. (adv. bd. emeritus), Phi Beta Kappa, Phi Eta Sigma, Beta Gamma Sigma. Republican. Roman Catholic.

ELLIMAN, CHRISTOPHER J. (KIM ELLIMAN), investment company executive; m. Nicole Bourgois; children: Isabel, Henry, Theodore, Claire. BA, Yale U., 1976. Co-founder, mng. editor Black River Tribune, Ludlow, Vt., 1976—78; asst. dir. Coun. Environment NYC, 1978—80; dir. environ. regulation & engring. Long Lake Energy Co., NY, 1981—82; CEO Overhills Group, 1982—2000; pres. Open Space Inst., 1992—99, CEO, 2003—; pres. Gray, Seifert & Co., Inc., 1999—2003; mng. dir. Barrett Assoc., 2003—. Chmn. Piggly Wiggly So., 1984—86; gen. ptnr. Elmrock Group, 1982—92; pres. Geraldine R. Dodge Found., Morristown, NJ, 1990—; bd. dirs. Toxics Targeting, Inc., Barrett Assoc., Inc., Open Space Inst.; with Gov. Cuomo's Environ. Adv. Com., NY, 1991—94; President's Commn. on Sustainable Devel. Hudson River Adv. Coun., NY, 1994—96. Bd. dirs. Adirondack Land Trust & Conservancy, NY, 1984—87, STRIVE/East Harlem Employment Svc., NYC, 1984—92, co-chmn., 1989—91, chmn., 1999—2003; bd. dirs. NY Environ. Planning Lobby, 1988—96, NY League of Conservation Voters, 1990—99, Environ. Def., 1987—2001, vice-chmn., 1989—93; bd. dirs. Adirondack Coun., NY, 1982—93, chmn. NY, 1986—90; bd. dirs. Coun. Environment NYC, 1983—, chmn., 1992—96; bd. dirs. Storm King Arts Ctr., 1999—, Dalton Sch., 2001—. Recipient Academy Award, Best Short Documentary, 1975, Media award in Econ. Understanding, 1978, Chevron Conservation award, 1999, NY Land Conservation award, 2000, NY State Parks & Conservation award, 2001. Mem.: Black Rock Forest Consortium, The Wilderness Soc. (chmn. 1992—97). Avocations: birdwatching, hiking, canoeing, history. Office: The Open Space Inst 1350 Broadway New York NY 10018 Office Phone: 212-629-3981. Office Fax: 212-244-3441. E-mail: kelliman@osiny.org.

ELLIN, DOUG, film producer, television producer, television director, writer; b. Bklyn, NY, Apr. 6, 1968; married; 2 children. Grad., Tulane Univ. Exec. prodr.: (TV series) Entourage, 2004— (Producers Guild award, 2006); dir. & writer: (films) The Pitch, 1993; The Waiter, 1993; dir.: Phat Beach, 1996, Kissing A Fool, 1998; writer: (TV series) Life with Bonnie. Mailing: Home Box Office Entourage 1100 Ave of the Americas New York NY 10036

ELLIN, MARVIN, lawyer; b. Balt., Mar. 6, 1923; s. Morris and Goldie (Rosen) E.; children: Morris, Raymond, Elisa; m. Marta I. Quintana, Aug. 15, 2001. JD, U. Balt., 1953. Bar: Md. 1953, U.S. Supreme Ct. 1978; diplomate Am. Bd. Forensic Examiners. Practice law, Balt., 1953—; pvt. practice, 1957—; specialist in med. malpractice law. Cons. on med. and legal trial matters; lectr. ACS, U. Md. Law Sch., U. Balt. City, Yale U. Sch. Medicine, Johns Hopkins Hosp., U. Calif., San Francisco, U. N.J.; former mem. chmn.'s adv. coun. com. on judiciary U.S. Senate. Mem. edit. adv. bd.: Ob/Gyn Malpractice Prevention; contbr. chpts. on med. malpractice to various profl. publs. including Radiation Therapy of Benign Diseases. Fellow Internat. Acad. Trial Lawyers; mem. ABA, Am. Soc. Law and Medicine. Home and Office: 300 W Pratt St Ste 400 Baltimore MD 21201 E-mail: marvinellinLaw@aol.com.

ELLINGBURG, C. MICHAEL, lawyer; b. Indianola, Miss., Jan. 27, 1951; m. Linda Jameson Ellingburg; 5 children. BA, Millsaps Coll., 1973; JD, Univ. Miss., 1976. Bar: Miss. 1976, Ala. 2003. Mem., prof. liability, comml. litigation Daniel Coker Horton & Bell, Jackson, Miss. Mem.: ABA, Fed. Bar Assn., Miss. Bar, Miss. Def. Lawyers Assn., Hinds County Bar Assn., Federalist Soc., Phi Delta Phi. Presbyterian. Office: Daniel Coker Horton & Bell PO Box 1084 4400 Old Canton Rd Jackson MS 39215-1084 Office Phone: 601-914-5230. Office Fax: 601-969-1116. Business E-Mail: mellingburg@danielcoker.com.

ELLINGHAUS, WILLIAM MAURICE, communications executive; b. Balt., Apr. 19, 1922; m. Erlaine Dietrich, May 30, 1942; children: Marcia A. Barone, Eric J., Douglas A., Barbara E. Gurne, Raymond W., Mark D., Christopher C., Jonathan P. LLD, Iona Coll., 1974, Pace U., 1976, St. John's U., 1976, Poly. Inst. N.Y., 1976; LL.D., W.Va. Wesleyan Coll., 1981; L.H.D., Manhattan Coll., 1975, Union Coll., 1982; D.BA, Curry Coll., 1978; D.Sc. (hon.), Washington Coll., 1979; D.Sc., NYU, 1981. With Bell System, 1940-84; comml. mgr. Chesapeake & Potomac Tel. Co. Md., Balt., 1950-51; pub. office mgr. Chesapeake & Potomac Tel. Co. Va., Norfolk, 1951-52, dist. comml. mgr. Culpeper, 1952-55; from gen. comml. supr. to v.p. dir. Chesapeake & Potomac Tel. Co. W.Va., Charleston, 1955-62; from v.p. accts. to v.p. pers. Chesapeake & Potomac Tel. Cos., Washington, 1962-65; from asst. v.p. planning to exec. v.p. AT&T, NYC, 1965-70, exec. v.p., 1970, vice-chmn. bd., 1976-79, pres., also bd. dirs., 1980-84, pres., 1970-76. Pres. N.Y. Telephone Co., 1970-76; exec. vice chmn. bd dirs. N.Y. Stock Exchange, 1984-86; 1st chmn. N.Y. Mcpl. Assistance Corp., 1975; mem. N.Y. Emergency Fin.Ctrl. Bd., 1975-76. Trustee Lawrence Hosp.; hon. trustee Mt. Sinai Med. Ctr. With USNR, 1943-45. Mem. Am. Soc. Corp. Execs., Monroe County Telecomm. Authority, Sovereign Order Knights of Malta, Equestrian Order Holy Sepulchre of Jerusalem. Home: Apt 3-H Stoneleigh 2 Bronxville NY 10708 Personal E-mail: wme419@aol.com.

ELLINGHAUSEN, JAMES R., construction executive; m. Joanie Ellinghausen; children: Chris, Lauren. Grad., Ohio State U., Columbus. Draft pick NBA Cleve. Cavaliers, 1980; profl. basketball player Europe; various human resources positions Frito-Lay divsn. PepsiCo; with Bristol-Myers Squibb Co., 1997, v.p., head human resources Worldwide Businesses Princeton, NJ; sr. v.p. human resources Pulte Homes Inc., 2005—06, exec. v.p. human resources, 2006—. Office: Pulte Homes Inc 100 Bloomfield Hills Pky Ste 300 Bloomfield Hills MI 48304-2946*

ELLINGSEN, RICHARD D., lawyer; BA magna cum laude, U. Wash., 1976; JD with distinction, Duke U., Durham, NC, 1979. Bar: Calif. 1979. Ptnr. Ellingsen, Christensen & Steinberg, 1985—90, Davis Wright Tremaine L.L.P., LA, 1990—, mng. ptnr., 2002—. Mem.: Calif. State Bar Assn., Phi Beta Kappa. Office: Davis Wright Tremaine LLP 865 S Figueroa St Ste 2400 Los Angeles CA 90017-2566 Office Phone: 213-633-6800. Office Fax: 213-633-6899. E-mail: rickellingsen@dwt.com.*

ELLINGTON, BETH ELDER, librarian; d. Wilton Kelly and Frances Rosser Elder; m. Amzi Jefferson Ellington III, Dec. 29, 1984; children: Frances Elizabeth, Rebecca Anne, Jefferson Wilton. BA, U. NC, Chapel Hill, 1978, postgrad., 2003—, MS in Info. Sci., 2005; MBA, Elon Coll., NC, 1991. Quality assurance coord. Miller Brewing Co., Reidsville, NC, 1979—93; prodn. supr. Reynolds Metals Co., Reidsville, 1994—96; CFO Jefferson Resources, Inc., Burlington, NC, 1996—99; prof. Appalachian State U., Boone, NC, 1999—2000, Elon U., 2000—04; libr. U. NC, Greensboro, 2004—. Quality assurance cons. Ellington Quality Resources, Burlington, 1993—94; rschr., author Sch. Info. and Libr. Sci. U. NC, Chapel Hill, 2005. Contbr. conf. proceedings; editor: book chpts. Vol. Turrentine Mid. Sch., Burlington, 1997—, Williams H.S., Burlington, 2000—. Grantee, NC State Libr., 2005. Mem.: ALA, Assn. Info. Sci. and Tech. Avocations: reading, writing, college sports, travel. Home: 808 Tarleton Ave Burlington NC 27215 Office Phone: 336-334-3741. Business E-Mail: veelling@uncg.edu.

ELLINGTON, CHARLES RONALD, lawyer, educator; b. Cuthbert, Ga., Sept. 3, 1941; s. Charles Bartlett and Annie Claire (Moore) E.; m. Jean Alice Spencer, Apr. 29, 1967; children— Gregory Spencer, Alicia Nicole. AB summa cum laude, Emory U., 1963; LL.B., U. Va., 1966; LL.M., Harvard U., 1978. Bar: Ga. 1967, D.C. 1967. Assoc. firm Sutherland, Asbill and Brennan, Atlanta, 1966-69; mem. law faculty U. Ga. Sch. Law, 1969—, prof. law, 1977—, Thomas R.R. Cobb prof. law, 1983-93, dean, 1987-93, J. Alton Hosch prof. law, 1993-99, A. Gus Cleveland prof. legal ethics and professionalism, 1999—, Josieh Meigs Disting. tchg. prof., 2007—. On leave as scholar in residence U.S. Dept. Justice, Washington, 1979-80; reporter Standards of the Profession Com., State Bar of Ga., mem. formal adv. opinion bd. Harvard U. fellow in law and humanities, 1973—74. Mem.: Am. Law Inst. Avocation: hiking. Office: Univ Ga Sch Law Herty Dr Athens GA 30602 Business E-Mail: cre@uga.edu.

ELLINGTON, MERCEDES, performing company executive, choreographer, director, producer, educator; b. NYC; d. Mercer Kennedy Ellington and Ruth Violet (Silas) Batts; granddaughter of Edward "Duke" Ellington. BS in Dance, Juilliard Sch. Music. Pres., artistic dir. DanceEllington Inc., NYC, 1986—. June Taylor dancer 7 seasons 10 Broadway shows; asst. choreographer on Broadway No No Nanette, Black Broadway, The Night That Made America Famous, Sophisticated Ladies; choreographer St. Louis No No Nanette, Cole Porter Hans Christian Andersen; asst. choreographer (Broadway) Sophisticated Ladies, 1980, choreographer, Birmingham, Ala., 1989; choreographer Body and Soul, Europe, 1988, Peter and the Duke, N.Y.C., 1989, Play On, (Black Theater Alliance award outstanding choreography, 1998, Garland award choreography, Pasadena Playhouse, 1999), Happiness, 2003, In Mahalia's Light, 2003, Vanqui, 2003, Crowns, Talk of the Town, 2006, Dreamgirls (Barrymore award outstanding choreography, 2006), Five Guys Named Moe, 2006. Bd. dirs. Capezio Dance Award, 1987, The Am. Tap Dance Found., NJTap; bd. gov. Friars Club. Recipient Gypsy Robe Actors' Equity Coun., 1982, Award of Recognition, Greater Cin. Jazz Soc., 1997, President's award, Soc. Singers, 2001, Legacy award, 2004; named Hon. Citizen Paris, Mayor of Paris, 2003, Woman of Yr. Boys' Town Italy, Inc., 2004; scholar Met. Opera Ballet Sch., N.Y. 1956. Mem. AFTRA (bd. dirs. N.Y. local 1977—, nat. bd. 1987—). Avocations: photography, ice skating, cross word puzzles, lionel trains, sewing. Office: DanceEllington Inc PO Box 20346 Park West Fin Sta New York NY 10025*

ELLINGTON, MILDRED L., retired librarian; b. Marion, Ohio, June 7, 1921; d. Edward J. and Julia Ellen (Oiler) E. BA, Olivet Nazarene Coll., Kankakee, Ill., 1943; MA in French, Ohio State U., 1952; MA in English, Bowling Green State U., Ohio, 1964; MLS, Rosary Coll., River Forest, Ill., 1976. Tchr. French, English, Morral HS, Ohio, 1944-49, Reddick HS, Ill., 1949-55; tchr. English, Bremen Cmty. HS, Midlothian, Ill., 1955-58, Bloom Twp. HS, Chicago Heights, Ill., 1958-60, Willowbrook HS, Villa Park, Ill., 1960-66; tchr. English, then libr. dir. Addison Trail HS, Ill., 1966-82; reference libr. Maywood Pub. Libr., Ill., 1982—2006; ret., 2006. Sunday sch. supt. Elgin (Ill.) Ch. of the Nazarene, 1985-92. Mem. Ill. Library Assn. Democrat. Mem. Ch. of the Nazarene. Avocations: opera, singing, genealogy, travel.

ELLINGTON II, MICHAEL L., lawyer; b. Marysville, Calif., Mar. 29, 1975; s. Michael L. and Deborah R. Ellington. BS in Indsl. Engring., Morgan State U., 1997; JD, 2003. Bar: U.S. Patent and Trademark Office 2004, Supreme Ct. N.J. 2003, N.Y. 2004. V.p. R36 Apparel, Newark, 1996—98; law clk. Superior Ct. N.J., Newark, 2003—04; atty. Law Offices

Michael L. Ellington II, Esq., Plainfield, NJ, 2004—. Recipient Entrepreneurial award, Morgan State U., 1997. Office: Law Offices of Michael L Ellington II PO Box 5649 400 Cleveland Ave St23 Plainfield NJ 07060 Office Phone: 908-769-0090. Office Fax: 908-769-0097.

ELLINGWOOD, BRUCE RUSSELL, structural engineer, educator; b. Evanston, Ill., Oct. 11, 1944; s. Robert W. and Carolyn L. (Ehmen) E.; m. Lois J. Drager, June 7, 1969; 1 son, Geoffrey D. BSCE, U. Ill., 1968, MSCE, 1969, PhD, 1972. Registered profl. engr., D.C. Structural engr. Naval Ship Rsch. and Devel. Ctr., Bethesda, Md., 1972—75; rsch. structural engr., leader structural engring. group Ctr. Bldg. Tech., Nat. Bur. Standards, Washington, 1975—86; prof. civil engring. Johns Hopkins U., Balt., 1986—2000, chmn. dept., 1990—97; chmn. sch. civil and environ. engring. Ga. Inst. Tech., Atlanta, 2000—02, prof. civil engring., 2002—. Lectr., cons. Editor Jour. Structural Safety; mem. editl. bd. Engring. Structures, Probabilistic Engring. Mechanics; contbr. articles to profl. jours. Recipient Dural Research prize U. Ill., 1968, Nat. Capital award for Engring. Achievement D.C. Joint Council Engring. and Archtl. Socs., 1980, Walter L. Huber prize ASCE, 1980, Silver medal U.S. Dept. Commerce, 1980, Markwardt Rsch. prize Forest Products Rsch. Soc., 1988, Lifetime Achievement award Am. Inst. Steel Constrn., 2006; named Engr. of Yr. of U.S. Dept. Commerce, Nat. Soc. Profl. Engrs., 1986. Mem. ASCE (pres. Md. sect. 1998-99, State of Art in Civil Engring. award 1983, 88, Norman medal 1983, 98, Moisseiff award 1988, Walter P. Moore award 1999, Nathan M. Newmark medal 2006), Am. Concrete Inst., Am. Nat. Stds. Inst., Am. Inst. Steel Constrn. (T.R. Higgins lectureship 1988, Lifetime Achievement award 2006), Nat. Acad. Engring., Sigma Xi, Chi Epsilon, Tau Beta Pi. Presbyterian. Achievements include administered the secretariat of American National Standard Committee A58 on minimum design loads from 1977-84 and was responsible for coordinating and directing revisions to the A58 Standard that culminated in the publication of ANSI A58.1-1982 (now ASCE Standard 7), the first load standard in the U.S. to contain probability-based load combinations for limit states. Such load combinations now are used in Canada, the U.S. and in the Eurocodes now being developed in the common market. Was instrumental in the move by the steel industry toward limit states design. Office: Ga Inst Tech Sch Civil and Environ Engring Dept Civil Engring Atlanta GA 30332-0355 Home Phone: 770-496-5744; Office Phone: 404-894-1635. Business E-Mail: bruce.ellingwood@ce.gatech.edu.

ELLINGWOOD, SUSAN, editor; BA, Dickinson Coll.; grad. study, St. Antony's Coll., Oxford. Researcher The New Yorker Mag., Washington; asst. mng. editor The New Republic mag.; news editor, fgn. desk Wall St. Jour., 1997—2000; sr. editor, fin., internat., polit. news Brill's Content; editl. dir. Com. to Protect Journalists; staff editor, Op-Ed desk NY Times, 2004—. Served with USAR. Office: Op-Ed Page NY Times 229 W 43rd St New York NY 10036 Office Phone: 212-556-8435. Office Fax: 212-556-4100, 212-556-3690. Business E-Mail: opedcity@nytimes.com.

ELLIOT, CAMERON ROBERT, lawyer; b. Portland, Oreg., Jan. 6, 1966; s. James Addison and Dianne Louise (Youngblood) Elliot. BS, Yale U., 1987; JD, Harvard U., 1996. Bar: Calif 1996, DC 1999. Jud. clk. US Dist. Ct., Reno, 1996-98; atty. civil divsn. US Dept. Justice, Washington, 1998—2001; asst. US atty., 2001—06; atty. Darby & Darby P.C., NYC, 2006—. Editor-in-chief: jour Harvard Environ Law Rev, 1995—96. Mem Reno Environ Bd, 1996—97. Lt USN, 1987—92. Home: 4 Lexington Ave Apt 12L New York NY 10010 Office: Darby & Darby PC 805 Third Ave New York NY 10022 Office Phone: 212-527-7635. Business E-Mail: cameron@justice.com.

ELLIOT, DAVID HAWKSLEY, geologist, educator; b. Chilwell, Eng., May 22, 1936; came to U.S., 1966; m. Ann Elliot, 1963. BA, Cambridge U., Eng., 1959; PhD, Birmingham U., 1965. Mem. faculty Ohio State U., Columbus, 1969—, prof. dept. geol. scis., 1979—, dir. Byrd Polar Reseach Ctr. (formerly Inst. Polar Studies), 1973-89. Mem. Geol. Soc. Am., Geol. Soc. London, Ohio Acad. Sci., Am. Geophys. Union, Sigma Xi. Office: Ohio State Univ Dept Geol Scis Columbus OH 43210 Business E-Mail: elliot.1@osu.edu.

ELLIOT, JARED, financial management consultant; b. Albany, NY, Oct. 15, 1928; s. Henry Melvin and Gladys Dolores (Richter) E.; children: Michael B., Lynn Elliot Sims, Blake R., Jared. B.C.E., Yale U., 1950; MBA, Stanford U., 1955. Mgr. electronic data processing and mfg. scheduling Lenkurt Electric Co. Inc., San Carlos, Calif., 1955-58; sec., treas. Spectracoat Inc., San Carlos, 1958-61; mng. asso. mgmt. services dept. Arthur Young & Co., San Francisco, 1961-69; v.p. Tex. Gas Resources Corp., Owensboro, Ky., 1969—, treas., 1979-84; v.p. fin. Lightnet, New Haven, 1984-86, ret., 1987; pvt. practice fin. mgmt. cons., 1987—92. Bd. dirs. United Way, Owensboro, 1969-80, pres., 1972; bd. dirs. Community Concert Assn., Owensboro, 1974-77. Served with USN, 1950-53. Democrat.

ELLIOT, JEFFREY M., political science professor, department chairman; b. LA, June 14, 1947; s. Gene and Harriet (Sobsey) E. BA, U. So. Calif., 1969, MA, 1970; ArtsD in Govt., Claremont Grad. Sch., 1978; LittD (hon.), Shaw U., 1985; LLD (hon.), City U. L.A., 1986; cert. in grantsmanship, Grantsmanship Tng. Ctr., 1980; cert. in internat. trade and devel., N.C. Ctrl. U., 1995; cert. in conflict resolution, Ctr. for Peace Edn., 1997. Rsch. asst. U. So. Calif., 1969-70; instr. polit. sci. Glendale Coll., 1970-72, Cerritos Coll., 1970-72; asst. prof. history and polit. sci. U. Alaska-Anchorage C.C., 1973-74; asst. prof. history and polit. sci., dean curriculum Miami-Dade C.C., 1974-76; asst. prof. polit. sci. Va. Wesleyan Coll., Norfolk, 1978-79; sr. curriculum specialist Edn. Devel. Ctr., Newton, Mass., 1979-81; prof. polit. sci. NC Ctrl. U., 1981—, dept. chair. Disting. advisor fgn. affairs Congressman Mervyn M. Dymally (Dem. Calif.), 1985-94. Author: 150 books, including Keys to Economic Understanding, 1976, Science Fiction Voices, 1979, Literary Voices, 1980, Analytical Congressional Directory, 1981, Deathman Pass Me By: Two Years on Death Row, 1982, Tempest in a Teapot: The Falkland Islands War, 1983, Kindred Spirits, 1984, Black Voices in American Politics, 1985, Urban Society, 1985, The Presidential-Congressional Political Dictionary, 1985, Fidel Castro: Nothing Can Stop the Course of History, 1986, The State and Local Government Political Dictionary, 1986, The Third World, 1987, The Arms Control, Disarmament, and Military Security Dictionary, 1988, Dictionary of American Government, 1988, Fidel, 1988, Conversations with Maya Angelou, 1988, Voices of Zaire: Rhetoric or Reality?, 1990, Brown & Benchmark Reader in American Government, 1991, Brown and Benchmark Reader in International Relations, 1991, The Trilemma of World Oil Politics, 1991, Starclimber: The Autobiography of Raymond Z. Gallon, 1991, Adventures of a Free-Lancer: The Autobiography of Stanton A. Coblentz, 1991, The Work of Jack Dann: An Annotated Bibliography and Guide, 1991, The Work of George Zebrowski: An Annotated Bibliography and Guide, 1991, Brown & Benchmark Reader in American Government, 1992, Brown & Benchmark Reader in International Relations, 1992, The Third World, 1992, Into the Flames: The Life Story of a Righteous Gentile, 1992, After All These Years: Sam Moskowitz On His Science Fiction Career, 1992, The Encyclopedia of African-American Politics, 1994, The Work of Raymond Z. Gallun: An Annotated Bibliography and Guide, 1994, Fidel By Fidel, 1994, The African-American Historical Atlas, 1994, The Historical Dictionary of OPEC, 1995, The Dictionary of State and Local Government, 1995, The Historical Dictionary of the Third World, 1995, The Work of Pamela Sargent: An Annotated Bibliography and Guide, 1996, The Work of George Zebrowski: An Annotated Bibliography and Guide, 1996, The Work of Jack Dann: An Annotated Bibliography and Guide, 1997; contbr. 550 articles and revs. to profl. and popular jours.; contbg. editor Negro History Bull., 1976-80, West Coast Writers' Conspiracy, 1978-80, Trumphet of Conscience, 2000—. Mem. cmty. svcs. adv. coun. Miami (Fla.) Comty. Svcs., 1974-76; mem. Los Angeles Mayor's Adv. Com., 1971-72; speechwriter, rsch. asst., campaign strategist U.S. Sen. Howard W. Cannon of Nev., 1969—; cons. Calif. Clean Environment Act, 1970-72; commr. Human Rels. Commn., Durham, N.C., 1999—; co-chmn. Sister Cities Program, Durham, 1999—; bd. dirs. Justice Policy Ctr., Durham, 1999—, N.C. Student Rural Health Projec, 1999—. Recipient 100 literary and scholarly awards including Fair Enterprise Medallion award, 1965, Outstanding Polit. Sci. Scholar citation, 1970, Outstanding Tchr. award, 1971, Outstanding Am. Educator citation, 1975, Disting. Svc. Through Community Effort award, 1976, Outstanding Rsch. prize, 1987, 91, Disting. Scholarship award, 1987, Outstanding Rsch. Prize, 1991, Nancy Susan Reynolds award, 1991, Disting Svc. award Acad. Help Ctr., 1992, Gen. News, Election Analysis Associated Press award, 1993, Documentary Profile Cmty. TV award, 1994, Excellence award, Soc. Internat. Develop., 1995, meritorious contributions for Human and Civil Rights award, City of Durham, NC, 2002. Mem. AAUP, ASCD, Cmty. Coll. Social Sci. Assn. (dir. 1970-77, pres. 1975-77), So. Assn. Coll. and Sch. (accreditation team 1974-76), Am. Polit. Sci. Assn., Nat. Coun. for Social Studies, Rocky Mountain Social Sci. Assn., Soc. Internat. Devel. Coun. Fgn. Affairs, Internat. Studies Assn., Assn. Third World Studies, Am. Hist. Assn., Pi Sigma Alpha, Phi Delta Kappa. Home: 511 N Water's Edge Dr Durham NC 27703-6722 Office: NC Cen Univ Dept Polit Sci Durham NC 27707 Office Phone: 919-530-5303. Personal E-mail: jmelliot@aol.com. *I have attempted to live those ideals which inspire me to fight for a more humane world love, honor, courage, integrity, and truth. I have also taken to heart the wisdom of the prophets who implore us to live and love as though life and love were one. Although this is a difficult and frustrating task, it is the only way to live. And finally, I have come to recognize that what matters most, after everything is said, are people-close family and friends who reach out and say in a host of ways, "I care".*

ELLIOTT, ANDREA, reporter; b. Washington, Dec. 14, 1972; married. BA, Occidental Coll., 1996; MS, Columbia U. Grad. Sch. Journalism, 1999. Reporter Miami Herald, 2000—03; met. reporter NY Times, 2003—. Dir., prodr., co-writer (documentaries) It's All Good, 1998. Recipient Pulitzer Prize for Feature Writing, 2007; Pulitzer Traveling fellowship, Columbia U. Grad. Sch. Journalism, 1999. Office: NY Times 229 W 43rd St New York NY 10036*

ELLIOTT, BILL, race car driver; b. Dawsonville, Ga., Oct. 8, 1955; m. Cindy Elliott; children: Starr, Brittany, Chase. Race car driver, 1974—. Named winner, Daytona 500, 1985, 1987, Coca-Cola 500, 1985, Winston 500, 1985, Budweiser 500, 1985, 1988, Van Scoy 500, 1985, Miller 400, 1985, 1986, 1989, Pocono 500, 1985, Champion Spark Plug 400, 1985, 1986, 1987, So. 500, 1985, 1988, Atlanta Jour. 500, 1985, 1987, The Winston, 1986, AC Delco 500, 1987, Oakwood Home 500, 1987, Talledaga 500, 1987, Busch Clash, 1987, Del 500, 1988, Summer 500, 1988, Firecracker 400, 1988, 1991, Valleydale 500, 1988, Autoworks 500, 1989, AC Spark Plug 500, 1989, Peak 500, 1990, Pepsi 400, 1991, GM Goodwrench 500, 1992, Pontiac Excitement 400, 1992, Motorcraft Quality PArts, 1992, Tran South 500, 1992, Hooters 500, 1992, So. 500, 1994, Winston Cup Champion, 1988, Most Popular Driver, 1991—2000; recipient Spirit of Ford award, 2000. Achievements include 40 career Winston Cup victories, 49 career pole positions.

ELLIOTT, BRADY GIFFORD, judge; b. Harlingen, Tex., Nov. 26, 1943; s. Clyde Andres Elliott and Mildred (Parker) Bounds; m. Rhea Elizabeth Ricks, May 15, 1967; children: Adrian Winthrope, Jason Lawrence. BBA, McMurray Coll., 1970; JD, South Tex. Coll. Law, 1973. Bar: Tex. 1973, US Dist. Ct. (so. dist.) Tex. 1974, US Tax Ct. 1974, US Ct. Appeals (5th cir.) 1974, US Supreme Ct. 1979, US Ct. Appeals (11th cir.) 1981. Asst. sec., asst. treas., asst. gen. counsel Gordon Jewelry Corp., Houston, 1973-79; sec., gen. counsel Oshman's Sporting Goods, Inc., Houston, 1979-82; sole practice, Sugar Land, Tex., 1982-88; legal counsel Ft. Bend C. of C., Sugar Land, 1982-88; mcpl. judge Missouri City, Tex., 1983-88; judge 268th Dist. Ct., Fort Bend County, Tex., 1988—; adminstrv. judge Bd. Dist. Judges, Fort Bend County, 2005-07. Bd. dirs. Ft. Bend chpt. Texans' War on Drugs, Sugar Land, 1981-94; bd. dirs. Ft. Bend Boys Choir, 1984-94. Mem. ABA, Houston Bar Assn., Fort Bend County Bar Assn., Masons, Rotary (treas. 1983-85). Republican. Methodist. Office: County Ct House Richmond TX 77469 Business E-Mail: elliobra@co.fortbendtx.us.

ELLIOTT, CAROLYN COLE, secondary school educator, department chairman; b. South Boston, Va., July 7, 1943; d. Raleigh Newmsn Cole and Gladys Ruth Newcomb; m. Clyde Clifton Elliott, Jan. 31, 1964; children: Natalie Elaine, Mark Landon. AA, Averett Coll., Danville, Va., 1964; BS, Longwood U., Farmville, Va., 1966; MEd, U. NC, Charlotte, 1999. Cert. tchr. NC. Tchr. Halifax County Sch., Halifax, Va., 1966—77, Granville County Schs., Oxford, NC, 1977—80, Allenstown Schs., NH, 1980—85, Manchester City Schs., NH, 1985—88, Iredell-Statesville Sch., Statesville, NC, 1988—, chmn. sci. dept., 2003—. Regional judge Exploravision/Nat. Sci. Teachers Assn., Arlington, Va., 2006—; master tchr. NCTeach, Charlotte, NC, 2000—05, SciLink, Raleigh, NC, 1994—2004, NC Leadership Network Earth Sci. Tchr., Charlotte, 1996—99; textbook reviewer Glencoe Pub., Columbus, Ohio, 2004—; presenter in field. Contbr. North Carolina Support Documents; contbr.: Support Document for Honors Physical Science, Resourse Guide for Oceanography and Coastal Processes. Pres. South Boston Bus. Women Club, Va.; mem. Oxford's Jr. Womens Club, NC. Named Tchr. of Yr., South Iredell HS, 2000; recipient State Presidential award for Excellence in Math. and Sci. Tchg., NSF, 2000—01, Nat. Tchr. award, Radioshack, 1999—2000, Dist. Tchr. of the Yr., Iredell-Statesville Sch. Sys., 2000-2001, Ben Craig Outstanding Educator award, First Union Bank, 2001. Mem.: Nat. Sci. Tchr. Assn. (awards and recognition com. 2005—, state coord. Bldg. Presence in Sci. program 2005—, dist. Outstanding Tchg. award 1995), NC Sci. Tchr. Assn. (life; dist. 7 dir., v.p., pres., past pres. 2004), Delta Kappa Gamma (1st v.p., 2d v.p. 1985—2007), Phi Kappa Phi (assoc.), Kappa Delta Pi (assoc.). Office: South Iredell HS 299 Old Mountain Rd Statesville NC 28677 Home Phone: 704-872-8980; Office Phone: 704-528-4536. Business E-Mail: celliott@iss.k12.nc.us.

ELLIOTT, DAVID DUNCAN, III, science company executive; b. LA, Aug. 4, 1930; s. David Duncan Elliott II and Mildred B. (Young) Mack; m. Arline L. Leckrone, Aug. 18, 1962; 1 child, Lauren Elliott Croft. BS, Stanford U., Calif., 1951; MS, Calif. Inst. Tech., Pasadena, 1953, PhD, 1959. Mem. tech. staff Lockheed Rsch. Lab., Palo Alto, Calif., 1959-61; postdoctoral fellow U. Paris., 1962; dept. head Aerospace Corp., El Segundo, Calif., 1962—70; sci. advisor Nat. Aeronautics and Space Coun., Washington, 1970-72; sr. staff mem. exec. office of pres. NSC, Washington, 1972-77; v.p. SRI Internat., Menlo Park, Calif., 1977-86; sr. v.p. Sci. Applications Internat. Corp., San Diego, 1986-91, Syst Control Tech., Palo Alto, Calif., 1991-94; corp. v.p. Sci. Applications Internat. Corp., Palo Alto, Calif., 1994-95; cons., 1995-99; cons. prof. Ctr. Internat. Security & Coop., Stanford U., Calif., 1999—. Mem. Army Sci. Bd., The Pentagon, Washington, 1982-89; cons. NRC, NAS, 1988—; mem. bd. visitors U. Calif., Davis, 1997-2003. Mem. editl. bd. Jour. Def. Rsch., 1988—. Recipient Outstanding Civilian Svc. award US Army, 1989. Mem. AIAA, AAAS, Am. Phys. Soc., Am. Geophys. Union. Home: 2434 Sharon Oaks Dr Menlo Park CA 94025-6829 Office: CISAC Encina Hall Stanford CA 94305-6165 Personal E-mail: ddelliott3@aol.com.

ELLIOTT, DAVID J., music educator; b. Toronto, Canada; MusB, U. Toronto, 1967—71, MusM, 1971—72, EdB, 1972—73; PhD, Case We. Res. U., Cleve., 1976—80. Prof. music edn. U. Toronto, 1974—2001, NY U., NYC, 2002—. Vis. prof. music Northwestern U., Evanston, Ill., 1983—84; vis. prof. music edn. Ind. U., Bloomington, 1986—87, U. N.Tex., Denton, 1995—96; vis. prof. U. Limerick, Ireland, 1996—97. Author: Music Matters: A New Philosophy of Music Education, 1995; editor: Praxial Music Education: Dialogues and Reflections; composer: No More Moon (1st Prize, US Assn. Jazz Educators, 1976). Office: NYU 35 W 4th St Ste 777 New York NY 10012 Office Phone: 212-998-5404. Business E-Mail: david.elliott@nyu.edu.

ELLIOTT, DAVID LEROY, mathematics and engineering educator; b. Cleve., May 29, 1932; m. Kiyoko Akaeda, Mar. 24, 1956 (div. 1980); children: Marguerite, Philip David; m. Pauline Wei-Ying Tang, Oct. 31, 1984. BA, Pomona Coll., 1953; MA, U. So. Calif., 1959; PhD, UCLA, 1969. Mathematician U.S. Naval Ocean Systems Ctr., Pasadena, Calif., 1955-69; lectr. UCLA, 1969-71; mem. faculty Washington U., St. Louis, 1971—, prof. dept. systems sci. and math., 1980-94, prof. emeritus, 1994—; with NSF, Washington, 1987-89. Vis. prof. Brown U., Providence, 1979, UCLA, 1987; vis. rsch. scientist U. Md., 1992—; sr. rsch. scientist NeuroDyne, Inc., 1993-99. Editor: Neural Systems for Control, 1997. Fellow IEEE; mem. Am. Math. Soc., Soc. Indsl. Applied Math., Math. Assn. Am., Sigma Xi. Avocations: music, science fiction. E-mail: delliott@umd.edu.

ELLIOTT, DIANE REID, history professor; b. Springfield, Mo, July 4, 1948; d. Robert F. and Rosemary L. Reid; m. Richard E. Elliott, Nov. 26, 1974; 1 child, Heather McAffrey; m. Gary D. Roney (div.); 1 child, Robert Reid Roney. BS in Edn., Mo. Southern State U., Joplin, 1971; MA in Hist., Mo. State U., Springfield, 1991; D in Hist., U. Arkansas, Fayetteville, 1998. New car dealer Fred Reid AMC/Jeep, Inc., Joplin, 1974—84; educator Mo. State U., 1991, Joplin R VIII Schs., 1992—97, Sarcoxie High Sch., Mo., 1998—, U. Mo., Kansas City, 2000—. Contbr. articles various profl. jours. Pres. Soroptimist Internat., Joplin, 1983—84. Named one of Outstanding Young Women Am., 1974. Mem.: Mo. State Tchrs. Assn., Nat. Coun. Social Studies. Democrat. Presbyn. Avocations: travel, reading, sewing, jewelry design. Home: 3105 E 11th St Joplin MO 64801 Office: Sarcoxie High Sch 101 S 17th St Sarcoxie MO 64862 Business E-Mail: delliott@sarcoxie.k12.mo.us.

ELLIOTT, DONNA LOUISE, artist; b. Oak Park, Ill., Sept. 2, 1931; d. Carl and Sarah Louise (Shelton) Reinecke; m. Gerald Morris Elliott, June 24, 1950. BS in Art Edn., U. Wis., Milw., 1966. Art tchr. Grafton H.S., Wis., 1969—70; instr. art Cardinal Stritch U., Fox Pt., Wis., 1990—95; leader workshop Wauwatosa Woman's Club, Wauwatosa, Wis., 1996; instr. workshop Art Mus. Wis., Wis., 1999, Peninsula Sch. Fine Arts, Fish Creek, Wis., 2002—03; instr. Art League Bonita Springs, 2004—05, Estero Art League, 2007—. One-woman shows include Firehouse Gallery, Cedarburg, Wis., 1972, Milw. Athletic Club, 1974, 1982, 1993, Sistermoon Gallery, Milw., 1978, Marine Bank, Fox Pt., 1987, Concordia Coll. Gallery, 1988, Firestation Gallery, Milw., 1989, Alexian Village Gallery, 1994, Metrix Co., Waukesha, Wis., 1997, The Andersen Arts Ctr., Kenosha, Wis., 1999, exhibitions include League of Milw. Artists Show, 1970—2003 (Best of Show, 1982, 1994), Wis. Watercolor Soc., 1989—2003, Wis. Women in Arts, Milw., 1970—90 (award of Excellence, 1982), Wis. Painters and Sculptors (various shows), 1995—2003 (1st place, 1998, Exhbn. award, 1999), Wustum Mus., Racine, Wis., 2002—03, Midwest Biennial New Visions Gallery, 2003, Art League of Bonita Springs, Fla., 2004, 2005, 2006, 2007, Represented in permanent collections Am. Internat. Supply Co., Tex., AT&T, Milw., Coopers & Lybrand, Northwestern Mutual Ins. Co. Vol. watercolor instr. North Shore Sch. Srs., United Meth. Sch., Whitefish Bay, Wis., 2001. Mem.: Naples Art Assn., Art League of Bonita Springs, Transparent Watercolor Soc. Am., Wis. Artists in All Media/Wis. Painters and Sculptors (life; chair S.E. chpt. 2001—03). Methodist. Avocations: weightlifting, walking, swimming, travel. Home: 9102 Windswept Dr Bonita Springs FL 34135-8187

ELLIOTT, EDWARD, investment executive, financial planner; b. Madison, Wis., Jan. 11, 1915; s. Edward C. and Elizabeth (Nowland) Elliott; m. Letitia Ord, Feb. 20, 1943 (div. Aug. 1955); children: Emily, Ord; m. Melita Uihlein, Jan. 1, 1958 (dec.); 1 child, Deborah; m. Sally Dodds Combs, Jan. 5, 2002. BS in Mech. Engring, Purdue U., 1936. Engr. Gen. Electric Co., Schenectady, 1936—37; with. Pressed Steel Tank Co., Milw., 1937-41, 46-58; v.p. sales Cambridge Co. div. Carrier Corp., Lowell, Mass., 1958-59; mgr. indsl. and med. sales Liquid Carbonic div. Gen. Dynamics Corp., Chgo., 1959-61; v.p. Haywood Pub. Co., Chgo., 1961-63; pres. Omnibus, Inc., Chgo., 1963-67; gen. sales mgr. Resistoflex Corp., Roseland, NJ, 1967-68; investment exec. Shearson, Hammill & Co., Inc., Chgo., 1968-74; v.p. McCormick & Co., Inc., 1974-75, Paine Webber, Inc., Naples, Fla., 1975-91, ret., 1991. Mem. pres.' coun. Purdue U. Lt. col. USAAF, 1941-46. Decorated officer Order Brit. Empire; inducted Indiana Basketball Hall of Fame. Mem.: ASME, Air Force Assn., Rotary, Family Club (San Francisco), Naples Yacht Club, Royal Poinciana Golf Club, Hole-in-Wall Golf Club, Naples Athletic Club, Phi Delta Theta. Episcopalian. Personal E-mail: eelliott@aol.com.

ELLIOTT, EDWIN DONALD, JR., lawyer, educator, federal agency administrator; b. Chgo., Apr. 4, 1948; s. Edwin Donald and Mary Jane (Bope) E.; m. Geraldine Gennet (div. 1980); m. Mary Ellen Savage, Nov. 22, 1980 (div. 1999); children: Eve Christina, Ian Donald; m. Gail Charnley. BA, Yale U., 1970, JD, 1974. Bar: D.C. 1975, U.S. Dist. Ct. D.C. 1975, U.S. Ct. Appeals (2d cir.) 1982. Law clk. to judge U.S. Dist. Ct. D.C., Washington, 1974-75, U.S. Ct. Appeals, Washington, 1975-76; assoc. Leva, Hawes et al, Washington, 1976-80; assoc. prof. law Yale U., New Haven, 1981-84, prof. law, 1984-89, 91-92; asst. adminstr., gen. counsel U.S. EPA, Washington, 1989-91; Julien & Virginia Cornell chair environ. law and litigation Yale U., New Haven, 1992-94, adj. prof. law, 1994—; cons. Fried, Frank, Harris, Shriver & Jacobson, NYC, Washington, 1991-93, ptnr., head of DC Environ. Practice Washington, 1993-96; ptnr., co-chair nat. environ. practice group Paul, Hastings, Janofsky & Walker, Washington, 1996—2003; ptnr., chair environ. dept. worldwide Willkie Farr & Gallagher LLP, Washington, 2003—. Adj. prof. law Georgetown U., Washington, 1997—; advisor Fed. Cts. Study Com., UN Environment Programme, 1993; cons. Asian Devel. Bank, 1994, Carnegie Com. Sci., Tech. and Govt., 1989-93, chair Role of Sci. and Risk Assessment; with Nat. Environ. Policy Inst., 1994—, Overseas Pvt. Investment Corp., Washington, 1983-85, Adminstrv. Conf. U.S., 1987-89, Aetna Ins. Co., 1987-89, G.D. Searle Co., 1988-89; spl. litigation counsel GE Co., Fairfield, Conn., 1985-89; gen. series editor Prentice Hall Environ. Series; bd. toxicology and environ. studies Nat. Acad. Scis., 2003. Co-author: Sustainable Environmental Law, 1993; bd. advisors Environment Law Reporter; mem. editl. bd. Jour. Indsl. Ecology. Resources for the Future fellow, 1989. Mem. ABA (vice chmn. com. on separation of powers 1985-89, jud. rev. 1992—, environ. values 1993—, chair govt. policy liaison), Environ. Law Inst., Gruter Inst. for Law and Behavioral Rsch. (adv. bd. 1986—), Nat. Environ. Policy Inst. (chair sci. and risk assessment), Yale Club N.Y.C., New Haven Lawn Club. Republican. Presbyterian. Address: 56 Beach Ave Milford CT 06460-8156 also: Yale Law Sch PO Box 208215 New Haven CT 06520-8215 Office: Willkie Farr and Gallagher LLP 1875 K St NW Washington DC 20006 Office Phone: 202-303-1120. E-mail: delliott@willkie.com.

ELLIOTT, EMERSON JOHN, education consultant, policy analyst; b. Ann Arbor, Mich., Nov. 13, 1933; s. Clarence Hyde and Ella Ruth (Kohl) E.; m. Joyce Ann Dodge, Aug. 19, 1956; children— Douglas, Stuart, Susan BA, Albion Coll., Mich., 1955; M.P.A., U. Mich., 1957. Chief edn. br. OMB, Washington, 1967-70, dep. chief human resources programs div., 1970-72; dep. dir. Nat. Inst. Edn., Washington, 1972-77; dir. ednl. staff seminar Inst. for Ednl. Leadership, Washington, 1977-79; dir. sch. fin. study U.S. Dept. Edn., Washington, 1979-81, dir. planning and evaluation, 1981-82, dir. issues analysis, 1982-84; head Nat. Ctr. for Edn. Stats., Washington, 1984-92; com. of edn. stats., 1992-95; dir. spl. projects Nat. Coun. Accreditation Tchr. Edn., Washington, 1995—. Recipient Disting. Alumnus award Albion Coll., 1975; Dirs. Superior Service award Nat. Inst. Edn., 1979; Presdl. Rank awards for Meritorious Service U.S. Govt., 1983, 91. Disting. Service U.S. Govt., 1987. Mem.: Am. Statistical Assn., Am. Ednl. Rsch. Assn. Office: Nat Coun Accred Tchr Edn Ste 500 2010 Massachusetts Ave NW Washington DC 20036-1023 Office Phone: 202-466-7496. Business E-Mail: emerson@ncate.org.

ELLIOTT, EMORY BERNARD, language educator, school system administrator; b. Balt., Oct. 30, 1942; s. Emory Bernard and Virginia L. (Ulbrick) E.; m. Georgia Ann Carroll, May 14, 1966; children: Scott, Mark, Matthew, Laura, Constance. AB, Loyola Coll., Balt., 1964; MA, Bowling Green State U., 1966; PhD, U. Ill., 1972. Instr. Cameron Coll., Lawton, Okla., 1966-67, U.S. Mil Acad., West Point, NY, 1967-69; from asst. prof. to prof. English, Princeton U., NJ, 1972-89, chmn. Am. studies program NJ, 1976-82, master Lee D. Butler Coll. NJ, 1982-86, chmn. English dept. NJ, 1987-89; Pres.'s chair English U. Calif., Riverside, 1989-91, disting. prof., 1992—, univ. prof., 2001—; dir. Ctr. for Ideas and Soc., 1996—. Writing cons. Bell Labs., Holmdel, NJ, 1975-79, RCA, Princeton, 1980-81; edn. cons. Western Electric Corp. Edn. Ctr., Hopewell, NJ, 1974-79; internat. adv. bd. Kennedy Inst. Am. Studies Free U. Berlin. Author: Power and the Pulpit in Puritan New England, 1975, Puritan Influences in American Literature, 1979, Revolutionary Writers: Literature and Authority in the New Republic, 1982, The Literature of Puritan New England in The Cambridge History of American Literature, Vol. 1, 1994, The Cambridge Introduction to Early American Literature, 2002, New Directions in American Literary Scholarship, 1980-2002, 2004; editor: Dictionary of Literary Biography, 3 Vols., 1606-1810, 1983-84; Columbia Literary History of the United States, 1988 (Am. Book award), American Literature: A Prentice Hall Anthology 3 Vols., 1990, Columbia History of The American Novel, 1991, The Jungle, 1991, Wieland, 1994, Huckleberry Finn, 1998, Aesthetics in a Multicultural Age, 2002; series editor Am. Novel Series, 1985—, Critical Studies in Contemporary Am. Fiction, 1987—; mem. editl. bd. Am. Quar., 1976-80, PMLA, 1990-92, Am. Lit., 1995—98, Modern Fiction Studies, 1993—, Ill. Studies Lang. Lit., 1993—, Studies in Am. Puritan Spirituality, 1991—; mem. adv. com. Gale Bibliography of Am. Lit., 1981—; editor-at-large Am. Studies Internat., 1993—. Served to capt. U.S. Army, 1966-69. Recipient Disting. Tchr. award U. Calif., Riverside, 1993, Outstanding Advisor/Mentor award , 2004, Rosemary Schaer Humanitarian award, 1997; fellow Woodrow Wilson Found., 1971-72, Am. Coun. Learned Socs., 1973, Guggenheim Found., 1976, Nat. Humanities Ctr. 1979-80, NEH, 1986-87, Inst. for Rsch. in the Humanities, 1991-92, Ford Found., 1998—2005, Rockefeller Found., 2000-03; Richard Stockton preceptor Princeton U., 1975-78; named to Acad. Disting. Tchrs., 2006. Mem. MLA (chmn. Early Am. lit. div., Am. lit. div. 1991, regional del.), Am. Studies Assn. (pres. 2006-07). Office: U Calif Dept English Riverside CA 92521-0001 Office Phone: 951-827-4332. Business E-Mail: emory.elliott@ucr.edu.

ELLIOTT, FRANK NELSON, retired college president; b. Dunkirk, NY, Mar. 18, 1926; s. Warren D. and Ima M. (Wilson) E.; m. Mary Elizabeth Neish, July 26, 1952; children: Robert Frank (dec.), Susan Marie, Ann Neish. BA cum laude with dept. honors, Alfred U., 1949, LL.D., 1972; MA, Ohio U., 1950; PhD, U. Wis., 1956; LLD (hon.), Rider U., 1994. Grad. asst. Ohio U., 1949-50; Draper fellow Wis. Hist. Soc., 1951-52, field rep., field supr., 1952-56; curator history, asst. prof. history Mich. State U., 1956-61; asso. dean Sch. Gen. Studies, Columbia U., 1961-64, acting dean, 1964; dir. div. arts and scis. State U. N.Y. Coll. at Cortland, 1964-65, acting dean, 1965-66; v.p. Hofstra U., Hempstead, NY, 1966-69; pres. Rider Coll., Lawrenceville, NJ, 1969-90. Contbr. articles to profl. jours. Mem. adv. coun. N.J. State Libr., 1972-87; bd. dirs. N.J. Coun. for Humanities, 1972-76, Deleware Valley United Way, 1986-92, Presbyn. Homes N.J., 1990-96, Granville Acad., Trenton, N.J., 1990-94; bd. dirs. Mercer Med. Ctr., 1980-97, chmn., 1992-95; trustee Alfred U., 1964-69; elder Presbyn. Ch. With AUS, 1944-46, PTO. Mem. Am. Assn. State and Local History (coun. 1960-62), Mich. Hist. Soc. (trustee 1959-61, award for TV lectures 1960), Mercer County C. of C. (dir. 1975-88, Citizen of Yr. 1990). Home: 46 Meadow Lakes Apt 8L Hightstown NJ 08520-3332

ELLIOTT, FRANK WALLACE, lawyer, educator; b. Cotulla, Tex., June 25, 1930; s. Frank Wallace and Eunice Marie (Akin) E.; m. Winona Trent, July 3, 1954 (dec. 1981); 1 child, Harriet Lindsey; m. Kay Elkins, Aug. 15, 1983. Student, N.Mex. Mil. Inst., 1947-49; BA, U. Tex., 1951, LLB, 1957. Bar: Tex. 1957, U.S. Supreme Ct. 1962, U.S. Ct. Mil. Appeals 1974, U.S. Dist. Ct. (no. dist.) Tex. 1987, U.S. Dist. Ct. (so. dist.) Tex. 2003, U.S. Ct. Appeals (5th cir.) 1988. Asst. atty. gen. State of Tex., 1957; briefing atty. Supreme Ct. Tex., 1957-58; prof. U. Tex. Law Sch., 1958-77; dean, prof. law Tex. Tech U. Sch. Law, 1977-80; pres. Southwestern Legal Found., 1980-86; ptnr. Baker, Mills & Glast, Dallas, 1987-88; of counsel Ramirez & Assocs., 1988—; dean Dallas/Ft. Worth Sch. Law, 1989-92; dean Sch. Law Tex. Wesleyan U., 1992-94, prof., dean emeritus, 1994—. Parliamentarian Tex. Senate, 1969-73; dir. rsch. Tex. Constl. Revision Commn., 1973 Author: Texas Judicial Process, 2d edit., 1977, Texas Trial and Appellate Practice, 2d edit., 1974, Cases on Evidence, 1980, West's Texas Forms, 20 vols., 1977—, West's Texas Practice, vol. 11, 1990, vol. 14, 1996. Served with U.S. Army, 1951-53, 73-74. Decorated Purple Heart. Mem. ABA, Judge Advs. Assn., Am. Judicature Soc., Am. Bar Found., Tex. Bar Found., Dallas Bar Found., Am. Law Inst., N.Mex. Mil. Inst. Alumni Hall of Fame. Home: 1609 Sunset Terr Fort Worth TX 76102 Office: 1515 Commerce St Fort Worth TX 76102-6572 Office Phone: 817-212-3926. Business E-Mail: felliott@law.txwes.edu.

ELLIOTT, GEORGE ARMSTRONG, III, artist, journalist; b. Wilmington, Del., July 24, 1929; s. George Armstrong Elliott Jr. and Amy Lewis (Rupert) Thomas; m. Shirley Barbara Henin, Oct. 16, 1965. BA, Colgate U., 1951; cert. in journalism, Columbia U., NYC, 1964. Reporter, copy editor, corr. local and nat. newspapers and news agys., 1950-66, Balt. Sun, 1955-62, N.Y. Herald Tribune, 1964, New York Daily News, 1965-66; adminstrv. asst./press sec. Spiro T. Agnew, Baltimore County Exec., Towson, Md., 1962-65, campaign press mgr., 1962; campaign press sec., speechwriter Spiro T. Agnew, Gov. of Md., 1966; pub. affairs dir. Md. State Rds. Commn., Balt., 1967-69; legis. asst. U.S. Congresswoman from Mass. Margaret M. Heckler, Washington, 1969-71; spl. asst. U.S. Sec. of Commerce Peter G. Peterson, Washington, 1972; campaign writer John H. Chafee for U.S. Senator, Providence, 1972; speechwriter Chmn. of FTC Lewis Engman, Washington, 1973; dir. nat. campaign for 55 m.p.h. speed limit U.S. Dept. Transp., Washington, 1976-77; spl. asst., speechwriter U.S. Congressman from Minn. Albert H. Quie, Washington and Mpls.-St. Paul, 1978; press sec. Rep. Margaret M. Heckler, Washington, 1979-81; prin. writer Nat. Alcohol Fuels Commn., Washington, 1980; writer Nat. Commn. on Air Quality, Washington, 1980-81; internat. pub. rels. counsel A. F. Sabo Assocs., Washington, 1981; Washington and East Coast corr. Jet Cargo News, Washington, 1984-93; profl. Chinese brush painting artist, 1993—. Writer former Md. Gov. Theodore R. McKeldin for Mayor, Balt., 1963; writer for numerous congrl. and local polit. campaigns, 1962-63. Exhibitions include M-Pac Fine Arts Works Shows, Sugarloaf Mt. Works Shows, Towson, Md., Invitational Art Exhibit, Waterford, Va., Art Mart and Garden tour, Wilmington, Brandywine Arts Festival, Sydney (NSW, Australia) Internat. Art Soc., 1996, Internat. Salon de Haute-Loire, Puy-en-Velay, France, 1997, 99, 7th St. Internat., Washington, 1997, 99, Lalit Kala Nat. Acad. Art, New Delhi, 1998, 99-2000, 2002, Overseas Chinese Culture and Art Festival, Wash., 2000, Internat. Cultural Union, Haifa, 2000-2001, Balt. City Hall Courtyard Galleries, 2000, Marlboro Gallery, , Largo, Md., 2000, Mus. Contemporary Art, Wash., 1996, 2001, 03, Russian Cultural Centre, Wash., 2002, 04, Acad. Arts and Design, Tsinghua U., Beijing and Capital Normal U., Beijing, 2002, The Warehouse, Washington, 2003, Gorohavaya 6 EGO Gallery, St. Petersburg, Russia, 2003, All India Fine Arts and Crafts Soc. Galleries, New Delhi, 2004, Vision Gallery, Washington, 2005, Al-Ahram Galleries, Cairo, Grand Gallery of Faculty Fine Arts, Luxor, Egypt, 2005, U.S. Capitol Rayburn Office Bldg., Washington, 2006, Mus. Americas, Miami, 2006, Chinese Artists Assn. Greater Washington D.C., Washington, 2006, Asian Fusion Gallery, NY, 2006, Florence Biennale, 2007. With U.S. Army, 1951-54. Ford Found. fellow in advanced internat. reporting Grad. Sch. Journalism, Columbia U., 1963-64. Mem. Nat. Assn. Govt. Communicators, Overseas Press Club Am., Washington Ind. Writers, Montgomery County Art Assn., Internat. Artists Support Group (pres. 1999-2001), Sumi-e Soc. Am., Harmonious Art Group. Address: 5826 Bradley Blvd Bethesda MD 20814-1128

ELLIOTT, GRAHAM JOHN, music educator, director; s. Charles and Kathleen Emily Elliott. BMus with honors, U. London, 1968; MA, U. Wales, 1982, PhD, 1985. Sub-organist Llandaff Cathedral, Cardiff, Wales, 1968—70; organist, master of the choristers St. Asaph Cathedral, 1970—81; dir. music Lowther Coll., St. Asaph, Wales, 1972—81; master music Chelmsford Cathedral, England, 1981—99; prof. Guildhall Sch. of Music and Drama, London, 1982—99; founder/dir. Chelmsford Cathedral Festival, England, 1983—99. Diocesan organ adviser Diocese of Chelmsford, England, 1981—99. Author (composer): (academic book) Benjamin Britten: The Spiritual Dimension, composer musical works various publ. for Mayhew. Recipient award, Royal Acad. of Music, 1985, Royal Sch. of Ch. Music, 1998; fellow, Royal Coll. Organists, 1967, Trinity Coll. Music, 1982, London Coll. Music, 1983, Guild of Ch. Musicians, 1999. Mem.: Am. Guild of Organists, Royal Soc. of Musicians, Assn. of Anglican Musicians, Royal Coll. of Organists, Athenaeum, London. Episcopalian. Avocations: swimming, architecture, reading. Office: St Paul's Episcopal Ch Rock Creek Ch Rd & Webster St NW Washington DC 20011 Home Phone: 301-445-7052; Office Phone: 202-726-2080. Office Fax: 202-726-1084; Home Fax: 202-726-1084. Personal E-mail: graham.elliott@rockcreekparish.org.

ELLIOTT, HOWARD, JR., lawyer, gas industry executive; b. St. Louis, July 4, 1933; s. Howard and Ruth Ann (Thomas) E.; m. Susan Jane Spoehrer, Sept. 2, 1961; children: Kathryn Elliott Love, Elizabeth Elliott Niedringhaus. Student Brown U., 1956; JD, Washington U., St. Louis, 1962. Bar: Mo. 1962. Assoc. Boyle, Priest, Elliott & Weakley, St. Louis, 1962-65, ptnr., 1965-67; mem. Mo. Pub. Svc. Commn., 1967-70, U.S. Postal Rate Commn., 1970—73; assoc. gen. counsel Laclede Gas Co., St. Louis, 1973-77, v.p. adminstrn., 1977-92, sr. v.p. adminstrn., 1992-93, cons., 1993-94, atty., counselor, 1994—. Mem. com. on electricity and nuclear energy Nat. Assn. Regulatory Utility Commrs., 1968-70, mem. exec. com., 1971-73. Charter mem. Com. of 30 for Adoption St. Louis and St. Louis County Jr. Coll. Dist., 1962. With U.S. Army, 1956-58. Mem.: ABA, Bar Assn. Met. St. Louis, Mo. Bar, Loblolly Golf Club (Hobe Sound, Fla.), Chevy Chase (Md.) Club, St. Louis Country Club, St. Louis Club. Republican. Presbyterian. Home: 46 Clermont Ln Saint Louis MO 63124-1351 also: 6820 SE Wood Lark Ln Hobe Sound FL 33455-8048 Personal E-mail: aceelliott@aol.com.

ELLIOTT, INGER MCCABE, apparel designer, consultant, textiles executive; b. Feb. 23, 1933; arrived in U.S., 1941, naturalized, 1946; d. David and Lova (Katz) Abrahamsen; m. Osborn Elliott, Oct. 20, 1973; children from previous marriage: Kari McCabe, Alexander McCabe, Marit McCabe. AB in History with honors, Cornell U., 1954; postgrad., Harvard U., 1955; AM, Radcliffe Coll., 1957. Photographer Photo Rschrs., 1960—98; pres. China Seas, Inc., NYC, 1972—91, Gifted Textile Collection to L.A. County Mus. Art, 1991—. Textile Exhibit L.A. County Mus. Art, 1996—96; cons. Sotheby's Inc., 1992—; mem. Coun. Fgn. Rels. Author: A Week in Amy's World, A Week in Henry's World, Exteriors, 1992; contbr.: photographic essays to Esquire, Vogue, Life, Newsweek, N.Y. Times, Infinity, House & Garden; author: Batik: Fabled Cloth of Java, 1985, 2004. Mem. East Asia vis. com. Harvard U.; trustee The Asia Soc., Am. Scandinavian Found. Recipient Roscoe awards, 1978—91. Mem.: Am. Soc. Mag. Photographers, Trust Historic Preservation, Com. of 200, Ellis Island Yacht Club (lt. comdr.), Cosmopolitan Club, Phi Beta Kappa. Home: 84 Water St Stonington CT 06378

ELLIOTT, J. RAYMOND, medical products executive; Graduate, Univ. We. Ontario. Pres. Far East div. Am. Hosp. Supply Corp.; pres. & CEO J.R. Elliott & Assoc., Cybex Inc., 1995—97; pres. Zimmer Inc., 1997—2001; chmn., pres. & CEO Zimmer Holdings Inc., Warsaw, Ind., 2001—07, chmn., 2007—. Dir. Centerpulse Ltd., 2003—. Dir. State of Ind. Workplace Devel. Bd.; dir., chmn. orthopaedic sect. AdvaMed; trustee Orthopaedic Rsch. & Edn. Found. Office: Zimmer Holdings Inc 345 E Main St Warsaw IN 46580*

ELLIOTT, JEAN ANN, retired library director; b. Martinsburg, W.Va., Jan. 18, 1933; d. Howard Hoffman and Dorothy Jean (Horn) E. AB in edn., Shepherd U., 1954; MS in libr. sci., Syracuse U., 1957; MS, Shippensburg U., Pa., 1974. Asst. libr. Fairmont U., W.Va., 1957-60; reference asst. U. Pitts., 1960-61; acting libr. Shepherd U., 1961-62, coord. libr. sci., 1962-97. Compiler Jefferson County Hist. mag., 1990. Nat. treas. Palatines of Am., Columbus, Ohio, 1986-88. Mem. ALA, AAUW, DAR (W.Va. treas. 1980-83, 86-89, 95-98, state regent 1998-2001, hon. state regent 2001—), W.Va. Libr. Assn. (election chmn. 1988-90), Jefferson County Hist. Soc., Nat. Soc. Daus. Am. Colonies (nat. libr. 1991-94, hon. state regent 1991—), Nat. Soc. Daus. 1812 (nat. libr. 1994-96), W.Va. Soc. Daus. 1812 (state pres. 1991-94, hon. state pres. 1994—), Nat. Soc. Daus. Colonial Wars (state pres. 2001—), Alpha Beta Alpha (nat. exec. sec. 1968-76), Phi Kappa Phi. Presbyterian. Avocations: genealogy, travel, knitting, computers. Home: PO Box 1649 Shepherdstown WV 25443-1649 E-mail: jaelliot@ix.netcom.com.

ELLIOTT, JOHN FOSTER, psychotherapist, writer; b. Pitts., Jan. 21, 1952; s. Victor and Ruth Elliott; m. Beth Tamara Kesselman, Dec. 18, 1982. MA, Internat. Coll., LA, 1981. Cert. clin. hypnotist Calif. Bd. Behavioral Scis., 1983. Founder, exec. dir. OD Drug Crisis Intervention, State College, Pa., 1972—74; founder, exec. dir., clin. dir. Sunrise Cmty. Counseling, LA, 1976—82; marriage and family therapist John F. Elliott & Assocs., North Hollywood, Calif., 1982—. Cons. LEAA, State College, Pa., 1971—72, Nat. Free Clinic Coun., Washington, 1974, Project Heavy, LA, 1976—78, Luth. Social Svcs., LA, 1979—82, Impact Ho., Pasadena, Calif., 1982—84, Calif. State Assembly, Sacramento, 1982, CA BBSE Orals Commn., LA, 1983, Pasadena HS Peer Counseling Program, 1983, mem. psychology grad. and undergrad. faculty Internat. Coll., 1983—85. Author: Grassroots Gestalt in Gestalt Therapy and Beyond, 1980, The Rock and Roll BIble of Collaborative Therapy in Heroic Clients, Heroic Agencies, Partners for Change, 2001, Directions In Life for the Occasionally Confused, 2004. Bd. dirs. LA County Drug Abuse Task Force, 1975, Kadima Conservatory of Music Inc., Sherman Oaks, Calif., 2003—. Recipient Eric Walker award for outstanding sr. grad., Pa. Sate U., 1974, Dist. Ten award, LA City Coun., 1979, Dist. Four award, 1982, citation, California State Assembly, 1979, Diogenes Lantern award, Psychjourney, 2004. Mem.: Calif. Assn. Marriage and Family Therapists (assoc.). Office: 6442 Coldwater Canyon Ste 114 North Hollywood CA 91606 Office Phone: 818-509-0600. Office Fax: 818-509-9536. Business E-Mail: jfelliott@aol.com.

ELLIOTT, JOHN MICHAEL, lawyer; b. Girardville, Pa., July 8, 1941; s. John T. and Clair C. E.; children: John P., Heather D., Kirwan B., Kyle M. AB in Econs. magna cum laude, St. Vincent Coll., 1963, LLD (hon.), 1985; LLB, Georgetown U., 1966. Bar: Pa. 1966, U.S. Dist. Ct. (ea., we. and mid. dists.) Pa. 1967, U.S. Ct. Appeals (3d cir.) 1967, U.S. Supreme Ct. 1968,. Chmn., CEO Elliott, Greenleaf & Siedzikowski, Phila., 1990—. Pa. counsel Del. River Port Authority, 1987-95; mem. Phila. Coal Rail Task Force, Rockefeller Commn., White House Coal Adv. Commn., 1980; bd. dirs. James A. Finnegan Fellowship Found., 1976-90; bd. dirs. Irish Edn. Devel. Found., Inc., chmn., 1986-2002; mem. Pa. Citizens Adv. Coun. Dept. Environ. Resources, 1970-78, chmn. urban com.; mem. environ. quality bd. Commonwealth of Pa., 1970-78; commr. Del. River Port Authority; rep. auditor Gen. Robert P. Casey; mem. Phila. City Planning Commn., 1970-75, Del. Valley Citizens Coun. for Clean Air; chmn. Disciplinary Bd. Supreme Ct. Pa., 1985-86, vice chmn., 1985, chmn. rules com., 1982, Pa. Bar Inst., 1988-94; mem. Commn. on Security and Coop. in Europe Conf. on the Human Dimension, Paris, 1989, Conf. on Dem. Instns., Oslo, 1991; mem. coun. of advisors Sch. of Humanities and Fine Arts; bd. trustee St. Vincent Coll., 2002. Contbr. articles to profl. jours. Bd. dirs. Mann Music Ctr., 1988—91, Walnut St. Theatre, 1988—93, Internat. League for Human Rights, 1988—95. Recipient St. Patrick's Coll. Maynooth Ireland Salamanaca Archives Dedication, Cahal B. Cardinal Daly, 1995, Gold medal, St. Patrick Desmond Cardinal Connell Dublin, 2001. Fellow Pa. Bar Found.; mem. ABA (lectr. on trial practice), Pa. Bar Assn. (ho. of dels. 1983-91, task force on civil ct. rules), Pa. Bar Inst. (bd. dirs. 1987-93, course planner, faculty), Am. Law Inst. (ABA appelate practice program), Nat. Inst. Trial Advocacy (lectr.), Phila. Bar Assn., Nat. Lawyers Com. for Civil Rights Under Law, Braehon Law Soc., Mil. History Soc. Ireland. Home: 1202 Penllyn Blue Bell Pike Blue Bell PA 19422-2108 Office: Elliott Greenleaf & Siedzikowski 925 Harvest Dr Blue Bell PA 19422-1956 Office Phone: 215-977-1004. Business E-Mail: jme@elliottgreenleaf.com.

ELLIOTT, KELLI JEANETTE, biology professor; d. James V. Flaagan and Vicki G. Beno, Richard D. Beno (Stepfather) and Carolyn Flaagan (Stepmother); m. Clay Elliott. BSc, San Diego State U., 1996; MSc, Calif. State U., Fullerton, 2000. Biology instr. Calif. State U., Fullerton, 1998—2005, Fullerton Coll., 2002—05, Orange Coast Coll., Costa Mesa, Calif., 2004—. Environ. club advisor Orange Coast Coll., Costa Mesa, 2006—. Recipient Travel award, Wilson Ornithol. Soc., 2000. Mem.: Audubon Soc. Office: Orange Coast Coll 2701 Fairview Rd Costa Mesa CA 90814 Home Phone: 562-826-9416; Office Phone: 714-432-5504. Business E-Mail: kelliott@occ.cccd.edu.

ELLIOTT, KENNETH YATES, theater educator; b. Indpls., June 15, 1955; s. Donald Finley and Dorothy Ann Elliott. BS, Northwestern U., Evanston, Ill., 1977; MA, Northwestern U., 1978; PhD, UCLA, 2004. Free-lance theatre dir., NYC, 1983—98; asst. prof. theatre Calif. State U., Bakersfield, 2004—. Founder, artistic dir. Theatre-in-Limbo, NYC, 1984—92. Dir.: (plays) Vampire Lesbians of Sodom, 1985, Psycho Beach Party, 1987, The Boys in the Band (revival), 1996. Mem.: Soc. of Stage Dirs. and Choreographers.

ELLIOTT, LARRY PAUL, radiologist, educator; b. Manhattan, Kans., Oct. 16, 1931; s. Leonard Paul and Mary Elizabeth (Myers) E.; m. Betty Lou Hawkins, June 23, 1956; children: Laurie Lou, Mary Elizabeth, Larry Paul. BS, U. Fla., 1954; MD, U. Tenn., 1957. Intern John Gaston Hosp., Memphis, 1957-58; resident in pediat. and pediat. cardiology U. Fla. Hosp., 1958-61; resident in cardiac pathology and cardiovasc. radiology U. Minn. Hosp., 1961-65; assoc. prof. cardiac radiology Washington U. Med. Sch., St. Louis, 1966-67; prof. cardiac radiology U. Fla. Med. Sch., 1967-76; prof. radiology, dir. divsn. cardiac radiology U. Ala. Med. Sch., Birmingham, 1976-81; prof., chmn. dept. radiology Georgetown U. Sch. Medicine, 1981—97, clin. prof., chmn. emeritus, 1996—; clin. prof. radiology Emory U. Med. Ctr., Atlanta, 1997—, Med. U. S.C., 1999—. Chmn. Fac. Practice Group, 1989—; clin. prof. Med. U. S.C., 1999—. Author: Pekannens, 1959, The X-Ray Diagnosis Heart Disease, 1968, 79; editor: Radiology, 1967—, Cardiovascular and Interventional Radiology, 1979—, The Fundamentals of Cardiac Imaging in Infants, Children and Adults, 1990; assoc. editor cardiovasc. sect. Taveras Radiology, 1986; contbr. over 200 articles to med. jours. Vol. Charleston Area Therapeutic Riding Group; camp counselor North Charleston Recreation Inner City Group; tutor Gethsesman's Cmty. Ctr., North Charleston, SC. Recipient Disting. Alumnus award U. Fla., 1981, Outstanding Alumnus award U. Tenn. Med. Sch., 1993; grantee cardiac radiology Nat. Heart Inst., 1968-76, Allied Health Profl. Act, 1970. Fellow N.Am. Soc. Cardiac Radiology (pres. 1977-78), Am. Coll. Cardiology; mem. Radiol. Soc. N.Am., Soc. Cardiac Angiography, Am. Heart Assn., Soc. Thoracic Radiology (founding mem., pres. faculty practice group 1989-93). Home: 3 Ocean Point Dr Isle Of Palms SC 29451-3852 *In my own success, I have found 5 key ingredients. (1) A mentor who ignited the switch or literally turned me on. (2) Superb training, especially in sound fundamental principles. (3) An obsessive enthusiasm, a prime feature I look for in all postgraduate students. (4) An element of discipline, which has prevented succumbing to the siren song of private practice. (5) Reward, the only fountain of youth that exists - a close association with each generation of students.*

ELLIOTT, MARIAN KAY, real estate manager; b. Wheatland, Wyo., Aug. 29, 1950; d. James Beal Jr. and Marian L. Angle; m. William Paul Elliott, June 1, 1978; children: Kenneth James Judd, L.R. Dedee Judd, William Paul, Joseph G., Christina Hope, Dennise Faith. Cert. Mont. Comml. Credit Mgmt. Assn.; therapeutic foster parenting Dept. Family Svcs.; lic. real estate agt. Wyo. Comml. credit mgr. Pacific Steel, Mills, Wyo., 1978—79; mgr. investment real estate Casper, Wyo., 1981—; real estate assoc. Associated Brokers, Casper, 1982—85. Local reporter National Voter; editor: (newsletter) Wyoming Recycler. Chair fundraising com. Casper Jaycee Jinx, 1974—76; Wyo. scholastic pageant judge Casper Jaycees, 1993; amb. Casper Area C. of C., 1995—96; guardian Youth in Crisis and Mentally Disabled Adults, Casper, 1996—2002; ct. apptd. spl. advocate for abused and neglected children CASA of Natrona County, Casper, 2002—05; vol. Blue Envelope Health/ Elem. Strep Prevention Program, Casper, 1975—78; vol. resource class aide Elem. Sch., Casper, 1975—76, PTA bd. mem., 1979—83; foster parent Dept. Family Svcs., Casper, 1986—96, spkr. new foster parent tng., 1987—98; advocate, lobbyist foster children's rights Foster Parents of Natrona County, Casper, 1989—91; v.p. St. Christopher's Presch. Guild, Casper, 1976; confirmation class tchr. St. Mark's Episcopal Ch., Casper, 1975—78. Mem.: Hat Club/ Resources for Women in Spl. Circumstances (pres. 1997—2001), Big Bros./ Big Sisters Ctrl. Wyo. (adv. coun. 2002—03). Democrat. Achievements include sued for and won the right to sue elected officials in the State of Wyoming; helped change Wyoming laws to allow earlier adoption of foster children. Avocations: gardening, fine arts. Home: 1434 S Beech St Casper WY 82601 Personal E-mail: chadelliott1@msn.com.

ELLIOTT, MARK LEE, lawyer; b. Wertzberg, Germany, July 28, 1956; BA, U. Va., 1977, JD, 1980. Bar: Ga. 1980. Assoc. Troutman Sanders LLP, Atlanta, 1980—87, ptnr., 1988—, practice group leader, comml. leasing dept. Mem. State Bar Ga. Office: Troutman Sanders 600 Peachtree St NE Ste 5200 Atlanta GA 30308-2216 Office Phone: 404-885-3603. Office Fax: 404-962-6551. Business E-Mail: mark.elliott@troutmansanders.com.

ELLIOTT, MISSY (MELISSA ARNETTE ELLIOT), musician; b. Portsmouth, Va., July 1, 1971; d. Ronnie and Pat Elliott. Grad., Manor H.S., Portsmouth, 1990. With Elektra Entertainment, 1996—; owner Gold Mind. Musician: Supa Dupa Fly, 1997 (Platinum), Da Real World, 1999 (Platinum), Miss E.So Addictive, 2001 (Platinum), Under Construction,

2002 (2 times Platinum), This Is Not A Test!, 2003, The Cookbook, 2005. Nominee 3 Grammy awards, 2002, 2 Grammy awards, 2003; named Best Female Hip-Hop Artist, BET, 2002, 15th of 50 Greatest Hip Hop Artists, VH1, 2003; recipient Best Video of Yr. for The Rain, Rolling Stone, 1997, Soul Train Lady of Soul award for Best R&B/Soul or Rap Music Video for Get Ur Freak On, 2001, Grammy award for Best Rap Solo for Get Ur Freak On, 2002, Soul Train Lady of Soul award for Best R&B/Soul or Rap Music Video for One Minute Man, 2002, Grammy award for Best Female Rap Solo Performance for Scream aka Itchin, 2003, Soul Train Music award for Best R&B/Soul or Rap Music Video for Work It, 2003, Soul Train Lady of Soul awards for Best Song and Best Music Video for Work It, 2003, Video of Yr., Best Hip Hop Video for Work It, 2003, Favorite Female Hip-Hop Artist, Am. Music Awards, 2003, 2005, Best Female Hip Hop award, Black Entertainment TV (BET), 2006, Video Spl. Effects award for We Run This, MTV Video Music Awards, 2006. Office: Elektra Entertainment 75 Rockefeller Plz New York NY 10019

ELLIOTT, OSBORN, journalist, educator, retired dean; b. NYC, Oct. 25, 1924; s. John and Audrey N. (Osborn) E.; m. Deirdre M. Spencer, May 8, 1948 (div. Dec. 1972); children: Diana, Cynthia, Dorinda; m. Inger McCabe, Oct. 20, 1973; stepchildren: Kari, Alexander, Marit. Grad., St. Paul's Sch., 1942; AB, Harvard U., Cambridge, Mass., 1946; LHD (hon.), Mich. State U., East Lansing, 1972; LittD (hon.), Marlboro Coll., Vt., 1996; LHD (hon.), Marymount Manhattan Coll., NYC, 1998. Reporter NY Jour. Commerce, 1946-49; contbg. editor Time mag., 1949-52, assoc. editor, 1952-55; sr. bus. editor Newsweek, 1955-59, mng. editor, 1959-61, editor, 1961-69, 72-75, editor-in-chief, vice chmn., pres., CEO, chmn. bd., 1969-76; former dir. Washington Post Co., A.S. Abell Co. (Balt. Sun); dep. mayor econ. devel. City of NY, 1976—77; dean Grad. Sch. Journalism, Columbia U., NYC, 1979-86, George Delacorte prof., 1986-94, pub. Columbia Journalism Rev., 1979-86. Author: Men At the Top, 1959, The World of Oz, 1980; editor: The Negro Revolution in America, 1964. Bd. overseers Harvard Coll., 1965—71; trustee NY Pub. Libr., 1968—72, 1977—79, St. Paul's Sch., 1969—73, Am. Mus. Natural History, 1958—80, Lincoln Ctr. Theater, 1987—92, Pulitzer Prize Bd., 1979—86; judge Livingston Journalism Awards; chmn. China Seas, Inc., 1973—90, Bernstein Book award N.Y. Pub. Libr.; chmn. bd. dirs. Citizens Com. for NYC, 1975—79, 1990—2003; bd. dirs. New Yorkers for Children, 1999—; organizer 250,000 person Save Our Cities! Save Our Children! March on Washington, 1992; life trustee Asia Soc. With USNR, 1944—46, Pacific Theatre. Named to Hall of Fame, N.Y.C. Deadline Club, 2000; recipient Carr Van Anda award, Ohio U., 1969, Frederick Douglass award, N.Y. Urban League, 1993, Editor's Hall of Fame award, Am. Soc. Mag. Editors, 1996, Creative Spirit award, Black Alumni Pratt Inst., 1997, Browning Sch. Alumni award, 2001. Fellow Am. Acad. Arts and Scis.; mem. Coun. Fgn. Rels. (trustee), Harvard Club, Century Assn., Ellis Island Yacht Club (commodore). Home: 84 Water St Stonington CT 06378

ELLIOTT, RICHARD HOWARD, lawyer; b. Astoria, NY, Apr. 30, 1933; m. Judith A. Kessler, Dec. 26, 1956 (dec. 1987); children: Marc Evan, Jonathan Hugh, Eve; m. Diane S. Schaefer, Nov. 18, 1978; children: Alexis, Sara Jane, Benjamin, David. BS, Lehigh U., 1954; JD cum laude, U. Pa., 1962. Bar: US Dist. Ct. (ea. dist.) Pa. 1962, Pa. Supreme Ct. 1962, US Ct. Appeals (3d cir.) 1963, US Dist. Ct. (mid. dist.) Pa. 1976. Assoc. Clark, Ladner, Fortenbaugh & Young, Phila., 1962—69, ptnr., 1970—75, Elliott & Magee, Doylestown, Pa., 1976—. Moderator Permanent Jud. Commn., Presbytery Phila.; v.p., dir. Bucks County Soc. Prevention Cruelty Animals; former pres., dir. Pa. Soc. Prevention Cruelty Animals; gen. counsel, dir. Fedn. Humane Socs. Pa., adj. faculty Bucks County CC; active Pa. Navigation Commn., 1977-80. Lt. USN, 1954-59. Mem. ABA, Pa. Bar Assn., Phila. Bar Assn., Bucks County Bar Assn. Republican. Home: 1205 Victoria Rd Warminster PA 18974-3923 Office: Elliott & Magee 11 Duane Rd PO Box 885 Doylestown PA 18901-0885 Office Phone: 215-230-9900. Personal E-mail: relli59360@aol.com.

ELLIOTT, SAM, actor; b. Sacramento, Aug. 9, 1944; m. Katharine Ross, 1984; 1 child, Cleo. Student, U. Oreg. Appeared in films including Butch Cassidy and the Sundance Kid, 1970, The Games, 1970, Frogs, 1972, Molly and Lawless John, 1972, Lifeguard, 1976, The Legacy, 1979, Mask, 1985, Fatal Beauty, 1987, Shakedown, 1988, Road House, 1989, Prancer, Sibling Rivalry, 1990, Rush, 1991, Gettysburg, 1993, Tombstone, 1993, The Big Lebowski, 1998, The Hi-Lo Country, 1998, The Contender, 2000, Pretty When You Cry, 2001, We Were Soldiers, 2002, Off the Map, 2003, Hulk, 2003, Thank You for Smoking, 2006, The Alibi, 2006, (voice) Barnyard: The Original Party Animals, 2006, Ghost Rider, 2007; appeared in TV movies including The Challenge, 1970, Assault on the Wayne, 1970, The Blue Knight, 1975, I Will Fight No More Forever, 1975, The Sacketts, 1978, The Shadow Riders, 1982, A Death in California, 1985, Gone to Texas: The Sam Houston Story, 1986, The Quick and The Dead, 1987, (also co-writer) Conagher, 1991, The Final Cut, 1995, Dog Watch, 1996, Rough Riders, 1997, Texarkana, 1998, You Know My Name, 1999, Fail Safe, 2000, Avenger, 2006; in TV series Mission Impossible, 1970-71, The Yellow Rose, 1983-84, You Know My Name, 1998, Fail Safe, 2000; in TV mini-series Once An Eagle, 1976-77, Aspen, 1977, Buffalo Girls, 1995. Address: care William Morris Agency 151 S El Camino Dr Beverly Hills CA 90212-2704*

ELLIOTT, SCOTT, minister, retired lawyer; b. San Jose, July 26, 1957; s. Roland Meredith and Sandra Gale (Deem) E.; m. Nancy Marie Oller, Apr. 6, 1979; children: Tristan Robin, Jordan Brook, Robin Sage, Forest Dream. BA in Drama magna cum laude, Calif. State U. Stanislaus, Turlock, 1979; JD, U. Oreg., 1987; MDiv, Eden Theol. Sem., 2006. Bar: Oreg. 1987, U.S. Dist. Ct. Oreg. 1988, U.S. Ct. Appeals (9th cir.) 1992. Assoc. Larry O. Gildea, Eugene, Oreg., 1987-88, Thorp, Dennet, Purdy & Golden, Springfield, Oreg., 1988; law clk. U.S. Dist. Ct. Nev., Las Vegas, 1988-89; ptnr. Green & Elliott, Lincoln City, Oreg., 1989-95; assoc. Thorp, Purdy, Jewett, Urness & Wilkinson, Springfield, Oreg., 1995-96, Wine, Weller, Ehrlich and Green, Lincoln City, 1996-98; pvt. practice Lincoln City, 1998—2003; seminarian Eden Theol. Sem., 2003—; youth dir. Eliot Chapel, 2003—04; student pastor Evangelical United Ch. of Christ, 2004—05; intern min. Lincoln City United Ch. of Christ, 2005; student pastor Crossroads Ch. of Christ, 2005—06; pastor Riviera United Ch. of Christ, Palm Bay, Fla., 2006—. Founder, artistic dir. Cmty. Family Players, 1997—2003; mem. choir Congl. Ch., 1997—2003. Recipient Commitment to Excellence in Art award, 4Cs, 2001; grad. tchg. fellow, U. Oreg. Theatre, 1979—80. Mem. Congl. Ch. Avocations: theology, gardening, theater, singing. Home: 451 Riviera Dr NE Palm Bay FL 32905 Business E-Mail: selliott@rivieraucc.org.

ELLIOTT, SCOTT D., lawyer; BA in Econs., U. Calif. Berkeley, 1988; JD, Hastings Coll. Law, 1992. Bar: Calif. 1992. Ptnr. Orrick, Herrington & Sutcliffe, Menlo Park, Calif., Ropes & Gray LLP, San Francisco, 2006—. Mem.: Calif. Bar Assn. Office: Ropes & Gray LLP One Embarcadero Ctr Ste 2200 San Francisco CA 94111-3627 Office Phone: 415-315-6379. Office Fax: 415-315-4834.*

ELLIOTT, STANLEY B., chemist, researcher; s. Louis Alexander Elliott and Nellie Cecilia Bennett; m. Elizabeth Marie Seitz, Aug. 2, 1958. Student, Wittenberg Coll., Springfield, Ohio, 1935—36; BA, Case We. Res. U., Cleve., 1939. Analytical chemist Harshaw Chem., Cleve., 1936—38, rsch. chemist, 1938—41, Ferro Corp. and U.S. O.S.R.D., Cleve., 1941—45, chem. engr., 1941—45; v.p. Ferro Chem., Cleve., 1945—48, pres., 1948—55; rschr. self-employed, Walton Hills, Ohio, 1955—. Author (A.C.S. Monograph No. 103): Metallic Soaps; contbr. articles Encylopedia of Chemistry 1973. Mem.: Sigma Xi, N.Y. Acad. of Sci., Am. Chem. Soc. Achievements include patents in field of Practical electrical superconductors of high temperature power and performance. Office: Management/Research 7125 Conelly Blvd Walton Hills OH 44146 Office Phone: 440-232-5139.

ELLIOTT, STEVEN G., bank executive; b. Delta, Colo. B in Fin., U. Houston; MBA, Northwestern U. V.p., corp. contr. First Interstate Bank Calif.; sr. v.p. Continental Ill. Nat. Bank; sr. v.p., corp. contr. Crocker Nat. Bank; exec. v.p., CFO First Commerce Corp.; exec. v.p., head fin. dept. Mellon Fin. Corp., Pitts., 1987-90, CFO, 1990—92, vice chmn., 1992-98, sr. vice chmn., 1998—2007; sr. vice-chmn., co-head integration Bank of NY Mellon, NYC, 2007—. Bd. dirs. UPMC Health Sys., Pitts. Cultural Trust. Mem. AICPA, Fin. Executives Inst., Fin. Svcs. Roundtable. Mailing: Bank of NY Mellon PO Box 2164 New York NY 10008-2164*

ELLIOTT, STUART JAY, editor, journalist; b. Bklyn., July 20, 1952; s. Eli and Sylvia (Perlo) E. BS in Journalism, Northwestern U., 1973, MS in Journalism, 1974. Reporter, copy editor, columnist The Times-Union, Rochester, NY, 1974-79; reporter, columnist Detroit Free Press, 1979-82; reporter, dep. N.Y. bur. chief Advt. Age, 1982-87; exec. editor Investment Dealers Digest, NYC, 1987; bus. reporter Gannett News Service, Washington, 1988; advt. and mktg. reporter USA Today, NYC, 1988-91; advt. columnist The NY Times, NYC, 1991—; advt. reporter Sta. WQXR-FM, 1991—2000. Office Phone: 212-556-1226.

ELLIOTT, SUSAN SPOEHRER, information technology executive; b. St. Louis, May 4, 1937; d. Charles Henry and Jane Elizabeth (Baur) Spoehrer; m. Howard Elliott Jr., Sept. 2, 1961; children: Kathryn Elliott Love, Elizabeth Elliott Niedringhaus. AB, Smith Coll., 1958. Systems engr. IBM, St. Louis, 1958-66; founder, chmn., CEO, SSE (Sys. Svc. Enterprises, Inc.), St. Louis, 1966—; systems analyst Mo. State Dept. Edn., Jefferson City, Mo., 1967-70; systems coord. Bank of Am. (formerly Boatmen's Nat. Bank), St. Louis, 1979-83. Bd. dirs., exec. com. Mo. Automobile Club; class C dir., dep. chmn. Fed. Res. Bd., St. Louis, 1996-98, chmn., 1999-2000; bd. dirs. Ameren Corp., Angelica Corp., Regional Bus. Coun., St. Louis Regional Commerce and Growth Assn., sec. bd. dirs., 1991-94; bd. dirs. AAA Mo. Trustee, vice-chmn. Mary Inst., St. Louis, 1976-89, Webster U., 1987-96; commr., vice-chmn. St. Louis Civil Svc. Commn., 1985-86, Mo. Lottery Commn., Jefferson City, 1985-87; bd. dirs. St. Louis Zoo, 1990-96, St. Louis Sci. Ctr., 1995-2004, 2006—; mem. pres.'s adv. coun. area coun., tech. com. Girl Scouts U.S.; chair women bus. owner's com. United Way, 1996-97. Mem. Internat. Women's Forum. Republican. Presbyterian. Avocations: golf, exercise. Office: SSE (Sys Svc Enterprises Inc) 77 West Port Plz Ste 500 Saint Louis MO 63146-3126 Home Phone: 314-997-0589; Office Phone: 314-439-4701. Business E-Mail: sselliott@SSEinc.com.

ELLIOTT, THOMAS MICHAEL, retired association executive, educator, consultant; b. Evansville, Ind., Aug. 4, 1942; s. Thomas Ira and Pauline (Dawson) E.; m. Susan M. Spiers, July 8, 1967 (div. Aug. 1975); 1 son, Christopher Michael; m. Loretta S. Glaze, Jan. 28, 1976. AB in Zoology, Ind. U., 1965, MS in Higher Edn., 1967, EdD, 1970. Asst. to pres. Purdue U., West Lafayette, Ind., 1972-73, asst. provost, 1973-74; exec. dir. Nat. Commn. United Meth. Higher Edn., Nashville, 1974-77; ptnr. Planning Mgmt. Services Group, Washington, 1976-82; dep. commr. Mo. Dept. Higher Edn., Jefferson City, 1977-79; exec. dir. Ark. Dept. Higher Edn., Little Rock, 1979-82; exec. dir., CEO IEEE Computer Soc., Washington, 1982-2000; ret., 2001—. Cons. numerous colls. and univs. Author: Computer Simulation System, 1975; contbr. articles to profl. jours. Bd. dirs., mem. exec. com. So. Regional Edn. Bd., Atlanta, 1980-82; mem. Cabinet of Gov. Bill Clinton and Gov. Frank White, State of Ark., 1979-82. Mem. IEEE (sr.), IEEE Computer Soc., State Higher Edn. Exec. Officers Assn., Am. Soc. Assn. Execs., Am. Mgmt. Assn., Assn. Computing Machinery. Democrat. Avocations: sailing, photography. Home: 1735 Q St NW Washington DC 20009-2407 E-mail: melliott@computer.org.

ELLIOTT, VIRGINIA F. HARRISON, retired anatomist, publisher, educator, investment advisor, kinesiologist, philanthropist; b. St. Louis, Mar. 15, 1918; d. George Benjamin and Florence Gertrude (McManus) H.; m. William Hector Marsh, Dec. 1, 1963 (dec. Dec. 1986); m. George William Elliott, Oct. 27, 1991; stepchildren: Carolyn Frances Roberts, George William II, Robert Bonner (dec. Apr. 1995), Cathrine Susan Dimino. BS, U. Wis., 1940, PhD, 1959; MA, Columbia U., 1944. Lectr. Columbia U., NYC, 1943-46; asst. prof. Mary Washington U., Fredericksburg, Va., 1946—48, Oreg. State U., Corvallis, 1948-50, assoc. prof., 1950-59; instr. Army Med. Acad./Brooks Army Med. Ctr., San Antonio, 1959-60, assoc. prof., 1960-64; lectr. Hadassah Med. Sch., Hebrew U. of Jerusalem, 1965; pvt. practice Washington, 1969—87; ret., 1987. Fashion model, 1936-47, with John Robert Powers Schs., Phila., Pitts., NYC, 1943-47; cons. U. Tex. Med. Sch., 1962-64, U.S. Pentathlon Team, San Antonio, 1960-64, Dentists for Treatment of Pain from Muscular Tension, San Antonio, 1960-64; vis. prof. grad. sch. U. Wash., Seattle, 1961; lectr. in field Contbr. articles to profl. jours. Bd. visitors Sch. Edn., U. Wis., Madison, 1992-95, now emeritus; mem. Washington com. Nat. Coun. on Women's Giving. Recipient Civilian Meritorious Svc. award U.S. Civil Svc., 1965; Amy Morris Homans fellow, 1958; hon. fellow U. Wis., 1956, 58, 59. Fellow AAHPERD, Tex. Acad. Sci.; mem. Am. Alliance Health, Phys. Edn., Recreation and Dance, Am. Assn. Anatomists divsns. Fedn. Am. Socs. for Exptl. Biology (emeritus), Cosmos Club (emeritus). Presbyterian. Avocations: designing clothing, furniture, landscaping and boats, sculpting, painting. Home: 6333 Cavalier Corridor Falls Church VA 22044-1301

ELLIS, ALFRED WRIGHT (AL ELLIS), lawyer; b. Cleve., Aug. 26, 1943; s. Donald Porter and Louise (Wright) E.; m. Kay Genseke, June 1965 (div. 1976); 1 child, Joshua Kyle; m. Sandra Lee Fahey, Feb. 11, 1989. BA with honors, U. Tex., Arlington, 1965; JD, So. Meth. U., 1971. Bar: Tex., U.S. Dist. Ct. (no., so., ea. and we. dists.) Tex., U.S. Ct. Appeals (5th cir.), U.S. Supreme Ct.; cert. personal injury and civil trial lawyer, Internat. Acad. Trial Lawyers. Capt. U.S. Army, 1965—69; atty. Woodruff, Kendall & Smith, Dallas, 1972; ptnr. Woodruff & Ellis, Dallas; pvt. practice Dallas, 1983-96; of counsel Howie & Sweeney, 1996—2003, Sommerman & Quesada, 2003—. Instr. So. Meth. U. Law Sch. Trial Advocacy; past pres. Law Focused Edn., Inc. Past mem. City of Dallas Urban Rehab. Stds. Bd., Dallas Assembly, Salesmanship Club, Dallas; trustee Hist. Preservation League, 1992—94; dir. Dallas Regional Golden Gloves Tournament, 1976—96; pres., bd. dirs. Dallas Coun. on Alcoholism, 1980; pres. Dallas All Sports Assn., 1980; bd. dirs. Dallas Habitat for Humanity, 1998—2002, 2005—. Named Boss of Yr., Dallas Assn. Legal Secs., 1978, Best Lawyer in Am., 2002—07; named one of Outstanding Young Men of Am., Jaycees, 1977, Nat.'s Leading Plaintiff Lawyers, Law Dragon, 2007; recipient Certs. of Recognition (8), Dallas Ind. Sch. Dist., 1971—83, Wall Street Jour. award, So. Meth. U. Law Sch., 1972, Hayward McMurray award, Dallas Jaycees, 1975—76, Spl. Recognition award, All Sports Assn., 1977, Cert. of Appreciation for Exceptional & Disting. Vol. Svcs., Gov. Mark White, 1983, Cmty. Spirit award, Dallas Bus. Jour., 1993, Disting. Svc. award, Dallas All Sports Assn., 1993, Nancy Garms Meml. award for Outstanding Contbns. to Law Focus Edn., 1996—, Leon Jaworski Tchg. Excellence in Law award, Dallas Minority Bar Assn., 2002; fellow, Roscoe Pound Found. Fellow: Dallas Bar Found., Tex. Bar Found. (sustaining life, Dan R. Price Meml. award 2003, "D" Mag. Best Personal Injury Lawyers, Dallas 2003, Tex. Monthly Super Lawyers 2003—06), Dallas Assn. Young Lawyers (life); mem.: ATLA, William Mac Taylor Inn of Ct. (Judith Sinclair Cmty. Svc. award 2007), Tex. Legal Svcs. Ctr. (bd. dirs. 1999—2002), Tex. Ctr. for Legal Ethics and Professionalism (bd. dirs. 1999—, chmn. 2002—04), Coll. State Bar of Tex. (bd. dirs. 1997—99), Am. Coll. Barristers, Tex. Equal Access to Justice Found. (bd. dirs. 1994—96), Tex. Trial Lawyers Assn. (bd. dirs. emeritus), Dallas Trial Lawyers Assn. (pres. 1977, Disting. Cmty. Svc. award 1990), Dallas Bar Assn. (bd. dirs. 1978, v.p. 1987—88, pres. 1990), State Bar Tex. (bd. dirs. 1991—94, lectr. seminars, Excellence in Diversity award 1994, Outstanding 3d Yr. Dir. award, Judge Sam Williams Local Bar Leadership award), Legal Svcs. of North Tex. (bd. dirs., Outstanding Svc. award 1990), Million Dollar Advocates Forum, Am. Bd. Trial Advocates (sec.-treas. Dallas chpt. 1998, pres. 1999, diplomate, Dayl Found. Excellence award 2004). Avocations: tennis, skiing. Office: 3811 Turtle Creek Blvd #1400 Dallas TX 75219-4461 Office Phone: 214-720-0720. Personal E-mail: al@textrial.com.

ELLIS, ANDREW JACKSON, JR., lawyer; b. Ashland, Va., June 23, 1930; m. Dorothy L. Lichliter, Apr. 24, 1954; children: Elizabeth E. Attkisson, Andrew C., William D. BA, Washington and Lee U., 1951, LLB, 1953. Bar: Va. 1952. Ptnr. Campbell, Ellis & Campbell, Ashland, 1955-70, Mays, Valentine, Davenport & Moore, Richmond, Va., 1970-88, Mays & Valentine, Richmond, 1988-96, sr. counsel, 1998—2002, Troutman & Sanders, Richmond, 2002—. Substitute judge County of Hanover (Va.) Ct., 1955—63, 15th Jud. Dist., 1990—96; commr. chancery cir. ct. Hanover County, 1955—63; commonwealth atty., 1963—70; county atty., 1970—78; judge 15th Dist. Juvenile and Domestic Rels. Ct., 1996—98; capital adv. bd. NationsBank Va., 1960—93. Mem. Ashland Town Coun., 1956—63; mayor Town of Ashland, 1958—63; trustee J. Sargent Reynolds CC, 1972—80. 1st lt. US Army, 1953—55. Fellow: Va. Law Found., Am. Coll. Trial Lawyers; mem.: S.R., Hanover Bar Assn. (past pres.), 15th Jud. Cir. Bar Assn. (past pres.), Richmond Bar Assn., Va. Trial Lawyers Assn., Va. State Bar (coun. 1968—74), Va. Bar Assn., Kiwanis. Episcopalian. Home: 15293 Old Ridge Rd Beaverdam VA 23015-1610 Office: PO Box 1122 Richmond VA 23218-1122

ELLIS, ANNE ELIZABETH, fundraiser; b. Orngestad, Aruba, Aug. 21, 1945; d. Thomas Albert and Anne Elizabeth (Belis) Wolfe; m. Earl Edward Ellis, Feb. 14, 1970. BS, La. State U., 1967. Fashion coord., Baton Rouge, 1962-67; textile researcher La. State U., Baton Rouge, 1965-67; buyer I.H. Rubensteins., Baton Rouge, 1967-68; fashion distbr. J.C. Penney, Inc., Arlington, Tex., 1969-70, asst. buyer Dallas, 1970-73; exec. dir. Nassau County Mus. Fine Art Assn., Roslyn, NY, 1985-88. Speaker C.W. Post U., Greenvale, NY, 1988—; cons. in field. Chmn., editor: (cookbook) Specialities of the House, 1981-83. Bd. dirs., com. chmn. Congregational Ch., Manhasset, NY, 1975-96; exec. v.p., bd. dirs., com. chmn. Jr. League Internat.; benefit gala chmn., com. chmn. Grenville Baker Boys & Girls Club, Locust Valley, NY, 1983-91; pres. bd., vice-chmn. cmty. outreach, benefit gala chmn. Tilles Performing Art Ctr. LI U., Greenvale, NY, 1985—; bd. dirs., benefit co-chmn. Nassau County Family Assn. Svcs., Hempstead, 1988-96; benefit vice-chmn. Glen Cove/North Shore Cmty. Hosp., 1989-93; mem. exec. bd., exec. v.p., trustee WLIW, LI Pub. TV, 1990-2001, chmn. bd. dirs., 1997-99; trustee Cmty. Found. of Oyster Bay, 1991-94; trustee Dowling Coll., Oakdale, NY, 1993-98, exec. bd., 1997-98; adv. bd. Westbury (NY) Gardens, 1993-97; chmn. adv. bd. Long Island chpt. Save the Children, 1995-2001; trustee LI U., 1998-2007. Recipient Vol. of Yr. award Jr. League LI, 1984, 85, Outstanding Vol. Svcs. and Commitment award County of Nassau, 1989, Juliette Low award Nassau County Girl Scouts, LI, 1991, Disting. Leadership award, LI, 1991, Outstanding Cmty. Vol. award Jr. League of LI, 1991-92, Disting. Svc. medal L.I. State Parks Found., 1999, Women of Achievement award Jr. League LI, 2000. Mem. P.E.O. (pres. 1985-87), The Creek Inc., Meadowbrook Club Inc., Lost Tree Club, Forest Creek Club, Brights Creek Club, Kappa Kappa Gamma (alumna pres. 1971-72). Republican. Congregationalist. Avocations: golf, gardening, needlepoint. Personal E-mail: aseellis@aol.com.

ELLIS, BERNICE, financial planner, investment advisor; b. Bklyn. d. Samuel and Clara H.; m. Seymour Scott Ellis; children: Michele, Wayne. BA, Bklyn. Coll., NYC; MS, Queens Coll., NYC, 1970. Cert. fin. planner NY, 1987, elem. educator NYC. Tchr. elem. L.I. Sch. Dists., Merrick, NY; tchr. reading N.Y.C. Bd. of Edn., Bklyn., 1972—73; coord. Reading is Fundamental, Lawrence, NY, 1973—75; pres., founder N.Y. State Assn. for Gifted and Talented, Valley Stream, NY, 1974—87; pres. Ellis Planning, Valley Stream, 1984—. Cons. Nassau County Bd. Coop. Ednl. Svcs., Westbury, N.Y., 1973-74; adminstrv. intern region II U.S. Office Edn., 1977-78; adj. asst. prof. Nassau C.C., Garden City, N.Y., 1975-91, adj. assoc. prof., 1991-94, adj. full prof., 1995—; fin. commentator Money Talk radio program WHPC FM; arbitrator NASD, 1996. Contbr. articles to profl. jours and fin. newsletters. Mem. adv. com. Ams. for Ams. for Hope, Growth and Opportunity, 1998; mem. Nat. Rep. Party, Valley Stream Rep. Party, N.Y. State Rep. Party. Recipient Ednl. Professions Devel. Act fellow CUNY Inst. for Remediations Skills for Coll. Pers., Queensborough C.C., 1970-73; named Business Person of Yr. Nat. Rep. Congl. Com., 2003. Mem. AAUW (North Shore bd., chmn. Money Talk 1991—), Nat. Assn. Securities Dealers (arbitrator 1996), Nat. Alliance of Sales Execs., Inst. for CFP, Inst. for CFP L.I. (bd. dirs.), Internat. Assn. Fin. Planners (legis. com. L.I. chpt. 1986-87), N.Y. State Reading Assn., Adj. Faculty Assn. Nassau C.C., L.I. C. of C., Rotary, Womens Nat. Republic Club. Avocations: reading, swimming. Office: Ellis Planning Inc 628 Golf Dr Valley Stream NY 11581-3594

ELLIS, BRET EASTON, writer; b. LA, Mar. 7, 1964; s. Robert Martin and Dale Jeffa (Dennis) E. BA, Bennington Coll., 1986. Author: Less Than Zero, 1985, The Rules of Attraction, 1987, American Psycho, 1991, The Informers, 1994, Zombies, 1996, Glamorama, 2000, Lunar Park, 2005; contbr. to periodicals including Rolling Stone, Wall St. Jour., Vanity Fair, Interview. Mem. Authors Guild. Office: c/o Amanda Urban ICM 40 W 57th St New York NY 10019-4001

ELLIS, COURTENAY, lawyer; b. Cottingham, Eng., Jan. 4, 1946; came to the U.S., 1970; BA, Oxford U., Eng., 1967, MA, 1974; LLM, George Washington U., 1972. Bar: D.C. 1973; cert. solicitor, Eng. Solicitor's articled clk. Field, Fisher & Co., London, 1968-69; solicitor Farrer & Co., London, 1970; assoc. atty. Covington & Burling, Washington, 1972-76, Akin, Gump, Strauss, Hauer & Feld, 1976-78, ptnr. Washington, 1979-98, Oppenheimer Wolff Donnelly Bayh, Washington, 1998-99, Murphy Ellis Weber, 2000—03, Ellis Weber, 2003—. Bd. dirs. The Episcopal Ctr. for Children, Washington, 1986-92. Mem. ABA, The Law Soc. London, Brit. Am. Bus. Assn. (bd. dirs., program chair 1997-98, pres. 1999-2001), Washington Fgn. Law Soc. (bd. govs., membership coord. 1993-95, program coord. 1995-96, pres. 1997-98), Fed. Bar Assn. (internat. law sect., chair 1996-98), Globalscot, Met. Club. Office: Ellis Weber Ste 1200 818 Connecticut Ave NW Washington DC 20006 Office Phone: 202-833-8220. Business E-Mail: cellis@ellisweber.com.

ELLIS, DAVID WERTZ, retired museum director, consultant, arbitrator; b. Huntingdon, Pa., Feb. 8, 1936; s. Calvert Nice and Elizabeth Oller (Wertz) E.; m. Marion Elizabeth Schmitt, June 24, 1961; children: Kathryn Dana, Lorna Beth, Audrey Heather. BA with honors in Chemistry, Haverford Coll., 1958; PhD in Chemistry, MIT, 1962; LLD (hon.), Lehigh U., 1979, Lafayette Coll., 1990; DSc (hon.), Susquehanna U., 1982, Ursinus Coll., 1985; LHD (hon.), Juniata Coll., 1989; DCL (hon.), U. of the South, 2000; DSc (hon.), Northeastern U., 2002. AMP cert. Advanced Mgmt. Program Harvard U. Graduate Sch. Bus. Adminstrn., 1989. Asst. prof. chemistry U. N.H., 1962-67, assoc. prof., 1967-78, acting asst. dean Grad. Sch., 1967, asst. dean coll. of Tech., 1968, assoc. acad. v.p., 1968-71, vice provost, v.p. acad. affairs, 1971-78; pres. Lafayette Coll., Easton, Pa., 1978-90, pres. emeritus, 1990—; pres., dir. Mus. of Sci., Boston, 1990—2002, pres. emeritus, 2003—; sr. fellow The Boston Found., 2003—04; pres The Mus Group, 2005—. Mem. Adv. Com. for The

Directorate on Edn. and Human Resources, NSF, 1998-2001, chmn., 2000, 2001. Co-author: Calculations of Analytical Chemistry, 1971; contbr. articles to scientific jours. Bd. dirs. Elderhostel, 1983—87, 1989—2000, chmn., 1990—95, 1996—2000; vice chmn. Nat. Assn. Ind. Coll. and Univs., 1987—88, chmn., 1988—89; bd. dirs., mem. Am. Coun. on Edn. Commn. on Leadership Devel., 1988—90; bd. dirs. Sci. Mus. Exhibits Collaborative, 1990—2002, sec.-treas., 1992—93, chmn., 1993—95; bd. dirs. Mus. Film Network, 1990—2002, chmn., 1993—97; bd. dirs. Sta. WGBH Pub. Broadcasting, 1990—2000, mem. exec. com., 1992—2000, chmn. audit com., 1993—2000, mem. tech. com., 2000—03; bd. dirs. Giant Screen Theater Assn., 1992—94, 1996—98, chmn. mktg. com., 1992—94, mem. liaison com., 1996—98; bd. dirs. Assn. Sci. Tech. Ctrs., 1992—93, 1995—2002, v.p., 1997—99; convener Nat. Health Scis. Consortium, 1994—96; mem. bd. overseers Tufts U. Coll. Arts and Sci., 1995—2001; bd. advisors Whitehead Inst., 1996—, Seacoast Sci. Ctr., 1998—, trustee, 2004—, Bermuda Biol. Sta. for Rsch., 1998—2004, Flaschner Inst., 2000—03, TERC, 2005—. Art Gallery, U. NH, 2006—, Bigelow Lab. of Ocean Scis., 2004—06; bd. dirs. U. NH Found., 1997—2006, vice chmn., 1999—2002; bd. dirs. MIT Mus., 2000—, chmn., 2005—, Rapport Inst., 2001—, Lemelson Ctr. of the Smithsonian Inst., 2003—06; mem. bd. visitors U. Maine, Machias, 2001—07; dir. Conservation Law Found., 2004—, Boston 4 Celebrations, 2001—. Mem. AAAS, Am. Chem. Soc., Am. Assn. Mus., The Mus. Group (pres. 2005—), Harvard Faculty Club, Conservation Law Found., Mus. Sci., NH Audubon, Seacoast Sci. Ctr. Mem. United Ch. of Christ. United Ch. Christ. Avocations: woodworking, cars. Office: 6 Canal Park #710 Cambridge MA 02141 Home Phone: 603-589-1123; Office Phone: 617-494-1123.

ELLIS, DONALD LEE, lawyer; b. Oct. 2, 1950; s. Truett T. and Rosemary (Tarrant) Ellis; children: Angela Nicole, Laura Elizabeth, Natalie Dawn, Donald Lee II. BS, U. Tulsa, 1973; JD, Okla. City U., 1976. Bar: Tex. 1979, Okla. 1977, U.S. Dist. Ct. (ea. dist.) Tex. 1978, U.S. Dist. Ct. (we. dist.) Okla. 1978, U.S. Ct. Appeals (5th cir.) 1984, U.S. Ct. Appeals (11th cir.), U.S. Supreme Ct. 1984. Spl. agt. FBI, Washington, 1976—78; asst. dist. atty. Smith County, Tyler, Tex., 1979—80; mem. firm Barron & Ellis, Tyler, 1980—85; pvt. practice, 1985—. Bd. dir. Mental Health Assn. Mem.: FBI Agents Assn., Tex. Trial Lawyers Assn., Soc. Former Spl. Agts. FBI, Smith County Bar Assn., Okla. Bar Assn., Tex. Bar Assn. Home: PO Box 131221 Tyler TX 75713-1221 Office: 3311 Woods Blvd Tyler TX 75707 Office Phone: 903-597-7777.

ELLIS, DORSEY DANIEL, JR., lawyer, educator; b. Cape Girardeau, Mo., May 18, 1938; s. Dorsey D. and Anne (Stanaland) E.; m. Sondra Wagner, Dec. 27, 1962; children: Laura Elizabeth, Geoffrey Earl. BA, Maryville Coll., 1960; JD, U. Chgo., 1963; LLD, Maryville Coll., 1998. Bar: N.Y. 1967, U.S. Ct. Appeals (2d cir.) 1967, Iowa 1976, U.S. Ct. Appeals (8th cir.) 1976. Assoc. Cravath, Swaine & Moore, NYC, 1963-68; assoc. prof. U. Iowa, Iowa City, 1968-71, prof., 1971-87, v.p. fin. and univ. svcs., 1984-87, spl. asst. to pres., 1974-75; dean Washington U. Sch. Law, St. Louis, Mo., 1987-98, prof. law, 1998-99; disting. prof. law, 1999—. Vis. mem. sr. common room Mansfield Coll., Oxford U., Eng., 1972-73, 75; vis. prof. law Emory U., Atlanta, 1981-82, Victoria U., New Zealand, 1999; vis. sr. rsch. fellow Jesus Coll. Oxford U., Eng., 1998; bd. dirs. Maryville Coll., 1989-98, 99—, vis. scholar U. Va., 2003. Contbr. articles to profl. jours. Trustee Mo. Hist. Soc., St. Louis, 1995-2000. Nat. Honor scholar U. Chgo., 1960-63; recipient Joseph Henry Beale prize, 1961, Alumni award Maryville Coll., 1988. Mem. ABA, Am. Law Inst., Bar Assn. Metro St. Louis, Mound City Bar Assn., Iowa Bar Assn., AALS Acad. Resource Corps., Order of Coif. Home: 6901 Kingsbury Blvd Saint Louis MO 63130 Office: Box 1120 1 Brookings Dr Saint Louis MO 63130-4862 E-mail: ellis@wulaw.wustl.edu.

ELLIS, DWIGHT HOLMES, III, lawyer; b. New London, Conn., Aug. 4, 1947; s. Dwight Holmes, Jr. and Rebecca Ruth (Perry) E.; m. Linda Dahl Martineau, Aug. 24, 1970; children: Jenny Rebecca, Stephanie Lynn. AB cum laude, Harvard U., 1969, JD cum laude, 1972. Bar: Mass. 1972, Wis. 1977, U.S. Mil. Appeals 1973. Atty.-at-law Whyte & Hirschboeck S.C., Milw., 1977—; shareholder Whyte Hirschboeck Dudek S.C., Milw., 1982—2004; pvt. practice Milw., 2004—05; of counsel Weiss Berzowski Brady, Milw., 2005—. Pres., dir. Friends of Art, Milw. Art Mus., 1992—; treas., dir. Literary Svcs. Wis., Milw., 1992—. Capt. USAF, 1973-77. With judge adv. gen. corps. USAF. Mem. Estate Counselors Forum, Wis. Retirement Plan Profls., Ltd., State Bars Wis., Mass. Bar Assn., Arizona Bar Assn., ABA, Milw. Bar Assn., fellow Am. Coll. Trust and Estate Counsel. Avocations: reading, golf. Office: Weiss Berzowski Brady 700 N Water St Ste 1400 Milwaukee WI 53202 Office Phone: 414-276-5800. Office Fax: 414-276-0458. Business E-Mail: dhe@wbb-law.com.

ELLIS, EDWARD R., career officer; BS in Bus. Mgmt., Va. Polytechnic Inst. and State U., 1968; MA in Bus. Stats., U. Ala., 1970; grad., Squadron Officer Sch., 1975, Air Command and Staff Coll., 1984, Air War Coll., 1986, Nat. Security Mgmt. Course, 1988, Nat. War Coll., Fort Lesley J. McNair, Washington, DC, 1991, Harvard Ukranian Nat. Security Program, John F. Kennedy Sch. Govt., Harvard U., 1999. Commd. 2d lt. USAF, 1971, advanced through grades to major gen., 1998; student, undergraduate pilot tng. Craig AFB, Ala., 1971—72; T-37 instr. pilot, 43rd Flying Tng. Squadron, later, flight examiner, 29th Flying Tng. Wing, 1972—77; F-4E pilot, asst. flight comdr. 18th Tactical Fighter Squadron, Elmendorf AFB, Alaska, 1977-80; sect. comdr., ops. officer for dir. student ops. Squadron Officer Sch., Maxwell AFB, Ala., 1980-83, exec. officer to comdt., 1980-83; F-4E pilot, asst. ops. officer then ops. officer 36th Tactical Fighter Squadron, Osan Air Base, Republic of Korea, 1984-86; exec. officer to comdr. 51st Tactical Fighter Wing, Osan Air Base, Republic of Korea, 1984-86; faculty instr., comdr. 3823rd Air Command and Staff Coll. Student Squadron, Maxwell AFB, 1986-88; comdr. 35th Flying Tng. Squadron, Reese AFB, Tex., 1988-90; chief Caribbean Basin br. then chief We. Hemisphere div. Directorate of Strategic Plans and Policy, Joint Staff, Pentagon, Washington, 1991-94; chief flying tng. div. Hdqs. Air Edn. and Tng. Command, Randolph AFB, Tex., 1994-95; comdr. 71st Flying Tng. Wing, Vance AFB, Okla., 1995-97; comdt. Squadron Officer Sch., Maxwell AFB, 1997; comdr. Air Force Accession and Tng. Schs., Maxwell AFB, 1997-99; dep. comdr. 5th Allied Tactical Air Force, Vicenza, Italy, 1999—2000, Combined Air Ops. Ctr. Seven, Larissa, Greece, 2000—01; comdr. Combined Task Force Operation Northern Watch, US European Command, Incirlik AB, Turkey, 2001—02; asst. chief of staff for ops. Hdqs. Allied Air Forces Southern Europe, NATO, Naples, Italy, 2002—04; comdr. 19th Air Force, Air Edn. and Tng. Command, Randolph AFB, Tex., 2004—. Decorated Defense Superior Svc. medal with two oak leaf clusters, Legion of Merit with oak leaf clusters, Meritorious Svc. medal with four oak leaf clusters, Air medal with oak leaf cluster, Aerial Achievement medal with oak leaf cluster, Air Force Commendation medal with oak leaf cluster, NATO medal with Bronze Star (Kosovo). Office: 12FTW/PA Randolph Afb TX 78150

ELLIS, ELDON EUGENE, retired surgeon; b. Washington, Ind., July 2, 1922; s. Osman Polson and Ina Lucretia (Cochran) E.; m. Irene Eaves Clay, June 26, 1948 (dec. 1968); m. Priscilla Dean Strong, Sept. 20, 1969 (dec. Feb. 1990); children: Paul Addison, Kathe Lynn, Jonathan Clay, Sharon Anne, Eldon Eugene, Rebecca Deborah; m. Virginia Michael Ellis, Aug. 22, 1992. BA, U. Rochester, NY, 1946, MD, 1949. Intern surgery Stanford U. Hosp., San Francisco, 1949—50, resident and fellow surgery, 1950—52, 1955; Schilling fellow pathology San Francisco Gen. Hosp., 1955; ptnr. Redwood Med. Clinic, Redwood City, Calif., 1955—87, med. dir., 1984—87; semi-ret. physician, 1987—2006; med. dir. Peninsula Occupl. Health Assocs., San Carlos, Calif., 1991—94, physician, 1995—99, Sequoia Med. Clinic, Redwood City, 1999—2006; ret., 2006. Asst. clin. prof. surgery Stanford U., 1970-80; dir. Sequoia Hosp., Redwood City, 1974-82. Pres. Sequoia Hosp. Found., 1983-92, bd. dirs.; pres., chmn. bd. dirs. Bay Chamber Symphony Orch., San Mateo, Calif., 1988-91; mem. Nat. Bd. Benevolence Evang. Covenant Ch., Chgo., 1988-93; mem. mgmt. com. The Samarkand Retirement Cmty., Santa Barbara, Calif., 1991-2000; past pres. Project Hope Nat. Alumni Assn., 1992-94, bd. dirs., 1994—; med. advisor Project Hope, Russia Commonwealth Ind. States, 1992. With USNR, 1942-46, 50-52. Named Outstanding Citizen of Yr., Redwood City, 1987; recipient Disting. Svc. award, San Mateo County Med. Assn., 2005. Mem.: AMA, Calif. Thoracic Soc., Cardiovasc. Coun., San Mateo Individual Practice Assn. (treas. 1984—97), Stanford Surg. Soc., San Mateo Surg. Soc., San Mateo County Comprehensive Health Planning Coun. (v.p. 1969—70), San Mateo Med. Soc. (pres. 1969—70, Disting. Svc. award 2005), San Mateo County Heart Assn. (pres. 1961—63), Calif. Heart Assn. (pres. 1965—66), Am. Heart Assn. (v.p. 1974—75), Am. Coll. Chest Physicians, Calif. Med. Assn. Republican. Mem. Peninsula Convenant Ch. Home: 2305 Wooster Ave Belmont CA 94002-1549 Personal E-mail: eldonellis@hotmail.com.

ELLIS, EUGENE JOSEPH, cardiologist; b. Rochester, NY, Feb. 23, 1919; s. Eugene Joseph and Violet (Anderson) E.; m. Ruth Nugent, July 31, 1943; children: Eugene J., Susan Ellis Renwick, Amy Ellis Miller. AB, U. So. Calif., LA, 1941; MD, U. So. Calif., 1944; MS in medicine, U. Minn., 1950. Diplomate Am. Bd. Internal Medicine and Cardiovascular Diseases. Intern L.A. County Hosp., 1944, resident, 1946; fellowship Mayo Clinic, Rochester, Minn., 1947-51; dir. dept. cardiology St. Vincent's Hosp., LA, 1953-55, Good Samaritan Hosp., LA, 1955-84, ret., 1984; prof. clin. medicine emeritus U. So. Calif., 1984—. Mem. Med. Bd. of Calif., 1984-91; pres., 1988; pres. Div. of Med. Quality, State of Calif., 1985-89; exec. com. trustees U. Redlands, 1976-86. Lt. USN, 1944-46. Contbr. articles to profl. jours. Bd. dirs. Cancer Found. Santa Barbara, Casa Dorinda Retirement Facility, Alcohol Coun. Santa Barbara; trustee Sansum-Santa Barbara Clinic, 2002-, Santa Barbara Mus. Natural History. Lt. USN, 1944-46. Fellow Am. Coll. Cardiology, Am. Heart Assn., Am Coll. Physicians; mem. L.A. Country Club, Birnam Wood Golf Club (bd. dirs. 1994-95), Valley Club of Montecito. Republican. Avocations: golf, fly fishing. Home: 300 Hot Springs Rd 208 Santa Barbara CA 93108

ELLIS, F. EARL, JR., lawyer; b. Walterboro, S.C., Apr. 12, 1950; BA, Davidson Coll., 1972; JD, U. S.C., 1975. Bar: S.C. 1975. Ptnr. Ellis, Lawhorne, & Sims, PA, Columbia, SC, mem. Workers' Compensation Practice Group, shareholder. Spkr. in field. Pres. Columbia Green and Columbia Film Soc., Nickelodeon Theatre. Mem.: SC Self-Insurers Assn. (past pres.), Def. Rsch. Inst., SC Def. Trial Attys. Assn. (chmn. workers compensation sect. 1992—94), SC Bar Assn. (mem. ho. of delegates 1982—, pres.-elect 2003, pres. 2004—05, founder, past pres. workers' compensation sect.), Richland County Bar Assn. Office: Ellis Lawhorne & Sims PA Floor 5 1501 Main St Columbia SC 29202 also: Ellis Lawhorne & Sims PA PO Box 2285 Columbia SC 29202 Office Phone: 803-254-4190. Office Fax: 803-779-4749. E-mail: eelliss@ellislawhorne.com.

ELLIS, FRANKLIN HENRY, JR., surgeon, educator; b. Washington, Sept. 20, 1920; s. Franklin Henry and Katherine (McClintock) E.; m. Mary Jane Walsh, Dec. 2, 1978; children: Katherine de Saulles, Elizabeth Dunston (Mrs. Joseph Browning), Franklin Henry III, Margot McClintock, Laura Lawson (Mrs. David Milliken), Marie-Armide Longer (Mrs. Charles Storey), Hedrick Watson, Michael Garrison. AB, Yale U., 1941; MD, Columbia U., 1944; PhD, U. Minn., 1951. Diplomate: Am. Bd. Surgery, Am. Bd. Thoracic Surgery. Intern Bellevue Hosp., NYC, 1944-45; fellow surgery Mayo Clinic, 1945-46, 48-52, fellow thoracic surgery, 1952-53, asst. to surg. staff, 1952-53, cons. surgery, 1953-70; mem. faculty Mayo Grad. Sch. Medicine, 1952-70, prof. surgery, 1964-70, chmn. thoracic surg. sect., 1966-70; chief cardiovascular surgery Lahey Clinic Found., Boston, 1970-75; chief thoracic and cardiovascular surgery Lahey Clinic Med. Ctr., 1975-86, sr. cons., 1986-90; chmn. dept. thoracic and cardiovascular surgery New Eng. Deaconess Hosp., Boston, 1971-90; lectr. surgery Harvard Med. Sch., 1970-74, asso. clin. prof. surgery, 1974-80, clin. prof. surgery, 1980-91, prof. emeritus, 1991—. Served with USNR, 1946-48. Mem. AMA (Billings Gold medal 1955), ACS, Am. Assn. Thoracic Surgery, Internat. Soc. Surgery, Boston Surg. Soc. (pres. 1985-86), New Eng. Surg. Soc., Soc. Clin. Surgery, Soc. Vascular Surgery (pres. 1971), Soc. Thoracic Surgeons (pres. 1977), Assn. Cardiothoracic Surgeons Gt. Britain and Ireland (hon.), Am. Surg. Assn., European Assn. Cardiothoracic Surgery, European Soc. Thoracic Surgeons (hon.), Internat. Soc. Diseases of Esophagus (hon.). Home: 21 Fairmount St Brookline MA 02445-5905 Office: BI-Deaconess Med Ctr 110 Francis St Ste 2A Boston MA 02215-5501 Home Phone: 617-232-3252; Office Phone: 617-632-8388. Business E-Mail: slerman@bidmc.harvard.edu.

ELLIS, GARY, medical products executive; BS in Acctg., U. SD, Vermillion, 1978. Sr. audit mgr. Price Waterhouse; asst. corp. contr. Medtronic, Inc., 1989—92, v.p. fin. Europe, 1992—94, v.p., corp. contr., 1994—2005, treas., 1999—2005, sr. v.p., CFO, 2005—. Bd. mem. Toro Co. Chmn. Am. Heart Assn. Bd., 2007—. Mem.: Minn. Soc. CPAs. Office: Medtronic Inc 710 Medtronic Pky Minneapolis MN 55432-5604 Office Phone: 763-514-4000. Office Fax: 763-514-4879.*

ELLIS, GEORGE EDWIN, JR., chemical engineer; b. Beaumont, Tex., Apr. 14, 1921; s. George Edwin and Julia (Ryan) E. BSChemE, U. Tex., 1948; MS, U. So. Calif., 1958, MBA, 1965, MS in Mech. Engring., 1968, MS in Mgmt. Sci., 1971, Engr. in Indsl. and Systems Engring., 1979. Rsch. chem. engr. Tex. Co., Port Arthur, 1948-51, Houston and Long Beach, Calif., 1952-53, Space and Info. Divsn., N.Am. Aviation Co., Downey, Calif., 1959-61, Magna Corp., Anaheim, Calif., 1961-62; chem. process engr. AiResearch Mfg. Co., LA, 1953-57, 57-59; chem. engr. Petroleum Combustion & Engring. Co., Santa Monica, Calif., 1957, Jacobs Engring. Co., Pasadena, Calif., 1957, Sesler & Assocs., LA, 1959; rsch. specialist Marquardt Corp., Van Nuys, Calif., 1962-67; sr. project engr. Conductron Corp., Northridge, Calif., 1967-68; info. systems asst. LA Dept. Water and Power, 1969-92. Instr. thermodynamics U. So. Calif., LA, 1957. With USAAF, 1943-45. Mem. ASTM, ASME, AIChE, Inst. Supply Mgmt., Nat. Contract Mgmt. Assn., Am. Inst. Profl. Bookkeepers, Am. Soc. Safety Engrs., Am. Chem. Soc., Am. Soc. Materials, Am. Electroplaters and Surface Finishers Soc., Nat. Assn. Corrosion Engrs., Inst. Indsl. Engrs., Am. Prodn. and Inventory Control Soc., Am. Soc. Quality, Soc. for Protective Coatings, Soc. Plastics Engrs., Inst. Mgmt. Accts., Soc. Mfg. Engrs., Fedn. Socs. for Coatings Tech., Assn. Finishing Processes, Soc. Tribologists and Lubrication Engrs., Soc. Human Resources Mgmt., Soc. Engring. and Mgmt. Systems, Nat. Fire Protection Assn., Assn. for Facilities Engring., Pi Tau Sigma, Phi Lambda Upsilon, Alpha Pi Mu. Home and Office: 1344 W 20th St San Pedro CA 90732-4408

ELLIS, GEORGIANA KEHR, internist, oncologist; b. Buffalo, Jan. 25, 1947; Undergrad., SUNY, Buffalo, NY; grad. cum laude in English Lit., U. Wash., 1977; BA, U. Wash., Seattle, 1977, MD, 1982. Diplomate Am. Bd. Internal Medicine. Intern U. Wash. Affiliate, Seattle, 1982-83, resident in internal medicine, 1983-85, fellow in med. oncology, 1985-88; asst. prof. U. Wash., Seattle, 1988—99, assoc. prof., 1999—. Office: Scca Seattle Cancer Care Alliance PO Box 19023 Seattle WA 98109-1023 Office Phone: 206-288-6711. Business E-Mail: gellis@u.washington.edu.

ELLIS, HELENE RITA, social worker; b. St. Paul, Sept. 20, 1935; d. Moe and Cele (Sidletsky) Weisman; m. Bernard M. Ellis, Sept. 30, 1956; children: Miriam, Arienne, Elia, Evie. BS, U. Minn., 1956; MSW, Loyola U., 1974; PhD, Inst. Clin. Social Work, Chgo., 1996. Lic. clin. social worker, Ill.; bd. cert. diplomate. Tchr. Roosevelt High Sch., Mpls., 1957-58, Barrington (Ill.) High Sch., 1958-59; social worker Dist. #39 Schs., Wilmette, Ill., 1974—2003; pvt. practice Wilmette, 1996—. Adj. prof. Loyola U. of Chgo., 1996—; chairperson Dist. 39 Health and Safety Curriculum Project, Wilmette, 1987-92. Named Ill. Sch. Social Worker of Yr., Ill. Assn. Sch. Social Workers, 1997-98. Mem. NASW, Sch. Social Work Assn. Am., Am. Group Psychotherapy Assn., Ill. Assn. Sch. Social Workers (Social Worker of Yr. 1997-98), Pi Lambda Theta, Phi Beta Kappa, Alpha Sigma Nu. Office: 3330 Old Glenview Rd Wilmette IL 60091 Office Phone: 847-800-4408. E-mail: ellish18@comcast.net.

ELLIS, HOMER GODSEY, mathematics professor, physicist, researcher; b. Paris, Tex., Sept. 29, 1933; s. Homer Chapman Ellis and Velma Bernhardine Godsey Ellis; m. Sally Peyton Ayres, June 8, 1957; children: Owen Godsey, Sarah Peyton Ellis Repine. BA, U. Tex., Austin, 1955, MA, 1958, PhD, 1961. Rsch. engr. Autonetics Divsn. North Am. Aviation, Downey, Calif., 1956—57, Fullerton, 1959—61; asst. prof. U. Utah, Salt Lake City, 1961—62, U. Wash., Seattle, 1962—65, U. Colo., Boulder, 1967—68, assoc. prof., 1968—. Vis. asst. prof. U. Colo., 1965—67; guest scientist Internat. Ctr. Theoretical Physics, Trieste, Italy, 1974—75. Contbr. articles to profl. jours. Fellow, U. Colo., 1968, 1974—75. Mem.: Internat. Soc. Gen. Relativity and Gravitation (life). Achievements include unified explanation of cosmic inflation, acceleration, dark matter, and dark 'energy'. Avocation: travel. Office: U Colo at Boulder Math Dept 395 UCB Boulder CO 80309-0395 Home Phone: 303-499-4027; Office Phone: 303-492-7754. Office Fax: 303-492-7707. Business E-Mail: ellis@euclid.colorado.edu.

ELLIS, HUBERT LEE, retired secondary school educator; b. Wilson, NC, Sept. 1, 1924; s. Oscar Matthew Ellis and Mamie Bynum; m. Sujette Victoria Jones, Mar. 15, 1949 (dec.); children: Carlotte, Maymette, Huberlette. BS, Livingstone Coll., Salisbury, NC, 1949; MS, NC Agrl. and Tech. U., Greensboro, NC, 1983. Middle sch. tchr. Scotland County Sch., Laurinburg, NC; HS tchr. Anson County Schs., Wadesboro, NC, Morton City Schs., NC; ret. Mem. bd. election Robeson County, Lumberton, 1995—97; mem. planning and zoning com. Maxton City, NC, 1990—. Cpl. US Army, 1944—45. Recipient Vol. Svc. award, K.B. Dean Sch., 1995, Founders award, 6th Dist. Omega Psi Phi, 1996. Democrat. Methodist. Avocation: photography. Home: 703 S Patterson St PO Box 755 Maxton NC 28364-0755

ELLIS, JAMES D., telecommunications industry executive, lawyer; b. Ottumwa, Iowa, 1943; BBA, U. Iowa, Iowa City, 1965; JD, U. Mo., Columbia, 1968. Bar: Mo. 1968, US Ct. Appeals (DC cir.) 1977, Tex. 1980. Atty. Long Lines AT&T, Kansas City, Mo., 1972-74, atty. Long Lines and gen. depts. NYC, 1974—79, v.p., gen. counsel centralized svcs. Basking Ridge, NJ, 1983-84; gen. atty. Southwestern Bell Tel. Co., San Antonio, 1979-83; v.p., gen. counsel Bellcore, 1984; v.p., gen. counsel Tex. divsn. Southwestern Bell Tel. Co., Dallas, 1984—86, v.p., gen. counsel, sec. St. Louis, 1986—88; sr. v.p., gen. counsel SBC Comm., San Antonio, 1988—89, sr. exec. v.p., gen. counsel, 1989—2005, AT&T Inc. (merger of SBC Comm. & AT&T Corp.), San Antonio, 2005—. With U.S. Army, 1968-72. Office: AT&T Inc 175 E Houston St Rm 1306 San Antonio TX 78299-2933

ELLIS, JAMES G., dean, finance educator; BBA, U. N.Mex; MBA, Harvard U. With Broadway Dept. Stores, 1970—83, v.p. merchandising and developing products; pres., CEO Am. Porsche Design, 1985—90; faculty mem. Marshall Sch. Bus., U. So. Calif., 1997—, vice dean external rels, assoc. dean undergraduate bus. programs, dean, Robert R. Dockson dean's chair in bus. adminstrn., 2007—; vice provost globalization U. So. Calif. Founding dir. Profl. Bus. Bank, Pasadena, Calif.; dir. fixed income funds The Capital Group, LA. Office: Marshall Sch Bus Office of Dean Mail Code: 0802 Los Angeles CA 90089 Office Phone: 213-740-6422. Office Fax: 213-740-5432. E-mail: jellis@marshall.usc.edu.

ELLIS, J(AMES) NICHOLAS, lawyer; b. Newport News, Va., Apr. 3, 1960; s. James Byrd and Loretta Shirley (Walker) E.; m. Susan Wilson Kuhn, May 16, 1987; 1 child, James Samuel. BS in Mktg., Va. Poly. Inst. & State U., 1982; JD, Wake Forest, 1986. Bar: N.C. 1986, U.S. Dist. Ct. (ea. dist.) N.C. 1987, U.S. Ct. Appeals 1988, US Supreme Ct. Tech. engr. N.N. Shipbuilding, Newport News, Va., 1982-83; law clk. Judge Thomas M. Moore, US Bankruptcy Ct. Ea. Dist. NC, Wilson, 1986-87; assoc. Ward & Smith, New Bern, NC, 1987—91; ptnr., bus. litig. Poyner & Spruill LLP, Rocky Mount, NC, 1991—. Instr. of basic law enforcement Craven Community Coll., New Bern, 1988; co-chmn. NC Gen. Assembly Civil Litig. Study Commn., 2000. Mem. ABA, NC Bar Assn. (chmn. litig. sect. 1999-2000, bd. gov. 2001-04), NC Assn. Def. Attys. (dir. 1998-2001, exec. v.p. 2002, pres. 2004), Craven County Bar Assn., Ea. NC Inn of Ct. (v.p. 2003-04, pres. 2005-06). Avocations: bicycling, running. Office: Poyner & Spruill LLP 130 S Franklin St Rocky Mount NC 27804 Office Phone: 252-972-7115. Office Fax: 252-972-7045. Business E-Mail: jnellis@poynerspruill.com.

ELLIS, JAMES OTTO, secondary school educator; b. Orange, Tex., Dec. 14, 1949; s. Eric A. and Bessie (Burkart) Ellis; m. Rhonda Gordon, Aug. 3, 1974; children: Erin, Daniel. BA in Govt., Lamar U., Beaumont, Tex., 1972, MA in Govt., 1977. Cert. secondary tchr. Tex. Grad. tchg. asst. Lamar U., 1972—74; tchr. West Hardin County Consolidated Ind. Sch. Dist., Saratoga, Tex., 1974—75, Humble Ind. Sch. Dist., Tex., 1975—. Adj. instr. North Harris County Coll., Houston, 1977—79, Houston CC Sys., 1978—. Mem. exec. com. Rep. Party Harris County, Houston, 1976—80, 1982—90; mem. exec. bd. Bapt. Gen. Convention Tex., Dallas, 1996—2002; deacon Woodridge Bapt. Ch., Humble, 2000—; bd. dirs. Harris County MUD # 109, Humble, 1988—96. Mem.: Assn. Tex. Profl. Educators, Masons. Office: Humble HS 1700 Wilson Rd Humble TX 77338-6118

ELLIS, JOE W., federal agency administrator; Asst. sec. adminstrn. and mgmt. HHS, 2005—. Office: US Dept Health and Human Services 200 Independence Ave SW Washington DC 20201 Office Phone: 202-690-7431. Office Fax: 202-401-5207. E-mail: Joe.Ellis@hhs.gov.

ELLIS, JOHN, retired school system administrator, writer; b. Amherst, Ohio, Sept. 15, 1929; s. Edward Pierson and Jean (Scott) E.; m. Carolyn Elizabeth Collier, Dec. 29, 1951; children: Linda Ellis Wieand, Jeanine Ellis Klausing, Jeanette Ellis Hale, John Edward. BS, Bowling Green State U., 1953; MA, Case Western Res. U., Cleve., 1958; EdD, Harvard U., 1964. Tchr. pub. schs., Lorain, Ohio, 1953-54, prin., 1957-61, from asst. supt. to supt. schs. Massillon, Ohio, 1963-66, supt. schs. Lakewood, Ohio, 1966-71, Columbus, Ohio, 1971-77; exec. dep. commr. edn. U.S. Office Edn., Washington, 1977-80; supt. schs. pub. schs., Austin, Tex., 1980-90; commr. NJ Dept. Edn., 1990—92. Adj. prof. ednl. adminstrn. Ohio State U., Columbus, 1971-77. Author: Bonville Search, 2006. Elder local Presbyn. Ch. With USAF, 1947-49, 54-57. Recipient Massillon Young Man of Yr. award, 1965; named to Saturday Rev. Honor Roll, 1977. Mem. Rotary, Phi Delta Kappa, Pi Kappa Alpha, Phi Alpha Theta, Kappa Delta Pi, Gamma Theta Upsilon. Home: 500 Leath Hollow Dr Wimberley TX 78676-5207

ELLIS, JOHN, urban designer; BA, MA, Cambridge U., Eng. Designer Anshen & Allen, San Fancisco; sr. designer Kaplan McLaughlin Diaz, San Francisco; ptnr. Solomon, ETC (a WRT Co.), San Francisco, 1996—99, prin., 2000—02, dir. urban design, 2002—. Adj. prof. Calif. Coll. Arts and Crafts, San Francisco, 1984; contbg. writer Arch. Rev., London, 1984;

designs include Oakland Fed. Bldg., Plaza Tower, Sacramento, Reno Fed. Courthouse, Flood Bldg. renovation. Mem.: RIBA, AIA. Office: Solomon ETC 1328 Mission St 4th Fl San Francisco CA 94103

ELLIS, JOHN HUBERT, retired history professor; b. Memphis, Sept. 29, 1931; s. John Hubert Ellis and Esther Verlin Sides; m. Wanda Ann Roper, July 1, 1949; children: Elaine Tucci, John, Suzanne Panick. BA, Memphis State Coll., 1955; MA, Memphis State U., 1958; PhD, Tulane U., 1962. Asst. prof. Memphis State U., 1960—64, Ga. State Coll., Atlanta, 1964—65; post-doctoral fellow Nat. Inst. of Gen. Med. Scis., New Orleans, 1965—67; assoc. prof. Georgetown Coll., Ky., 1967—71; prof. Lehigh U., Bethlehem, Pa., 1971—93; ret. Dir. Ctr. for Health Scis., Lehigh U., Bethlehem, 1971—77. Bd. of editors Chiropractic Hist. Jour., Davenport, Iowa, 1987—92; author: Medicine in Kentucky, 1977, Yellow Fever & Public Health in New South, 1992 (Book of Yr., 1992). Sgt. USAF, 1948—51. Danforth fellow, Danforth Found., 1980—86, Penrose Summer fellow, Am. Philos. Soc., 1975. Mem.: Nat. Assn. of Scholars, So. Hist. Assn. Avocations: reading, gardening.

ELLIS, JOSEPH JOHN MICHAEL, III, historian, professor; b. Washington, July 18, 1943; s. Joseph J. and Jeanette H. (Sigafoose) E.; m. Ellen Wilkins; children: Peter, Scott. BA, William and Mary Coll., 1965; MA, Yale U., 1967, PhD, 1969. Asst. prof. U.S. Mil. Acad., West Point, N.Y., 1969-72, Mount Holyoke Coll., South Hadley, Mass., 1972-75, assoc. prof., 1975-79, prof. history, 1979—, dean, 1980—90. Bd. dirs. Progressive Policy Inst. Author: The New England Mind in Transition: Samuel Johnson of Connecticut, 1696-1772, 1972, School for Soldiers: West Point and the Profession of Arms, 1974, After the Revolution: Profiles of Early American Culture, 1979, Passionate Sage: The Character and Legacy of John Adams, 1993, American Sphinx: The Character of Thomas Jefferson (Nat. Book award, 1997), 1997, Founding Brothers: The Revolutionary Generation (Pulitzer prize, 2001), 2000, His Excellency George Washington, 2004. Mem. exec. com. Mass. Found. for Humanities, 1978-81. Served to capt. U.S. Army 1969-72. Nat. Endowment for Humanities fellow, 1976-77, Guggenheim fellow, 1988-89. Mem. Am. Hist. Assn., Inst. Early Am. History and Culture, Nat. Humanities Faculty, William and Mary alumni Assn. (bd. dirs.), Progressive Policy Inst., Phi Beta Kappa.

ELLIS, JOSEPH NEWLIN, retired wholesale distribution executive; b. Tenn., Oct. 19, 1928; s. Richard M. and Pearl A. (Fuqua) E.; m. Barbara Harpster, Sept. 17, 1955; 1 child, Patricia Anne. BS, Northwestern U., 1954. Co-founder LaSalle-Deitch Co., Inc., Elkhart, Ind., 1963, exec. v.p., 1969-72, pres., CEO, 1972—89, chmn. of the bd., CEO, 1989-94; ret., 1994. With U.S. Army, 1950-52. Home: 1160 Benders Ferry Rd Gallatin TN 37066-5703

ELLIS, KATHERYN, finance company executive; b. Indpls., 1975; d. David William and Monica Ann Ellis. BA, Ind. U., Bloomington, 1998; MBA, U. Chgo., 2005. Commd. examiner Fed. Res. Bank Chgo., 1998—2006; sr. fin. analyst Fed. Res. Bd. Govs., Washington, 2006—. Mem.: Smithsonian Young Benefactors (assoc.). Office: Federal Reserve Board of Governors 20th and C St NW Washington DC 20551 Home Phone: 773-860-3343; Office Phone: 202-452-5276. Personal E-mail: kellis@alumni.uchicago.edu.

ELLIS, LAUREL GLYNN, retired entrepreneur; s. Otis Vernon and Adeline Ellis; m. Myra June Horten, Oct. 5, 1956; children: William Gregory, Catherine DeAnn, Judith Carol, Kimberly June. BA, E.Tex. State U., Commerce, 1956. Salesman Weyenberg Shoe Mfg. Co., Tex., 1956—70; owner Fairway Shoe Store, Wills Point, Tex., Fairway Security, Wills Point, Tex., Wills Point Investment Grp., Ellis Glen Longhorn Registered Cattle Co., Wills Point. Chmn. bd. Citizen Nat. Bank, Wills Point. Pres. Wills Point Hist. Soc.; trustee Wills Point ISD; councilman Wills Point City Coun.; elder Wills Point Ch. Christ; bd. dirs. Wills Point C. of C.; pres., v.p. Econ. Devel. Com., Wills Point; bd. mem. Rock Hill Cemetery Assn., Wills Point, White Rose Cemetery, Tex. Sgt. USMC, 1951—54, N. Korea. Decorated Battle Star USMC; named Outstanding Citizen, Vanzandt County; recipient Purple Heart, USMC, Campaign ribbon, Disting. Vets. award, Washington. Mem.: Marine Corps. Heritage Found., VFW, Disabled Veterans Assn. (life), 1st Marine Divsn. Veterans Assn. (life), Wills Point Hist. Soc., Wills Point Rotary Club, Wills Point Antique Tractor Club, Am. Legion. Personal E-mail: glynn68@sbcglobal.net.

ELLIS, LAWRENCE DOBSON, internist, educator; b. Pitts., Oct. 11, 1932; s. Robert S. and Elizabeth (Dobson) E.; m. Jacqueline Coogan, June 8, 1954; children: Christine, Thomas, Holly Anne, Jerome. BS, U. Notre Dame, 1954; MD, U. Pitts., 1958. Diplomate Am. Bd. Internal Medicine. Intern in internal medicine U. Pitts. Health Center Hosps., 1958-59; resident in internal medicine Presbyn.-Univ. Hosp., Pitts., 1959-60, 62-63, fellow in hematology, 1963-64; practice medicine specializing in internal medicine, hematology and oncology Pitts., from 1964; clin. asst. prof. medicine U. Pitts., 1966-71; clin. assoc. prof. U. Pitts, 1971-81; clin. prof. U. Pitts., from 1981; prof. medicine Presbyn.-Univ. Hosp., 1994—, mem. active staff, sec., treas. med. staff, 1972-76, v.p. med. staff, 1976-78, pres., from 1978. Mem. cons. staff Shadyside Hosp., Pitts., from 1964, Allegheny County Bd. Health, from 1976; bd. commrs. Health Edn. Ctr., Pitts., from 1976; mem. Pa. State Bd. Medicine, from 1986, vice chmn. 1987; mem. active staff Montefiore Hosp. Contbr. articles to profl. jours., chpts. to med. books. Trustee Leukemia Soc. Am., from 1972, chmn. profl. edn., from 1973, nat. pres., 1985-87; trustee Presbyn.-Univ. Hosp., from 1981, U. Pitts., from 1986. Served to lt. M.C. USN, 1960-62. Recipient Bicentennial medallion of distinction U. Pitts., 1987, honors convocation, 1989. Fellow ACP, Royal Soc. Medicine London; mem. AMA, Pa. Med. Soc. (del. 1974), Allegheny County Med. Soc. (pres. 1976, chmn. bd. 1977, bd. dirs. from 1970, Frederick M. Jacob Physician of Merit award 1981), Pitts. Acad. Medicine (pres. 1984), Royal Soc. Medicine, N.Y. Acad. Scis., Am. Soc. Hematology, Leukemia Soc. Am. (exec. com. from 1978, John J. Kenny award 1981, Spiral of Life award 1988), Med. Alumni Assn. U. Pitts. (pres. 1979-80), Alpha Omega Alpha. Clubs: Pitts. Field, Univ., Pitts. Athletic Assn. Republican. Roman Catholic. Office Phone: 412-687-1210.

ELLIS, LESLIE ELAINE, psychotherapist; d. Ira Milton and Evelyn Fogel Marks; m. Clyde Arthur Ellis, Jr., Feb. 16, 1969; children: David Michael, Eric Arthur. BA in Psychology, U. Fla., 1969, MA in Rehab. Counseling, 1972; PhD in Theatre, Fla. State U., 1982; MA in Psychology, Fielding Grad. Inst., 2002, PhD in Clin. Psychology, 2004. Cert. Rehab. Counselor Commn. Rehab. Counselor Certification, Rolling Meadows, Ill., Clin. Supr. Fla., lic. Mental Health Counselor, qualified rehab. profl. Instr. acting Fla. State U., 1982; instr. speech North Fla. Jr. Coll., Madison, Fla., 1983; dir. academic svcs. Profl. Employment Tng. Inc., Svcs., Clearwater, Fla., 1988—91; intern rehab. counseling Cognitive Rehab. Inst., Tampa, Fla., 1994—95; pvt. practice counselor, 1995—2003; intern clin. counseling Bay Area Psychol. Svcs., St. Petersburg, Fla., 1996—98; with Wein Ctr. Memory Disorders Mt. Sinai Hosp., Miami, Fla., 2001; intern neuropsychology Rehab. Solutions, Tampa, 2002—03; intern clin. psychology Counseling Ctr. U. South Fla., 2002—03; clin. dir. Genesis Behavioral Healthcare, Tampa; pres., clin. dir. Nat. Ednl. Training Sys. Inc., Lutz, Fla. Adj. instr. St. Petersburg (Fla.) Coll., 1991—94; adj. faculty Argosy U., Tampa, 2004—; mem. com. Nat. Rehab. Counselors Cert. Exam, Princeton, NJ, 2002, Princeton, 04; cons. in field; presenter in field. Author: Lose Weight By Surgery, 1974, Nutrition Guide to Brand Name Baby Foods, 1977, Teacher's Guide to Dramatic Techniques for Use with Handicapped Students, 1982; actor(dancer): (plays) Desire Under the Elms, 1979; author (dir.): (films) Teenaged and Pregnant, 1982, (plays) Merfel's Magic Wand, 1982; dir.: (plays) Ghost of Canterville Hall, 1984; author: (songs) Theme Song Leon County Spl. Olympics, 1983; co-author: (plays) The Trial of Ruby McCollum, 2003 (Honorable Mention award Sundance, 2003); contbr. articles to profl. jours., newspapers, mags. Mem. spl. events com. Fla. State Spl. Olympics, 1980—83; adv. bd. Thomas County Schs., 1985—86; adv. com. Career Devel. Ctr. Thomas Area Tech. Sch., 1985; chmn. pubs. Am. Theatre Assn., 1982—83. Recipient Disting. Performance Design Spl. Needs Program, Nat. Alliance Bus., 1987, Outstanding Performance award, Gov. Ga., 1987, Gov. Fla., 1989. Mem.: APA (student sci. com. 1999—2003), Phi Kappa Phi, Eta Rho Pi. Democrat. Jewish. Achievements include patents for book hanging device. Office: Nat Ednl Training Sys Inc 207 Crystal Grove Blvd Lutz FL 33548 Personal E-mail: lesliee@tampabay.rr.com.

ELLIS, LESTER NEAL, JR., lawyer; b. Washington, Aug. 1, 1948; s. Lester Neal and Marie (Brooks) E. BS, U.S. Mil. Acad., 1970; JD, U. Va., 1975. Bar: Va. 1975, U.S. Ct. Appeals (5th cir.) 1977, D.C. 1978, U.S. Ct. Appeals (4th and D.C. cirs.) 1979, U.S. Ct. Appeals (11th cir.) 1982, N.C. 1985, U.S. Supreme Ct. 2000, U.S. Dist. Ct. (ea., mid., we. dists.) N.C., U.S. Dist. Ct. (ea., we. dists.) Va., U.S. Ct. Claims. Trial atty. litig. divsn. Office of JAG, U.S. Dept. Army, Washington, 1975-78; assoc. Hunton & Williams, Richmond, Va., 1978-84, ptnr. Raleigh, NC, 1984—. Maj. U.S. Army, 1970-78, col. USAR, 1993-99. Recipient Judge Paul Brosman award U.S. Ct. Mil. Appeals, 1975. Mem.: ABA (chair tort and trial practice steering com., editor-in-chief Tort Source, chair comml. torts commn., chair trial techniques com., tort and ins. practice sect., editor-in-chief Tort and Ins. Law Jour., coun. mem., sect. coun.), D.C. Bar Assn. (Wake County bd. elections 1986—93, chmn. 1987—93, ct. rules com.), Va. Bar Assn. (spl. issues com. 1982), Phi Kappa Phi. Republican. Presbyterian. Home: 1116 Wagon Ridge Rd Raleigh NC 27614 Office: Hunton & Williams One Bank of Am Plz PO Box 109 Raleigh NC 27602-0109 Office Phone: 919-899-3019. Business E-Mail: nellis@hunton.com.

ELLIS, LISA, music company executive; BS in Mktg., Univ. Md., 1991. Mktg. mgr. Pepsi-Cola Co., 1990—92; promotions mktg. dir. WPGC CBS Radio, Washington, 1992—94; sports mktg. mgr. Reebok Internat., 1994—95; local promotion mgr. Columbia Records, 1995—98, nat. dir., crossover promotion, 1998—2000, v.p. nat. promotion West Coast and v.p. crossover promotion, 2000—02, sr. v.p. R&B/rhythm crossover promotion, 2002—03; sr. v.p. strategic mktg., music licensing Sony Music, 2003—04; gen. mgr. to pres. Sony Urban Music, 2004—05; pres. Sony Music Label Group, 2005—. Named Local Promotion Mgr. Yr., Street Info. Network, 1997, Crossover Exec. Yr., 1998, 1999, Gavin's Crossover Exec. Yr., 1998, 1999, FMQB's Crossover Exec. Yr., 1999; named one of America 's Top Women in Bus.-Game Changers, Pink mag. & Forté Found., 2007; recipient Radio Music award for Crossover Exec. Yr., 2000. Office: Sony Music Label Group 550 Madison Ave New York NY 10001*

ELLIS, LLOYD H., JR., emergency physician, art historian; b. Denver, Apr. 7, 1936; s. Lloyd Harris and Lura Lou (Wallace) E.; m. Nancy Kay Greenamyre, June 4, 1962 (div. June 1979); children: Peter, Amanda Hunt Thurber; m. Eva Marie Bevan, Sept. 1, 1984; children: Gwendolyn Ruth, David Bevan. Grad., Candiate Sch., 1957; BA, Yale U., New Haven, Conn., 1960, MA, 1961; MD, Case Western Reserve U., Cleve., 1970; MA, Case Western Reserve U., 1990, PhD, 2002. Diplomate Am. Bd. Emergency Medicine. Farm mgr., Hastings, Nebr., 1961-62; vice consul Dept. of State, Lourenco Marques, Mozambique, 1963-64, intelligence analyst Washington, 1965-66; intern, resident Case Western Res. U. Hosps., 1970—74, thoracic surgery resident, 1975—76; dir. emergency dept. Univ. Hosps., Cleve., 1976-84, emergency physician, 1985-94, Emergency Profl. Svcs., Wooster, Ohio, 1995-96, Chardon, Ohio, 1997, Warren, Ohio, 1998. Instr. in surgery Case Western Reserve U., Cleve., 1976-78, asst. prof. surgery, 1979-94; mng. ptnr. Ellis Family Ltd. Partnership, 1992—. Med. dir. Cleve. Emergency Svc., 1976-94; pres. Jeffrey Wallace Ellis Found., Hastings, 1993—; sr. warden Good Shepard, Lyndhurst, Ohio, 1985-86; jr. warden St. Christopher's, Gates Mills, 1998, sr. warden, 1999, Diocesan Coun., 1999-2002; trustee Lura Lou Wallace Ellis Trust, 1992-. 1st Lt. Armor, 1956-59. Recipient Ford scholar Ford Found., New Haven, 1952-55. Mem. Am. Coll. Emergency Physicians, Am. Acad. Emergency Medicine, Rowfant Club. Republican. Episcopalian. Home and Office: 32250 Woodsdale Ln Cleveland OH 44139-1335

ELLIS, LYNN WEBSTER, retired finance educator, telecommunications consultant; b. San Mateo, Calif., Feb. 27, 1928; s. Lynn Webster, Sr. and Mary Eleanor (Barstow) Ellis; m. Eileen Mary Gallagher; children: Lynn W. Jr., Margaret, Katherine. BEE, Cornell U., 1948; MS, Stevens Inst. Tech., 1954; D Profl. Studies in Mgmt., Pace U., 1979. Exec. ITT Corp., 1948-79; v.p. engring. Bristol Babcock Co., Waterbury, Conn., 1980-82; cons. Lynn W. Ellis Assocs., Westport, Conn., 1982-85; prof. U. New Haven, West Haven, Conn., 1985-94, scholar-in-residence, 1994-97, prof. emeritus, 1997—. Author: Evaluating R&D Processes, 1996, Financial Side of Industrial Research Management, 1984; contbr. articles to profl. jours.; patentee in field. Mem. five panels and coms. NRC, Washington, 1970—95; chmn. adv. com. Dept. of Commerce, Washington, 1973—75. Capt. US Army, 1948—52. Fellow: AAAS, IEEE (Internat. Communication award 1983).

ELLIS, MARY LOUISE HELGESON, retired healthcare technology company executive; b. Albert Lea, Minn., May 29, 1943; d. Stanley Orville and Neoma Lois (Guthier) Helgeson; m. David Readinger, Nov. 5, 1994; children from previous marriage: Christopher, Tracy. BS in Pharmacy, U. Iowa, 1966; MA in Pub. Adminstrn., Iowa State U., 1982, postgrad., 1982—83. Faculty Duquesne U., Pitts., 1977; cons. in pharmacy Colville, Wash., 1978—79; dir. pharmacy Mt. Carmel Hosp., Colville, 1978—79; clin. pharmacist Iowa Vets. Home, Marshalltown, 1980—81; instr. Iowa Valley C.C., Marshalltown, 1981—83; dir. Iowa Dept. Substance Abuse, Des Moines, 1983—86, State of Iowa Pub. Health, Iowa Dept. Pub. Health, Des Moines, 1986—90; spl. cons. health affairs Blue Cross/Blue Shield of Iowa, 1990—91; v.p. Blue Cross/Blue Shield of Iowa and S.D., 1991—2000, ret., 2000; pvt. practice cons. in field, 2001—05; v.p. Medicare, Affiliated Computer Svcs., 2005—07, ret., 2007. Chair Iowa Health Data Commn., Des Moines, 1986—90; bd. dirs. Health Policy Corp. Iowa, 1986—90; adj. asst. prof. U. Iowa, Iowa City, 1984—; commd. officer U.S. FDA, 1989—90; mem. alumnae bd. dirs. U. Iowa Coll. of Pharmacy, 1989—; chair Nat. Commn. Accreditation of Ambulance Svcs., 1992—97; commencement spkr. U. Iowa, Coll. Pharmacy, Iowa City, 2003. Mem. Iowa State Bd. Health, 1981—83, v.p., 1982—83; mem. adv. coun. Iowa Valley C.C., 1983—85. Named Alumnae of Yr., U. Iowa Coll. Pharmacy, 2005; recipient Woman of Achievement award, Des Moines YWCA, 1988. Mem.: APHA, Iowa Pub. Health Assn. (bd. dirs., Henry Albert award 1990), Iowa Pharmacists Assn., Pi Sigma Alpha, Phi Kappa Phi, Alpha Xi Delta. Republican. Home: 212 Lariat Ct Spearfish SD 57783

ELLIS, MISSIE LYNNE, music educator; b. Pitts., July 22, 1975; d. Gary Edward and Linda Clymer Ellis. B in Music Edn., Fla. So. Coll., 1998. Dir. bands Meadowbrook Mid. Sch., Orlando, Fla., 1998—2001, Lakeview Mid. Sch., Winter Garden, Fla., 2001—. Dir. all-county honors band Orange County Pub. Schs., 2005—. Deacon Wekiva Presbyn. Ch., Longwood, Fla., 2005—. Named Tchr. of Yr. at Meadowbrook Mid. Sch., Orange County Pub. Schs., 2002. Mem.: Nat. Assn. for Music Edn., Fla. Music Educators Assn., Fla. Band Masters Assn. Republican. Presbyterian. Avocations: golf, walking, reading, shopping, computers. Office: Lakeview Mid Sch 1200 W Bay St Winter Garden FL 34787 Home Phone: 407-963-3792; Office Phone: 407-877-5010 ext 275. Office Fax: 407-877-5019. Business E-Mail: ellism4@ocps.net.

ELLIS, MONTA, professional basketball player; b. Oct. 26, 1985; s. Rosa Ellis. Diploma, Lanier HS, Jackson, Miss., 2005. Player Golden State Warriors, Calif., 2005—. Named EA Sports Player of Yr., 2005, Mr. Basketball, Miss., 2005, Nat. Co-Player of Yr., Parade Mag., 2005, Most Improved Player, NBA, 2007. Mailing: Golden State Warriors 1011 Broadway Oakland CA 94607*

ELLIS, BROTHER PATRICK (H. J.), academic administrator; b. Balt., Nov. 17, 1928; s. Harry James and Elizabeth Alida (Evert) E. AB, Cath. U. Am., Washington, 1951; AM, U. Pa., Phila., 1954, PhD, 1960; postgrad., Barry Coll., 1963-64, Inst. Catholique, Paris, 1958; LHD (hon.), Assumption Coll., Worcester, Mass., 1982, La Salle U., Phila., 1992; HHD (hon.), King's Coll., 1987; LLD (hon.), U. Scranton, Pa., 1988, C.C. Phila., 1992, Quincy U., Ill., 1993; PdD, Manhattan Coll., Riverdale, NY, 1993; DEd, Anna Maria Coll., Paxton, Mass., 1993, Loyola U., 1997; LHD (hon.), Villa Julie Coll., Stevenson, Md., 2002. Joined Bros. of Christian Schs., Roman Cath. Ch., 1946. Tchr. English dept. West Cath. High Sch. for Boys, Phila., 1951-60, chmn. English dept., 1956-58, guidance dir., 1959-60; dir. practice teaching, sch. prin. St. Gabriel's Hall, Phoenixville, Pa., summers 1960-61, 65-66; asst. prof. English La Salle U., Phila., 1960-62, assoc. prof., 1968-73, prof., 1973—, dir. housing, 1961-62, dir. honors program, 1964-69, dir. devel., v.p., 1969-76, pres., 1977-92; prin. La Salle HS, Miami, Fla., 1962—64; pres. Cath. U. Am., Washington, 1992-98. Author: Called To Teach: Persons Are Forever, 2001; condg. author: series for How To Read Gt. Books, U. of the Air, WFIL-TV, Phila., 1961, 65; contbr. opinion column to Balt. Cath. Rev., articles to profl. publs. Trustee Manhattan Coll., NYC, Calvert Hall H.S., Balt., to 2001, St. Mary's Coll. Calif, St. Mary's U. Minn.; bd. dirs. Cathedral Found. Balt., 2004-, Phila. Cath. Charities, 1986-92, Greater Phila. Urban Coalition, Police Athletic League, Phila., Free Libr. Phila., 1991-92, Del. Valley Citizens Crime Commn., Fed. City Coun., DC Econ. Club, DC Bd. Trade; former trustee Cmty. Leadership Seminars, BBB; mem. recognition com. Coun. for Higher Edn. Accreditation, 1999-2001 Recipient Lindback award for disting. teaching LaSalle Coll., Phila., 1965 Mem. Sunday Breakfast Club (Phila.), Phila. Club, Univ. Club (Washington), Phi Beta Kappa, Knights of Holy Sepulchre. Home and Office: Calvert Hall HS 8102 La Salle Rd Baltimore MD 21286-8022 Office Phone: 410-296-6031. E-mail: brotherpatrickellis@erols.com.

ELLIS, RAYMOND CLINTON, JR., retired hotel executive; b. Chgo., May 11, 1921; s. Raymond Clinton and Frances Geraldine (Hersma) Ellis. Grad. cert. Pers. Psychology, Ohio State U., 1943; PhB, U. Chgo., 1950, MBA, 1953; grad. cert. Orgn. Mgmt., Syracuse U., 1962. Cert. hospitality tech. profl.; cert. lodging security dir.; cert. hospitality educator. Various positions Marshall Field & Co., Chgo., 1938-52, safety dir., 1953-55; staff rep., dir. small bus. program Nat. Safety Coun., Chgo., 1955-61; dir. mem. rels. Variety Stores Assocs., NYC, 1961-64; fleet safety coord. Am. Ins. Assn., NYC, 1964-67; group adminstr. Hotel Safety Group, NYC, 1967-77; dir. risk mgmt. and ops. Am. Hotel and Motel Assn., NYC, 1977-92; exec. v.p. Am. Hotel and Motel Assn. Gen. Agy., Inc., NYC, 1977-92; sec., project dir. Am. Hotel and Motel Assn. Rsch. Found., NYC, 1977-92; tchr. facilities mgmt loss prevention mgmt. Conrad N. Hilton Coll. Hotel Restaurant Mgmt., U. Houston, 1994—2007; ret., 2007. Sec. bd. trustees Hotel Assn. Group Trust, 1977-2003; mem. occupational safety and health com. Bus. Rsch. Adv. Coun., Bur. Labor Stats., U.S. Dept. Labor, 1971—; mem. overseas security adv. coun. U.S. Dept. State, 1989-2005; security cons. to lodging industry, 1993-94; ops. cons. Am. Hotel and Motel Assn., 1993-94; apptd. adj. prof. hotel and restaurant mgmt. Conrad N. Hilton Coll. of Hotel and Restaurant Mgmt., U. Houston, 1994—07, dir. tech. rsch. and edn. ctr., 1994-97, dir. loss prevention mgmt. inst., 1994—; mem. consumer adv. coun. Underwriters Labs., 1984-2006. Author: Security and Loss Prevention Management for the Lodging Industry, 1985, 2d edit., 1999; editor: Student Manual-Security Course, 1978, Security and Loss Prevention Management Manual, 1996, A Guide to Occupational Safety and Health Standards Compliance for the Lodging Industry, 1997; contbr. articles to profl. jours.; mem. tech. bd. Hotel & Motel Mgmt. Mag., 1988-97; mem. editl. bd. Hospitality Law, 1990-2001, 05—; pub. monthly loss prevention bull. Am. Hotel and Lodging Assn., 1995—, prevention sect. Lodging Law, 1998-07; photos shown at The Midway Club, U. Chgo. Grad. Sch. of Bus., 2004 Elder N.Y. Ave. Presbyn. Ch., Washington. With USAAF, 1943-46, ATO. Named to Hospitality Tech. Hall of Fame, Hospitality Fin. and Tech. Profls., 1989, Lamp of Knowledge award for Outstanding Educator, Edn. Inst. Am. Hotel & Motel Assn., 1999, Dean's award for teaching excellence Conrad N. Hilton Coll., U. Houston, 2002, Ray Ellis, Jr. Endowment, Conrad H. Hilton Coll., Hospitality Fin. & Tech. Profls., 2004. Mem. ASTM, Am. Soc. Safety Engrs. (Appreciation Plaque 2004), Vets. of Safety, Nat. Fire Protection Assn. (mem. exec. com. and dir. lodging sect., dir. emeritus 2004), Nat. Safety Coun. (hon. life; Disting. Svc. to Safety award 1986, mem. exec. com. svcs. 1994-04, retail and logistics divsn.), Am. Soc. Indsl. Security (mem. lodging sect. 2000-05, Ray Ellis Jr. Lodging Security ann. award named in his honor 2000-05), Phi Beta Delta. Independent. Avocation: travel. Home: 4444 Cullen Blvd Apt 105 Houston TX 77004-2624 E-mail: rellis@uh.edu.

ELLIS, RICHARD W., lawyer; b. Raleigh, NC, Apr. 20, 1942; AB, U. N.C., 1964, JD with high honors, 1969. Bar: N.C. 1969. Mem. Ellis & Winters, Raleigh. Assoc. editor N.C. Law Rev., 1968-69. With USNR, 1964-66. Mem. Am. Coll. Trial Lawyers, Interant. Assn. Def. Counsel, Def. Rsch. Inst., N.C. Assn. Def. Attys., Order of Coif. Office: Ellis & Winters LLP PO Box 33550 Raleigh NC 27636 Office Phone: 919-865-7007. Business E-Mail: dick.ellis@elliswinters.com.

ELLIS, ROBERT HARRY, retired broadcast executive, academic administrator; b. Cleve., Mar. 2, 1928; s. John George Ellis and Grace Bernice (Lewis) Ellis Kline; m. Frankie Jo Lanter, Aug. 7, 1954; children: Robert Harry Jr., Kimberley Kay Ellis Murphy, Shana Ellis Antonio. BA, Ariz. State U., 1953; MA, Case Western Res. U., 1962. Newswriter, announcer Sta. KOY, Phoenix, 1953-55, continuity dir., 1955-61; dir., radio ops. Ariz. State U., Tempe, 1959-61; gen. mgr. Sta. KAET-TV, Tempe, 1961-87; assoc. v.p. Ariz. State U., Tempe, 1986-90. Exec. com. bd. dirs. Pub. Broadcasting Svc., Washington, 1972-77, 80-86; founder Pacific Mountain Network, Denver, 1972, pres., 1973-75; mem. ednl. telecomm. com. Nat. Assn. Ednl. Broadcasters, Washington, 1973-77, 80-86. Mem. Sister City, Tempe, Tempe Ctr. For the Handicapped, East Valley Mental Health Alliance, Mesa, Ariz., Ariz. Acad., State Ariz. Behavior Health Bd. of Examiners, 1991-92. Recipient Bd. Govs. award Pacific Mountain Network, 1987, achievement award Ariz. State U., 1997; named to Ariz. Broadcasters Hall of Fame, 1999. Mem. Nat. Assn. TV Arts and Scis. (life, v.p., bd. trustees 1969-70, bd. dirs. Phoenix chpt. 1986, silver circle award 1992), Nat. Assn. Pub. TV Stas. (bd. dirs. 1988-94), Tempe C. of C. (diplomate, bd. dirs. 1987-90), Sundome Performing Arts Assn. (bd. dirs. 1986-90), Ariz. Zool. Soc. (bd. dirs., sec. 1984-90), Ariz. State U. Alumni Assn. (life), Ariz. State U. Retirees Assn. (founder, pres. 1991-92), Tempe Conv. and Visitors Bur. (founder, sec./treas. 1988-93), Tempe Sports Authority (founder 1989-95), ASU Faculty Emeritus Orgn. (pres. 1992-93). Methodist. Avocations: tennis, bridge. E-mail: bobhellis@cox.net.

ELLIS, ROSEMARY, editor-in-chief; Sr. editl. positions Working Woman, Self, Travel & Leisure; exec. editor Time Inc. Interactive, Time Inc. New Media; web site dir, exec. editor Expedia Travels; cons. Real Simple, AOL Web Properties divsn.; sr. v.p., editl. dir. Prevention Mag., 2003—06; editor-in-chief Good Housekeeping, 2006—. Mem.: Am. Soc. Mag. Editors (bd. dirs. 2007—). Office: Good Housekeeping Hearst Corp 300 W 57th St New York NY 10019-5288 Office Phone: 212-649-2200.*

ELLIS, ROSS, non-profit organization executive; Co-owner Visions & Images; pres. Elegant Events; v.p., dir. corp. affairs and events pharm. comm. co.; dir. resource devel. child abuse prevention group; founder, CEO Love Our Children, USA, 1999—. Active with Starlight Children's Found.; mem Phillip Morris Domestic Violence Coun. Mem.: NY Entertainment Publicists Soc. (bd. dirs.), NY Women's Agenda, NY Women in Comm. (bd. dirs.). Achievements include created and ran Dreams Come True program at Mt. Sinai Med. Ctr. Office: Love Our Children USA 220 E 57th St New York NY 10022 Home Phone: 212-465-3338; Office Phone: 888-347-5437. Business E-Mail: info@loveourchildrenusa.org.

ELLIS, SCOTT, theatrical director; Grad., Goodman Sch. of Drama, Chgo. Assoc. artistic dir. Roundabout Theatre Co. Dir. plays 1776 (Drama Desk, Outer Critics Circle and Tony nominations), Steel Pier (Drama Desk, Outer Critics Circle and Tony nominations), Company, She Love Me (Tony nomination, Outer Critics Circle award Best Dir., Best Revival, Olivier award), Picnic (Outer Critics Circle nomination), A Month in the Country, Dark Rapture, The World Goes Round: The Music of Kander and Ebb (Drama Desk, Outer Critics Circle awards Best Director, Best Musical Revue), Flora, the Red Menace, 110 in the Shade, A Little Night Music (Drama Desk award Best Director, Best Revival), Sondheim: A Celebration at Carnegie Hall, The Boys from Syracuse, 2002, Tartuffe, 2003, A Day in the Dearth of Joe Egg, 2003, Nine, 2003, The Look of Love, 2003, Master Harold and the Boys, 2003, Big River, 2003, Assassins, 2004, Twentieth Century, 2004, After the Fall, 2004, Twelve Angry Men, 2004, The Little Dog Laughed, 2005, Curtains, 2006. Office: Roundabout Theatre Co Ste 1200 231 W 39th St New York NY 10018

ELLIS, SOPHIA (LUGENE) HOLLEY, retired secondary school educator; b. Detroit, Jan. 30, 1927; d. Major Quincy and Ethel Lee (Jones) Holley; m. James Thomas Ellis, Feb. 17, 1968 (div. Feb. 1988); children: John Thomas, Holley Elizabeth. BA in Biology and German, U. Mich., 1949, MS in Botany, 1950, MA in German, 1964. Mid. sch. tchr. English, Oxnard (Calif.) Pub. Schs., 1968-69; elem. sch. tchr. sci. Cambridge (Mass.) Pub. Schs., 1969-71, City Sch. Detroit, 1973-75; instr. zoology Wayne County Community Coll., Detroit, 1976-77; elem. and high sch. tchr sci., biology and earth sci. Detroit Bd. Edn. Pub. Schs., 1950-68, high sch. tchr. biology and horticulture, 1978-85, tchr. sci. and lang., 1985-86, tchr. German, 1986—2006; ret., 2006. Book and sch. evaluator North Ctrl. Assn., 1984, 85, 89; cons. Ea. Mich. U. World Coll. in Germany, Ypsilanti, 1989—; mem. Am. Coun. for the Tchg. of Fgn. Lang.; mem. AATG-Cultural Diversity; mem. tng. trainers for tchg. German Goethe Inst., Ann Arbor, mem. multiculturism in the German classroom Ohio Dept. of Edn., spkr.; coord. German Student Exch. Programs Martin Luther King H.S., 1985—; spkr. in field. Coord. United Found., Detroit, 1973-77; pres. black leadership alumni coun. U. Mich., Ann Arbor; apptd. tchr. adv. bd. Detroit Hist. Mus., 1992; bd. dirs. Lisle Fellowship, Inc.; mem. Metro Detroit Visitors Coun.; bd. dirs. Internat. Visitors Coun., U.S. State Dept. Named Tchr. of Yr. (western div.), Newsweek mag., 1988, Outstanding Educator, Booker T. Washington Bus. Assn., Met. Detroit, 1991, Phyllis Layton Perry Educator of Yr., Nat. Coun. Internat. Visitors, 2006; recipient Golden Apple awards Wayne County Intermediate Sch. Dist., 1988, Bundesverdienstkreuz, Pres. Germany, 1995, Educators award Am. Legion, 2006, Septima P. Clark award in edn. So. Christian Leadership Com., 2007, Commendation of Svc. award in Edn., U.S. Sen. Carolyn Cheeks Fitzpatric, Commendation for Citizen Diplomacy Outreach; Student Aid Found. scholar, 1945-50. Mem. Am. Assn. Tchrs. German (pres. Mich. chpt. 1991-92, Cert. Merit 1997), Mich. Fgn. Lang. Assn., Met. Detroit Fgn. Lang. Assn., U. Mich. Alumni Assn. (life, family camping bd. 1977-79), Alpha Kappa Alpha, Phi Sigma. Democrat. Anglican. Avocations: gardening, travel, lapidarist, folk dancing, organ and harmonica.

ELLIS, STEPHEN A., engineering executive, consultant; b. Danville, Pa., June 4, 1966; s. Stephen F. Ellis and Sharon R. Foresman; m. Heidi A Baumgartner, Mar. 21, 1986; children: Krista M, Andrew R. Cert. in Mech. and Elec. Engring. Techn., Air Force, Wright Patterson AFB, 1991. Gis coord. Pa. Dept. Transp., Montoursville, Pa., 1992—2001; v.p. GeoDecisions, Camp Hill, Pa., 2001—. Mem.: Am. Soc. Hwy. Engrs. (assoc.), Am. Legion (life), VFW Am. (life), NRA (life). Office: GeoDecisions 209 Senate Ave Camp Hill PA 17011 Home Phone: 570-893-1636; Office Phone: 717-763-7211. Office Fax: 717-763-1850. Business E-Mail: sellis@geodecision.com.

ELLIS, STEPHEN CHARLES, lawyer; b. Portland, Oreg., Apr. 17, 1945; s. Donald E. Ellis and Francis E. (Shainholts) Cordiner; m. Helen Stevens, Jan. 1, 1981; children: Donald, Peter. BA cum laude, U. Wash., 1967; JD cum laude, U. Mich., 1970. Bar: Wash., 1970, U.S. Dist. Ct. (We. dist. Wash.). Assoc. Reed McClure Moceri & Thonn, Seattle, 1970—73, ptnr., 1973—86; mng. ptnr., pres. Weiss Jensen Ellis & Botteri (later Weiss Jensen Ellis & Howard, combined with offices Holland & Knight LLP), Seattle, 1986—2001; ptnr. Holland & Knight LLP, Seattle, profl. devel. and recruiting. Chmn. Com. of Law Examiners, Seattle, 1983-86; mem. WSBA Character and Fitness Com., Seattle, 1985-91. Contbr. articles to profl. jours. Bd. trustee Seattle Chidren's Home, 1987-91, King County Bar Found., 2004—; bd. trustee, sec. N.W. Theol. Union, Seattle, 1986-1994; bd. dir., pres. Village Theatre Issaquah, Wash., 1994-2002 Mem. ABA (mem., sect. on corp., banking and bus. law), Wash. State Bar Assn. (bar examiners com. mem. 1975-86, chmn., com. law examiners, 1983-86, law clerk com. 1983-97, corp., banking law and internat. law, sect. mem., character and fitness com. 1986-91), Seattle-King County Bar Assn., King County Bar Found. (trustee 2004—), Athletic Club, Harbor Club. Avocations: racquetball, book collecting, writing. Home: 12225 188th St SE Snohomish WA 98296-8153 Office Phone: 206-340-9573. Business E-Mail: stephen.ellis@hklaw.com.

ELLIS, STEVEN GEORGE, public relations/corporate communications executive; b. Mar. 14, 1949; s. George G. and Betty (Chew) E.; m. Sylvia Regina Ellis; children: Steven Andrew, Christopher John, Katharine Marie. BA, U. Ga., 1971. V.p. Burson-Marsteller, Washington, 1976-83; v.p., gen. mgr. Earle Palmer Brown Pub. Rels., Bethesda, Md., 1983-84, pres., 1987-88; v.p. corp. comms. RKO Gen. Co. subs. GenCorp, Inc., NYC, 1984-86; pres. Steve Ellis Comms. Inc., 1988-95; sr. v.p. Jefferson-Waterman Internat., Washington, 1995-98; dir. corp. comms. SAGA Software, Inc., 1998-2000; v.p. global corp. comm. Metiom, Inc., NYC, 2000-01; sr. dir. global corp. comm. Think Tools AG, Zurich, Switzerland, 2001—02; prin. Ellis Internat. Comm., 2003—06; v.p. Levick Strategic Comms., Washington, 2006—. Mem. adv. bd. Henry W. Grady Coll. Journalism and Mass Comm. Recipient Gold Key award Pub. Rels. News, 1985, 86. Office Phone: 202-973-1317. E-mail: steve.ellis@levick.com.

ELLIS, WILLIAM GRENVILLE, academic administrator, management consultant; b. Teaneck, NJ, Nov. 29, 1940; s. Grenville Brigham and Vivian Lilian (Breeze) E.; m. Nancy Elizabeth Kempton, 1963; children: William Grenville, Bradford Graham. BS in Bus. Adminstrn., Babson Coll., 1962; MBA, Suffolk U., 1963; MEd, Westfield State Coll., 1965; EdD, Pa. State U., 1968; MS, Concordia U., 1991; MLE (Sears Roebuck Found. scholar), Harvard U., 1980; postgrad., U. Chgo., 1983, MIT, 1984, Harvard U., 1988-96. Asst. prof. bus. Rider U., 1968-69; dir. dir., assoc. prof. Castleton (Vt.) State Coll., 1969-72; exec. v.p., prof. St. Joseph Coll. in Vt., Rutland, 1972-73; acad. v.p., dean grad. sch. Thomas Coll., Waterville, Maine, 1973-82; pres. Wayland Acad., Beaver Dam, Wis., 1982-95, New Eng. Coll., Henniker, N.H., 1995-97; dean Sch. Bus. and Legal Studies, Concordia U. Wis., Mequon, 1997—. Mem. adv. bd. CFX Bank, 1996-97; corporator 1st Consumers Savs., 1974-81, Maine Savs., 1981-82, BankOne, 1983-95. Author: The Analysis and Attainment of Economic Stability, 1963, The Relationship of Related Work Experience to the Teaching Success of Beginning Business Teachers, 1968, Marketing for Educational Administrators, 1991, A Gunner's Moon, 1997; contbr. numerous articles and abstracts to profl. jours. Trustee C.C. Vt., 1972-73, Marian Coll., 1988-91, Wayland Acad., 1982-95, New Eng. Coll., 1995-97; auditor Town of Castleton, 1969-71; pres. Kennebec Valley Youth Hockey, Augusta, Maine, 1975-77; pres. Beaver Dam C. of C., 1985, 86, Midwest Classic Athletic Conf., 1989, Wis. Assn. Ind. Schs., 1984-86; chair bd. dirs. Beaver Dam Cmty. Hosp., 1985-95; dir. North Ctrl. Assn. Colls. and Secondary Schs., 1991-94, Ind. Schs. Ctrl. States, 1991-95; dir. N.H. Coll. and Univ. Coun., 1995-97; dir. Ozaukee County Indsl. Devel. Corp., 2003-04, Internat. Assembly Collegiate Bus. Edn., 2004-. Recipient Cmty. Svc. award Rutland C. of C., 1973, Disting. Svc. citation Wayland Acad., 1995, Excellence in Edn. award Pa. State U., 2001; named Cons. of Yr., SBA, 1975, 77, Prof. of Yr. Concordia U. Wis., 1999. Mem. APA, Nat. Assn. Intercollegiate Athletics (cert. of merit 1979), Soc. for Advancement of Mgmt., Cum Laude Soc., Pheasant City Club, Rotary, Alpha Chi, Pi Omega Pi, Alpha Delta Sigma, Delta Pi Epsilon, Phi Delta Kappa. Home: 8655 N Regent Rd Fox Point WI 53217-2362 Office: Concordia U Sch Bus & Legal Studies 12800 N Lake Shore Dr Mequon WI 53097-2418 E-mail: william.ellis@cuw.edu.

ELLISON, CYNTHIA KUEHL, music educator, musician; b. Sioux Falls, SD, Aug. 30, 1957; d. Kenneth LeRoy and Corrine Jean Kuehl; m. David Morris Ellison, Dec. 23, 1979; children: Kjersti Noelle, Alexandra Ellison Rodasti, Lindsay Elise, Annika Leigh. BFA in Edn. and Instrumental and Vocal Music, U. SD, Vermillion, 1979, MusM, 1993. Cert. tchr. in instrumental and vocal music K-12 Minn. Dept. Edn., 2004, SD Dept. Edn., 2004. Elem. band and vocal music Brookings Pub. Schs., SD, 1988—94; music edn. instr. U. Sioux Falls, SD, 1999; k-8 vocal music Harrisburg Pub. Schs., Harrisburg, SD, 1994—95; co-founder, artistic dir., mgr. Sioux Falls Girls Chorale, 1995—2000; grades 4-8 instrumental music instr. Christian Ctr., Christian Liberty Acad., Good Shepherd Luth., 1995—97; elem. instrumental and vocal instr. Sioux Falls Cath. Schs., 1996—98; elem. and mid. sch. instrumental instr. Sioux Falls Pub. Schs., 1997—2004; grades 5 and 6 instrumental and classroom music instr. Eden Prairie Pub. Schs., Eden Prairie, Minn., 2004—04; mid. sch. vocal music instr. Anoka-Hennepin Pub. Schs., Champlin, Minn., 2004—05, Fridley Pub. Schs., Minn., 2005—, Centennial Pub. Schs., Minn., 2006—. Youth choirs dir. Trinity Luth. Ch., Vermillion, SD, 1978—85, Incarnation Luth. Ch., North Oaks, Minn., 2005—; pvt. music instr. self-employed, Lino Lakes, Minn., 1978—; choral clinician Minn. Music Educators Assn., Minn., 2001; clinician Siouxland Choristers Guild, SD, 1996—2004; youth choirs dir. First Luth. Ch., Brookings, SD, 1985—94; brookings civic symphony and cmty. band mem. SD State U., 1986—93, all-state music camp clinician, 1993—94; mem. Dakota Vocal Works, Sioux Falls, 1997—99; symphony chorus mem. SD Symphony, 1994—2000; youth choirs dir. Gloria Dei Luth. Ch., 1994—2004; rehearsal accompanist SD Am. Choral Dirs. Assn., Sioux Falls, SD, 2000—04; band mem. Sioux Falls Mcpl. Band, 1994—2003; band. mem. Shorview No. Lights Variety Band, SD, 2007—. Bd. mem. Brookings Area Arts Coun., SD, 1988; jr. music festival coord. Vermillion Music Club, SD, 1983—85; pre-sch. bd. pres. First Luth. Ch., 1987—88; pres., ch. women's orgn. Trinity Luth. Ch., 1984—85, ch. coun., 1984—85. Recipient Outstanding Young Women in Am., 1989; scholar Presdl. Alumni award, U. SD, 1975—79; Presdl. Alumni scholar, 1975—79. Mem.: NEA (assoc.), Choristers Guild (assoc.; sec. 1996—2004), Music Educators Nat. Conf. (assoc.; elem. honors choir audition 1999—2003), Am. Choral Dirs. Assn. (assoc.; sd state newsletter editor and exec. bd. 1999—2003), Nat. Fedn. of Music Clubs (assoc.; exec. bd. mem., state pres., v.p. 1986—90), Sons Norway (assoc.). Lutheran. Avocations: gardening, reading, writing, walking, running. Office: Fridley Pub Schs 6100 West Moore Lake Rd Fridley MN 55432

ELLISON, EARL OTTO, computer scientist; b. Elizabeth, NJ, Apr. 26, 1938; s. Thorleif and Reidun E. (Anderson) Ingeborg; m. Judith Roque Impoc, Feb. 2, 1997; children: Reidun Impoc, Arnfinn Alejandro. BS, Am. U., Washington, 1964, postgrad., 1964—66. Head supplies and equipment at Pentagon C & P Telephone Co. (now Verizon), Arlington, Va., 1956—62; tax acct. Trust Dept. Nat. Bank Washington, 1964—65; methods analyst Automation Industries, Consol. Am. Svcs. Mgmt. Cons. Subs., Washington, LA, 1965; mgmt. instr. fed. supply svc. GSA, Washington, 1965—67, contract negotiator info. tech. svc., 1967—77, computer sys. contracting officer, 1977—97; pres. Teledesic Svcs., Inc., Washington, 1997—; network security cons. Northrop Grumman-Mission Systems, McLean, Va., 2002—. Author: Revenue Code of 1962: Effects on the Multi-National Firm, 1965. Judge ballroom dancing US Ballroom Dancing Assn., Ea. seaboard, 1986—; swimming and diving coach Pike Br. Swim and Tennis Club, Alexandria, Va., 1966-2001. With USNR, 1961-62. Mem. Beethoven Soc. Am. (exec. bd. 1993—), Norwegian Soc., Sons of Norway (prin. bldg. fund 1985—2007, Washington chpt. pres. 1994, 95, counselor 1993, 96, 97, investment adv. 1979—, internat. del. to conv. 1988, 94, v.p. 1993, pres. 1994-95, trustee 2002—) Presbyterian. Avocations: swimming, diving, ballroom dancing. Home: 6324 Telegraph Rd Alexandria VA 22310-2969 also: Rosfjord 4580 Lyngdal Norway Office: Northrop Grumman-Mission Systems 7598 Coleshire Dr Mc Lean VA 22102

ELLISON, EDWIN CHRISTOPHER, surgeon, educator; b. Columbus, Ohio, Jan. 10, 1950; s. Edwin Homer and Molly (Scheeler) E.; m. Mary Pat Borgess, Dec. 23, 1978; children: Jonathan Scott, Eric Christopher. BS, U. Wis., 1972; MD, Med. Coll. Wis., 1976. Diplomate Am. Bd. Surgery. Resident surgery Ohio State U., Columbus, 1976—83, asst. prof. surgery, 1983—93, assoc. prof., 1993—99, prof., 1999—; chief divsn. gen. surgery, bd. dirs. Ohio Digestive Disease Inst., Columbus, 1987—93; chief of staff Ohio State U. Med. Ctr., Columbus, 1999—2000, vice chmn. dept. surgery, 1996—99, 1interim chair surgery, 0999—2000, chmn. surgery, 2000—, assoc. v.p. health sci., 2002—, vice dean clin. affairs, 2002—. Fellow ACS. Office: 327 Means Hall 1654 Upham Dr Columbus OH 43210-1240 Office Phone: 614-293-8701.

ELLISON, GLENN, finance educator; AB summa cum laude in Math., Harvard Univ., 1987; MPhil in Econ., Cambridge Univ., 1988; PhD, MIT, 1992. Assoc. Charles River Assoc., 1988—89, sr. assoc., 1989; asst. prof., economics Harvard Univ., 1992—94; Ford Career Devel. assoc. prof., economics MIT, 1994—97, prof., 1997—2007, assoc. head, economics, 2000—01, Gregory K. Palm prof. economics, 2007—; rsch. assoc. Nat. Bur. Economic Rsch., 1997—. Editor: Rand Jour. Economics, 1995—99, Econometrica, 2000—03. Grantee Alfred P. Sloan Rsch. Fellowship, 1996—2000. Fellow: Econometric Soc., Am. Acad. Arts & Scis.; mem.: Inst. for Adv. Study. Office: Dept Econ MIT E52-380A 50 Memorial Dr Cambridge MA 02142 Office Phone: 617-253-8702. Office Fax: 617-253-1330. Business E-Mail: gellison@mit.edu.*

ELLISON, HENRY PHILLIPS, military officer; b. Columbia, SC, Sept. 26, 1969; s. David Gaillard Ellison Jr. and Cornelia (Fleming) Mayer. BS in Geopolitics, U.S. Mil. Acad., West Point, NY; MBA, St. Martin's Coll., 2002. Commd. 2d lt. U.S. Army, Ft. Benning, Ga.; 1994-97, advanced through grades to capt., 1997, capt. 51st Fighter Wing, 1997-98, capt. G3 I Corps Ft. Lewis, Wash., 1998-2000, capt., BN intelligence officer 218 FA, 2000—01. Episcopalian. Avocations: college football, stamp collecting/philately, music. Home: 500 Springair Rd Columbia SC 29206

ELLISON, HERBERT JAY, historian, educator; b. Portland, Oreg., Oct. 3, 1929; s. Benjamin F. and Esther (Anderson) Ellison; m. Alberta M. Moore, June 13, 1952; children: Valery, Pamela. BA, U. Wash., 1951, MA, 1952; PhD (Fulbright fellow), U. London, 1955. Instr. history U. Wash., 1955—56, prof. Russian and Ea. European studies, 1968—, dir. divsn. internat. programs, 1968—72, vice provost for ednl. devel., 1969—72, dir. Inst. Comparative and Fgn. Area Studies, 1973—78, chmn. Russian and East European studies, 1979—83; asst. prof. U. Okla., 1956—62; assoc. prof. history, chmn. Slavic studies program U. Kans., 1962—67, prof., 1965—68, dir. NDEA Lang. and Area Ctr. Slavic Studies, 1965—67, assoc. dean faculties internat. programs, 1967—68; sec. Kennan Inst. Advanced Russian Studies, Washington, 1983—85. Trustee Nat. Coun. Russian and E. European Rsch., 1983—87; dir. Russian rsch. Nat. Bur. Asian Rsch., 1990—, bd. dirs., 1993—; chmn. bd. dirs. Internat. Rsch. and Exchs. Bd., 1992—98; dir. new Russia in Asia rsch. and conf. project, 1993—96; chmn. acad. coun. Kennan Inst. Advanced Russian Studies, 1997—2001; bd. govs. Blakemore Found., 1998—. Author: History of Russia, 1964, Sino-Soviet Conflict, 1982, Soviet Policy Toward Western Europe, 1983, Japan and the Pacific Quadrille, 1987, Boris Yelstin and Russian Democratization, 2006; co-author: Twentieth Century Russia, 1999; contbr. articles to profl. jours.; chief cons., exec. dir. (TV series) Messengers from Moscow, 1995, Yeltsin, 2000. Named Ellison Ctr. Russian, East European and Ctrl. Asian Studies Ctr. and Ellison Disting. Professorship Russian History, U. Wash., 2005. Mem.: AAUP, Am. Assn. Advancement Slavic Studies, Am. Hist. Assn., Univ. Club. Home: 12127 SE 15th St Bellevue WA 98005-3821 Office: Univ Wash Jackson Sch Internat Study PO Box 353650 Seattle WA 98195-3650 Business E-Mail: hellison@u.washington.edu.

ELLISON, KEITH, Congressman-elect, lawyer; m. Kim Ellison; 4 children. JD, Univ. Minn., 1990. Assoc. Linquist & Vennum; exec. dir. Legal Rights Ctr.; atty. Hassan & Reed Ltd.; atty., private practice Mpls.; mem., Dist. 58B Minn. Ho. Reps., 2003—; Congressman-elect 5th Dist. Minn., 2006. Democrat. Islam. First Muslim elected to U.S. Congress; first African-Am. elected to Congress from Minn. Office: House of Representatives 229 State Office Bldg 100 Rev Dr Martin Luther King Jr Blvd Saint Paul MN 55155*

ELLISON, LARRY (LAWRENCE JOSEPH), computer software company executive; b. Chgo., Aug. 17, 1944; m. Ada Quinn, 1967 (div. 1974); m. Nancy Wheeler, 1976 (div. 1977); m. Barbara Boothe, 1983 (div. 1986); m. Melanie Craft, Dec. 18, 2003; 2 children. Student, U. Ill., U. Chgo. With Amdahl, Inc., Santa Clara, Calif., 1967—71, systems arch.; pres. systems divsn. Omex Corp., 1972—77; co-founder (with Bob Miner & Ed Oates) Oracle Corp. (formerly Software Devel. Labs.), Redwood, Calif., 1977; CEO Oracle Corp., Redwood, Calif., 1977—, pres., 1978—96, chmn., 1990—92, 1995—2004. Bd. dirs. Oracle Corp., 1977—, Apple Computer, Inc., 1997—2002. Named Entrepreneur of Yr., Harvard Sch. Bus., 1990, Bio-IT Champion, Bio-ITWorld, 2002; named one of World's Richest People, Forbes Mag., 1999—, Forbes Richest Ams., 2006, 50 Who Matter Now, CNNMoney.com Bus. 2.0, 2006; recipient Leadership Award for Global Integration, 1994, Disting. Info. Scis. award, Assn. Info. Tech. Profls., 1996, Industry Achievement award, 1997. Avocation: yachting. Office: Oracle Corp 500 Oracle Pky Redwood City CA 94065-1675*

ELLISON, LOIS TAYLOR, internist, educator, medical association administrator; b. Fort Valley, Ga., Oct. 28, 1923; d. Robert James and Annie Maude (Anderson) Taylor; m. Robert Gordon Ellison, Feb. 11, 1945; children: Robert Gordon, Gregory Taylor, Mark Frederick, James Walton, John Charles. BS, U. Ga., 1943; MD, Med. Coll. Ga., 1950. Fellow, Univ. Hosp., Augusta, Ga., 1950-51; mem. faculty Med. Coll. Ga., Augusta, 1951—, prof. medicine and surgery, 1971—2000, assoc. dean, 1974-75, provost, 1975-84, assoc. v.p. planning (hosps. and clins.), 1984—2000, prof. emeritus medicine and surgery, 2000, med. historian, provost emeritus, 2000—. Attending VA Med. Ctr., Augusta; civilian cons. Eisenhower Army Med. Ctr., Fort Gordon, Ga.; mem. coal mine health research adv. council Nat. Inst. Occupational Safety and Health, 1972-75; bd. dirs. East Central Ga. Health Systems Agy., 1975-79, treas., 1979—; bd. dirs. Oak Ridge Associated Univs., 1978-84; mem. adv. council Univ. Systems Ga., 1975-84; mem. exec. com. Ga. Health Coordinating Council, 1980 Contbr. articles to profl. jours. Bd. dirs. United Way Greater Augusta, 1975-78, chair div. hosp. and health, 1978, chair div. colls. and univs., 1980; mem. adminstrv. bd. Trinity-on-the-Hill United Methodist Ch., Augusta, 1974-77, mem. pastor-parish com., 1978— NIH grantee, 1963-68; included in NIH Nat. Libr. Medicine exhbn., 2003. Fellow Am. Coll. Chest Physicians; mem. Am. Physiol. Soc., Am. Med. Women's Assn., AMA, Assn. Am. Med. Colls., Am. Lung Assn. (dir. 1967— , sec. 1982-85, pres.-elect 1985-86, pres. 1986-87), Am. Heart Assn. (pres. Ga. affiliate chpt. 1982-83, dir. 1979—), So. Soc. Clin. Investigation, Am. Lung Assn. of Ga. (pres. 1984-85), Ga. Heart Assn. Office: Med Coll Ga 1120 15th St AE-3055 Augusta GA 30912 Office Phone: 706-721-4013. Business E-Mail: ellisonl@mcg.edu.

ELLISON, LUTHER FREDERICK, oil industry executive; b. Monroe, La., Jan. 2, 1925; s. Luther and Gertrude (Hudson) E.; m. Frances Williams, July 18, 1948 (dec.); children; Constance Elizabeth, Carolyn Williams; m. Patsy Hunter, Nov. 23, 1996. Student, Emory U., 1943-44; BS in Petroleum Engring., Tex. A&M U., 1949, BS in Geol. Engring., 1950. Registered profl. engr., Tex., La. Jr. petroleum engr. Sun Prodn. Co., Kilgore and McAllen, Tex., 1950-52, area petroleum engr. Garcia Field, Tex., 1952-54, Delhi (La.) unit engr., 1954-60, asst. region supt. Dallas, 1960-62, dist. drilling engr. Corpus Christi, 1962-63, dist. engr. McAllen, 1963-65, supr. engring. Dallas, 1965-66, div. chief petroleum engr., 1966-70, regional mgr. engring., 1970-75, region mgr., 1975-78, dir. devel., 1978-80, v.p. devel., 1980-84; div. v.p., dir. Sun Exploration and Prodn. Co., 1984-86, pres., bd. dirs., 1986—; pres., chief exec. officer Oil & Gas Experts, Inc., Dallas, 1986—, Am. Energy Enterprises Inc., Dallas, 1988—. Pres., dir., mem. exec. com. Nabors-Sun Drilling Co.; dir., mem. exec. com. East Tex. Salt & Water Disposal Co.; CEO, pres. Oil & Gas Experts Inc., 1986; spkr. and writer in field. V.p. Northwood Jr. H.S. PTA, Dallas, 1967—68, pres., 1968—69; elder, trustee Preston Hollow Presbyn. Ch. Found.; sr. trustee, 2005—; bd. dirs. Glen Lakes Assn. With USN, 1943—46. Mem. Tex.-Mid-Continent Oil and Gas Assn. (Outstanding Achievement award 1964, chmn. area 1964-65, mgr. north region, operating com., Outstanding Performance award 1985—), Am. Petroleum Inst., Soc. Petroleum Engrs., Dallas Engrs. Club, Petroleum Engrs. Club, Dallas Petroleum Club, Park City Club, Northwood Club (Dallas), Lions Club, Premier Club (Dallas), Parents League, Sigma Alpha Epsilon (pres. 1944-45). Home: 526 Preston Trail Loop Kerrville TX 78028-6406 Office: PO Box 219 High Rolls Mountain Park NM 88325 Office Phone: 830-896-6809.

ELLISON, NICHOLAS HOWELL, literary agent; b. NYC, Mar. 18, 1948; s. William and Virginia (Howell) Soskin; children: Gustave Nicholas, Catherine Hannah. BA, Boston U., Sorbonne, 1969. Sr. editor Thomas Y. Crowell Pub. Co., NYC, 1972-76; sr. editor Harper & Row Pubs., NYC, 1976-79; editor-in-chief Delacorte Press, NYC, 1979-81; pres., found. ptnr. Nicholas Ellison, Inc., 1983—. Prof. writing Fairfield U., 1980—; dir. Verreaux Enterprises. Editor numerous books; contbr. articles to numerous profl. jours. Pres. Bell Island Assn., Rowayton, Conn., 1972. Recipient Outstanding Achievement award Folio Mgmt. Tng. Seminars, 1979 Mem.: Shore and Country (Norwalk, Conn.). Congregationalist. Home: 92 Mather Rd Stamford CT 06903-3026 Office: 55 5th Ave New York NY 10003-4301

ELLISON, PAMELA ION, secondary school educator, consultant; b. Copiaque, NY, Sept. 14, 1957; d. James Monroe and Ruby Louise (Miles) E.; divorced; 1 child, Bravetta Elizabeth. BS in Elem. Edn. and Spl. Edn., Hampton U., 1980; MA in Elem. and Secondary Adminstrn., George Washington U., 1992. Cert. tchr., Va. Elem. tchr. Fairfax County Pub. Schs., Alexandria, Va., 1980—, mid. sch. tchr. sci., 1993—. Peer observer performance evaluation program Fairfax Co. Pub. Schs., Fairfax, 1988—, writer sci. curriculum, 1987, 90, 93, 94, sci. lead tchr., 1985—; coord.

elem. sch. sci. Hayfield Elem. Sch., Alexandria, 1987-93; cons. on sci. curriculum Nat. Sci. Resource Ctr., Washington, 1994; sci. lead tchr., cons. Va. Quality Edn. in Scis. and Tech., Blacksburg, 1994; workshop presenter in field. Telethon vol. United Negro Coll. Fund, Washington, 1995; vol. Girl Scouts U.S.A., Alexandria, 1992, 93; mem. PTA. Scholar Fairfax Edn. Assn., 1991, Columbian Women scholar George Washington U., 1991. Mem. ASCD, NEA, FEA, AAUW, Nat. Coun. of Negro Women, Inc. Baptist. Avocations: writing, improving science education, crafts, painting, bowling. Home: PO Box 15419 Alexandria VA 22309-0419

ELLISON, PETER THORPE, anthropology professor; b. Tucson, June 2, 1951; s. John William and Mary Thorpe Ellison; m. Pippi Lindsay Lindsay, July 30, 1972; children: Samuel, Silas. BA, U. Vt., 1975; MS, U. Mass., 1980; PhD, Harvard U., 1983. Asst. prof., anthropology Harvard U., Cambridge, Mass., 1983—88, Thomas D. Cabot assoc. prof. Anthropology, 1988—90, prof. anthropology, 1990—2003, John Cowles prof. anthropology, 2003—. Chmn., dept. anthropology Harvard U., 1992—98; assoc. dean faculty Harvard U., Sch Arts and Scis., 1994—2000, dean, 2000—05; assoc. Kirkland House; curator human biology Peabody Mus. Archaeology and Ethnology, Cambridge. Editor (editor-in-chief): American Journal of Human Biology, 2002—; author: On Fertile Ground; editor: Reproductive Ecology and Human Evolution. Award, John Simon Guggenheim Found., 1998—99. Fellow: NY Acad. Scis.; mem.: AAAS, NAS, Am. Anthropology Assn., Soc. for Study Reprod., Soc. for Study Human Biology, Soc. Behavioral Neuroscience, Population Coun., Human Biology Assn., Endocrine Soc., Am. Fertility Soc., Am. Assn. Phys. Anthropologists, Phi Beta Kappa. Office: Harvard U Peabody Museum 11 Divinity Ave Cambridge MA 02138 Business E-Mail: pellison@fas.harvard.edu.

ELLISON, WILLIAM THEODORE, marine engineer; b. Wilmington, NC, Nov. 30, 1941; s. Robert Jay and Marie Catherine E.; m. Annelise Manecky, Dec. 18, 1987; children: Britt Kirsten, Hans Salter, Katerina Astri-Marie. BS, U.S. Naval Acad., 1963; MSME, MIT, 1968, PhD, 1970. Scientist, v.p. Cambridge Acoustical Assn., Inc., Mass., 1974—83; pres., CEO Marine Acoustics, Inc., Newport, R.I., 1983—. Bd. dirs. Lab. Ornithology, Cornell U., 2007—. Contbr. articles to profl. jours. Capt. USNR, ret. Named Disting. Alumni of Yr. The Breck Sch., 2001. Fellow Acoustical Soc. Am., Explorers Club; mem. Tau Beta Pi, Sigma Xi. Achievements include design of passive acoustical whale tracking system for population assessment of endangered species in the Arctic; pioneering work in impact of underwater sound on marine resources, breakthrough tech. in handheld voice translation sys. Office: Marine Acoustics Inc 809 Aquidneck Ave Middletown RI 02842

ELLMANN, DOUGLAS STANLEY, lawyer; b. Detroit, July 15, 1956; s. William Marshall and Sheila Estelle Ellmann. AB, Occidental Coll., 1978; JD, U. Mich., 1982. Bar: Mich. 1982, U.S. Dist. Ct. (ea. dist.) Mich. 1982, U.S. Ct. Appeals (6th cir.) 1982. Prin. Ellmann & Ellmann, P.C., Ann Arbor, Mich., 1989—. Spl. asst. atty. gen., 1986; trustee U.S. Panel, 1989—; sec. bankruptcy trustee assoc. U.S. Bankruptcy Ct. (ea. dist.) Mich., 1993—. Author: Selected Issues in Asset Protection, 1994, My Advice: Next Time Go Solo, 1994, LWUSA; co-author: Winning Labor Arbitrations, 1987. Mem. U. Mich. Law Sch. Fund, 1986—87. Mem.: ABA (vice chair bankruptcy com. 1995—2001), Washtenaw County Bar Assn. (chmn. banking, bus., bankruptcy com. 1995—2000), State Bar Mich. (mem. manditory CLE com. 1989—96, chmn. 1995—96, mem. jud. qualifications com. 2000—), Mich. Bar Assn. (rep. assembly 1983—89, 1990—92, 1998—, exec. counsel young lawyers sect. 1985—87, mem. client security fund com. 1987—95). Office: 308 W Huron St Ann Arbor MI 48103-4204 Office Phone: 734-668-4800. Business E-Mail: dse@ellmannlaw.com.

ELLMANN, SHEILA FRENKEL, investment company executive; b. Detroit, June 8, 1931; d. Joseph and Rose (Neback) Frenkel; m. William M. Ellmann, Nov. 1, 1953 (dec. Jan. 16, 2002); children: Douglas Stanley, Carol Elizabeth, Robert Lawrence. BA in English, U. Mich., 1953. Dir. Advance Glove Mfg. Co., Detroit, 1954—78; v.p. Frome Investment Co., Detroit, 1980—96, pres., 1996—. Mem.: U. Mich. Alumni Assn., Nat. Trust Hist. Preservation, VFW Aux. Home: 28000 Weymouth Dr Farmington Hills MI 48334 Personal E-mail: sheilaellmann@yahoo.com.

ELLNER, JERROLD JAY, infectious diseases specialist; b. 1945; MD, Johns Hopkins U., 1970. Diplomate Am. Bd. Internal Medicine, Am. Bd. Infectious Disease. Resident in internal medicine Johns Hopkins Hosp., Balt., 1970—72; formerly with Case Western Res. U. Med. Sch., Cleve.; chair dept. medicine, prof. medicine N.J. Med. Sch., 2000—, head Inst. for Emerging Pathogens; dir. Ctr. for Emerging Infectious Diseases U. Medicine and Dentistry N.J., 2000—. Founding mem. Acad. Alliance for AIDS Care and Prevention in Africa, 2001. Named one of Top Drs. in N.Y. Metro Area, Castle Connolly, Top Drs. 2003, N.J. Monthly Mag. Office: UMDNJ Med Sch Dept Medicine MSB Rm I 506 185 S Orange Ave Newark NJ 07103 E-mail: ellnerjj@umdnj.edu.

ELLNER, MICHAEL WILLIAM, art educator; b. NYC, Apr. 1, 1938; s. Charles and Sylvia May (Golub) E.; m. Josephine Helene Bilello, Aug. 24, 1957; children: Eileen Lorraine, Deborah Lynn, Laurence Steven. AA in Engring., San Jose City Coll., 1963, AA in Art, 1966; BA, Notre Dame De Namur U., 1970; MA, San Jose State U., 1971, postgrad., 1973-74, U. Calif., Santa Cruz, 1980. Cert. secondary art tchr., c.c. art tchr., Calif. Chair art dept. John Muir Jr. High Sch., San Jose, Calif., 1973-80; assoc. prof. art San Jose State U., 1974; chair art dept. Willow Glen Edn. Park, San Jose, 1980-91; visual arts coord. A. Lincoln AVPA Magnet High Sch., San Jose, 1991-96. Cons. Coll. Bd., San Jose, 1989-97, San Jose Unified Sch. Dist., Saturday Acad., San Jose, 1996-2007; prof. art San Jose City Coll., 1996—; advisor Nat. Art Honor Soc., San Jose, 1991-2007; intern advisor Casa Program, San Jose, 1991-2007; co-convenor Lincoln HS Magnet Curriculum Coun., San Jose, 1991-96; mentor tchr. San Jose Unified Sch. Dist., 1985-94; adv. art club San Jose C.C., 2006-07. Paintings included in more than 200 collections including San Jose Mus. Art, Calif., De Saisset Mus., Santa Clara, Calif., Foot Mus., Long Beach, Calif., Coll. Notre Dame De Namur U., Belmont, Calif.; guest curator Egyptian Mus. Art Gallery, San Jose, Calif., New World Gallery, San Jose, Calif., San Jose Art League, Calif.; guest curator Macla Gallery, San Jose, Calif., Genesis Gallery, San Jose, Calif., 1970—; exhibited in more than 300 group and one-person shows; created 21 cmty. murals; curator over 100 art exhbns.; represented in several art books on painting, and murals and poetry. Past pres. San Jose Art League; past treas. Cambrian Art League; mem. Anti-Graffiti Program, San Jose. Recipient Program Stds. award Nat. Art Edn. Assn., 1993, 94, 95, 96, Art grant City of San Jose, 1994, Mural grant Rose Garden Assn., San Jose, 1996, grant Nat. League Am. Pen Women, 1996, 97, 98, 99, Program awards Nat. Blue Ribbon Sch., 1998, Magnet Sch. of Am., 1991, 92, 93, Calif. Disting. Sch. award, 1992, 96, Golden Bell award, 1994, Kennedy Ctr. award for the arts, 1995, State Farm Good Nieghbor award Nat. Art Edn. Assn., 1996; inductee Calif. State Senate Youth Mentor's Hall of Fame award, 1999, Excellence in Edn. award City of San Jose, 2000, Youth Focus award, 1999; named Tchr. of Yr., Willow Glen Edn. Park PTA, 1985, San Jose Shrine, 1986. Mem. Calif. Tchrs. Assn., NEA, San Jose Tchrs. Assn., San Jose Inst. Contemporary Art, Artists Alliance Calif., South Bay Artists Assn. (adv. com.), Cmty. Partnership Santa Clara County, San Jose Art League (past pres.), Cambrian Art League (past treas.), Phi Kappa Phi. Avocations: painting, poetry, murals. Home: 1429 Scossa Ave San Jose CA 95118-2456

ELLNER, PAUL DANIEL, retired microbiologist; b. NYC, May 2, 1925; s. George and Cele (Weis) Ellner; m. Estelle Ziswasser, 1948 (div. 1960); 1 child, Diane; m. Cornelia Johns, Jan. 15, 1965; children: David, Jonathan. BS, LI U., 1948; MS, U. So. Calif., 1952; PhD, U. Md., 1956. Diplomate Am. Bd. Med. Microbiology, cert. clin. lab. dir. NYC Dept. Health. Clin. bacteriologist LA hosps., 1948-52; rsch. asst. Mt. Sinai Hosp., NYC, 1952-53; instr. microbiology U. Fla. Coll. Medicine, 1956-60; asst. prof. U. Vt. Coll. Medicine, 1960-63, Columbia U. Coll. Physicians and Surgeons, NYC, 1963-66, assoc. prof., 1966-70, prof., 1971-78, prof. microbiology and pathology, 1978—89, prof. emeritus, 1989, dir. clin. microbiology svc., 1971-89; assoc. microbiologist Presbyn. Hosp., NYC, 1966-70, attending staff, 1971-89; ret., 1989. Cons. in field; vis. prof. NY Med. Coll., Valhalla, 1979, ASM Latin Am., Medellin, Colombia, 1982, Am. Bur. Med. Advancement, Taiwan, 1982; regional coord. Nat. Disaster Med. Sys.; v.p. Am. BioSci. Cons. Author: Current Procedures in Clinical Bacteriology, 1978, Understanding Infectious Disease, 1992, The Biomedical Scientist as Expert Witness, 2006; editor: Infectious Diarrheal Diseases: Current Concepts and Laboratory Procedures, 1984; mem. editl. bd. Sexually Transmitted Diseases, 1982—84, European Jour. Clin. Microbiology, 1985—89; contbr. chapters to books, articles to profl. jours. With AC USN, 1943—44, served to capt. USPHS Res., health project officer USCG, 1982—91. Rsch. fellow, USN, 1954—56. Fellow: Infectious Diseases Soc. Am., Assn. Clin. Scientists, NY Acad. Medicine (assoc.), Am. Acad. Microbiology; mem.: AMA (spl. affiliate), Am. Venereal Disease Assn., Acad. Clin. Lab. Physicians and Scientists, Am. Soc. Microbiology (chmn. clin. divsn. 1980—81, Sonnerwirth Meml. award 1992), Sigma Xi. Republican. Jewish. Avocations: fishing, gardening, photography. Home Phone: 860-496-1207. Personal E-mail: pdel@columbia.edu. *The greatest satisfaction for the scientist is recognition by his peers for honesty and integrity in his studies, fairness and impartiality to his colleagues, and guidance and encouragement to his students.*

ELLROY, JAMES, writer; b. LA, Mar. 4, 1948; s. Geneva (Hillaker) E.; m. Mary Doherty, 1988. Author: (novels) Brown's Requiem, 1981, Clandestine, 1982, Blood on the Moon, 1984, Because the Night, 1984, Killer on the Road (formerly Silent Terror) 1986, Suicide Hill, 1986, The Black Dahlia, 1987, The Big Nowhere, 1988 (Prix Mystere award 1990), L.A. Confidential, 1990, White Jazz, 1992, Hollywood Nocturnes, 1994, Dick Contino's Blues, American Tabloid, 1995, My Dark Places, 1996, Crime Wave, 1999, The Cold Six Thousand, 2001, Destination Morque, 2003, (non-fiction) Scene of the Crime: Photographs from the LAPD Archive, 2004; contbr.: Fallen Angels: Six Noir Tales Told for Television, 1993; contbr., editor: Best American Mysteries, 2002. Office: care Warner Books Publicity Dept 1271 Ave of Americas New York NY 10020*

ELLSWEIG, PHYLLIS LEAH, retired psychotherapist; b. Irvington, NJ, Apr. 19, 1927; d. Sumar and Jeanette (Geffner) Schwartz; m. Martin Richard Ellsweig, Dec. 25, 1947; children: Bruce, Steven. BS, East Stroudsburg U., Pa., 1947; EdM, Lehigh U., 1966, EdD, 1972. Tchr. Stroud Union High Sch., 1963-66; guidance counselor East Stroudsburg (Pa.) Schs., 1966-68; asst. prof. edn. East Stroudsburg U., 1968; staff psychologist, outpatient supr. Mental Health Center Carbon, Monroe and Pike Counties, Stroudsburg, Pa., 1968-80; pvt. practice in psychotherapy and clin. hypnosis Stroudsburg, 1969-87. Mem. staff Pocono Hosp., 1968—80; pub. spkr. in field; cons. to schs. and pvt. orgns.; tchr. adult edn., Palm Beach County, Fla. Mem. Am. Soc. Clin. Hypnosis, Internat. Soc. Hypnosis, NOW (profl. cons. 1973—). Home: 2584 NW 12th St Delray Beach FL 33445-1353

ELLSWORTH, BRAD (BRADLEY ELLSWORTH), congressman, former police officer; b. Jasper, Ind., Sept. 11, 1958; m. Beth Ellsworth; 1 child, Andrea. BA in Sociology, Ind. State U., 1981, MA in Criminology, 1993; grad., FBI Nat. Acad., 1995. Dep. sheriff Vanderburgh County, Ind., 1982—98, D.A.R.E officer Ind., sheriff Ind., 1998—2007; mem. US Congress from 8th Ind. dist., 2007—, mem. armed svcs. com., agrl. com., small bus. com. Named Outstanding Alumni, U. Southern Ind. Mem.: Ind. Sheriff's Assn. (pres.), Blue Dog Coalition. Democrat. Roman Catholic. Office: 153 Cannon House Office Bldg Washington DC 20515 also: 101 NW Martin Luther King Blvd Rm 124 Evansville IN 47708 Office Phone: 812-434-6766.*

ELLSWORTH, FRANK L., not-for-profit executive; b. Wooster, Ohio, May 20, 1943; s. Clayton Sumner and Frances (Fuller) E.; 1 child, Kirstin Lynne. BA, Western Res. Coll., 1965; MEd, Pa. State U., 1967; MA, Columbia U., 1969; PhD, U. Chgo., 1976; LLD, Pepperdine U., 1997, Southwestern U., 2004. Asst. dir. devel. Columbia Law Sch., 1968-70; dir. spl. projects, prof. lit. Sarah Lawrence Coll., NY, 1971; asst. dean Law Sch., U. Chgo., 1971-79, instr. social sci. collegiate div., 1975-79; pres., prof. polit. sci. Pitzer Coll., Claremont, Calif., 1979-91; pres. Ind. Colls. So. Calif., LA, 1991-97; v.p. Capital Rsch. & Mgmt. Co., 1997—2003; pres. Japan Soc., 2003—06, Ellsworth Collection, 2006—. Author: The Foundation of the 21st Century, 2002, Law on the Midway, 1977, Student Activism in American Higher Education; contbr. articles to profl. jours. Trustee Japanese Am. Nat. Mus., Give2Asia, Pitzer Coll., Southwestern U.; chmn. Global Ptnrs. Inst., Can., Ctr. for the Preservation of Democracy; trustee Am. Friends Nat., Portrait Gallery, London. Recipient Disting. Young Alumnus award Case Western Res. U., 1981, Tree of Life award United Jewish Fund, 1991. Mem. Grolier Soc., Young Pres.'s Orgn., Asia Soc., Japanese Art Soc. Home: 2935 Sequoia Dr S Palm Springs CA 92262

ELLSWORTH, JAMES BYRON, national security educator; s. James B. and Shirley A. Ellsworth; m. Lynne Phillips-Ellsworth, June 7, 2000. BS, Clarkson U., 1986; MBA, Syracuse U., NY, 1988, PhD, 1998; MA, U.S. Naval War Coll., 2003. Student dir. ednl. computing Clarkson U., Potsdam, NY, 1983—86; grad. asst. Sch. Mgmt. Syracuse (N.Y.) U., 1986—88, grad. asst. Computing and Network Svcs., 1988—89; edn. specialist, dir. tng. and doctrine U.S. Army Armor Ctr. and Sch., Fort Knox, Ky., 1989—91; instrnl. design specialist, dir. evaluation and standardization U.S. Army Intelligence Sch., Fort Devens, Mass., 1991—92, instrnl. sys. adv., intelligence and elec. warfare dept., 1992—94; chief tng. support co. C/305th mil. intelligence bn. U.S. Army Intelligence Ctr., Fort Huachuca, Ariz., 1994—95, chief WWW, 1995—97, chief evaluation rsch., office of registrar, 1997—2000, chief automation and performance tech., office of registrar, 1999—2000; prof. Coll. Distance Edn. U.S. Naval War Coll., Newport, RI, 2000—. Sec., distance learning coordinating com. Mil. Edn. Coordination Coun., Washington, 2002—, bd. dirs.; mem. intelligence adv. coun. Am. Mil. U., 2005—. Author: (weblog) Education * Innovation * National Security, SURVIVING CHANGE: A Survey of Educational Change Models; co-author: Sustaining Distance Training, Educational Media and Technology Yearbook; contbr. articles to profl. jours.; author: SysAdmin: Toward Barnett's Stabilization and Reconstruction Force. Planning and zoning commn. observer Mayor's Youth Adv. Coun., Oneida, NY, 1982—83; student senator Clarkson U. Student Govt., Potsdam, NY, 1984—86; comm. dir. Coll. Rep. Syracuse (N.Y.) U., 1986—89; sec. pastoral coun. Holy Family Cath. Parish, Fort Huachuca, 1997—99; mem. choir St. Catherine Cath. Parish, Warwick, RI, 2001—02, St. Anthony Cath. Parish, Portsmouth, 2002—. Decorated Gen. Carl A. Spaatz award USAF Aux., Army Achievement medal Civilian Svc.; fellow, Inter-U. Seminar Armed Forces and Soc., Proteus Mgmt. Group, 2006—; grantee, Ednl. Comm. and Tech. Found., 1998. Mem.: U.S. Army Mil. Intelligence Corps Assn. (sr. intelligence officer Patriots chpt. 2003—, Lt. Col. Thomas Knowlton award 1995), Internat. Soc. Performance Improvement (pres. armed forces chpt. 2001—02), Assn. Ednl. Comm. and Tech. (bd. dirs. 2000—02, pres. divsn. sysematic change 2001—02, bd. dirs. 2005—06), Am. Ednl. Rsch. Assn., Assn. U.S. Army (life). R-Liberal. Roman Catholic. Achievements include one of the first to use the worldwide web as an educational medium; development of unifying framework for the major models of educational change and innovation; design of strategic architecture for the Naval War College's award-winning Web-enabled correspondence Program; research in adaptation of United States military organizations and doctrinal concepts to the post-cold-war security environment; design of evaluation strategy for US Army intelligence center and school. Avocations: running, poetry, computers. Home: Post Office Box 5162 Newport RI 02841-0102 Office: US Naval War College 686 Cushing Road (Code 1GA-4) Newport RI 02841-1207 Home Phone: 401-683-6809; Office Phone: 401-841-2215. Office Fax: 401-841-2457; Home Fax: 401-683-9569. Personal E-mail: jbellsworth@aol.com. E-mail: james.ellsworth@nwc.navy.mil.

ELLSWORTH, LAURA E., lawyer; b. NYC; BA, Princeton Univ., 1980; JD magna cum laude, Univ. Pitts., 1983. Bar: Pa. 1983. Ptnr.-in-charge Pitts. office Jones Day. Adv. com. for study of rules and practices US Dist. Ct., Western Dist. of Pa., 2003; adj. prof. law Univ. Pitts. Sch. of Law. Named a Leader in the Law, Legal Intelligencer, 2004; named one of the top female litigators in Pa., Pa. Law Weekly, 2004; recipient President's award, Pa. Bar Assn., 2002. Fellow: Am. Bar Assn.; mem.: Acad. of Trial Lawyers of Allegheny County, Pa. Bar Assn. (bd. mem.), Order of Coif. Office: Jones Day One Mellon Bank Ctr 31st Fl 500 Grant St Pittsburgh PA 15219 Office Phone: 412-394-7929. Office Fax: 412-394-7959. Business E-Mail: leellsworth@jonesday.com.

ELLSWORTH, PHOEBE CLEMENCIA, psychology professor; b. Hartford, Conn., Jan. 22, 1944; d. John Stoughton and Edith (Noble) E.; m. Samuel Raymond Gross, Nov. 7, 1979; children: Alexandra Ellsworth, Emma Beth Ellsworth. AB, Harvard U., 1966; PhD, Stanford U., 1970. Asst. prof. Yale U., New Haven, 1971-75, assoc. prof., 1975-79, prof., 1979-81, Stanford U., 1981-87; prof. psychology and law U. Mich., Ann Arbor, 1987—, Frank Murphy Disting. U. Prof. law and psychology, 2003—. Assoc. editor JESP, 1977-80; mem. social sci. rev. com. NIMH, 1973-77, com. on law and social sci. SSRC, 1975-84, rev. panel on law and social sci. NSF, 1983-85; mem. rev. bd. Am. Bar Found., 1987-91; bd. trustees Russell Sage Found., 1992-2002. Author: (with others) Emotions in the Human Face: Guidelines for Research And a Review of the Findings, Methods of Research in Social Psychology, Person Perception; contbr. articles to profl. jours. Fellow APA, Am. Acad. Arts and Scis.; mem. Soc. Exptl. Social Psychology, Am. Psychology Law Assn., Internat. Soc. Research on Emotion (charter)., Law and Soc. Assn. Home: 442 Huntington Pl Ann Arbor MI 48104-1800 Office: U Mich Sch Law 970 Legal Rsch 625 S State St Ann Arbor MI 48109-1215 Office Phone: 734-763-5781. E-mail: pce@umich.edu.

ELLSWORTH, ROBERT FRED, investment executive, former government official; b. Lawrence, Kans., June 11, 1926; s. W. Fred and Lucile (Rarig) E.; children: Robert William, Ann Elizabeth; m. Eleanor L. Biscoe, July 14, 2002 BS, U. Kans., 1945; JD, U. Mich., 1949. Bar: D.C., Mass., Kans., U.S. Supreme Ct. Mem. 87th to 89th Congresses from 2d and 3d Dist., Kans., 1961-67; asst. to Pres. of U.S., Washington, 1969; U.S. ambassador to NATO, 1969-71; gen. ptnr. Lazard Freres & Co., NYC, 1971-74; asst. sec. for internat. security affairs U.S. Dept. Def., Washington, 1974-75, dep. sec. Def., 1975-77. Bd. dirs. Price Comm. Corp.; founder Hamilton Bio Ventures, L.P. Lay reader Episcopal Ch. Knight Honor Johanniterorden. With USNR, 1944-46, 50-53. Recipient Presdl. Nat. Security medal, 1977. Mem. Coun. Fgn. Rels., Internat. Inst. Strategic Studies (v.p.), Atlantic Coun. of the U.S. (dir.), Coun. of Am. Amb. Home: 2505 Caminito del Barco Del Mar CA 92014 Office: 990 Highland Dr Ste 314 Solana Beach CA 92075 Home Phone: 858-509-2707; Office Phone: 858-314-2353. Business E-Mail: rellsworth@hamiltonbioventures.com.

ELLWANGER, ALBERT THOMPSON, III, secondary school educator; b. Richmond, Va., Aug. 5, 1948; s. Albert Thompson Ellwanger, Jr. and Frances Henrietta Sadler. BFA, Pratt Inst., 1970; MFA, George Washington U., 1981. Tchr. Richmond (Va.) Pub. Schs., 1970; designer Scan Furniture, Greenbelt, Md., 1972—74; educator Montgomery County Pub. Schs., Rockville, Md., 1974—. Dir. Visual and Performing Arts Acad., Kensington, Md., 2001—02. Benefactor Am. Arch. Found., Mariners' Mus., Newport News, Va., Nassau County (N.Y.) Mus. Art; founder Sadler Collection, Va. Mus., Richmond, 1974, Ellwanger-Mescha Collection, Nat. Gallery of Art; vestry mem. St. Bartholomew's Ch., Balt. With US Army, 1970—72. Named Silver Spring (Md.) Tchr. of Yr., Silver Spring C. of C., 1994, Montgomery County Art Tchr. of Yr., Md. Art Edn. Assn., 1998. Mem.: Assn. Supr. and Curriculum Development, Legacy Cir. Nat. Gallery Art (charter), Nat. Art Edn. Assn. Democrat. Episcopalian. Home: 2517 Pickwick Rd Baltimore MD 21207 Office: Albert Einstein HS 11135 Newport Mill Rd Kensington MD 20895 Office Phone: 301-962-1058.

ELLWANGER, THOMAS JOHN, lawyer; b. Summit, NJ, Feb. 26, 1949; s. James Warren and Lorean (Nicholson) E.; m. Sabine S. Ellwanger; children: James Hunter, Margaret Lorean, Stephanie M. Sperando, Jennifer A. Bell. BA, Northwestern U., 1970; JD, U. Fla., 1974. Bar: Fla. 1975, U.S. Dist. Ct. (mid. dist.) Fla. 1976, U.S. Ct. Appeals (11th cir.) 1976, U.S. Dist. Ct. (so. dist.) Fla. 1977, U.S. Tax Ct. Mem. Fowler, White, Gillen, Boggs, Villareal & Banker P.A. (now Fowler, White, Boggs, Banker P.A.), Tampa, Fla., 1975—. Instr. law U. Fla., Gainesville, 1975; adj. prof. Stetson U. Coll. Law, 1997-2000. Editor: Gadsden County Times, 1970-72. Fellow Am. Coll. Trust and Estate Counsel, Fla. Bar (cert. tax lawyer), Hillsborough County Bar Assn. (chmn. com. probate liaison 1985-86, real property probate and trust law sect. 1987-89, 2004-05), Tampa Bay Estate Planning Counsel (pres. 1994-95). Avocations: music, literature, sports. Office: Fowler White Boggs Banker PA 501 E Kennedy Blvd Ste 1700 Tampa FL 33602-5239 Home Phone: 813-250-1606; Office Phone: 813-222-1161. E-mail: tellwang@fowlerwhite.com.

ELLWOOD, DAVID TABOR, dean, public policy educator; b. Mpls., Sept. 16, 1953; s. Paul and Ann Ellwood; m. Marilyn Rymer. AB in Econs. summa cum laude, Harvard U., 1975, PhD in Econs., 1981. Rsch. asst. to prof. Martin S. Feldstein Harvard U., Cambridge, Mass., 1974-75, 77; rsch. assoc. health policy program U. Calif., San Francisco, 1975-76; tchg. fellow labor econs. Harvard U., Cambridge, 1977-79; rsch. asst. Nat. Bur. Econ. Rsch., Cambridge, 1978-80; asst. prof. pub. policy John F. Kennedy Sch. Govt., Harvard U., Cambridge, 1980-84, assoc. prof. pub. policy, 1984-88, prof. pub. policy, 1988-92, Malcolm Wiener prof. pub. policy, 1992-98, Lucius N. Littauer prof. polit. economy, 1998—2003, Scott M. Black prof. polit. economy, 2003—; co-dir. Malcolm Wiener Ctr. Pub. Policy, Harvard U., Cambridge, 1992-93; acad. dean John F. Kennedy Sch. Govt., Cambridge, 1992-93, 95-97, dean, 2004—; asst. sec. planning and evaluation US Dept. HHS, Washington, 1993-95. Rsch. assoc. Nat. Bur. Econ. Rsch., 1984-93; faculty mem. retreat U.S. House Ways and Means com.; panel mem. Work and Welfare Demonstration Manpower Demonstration Rsch. Corp., 1985-93, 95—; bd. overseers panel study income dynamics, 1986-88; dir. domestic strategy group The Aspen Inst., 1998—2003; bd. dirs. Abt Assocs.; cons. in field. Author: Poor Support: Poverty and the American Family, 1988 (notable books N.Y. Times Book Review 1988, outstanding book 1988 Policy Studies Orgn.); co-editor Welfare Policies for the 90s; co-author Welfare Realities: From Rhetoric to Reform, 1994; contbr. numerous articles, book reviews to profl. jours. Panel Com. Status Black Ams., NAS, 1986-91; adv. bd. Children's Program Edna McConnell Clark Found., 1989-93; mem. Nat. Forum Future Children and Their Parents, Nat. Rsch. Coun., 1988-91; mem. Task Force Poverty and Welfare Mario Cuomo, gov. State N.Y., 1986-87, Project Welfare Families Bruce Babbitt, gov., State Ariz., 1986-87. Named Hon. Prof., Grad. Sch. Chinese Acad. Scis.; recipient George Kerschaw award, Assn. Pub. Policy Analysis and Mgmt.; Lehman fellow, Harvard U. Fellow

Am. Acad. Arts and Scis.; mem. NAS (panel poverty and family assistance), Phi Beta Kappa. Office: Harvard U John F Kennedy Sch Govt 79 John F Kennedy St L-218 Cambridge MA 02138-5801 Office Phone: 617-495-1122.

ELLWOOD, SCOTT, lawyer; b. Boston, July 8, 1936; s. William Prescott and Doris (Cook) E.; m. Suzanne M. Timble; children: Victoria, William Prescott II, Marjorie. Student, Williams Coll., 1954-56; AB, Eastern Mich. U., 1958; LLB, Harvard U., 1961. Bar: Iowa 1961, Ill. 1961, U.S. Dist. Ct. (no. dist.) Ill., 1961. Assoc. McBride & Baker, Chgo., 1961-67, ptnr., 1968-84, McDermott, Will & Emery, Chgo., 1984-99. Pres. Miller Investment Co., 1973-93, bd. dirs.; pres. SMI Investment Corp., 1978—. Pres., bd. dirs. 110 N Wacker Dr Found., 1974-84, Northfield Found., 1978-84, Leadership Found., 1979-84, Woodbine Found., 1980-84, The Cannon River Found., 1982-84, L.M. McBride Found., 1982-84, Bellarmine Found., 1982-84, Mark Morton Meml. Fund, 1982—. Mem. Iowa Bar Assn., Ill. State Bar Assn., Harvard Law Soc. Ill. (bd. dirs. 1983-98, treas. 1987-88, sec. 1988-89, v.p. 1989-93, pres. 1993-95), Harvard Club Chgo. (bd. dirs. 1993-95), Monroe Club (bd. dirs. 1988-98), Skokie Country Club (Glencoe, Ill.). Republican. Episcopalian. Home: 1296 Hackberry Ln Winnetka IL 60093-1606 Office: 1296 Hackberry Lane Winnetka IL 60093

ELLYN, LYNNE, energy executive; Degree in computer sci. and mgmt., Oakland U., 1979; MBA, Mich. State U. Various positions to mgr. advanced tech. devel. Chrysler Corp.; dir. bus. systems devel., acting v.p. global systems deployment Xerox Corp., 1993-96; v.p. bus. applications Netscape Comm. Corp., 1996-98; named v.p. info. systems orgn. Detroit Edison Co., 1998; now sr. v.p., chief info. officer DTE Energy Co., Detroit. Fellow Cutter Bus. Tech. Coun. Mem. dean's adv. bd. Oakland U. Decision and Info. Sciences Sch. Named one of 100 Most Influential Women Bus. Leaders, Crain's Detroit Bus., 2002, Top Mich. Women in Computing, Assn. for Women in Computing, 2003, Premier 100 IT Leaders, Computerworld, 2005. Office: DTE Energy Co 2000 2nd Ave Detroit MI 48226-1279

ELLZEY, WAYNE EWELL, retired accountant; b. Laurel, Miss., Apr. 13, 1949; s. Ewell William and Mildred Mae Ellzey. BS, U. Southern Miss., Hattiesburg, 1971, BA, 1976. Auditor Miss. Dept. Audit, Jackson, 1976—96; ret., 1997. Sgt. USMC, 1971—74. Mem.: Am. Legion, South Miss. Mensa (treas. 2006—). United Methodist. Avocations: farming, gardening, antiques, hiking. Home: 6505 Plantation Ct Mobile AL 36695 Personal E-mail: ellzeya@aol.com.

ELMA, BAYANI BORJA, physician; b. Manila, Philippines, Nov. 3, 1942; s. Medardo Romero Elma and Hiwaga Rada Borja E.; m. Maria Mercado Chavez-Elma, July 4, 1971; children: Michael Anthony, Mary Anne. Degree in preparatory medicine, U. Philippines, 1963; MD, U. of the East, Quezon City, Philippines, 1968. Diplomate Am. Bd. Quality Assurance, Utilization Review Physicians. Vice-chief of staff Md. Gen. Hosp., Balt., 1985-90, dir., trustee, 1988-95, chmn., prof. affairs com., 1992-95. Panel editl. advisers Internal Medicine for the Specialist, Livingston, NJ, 1990-2003. Mem. editl. bd.: Md. Med. Jour., 1993—96. Pres. U. East Med. Alumni Assn., 1992-94, Assn. Philippine Physicians in Md., 1997-99.; dir., trustee U. East Med. Alumni Found, 1994-2006; vice-chmn. Govs. Commn. on Asian-Pacific Am. Affairs, Balt., 1992-2003; alt. del. House Del. Balt. City Med. Soc., 1997-99; vice-chmn. bd. trustees U. East Med. Alumni Found., 1998-2003, chmn. bd. trustees, 2003-06, chmn. emeritus, 2006—; trustee Found. for Aid to Philippines, Inc., 2002—. Named One of the Twenty Outstanding Filipino Am. US and Can. Filipino Image mag., 1998-99 Mem.: Am. Coll. Physician Execs. Republican. Roman Catholic. Avocations: reading, writing, travel. Home: 10907 Tony Dr Lutherville MD 21093-3618 Office Phone: 410-296-0573. Personal E-mail: bbelmamd@earthlink.net.

EL MALLAKH, DOROTHEA HENDRY, editor, publishing executive; b. Emmett, Idaho, July 16, 1938; d. David Lovell Parker and Lygia Teressa (Dalton) Hendry; m. Ragaei William El Mallakh, Aug. 26, 1962 (dec. Mar. 19, 1987); children: Helen Alise, Nadia Irene. BA in Modern Langs., Lewis and Clark Coll., 1960; MA in History, U. Colo., 1962, PhD in History, 1972; postgrad., Georgetown U., 1962-63. Exec. adminstr., treas. Internat. Rsch. Ctr. Energy & Econ. Devel., Boulder, Colo., 1973-87, exec. dir., 1987—. Assoc. editor Jour. Energy & Devel., Boulder, 1975-87, mng. editor, 1987—; bd. dirs. Rocky Mountain Eye Found., Boulder. Author: The Slovak Autonomy Movement, 1979; author (with others): The Genius of Arab Civilization, 1983, Gulf Oil in the Aftermath of the Iraq War: Strategies and Policies, 2005; editor: The Energy Watchers I-IX, 1990-98; author and editor: Saudi Arabia, 1982. Perrine Meml. fellow, U. Colo., 1960-61, Rare Lang. fellow, U.S. Govt., U. Colo., 1961-62, Rotary Internat. fellow, Boise, Idaho, 1962. Mem. Internat. Assn. Energy Econs. (v.p. internat. affairs 1989-91, sec. 1988-89). Office: ICEED 850 Willowbrook Rd Boulder CO 80302-7439 Office Phone: 303-442-4014. Business E-Mail: iceed@colorado.edu.

ELMAN, GERRY JAY, lawyer; b. Chgo., Oct. 7, 1942; s. Earl Samuel and Lucille Paulyne Elman; m. Lois Suzanne Bermet Levine; children: Jason Farrel, Floren Haley. BS, U. Chgo., 1963; MS in Chemistry, Stanford U., 1964; JD, Columbia U., 1967. Bar: N.Y. 1969, Pa. 1969, U.S. Dist. Ct. (so. and ea. dists.) N.Y. 1971, U.S. Dist. Ct. (ea. dist.) Pa. 1973, U.S. Dist. Ct. (mid. dist.) Pa. 1974, U.S. Ct. Appeals (Fed. cir.) 1987, U.S. Ct. Appeals (3d cir.) 1989, U.S. Patent Office, 1967, U.S. Supreme Ct. 1973, U.S. Dist. Ct. Colo. 2002. Assoc. Hubbell, Cohen & Stiefel, NYC, 1967-68; patent atty., enzymes and health products Rohm and Haas Co., Phila., 1968-72; dep. atty. gen. Pa. Dept. Justice, Harrisburg, 1972-76; trial atty. Mid. Atlantic office antitrust divsn. U.S. Dept. Justice, Phila., 1976-82; pvt. practice Phila., 1982-83; mem. Elman Assocs., Phila., 1984-88, Lipton, Famiglio & Elman, Media, Pa., 1988-89, Elman Wilf & Fried, Media, 1990-95, Elman & Fried, Media, 1995-96, Elman & Assocs., Media, 1996—2002, Elman Tech. Law, P.C., Swarthmore, Pa., 2002—. Instr. short course in computer law Temple U., Phila., 1984; faculty in intellectual property mgmt. U. Phoenix Online Campus, 1995-98; webmaster Stanford Club of Phila., 2001-. Contbg. author: Lawyers' Microcomputer Users Group Jour., 1985-88; editor: Columbia Jour. Transnat. Law, 1966-67; mem. editl. bd. Jour. Trademark Reporter, 1968, Jour. Computer Law Reporter, 1983-90, BNA Spl. Reports Biotech., 1989-90, Licensing Jour., 1998—; founder, editor in chief Biotech. Law Report, 1982—; mem. bd. advisors Santa Clara Computer and High Tech. Law Jour., 1994-2003; mem. Global CyberLaw Network, 1997-2002, World Tech. Network, 2001-. Chmn. Three Steps Nursery Sch., Phila., 1977; arbitrator Phila. Ct. Common Pleas, 1971-72, 83-88, U.S. Dist. Ct. (ea. dist.) Pa. 1983—, Am. Arbitration Assn., 1987-96, Delaware County Ct. Common Pleas, Pa., 1993—, Forum Sysop, CompuServe online svc., 1994-99. Mem. ABA, Licensing Execs. Soc., Am. Intellectual Property Law Assn., Phila. Bar Assn. (chmn. jurimetrics com. 1975-77), Phila. Intellectual Property Law Assn. (chmn. biotech. subcom. 1982-86, continuing legal edn. com. 1995-97, patent legis. coord. com. 2003—), Delaware County Bar Assn., Internat. Tech. Law Assn., Benjamin Franklin Am. Inn of Ct. (mem. bd. govs. 2004-), Converging Techs. Bar Assn. Home: 406 Yale Ave Swarthmore PA 19081-2024 Office: Elman Tech Law PC 406 Yale Ave PO Box 209 Swarthmore PA 19081-0209 Office Phone: 610-892-9942. E-mail: elman@elman.com.

ELMAN, JEFFREY LOCKE, cognitive sciences educator; b. LA, Jan. 22, 1948; s. Irving and Mildred Mae E.; m. Margaret Ravel, Aug. 5, 1972 (div. Nov. 1995); children: Emily, Jeremy. AB cum laude, Harvard Coll., 1969; PhD in Linguistics, U. Tex., Austin, 1977; D honoris causa (hon.), New Bulgarian U., 2002. Asst. prof. dept. linguistics U. Calif., San Diego, 1977—83, assoc. prof., 1983—89, assoc. prof. dept. cognitive sci., 1988—89, prof. dept. linguistics, 1989—94, prof. dept. cognitive sci. San Diego, 1989—2006, disting. prof., 2006—. Founding mem. dept. cognitive sci. U. Calif., San Diego, dir. Ctr. Rsch. in Lang., 1985—94, 2003—04, assoc. dir. Ctr. Rsch. in Lang., 1994—2003, chair dept. cognitive sci., 1995—98, assoc. dean divsn. social scis., 2002—06, acting dean divsn. social scis., 2006—, founding co-dir. Kavli Inst. Brain and Mind, 2004—; cons., bd. dirs. Ecco Industries, Boston, 1987—90; co-dir. Ctr. Cognitive Sci. New Bulgarian U.; mem. external adv. bd. Inst. Cognitive Sci. U. Colo., Boulder; cons. La. State Bd. Regents; mem. sci. adv. bd. Artificial Life VI. Contbr. articles to profl. jours.; sr. editor: Jour. Cognitive Sci. Soc., 1992—95; co-author: Rethinking Innateness, 1996; mem. editl. bd.: Neural Computation, Connection Sci., Internat. Jour. Neural Systems, Neural Networks, Lang. and Cognitive Processes, Neural Computing Surveys, Bilingualism, Lang. & Cognition. Recipient David E. Rumelhart prize, 2007. Fellow: Cognitive Sci. Soc. (bd. govs. 1994—2000, pres. 1999—2000); mem.: IEEE Acoustics, Speech and Signal Processing Soc., Assn. Computational Linguistics, Lang. Devel. Soc. (mem. exec. bd.), Acoustical Soc. Am. Office: Dept Cognitive Sci U Calif San Diego Rm 0515 La Jolla CA 92093-0515 E-mail: jelman@ucsd.edu.

ELMENDORF, STEVEN A., political strategist; b. NJ; Ed., Trinity Coll. Field organizer Mondale for Pres. campaign; exec. asst. Sen. Brock Adams; chief of staff Rep. Dennis Eckart; sr. adv. to Dick Gephardt, 1992—2004; chief of staff to Dick Gephardt, 1997—2004; dep. campaign mgr. Sen. John Kerry for Pres. campaign, 2004; pres. Bryan Cave Strategies, Washington, Elmendorf Strategies, LLC, Washington. Lectr. Inst. Politics Harvard U., Trinity Coll.; frequent guest Hardball with Chris Matthews, Capitol Report CNBC, Fox News, Crossfire CNN. Named one of 50 most powerful staff people on capitol hill, Roll Call newspaper, 1992—2004. Office: Elmendorf Strategies LLC 1455 Pennsylvania Ave NW Ste 400 Washington DC 20004 Office Phone: 202-737-1010.

ELMER, BRIAN CHRISTIAN, lawyer; b. Washington, Apr. 18, 1936; s. Arthur Christian and Kathryn Aleen (O'Brien) E.; m. Sonja Kay Glass, Sept. 3, 1966; children: Mark Christian, Kimberly Kay, Robin Ann. BA in Arts and Sci., Cornell U., 1960; JD, U. Mich., 1962. Bar: D.C. 1963. Law clk. U.S. Ct. Appeals for D.C. Cir., Washington, 1962-64; ptnr. Jones, Day, Reavis and Pogue, Washington, 1964-79, Crowell and Moring, LLP, Washington, 1979—. Author: Fraud in Government Contracting, 1985; contbr. articles to profl. jours. Mem. ABA, D.C. Bar Assn., Met. Club. Office: Crowell & Moring LLP 1001 Pennsylvania Ave NW Washington DC 20004-2595 Home Phone: 703-527-8340; Office Phone: 202-624-2550. E-mail: belmer@crowell.com.

ELMER, LAWRENCE WILLIAM, neurologist, researcher; b. Gainesville, Fla., Jan. 31, 1958; s. Joseph William and Jean (Maguire) Elmer; m. LeAnn Wolitarsky, Jan. 17, 1953; children: Stephen William, Caroline Grace. BA, Davidson Coll., NC, 1980; MS, Fla. State U., 1983; MD, U. Fla., 1987, PhD, 1988. Diplomate Am. Bd. Psychiatry and Neurology. Asst. prof. U. Mich., Ann Arbor, 1994—98, Med. Coll. Ohio, Toledo, 1998—2004; assoc. prof. Med. U. Ohio, Toledo, 2004—. Dir., Parkinson's Disease and Movement Disorders program Med. U. Ohio, Toledo, 1998—, dir. ctr. for neurol. disorders, 2003—, pres.-elect faculty senate, 2004—05. V.p. Washtenaw Christian Acad., Saline, Mich., 2000—02; bd. dirs. ctrl. Ohio chpt. Huntington's Disease Soc., Columbus, 1999—2001, bd. dirs. Mich. chpt. Lansing, 2001—03; med. dir. NW Ohio Parkinson's Found., Toledo, 1998—2005; APMCO credentials com. mem. Med. Coll. Ohio, Toledo, 2000—04, chair, clin. rsch. ctr. subcom., 2004—04. Named one of Am. Best Doctors, 2004—07; recipient Nat. Rsch. Svc. award, NIH, Baylor Coll. Medicine, 1987—88, Humanism in Medicine award, Med. Sch. Class of 2003, 2002, Golden Apple Tchg. award, 2003—07, Dean's Tchg. award, Dean's Office, Sch. Medicine, 2003; fellow, U. Fla. Sch. of Medicine, 1983—87; scholar, Pfizer Pharms., 1995—97. Mem.: Soc. for Neuroscience, NY Acad. Sci., Am. Acad. Neurology. Office: U Toledo Health Sci Campus 3000 Arlington Ave Mail Stop 1195 Toledo OH 43614-2598 Office Phone: 419-383-3544.

ELMER, MICHAEL BENDIK, legal administrator; b. Feb. 26, 1949; life ptnr. Annette Andersen; 1 child. Cand. jur., U. Copenhagen, 1973. Civil servant Min. of Justice, 1973-76, 77-82, head of divsn., 1982-87, 88-91; dep. judge Hillerød, 1976-77; high ct. judge Eastern High Ct., Copenhagen, 1987-88; v.p. a.i. Maritime and Comml. Ct., Copenhagen, 1988; dep. permanent sec. for justice, head of cmty. law and human rights dept., 1991-94; advocate gen. EC Ct. of Justice, Luxembourg, 1994—97; v.p. Maritime & Comml. Ct., Copenhagen, 1998—. Assoc. prof. U. Copenhagen, 1975-85; asst. pub. prosecutor, 1980-81; part time judge Ct. of Ballerup, 1981-82; external examiner Danish law schs., 1985—; internat. comml. arbitrator, 2000—; chmn., mem. numerous govt. and internat. orgns. Author of several books and articles, especially on property law, cmty. law and penal law. Recipient Grand Cross, Order of Merit, Luxembourg, Knight of the Order of Dannebrog, Denmark. Mem.: UNIDROIT (governing coun.), Assn. of European Competition Law Judges (London) (v.p.). Home: Skovalléen 16 DK-2880 Bagsvaerd Denmark Office: Maritime & Comml Ct Bredgade 70 DK-1260 Copenhagen Denmark Home Phone: +45 35 55 4963; Office Phone: +45 33 47 9203. E-mail: michael@elmer.as.

ELMER, RUSSELL S., diversified financial services company executive, lawyer; BA in Polit. Sci. and Internat. Rels., Stanford U.; JD, U. Calif., Berkeley, Calif., 1990. Ptnr. Gray, Cary, Ware & Freidenrich, 1990—2000; asst. gen. counsel E*TRADE Fin. Corp., Menlo Pk., Calif., 2000—01, gen. counsel, corp. sec., 2002—. Office: 135 E 57th St New York NY 10022 also: E*TRADE Financial Corp 4500 Bohannon Dr Menlo Park CA 94025*

ELMES, DAVID GORDON, psychologist, educator; b. Newton, Mass., Feb. 15, 1942; s. Leslie and Ruth (Adams) E.; m. Anne Louise Lawrence, June 7, 1963; children: Matthew David, Jennifer Anne. BA, U. Va., Charlottesville, 1964, MA, 1966, PhD, 1967. Mgmt. trainee C & P of Va., 1963; asst. prof. psychology Washington and Lee U., Lexington, Va., 1967-71, assoc. prof., 1971-74, prof., 1975—2007, prof. emeritus, 2007—, head dept. psychology, 1990-2000, co-dir. cognitive sci., 1987-2000. Rsch. assoc. Human Performance Ctr., U. Mich., 1973-74; vis. fellow Univ. Coll., Oxford U., Eng., 1987. Author: Readings in Experimental Psychology, 1978, Research Methods in Psychology, 2005; contbr. articles to profl. jours. Bd. dirs. Rockbridge Mental Health Clinic, 1968-73. Fellow Am. Psychol. Soc.; mem. Psychonomic Soc., Va. Acad. Sci., Coun. on Undergrad. Rsch. (past pres.), Phi Beta Kappa. Office: Washington and Lee U Dept Psychology Lexington VA 24450-0303 Business E-Mail: elmesd@wlu.edu.

ELMORE, BRUCE ALEXANDER, JR., lawyer; b. Asheville, NC, Nov. 1, 1952; s. Bruce Alexander and Sadie June Elmore; m. Virginia Anne Healy, Nov. 4, 2006; m. Martha Parker, Dec. 28, 1974 (div. Dec. 15, 1990); children: Scott Alexander, Rebecca Anne. BA, U. NC, Chapel Hill, 1974, JD, 1976. Bar: NC 1976. Ptnr. The Elmore Law Firm P.A., Asheville, 1976—2006, Cloninger, Elmore, Hensley &Searson PLLC, Asheville, 2006—. Mem.: ATLA (sustaining mem.), Nat. Assn. Criminal Def. Lawyers (presidents club), NC Acad. Trial Lawyers (benefactor), Million Dollar Advocates Forum, NC Chpt. ACLU (pres. 2006—), Western NC ACLU (bd. mem. 2002—07). Liberal. Avocation: motorcycle travel. Home: 169 Windsor Rd Asheville NC 28804 Office: Cloninger Elmore Hensley & Searson Pllc 366 Merrimon Ave Asheville NC 28801 Home Phone: 828-255-0979; Office Phone: 828-252-1786. Office Fax: 828-252-1874. Business E-Mail: elmore@cehslawfirm.com.

ELMORE, CENIETH CATHERINE, music educator; b. Wilson, NC, July 4, 1930; d. Thomas Onestrus Elmore and Effie Lee Morris. MusB in Theory, U. N.C., Greensboro, 1953; MusM in Composition, U. N.C., 1962, MA in Musicology, 1963, PhD in Musicology, 1972. Piano tchr. pub. sch., Fuquay Springs, NC, 1953—57, Louisburg, NC, 1957—60; grad. asst. piano tchr. U. N.C., Chapel Hill, 1960—63; music prof. Campbell U., Buies Creek, NC, 1963—94, prof. emeritus, 1994—. Lectr. in field; pvt. piano tchr., 1998—. Active Franklin County Arts Coun., Louisburg, NC, 1970—, Franklin County Person Place Preservation Soc., Louisburg, 1980—; judge Franklin County Arts Coun. Whistlers Conv., Louisburg, 1989—96, Internat. Whistlers Conv., Louisburg, 1997—99, 2003—05, 2007, asst. to judges, 2000—02; active Perry's Chapel Bapt. Ch., Franklinton, NC, 1948—. Named Artist of Yr., Franklin County Arts Coun., 1995. Mem.: NC Music Tchrs. Assn. (bd. dirs., chair arts awareness and advocacy 2006—), Am. Musicological Soc., Raleigh Piano Tchrs. Assn. (first v.p. 1996—98, 2000—02, pres. 2002—04, chair young artist auditions composition competition 2004—). Republican. Achievements include research in a structural analysis of Schoenberg's 15 Gedichte aus "Das Buch Der Hargenden Garten" von Stefan George; stylistic considerations in the piano sonatas of Nicholai Medtner. Avocations: painting, reading, gardening, travel, internet. Home: 981 Perry's Chapel Church Rd Franklinton NC 27525-8263 Personal E-mail: ceniethelmore@aol.com.

ELMORE, JAMES WALTER, architect, educator, retired dean; b. Lincoln, Nebr., Sept. 5, 1917; s. Harry Douglas and Marie Clare (Minor) E.; m. Mary Ann Davidson, Sept. 6, 1947; children: James Davidson, Margaret Kay. AB, U. Nebr., 1938; MS in Architecture, Columbia U., 1948. Mem. faculty Ariz. State U., 1949-86, prof. architecture, 1959-86, founding dean Coll. of Architecture, 1964-74. Cons. architect, 1956— Trustee Heard Museum, Phoenix, 1968-79; bd. dirs. Valley Forward Assn., 1969-89 , pres., 1985; bd. dirs. Central Ariz. chpt. Ariz. Hist. Soc., 1973-89; bd. dirs. Ariz. Architects Found., 1978-86, Rio Salado Devel. Dist., 1980-87. Served to col., C.E. U.S. Army, 1940-46. Decorated Bronze Star. Fellow AIA; mem. Ariz. Acad. Home: 7550 N 16t St #6304 Phoenix AZ 85020-4618

ELMORE, LEONARD JOSEPH, lawyer; b. Bklyn., Mar. 28, 1952; s. Moses Leonard and Gladys (Henson) E.; m. Gail Segal, Sept. 5, 1987; 1 child, Stephen. BA in English, U. Md., 1978; JD, Harvard Law Sch., 1987. Bar: N.Y. 1988. Asst. dist. atty. Kings County Dist. Atty., Bklyn, 1987-90; pres., CEO Test U., 2001—03; sr. counsel LeBoeuf, Lamb, Green & MacRae. Basketball player NBA, 1974—84; commentator Nat. Pub. Radio, Washington; basketball analyst CBS Sports, NYC, Jefferson Pilot/Raycom Sports, Charlotte, NC, 1985—92; coll. basketball analyst ESPN. Com. mem. Chancellor's Task Force on Academics., U. Md., 1986; bd. mem. Univ. Sys. of Md. Found., 1990—98; mem. Tourism Devel. Bd. U. Md., College Park, 1998—; bd. mem. 1 800 Flowers.com, NBA Retired Players Assn., John and James L. Knight Found.'s Knight Commn. on Intercollegiate Athletics, 2003—. Recipient Citizenship award U. Md., 1974, Alumni Achievement award Black Alumni Assn. U. Md., 1988. Mem. N.Y. Bar Assn. (Sports and Entertainment Com.), Sport Lawyers Assn. (bd. mem.) Avocations: cinema, baseball, literature, history, politics. Office: LeBoeuf, Lamb, Greene & MacRae LLP 125 W 55th St New York NY 10019-8000 Office Phone: 212-424-8000. E-mail: lelmore@llgm.com.

ELMORE, WALTER A., electrical engineer, consultant; b. Bartlett, Tenn., Oct. 2, 1925; s. Walter Alcorn and Lucile (Tapp) E.; m. Jane Ann Huey, June 3, 1950; children: Robin, Jamie, Laura. BSEE, U. Tenn., 1949. Registered profl. engr., Fla. Mgr. cons. engring. sect. Protective Relay div. Westinghouse Elec. Corp., Newark, 1951-79, Protective Relay div. ABB Power T & D Co., Coral Springs, Fla., 1979-89; mgr. cons. engring. sect. protective relay divsn. ABB Power T&D Co., Coral Springs, Fla., 1989-94, cons. engr. high voltage protection, 1994-96, ret., 1996. Author: (with others) Applied Protective Relaying, 1976, Protective Relaying Theory and Application, 1994, Pilot Protective Relaying, 1999. Fellow IEEE (chmn. IEEE/PES tech. coun. 1988-89, Gold medal for engring. excellence 1989); mem. NAE, Tau Beta Pi, Eta Kappa Nu, Phi Kappa Phi. Republican. Home: 104 Macgregor Dr Blue Ridge VA 24064-1526

EL-MOSLIMANY, ANN PAXTON, paleoecologist, educator, writer; b. Fullerton, Calif., Aug. 2, 1937; d. Donald Dorn and Sarah Frances (Turman) Paxton; m. Mohammed Ahmad El-Moslimany, May 31, 1962 (dec.); children: Samia, Ramsey, Rasheed. BS, N.Mex. State U., 1959; MS, Am. U., Beirut, 1961; PhD, U. Wash., 1983. Tchr. various schs., 1959-83, Kuwait U., 1984—86, Seattle Ctrl. C.C., 1986-90; prin., tchr. Islamic Sch. Seattle, 1989-99, curriculum coord., 1999—. Paleoecological rschr. Palynological Consultants, 1987—; founding dir. Islamic Sch. of Seattle; adv. bd. Islamic Sch. League Am. Author: Zaki's Ramadan Fast, 1994; contbr. articles to sci. jours.; mem. adv. bd. Aziah mag. Speaker Children of Abraham Organization. Mem. Amnesty Internat., Am. Quaternary Assn., Islamic Sch. League. Muslim. Avocations: travel, literature, history. Office: Islamic Sch Seattle 720 25th Ave Seattle WA 98122-4902 Mailing: PO Box 367 Seahurst WA 98062 Personal E-mail: annelmoslimany@yahoo.com.

EL-MOURSY, MAGDY, electronics engineer; b. Cairo, Giza, Egypt, Oct. 16, 1974; s. Ali El-Moursy and Naima Ahmed; m. Amira Malek; 1 child, Ziad Magdy. BS in Electronics and Comm. Engring. with honors, Cairo U., Egypt, 1996, MS in Computer Networks, 2000; MS in high performance VLSI/IC design, U. Rochester, NYC, 2001, PhD in high performance VLSI/IC design, 2004. Rsch. asst. Nat. Inst. Standards, Cairo, Giza, 1997—99; software developer Internat. Computer and Communication Consultants (ICCC), Giza, 1999—2000; rsch. asst. Electronics Rsch. Inst., Giza, 1999—2000; tchg. asst. U. Rochester, NY, 2000—01, rsch. asst., 2001—04; integrated circuit designer STMicroelectronics Corp., San Diego, 2003; sr. design elec. engr. Intel Corp., Portland, Oreg., 2004—06; asst. prof. info. engring. and tech. dept. German U., Cairo, 2006—. Contbr. chapters to books, scientific papers to profl. jours. Tchr. Bilal Masjed, Portland, Oreg., 2005—06, Islamic Ctr. Rochester, Rochester, NY, 2003. Recipient Advanced Design Divisional award, Logic Tech. Devel., 2006. Mem.: IEEE. Moslem. Avocations: reading, exercise. Personal E-mail: magdyaelmoursy@gmail.com.

ELMS, BEN, actor, theater director; b. Syracuse, NY, July 1, 1935; s. Benjamin Charles and Sarah Mildred (Nourse) E. BA, Syracuse U., 1957. Appeared in TV shows including Unsolved Mysteries, 1990; films include Man Who Knew Too Much, 1985, The Judgement, 1990, The Town With No Name, 2000; musicals include The Fantasticks, 1987, Jesus Christ Superstar, 1987, Phantom, 1997, Hello Dolly, 1998, Annie, 2004, Beauty And The Beast, 2005; plays include Death of a Salesman, 1989, Foxfire, 1991, Noises Off, 1996, Hamlet, 1997, Our Town, 1999, Julius Caesar, 2000, The Diary of Anne Frank, 2001, The Miracle Worker, 2002, Joseph & The Amazing Technicolor Dreamcoat, 2002, The Crucible, 2002, Jekyl & Hyde, 2003, Alice in Wonderland, 2003, Midsummer Night's Dream, 2003, Romeo and Juliet, 2004; dir. plays including Butterflies Are Free, 1978, Extremities, 1987; also commls. Capt. U.S. Army, 1958-60. Mem. SAG, Actors Equity Assn. Republican. Roman Catholic. Home: 60 Presidential Plz #1506 Syracuse NY 13202-2292

ELRAHMAN, O. ABD, environmental and transportation engineer, educator; m. Dina H. Refki, Aug. 1, 1985; children: Rhani A., Jaylan A. BEng in Urban and Regional Planning, AUC, Cairo, 1978; MSc in Transp. Planning and Engring., Polytechnic U., NYC, 1983; PhD in Urban and Environ. Studies, Rensselaer Polytechnic Inst., Troy, NY, 1989; cert. in Mgmt. Devel. Studies, Cornell U. Head R&D adminstrn. and mgmt. support sect. Transp. R&D NY State Dept. of Transp., Albany, 1996—. Prof. Union Coll., Schenectady, NY. Mem. editl. bd.: Jour. Tech. Transfer.

Recipient Excellence in Engring. award, NY State Transp. R&D, 1999. Mem.: NAS, Transp. Rsch. Bd. Office: NY State Dept of Transportation 16 Meadowbrook Rd Watervliet NY 12189 Business E-Mail: oelrahman@gw.dot.state.ny.us.

ELRICK, DONALD, retired literature educator; b. Cleve., May 27, 1940; s. Robert Donald and Hilda Freda Elrick; BA, Hiram Coll., Ohio, 1964; attended, U. Akron, Ohio, 1970. Cert. State of Ohio, 1964. English tchr. Medina City Schs., Ohio, 0964—1980, Lake Cath. High Sch., Mentor, Ohio, 1980—81, Lorain C.C., Ohio, 1981—83, Lakewood City Schs., Ohio, 1983—95; ret., 1995. Advanced placement reader Ednl. Testing Svc., Princeton, NJ, 1976—81; advanced placement cons. Coll. Entrance Exam. Bd., Chgo., 1980—81. Mem. Kiwanis, Seville, Ohio, 2002—06. Mem.: Ohio End. Assn., Nat. Edn. Assn., First Universalist Unitarian Ch. Westfield Ctr. (trustee 2005—), Seville Hist. Soc. and Mus. (pres. 2001—). Unitarian. Avocations: house restoration, antiques, reading, gardening.

ELRIFI, IVOR R., lawyer; b. 1961; BS in Biology, Queen's U. at Kingston, Can., 1982, PhD in Biology, 1986; LLB, Osgood Hall Law Sch., Toronto, Can., 1989. Bar: Can. 1991, NY 1991, ON 1991, Mass. 1998, US Ct. Appeals. (Fed. Cir.), registered: US Patent & Trademark Office. Assoc. Fish & Neave, NY; patent counsel CytoThearapeutics Inc., Providence, gen. counsel & v.p.; patent counsel Modex Therapeutics, Lausanne, Switzerland; ptnr. Mintz Levin Cohn Ferris Glovsky & Popeo PC, Boston, mem. policy com., co-chmn., Intellectual Property Sect. Mem.: Law Soc. Upper Can. Office: Mintz Levin Cohn Ferris Glovsky & Popeo PC One Financial Ctr Boston MA 02111 Office Phone: 617-348-1714. Office Fax: 617-542-2241. Business E-Mail: irelrifi@mintz.com.

ELROD, BEN MOODY, academic administrator; b. Rison, Ark., Oct. 13, 1930; s. Benjamin Searcy and Frances Othello (Sadler) E.; m. Betty Lou Warren, Aug. 7, 1951; children: Cynthia Lou, William Searcy. BA, Ouachita Baptist U., 1952; ThD, Southwestern Bapt. Theol. Sem., 1962; EdD, Ind. U., 1975. Ordained to ministry Baptist Ch., 1950; pastor First Bapt. Ch., Atkins, Ark., 1951-53, Tioga, Tex., 1955-57, Marlow, Okla., 1957-60, South Side Bapt. Ch., Pine Bluff, Ark., 1960-63; pres. Oakland City (Ind.) Coll., 1968-70, Georgetown (Ky.) Coll., 1978-83, Ind. Colls. of Ark., 1983-88; v.p. devel. Ouachita Bapt. U., Arkadelphia, Ark., 1963-68, 70-78, pres., 1988-97, chancellor, 1998—. Commr. Ark. Econ. Devel. Commn., 2002—, chmn., 2007; vis. lectr. in field; cons. in higher edn. Contbr. articles to religion jours. Page U.S. Ho. of Reps., 1946-47; trustee Clark County (Ark.) Hosp., 1973-77, chmn., 1975-77; trustee Ark. Bapt. Med. System, 1978, 1989-2001. Mem. Nat. Assn. Ind. Colls. and Univs. (chmn. tax policy commn. 1993), Ark. State C. of C. (bd. dirs. 1990-98), Assn. So. Bapt. Colls. and Schs. (pres. 1996-97), Consortium for Global Edn. (chmn. bd. dirs. 1997-99, mem. exec. com. bd. dirs. 1997-2002). Achievements include having Ben M. Elrod Center for Family and Community at Ouachita Baptist U. named in his honor. Home: 1008 Village Dr Arkadelphia AR 71923-2922 Office: Ouachita Bapt Univ Elrod Ctr for Family and Cmty Box 3790 Ouachita Sta Arkadelphia AR 71923-3221 Office Phone: 870-245-5320. Personal E-mail: belrodus@yahoo.com.

ELROD, DEBORAH LEE, special education educator; b. Bradford, Pa., June 27, 1952; d. Richard Irving McKelvey and Betty Jean Slingerland McCarty; m. Allen Wayne Elrod, Dec. 17, 1978. BS in Edn., Stephen F. Austin State U., 1974; MEd, Sam Houston State U., 1985. Cert. profl. reading specialist, provisional elem. edn., provisional elem. reading, provisional lang. and/or learning disabilities, provisional physically handicapped. Resource tchr. spl. edn. Newton (Tex.) Ind. Sch. Dist.; spl. edn. resource tchr. Aldine Ind. Sch. Dist., Houston; tchr. Hoffman Mid. Sch., 2000—. Instr. No. Harris County Coll., Houston, 1990-92; coord. dyslexia program Hoffman Mid. Sch., 2001— Named Tchr. of Year, Carmichael Elem. Sch., 1993; Fund for Tchr. Grantee, 2006. Mem. Ice Skating Inst., US Figure Skating Assn., Delta Kappa Gamma Avocation: figure skating. Home Phone: 713-937-3877; Office Phone: 713-613-7670. Personal E-mail: debonice@msn.com.

ELROD, EUGENE RICHARD, lawyer; b. Roanoke, Ala., May 14, 1949; s. James Woodrow and Selma Fromer (Steinbach) E. AB, Dartmouth Coll., 1971; JD, Emory U., 1974. Bar: Ga. 1974, DC 1976, US Ct. Appeals (DC cir.) 1985, US Ct. Appeals (5th cir.) 1987, US Dist. Ct. DC 1987, US Ct. Appeals (11th cir.) 1987, US Supreme Ct. 1987, US Ct. Appeals (10th cir.) 1997. Trial atty. Fed. Power Com., Washington, 1974-76; atty.-advisor Fed. Energy Adminstrn., Washington, 1977; assoc. Sidley & Austin, Washington, 1977-80, ptnr., 1981—. Adv. bd. Inst. for Energy Law, 2004-. Contbr. chapters to books. Mem. selection com. for Woodruff scholars Emory U. Law Sch., Dartmouth '71 Exec. Com. Mem. ABA (mem. coun. group pub. utility, comms. and transp. law 2007-), DC Bar Assn., Ga. Bar Assn., Energy Bar Assn. (chmn. oil pipeline com. 1982-83, tax com. 1980-81, 92-95, liaison with adminstrv. law judges 1986-87, ethics com. 1997-2001, bd. dirs. 2000-03, bd. dirs. Charitable Found. 2005-), Dartmouth Club (exec. com. class of 1971), Book Club of Calif. Avocations: running, book collecting, gardening. Home: 4330 Hawthorne St NW Washington DC 20016-3571 Office: Sidley Austin LLP 1501 K St NW Ste 900 Washington DC 20005 Office Phone: 202-736-8206. Business E-Mail: eelrod@sidley.com.

ELROD, LINDA DIANE HENRY, lawyer, educator; b. Topeka, Kans., Mar. 6, 1947; d. Lyndus Arthur Henry and Marjorie Jane (Hammel) Allen; divorced; children: Carson Douglas, Bree Elizabeth. BA in English with honors, Washburn U., 1969, JD cum laude, 1971. Bar: Kans. 1972, U.S. Supreme Ct. 2004, cert.: U.S. Supreme Ct. (domestic mediator) 1999. Instr. U. SD, Vermillion, 1970—71; research atty. Kans. Jud. Coun., Topeka, 1972—74; asst. prof. Washburn U., Topeka, 1974—78, assoc. prof., 1978—82, prof. law, 1982—93, disting. prof., 1993—2006, dir. Children and Family Law Ctr., 2001—, Richard S. Righter disting. prof. law, 2006—. Vis. prof. law U. San Diego, Paris Summer Inst., 1988, 90, Washington U. Sch. Law, St. Louis, 1990, 98, summer 1991, 93, Fla. State U. Law Sch., spring, 2000. Author: Kansas Family Law Handbook, 1983, rev. edit., 1990, supplement, 1993, Child Custody Practice and Procedure, 1993, supplements, 1994-2006; co-author: Principles of Family Law, 1999, 6th edit., 2007, Kansas Family Law Guide, 1999, supplements, 2000-06; editor Family Law Quar., 1992—; mem. joint editl. bd. on uniform family law Nat. Conf. Commrs. on Uniform State Laws; reporter Uniform Child Abduction Prevention Act, 2004-06; contbr. articles to profl. jours. Pres. YWCA, Topeka, 1982-83; vice-chair Kans. Commn. on Child Support, 1984-87, Supreme Ct. Commn. on Child Support, 1987—; chair Kans. Cmty. Svc. Orgn., 1986-87; adv. bd. CASA, 1997—; bd. dirs. Appleseed, 2000-05; elder Westminster Presbyn. Ch., 2006—; mem. permanent jud. commn. Presbytery No. Kans. Recipient Disting. Svc. award Washburn Law Sch. Assn., 1986, Washburn Alumni Assn., 2005; named YWCA Woman of Distinction, 1997; Woman of the Yr. scholar Am. Bus. Women's Assn., 2006. Mem. ABA (coun. family law sect. 1988, sec. 1998, vice-chair, 1999, chair-elect 2000, chair 2000-01, chair Schwab Meml. Grant Implementation 1984-87, co-chair Amicus Curiae com. 1987-92, co-chair pro bono child custody project adv. bd. 2001-2005, steering com. on unmet legal needs of children 2002-2005), Topeka Bar Assn. (sec. 1981-85, v.p. 1985-86, pres. 1986-87), Kans. Child Support Enforcement Assn. (bd. dirs. 1988—, Child Support Hall of Fame 1990), Kans. Bar Assn. (sec.-treas. 1988-89, com. ops. and fin. 1988, pres. family law sect. 1984-86, Disting. Svc. award 1985), NoNoSo, Phi Kappa Phi, Phi Alpha Delta Alumni Assn. (justice 1976-77), Phi Beta Delta, Kappa Alpha Theta (pres. alumnae chpt. 1995-97). Presbyterian. Avocations: bridge, reading, quilting. Office: Washburn U Law Sch 17th and College Topeka KS 66621 E-mail: linda.elrod@washburn.edu.

ELROD, LU, music educator, actress; b. Chattanooga, Apr. 23, 1935; d. John C. Elrod and Helen Pauline (Kohn). MusB, Ga. State U., 1960; M in Music Edn., U. Ga., 1970, EdD, 1971; PhD, U. London, 1975. Prof. music, music coach U. Md., Balt., 1972-78, Calif. State U., LA, 1978—2004, now prof. emerita. Singer with Dallas Opera, 1957. Appeared in movies Charly, 1969, Brewster's Millions, 1986, Major Pettigrew and Me, 1976, Seduction of Joe Tynan, 1977, Atlanta Child Murders, 1985, Children Don't Tell, 1986, For Love or Money, 1986, High School High, 1996, Wag the Dog, 1997, The Big Lebowski, 1998, Primary Colors, 1998, Lloyd the Ugly Kid, 1999, Beautiful, 1999, Glory Days, 2001, Freaky Friday, 2004, Kicking and Screaming, 2005, A River Reborn, 2006; appeared on TV in Lazarus Syndrome, 1980, Hill Street Blues (Emmy award), 1988, Superior Court, 1988, TV Bloopers, 1989, Beakman's World (Emmy award), Dream On, 1993, Misery Loves Company, 1995, Caroline in the City, 1995, Louie, 1996, George and Alana, 1996, Maggie, 1998, Two Guys and a Girl, 2000, Glory Days, 2001, I Love the 90's, 2004; appeared in TV commls Recipient Gold medal, Silver medal swimming Am. Atheletic Union, 1955, Leadership Devel. award Ford Found., 1967, Leadership Fellows award Ford Found., 1968, Nat. Philanthropy award, 2006; Tift Coll. voice scholar, 1953, Baylor U. voice scholar, 1956; Lu Elrod scholarship named at Calif. State U., LA, 1989; named to Calif. State U., L.A. Wall of Fame, 1993; named Disting. Prof. Arts and Letters, 1993. Mem. AAUP, AFTRA, SAG, Am. Guild Variety Artists, Calif. Faculty Assn., Coll. Music Soc. Achievements include established 32 music, theatre, communication studies scholarships through fundraising activities, collective bargaining, social work, and athletics 1978-2006. Office: Calif State Univ 5151 State University Dr Los Angeles CA 90032-4226 Business E-Mail: lelrod@calstatela.edu.

ELS, ERNIE (THEODORE ERNEST ELS), professional golfer; b. Kempton Park, South Africa, Oct. 17, 1969; s. Cornelius and Hester E. Diploma, Jan de Klerk Tech. Coll. Golf Course Designer Mem. nat. teams Dunhill Cup, 1992, 93, 94, 95, 96, 97, 98, 99, 2000, World Cup, 1992, 93, 96, 97, 2001 Pres.'s Cup, 1996, 98, 2000, 2003, host, Ernie Els Invitational, South Africa. Established the Ernie Els Foundation for Children 1999 Winner, 15 Career PGA Tour Victories, US Open, 1994, 97, British Open, 2002, 43 Career Internat. Victories; named PGA European Player of Yr., 1994; South African Sportsman of the Yr., 1994, recipient, Lifetime membership, PGA European Tour, 1998. Mem. Ocean Club (Paradise Island, The Bahamas). Avocations: squash, movies, winemaking. Mailing: PGA Tour 112 PGA TOUR Blvd Ponte Vedra Beach FL 32082*

ELSAS, LOUIS JACOB, II, medical educator; b. Atlanta, Feb. 10, 1937; s. Herbert R. and Edith (Levy) E.; m. Nancy Terrell, July 15, 1961; children: Nancy Louise, Margaret Edith, Louis Jacob, III. BA, Harvard U., 1958; MD, U. Va., 1962. Diplomate Am. Bd. Internal Medicine, Am. Bd. Med. Genetics. Intern Yale-New Haven Hosp., 1962-63, resident in internal medicine, 1963-65; NIH postdoctoral fellow in med. genetics Yale U., 1965-68, from instr. to asst. prof. sect. genetics, dept. medicine and pediatrics, 1968-70; faculty Emory U. Med. Sch., Atlanta, 1970—2002, prof. pediatrics and biochemistry, 1977—2002, prof. emeritus, 2002—. Dir. Ga. Comprehensive Genetic System, 1978; vis. prof. Japan Soc. Promotion Sci., 1976; Professore a contratto, Italy, 1985—; U.S. advisor Congress of Inborn Errors of Metabolism, 1980-2000; bd. dirs. The Howard Sch., 1994—; prof., dir. Dr. John T. MacDonald Found. Ctr. Med. Genetics U. Miami, 2002-. Contbr. numerous articles to profl. jours. Mem. alumni coun. Phillips Acad., 2001—. Recipient Rsch. Career Devel. award NIH, 1972-77, John Horsley Meml. prize U. Va. Med. Sch., 1972, A.E. Levy Faculty Rsch. award Emory U., 1989, Big Heart award Civitans, 1992, Claude Fuess award Phillips Acad., 2000; named hon. citizen Interlaken, Switzerland, 1980. Fellow Am. Acad. Pediat., Am. Coll. Med. Genetics (founder, bd. dirs. 1996—); mem. UNICEF, Soc. Inherited Metabolic Disorders (founding pres.), Am. Soc. Clin. Investigation, Soc. Pediat. Rsch., Am. Soc. Biol. Chemistry, Am. Soc. Human Genetics, Assn. Am. Physicians, Assn. Profs. Human and Med. Genetics (pres. 1998-2001), S.E. Genetics Group (chmn. 1983-94), Coun. Regional Networks (pres. 1994-2001), Emory U. Faculty Club, Druid Hills Golf Club, The Temple, Sigma Xi (past chpt. pres.). Clubs: Emory U. Faculty, Druid Hills Golf, Civitan (Humanitarian award 1979, Big Heart award 1992). Office: Dr John T Macdonald Found Ctr Med Genetics U Miami Sch Medicine Rm 6001 MCCD Bldg 1601 NW 12 Ave Miami FL 33136 Home: 3940 Braganza Ave Miami FL 33133-6355 Business E-Mail: lelsas@med.miami.edu. *The successful biomedical scientist must develop a personal balance between science and humanism; innovation and application; learning and teaching. This goal can be met if one starts at an early age and continues as a student of fundamental science; is curious and tests central dogma; uses truth and the scientific method as standards of conduct and is sympathetic to the needs of individuals and society.*

ELSASSER, GLEN ROBERT, journalist; b. Marion, Ohio, Oct. 18, 1935; s. Glen Robert and Mary Louise (Hogan) E.; m. Katharine Macy Kersting, Sept. 8, 1973; 1 child, Daniel. BA, Ohio State U., 1957; MS, Columbia U. Sch. Journalism, 1961. Reporter UPI, Louisville, 1957-58; reporter, writer Indpls. Star, 1961-63; reporter, writer, editor Chgo. Tribune, Chgo., NYC, Washington, 1963—. With U.S. Army, 1958-60, Kansas City, Mo. Recipient Gavel award ABA, 1979. Home: 319 C St NE Washington DC 20002-5709 Office: Chgo Tribune 1325 G St NW Ste 200 Washington DC 20005-3129

EL-SAYED, IVAN HOMER, otolaryngologist, researcher; s. Mostafa Amr and Janice El-Sayed; m. Belinda Hahn; 1 child, Ava Alexandria. MD (hon.), Boston U., 1996. Diplomate Am. Bd. Otolaryngology, 2002. Attending physician U. Calif., San Francisco, 2002—. Mem. Comprehensive Cancer Ctr. U. Calif., 2002—. Mem.: Am. Acad. Nanomedicine, Am. Acad. Otolaryngology, Alpha Omega Alpha. Achievements include patents for Spectroscopic Diagnosis for Bacteria in Biologic Fluid; patents pending for Detection of Cancer with Metallic Nanopartilces; invention of Photothermal Destruction of Cancer with Immunotarged Nanoparticles. Office: U Calif 400 Parnassus Ave San Francisco CA 94143 Office Phone: 415-353-2757. Office Fax: 415-353-2603.

ELSBERG, JOHN WILLIAM, publishing executive, writer; b. NYC, Aug. 4, 1945; s. John Christian and Paula Hutter E.; m. Constance Waeber, June 17, 1967; 1 child, Stephen John. BA in History magna cum laude, Columbia Coll., 1967; BA in History with honors, Cambridge U., 1969, MA in History, 1973. Editor U.S. Army Ctr. Mil. History, Washington, 1974-80, acting chief editl. br., 1981, chief editl. br., 1982, editor-in-chief, 1983, chief prodn. svcs. divsn., 1988—2005. Judge numerous writing competitions; lectr. Manassas campus Am. history and We. civilization No Va. C.C., 1974-75, 75-76; freelance rschr. bicentennial project Nat. Pub. Affairs Ctr. T.V., 1974; adj. prof. European div. U. Md., 1970-73; counselor, adminstr. residential Upward Bound program Columbia U., 1965-67. Editor (fiction): Gargoyle, 1977—80; editor: Bogg: A Jour. Contemporary Writing, 1980—, author numerous poems, 17 books and chapbooks of poetry, 6 historical titles; mem. editl. bd. Del. Poetry Rev., 2006—, Delmarva Rev., 2007—, Broadskill Rev., 2007—; contbr. book revs. to profl. jours. MC poetry readings, chair various pub. panel discussions The Writer's Ctr., Bethesda, Md; former mem. poetry com. Folger Shakespeare Libr., Washington. Kellett fellow U. Cambridge. Fellow Va. Ctr. Creative Arts; mem. Coun. Lit. Mags. and Pubs., Poets and Writers, Columbia U. Club Washington, Phi Beta Kappa. Avocations: bicycling, writing, travel, raising dogs. Home: 422 N Cleveland St Arlington VA 22201 Personal E-mail: boggmag@aol.com.

ELSE, CAROLYN JOAN, retired library director; b. Mpls., Jan. 31, 1934; d. Elmer Oscar and Irma Carolyn (Seibert) Wahlberg; m. Floyd Warren Else, 1962 (div. 1968); children: Stephen Alexander, Catherine Elizabeth. BS, Stanford U., 1956; MLS, U. Wash., 1957. Cert. profl. libr. Wash. Libr. Queens Borough Pub. Libr., NYC, 1957—59, U.S. Army Spl. Svcs., France, Germany, 1959—62; info. libr. Bennett Martin Libr., Lincoln, Nebr., 1962—63; br. libr. Pierce County Libr., Tacoma, 1963—65, dir., 1965—94; ret., 1994. Wellness cons. Nikken, Inc., 1994—. Mem. Higher Edn. Coun., South Puget Sound, 1988—92; bd. dirs. Tacoma Philharmonic, 2005—; mem. distbn. com. Greater Tacoma Cmty. Found., 2005—; mem. study commn. Wash. State Local Governance, 1985—88; bd. dirs. Campfire, Tacoma, 1984—92, Cmty. Health Care, 1997—2003. Mem.: Pacific N.W. Libr. Assn. (sec. 1969—71), Wash. Libr. Assn. (v.p. 1969—71), ALA, Tacoma Rotary #8 Club (bd. dirs. 1995—97), City Club (Tacoma). Home Phone: 253-565-9635. Personal E-mail: carolyn.else@stanfordalumni.org. E-mail: cjelse@harbornet.com.

ELSEN, JON, editor; b. NYC, Dec. 26, 1959; s. Sheldon H. and Gerri (Sharfman) E.; m. Ellen Hogan; children: Margaret, Benjamin, Rebecca. BA, Columbia U., 1981. Reporter Jour. Inquirer, Manchester, Conn., 1981-86, The Hartford Courant, 1986-89, The Record, Hackensack, NJ, 1989-90; editor NY Times New Media Group, NYC, 1991-95; reporter, editor Investment Dealer's Digest, NYC, 1995-97; media reporter NY Post, NYC, 1997-99, dep. bus. editor, 1999-2000, bus. editor, 2000—04; asst. editor NY Times, NYC, 2005—. Office: NY Times 620 Eighth Ave New York NY 10018-1405 Office Phone: 212-556-1234. Business E-Mail: jonelsen@nytimes.com.

ELSEN, SHELDON HOWARD, lawyer; b. Pitts., May 12, 1928; m. Gerri Sharfman, 1952; children: Susan Rachel, Jonathan Charles. AB, Princeton U., 1950; AM, Harvard U., 1952, JD, 1958. Bar: NY 1959, US Supreme Ct. 1971. Ptnr. Orans, Elsen & Lupert LLP, NYC, 1965—. Adj. prof. law Columbia U. Law Sch., 1969—; chief counsel NY Moreland Act Commn. on UDC, 1975-76; asst. US atty. So. Dist. NY, 1960-64; cons. Pres.'s Commn. Law Enforcement Adminstrn. Justice, 1967; mem. faculty Nat. Inst. Trial Advocacy, 1973; panel chair 1st dept. disciplinary com. NY, 1992-96; arbitrator and mediator JAMS, 2006—. Contbr. articles to profl. jours. Fellow Am. Coll. Trial Lawyers; mem. Assn. Bar City NY (v.p. 1988-89, chmn. com. on fed. legislation 1969-72, chmn. com. on fed. cts. 1983-86, chmn. nominating com. 1986-87, chmn. com. amenities in land use process for NYC 1987-88), Am. Law Inst. (adviser Principles of Transnat. Rules of Civil Procedure 1999-2005), Phi Beta Kappa. Office: 875 Third Ave 28th Fl New York NY 10022 Office Phone: 212-586-2211. Business E-Mail: selsen@oellaw.com.

ELSENER, G. DALE, lawyer; b. Frederick, Okla., Mar. 26, 1951; s. Gordon Lee and Anita Lois (Vaughan) Elsener; m. Ann Skidmore; children: Hayley Lynn, Garrett Dale. BS, Okla. State U., 1973; JD, Okla. U., 1976. Bar: Okla. 1976, U.S. Dist. Ct. (ea. and we. dists.) Okla. 1984. Assoc. Richard S. Roberts, Wewoka, Okla., 1976-78; ptnr. Roberts & Elsener, Wewoka, 1979-86; sole practice, 1986-90. City atty. City of Wewoka, 1986—. Chmn. bd. trustees Seminole County Law Libr., 1986; chmn. Seminole County Econ. Devel. Adv. Com., 1986; bd. dirs. Rural Water Dist. 3, Cromwell, Okla., 1982—90; mem. Seminole Econ. Devel. Coun., 1997—2000. Mem.: Seminole County Bar Assn., Okla. Bar Assn. (real property and mineral law sects.), Wewoka C. of C. (pres. 1987), Seminole State Coll. Edn. Found. (trustee), Seminole C. of C. (pres. 1998). Office: Elsener & Hargrave PO Box 32 Seminole OK 74818-0032 Office Phone: 405-382-1204. Personal E-mail: delsener@swbell.net.

ELSEY, GEORGE MCKEE, retired foundation administrator; b. Palo Alto, Calif., Feb. 5, 1918; s. Howard McKee and Ethel May (Daniels) E.; m. Sally Phelps Bradley, Dec. 15, 1951; children: Anne Kranz, Howard McKee. AB, Princeton U., 1939; A.M., Harvard U., 1940; L.H.D., Am. Internat. Coll., 1982. Asst. to spl. counsel to Pres. The White House, 1947—49, adminstrv. asst. to Pres., 1949—51; asst. to dir. Mutual Security Agy., 1951—53; with ARC, 1953-61, v.p., 1958-61; with various divs. Pullman Inc., 1961-65, asst. to chmn. and pres., 1966-70; pres. Am. Nat. Red Cross, 1970-82, pres. emeritus, 1983—. Mem. Washington adv. bd. MNC Fin., 1991-93; bd. dirs. The White House Hist. Assn., pres., 1990-95, dir. emeritus 1995— Author: An Unplanned Life: A Memoir, 2005 Pres. Meridian House Internat., Washington, 1961-66, vice chmn., 1967-68, counselor, 1971—; trustee Brookings Instn., 1971-83, George C. Marshall Rsch. Found., 1973-83, Harry S. Truman Libr. Inst., 1973-95, PCC Charitable Found., 1997-2005; mem. Nat. Archives Adv. Coun., 1974-79, mem. com. on presdl. librs., 1988-95; trustee emeritus Nat. Trust Hist. Preservation, 1976—; fin. chmn. League Red Cross and Red Crescent Socs., Geneva, 1977-87; mem. adv. bd. Nature's Best Found., 1999—; bd. dirs. U.S. Capitol Hist. Soc., 1993-95. Comdr. USNR, 1941-47. Decorated Legion of Merit, Order Brit. Empire, medals from Red Cross Socs. Finland, Korea, Greece, Netherlands, Fed. Republic Germany, Can. and Magen David Adom (Israel), comdr. Order of St. John; recipient Disting. Pub. Svc. medal Dept. Def. Internat. Humanitarian award Am. Red Mogen David for Israel, Henry Dunant medal Internat. Red Cross and Red Crescent, 1989. Mem. Hist. Soc. Washington, Nat. Geog. Soc. (trustee 1977-93), Met. Club (Washington), City Tavern Club (Washington), White House Mil. Aides Assn. (hon. chmn. 1998—), Phi Beta Kappa. Presbyterian. E-mail: georgeelsey@aol.com.

EL SHAHAWY, MAHFOUZ, internist, educator, cardiologist; b. Cairo, Aug. 1, 1936; came to U.S., 1967, naturalized U.S. citizen; married; 2 children. MD summa cum laude, U. Vienna, Austria, 1962, diploma cardiovasc. dis., 1966; MSc in Medicine and Cardiovasc. Diseases, U. Minn., Rochester, 1971. Cert. Fla. State Bd. Med. Examiners, 1973, Ga. State Bd. Med. Examiners, 1973, Can. Bd. Internal Medicine, 1975, Am. Bd. Internal Medicine, 1977, Am. Bd. Cardiovasc. Disease, 1981. Resident in medicine and cardiology U. Vienna-Algemeines Krankenhaus, 1962—67; rotating intern Flushing Hosp. and Med. Ctr., NYC, 1967—68; fellow in medicine Mayo Clinic, Rochester, 1968—70, rsch. fellow in medicine and cardiovasc. disease, 1970—71; fellow, tchg. fellow, instr. cardiology Med. Coll. Ga., Augusta, 1971—73; asst. prof. medicine and cardiology U. Fla., Gainesville, 1973—75, asst. clin. prof. medicine and cardiology, 1976—78, asst. clin. prof. medicine, 1976—95, assoc. clin. prof. medicine, 1995—97, clin. prof. medicine, 1997—, Lake Wood Ranch Med. Ctr., Bradenton, Fla., 2004—; pvt. practice, Sarasota, Fla., 1976—. Dir. adult cardiac catheterization lab., dir. heart sta. Shands Tchg. Hosp.-U. Hosp., 1973-74, dir. CCU, 1974-75; mem. staff Sarasota Meml. Hosp., 1975-83, mem. cardiac com., 1975-83, code C com., 1978-81, instnl. review bd., 1990-92, mem. staff Columbia-HCA Doctors Hosp., Sarasota, 1975—; chief medicine Doctors Hosp., Sarasota, 1980-81, trustee, 1986-90, vice chmn. bd., 1987-88, chmn. bd. 1980-83, 87-89, med. dir. cardiac catheterization lab., 1995—, chmn. continuing med. edn. com., 1980-, electrocardiography reading panel, 1980-2000, cardiology adv. coun., 1994-2000, mem.cardiac intensive care, 1976-84, utilization com., 1980-82, med. privileges com., 1980-83, 88-90, bylaws com., 1984-85, credentials com., 1984-87, radiation safety com., 1992-, instl. review bd., 1994-2000, med. staff credentials com., 1995-98, pharmacy and therapeutic com., 2005-; asst. clin. prof. medicine and cardiology U. South Fla., Tampa, 1976-78; chmn. long term investment com. Sarasota County Pub. Hosp., 1991-92, trustee, 1990-92; pres. Cardiovasc. Inst. Sarasota, 1989-95, Cardiovasc. Ctr. Sarasota Found. for Edn. and Rsch., 1995—; mem. Rehab. Inst. Sarasota, Health South, 1986—; presenter to nat. and internat. meetings, 1971—; organizer, dir. nat. and internat. cardiovasc. symposia, 1988—. Contbr. articles and abstracts to med. jours., including Chest, Circulation, Jour. Fla. Med. Assn., Brit. Heart Jour., Cardiovasc. Rsch. Jour., Am. Heart Jour., Jour. Med. Assn. Ga., Jour. AMA, Lancet,

Circulation Rsch. Supplement, Clin. Rsch.; mem. internat. adv. bd. Egyptian Heart Jour. Bd. dirs. YMCA, Ringling Mus., Selby Gardens, Sarasota Opera Soc., New Coll. Libr. Assn., Boys Club Sarasota, Sarasota County Pub. Health Clinic, Sun Coast Heart Assn. United Arab Republic scholar, 1962-67; nominated for Mayo Clinic Alumnus award, 1998, Physician of Yr. Nat. Rep. Congl. Com. Adv. Bd., 2002; recipient Ring of Honor Austrian Pres., Achievement award Egyptian Pres., Mayor Citation and Proclamation for Cmty Svc. City of Sarasota, 2006. Fellow ACP, Am. Coll. Chest Physicians (coun. on critical care), Am. Coll. Cardiology (mem. continuing edn. com. Fla. chpt., 1997-), Am. Heart Assn. (fellow coun. on clin. cardiology, bd. dirs. Fla./PR chpt., co chmn. Manatee/Sarasota Heart Ball, 2005, mem. Counsel for High Blood Pressure Rsch.), Am. Soc. Echocardiology, European Soc. Cardiology; mem. AMA, Internat. Soc. for Holter and Non-Invasive Electrocardiology, Am. Med. Soc. Vienna (life), Am. Soc. Hypertension in Black, Fla. Med. Assn. (named Disting. Physician 2004), Egyptian Soc. Hypertension (hon.), Sarasota County Med. Soc. (mem. CME com. 1990-, ednl. com. 1992-), NY Acad. Scis., Mayo Clinic Cardiovasc. Alumni Assn., Mayo Doctors Soc. (life), Plummer Soc. (charter mem.), Sarasota County C. of C. (bd. dirs.) Century Club Meml. Hosp., Longboat Key Club. Achievements include research in diabetic heart disease; Dysmetabolic Cardiac Syndrome; acute and chronic coronary syndroms; heart failure; hypertension; atrial fibrillation and stroke prevention; echocardiography/Doppler; Cardiac Hemodynamics-Catheterization; thyrocardiac disorders; HIS Bundle Electrophysiology; cardiomyopathies with particular reference to the role of electrolytes and trace metals, such as magnesium and potassium; Renin-Angiotensin-Aldosterone System; Peripheral Arterial Disease; the use of newer drugs in the treatment of: CAD, CHF:, Arrhythmias, Hypertension, Diabetic Heart Disease, Peripheral Arterial Disease and Renal Disease. Office: Cardiovasc Ctr Sarasota 1851 Arlington St Ste 206 Sarasota FL 34239-3517 Office Phone: 941-366-9800. Fax: 941-366-2781. Business E-Mail: mshahawy@cardiologycenter.net.

EL-SHANTI, HATEM ISAM, pediatrician, geneticist; b. Tripoli, Libya, Jan. 1, 1960; s. Isam and Samiha (Adili) El-Shanti; m. Sohair Abul-Haija, Sept. 22, 1994; children: Jawa, Rina. MD, Cairo U., 1983; MSc, Ind. U., 1989. Diplomate Am. Bd. Pediat.; diplomate in clin. genetics and cytogenetics Am. Bd. Med. Genetics. House officer, gen. practitioner Cairo U. Hosps., 1984—85; tchg. asst. Jordan U. Sci. and Tech., Irbid, 1985—87; resident, fellow U. Iowa, Iowa City, 1989—93; asst. prof. Jordan U. Sci. and Tech., 1993—98, assoc. prof., 1998—2002, dir. Cytogenetics Lab., 1993—2002; assoc. prof. U. Iowa Coll. Medicine, Iowa City, 2003—. Dir. Shafallah Genetics Med. Ctr., Doha, Qatar, 2007—. Fellow Am. Acad. Pediat., Am. Coll. Med. Genetics; mem. European Soc. Human Genetics. Avocations: reading, sports, history of science and medicine. Office: U Iowa Hosps and Clinics Pediatrics/Med Genetics Iowa City IA Home: 830 Evergreen Ct Iowa City IA 52245-3541 Office Phone: 319-356-2674. Business E-Mail: hatem-el-shanti@uiowa.edu.

ELSHARYDAH, AHMAD, anesthesiologist; MD, Damascus U., Syria, 1990. Diplomate Am. Bd. Anesthesiology, 2004. Asst. prof. anesthesiology La. State U. Health Sciences Ctr., Shreveport, 2002—06, Ohio State U. Med. Ctr., Columbus, 2006—. Dir. vascular anesthesia La. State U. Health Sciences Ctr., Shreveport, 2000—05. Contbr. articles to profl. jours. Mem.: La. Soc. Anesthesiologist, Internat. Anesthesia Rsch. Assn., Am. Soc. Anesthesiologist. Achievements include research in calcium. Office: Ohio State Univ Comprehensive Spine Ctr 2050 Kenny Rd 7th Fl Columbus OH 43221 Home Phone: 614-850-9427; Office Phone: 614-293-2225.

ELSHTAIN, JEAN BETHKE, social sciences educator; b. Windsor, Colo., Jan. 6, 1941; d. Paul G. and Helen L. Bethke; m. Errol L. Elshtain, Sept. 3, 1965; 1 adopted child, Bobby Bethke children: Sheri, Heidi, Jenny, Eric. BA in History, Colo. State U., 1963; MA in History, U. Colo., 1965; PhD in Politics, Brandeis U., 1973; LLD (hon.), Gonzaga U., 1996; DHL (hon.), Valparaiso U., 1996, Grinell Coll., 1997, Maryville U., 1997, Messiah Coll., 1999, Carthage Coll., 2000, Lake Forest Coll., 2001, Siena Coll., 2002, North Park Coll., 2002, U. West Timisoara, Romania, 2005. Prof. polit. sci. U. Mass., Amherst, 1973-88, Vanderbilt U., Nashville, 1988-94; vis. prof. Harvard U., Cambridge, Mass., 1994; prof. ethics U. Chgo., 1995—. Lectr. in field. Author: Public Man, Private Woman: Women in Social and Political Thought, 1982, 2d edit., 1992 (Top Choice Acad. Book), Czech transl., 1999, Ukranian transl., 2002, Women and War, 1987, Japanese transl., 1994, Power Trips and Other Journeys, Essays on Feminism as Civic Discourse, 1990, Meditations on Modern Political Thought: Masculine/Feminine Theme Luther to Arendt, 1992, Democracy on Trial, 1995 (N.Y. Times Notable Book, 1995), Augustine and the Limits of Politics, 1996; co-author: But Was It Just? Reflections on the Morality of the Gulf War, 1992; editor: The Family in Political Thought, 1982, Just War Theory, 1991, The Jane Addams Reader, 2002, Just War Against Terror: The Burden of American Power, 2003 (One of the Best Non-Fiction Books of 2003 Pub. Weekly); co-editor: Women, Militarism and War, 1990, Politics and the Human Body, 1995, Promise to Keep, Decline and Renewal of Marriage in America, 1996, Real Politics, Political Theory and Everyday Life, 1997, New Wine in Old Bottles: International Politics and Ethical Discourse, 1998 (Top Choice Acad. Book), Who are We? Critical Reflection, Hopeful Possibilities, 2000 (Best Acad. Book Am. Theol. Booksellers Assn., 2000), Jane Addams and the Dream of American Democracy, 2002, Just War Against Terror: The Burden of American Power in a Violent World, 2004 (Named One of Top Non-Fiction Book of Yr. Pubs. Weekly). Bd. dirs. Nat. Endowment Democracy, 2002—; trustee Inst. Advanced Study, 1994—99, Nat. Humanities Ctr., NC, 1996—2005; chair Coun. Civil Soc., NYC, Chgo., 1995—, Coun. Families Am., NYC, 1995—; apptd. Coun. of Nat. Endowment for Humanties, 2006—. Recipient award for Disting. Lifetime Contbn. to Faith and Scholarship, C.S. Lewis Soc., 2005, Jane Addams medal for lifetime scholarly achievement, Rockford Coll., 2005, Ind. Humanties award, 2006. Fellow: AAAS; mem.: Am. Soc. Polit. and Legal Philosophy (v.p. 1996—97), Am. Polit. Sci. Assn. (v.p. 1998—99, Maguire chair ethics Libr. Congress 2003—04, Goodnow award for Lifetime Svc. 2002, Gifford lectr. 2006). Avocations: movies, reading. Home: 4010 Wallace Ln Nashville TN 37215-2308 Office: U Chgo Div Sch 1025 E 58th St Chicago IL 60637-1509 Office Phone: 773-702-7252. Business E-Mail: jbelshta@uchicago.edu.

ELSILA, DAVID AUGUST, editor; b. Detroit, Feb. 2, 1939; s. Edward J. and Sylvia (Mikkola) E.; m. Kathlyn Deutch, July 17, 1965; children: Mikael, Jamie and Kari (twins). BA, Eastern Mich. U., 1960, postgrad., 1962. Tchr. pub. schs., Livonia, Mich., 1960-64; editor-in-chief Livonia Observer, 1964-65; dir. publs., editor Am. Tchr., also, Changing Edn., Am. Fedn. Tchrs., Washington, 1965-76; editor UAW Solidarity, 1976—98; asst. dir. pub. rels. and publs. dept. UAW, 1976-98; sr. editor Working USA, 1997—99. Editor ofcl. publs. ACLU, Mich., 1964—67; del. Greater Washington Ctrl. Labor Coun., AFL-CIO; mem. adv. bd. (TV show) We Do The Work, 1992—2001; instr. Labor Studies Ctr., Wayne State U., 1999—2007, Nommos Ednl. Svcs., 1999—2001, Labor Educators Inc., 2005—07. Co-author: Union Town: A Labor History Guide to Detroit, 1980; contbg. author: Working Detroit, 1986, The New Labor Press, 1992; exec. prodr. Forgotten: A Jazz Opera, 2004, 05. Nat. sec. Workers Edn. Local 189, 1978—86, Great Lakes bd. mem., 1986—88, Mich. chpt. bd. mem., 1992—99, exec. bd., 1994—99; co-chair Detroit Laborfest, 1997—2000; coord. Mich. Labor Legacy Project, Inc., 2001—; trustee Cranbrook Peace Found., 2001—; treas. SE Mich. Jobs. with Justice, 2002—; exec. bd. mem. Dem. Socialists of Am. SE Mich. Recipient Page 1 award, Chgo. Newspaper Guild, 1967, 1st awards in journalism, Internat. Labor Comm. Assn., 1968—69, 1972—73, 1975—76, 1983—97, Ednl. Press Assn. Am., 1968—76, Joady award, Film Arts Found., 1991, Pollie award, Am. Assn. Polit. Cons., 1992, Max Steinbock award, Saul Miller award, Internat. Labor Comm. Assn., 1996, Eugene V. Debs award, Dem. Socialists Am., 1998, Solidarity award, UAW, 1998, Communicator of Yr. award, Met. N.Y. Labor Comm. Coun., 2000, Eugene V. Debs award, Midwest Labor Press Assn., 2000, Journalism award, Mich. Labor Press, 2001, Spl. award, Matrix Theatre Co., 2001. Mem. Washington-Balt. Newspaper Guild (mem. exec. bd. 1970-71), Detroit Newspaper Guild, Ednl. Press Assn. Am. (pres. Washington chpt. 1971), Internat. Labor Comms. Assn. (v.p. 1983-89, sec.-treas. 1990-91), ACLU (mem. exec. bd. Detroit chpt. 1993—, sec. 1999-2003, v.p. 2004-05, exec. sec. 2005-06, v.p. 2006-), Mich. Labor History Soc. (program com. 2002—, editor publ. 2003—, trustee 2006—), Phi Delta Kappa. Home: 1411 Three Mile Dr Grosse Pointe Park MI 48230-1125 Personal E-mail: davelsi@aol.com.

ELSMAN, JAMES LEONARD, JR., lawyer; b. Kalamazoo, Sept. 10, 1936; s. James Leonard and Dorothy Isabell (Pierce) E.; m. Janice Marie Wilczewski, Aug. 6, 1960; children— Stephanie, James Leonard III. BA, U. Mich., 1958, JD, 1962; postgrad., Harvard Div. Sch., 1958-59. Bar: Mich. 1963. Clk. Mich. Atty. Gen.'s Office, Lansing, 1961; atty. legal dept. Chrysler Corp., Detroit, 1962-64; founding ptnr. Elsman, Young, O'Rourke, Bruno & Bunn, Birmingham, Mich., 1964-72; pvt. practice Elsman Law Firm, Birmingham, 1972—. Owner Radio Sta. WOLY, Battle Creek, Mich. Author: The Seekers, 1962; screenplay, 1976, 200 Candles to Whom?, 1973; contbr. articles to profl. jours.; Composer, 1974, 76; talk show host Citizen's Court, TV-48, Detroit. Mem. Regional Export Expansion Coun., 1966-73, Mich. Ptnrs. for Alliance for Progress, 1969-80; cand. U.S. Senate, 1966, 76, 94, 96, U.S. Ho. of Reps., 1970; internat. evangelist Jseus Christ's Army Ch. Warfare. Rockefeller Bros. Found. fellow Harvard Div. Sch., 1959. Mem. ABA, Am. Soc. Internat. Law, Econ. Club Detroit, World Peace Through Law Center, Full Gospel Businessmen, Bloomfield Open Hunt Club, Pres. Club (U. Mich.), Circumnavigators Club, Naples Bath and Tennis, Rotary. Republican. Mem. Christian Ch. Home: 4811 Burnley Dr Bloomfield Hills MI 48304-3781 Office: 635 Elm St Birmingham MI 48009-6768 Office Phone: 248-645-0750. Personal E-mail: elsmanlawfirm@aol.com. *Christianity is not a religion. It is knowing Jesus, i.e. God, personally. It does not hinge on man's works or effort. Christianity is the only way to God, as Christ is the only Mediator between God and man. Choose! You can be sincerely wrong and still go to Hell eternally. Just a country lawyer in a big city, representing the common man in mass tort and class actions and other litigation, whose priority client is Jesus.*

ELSNER, JAMES BRIAN, meteorologist, educator; b. Milw., Oct. 16, 1959; s. Roger Allen and Diane Lucille (Richard) E.; m. Svetoslava Chtilianova Kavlakova, Jan. 7, 1989; children: Ian James, Diana Michelle. BSc, U. Wis., Milw., 1981, MSc, 1984, PhD, 1988. Rsch. scientist U. Wis., Milw., 1989, lectr., 1989-90; asst. prof. dept. meteorology Fla. State U., Tallahassee, 1990-95, assoc. prof., 1995—98, assoc. prof. dept. geography, 1998—2001, prof., 2001—; pres. Climatek Inc., 2001—. Cons. Risk Prediction Initiative, Bermuda, 1995. Co-author: Singular Spectrum Analysis: A New Tool in Time Series Analysis, 1996, Hurricanes of the North Atlantic: Climate and Society, 1999; contbr. articles to profl. jours, chapters to books. Grantee NOAA, 1992, NSF, 1993, 95, 97. Mem. Am. Meteorol. Soc., European Geophys. Soc., Am. Assn. Geographers, Xi Epsilon Pi. Avocations: biking, butterflies, reading. Office: Dept Geography Fla State U Tallahassee FL 32306-2190 E-mail: jelsner@garnet.fsu.edu.

ELSON, ALEX, lawyer, educator, arbitrator; b. nr. Kiev, Russia, Apr. 17, 1905; came to U.S., 1906, naturalized, 1913; s. Jacob and Rebecca (Brodsky) E.; m. Miriam Almond, July 6, 1933; children: Jacova Silverthorne (dec.), Karen O'Neil. PhB, U. Chgo., 1925, JD, 1928. Bar: Ill. 1928. Bill drafter Legislative Reference Bur., Springfield, Ill., 1929; atty. Legal Aid Bur., Chgo., 1929-34; assoc. atty. Tolman, Chandler & Dickinson, 1934-38; regional atty. Wage-Hour Div., Chgo., 1938-41; regional atty., asst. gen. counsel OPA, 1941-45; sr. ptnr. Elson, Lassers & Wolff, 1952—79. Of counsel Rosenthal & Schanfield, 1979-99; lectr. U. Chgo., intermittently 1933-48, 79-99, Yale Law Sch., 1946, seminar-labor rels. Northwestern U. Sch. Law, 1961-65; seminar constl. law Ariz U., 1971 Author: Civil Practice Forms, 1934; co-author: Civil Practice Forms, Illinois-Federal, 1952, rev., 1965; contbr.: articles to profl. jours., also to Ency. Brit. Former pub. mem. Regional War Labor Bd.; former chmn. Chgo. Rent Commn.; pres. Fund for Justice, 1972-76; former chmn. Ill. divsn. ACLU (hon. mem. bd. dirs. Ill. divsn.); former vice chmn. Ill. Commn. on Children; former chmn. Bd. Mental Health Commrs. State Ill., 1960-69; v.p. Law in Am. Soc. Found.; pres. Nat. Acad. Arbitrators Rsch. and Edn. Found., 1987-90; bd. govs. Orthogenic Sch., U. Chgo.; mem. instnl. rev. bd. divsn. social sci. U. Chgo., 1994-97; cons. Ford Found., 1963-68; bd. dirs. Hull House Assn., 1955-65. Fellow Am. Bar Found., Emeritus fellow Coll. of Labor and Employment Lawyers, 1998—; mem. ABA, Ill. Bar Assn., Chgo. Bar Assn. (bd. mgrs.), Am. Law Inst. (life), Nat. Acad. Arbitrators (hon. life mem., v.p. 1983-85), Inst. Psychoanalysis (pres. 1976-79) Home: 5550 South Shore Dr Chicago IL 60637

ELSON, CHARLES MYER, law educator; b. Atlanta, Nov. 12, 1959; s. Edward Elliott and Suzanne (Goodman) E.; m. Aimee F. Kemker, Dec. 18, 1993; children: Caroline Kemker, Charles MacKenzie. AB magna cum laude, Harvard U., 1981, postgrad., 1981—82; JD, U. Va., 1985. Bar: N.Y. 1987, D.C. 1988, U.S. Dist. Ct. (so. and ea. dists.) N.Y. 1987, U.S. Ct. Appeals (11th cir.) 1987. Law clk. to judge U.S. Ct. Appeals (11th cir.), Atlanta, 1985—86; assoc. Sullivan & Cromwell, NYC, 1986—90; asst. prof. Stetson U. Coll. Law, St. Petersburg, Fla., 1990—93, assoc. prof., 1993—96, prof., 1996—2001; Edgar S. Woolard Jr. prof. corp. governance U. Del., 2000—, dir. John L. Weinberg Ctr. for Corp. Governance, 2000—. Vis. prof. law U. Ill., Champaign-Urbana, 1995, Cornell U. Law Sch., Ithaca, NY, 1996, U. Md. Law Sch., Balt., 1998; cons. Holland & Knight, 1995—, Towers, Perrin, 1998; bd. dir. Auto Zone, Inc., Health South Corp. Bd. dir. Big Apple Circus, Ltd., NYC, 1987-93, Circon Corp., 1997-99, Sunbeam Corp., 1996-2002, Alderwoods Group, 2001-06; trustee Talladega Coll., 1994-2001, Tampa Bay Performing Arts Ctr., 2000-2004, Tampa Mus. Art, 1993-99, Christiana Care Health Sys., 2006—, Del. Mus. Natural History, 2003—; ind. goverance adv. panel ARC, 2006. Salvatori fellow Heritage Found., 1993-94. Mem.: ABA (vice chair com. on corp. governance, mem. com. on corp. laws), Nat. Assn. Corp. Dirs. (commn. dir. compensation 1995, commn.dir. professionalism 1996, com. on securities litig. reform and fraud detection 1997, adv. coun. 1997—, com.on succession planning 1998, com. on audit coms. 1999, com on role of bd. in strategic planning 2000, com. on dir. evaluation 2001, com. on exec. compensation 2003, com. on bd. leadership 2004, com. on governance com. 2007), Assn. of Bar City of N.Y., Am. Law Inst., Century Assn., Univ. Club NYC, Down Town Assn., Harvard Club NYC, Chevaliers du Tastevin. Office: U Del Coll Bus and Econs Alfred Lerner Hall Newark DE 19716 Home: 1002 Westover Rd Wilmington DE 19807 Office Phone: 302-831-6157. Business E-Mail: elson@lerner.udel.edu.

ELSON, EDWARD ELLIOTT, diplomat; b. NYC, Mar. 8, 1934; s. Harry and Esther (Cohn) E.; m. Suzanne Wolf Goodman, Aug. 24, 1957; children: Charles Myer, Louis Goodman, Harry Elson II. Grad., Phillips Acad., 1952; BA in Polit. Sci. with honors, U. Va., 1956; JD, Emory U., 1959; DHL (honoris causa), Talladega Coll., 1995; JD (hon.), Brenau U., 1997. With Atlanta News Agy., Inc., 1959-86, pres., 1967-82, chmn. bd. dir. and pres., 1982—85, chmn. bd. dir., 1985—86; pres. Airport News Corp., Atlanta, 1961-82, chmn. bd. dir., 1982—85; pres. Elson's, Atlanta, 1963-82, chmn. bd. dir., 1982—86; chmn. Gordon County Bank, 1979-83; chmn. bd. dir. W.H. Smith & Son Holdings, PLC, 1985—88; amb. to Denmark U.S. Dept. State, 1993—. Bd. dirs. NationsBank of Ga., Citizens and So. Ga. Corp., Atlantic Am. Corp., Citizens and So. Trust Co., Inc., Genesco Inc., Specialty Coffee Holdings Inc., Mitre Sports Internat. Ltd., RF & P Corp., New & Lingwood Holdings Ltd., Thorkild Kristensen AG, Köllmann AG, Hamton Investment Funds; chmn. W.H. Smith Group PLC, 1986—, Majestic Wine Corp., 1988; hon. pres. Am. Club, Copenhagen, 1993-98; mem. hon. com. European Assn. Jewish Studies' 5th Cong., 1993—; vis. prof. Aalborg (Denmark) U. Mem. publs. com. Commentary Mag., 1967—, chmn., 1975-80. Dir., Am. Coun. Ambs.; bd. dir. So. Regional Coun., 1966—, exec. com., 1986—; bd. govs. Am. Jewish Com., 1966—, trustee, 1977—, chmn. bd. trustees, 1986-89, v.p., 1982-84, treas., 1984-86; v.p. Nat. Found. Jewish Culture, 1990—; mem. Presdl. Commn. on Obscenity and Pornography, 1967-71, Nat. Adv. Commn. Pub. Edn. and Desegregation, 1976-77; mem. funds appeals rev. bd. City of Atlanta, 1971-73, Atlanta-Fulton County Recreation Authority, 1973-80, vice chmn., 1975-80; adv. com. to U.S. Commn. on Civil Rights, State of Ga., 1974—, chmn., 1974-82; chmn. bd. dir. Nat. Pub. Radio, 1977-80, chmn., 1992—; chmn. Nat. Pub. Radio Found.; chmn. so. regional adv. com. to U.S. Commn. on Civil Rights, 1978, U. Va. Bayley Mus., 1986—; pres.'s coun. Brandeis U., 1967—, dir. Reading is Fundamental program, 1975-86, fellow, 1979; trustee Am.-Skandanavian Found., 1998—; bd. visitors U. Va., 1984-92, rector, 1990-92, exec. com. Health Sci. Coun., 1989—, chmn. Real Estate Found., 1990-92; bd. visitors Clark Coll., 1973—, chmn., 1982; trustee Brown U., 1988—, U. Va. Med. Ctr., 1987—, exec. com., 1987—; trustee Am. Briends Brit. Mus., Talladega Coll., 1973—, U. Mid-Am., 1979-82, Am. Fedn. Arts, 1985—, Brenau Coll., 1986—, Hampton Inst., 1986—, Hebrew Union Coll., 1992—, Spellman Coll., 1992—, Jewish Mus., 1992—, Glyndebourne Assn. Am., 1992—; mem. alumni coun. Phillips Acad., Andover, Mass., 1973-76, charter trustee, 1997; pres. coun. Agnes Scott Coll., 1973-82, chmn., 1975-82; mem. coun. White Burkett Miller Ctr. Pub. Affairs, 1990—; dean's adv. bd. Columbia U. Sch. Internat. Affairs and Pub. Affairs; chmn. adv. bd., bd. dir. Southeastern Ctr. Contemporary Art, 1976—; chmn. bd. vis. Emory U. Mus. Art and Archaeology, 1985-92; resource planning com. Nat. Gallery, Washington, 1986—, trustee's coun., 1990—, dir. Coun. Am. Ambs.; chmn. U. Va. Real Estate Found., 1990-92; presdl. del. returning Crown of Stephen to Hungary, 1978; exec. com. U. Va. Health Sci. Coun., 1989—; gov. J.C. Brown Libr., R.I., 1989—; bd. dir. Acad. Corp. Governance, Fordham U.; chmn. bd. trustees Jeffersonian Restoration, 1992—; trustee Nat. Symphony Orch., 1992—; hon. pres. Copenhagen Theatre Cir., 1993-98; exec. com. Assn. Friends Hans Christian Andersen Mus., 1993-98; active Internat. Inst. Strategic Studies, 1995—; assoc. dir. Met. Opera, 2000—; trustee Game Conservancy, Preservation Soc. Palm Beach, 2004—, Soc. of Four Arts, 2004—; gov. Addison Gallery Am. Art; chmn. Inst. Study of Europe Col. U., 2002—. Recipient Robert B. Downs award Grad. Sch. Library Sci., U. Ill., 1971, Human Relations award Am. Jewish Com., 1975, Disting. Service award Nat. Pub. Radio, 1979, Inst. Human Relations award, 1982, Merkonom award, 1997, Outstanding Alumnus award Emory U. Law Sch., 2002; Guggenheim fellow, 1994. Mem. Ga. Bar Assn., L.Q.C. Lamar Soc. (v.p. 1973-74, chmn. bd. dirs. 1974-80), Jewish Publ. Soc. (trustee 1974-82, 85—, v.p. 1986-87, pres., 1987-90, chmn. 1990—), Asia Soc. (trustee exec. com. 1999—), Am. Jewish Hist. Soc. (exec. com. 1980—, v.p. 1982-85), Am. Scandinavian Found. (vice chmn. 1998—, St. George's House coun.), Muscular Dystrophy Assn. Am. (v.p. 1972-73, corp. 1973-74), U. Va. Alumni Assn. (bd. mgrs. 1982-84), Soc. for the Four Arts (vice chmn. 2007—), Assn. Governing Bds. Univs. and Colls. (bd. dir.), Nat. Peace Garden Found. (dir., trustee), Royal Acad. U.K. (chair Am. bd.), Inst. Study Europe (co-chair 1999—), European Assn. Jewish Studies (hon. com. 5th congress 1993-98), Coun. Fgn. Rels., Royal Copenhagen Shooting Soc. and Danish Brotherhood, Farmington Country Club, Univ. Club (N.Y.C.), Century Assn., Game Conservancy, USA (trustee), Palm Beach Country Club, Sailfish Club (Palm Beach, Fla.), Whites Club (London), The Beach Club (Palm Beach). Home Fax: 561-833-5044.

ELSON, JAMES MARTIN, retired landmark director; b. NYC, Nov. 25, 1932; s. John James and Elizabeth Jane (Slights) E.; m. Joan Mary Scott Elson, Aug. 21, 1965 (dec. Feb. 15, 1991); children: Elizabeth Joan Elson, Christina Marie Elson, James Scott Elson; m. Karen Sue Porter Elson, Aug. 22, 1992. BA, U. Tenn., 1955; MS, The Juilliard Sch., 1961; Mus. AD, W.Va. U., 1970. Chmn. vocal dept. Dana Sch. Music, Youngstown (Ohio) State U., 1962-68; grad. asst. Creative Arts Ctr., W.Va. U., Morgantown, 1968-70; chmn., vocal dept. Sch. Music, Winthrop U., Rock Hill, 1970-72; chmn., dept. visual and performing arts Huntingdon Coll., Montgomery, Ala., 1972-76; chmn., dept. fine arts High Point (N.C.) U., 1976—83; exec. dir. Acad. of Music Theatre, Lynchburg, Va., 1984-88; exec. v.p. Patrick Henry Meml. Fdn., Brookneal, Va., 1988-2000, exec. v.p. emeritus, 2000—. Performing arts critic High Point (N.C.) Enterprise, 1977-83. Author: Academy of Music, Lynchburg, Virginia: The Golden Age of Live Performance, 1993, Lynchburg, Virginia: The First Two Hundred Years, 1786-1986, 2004; author, editor: Patrick Henry Essays, 1994, Patrick Henry and Thomas Jefferson, 1997, Patrick Henry in His Speeches and Writings, 2007; editor Lynch's Ferry Mag., 2000-05; contbr. articles to profl. jours. 1st lt. U.S. Army, 1955-57; col. USAR, ret. Grantee, Fulbright Commn., 1961—62. Mem. Coll. Music Soc. (life), Res. Officers Assn. (life), Kappa Sigma. Episcopalian. Home: 34 N Princeton Cir Lynchburg VA 24503-1547 Office Phone: 434-845-0452. E-mail: jelson@inmind.net.

ELSON, JOHN S., law educator; b. 1943; AB, Harvard U., 1964, JD, 1967; MA, U. Chgo., 1968. Bar: Ill. 1967. Staff lawyer Mandel Legal Aid Clinic, U. Chgo., 1971-75; assoc. prof. Northwestern U. Law Sch., Chgo., 1976-79, prof., 1979—. Contbr. articles to profl. jours. Mem.: Chgo. Coun. Lawyers (chair Chair, Com. Ethics and Profl. Responsibility 1998—). Office: Northwestern U Law Sch 357 E Chicago Ave Chicago IL 60611-3069 Office Phone: 312-503-8573. Office Fax: 312-503-8977. E-mail: j-elson@law.northwestern.edu.

ELSON, SUZANNE GOODMAN, social services administrator; b. Memphis, Oct. 17, 1937; d. Charles F. and Isabel (Ehrlich) Goodman; m. Edward Elliott Elson, Aug. 24, 1957; children: Charles Myer, Louis Goodman, Harry II. Student, Randolph-Macon Women's Coll., Lynchburg, Va.; BA, Agnes Scott Coll., 1959. Sec. Nat. Coun. Jewish Women, NYC, 1977-79; pres. Nat. Mental Health Assn., 1980-82; trustee emeritus Randolph Macon Women's Coll., 1988-98, 99. Chmn. Am. Craft Coun., 1989-92, hon. chmn., 1992-94, hon. trustee, 1994-; bd. dirs. Rosalynn Carter Inst., 1990-, Nat. Coun. Medicine Emory U., 1990-95; trustee Va. Mus. of Fine Art., 1992-96, High Mus. Fine Art, 1972-92, Am. Craft Mus., 1999-; bd. regents U. System of Ga., 1993-97; adv. bd. Breast Cancer Rsch. Found., 1998-; bd. dirs. Friends of Art and Preservation in Embassies, 1999- (trustee 1998); bd. govs. Mus. of Arts, 1998-; trustee Soc. for the Four Arts, 2003-, Preservation Soc. of Palm Beach, 2004- Home: 180 Cocoanut Row Palm Beach FL 33480-4121

ELSTAD, CATHERINE ANN, dean; b. Jamestown, ND, Sept. 29, 1953; BA, Jamestown Coll., ND, 1975; MS, U. Wis., La Crosse, 1977; PhD, Wash. State U., Pullman, 1983. Postdoctoral rsch. assoc. Wash. State U., Pullman, 1984—87; clin. asst. prof. Wash. State U. Coll. Pharmacy, Pullman, 2002—05, clin. assoc. prof., 2005—, assoc. dean student svcs., 2004—. V.p. Mathison Immuno Sci., Inc., Pullman, 1993—; bd. dirs. Critter Creek Therapeutic Riding Program, Moscow, 2002—05. Recipient Tchr. Yr., Wash. State U. Coll. Pharmacy, 1993—2006. Mem.: Kappa Psi Pharm. Frat., Am. Soc. Pharmacology and Exptl. Therapeutics, Am. Assn. Colls. Pharmacy, Metastasis Rsch. Soc., Am. Assn. Cancer Rsch. Office: Wash State Univ Coll Pharmacy Wegner Hall 155 Pullman WA 99164-6510 Office Phone: 509-335-8030.

ELSTON, JOAN WILMA, adult education educator, real estate agent; b. Kansas City, Mo., Sept. 20, 1938; d. William Hamilton Elston and Alyce Jean (Clark) Elston, Jones; m. Paul Wesley Sweeney, Sept. 10, 1968 (div.). BS, U. Kans., Lawrence, 1960; MS, U. So. Calif., LA, 1972. Cert. spiritual practitioner United Ch. of Religious Sci., 2000; tchr. Calif., 1960, reading tchr. Calif., 1968, C.C. student personnel worker Calif., 1976, C.C. instr. Calif., 1976, supr. Calif., 1976, adminstr. Calif., 1978, lic. real estate agt. Calif., 1989. Tchr. Compton Unified Sch. Dist., Calif., 1960—80; instrnl. designer DeJean Designs, Norwalk, Calif., 1985—90; instr. Cerritos C.C., Calif., 1989—90, Nat. U., Irvine, Calif., 1989—90; realtor Remax Real Estate Specialist, Long Beach, Calif., 1992—2000; tchr. Lynwood Unified Sch. Dist., Calif., 1996—2004; realtor Main St. Realtors, Long Beach, Calif., 2000—; instrnl. facilitator U. of Transformational Studies and Leadership, Culver City, Calif., 2000—. V.p. Compton Edn. Assn., Calif., 1969—70; treas. Mid-Cities chpt. Internat. Reading Assn., Compton, Calif., 1973—74; conv. del. NEA, Dallas, 1979; mem. leadership team Mark Twain Elem. Sch., Lynwood, Calif., 2001—04; mem. supt.'s adv. bd. Lynwood Unified Sch. Dist., Calif., 2001. Contbr. articles to profl. jours. Pres. Mid-Cities Schs. Credit Union, Compton, Calif., 1973—80. Named to Pres.'s Club, Re/Max Real Estate Internat., 1994. Mem.: Calif. Assn. of Realtors, Nat. Assn. Realtors (assoc.), Calif. Tchr.'s Assn. (life), Am. Contract Bridge League (assoc. Jr. Master 2005-2006). Achievements include development of a Reading Instructional guide for K-6, 1967; design of multi-media presentation that was used to instruct graduate students @ University of Southern California, 1971 & presented at a National Educational Conference, 1972; conducted workshops for The Loyola Television Conference, 1972 and for The California Teacher's Association, 1978; chaired a committee charged with reforming Math Instructional methods, 1977; created and implemented a homework program where students made 1.5 months growth for each month of instruction on The California Test of Basic Skills, 1975-1976; produced A Multi-Media Programmed Module That When Field Tested, Students Showed Significant Growth In Their Ability To Select And Sequencially Organize The Main Ideas Of A Story , 1971. Avocations: traveling, swimming, playing bridge, writing, reading. Office: Main Street Realtors 244 Redondo Ave Long Beach CA 90803 Home Phone: 562-754-2516; Office Phone: 562-719-2311. Office Fax: 562-719-2211; Home Fax: 562-438-5560. Personal E-mail: realgodjw@yahoo.com.

ELSTON, ROBERT C., medical educator; BA with honors, Cambridge U., Eng., 1955, diploma in agr., 1956, MA, 1957; PhD, Cornell U., 1959; postgrad., U. N.C., 1960. Asst. prof. U. N.C., Chapel Hill, 1960-62, assoc. prof., 1964-69, prof., dir. genetics lab. Sch. Pub. Health, 1969-79; sr. rsch. fellow biometric medicine U. Aberdeen, 1962-64; prof., head dept. biometry & genetics La. State U. Med. Ctr., New Orleans, 1979-95; prof. dept. epidemiology and biostats. Case Western Res. U., Cleve., 1995—. Vis. prof. Yale U., 1965-66, London U., 1967, Cambridge U., 1970, Fourth Mil. Med. Coll. Xian, China, 1987, U. Calif., Irvine, 1988-89; dir. Ctr. Molecular & Human Genetics La. State U. Med. Ctr., 1991-95; mem. internat. adv. bd. Genetics Selection Evolution, 1992-97; exec. com. mem. teaching of stats. in health scis. sect. Am. Stats. Assn., 1992-94, chair, 1993; pres. Internat. Genetic Epidemiology Soc., 1997. Assoc. editor Biometrics, 1967-71, 1984-88, Am. Jour. Human Genetics, 1974-82, Stats. in Medicine, 1997—; editl. bd. Thrombosis Rsch., 1972-76, Neuropsychobiology, 1974-79, Am. Jour. Med. Genetics, 1977-99, Genetic Epidemiology, 1984-96, T. Human Genetics, 2000; contbr. articles to profl. jours. Recipient Career Devel. award NIH, 1966-76, Rsch. Scientist award, NIMH, 1977-79, Hoch award Am. Psychopath. Assn., 1992, Wick R. Williams Meml. award Fox Chase Cancer Ctr., 1994, Leadership award Internat. Genetic Epidemiology Soc., 1995, William Allan Meml. award Am. Soc. Human Genetics, 1996, Merit award NIH, 1998, Marvin Zelen Leadership award statis. sci. Sch. Pub. Health, Harvard U.; King George VI Meml. fellow, 1956-57, John Simon Guggenheim Meml. fellow, 1973-74; Coulthurst scholar, 1955-56, Cornell scholar, 1956-59. Fellow Am. Stats. Assn. Office: Case Western Res U Wolstein Rsch Bldg 2103 Cornell Rd Rm 1303 Cleveland OH 44106-7281 Office Phone: 216-368-5630. E-mail: rce@darwin.cwru.edu.

ELSWIT, ROBERT, cinematographer; Cinematographer: (films) Waltz Across Texas, 1982, The End of August, 1982, Summerspell, 1983, Tiger Town, 1985, Moving Violations, 1985, The Sure Thing, 1985, Desert Hearts, 1985, Trick or Treat, 1986, Amazing Grace and Chuck, 1987, Return of the Living Dead Part II, 1988, Heart of Dixie, 1989, How I Got into College, 1989, Bad Influence, 1990, Paris Trout, 1991, Waterland, 1992, The Hand that Rocks the Cradle, 1992, The River Wild, 1994, Sydney, 1996, The Pallbearer, 1996, Boys, 1996, Boogie Nights, 1997, Tomorrow Never Dies, 1997, Richard Lester!, 1998, 8MM, 1999, Magnolia, 1999, Bounce, 2000, Heist, 2001, Punch-Drunk Love, 2002, Behind the Red Door, 2002, Gigli, 2003, Runaway Jury, 2003, Goodnight, and Goodluck, 2005 (winner Best Cinemetography, Spirit Awards, 2006), Syriana, 2005, American Dreamz, 2006, (TV movies) Margaret Bourke-White, 1989, Killing in a Small Town, 1989, Opposites Attract, 1990, A Murderous Affair: The Carolyn Warmus Story, 1992, (TV pilots) Dreamstreet, 1989. Office: care Spyros Skouras Sanford Skouras Gross & Assocs 1015 Gayley Ave Fl 3 Los Angeles CA 90024-3424

ELTAYEB, EMIL, pharmacist, researcher; b. Salzburg, Austria, May 24, 1975; arrived in U.S., 1975; s. Ali and Maia Eltayeb. BS cum laude, St. John's U., 1998, PharmD, 2002. Intern Mary Immaculate Hosp., Jamaica, NY, 1995—97, Rite Aid, Jamaica, NY, 1999—2000. Author: The Mystery of Cancer and Alzheimer's Disease is Revealed, 2005. Mem.: Am. Chem. Soc., N.Y. Acad. Scis., Rho Chi, Golden Key. Achievements include research in application of Einstein's theory of relativity, law of conservation of energy, and quantum mechanics to the understanding of the pathophysiology of various diseases and their treatment. Avocation: reading. Personal E-mail: Meltayeb@msn.com.

ELVERUM, GERARD WILLIAM, JR., retired electronics and aerospace transportation executive; b. Mpls., Sept. 29, 1927; m. Mary Jean Proverbs, Dec. 28, 1948. Student, U. Nebr., Lincoln, 1945, SD State U., Brookings, 1945; B in Physics, U. Minn., Mpls., 1949. Engr. Jet Propulsion Lab., Pasadena, Calif., 1949-59; sect. head, mgr. dept. Space Tech. Lab., El Segundo, Calif., 1959-62; dir. lab. Systems Group TRW, Redondo Beach, Calif., 1963-66, mgr. ops. Def. and Space Systems Group, 1969-81, v.p., gen. mgr. Applied Tech. Div./Space and Tech. Group, 1981-91, ret., 1991. Mem. adv. panel NASA/Aerospace Safety Bd., Washington, 1982-91; mem. NASA Access to Space Panel, 1995-2001; mem. space studies bd., NRC, 1996-99, com. AF Dept. Def. Aerospace Propulsion, 2005-06; mem. space transp. subcom. NASA adv. coun., 1996-2002. Contbr. articles to profl. jours.; patentee in field. Commr. Commn. on Engring. and Tech. Systems, Nat. Rsch. Coun., 1991-94. Served with USAF, 1944-46. Named Outstanding Engr., Inst. Advancement Engring., 1972; recipient Spl. Achievement award, ASME, 1971. Fellow AIAA (James H. Wyld Propulsion award 1973); mem. Am. Def. Preparedness Assn., Nat. Acad. Engring. Personal E-mail: jerrywelverum@msn.com. *Preparation, perseverance, patience with others, and absolute integrity will create the career opportunities that many will simply attribute to being at the right place at the right time.*

ELVIDGE, CHRISTINA MARIE, director; d. John and Rose Ann Elvidge. MA, U. Scranton, Pa., 1995; student, Ind. U. Pa., Indiana, Pa., 1998—. Lectr. English dept. Luzerne County CC, 1995—97; lectr. English Marywood U., Scranton, Pa., 1997—, dir. hons. and fellowships, 2004—. Advisor Kappa Gamma Pi, Nat. Cath. Coll. Grad. Honor Soc., Scranton, Pa., 2004. Mem.: Pa. Coll. English Assn. (pres. 2004—05), Kappa Gamma Pi (adv. 2004—). Democrat. Avocations: reading, writing. Office: Marywood University 2300 Adams Avenue Scranton PA 18509 Home Phone: 570-457-8268; Office Phone: 570-348-6211. Business E-Mail: elvidge@marywood.edu.

ELVIN, GEORGE, architecture educator; b. Washington, Sept. 9, 1958; m. Meg Calkins, May 30, 1998; children: Jackson Calkins, Annabel Calkins. BS, U. Md., 1991; MA in Architecture, U. Calif., Berkeley, 1995, PhD, 1998. Asst. prof. U. Ill., Urbana, 1999—2005; assoc. prof. Ball State U., Muncie, Ind., 2005—. Author: Integrated Practice in Architecture, 2007; contbr. The Architect's Guide to Design-Build Services, 2003. Dir. Green Tech. Forum. Fellow, Inst. for Advanced Study in Humanities, U. Edinburgh, 2005. Achievements include research in nanotechnology, bio-technology, architecture, and design. Office: 9801 Fall Creek Rd #402 Indianapolis IN 46256 Home Phone: 765-717-0797. Personal E-mail: elvin@greentechforum.net.

ELWAY, JOHN ALBERT, retired professional football player; b. Port Angeles, Wash., June 28, 1960; s. Jack Elway; m. Janet Elway; children: Jessica Gwen, Jordan Marie. BA in Econs., Stanford U., 1983. Quarterback Denver Broncos, 1983—98; ret., 1998; owner John Elway AutoNation; quarterbacks coach Cherry Creek HS, Greenwood Village, Colo., 2007—. Mem. Mayor's Coun. on Phys. Fitness City of Denver; chmn. Rocky Mountain regional Nat. Kidney Found. Named first overall pick in NFL draft by Balt. Colts, 1983, NFL MVP/Player of Yr., Associated Press, 1987, Am. Football Conf. Offensive MVP/Player of Yr., 1987, 1993, Super Bowl MVP, 1998; named to Sporting News Coll. All-Am. Team, 1980, 1982, Sporting News NFL All-Pro Team, 1987, Am. Football Conf. Pro Bowl Team, 1987, 1988, 1990, 1992, 1994, 1995, 1997—99, 1990's All-Decade Team. Achievements include winning Super Bowls XXXII and XXXIII (with Denver Broncos), 1997, 1998; inducted in NFL Hall of Fame, 2004. Office: Cherry Creek HS Football Program 9300 E Union Ave Greenwood Village CO 80111 Office Phone: 720-554-2285.*

ELWIN, JAMES WILLIAM, JR., lawyer; b. Everett, Wash., June 28, 1950; s. James William Elwin and Jeannette Georgette (Zichy-Litscheff) Sherman; m. Regina K. McCabe, Oct. 25, 1986. BA, U. Denver, 1971, MA, 1972; JD, Northwestern U., 1975. Bar: Ill. 1975, US Dist. Ct. (no. dist.) Ill. 1975, US Ct. Appeals (7th cir.) 1977, US Supreme Ct. 1980, US Ct. Fed. Claims 1989. Trial atty. antitrust divsn. US Dept. Justice, Chgo., 1975-77; asst. dean Sch. Law Northwestern U., Chgo., 1977-82, assoc. dean, 1982-2000; dir. profl. devel. and tng. Shearman & Sterling, NYC, 2000—04; chief learning officer Sonnenschein Nath & Rosenthal LLP, Chicago, 2004—. Exec. dir. Corp. Counsel Ctr., 1984-2000; planning dir. Corp. Counsel Inst., Garrett Corp. and Securities Law Inst., Chgo., 1983-2000; dir. Short Course for Pros. Attys., 1981-2000, Short Course for Def. Lawyers in Criminal Cases, Chgo., 1979-2000. Bd. dirs. Legal Assistance Found. of Chgo., 1985-97; vice chmn. Gov.'s Adv. Coun. on Criminal Justice Legis., 1986-91. Fellow German Acad. Exch. Svc., 1986; Fulbright scholar, Germany, 1990. Mem. Chgo. Coun. Fgn. Rels. (mem. Chgo. com.), Chgo. Bar Assn. (bd. mgrs. 1983-85), Chgo. Bar Found. (bd. dirs. 1985-93, pres. 1989-91), Ill. Inst. Continuing Legal Edn. (bd. dirs. 1978-90, chmn. 1987-88), Am. Law Inst., Legal Club (pres. 1991-92), U. Club, Lawyers Club Chgo., Phi Beta Kappa, Pi Gamma Mu.

ELWOOD, PATRICIA COWAN, city official, political scientist, consultant; b. Haverhill, Mass., Oct. 22, 1941; d. Raymond Bernard and Florence Eva Cowan; children: Robert Michael, Douglas Matthew. BS, Tufts U., 1963; MS in Edn., Boston U., 1965; PhD, U. Md., 1978. Tchr./trainer Boston Pub. Schs., 1964-67; dir. Head Start Program, various cities, Mass., 1968; adminstrv. asst. dept. child study Tufts U., Medford, Mass., 1967-68; diagnostician, tchr./counselor Program for Hearing Impaired Richmond (Calif.) Pub. Schs., 1968-69, supr., 1970-73; asst. to dir. Berkeley (Calif.) Profl. Studies Abroad Program, New Delhi, 1969-70; curriculum writer Prince Georges County Pub. Schs., Upper Marlboro, Md., 1974, learning problems and hearing specialist, 1976—2005; chief of protocol, sec. internal affairs DC Govt., 2005—07, chief internat affairs, protocol, 2007—. Lectr. Trinity Coll., Washington, 1980-84; cons. Pan Am. Health Orgn., Caribbean, 1978-80; coord. state conf. early childhood edn., grad. asst., 1978; cons. in field. Author: From a Professional Parent's Prospective, 1994; co-author: Social and Emotional Development of Young Children, 1968, Alameda County California Public Schools Health Curriculum, 1969, Piaget's Theory as It Relates to Early Childhood Curricula, 1979; co-editor: Parent-Centered Programs for Young Hearing Impaired Students, 1976; implemented approved self-authored grant for one of first Parent-Infant Programs in the U.S.; contbr. articles to profl. jours. Apptd. mem. Inst. for Dist. Affairs, U. DC, 1981-82; fin. com. Sidwell Friends Sch., 1985-90; elected mem. Dem. State Com., Washington, 1985—, fin. chmn., 1988-90; parent bd. St. Albans Sch., 1993-94; 1st vice chmn. Ward III Dem. Com., Washington, 1988-91, 95-99, fin. sec., 1994-95, treas., 1986-88, elected vice chair 1999-2006; past fin. and policy com. presdl., senate, ho. reps., gubernatorial campaigns; campaign co-chmn., ward chmn. steering com. DC and Greater Washington area polit. candidate campaigns, 1980—; co-founder DC Soccer, 1978, DC Baseball Connection, 1994-95; head com. to bring Am. Legion Baseball to DC, 1994-95; bd. dirs. Babe Ruth League, Little League and Boys and Girls Club, 1986-91, Nat. Child Rsch. Ctr., 1977-82, Washington Hearing and Speech Ctr., 1982-87, Washington Tufts Alliance, co-chair, 1986-88, vice-chair, 1985-86, treas., 1988—, chair interviewing com., 1990—; apptd. Coun. Govts. Task Force Com. on Growth and Transp., 1990-92; commr. Mayoral Appointee, Nat. Capital Planning Commn., 1987-2007, exec. com., 1993-2007, vice chair, 1995-2007; nominating com., trustee U. DC, 1988-92; presdl. appointee Selective Svc. Bd., 1988-91, 2004-06; bd. dirs. Ft. Myer Swim Team, 1983-85, 89-90; elected mem. alumni coun. Tufts U., 1988—; bd. trustees City Lights Sch., 1993-97, soccer adv. com., 1995-96; bd. dirs. DC Mental Health Assn., Anacostia Coord. Com., African-Am. Mus.; adv. coun. Hist. Soc. Washington, 1998; adv. com. Y-Care 2000 Found.; adv. bd. Hist. Preservation Soc., 1998-2001; active DC Agenda; founding mem. DC Baseball PAC, 2004-05. Named Outstanding Young Woman in Am., 1966. Mem. Nat. Assn. for Edn. Young Children, World Affairs Coun., Nat. Trust for Historic Preservation, Internat. Bus. Coun. (bd. dirs.), Citizens Against Gun Violence. Democrat. Avocations: politics, swimming, walking, baseball. Office: Office Dist Sec 1350 Pennsylvania Ave NW Ste 419 Washington DC 20004 Office Phone: 202-727-6306. E-mail: patricia.elwood@dc.gov.*

ELWOOD-AKERS, VIRGINIA EDYTHE, librarian, retired archivist; b. LA, Nov. 9, 1938; d. George Henry and Eileen Edythe Elwood; m. Roy Stanley Akers, Apr. 12, 1980 (widowed May 2003). BA, UCLA, 1964; MLS, U. Oreg., 1972; MA in Mass. Comm., Calif. State U., Northridge, 1981. Editor UCLA, LA, 1970-71, writer, 1971-72; libr., archivist Calif. State U., Northridge, 1972—2001, ret., 2001. Reader Huntington Libr., San Marino, Calif., 1990—. Author: Women War Correspondents in the Vietnam War, 1988; contbr. articles to profl. jours. Calif. State U. Found. grantee, Northridge, Calif. State U. Libr. grantee. Mem. Western Assn. Women Historians, Soc. Calif. Archivists. Democrat. Episcopalian. Avocations: travel, musical theater. Personal E-mail: virgoea@aol.com.

ELY, DEBORAH D., elementary school educator; b. Boston, May 17, 1953; d. John Merton Gardner and Elsie Mable Hilyard; m. David Marion Ely, Sept. 24, 1977; 1 child, Ryan David. AA in christian edn., Eastern Nazarene Coll., 1974, BS in edn., 1976; M, Mich. State, 1983. Tchr. Airport Cmty. Sch., 1979—2006. Chmn., sch. improvement team Airport AIMS, Carleton, Mich.; team MEAP coord. Airport Cmty. Sch., Carleton, 2001—03. Ch. pianist Bapt. Ch. Recipient Whole Apple award, Monroe Intermediate Sch., 1993, 1998. Republican. Baptist. Avocations: painting, camping, piano, crafts. Home: 147 W Newburg Rd Carleton MI 48117 Office Phone: 734-654-6205. Business E-Mail: dely@airport.k12.mi.us.

ELY, DONALD J(EAN), retired clergyman, secondary school educator; b. Frederick, Md., July 15, 1933; s. George Kline and Jennie Mabel (Boyer) E. m. Lois Jean Kirkpatrick, Aug. 27, 1967; children: Kathleen Rose, Stephen David, Yvonne Elaine. AB, Gettysburg Coll., 1955; BD, Lancaster Sem., 1958; MEd, Bloomsburg U., 1972. Ordained to ministry Evang. and Reformed Ch., 1958. Pastor St. John Evang. and Reformed Ch., Riegelsville, Pa., 1958-61, Zion's Reformed Ch., Ashland, Pa., 1961-64, Augusta Reformed Parish, Sunbury, Pa., 1964-74, Salem United Meth. Ch., Middleburg, Pa., 1974-79, Salem Ind. Brethren Ch., Middleburg, 1979-83; tchr. social studies Shikellamy H.S., Sunbury, 1966-98; ret., 1998. Bd. dirs. Sunbury Area YMCA, 1966—, sec., 1973-80, 88-2000; bd. dirs. Greater Susquehanna Valley YMCA, 1993—, sec. 1999—; bd. dirs. Northumberland County unit Am. Cancer Soc., 1971-74, Snyder County unit, 1974-84; rep. candidate state legis., 1982; vice chmn. Govt. Study Commn. of City of Sunbury, 1989-91; mem. Northumberland County Rep. com., 1987—, state committeeman, 1992—. Mem.: SAR (chaplain 1971—, chpt. pres. 1981—86, 1992), Pennsylvanians for Effective Govt., Greater Susquehanna Valley C. of C., Intercollegiate Studies Inst., Heritage Found., Federalist Soc., Am. Conservative Union, Hist. Soc. Evang. and Ref. Ch., Northumberland County Hist. Soc. (life; trustee 1972—83), Snyder County Hist. Soc. (life; pres. 1980—83), Union County Hist. Soc., Hereditary Register of U.S., Commonwealth Found., Susquehana Valley Country Club, Rolls Royce Owners' Club, Antique Auto Club Am., Masons. Home and Office: PO Box 765 Sunbury PA 17801-0765 Fax: 570-286-4444.

ELY, DUNCAN CAIRNES, social services administrator; b. Phila., Apr. 3, 1951; s. Donald and Barbara Dercum (Mifflin) E.; m. Elizabeth Caroline Wickenberg, June 14, 1984; 1 child, Penn Wickenberg Ely. BA, U. Ariz., 1974; MDiv, Gen. Theol. Sem., NYC, 1988; cert. mentor Edn. for Ministry, U. of South, 1985. Cert. in clin. pastoral edn. Bapt. Med. Ctr., 1985; cert. human svcs. adminstrn. Human Svcs. Inst., 1991. Nat. exec. dir. Assn. for Independence of Disabled, Inc., Tucson, 1974-77; exec. dir. Frat. of Alpha Kappa Lambda, Inc., Indpls., 1977-79; asst. St. Stephen's Episcopal Ch., Phila., 1979-80; exec. dir. The Youth Alternatives Camps, Inc., Tucson, 1980-83, Crisis Assistance Clothing Ministry, Charlotte, N.C., 1989-93, N.C. Harvest, Inc., Charlotte, 1993-96, Spartanburg (S.C.) Cmty. Events, Inc., 1996-98; dir. Camp Gravatt, Aiken, S.C., 1998—. Chmn. bd. advisors Expanded Foods and Nutrition Edn. Program N.C. State U., 1989-96; mem. foster care rev. bd. child protective svcs. Dept. Social Svcs., Charlotte, 1991-96. Author, editor: The Truth and the Word, 1978; also numerous articles in books, jours., mag. and newspapers. Past pres. Ely Assn., Inc., N.Y.C.; trustee Wildlife Guard, Inc., 1973—, past nat. pres., also past chmn. bd. advisors The Relatives, Inc., Charlotte, 1989-96, Ret. Sr. Vol. Program, Charlotte, 1990-96, Vol. Ctr. Charlotte, 1990-96; bd. dirs. Charlotte Emergency Housing, Inc., 1989-96, Met. Music Ministries, Inc., 1993-96, Piedmont Area Girl Scouts, Inc., 1997—, S.C. Inst. Nonprofit Leadership, Share the Vision resource com. City of Spartanburg, 1997—; mem. Vol. Leadership Devel. Program, Charlotte, 1991; grad. class XIII, Leadership Charlotte, 1991; grad. class III Carolinas Leadership Program, 1994; grad. class I Leadership N.C., 1995; chmn. bd. dirs. Spartanburg Caregivers, Inc., 1996—; grad. class 17 Leadership Spartanburg, 1997; grad. class 19 Leadership S.C., 1998; commr. for nat. and cmty. svc. State of N.C.; mem. N.C. Gov.'s Commn. on Nat. and Cmty. Svc.; mem. christian formation steering com. Episcopal Diocese Upper S.C., 1998—, mem. mission and outreach steering com., 1998—, mem. peer ministry conf., 1998. Recipient gold pin Phila. State Hosp., 1973, One of Nine Who Care award Sta. WSOC-TV and United Way, Charlotte, 1991, 94. Mem. S.R., Internat. Festivals and Events Assn., Nat. Soc. Am. Royal Descent, Barorial Order Magna Charta, Colonial Order of the Crown, Soc. Mayflower Descendants, Am. Mgmt. Assn., Am. Soc. Assn. Execs., Nat. Christian Counselors Assn. (lic. pastoral counselor), Metrolina Assn. for Vol. Adminstrn. (past pres.), N.C. Assn. Vol. Adminstrs. (past v.p.), S.C. Festival Assn., Penn Laurel Poets, Soc. Nonprofit Execs., Soc. Cin., Pen and Pencil Club, Alpha Kappa Lambda (past pres.), Alpha Phi Omega (past pres.), Theta Kappa Psi (past pres.), Theta Omega (past pres.), Psi Chi (past pres.), Country Club of Spartanburg, Piedmont Club, Fripp Island Club (S.C.), numerous others. Republican. Episcopalian. Avocations: arts, genealogy, horticulture, reading, sports. Office: Camp Gravatt 1006 Camp Gravatt Rd Aiken SC 29805-8730 Office Phone: 864-415-6338. E-mail: DuncanEly@Hotmail.com.

ELY, GARY G., utilities company executive; Grad., Brigham Young U.; postgrad., U. Idaho, Stanford U., Edison Elec. Inst. Leadership. With Avista Corp., Spokane, Wash., 1967—, v.p. mktg., 1986-91, v.p. natural gas, 1991-95, sr. v.p., 1996-97, chmn., CEO, 1997—. Mem. State Bldg. Code Coun. Mem. Pacific Coast Gas Assn. (chmn. gas mgmt. exec. com., chmn. mktg. exec. com., bd. dirs.), N.W. Electric Light and Power Assn. (bd. dirs.), Spokane Valley C. of C. (exec. bd.), N.W. Gas Assn. (bd. dirs.). Office: Avista Corp 1411 E Mission Ave Spokane WA 99220-3727

ELY, PARRY HAINES, dermatologist, educator; b. Washington, Sept. 19, 1945; s. Northcutt and Marica (McCann) E.; m. Elizabeth Magee, June 24, 1969 (div. June 1998); children: Sims, Rebecca, Meredith, Tess; m. Kathleen O'Brien, May 3, 2000 AB, Stanford U., 1967; MD, U. So. Calif., 1971. Diplomate Am. Bd. Dermatology, Am. Bd. Pathology; lic. dermatologist, Calif. Intern medicine U. So. Calif.-L.A. County Med. Ctr., 1971—72, resident dermatology, 1972—75; clin. prof. dermatology U. Calif., Davis, 1975—. Bd. dirs. Nevada City Wineries Mem. editl. bd. Calif. Physician, 1994—; manuscript reviewer Archives Internal Medicine, 1988—, Annals Internal Medicine, 1980—, Archives Dermatology, 1977—; contbr. articles to med. jours Fellow Am. Acad. Dermatology (asst. editor jour. 1988-94, manuscript reviewer 1994—), Am. Soc. Dermatopathology; mem. AMA, Internat. Soc. Tropical Dermatology, Am. Fedn. Clin. Rsch., Am. Soc. Dermatologic Surgery, N.Am. Clin. Dermatologic Soc., Calif. Med. Assn. (alt. del. 1995—, rep. to Calif. Telehealth/Telemedicine coord. project planning com. 1996—), Pacific Dermatologic Soc. (Nelson Paul Anderson Meml. Essay 1st pl. award 1979, Mini Presentation of Yr. award 1984), Noah Worcester Dermatol. Soc., Cutaneous Therapy Soc., Soc. Investigative Dermatology, Sacramento Valley Dermatol. Soc. (pres. 1990-91), Placer Nev. Med. Soc. (bd. dirs. 1978-79, 91-93, v.p. 1994, pres. 1995), Skin Cancer Found. (med. coun. 1987—), Tri-County Am. Cancer Soc. (bd. dirs. 1978-79, 91-92), Royal Soc. Medicine (London), Dermatology Found., Space Dermatology Found. (founding), Shivas Irons Soc. (founding) Office: 565 Brunswick Rd Ste 7 Grass Valley CA 95945-9053 E-mail: haines@netshel.net.

ELY, ROBERT EUGENE, lawyer, author, educator; b. Ft. Wayne, Ind., Aug. 18, 1949; s. Virgil Eugene and Alberta Irene (Steiner) E.; m. Jackline Sue Meyer, Apr. 14, 1973; 1 child, Elizabeth Vanessa. BA, Manchester Coll., 1971, MA, 1975; JD, Ind. U., 1983. Bar: Ala. 1985, U.S. Dist. Ct. (mid. dist.) Ala. 1988. Sales promotion cons. Lincoln Nat. Corp., Ft. Wayne, 1971-73; asst. dir. humanities Manchester Coll., North Manchester, Ind., 1973-75; assoc. instr. English Purdue U., West Lafayette, Ind., 1975-77; instr. English Ala. State U., Montgomery, 1977-81, dir. honors, 1984-86, asst. v.p., 1984-85, assoc. prof. English, 1986—; pvt. practice law Montgomery, 1985—. Communications cons. Cummins Internat., Columbus, Ind., 1982; adj. prof. paralegalism Auburn (Ala.) U., 1990-95. Author: The Humanities, 1979, (children's verse) Mose T.'s Slapout Family Album, 1996 (Shaw-Montgomery prize for poetry 1985), Encanchata, 2001, (novel) Hallelujah, Alabama!, 2006; contbr. articles to profl. jours. Named to Order of Reyes del Monte do Gozo; fellow Summer Inst., NEH, 1981, Rsch. fellow, Ala. State U., 1978, for Islamic Studies in Turkey, Mobil Found., 1999, for East-West studies U. Hawaii, Henry Luce Found., 2000, for ancient and modern studies in Egypt, Fulbright Found., 2002. Mem. ABA, Ala. Bar Assn., Montgomery County Bar Assn., Am. Acad. Poets, Nat. Coun. Tchrs. English, Lower Audubon Brook Soc., Coventry Motoring and Aviation Soc., The Writs. Democrat. Presbyterian. Avocations: serious and light verse, fishing, folk art, sports cars. Home: 3212 LeBron Rd Montgomery AL 36106-2334 Office: 625 S Hull St Montgomery AL 36104-5807 Office Phone: 334-265-2002. Personal E-mail: relylaw@juno.com.

ELYN, MARK, retired vocalist; b. Seattle, Feb. 4, 1932; s. Isadore and Goldie Elyn; m. Jaclyn Rendall, 1956. Student, U. Wash., 1948-51, Seattle U., 1951-52; student of Robert Weede. Bd. mem. Bel Canto Inst., NY. Debut, N.Y.C. Opera, 1956, leading roles, San Francisco Opera, NBC Opera, Phila. Lyric Opera, leading bass, Cologne, Munich, Hamburg, Stuttgart, Vienna, Monte Carlo, Geneva, Barcelona; roles include: Don Giovanni, Sarastro in The Magic Flute, Philip II in Don Carlo, Figaro in The Marriage of Figaro; prof. music, U. Ill., Urbana, 1977—, chmn. voice dept., 1990-98, prof. emeritus, guest lectr., 1998—. Mem. Am. Guild Mus. Artists, Deutsche Buehnengenossenschaft, Nat. Assn. Tchrs. of Singing. Home: 1238 10th Ave E Seattle WA 98102-4324

ELY-RAPHEL, NANCY, diplomat; b. NYC, Feb. 4, 1937; d. Thomas Clarkson and Margaret (Merritt) Halliday; widowed; children: John Duff Ely, Robert Duff Ely, Stephanie Joyce Raphel. AB, Syracuse U., 1957; JD, U. San Diego, 1968. Bar: Calif. 1968, U.S. Supreme Ct. 1976. Dep. city atty. City of San Diego, 1969—70; asst. U.S. atty. So. Dist. Calif., 1970—71; assoc. Tyler, Cooper, Grant, Bowerman and Keefe, New Haven, 1971—72; from asst. to assoc. dean Sch. Law Boston U., 1972—75; atty.-advisor U.S. Dept. State, Washington, 1975—77; spl. atty. Boston Strike Force U.S. Dept. Justice, 1977—78; asst. legal advisor African Affairs U.S. Dept. State, Washington, 1978—87, asst. legal advisor Nuclear Affairs, 1988—89; dep. asst. Sec. of State Bur. Democracy, Human Rights and Labor Affairs, Washington, 1878—83, prin. dep. asst., 1993—95; Balkan coord. Bur. European and Can. Affairs, Washington, 1995—98; U.S. amb. to Slovenia, Am. Embassy, Ljubljana, 1998—2001, sr. advisor to sec., 2001—03; counselor on internat. law, 2003; v.p. Save the Children, Washington, 2003—. Mem. Coun. on Fgn. Rels., 1990—. Recipient Outstanding Alumni award U. San Diego Law Sch., 1979, Superior Honor award U.S. Dept. State, Washington, 1983, 84, Presdl. Meritorious Svc. award U.S. Govt., Washington, 1986, 94, 98, Presdl. Disting. Svc. award, 1992, Author Hughes Career Achievement award, 2001, U.S. Dept. State Dir. Gen.'s Cup, 2004. Home: 1304 30th St NW Washington DC 20007-3343 E-mail: nancyelyraphel@earthlink.net.

ELZA, BETTY ANN, retired librarian; b. Wymer, W.Va., Feb. 27, 1944; d. Floyd and Gertrude (Snyder) E. BS, Clarion U., 1966, MSLS, 1971, postgrad., 1971—, U. Dundee, Scotland, Summer 1969. Libr. Brookville (Pa.) Area Sch. Dist., 1966—97, mem. steering com. for self study for evaluation, 1976—77; ret, 1997. Presenter workship on parliamentary procedure Tall Tree Coun. Boardmanship Tng., Clarion Holiday Inn, June 1991; mem. task force Pa. Guidelines for Media Programs, 1975-76; chairperson joint rev. com. Pa. Libr. Master Plan Report, 1975; vis. faculty Clarion U. Pa., 1972-73; inst. adviser U. Pitts., 1976. Contbr. articles to profl. publs. Organizer parish libr. Immaculate Conception Ch., Brookville, 1968-69, First Bapt. Ch., Brookville, 1976-77; mem. steering com. for strategic planning Brookville Sch. Dist., 1994-95; mem. capital stewardship campaign Immaculate Conception, Brookville, 2002; bd. trustees Summerville Pub. Libr., 1997-2003. Mem. Nat Soc. DAR (compiled lineage book of Clarion County chpt. 2006, Compiled Revolutionary War Patriots Book, 2007), Nat. Soc. Daus. Am. Colonists, Pa. Sch. Librs. Assn. (chair profl. stds. com. 1974-76), Embroiderers' Guild Am. (Nydill chpt.), Pa. Assn. Sch. Retirees, Jefferson County History Ctr., Clarion County Hist. Soc., Alpha Delta Kappa. Roman Catholic. Avocations: crafts, reading, travel, photography. Home: 618 Simpson Rd Corsica PA 15829-9409

ELZAY, RICHARD PAUL, retired dean, dental educator, department chairman; b. Lima, Ohio, Dec. 6, 1931; s. Paul William and Edna Virginia (Moyer) E.; 1 child, Mark S. BS, Ind. U., Indpls., 1957, DDS with honors, 1960, MS in Dental Surgery, 1962. Diplomate Am. Bd. Oral Maxillofacial Pathology. Gen. practice dentistry, Brownsburg, Ind., 1960-62; instr. dept. oral pathology Med. Coll. Va. Sch. Dentistry, Richmond, 1962-64; asst. prof. Sch. Dentistry Med. Coll. Va., Richmond, 1964-66, assoc. prof., 1966-69, prof., 1969—, chmn. dept. oral pathology, 1969-86, asst. dean acad. affairs, 1970-74; prof., dep. v.p. for health scis., dean Sch. Dentistry U. Minn., Mpls., 1986-96.

ELZER, ROBERT W., lawyer; b. 1951; BA with high distinction, Ind. U., 1973; JD cum laude, Harvard U., 1976. Bar: Ind. 1976. Ptnr. Baker & Daniels, Indpls. Bd. mem. Indianapolis Civic Theatre; mem. (planned giving com) Am. Heart Assn., Ind. Mem. ABA, 7th Cir. Bar Assn., Ind. State Bar Assn., Ind. Estate Planning Coun., past chair Indpls. Bar Assn., Phi Beta Kappa, fellow Am. Coll. (trust and estate counsel). Office: Baker & Daniels 600 E 96th St Ste 600 Indianapolis IN 46240 Office Phone: 317-569-4660. Office Fax: 317-569-4800. Business E-Mail: robert.elzer@bakerd.com.

ELZINGA, KENNETH GERALD, economics professor; b. Coopersville, Mich., Aug. 11, 1941; s. Clarence Albert and Lettie (Albrecht) E.; m. Barbara Ann Brunson, June 17, 1967 (dec. 1978); m. Terry M. Maguire, Aug. 9, 1981. BA, Kalamazoo Coll., 1963; MA, Mich. State U., 1966, PhD, 1967; LHD, Kalamazoo Coll., 2000. Rsch. economist Senate Antitrust and Monopoly Subcom., 1964; asst. instr. Mich. State U., 1965-66; asst. prof. U. Va., Charlottesville, 1967-71, assoc. prof., 1971-73, prof., 1973—; fellow in law and econs. U. Chgo., 1974; vis. prof. econs. Trinity U., 1984; Thomas Jefferson fellow Cambridge U., 1990, Cavaliers Disting. Tchg. Professorship, 1992-97, Robert C. Taylor prof. econ., 2002—. Spl. econ. advisor to asst. atty. gen., antitrust divsn. Dept. Justice, 1970-71; trustee Hope Coll., 1983-90, Inter-Varsity Christian fellowship, 1992-2000; mem. editl. bd. Antitrust Bull., 1977—; Univ. Disting. vis. prof. Pepperdine U., 2004; Vernon F. Taylor vis. rshc. prof. Trinity U., San Antonio, 2006, Disting. vis. prof. Pepperdine U., 2005. Author: (with others) The Antitrust Penalties, 1976, The Fatal Equilibrium, 1985, Murder at the Margin, 1993, A Deadly Indifference, 1995, The Antitrust Casebook, 3rd edit. 1996. Recipient Thomas Jefferson award U. Va., 1992, Commonwealth of Va. Outstanding Faculty award, 1992, Kenan Enterprise award for tchg. econs., William R. Kenan Jr. Charitable Trust, 1996, Templeton Honor Roll award for Edn. in a Free Soc. John Templeton Found., 1997, Disting. Alumni award Mich. State U., 1999; named Tchr. of the Yr. Phi Eta Sigma, 1992. Mem. ABA, Am. Econs. Assn., Mystery Writers of Am., Am. Law and Econs. Assn., So. Econ. Assn (pres. 1991), Internat. J.A. Shumpeter Soc., Indsl. Orgn. Soc. (pres. 1979). Presbyterian. Avocations: water-skiing, travel. Office: U VA Dept Econs PO Box 400182 Charlottesville VA 22904-4182 Business E-Mail: elzinga@virginia.edu.

EMANO, DENNIS JOSE MARMOL, psychology professor; b. Sorsogon, Philippines, Nov. 7, 1967; s. Nestor D and Enemina M Emano; life ptnr. Pedro M Garcia-Alonso. BA, U. Ill., Chgo., 1991; MA, Roosevelt U., 1995; PhD, Loyola U., Chgo., 2006. LCPC Dept. of Profl. Regulation, Ill., 1997. Staff therapist Cmty. Counseling Ctrs. Chgo., 1994—98; cons. Meth. Hosp. Chgo., 1999—2002; pre-doctoral psychology intern U. So. Calif., LA, 2002—03; adj. faculty Oakton CC, Des Plaines, Ill., 2003—06; counselor, asst. prof. Coll. DuPage, Glen Ellyn, 2006—. Cons. Youth Guidance, 2004—05; psychotherapist Ctrs. Family Change, 2005—06. Bd. dirs. Ch. of the Resurrection, MCC, Chgo., 1993—97. Recipient Outstanding Svc. to Internat. Students, Roosevelt U., 1993;, Ill. Consortium for Ednl. Opportunity Program fellow, 1999—2003, Anonymous Donor scholar, Roosevelt U., 1992—93, Tuition scholar, Wright Coll., 1987, First Prize scholar, Am. Acad. Art, 1986—87. Mem.: APA, ACA, Soc. Psychol. Study of Ethnic Minority Issues, Ill. Counseling Assn., Am. Mental Health Counselors Assn., Soc. Gay, Lesbian and Bisexual Issues. Democrat. Avocations: surfing, martial arts, weightlifting, camping, travel. Office: Coll DuPage 425 Fawell Blvd Glen Ellyn IL 60137-6599 Office Phone: 630-942-3062.

EMANUEL, ARI (ARIEL Z. EMANUEL), talent agent; b. Mar. 1961; m. Sarah Emanuel; 3 children. Grad., Macalester Coll. Agent trainee Creative Artists Agency; sr. agent Internat. Creative Mgmt.; ptnr. InterTalent; co-founder, ptnr. Endeavor Agy., Beverly Hills, Calif., 1995—. Blog contbr. The Huffington Post. Democrat. Office: Endeavor Agency 9601 Wilshire Blvd # 3 Beverly Hills CA 90210 Office Phone: 310-248-2000. Office Fax: 310-248-2020.*

EMANUEL, EZEKIEL J., oncologist, bioethicist; BA, Amherst Coll., 1979; MSc, Oxford U., Exeter Coll., 1981; MD, Harvard U. Med. Sch., 1988; PhD, Harvard U., 1989. Lic. Mass., diplomate med. oncology, internal medicine. Fellow in ethics & the professions Harvard U., Kennedy Sch. Govt., Cambridge, Mass., 1987—88; med. intern Beth Israel Hosp., Boston, 1988—89, med. resident, 1989—90; med. clin. fellow Harvard Med. Sch., Boston, 1990—92; fellow, med. oncology Dana-Farber Cancer Inst., Boston, 1990—92; instructor Harvard Med. Sch., Boston, 1992—94, asst. prof. medicine, clin. medicine, clin. epidemiology, 1994—97, assoc. prof. social medicine, 1997—98; chair dept. clin. bioethics, Warren G. Magnuson Clin. Ctr. NIH, 1998—. Internat. adv. bd. on bioethics Pan. Am. Health Orgn., 1999—; med. adv. bd. Cancer Care, Inc., 2000—; chair, Com. to Develop Ethical Guidelines Academy/Health, 2002—; adj. lectr. pub. policy John F. Kennedy Sch. Govt., Harvard U., 2002—03; assoc. editor Jour. Clinical Ethics, Jour. Health Comm.; bd. editors Lancet Oncology, Jour. Law, Medicine & Ethics, Am. Jour Bioethics; editorial adv. bd. BioMed Ctrl., Medicine, Health Care & Philosophy. Author: The Ends of Human Life, 1991; co-author: No Margin, No Mission, 2003; co-editor: Clinical & Epidemiol. Aspects of End-of-Life Decision-Making, 2001. Recipient Career Devel. award, Am. Cancer Soc., 1992, Baruj Benacerraf Clin. Investigator award, 1994, Clin. Ctr. Dir.'s award, 2000, AMA/Burroughs Welcome Leadership award, 1990, Danforth Teaching award, 1984—86. Fellow: Hastings Ctr.; mem.: Am. Soc. Clin. Oncology (mem. task force on oversight of clin. rsch. 2000—, chair task force on quality of cancer care 2000—, chair ethics com. 2003—04), Inst. Medicine, Phi Beta Kappa. Office: NIH Dept Clin Bioethics Bldg 10 Rm 1C118 10 Ctr Dr Bethesda MD 20892 E-mail: eemanuel@nih.gov.

EMANUEL, JOHN F., lawyer; BBA in Acctg. with honors, U. Wis., 1975; JD, Stanford U., 1978. Bar: Wis. 1978. Atty. Whyte Hirschboeck Dudek SC, Milw. Bd. dirs. Wiscraft, Inc.-Wis. Enterprises for the Blind, Associated Industries for the Blind, Am. Lung Assn. of the Upper Midwest. Mem.: State Bar Wis. Office: Whyte Hirschboeck Dudek SC 555 Wells St Ste 1900 Milwaukee WI 53202-3819 Office Phone: 414-978-5430. Business E-Mail: jemanuel@whdlaw.com.

EMANUEL, KERRY ANDREW, meteorologist, oceanographer, educator; b. Cin., Apr. 21, 1955; s. Albert II and Marny Catherine (Schonegevel) E.; m. Susan Boyd-Bowman, Dec. 29, 1990; 1 child, David Tristan Emanuel. SB in Earth and Planetary Scis., MIT, 1976, PhD in Meteorology, 1978. Adj. asst. prof. to asst. prof. dept. atmospheric scis. UCLA, 1978-81; postdoctoral fellow U. Okla. Coop. Inst. Mesoscale Meteorol. Studies, 1979; asst. prof. dept. meteorology and phys. oceanography MIT, 1981-83, asst. prof. to assoc. prof. ctr. meteorology and phys. oceanography and dept. earth, atmospheric & planetary scis., 1983-87, prof., 1987—, dir., 1989-97. Contbr. articles to profl. jours., textbooks, monographs; author: Divine Wind: The History and Science of Hurricanes, 2005. Named one of 100 Most Influential People, Time Mag., 2006. Fellow Am. Meteorol. Soc. (Meisinger award 1986, Banner I. Miller award with Richard Rotunno, 1992); mem. NAS, Sigma Xi, Phi Beta Kappa. Avocations: sailing, classical music. Office: MIT Dept Earth Atmospheric and Planetary Scis Rm 54-1620 77 Massachusetts Ave Cambridge MA 02139-4301 Office Phone: 617-253-2462. Office Fax: 617-253-6208. E-mail: emanuel@texmex.mit.edu.*

EMANUEL, RAHM, congressman; b. Chgo., Nov. 29, 1959; m. Amy Rule; 3 children. BA in Liberal Arts, Sarah Lawrence Coll., 1981; MA in Speech and Comm., Northwestern U., 1985. Nat. campaign dir. Dem. Congl. Campaign Com., 1988; sr. advisor, chief fundraiser Mayoral Campaign Richard M. Daley, 1989; nat. fin. dir. Clinton/Gore Campaign, 1991—92; asst. to Pres., dir. polit. affairs, dep. dir. comm. The White House, Washington, 1993-99, dir. spl. projects, sr. advisor for policy & strategy, 1995—98; mng. dir. Dresdner Kleinwort Wasserstein, Chgo., 1999—2002; mem. US Congress from 5th Ill. dist., 2003—. Co-author (with Bruce Reed): The Plan: Big Ideas for America, 2006. Recipient Alumni Achievement Citation, Sarah Lawrence Coll., 2001. Democrat. Jewish. Office: US Ho Reps 1319 Longworth House Office Bldg Washington DC 20515-1305 also: Dist Office 3742 W Irving Park Rd Chicago IL 60618*

EMANUEL-SMITH, ROBIN LESLEY, special education educator; m. Allen Weston Smith, Apr. 14, 1983; children: David, Ariel, Weston. BS in Engring., U.S. Mil. Acad., 1981; BS in Health-Phys. Edn. summa cum laude, Cameron U., Lawton, Okla., 1992; M Spl. Edn., Coll. of St. Rose, Albany, 1995. Cert. spl. edn., health and phys. edn. tchr., N.Y. Enlisted U.S. Army, 1974-76, commd. 2nd lt., 1981, advanced through grades to capt., 1984, resigned, 1990; tchr. spl. edn. Ulster County Bd. Coop. Ednl. Svcs., Port Ewen, NY, 1992—. Roman Catholic. Avocations: weightlifting, coaching and officiating youth soccer, softball and baseball. Office: Ulster County Bd Coop Ednl Svs Rt 32 New Paltz NY 12561 Personal E-mail: prteacher@msn.com.

EMANUELSON, JAMES ROBERT, retired insurance company executive; b. Hammond, Ind., Sept. 12, 1931; s. Clarence Harry and Ethel Janet (Anderson) E.; m. Dolores Patricia Fordyce, Aug. 10, 1957; children: James Robert, John Thomas, Karen Lynn. BS, Denison U., 1953. With Midland Mut. Life Ins. Co., Columbus, Ohio, 1953-67, mgr. gen. accounting, 1957-62, dir. cost accounting, 1962-67; with Columbus Mut. Life Ins. Co., 1967—, comptroller, 1969—, apptd. v.p., 1970-76, v.p., elected officer, 1976-91, v.p., comptroller, treas., 1991-93, ret., 1993—. Mem. Ins. Acctg. and Statis. Assn. (chpt. pres. 1954-69, pres. 1966-67, mem. interco. fin. rev. com. 1972-82, chmn. com. 1978-82, mem. fin. planning and control coun. 1978-91, cost acctg. com. 1982-91), Sigma Chi. Republican. Home: 3635 Cedar Circle Powell OH 43065-9148

EMBER, CAROL R., anthropology educator, writer; b. Bklyn., July 7, 1943; d. Hy and Elsie (Kardonsky) Ruchlis; m. Lawrence Baldwin, 1963 (div. 1969); m. Melvin Ember, Mar. 21, 1970; children: Katherine Ann, Julie Beth. BA, Antioch Coll., 1965; postgrad., Cornell U., 1965-66; PhD, Harvard, 1971. Lectr. Hunter Coll. CUNY, 1970-71; from asst. prof. to assoc. prof. CUNY, 1971-80; prof. Hunter Coll., 1981-97; exec. dir. Human Rels. Area Files Yale U., New Haven, 1997—. Author: Anthropology, 1973, Anthropology: A Brief Introduction, 1991; co-author: Cultural Anthropology, 1973; co-author: (with Burton Pastemak and M. Ember) Sex, Gender and Kinship: A Cross-Cultural Perspective, 1997;: 12th edit., 2007;; co-author: (with M. Ember) Marriage, Family and Kinship: Comparative Studies of Social Organization, 1983; co-author: 5th edit., 2003, Cross-Cultural Research Methods, 2001; co-editor: Cross-Cultural Research for Social Science, 1998, Research Frontiers in Anthropology, 1998, Portraits of Culture, 1998, Countries and Their Cultures, 2001, New Directions in Anthropology, 2004, Encyclopedia of Medical Anthropology, 2004, Encyclopedia of Sex and Gender, 2004, Encyclopedia of Diasporas, 2005. Woodrow Wilson Fellow, 1965-66, predoctoral fellow NIMH, 1969-70; rsch. grantee NSF, 1983-84, 86-98, U.S. Inst. Peace, 1990-92. Mem.: Human Behavior and Evolution Soc., Soc. for Psychol. Anthropology, Soc. for Cross-Cultural Rsch. (pres. 1985), Am. Anthrop. Assn. Office: Yale U Human Rels Area Files 755 Prospect St New Haven CT 06511-1225

EMBER, MELVIN LAWRENCE, anthropologist, educator; b. NYC, Jan. 13, 1933; s. Martin William and Ida F. (Trebuchovskaya) E.; m. Irma Stalberg, July 11, 1954 (div. Jan. 1970); children: Matthew, Rachel; m. Carol Lee Ruchlis, Mar. 21, 1970; children: Katherine, Julie. BA, Columbia Coll., 1953; PhD, Yale U., 1958. Postdoctoral fellow Yale U., New Haven, 1958-59; rsch. anthropologist NIH, Bethesda, Md., 1959-63; from asst. to assoc. prof. anthropology Antioch Coll., Yellow Springs, Ohio, 1963-67; assoc. prof. Hunter Coll., CUNY, 1967-70, prof., 1971-87; pres. Human Rels. Area Files, Inc., Yale U., New Haven, 1987—. Chmn. dept. anthropology Hunter Coll., CUNY, 1968-73, exec. officer PhD program in anthropology Grad. Sch., 1973-75. Co-author: Anthropology, 1973, Cultural Anthropology, 1973;: 12th edit., 2007, Marriage, Family and Kinship, 1983, Anthropology: A Brief Introduction, 1992, 5th edit., 2003, Sex, Gender and Kinship: A Cross-Cultural Perspective, 1997, Cross-Cultural Research Methods, 2001; co-editor: Portraits of Culture, 1998, Research Frontiers in Anthropology, 1998, Cross-Cultural Research for Social Science, 1998, Encyclopedia of Cultural Anthropology, 1996, American Immigrant Cultures: Builders of a Nation, 1997, Cultures of the World, 1999, Countries and Their Cultures, 2001, Encyclopedia of Prehistory, 2001—02, Encyclopedia of Urban Cultures, 2002, Archaeology: Original Readings in Method and Practice, 2002, Physical Anthropology: Original Readings in Method and Practice, 2002, Encyclopedia of Sex and Gender, 2004, Encyclopedia of Medical Anthropology, 2004, Encyclopedia of Diasporas, 2005; editor: Cross-Cultural Rsch.: The Jour. of Comparative Social Sci., 1982—. Fellow AAAS, Am. Anthrop. Assn.; mem. Soc. for Cross-Cultural Rsch. (pres. 1981-82). Office: Yale U Human Rels Area Files Inc 755 Prospect St New Haven CT 06511-1225 Home Phone: 203-772-1803; Office Phone: 203-764-9401.

EMBERGHER, MARY LOUISE, elementary school educator; b. Bklyn., July 22, 1943; d. Joseph and Anna Buonfiglio E. BS in Elem. Edn., St. John's U., 1964; MS in Elem. Edn., Bklyn. Coll. U. of N.Y., 1966. Cert. elem. tchr., Fla. Tchr. N.Y.C. Pub. Schs., Ozone Park, 1964-68, Broward County Pub. Schs., Pembroke Pines, Fla., 1968—. Adminstr. summative for master tchr. program State of Fla., Pembroke Pines, 1984-87; mem. tchr. rep. Broward county Quality Incentive coun. Broward County Pub. Sch. Bd., Ft. Lauderdale, 1983-84, peer tchrs., coach for new tchrs. Broward County Pub. Schs., Pembroke Pines, 1980-98; supr. tchr. for intern tchrs., 1970-98. Publicity chmn. Greater Hollywood Young, Fla., 1969; sec. Reps., 1970. Named Outstanding Young Educator Pembroke Pines Jaycees, 1973, Fla. Master Tchr. State of Fla., 1984-87; recipient Achievement in Edn. award Pembroke Pines Optimist Club. Mem. Women Educators (chpt. pres. 1980-82), Delta Kappa Gamma (yearbook chair 1972-73, chpt. 1st v.p. 1978-80). Republican. Roman Catholic. Avocations: travel, reading, music, politics. Office: Lakeside Elem Sch 900 NW 136th Ave Pembroke Pines FL 33028 Home Phone: 954-981-3284; Office Phone: 754-323-6400.

EMBLETON, TONY FREDERICK WALLACE, retired Canadian government official; b. Hornchurch, Essex, Eng., Oct. 1, 1929; emigrated to Can., 1952; s. Frederick William Howard and Lucy Violet Muriel (Wallace) E.; m. Eileen Loraine Blackall, Nov. 14, 1953; 1 dau., Sheila. B.Sc. with honours, U. London, 1950, PhD in Physics, 1952, D.Sc., 1964. Postdoctoral fellow NRC, Ottawa, Ont., Canada, 1952-53, asst. research officer, 1954-57, asso. research officer, 1957-62, sr. research officer, 1962-74, prin. research officer, 1974-90, ret., 1990. Vis. lectr. U. Ottawa, 1959-69, MIT, 1964, 67, 72; John Wiley Jones award lectr.Rochester Inst. Tech., 1976; adj. prof. Carleton U. 1977-90. Patentee in field; contbr. articles to profl. jours. Mem. Rockcliffe Park Pub. Sch. Bd., 1966-69; bd. dirs. Youth Sci. Found., 1967-72. Recipient Arch T. Coldwell award Soc. Automotive Engrs., 1974 Fellow Acoustical Soc. Am. (assoc. editor jour., exec. coun., v.p. 1977-78, pres. 1980-81, stds. dir. 1993-97, Biennial award 1964, Silver medal in Noise 1986, Gold medal 2002), Royal Soc. Can. (hon. treas. 1982-85); mem. NAE (fgn. assoc.), Can. Acoustical Assn. (founding sec. 1961-64, founding editor jour. 1971-74), Inst. Noise Control Engring. (dir. tech. group 1983-87, editl. bd. jour. 1983-93), Internat. Inst. of Noise Control Engring. (bd. dirs. 1992-2003, v.p. devel. 1998-2002). Home: PO Box 786 80 Sheardown Dr Nobleton ON Canada L0G 1N0

EMBREE, AINSLIE THOMAS, history professor; b. NS, Can., Jan. 1, 1921; came to U.S., 1958, naturalized, 1965; s. Ira Thomas and Margaret (Langley) E.; m. Suzanne Helene Harpole, May 24, 1947; children: Ralph Thomas, Margaret Louise. BA, Dalhousie U., Halifax, NS, 1941; BD, Pine Hill Theol. Sem., Halifax, 1946; MA, Union Theol. Sem., 1947, Columbia U., 1955, PhD, 1960; LLD (hon.), Juniata Coll., 1982. Prof. history Indore (India) Christian Coll., 1948-58; asst. prof., assoc. prof. history Columbia U., 1958-69, prof., 1972-91, prof. emeritus, 1991; assoc. dean Sch. Internat. Affairs, 1972-78, chmn., 1982-85, acting dean, 1989-90. Prof. Duke U., 1969-72; counsellor for cultural affairs Am. Embassy, New Delhi, 1978-80, cons., 1994-95; vis. disting. prof. Brown U., 1996-97, vis. prof. Sch. Advanced Internat. Studies, Johns Hopkins U., 2002-04. Author: Charles Grant and British Rule in India, 1962, India, 1967, India's Search for National Identity, 1971; editor: The Hindu Tradition, 1966, Alberuni's India, 1971, Pakistan's Western Borderlands, 1978, Sources of Indian Tradition rev., 1988; editor in chief: Encyclopedia of Asian History, 4 vols., 1988, Imagining India, 1989, Utopias in Conflict, 1990; co-editor: Asia in Western and World History, 1997, India's Worlds and U.S. Scholars, 1998. With RCAF, 1942—45. Recipient Van Doren award, 1985, Bancroft award, 1991, T. Das award, 1999, Tannenbaum award, 1999; Can. Council fellow, 1953-54; Am. Council Learned Socs. fellow, 1967; Am. Inst. Indian Studies fellow, 1968-69, 85-86; NEH fellow, 1977. Fellow AAAS; mem. Council Fgn. Relations, Assn. Asian Studies (pres. 1982-83), Am. Hist. Assn., Am. Inst. Indian Studies (pres. 1970-73), Cosmos Club. Home: 10450 Lottsford Rd Apt 1008 Mitchellville MD 20721-2745 Personal E-mail: atembree@aol.com.

EMBREE, MARY EVELYN, retired secondary school educator; b. Columbus, Ohio, May 10, 1940; d. Francis Marion and Mary Edith (Howdyshell) E. BFA, Ohio U., 1962; MS, Nova Southeastern U., 1982; postgrad., Oxford U., Eng., 1987—96. English tchr. Chillicothe (Ohio) Pub. Schs., 1962-67, Columbus (Ohio) Pub. Schs., 1967-74, Palatka (fla.) H.S., 1974—99, chair dept., 1994—99. Coach acad. competition Palatka H.S., 1996-97; adj. faculty mem. St. Johns River C.c., Palatka, 1990-94. Mem. Sch. Improvement Team, Palatka, 1990-92. Tchrs. as Advisors grantee State of Fla., 1989-91. Mem.: Putnam Fedn. Tchrs., Nat. Coun. Tchrs. English, Pi Lambda Theta, Alpha Delta Kappa (internat. dist. officer 1994—96). Democrat. Methodist. Avocations: world study courses, travel, writing. Office: Palatka HS 302 Mellon Rd Palatka FL 32177-4018 E-mail: embree@teacher.com.

EMBRY, MICHAEL DALE, writer, editor, educator; b. Louisville, Oct. 30, 1948; s. G.T. Dale and Dolores Lorraine (Colburn) E.; m. Mary Elizabeth Frederick, Aug. 7, 1971; children: Justin Michael, Sean Russell. AB in journalism, Ea. Ky. U., 1975. Sports editor Messenger, Madisonville, Ky., 1975-77; sports writer Lexington (Ky.) Herald, 1977-80; newsman AP, Louisville, 1980-82, sports writer NYC, 1982-83, state sports editor Milw., 1983-85, corr. Lexington, 1985—98; editor Ky. Mo., 1998—. Mem. adv. bd. Ea. Ky. U. Dept. Comms., 1990-2005, Ea. Ky. Progress,

1990-2005; judge Ky. Lit. Awards, 2005-06. Author: Basketball in the Bluegrass State, 1983, March Madness, 1985, The Touch, 1999, Baron of the Bluegrass, 2000, A Long Highway, 2001; contbr. articles to profl. publs. With USAF, 1969-73. Recipient Writing award Ky. chpt. Am. Cancer Soc., 1986-87, 89-90, 93, Ea. Ky. U. Comms. Alumni of Yr. 1983, DeDe award Ky. Devel. Planning Coun., 1988, numerous writing awards Ky. Press Assn., Louisville chpt. Soc. Profl. Journalists. Mem. AARP, Nat. Sportscasters and Sportswriters Assn., Blue Grass Soc. Profl. Journalists (pres. 1985-86), Ky. Romance Writers, Romance Writers of Am., Amnesty Internat., U.S. Basketball Writers Assn., Basketball Writers Assn. (pres. Milw. chpt. 1983), Milw. Pen and Mike Club (2nd v.p. 1985), Coun. Exceptional Children, Sierra Club, Friends of Paul Sawyer Libr. (pres. 2006-07), Nat. Wildlife Fedn., Hon. Order of Ky. Cols., Ky. Athletic Hall of Fame (selection com.). Avocations: tennis, music, reading, hiking, travel. Home: 152 Skyview Dr Frankfort KY 40601-8376 E-mail: membry@fewpb.net.

EMBRY, STEPHEN CRESTON, lawyer; b. Key West, Fla., Feb. 13, 1949; s. Jewell Creston and Julia Martine (Taylor) E.; m. Priscilla Mary Brown, Aug. 21, 1971; children: Nathaniel, Julia, Jessamyn. BA, Am. U., 1971; JD, U. Conn., 1976. Bar: Conn. 1976, U.S. Dist. Ct. Conn. 1976, U.S. Ct. Appeals (2d, 5th and 9th cirs.). Staff aide to Pres. The White House, Washington, 1969-72; assoc. Turner & Hensley, Great Bend, Kans., 1976, O'Brien, Shafner, Bartinik, & Stuart, Groton, Conn., 1976-85, Embry and Neusner, Groton, Conn., 1985—. Editor: Longshore and Harborworkers Textbook; mem. editl. bd. Matthew Bender, BRB Reporter; contbr. articles to profl. publs. Mem. Groton Rep. com., 1976-83, North Stonington Rep. com., 1984-88; chmn. Groton Housing Authority, 1979-80; mem. dean's adv. coun. Am. U. Sch. Internat. Svc., 2002—. Mem. ATLA (chair workers compensation sect. 1984-85, bd. dirs. workplace injury litigation group, sec. 1999-2000, pres.-elect 2001-02, pres. 2002-03), Maritime Claimants Attys. Assn. (bd. dirs.), Conn. Trial Lawyers, Conn. Bar Assn. (exec. bd.), Thames Club, Grange. Democrat. Office Phone: 860-449-0341.

EMDEN, CRAIG A., lawyer; b. Cin., Apr. 10, 1955; BS magna cum laude, Miami U., 1977; JD with honors, George Washington U., 1980; LLM in Taxation, Georgetown U., 1984. Bar: DC 1980, US Tax Ct. Ptnr., nonprofit org., real estate & taxation Venable LLP, Washington, 1999—. Author: (journal articles) Current Decision, Redding v. Commissioner, 1979; co-author: The Low-Income Housing Credit Provides Shelter from the Cold and Taxes, 1995, IRS Rulings May Significantly Reduce Eligible Basis in Tax Credit Transactions, 2001. Mem.: ABA (mem. taxation section, affordable housing forum), DC Bar Assn. Office: Venable LLP 575 7th St NW Washington DC 20004 Office Phone: 202-344-8521. Office Fax: 202-344-8300. Business E-Mail: caemden@venable.com.

EMEAGWALI, GLORIA THOMAS, humanities educator; b. Trinidad, West Indies, Feb. 6, 1950; came to U.S., 1991; BA, U. W.I., 1973; edn. dipl., London U., 1975; MA, Toronto U., 1976; PhD, Ahmadu Bello U., Zaria, Nigeria, 1986. Asst. prof. Ahmadu Bello U., Zaria, Nigeria, 1979-86; assoc. prof. Nigerian Def. Acad., 1986, Ilorin U., Nigeria, 1986-89; vis. prof. U. W.I., Trinidad, 1989, Oxford U., U.K., 1990-91; assoc. prof. history and African studies Conn. State U., New Britain, 1991-96, tenured prof. history and African studies, 1996—. Vis. prof. Internat. Devel. Ctr., Oxford (Eng.) U., spring 2000; mem. editl. bd. Review of African Political Economy, U.K, chief editor Africa Update, CCSU.; mem. adv. bd. Encyclopedia of the History of Science, Technology and Medicine, Hampshire Coll., Amherst; reviewer profl. jours.; spkr. in field. Editor: Historical Development of Science and Technology in Nigeria, 1992, Science and Technology in African History, 1992, African Systems of Science Technology and Art, 1993, Women Pay the Price: Structural Adjustment in Africa and the Caribbean, 1995, African Civilization, 1997, Africa and the Academy: Challenging Hegemonic Discourse on Africa, 2006; co-editor: The African Experience, Past, Presnt and Future, 2006. Recipient UNESCO award, 1999; Oxford U. fellow, 1990; grantee Old Dominion U., 1986, 88. Mem. AAUP (Conn. state award 1992, 97, 2002), Internat. Soc. for Study of Comp. Civilization (mem. governing body, exec. com. 1992—), World Anthrop. Soc., World Archeaol. Congress, Am. Hist. Assn., African Studies Assn. Avocations: keyboard playing, ping pong/table tennis. Office: Cen Conn State U History/African Studies Dept New Britain CT 06050 Home Phone: 860-224-3450; Office Phone: 860-832-2815. Business E-Mail: emeagwali@mail.ccsu.edu.

EMEK, SHARON HELENE, risk management consultant; b. Bklyn., Oct. 23, 1945; d. Hyman Sampson and Cynthia Gertrude (Roth) Rabinowitz; children: Aleeza Judith, Joshua Michael, Elana Yael. BA, CCNY, 1967; MA, Bklyn. Coll., 1970; EdD, Rutgers U., 1977. Cert. ins. counselor. Dir. preliminary program for small coll. Bklyn. Coll., 1969—71, 1973—74; dir. Am. Ctr. Reading Skills, Tel Aviv, 1972; asst. prof. Brookdale C.C., Lincroft, NJ, 1975—77, Rutgers U., New Brunswick, NJ, 1977—82; pres. Emek Group, Inc., NYC, 1980—98, CEO Metro Ptnrs., Inc., NYC, 1998—2001; ptnr. CBS Coverage Group, Inc., 2001—. Bd. mem. Women's Builders Coun., 2007—; mem. AETNA Minority and Women's Adv. Coun., 2007—; spkr. profl. meetings. Author: Answers for Managers, 1986, Dealing Successfully with key Management Issues, 1986; contbr. articles to profl. jours. Mem. Mayor's Small Bus. Adv. Bd., NYC, 1998—2001, Small Bus. Rsch. and Tech. Adv. Coun. IBM, 1998—2000; bd. dirs. Ctr. Women's Bus. Rsch., 2006—; mem. adv. coun. Women's Fin. Network Siebert, 2000—02; founding bd. dirs. Nat. Mus. Women's History, 1997—2002; bd. dirs. Ctr. Women's Bus. Rsch., 2000—, Family Bus. Coun. Greater N.Y., 1997—98, Women's Econ. Devel. Task Force, NYC, 1999—2001; bd. dirs., v.p. N.Y. Women's Agenda, 2000—04; bd. dirs. Women's Builders Coun., 2007—; vice chair bd. dirs. Inst. Student Achievement, 1999—; mem. adv. bd. Women's Leadership Exch., 2002—; chmn. Ind. Ins. Agents & Brokers, NY, 2006—, bd. dirs., 2003—. Recipient Promising Rsch. award, Nat. Coun. Tchrs. English, 1978, Woman of Power and Influence award, NOW, 1999, Disting. Svc. award, Ind. Ins. Agts. and Brokers, NY, 2005—06. Mem.: Ind. Ins. Agts. and Brokers NY, Coun. Ins. Brokers Greater NY, Women's Pres. Orgn., Assn. Profl. Ins. Women, Nat. Assn. Ins. Women (Helen Garvin Outstanding Achiever in Ins. Industry award 1999), Coun. Ins. Brokers Greater NY, Nat. Assn. Women Bus. Owners (bd. dirs., pres. 1997—98, Mem. of Yr. 1997), Profl. Ins. Agts. Assn., Ind. Ins. Agts. and Brokers Am. (chair elect bd. dirs., Disting. Svc. award 2006, Sidney O. Smith Govt. Affairs award 2007), Emily List (majority coun.). Avocations: writing, reading, jogging, tennis, travel. Home Phone: 201-866-4467; Office Phone: 212-684-5670 x 101. Business E-Mail: semek@cbsinsurance.com.

EMELETT, STEPHEN JOHN, electrical engineer, researcher; b. Nanticoke, Pa., Feb. 3, 1977; s. Edward Eugene and Ann Marie Emelett. BS in Physics and Philosophy, U. Scranton, Pa., 1999; MS in Physics, U. Mass., Lowell, 2003; MEng in Elec. Engring., Cornell U., Ithaca, NY, 2006. Tchg. asst. physics U. Scranton, Pa., 1999, U. Mass., Lowell, Mass., 2000—02, rsch. asst., 2001—03, contracting scientist, 2003, Air Force Rsch. Lab, Bedford, Mass.; rsch. scientist Solid State Sci. Corp., Hollis, NH, 2003; tchg. asst. electrical engring. Cornell U., Ithaca, NY, 2005—. Mem.: Optical Soc. Am., Internat. Soc. Optical Engring., IEEE, Am. Phys. Soc. Republican. Roman Catholic. Achievements include invention of and synthesis of linear optical modulator, invention of single barrier resonant photodiode; co-patent pending for room temperature phonon assisted silicon microresonator laser invention; research in and publications on optical switching, modulation and filtering in silicon. Home: 181 Ludlowville Rd Lansing NY 14882 Home Phone: 607-533-7182. Personal E-mail: sje24@cornell.edu.

EMELY, CHARLES HARRY, trade association executive, consultant; b. Phila., Oct. 30, 1943; s. Charles Walter and Jane Beatty (Stott) E.; m. Susan Elizabeth Lawton, June 18, 1966 (dec. Mar. 1977); 1 child, Charles Walter II; m. Mary Ann Horvath, Sept. 1, 1979; 1 stepchild, Wendy A. Vellrath. Student, Drexel Inst. Tech., 1961-62; BA, Temple U., 1967; MA, Fairfield U., 1974; postgrad., NYU, 1974-76; PhD, Calif. Western U., 1978; postgrad., Ohio U., 1981-82. Adminstrv. asst. City of Phila., 1966-68; nat. rep. ARC, Washington, 1968-70; exec. dir., chief exec. officer Bridgeport, Conn., 1970-77; pres., chief exec. officer Comprehensive Bus. Cons., Ft. Washington, Pa., 1977-86; exec. v.p., chief exec. officer Adhesive & Sealant Council, Washington, 1987-88; pres., CEO Comprehensive Bus. Cons., Inc., Fairfax, Va., 1988—; exec. dir., CEO Internat. Assn. Law Firms, 1988—; exec. dir., COO Am. Soc. Hort. Sci., Alexandria, Va., 1994-97; CEO Am. Railway Engring. and MOW Assn., Landover, Md., 1998—. Chmn. Cmty. Cons. Corps, Ft. Washington, 1980—; sr. cons. Philippine Nutrition Ctr., Manila, 1980; adj. faculty Ohio U., Athens, 1982-83, bd. dirs. ICM Internat., Inc.; comunications officer, U.S.A. Nat. Disaster Med. Sys., 1992—. Mem. bd. mgrs. YMCA, Fairfield, Conn., 1971-75; bd. dirs. Hope Ctr., Inc., Bridgeport, 1972-76, Comprehensive Health Planning Agy., Bridgeport, 1973-74, Found. for Internat. Meetings; mem. Mayor's Energy Adv. Com., Bridgeport, 1973-74, Fayetteville (N.Y.) United Meth. Ch., 1985; trustee, v.p. Mental Health Assn. Conn., 1973-77; mem. adminstrv. bd. Nichols United Meth. Ch., Trumbull, Conn., 1975-77; adv. com. campaign coun. Rep. Nat. Com.; mem. Patriots Soc. Germantown Acad., Ft. Washington, 1978-80; pres. Ambler (Pa.) Symphony Orchestra, 1979-80; mem. Pvt. Industry Council, Ambler, 1979-80, Zanesville, Ohio, 1981-83; mem. parents council Hartwick Coll., Oneonta, N.Y., 1987. Mem.: Associated Pub. Safety Comm. Officers, Found. for Internat. Meetings, Am. Railway Engring. and Maint. of Way Assn. (CEO 1998—), Nat. Assn. Corp. Dirs. (sec./treas. Washington chpt.), Am. Soc. Assn. Execs. (cert. assn. exec. 1977), Adminstrv. Mgmt. Soc., Am. Mgmt. Assn., Heritage Found., Officers Club Marine Corps Base Quantico, U. Conn. Alumni Assn. (life), Mensa, Officers Club Nat. Naval Med. Ctr. (Bethesda), Am. Radio Relay League, Heritage Found. (exec. com.), Rep. Nat. Com. Campaign Coun., Armed Forces Comms. and Electronics Assn., Aircraft Owners and Pilots Assn., Renewable Natural Resources Found. (bd. dirs.), Rotary, Nat. Assn. Execs. Club, City of Washington Club, Univ. Club, Vesper Club, Phila. Aviation Country Club, Rep. Nat. Com. Pres.'s Club, Elks, Shriners, Masons. Avocations: music, amateur radio, aviation, stamp collecting/philately, travel. Home: 7 Beaver Ridge Rd Stafford VA 22556-6677 Office: Comprehensive Bus Cons Inc PO Box 545 Garrisonville VA 22463-0545 Business E-Mail: chemely@cbc.org.

EMELY, MARY ANN, association executive; b. Bridgeport, Conn., Aug. 10, 1947; d. John and Stefanie Maria (Hutta) Horvath; m. Timothy Vellrath, Sept. 7, 1968 (div. Mar. 1975); 1 child, Wendy Amethyst Mackay; m. Charles H. Emely, Sept. 1, 1979. BA, U. Conn., 1969; postgrad., U. Bridgeport, 1975-76, Ohio U., 1982-83. Adminstrv. asst. ARC, Bridgeport, 1973-78; dir. mem. svcs. Comprehensive Assn. Cons., Ft. Washington, Pa., 1978-81; exec. dir. Muskingum County Respiratory Disease, Zanesville, Ohio, 1981-83; assoc. exec. dir. The Vol. Ctr., Syracuse, N.Y., 1984-86; dir. mem. programs NEA, Rockville, Md., 1986-91; dir. mem., mktg. Am. Geophys. Union, Washington, 1991-93; sr. dir. membership Coun. for Exceptional Children, Reston, Va., 1993-94; dep. exec. dir. Spl. Librs. Assn., Washington, 1994-95; exec. dir. Fedn. Govt. Info. Processing Couns., Fairfax, Va., 1995-99; mng. dir. Nat. Assn. Profl. Employer Orgns., Alexandria, Va., 2000—01; v.p. ops. Am. Coun. Engring. Cos., 2001—. Editor Husky P.A.W. Print, 1995-96, Fedn. Facts, 1995-99; columnist Female Exec., 1994-95. Bd. dirs. Pub. Employees Roundtable, Washington, 1995-99; mem. Nat. Rep. Coalition for Choice, Washington, 1993—, Jr. League of Washington, 1986—. Mem. NAFE, Am. Soc. Assn. Execs. (cert., mentor diversity programs 1994-95), Am. Radio Relay League, Greater Washington Soc. Assn. Execs., Found. for Internat. Meetings (bd. dirs. 2007—), Comprehensive Assn. Consultants, Mercedes Benz Club of Am., U. Conn. Alumni Assn. (chpt. pres. 1996-99, nat. bd. dirs. 2002-, nat. fundraising com. 2001-06), Kappa Alpha Theta. Methodist. Avocations: gardening, flower arranging, reading, travel. Home: PO Box 96 Garrisonville VA 22463-0096 Office: 1015 15th St NW Washington DC 20005

EMENHISER, JEDON ALLEN, political science professor, dean; b. Clovis, N.Mex., May 19, 1933; s. Glen Allen and Mary Opal (Sasser); m. Patricia Ellen Burke, Jan. 27, 1954; 1 child, Melissa Mary Emenhiser Westerfield. Student, Am. U., Washington, DC, 1954; BA, U. Redlands, Calif., 1955; PhD, U. Minn., 1962. Cert. community coll. adminstr. Calif. Instr. to prof. polit. sci. Utah State U., Logan, 1960-77, acting dean, 1973-74; prof. Humboldt State U., Arcata, Calif., 1977—, dean, 1977-86, acting v.p., 1984; chair Social Sci. Rsch. and Instrnl. Coun. Calif. State U., 1994-95; prof. Jr. Statesmen Summer Sch., Stanford U., 1989—2002, 2005. Vis. instr. U. Redlands, Calif., 1959—60; vis. prof. U. Saigon, Vietnam, 1964—65, U. Mons-Hainaut, Belgium, 2003; dir. Bur. Govt. and Opinion Rsch., Logan, 1965—70; staff dir. Utah Legislature, Salt Lake City, 1967, cons., 1968—77, USCG, McKinleyville, Calif., 1982; v.p. Exch. Bank, New Franklin, Mo., 1970—76; asst. dean Colgate U., Hamilton, NY, 1972—73; reader advanced placement exam. US Govt. Coll. Bd., 1990—98; vis. fellow govt. divsn. Congl. Rsch. Svc., Libr. of Congress, 1996; vis. fellow Nat. U. Ireland, Galway, 2002; vis. prof. Am. studies Royal Libr., Belgium, 2003. Author: Utah's Governments, 1964, Freedom and Power in California, 1987; editor, contbr. Dragon on the Hill, 1970, Rocky Mountain Urban Politics, 1971; producer, dir. TV broadcasts The Hawks and the Doves, 1965-66; contbr. articles to profl. jours. Sec. Cache County Dem. Party, Logan, 1962-63; chmn. Mayor's Commn. on Govt. Orgn., Logan, 1973-74; campaign mgr. various candidates and issues, Logan, 1965-75; bd. dirs. Humboldt Connections, Eureka, Calif., 1986-96, pres., 1989-92; elder Presbyn. ch. Sr. Fulbright-Hays lectr. Com. Internat. Exch. of Persons, Vietnam, 1964-65; Adminstrv. fellow Am. Coun. Edn., Colgate U., 1972-73; Paul Harris fellow Rotary Internat.; Fulbright prof., Belgium, 2003. Mem.: Phi Beta Kappa, Omicron Delta Kappa. Presbyterian. Avocations: gardening, photography, travel. Home: 2898 Sand Pointe Dr Mckinleyville CA 95519 Office: Humboldt State U Dept Polit Sci Arcata CA 95521 Office Phone: 707-826-4117. Personal E-mail: jaepat@suddenlink.net. Business E-Mail: jae1@humboldt.edu.

EMERICK, JOHN L., library director; b. Fleetwood, Pa., Apr. 26, 1937; s. Leo J. and Rachael E. Emerick; divorced; 1 child, Michael J. BS in Libr. Sci., Kutztown U., 1959; MLS, Villanova U., 1965; media cert., Temple U., 1969. Librarian, English tchr. Daniel Boone Sch. Dist., Birdsboro, Pa., 1959-62; English tchr. Fleetwood Area Sch. Dist., 1962-65; librarian, head dept. Muhlenberg Sch. Dist., Laureldale, Pa., 1965-72; dir. sch. libs. Boyertown (Pa.) Area Sch. Dist., 1972-93; dir. sch. libr. media svcs. Pa. Dept. Edn., Harrisburg, 1993—. Mem. adv bd. dept. libr. sci. Kutztown U., 1984—; cons. Phila. Sch. Dist., 1994-95, Ctrl. Bucks Sch. Dist., Doylestown, Pa., 1992-94. Contbr. articles to profl. jours. Pres. Berks County (Pa.) Sch. Librarians, 1982-84, Berks County Libr. Assn., 1990-92; mem. sch. bd. Oley (Pa.) Valley Sch. Dist., 1984-90; supr. Ruscomb Manor Twp., Fleetwood, 1983-87, Mem. ALA (mem. com. 1976-80), Am. Assn. Sch. Librarians (mem. com. 1982-86), Pa. Assn. for Ednl. Comms. and Tech. (chmn. com. 1989-91, award 1997), Pa. Sch. Librarians (chmn. com. 1990-93, award 1999), Pa. Ednl. Tech. (planning com. 1993—, Spl. Svc. award 1997). Democrat. Lutheran. Avocations: travel, swimming, reading, biking, camping. Home: 315 Charleston Ln Wyomissing PA 19610 Office: Pa Dept Edn 333 Market St Harrisburg PA 17126 Home Phone: 610-670-4905; Office Phone: 717-783-9542. E-mail: jemerick@state.pa.us.

EMERLING, CAROL G., management consultant; b. Cleve., Sept. 13, 1930; d. Bernard and Florence A. Greenbaum; m. Norton Harvey Noll, Oct. 1, 1950 (dec. July 1951); m. Stanley Justin Emerling, May 2, 1953 (div. Aug. 1971); children: Keith S., Susan C.; m. Jerrold A. Fadem, Aug. 24, 1974 (div. Oct. 1977). Student, Vassar Coll., 1948-49, Case Western Res. U., 1949-50; LL.B. summa cum laude, Cleve. State U., 1955. Bar: Ohio 1955, Calif. 1975, NY 1982, US Supreme Ct. 1975. Instr. Cleve. Coll., 1956-59; from staff atty. to atty.-in-charge Legal Aid Defenders Office, Cleve., 1962-70; regional dir. FTC, Cleve., 1970-74, LA, 1974-78; sec. Am. Home Products Corp., NYC, 1978-96; chmn. bd. Global Health Coun., 1998—2002. Adv. com. criminal rules Supreme Ct. Ohio, 1970-73; chmn. Cleve. Fed. Exec. Bd., 1973; internat. health policy cons.; mem. nat. adv. com. Cleve. State U. Law Sch., Inner-City Arts. Co-author: The Allergy Cookbook, 1969; contbr. articles to legal jours. Founder Pepper Pike Civic League, Ohio, 1959; sec. Pepper Pike Charter Commn., 1966. Recipient Claude E. Clarke award Legal Aid Soc., 1967, Disting. Svc. award FTC, 1972. Mem. State Bar Calif., State Bar Ohio, State Bar NY Personal E-mail: cgemerling@earthlink.net.

EMERSON, ANNE DEVEREUX, museum administrator; b. Boston, Oct. 6, 1946; d. Kendall and Margaret (Drew) E.; (div. 1980); children: Josephine, Hannah; m. Peter Alexander Altman, 1992. BA magna cum laude, Brown U., 1968; MA, Fletcher Sch. Law and Diplomacy, Tufts U., 1969; MBA, Boston U., 1990. Exec. asst. to v.p. adminstrn. Boston U., 1977—85, dir. adminstrn., program devel., 1985—88; exec. dir. Ctr. for Internat. Affairs Harvard U., Cambridge, 1988—98, acting exec. dir. David Rockefeller Ctr. for L.Am. Studies, 1995—96; pres. Bostonian Soc., Boston, 1998—2002; exec. dir. The Boston History Ctr. and Mus., Inc., 1999—, pres., 2004—. Bd. dirs. Integrated Foster Care, Cambridge, 1985-89; trustee Winsor Sch., 1989-91, Internat. Honors Program, 1995-2003; bd. dirs. World Affairs Coun., Boston, 1991-94, Urban Edge, 2003-06; exec. com. Boston Com. Fgn. Affairs, 1997-99. Mem.: Phi Beta Kappa. Office: The Boston Mus 55 Court St Boston MA 02108

EMERSON, CARTER WHITNEY, lawyer; b. Oak Park, Ill., Mar. 18, 1947; s. Garner P. and Daisy M. (Carter) Emerson; m. Susan D. Emerson, June 28, 1969. BS in Fin., Miami U., Oxford, Ohio, 1969; JD magna cum laude, Northwestern U., 1972. Bar: Ill. 1972. Law clk. to judge US Dist. Ct. (no. dist.) Ill., 1972-73; assoc. Kirkland & Ellis, Chgo., 1974-78, ptnr., 1978—. Dir. Chgo. Coun. Fgn. Rels. Mem. ABA (business corps. and banking sect.), Internat. Bar. Assn., Order of Coif. Clubs: Mid-Am. (Chgo.). Office: Kirkland & Ellis 200 E Randolph Dr Fl 54 Chicago IL 60601-6636 E-mail: cemerson@kirkland.com.

EMERSON, CHARLES LEROY, religious studies educator; b. Eugene, Oreg., Sept. 17, 1936; s. Anor Cornelius Emerson and Gunhild Maria Lindberg; m. Wilma Jean Basnett, Apr. 6, 2002; 1 child, Richard Charles. BA, NW Christian Coll., Eugene, 1958; MDiv, Christian Theol. Sem., Indpls., 1961; MA, Butler U., Indpls., 1962; D of Religion, Claremont Sch. Theology, Calif., 1965. Ordained Christian Chs. So. Calif., 1961. Min. First Christian Ch., Barstow, Calif., 1962—67; chaplain, asst. prof. religion Eureka Coll., Ill., 1967—69; min. First Christian Ch., Pittsfield, Ill., 1969—74; sr. min. Vine St. Christian Ch., Nashville, 1974—77, Phoenix Ctrl. Christian Ch., 1978—92; faculty assoc. religious studies Ariz. State U., Ariz., 1981—. Pres. Rotary Club Phoenix, 2000—01. Mem.: Western Assn. for Theol. Discussion (pres. 2005—06). Democrat. Mem. Disciples Of Christ. Avocations: piano, reading, travel. Home: 25 W San Juan Ave Phoenix AZ 85013 Office: Arizona State University PO Box 873-104 Tempe AZ 85287-3104 Home Phone: 602-264-9384; Office Phone: 480-965-7145. Home Fax: 602-264-9385. Personal E-mail: charles.emerson@asu.edu.

EMERSON, CHARLES P., research scientist; PhD. Dir. Boston Med. Rsch. Inst., 2003—, Penn Ctr. Devel. Biology, 1999—2003; prof., dept. chair cell and devel. biology U. Pa. Sch. Medicine, 1994—2003. Author: Methods in Muscle Biology, 1997. Office: Boston Biomedical Rsch Inst 64 Grove St Watertown MA 02472 Business E-Mail: emersonc@bbri.org.

EMERSON, CLAUDIA, poet, language professor; b. Chatham, Va., 1957; d. Claude and Mollie E.; m. Kent Ippolito, 2000. BA in English, U. Va., 1979; MFA in Creative Writing, U. NC, Greensboro, 1991. Acad. dean Chatham Hall, Chatham, Va., 1996—98; assoc. prof. English U. Mary Washington, Fredericksburg, Va., 1998—. Bd. trustees Chatham Hall, Chatham, Va., 1998—2004. Contbg. adv. editor Shenandoah, guest editor Visions Internat.; author: (poetry collections) Pharaoh, Pharaoh, 1997 (Pulitzer Prize nomination), Pinion, An Elegy, 2002, Late Wife, 2005 (Pulitzer Prize for poetry, 2006). Recipient Associated Writing Program's Intro award, 1991, Acad. of Am. Poets Prize, 1991, Mary Washington Coll. Alumni Assn. Outstanding Young Faculty award, 2003; grantee Nat. Endowment for Arts fellowship, 1994, Va. Commn. for Arts Individual Artist Fellowship in Poetry, 1995, 2002, Witter Bynner Found. fellowship in poetry, Libr. of Congress, 2005.

EMERSON, DANIEL EVERETT, retired communications company executive; b. Passaic, NJ, Oct. 22, 1924; s. Daniel T. and Jennie (VanBeveren) E.; m. Patricia Thorston, June 14, 1947; children— Patricia Sue, Nancy Ellen, Pamela Thorston. B.E.E., Cornell U., 1949; postgrad., George Washington U., Boston U., N.Y. U., 1951-56, Dartmouth Coll., 1956, U. Pa., 1959-60. With A.T.&T., 1949—, v.p. fed. relations, 1968-74; v.p. network ops. N.Y. Telephone, NYC, 1974-75, v.p. ops. analysis and methods, 1975-76, exec. v.p. corp. devel., dir., 1976-83; exec. v.p. NYNEX Corp., 1983-86; chmn. bd. NYNEX Mobile Communications Co., 1983-86, NYNEX Info. Resources Co., 1983-86. Bd. dirs. Adams Express Co., Petroleum and Resources Corp. Former mem. bd. dirs., chmn. YMCA U.S.A.; former dir., trustee, chmn. YMCA of Greater N.Y.; former trustee, pres. Kent Pl. Sch., Summit, N.J. 1st lt. USAAF, 1943-45. Decorated Air medal. Mem. U.S. C. of C. (communications com. 1972-74), Canoe Brook Country Club (Summit), Vero Beach (Fla.) Country Club, Cornell Club (N.Y.C.), Vero Beach Yacht Club, Tau Beta Pi, Eta Kappa Nu, Theta Xi.

EMERSON, JO ANN H., congresswoman; b. Washington, Sept. 16, 1950; d. Ab and Sylvia Hermann; m. Bill Emerson, 1975 (dec.); children: Victoria, Katharine; m. Ron Gladney, 2000; stepchildren: Elizabeth, Abigail, Alison, Jessica, Stephanie, Sam. BA in Polit. Sci., Ohio Wesleyan U., 1972; DHL (hon.), Westminster Coll., Fulton, Mo. Mem. US Congress from 8th Mo. dist., 1996—, mem. appropriations com., 1998—. Sr. v.p. pub. affairs Am. Ins. Assn.; dir. state rels. and grassroots progs. Nat. Restaurant Assn.; dep. dir. comm. Nat. Rep. Congl. Com. Mem. PEO Womens's Svc. Grp. (FY chpt.), Cape Girardeau; mem. adv. bd. Arneson Inst. Practical Politics and Pub. Affairs, Ohio Wesleyan U.; co-chair Congl. Hunger Ctr.; bd. dirs. Bread for the World; hon. and life trustee Westminster Coll.; bd. dirs. Presbyn. Children's Home, Farmington, Mo. Recipient Rural Housing Legislator of Yr., Nat. Assn. Home Builders, 2001, Schwarz Pharma Leadership in Pharmacy award, Nat. Assn. Chain Drug Stores, 2002, Ground Water Protector award, Nat. Ground Water Assn., 2005. Mem.: Copper Dome Soc., S.E. Mo. State U. Republican. Presbyn. Office: US House Reps 2440 Rayburn Ho Office Bldg Washington DC 20515-2508 Office Phone: 202-225-4404.*

EMERSON, NORENE ROGERS, music educator; b. Ogden, Utah, May 14, 1931; d. Cecil Clay Rogers and Idella Ethel Carter; m. Raymond Maurice Emerson, Sept. 17, 1954. BA with high honors, U. Utah, 1953. Pvt. piano tchr., Salt Lake City, 1946—. Piano soloist Utah Artist, Utah Concerts Coun., Salt Lake City, 1963—64. Mem. Temple Sq. Concert Series Com., Salt Lake City, 1996—; organizer downtown outdoor concert series, Salt Lake City; bd. trustees Gina Bachauer Internat. Piano Found. Recipient Piano Tchr. Recognition award, Keith Jorgensen Music Co., Salt Lake City, 1992. Mem.: Music Circle, Utah Music Tchrs. Assn., Nat. Fedn.

Music Clubs, Piano Club, Mu Phi Epsilon Internat., Phi Beta Kappa. Republican. Mem. Lds Ch. Avocation: photography. Home and Studio: 3543 Monte Verde Dr Salt Lake City UT 84109 Personal E-mail: norbird70@aol.com.

EMERSON, ROGER HILL, JR., orthopeadist; b. NYC, Sept. 17, 1948; s. Roger Hill Sr. E.; m. Patricia P. Emerson; children: Caroline, Christopher, Cara. BA, Dartmouth Coll., 1970; MD cum laude, Yale Med. Sch., 1974. Diplomate Am. Bd. Orthop. Surgery; cert. advanced trauma life support. Intern Beth Israel Hosp., Boston, 1974-75; resident in orthop. Harvard U., 1977-79; chief resident Childrens Hosp. Med. Ctr., Boston, 1979, Mass. Gen. Hosp., Boston, 1980; Otto Aufranc fellow New Eng. Baptist Hosp., Boston, 1980; staff Mass. Gen. Hosp. Orthop. Assoc., Boston, 1981-86, Reconstructive Orthop. Surgeons, Dallas, 1986—; orthop. surgeon Tex. Ctr. for Joint Replacement, Plano. Instr. orthop. surgery Tufts U., Boston, 1980, Harvard Med. Sch., 1981-86; clin. asst. prof. U. Tex. Southwestern Med. Sch., Dallas, 1986-89, clin. assoc. prof. orthop., 1989—; chief orthop. surgery Cambridge Hosp., 1981-86; staff Gaston Hosp., Dallas, 1986-88, Presbyn. Hosp., Dallas, 1988—, Plano, 1993—; asst. in orthop. Mass. Gen. Hosp., 1980-84, asst. orthop. surgeon, 1984-86; cons. Youville Rehab. Hosp., 1984-86; courtesy staff South Shore Hosp., Weymouth, Mass., 1977-87, Parkland Hosp., Dallas, 1986—;assoc. attending Childrens Hosp. Med. Ctr., Dallas, 1988-89; med. adv. bd. Orthographics, 1993; presenter and lectr. in field. Co-author: (with R.H. Turner) Revision Hip Arthroplasty, 1982; (with R.H. Turner, A.D. Scheller) The Hip, 1984; mem. editl. bd. Jour. Bone & Joint Surgeons, 1991—; contbr. articles to profl. jours. Bd. incorporators South Weymouth Savs. Bank, 1983-86; active Waterville (N.H.) Valley Med. Assoc., 1985—; bd. dirs. Mass. Orthop. Soc., 1985-86. Recipient Stinchfield award Hip Soc., 1992. Mem. Am. Med. Soc., Am. Acad. Orthop. Surgery, Tex. Orthop. Assn., Mass. Med. Soc., New Eng. Med. Assn., Dallas County Med. Soc., Assn. for Arthritic Hip and Knee Surgery, Phi Beta Kappa. Office: Tex Ctr Joint Replacement 5940 W Parker Rd #100 Plano TX 75093 Office Phone: 214-609-8868.*

EMERSON, STEPHEN G., academic administrator, oncologist, hematologist, educator; b. NYC, Oct. 21, 1953; BA summa cum laude, Haverford Coll., 1974; MS in Molecular Biophysics, Yale U., 1976, PhD in Cell Biology and Immunology, 1980, MD, 1980; MA (hon.), U. Pa., 1994. Intern, resident Mass. Gen. Hosp., Boston, 1980—82; fellow Brigham & Women's Hosp., Dana-Farber Cancer Inst., Children's Hosp., Boston, 1982—86; asst. to assoc. prof. medicine U. Mich., Ann Arbor, 1986—94; prof. medicine U. Pa., Phila., 1994—2007, chief Div. Hematology/Oncology, 1994—2007, assoc. dir. clin./tanslational rsch., Francis C. Wood prof. medicine, pathology and pediatrics; pres. Haverford Coll., Pa., 2007—. Founder Astrom Biosci., Inc., Ann Arbor, 1989. Mem. editl. bd. Jour. Experimental Medicine, Stem Cells, Journal of Clin. Investigation; contbr. articles to profl. jours. Named one of Top Docs, Philadelphia Mag., 2002, 2005, 2006; recipient Med. Scientist Trainee Prize, Yale U.; Career Achievement award, Rolex Corp., 1999, Stohlman Award, Leukemia and Lymphoma Soc., Bai-Yu Lan Prize, City of Shanghai; scholar, Leukemia Soc. Am., 1987—92. Fellow: ACP; mem.: Am. Soc. Blood and Marrow Transplantation (mem. leadership coun.), Am. Soc. Hematology (mem. leadership coun.), Internat. Clin. Club, Am. Assn. Physicians. Office: Haverford Coll Office of Pres 370 Lancaster Ave Haverford PA 19041 Office Phone: 215-662-2359. Fax: 215-349-5866. E-mail: emersons@mail.med.upenn.edu.*

EMERSON, STERLING JONATHAN, lawyer; b. Pasadena, Calif., July 2, 1929; s. Sterling H. and Mary Foote (Randall) E.; m. Virginia Beabes, July 3, 1954; children: Margaret Ellen, Henry Rollins, Peter Randall. BA in Econs. with honors, U. Calif., Berkeley, 1955; JD, U. Mich., 1957. Bar: Pa. 1958, U.S. Dist. Ct. (ea. dist.) Pa. 1958, U.S. Ct. Appeals (3d cir.) 1958. Assoc. Montgomery, McCracken, Walker & Rhoads, Phila., ptnr., 1966-97; pvt. practice Media, Pa., 1998—. Asst. editor: Law Rev. U. Mich., 1957. With third inf. divsn. US Army, 1950—52, Korea. Fellow Am. Coll. Trust and Estate Counsel; mem. ABA, Fiduciary Law Soc., Pa. Bar Assn., Phila. Bar Assn. (former bd. govs., former chmn. sect. on probate and trust law), Delaware County Bar Assn. Avocations: tennis, gardening, travel. Home: 16 Oberlin Ave Swarthmore PA 19081-1512 Office: Monroe Profl Bldg 117 N Monroe St Media PA 19063-3037

EMERSON, WILLIAM ALLEN, retired investment company executive; b. Columbia, Tenn., July 13, 1921; s. Henry Houston and Mabel N. (Allen) E.; m. Jane Stannard, Oct. 5, 1944; children: Marshal Henry, Shelley, Stacey, Kimberly. AA, St. Petersburg Jr. Coll., 1941; BSBA, U. Fla., 1946. With Merrill Lynch, Pierce, Fenner & Smith, Inc., 1947-87, dir. gen. services div. NYC, 1968-72, Southeast regional dir., corp. dir. Atlanta, 1972-81, sr. v.p., nat. sales dir., 1981-86; dir. Merrill Trust Co. Past vice chmn. bd. trustees St. Joseph-St. Anthony Health Sys. Trustee Oglethorpe U., Atlanta, Mus. Fine Arts, St. Petersburg, Salvadore Dali Mus., St. Petersburg; trustee, past pres. U. Fla. Found. Pilot with USMC, 1942-45. Named Emerson Alumni Hall at U. Fla. in his honor, 2003. Mem.: Feather Sound Country Club (St. Petersburg), St. Petersburg Yacht Club, Capital City Club, Masons. Republican. Baptist. Home: 3050 82nd Way N Saint Petersburg FL 33710-2220 *I believe that what you give away returns to bless you in many ways, and that what you have left is worth more than before the gift.*

EMERSON, WILLIAM HARRY, retired lawyer; b. Rochester, NY, Jan. 13, 1928; s. William Canfield and Alice Sarah (Adams) E.; m. Jane Anne Epple, Dec. 27, 1956; children: Elizabeth Anne, Carolyn Jane. BA, Cornell U., 1951, LLB, 1956. Bar: Ill. 1974. Atty. Amoco Corp., 1956-91; sec., dir. Amoco Gas Co., 1979-91. Pres., dir. Undercroft Montessori Sch., Tulsa, 1965-67, Tulsa Figure Skating Club, 1969; bd. dirs. Lake Forest (Ill.) Found. for Hist. Preservation, 1983-2001; mem. vestry Ch. Holy Spirit, Lake Forest, 1988-91. Home: 593 Greenvale Rd Lake Forest IL 60045-1526

EMERSON, WILLIAM KARY, engineering company executive; b. Enid, Okla., July 15, 1941; s. Kary Cadmus and Mary Rebecca (Williams) E.; m. Marcie Louise Stogner, Mar. 13, 1965; children: Rebecca A., Phillip W. BS, Okla. State U., 1965, MS, 1974; diploma, Command and Gen. Staff Coll., 1979, Def. Systems Mgmt. Coll., 1980. Commd. 2d lt. US Army, 1965, advanced through grades to lt. col., 1985; prin. program mgr. Honeywell, Inc., Minnetonka, Minn., 1985-90; sr. program mgr. Alliant Techsystems, Inc., Minnetonka, 1990-92; dep. dir. engring. Teledyne Brown Engring. Co., Huntsville, Ala., 1992-96, dir. advanced engring., 1996-97; sr. program mgr. PEI Electronics, Huntsville, 1997-2001; pres. Emerson Consulting, Inc., 2001—. Bd. dirs. Invetex Corp., 2007-; disting. guest lectr. Def. Systems Mgmt. Coll., 1997. Author: Chevrons, 1983, Encyclopedia of Insignia, 1995, Marksmanship in the U.S. Army, 2004, U.S. Army Badges, 2006, An Introduction To Insignia Collecting, 2006; contbr. articles to profl. jours.; chpts. to books. Adv. com. Dist. 281 Sch. Bd., Minn., 1986-88, summer sch. concept com., 1988-89; mem. Huntsville Land Trust, 1994-2004; chmn. recycling com. N. Ala. Sierra Club, 1994-98; citizen mem. City of Huntsville Ordinance Rewrite Com., 1995-97; lay leader Asbury Meth. Ch., 1997-00, chair adminstrv. bd., 2000-02; bd. mgmt. Anne S.K. Browne Collection, Brown U., Providence, 1998—; pres., bd. dirs. Non Profit Counseling Ctr., 2000-02. Decorated Legion of Merit, Bronze Star with V and one oak leaf cluster, Purple Heart with two oak leaf clusters; inducted into Madison County Hall of Heroes, Ala., 1996. Fellow Co. Mil. Historians (bd. dir. 1983-86, 2000-06, editor 1986-92, pres. 2003-06, Miller award 1977, 2004); mem. VFW (life), Am. Soc. Mil. Insignia Collectors (editor jour. 1993—, Best Nat. Display award 1984, 2006), Am. Def. Preparedness Assn., Assn. US Army, Am. Assn. Mil. Uniform Collectors (Writing award 1999, 2000, Achievement medal 2002), Orders and Medals Soc. Am. (bd. dir. 2003-04, chmn. publs. 2003—, Lit. award 1998, 2005, Silver medal 2000, 02, 07, Commendation medal 2005, Meritorious Svc. medal, 2007), Mil. Order Purple Heart, Sierra Club (local chmn. recycling com.). Lutheran. Avocations: running, fishing, racquetball, swimming. Office: Emerson Cons Inc 124 Kensington Dr Madison AL 35758

EMERY, CHARLES CHRISTIAN, JR., health care and information systems executive; b. Pitts., Oct. 11, 1946; s. Charles C. and Gloria V. (Nutridge) E.; m. Marcia A. Balestrino, May 7, 1988; children: Charles C. III, Sandra J. BSME in Aero. Engring., U. Pitts., 1968, MS, 1972, MBA, 1982; PhD in Mgmt., Claremont U., 1990. Engr. AVCO Lycoming, Bridgeport, Conn., 1968-69, Westinghouse Co., Pitts., 1969-71; systems mgr. U. Pitts., 1971-72; v.p. hosp. info. systems Monsour Hosp. and Clinic, Jeannette, Pa., 1972-73; assoc. exec. dir., chief fin. officer St. Elizabeth Hosp. Med. Ctr., Youngstown, Ohio, 1973-85; v.p. info. svcs. Samaritan Health Svc., Phoenix, 1985--; chief info. officer U. Tex. M.D. Anderson Cancer Ctr., Houston, Sisters of the Humility of Mary, Ohio; v.p. & chief info. officer Horizon Blue Cross Blue Shield of N.J., 1996—99, sr. v.p. & chief info. officer, 1999—. Fellow Coll. of Healthcare Info. Mgmt. Executives. Bd. dirs. YW-YMCA, Phoenix, 1987. Recipient Award for Excellence in Healthcare Info. Tech., 1993, John E. Gall Jr. CIO of Yr. award, Healthcare Info. Mgmt. Sys. Soc. and Coll. of Healthcare Info. Mgmt. Executives, 2001. Mem. Am. Coll. Healthcare Execs., Healthcare Fin. Mgmt. Assn. (adv. mem.), Moon Valley Country Club. Methodist. Avocation: golf. Office: SVP & CIO Horizon Blue Cross Blue Shield PO Box 820 Newark NJ 07101

EMERY, HERSCHELL GENE, lawyer; b. Hobart, Okla., Oct. 19, 1923; s. W. Herschell and L. Noreen Emery; m. Charlotte Chrisney, Oct. 29, 1948; children: Kathy Emery Miller, Steve. AB, U. Ill., 1945; LLB, Harvard U., 1948. Bar: Ind. 1949, Tex. 1955, U.S. Tax Ct. 1956, U.S. Ct. Appeals (5th cir.) 1980, U.S. Ct. Claims 1980. Assoc. Ross McCord Ice & Miller, Indpls., 1948—55; assoc. to ptnr. Thompson Knight Wright & Simmons, Dallas, 1955—65; ptnr. Rain, Harrell Emery Young & Doke, Dallas, 1965—87, Locke Purnell Rain Harell, 1987—98, Locke Liddell & Sapp, 1999—2000, of counsel, 2002—. Fellow: Am. Coll. Tax Counsel; mem.: ABA, Dallas Bar Assn., Tex. Bar Assn., Am. Coll. Trust and Estate Counsel, Birnam Wood Club, Dallas Petroleum Club, Dallas Country Club, Phi Beta Kappa. Presbyn. Office: Locke Liddell & Sapp 2200 Ross Ave Ste 2200 Dallas TX 75201-6776 Home Phone: 214-357-5174; Office Phone: 214-740-8405.

EMERY, JOHN EDWARD, plastic surgeon, vintner; b. Montreal, Que., Canada, Jan. 4, 1932; arrived in U.S., 1965; s. Herbert James and Phyllis Gwyndolyn (Young) Emery; m. Deborah Mae Nelson, Oct. 17, 1980; children: Tamera, Allison, Forest Meadow Spring, John Edward. MD, Queens U., Kingston, Ont., Canada, 1957. Diplomate Am. Bd. Plastic Surgeons. Rotating intern in medicine and surgery, Vancouver, BC, Canada; resident in orthopedic surgery Sun Valley, Idaho; resident in pathology Munich; registrar gen. surgery Northampton, England; resident plastic surgeon Oxford, England, Glasgow, Scotland, Toronto, Ont., Canada; resident gen. surgery San Francisco; plastic surgeon San Francisco and Sonoma, Calif., 1966—. Mem. staff St. Mary's Hosp., San Francisco, 1970—2002, Sonoma Valley Hosp., 2000—; founder Emery Med. Ctr. and Spa, Sonoma, Calif., 2000—; owner, mgr. Emery Estate Vineyards, 2001—. Lt. Canadian Navy, 1953—57. Named Man of Yr., Leukemia Soc., 1997; named to, Sports Hall of Fame, Canada, 1964; recipient Stubbs trophy for Best Athlete, U. Naval Tng. Divsn., 1956, Gold medal for bobsled team, Innsbruck Olympics, 1964. Fellow: ACS, Internat. Acad. Cosmetic Surgery, Royal Coll. Surgeons, Can.; mem.: AMA, Aesthetic Surgery Edn. and Rsch. Found., Oculoplastic Fellowship NY, Lipoplasty Soc. N.Am., Canadian Aesthetic Soc., Am. Soc. Plastic and Reconstructive Surgeons, Rotary. Republican. Mem. Ch. Of England. Home: 16600 Gehricke Rd Sonoma CA 95476 Office: Emery Med Ctr 27 E Napa St Sonoma CA 95476 Office Phone: 707-933-1611. Personal E-mail: silveremo@emerywines.com.

EMERY, NANCY BETH, lawyer; b. Shawnee, Okla., July 9, 1952; d. Paul Dodd Finefrock and Kathryn Jo (Saling) Hutchens; m. Lee Monroe Emery, May 18, 1974. BA with highest honors, U. Okla., 1974; JD, Harvard U., 1977. Bar: D.C. 1981. Atty. advisor Office Gen. counsel, USDA, Washington, 1977-79; legal advisor Fed. Energy Regulatory Commr. Matthew Holden, Jr., Washington, 1979-81; assoc. Pierson, Ball & Dowd and predecessor Sullivan & Beauregard, Washington, 1981-83, Paul Hastings, Janofsky & Walker, Washington, 1983-87, ptnr., 1987-93, Sutherland, Asbill & Brennan, Washington, 1993-97; v.p., gen. counsel, corp. sec. Calif. Ind. Sys. Operator Corp., 1997-99; ptnr. Hopkins & Sutter, Washington, 1999-2001, Ballard, Spahr, Andrews & Ingersoll, LLP, Washington, 2001—03; sr. v.p., gen. counsel, corp. sec. CPS Energy, San Antonio, 2003—. Nat. adv. bd. USAID Tng. Program, 1994—98. Bd. dirs., sec. Park Place Condominium Assn., Inc., Washington, 1982—84; page Continental Congress DAR, 1978—82, chpt. del., 1981, 1984; bd. dirs. New Hope Housing, Inc., Alexandria, Va., 2001—03, chmn. strategic planning com., 2002—03, exec. com., 2003; bd. dirs. Carver Cultural Arts Ctr. Devel. Bd., 2005—. Mem.: ABA (natural resources energy and eviron. law sect. 1990—98, bd. editors Natural Resources & Environment 1990—98, pub. utility law sect., vice chmn. electricity com. 1998—, chmn. program com. 2000—01, chmn. mem. com. 2001—02, chmn. strategic planning com. 2001—02, mem. coun. 2002—, chmn. cmty. involvment 2002—04), Soc. Profl. Journalists, Fed. Energy Bar Assn. (chair tax com. 1986—87, chair FERC ops. and adminstrn. com. 1991—93, chair elec. utility regulation com. 1995—97, chair program com. 1997—98), Mortar Bd., Phi Beta Kappa. Democrat.

EMERY, PAUL EMILE, psychiatrist; b. Montreal, May 2, 1922; arrived in U.S., 1951; s. Esdras Fernand and Julia (Benoit) E.; m. Virginia Olga B. Kennick, July 27, 1979. BA, U. Montreal, 1942, MD, 1948. Diplomate in gen. psychiatry and forensic psychiatry, Am. Acad. Experts in Traumatic Stress. Staff psychiatrist Austen Riggs Ctr., Stockbridge, Mass., 1958-60; chief mental hygiene VA, Bridgeport, Conn., 1960-62, staff psychiatrist, chief of psychiatry Manchester, NH, 1988-99; pvt. practice Concord, NH, 1962-85, 99—; clin. dir. Ctr. for Stress Recovery, Brecksville, Ohio, 1985-87, dir., 1987-88. Med. dir. forensic unit N.H. Hosp., Concord, 1980-82; cons. VA med. Ctr., Manchester, 1962-64, 82-85, pub. health State of N.H., Concord, 1962-71, St. Paul's Sch., Concord, 1971-78; mem. faculty Dartmouth Coll. Med. Sch., 1971—, Western Res. Sch. Medicine, 1985—. Contbr. articles to profl. jours.; author: Trauma Psychology Model of the Mind, 1993. Sec. adv. commn. health and welfare State of N.H., Concord. Capt. U.S. Army, 1953-55. Recipient Salutation plaque N.H. Program on Alcoholism, 1971, cert. honor for scholarly achievement Internat. Assn. Psychohistory, 1998. Fellow Am. Psychiat. Assn. (life, disting., founder N.H. dist. br. 1972, chair ethics com.), Am. Acad. Experts in Traumatic Stress; mem. N.H. Med. Soc. (cert. commendation 1972), Mass. Psychiat. Soc. (pres. 1965), N.H. Psychiat. Soc. (pres. 1980). Office: 15 Buckingham Dr Bow NH 03304-5207

EMERY, RAY, professional hockey player; b. Cayuga, Ont., Can., Sept. 28, 1982; Goalie Binghamton Senators (Am. Hockey League), 2002—05, Ottawa Senators, 2005—. Named to All-Rookie Team, Am. Hockey League, 2003. Achievements include tying NHL record for most wins in a single month with 12, 2006. Office: Ottawa Senators Scotiabank Place 1000 Palladium Dr Kanata ON K2V 1A5 Canada*

EMERY, ROBERT ALLAN, minister; b. Rutland, Vt., Aug. 17, 1943; s. Dexter Scott and Frances Elizabeth (Cook) Emery; m. Mary Ann Whiteford, Sept. 1, 1979; children: Allan, Kimberly, Steven, Scott, Gregory. BRE, Northeastern Bible Coll., Essex Fells, NJ, 1965; MA with honors, Dallas Theol. Sem., 1976. Ordained to ministry Bapt. Ch., 1971. Assoc. pastor 1st Bapt. Ch., Foxboro, Mass., 1965-67; pastor Grace Bapt. Ch., Attleboro, Mass., 1967-69, Vance Bible Ch., Bristol, Tenn., 1970-71; assoc. pastor 1st Bapt. Ch., Wayne, Mich., 1971-78; chaplain Syracuse (N.Y.) Rescue Mission, 1979-85; assoc. pastor North Syracuse (N.Y.) Bapt. Ch., 1985—. Pres. Search the Scriptures Ministries, Liverpool, NY, 1986—; mem. bd. reference Evang. Counseling Ctr., 1987—88; founder, pres. Greater Syracuse Singles Fellowship, 1990—; lectr. Internat. Leadership, Moscow, Chennai, India, Syracuse U. Author: Divorce Recovery, 1985, How to Study the Bible, 1986. Chief arbitrator Wayne-Westland Sch. Sys., 1976; bd. dirs. Syracuse Rescue Mission, 1986—87. Staley Found. Disting. Christian scholar, lectr., 1988. Republican. Office: North Syracuse Bapt Ch 420 S Main St Syracuse NY 13212-2861 Office Phone: 315-458-0271. Business E-Mail: pastoremery@usadatanet.net. *In life the only constant has been Jesus Christ. He has been Lord and friend, my source of joy and strength.*

EMERY, VINCE, writer, educator; b. Mpls., Oct. 29, 1951; Advt. dir. Harkins Amusement Enterprises, Scottsdale, Ariz., 1972-75; mng. editor CableVision Guide, San Francisco, 1976; west coast creative dir. World Wide Advt. and J. Walter Thompson, Los Angeles, 1978-80; dir. advt. and publicity Jerry Gross Orgn., Inc., Los Angeles, 1980-81; advt. dir. PBL Assocs., Point Richmond, Calif., 1983-92; pres. Vince Emery Prodns., San Francisco, 1985—; advt./publicity dir. Kedwell Software, Novato, Calif., 1992; mktg. mgr. Computer Literacy Bookshops, San Jose, Calif., 1992-94; dir. creative svcs. Blaze Software/Brokat, 1999—2001, Blue Pumpkin Software, Sunnyvale, 2001—02; dir. mktg. comms. Trados/SDL Internat., 2003—05. Editorial cons. Magical Bend mag., San Francisco, 1982-84; guest lectr. Film Arts Found., San Francisco, 1982, Media Alliance, San Francisco, 1983; lectr., workshop facilitator U.S. and abroad. Author: (books) Guide to Non-Stop Fun at Walt Disney World, 1984, How to Grow Your Business on the Internet, 1995, 3d edit., 1997, All-in-One Internet Business Success Pack, 1995, Free Business Stuff from the Internet, 1996; editor: (book) Lost Stories of Dashiell Hammett, 2005; prodr.: (albums) The Boogeyman, 1980, Star Trek Comedy-The Unofficial Album, 1986, Jim Samuels: Dean of Comedy, 1988, The Funniest Computer Songs, 1990; contbr. more than 200 articles to mags., jours. and newspapers. Recipient Best Poster award Creative Concepts, 1979-80, Best Mag. Campaign award Creative Concepts, 1980. Mem.: Film Arts Found. Office: Vince Emery Prodns PO Box 460279 San Francisco CA 94146

EMERY, VIRGINIA OLGA BEATTIE, psychologist, researcher; b. Cleve., Apr. 9, 1938; d. W. Joseph P. and Antoinette Pauline (Misjak) Kennick; m. Paul Hamilton Beattie Sr., 1960 (div. 1975); children: Tamsan Beattie Tharin, Paul Hamilton Beattie Jr.; m. Paul E. Emery, 1979. BA, U. Chgo., 1962, PhD, 1982; MA, Ind. U., 1973. Diplomate Am. Bd. Disability Analysts, Am. Acad. Traumatic Stress; lic. psychologist, NH, Ohio; cert. brief therapist Nat. Acad. Brief Therapists; cert. cognitive therapist Nat. Bd. Behavioral Therapists, cert. domestic violence counselor endorsement; cert. expert traumatic stress, cognitive therapist. Asst. prof. psychology Case Western Res. U., Cleve., 1986—89, asst. clin. prof. psychiatry, 1986—89; sr. faculty assoc. Ctr. on Aging and Health, Concord and Hanover, NH, 1986—89, dir., 1989—; adj. clin. asst. prof. psychiatry Dartmouth Med. Sch., Lebanon, NH, 1983—85, clin. assoc. prof., 1989—. Mem. com. human devel. NIMH, Adult Devel. and Aging Traineeship, U. Chgo., 1974-76; sub-project dir. Case Western Res. U. Sch. Medicine, 1986-90; sec. women's faculty assn. Case Western Res. U., 1987-89; cons. Vets. Affairs Med. Ctr., Manchester, NH, 1989—; sub-project dir. NIMH Mental Health Clin. Rsch. Ctr. Grant, Case Western Res. U. Sch. Medicine, 1986-90; mem. Dartmouth Coll. and Dartmouth Med. Sch. Neurosci. Group, 1990—; Dunaway-Burnham vis. scientist Dartmouth Med. Sch., 2005; Paul Janssen lectr. U. Goteberg, Sweden, 1997; Dunaway-Burnham vis. scientist Dartmouth Med. Sch., 2005; lectr. 4th Internat. Congress Vascular Dementia , Porto, Portugal, 2005; lectr. in field. Author: Language and Aging, 1985, Pseudodementia: A Theoretical and Empirical Discussion, 1988, Language Impairment in Dementia of the Alzheimer Type: A Hierarchical Decline, 2000, Interface between Vascular Dementia and Alzheimer Syndrome: Nosologic Redefinition, 2000, Retrophylogenesis of Memory in Dementia of the Alzheimer Type: A New Evolutionary Memory Framework, 2003, Noninfarct Vascular Dementia and Alzheimer Syndrome Spectrum, 2005; editor: Dementia: Presentations, Differential Diagnosis, and Nosology, 1994, 2d edit., 2003; contbr. chapters to books, articles to profl. jours. Bd. dirs. Frontiers of Knowledge Civic Trust, Concord, 1990—, pres. 1990-95. Recipient Adult Devel. and Aging grant, traineeship NIH/NIMH, 1974-76, Rsch. prize Am. Aging Assn., 1983, Havighurst prize for aging rsch. U. Chgo., 1984, NH Hosp. award for outstanding rsch. in dementia, 2003; named Frontiers of Knowledge Atlee Zellers lectr., 1994, Paul Janssen Med. Inst. lectr., 1997; rsch. grantee Western Res. Coll., 1986-87, NIMH Mental Health Clin. rsch. grantee, 1986-89. Fellow Gerontol. Soc. Am. (Disting Creative Contbn. award 1989; clin. medicine membership com. state liaison 1998—; lectr. Boston 2002), Am. Psychol. Assn., NH Psychol. Assn. (bd. dirs. 1991-93, chair com. acad. rsch. interests 1992-94, sec. 1994—, Riggs Disting. Contbn. award 1991, chmn. Women and Minorities com. 2001—), APA (student rsch. award 1984), Am. Acad. Experts in Traumatic Stress; mem. AAAS, AAUW, Internat. Psychiat. Rsch. Soc., Internat. Psychogeriatric Assn. (Pfizer lectr. 1997, 2d place award for rsch. paper 1995, 2nd Pl. Rsch. award in psychogeriatrics for paper 1995, IPA/Bayer Rsch. award in psychogeriat. 1995), Boston Soc. Gerontol. Psychiatry, Acad. Psychosomatic Medicine, NY Acad. Scis., Am. Acad. Experts in Traumatic Stress, Assn. Alzheimer's Disease Scientists, Am. Mensa Ltd. Home: 15 Buckingham Dr Bow NH 03304-5207 Office: Dartmouth Med Sch Dept Psychiatry Box HB 7750 Lebanon NH 03756 Personal E-mail: vobemeryphd@aol.com. Business E-Mail: v.olga.emery@dartmouth.edu.

EMERY, WILLIAM DAVID, consulting company executive; b. Chgo., Jan. 31, 1948; s. Elbert Raney and Marjorie Ann Emery; m. Janice Eleanor Obenauf, June 8, 1974; children: Kimberly, Brenna Williams. BS in Indsl. Mgmt., Purdue U., West Lafayette, Ind., 1970; MBA, Lake Forest Coll., Ill., 1983. Owner Towing Co. and Svc. Sta., Deerfield, Ill., 1974—79; pers. mgr. Corcom, Inc., Libertyville, Ill., 1979—83; mgr. US sales Apple Computer Inc., Cupertino, Calif., 1983—91; v.p. ops. LDDS WorldCom, Jackson, Miss., 1991—94; v.p. sales and mktg. Conf. Source Internat., Atlanta, 1994—96; pres., CEO Laser Atlanta Optics, Inc., Atlanta, 1996—97; sr. v.p. Premiere Tech. Inc., Atlanta, 1997—2000; COO FiWare Inc., Norcross, Ga., 2001—02, Tavilo, Inc., Norcross, Ga., 2003—05; owner, cons. Emery Consulting Corp., Norcross, 2006—07. Lt. j.g. USN, 1970—74. Office: Emery Consulting Corporation 5519 Folly Pl Norcross GA 30092 Office Phone: 770-446-2249. Personal E-mail: billemery@comcast.net.

EMIGH, REBECCA JEAN, social sciences educator; BA in Sociology summa cum laude, Barnard Coll., 1984; PhD, U. Chgo., 1993. Assoc. prof. dept. sociology UCLA, 1993—. Author: (multimedia project) The Unmaking of Markets: A Composite Visual History (Opened at the Mus. Contemporary Art, L.A., 2005), articles in profl. jours. Recipient Hon. Mention Barrington Moore Prize for Best Article, Am. Sociol. Assn., 1999. Office: UCLA Dept Sociology 264 Haines Hall Box 951551 Los Angeles CA 90095-1551 Business E-Mail: emigh@soc.ucla.edu.

EMILIO, GARRIDO SANABRIA RAFAEL, science educator, researcher; b. Havana, Cuba, July 29, 1970; s. Emilio Garrido and Carmen De la Caridad Sanabria; m. Lucianna D'Andrea Sanabria, Nov. 11, 1974; children: Rafael D'Andrea Garrido, Daniel D'Andrea Garrido. MD, Inst. Med. Scis., Havana, 1994; PhD, U. Fed. Sao Paulo, UNIFESP, Brazil, 1999. Asst. prof. anatomy and neurobiology U. Md., Balt., 2001—04; asst. prof. U. Tex., Brownsville. Contbr. articles to profl. jours. Recipient Young Investigator award, Soc. for Clin. Investigation at the FESBE, Brazil, 1996, Neurology Rsch. award, XVII Congresso Brasileiro de Neurologia, Curitiba. Brazil, 1996; GLAXO Traveling Jr. fellow, World Fedn. Neurology, 1995. Mem.: Soc. for Neuroscis. (assoc.). Office: University of Texas at Brownsville 80 Fort Brown Brownsville TX 78520 Office Phone: 956-882-5053. Office Fax: 956-882-5043. Business E-Mail: emilio.garridosanabria@utb.edu.

EMILSON, HENRY BERTIL, artist; b. Sundals-Ryr, Dalsland, Sweden, June 1, 1933; came to US, 1951; s. Harry Cristoffer Emilsson and Hanna (Nilsson) Svensson. BFA, Okla. U., 1960; MFA, Inst. Allende San Miguel, Mexico, 1967. Dir. US Army Arts and Crafts Recreation Svcs., US and Overseas, 1962-88; artist Bollungsnas, Bralanda, Sweden, 1988—. Exhibited in one-man shows in Erlangen, Germany, 1979, Bad Windsheim, Germany, 1981, Gothenburg, Sweden, 1990, Vanersborg, Sweden, 1994, also others; represented in nat. and internat. pub. and pvt. collections. With USAF, 1952-56. Office: Bollungsnaset 120 460 65 Bralanda Sweden Office Phone: 521-35383.

EMIN, DAVID, physicist; b. NYC, Oct. 2, 1941; s. Irving and Sonia Emin; m. Shirley Lynne Hirshey, Aug. 15, 1963. Student, U. Chgo., 1958—60; AB in Physics, Fla. State U., 1961—62; PhD, U. Pitts., 1968. Asst. rsch. physicist UCLA, 1968—69; mem. tech. staff Sandia Nat. Labs., Albuquerque, 1969—83, disting. mem. tech. staff, 1983—97; rsch. prof. U. N.Mex, Albuquerque, 1997—. Author: 208 refereed jour. articles and book chpts. Recipient Significant Implications for Dept of Energy Related Technologies, U.S. Dept. Energy, 1988. Fellow: Am. Phys. Soc. (life). Achievements include research in theory of polaron formation and motion; electronic and thermal transport in boron-rich solids; polaron transport in magnetic semiconductors; theory of Hall Effect for hopping conduction; theory of light interstitial diffusion in metals; theory of the Seebeck Effect in hopping conduction; theory of superconductivity of large bipolarons; small-polarons in noncrystalline semiconductors; patents for fast opening switch; radiation tolerant icosahedral boride beta-voltaic cell; patents pending for icosahedral boride solid-state neutron detector. Office: Univ New Mexico Dept Physics and Astronomy Albuquerque NM 87131 Home Phone: 505-232-2128; Office Phone: 505-277-2210. Office Fax: 505-277-1520. Business E-Mail: emin@unm.edu.

EMINEM, (MARSHALL MATHERS III), rap artist; b. St. Joseph, Mo., Oct. 17, 1973; m. Kimberly Ann Scott, June 14, 1999 (div. Oct. 11, 2001), remarried Jan. 14, 2006 (div. Dec. 19, 2006); 1 child Hailie Jade. Founder Shady Records, NYC, 1999—; performer D12. Performer: (albums) Infinite, 1997, The Slim Shady LP, 1999, The Marshall Mathers LP, 2000, The Eminem Show, 2002 (Best Selling Album in U.S., 2002), Encore, 2004, Curtain Call, 2005, The Re-Up, 2006, with D12: (albums) Devil's Night, 2001, D12 World, 2004; prodr.: albums My Band (D12), 2004; actor: (films) 8 Mile, 2002. Nominee 5 Grammy awards, 2003; recipient 2 Grammy awards, 1999, 3 Grammy awards, 2000, 2 Grammy awards, 2002, Favorite Male Rap Artist, Am. Music Awards, 2005, 2006, Best-Selling Pop/Rock Artist, World Music Awards, 2005, Best-Selling Rap/Hip-Hop Artist, Favorite Hip-Hop Song-Shake That, People's Choice Awards, 2007. Office: Interscope Records 2220 Colorado Ave Santa Monica CA 90404*

EMISON, EWING RABB, JR., lawyer; b. Vincennes, Ind., Feb. 3, 1925; s. Ewing and Tuley (Sheperd) E.; m. Kathleen M. Crowley, Nov. 28, 1952; children: Susan, Anne Emison Wishard. AB, DePauw U., 1947; JD, Ind. U., 1950. Bar: Ind. 1950. Of counsel Emison Doolittle Kolb & Roellgen, Vincennes; dep. atty. gen. State of Ind., 1968—69. Lectr. CLE seminars, ABA Nat. Conf. for Diversity, 2002. Contbg. columnist Res Gestae, Ind. State Bar mag., 1987—. Mem. Wabash Valley Interstate Commn., 1959-62, Ind. Flood Control and Water Resources Commn., 1961-65; mem. bd. visitors Ind. Univ. Sch. Law, 1984-87. With USN, 1943-46, 52-53. Mem. ABA (Spirit of Excellence award commn. on racial and ethnic diversity in the profession 2003), Nat. Bar Assn., Ind. State Bar Assn. (bd. of mgrs. 1975-77, chmn. ho. of dels. 1979, pres. 1986-87), Phi Delta Phi, Phi Kappa Psi. Republican. Presbyterian. Avocations: golf, assistance to minority law students, military history. Office: Emison Doolittle Kolb & Roellgen PO Box 215 8th and Busseron Sts Vincennes IN 47591 Office Phone: 812-882-2280. Office Fax: 812-885-2308. Personal E-mail: rabbem@sbcglobal.net. Business E-Mail: emison@emisonlaw.com.

EMLEN, STEPHEN THOMPSON, zoology educator; b. Sacramento, Aug. 21, 1940; s. John Thompson and Virginia (Merritt) E.; m. Natalie Jean Demong, June 29, 1973; children: Douglas John, Katharine Merritt. BA with distinction, Swarthmore Coll., 1962; MS, U. Mich., 1964, PhD, 1966. Asst. prof. animal behavior Cornell U., 1966-70, assoc. prof., 1970-76, Jacob Gould Schurman prof., 1976—. Bd. dirs. Cornell Lab. Ornithology. John Simon Guggenheim fellow, 1973; Nat. Geog. Soc. fellow, 1973, 75; fellow Ctr. for Advanced Study in Behavioral Scis., 1980. Fellow AAAS, Am. Acad. Arts & Scis., Am. Ornithologists Union (William Brewster medal 1984), Animal Behavior Soc., Deutschen Ornithologen-Gesellschaft (corr.); mem. Brit. Ornithologists Union, Am. Soc. Naturalists, Cooper Ornithol. Soc., Wilson Ornithol. Soc., Ecol. Soc. Am., Sigma Xi (nat. lectr. 1989-91). Office: Cornell U Neurobiology And Behav Ithaca NY 14853*

EMLEN, WARREN METZ, retired computer company executive; b. Elizabeth, NJ, Oct. 12, 1932; s. Andrew Arnberg and Dorothy Emma (Metz) E.; m. Carol Ringold Taylor, Sept. 28, 1958; children: Deborah Emlen Baker, David Taylor, Anne Emlen Donohue. BS in Forestry, U. Calif., Berkeley, 1955; BSEE, Pa. State U., 1963; MS in Systems Mgmt., U. So. Calif., 1973; MA in Pub. Adminstrn., U. N.Mex., Albuquerque, 1980. Jr. forester U.S. Forest Service, Klamath, Calif., 1955-56; electronic engr. USAF, Griffiss AFB, NY, 1967-87; cons. forester, ptnr. L&E Environ. Cons., Rome, NY, 1965-87; v.p., adminstrv. asst. BPLW Architects & Engrs., Inc., Albuquerque, 1988-94; adminstrv. asst. Lovelace Health Systems, 1994-95; adminstrv. coord. Molzen-Corbin & Assocs. P.A., 1995-96; sole propr. Bus. Solutions and Svcs., 1998—2003; ret., 2004. Trustee DEDANE Trust, ANDOREM Trust; co-chmn. Industry Looks at Rome Air Devel. Ctr., Griffiss AFB, 1981; sec. Def. Intelligence Tech. forum, Washington, 1981-86; automated data processing cons., 1987-88, 96-97; adminstrv. asst., v.p. BPLW Architects& Engrs., Inc., Albuquerque, 1988-94; adminstrv. coord. Molzen-Corbin & Assocs., P.A., 1995-96; cons. in field. Contbr. numerous articles to profl. jours. Served to capt. USAF, 1956-67. Mem. IEEE (sr. life, chmn. engring. mgmt. group Mohawk Valley sect. 1975-76), Armed Forces Comm. and Electronics Assn. Republican. Methodist. Avocations: stamp and coin collecting, investments, hiking, reading. Home: 4871 Quail Ct Frederick CO 80504-5553

EMMANOUILIDES, GEORGE CHRISTOS, physician, educator; b. Drama, Greece, Dec. 17, 1926; came to U.S., 1955; s. Christos Nicholas and Vassiliki (Jordanopoulos) E.; married; children: Nicholas, Elizabeth, Christopher, Martha, Sophia MD, Aristotelion U., 1951; MS in Physiology, UCLA, 1963. Diplomate in pediatric cardiology and neonatal-perinatal medicine Am. Bd. Pediat. Asst. prof. UCLA, 1963-69, assoc. prof., 1969-73, prof., 1973-95, prof. emeritus, 1995—. Chief divsn. pediat. cardiology Harbor UCLA Med. Ctr., Torrance, Calif., 1963-95 Co-author: Practical Pediatric Electrocardiography, 1973; co-editor: Heart Disease in Infants, Children and Adolescents, 2d edit., 1977, Moss' Heart Disease in Infants, Children and Adolescents, 5th edit., 1995, Neonatal Cardiopulmonary Distress, 1988; contbr. more than 70 articles to profl. jours. and 25 chpts. to books Served as 2d lt. M.C., Greek Army, 1953-55 Recipient Sherman Mellincoff award UCLA Sch. Medicine, 1982, Rsch. award Am. Heart Assn., 1965-83. Fellow Am. Acad. Pediat. (cardiology sect., chmn. 1978-80, Founders award 1996), Am. Coll. Cardiology; mem. Am. Pediatric Soc., Soc. for Pediatric Rsch., Hellenic-Am. Med. Soc. (pres.), Acad. of Athens (corr.), Hellenic Univ. Club (LA, bd. dirs.) Democrat. Greek Orthodox. Avocation: gardening. Home: 4619 Browndeer Ln Rolling Hills Estates CA 90275-3911 Office: Harbor-UCLA Med Ctr 1000 W Carson St Torrance CA 90502-2004

EMMANUEL, JORGE AGUSTIN, chemical engineer, environmental consultant; b. Manila, Philippines, Aug. 28, 1954; came to U.S., 1970; s. Benjamin Elmido and Lourdes (Orozco) E.; 1 child, Andres Layanglawin. BS in Chemistry, N.C. State U., 1976, MSChemE, 1978; PhD in Chem. Engring., U. Mich., 1988. Registered profl. engr., Calif., environ. profl.; cert. hazardous materials mgmt. U. Calif., Berkeley, 1993; cert. pub. health U. Iowa, 2006. Process engr. Perry Electronics, Raleigh, N.C., 1973-74; rsch. asst. N.C. State U., Raleigh, 1977-78; rsch. chem. engr. GE Corp. R & D Ctr., Schenectady, N.Y., 1978-81; Amoco rsch. fellow U. Mich., Ann Arbor, 1981-84; sr. environ. analyst TEM Assocs., Inc., Emeryville, Calif., 1988-91; pres. Environ. & Engring. Rsch. Group, Pinole, Calif., 1991—. Environ. cons. to the Philippines, UN Devel. Program, 1992, 94; rsch. assoc. U. Calif., Berkeley, 1988-90; adj. prof. chem. engring. U. Philippines-Diliman. Contbr. articles to profl. jours. Mem. Assn. for Asian Studies, Ann Arbor, 1982-88; sec. Alliance for Philippine Concerns, L.A., 1983-91; assoc. Philippine Resource Ctr., Berkeley, 1988-92; bd. dirs. ARC-Ecology, San Francisco, 1990-2005, Asia Pacific Ctr., Washington, 1995-2000; bd. advisors Urban Habitat, 1995-2002; chmn. bd. Filipino-Am. Coalition for Environ. Solutions, 2001-03; internat. cons. WHO, UN Devel. Program, Healthcare Without Harm, 2005—. Grantee, NC State U., 1976; Phoenix grant, U. Mich., 1982. Mem. NSPE, AAAS, APHA, Air and Waste Mgmt. Assn., Assn. Profl. in Infection Control and Epidemiology, Calif., Scis., N.Y. Acad. Sci., Filipino-Am. Soc. Architects and Engrs. (exec. sec. 1989-90, Svc. award 1990). Avocations: classical guitar, ethnomusicology, asian studies. Office: Environ & Engring Rsch Group 2550 Appian Way Ste 202 Pinole CA 94564 Office Phone: 510-758-2525.

EMME, (EMME ARONSON), model, apparel designer; b. NYC; Degree in speech comm., Syracuse U. Reporter, Flagstaff, Ariz.; morning anchor NBC affiliate Sta. KNAZ-TV; spokesperson Revlon and numerous fashion houses; clothing designer Emme; supermodel. Lectr. in body image and self-esteem at h.s. and univs.; first model invited to speak to a congressional subcom. on eating and body-image disorders, Washington. Host Fashion Emergency, E! Entertainment TV; author: True Beauty-Positive Attitudes & Practical Tips from the World's Leading Plus Size Model, Life's Little Emergencies, 2003; columnist: Ask Emme. Hon. bd. dirs. Eating Disorders & Awareness Prevention, Am. Anorexia & Bulimia Assn.; ambassadors Mutiple Sclerosis Soc. Named Woman of Yr., Glamour Mag., 1997; named one of 50 Most Beautiful People, People Mag., 1994, 1999, Most Fascinating Woman of Yr., Ladies Home Jour., 1997, Most Important Women in Am., 1999; named to Orange Plus Hall of Fame, Syracuse U.; scholar Full athletic scholar, Syracuse U., Rowing Team. Studio: William Morris Agency Brian Dubin 1325 Ave of Americas Flr 15 New York NY 10019

EMMELUTH, BRUCE PALMER, investment company executive, venture capitalist; b. LA, Nov. 30, 1940; s. William J. and Elizabeth L. (Palmer) E.; children: William J. II (dec.), Bruce Palmer Jr., Carrie Elaine; m. Canda S. Samuels, Mar. 29, 1987. Sr. investment analyst corp. fin. dept. Prudential Ins. Co. Am., LA, 1965—70; with Seidler Amdec Securities, Inc., 1970—90, sr. v.p., mgr. corp. fin. dept., 1974—90; gen. ptnr. VK Ventures, VK Capital, 1990—99; exec. v.p., sr. mng. dir. investment banking Van Kasper & Co., LA, 1990—99, First Security Van Kasper, 1999—2000; exec. v.p., sr. mng. dir. Wells Fargo Van Kasper, LA, 2000—01; exec. v.p., sr. mng. dir. investment banking Wells Fargo Securities, 2001—03; pvt. investor, 2004—. Pres., bd. dirs. SAS Capital Corp., venture capital subs. Seidler Amdec Securities, 1974-90, Van Kasper & Co., 1990-99, First Security Van Kasper, 1999-2000; bd. advisors Entreprenurial Studies program Anderson Grad. Sch. Mgmt. UCLA, 1985-2006. With U.S. Army N.G., 1965-71. Presbyterian. Home: 16 Augusta Ln Santa Barbara CA 93108

EMMER, BARBARA LOUISE, librarian; b. Charleroi, Pa., Apr. 11, 1947; d. William John and Helen Martha E. BS in Edn., Clarion U. Pa., 1969, cert. advanced studies, 1989; MLS, U. Pitts., 1978. Libr. dir. Pa. State U., DuBois, 1984-89; libr. Ridgway (Pa.) Area Sch. Dist., 1969-84, Brockway (Pa.) Area Sch. Dist., 1989—2005, Mengle Meml. Libr., 2006—. Sec. Riverview Libr. Consortium, Shippenville, Pa., 1990-93, chmn., 2001-03; reviewer, cons. Choice 1985-89. Pres. Friends of the Libr., DuBois, 1989-91; mem. hosp. aux. DuBois Regional Med. Ctr., 1985—. Mem. AAUW (bd. dirs. 1979—, legis. chair 1990—, Woman of Yr. 1991), NEA, ALA (chair off-campus libr. svcs. 1988-89), Pa. State Edn. Assn., Pa. Sch. Librs. Assn. (regional rep. 1996-2005), Brockway Area Edn. Assn. (sec. 1991-93), DuBois Area Coun. on the Arts, DuBois Hist. Soc. (print libr. and property com. 1994—, Woman of Yr. award 2005), Delta Kappa Gamma Soc. (Woman of Distn. award 2005), Beta Phi Mu, Alpha Alpha (hist. records com.). Home: 526 1st St Du Bois PA 15801-3059

EMMERICH, ADAM OLIVER, lawyer; b. NYC, Dec. 15, 1960; s. André and Constance Ruth (Marantz) E.; m. Pamela Anne Nadler, Dec. 8, 1991; children: Sarah Abigail, Rebecca Elizabeth, Benjamin Ezekiel. BA, Swarthmore Coll., 1981; JD with honors, U. Chgo., 1985. Bar: NY 1987. Law clk. to Abner J. Mikva U.S. Cir. Ct., Washington, 1985-86; assoc. Wachtell, Lipton, Rosen & Katz, NYC, 1986-91, ptnr., 1992—. Mem. ABA, N.Y. State Bar Assn., N.Y. County Lawyers Assn., Assn. Bar City N.Y. Democrat. Jewish. Avocations: running (marathons), squash. Office: Wachtell Lipton Rosen & Katz 51 W 52nd St New York NY 10019-6150 Office Phone: 212-403-1234. Business E-Mail: aoemmerich@wlrk.com.

EMMERICH, TOBY, film company executive; b. NYC, Feb. 8, 1963; s. Anacé and Constorte (Morombs) E. BA, Wesleyan U., Middletown, Conn., 1985. Artist and repertoire rep. Atlantic Records, NYC, 1987—92; pres. New Line Cinema Productions, 1992—. Prodr., writer: (films) Frequency, 2000; exec. prodr.: Rush Hour 2, 2001, All About the Benjamins, 2002, Blade II, 2002, Austin Powers in Goldmember, 2002, Friday After Next, 2002, Highwaymen, 2003, Final Destination 2, 2003, Willard, 2003, Dumb and Dumberer: When Harry Met Lloyd, 2003, How to Deal, 2003, Seconhand Lions, 2003, Elf, 2003, The Butterfly Effect, 2004, Laws of Attraction, 2004, The Notebook, 2004, Cellular, 2004, Raise Your Voice, 2004, After the Sunset, 2004; exec. prodr.: (films) Blade: Trinity, 2004; exec. prodr.: (films) Son of the Mask, 2005, King's Ransom, 2005, Monster-in-Law, 2005, A History of Violence, 2005, Wedding Crashers, 2005, The Man, 2005, Domino, 2005, Just Friends, 2005, The New World, 2005, Final Destination 3, 2006, Snakes on a Plane, 2006, Little Children, 2006, The Texas Chainsaw Massacre: The Beginning, 2006; exec. prodr.: (films) The Number 23, 2007, Fracture, 2007; writer: (films) The Last Mimzy, 2007. Mem. Phi Beta Kappa. Office: New Line Cinema Corp 888 7th Ave Fl 19 New York NY 10106*

EMMERICH, WERNER SIGMUND, physicist, educator; b. Dusseldorf, Germany, June 3, 1921; s. Adolph and Julia (Frank) E.; m. Eva G. Pauson, June 13, 1953; children— Fay Lillian, Ralph Austin, Bertram Frank BS, Ohio State U., 1949, MS, 1950, PhD, 1953. Research physicist Westinghouse Research and Devel. Ctr., Pitts., 1954-57, adv. physicist, 1957-64, mgr. arc and plasma research, 1964-73, dir. applied physics, 1973-75, dir. corp. research, 1975-79, dir. power systems, 1979-83, dir. corp. and comml. research, 1983-86; retired, 1986. Author: Fast Neutron Physics, 1963; patentee in field Served with AUS, 1942-46, ETO Fellow Am. Phys. Soc.; mem. AAAS (life), Sigma XI, Phi Beta Kappa, Zeta Beta Tau Home: 1883 Beulah Rd Pittsburgh PA 15235-5004 Personal E-mail: wemrick@aol.com.

EMMERSON, ARCHIE ALDIS (RED EMMERSON, A.A. EMMERSON), sawmill owner; b. 1929; Mgr. R.H. Emmerson & Son, 1949—52, 1954—69; pres. Sierra Pacific Industries, Redding, Calif. Named one of Forbes' Richest Americans, 2006; recipient Harry A. Merlo award, 2002. Office: Sierra Pacific Industries 19794 Riverside Ave Redding CA 96007 also: PO Box 496028 Redding CA 96049-6028

EMMERT, GILBERT ARTHUR, retired engineering educator; b. Merced, Calif., June 2, 1938; s. Allan Valentine and Mildred (Vanderbilt) E.; m. Nancy Sue Johnson, June 12, 1964; children: David Allan, Daniel Andrew. BS, U. Calif., Berkeley, 1961; MS, Rensselaer Poly. Inst., Troy, NY, 1964; PhD, Stevens Inst. Tech., Hoboken, NJ, 1968. Analytical engr. United Tech. Corp., East Hartford, Conn., 1961-64; asst. prof. U. Wis., Madison, 1968-72, assoc. prof., 1972-79, prof., 1979—2001, prof. emeritus, 2001—, dept. chair, 1992-01. Contbr. articles to profl. jours. Mem. AIAA, Am. Physical Soc., Am. Nuclear Soc. Office: U Wis Dept Engring Physics 1500 Engineering Dr Madison WI 53706-1609 E-mail: emmert@engr.wisc.edu.

EMMERT, MARK ALLEN, academic administrator, educator; b. Tacoma, Dec. 16, 1952; s. Chester Eugene and Naomi Abigale E.; m. DeLaine Sharon Smith, June 24, 1977; children: Stephen Kenneth, Jennifer Ashley. BA in Polit. Sci., U. Wash., 1975; MPA, Syracuse U., 1976, PhD in Pub. Adminstrn., 1983. Fellow, rsch. asst. Syracuse U., 1980—83; asst. prof. dept. polit. studies Northern Ill. U., DeKalb, 1983-85; assoc. dean grad. sch. pub. affairs U. Colo., Denver, assoc., asst. prof., grad. sch. pub. affairs, assoc. vice chancellor academic affairs, 1985—92; provost, v.p. academic affairs Mont. State U., Bozeman, 1992—95; chancellor, prof. U. Conn., Storrs, 1994-99, La. State U., Baton Rouge, 1999—2004; pres. U. Wash., Seattle, 2004—, prof. Evans Sch. Pub. Affairs, 2004—. Contbr. articles to profl. jours. Bd. dirs. Boy Scouts Am., Baton Rouge, 1999, La. Rsch. Park, 1999, LUMCON, 1999—; coun. chmn. Nat. Assn. State Univ. and Land Grant Coll., 1998-99; mem. Seattle Cmty. Devel. Roundtable, 2005-, Governor's Global Competitiveness Coun., 2005-; co-chair Prosperity Partnership, 2005-; bd. trustees Greater Seattle Chamber of Commerce, 2006- Am. Coun. on Edn. fellow U. Colo., 1988, Fulbright fellow, Germany, 1990-91; recipient Good Growth award, Baton Rouge Bus. Report & Growth Coun., 2003; named Marketer of Yr., Sales and Mktg. Executives Assn., 2003 Mem. Rotary, Phi Kappa Phi, Golden Key Honor Soc., Alpha Lambda Delta, Assn. Am. Universities, Coun. Presidents, Am. Coun. on Edn., Coun. Fellows, Assn. Governing Boards of Universities and Colleges Avocations: reading, golf, scuba diving, fly fishing. Office: Office of the Pres Box 351230 301 Gerberding Hall Seattle WA 98195-1230 E-mail: pres@u.washington.edu.*

EMMERT, RICHARD EUGENE, retired industrial and professional association executive; b. Iowa City, Iowa, Feb. 23, 1929; s. Frank Thomas and Okie Leona (Seydel) E.; m. Marilyn Ruth Marner, June 19, 1949; children: Debra Sue Emmert Warrington, Andrea Gale Emmert Mazzuca, Lisa Alison Emmert Grant. BS, U. Iowa, 1951; MS, U. Del., 1952, PhD, 1954; DSc (hon.), Manhattan Coll., 1992. Supt. mfg. textile fibers dept. E.I. du Pont de Nemours & Co., Martinsville, 1966-67, mgr. engring. tech. and materials rsch. Wilmington, 1969-73; dir. rsch. and devel. pigments dept., 1973-75, dir. instrument products, photo products dept., 1975-77, dir. electronic products, photo products dept., 1977-79, gen. mgr. textile fibers dept., 1979-80, v.p. corp. plans, 1980-83, v.p. electronics dept., 1984-87; exec. dir. AIChE, NYC, 1988-96, ret., 1996. Trustee U. Del. Rsch. Found., Newark, 1987—, pres., 1994-2000; commencement spkr. Coll. Engring., U. Iowa, 1995. Author: Gas Absorption and Solvent Extraction, 1963; contbr. articles to profl. jours. Vice chmn. Stanton Sch. Bd., Del., 1961-64; chmn. adv. bd. Coll. Engring., U. Iowa, Iowa City, 1974-80; chmn. adv. bd. dept. chem. engring. U. Calif., Berkeley, 1978-87, chmn., 1982-83; co-chmn. adv. bd. dept. chem. engring. U. Del., Newark, 1984-88, mem. Coll. Engring. adv. coun., 1995—; mem. Coll. Engring. adv. coun. Villanova U., 2003—; trustee Christiana Care Health Sys., Wilmington, 1983—; pres. Del. Found. for Phys. Edn. (now Del. Tennis Found.), Wilmington, 1984-86. With U.S. Army, 1954-56. Recipient 1st Disting. Engring. Alumni award U. Del., 1984, Medal of Distinction, U. Del., 1993, Disting. Alumni award U. Iowa, 1988, Kenneth Andrew Roe award Am. Assn. of Engring. Socs., 1996, Disting. Engring. Alumni Acad. award U. Iowa, 1996. Fellow AIChE (Van Antwerpen award 1998); mem. Nat. Acad. Engring., Del. Tennis Assn. (pres. 1982-83), United Engring. Found. (trustee 1988-2001), Chem. Heritage Found. (dir. 1998—), Tau Beta Pi, Sigma Xi, Phi Eta Sigma. Republican. Presbyterian. Avocation: tennis. Home: 24 Brandywine Falls Rd Wilmington DE 19806-1002 E-mail: emmertr@comcast.net.

EMMET, THOMAS ADDIS, JR., college administrator, consultant; b. Detroit, July 26, 1930; s. Thomas Addis and Leona Marguerete (Schneider) E.; m. Anne Marie Baker, Mar. 3, 1972 (dec. Sept. 19, 2001); children: Lynn, Anthony, William Novitsky. PhB, U. Detroit, 1952, MA, 1954; EdS, EdD, U. Mich., 1963; LLD (hon.), St. Norbert Coll., 2001; DHL in Ednl. Leadership (hon.), Quincy U., 2001. Asst. dean U. Detroit, 1953-57, dean men, 1957-64, dean evening coll. arts and scis., 1964-66, asst. prof. higher edn., 1964-67, assoc. v.p. acad. affairs, 1966—67; spl. asst. to pres., prof. edn. Regis U., Denver, 1972-91, pres. higher edn. exec. assocs., 1967-72, 84-86, 89—, sr. adv. to pres., 1991—. Adj. prof. higher edn. Wayne State U., Detroit, 1968-70; chmn. bd. Higher Edn. Group, 1986-89; pres. Thomas A. Emmet & Assos., 1972-84; cons. collective negotiations in higher edn. Edn. Commn. of States, 1971-84; cons. higher edn. Opinion Rsch. Corp., 1984-86; dir. leadership seminars, sr. adviser Am. Council on Edn., 1979-93. Editor: The Acacemic Department and Division Chairman, 1972-94, Collective Bargaining in Postsecondary Institutions: The Impact on the Campus and the State, 1974; assoc. editor Coll. and Univ. Bus., 1969-71; pub. The Department ADvisor, 1985-92. Staff dir. Mich. State Senate Student Unrest Com., 1968-69; exec. sec. Conf. Jesuit Student Personnel Adminstrs., 1956-64; sec. Coun. Student Personnel Assns. in Higher Edn., 1966-69. Recipient Bernard Webster Reed award, 1963, John P. McNichols award U. Detroit, 1986, Alan P. Splete award Coun. Ind. Colls., 2005. Mem. Adult Student Personnel Assn. (v.p. 1961-64), Nat. Assn. Student Personnel Adminstrs. (mem. exec. com. 1961-67, editor Jour. 1962-63), Phi Kappa Phi, Alpha Sigma Nu, Alpha Sigma Lambda, Phi Delta Kappa, Phi Eta Sigma. Office: Regis U New Ventures 3333 Regis Blvd Denver CO 80221-1154 Home: 520 Fifth St Castle Rock CO 80104 Office Phone: 720-560-0447. E-mail: heea@aol.com.

EMMETT, BRIAN, software developer; b. Herndon, Va. B in Computer Sci., Va. Polytechnic Inst. and State Univ. (Va. Tech.), 1998. Intern Boeing; sr. software developer, endoscopy divsn. Stryker Corp., San Jose, Calif. Won the 2005 Oracle Space Sweepstakes (N.Am.) once-in-a-lifetime trip 62 miles above the surface of the Earth, but decided to forfeit the Grand Prize because of the cost of taxes on the contest prize. Second chance to receive such an opportunity by serving as a test passenger (free ride) for a space flight in 2008 through the company Benson Space Company. Office: Stryker Endoscopy 5900 Optical Ct San Jose CA 95138 Office Phone: 408-754-2000.

EMMETT, JAMES ROBERT, retired lawyer; b. Gary, Ind., Jan. 24, 1940; s. Robert Gerald and Jeannette Louise (Pinkerton) E.; m. Marian

Carol Yanney, Jan. 28, 1967; children: Jennifer Kathleen, Robert Yanney. BCE, Purdue U., 1963; JD, Ind. U., 1966. Bar: Ind. 1967, U.S. Dist. Ct. (so. dist.) Ind. 1967, U.S. Ct. Internat. Trade 1993, U.S. Supreme Ct. 1993. Engr. design GE Snyder & Assocs., Jackson, Mich., 1968-70; atty. real estate Amoco Oil Co., Chgo., 1970-72; rep. property tax Amoco Corp., Chgo., 1972-74, atty. state tax, 1974-86, sr. tax atty., 1986—2000; ret., 2000. Bd. dirs. St. Charles Singers, Ill., 2002—. Avocations: golf, guitar, horses, reading, drums.

EMMETT, JOHN COLIN, retired inventor, consultant; b. Bradford, Yorkshire, Eng., Apr. 27, 1939; BS, PhD, London U. Former rsch. team leader SmithKline Beecham Corp.; cons. Euromedica Ltd.; freelance cons., 2001—. Co-inventor over 100 patents in field. Named to National Inventors Hall of Fame, 1990. Office: Nat Inventors Hall of Fame 221 S Broadway St Akron OH 44308-1505

EMMETT, RITA, professional speaker; b. Chgo., Apr. 12, 1943; d. Thomas Henry Dorney and Helen Fischer; m. Bruce Karder, May 21, 1994; children: Robb Sean, Kerry Shannon. BA in English, Northeastern Ill. U., 1979; MS in Adult and Cont. Edn, Nat. Louis U., Evanston, Ill., 1985. Coord. edn. programs Leyden Family Svc., Franklin Park, Ill., 1977-95; pres. Emmett Enterprises, Inc., Des Plaines, 1984—. Adj. faculty Triton Coll., River Grove, Ill., 1977-99, Wright Coll., Chgo., 1985-99; presenter in field. Author: The Procrastinator's Handbook: Mastering the Art of Doing It Now, 2000; The Procrastinating Child: A Handbook for Adults to Help Children Stop Putting Things Off, 2002, The Clutter-Busting Handbook, 2005, Great Speakers Anthology; contbr. articles to newspapers and mags. Pres. Parent's Club, River Grove, 1987-88; keynote spkr. Gov.'s Mansion, Springfield, Ill. Mem. Bus. and Profl. Women (Achievement award 1986), Assn. Consultation and Edn. (sec.), Ill. Prevention Network, Century Club, Nat. Spkrs. Assn., Profl. Spkr.'s of Ill. (bd. dirs. 1995-96, 2002-03). Roman Catholic. Avocations: reading, writing, travel. Office Phone: 847-699-9950. Personal E-mail: rita@ritaemmett.com.

EMMONS, ROBERT DUNCAN, diplomat; b. LA, Mar. 1, 1932; s. Richard Norman and Margaret Houston (Kelly) E.; m. Susan Mary Likeman, Aug. 23, 1958; 1 child, Robert Campbell; m. Carolyn Elizabeth Kingsley, Sept. 27, 1995. BA, UCLA, 1954, LL.B., 1957. Contract adminstr. N.Am. Aviation, Inc., Los Angeles, 1958-60, 62-63; contract adminstr. Litton Industries, Los Angeles, 1961; fgn. service officer Dept. State, Washington, 1963-88; vice consul, 3d sec. Am. embassy, Beirut, 1963-65; consul Am. consulate, St. John, N.B., Canada, 1966-68; program officer AID, Saigon, Vietnam, 1968-70; sr. watch officer Dept. State, Washington, 1970-71; chief consular sect. Am. embassy, Warsaw, 1972-74, counselor of embassy Copenhagen, 1974-76, consul gen. Kingston, Jamaica, 1976-78; office dir. Dept. State, Washington, 1978-80; chief immigration br. Am. embassy, London, 1980-84; consul gen. Am. consulate gen., Tijuana, Mexico, 1984-87; retired, 1988. Recipient Vietnam award, Dept. State, 1969. Mem.: Calif. State Bar.

EMMONS, ROBERT JOHN, corporate executive, poet; b. Trenton, NJ, Sept. 18, 1934; s. Charles Glunk and Ruth Marie (Heilhecker) E.; m. Christine Young Bebb, July 13, 1980; children: Bradley Thomas, Cathy Lynne, Christopher Robert, Ryan Hunter. AB in Econs, U. Mich., 1956, MBA, 1960, JD, 1964. V.p. Baskin-Robbins Co., Burbank, Calif., 1964-68; pres. United Rent-All, Los Angeles, 1968-69, Master Host Internat., Los Angeles, 1969-71; prof. Grad. Sch. Bus., U. So. Calif., 1971-82; pres. LTI Corp., Monterey, Calif., 1982-84; chmn., CEO, dir. Casino USA/SFI Corp., Santa Barbara, Calif., 1984-98; mng. ptnr. Emmons Capital Investments, Santa Barbara, Calif., 1999—. Author: The American Franchise Revolution, 1970, The American Marketing Revolution, 1980; poetry Other Places, Other Times, 1974, Love and Other Minor Tragedies, 1980, The Road to Paradise, 2003, The Wanderer, A Poet's Journey, 2005, Seafarer, Poems of the Sea, 2007. Mem. AAUP, Am. Mktg. Assn., European Mktg. Assn., Am. Econ. Assn., Calif. Yacht Club (L.A.), Hawaii Yacht Club (Honolulu), The Valley Club of Montecito (Calif.), Useppa Island Club (Fla.), St. Petersburg Yacht Club (Fla.), The Calif. Club (LA), Ocean Reef Club (Fla.), Beta Gamma Sigma, Pi Kappa Alpha. Office: Emmons Capital Investments PO Box 50243 Santa Barbara CA 93150-0243

EMMRICH, STUART J., editor; b. 1955; Degree in journalism, U. Florida. Reporter Atlantic Constn.; dep. bus. editor Daily News; exec. editor, editor Smart Money, 1992—99; exec. editor Offspring mag., 1999—2002; Escapes sect. editor NY Times, 2002—04, Travel sect. editor, 2004—. Mem. adv. bd. Smoke Farm Sch., Wash., 2003. Office: NY Times 229 W 43rd St New York NY 10036 Office Phone: 212-556-1601. Office Fax: 212-556-1604. E-mail: emmrich@nytimes.com.

EMR, SCOTT DAVID, molecular biologist, director; b. Jersey City, Feb. 8, 1954; s. John Frank and Evelyn Grace (Metzger) E.; m. Michelle Christine Therrien, July 16, 1977; children: Bryanna Michelle, Kevin Scott. BS in Biology, U. RI, Kingston, 1976; PhD in Microbiology & Molecular Genetics, Harvard U., 1981. Tchg. fellow dept. microbiology & molecular genetics Harvard Med. Sch., Boston, 1976—79; vis. scholar Pasteur Inst., Paris, 1978; traveling scholar cancer rsch. prog. Nat. Cancer Inst.-Frederick Cancer Rsch. Facility, Md., 1980—81; postdoctoral fellow biochemistry and cell biology Miller Rsch. Inst. U. Calif., Berkeley, 1981—83; asst. prof. to assoc. prof. divsn. biology Calif. Inst. Tech., Pasadena, 1983—91; prof. divsn. cellular & molecular medicine U. Calif., San Diego, 1991—2007, adj. prof. dept. biology, 1996—2007; investigator Howard Hughes Med. Inst., 1991—; Frank H.T. Rhodes Class of '56 endowed dir. Inst. Cell and Molecular Biology Cornell U., Ithaca, NY, 2007—. Spl. reviewer NIH Microbial Physiology and Genetics Study Sect., 1986, ad hoc reviewer, 90; mem. NIH Biol. Scis. Study Sect., 1990—93, FASEB Rsch. Confs. Adv. Com., 1994—96; mem. grants rev. panel Am. Cancer Soc., 1994—96; mem. Searle Scholars Prog. Sci. Adv. Bd. and Rev. Panel, 2001—02, Pew Scholars in Biomedical Scis. Adv. Bd. and Rev. Panel, 2003—. Contbr. articles to profl. jours. Named Presdl. Young Investigator NSF, 1985-90; Searle Scholars Prog. grantee, 1984-87; recipient Hansen Found. Gold medal prize and lecture, Copenhagen, Denmark, 2003. Fellow: AAAS, Am. Acad. Microbiology, Am. Acad. Arts & Scis.; mem.: NAS, Genetics Soc. Am., Am. Soc. Cell Biology, Am. Soc. Microbiology, Phi Kappa Phi. Office: Dept Molecular Biology and Genetics Cornell U Biotechnology Bldg Ithaca NY 14853 Office Phone: 858-534-6462, 858-534-7673, 607-255-0816. Office Fax: 858-534-6414. Business E-Mail: semr@ucsd.edu. E-mail: sde26@cornell.edu.*

EMRICK, CHARLES ROBERT, JR., lawyer; b. Lakewood, Ohio, Dec. 19, 1929; s. Charles R. and Mildred (Hart) E.; m. Lizabeth Keating; children— Charles R. III, Caroline K. B.S., Ohio U., 1951, M.S., 1952; J.D., Cleve. State U., 1958. Bar: Ohio 1958. Ptnr. Calfee, Halter & Griswold, Cleve., 1965—2000, ret.; v.p. Transaction Group, Cleve., 2000-; lectr. U. Services Bus. Ctr., John Carroll U., 1970—; former Cleve. dir. Best Sand Co., Fairmount Minerals, Gt. Lakes Lithograph, Clamco Corp., Hunter Mfg. Co., Ken-Mac Metals, S & H Industries, Somerset Techs., Inc., Wedron-Silica Sand Co. Former trustee, br. bd. chmn. YMCA; former officer, trustee Lake Erie Jr. Nature and Sci. Ctr.; former adj. prof. Baldwin Wallace U.; adv. mem. Hartzell Propeller, Lake Erie Elec. Co., Bil-Jac Dog Food Co.; lectr. Chartered Life Underwriters Assn.; former adj. lectr. Case Western Res. U.; trustee Rocky River Pub. Library; trustee, treas. Cleve. Area Devel. Fin. Corp.; trustee Fairview Gen. Hosp., prin. enterprise bd. Cleve. Zool. Soc., Lake Ridge Acad.; former mem. nat. policy adv. com. New Eng. Mut. Life Ins. Co.; mem. vis. com. Cleve. State Law Sch.; mem. vis. com. Cleve. State Law Sch.; bd. dirs. N.E. chpt. Am. Cancer Soc. Mem. Nat. Assn. Corp. Dirs. (sec., bd. dirs.); dir., adv. bd. Great Lakes Fastener LLC, Willow Hill Corp., Austin Capital, Westney Corp., C.E. White; trustee Ohio U. (bd. chair), ohio U. Found. (medal of merit, founders medal, Baker award), O.U. Cutler Scholar bd.; dir. Cleve. Clinic Urology Inst., Cleve. Orch. Planned Giving Comm. Recipient Alumnus of Yr., Ohio U. Coll. Bus. award, also Cleve. State Marshall Sch. Mem. Westwood Country Club (former sec., legal counsel), Union Club, Cleveland Yachting Club, The Clifton Club. Methodist. Office: Calfee Halter & Griswold 800 Superior Ave E Ste 1800 Cleveland OH 44114-2688 Address: Transaction Group 1422 Euclid Ave Cleveland OH

ENABNIT, TED, retired lawyer; b. Mason City, Iowa, Sept. 2, 1927; s. Elgin and Clarice Enabnit; m. Carol Schrage, May 1, 1969 (dec.); children: Karen, Jeffrey, Kevin, Brian, Jill. BA, U. Iowa, 1950, JD, 1952. Bar: Iowa 1952, U.S. Dist. Ct. (so. dist.) Iowa 1960, U.S. Supreme Ct. 1980. Ptnr. Levinson and Enabnit, Mason City, Iowa, 1959—70; sr. ptnr. Enabnit, Keen, Mason City, Iowa, 1970—90; pres. Ted Enabnit PC, Mason City, Iowa, 1990—96; ret., 1996. Chmn. No. Iowa Cmty. Auditorium FD, Mason City, 1974—84; v.p., counsel Mason City Found., 1990—2006. With USNR, 1945—51, with US Army, 1952—54. Mem.: Kiwanis (pres. 1972), Am. Legion (comdr. 1970), Masons (Master 1967). Lutheran. Avocations: Rving, golf, travel. Home: 2515 S Lakeview Ct Clear Lake IA 50428

ENAM, SYED ATHER, neurosurgeon, researcher; b. Sindri, Bihar, India, Nov. 21, 1961; s. Syed Enamul Haque and Razia Enam; m. Kishwar Fakhar, Jan. 1, 1989; children: Syed Faaiz, Syed Zayd, Syed Usman. MBBS, Dow Med. Coll., Karachi, Pakistan, 1987; PhD, Northwestern U., 1991. Diplomate Am. Bd. Neurol. Surgeons. Resident in gen. surgery SUNY, Buffalo, 1991-92; resident in neurosurgery Henry Ford Hosp., Detroit, 1992—97, chief resident in neurosurgery, 1997—98; chief Neurosurgery Assocs. of Macomb, 1998—2003; vice chmn. Dept. Neurosurgery Henry Ford Hosp., 2001—03; attending neurosurgeon William Beaumont Hosp., 2001—03, Oakwood Hosp. Med. Ctr., 2001—03; dir. clin. rsch. St. Joseph Mercy of Macomb Hosp., Mich., 2003; dir. neurosurg. svcs. William Beaumont Hosp., Troy, Mich., 2003; head, divsn. neurosurgery Aga Khan U., Karachi, Pakistan, 2003—. Contbr. chpts. to textbooks, articles to profl. jours. Recipient Physician of the Yr. award St. Joseph's Mercy of Maycomb Hosp, 2002, Outstanding Resident award Henry Ford Med. Assn., 1998, 1st prize Midwest Soc. Electron Microscopists, 1991; Am. Health Assn. Found. fellow, 1990, Northwestern U. Dean's fellow, 1987; Quaid-e-Azam scholar/medal Bd. of Edn., Punjab, 1977. Fellow: ACS, Royal Coll. Surgeons Ireland, Royal Coll. Physicians and Surgeons Can.; mem.: Congress of Neurol. Surgeons, Rsch. Soc., World Fedn. Neurology, Am. Assn. Neurol. Surgeons, Soc. Neurosci., Sigma Xi (Grad. Rsch. Symposium award). Muslim. Achievements include research on cell biology of Alzheimer's Disease, neuron interaction and neuronal development, cell biology of brain tumor invasion; Immunotherapy for brain tumors. Home: E-138 Block 7 Gulshan Iqbal Karachi Pakistan Office: Henry Ford Hosp Dept Neurosurgery 2799 W Grand Blvd Detroit MI 48202-2689 also: Divsn Neurosurgery Aga Khan U Karachi Pakistan Home: 5225 Chablis Cir Irvine CA 92604-3168

ENCARNACIÓN, JOSE M. IZQUIERDO, construction executive, former Puerto Rico secretary of state; Sec. transp. and pub. works Puerto Rico, sec. of state, 2004, acting gov., 2004; pres. Am. Concrete Inst., Farmington Hills, Mich., 2006—. Pres. Am. Concrete Inst., Farmington Hills, Mich., 2003.

END, WILLIAM THOMAS, marketing executive; b. Milw., Oct. 31, 1947; s. Jack Arthur and Cecil (O'Brien) E.; m. Nancy Kolb, June 10, 1969 (div. 1974); 1 child, Laura; m. Elyse Soucy, Feb. 23, 1980; children— Alison, David BA, Boston Coll., 1969; student, U. Vienna, Austria, 1967-68; MBA, Harvard U., 1971. Group product mgr. Gillette Toiletries, Boston, 1971-75; exec. v.p. L.L. Bean, Inc., Freeport, Maine, 1975-90, Lands' End, Inc., Dodgeville, Wis., 1991-92, pres., CEO, 1992-95; chmn., CEO Cornerstone Brands Inc., Portland, Maine, 1995—, also bd. dirs. Bd. dirs. Hannaford Bros. Co., Scarborough, Maine, Ariel, Inc., Augusta, Maine, Cinmar, Cin., Travel Smith, San Rafael, Calif., Internat. Cornerstone Group, The Territory Ahead, Santa Barbara, Calif., Garnet Hill, Franconia, N.H., Ballard Designs, Atlanta. Republican. Roman Catholic. Avocations: hunting, fishing, camping, canoeing, skiing. Home: PO Box 339 34 Castle Rd South Freeport ME 04078 Office: Cornerstone Brands Group Inc 5568 W Chester Rd West Chester OH 45069-2914

ENDAHL, ETHELWYN MAE, elementary education educator, consultant; b. Duluth, Minn., May 27, 1922; d. Herman and Florence Jenny (Mattson) Johnson; m. John Charles Endahl Sr., Nov. 27, 1943; children: Merrilee Jean, Marsha Louise, John Charles Jr., Kimberly Ann. BS in Library Science, U. Minn., Mpls., 1943; MA in Edn., Fairfield U., 1978; attended, Elmhurst Coll., Ill., 1966-68, U. Bridgeport, Conn., 1981-83, Northeastern U., Martha's Vineyard, Mass., 1982-85, U. Conn., 1971. Cert. Tchr. Conn. Librarian children's hosp. Davenport (Iowa) Pub. Library, 1943-44; librarian Omaha (Nebr.) Pub. Library, 1944; tchr. 4th gr. Center Elem. Sch., New Canaan, Conn., 1968-81, writing coord., 1981-83; staff devel. Dept. Edn. State of Conn., 1986-88; writing coord. East Elem. Sch., New Canaan, 1986-88; instr. Grad. Sch. Edn. Simmons Coll., Boston, 1989. Leader Reminiscence Writing Courtland Gardens Nursing Home, Stamford, Conn., 1985-86; leader adult writing group Charlotte Hobbs Library, Lovell, Maine, 1987-89; leader writing process-children's group Cmty. Ctr., Boca Grande, Fla., 1994; cons. writing process Banyan Elem. Sch., Sunrise, Fla., 1995-96; writing tchr. John Knox Village Retirement Ctr. Mem. AAUW, Nat. League of Pen Women, Older Women's League. Democrat. Mem. Soc. Of Friends. Avocations: women's studies, reading, writing, hiking. Home: 528 Village Dr Pompano Beach FL 33060-7718 Personal E-mail: emendahl@comcast.net.

ENDERS, ALLEN COFFIN, anatomy educator; b. Wooster, Ohio, Aug. 5, 1928; s. Robert Kendal and Abbie Gertrude (Crandell) E.; m. Alice Hay, June 15, 1950 (div. Dec. 1975); children: Robert H., George C., Richard S., Gregory H.; m. Sandra Jean Schlafke, Aug. 5, 1976. AB, Swarthmore Coll., 1950; AM, Harvard U., 1952, PhD, 1955. From asst. prof. to assoc. prof Rice Inst., Houston, 1954-63; from assoc. prof. to prof. Washington U., St. Louis, 1963-75; prof., chmn. dept. human anatomy U. Calif., Davis, 1976-86, prof. cell biology and human anatomy, 1986—. Cons. NIH, Bethesda, Md., 1964-68, 70-73, 76-80, 83-93. Author: (with others) Bailey's Microscopic Anatomy, 1984; editor: Delayed Implantation, 1964; contbr. numerous articles on anatomy and reproduction to profl. jours. Nat. pres. Perinatal Rsch. Soc., 1981. Grantee NIH, 1959-99. Fellow AAAS; mem. Am. Assn. Anatomists (v.p. 1980-82, pres. 1983-84), Pioneer Reprodn. Res. Home: 39707 Barry Rd Davis CA 95616-9415 Office: U Calif Sch Medicine Cell Biology & Anatomy Davis CA 95616

ENDERS, ELIZABETH MCGUIRE, artist; b. New London, Conn., Feb. 18, 1939; d. Francis Foran and Helen Cuseck (Connolly) McGuire; m. Anthony Talcott Enders, June 9, 1962; children: Charles Talcott, Alexandra Eustis, Camilla, Ostrom II. BA, Conn. Coll., 1962; MA, NYU, 1987. Trustee Artists Space, NYC, 1986-95, Conn. Coll., New London, 1988-93; assoc. dept. prints and illustrated books Mus. Modern Art, 1993—, Lyman Allyn Art Mus., 1994—. One-woman shows include Paul Schuster Gallery, Cambridge, Mass., 1966, Ulysses Gallery, NYC, 1992, 1994, Lyman Allyn Art Mus., New London, Conn., 1994—2006, Charles Cowles Gallery, NYC, 1995, Norbert Considine Gallery, Princeton, NJ, 1997, Artists Space, NYC, 2001, Charles Shain Libr., Conn. Coll., 2004, 2006, Alva Gallery, New London, 2006, Represented in permanent collections Wadsworth Atheneum, Hartford, Conn., exhibited in group shows at Boston Symphony Orch., 1982, NYU, 1983, Conn. Coll., 1988, Bronx Coun. on Arts, 1990—91, Addison Gallery Am. Art, 1993, 2006, Angel Art, LA, 1993, Lyman Allyn Art Mus., New London, Conn., 1994—95, 1998, 1999, 2006—07, one-woman shows include Real Art Ways, Hartford, Conn., 2004, 2006, exhibited in group shows at So. Alleghenies Mus. Art, Loretto, Pa., 1994, Artists Space Multiple, 1995, New Mus. Contemporary Art, NYC, 1995, Denise Bibro Fine Art, 1995, 1998, NY Studio Sch., 1995, 2002, Divine Design '95, LA, Spring Benefit Raffle, Sculpture Ctr., NYC, 1996, 1997, 1998, 2000, 2003, 2004, 2005, Charles Cowles Gallery, 1996, 1998, 2000, 2001, 2002, 2003, 2005—06, Fax Art Week, Copenhagen, Assn. Danish Graphic Artists, 1996, Open Studio, Downtown Arts Festival, NYC, 1997, 1998, Dieu Donne Papermill, 1997, 1999, 2001, Robert Brown Gallery, Wash., DC, 1999, 2001, 2002, 2003, 2004, Brand X, NYC, NY Acad. of Art Benefit Auction, 1999, Cooley Gallery, Old Lyme, Conn., 1999, 2002, (Benefit for the Nature Conservancy), Nielsen Gallery, Boston, 2001, Artwalk, Coalition for the Homeless, 2001, Pfizer Inc., 2004, 2005, Incognito Santa Monica Mus. of Art, 2005, 2007, Florence Griswold Mus., 2006, traveling group show Artists Space, 1992, 1994, Southeastern Ctr. Contemporary Art, Winston-Salem, N.C., 1993, Allentown Art Mus., Pa., 1994, Cleve. Ctr. Contemporary Art, 1994, Salt Lake Art Ctr., Salt Lake City, 1995, Kemper Ctr. Contemporary Art and Design, Kansas City, Mo., 1996, Bass Mus. of Art, Miami Beach, Fla., 1997, Flint Inst. Arts, Mich., 1998, Blaffer Gallery, U. Houston, Tex., 1998, Contemporary Art Ctr., Va. Beach, 1998, Tampa Mus. of Art, 1998—99, Art Mus. of Southeast Tex., 1999, Fresno Metropolitan Mus., Calif., 2000, www.sfnbotanicalart.com, 2003, 2004, 2005, Represented in permanent collections, Addison Gallery of Am. Art, Andover, Mass., Brooklyn Mus., Internat. House, Florence Griswold Mus., Old Lyme, Dow Jones, NYC, Agnes Gund, Lyman Allyn Art Mus., Conn. Coll., New London, Pfizer Inc. Recipient Conn. Coll. medal, 1993. Mem. The Bklyn. Mus., Contemporary Art Coun. Home: 530 E 86th St New York NY 10028-7535

ENDERS, THOMAS, air transportation executive; b. Dec. 21, 1958; married; 4 children. BA in Econ., Polit. Sci. & History, Univ. of Bonn, 1983; PhD in Polit. Sci., UCLA, 1987. Asst. German Fed. Parliament, 1982—85; rsch. assoc. Institute of the Konrad Adenauer Found., St. Augustin, 1985—87, Rsch. Inst. of the German Coun. on Fgn. Affairs, Bonn, 1988—90; sr. rsch. assoc. Internat. Inst. for Strategic Studies, London, 1988—90; mem. planning staff German Minister of Def., Bonn, 1989—91; various mktg. posts (Messerschmitt-Boelkow-Blohm)MBB/(DaimlerChrysler Aerospace AG) DASA, 1991—95; corp. sec., head chairman's office DASA, 1995—96, dir., corp. strategy and tech., 1996—2000; exec. v.p., mem. bd. mgmt., CEO def. and security sys. divsn. European Aeronautic Def. and Space Co. EADS, 2000—05, co-chair, exec. com., 2000—05, CEO, 2005—. Chair Atlantik-Brücke e.V., 2005—, pres.; bd. dir. EADS Participations B.V., CEO; chmn. supervisory bd. EADS Deutschland GmbH, Dornier GmbH, DADC Luft und Raumfahrt Beteiligungs AG, 2000—05, Industrieanlagen-Betriebsgesellschaft mbH (IABG), 2000—05; mem. shareholders com. Airbus S.A.S.; chmn. supervisory com. Eurocopter S.A.S.; mem. supervisory bd. Deutsche BP; bd. dir. EADS N.Am. Inc., Deutsche Gesellschaft für Auswärtige Politik (DGAP), Stichting Administratiekantoor EADS. Airborne officer, maj. of reserve first airborne divsn. German Bundeswehr, 1977—78. Mem.: Aerospace and Def. Industries Assn. Europe (pres.), German Aerospace Industries Assn. (pres., Bundesverband der Deutschen Luft (BDLI) 2005—). Office: European Aeronautic Def & Space Co EADS NV Le Carré Beechavenue 130-132 1119 PR Schiphol Rijk Netherlands Address: EADS Deutschland GmbH 81663 Munich Germany

ENDICO, MARY ANTOINETTE, artist; b. Bronx, NY, June 13, 1954; d. Felix and Katherine (Gluck) E.; m. Robert W. Fugett. BFA, Boston U., 1976. Artist cons. D'Arches Fine Art Paper, France, 1983; demonstrator, lectr. art groups N.Y. State, 1980-97; sec. Sugarloaf (N.Y.) Guild, 1980-88. Self-employed artist, Sugar Loaf, 1977—; group shows include Art of Orange and Rockland N.Y. Invitational, 1986, Aqueous Annual, Ky., 1987, 88, 89, 94, Nat. Exhibit Am. Watercolors, N.Y., 1989, 90, 91, N.E. Watercolor Annual, N.Y., 1991, Nat. Watercolor Soc., Calif., 1992, 2001, San Diego Internat., 1997, Am. Watercolor Soc., 2006, Am. Watercolor Soc., 139th Annual; permanent collections include Del Monte Corp., N.Y., IBM Corp., N.Y., The Ambra Found., N.H., Ashville (N.C.) Mus., Ky. Mus., Bowling Green. Mem. Nat. Watercolor Soc. (signature), Northeast Watercolor Soc. (co-founder 1991), Knickerbocker Artists, Orange County Watercolor Soc., Salmagundi Club, Ky. Watercolor Soc.(signature mem.) Avocation: road cycling. Office: Endico Watercolor Originals PO Box 31 1386 Kings Hwy Sugar Loaf NY 10981 Home Phone: 845-469-9272; Office Phone: 845-469-9272.

ENDICOTT, WILLIAM F., journalist; b. Harrodsburg, Ky., Aug. 26, 1935; s. William O. and Evelyn E.; m. Mary Frances Thomas, Dec. 27, 1956; children: Gene, Fran, Greg. Student, Am. U., 1955; BA in Polit. Sci., Transylvania U., 1957. With Lexington (Ky.) Leader, 1957; sports writer Louisville Courier-Jour., 1958-62; reporter Tulare (Calif.) Advance-Register, 1963; reporter, city editor Modesto (Calif.) Bee, 1963-66; city editor Sacramento Union, 1966-67; with Los Angeles Times, 1968-85; Capitol bur. chief Sacramento Bee, 1985-95, asst. mng. editor, 1995-98, dep. mng. editor, 1998-2000, ret. Hearst vis. profl. U. Tex., 1993. Served with USMCR, 1957-58. Recipient various journalism awards Disting. Alumnus award Transylvania U., 1980 Episcopalian.

ENDRENYI, JANOS, research engineer, educator; b. Budapest, Hungary, Nov. 9, 1927; came to Can., 1957; s. Sandor and Lilly (Szegvari) E.; m. Edith Bernat, Dec. 5, 1956. Diploma in Engring., Tech. U., Budapest, 1951; MASc, U. Waterloo, Ont., Can., 1965; PhD, U. Toronto, Ont., 1972. Registered profl. engr., Ont., Can. Tchg. asst. Tech. U., Budapest, 1949—52; rsch. engr. Rsch. Inst. for Electric Power, Budapest, 1952-56; engr. Toronto Hydro, 1957-59; rsch. engr. rsch. divsn. Ont. Hydro, Toronto, 1959-79, head reliability and stats. sect., 1979-90, prin. rsch. engr., 1990-92, prin. scientist emeritus, 1992—. Lectr. U. Toronto, 1972-80, adj. assoc. prof., 1980-83, adj. prof., 1983—; spkr. at seminars worldwide. Author: Electric Shock Prevention (in Hungarian), 1956, Reliability Modeling in Electric Power Systems, 1978 (translated into Russian and Chinese); contbr. papers to profl. jours. Fellow IEEE; mem. Toronto Mozart Soc. (pres. 2001—, bd. dirs.). Home: 80 Front St E Apt 201 Toronto ON Canada M5E 1T4 Office: Kinectrics Inc 800 Kipling Ave Toronto ON Canada M8Z 6C4 Personal E-mail: john.endrenyi@rogers.com.

ENDRES, ARTHUR P. (SKIP ENDRES), rail transportation executive; BA, Univ. Md.; JD, Cath. Univ. Sch. of Law. Held various positions in house com. including staff dir. of the full com., House Judiciary Com., exec. dir. and gen. counsel Congl. Commn. on Internat. Migration and Coop. Econ. Devel., 1970—94; majority staff dir. sub com. on transp. and hazardous material House Energy and Commerce Com.; spl. coun. to the sub com. on Commerce and Consumer Protection; asst. v.p. govtl. affairs Burlington No. Santa Fe, 1994—96, v.p. govtl. affairs, 1996—. Office: Burlington Northern Santa Fe Corp 2650 Lou Menk Dr 2nd Fl PO Box 961057 Fort Worth TX 76161-0057

ENDRIZ, JOHN GUIRY, retired electronics executive; b. Oak Park, Ill., Jan. 10, 1942; s. John Daniel and Florence (Guiry) E.; m. Sally Jean Doubleday, July 19, 1975. BSEE, MSEE, MIT, 1965; PhD in EE, Stanford U., 1970. Guest rschr. Linkoping (Sweden) U., 1970-72; project mgr. R.C.A. Rsch. Lab., Princeton, NJ, 1972-77; engring. mgr. Varian Assocs., Palo Alto, Calif., 1977-88; v.p. engring. S.D.L., Inc., San Jose, Calif., 1988-97, v.p. power delivery bus. unit, 1997-99; ret., 2000. Contbr. 53 articles to profl. jours.; patentee more than 30 inventions. Home: 5 Heritage Ct Belmont CA 94002-2944

ENENBACH, MARK HENRY, community action agency executive, educator; b. Chgo., July 28, 1949; s. Joseph Henry and Antonette Regina

(Kasko) E.; children: Joy Elizabeth, Erin Regina; m. Kai Lindquist Bergin, Sept. 28, 1985; 1 child, Faith Marie. BA in Polit. Sci. with honors, Loyola U., Chgo., 1971, MA in Urban Studies with honors, 1973. Cmty. resource specialist Model Cities, Chgo., 1974—79; grad. prof. Govs. State U., Park Forest South, Ill., 1977—89; dir. energy program City of Chgo., 1980—83; prof. St. Augustine's Coll., Chgo., 1981—82; coord. cmty. svcs. Dept. Human Svcs., Chgo., 1984—91; prof. urban planning and pub. adminstrn. DePaul U., Chgo., 1987—; dir. cmty. svcs. block grant programs Cmty. and Econ. Devel. Assn. Cook County, Inc., Chgo., 1992—96, v.p./COO, 1997—; CEO CEDA Neighborhood Devel. Corp., Chgo., 2000—05. Mem. adv. bd. City Colls. Chgo., 1984-88; spkr. Nat. Headstart Assn., Washington, 1995; mem. task force Ill. Dept. Commerce and Cmty. Affairs, Springfield, 1996—; spkr. Nat. Assn. Cmty. Action Agys., 1996-2000, Nat. Assn. State Cmty. Svcs. Programs, 2000. Pres. Lincoln Park Interagy. Coun., Chgo., 1986-91; mem. adv. bd. Salvation Army, Chgo., 1987-91. Grad. rsch. fellow Loyola U., 1972-73. Mem. Nat. Assn. Cmty. Action Agys., Ill. Assn. Cmty. Action Agys. Avocations: urban research, writing and travel in over 40 countries. Office: Cmty and Econ Devel Assn 208 S Lasalle St Ste 1900 Chicago IL 60604-1119 Business E-Mail: menebach@cedaorg.net.

ENFIELD, DONALD MICHAEL, insurance company executive; b. LA, Jan. 24, 1945; s. Fred Donald Jr. and Suzanne Arden (Hinkle) Enfield; children: Susan Ann, Michael David, Peter Christian. BA in Polit. Sci., U. San Francisco, 1967. Mgmt. trainee Marsh & McLennan, Inc., San Francisco, 1967-70, acct. exec., 1970-77, asst. v.p., 1977-79, v.p., 1979-81, sr. v.p., 1981-82, mng. dir., 1982-89; chmn., CEO Frank B. Hall & Co. of No. Calif., San Francisco, 1989-92; founder, chmn., CEO Metro/Risk, Inc., San Francisco, 1992—. Cons. in field. Contbr. articles to profl. jours. Bd. dirs. Ronald McDonald Ho., San Francisco, 1989—92, Philharmonica Baroque Orch., San Francisco, 2003—; chmn. bd. dirs. Midsummer Mozart Festival, San Francisco, 1985—90; trustee Lamplighters Music Theater, 1996—2003. Mem.: Wine Adv. San Francisco (founder), San Francisco C. of C. (dir. bus./arts coun. 1987—93), The Family, San Francisco, Club des Oenophiles Gastronome de Paris (dep. pres. 2000—), Olympic Club San Francisco, City Club of San Francisco, Lotus Club N.Y., Soc. Calif. Pioneers (county v.p. 1974—2004). Avocation: classical music. Office: Metro/Risk Inc 153 Townsend St San Francisco CA 94107 Home Phone: 415-341-5880; Office Phone: 415-249-0111. Business E-Mail: enfield@metrorisk.com.

ENG, ADRIENNE ROSE, corporate financial executive; d. Victor and Marie Madison Metoyer; m. Kenneth Gunn Eng, Aug. 23, 1997; children: Kimberly Marie, Nicole Kendra Cahlander. AB, Brown U., Providence, 1981; MBA, U. Calif., Berkeley, 1989. Fin. analyst Hewlett Packard, Santa Rosa, Calif., 1988—92, Mountain View, Calif., 1992—94; sr. analyst William M, Mercer, Inc., San Francisco, 1996—97; sr. compensation analyst Radford Associates/Aon Cons., San Jose, Calif., 1997—99; compensation cons. SGI, Inc., Mountain View, 1999—2000; compensation program mgr. Yahoo!, Sunnyvale, Calif., 2000—04, Network Appliance, Inc., Sunnyvale, Calif., 2004—. Mem.: World at Work (cet. compensation professional). Home Phone: 510-745-7326; Office Phone: 408-822-3551.

ENG, CATHY, oncologist, educator; BA, NYU, 1990; MD, Hahnemann U. Sch. Medicine, 1994. Asst. prof. M.D. Anderson Cancer Ctr., Houston, 2002—. Physician, clin. rschr. M.D.Anderson Cancer Ctr., Houston, 2002—. Achievements include research in Clinical Trials. Office: MD Anderson Cancer Center 1515 Holcome Blvd Unit 426 Houston TX 77030 Office Phone: 713-792-2828. Office Fax: 713-745-1163.

ENG, CHARIS EU LI, oncologist, geneticist; b. Singapore, Jan. 17, 1962; s. SooPeck and Siok Mui (Lee) E. BA, U. Chgo., 1982, PhD, 1986, MD, 1988. Diplomate Am. Bd. Internal Medicine and Med. Oncology. Med. resident Beth Israel Hosp., Boston, 1988-91; clin. fellow Dana-Farber Cancer Inst., Boston, 1991-95, Harvard Med. Sch., Boston, 1988-93; CRC Dana-Farber fellow U. Cambridge, Eng., 1992-95; instr. Harvard Med. Sch., Boston, 1994-95, asst. prof. medicine, 1995-98; staff physician Dana-Farber Cancer Inst., Boston, 1995-98; assoc. prof. medicine Ohio State U., Columbus, 1999—2002, dir. clin. cancer genetics, 1999—2005, prof. medicine, 2002—05, Dorothy E. Klotz chair cancer rsch., 2002—05, dir. divsn. human genetics, dept. internal medicine, 2002—05; chmn., dir. Genomic Medicine Inst., Cleve. Clinic Found., 2005—. Prof., vice-chmn. genetics Case Western Reserve U., Cleve., 2005—. N.Am. editor, cancer genetics editor Jour. Med. Genetics, 1998—2005; assoc. editor Cancer Rsch., 2001-03, sr. editor, 2004—; assoc. editor Jour. Clin. Endocrinol. Metab., 2005—. Recipient Upjohn travel award, 1991, ATA Van Meter award, 2005, Ernst Oppenheimer award, 2006. Fellow ACP, AAAS; mem. Assn. Am. Physicians, Am. Soc. Clin. Investigation, Alpha Omega Alpha, Phi Beta Kappa, Sigma Xi. Office: Genomic Medicine Inst Cleve Clinic Found 9500 Euclid Ave NE 50 Cleveland OH 44195 Office Phone: 216-444-3440. Business E-Mail: engc@ccf.org.*

ENG, GLORIA D., retired pediatrician; b. Milw., Jan. 23, 1930; d. Jack M. Eng and Wanda Sophie Andryszyk; m. C. James Duke, Nov. 24, 1956; children: Jacqueline, Christopher, Teresa, Paula. At, Marylhurst Coll., Oreg., 1948—50; MD, Marquette U. Sch. Medicine, Milw., 1955; MD (hon.), George Washington U., Washington, 1960. Lic. physician Md., DC, diplomate Am. Bd. Pediat., 1960, Am. Bd. Phys. Medicine and Rehab., 1969, Am. Bd. Electrodiagnostic Medicine, 1989. Intern Phila. Gen. Hosp., Phila., 1955—56; resident Children's Nat. Med. Ctr., Washington, 1956—58, fellow in hematology, 1958—60, dir. phys. medicine and rehab., 1966—98, chmn. dept. phys. medicine and rehab., 1966—92, prof., 1966—98, chmn. emeritus dept. phys. medicine and rehab., 1992; pvt. practice pediat. Md., 1960—64; post- doctoral fellow phys. medicine and rehab. George Washington U., Washington, 1964—66, prof., 1966—98, ret., 1998. Med. cons. rehab. medicine Montgomery County Child Ctr., Md.; dir. muscular dystrophy clinic Children's Hosp. Med. Ctr., Washington, mem. home care adv. com., mem. inpatient unit devel. com.; mem. program com. Am. Assn. Electromyography and Electrodiagnosis, 1989; mem. editl. bd. Archives of Phys. Medicine and Rehab.; mem. Nat. Advisory Bd. Med. Rehab. Rsch. NIH, Bethesda, Md., 1999—2001; lectr. in field. Contbr. chapters to books, articles to profl. jours. Fellow: Am. Acad. Pediat.; mem.: Am. Bd. Phys. Medicine and Rehab. (mem. com. to devel. exam items 1986—89), Am. Pediat. Soc., Am. Acad. Cerebral Palsy and Devel. Disabilities, Am. Assn. Electrodiagnostic Medicine, Am. Congress Rehab. Medicine (mem. program com. 1989), Am. Acad. Phys. Medicine and Rehab. (chmn. spl. interest group pediat. rehab. 1990—93, Distinguished Clinician award 1994). Roman Catholic. Achievements include first to establish home care services, Children's Nat. Med. Ctr. Avocations: writing, painting, golf, babysitting. Home: 3507 Dunlop St Chevy Chase MD 20815-5937

ENG, HOLLY S.A., lawyer; b. 1966; BA in English & Econ., St. Cloud State Univ., 1989; JD, Georgetown Univ., 1993. Bar: Minn. 1993. Atty. Dorsey & Whitney LLP, Mpls., 1993—2001, ptnr., labor, employment practice group, 2001—; spl. assignment Mpls. City Atty. Off., 1997. Guardian ad Litem Minn. Guardian ad Litem Program; instr. Univ. St. Thomas Grad. Sch. Bus., 1999—2001. Grantee Nat. Lawyer's Guild Fellowship, Georgetown Univ. Mem.: Minn. Women Lawyers. Office: Dorsey & Whitney LLP Ste 1500 50 S Sixth St Minneapolis MN 55402-1498 Office Phone: 612-343-2164. Office Fax: 612-340-2868. Business E-Mail: eng.holly@dorsey.com.

ENGARD, NICOLE C., library and information scientist; b. June 27, 1979; d. Cheryl A. and Nicholas Dirato; m. Brian T. Engard. BA, Juniata Coll., 2001. Libr. asst., HR asst., help desk asst. & webmaster Juniata Coll., Huntingdon, Pa., 1997—2001; web asst. Jenkins Law Libr., Phila., 2001—03, web mgr., 2003—07; metadata libr. Princeton Theol. Sem., 2007—. Contbr. articles to profl. jours. Webmaster Patchwork Shelties Rescue, 2005—; bd. mem. & webmaster Upper Darby (Pa.) Adult Evening Program, 2005—, web design instr., 2005—06. Named one of the Movers & Shakers, Libr. Jour., 2007; recipient TBAC Appreciation award for Outstanding Svc., 2007; Code4lib Conf. Scholarship for Women, 2007. Mem.: ALA, Greater Phila. Law Libr. Assn. (Electronic Svcs. Group 2006—, webmaster 2007—), Pa. Libr. Assn., Libr. & Info. Tech. Assn., Spl. Libr. Assn. (Phila. Tech. Task Force 2007, Drexel Student ch. co-newsletter editor 2006—07), Tail Blazers Agility Club. Office: Princeton Theol Sem Librs Mercer St & Libr Place PO Box 111 Princeton NJ 08542-0111 Office Phone: 609-497-2773. E-mail: nengard@gmail.com, nicole.engard@ptsem.edu.

ENGAU, ALEXANDER, research scientist; b. Herford, Germany, Jan. 30, 1980; s. Herwigh and Annette Margarete Gisela Engau. MS, Clemson U., SC, 2004, PhD, 2007; Diploma, U. Kaiserslautern, Germany, 2005. Grad. rschr. Fraunhofer's Inst. Indsl. Math., Kaiserslautern, 2002—03; tchg. asst. Clemson U., 2003—04, tchr. of record, 2006—07; grad. rschr. Automotive Rsch. Ctr., Clemson, SC, 2004—06; postdoctoral fellow U. Waterloo, Ont., Canada, 2007—. Tchg. asst. Dresden U. Tech., Germany, 2001—02. Scholar, German Nat. Academic Found., 2001—05; Hoelderlin Fgn. Studies scholar, SAP, 2003—04. Mem.: Soc. Indsl. and Applied Math. (Travel award 2005, travel grantee 2007), Am. Math. Soc., Inst. Ops. Rsch. and Mgmt. Scis., Internat. Soc Multiple Criteria Decision Making, Math. Programming Soc. Protestant. Avocations: music, travel, sports. Home: Donatusstrasse 7 Korschenbroich 41352 Germany

ENGBER, CHERYL ANN, retired language educator, linguist; b. East Chicago, Ind., Oct. 12, 1945; d. James Ward and Beryl Ann (Crowe) Biddle; m. Michael David Engber, Nov. 25, 1967; children: Sara Ann, Kimberly Sue. BA in Spanish with honors, Ind. U., Bloomington, 1967, MA in Spanish, 1974; MA in Tchg. ESL, Ball State U., Muncie, Ind., 1979; PhD in Linguistics, Ind. U., Bloomington, 1992. Instr. Spanish Anderson (Ind.) U., 1979-82; assoc. instr. intensive English program Ind. U., Bloomington, 1983-86, adminstrv. asst. com. for R & D, 1989-91, instr. semi-intensive English program, 1991-93; assoc. prof. linguistics Truman State U., Kirksville, Mo., 1993—2004; ret., 2004; adminstrv. asst. Rotary Club, Bloomington, 2005—. Instr. ESL Ind. U., Kuala Lumpur, Malaysia, 1985—86; grader for Test of Written English Ednl. Testing Svc., Princeton, NJ, 1989—98, reader for AP exams, 2001—03; asst. to editor Studies in Second Lang. Acquisition Ind. U., 1987—89; spkr. in field. Contbr. Understanding English: A Listening Approach to ESL, 1983; contbr. articles to profl. jours. Founder Muncie (Ind.) Internat. Ctr., 1974; vol. tchr., founder internat. summer workshops for children, Muncie, 1977; deacon, elder, mem. com. First Christian Ch., Bloomington, Ind., 1987-92, 2004—; advanced master gardner Monroe County Assn. Ind. U. fellow, 1982; Truman State U. grantee, 1994, 2001. Mem. Linguistic Soc. Am., Tchrs. ESL, Am. Assn. for Applied Linguistics, Ind. Hist. Soc, Friends of Lilly Libr. Ind. U., Friends Music Ind. U., Frineds of Music Ind. U., Nature Conservancy, Phi Beta Kappa, Phi Kappa Phi. Achievements include Purdue U. advanced master gardener. Avocations: travel, gourmet cooking, gardening. Home: 4672 Compton Blvd Bloomington IN 47401 Personal E-mail: cmengber@att.net.

ENGDAHL, BRIAN EDWARD, psychologist; b. Owatonna, Minn., July 3, 1952; s. Gilbert Donald and Marion Eloise (Scofield) E.; m. Raina Elaine Eberly, July 9, 1977; 1 child, Rebecca Raina. PhD, U. Minn., 1980. Psychologist, coord. VA Med. Ctr., Mpls., 1980—; clin. asst., assoc. prof. Dept. Psychology U. Minn., Mpls., 1980—. Contbr. chpts. to books and articles to profl. jours. Grantee VA 1989-91, 91-94. Mem. AAAS, APA, Am. Psychol. Soc. Home: 1376 Summit Ave Saint Paul MN 55105-2218 Office: VA Med Ctr Psychology One Veterans Dr Minneapolis MN 55417

ENGDAHL, TODD PHILIP, editor; b. Jamestown, NY, Feb. 8, 1950; s. George Philip and Janice Marie (Wallin) E.; m. Caroline C.N. Schomp, Dec. 29 , 1973; children: Anders Justus Schomp, Mats Philip Schomp. BA, Pomona Coll., 1971; MS, Northwestern U., 1972. Reporter Oregonian, Portland, 1972—75, Denver Post, 1975—80, asst. city editor, 1980—83, night city editor, 1983—85, Sunday editor, 1985—86, city editor, 1986—90, exec. city editor, 1990—95, website editor, 1995—2003, perspective editor, 2003—07. Lectr. journalism Portland State U., 1974. Democrat. Lutheran. Avocations: reading, gardening, woodworking. Office: Denver Post 101 W Calfax Ave Denver CO 80202 Personal E-mail: tengdahl@comcast.net.

ENGE, PER KRISTIAN, engineering educator; MS, I. Ill., 1979, PhD in Elec. Engring., 1983. Prof. aeronautics and astronautics, dept. chair Sch. Engring., Stanford U., Kleiner Perkins, Mayfield, Sequoia Capital prof.; dir. Stanford Ctr. for Position Navigation and Time. Fellow: IEEE, Inst. of Navigation (Kepler, Burka, and Thurlow Awards); mem.: NAE. Office: Stanford U Sch Engring Durand 023B / Mailcode 4035 Stanford CA 94305 Office Phone: 650-723-3853. Office Fax: 650-725-8132. E-mail: per.enge@stanford.edu.

ENGEBRETSON, DOUGLAS KENNETH, architect, interior designer; b. Dawson, Minn., Nov. 5, 1946; s. Melvin Kenneth and Mary Louise (Jackson) Engebretson; m. Kathleen Stella Jefferies, June 14, 1969; children: Leif Erik, Kristin Ann. BArch, U. Ariz., 1969. Registered arch., Mass., Vt., N.H., Conn., N.Y., R.I., Maine. Draftsman William B. Tabler, FAIA, NYC, summer 1969, Wheeler Petterson Coffeen, Tucson, 1968-69; assoc. Alderman & MacNeish, West Springfield, Mass., 1970-78; pres. Tessier Assocs., Springfield, 1978—. Mem. Mass. Bd. Registration Archs., 1996—, chair, 2002—; dir. Nat. Coun. Archtl. Registration Bds., 2000—03, nat. sec., 2003—05, 2nd v.p., 2005—06, 1st v.p., 2006—07, pres., 2007—; corporator Chicopee Savs. Bank, Mass., 1996—, trustee, 2000—06, mem. bd. investment, 2005—06, dir., 2006—. Prin. works include Putnam Vocat. Tech. Sch., Springfield, Palmer HS and Elem. Schs., Cmty. Savs. Bank, South Hadley, Mass., Ring Nursing Home, Springfield, Mt. Everett Regional Sch., Sheffield, Mass., Heritage Bank Hdqrs., Holyoke, Mass.; co-author: Norway, 1978. Mem. Zoning Bd. Appeals, Southampton, Mass., 1976—84, Pers. Policy and Procedures Bd., 1983—85; trustee Brightside Families and Chidren, West Springfield, 1992—96; trustee, bd. tribunes Sta. WGBY-TV, Springfield, 1992—2001, chmn., 2000; trustee Colony Club, 2001—, bd. govs., 2002—; bd. dirs. Sisters Providence Health Sys. Found., 1999—2005; trustee Bay Path Coll., Longmeadow, Mass., 1991—2007. Recipient Philanthropist to Distinction award, Nat. Soc. Fundraising Execs., 1996. Fellow: AIA (nat. dir. 1986—89, nat. sec. 1991—92, pres. New Eng. regional coun. 1985—86, pres. western Mass. chpt. 1980—82, Richard Upjohn fellow 1992); mem.: Mass. State Assn. Archs. (pres. 1982—83), Rotary (pres. 1985—86, Group Study Exch. award to Norway 1978). Republican. Lutheran. Home: 6 Madison Ave Southampton MA 01073-9520 Office: Tessier Assoc Inc Tower Sq Ste 250 1500 Main St PO Box 15169 Springfield MA 01115-5169 Office Phone: 413-736-5857. Business E-Mail: douglase@tessierarchitects.com.

ENGEL, ALISON LANGE, marketing executive; b. 1973; Grad., Wharton Sch. of Bus. Former investment banker Goldman Sachs; mktg. dir. Massive Inc. Named one of 40 under 40, Advt. Age, 2007. Mem.: The Advt. Women of NY. Office: Massive Inc 632 Broadway 8th Fl New York NY 10018 Office Phone: 212-228-2296. Office Fax: 212-228-2161.*

ENGEL, AMY J., corporate financial executive; BS in Bus., SUNY, Buffalo, 1977, MBA in Fin., 1978. Treasury analyst Kennecott Cooper, Stamford, Conn., Perkin Elmer, Tinton Falls, NJ, Carborundum Co., Niagara Falls, NY; with Philip Morris Internat., 1981, supr. treas. ops., mgr. fin. planning and analysis, asst. treas.; dir. corp. financing Philip Morris Mgmt. Corp., 1990, asst. treas. corp. financing, mng. dir. global corp. fin., mng. dir. global risk mgmt., 1999; v.p., treas. Altria Grp., Inc., 2002—. Office: Altria Grp Inc 120 Park Ave New York NY 10017

ENGEL, ANDREW GEORGE, neurologist; b. Budapest, Hungary, July 12, 1930; s. Alexander and Alice Julia (Gluck) E.; m. Nancy Jean Brombacher, Aug. 15, 1958; children: Lloyd William, Andrew George. BSc, McGill U., Montreal, 1953, MD, 1955. Diplomate: Am. Bd. Internal Medicine, Am. Bd. Psychiatry and Neurology. Intern Phila. Gen. Hosp., 1955—56; sr. asst. surgeon, clin. asso. USPHS, NIH, Bethesda, Md., 1958-59; fellow in neuropathology Columbia U., NYC, 1962-64; with Mayo Clinic, Rochester, Minn., 1956-57, 60-62; cons. Rochester, Minn., 1965—; prof. neurology Mayo Med. Sch., Rochester, 1973—, William L. McKnight-3M prof. neurosci., 1984—; disting. investigator Mayo Clinic, 1995—. Mem. sci. adv. com. Muscular Dystrophy Assn., 1973-99; mem. rev. com. NIH, 1977-81. Mem. editl. bd. Neurology, 1973-77, Annals Neurology, 1978-84, 90-95, Muscle and Nerve, 1978-97, 00-, Jour. Neuropathology, 1981-83, 96-00, European Neurology, 1989-2005, Jour. Neuroimmunology, 1991-98, Molecular Neurobiology, 1997—; assoc. editor Neuromuscular Disorders, 1998-2006, Neurology, 2007—; contbr. over 350 articles to med. jours. Served with USPHS, 1957-59. Mem. Am. Acad. Neurology (hon.), Am. Neurol. Assn. (hon.), Am. Soc. Cell Biology, Soc. Neurosci., AAAS, Inst. of Medicine of Nat. Acad. Sci., 2004, European, German and Spanish Neurologic Assoc. (hon.) Home: 2027 Lenwood Dr SW Rochester MN 55902-1051 Office: Mayo Clinic 200 1st St SW Rochester MN 55905-0002

ENGEL, BARBARA ALPERN, history professor; BA in Russian Studies, CCNY, 1965; MA in Russian Studies, Harvard U., 1967; PhD in Rusian History, Columbia U., 1974. Part-time instr. Drew U., Madison, NJ, 1972—73; instr. Columbia U., NYC, 1974; asst. prof. Sarah Lawrence Coll., 1974—76, U. Colo., Boulder, 1976—82, assoc. prof., 1982—92, prof., 1992—, disting. prof., dir. Ctrl. and Ea. European studies, 1993—95, chair dept. history, 1995—98. Author, co-editor: Five Sisters: Women Against the Tsar, 1975; author: Spanish transl., 1980, new edit., 1992, Mothers and Daughters: Women of the Intelligentsia in Nineteenth Century Russia, 1983; author, co-editor: Russia's Women: Accomodation, Resistance, Transformation, 1991; author: Between the Fields and the City: Women, Work and Family in Russia, 1861-1914, 1994, paperback edit., 1996; co-editor: A Revolution of their Own. Voices of Women in Soviet History, 1998; cons. editor Feminist Studies, 1979—98, mem. editl. bd. Frontiers, 1980—86, Slavic Rev., 1996—2001; contbr. articles. Recipient Heldt Article award, 1991, cert. tchg. excellence, Mortar Bd. Sr. Honor Soc., 1994, Heldt prize for Outstanding Achievement in Slavic Studies, AWSS, 1996, numerous other awards, grants; Wallenberg fellow, Rutgers Ctr. Hist. Analysis, 1995, fellow, John Simon Guggenheim Meml. Found., 2003, Sr. Exch. grant with the Soviet Union, IREX, 1985, 1987, 1991, Fulbright-Hays tng. grant, Faculty Rsch. Abroad program, 1987, Woodrow Wilson fellow, 1991, John D. and Catherine T. MacArthur Found. grantee, 1993—95, NEH fellow, 2003—. Mem.: Am. Assn. for Advancement of Slavic Studies, We. Assn. Women Historians (book prize com. 1990), Internat. Fedn. Socs. Rsch. Women's History (mem. U.S. com. 1988—91), Am. Hist. Assn. (com. on women historians 1987—89, mem. profl. divsn. 1990—92, mem. program com. 1994—95), Phi Beta Kappa. Office: Univ Colo Dept History 234 UCB Boulder CO 80309-0234 Office Phone: 303-492-6831. E-mail: barbara.engel@colorado.edu.*

ENGEL, BERNARD THEODORE, psychologist, educator; b. Chgo., Apr. 18, 1928; s. Marvin I. and Hannah (Hollander) E.; m. Rae Goldberg, Mar. 10, 1951; children: Sandra E., Jeffrey P., Lauren C. BA, UCLA, 1954, PhD, 1956. Jr. rsch. psychologist UCLA, 1956; rsch. psychologist Inst. Psychosomatic and Psychiatric. Research and Tng., Michael Reese Hosp., Chgo., 1957-58; lectr. med. psychology, mem. sr. staff Cardiovasc. rsch. Inst., Sch. Medicine U. Calif., San Francisco, 1959-67; chief behavioral physiology sect., chief Lab. Behavioral Scis. Gerontology Research Center, Nat. Inst. Aging, NIH, Balt., 1967-95; assoc. prof. behavioral biology Johns Hopkins Sch. Medicine, Balt., 1970-82, prof., 1982—. Bd. dirs. Insts. for Behavioral Resources, Inc.; adj. prof. psychiatry and behavioral scis. Duke U. Sch. Medicine, Durham, N.C., 1999—. Contbr. 175 articles to sci. jours.; editorial bds. Applied Psychophysiology and Biofeedback, Jour. of Behavioral Medicine, Psychosomatic Medicine. Served US Army, 1950—52. Recipient award Pavlovian Soc., 1979; cert. of Appreciation, N.C. State Hwy. Patrol, 2003. Fellow AAAS, Gerontol. Sci.; mem. Soc. Psychophysiol. Rsch. (pres. 1970-71), Assn. Applied Psychophysiology and Biofeedback (pres. 1981-82, Disting. Scientist award 2001), Am. Psychosomatic Soc. (sec.-treas. 1981-85, pres. 1985-86, Patricia R. Barchas award in sociophysiology 1999), Gerontol. Soc. Am., Acad. Behavioral Medicine Rsch., Sigma Xi. Personal E-mail: btere@aol.com.

ENGEL, BRADFORD CHARLES, educational association administrator, secondary school educator; b. Washington, Feb. 28, 1959; s. Jane and W. King Engel, Wala Askanas (Stepmother); m. Jackie Engel, Sept. 15, 2001; children: Ryan Bender, Rachel Bender, Bradford. BA, U. of Md. Balt. County, 1982—89. Advanced Profl. Tchg. Cert. Md., 1999. Tchr. Kent Island H.S., Stevensville, Md., 1989—, v.p., 2005—; leadership devel. coord. Md. State Dept. of Edn., Balt., 1999—. Founder Mentor Adv. Program(M.A.P.), Stevensville, Md., 2001—. Author: (textbook) The 4 Challenges of Leadership, 2001, (book) Closing the Character Gap, 2002, (classroom management system) Quality Classroom Customer Service, 2003, Opportunity Dynamics, (children's book) Forever's Wish, 2006. Coord. Hand in Hand Project, The Achievement Challenge, Leadership Olympics, Stevensville, Md., 1989—. Named Md. Tchr. of Yr., Md. State Dept. of Edn., 2005—; recipient Kent Island H.S. Tchr. of the Yr., Kent Island H.S. Adminstrn., 1999, Queen Anne's County Tchr. of the Yr., Queen Anne's County Bd. of Edn., 2004. Achievements include founder of the leadership honors program for the state of Maryland. Office: Kent Island HS 900 Love Point Rd Stevensville MD 21666 Home Phone: 410-804-5448; Office Phone: 410-604-2070 4021. Business E-Mail: engelB@qacb.k12.md.us.*

ENGEL, DAVID LEWIS, lawyer; b. NYC, Mar. 31, 1947; s. Benjamin and Selma (Fruchtman) Engel; m. Edith Greetham Smith, June 9, 1973; children: Richard William, Jonathan Martin. AB in Gen. Studies in Econ. cum laude, Harvard U., 1967, JD magna cum laude, 1973; Disting. Naval grad., U.S. Naval Officer Candidate Sch., 1969. Bar: Mass. 1975. Law clk. to Judge Henry J. Friendly U.S. Ct. Appeals (2d cir.), NYC, 1973—74; assoc. Goodwin, Procter & Hoar, Boston, 1974—76, 1979—80; asst. prof. law Stanford U., Calif., 1976—79; ptnr. Berman, Dittmar & Engel, PC, Boston, 1980—84, Bingham McCutchen LLP, Boston, 1984—2005, co-chmn. corp. practice area, 2002—05, of counsel, 2005—. Pres. Harvard Law Rev., 1972—73. Mem. bd. visitors Stanford U. Law Sch., 1982—84; bd. dirs. Project Joy, 1995—2001. Lt. j.g. USNR, 1969—71. Recipient Sears prize, 1968, John Bingham Hurlbut award, 1979; John Harvard scholar, Harvard Coll. scholar, Nat. Merit scholar, 1964—67. Mem.: ABA, Boston Bar Assn. (working group of task force on revision of Mass. corp. statute 1987—2001), Phi Beta Kappa. Office: Bingham McCutchen LLP 150 Federal St Boston MA 02110-1713 Home Phone: 617-484-4382. Business E-Mail: david.engel@bingham.com.

ENGEL, DAVID WAYNE, lawyer, federal official; b. Salisbury, Md., Nov. 29, 1956; s. Robert Peter Engel and Joan (King) Bradshaw; m. Laura Marie Tuck, June 25, 1983; children: Michael Andrew, Jennifer Lynn, Matthew Alan. AB, William & Mary Coll., 1978; JD, Washington & Lee U., 1981; LLM, Judge Advocate Gen.'s Sch., Charlottesville, Va., 1988. Bar: Va. 1981, U.S. Dist. Ct. (ea. and we. dists.) Va. 1981, U.S. Ct. Mil. Appeals 1981, U.S. Ct. Appeals (4th cir.) 1981, U.S. Tax Ct. 1982, U.S. Ct. Appeals (5th cir.) 1985, Tex. 1985, U.S. Dist. Ct. (we. dist.) Tex. 1985, U.S. Supreme Ct. 1988, U.S. Ct. Appeals Vets. Claims 1990, U.S. Ct. Appeals (Fed. cir.) 1991, U.S. Ct. Appeals (10th cir.) 1998, U.S. Dist. Ct. (no. dist.) Okla. 1998. Capt. U.S. Army, 1981-89, active duty, 1989, USAR, 1989-97; appellate litigation atty. U.S. Dept. Vets. Affairs, Washington, 1989-92, spl. asst. to acting asst. gen. counsel, 1992-93; deputy asst. Gen. Coun., 1993-97; U.S. adminstrv. law judge Social Security Adminstrn., Office Hearings & Appeals, Tulsa, Okla, 1997—; col. USAF Res., 1997—; hearing office chief judge, 2002—. Office: 2 W 2nd Ste 450 Tulsa OK 74130-3111 Business E-Mail: david.engel@ssa.gov.

ENGEL, ELIOT LANZE, congressman; b. NYC, Feb. 18, 1947; s. Philip and Sylvia (Bleend) Engel; m. Patricia Ennis Engel; 3 children. BA in Hist., Hunter-Lehman Coll., 1969; MS in Guidance and Counseling, CUNY Herbert H. Lehman Coll., 1973; JD, NY Law Sch., 1987. Counselor, adv. NY Urban Corps, 1968; tchr., dept. chmn. NY Bd. Edn., 1969-76; guidance counselor NY Pub. Schs., 1973-75; mem. NY State Assembly, 1977—88, US Congress from 17th NY dist., 1989—, mem. energy and commerce com., mem. fgn. affairs com., chmn. western hemisphere subcommittee, vice chair Dem. homeland security task force, founder, co-chair oil and nat. security caucus, mem. Dem. health task force, mem. human rights caucus, mem. Hudson Valley caucus. Columnist Co-op City News, 1972. V.p. Park-East Ind. Dem. Club, NY, 1970-71; del. Bronx Com. for Dem. Voters, 1971-76, v.p., 1975-76; del., mem. steering com. Youth Caucus, Dem. Nat. Conv., 1972; v.p. Ind. Dems. of Co-op City, 1972-73, pres., 1974-75; committeeman Bronx County Dem. Com., NY, 1972; mem. exec. coun. NY State New Dem. Coalition, 1973-75; founder New Dem. Club Co-op City, 1975, pres., 1975-76; jud. del. NY Supreme Ct. Conv., 1st Jud. Dist., 1975-76, dist. leader, 1976. Recipient Man of Yr. award, FDR Ind. Dem. Club, 1976, Legislator of Yr., Children are Precious, 1990, Disting. Svc. award, Coun. Negro Women, Inc., Humanitarian award, United Field Reps. and Staff Union, Notable Ams. award, Historic Preservation of Am. Mem. United Fund Tchrs., Ams. for Dem. Action (bd. dirs. NY 1974), Zionist Orgn. Am., KP Democrat. Jewish. Office: US House Reps 2161 Rayburn House Office Bldg Washington DC 20515 Office Phone: 202-225-2464. Office Fax: 202-225-5513.*

ENGEL, FELIX BENEDIKT SALOMON, cell biologist, researcher; b. Berlin, July 5, 1971; s. Juergen Nast and Siegrid Engel. Degree, Walther-Rathenau-Oberschule, Berlin, Germany, 1990; diploma in Engring., Tech. U., Berlin, Germany, 1996, PhD, 2001. Postdoctoral fellow med. sch. Harvard U., Boston, 2001—05; jr. rsch. group leader Max-Planck-Inst. Heart and Lung Rsch., Bad Nauheim, Germany, 2006—. Co-founder, mem. sci. bd. bcd GmbH, Berlin, 1998—2003; instr. pediat. med. sch. Harvard U., 2005—; assoc. sci. rschr. Children's Hosp. Boston, 2005—; cons. in field. Contbr. articles to profl. jours. Recipient Trainee Abstract award, Am. Heart Assn., 2001; grantee, Charles H. Hood Found., 2006—07; Sofja Kovalevskaja grantee, Alexander von Humboldt Found., 2006—. Mem.: German Soc. Cell Biology, Am. Heart Assn. Achievements include patents for method to induce cardiomyocyte proliferation; research in 2-drug therapy in a rat model to treat myocardial infarction; discovery of p38 MAP kinase is a key negative regulator of cardiomyocyte proliferation; adult mammalian cardiomyocytes can undergo cell division. Home: Liebigstrasse 12 Bad Nauheim 61231 Germany Office: Max Planck Inst Heart and Lung Parkstrasse 1 Bad Nauheim 61231 Germany Home Phone: 011-49-6032-705248; Office Phone: 011-49-6032-705248. Business E-Mail: felix.engel@mpi-bn.mpg.de.

ENGEL, GERALD L., engineering educator; m. Doris Evelyn Smith, Aug. 22, 1964; children: Samantha Emily, Shannon Elliott. BS, Hampden-Sydney Coll., Va., 1964; MA, La. State U., Baton Rouge, 1965; EdD, Pa. State U., Univ. Park, 1974. Assoc. prof. Christopher Newport U., Newport News, Va., 1979—84, Old Dominion U., Norfolk, Va., 1978—79; head computing and stats. Va. Inst. Marine Sci., Gloucester Point, 1973—77; Leonhardt prof. of computer sci. and engring. U. Conn., Stamford, 1984—. Dir. CSAB Inc., Stamford, Conn., 1985—93, ABET Inc., Balt., 2001—06, Faulk Found., Middlebury, Conn., 2005—07; dep. divsn. dir. NSF, Arlington, Va., 1991—95. Soccer official Western Conn. Soccer Ofcls. Assn., 1988—2002; softball official Naugatuck Watersburg Softball Umpires Assocs., 1987—. Recipient Third Millennium Medal, IEEE, 2000, Meritorious Achievement Award in Accreditation Activities, IEEE Ednl. Activities Bd., 2003, Meritorious Svc. Award, IEEE Edn. Soc., 1999, Golden Core Award, IEEE Computer Soc., 1996. Fellow: IEEE (dir. Piscataway, NJ chpt. 1992—93, chair, conferences com. 2007—, pres. Computer Soc. 2005—05, pres. Soc. Social Implications of Tech. 1999—2000, Merwin Medal, IEEE Computer Soc. 2000), CSAB, Inc (pres. 2001—02), Assn. for Computing Machinery (Disting. Svc. award 1991); mem.: AAUP, Nat. Coun. Tchrs. of Math., Math. Assn. Am., Western Conn. Soccer Ofcls. Assn., Naugatuck-Waterbury Softball Umpires Assn. Avocation: travel. Office: U Conn Stamford 1 University Pl Stamford CT 06901-2315 Home Phone: 203-723-2651; Office Phone: 203-251-8431. Personal E-mail: g.engel@computer.org. Business E-Mail: gerald.engel@uconn.edu.

ENGEL, JEFFREY MARK, musician, music educator; b. NYC, Nov. 7, 1947; s. Walter Engel and Marianne Eisler. BA in Music, Ithaca Coll., NY, 1969; cert. in French lang., U. de la Sorbonne Nouvelle, Paris, 1976. Instrumental, vocal and classroom music tchr. Brooklyn Elem. and Jr. HS, Conn., 1969—71; cellist RI Philharmonic, Providence, 1971—72, Concerts Pasdeloup, Paris, 1976—86, Santa Fe Opera, 1981, 1983; cello instr. Indian Mountain Mid. Sch., Lakeville, Conn., 2001—06; adj. prof. Northwestern Conn. CC, Winsted, 2004—, U. Conn.-Torrington br., 2007—. Author: Singing Games & Singing Fun, 1972. Avocation: collecting books. Home: 123A Sharon-Goshen Turnpike West Cornwall CT 06796

ENGEL, JEROME, JR., neurologist, neuroscientist, psychiatry professor; b. Albany, NY, May 11, 1938; s. Jerome and Pauline (Feder) E.; m. Catherine Margaret Lambourne, Feb. 26, 1967; children: Sean, Jesse, Anasuya. BA, Cornell U., 1960; MD, Stanford U., 1965, PhD in Physiology, 1966. Diplomate Nat. Bd. Med. Examiners, Am. Bd. Qualification in EEG, Nat. Bd. Psychiatry and Neurology. Intern Ind. U., Indpls., 1966-67; resident in neurology Albert Einstein Coll. Medicine, Bronx, N.Y., 1967-68, 70-72; resident in EEG Nat. Hosp. Nervous and Mental Disease Queen Sq., London, 1971, Maudsley Hosp., London, 1972; attending neurologist, dir. electroencephalography labs. Bronx Mcpl. Hosp. Ctr., Hosp. Albert Einstein Coll. Medicine, 1972-76; attending neurologist, chief of epilepsy, clin. neurophysiology UCLA Hosp. and Clinics, 1976—; assoc. investigator lab. nuclear medicine of Lab. Biomed. and Environ. Scis. UCLA Med. Ctr., 1981—; dir. UCLA Seizure Disorder Ctr., 1994—; prof. psychiatry and biobehavioral medicine UCLA Sch. Medicine, 2005—. Staff assoc. NINDS NIH Lab. Perinatal Physiology, San Juan, P.R.; vis. asst. prof. dept. physiology and biophysics U. P.R. Sch. Medicine, 1968-69, Lab. Neural Control, Bethesda, Md., 1969-70; asst. prof. neurology Albert Einstein Coll. Medicine, Bronx, 1972-76, asst. prof. neurosci., 1974-76; assoc. prof. neurology UCLA Sch. Medicine, 1976-80, assoc. prof. anatomy, 1977-80, prof. neurology, neurobiology (formerly anatomy and cell biology), 1980—; assoc. investigator Lab. Nuclear Medicine, Lab. Biomed. and Environ. Scis., 1981—; chmn. internat. and coop. projects study sect. NIH, 1989-90, mem. biomed. scis. study sect., 1985-89, chmn., 1988-89; vis. prof. dept. anatomy Sydney U., 1984, Jonathan Sinay prof., 2002—; prof. psychiatry and behavioral scis., 2005—. Author: Epilepsy and Positron CT, Clinical Relevance for Diagnosis of Epilepsy, 1985, Surgical Treatment of the Epilepsies, 1987, Seizures and Epilepsy, 1989, Surgical Treatment of Epilepsies, 1993, (with others) Neurotransmitters, Seizures and Epilepsy II, 1984, Neurotransmitters, Seizures and Epilepsy II, 1984, Neurotransmitters, Seizures and Epilepsy III, 1986, The Epileptic Focus, 1987, Fundamental Mechanisms of Human Brain Function, 1987, Clinical Use of Emission Tomography in Focal Epilepsy, Current Problems in Epilepsy, Vol. 7, 1990, Neurotransmitters in Epilepsy, 1992, Molecular Neurobiology and Epilepsy, 1992, The Progressive Nature of Epilepsy, 1996, Epilepsy: a Comprehensive Textbook, 1998, Parallel Studies of Epileptogenesis in Human Tissue and Animal Models, 1998, Brain Plasticity and Epilepsy, 2000, 01, The Goal of Epilepsy Surgery, No Seizures, No Side Effects, As Soon As Possible, 2004, Atlas of EEG Patterns, 2004, Epilepsy: Global Issues for the Practicing Neurologist, 2005, Generalized Seizures, From Clinical Phenomenology to Underlying Systems and Networks, 2006; chief editor: Advances in Neurobiology of Epilepsy, 1989-91, World Federation of Neurology, Seminars in Neurology, 2006-; assoc. editor: Jour. Clin. Neurophysiology, 1983—, Epilepsy Rsch., 1985—, Epilepsy Advances, 1985-87, Brain Topography, 1990—, Epilepsia, 1994—; contbr. over 140 chpts. to books including Functional Brain Imaging, 1988, Anatomy of Epileptogenesis, 1989, EEG Handbook, rev. series vol. 4, 1990, Comprehensive Epileptology, 1990, Generalized Epilepsy, 1990, Neurotransmitters in Epilepsy, Epilepsy Research (Supplement), 1992, Molecular Neurobiology and Epilepsy;, Encyclopedia of the Neurological Sciences, 2003, The Goal of Epilepsy Surgery, 2004; contbr. over 240 articles to profl. jours. including New Issues in Neurosci., Neurology, Jour. Neurosurg., Jour. Epilepsy, Epilepsia, Can. Jour. Neurol. Sci., Radiology, Jour. Cerebral Blood Flow Metabolism, Acta Neurochirugica, Jour. Clin. Psychiatry. Active profl. adv. bd. Epilepsy Found. Internat. League Against Epilepsy, 1988—. N.Y. State Regents scholar, 1956-60, NIH traineeship, summer 1962, predoctoral fellowship, 1964, postdoctoral fellowship, 1965-66, career devel. award 1972-76; recipient Epilepsy Found. Am. award, 1963, Stiftung Michael prize, 1982; Fulbright scholar, 1971-72, fellow in neurology Sch. Medicine Stanford U., 1965-66, Lab. Applied Neuophysiology, C.N.R.S., Marseilles, France, 1966, Dagan Lectr. Winter Conf. on Brain Rsch., 1981, John Guggenheim fellow, 1983-84, Hanna lectr. Case-Western Reserve, 1983, First Aird lectr. U. Calif. San Francisco, 1985, First Cox lectr. Albert Einstein Coll. Medicine, 1985, First Vaajasalo lectr. and award, Kuopio, Finland, 1987, Aring lectr. U. Cin. Med. Ctr., 1987, First Hans Berger lectr. Internat. Congress of EEG and Clin. Neurophysiology, 1990; Covy Williams lectr. Cleve Clinic, 1992; Hans Berger lectr. Med. Coll. Va., 1993, Javits Investigator award, NIH, 2003. Fellow: Am. Acad. Neurology (self assessment epilepsy task force chair 1990—96, Mythili Oration 2000, Hoyer lectr. 2002, Mary Ann Lee lectr. U. Calgary); mem.: AAAS, Liga Chilena contra la Epilepsia, Hong Kong Neurol. Soc., Western Electroencephalography Soc. (Wilder Penfield lectr. 2000), Soc. for Neurosci. (neurobiology of disease workshop organizing com. 1989—90), Nat. Assn. Epilepsy Ctrs. (bd. dirs. 1988—, treas. 1990—94), Ea. Assn. Electroencephalographers (Kershman lectr. 1994, first Judith Hoyer lectr. 2002, Dreifuss lectr. 2003), Internat. Soc. Cerebral Blood Flow and Metabolism, Epilepsy Support Assn. Ethopia (hon.), Australian Assn. Neurologists (hon.), Can. Soc. Clin. Neurophysiologists (hon.), Turkish Epilepsy Soc. (hon.), All-Russian Assn. Neurologists (hon.), Yugoslavian League Against Epilepsy (hon.), Internat. League Against Epilepsy (program com. 1986—88, commn. on epilepsy surgery 1989—93, chmn. commn. on neurobiology of epilepsy 1989—93, treas. 1994—97, pres. 1997—2001, co-chair global campaign against epilepsy 2001—05, amb. for epilepsy award 1991), Internat. Fedn. EEG and Clin. Neurophysiology Socs. (program com. 1988—90, chmn. com. on guidelines for long-term monitoring for epilepsy 1989—), Internat. Brain Rsch. Orgn., Am. Physiol. Soc., Am. Neurol. Assn. (mem. program com. 1987—90), Am. Epilepsy Soc. (sec. 1979—82, 2nd v.p. 1982—83, 1st v.p. 1983—84, pres. 1984—85, councillor 1985—86, v.p. to Internat. League Against Epilepsy 1990—93, William G. Lennox lectr. 1990, Clin. Investigator award 1996, William Lennox award 1999), Am. EEG Soc. (councillor 1984—87, chmn. rsch. fellowship com. 1988—91, pres. elect 1991—92, pres. 1992—93, Pierre Gloor award 1999), Russian League Against Epilepsy. Achievements include research on basic mechanisms of epilepsy and epilepsy related behavior, particularly involving surgical treatment of partial seizures and use of new technology such as positron emission tomography and advanced EEG telemetry. Home: 10521 Seabury Ln Los Angeles CA 90077-2441 Office: UCLA Sch Medicine Reed Neurol Rsch Ctr # 1250 710 Westwood Plz Los Angeles CA 90095-8353 Home Phone: 310-441-7783; Office Phone: 310-825-5745. Business E-Mail: engel@ucla.edu.

ENGEL, JOHN, lawyer; b. NYC, Mar. 8, 1943; s. Ralph and Ann (Unterman) E.; m. Gayle Iselin, May 25, 1980; children: Samuel Albert, Maxwell Robert. BA, Yale U., 1965; JD, Georgetown U., 1971. Bar: D.C. 1971, Va. 1984. Atty. The Rouse Co., Columbia, Md., 1971-75, Shaw Pittman Potts & Trowbridge, Washington, 1976-84, ptnr., 1984—2005; ptnr., Real Estate practice Pillsbury Winthrop Shaw Pittman, Washington, 2005—. Mem. regional adv. bd. Chgo. Title Ins. Co. Chmn. Va. Govt. affairs Internat. Coun. of Shopping, 1987-89; mem. task force City of Alexandria, Va.; bd. dirs. Family Respite Ctr. Mem. ABA, No. Va. Bldg. Industry Assn., DC Bldg. Industry Assn., Internat. Council of Shopping Ctrs. Office: Pillsbury Winthrop Shaw Pittman 2300 N St NW Washington DC 20037-1128 Office Phone: 202-663-8863. Office Fax: 202-663-8864. Business E-Mail: john.engel@pillsburylaw.com.

ENGEL, RALPH MANUEL, lawyer; b. NYC, May 13, 1944; s. Werner Herman and Ruth Fredericke (Friedländer) E.; m. Diane Linda Weinberg, Aug. 10, 1968; children— Eric M., Daniel C., Julie R. BA in Econs. with highest honors, NYU, 1965, JD, 1968. Bar: N.Y. 1968, U.S. Supreme Ct. 1972. Assoc. Gilbert, Segall and Young, NYC, 1968—71, Trubin Sillcocks Edelman & Knapp, NYC, 1971—76; assoc., then ptnr. Summit Rovins & Feldesman and predecessor firms, NYC, 1976—91; ptnr. Rosen & Reade, LLP, NYC, 1991—2001, Sonnenshein Nath & Rosenthal LLP, NYC, 2001—. Lectr. Sch. Law, Fordham U., 1990—91. Contbr. articles to legal and other publs.; editor-in-chief The Commentator, NYU, 1968. Mem. Planning Bd., Larchmont, NY, 1992—. Fellow Am. Coll. Trust and Estate Counsel; mem. N.Y. State Bar Assn. (trust and estate law sect. com. on practice and ethics 1991—, vice-chmn., 2006—, elder law sect., com. on guardianships and fiduciaries 1991-97, com. on estates and tax planning 1997—), Estate Planning Coun. Westchester County (bd. dirs. 1985-91). Jewish. Home and Office: 6 Rockwood Dr Larchmont NY 10538-2537 Office: Sonnenschein Nath & Rosenthal LLP 1221 Ave of the Americas New York NY 10020 Office Phone: 212-768-6700, 914-834-6576. Personal E-mail: engelesq@yahoo.com. Business E-Mail: rengel@sonnenschein.com.

ENGEL, RICHARD L., career officer; b. LA, July 2, 1946; s. Richard Leroy and Margret Ellen (Wilson) E.; m. Connie Jean Ricks, Sept. 8, 1973; children: Lindsey, Jennifer, Shelly. BS in Mech. Engring., Tex. A&M U., 1968; MS in Indsl. and Sys. Mgmt. Engring., Ariz. State U., Tucson, 1975; student, Air Force Test Pilot Sch., 1976-77, Armed Forces Staff Coll., 1981; M in Nat. Security Strategic Studies, Naval War Coll., 1988. Commd. 2d lt. USAF, 1968, advanced through grades to maj. gen., 1996, pilot spl. ops. South Vietnam, 1970-71, instr. pilot Williams AFB, Ariz., 1971-74; air staff officer Hdqs. Air Tng. Command, Randolph AFB, Tex., 1974-76; advanced simulator rsch. flight test officer Air Force Human Resources Lab., Williams AFB, 1978-81; chief of acads. Air Force Test Pilot Sch., Edwards AFB, Calif., 1981-83; dep. dir. F-16 LANTIRN Test Program, Edwards AFB, 1983-85; comdr. F-16 and LANTIRN Combined Test Forces, Edwards AFB, 1985-87; divsn. chief weapons sys. divsn. Office of Legis. Liaison for Sec. of Air Force, Washington, 1988-89; comdr. 3246th Test Wing, Air Force Devel. Test Ctr., Eglin AFB, Fla., 1989-92, 412th Test Wing, Edwards AFB, 1992-93, Air Force Flight Test Ctr., Edwards AFB, 1993-98; commandant Indsl. Coll. of the Armed Forces, Ft. McNair, 1998—2000; ret. Decorated Legion of Merit, D.F.C. with two oak leaf clusters, Air medal with nine oak leaf clusters, Air Force Commendation medal. Mem. AIAA, Soc. Exptl. Test Pilots.

ENGEL, TALA, lawyer; b. NYC; d. Volodia Vladimir Boris and Risia (Modelevska) E.; m. James Colias, Nov. 22, 1981 (dec. Nov. 1989). AA, U. Fla., 1952; BA in Russian and Spanish, U. Miami, 1954; JD, U. Miami, Coral Gables, Fla., 1957; postgrad., Middlebury Coll., 1953. Bar: Fla. 1957, Ill. 1962, D.C. 1982, U.S. Dist. Ct. (so. dist.) Fla. 1957, U.S. Dist. Ct. (no. dist.) Ill. 1962, U.S. Supreme Ct., 1965. Pvt. practice in immigration law, Miami, Fla., 1957—61, Chgo., 1966—86, Washington, 1987—89, Chgo., 1990—93, Washington, 1993—2002, Miami, Fla., 2002—. Atty. Immigration and Naturalization Svc., Chgo., 1961-62; parole agt. Ill. Youth Commn., Chgo., 1963-66. Author: The Memoirs of a Woman Traveling to the Ukraine to find Relatives, 2002, The Janitor and the Junkman, 2006; editor The Lawyer, 1956; mem. editl. bd. Miami Law Quar., 1955-57, 10 ML Q 110 Criminal Law, 10 ML Q 608 Ins. Law, 1955-56. Bd. dirs. Cordi-Marian Settlement, Chgo., 1977-93, Kiwanis Internat., 2006-. Mem.: Fla. Bar Assn., Fed. Bar Assn., Chgo. Bar Assn. (entertainment com. 1971—72, devel. of law com. 1985—87), Ill. Bar Assn. (gen. assembly 1984—86), Fla. Bar Found. (life), Chgo. Bar Found. (life), Nu Beta Epsilon, Alpha Lambda Delta. Avocations: theater, singing, computers, Russian and Spanish languages, travel in 102 countries. Home: 601 Three Islands Blvd #215 Hallandale Beach FL 33009 Office Phone: 954-455-7044. Personal E-mail: talaengel@aol.com.

ENGEL, THOMAS WALTER, chemistry professor; b. Yokohama, Japan, Apr. 2, 1942; came to U.S., 1947; s. George Walter and Juliane (Urban) E.; m. Esther Neeser, Aug. 23, 1979; 1 child, Alex. BS, Johns Hopkins U., 1963, MS, 1964; PhD, U. Chgo., 1969; Dr. rer. nat. habil., U. Munich, Fed. Republic Germany, 1979. Instr. Tech. U. Clausthal, Clausthal-Zellerfeld, Fed. Republic Germany, 1969-75, U. Munich, 1975-78; staff mem. IBM Rsch. Lab., Zurich, Switzerland, 1978-80; assoc. prof. chemistry U. Wash., Seattle, 1979-84, prof., 1984—, chmn. dept. chemistry, 1987-90. Contbr. papers and book chpts. to profl. publs. Recipient numerous grants NSF, Air Force Office Sci. Rsch., Office Naval Rsch, Am. Chem Soc. award in Colloid or Surface Chemistry, 1995; sr. rsch. award, Alexander von Humboldt Found. Mem. Am. Chem. Soc. (Surface Chemistry award 1995), Am. Vacuum Soc. Office: U Wash Dept Chemistry Box 1700 Seattle WA 98195 Business E-Mail: engel@chem.washington.edu.

ENGEL, WALBURGA See VON RAFFLER-ENGEL, WALBURGA

ENGEL, WILLIAM KING, neurologist, educator; b. St. Louis, Nov. 19, 1930; s. William Ernst and Opal (King) E.; m. Valerie Askanas; children: W. Keith, Peter J., Bradford C., Eve M. Kerr. BA, Johns Hopkins U., 1951; MD, C.M., McGill U., 1955; MD (hon.), L'univ. d'Aix Marseille II, 1987. Diplomate: Am. Bd. Neurology and Psychiatry, Pan. Am. Med. Assn. (hon. life mem.). Intern U. Mich. Hosp., 1955-56; clin. assoc. Nat. Inst. Neurol. Diseases and Blindness, 1956-59; clin. clk. Nat. Hosp., London, 1959-60; with Nat. Inst. Neurol. Diseases and Stroke, 1960-81, chief med. neurology, 1963-78, chief neuromuscular diseases, 1978-81; clin. prof. neurology George Washington U., 1969-81; prof. neurology and pathology, chief div. neuromuscular diseases, dept. neurology U. So. Calif. Sch. Medicine, Los Angeles, 1981—; mem. med. bd. NIH, 1968-69; founding dir. U. So. Calif. Neuromuscular Center, Hosp. of Good Samaritan, 1981—. Mem. med. adv. bd. St. Jude's Children's Rsch. Hosp., Memphis, 1970-76, Myasthenia Gravis Found., 1970—, L.A. chpt. Muscular Dystropy Assn., 1981—, Amyotrophic Lateral Sclerosis Nat. Found., 1971-85, Amyotrophic Lateral Sclerosis Soc. Am., 1980-85, mem. sci. adv. bd., 1982-85; vis. prof., invited lectr., advisor internat. congresses in Europe, S.Am., Can., Australia, Far East; cons. Nat. Naval Med. Ctr. Former mem. editl. bd. Archives of Neurology; contbr. over 800 articles to profl. jours., poems to mags. Past pres. Citizens Assn., Bethesda, Md., Longhouse chief YMCA Indian Guides, 1965-66; past chmn. troop com. Boy Scouts Am.; mem. edn. adv. bd. Phronesis, Spain; nat. corp. mem. Muscular Dystrophy Assn., 1985-88, nat. v.p. 1988— , med. adv. bd. Los Angeles chpt., 1981—, bd. dirs. 1985—, chmn., 2001—; mem. med. bd. The Myositis Assn., 1995—, mem. med. adv. bd., 1997—. Recipient Meritorious Service medal USPHS, 1971, Gaetano Conte Gold medal for clin. rsch., 1999, Lifetime Achievement award World Fedn. Neurology, 2002, Lifetime Achievement award Neuropathy Assn., 2006, various awards from Italian me. socs. Fellow Am. Acad. Neurology (S. Weir Mitchell award 1962; pres. VI Internat. Congress Neuromuscular Diseases 1986); mem. AMA, Histochem. Soc., Am. Soc. Cell Biology, Soc. Neurosci., Am. Assn. Neuropathologists, Soc. for Neurosci., World Commn. Neuromuscular Disease (exec. com.), Am. Neurol. Assn., LA County Med. Assn., Societè Belge d'Electromyographie (assoc.), Asociación de Distrofia Muscular de la Republica Argentina (hon. pres.), Societè Française de Neurologie (hon.). Office: U So Calif Neuromuscular Ctr Good Samaritan Hosp 637 Lucas Ave Los Angeles CA 90017-1912 Office Phone: 213-975-9950.

ENGELAGE, JAMES ROLAND, management consultant; b. Springfield, Mo., Dec. 5, 1945; s. Roland C. and Dorothy (Dixter) E.; m. Marcia Cooley, July 5, 1968. BS, S.W. Mo. State U., 1965; MS, Troy U., 1968; PhD, St. Louis U., 1977; MA, Ctrl. Mich. U., 1978. Dept. chmn. Montgomery (Ala.) Pub. Schs., 1968-69; asst. prin. Francis Howell Sch. Dist., St. Charles, 1969-74, asst. supt., 1974-75; commd. 2d lt. U.S. Army, 1975—93, advanced through grades to col., 1987; dean Randolph Macon Acad., Front Royal, Va., 1993-94; CEO JAMARC Mgmt. Corp., Winchester, Va., 1994—2003. Evening dir. Temple Schs., Silver Spring, Md., 1982-84; adj. prof. Park Coll., Ft. Myer, Va., 1980-82. Editor: Operation Desert Shield, 1992; contbr. articles to publs. Recipient legion of merit award Dept. Army, Washington, 1993. Mem. Res. Officers Assn. (pres. Chgo. chpt. 1992, Louisville chpt. 1993), Civil Air Patrol (capt. 1973-74), Lions Club (charter 1970-71), Civitans. Republican. Home: 411 Windsor Ln Winchester VA 22602-2333

ENGELBERG, GAIL MAY, fine arts patron; m. Alfred B. Engelberg, May 5, 1990. Trustee Engelberg Charitable Found.; bd. trustee Solomon R. Guggenheim Mus., NYC; bd. dir. Jazz at Lincoln Ctr., NYC. Office: Guggenheim Mus Trustees 1071 Fifth Ave New York NY 10128-0173 also: The Engelberg Foundation 1050 N Lake Way Palm Beach FL 33480-3252 Office Phone: 212-877-4050.

ENGELBRECHT, RUDOLF, electrical engineering educator; b. Atlanta, Apr. 18, 1928; s. Walter and Dorothea Engelbrecht; m. Christel M. Kluth, Sept. 10, 1050; children: Richard, Rolf, Erika. BS, Ga. Inst. Tech., 1951, MSEE, 1953; PhD in Elec. Engring., Oreg. State U., 1979. Mem. tech. staff Bell Labs., Whippany, N.J., 1953—60, supr. Murray Hill, N.J., 1961—63, dept. head, 1964—69; dir. RCA Tech. Ctr., Somerville, N.J., 1970—72; group leader RCA Labs., Zurich, Switzerland, 1972—77; assoc. prof. Oreg. State U., Corvallis, 1977—93. Co-author: Microwave Devices, 1969; contbr. articles to profl. jours. Named to Oreg. State U. Engring. Hall of Fame, 1998. Fellow: IEEE (life Centennial award 1984, Third Millennium medal 2000); mem.: Sigma Xi. Achievements include patents in field. Office: Oreg State U Dept Elec Computer Eng Corvallis OR 97331

ENGELBREIT, MARY, art licensing entrepreneur; b. St. Louis, 1952; m. Phil Delano, 1977; 2 children. Illustrator greeting card cos., 1983; founder, pres. Mary Engelbreit Studios Retail and Pub. Cos., St. Louis, 1983—; founder, head The Mary Engelbreit Store; founder, creator Mary Engelbreit's Home Companion mag., 1996—. Illustrator The Snow Queen, 1993, The Night Before Christmas, 2001. Office Phone: 314-726-5646.

ENGELHARDT, ALBERT GEORGE, physicist; b. Toronto, Ont., Can., Mar. 17, 1935; came to U.S., 1957, naturalized, 1965; s. Samuel and Rose (Menkes) E.; m. Elzbieta Szajkowska, June 14, 1960; children— Frederick, Leonard, Michael. BASc., U. Toronto, 1958; MS, U. Ill., 1959, PhD (grad. fellow), 1961. Rsch. asst. elec. engring. U. Ill., Urbana, 1958-61; staff rsch. and devel. ctr. engr. Westinghouse Electric Co., Pitts., 1961-70, mgr., 1966-69, fellow scientist, 1969-70; sr. rsch. scientist, group leader Hydro-Que. Rsch. Inst., Varennes, Canada, 1970-74; mem. staff Los Alamos Sci. Lab., 1974-86; adj. prof. elec. engring. Tex. Tech. U., Lubbock, 1976—; pres., chief exec. officer, founder Enfitek, Inc., Los Alamos, N.Mex., 1982—. Vis. prof. U. Que., 1970-77 Contbr. articles to profl. jours. Group leader Boy Scouts Can., 1972-74. Mem. IEEE Nuclear and Plasma Scis. Soc., Am. Phys. Soc. Home and Office: 549 Bryce Ave Los Alamos NM 87544-3607 *Since 1959 my basic research interest has been plasma physics and concomitantly nuclear fusion. The importance of the latter is that it shows great promise for providing us with renewable energy resources with acceptably small environmental and ecological perturbation.*

ENGELHARDT, HUGO TRISTRAM, JR., physician, educator; b. New Orleans, Apr. 27, 1941; s. Hugo Tristram and Beulah Engelhardt; m. Susan Gay Malloy, Nov. 25, 1965; children: Elisabeth, Christina, Dorothea. BA, U. Tex., Austin, 1963, PhD, 1969; MD with honors, Tulane U., New Orleans, 1972; Dr (hon.), U. Medicine and Pharmacy Gr. T. Popa, Iasi, Romania, 2005. Asst. prof. U. Tex. Med. Br., 1972-75, assoc. prof., 1975-77; mem. Inst. Med. Humanities, 1973-77; Rosemary Kennedy prof. philosophy of medicine Georgetown U., 1977-82; sr. rsch. scholar Kennedy Inst. Ctr. for Bioethics, Washington, 1977-82; prof. depts. internal medicine, cmty. medicine and ob-gyn. Baylor Coll. Medicine, Houston, 1983-2001, prof. emeritus, 2001—; mem. Ctr. for Med. Ethics and Health Policy, Houston, 1983-2001; prof. dept. philosophy Rice U., Houston, 1983—. Chmn. adv. panel on infertility prevention and treatment for office of tech. assessment of the U.S. Congress, 1986-87; vis. scholar Internat. Akad. für Philosophie, Liechtenstein, 1997, Liberty Fund, spring, 1998. Author: Mind Body: A Categorial Relation, 1973, The Foundations of Bioethics, 1986, rev. edit., 1996, Bioethics and Secular Humanism, 1991, The Foundations of Christian Bioethics, 2000; co-author: Bioethics: Readings and Cases, 1987; assoc. editor Ency. of Bioethics, 1978—83; assoc. editor Jour. Medicine and Philosophy, 1974—84; mem. editl. adv. bd.: Teaching Philosophy, 1975; mem. editl. bd. Poiesis & Praxis, 2001—, Chinese and Internat. Philosophy Medicine, 1998—; editor: Jour. Medicine and Philosophy, 1984—, (series) Philos. Studies in Contemporary Culture, 1992, Philosophy and Medicine series, 1974—, Clin. Med. Ethics, 1987—2002, Evaluation and Explanation in the Biomedical Sciences, 1975, Philosophical Medical Ethics, 1977, Mental Health, 1978, Clinical Judgment, 1979, Concepts of Health and Disease, 1981, New Knowledge in the Biomedical Sciences, 1982, Scientific Controversies, 1987, The Use of Human Beings in Research, 1988, Sicherheit und Freiheit, 1990, Hegel Reconsidered, 1994, The Philosophy of Medicine, 2000, Allocating Scarce Medical Resources, 2002, Global Bioethics, 2006; senior editor: Christian Bioethics, 1995—. Mem. bioethics com. Nat. Found. March of Dimes, 1975—. Recipient McDonald-Merrill-Ketcham Meml. Excellence award in law and medicine, 2003; Fulbright fellow, 1969-70, Woodrow Wilson vis. fellow, 1988; fellow Inst. for Advanced Studies, Berlin, 1988-89. Mem. Am. Philos. Assn., European Acad. Scis. and Arts. Office: Rice U Dept Philosophy PO Box 1892 Houston TX 77251-1892 Office Phone: 713-348-2491. Business E-Mail: htengelh@rice.edu.

ENGELHARDT, IRL F., coal company executive; b. Oct. 19, 1946; m. Suzanne C.; children: Joel, Erin, Evan. BS in Acctg., U. Ill., 1968; MBA, So. Ill. U., 1971. From mem. staff to pres., CEO Peabody Energy, St. Louis, 1979-90, pres., CEO, 1990—98, chmn., CEO, 1998—2005, chmn., 2006—. Bd. dir. Williams Cos.; bd. dir. Fed. Reserve Bank of St. Louis, dep. chmn. 2006. Mem. Nat. Mining Assn. (bd. dirs., chmn. 1995-96), Nat. Coal Assn. (chmn. 1995-96), Internat. Energy Agy. (coal industry adv. bd., chmn., special com. mem.), Nat. Assn. Mfrs. (bd. dirs.), Coal Utilization Rsch Group (co-chmn.), Coal Based Stockholders Group (co-chmn.), St. Louis Arts and Edn. Council, St. Louis Area Council (exec. bd.), Boy Scouts of Am. Office: Peabody Energy 701 Market St Saint Louis MO 63101 Fax: 314-342-7797. E-mail: lengelhardt@peabodyenergy.com.*

ENGELHARDT, JOHN HUGO, lawyer, bank executive; b. Houston, Feb. 3, 1946; s. Hugo Tristram and Beulah Lillie (Karbach) E.; m. Jasmin Inge Nestler, Nov. 12, 1976; children: Angelique D., Sabrina N. BA, U. Tex., 1968; JD, St. Marys U., San Antonio, 1973. Bar: Tex. 1973. Tchr. history Pearsall HS, Tex., 1968-69; pvt. practice New Braunfels, Tex., 1973-75, 82—; exam. atty. Comml. Title Co., San Antonio, 1975-78, San Antonio Title Co., 1978-82. Adv. dir. M Bank Brenham, Tex., 1983-89. Fellow Coll. State Bar Tex.; mem. ABA, Pi Gamma Mu. Republican. Roman Catholic.

ENGELHARDT, LEROY A., retired paper company executive; b. Saginaw, Mich., Mar. 15, 1924; s. Herman J. and Alma (Engelhard) E.; m. Arlene L. Papineau, July 12, 1947; children— Richard C., Kay C., Douglas R. BBA, U. Mich., 1949, MBA, 1950. Plant, div. or subsidiary controller Chrysler Corp., 1950-60; mgmt. controls cons. Diehl K.G., Nuremberg, Germany, 1960-63; sec. Genesee Brewing Co., Rochester, N.Y., 1963-67; v.p. fin. Consol. Papers, Inc., Wisconsin Rapids, Wis., 1967-89, also ret. dir. Served with AUS, 1943-46. Home: 444 Two Mile Ave Wisconsin Rapids WI 54494-6559 E-mail: arlroy@wctc.net.

ENGELHARDT, THOMAS ALEXANDER, editorial cartoonist; b. St. Louis, Dec. 29, 1930; s. Alexander Frederick and Gertrude Dolores (Derby) E.; m. Katherine Agnes McCue, June 25, 1960; children— Marybeth, Carol Marie, Christine Leigh, Mark Thomas. Student, Denver U., 1950-51, Ruskin Sch. Fine Arts, Oxford U., Eng., 1954-56, Sch. Visual Arts, NYC, 1957. Free-lance cartoonist, comml. artist, N.Y.C., 1957-60, Cleve., 1961-62, asst. editl. cartoonist, Newspaper Enterprise Assn., Cleve., 1960-61; editl. cartoonist St. Louis Post-Dispatch, 1962-97; freelance cartoonist, 1998—; one-man exhbns. of cartoons at Fontbonne Coll. Art Gallery, St. Louis, 1972, Old Courthouse (Jefferson Nat. Meml.), St. Louis, 1981, Mark Twain Bank, Frontenac, Mo., 1989; group exhbns. Washington U., St. Louis, 2000, Nat. Press Club, Washington, 2001, St. Louis Artists Guild, 2001. Served with USAF, 1951-53. Recipient Ethical Humanist of Yr. award St. Louis Ethical Soc., 1986, Kay and Leo Drey Environ. Leadership award Mo. Coalition for Environment, 1999. Roman Catholic. Office: 7830 Lafon Pl Saint Louis MO 63130-3805 Home Phone: 314-863-1165; Office Phone: 314-863-1165. Personal E-mail: tomeng@sbcglobal.net.

ENGELKE, CHARLES EDWARD, physics professor; b. NYC, July 26, 1930; s. John and Anna Margaret (Burnham) E.; m. Evelyn Viola Bieling, oct. 8, 1955; children: Charles W., Lynne M., Karen A. Lee. BS, Queens Coll., 1951; MA in Physics, Columbia U., 1953, PhD in Physics, 1961. Rsch. asst. Columbia U., NYC, 1952-53, 56-61, rsch. assoc., 1961-65; asst. prof. Hunter Coll., NYC, 1961-66; assoc. prof. Grad. Faculty CUNY/Lehman Coll., NYC, 1966-95, prof. emeritus, 1995—. 1st lt. USAF, 1953-56. Mem. Am. Phys. Soc., Sigma Xi. Achievements include the devel. of high pressure gas scintillation counters for energy sensitive neutron detection; performance of precision measurements of the neutron-proton total cross sect., determining the best existing value of the neutron-proton singlet effective range; designed economically competitive cmy. total energy system exploiting interseasonal thermal storage, near ideal realization of Einstein's which-path experiment; proposed causal interpretation of relativistic Quantum Electrodynamics. Home: 4 Chemung Pl Jericho NY 11753-1502 Office: Lehman Coll of CUNY Bedford Park Blvd Bronx NY 10468 Personal E-mail: lengelke@verizon.net.

ENGELKER, LYNSEY L., athletic trainer, professional athletics manager; b. Denver, May 4, 1978; d. Herman L. and Karen L. Engelker. AS, Northeastern Jr. Coll., Sterling, Colo., 1998; BS, U. Nebr., Kearney, 2000; MS, Ariz. State U., Tempe, 2003. Cert. athletic trainer Nat. Athletic Trainers Assn., 2001, strength & conditioning specialist Nat. Strength & Conditioning Assn., 2000, first aid/CPR/AED Am. Heart Assn., 2005. Athletic tng. internship Nokia Sugar Bowl, Coral Gables, Fla., 2000—01, U. Miami, Coral Gables, 2000—01; grad. asst. athletic trainer Ariz. State U., Tempe, 2001—03; head athletic trainer Greek Softball Fedn., Athens, Greece, 2002—04; clin. athletic trainer & HS head athletic trainer SW Sports Medicine & Rehab., Mesa, Ariz., 2003—04; account mgr. RS Med., Phoenix, 2004—. Participant Women's NCAA Coll. World Series, Oklahoma City, 2001—02; head athletic trainer European championships Greek Softball Fedn., Saronno, Italy, 2002—03, head athletic trainer U.S. cup women's softball, Honolulu, 2002—03, head athletic trainer and med. dir. summer Olympics, Athens, Greece, 2002—04, head athletic trainer Greece cup, 2002—03. Home: 9020 S 4th St Phoenix AZ 85042 Office: RS Medical 14001 SE First St Vancouver WA 98684 Home Phone: 480-797-3560; Office Phone: 866-849-6160. Office Fax: 602-243-1978; Home Fax: 602-243-1978. Personal E-mail: lengelker@yahoo.com. Business E-Mail: lengelke@rsmedical.com.

ENGELL, JAMES THEODORE, language educator, department chairman; b. Danville, Pa., Sept. 6, 1951; s. Frederick Jacob and Ruth Louise Engell; m. Ainslie Sheridan Brennan, June 2, 1984; children: Marleny Brennan, Alexander E. BA, Harvard Coll., 1973; PhD, Harvard U., 1978. From asst. prof. to prof. Harvard U., Cambridge, Mass., 1978—83, prof. English and comparative lit., 1983—, chmn. English and Am. lit. and lang., 2004—. Author: The Creative Imagination, 1981 (Thomas Wilson prize 1982), Forming the Critical Mind, 1989, The Committed Word: Literature and Public Values, 1999; co-author: Saving Higher Education in the Age of Money, 2005; editor: Coleridge: The Early Family Letters, 1994, Coleridge, Poetry for Young Readers, 2003; co-editor: Coleridge, Biographia Literaria, 1983; editor, contbr.: Johnson and His Age, 1984, Teaching Literature: What Is Needed Now, 1988; editl. advisor Jour. History of Ideas, 1986—, Coll. Lit., 1990-, 1650-1850 Ideas, Aesthetics, and Inquiries in the Early Modern Era, Eighteenth-Century Thought, Literature and Religion. Corporator Emerson Hosp. and Health Sys., Concord, Mass., 1989-94. Recipient Levenson Tchg. prize, 1995, Roslyn Abramson Tchg. award, 1997, Coun. for Advancement and Support Edn. Gold award, 1999, Phi Beta Kappa Tchg. award, 2002, John Marquand Advising prize, 2003, Frederic W. Ness Book award AAC&U, 2007; grantee Ford Found., 1978, Baker Found., 2002-04; Cabot fellow, 2001. Mem. AAAS, MLA, Am. Soc. 18th Century Studies, Johnsonians (chair 1990-91), Assn. Lit. Scholars and Critics (pres. 2001-02, sec. 2002-04), Friends of Coleridge. Avocations: travel, sports, music. Office: Harvard U Barker Ctr Dept English 12 Quincy St Cambridge MA 02138-3804

ENGELMAN, DONALD MAX, molecular biophysics and biochemistry educator; b. LA, Jan. 25, 1941; s. Francis Leopold and Mildred Lillian (Bordsen) E.; m. Pamela Alice Rackliff, Dec. 14, 1963 (div. 1986); children: Ian Kenton, Bevin Page; m. Susan Froshauer, Jan. 1, 1994. BA, Reed Coll., Portland, Oreg., 1962; MS, Yale U., 1964, PhD, 1967. Postdoctoral fellow U. Calif., San Francisco, 1967-68, Kings Coll., London, 1968-70; asst. prof. Yale U., 1970-74, assoc. prof., 1974-78, prof. molecular biophysics and biochemistry, 1978—, Eugene Higgins prof., 1995—, chmn. dept., 1987-92; acting dean Yale Coll., 1992-93; prof. de recherche Blaise Pascal, Ile de France, 1997—. Bd. dirs. Stryker Corp., Kalamazoo, Mich.; vis. prof. Coll. de France, 1993; editor-in-chief Ann. Rev. Biophysics, 1982-92; vis. prof. Cambridge U., Eng., 1978-79, Stanford U., 1984; Swiss Nat. lectr., 1993; guest biophysicist Brookhaven Nat. Lab., Upton, N.Y., 1974—, chair sci. and tech. steering com., 1998—; series cons. U.S. News Books, Washington, 1980-82. Editor: Biophysics Jour., Jour. Membrane Biology, Jour. Cell Biology, Biosci. Report, Proteins: Structure and Function; editor-in-chief: Ann. Rev. Biophysics, 1982-92; contbr. numerous articles to internat. jours., sci. jours. Guggenheim fellow, 1978-79; NSF, NIH research grantee, 1970— Mem. AAAS, NAS, Orgn. Biophys. Soc., Am. Chem. Soc., Conn. Acad. Arts and Scis.; Fellow Am. Acad. Arts & Sci. Office: Yale U PO Box 208114 New Haven CT 06520-8114 E-mail: Donald.engelman@yale.edu.

ENGELMAN, KARL, physician; b. NYC, June 23, 1933; s. Samuel and Lillian (Wachs) E.; m. Elaine Kaufman, June 10, 1956; children— Harold Kent, Ross Mitchell, Jeffrey Steven. BS, Rutgers U., 1955; MD, Harvard U., 1959; MA (hon.), U. Pa., 1971. Diplomate Am. Bd. Internal Medicine. Intern, asst. resident, resident in medicine Mass. Gen. Hosp., Boston, 1959-64; clin. asso., sr. investigator, attending physician Nat. Heart Inst., NIH, Bethesda, Md., 1961-70; assoc. prof. medicine and pharmacology Sch. Medicine U. Pa., Phila., 1971-95; chief hypertension sect., dir. clin. research center Sch. Medicine U. Pa. Cons. physician Phila. VA Hosp., 1971-95, Children's Hosp., Phila., 1971-95; clin. prof. medicine Med. U. of S.C., 1996—; cons. Beaufort-Jasper Comprehensive Health Svcs., 1996—, Vols. in Medicine, 2002—. Patentee in field. Med. staff Vols. in Medicine, 2002--. Served with USPHS, 1961-63. Mem. ACP, Am. Coll. Clin. Pharmacology, Internat. Soc. of Hypertention (sci. coun. on hypertension), U.S. Pharmacopeia and Nat. Formullary (adv. coun.), Coun. for High Blood Pressure Rsch. (adv. bd.), Am. Heart Assn., Phila. Doctors Golf Assn., Sea Pines Club. Jewish. Home: 20 Turnberry Ln Hilton Head Island SC 29928-4108

ENGELMAN, MELVIN ALKON, retired dentist, dental products executive; b. Waterbury, Conn., July 27, 1921; s. Herman B. and Marion (Halpern) E.; m. Muriel Phillips, Aug. 27, 1949; children: Curtis Land, Suzanne Ruth. AB, Ohio U., 1942; DDS, Case Western Res. U., 1944. Diplomate: Am. Bd. Oral Electrosurgery. Pvt. practice dentistry, Wappingers Falls, NY, 1949-89; chmn. oral diagnosis and oral pathology sect., dir. oral diagnostic ctr. St. Francis Hosp., Poughkeepsie, NY, 1963-77, attending dentist, 1963-89, dir. dept. dentistry, 1967, 71-74, 78, hon. staff, 1989—; pres. Di-Equi Dental Products Inc., 1980-99, Dentifax Internat. Inc., 1982-99. Dir. 1st regional sci. fair, Dutchess County, NY, 1960-61; observer Meml. Hosp. Cancer and Allied Diseases, NYC, 1962-66; adv. bd. Dutchess CC, 1963-69; project dir. USPHS cmty. cancer demonstration project, St. Francis Hosp., 1963-66; asst. chief med. officer Dutchess County NY CD, 1963-68; cons. Nat. Cancer Inst., clin. cancer tng. com., 1968-71, profl. edn. com. for cancer control, 1972-73; attending dentist Central Dutchess Nursing Home, 1970-85; cons. VA Hosp., Castle Point, NY, 1976-77, Lactona Corp., divsn. Warner Lambert, 1976-80; lectr. in field Co-author: Oral Cancer Examination Procedure, 1967, 16th edit., 83; contbr. articles to profl. jours. Chmn. Wappinger Red Cross Fund Drive, 1956; troop com. mem., Boy Scouts Am., Chelsea, NY, 1963-67; pres. Dutchess County unit Am. Cancer Soc., 1969-71. With USNR, 1942—81, lt. (j.g.) dental corps USNR, 1944, ret. lt. comdr. USNR, 1981. Fellow AAAS (life), Royal Soc. Health (Eng.), Am. Pub. Health Assn., Acad. Gen. Dentistry; mem. ADA (life), Internat. Assn. Dental Rsch., Mil. Officers Assn., Assn. Mil. Surgeons (life), 9th Dist. Dental Soc. (life), Dutchess County Dental Soc. (pres. 1965), Am. Acad. Dental Electrosurgery (pres. 1983), Wappinger Conservation Assn. (v.p. 1970-71), Wappingers Falls C. of C. (pres. 1952-54), Masons (32 degree), Shriners, B'nai B'rith (pres. So. Duchess lodge 1963-64), Am. Legion, Jewish War Vets., Navy Reserve Assn., Marine Corps League, Alpha Omega Achievements include patents for feeder bar, spruing assembly, sprue pin, and hollow movable reservoir. Home: 5720 Cottonwood St Bradenton FL 34203-8806

ENGELMAN, ROSALYN ACKERMAN, artist; b. Liberty, NY, Jan. 2, 1938; d. Nathan and Lillie (Schultz) Ackerman; m. Irwin Engelman, Nov. 24, 1956; children: Madeleine Florence, Marianne Leslie. BA, CCNY, 1958; MS, U. Rochester, 1978. Tchr. art, NYC, 1958, N.J., 1964-66; lectr., fund raiser, docent Meml. Art Gallery, Rochester, N.Y., 1972-74; rschr. Meml. Arts Gallery, Rochester, 1975-78; co-chair arts Westport (Conn.) Bicentennial Com., 1975-76; mem. Met. Arts Resources Com., Rochester, 1977-78; pres. Westport-Weston Arts Coun., 1980-81; devel. officer Conn. Pub. TV, 1982-83; v.p. mktg. Praxis Media, 1984—. Exhbns. include regional N.J. galleries, Gronsky Gallery, Kravetz Gallery, Rochester, Temple Israel, N.Y.C., 1997, T-Zart Gallery, N.Y.C., 1994, Baruch Coll., N.Y.C., 1998, Nigerian Embassy, 1998, Nat. Arts Club, N.Y.C., 1999, Adelphi Univ. Gallery, 1999, Masters Mystery Show, Fla. Internat. U., 2004, Norwalk (Conn.) Symphony, 2004; one woman shows: Nat. Arts Club, 1999, Mishkin Gallery Baruch Coll., 2001, Nico Gallery Seattle, 2001, All Commemorative Show NAC NY, 2002, Earthplace Westport, 2003, Thomas Walsh Art Gallery Fairfield U., 2003, Barbara Gillman Gallery, Miami, Fla., 2004, Art Miami Fla., 2004, Caelum Gallery, N.Y.C., 2004, 05, 06, Masters Mystery Show, Miami, 2004, 05, 06, Art Miami Gillman Gallery, 2005, Queensborough C.C. Art Gallery, Bayside, NY, 2005, Phthalo Gallery, Bay Harbor, Fla., 2005, Etra Fine Arts, Gallery, Miami, 2005-07, Compton Goethals Gallery, N.Y.C., 2006, 07, Art Basel-Etra Gallery, Miami, 2006, Biennale Citta di Firenze, 2007, Delorenzo Gallery, NYC, 2007—, Kaller Fine Arts, Mt., 2007; commns.: Substantive and Procedural Aspects of Internat. Criminal Law, The Hague Netherlands, 2000. Bd. dirs. Long Wharf Theatre, 1980-83, Performers Conn., 1980-84, Mus. Art Sci. and Industry, Bridgeport, Conn., 1990; chair bd. dirs. Westport-Weston Arts Coun., 1982—; bd. dirs. Nat. Corp. Theatre Fund, 1981-88, treas., 1982, pres., 1984. Recipient citation Town of Westport, 1981, Gold medal Grumbacher award, 1998, Painting award Nat. Arts Club, 2007. Mem. Alumni Assn. U. Rochester, Nat. Arts Club. Home Phone: 212-861-3134; Office Phone: 212-213-3879. Personal E-mail: ra936@aol.com.

ENGELS, BEATRICE ANN, artist, poet, retired real estate company executive; b. NYC, Oct. 1, 1925; d. Sydney and Marguerite Agnes (Carroll) Jonap; m. James J. Engels, May 10, 1944 (dec.); children: James J. Jr.(dec.) , Edward R., Marguerite Mary McHale. Brokers degree, Dowling Coll., 1970. Agt. real estate sales Kathleen Hart Real Estate, Bayport, NY, 1969—70; pres., real estate broker Beatrice A. Engels Realty, Patchogue, NY, 1970—76, Blue Point, NY, 1976—95; dir., pres. Beatrice A. Engels Art Gallery, Patchogue, 1970—76, Petite Pallette Art Gallery, Bayport, 1989—91; ret., 1995. Mem. real estate bd. Suffolk County, 1970—80; ecology adv., Blue Point, 1974—94; columnist LI Advance, Patchogue, NY, 1971—75, Suffolk County News, Sayville, NY, 1971—75. Author: Morning Song, 1996 (Editor's Choice award, 1996), Sea Sonnets and Other Poems, 1997, Endless Skies of Blue (Editor's Choice award, 1997), Best Poems of 1997, Celebration of Poets, 1997, Outstanding Poets of 1998 (Editor's Choice award, 1998), Best Poems of 1998; author: (compiled by Famous Poets Press) Our 100 Most Famous Poets, 2004; author, illustrator: Marguerite, The Story of a Dolly, 2003; author: (songs) Best Christmas Present, 1998. Mem. Blue Point Rep. Club, 1970—88. Mem.: Famous Poets Soc., Rosary Soc. (pres.), Internat. Soc. Poets (life), Wet Paints Studio Group (life). Roman Catholic. Achievements include ecological efforts that helped to save the wetlands near Blue Point, N.Y. E-mail: beabysea@bellsouth.net.

ENGELS, LAWRENCE ARTHUR, retired metal products executive; b. Darlington, Wis., Sept. 26, 1933; s. Henry Morris and Nell Ellen (O'Connor) E.; m. Marilyn Rae Stellick, Sept. 6, 1958; children: Laurie, Michael, Thomas, Stephen BBA, U. Wis., 1959; MBA, Northwestern U., 1970. Dist. credit mgr. U.S. Steel Corp., Chgo., 1959-69; asst. treas. Nat. Can Corp., Chgo., 1969-77; corp. treas. Comml. Metals Co., Dallas, 1977—, chief fin. officer and treas., 1979—, v.p., treas., chief fin. officer Dallas, 1981-99, retired, 1999. Served with USN, 1952-55. Fellow Nat. Inst. Credit; mem. Cash Mgmt. Practitioners Assn. (Chgo. sec. 1975), Chgo. Midwest Credit Mgmt. Assn. (dir. 1973-75), Chgo. Midwest Credit Service Corp. (dir. 1975), Fin. Execs. Inst., Nat. Assn. Corp. Treas.

ENGER, EDWARD HENRY, JR., retired editor, writer; b. Mpls., Mar. 16, 1930; s. Edward Henry Sr. and Anastasia (Barber) E.; m. Carolyn Sue Bush, June 1, 1964. BS in Edn., U. Minn., 1952. Cert. tchr., Calif. Tchr. Downers Grove (Ill.) Pub. Sch., 1956-58; editor Harper & Row, Evanston, Ill., 1958-62, author NYC, 1975—78; editor Silver Burdett Co., Morristown, N.J., 1962-68, Dell Pub. Co., NYC, 1968-75; author Nat. Textbook Co., Chgo., 1979-81; editl. dir. Amsco Sch. Publs., NYC, 1982-97; ret., 1997. Author: Writing by Doing, 1981, (textbook series) Language Basics, 1975-78. Served to cpl. U.S. Army, 1954-56, Korea. Mem. Nat. Council Tchrs. English. Democrat. Avocations: gardening, cooking, hiking, jogging.

ENGER, SHELLEY MCCLELLAND, epidemiologist, researcher; b. LA, May 14, 1964; m. William K. Enger; children: Matthew W., Anna E., Katherine R., Julia M. MPH, U. Calif., LA, 1991, PhD, 1995. Postdoctoral fellow U. So. Calif., 1995—97; rsch. scientist Kaiser Permanente So. Calif., Pasadena, Calif., 1997—2005; adj. rsch. asst. prof. U. So. Calif., 1997—2005. Mem. breast cervical cancer master plan Calif. Dept. Health Svcs., Sacramento; faculty, project lead Nat. Breast Cancer Coalition, Washington, 1999—2003. Contbr. numerous articles on breast cancer to profl. jours. Grantee, Ctrs. Disease Control and Prevention, 1999—2003, Calif. Cancer Rsch. Program, 2000—02; grants, Breast Cancer Rsch. Program Calif., 1995—2002, Nat. Cancer Inst., 2001—. Mem.: Am. Cancer Soc. (nat. breast cancer prevention forum). Home Phone: 626-793-9680. Home Fax: 626-792-7953. Personal E-mail: shelleyenger@yahoo.com.

ENGERRAND, DORIS DIESKOW, retired business educator; b. Chgo., Aug. 7, 1925; d. William Jacob and Alma Louise Willhelmina (Cords) Dieskow; m. Gabriel H. Engerrand,Oct. 26, 1946 (dec. June 1987); children: Steven, Kenneth, Jeannine. BS in Bus. Adminstrn., N. Ga. Coll., 1958, BS in Elementary Edn., 1959; M. Bus. Edn., Ga. State U., 1966, PhD, 1970. Tchr., dept. chmn. Lumpkin County H.S., Dahlonega, Ga., 1960-63, 65-68; tchr. Gainesville, Ga., 1965; asst. prof. Troy (Ala.) State U., 1969-71; asst. prof. bus. Ga. Coll. and State U., Milledgeville, 1971-74, assoc. prof., 1974-78, prof., 1978-90, chmn. dept. info. sys. and comms., 1978-89; retired, 1990. Contbr. articles on bus. edn. to profl. publs. Named Outstanding Tchr. Lumpkin County Pub. Schs., 1963, 66; Outstanding Educator bus. faculty Ga. Coll., 1975, Exec. of Yr. award, 1983. Fellow Assn. for Bus. Communication (v.p. S.E. 1978-80, 81-84, 89-92, bd. dirs.), Nat. Bus. Edn. Assn., Ga. Bus. Edn. Assn. (Postsecondary Tchr. of Yr. award 10th dist. 1983, Postsecondary Tchr. of Yr. award 1984), Am. Vocat. Assn., Ga. Vocat. Assn. (Educator of Yr. award 1984, Parker Liles award 1989), Profl. Secs. Internat. (pres. Milledgeville chpt. 1996-97), Ninety-nines Internat. (chmn. N. Ga. chpt. 1975-76, named Pilot of Yr. N. Ga. chpt. 1973). Methodist. Home: 1674 Pine Valley Rd Milledgeville GA 31061-2465

ENGERRAND, KENNETH G., lawyer, educator; b. Atlanta, June 30, 1952; s. Gabriel H. and Doris A. (Dieskow) E.; m. Anne Walts, Mar. 16, 1985; children: Caroline Elizabeth Turner, Catherine Anne Denton. BA, Fla. State U., 1973; JD, U. Tex., 1976. Bar: Tex. 1976, U.S. Dist. Ct. (so.

dist.) Tex. 1977, U.S. Ct. Appeals (5th cir.) 1978, U.S. Supreme Ct. 1980, U.S. Ct. Appeals (11th cir.) 1981, U.S. Dist. Ct. (ea. dist.) Tex. 1987. Assoc. Royston, Rayzor, Vickery & Williams, Houston, 1976-80, Brown, Sims & Ayre, Houston, 1980; v.p., gen. counsel Huthnance Offshore Corp., Houston, 1980-86; ptnr. Brown, Sims, Wise & White, Houston, 1986-2000, Brown Sims PC, Houston, 2000—. Adj. prof. law S. Tex. Coll. Law, 1978-93; columnist The Reporter, 1984-87; contbr. articles to profl. jours.; faculty advisor to spl. maritime edits. S. Tex. Law Jour., 1981-86. Fund drive vol. Houston Grand Opera, 1985-93, trustee, 1986-93; trustee Judge John R. Brown Scholarship Found., 1994—. Recipient outstanding contbn. to cmty. award Houston Jaycees, 1983. Mem. ABA (vce chmn. admiralty and maritime law com., tort and ins. practice sect. 1986-89), Def. Rsch. Inst., Maritime Law Assn., Coll. of State Bar Tex., Order of Coif, Phi Beta Kappa, Phi Delta Phi. Republican. Episcopalian. Avocations: legal writing, cultivating roses. Home: 3511 Durness Way Houston TX 77025 Office: Brown Sims PC 1177 West Loop S STE 1000 Houston TX 77027-9083 Business E-Mail: kengerrand@brownsims.com.

ENGH, N. ROLF (ROLF ENGH), lawyer; b. Scotts Bluff, Nebr., Oct. 26, 1953; s. N.A. and Dolcie (Cuplin) E.; m. Nancy A. Carroll, Jan. 17, 1986. BA, U. Minn., 1976; JD cum laude, William Mitchell Coll., 1982. Bar: Minn. 1982. Grain merchandiser Cook Industries, Memphis, 1976-78; assoc. corp. dept. Lindquist & Vennum, Mpls., 1982-86, ptnr. corp. dept., 1986-93; gen. counsel The Valspar Corp., Mpls., 1993—. Trustee Breck Sch. Mem. ABA, Minn. State Bar Assn., Hennepin County Bar Assn., Mpls. Club, Westminster Church, Phi Beta Kappa. Home: 1928 Humboldt Ave S Minneapolis MN 55403-2815 Office: The Valspar Corp 1101 S 3rd St Minneapolis MN 55415-1259 Business E-Mail: rengh@valspar.com.*

ENGIBOUS, THOMAS JAMES, electronics executive; b. St. Louis, Jan. 31, 1953; s. James C. and Emma E. (Buck) E.; m. Wendy; children: Ryan T., Mandie, Christopher Megan. B of Elec. Engring., Purdue U., West Lafayette, Ind., 1975, M of Elec. Engring., 1976, DEng (hon.), 1997. Design engr. SCG, Tex. Instruments, Dallas, 1976-80, dept. mgr., 1980-86, v.p., 1986-91, sr. v.p., 1991-93; exec. v.p., pres. semi-condr. group Tex. Instruments Inc., Dallas, 1993-96, pres., CEO, 1996-98, chmn., pres., CEO, 1998—2004, chmn., 2004—. Mem. vis. com. Purdue U. Engring., 1995—; bd. dirs. J.C. Penny Co., Catalyst, US-Japan Bus. Coun., Nat. Ctr. Ednl. Accountability. Dir. Dallas Citizens Coun., 1996—; trustee So. Meth. U.; bd. dir. SW Med. Found. Mem. IEEE, Bus. Roundtable, Bus. Coun., NAE. Roman Catholic. Avocations: boating, water sports, skiing. Office: Tex Instruments Inc PO Box 660199 Dallas TX 75266-0199 Office Phone: 972-995-2011. Office Fax: 972-995-4360.*

ENGLAND, ANTHONY WAYNE, engineering and science educator, dean; b. Indpls., May 15, 1942; s. Herman U. and Betty (Steel) E.; m. Kathleen Ann Kreutz, Aug. 31, 1962. SB, MIT, 1965, PhD, 1970, SM, 1965. With Texaco Co., 1962; field geologist Ind. U., 1963; scientist-astronaut NASA, 1967-72, 79-88; with U.S. Geol. Survey, 1972-79; crewmember on Spacelab 2, July, 1985; adj. prof. Rice U., Houston, 1987-88; prof. elec. engring. and computer sci. U. Mich., Ann Arbor, 1988—, prof. atmospheric, oceanic and space sci., 1989—, assoc. dean Rackham Grad. Sch., 1995-98, assoc. dean Coll. Engring., 2004—. Mem. space studies bd. NRC, 1992-98. Assoc. editor Jour. Geophys. Rsch. Recipient Antarctic medal, Spaceflight medal NASA, Spaceflight award Am. Astron. Soc., Outstanding Scientific Achievement medal NASA. Fellow IEEE; mem. Am. Geophys. Union. Home: 7949 Ridgeway Ct Dexter MI 48130-9700 Office: U Mich Dept Elec Engring-Comp Sci Ann Arbor MI 48109-2122

ENGLAND, ARTHUR JAY, JR., lawyer, former state justice; b. Dayton, Ohio, Dec. 23, 1932; s. Arthur Jay and Elsbeth (Weiskopf) E.; m. Morley Tenenbom, June 24, 1959 (div.); children: Andrea, Pamela, Ellen, Karen; m. Deborah J. Miller, Mar. 31, 1984; children: Rachel, Aaron. BS, U. Pa., 1955, LLB, 1961; LLM, U. Miami, 1971; LLD (hon.), John B. Stetson Coll. Law, 1979, Nova U., 1982. Bar: Fla. 1961, N.Y. 1962, Colo. 1997. Assoc. Dewey, Ballantine, Bushby, Palmer & Wood, NYC, 1961-64; ptnr. Culverhouse, Tomlinson, Taylor & DeCarion, Miami, Fla., 1964-69, Scott, McCarthy, Steel, Hector & Davis, Miami, 1969-70; spl. tax counsel Fla. Ho. Reps., 1971-72; consumer adviser, spl. counsel to gov. Fla., 1972-73; ptnr. Paul & Thomson, Miami, 1973-74; justice Supreme Ct. Fla., 1975-81, chief justice, 1978-80; ptnr. Steel, Hector & Davis, Miami, Fla., 1981-84, Fine Jacobson Schwartz Nash Block England, Miami, 1984-92, pres., CEO, 1988-89; shareholder Greenberg Traurig, P.A. (and predecessor firm), Miami, 1992—, and head Appellate Practice Group. Dep. chmn. Conf. of Chief Justices, 1978-80; chmn. Coun. of State Ct. Reps., Nat. Ctr. for State Cts., 1979-80; mem. Commn. on Interest on Lawyers' Trust Accounts, 1986-90, chmn., 1989-90; chmn. adv. bd. Nat. Interest on Lawyers' Trust Accounts Clearinghouse, 1983-86; adj. prof. Coll. Law, Fla. State U. Contbr. articles to legal jours. With AUS, 1955-57. Recipient Medal of Honor, Fla. Bar Found., 1983, Herbert Harley award Am. Judicature Soc., 1986, Jurisprudence award Anti-Defamation League, 1991. Mem. ABA (Pro Bono Pub. award 1988, Second Pl. Law Day Speech award 2004), Am. Acad. Appellate Lawyers (pres. 1990-92), Am. Law Inst. (life), Fla. Bar Assn. (chmn. appellate practice cert. com. 1993-94, cert. appellate lawyer), N.Y. State Bar Assn., Colo. State Bar Assn., Fla. State Bar Assn., Order of Coif, Beta Gamma Sigma. Jewish. Office: Greenberg Traurig LLP 1221 Brickell Ave Miami FL 33131-3224 Office Phone: 305-579-0605. Office Fax: 305-579-0717. Business E-Mail: englanda@gtlaw.com.

ENGLAND, DIANA WHITTEN, elementary school educator; b. Cleve., June 12, 1951; d. George Herbert Whitten and Evelyn Mixon Herring; m. Henry England Jr., Sept. 26, 1971. BS in Elem. Edn., Kent State U., 1974; MEd, Cleve. State U., 1984, postgrad., 1992. Cert. tchr. gifted and talented, supr. gifted and talented, Ohio. Classrm. tchr. East Cleveland (Ohio) Bd. Edn., 1974—79, tchr. gifted and talented students, 1979—89, math. coach, 1991—2001, supr. curriculum and instrn., 2001—; vis. instr. Cleve. State U., 1989—91, coord. Gov.'s Summer Inst., 1991—. Family math. presenter Kent (Ohio) State U., 1991—; coord. L.E.A.P., East Cleveland Bd. Edn., 1993, 94, 95. Elder, St. Mark's Presbyn. Ch., Cleve., 1990-92; moderator St. Mark-Elizabeth Clarke Scholarship, Cleve., 1983—. Nominee Ohio Tchr. of Yr., East Cleveland Bd. Edn., 1989; named Educator of Yr., East Cleveland PTA, 1988, Eisenhower Exemplary Tchr., Ohio Dept. Edn., 1994; recipient Martha Holden Jennings scholar, 1991. Mem. Nat. Coun. Tchrs. of Math., Ohio Assn. for Gifted Children (Cert. of Merit 1986), Ohio Coun. Tchrs. of Math., Nat. Coun. Suprs. of Math., Met. Cleve. Alliance Black Sch. Educators (1st v.p.), Phi Delta Kappa (pres. 1990-91, Svc. Key 1993). Presbyterian. Avocations: reading, collecting african-american art. Home: 15924 Glynn Rd East Cleveland OH 44112-3533 Office: East Cleveland Bd Edn 15305 Terrace Rd East Cleveland OH 44112-2933 Office Phone: 216-268-6605. E-mail: dengland@east-cleveland.k12.oh.us.

ENGLAND, GORDON RICHARD, federal agency administrator; b. Balt., Sept. 15, 1937; m. Dorothy England. BS in Elec. Engring., U. Md., 1961; MBA, Tex. Christian U., 1975. Engr. Honeywell Internat., 1961—66; with Gen. Dynamics Corp., 1966—2001, v.p., pres., land systems Falls Church, Va., 1986—91, pres. aircraft sys. Ft. Worth divsn., exec. v.p., 1991, exec. v.p. Falls Church, Va., 1991—93, pres. Lockheed Ft. Worth, 1993-95; owner consulting co., 1995-97; exec. v.p. combat sys. group Gen. Dynamics Corp., Falls Church, Va., 1997—2001; sec. USN, Washington, 2001—03, 2003—06; dep. sec. US Dept. Homeland Security, Washington, 2003; acting dep. sec. US Dept. Def., Washington, 2005—06, dep. sec., 2006—. Mem. Def. Sci. Bd. Vice-chmn. Goodwill Internat.; bd. govs. USO; bd. visitors TCU. Recipient award, Boy Scouts Am., Nat. Def. Indsl. Assn., Nat. Mgmt. Assn., Centennial award, IEEE, inductee, Aviation Hall of Fame. Mem.: Beta Gamma Sigma, Omicron Delta Kappa, Eta Kappa Nu. Office: US Dept Def 1010 Def Pentagon Rm 3E944 Washington DC 20301

ENGLAND, JOHN F., lawyer; b. Nov. 1961; m. Gail Crosthwait; 2 children. BA cum laude, U. Miss., 1984; JD with distinction, Miss. Coll., 1990; LLM in Taxation, U. Fla., 1992. CPA; bar: Miss. 1991. Mem. Pub. Law and Fin. Group Butler, Snow, O'Mara, Stevens & Cannada, PLLC, Jackson, Miss. Adj. prof. Miss. Coll. Sch. Law. Named a Dealmaker of Yr., Am. Lawyer Mag., 2006. Mem.: ABA, Miss. Bar (past chmn. Judiciary Com., mem. Taxation Com. for Young Lawyer Div., bd. dirs.), Nat. Assn. Bond Lawyers, Miss. Soc. Certified Pub. Accountants, River Hills Club, Rotary Club of Jackson. Office: Butler, Snow, O'Mara, Stevens & Cannada, PLLC 17th Fl, AmSouth Plaza, 210 E Capitol St PO Box 22567 Jackson MS 39225-2567 Office Phone: 601-985-4563. Office Fax: 601-985-4500. E-mail: john.england@butlersnow.com.

ENGLAND, JOHN MELVIN, lawyer, clergyman; b. June 29, 1932; s. John Marcus and Frances Dorothy (Brown) E.; m. Jane Cantrell, Aug. 2, 1953; children: Kathryn Elizabeth, Janette Evelyn, John William, Kenneth Paul, James Andrew, Samuel Robert. Student, Ga. State U., 1951-53; JD, U. Ga., 1956; BD magna cum laude with honors Theology, Columbia Theol. Sem., Decatur, Ga., 1964. Bar: Ga. 1959, U.S. Dist. Ct. (no. dist.) Ga. 1967, U.S. Ct. Mil. Appeals 1976, U.S. Ct. Appeals (5th cir.) 1967, U.S. Ct. Appeals (11th cir.) 1981, U.S. Supreme Ct. 1977, U.S. Dist. Ct. (mid. dist.) Ga. 1986, U.S. Dist. Ct. (so. dist.) Ga. 1991, U.S. Dist. Ct. (no. dist.) Tex. 1991; ordained to ministry Presbyn. Ch., 1964. Spl. agt. FBI, Washington, 1956-57, Indpls., 1957-59, Charlotte, N.C., 1959, Greenville, S.C., 1959-60; student supply pastor Bethel and Buford Presbyn. Chs., Atlanta, 1960-63; pastor Mullins (S.C.) Presbyn. Ch., 1964-67; asst. dist. atty. Fulton County, Ga., 1967-75; sr. ptnr. England and Weller, Atlanta, 1975-88, England, Weaver & Kytle, 1988-94, England & McKnight, 1994-2000, England & England, 2000—. Legal seminar lectr. and spkr. throughout the country under auspices of Christian orgns.; spl. pros. for gov. Ga., 1976-79; spl. cons. on appellate reform Supreme Ct. Ga., 1979-80; state bar rep. to Superior Ct. Uniform Rules Com. Coun. Superior Ct. Judges, 1984, Uniform Rules Com. State Bar Ga., 1993—. Elder, tchr., evangelism coord. Presbyn. Ch. USA; chmn. Christian Bus. Men's Coms. of U.S.A., Atlanta, 1971-73, chmn. internat. conv., Atlanta, 1979, bd. dirs., 1971-81. Mem. ABA, ATLA, State Bar Ga., Atlanta Bar Assn., Lawyers Club Atlanta, Ga. Trial Lawyers Assn., Nat. Assn. Criminal Def. Lawyers, Ga. Assn. Criminal Def. Lawyers, North Fulton Bar Assn. Office: England & England 201 Bombay Ln Roswell GA 30076 Office Phone: 770-641-6010. Business E-Mail: england_england_11p@hotmail.com.

ENGLAND, JULIE SPICER, computer company executive; BS in Chem. Engring., Tex. Tech. U., 1979. First line engr. Tex. Instruments, 1979—89, sr. mem. tech. staff, 1989—94, v.p. quality Semiconductor Group, 1994—98, v.p., 1994—, gen. mgr. radio frequency identification bus., 2004—. Former bd. dir. Panja, Inc., Dallas Forum; bd. dir. Fed. Reserve Bank Dallas; spkr. in field. Mem. bus. adv. coun. Tex. Tech. Rawl Coll.; founder 3/2 program Tex. Women's U. Recipient Women of Achievement award Richardson Tex. YWCA, Henry Laurence Gantt Medal, ASME, 2004; inductee Hall of Fame Women in Tech. Internat., 1998. Mem. IEEE (sr.), Soc. Women Engrs. (life), Dallas C. of C. (mem. exec. women's roundtable), Dallas Women's Found. (circle of honor award). Achievements include patents for related to infrared focal plane array process technology. Office: Tex Instruments Inc 12500 TI Blvd Dallas TX 75243-4136 Fax: 972-995-4360.

ENGLAND, LYNNE LIPTON, lawyer, pathologist; b. Youngstown, Ohio, Apr. 11, 1949; d. Sanford Y. and Sally (Kentor) Lipton; m. Richard E. England, Mar. 5, 1977. BA, U. Mich., 1970; MA, Temple U., 1972; JD, Tulane U., 1981. Bar: Fla. 1982, U.S. Dist. Ct. (mid. dist.) Fla. 1982, U.S. Ct. Appeals (11th cir.) 1982; cert. clin. competence in speech pathology and audiology. Speech pathologist Rockland Children's Hosp., N.Y., 1972-74, Jefferson Parish Sch., Gretna, La., 1977-81; audiologist Rehab. Inst. Chgo., 1974-76; assoc. Trenam, Simmons, Kemker, Scharf, Barkin, Frye & O'Neill, Tampa, Fla., 1981-84; asst. U.S. atty. for Middle Dist. Fla. Tampa, 1984-87; asst. U.S. trustee, 1987-91; ptnr. Stearns, Weaver, Miller, Weissler, Alhadeff & Sitterson, P.A., 1991-94, Prevatt, England & Taylor, Tampa, Fla., 1994-99; pvt. practice Brandon, Fla., 1999—. Editor Fla. Bankruptcy Casenotes, 1983. Recipient clin. assistantship Temple U., 1972-74. Mem. Comml. Law League, Am. Speech and Hearing Assn., Tampa Bay Bankruptcy Bar Assn. (dir. 1990-95), Am. Bankruptcy Inst., Fla. Bar Assn., Hillsborough County Bar Assn., Order of Coif. Jewish. Avocations: tennis, golf, playing french horn and piano. Office: 1463 Oakfield Dr Ste 125 Brandon FL 33511-0802 Home Phone: 813-689-2987; Office Phone: 813-661-6464. Business E-Mail: englandlawoffice@aol.com.

ENGLAND, ROBERT STOWE, writer; b. York, SC, Jan. 14, 1944; s. Hershel Stowe and Myrtle Lorene (Deal) E. BA in English, Duke U., 1967. Reporter Hartford (Conn.) Times, 1967-68; editor, pub. Washington, A Tabloid Rev., 1973-76; editor Del. Valley Bus. Mag., Phila., 1976-77; sr. editor Ingersoll-Rand Co. Corp. Mag., Washington, N.J., 1977-79; editor Metro Newark Mag., 1982-84; writer Insight Mag., Washington, 1985-88; ind. writer bus., fin. and polit. mags., Arlington, Va., 1988—. Adj. fellow, dir. rsch. for global aging initiative, Ctr. for Strategic and Internat. Studies, Washington, 1999-2003. Author: The Fiscal Challenge of an Aging Industrial World, 2002 (One of the 25 Best Books, World Future Soc., 2002), Global Aging and Financial Markets: Hard Landings Ahead?, 2002, The Macroeconomic Impact of Global Aging: A New Era of Economic Frailty?, 2002, Aging China: The Demographic Challenge to China's Economic Prospects, 2005. Pres. Harsimus Cove Neighborhood Assn., Jersey City, 1982-84. Recipient Blue Smoke and Mirrors award Insight mag., Washington, 1986. Mem. Washington Ind. Writers, Folklore Soc. Greater Washington. Anglican. Avocations: piano, genealogy. Home: 3116 Military Rd Arlington VA 22207-4136 Office Phone: 703-522-7847. Personal E-mail: rengland@us.net.

ENGLANDER, ISRAEL A., financier; m. Caryl Englander; 3 children. BA, NYU. Ptnr. Aegis Ptnrs.; pres. Englander Capital Corp. Capital Corp., 1984—90; co-founder Jamie Securities, 1985—89; founder Israel A. Englander & Co.; CEO First Millennium Ptnrs., Inc., 1990—; mng. gen. ptnr. Millennium Ptnrs. LLC; sole mgr. Millennium Mgmt. LLC. Mem. bd. govs. AMEX. Bd. mem. Met. NY Coordinating Coun. Jewish Poverty, Mt. Sinai Children's Ctr. Found. Named one of Forbes' Richest Americans, 2006. Office: First Millennium Ptnrs Inc 666 Fifth Ave 8th Fl New York NY 10103*

ENGLANDER, JOHN C., lawyer; BS, Cornell Univ., 1980; JD, Boston Univ., 1983. Bar: Mass. 1984. Law clerk, Hon. Bailey Aldrich US Dist. Ct. Appeals (1st cir.); law clerk, Justice William H. Rehnquist US Supreme Ct.; ptnr., comml. litig. Goodwin Procter, LLP, Boston, co-chair, litig. group, mem. exec. com. Office: Goodwin Procter LLP Exchange Pl 53 State St Boston MA 02109 Office Phone: 617-570-1268. Office Fax: 617-523-1231. Business E-Mail: jenglander@goodwinprocter.com.

ENGLANDER, ROGER, television producer, director; b. Cleve., Nov. 23, 1926; s. Will C. and Frieda (Osteryoung) E. Student, Chgo. Mus. Coll., 1945-48; PhB, U. Chgo., 1946; postgrad., Goodman Theater of Art Inst. Chgo., 1947-48, U. Chgo., 1947-49. Freelance TV producer, dir. for Leonard Bernstein N.Y. Philharm. Young People Concerts, 1958-75; asst. to gen. mgr. Chgo. Opera Co., 1946-47; asst. to Gian Carlo Menotti NYC, 1947-49; assoc. dir. ABC-TV, NYC, 1949-50; producer, dir. CBS-TV, NYC, 1950-75; freelance TV producer, dir., writer major networks, theatrical orgns., U.S., Eng., Israel, Italy, Japan, 1975—. Chmn. panel Nat. Endowment for the Arts, Washington, 1962-72; tchr. broadcasting NYU, Fairfield U.; founder Am. Dance Theater, N.Y.C., 1964-66; producer N.Y. Philharm. Promenade Concerts, N.Y.C., 1963-67; dir. Music Theater of Lincoln Ctr., N.Y.C., 1964-65. Author: Opera: What's All the Screaming About?, 1983. Pres. St. Lukes Pl. Assn., N.Y.C., 1970-90; mem. vis. com. U. Chgo., 1982—. Recipient Emmy award NATAS, 1961, 63, 65, 69, 73, Peabody award, 1979, Dirs. Guild Am. award, 1980, Profl. Achievement award U. Chgo., 1980. Avocation: writing. Home: 15 Moorland Farm 15 Hammersmith Rd Newport RI 02840-7303

ENGLANDER, SOL WALTER, biochemistry and biophysics educator, medical educator; BS in Physics/Math., U. Md., 1951; MS in Biophysics, U. Pitts., 1953, PhD in Biophysics, 1958. Instr. in biochemistry Dartmouth Med. Sch., NH, 1960-63, asst. prof. biochemistry NH, 1963-66; assoc. prof. biochemistry U. Pa., Phila., 1967-73, prof. biochemistry & biophysics, 1974—, assoc. chmn. dept. biochemistry & biophysics, 1979-82, Jacob Gershon-Cohen prof. med. sci., 1990—. Vis. scientist Danish AEC Rsch. Establishment, 1965; Charles Sabat Disting. lectr. Rutgers U., 1990, Hugh Clark Disting. lectr. U. Conn., 1994. Contbr. articles to profl. jours. Predoctoral fellow USPHS, 1957; Postdoctoral fellow Am. Cancer Soc., 1959-60; postdoctoral NIH, 1960; recipient Excellence in Rsch. award Am. Chem. Soc., 1994. Mem. Nat. Acad. Scis., Protein Soc. (exec. coun. 1997), Phi Kappa Phi, Sigma Xi, Pi Sigma, Phi Kappa Phi; fellow Am. Acad. Arts & Sciences Office: U Pa Sch Medicine 1005-09 Stellar-Chance Lab 422 Curie Blvd Philadelphia PA 19104 Office Phone: 215-898-8042. Office Fax: 215-898-2415. E-mail: Walter@HX2.Med.UPenn.edu.

ENGLAR, JOHN DAVID, finance educator, textiles executive, lawyer; b. Baldwin, NY, Feb. 19, 1947; s. Jack Donald and Edith (Blackwell) E.; m. Linda Meter, May 10, 1986. BA magna cum laude, Duke U., 1969, JD, 1972. Bar: N.Y. 1973. Assoc. Davis Polk and Wardwell, NYC and Paris, 1972-78; corp. atty. Burlington Industries, Inc., Greensboro, NC, 1978—, v.p., gen. counsel, sec., 1984-93, CFO, 1994-96, sr. v.p. corp. devel. and law, 1995—2003, also bd. dirs., 1990—2003; exec. in residence Fuqua Sch. Bus., Duke U., 2004—, UNCG Bryan Sch. of Bus., 2005—. Bd. dirs. Delphi Corp. Chmn. bd. trustees Cen. N.C. chpt. Nat. Multiple Sclerosis Soc., 1984-86, mem. nat. adv. coun., 1988-89; mem. bd. visitors Wake Forest U. Sch. Law, 1984-95, Duke U. Fuqua Sch. Bus., 1995—2005; mem. sch. bd. Our Lady of Grace, 2006—, mem. parish fin. coun., 2006—. Mem. Order of Coif, Phi Beta Kappa. Home: 215 Ridgeway Dr Greensboro NC 27403-1526

ENGLAR, NANCY ELLEN, nurse, consultant, nursing educator; b. Excelsior Springs, Mo., Jan. 23, 1955; d. Billy Paul and Mary Helen Slater; m. Jack M. Englar, Jan. 22, 1972; children: Brian, Nathan, Sara. A in Nursing, Frederick CC, Md., 1985; BSN, U. Md., 2001; M Health Law, Nova Southeastern U., 2004. Cert. clin. transplant coordinator, Am. Bd. Transplant Coordinators, oncology nurse, Oncology Nursing Soc., 2005. Transplant coord. NIH, 1990—2000, clin. nurse Bethesda, Md., 2000; transplant coord. U. Md. Med. Ctr., Balt., 1998—2000; clin. nurse Johns Hopkins Hosp., Balt., 1989—90; clin. nurse oncology Frederick (Md.) Meml. Hosp., 1985—89; legal nurse cons. NSE Legal Nurse Cons., Mount Airy, Md.; nurse cons., project mgr. Nat. Insts. Allergy and Infectious Diseases, Bethesda, 2004—05, project mgr., transplant coord., 2005—. Mem.: Assn. Clin. Rsch. Profls., Am. Assn. Legal Nurse Cons., N.Am. Transplant Coord. Orgn., Oncology Nursing Soc. Office: U Md Dept Nuclear Medicine 22 S Green St Baltimore MD 21201 Home Phone: 301-829-2365; Office Phone: 410-328-7803. Business E-Mail: nenglar@umm.edu.

ENGLE, CAROLE RUTH, aquaculture economics professor; b. Harrisburg, Pa., July 7, 1952; d. Morris Mumma Engle and Mildred Evelyn (Orris) Wambold; m. Nathan Mayhew Stone, May 30, 1981; children: Reina, Eric, Cody. BA, Friends World Coll., 1975; MS, Auburn U., 1978, PhD, 1981. Vis. prof. U. Centroamericana, Managua, Nicaragua, 1981-83; fisheries economist Inter-Am. Devel. Bank, Santiago, Panama, 1984-85; asst. prof. econs. Auburn U., Montgomery, Ala., 1985-88; assoc. prof. aquaculture econs. U. Ark., Pine Bluff, 1988-94, prof., 1994—; dir., Aguacultural Fisheries Ctr., U. Ark., Pine Bluff, 1989—. Aquaculture coord. U. Ark., Pine Bluff, 1989—; cons. FAO, Rome, 1986, 88. Contbr. articles to profl. jours.; editor conf. proceedings. Mem. World Aquaculture Soc., Am. Fisheries Soc., Am. Assn. Agriculture Econs., So. Agriculture Econs. Assn., Ark. Acad. Scis. Avocations: gardening, reading, swimming. Office: U Ark PO Box 108 1200 University Dr Pine Bluff AR 71601-2799 Business E-Mail: cengle@uaex.edu.

ENGLE, DONALD EDWARD, retired rail transportation executive, lawyer; b. St. Paul, Mar. 5, 1927; s. Merlin Edward and Edna May (Berger) E.; m. Nancy Ruth Frank, Mar. 18, 1950; children: David Edward, Daniel Thomas, Nancy Ann. BA, Macalester Coll., St. Paul, 1948; JD, U. Minn., Mpls., 1952, BSL., 1950. Bar: Minn. 1952, Mo. 1972. Law clk., spl. atty. Atty. Gen.'s Office Minn., 1951-52; atty., asst. gen. solicitor, asst. gen. counsel G.N. Ry., St. Paul, 1953-70; asso. gen. counsel Burlington No., Inc., 1970-72; v.p., gen. counsel S.L.-S.F. Ry., St. Louis, 1972-80, v.p. law, sec., 1979-80; v.p. law Burlington No., Inc., St. Paul, 1980-81, Burlington No. Ry., St. Paul, 1981-83, sr. v.p. law and govt. affairs, sec., 1983-86, also dir.; ptnr., chmn., chief exec. officer Oppenheimer, Wolff & Donnelly, 1986-93, chmn., chief exec. officer, 1991-93, of counsel, 1993—2004; ret., 2004. Continuing edn. lectr. U. Minn.; bd. dirs. Regions Hosp. Found., 2001—05. Bd. dirs. YMCA, St. Paul, 1981-84, ARC, 1981-84, Boy Scouts Am., 1991-2005. Mem. ABA, Mo. Bar Assn., Minn. Bar Assn., Ramsey County Bar Assn., St. Louis Bar Assn., St. Paul C. of C. (bd. dirs. 1994-97), North Oaks Golf Club, Phi Delta Phi. Republican. Lutheran. Home: 5919 Centerville Rd Apt 208 North Oaks MN 55127 Home Phone: 651-762-6574. Personal E-mail: engleone@aol.com.

ENGLE, HOWARD A., retired pediatrician; b. Wis., Sept. 11, 1919; married; three children. BS, U. Wis., 1939, MS, 1941, MD, 1943. Diplomate Am. Bd. Pediatrics. Intern Michael Reese Hosp., Chgo., 1943, resident in pediatrics, 1943-44; pvt. practice Miami Beach, Fla., 1947—; assoc. clin. prof. U. Miami Sch. of Medicine, assoc. prof. pediatrics emeritus. Sr. cons., past chmn. dept. pediatrics, Mount Sinai Med. Ctr., Miami Beach; com. mem., operation newborn U. Miami Sch. of Medicine; instr. dept. pediatrics U. Fla. Sch. of Nursing; pediatric preceptor Fla. Internat. U. Sch. Nursing; sr. cons. pediatrics Mount Sinai Med. Ctr.; courtesy staff Miami Childrens Hosp.; sr. attending pediatrics Jackson Mem. Hosp.; cons. Fla. Atlantic U. Dept. Spl. Edn., neuropediatrics, Childrens Home Soc. of Fla.; cons., lectr. Dupont de Nemours Found., State Miss.; cons. pediatric neurology Hope Sch.; dir. Symposium Cerebral Palsy, Miami; med. rep. Symposia Cerebral Palsy, State of Tex.; lectr. in field. Contbr. articles to profl. jours. Com. mem. Edn. and Therapy for the Handicapped, Dade County Sch. Bd.; past med. dir. United Cerebral Palsy of Miami; cons. neuropediatrics United Cerebral Palsy of Fla.; past. mem. clin. adv. bd. United Cerebral Palsy; nat. del. World Commn. on Cerebral Palsy, Copenhagen, 1963; med. cons. divsn. exceptional student edn. Miami-Dade County Sch. Bd. Recipient Ralph Hawley award for 50 yrs. svc. to medicine and the cmty. U. Wis., 1993. Mem. Am. Acad. Pediat., Child Neurology Soc., Am. Acad. Cerebral Palsy (exec. com.), Am. Acad. Neurology, Am. Assn. on Mental Retardation, Am. Population and Reproduction Assn. (pres., founder), Fla. Rehab. Assn., Internat. Soc. for Rehab. of Crippled and Disabled, Am. Acad. Phys. Medicine and Rehab., Internat. Soc. for Cerebral Palsy, Internat. Child Neurology Assn. (assoc.), Japanese

Soc. Child Neurology, Dade County Med. Assn., Fla. Med. Assn., Fla. Pediatric Soc., Miami Pediatric Soc. (past pres.), Southeastern Med. Assn., European Paediatric Neurology Soc., World Med. Assn., Internat. Population and Reproduction Com. (chmn. edn. programs, bd. dirs., past pres. 1981-82), Alpha Omega Alpha, Sigma Sigma.

ENGLE, JAMES BRUCE, ambassador; b. Billings, Mont., Apr. 16, 1919; s. Bruce Wilmot and Verbeaudah Margaret (Morgan) E.; m. Priscilla Joyce Wright, June 10, 1950; children: Stephen, Judith, Philip, Susan, John, Peter. Diploma, Burlington Jr. Coll., Iowa, 1938; BA, U. Chgo., 1940, postgrad., 1940-41, 46; diploma, Grad. Sch. Bus. Adminstrn., Harvard, 1945; Honours BA (Rhodes scholar), Oxford U., Eng., 1950, Honours MA, 1954; diploma, U. per Stranieri, Perugia, Italy, 1949; Fulbright scholar, Istituto Italiano Studi Storici, Naples, 1950-53; postgrad., Am. U., Washington, 1956-58; diploma, Goethe Institut, Germany, 1958; postgrad., King's Coll., Cambridge U., Eng., 1958-59. Dept. State liaison officer with Bd. Econ. Warfare, Washington, 1941-42; vice consul Quito, Ecuador, 1942-44, Rio de Janeiro, 1946-47, Naples, 1951-53; 2d sec. Am. embassy, Rome, 1953-54; Italian desk officer Dept. State, Washington, 1955-58; 1st sec. Am. embassy, London, 1958-59; consul Frankfurt, Germany, 1959, Duesseldorf, Germany, 1959-60; labor attache Am. embassy, Bonn, Germany, 1960-61, 1st sec. Accra, Ghana, 1961-62, acting dep. chief mission, 1962-63, charge d'affaires, 1963; dep. chief mission, counselor embassy Managua, Nicaragua, 1963-67; charge d'affaires, 1967; mem. sr. seminar in fgn. policy Dept. State, Washington, 1967-68; dep. chief reports and analysis div. CORDS, Mil. Assistance Command, Saigon, Vietnam, 1968; province sr. advisor Phu Yen mil. region II, Tuy Hoa, Vietnam, 1969-70; dir. Vietnam working group Dept. State, sec. Nat. Security Council com. on Indochina, Washington, 1970-71; spl. advisor to ambassador-at-large on trade and currency negotiations, 1971-72; diplomatic advisor to sec. of treasury, 1972; spl. asst. to U.S. ambassador to North Atlantic Council, Brussels, 1972; exec. sec. spl. interdepartmental task force on Indochina Dept. State, Washington, 1972-73; consul gen. Nha Trang, Vietnam, 1973; dep. chief mission, counselor of embassy Phnom Penh, Cambodia, 1973-74; charge d'affaires, 1974; ambassador to People's Republic of Bénin (Dahomey), Cotonou, 1974-76; polit. advisor with rank of ambassador to U.S. Comdr.-in-Chief Atlantic and Supreme Allied Comdr. Atlantic, 1976-78; sr. fgn. service insp. Dept. State, Washington, 1978-82; cons. on war gaming, 1983-84; dir. U.S. representation U.S.—Saudi Arabian Joint Commn. on Econ. Cooperation Riyadh, Saudi Arabia, 1984-85; Joint Commn. Advisor to Sr. Level Coms. U.S. and Saudi Arabian govts., 1985-87; cons. on fgn. affairs, 1987—; pres. Vermont Coverts: Woodlands for Wildlife, 1991-96, chmn. bd., 1996—2001, pres. emeritus, 2001—. Mem. Vt. Forestry Communications Coun., 1991-95. Mem. Vt. Citizens Adv. Com., No. Forest Lands Coun., 1992-94, U. Vt. Extension Adv. Coun., 1993—. Served to lt. (j.g.) USN, 1944-46; mil. govt. officer Japan, 1945-46. Named winner over-60 group, Nat. Heart Run, 1981, Tree Farmer of Yr., Caledonia County, Vt., 1997, Vt. Tree Farmer of Yr., 2001; recipient Rockefeller Pub. Svc. award, 1958. Mem. The Oxford Union, Phi Beta Kappa. Congregationalist. Achievements include leading 11 U.S. Andean expdns. in Ecuador, 1942-43. Home: PO Box 64 Peacham VT 05862-0064 Mailing: 443 Bayley Hazen Rd Peacham VT 05862-0064

ENGLE, KATHLEEN FAYE, elementary education educator; b. Rapid City, SD, July 8, 1958; d. Frank Denton and Marie Lucille (Coffield) Packard; m. Steven S. Engle, June 1, 1984; children: Kirstin Marie, Kalin Kathleen. BS in Edn., Black Hill State Coll., 1980. Tchr. physical edn. Campbell County Sch. Dist., Gillette, Wyo., 1980-84, Weston County Sch. Dist., Newcastle, Wyo., 1985—. Mem. evaluatin team Conestiga Rep., Gillette, 1982-83; mem. adv. team Newcastle Mid. Sch., 1981—, evaluation team, 1992—. Middle Sch. Physical Edn. Teacher or the Year, Nat. Assn. for Sport & Phys. Edn., 1995. Mem. Wyo. Edn. Assn., Wyo. Alliance Physical Edn. Health Recreation and Dance, Wyo. Coaching Assn., Newcastle Edn. Assn., Delta Kappa Gamma. Avocations: aerobics, weightlifting. Office: Newcastle Mid Sch 116 Casper Ave Newcastle WY 82701-2705

ENGLE, MARY ALLEN ENGLISH, retired physician; b. Madill, Okla., Jan. 26, 1922; d. Russell C. and Vera (Apperson) English; m. Ralph Landis Engle, Jr., June 7, 1945 (dec. Oct. 2000); children: Ralph Landis III (dec.), Marilyn Elizabeth. AB cum laude, Baylor U., Waco, Tex., 1942; MD, Johns Hopkins U., Balt., 1945; D.Sc. (hon.), Iona Coll., New Rochelle, NY, 1982. Diplomate: in pediatric cardiology Am. Bd. Pediatrics. Intern pediatrics Johns Hopkins Hosp., 1945-46, asst. dir. pediatrics out-patient dept., 1946-47, fellow pediatric cardiology, 1947-48; instr. pediatrics Johns Hopkins U., 1946-48; asst. resident Sydenham Hosp. Contagious Diseases, Balt., 1946, N.Y. Hosp., 1948-49, asst. attending pediatrician, 1952-60, assoc. attending pediatrician, 1960-62, attending pediatrician, 1962-92, hon. staff, 1992—; fellow in pediatrics Cornell U., NYC, 1949-50, mem. faculty, 1950-92, prof., 1969-92, prof. emeritus, 1992—, Stavros S. Niarchos prof. pediatric cardiology, 1979-92, emeritus, 1992—. Med. dir. Insts. in Care Premature Infant, 1952-55, dir. pediatric cardiology, 1963-92. Recipient Spence-Chapin award for contbns. to pediatrics, 1958, award of merit Philoptochos Soc. N. and S. Am., 1978, Woman of Conscience award Nat. Council Women, 1979, citation Nat. Bd. Med. Coll. Pa., 1979, Disting. Achievement award Baylor U., 1981, Disting. Alumna award Baylor U., 1988, Maurice Greenberg Disting. Svc. award N.Y. Hosp.-Cornell Med. Ctr., 1991; hon. fellow Cornell U. Med. Coll. Alumni, 1984; Mary Allen Engle Div. Pediatric Cardiology, N.Y. Hosp.-Cornell U. Med. Coll. dedicated in her honor, 1992, Johns Hopkins U. Soc. Scholars award, 1992, Alumni Assoc. Detlev Bronk award, 1993, Disting. Alumna award, 2002. Mem. Am. Acad. Pediat. (charter mem. sect. cardiology, Founder's award cardiology sect. 1983), Am. Clin. and Climatological Assn. (recorder 1992-2000, pres. 2003-04), Am. Heart Assn. (bd. dirs. 1975-78, award of merit 1975, Helen B. Taussig award 1976), N.Y. Heart Assn. (bd. dirs. 1980-86), N.Y. Acad. Medicine, N.E. Pediatric Cardiology Soc., Harvey Soc., Soc. Pediatric Rsch., Assn. European Pediatric Cardiologists (corr.), Royal Soc. Medicine (bd. dirs. Found. 1983-92, hon. bd. dirs. 1992-2000), Am. Coll. Cardiology (master tchr. 1969, 73, 76, trustee 1974-79, bd. govs. 1990-94, pres. N.Y. State chpt. 1991-92, Theodore and Susan Cummings Humanitarian award 1973, 76), Am. Pediatric Soc., Pediatric Cardiology Soc. Greater N.Y., N.Y. Cardiology Soc. (bd. dirs., pres. 1986-87), Scon. Scholars, Phi Beta Kappa, Alpha Omega Alpha. Presbyterian.

ENGLE, RICHARD VICTOR, publishing executive; b. Chicago, Oct. 7, 1961; s. Frank J. and Margaret Anne (Fogarty) Wenglewski; m. Denise Marie Denning, July 23, 1985; 1 child, Destiny René. AD, Christ for the Nations Inst., Dallas, 1983. Commr. of archives and records State of Okla., 1998—; pub. BellWest, Am. Bethany-Warr Acres, Nichols Hills Quail Creek Tel. Directories, others, Okla., 2000—. Mem. City Coun., Bethany, Okla., 1998—2002; pres. Nat. Fedn. Rep. Assemblies, 2003—, Assembly Edn. Fund, 2004—; v.p. Okla. Conservative PAC, 2000—; chmn. Okla. Fedn. Young Rep., 1997—2001; alt. del. Rep. Nat. Conv., Okla., 1996, del., mem. nat. rules com. Okla., 2000; chair Rep. Victory Fund. Mem. Okla. Press Assn., (legis. affairs com. 1998-2001). Republican. Home: 4034 Coronado Pl Warr Acres OK 73122-3114 Home Phone: 405-577-2999; Office Phone: 405-787-6372. Business E-Mail: president@GOPwing.com.

ENGLE, ROBERT F., finance educator; b. Syracuse, NY, Nov. 10, 1942; m. Marianne Eger, Aug. 10, 1969; children: Jordan, Lindsey. BS in Physics with honors, Williams Coll., 1964; MS in Physics, Cornell U., 1966, PhD in Economics, 1969. Asst. prof. MIT, Cambridge, 1969—74, assoc. prof., 1974—75, U. Calif., San Diego, 1975—77, prof. economics, 1977—2003, chair economics dept., 1990—94, prof. emeritus and rsch. prof., 2003—; vis. prof. fin. NYU Stern Sch. Bus., 1999, Michael Armellino prof. mgmt. fin. services, affiliated prof., Stats Group, 2000—. Rsch. assoc. Nat. Bur. Econ. Rsch., 1987—. Editor: Cointegration, Casuality, and Forecasting: A Festschrift in Honour of Clive W.J. Granger, 1999; co-editor: Jour. Applied Econometrics, 1985—89; assoc. editor:, 1988—, Jour. Regional Sci., 1978—, Jour. Forecasting, 1985—, mem. editl. bd.: Real Estate Econs., 2004—. Recipient Excellence in Tchg. Award, MIT Grad. Econ. Assn., 1974—75, Nobel Prize for Econ. Sciences, 2003. Fellow: Am. Econ. Assn., Am. Statis. Assn., Econometric Soc. (coun. mem. 1994), Am. Acad. Arts and Sciences; mem.: NAS. Office: NYU Kaufman Mgmt Ctr-KMC 9-62 44 W Fourth St New York NY 10012-1126 Office Phone: 212-998-0710. Office Fax: 212-995-4220. Business E-Mail: rengle@stern.nyu.edu.*

ENGLE, ROBERT IRWIN, music educator, translator; b. New Kensington, Pa., Feb. 11, 1945; s. Dale Clair Engle and Rosalyn Imogene (Timblin) Erickson, 1 child, adopted Emmanuel Glémaud. BS in Music Edn., U. Cin., 1967; postgrad., Stanford U., 1967-68, Ind. U., 1969, U. So. Calif., 1969-71; MA in Music, U. Hawaii, 1973, cert. in Samoan, 1986; PhD in Music, U. Wash., 1994; postgrad., U. San Diego, 2006. Cert. tchr. music grades K-12, Calif. Choral instr. Terminal Island Prison, San Pedro, Calif., 1969-71, Oahu Cmty. Correction Ctr., 1974; choral music tchr. Palos Verdes (Calif.) High Sch., 1968-72; dir. music Makiki Christian Ch., Honolulu, 1978-84, 1st United Meth. Ch., Honolulu, 1986-88; tchr. music and French Redemption Acad., Kailua, Hawaii, 1988-91; dir. music Kapiolani C.C., Honolulu, 1975-99; dir. choral activities U. Hawaii, Hilo, 1995-96; asst. dir. music Hilo First Samoan Assembly of God, 1995-96; dir. music Good Samaritan Samoan Ch., Honolulu, 1997-98, Tacoma, 1999-2001, San Diego, 2001—02; chair music dept. Northwest Coll., Kirkland, Wash., 1999-2001; choral music tchr. Mt. Carmel H.S., San Diego, 2001—03; artistic dir. San Diego Men's Chorus, 2002—03; music tchr., French tchr., drama tchr. Century HS, Santa Ana, Calif., 2003—; asst. dir. music, lay preacher, tchr. Sunday sch., dir. missions program Long Beach First Samoan Assembly of God, 2005—, also bd. dirs. Cons. Performing Arts Abroad, Kalamazoo, 1979-99, Pacific Basin Choral Festival in Hawaii, Berkeley, Calif., 1989, Gateway Music Festivals, 1997-99; tchr. music theory, piano South Seattle C.C., 1993-94; choral music tchr. Inglemoor H.S., Bothell, Wash., 1994; prof. Polynesian music and dance U. Pitts., summer 1996; spkr. Internat. Soc. Music Edn. Conv., Tampa, Fla., 1994, Pretoria, South Africa, 1998; spkr. nat. conf. Soc. Ethnomusicology, L.A., 1995, Music Educators Nat. Conf., Kansas City, 1996; spkr. in field.; accompanist Honolulu Boy Choir, 1996; coord. summer course in Tahitian dance and music, Papeete, Tahiti, 1998; dir. model choir, State Conv. Calif. Music. Edn. Assn., 2003; dir. various choirs, Internat. Festival L.A., 2003-07, Gospel Piano Seminars, 2005—. Author: Taking Note of Music, 1988, Piano is My Forte, 1989; editor: Pacific Island Choral Series, 1995—99; composer: Tatalo A Le Alii, 1984 (3d pl. state competition); composer, rec. artist Pese Pa'ia, 1988, (rec.) Music at Northwest, 2000, '01 In the Spirit, 2001, profl. rec. Christmas Aloha, dir., composer of new repertoire New Samoan Ch. Choir Repertoire Project, Am. and Western Samoa, 1997; contbr. articles to profl. jours. Founder E Himeni Kakou Colls. Choral Festival, Honolulu, 1976-99; founder, dir. Maile Aloha Singers, Honolulu, 1973-92, Carols at the Centerstage Festival, Honolulu, 1989-99, Lokahi Choral Festival, Honolulu, 1989-99, Aloha, America! Invitational Choral Festival, Honolulu, 1995; dir. Northwest Singers, Kirkland, 1999-2000, Northwest A Cappella, 2000-01; founder Wash. Collegiate Choral Festival, Seattle, 1999-2001, CANTATE! Mid. Schs. Honor Choir, 2002; Gospel piano seminars, Samoa, 2005—, Long Beach, Calif., 2007. Dir. mus. group representing Hawaii, Cultural Office for Territorial Activity, Papeete, Tahiti, 1982, World U. Games, 1983, Casa De La Cultura, Southeastern Mex., 1984, La. World EXPO, 1984, EXPO '86, Vancouver, Hawaiian Airlines, 1987, Goodwill Tour Am. Samoa, 1989, Artists in the Schs. Auckland, N.Z., 1991, Paris, 1999, Detroit, 2000; dir. mus. group representing U.S.A., U.S. Dept. State, EXPO '85, Tsukuba, Japan, 1985; Dir. award 2d pl. group Collegiate Showcase, Chgo., 1988, Dir. award 1st place Choral Groups All Am. Festival, Orlando, Fla., 1994, 7 NW States H.S. Honor Choir, 2000, Nat. Samoa Pastors Choir, Denver, 2005, Samoa, 2006. Mem. AAUP, Am. Choral Dirs. Assn. (Hawaii chpt. 1978-99, editor newsletter 1987-89, 97-99, state pres. 1989-91, state sec. 1997-99, ethnic music chair NW divsn.), Samoa Fealofani Club, Delta Tau Delta (life). Republican. Mem. Pentecostal Ch. Avocations: languages, weightlifting, dance, drums, translating. Home: 4141 Hathaway Ave 23 Long Beach CA 90815-5130 Personal E-mail: drrobertengle@hotmail.com. Business E-Mail: bengle@hawaii.edu.

ENGLE, STEVE EUGENE, artist; b. Honolulu, Dec. 27, 1950; BFA in Sculpture, Santa Barbara Art Inst., 1973; MFA in Sculpture, Ind. U., 1980; postgrad., Pa. Acad. Fine Art, 1982-84. One-man exhbns. include Lisa Harris Gallery, Seattle, 1990, 92, The Contemporary Mus., Honolulu, 1996, Davis/Cline Gallery, Ashland, 2000, Thorndike Gallery, So. Oreg. U., Ashland, 2001, Hypotenuse Gallery, Sinclair C.C., Dayton, Ohio, 2001, Rogue Gallery and Art Ctr., Medford, Oreg., 2006; exhibited in group shows Contemporary Arts Ctr., Honolulu, 1981, Honolulu Acad. Art, 1982, Shreveport (La.) Art Guild, 1984, Woodmere Art Mus., Phila., 1985, U. Del., Newark, 1986, Roger Lapelle Gallery, Phila., 1987, Phila. City Hall, 1988, Bellevue (Wash.) Art Mus., 1988, 92, U. Wash. Med. Ctr., Seattle, 1990, Port Angeles (Wash.) Fine Arts Ctr., 1990, Seattle Ctr., Modern Art Pavillion, 1990, Alt. Mus., N.Y.C., 1991, Whatcom Mus., Bellingham, Wash., 1991, 92, Honolulu Advt. Gallery, 1991, Microsoft Corp., Redmond, Wash., 1992, WestOne Bancorp, Wash., Oreg., and Idaho, 1992, Seattle Ctr. Pavillion, 1993, Jonson Gallery, U. N.Mex., Albuquerque, 1999, Shepparton Art Gallery, Victoria, Australia (Sidney Myer Fund Internat. Ceramic Exhbn.), 2006; represented in permanent collections WestOne Bancorp, Boise, Microsoft Corp., Redmond, Wash. State Arts Commn. Collection, Sch. Dist. Lacey, Wash., Seattle Arts Commn., Portable Works Collection, 1st Hawaiian Bank, Honolulu, Linda and Robert Kanter, Seattle, Hirschl Adler, N.Y.C., Contemporary Arts Ctr., Honolulu, Laila and Thurston Twigg-Smith, Honolulu, others; works included in publs. Jour. Am., The Herald, Seattle Times, Alt. Mus. Exhbn. Catalog, The Weekly, Artweek, Star-Bull, Impact Weekly, Dayton, Ohio, Sunday Jour., Albuquerque, Contemporary Mus. News, Honolulu. Recipient Betty Bowen Meml. Recognition award Seattle Art Mus., 1989, Juror award Bellevue Art Mus., 1992, Best of Category award Paris Gibson Sq. Mus. Art, 1993, Anita Chadwick award Chautauqua Ctr. Visual Arts, N.Y., 1997; tuition scholar Santa Barbara Art Inst., 1972-73; Ford grantee N.Y. Sch. Painting, Drawing and Sculpture, 1979, Nat. Endowment for Arts visual artists fellowship grantee in sculpture, 1990; Seattle Artists project grantee Seattle Arts Commn., 1990. E-mail: sengleart@yahoo.com.

ENGLE, STEVEN B., biotechnology company executive; BSEE, MSEE, U. Tex. Mgmt. cons. Strategic Decisions Group, 1979—84, SRI Internat., 1979—84; v.p. mktg. and divsnl. gen. mgr. Micro Power Systems, 1984—87; CEO Quantum Mgmt. Co., 1987—91; v.p. mktg. Cygnus Inc., 1991—93; exec. v.p., COO La Jolla Pharm. Co., San Diego, 1993—94, pres., dir., sec., 1994—95, CEO, 1995—2006, chmn. bd., 1997—2006. Chmn. BIOCOM; dir. CareLinc Corp.

ENGLEMAN, EPHRAIM PHILIP, rheumatologist; b. San Jose, Calif., Mar. 24, 1911; s. Maurice and Tillie (Rosenberg) E.; m. Jean Sinton, Mar. 2, 1941; children: Ephraim Philip, Edgar George, Jill. BA, Stanford U., 1933; MD, Columbia U., 1937. Intern Mt. Zion Hosp., San Francisco; resident U. Calif., San Francisco, Jos. Pratt Diagnostic Hosp., Boston; rsch. fellow Mass. Gen. Hosp., Boston, 1937-42; practice medicine specializing in rheumatology San Francisco, 1948—; mem. faculty U. Calif. Med. Ctr., San Francisco, 1949—, clin. prof. medicine, 1965—; dir. Rosalind Russell Arthritis Ctr., 1979—. Staff U. Calif. Hosp.; chmn. Nat. Commn. Arthritis and Related Diseases, 1975-76. Author: The Book on Arthritis: A Guide for Patients and Their Families, 1979; also articles, chpts. in books. Served to maj. M.C. USMCR, 1942—47. Recipient medal of Honor, U. Calif., San Francisco, 1999, citation Arthritis Found., 1973, Gold medal for excellence in clin. medicine Columbia U. P&S Alumni, 2007; Ephraim P. Engleman Disting. Professorship in Rheumatology named in his honor U. Calif., San Francisco, 1991; Nat. Inst. Arthritis grantee. Fellow ACP; mem. Internat. League Against Rheumatism (pres. 1981-85), Am. Coll. Rheumatology (founding fellow, master, pres. 1962-63, Presdl. Gold medal 2002), Nat. Soc. Clin. Rheumatologists, AMA, Am. Fedn. Clin. Rsch.; mem. Japanese Rheumatism Soc. (hon.), Spanish Rheumatism Soc., Uruguay Rheumatism Soc., Australian Rheumatism Assn., Chinese Med. Assn., French Soc. Rheumatology, Internat. League against Rheumatism, Gold-Headed Cane Soc. (U. Calif. San Francisco), Family Club (San Francisco). Republican. Jewish. Office: U Calif Rosalind Russell Med Rsch Ctr Arthritis 350 Parnassus Ave Ste 600 San Francisco CA 94117-3608 Business E-Mail: ephraim.engleman@ucsf.edu.

ENGLEMAN CONNORS, ELLEN GAYLE, former federal agency administrator; b. Indpls., Sept. 21, 1959; BA in Eng. and Comm., Ind. U., 1983, JD, 1987; MPA, Harvard U., 1994. Bar: Ind. 1987, U.S. Dist. Ct. (no. and so. dists.) 1987. Pub. affairs exec. GTE, 1987—92; pres., CEO Electricore, Ind., 1994—2001; adminstr. rsch. and spl. programs adminstrn. U.S. Dept. Transp., Washington, 2001—03; mem. Nat. Transp. Safety Bd. (NTSB), Washington, 2003—06, chmn., 2003—05. Dir. Corporate & Govt. Affairs, Direct Relief Internat., 1993—94. Bd. dirs. Direct Relief Internat., dir. corp. & govt. affairs. Lt. USNR, 1999—. Recipient Disting. Pub. Svc. award, USCG, 9/11 medal, U.S. Dept. Transp., 2003 Laurel, Aviation Week. Mem.: Pub. Rels. Soc. Am. (cert. pub. rels.). Home: 11432 Divers Cove Ct Indianapolis IN 46236-8601*

ENGLER, BRIAN DAVID, professional society administrator; b. Palmerton, Pa., Oct. 9, 1947; s. David James and Doreen Estelle (Sheldon) Engler; m. Margaret Mary Hurlock, Dec. 31, 1969 (div. Apr. 1981); children: Donna, David; m. Maxine Sue Richard, May 24, 1981; children: Rachel, Stacey. BS with merit, US Naval Acad., 1969; MS in Ops. Rsch., Naval Postgrad. Sch., Monterey, Calif., 1978; MBA in Fin., Acctg., Marymount U., 1986. Commd. ensign USN, 1969, advanced through grades to comdr., 1983, naval flight officer, mission comdr., ops. analyst, 1969-89, ret., 1989; ops. analyst, project leader Systems Planning and Analysis., Alexandria, Va., 1989-90, asst. program mgr., 1990-91, program mgr., 1991-2000; exec. v.p. Mil. Ops. Rsch. Soc., 2000—. Assoc. editor: alumni newsletter O.R. News, 1976—78. Mem. Big Bros./Big Sisters of Balt., Annapolis, Md., 1968—69; sec.-treas. bd. dirs. Gov.'s Sq. Homeowners Assn., Williamsburg, Va., 1989—97. Decorated Navy Commendation medals (2), Meritorious Svc. medal; recipient cert. of Proficiency, Civil Air Patrol, 1963, Juvenile Decency award, Kiwanis Club, 1965, Best Cadet award, Temple U., 1965. Mem.: VFW (post comdr. 2002—05), Washington Inst. Ops. Rsch. and Mgmt. Sci., Inst. Ops. Rsch. and Mgmt. Sci., Mil. Applications Soc., Mil. Ops. Rsch. Soc. (bd. dirs. 1991—, sec.-treas. 1993—94, v.p. adminstrn. 1995, v.p. fin. and mgmt. 1999—2000), Greater Washington Soc. Assn. Execs., Am. Soc. Assn. Execs., Am. Legion, Delta Epsilon Sigma. Avocations: running, sailing, reading, music, fencing, bowling. Home: 5918 Clermont Landing Ct Burke VA 22015-2565 Office: Mil Ops Rsch Soc Ste 450 1703 N Beauregard St Alexandria VA 22311-1745 E-mail: brian@mors.org.

ENGLER, EVA KAY, dental and veterinary products company executive; b. Czechoslovakia, May 7, 1927; m. Alfred Engler (dec. 1979); children: Raya, Michael David. Pres., founder med. and dental mfg. co. Engler Engrng. Corp., Hialeah, Fla., 1964—. Avocations: languages, painting. Office: Engler Engrng Corp 1099 E 47th St Hialeah FL 33013-2139 Office Phone: 305-688-8581. Office Fax: 305-685-7671. Personal E-mail: eengler@bellsouth.net.

ENGLER, JOHN M., trade association administrator, former governor; b. Mt. Pleasant, Mich., Oct. 12, 1948; s. Mathias John and Agnes Marie (Neyer) E.; m. Michelle; children: Margaret Rose, Hannah Michelle, Madeleine Jenny; B.S. in Agrl. Econs., Mich. State U., 1971; J.D., Thomas M. Cooley Law Sch., 1981. Mem. Mich. Ho. of Reps., 1971-78; mem. Mich. Senate, 1979-90, Republican leader, 1983, senate majority leader, 1984-90; gov., 1991-2003; pres. state and local govt. EDS, 2003-04; pres., CEO, Nat. Assn. Mfrs., 2004—; bd. dirs. Dow Jones & Co., 2005-, Northwest Airlines, Universal Forest Products, Munder Capital; trustee Annie E. Casey Found.; U.S. Trade Reps.' Intergovernmental Policy Adv. com., 1988, Intergovernmental Adv. Coun. on Edn., 1988; chmn. Presdl. Scholars, 1991-92; One of 5 Outstanding Young Men of Mich., Mich. Jaycees, 1983, Governing Magazine Public Official of the Yr. pres. Gerald R. Ford Found.; mem. Nat. Gov.'s Assn. (welfare reform task force 1993-96, edn. goals panel 1993-2002, chair 2001-02). Republican. Roman Catholic. Office Phone: 202-637-3106.

ENGLER, RENATA JOHANNA MARTHA, allergist, immunologist, internist, educator; b. Frankfurt, Germany, 1949; MD, Georgetown U., 1975. Diplomate Am. Bd. Internal Medicine, Am. Bd. Allergy and Immunology (bd. dirs.). Intern Nat. Naval Med. Ctr., Bethesda, Md., 1975-76, resident in internal medicine, 1978-80; fellow in allergy and immunology Walter Reed Army Med. Ctr., Washington, 1980-82, mem. staff, 1982—, chief allergy & immunization svcs. Assoc. prof. Uniformed Svcs. U. Health Sci., Bethesda. Mem. ACP, Am. Acad. Allergy and Immunology, Am. Coll. Allergy, Am. Fedn. Clin. Rsch. Home: 1900 Wallace Ave Silver Spring MD 20902-1302 Office: Sair Hosp and Clinic Allergy-Immunology Dept Walter Reed Army Med Ctr Washington DC 20307-0001

ENGLERT, PETER, academic administrator, director; Grad., U. Cologne, Germany. Faculty mem., adminstr. San Jose State U., Calif.; pro vice chancellor, dean sci., architecture and design Victoria U., Wellington, New Zealand, 1995—2002, U. Hawaii, Manoa, 2005—, CEO, chancellor, 2002—05. Founder support group Maori and Pacific nation students U. Victoria; elected adminstrv. bd. Internat. Assn. Univs. (IAU), 2004—. Office: U Hawaii Hawai Inst Geophysics and Plan 1680 E-W Rd, Post 602 Honolulu HI 96822 Home Phone: 808-595-0119; Office Phone: 808-956-5033. Office Fax: 808-965-6322. Business E-Mail: penglert@hawaii.edu.

ENGLERT, ROY THEODORE, lawyer; b. Nashville, Sept. 11, 1922; s. Roy T. and Ruth Rowe (Tindall) E.; m. Helen Frances Wiggs, Sept. 25, 1948; children: Lee Ann, Roy Jr. BA, Vanderbilt U., 1943; JD, Columbia, 1951; LLM, George Washington U., 1953. Bar: Tenn. 1951, US Dist. Ct. DC 1951, US Supreme Ct. 1955, Internat. Trade 1975. Asst. counsel Office Comptroller of Currency, U.S. Treasury Dept., 1951-58, chief counsel, 1958-62, asst. gen. counsel of dept., 1962-66, dep. gen. counsel, 1966-73; sole practice Washington, 1973-96. Bd. dirs., sec. Walker/Potter Assocs., Inc., Washington, 1973-96; mem. Sr. Seminar in Fgn. Policy, Dept. State, 1963-64, US Assay Commn., 1975; lectr., writer on banking law. Contbr. articles to profl. jours. Judo tech. ofcl. Atlanta Olympics; bd. dirs. Westminster at Lake Ridge, Ingleside at Rock Creek, Westminster Ingleside Found. Lt. USNR, 1943—46, participated in D-Day invasion at Normandy. Recipient Exceptional Service award U.S. Treasury, 1972, Gen. Counsel's award, 1973; winner 19 nat. championships in master track events. Mem. ABA, Tenn. Bar Assn. Presbyterian. Home: 12183 Cathedral Dr Woodbridge VA 22192-2227 Office: 6720 Bellamy Ave Springfield VA 22152-3023

ENGLERT, WALTER GEORGE, classics and humanities educator; b. Oakland, Calif., June 30, 1952; s. Walter George and Isobel Ann (O'Hearne) E.; m. Mary Ellen Mecchi; children: Francesca, Molly. BA summa cum laude, St. Mary's Coll. Calif., 1974; MA, U. Calif. Santa

Barbara, 1976; postgrad., Am. Sch. Classical Studies, Athens, 1979; PhD, Stanford U., 1981. Teaching asst. U. Calif., Santa Barbara, 1974-76, Stanford U., 1977-78; vis. lectr. U. Mich., Ann Arbor, 1980-81; vis. assoc. prof. U. Calif., Berkeley, 1986, Intercollegiate Ctr. Classical Studies, Rome, 1992-93, 2007—; Omar and Althea Hoskins prof. Reed Coll., Portland, Oreg., 1981—. Organizer and lectr. Reed Latin Symposium for H.S. Students, 1988-2006; participant TAG Spring Interdisciplinary confs., 1988; tchr. Paideia Class, 1989, 91, 96, 97, Reed MALS Seminar, 1988, 93, 97, 2001, 05, Reed Elderhostel Program, 1989; mem. faculty Reed Alumni Coll., 1989, 95; lectr. Seattle Reed Alumni Group, 1991; guest Town Hall TV show, 1991. Contbr. articles to profl. jours. Grantee NEH, 1983, 95, Mellon Faculty Seminar, 1986-87, Sloan Found., 1987-88. Office: Reed Coll 3203 SE Woodstock Blvd Portland OR 97202-8138 Home Phone: 503-775-8470; Office Phone: 503-517-7310. Business E-Mail: walter.englert@reed.edu.

ENGLES, ERIC WILLIAM, editor, writer; b. Albany, NY, Dec. 28, 1958; s. Robert William and Margaret Engles; m. Lisa Frankel, Jan. 2002. BA in Environ. Studies and Biology, U. Calif., Santa Cruz, PhD in Sociology, 1991. Editor Addison-Wesley Pub. Co., 1985—86; prin., sole propr. EditCraft Editl. Svcs., Grass Valley, Calif., 1991—. Editor: (book) Tending the Wild: Native American Knowledge and the Management of California's Natural Resources, New Guardians for the Golden Gate: How America Got a Great National Park, (textbook) Agroecology: The Ecology of Sustainable Food Systems. Mem., bd. dirs. Foothill Country Dancers, Nevada City, Calif., 2001. Mem.: Bay Area Editors' Forum, Nat. Assn. Sci. Writers. Democrat-Npl. Avocations: gardening, botany, travel, dance. Home and Office: EditCraft 422 Pine St Grass Valley CA 95945 Business E-Mail: eric@editcraft.com.

ENGLES, GREGG L., food products executive; b. Durant, Okla., Aug. 16, 1957; AB, Dartmouth Coll., 1979; JD, Yale Univ., 1982. Law clk. Judge Anthony Kennedy, US Ct. Appeals, 1982—83; pres. Engles Capital Corp., 1988—92; chmn., CEO Reddy Ice Co., 1988—95; pres. Engles Mgmt. Corp., 1993—94, Suiza Dairy, San Juan, 1993—95; chmn. Velda Farms, 1994—95; founder, chmn., CEO Suiza Foods, Dallas, 1995—2001; vice-chmn., CEO Dean Foods Co., Dallas, 2001—02, chmn., CEO, 2002—. Bd. dir. Grocery Manufacturers Am. Bd. mem. Southwestern Med. Found., So. Methodist Univ., Dallas Citizens Council, TreeHouse Foods; mem. Dartmouth President's Leadership Council. Mem.: Dallas CEO Roundtable, Young Presidents Org. Office: Dean Foods Co Ste 1200 2515 McKinney Ave Dallas TX 75201-1945*

ENGLESE, DAMON JOSEPH, director; b. Secaucus, NJ, Aug. 8, 1979; s. Dennis L. and Theresa Englese. BS, Seton Hall U., 2001; MA in Edn., St. Peter's Coll., 2003. Tchr. Union City Bd. Edn., NJ, 2001—03, whole sch. reform facilitator, 2003—. Chair Sch. Leadership Coun., Union City, 2003—05. Democrat. Roman Catholic. Avocations: golf, travel. Office: Union City Bd Edn 1401 Central Ave Union City NJ 07087 Home Phone: 201-943-5971; Office Phone: 201-348-5602.

ENGLESMITH, TEJAS, actor, television producer, curator; b. London, Nov. 28, 1941; came to U.S. 1957; s. George and Lydia Julia (Johnson-Briet) E. Student in art history, U. St. Thomas, Houston, 1959-63. Asst. dir. Whitechapel Gallery, London, 1963-69; curator Contemporary Art Jewish Mus., NYC, 1969-70; dir. Leo Castelli Gallery, NYC, 1970-76, Max Hutchinson Gallery, Houston, 1976-78; pvt. art cons. Houston, 1978-80; auction mgr. Sta. KUHT-TV, Houston, 1980-84, exec. prodr., 1980-86, assoc. dir., devel. managing editor Public Times, 1984-86; prodr., announcer Sta. KUHF-FM, Houston, 1987-90; ind. broadcast cons. and prodr. Houston, 1990—; subscriber svcs./pub. rels. rep. Theatre Under the Stars, Houston, 1992-99; prin. Dean James. Judge Roanoke (Va.) Art Festival, 1972; judge, lectr. S.W. Tex. State U., San Marcos, 1978. Narrator: (film) Pas de Deux: A Dance of Two Countries: China and America, 1980, Just a Closer Walk With Thee, 1989, The English Countryside, 1992 (Silver Telly award narration 1994), Hall of the Americas, 1998, Voyages of Discovery, 2000, Houston Mus. of Natural Sci., numerous travel and indsl. videos; actor (TV series) Gamera 2: Region shurai, 1996, Kino no tabi, 2003; interviewee: Inflatable Sculpture, CBS-TV, 1969, Views on Art, Sta. WNYC-FM, 1975, Curtain!, Sta. KUHT-TV, 1980-81; prodr./host: Conversations with People in Arts, Sta. KPFT-FM, 1977; exec. prodr. 30th Anniversary Sta. KUHT Sock Hop, 1983; writer mus. catalogues; organizer various exhbns. Mem. selection com. N.Y. Drawing Soc., 1970; reader Taping For the Blind, 1987—; adv. bd. Cultural Arts Council Houston, 1978. Recipient Silver award Assn. for Community TV, 1981, Gold award Assn. for Community TV, 1982. Fellow Royal Soc. Arts. Clubs: TLC Four Seasons. Home: 7839 Fondren Rd Houston TX 77074-4601 Office: Pastorini/Bosby Talent Agy 3013 Fountain View Dr Houston TX 77057-6124 Office Phone: 713-266-4488. Personal E-mail: tejase@sbcglobal.net. *The learning and practice of good manners would alleviate most of the problems we face today... and tomorrow.*

ENGLISH, BRUCE VAUGHAN, environmentalist, consultant; b. Richmond, Va., Aug. 6, 1921; s. Pollard and Lucy Kelly (Rice) E.; m. Virginia Tejas McCall Shaw, Feb. 6, 1949. BS in Physics and Math., Randolph-Macon Coll., 1942; MS in Physics and Math., Ind. U., 1943; PhD in Physics, U. Va., 1958. Grad. asst. instr. army specialized tng. program/rsch. asst. Manhattan Dist. Engrs. Project; physics instr. Ind. U., Bloomington; asst. prof. physics army specialized tng. program Randolph-Macon Coll., Ashland, Va., 1943-44, assoc. prof., acting chmn. dept. physics, 1948-58, prof., chmn. dept., 1958-64; physicist, head high pressure lab. US Navy Underwater Sound Reference Lab., Orlando, Fla., 1946-48; physicist, cons. historic preservation, pollution control and environment Ashland, 1964—; dir. Poe Found., Inc., Richmond, 1968-97, pres., 1973-92, life hon. pres., 1998—; pres., dir. Edgar Allan Poe Mus., Richmond, 1973-92. Pres. Pollution Control Assocs., Richmond, 1967-70. Pub.: Conway Thompson, A Retrospective, 2000; co-pub.: Poe's Richmond, 1978; columnist Herald-Progress, 1971—; contbr. articles to Poe Messenger mag. Founding mem. Richmond Symphony, 1956; mem. Patrick Henry Scotchtown Com., Hanover County, Va., 1958—; pres. Hist. Richmond Found., 1967-70; bd. dirs. Church Hill Model Neighborhood Bd., Richmond, 1968-73; chmn. Bicentennial Com. for Hanover County, 1974-92, Drainage Com., Ashland, 1980s, Courthouse Com. for Hanover County, 1985—; lay reader, mem. vestry St. John's Ch., Church Hill, Richmond, Va., 1969-70; hon. pres. Poe Found., Inc., 1998. With USN, 1944-45. Named Hon. Citizen State of Md., 1990; Ford Faculty fellow, 1951-52, Danforth fellow, 1956-57, du Pont fellow, 1957-58; recipient Smithey Math Gold medal, 1942. Mem. AAAS, Am. Phys. Soc., Va. Acad. Sci., Va. Hist. Soc., Nat. Trust for Hist. Preservation, Irish Georgian Soc., Cousteau Soc. (founding), Air and Waste Mgmt. Assn., Nat. Soc. for Clean Air Gt. Britain, Soc. Descs. of Peter Francisco (founder, advisor), Nat. D-Day Mus. WWII (charter), City Tavern Club, Commonwealth Club, Farmington Country Club, Downtown Club, Phi Beta Kappa, Sigma Xi, Omicron Delta Kappa, Chi Beta Phi, Pi Delta Epsilon. Episcopalian. Achievements include research in project developing atomic bomb, increasing awareness of hazards of pollution since 1955, of Edgar Allan Poe's cosmology, cryptography, and other scientific writings.

ENGLISH, CARL L., electric power industry executive; m. Linda English; 2 children. B in Chem. Engring., Mich. State U., East Lansing, 1968, MBA, 1969. With Consumers Energy, Jackson, Mich., 1969, head statewide electric transmission and distbn. ops. and customer svc. activities, pres., CEO gas divsn., 1999; pres. AEP Utilities Am. Electric Power Svc. Corp. Mem. Columbus Downtown Devel. Adv. Bd., Columbus Downtown Housing Investment Funds Bd., Directions for Youth & Families Bd. Office: Am Electric Power Svc Corp 1 Riverside Plz Columbus OH 43215-2373 Office Phone: 614-716-1000.*

ENGLISH, FLOYD LEROY, telecommunications industry executive; b. Nicholas, Calif., June 10, 1934; s. Elvan L. and Louise (Corliss) E.; children from previous marriage: children: Roxane, Darryl; m. Elaine Ewell, July 3, 1981; 1 child, Christine. AB in Physics, Calif. State U., Chico, 1959; MS in Physics, Ariz. State U., 1962, PhD in Physics, 1965; DSc (hon.), Calif. State U., Chico, 2005. Divsn. supr. Sandia Labs., Albuquerque, 1965-73; gen. mgr. integrated cirs. divsn. Rockwell Internat.-Collins, Newport Beach, Calif., 1973—75; pres. Darcom, Albuquerque, 1975-79; cons in energy mgmt. and acquisitions Albuquerque, 1980-81; v.p. U.S. ops. Andrew Corp., Orland Park, Ill., 1981-82, pres., 1981-82, COO, 1981-82, CEO, 1983-92, also bd. dirs., 1982—, chmn. bd. dirs., pres., CEO, 1992—2000, 2000—01, chmn., bd. dirs., CEO, 2001—02, chmn. bd. dirs., 2002—04, chmn. emeritus, 2004. Contbr. articles to profl. jours. 1st lt. U.S. Army, 1954-57; capt. Res., 1957-69 Mem.: IEEE, Internat. Engring. Consortium (bd. dirs. 1984—2002), Exec. Club Chgo. (bd. dirs. 1983—2004). Republican. Presbyterian. Home Phone: 956-772-9511. Personal E-mail: eee81@comcast.net.

ENGLISH, JAMES FAIRFIELD, JR., former college president; b. Putnam, Conn., Feb. 15, 1927; s. James Fairfield and Alice Bradford (Welles) English; m. Isabelle Spotswood Cox, July 9, 1955; children: Alice, James Fairfield, Margaret, William. Grad., Loomis Sch., 1944; BA, Yale U., 1949; MA, Cambridge U., Eng., 1951; JD, U. Conn., 1956; HLD, Northeastern U., 1982, Trinity Coll., 1989; LLD, U. Hartford, 1971, St. Joseph Coll., West Hartford, Conn., 1982. With Conn. Bank & Trust Co., Hartford, 1951—, sr. v.p., 1961-63, exec. v.p., 1963-66, pres., 1966-70, chmn. bd., 1970-80; v.p. fin. and planning Trinity Coll., Hartford, 1977-81, pres., 1981-89. Trustee emeritus Loomis Chaffee Sch., Mystic Seaport Mus.; bd. dirs. Cmty. Found. S.E. Conn. With AUS, 1944—46. Episcopalian. Home: 31 Potter St Groton CT 06340-5734 also: 777 Prospect Ave West Hartford CT 06105-4204

ENGLISH, JOHN DWIGHT, lawyer; b. Evanston, Ill., Mar. 28, 1949; s. John Francis English and Mary Faye (Taylor) Butler; m. Claranne Kay Lundeen, Apr. 22, 1972; children: Jennifer A., Katharine V., Margaret E. BA, Drake U., 1971; JD, Loyola U., 1976. Bar: Ill. 1976, U.S. Dist. Ct. (no. dist.) Ill. 1976, U.S. Tax Ct. 1977. Assoc. Bentley DuCanto Silvestri & Forkins, Chgo., 1976-79; ptnr. Silvestri Mahoney English & Zdeb, Chgo., 1979-81; assoc. Coffield Ungaretti Harris & Slavin, Chgo., 1981-83; ptnr. Ungaretti & Harris, Chgo., 1983—. Instr. estate planning Loyola U., Chgo., 1982-87; instr. Ill. Inst. Continuing Edn. Estate Planning Short Course, 1998, 2001. Bd. dirs. Prince of Peace Luth. Sch., Chgo., 1977-83, Bethesda Home for the Aged, Chgo., 1981-89, 2000-03, Luth. Family Mission, Chgo., 1985-91; alderman Park Ridge (Ill.) City Coun., 1991-95; pres. congregation coun. St. Luke's Luth. Ch., Park Ridge, 2000-03, 05-06. Mem.: Chgo. Bar Assn. (former chmn. divsn. II probate practice com.), Ill. State Bar Assn., Phi Beta Kappa. Lutheran. Home: 631 Wisner St Park Ridge IL 60068-3428 Office: Ungaretti & Harris 3500 Three 1st Nat Bank Plz Chicago IL 60602 Office Phone: 312-977-4401. Business E-Mail: jdenglish@uhlaw.com.

ENGLISH, MARK, artist; b. Hubbard, Tex., 1933; Attended, U. Tex.; grad., Art Ctr. Coll., LA, 1960; D (hon.), Acad. Art Coll., San Francisco, 2005. One-man shows include Johnson County Mus., Kansas City, 1992, Am. Legacy Gallery, 1999, 2002, 2004, Richard McDonald Gallery, Santa Fe, 2001, Laguna Beach, Calif., 2001, Eleanor Ettinger Gallery, NYC, 2001, 2002, 2005, exhibitions include Hanson Gallery, New Orleans, Telluride Gallery, 1999, 2001, 2004, Linda Beutner Gallery, Denver, Eleanor Ettinger Gallery, NYC, 1999—2000, 2003, 2004, 2007, Albemarle Gallery, London, 2003—04; works published in Good Housekeeping, The Ladies' Home Jour., McCall's, Redbook, Saturday Evening Post, Sports Illustrated, Time mag. Named Artist of Yr., Guild of NY, 1967. Mem.: Soc. of Illustrators (Hall of Fame 1983, Hamilton King award 1967). Achievements include designing thirteen US Postal stamps. Office: c/o Eleanor Ettinger Gallery 19 Spring St Ground Fl New York NY 10012*

ENGLISH, MARLENE CABRAL, management consultant; b. Lawrence, Mass., Apr. 28, 1954; d. Amick John and Mary Rose (Vasconcelos) Cabral; m. Richard Gayle English, June 24, 1978. BBA, U. Mass., 1976. Acct. mgr. Revlon, Inc., NYC, 1977—79; tech. rep. Rapidata, Inc., NYC, 1979—80; mgr. acctg. sys. group Pannell, Kerr, Forster, Dallas, 1980—83; mgmt. cons. Blythe/Nelson, Dallas, 1983—84, Prism Cons., Arlington, Tex., 1984—. Sec., treas. Highland-Avery Industries, Inc., Dallas, 1988—95. Author: And God Created Woman, 1995, Fit for a King: The Proverbs 31 Woman, 2005. Sys. cons. Van Cliburn Internat. Piano Competition, Ft. Worth, 1985; tech. sys. procurement and installation Rep. Nat. Conv., Dallas, 1984; dir. Faith Harvest Ministries, Inc., Dallas, 1990—95. Roman Catholic. Avocations: victorian studies, antique linen restoration, gardening, writing, piano. Home and Office: 4320 Rambling Creek Dr Arlington TX 76016-3418 Personal E-mail: jicky@sbcglobal.net.

ENGLISH, MICHELA, entertainment company executive; married; 2 children. BA in Internat. Affairs, Sweet Briar Coll.; M Pub. and Pvt. Mgmt., Yale U. Policy analyst Fed. Energy Adminstrn.; sr. mgr. McKinsey & Co.; v.p. corp. planning and bus. devel. Marriott Corp.; sr. v.p. Nat. Geog. Soc.; pres. Discovery.com, Bethesda, Md. Bd. dirs. Riggs Nat. Corp., Washington; cons. in field. Bd. dirs. Sweet Briar (Va.) Coll. Mem. Nat. Found. for Improvement of Edn. (bd. dirs.). Office: Discovery.com 7700 Wisconsin Ave Fl 5 Bethesda MD 20814-3557 Fax: 301-986-4826.

ENGLISH, NICHOLAS CONOVER, lawyer; b. Elizabeth, NJ, Apr. 12, 1912; s. Conover and Sara Elizabeth (Jones) E.; m. Agnes N. Perry, Mar. 18, 1939 (div. 1947); children— Henry H. P., Ann Whitall (Mrs. Edward J. Wardwell); m. Eleanor Morss, May 1, 1948; children— Priscilla English Vincent, Sara (dec.), Sherman, Eleanor English Folta. Grad., Pingry Sch., 1929; AB magna cum laude, Princeton, 1934; LL.B., Harvard, 1937. Bar: N.J. 1937. Since practiced in, Newark; partner firm McCarter & English, 1947-77, of counsel, 1978—. Bd. dirs. Summit (N.J.) YMCA, 1950-57, pres., 1953-55; bd. dirs. Newark YMWCA, also pres.; chmn. exec. com. Ctrl. Atlantic Area YMCA, 1957-63; mem. nat. coun. YMCA, 1954, 58-81, v.p., 1959-60, mem. nat. bd., 1960-71, 73-81, vice chmn., 1969-71, treas., 1977-81; trustee N.J. Nat. Land Trust, 1983-93, Kent Place Sch., 1959—, pres., 1961-72, Pingry Sch., 1954-73; bd. dirs. Nat. Legal Aid Assn., 1953-56. Lt. USNR, 1943—45. Mem. ABA (ho. of dels. 1957-58), N.J. Bar Assn., Essex County Bar Assn., Am. Bible Soc. (bd. trustees 1964-93, sr. trustee 1993—), Am. Law Inst. Congregationalist. Home: 46 Meadow Lks Apt 04L Hightstown NJ 08520-3332 Office: McCarter & English 4 Gateway Ctr 100 Mulberry St Newark NJ 07102-0652 Home Phone: 609-426-6296.

ENGLISH, PATRICIA DORZELL, women's health nurse practitioner; d. Robert William and Irma Mary English. BSN, St. Xavier U., 2000. RN State Ill. Dept. Regulation and Edn., 2002, lic. practical nurse, State Ill. Dept. Regulation and Edn., 1983, cert. childbirth educator, ARC, 1983. Nurse Daniel Hale Williams Med. Ctr., Chgo., 1984, St. Francis Xavier Cabrini Hosp., Chgo., 1985—86, Michael Resse Health Plan, Chgo., 1986—89, Rush Presbyn. St. Luke's Med. Ctr., Chgo., 1989; educator, couselor South Side Pregnancy Ctr., Oak Lawn, Ill., 2004—; pvt. tchr., 1989—2004. Editor Block Club, Chgo., 1994—97. Recipient Outstanding Vol. Svc. award, Oak Forest Hosp., 1980—90, Vol. award, ARC, 1983—89. Mem.: Sigma Theta Tau. Avocations: ceramics, sewing, crafts, singing, writing poetry.

ENGLISH, PHILIP SHERIDAN, congressman; b. Erie, Pa., June 20, 1956; s. John Sr. and Otilie English; m. Christiane Weschler. BA in Polit. Sci., U. Pa., 1978; D (hon.), Erie Coll. Osteopathic Medicine; LLD (hon.), Thiel Coll. Contr., Erie, Pa., 1986-90; chief of staff Staff of Pa. State Senator Melissa Hart, Harrisburg, Pa., 1990-92; minority exec. dir. Pa. State Senate Fin. Com., Harrisburg, 1992-94; exec. dir. Pa. State Senate Transp. Com.; rsch. dir. Pa. State Senate Labor and Industry Com.; mem. US Congress from 3rd (formerly 21st) Pa. dist., 1995—, mem. ways and means com., mem. joint econ. com., 2001—, mem. Rep. Policy Com., vice chmn. Congl. Steel Caucus. Named Erie County Young Rep. of Yr., 1995, Congl. Legislator of Yr., Pa. Assn. Home Health Agencies, 1996, Friend of the Nat. Pks., Nat. Pk. Conservancy Assn., Friend of the Shareholder, Am. Shareholders Assn., Champion of Small Bus., Small Bus. Survival Ctr., Nat. Fedn. Ind. Bus., Super Friend of Seniors, 60 Plus Assn.; recipient Guardian of Medicare award, Coalition Responsible Medicare Reform, 1995, Campaign to Keep Am. Warm award, 1996, Friend of the Family award, Christian Coalition, 1996, Congressman of Yr. award, Coun. Devel. Fin. Agencies, 1996, Pres.'s award for Legis. Excellence, Nat. Beer Wholesalers Assn., 1996, Pub. Svc. award, Greater Erie Cmty. Action Com., 1996, Thomas Jefferson award, Food Distbrs. Internat., 1996, 2004, 2006, Coalition to Save Medicare award, 1997, Pub. Svc. award, Soc. Am. Archaeology, 1997, Beacon award, Am. Soc. Assn. Execs., 1999, Am. Occupl. Therapists Assn. award, Excellence in Leadership, 2003, Ben Franklin award, 60 Plus Assn., 2004, Mfrs. Adv. of Yr. award, Am. Bus. Coun., 2005, Award for Advocacy of Ind. Higher Edn., Nat. Assn. Ind. Colls. and Univs., 2005, Superhero award, Nat. Assn. Cmty. Health Ctrs., 2006, Oncology Medal of Honor award, Hero of the Taxpayer award, Ams. for Tax Reform, Legis. Leadership award, Nat. Assn. Realtors, Small Bus. Adv. award, Small Bus. Survival Com., Disting. Svc. award, Lake Erie Health Edn. Ctr., Roger Williams award, Zeta Beta Tau Frat., Spirit of Enterprise award, US C. of C., Jefferson award, Citizens for a Sound Economy, Paul Harris award, Rotary Internat., Am. Coll. Pharmacy Physicians award, Neal Coughlin award, Erie County Rep. Party, Robert Parker award, Legis. Excellence award, Nat. Mfrs. Assn., Appreciation award, Make-a-Wish Found., Pro-Sr. Tax Cut award, United Srs. Assn., 24/7 award, Am. Coll. Emergency Physicians, Humane Adv. award, Human Soc. US. Republican. Roman Catholic. Avocations: hiking, history, archaeology. Office: City Annex Bldg 900 N Hermitage Rd Hermitage PA 16148 Office Phone: 202-225-5406, 724-342-6132. Office Fax: 724-342-6219.*

ENGLISH, RAY, library administrator; b. Brevard, NC, Dec. 11, 1946; s. Daniel Leon and Lois (Dorsett) E.; m. Allison Scott Ricker, Oct. 19, 1985; children: John, Michael. AB with honors in German, Davidson Coll., 1969; MA in German Lit., U. N.C., 1971, MSLS, 1977, PhD, 1978. Teaching asst. German dept. U. N.C., Chapel Hill, 1970-73, 74-75, rsch. asst., 1976; reference libr. Alderman Libr. U.Va., Charlottesville, Va., 1977-79; head reference libr. Oberlin (Ohio) Coll. Libr., 1979-89, assoc. dir., 1986-90; dir. libraries, Oberlin (Ohio) Coll., 1990—, acad. advisor, 1980—. Lectr. in German, 1986—2000; vis. lectr. Sch. Libr. Sci., U. N.C., Chapel Hill, 1981; steering com. Scholarly Pub. and Acad. Resources Coalition, 1999—, chair, 2006—; spkr. in field. Mem. editl. bd. Portal: Libraries and the Academy; contbr. articles to profl. jours. German Acad. Exchange Svc. fellow, 1973-74. Mem.: ALA, Acad. Libr. Assn. Ohio, Libr. Adminstrn. and Mgmt. Assn., Assn. Coll. and Rsch. Librs. (bd. dirs., exec. com. 1996—98, chair scholarly comm. com. 2002—06, Acad. Rsch. Libr. of the Yr. 2006). Home: 83 S Cedar St Oberlin OH 44074-1559 Office: Oberlin Coll Library 148 W College St Oberlin OH 44074-1575 Office Phone: 440-775-8287. E-mail: ray.english@oberlin.edu.

ENGLISH, RICHARD ALLYN, sociologist, educator; b. Winter Park, Fla., Aug. 29, 1936; s. Wentworth and Mary English; m. Ireita Geraldine Williams, June 29, 1978 AB, Talladega Coll., 1958; MA (Woodrow Wilson fellow), U. Mich., 1959, MSW, 1964, PhD, 1970. Cert. Oxford U., Internat. Summer Sch. Forced Migration Refugee Ctr., Queen Elizabeth Hse, Oxford, England, 2001. Dir. vocat. and youth services Flint Urban League, Mich., 1959-61, acting exec. dir., 1961-62; social group worker Neighborhood Service Orgn., Detroit, 1963-65; mem. faculty Sch. Social Work, Wayne State U., 1965-67; lectr. U. Mich., Ann Arbor, 1967-70, asst. prof. social work, 1970-72, assoc. prof., 1972-83, prof., 1983—85, assoc. v.p. acad. affairs, 1974-81; dean Howard U. Sch. Social Work, 1985—2000, prof., 1985—; interim provost and chief acad. officer Howard U., 2003—04, provost and chief acad. officer, 2004—. Vis. scholar Paul Baerwald Sch. Social Work, Hebrew U., Jerusalem, 1975; vis. prof. Howard U., fall 1981; Am. Psychol. Assn.-Nat. Inst. Edn. fellow, 1981; Robert L. Sutherland chair in mental health and social policy U. Tex.-Austin Sch. Social Work, 1983-84, 84-85; cons. to various schs., social work, public sch. dists. and pvt. founds., 1969—; pres. Council on Social Work Edn., 1981-84; bd. dirs. Nat. Resource Ctr. for Spl. Needs Adoption, Spaulding Sch. for Children, Chelsea, Mich., 1986—, Nat. Coun. Aging. Author: (with others) Inheriting the Earth: Child Welfare Policies and Practices for Minority Children, 1990; co-editor: Human Service Organizations: A Book of Readings, 1974; The Challenge for Mental Health: Minorities and Their World Views, 1984, (with W. Allen and J. Hall) Black Families, 1960-84: A Classified, Selectively Annotated Bibliography, 1986; co-editor: (with C. Guzzetta and A.J.Katz) Education for Social Work Practice: Selected International Models; The Professional School Dean: The Roles of Leadership (co-editor with M.J. Austin and F.L. Ahearn), 1997; mem. editorial bd. Black Caucus: Jour. Nat. Assn. Black Social Workers; contbr. articles to profl. jours. Mem. adv. panel Refugee Policy Group, mem. adv. bd. Nat. Assembly; bd. visitors Sch. Social Work U. Pitts.; bd. dirs. Youth for Understanding Internat. Exch., 1991—, Coalition for the Homeless; bd. advisors Ill. Inst. Mil. and Occupational Studies; adv. bd. Enterprise Found.; mem. vestry St. Mary's Episcopal Ch. Recipient Outstanding Service award Nat. Assn. Black Social Workers, 1983; Nat. Assn. for Equal Opportunity in Higher Edn. Disting. Alumni award, 1985, Presdl. award for Excellence in Social Work Edn., 1997; Whitney Young, Jr. scholar, Western Mich. U., 1988. Mem. Nat. Assn. Social Workers, Nat. Coun. Family Rels., Am. Sociol. Assn., Internat. Council Social Welfare, Internat. Assn. Schs. Social Work (bd. dirs.), ACLU (bd. dirs. nat. capitol area 1986—), The Emeritus Found. (bd. dirs.), Dept. Human Svcs. Commn., D.C. Govt., Nat. Network for Social Work Mgrs. (adv. bd.), Internat. Coun. Social Welfare (U.S. com., internat. bd.), Coun. on Social Work Edn., Nat. Assn. Black Social Workers. Home: 2724 Abilene Dr Chevy Chase MD 20815-3051 Office: Howard U Office of Provost 2400 6th St Ste 405 Washington DC 20059-0001 Business E-Mail: renglish@howard.edu.

ENGLISH, ROBERT JOSEPH, electronics executive; b. Jersey City, Dec. 5, 1932; s. John Joseph and Mary (Budrawiz) E.; m. Robyn Adele Allan, Dec. 27, 1958; children: Robert Joseph, Mark Allan, John Frederick. BS, St. Peters Coll., 1954; LL.B.; Georgetown U., 1958; MBA, NYU, 1963. Bar: DC 1958, NJ 1959, NY 1984. Subcontract adminstr. ITT Fed. Labs. div., Nutley, NJ, 1959-60; with Fed. Electric Corp., Paramus, NJ, 1960—, sec., gen. counsel, 1964-66, dir. legal contracts, 1967-70; gen. counsel ITT Govt. and Comml. Services Group, 1970-72; v.p., sec., gen. counsel ITT Def. Communications and ITT Avionics divs., Nutley, 1972—; sec., gen. counsel Internat. Electric Corp., 1972—. Dir. ITT Fed. Support Services Inc., ITT Tech. Services Inc., Intelex Systems Inc., Providence, Base Services Inc., Paramus, Internat. Standard Engring. Inc., Paramus. Author: Business Contract Forms, Federal Government Subcontract

Forms; contbr. articles to profl. jours. Trustee Mahwah Hist. Soc., N.J., 1978—. Served to 1st lt., Chem. Corps, U.S. Army, 1954-56. Mem. Am., Bergen, NJ, DC, NY Bar Assns., Phi Delta Phi. Home: 36 Sunnyside Rd Mahwah NJ 07430-1418 Office: 492 River Rd Nutley NJ 07110-3609 Personal E-mail: esquire@aol.com.

ENGLISH, STEPHEN FRANCIS, lawyer; b. Portland, Oreg., Jan. 17, 1948; BA, Hons. Coll., U. Oreg., 1970; JD, U. Calif., San Francisco, 1973. Bar: Oreg. 1973; U.S. Dist. Ct. Oreg. 1973; U.S. Ct. Appeals (9th cir.) Oreg. 1980; U.S. Supreme Ct. 1982. Ptnr. Bullivant Houser Bailey, Portland, Oreg., 1983—. Mem. faculty Hastings Coll. Trial Advocacy, 1998—; mem. Bus. Litigation Inst., 2000; bd. dirs. Dr. Martens AirWair USA, 2002—, Fellow Am. Coll. Trial Lawyers; Mem. ABA (vice-chair products liability com., 1996—, chair self insurers and risk mgrs. com. 1994-95, editor Self Insurers Newsletter 1987-89, chair non-profit, charitable and religious orgns. com. 1990-92, mem. Tort and Insurance Practice Sect.), Multnomah County Bar Assn., Oreg. State Bar Assn. (chair litigation sect. 1990-91, exec. com. 1987-91), Am. Bd. Trial Adv. (treas. Oreg. chpt. 1996-98, bd. dirs. 1997—, sec. 1998—, pres. 2002-, pres. Oreg. chpt., 2003-04), Oreg. Assn. Def. Counsel (chair products liability practice group 1997-98), Def. Rsch. Inst., Oreg. State Bar Masters of Trial Advocacy. Office: Bullivant Houser Bailey 300 Pioneer Tower 888 SW 5th Ave Portland OR 97204-2089 E-mail: steve.english@bullivant.com.

ENGLISH, STEPHEN RAYMOND, lawyer; b. Key West, Fla., Nov. 25, 1946; s. Jack Raymond and Jean Clyde (Peightal) E.; m. Molly Munger, Oct. 7, 1978; children: Nicholas, Alfred. BA, UCLA, 1975; JD, Harvard U., 1975. Bar: Calif. 1975, U.S. Dist. Ct. (ctrl. dist.) Calif. 1976, U.S. Dist. Ct. (so. dist.) Calif. 1978, U.S. Dist. Ct. (ea. dist.) Calif. 1988, U.S. Ct. Appeals (9th cir.) 1992. Assoc. Agnew, Miller & Carlson, LA, 1975-78, Morgan, Lewis & Bockius, LA, 1978-85, ptnr., 1985-98, English, Munger & Rice, LA, 1998—, co-dir. Advancement Project, 2000—. Lawyer rep. Ninth Cir. Jud. Conf., 1996-97. Pres. bd. dirs. Pub. Counsel, L.A., 1988-89, Inner City Law Ctr., L.A., 1992-93; mem. L.A. Legal Aid Found., pres., 2006—. Mem. L.A. County Bar Assn. (mem. barristers exec. com. 1980-82, trustee 1990-92, chair pro bono coun. 1990-92, chair legal svcs. for poor 1993-95, mem. exec. com. litig. sect. 1994-2005, chair litig. sect. 2003-04), L.A. County Bar Found. (pres. 1998-99).

ENGLISH, THOMAS FRANCIS, lawyer; b. Washington, Mar. 8, 1958; s. Joseph Martin and Dorothea Mary (Jackal) E.; m. Margaret Catherine Hitselberger, May 29, 1982; children: Carolyn Sara, Pamela Marie, Thomas Francis Jr., Gregory Joseph. AB, Georgetown U., 1980, JD, 1983. Bar: Mass. 1983, DC 1988, NY 2000, U.S. Dist. Ct. Mass. 1985. Atty. Mass. Mut. Life Ins., Springfield, Mass., 1983-85, asst. counsel, 1985-88, counsel, 1988—90, second v.p., gen. counsel, v.p., assoc. gen. counsel, 1996—2000; v.p., dep. gen. counsel NY Life, NYC, 2000, sr. v.p., dep. gen. counsel, 2000—05, sr. v.p. gen. counsel, 2005—. Mem. Assn. Life Ins. Counsel, DC Bar, Knights of Columbus. Republican. Roman Catholic. Office: New York Life Ste 10 SB 51 Madison Ave New York NY 10010 Business E-Mail: tenglish@newyorkerlife.com.*

ENGLISH, TODD, food company executive, chef; b. Amarillo, Tex., Aug. 29, 1960; m. Olivia; children: Oliver, Isabelle, Simon. Student, Guildord Coll., NC, Culinary Inst. Am., Hyde Park, NY, 1982; apprenticeship, Dal Pescatore, Canto Sull, O'lio, Italy, Paraccuchi, Locando D'Angello, Italy. Ptnr. Michela's, Cambridge, Mass., 1984-88; exec. chef, owner Olives, Charlestown, Mass., 1989—, owner NYC, Las Vegas, Washington, Aspen, Tokyo, 2003, Figs, Boston, NYC, Tuscany, Mohegan Sun, Conn., Bonfire, Boston, KingFish Hall, Boston, Fish Club, Seattle, 2003, Todd English, Queen Mary 2, 2004—, BlueZoo, Dolphin Hotel, Walt Disney World, 2004—, Riche, Harrah's Hotel, New Orleans. Host (TV series) Cooking In with Todd English, Conn. Pub. TV, guest appearances include Iron Chef USA, Martha Stewart Living, Chef du Jour, The Main Ingredient, Good Morning America, In Food Today, Bobby Flay's Food Nation, CBS This Morning, Live with Regis and Kelly, The Today Show, Great Chefs of the Northeast series, Hot Off the Grill; author: (cookbooks) The Olives Table, 1997, The Figs Table, 1998, The Olives Dessert Table, 2000. Involved with Big Brother, Anthony Spinazzola Found., Cmty. Servings, Share Our Strength, Boys and Girls Club, City Yr. Named Nat. Rising Star Chef, James Beard Found., 1991, Best Chef in Northeast, 1994, Restaurateur of Yr., Bon Appetit, 2001; named one of Top 50 Tastemakers, Nation's Restaurant News, 1999, 50 Most Beautiful People, People Mag., 2001; named to Who's Who of Food and Beverage in Am., James Beard Found., 2004; recipient Robert Mondavo Award for Culinary Excellence. Office: Olives 10 City Sq Charlestown MA 02129-3714*

ENGLISH, WILLIAM DESHAY, lawyer, director; b. Piedmont, Calif., Dec. 25, 1924; s. Munro and Mabel (Michener) E.; m. Nancy Ames, Apr. 7, 1956; children: Catherine, Barbara, Susan, Stephen. AB in Econs., U. Calif., Berkeley, 1948, JD, 1951. Bar: Calif. 1952, D.C. 1972. Trial atty., spl. asst. to atty. gen. U.S. Dept. Justice, Washington, 1953-55; sr. atty. AEC, Washington, 1955-62; legal advisor U.S. Mission to European Communities, Brussels, 1962—64; asst. gen. counsel internat. matters COMSAT, Washington, 1965-73; counsel Internat. Telecomm. Satellite Orgn., 1965-73; v.p., gen. counsel, dir. COMSAT Gen. Corp., 1973-76; sr. v.p. legal and govtl. affairs Satellite Bus. Sys., McLean, Va., 1976-86; v.p., gen. counsel Satellite Transponder Leasing Corp. (IBM), McLean, Va., 1986-87; pvt. practice Washington, 1987—; counsel Am. Space Transp. Assn., 1987-93, Washington Space Bus. Roundtable; gen. counsel Iridium, LLC, 1992-96, spl. counsel, 1996-2000. With USAAF, 1943-45. Decorated Air medal. Fellow Coun. on Econ. Regulation, 1985-91; mem. ABA, AIAA (chmn. com. legal aspects aeronautics and astronautics,1993-2000, chmn. allocation space launch risks subcom. 1987, chmn. orbital debris legal subcom.), Am. Competitive Telecomm. Assn. (bd. dirs. 1976-84, pres. 1983), D.C. Bar Assn., Fed. Comm. Bar Assn., State Bar Calif., Fgn. Policy Discussion Group, Met. Club, Chevy Chase Club. Home: 7420 Exeter Rd Bethesda MD 20814-2352 Personal E-mail: w.english2@verizon.net.

ENGLISH-ANDERSON, SAN DEI, minister; b. Jacksboro, Tex., Aug. 27, 1945; d. Robert March English and Ressie English; m. Donald Loren Anderson, Dec. 19, 2001; children: Traci Dixon, Tiara Cunningham, Joshua English. AA, Jarvis Christian Coll., Hawkins, Texas, 1965. Minister, assoc. pastor New Creation Outreach, Anaheim, Calif., 2001—02; producer/host Sonic Cable TV, San Luis Obispo, Calif., 1982—86; CEO Tiara Prodns., Mission Viejo, Calif., 1987—2002; v.p. pub. rels. Busk Entertainment. V.p. ways & means Laguna Niguel Rep. Women Federated, 2000—01. Served USAF, 1964—65. Named Model of Yr., Foxes and Hares Model Assn., 1967, Ms. Royal Ambassador 2002, Mrs. Orange County Am., 2003, Mrs. Irvine Am., 2004. Mem.: Ctr. Stage/ Performing Arts Guild, Phenomenal Women Orgn. (founding pres.). Avocation: writing, sewing, reading, dancing, meditating. Personal E-mail: goldeneyes@fastmail.fm.

ENGLUND, GAGE BUSH, dancer, educator; b. Sept. 7, 1931; d. Morris Williams and Margaret Wallace (Gage) Bush; m. Richard Bernard Englund, Dec. 1, 1959; children: Alixandra Gage, Rachel Rutherford. Student, Sch. Am. Ballet, 1960. Founder Birmingham Civic Ballet, 1952; mem. Robert Joffrey Ballet, NYC, 1957-60, soloist, 1959-60; mem. Am. Ballet Theatre, NYC, 1960-63, Huntington Dance Ensemble, LI, N.Y., 1968-69; soloist Dance Repertory Co., 1969-72; tchr. ballet, assoc. chmn. Friends of Am. Ballet Theatre, NYC, 1972—. Dir. Ala. By-Products Corp., 1971—77; rehearsal coach Am. Ballet Theatre II, 1973—85; mem. scholarship com. Am. Ballet Theatre Sch., NYC, 1974—; rehearsal coach Joffrey Ballet II, 1985—95, Am. Ballet Theatre Studio Co., 1995—. Trustee Ballet Theatre Found., 1974—87, v.p., 1980—81; trustee Chapin Sch., 1982—2003, Animal Med. Ctr., NYC, 1982—, Cancer Rsch. Inst., 1984—, Episcpoal Sch. N.Y., 1979—83; bd. dirs. Children's Hosp. Clinic, Birmingham, 1955—57, Spoleto Festival, U.S.A., 1980—83, Ala. State Ballet, 1967—, Birmingham Civic Ballet, 1952—67. Named Queen, Birmingham Festival Arts, 1957; recipient Silver Bowl award, 1957, Lucia Chase award for svcs. to Am. Ballet Theatre, Soc. Fine Arts U. Ala., 2001, Patron of the Arts award, 2002; Ford Found. scholar, 1960. Mem.: Am. Guild Mus. Artists, Jr. League N.Y.C., Colonial Dames Ala., Colony Club, Lakewood Country Club. Episcopalian. Home: PO Box 469 17367 Scenic Hwy 98 Point Clear AL 36564

ENGLUND, ROBERT, actor, director, producer; b. Glendale, Calif., June 6, 1949; s. C. Kent and Janice (McDonald) E.; m. Nancy Ellen Booth, Oct. 1, 1988. Student, Oakland U., U. Calif., Northridge, UCLA, Royal Acad. Dramatic Arts, Rochester, Mich. Actor, dir., producer; resident artist Meadow Brook Theatre, Rochester, 1969-72, guest artist, 1973; resident actor Gt. Lakes Shakespeare Festival, Cleve., 1970—71; resident actor Judas in Godspell, Cleve., 1971. Appeared as Freddy Krueger in A Nightmare on Elm Street, 1984, A Nightmare on Elm Street, Part 2: Freddy's Revenge, 1985, A Nightmare on Elm Street 3: Dream Warriors, 1987, A Nightmare on Elm Street 4: The Dream Master 1988, A Nightmare on Elm Street 5: The Dream Child, 1989, Freddy's Dead: The Final Nightmare, 1991, Wes Craven's New Nightmare, 1994, Freddy vs Jason, 2003; also appeared in films Buster and Billie, 1973, Hustle, 1974, Last of the Cowboys, 1976, Stay Hungry, 1975, A Star Is Born, 1976, Bloodbrothers, 1977, Big Wednesday, 1978, Galaxy of Terror, 1980, Dead and Buried, 1981, Don't Cry, It's Only Thunder, 1982, Never Too Young to Die, 1986, Phantom of the Opera, 1989, Dance Macabre, 1992, Steven King's The Mangler, 1995, Tobe Hoopers Night Dreams, 1992, Ford Fairlane, 1990, Killer Tongue, 1996, Wishmaster, 1997, Disney's Meet the Deedles, 1997, Dee Snyder's Strangeland, 1997, Urban Legend, 1998, Nobody Knows Anything, 1999, The Prince and the Surfer, 1999, Wish You Were Dead, 2000, The Return of Caligostro, 2000, Python, 2000, Cold Sweat, 2000, Windfall, 2001, Like A Bad Dream, 2002, 2001 Maniacs, 2002, Behind The Mask, 2004, Hatchet, 2005, Heart STopper, 2005, Jack Brooks: Monster Slayer, 2006, Red, 2006, others; dir. 976-EVIL, 1988; appeared on TV in series Downtown, 1986-87, Freddy's Nighymares, 1987-89, Nightmare Cafe, 1992-93, Young Joe, the Forgotten Kennedy, 1977, The Ordeal of Patty Hearst, 1979, V, 1983, Hobson's Choice, 1983, I Want to Live, 1983, Hunter, 1985, Knight Rider, 1986, MacGyver, 1986, also on Police Woman, Soap, Charlie's Angels, Police Story, Married With Children, also others; TV films Mortal Fear, 1995, Unspoken Truth, 1996; dir. (films) Killer Pad, 2006; master of horror Showtime, 2005; also stage actor and producer. Mem. SAG, AFTRA, Actors Equity Assn., Dirs. Guild Am.

ENGSBERG, JACK ROBERT, science educator, researcher; b. Lake Mills, Wis., Nov. 28, 1950; s. Philip E. and Eileen P. Engsberg; m. Susan Kathleen Grimston, July 14, 1982; children: Kathleen Susan, Christopher Peter. BS, U. Wis., LaCrosse, 1973, MS, 1979; PhD, U. Iowa, Iowa City, 1985. Tchr. math. Wisconsin Dells H.S., Wis., 1973—78; asst. prof. U. Denver, 1979—83, U. Calgary, Canada, 1988—93; assoc. prof. Washington U. Sch. Medicine, St. Louis, 1993—2005, St. Louis U., 2005—. Contbr. articles to profl. jours. Recipient Tchg. Excellence award, U. Calgary, 1991. Mem.: Am. Soc. Gait and Clin. Movement Analysis, Am. Acad. Cerebral Palsy and Devel. Medicine, Internat. Soc. Biomechanics. Achievements include patents for laser digitizing system for prosthetics and orthotics; surgical apparatus for determining ligament and tendon tension; surgical apparatus for controlling ligament lengthening. Home: 9 North Trail Eureka MO 63025 Office: Saint Louis University 3437 Caroline St Saint Louis MO 63104 Home Phone: 636-938-5311; Office Phone: 314-977-8532. Office Fax: 314-977-8513. E-mail: jengsber@slu.edu.

ENGSTRAND, BEATRICE C., neurologist, educator; b. Oceanside, NY, July 16, 1960; d. Donald Daniel and Claudia Helen Engstrand. BA, Lehigh U., 1982, doctorate (hon.); MD, Med. Coll. Pa., 1984. Diplomate Am. Bd. Psychiatry and Neurology, bd. cert. in neurology; lic. physician, NY. Resident in medicine North Shore U. Hosp., Manhasset, NY, 1984—85; resident in neurology NY Hosp., NYC, 1985—86, SUNY Health Sci. Ctr., Bklyn., 1986—88; attending physician Met. Hosp., NYC, 1988—92; asst. prof. neurology NY Med. Coll., Valhalla, 1988—; pvt. practice Huntington, NY, 1992—. Founder, pres. Neuro-Degenerative Disease Found., 1993—; radio host Sta. WOR; mem. Geriatric Bd. Ethics; presenter and lectr. in field. Author: (book) A Gift of Healing—A Legacy of Hope, 1990; host, prodr. WOR Radio Mem. adv. bd. arts and sci. Lehigh U., Bethlehem, Pa., 1992—, women's adv. study bd., 1993—; mem. legis. com. Suffolk County Med. Soc., 1994-97; com. fundraiser Gov. George Pataki Election, 1995; mem. People for Ethical Treatment of Animals, Physicians for Responsible Medicine, other animal rights groups. Recipient Woman of Distinction award Soroptomist Internat.; named one of Outstanding Young Woman of Am., 1997. Fellow Am. Acad. Neurology (diplomate); mem. AMA, ACP, Am. Med. Student Assn., Am. Acad. Neurology, Nat. Bd. Med. Examiners (diplomate), Med. Soc. NY State, NY County Med. Soc. (pub. rels. com.), Westchester County Med. Ctr. (bioethics com.), Bklyn. Neurol. Soc., Med. Coll. Pa. Alumni Assn., Cornell U. Alumni Assn., Rotary Club Upper Manhattan (v.p. 1990-91, pres. 1991-92, Paul Harris award 1991). Republican. Avocations: travel, animals, languages, opera, writing. Office: 76 E Main St Ste 1 Huntington NY 11743-2837 Office Phone: 631-423-2100. Personal E-mail: neurologydoctor@aol.com.

ENGSTROM, ERIK, publishing executive; b. Taby, Stockholm, Sweden; s. Kjell and Alice (Klarstrom) E. BS in Econs. & Bus. Adminstrn., Stockholm Sch. Econs., 1986; MS in Engring., Royal Inst. Technology, 1986; diploma Internat. Mgmt. Program, Ecole des Hautes Etudes Comml., Paris, 1986; MBA, Harvard U., 1988. Cons. and engagement mgr. McKinsey & Co., NYC, 1988-91; v.p. corp. devel. Bantam Doubleday Dell Pub. Group, Inc., NYC, 1991-92, sr. v.p., CFO, 1992-93, exec. v.p., chief adminstrv. officer, 1993-94, exec. v.p., COO, 1994-96, pres., COO, 1996-98; pres., CEO BDD N.Am., 1998; pres., COO Random House Inc., NYC, 1998-2001; ptnr. Gen. Atlantic Ptnrs., Greenwich, Conn., 2001—04; CEO Elsevier, 2004—. Bd. dirs. Reed Elsevier PLC, 2004—, Internat. Assn. Sci., Tech. and Medical Pubs., 2005—, Pub. Assn., 2005—. Mem. bus. com. Met. Mus. of Art, 1998—. Sgt. Swedish Army, 1983-84. Scholar Fulbright Commn., 1986. Office: Elsevier 360 Park Ave S New York NY 10010

ENGSTROM, MARLENE MAE, volunteer; b. McIntosh, SD, June 4, 1932; d. Alfred Palmer Hustad and Cora Alberta Haugen; m. E. Duane Engstrom, July 24, 1954; children: Christine, Peter, Rolf. BA, St. Olaf Coll., 1954. Receptionist, sec. Luth. Ch. of the Good Shepherd, Mpls., 1954-55; acting dir. stewardship Am. Luth. Ch. Women, Mpls., 1979, interim dir. for edn., 1980-81, vol. nat. pres., 1984-87; receptionist, devel. Crossways Internat., Mpls., 1990-91. Tape transcriber Minn. State Svc. for the Blind, St. Paul, 1964-78; bd. dirs. Luth. Deaconess Hosp., Mpls., 1972-83, Luther Theol. Sem./Am. Luth. Ch., St. Paul, 1974-82, Luther N.W. Theol. Sem./Am. Luth. Ch./Luth. Ch. Am./Evangelical Luth. Ch. Am., 1982-88; chmn. bd. regents Luther Sem., 1981, Luther N.W. Theol. Sem., 1982-84; v.p. Mpls. Area Synod/Evang. Luth. Ch. Am., Mpls., 1988-92; trustee Luth. Sem. Found., St. Paul, 1991-99. Recipient Disting. Alumni award St. Olaf Coll., Northfield, Minn., 1981. Mem. AMA Alliance, Minn. Med. Assn. Alliance (treas., 2nd v.p., Disting. Svc. award 1996), Hennepin Med. Soc. Alliance (pres. 1991-93), Phi Beta Kappa. Avocations: genealogy, memoir writing, reading, photography.

ENGVALL, BILL, comedian, actor; b. Galveston, Tex., July 27, 1957; m. Gail Engvall; 2 children. Comedian Blue Collar Comedy Tour, 2000—03. Author: You Don't Have To Be Dumb To Be Stupid; comedian (albums) Here's Your Sign, 1996, Dorkfish, 1998, Here's Your Christmas Album, Now That's Awesome, Cheap Drunk: An Autobiography, 2002, Here's Your Sign: Reloaded, 2003, 15 degrees Off Cool, (DVDs) Here's Your Sign, Live, 2004, (films) Blue Collar Comedy Tour: The Movie, 2003, Blue Collar Comedy Tour Rides Again, 2004, (TV specials) Pair of Jokers with Rosie O'Donnell & Bill Engvall, 1989, Comedy Central's Last Laugh '04, 2004, Comedy Central Roast of Jeff Foxworthy, 2005; actor: (films) Split Image, 1982, Not for Publication, 1984; (TV series) Delta, 1992, The Jeff Foxworthy Show, 1996—97, Blue Collar TV, 2004—, The Bill Engvall Show, 2007; host (TV specials) American Originals, 1997, host, prodr. Mobile Home Disaster, 2005, writer BIll Engvall: 15 degrees Off Cool, 2007. Named Funniest Male Stand-Up Comic, Am. Comedy Awards, 1992. Office: c/o Parallel Entertainment Ste 1040 9255 Sunset Blvd Los Angeles CA 90069

ENHORNING, GORAN, obstetrician, gynecologist; b. Birkdale, Eng., Mar. 18, 1924; came to US 1986; s. Emil Augustin and Maria Rosina (von Haartman) E.; m. Louise Christina Carlberg, Apr. 16, 1955; children: Ulf, Dag and Peder (twins), Marianne. MD, Karolinska Inst., Stockholm, 1952, PhD in Physiology, 1961. Asst. prof. ob-gyn. Karolinska Inst., Stockholm, 1952—61; Fulbright scholar U. Utah, Salt Lake City, 1961—63, UCLA, 1963—64; assoc. prof. ob-gyn. Karolinska Inst., 1964—71, U. Toronto, Ont., Canada, 1971—75, prof. ob-gyn., 1975—86; prof. ob-gyn. and physiology SUNY, Buffalo, 1986—2002. Contbr. articles to profl. jour. initiation of concept that symptoms of asthma and infectious bronchiolitis may be due to a surfactant dysfunction, caused by airway inflammation, an allergic reaction, an inhalation of cold air, or a hydrolysis of surfactant phospholipids, catalyzed by phospholipase A2 (PLA2) and by lysophospholipase (LPL) from eosinophils. The way the surfactant dysfunction causes airway blockage, and thus breathing difficulties is demonstrated with the Capillary Surfactometer, a new instrument developed to simulate surfactant function in terminal airways. Business E-Mail: gee1@buffalo.edu.

ENKE, CHRISTIE GEORGE, chemistry professor, consultant; b. Mpls., July 8, 1933; s. Alvin Christie Enke and Mae Eileen (Ferris) Nichols; m. Mary Crane, June 23, 1956; children: Paul F. (dec.), David M., Anne; m. Bea Reed, Dec. 24, 1988; 1 stepchild, Gillian. BA, Principia Coll., 1955; PhD, U. Ill, 1959. Instr. to asst. prof. Princeton U., 1959-66; assoc. to prof. chemistry Mich. State U., East Lansing, 1966-94; prof. emeritus, 1994; prof. chemistry U. N.Mex., Albuquerque, 1994—2006, prof. emeritus, 2006—. Author: Electronics and Instrumentation, 1982; patentee in field. Sloane Found. fellow, 1969. Fellow AAAS, Am. Chem. Soc. (chmn. divsn. computers, chair analytical divsn. 2006, Chem. Instrumentation award 1974, Computers in Chemistry award 1989, J.C. Gidding award for Excellence in Edn. 2003); mem. Am. Soc. Mass Spectrometry (pres. 1994-96, Disting. Contbn. award 1994). Avocation: stained glass. Office: U NMex Clark Hall Albuquerque NM 87131 Office Phone: 505-277-3159. Business E-Mail: enke@unm.edu.

ENLOW, DONALD HUGH, retired anatomist, dean; b. Mosquero, N.Mex., Jan. 22, 1927; s. Donald Carter and Martie Blairene (Albertson) E.; m. Martha Ruth McKnight, Sept. 3, 1945; 1 child, Sharon Lynn. BS, U. Houston, 1949, MS, 1951; PhD, Tex. A&M U., 1955. Instr. biology U. Houston, 1949-51; asst. prof. biology West Tex. State U., 1955-56; instr. anatomy Med. Coll. S.C., 1956-57; asst. prof. U. Mich. Med. Sch., Ann Arbor, 1957-62, assoc. prof., 1962-67, prof. anatomy, 1969-72; dir. phys. growth program Center for Human Growth and Devel., 1966-72; prof., chmn. dept. anatomy W.Va. U. Sch. Medicine, Morgantown, 1972-77; Thomas Hill disting. prof., chmn. dept. orthodontics Case Western Res. Sch. Dentistry, Cleve., 1977-89, prof. emeritus, 1989—, asst. dean for rsch. and grad. studies, 1977-85, acting dean, 1983-86. Adj. prof. U. NC, 1992—; lectr. in field in 32 fgn. countries. Author: Principles of Bone Remodeling, 1963, The Human Face, 1968, Handbook of Facial Growth, 1975, 3d edit., 1990, Essentials of Facial Growth, 1996; contbr. chpts. to 30 books, numerous articles to profl. jours. Served with reserves USCG, 1945—46. Recipient Outstanding Research award Tex. Acad. Sci., 1952, Dewel award, 2006, Thomas Graber award, 2006. Fellow Royal Soc. Medicine, Am. Assn. Anatomists, Internat. Assn. Dental Research; hon. mem. Am. Assn. Orthodontists (Mershon Meml. lectr. 1968, Spl. Merit award 1969, award for outstanding contbns. to orthodontia, 1984, Thomas Grober award 2003), Gt. Lakes Orthodontic Soc., Cleve. Dental Soc., Cleve. Orthodontic Soc., Omicron Kappa Upsilon. Republican. Methodist. Home: 4940 Monarch Rd Milton WI 53563 Personal E-mail: donnlo@charter.net.

ENNIS, BRUCE CLIFFORD, retired lawyer; b. Dover, Del., Mar. 22, 1941; s. Clifford Morgan and Mary Elizabeth (Jones) E.; m. Diane Wallace, July 19, 1969; 1 child, Heather Diane. BA, W.Va. Wesleyan Coll., 1963; JD, Dickinson Law Sch., 1966. Bar: Del. 1969, U.S. Dist. Ct. Del. 1971. Ptnr. Schmittinger & Rodriguez, P.A., Dover, 1969—2001; ret. Instr. Wesley Coll., Dover, 1970-78, Del. Tech. and C.C., Dover, 1978-98. Active United Meth. Ch., Dover. With U.S. Army, 1966-68. Mem. Del. State Bar Assn., Kent County Bar Assn. Home: 444 Troon Rd Dover DE 19904-2343

ENNIS, CAROL ROBBINS, retired music educator; b. Niagara Falls, Ont., Can., July 5, 1934; arrived in US, 1954; d. George Burt Robbins and Mabel Marie Hallman; m. Harold David Jamieson Jr. (dec.); children: Stephen Jamieson(dec.) , Robin Jamieson, Glenn Jamieson; m. George Vernon Ennis. BFA, SUNY, Buffalo, 1967, MEd, 1971. Pvt. piano tchr., 1957—67; ch. organist, various chs., 1959—88; music tchr. Tonawanda Pub. Schs., NY, 1967—96; music dir., organist, choir dir. Bacon Meml. Presbyn. Ch., Niagara Falls, NY, 1988—. Reader Radio Reading for Blind, Cheektawaga, NY, 1997—2005; leader music combo Amherst Sr. Ctr.; leader Drama Club formation; election polling inspector Erie County Bd. Elections, Amherst Town Bd., NY, 1998—. Named Voices of Tomorrow winner, WBEN-TV, Buffalo, 1958; scholar, Kiwanis Music Festival, Niagara Falls, Can., 1952—53. Mem.: NY State United Tchrs., U. Buffalo Women's Club, U. Buffalo Alumni Assn. Avocations: travel, tennis, current event discussion groups, genealogy, jazz. Home: 279 Brockmore Dr PO Box 152 East Amherst NY 14051

ENNIS, EDGAR WILLIAM, JR., lawyer; b. Macon, Ga., May 20, 1945; s. Edgar W. and Nelle (Branan) E.; m. Judith Anne Godfrey, June 29, 1974; children: William, Branan. BS in Engring. Sci., USAF Acad., Colorado Springs, Colo., 1967; JD, U. Ga., 1971. Bar: Ga. 1971. Commd. 2d lt. USAF, 1967, advanced through ranks to capt., 1970, resigned, 1975; asst. U.S. atty. U.S. Atty.'s Office-Mid. Dist. of Ga., Macon, 1975-88; U.S. atty. U.S. Dept. Justice, Macon, 1988-93; of counsel Haynsworth, Baldwin, Johnson & Harper, Macon, 1993-97; ptnr. Haynsworth, Baldwin, Johnson & Greaves LLC, Macon, 1998-99, Constangy, Brooks & Smith LLC, Macon, 1999—. Office: Constangy Brooks & Smith LLC 577 Mulberry St Ste 710 Macon GA 31201-8588 Office Phone: 478-750-8600. Personal E-mail: eennis@constangy.com.

ENNIS, RONALD DOV, radiation oncologist; b. Boston, Jan. 22, 1962; s. Herbert L. and Judith W. (Wolper) E.; m. Pamela S. Finson, May 31, 1987; children: Ariel, Kivi, Avi. BA, Columbia U., 1985; MD, Yale U., 1990. Diplomate in radiation oncology Am. Bd. Radiology. Intern L.I. Jewish Med. Ctr., New Hyde Park, N.Y., 1990-91; resident in therapeutic radiology Yale U. Sch. medicine, New Haven, 1991-94; asst. attending Columbia Presbyn. Med. Ctr., NYC, 1994—; asst. prof. Columbia U. Coll. Phys. and Surg., NYC, 1994—. Contbr. chpt. to book, articles to profl. jours. Mem.

AMA, Am. Soc. Therapeutic Radiology and Oncology, Am. Soc. Clin. Oncology, Am. Coll. Radiation Oncology. Office: Columbia Presbyn Med Ctr Dept Radiation Oncology 622 W 168th St New York NY 10032-3720

ENNIS, THOMAS MICHAEL, management consultant; b. Morgantown, W.Va., Mar. 7, 1931; s. Thomas Edson and Violet Ruth (Nugent) E.; m. Julia Marie Dorety, June 30, 1956; children: Thomas John, Robert Griswold (dec.). Student, W.Va. U., 1949-52; AB, George Washington U., 1954; JD, Georgetown U., 1960. With Gov. Employees Ins. Co., Washington, 1956, 59, Air Transport Assn. Am., Washington, 1959-60; dir. ann. support program George Washington U., 1960-63; nat. dir. devel. Project HOPE, People to People Health Found., Inc., Washington, 1963-66; nat. exec. dir. Epilepsy Found. Am., Washington, 1966-74; exec. dir. Clinton, Eaton, Ingham Community Mental Health Bd., Lansing, Mich., 1974-83; nat. exec. dir. Alzheimer's Disease and Related Disorders Assn., Inc., Chgo., 1983-86; exec. dir., pres. The John Douglas French Alzheimers Found., LA, 1986-96, pres. emeritus, 1996—. Clin. instr. dept. cmty. medicine and internat. health Georgetown U., 1967-74; adj. assoc. prof. dept. psychiatry Mich. State U., 1975-84; lectr. Univ. Ctr. for Internat. Rehab., 1977; cons. health and med. founds., related orgns.; cons. Am. Health Found., 1967-69, Reston, Va.-Georgetown U. Health Planning Project, 1967-70. Editl. bd.: Am. Jour. Alzheimer's Disease, 1997—; exec. prodr. Heartland Pictures, 2007—. Mem. adv. bd. Nat. Center for the Law and the Handicapped, 1971-74; advisor Nat. Reye's Syndrome Found.; mem. Nat. Com. for Research in Neurol. Disorders, 1967-72; mem. nat. adv. bd. Developmental Disabilities/Tech. Assistance System, U. NC, 1971-78; nat. trustee Nat. Kidney Found., 1970-74, mem. exec. com. and bd. Nat. Capitol Area chpt., pres., 1972-74; bd. dirs. Nat. Assn. Pvt. Residential Facilities for Mentally Retarded, 1970-74; bd. dirs., mem. exec. com. Epilepsy Found. Am., 1977-84, Epilepsy Center Mich., 1974-83; nat. bd. dirs. Western Inst. on Epilepsy, 1969-72; bd. dirs., pres. Mich. Mid-South Health Systems Agy., 1975-78; sec. gen. Internat. Fedn. Alzheimer's Disease and Related Disorders, 1984-86; mem. panel Alzheimer's Disease Edn. and Referral Ctr., 1990-93; mem. Calif. State Coun. on Developmental Disabilities, 1997—2003; med. adv. bd. EdenCare Sr. Living Svcs., advisor Ctr. Aging, Washington, 1998—. World Rehab. Fund fellow Norway, 1980. Mem. Nat. Epilepsy League (bd. dirs. 1977-78), Mich. Assn. Cmty. Mental Health (pres. 1977-79), Nat. Coalition Rsch. Neurol. Disorders (dir. at-large 1991—), Scan Health Plan (bd. govs.), Phi Alpha Theta, Phi Kappa Psi. Home and Office: 23740 Killion St Woodland Hills CA 91367-5822 Office Phone: 818-999-2273. Personal E-mail: ennisinis@aol.com.

ENO, AMOS STEWART, natural resource foundation administrator; b. Princeton, NJ, Jan. 26, 1950; s. Amos and Alice Pardee (Stewart) E.; m. Marjorie Theresa Belli, Sept. 18, 1982; children: Amos Pinchot L., Angus Connelly. BA, Princeton U., 1972; MA, Cornell U., 1977. Staff asst. to asst. sec. U.S. Dept. Interior, Washington, 1974-76, spl. asst. to chief, office of endangered species, 1978-81; asst. dir. wildlife affairs Nat. Audubon Soc., Washington, 1981-82, dir. wildlife programs, 1982-86; dir. conservation programs Nat. Fish and Wildlife Found., Washington, 1986-91, exec. dir., 1991-99; pres. Resources First Group, South Freeport, Maine, 2000—. Pres. Resources First Found.; exec. dir. New Eng. Forestry Found., 2002—05; bd. dirs. Strategic Environ. Rsch. and Devel. Program, U.S. Dept. Def., LightStream Corp., Hydrophilix Corp.; mem. coun. N.Am. Wetlands Conservation Coun., U.S. Dept. Interior. Editor FY 1987-93 Federal Agency Needs Assessment; editor reports. Recipient Frederick Douglas award, Princeton, 1972, Profl. Conservationist award Chevron, 1992, Pres. Conservation Achievement Awd., 1993, Nature Conservancy. Mem. Ivy Club, Met. Club. Avocations: tennis, running, photography. E-mail: amoseno@aol.com.

ENOCH, CRAIG TRIVELY, retired judge; b. Wichita, Kans., Apr. 3, 1950; BA, So. Meth. U., 1972, JD, 1975; LLM, U. Va., 1992. Bar: Tex. 1975, U.S. Dist. Ct. (no. & we. dist.) Tex. 1976, U.S. Ct. Appeals (5th cir.) 1979; cert. Civil Trial Law. Assoc. Burford, Ryburn & Ford, Dallas, 1975-77; ptnr. Moseley, Jones, Enoch & Martin, Dallas, 1977-81; judge 101st Dist. Ct., Dallas, 1981-87; chief justice Tex. Ct. Appeals (5th dist.), 1987-92; justice Tex. Supreme Ct., Austin, 1993—2003; chair appellate practice, mem. litigation and govt. rels. sects. Winstead PC, Austin, 2003—. Pres. Appellate Judges Edn. Inst., 2002—; guest commentator various TV programs. Mem. exec. bd. Dedman Sch. Law So. Meth. U., 1990—. Capt. USAFR, 1973-81. Recipient Outstanding Young Lawyer in Dallas, 1985, Disting. Alumni award for judicial svc. So. Meth. U. Dedman Sch. Law, 1999, J. Edward Finch Law Day Speech award, 2001, Disting. Alumni award So. Meth. U., 2006, Outstanding Lead Article award Tex. Tech. Law Rev., 2006-07. Fellow: Dallas Bar Found., Tex. State Bar Found., Am. Bar Found.; mem.: ABA (past chair exec. bd. appellate judges conf. jud. divsn.), Tex. Supreme Ct. (liaison to State Bar of Tex. 1999—2003), Am. Law Inst. Episcopalian. Office Phone: 512-370-2883. Business E-Mail: cenoch@winstead.com.

ENOCH, JAY MARTIN, optometrist, research scientist, educator; b. NYC, Apr. 20, 1929; s. Jerome Dee and Stella Sarah (Nathan) E.; m. Rebekah Ann Feiss, June 24, 1951; children: Harold Owen, Barbara Diane, Ann Allison. *Grandchildren, Jordan Michael and Ryan Samuel Enoch, David Jacob Dryfoos, and Julia Rose and Maxwell Jay Perry. Enoch's career stems from inspiration received at the Bronx High School of Science. Stimuli were provided by mentors at Columbia U. by Isidore Finkelstein and George Smelser, at OSU by Glenn Fry, at NPL in Teddington, England, by Walter Stanley Stiles, at Washington U. in St. Louis by Bernard Becker, in Berne by Hans Goldmann, and at U. Florida by Herbert Kaufman. Throughout, he was encouraged by his parents, grandfather Harry Nathan, and his wife.* BS in Optics and Optometry, Columbia U., 1950; post grad., Inst. Optics U. Rochester, 1953; PhD in Physiol. Optics, Ohio State U., 1956; DSc (hon.), SUNY, 1993, U. Politecnica Catalunya, Barcelona, Spain, 2002. Asst. prof. physiol. optics Ohio State U., Columbus, 1956-58; assoc. supr. Ohio State U. (Mapping and Charting Rsch. Lab.), 1957-58; fellow Nat. Phys. Lab., Teddington, England, 1959-60; rsch. instr. dept. ophthalmology Washington U. Sch. Medicine, St. Louis, 1958-59, rsch. asst. prof., 1959-64, rsch. assoc. prof., 1965-70, rsch. prof., 1970-74; fellow Barnes Hosp., St. Louis, 1960-64, cons. ophthalmology, 1964-74; rsch. prof. dept. psychology Washington U., St. Louis, 1970-74; grad. rsch. prof. ophthalmology and psychology Coll. Medicine U. Fla., Gainesville, 1974-80, grad. rsch. prof. physics, 1979-80; dir. Ctr. for Sensory Studies, 1976-80; dean Sch. Optometry, chmn. Grad. Group in Vision Sci. U. Calif., Berkeley, Calif., 1980-92, prof. optometry and vision sci., 1980-94, prof. of Grad. Sch., 1994—; prof. physiol. optics in ophthalmology U. Calif., San Francisco, 1980—. Mem. exec. sec. subcom. on vision and its disorders of nat. adv. Neurol. Diseases and Blindness Coun., NIH, 1963-66; chmn. subcom. contact lens stds. Am. Nat. Std. Inst., 1970-77; mem. nat. adv. eye coun. Nat. Eye Inst., NIH, 1975-77, 80-84; exec. com., com. on vision NAS-NRC, 1973-76; mem. US Nat. Com. Internat. Commn. Optics, 1976-79, health sci. com. Systemwide Adminstrn. U. Calif., 1989-93, co-chmn. subcom. on immigrant health in Calif., 1993-94, sci. adv. bd. Fight-for-Sight, 1988-92, Allergan Corp., 1991-95, mem. Lighthouse Internat., NY, 1991-95, 2001-05, chair, 1995, Pisart award com., bd. dir. 2001-06, com. on Refractive Errors WHO, 2002-; founder Elite Sch. Optometry, Chennai, Tamil Nadu, India, dedication lectr., 1985, plenary spkr. 20th Ann., 2005; Enoch Lecture on Vision Sci., Washington U. St. Louis, 2007. *As Executive Secretary of the Subcommittee on Vision and its Disorders, Enoch had opportunity to draft the plan for the future National Eye Institute, NIH. With modifications, this proved to be a seminal document. Enoch served for decades as liaison between ophthalmology and optometry, helped develop the infrastricture of modern visual and ophthalmic science, and aided in organizing modern optometry in India. He derived satisfaction during years in neonatal vision-care practice, as well as from his research on retinal receptor optics, etc., during his service as Dean at Berkeley, and in development of low vision services in the U.S.A. and India.* Mem. editl. bd.: Investigative Ophthalmology and Vision Sci., 1965—75, 1983—88, Vision Rsch., 1974—80, Sight-Saving Rev., 1974—84, Sensory Processes, 1974—80, Internat. Ophthalmology, 1977—93, mem. editl. bd. optical scis.: Springer-Verlag, 1978—87, mem. editl. bd.: Binocular Vision, 1984—2004, Clin. Vision Sci., 1986—93, Biomed. Optics, 1988—90, mem. editl. bd. biomed. scis.: Springer-Verlag, 1988—95, mem. editl. bd.: Annals of Ophthalmology, 1997—2006, assoc. editor for vision: Handbook of Optics, Optical Soc. Am., 1997—, mem. internat. editl. bd.: Ophthalmic and Physiol. Optics, 2002—; contbr. chpts. and articles on visual sci., photoreceptor optics, perimetry, contact lenses, infant and aged vision, myopia, history of earliest lenses and mirrors to profl. jours. Nat. sci. adv. bd. Retinitis Pigmentosa Found., 1977-95; US rep. Internat. Perimetric Soc., 1974-90, also exec. com., chmn. Rsch. Group Standards; bd. dirs. Friends of Eye Rsch., 1977-88, Lighting Rsch. Bd., 1988-95; trustee Illuminating Engring. Rsch. Inst., 1977-81; mem. bd. counselors U. Calif. San Francisco Sch. Dentistry, 1995-2003. 2d lt. US Army, 1951-52. Named one of 250 Alumni Ahead of Their Time, Columbia Univ., 2004; recipient Career Devel. award, NIH, 1963—73, Everett Kinsey award, Contact Lens Soc. Ophthalmologists, 1991, Berkeley citation, Festschrift U. Calif. Berkeley, 1996, Pisart award, Lighthouse Internat., 2001, Gaspar de Portola award, U. Calif. and Govt. of Catalunya, 2001, 2004, US Congl. Recognition award, 2005, Spl. Recognition award, Friends Indo-Am. Cmty., 2005. Fellow AAAS, Am. Acad. Optometry (co-founder eye disease sect., Glenn A. Fry award 1972, Charles F. Prentice medal award 1974, 50 Yr. award 2004), Optical Soc. Am. (chmn. vision tech. sect. 1974-76, mem. book pub. com. 1996-2000), Am. Acad. Ophthalmology (low-vision com., honor award 1985); mem. Assn. for Rsch. in Vision and Ophthalmology (trustee 1967-73, pres. 1972-73, Francis I. Proctor medal 1977), Concilium Ophthalmologicum Universale (chmn. visual functions com. 1982-86), Am. Optometric Assn. (low vision sect., Vision Care award 1987), Internat. Perimetric Soc. (hon. mem., chair com. stds.), Ocular Heritage Soc. (medal 1997), Cogan Ophthalmic History Soc., Optometric Hist. Soc. (trustee 2000-02, 2006—, v.p. 2002-04, pres. 2005), Cosmos Club (Washington), Sigma Xi. Office: U Calif Sch Optometry Berkeley CA 94720-2020 Home Phone: 925-631-0198; Office Phone: 510-642-9694. Business E-Mail: jmenoch@berkeley.edu.

ENOMOTO, DAISUKE (DICE-K), entrepreneur, investor; b. Matsudo City, Apr. 22, 1971; 2 children. Founder, head EXA Co., Ltd., Tokyo, 1994—96, EXasia Hong Kong Ltd., Hong Kong, 1996—98, Pro-G Group Co. Ltd. (acquired by Liverdoor Co.), Tokyo, 1998; exec. v.p., chief strategic officer, also bd. dir. Liverdoor Co., 1998—2003; independent investor (provides services to companies such as, NetVillage & Astrix Capital Partners). Tng. for private space flight Star City, Russia, 2005—. will be the fourth private cosmonaut to fly in space on the Russian Spacecraft Soyuz TMA-9 (flying to the International Space Station, lift off from Baikonur Cosmodrome in Kazakhstan in Fall, 2006). In August, 2006 was medically disqualified from flying the Soyuz TMA-9 mission in September.; would have been the first private cosmonaut from Japan and Asia.

ENOS, PAUL, geologist, educator; b. Topeka, July 25, 1934; s. Allen Mason and Marjorie V. (Newell) E.; m. Carol Rae Curt, July 5, 1958; children: Curt Alan, Mischa Enos Martin, Kevin Christopher, Heather Enos Wohlert. BS, U. Kans., 1956; postgrad., U. Tübingen, W.Ger., 1956-57; MS, Stanford U., 1961; PhD, Yale U., 1965. Geologist Shell Devel. Co., Coral Gables, Fla., 1964-68, research geologist Houston, 1968-70; from assoc. prof. to prof. geology SUNY, Binghamton, 1970-82; Haas Disting. prof. geology U. Kans., Lawrence, 1982-2000, prof., 2001—03, Disting. prof. emeritus, 2003—. Cons. to industry; sedimentologist Ocean Drilling, 1975, 92; rsch. vis. Oxford U., 1989, U. Erlangen, Germany, 1995-96; fgn. scientist Ministry Geology, People's Republic China, 1988; with Global Sedimentary Geology Project, 1988—, co-convener Working Group 4, 1992-2000. Co-author: Quaternary Sedimentation of South Florida, 1977, Mid-Cretaceous, Mexico, 1983, Triassic Evolution of Yangtze Platform, 2006; editor: Field Trips: South-Central New York, 1981, Deep-Water Carbonates, 1977; contbr. articles to sci. jours. Served to 1st lt. C.E., U.S. Army, 1957-59. Recipient Pettijohn medal Sedimentology, 2001, Excellence in Tchg. award, Geology Dept., 2003; fellow U. Liverpool, 1976-77, NSF, 1959-62, Fulbright, 1956-57; Summerfield scholar, 1954-56. Mem. Soc. Sedimentary Geology (assoc. editor 1976-80, 83-87, Best Paper award 1969), Internat. Assn. Sedimentologists (assoc. editor 1983-87), Am. Assn. Petroleum Geologists, Geol. Soc. Am., Omicron Delta Kappa. Avocations: photography, diving, bicycling, history. Office: U Kans Dept Geology Lawrence KS 66045-2124 Home: 1825 Castle Pine Court Lawrence KS 66047-2017 Office Phone: 785-864-2744.

ENOS, RANDALL, cartoonist, illustrator; b. New Bedford, Mass., Jan. 30, 1936; s. Eugene and Isabel (Da Costa) E.; m. Leann Walker, June 23, 1956. Student, Boston Mus. Sch. Fine Arts, 1954-55. Art tchr. Famous Artists Schs., Inc., Westport, Conn., 1956-64; film designer Pablo Ferro Films, Inc., NYC, 1964-66; free-lance illustrator and film designer Westport, 1966—; part-time tchr. Parsons Sch. Design, NYC, 1975-84; lectr., tchr. Syracuse U. Designed films for maj. Am. corps.; illustrator for maj. publs. including N.Y. Times, Time Mag., also children's books, posters; represented in numerous illustrators and art dirs. anns., other anthologies and mus. collections; created comic strips. Recipient Cannes TV award, 1964. Mem. Soc. of Illustrators. Democrat. Avocations: collecting antique harpoons and other whale craft, studying history of American whaling, creating limited edition prints of whaling subjects. Home: 402 N Park Ave Easton CT 06612-1248 Office Phone: 203-445-8376. E-mail: renos@optonline.net.

ENQUIST, BRIAN JOSEPH, ecologist, educator; b. Mar. 4, 1969; BA in Biology with distinction, Colo. Coll., Colo. Springs, 1991; MS in Biology, U. N.Mex., Albuquerque, 1994, PhD in Biology, 1998. Rsch. asst. prof. dept. biology U. N.Mex., 1998—2001; NSF postdoctoral fellow Santa Fe Inst., 1998—99; NSF postdoctoral fellow Nat. Ctr. Ecol. Analysis and Synthesis U. Calif., Santa Barbara, 1999—2000; asst. prof. dept. ecology and evolutionary biology U. Ariz., Tucson, 2001—05, assoc. prof., 2005—. Contbr. articles to sci. jours. Named an Brilliant 10, Popular Sci. mag., 2004; recipient CAREER award, NSF, 2002—. Mem.: Bot. Soc. Am. (mem. ecol. and tropical biology sects.), Ecol. Soc. Am. (mem. theoretical sect., George C. Mercer award 2001), Am. Soc. Naturalists, AAAS. Office: Dept Ecology and Evolutionary Biology U Ariz BioSciences West Tucson AZ 85721 Office Phone: 520-626-3329. Office Fax: 520-621-9190. E-mail: benquist@u.arizona.edu.*

ENQUIST, LYNN WILLIAM, molecular biologist; b. Denver, Oct. 23, 1945; s. Clarence Andrew and Doris Alice (Hajenga) E.; m. Kathleen Marie Siverson, Aug. 10, 1968; 1 child, Brian Joseph. BS, S.D. State U., 1967; PhD, Va. Commonwealth U., 1971. Postdoctoral fellow Roche Inst. of Molecular Biology, Nutley, N.J., 1971-73; staff fellow NIH, Bethesda, Md., 1973-77, staff scientist, 1977-81; rsch. dir. Molecular Genetics Inc., Minnetonka, Minn., 1981-84; rsch. leader DuPont Cen. Rsch., Wilmington, Del., 1984-90; sr. rsch. fellow DuPont Merck Pharm. Co., Wilmington, 1991-93; prof. molecular biology Princeton (N.J.) U., 1993—, assoc. chair dept. molecular biology, 2003—04, chair dept. molecular biology, 2004—. Mem. Nat. Sci. Adv. Bd. for Biosecurity, 2005—. Editor Jour. Virology, 1994-2001, editor in chief, 2002--; mem. editorial bd. Jour. of Virology, 1979-81, 89-91, 91-94, Virology, 1992-94; contbr. numerous articles to profl. jours.; patentee in field; author: Experiments with Gene Fusions, 1984, Principles of Virology: Molecular Biology, Pathogenesis and Control, 2000, 2d edit., 2004. Named Disting. Alumnus, Va. Commonwealth U., 1983, S.D. State U., 1984; recipient Pres.'s award Disting. Tchg. Princeton U., 2001. Mem. AAAS (bd. dirs. 2005—), Am. Acad. Microbiology, Am. Soc. for Microbiology, Am. Soc. for Virology, Soc. for Neurosci. Avocations: fishing, skiing, reading, music, gardening. Office: Dept Molecular Biology Princeton U 314 Schultz Lab Princeton NJ 08544-0001 Home Phone: 609-497-4589. Business E-Mail: lenquist@princeton.edu.

ENRICO, ROGER A., film and retired soft drink company executive; b. Chisholm, Minn., Nov. 11, 1944; m. Rosemary Margo, 1969; 1 child. BA, Babson Coll., 1965. Former v.p. sales and mktg. Pepsi-Cola Metropol Bottling Co. Inc., Purchase, NY; chmn., CEO PepsiCo Worldwide Beverages, Purchase, 1987; CEO, chmn. PepsiCo, Inc., 1996—2001, vice-chmn, 2001—02; chmn. DreamWorks Animation SKG Inc., 2004—. Bd. dirs. Belo Corp., 1995—, Electronic Data Systems Corp., 2000—. Office: Dream Works Animation SKG Inc 1000 Flower St Glendale CA 91201*

ENRIGHT, STEPHANIE VESELICH, investment company executive, financial consultant; b. LA, Mar. 24, 1934; d. Stephen P. and Violet (Guthrie) Veselich; m. Robert James Enright (dec. Sept. 1982); children: Craig James, Brent Stephen, Erin Suzanne, Kyle Stephen. BA, U. So. Calif., LA, 1952, MS, 1975. Fin. and engring. cons. Orange County, Santa Ana, Calif., 1976—79; fin. cons. The Sim-Ehrflo Group, Newport Beach, Calif., 1979—81; pres. Enright Premier Wealth Advisors, Torrance, Calif., 1981—; fin. columnist Copley/Daily Breeze Newspaper, Torrance, Calif., 1982—. Adj. faculty mem. UCLA, U. So. Calif.; pres. Pacific Home Builders. Author: Family Wealth Counseling: Getting to the Heart of the Matter, 1999, Strictly Business, 2001; contbr. articles to profl. jours. Mem. Com. Assn. of the Peninsula, Palos Verdes, Calif., 1986; found. dir. Little Co. of Mary Hosp., Torrance; dir. endowment com. Pa. Art Assn.; adv. bd. Assistance League; bd. dirs. Pa. Symphony Soc., 1991, El Camino Coll. Found., Torrace Libr. Found.; adv. bd. Switzer Ctr. Bloombergs Top Wealth Mgnr., 2002-06. Mem. Fin. Planning Assn. (bd. dirs., officer 1982-84, Planner of Month award 1984), Nat. Assn. Women Owners, Nat. Assn. Fin. Edn., Registry Profl. Planners, Fin. Planning Assn., Torrance C. of C., Assistance League (bd. dirs. South Bay), Women in Constrn., Trojan Club and League (bd. dirs. 1978-79, 91—). Republican. Avocations: travel, writing. Office: 21515 Hawthorne Blvd Ste 1200 Torrance CA 90503-6517 Home Phone: 310-541-3013; Office Phone: 310-543-4559, 800-272-2328. Business E-Mail: senright@enrightpremier.com.

ENRIGHT, WILLIAM GERALD, religious institute administrator; b. Peoria, Ill., Dec. 5, 1935; s. William Gerald and Lucille Mae (Strubhar) E.; m. Edith Strai, June 13, 1959; children: Scott, Kirk. BA, Wheaton Coll., Ill., 1958; MDiv, Fuller Theol. Sem., Pasadena, Calif., 1961; ThM, McCormick Theol. Sem., Chgo., 1965; PhD in Church History, U. Edinburgh, Scotland, 1968; DD (hon.), Hanover Coll., Ind., 1983, Dubuque Theol. Sem., Iowa. Ordained to ministry Presbyn. Ch. (U.S.A.), 1963. Asst. pastor Roseland Presbyn. Ch., Chgo., 1963-65; pastor 1st Presbyn. Ch., Glen Ellyn, Ill., 1968-80, 2d Presbyn. Ch., Indpls., 1981—2003; exec. dir. Lake Family Inst. on Faith and Giving Ctr. Philanthropy at Ind. U., Indpls., 2004—. Author: (books) Channel Markers: Wisdom from the Ten Commandments and the Sermon on the Mount, 2001. Bd. dirs. Lilly Endowment, Inc., Indpls., The Wishard Hosp. Found.; trustee Hanover Coll. Mem. Soc. Am. Ch. History, Soc. for Sci. Study Religion, Rotary. Office: Ctr Philanthropy at Ind U Ste 301 550 W North St Indianapolis IN 46202 Office Phone: 317-278-8930. E-mail: wenright@iupui.edu.

ENRIQUEZ, CAROLA RUPERT, museum director; b. Washington, Jan. 2, 1954; d. Jack Burns and Shirley Ann (Orcutt) Rupert; m. John Enriquez, Jr., Dec. 30, 1989. BA in History cum laude, Bryn Mawr Coll., 1976; MA, U. Del., 1978, cert. in mus. studies, 1978. Pers. mgmt. trainee Naval Material Command, Arlington, Va., 1972-76; tchg. asst. dept. history U. Del., Newark, 1976-77; asst. curator/exhibit specialist Hist. Soc. Del., Wilmington, 1977-78; dir. Macon County Mus. Complex, Decatur, Ill., 1978-81, Kern County Mus., Bakersfield, Calif., 1981—. Pres. Kern County Mus Found., 1991-02; advisor Kern County Heritage Commn., 1981-88; chmn. Hist. Records Commn., 1981-88; sec.-treas. Arts Coun. of Kern, 1984-86, pres., 1986-88; county co-chmn. United Way, 1981, 82; chmn. steering com. Calif. State Bakersfield Co-op Program, 1982-83; mem. cmty. adv. bd. Calif. State U.-Bakersfield Anthrop. Soc., 1986-88; bd. dirs. Mgmt. Coun., 1983-86, v.p., 1987, pres., 1988; bd. dirs. Calif. Coun. for Promotion of History, 1984-86, v.p., 1987-88, pres., 1988-90; mem. cmty. adv. bd. Calif. State U.-Bakersifled Sociology Dept., 1986-88; mem. women's adv. com. Girls Scouts U.S., 1989-91; bd. dirs. Greater Bakersfield Conv. and Visitors Bur., 1993-95; co-chair 34th St. Neighborhood Partnership, 1994-01. Hagley fellow Eleutherian Mills-Hagley found., 1977-78; Bryn Mawr alumnae reg. scholar, 1972-76. Mem. Calif. Assn. Mus. (regional rep. 1991—2002, v.p. legis. affairs 1992—2002), Am. Assn. State and Local History (chair awards com. Calif. chpt. 1990, regional vice chair 1999—2002). Presbyterian. Office: Kern County Museum 3801 Chester Ave Bakersfield CA 93301-1345

ENRIQUEZ, CRISTINO CATUD, radiologist, internist, cardiologist; b. Batangas, Philippines, 1941; MD, U. of the East, Philippines, 1964. Diplomate Am. Bd. Radiology. Internist St. Mary's Hosp., Waterbury, Conn., 1965-66; res. internal med. Hosp. St. Raphael, New Haven, Conn., 1966-68; res. diagnostic radiol. Jackson Meml. Med. Ctr. U Miami, 1974-77; fellow in cardiology Baylor U., 1969-70; fellow in pulmonary disease Yale U. Hosp., 1971-72. Co-founder Rapha Health Inst.; lectr. in field. Author: Untruths & Conscance, 1991, We Don't Die, 2002, Healty Life, 2004. Chmn. bd. Mission Compassion. Fellow Am. Coll. Internat. Physicians; mem. AMA, Internat. Third World Leaders Assn. (mem. exec. coun.), Am. Coll. Cardiology, Am. Coll. Radiology, Interam. Coll. Radiology, Assn. Philippine Physicians in Am., Full Gospel Businessmen's Fellowship, Christian Med. and Dental Assn. Office: Apt 3606 848 Brickell Key Dr Miami FL 33131-3707

ENRIQUEZ, MANUEL HIPOLITO, physician; b. Angeles City, Philippines, Aug. 19, 1953; came to U.S., 1982; s. Antonio S. and Milagros D. (Hipolito) E.; m. Mary Diane Maloney, June 22, 1985; children: Steven, Katie. BS, U. of the East, 1974, MD, 1979; MPH, Med. Coll. Wis., 2004. Diplomate internal medicine, pulmonary disease, critical care medicine, and occupational medicine. Intern Philippine Gen. Hosp., Manila, 1980; resident Mercy Hosp., Buffalo, 1982-85; fellow Wayne State U. Sch. Medicine, Detroit, 1985-87; dir. respiratory therapy Humana Hosp. Clinch Valley, Richlands, Va., 1987-88; staff pulmonologist VA Med. Ctr., Asheville, NC, 1989—99, also dir. med. ICU, 1990—99, med. dir. respiratory therapy, 1997—99; staff physician VA Outpatient Clinic, Chattanooga, 1999—2001; flight surgeon USAF Clinic, Charleston AFB, SC, 1991—99; cons. assoc. Duke U. Med. ctr., Durham, NC, 1989-99; sr. physician TVA Nuclear, Chattanooga, 2001—06; sr. flight surgeon 134th Med. Squadron McGhee Tyson Air NG Base, Tenn., 1999—2006; chief pulmonary disease sect., med. dir. respiratory therapy VA Med. Ctr., Hampton, Va., 2007—. Med. officer 192d Med. Group Va. Air N.G., 2007—; asst prof. clin. internal medicine Ea. Va. Med. Sch., Norfolk, 2007—; cons. in field. Med. officer CAP, Asheville, 1990-99, sr. programs officer, 1993-99. Fellow: ACP, Am. Coll. Chest Physicians; mem.: Am. Coll. Physician Execs., Res. Officers Assn., Aerospace Med. Assn. Roman Catholic. Avocations: flying, jogging, reading, computers. Office: VA Med Ctr 100 Emancipation Dr Hampton VA 23667 Home: 300 Piccadilly Loop Apt K Yorktown VA 23692

ENROTH-CUGELL, CHRISTINA ALMA ELISABETH, neurophysiologist, educator; b. Helsingfors, Finland, Aug. 27, 1919; came to US,

1956, naturalized, 1962; d. Emil and Maja (Syren) Enroth; m. David W. Cugell, Sept. 5, 1955. MD, Karolinska Inst., 1948, PhD, 1952; Hon. Doctors Degree, U. Helsinki, Finland, 1994. Resident in ophthalmology Karolinska Sjukhuset, 1949-52; intern Passavant Meml. Hosp., 1956-57; with Northwestern U., Evanston, Ill., 1959-91, prof. emeritus, 1991—, prof. dept. neurobiology and physiology and dept. biomed. engring., 1974—78; mem. vision rsch. program com. Nat. Eye Inst., 1974-78, mem. nat. adv. eye coun., 1980-84. Contbr. articles to profl. jours. Recipient Ludwig von Sallman award Internat. Assn. Rsch. in Vision and Ophthalmology, 1982. Fellow Am. Inst. Med. and Biol. Engring., Am. Acad. Arts and Sci.; mem. Am. Assn. Rsch. in Vision and Ophthalmology (co-recipient Friedenwald award 1983, recipient W.H. Helmerich III award 1992), Soc. Neurosi., Am. Physiol. Soc., Physiol. Soc. (U.K.) Office: Northwestern U McCormick Sch Engring Technl Inst 2145 Sheridan Rd Evanston IL 60208-0834 Business E-Mail: enroth@northwestern.edu.

ENSCOE, JON, lawyer; b. Astoria, Oreg., June 8, 1949; AB cum laude, Harvard U., 1971, JD, 1975. Bar: Calif. 1975. Ptnr. Landels, Ripley & Diamond, San Francisco, 1975—2000; sr. ptnr. Barg Coffin Lewis & Trapp, LLP, San Francisco, 2000—. Named Super Lawyer, by San Francisco mag., 2005, 2006. Mem. ABA, The State Bar of Calif. Office: Barg Coffin Lewis & Trapp LLP 1 Market Steuart Tower Ste 2700 San Francisco CA 94105-1475 Office Phone: 415-228-5400. Office Fax: 415-228-5450. Business E-Mail: je@bcltlaw.com.

ENSENAT, DONALD BURNHAM, ambassador, lawyer; b. New Orleans, Feb. 4, 1946; s. A.G. and Genevieve (Burnham) E.; m. Taylor Harding, June 5, 1976; children: Farish, Will. BA, Yale U., 1968; JD, Tulane U., 1973. Bar: La. 1973, U.S. Ct. Appeals (5th cir.) 1974, U.S. Supreme Ct. 1975, U.S. Ct. Appeals (11th cir.) 1982, Tex. 1991. Legis. asst. Congressman Hale Boggs, U.S. Ho. of Reps., Washington, 1969-70, legis asst. Congresswoman Lindy Boggs, 1973-74; personal aide Hon. George Bush, Houston, 1970; asst. atty gen. State of La., New Orleans, 1975-80; assoc., dir., mng. dir. Carmouche, Gray, & Hoffman, A.P.L.C., New Orleans, 1981-89; mng. dir. Hoffman Sutterfield Ensenat, A.P.L.C., New Orleans, 1989-92, sr. dir., 1994-97; of counsel Locke Liddell & Sapp, PC, New Orleans, 1997-2001; U.S. Chief of Protocol Washington, 2001—. U.S. amb. to Brunei, 1992-93. Bd. dirs. World Trade Ctr., New Orleans, chmn. fin. com., 1990-92, exec. com., 1993-2001, pres.-elect, 1995, pres., 1996, chmn. bd. dirs., 1997. With USAR, 1968-74. Mem. State Bar Tex., La. State Bar Assn., Maritime Law Assn. U.S., Yale Alumni Assn. La. (bd. dirs. 1976-92, 94—, pres. 1980-82), Assn. Yale Alumni (rep. 1976-79). Republican. Roman Catholic. Avocation: sports. Home: 5527 Hurst St New Orleans LA 70115 Office: US State Dept S/CPR 2201 C St NW Washington DC 20520

ENSIGN, JOHN ERIC, senator, former congressman; b. Roseville, Calif., Mar. 25, 1958; s. Mike and Sharon Ensign; m. Darlene Sciarretta; 3 children. Student, U. Nev., Las Vegas, 1979; BS in Gen. Sci., Oreg. State U., 1981; D of Veterinary Medicine, Colo. State U., 1985. Intern West LA Vet. Med. Group; owner West Flamingo Animal Hosp., Las Vegas, 1987—94, South Shores Animal Hosp., Las Vegas, 1994—; gen. mgr. Gold Strike Hotel & Casino, 1991, Nev. Landing Hotel & Casino, 1992; mem. U.S. Congress from 1st Nev. dist., Washington, 1995—99; US Senator from Nev., 2001—. Mem. com. veterans' affairs US Senate, mem com. health, edn., labor and pensions, mem com. commerce, sci., transp., mem. com. budget, mem. com. armed forces. Recipient Taxpayers' Friend award, Nat. Taxpayers Union, 2003, Thomas Jefferson award, Food Marketing Inst. and Internat. Foodservice Distributors Assn., 2004, Legis. of Yr., Info. Tech. Industry Coun., 2004, Cyber Champion award, Bus. Software Alliance, 2005. Republican. Christian. Office: US Senate 356 Russell Senate Office Building Washington DC 20510 also: Lloyd George Federal Bldg Ste 8203 333 Las Vegas Bvld South Las Vegas NV 89101 Office Phone: 202-224-6244, 702-388-6605. Office Fax: 202-224-2193, 702-338-6501.*

ENSIGN, MICHAEL S., resort company executive; Gen. mgr. Circus Circus-Las Vegas; COO, exec. v.p. Circus-Circus Enterprises; also bd. dirs.; rejoined as COO, vice-chmn., 1995-98; CEO, chmn., 1998; CEO, COO, chmn. Mandalay Resort Group, Las Vegas, 1998—. Office: Mandalay Resort Group 3950 Las Vegas Blvd S Las Vegas NV 89119

ENSIGN, RICHARD PAPWORTH, transportation executive; b. Salt Lake City, Jan. 20, 1919; s. Louis Osborne and Florence May (Papworth) E.; m. Margaret Anne Hinckley, Sept. 5, 1942; children: Judith Ensign Lantz, Mary Jane Ensign Hofmeister, Richard L., James R., Margaret. BS, U. Utah, 1941. With Western Air Lines, 1941-70, v.p. in-flight service, 1963-70, v.p. passenger service, 1970, Pan Am. World Airways, 1971, sr. v.p. field mgmt., 1972-74, sr. v.p. mktg., 1974-75; exec. v.p. Western Airlines, 1975-82; pres. R.P. Ensign & Assocs., 1982—; spl. asst. to pres. Marriott-Host, Marriott Corp., 1990-91; spl. asst. to chmn. Caterair Internat. Corp., 1991-96. Chmn. Utah Nat. Adv. Coun., 1984-86; bd. dirs. Western Airlines, 1980-81, Pacific Area Travel Assocs., 1976-81, Marriott Airport Svc. Co., Osaka, Japan, 1986-92; resident dir. Marriott Internat. Corp., Seoul, People's Republic of Korea. Patentee in field. Nat. fund raising chmn. U. Utah, 1982-83, 83-84. Recipient Disting. Service award Fla. Internat. U., 1973; named Disting. Alumnus U. Utah, 1976, 86, recipient merit award of honor, 1985. Mem. Nat. Aeros. Assn. Clubs: Lochinvar. Republican. Mem. Lds Ch. Home: 3848 Malibu Country Dr Malibu CA 90265-4717

ENSLEN, PAMELA CHAPMAN, lawyer; b. Detroit, Dec. 29, 1953; d. Ralph Nicholas Chapman and Roberta Margaret Clarke McLaughlin; m. Richard Alan Enslen, Nov. 20, 1985; 1 child, Alan Gennady Robert. BMus, U. Mich., 1976, MMus, 1977; JD, Wayne State U., 1981. Bar: Mich. 1981, Calif. 1996, U.S. Dist. Ct. (ea. and we. dists.) Mich. 1981, U.S. Ct. Appeals (6th cir.) 1983, U.S. Supreme Ct. 1983. Pre-hearing atty. Mich. Ct. Appeals, Detroit, 1981-83; fed. law clk. U.S. Dist. Ct., We. Dist. Mich., Kalamazoo, 1983-85; sr. ptnr. Miller, Canfield, Paddock & Stone, Kalamazoo, 1985-2001; fed. pub. defender We. Dist. Mich., Kalamazoo, 2001—03; sr. counsel Miller, Canfield, Paddock & Stone, Kalamazoo, 2003—07, ptnr., 2007—. Lectr., cons., arbitrator and mediator in field; standing com. on US cts. State Bar Mich., Mich., 2004—. Co-founder, bd. dirs. Cmty. Dispute Resolution Ctr. Kalamazoo County, 1988—; bd. dirs. Am. Cancer Soc., Kalamazoo, 1991—. Named Mich. Lawyer of Yr., Mich. Lawyers Weekly, 1998; named one of Mich. Super Lawyers, 2006, Top 50 Mich. Women Super Lawyers, 2006. Master: Am. Inns of Ct.; fellow: ABA (standing com. on dispute resolution 1990—93, governing coun. dispute resolution sect. 1994—97, chair dispute resolution sect. 1997—98, sect. del. Ho. of Dels. 1999—, standing com. on fed. jud. improvements 2001—04, standing com on jud. independence 2004—), Am. Bar Found.; mem.: ATLA, Fed. Bar Assn. We. Mich. (governing bd. 2003—, bd. dirs.), Nat. Order of Barristers (John Marshall award com. 2003), Women Lawyers of Mich. (regional rep. 1989—90), Kalamazoo Trial Lawyers Assn., Kalamazoo County Bar Assn. (chair law day com. 1989, bd. dirs. 1996—99, 2007—), Mich. Bar Assn. (counsel sect. on arbitration and alternative dispute resolution 1985—98), Am. Mensa, Pi Kappa Lambda. Democrat. Avocations: reading, music. Office: Miller Canfield 444 W Michigan Kalamazoo MI 49007

ENSLEN, RICHARD ALAN, federal judge; b. Kalamazoo, May 28, 1931; s. Ehrman Thrasher and Pauline Mabel (Dragoo) E.; m. Pamela Gayle Chapman, Nov. 2, 1985; children— David, Susan, Sandra, Thomas, Janet, Joseph, Gennady. Student, Kalamazoo Coll., 1949-51, Western Mich. U., 1955; LL.B., Wayne State U., 1958; LL.M., U. Va., 1986; Doctorate (hon.), Western Mich. U., 2006. Bar: Mich. 1958, U.S. Dist. Ct. (we. dist.) Mich. 1960, U.S. Ct. Appeals (6th cir.) 1971, U.S. Ct. Appeals (4th cir.) 1975, U.S. Supreme Ct 1975. Mem. firm Stratton, Wise, Early & Starbuck, Kalamazoo, 1958-60, Bauckham & Enslen, Kalamazoo, 1960-64, Howard & Howard, Kalamazoo, 1970-76, Enslen & Schma, Kalamazoo, 1977-79; dir. Peace Corps, Costa Rica, 1965-67; judge Mich. Dist. Ct., 1968-70; U.S. dist. judge Kalamazoo, 1979—; chief judge, 1995-2001. Mem. faculty Western Mich. U., 1961-62, Nazareth Coll., 1974-75; adj. prof. polit. sci. Western Mich. U., 1982— Co-author: The Constitutional Law Dictionary: Volume One, Individual Rights, 1985; Volume Two, Governmental Powers, 1987, Constitutional Deskbook: Individual Rights, 1987, (with Mary Bedikian and Pamela Enslen) Michigan Practice, Alternative Dispute Resolution, 1998. Served with USAF, 1951-54. Named Person of the Century-Law and Courts, The Kalamazoo Gazette, 1999; named to Great Am. Judges, ABC-Clio, 2003; recipient Disting. Alumni award, Wayne State Law Sch., 1980, Western Mich. U., 1982, Outstanding Practical Achievement award, Ctr. Pub. Resources, 1984, award for Excellence and Innovation in Alternative Dispute Resolution and Dispute Mgmt., Legal Program; scholar, Jewel Corp., 1956—57, Lampson McElhorne, 1957. Mem. ABA (standing com. on dispute resolution 1983-90), Mich. Bar Assn., Am. Judicature Soc. (bd. dirs. 1983-85), Sixth Cir. Jud. Coun. Office: US Dist Ct 410 W Michigan Ave Kalamazoo MI 49007-3757 Office Phone: 616-343-7542.

ENSLER, EVE, playwright, actress; b. NYC, May 25, 1953; m. Richard McDermott, 1978 (div. 1988); adopted stepson Dylan McDermott; life ptnr. Ariel Orr Jordan. BA, Middlebury Coll., Vt., 1975; LittD (hon.), Middlebury Coll., 2003. Founder V-Day, 1998; leader writing group Beford Hills Correctional Facility for Women, 1998—; faculty mem. Omega Inst. Playwright Coming From Nothing, The Vagina Monologues, 1997 (Obie Award, 1997), Necessary Targets, 2002, Conviction, Lemonade, The Depot, Floating Rhoda and the Glue Man, Extraordinary Measures, The Good Body, 2004, The Treatment, 2006; exec. prodr.: (documentaries) What I Want My Words to Do to You: Voices From Inside a Women's Maximum Security Prison, 2003; author: Vagina Warriors, 2005. Trustee PEN Am. Ctr., chair, Women's Com. Recipient Berrilla-Kerr Award playwriting, Elliot Norton Award outstanding solo performance, Jury Award theater, US Comedy Arts Festival, Media Spotlight Award for leadership, Amnesty Internat., 2002, Matrix Award, 2002; Guggenheim Fellowship in playwriting. Vagina Monologues has been translated into over 35 languages & enlists many celebrities as performers/activists. Mailing: PEN American Ctr 588 Broadway Ste 303 New York NY 10012 also: Omega Institute 150 Lake Dr Rhinebeck NY 12572

ENSLIN, THEODORE VERNON, poet; b. Chester, Pa., Mar. 25, 1925; s. Morton Scott and Ruth May (Tuttle); m. Mildred Marie Stout, Aug. 1, 1945 (div.); children— Deirdre, Jonathan Morton; m. Alison Jane Jose, Sept. 14. 1969; 1 son, Jacob Hezekiah. Studied mus. composition with Nadia Boulanger, Cambridge, Mass., 1943-44. Author: New Sharon's Prospect, 1965, To Come To Have Become, 1966, Forms (5 vols.), 1970-74, The Country of Our Consciousness, 1971, The Median Flow, 1975, Synthesis, 1975, Carmina, 1976, Ranger, 2 vols., 1978-80, Music for Several Occasions, 1985, Small Suite for Solo Flute, 1985, The Weather Within, 1986, Case Book, 1987, From Near the Great Pine, 1988, Love and Science, 1990, Little Wandering Flake of Snow, 1991, Gamma-UT, 1992, The House of the Golden Windows, 1993, Music in the Key of C, 1995, Communitas, 1996, Propositions for John Taggart, 1996, Thumbprint on Landscape, 1997, Skeins, 1998, Then and Now Selected Poems, 1999, Sequentiae, 1999 (in tandem 2003), A Folder for LN, 2003, Nine, 2004, One Day and How it Was, 2005; artist 20 CD Set Recordings As An Overview of Work 1943-2000, 2000; readings and seminars various colls. and univs. Recipient Niemann award for weekly newspaper column The Cape Codder, 1955, Hart Crane Meml. award, 1969, Fortner award St. Andrews Coll., 2006; Disting. vis prof. Bowling Green State U., 1989. Mem. Am. Found. for Homeopathy. Address: 379 Kansas Rd Milbridge ME 04658

ENSMINGER, DALE, retired mechanical and electrical engineer; b. Mt. Perry, Ohio, Sept. 26, 1923; s. Charles Henry and Mary Elpha (Koehler) Ensminger; m. Lois Elizabeth Hamilton, Mar. 25, 1948; children: Martha Jean, Laura Lee, Charles Robert, Jonathan Dale, Mary Ann, Daniel Joseph; m. Patricia Ann Evans, June 7, 2002. BSME, BSEE, Ohio State U., 1950, postgrad., 1950-53. Registered profl. engr., Ohio. Rschr. Battelle Meml. Inst., Columbus, Ohio, 1950, prin. rschr.; sr. rschr. Battelle Columbus Labs., mgr. ultrasonics, sr. rsch. scientist, 1984—88, ret., 1988. Cons. in field. Author: Ultrasonics, 1973, 2d edit., 1988; editor, author: Ultrasonics Data and Equations, 2006—; contbr. articles to profl. jours., chapters to books; reviewer Am. Society Non-Destructive Testing Handbook, 1989—. Sec. Columbus Prison Assn., 1950—; dean, dir. Columbus Bible Inst., 1952—97; mem. bd. Fundamental Bapt. Mission Trinidad and Tobago, emeritus mem., 2006; mem. session governing body Calvary Bible Ch., 1953—89, clk.session, 1953—84. With US Army, 1943—46. Decorated Bronze Star; recipient Recognition cert., NASA, 1975. Mem.: ASM, Ultrasonic Industry Assn., Soc. for Non-Destructive Testing, Acoustical Soc. Am., Am. Registry Outstanding Profls. (life). Achievements include patents in field. Home: 322 N Sunnyvale Ave Sunnyvale CA 94085-4317 Personal E-mail: patdens@earthlink.net.

ENSMINGER, JOHN JAY, writer, poet, minister, counselor, playwright; b. June 25, 1945; m. Cynthia Re Fugate, Feb. 18, 1983. BTh, Southwest Bible Sem., Springfield, Mo., 1967; PhD, Univ. Metaphysics, Studio City, Calif., 1997. Caseworker State of Mo., 1974—2002; ret., 2002; jewelry designer and gem collector Ageless Wonders, St. Joseph, Mo., 1984—2003; metaphys. min. U. Metaphysics, Studio City, Calif., 1996—. Pub. On Earth Newsletter. Author: On Earth as it is in Heaven, 2003, Joy on Joy, 2005, The Darkness of 10,000 Stars, 2007, The Slightly-Divine Comic-Opera of Unrehearsed Chimes, 2006, How God Is, 2007; photographer (exhibitions) The Faces of Majesty Collection, 2005, Swansong Family Album Collection; exhibitions include Wyeth-Tootle Mansion Midwest Artist Assn., St. Joseph, Mo., 2006, multiple displays in St. Joseph's. Named Artist of Mo., Midwest Artist Assn., St. Joseph, 2007. Mem.: Albrecht-Kemper Art Mus., Midwest Artist Assn. (1st prize in photography 2005, May Artist of the Month 2005, Sept. Artist of the Month 2005), Acad. Am. Poets. Avocations: antiques, collecting rocks and gems, rare books. Personal E-mail: ensco7@stjoelive.com.

ENSMINGER, LUTHER GLENN, retired chemist; b. Mt. Perry, Ohio, Oct. 17, 1919; s. Charles Henry and Mary Elfa (Koehler) E.; m. Emma Jean Couch, May 12, 1951 (div. Apr. 1973); children: Luther, Douglas, Phillip, Deborah; m. How Leng Cheng, Nov. 11, 1983 (div. Dec. 1988); m. Lee Rose Olson, Oct. 19, 1992. BSc, Ohio State U., 1942, BSc with honors, 1948. Chemist FDA, Cin., 1948-56, chemist, lab. supr. LA, 1956-59, sci. adminstr. Washington, 1959-79, ret., 1979; sci. cons. Arlington, Va., 1979—. Vol., tutor for immigrant high sch. and coll. students (YMCA awards for outstanding tutoring work 1992, 93). Contbr. articles to profl. jours. Sec. Lee-Ballston Citizens Assn., 1965-75; coach Little League Softball, Arlington, Va. With US Army, 1943—45, WW II, North Africa, Italy. Decorated 2 Bronze Battle Stars US Army; recipient Seven Who Care award, 1990, Letter of Commendation award, Commonwealth Va. Bd Edn., 1990, Outstanding Svc. to Cmty. award, YMCA Met. Washington, 1996. Fellow Assn. Ofcl. Analytical Chemists (exec. sec. 1967-79, mem. exec. com. 1960-79), Beta Gamma Sigma; mem. Am. Shoppers Panel, Nat. Family Opinion World Group. Republican. Presbyterian. Achievements include supervising development of analytical methods for government regulatory purposes in 60 subject areas world-wide; organizing annual scientific meetings for adoption of methods. Avocations: gardening, coin collecting/numismatics, clarinet, ballroom dancing.

ENSTROM, JAMES EUGENE, epidemiologist; b. Alhambra, Calif., June 20, 1943; s. Elmer Melvin, Jr. and Klea Elizabeth (Bissell) E.; m. Marta Eugenia Villanea, Sept. 3, 1978. BS, Harvey Mudd Coll., Claremont, Calif., 1965; MS, Stanford U., 1967; PhD in Physics, 1970; M.P.H., UCLA, 1976. Research assoc. Stanford Linear Accelerator Center, 1970-71; research physicist, cons. Lawrence Berkeley Lab. U. Calif., 1971-75; Celeste Durand Rogers cancer research fellow Sch. Pub. Health, UCLA, 1973-75; Nat. Cancer Inst. postdoctoral trainee, 1975-76; cancer epidemiology researcher, 1976-81; assoc. research prof., 1981—. Program dir. for cancer control epidemiology Jonsson Comprehensive Cancer Center, 1978-88, research epidemiologist, 1988—, sci. dir. tumor registry, 1984-87, mem. dean's council, 1976—; cons. epidemiologist Linus Pauling Inst. Sci. and Medicine, 1976-94; cons. physicist Rand Corp., 1969-73, R&D Assos., 1971-75; mem. sci. bd. Am. Council on Sci. and Health, 1984—. Author papers in field. NSF predoctoral trainee, 1965-66; grantee Am. Cancer Soc., 1973—, Nat. Cancer Inst., 1979—; Preventive Oncology Acad. award, 1981-87. Fellow Am. Coll. Epidemiology; mem. Soc. Epidemiologic Research, Am. Heart Assn., Am. Pub. Health Assn., Am. Phys. Soc., AAAS, N.Y. Acad. Scis., Galileo Soc. Office: U Calif Sch Pub Health Los Angeles CA 90024

ENTEMAN, WILLARD FINLEY, retired philosopher; b. Glen Ridge, NJ, Oct. 21, 1936; s. Verling Clair and Elizabeth Vance Rutherford (Dailey) E.; m. Kathleen Ffolliott, June 18, 1960; children: Sally Holyoke, David Finley. BA, Williams Coll., 1959, LL.D. (hon.), 1978; MBA, Harvard U., 1961; MA, Boston U., 1962, PhD, 1965; LL.D. (hon.), Colby Coll., 1980. Instr. in philosophy Wheaton Coll., 1963-65, asst. prof., 1965-69, assoc. prof., 1969-70; assoc. prof., chmn. dept. philosophy Union Coll., Schenectady, 1970-72, provost and assoc. prof., 1972-78; pres., prof. Bowdoin Coll., 1978-81; provost, v.p. acad. affairs R.I. Coll., Providence, 1982-90, prof. philosophy, 1982—2005, prof. emeritus, 2005—; exec. v.p., dir. Bibliotech, Inc., 1984-96. Mem. New Eng. Bd. Higher Edn., 1978-81; 2d v.p., trustee Colby-Bates-Bowdoin Ednl. Telecasting Corp., 1978-81. Author: Managerialsim: The Emergence of a New Ideology, Retirement 101: How TIAA-CREF Members Should Deal with the Dramatic Changes in Their Pensions; editor: The Problem of Free Will, 1967; contbr. articles to profl. publs. Trustee Regional Meml. Hosp., Brunswick, Maine, 1978-81, Hotchkiss Sch., 1980-90, Eckerd Coll., 1987—; mem. long-range planning com. Portland (Maine) Sch. Art, 1979-81; vice chmn. bd. trustees R.I. Coun. on Econ. Edn.; bd. dirs. Sr. Initiative, 2006—. Named One of 100 Top Young Leaders in Higher Edn., Change mag., 1978. Mem. Nat. Assn. Ind. Colls. and Univs. (dir.), Brunswick C. of C. (trustee 1978-81) Home: 30 Abbotsford Ct Providence RI 02906-2403 Home Phone: 401-831-1242; Office Phone: 401-456-9766. Business E-Mail: wenteman@ric.edu.

ENTHOVEN, ALAIN CHARLES, economist, educator; b. Seattlle, Sept. 10, 1930; s. Richard Frederick and Jacqueline E.; m. Rosemary Fenech, July 28, 1956; children: Eleanor, Richard, Andrew, Martha, Nicholas, Daniel. BA in Econs., Stanford U., 1952; M.Phil. (Rhodes scholar), Oxford U., Eng., 1954; PhD in Econs, MIT, 1956. Instr. econs. MIT, Cambridge, 1955-56; economist The RAND Corp., Santa Monica, Calif., 1956-60; ops. research analyst Office of Dir. Def. Research and Enging., Dept. Def., Washington, 1960; dep. comptroller, dep. asst. sec. U.S. Dept. Def., Washington, 1961-65, asst. sec. for systems analysis, 1965-69; v.p. for econ. planning Litton Industries, Beverly Hills, Calif., 1969-71; pres. Litton Med. Products, Beverly Hills, 1971-73; Marriner S. Eccles prof. pub. and pvt. mgmt. Grad. Sch. Bus. Stanford (Calif.) U., 1973-2000, prof. health care econs. Sch. Medicine, 1973-2000; sr. fellow Ctr. for Health Policy, Stanford U., 2000—. Cons. The Brookings Instn., 1956-60; vis. assoc. prof. econs. U. Wash., 1958; mem. Stanford Computer Sci. Adv. Com., 1968-73; cons. The RAND Corp., 1969—; mem. vis. com. in econs. MIT, 1971-78; mem. vis. com. on environ. quality lab. Calif. Inst. Tech., 1972-77; mem. Inst. Medicine, Nat. Acad. Scis., 1972—; mem. vis. com. Harvard U. Sch. Pub. Health, 1974-80; cons. Kaiser Found. Health Plan, Inc., 1973—; vis. prof. U. Paris, 1985, London Sch. Hygiene and Tropical Medicine, 1998-99; vis. fellow St. Catherine's Coll., Oxford U., Eng., 1985, New Coll., 1998-99; dir. Hotel Investors Trust, 1986-87, PCS Inc., 1987-90, Caresoft, 1996-2002, Rx Intelligence, 2000-03, eBenX Inc, 2001-03. Author: (with K. Wayne Smith) How Much is Enough? Shaping the Defense Program 1961-69, 71, 2d edit., 2005, Health Plan: The Only Practical Solution to the Soaring Cost of Medical Care, 1980; editor: (with A. Myrick Freeman III) Pollution, Resources and the Environment, 1973, Theory and Practice of Managed Competition in Health Care Finance, 1988, In Pursuit of an Improving National Health Service, 1999, (with Laura A. Tollen) Toward a 21st Century Health System: The Contributions and Promise of Prepaid Group Practice, 2004; contbr. articles to profl. jours. Bd. dirs. Georgetown U., Washington, 1968-73, Jackson Hole Group, 1993-96; bd. regents St. John's Hosp., Santa Monica, 1971-73; chmn. Gov's Taskforce Managed Health Care Improvement, 1997-98, vis. com. Harvard U. Kennedy Sch. Govt., 1998-2003. Recipient President's award for disting. fed. civilian svc., 1963, Disting. Pub. Svc. medal Dept. Def., 1968, Baxter prize for health svcs. rsch., 1994, Bd. Dirs.' award Healthcare Fin. Mgmt. Assn., 1995, Ellwood award Found. for Accountability, 1998, Rock Carling fellow, Nuffield Trust, 1999. Mem. Am. Assn. Rhodes Scholars, Am. Acad. Arts and Scis., Integrated Healthcare Assn. (bd. dirs. 1999—), Phi Beta Kappa. Home: 1 McCormick Ln Atherton CA 94027-3033 Office: Stanford Univ Grad Sch Business 518 Memorial Way Stanford CA 94305-5015 Office Phone: 650-723-0641. Business E-Mail: enthoven@stanford.edu.

ENTMAN, ROBERT MATHEW, communications educator, consultant; b. Bklyn., Nov. 7, 1949; s. Bernard and Rose (Jacobson) E.; m. Francie Seymour, June 1, 1979; children: Max, Emily. AB, Duke U., 1971; PhD, Yale U., 1977; M in Pub. Policy, U. Calif., Berkeley, 1980. Asst. prof. Dickinson Coll., Carlisle, Pa., 1975-77, Duke U., Durham, NC, 1980-89; postdoctoral fellow U. Calif., 1978-80; assoc. prof. comm. Northwestern U., Evanston, Ill., 1989-94; prof. comm. N.C. State U., Raleigh, 1994—2005, dir. Ctr. for Info. Tech. and Policy, 1999—2003; Shapiro prof. media and pub. affairs George Washington U., Washington, 2005—. Adj. prof. U. N.C., Chapel Hill, 1995-98; Lombard vis. prof. Harvard U., 1997; cons. subcom. on telecom. U.S. Ho. of Reps., Washington, 1982, Nat. Telecom. and Info. Adminstrn., Washington, 1984-85, Aspen Inst., Washington and Aspen, Colo., 1986—; mem. working group Commn. on TV Policy, 1990-96; guest scholar Woodrow Wilson Ctr., Washington, 1989. Author: Democracy without Citizens, 1989, (monograph) Blacks in the News, 1991, Diversifying Broadcast Media, 1998, The Black Image in the White Mind, 2000 Projections of Power, 2004; co-author: Media Power Politics, 1981; co-editor Mediated Politics: Communication in the Future of Democracy, 2000, (book series) Communication, Society and Politics, 1998—; also articles. Recipient McGannon award for comm. policy rsch., 1993, Mott award, 2000, Lane award, 2000, Goldsmith Book prize, 2002, Woolbert award Nat. Comm. Assn., 2005, Edelman Disting. Career award, Am. Political Sci. Assn., 2006; rsch. grantee Markle Found., 1984, 1986, 1988, 1995, Chgo. Cmty. Trust, 1989-92, 1995-97; rsch. grantee Carnegie-Knight Task Force on Future of Journalism, 2007; rsch. fellow Ameritech., 1989-90. Mem. Am. Polit. Sci. Assn. (coun. polit. com. sec. 1990-91, mem. editl. bd. Polit. Comm. 1992—, Jour. Comm. 1994-98, Comm. Law and Policy 1994-2002, Critical Studies in Media Comm., 2002- , Comm. Rev., 2001- , sec.-treas. polit. com. sec. 1996-99, vice chair 1999-2000, chair 2000-01), Social Sci. Rsch. Coun. (mem. working group on media and fgn. policy 1990-93). Avocations: wine collecting and tasting, tennis. Office: George Washington Univ Sch Media and Pub Affairs 805 21st St NW Washington DC 20052

ENTORF, RICHARD CARL, retired management consultant; b. Gettysburg, SD, Feb. 11, 1929; s. Carl Luke and Violet (Carr) E.; m. Dorothy Ann Alexander, Nov. 23, 1951; children: Mark, Kimberly. BS, U. Calif., Berkeley, 1952. Methods engr. Boeing Aircraft Corp., 1957; successively prodn. mgr., dir. mfg., v.p. ops., v.p., gen. mgr., pres. Riverside Cement Co. div. Amcord, Inc., Los Angeles, 1957-75; successively v.p., gen. mgr. Fla. div., sr. v.p. Gen. Portland Inc., Dallas, 1975-81; sr. v.p. Fla. Crushed Stone Co., Leesburg, Fla., 1982-84, pres., 1984-89; pvt. practice mgmt. cons. Leesburg, 1989-99; retired, 1999. Served with USAF, 1953-57. Home: 248 Island Pointe Dr Medford OR 97504-9453

ENTWISTLE, ANDREW JOHN, lawyer, consultant; b. Rockville Centre, NY, Apr. 13, 1959; s. Michael Joseph and Frances (Deluca) E. BA in Govt. and Internat. Relations, U. Notre Dame, 1981; JD, Syracuse U., 1984. Bar: NY 1985, NJ 1986, US Dist. Ct. (ea. and so. dists.) NY 1986, US Ct. Appeals (2d cir.) 1986, US Dist. Ct. NJ 1987, US Ct. Appeals (3d cir.) 1989, US Dist. Ct. (no. dist.) NY 1993, US Supreme Ct. 1993, Ill. 2001, DC 2001, Tex. 2002, Colo. 2004. Assoc. D'Amato & Lynch, NYC, 1984—86, Wilson, Elser, Moskowitz, Edelman & Dicker, NYC, 1986—89, Mudge Rose Guthrie Alexander & Ferdon, NYC, 1989—91; ptnr., chmn. litigation dept. Wohl & Entwistle, LLP, NYC, 1992—98; mng. ptnr. Entwistle & Cappucci LLP, NYC, 1998—. Chmn. Nattech Security Svcs., 2003-; spl. mediator US Bankruptcy Ct. for So. Dist. NY; NE regional editor The Bus. Suit, Def. Rsch. Inst., 1997—. Mem. exec. com. bd. Cath. Big Sisters and Big Bros. of NY, 1995-98, bd. dirs., 1998-05, co-chair adv. bd., 2005—; mem. Housing Bd. Town of North Salem, NY, 1996-00; chmn. Sports Buddies, Inc., 1998-05; dir. Linden Hill Sch., 2001-02, Guiliani Ctr. Urban Leadership, 2003-. Mem. ABA, NY Bar Assn., NJ Bar Assn., Ill. State Bar Assn., DC Bar Assn., Assn. Trial Lawyers Am., Nat. Assn. Pension Plan Attys., Coun. Instnl. Investors (edn. sustainer), Nassau County Bar Assn., NY Trial Lawyers Assn., Westchester County Bar Assn., Assn. Bar City NY, Fed. Bar Coun., Def. Rsch. Inst. Avocations: golf, skiing, fly fishing, hunting. Office: 280 Park Ave 26th Fl W New York NY 10017 Home: 35 Mianus River Rd Bedford NY 10506-2805 Home Phone: 914-234-4486; Office Phone: 212-894-7200. Business E-Mail: aentwistle@entwistle-law.com.

ENTZI, KAREN RUSSELL, orchestra educator; d. John A. and Angeline Noe Russell; m. John A. Entzi, Jan. 4, 1989; 1 child, Angeline Lorraine Bumgardner. MusB, U. NC, Greensboro, 1973; MS in Tchg., N.W. Mo. State U., 1995. Tchr. Richland Dist. I and II, Columbia, SC; orch. tchr. Charlotte (NC) Mecklenburg Sch.; tchr. Lexington (SC) Sch. Dist. #2, Lancaster (SC) County Sch.; orch. tchr. Johnston County Sch., Smithfield, NC, 2002—, Cumberland County Schs., Fayetteville, NC. Condr. Johnston County Youth Orch., Smithfield, NC, 2003—; adj. tchr. violin U. NC, Pembroke. Musician: various profl. performances. Mem.: NC Music Educators Assn., Am. String Tchrs. Assn., Nat. String Orch. Assn. Home: 27 Due West Dr Leicester NC 28748 Office Phone: 919-345-6702. Personal E-mail: karenentzi@hotmail.com.

ENTZMINGER, JOHN NELSON, JR., federal agency administrator, electrical engineer; b. Memphis, Dec. 17, 1936; s. John Nelson and Josephine Chambers (Marshall) Entzminger; m. Nancy May Burg, Sept. 9, 1961; children: David Marshall, Rebecca Louise. BSEE magna cum laude, U. S.C., 1959; MSEE, Syracuse U., 1968. Elec. engr. Bell Telephone Labs., Winston-Salem, NC, 1959; project engr. Rome Air Devel. Ctr., Griffiss AFB, NY, 1960-66, sect. chief, communications, 1966-73, br. chief, communications and control, 1973-81, tech. dir. intelligence and reconnaissance, 1981-83; dir. tactical tech. Def. Advance Rsch. Project Agy., Washington, 1983-91, chief advanced tech., 1991—93, dir. joint uav program off, 1993—96; sr. staff mem. Inst. for Def. Analyses, Alexandria, Va., 1996-98; dep. for technology Def. Airborne Reconnaissance Office, Washington, 1996-98; pres. Entzminger Assocs. Consulting Firm, 1998—. Contbr. articles to profl jours. Elder Christian Assembly, Vienna, Va., 1985—. Recipient Decoration for Exceptional Civilian Svc., USAF, 1974, Medal for Meritorious Civil Svc., Dept. Defense, 1995, Laurels award, Aviation Week and Space Tech., 1995, Pioneer award, Assn. for Unmanned Vehicle Sys. Internat. Fellow: IEEE (AES pioneer award 1998, W. D. White award for Excellence in Radar Engrng. 2005), AIAA (assoc.); mem.: Phi Beta Kappa, Tau Beta Pi. Republican. Achievements include patents in field. Avocations: flying, carpentry, mechanics, skiing. Home: 3203 Dominy Ct Oakton VA 22124-2008 Personal E-mail: jentzminger@ieee.org.

ENYA, (EITHNE NI BHRAONAIN, ENYA BRENNAN), musician; b. Gweedore, Ireland, May 17, 1961; With Clannad, 1980—82; solo career, 1982—. Musician: (albums) The Frog Prince, 1985, Enya, 1987, Watermark, 1988, Shepherd Moons, 1991 (Grammy award for Best New Age Album, 1992), The Celts, 1992, The Memory of Trees, 1995 (Grammy award for Best New Age Album, 1996), Paint the Sky with Stars, 1997, A Day Without Rain, 2000 (Grammy award for Best New Age Album, 2001), Amarantine, 2005 (Grammy award for Best New Age Album, 2007), (singles) I Want Tomorrow, 1987, Evening Falls, 1988, Orinoco Flow, 1988, Storms in Africa, 1989, 6 Tracks, 1989, Oiche Chiun (Silent Night), 1989, 3 Tracks EP, 1990, Exile, 1991, Caribbean Blue, 1991, How Can I Keep from Singing?, 1991, Book of Days, 1992, The Celts, 1992, Marble Halls, 1994, The Christmas EP, 1994, Anywhere Is, 1995, On My Way Home, 1996, Only If, 1997, Only Time, 2000, Wild Child, 2001, Only Time (remix), 2001, May It Be, 2002, Amarantine, 2005. Recipient Best-Selling Irish Artist award, World Music Awards, 2007. Office: Warner Music The Warner Bldg 28 Kensington Church St London W8 4EP England*

ENYEDY, GUSTAV, JR., chemical engineer; b. Cleve., Aug. 23, 1924; s. Gustav and Mary (Silay) E.; m. Zoe Agnes Zachlin, Aug. 25, 1956 (div.); children: Louise Elaine, Roseann Marie, Arthur Gustav, Lillian Alice, Edward Anthony; m. Barbara Martha Ludwig Holley, May 9, 1987. BS in Chem. Engring., Case Inst. Tech., Cleve., 1950, MS, 1955. Registered profl. engr., Ohio. Engr., Rayon Tech. div. E.I. duPont, Richmond, Va., 1950-51; project engr. Grasselli Chem. Div., Cleve., 1951-54; devel. engr. Diamond Alkali (Soda Products), Painesville, Ohio, 1954-60; process engr. Central Engring., Cleve., 1960-61, staff engr. research dept. Painesville, 1961-65, supr. computer services, 1965-68; mgr. Diamond Shamrock Corp., Painesville, 1968-73; engring. cons., 1973-85; pres. PDQS, Inc., 1975—. Lectr. chem. engring. Fenn Coll., Cleve., 1957-61, Cleve. State U., 1975-76 Contbr. articles to tech. jours., textbooks. Treas., cubmaster, chmn. Gates Mills Cub Scout Pack, 1970-71, 75-78. Served with AUS, 1943-46. Decorated Bronze Star medal, Combat Inf. badge. Fellow Am. Inst. Chem. Engrs., Am. Assn. Cost Engrs. (tech. v.p. 1966-68, pres. 1969-70, speakers' bur. program 1971-89, O.T. Zimmerman Founder's award and hon. life mem., 1992); mem. Hungarian Geneal. Soc. of Greater Cleve. (founder 1996), Tau Beta Pi, Pi Delta Epsilon. Home and Office: 7830 Sugarbush Ln Gates Mills OH 44040-9317 Home Phone: 440-423-3469; Office Phone: 440-423-3520. Personal E-mail: gusenyedy@aol.com. *Do each job with complete integrity. Do not gain favor by giving in to outside pressure to slant results.*

ENZENAUER, KIRK KARL, elementary school educator; b. RushCity, Minn., Nov. 1, 1960; s. Harlan and Gladys Enzenauer; m. Sheila Barrett, Dec. 12, 1963; children: Sara Helena, Katherine Marie. BS, U. Minn., Mpls., 1985, MS in Edn., 1994. Sci. tchr. Coon Rapids Mid. Sch., Minn., 1985—. Basketball and track coach Coon Rapids Mid. Sch., 1985—94, athletic trainer, 1985—2000. V.p., pres. Monroe Elem. PTO, Brooklyn Park, Minn., 2004—07; bd. mem., treas. Heart of Edinburgh Homeowners Assn., 1998—. Mem.: Nat. Assn. Geosci. Tchrs. (Tchr. Yr. award 2006), Minn. Earch Sci. Tchrs. Assn. (bd. mem. 1996—, pres. 2003—05). Democrat. Roman Catholic. Office: Coon Rapids Mid Sch 11600 Raven St NW Coon Rapids MN 55433

ENZI, MICHAEL BRADLEY, senator, accountant; b. Bremerton, Wash., Feb. 1, 1944; s. Elmer Jacob and Dorothy (Bradley) E.; m. Diana Buckley, June 7, 1969; children: Amy, Bradley, Emily. BBA, George Wash. U., 1966; MBA, Denver U., 1968. Cert. profl. human resources, 1994. Mayor City of Gillette, Wyo., 1975—82; pres. NZ Shoes, Inc., Gillette, Wyo., 1969-95, NZ Shoes of Sheridan, Inc., Wyo., 1983-96; acctg. mgr. Dunbar Well Svc., Inc., Gillette, 1985-97; mem. Wyo. Ho. of Reps., Cheyenne, 1986—91. Wyo. State Senate, Cheyenne, 1991-96; commr. Western Interstate Commn. for Higher Edn., 1995—96; US Senator from Wyo., 1997—. Mem. Edn. Commn. of States, 1989—93, Western Interstate Commn. Higher Edn., 1995—96; mem. com. banking, housing, and urban affairs US Senate, com. budget, chmn. com. health, edn., labor, and pensions, com. small business and entrepreneurship. Pres. Wyo. Assn. Mcpls., Cheyenne, 1980-82; chmn. bd. dirs. 1st Wyo. Bank, Gillette, 1978-88, bd. dirs. Black Hills Corp., 1992-96. Served as Sgt. Wyo. Air NG, 1967—73. Recipient W. Stuart Symington award, Air Force Assn., 2001, Small Investor Empowerment award, Nat. Assn. Real Estate Investment Trusts, 2002, Legis. of Yr., Am. Soc. Consultant Pharmacists, 2004, Biotechnology Industry Orgn., 2005, Congressional Leadership award, Food Industry Assn., 2005, Leadership award, Nat. Orgn. Fetal Alcohol Syndrome, 2005, Policy Maker of Yr., Assn. Career and Technical Edn., 2005, TechNet Founders Cir. award, 2005. Mem. Wyo. Order of DeMolay (state master councilor 1963-64), Wyo. Jaycees (state pres. 1973-74), Masons (Sheridan and Gillette lodges), Scottish Rite, Shriners, Lions, Sigma Chi. Republican. Presbyn. Avocations: fishing, bicycling, soccer, hunting. Office: US Senate 379A Senate Russell Bldg Washington DC 20510-0001 also: District Office Ste 303 400 South Kendrick Ave Gillette WY 82716-3803 Office Phone: 202-224-3424, 307-682-6268. Office Fax: 202-228-0359, 307-682-6501. Business E-Mail: senator@enzi.senate.gov.

EO, SURAK, plastic surgeon, educator; b. Gwangju, Republic of Korea, Feb. 14, 1968; s. JaeHong Eo and OkSoon Ju; m. InA Jeong; children: DoYang, Douglas Ford. MD, Chonnam Nat. Med. Sch., Gwangju, 1993; MS, Chonnam Nat. U., Gwangju, 1999, PhD, 2002. Diplomate Korea, 1993. Intern Chonnam Nat. U. Med. Ctr., 1993—94, resident in plastic surgery, 1998—2002, fellow in plastic surgery, 2002—03; gen. physician Dr. Cho's Internal Medicine Clinic, GwangJu, Republic of Korea, 1997—98; internat. fellow UCLA Med. Ctr., 2003—05; asst. prof. Hallym U. Med. Ctr., Seoul, Republic of Korea, 2005. Contbr. articles to profl. jours. Lt. Korean Army, 1994—97. Recipient Young Plastic Surgeon award, Korean Soc. Plastic Surgeons, 2006. Mem.: Korean Soc. Plastic and Reconstructive Surgery. Presbyterian. Home: 827 Levering Ave Apt 508 Los Angeles CA 90024 Office: UCLA Med Ctr 10945 Le Conte Ave Ste 3355 Los Angeles CA 90095 also: DongGuk U Internat Hosp Dept Plastic Sugery 814 SikSa-dong Sandong-gu 410773 Goyang-si Republic of Korea Office Phone: 82-31-961-7330. Personal E-mail: u9998185kr@yahoo.com.

EPCAR, RICHARD MICHAEL, actor, writer, film director; b. Denver, Apr. 29, 1955; s. George Buck and Shirley (Learner) E.; m. Ellyn Jane Stern, Aug. 15, 1982; children: Jonathan Alexander, Jacqueline Elizabeth. BFA in Performing Arts, U. Ariz., 1978; postgrad., U. So. Calif., LA, 1980, U. Calif., 1981, Am. Film Inst., 1982. Pres. Epcar Entertainment, LA, 1986—. Actor (films) including Memoirs of an Invisible Man, DC Collins, Incident of War, Street Hawk, Escape to Love, Not of This World, Three Putts, (TV series) Diagnosis Murder, Columbo, Beverly Hills 90210, Cheers, General Hospital, Guns of Paradise, Matlock, Who's the Boss?, Sonny Spoons, Moonlighting, Highway to Heaven, Amazing Stories, Fast Times, Crazy Like a Fox, Hell Town, Stir Crazy, Santa Barbara, Days of our Lives, (animated series) Teknoman 2 Lead Voices; author 7 episodes, co-dir. Ghost in the Shell (film & lead voice- series), Transformers (co-author and lead voice), Digimon (dir. first season), Lupin the Third (dir. and lead voice), Fighting Spirit (dir. and lead voice), Storm Force, Noein (dir. and lead voice), Cyborg 009 (author and lead voice), Daigunder (author and lead voice), Robotech, (lead voice) Shadow Cronicles, Shark Bait, (dir., lead voice) Toy Warrior, (dir.) Pat Labor III, (dir.) Tae Guk Gi, (dir.) Old Boy, (voice) Curious George, (lead voice) Avenging Apes, Bo-Bo-B0-B0, Prince of Egypt, Honey Bee Hutch, Mr. Men, X-Men; dir., voice Crimes of Father Amaro (acad. award nomination); dir and author, Betty Blue, Warriors of Heaven and Earth, The Code, The Returner, Widow of St. Pierre (acad. award nomination) Mostly Martha, Emperor and Assassin, Iron Monkey, Mission Kashmir, Shiri, Double Vision, and Omhyosi; dir. The Pearl, Toy Warrior, Shadow Hearts II, Robotech The Game; Onmyoji dir., author, lead voice Eagle Riders, 2 lead voices Digimon, lead voice Flint; co-dir., co-author, lead voices Samurai X; TV and film voice Gladiator, Gods and Generals, Riddick, Independence Day, Seven, Hell Raiser III & IV, Resident Evil III, Hard Target, Crime Story, Power Rangers, Jack, E.R., Nash Bridges, Xena, Hercules; (on stage) Why a Hero, Dracula, An Evening with Lincoln, Rumors, Real Inspector Hound, Richard II; actor, writer (play) (on stage) The Vow, Take My Wife.Please!, 1980; wrote and directed English adaptation of Acad. award winning Cinema Paradisco, Belle Epoque (Acad. Award winner), Women on the Verge of a Nervous Breakdown (Acad. Award nomination), Eat Drink Man Woman (Acad. Award nominated), Fencing Master (Acad. Award nominated); internat. supr. Gladiator, Galaxy Quest, Chicken Run, El Dorado, E.T.; CD-ROM lead voice Medal of Honor, Blackhawk Down, Samurai Warriors, Dynasty Tactics II, Waterworld, Xena-Saga I & II, Aero Wings, Wetlands, Jade Cacoon, Dynasty Warriors IV, Kingdom Hearts II, Star Wars: Empire at War, Shadow Hearts II (lead voice, dir.), Hack I, II, II (lead voice), Generation of Kaos I, II, Splinter Cell, Blue Dragon (lead voice, dir.), Sylpheed (cast), Dead Head Fred (dir.), Jackass the Game (lead voice, dir.), dir. Fighting Spirit, dir., lead voice Lupin III, Covenant, others. Mem. L.A. Zoo Assn., 1983-90, 91, 94, Natural History Mus., L.A., 1989-91, Earth Save, L.A., 1990, L.A. Mus. Art, 1991; host fall festival Sta. KCET-Pub. TV, L.A., 1980; active Am. Cancer Soc. Recipient Haldeman Found. scholarship, U. Ariz., 1973-78; named Nat. Best Actor of Yr., Nat. Players, 1977, CPC Repertory Group, 1980; recipient Irene Ryan Soloist award, 1978. Avocations: weightlifting, tennis, music, art. Office Phone: 818-426-3415. E-mail: tallactor@richardepcar.com.

EPHRON, NORA, writer; b. NYC, May 19, 1941; d. Henry and Phoebe (Wolkind) E.; m. Dan Greenburg (div.); m. Carl Bernstein (div.); children: Jacob, Max; m. Nicholas Pileggi. BA, Wellesley Coll., 1962. Reporter N.Y. Post, 1963-68; free-lance writer, 1968—; contbg. editor, columnist Esquire mag., 1972-73, sr. editor, columnist, 1974-78; contbg. editor N.Y. mag., 1973-74. Author: Wallflower at the Orgy, 1970, Crazy Salad, 1975, Scribble Scribble, 1978, Heartburn, 1983, Nora Ephron Collected, 1991, I Feel Bad About My Neck: And Other Thoughts on Being a Woman, 2006; screenwriter: (with Alice Arlen) Silkwood (nominated Acad. award for best original screenplay), 1983, Heartburn, 1986, Cookie, 1989, When Harry Met Sally (nominated Acad. award, BAFTA award for best screenplay), 1989, My Blue Heaven, 1990; dir., screenwriter (with Delia Ephron) This Is My Life, 1992, Mixed Nuts, 1994, Michael, 1996, You've Got Mail, 1998; co-screenwriter, dir. Sleepless in Seattle (nominated Acad. award for best original screenplay), 1993; prodr., dir. Lucky Numbers, 2000; screenwriter, prodr. Hanging Up, 2000; playwright Imaginary Friends, 2002; screenwriter, dir., Bewitched, 2005. Mem. Writers Guild Am., Authors Guild, Dirs. Guild of Am., Acad. Motion Picture Arts and Scis.

EPLER, GARY ROBERT, physician, author, educator; b. Chico, Calif., Apr. 5, 1944; s. Deane Chandler and Kathryn Louise (McNeil) E.; m. Joan Susan Weidman, Sept. 10, 1983; children: Gregory C., Brett H. MD, Tulane U., 1971; MPH, Harvard U., 1978. Diplomate in internal medicine and pulmonary medicine Am. Bd. Internal Medicine. Intern Harlem Hosp., Columbia U., 1971-72; resident U. Hosp., Boston, 1974-76, pulmonary medicine fellowship, 1975-78; asst. prof. medicine Sch. Medicine Boston U., 1978-85, assoc. clin. prof. medicine, 1985-96, Harvard U., Boston, 1995—; med. dir. respiratory therapy, chmn. dept. medicine New England Bapt. Hosp., Boston, 1983-98, med. dir. rehab. unit, 1983-98. Parasitology rsch. fellow Tulane U., Cali, Colombia, 1969-70, USPHS, Ctrs. Disease Control, 1972-74; tuberculosis cons. CDC Vietnamese Refugee Camps, Eglin AFB, Fla. and Indiantown Gap, Pa., 1975, Cuban Refugee Camp, Indiantown Gap, 1980; med. cons. CDC, Vietnamese Refugee Programs in Hong Kong, Thailand, Philippines, Malaysia, Indonesia; vis. attending physician U. Hosp., Boston City Hops. and Boston VA Hosp., 1978-98, Brigham and Women's Hosp., Boston, 1999—; med. dir. Occupational Health Ctr., Wilmington, Mass; vis. prof. Kyoto (Japan) U., 1990; many others. Author book on diseases of bronchioles, 1994; editor book on occupational lung diseases; editl. reviewer New England Jour. Medicine, Annals of Internal Medicine, Jour. AMA, Am. Rev. Respiratory Diseases, Chest, Jour. Respiratory Medicine, Jour. Western Medicine, Jour. Rheumatology, European Respiratory Jour.; contbr. chpts. to books, more than 85 articles to sci. jours. Lt. comdr. USPHS, 1972-74. Recipient cert. of appreciation Am. Lung Assn. Mass.; named one of Outstanding Med. Specialists in U.S., Town and Country Mag., 1989. Fellow ACP, Am. Coll. Chest Physicians (chmn. com. on occupational and environ. health 1987-88, v.p. New England States chpt. 1989-91, pres. chpt. 1991-93); mem. AMA (alt. del. 1987-93), Am. Soc. Law and Medicine (treas. 1983-85, Disting. Svc. award 1985), Am. Coll. Physician Execs., Mass. Thoracic Soc. (mem. coun. 1980-84, sec.-treas. 1984-85, pres. 1986-88), Mass. Med. Soc. Office: Brigham and Women's Hosp Pulmonary/Critical Care Med 75 Francis St Boston MA 02115-6106

EPLEY, LEWIS EVERETT, JR., retired lawyer; b. Ft. Smith, Ark., Apr. 28, 1936; s. Lewis Everett and Evelyn (Wood) E.; m. Donna Louise Swopes, Feb. 24, 1962. BS, JD, U. Ark., 1961. Bar: Ark. 1961. Formerly practiced in Eureka Springs, Ark.; city atty., 1969-71; chmn. bd. Bank of Eureka Springs, Ark., 1990-93, vice-chmn., 1993—2005; ret., 2005. Bd. dirs. Bank of Eureka Springs, 1964—; del. Ark. Constl. Conv., 1969-70; apptd. spl. assoc. justice Ark. Supreme Ct., 1984; bd. adv. U. Ark., 2006—, exec. com.; adv. bd. U. Ark. Med. Sci. Reynolds Inst. on Aging, 2006—. Ark. Bldg. Svcs. Coun., 1975-80, chmn., 1976-78; Carroll County Cen. Dem. Com., 1964-68, Beaver Lake Adv. Com., 1982-89; bd. dirs. Eureka Springs Ozark Folk Festival, 1964-69, Ark. Cancer Rsch. Ctr., N.W. Ark. Radiation Therapy Inst., 1984-91, pres. bd. dirs., 1989; chmn. adv. bd. Eureka Springs Mcpl. Hosp., 1963-71; trustee U. Ark., 1989-99, chmn. bd. trustees, 1996-98; bd. dirs. U. Ark. Found., 1994—, chmn., 2004-06; bd. dirs. Mashburn Scholarship Found., 1993-2002, S.W. Energy Co., 1998—; past dir., past mem. Washington Regional Med. Found.; mem. Carroll County Com. for Study of Long-Term Health Care Needs, 1990-93; devel. coun. Eureka Springs Hosp., 1997-2001. Fellow Ark. Bar Assn. (del. 1975-78), Am. Inns of Ct. (mem. emeritus W. B. Putnam chpt. 1990-97), Carroll County Bar Assn. (past pres.), Eureka Springs C. of C. (dir., past pres.), Fayetteville Rotary Club, Phi Alpha Delta, Kappa Kappa Psi. Baptist. Home: 3620 N Brodie Station Fayetteville AR 72703 E-mail: epleyoff@sbcglobal.net.

EPLING, RICHARD LOUIS, lawyer; b. Waukegan, Ill., Aug. 16, 1951; s. Carrol Franklin and Mary Teresa Epling; m. Suzanne Braley, Aug. 4, 1973. BA in English and History magna cum laude, Duke U., 1973; JD, U. Mich., 1976. Bar: Ill. 1977, US Dist. Ct. (no. dist.) Ill. 1977, US Ct. Appeals (7th cir.) 1979, Ariz. 1981, US Dist. Ct. Ariz. 1981, US Ct. Appeals (9th cir.) 1982, NY 1988, US Ct. Appeals (2d cir.) 1988, US Ct. Appeals (3rd cir.) 2005, US Dist. Ct. (ea. and so. dists.) NY 1989. Law clk. to presiding justice Mich. Supreme Ct., Southfield, 1976-77; assoc. Katten, Muchin & Zavis, Chgo., 1977-81; ptnr. Brown & Bain, P.A., Phoenix, 1981-88, Sidley & Austin, NYC, 1988-92, Pillsbury Winthrop Shaw Pittman LLP and predecessor firm, NYC, 1992—, ptnr., leader Insolvency and Restructuring practice, 2005—. Assoc. conferee Nat. Bankruptcy Conf., Washington, 1985-93. Contbr. articles to profl. jours. Mem. Am. Bankruptcy Inst., Phi Beta Kappa. Office: Pillsbury Winthrop Shaw Pittman 1540 Broadway New York NY 10036 Office Phone: 212-858-1649. Office Fax: 212-858-1500. Business E-Mail: richard.epling@pillsburylaw.com.

EPNER, STEVEN ARTHUR, computer consultant; b. Buffalo; s. Robert and Rosann (Krohn) E.; m. Louise Berke, June 20, 1970; children: Aaron J., Brian D. BS, Purdue U., 1970. Computer operator/programmer Union Carbide, Chgo. and London, 1966-68; system analyst process design III, Chgo., 1969; analyst, sr. systems analyst Monsanto Co., St. Louis, 1970-74; lead analyst Citicorp., St. Louis, 1974-76; cons., pres. The User Group, Inc. (name changed to BSW Consulting, Inc. 1995), St. Louis, 1976—. Lectr. U. Mo., St. Louis Bus. Program, AICPA, Mo., 1983-93; SBA Task Force on Small Bus.; dir. Programming and Systems Cons., Inc. Editor: The Independent, 1977-84; contbg. editor St. Louis Bus. Jour., St. Louis Computing; contbr. articles to profl. jours. Trustee Steven A. Epner/ICAA Scholarship fund; mem. tech. com., founding rep. EDI Coalition of Assns. Mem. Ind. Computer Cons. Assn. (dir., pres. chpt., nat. pres.), Nat. Cons. Council, Nat. Spkrs. Assn. (Cert. Spkg. Profl. award 2000), Internat. Brotherhood Magicians. Office: BSW Cons Inc 1050 N Lindbergh Blvd Saint Louis MO 63132-2912 *I am often asked about starting businesses. My normal reply is, "If it were easy and guaranteed, then it would already be done." Therefore, building a successful organization takes time, effort, and risk.*

EPP, DIANNE NAOMI, secondary school educator; b. Yankton, SD, Oct. 1, 1939; d. Willard H. and Florence A. (Leigh) Waltner; m. Anthony R. Epp, Aug. 18, 1964; children: Alain-René Epp Weaver, Rachel Epp Buller. BA in Chemistry, Bethel Coll., 1961; MA, U. Mo., 1963; cert. etudes, L'Ecole d'Administration, Brussels, 1965. Chemistry instr. Bethel Coll., North Newton, Kans., 1963-64; sci. tchr. Ecole Secondaire, Sundi-Lutete, Zaire, 1965-67; rsch. chemist FMC Glass Lab., Golden, Colo., 1967-70; vis. instr. Nebr. Wesleyan U., Lincoln, 1973-74, 77-79, 1980-81; chemistry tchr. East High Sch., Lincoln, 1982—93, 1994—2005; vis. scholar Miami U., Oxford, Ohio, 1993-94. Cons. NSF Doing Chemistry Videodisc, 1988; cons. small scale CD ROM Synapse Corp., Lincoln, 1993. Author: Chemical Manfacturing: The Process of Mixing, 2000, Experimental Design: The Chemistry of Adhesives, 1998, Product Testing: The Chemistry of Ice Cream, 1998; cons. editor: Starting at Ground Zero, 1989; author: (monograph series) A Palette of Color, 1995; contbr. articles to profl. jours. Recipient Excellence in Teaching award Cooper Found., 1990, Excellence in High Sch. Chemistry Teaching award Am. Chem. Soc., 1990, 91, Presdl. award for Excellence in Sci. and Math. Teaching NSF, 1994, Kiewit Found. Tchg. award, 1997, 01, Christa McAuliffe award, 2005. Personal E-mail: depp@huskeraccess.com.

EPP, ELDON JAY, religion educator; b. Mountain Lake, Minn., Nov. 1, 1930; s. Jacob Jay and Louise (Kintzi) E.; m. ElDoris Balzer, June 13, 1951; children: Gregory Thomas, Jennifer Elizabeth. AB magna cum laude, Wheaton Coll., 1952; BD magna cum laude, Fuller Theol Sem., 1955; STM, Harvard U., 1956, PhD, 1961. Spl. rsch. asst. Princeton Theol. Sem., 1961-62; vis. instr. Drew U. Theol. Sch., 1962; asst. prof. religion U. So. Calif. Grad. Sch. Religion, 1962-65, assoc. prof., 1965-67, assoc. prof. classics, 1966-68; assoc. prof. religion Case Western Res. U., Cleve., 1968-71, prof. religion, Harkness prof. bibl. lit., 1971-98, prof. emeritus, 1998—, dean humanities and social scis., 1977-85, dean emeritus, 1998—, chmn. dept. religion, 1982-98; acting dean Western Res. Coll., Cleve., 1984. Lectr. Harvard Divinity Sch., 2001-02, vis. prof., 2002-03, 04-05,

06-07; Am. exec. com. Internat. Greek New Testament Project, 1968-88; mem. N.Am. Com., 1989—; mem. accreditation rev. coun. North Ctrl. Assn. Commn. on Insts. Higher Edn., 1986-90, mem. appeals panel, 1992-95, cons. evaluator corps, 1983-98; panelist NEH, 1978, 80, 90, 00; reader John Simon Guggenheim Meml. Found., 1991-94; Kenneth W. Clark lectr. Duke U., 1986; Ratner lectr. Case Western Res. U., 1998; bd. dirs. New Testament Lang. Project, 1999—. Author: The Theological Tendency of Codex Bezae Cantabrigiensis in Acts, 1966, Perspectives on New Testament Textual Criticism, 2005, Junia, First Woman Apostle, 2005; co-author: Studies in the Theory and Method of New Testament Textual Criticism, 1993; co-editor: New Testament Textual Criticism: Its Significance for Exegesis, 1981, The New Testament and Its Modern Interpreters, 1989, New Testament Tools, Studies, and Documents, 2007; assoc. editor Jour. Bibl. Lit., 1971-90; editor Critical Rev. of Books in Religion, 1991-94, Studies and Documents, 1991-07; mem. editl. bd. Soc. Bibl. Lit. Monograph Series, 1969-72, Soc. Bibl. Lit. Centennial Publs., 1975-86, Studies and Documents, 1971-06, Critical Rev. of Books in Religion, 1987-94; exec. sec. Hermeneia: A Critical and Historical Commentary on the Bible, 1962—, mem. editl. bd., 1966—; contbr. about 50 scholarly articles to profl. jours. Active Boy Scouts Am., 1975-78; bd. mgrs. St. Paul's Episcopal Cathedral, LA, 1964-68, clk., 1967-68. Harvard Faculty Arts and Scis. fellow, 1958-59, Rockefeller doctoral fellow in religion, 1959-60; postdoctoral fellow Claremont Grad. Sch., 1966-68; Guggenheim fellow, 1974-75; NEH grant, 1988. Mem. AAUP 1963-98 (mem. chpt. exec. com. 1970-72), Am. Acad. Religion 1961-98(sect. pres. 1965-66), Soc. Bibl. Lit. (chmn. textual criticism seminar 1966, 71-84, mem. permanent Centennial com. 1975-80, mem. coun. 1980-82, 85-87, 2002-03, del. Coun. on Study of Religion 1980-82, chair nominating com. 1985-87, mem. fin. com. 1997—, v.p. 2002, pres. 2003, chmn. com. on programs and initiatives 2003-05), Studiorum Novi Testamenti Societas, Cath. Bibl. Assn., Am. Soc. Papyrologists, New Testament Colloquium (chmn. 1974), Soc. Mithraic Studies, Egypt Exploration Soc., Phi Beta Kappa. Personal E-mail: eepp@erols.com. *Personal philosophy: Two essentials for life and livelihood are integrity and maturity. Integrity, in the abstract, is soundness, but in practical terms means incorruptibility, while maturity is basically the capacity to tolerate ambiguity. As individuals and as a society, we cannot afford to abandon integrity or to stifle maturity.*

EPP, GARRETT WAYNE, music educator; b. Reedley, Calif., July 4, 1944; s. William Howard and Verna Myrtle (Janzen) E.; m. Teresa R. Pruett-Epp; 1 child, Caroline Mackenzie BA in Music Edn., Bethel Coll., 1967; MusM, So. Meth. U., 1975, M in Sacred Music, 1975; MusD, U. Mo., Kansas City, 1993. Cert. elem., secondary tchr., Ind., Kans. Choral dir. grades 4-12 Stockton (Kans.) Unified Sch. Dist., 1967-70; edn. coord., counselor, tchr. Mpls. City Workhouse, 1970-73; supr. music, choral dir. grades 7-12 South Adams Schs., Berne, Ind., 1975-88; pvt. voice tchr. part-time Shawnee Mission South H.S., Overland Park, Kans., 1990-91; artist-in-residence/pvt. voice instr. Paseo Acad. Fine & Performing Arts, Kansas City, Mo., 1991-93; adj. faculty, pvt. voice instr. Kansas City (Kans.) C.C., 1993; secondary choral coord., choral dir. Olathe (Kans.) North H.S., 1993—. Profl. singer Kansas City (Mo.) Chorale, 1998—; profl. singer, sect. leader St. Michael's & All Angels Episcopal Ch., Overland Park, 2000—; dir. music Trinity United Meth. Ch., Kansas City, Kans., 1989-93; founder, music dir. Kansas City Singers, 1991; guest condr. Kansas City Symphony Chorus, 1991. Ch. choir director various Kans., Ind. chs., 1966-93; founder, music dir. Stockton (Kans.) Cmty. Chorus, 1967-70; dir., condr. other singing groups, 1970-93; soloist with several maj. choruses, others Recipient U. Mo. Kansas City Chancellor's Non-Resident award, 1988-90, Perkins Sch. Theology Tuition award, 1974-75, Bethel Coll. Music Theory assistantship, 1965-67; named one of 160 singers to perform in Carnegie Hall with the Robert Shaw/Carnegie Hall Festival Chorus, 1990, 92, 94, 99 Mem. Internat. Fedn. Choral Music, Am. Choral Dirs. Assn., Music Educators Nat. Conf., Nat. Assn. Tchrs. of Singing, Nat. Educators Assn., Coll. Music Soc., Phi Kappa Phi, Pi Kappa Lambda. Mennonite. Avocations: biking, hiking, racquetball, cultural activities. Office: Olathe North H S 600 E Prairie St Olathe KS 66061-3355 Home Phone: 913-712-8452; Office Phone: 913-780-7140. Business E-Mail: geppon@olatheschools.com.

EPP, MARY ELIZABETH, retired technologies consultant; b. Buffalo, Aug. 7, 1941; d. John Conrad and Gertrude Marie (Murphy) Winkelman; m. Harry Francis Epp, Aug. 31, 1963. BA in Math., D'Youville Coll., 1963; MS in Math., Xavier U., 1974, MBA in Fin., 1981, MBA in Mktg., 1987. Systems analyst GE, Evendale, Ohio, 1965-71, Palm Beach Co., Cin., 1972-73; hardware systems engr. Procter & Gamble, Cin., 1973-76; systems engr. CalComp Inc., Anaheim, Calif., 1980-84; software engr. SDRC Inc., Cin., 1984-86; advanced systems project mgr. SAMI/Burke Mktg., Cin., 1986-89; ptnr., dir. strategic planning Info. Advantage, Inc., Cin., 1989-91; internat. product control specialist Cincom Systems Inc., Cin., 1991-94; corp. profl. svcs., mgr. methods & tools, prin. cons. Sybase, Inc., Cin., 1995—2002. Cons. Shelley & Sands, Zanesville, Ohio, 1983-85. Contbr. articles to profl. jours. Active Fairfield Charter Rev. Commn., 1981-83, Hamilton-Fairfield Symphony Choral. Mem. AAUW (br. treas. 1975-79, state women's chair 1979-80, state treas. 1980-82) Republican. Roman Catholic. Avocations: bridge, skiing, music, fishing, travel, dog training and showing. Home: 4242 Stahlheber Rd Hamilton OH 45013-8911

EPPEN, GARY DEAN, business educator; b. Austin, Minn., Apr. 28, 1936; s. Marldene Fredrick and Elsie Alma (Wendorf) E.; m. Ann Marie Sathre, June 14, 1958; children: Gregory, Peter, Paul, Amy. AA, Austin Jr. Coll., 1956; BS, U. Minn., 1958, MSIE, 1960; PhD, Cornell U., Ithaca, NY, 1964; Doctorate (hon.), Stockholm Sch. Econs., 1998. Prof. mgmt. European Inst. Advanced Studies, Brussels, 1972-73; assoc. dean Grad. Sch. Bus., U. Chgo., 1969-75, prof. indsl. adminstrn., 1970—, assoc. dean PhD studies, 1978-85, dir. internat. bus. exchange program, 1977-92, dir. Life Officers Investment Seminar, 1975-88, dir. Fin. Analysts Seminar, 1982-88, Robert Law prof., 1989-97, dir. exec. program, 1989-94, Keller Disting. Svc. prof., 1997-2001, dep. dean part-time programs, 1998-2001, Keller Disting. Svc. prof. emeritus, 2001—. Francqui prof. Cath. U. Leuven, Belgium, 1979; Urwitz vis. prof. Stockholm Sch. Econs., 1994; external examiner U. W.I., 1979-82; dir. Hub Group, Inc., Hornet Capital, LLC. Author: (with F.J. Gould) Quantitative Concepts for Management, 1979, (with Metcalfe and Walters) The MBA Degree, 1979, (with F.J. Gould and C.P. Schmidt) Introductory Management Science, 1984; editor: Energy the Policy Issues, 1975; contbr. articles to profl. jours. FMC Faculty Rsch. scholar, 1986—89. Home: 3107 N Snead Dr Goodyear AZ 85338 Business E-Mail: gary.eppen@chicagogsb.edu.

EPPERSON, ERIC ROBERT, finance executive, film producer; b. Oregon City, Oreg., Dec. 10, 1949; s. Robert Max and Margaret Joan (Crawford) E.; m. Lyla Gene Harris, Aug. 21, 1969; 1 child, Marcie. BS, Brigham Young U., 1973, M of Acctg., 1974; MBA, Golden Gate U., 1977, JD, 1981. Instr. acctg. Brigham Young U., Provo, Utah, 1973-74; supr. domestic taxation Bechtel Corp., San Francisco, 1974-78; supr. internat. taxation Bechtel Power Corp., San Francisco, 1978-80; mgr. internat. tax planning Del Monte Corp., San Francisco, 1980-82, mgr. internat. taxes, 1982-85; internat. tax specialist Touche Ross & Co., San Francisco, 1985-87; dir. internat. tax Coopers & Lybrand, Portland, Oreg., 1987-89; exec. v.p., CFO Epperson Dayton Sorenson Prodns., Inc., Salt Lake City, 1989-90, Epperson Prodns., 1990-92; exec. dir. The Oreg. Trail Found., Inc., Oregon City, 1992-93; pres., chmn. bd. MFD Ltd., Portland, 1993—; pres. Oreg. Trail Films, Ltd., 1998—, Morgan's Ferry Prodns., LLC, 1988—2007, Lakeboat Prodns., LLC, 1999—2007, Oregon Trail TV, Ltd., 1999—2006, Oregon Trail Promotions, Ltd., 1999—2006; COO, CFO Whitlock Training Group Corp., 2006—. Estate executor in field, 2005—; CFO/COO Crimeline and Whitlock Training Group Corp., 2006. Author: (with T. Gilbert) Interfacing of the Securities and Exchange Commission with the Accounting Profession: 1968 to 1973, 1974; prodr. (film) Without Evidence, 1995, Morgan's Ferry, 1999, Lakeboat, 2000; exec. prodr. (film) Dream Machine, 1989, Live & Learn, 2001, (TV series) Live & Learn, 2000, Dixie Chick Fly Tour, 2000. Scoutmaster Boy Scouts Am., Provo, 1971-73, troop committeeman, 1973-74, 83—, vice-chmn. ranch devel. com., Butte Creek; mem. IRS Vol. Income Tax Assistance Program, 1972-75; pres. Youth First Found. Inc., 2000-, Mut. Improvement Assn., Ch. Jesus Christ of Latter-day Saints, 1972-74, pres. Sunday sch., 1977-79, tchr., 1974-80, ward clk., 1980-83, bishopric, 1983-87; bd. dirs. Oreg. Art Inst. Film Ctr., Oreg. Trail Coordinating Coun., Hist. Preservation League of Oreg. Mem. World Affairs Coun., Japan/Am. Soc., Internat. Tax Planning Assn., Internat. Fiscal Assn., Oreg. Trail Coordinating Coun. (exec. bd.), Oreg. Hist. Soc., U.S. Rowing Assn., Oreg. Calif. Trail Assn., Royal Photog. Soc., Commonwealth Club, Multnomah Athletic Club, Exec. Officers Club. Republican. Office: PMB 180 25 NW 23d Pl Ste 6 Portland OR 97210-5599

EPPERSON, ROBERT DALE, farmer; b. Santa Maria, Calif., Jan. 12, 1947; s. Joseph Cary and Lina Marcille Epperson; m. Loretta Jolan Lambrecht, July 20, 1968; children: Andrea, David, Sara, Mary. BS, Calif. State U., Fresno, 1968, MS, 1970. Farmer, Kerman, Calif., 1974—; v.p. Epperson's Market, Inc., Kerman, 1974-79; dir. grants and contracts Calif. State U., Fresno, 1984-89; sr. environ. planner Calif. Dept. Transp., Fresno, 1989-2000; resource mgr. U.S. Bur. Reclamation, Fresno, 2000—. Mem. Nat. Agrl. Stats. Adv. Com., Washington, 1999-2004, mem. mktg. and strategic planning com. Sun-Maid Growers Bd. Dirs., Kingsburg, Calif., 1987—, mem. fin. com., 1987—, mem. pers. com., 1990—, chair fin. com., 1996—, chair ethics com., 1997—, chair mktg. and strategic planning com., 1990-96; dir. Sun-Diamond Growers, Pleasanton, Calif., 1988-97, mem. audit com., 1995-97, mem. ethics com., 1996-97: mem. Raisin Adminstrv. Com., Fresno, 1985—; mem. audit com. Raisin Adminstrv. Com., Fresno, 1995, vice-chair grades and stds. com., 1992-96. Chair safety and environ. protection subcom. Joint Army, Navy, NASA and Air Force Com. on Rocket Propulsion, LA, 1979-83; admissions liaison officer USAF Acad., Colorado Springs, 1993-99; youth group leader St. Olaf Luth. Ch., Garden Grove, Calif., 1980-83, Hope Luth. Ch., Fresno, 1984-88; youth group leader Bethel Luth. Congregation, Fresno, 1974-79, pres., 1977-79; v.p. Hope Luth. Ch., Fresno, Calif., 2004—. Explorer Scout liasion Air Force Armament Lab., Eglin AFB, Fla., 1972-74; planning commr. City of Kerman, Calif., 2006—, chmn. planning commn., 2007—. Capt. USAF, 1979-83. Mem. Am. Chem. Soc. Republican. Avocations: genealogy, history, plant physiology, travel, reading. Home: 15615 W Dakota Ave Kerman CA 93630 Office: US Bur Reclamation 1243 N St Fresno CA 93721-1813 Personal E-mail: r-epperson@comcast.net. Business E-Mail: repperson@kermantel.net.

EPPERSON, STUART W., religious raido broadcaster; b. 1935; m. Atsinger Nancy Epperson; 4 children. BA radio/television broadcasting, Bob Jones U., Greenville South Carolina, MA communications. Co-founder, chmn. Salem Communications, 1986—. Mem. bd. of dir. Nat. Religious Broadcasters Assoc. Mem. Coun. for Nat. Policy, 1996—. Named one of 25 most influential evangelicals in America, Time Magazine. Baptist. Achievements include being the leading U.S. radio broadcaster focused on religious and family themed programming with 92 radio stations in 36 radio markets. Office: Salem Comm Corp 4880 Santa Rosa Rd Camarillo CA 93012 Office Phone: 805-987-0400. Office Fax: 805-384-4520.*

EPPES, THOMAS EVANS, advertising and public relations executive; b. NYC, Aug. 10, 1952; s. Benjamin F. and Eileen (Evans) E.; m. Jennie Spradling, Aug. 2, 1980; children: Benjamin, Jared, Michael. BS, U. So. Miss., 1974. Reporter Jackson (Miss.) Daily News, 1974-75, 76-77, Clearwater (Fla.) Sun, 1975-76; pub. info. coord. Miss. Rsch. and Devel. Ctr., Jackson, 1976-78; press sec. Gov. Bill Waller for U.S. Senate, Jackson, 1978, Maurice Dantin for U.S. Senate, Jackson, 1978; dir. pub. rels. Days Inns Am., Atlanta, 1978-82, Mgmt. Sci. Am., Atlanta, 1982-85; pres., pub. rels. Eric Mower & Assocs. (formerly Price-McNabb), Charlotte, NC, 1985-91, pres., CEO, 1992—94, pres., 1994—, sr. ptnr., bd. dirs. Spkr. nat. confs. on comms. and mktg. Bd. dirs., comms. chmn. United Way of Asheville and Buncombe, 1986-87; campaign dir. Jacksonians for Mayor, Jackson, 1976; bd. advisors U. Colo., Boulder Inc. Sch. Fellow Pub. Rels. Soc. Am. (counselor's acad., exec. bd. counselor's acad. 1998-2000, Coll. of Fellows 2000, Silver Anvil award 1993), Internat. Assn. Bus. Communicators (Gold Quill award 1980, 81), Internat. Comms. Agy. Network (v.p. 2002), Charlotte C. of C. (bd. dirs. 1997), Charlotte Pub. Rels. Soc. Am. (nat. assembly del., bd. dirs. 2005-06, nat. bd. 2006-, Infinity award 2006). Avocation: golf. Office: Eric Mower & Assocs 1001 Morehead Square Dr 5th Flr Charlotte NC 28203-4253

EPPES, WILLIAM DAVID, arts and humanities advocate; s. Talmadge DeWitt and Annie Lou (McCord) E AB, Coll. of William and Mary, 1939; BS in LS, Vanderbilt U., 1940; student, U. Manchester, Eng., 1950, Columbia U., 1950; MA, NYU, 1959; student, U. Durham, Eng., 1987. Reference asst. George Washington U., 1944—48, Calif. State U., San Francisco, 1948—49; head, stack personnel Butler Libr. Columbia U., NYC, 1954-58; assoc. prof. Kean State Coll., NJ, 1958-61; asst. libr. Cooper Union, NYC, 1961-70. Founder Film Classics League, St. Petersburg, Fla., 1950; co-founder Backstage Gallery, St. Petersburg Jr. Coll., 1950, Littlebury Eppes Meml. Libr., Westover Ch., Va.; adv. bd. Coral Gables (Fla.) Hist. Preservation Bd. Rev., 1979-81; trustee Greenwich Village Trust for Hist. Preservation, Inc., 1980, pres., 1980-84, 1984-90; cons. Hist. Buckingham (Va.) Inc., 1987—; hon. commr. Eleanor Roosevelt Monument Fund, Inc., N.Y.C Author: The Empire Theatre (1893-1953), 1978, Gertrude Michael-A Star of the Golden Age of Hollywood, 1985, Montgomery (Ala.) Theatre 1822-1985, 1986, The House Off Main Street, A Chronicle of the McCord-Eppes Family; contbr. articles to mags. and hist. jours. Bd. dirs. St. Petersburg Symphony Orch., 1950-54; exec. bd. Assn. Village Homeowners, N.Y.C., 1969-82, Assocs. of Earl Gregg Swem Libr., Coll. of William and Mary, 1973-86; benefactor Jonathon Daniels Sch., Keene, N.H., 1998, Apple Hill Chamber Orch., Sullivan, N.H., 1998, Kean State Coll., 1999—; benefactor, hist. cons. Redfern Performing Arts Ctr. Keene (N.H.) State Coll., 2000—; pres. coun. Va. Hist. Soc., 1982; profl. advisor McLeod Plantation, Sea Island Hist. Soc., SC. Mem. Theater Hist. Soc. (rsch. and reference com. 1977-81), Author's Guild, Inc., W&M Choir, Va. Hist. Soc. (pres.'s coun. 1993—, exec. coun. 1995), Sea Island Hist. Soc. (profl. adv. bd. 2000) Episcopalian. Home: 14 Rivermead Rd Peterborough NH 03458-1701 Personal E-mail: jonietc@earthlink.net.

EPPINGER, FREDERICK H., JR., insurance company executive; Grad., Coll. Holy Cross, 1981; MBA, Dartmouth Coll., 1985. CPA. Acct. Coopers & Lybrand; ptnr. fin. instn. group McKinsey & Co., 1985—2000; exec. v.p. mktg. and svc. ops. ChannelPoint, Inc., 2000—01; from sr. v.p. strategic mktg. to exec. v.p The Hartford, 2001—02; pres., CEO Hanover Ins. Group (formerly Allmerica Fin. Corp.), Worcester, Mass., 2003—. Edward Tuck scholar. Office: Hanover Ins Group 440 Lincoln St Worcester MA 01653*

EPPINK, JOSEPH A., music educator; b. Grand Rapids, Mich., Feb. 10, 1965; s. Marvin Jay Eppink and Ellen June DeVries; life ptnr. Ralph Panelli; children: Ralphie Panelli, Natalia Panelli. MusB, We. Michigian U., Kalamazoo, 1989; MS in Edn., Ind. U., South Bend, 1995; D in Arts, Ball State U., Muncie, Ind., 2002. Elem. music specialist Elkhart Cmty. Schools, Elkhart, Ind., 1989—99; assoc. prof./coord. of music edn. The Coll. of St. Rose, Albany, NY, 2002—. Condr., founder Elkhart Boys Choir, Ind., 1990—2000; organist St. John's Episc. Ch., Elkart, 1990—2002, choirmaster, 1990—2002; organist St. Andrews Episc. Ch., Albany, NY, 2003—, choirmaster, 2003—; condr. Capital Pride Singer, Albany, 2003—. Contbr. articles to profl. jours. Grantee, The Coll. St. Rose, 2006. Mem.: Berkshire-Hudson Orff Assn. (v.p. 2003—06), Music Educators Nat. Conf. (rep. ea. divsn. 2006—), Anglican Musician Assn., Coll. Music Soc. (coll. rep. 2003), Am. Choral Dir.'s Assn., Am. Guild Organists (bd. dirs. 2004—06), NY State Sch. Music Assn. (adjudicator 2006—), Phi Mu Alpha. Democrat. Episcopalian. Avocations: travel, cooking. Office: The Coll Saint Rose 432 Western Ave Albany NY 12203 Office Phone: 518-454-5286. Office Fax: 518-454-2146. Business E-Mail: eppinkj@strose.edu.

EPPLER, JEROME CANNON, investment advisor; b. Englewood, NJ, Mar. 16, 1924; s. William E. and Aileen (Vaughan) E.; m. Debora Nye Eppler; children: Stephen Vaughan, William Durand, Margaret Nye, Elizabeth Scott, Edward Curtis. BSME, Tex. A&M U., 1946; MBA, U. Pa., 1949. Mem. N.Y. Stock Exch. With Gen. Electric Supply Corp., Newark, 1949-50; investment banker Equitable Securities Corp., Nashville, mgr. Houston, 1950—53; gen. ptnr. Cyrus J. Lawrence & Sons, NYC, 1953—61; owner Eppler & Co., Denver, 1961; chmn. bd. United Screen Arts, Inc., LA, 1966—73; chmn. bd. dir. Life Ins. Co. Calif., 1967—77, I.S.I. Corp., 1967—77, Tessco Techs. Inc., Hunt Valley, Md., 1982—2007, World Wide Life Assurance Co., London, 1972—77; ltd. ptnr. Alex Brown & Sons, Balt., 1982—84; prin. Olympic Capital Ptnrs., Seattle, 1995—2000. Mem. indsl. adv. com. U. Calif., San Diego, 1978—93; mem. N.Y. Stock Exch.; chmn. Global Leadership Coun. Coll. Bus. Colo. State U., Ft. Collins, Colo.; dir. emeritus Tessco Techs. Inc., Hunt Valley. Trustee emeritus Scripps Clinic and Research Found., La Jolla; former trustee Drew U. (N.J.), 1966-67, Morris Mus. Arts & Scis. (N.J.), 1954-76, Met. Opera Assn., 1980-82, Wharton Grad. Sch. Bus. N.Y., 1972-86. Lt. (j.g.) USNR, 1942-46. Mem. Wharton Grad. Bus. Sch. Club, Castle Pines Golf Club, River Bend Country Club (Tequesta, Fla.). Presbyterian. Home: 2800 S University Blvd #22 Denver CO 80210

EPPLEY, FRANCES FIELDEN, secondary school educator, writer; b. Knoxville, Tenn., July 18, 1921; d. Chester Earl and Beulah Magnolia (Wells) Fielden; m. Gordon Talmage Cougle, July 25, 1942; children; Russell Gordon Eppley, Carolyn Eppley Horseman; m. Fred Coan Eppley, Mar. 8, 1953; 1 child, Charlene Eppley Sellers. BA in English, Carson Newman Coll., 1942; MA, Winthrop U., 1963. Tchr. East Corinth (Maine) Acad., 1942-43, pub. schs., Charlotte, NC, 1950-53, 59-83, Greenville, SC, 1954-56, Spartanburg, SC, 1957-58; Head Start tchr., summers 1964-68. Author: First Baptist Church: Its Heritage, 1982, Flint Hill Church, 1984, Religion and Astrology, 1991, Astrology and Prophecy, 1992, Sammy's Song, Jericho, Aunt Lillian's Sea Foam Candy, The First Astrologer, 1993, The Story of William Fielden, 1998, Search for an Ancestor, 1999, Christmas Magnus, Stella and the Sitting Stone, Messiah, An Immediate Family, 1999, The Signs of Your Life, 2000, Another Mary, 2000, The Winter Solstice, 2001, Of Course Your Child Can Read!, 2002, Columbus: The Race Home, 2003, Canada Trilogy, 2003;: To A Japanese Friend, 2002, Wacky Kings and Mystic Things, 2003, The Yellow River, 2003, To A Japanese Friend, 2004. Mem. hist. com. N.C. Bapt. Conv., 1985-88. Alpha Delta Kappa Grantee, 1970. Mem. NEA, N.C. Social Studies Conf., Writers Assn., Alpha Delta Kappa, Pi Kappa Delta, Alpha Psi Omega. Baptist. Home: 1421 Delane Ave Apt 5N Charlotte NC 28211-2564

EPPOLITO, MARY, assistant principal, educator; b. Bklyn., Feb. 10, 1975; d. Nicholas Joseph and Maria Silecchia; m. Joseph Eppolito Jr., Aug. 5, 2000. BA in Elem. Edn. magna cum laude, Bklyn. Coll., 1997; MS in Reading, Adelphi U., 1999; profl. diploma, L.I. U., 2003. Cert. sch. adminstr. N.Y., 2003, elem. edn. N.Y., 1997, reading specialist N.Y., 1999. Reading specialist Monroe-Woodbury Ctrl. Sch. Dist., Central Valley, NY, 2000—03; elem. asst. prin. Minisink Valley Ctrl. Sch. Dist., Slate Hill, 2003—05; asst. prin. Monroe-Woodbury Sch. Dist., 2005—. Adj. prof. SUNY, New Paltz, 2003—04, Rockland Tchrs. Ctr., 2004—. Mem.: Golden Key Honor Soc., Kappa Delti Pi (life Honors in Edn. 1997). Roman Catholic. Avocation: travel. Home Phone: 845-928-8609.

EPPS, ANNA CHERRIE, immunologist, educator, dean; b. New Orleans, July 8, 1930; d. Ernest and Anna L. (Johnson) Cherrie; m. Joseph M. Epps, Sr., Nov. 23, 1968. BS, Howard U., 1951, PhD, 1966; MS, Loyola U., New Orleans, 1959. Technologist clin. lab. dept. Our Lady of Mercy Hosp., Cin., 1953-54; asst. prof., acting chmn. dept. med. tech. Xavier U., New Orleans, 1954-60; technologist dept. medicine La. State U. Sch. Medicine, New Orleans, 1954-60; asst. prof. microbiology Coll. Medicine Howard U., Washington, 1961-69; fellow dept. medicine Sch. Medicine Johns Hopkins U., Balt., 1969; asst. prof., USPHS faculty fellow dept. medicine Tulane U. Sch. Medicine, New Orleans, 1969-71, assoc. prof., 1971-75, prof., 1975—97, assoc. dean student svcs., 1970—97; dir. med. edn. reinforcement and enrichment program Tulane U. Med. Ctr., New Orleans, 1969—97; acting dean, v.p. acad. affairs Meharry Med. Coll., Nashville, 1994—96, dean sch. med., sr. v.p. acad. affairs, 1997—2002, dean emerita, sr. advisor to pres., 2002—. Co-author: Medrep, Tulane U.; co-editor: Medical Education: Responses to a Challenge; mem. editorial bd. Jour. Med. Edn., 1980—; contbr. articles to med. jours. Trustee Children's Hosp., New Orleans, 1977-79; regent Georgetown U., Washington, 1975—; bd. dirs. Diabetes Assn. Greater New Orleans, 1978; mem. La. Bd. Health and Rehab. Svcs., 1972; adv. mem. Kellogg Nat. Fellowship Program, 1981. Recipient award for meritorious rsch. Interstate Postgrad. Med. Assn. N.Am., 1966, Scroll of Merit, Nat. Med. Assn., 1980, Herbert W. Nickens award, AAMC, 2003. Mem. Am. Soc. Clin. Pathologists (cert. in med. tech. and blood banking), Am. Soc. Med. Technologists, Am. Assn. Blood Banks (cert. in blood banking), Am. Soc. Tropical Medicine and Hygiene, AAUP, Musser-Burch Soc., Albertus Magnus Guild, Washington Helminthol. Soc., Am. Soc. Bacteriologists, Sigma Xi. Home: 769 Sinclair Cir Brentwood TN 37027-2921 Office: Meharry Med Coll 1005 D B Todd Blvd Nashville TN 37208 Home Phone: 615-371-2404; Office Phone: 615-327-5935. Business E-Mail: acepps@mmc.edu.

EPPS, CHARLES HARRY, JR., retired orthopaedic surgery educator, dean; b. Balt., July 24, 1930; BS magna cum laude, Howard U., 1951, MD, 1955. Intern Freedmen's Hosp., 1955-56, resident, 1956-57, mem. staff, 1961—2001; resident D.C. Gen. Hosp., Washington, 1958-60, vis. staff, 1961-98, orthopaedic med. officer for handicapped and crippled children's svc., 1961-98; instr. orthopaedic surgery Howard U., Washington, 1961-64, asst. prof., 1964-68, assoc. prof., 1968-73, prof., 1973-96, prof. emeritus, 1996—2001, chief divsn. orthopaedic surgery, 1968-88, dean Coll. Medicine, 1988-94, exec. dean Coll. Medicine, 1994-95; v.p. health affairs, acting exec. dir., CEO Howard U. Hosp., Washington, 1994-96; spl. asst. to pres. for health affairs Howard U., 1996-2001; ret., 2001. Assoc. prof. Johns Hopkins U., 1971; mem. staff VA Hosp., Washington, Cafritz Meml. Hosp., Providence Hosp.; cons. USN Med. Ctr., Bethesda, Md., Walter Reed Army Med. Ctr. Capt. M.C., U.S. Army, 1961-62. Fellow ACS; mem. AMA, Nat. Med. Assn., Ea. Orthop. Assn., Am. Orthop. Assn., Am. Acad. Orthop. Surgery.

EPPS, HARLAND WARREN, astronomy educator, optical design consultant; b. Hawthorne, Calif., July 29, 1936; s. Harland Garner and Nydia Dolly (Gall) E.; m. Louise Rodney Daniels, June 5, 1962 (div. Jan. 1970); m. Susan Lou Markowitz, Oct. 10, 1976 (div. Feb. 1983); children: Melody Amanda, Brenden Putty; m. Johanna Helen Archer, Nov. 23, 1991; children: Helena Dolly, Naomi Lauren. Student, U. Vienna, Austria, 1956—57; BA, Pomona Coll., 1959; MS, U. Wis., 1961, PhD, 1964. Asst. prof. astronomy San Diego State U., 1964-65, UCLA, 1965-70, assoc. prof., 1970-76, prof., 1976—89; astronomer, prof. astronomy Lick Obs.,

Santa Cruz, Calif., 1989—, U. Calif., Santa Cruz, 1989—. Cons. Steward Obs., Tucson, 1972—, Lick Obs., 1970—, Smithsonian Astrophys. Obs., Cambridge, Mass., 1984—, Los Alamos (N.Mex.) Nat. Lab., 1984—, Mount Wilson and Las Campanas Observatories, 1987—, Calif. Inst. Tech., 1988—. Assoc. editor for instrumentation: Publs. of Astron. Soc. of the Pacific, 2003—; contbr. articles to profl. jours. Mem. USAF Sci. Adv. Bd., 1989-93. Grantee NSF, Air Force Cambridge Rsch., U. Calif. Regents Opportunity Fund, NASA. Mem. Am. Astron. Soc., Internat. Astron. Union, Soc. Photooptical Instrumentation Engrs., Sigma Xi. Avocation: classical and flamenco guitar. Office: U Calif UCO/Lick Obs Natural Scis 2 Rm 191 Santa Cruz CA 95064 Office Phone: 831-459-3454. Business E-Mail: epps@ucolick.org.

EPPS, JAMES HAWS, III, lawyer; b. Johnson City, Tenn., Sept. 15, 1936; s. James Haws and Anne Lafayette (Sessoms) E.; m. Jane Mahoney, Oct. 9, 1976; children from previous marriage: James Haws IV, Sara Stuart. BA, U. NC, Chapel Hill, 1959; JD, Vanderbilt U., Nashville, 1962. Bar: Tenn. 1962, U.S. Dist. Ct. Tenn. 1962, U.S. Ct. Appeals (6th cir.) 1971, Interstate Commerce Commn. Bar 1962, U.S. Supreme Ct. 1967. Prin. Epps & Epps, Johnson City, Tenn. City atty. Johnson City, 1966—, Johnson City Bd. Edn., 1967-86; spl. counsel State of Tenn., 1966-70; former gen. counsel Appalachian Flying Svc. Inc., ET&WNC Transp. Co., Inc. First bd. govs. Transp. Law Jour. Past bd. dirs. Washington County Mental Health Assn., East Tenn. and Western N.C. Transp. Co., East Tenn. and Western N.C. R.R., Tennolina Corp., Appalachian Air Lines, Inc., Appalachian Flying Svc., Inc., Farmers and Mchts. Bank, Limestone, Tenn., budget com. United Way of Johnson City, 1964-68, Assault Crime Counsel Early Support Svcs. Inc., Safe Passage Inc., Johnson City Homeless Coalition, Home Base Adv. Coun., Johnson City/Washington County Health Coun. adv. com.; former legal adviser Appalachian coun. Girl Scouts USA; mem. Tenn. Law Revision Commn., 1970-71; legal counsel Salvation Army, mem. adv. bd. 1974—, exec. com. 1977—, 1st v.p. adv. bd. 1991, pres. adv. bd. 1993, 94, mem. property com., nominating com.; chmn. Family Violence Coun.; legal counsel Washington County Humane Soc., Inc.; mem. Civil Def., 1967—; chmn. Washington County Tenn. Leukemia Soc., 1991; mem. exec. com. Washington County Dem. Party, Tenn. Bicentennial Commn., exec. and fin. coms.; past mem. bd. dirs. Tenn. Mental Health Assn. Fellow Tenn. Bar Found.; mem. ABA, Fed. Bar Assn., Nat. Orgn. Legal Problems Edn., Am. Counsel Assn., Nat. Assn. R.R. Trial Counsel, Nat. Inst. Mcpl. Law Officers, Internat. Mcpl. Lawyers Assn. (bd. dirs. 1992-04, state chmn. Tenn. 1988-89, ethics and environ. coms. 1989—, regional v.p. 1989-92, chmn. resolutions com. 1989-90, lectr., trustee, 1992—, chmn. dues and alternative revenue 1996-97, budget and fin., federalism com. 1996—, state league counsel rev. com. 1997, awards com., 1999—, bd. mem. policy adv. com. 2000, 1st v.p. 2001, pres. 2002-03), Nat. Legal Aid Defender Assn., Tenn. Bar Assn., Am. Judicature Soc., Washington County Bar Assn. (past pres.), Tenn. Mcpl. Attys. Assn., Assn. ICC Practitioners (past com. profl. ethics and grievences), Transp. Lawyers Assn., Motor Carrier Lawyers Assn., Johnson City C. of C. (Disting. Svc. award 1968), Internat. Platform Assn., Lawyers Com. Civil Rights Under Law, World Peace Through Law Ctr., Tenn. Lung Assn., Tenn. Correctional Assn., Tenn. Taxpayers Assn. (past bd. dirs.), Tennesseans for Better Transp., U.S. Supreme Ct. Hist. Soc. (charter mem.), Def. Rsch. Inst., Tipton Haynes Hist. Assn. (past dir.), Hurstleigh Club, Unaka Rd. and Gun Club, Highland Stable Club, North Johnson City Bus. Club (dir., past pres. 1966-67), Nat. Lawyers Club, East Tenn. State U. Century Club, Boys'Club (charter, Johnson City/Washington County), Masons, Elks (legal counsel 1963-67), Phi Delta Phi, Phi Delta Theta. Episcopalian. Office: 115 E Unaka Ave Johnson City TN 37601-4623 also: PO Box 2288 Johnson City TN 37605-2288

EPPS, OMAR, actor; b. Bklyn., July 23, 1973; m. Keisha Spivey; 1 child, K'mari Mae. Actor: (films) Juice, 1992, The Program, 1993, Major League II, 1994, Higher Learning, 1995, Don't Be a Menace to South Central While Drinking Your Juice in the Hood, 1996, Blossoms and Veils, 1997, Scream 2, 1997, Breakfast of Champions, 1999, The Mod Squad, 1999, The Wood, 1999, In Too Deep, 1999, Love & Basketball, 2000, Brother, 2000, Dracula 2000, 2000, Perfume, 2001, Big Trouble, 2002, Against the Ropes, 2004, Alfie, 2004, (TV films) Daybreak, 1993, Deadly Voyage, 1996, First Time Felon, 1997, Conviction, 2004 (TV series) House M.D., 2004-(Supporting Actor in a Drama Series, NAACP Image awards, 2007); TV appearances include Here and Now, 1992, Street Justice, 1993, ER, 1996, 97. Office: The Gersh Agy 232 N Canon Dr Beverly Hills CA 90210-5302*

EPPS, ROSELYN ELIZABETH PAYNE, pediatrician, educator; b. Little Rock, Dec. 11, 1930; d. William Kenneth and Mattie Elizabeth (Beverly) Payne; m. Charles Harry Epps, Jr., June 25, 1955; children: Charles Harry III (dec.), Kenneth Carter, Roselyn Elizabeth, Howard Robert. BS, Howard U., 1951, MD, 1955; MPH, Johns Hopkins U., 1973; MA, Am. U., 1981. Intern Freedmen's Hosp., Howard U., Washington, 1955-56, pediatric resident, 1956-59, chief resident, 1958-59; practice medicine specializing in pediatrics Washington, 1960; med. officer, pediatrics D.C. Dept. Pub. Health, Washington, 1961-64, dir. Clinic for Retarded Children, 1964-67, chief Infant and Pre-Sch. div., 1967-71, dir. children and youth project, 1970-71, dir. maternal and crippled children services, 1971-75; chief Bur. Clin. Services D.C. Dept. Human Services, Washington, 1975-80, acting commr. pub. health, 1980; instr., asst. research investigator Howard U. Coll. Medicine, Washington, 1960-61, prof. Dept. Pediatrics and Child Health, 1980-98, chief divsn. child devel., dir., 1985-89, dir. Child Devel. Ctr., 1985-89; rsch. assoc., vis. scientist smoking tobacco and cancer program, div. cancer prevention and control Nat. Cancer Inst. NIH, Washington, 1989-91; expert Nat. Cancer Inst. NIH, Pub. Health Applications Br., Bethesda, Md., 1991-97; scientific program adminstr. Nat. Cancer Inst. Pub. Health Applications Branch, Bethesda, Md., 1997-98; med. pub. hlth cons., 1998—; sr. program advisor for women's health programs Women's Health Inst., Howard U., Wash., 1999—. Chmn. task force to prepare comprehensive child care plan for D.C. Dept. Human Services, 1973-74; mem. nat. task force on pediatric hypertension Heart, Lung and Blood Inst., NIH, 1975; chmn. rsch. grants rev. com. maternal and child health and crippled children's svcs. HEW, Rockville, Md., 1978-80; sec. Commn. Licensure to Practice Healing Arts, Washington, 1980; trustee med. svc. D.C. Blue Shield Plan Nat. Capital Area, 1980; chmn. sec.'s adv. com. on rights and responsibilities of women HEW, Washington, 1981; dir. high-risk young people's project Howard U. Hosp., 1981-85; Washington coord. Know Your Body Program Am. Health Found., N.Y.C., 1982-91; mem. bd. advs. Coll. Home Econs. Ohio State U., Columbus, Ohio, 1983-87; adv. com. Nat. Ctr. for Edn. in Maternal and Child Health Georgetown U., Washington, 1983-89; nat. steering com., subcom. chmn. Healthy Mothers, Healthy Babies Coalition, Washington, 1983-90, mem. nominating com., 1991; cons. sickle cell disease NIH, 1984-88, Govt. Liberia and World Bank, 1984, UN Fund for Population Activities, N.Y. and Caribbean, 1984, filmstrip Miriam Berg Varian/Parents Mag. Films, 1978; bd. dirs. Vis. Nurse Assn., Inc., Washington, 1983-89; pres. bd. dirs. Hosp. for Sick Children, Washington, 1986-90, bd. dirs., 1984-94; frequent guest lectr. Weekly columnist Your Child's Health, Afro-Am. Newspaper, Washington, 1960-63; contbr. articles syndicated column Nat. Newspaper Pubs. Assn., 1982, Nat. Newspaper Assn., 1986-87; co-author audiocassettes; exhibitor sci. program; exhibit: Women Chage the Faces of Medicine; contbr. more than 90 articles to profl. jours. US trustee Children's Internat. Summer Villages, Casstown, Ohio, 1969—76, pres., 1974—75; trustee nat. bd. Palmer Meml. Inst., Sedalia, NC, 1969—71, Ford's Theater, Washington, 1973—79; bd. mgrs. YWCA of DC, 1970—83, vice chmn., 1975—76; v.p. Jack and Jill of Am., Inc., Washington, 1970—71; nat. bd. dir. Ctr. Population Options, Washington, 1980—86, Alexander Graham Bell Assn. for Deaf, Washington, 1974—78; bd. dir. Washington Performing Arts Soc., 1971—81, v.p., 1979—81, hon. dir., 1981—. Recipient Leadership and Meritorious Service in Medicine award Palmer Meml. Inst., 1968, 14th Ann. Fed. Women's award CSC, Washington, 1974, Superior Performance award D.C. Govt., 1975, Meritorious Community Service award Howard U. Sch. Social Work Alumni Assns. and vis. com., 1980, Cert. Commendation Mayor of DC, 1981, Roselyn Payne Epps M.D. Recognition Resolution of 1983 Council DC, 1983, Disting. Vol. Leadership award March of Dimes Birth Defects Found., 1984, Community Svc. award DC Hosp. Assn., 1990, Physician of Yr. award Women's Med. Assn. N.Y.C., 1990, 91; named Outstanding Vol. in Leadership category YWCA Nat. Capital Area, 1983; inducted into DC Women's Hall of Fame DC Commn. for Women, 1990, Hall of Fame, DC, 2005; grantee Robert Wood Johnson Found., Princeton, N.J., 1982, div. maternal and child health HHS, Rockville, Md., 1986; honored Tribute Resolution of 1981 declaring Feb. 14 Dr. Roselyn Payne Epps Day, Council of D.C., 1981; recipient Ophelia Settle Egypt award Planned Parenthood of Met. Washington, 1991, Advocacy award Soc. Advancement Women's Health, 1996, Horizon award Nat. Assn. Negro Bus. and Profl. Women's Clubs, 1999, Dorothy I Height award, Nat. Coun. of Negro Women, 2001, Lifetime Achievement award, Girls Inc., 2003. Fellow Am. Acad. Pediatrics (alt. state chmn. D.C. 1973-75, exec. com. D.C. chpt. 1983-94, pres. D.C. chpt. 1988-91, sec. cmty. pediatrics sect. 1973-75, cert. appreciation 1979, mem. coun. of child and adolescent health, cmty. and internat. health sect., charter mem., exec. com. 1992-94); mem. Acad. Medicine, AMA (alt. del. Nat. Med. Assn. 1983-85), Am. Med. Women's Assn. (chmn. pub. health com. 1973-75, pres. br. 1 1974-76, sec. 1988, v.p. 1989, pres-elect nat. 1990, pres. 1991, found. founding pres. 1992, bd. dirs. 1992-97, chmn. nominating com. 1993, Physician of Yr. award 1991, Cmty. Svc. award 1990, Elizabeth Blackwell award 1992), Women's Forum Washington, Med. Soc. D.C. (exec. bd. 1990, sec. 1990, pres.-elect 1991, pres. 1992, chair exec. bd. 1993, ann. Cmty. Svc. award 1982), Am. Pediatric Soc., D.C. Hosp. Assn. (Cmty. Svc. award 1990), Am. Pub. Health Assn. (action bd. 1977-79, joint policy com. 1978-79, gov. council 1978-81), Met. Washington Pub. Health Assn. (gov. council 1975-78, 81-83, ann. award 1981), Nat. Med. Assn. (chmn. pediatric sect. 1977-79, Ross Labs. award 1979, Outstanding Svcs. to Children during Internat. Yr. of Child award 1979, Meritorious Service Appreciation award 1979, W.M. Cobb co-lectr. 1985, mem. Coun. on Maternal and Child Health, 1974-92, chmn. 1979-89, ann. Roselyn Payne Epps Symposium 1994—, Grace Marilyn James award for Disting svc. Pediatric sect. 1991, Achievement award 1993, ann. Roselyn Payne Epps symposium 1994—), Am. Hosp. Assn. (maternal and child health sect. governing coun. 1989, 1992-94, maternal and child health nominating com. 1991), Soc. for the Advancement of Women's Health Rsch. (award for advocacy 1996), The Women's Forum of Washington, Alpha Omega Alpha, Delta Omega, Alpha Kappa Alpha. Mem. United Ch. of Christ. Clubs: Pearls (pres. 1984-86), Carrousels (corr. sec. 1978-80), Links (pres. Met. chpt. 1986-89) (Washington), Cosmos. Lodge: Zonta, Internat. Women's Forum. Home and Office: 1775 N Portal Dr NW Washington DC 20012-1014

EPSEN, ROBERT A., lawyer; b. Omaha, May 25, 1939; AB, Princeton U., 1961; JD, Stanford U., 1971. Bar: Calif. 1971. Atty. Heller, Ehrman, White & McAuliffe, San Francisco, 1971—, gen. coun. Mem. ABA. Office: Heller Ehrman White & McAuliffe 333 Bush St San Francisco CA 94104-2806 Office Phone: 415-772-6042. Office Fax: 415-772-6268. E-mail: repsen@hewm.com.

EPSTEIN, ADAM, theater producer; b. Miami, 1975; BA, NYU, 1996. Pres. & CEO Adam Epstein Co., NYC. Assoc. prodr.: (Broadway plays) The Life, 1997; A View from the Bridge, 1997; prodr.: Amadeus, 1999, The Crucible, 2002, Hairspray, 2002 (Tony award for Best Musical, Drama Desk award for Outstanding New Musical, 2003), The Wedding Singer, 2006. Named one of 40 Under 40, Crain's NY Bus., 2007; recipient Tony award, 2003.*

EPSTEIN, ALAN BRUCE, lawyer; b. Passaic, NJ, Sept. 20, 1944; s. Jerome P. and Stella M. (Goldfinger) E.; m. Eve Teichholz, June 21, 1966; children: Jason, Dylan. BA, Temple U., 1967, JD, 1969. Bar: Pa. 1970, U.S. Dist. Ct. (ea. dist.) Pa. 1970, U.S. Ct. Appeals (3d cir.) 1972, U.S. Ct. Appeals (5th cir.) 1977, U.S. Dist. Ct. (cen. and we. dists.) Pa. 1987, U.S. Supreme Ct. 1988, U.S. Ct. Appeals (9th cir.) 2000. Assoc. firm Freedman, Borowsky & Lorry, Phila., 1969-77; ptnr. firm Jablon, Epstein, Wolf & Drucker, Phila., 1977-99; shareholder Spector, Gadon & Rosen, Phila., 1999—. Pres. Judicate Nat. Pvt. Ct. System, Phila., 1983-88. Fellow Pa. Bar Found., Coll. Labor and Employement Lawyers; mem. ABA, AAJ, Pa. Bar Assn., Phila. Bar Assn., Temple Am. Inn Ct. (bd. dirs. 1994—, pres. 2001—, nat. edn. chair 2000—) Jewish. Home: 404 S Camac St Philadelphia PA 19147-1112 Office: Spector Gadon & Rosen PC Seven Penn Ctr 1635 Market St Fl 7 Philadelphia PA 19103-2217 Home Phone: 215-546-5223; Office Phone: 215-241-8888. Business E-Mail: aepstein@lawsgr.com.

EPSTEIN, ALVIN, actor, performance artist, theater director, make-up artist; b. Bronx, NY, May 14, 1925; s. Harry and Goldie (Rudnick) E. Student, Queens Coll., 1941-43, Ecole de Mime Etienne Decroux, Paris, 1947-51, Sanford Meisner Profl. Class, NYC, 1951-52. Tchr. Chamber Theatre, Israel, Neighborhood Playhouse, NYC, Circle in Sq. Theatre Sch., NYC, Yale Drama Sch., 1968-77, Am. Repertory Theatre Inst.; acting artistic dir. Yale Repertory Theatre, 1972-73, assoc. artistic dir., 1973-77; artistic dir. Guthrie Theatre, Mpls., 1978-79. Mem. faculty Salzburg Am. Seminar, 1972, Aspen Music Festival, 1980-82. Actor Theatre de Mime Etienne Decroux, Paris, 1947-51, Habima Theatre, Israel, 1952-55; Am. profl. debut with Marcel Marceau, Phoenix Theatre, NYC, 1955; appeared in Broadway, off-Broadway touring and regional prodns. including King Lear, NYC, 1956, Waiting for Godot, 1956, A Midsummer Night's Dream, Empire State Music Festival, NY, 1956, Purple Dust, NYC, Endgame, NYC, No Strings, NYC, lead actor Enrico IV, Milw., Chgo., The Pedestrian in the Air, Chgo., A Midsummer's Night Dream, NYC, Clerambard, NYC; actor Postmark Zero, NYC, The Latent Heterosexual, LA, Dynamite Tonite, NYC, Whores, Wars and Tin Pan Alley, Chgo., New Haven, NYC, Easthampton, A Place Without Doors, Long Wharf Theatre, New Haven, Staircase Theatre, NYC, Goodman Theatre, Chgo., on U.S. tour, LA, Washington, 3 Plays by Samuel Beckett, Harold Clurman Theater NYC, 1983-84, Mark Taper Forum LA, Library of Congress, Washington, 1984, Jerusalem Festival, 1985, Howard Katz, 2007, King Lear Actors Shakespear Project, Boston, 2005, LaMama Theatre, NYC, Your Dada, Wooster Group at Mus. Modern Art, NYC, Black Snow, Yale Repertaory Theatre, Howard Katz, Roundabout Theatre, NYC; dir., actor Endgame, Samuel Beckett Theatre, Cherry Ln. Theater, NYC, New Mayfair Theater, LA, Jerusalem Festival, 1985; mem. Yale Repertory Theatre, New Haven, 1968-77; lead actor Dynamite Tonite, God Bless, Story Theatre, The Bacchae, Greatshot, Crimes and Crimes, Olympian Games, Gimpel the Fool, Woyzeck, Don Juan, Macbett, The Tempest, Happy End, The Possessed, Bingo, Ivanov. Crossing Niagara, NYC Manhattan Theatre Club, Ghosts, Three Sisters, School for Scandal, Good Woman of Setzuan, 6 Characters in Search of an Author, Right You Are (If You Think You Are), Uncle Vanya, King Stag, Platanov, Mastergate, In Twilight (Chekhov Short Stories), The Miser, Once In A Lifetime, When We Dead Awaken, Gloucester in King Lear, Polonius in Hamlet, Lord Summerhays in Misalliance, Media Amok, Judge Brack in Hedda Gabler, Dr. Lombardi in The Servant of Two Masters, Dream of the Red Spider, Iva Vasilyevich in Black Snow, Silence, Cunning, Exile; dir., actor Macbeth, Henry IV Parts 1 & 2, What the Butler Saw, Firs in the Cherry Orchard, A Touch of the Poet, Krapp's Last Tape, Ohio Impromptu, Agamemnon, Waiting for Godot, Henry V, Threepenny Opera, Beckett Trio: Eh Joe, Ghost Sonata, Nacht Und Träume, The Tempest, Tartuffe, Slaughter City, Am. Repertory Theatre, Cambridge, Mass., Value of Names, Androcles and the Lion, Hartford Stage Co., Waltz of the Toreadors, Roundabout Theatre, NYC, Peachum in Three Penny Opera, Lunt-Fontanne Theatre, 1989; dir. The Rivals, Caligula, Seven Deadly Sins, Bourgeois Gentleman, Rise and Fall of the City of Mahagonny, The Tempest, A Midsummer Night's Dream, Troilus and Cressida, Julius Caesar, Old Times, Marriage of Figaro, Boys From Syracuse, Endgame, Importance of Being Earnest, Heartbreak House, others at Yale Repertory Theatre, Am. Repertory Theatre, Williamstown Theatre Festival, Richard III, Becket Trio; narrator Oedipus Rex, Cantata Singers; appeared in TV shows including The Doctors, 1981-82, Doing Life, 1986; dir. The Pretenders, Beggars Opera, Colette, Berkshire Theatre Festival, Stockbridge, Mass., 1974; appeared in Marriage, A Kurt Weill Cabaret for Guthrie Theatre, with Martha Schlamme in A Kurt Weill Cabaret for Bijou Theater, NYC, on tour throughout U.S., Argentina, Brazil, Israel, 1979-85; co-founder, actor Berkshire Theatre Festival, Stockbridge, Mass., 1966; actor Skin of Our Teeth, Shylock in Merchant of Venice, Schlammeand Epstein Sing Bernstein and Blitzstein, Aspen Music Festival, HB Studio NYC, Am. Repertory Theatre, Cambridge, Mass., 1981, When the World Was Green, Olympic Arts Festival, The Cabinet of Dr. Caligari, Man and Superman; (film) Never Met Picasso, The Wizard of Menlo Park with Boston Pops,Stravinsky's Soldier's Tale, Jordan Hall, Boston, Alice Tully Hall, NYC, GBS in Dear Liar, Cadmus in The Bacchae, In The Jungle of Cities, Nobody Dies on Friday, When The World was Green, Internat. Festival, Moscow Art Theatre, Russia, 1997-98; narrator Philosopher's Stone by Mozart et al, Boston Baroque, Jordan Hall, Boston, Charlie in The House of Rue, American Repertory Theatre, Cambridge, Leonard in film The Living Room Waltz, 1998-99; roles in series of Samuel Beckett Radio Plays, 1987-88; voice-overs (documentary) Africans in America, Merchant of Venice, Am. Repertory Theatre, Cambridge Mass., Walt Disney's Beauty and the Beast, 1991, The Gentleman from Boston (film), Passionada (film), Count Shabelsky in Ivanov (Indep. Reviewers New England award: Best Supporting Actor 1999), McLeavy in Loot, Full Circle, The Winters Tale, Sophocles' Antigone, Chekhov's The Wedding, Shaw's The Doctor's Dilemma, Richard II, American Repertory Theatre, 1999-2001, Kurt Weill Songs Dengenerate and Otherwise Market Theatre, Cambridge, 2001, Ragpicker in The Madwoman of Chaillot, Neighborhood Playhouse, NYC, Marat/Sade, Lysistrata, Am. Repertory Theatre; Psychoanalysis Changed My Life (film), Tuesdays with Morrie, NY Stage and Film Co., Vassar Coll., 2001-02, Minetta Lane Theatre, NYC, 2002-03, Seattle Repertory Theatre, Twenty Four Evenings of Wit and Wisdom, Colleague's Theatre, NYC, 2003, Law and Order, 2004; (concert appearance) 92nd St. Y, Bryn Mawr Coll., 2003, Firs in the Cherry Orchard, Atlantic Theater Co., NYC, 2005, Synecdoche NY, 2007. Bd. dirs. Theatre Communications Group, N.Y.C., 1975-77. Served with AUS, 1943-46, ETO. Recipient Brandeis Creative Arts award, 1966, Obie award for Dynamite Tonite, 1967, Torch of Hope award, 1994, Elliot Norton prize, Boston Theatre Critics, 1996, Jason Robards award, 2001, Best Cabaret award Ind. Reviewers of New Eng., 2002, Spencer Cherashore Lifetime Dedication to Not-for-profit Theatre award, 2003, Obie award, 2007; Ford Found. grantee, 1959-60; Trumbull Coll. fellow Yale U., Beinecke fellow Yale U., 2006; named Most promising Actor, Variety poll, 1956, Best Supporting Actor award Ind. Reviewers New Eng., 1999. Office: 57 Montague St Brooklyn NY 11201

EPSTEIN, ANTHONY CHARLES, lawyer; b. NYC, June 17, 1952; m. Karen K. Epstein; children: Katherine, Claire. BA summa cum laude, Yale U., 1974, JD, 1977. Bar: DC 1978, Md., US Dist. Ct. DC (1978), US Dist. Ct. Md. (1988), US Ct. Appeals (DC & 4th cirs.), US Supreme Ct. Law clk. to presiding justice, San Francisco, 1977-78; atty. antitrust div. U.S. Dept. Justice, Washington, 1978-80, spl. asst. to dep. atty. gen., 1980-81; spl. asst. U.S. atty. U.S. Dist. Ct. (ea. dist.) Va., Alexandria, 1981; assoc. Leva, Hawes, Symmington, Martin & Oppenheimer, Washington, 1981-83, Jenner & Block, Wash., 1983; ptnr. Steptoe & Johnson LLP, Wash., DC. Mem. ABA, Phi Beta Kappa, DC Bar, State Md. Bar, numerous fed. Cts. Office: Steptoe & Johnson LLP 1330 Connecticut Ave NW Washington DC 20036 Office Phone: 202-429-8065. Office Fax: 202-261-7507. Business E-Mail: aepstein@steptoe.com.

EPSTEIN, ARNOLD M., medical educator; MD, Duke U., 1976. John H. Foster prof. health policy and mgmt. Harvard Sch. Pub. Health, Boston, chair dept. health policy and mgmt., prof. medicine; chief sect. on health svcs. and policy rsch. Brigham & Women's Hosp.; assoc. editor New England Jour. Medicine, Boston. Adv. coun. on performance measurement Joint Commn. on Accredidation of Healthcare Org.; bd. dirs. Academy-Health, Washington. Contbr. articles; author: Falling Through the Safety Net: Insurance Status & Access to Health Care (Kulp Wright award, Am. Risk & Ins. Assn., 1994). Health care delivery sys. quality & mgmt. advisor at the White House, Washington, 1993—94; vice chair Com. on Developing a Nat. Report on Health Care Quality, Inst. of Medicine. Mem.: Inst. Medicine. Achievements include research on access and quality of care especially for disadvantaged populations. Office: Harvard Sch Pub Health 677 Huntington Ave Boston MA 02115-6028 also: New England Journal of Medicine 10 Shattuck St Boston MA 02115-6094 Fax: 617-432-3417. E-mail: aepstein@hsph.harvard.edu.

EPSTEIN, ARTHUR JOSEPH, physics and chemistry educator; b. Bklyn., June 2, 1945; s. Benjamin and Esther F. (Fellner) Epstein; m. Paulayne Tina Sklarsky, Aug. 3, 1969; children: Melissa Ann, Dana Michelle. BS cum laude in Physics, Poly. Inst. Bklyn., 1966; MS in Physics, U. Pa., Phila., 1967, PhD in Physics, 1971. Mem. tech. staff MITRE Corp., McLean, Va., 1971-72; prin. scientist Xerox Webster Rsch. Ctr., NY, 1972-85; prof. physics and chemistry Ohio State U., Columbus, 1985—, dir. Ctr. Materials Rsch., 1989—, disting. univ. prof., 1997—. Vis. prof. UCLA, 1977-78, 79-80, U. Paris, 1980, 88, 90, 92, Technion, 1984-85; cons. DuPont Co., Wilmington, Del., Xerox Corp., Webster, 1985—, NCR, Cambridge, Ohio, 1991, Eeonyx Corp., Pinole, Calif., 1993—; expert in polymer elec. conductivity, electronic and optical properties of molecular and polymeric magnets; co-organizer Internat. Conf. on Synthetic Metals, 1977, 81, 88, 96; Frontiers of Sci. lectr. U. Fla., 1984, 96; vis. scholar, lectr. U. R.I., 1987. Regional editor Jour. Synthetic Metals, 1982—; contbr. more than 500 articles to sci. jours. Recipient Disting. Scholar award Ohio State U., 1991. Fellow Am. Phys. Soc. (mem. applications com., James C. McGroddy prize for New Materials, 2007); mem. Am. Chem. Soc., Materials Rsch. Soc., Nat. Inst. Emerging Techs. (hon. mem. exec. com. 1990—). Achievements include patent for technologies for electronic uses of plastics, 15 others; co-discovery of first molecular ferromagnet and first room temperature molecular based magnet, first self-doped water soluble electrically conducting polymer. Office: Dept Physics Ohio State U 191 W Woodruff Ave Columbus OH 43210-1117 Office Phone: 614-292-1133. Office Fax: 614-292-3706. E-mail: epstein.2@osu.edu.*

EPSTEIN, BENNETT L. (BUZZ EPSTEIN), lawyer; BA with distinction, U. Mich., 1972; JD, Washington U., 1975. Bar: Ill. 1975, Mo. 1976, US Ct. Appeals (7th cir.) 1979, US Dist. Ct. (no. dist. Ill., trial bar) 1983, US Dist. Ct. (ctrl. dist. Ill.) 1992. Assoc. editor Urban Law Ann., 1974—75; trial atty. NLRB, Chgo., 1975—78; ptnr. Foley & Lardner, Chgo., 1978—. Bd. mgr. Family Care, Ill. Mem.: ABA. Office: Foley & Lardner Suite 2800 321 N Clark St Chicago IL 60610 Office Phone: 312-832-5193. E-mail: bepstein@foley.com.*

EPSTEIN, BROOKE C., lawyer; 2 children. BA, Columbia U. Barnard Coll., 1992; JD, So. Meth. U., 1998. Bar: Tex. 1998. Assoc. gen. counsel Barrett, Burke, Wilson, Castle, Daffin & Frappier, L.L.P., Addison, Tex.

Named a Rising Star, Tex. Super Lawyers mag., 2006. Mem.: ABA, Dallas Bar Assn. Office: Barrett Burke Wilson Castle Daffin & Frappier LLP 15000 Surveyor Blvd Ste 100 Addison TX 75001 Office Phone: 972-386-5040.*

EPSTEIN, CHARLES JOSEPH, pediatrician, geneticist, biochemist, educator; b. Phila., Sept. 3, 1933; s. Jacob C. and Frieda (Savransky) E.; m. Lois Barth, June 10, 1956; children: David Alexander, Jonathan Akiba, Paul Michael, Joanna Marguerite. AB, Harvard U., 1955, MD, 1959; DS, Northeastern Ohio U., 1997. Diplomate Am. Bd. Med. Genetics. Intern in medicine Peter Bent Brigham Hosp., Boston, 1959-60, asst. resident in medicine, 1960-61; research assoc., med. officer and sect. chief Nat. Heart Inst. and Nat. Inst. Arthritis and Metabolic Diseases, NIH, Bethesda, Md., 1961-67; rsch. fellow in med. genetics U. Wash., 1963-64; assoc. prof. pediat. and biochemistry U. Calif., San Francisco, 1967-72, prof., 1972—2005, prof. emeritus, 2005—, chief divsn. med. genetics. dept. pediat. San Francisco, 1967—, co-dir. program in human genetics, 1997—2004. Investigator Howard Hughes Med. Inst., 1976-81; mem. human embryology and devel. study sect. NIH, 1971-75; mem. mental retardation rsch. com. Nat. Inst. Child Health and Devel., 1979-83, chmn., 1981-83; mem. com. for study inborn errors of metabolism NRC, 1972-75; mem. sci. adv. bd. Nat. Down Syndrome Soc., 1981-99, chmn., 1984-99, mem. nat. adv. bd., 1999-2006, hon. bd. govs., 2007—, also bd. dirs.; mem. recombinant DNA adv. com. NIH, 1985-90, mem. human gene therapy subcom., 1987-91, chmn. residency rev. com. med. genetics, 1993-99; mem. sci. adv. bd. Buck Inst., 2002-, chmn., 2004-, trustee, 2004-; mem. sci. steering com., Pediatric Biobank, 2006-; Stanley Wright Meml. lectr. Western Soc. Pediatric Rsch., 1986; William Potter lectr. Thomas Jefferson U., 1987; George H. Fetterman lectr. U. Pitts., 1989; faculty rsch. lectr. U. Calif., San Francisco, 1994; Mary Hulings Edens lectr. U. Tex. Med. Br., Galveston, 1996; Ida Cordelia Beam lectr. U. Iowa, 1998; Donald L. Thurston meml. lectr. Washington U., St. Louis, 1999, others. Author: The Consequences of Chromosome Imbalance: Principles, Mechanisms and Models, 1986; editor: Human Genetics, 1984-95, The Neurobiology of Down Syndrome, 1986, Oncology and Immunology of Down Syndrome, 1987, Am. Jour. Human Genetics, 1987-93, Molecular and Cytogenetic Studies of Non-disjunction, 1989, Molecular Genetics of Chromosome 21 and Down Syndrome, 1990, Morphogenesis of Down Syndrome, 1991, Down Syndrome and Alzheimer Disease, 1992, Phenotypic Mapping of Down Syndrome and other Aneuploid Conditions, 1993, Etiology and Pathogenesis of Down Syndrome, 1995, Inborn Errors of Development. The Molecular Basis of Clinical Disorders of Morphogenesis, 2004; assoc. editor Rudolph's Textbook of Pediatrics, 18th edit., 1986, 20th edit., 1996; mem. editl. bd. Biology Reproduction, 1974-78, Cytogenetics and Cell Genetics, 1975-80; mem. editl. bd. Am. Jour. Med. Genetics, 1977—, sr. editor, 1995-99, adv. editor, 2000—; mem. editl. bd. Devel. Genetics, 1983-85, Jour. Embryology and Exptl. Morphology, 1983-85, Human Gene Therapy, 1990-98, Human Mutation, 1992-99, Human Genetics, 1995-99, Down Syndrome Quar., 1996—2004, Trends in Genetics, 1997—, Cmty. Genetics, 1998—, Ann. Rev. of Human Genetics and Genomics, 1999—2004, Mechanisms of Aging and Devel., 2000—; contbr. numerous rsch. articles on human and med. genetics, devel. genetics and biochemistry to profl. publs. Served with USPHS, 1961-63. Named to Hall of Fame, Central High Sch. of Phila., 2001; recipient Henry A. Christian award, Harvard Med. Sch., 1959, Rsch. Career Devel. award, NIH, 1967—72, Nancy and Daniel Weisman Charitable Found. award, 1990, Lifetime Achievement award in genetic scis., March of Dimes Birth Defects Found., Col. Harland Sanders, 1995, 6th World Congress on Down Syndrome award, 1997, Disting. Rsch. award, The Arc of the U.S., 1998, Premio Internat. Phoenix-Anni Verdi Perle Rsch. Genetiche, Italian Soc. Human Genetics, 1999, Allan award, Am. Soc. Human Genetics, 2001. Fellow AAAS, Am. Acad. Arts and Scis.; mem. AMA, Am. Bd. Med. Genetics (bd. dir. 1988-93, v.p. 1989, pres. 1990-91), Genetics Soc. Am., Am. Fedn. Clin. Rsch., Am. Soc. Human Genetics (bd. dir. 1972-75, 87-93, 97-98, pres.-elect 1995, pres. 1996), Am. Soc. Biochemistry and Molecular Biology, Soc. Pediatric Rsch. (coun. 1972-75), Am. Coll. Med. Genetics (pres.-elect 2001-02, pres. 2003-05, past pres., 2005-07), Western Soc. Clin. Investigation, Western Soc. Pediatric Rsch., Am. Soc. Clin. Investigation, Am. Soc. Cell Biology, Soc. Devel. Biology, Am. Pediatric Soc., Western Assn. Physicians (coun. 1993-95), Assn. Am. Physicians, Soc. Inherited Metabolic Disorders, Inst. Medicine of NAS, Calif. Acad. Medicine (exec. com. 2002- , v.p. 2004-05, pres. 2006-07), Phi Beta Kappa, Alpha Omega Alpha. Jewish. Office: U Calif Dept Pediat Rock Hall RH584B 1550 4th St San Francisco CA 94143-2911 Home Phone: 415-435-1919; Office Phone: 415-476-2981.

EPSTEIN, CYNTHIA FUCHS, sociology educator, writer; BA in Polit. Sci., Antioch Coll., 1955; postgrad., U. Chgo. Law Sch., 1955—56; MA in Sociology, New Sch. Social Rsch., 1960; PhD, Columbia U., 1968. Instr. anthropology Finch Coll., 1961—62; assoc. in sociology Columbia U., 1964—65, instr. Barnard Coll., 1965; instr. sociology Queens Coll., NYC, 1966—67, asst. prof., 1968—70, assoc. prof., 1971—74, prof., 1974—84; prof. grad. ctr. CUNY, 1974, Disting. prof. Grad. Ctr., 1990; resident scholar Russell Sage Found., 1982—88; co-dir. Program in Sex Roles and Social Change Ctr. Social Scis., Columbia U., 1977—82, co-dir. NIMH tng. grant on sociology and econs. of women and work Grad. Ctr., disting. prof. Grad. Ctr., 1990—. Vis. prof. Health Sci. Ctr. SUNY, Stony Brook, 1975, Stanford Law Sch., 1997; vis. fellow, 2002; vis. scholar Stanford U., 1991, Columbia Law Sch., 2004, Phi Beta Kappa, 1991-92; com. on women's employment and related social issues NRC-NAS, 1981-88; adv. com. on econ. role of women Pres.' Coun. Econ. Advisers, 1973-74; cons., lectr. and spkr. in field. Author: Woman's Place: Options and Limits in Professional Careers, 1970, Women in Law, 1981, 2d edit., 1993, Deceptive Distinctions: Sex, Gender and the Social Order, 1988, The Part-time Paradox: Time Norms, Professional Life, Family and Gender, 1999; editor: (with William J. Goode) The Other Half: Roads to Women's Equality, 1971; (with Rose Laub Coser) Access to Power: Cross-National Studies of Women and Elites, 1981, (with A. Kalleberg) Fighting for Time, 2004, Shifting Boundaries of Work and Social Life, 2004; mem. editl. bds. Signs, Women's Studies, Internat. Jour. Work and Occupations, Sociol. Focus, Women 1974, Dissent, Am. Jour. Sociology, CUNY Mag., Gender and Soc.; contbr. chpts. to books, articles to profl. jours. Trustee Antioch U., 1984—97. Recipient Award for Disting. Contbn. to Study of Sex and Gender, ASAN, 1994, Rebecca Rice award Antioch Coll., 1997; grantee Inst. Life Ins., 1974, Ford Found., 1975-77, Rsch. Found. City of N.Y., 1974-76, 90-93, Guggenheim Meml. Found., 1976-77, Ctr. Advanced Study in Behavioral Scis., 1977-78, 2005, Russell Sage Found., 1982-90, Sloan Found., 1995—; fellow NIH, 1963-66, MacDowell Colony, 1973, 74, 77, 80, Guggenheim Found., 1976-77, Ctr. Advanced Study in Behavioral Sci., 1977-78, Va. Ctr. Creative Arts, 1984. Mem. AAAS, Ea. Sociol. Soc. (v.p. 1977-79, exec. coun. 1973-74, pres. 1983-84, I Peter Gellman award, Outstanding Contbn. to Discipline Merit award 2004), Am. Sociol. Assn. (coun. 1974-77, com. exec. office and budget 1978-81, chmn. sect. on orgns. and occupations, chmn. sect. on sociology of sex roles 1973-74, chair culture sect. 2000-01, pres.-elect, 2004-05, pres. 2006—, Jessie Bernard award 2003), Social Rsch. Assn., Internat. Sci. Commn. on Family. Jewish. Office: CUNY Grad Ctr 365 5th Ave New York NY 10016-4309 Home Phone: 212-666-0342. Business E-Mail: cepstein@gc.cuny.edu.

EPSTEIN, DANIEL MARK, poet, dramatist, biographer; b. Washington, Oct. 25, 1948; s. Donald David and Louise Marietta (Tillman) E.; m. Wendy Roberts, May 29, 1976 (div. 1994); children: Johanna Ruth, Benjamin Robert; m. Jennifer Bishop, 1994; children: Theodore John, Nathaniel David. AB magna cum laude with highest honors in English, Kenyon Coll., 1970; postgrad., U. Va., 1970-71; M.F.A. h.c., Norwich U. Asst. mgr. Automatic Enterprises, Washington, 1967-70; disting. scholar-in-residence Randolph-Macon Woman's Coll., 1982; writer-in-residence Towson State U., 1983-90. Cons. lit. div. Nat. Endowment for Arts, Washington, 1973; lectr. USIS tour German univs., 1977, tour, Africa, 1978; asst. prof. Johns Hopkins U.; bd. dirs. Balt. Theatre Project; co-founder Balt. Poet's Theatre. Poet-in-residence, NDEA grantee, Garrett County, Md., 1972; master poet Md. Arts Coun. Artists-in-the Schs. program, 1974-77; appeared in numerous poetry readings; books of poetry include Appearances, 1969, No Vacancies in Hell, 1973, The Follies, 1977, Young Men's Gold, 1978, The Book of Fortune, 1982, Spirits, 1987, The Boy In The Well, 1995, The Traveler's Calendar, 2002, stories and essays include Star of Wonder, 1986, Love's Compass, 1990; biographies include Sister Aimee, 1993, Nat King Cole, 1999, Edna St. Vincent Millay, 2001, Lincoln and Whitman, 2004; plays include Jenny and the Phoenix, 1977, The Midnight Visitor, 1981, The Leading Lady 1999, others; translator Euripides' The Bacchae, 1998. Recipient Robert Frost prize, 1969, Acad. award Acad. Arts and Letters, 2006; Prix de Rome AAAL, 1977; Danforth Found. grantee, 1971; Nat. Endowment for Arts fellow, 1974; Guggenheim fellow, 1983 Fellow Am. Acad. in Rome; mem. Phi Beta Kappa. Address: 843 W University Pkwy Baltimore MD 21210-2911

EPSTEIN, DAVID STANLEY, educator, consultant; b. NYC, Apr. 17, 1948; s. Mortimer and Shirley Ruth (Silver) E. BA, Adelphi U., 1970, MS, 1972; PhD, St. John's U., Jamaica, NY, 1979. Cert. tchr., NY. Rsch. scientist NY State Inst. Basic Rsch., SI, 1979-80; tchr. NYC Bd. Edn., 1981—99; tchr., Richmond Pub. Schs., 1999-2000; lectr. J. Sargeant Reynolds CC, 2002-04, asst. prof. natural sci., 2004—; cons. in field. Contbr. articles to profl. jours., 1972-81. Mem. Am. Soc. Microbiologists, Am. Soc. Zoologists, Chemistry Tchr.'s Club NY, Sigma Xi. Democrat. Jewish. Avocation: collecting books. Home: 1502 Autumn Honey Ct Apt C Richmond VA 23229 Personal E-mail: dvepstn@aol.com.

EPSTEIN, EDWARD LOUIS, lawyer; b. Walla Walla, Wash., Jan. 10, 1936; s. Louis and Marie (Barger) E.; m. Marilyn K. Young, Dec. 29, 1962; children: Lisa Marie, Rachel Ann. BA with great distinction, Stanford U., 1958; LLB magna cum laude, Harvard U., 1961. Bar: Oreg. 1962, U.S. Dist. Ct. Oreg. 1962, U.S. Ct. Appeals (9th cir.) 1963. Assoc. Stoel Rives LLP, Portland, Oreg., 1962-67, ptnr., 1967—. Past sec., bd. dirs. Portland Hosp. Facilities Authority; trustee Good Samaritan Hosp. and Med. Ctr., Portland, 1972-78, pres., 1978; past trustee Morrison Ctr. for Youth and Family Svcs., Oreg. Assn. Hosps. Found.; bd. dirs. Banner Corp., Banner Bank. Mem. ABA, Am. Bar Found., Am. Health Lawyers Assn., Oreg. Bar Assn., Multnomah County Bar Assn., Multnomah Athletic Club, Univ. Club, Harvard Law Rev., Phi Beta Kappa. Office: Stoel Rives LLP 900 SW 5th Ave Ste 2600 Portland OR 97204-1268 Home Phone: 503-223-1790; Office Phone: 503-294-9245. Business E-Mail: elepstein@stoel.com.

EPSTEIN, EMANUEL, plant physiologist; b. Duisburg, Germany, Nov. 5, 1916; came to U.S., 1938, naturalized, 1946; s. Harry and Bertha (Lowe) E.; m. Hazel L. Leask, Nov. 26, 1943; children: Jared H. (dec.), Jonathan H. BS, U. Calif., Davis, 1940, MS, 1941; PhD, U. Calif., Berkeley, 1950. Plant physiologist Dept. Agr., Beltsville, Md., 1950-58; lectr., assoc. plant physiologist U. Calif.-Davis, 1958-65, prof. plant nutrition, plant physiologist, 1965-87, faculty rsch. lectr., 1980, prof. botany, 1974-87, prof. and plant physiologist emeritus (active), 1987—. Cons. in field. Author: Mineral Nutrition of Plants: Principles and Perspectives, 1972, 2d edit. (with A.J. Bloom), 2005; mem. editl. bd. Plant Physiology, 1962-71, 76-92, CRC Handbook Series in Nutrition and Food, 1975-84, The Biosaline Concept: An Approach to the Utilization of Underexploited Resources, 1978, Saline Agriculture: Salt-Tolerant Plants for Developing Countries, 1990, Plant Sci., 1981-89, Advances in Plant Nutrition, 1981-88; contbr. articles to profl. jours. With US Army, 1943—46. Recipient Gold medal Pisa (Italy) U., 1962; Guggenheim fellow, 1958; Fulbright sr. research scholar, 1965-66, 74-75, award of honor, Am. Soc. Agronomy Calif. Chapter, 2002. Fellow AAAS (pres. Pacific divsn. 1990, Fifty-Yr. Life mem. award 1999); mem. Nat. Acad. Scis., Am. Soc. Plant Biologists (Charles Reid Barnes Hon. Life Membership award 1986), Am. Soc. Agronomy Calif. (award of honor, 2002), Common Cause, Save-the-Redwoods League, U. Calif. Davis Club, Calif. Aggie Alumni Assn. (Alumni citation for Excellence, 1999), Nature Conservancy, Sigma Xi. Achievements include rsch. in ion transport in plants, mineral nutrition and salt rels. of plants, salt tolerant crops, and silicon in plant biology. Office: UC Soils & Biogeochemistry-Land Air & Water Resources One Shields Ave Davis CA 95616-8627 Home Phone: 530-753-2620; Office Phone: 530-752-0197. Business E-Mail: eqepstein@ucdavis.edu.

EPSTEIN, ERVIN HAROLD, JR., dermatologist, educator, researcher; b. Oakland, Calif, Mar. 6, 1941; s. Ervin Harold Sr. and Selma E.; m. Sally Ann Fain, Aug. 11, 1963; children: Adam, Stephanie, Emily. AB, Harvard Coll., 1962; MD, U. Calif., San Francisco, 1966. Diplomate Am. Bd. Dermatology. Intern Barnes Hosp., Washington U., St. Louis, 1966-67; resident in dermatology Harvard U., Boston, 1967-68; clin. assoc. dermatol. br. NIH, Bethesda, Md., 1968-70, resident fellow in biochemistry, 1970-71; resident in dermatology NYU Med. Sch., 1971-72; asst. to clin. prof. dept. dermatology U. Calif. Med. Sch., San Francisco, 1972—, asst. to rsch. dermatologist, 1972—2007; scientist Children's Hosp. Oakland Rsch. Inst., Calif., 2007—. Prin. investigator various rsch. grants NIH Bethesda, 1972—; mem. gen. medicine study sect. 1987-91, mem. adv. coun. Nat. Inst. Arthritis, Musculoskeletal and Skin Diseases, 1993-96. Co-editor: Skin Surgery, 1977, 3rd edit., 1988; editor: Progress in Dermatology, 1982-87; assoc. editor: (audio tape) Dialogues in Dermatology, 1977-84; author numerous rsch. papers, 1966—. Lt. USPHS, 1968-70. Recipient Marian Sulzbergen award, Am. Acad. Dermatology, 1998, Lifetime Achievement award, Am. Skin Assn., 2005. Mem. Soc. Investigative Dermatology (sec.-treas. 1984-89, pres.-elect 1990-91, pres. 1991-92), Dermatology Found. (trustee 1981-83, 84-91), Am. Dermatol. Assn. (treas. 1992-96), Harvard Club San Francisco (v.p.). Jewish. Office: Children's Hosp Oakland Rsch Inst 400 30I St 205 Oakland CA 94609

EPSTEIN, FRANKLIN HAROLD, internist, educator; b. Bklyn., May 5, 1924; s. Max and Fannie (Geduld) E.; m. Sherrie Spivack, Aug. 12, 1951; children: Mark, Ann, Sara, Jonathan. BA, Bklyn. Coll., 1944; MD, Yale U., 1947; Doctor Honoris Causa, Med. Acad., Gdansk, 1992. Diplomate: Am. Bd. Internal Medicine (chmn. subsplty. bd. in nephrology 1969-72). Asst. prof. medicine Yale U., 1954-59, assoc. prof., 1959-66, prof. medicine, 1966-72, chief, divsn. metabolism, 1965-72; prof. medicine Harvard U., 1972—, H.L. Blumgart prof. medicine, W. Applebaum prof. medicine; dir. Thorndike Meml. Lab., Boston City Hosp., 1972; physician-in-chief Beth Israel Hosp., 1973-80, dir. renal divsn., 1980-93; Macy Found. fellow and vis. scientist Oxford (Eng.) U., 1980-81. Cons. to surgeon gen. U.S. Army, 1964-80; mem. metabolism study sect. USPHS, 1962-66; pres. Mt. Desert Island Biol.Lab., 1986-95. Editor: Yearbook of Medicine, 1967-96; assoc. editor: Jour. Clin. Investigation, 1957-62, New Eng. Jour. Medicine, 1982-2001, Quar. Jour. Medicine, 1984-93; contbr. papers, book chpts. on renal physiology, disease of kidneys. Capt. M.C., U.S. Army, 1950-53. Recipient Rsch. Career award, USPHS, 1964, John P. Peters award, Am. Soc. Nephrology, 1985, Bywaters award, Internat. Soc. Nephrology, 1999, David Hume award, Nat. Kidney Found., 2003, Gibbs award, NY Acad. Medicine, 2007. Fellow AAAS, Assn. Physicians Gt. Britain and Ireland, Royal Coll. Physicians; mem. Am. Soc. Clin. Investigation (v.p. 1970), Assn. Am. Physicians, Interurban Clin. Club, Sigma Xi, Alpha Omega Alpha. Jewish. Home: 294 Buckminster Rd Brookline MA 02445-5801 Office: 330 Brookline Ave Boston MA 02215-5400 Office Phone: 617-667-4104. Business E-Mail: fepstein@bidmc.harvard.edu.

EPSTEIN, GARY M., lawyer; b. Newark, Feb. 19, 1948; BA summa cum laude, Yeshiva U., 1969; MA in English and Am. Lit., NYU, 1970; JD, Harvard U., 1980. Bar: Fla. 1980, US Ct. Appeals (11th cir.) 1980, US Dist. Ct. (so. dist.) Fla. 1981. Shareholder, chair nat. corp. and securities practice, co-chair Israel Initiative Greenberg Traurig LLP, Miami, Fla. Mem.: Fla. Bar Assn. Office: Greenberg Traurig LLP 1221 Brickell Ave Miami FL 33131 Office Phone: 305-579-0500. Office Fax: 305-579-0717. Business E-Mail: epsteing@gtlaw.com.

EPSTEIN, GARY MARVIN, lawyer; b. Bklyn., Nov. 28, 1946; s. Arthur and Juliett (Winick) E.; m. Jeralyn Needel, June 29, 1969; children: Daniel, Deborah. BSEE, Lehigh U., 1968; JD, Harvard U., 1971. Bar: D.C. 1971, U.S. Ct. Appeals (3d cir.) 1973, U.S. Supreme Ct. 1975, U.S. Ct. Appeals (9th cir.) 1988. Engr. Gordon Engring. Co., Wakefield, Mass., 1967-70; assoc. Arent, Fox, Kinter, Plotkin & Kahn, Washington, 1971-79, ptnr., 1979-81; chief Common Carrier Bur. FCC, Washington, 1981-83; ptnr., head telecom. group Latham & Watkins, Washington, 1983—. Pub. mem. Adminstrv. Conf. U.S., 1983-86; chmn. adv. com. reduced orbital spacing FCC, 1983-86; chmn. adv. com. World Radiocomms. Conf., FCC, 1994-96; dir. D.C. Appleseed Ctr., 2001—, vice chmn., 2002—, vice chair, 2003-, Appleseed Found., 2002-, v.p., 2002-. Bd. dirs. Appleseed Found., 2002—. Mem. ABA, D.C. Bar Assn., Eta Kappa Nu, Tau Beta Pi. Home: 1111 23d St NW Apt PH1F Washington DC 20037-2809 Office: Latham & Watkins 555 11th St NW Washington DC 20004-2585 Office Phone: 202-637-2249. Business E-Mail: Gary.Epstein@lw.com.

EPSTEIN, GERALD LEWIS, technology and security policy analyst; b. Washington, Dec. 13, 1956; s. Joseph Bernard and Rosalie E.; m. Ellen Mika, June 30, 1985; children: Alanna, Nathan. SB, MIT, 1978; MA, U. Calif., Berkeley, 1980, PhD in Physics, 1984. Analyst Office Tech. Assessment, Washington, 1983-87, sr. analyst, 1987-89, 91-95, sr. assoc., 1995; project dir. Kennedy Sch. Govt., Harvard U., Cambridge, Mass., 1989-91; sr. policy analyst White House Office Sci. and Tech. Policy, 1996-2000, asst. dir. for nat. security, 2000—01; sr. dir. for sci. and tech. Nat. Security Coun. Staff, 2000—01; rschr. Inst. Def. Analyses, 2001—03; sr. fellow sci. and security Ctr. Strategic & Internat. Studies, 2003—. Vis. lectr. pub. and internat. affairs Princeton U., 1992; mem. adv. bd. Chem. and Engring. News, 1994—97; mem. editl. bd. Biosecurity and Bioterrorism, 2003—; adj. prof. security studies program Georgetown U., 2004—; mem. biol. threats panel Nat. Acad. Sci. Com. on Internat. Security and Arms Control. Co-author: Beyond Spinoff: Military and Commercial Technologies in a Changing World, 1992; project dir.: Starpower: The U.S. and the International Quest for Fusion Energy, 1987, Proliferation of Weapons of Mass Destruction: Assessing the Risks, 1993. Fannie and John Hertz Found. fellow, 1978-83; Congl. fellow Office Tech. Assessment, 1983. Fellow: Am. Phys. Soc. (exec. com. forum on physics and soc. 1994—97, com. on internat. sci. affairs 2005—); mem.: AAAS, Tau Beta Pi, Sigma Xi, Phi Beta Kappa. Home: 6008 Anniston Rd Bethesda MD 20817-3404 Office: Ctr for Strategic and Internat Studies 1800 K St NW Washington DC 20006 Office Phone: 202-775-3125. Business E-Mail: gepstein@csis.org.

EPSTEIN, IRVING ROBERT, chemistry professor; b. Bklyn., Aug. 9, 1945; s. Milton and Marion (Hillsberg) E.; m. Ellen Bea Fisher, Oct. 31, 1971; children: David, Peter. AB, Harvard U., 1966, MA, 1968, PhD, 1971; diploma, Oxford U., 1967. NATO postdoctoral fellow Cambridge U., 1971; asst. prof. dept. chemistry Brandeis U., Waltham, Mass., 1971-75, assoc. prof., 1975-81, prof., 1981—, Helena Rubinstein prof., 1989—94, chmn., 1983-87, dean arts & scis., 1992-94, provost, sr. v.p. for acad. affairs, 1994-2001, Howard Hughes Med. Inst. prof., 2006—, Henry F. Fischbach prof., 2006—. NSF faculty profl. devel. fellow Max Planck Inst., Göttingen, Germany, 1977-78. Editl. adv. bd. Jour. Phys. Chemistry, 1982-89; assoc. editor Chaos, 1990—; editl. bd. Interjour. Complex Sys., 1995—; contbr. articles to profl. jours. Recipient tchr.-scholar award Dreyfus Found., 1973; Nat. Merit scholar, 1962-66, Marshall scholar, 1966-67, Woodrow Wilson fellow, 1968, Guggenheim fellow, 1977, 87, Humboldt fellow, 1977, NSF fellow, 1977-78. Mem. Am. Chem. Soc. (Liebmann award), Phi Beta Kappa. Home: 28 Otis St Newton MA 02460-1803 Office: Brandeis U MS 015 Waltham MA 02454-9110 Office Phone: 781-736-2503. Business E-Mail: epstein@brandeis.edu.

EPSTEIN, JASON, publishing company executive; b. Cambridge, Mass., Aug. 25, 1928; s. Robert and Gladys (Shapiro) E.; children: Jacob, Helen. BA, Columbia U., 1949, MA, 1950. Editor Doubleday & Co., 1951-58; v.p., editorial dir. Random House, Inc., NYC, 1968—97; co-founder On Demand Books. Co-founder N.Y. Rev. Books; founder Libr. of Am.; founder Reader's Catalog. Author: The Great Conspiracy Trial, 1970; co-author: Easthampton, a history and guide, 1975, Book Business, 2001; contbr. articles to various publs. Recipient John Jay award Columbia Coll., 1988, Lifetime Achievement award Nat. Book Award, 1988, Curtis Benjamin award Assn. Am. Pubs., 1993, Lifetime Achievement award Guld Hall, 2001, Lifetime Achievement award Nat. Book Critics Cir., 2002. Mem. Coun. on Fgn. Rels., Phi Beta Kappa. Home: PO Box 1143 Sag Harbor NY 11963-0039 Personal E-mail: jasepstei@aol.com.

EPSTEIN, JAY STUART, federal agency administrator; married; 2 children. BA cum laude, Harvard U., 1969; MD, Downstate Med. Coll., 1976. Resident internal medicine George Washington U. Hosp., Washington, 1976-79, clin. fellow infectious diseases, 1979-81; sr. staff fellow rsch. divsn. virology office biologics rsch. & review FDA, Rockville, Md., 1981-85, chief immunochemistry lab., 1984-86, chief retrovirology lab. divsn. transfusion sci., 1986-92, acting dept. dir., 1990-92, dir. divsn. transfusion transmitted diseases, 1993-95, acting. dir. Office Blood Rsch. and Rev., 1993-95, dir., 1995—. Rsch. asst. Moffit Hosp., San Francisco, 1971-73; part time physician Potomac (Md.) Village Med. Ctr., 1981-83; part time house physician Capitol Hill Hosp., Washington, 1981-83. With USPHS, 1985-88. Nat. Merit scholar, 1965, Harvard Coll. scholar, 1965, N.Y. State Regents Medicine scholar, 1969. Mem. AAAS, Infectious Diseases Soc. Am., Alpha Omega Alpha. Home: 1922 Foxhall Rd Mc Lean VA 22101-5535 Office: Office Blood Rsch & Review FDA CBER HFM-300 1401 Rockville Pike Rockville MD 20852-1448 Office Phone: 301-827-3518. Business E-Mail: jay.epstein@fda.hhs.gov.

EPSTEIN, JEREMY G., lawyer; b. Chgo., Sept. 28, 1946; s. Joseph and Gayola (Goldman) E.; m. Amy Kallman, Sept. 15, 1968; children: Joshua, Abigail. BA summa cum laude, Columbia U., 1967; BA, Cambridge U., Eng., 1969, MA, 1973; JD, Yale U., 1972. Bar: N.Y. 1973. Law clk. to judge Arnold Bauman U.S. Dist. Ct. (so. dist.) N.Y., 1972-74; asst. U.S. atty. So. Dist. N.Y., 1974-78; ptnr. Shearman & Sterling, NYC, 1982—. Vol. Lawyers for the Arts; bd. dirs. Fund for Modern Cts, City Bar Fund, Inc. Fellow Am. Coll. Trial Lawyers, Phi Beta Kappa. Office: 599 Lexington Ave Fl C2 New York NY 10022-6030 Home Phone: 718-237-0993; Office Phone: 212-848-4169. Business E-Mail: jepstein@shearman.com.

EPSTEIN, JOHN HOWARD, dermatologist; b. San Francisco, Dec. 29, 1926; s. Norman Neman and Gertrude (Hirsch) E.; m. Alice Thompson, Nov. 1953; children: Norman H., Janice A., Beverly A. BA, U. Calif., Berkeley, 1949, MD, 1952; MS, U. Minn., 1956. Diplomate Am. Bd. Dermatology (dir. 1974-84, pres. 1981-82). Intern Stanford U. Med. Ctr., 1952-53; resident in dermatology Mayo Clinic, Rochester, Minn., 1953-56; practice medicine specializing in dermatology San Francisco, 1956—; chief dermatology Mt. Zion Hosp., 1970-80. Clin. prof. U. Calif. Med. Sch., San Francisco, 1972—; cons. Letterman Army Med. Center, U.S. Naval Hosp., San Diego. Chief editor Archives of Dermatology, 1973-78; asst. editor Jour. Am. Acad. Dermatology, 1978-88; contbr. over 275 articles to profl. jours. With USNR, 1944-46. Recipient Finsen medal, Internat. Soc. Photobiology, 2004. Fellow ACP; mem. Am. Acad. Dermatology (pres. 1981-82, Silver award for exhibit 1962, Gold award 1969), Soc. Investigative Dermatology (v.p. 1979-80), Am. Dermatol. Assn. (bd. dirs. 1983-88, pres. 1990-91), N.Am. Dermatology Soc., Pacific Dermatol. Assn. (pres. 1985-86), Brit. Dermatol. Soc., Danish Dermatol. Soc., Polish Dermatol. Soc., San Francisco Dermatol. Soc. (pres. 1963-64), Am. Soc. Photobiology (councilor 1983-86), Academia Mexicana and Dermatologia (hon.), European Acad. Dermatology and Venerology (hon.), La Societe Francaise de Dermatologie & de Syphiligraphie, Spanish Dermatol. Soc. Office: 450 Sutter St Rm 1306 San Francisco CA 94108-4002 Office Phone: 415-781-4083.

EPSTEIN, LEE JOAN, political science and law professor; b. NYC, Mar. 17, 1958; d. Kenneth Maurice and Ann (Buxbaum) Spole BA with high honors, Emory U., Atlanta, 1980, MA, 1982, PhD, 1983. Mallinckrodt Disting. Univ. prof. polit. sci. Washington U., St. Louis, 1998—2006, prof. law, 2000—06; Beatrice Kuhn prof. law Northwestern U., 2006—. Author: Conservatives in Court, 1985; co-author: Supreme Court and Legal Change, 1992, The Choices Justices Make, 1998, Advise and Consent, 2005, Constitutional Law for a Changing America, 2006, The Supreme Court Compendium, 2006; contbr. articles to profl. jours., chpts. in books. Fellow Am. Acad. Polit. and Social Sci., Am. Acad. Arts and Scis.; mem. Am. Polit. Sci. Assn., Midwest Polit. Sci. Assn., Law and Soc. Assn., Pi Sigma Alpha, Alpha Epsilon Phi. Jewish. Avocations: skiing, tennis. Office: Northwestern U Sch Law 357 E Chgo Ave Chicago IL 60611-3069 Home Phone: 314-440-8624; Office Phone: 312-503-1838. Business E-Mail: lee-epstein@northwestern.edu.

EPSTEIN, MARK ROBERT, electronics executive; b. NYC, Feb. 7, 1943; s. Albert David and Edith (Prager) Epstein; children: Paul, Jeff. BS, MIT, 1963, MS, 1964; PhD, Stanford U., 1968. Rsch. assoc. Stanford Electronic Labs., 1967—68; mgr. R&D Northrop Page Engrs. Inc., Vienna, Va., 1968—74; program dir. Computer Sci. Corp., Falls Church, Va., 1974—76; staff asst. Theater C3 Office Sec. Def., Washington, 1976—80; dep. C3 and intelligence Office Sec. Army, Washington, 1980—86; sr. v.p. Qualcomm Inc., San Diego, 1986—. Chmn. cirs. bd. Kennedy Ctr. Performing Arts, Washington, 2003—04; chmn. Washington Com. for Arts, 2004—06; mem. Wilson coun. Woodrow Wilson Internat. Ctr. Scholars, 2002—; mem. MIT Corp., 2002—. Mem. IEEE (sr.), MIT Club Washington (bd. dirs. 1998—, pres. 2002-03), Sigma Xi. Avocations: swimming, piano, dance, golf. Home: 9209 Fox Meadow Ln Potomac MD 20854 Office: Qualcomm Inc 9209 Fox Meadow Ln Potomac MD 20854 Office Phone: 301-365-6963. Business E-Mail: mepstein@qualcomm.com.

EPSTEIN, MARSHA ANN, public health service officer, physician; b. Chgo., Feb. 4, 1945; 1 child, Lee Rashad Mahmood. BA, Reed Coll., 1965; MD, U. Calif., San Francisco, 1969; MPH, U. Calif., Berkeley, 1971. Diplomate Am. Bd. Preventive Medicine. Intern French Hosp., San Francisco, 1969-70; resident in preventive medicine Sch. Pub. Health, U. Calif., Berkeley, 1971-73; fellow in family planning dept. ob-gyn. UCLA, 1973-74; med. dir. Herself Health Clinic, LA, 1974-79; pvt. adult gen. practitioner LA, 1978-82; dist. health officer Los Angeles County Pub. Health, LA, 1982—2001, area med. dir., 2001—. Part-time physician U. Calif. Student Health, Berkeley, 1970—73; co-med. dir. Monsenior Oscar Romero Free Clinic, LA, 1992—93. Mem.: APHA, Calif. Acad. Preventive Medicine, So. Calif. Pub. Health Assn., LA-Am. Med. Women's Assn., Am. Med. Women's Assn., Am. Coll. Physician Execs. Democrat. Jewish. Avocations: dance, native plants, meditation. Office: Tucker Health Ctr 123 W Manchester Blvd Inglewood CA 90301 Home Phone: 310-390-6430; Office Phone: 310-419-5301. Business E-Mail: mepstein@ph.lacounty.gov.

EPSTEIN, MARVIN MORRIS, retired construction company executive; b. Cleve., June 2, 1928; s. Isadore Elchanan and Rose (Gevelber) E.; m. Lois M. DeSure, June 10, 1956; children: Deborah L. Moskoff, David A. BA with highest honors, U. Mich., 1951; attended, Western Res. U., 1947-49, Ohio State U., 1953, Cleve. State U., 1995-98. Reporter Cleve. Plain Dealer, 1951-52; editor AP, Columbus, Ohio, 1953-55; asst. mng. editor Times-Star, Cin., 1956-57; editor internat. news Milw. Jour., 1958—59; cons. Eden & Assocs., Cleve., 1959-60; sr. exec. The Austin Co., Cleve., 1961-93, sr. v.p., 1990—93, ret., 1993. Contbr. articles to profl. jours. Active Greater Cleve. Growth Assn., 1975-90; mem. bd. overseers, visiting com. Case Western Res. U., Case Inst. Tech., Cleve., 1981-85; bd. dirs. The Stearns Collection, Ann Arbor, Mich., 1990-93; bd. dirs. World Affairs Coun. of Desert, 2000-04; trustee Cleve. Music Sch. Settlement, 1989-90; mem. Presdl. Societies, Univ. Mich., 1980—, Vis. Com. Coll. Lit., Sci. and the Arts, U. Mich., 1989-92; trustee Cleveland Heights-University Heights Pub. Libr., 1997-99. With U.S. Army, 1946-47. Recipient McNaught Gold medal U. Mich., 1951, Disting. Svc. award, 1998. Mem. Soc. Profl. Journalists (life), U. Mich. Alumni Assn. (pres. Cleve. chpt. 1975-76), Heights Regional C. of C. (pres. 1992). Democrat. Home: 36598 Fan Palm Way Palm Desert CA 92211-2383 Office Phone: 760-360-2942. Personal E-mail: mmebrain@aol.com.

EPSTEIN, MATTHEW, opera company director; b. NY; Grad., U. Pa., 1969. Artistic dir. opera programme Bklyn. Acad. Music, 1987-91; gen. dir. Welsh Nat. Opera, Cardiff, Wales, 1991-94; v.p. Columbia Artists Mgmt., NYC, 1973—99, dir., vocal divsn., 2005—; artistic dir. Lyric Opera Chgo., 1999—2005. V.p., spl. cons. Columbia Artists Mgmt.; artistic cons. San Francisco Opera, Santa Fe Opera, Lyric Opera Chgo., BMG Classics/RCA Records, Sony Classical, Carnegie Hall, 1982-86 Mem. jury panel Cardiff Singer World Competition, 1989, 91, 93. Office: Columbia Artists Management Llc 1790 Broadway # 6 New York NY 10019-1412

EPSTEIN, MELVIN, lawyer; b. Passaic, NJ, Jan. 4, 1938; s. Hyman and Lillian (Rozenblum) E.; m. Rachel Judith Stein, Dec. 20, 1964; children: Jonathan Andrew, Emily E. Landau. AB, Harvard U., 1959, LLB, 1962. Bar: N.Y. 1963. Assoc. Stroock & Stroock & Lavan LLP, NYC, 1962-71, ptnr. securities & corp. fin., 1972—. Mem. schs. com. Harvard U., 1984—; bd. dirs. Manhattan Class Co. Theater, 2005—. Mem. N.Y. State Bar Assn., Assn. of Bar of City of N.Y. Democrat. Jewish. Office: Stroock & Stroock & Lavan LLP 180 Maiden Ln New York NY 10038-4925 Home Phone: 718-624-7610; Office Phone: 212-806-5864. Office Fax: 212-806-6006. Business E-Mail: mepstein@stroock.com.

EPSTEIN, MICHAEL ALAN, lawyer; b. NYC, June 26, 1954; s. Herman and Lillian (King) E. BA, Lehigh U., 1975; JD, NYU, 1979. Bar: NY, 1980, US Dist. Ct. (So. & Ea. Dists.) NY, 1980. Ptnr. Weil, Gotshal & Manges LLP, NYC, 1979—. Lectr. in field. Author: Modern Intellectual Property, 1984, 3rd edit., 1994, International Intellectual Property, 1992, Epstein on Intellectual Property, 4th edit., 2001, 5th edit., 2006; editor: Corporate Counsellors Deskbook, 1982, 3rd edit., 1990, Biotechnology Law, 1988, The Trademark Law Revision Act, 1989, Trade Secrets, Restrictive Covenants and Other Safeguards, 1986, Online-Internet Law, 1997, others; mem. editl. bd. Computer Lawyer 1984-, Intellectual Property Strategist 1994-, Cyberspace Lawyer 1996-; co-editor-in-chief, bd. editor Jour. Proprietary Rights 1988-; contbr. articles to profl. jours. Trustee Jonas Salk Found., North Shore-LIJ Health Sys., Jewish Bd. of Family and Children's Svcs. Donald L. Brown fellow in trade regulation NYU Sch. Law, 1978-79. Mem. ABA, NY State Bar Assn. Home: 1020 Park Ave New York NY 10028-0913 Office: Weil Gotshal & Manges LLP 767 5th Ave New York NY 10153 Office Phone: 212-310-8432. Office Fax: 212-310-8007. Business E-Mail: michael.epstein@weil.com.

EPSTEIN, NORMAN B., psychologist, marriage and family therapist, educator; b. Worcester, Mass., July 15, 1947; s. Paul (Stepfather) and Irene R. Sherman, Max L. Epstein; m. Carolyn R. Smith, May 24, 1985; children: Meredith B., Christine E. BA, UCLA, 1969, PhD, 1974. Lic. psychologist Md. State Bd. Examiners of Psychologists, 1984, marriage and family therapist Md. State Bd. Profl. Counselors and Therapists, 2002, diplomate Am. Bd. Assessment Psychology. Asst. prof. psychology SUNY, Buffalo, 1974—78; asst. prof. psychology in psychiatry U. Pa. Sch. Medicine, Phila., 1978—83; asst. prof. family studies U. Md., College Park, 1983—86, assoc. prof. family studies, 1986—92, prof. family studies, 1992—. Pvt. practice clin. psychology, Rockville, Md., 1976—. Author: Cognitive-Behavioral Marital Therapy, 1990, Enhanced Cognitive-Behavioral Therapy for Couples: A Contextual Approach, 2002; editor: Depression in the Family, 1986, Cognitive-Behavioral Therapy with Families, 1988; contbr. chapters to books, articles to profl. jours. Grantee, Substance Abuse and Mental Health Services Adminstrn., 2002—03, Substance Abuse and Mental Health Svc. Adminstrn., 2003—04. Fellow: APA; mem.: Groves Conf. on the Family, Assn. for Advancement Behavior Therapy, Am. Assn. for Marriage and Family Therapy. Achievements include development of questionnaires for assessing individuals' cognitions regarding their marital relationships; research in assessment and treatment of marital problems; cross-cultural comparison of marital standards and marital satisfaction of couples in mainland China and in the United States; evaluating couple therapy for domestic abuse; family psychoeducation for families with a member diagnosed with Schizophrenia. Avocations: travel, reading, cooking, running. Office: Dept Family Studies University of Maryland College Park MD 20472 Office Phone: 301-405-4013. E-mail: nbe@umd.edu.

EPSTEIN, RAYMOND, engineering and architectural executive; b. Chgo., Jan. 12, 1918; s. Abraham and Janet (Rabinowitz) Epstein; m. Betty Jadwin, Apr. 7, 1940; children: Gail, David, Norman, Harriet. Student, MIT, 1934-36; BS, U. Ill., 1938. Registered architect registered profl. engr. With A. Epstein & Sons Internat., Inc., Chgo., 1938—, chmn. bd., 1961-83, chmn. exec. com., 1983—. Bd. dirs., life trustee United Israel Appeal; past sec., hon. dir. Am. Jewish Joint Distbn. Com.; mem. exec. com. Nat. Jewish Cmty. Rels. Adv. Coun.; v.p. nat. bd. Jewish Telegraphic Agy.; mem. citizens bd. Loyola U.; past pres. Coun. Jewish Fedns., Welfare Funds, Inc., Jewish Welfare Fund Met. Chgo., Jewish United Fund, Young Men's Jewish Coun.; past sec. Jewish Fed. Met. Chgo.; past chmn. budget com., bd. govs. Jewish Agy.; past trustee Chgo. Med. Sch; past bd. dirs. United Jewish Appeal; past exec. com. Meml. Found. Jewish Culture; past chmn. pub. affairs com., past chmn. campaign Jewish United Fund Met. Chgo.; past. sec. Welfare Coun. Met. Chgo.; past bd. dirs. Chgo. Bldg. Congress; life dir. Mt. Sinai Med. Rsch. Found.; trustee, past dir. Ampal-Am. Israel Corp. Decorated comdr. Legion of Honor Ivory Coast, 1982; recipient Disting. Alumnus award U. Ill., 1974, Julius Rosenwald Meml. award Jewish Fedn. Chgo., 1974, Citation Brandeis U., 1992; named to City of Chgo. Sr. Citizens Hall of Fame, 1991. Fellow Soc. Civil Engr. France, Soc. Am. Registered Architects; mem. NSPE, ASCE, Am. Concrete Inst., Western Soc. Engrs., Assn. Engrs. and Architects in Israel, French Engrs. in the U.S., Inc., Pi Lambda Phi. Clubs: Standard (past trustee), Illini, MIT, Caxton (Chgo.). Home: 4950 S Chicago Beach Dr Chicago IL 60615-3207 Office: 600 W Fulton St Chicago IL 60661-1100 Home Phone: 773-752-4140. Business E-Mail: ray@rayepstein.com.

EPSTEIN, ROBERT, professional sports team owner, real estate company executive; m. Esta Epstein. Mng. ptnr., mem. exec. com. Boston Celtics, 2002—; ptnr., CEO Abbey Grp., Boston. Recipient Sam Cohen Sportsman of Yr., New Eng. Sports Lodge, 2005. Jewish. Office: Abbey Grp 575 Boylston St #8R Boston MA 02116 Office Phone: 617-266-8860.*

EPSTEIN, ROBERT HARRY, lawyer; b. St. Louis, June 22, 1958; s. I. Robert and Marcia Ruth (Marglous) Epstein; m. Donna Jean Brafman, June 21, 1986; children: Jeffrey Evan, Leslie Ellen. BA in History and Polit. Sci. cum laude, Boston U., 1980; JD, Washington U., St. Louis, 1983. Bar: Mo. 1983, Ill. 1984, US Dist. Ct. (ea. and we. dists.) Mo. 1983, US Ct. Appeals (8th cir.), US Supreme Ct. 1991. Assoc. Susman, Schermer, Rimmel & Shifrin, predecessor firms, St. Louis, 1983-89, ptnr., 1989-2000; mem. Gallop, Johnson & Neuman, L.C., 2001—, chmn. real estate dept. Mem.: ABA, Ill. Bar Assn., Bar Assn. Met. St. Louis, Mo. Bar Assn. (mem. real estate com. 1985—). Avocations: coin collecting/numismatics, softball, golf, reading. Office: Gallop Johnson & Neuman LC 101 South Hanley Fl 17 Saint Louis MO 63105 Home Phone: 636-227-0897; Office Phone: 314-615-6000. Business E-Mail: rhepstein@gjn.com.

EPSTEIN, ROBERT MARVIN, anesthesiologist, educator; b. NYC, Mar. 10, 1928; s. Nathan B. and Rebecca Epstein; m. Lillian Ray Cohen, Dec. 31, 1950; children: Judith Susan, Neal Myron, Charles Benjamin. BS with distinction, U. Mich., 1947, MD cum laude, 1951. Diplomate Am. Bd. Anesthesiology (dir. 1972-84, pres. 1979-80). Intern U. Mich. Hosp., 1951—52; resident in anesthesiology Presbyn. Hosp., NYC, 1952—53, 1955—56; instr. in anesthesiology and fellow in medicine Columbia U., NYC, 1956—57, assoc., 1957—59, asst. prof., anesthesiology, 1959—65, assoc. prof., 1965—70, prof., 1970—72, U. Va., Charlottesville, 1972—74, Alumni prof., 1974—87, Disting. prof., 1987—92, Harold Carron prof., 1992—2002, dept. chmn., 1972—96, Harold Carron prof. emeritus, 2002—. Mem. anesthesiology tng. com. Nat. Inst. Gen. Med. Scis., NIH, 1966—69; mem. com. on anesthesia NRC, 1970—71; mem. Nat. Bd. Med. Examiners, 1982—90, Am. Bd. Med. Specialities, 1974—95. Editor: Anesthesiology, 1974—79; contbr. numerous articles to profl. jours. Bd. dirs., sec. U. Va. Health Svcs. Found., 1980—90, pres., 1990—93; trustee Ednl. Commn. for Fgn. Med. Grads., 1991—95, vice chmn., 1993—95; bd. dirs. QualChoice of Va., 1997—2000. With US Army, 1953—55. Fellow Guggenheim fellow, Oxford U., England, 1966—67, NY Heart Assn., 1956—57; scholar in-residence, Inst. Medicine NAS, 1997, sr. scholar, Va. Health Policy Ctr., 1997—2002. Fellow: Royal Coll. Anaesthetists (Eng.); mem.: W.T.G. Morton Soc., Assn. Univ. Anesthesiologists (pres. 1973—74), Anaesthetic Rsch. Soc. (U.K.), Am. Soc. Pharmacology and Exptl. Therapeutics, Soc. Acad. Anesthesia Chmn. (rep. to Coun. Acad. Soc. Assn. Am. Med. Coll. 1984—91, mem. coun.), Am. Soc. Anesthesiologists, Am. Physiol. Soc., Inst. Medicine NAS, AAAS, Alpha Omega Alpha, Sigma Xi, Phi Beta Kappa. Avocations: sailing, photography. Office: Dept Anesthesiology PO Box 800710 Charlottesville VA 22908-0710

EPSTEIN, SAMUEL ABRAHAM, sales executive; b. NYC, Sept. 14, 1956; s. Isidore and Mamie (Kosofsky) E.; m. Peggy Ann Eisenberg, July 4, 1979; children: David, Daniel, Rebecca. BS in Geology, Bklyn. Coll., 1977; MS in Geology, Rensselear Poly. Inst., Troy, NY, 1979. Rsch. asst. Steinetz Marine Lab., Elat, Israel, 1978-79; petroleum geologist Cities Svc. Co., Houston, 1979-82; sr. petroleum geologist Getty Oil Co./Texaco, Houston, 1982-85; with Morgan Stanley, Houston, NYC, 1985—, first v.p. investments, retirement planning specialist NYC, 1998-99, World Trade Ctr. br. taxable fixed income coord., 1996-98, CPA continuing edn. instr. N.Y. State Investment Adv. Svcs., 1996-97, br. equity and taxable fixed income coord., 1999, sales mgr. World Trade Ctr. Office, 1999—2001, sales mgr. Penn Plz., 2001—02, 1st v.p./retiring planning specialist, 2002—. Author articles on interest rates, global sea level changes; contbr. articles to petroleum industries profl. publs. Mem. Prime Mins. Club State of Israel Bonds, 1987-92; bd. overseers Lander Coll. for Touro Coll.; bd. dirs. Ohav Zedek, Queens, NY. Recipient Bklyn. Coll. Disting. Geol. Alumni award, CUNY, 1990. Mem. Am. Assn. Petroleum Geologists (cert.), NY Acad. Scis. (co-chmn. geol. scis. sect. 1998-2002), Morgan Stanley Dirs. Club, Pres. Club, Equity Club. Jewish. Avocations: weightlifting, walking, geology, oceanography. Home: 173 Beach 134 St Far Rockaway NY 11694-1965 Office Phone: 212-613-6701. Business E-Mail: sam_epstein@morganstanley.com.

EPSTEIN, SIDNEY, architect, civil engineer; b. Chgo., 1923; m. Sondra Berman, Sept. 4, 1987; children from previous marriage: Donna Epstein Barrows, Laurie Epstein Lawton. BS in Civil Engring. with high honors, U. Ill., 1943. Various positions A. Epstein & Sons Internat.; bd. mem. A. Epstein & Sons Internat., Inc., Chgo. Bd. dirs. Polk Bros. Found.; trustee emeritus Northwestern Mut. Life Ins. Co. Founder, bd. dirs., past chmn. Chgo. Youth Ctrs.; past chmn. bd. trustees Michael Reese Hosp. and Med. Ctr.; bd. govs., life mem. U. Chgo. Hosps. and Clinics; life trustee Orchestral Assn. Chgo. Mem.: Standard Club (life; past pres.), Chi Epsilon, Phi Eta Sigma, Phi Kappa Phi, Sigma Tau, Tau Beta Pi, Sigma Xi. Home: 1430 N Lake Shore Dr Chicago IL 60610-6682 Office: A Epstein & Sons Internat Inc 600 W Fulton St Chicago IL 60661-1100 Office Phone: 312-429-8000. Business E-Mail: sidneyepstein@epstein-isi.com.

EPSTEIN, STEPHEN ROGER, financial executive; b. Chgo., Nov. 25, 1947; s. Maurice and Gertrude (Ades) E.; m. Christine Marie Kudrys, June 10, 1979; 1 child, Jorie Anne. Student, U. Ill., 1965-69; BSBA, Roosevelt U., 1977. Mgr. collection and billing Field Enterprises Ednl. Corp., Chgo., 1971-73; asst. mgr. cost acctg. dept. Sun Electric Corp., Crystal Lake, Ill., 1973-77; fin. analyst Wilson Sporting Goods Co., River Grove, Ill., 1978-79; mgr. cost acctg. dept. Salerno-Megowen Biscuit Co., Niles, Ill., 1980-81; mgr. fin. planning dept. Nachman Corp., Des Plaines, Ill., 1981-82, controller, 1982-83; controller ops. div. Helene Curtis, Inc., Chgo., 1983-88, dir. cost mgmt., 1988-90; dir. cost and performance mgmt. svcs. Checkers, Simon & Rosner, Chgo., 1990-93; sr. mgr., practice leader advanced cost mgmt. Grant Thornton, Chgo., 1993-95; CFO Aquion Ptnrs., L.P., Elk Grove Village, Ill., 1995-97, CIO, 1998; dir. mfg. cons. FERS Bus. Svcs., Inc., Chgo., 1998-99; v.p., CFO Perfection Spring and Stamping Co., Mt. Prospect, Ill., 1999—. Speaker in field. Assoc. mem. Leukemia Rsch. Found., Chgo., 1974—. Staff sgt. Ill. N.G., 1970-77. Mem. Inst. Mgmt. Accts., Am. Prodn. and Inventory Control Soc., Inst. Mgmt. Cons., Am. Mgmt. Assn., Am. Radio Relay League. Avocations: electronics, photography, physical fitness. Office: 1449 E Algonquin Rd Mount Prospect IL 60056 Home Phone: 773-631-1643. E-mail: stephene@pss-corp.com.

EPSTEIN, STUART JOEL, investment banker; b. 1963; s. Edwin E. Epstein; m. Randi Hutter, Mar. 31, 1990. BS cum laude, U. Pa., 1984; MBA, Stanford U. Assoc. O'Connor Group; mng. dir. Morgan Stanley, NYC, co-head, global media and comm. group, 2006—. Named a Top Dealmaker, Dealmaker mag., 2006. Office: Media & Comm Morgan Stanley 1585 Broadway New York NY 10036 Office Phone: 212-761-4000.*

EPSTEIN, THEO N., professional sports team executive; b. NYC, Dec. 29, 1973; s. Leslie and Ilene Epstein; m. Marie Whitney, 2007. BA in Am. Studies, Yale U., 1995; JD, U. San Diego, 1998. Summer intern, media rels. San Diego Padres, 1992—98, baseball ops. asst., 1998—2000, dir. baseball ops., 2000—02; gen. mgr. Boston Red Sox, 2002—05, 2006—. Achievements include being the youngest general manager in major league baseball history, 2002. Office: Boston Red Sox 4 Yawkey Way Boston MA 02215

EPSTIEN, JAY ALAN, lawyer; b. Newark, May 23, 1951; s. Leonard and Lorraine (Pedd) E.; children: Jessica, Shira; m. Nancy Elizabeth Kirsch, June 1, 1996. BS, Case Western Res. U., 1973; JD, Cornell U., 1976. Bar: D.C. 1976, N.J. 1976, U.S. Supreme Ct. 1977. Indsl. engr. Ortho Pharm., Somerset, NJ, 1973, Shaw, Pittman, Potts & Trowbridge, Washington, 1976—2000, ptnr., 1984—96, chmn. bus. dept., 1994-95; mng. ptnr. Rudnick, Wolfe, Epstien & Zeidman, Washington, 1996-99; DC co-mng. ptnr. Piper Rudnick LLP, Washington, 1999—2003, chmn. US real estate dept., 2003—; co-chmn. global real estate dept. DLA Piper US LLP, Washington, 2005—. Mem. adv. bd. Advanced Comml. Leasing Inst., Georgetown Univ. Law Ctr., 1998—2001. Editor: Cornell Law Rev., 1975—76. Bd. dirs. greater Washington region Am. Heart Assn., 1998—2001. Named Top Real Estate Lawyer in Washington, Washington Bus. Jour., 2004; named one of Top Lawyers in Washington, Washingtonian Mag., 2004. Mem.: Anglo-Am. Real Property Inst., Am. Coll. Real Estate Lawyers (bd. govs. 2001—), Internat. Coun. Shopping Ctrs. (chmn. D.C. govt. affairs 1989—96), Fed. City Council. Avocation: golf. Office: DLA Piper 1200 19th St NW Fl 7 Washington DC 20036-2412 Office Phone: 202-861-3850. Office Fax: 202-223-2085. Business E-Mail: jay.epstien@dlapiper.com.

ERASMUS, CHARLES JOHN, anthropologist, educator; b. Pitts., Sept. 23, 1921; s. Percy Thomas and Alice E.; m. Helen Marjorie O'Brien, Feb. 18, 1943; children: Thomas Glen, Gwendolyn. BA, UCLA, 1942; MA, U. Calif., Berkeley, 1950, PhD, 1955. Field ethnologist Smithsonian Instn., Colombia, 1950-52; applied anthropologist AID, Western S.Am., 1952-54; research assoc. culture exchange project U. Ill., Champaign-Urbana, 1955-59; vis. prof. anthropology Yale U., New Haven, 1959-60; assoc. prof. U. N.C., Chapel Hill, 1960-62, U. Calif., Santa Barbara, 1962-64, prof., 1964-87, prof. emeritus, 1987—, chmn. dept. anthropology, 1964-68. Author: Man Takes Control: Cultural Development and American Aid, 1961, In Search of the Common Good: Utopian Experiments Past and Future, 1977, Contemporary Change in Traditional Communities of Mexico and Peru, 1978. Served with USN, 1942-45. Home: 6190 Barrington Dr Santa Barbara CA 93117-1758 Office: U Calif Dept Anthropology Santa Barbara CA 93106

ERB, BETTY JANE, retired real estate agent; b. Balt., July 10, 1930; d. Edgar Smith Shanks and Delora Hickman Cockrum; m. William Cornelius Smith, Oct. 14, 1950 (div. Aug. 11, 1966); children: Stephen Cole Smith, Scott Douglas Smith(dec.) , Cindy Lynn Smith(dec.); m. George Lewis Erb, Apr. 30, 1982. Mainframe computer operator Svc. Bur. Corp., Balt., 1974—86; real estate agt. Carroll County Assn. Realtors, Westminster, Md., 1988—2002. Author: Taming the Donkeyphant, 2007; contbr. articles to various pubs. Mem.: Carroll County Coin Club (pres., v.p., sec., bd. dirs.). Baptist. Home: 402 Barnes Ave Westminster MD 21157

ERB, DONALD, composer; b. Youngstown, Ohio, Jan. 17, 1927; s. Tod and Janet (Griffith) E.; m. Lucille Hyman, June 10, 1950; children: Christine, Matthew, Stephanie, Janet. BS, Kent State U., 1950; MusM, Cleve. Inst. Music, 1953, MusD (hon.), 1984; MusD, Ind. U., 1964. Tchr. Cleve. Inst. Music, 1953-61, composer-in-residence, 1966-81, disting. prof. of composition, 1987-96; prof. of composition Ind. U., 1984—87; Meadows prof. composition So. Meth. U., 1981-84; composer-in-residence St. Louis Symphony, 1988-91; resident composer Am. Acad., Rome, 1991. Vis. asst. prof. rsch. electronic music Case Inst. Tech., 1965-67; composer-in-residence Dallas Symphony, 1968-69, Aspen Music Festival, 1993, Schweitzer Inst., 1994, 95; vis. prof. Ind. U., 1975-76, Calif. State U., L.A., 1977; staff composer Bennington Composers Conf., 1969-73; resident composer June in Buffalo, 1984-96, composer-librettist panelist Nat. Endowment for Arts, 1973-79, chmn., 1977-79; performed at Warsaw Autumn Festival, 1971, 73, 94—; artist-in-residence Atlantic Ctr. for Arts, 1995. Composer: Dialogue for Violin and Piano, 1958, Correlations for Piano, 1959, Music for Violin and Piano, 1959, String Quartet No. 1, 1960, Sonata for Harpsichord and String Quartet, 1962, Chamber Concerto, 1961, Sonneries for Brass Choir, 1961, Four for Percussion, 1962, Bakersfield Pieces, 1962, Cumming's Cycle, 1963, Concertant for Harpsichord and Strings, 1963, Symphony of Overtures, 1964, VII Misc, 1964,

Fallout?, 1964, Reticulation, 1965, Phantasma, 1965, Concert Piece 1, 1966, Diversion for Two, 1966, Stargazing, 1966, Concerto for Solo Percussion and Orchestra, 1966, Andante for Piccolo, Flute and Alto Flute, 1966, String Trio, 1966, Summermusic, 1966, Kyrie, 1967, Reconnaissance, 1967, In No Strange Land, 1968, the Seventh Trumpet, 1969, Basspiece, 1969, Klangfarbenfunk I, 1970, God Love You Now, 1971, Fanfare, 1971, The Purple-Roofed Ethical Suicide Parlor, 1972, Harold's Trip to the Sky, 1972, Concerto for Trombone and Orchestra, 1976, Quintet, 1976, Music for a Festive Occasion, 1976, Concerto for Violoncello and Orchestra, 1976, The Hawk, 1979, Cenotaph, 1979, Sonata for clarinet and percussino, 1980, Concerto for trumpet and orch., 1980, The Devil's Quickstep, 1982, Prismatic Variations, 1983, Concerto for clarinet and orch., 1984, The Rainbow Snake, 1985, The Dreamtime, 1985, Concerto for orch., 1985, Concerto for brass and orch., 1986, Three Poems for violin and piano, 1987, Solstice, 1988, Woody, 1988, Symphony for winds, 1989, String Quartet # 2, 1989, Five Red Hot Duets, 1989, Ritual Observances, 1991, Drawing down the Moon, 1991, Concerto for violin and orch., 1992, Evensong, 1993, Sonata for solo violin, 1994, Remembrances, 1994, Changes, 1994, Sonata for harp, 1995, Sunlit Peaks and Dark Valleys, 1995, String Quartet # 3, 1995, Suddenly It's Evening, 1997, Dance, You Monster, To My Soft Song, 1998, others. With USN, 1945—46, USS Balt. Recipient Disting. Alumni award Ind. U. Sch. Music, Naumberg Rec. award, 1974, Disting. Alumnus award Kent Sate U., 1982, Ohioana citation, 1978, award Am. Acad. Inst. Arts and Letters, 1985, Libr. of Congress Commn., 1987, Grammy nominee, 1994, Koussevitzky Commn., 1994, Fromm Found. Commn., 1994, Meet the Composer Commn., 1994, Ohioana Libr. Career award 1998, letter of distinction Am. Music Ctr., 2001; Ford Found. composer-in-residence Bakersfield, Calif., 1962-63; Rockefeller Found. grantee for performance Symphony of Overtures, 1965, grantee Nat. Coun. on Art, 1967-68, Nat. Endowment for Arts, 1980, 84, 91; Guggenheim fellow, 1965-66, fellow Bellagio Study and Conf. Ctr., 1979, 89, USA-Can. fellow NEA, 1995. Mem. Am. Music Center (pres. 1982-85), Broadcast Music, Cleve. Composers Guild, League ISCM (nat. adv. bd.). Home: 4073 Bluestone Rd Cleveland OH 44121-2465 Personal E-mail: donalderb@aol.com.

ERB, JAMES BRYAN, conductor, musicologist, educator; b. La Junta, Colo., Jan. 25, 1926; s. Tillman Harvey and Phebe Ann (King) E.; m. Ruth Hildegard Esther Urbancic, Mar. 1, 1952; children: Martin Georg, Paul David, Christina Elizabeth, Jonathan Tillman. BA, Colo. Coll., 1950; Staatszeugnis (Gesang), Staatsakademie Musik, Vienna, Austria, 1952; MM in Singing, Ind. U., 1954; MA, Harvard U., 1964, PhD, 1978. Tchr. City Schs., Cheyenne, Wyo., 1952-53; from instr. to assoc. prof. music U. Richmond, Va., 1954-78, prof. Va., 1978-94, prof. emeritus Va., 1994—. Music dir. Cafur, Richmond, 1966-94; chorus master Richmond Symphony Chorus, 1971-2007. Arranger (choral adaptation) Shenandoah, 1975; editor: O. diLasso Sämtl-Werke, Neue Reihe, vols. 13-17, 1981-88; author: O. diLasso, A Guide to Research, 1990. With U.S. Army, 1944-46. Named Outstanding Educator, Va. Coun. Higher Edn., 1993; Tchr. study grantee Danforth Found., 1962-65, Study grantee Martha Baird Rockefeller Fund Music, 1968-69. Mem. Am. Musicological Soc., Am. Brahms Soc., Gesellschaft Für Bayerische Musikgeschichte.

ERB, KARL ALBERT, physicist, government official; b. Chgo., June 30, 1942; s. Edgar Gillette and Dorothy (Carsten) E.; children: Janet, Margaret. BA, NYU, 1965; MS, U. Mich., 1966, PhD, 1970. Instr. U. Pitts., 1970-72; instr., asst. prof., assoc. prof. Yale U., New Haven, 1972-80; staff scientist Oak Ridge Nat. Lab., Tenn., 1980-86; program dir. NSF, Washington, 1986-89, dep. dir. physics divsn., 1991; asst. dir. White House Office Sci. and Tech. Policy, Washington, 1989-91; acting assoc. dir. for phys. scis. and engring. White House Office of Sci. and Tech. Policy, Washington, 1991-92, assoc. dir. for phys. scis. engring., 1992-93; sr. sci. advisor NSF, 1993-98; dir. office of polar programs NSF and US Antarctic Program, 1998—. Exec. sec. Pres.'s Com. for the Nat. Medal of Sci., 1993-99; exec. com. Fed. Demonstration Partnership, 1996-99; chmn. Coun. Mgrs. Nat. Antarctic Program, 2000-04; U.S. rep. Arctic Sci. Coun. Regional Bd.; vice chair APS Com. on Internat. Sci., 1999-2002, mem. U.S. Nuc. Sci. Adv. Com., Washington, 1983-86; vis. prof. J.W. Goethe U., Frankfurt, 1978; bd. govs. U.S.-Indo. S&T forum, 2001-02. Contbr. articles to physics jours. and encys., chpts. to books. Recipient Pres. Sr. Exec. Svc. Meritorious award, 1998, 2003, Pres.'s Disting. Svc. award, 2006, New Zealand Antarctic medal, 2007. Fellow AAAS, Am. Phys. Soc. Office: NSF 4201 Wilson Blvd Arlington VA 22230-0001 Business E-Mail: kerb@nsf.gov.

ERB, RICHARD LOUIS LUNDIN, resort and hotel executive; b. Chgo., Dec. 23, 1929; s. Louis Henry and Miriam (Lundin) E.; m. Jean Elizabeth Easton, Mar. 14, 1959; children: John Richard, Elizabeth Anne, James Easton, Richard Louis II. BA, U. Calif., Berkeley, 1951, postgrad., 1952; student, San Francisco Art Inst., 1956. Cert. hotel adminstr. Asst. gen. mgr. Grand Teton Lodge Co., Jackson Hole, Wyo., 1954-62; mgr. Mauna Kea Beach Hotel, Hawaii, 1964-66; v.p., gen. mgr. Caneel Bay Plantation, Inc., St. John, V.I., 1966-75; gen. mgr. Williamsburg Inn, Va., 1975-78; exec. v.p., gen. mgr. Seabrook Island Co., Johns Island, SC, 1978-80; v.p., dir. hotels Sands Hotel and Casino, Inc., Atlantic City, 1980-81; v.p., gen. mgr. Disneyland Hotel, Anaheim, Calif., 1981—82; COO Grand Traverse Resort, Grand Traverse Village, Mich., 1982—93; gen. mgr. Stein Eriksen Lodge, Deer Valley, Utah, 1993-96; pres. The Erb Group, 1996—. Pres. Spruce-Park Mgmt. Co., 1989; mem. adv. bd. travel and tourism Mich. State U., 1992-96; vice-chmn. Charleston (S.C.) Tourism Coun., 1979-81; bd. dirs. Anaheim Visitors and Conv. Bur., 1981-82, Grand Traverse Conv. and Visitors Bur., 1985-90, U.S. 131 Area Devel. Assn., 1983-93; sr. cons. Cayuga Hosp. Advisors, 1996—. Contbr. articles to trade jours. Vice-pres. V.I. Montessori Sch., 1969-71, bd. dirs., 1968-76; bd. dirs. Coll. of V.I., 1976-79; adv. bd. U. S.C., 1978-82, Calif. State Poly. Inst., 1981-82, Orange Coast C.C., 1981-82, Northwestern Mich. Coll., 1983-93; adv. bd. hospitality mgmt. program Ea. Mich. U., 1989-93; trustee Munson Med. Ctr., Traverse City, 1985-93; bd. dirs. Traverse Symphony Orch., 1984-88, N.A. Vasa, 1987-89; adv. panel Mich. Communities of Econ. Excellence Program, 1984-88; mem. hospitality adv. bd. Utah Valley State Coll., 1994-98. Lt. arty. U.S. Army, 1952-54. Named hon. prof. Mich. State U. Hotel Sch., 1992—. Fellow Edn. Inst.; mem. Am. Hotel and Motel Assn. (dir. 1975-77, , 90-94, exec. bd. 1991-94, Service Merit award 1976, Lawson Odde award 1993, Gold Medalist Membership award 1993, trustee Ednl. Inst. 1977-83, mktg. com., exec. com. 1978-83, chmn. projects and programs com. 1982-98, AH&MA resort com. 1986-96, AH&MA condominium com. 1985-96, chmn. ratings com. 1988-96, Ambassador award 1986, Blue Ribbon task force 1988-89, Resort Exec. of Yr. 1988), Caribbean Hotel Assn. (1st v.p. 1972-74, dir. 1970-76, hon. life mem., Extraordinary Service Merit award 1974), V.I. Hotel Assn. (pres. chmn. bd. 1971-76, Merit award 1973), Calif. Hotel Assn. (dir. 1981-82), Caribbean Travel Assn. (dir. 1972-74), Internat. Hotel Assn. (dir. 1971-73), S.C. Hotel Assn. (dir. 1978-82), Am. Hotel Assn. Edn. Inst., (Lamp of Knowledge award 1988), Va. Hotel Assn., Williamsburg Hotel Assn. (bd. dirs. 1975-78), Atlantic City Hotel Assn. (v.p. 1981-82), Atlantic City Casino Assn. (dir. 1981-82), Cornell Soc. Hotelmen, Mich. Travel and Tourist Assn. (bd. dirs. 1983-94, treas. 1986, sec. 1987, v.p. 1988, mktg. com. 1986-93, govtl. affairs com. 1986-93, chmn. edn. com. 1983-84, chmn. bd. 1989-90, Mich. Hotelier of Yr. 1991), Mich. Restaurant Assn. (bd. dirs. 1989-91, chmn. adminstrv. com. 1989-90), Mich. Gov.'s Task Force on Tourism, 1986-87, Grand Island Adv. Commn., Traverse City C. of C. (bd. dirs. 1984-89), Nat. Restaurant Assn., Utah Hotel and Motel Assn. (bd. dirs. 1994-96, treas. 1996), Leadership Grand Traverse (exec. com. 1984-92, fellow 1992), Park City Lodging Assn. (bd. dirs. 1993-96), Park City C. of C. (bd. dirs. 1994-97), Tavern Club, Rotary (Paul Harris fellow 1990), Beta Theta Pi. Congregationalist. Office Phone: 435-649-5605. Personal E-mail: richarderb@aol.com.

ERB, ROBERT ALLAN, physical scientist; b. Ridley Park, Pa., Jan. 30, 1932; s. John Walter and Roma (Chapman) E.; m. Doretta Louise Barker, June 27, 1953; children: Sylvia Ann, Susan Doretta, Carolyn Joy. BS in Chemistry, U. Pa., 1953; MS, Drexel Inst. Tech., 1959; PhD, Temple U., 1965. Chemist Gates Engring. Co., Wilmington, Del., 1953-54; with Franklin Rsch. Ctr., divsn. Franklin Inst. (later divsn. Arvin/Calspan), Phila., 1954-93, sr. staff chemist, 1965-68, prin. scientist, 1968-81, Inst. fellow, 1981-84, staff scientist, 1985-93; tech. dir. SiliClone Studio, Valley Forge, Pa., 1993—. Faculty mem. Silicone Prosthetic Inst., 2007—. Mem. AAAS, Am. Anaplastology Assn. (pres. 1996-97), Am. Chem. Soc., Soc. Plastics Engrs., The Franklin Inst., Sigma Xi. Presbyterian. Inventor human simulators, medical and prosthetic devices, solar collectors, permanent systems for dropwise condensation, contraceptive systems, composites using waste plastics. Home and Office: PO Box 86 Valley Forge PA 19481-0086 *Success is to know God's will for your life and to do it.*

ERB, THOMAS OWEN, education educator; m. Karen Simmons, 1971; children: Christopher, Gregory, Brian, Emily. BA, DePauw U., 1967; MAT, Northwestern U., 1968; PhD, U. Fla., 1977. Mid. sch. core curriculum tchr. Wilmette (Ill.) Pub. Schs., 1967—71; mid. sch. social studies tchr. U. Chgo. Lab. Sch., 1971—72; lead tchr.mid. sch. social studies Escola Inglesa de Luanda, Angola, 1972—74; outreach coord. Ctr. for African Studies, U. Fla., 1976—78; asst. prof. edn. U. Fla., 1978; asst. prof. curriculum and instrn. U. Kans., 1978—84, assoc. prof., 1984—94, prof. tchg. and leadership, 1994—2005; Elizabeth P. Allen disting. prof. edn. studies DePauw U., Greencastle, Ind., 2005—06. Liaison profl. devel. Ctrl. Jr. HS, Lawrence, Kans., 1997—2005; cons. in field; presenter in field. Author: This We Believe and Now We Must Act, 2001, This We Believe in Action: Implementing Successful Middle Level Schools, 2005; co-author: Team Organization: Promise--Practices & Possiblilities, 1989, We Gain More Than We Give: Teaming in Middle Schools, 1997, Dilemmas in Talent Development in the Middle Grades: Two Views, 1997; editor: Mid. Sch. Jour., 1994—; contbr. chapters to books, articles to profl. jours. Named Thomas O. Erb Tchg. award, Kans. Assn. Mid. Level, 1993; recipient Career Tchg. award, U. Kans., 1994; grantee 10 grants from various orgns., 1979—97. Mem.: Am. Ednl. Rsch. Assn. (mem. program com. 1978—), Nat. Mid. Sch. Assn. (trustee 1978—), Phi Beta Kappa, Phi Delta Kappa (pres. chpt. 1968—). Avocations: travel, photography, theater, films. Business E-Mail: thomaserb@ku.edu.

ERBAN, JOHN KALIL, III, medicine educator, cancer specialist, researcher; b. Boston, Aug. 26, 1955; s. John Kalil and Najla Teresa (Maloof) E.; m. Lisa Ann Benoit, Sept. 4, 1982; children: Laura Elizabeth, John Kalil IV, Stephen Benoit. AB, Harvard U., 1977; MD, Tufts U., 1981. Diplomate Am. Bd. Internal Medicine. Intern U. Pa., 1981—82, resident, 1982—84, 1986—87; assoc. prof. medicine New Eng. Med. Ctr., Tufts U. Sch. Medicine, Boston, 1990—, dir. med. oncology breast cancer program, 1992—, chief divsn. hematology oncology, 1998—; with Pub. Health Svcs., 1984—86. Med. editor Tufts Medicine, 1991—; contbr. articles to sci. and med. jours. Recipient Disting. Alumni award, Tufts Univ. Sch. Medicine, 2006. Mem. Mass. Soc. Clin. Oncology (pres. 2001). Office: New Eng Med Ctr Box 245 750 Washington St Boston MA 02111-1526 Business E-Mail: jerban@tufts-nemc.org.*

ERBAY, NAZLI, radiologist; b. Ankara, Turkey, July 11, 1961; arrived in U.S., 1974; d. Engin and Honorata Oktay; m. Sami H. Erbay, Nov. 26, 1988; children: Kaan D., Leila A. MS in Biology, Chemistry, U. Irvine, 1984; MD, Drexel U., 1988. Diplomate Am. Bd. Radiology. Intern in internal medicine Portsmouth Naval Hosp., Conn., 1988—89; resident in nuclear medicine U. Conn., Farmington, 1995—97; resident in radiology Hartford Hosp., Conn., 1997—98; resident radiology Boston U., 1998—2000; fellow imaging Beth Israel Deaconess Hosp., Boston, 2000—01; radiologist Lahey Clinic, Burlington, Mass., 2001—; with Cambridge Health Alliance, Dept. Radiology, Mass., 2006—. Lt. USNR, 1988—93. Mem.: Am. Roentgen Ray Soc., Radiol. Soc. N.Am. E-mail: nazlierbay@gmail.com.

ERBER, THOMAS, mathematics and physics professor; b. Vienna, Dec. 6, 1930; m. Audrey Burns. BSc, MIT, 1951; MS, U. Chgo., 1953, PhD in Physics, 1957. Asst. prof. physics Ill. Inst. Tech., Chgo., 1957-62, assoc. prof., 1962-69, prof., 1969—, prof. math., 1986—, disting. prof., 1999—. Vis. scientist Stanford Linear Accelerator Ctr., 1970; prof. physics U. Graz, 1971, 82, hon prof., 1971—; prof. physics UCLA, 1978-79, 84-85, 87-92, 2006, U. Grenoble, 1982; prof. physics U. Chgo., 1998-99; adv. bd. rsch. corp. Mem. editl. bd. Acta Physica Austriaca. Rsch. fellow, Brussels, Belgium, 1963-64. Fellow: Inst. Physics (U.K.), Am. Math. Soc., Am. Phys. Soc.; mem.: IEEE (life sr.), Nuclear, Plasma & Magnetics Soc., Am. Acad. Mechanics, Am. Radio Relay League, Magnetics Soc., Oesterreichische Physikalische Gesellschaft, European Phys. Soc. Office: Ill Inst Tech Dept Physics Chicago IL 60616

ERBER, WILLIAM FRANKLIN, gastroenterologist; b. NYC, June 1, 1941; s. Sigmund and Marcia (Picard) E.; m. Ingrid Amelia Friedler, Dec. 25, 1967; children: Gregory, Karina, Jonathan, Joanna, Jeremy. BS, Muhlenberg Coll., 1963; MD, U. Health Sci., Chgo., 1967. Diplomate Am. Bd. Internal Medicine and Gastroenterology. Intern Maimonides Hosp., 1967-68, resident, 1968-69, 71-72; fellowship in gastroenterology Albert Einstein Coll. of Medicine, 1973-75; rsch. fellow Hadassah Hosp., Jerusalem, 1971-72; clin. asst. prof. Health Sci. Ctr., Bklyn., 1975—. Cons. Crohn's Colitis Found., N.Y.C., 1975—, H.I.P., N.Y.C., 1975—; attending gastroenterologist Maimonides Med. Ctr., Bklyn., 1975—. Author: Internal Medicine Review, 1979; contbr. articles to profl. jours. Maj. USAF, 1969-71. Fellow: ACP, Am. Coll. Gastroenterology; mem.: Am. Soc. Gastroenterol. Endoscopy, Am. Gastroenterol. Assn. Avocations: music, piano, skiing. Office: 591 Ocean Pkwy Brooklyn NY 11218-5913 Home: 159 Beach 147th St Neponsit NY 11694 Home Phone: 718-474-2233; Office Phone: 718-972-8500. Personal E-mail: ef591@aol.com.

ERBIL, CAN, economist, educator; BA in Econs., Bogazie U., 1992; MA in Econs., Boston Coll., 1996, PhD in Econs., 2002. Rsch. fellow EcoMod, Brussels, 2000—; asst. prof. econs. Brandeis U., Waltham, Mass., 2002—. Rsch. assoc. Econ. Rsch. Forum, Cairo, 2007—. Contbr. articles to profl. jours. Grantee, Brandeis U., 2005—06. Fellow: Econ. Rsch. Forum (assoc.); mem.: Turkish Econ. Assn., Turkish-Am. Scientists and Scholars Assn., European Econ. Soc., Am. Econ. Assn. Avocation: bridge. Office: Brandeis U Dept Econs 415 South St Sachar 215 MS 021 Waltham MA 02454 Home Phone: 617-407-4504; Office Phone: 781-736-2238.

ERBSEN, CLAUDE ERNEST, retired journalist; b. Trieste, Italy, Mar. 10, 1938; came to U.S., 1951, naturalized, 1956; s. Henry M. and Laura Elena (Treves) E.; m. Jill J. Prosky, July 16, 1959; 1 dau., Diana Lisa; m. Hedy Miriam Cohn, Apr. 7, 1970; children: Allan Henry, Michael David. BA cum laude, Amherst Coll., 1959; Inter-Am. Press Assn. scholar, U. Andes, Bogota, Colombia, 1960. Reporter-printer Amherst Jour.-Record, 1955-57; staff reporter El Tiempo, Bogota, 1960; with AP, 1960-1965, newsman in NYC, Miami, Fla., Washington; to chief of bur. Brazil, 1965—69; exec. rep. for Latin Am., 1969—70; bus. mgr., adminstrv. dir. AP-Dow Jones Econ. Report, London, 1970—75; dep. dir. world services AP, NYC, 1975-80; v.p., dir. AP-Dow Jones News Svcs., London, 1980—87; v.p., dir. world services AP, NYC, 1987—2003, ret., 2003; sr. cons., dir. Innovation Internat. Media Cons. Group, 2003—. Bd. dirs. World Press Inst., St. Paul. Served to lt. USNR, 1961-65. Recipient San Giusto D'Oro award City of Trieste, 1995. Mem. Internat. Press Inst., Coun. Fgn. Rels., World Assn. of Newspapers. Home: 27 Stratton Rd Scarsdale NY 10583-7556

ERCKLENTZ, ALEXANDER TONIO, investment company executive; b. NYC, July 13, 1936; s. Enno Wilhelm and Hildegard (Schlubach) E.; m. Harriet Fidoan-Green; children: Alexander Tonio Jr., Christina Titaua, Nicholas Ley. BA, Yale U.; postgrad, NYU. Various positions Brown Brothers Harriman & Co., NYC, 1959-77, ptnr., 1978—. Bd. dirs. AXA Art Ins. Corp., Stinnes Corp. Trustee The Opera Found., Am. U. Beirut; chmn. Friends Atlantik-Bruecke e.V., Am. Friends Covent Garden. Mem.: Field Club, Stanwich Club, The Links. Roman Catholic. Office: Brown Brothers Harriman & Co 140 Broadway New York NY 10005-1101 Office Phone: 212-493-7822.

ERCKLENTZ, ENNO WILHELM, JR., lawyer; b. NYC, Jan. 27, 1931; s. Enno Wilhelm and Hildegard (Schlubach) E.; m. Mai A. Vilms, Sept. 20, 1969; children: Cornelia, Stephanie. AB, Columbia U., 1954; JD, Harvard U., 1957. Bar: N.Y. 1958. Assoc. Curtis, Mallet-Prevost, Colt & Mosle, NYC, 1957-60; sec., gen. counsel Channing Fin. Corp., NYC, 1960-69; v.p., sec., gen. counsel Inverness Mgmt. Corp., NYC, 1969-75; pvt. practice NYC, 1975-78; ptnr. Whitman & Ransom, NYC, 1978-87, Greeven & Ercklentz, NYC, 1987-98; pvt. practice NYC, 1998—. Author: Modern German Corporation Law, 1979. Chmn. bd. German Sch. N.Y., White Plains, 1993—99. Mem. ABA, N.Y. State Bar Assn., Assn. of Bar City of N.Y., Am. Fgn. Law Assn. Republican. Roman Catholic. Office: Enno W Ercklentz Jr PC 620 Fifth Ave 6th Fl New York NY 10020-2457 Office Phone: 212-632-3560. Business E-Mail: ennoerck@aol.com.

ERDELYI, EILEEN EDITH, financial planner and advisor; m. Alex Erdelyi, Jr., Dec. 11, 1971; children: Stephen Alex, Diana Lynn. Cert. real estate salesperson, Lumbleau Real Estate Sch., LA, 1985; stock market investment cert., Pacific Sch. Fin., Pasadena, Calif., 1985; cert. fin. planning program, U. So. Calif., 1987; cert. fin. planner, Coll. Fin. Planning, Denver, 1988; AAS, Palomar Coll., San Marcos, Calif. CFP; lic. series 63 and 7 Nat. Assn. Securities Dealers; lic. in health and disability ins., life agt. Calif. Supervising clk. dept. pub. social svcs. and dept. probation Los Angeles County, LA, 1969-75; broker assoc. Red Carpet Real Estate, Tujunga, Calif., 1986-88; assoc. fin. advisor prudent planning-alliance adv. group NBC Employees Fed. Credit Union, Burbank, Calif., 1988-89; fin. advisor, affiliate Alliance Adv. Group, Inc., Chatsworth, Calif., 1989-94; real estate sales assoc. Key Real Estate, Escondido, Calif., 1989-94; fin. advisor Capital Planning Concepts, San Diego, 1994-95; sr. fin. advisor Alliance Adv. and Securities, Inc., Westlake Village, Calif., 1995—. Former press chmn., treas., v.p., pres. Sunland Woman's Club Jrs. of Calif. Fedn. Woman's Clubs, 1978-88, also former bd. dirs. Verdugo Met. dist. Named Jr. of Yr., Woman's Club Jrs., 1981. Mem.: Kingdom Advisors, Fin. Planning Assn. Avocations: gardening, water sports, creative writing. Address: PO Box 2262 Temecula CA 92593 Office: Alliance Adv and Securities Inc 3390 Auto Mall Dr Westlake Village CA 91362 Office Phone: 951-587-9130.

ERDEM, NURUM FILIZ, geriatrician; b. Livonia, Mich., July 1, 1968; d. Mehmet Emin and Nurhan Erdem; m. Seth Allen Richards, Sept. 18, 1999; children: Taner Allen Richards, Ayla Erdem Richards. BS in Psychology, U. Mich., Ann Arbor, 1990, MPH in Toxicology, 1992, MD, 1996. Diplomate Am. Bd. Interna. Medicine and Geriatric Medicine. Intern internal medicine Duke U. Med. Ctr., Durham, NC, 1996—97, resident internal medicine, 1997—99, cons. assoc. dept. medicine, 1999—2003; geriatric medicine fellow U. N.C., Chapel Hill, 2003—05, asst. clin. prof. divsn. geriatric medicine, 2005—. Presenter in field. Contbr. articles to profl. jours. Chair Reach Out to Srs. Campaign Jr. League Durham and Orange Counties, NC, 2001—05; bd. mem. Adelaide Walters Apt., Chapel Hill, NC, 2004—05, 2005—06, sr. pharmacist formulary com., 2005—06. Mem.: AMA (Physicians Recognition award 2003—06), ACP (assoc.), Gerontol. Soc. Am., Am. Med. Dirs. Assn. (Found. Futures Scholarship 2005), Am. Geriat. Soc. (Geriatric Recognition award 2005). Achievements include research in racial disparities in the nursing home management of urinary incontinence in the Southeastern United States. Office: Univ North Carolina Hosps Sch Medicine 141 MacNider Bldg CB 7550 Chapel Hill NC 27599-7550

ERDEN, SYBIL ISOLDE, artist; b. NYC, Nov. 30, 1950; d. Mark and Annelise (Stautner) E.; m. Philip M. Freund, July 7, 1970 (div. 1978); m. Jerry Buley, June 15, 1991 (div. 1998). Student, Acad. of Art, San Francisco, 1970-71, San Francisco Art Inst., 1971-73, Ariz. State U., 1992-93. Lectr. Calif. Coll. Arts and Crafts, 1978, Tempe Fine Art Ctr., 1985, Collins Gallery, San Francisco, 1986, Collage Art Appreciation Group, Colorado Springs, Colo., 1987, South Park Sch. Dist., Fairplay, Colo., 1987, Al Collins Sch. Graphic Design, 1989-90, Cerro Coso C.C., Calif., 1991, Chico State U., 1991; tchr. workshops City of Phoenix, 1991, Cerro Coso C.C., Calif., 1991, Chico State U., 1991, Phoenix Coll., 1992-94, Cochise Coll., 1993; guest spkr. Tempe Art Ctr. Seminar for Artists, 1993, Mesa C.C., 1994-96; invited spkr. Animal Rights 2003, L.A., 2003, Ann Arbor Bird Club, 2005, Salt Lake Bird Club, 2005, Las Vegas Agr. Soc., 2005, Pittsburgh Bird Club, 2003, Pet Bird Report Conf., 1998, 2001, Long Island Parrot Soc. Conf., 2000, 03, West LA Bird Club, 2000, Las Vegas Avicultural Soc., 1999, TARA (Tucson Avian Rescue and Adoption, 2002, Manhattan Bird Club, 2004, others. Exhibited in group shows including San Francisco Art Inst., 1973, The Bush Street Gallery, San Francisco, 1977, The Top Floor Gallery, San Francisco, 1979, I-Beam, San Francisco, 1980, Diablo Valley Coll., Walnut Creek, Calif., 1980, The Stable, San Francisco, 1982, Tempe Fine Arts Ctr., 1985, Collins Gallery, San Francisco, 1986, 89—, Berkeley (Calif.) Art Ctr., 1986, The Cave, San Francisco, 1981, Alwun House, Phoenix, 1985, 87-93 (award 1989), Grand Canyon Coll., Phoenix, 1988, N.Mex. Jr. Coll., 1988, 90 (award 1990), San Francisco State U., 1988, Pa. State U., 1989, Ohio State U., 1989, Mendocino Art Ctr., 1990, Jewish Cmty. Ctr., Denver, 1990, Cerro Coso C.C., Kern County, Calif., 1990-91, Chico State U., 1991, Sierra Arts Found., 1991, Ea. N.Mex. U., 1992, Shemer Art Ctr., Phoenix, 1991, Chico (Calif.) State U., 1992, Sierra Arts Found., Reno, 1992, IOA Artspace, Oklahoma City, 1995, Ariz. State U., 1996, Tempe Pub. Libr., 1996, La Bandera Vieja nat. traveling exhibit Ariz. Commn. on Arts; executed mural office of Dr. Peter Eckman, San Francisco, 1977, HandBall Express, San Francsico, 1981; archived by Smithsonian Mus. Archive Am. Art, Washington; columnist Cages Bird Hobbyist, 1996—, Companion Bird Quar., 1998-; contbr. articles to popular mags. Founder, dir., pres. Oasis Sanctuary Found., 1996—; co-founder/ bd. dirs. Avian Welfare Coalition, 1999—2002; nat. rescue coord. Avian Welfare Coalition Rescue Network, 2003. Mem. Am. Surrealist Initiative, Ariz. Visionary Alternative (founder, dir. 1984-85, 87-95), Movemiento Artistico del Rio Salado Artspace (artist mem. 1995-98), LIC Rehabber For the Birds, Avian Veterinarians, Am. Sanctuary Assn. (bd. dirs., sec. 2003-), The Assn. of Sanctuaries. Democrat. Jewish. Avocation: rescue work. Mailing: 5411 N Teran Rd Benson AZ 85602 Office Phone: 520-212-4737.

ERDMAN, DAVID WILLIAMS, lawyer; b. Camp Lejeune, NC, July 4, 1949; s. Lawrence Huntington and Marian (Williams) E.; m. Lynn Kendrick, Feb. 4, 1984; children: Natalie, Emily. BSE, Duke U., 1971; JD, Georgetown U., 1975. Bar: NC 1975. Rsch. staff asst. Watergate com. U.S. Senate, Washington, 1973; atty. N.C. State Bd. Edn., Raleigh, 1975-76; mem. campaign staff Jim Hunt for Gov. of N.C., Raleigh, 1976; assoc. Wardlow, Knox & Knox, Charlotte, NC, 1977-81; ptnr. Erdman and Hockfield LLP, Charlotte, 1981—. Composer, performer 45 RPM recording On My Knees, 1967; developer Juriscan computer program, 1974. Mem.-at-large Charlotte City Coun., 1999; mem. N.C. Employment Security Commn., Raleigh, 1978-82. Angier B. Duke scholar, 1967. Mem. Met. Bus. Coun., Charlotte C. of C. (bd. advisors 2001), Myers Park

Country Club. Democrat. Baptist. Avocation: guitar. Home: 251 Huntley Pl Charlotte NC 28207 Office: Erdman and Hockfield LLP 2300 E 7th St Charlotte NC 28204-4366 Office Phone: 704-333-7800. Business E-Mail: erdman@charlotte-nc-law.com.

ERDMAN, JOHN W., nutritionist, educator; m. Edie Erdman; children: Carolyn, Jackie. PhD, Rutgers U., 1975. Asst. prof. Dept. Food Sci. U. Ill., Urbana, prof. Food Sci. and Human Nutrition. Dir. Nutritional Scis. divsn. U. Ill., Urbana, 1989—99, asst. dean Coll. Office Rsch., 1995—99. Contbr. more than 130 articles to profl. jours. Recipient award, Am. Soc. Nutritional Scis. Fellow: Inst. Food Technologists (Babcock-Hart award 1999); mem.: NAS, Inst. Medicine, 2004, Am. Assn. Nutritional Scis. (pres.-elect 2000—01). Office: Univ Illinois Divsn Nutritional Scis 451 Bevier Hall MC-186 905 S Goodwin Ave Urbana IL 61801

ERDMAN, MARIE MIMMIE, small business owner; b. Balt., May 22, 1925; d. Harry Aaron and Sophie (Weiner) Fox; m. Albert Aaron Erdman, Feb. 25, 1945 (dec.); children: Jay Elliott, Elaine Deborah Gordon. Lic. cosmetic and skin care demonstrator Md., 1972. Supr. Adm. Auto Ins., Balt., 1956—71; leader sales Shaklee US, Pleasanton, Calif., 1971—, nutritional cons., 1971—. Judge elections City Balt., 1946—96. Mem.: Nat. Assn. Women Bus. Owners (pres., founder, named Woman of Yr., Balt. regional chpt. 1982), Sr. Corp. Ret. Execs. (counselor 2002—06), Jewish Women Internat. (assoc.; pres. 1955—56), Hadassah (life). Jewish. Avocations: knitting, painting, mahjong. Home: 2026 West Rogers Ave Baltimore MD 21209 Home Phone: 410-664-7861.

ERDMANN, CHARLES EDGAR (CHIP ERDMANN), federal judge, former state supreme court justice; b. June 26, 1946; married; 4 children. Student, Mont. State U., 1964-66; BS in Bus./Econs., Eastern Mont. Coll., 1972; JD, U. Mont., 1975. Bar: Mont., U.S. Dist. Ct. Mont., U.S. Ct. Appeals (9th cir.), U.S. Mil. Ct. Appeals. Legal intern Cascade County (Mont.) Atty.'s Office, 1974; asst. atty. gen. Mont. Atty. Gen.'s Office, 1975-76, chief state atty., 1978-79; chief counsel Mont. State Auditor's Office, 1976-78; bur. chief/atty. Medicaid Fraud Control Bur., State of Mont., 1979-82; staff atty. Mont. Sch. Bds. Assn., 1982-86; pvt. practice Helena, Mont., 1986-95; justice Mont. Supreme Ct., Helena, 1995—97; head Human Rights & Law Dept. Office of the High Rep. in Bosnia, 1999—2000; chmn., chief judge Bosnia Election Ct., 2000—02; judge US Ct. Appeals for the Armed Forces, Washington, 2002—. Sgt. USMC, 1967-69, lt. col. Mont. Air NG, 1980—. Pre-Law scholar Yellowstone County Bar Assn., Cascade County Bar Assn. scholar, 1973-74, Albyn F. McCulloch scholar, 1974-75. Mem. Mont. State Bar Assn., Alpha Psi Kappa, Phi Delta Phi. Office: US Ct Appeals Armed Forces 405 E St NW Washington DC 20442*

ERDMANN, JAMES BERNARD, educational psychologist; b. Oct. 27, 1937; s. George C. and Emma (Hiltebrand) E.; m. Rebecca Susan Lindsay; children: Theodore Michael, Carolyn Louise, Christopher Joseph, Timothy James. Grad. cum laude, Pontifical Coll., Josephinum, 1959; MA, Loyola U., Chgo., 1964, PhD, 1966. Rsch. asst. Psychometric Lab. Loyola U., 1960-63, rsch. assoc., project dir., 1963-65, acting dir., 1965-66, assoc. dir., 1967-69, instr. dept. psychology, 1964-66, asst. prof. measurement program, 1967-69; assoc. prof. Sch. Edn. and Sch. Human Medicine, eval. coord. Office Med. Edn., R & D, Mich. State U., 1969-70; dir. divsn. ednl. measurement and rsch. Assn. Am. Med. Colls., Washington, 1970-87; clin. assoc. prof. psychiatry and behavioral scis. George Washington U. Sch. Medicine and Health Scis., 1973-87; assoc. dean adminstrn. and spl. projects Jefferson Med. Coll., Thomas Jefferson U., Phila., 1987-89, assoc. dean adminstrn. and univ. registrar, 1990-2001, prof. medicine (edn.) dept. medicine, 1993—, sr. assoc. dean faculty affairs, 2001—; dean Jefferson Coll. Health Professions Thomas Jefferson U., Phila., 2002—. Contbr. articles to profl. jours. Mem. Am. Ednl. Rsch. Assn., Assn. Schs. of Allied Health, Assn. Am. Med. Coll. Roman Catholic. Home: 408 Bickmore Dr Media PA 19086-6909 Office: 130 S 9th St Philadelphia PA 19107-5233 Office Phone: 215-955-4481. Business E-Mail: james.erdmann@jefferson.edu.

ERDMANN, JOACHIM CHRISTIAN, retired physicist; b. Danzig, June 5, 1928; s. Franz Werner and Maria Magdalena (Schreiber) E.; m. Ursula Maria Wedemeyer, Aug. 24, 1957; children: Michael Andreas, Thomas Christian, Maria Martha Dorothea D, Tech U. Braunschweig, Germany, 0958. Physicist Osram Labs., Augsburg, Germany, 1954—60; sr. rsch. scientist Boeing Sci. Rsch. Labs., Seattle, 1960—72, Boeing Aerospace Co., Seattle, 1972—73; prin. engr. Boeing Comml. Airplane Co., Seattle, 1973—81, sr. prin. engr., 1981—84, Boeing Aerospace (Boeing Def. and Space Group), Seattle, 1984—90; tech. cons., 1990—2003; ret., 2003. Vis. prof. Max Planck Inst. for Metals Rsch., Stuttgart, Germany, 1968-69; lectr. Tech. U. Stuttgart, 1968-69; pres. Optologics Inc., Seattle, 1973-94 Author: Heat Conduction in Crystals, 1969; contbr. articles to profl. jours Mem. Am. Phys. Soc., Optical Soc. Am., Soc. Photo Optical Instrumentation Engrs Achievements include research in cryogenics, statistical physics and opto electronics. Personal E-mail: jo@joejuerdmann.com.

ERDNER, JON W., small business owner, securities trader; b. Pitts., Nov. 4, 1942; s. William John and Marie Dorothy (Filipietz) E.; m. Joyce Ann Girouard, Dec. 1, 1990; children: Niki Lee, Kassandra Marie. Student, U. Pitts., 1961-64; BA in Psychology, Kent State U., Ohio, 1967. Pres. Erdner Enterprises, Inc., Pitts., 1967—; exec. v.p. Investment Timing Svcs., Inc., Washington, Pa., 1978-88, pres., owner, 1988-95, also bd. dirs.; owner Stormy Acres Farm & Stable, Washington, 1984—, ITS AssetMgmt., 1995—; pres., owner Erdner Enterprises, Inc., Washington, Pa., 1995—; owner Atlas Brokerage Co., Washington, Pa., 1998—2003; prin., owner Four Coins Fin. Svcs., L.P., 2005—. Mem. N. Strabane Township Planning Commn., 2005. Mem. Internat. Assn. Fin. Planners, U.S. Trotting Assn., Pa. Harness Horse Assn., Meadows Standardbred Owners Assn., Masons, Shriner. Republican. Avocations: radio, classical music, bridge. Home: 52 Hatfield Ln Canonsburg PA 15317-4918 Office: ITS Asset Mgmt LP & Erdner Enterprises Inc 1720 Washington Rd Washington PA 15301-8919 Office Phone: 724-745-2300.

ERDOES, MARY CALLAHAN, bank executive; m. Philip Erdoes. BS in Math., Georgetown Univ.; MBA, Harvard Univ., 1993. With Bankers Trust; portfolio mgr. Meredith, Martin & Kaye; head, fixed income group, JPMorgan Flemming Investment Mgmt Divsn. JPMorgan Private Bank, 1996—2002, mng. dir., global head, investments, 2002, now CEO. Bd. dir. UNICEF, 2005—. Named one of 100 Most Powerful Women in World, Forbes mag., 2005. Office: JP Morgan Pvt Banking 345 Park Ave New York NY 10154 E-mail: mary.erdoes@jpmorgan.com.

ERDOS, JOANNA E., school counselor, secondary school educator; d. Paul Thomas and Eva Judith Erdos. AA in Theatre Arts, LA City Coll., 1973; BA in Theatre Arts, UCLA, 1975; MSc in Counseling and Guidance, Calif. Luth. U., 2001. Cert. Secondary Edn. Tchr. UCLA, 1975, English Tchr. UCLA, 1976, in Cross Cultural Lang. and Academic Devel. LA Unified Sch. Dist., 1994, Pupil Pers. Svcs. Credential Calif. Luth. U., 2001. Substitute tchr. LA Unified Sch. Dist., 1976—77, mentor tchr., 1997—99, all dist. speech tournament founder, dir., academic decathlon judge, newspaper editor, asst. proofreader, textbook selection com. mem., write test reader; tchr. John Marshall HS, 1977—2003, master tchr., 1992—95, counselor, 2003—, asst. coach speech and debate team, 1979—80, coach speech and debate team, 1980—92, co-chairperson performing arts, 1995—97, stds. based assessment coord., 1999—2000, accreditation com., focus group leader, sec. booster club, mem. 50th anniversary organizing com., chairperson 65th anniversary organizing com., chairperson 70th anniversary organizing com., co-chairperson 75th anniversary organizing com. Restructuring team leader Coalition Essential Schs.; tutor in field. Supporting mem. LA Conservancy, 1988—; chaperone LA Olympics Amateur Athletics Assn.; mem. Los Feliz Improvement Assn., Cultural Heritage Found., Nat. Trust Hist. Preservation. Nominee Tch. of Yr., John Marshall HS, 1988; named Outstanding Young Educator LA, Bayanihan Jaycees, 1986; recipient Appreciation award, Masonic Lodge, 1977, Lions Club, 1981, 1982, 1983, 1984, 1985, 1986, 1989, 1991, 1992, 1994, Cheerleaders Spirit award, John Marshall HS, 1984, Baseball Team Appreciation award, 1984, Basketball Team Appreciation award, 1985, Student Coun. Cmty. Svc. award, 1985, 1986, 1987, 1988, Academic Decathlon Appreciation cert., 1990, Nat. Excellence in Speech award, Nat. Forensic League, 1984, Degree Spl. Distinction, 1986, Degree Outstanding Distinction, 1991, Diamond Coach award, 1993, Outstanding Young Educator Calif., Calif. Jr. C. of C., 1987, Fellowship award, Am. Legion Freedoms Found., 1988. Mem.: NEA, Western Assn. Coll. Admissions Counselors, LA City Coll. Theatre Alumni and Assocs. (charter mem., bd. dirs., sec.), Theatre West, Internat. Thespian Soc., Drama Tchrs. Assn. So. Calif., Nat. Coun. Tchrs. English, English Coun. LA (workshop presenter), Calif. Tchrs. Assn., John Marshall HS Faculty Assn. (pres., sec.), Nat. Forensic League (dist. tournament ofcl.), Calif. HS Speech Assn. (state coun. mem., area chairperson, state tournament ofcl.), United Tchrs. LA, Western Bay Forensic League (pres., sec.), Sr. High Assn. Speech Educators (pres., co-founder), John Marshall Parent Tchr. Student Assn. (Hon. Svc. award 1990, Appreciation cert. 1983), John Marshall HS Alumni Assn. (founding mem. 1979—, v.p. faculty liaison 1979—, variety show prodr. and performer, newsletter editor), LA City Coll. Theatre Alumni Assn. (bd. mem. 1993), Culinary Historians So. Calif. (membership com. co-chair), UCLA Alumni Assn. (life), Sigma Tau Sigma, Pi Lambda theta. Avocations: reading, travel, Scrabble, history, cooking. Office: John Marshall HS 3939 Tracy St Los Angeles CA 90027

ERDRICH, LOUISE (KAREN ERDRICH), writer, poet; b. Wahpeton, ND, June 7, 1954; d. Ralph Louis and Rita Joanne (Gourneau) E.; m. Michael Anthony Dorris, Oct. 10, 1981 (dec. Apr. 1997); children: Abel (dec.), Sava, Madeline, Persia, Pallas, Aza. BA, Dartmouth Coll., 1976; MA, Johns Hopkins U., 1979. Vis. poet, tchr. ND State Arts Coun., 1977-78; tchr. writing Johns Hopkins U., Balt., 1978-79; communications dir., editor Circle-Boston Indian Council, 1979-80; textbook writer Charles Merrill Co., 1980; owner BirchBark Books and Native Arts, Mpls., 2000—; founder BirchBark Books Press, Mpls. Author: (textbook) Imagination, 1981; (poetry) Jacklight, 1984, Baptism of Desire, 1989; (novels) Love Medicine, 1984 (Nat. Book Critics Circle award for fiction 1984, Virgina McCormick Scully prize 1984, LA Times award for best novel 1985, Sue Kaufman prize for first fiction Am Acad. and Inst. of Arts and Letters 1985), The Beet Queen, 1986, Tracks, 1988, (with Michael Dorris) The Crown of Columbus, 1991, (with Dorris) Route 2, 1991, The Bingo Palace, 1994, The Blue Jay's Dance: A Writer's Year with Baby, 1995, Tales of Burning Love, 1996, The Antelope Wife, 1998, Last Report on the Miracles at Little No Horse, 2001, The Master Butchers Singing Club, 2003, Four Souls, 2004, The Painted Drum, 2005; (children's) Grandmother's Pigeon, 1997, The Birchbark House, 1999 (Am. Indian Youth Lit. award, 2006), Game of Silence, 2005; contbr. short stories, essays and poems to popular mags., other publs. Johns Hopkins U. teaching fellow, 1979; Macdowell Colony fellow, 1980; Yaddo Colony fellow, 1981; vis. fellow Dartmouth Coll., 1981; Guggenheim fellow, 1985-86; recipient numerous awards for profl. excellence including Nelson Algren award, 1982, Pushcart prize, 1983, Nat. Mag. Fiction award, 1983, 87, First prize O. Henry awards, 1987. Mem. PEN (exec. bd. 1985-90), Am. Acad. Arts and Letters, Authors Guild, Western Lit. Assn. Address: c/o Wylie Aitken & Stone Inc 250 W 57th St Ste 2114 New York NY 10107-2199 Office: Birchbark Books and Native Arts 2115 W 21st St Minneapolis MN 55405

ERDTMANN, FREDERICK J., physician, retired military officer; b. Mineola, NY, July 28, 1944; m. Jean Erdtmann. BS, Bucknell U.; MD, Temple U. Sch. Medicine, 1970; MPH, U. Calif., Berkeley; grad., Armed Forces Staff Coll., Indsl. Coll. Armed Forces. Intern Allentown Gen. Hosp., Pa., 1970—71; advanced through grades to col. U.S. Army; resident, preventive medicine Walter Reed Army Inst. Rsch., 1974—75; chief, preventive medicine svc. Fitzsimmons Army Med. Ctr., Frankfurt Army Med. Ctr., Germany, Madigan Army Med. Ctr.; divsn. surgeon 2d Infantry Divsn., Tongduchon, Republic of Korea; several tours Office of the Surgeon Gen.; hosp. cmdr. Walter Reed Army Med. Ctr., 1998—99; dir. Bd. on Mil. and Veterans Health Inst. Medicine Nat. Acads., 2003—. Decorated 5 Legions of Merit, Order of Military Med. Merit, George Sternberg Medal for Excellence in Preventive Medicine. Office: Inst Medicine 500 Fifth St NW Washington DC 20001 Office Phone: 202-334-1925. Business E-Mail: rerdfmann@nas.edu.

ERENBERG, SAMUEL JOSEPH, artist; b. LA, Sept. 26, 1943; s. Arthur and Adele Irene Erenberg; m. Elena Mary Siff, July 16, 1967; children: Noah, Ravelle. BA, Calif. State U., Northridge, 1974; MFA, U. Calif., Santa Barbara, 1976. Instr. Oxnard CC, Calif., 1977—78. Vis. instr. Ohio State U., Columbus, 1979—80; vis. lectr. C.W. Post Coll., LI U., North Hempstead, NY, 1982, SUNY, Purchase, 1984, Brigham Young U., Provo, Utah, 1992, Utah State U., Logan, 2000; vis. fellow Va. Ctr. Arts, Sweet Briar, 2001. Represented in permanent collections Mus. Modern Art, NYC, Sheldon Meml. Art Gallery, Kurst Mus., Bern, Switzerland, U. Calif. Berkeley Art Mus., Long Beach Mus. Art, Calif., Mus. Fine Arts, Santa Fe, N.Mex., Palm Springs Desert Mus., Santa Barbara Mus. Art, numerous others. Mem. med. art com. UCLA Hosps. and Clnics, 1998; bd. dirs. Santa Barbara Contemporary Arts Forum, 1979—81, Waves, Music of Present Day, Santa Barbara, 1982—85. Grantee, Nat. Endowment Arts, 1981, Durfee Found., Santa Monica, Calif., 2003; artist's fellow, Calif. Arts Coun., 1994. Mem.: Am. Assn. Museums.

ERENS, JAY ALLAN, lawyer; b. Chgo., Oct. 18, 1935; s. Miller S. and Annette (Goodman); m. Patricia F. Brett, Aug. 21, 1960 (div. May 1985); children: Pamela B., Bradley B.; m. Patrice K. Franklin, June 15, 1985; 1 child, Cameron Jay. BA, Yale U., 1956; LLB, Harvard U., 1959. Bar: Ill. 1960. Law clk. to Justice John M. Harlan U.S. Supreme Ct., Washington, 1959-60; pvt. practice Chgo., 1960-64; founding and sr. ptnr. Levy and Erens (name changed to Erens and Miller 1985), Chgo., 1964-86; sr. ptnr. Hopkins & Sutter, Chgo., 1986-2001; with Foley & Lardner, Chgo., 2001—. Lectr. law Northwestern U., Chgo., 1961-63; spl. asst. atty. gen. State Ill., Chgo., 1964-70. Trustee Latin Sch. Chgo., 1975—80. Mem.: ABA, Chgo. Bar Assn. Office: Foley & Lardner 321 N Clark St Chicago IL 60610 Home Phone: 312-944-6197; Office Phone: 312-832-4536. Business E-Mail: jerens@foley.com.

ERENSTEIN, ALAN, emergency nurse practitioner, nursing consultant; Grad., Aliquippa Hosp Sch. Radiology, Pa., 1974; student, Aliquippa Hosp. Sch. Radiology, New Wilmington, Pa., 1974; AA in Gen. Studies, LPN, Beaver County C.C., Monaca, Pa., 1977, AS in Nursing, RN, 1979. RN, Fla.; registered radiologic technologist, cert. legal nurse cons. LPN Hamot Med. Ctr., Erie, Pa., 1977-78; team leader Trauma-Neuro ICU and Stepdown Unit Allegheny Gen. Hosp., Pitts., 1979-81, staff nurse Emergency Room, 1981; flight nurse LifeWATCH HCA Wesley Med. Ctr., Wichita, Kans., 1981-91, contigency and float pool, 1991-92, hyperbaric nurse, 1991-92; ER nurse, relief charge nurse, clin. coord., team leader JFK Med. Ctr., Atlantis, Fla., 1992-95; aeromed. specialist Bizjet Air Ambulance, West Palm Beach, Fla., 1994-95; med. edn. cons. Med. Edn. Cons. Am., Tampa, 1994-97; with disaster team Cutler Ridge (Fla.) Field Hosp., 1992; response team Kans. Tornado Wesley Med. Ctr., Wichita, 1991; emergency rm./trauma nurse DelRay Med. Ctr., 1996—. Paramedic clin. coord. Hutchinson (Kans.) C.C., 1989; skills lab coord. Advanced Trauma Life Support Course, HCA Wesley Med. Ctr., Wichita, 1989-92; lectr.in field; cons. in field. Author: Trauma in Pregnancy, 1990; co-author: LifeWATCH Transport Manual, 1988; contbr. Society Trauma Nurses: Instructor's Resource Manual for Trauma Nursing, The Pregnant Trauma Patient Module, 1998.

ERGEN, CHARLES W., communications professional; b. Oak Ridge, Tenn., Mar. 1, 1953; m. Cantey Ergen; 5 children. BS in Bus. and Acctg., U. Tenn., Knoxville; MBA, Wake Forest U. Fin. analyst Frito-Lay; profl. blackjack player Las Vegas, Nev.; founder, chmn., CEO Echostar Communications Corp. (DISH Network), Littleton, Colo., 1980—. Co-founder Satellite Broadcasting Comm. Assoc. Named Master Entrepreneur of the Year for the Rocky Mountain region, INC. Mag., 1991, Business Person of the Year, Rocky Mountain News, 1996, 2001, Space Industry Business Man of the Year, Aviation Week Mag., 2000; named one of Forbes Richest Americans, 1999—, Forbes World's Richest People, 2000—; recipient Star award, Home Satellite TV Assn., 1988, CEO of the Year, Frost & Sullivan, 2001. Achievements include leading figure in the movement for the Satellite Home Viewer Improvement Act in 1999 which gave American consumers the right to watch local TV channels via satellite; testified before Congress regarding other video competition issues on several occasions. Avocations: mountain climbing, poker, basketball. Office: Echostar Comms 5701 S Santa Fe Littleton CO 80120*

ERHARDT, WALTER L., JR., medical association administrator; m. Carolyn Erhardt; children: Trish, Abbie. BS cum laude, Roanoke Coll., Salem, Va., 1969; MD, U. Va. Sch. Medicine, Charlottesville, 1973. Diplomate Am. Bd. Plastic Surgery 1980, lic. Ga., Va. Resident, gen. surgery, plastic and reconstructive surgery Vanderbilt U., Nashville; chief of surgery Phoebe Putney Meml. Hosp., Albany, Ga., chmn., divsn. plastic surgery; solo private practice Albany, Ga., 1979—. Adv. bd. Consumer Guide to Plastic Surgery; examinar Am. Bd. Plastic Surgery, 1996—, dir., chair, written examination com. Editor: Plastic Surgery News, 1995—99; assoc. adv. editor Plastic Surgery News, 1992—95. Mem. med. mission teams to India and El Salvador. Fellow: ACS; mem.: Southeastern Soc. Plastic and Reconstructive Surgeons, Dougherty County Med. Soc., Med. Assn. Ga., Am. Soc. Plastic and Reconstructive Surgeons (bd. dir. 1992—93, mem. publications com. 1992—, mem. fin. com. 1992—, mem. CPT com. 1992—, bd. dir. 1995—, treas. 1996—98, v.p. 1998—99), Am. Soc. Plastic Surgeons (pres. 2000—01, past pres. 2002), Ga. Soc. Plastic Surgeons, Am. Soc. Aesthetic Plastic Surgery, AMA (mem. specialty soc. adv. com., alternate del. 1992—). Office: 506 West 4th Ave Albany GA 31701 Office Phone: 229-432-9325. Office Fax: 229-439-4396.*

ERHART, SUE A., lawyer; b. Cin., Oct. 6, 1971; BS, Xavier U., 1993; JD, U. Cin. Coll. Law, 1996. Bar: Ohio 1996, Ind. 1999. Law clerk Hon. Robert L. Miller, Jr., US Dist. Ct. Northern Dist. Ind., Hon. David A. Nelson, US Ct. of Appeals Sixth Cir.; ptnr. Keating, Muething & Klekamp PLL, Cin. Named one of Ohio's Rising Stars, Super Lawyers, 2005, 2006. Fellow: Cin. Acad. Leadership for Lawyers; mem.: Potter Stewart Am. Inn of Ct., Ind. State Bar Assn., Ohio State Bar Assn., FBA, Cin. Bar Assn. Office: Keating Muething &Klekamp PLL One E Fourth St Ste 1400 Cincinnati OH 45202 Office Phone: 513-579-6400. Office Fax: 513-579-6457.

ERIC, BECHHOEFER ROBERT, technologist; b. Singapore, Nov. 17, 1962; s. Arthur Sharfield Bechhoefer and Margot Klare Wilson (Stepfather); m. Susan Leslie Swartz; children: Zachary Eric Bechhoefer, Joshua Theodore Bechhoefer. BS in Biology, U. Mich., Ann Arbor, 1984; MS in Ops. Rsch., Naval Postgraduate Sch., Monterey, Calif., 1992; PhD in Gen. Engring., Kennedy-Western U., LA, 2003. Tactical coord., NFO Patrol Squadron Six, Barbers Pt., Hawaii, 1986—90; tactical action officer USS Dwight D. Eisenhower, Norfolk, 1992—94; signal processing engr. MITRE Corp, Reston, Va., 1999—2000; sr. technologist Goodrich Sensors and Integrated Sys., Vergennes, Vt., 2000—. Tech. adv. com. Ctr. for Rotorcraft Innovation, Media, Pa., 2005—. Maintenance Bridge Sch., Middlebury, Vt., 2002—. Lt. USN, 1984—94. Mem.: Am. Helicopter Soc., IEEE. Achievements include 9 patents for health and usage monitoring; 2 Patents for detection and classification of faults on wire; patents pending for wireless proximity sensing. Avocations: sailing, farming, skiing. Office: Goodrich Sensor and Integrated Sys 100 Panton Rd Vergennes VT 05491 Home Phone: 802-877-4875; Office Phone: 802-877-4875. Office Fax: 802-877-4444; Home Fax: 802-877-4444.

ERICHSEN, PETER CHRISTIAN, foundation administrator; b. Kentfield, Calif., Aug. 4, 1956; s. Hans Skabo and Ruth Elsie (Henderson) E. AB magna cum laude, Harvard U., 1978, JD cum laude, 1981. Bar: Mass. 1981, Pa. 2000. Assoc. Ropes & Gray, Boston, 1981-90, ptnr., 1990-93; dep. asst. atty. gen. U.S. Dept. Justice, Washington, 1993-96; assoc. counsel to Pres. The White House, 1996-97; v.p., gen. counsel U. Pa., U. Pa. Health Sys., 1997—2001; v.p., gen. counsel, sec. J. Paul Getty Trust, 2001—. Bd. govs. Phila. Stock Exch., 1999—; bd. dirs. Music Ctr. Performing Arts Ctr., LA, 2004-; mem. exec. com. LA Appleseed, Appleseed Found., Washington, DC, 2003-, Recording for Blind and Dyslexic, Inc., NJ, 2005-; trustee Samuel Courtauld Trust, London, 2003—; dir. Claymore Western Asset Treas. Inflation Protected Securities Funds, 2004—. Vestryman Trinity Ch., Boston, 1987-91, 92-93; founding dir. Trinity Hospice, Boston, 1988-93. Office: 1200 Getty Ctr Dr Los Angeles CA 90049-1681 E-mail: perichsen@getty.edu.

ERICHSON, ROBERT B., hematologist, oncologist; b. Bklyn., Aug. 23, 1935; s. Harry L. Erichson and Betty Reichlin; m. Elaine Greenberg, June 15, 1958; children: Laura, Howard. BA, Columbia U., 1956; MD, Cornell U., 1960. Adj. attending physician Montefiore Hosp., Bronx, NY, 1965; instr. medicine Albert Einstein Coll. Med., 1966; cons. to US Army Transfusion Service, Europe, 1966-69; clin. asst. prof. medicine Yale Med. Sch., New Haven, 1974-80; clin. prof. medicine NY Med. Coll., NYC, 1981—; clin. prof. medicine Columbia U., 1998—, dir. hematology Stamford Hosp., Conn., 1973-, physician-in-chief, 1972-73, pres. med. staff, 1979-82, bd. trustees, 1979-83; bd. dirs. Ctr. for Continuing Care, 1986—; dir. Bennett Cancer Ctr., 1996—. Author: Hematologic Problems in Surgery, 1970. Contbr. articles to profl. jours. Served to maj. US Army, 1966-69. Fellow ACP; mem. Am. Soc. Clin. Oncology, Am. Soc. Hematology (publs. com. 1980-). Democrat. Jewish. Office: Hematology-Oncology PC 34 Shelburne Rd Stamford CT 06902-3658 Office Phone: 203-325-2695. E-mail: bobbye2@optonline.net.

ERICKSEN, JERALD LAVERNE, retired science engineering educator; b. Portland, Oreg., Dec. 20, 1924; s. Adolph and Ethel Rebecca (Correy) E.; m. Marion Ella Pook, Feb. 24, 1946; children: Lynn Christine, Randolph Peder. BS, U. Wash., 1947; MA, Oreg. State Coll., 1949; PhD, Ind. U., 1951; DSc (hon.), Nat. U. Ireland, 1984, Heriot-Watt U., 1988. Mathematician, solid state physicist U.S. Naval Rsch. Lab., 1951-57; faculty Johns Hopkins U., 1957-83, prof. theoretical mechanics, 1960-83; prof. mechanics and math. U. Minn., Mpls., 1983-90; cons. Florence, Oreg., 1990—. Served with USNR, 1943-46. Recipient Bingham medal, 1968, Timoshenko medal, 1979, Engring. Sci. medal, 1987. Mem. Internat. Liquid Crystal Soc. (hon.), NAE, Soc. Rheology (Panetti-Ferrari prize and Gold medal 2003), Soc. Natural Philosophy, Soc. Interaction Mechanics and Math., Soc. Engring. Sci., Royal Irish Acad. (hon.). Home: 5378 Buckskin Bob Dr Florence OR 97439-8320

ERICKSON, ALAN ERIC, librarian; b. Boston, Feb. 6, 1928; s. Elmer Eric and Ethel M (Winch) Erickson; m. June Andersen, July 14, 1951; children: Kim, John, Martha, William. AB, Middlebury Coll., 1949; MA, Boston U., 1955, PhD, 1960; MS in L.S., Simmons Coll., 1969. Cert. tchr.

Mass. Instr. Boston U., 1954-60; staff scientist Worcester Found. for Exptl. Biology, Shrewsbury, Mass., 1960-66; sci. specialist library Harvard U., Cambridge, Mass., 1966-91; librarian Cabot Sci. Library, 1973-91; assoc. librarian for adminstrn. Harvard Coll., Cambridge, Mass., 1970-72; assoc. librarian Harvard Coll. Sci., 1984-91; ret., 1991. Consult Marine Biol Labs, Wood Hole, Mass., 1981—82; trustee BIOSIS Info Serv, 1988—93, chmn bd dirs, 1993; tchr. ESL. Contbr. articles to profl jours. Trustee David Turner Scholarship Fund, Needham, Mass., 1970—; bd. govs. Greater Boston 32 degree Masonic Learning Ctr. for Children, Inc., 2001—04; trustee Carter Mem Meth Ch, Needham, Mass., 1964—66. Lt col USAFR, 1951—73, ret USAFR. Recipient Woolsey Bible Prize, Middlebury Col, Vt, 1949. Mem.: Harvard U. Retirees Assn. (pres. 1995—97), Needham Ret. Men's Club (pres. 1999, 2000). Avocations: gardening, woodworking, baking.

ERICKSON, ARTHUR CHARLES, architect; b. Vancouver, BC, Can., June 14, 1924; s. Oscar and Myrtle (Chatterson) Erickson. Student, U. BC, Vancouver, 1942-44, LittD (hon.), 1985; BArch, McGill U., Montreal, Que., Can., 1950, DEng (hon.), 1971; LLD (hon.), Simon Fraser U., Vancouver, 1973, U. Man., Winnipeg, Can., 1978, Lethbridge U., 1981; LittD (hon.), Frank Lloyd Wright Sch. Arch., 2001, MArch (hon.), 2001. Asst. prof. U. Oreg., Eugene, 1955-56; assoc. prof. U. B.C., 1956-63; ptnr. Erickson-Massey Architects, Vancouver, 1963-72; prin. Arthur Erickson Architects, Vancouver, 1972-91, Toronto, Ont., Can., 1981-91, Los Angeles, 1981-91, Arthur Erickson Archtl. Corp., Vancouver, 1991—. Prin. works include, Simon Fraser U., Lethbridge U. Alta., Bloedel Bldg., Can. Pavilion Expo '70, Osaka (1st prize nat. competition, Archtl. Inst. Japan award for best pavillion), Robson Sq./Law Cts. (honor award), Mus. Anthropology (honor award), Eppich Residence (honor award), Habitat Pavillion (honor award), Sikh Temple (award of merit), Champlain Heights Cmty. Sch. (award of merit), San Diego Conv. Ctr., Calif. Plz., LA, Fresno City Hall, Can. Embassy, Washington, Roy Thompson Hall, Toronto, Bank of Can., Ottawa, Koerner Libr., Liu Internat. Conf. Ctr., U. BC, Scotibank Dance Ctr., Internat. Glass Mus., Tacoma, 2003. Mem. com. urban devel. Coun. of Can., 1971; bd. dirs. Can. Conf. Arts, 1972; mem. design adv. coun. Portland Devel. Commn., Can. Coun. Urban Rsch.; trustee Inst. Rsch. Pub. Policy; mem. internat. coun. Mus. Modern Art, NYC, 1982—86. Capt. Can. Intelligence Corps., 1945—46. Decorated officer Order of Can., companion; recipient Molson prize, Can. Coun. Arts, 1967, Triangle award, Nat. Soc. Interior Design, Royal Bank Can. award, 1971, Gold medal, Tau Sigma Delta, 1973, Residential Design award, Can. Housing Coun., 1975, August Perret award, Internat. Union Archs. Congress, 1975, Pres. award Excellence, Am. Soc. Landscape Archs., 1979, Chgo. Architecture award, 1984, Gold medal, French Acad. Architecture, 1984. Fellow: AIA (Pan Pacific citation Hawaiian chpt. 1963, Gold medal 1986), Royal Archtl. Inst. Can. (award 1980, Gold medal 1984), Royal Inst. Scottish Archs. (hon.), Royal Inst. Brit. Archs. (hon.), Frank Lloyd Wright Found. (hon.); mem.: Royal Can. Acad. Arts (academician), ARCAB Wash. State Archtl. Assn., Coll. d'arquitectos de España (hon.), Coll. d'architectos de Mex. (hon.), Archtl. Inst. BC, S.F.U. Faculty Club. Office: Arthur Erickson Archtl Corp 303-375 W 5th Ave Vancouver BC Canada V5Y 1J6 Office Phone: 604-737-6091. E-mail: arthurerickson@lynx.bc.ca, arthurerickson@telut.net.

ERICKSON, BARBARA MARTHA, historian, writer; b. Knoxville, Tenn., July 17, 1932; d. William Vivian and Elza Cleo (Nichols) Slatery; m. Eugene William Erickson, Aug. 21, 1954; children: Randall William, Jacqueline Barbara. BA, U. Tenn., 1954. Asst. bridal cons. LeGrands Jewelers, Chattanooga, Tenn., 1952-54; organizer patient file room Erlanger Hosp., Chattanooga, 1954; floral arranger Stevens Florists, Spring Valley, N.Y., 1956-58; sec. treas. Erickson Olds, Inc., Monsey, N.Y., 1968-92, Toyota of Rockland, Monsey, 1992. Floral arranger Schweizers Florist, Pearl River, N.Y., Dykstras Florists, Spring Valley, N.Y. Author: (children's hist. drama) Lure of the Kakiat, 1956, 200 Years of Brick Church History, 1974, What in the World is a Rotary Ann?, 1983, Diary of the West New Hempstead Dutch Reformed Church, 2000, Sergent. Richard M. Masterson, Life of a Tennessee Farmer and Soldier in the Union Army, 2004; editor Rockland Rep. Reporter Rockland County Young Rep. Club, 1950's, 60's, The Tempo of Brick Church West New Hempstead Reformed Ch., Spring Valley, N.Y., 1958-98; contbr. articles to mags., jours., chpt. to book. Historian West New Hempstead Reformed Ch., 1961-2002; co-chmn. bi-centennial Town of Ramapo, N.Y., 1976; sponsor, participant Canine Companions for Independence, 1990—, Ramapo Children of Chernobyl project, 1998-2000. Recipient Gov.'s Newsletter award Dist. Gov. Rotary Internat., 1984, Town Svc., Humanitarian awards Town of Ramapo, 1991; named First Families of Tenn. East Tenn. Hist. Soc., 1995; Paul Harris fellow, 1981, Fred. Ellen Am. Legion Aux. Mem. Valley Garden Club (hon., pres. 1962-65), Valley Star Order of the Ea. Star (matron, pres. 1960), Suffern Woman's Club (mem. exec. bd. 1996-2002), Sons of Norway (Tubfrim chmn. Norrona chpt. 2001—, exec. bd., 1996-2002), Atlantic Coast Old Timers Racing Assn., Rockland County German-Am. Club (sec. 2002-03), NSDAR American Heritage (NY state chmn., Hudson Valley Coun. sec., NSDAR chair 2006-07, NY State womens issues chmn. 2007-), DAR (chpt. scrapbook chmn. 2003, regent Shatemuc, N.Y. chpt., 2005—, pub. rels. chmn. 2003, assoc. Mary Blount chpt.), Pearl River Rotary Club, German-Am. Club, Phi Mu. Mem. Reformed Ch. in Am. Avocations: writing, golf, scuba diving, camping, travel. Home: 179 W Maple Ave Monsey NY 10952-1733

ERICKSON, CAROL JEAN, literature and language professor; b. St. Cloud, Minn., Dec. 25, 1943; d. Clarence Joseph and Lucille Frances Reiter; m. Eric Bruce Erickson, Aug. 13, 1966 (dec. July 2004); children: Holly Lynn, Kirk Adam. BS in English, St. Cloud State U., Minn., 1962—66; MA in Tchg. and Learning, St. Mary's U. Minn., Winona, 1996—98. Lang. arts educator Sch. Dist. 728, Elk River, Minn., 1966—. Speech coach VandenBerge Jr. High, Elk River, Minn., 1966—2000, lang. arts chair, 1968—85, site coun. chair, 2000—03; past sec., faculty rep., and parliamentarian Elk River Edn. Assn., Minn., 1968—78; lang. arts dist. 728 curriculum com. Dist. 728, Elk River, Minn., 2001—03. State v.p. Jaycee Women, Minn., 1975—76; founder, past chair, bd. mem. Rivers of Hope, Monticello, Minn., 1989—2005. Nominee Tchr. of Yr., Elk River Edn. Assn., 1980; recipient Key Woman, Minn. Jaycee Women, 1977, Minn. Tchr. Excellence, Minn. Edn. Assn., 1983. Mem.: NEA, Edn. Minn., Elk River Edn. Assn., Delta Kappa Gamma (past chair, past parliamentarian, current mem.). Roman Catholic. Avocations: gardening, reading, travel. Home Phone: 763-441-2569; Office Phone: 763-241-3400.

ERICKSON, DENNIS, college football coach, former professional football coach; b. Everett, Wash., Mar. 24, 1947; m. Marilyn Erickson; children: Bryce, Ryan. BS Phys. Educ., Montana State U. Grad. asst. coach Montana State U. Bobcats, 1969, backfield coach, 1971-73; grad. asst. coach Washington State U. Cougars, 1970; head football coach Billings Central H.S., Billings, Mont., 1970; offensive coord., head football coach U. Idaho Vandals, 1974-75, 1982-85; offensive coord. Fresno State U. Bulldogs, 1976-78, San Jose State U. Spartans, 1979-81; head football coach U. Wyoming Cowboys, 1986, Washington State U. Cougars, 1987-88, U. Miami Hurricanes, 1989-95, Seattle Seahawks, 1995-98, Oreg. State U. Beavers, 1999—2003, S.F. 49ers, 2003—04, U. Idaho Vandals, 2006, Ariz State U. Sun Devils, Tempe, 2007—. won Nat. Championship, 1989, 1991. Office: Ariz State U 1200 S Forest Ave Tempe AZ 85281*

ERICKSON, EDWARD LEONARD, biotechnologist, consultant; s. Leonard Gerald and Eleanore Antoinette E.; m. Helen Leonora Masten, Dec. 29, 1979. BS in Math., Ill. Inst. Tech., 1968, MS in Math., 1970; MBA in Gen. Mgmt., Harvard U., 1980. Mktg. rep. IBM, Miami, Fla., 1975-76; sr. systems engr. Advanced Tech., Inc., McLean, Va., 1976-78; cons. Bain & Co., Boston, 1979-80; sr. assoc. Resource Planning Assocs., Washington, 1980-82; dir. RPA Mgmt. Cons., London, 1982-83; dir. corp. devel. Amersham Internat. plc., Little Chalfont, Eng., 1983-86, gen. mgr. internat. ops., 1986-88; v.p. fin. ops. The Ares-Serono Group, Boston, 1988-90; pres. Serono-Baker Diagnostics (The Ares-Serono Group), Allentown, Pa., 1990-91; pres., CEO, dir. Cholestech Corp., Hayward, Calif., 1991-93, DepoTech Corp., La Jolla, Calif., 1993-98; chmn. Immunicon Corp., 1998—2007. Venture ptnr. University City Sci. Ctr.; bd. dirs. BioTrove, Inc., Barrier Therapeutics, StageMark, Inc., Immunotope Inc., Lazarus Therapeutics, Inc. Lt. USN, 1970—75. John L. Loeb fellow Harvard U., 1980, George F. Baker scholar, 1980, NASA fellow, 1968-70. Mem. AAAS, Am. Assn. Pharm. Scientists. Republican. Avocations: tennis, skiing. Office Phone: 215-297-8493. Personal E-mail: elerickson@comcast.net.

ERICKSON, GERALD MEYER, classical studies educator; b. Amery, Wis., Sept. 23, 1927; s. Oscar Meyer and Ellen Claire (Hanson) E.; m. Loretta Irene Eder, Feb. 11, 1951; children: Rachel, Viki, Kari BS, U. Minn., 1954, MA, 1956, PhD, 1968. Cert. secondary sch. tchr., Minn. Tchr. Edina-Morningside Pub. Sch., Minn., 1956-65, 66-67; vis. lectr. U. Minn., Mpls., 1965-66, asst. prof., 1968-71, assoc. prof., 1971-83, prof. classical studies, 1983-95, prof. emeritus, 1995—. Exchange prof. Moscow State U., 1980, 86; vis. prof. U. Ill., 1967, 68, Coll. of William and Mary, 1984; bd. regents La. Univ. System, 1981, chmn. evaluation team for classics programs; reader Coll. Bds. Advanced Placement Program, 1975-77, chief reader, 1978-81; cons., lectr. in field Assoc. editor, mem. editorial staff Nature, Society and Thought, 1987—; author, lectr. various TV and radio courses Served with U.S. Mcht. Marine, 1945-46, U.S. Army, 1946-47, PTO; served to capt. USAF, 1951-53 NEH grantee, 1977-79; recipient award Horace T. Morse Amoco Found., 1984 Mem. Minn. Classical Conf. (pres. 1971-74), Minn. Humanities Conf. (pres. 1974-75), Classical Assn. Midwest/South (Ovatio award 1971). Avocations: bicycling, short-wave radio. Home: 121 E 51st St Minneapolis MN 55419-2605 E-mail: erick002@umn.edu.

ERICKSON, HOWARD HUGH, veterinarian, physiology educator; b. Wahoo, Nebr., Mar. 16, 1936; s. Conrad and Laurene (Swanson) E.; m. Ann E. Nicolay, June 6, 1959; children: James, David. BS, DVM, Kans. State U., 1959; PhD, Iowa State U., 1966. Commd. 1st lt. U.S. Air Force, 1959, advanced through grades to col., 1979; veterinarian England, 1960-63; vet. scientist Sch. Aerospace Medicine, Brooks AFB, Tex., 1966-75, Air War Coll., Maxwell AFB, Ala., 1975—76; dir. rsch. and devel. aerospace med. divsn. Brooks AFB, 1976—81; prof. physiology Kans. State U., Manhattan, 1981—, acting head dept. anatomy and physiology, 1989—90, Roy W. Upham prof. vet. medicine, 2001—04. Sci. adv. bd. Morris Animal Found., Englewood, Colo., 1990-93; cons. Tex. Higher Edn. Coordination Bd., Austin, 1990-91; clin. asst. prof. U. Tex. Health Sci. Ctr., San Antonio, 1972-81; vis. mem. grad. faculty Tex. A&M U., College Station, 1967-81; affiliate prof. Colo. State U., Fort Collins, 1970-75. Editor: Animal Pain, 1983; contbr. articles to profl. jours. Founding mem. Kans. State U. Golf Course Rsch. and Mgmt. Found.; trustee Meadowlark Hills Cmty. Found., 1998—2007. Recipient Alumni Achievement award Midland Luth. Coll., Fremont, Nebr., 1977, Merck award for Creativity, 1993, Bayer Excellence in Equine Rsch. award Am. Vet. Med. Assn. Coun. on Rsch., 2000, E.R. Frank award Kans. State U., 2006, Animal Health Tchg. Excellence award IVX, 2006. Fellow AAAS, Royal Soc. Health, Aerospace Med. Assn. (assoc.); mem. Am. Vet. Med. Assn. (chmn. coun. on rsch. 1984), Am. Physiol. Soc., Optimists Club. Republican. Lutheran. Home: 1700 Kings Rd Manhattan KS 66503-7550 Office: Kans State U Coll Vet Medicine Dept Anatomy and Physiology Manhattan KS 66506 Business E-Mail: erickson@vet.ksu.edu.

ERICKSON, JACKIE MAHI, lawyer, electric power industry executive; BFA, U. Denver, 1962; JD, U. Hawaii, 1977. Bar: Hawaii 1977. Law clk. Supreme Ct. of Hawaii; dept. atty. gen. State of Hawaii; corp. counsel Hawaiian Electric Co., Inc., Honolulu, 1981—91, v.p., gen. counsel, 1992—95, v.p. govt. rels., gen. counsel, 1995—98, v.p., gen. counsel, 1998—. Office: Hawaiian Electric Co PO Box 2750 Honolulu HI 96840-0001 Office Phone: 808-543-7300. E-mail: jackie.erickson@heco.com.

ERICKSON, MITCHELL DRAKE, chemist, environmental scientist; b. Chgo., Aug. 31, 1950; s. Charles O. and Jane (Drake) E.; m. Colleen M. Erickson, June 12, 1976; children: Adam M., Carl J., Brendan C. AB in Chemistry, Grinnell Coll., 1972; PhD in Analytical Chemistry, U. Iowa, 1976. Chemist Research Triangle Inst., Research Triangle Park, NC, 1976-81; prin. chemist Midwest Rsch. Inst., Kansas City, Mo., 1981-87; group leader Argonne (Ill.) Nat. Lab., 1987-89, 93-97, assoc. dir. R & D program office, 1989-93; lab. dir. Environ. Measurements Lab. U.S. Dept. Energy, NYC, 1997—. Sci. adv. com., Hazardous Substance Rsch. Ctr. for Fed. Regions 7 and 8, Kans. State U., Manhattan, 1991—, chmn., 1994-98. Author: Analytical Chemistry of PCBs, 1986, 2d edit., 1997, Remediation of PCB Spills, 1993; contbr. articles to profl. jours. Recipient R&D Mag. 100 award, 1996, Fed. Lab. Consortium award for excellence in tech. transfer, 1997. Mem. Am. Chem. Soc., Soc. Applied Spectroscopy, Sigma Xi. Office: US Dept Homeland Security Environmental Measurements Lab 5th Fl 201 Varick St New York NY 10014-7447 Fax: 212-620-3651. E-mail: mitchell.erickson@dhs.gov.

ERICKSON, PHYLLIS TRAVER, marketing executive; b. NYC, Mar. 31, 1952; d. Harold August and Barbara Lucille (Seifert) T.; m. C. Carl Muscari, June 30, 1979 (div. Nov. 1982); m. Roger C. Erickson, July 8, 1995. BA, Northwestern U., 1974; MBA, Harvard U., 1978. Dir. rsch. Staub, Warmbold and Assocs., NYC, 1974-75; dir. rsch., assoc. cons. Coopers and Lybrand, NYC, 1975-76; asst. product mgr. Nestle Food Corp., White Plains, N.Y., 1978-79, product mgr., mktg. mgr., 1979-83, bus. dir. Purchase, N.Y., 1983-90; pres. PT Ventures, 1990—, Barrier Systems, Inc., Greenwich, Conn., 1991-92; v.p. mktg. Homeview, Inc., Needham, Mass., 1992-94, Media One, Boston, 1995-99. Pres. Erickson Cons., 1999—. Contbr. articles to mktg. jours. Named to Acad. Women Achievers YWCA. Mem. Harvard U. Bus. Sch. Club. Republican. Episcopalian. Home and Office: 133 Washington St Duxbury MA 02332-4520 E-mail: perickson@adelphia.net.

ERICKSON, RANDALL J., lawyer; b. 1960; Atty. securities practice group Godfrey & Kahn, 1990—2002; sr. v.p., gen. counsel, corp. sec. Marshall & Ilsley Corp., 2002—. Mem. bd. Marshall & Ilsley Bank FSB, Marshall & Ilsley Community Devel. Corp., SWB Holdings, Inc., Marshall & Ilsley Capital Markets Group, Marshall & Ilsley Ventures. Mem. bd. dirs. Wis. Banking Assn. Office: Marshall & Ilsley Corp 770 N Water St Milwaukee WI 53202

ERICKSON, RAY CHARLES, retired wildlife biologist; b. St. Peter, Minn., Jan. 30, 1918; s. Isaac and Martha Ernestina (Ziebarth) Erickson; m. Patricia Katherine Miles, Jan. 8, 1950 (div. Nov. 8, 1951); 1 child, Susan Eileen; m. Helen Josephine Haworth, Sept. 10, 1953 (dec. Nov. 16, 1996); children: Joanne Louise, David Wayne, Thomas Alan; m. Grace Marjorie Hayes, May 2, 2001. Student, George Washington U., 1939—40; AB, Gustavus Adolphus Coll., St. Peter, Minn., 1941; MS, Iowa State U., Ames, 1942, PhD, 1948. Wildlife biologist U.S. Fish and Wildlife Svc., Burns, Oreg., 1948—57, rsch. staff specialist divsn. wildlife rsch. Washington, 1957—65, supr. endangered wildlife rsch. program Laurel, Md., 1965—80; ret., 1980. Mem., scientist Oreg. Natural Heritage Adv. Coun., Salem, 1990—2002. Contbr. articles to profl. publs. Officer boat divsn. USN, 1943—46, PTO. Named Disting. Alumnus, Gustavus Adolphus Coll., 1991; recipient Disting. Svc. award, U.S. Dept. of Interior, 1968, Spl. Conservation award, Nat. Wildlife Fedn., 1975, Wildlife Conservation award, Zool. Soc. San Diego, 1979. Mem.: Whooping Crane Conservation Assn. (life), Washington Biologists' Field Club (pres. 1967—70). Lutheran. Achievements include federal refuge management studies of the role of grazing and other agricultural practices in wetland wildlife production; conceiving and directing endangered species research involving coordinated laboratory and ecological investigations; captive propagation to preserve and restore viable wild populations. Avocations: nature watching, fishing, photography, travel. Home: 3010 Twin Oak Pl NW Salem OR 97304

ERICKSON, RICHARD AMES, physicist, emeritus educator; b. Bryant, SD, Sept. 12, 1923; s. Ray and Mabel Gabriella (Arneson) E.; m. Frances Irene Boyd, June 13, 1943; children: Donna Mae, Jeanne Marie (Mrs. Paul Mahoney), David Ray, Kristine Ann (Mrs. Scott Stewart). B.Sc., S.D. Sch. Mines and Tech., 1944; PhD, Tex. A. and M. U., 1952. Predoctoral fellow Oak Ridge Inst. Nuclear Studies, 1949-51; asst. prof. physics U. Tenn., 1951-54; asst. prof. Ohio State U., 1954-61, assoc. prof., 1961-74, prof., 1974-79, prof. emeritus, 1979—; prof. of physics Ind. U. (ITM/MUCIA), Shah Alam, Malaysia, 1987-89; sec. faculty Ohio State U., 1975-77. Cons. Lockheed Research Lab., Palo Alto, Calif., 1964, AID, India, 1965; Mem. Univ. Area Commn., Columbus, Ohio, 1973-74 Contbg. author: Methods of Experimental Physics, vol. 3, 1961; Contbr. articles to profl. jours. Served with USNR, 1944-46. Home: 325 W Grant St Spearfish SD 57783-2334 Personal E-mail: fizit43@cox.net.

ERICKSON, ROBERT PORTER, genetics researcher, educator, clinician; b. Portland, Oreg., June 27, 1939; s. Harold M. and Marjorie S. (Porter) Erickson; m. Sandra De'Ath, June 20, 1964; children: Andrew Ian, Colin De'Ath, Tanya Nadene, Tracy Lynn, Michelle Lee, Christof Phillipe. BA, Reed Coll., Portland, 1960; MD, Stanford U., Calif., 1965. Diplomate Am. Bd. Pediat., Am. Coll. Med. Genetics. Asst. prof. pediatrics U. Calif.-San Francisco Med. Sch., 1970-75; vis. scientist Institut Pasteur, Paris, 1975-76; assoc. prof. human genetics and pediat. U. Mich., Ann Arbor, 1976-80, prof., 1980-90, dir. divsn. pediat. genetics, 1985-90. Vis. scientist Imperial Cancer Rsch. Fund, London, 1983-84; Holsclaw Family prof. human genetics and inherited diseases dept. pediat. U. Ariz., 1990—; vis fellow Hughes Hall, U. Cambridge, 1996-97. Mem. editl. bd. Jour. Reproductive Immunology, 1978-89, Dictionary of Lab. Tech., 1983, Molecular Reprodn. and Devel., 1989-99, Antisense R&D, 1992-2005, Jour. Rare Diseases, 1995-98, Jour. Applied Genetics, 2000—, Reviews in Mutation Rsch., 2001—; contbr. over 300 articles to sci. jours. and books. With USPHS, 1967-69. Guggenheim fellow, Paris, 1975, Eleanor Roosevelt fellow, London, 1983; Fogarty Sr. Internat. fellow, 1996, Burroughs Wellcome travel fellow, 1996; Fulbright grantee, London, 1983, NIH grantee, 1971—. Mem. Am. Soc. Human Genetics, Soc. Pediat. Rsch., Am. Pediat. Soc. Avocations: hiking, enology. Home: 5200 N Camino Real Tucson AZ 85718-5029 Office Phone: 520-626-5483. Business E-Mail: erickson@peds.arizona.edu.

ERICKSON, RUTH ALICE, poet, artist; b. Green Bay, Wis., Apr. 9, 1933; d. Walter Byron and Verona Ann (Giese) Kottke; m. Clyde Gordan Hansen, Oct. 15, 1949 (dec. Dec. 1965); children: Gary Hansen, Gloria Hansen, Debora Hansen, Dale Hansen; m. Norton M. Erickson, July 31, 1977. Nursing asst., Nursing Acad. Green Bay, 1966. Choir dir. St. John's Luth. Ch., Green Bay, 1954—66; nurse Nursing Home, Hosp., DePere, Wis., 1966—79; poet Green Bay, 2001—. Author: Spiritual Lyrics and Poems, 2001, Hidden Haven, 2003, (chapbook) Its for the Berries, 2004, A Christmas Journey in Poetry, 2004, (poetry) A Kaleidoscope of Poetry, 2005. Mem. Leadership Coun. on Human Rights. Recipient Merit Silver Bowl award, Internat. Soc. Poets, 2002, Two Bronze Medallions, 2003, Silver Cup award, 2003. Home: 2139 Packerland Dr Green Bay WI 54304 Personal E-mail: Ruthae92@msn.com.

ERICKSON, SUE ALICE, health educator, consultant, nurse; b. Sailor Springs, Ill., Feb. 3, 1938; d. Charles Ashby and Myra Estella (McPherson) Inskeep; m. Dale Gilbert Erickson, Sept. 25, 1959; children: Erin Erickson Fonken, Kelly, Sean B. Diploma in Profl. Nursing, St. Luke's Hosp., 1959; BA, Stephens Coll., 1981; MS in Cmty. Health Edn., U. N.Mex., 1987, PhD in Cmty. Health Edn., 1992. RN; cert. health edn. specialist. Nurse, health educator Sandia Nat. Labs., Albuquerque, 1985-88; cons. Cuidandos Los Ninos, Albuquerque, 1988-90; cons., bd. dirs., speaker Pioneer Bible Translators, Duncanville, Tex., 1983—95, vice chmn. bd. dirs., 1993—94; owner SAE Health Comms., LLC, 1993—. Asst. matron, health educator Chidamoyo Christian Hosp., Karoi, Rhodesia, 1968-70, vol. nurse tchr., Zimbabwe, 1991; instr. Pioneer Missions Inst., 1982-94; vis. lectr. dept. medicine U. Zimbabwe, 1995, 97-2000, 01, 04; adj. health instr. Equip, Inc., 1994-04; adj. prof. health edn. U. N.Mex., 2001; adj. prof. bioethics Lincoln Christian Sem., Ill., 1996, 2001, 03, 07, Hope Internat. U., Fullerton, Calif., 1997; bd. dirs. Best Choice Ednl. Svc., 2001-06; mem. adv. coun. abstinence edn. State N.Mex., 2004—; adv. coun. Carenet, Inc., Albuquerque, N.Mex., 2003—; pres. TTL Care Assessment and Edn., LLC, 2006—; instr. primary health care Pioneer Bible Translators, Ducanville, Tex. 2005—; nurse tng. cons., provider Aegin Place Home Care, Footprints Homecare, Albuquerque 2005—; mem. bd. N.Mex. Family Coun., 2006—. Author: (course for HS students/pregnancy crisis ctrs.) After Abstinence, 2005. Vol. nurse educator New Heart, Inc., Albuquerque, 1975-80; mem. bd. dirs. Covenant Christian Fellowship, Albuquerque, 1984-88; dir. Christian Edn., Hts. Christian Ch., 1992-96; adv. Boy Scouts Am., 1978-86; organize dir. Fibromyalgia Support Group Albuquerque, 1989-95. St. Luke's Hosp. Sch. Nursing scholar, 1959; named Disting. Alumnus, Mt. Vernon Township H.S., 2006. Mem. ACA, AAHPERD, Christian Med. and Dental Assn., N.Mex. Abstinence Edn. Coalition, Nat. Abstinence Edn. Assn., Health Vols. Overseas, Nat. Abstinence Edn. Assn. Republican. Avocations: backpacking, running, biking, skiing, music. Home: 2904 Calle Grande NW Albuquerque NM 87104-3146 Office Phone: 505-344-3570. Personal E-mail: saede2@cs.com.

ERICKSON, W(ALTER) BRUCE, business and economics educator, entrepreneur; b. Chgo., Mar. 4, 1938; s. Clifford Eric and Mildred B. (Brinkmeier) E. BA, Mich. State U., 1959, MA, 1960, PhD in Econs., 1965. Rsch. assoc. subcom. on antitrust and monopoly U.S. Senate, 1960-61; asst. prof. econs. Bowling Green (Ohio) U., 1964-66; asst. prof. bus. and govt. Coll. Bus. Adminstrn., U. Minn., Mpls., 1966-70, assoc. prof., 1971-75, prof. dept. mgmt., 1975—, prof., chmn. dept. mgmt., 1977-80, co-chmn., then chmn., 1988-92. Bd. dirs. various bus., non-profit and venture capital orgns.; cons. rock salt antitrust cases for atty. gens. Mich., cons. rock salt antitrust cases for atty. gens. Calif., Ill., Wis., Minn.; cons. U.S. Justice Dept. Author: An Introduction to Contemporary Business, 4th edit., 1985, Government and Business, 1980, 2d edit., 1984, International Business, 1998; co-author: International Business, 1998; bd. editors Antitrust Law and Econs. Rev., Jour. Indsl. Orgn.; contbr. articles to profl. jours. Bd. dirs. Found. for Constl. Edn. and the Citizens League, 1991-92; mem. ethics com. Ebenezer System, Minn. Mem. Am. Econ. Assn., Royal Econ. Soc. Office: Carlson Sch Mgmt 321 19th Ave S Minneapolis MN 55455-0438

ERICKSON, WILLIAM HURT, retired state supreme court justice; b. Denver, May 11, 1924; s. Arthur Xavier and Virginia (Hurt) E.; m. Doris Rogers, Dec. 24, 1953; children: Barbara Ann, Virginia Lee, Stephen Arthur, William Taylor. Degree in petroleum engring., Colo. Sch. Mines, 1947; student, U. Mich., 1949; LLB, U. Va., 1950; PhD in Engring. (hon.), Colo. Sch. of Mines, 2002. Bar: Colo. 1951. Pvt. practice, Denver; state supreme ct. justice Colo. Supreme Ct., 1971-96, state supreme ct. chief justice, 1983-86; faculty NYU Appellate Judges Sch., 1972-85. Mem. exec. Commn. on Accreditation of Law Enforcement Agys., 1980-83; chmn. Pres.'s Nat. Commn. for Rev. of Fed. and State Laws Relating to

Wiretapping and Electronic Surveillance, 1976. Chmn. Erickson Commn., 1997, Limitations on use Deadly Force by Police; chmn. gov.'s Columbine Rev. Commn., 1999-2001. With USAAF, 1943. Recipient Disting. Achievement medal Colo. Sch. Mines, 1990. Fellow Internat. Acad. Trial Lawyers (former sec.), Am. Coll. Trial Lawyers (state chmn. 1970), Am. Bar Found. (chmn. 1985), Internat. Soc. Barristers (pres. 1971); mem. ABA, (bd. govs. 1975-79, former chmn. com. on standards criminal justice, former chmn. coun. criminal law sect., former chmn. com. to implement standards criminal justice, mem. long-range planning com., action com. to reduce ct. cost and delay), Colo. Bar Assn. (award of merit 1989), Denver Bar Assn. (past pres., trustee), Am. Law Inst. (coun. 1973—), Practising Law Inst. (nat. adv. coun., bd. govs. Colo.), Freedoms Found. at Valley Forge (nat. coun. trustees, 1986—), Order of Coif, Scribes (pres. 1978). Home: 10 Martin Ln Englewood CO 80113-4821 Personal E-mail: bnderickson@yahoo.com.

ERICSON, BRUCE ALAN, lawyer; b. Buffalo, Feb. 28, 1952; s. Carl H. and Jean (Herman) E.; m. Elizabeth Whitney Burton, Feb. 6, 1988; children: John Cotton, Whitney Burton. AB, U. Pa., 1974; JD, Harvard U., 1977. Bar: Calif. 1977, U.S. Dist. Ct. (no. dist.) Calif, 1977, U.S. Dist. Ct. (ea. dist. and so. dist.) Calif. 1988, U.S. Dist. Ct. Ariz. 1992, U.S. Ct. Appeals (9th cir.) 1981, U.S. Ct. Appeals (11th cir.), 1991, U.S. Ct. Appeals (D.C. cir.) 1994, U.S. Supreme Ct. 1982. Assoc. Pillsbury, Madison & Sutro, San Francisco, 1977-84, ptnr., 1985—2001, Pillsbury Winthrop LLP, San Francisco, 2001—05; ptnr., chmn. Securities Litigation practice, head litig. sect. Pillsbury Winthrop Shaw Pittman, San Francisco, 2005—. Judge pro tem. San Francisco Mcpl. Ct., 1984—. Contbr. articles to profl. jours. Named No. Calif. Super Lawyer, San Francisco mag., 2004, 2006. Mem. ABA, San Francisco Bar Assn., Phi Beta Kappa. Clubs: Olympic (San Francisco). Republican. Avocation: skiing. Office: Pillsbury Winthrop Shaw Pittman 50 Fremont St San Francisco CA 94105 Office Phone: 415-983-1560. Office Fax: 415-983-1200. Business E-Mail: bruce.ericson@pillsburylaw.com.

ERICSON, DAVID FRANK, political scientist, educator; b. Chgo., June 18, 1950; s. Arthur Edward Ericson and Ruth Irene Kessel. BA in Polit. Sci., Wayne State U., 1972; MA in Polit. Sci., U. Mich., 1973, MA in Journalism, 1976; PhD in Polit. Sci., U. Chgo., 1987. Journalist Jackson (Mich.) Citizen-Patriot, 1977, Detroit News, 1978-80; instr. Oberlin (Ohio) Coll., 1986-87; prof. Wichita (Kans.) State U., 1992—. Vis. prof. Washington U., St. Louis, 1987—89, U. Chgo., 1990—91; rsch. fellow Princeton U., James Madison Ctr. Study Am. Ideals and Instns., 2007—. Author: (book) The Shaping of American Liberalism: The Debates Over Ratification, Nullification, and Slavery, 1993, The Debate Over Slavery: Antislavery and Proslavery Liberalism in Antebellum America, 2001; editor: The Liberal Tradition in American Politics: Reassessing the Legacy of Amercian Liberalism, 1999; contbr. articles to profl. jours. Grantee Summer Rsch., NEH, 1994, James Madison Ctr. Study of Am. Instns. and Ideals Princeton U., 2007—; Postdoctoral fellow, John M. Olin Ctr. Study History Polit. Culture, U. Chgo., 1989—90. Mem.: Social Sci. History Assn., Midwest Polit. Sci. Assn., Am. Polit. Sci. Assn., Phi Beta Kappa, Pi Sigma Alpha. Avocations: tennis, hiking. Home: 105 Melrose Ave Albany NY 12203 Personal E-mail: david.ericson@wichita.edu. Business E-Mail: dericson1@uamail.albany.edu.

ERICSON, JON MEYER, academic administrator, language educator; b. Three Forks, Mont., Aug. 1, 1928; s. George Edward and Olga Young (Meyer) E.; m. Amy Knutson, Aug. 19, 1951; children: Jon, Beth, Joel, Ingrid. BA, Pacific Luth. Coll., 1952; MA, Stanford U., 1953, PhD, 1961. Instr. argumentation, pub. speaking, rhetorical theory and criticism Tex. Luth. Coll., Seguin, 1953-54; asst. prof. Pacific Luth. Coll., Tacoma, 1954-57; instr., dir. forensics Stanford (Calif.) U., 1959-61, asst. prof., 1961-64; from assoc. prof. to prof., dept. head Cen. Wash. State U., Ellensburg, 1964-70, prof. dept. speech communication, 1970—88; dean sch. liberal arts Calif. Poly. State U., San Luis Obispo, 1988—95, dept. dir. London Study Program, 1984-96. Co-author: The Debater's Guide, 1961; contbg. author: Demosthenes on the Crown, 1967, Public Speaking as Dialogue, 1970; contbr. articles to profl. jours. and books Pres. Pacific Forensic League, 1961-62, No. Calif. Forensic Assn., 1962-63; mem., trustee Pacific Luth. Theol. Sem., Berkeley, 1961-64. Served with USN, 1946-48. Danforth tchr., 1957; Univ. Honors scholarship Stanford U., 1957-61. Lutheran. Avocations: tennis, gardening. Home: 741 Pasatiempo Dr San Luis Obispo CA 93405-1033

ERICSON, ROBERT WALTER, lawyer; b. Highland Park, Ill., June 24, 1948; BA, Johns Hopkins U., 1970, MA, 1971; JD, U. Va., 1976. Bar: Ill. 1976, N.Y. 1992. Ptnr. Winston & Strawn, NYC. Mem.: N.Y. State Bar Assn. Office: Winston & Strawn 200 Park Ave 42nd Fl New York NY 10166-4401 Home Phone: 203-966-4091; Office Phone: 212-294-6741. Business E-Mail: rericson@winston.com.

ERICSON, ROGER DELWIN, lawyer, forest resource company executive; b. Moline, Ill, Dec. 21, 1934; s. Carl D. and Linnea E. (Challman) E.; m. Norma F. Brown, Aug. 1, 1957; children: Catherine Lynn, David. AB, JD, Stetson U., DeLand, Fla., 1958; MBA, U. Chgo., 1971. Bar: Fla. 1958, Ill. 1959, Ind. 1974. Atty. Brunswick Corp., Skokie, Ill., 1959-62; asst. sec., asst. gen. counsel Chemetron Corp., Chgo., 1962-73; asst. v.p. Inland Container Corp., Indpls., 1973-75, v.p., gen. counsel, sec., 1975-83, Temple-Inland, Inc., 1983-94, of counsel, 1994—. V.p., sec. bd. dirs. Inland Container Corp.; dir., pres., co-CEO Kraft Land Svcs., Inc., Atlanta, 1978-88; bd. dirs., v.p. Guaranty Holdings Inc., Dallas; v.p. Temple-Inland Fin. Svcs., Inc., Austin, 1990-94; bd. dirs. Temple-Inland Forest Products, Temple-Inland Real Estate Investment, Inc., Temple-Inland Realty Inc. Trustee Chgo. Homes for Children, 1971-74; mem. alumni coun. U. Chgo., 1972-76; mem. Palatine Twp. Youth Commn., 1969-72; sect. chmn. Chgo. Heart Assn., 1972, 73; alumni bd. dirs. Stetson U.; bd. dirs. Temple-Inland Found; past mem. Safe and Drug-Free Comm. Collier County Sch. Bd. Mem. ABA, Am. Arbitration Assn. (past nat. panel comml. arbitrators), Am. Soc. Corp. Secs., Am. Forest Products Assn. (past mem. govt. affairs com. and legal com.), Am. Corp. Counsel Assn., Ind. Bar Assn., Fla. Bar Assn., Chgo. Bar Assn., Indpls. Bar Assn. (chmn. corp. counsel sect., mem. profl. responsibility com. 1982), Collier County Bar Assn., Indpls. C. of C. (govt. affairs com.), Plum Grove Club (pres. 1967), The Floridian Club, Omicron Delta Kappa, Phi Delta Phi. Office: PO Box 110218 Naples FL 34108-0104 *Concentrate on the desired final result of any activity. Never forget your family, co-workers, friends.*

ERICSSON, APRILLE JOY, aerospace engineer; b. Bklyn. BS in Aeronautical/Astronautical Engring, MIT; MSEE, Howard U., PhD in Mech. Engring. Aerospace Option; DSc (hon.), Medger Evers Coll., Bklyn., NY, 2001. Aerospace engr. in Guidance Navigation and Control Ctr. NASA Goddard Space Flight Ctr., Greenbelt, Md. Adj. prof. math. dept. Bowie State U.; adj. prof. mech. engring. dept. Howard U. Featured on NBC Nightly News, Women to Watch, iVillage.com as a Women Who Rules, ScienceMaster.com, thetechmag.com, featured in Essence Mag., You Done Good Girl, Yahoo Internet Life Mag., America Uses the Net, Howard U. Mag., Emerging Markets Mag., Jet, Biography Journal, Caribbean Life Mag., Rolling Out Mag. Recipient Top 50 Minority Women in Sci. and Engring. Nat. Tech. Assn., 1996, 97, Women in Sci. and Engring. award, 1998, Spl. Recognition award Black Engrs. award Conf., 1998, Cmty. Svc. award Fed. Exec. Bur. Md., 1999, Fed. Career award, Fed. Exec. Md., 1999, Centurion of Tech. award, Women of Color Tech. award conf., 1999, Giant in Sci. award Quality Edn. for Minorities Network, 2000, Howard U. Coll. Engring., Arch. & Computer Sci. Alumni Excellence award, 2002. Mem. NASA Goddard Space Flight Ctr. Spkrs. Bur., Women of NASA. first African American female to receive a Ph.D. in Mechanical Engineering from Howard University; the first American to receive a Ph.D. in Mechanical Engineering, the Aerospace option from Howard University; and the first African American female to receive a Ph.D. in Engineering at NASA Goddard Space Flight Center. Office: NASA Code 556 Inst Sys Branch Goddard Space Flight Ctr Greenbelt MD 20771-0001*

ERICSSON, SALLY CLAIRE, not-for-profit consultant; b. Madison, Wis., Jan. 16, 1953; d. William H. and JoAnn (Finnell) Ericsson; m. Thomas A. Garwin, Oct. 7, 1979; children: Rachel Garwin, Benjamin Garwin. B in Urban and Regional Planning, U. Ill., 1976; M in Pub. Policy, Harvard U., 1981. Legis. analyst Dem. Steering and Policy Com, Washington, 1982-87; adminstr. asst. Rep. Sam Geidenson U.S. Ho. Reps., Washington, 1987-89; legis. asst. to Sen. John F. Kerry U.S. Senate, Washington, 1989-90; asst. to pres. for policy and rsch. Svc. Employees Internat. Union, Washington, 1990-93; assoc. under sec. for econ. affairs U.S. Dept. Commerce, Washington, 1993-96, dep. chief of staff, 1996-97; assoc. dir. natural resources Coun. Environ. Quality, Exec. Office of the Pres., 1997-99; dir. outreach Pew Ctr. Global Climate Change, Arlington, Va., 1999—2005; cons., 2005—. Home: 1805 Monroe St NW Washington DC 20010-1014

ERIKSEN, BARBARA ANN, writer, researcher; b. Mason City, Iowa, Sept. 13, 1931; d. Arthur Charles Beckel and Katherine Irma Konvalinka; m. Charles Walter Eriksen, Apr. 3, 1971; 1 stepchild, Kathy; m. Wesley Clemence Becker (div.); children: Jill, Jeffrey, Linda, James. BA, U. Ill., 1970, MA, 1972. Rsch. asst. dept. psychology U. Ill., Champaign-Urbana, 1968—72, rsch. assoc. dept. psychology, 1972—87; author Harlequin Romances, 1988—93. Editor: Perception and Psychophysics, 1975—87; author: The Practical Princess, 1980, 15 Romance Novels, 1985—93 (named Best Harlequin Romance for Cinderella Wife, Romantic Times Mag., 86); contbr. articles to profl. jours. Dir. mktg. Oakland (Ill.) Econ. Devel. Found., 1980. Recipient ranked 9th nationally, Jr. Ladies US Lawn Tennis Assn., 1949. Mem.: Ladies Aux. Oakland VFW, United Meth. Women, Oakland Lions Club. Avocations: gardening, tennis, cooking, painting, birdwatching. Home: 22485 State Hwy 133 Oakland IL 61943-6812 Personal E-mail: erikbarb@consolidated.net.

ERIKSEN, CHARLES WALTER, psychologist, educator; b. Omaha, Feb. 4, 1923; s. Charles Hans and Luella (Carlson) E.; m. Garnita Tharp, July 22, 1945 (div. Jan. 1971); children: Michael John, Kathy Ann; m. Barbara Becker, Apr. 1971. BA summa cum laude, U. Omaha, 1943; PhD, Stanford, 1950. Asst. prof. Johns Hopkins U., Balt., 1949-53, research scientist, 1954-55; lectr. Harvard U., Cambridge, Mass., 1953-54; mem. faculty U. Ill., Urbana, 1956—, prof., 1959-93, prof. emeritus, 1993—. Rsch. cons. VA, 1960-80; mem. psycho-biology panel NSF, 1963; mem. exptl. psychology study sect. NIH, 1962-66, 66-70; Pillsbury Meml. lectr. Cornell U., 1966; keynote address 1st Internat. Congress on Visual Search, U. Durham, U.K., 1988, European Congress for Cognitive Psychology, Elsinore, Denmark, 1993; invited lectr. Max Plank Inst., Munich, 1993, Universidad Autonoma de Madrid, 1993, U. of Salamanca, Spain, 1993. Author: Behavior and Awareness, 1962; editor Am. Jour. Psychology, 1968; prin. editor Perception and Psychophysics, 1971-93; cons. editor Jour. Exptl. Psychology, 1965-71, Jour. Gerontology, 1980—; contbr. articles to profl. jours. Recipient Stratton award Am. Psychopath. Assn., 1964, NIMH Research Career award, 1964 Fellow AAAS; mem. Am. Psychol. Soc., Psychonomic Soc., Soc. Exptl. Psychologists, Midwestern Psychol. Assn., Sigma Xi. Home: 22485 State Highway 133 Oakland IL 61943-6822 Office: U Ill Psychol Bldg 603 E Daniel St Champaign IL 61820-6232 Personal E-mail: erikbarb@consolidated.net.

ERIKSEN, ERIK FINK, endocrinologist, internist, researcher; b. O. Jerstal, Denmark, Aug. 2, 1953; s. Christian Frede and Signe Fink Eriksen; m. Catherine Barbara Sundt (Andersen), Mar. 12, 2002; 1 child, Barbara S. Fink stepchildren: Celia Sundt, Athena B. Sundt, Sander N. Sundt;children from previous marriage: Morten Fink, Mads Fink. MD, Aarhus U., Denmark, 1980; MD in Med. Sci., Aarhus U., 1989. Diplomate Endocrinology and Internal Medicine. Cons. Aarhus U. Hosp., Denmark, 1980-82; rsch. fellow Aarhus Amtssygehus, 1982-85; postdoctoral fellow Mayo Clinic, Rochester, Minn., 1985-87; clin. fellow Aarhus U. Hosp., 1987-89, asst. prof. internal medicine, 1989-96, assoc. prof. internal medicine, 1996—2002, cons. endocrinology and internal medicine, 1994—2001, chmn. dept. endocrinology, 1995—2002; med. dir. Eli Lilly & Co., Indpls., 2002—05, Novartis Pharma A.G., Basel, Switzerland, 2005—, Global Brand. Author: Osteoporosis, 1992, 2002, Histomorphometry, 1993; mem. editl. bd. Osteoporosis Int., 1989, Bone, 1988, Bone Mineral Rsch., 1988-98, Scandinavian Jour. Musculoskeletal Rsch., 1992; sci. editor European Jour. Clin. Investigation; contbr. chpts. to books, articles to profl. jours. Mem. European Calcified Soc., Danish Soc. Internat. Medicine, Danish Endocrine Soc. (bd. dirs.), Am. Soc. Bone and Mineral Rsch. (Young Investigator award 1987), Danish Bone and Tooth Soc. (chmn.), Internat. Osteoporosis Found. (mem. sci. adv. com.). Office: Novartis Pharma AG CH-4002 Basel Switzerland Office Phone: +41-61-324-4389. Business E-Mail: erik_fink.eriksen@novartis.com.

ERIKSON, G(EORGE) E(MIL) (ERIK ERIKSON), information specialist, anatomist, archivist, science historian; b. Palmer, Mass., May 3, 1920; s. Emil and Sofia (Gustafson) Erikson; m. Suzanne J. Henderson, Apr. 23, 1950; children: Ann, David, John, Thomas. BS, U. Mass., 1941; MA in Biology, Harvard U., 1946, PhD in Biology, 1948. Reader in history of sci. and learning Harvard U., 1943—45, asst. prof. gen. edn. in biology, 1949—52, lectr. anthropology, 1965; instr. anatomy Harvard Med. Sch., 1947—49, rsch. fellow anatomy, 1949—52, assoc. in anatomy, 1952—55, asst. prof. anatomy, 1955—65, assoc. curator Warren Anat. Mus., 1961—65; prof. med. sci. Brown U., Providence, 1965—90, chmn. sect. morphology, 1968—85, co-chmn. sect. population biology, morphology & genetics and chmn. for anatomy, 1985—90, prof. emeritus, 1990—; vis. prof., Dept. Anatomy and Cellular Biology Harvard U. Med. Sch., 1990—91; vis. lectr. in surgery Med. Sch. Harvard U., 1990—99; anatomist dept. surgery Mass. Gen. Hosp., Boston, 1990—2004; pres. Erikson Biog. Inst., Inc., Providence, 1990—. Adv. bd. Reed Elsevier, 1990; anatomist various Boston Hosps., 1952—82, Mass. Gen. Hosp. Sch. Med. Illus., 1947—60, Mass. Gen. Hosp., 1990—, Lahey Clinic, Boston, 1947—60; anatomist depts. surgery, orthopedics, rehab. and neurosurgery R.I. Hosp., 1967—; cons. anatomist Surg. Techniques Illus., 1976—80; cons. Dorlands Illus. Med. Dictionary, Rockefeller Found. med. and pub. health, S. Am., 1949; specialist State Dept., Brazil, 1962; adj. mem. faculty R.I. Sch. Design, 1970—; Kate Hurd Mead lectr. Coll. Physicians Phila., 1977; Raymond C. Truex lectr. Hahnemann U. Sch. Med., 1985. Fellow Sheldon Traveling, Harvard Ctrl. Am., 1946, Guggenheim, S. Am., 1949, Fulbright, Brazil, 1962. Mem.: Assn. of Anatomy Chairmen (emeritus), Oral History Medicine, Am. Assn. History Medicine (coun. 1972—74), Am. Assn. Anatomists (historian and archivist 1972—86, archivist 1986—90, historian and archivist 1990—), Am. Assn. Phys. Anthropologists (archivist and co-historian 1981—), History Sci. Soc. (life), Alpha Omega Alpha Honor Med. Soc. (faculty election 1957). Achievements include research in new world primates and gen. intellectual history, especially biology and medicine; development of of database foundation of Erikson Biographical Institute, 1990, with database of 450,000 individuals. also: Erikson Biog Inst 242B Meeting St Providence RI 02906-2221 Office Phone: 401-861-8848. Business E-Mail: gee@biographical.org.

ERIKSON, KAI, sociologist, educator; b. Vienna, Feb. 12, 1931; came to U.S., 1933, naturalized, 1937; s. Erik H. and Joan (Serson) E.; m. Joanna M. Slivka, Jan. 27, 1961; children: Keith S., Christopher J. BA, Reed Coll., 1953; MA, U. Chgo., 1955, PhD, 1963. Instr. psychiatry U. Pitts., 1959-63; assoc. prof. Emory U., Atlanta, 1963-66; prof. sociology and Am. studies Yale U., New Haven, 1966, master Trumbull Coll., 1969-73; editor Yale Rev., 1979-89. Author: Wayward Puritans, 1966, Everything in Its Path, 1976, A New Species of Trouble, 1994. With AUS, 1955-57. Fellow Am. Sociol. Assn. (MacIver award 1967, Sorokin award 1977, pres. 1984-85); mem. Soc. Study Social Problems (pres. 1970-71), Eastern Sociol. Soc. (pres. 1980-81) Home: 53 Quarry Dock Rd Branford CT 06405-4655 Office: Yale U Dept Sociology PO Box 208265 New Haven CT 06520-8265 Business E-Mail: kai.erikson@yale.edu.

ERIKSON, RAYMOND LEO, biology professor; b. Eagle, Wis., Jan. 24, 1936; m. 1958. BS, U. Wis., 1958, MS, 1961, PhD in Molecular Biology, 1963. Asst. prof. to assoc. prof. U. Colo., Denver, 1965-72, prof. pathology, 1972-82; John F. Drum Am. Cancer Soc. Prof. Cellular and Devel. Biology Harvard U., Cambridge, Mass., 1982—. Mem. adv. coun. GM Cancer Rsch. Found. Contbr. articles to profl. jours. USPHS fellow, 1963-65; recipient Papaicolau award, 1980, Albert Lasker Basic Med Rsch. award, Lasker Found., 1982, Robert Koch prize, 1982, Alfred P. Sloan Jr. prize GM Cáncer Rsch. Found., 1983, Hammer Cancer Rsch. prize, 1984. Mem. NAS, Am. Academia of Arts and Scis., Am. Soc. Biol. Chemists, Am. Soc. Microbiology. Office: Harvard U 16 Divinity Ave Rm 2048 Cambridge MA 02138-2020 Office Phone: 617-495-5386. Business E-Mail: erikson@mcb.harvard.edu.*

ERIKSON, ROBERT S., political science professor; BA, Lake Forest Coll., 1963; MA, Univ. Ill., 1966, PhD, 1969. Prof., polit. sci. Univ. Houston, 1978—99, disting. prof., 1991—99; prof. Columbia Univ., 1999—. Editl. bd. American Political Science Rev., American Journal of Political Science, 1978—81, 1986—88, 2001—; editor: Political Analysis, 2003—. Fellow: Am. Acad. Arts & Scis.; mem.: Southwestern Polit. Sci. Assn. (pres. 1989—90), Midwest Polit. Sci. Assn., Am. Polit. Sci. Assn. Office: Polit Sci Columbia Univ Internat Affairs Bldg Fl 7 420 West 118th St New York NY 10027 Office Phone: 212-854-0036. Office Fax: 212-222-0598. Business E-Mail: rse14@columbia.edu.*

ERIKSON, SHELDON R., oil industry executive; b. Chgo., Sept. 23, 1941; s. Roy A. and Florence Mary (Sheldon) E.; children: Steven, Michael. MBA, Harvard U., 1970. Assoc. Booz, Allen & Hamilton, Cleve., 1970-75; gen. mgr. Gen. Electric Co., Houston, 1975-80; group v.p. plastics and chems. Hoover Universal, Ann Arbor, Mich., 1980-82; pres. oilfield services group NL Industries, Houston, 1982-86; pres. Joy Petroleum Equipment Co., Houston, 1986-87; pres., chief exec. officer The Western Co. of N.Am., Ft. Worth, 1987-88, also bd. dirs., 1987-95, chmn., pres., chief exec. officer, 1988-95; pres., CEO Cameron Internat. Corp., Houston, 1995—96, chmn., pres., CEO, 1996—. Bd. dirs. Harvard Bus. Sch. Club, Houston. Office: Cooper Cameron Corp 515 Post Oak Blvd Houston TX 77027-9482*

ERIKSSON, STEVEN, social studies educator; BA, U. Colo., 1980, MA, 1984, postgrad., 1992. Social studies tchr. Denver Pub. Schs., 1989—. Chair dept. social studies Denver Pub. Schs., 2001—, mem. social studies adv. coun., 2005—06, theater dir., 2000.

ERISTOFF, ANDREW S., state agency administrator; b. NYC, Feb. 20, 1963; m. Catherine E. Baxter; 3 children. BA cum laude, Princeton U., 1985; JD cum laude, Georgetown U., 1989. Legis. analyst N.Y. State Senate, 1987; assoc. Webster & Sheffield Law Firm, 1989-91; counsel to Senator Roy M. Goodman, 1991-93; councilman dist. 4 City of N.Y., 1993—99; commr. NYC Dept. Fin., 1999—2002, New York State Dept. Tax and Fin., 2003—. Mem.: Assn. Bar City N.Y. Office: W A Harriman Campus Albany NY 12227 Office Phone: 518-457-2244. Fax: 518-485-8593. Business E-Mail: andrew_eristoff@tax.state.ny.us.

ERKAMP, RAMON QUIDO, medical researcher, consultant; s. Henri Victor and Ursula Erkamp. BSEE, Hogeschool Enschede, The Netherlands, 1992; MS in Biomed. Engring., U. Mich., Ann Arbor, 1995, MSE in Elec. Engring., 1997, PhD in Biomed. Engring., 2003. Rsch. asst. U. Mich., Ann Arbor, 1993—2003, postdoctoral rsch. fellow, 2003—05; rsch. scientist Philips Rsch., Briar Cliff Manor, NY, 2005—. Office: Philips Rsch 345 Scarborough Rd Briarcliff Manor NY 10510 Home: 3 Gloria Way Purdys NY 10578 Home Phone: 734-587-6472; Office Phone: 734-647-0846. E-mail: erkamp@umich.edu.

ERKES, JASON, sports association executive; b. 1969; Pres. Sports & Social Clubs, Inc., Chgo., 2005. Named one of 40 Under Forty, Crain's Bus. Chgo., 2005. Office: Sports & Social Clubs Inc 1516 Fremont Chicago IL 60622 Office Phone: 312-335-9596. Office Fax: 773-883-9978.*

ERKKILA-RICKER, BARBARA HOWELL, writer, photographer; b. Boston, July 11, 1918; d. John William and Adelia Parsons (Jones) Howell; m. Onni R. Erkkila, Apr. 27, 1941 (dec. 1981); children: John W., Kathleen L., Marjorie A.; m. G. Ashton Ricker, FEb. 5, 2000. Student, Boston U. Evening Coll., 1959—62. Corr. Gloucester (Mas.) Daily Times, 1936-53, feature writer, 1953—, women's editor, 1967-72, cmty. news editor, 1972-74. Editor weekly mag. Essex County Newspapers, Gloucester, 1973, editl. asst., 1974-85, writer, photographer, 1970—; tchr. Russian, Ipswich (Mass.) Pub. Schs., evenings, 1962-63; jewelry designer; quarry historian. Author: Hammers on Stone, 1981, Village at Lane's Cove, 1989; editor Lane's Cove Cook Book, 1954; contbr. articles to popular mags. Asst. traffic mgr. Lepage's, Inc., 1936-40; price panel OPA, 1944-46; ARC nurse's aide class Addison Gilbert Hosp., 1942-43; active Gloucester Hist. Commn., 1967-69, 93-2000; formerly active Girl Scouts U.S.A.; sec. Lanesville CC, 1957-94; apptd. granite industry cons. Cape Ann Hist. Assn. Mus., Mass., 1997. Recipient 2d prize for feature writing UPI, 1970, historian award Town of Rockport, 1978, First Walker Hancock award City of Gloucester, 1999. Mem. Sandy Bay Hist. Soc., Ohio Geneal. Soc., Westford Hist. Soc., Cape Ann Hist. Assn., North Shore Rock and Mineral (charter), North Shore Button Club. Congregationalist. Home and Office: 7 School St North Chelmsford MA 01863-2109 Office Phone: 978-251-3578. E-mail: barickgran@aol.com.

ERKONEN, WILLIAM EDWARD, radiologist, medical educator; BS, U. Iowa, 1955, MD, 1958. Diplomate Am. Bd. Radiology. Intern U. Oreg., Portland, 1959; family practice, 1961—68; pvt. practice, 1971-87; resident in radiology U. Iowa Coll. Medicine, Iowa City, 1968-71, faculty, 1988-94, asst. prof. radiology, 1994-98, assoc. prof., 1995-98, co-dir. Electric Differential Multimedia Lab., 1993—, assoc. prof. emeritus, 1998—. Rschr. in med. informatics and med. student instrn. and edn.; mem. anatomy and interdisciplinary com. Nat. Bd. Med. Licensure Exam., 1999—2001. Editor: (textbook) Radiology 101 1st edit., 1998, 2d edit., 2005; contbr. articles to profl. jours.; developer electronic med. textbooks. Capt. US Army, 1959—61. Recipient numerous certs. of merit Radiology Soc. N.Am.; named Tchr. of Yr., U. Iowa Coll. Med., 1990, 93, 96; recipient Disting. Tchr. award for jr. faculty in clin. scis. Alpha Omega Alpha. Fellow Am. Coll. Radiology.

ERLA, KAREN, artist, painter, collagist, printmaker; b. Pitts., Nov. 17, 1942; d. Jack and Lenore (Kamons) Franklin; children: Stephanie, Joan. BFA, George Washington U., 1965; postgrad., Parsons Sch. Design, 1979-81, Carnegie Inst., 1958-59, Boston U., 1960-62, Pratt Inst., 1980-82, NYU, 1982. Solo exhbns. include Phoenix Gallery, N.Y.C., 1985, E.L. Stark Gallery, N.Y.C., 1988, Bertha Urdang Gallery, N.Y.C., 1986, Bennett and Siegel Gallery, 1989, 90, U. of South, Sewanee, Tenn., Manhattanville Coll., Purchase, N.Y., 1982, Printmaking Council of N.J., 1982, Bennet

Siegel Gallery, N.Y.C., 1990, Bryant Gallery, N.Y.C., 1990, Queens Coll., N.Y.C., 1991; group shows include Herbert Johnson Mus. Art, Atlanta Coll. Art, Van Straaten Gallery, Chgo., Greene Gallery, Guilford, Conn., Nat. Mus. of Am. Art, Washington, D.C., Fine Arts Museum of L.I., N.Y., Zimmerli Mus., New Brunswick, N.J., Printmaking Council of N.J., Somerstown Studios and Gallery, Somers, N.Y., Cork Exhbn. in Lincoln Ctr., Fay Gold Gallery, Atlanta, 1984, Boston Printmakers 37th Nat. Exhbn., 1985, The Print Club's 61st Internat. Juried Exhbn., Phila., Schering-Plough Corp. Gallery, Madison, N.J., New Brunswick, N.J., Australian Nat. Gallery, 1989, E.L. Stark Exhbn., 1990, Am. Embassy, 1990, others; represented in permanent collections at Balt. Mus. of Art, Herbert F. Johnson Mus., Cornell U., Bklyn. Mus. Art, Huntsville Mus. Art, Ala., L.A. County Mus. Art, Met. Mus. Art, N.Y., Nat. Museum Am. Art, Australian Nat. Gallery, Smithsonian Inst., New Orleans Mus. Art, Phila. Mus. Art, Tampa Mus., Fla.; featured in Monograph of Karen Erla (text by Ronnie Cohen) 1988, Monoprints Karen Erla (text by Dr. Mary Lee Thompson), Paintings: Karen Erla (text by Bertha Urdang and E.L. Stark); featured in Newsday as New Yorker mag.; solo exhibitions E.L. Stark Gallery, Bertha Urdang Gallery, N.Y.C. Harrison Library, Harrison, N.Y. Manhattanville Coll., Purchase, N.Y., Sound Shore Gallery, N.Y.C., The Print Club 62d Internat., Phila. Recipient Nat. Art award, Pa., 1959, award Herbert F. Johnson Mus., Cornell U., award Mamroneck Artists Guild, 1983, Outstanding Svc. award N.Y. State Assembly, 2004, Outstanding Svc. award Westchester County Bd. Legislators, 2004, Outstanding Svc. award White Plains Bd. Legislators, 2004, Outstanding Svc. award N.Y. Bd. Legislators, 2004. Mem. World Print Council, Printmaking Council N.J., Artists Equity, Pratt Graphic Ctr., L.A. Printmaking Soc. Avocations: music, reading, travel. Address: PO Box 202 North White Plains NY 10603-0202

ERLANDSON, DAVID ALAN, education administration educator; b. Chgo., Jan. 10, 1936; s. Gerald Kenneth and Anna Marie Schlichting E.; m. Gwyneth Ellen Jones, Sept. 21, 1957; children: Paul William, Linda Ann, Daniel Lindsay, Charles David. AB, Wheaton Coll., Ill., 1956; MS, No. Ill. U., 1962; EdD, U. Ill., 1969. Cert. supr. all grades, Ill. Tchr. jr. high sch. Geneva (Ill.) Pub. Schs., 1959-62, Unit 4 Schs., Champaign, Ill., 1962-63, dir. gifted program, 1965-68, asst. prin., 1969-71; tchr. Univ. High Sch., Urbana, Ill., 1963-64; asst. prof. SUNY, Buffalo, 1964-65; dir. Ctr. for Upgrading Ednl. Services, Champaign, 1968-69; asst. prof. Queens Coll. CUNY, Flushing, 1971—77; prof. ednl. adminstrn. Tex. A&M U., College Station, 1977—2006, prof. emeritus, 2006—, head dept. ednl. adminstrn., 1984-92. Dir. Prins.' Ctr., Tex. A&M U., 1983-85, 93-01. Author: Strengthening School Leadership, 1976, Doing Naturalistic Inquiry, 1993, Organizational Oversight, 1996; co-author: School Special Services, 1979, Measurement and Evaluation, 1999, The Emerging Principalship; co-editor School Leadership Library; contbr. 130 articles to books and profl. jours. Served to 1st lt. USMC, 1956-59. Mem. Nat. Assn. Secondary Sch. Prins. (commn. on standards for principalship 1985-88), Am. Ednl. Rsch. Assn., Phi Delta Kappa, Phi Kappa Phi. Democrat. Home: 1107 Glade St College Station TX 77840-4434 Office: Tex A&M U Dept Ednl Adminstrn College Station TX 77843-4226 Business E-Mail: d-erlandson@neo.tamu.edu.

ERLANDSON, PATRICK J., health products executive; Ptnr. Arthur Andersen; v.p. Process, Planning, and Info. Channels UnitedHealth Grp., Minnetonka, Minn., 1997—98, corp. contr., chief acctg. officer, 1998—2000, CFO, 2001—06, operational position, 2006—. Office: UnitedHealth Group 9900 Bren Rd E Minnetonka MN 55343*

ERLANGER, BERNARD FERDINAND, biochemist, educator; b. NYC, July 13, 1923; s. Leo and Frieda (David) E.; m. Rachel Fenichel, June 23, 1946; children: Laura, Louis, Leon. BS with highest honors, CCNY, 1943; MA, NYU, 1949; PhD, Columbia U., NYC, 1951. Chemist US Indsl. Chems. Co., Inc., Newark, 1943-44; tech. adviser Manhattan Project, US Army, Los Alamos, 1944-46; prodn. mgr. Hexagon Labs., Inc., NYC, 1946-48; faculty Columbia, 1951—, prof. microbiology, 1966—; vis. scientist Instituto Superiore di Sanita, Rome, 1961-62, Inst. Cell Biology, Shanghai, People's Republic of China, 1978. Mem. Fulbright-Hays Award Com., 1966-72; invited expert analyst biochem. and molecular biology edit. Chemtracts; mem. study sect. neurol. C, NIH, 1985-88. Recipient 600th Anniversary medal Copernican Med. Acad., Cracow, Poland, 1979,Sigma Alpha/Mu Gamma award NY Heart Assn., Townsend Harris medal CUNY, 1995; Fulbright scholar U. Republic of Uruguay, 1967, Guggenheim fellow Inst. Phys.-Chem. Biology, Paris, 1969, Am. Cancer Soc. scholar Pasteur Inst., Paris, 1979. Recipient Physicians and Surgeons Disting. Svc. award Columbia U., 1996. Mem. Am. Chem. Soc., Am. Soc. Biol. Chemists, Biochem. Soc., NY Acad. Scis. (mem. conf. com. 1978), Soc. Exptl. Biol. Medicine (assoc. editor proceedings 1981-88), Harvey Soc., Am. Soc. Immunologists, NY Heart Assn., Am. Soc. Photobiology, Phi Beta Kappa, Sigma Alpha Mu (Gamma award). Achievements include research in mode of action of antibiotics and on cancer; investigation of mechanisms of enzyme catalysis; investigation of macromolecules concerned with genetics, immunology of fullerenes, photoregulation, biological receptors; investigation of immunochemistry of buckminsterfullerenes, nanobiotechnology. Office: Columbia U 701 W 168th St New York NY 10032-2704 Home: 333 E 30 St Apt 2C New York NY 10016 Office Phone: 212-305-3740. Business E-Mail: bfe1@columbia.edu. *The scientist, like the artist, contributes most when he allows his work to be an extension of his individuality. The risks to his ego and security are great, but success brings with it the satisfaction of making a personal imprint on the future of society.*

ERLEBACHER, ARLENE CERNIK, retired lawyer; b. Chgo., Oct. 3, 1946; d. Laddie J. and Gertrude V. (Kurdys) Cernik; m. Albert Erlebacher, June 14, 1968; children: Annette Doherty, Jacqueline McCarthy. BA, Northwestern U., 1967, JD, 1973. Bar: Ill. 1974, U.S. Dist. Ct. (no. dist.) Ill. 1974, U.S. Ct. Appeals (7th cir.) 1974, Fed. Trial Bar 1983, U.S. Supreme Ct. 1985. Assoc. Sidley & Austin, Chgo., 1974-80, ptnr., 1980-95, ret., 1996. Fellow Am. Bar Found.; mem. Order of Coif.

ERLEBACHER, MARTHA MAYER, artist, educator; b. Jersey City, Nov. 21, 1937; d. Desiderius and Mary Mayer; m. Walter Erlebacher, June 26, 1961 (dec. Aug. 1991); children: Adrian Immanuel, Jonah Daedalus. Student, Gettysburg Coll., Pa., 1955-56; B of Indsl. Design, Pratt Inst., 1960, MFA, 1963; DFA (hon.), NY Acad. Art, 2006. Indsl. designer, illustrator Arthur Wagner Assocs., NYC, 1956-61; tchr. anatomy and figure drawing U. of Arts, Phila., 1978-94. Tchr. Phila. Coll. Art, 1966-68, 78-94; tchr. anatomical drawing and painting Grad. Sch. Figurative Art, N.Y. Acad. Art, N.Y.C., 1992-2006, others; guest lectr. Grad. Sch. Art Yale U., 1974, Vassar Coll., Poughkeepsie, N.Y., 1975, Phila. Coll. Art, 1976, U. Conn., Storrs, 1977, Tyler Sch. Art Temple U., 1978, Med. Coll. Pa., Phila., 1987, N.Y. Acad. Art, 1990, others; vis. artist colls. and univs. including U. Wis., Oshkosh, 1979, Syracuse U., 1986-87, U. Mich., 1988, Calif. State U., 1989, 91, Tulane U., New Orleans, 1992, Kalamazoo Inst. Arts, 1989; panelist arts shows, 1978—; juror U. Del., 1979, N.Y. Statewide Bi-Annual, Trenton, 1984, Moss Rehab. Hosp., Phila., 1985, Tex. Nat. '98, Nacogdoches. Exhibited in one-person shows at Robert Schoelkopf Gallery, N.Y.C., 1973, 75, 78, 80, 82, 85, Dart Gallery, Chgo., 1976, 78, 83, Koplin Gallery, L.A., 1989, 91, Kalamazoo Inst. Arts, 1989, Fischbach Gallery, N.Y.C., 1993, 95, The More Gallery, Phila., 1993, 97, 2000, Hackett-Freedman Gallery, San Francisco, 1999, 2002, Arnot Mus., Elmira, NY, 2001, Forum Gallery, N.Y.C., 2003, Seraphin Gallery, Phila., 2005, U. NC, Wilmington, 2007, others; exhibited in group shows Bklyn. Mus., 1960, Phila. Art Alliance, 1967, Suffolk Mus., Stony Brook, N.Y., 1971, Pratt Manhattan Ctr., 1971, Am. Acad. Arts and Letters, N.Y.C., 1973, 76, 87, Yale U. Art Gallery, 1973, Phila. Civic Ctr., 1974, Mus. Art, Penn. State U., 1974, 76, N.Y. Cultural Ctr., 1975, Libr. Congress, 1975, U. Notre Dame, 1976, Ringling Mus. Art, Sarasota, Fla., 1976, Fogg Art Mus. Harvard U., Cambridge, Mass., 1976, Art Gallery Boston U., 1977, Penn. Acad. Fine Arts, 1978, 81, 82, Phila. Mus. Art, 1979, Centro Colombo Americano, Bogota, Colombia, 1979, Fendrick Gallery, Washington, 1980, Print Club, Phila., 1980, 88, Albright-Knox Gallery, Buffalo, 1981, Woodmere Art Gallery, Phila., 1982, Univ. Art Mus., Santa Barbara, Calif., 1983, N.J. State Mus., Trenton, 1984, Hudson River Mus., Yonkers, N.Y., 1986, Sch. Fine Arts Gallery Ind. U., 1987, Sherry French Gallery, N.Y.C., 1988, 91, 92, Jack Wright Gallery, Palm Beach, Fla., 1992, Contemporary Realist Gallery, San Francisco, 1993, 94, Gerald Peters Gallery, Sante Fe, 1993, Fletcher Gallery, Sante Fe, 1994, Arnot Mus., Elmira, 2000, So. Allegheny Mus. Fine Art, Altoona, Pa., many others; represented in pvt. and pub. collections including Cleve. Mus. Art, Ball State U., Muncie, Ind., AT&T Co., Inc., Chgo., U. Notre Dame, Art Inst. Chgo., Fogg Mus. of Art, Fed. Reserve Bank, N.Y.C., Penn. Acad. Fine Arts, Phila., Valparaiso U., Phila. Mus. Art, Libr. Congress, Flint Inst. Arts, N.J. State Mus., others. Recipient Bertha Shay award Cheltenham Art Ctr., 1967, Netsky-Sernaker Meml. prize, 1973, Vivian and Meyer P. Potamkin prize, 1974; Yaddo fellow, 1966, 73, sr. fellow Nat. Endowment for Arts, 1982, fellow Pa. Coun. on Arts, 1988; grantee Ingram Merrill Found., 1978, Mellon Venture Fund, 1987; also other grants and awards. Home: 7733 Mill Rd Elkins Park PA 19027-2708 Personal E-mail: mmayererlebacher@aol.com.

ERLENBACH, JULIUS E., academic administrator, musician; AB, Oberlin Coll., BA in Music; M, PhD, Northwestern U. Acting v.p. academic adminstrn. Drake U., dean Coll. Fine Arts; chmn. dept. music U. Wis., Stevens Point, provost, vice chancellor La Crosse, chancellor Superior, 1996. Bd. dir. Superior-Douglas County Devel. Assn., United Way of Superior, Duluth-Superior Symphony Orch., C. of C., Superior-Douglas County. Office: Uni Wis Office Chancellor Main 202 Belknap and Catlin PO Box 2000 Superior WI 54880-4500 Office Phone: 715-394-8221. E-mail: jerlenba@uwsuper.edu.

ERLENMEYER-KIMLING, L., psychiatrist, researcher; b. Princeton, NJ; d. Floyd M. and Dorothy F. (Dirst) Erlenmeyer; m. Carl F. E. Kimling. BS magna cum laude, Columbia U., 1957, PhD, 1961; DSc (hon.), SUNY, Purchase, 1997. Sr. rsch. scientist N.Y. State Psychiat. Inst., NYC, 1960-69, assoc. rsch. scientist, 1969-75, prin. rsch. scientist, 1975-78, dir. div. devel. behavioral studies, 1978—, chief med. genetics, 1991—; asst. in psychiatry Columbia U., 1962-66, rsch. assoc., 1966-70, from asst. prof. to assoc. prof. psychiatry and genetics, 1970—78, prof., 1978—. Adj. prof. psychology New Sch. Social Rsch., 1971—97; mem. peer rev. group NIH, 1976—80; mem. work group guidance and counseling Congl. Commn. Hungtinton's Disease, 1976—77; mem. task force intervention Pres.'s Commn. Mental Health, 1977—78; mem. initial rev. group NIMH, 1981—85; mem. adv. bd. Croatian Inst. Brain Rsch., 1991—93. Editor: Life-Span Research in Psychopathology, 1986; issue editor: Differential Reproduction, Social Biology, 1971, Genetics and Mental Disorders, Internat. Jour. Mental Health, 1972, Genetics and Gene Expression in Mental Illness, Jour. Psychiat. Rsch., 1992, Measuring Liability to Schizophrenia: Progress Report, 1994; mem. editl. bd. Social Biology, 1970—79, Schizophrenia Bull., 1978—2004; issue editor: Schizophrenia Bull., 1994; mem. editl. bd. Jour. Preventive Psychiatry, 1980—84, Croatian Med. Jour., 1991—, Neurology/Psychiatry/Brain Rsch., 1991—97, Am. Jour. Med. Genetics: Neuropsychiat. Genetics, 1992—2007. Recipient Merit award, NIMH, 1989—96, William K. Warren Schizophrenia Rsch. award, Internat. Congress Schizophrenia Rsch., 1995, Disting. Investigator award, Nat. Alliance Rsch. on Schizophrenia and Depression, 1996, Lifetime Achievement award, Internat. Soc. of Psychiatric Genetics, 2002; grantee, NIMH, 1966—69, 1971—, Scottish Rite Com. Schizophrenia, 1970—74, 1984—87, 1989—94, W. T. Grant Found., 1978—86, MacArthur Found., 1981, Stanley Found., 1995—2001, Nat. Alliance Rsch. on Schizophrenia and Depression, 1996—2000. Fellow: APA, Am. Psychol. Soc., Am. Psychopath. Assn. (Joseph Zubin award 2005); mem.: ACLU, AAAS, Soc. Study Social Biology (bd. dirs. 1969—84, sec. 1972—75, pres. 1975—78, bd. dirs. 1992—96), N.Y. Acad. Scis., Internat. Soc. Psychiat. Genetics (Lifetime Achievement award 2002), Behavior Genetics Assn. (mem.-at-large 1972—74, Theodosius Dobzhansky award 1985), Am. Soc. Human Genetics, Nat. Resources Defense Coun. (pres.'s coun. 2006—), NY Presbyterian Hosp., Earth Justice, Animal Legal Def. Fund, Animals and Soc. Inst. (bd. dirs. 2005—), Interfaith Alliance, People for Am. Way (pres. coun. 2006—), John Lennox Soc., Greenpeace, Planned Parenthood, Defenders of Wildlife (pres.'s coun. 2003—), Earth Island, Environ. Def., Sigma Xi, Phi Beta Kappa. Office: NY State Psychiat Inst Dept Med Genetics 1051 Riverside Dr Mail Unit 6 New York NY 10032-2603 Business E-Mail: le4@columbia.edu.

ERLICHT, LEWIS HOWARD, broadcasting company executive; b. NYC, Aug. 6, 1939; s. Harry and Estelle (Silk) E.; m. Wilma Binder, June 10, 1961; children: Paul Jon, Jamie Blake. BA in Psychology, L.I. U., 1962. With ABC-TV, 1962—, account exec., 1965-70; sales mgr. Sta. WABC-TV, 1970-73, gen. sales mgr., 1973-74; gen. mgr. Sta. WLS-TV, Chgo., 1974-77, v.p. programming NYC, 1977-79; v.p., asst. to pres. ABC Entertainment, Los Angeles, 1979-80, sr. v.p., asst. to pres., 1980-81, sr. v.p. prime time programming, 1981-83, pres., 1983-85, ABC Circle Films, 1985-86; pres., chief operating officer New World Broadcasting, Los Angeles, 1986-87; pres. LHE, Inc., 1986—. Cons. Scandinavian Broadcasting Systems, 1989-91. Served with USAF, 1956-60.

ERLUND, CECILIA WHARTON, psychology professor, small business owner; b. Nacogdoches, Tex., Nov. 7, 1943; d. John Cecil Wharton, Sr. and Merrian McLeroy Wharton; m. Otheil Justus Erlund, Sr., Aug. 1, 1976; m. Tony Mac Price, Feb. 14, 1965 (div. July 15, 1975); children: Merrie Daune Price, John McClure Price. BS in Vocat. Home Econs., Stephen F. Austin State Coll., Nacogdoches, Tex., 1964; MEd in Counseling, Stephen F. Austin State U., Nacogdoches, Tex., 1969; EdD in Counseling and Psychology, Tex. A&M U., Commerce, 1984. Lic. profl. counselor Tex. Edn. Agy., 1969, profl. ednl. diagnostician Tex. Edn. Agy., 1982, spl. edn. counselor Tex. Edn. Agy., 1984, profl. vocat. counselor Tex. Edn. Agy., 1984. Tchr. vocat. homemaking LaPoynor H.S., LaRue, Tex., 1966—72; dir. guidance svcs. Trinity Valley C.C., Athens, Tex., 1972—74; dir. testing Ctrl. Tex. Coll., Killeen, Tex., 1975—76; office mgr. Group Enterprises, Austin, Tex., 1976—77; ednl. diagnostician Shelby County Spl. Edn. Coop., Ctr., Tex., 1979—81; tchr. spl. edn. classroom Carthage Ind. Sch. Dist., Carthage, Tex., 1981—84; ednl. diagnostician Belton Ind. Sch. Dist., Tex., 1984—85; dir. spl. edn. U. Mary Hardin-Baylor, Belton, Tex., 1985—90, dir. counseling and testing, 1990—95, chmn. dept. psychology and counseling, 1995—97, prof. psychology, 1997—. Prin., owner Esquire Limousines, 1995—. Named Notable Women Tex., 1984. Republican. United Methodist. Avocations: cooking, reading, gardening. Home: 12961 Fm 2601 Moody TX 76557 Office: Univ Mary Hardin-Baylor 900 College St Belton TX 76513 Home Phone: 254-853-9400; Office Phone: 254-295-4552. Office Fax: 254-295-4550; Home Fax: 254-853-9872. Personal E-mail: cerlund@sbcglobal.net. Business E-Mail: cerlund@umhb.edu.

ERMAN, AILA, small business owner; b. State Island, NY, Mar. 8, 1941; d. Theodor Diatlo and Selma Eva (Anderson) Erman; m. Marvin Ross Cutson, Nov. 2, 1962 (div. Oct. 31, 1981); children: Craig Bernard, Jaana Erman Cutson; m. Jospeh McEwen, Nov. 19, 1983 (div. Jan. 6, 2004). BS in Mktg., Fla. State U., 1962; MLA, U. Pa., 1992. Asst. dept mgr. Sears Roebuck, Tampa, Fla., 1962; social worker State of Fla., Tampa, 1962-64; owner Aila's Decorative Hardware & Bath Gallery, St. Petersburg, Fla., 1965—79; v.p., sec. So. Lock & Supply Co., Inc., St. Petersburg, 1968-81; pres. Mills Travel Svc., Inc., St. Petersburg, 1983—2004; jewelry designer Saint Petersburg, Fla., 2004—. Bd. dirs. PAVA, Guatemala Highland Maya assistance group; docent Mus. Fine Arts, St. Petersburg, 1982. Mem.: N.C. Friendship Force, Fla. Goldsmith, Assn. Sr. Profls. Eckerd Coll., Dali Mus., Am. Stage Theater, Ctr. Against Spouse Abuse, Arts Ctr., Suncoast Friendship Force, Am. Soc. Goldsmiths, Fla. Suncoast Club, St. Petersburgh Yacht Club, Tiger Bay Club (founding mem.), Fla. State U. Pres.'s Club, Century Travel Club, Alpha Chi Omega (past pres. Delta Sigma chpt.). Democrat. Jewish. Avocations: travel, creative decorative arts, gardening. Home: 1910 Kansas Ave NE Saint Petersburg FL 33703-3430 Home (Summer): 309 Old Forbes Rd Bakersville NC 28705

ERMOLAEV, HERMAN SERGEI, Slavic languages educator; b. Tomsk, Russia, Nov. 14, 1924; came to U.S., 1949, naturalized, 1956; s. Sergei and Vera (Kozminykh) E.; m. Tatiana Kuzubova, June 8, 1975; children: Michael, Natalia, Katherine. Student, U. Graz, Austria, 1949; BA, Stanford U., Calif., 1951; MA, U. Calif.-Berkeley, 1954, PhD, 1959. Mem. faculty Princeton U., 1959—, prof. Slavic langs. and lits., 1970—. Author: Soviet Literary Theories, 1917-1934, The Genesis of Socialist Realism, 1963, 77, Mikhail Sholokhov and His Art, 1982, Censorship in Soviet Literature, 1917-1991, 1997, Mikhail Sholokhov and His Art (in Russian), 2000, Tikhii Don and Political Censorship, 1928-1991 (in Russian), 2005; co-author: Sholokhov's Tikhii Don, A Commentary, 1997; also articles; translator: Untimely Thoughts (Gorky), 1968, 95. McCosh fellow, 1967-68 Mem. Am. Assn. Advancement Slavic Studies, Am. Assn. Tchrs. Slavic and East European Langs. (pres. 1971-72) Home: 206 Moore St Princeton NJ 08540-3404 Business E-Mail: ermolaev@princeton.edu.

ERNEST, J. TERRY, ocular physiologist, educator; b. Sycamore, Ill., June 26, 1935; married (div.); 1 child. BA, Northwestern U., 1957; MD, U. Chgo., 1961, PhD in Visual Sci., 1967; Postgrad. Diploma in Health Care Ethics and Law, Manchester U., Eng., 2005. Prof. ophthalmology U. Wis., 1977-79; prof., chmn. ophthalmology Ind. U., 1980-81; prof. ophthalmology U. Ill., 1981-85; prof., chmn. ophthalmology U. Chgo., 1985—2004, Cynthia Chow prof., 2002—. Mem visual sci. A study sect., NIH, 1975-78, chmn. 1978-79, chmn. visual disorders study sect., 1979-80; rsch. prof. Rsch. to Prevent Blindness, Ind., 1981-84; mem. Vision Rsch. Program Com., 1982-84. Founding editor, Key, 1986-88; editor, Year Book of Ophthamology, 1982-88, Investigative Ophthalmology and Visual Sci., 1988-92. Recipient Rsch. Career Devel. award NIH, 1972. Mem. AAAS, Am. Ophthalmol. Soc., Am. Acad. Ophthalmology (Honor award 1982), Assn. Rsch. Vision and Ophthalmology. Achievements include research in ocular circulation with special emphasis on glaucoma and diabetic retinopathy using various methods of in vivo blood flow measurements. Office: U Chgo Visual Sciences Ctr 5841 S Maryland Ave MC2114 Chicago IL 60637-1454 Home Phone: 773-667-9203; Office Phone: 773-702-8888. E-mail: jernest@bsd.uchicago.edu.

ERNEST, ROGER CRAIG, language educator; s. Robert Howell Ernest; m. Jennifer Louise Strauch, Aug. 31, 1968. MA in English Lit., Calif. State U. Dominguez Hills, Carson, 1993, cert. in rhetoric and composition, 1994. Actor Universal Pictures and United Artists, Calif., 1974—76; freelance screenwriter Long Beach, Calif., 1974—88; show design writer, dir. Universal Studio Tours, Universal, Calif., 1984—87; freelance artist Long Beach, 1988—92; English prof. Cerritos Coll., Norwalk, Calif., 1994—. Actor: Sugarland Express, Close Encounters of the Third Kind; Exhibited in group shows at Arts for the Parks, 1992 (Judges' Merit award). Decorated Air Force Commendation medal Dept. of the Air Force; named Outstanding Faculty Mem., Cerritos Coll., 2004—05; recipient Who's Who Among America's Tchrs., Ednl. Comm., 2003—06. Mem.: SAG, Writers Guild of Am. West (life), Phi Kappa Phi, Theta Chi. Office: Cerritos Coll 11110 Alondra Blvd Norwalk CA 90650 Office Phone: 562-860-2451 ext 2893. Business E-Mail: rernest@cerritos.edu.

ERNST, CALVIN BRADLEY, retired vascular surgery educator; b. Detroit, May 12, 1934; s. Edward William and Irene Marie (Doelker) E.; m. Elizabeth Abbott, Dec. 21, 1957; children: Lisa Anne, Matthew Abbott, David William, Susan Elizabeth. MD, U. Mich., 1959. Diplomate Am. Bd. Surgery (bd. dirs. 1991-97). Intern Ohio State U. Med. Ctr., Columbus, 1959-60; resident U. Mich. Med. Ctr., Ann Arbor, 1960-65; instr. surgery U. Mich., 1968-69, asst. prof., 1969-72, assoc. prof., 1972, U. Ky., Lexington, 1972-74, prof., 1974-79; prof. surgery Johns Hopkins U., 1979-85, surgeon hosp., 1979-85; chmn. surg. scis. Balt. City Hosps., 1979-85; clin. prof. surgery U. Mich., Ann Arbor, 1985-97; prof. surgery Case Western Res. U., Cleve., 1994-97; head vascular surgery Henry Ford Hosp., Detroit, 1985-97; prof. surgery, chief vascular surgery Med. Coll. Pa., Hahnemann Univ., Phila., 1997-99. Cons. surgeon Loch Raven VA Hosp., Balt., 1979-85. Assoc. editor Jour. Vascular Surgery, 1986-91, editor, 1991-97, emeritus editor, 1997—; mem. editl. bd. Archives of Surgery, 1983-93, Surgery, 1983-93; editor 7 vascular surgery textbooks; contbr. chpts. to books. Dir. Am. Bd. Surgery, 1991-97. Served to capt. U.S. Army, 1966-68. Fellow ACS; mem. Soc. Vascular Surgery (sec. 1984-88, pres.-elect 1989-90, pres. 1990-91, Am. Surg. Assn., Internat. Cardiovascular Soc. (recorder 1977-82), So. Assn. Vascular Surgery (sec. treas. 1976-81, pres. 1982-83), Alpha Omega Alpha. Home: 3904 N Farway Dr Jupiter FL 33477 E-mail: cbernst@earthlink.net.

ERNST, DAVID A., lawyer; b. Portland, Oreg., Oct. 2, 1960; BS, Oreg. State U., 1982; JD, Lewis & Clark Coll., 1985. Bar: Oreg. 1985, U.S. Dist. Ct. Oreg. 1985, Wash. 1990, U.S. Dist. Ct. Wash. (we. dist.). Shareholder, bd.dirs. Bullivant Houser Bailey PC, Portland, Oreg., 1997—2002, 2006—, shareholder in charge, 2002—05, pres., 2006—, chmn. food & beverage industry group. Pres. Fed. Bar Assn. (Oreg. Chpt.), 1996—97; chmn. 9th Cir. Lawyer Representatives, 2001; pres. alumni bd. Lewis and Clark Law Sch., 2001—02; program chmn. First Ann. DRI Conf. on Food Liability, St. Louis, 2005; bd. dirs. Multnomah Bar Found., Northwest Bus. Culture and Arts; bd. visitors Lewis and Clark Law Sch.; spkr. in field. Office: Bullivant Houser Bailey PC 300 Pioneer Tower 888 SW Fifth Ave Portland OR 97204-2089 Office Phone: 503-499-4634. Office Fax: 503-295-0915. E-mail: dave.ernst@bullivant.com.

ERNST, EDWARD WILLIS, retired electrical engineering educator; b. Great Falls, Mont., Aug. 28, 1924; s. Paul Wilson and Grace Vio (Woodmore) E.; m. Helen Kitty Todd, Jan. 29, 1950 (dec. Mar. 1975); children: Deborah Kitty, Thomas Edward (dec.); m. Margaret Frances Patton, Sept. 13, 1975 (dec. Feb. 2002); children: Alan Harmon, Ruth Margaret, Betty Carol; m. Barbara Allen Moye, Apr. 26, 2003. BSEE, U. Ill., 1949, MSEE, 1950, PhD in Elec. Engring., 1955. Rsch. engr. GE, Syracuse, NY, 1955, Stewart-Warner, Chgo., 1955-58; assoc. prof. U. Ill., Urbana, 1958-68, prof., 1968-89, assoc. head elec. engring., 1970-85, assoc. dean engring., 1985-89; Allied-Signal prof. engring. U. S.C., Columbia, 1990-2000, disting. emeritus engring. prof., 2000; ret., 2000. Program dir. NSF, Washington, 1987-90; chmn. Engring. Accreditation Commn., Accreditation Bd. for Engring. Tech., N.Y.C., 1985-86, pres., 1989-90. Pres. Mckinley Found., Champaign, Ill. 1968-72. Recipient Linton Grinter award Accreditation Bd. Engring. and Tech., 1992. Fellow IEEE (v.p. 1981-82, Centennial medal 1984, EAB Meritorious Achievement award in accreditation activities 1985), AAAS, Accreditation Bd. for Engring. Tech., Internat. Engring. Consortium (bd. dirs.), Am. Soc. for Engring. Edn. (editor Jour. Engring. Edn. 1992-96). Presbyterian. Avocations: photography, reading. Personal E-mail: eernst1@charter.net.

ERNST, JAMES ALLAN, safety engineer, consultant; b. Pittsburgh, Pa., Feb. 15, 1943; s. Charles Joseph and Ellen Black McKenzie Ernst; m. Tamara Sue Kugel, July 28, 1947; children: Tina Rae Evans, Tela Fae Cooper. BS Mgmt., Cardinal Stritch U., Edina, Minn. Campus, 1997—99; AAS Electronic Engring. Tech., CC Of The Air Force, Maxwell Air Force Base, AL, 1978—81. Cert. paramedic NY, 1985. Electronics technician USAF, 1961—81; sys. safety/human factors engr. GE/Martin

Marietta/Lockheed Martin, Syracuse, NY, 1981—95; paramedic Syracuse U. (Carrier Dome), 1987—95; EMT instr. NY State Dept. of Health, Syracuse, 1990—95; EMT/paramedic Greater Baldwinsville Ambulance Corps, Baldwinsville, NY, 1983—95; project safety engr. United Def. LP, Mpls., 1995—2004; system safety engring. cons., 2005—. Dir. of ops. Greater Baldwinsville Ambulance Corps, Baldwinsville, 1992—92. Firefighter Jefferson Twp Vol Fire Dept., Bowersville, Ohio, 1967—70, Ocean Springs Fire Dept., Ocean Springs, Miss., 1970—71; aux. police officer Chelmsford Aux. Police Force, Chelmsford, Mass., 1979—81; deacon Bklyn Ctr. Ch. Of Christ, Brooklyn Center, Minn., 1998—2001; boy scout leader BSA, Chelmsford, Mass., 1976—81. Msgt (e7) USAF, 1961—81, Various. Decorated AFCM w/ 1 oak cluster, Humanitarian Svc. Medal w/ 1 oak cluster, AFLSM w/ 4 oak clusters, NDSM, AF Orgnl. Excellence Award USAF, NCO Acad. Grad. Ribbon, AFGCM w/ 5 oak clusters. Mem.: Human Factors and Ergonomics Soc., Internat. Sys. Safety Soc. Christian. Avocations: travel, camping, woodworking. Home: 1730 Van Ct Alamogordo NM 88310 E-mail: je43@prodigy.net.

ERNST, JOHN LOUIS, management consultant; b. Pine Bluff, Ark., Dec. 24, 1932; s. Albert C. and Christine (Vinent) E.; m. Lois R. Geraci, June 12, 1971; children: Ann Marie, Catherine Teresa, Laura Elizabeth, Christine Margaret. BS, Spring Hill Coll., Mobile, Ala., 1954; postgrad., Georgetown U. Law Sch., 1956-57. Stockbroker Washington Planning Co., 1957-58; pub. rels.-sales exec. Am. Airlines, Washington, Phila. and NYC, 1958-62; account exec. Ted Bates Advt. Agy., NYC, 1962-65; sr. v.p., mgmt. dir. Marschalk Advt. Agy., NYC, 1965-68; dir. Interpub. Svc. Corp., 1967-69; sr. v.p., mng. dir. McCann-Erickson Advt. Agy., NYC, 1969-70; pres. Ernst-Van Praag, NYC, 1970-75; chmn. bd. A.V.E. Corp., NYC, 1974-75, Advt. to Women, Inc., NYC, 1975-86; pres. Bellvinent Communications, Inc., NYC, 1986—, Art Vault Internat., NYC, 1996—. Capt. USMC, 1954-57. Mem. Amyotrophic Lateral Sclerosis (Lou Gehrig's Disease) Assn. (chmn. bd. dirs., CEO Greater N.Y.C. chpt. 1997—), Players Club. Home: 644 Broadway Apt 5w New York NY 10012-2324

ERNST, MARK A., diversified financial services company executive; m. Annette Ernst; two children. Degree in Acctg. & Fin. summa cum laude, Drake U.; MBA, U. Chgo. With tax, investment and corp. adv. svcs. dept. Coopers & Lybrand; v.p., gen. mgr. tax and bus. svcs. divsn. Am. Express Co., Mpls., sr. v.p. workplace fin. svcs., sr. v.p.; exec. v.p., COO H&R Block, Inc., 1998-99, pres., COO, 1999—2001, pres., CEO, 2001—, chmn., 2002—. Adv. Initiative Fin. Security Aspen Inst.; bd. trustees U. Mo. Kans. City; bd. dirs. Great Plains Energy, Knight-Ridder Inc., 2004—. Bd. dir. Civic Coun. Greater Kans. City, Greater Kans. City Area C. of C., Kansas City Area Devel. Coun., H&R Block Found., Am. Royal. Office: H&R Block 4400 Main St Kansas City MO 64111-1812*

ERNST, RICHARD ROBERT, chemist, educator; b. Winterthur, Zurich, Switzerland, Aug. 14, 1933; s. Robert and Irma (Brunner) E.; m. Magdalena Kielholz, Oct. 9, 1963; children: Anna Magdalena, Katharina Elisabeth, Hans-Martin Walter. Diploma Chemistry, ETH-Zurich, 1956, DSc in Tech., 1962; PhD (hon.), ETH-Lausanne, Switzerland, 1986, Technische Hochschule, Munich, 1989, U. Zurich, 1994, U. Antwerp, 1997, U. Cluj-Napoca, 1998, U. Montpellier, 1999, Charles U., Prague, 2002, Babes-Bolyai U. Scientist ETH-Zurich, 1962-63, privatdozent, 1968-70, asst. prof., 1970-72, assoc. prof., 1973-76, prof., 1976—, dir. Phys. Chemistry Lab., pres. Rsch. Coun.; scientist Varian Assocs., Palo Alto, Calif., 1963-68. Cons. Spectrospin AG, Fällanden, Switzerland, 1978—, v.p. bd. dirs. Editl. bd. mem. of 10 sci. jours; numerous inventions, patents in field. 1st lt. ACS-Dienst, 1953-88, Swiss mil. Recipient Silver medal ETH-Zurich, 1962, Ruzicka prize, 1968, Gold medal Soc. Magnetic Resonance in Medicine, San Francisco, 1983, Benoist prize Swiss Fedn. Confedn., Berne, 1986, Kirkwood award Yale U., 1989, Ampere prize, 1990, Wolf prize in chemistry, Wolf Found., Israel, 1991, Louisa Gross Horwitz prize Columbia U., 1991, Nobel prize in chemistry, 1991, award for Achievements in Magnetic Resonance EAS, 1992. Mem. NAS (India), Deutsche Akademie Leopoldina, Acad. Europaea, Schweizerische Chemische Gesellschaft, Royal Soc. London, Österreichische Gesellschaft für Analytische Chemie, Am. Phys. Soc., U.S. Nat. Acad. Sci., Am. Acad. Arts and Scis., Schweizerische Akademie d. Tech. Wiss., Russian Acad. Scis, IOM (elected 2004), Swiss Sci. Coun., COST Com., Found. Marcel Benoist (prize, 1986). Avocations: tibetan art, music. Office: Lab F Phys Chem ETH-Honggerberg 8093 Zurich Switzerland Home Phone: 41 52 242 7807; Office Phone: 41 1 632 4368. E-mail: ernst@nmr.phys.chem.ethz.ch.

ERNST, SUZANNE, academic administrator, educator; d. Leslie Rudolph Schwartz and Bernice Mary Sheridan; m. William R. Ernst, Aug. 25, 1957 (div.); children: Dawn L., Mark H., Erin R.(dec.) , Lori S. Ernst-Furtmann, Paul W. BS, U. Nev., Reno, 1958; MEd, U. Nev., 1974. Asso. in Social Work Nev. State Bd. Examiners for Social Workers, 1988; cert. retirement planner U. So. Calif., Percy Andrus Gerontology Ctr., 1981, jr. h.s. tchr. Nev. State Bd. Edn., 1958. Tchr. Washoe County Sch. Dist., Reno, 1958—59, Burlingame Sch. Dist., Millbrae, Calif., 1959—60, San Rafael Sch. Dist., Vallecito, Calif., 1960—61; sr. svcs. dir., sr. nutrition program Cath. Charities So. Nev., Las Vegas, 1974—77; field rep. State of Nev., Divsn. for Aging Svcs., Las Vegas, 1977—82, dep. adminstr., 1982—88, adminstr., 1988—96; dep. to chancellor Nev. Sys. Higher Edn., Las Vegas, 1996—99, chief adminstrv. officer, 1999—2005, spl. asst. to chancellor, 2006—. Columnist Sr. World and Sr. Spectrum, Las Vegas, 1980—96; prodr., host, action srs. KVBC, Las Vegas, 1982—89; bd. dirs. Nat. Assn. State Units on Aging, Washington, 1990—96; del. White Ho. Coun. on Aging, Washington, 1995. Commr. City of Las Vegas Housing Authority, Las Vegas, Nev., 1989—93; bd. mem. Nev. Bd. of Examiners for Long-Term Care Adminstr., Las Vegas, Nev., 1990—96, Cmty. Housing Resource Bd., Las Vegas, Nev., 1986—88, State of Nev. Employee Mgmt. Com., Nev., 1986—2002, Clark County, City of Las Vegas Citizens' Govt. Efficiency Com., Las Vegas, Nev., 1992—92, Clark County Cmty. Devel. Adv. Com., Las Vegas, Nev., 1989—2006, Nev. Pub. Health Found., Inc., Las Vegas, Nev., 1996—2005; grand jury mem. Fore-Person Fed. Grand Jury on Organized Crime, Las Vegas, Nev., 1987—89. Named Outstanding Alum, Gamma Phi Beta Alumni, U. Nev., Reno, 1970, Outstanding Citizen, B'nai B'rith, 1989, Disting. Woman So. Nev., 1989—, Mother of Yr., Nev. Silver State, 1993, Outstanding Alumnus, U. Nev., Las Vegas, Coll. Edn., 1998; recipient Cmty. Achievement award, Adminstrn. on Aging, 1989; grantee, Fleishman Found., 1976. Mem.: Phi Kappa Phi. Democrat. Roman Catholic. Avocations: travel, reading. Office: Nev Sys Higher Edn 5550 W Flamingo Rd Ste C-1 Las Vegas NV 89103 Office Phone: 702-889-8426. Business E-Mail: ernsts@nevada.edu.

ERNST, WALLACE GARY, geology educator, dean; b. St. Louis, Dec. 14, 1931; BA, Carleton Coll., 1953; MS, U. Minn., 1955; PhD, Johns Hopkins U., 1959. Geologist U.S. Geol. Survey, Washington, 1955-56; fellow (Geophys. Lab.), Washington, 1956-59; mem. faculty UCLA, 1960-89, prof. geology and geophysics, 1968-89, chmn. geology dept. (now earth and space scis. dept.), 1970-74, 78-82, dir. Inst. Geophysics and Planetary Physics, 1987-89; dean Stanford Sch. of Earth Scis., 1989-94; prof. geol. and environ. scis. Stanford (Calif.) U., 1989—, Benjamin M. Page prof., 1999—, dean Sch. of Earth Scis., 1989-94. Author: Amphiboles, 1968, Earth Materials, 1969, Metamorphism and Plate Tectonic Regimes, 1975, Subduction Zone Metamorphism, 1975, Petrologic Phase Equilibria, 1976, The Geotectonic Development of California, 1981, The Environment of the Deep Sea, 1982, Energy for Ourselves and Our Posterity, 1985, Cenozoic Basin Development of Coastal California, 1987, Metamorphic and Crustal Evolution of the Western Cordillera, 1988, The Dynamic Planet, 1990, Integrated Earth and Environmental Evolution of the Southwestern United States, 1998, Planetary Petrology and Geochemistry, 1999; editor: Earth Systems: Processes and Issues, 2000, (with R.G. Coleman) Tectonic Studies of Asia and the Pacific Rim--A Tribute to Benjamin M. Page, 2000, (with J.G. Liou) Ultrahigh-Pressure Metamorphism and Geodynamics in Collision-Type Orogenic Belts, 2000, Frontiers in Geochemistry, 2002, (with S.L. Klemperer) The Lithosphere of Western North America, 2004, Serpenite and Serpentinites, 2004. Trustee Carnegie Instn. of Washington, 1990—. Recipient Miyashiro medal Geol. Soc. Japan, 1998, Penrose medal, Geol. Soc. Am., 2004, Roebling medal, Mineralogical Soc. Am., 2006. Mem. NAS (chmn. geology sect. 1979-82, chair class I 2000—), AAAS, Am. Philos. Soc., Am. Geophys. Union, Am. Geol. Inst., Geol. Soc. Am. (pres. 1985-86), Am. Acad. Arts and Sci., Geochem. Soc., Mineral Soc. Am. (recipient award 1969, pres. 1979-80). Office: Stanford U Dept Earth & Environ Scis Green Earth Sci #209 Palo Alto CA 94303-1823

EROMON, DAVID IGHOGBOYA, electronics engineer, educator; b. Ujemen-Ekpoma, Edo, Nigeria, June 25, 1963; arrived in US, 1998; s. Emmanuel and Omomene Eromon. BSEE, U. Sci. and Tech., Port-Harcourt, Nigeria, 1987; MSc, U. Benin, Nigeria, 1990, PhD in Elec. and Computer Engring., 1999. Cert. elec. instr., indsl. maintenance instr., core curricula instr. Nat. Ctr. Constrn. and Edn. and Rsch., Proctor instr. Nat. Assn. Radio and Telecomms. Engrs. Elec. design and planning engr. Ministry Works and Transp., Benin, 1989—91; svc. mgr., svc. engr. Wayne Dresser Internat., Lagos, Nigeria, 1995—97; engr. Skotec Engring., Inc., Schaumburg, Ill., 1998; vis. asst. prof. So. Ill. U., Carbondale, 1999—2001; asst. prof., coord. electronics tech. Denmark Coll., SC, 2000—03; asst. prof. electronics, computer and info. tech. NC A&T State U., Greensboro, 2003—. Faculty summer rsch. fellow engring. sci. and tech. divsn. Oakridge Nat. Lab., Tenn., 2004; presenter, cons. in field. Recipient Engring. Sci. and Tech. Divsn. award, Oakridge Nat. Lab., 2004, Young Rsch. Investigator of Yr. award, NC A&T State U., 2006, cert. of appreciation, Internat. Jour. Modern Engring., 2006; grantee, US Dept Energy, 2004, NC Space Grant Consortium, NC State U., 2005, ABET/TEI, 2004, 2006, NSF, 2006. Mem.: IEEE, Nigeria Soc. Engrs., Coun. Regulation and Engring. Bodies Nigeria, IEEE Power Engring. Soc., IEEE Electromagnetic Compatability Soc., IEEE Commn. Engring. Soc., IEEE Control Sys., CIGRE, Am. Soc. Engring. Edn. Achievements include research in energy systems and controls, power electronics, microelectromechanical systems and neuronetworks. Office: NC A&T State U Dept Electronics and Computer Engring Greensboro NC 27411-0001 Personal E-mail: eromon9@aol.com. Business E-Mail: dieromon@ncat.edu.

ERON, LEONARD DAVID, retired psychology professor; b. Newark, Apr. 22, 1920; s. Joseph I. and Sarah (Hilfman) E.; m. Madeline Marcus, May 21, 1950; children: Joan Hobson, Don, Barbara Christensen. BS, CCNY, 1941; MA, Columbia U., NYC, 1946; PhD, U. Wis., Madison, 1949. Diplomate Am. Bd. Profl. Psychology. Asst. prof. psychology and psychiatry Yale U., New Haven, 1948-55; rsch. assoc. prof. Yale U. Sch. Medicine, New Haven, 1955—69; dir. rsch. Rip Van Winkle Found., 1955-62; prof. psychology U. Iowa, Iowa City, 1962-69, dir. grad. tng. clin. psychology; rsch. prof. U. Ill.-Chgo., 1969-89, emeritus rsch. prof. of the social sci. in psychology, 1989—2007; rsch. scientist, prof. psychology Inst. for Social Rsch., U. Mich., Ann Arbor, 1992—2003; assoc. dean rsch. Sch. Social Work U. Mich., Ann Arbor, 2001—03. Cons. Chgo. Bd. Edn., 1981—89. Author 8 books; editor Jour. Abnormal Psychology, 1973-80; assoc. editor Am. Psychologist, 1986-90; mem. editl. bd. Guggenheim Found. Rev. on Violence and Aggression, 1996-2003; contbr. numerous articles to profl. jours. Served to 1st lt. US Army, 1942—45. Fulbright lectr., Free U. Amsterdam, 1967-68; recipient Fulbright Sr. Scholar award, Queensland U., Australia, 1976-77, James McKeen Cattell Sabbatical award, U. Rome, 1984-85. Fellow AAAS, APA (chair commn. violence and youth 1991-93, Disting. Contbns. to Knowledge award 1980, Gold medal award for Life Contbn. to Psychology in the Pub. Interest 1995, Lifetime Contbn. to Media Psychology award 2003), Am. Orthopsychiat. Assn.; mem. NIMH, Midwestern Psychol. Assn. (pres. 1985-86), Internat. Soc. for Rsch. in Aggression (pres. 1989-90), Nat. Rsch. Coun. (panel understanding and control violent behavior, 1987-1992), Commn. Social Scis. and Humanities, Am. Coun. Learned Socs. Home: Lindenhurst, Ill. Died May 3, 2007.

ERON, MADELINE MARCUS, psychologist; b. New Brunswick, NJ, Sept. 8, 1919; d. Israel and Rae (Becker) Marcus; m. Leonard David Eron, May 21, 1950; children: Joni Eron Hobson, Don Marcus, Barbara Eron Christensen. Student, U. Mich., 1937-39; BA, NYU, 1941; MA, Columbia U., 1942. Lic. psychologist, Ill., N.Y.; nat. cert. Sch. Psychologist. Intern in psychology Phila. State Hosp., 1942-43; psychology extern Neurol. Inst. Columbia Presbyn. Med. Ctr., NYC, 1943-44; sr. clin. psychologist Inst. Crippled and Disabled, NYC, 1944-51; cons. psychologist New Haven, 1951-55; clin. psychologist Rip Van Winkle Clinic and Found., Hudson, N.Y., 1958-62; chief psychologist Berkshire Farm for Boys, Canaan, N.Y., 1961-62; pvt. practice psychology specializing in retng. the brain injured Iowa City, 1962-63; cons. Cedar Rapids (Iowa) Community Sch. Dist., 1963-67; dir. psychol. svcs. Comprehensive Evaluation-Rehab. Ctr., U. Iowa Med. Sch., Iowa City, 1968-69; sch. psychologist Winnetka, Glencoe and Skokie (Ill.) Elem. Sch. Dists., 1969-72, Evanston (Ill.) Twp. High Sch., 1972-90. Bd. dirs. Lincoln Ctr. Clin. Services, Highland Park, Ill. Mem. APA (divsn. sch. psychology, rehab. psychology, child and youth service), Iowa Psychol. Assn. (sec. 1965-67), Midwestern Psychol. Assn., Nat. Assn. Sch. Psychologists (charter), Ill. Sch. Psychologists Assn. (charter), Assn. Advancement Psychology, N.Y. State Psychol. Assn., Psi Chi. Home: 1075 E Victory Dr Ste 241 Lindenhurst IL 60046-7911

EROZAN, YENER SAHIR, pathologist, educator; arrived in U.S., 1959; s. Celal Sahir and Sevim Erozan; m. Brenda Martin, July 7, 1966. MD, Istanbul U., Turkey, 1954. Cert. practice medicine and surgery Bd. Med. Examiners State Md., 1971, anatomic pathology Am. Bd. Pathology, 1974, added qualification in cytopathology Am. Bd. Pathology, 1989. Resident in pathology Haydarpasa Numune Hosp., Istanbul, 1956—59, Suburban Hosp., Bethesda, Md., 1959—62; fellow in pathology Johns Hopkins U., Balt., 1962—64; instr. pathology Johns Hopkins U. Sch. Medicine, Balt., 1964—65, asst. prof. pathology, 1969—75, assoc. prof. pathology, 1975—95, prof. pathology, 1995—; asst. prof. pathology Hacettepe U. Sch. Medicine, Ankara, Turkey, 1965—68. Dir. The John K. Frost cytopathology lab. The Johns Hopkins Hosp., Balt., 1989—95. Editor: (book) Fine Needle Aspiration of Subcutaneous Organs and Masses, 1996. Named Otago Trust Vis. Prof., Dunedin Sch. Medicine, New Zealand, 1998; recipient Disting. Svc. award, Am. Soc. for Clin. Pathology, 2002, L. C. Tao award - Educator of Yr., Papanicolaou Soc. Cytopathology, 2004; Yener S. Erozan, M.D. fellowship established in his name, Johns Hopkins U. Sch. Medicine Dept. Pathology, 2003. Fellow: Am. Coll. Chest Physicians, Internat. Acad. Cytology (Maurice Goldblatt award 2007), Coll. Am. Pathologists; mem.: AMA, Md. Soc. Pathologists, The Johns Hopkins Alumni and Faculty Assn., Am. Soc. Cytopathology (pres. 1985—86, Papanicolaou award 1997), Johns Hopkins Club. Avocations: photography, travel, swimming. Office: The Johns Hopkins Hosp 600 North Wolfe St Baltimore MD 21287 Office Phone: 410-955-1180. Business E-Mail: yerozan@jhmi.edu.

ERRICO, R. CHRISTOPHER, investment advisor; m. Lisa Jane Krupnick, 2001. BA, LeMoyne Coll. Investment advisor Lehman Bros., NYC, PaineWebber, NYC; sr. v.p. investments Morgan Stanley, NYC, 1999—2006, mng. dir., 2006—. Named one of Top 100 Fin. Advisors, Barron's Mag. Office: Morgan Stanley 1585 Broadway New York NY 10036*

ERRINGTON, JAMES JOSEPH, anthropology educator; b. Bloomington, Ind., Oct. 12, 1951; s. Joseph and Frances Claire (Smyth) E.; m. Elizabeth P. Ford; children: Clela Alice, Sarah Rose. BA in Linguistics, Wesleyan U., 1973; MA in Linguistics, U. Chgo., 1976, PhD in Linguistics and Anthropology, 1981. Asst. prof. anthropology dept. Yale U., New Haven, 1982—85, assoc. prof. anthropology dept., 1986—94, prof. anthropology dept., 1994—. Chair council Southeast Asian studies Yale U., 1988—2007. Author: Language & Social Change in Java, 1985, Structure & Style in Javanese, 1988, Shifting Languages: Interaction & Identity in Javanese Indonesia, 1998, Colonial Linguistics: A Story of Language, Meaning and Power, 2007. Mem. Am. Anthropol. Assn., Assn. for Asian Studies, Linguistic Soc. Am., Soc. Linguistic Anthropol. (pres.). Office: Yale U Dept Anthropology PO Bos 208277 New Haven CT 06520-8277 Office Phone: 203-432-3672. Office Fax: 203-432-3669. E-mail: j.errington@yale.edu.

ERSEK, GREGORY JOSEPH MARK, lawyer; b. Cleve., Aug. 30, 1956; s. Joseph Francis and Mary H. (Hurchanik) E. AB, Columbia U., 1977; MBA, U. Pa., 1979; JD, U. Fla., 1984; cert. cir. civil mediator, Fla. Internat. U., 1998. Bar: Fla. 1986, US Dist. Ct. (so. dist.) Fla. 1987, US Ct. Appeals (11th cir.) 2006, US Supreme Ct. 2006. Cons. fin. valuation Am. Appraisal Co., Princeton, N.J., 1979-80; mgr. import-export Marie L. Veslie Co., Coral Gables, Fla., 1980-85; dir. corp. fin. dept. and capital markets group Dunhill Diversified, Ltd., LA, 1980—2001; assoc. Lunny, Tucker, Karns & Brescher, Ft. Lauderdale, Fla., 1986; dir. legal dept. Horizons Rsch. Labs. Inc., Ft. Lauderdale, 1986-89, sr. corp. planner, 1988-89; gen. counsel Unisco Corp., Ft. Lauderdale, 1989-93, TRICORD Corp., Ft. Lauderdale, 1990-93, Irish Times, Inc., Ft. Lauderdale, 1993-97; dir. corp. fin. dept. & sr. corp. counsel Canton Fin. Svcs. Corp., subs. Cyber Am. Corp., Salt Lake City, 1995-96; gen. counsel Greenstreet Capital Corp., Investment Bankers, Las Vegas, 1996-99, Gaelic Pub. Devel., Inc., Ft. Lauderdale, 1998—2002, Premier Fin. Corp., Jacksonville, 1998—2002. Rsch. asst. jurisprudence U. Fla., 1982-84; tchg. fellow U. Fla. Law Sch., 1983; sec.-treas. Sorkar Group, Inc., Ft. Lauderdale, 1987-89; CEO Am. CompuShopper, Inc., 1989-98; with legal dept. Pfizer Inc., NYC, 1983; co-founder, mgr. Poland/US Trade and Mktg. Consortium, 1989—; mem. Philip C. Jessup Internat. Moot Ct. team, 1983; gen. counsel Biltmore Vacation Resorts, Inc., f/k/a Cyber Info., Inc., Las Vegas, 1997-99, Avalon Group, Inc., Cedar Rapids, Iowa, 1997-99; rsch. asst. in jurisprudence to Prof. Robert Moffat, U. Fla., 1982-84; gen. counsel HLO Custom Internat. Tours, Orlando, 1992—, Custom Archtl. Builders, Inc., Boca Raton, 2002—; rschr. Ctr. of Excellence in Functional Recovery in Chronic Spinal Cord Injury, Miami VA Med. Ctr., 2004-06; mem. Miami Project to Cure Paralysis, 2004—. Editor Medscanner, med. industry newsletter, 1987-89. Mem. venture coun. forum; alumnus Internat. House, NYC, 1984; mem. South Fla. Regional Spinal Cord Injury Model Sys., 2004—. Tchg. fellow, U. Fla. Law Sch., 1983. Mem.: Minn. State Bar Assn., Nat. Register Practicing Lawyers with Spinal Injury, Nat. Assn. Disabled Attys., Execs. and Dirs., Fla. Bar Assn., Nat. Assn. Securities Dealers (nat. arbitration com. 1991—98), Assn. Disabled Attys., Coun. on Fgn. Rels. (local com.), United Spinal Assn., Corp. Execs. and Dirs. Pub. Cos. with Spinal Cord Injury, Wharton Club South Fla., Phi Delta Phi. Avocations: travel, books. Home and Office: 17820 NW 18th Ave Miami Gardens FL 33056-4949

ERSEK, ROBERT ALLEN, plastic surgeon; b. Ridley Twp., Pa., June 19, 1938; s. Joseph Martin and Theda Louise (Kromes) E.; m. Gerry Avenelle Mullins, Mar. 28, 1958; children: Stephanie Louise, Cynthia Leigh. BS, Morris Harvey Coll., 1961; MD, Hahnemann Med. Coll., 1966. Diplomate Nat. Bd. Med. Examiners; cert. Am. Bd. Plastic Surgery. Intern surgery U. Minn. Hosps., Mpls., 1966-67; research fellow U. Pa., 1962, Hahnemann Med. Coll., Phila., 1963-65; med. fellow dept. surgery U. Minn., 1967-73; resident dept. plastic and reconstructive surgery Tulane U., New Orleans, 1975-77; fellow in plastic surgery U. Miss., Jackson, 1978; clin. instr. plastic surgery U. Tex. Health Sci. Center, San Antonio, 1979. Chmn. bd., dir. Med. Gen. Inc., 1969—; dir., med. dir. Genetic Labs., 1970— , Emerald Airlines, Inc.; chmn. bd. Remedco, 1980—; bd. dirs., med. dir. Genetic Labs Wound Care; chmn. Personique Inc., 1996; bd. dirs. Plastic Surgery Co.; dean Lipoplasy Univ. Author: Pain Control, 1981; Co-editor: Organ Perfusion and Preservation, 1969; contbr. articles to med. jours.; patentee numerous surg. devices. Bd. dirs. Austin Civic Ballet. Served to maj. USAF, 1973-75. Recipient Alan Edelsohn prize Hahnemann Med. Coll., 1966; Grand award for exhibit Student Am. Med. Assn. Squibb Nat. Contest, 1967; award of excellence in med. writing Minn. Medicine, 1970 Fellow ACS; mem. AMA, AAUP, NAS, Am. Coll. Emergency Physicians, La. Med. Soc., Soc. for Cryosurgery, Am. Soc. Plastic and Reconstructive Surgeons, Am. Soc. Artificial Internal Organs, Am. Med. Writers Assn., Smithsonian Inst., Nat. Assn., Flying Physicians, Am. Trauma Soc., Tex. Med. Assn., Travis County Med. Soc., Am. Burn Assn., Lipoplasty Soc. N.Am. (bd. dirs.), Serpent Soc., Aesculpulation Soc., Austin Knights of Symphony (chmn. Personique Inc. 1996), Phi Kappa Delta. Achievements include patents in field; patents pending in field. Office: 630 W 34th St Austin TX 78705-1229 Home Phone: 512-970-9676; Office Phone: 512-459-6800. Personal E-mail: ersek@ensek.com. E-mail: personique@hotmail.com.

ERSHLER, WILLIAM BALDWIN, biogerontologist, educator; b. Syracuse, NY, Jan. 13, 1949; s. Irving Leonard and Eunice (Baldwin) E.; m. Joan Lipstein, Nov. 6, 1971; children: Rachel Eve, Leah Rose. BA, Case Western Res. U., 1970; MD, SUNY Upstate Ctr., Syracuse, 1974. Diplomate Am. Bd. Internal Medicine, Am. Bd. Med. Oncology, Am. Bd. Hematology. Asst. prof. U. Vt., Burlington, 1980-85; assoc. prof. U. Wis., Madison, 1985-89, prof. medicine, 1989-96, dir. U. Wis. Inst. on Aging, 1989-96, head geriatrics, 1989-96; dir. geriatric rsch. Edn. and Clin. Ctr. William Middleton VA Hosp., Madison, 1991-96; prof. medicine, dir. Glennan Ctr. Geriatrics & gerontolog Eastern Va. Medical Sch., Norfolk, 1996-97; dir. Inst. Advanced Studies in Aging and Geriatric Medicine, Washington, 1998—, Nat. Geriatrics Rsch. Consortium, 1998—; rsch. edn. dir. Extended Care Info. Network, 1999—. Dir. Geriatric Oncology Consortium, 2001—; sr. investigator Nat. Inst. Aging, NIH, dep. clin. dir., 2007—. Editor Jour. Gerontology, 1996-2000; contbr. articles to profl. jours. Recipient Geriatric Leadership award NIH, 1990-96; NIH grantee, 1989—. Fellow Gerontologic Soc. Am.; mem. Am. Geriatrics Soc., Am. Assn. Cancer Rsch., Am. Soc. Clin. Oncology, Am. Soc. Hematology, Assn. Dirs. Acad. Geriatrics (councilor). Jewish. Avocations: running, photography, travel. Office: 1700 Wisconsin Ave NW Washington DC 20007 Business E-Mail: ershlerwi@mail.nih.gov.

ERSKINE, JAMES LORENZO, physics professor; b. Seattle, Oct. 25, 1942; s. Lawrence A. and Elizabeth (Woodbury) E.; m. Julie Ann Grant; children: Michael Grant, John Lawrence. BSEE, U. Wash., 1964, MSEE, 1966, PhD in Physics, 1973. Sr. engr. and cons. Boeing Co., Seattle, 1967-74; rsch. asst. prof. dept. physics U. Ill., Urbana, 1974-77; asst. prof. dept. physics U. Tex., Austin, 1977-82, assoc. prof., 1982-86, prof., 1986—. Trull Centennial prof. Trull Found. U. Tex., 1986. Contbr. numerous articles in fields of solid state physics, magnetism and magnetic materials, surface physics, surface chemistry, and instrumentation. Grantee NSF, R.A. Welch Found., other fed. and pvt. agys. Fellow Am. Phys. Soc.; mem. Am. Vacuum Soc. Office: U Tex Grad Sch Dept Of Physics Austin TX 78712 Office Phone: 512-471-1464. Business E-Mail: erskine@physics.utexas.edu.

ERSKINE, RODNEY D., oil industry executive; m. Jackie Erskine. BS in petroleum engring., Tex. A&M U., 1966. With Union Tex. Petroleum, 1975—91; pres. and CEO Nerco Oil & Gas, Inc.; with Coastal Oil & Gas (merged with El Paso Corp. 2001), 1994—97, sr. v.p., 1997—2001, pres., 2001; pres. prodn. El Paso Corp., Houston, 2001—.

ERSKINE, WILLIAM CRAWFORD, retired academic and health facility administrator, accountant; b. Seattle, Feb. 29, 1924; s. Alwin Crawford and Emilie Hildred (Davies) E.; m. Mary Jean Hopkins, Feb. 28, 1946; children: Scott Crawford, Nancy Page. BA in Bus. Adminstrn., U. Wash., 1950. CPA, Wash. Auditor Arthur Andersen & Co., 1950-54; sr. auditor Ansell Johnson & Co., CPAs, Seattle, 1956-59; contr. Food Giant Stores, Seattle, 1959-64; comptr. U. Wash., Seattle, 1964-70; v.p. bus. U. Colo., Boulder, 1970-74; exec. v.p. U. Nebr. Sys., Lincoln, 1974-80; v.p. bus. affairs U. Tex., El Paso, 1980-88; ret., 1988. Dir. West Tex. Higher Edn. Authority, El Paso, 1982-88; cons. Educator Cons. Panel GAO, 1978-86. Treas. St. Francis on the Hill Episcopal Ch., 1996-99; mem. exec. com. Nat. Assn. State Univs. and Land Grant Colls., 1977-80. With U.S. Air Corps, WWII. Mem.: Coronado Country Club (treas. 1990—93). Home: 6136 Los Robles Dr El Paso TX 79912-1933 Personal E-mail: werskine@elp.rr.com.

ERTL, WOLFGANG, German language and literature educator, artist; b. Sangerhausen, Germany, May 27, 1946; came to U.S., 1969; m. Mary R. Clough, Aug. 30, 1969. BA equivalent in German and English, Philipps U., Marburg, Germany, 1969; MA in German, U. N.H., 1970; PhD in Germanic Langs. and Lits., U. Pa., 1975. Lectr. German U. Pa., Phila., 1974-76; asst. prof. German Swarthmore (Pa.) Coll., 1976-77, U. Iowa, 1977-82, assoc. prof., 1982-88, prof. Iowa City, 1988—2006, chmn. dept. German, 1988—96, prof. emeritus, 2006—. Author: Stephan Hermlin and Tradition, 1977, Nature and Landscape in the Poetry of the GDR: Walter Werner, Wulf Kirsten, and Uwe Gressmann, 1982, (with Christine Cosentino) On Volker Braun's Lyric Poetry, 1984; co-editor: GDR Poetry in Context, 1988; co-editor Glossen: An Internat. Bi-Lingual Scholarly Jour. on Lit., Film, and Art in the German Speaking Countries After 1945; co-editor (with C. Cosentino and W. Muller) Taking Stock--German Literature after Unification: Contributions to the 1st Carlisle Symposium on Modern German Literature, Glossen 10, 2000-, Crosscurrents--German Literature(s) and the Search for Identity: Selected Papers from the 2d Carlisle Symposium on Modern German Literature, Glossen 15, 2002; co-editor At the Milennium: Focus on German Literature, 2003; co-editor, America in German Literature and Film: Selected Papers from the 3rd Carlisle Sympsium on Modern German Literature, Glossen 19, 2004; contbr. chpts. to books, revs. and articles to profl. jours. Resident dir., Academic Year In Freiburg, Germany, 2000-01, 04-05. May Brodbeck Humanities fellow, 1987. Mem. MLA, N.E. MLA, Am. Assn. Tchrs. German, German Studies Assn. Office: U Iowa Dept German 526 Phillips Hall Iowa City IA 52242-1323

ERVIN, BILLY MAXWELL, retired military officer; b. Dante, Va., July 29, 1933; s. Willie Beldon and Ollie Lowel (Biggs) Ervin; m. Barbara Frances Walsh, June 27, 1971; 1 child, Honore McDonough 1 stepchild, Kerry Thompson; 1 child from previous marriage, Michael. BS, US Naval Acad., Annapolis, Md., 1955; grad., Navy Nuclear Power Training, Vallejo, Calif., 1961, Navy Nuclear Power Training, Idaho Falls, 1961, Naval War Coll., Newport, RI, 1971; M in Marine Affairs, U. RI, Kingston, 1971; postgrad., U. Mass., Amherst, 1989. Commd. ensign USN, 1955, advanced through grades to capt., 1975, chief engr. aircraft carrier Pacific, 1969-70, destroyer capt. Atlantic/Pacific, 1971-73, project mgr. Washington, 1973-78, head logistics br., 1978-80, head rsch. and devel. br., 1980-82, insp. gen. Europe London, 1982-85, ret., 1985; adminstr. Baystate Eye Care, P.C., Springfield, Mass., 1986-88; mgr. engring. adminstrn. and planning Kaman Aerospace Corp., Bloomfield, Conn., 1990-92; chief oper. officer Conn. Orthopaedic and Sports Medicine Ctr., Vernon, CT, 1992-97; bus. mgr. engring. Kaman Aerospace Corp., Bloomfield, 1997-2000; mgmt. cons. Bloomfield, 2000—05; ret., 2005—. Decorated Bronze Star; recipient Meritorious Svc. Medal award Pres. of the U.S., 1985. Mem. Naval War Coll. Found., Navy League, St. Andrew's Soc., Clan Irwin Assn. Avocations: antique cars, genealogy. Home: 20 Magnolia Ter Springfield MA 01108-2512 Personal E-mail: max.ervin@1955.usna.com.

ERVIN, CHARLES PHIFER, JR., education educator, retired military officer; b. Morganton, NC, Nov. 30, 1942; s. Charles P. Ervin Jr. and Eunice (Cuthbertson) Ervin; m. Margie Berry Ervin, Sept. 10, 1962 (div. Aug. 1989); children: Eunice Anita, Charles III, Todd. BS in Sociology, N.C. A&T State U., 1965; MA in Mgmt., Ctrl. Mich. U., 1978; PhD in Social Found. of Edn., Ga. State U., 2001. Commd. 2d lt. US Army, 1965, advanced through grades to lt. col., chief pers. svcs. officer Ft. Bragg, NC, 1980—81, insp. gen., auditor Camp Casey, Republic of Korea, 1983—84, manpower staffing officer, Pentagon, 1984—87, dep. cmty. comdr., resource mgr. Camp Red Cloud, Republic of Korea, 1987—89, ret., 1993; prof. mil. sci. SROTC Ft. Valley State Coll., Ga., 1989—93; sr. army ROTC instr. Northeast HS, Macon, Ga., 1993—96; state coord. edn. homeless children and youth program, Fla. Dept. Edn. Fla. A&M U., Tallahassee, 1996—2003, asst. prof., 2001—. Bd. dirs. Tallahassee Coalition for Homeless, 1997—, Fla. Coalition for Homeless, Orlando, 1998—2004; chmn. dept. secondary edn. Fla. A&M U., 2006—. Named one of 100 Black Men of Mid. Ga., CME Ch., Warner Robins, Ga., 1991; Fulbright scholar, Turkey, 2004. Mem.: NAACP, Ret. Officers Assn., Nat. Assn. for Edn. Homeless Children & Youths, Urban League, Mason, Phi Delta Kappa, Phi Lambda Theta, Kappa Delta Pi, Alpha Phi Alpha. Democrat. Methodist. Avocation: running. Home: 8691 Alexandrite Ct Tallahassee FL 32309 Office: Fla A&M Univ Dept Secondary Edn Coll Edn Tallahassee FL 32301 Office Phone: 850-412-7190. Personal E-mail: cervin42@aol.com.

ERVIN, CLARK KENT, former federal agency administrator; b. Apr. 1, 1959; m. Carolyn A. Harris. BA in Govt., Harvard Coll., 1980, LLD, 1985; MA, Oxford U., 1982. Atty Vinson & Elkins, 1985—89; assoc. dir. policy Office of Nat. Svc., 1989—91; atty. Locke, Liddell & Sapp, 1993—95; asst. sec. of state State of Tex., 1995—99; dep. atty. gen., gen. counsel, dir. adminstrn. Tex. Atty. Gen.'s Office, 1999—2001; insp. gen. US Dept. State, Washington, 2001—03; acting insp. gen. US Dept. Homeland Security, Washington, 2003, insp. gen., 2003—04; Paul H. Nitze Fellow, dir. Homeland Security Initiative The Aspen Inst., Washington, 2005—. Author: Open Target: Where America is Vulnerable to Attack, 2006. Scholar Rhodes scholar. Office: The Aspen Inst One DuPont Cir NW Ste 700 Washington DC 20036*

ERVIN, KATHLEEN GWEN, journalist; b. Owosso, Mich., Aug. 23, 1947; d. Joseph Hanastede, Jr. and Barbara Ann Curenico; m. Samuel David Ervin, Jr. (div.); 1 child, Sara Theresa. BA, Rutgers U., New Brunswick, NJ, 1969. Freelance journalist The Economist, London, Phila. Weekly. Mem.: Mensa. Republican. Avocations: writing, philosophy.

ERVIN, PATRICK FRANKLIN, nuclear engineer; b. Kansas City, Kans., Aug. 4, 1946; s. James Franklin and Irma Lee (Arnett) E.; m. Rita Jeanne Kimsey, Aug. 12, 1967; children: James, Kevin, Amber. BS in Nuclear Engring., Kans. State U., 1969, MS in Nuclear Engring., 1971; postgrad., Northeastern U., 1988. Registered profl. engr., Ill., Colo., Calif., Idaho, Wash.; cert. paleontology paraprofl., Colo. Reactor health physicist Dept. Nuclear Engring. Kans. State U., Manhattan, 1968-69, rsch. asst. Dept. Nuclear Engring., 1969-72, sr. reactor operator, temp. facility dir. Dept. Nuclear Engring., 1970-72; system test engr. Commonwealth Edison Co., Zion, Ill., 1972—74, shift foreman, 1973, shift foreman with sr. reactor operator lic., 1974-76, prin. engr., 1976-77, acting operating engr., 1977, tech. staff supr. Byron, Ill., 1977-81; lead test engr. Stone & Webster Engring. Corp., Denver, 1982-83, project mgr., 1982-95, ops. svcs. supr., 1982-86, asst. engring. mgr., 1986-89, cons. engr., 1989-94; sr. cons., 1994—96; decommisioning program mgr. Rocky Flats Closure project Kaiser-Hill Co., Denver, 1996—2001; prin. project mgr. CH2M Hill Constructors, Inc., Denver, 2001—04; Windscale piles decommission program mgr. CH2M Hill Internat. Nuc. Svcs., 2004—. Contbr. articles to profl. jours. Served with U.S. Army N.G., 1971-77. Mem. Am. Nuclear Soc. (Nat. and Colo. chpts.), Am. Nat. Standards Inst. (working group on containment leakage testing). Independent. Roman Catholic. Avocations: paleontology, hunting, fishing, camping, stamp collecting/philately. Office: 9189 S Jamaica St Englewood CO 80112 Home: PO Box 24548 Denver CO 80224 Office Phone: 720-286-2550. Business E-Mail: pervin@ch2m.com.

ERVIN, ROBERT MARVIN, lawyer; b. nr. Ocala, Fla., Jan. 19, 1917; s. Richard William and Carrie (Phillips) Ervin; m. Frances Ann Cushing, Dec. 25, 1941; children: Anne Cushing, Robert Marvin. BSBA, U. Fla., 1941, LLB, 1947. Bar: Fla. 1947. Of counsel Ervin, Kitchen & Ervin, Tallahassee, 1947—; part-time US referee in bankruptcy US Dist. Ct. (no. dist.) Fla., 1952-72. Mem. Fla. Constn. Revision Commn., 1966—68; trustee U. Fla. Law Ctr. Assn.; mem. founders com., mem. bd. visitors Fla. State U. Coll. Law. With USMC, 1941—45. Named to Fla. Housing Hall of Fame, 1993; recipient Disting. Svc. award for Legal Edn., John B. Stetson U., 1966, Disting. Svc. award, Armed Forces League, 1966, Medal of Hon. award, Fla. Bar Found., 2003. Fellow: Am. Bar Found. (chmn. 1989—90); mem.: ABA (ho. dels. 1966—91, chmn. sect. criminal justice 1975—76, bd. govs. 1979—82, vice chmn. sr. lawyers divsn., chmn. spl. com. fiscal policy 1984—85, mem. resource devel. coun., mem. audit com.), Nat. Conf. Referees Bankruptcy (pres. 1963—64), Fla. Supreme Ct. Hist. Soc. (pres. 1986—87, chmn. trustees 1987—98), Fla. Bar (pres. 1965—66, Disting. Svc. award 1966), Am. Judicature Soc., Am. Law Inst., Am. Coll. Trial Lawyers (bd. regents 1983—84), Ret. Officers Assn., Am. Bar Retirement Assn. (pres. 1980—82), Fla. Blue Key, Elks, Alpha Kappa Psi, Phi Alpha Delta. Baptist. Home: 530 North Ride Tallahassee FL 32303-5127 Office: PO Box 1170 Tallahassee FL 32301-1811 Office Phone: 850-386-5502. Personal E-mail: ervin090@comcast.net.

ERVIN, SPENCER, lawyer; b. Bala, Pa., Nov. 25, 1932; s. Spencer and Miriam Williams (Roberts) E.; m. Florence Wetherill Schroeder, Sept. 12, 1964; children: Margaret, Mary, Miriam, Helen. AB, Harvard U., 1954, JD, 1959. Bar: Pa. 1960, Maine 1995, US Supreme Ct. 1963. Staff counsel Philco Corp., Phila., 1959-62; assoc. Ringe & Dewey, Phila., 1962-64; ptnr. Ringe, Tate & Ervin, Phila., 1964-72, Gratz, Tate, Spiegel, Ervin & Ruthrauff, Phila., 1972-92, Hepburn, Willcox, Hamilton & Putnam, Phila., 1992-96, Largay Law Offices, Bangor, Maine, 1996-97; pvt. practice, Bass Harbor, Maine, 1998—. Bd. dirs. Mt. Desert Island Biol. Lab. Bd. dirs., officer Neighborhood Club, Bala Cynwyd, Pa., 1969-89. Lt. USNR, 1954-56. Republican. Episcopal. Home and Office: PO Box 383 Bass Harbor ME 04653-0383 Office Phone: 207-244-3289. E-mail: law@spencerervin.com.

ERVING, JULIUS (WINFIELD), (II), retired professional basketball player, business executive; b. East Meadow, NY, Feb. 22, 1950; s. Callie Erving Lindsey; m. Turquoise Erving; 4 children. Grad., U. Mass., 1986; doctorate (hon.), U.Mass., 1983, Temple U., 1983. With Va. Squires, Am. Basketball Assn., 1971-73, N.Y. Nets, Am. Basketball Assn., 1973-76, Phila. 76ers, NBA, 1976-87; mem. NBA Championship team, 1983; broadcaster NBC, 1993; exec. v.p. Orlando Magic, 1997—; v.p. RDV Sports, Orlando, 1997—. Bd. dirs. Meridian Bancorp, Phila. Coca-Cola Bottling Co., DJ Group, Inc.; pres. mgmt. and mktg. firm JDREGI; spokesman Coca-Cola Co., Converse Shoe Co., Advanced Golf Techs., Hardee's. Appeared in film The Fish That Saved Pittsburgh, 1979. Trustee NBA Internat., Basketball Hall of Fame; bd. dirs. N.Y. State Sports Commn. Named Rookie of Yr. Am. Basketball Assn., 1972, Most Valuable Player Am. Basketball Assn., 1974, 76 and mem. championship team, 1974, 76; named to NBA 35th Anniversary All-Star Team, 1980; named Most Valuable Player NBA, 1981, Most Valuable Player All-Star Game NBA, 1971, 83; recipient Cert. Appreciation Easter Seals, 1982, Best Friend award Police Athletic League Phila, 1982, Walter Kennedy Citizenship award, 1983, Jackie Robinson award for Am. Black Achievement Ebony mag., 1983, Whitney M. Young award Urban League, 1984, Father Flanagan award Boys Town Nebr., 1984, Biddy Basketball award, 1984, Sports award Big Bros. Inc., N.Y.C., 1985, Man of Yr. award Am. Express, 1985, Appreciation award Lupus Found. Am., 1985, Sportsman of Yr. award David Zinkoff Meml. Found., 1986; presented Liberty Bell award Mayor Frank Rizzo, Phila., 1978; named to Hall of Fame, U. Mass., 1980, Basketball Hall of Fame. One of 3 players to score 30,000 points in his profl. basketball career; holds NBA All-Star game record for most free-throws attempted in one half, 11, in 1978; shares NBA All-Star game record for most free-throws made in one half, 9, in 1978; one of 7 players to average over 20 points and 20 rebounds per game during NCAA career. Office: care Erving Group Inc PO Box 8269 Cherry Hill NJ 08002-0269

ERWIN, BARBARA F., school system administrator; b. Chgo. married; 2 children. BS in Spl. Edn., Ind. U., Bloomington; MS in Sch. Adminstrn., Purdue U., West Lafayette, Ind.; PhD in Sch. Adminstrn., Ind. U., Bloomington. Mid. sch. spl. needs tchr.; Title IV-C cons. Ind. Dept. Pub. Instrn.; spl. edn. diagnostician; tchr.; elem. sch. prin.; supt. Ind., Tex., Allen Ind. Sch. Dist., Tex., 1994—2000, Scottsdale Pub. Sch., Ariz., 2000—04; school supt. St. Charles, Ill., 2004—07; commr. edn. Ky. Dept. Edn., 2007—. Nominee Nat. Supt. of Yr., 1999; named Supt. of Yr., Tex. Assn. of Sch. Bds., 1997, Tex. Assn. Sch. Adminstrs., 1998; recipient Top Suburban Supt. Leadership Learning award, Am. Assn. of Sch. Adminstrs., 1996. Office: Ky Dept Edn 500 Mero St, 1st Fl CPT Frankfort KY 40601*

ERWIN, DONALD CARROLL, plant pathology educator; b. Concord, Nebr., Nov. 24, 1920; s. Robert James and Carol Erwin; m. Veora Marie Endres, Aug. 15, 1948; children: Daniel Erwin, Myriam Erwin Casey. Student, Wayne State Coll., Nebr., 1938-39; BSc, U. Nebr., 1949, MA, 1950; PhD, U. Calif.-Davis, 1953. Jr. plant pathologist U. Calif., Riverside, 1953-54, asst. plant pathologist, 1954-60, assoc. plant pathologist, 1960-66, prof. plant pathology, 1966—, emeritus prof., 1991. Sr. author: Phytophthora Diseases Worldwide, 1996; editor: Phytophthora: Its Biology, Taxonomy, Ecology and Pathology, 1983; contbr. articles to profl. jours. With U.S. Army, 1942-46; ETO. Nathan Gold fellow, 1949, Guggenheim fellow, 1959 Mem.: Am. Phytopathol. Soc. (fellow), Sigma Xi.

ERWIN, DOUGLAS HAMILTON, museum director, paleobiologist; b. LA, Mar. 27, 1958; s. John Daniel and Ann E. AB, Colgate U., 1980; PhD, U. Calif., Santa Barbara, 1985. Asst. prof. dept. geol. sci. Mich. State U., East Lansing, 1985-90; assoc. curator dept. paelobiology U.S. Nat. Mus. Natural History, Washington, 1990-93, curator dept. paelobiology, 1993—; interim dir. Natural Mus. of Natural History, 2002—03. Mem. Paleontol. Soc., AAAS, Geol. Soc. Am.

ERWIN, ELMER LOUIS, vintager, consultant; b. Visalia, Calif., Oct. 6, 1926; s. Louis Nelson and Myra Erla (Hector) E.; m. Jeanne Prothero, Feb. 27, 1954; children: Catherine Lynn, Christopher Lawrence. BS, U. Calif.-Berkeley, 1950. Registered profl. engr., Calif. With Kaiser Cement Corp., Oakland, Calif., 1957-80, v.p. mfg. and distbn., 1980-87; freelance vintager. Cons. internat. cement plant projects.

ERWIN, FRANK WILLIAM, human resources consultant; b. Elizabeth, NJ, Nov. 22, 1931; s. Frank J. and Jessie (Rugero) E.; m. Bridget E. Taddeo, June 26, 1965. BA cum laude, NYU, 1957. With MBS, 1957-62, asst. to pres., asst. sec. to bd. dirs., 1960-62; dep. dir. div. selection, dir. recruiting ops. Peace Corps, 1962-65; exec. asst. to sec. labor, 1965-68; pres., chmn. Richardson, Bellows, Henry & Co., Inc., 1968-99; advisor FBI, 1995—, ePredix, Inc., 1999—2005, Nat. Skills Stds. Bd., 2001—03, PreVisor, 2005—. Chmn. fin. com. Our Lady of Lourdes Ch.; pres. Ridge House Condominium, 2002-05; v.p. Ridge House Condominium, 2001-02. With US Army, 1949—52. Mem. APA, Internat. Assn. for Advancement Pschology, Soc. for Indsl. and Orgnl. Psychology (Disting. Profl. Contbn. award, 2005), Pers. Testing Coun. Met. Washington. Home and Office: 2310 S Rolfe St Arlington VA 22202-1545 Office Phone: 703-521-6264. E-mail: niwre@ix.netcom.com.

ERWIN, GREGORY SCOTT, lawyer; b. Baton Rouge, May 10, 1949; s. Scott Wilson and Anne (Sanders) E.; m. Terry Williams, May 7, 1971; children— Amy, Gregory Scott. B.A., La. State U., 1971, J.D., 1974. Bar: La. 1974, U.S. Dist. Ct. (we., mid. and ea. dists.) La. 1974, U.S. Ct. Appeals (5th cir.) 1974, U.S. Ct. Appeals (11th cir.) 1981, U.S. Supreme Ct. 1984. Ptnr. Bolen & Erwin, Ltd., Alexandria, La., 1974—99; sole practitioner, 1999—; mem. products liability com. Def. Rsch. Inst., Chgo., 1984—. Profl. liaison United Givers of Rapides Parish, Alexandria, La., 1982; mem. Indsl. Devel. Bd. of Cenla, Alexandria, 1984. Served to capt. U.S. Army, 1967-74. Mem. La. Assn. Def. Counsel (bd. dirs. 1982-84), La. State Bar Assn., La. Trial Lawyers Assn. (Robert Lee Tullos Meml. award 1974), Alexandria Bar Assn., Alexander/Pineville C. of C. (city govt. liaison com. 1983), Lions (bd. dirs. 1981-82), Rotary Internat. Republican. Baptist.

ERWIN, H. ROBERT, lawyer; b. LA, May 19, 1945; s. Howard R. and Nina B. Erwin; m. Nancy Smick, Sept. 9, 1967; children: Meghan, Kate, Benson, Carter. BA, Purdue U., 1967; JD, Georgetown U., 1972. Bar: Md. 1973, D.C. 1972, U.S. Dist. Ct. Md. 1973, U.S. Ct. Appeals (4th cir.) 1985. Dir. Consumer Law Ctr. Legal Aid Bur., Balt., 1972-78; cons., Office of Consumer Affairs U.S. Dept. Energy, Washington, 1978; chief Consumer Protections Divsn. Office of Atty. Gen., Balt., 1979-82; ptnr. Pretl & Erwin, P.A., Balt., 1983-95, The Erwin Law Firm, P.A., Balt., 1996—. Guest lectr., moot ct. judge U. Md. Sch. Law, Balt., 1988, 91-94; adv. bd. St. Ambrose Legal Svcs., Balt., 1994—. Contbr. chpt. to book. Pres., bd. mem. League for the Disabled, Balt., 1989-98; chpt. mem. Cathedral of the Incarnation, Balt., 1987-89. With U.S. Army, 1969-71. Mem. Md. State Bar Assn., Nat. Assn. Consumer Advocates, Engring. Soc. Office: The Erwin Law Firm PA Side 10 W Madison St Baltimore MD 21201-2398 Office Phone: 410-385-6000.

ERWIN, LINDA MCINTOSH, retired librarian; b. Austin, Tex., June 22, 1939; d. William Erwin and Martha (Ferguson) McIntosh; m. Kenneth James Erwin, June 7, 1962 (div. Feb. 1986); 1 child, Jason Emerson. BA magna cum laude, U. Tex., 1961, MLS, 1968. Tchr. Spanish, Victoria (Tex.) H.S., 1961-62, El Campo (Tex.) H.S., 1962-63, Del Valle (Tex.) H.S., 1963-66; libr. U. Tex., Austin, 1968-69, Corpus Christi Pub. Librs., 1981-89; cons. South Tex. Libr. Sys., Corpus Christi, 1989-99, asst. coord., 1999—2006; ret., 2006. Ford Found. scholar, 1966-67. Mem. Tex. Libr. Assn., Phi Beta Kappa, Alpha Phi, Sigma Delta Pi.

ERWIN, MARK A., air transportation executive; Sr. v.p. airport svcs. Continental Airlines, Inc., 1995—2002, dir., pres., CEO Continental Micronesia, Inc., 2002—, sr. v.p. Asia/Pacific & corp. devel., 2004—. Dir. Copa Airlines and Copa Holdings, 2004—. Office: Continental Airlines Inc PO Box 4607 Houston TX 77210 Office Phone: 713-324-8601. Office Fax: 713-324-3099. E-mail: mark.erwin@coair.com.*

ERWIN, MARY R., investment advisor; b. Chgo., Apr. 24, 1979; d. Jacklien and Bill Erwin. BA, U. Fla., Gainesville. Instl. equity sales/trading asst. Raymond James & Assocs., St. Petersburg, Fla., 2003—05; LSAT instr./braintrust mem. Kaplan Test Prep, Tampa, 2003—06; portfolio specialist BlackRock, St. Petersburg, Fla., 2006—. Mem.: Tampa Gator Club, Am. Mensa. Home Phone: 352-219-6915.

ERWIN, RAYMOND MAURICE, educator; b. Ames, Iowa, Dec. 8, 1924; s. Maurice Weir and Ruth (Martin) E.; m. Gloria Yvonne Crews, June 18, 1949; m. 2d, Marion Emma Schwarting, Oct. 14, 1972; m. 3d Vivian Elaine Johnson, Aug. 4, 1996. BS, ND State U., 1948; BS, U. Minn., 1954, MA, 1971. Cert. vocat. agr., agribus. tchr., audio-visual dir. Minn. Vets. instl. on-farm instr. Minot State Coll., ND, 1948-51; vocat. agr. instr. Stillwater HS, Minn., 1954—84; agr. adv. Lam Dong province South Viet Nam, AID, 1966-67; freelance comml. photographer. Baytown twp. supr., Washington County, Minn., 1963-66. Served to col. USMCR, 1942-84. Sears Coll. scholar ND State U., 1942. Contbr. articles to profl. jours. Mem. NEA, Future Farmers of Am. (hon. Am. Farmer, life alumni), Minn. Edn. Assn., Minn. Vocat. Agr. Instrs. Assn. (dist. dir., sec., editor Ag Man), Am. Vocat. Assn., Minn. Vocat. Assn., Marine Corps Assn., Marine Corps Res. Officers Assn., Res. Officers Assn., Kappa Delta Pi, Alpha Zeta, Alpha Tau Alpha, Alpha Phi Gamma, Phi Delta Kappa, Rotary, SAR. Republican. Methodist. Home: 5225 Northbrook Blvd N Stillwater MN 55082-2106 Personal E-mail: rerwin3957@aol.com.

ERXLEBEN, WILLIAM CHARLES, lawyer, data processing executive; b. Chgo., Dec. 18, 1942; s. Walter Oscar and Sarah Louise (Githens) E.; m. Gayle Amelia Reichmuth, Aug. 28, 1965; children: David William, Jennifer Renée. BS in Bus., Miami U., Oxford, Ohio, 1963; JD, Stanford U., 1966. Bar: Wash. 1969. Asst. state atty. gen. Wash. State Atty. Gen.'s Office, Olympia, 1968-70; exec. asst. U.S. atty. Dept. Justice, Seattle, 1970-72; regional dir. FTC, Seattle, 1972-79; lectr. Grad. Sch. Bus., U. Wash., Seattle, 1979-85; ptnr. Foster, Pepper & Shefelman, Bellevue, Wash., 1985-91, Lane Powell Spears Lubersky, Olympia, 1991-93; pres., CEO, Data I/O Corp., Redmond, Wash., 1993-98, bd. dirs., 1979-98. Chmn., dir. Advanced Digital Tech., Bellevue, 1983-85. Contbr. articles to law revs. Counsel Wash. Assn. for Children and Adults with Learning Disabilities, Seattle, 1985-93; chmn. Portwatch, Seattle, 1985; mem. advt. rev. com. BBB, Seattle, 1982; bd. dirs. Wash. Citizens for Recycling, Seattle, 1980-84; Dem. nominee for Wash. State Atty. Gen., 1988, Wash.Ho. of Reps., 1982; mem., chmn. Newcastle City Planning Commn., 2002—; mem. Newcastle City Coun., 2002—. Recipient Excellence in Supervision award FTC, 1975, Disting. Svc. award, 1979; Sloan exec. fellow Stanford U. Grad. Sch. Bus., 1975-76. Mem. ABA, Wash. State Bar Assn. (sec.-treas. antitrust subcom 1981-83). Home: 7625 120th Pl SE Newcastle WA 98056-1791 E-mail: billerx3@yahoo.com.

ERZINGER, KATHY MCCLAM, nursing educator; b. Lake City, SC, July 14, 1951; d. Curtis Brown and Parneace Ora (Timmons) McClam; m. Dennis Eugene Erzinger, Sr., June 22, 1974; children: Amberlyn Marie, Dennis Eugene Jr. AA, Brevard C.C., 1971; BS in Vocat. Edn., Carson-Newman Coll., 1974; degree in Vocat. Nursing, Simi Valley Adult Sch., 1997. Lic. vocat. nurse, cert. intravenous therapy and blood withdrawal; staff devel. Tchr. First Bapt. Acad., Thousand Oaks, Calif., 1988—90, Hillcrest Christian Sch., Thousand Oaks, 1990—93; charge nurse Victoria Care Ctr., Ventura, Calif., 1997—98; per diem charge nurse Thousand Oaks (Calif.) Health Care, 1998—2007; dir. staff devel. Westlake Healthcare Ctr., Westlake Village, Calif., 2001—02; instr. Simi Valley Adult Sch., Simi Valley, Calif., 2000—. Vol. Am. Cancer Assn., Simi Valley, 2003. Mem.: NEA, Calif. Vocat. Educators, Calif. Coun. for Adult Edn., Simi Educators Assn., Calif. Tchrs. Assn., Health Occupations Students of Am. Republican. Avocations: painting, baking, walking, music, gardening. Office: Simi Valley Adult School 1880 Blackstock St Simi Valley CA 93065 Office Phone: 805-579-6200 x 1078. Personal E-mail: erzingerk@msn.com.

ESAKI, LEO (ESAKI LEONA), physicist, foundation executive, university president; b. Osaka, Japan, Mar. 12, 1925; arrived in U.S., 1960, permanent resident; s. Soichiro and Niyoko (Ito) Esaki; m. Masako Araki, 1959; children: Nina Yvonne, Anna Eileen, Eugene Leo; m. Masako Kondo, May 31, 1986. BS, U. Tokyo, 1947, PhD, 1959. With Sony Corp., Japan, 1956—60; with Thomas J. Watson Research Center, IBM, Yorktown Heights, NY, 1960—92, IBM fellow, 1967—92, mgr. device research, 1965—92; dir. IBM-Japan, 1975—92; pres. U. Tsukuba, Ibaraki, Japan, 1992—98; chmn. Sci. and Tech. Found. of Ibaraki, 1998—; exec. dir. Tsukuba Internat. Congress Ctr., 1999—; pres. Shibaura Inst. of Tech., Tokyo, 2000—05. Dir. Yamada Sci. Found., 1976—. Contbr. numerous articles to professional journals. Decorated Order of Culture Govt. of Japan, Grand Cordon Order of Rising Sun (First Class); recipient Nishina Mem. Prize, 1959, Asahi Press award, 1960, Toyo Rayon Found. award, 1961, Morris N. Liebmann Mem. prize, 1961, Stuart Ballantine medal, Franklin Inst., 1961, Japan Acad. award, 1965, Nobel prize in Physics, 1973, Sci. Achievement award, US-Asia Inst., 1983, Internat. Prize for New Materials, Am. Physical Soc., 1985, Medal of Honor, IEEE, 1991. Fellow: IEEE (Morris N. Liebman Meml. prize 1961, medal of Honor 1991), Am. Vacuum Soc. (bd. dirs. 1973—74), Japan Phys. Soc., Am. Phys. Soc. (councillor-at-large 1971—74); mem.: NAE (fgn. assoc.), NAS (fgn. assoc.), Japan Acad., Russian Acad. Scis. (fgn.), Academia Nacional de Ingenieria Mex. (corr.), Max-Planck Gesellschaft, Am. Philos. Soc., Am. Acad. Arts and Scis. Achievements include discovery of Esaki tunnel diode, 1957; pioneering research in semiconductor superlattices and quantum wells. Home: PO Box 851 Katonah NY 10536-0851 Office: Esaki Tokyo Office 25-17 Sakuragaokacho Shibuya Tokyo 150 0031 Japan also: Tsukuba Internat Congress 2-20-3 Takezono Tsukuba 305 0032 Japan E-mail: leoesaki@epochal.or.jp.

ESAMANN, DOUGLAS F., utilities executive; m. Kimberly Esamann; children: Regan, Kalee, Conley. BS, Ind. U., 1979. Various positions to tax mgr. Pub. Svc. Indiana (now subs. of Cinergy), Ind., 1979—94; project mgr., corp. devel. Cinergy Corp., Cin., 1994—96, fin. team, comml. bus. unit, 1996—98, gen. mgr., bus. devel. Cin., 1998—99, v.p., CFO, comml. bus. unit, 1999—2001, pres. Pub. Svc. Ind. Inc., 2001—04, sr. v.p., Energy Portfolio Strategy and Mgmt., Comml. Bus. Unit. Cin., 2004—. Bd. dir. Ctrl. Ind. Corp. Partnership, Ind. Fiscal Policy Inst. Mem.: Ind. Mfrs. Assn. (bd. dir.), Ind. C. of C. (bd. dir.), Indpls. (Ind.) C. of C. (bd. dir.). Office: Cinergy Corp 139 E 4th St Cincinnati OH 45202

ESBECK, EDWARD S., retired education educator; b. Kimballton, Iowa, June 30, 1932; s. Edward Theodore and Gudrun Marie Esbeck; m. Rosemary J. Hastings, Aug. 15, 1998; m. Janet Marie Thuesen, June 30, 1957 (div. July 1, 1976); children: E. Scott, Jill Marie Esbeck-Kearns, Karen Marie James. AA, Grandview Coll., 1953; BA in Bus. Adminstrn., Drake U., 1957; MEd in Bus., U. Iowa, 1962; PhD in Orgnl. Behavior, Case Western Res., 1972. Assoc. prof. bus. U. No. Iowa, Cedar Falls, 1976—78; prof. mgmt. Ctrl. Wash. U., Ellensburg, 1978—98. Dir., orgn. devel. Hillsdale Coll., Mich., 1972—74. Author: (article) Adminstrv. Sci. Quarterly, Jour. Police Sci. & Adminstrn., Jour. Mgmt. Edn. Planning/organizing team White Anti-Racism Conf., Seattle, 2005. Cpl. US Army, 1953—55, Fort Hood, Tex. Mem.: Pacific NW Orgn. Devel. Network (bd. dirs. 1981—2006). D-Liberal. Lutheran. Avocations: sailing, woodworking, metalworking. Home: 1322 11th Ct SW Olympia WA 98502-5807

ESCALANTE, JUAN, performing company executive; children: Juan, Eduardo. Devel. mgr., human resources dir. Miami City Ballet; asst. dir. fin. N.Y.C. Ballet; mng. dir. Ballet of Fla., Fla., 2002—. Mem. bd. trustees Chaminade-Madonna Coll. Prep. , Hollywood, Fla. Business E-Mail: Jescalante@balletflorida.com.

ESCALANTE, JUDSON ROBERT, business consultant; b. Schenectady, NY, Jan. 31, 1930; s. James S. and Katherine H. (Judson) E.; m. Charlotte D. Carpenter, June 7, 1958; children: David J., Katherine Anne. BA, Union Coll., 1953. Asst. estate planning officer Nat. Comml. Bank, Albany, NY, 1955-65; founder, v.p., sec., dir. Fidelity Bank of Colonie, Latham, NY, 1966-69; area dir. Gen. Bus. Svcs., Latham, 1969-81, Micro Bus. Svcs., 1981—2003. V.p. fin. Gad Cruise Lines, Inc., 1987-88; instr. in field. Bd. dirs., treas. Capital Artists Opera Co., 1970-74, 79; mem. fund dr. com. Union Coll., 1979-80; vestryman, treas. Episcopal Ch.; treas., chief fin. officer Chatham Vis. Nurse Assn., 1983-89; trustee Chatham Vis. Nurse Assn. Profit Trust, 1985-96; auditor Chatham Conservation Found., 1985-95. With U.S. Army, 1953-55. Mem. Colonie C. of C. (treas., bd. dirs. 1972-76), Union Coll. Alumni Soc. (pres. 1971-73, Alumni Gold medal 1978), Dutch Settlers Soc. Albany. Home: 400 Old Comers Rd Chatham MA 02633-1315 E-mail: judcape@capecod.net.

ESCARRAZ, ENRIQUE, III, lawyer; b. Evergreen Park, Ill., Aug. 30, 1944; s. Enrique Jr. and Mary Ellen (Bandy) E.; children from previous marriage; Erin Christine, Martina Mary; m. Patricia Jane Escarraz; children: Sarah Ellen, James Lee, Jason F. BA, U. Fla., 1966, JD, 1968. Bar: Fla. 1969, US Dist. Ct. (so. and mid. dists.) Fla. 1969, US Ct. Appeals (5th cir.) 1971, US Ct. Appeals (11th cir.) 1981. VISTA atty. Community Legal Counsel, Chgo., 1968-69; mng. atty. Fla. Rural Legal Svcs., Ft. Myers, 1969-71; pvt. practice law St. Petersburg, Fla., 1971-82, 85-87, 88—; ptnr. Anderson & Escarraz, St. Petersburg, 1982-85; asst. gen. counsel U. South Fla., 1987-88; assoc. James L. Eskald Law Office, Largo, Fla., 1988. Part-time atty. Pub. Defender's Office Fla. 6th Cir., St. Petersburg, 1973-74; bd. dirs. Gulf Coast Legal Svcs., Inc., 1989—, pres., 1994-96. Vol. Cmty. Law Prog., Inc.; coord. James B. Sanderlin for Judge, Pinellas County, Fla., 1972-76; mem. ACLU Legal Panel, St. Petersburg, 1972—; cooperating atty. NAACP Legal Def. Edn. Funds, Inc., NYC, 1973—; pres. Creative Care, Inc., Clearwater, Fla., 1974-80; mem. allocations com. United Way, Pinellas County, 1976, 1978-81; pres., treas. Cmty. Youth Svcs., Inc., St. Petersburg, 1977-82; co-chmn. Blue Ribbon Com. Pinellas County Dem. Exec. Com., 1977-82; mem. Fla. HRS Dist. V Adv. Coun., Pinellas County, 1982, St. Petersburg Human Rels. Rev. Bd., 1984, 90—, St. Petersburg Adult Cmty. Band, 1989-2003, Greater St. Petersburg Second Time Around Marching Band, 1990-92; mem. adv. bd. Jacquelyn Elvera Hodges Johnson Fund, 1990-2007. Mem.: ATLA, ABA, St. Petersburg Bar Assn. (pro bono com. 1988, 1995—2001, diversity com. 2000—07), Nat. Assn. Social Security Claimant Reps., Fla. Bar Assn., Show Me the Money Investment Club Pinellas (founding mem., 1st pres. 2002, v.p. 2005), Greater Pinellas County Dem. Club (sec.-treas. 1989—97, bd. dirs. 1997—2001). Office: 2101 5th Ave N Saint Petersburg FL 33713-8013 also: PO Box 847 Saint Petersburg FL 33731-0847 Home Phone: 727-822-0309; Office Phone: 727-327-6600. Personal E-mail: rattorne@tampabay.rr.com.

ESCHBACH, JOSEPH WETHERILL, nephrology educator; b. Detroit, Jan. 21, 1933; s. Joseph William and Marguerite (Wetherill) E.; m. Mary Ann Charles, June 16, 1956; children: Cheryl Louise, Ann Elizabeth, Joseph Charles. BA, BS, Otterbein Coll., 1955; MD, Jefferson Med. Coll., 1959. Practitioner nephrology and internal medicine Minor and James Med., Seattle, 1965—2003; dir. home dialysis U. Wash., Seattle, 1965-72, clin. asst. prof. div. nephrology, 1967-70, clin. assoc. prof. div. nephrology, 1970-75, clin. prof. div. nephrology, 1975-85, clin. prof. divs. nephrology and hematology, 1985—2003. Cons. Ortho Pharm., Raritan, N.J., 1987-88, Amgen, Thousand Oaks, Calif., 1985-91. Co-editor: Erythropoietin: Molecular, Cellular and Clinical Biology, 1991; contbr. articles to jours. in field, chpts. to textbooks. Trustee First Ave. Svc. Ctr., 1976-86; pres. bd. trustees Northwest Kidney Ctr., Seattle, 1985-87 (Haviland award 1991). Recipient Disting. Svc. award Seattle Jaycees, 1979, Alumni Achievement award Otterbein Coll., 1991. Fellow: ACP; mem.: AMA, Washington Assn. Biomed. Rsch. (pres. 1999—2001), King County Med. Soc. (pres. 1987), Internat. Soc. Nephrology, Am. Soc. Nephrology, Inst. Medicine of NAS. Presbyterian. Avocations: squash, woodworking, singing. Home: 101-101st Ave SE 301A Bellevue WA 98004-6502 Office: U Wash NW Kidney Ct 700 Broadway Seattle WA 98122

ESCHELBECK, GERHARD, information technology executive; MS, PhD, Univ. Linz, Austria. Founder IDS GmbH (acquired by McAfee); v.p. engring. anti-virus products McAfee Assoc.; v.p. engring. security products Network Assoc.; v.p. engring, chief tech. officer Qualys, Inc.; sr. v.p. engring., chief tech. officer Webroot Software Inc., 2006—. Named one of Top 25 Most Influential CTOs, InfoWorld, 2003, 2004, 2006. Achievements include being one of the inventors of the Common Vulnerability Scoring Sys. (CVSS); holds numerous patents in the field of managed network security. Office: Webroot Adv Tech Ctr 515 Ellis St Mountain View CA 94043 also: Webroot HQ 2560 55th St PO Box 19816 Boulder CO 80308-2816*

ESCHENBACH, CHRISTOPH, conductor, musician, music director; b. Breslau, Silesia, Germany, Feb. 20, 1940; Attended, Hamburg Conservatory, Germany, State Conservatory Music, Cologne, Germany; D, U. Houston. Performed with leading orchs. including Concertgebouw, Amsterdam, The Netherlands, Paris Orch., London Symphony, Berlin Philharm., Carnegie Hall debut with Cleve. Orch., 1969, toured Europe, N.Am. and S.Am., Israel, Japan, appeared at festivals including, Salzburg, Austria, Lucerne, Switzerland, Bonn, Germany, Aix-en-Provence, France, Pacific Music Festival, 1990—94, chief condr. Staatsphilharmonie Rheinland-Pfalz, Germany, 1979, first prin. guest condr. Tonhalle Orch., Switzerland, 1981, chief condr., 1982, rec. artist Deutsche Gammophon, Polydor, EMI, Virgin Classics, London, 1989, artistic dir. Schleswig-Holstein Music Festival, Germany, music dir. Hamburg NDR Symphony Orch., Orch. de Paris, 2000, Houston Symphony, 1988—99, Phila. Orch., 2003—. Decorated officers cross German Order Merit, comdrs. cross; named artistic dir., Ravinia Music Festival, 1995, award, Munich Internat.; recipient Leonard Bernstein award, Pacific Music Festival, 1993. Office: Columbia Artists Management Llc 1790 Broadway # 6 New York NY 10019-1412 also: Phila Orch Kimmel Ctr Performing Arts 260 S Broad St Philadelphia PA 19102*

ESCHENMOSER, ALBERT, chemist; b. Erstfeld, Aug. 5, 1925; s. Alfons and Johanna (Oesch) E.; m. Elizabeth Baschnonga, 1954; 3 children. Dr. Nat. Sci., Swiss Fed. Inst. Tech., 1951; student Collegium Altdorf, Kantonsschule St. Gallen, ETH Zurich; Dr.rer.nat. (hon.), U. Fribourg, 1966; DSc (hon.), U. Chgo., 1970, U. Edinburgh, 1979, U. Bologna, 1989, U. Frankfurt, 1990, U. Strasbourg, 1991, Harvard U., 1993, Scripps Rsch. Inst., La Jolla, Calif., 2000. Privatdozent organic chemistry Swiss Fed. Inst. Tech., 1956, assoc. prof., 1960, prof. organic chemistry, 1965; prof. Skaggs Inst. Chem. Biology Scripps Rsch. Inst., La Jolla, Calif., 1996. Contbr. articles to profl. jour. Recipient Kern award, Swiss Fed. Inst. Tech., 1949, Werner award, Swiss Chem. Soc., 1956, Ruzicka award, Swiss Fed. Inst. Tech., 1958, Fritzsche award, Am. Chem. Soc., 1966, Marcel Benoist prize, Swiss Govt., 1973, R.A. Welch award in Chemistry, Houston, 1974, Kirkwood medal, Yale, 1976, A.W.V. Hofmann-Denkmünze, GDCh., 1976, Dannie Heinemann prize, Akademie der Wissenschaften Göttingen, 1977, Davy medal, Royal Soc. London, 1978, Tetrahedron prize, Pergamon Press, 1981, G. Kenner award, U. Liverpool, 1982, Arthur C. Cope award, Am. Chem. Soc., 1984, Wolf prize for chemistry, Wolf Found., Israel, 1986, Cothenius medal, Leopoldina Halle, 1991, Orden Pour le mérite für Wissenschaften und Künste, Berlin, 1992, Oesterreichisches Ehrenzeichen für Wissenschaft und Kunst, 1993, Nakanishi prize, Chem. Soc. Japan, 1998, Paracelsus prize, Swiss Chem. Soc., 1999, Grande Medaille d'Or, Acad. de Sci., Paris, 2001, A.I. Oparin medal, Internat. Soc. Study Origin of Life, 2002, Roger Adams award, Am. Chem. Soc., 2003, F. H. Westheimer medal, Harvard U., 2004, F. A. Cotton medal, Tex. A&M U., 2004, Sir Derek Barton medal, Royal Soc. Chemistry, London, 2004. Mem. Am. Acad. Arts and Sci. (fgn.), Nat. Acad. Sci. US (fgn. assoc.), Akademie der Wissenschaften (corr. mem. Göttingen), Deutsche Akademie der Naturforscher Leopoldina (Halle), Royal Soc. (fgn. London), Pontificial Acad. (Vatican), Acad. Europe (London), Croatian Acad. Sci. Arts (corr. mem. Zagreb), European Acad. Scis. (Brussels). Home: Bergstrasse 9 8700 Kusnacht Switzerland Office: ETH Hönggerberg HCI H309 CH-8093 Zurich Switzerland Business E-Mail: eschenmoser@org.chem.ethz.ch.

ESCHWEILER, PETER QUINTUS, planning consultant; b. Milw., Nov. 2, 1932; s. Alexander Chadbourne Jr. and Dorothy Quincy (Adams) E. m. Mickie Pauline Symonds, Aug. 13, 1955; children Susan Marie, Steven Adams. BA, Cornell U., 1955, M of Regional Planning, 1957. Assoc. planner Frederick P. Clark & Assocs., Rye, NY, 1960—66; chief planner Westchester County, White Plains, NY, 1967, dep. commr. of planning, 1968—69, commr. of planning, 1969—91; advisor Greenway Cmty. Coun. Hudson River Valley, NY, 1991—2000; advisor Nassau County Planning Commn., NY, 1997—98. Pres. Pleasantville (N.Y.) Housing Devel. Fund Co., Inc., 1997—2002, sec., 2003—; mem. Mt. Pleasant Pub. Libr. Men's Group, 1991—, chmn., 2002—; dir. Westchester County Hist. Soc., 2001—07; pres. Pleasantville Cmty. Housing Devel. Orgn., Inc., 2002—03, sec., 2005—; mem. Pleasantville Bus. Support Coun., 2004—; chmn. Westchester County Drought Mgmt. Task Force, 1991—2002, Westchester County Geographic Info. Sys. Task Force, 1998—; mem. mission planning task force Presbytery of Hudson River, 1994, 1997, 2002, chmn. mission planning task force, 1997. Lt. USAF, 1957—60. Recipient Lifetime Achievement award, Westchester Mcpl. Planning Fedn., 2004, Outstanding Cmty. Svc. award, Pleasantville C. of C., 2004, Top Honor award, Westchester County Sr. Citizens Hall Fame, 2005. Mem. Am. Inst. Cert. Planners, Nat. Assn. County Planning Dirs. (pres. 1984-85), N.Y. State Assn. Counties (pres. 1980-81, Recognition award 1991), N.Y. Assn. County Planning Dirs. (pres. 1970, bd. dirs. 1969-91), Nat. Assn. Counties (bd. dirs. 1987-89), Nat. Assn. Regional Couns. (bd. dirs. 1988-89), Am. Soc. for Photogrammetry and Remote Sensing (bd. dirs. North Atlantic region 1987-97, 99—, sec.-treas. 1988-97, Bausch and Lomb Photogrammetric award 1957, Meritorious Svc. award 1997), Cornell Club (N.Y.C.), Rotary (pres. White Plains 1985-86), Sigma Chi. Presbyterian. Avocations: skiing, photography, computers. Home and Office: 36 Wilton Rd Pleasantville NY 10570-2022 Home Phone: 914-769-4477; Office Phone: 914-747-1445. E-mail: PQuintus@aol.com.

ESCOBAR, ANTHONY, marketing professional, consultant; b. Liverpool, England, Aug. 29, 1948; s. Antonio and Joyce Escobar; m. Randi Medlock, Jan. 3, 1970; children: Danielle Lisa Coletti, Anthony Brandon, Andrea Marie Clawson, Sean Anthony. Concept product designer Total Health Solutions, Salt Lake City, 1991—; rep. Isagenix Internat., Tempe, Ariz., 2002—. Cons. and seminar spkr. Anthony Escobar & Assoc., Salt Lake City, 1992—; herbalist, nutritionist; cons. to network mktg. industry. Author network mktg. ednl. materials; editor: Cleansing Times Newsletter. Mem.: Women's Health Rsch. Soc., N.Y. Acad. Scis., Christopher Reeve's Paralysis Found., Nat. Health Mus. Achievements include having broken every record in network mktg., income and recruiting. Home: 12913 Boulter St Draper UT 84020-9167 Home Phone: 801-381-1925; Office Phone: 801-381-1925. E-mail: tony@tonyescobar.com.

ESCOBAR, JAVIER IGNACIO, psychiatrist; b. Medellin, Colombia, July 26, 1943; came to U.S., 1969; s. Ignacio and Ines (Soto) E.; m. Luz M. Zapata, July 7, 1967; children: Javier I. Jr., Linda. BS, San Ignacio de Loyola, Medellin, 1960; MD, U. Antioquia, Medellin, 1967; M Psychiatry, U. Minn., 1973. Diplomate, Am. Bd. Psychiatry and Neurology. Resident in psychiatry U. Minn., Mpls., 1969-73, asst. prof. dept. psychiatry, 1973-76; prof., vice-chmn. dept. psychiatry U. Conn. Health Ctr., Farmington, 1986—; prof., acting chmn. dept. psychiatry U. Conn. Sch. Medicine, Farmington, 1992-94; prof., chmn. dept. psychiatry UMDNJ-Robert Wood Johnson Med. Sch., Piscataway, NJ, 1994—. Adj. prof. Rutgers U., Piscataway, N.J., 1995—; assoc. prof. depts. pharmacology, psychiatry, U. Tenn., Memphis, 1976-79; assoc. prof. dept. psychiatry, UCLA, 1979-85, prof., 1985-86; chief, VA Neighborhood Clinic, L.A., 1979-82, Clin. Rsch. Ctr. at Brentwood VA Hosp., L.A., 1984-86; mem. adv. com. on psychiat. drugs, FDA, Washington, 1989-95; mem. NIMH Rsch. Com., Washington, 1989-93; mem. tech. adv. group, VA, Washington, 1987-89; sr. advisor to the dir. NIMH, 2003—. Co-author: Mental Health and Hispanic Americans, 1982; contbr. to over 200 med. publs. Fellow Am. Psychiat. Assn. (disting., mem. DSM-V task force, 2006-, Simon Bolivar award, 1998), Am. Assn. Social Psychiatry, Am. Coll. Psychiatry, Am. Soc. Hispanic Psychiatry (past. pres.) Am. Coll. Clin. Psychopharmacology, Am. Psychosomatic Soc., Acad. Psychosomatic Medicine. Democrat. Roman Catholic. Avocations: running, bicycling, guitar, music, singing. Office: UMDNJ-RWJMS Dept Psychiatry 675 Hoes Ln Piscataway NJ 08854-5627 Home: 1 Spring St Apt 1601 New Brunswick NJ 08901 Office Phone: 732-235-4440.

ESCOLAR, DIANA M., neurologist, researcher; b. San Juan, Argentina, Dec. 29, 1961; m. Adrian G. Becher, Oct. 25, 1987; children: Nicole A. Becher, Melanie K. Becher. MD magna cum laude, U. Buenos Aires, 1987. Bd. cert. Am. Acad. Neurology and Psychiatry, cert. neurophysiology Am. Acad. Neurology and Psychiatry, electrodiagnostic medicine Am. Acad. Electrodiagnostic and Neuromuscular Medicine; ballat tchr. 1979. Profl. ballet dancer Colon Theatre Chamber Ballet, Buenos Aires, 1979—82; asst. prof. neurology and pediat. Children's Nat. Med. Ctr, George Washington U., Washington, 1993—2002, assoc. prof. neurology and pediat., 2002—; med. dir. coop. internat. neuromuscular rsch. group Multi-Ctr. Orgn. Hdqrs. Children's Nat. Med. Ctr., Washington, 1999—, dir. neuromuscular program and Muscular Dystrophy Assn. clinic, 2000—. Mem. steering com. SMA Project NIH, Bethesda, Md., 2002—; mem. NIH sci. review com., 2002—; mem., clinical advisory bd. Muscular Dystrophy Assn., 2003—; editl. bd. Clinical Neuromuscular Disorders Jour.; reviewer several profl. jours. and assocs.; cons. Genzyme Inc., Faust Pharm., Wyeth. Mem. Kennedy Ctr. Grantee, NIH, 2001—06, 2005—, Clin. Trial of Prednisone in DMD, Muscular Dystrophy Assn., 2002—06, Assn. Française contre les miopaties, 2002—04, Found. to Erradicate Duchenne, 2003—04. Mem.: Am. Acad. Neurology (assoc.). Achievements include development and validation of a quantitative muscle testing system for use as outcome measures in clinial trials for pediatric neuromuscular diseases; successfully designed, launched, completed and published several clinical trials of new compunds for Duchenne Muscular Dystrophy. Avocations: dance, photography, running, classical music. Office: Childrens Nat Medical Ctr 111 Michigan Ave NW Washington DC 20010 Office Phone: 202-884-4110. Business E-Mail: descolar@cnmcresearch.org.

ESCOTO, CARLOS AURELIO, psychology professor, researcher; b. LA, Sept. 7, 1962; s. Carlos Aurelio Escoto and Marta Elva Lopez. AA with hons., Irvine Valley Coll., Calif.; BA with hons., Chapman U., Orange, Calif., 1994; PhD in Exptl. Psychology, Loma Linda U., Calif., 2002. Vis. prof. Miss. State U., Starkville, Miss., 2001—02; asst. prof. Ea. Conn. State U., Willimantic, Conn., 2002—07, assoc. prof., 2007—, asst. chmn. dept. psychology, 2007—. Adj. faculty Calif. State U., San Bernardino, 1996—2001, Riverside C.C., Calif., 1996—2001, Chapman U., 1996—2001. Contbr. chapters to books, articles to profl. jours. Mem. HIV planning adv. coun. Orange County, Santa Ana, Calif., 1992—94; sec. Laguna Shanti, Laguna Beach, Calif., 1992—94. Named Psychology Student of Yr., Chapman U., 1993, 1994, Prof. of Yr., Calif. State San Bernardino Panhellenic Soc., 2001; recipient Selma Andrews Resarch award, Loma Linda (Calif.) U., 1998, 2001, Competitive Realease Time award, Ea. Conn. State U., 2004; scholar, Irvine Valley Coll., 1991. Mem.: APA (regional trainer 2005—), PNI Rsch. Soc., Am. Psychol. Soc., Psi Chi (Prof. of Yr. Ea. Conn. State U. 2006—07). Office: Eastern Connecticut State University 83 Windham Street Willimantic CT 06226 Office Phone: 860-465-0263. Office Fax: 860-465-4541. Business E-Mail: escotoc@easternct.edu.

ESENALIEV, RINAT OROZBEKOVICH, science educator, lab administrator; b. Frunze, USSR, May 7, 1964; s. Orozbek Esenaliev and Raisa Esenalieva; m. Rauza Tartykova, Mar. 27, 1993; children: Alina, Timur, Arthur. BS in Physics, Moscow Inst. Physics and Tech., 1984, MS in Biophysics, 1987; PhD, Russian Acad. Scis., Inst. Spectroscopy, 1992. With Inst. Spectroscopy, Moscow, 1987—93; faculty Rice U., Houston, 1993—97; staff M.D. Anderson Cancer Ctr., Houston, 1995—96; asst. prof. U. Tex. Med. Br., Galveston, Tex., 1997—2002, assoc. prof., 2002—06, prof., 2006—. Contbr. articles to profl. jours. Mem.: SPIE, Internat. Soc. Therapeutic Ultrasound. Achievements include patents for drug delivery, optics, ultrasound, glucose monitoring, oxygenation and hemoglobin monitoring. Office: U Tex Med Branch 301 University Blvd Galveston TX 77555-0456 Home Phone: 281-554-6997; Office Phone: 409-772-8144. Office Fax: 409-772-8144.

ESFANDIARY, MARY S., physical scientist, operations consultant; b. Passaic, NJ, June 27, 1929; d. Peter J. and Veronica R. (Kida) Nieradka; m. Mohsen S. Esfandiary; children: Homayoun Austin, Dara S. BS in Chemistry, St. John's U., 1951; postgrad., Polytechnic Inst. N.Y., 1955-56. Research chemist Picatinny Arsenal, Dover, N.J., 1951-56; supr. phys. sci. Bur. Mines, Washington, 1956-61; asst. to dir. research Nat. Iranian Oil Co., Tehran, 1961-64; lectr. U. Tehran and Aryamehr Inst. Tech., Tehran, 1961-64, 69-73; dir. internat. affairs Acad. of Scis., Tehran, 1977-79; chief geog. names br. Def. Mapping Agy., Washington, 1981-86, chief prodn. mgmt. office, 1986-87, chief support div., chief inventory mgmt. div., 1987-90, chief product mgmt. dept., 1990-92, dep. dir. distbn. mgmt. ops. Combat Support Ctr., 1993, chief, co-prodn. mgmt. divsn., 1993-94, chief divsn. internat. ops. coprodn. mgmt., 1993-96; ops. mgmt., 1996; dir. MS svcs. Washington, 1997—. Contbr. papers and articles to tech. jours., 1952-78. Pres. UN Delegations Women's Club, N.Y.C., 1967-69, v.p., program dir., 1964-67; pres. Diplomatic Corps. Com. for Red Cross, Bangkok, Thailand, 1974-76; v.p., bd. dirs. Found. for Blind of Thailand, Bangkok, 1973-77. Recipient Badge of Honor for Social Service, Thailand, 1975, 1st Class medal Red Cross, Thailand, 1976. Home and Office: 4401 Sedgewick St NW Washington DC 20016-2713

ESHBAUGH, W(ILLIAM) HARDY, botanist, educator; b. Glen Ridge, NJ, May 1, 1936; s. William Hardy Eshbaugh Jr. and Elizabeth (Wakeman) Henderson; m. Barbara Keller, Sept. 6, 1958; children: David Charles, Stephen Hardy, Elizabeth Wendy Brown, Jeffrey Raymond. BA, Cornell U., 1959; MA, Ind. U., 1961, PhD, 1964. Lectr. in botany Ind. U., Bloomington, 1962; spl. asst. to chief ecology and epidemiology br. Dugway Proving Ground, Utah, 1964-65; asst. prof., curator herbarium So. Ill. U., Carbondale, 1965—67; from asst. prof. to prof. botany Miami U., Oxford, Ohio, 1967—98, chmn. dept. botany, 1983-88, prof. emeritus, 1998. Cur., Willard Sherman Turrell Herbarium, Miami U., 1967-82; assoc. program dir. NSF, Washington, 1982-83; co-chmn. steering com. Systematics Agenda 2000-Charting the Biosphere; adv. bd. Am. Bot. Coun., 1996—; instr. Internat. Rainforest Workshops, 1991-99; pres., bd. dirs. Avian Rsch. and Edn. Inst., 2005—. Co-author: (Book) The Vascular Flora of Andros Island, Bahamas, 1988; contbr. articles to profl. jours. Bd. dirs. Childrens Environ. Trust Found., 1992-94, Hawk Mtn., 2007—; pres. Elizabeth Wakeman Henderson Charitable Found., 1997—; mem. Penobscot Leadership Coun., 2006—. Capt. U.S. Army, 1964-65. Named Citizen of Yr., Oxford, Ohio, 2002, Man of Yr., St. Mary's River Assn., 2006; recipient Herbert Robinson award, Ohio Biol. Survey, 2006, Outstanding Communicator award, Ohio Ornithological Soc., 2007. Fellow: AAAS, Inst. Environ. Scis., Ohio Acad. Sci.; mem.: Ohio Biol. Survey (Herbert Osborn award 2006), Internat. Field Studies (trustee 1989—95), Internat. Orgn. Plant Biosytematists (coun. 1987—89, ad hoc com. 1989—92, N. Am. treas. 1992—95), Assn. Systemic Collections (bd. dirs. 1981—84, rep.-at-large), Nature Conservancy (vice chmn. Ohio chpt. 1970—75, trustee 1970—77), Atlantic Salmon Fedn. (bd. dirs. 2002—), Bot. Soc. Am. (pres. 1988—89, Merit award 1992, Centennial medal 2006), Soc. Econ. Botany (v.p. 1982—83, pres. 1983—84, Disting. Econ. Botanist 2007), Am. Soc. Plant Taxonomists (pres. 1991—92), Am. Inst. Biol. Scis. (pres. 1995), Nat. Audubon Soc. (bd. dirs. 1993—2006, vice-chmn., Great Egret award 2005), Explorer's Club. Methodist. Avocations: camping, fly fishing, photography, sailing, swimming. Home: 209 Mckee Ave Oxford OH 45056-9059 Office: Miami U Dept Botany Oxford OH 45056 Home Phone: 513-523-8305; Office Phone: 513-529-4200. Business E-Mail: eshbauwh@muohio.edu.

ESHELMAN, RALPH ELLSWORTH, historian, consultant, paleontologist; b. Mt. Holly, NJ, Mar. 20, 1947; s. Ralph Mengel and Grace Elizha (Bozarth) E.; m. Evelyne Margaret Herman, May 3, 1974; 1 child, Erich Ellsworth. AA, Prince George's C.C., 1967; BS, SUNY, Stony Brook, 1969; MS, U. Iowa, 1971; PhD, U. Mich., 1974. Phys. sci. aide U.S. Geol. Survey, Washington, 1965-69; dir. Calvert Marine Mus., Solomons, Md., 1974-90; rsch. assoc. Smithsonian Inst., Washington, 1976—2005. Owner Eshelman & Assocs., 1994—; cons. Nat. Maritime Initiative, Nat. Park Svc., 1993-00, USCG, 1995-98; project dir. Md. War of 1812 Initiative, 1998-2002; cons. Am. Battlefield Protection program Nat. Park Svc., 1999-02, cons. Star-Spangled Nat. Historic Trail study, 2002—; lectr. on expedition cruise ships, 1991—; study leader for nat. and internat. trips Smithsonian Instn., 1998-03; dir. palenotological field camp Mus. of Middle Appalachians, 2000-03. Contbr. articles to profl. jours. Grantee Sigma Xi, 1972, Nat. Geog. Soc., 1981, 86. Mem. Nat. Maritime Preservation Task Force (vice chmn. 1983-84), Md. Soc. Underwater Archeology (trustee 1984-86), Md. Historical Trust (bd. mem. 1984—), Md. Humanities Coun. (trustee 1984-89, 2d v.p. 1987-89), Coun. Am. Maritime Mus. (exec. com. 1983-89, v.p. 1988-89, pres. 1990), Solomons Environ. and Archeol. Rsch. Consortium (founding chmn. 1987), Nat. Maritime Alliance (co-chair 1994-95), Nat. Lighthouse Mus. (pres. steering com., trustee 1998-2003, 2nd v.p.), The Nature Conservancy (Md. chpt. v.p. sci. and stewardship 1996-2001), Natural History Soc. Md. (trustee 2003—), Patuxent Riverkeeper (trustee 2003—). Avocations: spelunking, snorkeling, kayaking, hiking, swimming. Home and Office: 12178 Preston Dr Lusby MD 20657-2905 Office Phone: 410-326-4877. E-mail: ree47@comcast.com.

ESHER, BRIAN RICHARD, manufacturing executive; b. NYC, Sept. 1, 1948; s. John Conrad and Elizabeth (Carley) E.; m. Christina M.; children: Justin John, Christopher Ryan. BS in Bus. Mgmt. magna cum laude, Fairleigh Dickinson U., Madison, NJ, 1971, MBA summa cum laude, 1975. Mgr. Litton Industries, Morristown, 1972-75; industry mgr. AT&T Long Lines, Somerset, NJ, 1975-77; v.p. Transaction Mgmt., Inc., Montgomeryville, Pa., 1977-79; dir. mktg. Burroughs Corp., Detroit, 1980-82, exec. office Detoit, 1982-84, v.p. Rochester, NY, 1984-85; sr. v.p., gen. mgr. ITEK Graphic Systems Divsn., 1985-88; exec. v.p. A.B. Dick Co., Chgo., 1988-89; chmn., pres., CEO Environ. Control Group, Inc., Maple Shade, NJ, 1989, pres., CEO, chmn., 1990-96; dir., chmn, CEO MLX Corp., 1990-96, also bd. dirs.; chmn, pres., CEO Pameco Corp., Norcross, Ga., 1992-96; prin. S.E. Tech. Opportunities Fund LLC., 1998—2000; chmn., CEO Storm Consulting LLC, 2000—; chmn., pres & CEO, Coe Mfg. Co., 2002—03, pres., chmn., 2003—04; chmn. Coe Newnes/McGehee, 2002—04, Ace Products Inc., 2003—04, CEO, 2003—04, Fibermark Inc., 2006—. With U.S. Army, 1967-69, Vietnam. Decorated D.S.C., Silver Star, Bronze Star, Purple Heart (3). Mem. Assn. of MBA Execs., Phi Omega Epsilon (Membership award 1971). Republican. Avocation: tennis.

ESHETU, GWENDELBERT LEWIS, retired social worker; b. Cairo, Ill., Mar. 22, 1940; d. Rassie A. and Naomi (Briggs) Lewis; m. Frederick O. Carr (div. 1976); 1 child, Melisande Caprice; m. Fisseha Eshetu, Feb. 17, 1984 (div. 1990). BA, U. Wis., Milw., 1966, MS, 1972. Caseworker Milw. County Dept. Social Services, 1966-70; social worker Ill. Dept. Children and Family Services, Cairo, 1971, Milw. Pub. Schs., 1972—97; ret., 1997. Instr. field placement for grad. students, Milw. Pub. Schs. and U. Wis., Milw., 1973-75. Mem. Nat. Assn. Social Workers, Nat. Assn. Black Social Workers, Milw. Sch. Social Workers Assn., Wis. Assn. Black Social Workers (office holder), Acad. Cert. Social Workers, NAACP (life), Mensa (life), Eta Phi Beta. Democrat. Avocation: writing fiction. Home: 3019 N 55th St Milwaukee WI 53210-1564

ESHLEMAN, VON RUSSEL, electrical engineering educator, aerospace scientist; b. Darke County, Ohio, Sept. 17, 1924; married; 4 children. BEE, George Washington U., 1949; MS, Stanford U., 1950, PhD in Elec. Engring., 1952. Rsch. assoc. Radio Propagation Lab. Stanford (Calif.) U., 1952-56, from instr. to prof. elec. engring., 1956-61, prof. elec. engring., co-dir. Ctr. Radar Astronomy, 1961-82, dir. Radioscience Lab., 1974-83. Cons. NAS, Nat. Bur. Stds., SRI Internat., Jet Propulsion Lab.; mem. Internat. Astronaut Congress, Internat. Astron. Union, Internat. Sci. Radio Union; dir. emeritus Watkins-Johnson Co.; mem. radio sci. teams for Viking, Pioneer, Mariner, Voyager, Galileo spacecraft studies of the planets. Fellow AAAS, IEEE, Am. Geophys. Union, Royal Astronomy Soc.; mem. NAE. Achievements include rsch. in radar astronomy, planetary exploration, ionospheric and plasma physics, radio wave propagation, astronautics. Office: Stanford U Radar Astronomy Ctr Packard EE Bldg 309 Stanford CA 94305-9515 E-mail: eshleman@stanford.edu.

ESHOO, ANNA GEORGES, congresswoman; b. New Britain, Conn., Dec. 13, 1942; d. Fred and Alice Alexandre Georges; children: Karen Elizabeth, Paul Frederick. AA with honors, Canada Coll., 1975. Chmn. San Mateo County Dem. Ctrl. Com., Calif., 1978-82; chair Human Rels. Com., 1979-82; mem. U.S. Congress from 14th Calif. dist., 1993—; at-large minority whip; mem. energy and commerce com., intelligence com. Chief of staff Calif. Assembly Spkr. Leo McCarthy, 1981; regional majority whip No. Calif., 1993-94. Co-founder Women's Hall of Fame; chair San Mateo County (Calif.) Dem. Party, 1980; active San Mateo County Bd. Suprs., 1982-92, pres., 1986; pres. Bay Area Air Quality Mgmt. Dist., 1982-92; mem. San Francisco Bay Conservation Devel. Commn., 1982-92; chair San Mateo County Gen. Hosp. Bd. Dirs. Democrat. Roman Catholic. Office: US House Reps 205 Cannon Ho Office Bldg Washington DC 20515-0514*

ESHOO, BARBARA ANNE RUDOLPH, non-profit administrator; b. Worcester, Mass., Sept. 27, 1946; d. Charles Leighton and Irene Isabella (Wheeler) Rudolph; divorced: 1 child, Melissa Clinton; m. Robert Pius Eshoo, July ll, 198l. Student, Morehead State U., 1964-66, U. N.H., 1974-75; BA, New England Coll., 1976. Asst. to dir. Currier Gallery Art, Manchester, NH, 1976-78, coord. pub. rels., 1979-82; dir. pub. rels. Daniel Webster Coll., Nashua, NH, 1982-87, chief advancement officer, 1988-95; v.p. instnl. advancement Ea. Conn. State U., Willimantic, 1995—2004; sr. v.p. advancement YMCA Greater Hartford Metro, Conn., 2004—. Mem. faculty Currier Art Ctr., Manchester, 1977-79; bd. advisers New Eng. Coll. Art Gallery, Henniker, N.H., 1989-91. Adv. planned giving United Way, Nashua, 1989-90; com. mem. Manchester Mayor's Task force on Youth Affairs, 1986-88, Manchester Bd. of Sch. Commn., 1986-90; del. N.H. Sch. Bds. Assn., 1988-90; trustee, bd. sec. Manchester Hist. Assn., 1990-95; mem. Mayor's Com. on Leadership, Manchester, 1988-91; bd. dirs. Swiftwater coun. Girl Scouts U.S., 1990-95; chair parents com. Bennington Coll.; mem. N.Am. devel. orgn. YMCA, 2004— Mem.: N.Am. YMCA Devel. Officers Orgn., Middlesex County C. of C., Assn. Fundraising Profls., Coun. Advancement and Support of Edn., Assn. Governing Bds. Univs. and Colls. (facilitator 1995—2003, planning com.), Conn. Com. on Planned Giving, Nat. Com. on Planned Giving, Am. Coun. on Edn. (state of Conn. rep. Office Women in Higher Edn.), Conn. Women in Higher Edn., Nat. Soc. Fundraising Execs. (bd. dirs., v.p. pub. affairs N.H./Vt. chpt. to 1995), Newcomen Soc. US, Newcomen Soc. Conn., Rotary (Nashua West chpt. 1990—95), Advt. Club N.H. (bd. dirs., v.p. 1980—82). Avocation: performing and visual arts. Office: YMCA Metrop Offices 241 Trumbull St 2d Fl Hartford CT 06103 Office Phone: 860-522-9622 x2308. Business E-Mail: barbara.eshoo@ghymca.org.

ESHRAGHI, ADRIEN A., head and neck surgeon, medical educator, researcher; b. Nov. 21, 1964; s. Khalil and Pari Eshraghi; m. Rebecca Eshraghi; 1 child, Nicolas. MS, U. Paris, 1993; MD, U. Paris, France, 1994; fellowship in otolaryngology (hon.), UCLA, 1995; DEA, U. Paris, 1997. Cert. otology, neurotology, otolaryngology U. Miami, 2002. Chef de clinique U. Paris, 1996—99; asst. prof. U. Miami Sch. Medicine, Fla., 2002—04, assoc. prof., 2005—; chief otolaryngology Miami VA Med. Ctr., 2004. Ethic adv. bd. West Palm Beach VA med. Ctr., Fla., 2003, laser safety com., 03; dir. Cochlear Implant Program and Rsch., Miami, 2003—05. Contbr. articles various profl. jours., chapters to books. Recipient First Prize Rsch. award, Shandler Soc., 2000, A.M.B. award, Le HumanityMission, 1990. Mem.: Assoc. for Rsch. in Otolarynology, Am. Acad. Otolarynology Head and Neck Surgery, Am. Neurotology Soc. Office: U Miami Miller Sch of Medicine Otolarynotology Dept 1666 NW 10th Ave Ste 306 Miami FL 33136 Home Phone: 954-384-7993; Office Phone: 305-585-7126. Business E-Mail: aeshraghi@miami.edu.

ESIASON, BOOMER (NORMAN JULIUS ESIASON), professional football player; b. West Islip, NY, Apr. 17, 1961; m. Cheryl Esiason. Student, U. Md. Football player Cin. Bengals, 1984-92, N.Y. Jets, 1993-97; broadcaster Monday Night Football ABC Sports, NYC, 1997—99; studio analyst Fox Sports NFL This Morning, 2001, CBS Sports, 2002—; host Boomer Esiason Show on MSG Network, 2002. Host In the Huddle with Boomer Esiason and Chris "Mad Dog" Russo, CBS Sports Radio/Westwood One, 1999—; played in Super Bowl XXIII, 1988. Author: A Boy Named Boomer, 1995; co-author: Toss, 1998; contbr. articles to numerous profl. jours., websites. Co-chmn. Boomer Esaison Found., 1993—. Named to Pro Bowl, 1986, 88, 89, 93; Sporting News All-Pro team, 1988; named Sporting News Player of Yr., 1988. Office: Boomer Esiason Found 200 B Armstrong Rd New Hyde Park NY 11040

ESKANDARIAN, EDWARD, advertising executive; b. Telford, Pa., Nov. 20, 1936; s. Michael and Katherine (Arslanian) E.; m. Nancy Rose Boujicanian, June 26, 1965; children: Wendy, Christopher, Jill. BS, Villanova U., 1958; MBA, Harvard, 1965. Engr. Pitman Dunn Labs., Phila., 1958-60; project engr. GE, Phila., 1961-63; v.p., account supr. Compton Advt., Inc., NYC, 1965-71; chmn., CEO HBM/Creamer Inc., Boston, 1971—89, Arnold Comm., Boston, 1989-2000, Arnold Worldwide Ptnrs., Boston, 2000—; vice chmn. Havas, 2005—. Bd. dirs. Engine, Ltd. Trustee U. Richmond, Dana Farber Cancer Inst.; bd. dirs. HAVAS, Getwell Network. With USAF, 1959-60. Mem. Am. Assn. Advt. Agys. (sec.-treas. 1988-89, ea. region gov.-at-large 1989-91), New Eng. Broadcasters Assn. (pres. 1982-83), Advt. Club Boston (pres. 1977-78, trustee 1980—), Harvard Bus. Sch. Assn. Boston (pres. 1984-85), Harvard Club, Algonquin Club, Weston Golf Club, Jupiter Hills Club, Oyster Harbors Club, Willowbend Club, Caves Valley Club. Home: 300 Boylston St Boston MA 02116-3923 Office: Arnold Worldwide Ptnrs 101 Huntington Ave Boston MA 02199-7606 Business E-Mail: ee@arn.com.

ESKENASI, PEGGY, retail executive; Various merchandising positions including v.p., gen. mgr. and sr. v.p., gen. mdse. mgr. accessories, intimate apparel, children's, cosmetics and shoes Frederick Atkins, Inc., 1980—96; sr. v.p. pvt. label and brand devel. Saks Inc., 1997—99, exec. v.p. pvt. label and brand devel. Proffitt's Merchandising Group, 1999, pres. pvt. label brand devel., 2002; exec. v.p. product devel. Kohl's Corp., Menomonee Falls, Wis., 2004—. Office: Kohls Corp N56 W17000 Menomonee Falls WI 53051-5660 Office Phone: 262-703-7000.*

ESKEW, HENRY LAWRENCE, JR., economist, consultant; b. Atlanta, July 31, 1937; s. Henry L. and Marian Gresham Eskew; m. Gloria Harrell Eskew (div.); children: Marian Kathryn Eskew Brown, Lauren Claire Eskew Kaniecki. BS in Indsl. Mgmt., Ga. Inst. Tech., 1959, MS in Indsl. Mgmt., 1963; MA in Econs., Am. U., Washington, 1966, PhD in Econs., 1988. Ops. analyst Tech. Ops. Inc., Ft. Belvoir, Va., 1963—66; sr. assoc. Planning Rsch. Corp., Washington, 1967—68; founder, pres., CEO Adminstrv. Sci. Corp., Alexandria, Va., 1968—83; prin. Booz Allen & Hamilton, Inc., Washington, 1984—85; rsch. staff, dep. dept. dir. Ctr. for Naval Analyses, Alexandria, 1985—2000; cons. economist, 2000—. Vis. prof. Naval Postgrad. Sch., Monterey, Calif., 1998; profl. lectr. George Washington U., Washington, 1985—95, Am. U., Washington, 1985—95. Contbr. articles to profl. jours. Mem. regional devel. coun. Ga. Inst. Tech., Washington, 1996—99. Commd. officer USAF, 1960—68. Mem.: Mil. Ops. Rsch. Soc., INFORMS, Am. Econ. Assn. Avocations: golf, bridge, sudoku. Office Phone: 704-875-3853. Personal E-mail: heskew@carolina.rr.com.

ESKEW, MICHAEL L., package distribution company executive; BS in Indsl. Engring., Purdue U., 1972; postgrad., Butler U., U. Pa. Various positions UPS, Inc., Germany, 1972-82, indsl. engring. mgr. northwest region, 1982-91, dist. mgr. Cen. Jersey dist., 1991-93, corp. indsl. engring. mgr., 1993, corp. v.p. indsl. engring, 1994—96, group v.p. engring., 1996—99, exec. v.p., 1999—2002, vice chmn., 2000—02, chmn., CEO, 2002—. Bd. dirs. 3M; Mem. Bus. Roundtable. Mem.: NAE. Office: UPS Inc 55 Glenlake Pkwy NE Atlanta GA 30328-3474*

ESKEW, SANDRA CAYE, elementary school educator; b. Cheyenne, Wyo., June 11, 1954; d. James and Dorothy Anne Roth; m. John Thomas Eskew, Jan. 1, 2000; children: Leslie Marie Akin, Shawn Michael Akin. BA in Edn., U. Wyo., Laramie, 1976; M Reading and Literacy, Walden U., Mpls., 2005. Cert. elem. and mid. sch. tchr. Wyo., 1976. 3d grade tchr. East Elem., Douglas, Wyo., 1976—79, West Elem., Douglas, 1979—92; 6th grade tchr. Ronan Mid. Sch., Mont., 1992—94, Oreg. Trail Elem., Casper, Wyo., 1994—. Sponsor Wyo. history day Nat. History Days, Washington, 2000—07; rep. Natrona County Sch. Dist. Employee Family Assistance Program, Casper, Wyo., 2000—. Finalist Nat. History Day Tchr. of Merit, 2004; named Significant Educator, Natrona County Sch. Dist., 2004, Dist. History Day Tchr. of Merit, 2004; recipient Wyo. History Day Tchr. of Merit, 2004. Mem.: Nat. Coun. Social Studies. Office: Natrona County Sch Dist # 1 970 North Glenn Rd Casper WY 82601 Home Phone: 307-265-3105; Office Phone: 307-577-0200.

ESKIN, JEFFREY LAURENCE, lawyer; b. NYC, May 10, 1952; s. Jordan Harlan Eskin and Charlette (Davies) Krane; m. Darla Lynn Gugel, Aug. 5, 1977; children: Jennifer, Jonathan, Emily, Lindy. BA, Yale U., 1974; JD, Emory U., 1978. Bar: Nev. 1978, U.S. Dist. Ct. Nev. 1979, U.S. Ct. Appeals (9th cir.) 1980, U.S. Supreme Ct. 1982. Law clk. Northern Ky. Legal Aid Soc., 1977; dep. atty. gen. State of Nev., Las Vegas, 1979-81; atty. Vargas, Bartlett & Dixon, Las Vegas, Nev., 1978-79, Eskin Law Offices, 1981—89, 1992—, Keefer, O'Reilly, Ferrario and Eskin, Las Vegas, 1989-92. Spl. prosecutor State of Nev., Las Vegas, 1982-84; legal coun. Gov. Richard Bryan's 1988 US Senate Campaign. Moderator Sun Youth Forum; vol. VISTA, 1974—75; coach Clark County Basketball League, 1989—93; baseball coach, 1990—94; softball coach, 1995—97; All-Stars coach, 1995—97; coach Silver State Girls Soccer League, 1989—97, 2003—; bd. dir. Green Valley Little League, 1992—93; mem. Employee Mgmt. Rels. Bd., Las Vegas, 1983—89, chmn., 1986—87. Mem. ABA, ATLA, Clark County Bar Assn., Assn. Yale Alumni (assembly 1980-83, class treas. 1989-94, alumni interviewer 1982-97). Democrat. Jewish. Home: 2431 Greens Ave Henderson NV 89014-3736 Office: Eskin Law Offices 3191 E Warm Springs Rd Las Vegas NV 89120 Office Phone: 702-933-4448. Business E-Mail: jeskin@eskinlawoffices.com.

ESKRIDGE, WILLIAM NICHOL, JR., law educator; b. Princeton, W.Va., Oct. 27, 1951; s. William Nichol Sr. and Elizabeth Beckwith (DeJarnette) E. BA, Davidson Coll., NC, 1973; MA, Harvard U., 1975; JD, Yale U., 1978. Bar: DC 1979. Law clk. to hon. judge Edward Weinfeld US Dist. Ct. (so. dist.) NY, NYC, 1978-79; assoc. Shea & Gardner, Washington, 1979-82; asst. prof. Law Sch. U. Va., Charlottesville, 1982-86; assoc. prof. Georgetown U. Law Ctr., Washington, 1987-90, prof., 1990—98; Garver Prof. of Jurisprudence Yale U., New Haven, 1998—. Vis. prof. NYU Law Sch., 1993, 2004, Harvard Law Sch., 1994, Stanford Law Sch., 1995, Yale Law Sch., 1995-98, Columbia U., 2003. Author: (with Philip Frickey) Statutes and the Creation of Public Policy, 1987, 3d edit., 2000, (with Daniel Farber and Philip Frickey) Constitutional Law: Themes for its third Century; Dynamic Statutory Interpretation, 1994, 3d edit., 2001, (with Philip Frickey) Hart and Sacks, The Legal Process, 1994, The Case for Same Sex Marriage, 1966, (with Sanford Levinson) Constitutional Stupidities, Constitutional Tragedies, 1998, Equality Practice: Civic Unions and the Future of Gay Rights, 2002, (with Darren Spedale) Gay Marriage: For Better or For Worse? What We Learned from the Evidence, 2006. Fellow Guggenheim, 1995; mem. ABA. Presbyterian. Office: Yale Law Sch PO Box 208215 New Haven CT 06520 E-mail: william.eskridge@yale.edu.

ESLAMBOLCHI, HOSSEIN, communications executive; BSEE with highest honors, U. Calif., San Diego, MSEE, PhD in Elec. Engring. Joined AT&T Bell Labs., 1986—; v.p. network ops. and chief compliance officer AT&T Corp., v.p., AT&T Data and Network Svcs., 2000, sr. v.p., Packet and Optical Network Svcs., 2000—01, interim pres. Excite@Home Broadband Networks, 2001, pres., AT&T labs, 2001—, pres., AT&T Global Networking Tech. Svcs., chief tech. officer, 2001—, chief information officer, chief tech. officer. Bd. dirs. Mindspeed Techs., Inc., 2003—, Nat. Action Coun. for Minorities in Engring., Wytec; mem. adv. bd., bd. dir. Nat. Alliance Bus.; serves as AT&T's Accessibility Champion President's Com. on Employment of People with Disabilities; bd. advisor The Catalyst Group, Inc., Pacific Broadband Comm., Conexant; bd. tech. advisors Compaq Computer Corp.; spkr. in field. Mem. editl. bd.: IEEE Jour. Network and Sys. Mgmt.; contbr. articles to profl. jours. Mem. adv. coun. John Hopkins U. Whiting Sch. Engring. Named Inventor of Yr., NJ Inventors Hall of Fame, 2001, Alumnus of Yr., U. Calif. San Diego, 2002; named one of Top Ten Innovators "Ten award", Exec. Coun. NY, 2003, 10 Internet Bus. Leaders, Cisco IQ Mag., 2003, Premiere 100 IT Leaders, Computerworld, 2004, Top 25 Most Influential CTOs of 2005, InfoWorld; recipient Thomas Alva Edison award, NJ R&D Coun., 1997; AT&T Fellow, 1999. Achievements include patents in field; invention of FASTAR (Fast Automated Restoration System), which instantly reroutes service on AT&T's SONET rings, eliminating or minimizing service outages for customers. Office: AT&T Corp One AT&T Way Bedminster NJ 07921

ESLINGER, KENNETH NELSON, social sciences educator; s. Kenneth N. and Pearl May E.; m. Denise Marie Juba, July 22, 1979. BA, Ind. State U., Terre Haute, Ind., 1963; MA, The Ohio State U., Columbus, 1968, PhD, 1971. Asst. prof. of sociology Ohio State U., Columbus, 1972—73, The Cleve. State U., 1973—80; asst. prof. sociology John Carroll U., University Heights, Ohio, 1980—85, assoc. prof. sociology, 1985—, acting chair dept. sociology, 1995—96, chair dept. sociology, 1997—2005. Contbr. articles to profl. jours. Mem. Dem. Nat. Com., 1993—2003; adv. com., congressman Cleve., 1983—84; organizer higher edn. field gubernatorial campaign, Cleve., 1982. Mem.: Am. Sociol. Assn., North Ctrl. Sociol. Assn. (v.p. 1997—99), Soc. Study Social Problems, Nat. Coun. Family Rels. Avocations: bass fishing, fly fishing. Office: John Carroll U 20700 North Park Blvd University Heights OH 44118 Office Phone: 216-397-4381.

ESLINGER-BROWN, VANESSA PAULINE, humanities educator; b. Murfreesboro, Tenn., Dec. 28, 1951; d. Walter Clarence and Clare Marie Eslinger; m. Wilbur Edwin Brown Jr., Nov. 28, 1987; children: Celeste Gabrielle Brown, Cameron Yates Brown, Savannah Clare Brown. B Speech and Comm., U. Mont., 1973; MEd, U. Va., 1983, EdD, 1986. Cert. secondary tchr. Va. Sub. tchr. Eugene Pub. Schs., 1976—78; coach, drama dir., English tchr. Matoaca HS, Ettrick, Va., 1978—82; rsch. asst. U. Va., Charlottesville, 1986—87; adj. lectr. Germanna CC, Locust Grove, Va., 1987—89; adj./asst. prof. No. Va. CC, Woodbridge, 1987—89; adj./sr. lectr. Mary Washington Coll., Fredericksburg, Va., 1990—94, 2006—, sr. lectr., 1994—95; prof. gen. studies Stayer U., Fredericksburg, 1996—2005, chmn. dept. gen. studies, 1999—2005, prof., assoc. dean, 2005—. Piano tchr., Fredericksburg, 1995—98; minority achievement com. Walker Grant Mid. Sch., Fredericksburg, 2003—04. Vol. magic cir. Women's Shelter for Help and Emergency, Charlottesville, 1982—87; Bible sch. tchr. Shiloh New Site Bapt. Ch., Fredericksburg, 1989—99. Recipient Outstanding Vol. award, Women's Shelter for Help and Emergency, 1985. Mem.: ASCD, So. Poverty Law Ctr., Fredericksburg Sister City Assn., Nat. Coun. Tchrs. English, Va. Assn. Tchrs. English, Nat. Forensics League, Thespians Soc. Democrat. Methodist. Avocations: swimming, piano, reading, cooking. Home: 10415 Edinburgh Dr Spotsylvania VA 22553 Office: Strayer U 150 Riverside Pkwy Fredericksburg VA 22406 Office Phone: 540-374-4321. Business E-Mail: veb@strayer.edu.

ESMOND, DONALD V., transportation executive; m. Cheryl Esmond; children: Mike, Dan, Chris. BSc in Bus. and Econs., Ill. Inst. Tech. With Ford Motor Co., 1970—82; from copr. fleet and truck mgr. to sr. v.p. and gen. mgr. Toyota Motor Sales, USA, Inc., Torrance, Calif., 1982—2003, sr. v.p., 2003—, gen. mgr., 2003—. Capt. USMC, Vietnam. Decorated Silver Star USMC, Disting. Flying Cross, Purple Heart; recipient Semper Fidelis award, 1999. Office: Toyota Motor Sales USA Inc 19001 South Western Ave Torrance CA 90509

ESNAULT, TONY, chef; b. Saumur, France; Attended, François Rabelais Culinary Sch. Cook Le Montparnasse 25, Paris, 1990, Carré des Feuillants, Paris, 1993, Auberge de L'Ill, Alsace, France; chef Louis XV Alain Ducasse Restaurant, Monte Carlo; sous chef Ritz-Carlton, San Francisco, 1996—2002, exec. chef Boston, 2002—05, Alain Ducasse at the Essex House, NYC, 2005—. Named Best Hotel Chef of Am., Food & Wine mag., 2004; named one of NYC's Rising Stars, StarChefs.com, 2006. Office: Alain Ducasse at the Essex House 155 W 58th St New York NY 10019 Office Phone: 212-265-7300.*

ESPAÑA, LOURDES MARIA, mathematics professor; d. Guillermo and Sylvia España. AA with highest honors, Miami-Dade CC, Fla., 1988; BS with honors, Fla. Internat. U., Miami, 1991, MS with honors, 1996. Substitute tchr. Miami Dade County Pub. Schs., 1990—2000, Hialeah HS, Fla., 1992, 1995; adj. math instr. Miami-Dade CC, 1992—2000; ESOL instr. Hialeah Adult & Cmty. Edn. Ctr., 1996—2000; assoc. prof. math. Miami-Dade Coll., 2001—. Recipient Outstanding Young Woman Am. award, Young Women Am., 1991, Wachovia Bank Endowed Tchg. Chair award, Miami-Dade Coll., 2006—. Mem.: Fla. Devel. Edn. Assn., Fla. Assn. Cmty. Colls., Nat. Coun. Tchrs. Math., Am. Math. Assn. Two-Yr. Colls., Math. Assn. Am., Phi Theta Kappa (Outstanding Alumnus &

Outstanding Mem. award). Office: Miami-Dade Coll 11380 NW 27th Ave Miami FL 33167 Business E-Mail: lespana@mdc.edu.

ESPARZA, RAUL, actor; b. Wilmington, Del., 1970; Actor: (Broadway plays) Cabaret, 2001, The Rocky Horror Picture Show, 2000 (Theatre World award, 2000), Short Talks on the Universe, 2002, Chess, 2003, Taboo, 2003 (Drama Desk award outstanding featured actor in a musical, 2004), Hair, 2004, Children and Art, 2005, Chitty Chitty Bang Bang, 2005, Company, 2006 (Drama Desk award outstanding featured actor in a musical, 2007, Outer Critics Cir. award outstanding actor in a musical, 2007), (Off-Broadway) The Normal Heart, Comedians, tick, tick.BOOM!, (nat. tour) Evita, (regional theatre) Mixed Blessings, Grease, Messiah, What the Butler Saw, Arcadia, The Washington-Sarajevo Talks, A Christmas Carol, Richard II, Beloved Country, Slaughterhouse-Five, Fur, Merrily We Roll Along, Sunday in the Park with George, Company; (films) Find Me Guilty. Recipient HOLA Jose Ferrer Acting award.*

ESPE, MATTHEW J., manufacturing executive; With GE, 1980—2002; pres. GE Plastics Netherlands, 1994—99, GE Plastics Europe, 1999—2000; pres., CEO GE Lighting, 2000—02, IKON Office Solutions, Inc., 2002—, chmn., 2003—. Office: 70 Valley Stream Pkwy Malvern PA 19355*

ESPENLAUB, MARGO LINN, women's studies educator, writer, artist; b. Decorah, Iowa, May 1, 1944; d. Lloyd Wilson and Margaret Mary (Seegmiller) Ruid; children: Arn R. Johnson, Cara C. Hubbell. BA in Philosophy, U. Colo., 1983, M in Humanities, 1985; PhD in Women's Studies, The Union Inst. Grad. Sch., 1995. Assoc. dir. student devel., mem. faculty U. Denver, The Women's Coll., 1999—. Mem. faculty senate Ctr. Tchg. and Learning; faculty coord. TWC Student Writer's Club, U. Denver. Co-author: Women's Studies: Thinking Women, 1993; gen. editor Voices of the Women's Coll.; editor The Weekender. Mem. biomed. ethics com. Kaiser Permanente, Denver, 1986-96. Mem.: NOW, Nat. Women's Health Network, Nat. Mus. Women in the Arts.

ESPER, SUSAN, diversified financial services company executive; BS in Acctg., Providence Coll., Rhode Island. CPA Mass. Ptnr., fin. svcs. industry practice Deloitte & Touche, Boston. Vol. Big Sister Assn. Greater Boston; mem. women's leadership com. United Way; corp. adv. bd. Commonwealth Inst. Mem.: Nat. Investment Co. Svc. Assn. Office: Deloitte Consulting 200 Clarendon St Boston MA 02116

ESPINO, ANA M., parasitology and immunology educator, researcher; b. Guanabacoa, Havana, Cuba, June 8, 1959; arrived in Puerto Rico, 2000; d. Enrique A. Espino and Fortuna J. Hernández; m. Carlos A. Morera, May 22, 1982 (div. June 22, 1999); life ptnr. Carlos A. Sariol, Oct. 5, 2001; 1 child, Jezabel Morera. BSc in Biochemistry, U. Havana, 1982; PhD in Med. Scis., Inst. Tropical Medicine Pedro Kourí, Havana, 1997. Jr. rschr. Inst. Tropical Medicine Pedro Kourí, Havana, 1982—85, asst. rschr., 1985—88, assoc. rschr., 1988—93, full rschr., 1993—98, head lab., 1988—98, head parasitology dept., 1990—94; post doctoral fellow, Lab of Parasite Immunology U. PR, San Juan, 2000—02, asst. rschr. dept. pathology, 2002—04, asst. prof. dept. microbiology, 2004—07, assoc. prof. dept. microbiology. Adj. prof. dept. biochemistry U. Havana, 1994—98; cons. Panamerican Health Orgn., Managua, Nicaragua, 1994—98; asst. prof. Ctrl. U. of the Caribbean, San Juan, 2004—; presenter in field. Contbr. chapters to books, over 30 articles to profl. and peer-reviewed jours. Recipient Nat. prize, Ministry Pub. Health, 1998, Nat. award for best sci. rsch. in vet. scis., 1999, Travel award, Rsch. Ctr. in Minority Instns. Program, 2003; grantee, Third World Acad. Sci. Orgn., 1997, Minority Biomed. Rsch. Support Program, 2004—, Rsch. Ctr. Minority Instns., 2006—; scholar, U. UN, Japan, 1998—99. Mem.: Am. Soc. Microbiologist (hon.), Am. Soc. Tropical Medicine and Hygiene (hon.), Latinoamerican Fedn. Parasitologist (assoc.). Achievements include patents for Monoclonal antibody FFH F7.8 (ES78) which recognize Fasciola hepatica ES antigens and Diagnostic Kit that contain this MAb; three GenBank reports about cDNA of Fasciola hepatica encoding proteins with immunoprophylactic potential; molecular cloning and characterization of a novel vaccine candidate against Fascioliasis. Avocations: jogging, reading, theater, travel, dance. Home: Estancias del Boulevard 166 Carr 844 San Juan PR 00926 Office: University of Puerto Rico School Medicine Dept Microbiology San Juan PR 00935 Office Phone: 787-758-2525 ext. 1318. Office Fax: 787-758-4808. Personal E-mail: amespino38@hotmail.com. Business E-Mail: aespino@rcm.upr.edu.

ESPINOSA, LEANDRO, composer, conductor, educator; b. Monterrey, Nuevo Leon, Mexico, Jan. 2, 1955; arrived in US, 1992; s. Leandro Espinosa and Enrriqueta Garay. Undergraduate studies, Formative Sch. Through Arts, Monterrey, Nat. Conservatory Music, Mexico City, Perfecting Sch. Life and Movement; MusM, Peabody Conservatory, Balt., 1999; D in Musical Arts, U. Mo., Kansas City, 2002. Asst. prof. Formative Sch. Through Arts, Monterrey, 1976—78; assoc. prof. music Superior Sch. Music and Dance Carmen Romano de Lopez Portillo, Monterrey, 1987—90; asst. prof. music Ea. Oreg. U., La Grande, 2002—. Music dir. chamber orch. Technol. Inst. Superior Studies of Monterrey, 1977—78, Superior Sch. Music and Dance Carmen romano de Lopez Portillo, Monterrey, 1987—89, U. Coahuila, Saltillo, 1987—89; asst. condr. Peabody camerata Peabody Conservatory, Balt., 1997—99; music dir., condr. musica nova ensemble U. Mo., Kansas City, 2001—02, vis. adj. prof. music., 2001—02; music dir., condr Grande Ronde Symphony Orch., La Grande, Oreg., 2002—. Composer: (musical composition) Homage, 1974—76 (Participation in the Internat. Festival Mex. a Work of Art, 1991), rev., 1979, The Dream of Daniel (for Organ), 1975, rev., 1978, Duo for Electric Bass and Piano, 1976, Duo for Cello and Piano, 1977, Canto (for Piano four hands), 1976, rev., 1980, Canto (for guitar), 1977 (Participation in the Internat. Cervantine Festival, 1991), rev., 1987—88, Canto (a capella choir), 1985, rev., 2004, Canto (choral-orchestral), 1986, Mass (four versions and orchestrations), 1978—85, Paramo (versions for ballet), 1979, Paramo (chamber ensemble), 1982, Paramo (orchestra), 1983, Landscape Ballet, 1980, rev., 1985, 2nd edit. for chamber orchestra, 1993, 3rd edit., 1999, Homage to W. Killmayer, 1981, 2nd edit., 1983, The Calling (five versions and orchestrations), 1981—88, Duo for Violin & Cello, 1983, 1994, Senso (ballet), 1984 (Participation in the Berchem Internat. Fesival of Choreography, and Brussels Gestes 85, 1985), Andante (for strings), 1986, String Quartet, 1987, rev., 1999, Small Concerto for Bassoon or French Horn and Strings, 1988, Opera Ifigenia Cruel, 1989—91 (Grant to the Creators and Intellectuals of Mex., 1989), Miniatura (for guitar), 1989, Piano Sonata, 1992, Nocturno (for guitar), 1992—93, Sinfonia II (for virtual orchestra), 1993, Sinfonia II (for great orchestra, part I), 1993, rev., 1995, Sinfonia II (for great orchestra, part II), 1999—2000, La Noche, 1995 (Commisioned by the Nat. Inst. of Fine Arts of Mex., 1995), Before the Tears (ballet), 1995, Small Concerto for Piano & Orchestra, 1999—2000, Dawn (virtual orchestra), 2001, Concerto for Oboe, Strings, and Percussion, 2001—02, (version for French Horn), 2003—04, Homage to Josquin, 2002—04. Recipient Chamber Music 2000, U. of Missouri-Kansas City, 2000, Grad. Asst. Excellence in Tchg. Award, U. of Mo., Kansas City, 2002, Faculty Scholars Award, Ea. Oreg. U., 2003—05; scholar To the Creators and Intellectuals of Mex., Nat. Fonds for Culture and the Arts of Mex., 1989. Mem.: ASCAP (assoc. Raymond Hubbell scholar 2001), Oxford Round Table (contbr. online rsch. paper). Achievements include research in an alternative system of music serialism; development of a computerized composition technique labeled "virtual orchestra". Office: Eastern Oregon Univ One University Blvd La Grande OR 97850 Home Phone: 541-962-8777. Personal E-mail: espinosaleandro@hotmail.com. Business E-Mail: lespinos@eou.edu.

ESPINOSA, NANCY SWEET, artist, anthropologist, curator; b. Jackson, Mich., Feb. 21, 1956; d. Harland Guy and Genevieve Kathryn Sweet; m. John P. Espinosa, 1978 (div. 1998). BFA in Two-Dimensional Art, BS in Anthropology, Ea. N.Mex. U., 1998, BS in Anthropology, 1998, MA in Anthropology, 2002. Comm. operator III N.Mex. State Police, Roswell, N.Mex., 1980—88; emergency comm. operator Roswell Police Dept., 1989—96; fellow Ea. N.Mex. U., 1999—2002, archaeol. collections mgr., 2000—02; curator Salmon Ruins Mus. and Rsch. Libr., Bloomfield, N.Mex., 2003—04, curator, edn. coord., 2004—. Exhibited in group shows at Clovis C.C./Ea. N.Mex. U., 1996, BFA Gallery, 1998. Home: 3105 Stanford Ave Farmington NM 87402-8845 Home Phone: 505-326-5145; Office Phone: 505-632-2013. Personal E-mail: espnart@hotmail.com.

ESPINOSA, PATRICIO SEBASTIAN, neurologist, researcher; s. Espinosa. MD, U. Ctrl. Ecuador, Quito; MPH, Johns Hopkins U., Balt.; B, El Sauce Quito, Ecuador, 1993. Cert. neurologist Ky., 2003. Intern, internal medicine U. Ky., Lexington, resident, neurology, MD, 2002—. Fellow Harvard Med. Sch. Epilepsy. Achievements include research in epidemiology of neurological disease. Office: Univ Ky 740 South Limestone Lexington KY Office Phone: 859-323-6702. Office Fax: 859-323-5943. Business E-Mail: ps.espinosa@gmail.com.

ESPINOZA, LUIS ROLAN, rheumatologist, researcher; b. Pisco, Peru, July 3, 1943; arrived in US, 1969, naturalized, 1992; s. Luis R. and Luz Lelia (Bernales) E.; m. Carmen G. Gonzalez, Dec. 20, 1969; children: Luis M., Gabriela M. MD, Cayetano Heredia, Lima, Peru, 1969. CPA; cert. Am. Bd. Internal Medicine, 1973, in rheumatology 1974, in allergy & immunology 1975, diagnostic & clin. immunology 1986. Intern Jersey City (N.J.) Med. Ctr., 1969-70; resident Washington U., St. Louis, 1970-72, rheumatlogy fellow, 1972-73, McGill U., Montreal, Can., 1973-74, asst. prof., 1976-78; immunology fellow The Rockefeller U., NYC, 1974-76; assoc. prof. U. South Fla., Tampa, 1978-83, prof. medicine, 1983-90, La. State U. Sch. Medicine, New Orleans, 1991—, also chief rheumatology sect. Editor: Infection in the Rheumatic Diseases, 1988, Psoriatic Arthritis, 1985, Immun Complexes, 1983; guest editor Infectious Arthritis Rheumatic Disease Clin. N. Am., 1993, 98. Chmn. Lupus Found. Am., Tampa, 1979-90; pres.-elect Pan Am. League Against Rheumatism. Recipient Rsch. award NIH, Tampa, 1981, Arthritis Found., Tampa, 1990. Fellow ACP, Am. Coll. Rheumatology; mem. Am. Assn. Immunologists, So. Soc. for Clin. Investigation, Soc. for Clin. Rsch., Can. Soc. Rheumatologists, Can. Soc. for Clin. Investigation. Avocations: music, swimming, chess. Home: 1212 Conery St New Orleans LA 70115-3340 Office: La State U Med Ctr 1542 Tulane Ave New Orleans LA 70112-2825 Home Phone: 504-899-8719; Office Phone: 504-568-4630. Business E-Mail: lespin1@lsuhsc.edu. E-mail: luisrolan@msn.com.

ESPIRICUETA, SYLVIA, counseling administrator; b. Chgo., June 17, 1960; d. Zeferino Sáenz and Maria Delua; m. Valentine Espiricueta, July 26, 1986; 1 child, Valentine IV. BS in Edn. magna cum laude, Pan Am. U., Edinburg, Tex., 1983; MS in Edn., Counseling, Guidance, U. North Tex., Denton, 1990. Cert. counselor Tex., tchr. Tex. Bilingual tchr. Mission Sch. Dist., Tex., Austin Ind. Sch. Dist., Tex., Irving Ind. Sch. Dist., Tex.; tchr. Spanish Mesquite Ind. Sch. Dist., Tex.; binlingual psychotherapist MHMR, Dallas, Galaxy Ctr., Garland, Tex.; elem. sch. counselor Grand Prairie Ind. Sch. Dist., Tex., Arlington Ind. Sch. Dist., Tex. Whole brain tutor, Dallas, Ft. Worth, 1998—; lectr. in field; bilingual storyteller Arlington Pub. Libr., 2002. Singer (songwriter): (CD) After the Rain Comes the Sun, 2003; author: Positive Choices, 1996, Teach to Reach, 2002, Choosing to Learn to Climb, 2002. Internat. singer, songwriter. Finalist, Festival Cancion Latin Am., Calif., 2003, Christian gospel, Song of Yr., 2007, Am. Idol Underground finalist, 2007; recipient 2d pl. singer/songwriter, Festival de la Cancion, 2004, Song of Yr., 2005, semi-finalist folk/country music, UK Internat. Song Competition, 2006, 2d place country music, Song of Yr., 2006, Song of Year finalist Christian Gospel, UK Internat. Song Competition, 2007. Mem.: ASCAP, LA Music Network, Ft. Worth Songwriters Assn. Office Phone: 682-365-2894. Personal E-mail: espiricuetasylvia@hotmail.com.

ESPLIN, J. KIMO, chemicals executive; BS in Acctg., Brigham Young U., Provo, Utah; MBA, Northwestern U. V.p. Investment Banking Divsn. Bankers Trust Co.; v.p., treas. Huntsman Corp., Salt Lake City, 1994—96, sr. v.p. to exec. v.p., CFO, 1997—. Dir. Nutraceutical Internat. Corp., 2004—. Office: Huntsman Corp 500 Huntsman Way Salt Lake City UT 84108 Office Phone: 801-584-5700.*

ESPOSITO, JENNIFER, actress; b. NYC, Apr. 11, 1973; m. Bradley Cooper, Dec. 30, 2006 (separated 2007). Actor: (films) A Brooklyn State of Mind, 1997, A Brother's Kiss, 1997, Kiss Me, Guido, 1997, No Looking Back, 1998, He Got Game, 1998, Side Streets, 1998, I Still Know What You Did Last Summer, 1998, Summer of Sam, 1998, Just One Time, 1999, The Bachelor, 1999, Dracula 2000, 2000, Backflash, 2001, The Proposal, 2001, Made, 2001, Don't Say a Word, 2001, Beyond City Limits, 2001, Welcome to Colinwood, 2002, The Master of Disguise, 2002, Breakin' All the Rules, 2004, Crash, 2004 (recipient Outstading Performance by a Cast in a Motion Picture, SAG awards, 2006), Taxi, 2004, Jesus, Mary, and Joey, 2006, American Crude, 2007; (TV films) Partners and Crime, 2003, The Sunshine Boys, 1995, Snow Wonder, 2005, More, Patience, 2006; (TV series) Law and Order, 1996—2000, Spin City, 1997—99, Judging Amy, 2004—05, Related, 2005—06, (guest appearances) The City, 1995, New York Undercover, 1998, Law & Order: Special Victims Unit, 2000.*

ESPOSITO, JOHN VINCENT, lawyer; b. Logan, W.Va., Dec. 25, 1946; s. Vito T. and Mary Frances (Lamp) E. BA magna cum laude, W.Va. U., 1968, JD, 1971. Bar: W.Va. 1971, S.C. 1980, D.C. 1994, Legis. aide to Congressman Ken Hechler, 4th Dist. W.Va., 1971; counsel to Hans McCourt, Pres. W.Va. State Senate, 1972; instr. So. W.Va. Community Coll., 1972-; founder, sr. ptnr. Esposito & Esposito, Logan, W.Va. and Hilton Head Island, S.C., formerly in Washington, D.C. and N.Y.C., 1972—; arbitrator United Mine Workers Am.-Coal Operators Assn.; spl. judge Cir. Ct. Logan County (W.Va.); commr. in chancery Cir. Ct. Logan County; judge Mcpl. Ct. City of Chapmanville (W.Va.); spl. pros. atty., W. Va.; Citizen Ambassador to People's Republic of China and Soviet Union for U.S. Legal Del.; Founder, Citizens Environ. Quality, 1983.; of coun. to several Nat. & Internat. law firms; coun. to various Internat., Nat., State, and Local leaders; Citizen's Amb. relative to U.S. Legal Sys.; spkr. for Nat. & Internat. Forums; fashion model for Elite Knot; 2d lt. U.S. Army. U. Calif.; Hastings Coll. Law Coll. Advocacy scholar; Mem. ABA, Assn. Trial Lawyers Am., Am. Judicature Soc., W.Va. State Bar, S.C. Bar, D.C. State Bar, U.S. Supreme Ct. Bar, Internat. Platform Assn., Acad. Am. Poets; assisted in formation of Internat. War Crimes Amb., in Democracies establishing their gov., including Solvenia, Bosnia, Romania; Co-author: Laws for Young Mountaineers, 1973-74; Author: Law & Sex Come Together in the 90's; featured in a coll. textbook, Public Speaking/Theory Into Practice by Dr. John Makay; Creator, Dir. & Host of TV program, Law USA. Office: Ste 303 WatersEdge at Shelter Cove Harbour PO Drawer 5705 Hilton Head Island SC 29938 Office Phone: 843-785-6959.

ESPOSITO, JOSEPH LOUIS, lawyer; b. New Haven, Nov. 2, 1941; s. Joseph Henry and Camille (Carrano) E.; m. Nancy Giller, June 17, 1967 (div. 1973); m. Maddalena Fiorillo, Dec. 17, 1977 (div. 1986); 1 child, Giulio; m. Katherine Valenzuela, Oct. 26, 1996. BS, Fairfield U., 1964; MA, NYU, 1968, PhD, 1970; JD, U. Ariz., 1986. Bar: Ariz. 1987, U.S. Dist. Ct. (9th cir.) Ariz. 1987, U.S. Supreme Ct. 1991, U.S. Ct. Appeals (fed. cir.) 1998. Assoc. prof. philosophy Bradley U., Peoria, Ill., 1968-70, prof. philosophy, 1970-76; editor, 1974-80; with various bus. ventures, 1981-88; assoc. Smitherman and Sacks, Tucson, 1987-88; ptnr. Smitherman, Sacks and Esposito, Tucson, 1988-89, Smitherman & Esposito, Tucson, 1989-91; pvt. practice Tucson, 1992—. Rsch. prof. Inst. for Studies in Pragmatism, Tex. Tech. U., Lubbock, 1975-84; vis. scholar U. Ariz., 2001-04, rsch. prof., 2005—. Author five philosophy books; contbr. articles to profl. jours. Mem. Am. Philos. Assn. Avocation: travel. Home: PO Box 31494 Tucson AZ 85751-1494 Home Phone: 520-298-1067. Personal E-mail: jlespo@comcast.net.

ESPOSITO, LOUIS, real estate developer; married; 3 children. Diploma in Engring., Manhattan Coll. With Turner Constrn., The Durst Orgn., NYC, 1990—, head constrn., 2000—06, COO, 2006—. Office: The Durst Orgn 1155 Avenue of the Americas New York NY 10036 Office Phone: 212-789-1155.

ESPOSITO, RICHARD JOSEPH, journalist, executive; b. NYC, Dec. 28, 1954; s. Richard and Marie (Croci) E.; m. Diana Claire von Mueffling, Aug. 29, 1992; 1 child, Tatiana Maria von Mueffling. BA with honors, NYU, 1975; postgrad., U. Calif., Berkeley, 1976-77. Clk. NY Daily News, 1977-80, reporter, 1980-81; police bur. chief Phila. Bull., 1981; asst. editor Crains Bus. Mktg., NYC, 1981-82; assoc. editor CBS Venture One, Fairlawn, NY, 1982-83; investigative reporter NY Post, 1983-86; police bur. chief NY Newsday, 1986-90, city editor, 1990-93; metro editor NY Daily News, 1993, Sunday editor, 1993-95; sr. v.p. Warner Music Group, NYC, 1995; exec. v.p., CEO Constant Mgmt. (formerly Maroley Media Group), 1995—. Lectr. in field. Author: Dead on Delivery, 1992—. Recipient Silurian award, 1992, AP award, 1990-94; co-recipient Pulitzer Prize city editor Newsday, 1992. Mem. NY Press Club, Internat. Crime Writers, Soc. Profl. Journalists. Avocations: skiing, tennis, sport fishing, shooting. Home: Apt 5A 245 E 72nd St New York NY 10021-4516

ESPOSITO, RICK ANTHONY, thoracic surgeon; b. Chgo., Feb. 24, 1954; s. Anthony and Marie Premetta Esposito; m. Margaret Rose Devito, May 12, 1984; children: Matthew James, Daniel Anthony, Katherine Anne. BS summa cum laude, U. Ill., Urbana-Champaign, 1975; MD with honors, U. Chgo., 1979. Cert. Am. Bd. Thoracic Surgery, 1996, Am. Bd. Surgery. Resident surgery NYU Med. Ctr., NYC, 1979—84, fellow cardiothoracic surgery, 1984—86, staff surgeon, 1986—2002, assoc. prof. surgery, 1996—2002; staff surgeon Bellevue Hosp. Ctr., NYC, 1986—2002; chief cardiothoracic surgery NY VA Med. Ctr., NYC, 1988—2002; faculty mem. North Shore U. Hosp., Manhasset, NY, 2002—, assoc. chmn. cardiothoracic surgery, 2005—. Dir. cardiac surgery quality assurance North Shore U. Hosp., Manhasset, 2002—, dir. cardiac surgery Intensive Care Unit, 2004—. Contbr. articles to profl. jours.; mem. editl. bd.: Jour. Cardiac Surgery; mem. editl. bd. Thoracic and Cardiovascular, Surgeon, ad hoc reviewer Annals Thoracic Surgery, Am. Heart Assn., Circulation and Chest. Recipient Bronze Tablet, U. Ill., 1975. Fellow: ACS, Am. Heart Assn., Am. Coll. Chest Physicians (life); mem.: AMA, Northeastern Cardiovasc. Surgery Assn., Med. Soc. NY State, NY Soc. Thoracic Surgeons, NY Assn. Thoracic Surgery (life), European Assn. Cardiothoracic Surgery, Soc. Thoracic Surgeons, Assn. and Soc. Alumni Bellevue Hosp. Achievements include research in heparin usage, reversal, myocardial protection, mitral valve surgery, mitral valve repair, minimally invasive surgery, surgery in the elderly. Office: North Shore Univ Hosp 300 Community Dr Manhasset NY 11030 Office Phone: 516-562-4970. Office Fax: 516-562-3786. E-mail: resposit@nshs.edu.*

ESPOSO, ARNEL, chef; b. Philippines; married. Degree in Culinary Arts, Balt. Internat. Coll. US representative Culinary Team Europe competition, 1989; chef tournant Kilkea Castle Hotel, Ireland; chef de partie Citronelle, Washinton, DC; sous chef Red Sage, Washinton, DC, Palette at the Madison Hotel, Washinton, DC, 2003, exec. chef. Cook US Army. Named one of Washington DC's Rising Stars, StarChefs.com, 2006. Office: Palette at the Madison 1177 15th St NW Washington DC 20005 Office Phone: 202-587-2700. Office Fax: 202-587-2705.*

ESPREE, MILDRED MICHELLE, language educator, writer; b. Houston, Dec. 13, 1954; d. Mitchell Cornelius and Eunice Vitalee (Delahoussaye) Barlow; m. Réne Jerome Espree; children: Jaréd Hilary, Genevieve Rachel. BJ, U. Tex., Austin, 1977; MEd, U. Houston, 1984. Newspaper reporter, feature writer Brazosport Facts, Clute, Tex., 1979—80; reporter Baytown Sun, Tex., 1980—81; English tchr. Houston Ind. Sch. Dist., 1985—. Adj. coll. English tchr. various cmty. colls., Houston, 1989, 96, 2000; adj. prof. St. Xavier U. Master's Program, Chgo.; cons., reader Coll. Bd. ETS, Princeton, NJ, 1998—2003; tchr. rep., coord. Houston Tchrs. Inst., 2000—; mem. supt. adv. bd. Houston Sch. Dist., 2002—03. Contbr. articles to profl. jours. Adult catechist St. Andrew Cath., 1991—98, lector, 1990—. Named Houston ISD Tchr. of Yr., 2002—03; recipient Joseph B. Whitehead Nat. Educator of Distinction award, Coca Cola, 2003; Walt Disney Tchr's. grant, Walt Disney Corp., 2001, At Challenge grant, DeBakey HS. Mem.: Assn. Supervision and Curriculum Devel., Nat. Coun. Tchrs. English, Kappa Delta Pi. Democrat. Roman Catholic. Avocations: reading, writing, cooking, travel, movies. Home: 303 Haymarket Ln Houston TX 77015 Office: DeBakey HS for Health Professions 3100 Shenandoah St Houston TX 77021 E-mail: mespree@houstonisd.org.

ESQUIBEL, EDWARD V., psychiatrist, health facility administrator; b. Denver, May 28, 1928; s. Delfino C. and Beatrice (Solis) E.; m. Elaine F. Telk (div. 1961); children: Roxanne, Cyndi, Allen, James; m. Lillian D. Robb, 1961; children: Amanda, Ramona. MD, U. Colo., 1958. Diplomate Am. Bd. Psychiatry and Neurology. Assoc. chief svc. Ill. State Psychiat. Inst., Chgo., 1964-66; dir. undergrad. program psychiatry, asst. prof. psychiatry Chgo Med. Sch., 1966-68; cons. and supr. group therapy Lake County Mental Health Clinic, Gary, Ind., 1968-72; pvt. practice Daytona Beach, Jacksonville, Fla., 1972-82; chief forensic svcs., dir. div. maximum security and inst. rsch. Colo. State Hosp., Pueblo, 1981; assoc. clin. prof. psychiatry Quillen-Dishner Coll. Medicine, Johnson City, Tenn., 1982-84; clin. psychiatrist VA Outpatient Clinic, Riviera Beach, Fla., 1984-86; mental health coord., supr. VA, Pensacola, Fla., 1986-88; assoc. chief staff, ambulatory care VA Med. Ctr., Ft. Lyon, Colo., 1988-90, Carl Vinson VA Med. Ctr., Dublin, Ga., 1990-91; staff physician VA Med. Ctr., Sheridan, Wyo., 1993—, chief psychiat. svcs. Lake City, Fla., 1993-94; contract physician, 1995—. Author: Healthcare Faction; Ticket to Nowhere: Toward Wiser Care of Veterans, 2005; contbr. articles to profl. jours. Sgt. U.S. Army, 1948-52. Recipient Plaque Recognition award Southeastern Psychiat. Inst., 1964, Internat. Pers. Creative award, 1972, Key to City Daytona Beach, 1975, Hosp. Dirs. commendation VA, 1991. Avocations: gardening, arts and crafts, reading. Home and Office: 801 Gospel Island Rd Inverness FL 34450-3592 E-mail: dreesquibel@wmconnect.com.

ESQUIVEL, AGERICO LIWAG, retired research physicist; b. Manila, June 5, 1932; came to U.S., 1957, naturalized, 1971; s. Enrique Frias and P. R. (Liwag) E. AB, Berchmans Coll., Manila, 1955; MA, Berchmans Coll., 1956; PhD, St. Louis U., 1963. Rsch. assoc. St. Louis U., 1961-63; rsch. scientist Research Inst. Advanced Studies, Balt., 1963, Materials Research Lab., Martin Co., Orlando, Fla., 1964-65; sr. rsch. engr. Materials Tech. Labs. Boeing Co., Seattle, 1965-71; postdoctoral fellow Advanced Research Projects Agy., U. So. Calif., LA, 1971-73; mem. tech. staff Hughes Aircraft Co., Culver City, Calif., 1973-76; mem. tech. staff Semicondr. Process and Device Ctr., Tex. Instuments Inc., Dallas, 1976-98. Presenter internat. symposia, U.S., Japan, Europe. Contbr. papers to jours. and procs. on X-ray, electron diffaction, radiation hardening, cathodoluminescence in GaAs, deep level transient spectroscopy, x-ray lithography, high density nonvolatile memories, trench isolated electronically programmable read-only memories (EPROMs), sub-0.25 micron Complementary Metal Oxide Semiconductor (CMOS) transistors and fabrication process, 0.18 micron CMOS logic transistor technology, Ultra Large Scale Integrated (ULSI) CMOS device process integration and characterization. NSF postdoctoral fellow, 1963. Mem. IEEE Elec. Devices Soc. (sr. mem.), Am. Phys. Soc., Electrochem. Soc., Sigma Xi, Pi Mu Epsilon. Achievements include 16 U.S. patents issued on submicron CMOS process integration, development, device characterization, process/device computer simulation, trench isolation, buried multilevel interconnect systems, nonvolatile memory devices.

ESREY, ELIZABETH GOVE GOODIER, chemist, biologist; b. West Chester, Pa., Mar. 25, 1964; d. Robert Egan and Mary Ellen (Winslow) Goodier; m. James David Esrey, Nov. 28, 1987; children: Briana, Steven. BA in Biology, Maryville Coll., 1986. Lab. tech. Franklin Co., Wilmington, Del., 1987, Stine Haskell Rsch. Labs., DuPont, Newark, Del., 1987-91, chemist, 1991-93, biochemist, 1993—, biochemist herbicide biomechanisms Agrl. Product Discovery, 1993-94, biologist plant and fungal biochemistry, 1994-97, biologist high throughput screening/assay devel. biol. leads, 1998-99, lead generation screening, lead characterization, 1999-2000, site of action assay devel., 2000—05, mem. safety resource team, 1996—98, 2003—05; biologist Chem. Genomics, 2005—07; sr. rsch. assoc. crop genetics DuPont Exptl. Sta., Wilmington, Del., 2007—. Owner Beth's Homemade Breads & Pies Middletown, Del., 1987—. Active Chesapeake Bay Girl Scouts, 1998—. Recipient DuPont Agr. Products Global Tech Divsn. Achievement award, 1997, 2000, Crop Protection R&D award, 2004; named to Outstanding Young Women of Am., 1987, 97, Accomplishment award DuPont Agr. and Nutrition R&D Divsn., 2007; named Outstanding Vol. Chesapeake Bay Girl Scout Coun., 2003. Republican. Episcopalian. Office: DuPont Exptl Sta Rte 141 Henry Clay PO Box 80353 Wilmington DE 19880-0353 Business E-Mail: elizabeth.g.esrey@usa.dupont.com.

ESREY, WILLIAM TODD, telecommunications company executive; b. Phila., Pa., Jan. 17, 1940; s. Alexander J. and Dorothy (B.) E.; m. Julie L. Campbell, June 13, 1964; children: William Todd, John Campbell. BA, Denison U., Granville, Ohio, 1961; MBA, Harvard U., 1964. With Am. Tel & Tel. Co., also N.Y. Tel. Co., 1964-69; pres. Empire City Subway Ltd., NYC, 1969-70; mng. dir. Dillon, Read & Co. Inc., NYC, 1970-80; exec. v.p. corp. planning United Telecommunications, Inc. (now Sprint), Westwood, Kans., 1980-81, exec. v.p., CFO, 1981-82, 84-85, CEO, 1985—90; chmn., CEO Sprint Corp., Westwood, Kans., 1990—2003. Bd. dirs. Duke Energy Corp., Gen. Mills, Inc.; chmn. bd. dirs. Japan Telecom Co., Ltd., 2003—04. Mem. Birnum Wood, Eagle Springs, Valley Club of Montecito, Phi Beta Kappa.

ESRICK, JERALD PAUL, lawyer; b. Moline, Ill., Oct. 1, 1941; s. Reuben and Nancy (Parson) E.; m. Ellen Feinstein, June 18, 1966; children: Sara Elizabeth, Daniel Michael. BA, Northwestern U., 1963; JD, Harvard U., 1966. Bar: Ill. 1966, U.S. Dist. Ct. (no. dist.) Ill. 1967, U.S. Supreme Ct. 1974, U.S. Ct. Appeals (9th cir.) 1985, U.S. Ct. Appeals (7th cir.) 1967. Law clk. U.S. Dist. Ct. (no. dist.) Ill., 1966-68; assoc. Wildman, Harrold, Allen & Dixon, Chgo., 1968-73, ptnr., 1973—, also chmn. firm mgmt. com., 1987-90. Lectr. Northwestern U., 1984-93, Coll. Arts and Scis. bd. visitors, 1993—, Nat. Panel Comml. Arbitrators, Am. Arbitration Assn. Pres. bd. trustees Nat. Lekotek Ctr., Evanston, Ill., 1989-93, U.S. Toy Libr. Assn., 1987-88; bd. dirs. Evanston Mental Health Assn., 1984-86, Fund for Justice, 1969-95, Lawyers' Com. for Civil Rights, 1974-84. Fellow Am. Coll. Trial Lawyers; mem. ABA, Ill. State Bar Assn., Chgo. Coun. Lawyers (bd. dirs., sec., founding mem.), Chgo. Bar Assn., Lawyers Club Chgo. Avocations: running, skiing, sailing, classical music, bicycling. Home: 1326 Judson Ave Evanston IL 60201-4720 Office: Wildman Harrold Allen & Dixon LLP 225 W Wacker Dr Ste 3000 Chicago IL 60606-1229 Office Phone: 312-201-2508. Business E-Mail: esrick@wildman.com.

ESSEN, RICHARD JOEL, lawyer; b. NYC, Jan. 28, 1939; s. Ben and Hazel Essen; m. Laura Barbara Ammerman, Sept. 7, 1968; children: Elena, Michael. BA, U. Miami, Fla., 1960, JD, 1963. Ptnr. Essen & Essen, PA, Miami, 1963—79, Essen & Spiegel, PA, Coral Gables, Fla., 1979—81; CEO Essen, Essen, Susaneck & Cohen (formerly Knomos Essen & Essen), Miami, 1969—; asst. state's atty. Dade County State Atty., Miami, 1967—68. Mem. editl. bd. DWI Jour: Law and Sci. Author: (jour.) Essen's Notebook; contbr. articles to profl. jours. Past chmn. Fla. Regional Bd. ADL, 1970; bd. regents Nat. Coll. DUI. Mem.: ATLA, ABA, Nat. Coll. DUI Lawyers, Nat. Exec. Com., ADL (life). Republican. Jewish. Home: 626 Coral Way # 301-302 Miami FL 33134 Office: Essen Essen Susaneck & Cohen PA 20801 Biscayne Blvd Ste 300 Miami FL 33180

ESSER, CARL ERIC, lawyer; b. Montclair, NJ, Feb. 12, 1942; s. Josef and Elly (Graber) E.; m. Barbara A. B. Stelzer, Oct. 12, 1968; children: Jennifer, Eric, Brian. AB, Princeton U., NJ, 1964; JD, U. Mich., 1967. Bar: Pa. 1967. Assoc. Reed Smith LLP, Phila., 1967-72, ptnr., 1973—2002; pvt. practice Phila., 2003—. With USMCR, 1960-66. Mem. ABA, Pa. Bar Assn., Pa. Lawyers Fund for Client Security (bd. dirs., chmn.), Octavia Hill Assn. (chmn. bd. dirs.), German Am. C. of C. (bd. dirs.); Racquet Club, Penllyn Club, Mfrs. Golf and Country Club. Republican. Office: 2500 One Liberty Pl Philadelphia PA 19103 Office Phone: 215-851-8181. Business E-Mail: cesser@reedsmith.com.*

ESSER, PATRICK J., communications executive; BA in Comm. Media, MA in Comm. Media, U. No. Iowa. Mem. mgmt. team for CableRep (now Cox Media, Inc.), 1981—90, dir. advertising sales, 1990—91, v.p. advertising sales, 1991—99; dir. programming, Hampton Roads Sys. Cox Communications, Inc., 1976, v.p. ops., 1999—2000, sr. v.p. ops., western divsn., 2000—01, exec. v.p. ops. Atlanta, 2004—06, COO, 2004—06, pres., CEO, 2006—. Co-founder, former bd. dir. Product Information Network; mem. telecommunications adv. bd. Compaq; bd. dir. C-SPAN, CableLabs, Cable in the Classroom. Recipient Heritage Honors Alumni Achievement award, U. No. Iowa, 2003, Cable TV Advertising Bur. President's award. Mem.: Cable TV Pub. Affairs Assn. (bd. advisor), Nat. Cable & Telecommunications Assn. (bd. dir.), Cable & Telecommunications Assn. for Mktg. Ednl. Found. (bd. dir.). Office: Cox Enterprises Inc 6205 Peachtree Dunwoody Rd Atlanta GA 30328 Office Phone: 404-843-5000. Office Fax: 404-843-5975.

ESSERMAN, SANDER L., lawyer; b. Chgo., Dec. 5, 1950; BA with distinction, DePauw U., Ind., 1973; JD, So. Meth. U. Sch. Law, Dallas, 1976. Bar: Tex. 1976. Law clk. to Hon. Nauman S. Scott US Dist. Ct. (we. dist. La.), 1976—77; atty. Stutzman, Bromberg, Esserman & Plifka, P.C., Dallas, 1984—, pres., 1996—. Mem. adj. faculty So. Meth. U. Sch. Law, Dallas, 1999—. Named one of Best Lawyers in Dallas, D Mag., 2005. Master: John C. Ford Am. Inn Ct.; mem.: Dallas Bar Assn., State Bar Tex. Office: Stutzman Bromberg Esserman & Plifka PC 2323 Bryan St Ste 2200 Dallas TX 75201 Office Phone: 214-969-4910. Office Fax: 214-969-4999. E-mail: esserman@sbep-law.com.*

ESSEX, JOSEPH MICHAEL, visual communication planner; b. Santa Barbara, Calif., May 27, 1947; Student, Montgomery Coll., Rockville, Md., Va. Commonwealth U., Richmond. Art dir. Met. Pitts. Pub. Broadcasting, 1970-73; sr. designer Ctr. for Comm. Planning, 1973-76; assoc. creative dir. Jim Johnston Advt., 1976; design dir. Burson-Marsteller Design Group, Chgo., 1976-86, v.p., dir. visual comm. planning Americas, 1980-88; prin. Design By Objectives, Chgo., 1986-88; ptnr. Essex Partnership, Chgo., 1988-89, Essex Two Inc., Chgo., 1989—. One man poster exhbn. Chgo., 1979; exhibited in group shows: Japan, 1976, Ireland, 1977, Cooper-Hewitt Mus., N.Y.C., 1981. Recipient Silver medals, Merit award Art Directors Club, N.Y.C., 1979, 80, over 300 other awards from design and advt. orgns. Office: Essex Two Inc 2210 W North Ave Chicago IL 60647-5430 Office Phone: 773-489-1400. E-mail: joseph@5x2.com.

ESSEX, MYRON ELMER, microbiology and virology educator; b. Coventry, RI, Aug. 17, 1939; s. Myron Elmer Essex and Ruth Hazel (Knight) Esses; m. Elizabeth Katherine Jordan, June 19, 1966; children: Holly Anne, Carrie Lisa. BS, U. R.I., Kingston, 1962; DVM, Mich. State U., East Lansing, 1967; MS, Mich. State U., 1967, DSc (hon.), 1988; PhD, U. Calif., Davis, 1970; MA (hon.), Harvard U., 1979; DSc (hon.), U. R.I., 1987; DSc (hon.), U. Madrid, 1989, U. Md., 1992; DSc (hon.), U. Kinshasa, Zaire, 1995. Research fellow Karolinska Inst., Stockholm, 1970—72; asst. prof. Harvard U., Cambridge, Mass., 1972—76, assoc. prof., 1976—78; prof., chmn. dept. microbiology Harvard Sch. Pub. Health, Cambridge, Mass., 1978—81, chmn. dept. cancer biology, 1981—97, chmn. dept. immunology and infectious diseases, 1997—, Mary Woodard Lasker prof. health scis., 1989—, John Laporte Given prof. infectious diseases, dept. immunology and infectious diseases, chmn. AIDS Inst., 1988—. Mem. sci. adv. bd. Cambridge Biosci. Corp., 1982—93, Virus Rsch. Inst., 1993—; cons. Diacrin, Cin. Co-editor: Viruses in Cancer, 1980, AIDS:Etiology, Diagnosis, Treatment and Prevention, 1992, 1997, Human T-cell Leukemia Viruses, 1984, AIDS in Africa, 1994; contbr. articles to profl. jours.; patentee test for human T leukemia virus infection and AIDS blood tests and vaccines. Bd. sci. counselors Nat. Cancer Inst., 1982—93; sci. adv. bd. ARC, 1985—89; v.p. sci. affairs Internat. Retrovirol. Assn. HTLV and Related Viruses, 1995—; sec. gen. Internat. Assn. Rsch. on Leukemia, 1995—97, pres., 1997; mem.Lasker award jury Albert & Mary Lasker Found., 1982—84, 1987—92; bd. dirs. Pierre Dick/Virbac Found.; mem. adv. bd. AIDS Assn., 1990—; mem. sci. adv. bd. Until There's A Cure, 1995—, Internat. AIDS Vaccine Initiative, Rockefeller Found., 1996—, Sabin Found., 1996—, Inst. for Internat. Vaccine Devel., 1997—, Virus Rsch. Inst., 1992—; bd. dirs. Hong Kong Cancer Ctr., 1994—. Recipient Bronze medal, Am. Cancer Soc., 1978, Ralston-Purina Rsch. award, 1985, Outstanding Investigator award, Nat Cancer Inst., 1985, Lifetime Rsch. award, 1995, Disting. Alumnus award, Mich. State U., Lasker award, 1986, Carnation Rsch. award, 1987, Disting. Alumnus award, U. Calif., Davis, 1987, Presdl. medal of honor, Govt. of Senegal, 1991, Ann. award, Am. Assn. Vet. Epidemiologists, 1992, Gold-Headed Cane award, 1995, Alumni Excellence award, U. R.I., 1994; scholar Leukemia Soc. Am., 1972, Am. Cancer Soc. Nat Cancer Inst., 1973—. Fellow: Infectious Disease Soc. Am., Am. Assn. Microbiology, AAAS; mem.: Internat. Retrovirology Assn. (v.p.), Leukemia Soc. Am. (adv. bd. 1978—83, 1985—), Am. Cancer Soc. (mem. rsch. com. Mass. br. 1975—86), Soc. Gen. Microbiology, Reticuloendothelial Soc., Nat. Acad. Practitioners, Am. Soc. Virology, Internat. Assn. Rsch. in Leukemia (pres.), Am. Assn. Immunologists, Am. Assn. Cancer Rsch., AVMA, Inst. Medicine of NAS. Office: Harvard Sch Pub Health Immunology & Infectious Dis FXB 402 651 Huntington Ave Boston MA 02115 Office Phone: 617-432-2334. Office Fax: 617-739-8348. Business E-Mail: messex@hsph.harvard.edu.*

ESSIEN, FRANCINE B., biologist, educator; BA in Biology, Temple U.; PhD in Genetics, Yeshiva U.; postgrad., U. Conn. Prof., Cell Biology & Neuroscience Dept. Rutgers U., New Brunswick, NJ, 1997—. Dir. Minority Undergrad. Sci. Programs, Rutgers U., 1988—, founder, co-founder Success in the Scis., Biomed. Careers Program, Rsch. Apprentice Program, ACCESS-MED, mem. adv. bd. Douglass Project for Rutgers Women in Math, Sci. and Engring.; mem. rev. panel NSF/NIH; cons. CUNY, Atlanta U.; lectr. in field. Contbr. articles to profl. jours. Fulbright scholar; recipient Spina Bifida Assn. Am. award, N.J. Women of Achievement award Woodrow Wilson Found. Instns.; named Black Achiever in Sci., Chgo. Mus. Sci. and Industry, U.S. Prof. of Yr. for Rsch. and Doctoral Univs., 1994, Carnegie Found. Advancement of Teaching.; Disting. Black Scholar-in-Residence, U. Cin., 1988; CASE Professor of the Yr. 1994-95; recipient W.E.B. DuBois award for edn. NAACP of Cen. N.J., 1997. Office: Rutgers U Cell Biology & Neuroscience Dept Nelson Lab C218 Busch 604 Allison Rd Piscataway NJ 08854-8000 Office Phone: 732-445-4145. Business E-Mail: fessien@rci.rutgers.edu.*

ESSIG, JACK, magazine publishing executive; b. 1970; Advt. dir. Men's Health Mag., 2002—03, assoc. pub., 2003—05, pub., v.p., 2005—. Named one of 40 under 40, Advt. Age, 2007. Office: Men's Health 733 Third Ave 15th Fl New York NY 10017 Office Phone: 610-967-5171. Office Fax: 212-949-9455. E-mail: jack.essig@rodale.com.*

ESSIGMANN, JOHN M., chemistry professor; b. Medford, Mass. m. Ellen Essigmann; children: Amy, Nolan. BS, Northeastern U., 1970; MS, MIT, 1972, PhD, 1976. William R. and Betsy P. Leitch prof. chemistry, dept. chemistry MIT, prof. toxicology, biomedical engring. divsn. Contbr. contbn. to prof. jour. Recipient Outstanding Investigator award, Nat. Cancer Inst., 1989, Arthur C. Smith award, 1998, Susan B. Komen Breast Cancer Found. award, 2000, Princess Chulabhorn Gold Medal, Thailand, 2004; Margaret Mac Vicar fellowship, 1997—2007. Mem.: Nat. Assn. Collegiate Scholars, Environ. Mutagen Soc., Am. Soc. Microbiology, Soc. Toxicology, Am. Assn. Cancer Rsch., Am. Chem. Soc. (Mutation Rsch. award for Sci. Excellence 2002). Office: Simmons Hall MIT 229 Vassar St Cambridge MA 02139*

ESSLINGER, ERIC JASON, web site designer; b. Fort Worth, Tex., Dec. 28, 1971; s. James and Velma Esslinger. AS, Motlow State CC, Tullahoma, Tenn., 1994. Web designer, developer Valley Internet, Inc., Fayetteville, Tenn., 1998—. Mem. Amateur Radio Emergency Svc., Fayetteville, 2006. Mem.: Lincoln County Amateur Radio Soc., Am. Mensa. Avocations: amateur radio, computer programing. Home: 38 Kelso-Mulberry Rd Mulberry TN 37359 Office: Valley Internet 102 E Maple St Fayetteville TN 37334 Home Phone: 931-227-7431; Office Phone: 931-433-1921.

ESSLINGER, JOHN THOMAS, lawyer; b. Ephrata, Pa., Aug. 11, 1943; s. Doster Alvin and Lucy Mildred (Ream) E.; 1 child, John David. BA, Yale U., 1965; JD, Georgetown U., 1973. Bar: D.C. 1973, U.S. Dist. Ct. D.C. 1974, U.S. Supreme Ct. 1974, U.S. Ct. Appeals (D.C. cir.) 1974. Assoc. Morgan, Lewis & Bockius, Washington, 1973-76; ptnr. Schmeltzer, Aptaker & Shepard, P.C., Washington, 1976—2006; gen. counsel Legum & Norman, Inc., Alexandria, Va., 2006—. Capt. USMC, 1966-70, Vietnam. Decorated Purple Heart, Bronze Star, Gold Star. Mem. ABA, Bar Assn. D.C., D.C. Bar Assn., Maritime Adminstrv. Bar Assn. Episcopalian. Avocations: golf, wine, baseball. Office: Ste 1200 4401 Ford Ave Alexandria VA 22302 Office Phone: 703-848-8544. Business E-Mail: tesslinger@legumnorman.com.

ESSMAN, ROBERT NORVEL, artist, graphics designer; b. St. Louis, Feb. 6, 1937; s. Paul M. and Rose (Solinsky) E. BFA, State U. of Iowa, 1959. Artist Simplicity Pattern Co., NYC, 1961-62, Life Mag., NYC, 1962-68, art dir., 1969, Show Mag., NYC, 1969-70, Bus. Week Mag., NYC, 1970-74; logo designer, creative dir. N.Y.C. Bicentennial Commn., NYC, 1974-76; art dir. People Weekly Mag., NYC, 1974-82; art dir., pres. Bob Essman: Design, The Cricket Press, NYC, 1982—. Pub., design dir.: Revival: Theatrical History Revisited, 1992—94; designer Time-Life Alumni Soc. Newsletter, 2006—. Mem. steering com. Vt. Gay Social Alternatives, 2007; bd. dirs. League for the Hard of Hearing, 1977—99, rec. sec., 1987—95, hon. bd., 1999—; bd. dirs. Hampton-Booth Theatre Libr., 1993—94, sec., 1994; bd. dirs., assoc. exec. dir. pub. rels. Champlain Adaptive Mounted Program Champ, 2005. Recipient Vol. of Yr. award League for the Hard of Hearing, 1990, Excellence of Design award Advt. Club NY, 1977, Art Dirs. Club of NY, 1978, Gen. Excellence Nat. Mag. award Am. Soc. Mag. Editors, 1973, Real Masson Founders award, Vt. Gay Social Alternatives, 2004. Mem.: Overseas Press Club (Designer Dateline 1991—92, New Club Logo 1994), Soc. Pub. Designers (bd. dirs. 1972—79, pres. 1976—79, Excellence of Design award 1972, 1973, 1975, 1976, 1978), Am. Inst. Graphic Arts (Excellence of Design award 1980), Dutch Treat Club (annual book designer 1989—, compiled membership history The Whole Who 1995, Gold medal 2003), The Players Club (bd. dirs. 1979—85). Home and Office: 344 Falcon Manor Williston VT 05495 Personal E-mail: bobessman@comcast.net.

ESSMYER, MICHAEL MARTIN, lawyer; b. Abilene, Tex., Dec. 6, 1949; s. Lytle Martin Essmyer and Roberta N. Essmyer Nicholson; m. Cynthia Rose Piccolo, Dec. 27, 1970; children: Deanna, Mike, Brent Austin. BS in Geology, Tex. A&M U., 1972; postgrad., Tex. Christian U., 1976; JD summa cum laude, South Tex. Coll. Law, 1980. Bar: Tex. 1980, U.S. Dist. Ct. (no., so., ea. we. dists) Tex. 1982, U.S. Ct. Appeals (5th cir.) 1981, U.S. Ct. Appeals (9th cir.) 1990, U.S. Ct. Appeals (1st cir.) 1993, U.S. Ct. Appeals (7th cir.) 1995, U.S. Ct. Appeals (fed. cir.) 1985, U.S. Ct. Claims, 1981, U.S. Supreme Ct. 1991. Briefing atty. Supreme Ct. Tex., Austin, 1980-81, Haynes & Fullenweider, Houston, 1981-89, Essmyer & Hanby, Houston, 1989-92; atty. Essmyer & Assocs., Houston, 1992-94; pres. Essmyer & Tritco, LLP, Houston, 1994-95, Essmyer, Tritco & Clary, LLP, Houston, 1995-99, Essmyer & Tritco, LLP, Houston, 1999—. Lead article editor South Tex. Law Jour., 1979. Dem. candidate for state rep., Bryan, Tex., 1972; del. Dem. Party, Houston, 1982, 84; precinct chmn. Harris County Dem. Exec. Com., Houston, 1983-86. Capt. USAF, 1972-78. Nat. Merit Scholar, 1968-72. Mem. ATLA, ABA, Houston Bar Assn. (co-chmn. lawyers in pub. schs. com. 2003-05, co-chair spkrs. com. 2005-06), Tex. Trial Lawyers Assn. (dir. 1996—), Harris County Trial Lawyers Assn. (dir. 1997—), Tex. Criminal Def. Lawyers Assn., Tex. Bar Found., Harris County Criminal Lawyers Assn. (dir. 1986-87), Fed. Bar Assn., Houstonian Club, The Petroleum Club of Houston, The Company Onstage (dir. 2001—). Roman Catholic. Home: 1122 Glourie Dr Houston TX 77055-7506 Office: Essmyer Tritico & Rainey LLP 5111 Center St Houston TX 77007-7328 Office Phone: 713-869-1155. Business E-Mail: messmyer@essmyertritico.com.

ESSNER, ROBERT ALAN, pharmaceutical executive; b. NYC, Oct. 26, 1947; s. Arthur and Charlotte (Levy) E.; m. Rosalind Esser, July 24, 1969 (div. June 1986); children: Elizabeth, Emily; m. Anne Essner, May 23, 1987; children: Elizabeth, Emily, Benjamin. Grad., Miami U., Oxford, OH; MA, U. Chicago. Various positions Sandoz Pharms. Corp., East Hanover, NJ, 1978-86, v.p., 1986-87, corp. v.p., COO bus. mgmt., 1987; pres. Sandoz Consumer HealthCare Group, Parsippany, NJ, 1987, Wyeth-Ayerst Labs., 1993—97, Wyeth-Ayerst Global Pharm., 1997; exec. v.p. Wyeth, Madison, NJ, 1997-2000, COO, 2000, pres., 2000—06, CEO, 2001—, chmn., 2003—. Bd. dirs. Mass. Mutual Life Ins. Comp., Pharm. Rsch. & Mfr. Am.; mem. Bus. Roundtable, Bus. Coun. Chmn. Children's Health Fund Corp. Coun.; trustee Penn Medicine. Recipient Prix Galien Suisse, 2003, Science/Tech. medal, R&D Coun. NJ, 2003. Mem.: Pharm. Mfr. Assn. Avocation: antique photography. Office: Wyeth 5 Giralda Farms Madison NJ 07940-0874*

ESTABROOK, ALISON, surgeon, educator; b. NYC, Oct. 29, 1951; d. Edwin Burke and Shirley (Butler) E.; m. William Harrington, June 12, 1982. BA, Barnard Coll., 1974; MD, NYU, 1978. Resident in surgery Columbia-Presbyn. Med. Ctr., NYC, 1978-81, 82-84, fellow in surgery, onocology, 1981-82, asst. prof. surgery, 1984—, dir. Breast Clinic, 1985—97, Florence Irving asst. prof., 1989-92, chief breast surgery, 1991-97, assoc. prof. surgery, 1992-95, prof. clin. surgery, 1995—; chief breast surgery St. Luke's Roosevelt Hosp., NYC, 1998—. Mem.: Am. Soc. Breast Disease (bd. dirs. 1996—2001), Soc. Surg. Oncology, N.Y. Surg. Soc., N.Y. Met. Breast Group, Assn. Women Surgeons, Am. Soc. Clin. Oncology, Sigma Xi (Kappa chpt.). Office: St Lukes Roosevelt Hosp 425 W 59th St New York NY 10019-1104 Home Phone: 914-777-0939; Office Phone: 212-523-7500. Business E-Mail: ae9@columbia.edu.

ESTABROOK, REED, artist, educator; b. Boston, May 31, 1944; s. F. Reed and Nancy (Vogel) E.; 1 son, August. BFA, R.I. Sch. Design, Providence, 1969; MFA, Art Inst. Chgo., 1971. Instr. U. Ill., 1971-74; asst. prof. U. No. Iowa, Cedar Falls, 1974-78, assoc. prof., 1978-83, head dept. photog. program, 1974-83; advisor visual arts Iowa Arts Coun., Des Moines, 1977-78, mem. art purchase com., 1977-78; chmn. photog. dept. Kansas City (Mo.) Art Inst., 1983—84, prof., coord. photography, 1984—92, 2005—; prof., coord. photo dept. San Jose (Calif.) State U., 1984—89. Bd. dirs. San Francisco Camera Work, 1987-90; Fulbright exch. tchr. Sheffield Poly., Eng., 1990-91. One-man shows include Sioux City Art Ctr., Iowa, 1981, Klein Gallery, Chgo., 1982, James Madison U., Harrisonburg, Va., 1983, Orange Coast Coll., Costa Mesa, Calif., 1983, Portland State U., Oreg., 1983, others, group shows, Isetan Mus. of Art, Tokyo, 1993, U. Colo., Boulder, 1977, 82, Mus. Modern Art, NYC, 1978, 82, 84, Santa Barbara Mus. Art, Calif., 1979, San Francisco Mus. Modern Art, 1982, 90, Hokkaido Obihito Mus. Art, Tokyo, 1993, Royal Coll. Art, London, 1994, Mus. Fine Art, Santa Fe, N.Mex., 1994, 96, San Jose Inst. Contemporary Art, 1996, San Francisco Mus. Modern Art, 1996, Sheppard Gallery U. Nev., Reno, others; represented permanent collections, Mus. Modern Art, NYC, Mpls. Inst. Arts, Hallmark Collection, Kansas City, Mo., Boise Gallery Art, Idaho, Walker Art Ctr., Mpls., RI Sch. Design, U. Colo., Fogg Mus. Art, Harvard U., Spencer Mus. Art, U. Kans., Lawrence, Internat. Mus. Photography, Rochester, NY, Art Inst. Chgo., Humbolt State U., Arcata, Calif., Smithsonian Instn., Washington, San Francisco Mus. Modern Art, J. Paul Getty Mus., Santa Monica, Calif., Honolulu Acad. Arts. W.R. French fellow Art Inst. Chgo., 1971; Nat. Endowment for Arts fellow, 1976. Fellow Soc. Contemporary Photo; mem. Soc. for Photog. Edn. Home: 482 Chetwood St Oakland CA 94610-2649 Office: San Jose State U Sch Art & Design San Jose CA 95192-0089 Home Phone: 510-763-0450. Personal E-mail: reed@reedestabrook.net.

ESTABROOK, ROBERT HARLEY, journalist; b. Dayton, Ohio, Oct. 16, 1918; s. Charles and Christianne M. (Harley) E.; m. Mary Lou Stewart, Dec. 22, 1942; children: John Stewart, James Ross, David Morse, Margaret Harley. AB, Northwestern U., 1939; postgrad., Am. Press Inst., Columbia, 1947; LHD (hon.), Colby Coll., 1972. Reporter Emmet County Graphic, Harbor Springs, Mich., 1936; editor Daily Northwestern, Northwestern U., 1938-39; reporter Cedar Rapids (Iowa) Gazette, 1939-40, editorial writer, 1940-42, Washington Post, 1946-53, editor editorial page, 1953-61, corr. London, 1961-62, chief fgn. corr., 1962-65, UN and Can. corr., 1966-71; editor, pub. Lakeville (Conn.) Jour., 1971-86, pub. emeritus, cons., 1987—. Lectr. journalism U. Md., 1948-49; India Editor Exchange Program, 1987. Author: Never Dull: From Washington Editor and Foreign Correspondent To Country Publisher, 2005. Served from pvt. to capt. AUS, 1942-46; in charge Army newspaper and radio sta. 1945, Brazil. Recipient John Peter Zenger award U. Ariz., 1979, Eugene Cervi award, 1980, Horace Greeley award, 1980, Yankee Quill award Acad. New Eng. Journalists, 1983; named to New Eng. Cmty. Newspaper Hall of Fame, 2000. Mem. Nat. Conf. Editorial Writers (founder, life mem. pres. 1951), Council Fgn. Relations, Conn. Council on Freedom of Info. (chmn. 1981-82, Stephen Collins award, 1989), New Eng. Press Assn. (pres. 1983), Rotary Club, Phi Beta Kappa, Sigma Delta Chi (award for best editorial 1954), Deadline Club (Pulitzer Prize juror 1987, 88, award for UN corr. 1969, Golden Quill award for best editorial 1973, 78, Herbert Brucker award 1977), Delta Tau Delta. Unitarian Universalist. Office: Lakeville Jour 33 Bissell St PO Box 1688 Lakeville CT 06039-9989 Office Phone: 860-435-9873. Personal E-mail: restabrook01@comcast.net.

ESTELL, JOHN K., computer science and engineering educator, department chair; s. Kent and Louise Estell; m. Melinda Geithmann, July 17, 1999. BS in Computer Sci. and Engring., The U. Toledo, 1984; MS in Computer Sci., U. Ill., 1987, PhD in Computer Sci., 1991. Asst. prof. computer sci. and engring. The U. Toledo, 1991—96; assoc. prof. computer sci. Bluffton U., 1996—2001; dept. chair, assoc. prof. computer engring. and computer sci. Ohio No. U., Ada, 2001—06, dept. chair, prof. computer engring. and computer sci., 2006—. Exec. com. mem. Western Lake Erie Sierra Club, Toledo, 1993—2007, chair, 1996—2000; vice chair Ohio Chpt. Sierra Club, Columbus, 1997—99; coun. sec. First Mennonite Ch., Bluffton, 1998—2000. Grad. Fellowship, NSF, 1984—87. Mem.: Elec. & Computer Engring. Dept. Heads Assn., Am. Soc. for Engring. Edn. (mem.-at-large, bd. dirs. computers in edn. divsn. 2006—), Assn. for Computing Machinery, IEEE (sr.; sr. mem.), Reed Organ Soc., Upsilon Pi Epsilon, Phi Kappa Phi, Eta Kappa Nu, Tau Beta Pi (Fellowship 1984—85). Mennonite. Office: Ohio Northern U 525 S Main St Ada OH 45810 Home Phone: 419-358-8202; Office Phone: 419-772-1849. Business E-Mail: j-estell@onu.edu.

ESTELLE, MARK, biology professor; BS in Genetics, U. Alta., Edmonton, 1978, PhD in Genetics, 1983. Rsch. assoc. Mich. State U.-US Dept. Energy Plant Rsch. Lab., East Lansing, 1983—86; faculty mem. Ind. U., Bloomington, 1986, Carlos O. Miller prof. plant devel. biology. Contbr. articles to sci. jours.; mem. editl. bd.: Plant Cell. Recipient Kumho Internat. Sci. prize, Kumho Cultural Found., Seoul, Korea, 2006. Fellow: AAAS; mem.: NAS. Office: Dept Biology Ind U 915 E Third St Bloomington IN 47405 Office Phone: 812-856-0485. Office Fax: 812-855-6082. E-mail: maestell@indiana.edu.

ESTEP, ARTHUR LEE, lawyer; b. Forsyth, Mo., Dec. 4, 1932; s. Raymond B. and Nancy Mabel (Melton) E.; m. Joan Marie Hayes, June 16, 1956; 1 child, Sallie Ann Estep Warren. BS, U. Mo., 1954; JD, U. Ariz., 1959, grad. (hon.), 1989. Bar: Ariz. 1959, Calif. 1959. Trust officer 1st Nat. Bank, San Diego, 1959-60; dep. city atty. City of San Diego, 1960-61; pvt. practice San Diego, 1961—. Bd. visitors U. Ariz., Tucson, 1986-96. 1st lt. USMC, 1950-56, Korea. Recipient Outstanding Svc. to Legal Profession award San Diego Bar Assn., 1986. Diplomate Am. Bd. Trial Advs. (pres. San Diego chpt. 1991, mem. nat. bd. dirs. 1990-96). Office: Hughes Nunn 401 B St Ste 1250 San Diego CA 92101-4235

ESTEP, MYRNA LYNNE, systems analyst, philosophy educator; b. Whitesville, W.Va., Jan. 7, 1944; d. Modest Schaeffer and Mary Magdalene E.; m. Richard Keith Schoenig, June 5, 1971; 1 child, Debora Lynne. BA, Ind. U., 1970, MS, 1971, PhD, 1975; postgrad., U. Tex., 1993. Assoc. instr. Ind. U., Bloomington, 1972-75; asst. prof. U. Tex., San Antonio, 1975-78; rsch. edn. specialist Acad. Health Scis., San Antonio, 1979-84; program systems analyst, field rschr. USMC, USN, Quantico, Va., 1984-87; grad. faculty, advisor U. Zimbabwe, 1987-89; rsch. systems analyst San Antonio, 1990—; adj. faculty in philosophy U. of Incarnate Word, San Antonio, 1996-99, Our Lady of the Lake U., San Antonio, 1996-98. Grad. faculty U. Zimbabwe, Harare; advisor to ministries of higher edn. and labour, manpower planning and social welfare, Zimbabwe, 1987-89. Author: The Relation Between Theoretical and Procedural Knowing, 1975, A Theory of Immediate Awareness: Self-Organization and Adaptation in Natural Intelligence, 2003, Self-Organizing Natural Intelligence: Issues of Knowing, Meaning and Complexity, 2006; co-editor (with E.S. Maccia and others): Women and Education, 1975; reviewer (for jours.); contbr. articles to profl. jours. including Applied Sys. and Cybernetics, Pergamon, Ferminista: The On-Line Jour. of Feminist Reconstrn. Recipient Best Paper award U. Vienna, Austria, 1992. Mem. Internat. Soc. Gen. Systems Rsch., Austrian Soc. Cybernetics, Math. Assn. Am., NY Acad. Sci., Phi Kappa Phi. Home: 16022 Oak Grove Dr San Antonio TX 78255-1128 Personal E-mail: emathematica@aol.com.

ESTEP, ROBERT LLOYD, lawyer; b. Marion, Va., Dec. 20, 1939; s. Lanson Eugene and Clara Nell (White) E.; m. Elizabeth Grayson Werth, July 10, 1971; 1 child, Laura White. BA with Honors, U. Va., 1962, JD, 1973. Bar: Ill. 1973, U.S. Dist. Ct. (no. dist.) Ill. 1973, Tex. 1984. From assoc. to ptnr. Isham, Lincoln & Beale, Chgo., 1973-83; ptnr. Jones Day, Dallas, 1983—, of counsel. Served to capt. U.S. Army, 1966-70, Vietnam. Woodrow Wilson fellow, U. Va., 1962. Mem. Tex. Bar Assn., Law Club Chgo., Spl. Forces Assn., Phi Beta Kappa. Republican. Lutheran. Office: Jones Day 2727 N Harwood St Dallas TX 75201-1515 E-mail: rlestep@jonesday.com.

ESTERLY, NANCY BURTON, retired physician; b. NYC, Apr. 14, 1935; d. Paul R. and Tanya (Pasahow) Burton; m. John R. Esterly, June 16, 1957; children: Sarah Burton, Anne Beidler, John Snyder, II, Henry Clark, II. AB, Smith Coll., 1956; MD, Johns Hopkins U., 1960. Intern, then resident in pediatrics Johns Hopkins Hosp., 1960-63, resident in dermatology, 1964-67; instr. pediatrics Johns Hopkins U. Med. Sch., 1967-68; instr., trainee La Rabida U. Chgo. Inst.; also dept. pediatrics U. Chgo. Med. Sch., 1968-69; asst. prof. Pritzker Sch. Medicine, U. Chgo., 1969-70, assoc. prof., 1973-78; asst. prof. dermatology Abraham Lincoln Sch. Medicine, U. Ill., 1970-72, assoc. prof. dermatology and pediatrics, 1972-73; dir. div. dermatology, dept. pediatrics Michael Reese Hosp. and Med. Ctr., Chgo., 1973-78; prof. pediatrics and dermatology Northwestern U. Med. Sch., 1978; head div. dermatology, dept. pediatrics Children's Meml. Hosp., Chgo., 1978-87; prof. pediatrics and dermatology Med. Coll. Wis., Milw., 1987—2004, prof. emeritus dermatology, 2005—; head div. dermatology, dept. pediatrics Children's Hosp. Wis., Milw., 1987—2004; ret., 2004. Editor-in-chief Pediatric Dermatology, 1983—; contbr. articles to profl. jours. Recipient David Martin Carter award, Am. Skin Assn., 2002, Lifetime Career Educator award, Dermatology Found., 2002, Disting. Svc. award, Med. Coll. Wis., 2004. Mem.: Wis. Pediat. Soc., Women's Dermatol. Soc. (Rose Hirschler award), Soc. Pediat. Dermatology (1st Lifetime Achievement award 1998), Soc. Pediat. Rsch., Am. Acad. Pediatrics, Soc. Investigative Dermatology, Wis. Dermatol. Soc., Am. Dermatol. Assn., Am. Acad. Dermatology, Internat. Soc. Pediat. Dermatology, Sigma Xi. Home Phone: 505-742-1427. Personal E-mail: nesterly@comcast.net.

ESTERN, NEIL CARL, sculptor; b. NYC, Apr. 18, 1926; s. Marc J. and Molly (Sylbert) E.; m. Anne Graham, May 27, 1947; children: Peter, Evan, Victoria. Student, Barnes Found., Merion, Pa., 1945—47; BFA, BS in Edn., Tyler Sch. Fine Arts, 1948. One-man shows include Scoville Meml. Libr., Salisbury, Conn., 1985; exhibited in group shows at Nat. Acad., N.Y.C., 1985-2007, Nat. Sculpture Soc., 1985-2007, Sharon Creative Arts Found., 1985, Bklyn. Mus., 1980, Kent, Conn., 1992, Fairfield, Conn., 1994, 96, Century Assn., 1995-2007; prin. works include J.F.K. Meml., Bklyn., 1966, Statue of Fiorello H. LaGuardia, LaGuardia C.C., 1983, LaGuardia Meml. Statue of Fiorello La Guardia, Greenwich Village, N.Y.C., 1994, FDR Meml. Statues of Eleanor, FDR and Fala, Washington, 1997, Nat. Cathedral Statue of Eleanor Roosevelt, Washington, 1998, Claude Pepper Meml., Tallahassee, 2003; portrait busts of Danny Kaye, Gov. Raymond Baldwin, Thomas Buechner, Jack Nicholson, Pres. Carter, Prince Charles, Lady Diana, David Levine, J. Edgar Hoover, Senator Robert Taft, Covington Hardee, Miguel de la Madrid. Recipient 1st prize sculpture Kent Art Assn., 1982,. Fellow Nat. Sculpture Soc. (pres. 1994-97, 2006—, Lindsey Morris prize 1984, Mildred Victor Meml. prize 1988); mem. NAD (John Gregory award 1964, Samuel F.B. Morse Gold medal 1970, Cert. of Merit 1979, 90, Dessie Green prize 1990, Daniel Chester French award), Century Assn. Avocation: tennis. Home: 432 Cream Hill Rd West Cornwall CT 06796 Office Phone: 860-824-5208. Personal E-mail: anneilestern@yahoo.com.

ESTEROW, MILTON, publishing executive; b. Bklyn., July 28, 1928; s. Bernard and Yetta (Barash) E.; m. Jacqueline Levine, Jan. 6, 1951; children: Judith, Deborah. Student, Bklyn. Coll., 1946-49. Reporter N.Y. Times, NYC, 1948-63, asst. to cultural news dir., 1963-68; assoc. dir. Kennedy Galleries, NYC, 1968-72; editor, pub. ARTnews, NYC, 1972—; pub. ARTnewsletter, 1975—; chmn. Esterow Communications Corp., 1981, Annellen Publs., 1982. Lectr. in field. Author: The Art Stealers, 1966. Office: ARTnews LLC 48 W 38th St Fl 9 New York NY 10018-6238

ESTES, ANDREW HARPER, lawyer; b. Pecos, Tex., Dec. 16, 1956; s. Bobby Frank and Gayle (Harper) E.; m. Deidre Dement, Mar. 19, 1976; children: Andrew Kimble, Jada Catherine. BA, Tex. Tech U., 1977; JD, Baylor Sch. Law, 1979. Bar: Tex. 1980, US Dist. Ct. (no. dist.) Tex. 1980, US Dist. Ct. (we. dist.) Tex. 1981, US Ct. Appeals (5th cir.) 1982, US Supreme Ct. 1983, US Tax Ct. Ptnr. Lynch, Chappell & Alsup P.C., Midland, Tex., 1980—. Mem. admissions com. Dist. 16, State Bar Tex., 1982-85, bd. dirs., 1999-2002. Mem. Tex. Tech. U. Coll. Edn. Devel. Coun., Lubbock, 1986-87; vol. Big Bros., Midland, 1983—, bd. dirs., 1985-89; bd. dirs. Hearthstone Temporary Children's Shelter, 1988-92; mem. bd. dirs. Tex. Book Festival, 2001-. Named Big Brother of Yr., Big Bros./Big Sisters of Midland, 1985; recipient Trimble Vol. Svc. award, Leadership Midland Alumni, 1986, Pro Bono Atty. award West Tex. Legal Svcs., 1991. Mem. ABA, Midland County Young Lawyers Assn. (sec., treas. 1987-88, Outstanding Young Lawyer of Midland County 1992), Midland County Bar Assn. (sec., treas. 1987-88, v.p. 1992-93, pres.-elect. 1993-94, pres. 1995-96), State Bar Tex. (Dist. 16B grievance com. 1990-93, chmn. 1992-93, bd. dirs. 1999-2002, pres.-elect 2007-), Tex. Young Lawyers Assn. (bd. dirs. 1987-89), Tex. Bd. Legal Specialization (cert.), State Bar Tex. (pres.-elect, 2007-), Phi Delta Phi. Presbyterian. Home: 1505 Princeton Ave Midland TX 79701-5760 Office: Lynch Chappell & Alsup PC The Summit Bldg 300 N Marienfeld St Fl 7 Midland TX 79701-4345 Office Phone: 432-683-3351. Business E-Mail: hestes@lynchchappell.com, hestes@lcalawfirm.com.

ESTES, CARL LEWIS, II, lawyer; b. Ft. Worth, Feb. 9, 1936; s. Joe E. and Carroll E.; m. Gay Gooch, Aug. 29, 1959; children: Adrienne Virginia, Margaret Ellen. BS, U. Tex., 1957, LL.B., 1960. Bar: Tex. 1960. Law clk. U.S. Supreme Ct., 1960-61; assoc. firm Vinson & Elkins, Houston, 1961-69, ptnr., 1970—2002. Bd. dirs. Houston Grand Opera Assn., Houston Arboretum. Fellow Am. Bar Found., Tex. Bar Found.; mem. ABA, Internat. Bar Assn., Am. Law Inst., Am. Coll. Probate Counsel, Tex. Bar Assn., Internat. Fiscal Assn., Internat. Acad. Estate and Trust Law. Fellow Am. Bar Found., Tex. Bar Found.; mem. ABA, Internat. Bar Assn., Am. Law Inst., Am. Coll. Probate Counsel, Tex. Bar Assn., Internat. Fiscal Assn., Internat. Acad. Estate and Trust Law, Asia Soc. (bd. dirs.).

ESTES, CARROLL LYNN, sociologist, educator; b. Ft. Worth, May 30, 1938; d. Joe Ewing and Carroll (Cox) E.; 1 child, Duskie Lynn Gelfand Estes. AB, STanford U., 1959; MA, So. Meth. U., 1961; PhD, U. Calif., San Diego, 1972; DHL (hon.), Russell Sage Coll., 1986. Rsch. asst., asst. study dir. Brandeis U. Social Welfare Rsch. Ctr., 1962-63, rsch. assoc., 1964-65, project dir., 1965-67; vis. lectr. Florence Heller Grad. Sch., 1964-65; rsch. dir. Simmons Coll., 1963-64; asst. prof. social work San Diego State Coll., 1967-72; asst. prof. in residence dept. psychiatry U. Calif., San Francisco, 1972-75, assoc. prof. dept. social and behavioral scis., 1975-79, prof., 1979-92, chair dept. social and behavioral scis., 1981-93, coord. human devel. tng. program, 1974-75; dir. Aging Health Policy Rsch. Ctr., 1979-85, Inst. for Health and Aging, 1985-99. Faculty rsch. lectr. U. Calif., 1993; LaSor lectr. Oreg. Health Scis. U, 2005; co-founder Concerned Scientists in Aging, 2005. Author: The Decision-Makers: The Power Structure of Dallas, 1963; co-author: Protective Services for Older People, 1972, U.S. Senate Special Committee on Aging Report, Paperwork and the Older Americans Act, 1978, The Aging Enterprise, 1979 Fiscal Austerity and Aging, 1983, Long Term Care of the Elderly, 1985, Political Economy, Health and Aging, 1984, The Long Term Care Crisis, 1993, The Nation's Health, 2001, 7th edit., 2003, Critical Gerontology, 1999, Social Policy and Aging, 2001, Social Theory, Social Policy and Aging, 2003, Health Policy, 5th edit., 2007; contbr. articles to profl. jours. Mem. Calif. Commn. on Aging, 1974-77; cons. U.S. Senate Spl. Com. on Aging from 1976, Notch Commn. U.S. Commn. Social Security, 1993-94; bd. dir. Nat. Com. to Preserve Social Security and Medicare, 2002—, vice chair, 2006-. Recipient Matrix award Theta Sigma Phi, 1964, award for contbns. to lives of older Californians, Calif. Commn. on Aging, 1977, Helen Nahm Rsch. award U. Calif., San Francisco, 1986, Woman Who Would Be Pres. League of Women Voters, 1998, Lifetime Achievement award Nat. Com. to Preserve Social Security and Medicare, 2006, Improvement of Status of Women award, U. Calif. San Francisco, 2007. Mem. Inst. Medicine of NAS, ACLU, Am. Sociol. Assn. (Disting. Scholar award Aging and Life Course 2000), Assn. Gerontology in Higher Edn. (pres. 1980-81, recipient Beverly award 1993, Tibbitts award 2000), Am. Soc. on Aging (pres. 1982-84, Leadership award 1986, Hall of Fame award, 2007), Geronotol. Soc. Am. (Kent award 1992, pres. 1995-96), Older Women's League (v.p. 1994-97), Soc. Study Social Problems, Alpha Kappa Delta, Pi Beta Phi. Office: U Calif San Francisco Inst Health & Aging 3333 California St Ste 340 San Francisco CA 94118-1944 Business E-Mail: carroll.estes@ucsf.edu.

ESTES, ELAINE ROSE GRAHAM, retired librarian; b. Springfield, Mo., Nov. 24, 1931; d. James McKinley and Zelma Mae (Smith) Graham; m. John Melvin Estes, Dec. 29, 1953. BSBA, Drake U., 1953, tchg. cert., 1956; MSLS, U. Ill., 1960. With Pub. Libr. Des Moines, 1956-95, coord. ext. svcs., 1977-78, dir., 1978-95, ret., 1995. Lectr. antiques, hist. architecture, librs.; mem. conservation planning com. for disaster preparedness for librs. Author bibliographies of books on antiques; contbr. articles to profl. jours. Mem. State of Iowa Cultural Affairs Adv. Coun., 1986—94, Nat. Commn. on Future of Drake U., 1987—88; chmn. Des Moines Mayor's Hist. Dist. Commn.; mem. nominations review com. Iowa State Nat. Hist. Register, 1983—89; chmn. hist. subcom. Des Moines Sesquecentennial Com., 1993, Iowa Sister State Commn., 1993—95; mem. com. 40th Anniversary Drake U. Alumni Weekend, 50 Yr. Drake Alumni Weekend, 2003; mem. July 4 com. Iowa Sesquecentennial; nat. exch. dir. Friendship Force, 1997; mem. nat. adv. bd. Cowles Libr., 1998—; mem. Gov.'s Iowa Centennial Meml. Found., 2003—; mem. acquisition com. Salisbury House, 2003; mem. cultural ctr. task force African Am. Hist. Mus., 1999—2003; mem. Iowa author com. Pub. Libr. Des Moines Found., 2001—; mem. Terrace Hill Commn., 2001—; bd. dirs. Des Moines Art Ctr., 1972—83, hon. mem., 1983—; bd. dirs. Friends of Libr. USA, 1986—92, Henry Wallace House Found., Iowa Libr. Centennial Com., 1990—91, Wagner Hall Preservation Project, 2004—. Recipient Recognition award Greater Des Moines, YWCA, 1975, Disting. Alumni award Drake U., 1979, Woman of Achievement award YWCA, 1989, Excellence in Hist. Preservation award City of Des Moines, 1994, Contbn. to Cmty. award Connect Found., 1995, Friend of Literacy award Pub. Libr. of Des Moines Found., 2003; named Textbook Project in her honor, Forest Libr., 2002; named to Wall of Fame, YWCA, 2003. Mem.: ALA (30th Anniversary Honor Roll for Intellectual Freedom 1999), Iowa Soc. Preservation Hist. Landmarks (bd. dirs. 1969—97), Libr. Assn. Greater Des Moines Metro Area (chmn. 1992, pres.), Iowa Urban Pub. Libr. Assn., Iowa Libr. Assn. (life; pres. 1978—79), Iowa Antique Assn., Terrace Hill (Gov.'s Mansion) Soc. (bd. dirs. 1972—, v.p. 1991—93, pres. 1993—96), Links Inc. (40th ann. com. 1997), Drake U. 50 Yr. Club, Questers Inc. Club (pres. 1982, state 2d v.p. 1984—86, 1st v.p. 1990—2000, pres. 1997, state pres. 2000—03, pres. 2001—03), Rotary (history com. 2001—06), Proteus Club (pres. 2003—04).

ESTES, ERNEST L., geologist, educator; b. Evanston, Ill., Mar. 21, 1942; s. Ernest L. and Berit Lillian Estes; m. Mary K. Kolb, Apr. 13, 1967; children: Aaron Judson, Erika Nichol. BS, Lawrence U., Appleton, 1965; MS, Duke U., Durham, NC, 1967; PhD, U. NC, Chapel Hill, 1971. Asst. prof. Lamar U., Beaumont, Tex., 1972—76; prof. Tex. A&M U., Galveston, 1976—. Recipient Achievement award, Tex. A&M U., Galveston, 1988, Faculty Disting. Achievement award, Assn. Former Students Tex. A&M U., Galveston, 2001. Mem.: Phi Kappa PHi. Avocations: sailing, travel, reading. Office: Tex A&M Univ at Galveston 200 Seawolf Pky Galveston TX 77553 Business E-Mail: estese@tamug.edu.

ESTES, JACK CHARLES, entrepreneur, oil industry executive, research scientist; b. Rogers, Ark., Apr. 7, 1935; s. Jack Russell and Merle Clara (White) E.; m. Sandra Jean Reeves, Nov. 10, 1961; children: Michael Lynn, David Russell, Cristi Yvonne. BS in Engring., U. Tulsa, 1965. Computer engr. Remington Rand Univac, Illion, NY, 1960; rsch. tech. Pan Am. Petroleum Corp., Tulsa, 1960-65, rsch. engr., 1965-76; rsch. supr. Amoco Prodn. Co., Tulsa, 1976-89; pres. Environ. Drilling Tech., Inc., Tulsa, 1990—; prin. Estes Consulting Group, Inc., Tulsa, 1999—. Founder Environ. Drilling Tech. Inc., Estes Consulting Group Inc, Intech. LLC, Ye Olde Shoppe LLC. Contbr. articles to profl. jours.; patentee in field. With USAF, 1955-59. Mem. ASME, N.E. Okla. Sq. Dance Assn. (bd. dirs. 1989-92), Am. Petroleum Inst. (chmn. internat. subcom. 13 1982-85, vice chmn. com. 13 1986-89, task group chmn. 1989—, Svc. award 1991), Internat. Drilling Contractors (chmn. drill bit standardization task group 1973-80), Am. Mgmt. Assn., Soc. Petroleum Engrs. (tech. editor Jour. Petroleum Tech. 1977-78, Svc. award 1985, program com. 1989-92), Am. Chem. Soc. (Svc. award 1984), Sci. Rsch. Soc. (internat. sci. fair judge), Sigma Xi. Office Phone: 918-251-8020. E-mail: edti@olp.net, jestes@olp.net.

ESTES, KENNETH WILLIAM, history professor, military officer; b. Seattle, Aug. 25, 1947; s. Victor Guy Estes and Lois Bernice Horth; m. Genevieve Perrin, Sept. 24, 2002; children: Caroline Estes Hougen, Gwendolyn Estes Haley. BSc, US Naval Acad., 1969; MA, Duke U., 1974; PhD, U. Md., 1984. Lt. col. USMC, 1969—93; prof. history various ednl. insts., 1974—2007. Cons. Computing Technologies, Inc., Falls Church, Va., 1996—2001; rsch. fellow Emirates Ctr. for Strategic Studies, 2002; sr. rsch. fellow Marine Corps U., Quantico, 2006—. Editor: (guide book) Marine Officer's Guide, (hand book) Handbook for Marine NCOs, (non-fiction) History in Dispute 18: The Spanish Civil War; author: Marines under Armor, Tanks on the Beaches, US Marine Corps Tank Crewman World War II, A European Anabasis, U.S. Army Soldier: Baghdad, 2003-2004, Into the Breach. Decorated Meritorious Svc. medal, Def. Meritorious Svc. medal, Cruz de Merito (Naval) con Distinctivo Blanco Kingdom of Spain; recipient 3d Pl. award as Outstanding Navy ROTC Instr., Am. Def. Preparedness Assn., 1983; European Acad. fellow, Fed. Republic of Germany, 1982. Mem.: US Naval Inst., Soc. for Mil. History, Am. Hist. Assn (Gutenberg-e prize 2001). Home: 19202 39th Ave S Seattle WA 98188-5316 Personal E-mail: ken_estes@compuserve.com.

ESTES, LESLIE KAREN, educator; b. Waco, Tex., Dec. 9, 1964; d. Curtis Alton Rothe and Myrl Janette Tull, Joann Rothe (Stepmother); m. Troy Bryant Estes, Oct. 16, 1982; children: Cody Bryant, Katrina Lane, LeslieAnne, Katelyn Jolene, Emma Annette, Daniel Curtis. BS, U. Mary Hardin-Baylor, Belton, Tex., 1993; MS in Edn., Baylor U., Waco, Tex., 1996—98, EdD, 2005. Cert. rchr. Tex. Edn. Agy., 1993. Lectr. Baylor U., Waco; asst. prof. U. Mary Hardin-Baylor, Belton, 2003—. Achievements include research in efficacy scale for teachers of reading. Office Phone: 254-295-4183.

ESTES, MARY K., virologist, researcher; BA, Elmira Coll.; PhD, U. NC, Chapel Hill. Postdoctoral rschr. Baylor Coll. Medicine, Houston, prof. molecular virology, microbiology & medicine. Adv. bd. Virology Jour., Burroughs Wellcome Fund; bd. dirs. Gulf Coast Consortia. Contbr. articles to profl. jours.; editor: (books) Viral Gastoenteritis (One Nation), 1997. Adv. com. Ctr. Biologistics Evaluation and Rsch. FDA, 1998—. Fellow: AAAS (chmn. med. scis. 1999—2001); mem.: NAS, Inst. Medicine. Achievements include cloning Norwalk virus & developing a vaccine. Office: Baylor Coll Medicine One Baylor Plz BCM 385 Houston TX 77030-3498 Office Phone: 713-798-3585. Office Fax: 713-789-3586. E-mail: mestes@bcm.tmc.edu.*

ESTES, NATHAN ANTHONY MARK, III, cardiologist, medical educator; b. Newport, RI, Aug. 20, 1949; s. Nathan Anthony Jr. and Ione (Lewis) E.; m. Noël Evangeline Thorbecke, June 22, 1974; children: Elise Thorbecke, N.A. Chace, Kathryn Elizabeth. BA cum laude, U. Pa., 1971; MD magna cum laude, U. Cin., 1977. Diplomate Am. Bd. Internal Medicine, Am. Bd. Cardiovascular Disease, Am. Bd. Cardiac Electrophysiology. Intern New Eng. Deaconess Hosp.-Harvard Med. Sch., Boston, 1977-78, resident, 1978-80; fellow in cardiology New Eng. Med. Ctr.-Tufts U., Boston, 1980-82; fellow in electrophysiology Mass. Gen. Hosp.-Harvard Med. Sch., Boston, 1982-83; dir. cardiac arrhythmia New. Eng. Med. Ctr. Svc., Boston, 1983-96, dir. heart station, 1983-91; assoc. prof. medicine Tufts U. Sch. Med., Boston, 1983-90, prof., 1990-96, chief New Eng. Cardiac Arrythmia Ctr., 1996-97; chief New. Eng. Arrhythmia Ctr., Boston, 1996—, Lifespan Cardiac Arrhythmia Consortium, Boston, 1998. Bd. dirs. Lifespan; ednl. cons., 1985-96; mem. internat. safety monitoring bd. 3M Pharms., Mpls., 1990-96; co-chmn. pubs. com. NIH, Bethesda, 1993-96; chmn. instl. rev. bd. Tufts U. Sch. Medicine, 1996-2001. Contbr. over 200 articles to profl. jours.; contbr. over 30 chpts. to books; editor books, 1994-96; mem. editl. bd. Jour. Interventional Electrophysiology, 1995—, Pacing and Cardiac Electrophysiology, 1995—, Jour. Cardiovasc. Electrophysiology, Am. Jour. Sports and Medicine, 1998, Am. Jour. Cardiology. Vestry mem. Trinity Ch., Newton, Mass., 1985-87; coach Baystate Tournament of Champions, Waltham, Mass., 1990-94; judge N.H. Racing Assn., Lincoln, 1993-95; bd. trustees Moses Brown Sch., Providence, R.I., 1997—. Fellow Am. Coll. Cardiology; mem. Am. Heart Assn. (chmn. bd. trustees Boston chpt. 1998, vice-chair New Eng. affiliate 1999, pres.-elect New Eng. affiliate 2000, coun clin. cardiology), N.Am. Soc. Pacing and Electrophysiology (chmn. publs. com., trustee 2001), New Eng. Electrophysiology Soc. (pres. 1994-97), Lifespan (bd. dirs. 2001), N.Am. Soc. Pacing and Electrophysiology (trustee 2001), Alpha Omega Alpha. Episcopalian. Avocations: sailing, skiing, tennis, running. Office: New Eng Med Ctr 750 Washington St Boston MA 02111-1526

ESTES, TODD A., historian; b. Akron, Ohio, Oct. 21, 1963; s. Glenn Elwood Estes and Elizabeth Ann Sexton; m. Kathleen Ann Pfeiffer, Nov. 26, 1999; children: Elizabeth, Brian. BA in History, U. Tenn., Knoxville, 1986; MA in History, U. Ky., Lexington, 1989, PhD in History, 1995. Tchg. asst. history U. Ky., Lexington, 1987—90, instr. history, 1990—92; asst. prof. history Oakland U., Rochester, Mich., 1995—2001, assoc. prof. history, 2001—. Author: The Jay Treaty Debate, Public Opinion, and the Evolution of Early American Political Culture, 2006; contbr. articles to profl. jours. Vestry mem. St. James Episcopal Ch., Birmingham, Mich., 2001—03, jr. warden, 2002, sr. warden, 2003. Recipient Chancellor's award for outstanding tchg. assts., U. Ky., 1990, Tchg. Excellence award, Oakland U., 2001. Mem.: New Eng. Hist. Assn., Soc. for Historians of the Early Am. Rep., Orgn. of Am. Historians, Am. Hist. Assn. Democrat. Episcopalian. Avocations: classical music, reading, basketball, jazz music. Home: 2979 Heidelberg Dr Rochester Hills MI 48309 Office: Oakland Univ Dept History 2200 Squirrel Rd Rochester MI 48309 Office Phone: 248-370-3534. Office Fax: 248-375-3528. E-mail: estes@oakland.edu.

ESTES, WILLIAM KAYE, psychologist, educator; b. Mpls., June 17, 1919; s. George D. and Mona Estes; m. Katherine Walker, Sept. 26, 1942;

children: George E., Gregory W. Mem. faculty Ind. U., 1946—62, prof. psychology, 1955—60, research prof. psychology, 1960—62; faculty research fellow Social Sci. Research Council, 1952—55; lectr. psychology U. Wis., 1949; vis. prof. Northwestern U., 1959; fellow Center Advanced Study Behavioral Scis., 1955—56; spl. univ. lectr. U. London, 1961; prof. psychology, mem. Inst. Math. Studies Social Scis., Stanford, 1962—68; prof. Rockefeller U., 1968—79, Harvard U., 1978—89, prof. emeritus, 1989—; prof. Ind. U., 1999—. Chmn. Office Sci. and Engring. Personnel NRC, 1982—85, chmn. com. on prevention of nuclear war, 1984—89. Author: An Experimental Study of Punishment, 1944, Learning Theory and Mental Development, 1970, Models of Learning, Memory and Choice, 1982, Statistical Models in Behavioral Research, 1991, Classification and Cognition, 1994; co-author: Modern Learning Theory, 1954; contbr. articles to profl. jours.; editor: Handbook of Learning and Cognitive Processes, 1962—68, Psychol. Rev., 1977—82, Psychol. Sci., 1990—94; Jour. Exptl. Psychology, 1958—62. With AUS, 1944—46. Recipient U.S. Nat. medal of Sci., 1997. Fellow: AAAS, APA (pres. divsn. exptl. psychology 1958—59, Disting. Sci. Contbn. award 1962, gold medal for lifetime achievement in psychol. sci. 1992), Am. Acad. Arts and Scis.; mem.: NAS, Fedn. Behavioral Psychol. and Cognitive Scis. (v.p. 1988—91), Midwestern Psychol. Assn., N.Y. Acad. Scis. (life), N.Y. Acad. Scis. (hon.), Soc. Exptl. Psychologists (Warren medal 1963). Home: 2714 E Pine Ln Bloomington IN 47401-4423 Office: Ind U Psychology Bldg Bloomington IN 47405 Home Phone: 812-339-3229. Business E-Mail: wkestes@indiana.edu.

ESTEVA, FRANCISCO JAVIER, physician, researcher; b. Bueu, Galicia, Spain, Jan. 16, 1964; came to U.S., 1990; s. Carlos Esteva and Anunciacion Lorenzo; m. Maria J. Pastoriza-Regueira, June 2, 1991; 1 child, Eduardo. MD, U. Zaragoza, Spain, 1988. Diplomate Am. Bd. Internal Medicine, Am. Bd. Med. Oncology. Resident in internal medicine Cooper Hosp./U. Med. Ctr., Camden, NJ, 1991-94; fellow in med. oncology Georgetown U., Washington, 1994—96, instr. medicine, 1997; asst. prof. medicine U. Tex. M.D. Anderson Cancer Ctr., Houston, 1997—2003, assoc. prof. medicine, 2003—. Mem. spkrs. bur. Genentech, Inc., San Francisco, 1998—, Astro-Zeneca, Wilmington, Del., 1998—. Author: Hormones and Growth Factors in Development and Neoplasia, 1998, Monoclonal Antibody-Based Therapy of Cancer, 1998, Hematology-Oncology Clinics in North America, 1999; contbr. articles to profl. jours. Recipient Rsch. award Nat. Cancer Inst., 1999—2004. Mem. ACP, Am. Soc. Clin. Oncology, Am. Assn. Cancer Rsch., Am. Soc. Breast Disease, European Soc. Med. Oncology. Avocations: travel, reading. Office: MD Anderson Cancer Ctr 1515 Holcombe Blvd Unit 1354 Houston TX 77030-4009

ESTEVEZ, CARLOS IRWIN See SHEEN, CHARLIE

ESTEVEZ, EMILIO, actor, writer, director; b. NYC, May 12, 1962; s. Martin and Janet Sheen; m. Paula Abdul, Apr. 29, 1992 (div. May 1994); children: Taylor, Paloma. Grad. high sch., Santa Monica, Calif. Actor: (stage prodn.) Mister Roberts, Burt Reynold's Dinner Theatre, Fla. (TV spls.) Seventeen Going on Nowhere, ABC, To Climb a Mountain, Making the Grade, (films) Tex, 1982, The Outsiders, 1983, Nightmares, 1983, Repo Man, 1984, The Breakfast Club, 1985, St. Elmo's Fire, 1985, That Was Then. This is Now, 1985 (also screenwriter), Maximum Overdrive, 1986, Stakeout, 1987, Young Guns, 1988, Never On Tuesday, 1989, Young Guns II, 1990, The Mighty Ducks, 1992, Freejack, 1992, National Lampoon's Loaded Weapon 1, 1993, Another Stakeout, 1993, Judgment Night, 1993, D2: The Mighty Ducks, 1994, D3: The Mighty Ducks, 1996, Mission Impossible, 1996, The War at Home, 1996, The Bang Bang Club, 1998, Killer's Head, 1999, Sand, 2000, Rated X, 2000, (voice) The 3 Wise Men, 2003, The LA Riot Spectacular, 2005; (TV films) In The Custody of Strangers, 1982, Nightbreaker, 1989, Dollar for the Dead, 1998, Late Last Night, 1999; actor, screenwriter, dir. Wisdom, 1987; writer, dir., actor: Men at Work, 1990, Bobby, 2006; prodr.: The Jerky Boys, 1995, The War at Home, 1996. Office: care UTA 9560 Wilshire Blvd Fl 5 Beverly Hills CA 90212-2401

ESTEVEZ, LUIS DE GALVEZ, designer, manufacturer; b. Havana, Cuba, 1930; came to U.S., 1944, naturalized, 1960; s. Luis Estevez y Navarro and Gloria Cortinas de Galvez y Benitez de Lugo; m. Betty Dew Menzies. Student, U. Havana, 1948-49, Traphagen Sch. Fashion, 1951-51. Display at Lord & Taylor, NYC, 1950, Jean Patou, Paris, 1951-52; prin. Grenelle-Estevez, NYC, 1955-58; prin., ptnr. Estevez, NYC, 1959-65, owner, operator Estevez/Gabor-Estevez/Estevez Resort Sports Wear, 1973-76; ptnr. with Neal Diamond Estevez Dress Firm, Los Angeles, from 1977; owner Estevez, Los Angeles. Designer for Pat Hartley, N.Y.C., 1953-54, Neal of Calif., Los Angeles, 1968-72, films and TV, Universal Studios, 1969-70; designer Betty Ford's wardrobe, 1975-77; designer home furnishings for Dan River, also houses and real estate devel.; presented fashion openings Broadway shows Hair, 1969, Hello Dolly, 1974; contbr.: articles on fashion to Phila. Inquirer, 1956-66. Recipient Fla. Sunshine award, 1955, Coty Am. Critics award, 1956, Chgo. Gold Coast awards, 1959, 60, 62, Denver Symphony award, Goldwaters Phynix award, Bambergers Fashion award, 1962, Silk award, Traphagen Fashion award, 1975, Am. Schiffli Embroidery award, 1963, Hispanic Designers Life Time Achievement award, 1990 Mem. Costume Designers Guild Los Angeles, Acad. Motion Pictures Arts and Scis., Council Fashion Designers Am. Roman Catholic. Office: Estevez 8810 Melrose Ave West Hollywood CA 90069-5604 *I believe that you should only wear what is flattering regardless what fashion dictates.*

ESTEVEZ, RAMON See SHEEN, MARTIN

ESTIN, HANS HOWARD, retired investment company executive; b. Prague, Czechoslovakia, Sept. 8, 1928; came to U.S., 1941, naturalized, 1946; m. Martha McCormick, Oct. 1990 (dec. 2006); children from previous marriage: Hilary Parker, Alexandra Howard; stepchildren: Sargent L. Goodchild, Jr., Abigail Goodchild, McKay Goodchild. AB, Harvard U., 1949; LL.D., Merrimac Coll., 1972, Boston U., 1977. Vice chmn., pres., chmn. bd. Harbor Nat. Bank, Boston, 1964-67; vice chmn. N.Am. Mgmt. Corp., Boston, 1974—2004, vice chmn. emeritus, 2004—. Trustee Putnam Group Mut. Funds, 1972-2001. Former trustee New Eng. Aquarium; chmn. bd. trustees Boston U., 1969-76; mem. Schepens Eye Rsch. Inst.; former bd. overseers Boys and Girls Clubs Boston, Inc. 1st lt. USAF, 1951-55. Decorated Knight, Order of Crown, Belgium, 1983, Order of Leopold, Belgium, 1990; named Hon. Consul of Belgium at Boston, 1970-90. Mem. Essex County Club (Manchester, Mass.). Home: 600 Summer St Manchester MA 01944-1626 Office: NAm Mgmt Corp Ten Post Office Sq Boston MA 02109 Business E-Mail: hestin@namcorp.com.

ESTIN-KLEIN, LIBBYADA, advertising executive, writer; b. Newark, July 13, 1937; d. Barney and Florence B. (Tenkin) Straver; m. Harvey M. Klein, Sept. 9, 1984. Student, Syracuse U., 1955—57; BS, Columbia, 1960; cert., NY Sch. Interior Design, 1962. RN 1960. Med. rsch. tech. writer, NYC, 1960-62; pres. Libbyada Estin Interiors, NYC, 1962-65; v.p. advt. and pub. relations Behrman/Estin Inc., NYC, 1965-67; account exec., dir. pub. rels. J.S. Fullerton, Inc., NYC, 1968-69, Kallir Philips Ross Inc., NYC, 1969-71; copy supr. William Douglas McAdams Inc., NYC, 1971-75, Sudler & Hennessey Inc., NYC, 1975-80; v.p., exec. adminstr., creative dir. Grey Med. Advt. Inc., NYC, 1980-84; founder, ptnr. Estin Sandler Comm. Inc., NYC, 1984; v.p. Barnum Comm. Inc., NYC, 1984-86; sr. v.p. ICE Comm., Inc., Rochester, N.Y., 1986-87; sr. cons. Nelson Comms., Inc., Sudler & Hennessy Inc., Worldwide Healthcare Comms., NYC, 1998—2003; pres. Estin-Klein Comm. Inc., Rochester and Pittsford, NY, 1987—2005, Ellicott City, Md., 2005—. Dir. health group Robert Comm., Inc., East Rochester, NY, 1993-95; bd. dirs., Perinatal Network of Monroe County, Pathways to Health. mem. PRSA Health Acad.; sr. cons. Nelson Comms., Ind., Sudler & Hennessy Inc., Worldwide Healthcare Comms. Inc., NYC, 1993-2004. Mem. Pub. Rels. Soc. Am./Health Acad., Advt. Women N.Y., Am. Advt. Fedn., Advt. Coun. Rochester, Rochester Sales and Mktg. Execs. Club, Mktg. Communicators Rochester, Am. Med. Writers Assn., Women in Comm., Healthcare Mktg. and Comms. Coun., Healthcare Bus. Women's Assn., Bus. Womens Network Howard County, Am. Nurses Assn., Allied Bd. Trade, Columbia-Presbyn. Hosp. Alumnae Assn., Columbia U. Alumnae Assn., Syracuse U. Alumnae Assn., Sigma Theta Tau, Delta Phi Epsilon. Office: Estin-Klein Comms 2769 Westminster Rd Ellicott City MD 21043 Home Phone: 410-251-9897; Office Phone: 410-480-4380. Personal E-mail: libbyada@aol.com.

ESTLUND, CYNTHIA, law educator; BA summa cum laude, Lawrence U., 1978; JD, Yale U., 1983. Law clk. to Juege Patricia Wald US Ct. Appeals (DC Cir.), 1983—84; assoc. Bredhoff & Kaiser, Washington, DC, 1985—89; asst. prof. law U. Tex. Sch. Law, 1989—93, prof., 1993—99, Leroy G. Denman, Jr., regents prof. law, 1994, assoc. dean academic affairs, 1995—98; Samuel J. Rubin vis. prof. law Columbia Law Sch., NYC, 1998, prof., 1999—2006, Isidor and Seville Sulzbacher prof. law, 2004—06, vice dean rsch., 2004; vis. prof. law NYU Sch. Law, 2005—06, Catherine A. Rein prof. law, 2006—. Contbr. articles to law jours. Office: NYU Sch Law 40 Washington Sq S, 314G New York NY 10012 Office Phone: 212-998-6184. Office Fax: 212-995-4881. E-mail: cynthia.estlund@nyu.edu.

ESTRADA, ERIK (HENRY ENRIQUE ESTRADA), actor; b. NYC, Mar. 16, 1949; m. Joyce Miller Nov. 25, 1979 (div. 1980), 1 child; m. Peggy Rowe Estrada Aug. 19, 1985 (div. 1990), children Anthony Erik, Brandon Michael-Paul; m. Nanette Mirkovich Sept. 20, 1997, 1 child Francesca Natalia. Student, Mus. Dramatic Acad., NYC. Actor: (feature films) The Cross and the Switchblade, 1967, Cactus Flower, 1969, John and Mary, 1969, Chrome and Hot Leather, 1971, The Ballad of Billy Blue, 1972, Parades, 1972, The New Centurions, 1972, Airport '75, 1974, Midway, 1976, Trackdown, 1976, The Line, 1980, Where is Parcifal?, 1983, The Repenter, 1985 Light Blast, 1985, Hour of the Assassin, 1987, Guns, 1990, The Lost Idol, 1990, A Show of Force, 1990, Twisted Justice, 1990, Night of the Wilding, 1990, Do or Die, 1991, Look at Me, America, 1991, The Last Riders, 1991, Spirits, 1991, The Sounds of Silence, 1992, The Naked Truth, 1992, The Divine Enforcer, 1992, Angel Eyes, 1993, Tuesday Never Comes, 1993, Loaded Weapon, 1993, Juana la Cubana, 1994, The Final Goal, 1995, The Misery Brothers, 1995, Visions, 1996, Shattered Dreams, 1998, The Modern Adventures of Tom Sawyer, 1998, Oliver Twisted, 2000, UP, Michigan!, 2001, Van Wilder, 2002, Border Blues, 2004 (TV series) CHiPs, 1977-83 (nominated Best TV Actor-Drama, Golden Globe, 1977), (soap opera) Dos Mujeres, Un Camino (Two Women, One Road), 1993, The Bold and the Beautiful, 2001, (TV movie) The Quest: The Longest Drive, 1976, Fire!, 1977, Honey Boy, 1982, Grandpa, Will You Run With Me?, 1983, The Dirty Dozen: The Fatal Mission, 1988, She Knows Too Much, 1989, Extralarge: Cannonball, 1991, Earth Angel, 1991, Panic in the Skies!, 1996, CHiPs '99, 1998 (also prodr.)(nomination Outstanding Actor in a Made-for-TV Movie or Mini-Series, ALMA award, 1998), Taylor Made, 2005, others, (off-broadway) True West, (TV reality show) Surreal Life, 2004; guest appearances (TV shows) Circus of the Stars, 1979 (Ringmaster), Tonight Show: Dinah!, Mike Douglas, Merv Griffin, Hawaii Five-0, 1973, Emergency!, 1974, Kojak, 1975, Six Million Dollar Man, 1975, Police Woman, 1975, Medical Center, 1975, Baretta, 1976, Barneby Jones, 1976, Delvecchio, 1977, The Love Boat, 1978, Hunter, 1987, LA Law, 1993, The Nanny, 1995, Burke's Law, 1995, Baywatch, 1997, Martin, 1997, The Wayans Bros., 1997, Sabrina, The Teenage Witch, 1997, Diagnosis Murder, 1997, (voice) King of the Hill, 1998, Tracey Takes On, 1998, (voice) Family Guy, 1999, Walker, Texas Ranger, 1999, Weakest Link, 2001, American Family, 2002, Lizzie McGuire, 2002, For Your Love, 2002, Spy TV, 2002, The Rerun Show, 2002, Scrubs, 2003, Hollywood Squares, 2004, Drake & Josh, 2004, Maya & Miguel, 2004, Discovery Health Celebrity Body Challenge, 2004, (voice) Sealab 2021, 2004, 2005, According to Jim, 2006, others; actor, assoc. prodr. Alien Seed, 1989, Caged Fury, 1989; host The Image Workshop, 1991, American Adventure, 1994; guest appearances in a number of TV commercials; reserve officer Muncie Ind. Police Dept. (TV reality show) Armed & Famous, 2007. Internat. Face of D.A.R.E.; spokesperson Calif. Highway Patrol Car Seat Inspection and Installation Prog., Smoke Signals Communications, California Pines Homesites and Acreage Parcels, 2003, Hot Springs Village Arkansas' homes, 2004, 21st Century Ins. and makes appearances nationwide promoting car seat safety for children, 2006; speaks out for the Heart Assn. and The United Way. Recipient Sour Apple, 1980, Star on the Hollywood Walk of Fame, 2007. Avocations: running, tennis, golf, workout at gym. Office: 103 Sinclair Ave Yorkville OH 43971 Business E-Mail: erikestrada@1st.net.

ESTRADA, ISABEL VICTORIA, obstetrician, gynecologist; b. San Juan, P.R., Nov. 17, 1918; d. Serafin and Elisa (Molinari) Estrada; children: Kenneth Wayne, Lisa Darlene. Attended, U. P.R., 1938; MD, Marquette U. Diplomate Am. Bd. Ob-Gyn. Intern St. Joseph's Hosp., Milw.; gen. practice medicine Santurce, PR, 1943—50; resident St. Luke's Hosp., New Bedford, Mass., 1950—51; fellow in ob-gyn pathology Free Hosp. Med. Women, Brookline, Mass., 1952; resident Mt. Sinai Hosp., Milw., 1952—54; USPHS fellow Rio Piedras, PR, 1956—62; practice medicine specializing in ob-gyn Whittier, Calif. Pres. pro tem Hispanic Rep. Women L.A. County. Recipient L.A. Med. Woman of Yr. Am. Med. Women's Assn., 1966, cert. of appreciation of vol. svc. Am. Coll. Obstreticians and Gynecologists and Indian Health Svc., 1981, Pope John XXIII award Italian Cath. Fedn., Shiprock, N.Mex., 1982. Fellow Am. Coll. Obstreticians and Gynecologists, ACS, L.A. Ob-Gyn Soc.; mem. Gynecol. Urological Soc., L.A. County Med. Women (pres. 1968), Calif. Hispanic Drs. Assn., P.R. Med. Soc., P.R. Ob-Gyn Soc., Assn. Marquette Univ. Women (dir. 1954-56), Flying Drs. of Mercy, Am. Med. Women's Assn., N.Y. Acad. Scis., AAAS, Women's Overseas Svc. League, Marquette U. Med. Alumni Assn. (bd. dirs. L.A. County), La Mirada Bus. and Profl. Women (Merit award 1983), Marquette U. Alumni Assn. (Merit award 1983), Baker-Channing Soc., Alpha Sigma Nu, Gamma Pi Epsilon. Office: 1201 W Lambert Rd La Habra CA 90631-6614

ESTRAIKH, GENNADY, humanities educator; b. Zaporozhe, Ukraine, Apr. 7, 1952; s. Yakov and Hesia Estraikh; m. Elena Dashevskaya; children: Anna Nuttall, Yakov. MSc with honors in Radio Engring., Zaporozhe Tech. U., 1974; PhD, U. Oxford, England, 1996. Mng. editor Sovetish Heymland, Moscow, 1988—91; rsch. fellow Inst. Yiddish Studies, Oxford, England, 1995—2001, lectr. yiddish lingusitics London, 1998—2002; Rauch assoc. prof. yiddish studies NY U., NYC, 2003—. Author: (collection of yiddish stories) The Red Ravine, Mocow Purim Plays, Yiddish-Russian Dictionary, (textbook) Intensive Yiddish, (monograph) Soviet Yiddish: Language Planning and Linguistic Development, In Harness: Yiddish Writers Romance with Communism; editor: Yiddish in the Contemporary World, David Bergelson: From Modernism to Socialist Realism, The Shtetl: Image and Reality, Yiddish and the Left; mng. editor: Di Pen, 1994—97; editor, 1997—98; co-editor: East European Jewish Affairs, 1999—, Tsukunft, 2007—; weekly columnist: Forverts, 2001—; editor: Vayter, 2006—. Home: 1311 Brightwater Ave Apt 11A Brooklyn NY 11235 Office: NY Univ Hebrew and Judaic 51 Washington Sq S Rm 101 New York NY 10012-1075 Home Phone: 347-401-3702; Office Phone: 212-998-9059. Office Fax: 212-995-4178. Business E-Mail: ge293@nyu.edu.

ESTREICHER, SAMUEL, lawyer, educator; b. Bergen, Democratic Republic Germany, Sept. 29, 1948; came to U.S., 1951; s. David and Rose (Abramowicz) E.; m. Aleta Glaseroff, Aug. 10, 1969; children: Michael, Hannah. BA, Columbia U., 1970, JD, 1975; MS in Labor Rels., Cornell U., 1974. Bar: N.Y. 1976, D.C. 1978, U.S. Dist. Ct. (so. and ea. dists.) N.Y., U.S. Ct. Appeals (2d and 11th cirs.), U.S. Supreme Ct. Law clk. to assoc. judge Harold Leventhal, U.S. Ct. Appeals (D.C. cir.), 1975-76; assoc. Cohn, Glickstein, Lurie, Ostrin & Lubell, NYC, 1976-77; law clk. to assoc. justice Lewis F. Powell Jr. U.S. Supreme Ct., Washington, 1977-78; prof. law NYU, 1978—; of counsel Cahill, Gordon & Reindel, NYC, 1984-98; labor and employment counsel O'Melveny & Myers LLP, NYC, 1998—2002; spl. counsel Morgan Lewis & Bockius LLP, NYC, 2002—03; of counsel Jones Day, NYC, 2003—. Vis. prof. law Columbia U., 1984-85; dir. NYU-Inst. Jud. Adminstrn., 1991—, Ctr. for Labor and Employment Law at NYU Sch. Law, 1996—; prof. law NYU Sch. Law, 1978—, Charles L. Denison chair, 2002-04, Dwight D. Opperman chair, 2004—. Author: Redefining the Supreme Court, 1986, Labor Law and Business Change, 1988, The Law Governing the Employment Relationship,1990, 2d edit., 1992, Labor Law: Text and Materials, 6th edit., 2007, Procs. of 49th NYU Annual Conference on Labor, 1997, Employee Representation in the Emerging Workplace: Alternatives/Supplements to Collective Bargaining, 1999, Sexual Harassment in the Workplace, 1999, Foundations of Labor and Employment Law, 2000, Employment Discrimination and Employment Law, 2000, 2d edit., 2004, Global Competition and The American Employment Landscape, 2000, Employment Law, 2004, Employment Law Discrimination, 2004, Global Issues in Labor Law, 2007,others; editor-in-chief Columbia U. Law Rev., 1974-75; contbr. articles to profl. jours. Pulitzer Fund scholar, 1966-70; Herbert H. Lehman fellow, 1970-72. Mem. ABA (labor and employment law sect. 1978—, sec. sect. on labor and employment law 2004—), N.Y. State Bar Assn. (labor and employment law sect. 1980—), Assn. Bar City N.Y. (chmn. labor and employment law com. 1984-87), Am. Law Inst. (chief reporter Restatement of Employment Law 2000—). Office: NYU Sch Law 40 Washington Sq S New York NY 10012 Office Phone: 212-998-6226. E-mail: samuel.estreicher@nyu.edu, sestreicher@jonesday.com.

ESTREN, MARK JAMES, communications executive, television producer, writer; b. NYC, July 12, 1948; s. Solomon and Elaine Estren; m. S. Amber Gordon, July 4, 1986; children: Meredith, Nicholas. BA in Classics and English cum laude, Wesleyan U., 1968; MS in Journalism, Columbia U., 1970; MA in English and Psychology, U. Buffalo, 1973, PhD in English and Psychology, 1978. Producer, reporter, anchor Stas. WBEN & WBEN-TV, Buffalo, 1971-75; exec. producer Stas. WCBS-Radio and TV, NYC, 1975-76, Sta. WCAU-TV, Phila., 1976-79; sr. producer ABC News, NYC and Washington, 1979-80; editor Phila. Inquirer, 1980-81, Miami (Fla.) Herald, 1980-81; exec. producer The Nightly Bus. Report, Miami, Fla., 1981-84; sr. v.p., gen. mgr. Fin. News Network, NYC and L.A., 1984-87; editor-in-chief High Tech. Bus. mag., Boston and NYC, 1987-89; exec. v.p. Infotechnology, Inc., NYC and Washington, 1987-90, UPI, Washington, 1988-90; founder, pres. UPI TV, Fairfax, Va., 1989-90; pres., chief exec. officer TransCentury Comm., Inc., Easton, Conn. and McLean, Va., 1984—. Adj. prof. Columbia U., 1987-89; webmaster www.infodad.com, 1999—; music critic Washington Post, 2005—. Author: A History of Underground Comics, 1974, rev. edit., 1987, 89, 93; co-author: In a Word, 1992; contbg. editor Miami Herald, Bottom Line/Personal, Bottom Line/Tomorrow, Boardroom Reports, Bottom Line/Business, Bottom Line/Health, Bottom Line/Retirement, Washington Office Mag., Moneysworth, Parent Weekly, Va. Parent News. Trustee Boston Cath. TV Ctr., 1987-89; vice chmn. Arthritis Found., Washington, 1992-94, chmn. commn. com., 1990-92. Pulitzer Found. fellow, 1970. Avocations: classical music, herpetology. Office: 1163 Old Gate Ct Mc Lean VA 22102-2532 Personal E-mail: infodad@gmail.com.

ESTRICH, SUSAN RACHEL, law educator; b. Lynn, Mass., Dec. 16, 1952; d. Irving Abraham and Helen Roslyn (Freedberg) E.; m. Martin Kaplan 1986; children: d. Isabel, s. James. BA with highest honors, Wellesley Coll., 1974; JD magna cum laude, Harvard U., 1977. Bar: Calif., DC, US Supreme Ct. Assoc. Covington & Burling, Wash., DC, 1977; law clk. to Hon. J. Skelly Wright U.S. Ct. Appeals, Washington, 1977-78; law clk. to Hon. John P. Stevens U.S. Supreme Ct., Washington, 1978-79; dep. nat. issues dir., spl. asst. Kennedy for Pres. campaign, Washington, 1979-80; sr. policy advisor Mondale-Ferraro campaign, 1984; of counsel Tuttle & Taylor, LA, 1986-87; campaign mgr. Dukakis for Pres. campaign, Boston, 1987-88; asst. prof. law Harvard Law Sch., Cambridge, Mass., 1981-86, prof. law, 1986-90; Robert Kingsley prof. law and polit. sci. USC Gould Sch. of Law, LA, 1990—. Host talk show Sta. KABC, L.A. Author: Real Rape, 1987, Making the Case for Yourself 1997, Getting Away with Murder 1998, Sex and Power 2000.; co-author: Dangerous Offenders, 1985; columnist LA Style mag.; weekly columnist USA Today; contbg. editor LA Times Opinion Sect.; pres. Harvard Law Rev.; contbr. articles to numerous jours. Mem. Dem. Nat. Com., Wash. 1984-88, ACLU (nat. bd.), pres. Boston chpt., 1985-86; mem. nat. governing bd. Common Cause 1983-89; Nat. Campaign mgr. Dukakis for President Campaign 1987-88; bd. trustees Ctr. for Early Edn. 1995 -2003, B'nai B'rith Youth orgn. Wash. DC, 1996 -2000.; vice chair Endowment com.; chair Legal Com.; bd. dir. Calif. Abortion Rights Action Leage 1992 — 1994, Victims Rights Law Ctr., Boston, Mass. Ethics Commn. City LA 1999 — 2001, Planned Parent LA 1991 — 1993 adv. bd. 1993 — 1995; Nat. Adv. bd. Inst. for Global Ethics 1999 —; chair USC Law Sch. 1995 -1996, adminstrn. and Fin. Com 1995 -1997. Durant Scholar, Disting. Alumni award 1989, fellow Nelson Rockefeller, Dartmouth Coll. 1999. Mem. DC Bar, Calif. Bar, US Supreme Ct. Bar, Phi Beta Kappa. Jewish. Pres. Harvard Law Review. Office: USC Gould Sch of Law Rm 306A 699 Exposition Blvd Los Angeles CA 90017 Office Phone: 213-740-7578. Office Fax: 213-740-5502. E-mail: sestrich@law.usc.edu.

ESTRIDGE, LARRY D., lawyer; b. Rock Hill, SC, Jan. 31, 1944; BA in Hist., cum laude, Furman U., 1966; JD, Harvard U., 1969. Bar: Ga. 1969, SC 1973, admitted to practice: US Dist. Ct., Dist. SC, Dist. Ga., US Ct. of Appeals (4th Cir.). Assoc. Alston, Miller & Gaines (now Alston & Bird), Atlanta, 1971—72, Wyche, Burgess & Parham, P.A., Greenville, SC, 1972—75, mem., 1975—98; mng. mem., econ develop. dept. and real estate dept. Womble Carlyle Sandridge & Rice, PLLC, Greenville, SC, mem. mgmt. com. Pro bono legal svcs. Habitat for Humanity; bd. dir. Evergreen Resources, Inc., 1988—; lectr. in field. Co-author (chpt.) Oral Advocacy, Apellete Practice Manuel. Former pres. Furman U. Alumni Assn.; SC chair Harvard Law Sch. Fund, 1973—76; legal divsn. chair Greenville United Way, 1974; pres. Citizens for Greenville (local polit. initiatives, 1975—77, Greenville Ctrl. Area Partnership (downtown revitalization), 1982—83; bd. trustee Carolina Piedmont Found. (U. SC-Spartanburg), 1989—96, Lees-McRae Coll., 1990—93; mem. Reedy River Basin Task Force (City of Greenville), 1990—91; bd. gov. Thornblade Club, 1990—2001, pres., 1990—2001; bd. trustee Furman U., 1996—2001, 2001—; bd. dir. Greater Greenville C.ofC., 1997—2000, general counsel, 1997; bd. dir., pres. Children's Mus. of the Upstate, 1998—2001. Capt. US Army, 1969—71, Ft. Jackson, SC, battalion def. counsel for courts martial US Army, S. Vietnam. Decorated Bronze Star, Vietnam Svc. medal. Mem.: ABA, Greenville County Bar Assn., Ga. Bar Assn., SC Bar Assn. (mem., pro bono program and real estate sect., House of Delegates), Southern Club (pres.), Blue Key Honor Soc. Office: Womble Carlyle Sandridge & Rice PLLC 700 Poinett Plz 104 S Main St PO Box 10208 Greenville SC 29603 Office Phone: 864-255-5401. Office Fax: 864-255-5481. Business E-Mail: lestridge@wcsr.com.

ESTRIN, DEBORAH LYNN, computer engineer, educator; d. Gerald and Thelma Estrin; 1 child, Joshua E. Skrzypek. BS in Electrical Engring., U. Calif., Berkeley, 1980; MS in Electrical Engring. and Computer Sci., MIT, Boston, 1982, PhD in Electrical Engring. and Computer Sci., 1985. Asst. prof. computer sci. dept. U. So. Calif., 1986—92, assoc. prof. computer sci. dept., 1992—98, prof. computer sci. dept., project leader, 1998—2000, prof. computer sci. dept., 2000—; founding dir. Ctr. for Embedded Networked Sensing, an NSF Sci. and Tech. Ctr., 2002—; prof. computer sci., electrical engring. UCLA, 2006—. Cons. scientist CISCO Sys., Inc., 1993—95; bd. dirs. Precept Software, Inc., 1995—98; mem. tech. adv. bd. Fast Forward Networks, Inc., 1998—2000, VitalSigns, Inc., 1998—2000; cons. prof. Intel Corp., 2001—03; mem. tech. adv. bd. Sensicast Inc., 2003—05. Contbr. chapters to books; assoc. editor ACM Transactions on Sensor Networks. Mem. ATS Tech. Adv. Bd., 2001—04, SEAS Dean Search Com., 2001—03, Computational Sci. and Engring. Adv. Bd., 2001—, CNS Dir. Search Com., 2001—03, Rsch. Adv. Coun. for UCLA, 2004—. Recipient Presdl. Young Investigator award, NSF, 1987—92, Award, Okawa Found., 1997; fellow, ACM, 2000, AAAS, 2001, IEEE, 2004. Fellow: ACM, IEEE, AAAS, Am. Acad. Arts & Scis.; mem.: The Nat. Academies Computer Sci. and Telecommunications (bd. mem.). Office: Ctr for Embedded Network Sensing 3563 Boelter Hall Los Angeles CA 90095 also: Computer Sci Dept 3531H Boelter Hall Box 951596 Los Angeles CA 90095-1596

ESTRIN, DEBORAH PERRY, human resources executive; b. Waynesboro, Va., Dec. 28, 1948; d. James William and Annie Lee (Miller) Perry; m. Abbott Simon Estrin, Feb. 6, 1982. BS in Humanities, U. Tenn., Knoxville, 1982; MBA, Fairleigh Dickinson U., Teaneck, NJ, 1988. Dir. human resources Ciba Geigy Pharms., Summit, NJ, 1983-89; v.p. human resources Geneva Pharms. divsn. Ciba Geigy Pharms., Broomfield, Colo., 1989-91, USPCI subs. Union Pacific, Houston, 1994-96, NY Power Authority, White Plains, 1994-96; sr. v.p. human resources Phila. Gas Works, 1996-98; v.p. human resources Maersk-Sealand, Inc., Madison, N.J., 1999-2000; dir. human resources Thames Water, London and N.J., 2001—04, Christies Inc., London and NYC, 2004—. Adj. prof. Audrey Cohen Coll., 1994—96; dir. SC Ctr. Dispute Resolution, 2001—04. Mem. Beaufort County Transp. Authority, 2001—04, bd. dirs. Personal E-mail: fitzaddison@aol.com.

ESTRIN, HERBERT ALVIN, financial consultant, film company executive; b. Jamaica, NY, May 4, 1925; s. Joseph and Minnie (Haskell) E.; m. Phyllis Glassman, Jan. 28, 1951; children— Myrna Hope, Richard Lawrence. BS in Acctg, N.Y. U., 1949. With Columbia Pictures Industries, Inc., NYC, 1953-73, v.p., 1971-73; v.p., treas., chief fin. officer Prudential Bldg. Maintenance Corp., NYC, 1973-79; v.p., treas. Bolt Corp., South Laguna, Calif., 1979; sr. v.p. fin. and adminstrn. Warner Home Video Inc. subs. Warner Communications, 1981-83; dir. ops. adminstrn. United Satellite Communications Inc., 1983-85; v.p. fin. and adminstrn. Rainbow Home Video div. Rainbow Program Enterprises Co., 1986-88; fin. cons., 1986—. Served with U.S. Army, 1943-46.

ESTRIN, JUDITH, computer company executive; m. Bill Carrico. BS in Maths. and Computer Sci., UCLA; MSEE, Stanford U. Co-founder Bridge Comms.; pres., CEO Network Computing Devices; chief tech. officer, sr. v.p. Cisco Sys., Inc., San Jose; chmn. Packet Design, Palo Alto, 2002—. Bd. dirs. Fed. Express, Sun Microsystems, Walt Disney Co. Named to, Women in Tech. Internat. Hall Fame. Office: Packet Design Inc 3400 Hillview Ave Bldg 3 Palo Alto CA 94304 Fax: 408-526-4100.

ESTRIN, KARI (KAREN RUTH ESTRIN), music producer, agent, consultant; b. Plainfield, NJ, Nov. 5, 1954; d. Herman Albert and Pearl (Simon) E. BA with honors, Ramapo Coll. of NJ, 1976. Founder, exec. dir. Black Sheep Concerts and Publs., Inc., Cambridge, Mass., 1980-86; artist mgr., agt. Tony Rice/Rounder Records, 1981-85; tour mgr. Suzanne Vega/A&M Records, 1985, Peter Murphy Tour/Island Records, 1987, Kevin Brown Ryko Disc/Chrysalis, 1991; founder, cons. Palomine Mgmt., 1984—92; asst. producer Newport Folk Festival Festival Prodns., Inc., NYC, 1987; artist and tour mgr. 3 Mustaphas 3/Ryko Disc, 1988-91; artist asst. Suzy Bogguss/Capitol Records, 1989; mgr. Kanda Bongo Man, 1991, 93; tour mgr. Irma Thomas/Rounder Records, 1993, Papa Wemba/Real World Records, 1995; booking & spl. events dir. Caffe Milano, 1998; owner. prin. Kari Estrin, Mgr., Cons., Nashville, 1995—. Nat. promoter Rounder Records, Cambridge, Mass., 1979; asst. to dir. Berkshire Mt. Bluegrass Festival, Hillsdale, NY, 1980—81; assoc. prodr. Gt. N.E. Prodns., Townsend, Mass., 1986, Pickin' for Merle series N,C, Pub. TV, Rsch. Triangle Park, 1992; chairperson events ECO, Nashville, 1990; bd. dirs., vol. Sta. WPLN, 1991—92, pres. vol bd. dirs., 1993—94; cons. Marie Watson Meml. Festival, Wilkesboro, NC, 1992—93, asst. festival dir., 1993; co-founder Chris Austin Songwriting Contest, Nashville/Wilkesboro, 1992—93; artist mgr. Wayland Patton, 1993—94, David Llewellyn, 2002—, Rob Lutes, 2003—05; talent coord. Pro Events Summer Lights, 1997; nat. advt. mgr. Sing Out ! mag., 1995—96; co-prodr. Americana Music Assn. Conv., Nashville, 2000; club booking agt. Radio Cafe, Nashville, 2000—01, 3rd and Lindsley, Nashville, 2002; prodr. Woody Guthrie Month, Nashville, 2003, Authentic Voice Compilation CD, 2004; local co-chair Folk Alliance Conf. Nat. Conf., Nashville, 2003; co-prodr. Nashville Sings Woody, 2003. Editor: How to be Your Own Booking Agent and Save Thousands of Dollars, 1997; editor Black Sheep Rev., 1982-85; co-prodr.: (album) Great Acoustics, 1985. Bd. dirs. Hey, Rube Folk Music Orgn., 1983-86, Folk Arts Network, Cambridge, 1983-85, Folk Arts Ctr. of New Eng., Cambridge, 1982-84; sec., newsletter editor Eastwood Neighbors Bd., 1995-97. Mem.: S.E. Regional Folk Alliance (pres. 2002—). Avocations: catering and cooking, travel, performing arts. Home and Office: 1415 Sumner Ave Nashville TN 37206-2533 Home Phone: 615-262-0883; Office Phone: 615-262-0883. Personal E-mail: kari@kariestrin.com.

ESTRIN, MELVYN J., computer products company executive; b. 1942; Co-chmn., co-CEO Nat. Intergroup, Inc., Carrollton, Tex., 1997—; co-chmn, co-CEO McKesson Health Corp., Carrollton, Tex., 1996; also bd. dirs.; chmn. U. Rsch. Corp., Bethesda, Md.; co-CEO Phar-Mor. Inc., Youngstown, Ohio. Mng. ptnr. Centaur Ptnrs., L.P.; chmn., pres., CEO Am. Health Svcs.; v.p., dir. Spectro Industries; founder First Women's Bank of Md.; pres. FWB Bancorporation, Rockville, Md.; chmn. FWB Bancorporation.; chmn. Estrin Internat., Inc.; with Estrin Realty and Devel. Corp.; bd. dirs. Washington Gas Light Co. Trustee U. Pa.; active Endowment Bd. of the Kennedy Ctr., The Econ. Club of Washington, The Washington Opera; nat. vice chmn. State of Israel Bonds; apptd. by Pres. Bush commr.Nat. Capital Planning Commn.; apptd. Nat. Coun. for the Performing Arts, John F. Kennedy Ctr. Recipient Eleanor Roosevelt Humanities award for Community Svc., 1986. Office: Phar-Mor Inc 20 Federal Plz W Ste 3 Youngstown OH 44503

ESTRIN, RICHARD WILLIAM, real estate and business broker, retired editor; b. NYC, Apr. 16, 1932; s. Max and Ruth (Lillienthal) E.; m. Alison Kiendl Stewart, Mar. 13, 1971. BA, CCNY, 1953; grad., Realtor Inst., 2000. Reporter Pk. Row News Svc., NYC, 1953-55; with Newsday, Inc., Long Island, NY, 1955-85, sucessl. Sunday news editor, Part II editor, sr. editor news, until 1983, exec. news editor N.Y.C. Newsday, 1983-85; weekend editor Herald-Tribune, Sarasota, Fla., 1985-86, news editor, 1986-90, asst. mng. editor, 1990-97; v.p. Longview Realty, Longboat Key, Fla., 1999-2001, pres., 2001—. Recipient First Place Lifestyle Journalism awards J.C. Penney-U. M., 1974, 75 Mem. Kiwanis, Phi Beta Kappa. Office Phone: 941-383-6112. Business E-Mail: longviewrealty@att.net.

ESTRUP, PEDER JAN, physics and chemistry professor; came to U.S., 1956; m. Faiza Fawaz, Sept. 15, 1960. M.Sc., Poly. Inst. Denmark, Copenhagen, 1954; PhD (Fulbright fellow, Sheffield Sci. fellow), Yale, 1959; Postdoctoral fellow, European Center Nuclear Research, Geneva, 1959-61. Mem. tech. staff Bell Telephone Labs., Murray Hill, NJ, 1961-64; rsch. scientist Bartol Rsch. Found., Swarthmore, Pa., 1964-67; prof. physics, chemistry Brown U., Providence, 1967—, chmn. dept. chemistry, 1989-96, Newport Rogers prof. chemistry and physics, 1992—, dean Grad. Sch. and Rsch., 1996—. Assoc. editor Jour. Vacuum Sci. and Tech., 1988-94; sr. editor Jour. Phys. Chemistry, 1990-95; mem. editorial bd. Progress in Surface Sci., 1982-97, Jour. Phys. and Chem. Reference Data, 1993—. Served to lt. Danish Army, 1954-56. Fellow Am. Phys. Soc., Am. Vacuum Soc. (exec. com. surface sci. divsn.); mem. Am. Chem. Soc. Research in physics and chemistry of surfaces. Office: Brown U Dept Physics Box 1843 Providence RI 02912

ESTY, DANIEL CUSHING, lawyer, educator; b. Boston, June 6, 1959; s. John Cushing and Katharine (Cole) E.; m. Elizabeth Henderson, Oct. 20, 1984. AB, Harvard U., 1981; BA, Oxford U., 1983; JD, Yale U., 1986. Bar: Calif. 1986, US Ct. Internat. Trade 1987, DC 1988, US Dist Ct. DC 1988, US Ct. Appeals (Fed. Cir.) 1988. With Arnold & Porter, Washington, 1986-89; spl. asst. to adminstr. EPA, Washington, 1989-90, dep. chief of staff, 1990-91, dep. asst. adminstr. for policy, 1991-93; sr. fellow Inst. for Internat. Econs., Washington, 1993-94; assoc. prof. Environ. Law and Policy Yale U., New Haven, 1994—2004, prof., 2001—, dir. Ctr. for Environ. Law and Policy, 1994—, assoc. dean Sch. Forestry and Environ. Studies, 1998—2002, dir. World Fellows Prog., 2001—. Vis. prof. INSEAD, Fontainebleau, France, 2000—01. Author: Greening the GATT: Trade, Environment, and the Future, 1994, Asian Dragons and Green Trade, 1996, Sustaining the Asia Pacific Miracle: Environmental Protection and Economic Integration, 1997, Thinking Ecologically: The Next Generation of Environmental Policy, 1997, Regulatory Competition and Economic Integration, 2001, Environmental Performance Measurement: The Global Report 2001-2002, 2002, Greening the Americas: NAFTA's Lessons for Hemispheric Trade, 2002, Global Environmental Governance: Options and Opportunities, 2002, Green to Gold: How Smart Companies Use Environmental Strategy to Innovate, Build Value, and Creak Competitive Advantage, 2006. Office: Yale Ctr for Environ Law and Policy 205 Prospect St New Haven CT 06511-2106 also: PO Box 208215 New Haven CT 06520 Office Phone: 203-432-1602. Office Fax: 203-432-8095.

ESTY, DAVID CAMERON, marketing and communications executive; b. Mt. Kisco, NY, May 26, 1932; s. John Cushing and Virginia (Place) E.; m. Elizabeth Gunn; children: Philip, Virginia, David Jr., Lisa, Jennifer, Gordon. BA, Amherst Coll., 1954. Sr. v.p. J. Walter Thompson, NYC, 1960-68; pres., CEO T.D.I., NYC, 1968-75; CEO Douglas Leigh, Inc., NYC, 1975-76; founder Catalyst Corp., 1976-78; CEO BIS Communications Corp., NYC, 1979-82; owner, CEO Esty Assocs., Inc., Darien, Conn.; COO The Alden Group, NYC, 1990-92; owner, CEO MarkeTeam, Inc., 1992—; prin. Adventure Assets, Inc., Cambridge, Mass., 1997—. Bd. dirs. World Sports Humanitarian Hall of Fame, Boise, Idaho, Inst. Internat. Sport., Kingston, RI, Summit Ventures NE, LLC, Warren, Vt., Pacific Beacon, Seattle. Author: Somebody Close to You is on Drugs, 1971. Mem. Nat. Ski Patrol, Sugarbush VT Ski Patrol; pres. Friends of Tuckerman Ravine, North Conway, NH; mem. Christ Episcopal Ch., Montpelier, Vt. Capt. USAFR, 1950—67. Recipient Disting. Svc. award, Nat. Ski Patrol, 1995, Amherst Coll., 1999. Mem. Ad Coun. (dir., mem. exec. com. emeritus), Young Pres. Orgn. (49er) Home: PO Box 756 Waitsfield VT 05673 Office Phone: 802-279-8818. Personal E-mail: davecesty@gmavt.net.

ESTY, JOHN CUSHING, JR., writer, educator, not-for-profit counsel; b. White Plains, NY, Aug. 9, 1928; s. John Cushing and Virginia (Place) E.; m. Katharine Woolsey Cole, Dec. 21, 1955; children: Daniel Cushing, Paul Cameron, Benjamin Cole, Joshua Dwight. BA, Amherst Coll., 1950, LHD (hon.), 1970; MA, Yale U., 1951; postgrad., U. Calif., Berkeley, 1959-60. Asst. dean, asst. dir. admissions Amherst Coll., 1953-58, asso. dean, 1958-63, lectr. math., 1958-63; headmaster Taft Sch., Watertown, Conn., 1963-72; research asso. in edn. Harvard U., 1972-73; scholar-in-residence U. Mass. Sch. Edn., 1972-73; sr. staff asso. Edn. Devel. Center, Newton, Mass., 1973-74; staff asso. Rockefeller Bros. Fund, NYC, 1973-78; pres. Nat. Assn. Ind. Schs., 1978-91; adj. lectr. U. Mass., 1978—2002. Pres. bd. Coun. for Am. Pvt. Edn., 1987-89. Author: Choosing Private School, 1974. Trustee Amherst Coll., 1970-76; trustee, bd. chmn. Greeley Found., Mass., 1991-2000; dir., founder Recruiting New Tchrs., Inc., 1988—2003. 1st lt. USAF, 1951-53. Mem. Phi Beta Kappa, Sigma Xi. Clubs: Univ. (N.Y.C.), Century Assn. (N.Y.C.).

ETCHEGOYEN LYNCH, MARTIN, lawyer, consultant; s. Julio Angel Etchegoyen and Maria Teresa Lynch; m. Geraldine Natalie Hamilton, Jan. 10, 1998; children: Theresa, Christina. M in Criminal Law, U. Cath. El Salvador, Buenos Aires, 1995, PhD in Criminal Scis., 1999. Cert.: Buenos Aires City Bar (lawyer) 1993, Calif. (arbitrator) 2004. Dist. atty., San Isidro, Argentina, 1998—2001; CEO, cons. criminal investigations, arbitrator Justicia Privada, Bellflower, Calif., 2001—. Mem. Presdl. Task Force, Washington, 2005—. Mem.: ABA (assoc.). Liberal. Personal E-mail: martinetchegoyen@hotmail.com.

ETCHEMENDY, JOHN, academic administrator, educator; b. Reno; m. Nancy Etchemendy; 1 child, Max. Bachelors Degree, Masters Degree, U. Nev.; PhD, Stanford U., 1982. Lectr. Princeton U., 1981—82, asst. prof., 1982—83; faculty philosophy dept. Stanford U., 1983—, sr. assoc. dean Sch. Humanities and Scis., 1993—97, provost, 2000—, mem. Symbolic Systems Program, sr. rschr. Ctr. for Study of Language and Info. Faculty mem. Symbolic Sys. Program Stanford U., sr. rschr. Ctr. for the Study of Lang. and Info. Author: Hyperproof, 1994, Language, Proof and Logic, 1999; editor; Jour. Symbolic Logic; mem. editl. bd. Synthese, Philosophia Mathematica. Mem.: Assn. for Symbolic Logic (mem. governing coun.), Am. Philos. Assn. Office: Office of the Provost Bldg 10 Stanford Univ Stanford CA 94305-2061 Office Phone: 650-724-4074. Office Fax: 650-725-1347. E-mail: etch@csli.stanford.edu.*

ETCHES-JOHNSON, AMANDA, library and information scientist; married. BA in English with honors, U. Western Ohio; MA in English, U. Toronto, M in Libr. and Info. Sci. Reference and user experience libr. McMaster U., Hamilton, ON, Canada. Named one of the Movers & Shakers, Libr. Jour., 2007. Avocation: knitting. Office: Mills Memorial Library L 212 1280 Main West St Hamilton L8S 4L8 Canada

ETCHISON, BRUCE, retired museum director, conservator; b. Wash., DC, Dec. 19, 1918; s. Page McKendree and Lucille Etchison; m. Martha Jane Esterline, Apr. 10, 1942; children: Craig, Jeanette, Page. BA, Am. U., 1941; BFA, Yale U., 1948, MFA, 1949. Dir. Wash. County Mus. Fine Arts, Hagerstown, Md., 1950—64, Abbey Aldrich Rockefeller Mus., Williamsburg, Va., 1964—66; art conservator Bear Pond Studio, Mercersburg, Pa., 1967—86; ret. Instr. arts appreciation Hagerstown Jr. Coll., 1953—57; TV art tchr. Washington County Bd. Edn., Hagerstown, 1954—59. Chief petty officer US Coast Guard, 1941—46. Mem.: Internat. Inst. for the Conservation of Mus. Art Objects, State of Md. Arts Commn. Avocations: painting, sculpting, graphic arts. Home: 3830 Farmstead Dr Fayetteville PA 17222

ETEFIA, FLORENCE VICTORIA, retired school psychologist; b. Alton, Ill., Feb. 13, 1946; d. Esau and Pearl (Taylor) Anthony. BA, Mich. State U., 1968; MAT, Oakland U., Rochester, Mich., 1972; EdS, Wayne State U., 1977, MA, 1987, postgrad. Cert. tchr. mentally impaired, Mich.; spl. edn. supr., Mich.; cert. tchr. mentally impaired, learning disabled, K-8 gen. edn., psychology, Mich. Spl. edn. tchr. Sch. Dist. of Pontiac, Mich. Mem. NEA, Mich. Edn. Assn., Pontiac Edn. Assn., Delta Sigma Theta. Home: 3035 Debra Ct Auburn Hills MI 48326-2044

ETESSAMI, HIRBOD (HIRI ETESSAMI), endodontist, educator; b. Tehran, Jan. 31, 1965; came to U.S., 1978; s. Abdollah and Mahin Etessami; m. Jacqueline Etessami, Aug. 21, 1993; children: Noah, Jonah. Student, Georgetown U., 1982-85; DDS, U. So. Calif., 1989, Cert. in Advanced and Surg. Endodontics, 1991. Pvt. practice, LA, 1991—. Clin. instr Sch. Dentistry, U. So. Calif., LA, 1991—, UCLA, 1993—; founder Mymoneysworth.com; chmn. bd. dirs. Qualte.com. Bd. dirs. Beth Jacob Congregation, Beverly Hills, Calif., 1995—; bd. dirs. L.A. Mozart Orch., 1995-96; mem. ethics com. U. So. Calif. Dental Sch., 1985-91. Mem. ADA, Calif. Dental Assn., Am. Assn. Endodontics, Alpha Omega (pres. chpt. 1989). Jewish. Avocations: playing santour (hammer/dulcimer), archeology, theology, politics. Office: 9201 W Sunset Blvd Ste 908 Los Angeles CA 90069-3710

ETGEN, ANN, performing arts educator, choreographer; b. Dallas; d. Eddy R. Etgen and Myrtle (Applegate) Etgen; life ptnr. Bill Atkinson, Aug. 16, 1961. Dance, active Arts Magnet Sch., 1980, 81, 82, 83. Dancer Met. Opera Ballet , NYC, 1958—60. Artistic dir. Etgen-Atkinson Sch. of Ballet, Dallas, 1962—, Dallas Met. Ballet, 1964—; dance panel Tex. Fine Arts Com., 1978—79. Dancer (Broadway musicals) Brigadoon, Carousel; guest dancer Omnibus History of Dance for Agnes De Mille, 1957, host S.W. Regional Ballet Festival, 1973, Creator (ballets) Dallas Met. Ballet. Recipient choreography plan award, Nat. Assn. Regional Ballet, 1983; grantee NEA choreography grantee, 1976, Tex. Fine Arts Commn., 1973, 1976—77, Mobile Oil, 1979, 500 Inc., 1978—79. Mem.: S.W. Regional Ballet Assn. (membership chmn. 1986—87), Nat. Assn. Regional Ballet. Presbyterian. Office: Etgen Atkinson Ballet School 6815 Hillcrest Ave Dallas TX 75205-1308

ETH, JORDAN DAVID, lawyer; BA, Swarthmore Coll., 1980; JD, Stanford U., 1985. Bar: Calif. 1985. Law clerk to Chief Judge Robert F. Peckham U.S. Dist. Ct. Calif. (No. dist.), 1985—86; economist U.S. Dept. Energy, U.S. Ho. of Reps., 1980—82; assoc. Morrison & Foerster LLP, San Francisco, 1986—92, ptnr., 1992—. Spkr. in field. Contbr. articles to profl. jours. Office: Morrison & Foerster LLP 425 Market St San Francisco CA 94105-2482 Office Phone: 415-268-7126. Office Fax: 415-268-7522. E-mail: jeth@mofo.com.

ETHAN, CAROL BAEHR, psychotherapist, psychoanalyst; b. NYC, May 30, 1920; d. Irving and Sadie (Goldman) Baehr; m. Sy Ethan, Mar. 18, 1955; children: Willa Capraro, Barbara Capraro Ethan. Trained, Greenwich Inst. Psychoanalytic Studies, 1965-70; BA in Psychology with honors, NYU, 1978; MA in Psychology, New Sch. Social Rsch., 1981. Tchr. Queens Coll., 1956-57; consumer psychology rschr., cons., 1950-70; staff psychotherapist Fifth Ave. Ctr. Counseling & Psychotherapy, 1965-70; psychotherapist-psychoanalyst pvt. practice, NYC, 1967—. Writer: Irvington (N.J.) Herald, 1946, Walt Framer Prodns., 1949—50, columnist: Rhinebeck Gazette-Advertiser, 1981—86. Vol. social rehab. program Queens County Mental Health Soc., 1965—66; Dem. committeewoman Queens County, 1960. Recipient Founders Day award, NYU, 1978; fellow Internat. Coun. Sex Edn. and Parenthood, Am. U. Fellow: Am. Orthopsychiat. Assn.; mem.: APA, Am. Counselors Assn., Nat. Assn. Advancement of Psychoanalysis (cert. psychoanalyst), Am. Psychotherapy Assn. (cert. diplomate), N.Am. Assn. Masters in Psychology (cert.), Internat. Acad. Behavioral Medicine, Counseling and Psychotherapy (clin. mem.), Family and Divorce Mediation Coun. N.Y., Am. Mental Health Counselors Assn., N.Y. State Assn. Practising Psychotherapists (cert.). Address: 235 W 76th St New York NY 10023-8217 Office Phone: 212-595-4657. E-mail: cethan@nyc.rr.com.

ETHELL, JUDY A., consulting company executive; b. St. Louis; BS, Ea. Ill. U. CPA. Various positions including tax ptnr. in charge PricewaterhouseCoopers, LLP; exec. v.p., chief acctg. officer BearingPoint, McLean, Va., 2005—, CFO, 2006—. Office: BearingPoint 1676 Internat Dr Mc Lean VA 22102 Office Phone: 703-747-3000.*

ETHERIDGE, BOB (BOBBY RAY ETHERIDGE), congressman; b. Lillington, NC, Aug. 7, 1941; m. Faye Cameron Etheridge; 3 children. BSBA, Campbell U., 1965; grad. student, NC State U.; degree (hon.), Fayetteville State U., Pfieffer Coll., Shaw U., Campbell U. Owner hardware store; tobacco farmer; commr. Harnett County, 1972—76; mem. NC Gen. Assembly, 1978—88; state supt. schs. NC, 1989—96; mem. US Congress from 2nd NC dist., 1997—, mem. agr. com., mem. homeland security com., mem. budget com., chmn. gen. farm commodities and risk mgmt. subcommittee, chmn. Dem. caucus edn. task force, co-chair Dem. rural working grp. Bd. trustees NC Symphony; mem. adv. bd. Math./Sci. Edn. Network; bd. dirs. NC Coun. Econ. Edn. With US Army, 1965—67. Recipient Legislator of Yr. award, Congl. Fire Svcs. Inst., 2004, Rising Champion of Sci. award, Sci. Coalition, Silver Beaver award, Boy Scouts Am. Democrat. Presbyterian. Office: US House Reps 1533 Longworth House Office Bldg Washington DC 20515-3302 Office Phone: 202-225-4531. Office Fax: 202-225-5662.*

ETHERIDGE, DIANA CAROL, internet business executive; b. Nebr., Mar. 18, 1940; d. Elvon Lynn and Enola Nadene Howe; m. Brian Newman Etheridge, May 30, 1940; children: Melissa Ann, Juliana Lynn Student, U. Geneva, Switzerland, 1960-61; BA, U. Denver., 1962; MA, Simmons Coll., 1981. Cert. tchr., Colo., Fla.; real estate lic., Fla., 1995. Tchr. French, science, English Denver Pub. Schs., 1962-63, 64-68; tchr. 7th grade, French tchr. preK-7th grade St. Anne's Episcopal Sch., Denver, 1974—76; tchr. 6th grade, French tchr. k-8th grade, co-founder Collegiate Sch., Denver, 1976—80; real estate broker Merrill Lynch, Prudential, Long & Foster, Treder Realty, Potomac, Md. and Titusville, Fla., 1982—, Vincent Keenan Realtors, Cape Canaveral, Fla. Mem. No. Va. Coun. Comml. Realtors, Fairfax, Va., 1993—95, Govtl. Internat. and Info. Svcs. Coms., Fairfax, Internat. Real Estate Inst., Alexandria, Minn., 1996—2007, World Trade Ctr. Inst., Balt., 1995; cert. internat. property specialist Nat. Assn. Realtors, 1994—2000, judge Who is Today's Realtor, 1995; pres., founder EDEA, Inc. The Idea Clearinghouse, Merritt Island, Fla., 1997—, Cybernastics, Inc., Merritt Island, 1999—, Flexystema/Flexhome, Merritt Island, 2000—. Editor: My Hawaii (by Jane Thomas). House bill proofreader Colo. State Legislature, Denver, 1970; campaign staff mem. U.S. Congressman Dave Weldon, Melbourne, Fla., 1996, 1998, 2000; hon. chmn. Fla. bus. adv. coun. Nat. Rep. Congl. Com., 2003. Recipient Lifetime award Prudential Preferred Properties, 1990 Mem.: Meridian Internat. Ctr., Md. Assn. Realtors, Fla. Bus. Adv. Coun., Montgomery Assn. Realtors (Lifetime award), Nat. Assn. Realtors, Nat. Assn. Home Builders, Nat. Assn. Women in Constrn., Meridian Internat., Hospitality and Info. Svcs. Internat. Club, Optimists Club (past pres. Capital City), Brevard County Newcomer's Club, Welcome to Washington Internat. Club, Long and Foster Pres.'s Club (life), Phi Beta Kappa, Pi Beta Phi. Achievements include patents for building construction; tensioned building system. Avocations: skiing, swimming, scuba diving, hiking, aerobics. Office Phone: 321-453-7665. E-mail: diana_etheridge@yahoo.com, info@edea.com.

ETHERIDGE, JACK PAUL, arbitrator, mediator, retired judge; b. Atlanta, Mar. 16, 1927; s. Anton Lee and Jessie Shephard (Brown) E.; m. Ursula Schlatter, Feb. 2, 1952; children: Jack Paul, Margaret Ann, Mary

Elizabeth. Grad., Darlington Sch., Rome, Ga., 1945; BS, Davidson Coll., 1949; JD, Emory U., 1955. Bar: Ga. 1955. Since practiced in, Atlanta; mem. firm Huie, Etheridge & Harland, 1959-66; mem. Ga. Gen. Assembly from Fulton County, 1963-66; judge Fulton Superior Ct., 1966-76, sr. judge, 1977—, litigation mgr., 1991; faculty Nat. Jud. Coll., Coll. Criminal Justice, Law Sch., U. S.C., 1977-80; assoc. dean Emory U. Law Sch., Atlanta, 1981-88; chief jud. officer Jud. Arbitration and Mediation Svcs., Inc., Atlanta, 1992-98, spl. master nat. class actions, 1999—. Mem. Ga. Crime Commn., 1971-73; bd. dirs. Atlanta Legal Aid Soc., 1960-70. Trustee Davidson Coll., 1966-75; trustee Arts Festival of Atlanta, 1971-74, Atlanta U., 1977-87; chmn. bd. dirs. Atlanta Neighborhood Justice, Inc., Wolfcreek Wilderness Schs., Inc.; Fellow Harvard Law Sch., 1980. Served with USNR, 1945-46; Served with with AUS, 1949-52. Named Young Man of Year in Professions Atlanta Jr. C. of C., 1962 Fellow ABA, Am. Bar Found., Ga. Bar Assn., Internat. Acad. Trial Judges, Ctr. for Pub. Resources; mem. Atlanta Bar Assn. (pres. 1962-63), Nat. Conf. State Trial Judges (chmn. 1978-79), Atlanta Hist. Soc. (trustee 1969-75), Nat. Acad. Pub. Adminstrn., Beta Theta Pi, Omicron Delta Kappa, Phi Alpha Theta. Presbyterian. Home: 4715 Harris Trl NW Atlanta GA 30327-4409 Office Phone: 770-240-1426. Personal E-mail: jetheridge@mindspring.com.

ETHERIDGE, JAMES RALPH, history professor; b. Nuremberg, Germany, Apr. 10, 1956; s. James Ralph Sr. and Flora Folendore Etheridge. BA in History, U. Ga., Athens, 1979; MEd, Columbus Coll., Ga., 1980; EdS in Social Sci., Ga. So. Coll., Statesboro, 1987. Tchr. social sci. and lang. arts Hinesville Mid. Sch., Ga., 1981—91; tchr. dept. head social sci. Liberty County HS, Hinesville, Ga., 1991—; adj. instr. history Ctrl. Tex. Coll., Ft. Stewart, Ga., 1998—, Columbia Coll. Mo., Ft. Stewart, Ga., 2005—. Coun. faculty mem. Liberty Co. State Govt., Hinesville, Ga., 2002—. Deputy voter registrar Liberty Ct. Govt., Hinesville, Ga., 1995—; rep. Selective Svc., Hinesville, 1995—. Recipient Golden Apple award, Knoxville News/Sentinel, 1985. Mem.: Assn. for Supervision and Curriculum Devel., Profl. Assn. Ga. Educators, Nat. Assn. Social Studies Studies. Republican. Methodist. Avocations: stamp collecting/philately, target shooting, camping. Home: PO Box 246 Walthourville GA 31333 Office: Liberty County HS 3216 E Ogle Thorpe Hwy Hinesville GA 31313 Office Phone: 912-876-4316. Personal E-mail: jetheridge@yahoo.com.

ETHERIDGE, MELISSA LOU, singer, lyricist; b. Leavenworth, Kans., May 29, 1961; d. John and Elizabeth Etheridge; m. Tammy Lynn Michaels, Sept. 22, 2003; children: Bailey, Beckett, Miller Steven, Johnnie Rose. Student, Berklee Coll. of Music, Boston, 1970. Wrote songs for the film, Weeds; albums include Melissa Etheridge, 1988, Brave and Crazy, 1989, Never Enough, 1992, Yes I Am, 1993, Your Little Secret, 1995, Breakdown, 1999, Skin, 2001, Lucky, 2004, Greatest Hits: The Road Less Traveled, 2005; songs include I Need to Wake Up (for film An Inconvenient Truth), 2006 (Oscar award for best song 2007). Named Entertainer of Year Can. Acad. Recording Arts and Scis., 1990; Grammy award, Best Female Rock Vocal for "Aint It Heavy," 1993, Female Rock Vocal Performance for "Come to My Window," 1994; named one of 100 Most Influential People, Time Mag., 2005. Address: MEIN PO Box 884563 San Francisco CA 94188-4563*

ETHERINGTON, CAROL A., medical association administrator; b. Tenn. married. MSN in Psychology and Mental Health. RN Tenn. With Internat. Med. Corps, Bosnia-Herzegovina, 1994; pres., bd. dirs. U.S. sect. Doctors Without Borders, 1999—; asst. prof. nursing Vanderbilt U. Med. Ctr., Nashville. Founder Victims Intervention Program, Nashville Police Dept., 1975—95; mem. internat. com. ARC, 1980, vol. for disaster relief. Recipient Internat. Achievement award, Florence Nightingale Internat. Found., Geneva, 2003, Florence Nightingale medal, Internat. Red Cross, 1997—98. Office: Vanderbilt Univ 336 First Hall 461 21st Ave S Nashville TN 37240

ETHERTON, REGINA PICONE, lawyer; BA magna cum laude, So. Meth. U., Dallas; JD, Loyola U., Chgo. Bar: Ill., US Dist. Ct. (no. and ea. divsns.) Ill. Assoc. Jay A. Baier, Ltd., Chgo., 1984—86; atty. Peter D. Kasdin, Ltd., Chgo., 1986—2005; dir. Regina P. Etherton & Associates, LLC, Chgo., 2005—. Mem. Com. Women's Issues, Chgo., 1983—84; mem. of tort litig. com. Chgo. Bar Assn., Chicago, Ill., 1984—86; apptd. Am. Del. Women Lawyers through Citizen Amb. program People to People Internat., 1987; ju; judge moot ct. competition Loyola Law Sch., guest lectr., 1988. Contbg. writer: Loyola U. Woman's Law Reporter. Named one of 500 Leading Plaintiffs' Lawyers in Am., Lawdragon Mag. and Lawdragon.com, 2006; Eastwood scholar, acad. scholar, So. Meth. U., Dad's Club scholar. Mem.: ABA, ATLA (judge mock trial final competition), Nat. Italian Am. Found., Women Trial Lawyers Caucus, Ill. Trial Lawyers Assn. (mem. legis. com. 1984), Ill. State Bar Assn. (mem. personal injury and med. malpractice referral panel 2005—, mentor 2005—), Chgo. Bar Assocation (mem. tord litigation com. 1984—86, mem. personal injury and med. malpractice referral panel 2005—), Justinian Soc. Lawyers, Million Dollar Advocates Forum (life). Home: 971 Newcastle Ln Lake Forest IL 60045 Office: Regina P Etherton & Associates LLC 303 W Madison Street Suite 1800 Chicago IL 60606 Home Phone: 847-615-1952; Office Phone: 312-529-5500. Office Fax: 312-529-5501; Home Fax: 847-615-1962. Business E-Mail: retherton@rpethertonllc.com.

ETHRIDGE, JOSEPH ALFRED, manufacturing executive; BBA in Acctg., U. N. Tex., 1963, MBA in Fin., 1967. Comptr. currency Asst. Nat. Bank Examiner, Dallas, 1968-69; staff acct. to mng. ptnr. Coopers & Lybrand, 1970-90; sr. v.p. fin., treas. Sammons Enterprises Inc., Dallas, 1990—. Office: Sammons Enterprises Inc 5949 Sherry Ln Ste 1900 Dallas TX 75225

ETHRIDGE, LARRY CLAYTON, lawyer; b. Houston, Feb. 27, 1946; s. Robert Pike and Gladys Jeannette (Grant) E.; m. Edith Kirkbride Gilbert, May 21, 1977; children: Elizabeth Kirkbride, Grant Harbin. BA, Duke U., 1968; JD cum laude, U. Louisville, 1975. Bar: Ky. 1975, U.S. Dist. Ct. (we. dist.) Ky. 1980, U.S. Ct. Appeals (6th cir.) 1981, U.S. Dist. Ct. (ea. dist.) Ky. 2003. Intern Adv. Commn. on Intergovtl. Rels., Washington, 1975-76; asst. dir. model procurement code project ABA, Washington, 1976-80; ptnr. Mosley, Clare & Townes, Louisville, 1980-97, Ackerson Mosley & Yann, 1998—2003, Ackerson & Yann, Louisville, 2003—. Cons. ABA model procurement code project, Washington, 1980-82; panel mem. N.Y. State Procurement Rev., 1984—. Co-author: Supplement to Annotations on the Model Procurement Code, 1991, Annotations, 3d edit., 1996. Elder Highland Presbyn. Ch., Louisville, clk. of session, 1989-90, 96-2001; vol. ARC; gen. counsel Mobile Riverine Force Assn., 1995—; mem. bd. overseers U. Louisville, 2003—. Lt. USNR, 1969, Vietnam, Cambodia, and Japan. Recipient Disting. Svc. award Nat. Inst. Govtl. Purchasing, 1987. Fellow Am. Bar Found. (life); mem. ABA (chmn. coord. com. on a model procurement code 1985-96, co-chmn. model procurement code revision project steering com. 1997—, coun. mem., state and local govt. law sect. 1988—, sect. publs. dir. 1990-93, comms. dir. 1993-95, sec. 1995-96, vice-chmn. 1996-97, chmn. elect 1997-98, chmn. 1998-99, Donald M. Davidson award), AAA Ky. (bd. dirs. 1990-96, sec., gen. counsel 1996—), Ky. Bar Assn., Louisville Bar Assn., Jefferson Fordham Soc., U. Louisville Law Alumni Assn. (pres. 1990-92), U. Louisville Alumni Assn. (exec. com., pres.-elect, pres. 2003-2004, Alumni Svc. award), Duke Club Ky. (pres. 1992-94), Waggener H.S. Alumni Assn. (pres. 1996-97, Hall of Fame), Univ. of Louisville Club (bd. dirs. 1997—, treas. 2000—, v.p. 2002-04, pres. 2004—). Republican. Presbyterian. Avocations: gardening, travel, golf, bicycling, reading. Home: 2402 Longest Ave Louisville KY 40204-2125 Office: Ackerson & Yann 401 W Main St Ste 1200 Louisville KY 40202-2806 Office Phone: 502-583-7400. E-mail: lethridge@ackersonlegal.com.

ETHRIDGE, MARK FOSTER, III, writer, publishing executive, consultant; b. Winston-Salem, NC, May 28, 1949; s. Mark F. Jr. and Margaret Burns (Furbee) E.; m. Kay Stover, Aug. 12, 1972; children: Emily Vigland, Mark Furbee. Grad., Phillips Exeter Acad., 1967; AB cum laude, Princeton U., 1971. Reporter AP, Boston, 1971-72, The Charlotte (N.C.) Observer, 1972-88, dep. metro editor, 1978-79, mng. editor, 1979-88; pub. The Bus. Jour. of Charlotte, 1989-98; pres. Carolina Parenting, Inc., 1991—, Cotter Group, Harrisburg, NC, 1998-2001. Bd. dirs. Bioethics Resource Group Ltd. Mem. exec. com. Princeton Alumni Coun., 2001—03; trustee Charlotte Country Day Sch., 2002—. Nieman fellow Harvard U., 1986. Presbyterian. Home: 5516 Gorham Dr Charlotte NC 28226-6414 Office: Carolina Parenting Inc 2125 South End Dr Charlotte NC 28203 Office Phone: 704-344-1980. Business E-Mail: methridge@charlotteparent.com.

ETO, HAJIME, retired information scientist, educator; b. Tokyo, June 16, 1935; s. Yoshio and Kikuko (Tamari) E. BA, U. Tokyo, 1959, MA, 1962; MS, U. Calif., Berkely, 1967; PhD, Tokyo Inst. Tech., 1979. Rschr. Hitachi Ltd., Tokyo, 1962-76; prof. U. Tsukuba, Japan, 1976-99, Chiba Keizai U., Japan, 1999—2006; prof. emeritus U. Tsukuba, 1999—. Author, editor: R & D Management Systems in Japanese Industry, 1984, R & D Strategies in Japan, 1993; mem. editl. bd. Scientometrics Jour., 1979—, Human Sys. Mgmt., 1980-84, Internat. Jour. of the Sci. of Scis., 1994—, Internat. Jour. Svc. Tech. & Mgmt., 1998—, Internat. Jour. Foresight and Innovation Policy, 2003—, Information and Management, 2004—, Internat. Jour. Bus. and Sys. Rsch., 2006-; contbr. sci. articles to profl. jours. Recipient Fulbright scholarship U.S.-Japan Edn. Com., 1966. Mem. AAAS, Internat. Soc. Scientometrics and Informetrics (mem. coun. 1993—, mem. editl. bd. 1995—), Japan Assn. for Philosophy Sci. (mem. coun. 1970-92), Japan Soc. for Sci. Policy (bd. dirs. 1994-96, coun. 1997—), Assn. of France on Cybernetics, Econs. and Tech. (mem. editl. bd. 1985—), NY Acad. Sci., Am. Chem. Soc. Buddhist. Home: Nakano 3-43-17-305 Nakano-ku Tokyo 164-0001 Japan Home Phone: 3-3384-2791. Personal E-mail: etohajime@peach.ocn.ne.jp.

ETRA, LIONEL, lawyer; b. NYC, July 22, 1942; s. Max Jacob and Reba (Zuckerbraun) E. AB, Columbia Coll., 1964; JD, Harvard U., 1967; LLM in Taxation, NYU, 1978. Atty. Karelsen Karelsen Lawrence & Nathan, NYC, 1969-77, Roberts & Holland, NYC, 1977—. Avocations: photography, flute, running. Home Phone: 212-595-4607; Office Phone: 212-903-8721. Business E-Mail: letra@rhtax.com.

ETRIS, SAMUEL FRANKLIN, trade association research consultant; b. Port Huron, Mich., Dec. 3, 1922; s. Samuel and Mildred Susan (Davis) E.; m. Mary Jane Lytle, June 29, 1957; children— Andrew Brooke, Edward Lytle. AB, Temple U., 1947; MS, Rutgers U., 1951. With Foote Mineral Rsch. Labs., Phila., 1947-49, spl. asst. to mng. dir. for nat. affairs, editor, 1967-80; editor ASTM, Phila., 1967-76. Sr. cons. Klein of Saks, Inc., Washington; mgrs. Silver Inst.; mem. numerical data adv. bd. NRC. Contbr. articles and editorials to profl. publs. Tchr. measurement course Phila. Pkwy. Sch.; Scoutmaster Boy Scouts Am., 1954-57, troop com. chmn., 1957-61; convenor 1st Internat. Conf. on Gold and Silver in Medicine, Bethesda, Md., 1987. Served to 1st lt. USAAF, 1944-46, CBI; Served to 1st lt. USAF, 1951-52. Recipient Scoutmaster's Key award, 1957 Mem. Am. Ceramic Soc. (emeritus). Home and Office: 115 Runnymede Ave Wayne PA 19087-4014 Home Phone: 610-688-7649. Personal E-mail: sfetris@erols.com.

ETTE, ENE IKPONG, clinical pharmacologist; b. Nwaniba, Akwa Ibom, Nigeria, Jan. 28, 1954; s. Ikpong Ikpong and Nkaepe Ebrewong Ette; m. Esther Awala Awala, Feb. 11, 1961; 6 children. BSc in Pharmacology, U. Ibadan, Nigeria, 1977; MS in Pharmacology, Obafemi Awolowo U., Nigeria, 1980; BS in Pharmacy, Northeastern U., 1983; PhD in Clin. Pharmacology, U. Glasgow, 1992. Cert. pharmacist Nigeria. Grad. asst. Obafemi Awolowo U., Ile-Ife, Oyo, Nigeria, 1977—78, juinor rsch. fellow, 1978—80. Asst. to assoc. prof. U. Lagos, Nigeria, 1983—92; reviewer to sr. reviewer, rschr. FDA, Rockville, Md., 1992—96, expert scientist (pharmacometrics), 1997; staff scientist Vertex Pharms., Inc., Cambridge, Mass., 1997, head of clin. pharmacology, 1999—2000, dir. to sr. dir. clin. pharmacology, 2002—. Author: Guidance on Population Pharmacokinetics for Industry (CDER(FDA) Excellence in Rev. Sci. Award, 1996). Ministering to the sick and the needy MetroWest Worship Ctr., Ashland, Mass., 1997—2004. Recipient Team Excellence award, Ctr. for Drug Evaluation, 1998; Glaxo Ltd. Travel fellow, Glaxo Nigeria Ltd., 1988, Overseas Rsch. Students awardee, U.K. Overseas Rsch. Students Scholarship, 1989—91. Fellow: Am. Coll. Clin. Pharmacy (Russell Miller award 1999, Therapeutic Frontiers award 2006); mem.: Am. Assn. Pharm. Scis. Achievements include patents in field; development of the process of discovering knowledge from population pharmacokinetics data sets; the methodology for estabilishing population model stability and performance; the importance of informative graphics in population pharmacokinetic modeling. Avocations: reading, Christian ministry. Office: Vertex Pharmaceuticals Inc 130 Waverly St Cambridge MA 02139 E-mail: ette@vrtx.com.

ETTEN, STEWART LOUIS, lawyer; b. Neenah, Wis., Oct. 18, 1955; s. Marvin Paul and June Janet Etten; m. Tracy Lor-Ell Clark, June 30, 1984; children: Clark, Treva. BBA, U. Wis., 1977, JD, 1980. Atty. Ruder Ware, L.L.S.C., Wausau, Wis., 1980—. Home: 210 Rainbow Ln Wausau WI 54401 Home Phone: 715-359-2439. Business E-Mail: setten@ruderware.com.

ETTENGER, ROBERT BRUCE, physician, pediatric nephrologist; b. Phila., Sept. 17, 1942; s. Ervin Earl and Sylvia (Goodstein) W.; m. Angela Joan Castellano; children: Allison, Jessica. BA, U. Pa., 1964; MD, 1968. Asst. prof. pediat. Children's Hosp. LA, 1976-80, Sch. Medicine UCLA, 1980-84, asst. prof., 1984-89, prof., 1989—, Casey Lee Ball Disting. prof. pediat., 2005—, head divsn. pediat. nephrology dept. pediat., 1990—2004, vice chmn. clin. affairs, 1990—2004; med. dir. pediat. renal transplant program UCLA Med. Ctr., 1983—, dir. historcompatibility lab., 1987—2001, vice chief med. staff, 2002—04, chief med. staff, 2004—06. Mem., chair sub-bd. nephrology Am. Bd. Pediat., Chapel Hill, N.C., 1986-91; cons. Immunosuppressive Adv. Com. Food and Drug Adminstrn., Bethesda, Md., 1994—, Biologics and Immune Response Modifiers, Food and Drug Adminstrn., Bethesda, 1994—; mem. biol. sci. adv. com. U.S. Renal Data Sys., Ann Arbor, Mich., 1993-2000, Data Safety Monitoring Bd., Dept. Transplantation, Nat. Inst. Immunology Transplant Adv. Group, Am. Soc. Nephrology. Assoc. editor Am. Jour. Transplantation; mem. editl. bd. Transplantation, Pediat. Nephrology, Pediat. Transplantation; contbr. articles to profl. jours. Coach, mem. exec. bd. AYSO Soccer, Santa Monica, Calif., 1994-2001, Bobby Sox Softball, 1995-97, YWCA Basketball, 1995-2000; mem. med. adv. bd. Nat. Kidney Found., LA, 1993—. Maj. US Army, 1971—73. Recipient Ortho Biotech Lectureship Urologic Soc. for Transplantation, 1990, Continuing Svc. award Nat. Kidney Found., L.A., 1991, 92, 94. Fellow Internat. Soc. Nephrology, Internat. Pediat. Nephrology Assn., Am. Acad. Pediat., Am. Soc. Transplant Physicians (pres. 1984-85), Am. Pediat. Soc., Am. Soc. of Nephrology, Am. Soc. Pediat. Nephrology, Soc. Pediat. Rsch., Transplantation Soc. (Best Drs. in Am. 1992-06, Am.'s Top Drs. 1998-06), United Network Organ Sharing (regional councillor at region 5, bd. dirs. 2000-02). Jewish. Avocations: distance running, youth sports. Office: UCLA Med Ctr A2-383 Dept Pediatrics 10833 Le Conte Ave Los Angeles CA 90095-3075

ETTENSOHN, FRANK ROBERT, geologist, educator; b. Cin., Feb. 6, 1947; s. Robert Frank and Aileen Frances (Keman) E.; children: Clare Marie, Marc Francis. BS, U. Cin., 1969, MS, 1970; PhD, U. Ill., 1975. Lic. profl. geologist Ky. Tchr. math. Greenhills-Forest Park City Sch. Dist., Ohio, 1971; from asst. prof. to prof. geology U. Ky., Lexington, 1975—87, prof., 1987—, chmn. dept. geol. sci., 1997—2005. Mem. geology adv. com. Coun. for Internat. Exch. Scholars, 1993-96, 2007-, chmn., 1994-96; bd. dirs., v.p. Ky. Mus. Natural History, 1991-; tech. adv. com. Ea. Oil Shale Symposium, 1992-94; dir. U. Ky. Geology Field Camp, 1977-81, 84-85, 92-93, 95, 97-98, 2001; adv. com. Ky. Water Resources Rsch. Inst., 1998-2001; faculty math. and sci. edn. program U. Ky. Coll. Edn., 1999-; adv. bd. Appalachian Math. Sci. Partnership, 2003-07, U. Ky. AMSTEMM Project, 2005-; vis. prof. China U. Geoscis., Beijing, 2005-06, Escuela Superior Politecnica del Litoral, Guayaquil, Ecuador, 2005-06.cons., expert witness in field. Editor (tech.): Jour. Paleontology, 1994—97; contbr. articles to profl. jours. Capt. C.E., AUS, 1970. Fenneman fellow, 1969-70; U. Ill. fellow, 1971-74; grantee US Dept. Energy, 1976-81, NSF, 1987-90, US Bur. Mines, 1990-91, Ky. Coun. on Higher Edn., 1998-2002, NSF/EPSCOR, 2002-05, Geol. Soc. Am.; Fulbright lectr. US Govt., Soviet Union, 1989, Nepal, 2006. Fellow Geol. Soc. Am. (jt. chmn., field trip chmn. ann. mtg. southeastern sect. 2001-02); mem. AAAS, Am. Geol. Inst., Am. Inst. Profl. Geologists, Paleontol. Soc., Paleontol. Assn., Paleontol. Rsch. Inst., Internat. Paleontol. Assn., Ky. Acad. Sci., Am. Geophys. Union, Nat. Assn. Geosci. Tchr., Nat. Earth Sci. Tchr. Assn., Fulbright Assn., Phi Beta Kappa, Sigma Xi, Phi Kappa Phi, Sigma Gamma Epsilon. Roman Catholic. Avocations: phlately, coin collecting/numismatics, scouting, soccer. Home: 1631 Duntreath Dr Lexington KY 40504-2352 Office: U Ky Earth and Environmental Sciences Lexington KY 40506-0053 Office Phone: 859-257-1401. Business E-Mail: fettens@uky.edu, f.ettensohn@uky.edu.

ETTER, DELORES M., civilian military employee; b. 1947; Student, Okla. State U., U. Tex., Arlington; BS in Math., Wright State U., Dayton, Ohio, 1970, MS in Math., 1972; PhD in Elec. Engring., U. New Mex., 1979. Mem. faculty dept. elec. and computer engring. U. N.Mex., 1979-89, assoc. chair dept., 1987-89, assoc. v.p. acad. affairs, 1989; prof. elec. and computer engring. U. Colo., Boulder, 1990-98; dep. under sec. for sci. and tech. US Dept. Def., Washington, 1998—2001, asst. sec. for rsch. devel., & acquisition, Dept. Navy, 2005—; disting. chair sci. & tech. office naval rsch. US Naval Acad., 2001—05. Mem. Naval Rsch. Adv. Com., 1991-97, chmn. 1995-97; vis. prof. info. sys. lab.Stanford U., 1983-84; bd. dirs. Def. Sci. Bd., 1995-98, Nat. Sci. Bd., 2002-2005; prin. U.S. rep. NATO rsch. and tech. bd., tech. cooperation program; mem. bd. vis. Nat. Def. U.; panel mem. numerous studies. Recipient Pub. Svc. award Dept. Navy, 1998, Fed. Women in Sci. and Engring. Lifetime Achievement award. Fellow IEEE (pres., acoustics, speech and signal processing soc. 1988-89, editor in chief Transactions on Signal Processing jour. 1993-95, Disting. lectr. 1996-97, Harriet Rigas award 1998), AAAS, Am. Soc. Engring. Edn.; mem. NAE. Office: US Dept Def 1000 Navy Pentagon Rm 4E739 Washington DC 20350

ETTER, ZANA CLAIRE, library director; b. Camden, NJ, June 6, 1950; d. Clair V. and Zana Irene Cathers; m. Markus Ernst Etter, May 28, 1988; 1 child, Erich. Student, U. Lausanne, Switzerland, 1970; BA in French, Rutgers U., 1972, MEd, 1979, MLS, 1986. Cert. French, German and ESL tchr., N.J. Cataloguer Princeton (N.J.) U., 1973-79; info. specialist Edn. Improvement Ctr., Princeton, 1979-82; supr., libr. assoc. Rutgers U. Tech. Svcs., New Brunswick, N.J., 1982-87; dir. media libr. univ. medicine and dentistry Robert Wood Johnson Med. Sch., Piscataway, N.J., 1987—. Tchr. ESL West Windsor-Plainsboro (N.J.) Schs., 1978, YMCA, Princeton, 1981; tchr. French East Windsor Adult Sch., Hightstown, N.J., 1981; pvt. practice tutoring English, Plainsboro, N.J., 1981-84. Contbr. articles to profl. jours. Mem. Med. Libr. Assn., Acad. Health Info. Profls. of Med. Libr. Assn. (sr. mem.), Health Scis. Libr. Assn. N.J. Avocations: travel, reading, writing. Office: Robert Wood Johnson Med Sch 675 Hoes Ln Piscataway NJ 08854-5627

ETTERER, SEPP, industrial relations specialist, consultant, application developer; b. Munich, Aug. 31, 1944; arrived in U.S., 1955, naturalized, 1962; s. Josef and Ingeborg Anna (Fierlings) Etterer; m. Judith Annette Shell, Feb. 25, 1978; children: Jonathan Sepp, Julia Anne, Joseph William;children from previous marriage: Victoria Marie, Christina Diane, Kurt. BSEE, Mich. State U., East Lansing, 1966. Lic. comml. pilot. Assoc. ele. engr. Boeing Co., 1966-67; pulp mill supr., plant safety engr. Procter & Gamble Co., 1970-76; sr. safety rep. Bechtel Power Co., 1976-77; plant safety supt. Hooker Chems. & Plastics Corp., 1977-78; indsl. relations dir. Interstate Lead Co. Inc., Leeds, Ala., 1978-85; regional personnel and safety dir. Structl. Steel Fabrication div. Trinity Industries, Inc., Birmingham, Ala., 1985-89; safety mgr. freight car div. Trinity Industries, Bessemer, Ala., 1989-94; pres. SMOsys, Birmingham, 1994—. Indsl. rels. software developer, cons.; v.p. Le Marche aux Fleurs, Inc., 1986—97. Author: (book) Take It-It's Yours, 1975, Sky Pig, 1976, Equity 5, 1980, (software) SMOsys M7 Indsl. Rels. Mgmt., 1991—2006. Capt. USAF, 1967—70. Mem.: Soc. Human Resource Mgmt., Am. Indsl. Hygiene Assn., Am. Soc. Safety Engrs. (past pres.). Home: 1315 Wickford Rd Birmingham AL 35216-2903 Office: PO Box 661333 Birmingham AL 35266-1333 Office Phone: 205-907-5632. Business E-Mail: sepp@smosys.com.

ETTERS, RONALD MILTON, retired lawyer, former government official; b. San Antonio, Nov. 6, 1948; s. Milton William and Ilse Charlotte (Ostler) E.; m. Anna Colleen Wesson, Feb. 12, 1977; children: William Lawrence, Elizabeth Charlotte, Margaret Lawreen. BA magna cum laude, Am. U., 1971, JD, 1976. Bar: Va. 1976, U.S. Ct. Appeals (D.C. cir.) 1977, U.S. Dist. Ct. (ea. dist.) Va. 1978, U.S. Ct. Appeals (4th and 9th cirs.) 1978, U.S. Supreme Ct. 1979, D.C. 1980, U.S. Dist. Ct. D.C. 1980, U.S. Ct. Appeals (1st and 2d cirs.) 1980, U.S. Ct. Appeals (7th cir.) 1981, U.S. Ct. Appeals (3rd, 11th and fed. cirs.) 1982, U.S. Ct. Appeals (5th cir.) 1983. Intern to gen. counsel Adminstrv. Office of U.S. Cts., Washington, 1970-71; fed. mgmt. intern IRS, Washington, 1971-72, labor rels. officer, 1972-75; ptnr. Nusbaum & Etters, Burke, Va., 1976-80; gen. counsel Nat. Mediation Bd., Washington, 1980—2002; ret., 2002. With Sigma Alpha, 1971; justice Phi Alpha Delta, 1975; professorial lectr. Am. U., Washington, 1978-83; adj. prof. law Georgetown U., Washington, 1985-88; vis. prof. George Mason U. Sch. Law, Arlington, Va., 1999, dir. Ctr. Advanced Study of Law and Dispute Resolution Processes, Arlington, 2000-2002. Sr. bd. editors The Railway Labor Act, 1991-2002. Mem. ABA (co-chmn. com. on railway and airline labor law 1987-93, 1999-2002), Christian Legal Soc., Nat. Lawyers Assn., Fed. Bar Assn. Home: PO Box 2374 Centreville VA 20122-2374 E-mail: etters5@etters.net.

ETTINGER, DAVID SEYMOUR, oncologist; b. Bklyn., Mar. 16, 1942; s. Harry and Frieda (Rose) E.; m. Phyllis Evellen Katz, June 4, 1964; children: Laura, Daniel, Kathryn. BA, Yeshiva Coll., 1963; MD, U. Louisville, 1967. Intern Albany (N.Y.) Med. Coll., 1967-68; fellow in medicine Mayo Clinic, Rochester, NY, 1968-71; fellow in med. oncology Johns Hopkins U. Sch. Medicine, Balt., 1973-75, instr. oncology, 1975-76, instr. medicine, 1975-77, asst. prof. oncology, 1976-81, asst. prof. medicine, 1977-81, assoc. prof. oncology, 1981-82, assoc. prof. medicine, 1981-93, prof. oncology, 1992—, prof. medicine, 1993—, Alex Grass prof. oncology, 2003—; assoc. dir. for clin. rsch. Johns Hopkins Oncology Ctr., Balt., 1992—. Mem. editorial bd. Oncology: Internat. Jour. of Cancer Rsch. and Treatment, Jour. Cancer Rsch. and Clin. Oncology, The Oncologist, Expert Rev. of Anticancer Therapy; editor-in-chief: Current Treatment Options in Oncology; contbr. chpts. to books, numerous articles to profl. jours. Pres. Md. divsn. Am. Cancer Soc., 1994-96. Maj. U.S. Army, 1971-73. Recipient Nat. Divisional award, St. George Medal, Am. Cancer Soc. 1997. Fellow ACP, Am. Coll. Chest Physicians; mem. Eastern Coop. Oncology Group, Radiation Therapy Oncology Group, Am. Soc. Clin. Oncology, Am. Assn. for Cancer Rsch., Internat. Assn. for Study of Lung

Cancer, Am. Soc. Therapeutic Radiology and Oncology, Connective Tissue Oncology Soc., Phi Delta Epsilon. Office: Bunting Blaustein CRB 1650 Orleans St Baltimore MD 21231 Office Phone: 410-955-8847. Business E-Mail: ettinda@jhmi.edu.*

ETTINGER, HARRY JOSEPH, retired industrial hygiene engineer, consultant; b. NYC, July 20, 1934; s. Morris and Pauline (Waxman) E.; m. June Kopf, June 14, 1958; children: Linda E., Steven E., Robert A. BCE, CCNY, 1956; MCE, NYU, 1958. Registered profl. engr., N.Mex.; cert. indsl. hygienist. San. engr. USPHS, Bethesda, Md., 1958-61; staff mem. Los Alamos (N.Mex.) Nat. Lab., 1961-71, alt. group leader, 1971-74, group leader, 1974-80, program mgr., 1981-87, tech. rsch. coord., 1989-91, program mgr., 1991-93, chief scientist environ., safety and health divsn., 1993-97, acting dep. divsn. dir., 1995-96, lab. assoc., 1997-99, cons., 1999—2004; project dir. Occupl. Safety and Health Adminstrn., Washington, 1987-89. Cons. divsn. reactor licensing USAEC, 1970-71, cons. EPA, 1972-74, various industries, 1970—; cons. to adv. com. on nuc. facility safety DOE, 1990-91; mem. adj. faculty U. Ark., Little Rock, 1969-90, San Diego State U., 1981-86; vis. faculty Tex. A&M U., College Station, 1981-99; faculty affiliate Colo. State U., Ft. Collins, 1983-2004; mem. exec. com. toxic substances rsch. and tchg. program U. Calif., 1984-90; mem. stds. steering group DOE Lab. Dirs. Environ. and Occupl. Health, 1990-96; mem. liaison com. NIOSH Nat. Occupl. Rsch. Agenda, 2000-03; reviewer Inst. Medicine, 2006. Mem. editl. bd. Jour. Occupl. and Environ. Hygiene, 2004-; contbr. jour. articles and tech. reports on indsl. hygiene, aerosol physics, respiratory protection. Active Los Alamos County Utility Bd., 1968-70, 78-82, chmn., 1970; vice chmn. Los Alamos County Planning and Zoning Commn., 1974-76, mem., 1972-76, 97-2001, 2004-2006. Fellow: Am. Indsl. Hygiene Assn. (chmn. aerosol tech. com. 1968—70, mem. aerosol tech. com. 1968—78, editl. rev. bd. 1979—87, aerosol tech. com. 1980—84, bd. dirs. 1987—90, editl. rev. bd. 1990—91, v.p. 1991—92, pres.-elect 1992—93, pres. 1993—94, editl. rev. bd. 1995—2003, respirator com. 1995—, Edward Baier award 1990, Donald Cummings Lectr. and award 2003, Henry Smyth Lectr. and award 2004); mem.: Internat. Occupl. Hygiene Assn. (bd. dirs. 1994—97), Internat. Soc. Respiratory Protection (bd. dirs. 1985—88, 1995—97, mem. editl. bd. NSC Jour. safety rsch. 2001—), Am. Conf. Govtl. Indsl. Hygiene (Meritorious Achievement award 1985), Am. Bd. Indsl. Hygiene (bd. dirs. 1979—85, chmn. 1983—85), Am. Acad. Indsl. Hygiene (editor newsletter 1997—2001). Democrat. Jewish. Office Phone: 505-662-7132. Personal E-mail: Junee@rt66.com.

ETTINGER, IRWIN R., insurance company executive; m. Arlene Ettinger; 1 child, Craig Jonathan. Grad., CUNY Baruch Coll., NYC, 1958. Ptnr. Arthur Young & Co. (now Ernst & Young); with Citigroup, 1987—2002, chief acctg. and tax officer, 1998—2002; vice chmn. TPC, 2002—04, Travelers Cos. Inc., 2004—. Office: Travelers Cos Inc 385 Washington St Saint Paul MN 55102 Office Phone: 651-310-7911.*

ETTINGER, JEFFREY M., food products executive, lawyer; BA, UCLA, 1980, JD, 1983. Law clk. Judge Arthur Alarcon, U.S. Ct. Appeals 9th cir.; v.p., gen. counsel Comar Mktg., LA; corp. atty. Hormel Foods Corp., Austin, Minn., 1989—95, product mgr. Hormel Chili, 1995—97, asst. treas., 1997—98, treas., 1998—99, v.p., pres. Jennie-O Foods, 1999—2001, pres., COO Jennie-O Turkey Store, 2001—03, CEO Jennie-O Turkey Store, 2003—04, pres., COO, 2004—05, pres., CEO, 2006, chmn., pres., CEO, 2007—. Office: Hormel Foods Corp 1 Hormel Pl Austin MN 55912-3680*

ETTINGER, JOHN RICHE, lawyer; b. NYC, June 12, 1951; s. Austen A. and Shirley (Riche) E.; m. Linda A. Simpson, Apr. 19, 1986; children: Katharine Simpson, John Tyler, William Riche. BA summa cum laude, Yale U., 1973; JD, Harvard U., 1978. Bar: N.Y. 1979. Atty. Davis Polk & Wardwell, 1979—86, ptnr. NYC, 1986—, chmn. mgmt. com. Rhodes scholar Oxford (Eng.) U., 1975. Office: Davis Polk & Wardwell 450 Lexington Ave Fl 31 New York NY 10017-3982 Office Phone: 212-450-4232. Office Fax: 212-450-3232. Business E-Mail: john.ettinger@dpw.com.

ETTINGER, JOSEPH ALAN, lawyer; b. NYC, July 21, 1931; s. Max and Frances E.; children: Amy Beth, Ellen Jane. BA, Tulane U., 1954, JD with honors, 1956. Bar: La. 1956, Ill. 1959. Asst. corp. counsel City of Chgo., 1959-62; pvt. practice, Chgo., 1962-73, 76-80; sr. ptnr. Ettinger & Schoenfield, Chgo., 1980-92; pvt. practice, Chgo., 1993—. Assoc. prof. law Chgo.-Kent Coll., 1973-76; chmn. Village of Olympia Fields (Ill.) Zoning Bd. Appeals, 1969-76; chmn. panel on corrections Welfare Coun. Met. Chgo., 1969-76; spl. state appellate defender State of Ill., 1997-98; delegate inauguration Michael M. Crow to Pres. Ariz. State U., Tulane U., 2002. Contbr. articles to profl. jours. Capt. JAGC US Army, 1956—59. Recipient svc. award, Village of Olympia Fields, 1976. Mem.: Assn. Criminal Def. Lawyers (gov. 1970—72), Chgo. Bar Assn. Office Phone: 312-326-1543. E-mail: joeett@aol.com.

ETTINGER, LAWRENCE JAY, pediatric hematologist, oncologist, educator; b. Bklyn., Dec. 17, 1947; s. Joseph and Blanche (Mittman) E.; m. Alice G. Renick. BA, Case Western Res. U., 1969, MD, 1973. Cert. in pediatrics Am. Bd. Pediatrics, 1978, in pediatric hematology-oncology Am. Bd. Pediatrics Sub-Bd. Pediatric Hematology-Oncology, 1978. Intern in pediatrics U. Md. Hosp., Balt., 1973-74, resident in pediatrics, 1974-75, Children's Hosp. Buffalo, 1975-76; fellow in pediatric hematology-oncology Roswell Park Meml. Inst. and Children's Hosp. Buffalo, 1976-78; asst. prof. pediatrics U. Rochester (N.Y.) Sch. Med. and Dentistry, 1978-81, U. So. Calif., LA, 1981-84; assoc. prof. U. Medicine and Dentistry N.J., Robert Wood Johnson Med. Sch., New Brunswick, chief div. pediatric hematology-oncology, 1984-98; lectr. in pediats. Coll. Physicians and Surgeons Columbia U., 1998-2000; chief divsn. pediat. hematology/oncology St. Peter's Univ. Hosp., 1998—; assoc. clin. prof. pediatrics Coll. Physicians and Surgeons Columbia U., 2000—04; clin. prof. pediat. Drexel U. Coll. Medicine, Phila., 2005—. Sickle cell adv. com. N.J. State Dept. Health, 1998—. Manuscript reviewer Cancer, Mayo Clinic Proceedings, Jour. Pediat. Hematology-Oncology, Brit. Jour. Cancer, Med. Pediat. Oncology, Am. Jour. Perinatology, Pediatric Blood & Cancer; contbr. articles to profl. jours Mem. adv. com. Pediatric Oncology Adv. Group, N.J. Commn. Cancer Rsch., 1986—; mem. med. adv. bd. Inst. for Children with Cancer and Blood Disorders, 1991-98; field reader Office of Orphan Products Devel. FDA, 1988—; mem. spl. rev. com. NIH, 1992, 95; mem. cancer ad hoc com. Ocean County (N.J.) Health Dept., 1996-98. Recipient Univ. Excellence award for patient care U. Medicine and Dentistry, N.J., 1991, Pride of N.J. award and Clara Barton Med. Svc. award Gov. of N.J., 1992, N.J. Pride award in health, 1993; grantee N.J. Commn. on Cancer Rsch., Trenton, 1987-89, Valerie Fund, Maplewood, N.J., 1985-90, The Upjohn Co., Kalamazoo, 1984-86, Wyeth-Ayerst Rsch., Phila., 1992-94, Enzon Inc., Piscataway, N.J., 1992-94, Amgen, Inc., Thousand Oaks, Calif., 1992-94, Inst. for Children with Cancer and Blood Disorders, 1991-98, Sanofi Winthrop, 1996; Jr. Faculty Clin.. Fellow Am. Cancer Soc., 1980-83. Fellow: Am. Acad. Pediat. (exec. com. sect. on hematology-oncology 1997—2000); mem.: Children's Oncology Group (prin. investigator 2004—), Internat. Soc. Pediat. Oncology, Children's Cancer Group (prin. investigator 1997—98), Am. Cancer Soc. (svc. and rehab. com. N.J. divsn. 1986—96, vice chmn. 1988—89, 1992—94, chmn. 1994—96, trustee, exec. com. 1994—96), Am. Soc. Pediat. Hematology-Oncology, Am. Soc. Hematology, Am. Soc. Clin. Oncology, Am. Assn. Cancer Rsch., Phi Beta Kappa. Avocations: photography, travel. Office: St Peter's U Hosp 254 Easton Ave PO Box 591 New Brunswick NJ 08903-0591 Home Phone: 908-755-0857; Office Phone: 732-745-6674. Business E-Mail: lettinger@saintpetersuh.com.

ETTINGER, MICHAEL SAUL, lawyer; b. 1961; s. Leon and Victoria S. Ettinger; m. Joyce Francine Katz, Aug. 18, 1984. BA, SUNY, Binghamton; JD, SUNY, Buffalo. Bar: 1986. Assoc. Arthur Andersen & Co., 1986—87, Bower & Gardner, 1988—94; v.p., gen. counsel, sec. Henry Schein Inc., Melville, NY, 1994—. Mem.: Nassau County Bar Assn. Office: Henry Schein Inc 135 Duryea Rd Melville NY 11747*

ETTLICH, WILLIAM F., electrical engineer; b. Spokane, Wash., Jan. 7, 1936; s. Fred Ernest Ettlich and Dorothy Sue (Olney) Nicholls; m. Alice Dianne Lawton, Aug. 24, 1958; children: Pamela, Daniel. BS, Oreg. State U.; PMD-25, Harvard U. Registered profl. engr., Oreg., Calif., Nev., Colo., Ohio. Project engr. CH2M-Hill Corp., Corvallis, Oreg., 1959-65; pres. Neptune Microfloc, Corvallis, 1965-74; v.p. Culp Wesner Culp, Cameron Park, Calif., 1974-86; exec. v.p. CWC-HDR, Inc., Cameron Park, 1986-88, HDR Engring., Inc., El Dorado Hills, 1988—. Pres. Cameron Estates CSD, Cameron Park, 1977-80. Contbr. tech. articles to jours.; patentee in field. Bd. dirs. Marshall Hosp.; trustee emeritus Marshall Hosp. Found. and Hosp. Bd. Mem. IEEE (sr.), Instrument Soc. Am., Rotary (pres. Cameron Park club 1987-88). Republican. Presbyterian. Avocations: skiing, woodworking. Home: 101 Flindell Way Folsom CA 95630 Office: HDR Engring 2365 Iron Point Rd Folsom CA 95630 Business E-Mail: bill.ettlich@hdrinc.com.

ETTORE, JOSEPH R., retired discount department store chain executive; B, St. Peter's Coll., Jersey City, NJ, 1961. Pres., COO, dir. Stuart's Dept. Store, Inc., 1989—92, chmn., CEO, 1992—93; pres., CEO, Jamesway Corp., 1993—94; pres., CEO Ames Dept. Stores Inc., Rocky Hill, Conn., 1994—99, chmn., 1999—2002; sr. exec. Management Capital LLC, Providence, 2004—. Recipient numerous industry awards and honors, including Humanitarian of Yr. award Housewares Charity Found., Retail Exec. of Yr. award Discount Merchandiser mag., Discounters in Svc. to Cmty. award Discount Store News, Bus. Leadership award U. Hartford, Corp. Leadership award Nat. Coun. on Aging, 1st award for edn. excellence Sch. and Home Office Products Assn. Found., 1999. Mem. Internat. Mass Retail Assn. (chmn.).

ETTRE, LESLIE STEPHEN, chemist; b. Szombathely, Hungary, Sept. 16, 1922; came to U.S., 1958, naturalized, 1965; s. Stephen and Mary Therese (Dunay) E.; m. Kitty Polonyi, May 16, 1953; 1 child, Julie Suzanne. Diploma Chem. Engring. U. Tech. Scis., Hungary, 1945, D.Tech. Scis. Chemist G. Richter Pharm. Works, Budapest, Hungary, 1946-49; rsch. chemist Rsch. Inst. for Heavy Chem. Industries, Veszprem, Hungary, 1949-51, head tech. office, 1951-53; sr. lectr. chemistry U. Veszprem, 1951-53; head indsl. dept. Research Inst. for Plastics Industry, Budapest, 1953-56; chemist Lurgi Cos., Frankfurt, Fed. Republic Germany, 1957-58; applications chemist Perkin-Elmer Corp., Norwalk, Conn., 1958-60, product specialist, 1960-62, chief applications chemist, 1962-68, sr. staff scientist, 1972-87, sr. scientist, 1987-90. Exec. editor Ency. Indsl. Chem. Analysis John Wiley & Sons, N.Y.C., 1968-72; rsch. assoc. dept. engring. and applied scis. Yale U., New Haven, 1977-78, adj. prof., 1989-95, rsch. affiliate, 1995—2004; adj. prof. U. Houston, 1978-88; chmn. various symposia on chromatography, intermittantly, 1972-93; co-chmn. Summer Symposium on Analytical Chemistry Miami U., Oxford, Ohio, 1973; lectr. in U.S., Can., Europe, Asia, Africa, Australia; participant lecture tours of Chromatography Coun. of Acad. Scis., USSR, 1976, 78, 79, 80, 81, 86, 88, Estonian Acad. Scis., 1979-81, Chinese Acad. Scis., 1980, 85, 87, Georgian Acad. Sci., 1981. Recipient Commemorative Chromatography medal Acad. Scis., USSR, 1978, M.S. Tswett award, 1978, L.S. Palmer award Minn. Chromatography Forum, 1980, A.J.P. Martin award Brit. Chromatography Discussion Group, 1982, Outstanding Svc. award Western Carolinas Chromatography Discussion Group, 1987, M.J.E. Golay award Internat. Symposium on Capillary Chromatography, 1992, Jubilee award, 1998, Golden Diploma U. Tech. Scis., Budapest, 1995, Diamond Diploma, 2005, Dimick award Pitts. Conf. on Analytical Chemistry and Applied Spectroscopy, 1998, Cs Horvath award Conn. Separations Sci. Coun., 2001. Fellow Am. Inst. Chemists; mem. ASTM (chmn. subcom. rsch. com. E-19, 1966-70, subcom. on nomenclature of com. E-19, 1970-73), Am. Chem. Soc. (award in chromatography 1985), Chromatography Soc. (exec. com. 1982-89), N.Y. Acad. Scis., Internat. Union Pure and Applied Chemistry (nomenclature com. 1981-91), Hungarian Chem. Soc. (hon.; Heureka award 2001). Office: 38 Boston Ave Middletown CT 06457-3562 Office Phone: 860-704-0221. E-mail: lsettre@comcast.net.

ETZEL, JAMES EDWARD, environmental engineering educator; b. Reading, Pa., Nov. 9, 1929; s. Edward John and Ruth Anna (Getrost) E.; m. Barbara Dawn Shoup, Sept. 3, 1950; children: Pamela Dawn, Gregory John, Mark Raymond, Scott Edward, Christopher James. BS in Sanitation Engring., Pa. State U., 1951; MSCE, Purdue U., 1955, PhD, 1957. Registered profl. engr., Ind. Engr. Capitol Engring. Co., Dillsburg, Pa., 1951, du Pont Co., Wilmington, Del., 1957-58; engr., dir. research Roy F. Weston, engrs., Newtown Sq., Pa., 1958-59; mem. faculty Purdue U., 1959-90, prof. environ. engring., 1964-90, Water Refining Co. prof., 1978-83, head environ. engring. area Sch. Civil Engring., 1971-90, prof. emeritus environ. engring., 1990—; v.p. Heritage Environ. Svcs., Inc., 1990—. Chmn. Tippecanoe County (Ind.) Solid Wastes Com., 1971-86; mem. W. Lafayette Environ. Commn., 1968-76; cons. to industry, 1960—. Patentee in field. Served with C.E., 1951-53, AUS. Named Outstanding Prof. in Civil Engring. Purdue U., 1979 Mem. Water Pollution Control Fedn. Ind. Water Pollution Control Assn. (past pres.) Lutheran. Home and Office: 710 Cardinal Dr Lafayette IN 47909-9036

ETZEL, RUTH ANN, pediatrician, epidemiologist, educator; b. Milw., Apr. 6, 1954; d. Raymond Arthur and Marian Dorothy Etzel. Student, St. Olaf Coll., 1972-73; BA in Biology summa cum laude, U. Minn., 1976; MD, U. Wis., 1980; PhD, U. N.C., 1985. Bd. cert. Am. Bd. Pediat., Am. Bd. Preventive Medicine. Resident in pediat. N.C. Meml. Hosp., Chapel Hill, 1980-83; adj. asst. prof. pediat. Emory U. Sch. Medicine, Atlanta, 1985-87; epidemic intelligence svc. officer Ctr. Environ. Health Ctrs. Disease Control, Atlanta, 1985-87, med. epidemiologist Ctr. Environ. Health and Injury Control, 1987-90, chief air pollution and respiratory health br., 1991-96, asst. dir. preventive medicine residency program, 1992-97; dir. divsn. epidemiology and risk assessment Office Pub. Health and Sci., Food Safety and Inspection Svc., USDA, Washington, 1998—2001; adj. prof. environ. and occupl. health George Washington U., Washington, 2000—. Mem. preventive medicine and pub. health test com. Nat. Bd. Med. Examiners, 1992—94; mem. US Med. Licensing Exam. Step 2 Preventive Medicine and Pub. Health Test Material Devel. Com., 1992—94; mem., trustee Am. Bd. Preventive Medicine, 1992—2001, vice chair pub. health and preventive medicine, 1997—2001; commissioned officer US Pub. Health Svc, 1985—2005. Editor: Am. Acad. Pediat., Pediat. Environ. Health, 1999—; assoc. editor: Current Problems in Pediatrics and Adolescent Healthcare, 2005—; contbr. articles to profl. publs. Recipient Arthur S. Flemming award, DC Jaycees, 1991; Robert Wood Johnson Clin. scholar, U. N.C., 1983—85, MacPherson scholar, 1972. Fellow: Am. Coll. Preventive Medicine, Am. Acad. Pediats. (Ctrs. Disease Control and Prevention liaison 1986—94, chmn. sect. epidemiology 1988—92, ex-officio 1993—94, chmn. com. environ. health 1995—99, mem. com. on native Am. child health 2003—, mem. exec. com. sect. epidemiology 2005—); mem.: Internat. Soc. Environ. Epidemiology, Ambulatory Pediatric Assn. (mem. rsch. com. 1987—, comms. dir. 2002—05), Delta Omega, Phi Beta Kappa. Office: 4501 Diplomacy Dr Anchorage AK 99508-5925 Personal E-mail: retzel@earthlink.net.

ETZIONI, AMITAI, sociologist, educator; b. Cologne, Germany, Jan. 4, 1929; s. Willi Falk and Gertrude Hannauer (Falk) E.; m. Minerva Morales, Sept. 14, 1965 (dec. Dec. 20, 1985); children: Ethan, Oren, Michael (dec.), David, Benjamin; m. Patricia Kellogg, Nov. 6, 1992. BA, Hebrew U., Jerusalem, 1954, MA, 1956; PhD in Sociology, U. Calif., Berkeley, 1958; LittD (hon.), Rider Coll., 1980, Gov.'s State U., 1987; LLD (hon.), U. Utah, 1991; LHD (hon.), Colo. Coll., 1994, Conn. Coll., 1994. Mem. faculty Columbia U., 1958-80; rsch. assoc. Inst. War and Peace Studies, 1961, prof. sociology, 1967, chmn. dept., 1969-78; dir. Ctr. for Policy Rsch., 1968—; guest scholar Brookings Instn., 1978-79; sr. advisor White House, 1979-80; univ. prof. George Washington U., Washington, 1980—, dir. Inst. for Communitarian Policy Studies, 1995—; Thomas Henry Carroll Ford Found. vis. prof., grad. sch. bus. Harvard U., Cambridge, Mass., 1987-89. Bd. dirs. Ctr. for Policy Rsch., Washington; mem. Econ. Forum The Conf. Bd., 1983-85; founder Ctr. for Comm. Policy Studies, George Washington U., 1995—; dir., founder Inst. Communitarian Policy Studies, 1995; developed organizational analysis, a typology based on means used to control participants in orgns., how orgns. change, survive and are integrated into larger social units. Author: A Comparative Analysis of Complex Organizations, 1961, Modern Organizations, 1964, Political Unification, A Comparative Study of Leaders and Forces, 1965, Studies in Social Change, 1966, the Active Society, 1968, Genetic Fix, 1973, Social Problems, 1975, An Immodest Agenda, 1982, Capital Corruption, 1984, The Moral Dimension, 1988, The Spirit of Community, 1993, The New Golden Rule, 1996, The Limits of Privacy, 1999, The Road to the Good Society, 2001, The Monochrome Society, 2001, My Brother's Keeper, 2003, From Empire to Community, 2004, How Patriotic is the Patriot Act, 2004; editor: The Responsive Community, 1990-2004; mem. editl. bd. Sci. Mag., 1969-71; contbr. numerous articles to profl. jours. With Israeli Army. Social Sci. Rsch. Coun. faculty fellow, 1960-61, 67-68; fellow Ctr. for Advanced Study in Behavioral Scis., 1965-66; Guggenheim fellow, 1968. Fellow AAAS; mem. Am. Sociol. Assn. (pres. 1995), Soc. for the Advancement Socio-Econs. (founder 1989), The Communitarian Network (founder 1993), Inst. Medicine. Office: George Washington U Rm 703 2130 H St NW Washington DC 20052-0001 Office Phone: 202-994-8190.

EUBANK, DAVID LYNN, lawyer, consultant; b. Lexington, Ky., May 3, 1950; s. Elbert H. and Thelma C. Eubank; m. Lenora A. Eubank, Apr. 12, 1980; 1 child, Mitchell. B of Cmty. Planning, U. Cin., 1974; MPA, JD, U. Dayton, 1989. Bar: Ohio 1989, U.S. Supreme Ct. 1996, U.S. Ct. Appeals (6th cir.) 1991, U.S. Dist. Ct. (so. dist.) Ohio 1990. Exec. dir. Longmont (Colo.) Downtown Devel. Authority, 1980-85; city atty. City of Beavercreek, Ohio, 1991-97; law dir. City of Kettering, Ohio, 1997—. Prin. SFDG Cons., Cin., 1975—80; adj. prof. Wright State U., 2005—. Mem. Montgomery County, Ohio Cmty. Human Svcs. Levy Rev. Bd., Dayton, 1990-96, mem. Montgomergy County Criminal Justice Council, Dayton, 2004—. Mem. Am. Inst. Cert. Planners. Office: City of Kettering Law Dept 3600 Shroyer Rd Kettering OH 45429

EUBANK, J. THOMAS, lawyer; b. Port Arthur, Tex., Mar. 17, 1930; s. J.T. and Ada (White) E.; m. Nancy Moore, Feb.10, 1956; children: John, Marshall, Stephen, Laura. BA, Rice U., 1951; JD, U. Tex., 1954. Bar: Tex. 1954, US Supreme Ct. 1960. With Baker Botts L.L.P., Houston, 1954-90, sr. ptnr., 1979-90, sr. counsel, 1999—; dir. Sentinel Trust Co., L.B.A., 1997—. Mem. joint editl. bd. Uniform Probate code, 1972-86. Bd. govs. Rice U., 1985-91. Mem. ABA (chmn. sect. real property, probate and trust law 1978-79), Am. Coll. Trust and Estate Counsel (pres. 1984-85, pres. Found. 1986-89, Trachtman lectr. 1986), State Bar Tex. (chmn. sect. real estate, probate and trust law 1972-73, Lifetime Achievement award 2003), Am. Bar Found., Tex. Bar Found. (Outstanding Fifty Yr. Lawyer 2007), Houston Philos. Soc., Rice U. Alumni Assn. (pres. 1979-80, Rice Gold medal 1992), Am. Law Inst., Internat. Acad. Estate and Trust Law, Houston Country, Coronado, Allegro, Thalia, Chevaliers du Tastevin. Home: 26 Liberty Bell Cir Houston TX 77024-6303 Office: 910 Louisiana St Houston TX 77002-4995 Office Phone: 713-229-1688. Business E-Mail: tom.eubank@bakerbotts.com.

EUBANKS, EUGENE EMERSON, education educator, consultant; b. Meadville, Pa., June 6, 1939; s. Nelson Eubanks and Emily (Princes) Jackson; m. Audrey Hunter, Aug. 4, 1962; children: Brian, Regina. BS, Edinboro U., Pa., 1963; PhD, Mich. State U., 1972. Tchr. Cleve. Pub. Schs., 1963-68, unit prin., 1968-70; asst. prof. U. Del., Newark, 1972-74; asst. dean U. Mo., Kansas City, 1974-79, dean, 1979-88, prof. edn. and urban affairs, 1988—; dept. supt. Kansas City Pub. Schs., 1984-85. Contbr. articles to profl. jours. Cons. Urban League, 1978—, legal def. fund NAACP, 1978, Cleve. Found., 1978, U. Wis., 1988; bd. dirs. Operation PUSH, 1982-87, Mid-Continent Girl Scouts, Kansas City, 1983—, Genesis Sch., 1984—; chair Desegration Monitoring Com., 1985—. Mem. Am. Assn. Coll. Tchr. Edn. (pres. 1988-89), Nat. Alliance Found. (chmn. 1984-85), Black Sch. Educators (edn. commn.). Home: 12737 Oakmont Dr Kansas City MO 64145-1140 Office: U Mo Sch Edn 5100 Rockhill Rd Kansas City MO 64110-2481 Office Phone: 816-235-2448. Business E-Mail: EubanksE@umkc.edu.

EUBANKS-POPE, SHARON G., real estate company executive, entrepreneur; b. Chgo., Aug. 26, 1943; d. Walter Franklyn and Thelma Octavia (Watkins) Gibson; m. Larry Hudson Eubanks, Dec. 20, 1970 (dec. Jan. 1976); children: Rebekah, Aimée; m. Otis Eliot Pope, June 7, 1977; children: O. Eliot Jr., Adrienne. BS in Edn., Chgo. Tchrs. Coll., 1965; postgrad., Ill. Inst. Tech., Chgo., 1967, John Marshall Law Sch., 1970, Governors State U., University Park, Ill., 1975-76. Educator, parent coord. Chgo. Bd. Edn., 1965-77; owner, ptnr. Redel Rentals, Chgo., 1977—. Realtor, 1990—. Adminstrv. bd. St. Mark United Meth. Ch., Chgo., 1967, bd. trustees, 1988; com. chair Englewood Urban Progress Ctr., Chgo., 1973; coord., educator LWV, 1975-76; chair comms. Marian Cath. H.S., 1999-2005, adv. bd.; mem. Cottage Grove Tax Increment Financing Bd., 2005—; mem. bd. The Princeton Group, Inc., 2007-, The Links Found., Inc., 2007-. Named Outstanding Sch. Parent Vol., Chgo. Bd. Edn., 1977; recipient Outstanding Cmty. Law Class award LWV, 1975-76, Christian Leadership award United Meth. Women, Chgo., 1985. Mem.: NAACP, NAFE, Nat. Assn. Realtors, Am. Soc. Profl. and Exec. Women, St. Mark Cmty. Devel. Corp. (v.p. 2003—), Links, Inc., Jack and Jill Am., Inc. (Chgo. chpt. journalist 1989—91, parliamentarian 1991, founder Parents for Parity in Edn. 1992, pres. Eubanks-Pope Devel. Co., Inc. 1993, Midwestern region sec.-treas. 1993—95, nat. treas. 1998—2000, Midwestern regional dir. 1995—97), Alpha Beta Gamma (female exec. del. to China People to People Amb. program 1998). Office: Redel Rentals 4338 S Drexel Blvd Chicago IL 60653-3536

EULLER, STEVEN C., lawyer; b. 1949; BA, Macalester Coll., 1971; JD, Harvard Univ., 1979. Bar: Minn. 1979. Sr. atty. Cargill Inc., Singapore, corp. v.p., gen. counsel, corp. sec. Minn. Named one of 50 most influential in-house counsel in N.Am., InsideCounsel, 2006. Office: Cargill Inc 15407 McGinty Rd W Eitzen MN 55931 Mailing: Cargill Inc PO Box 9300 Minneapolis MN 55440-9300 Office Phone: 952-742-4771. Office Fax: 952-742-7393. E-mail: steve_euller@cargill.com.

EURICH, JUDITH, art appraiser, printmaker; Tchr. Acad. Art Coll., Hearst Art Gallery, St. Mary's Coll., Moranga, Calif., Univ. Calif. Ext., San Francisco; curatorial asst., asst. curator, curator, prints, drawings, 19th century photogs. San Francisco Arts Mus. Achenbach Found. for Graphic Arts, 1981—92; specialist to dir., print dept. Butterfield & Butterfield (now Bonhams & Butterfields), San Francisco, 1995—. Lectr. in field. Office: Bonhams & Butterfields 220 San Bruno Ave San Francisco CA 94103 Home Phone: 415-452-9737; Office Phone: 415-503-3259. Office Fax: 415-861-8951. Business E-Mail: judith.eurich@bonhams.com.

EURICH, RICHARD REX, lawyer; b. Lancaster, Pa., Apr. 12, 1947; s. Richard Roy and Mary Elizabeth (Kiehl) E.; m. JoAnn Samsa, June 27,

1970; 1 child, Richard. BA cum laude, Am. U., 1969; JD cum laude, Harvard U., 1972. Bar: Mass. 1972, U.S. Dist. Ct. Mass. 1973, U.S. Ct. Appeals (1st cir.) 1975. Assoc. Morrison Mahoney, LLP, Boston, 1972-76, ptnr., 1976—. Elected Town Meeting Mem., Town of Lexington, 1996-99; mem. exec. bd. Lexington Town Meeting Mems. Assn., 1998-99, Lexington Appropriation Com., 2000— Fellow Mass. Bar Found.; mem. ABA, Mass. Bar Assn. (mem. budget and fin. com., chmn. ins. com.), Def. Rsch. Inst., Mass. Def. Lawyers Assn., Internat. Assn. Def. Counsel. Roman Catholic. Home: 7 Pitcairn Pl Lexington MA 02421-7108 Office: Morrison Mahoney LLP 250 Summer St Fl 1 Boston MA 02210-1181 Office Phone: 617-439-7508. E-mail: reurich@morrisonmahoney.com.

EURICH LAZARUS, NELL P., education educator; b. Norwood, Ohio, July 28, 1919; d. Clayton W. and Adah (Palmer) Plopper; m. Alvin C. Eurich, Mar. 15, 1953 (dec. 1987); children: Juliet Ann, Donald Alan; m. Maurice Lazarus, 1988. AA, Stephens Coll., 1939; BA, Stanford U., 1941, MA, 1943; PhD, Columbia U., 1959. Dir. student union U. Tex., 1942-43; resident counselor Barnard Coll., 1944-46; asst. to pres. Woman's Found., 1947-49; officer charge pub. relations State U. N.Y., 1949- 52; acting pres. Stephens Coll., 1953-54; asst. prof. English NYU, 1959-64; academic dean New Coll., Sarasota, Fla., 1965; dir. project to reorganize curriculum Aspen (Colo.) Pub. High Sch., 1966; dean faculty, prof. English Vassar Coll., 1967-70; provost, dean faculty, prof. English, v.p. acad. affairs Manhattanville Coll., NY, 1971-75; sr. cons. Internat. Council for Ednl. Devel., 1975-82, Acad. for Ednl. Devel., 1982-88. Mem. nat. selection com., chmn. Rocky Mountain regional com. Nat. Endowment Humanities, 1966-67, cons., 1970-71; mem. Middle States commn. Marshall Scholarships, 1967-68; chmn. Northeastern region, 1969-71; mem. U.S. Commn. on Ednl. Tech., HEW, 1968-69; mem. overseer's vis. com. on summer sch. and univ. extension Harvard, 1969-75; mem. panel of judge's Fed. Woman's award, 1969; cons. Acad. for Ednl. Devel., 1970-71; mem. career minister rev. bd. U.S. Dept. State, 1972; participant Ditchley Conf. V, 1973; mem. Rhodes Scholarship Selection Com., 1976; moderator exec. seminar Aspen Inst. for Humanistic Studies, 1977, 79, 80; dir. Adult Learning Project Carnegie Found. for Advancement Teaching, 1985-90; advisor Nat. Acad. of Engring., 1987-88; vis. com. Neuro Scis., Mass. Gen. Hosp. Author: Science in Utopia, 1967, Higher Education in Twelve Countries: A Comparative View, 1981, (with B. Schwenkmeyer) Great Britain's Open University, 1971, Corporate Classrooms, 1985, The Learning Industry, 1991; contbg. author: (Alvin Toffler) Learning for Tomorrow, 1974, From Parnassus: Essays for Jacques Barzun, 1976; contbr. articles to profl. jours. Past trustee Bank Street Coll., Salisbury Sch., Hudson Guild Neighborhood House, Colo. Rocky Mountain Sch., Bennington Coll.; trustee Carnegie Coun. on Policy Studies in Higher Edn., 1977—80, Carnegie Found. for Advancement of Teaching, 1978—84; trustee emeritus New Coll. Found., 1964—2001. Mem. MLA, Am. Assn. Colls. (spl. com. on liberal studies 1966-70), World Soc. Ekistics, Nat. Coun. Women (hon.), Century Assn. N.Y.C. Home: 144 Brattle St Cambridge MA 02138-2202

EUSDEN, JOHN DYKSTRA, theology studies educator, minister; b. Holland, Mich., July 20, 1922; s. Ray Anderson and Marie (Dykstra) E.; m. Joanne Reiman, June 14, 1950; children: Andrea Bonner, Alan Tolles, John Dykstra Jr., Sarah Jewell. AB, Harvard U., 1943; postgrad., Harvard Law Sch., 1946; BD cum laude, Yale U., 1949, PhD in Religion, 1954. Ordained to ministry United Ch. of Christ, 1949. Instr. in religion Yale U., 1953-55, asst. prof., 1955-60; assoc. prof. religion, chaplain Williams Coll., Williamstown, Mass., 1960-70, Nathan Jackson prof. Christian theology, 1970-90, vis. prof. environ. studies, 1990-92; vis. prof. religion and Asian studies Mt. Holyoke Coll., Mass., 1992—93; min. 1st Congl. Ch., Bennington, Vt., 1991—; cons. Asian programs and environ. studies Williams Coll., Williamstown, Mass., 1992—. Lectr., research fellow Kyoto U., 1963-64, 76, 81-82; theologian-in-residence Am. Ch. in Paris, 1972; lectr. Doshisha U., Kyoto, Japan, 1976, 82; bd. dir. Associated Kyoto Program, Japan. Author: Puritans, Lawyers and Politics in Early 17th Century England, 1958, 68, Zen and Christian: The Journey Between, 1981, (with John H. Westerhoff III) The Spiritual Life: Learning East and West, 1982, (with Westerhoff) Sensing Beauty: Aesthetics, the Human Spirit, and the Church, 1998, Thirsting for Healing and Wholeness, 2007; contbr. articles to profl. jours.; translator, editor, author introduction: The Marrow of Theology (William Ames), 1975, 86; author introduction: Zen Buddhism and Christianity in Y. Takeuchi Festschrift (Japanese edition), 1993, Christology: The Dialogue of East and West in Christology in Dialogue, 1993, Chinese Healing: A Practical Mysticism in John Sahadat Festschrift, 2002. Adv. coun., campus ministry program Danforth Found., 1966-70; bd. dirs. Wellesley Coll. Parents Assn., 1972-75, pres., 1974-75; rsch. fellow Ctr. for Study of Japanese Religion, Kyoto, 1976-94; trustee Lingnan Found., NYC, 1964—, Buxton Sch., Williamstown, Mass., 1970-83, Chewonki Found., Wiscasset, Maine, 2002—; leader trips, People's Republic of China, 1978, 81, 86, 88, 90, 94. 1st lt. USMCR, 1943-45. Scholar Harvard U.; faculty fellow Am. Assn. Theol. Schs., 1958-59, Sterling fellow Yale U., 1950-53, fellow Folger Shakespeare Libr., 1958-59, 71-72; Lilly postdoctoral grantee, 1963-64, Danforth campus ministry grantee, 1963-64; fellow Am. Council Learned Socs., 1967-68; Fulbright rsch. travel grantee, 1967-68; research fellow U. Utrecht, Netherlands, 1968; rsch. grantee Williams Coll., 1976. Mem. AAUP, Am. Acad. Religion, Am. Soc. Ch. History, Am. Soc. Christian Ethics, Nat. Assn. Coll. and Univ. Chaplains, Soc. Values in Higher Edn., Appalachian Mountain Club, Randolph Mountain Club (pres. 1973-75). Home: 75 Forest Rd Williamstown MA 01267-2028 Office Phone: 413-597-2241. Personal E-mail: jeusden@sover.net.

EUSTACE, ALAN, information technology executive; BS, MS, U. Ctrl. Fla., PhD in Computer Sci. With Western Rsch. Lab., Hewlett Packard, 1987—2002, dir., 1999—2002; v.p. engring. Google Inc., Mountain View, Calif., 2002—06, sr. v.p. engring & rsch., 2006—. Vol. Harvest Food Bank, Anita Borg Scholarship Fund. Mem.: Internet Soc. Avocations: flying, bicycling. Office: Google Inc 1600 Amphitheatre Pkwy Mountain View CA 94043 Office Phone: 650-253-0000. Office Fax: 650-253-0001.*

EUSTACE, DUDLEY GRAHAM, diversified financial services company executive; b. July 3, 1936; m. Carol Diane Zakrajsek; 2 children. BA in Econs., U. Bristol. Chartered acct. With John Barrit & Son, Hamilton, Bermuda, 1962, Internat. Resort Facilities, Ont., 1963, Alcan Aluminium, Ltd., Montreal, Vancouver, Buenos Aires, Rio de Janeiro, Madrid & U.K., 1964-87, Brit. Aerospace plc, 1987, fin. dir., 1988-92; mem. group mgmt. com. Philips, 1992—2001, exec. v.p. fin., 1993-97, vice chmn. Amsterdam, 1997—; chmn. Smith & Nephew plc, London, 2000—06. Mem. coun. dept. exports, credits guarantee Resigweb, 1992; chmn. Sendo PLC, 2001-2005; chmn. supervisory bd. Aegon N.V., chmn. KPN N.V., Hagemeyer N.V., 1999-2004. Avocations: stamp collecting/philately, gardening, reading. Office: Smith & Nephew plc 15 Adam St London WC2N 6LA England Business E-Mail: dudley.eustace@smith-nephew.com.

EUSTER, JOANNE REED, retired librarian; b. Grants Pass, Oreg., Apr. 7, 1936; d. Robert Lewis and Mabel Louise (Jones) Reed; m. Stephen L. Gerhardt, May 14, 1977; children: Sharon L., Carol L., Lisa J. Student, Lewis and Clark Coll., 1953-56; BA, Portland State Coll., 1965; MLibrarianship, U. Wash., 1968, MBA, 1977; PhD, U. Calif., Berkeley, 1986. Asst. libr. Edmonds C.C., Lynnwood, Wash., 1968-73, dir. libr.-media ctr., 1973-77; libr. Loyola U., New Orleans, 1977-80; libr. dir. J. Paul Leonard Libr., San Francisco State U., 1980-86, Rutgers State U. N.J., New Brunswick, 1986-89, v.p. info. svcs., 1989-91, v.p. univ. librs., 1991-92; libr. dir. U. Calif., Irvine, 1992-97; ret., 1997. Mem. adv. coun. Hong Kong U. Sci. and Tech. Librs., Princeton U. Libr., U. B.C., Can.; cons. in field Author: Changing Patterns of Internal Communication in Large Academic Libraries, 1981, The Academic Library Director, Management Activities and Effectiveness, 1987; columnist Wilson Libr. Bull., 1993-95; contbr. articles to profl. jours. Pres. Seattle Repertory Orgn.; trustee Seattle Repertory Theatre. Mem. ALA, Calif. Libr. Assn., Assn. Coll. and Rsch. Librs. (pres.), Rsch. Librs. Group (chair bd. dirs.).

EUSTICE, FRANCIS JOSEPH, lawyer; b. LaCrosse, Wis., Feb. 2, 1951; s. Frank R. and Cecelia T. (Babler) E.; m. Mary J. McCormick, July 28, 1971; children: Cristen L., Tara L. BS in Chemistry, Kansas Newman Coll., 1976; JD, U. Wis., 1980. Bar: Wis. 1980, U.S. Dist. Ct. (ea. and we. dists.) Wis. 1980, U.S. Tax Ct. 1981, U.S. Ct. Appeals (7th cir.) 1990, U.S. Dist. Ct. (no. dist.) Ill. 1993. With Eustice, Laffey, Sebranek & Auby, S.C. and predecessor firms, Sun Prairie, Wis., 1980—. Bd. dirs., pres. Sun Prairie Devel. Corp., 1989—. Bd. dirs. Exch. Ctr. for Prevention of Child Abuse, Inc., Dane County, Wis., 1984-95. Sgt. USAF, 1973-77. Mem. Wis. Bar Assn., Dane County Bar Assn., Sun Prairie C. of C. (bd. dirs., pres., amb. 1987—), Sun Prairie Exch. Club (sec., pres., bd. dirs. 1980—). Office: PO Box 590 100 Wilburn Rd Ste 202 Sun Prairie WI 53590-0590 Home Phone: 608-837-2770; Office Phone: 608-837-7386. Business E-Mail: f.eustice@els-law.com.

EUSTIS, ALBERT ANTHONY, lawyer, diversified financial services company executive; b. Mahanoy City, Pa., Nov. 8, 1921; m. Mary Hampton Stewart, Apr. 25, 1959; children: Thomas Stewart, David Anthony. BS, Columbia U., 1948; LLB, Harvard U., 1951. Bar: N.Y. 1952, U.S. Dist. Ct. (So. dist.) N.Y 1955. Atty. firm Kelley, Drye & Warren, NYC, 1951—61; atty. W.R. Grace & Co., NYC, 1961—66, asst. gen. counsel, 1966—76, v.p., gen. counsel, sec., 1976—78, sr. v.p., gen. counsel, sec., 1978—82, exec. v.p., gen. counsel, sec., 1982—87; of counsel Holland & Knight, Washington, 1987—. Chmn. bd. trustees, spl. counsel Found. for President's Pvt. Sector Survey on Cost Control; adj. prof. law Fordham Law Sch. Served with AUS, 1942-46. Mem. ABA, Am. Arbitration Assn. (bd. dirs., comml. arbitration panel)

EUSTIS, JOANNE D., university librarian; BA in English Lit., Ind. U., 1974, MLS, 1974, MA in English Lit., 1979. Various libr. positions Va. Poly. Inst. and State U., 1974—98, interim libr. dir., 1992—94; univ. libr. Case Western Res. U., Cleve., 1998—. Office: Kelvin Smith Libr Case Western Res U 11055 Euclid Ave Cleveland OH 44106-7151 Office Phone: 216-368-2992. E-mail: joanne.eustis@case.edu.*

EUSTIS, RICHMOND MINOR, lawyer; b. New Orleans, Nov. 24, 1945; s. David and Molly Cox (Minor) Eustis; m. Catherine Luise Baños, Apr. 15, 1971; children: Richmond Minor Jr., Julie Bransford, Joshua Leeds, Molly Minor. BA in Econs., U. Va., Charlottesville, 1967; JD, Tulane U., New Orleans, 1970. Bar: La. 1970. Assoc. Phelps Dunbar, New Orleans, 1970-75; ptnr. Monroe and Lemann, New Orleans, 1975-96; founder, ptnr. Eustis, O'Keefe & Gleason LLC, New Orleans, 1996—. Bd. dirs. New Orleans Bd. Trade. Bd. dirs. Children's Bur., 1976—88, treas., 1984. Mem.: Am. Inns of Ct., S.E. Admiralty Law Inst., Maritime Law Assn., New Orleans Bar Assn. (chmn. torts and ins. com. 1992—95), La. Bar Assn., La. Club, Boston Club. Republican. Episcopalian. Avocation: fishing. Office: Eustis & O'Keefe 228 Saint Charles Ave Ste 700 New Orleans LA 70130-2686 Office Phone: 504-524-0681. Personal E-mail: richmond_eustis@msn.com.

EUSTIS, ROBERT HENRY, design company executive, mechanical engineer; b. Mpls., Apr. 18, 1920; s. Ralph Warren and Florence Louise E.; m. Katherine Vik Johnson, Mar. 20, 1943; children: Jeffrey Nelson, Karen V. B in Mech. Engring., U. Minn., 1942, MS, 1944; ScD, MIT, 1953. Instr. U. Minn., 1942-44; rsch. scientist NASA, 1944-47; asst. prof. MIT, 1947-51; chief engr. Thermal Rsch. and Engring. Corp., 1951-53; mgr. heat and mech. sect. S.R.I. Internat., 1953-55; mem. faculty dept. mech. engring. Stanford (Calif.) U., 1955-90, prof., 1962, dir. high temperature gasdynamics lab., 1961-80, assoc. dean engring., 1984-88; pres. Menlo Furniture Designs, 2004—. Chmn. tech. adv. coun. Emerson Electric Corp.; prin. Eustis Designs, 1990-00. Contbr. articles to profl. jours. Recipient medal Soviet Sci. Acad., 1973. Fellow: AAAS, ASME, AIAA. Home: 862 Lathrop Dr Palo Alto CA 94305-1053 Office: Stanford Univ Dept Mech Engring Stanford CA 94305 Home Phone: 650-857-0623. Business E-Mail: rheustis@stanford.edu.

EUWER, REBECCA L., dermatologist; b. Wichita, Kans., Apr. 7, 1955; d. Robert Lee and Barbara Daniel Euwer; m. Robert Stevens; children: Brittany, Max. BA in Biology and Psychology, Western State Coll., Gunnison, Colo., 1978; MD, U. Colo., Denver, 1986. Cert. Am. Bd. Dermatology. Rsch. cons. Nat. Jewish Hosp., Denver, 1978—82; rsch. asst. Eastside Health Clinic, Denver, 1983—86; intern internal medicine Baylor U. Med. Ctr., Dallas, 1986—87; resident dermatology Parkland Hosp., Dallas, 1989—90; dermatologist Dermatology Cons., Dallas, 1990—. Clin. assoc. prof. U. Tex. Southwestern Med. Ctr., Dallas, 1990—; cons. med. staff Parkland Hosp.; presenter in field. Contbr. articles to profl. jours. Room mother, Sunday sch. tchr. Highland Park Meth. Ch.; leader Campfire Girls, 1992—96; vol. Ann. Skin Cancer Screening Program, 1990—, D-Tag Program. Recipient Janet M. Glasgow Meml. Achievement citiation for scholastic achievement, Robert W. Goltz award for outstanding performance in dermatology, Residency in Silver award, 1989, Best Tchr. of Yr. award, U. Tex. Southwestern Med. Sch., 2001. Fellow: Am. Soc. for Laser Medicine and Surgery, Inc.; mem.: AMA (Continuing Edn. award), Am. Soc. for Mohs Surgery, Am. Soc. for Laser Medicine and Surgery, Leaders Soc. Dermatology Found., Women's Dermatol. Soc., Assn. Acad. Dermatologic Surgeons, Am. Soc. Dermatologic Surgery, Dallas County Med. Soc., Tex. Med. Assn., Tex. Dermatol. Soc. (trustee 2005—), Dallas Dermatol. Soc. (sec. 1996—97, pres. 1997—99), Am. Acad. Dermatology (Continuing Edn. award). Avocation: tennis.

EVAN, AMATO TOMAS, climate scientist; b. San Jose, Calif., Apr. 3, 1975; s. Tom Joseph Evan and Kitty Jane Moore; m. Maria Paula Di Dio. BS in Physics, Oreg. State U., Corvallis, 1999—2003; MS in Atmospheric & Oceanic Scis., U. Wis., Madison, 2003—05. Climate scientist U. Wis., Madison, 2005—. Achievements include discovery of a climatological relationship between African dust storms and hurricanes in the Atlantic Ocean; led effort to incorporate real time weather satellite data and products into Google Earth for broader dissemination. Office: Univ Wis CIMSS 1225 W Dayton St Madison WI 53706

EVAN, WILLIAM MARTIN, sociologist, educator; b. Ostrow, Poland, Dec. 17, 1922; BA, U. Pa., 1946; PhD, Cornell U., 1954. Instr. sociology Princeton U., 1954-56; asst. prof. Columbia U., 1956-59; research sociologist Bell Telephone Labs., Murray Hill, NJ, 1959-62; assoc. prof. sociology and mgmt. MIT, 1962-66; prof. U. Pa., Phila., 1966—. Ford vis. prof. sociology Grad. Sch. Bus., U. Chgo., 1971-72; vis. fellow Wolfson Coll., U. Oxford, 1978-79; cons.in field Author: (with others) Preventing World War III, 1962, Law and Sociology, 1962, Organizational Experiments, 1971, Interorganizational Relations, 1976, Organization Theory, 1976, Frontiers in Organization and Management, 1980, The Sociology of Law, 1980, Knowledge and Power in a Global Society, 1981, The Arms Race and Nuclear War, 1987, Social Structure and Law, 1990, Organization Theory: Research and Design, 1993, (with Ved P. Nanda) Nuclear Proliferation and the Legality of Nuclear Weapons, 1995, (with Mark Manion, in Chinese) Minding the Machines: Preventing Technological Disasters, 2002, War and Peace In An Age of Terrorism, 2005. Social Sci. Rsch. Coun. tng. fellow, 1951-52, Fulbright fellow, 1952-53; Russell Sage Found. resident, 1956-58. Fellow AAAS; mem. Am. Sociol. Assn., Internat. Sociol. Assn., Internat. Inst. Mgmt. Scis., Law and Soc. Assn., Internat. Studies Assn., Fulbright Assn., U. Pa. Faculty Club, Phila. Art Alliance. Home: 200 Harvard Ave Swarthmore PA 19081 Office: Dept Sociology and Dept Mgmt Univ Pa Philadelphia PA 19104 Office Phone: 215-898-7668. Business E-Mail: evanw@wharton.upenn.edu.

EVANGELIST, SHANE, advertising executive; b. 1973; MBA, So. Meth. U., 2000. Sr. v.p., gen. mgr. Blockbuster Online. Named one of 40 under 40, Advt. Age, 2007. Office: Blockbuster Videos Inc 1201 Elm St Dallas TX 75270*

EVANGELISTA, ALLAN, surgeon, medical researcher; b. Quezon City, Manila, The Philippines, June 23, 1970; came to U.S., 1990, naturalized, 2003. s. Go Guan and Ana Evangelista; m. Julia Ann Adams, Nov. 9, 2002; children, Christian Allan, Ryan Connor. BA in Biology, U. La Verne, Calif., 1991; MDiv in Family, Pastoral Care and Counseling, Fuller Theol. Sem., Calif., 1996; MPH in Epidemiology, Loma Linda U., Calif., 1998; D of Podiatric Medicine, Temple U., Phila., 2002. Tchg. asst. U. La Verne, Calif., 1991; project supr., computer graphic designer Interior Corner, Monterey Park, Calif., 1992-93; assoc. pastor New Life Christian Ctr., El Monte, Calif., 1992—98; rsch. assoc. U. So. Calif. Cardiovasc. Lab., LA, 1993—98; inter libr. loan processor Fuller Sem. Libr., Pasadena, Calif., 1995-96; intern VA, West Los Angeles, Calif., 2002—03; resident VA-Tampa, Fla., 2003—05; fellow in reconstructive surgery of foot, ankle and leg Sarasota (Fla.) Orthop. Assocs., 2005—06; foot and ankle surgeon Kaiser Permanente Riverside Med. Ctr., 2006—. Fin. trustee New Life Christian Ctr., El Monte, 1994—98; pastoral care/marriage counselor First Assembly of God Ch., El Monte, 1994—98. Contbr. articles to med. jours. Vol. San Gabriel Valley Med. Ctr., 1992; med. outreach coord. First Assembly of God Ch., El Monte, 1994—98; youth pastoring/Bible tchr. Christian Reform Ch., West Covina, Calif., 1995—97; chaplain UCLA Med. Ctr., Westwood, 1996. Recipient Ednl. Excellence award Alpha Kappa Alpha, Chgo., 1995; Harding Found. scholar, 1995-96, Fuller Theol. Sem. scholar, 1995-96. Mem.: APHA, ACA, AAAS, Am. Coll. Foot and Ankle Surgeons, Am. Diabetes Assn., Am. Heart Assn. (rsch. coun. 1999), Am. Podiatric Med. Assn., Internat. Assn. Marriage and Family Counselors, Am. Fedn. Med. Rsch. (trainee investigator award 1994). Avocations: basketball, swimming, drawing, travel, cooking. Home: 16222 Perrin Cir Riverside CA 92503-5986 Home Phone: 951-687-7237. Personal E-mail: allevan@hotmail.com.

EVANGELISTA, ANITA LORETTA, freelance/self-employed writer, publishing executive, psychologist, nurse; b. LA, Nov. 9, 1952; d. Carl A. and Etta L. (Erickson) Anderson; m. Nick F. Evangelista, 1979; children: Jamie, Justin. Student, Pepperdine U., 1970-71, U. So. Calif., 1972; BSN, S.W. Mo. State U., Springfield, 2001; MSN, S.W. Mo. State U., 2004; postgrad. in Nursing, Duquesne U., 2004—; MS in Psychology, Mo. State U., 2007. RN; cert. family nurse practitioner; cert. clin. hypnotherapist, transcultural nursing; bd. cert. advanced practice registered nurse and advanced holistic nurse. Asst. to dir. internat. fin. Max Factor, LA, 1972-73; asst. to 2d mgr. steel dept. Sumitomo Shoji, LA, 1973-75; freelance writer, 1975—; columnist Mo. Farm Mag., Clark, 1984-87; adminstr. West Plains (Mo.) Coun. on Arts, 1986-91; editor Ranch Dog Trainer mag., West Plains, 1990-92; mng. editor Fencers Quar., 1999—; family nurse practitioner Cox Health, Mo., 2004—06; owner, dir. Basic Care Clinic LLC, Springfield, Mo., 2006—; adminstr. Auctoritas Pub. LLC, 2007—. Spkr., lectr. Mid West Hypnosis Conv., Chgo., 1983; cons. film dir. R. Wise, Hollywood, Calif., 1977; reader Llewellyn Pub., 1997—. Author: Hypnosis-A Journey into the Mind, 1980, Dictionary of Hypnotism, 1991, How to Develop a Low-Cost Family Food Storage System, 1995, How To Live Without Electricity and Like It, 1997, Backyard Meat Production, 1997, (with N. Evangelista) Blood Lust Chickens and Renegade Sheep: A First Timer's Guide to Country Living, 1999, (with N. Evangelista) Country Living is Risky Business, 2000, (with N. Evangelista) The Women Fencer, 2001, The Survivial Gene: Guide to Surviving The Collapse of Civilization, 2007; indexer: Tikkum Olam, 1996; contbr. articles to mags., periodicals including Mother Earth News, Sci. Digest, Reason, Chronicles, Backwoods Home, Small Farmers Jour., Practical Farmer of Iowa, Fate, Maine Organic Gardner, Dairy Goat Jour., numerous others. Vol. Ozark Med. Ctr., West Plains, 1995-98, ARC, 1999; founder Master Kennel Club, 2004. Recipient TZ 1st prize Twilight Zone Mag., 1989, 1st place Fine Arts Heart of the Ozarks Fair, 1989. Mem.: Transcultural Nursing Soc., Am. Acad. Nurse Practitioners (poster presenter conf. 2007), Soc. Sci. Exploration, Advanced Practice Nurses of the Ozarks (treas. 2005—, conf. planning poster com. 2006—), Parapsychology Assn., Mo. Psychol. Assn., Cath. Med. Assn., Ozark Area Psychol. Assn., Am. Psychol. Soc., Internat. Assn. Clin. Hypnotherapists, Calif. Profl. Hypnotist Assn. (chpt. pres. L.A. 1976—82), Am. Holistic Nurses Assn., Am. Soc. Psychical Rsch., Sigma Theta Tau, Psi Chi, Alpha Sigma Lambda, Phi Theta Kappa. Roman Catholic. Achievements include research in apolipoprotein E4 in Alzheimer's linguistic expression; Parkinson's disease and visual scanning; Alzheimer's disease and divorce; assessing single-question screening tool for problem drinking; improving hypnotizability; nurse license disciplinary actions; male nurse characteristics and issues; gender disparities in nursing. Office Phone: 417-869-1170. E-mail: director@basiccareclinic.com.

EVANGELISTA, NICK FORREST, fencing master, writer, illustrator, publisher; b. Glendale, Calif., Jan. 25, 1949; s. Joseph Norman and Marianne (Williamson) E.; m. Anita Loretta Evangelista, Aug. 5, 1979; children: Jamie Alexandre, Justin Alyn. Student, Mo. State U., Springfield, 2001—. Fencing master Faulkner Sch. Fencing, LA, 1973-81, Evangelista Sch. Fencing, LA, 1981-85, Peace Valley, Mo., 1985—2000, Springfield, Mo., 2001—06, St. Louis Classical Fencing Soc., 1998—2003, Mo. State U. Fencing Soc., 2001—, Evangelista Fencing Acad., 2007—; farmer Peace Valley, 1985—2006; historian, 1989—. Author: The Encyclopedia of the Sword, 1995, The Art and Science of Fencing, 1996, Fighting with Sticks, 1998, Blood-Lust Chickens and Renegade Sheep, 1999, The Inner Game of Fencing, 2000, Country Living Is Risky Business, 2000, The Woman Fencer, 2001; pub., editor-in-chief Vet. Fencers Quar. aka Fencers Quarterly Mag., 1999—; fencing editor Ency. Brit., 2000—; contbr. articles to profl. jours. Fundraiser West Plains (Mo.) Coun. on Art, 1987-91. Recipient 1st Ann. Fiction awards Crosscurrents Mag., 1981. Mem. U.S. Fencing Assn., Nat. Soc. Collegiate Scholars, Phi Alpha Theta, Alpha Sigma Lambda, Golden Key Internat. Honor Soc. Roman Catholic. Avocations: paleontology, book collecting, cartooning, Latin. E-mail: evangel@atlascomm.net.

EVANICH, KEVIN REESE, lawyer; b. 1955; BA, U. Wis., Milw., 1976; JD, Northwestern U., 1980. Bar: Ill. 1980. Assoc. Kirkland & Ellis LLP, Chgo., 1983—86, ptnr., mem. firm mgmt. com., 1995—. Named one of World's Leading Lawyers in Corp. M&A, Chambers Global, 2002—06; recipient Award for Excellence in Pvt. Equity, Chambers & Partners, 2006. Mem.: Phi Beta Kappa. Office: Kirkland & Ellis LLP 200 E Randolph Dr Chicago IL 60601 Office Phone: 312-861-2076. Office Fax: 312-861-2200. Business E-Mail: kevanich@kirkland.com.

EVANOFF, GEORGE C., retired consumer products company executive; b. West Deer, Pa., June 5, 1931; s. Christ and Luba Evanoff; m. Mary E. Yelavich, Nov. 21, 1964; 1 son, Michael. BS cum laude, U. Detroit, 1952, MBA, 1956. Engr. GM, Detroit, 1953—57; supervisory, mgmt. and exec. positions in sales, mktg., and product devel. Ford Motor Co., Dearborn, Mich., 1957—68; staff v.p. mktg., v.p. corp. planning, v.p. corp. devel. RCA Corp., NYC, 1968—76; with Norton Simon, Inc., LA and NYC, 1977—82; v.p. corp. planning, interim pres. Max Factor & Co., 1977—78; pres. Max Factor Internat., 1979—82; pres., CEO Cordura Publs., Inc., San Diego, 1984—86, mgmt. cons., 1987—88; pres., CEO Tago, Inc., Burlingame, Calif., 1989—92; ret., 1992. Ind. cons., pvt. investor, 1993—96. Comms. officer USAF, 1952—53, capt. Res. USAF. Roman Catholic. Home: 10 Ronsard Newport Coast CA 92657-0113

EVANOVICH, JANET, writer; Attended, Douglass Coll. Author: (Stephanie Plum series) One For the Money, 1994, Two For the Dough, 1996, Three to Get Deadly, 1997, Four to Score, 1998, High Five, 1999, Hot Six, 2000, Seven Up, 2001, Hard Eight, 2002, Visions of Sugar Plums, 2002, To the Nines, 2003, Ten Big Ones, 2004 (Publishers Weekly Bestseller list, 2004), Eleven on Top, 2005 (No. 1 NY Times Bestseller hardcover fiction list, 2005, No. 1 Publishers Weekly Bestseller hardcover fiction list, 2005, Quills award for mystery/suspense/thriller, 2005), Lean Mean Thirteen, 2007, (Romance novels written under pseudonym Steffie Hall) Hero at Large, 1987, Foul Play, 1989, (Romance novels) The Grand Finale, 1988, Thanksgiving, 1988, Manhunt, 1988, Ivan Takes a Wife, 1989, Back to the Bedroom, 1989, 2005, Wife for Hire, 1990, Smitten, 1990, The Rocky Road to Romance, 1991, Naughty Neighbor, 1992, Plum Lovin', 2007, Metro Girl, 2004, (novels) Twelve Sharp, 2006 (The Quill award for Mystery/Suspense/Thriller, 2006); co-author (with Charlotte Hughes): (Full series) Full House, 2002, Full Speed, 2003, Full Tilt, 2003, Full Blast, 2004, Full Bloom, 2005. Mem.: Mystery Writers Am. (pres. 2006). Address: c/o Robert Gottleib Trident Media Group 36th Fl 41 Madison Ave New York NY 10010*

EVANS, ALFRED LEE, JR., advertising executive; b. Kansas City, Mo., Sept. 16, 1940; s. Alfred Lee and Laura Edith (Redman) E.; m. Jean Perpetua Corcoran, Aug. 29, 1970 (div. Mar. 1994); children: Amanda Corcoran, Cynthia Redman, Cassandra Lee, Nicholas Carpenter; m. Georgiana Coyle Mundy, July 9, 1994. BA, Princeton U., 1962. Account exec. Ted Bates & Co., NYC, 1963-66, Papert Koenig Lois Inc., NYC, 1967-68; v.p. account supr. Lois Holland Callaway, Inc., NYC, 1969-74, v.p. mgmt. supr., 1975, sr. v.p. mgmt. supr., 1976, Norman Craig & Kummel, NYC, 1977-80, Laurence, Charles, Free & Lawson, NYC, 1981-84, 85—, exec. v.p., mem. ops., 1988-95, mem. bd. dirs.; sr. v.p. Wolf Group, NYC, 1995-2000, Bates USA, NYC, 2000—03; sr. ptnr., dir. in charge J. Walter Thompson, NYC, 2004—. Recipient summer travel award Carnegie Found., 1960; scholar Princeton U., 1958-62. Episcopalian. Home: 1530 Palisade Ave Fort Lee NJ 07024-5470 Office: J Walter Thompson 466 Lexington Ave New York NY 10017 Home Phone: 201-585-7006; Office Phone: 212-210-7186. E-mail: al.evans@jwt.com.

EVANS, ALLAN JOSEPH, research scientist, educator; s. Larry Eugene and Nancy Cooper Evans. BSEE, Northwestern U., Evanston, Ill., 1999, PhD, 2007. Engr. MCIWorldcom, Tulsa, 1999, United Parcel Svc., Hodgkins, Ill., 2000—01; rschr. Ctr. for Quantum Devices, Evanston, 2001—. Presenter in field. Contbr. articles to profl. jours. V.p. housing affairs Northwestern U. Alumni of Lambda Chi Alpha, Evanston, 2002—07; pres. Northshore Pl. Condominium Assn., Chgo., 2005—07; capital campaign coord. Northwestern U. Alumni of Lambda Chi Alpha, Evanston, 2005—07. Nominee Cyril F. Duke Flad Outstanding Undergraduate award, Lambda Chi Alpha Ednl. Found., 2002; recipient Motorola Undergraduate Rsch. award, Motorola Corp., 2002, Impact Leadership award, Lambda Chi Alpha Ednl. Found., 2002; Ednl. scholar, Internat. Soc. for Optical Engring., 2003—04, Walter P. Murphy Grad. fellow, Northwestern U., 2004. Mem.: IEEE, Internat. Soc. for Optical Engring. (Optoelectronics Best Paper award 2005), Lambda Chi Alpha (bd. dirs., risk mgr., ho. mgr., standards chmn. 2001—03). Episcopalian. Achievements include development of high power continuous-wave mid-infrared quantum cascade lasers operating above room temperaure, widely tunable continuous-wave quantum cascade lasers, portable quantum cascade laser module; research in reliability testing of quantum cascade lasers. Home Phone: 847-877-6329.

EVANS, ANTHONY GLYN, materials scientist, educator; b. Porthcawl, Eng., Dec. 4, 1942; came to US, 1967; BSc with first class honors in Metallurgy, U. London Imperial Coll., 1964, PhD in Metallurgy, 1967. Ceramics project leader Atomic Energy Rsch. Establishment, Harwell, 1968—72, Nat. Bur. Standards, Washington, 1972—74; grp. leader Rockwell Internat. Sci. Ctr., Thousand Oaks, Calif., 1974-78; prof. dept. materials sci. and mineral engring. U. Calif., Berkeley, 1978-85, Alcoa prof. and chair materials dept. Santa Barbara, 1985-91, Alcoa prof. and co-dir. high performance composites ctr., 1985—97, prof. depts. mech. engring. and materials; Gordon McKay prof. materials engring. divsn. applied scis. Harvard U., Cambridge, Mass., 1994-98; dir. Materials Inst. Princeton U., NJ, 1998, Gordon Wu prof. mech. and aerospace engring., 1998. Cons. and mem. Materials Rsch. Coun., 1974—; mem. Nat. Materials Adv. Bd., 1976—. Contbr. articles to profl. jours. Recipient Griffith medal and prize, Inst. Materials, 1994, Peterson award, Soc. Exptl. Mechanics, 1998, Turnbull award, Materials Rsch. Soc., 2000. Fellow: Am. Acad. Arts & Scis., Internat. Congress on Fracture (hon.); mem.: NAE, Am. Ceramic Soc. (life; v.p. 1984—88, Ross Coffin Purdy prize 1974, John Jeppson medal 1988, Hobart N. Kraner award 1986, Robert Sosman award 1980, Richard M. Fulrath 1979). Achievements include contributions to knowledge of mechanical properties of brittle materials, particularly fracture of ceramics under conditions of impact, thermal and mechanical stress; failure prediction based on non-destructive evaluation; properties of thin films and multilayer materials. Office: Dept Materials Engr II Rm 2361A U Calif Santa Barbara Santa Barbara CA 93106-5070 E-mail: agevans@engineering.ucsb.edu.

EVANS, BARTON, JR., retired analytical instrument company executive; b. Washington, Dec. 11, 1947; s. Barton and Viola (Gompf) E.; m. Harriet Andrea Neves, Nov. 20, 1983. BA in Econs., Claremont McKenna Coll., Calif., 1970; BS in Engring., MS in Engring., Stanford U., Calif., 1972. Sr. instr. Ctrl. Tex. Coll., 1974—75; sr. engr. Lockheed Missiles and Space Co., Sunnyvale, Calif., 1976-77, Dionex Corp., Sunnyvale, 1977-79, engring. mgr., 1979-81, dir. engring., 1981-83, v.p. engring., 1983-84, v.p. ops., 1984-93, sr. v.p. ops., 1993-2001, exec. v.p. and COO, 2001—05; pvt. practice, 2005—. Trustee Claremont McKenna Coll., 2005—, chair Info. Tech. adv. bd., 2005—. 1st lt. US Army, 1972—75, col. USAR, 1976—2002, ret. Mem.: ASME, Res. Officers Assn., Assn. U.S. Army, Psychol. Ops. Assn., Civil Affairs Assn. (dir.). Progressive. Achievements include co-inventor conductivity detector. Home Phone: 650-357-6971. Personal E-mail: barton.evans@comcast.net.

EVANS, BERNARD WILLIAM, geologist, educator; b. London, July 16, 1934; came to U.S., 1961, naturalized, 1977; s. Albert Edward and Marjorie (Jordan) E.; m. Sheila Campbell Nolan, Nov. 19, 1962. BSc, U. London, 1955; PhD, Oxford U., Eng., 1959. Asst. U. Glasgow, Scotland, 1958-59; departmental demonstrator U. Oxford, 1959-61; asst. research prof. U. Calif., Berkeley, 1961-65, asst. prof., 1965-66, assoc. prof., 1966-69; prof. geology U. Wash., Seattle, 1969—2001, chmn. dept. geol. scis., 1974-79; emeritus prof. U. Washington, 2001—. Contbr. articles to profl. jours. Recipient U.S. Sr. Scientist award Humboldt Found., Fed. Republic Germany, 1988-89; Fulbright travel award, France, 1995-96. Fellow Geol. Soc. Am., Mineral Soc. Am. (pres. 1993-94, award 1970), Geochem. Soc., Geol. Soc. London, Mineral. Soc. Gt. Britain. Home: 8001 Sand Point Way NE Apt C55 Seattle WA 98115-6399 Office: U Wash Dept Earth and Space Scis PO Box 351310 Seattle WA 98195-1310 Office Phone: 206-543-1163. Business E-Mail: bwevans@u.washington.edu.

EVANS, BETH, library and information scientist; married; 4 children. MLS, Queens Coll., CUNY, 1994; MA in English, Brown U., Providence. Assoc. prof., reference libr., elec. info. specialist Brooklyn Coll. Library, 1994—. Named one of the Movers & Shakers, Libr. Jour., 2007. Mem.: Metropolitan NY Library Coun., Library Assn. CUNY, Assn. Coll. Rsch. Libraries, Am. Library Assn. Office: Brooklyn College Library 2900 Bedford Ave Brooklyn NY 11210

EVANS, BETTY VAUGHN, minister; b. Campbell, Ala., Sept. 3, 1954; children: Robert, Rochelle, James. D in Ministry, Victory Bible Coll., 2003. Ordained evanglist Ch. God in Christ, 1985, ordained minister Ch. God in Christ, 1986, ordained pastor Whole Lifw Christian Ch./TX, 1995, cert. restorative therapist Faith Based Counselor Tng. Inst. Tex., 2000. Pastor Storehouse Ministry Fellowship, Inc., San Antonio, 1995—. Spkr. in field. Chmn. bus. adv. coun. Tex. chpt. Nat. Rep. Congl. Com., 2005—. Nominee Black Achievement award, San Antonio, Tex., 2003; named Pioneer Woman Pastor, San Antonio Express News, 2003. Office: Storehouse Ministry Fellowship Inc 14100 Nacogdoches Rd San Antonio TX 78247 Home Phone: 210-599-8136; Office Phone: 210-599-8136. E-mail: storehousemf.org.

EVANS, BOB (ROBERT EVANS), publishing executive; Founding editor Computer Reseller News; with CMP Media Inc., Manhasset, NY, 1983—, v.p., 1989—, v.p. product devel., 1993—, editor-in-chief Info. Week, 1996—2005, mng. dir. Info. Week; editl. dir. CMP Media Inc, 1999—, sr. v.p., web tech., 1999—. Office: CMP Media Inc 600 Community Dr Ste 1 Manhasset NY 11030-3875 E-mail: bevans@cmp.com.*

EVANS, BRUCE DWIGHT, lawyer; b. Mt. Hope, W.Va., May 27, 1934; s. M. Albert and Eleanor E. (Fowler) E.; m. Sallie Lee Hazen, Aug. 24, 1957 (div. Jan. 1974); children: Scott C., Leigh F., Randolph D.; m. Doris M. Stritzinger Webster, Sept. 2, 1978. AB, Princeton U., 1956; LL.B., Harvard U., 1959. Bar: N.Y. 1960, Pa. 1970. Assoc. Debevoise, Plimpton, Lyons & Gates, NYC, 1959-68; ptnr. Reed Smith Shaw & McClay, Pitts., 1969-96. Trustee Ellis Sch., Pitts., 1972-78. Mem. ABA, Pa. Bar Assn., Allegheny County Bar Assn., Rivers Club, Phi Beta Kappa Republican. Episcopalian. Office: One Oxford Centre Ste 4300 301 Grant St Pittsburgh PA 15219 Personal E-mail: bruce_evans@pobox.com.

EVANS, CAROL ANN, reading specialist; b. Meridian, Miss., Aug. 1, 1947; d. Charles and Anne Bishop Easterling; m. Robert David Evans, Aug. 23, 1969; children: Kelly Sinclair, David Robert. BS in Edn., Miss. State U., Starkville, 1969, MA in Edn., 1970. Cert. elem. tchr. Ariz., reading specialist Ariz. Tchr. Lowndes County Elem. Sch., 1969—71, Miss. Pub. Sch. Sys., 1973—74, Olive Tree Day Sch., 1974—75, Palo Alto Presch., 1975—80, U. Nev., Las Vegas, 1979—80, Clark County Pub. Schs., 1980—83, Dept. of Def. Sch., 1983—84, Saudi Arabia Internat. Sch., 1984—86, Village Meadows Elem., 1986—87, New River Elem. Sch., 1987—94, Desert Mountain Sch., 1994—. Coord. ann. fund drive Am. Kidney Found.; officer PTA, Gene Ward Elem. Sch., Las Vegas. Recipient award, Phoenix Ednl. Trust, 1997, Mid. Sch. Educator of Yr. award, Desert Mountain Mid. Sch., 1999, Pride award, Deer Valley Unified Sch. Dist., 2006; grantee, Wells Fargo Bank, 1997, 1999; Lit. Classroom grant, Phoenix West Feading Coun., 1999. Mem.: Ariz. Assn. Curriculum Devel., Ctrl. Ariz. Mid. Level Assn., Phoenis West Reading Assn., Nat. Coun. Tchrs. of English, Internat. Reading Assn., Ariz. Desert Land Trust Coun. Republican. Methodist. Avocations: travel, reading, child advocacy projects, art council. Home: 11002 E Lovingtree Ln Scottsdale AZ 85262 Office: Desert Mountain Sch 35959 N 7th Ave Desert Hills AZ 85086 Office Phone: 623-445-3549. E-mail: Carol.Evans@dm.dvusd.org.

EVANS, CAROL ROCKWELL, nursing administrator; b. New Orleans, Jan. 8, 1953; d. Daniel Raymond Sr. and Helen (Fischer) Rockwell; divorced; children: Nikki Elizabeth, Mimi Michelle. ADN, La. State Med. Ctr., 1990. RN, La.; cert. ACLS, BLS, cert. case mgr.; lic. life and health ins. agent. Life and health ins. agt. La. Ins. Agts. Assn., New Orleans, 1975-95; dir. case mgmt. and utilization rev. Associated Med. Rev. Svcs., Metairie, La., 1986-95; charge nurse med-surg. telemetry unit Elmwood Med. Ctr., Jefferson, La., 1990—; RN specialist III ICU dept. St. Charles Gen. Hosp., New Orleans, 1993—; dir. med. mgmt. Nat. Health Resources, Inc., Metairie, La., 1995-99, Med. Care Solutions, Inc., 1999—2002; owner Case Mgmt. Svcs., Metairie, 2002—. Nurse and managed care liaison St. Charles Splty. Hosp., 2005; dir. nursing Canon Hospice, 2005; dir. program and resource devel. Vital Healthcare Group, 2007; nurse liaison bus. devel. Gulf States Healthcare. Lobby La. Health Care, Baton Rouge, 1991. Mem. ANA, NAFE, Case Mgmt. Soc. Am., Individual Case Mgmt. Assn., Assn. Respiratory Care, New Orleans Continuity Care, La. Managed Healthcare Assn. (Great Nurses award 1997). Republican. Roman Catholic. Avocations: sports, dance, swimming, travel, theater. Home: 6316 York St Metairie LA 70003-3557 Office: Case Mgmt Svcs PO Box 74137 Metairie LA 70033-4132 Office Phone: 504-818-2723. Personal E-mail: crocky108@aol.com.

EVANS, C(AROLINE) SUE, education educator; b. Bethel, Ohio, July 14, 1948; d. Raymond George Brown and Relva Olive Spears-Brown; m. Gary W. Evans, June 18, 1966; children: Rhonda Fannin, Gary Lee, Daniel Ray, Rebekah Drury, David Jonathan Assoc. of Applied Bus., So. State C.C., Hillsboro, Ohio, 1989; BS, Wilberforce U., 1999. Leader, lectr. Weight Watchers, Inc., West Union, Ohio, 1974—80; lab. asst. So. State C.C., Sardinia, Ohio, 1989—92, 1993—99, dir., instr., 1999—; project sec. Ford Motor Co./Morrison Knuedson, Contractor, Batavia, Ohio, 1992—93; adminstrv. asst. So. Ohio Ctr. of Excellence, Ohio Coll. Access Network, 2005—. Mem. adv. bd. Your Place, Sardinia, Family/Cons. Sci., Seaman, Ohio. Author: Broken Wings Fly, 2003, Your Place for the Adult Learner Workbook, 2007. Bd. dirs. United Ch. of God, Portsmouth, Ohio, Adam Brown Counties Econ. Opportunities Inc.; leader Take Off Pounds Sensibly. Office: So State CC 12681 US 62 Sardinia OH 45171 Home Phone: 937-386-2430; Office Phone: 937-695-0307 3540. Business E-Mail: sevans@sscc.edu.

EVANS, CHARLES H., federal judge; b. 1922; BA, U. Ill., 1947, JD, 1948. Asst. atty. gen. State of Ill., 1949—56, 1957—62; pvt. law practice, 1962—77; magistrate judge Ill. Ctrl., Springfield, 1977—. With USAAF, 1942—45. Office: 110 US Courthouse 600 E Monroe St Springfield IL 62701-1626

EVANS, CHARLES L., bank executive; b. Jan. 15, 1958; married; 2 children. BA in Econ., U. Va., 1980; MA in Econ., Carnegie-Mellon U., 1985, PhD. in Econ., 1989. Asst. prof. Dept. Econ., U. SC, 1988—91; economist Fed. Res. Bank Chgo., 1991—92, sr. economist, 1992—93, sr. rsch. economist, rsch. officer, 1993—94, asst. v.p., sr. economist, 1994—98, v.p. & econ. adv., 1998—2003, sr. v.p. & dir. rsch., 2003—07, dir. rsch., sr. v.p., 2007, pres., CEO, 2007—. Adj. prof. Grad. Sch. of Bus., U. of Chgo., 1995; visiting prof. Dept. of Econ., W. of Mich., 1999; assoc. economist Fed. Open Market Com., 2003, 05, 07. Contbr. articles to profl. jours. Mem.: Econ. Club of Chgo., exec. bd., Met. Chgo. Info Ctr., pres. coun., Chgo. Coun. on Fgn. Rels. Office: Fed Res Bank of Chgo Rsch Dept 230 S LaSalle St Chicago IL 60604 Office Phone: 312-322-5800. E-mail: charles.l.evans@chi.frb.org.*

EVANS, CHARLES WAYNE, II, biologist, researcher; b. Athens, Ohio, Aug. 9, 1929; s. Charles Wayne Evans and Florence Louise (Sheets) Evans Claypool; m. Jo F. Burt, 1948 (div. 1959); children: Charles Wayne III, James Friedrich(dec.) , John Burns, Elizabeth Burt; m. Patricia Anne Baker, 1971; children: Debbie Jo(dec.) , Caralyn Michele. Student, Tex. A&M U., 1947-51, BA, 1957, postgrad., 1963-65, U. Houston, 1969-70. Seismologist Universal Seismic Expt., Beaumont, Tex., 1958-65; marine biologist CRI/VIERS, St. Thomas, U.S. Virgin Islands, 1965-71; geologist Dr. C. B. Claypool, Beaumont, Tex., 1971-76; research biologist Panthera-Marine-Internat., Ltd., Belize, C.A., Beaumont; pres., CEO Panthera-Marine-Internat., Ltd., Belize, 1976—; rsch. biologist Synetics Inc., Las Vegas, 1979-82; bd. dirs., treas. Las Vegas, 1979; rsch. biologist SAC Research Ctr., 1982-88; pres. Jordhammer, Inc., Las Vegas, 1980—; bd. dirs. Ant Fire, Inc., Beaumont, 1985-89, Caribbean World enterprises, Ltd., New Orleans & Belize, 1987—; pres., dir. rsch. Invicta Corp., 1988. Cons. I.Q. Tech., Houston, 1994—96, Eradicator Corp., Houston, 1994—98, Aire-Mate Inc., Westfield, Ind., Terminator Techs., Inc., San Jose, Calif., 1999. Co-inventor Jordhammer, 1982, Earthfire Injection System, 1988. Sus. mem. Rep. Nat. Com., Washington, 1982; charter mem. Ellis Island Found., N.Y.C., 1983—; founder, pres. Caribbean Inst. Natural Sci., St. Thomas, 1967-70; with N.G., 1945-47. SAC Research Ctr. grantee, 1983, Dr. C.B. Clayppol grantee, 1963, 78. Mem. AAAS, Smithsonian Asocs., Am. Mus. Natural History (assoc.), N.Y. Acad. Sci., Internat. Oceanographic Found., Entomol. Soc. Am., World Wildlife Fund, Aggie Club, Century Club, Lions. Avocations: music, chess, big game fishing. Office: 5380 Grain Mill Rd Pahrump NV 89061 E-mail: Solenopsis@aol.com.

EVANS, CLEVELAND KENT, psychology professor; b. Charlottesville, Va., July 10, 1951; s. Kent Evans, Jr. and Leona Frances Lively. BA, Duke U., Durham, NC, 1973; PhD, U. Mich., Ann Arbor, 1985. Assoc. prof. psychology Bellevue U., Nebr., 1986—. Author: (non-fiction book) The Great Big Book of Baby Names, Unusual & Most Popular Baby Names; author: (non-fiction book) the ultimate baby name book. Commr. 213th Gen. Assembly Presbyn. Ch. USA, Louisville, 2001—01; bd. mem. Presbyterians Lesbian/Gay Concerns, 1988—92; elder Lowe Ave. Presbyn. Ch., Omaha, 1988—2007, Northside Presbyn. Ch., Ann Arbor, Mich., 1975—86. Mem.: APA, Nebr. Psychol. Assn., Nebr. Psychol. Soc. (pres. 2001—02), Assn. for Psychol. Sci., Am. Name Soc. (pres. 2005—07), Phi Beta Kappa. Presbyterian. Achievements include research in given names and fashions in the USA. Avocations: reading, swimming. Home: 3810 S 13th St #22 Omaha NE 68107 Office: Bellevue U 1000 Galvin Rd S Bellevue NE 68005-3098 Home Phone: 402-733-1360; Office Phone: 402-557-7524. Business E-Mail: cleveland.evans@bellevue.edu.

EVANS, DAMON, university athletics director; m. Kerri Budd; 2 children. BS in Fin., Univ. Ga., 1992, MBA in Sports Mgmt., 1994. Asst., dept. compliance and acad. affairs Southeastern Conf. (SEC), 1993—94; dir. compliance ops. Univ. Mo., 1994—95; asst. commr. compliance SEC, 1997—98; assoc. athletics dir. University Georgia, 1998—2000, sr. assoc. athletics dir., 2000—05, athletics dir., 2005—. Spkr. in field. Achievements include being first black athletic dir. in Univ. Ga. History. Office: Dept Athletics UGA Athens GA 30609*

EVANS, DANIEL A., pediatrician, educator; s. Norman and Janice Evans; m. Sally Sager, Jan. 19, 1991; children: Anna, Joseph, Abigail. BA, Wright State U., Dayton, Ohio, 1982—86, MD, 1986—90. Lic. pediatrics Am. Bd. Pediat., 1993, pediatric pulmonology Am. Bd. Pediat., 1996. Asst. prof. pediat. dept. pediat. Pa. State Coll. Medicine, Hershey, 1996—98; asst. clin. prof. dept. pediat. & emergency medicine Wright State U. Sch. Medicine, 1998—. Pediatric residency Children's Med. Ctr., Dayton, Ohio, 1990—93; pediatric pulmonary medicine fellowship Children's Hosp. Med. Ctr., Cincinnati, Ohio, 1993—96. Contbr. chapters to books, articles to profl. jours. Grantee Fellowship Tng. grant, Am. Lung Assn., 1995—96. Mem.: AMA. Home Phone: 937-431-8545.

EVANS, DANIEL E., manufacturing executive, restaurant chain company executive; b. Gallipolis, Ohio, Aug. 24, 1936; With Bob Evans Farms Inc., Columbus, Ohio, 1957—; chmn. bd., sec., CEO, dir., 1971—. Office: Bob Evans Farms Inc 3776 S High St Columbus OH 43207-4000

EVANS, DAVID ALBERT, chemistry professor; b. Washington, Jan. 11, 1941; s. Albert Edward and Iris (Hill) Evans Yohe; m. Selena Anne Welliver, Dec. 27, 1962; 1 child, Bethan Hill AB in Chemistry, Oberlin Coll., Ohio, 1963; PhD in Chemistry, Calif. Inst. Tech., Pasadena, 1967; MA (hon.), Harvard U., Cambridge, 1983. Asst. prof. chemistry UCLA, 1967-72, assoc. prof. chemistry, 1972-73, prof. chemistry, 1974, Calif. Inst. Tech., Pasadena, 1974-83, Harvard U., Cambridge, 1983—90, Abbott and James Lawrence prof. chemistry, 1990—, chmn., dept. chemistry and chem. biology, 1995—98. Mem. com. on chem. scis. NRC; cons. Upjohn Co., 1972-74, Eli Lily Co., 1974-89, Merck Rsch. Lab. 1989-, Oxford Asymmetry Ltd., Oxon, Eng., 1994-2001, Bristol-Myers Squibb Pharma Co., 1994-2002, Amgen, 2002-; lectr. in field Contbr. several articles of profl. jours.; hon. editor Tetrahedron and Tetrahedron Letters, 1981—; mem. adv. bd. Jour. Organic Chemistry, 1974-78; hon. editl. adv. bd., Tetrahedron and Tetrahedron Letters, 1981-; mem. editorial adv. bd. Jour. Am. Chem. Soc., 1983—88, Topics in Stereoschemistry, 1989-, Chemical Reviews, 1993-96, , Organic Letters, 1999-, Accounts Chem. Rsch., 2003-; mem. editl. bd., Current Opinion in Bio-organic Chemistry, London, UK, 1996-; mem. adv. bd., Office of Chemistry and Chem. Technology, NRC, 1981-84; mem. com. on chem. sciences, NRC, 1981-85 Recipient Camille and Henry Dreyfus Tchr.-Scholar award Dreyfus Found., 1971-76; Disting. Teaching award UCLA Alumni Assn., 1973, Allen R. Day award, Phila. Organic Chemists Club, 1984, C.S. Hamilton award, Univ. Nebr., 1992, Mack award, Ohio State Univ., 1992, Pfizer Rsch. award for Synthetic Organic Chemistry, Pfizer, Inc., 1992, Yamada prize, Univ. Tokyo, Japan, 1997, Tetrahedron award, 1998, Prelog Medal, ETH, Zürich Switzerland, 1999, Calif. Inst. Tech. Disting. Alumni award, 2002, Nagoya medal, Nagoya Univ., Japan, 2003, Karl Ziegler prize, Max Planck, Muelheim, Germany, 2003, Ryoji Noyori prize, Soc. Synthetic Organic Chemistry, Japan, 2006, Thomson Scientific Laureate in Chemistry, Thomson Scientific, 2006, Glenn T. Seaborg medal, UCLA, 2006; Alfred P. Sloan Found. fellow, 1972-74. Mem. Am. Chem. Soc. (award for creative work in synthetic organic chemistry 1982, Arthur C. Cope Award, 2000, Remsen award, Md. sect., 1996, Willard Gibbs medal, Chgo. Sect., 2005, Herbert C. Brown award for Creative Rsch. in Synthetic Methods, 2007), NAS (award 1984), Royal Soc. Chem. (Robert Robinson award, 1998); fellow Am. Acad. Arts and Sciences. Home: 39 Pine Hill Ln Concord MA 01742-4414 Office: Harvard U Dept of Chemistry & Chemical Biology 12 Oxford St Cambridge MA 02138-2902 Office Phone: 617-495-2949. Office Fax: 617-495-1460. Business E-Mail: evans@chemistry.harvard.edu.*

EVANS, DAVID ALLAN, language educator; b. Sioux City, Iowa, Apr. 11, 1940; s. Arthur Clarence and Ruth (Lyle) Evans; m. Janice Kay Johnson, July 4, 1958; children: Shelly Evans Moreau, David Allan Jr., Karlin. BA, Morningside Coll., 1962; MA, U. Iowa, 1964; MFA, U. Ark., 1973. Asst. U. Iowa, Iowa City, 1965, U. Ark., Fayetteville, 1971-72; asst. prof. English, Adams State Coll., Alamosa, Colo., 1966-68, S.D. State U., Brookings, 1968-78, prof., 1978—, writer-in-residence, 1997—; poet laureate SD, 2002. Faculty exch. prof. Yunnan Normal U., Kunming, China, 1988—89; faculty leader Seminar Abroad S.D. State U., Yunnan Province, China, 2001, Phi Kappa Phi lectr., 03; poet laureate, SD, 2002—. Author: (poetry chapbook) Among Athletes, 1970, (poetry) Train Windows, 1976, Real and False Alarms, 1980, Hanging Out with the Crows, 1990, Decent Dangers, 2001, Bull Rider's Advice: New and Selected Poems, 2004, (essays) Remembering the Soos, 1982; (with Jan Evans) Double Happiness: Two Lives in China, 1995; co-editor: From Language to Idea, 1970, Statement and Craft, 1972, The Sport of Poetry/The Poetry of Sport, 1979; editor: New Voices in American Poetry, 1973; gen. editor, writer What the Tall Grass Says, 1982. Writing mentor S.D. State Prison, Sioux Falls, 2001—; mem. steering com. Brookings Arts Coun., 2001—; active participant artist in schs. SD Arts Coun. Named S.D. Centennial Poet, 1989, Alumni Educator of Yr., Morningside Coll., Sioux City, Iowa, 2003, S.D. Author of Yr., S.D. Coun. Tchrs. English, 2005; recipient Exemplary Tchr. award Guangdong U. Fgn. Studies, 1999, Spl. Recognition, Sports Hall of Fame Banquet, Augustana Coll., 2004, Mayor's award for the arts Excellence in Lit. Arts in Sioux Falls, 2007; athletic scholarship Augustana Coll., 1958-60, Breadloaf scholar, Vt., 1973, Fulbright scholar, China, 1992-93, 98-99; writing grantee Nat. Endowment for Arts, 1975, 80, grantee S.D. Arts Coun., 1981, artist grantee Bush Found., 1990. Mem. Soc. Midland Authors, Acad. Am. Poets, Sports Lit. Soc., Poetry Soc. Am. (S.D. Poet of Yr. 2004), S.D. Coun. Tchrs. English (S.D. Author of Yr. 2005, Mayor's award 2007), Fulbright Assn., Sigma Tau Delta (hon. mem. Alpha Chi chpt.). Democrat. Avocations: racquetball and other exercise, reading, travel. Office: SD State U Scobey Hall 008 Box 504 Brookings SD 57007 Home: 2812 S Williams Ave Sioux Falls SD 57105 Business E-Mail: evanspl@sio.midco.net.

EVANS, DAVID C., lawyer; b. Nov. 10, 1945; BS in Bus. Mktg., Ind. U., 1968, JD, 1971. Bar: Ind. 1971, DC 1972, Supreme Ct. Ind. 1971, US Dist. Ct. DC 1972, US Ct. Appeals DC Cir. 1972. Mem. Reed Smith Shaw & McClay (now Reed Smith LLP), Washington, 1971—, dir. practice devel., 1991-95, former mng. ptnr., Washington office, former practice group leader Govt. Services Group, now ptnr., practice group leader, Real Estate Group, 2005—, also treas. polit. action com. Sec. bd. trustees Nat. Bldg. Mus., Washington. Recipient Outstanding Young Alumnus Award, Ind. U. Mem.: Am. Soc. Assn. Executives (mem. legal sect. coun.), ABA, Fed. City Coun., Nat. Eagle Scout Assn., Econ. Club Wash., Chevy Chase Club, Annapolis Yacht Club, Ocean Reef Club. Office: Reed Smith LLP 1301 K St NW Ste 1100 - East Tower Washington DC 20005 Office Phone: 202-414-9221. Office Fax: 202-414-9299. Business E-Mail: devans@reedsmith.com.

EVANS, DAVID HOWELL See THE EDGE

EVANS, DAVID LYNN, management consultant; b. Red Oak, Iowa, June 26, 1941; s. John Louis and Margaret Alice (Young) E.; m. Mary Susan Ricke, Aug. 4, 1963; children: John Louis, Mary Lynn, Sarah Leigh, Michael Ricke. BS, Iowa State U., 1964; MBA, U. Pa., 1966. Various positions Deere & Co., Moline, Ill., 1964-92; exec. v.p. Rocky Mountain Internet Inc., Denver, 1997-98; CFO Netbeam. Inc., Breckenridge, Colo., 1999-2000; CEO Evanwood Corp., Evergreen, Colo., 1992—, Rose Creek Ridge LLC, Evergreen, Colo., 2003—. Bd. dirs. John Deere Receivables, Inc., 1996—; bd. dirs., chmn. audit com. Pearl Mut. Funds, 1977—; chmn. audit com. Data Transmission Network Corp., 1986-95; mng. dir. Evans Farms, 1972—; dir. World Federalists Assn., 1980-90, v.p. midwest region 1977-82; dir. Campaign for UN Reform, 1979-82, 1980-81, treas, 1982-88; trustee John Deere Dealer Group Ins. Trust, 1981-85; chmn. fin. rels. com. Am Fin. Svcs. Assn., 1991-92; chmn. Nat. Assn. Corp. Dirs., 1991—; cons. corp. fin. N.Am., India and China. Elder Presbyn. Ch.; dir. Colo. Foothills World Affairs Coun., 2007—. Mem.: Iowa Mfrs. Assn. (chmn. econ. edn. com. 1979—81), Inst. Internat. Edn. (mem. adv. bd. Rocky Mtn. region 2003—), Denver World Affairs Coun. (chair 2004—), Denver Coun. Fgn. Rels., UN Assn., Am. Econ. Assn., Quad Cities World Affairs Coun. (pres. 1984, 1992). Republican. Home and Office: Evanwood Corp 32500 El Diente Ct Evergreen CO 80439-9773

EVANS, DENNIS HYDE, chemist, educator; b. Grinnell, Iowa, Mar. 28, 1939; s. Leonard Hyde and Clara Ethel (Parmley) E.; m. Ruth Elizabeth Turnbull, June 28, 1958 (div. July 1986); children: Susan Katherine, John Hyde, Andrew Turnbull; m. Mary Jean Wirth, Aug.2, 1986. BS, Ottawa U., 1960; AM, Harvard U., 1961, PhD, 1964. Instr. chemistry Harvard U., Cambridge, 1964-66; asst. prof. chemistry U. Wis., Madison, 1966-70, asso. prof., 1970-75, prof., 1975-84, Meloche-Bascom prof. chemistry, 1984-86, chmn. dept., 1977-80, assoc. dean Coll. of Letters and Sci., 1983-86; prof. chemistry U. Del., Newark, 1986—2004, U. Ariz., Tucson, 2004—. Contbr. articles to profl. jours. Danforth fellow, 1960-64, NIH fellow, 1961-64; recipient C.N. Reilley award Soc. for Electroanalytical Chemistry, 1993. Fellow Electrochem. Soc. (M.M. Baizer award Organic and Biol. Electrochemistry Divsn. 2004); mem. Am. Chem. Soc., Internat. Soc. Electrochemistry, Soc. for Electroanalytical Chemistry (pres. 1993-95). Baptist. E-mail: dhevans@email.arizona.edu.

EVANS, DICK, artist; b. Roswell, N.Mex., July 10, 1941; s. Harvey Lee and Byrd Seymour Evans; m. Susan Elizabeth Stamm, Aug. 19, 1975; children: Stephanie Karen, Katherine Suzanne Schwarz. MFA, U. Utah, 1966. Instr. art Tex. Tech U., Lubbock, 1966—70; asst. prof. art U. Tenn., Knoxville, 1971—72, U. N.Mex, Albuquerque, 1972—75; prof. art U. Wis.-Milw., 1975—87, assoc. dean, sch. of fine arts, 1981—83. One-man shows include Joyce Robins Gallery, Santa Fe, 1996—2006, Shadid Fine Art, 2003—06, Tory Folliard Gallery, 1993, 1995, 2006, Elaine Horwitch Galleries, 1990, Represented in permanent collections Smithsonian Inst., Milw. Art Mus., Mint Mus., Cornell U., Albuquerque Art Mus., Ariz. State U., U. N. Mex., reviewed in, Art News, 2002, "The" mag., 2003, Southwest Art, 2003, 2004, The Santa Fean, 2004, Art & Antiques, 2005. Avocation: fly fishing. Home: 47 Coyote Mountain Rd Santa Fe NM 87505-8179 Personal E-mail: dickevans@grappawireless.com.

EVANS, DONALD LOUIS, think-tank executive, former secretary of commerce; b. Houston, July 27, 1946; m. Susan Marinis Evans; three children: Lisa Moon, Jennifer, Donald L. BS in Mech. Engring., U. Tex. Austin, 1969, MBA, 1973; LHD (hon.), U. SC, 2001. Mgmt. to chmn. bd. dirs. Tom Brown, Inc., Denver, 1975-2001, CEO, 1985—2001; sec. U.S. Dept. Commerce, Washington, 2001—05; CEO Fin. Services Forum, 2005—. Bd. dirs. TMBR/Sharp Drilling, Inc., bd. regents U. Tex., 1995-2001, chmn. bd., 1997-2001. Bd. Trustees Meml. Hosp. & Med. Ctr., 1990-94; bd. dirs. The Gladney Fund, 1992-96, Scleroderma Rsch. Found., 1992-2000; campaign chair United Way of Midland, 1981, pres., 1989; bd. dirs. Scleroderma Rsch. Found; active United Way, campaign chair, 1981, pres., 1989; mem. Gov. Bush gubernatorial campaign, 1994, 98; chmn. Bush/Cheney Presdl. campaign, 2000. Named to U. Tex. Red McCombs Sch. Bus. Hall of Fame, 2002; recipient Disting. Alumnus award, U. Tex., 2002. Mem. Independent Petroleum Assn. Am., Young Presidents Orgn., Rocky Mtn. Oil & Gas Assn., Permian Basin Petroleum Assn., All-Am. Wildcatters, Nat. Petroleum Council. Republican. Methodist. Office: Financial Services Forum 601 Thirteenth St NW Ste 750 S Washington DC 20005*

EVANS, DOUGLAS HAYWARD, lawyer; b. Providence, July 21, 1950; s. Jerrold Merton and Gladys Jean (Snelgrove) E.; m. Sarah Edwards Cogan, May 28, 1983; children: Anne Morrill, Thomas Taylor Seelye, Elizabeth Hayward. AB, Franklin and Marshall Coll., 1972; JD, Cornell U., 1975. Bar: N.J. 1975, U.S. Dist. Ct. N.J. 1975, N.Y. 1976, U.S. Dist Ct. (so. dist.) N.Y. 1991. Assoc. Windels, Marx, Davies & Ives, NYC, 1975-85, Sullivan & Cromwell, NYC, 1985-90, spl. counsel, 1990—. Faculty NYU Inst. Fed. Taxation, NYC, 1984; counsel, treas., pres. St. David's Soc. State of N.Y., NYC, 1985—; bd. dirs. Friends of Washington Sq. Park, 1989—, chmn., 2004—; bd. dirs. Washington Sq. Assn., 1992—, chmn., 2004—; bd. dirs. 1st Presbyn. Ch. Nursery Sch., 1999—2003. Co-Author: Estate Accounting, 1980, Probate and Estate Administration, 1982, Administration of Estates, 1985, Settling An Estate, 1989; editor-in-chief, co-author: Probate and Administration of New York Estates, 1995, 2d edit., 2001; contbr. articles to profl. jours. Trustee Franklin and Marshall Coll., 1994—, Grace Ch. Sch., N.Y.C., 1997—, vice chmn., 2000-01, chmn., 2001—; mem. Ch. Club of N.Y., Salmagundi Club, N.Y.C. Fellow: Am. Coll. Trust and Estate Counsel; mem.: ABA, NYC Bar Assn. (mem. com. estate and gift taxation 2001—04, mem. com. non-profit orgs. 2004—), NY County Lawyers Assn. (mem. not-for-profit com.), NY State Bar Assn. (chmn. 1991—94, mem. com. CLE, mem. estate litig. and adminstrn. trusts and estates com.), NJ Bar Assn., Order of St. John (serving brother), Pi Gamma Mu, Phi Alpha Theta, Phi Delta Phi, Phi Beta Kappa. Episcopalian. Home: 43 Fifth Ave New York NY 10003-4368 Office: Sullivan & Cromwell 125 Broad St Fl 28 New York NY 10004-2489

EVANS, DOUGLAS MCCULLOUGH, surgeon, educator; b. Vandergrift, Pa., July 31, 1925; s. Archibald Davis and Helen Irene (McCullough) E.; m. Thelmajean Volkers, Aug. 1, 1959; children: Matthew Kirk, Daniel Scott. MD, Western Res. U., 1952; postgrad., U. Mich., 1956-58. Diplomate Am. Bd. Surgery. Resident in surgery Henry Ford Hosp., 1952-57, chief resident in surgery, 1957-58, mem. surgery staff, 1959-60, Akron (Ohio) Gen. Hosp., 1960-70; chmn. dept. surgery Akron Gen. Med. Ctr., 1971-90, rsch. cons.; prof. and chmn. surgery emeritus Northeastern Ohio U. Coll. Medicine. Served with AUS, 1943-46. Fellow: ACS; mem.: AAAS, AMA, N.Y. Acad. Scis., Ohio Med. Assn., Midwest Surg. Soc., Soc. Critical Care Medicine, Metastasis Rsch. Soc., Am. Assn. Cancer Rsch. Republican. Presbyterian. Office: 400 Wabash Ave Akron OH 44307-2433

EVANS, DWIGHT H., utilities executive; b. 1948; B in Civil Engring., Ga. Inst. Tech., Atlanta, M in Environ. Engring.; JD, Atlanta Law Sch. Design and environ. engr. Ga. Power Southern Co., 1970, various exec. positions in external affairs and public affairs, pres., CEO Miss. Power, 1995—2001, exec. v.p., 2001—. Bd. dirs. Cellnet Tech., Inc., 2006—; bd. dirs., chair environment and energy com. US C. of C. Bd. mem. US Inst. Environ. Conflict Resolution. Office: Southern Co 30 Ivan Allen Jr Blvd NW Atlanta GA 30308 Office Phone: 404-506-5000.*

EVANS, ELIZABETH ANN WEST, retired real estate agent; b. Xenia, Ohio, Mar. 28, 1933; d. Millard Stanley and Elizabeth Denver (Johns) West. BA, Ohio U., Athens, 1966, MA, 1968. Cert. GRI, 1993. Sec. various orgns., Ohio, 1952-61; tchr. Ohio U., Athens, 1966-67, Zanesville, 1968-72, Collier County Pub. Schs., Naples, Fla., 1972-77; sales Helen's Hang Ups, Naples, 1978-79; mgr. pvt. practice Wilmington, Ohio, 1979-87; adminstrv. asst. Powell Assocs., Cambridge, Mass., 1987-90; real estate agt. Bill Evans Realty, Inc., Naples, 1989-90, Howard Hanna Real Estate Svcs., Naples, 1991—93, Downing-Frye Realty, Inc., Naples, 1993—97, Downing-Frye Referral Network Realty Inc., Naples, 1997—2002; ret., 2002. Cape May resident rep. to Ohio Presbyn. Retirement Svcs., 2004—. Fellow: Phi Beta Kappa; mem.: DAR (chaplain 1988—90, chmn. Motion, Picture, Radio and TV 1992—94, asst. chaplain 1994—96, chaplain 2000—01, chmn. pub. rels. 2003—05), Kappa Alpha Theta (50-yr. mem.), Phi Kappa Phi, Phi Sigma Iota. Republican. Presbyterian. Home: 182 Cape May Dr Wilmington OH 45177

EVANS, ERIC ALAN, retired lawyer; b. Bend, Oreg., Mar. 17, 1949; s. Byron Fletcher and Margaret Jeanette Evans; m. Anne Van Vechten Myers Evans, July 26, 1975; children: Ryan, Katharine, Andrew. BA, U. of Pa., 1971; JD, Albany Law Sch. of Union U., NYC, 1976. Bar: N.Y. 1977, Fed. 1977. Banking & comml. lawyer Harter, Secrest & Emery LLP, Rochester, NY, 1976—78, mgmt. labor lawyer, 1978—, chair, labor dept., 1992—95, unit mgr., bus., 1998—2000, mng. ptnr., 2000—06; ret., 2006. Bd. mem. Kirkhaven, Rochester, NY, 1994—2000; nominating com. United Way of Greater Rochester, NY, 2002; bd. mem. Rochester Bus. Alliance, NY, 2003. Mem.: Mgmt. Attorneys Conf., Genesee Valley Club. E-mail: eevans@hselaw.com.

EVANS, ERSEL ARTHUR, engineering executive, consultant; b. Trenton, Nebr., July 17, 1922; s. Arthur E. and Mattie Agnes (Perkins) E.; m. Patricia A. Powers, Oct. 11, 1945 (div.); children: Debra Lynn (dec.), Paul Arthur. BA, Reed Coll., Portland, Oreg., 1947; PhD, Oreg. State U., 1950. Registered profl. engr., Calif. With Gen. Electric Co., 1951-67, supr. ceramics research and devel. Hanford, Wash., 1961-64; mgr. plutonium devel. Vallecitos Lab., Pleasanton, Calif., 1964-67; mgr. fuels and materials dept. Battelle Meml. Inst., Richland, Wash., 1967-70; with Westinghouse Electric Corp., 1970-87; v.p. Westinghouse Hanford Co., Richland, 1972-87, v.p., lab. tech. dir., 1985-87, ret., 1987, cons., 1987—. Mem. Tech. Assistance Adv. Group for Three Mile Island Recovery, 1981-86; mem. rev. Com. EBR-II, U. Chgo., 1989-91, 94—; mem. Japan Tech. Panel for Nuclear Power, NSF, 1989-90; mem. alt. applications of laser isotope separations tech. com. NRC, 1991-92, separations and tech. study, 1991-95, 96; del. Atlantic Coun. U.S.-Japan Conf. on Global Energy Issues, Maui, 1994, 96. Chmn. vis. com. U. Wash. With USNR, 1943—45. Recipient Westinghouse Order of Merit; DuPont fellow, 1950-51; recipient Mishima award Am. Nuclear Soc., 1995. Fellow Am. Nuclear Soc. (Spl. Merit award 1964, Spl. Performance award 1980 Presidential Design Achievement award 1991, Walker Cisler medal 2001), Am. Inst. Chemists, Am. Soc. Metals, Am. Ceramic Soc.; mem. NAE, Phi Kappa Phi, Sigma Xi. Achievements include patents in field. Home and Office: 4152 Providence Point Dr SE 106 Issaquah WA 98029 Home Phone: 425-373-6812; Office Phone: 425-369-2320. *Inspiration and guidance for my career have often been provided by Justice Oliver Wendell Holmes, "certainty generally is illusion, and repose is not the destiny of man." (Harvard Law Review 1897).*

EVANS, FAITH, singer; b. Fla., June 10, 1973; m. Christopher Wallace (The Notorious B.I.G.), 1995 (dec.); 1 child, Christopher Wallace Jr., 1996. Student, Fordham U. Singer: (albums) Faith, 1995, Keep The Faith, 1998 (Grammy award for best rap performance, 1998), Faithfully, 2001, The First Lady, 2005; singer: (background vocals) (Mary J. Blige) My Life, 1994, Ballads, 2001, (Hi-Five) Keep it Goin On, 1992, (Frankie) My Heart Belongs to You, 1997, (The Notorious B.I.G.) Life After Death, 1997, (Eric Benet) Day in the Life, 1999, (Jon B.) Pleasures U Like, 2001, (Kelly Price) Priceless, 2003, and others; singer: (background vocals, assoc. prodr.) (LSG) Levert, Sweat, Gill, 1997.

EVANS, FRANK BERNARD, retired historian; b. Aug. 21, 1927; BA, Pa. State Coll., 1949; MA, U. Pa., Phila., 1950; PhD, Pa. State U., Univ. Park, 1962. Cert. archivist Acad. Cert. Archivists. Faculty Pa. State U., Coll. Park, 1950—58; assoc. archivist Pa. Historical and Mus. Commn., Harrisburg, 1958—61, state archivist, 1961—63; dir. archival training Nat. Archives and Records Svcs., Washington, 1963—76, dir. archival projects, 1965—66, divsn. dir., 1966—68, deputy asst. archivist, 1968—72, asst. to US archivist, 1972—74, regional commr., 1974—76; program specialist, sr. officer UNESCO, Paris, 1976—84; deputy asst. archivist Nat. Archives and Records Adminstrn., 1984—95. Lectr. Am. U., Washington, 1963—66, adj. prof., 1966—76; mgmt. cons., Washington, 1963—97. Author: Pennsylvania Politics, 1872-77: A Study in Political Leadership, 1964; editor: The Administration of Archives: A Select Bibliographic Guide, 1970, Guide to the National Archives of the United States, 1974, Modern Archives and Manuscripts: A Select Bibliographic Guide, 1975, The History of Archives Administration: A Select Bibiliography, 1979; co-editor: Research in the Administration of Public Policy, 1975; co-author: Dictionary of Archival Terminology, 1984; contbr. articles to profl. jours. Advisory com. Bowie Sr. Ctr. Served with USN, 1945—48. Recipient Achievement award, US Archivists, 1985, 1987, 1995, Everett O. Alldredge award, Info. Resources Mgmt. Coun., 1990, Emmett J. Leahy award, Inst. Cert. Records Mgr., 1995. Fellow: Acad. Cert. Archivists (pres. 1994—95), Soc. Am. Archivists (pres. 1988—89); mem.: Nat. Assn. Ret. Fed. Employees, Internat. Coun. Archives (hon.), Knights of Columbus Coun., St. Vincent de Paul Soc. (pres.), Pi Gamma Mu, Phi Alpha Theta.

EVANS, FREDERICK JOHN, psychologist; b. Wollongong, Australia, Nov. 17, 1937; came to U.S., 1963; s. Frederick John and Phyllis Lurline (Wiffen) E.; m. Barbara Joan Marcelo, June 8, 1968 (div. 1990); children: Christopher Arthur, David Troy, Mark Fredrick (dec.), Diana Joy; m. Patricia E. Burns, Nov. 26, 1993; children: Mariefred Joy, Ellen Blessing. BA Honors Class I, U. Sydney, Australia, 1959, PhD, 1966. Tchg. fellow U. Sydney, 1959-63; rsch. psychologist Mass. Mental Health Center, 1963-64; from instr. psychology in psychiatry U. Pa. Sch. Medicine, Phila., 1965-66, to assoc. prof. psychiatry, 1972-81, assoc. prof. psychology, 1974-79; sr. rsch. psychologist Unit for Exptl. Psychiatry Inst. of Pa. Hosp., Phila., 1964-79; cons. psychologist pain mgmt. ctr. Med. Ctr. Princeton, NJ, 1998—; mem. cons. staff dept. psychiatry Princeton House, 1998—; cons. psychologist Pain Care Inst., Phila., 1999—, Arthritis Osteoporosis Ctr., West Reading, Pa. Vis. fellow psychology Yale U., 1970-71; trustee Inst. Exptl. Psychiatry, Boston, 1970-79; adj. prof. U. Medicine and Dentistry N.J.-Robert Wood Johnson Med. Sch., 1979-88; dir. rsch. divsn. Carrier Found., Belle Mead, N.J., 1979-88; v.p. Tex. Inst. Behavioral Medicine and Neurosci., 1989-96; pres. Pathfinders, Cons. in Human Behavior; dir. Pain Mgmt. Behavioral Medicine Svcs., Reading, Pa.; consulting psychologist The Elms Nursing Home, 1995—, The Back Rehab. Inst., Cranbury, N.J., Hamilton, N.J., 1997—; dir. psychol. svcs. Pain Mgmt. Ctr. The Med. Ctr. at Princeton, 1998—. Adv. editor: Internat. Jour. Clin. and Exptl. Hypnosis, 1968-69, assoc. editor, 1969—; assoc. editor: Am. Jour. Clin. Hypnosis, 1986-91, 95—; cons. editor: Jour. Abnormal Psychology, 1979-87, assoc. editor, 1989-91; co-editor: Functional Disorders of Memory, 1979, Springer Series in Behavior Modification and Behavioral Medicine, 1980-86; contbr. chpts. to textbooks, articles to profl. jours. Mem. Montgomery County Sch. Bd., 1983-89. Served to capt. Australian Army, 1961-63. Fulbright grantee, 1963-66 Fellow AAAS, APA (divsn. 30 program chmn. 1972, sec-treas. 1973-75, pres. 1978-79), Am. Soc. Clin. Hypnosis (chmn. liaison com. 1975-77, 88-89, cert. cons. 1993—), N.J. Psychol. Soc., Pa. Psychol. Soc., Soc. Clin. and Exptl. Hypnosis (co-chmn. sci. program 1970, 99, chmn. rsch. workshop, 1971, 76, 79, 80, 87-90, 97-2000, sec. 1973-86, co-chmn. publs. com. 1975-77, v.p. 1979-81, pres. 1981-83, chmn. budget com. 1987-89); mem. Am. Pain Soc. (founding dir. 1977-80), Internat. Soc. Hypnosis (sec.-treas. 1973-79, co-chmn. 7th Internat. Congress Hypnosis 1976, vice chmn. bd. dirs. organizing com. 10th Internat. Congress 1985, pres.-elect 1986-88, pres. 1987-91, immediate past pres. 1991-94, chair nominations and election com. 1991-94), Nat. Pain Found. (pres. 1989-92), Royal Soc. Medicine, Internat. Soc. Inner Mental Tng. (v.p. 1993-96). Home and Office: 102 Slack Ave Lawrenceville NJ 08648-4304 Office Phone: 609-637-0717. E-mail: aussiedr@aol.com.

EVANS, GERALD WILLIAM, engineering educator, consultant; b. New Albany, Ind., Sept. 29, 1950; s. Robley Warren and Ruth Ann Evans; m. Linda Marie Napierala, May 4, 1974; children: Matthew, Brian. BS in Math., Purdue Univ., West Lafayette, Ind., 1972; MS in Indsl. engring., Purdue Univ., 1974, PhD in Indsl. engring., 1979. Indsl. engr. Rock Island Arsenal, Ill., 1974—75; sr. rsch. engr. Gen. Motors Rsch. Labs, Warren, Mich., 1978—81; asst. prof. U. Louisville, Ky., 1981—87, assoc. prof., 1987—93, prof., 1993—; NSA ASEE faculty fellow Langley Rsch. Ctr., Hampton, Va., 1987; NASA ASEE faculty fellow Kennedy Space Ctr., Cape Canaval, Fla., 1995. Editor (with others): Applications of Fuzzy Set Methodologies Industrial Enggineering, 1989, Proceedings of the 1993 Winter Simulation Conference, 1993, Proceedings of the 1999 Winter Simulation Conference, 1999. Mem.: Inst. Ops. Rsch. and Mgmt. Scis. (Moving Spirit award 2005), Inst. Insdl. Engrs. (v.p. 1995—97, Divsn. award 1996).

EVANS, GERALDINE ANN, former academic administrator; b. Zumbrota, Minn., Feb. 24, 1939; d. Wallace William and Elda Ida (Tiedemann) Whipple; m. John Lyle Evans, June 21, 1963; children: John David, Paul William. AA, Rochester Community Coll., 1958; BS, U. Minn., 1960, MA, 1963, PhD, 1968. Cert. tchr., counselor, prin. and supt., Minn. Tchr. Hopkins (Minn.) Pub. Schs., 1960-63; counselor Anoka (Minn.) Pub. Schs., 1963-66; cons. in edn. Mpls., 1966-78; policy analyst Minn. Dept. Edn., St. Paul, 1978-79; dir. personnel Minn. Community Coll. System, St. Paul, 1979-82; pres. Rochester (Minn.) Community Coll., 1982-92; chancellor Minn. C.C. System, St. Paul, 1992-94; exec. dir. Ill. C.C. Bd., Springfield, 1994-96; chancellor San Jose (Calif.) Evergreen C.C. Dist., 1996—2004; ret., 2004. Mem. San Jose Workforce Investment Bd., 2000—; mem. legis. and adv. com. Calif. C.C. League, 1998-2002. Mem. Gov.'s Job Tng. Coun., St. Paul, 1983—94, chair, 1992—94; mem. Silicon Valley Pvt. Industry Coun., 1997—2000, Workforce Silicon Valley, 1998—2002; trustee Golden Gate U., 1997—; chair Rochester (Minn.) United Way, 1985—86; mem. campaign cabinet United Way of Silicon Valley, 2003—; moderator Mizpah United Ch. Christ, Hopkins, 1982; mem. complete count com. U.S. Census, Santa Clara County, 2000; vice chair, bd. dirs. Wayzata (Minn.) Sch. Bd., 1980—83; bd. dirs. Minn. Tech. Ctr., Rochester, 1991—92; bd. mem. Boy Scouts San Clara Coun., 2004—; sec.-treas. Coun. North Ctrl. Cmty. and Jr. Colls., 1990—92; mem. ACE Commn. on Edn. Credit and Credentials, 1992—96. Winner Rochester C. of C. Athena award, 1990, San Jose YWCA Exec. award, 1998; Inst. Ednl. Leadership fellow, Washington, 1978-79. Mem. Nat. League Nursing (bd. assoc. degree accreditation rev. 1990-93, exec. com. 1993-96), Am. Assn. Cmty. Colls. (workforce commn. 2000-03), Am. Assn. Cmty. Jr. Colls. (bd. dirs. 1984-87), North Ctrl. Assn. Cmty. and Jr. Colls. (evaluator 1985-96), Silicon Valley C. of C. (bd. dirs. 2001-04), La Raza Roundtable, Rotary. Congregationalist. Avocations: travel, gardening.

EVANS, GREG, cartoonist; b. LA, 1947; m. Betty Evans; 3 children. Syndicated by King Features, 1987—96, United Feature Syndicate, 1996—. Author & artist (comic strips) Luann, 1985—. Mem.: Nat. Cartoonists Soc. (1st v.p. 2007—09, chmn. San Diego ch., Reuben award 2003). Office: c/o United Media 200 Madison Ave New York NY 10016 also: Nat Cartoonists Soc Ste 201 1133 W Morse Blvd Winter Park FL 32789

EVANS, GREGORY HINOJOSA, lawyer; BS in Pub. Affairs, U. So. Calif., 1984; MSW, U. Calif., Berkeley, 1986; JD, U. Notre Dame, 1989. Bar: Calif. 1990, US Dist. Ct. (all dists. Calif.), US Ct. Appeals (7th and 9th cirs.), Calif. Supreme Ct., Wash. Supreme Ct. Dep. counsel Nat. Coalition Homeless, Washington; ptnr. Orrick, Herrington & Sutcliffe, LLP, LA, Milbank, Tweed, Hadley & McCloy, LLP, LA, 2006—. Fellowship US Dept. Justice, 1987; mem. Nat. Assn. Elected and Appointed Officials Ednl. Fund; bd. dirs. Leadership for Environment and Devel., USA. Contbr. articles to law jours. Bd. trustees Cath. Charities LA; bd. dirs. YMCA, San Francisco, NAACP Legal Def. and Ednl. Fund, Inc., LA County Bar Found. Named one of Am. Top 45 Young Lawyers, The Am. Lawyer mag., 2003. Mem.: Nat. Assn. Latino Elected and Apptd. Ofcls., State Bar Calif. (Wiley W. Manuel award 1993). Office: Milbank Tweed Hadley & McCloy LLP 601 S Figueroa St 30th Fl Los Angeles CA 90017 Office Phone: 213-892-4488. E-mail: gevans@milbank.com.*

EVANS, H. TODD, music educator; b. Pittsfield, Ill., June 25, 1966; s. Harold Dean and Myra Karen Evans; m. Alicia Dawn Shelton-Evans, July 6, 2002; 1 child, Logan Aleczander. AA, John Wood CC, Quincy, Ill., 1986; BS in Edn., Hannibal-LaGrange Coll., Mo., 1989; MA in Legal Studies, U. Ill., Springfield, 1998. Cert. Tchr. Ill. Bd. Edn., 2006. Vocal music dir. Shelby County R-IV Schs., Shelbing, Mo., 1989—90, West-Pike Schs., Kinderhook, Ill., 1990—95, Griggsville Perry Schs., Griggsville, 1996—. Adj. faculty John Wood CC, Pittsfield, Ill., 2001—; jr. class sponsor Griggsville-Perry Schs., 2006. Actor, rehearsal pianist, pageant judge, speech judge:, and state music contest judge:. Vol. Skinner House Com., Griggsville, 2005—06; pianist Pleasant Hill Bapt. Ch., 1999—; mem. homecoming com. Bethel Ch., Rural Griggsville, 2006; mem./rep. scholarship com. Pike County Educators Assn., Pittsfield, 2006—. Mem.: Pittsfield Masonic Lodge, Ea. Star (organist, past patron). Democrat. Baptist. Office: Griggsville-Perry Schs Stanford & Liberty Sts Griggsville IL 62340 Address: PO Box 155 Griggsville IL 62360-0155

EVANS, HAROLD EDWARD, retired banker; b. Detroit, Apr. 23, 1927; s. Harold J. and Mary Esther (Keenoy) E.; m. Patricia Mae Persons Willy, Mar. 28, 1982; children by previous marriage: D'lorah Ann, M'liss Lorraine, David Keenoy, Craig Edward. BBA, U. Mich., 1950; cert., Bank Adminstrn. Inst., U. Wis., 1968, Rutgers U., 1975. Auditor Second Nat. Bank Saginaw, Mich., 1952-61, controller Mich., 1961-73, sr. v.p., cashier, sec., chief fin. officer Mich., 1973-92; founder, chmn. art collection, 1976-92; mem. selection com., 1992-2001; v.p. loan rev. officer Citizens Banking Corp., Flint, Mich., 1986-92. Sec.-treas. 2d Nat. Corp., 1973-88, Century Life Ins. Co., Mich., 1973-93; lectr. Robert Perry Sch. Banking, Ctrl. Mich. U. Mem. Saginaw Citizens Coun. for Ctrl. Bus. Dist., 1970-89; mem. adv. bd. Urban Renewal, chmn. econ. base study com., 1954-55; chmn. Downtown Saginaw Beautification Commn., 1968-83, Greater Saginaw Beautification Residential Com., 1965-68, 1988-97; chmn. Saginaw Valley State U. Humanities Series Com., 1990—06; sec., trustee Saginaw Osteo. Hosp., 1960-84; treas., trustee Saginaw Symphony Orch., 1965-72; past trustee Saginaw His. Mus.; treas., dir. United Rehab. Svcs., 1954-65, Temple Theater Arts Assn., 1980-87; fin. officer Saginaw CAP, 1978-84; trustee, treas. Saginaw Valley Dancers, 1977-93; trustee Hartley Nature Ctr. Found., 1987—, Saginaw Hall of Fame, 1989—; mem. adv. bd. Health Source Saginaw, Inc., 1991—, sec. adv. bd., 1993, 96, vice chmn., 1997, chmn., 1998; mem. steering com. Cathedral Dist. Renewal, 1990—; mem. com. for advancement Saginaw Valley State U., 1992—, mem. com. Stuart and Vernice Gross History Lit. award, 1996-2000; mem. com. for advancement Saginaw Area Enrichment Commn., 1992-2002, Saginaw Twp. Art in Pub. Place Commn., 1991-2007, Delta Coll. Pub. Radio Fund Raiser Com., 1990-97, Temple Theater Film Selection com., 1998-2003; mem. awards panel Theatre Guild Midland Ctr. for the Arts; bd. trustees Mideastern Libr. Coop., 2003—, treas., 2006—. With USNR, 1945—46. Recipient Saginaw Arts award Community Enrichment Commn., 1992; nominee Gov's. Art award, 1996. Mem. Saginaw C. of C., Bank Adminstrn. Inst. (life; pres. Ea. Mich. conf. 1955-56, v.p. Mich. chpt. 1958-59), Valley Film Soc. (bd. dirs. 1991—), Tri-County Econ. Club, Econ. Club Detroit, Internat. Torch Club (Saginaw Valley chpt. 1993—), U. Mich. Alumni Club (Saginaw chpt.), Optimists (bd. dirs. Breakfast Club 1960-80, treas. 1961-63, pres. 1970-72), Mich. Women's Hall of Fame (elector 1992-93), Friends Theodore Roethke, U.S. Navy League. Home: 17 Riverside Blvd Saginaw MI 48602-1077 also: 1710 N Charles St Saginaw MI 48602-4848

EVANS, SIR HAROLD MATTHEW, editor, publisher, writer; b. Manchester, Eng., June 28, 1928; arrived in US, 1984, naturalized, 1993; s. Frederick Albert and Mary Hannah (Haselum) Evans; m. Enid Parker, Apr. 15, 1953 (div. 1978); children: Ruth, Katherine, Michael; m. Tina Brown, Aug. 20, 1981; children: George, Isabel. BA in Politics, Econ. (hon.), Durham U., London, 1952; MA, Durham U., 1966; PhD (hon.), Sterling U., 1982; DCL (hon.), Durham U., 1998; DLitt (hon.), U. Teesside, 2000, London Inst., 2001. Reporter, Ashton-under-Lyne; reporter, editl. writer Manchester Evening News, England, 1952—56, asst. editor, 1958—61; editor Northern Echo, Darlington, England, 1961—67, The Sunday Times, London, 1967-81, The Times, London, 1981-82; dir., exec. bd. Goldcrest Films & TV, London, 1982—84; editor-in-chief Atlantic Monthly Press, NYC, 1984; editorial dir. US News & World Report, Washington, 1984-86, contbg. editor, 1984—; founding editor-in-chief Conde Nast Traveler, NYC, 1986-90; pres., pub. Random House Trade Pub. Group, NYC, 1990-97; vice chmn., edit. dir. US News and World Report, NY Daily News, Atlantic Monthly, Fast Company, 1997-99; author Little, Brown and Co., NYC, 2000—; editor-at-large The Week Mag., NYC. Vis. prof. City U., London, 1978-82, Poynter Inst., St. Petersburg, Fla., 1982, Duke U., NC, 1984. Author: Eye Witness, 1981, Good Times Bad Times, 1983, Editing and Design (5 vols.), 1977-78, (with others) We Learned to Ski, 1976, Suffer the Children, 1979, The American Century, 1998, They Made America: From the Steam Engine to the Seach Engine: Two Centuries of Innovators, 2004; exec. producer: (TV prog.) We Learned to Ski, 1983; writer (TV series) WGBH. Served to cpl. RAF, 1946-49. Named one of 50 World Press Heroes, Internat. Press Inst., 2000; recipient Internat. Editor of Yr. award, World Press Rev., 1974, Editor of Yr. award, Granada Press Awards, 1982, Lifetime Achievement award, Internat. Ctr. Photography, 1999, Gold award lifetime achievement, Brit. Press Awards, 2000; Harkness Commonwealth Fund fellow in journalism, U. Chgo. and Stanford U., 1956—57, knighted svcs. to journalism, Queen Elizabeth II, 2004. Fellow Soc. Indsl. Designers, Inst. Journalists (European Gold Medal 1978); mem. Royal Photographic Soc. (Hood Medal 1980), Nat. Press Photographers of Great Britain (honoree 1986), Garrick Club (London), Century Club (NY), Yale Club (NY). Avocations: music, swimming, ping pong/table tennis. Office: The Week Mag 1040 Ave of Americas New York NY 10018 E-mail: hardd37@aol.com.

EVANS, HARRY LAUNIUS, pathology educator; b. Mobile, Ala., June 11, 1948; s. Aurelius A. and Anne (Hathaway) E.; m. Cheryl J. Winfrey, June 6, 1970 (div. Dec. 1990); children: Thomas H., Sarah S. BS, Stetson U., 1970; MD, U. Fla., 1974. Diplomate Am. Bd. Pathology. Resident in pathology Vanderbilt U. Med. Ctr., Nashville, 1974-75; fellow in dermatopathology Mayo Clinic, Rochester, Minn., 1977-78; fellow in pathology U.Tex.-M.D. Anderson Cancer Ctr., Houston, 1975-77, asst. prof. pathology, 1978-82, assoc. prof., 1982-90, prof., 1990—. Contbr. articles to med. jours. Mem. U.S.-Can. Acad. Pathology, Arthur Purdy Stout Soc. Surg. Pathologists. Avocations: mountain climbing, music, crossword puzzles. Office: U Tex-MD Anderson Cancer Ctr Dept Pathology 1515 Holcombe Blvd Houston TX 77030-4009 Office Phone: 713-792-3152. E-mail: hevans@mdanderson.org.

EVANS, HEIDI, journalist; m. Josh Getlin; 1 child, Alex. M. in journalism, Columbia U., 1984. Reporter LA Times, 1984—87, NY Daily News, 1987—93, 1999—; nat. urban affairs writer Wall St. Jour., 1993—96; reporter Newsday, 1998—99. Co-recipient George Polk award, 2001, Selden Ring award for Investigative Reporting, 2002, Daniel Pearl award for Investigative Reporting, 2006, Pulitzer Prize for Editl. Writing, 2007; recipient George Polk award, 1990; Nieman fellow, 1993. Office: NY Daily News 450 W 33 St New York NY 10001 Office Phone: 212-210-6394. Office Fax: 212-210-2921. E-mail: evansheidi@aol.com.*

EVANS, HUGH E., pediatrician, educator; b. NYC, July 6, 1934; s. David and Geraldine (Krebs) E.; m. Ruth L. Orloff, June 5, 1960 (dec. Mar. 1999); children: Margo Lynn Evans Manspeizer, Marc Douglas. AB cum laude, Columbia U., 1954; MD, SUNY Downstate Med. Center, 1958. Intern Johns Hopkins Hosp., Balt., 1958-59, asst. resident, 1959-60; sr. asst. resident NIH, Bethesda, Md., 1960-62, chief resident outpatient dept., 1962-63; pvt. practice Bellaire, Ohio, 1963-66; assoc. dir. pediatrics Harlem Hosp. Center, NYC, 1966-73; dir. dept. pediatrics Jewish Hosp. and Med. Center, Bklyn., 1973-85; prof. pediatrics U. Medicine and Dentistry of N.J., Newark, 1985—, prof. preventive medicine and community health, 1991—, chmn. dept. pediatrics, 1985-90; dir. dept. pediatrics U. Hosp., Newark, 1985-90, mem. attending staff, 1985—. Assoc. clin. prof. pediatrics Columbia U., 1968-73; prof. pediatrics SUNY Downstate Med. Center, Bklyn., 1973-85; trustee Bergen-Passiac County Lung Assn., 1973-85. Author: (with Leonard Glass) Perinatal Medicine, 1976, Lung Diseases of Children, 1979, 2d edit., 1985, The Hidden Campaign: The Medical History of President Franklin D. Roosevelt and the 1944 Election, 2002; editor: Hospital Care of Children and Youth, 1986, Jour. Perinatology, 1985-2000; contbr. articles to profl. jours., chpts. to textbooks; TV appearances include C-Span, History Channel, Discovery Channel. Trustee Englewood Hosp. and Med. Ctr., NJ, 2005—, NJ State Opera, 2005—. Served to sr. asst. surgeon USPHS, 1960-62. Named Faculty of Yr., NJ Med. Sch., 2007, Hon. Alumnus of Yr., 2007; recipient Richard L. Day award in pediats., 2003; fellow, Sabin Vaccine Inst., 2004—. Mem. AAUP (bd. govs. 2001—, v.p. 2003-05, pres. 2005—), Soc. Pediat. Rsch., Harvey Soc., Am. Soc. Microbiology, Am. Acad. Pediat. (com. on hosp. care 1982-85, chmn. 1985-88, task force on pediat. AIDS 1987-92), Am. Thoracic Soc., Am. Pediat. Soc., Soc. Exptl. Biology and Medicine, N.Y. Pediat. Soc. (pres. 1982-83), Am. Polit. Sci. Assn., Bklyn. Acad. Pediat. (v.p. 1976, pres. 1977), Infectious Diseases Soc., Med. Soc. N.J. (mem. spl. com. AIDS 1993-95), Rotary Internat., Palm Beach Found Table (bd. dirs. 2007), Sigma Xi, Alpha Omega Alpha. Home: 49 Nelson Pl Tenafly NJ 07670 Office: U Medicine and Dentistry NJ MSB-F586 185 S Orange Ave Newark NJ 07103-2757 Office Phone: 973-972-6530. Business E-Mail: evanshe@umdnj.edu.

EVANS, JACK R. (J. GLENN), writer, poet; b. Wewoka, Okla., Dec. 21, 1930; s. John and Jimmie Devonia (Gordon) Glenn; m. Lucille Wallace, May 28, 1957 (div. 1967); m. Barbara Ann Lubic Conroy, Oct. 26, 1968; 1 stepchild, Barbara Ann Conroy. BS, East Ctrl. U., Ada, Okla., 1956. Stockbroker Hinton Jones Co., Seattle, 1966-68; stockbroker, v.p. Fox Roff Co., Seattle, 1968-70, John R. Lewis Co., Seattle, 1970-73; stockbroker, pres. Securities Exch., Seattle, 1973-76; pres., stockbroker, investment banker Securities Corp. of Wash., Seattle, 1976-84; pub. SCW Publs., Seattle, 1984—; poetry editor, pub. PoetsWest Online, Seattle, 1998—; freelance poet, writer, historian Seattle, 1986—; poetry curator Seattle City Coun. "Words' Worth", 2001. Bd. dirs. Seattle Freelances, 1995-2002, pres. 2004-05; mem. adv. bd. U. Wash. Writers Program; prodr., host weekly radio program Poets West at KSER 90.7 FM, 2005; founder SCW Shirt Pocket Book series, 2005. Author: Little History of Renton Washington, 1987, Little History of Bothell Washington, 1988, Little History of Gig Harbor Washington, 1988, Little History of North Bend-Snoqualmie, 1990, Levant F. Thompson: Hop King, Banker, Senator, 1992, Little History of Pike Place Market, 1991, Swedes From Whence They Came, 1993, Window in the Sky, 1996, Seattle Poems, 1996, (CD) Window in the Sky, 1999, Broker Jim, 2002, Chasing His Dreams: Life of Entrepreneur, 2002, Buffalo Tracks, 2003, Dear Editor, 2005, Serious Business, 2005, I Was There, 2005, Sacred Moments, 2005, How Came it Came to Be, 2005, The New Philosphy, 2005, A Little Thinkin', 2006, Hard Times, 2006, People's Manifesto, 2006; editor: Klondike Gold Rush Centennial Anthology, 1997. Contest dir., bd. dirs. Klondike Gold Rush Centennial Celebration, Wash. State, 1997. Cpl. USAF, 1954. Recipient Faith Beamer Cooke award Wash. Poets Assn., 1999, Seattle FreeLances Outstanding Writer award, 2003, Nat. winner Rock River Poetry Contest, 2003, 2d pl. winner William Stafford award, 2002. Mem. Assn. King County Hist. Orgn. (past pres.), Pacific N.W. Hist. Guild (past v.p.), Wash. Poets Assn. (bd. dirs. 1997-2004), PoetsTable (founding mem.), Activists For a Better World (founding mem., mng. dir. 2007-). Avocations: history, reading, poetry reading. Office Phone: 206-682-1268. Business E-Mail: info@poetswest.com.

EVANS, JAMES E., lawyer; b. 1946; BA, Mich. State U., 1968; JD, Ohio State U., 1970. Bar: Ohio 1971. Assoc. Keating, Muething & Klekamp, 1970—76; named v.p., gen. counsel Am. Fin. Corp. (former subsid. Am. Fin. Group Inc.), Cin., 1976; sr. v.p., gen. counsel, dir. Am. Fin. Group Inc., Cin., 1995—. Mem.: Cin. Bar Assn., Ohio Bar Assn., ABA. Office: Am Fin Group Inc 1 E 4th St Cincinnati OH 45202*

EVANS, JAMES HANDEL, academic administrator, architect; b. Bolton, Eng., June 14, 1938; came to U.S., 1965. s. Arthur Handel and Ellen Bowen (Ramsden) E.; m. Carol L. Mulligan, Sept. 10, 1966; children: Jonathan, Sarah. Diploma of Architecture, U. Manchester, Eng., 1965; MArch., U. Oreg., 1967; postgrad., Cambridge U., Eng., 1969-70. Registered architect, Calif., U.K.; cert. NCARB. Assoc. dean. prof. architecture Calif. Poly. State U., San Luis Obispo, 1967-78; prof. art and design San Jose (Calif.) State U., 1979—, assoc. exec. v.p., 1978-81, interim exec. v.p., 1981-82, exec. v.p., 1982-91, interim pres., 1991-92, pres., 1992-95; sr. adminstr. Calif. State U., Monterey Bay, 1991—94; vice chancellor Calif. State U System, Long Beach, Calif., 1995-96; planning pres. Calif. State U. Channel Islands, Ventura, 1996-2001; pres. HE Cons. Inc., 2001—. Cons. Ibiza Nueva, Ibiza, Spain, 1977-80; vis. prof. Ciudad Universitaria, Madrid, 1977; vis. lectr. Herriott Watt U., Edinburgh, 1970; mem. adv. com. Army Command Staff Coll., Ft. Leavenworth, Kans., 1988. Trustee Good Samaritan Hosp., San Jose, 1987-90; bd. dirs. San Jose Shelter, 1988-90; dir. San Jose C. of C., 1991-94, Ventura County Mus. History and Art. Sci. Rsch. Coun. fellow Cambridge U., 1969-70. Fellow AIA; mem. Royal Inst. Brit. Architects, Assn. Univ. Architects. Avocation: golf. Home Phone: 805-384-8151. Personal E-mail: jhevans@adelphia.net. Business E-Mail: hhevans@vcccd.net.

EVANS, JAMES HURLBURT, retired transportation and natural resources executive; b. Lansing, Mich., June 26, 1920; s. James L. and Marie (Hurlburt) E.; m. Mary Johnston Head, 1984; children by previous marriage: Eric B. (dec. 1996), Carol E. Jepperson, Joan E. Madsen. AB, Centre Coll., 1943, DHL (hon.), 1987; JD, U. Chgo., 1948; LLD (hon.), Millikin U., 1978. Bar: Ill. 1949. Atty., loan officer Harris Trust & Savs. Bank, Chgo., 1948-56; sec.-treas. Reuben H. Donnelley Corp., Chgo., 1956-57; v.p., dir. Reuben H. Donnelley Corp. (merged with Dun & Bradstreet 1961), NYC, 1957-62; v.p. fin. Dun & Bradstreet, 1962-65, also bd. dirs.; pres. Seamen's Bank for Savs., NYC, 1965-68, chmn. bd., 1968, trustee, 1965-78; pres. Union Pacific Corp., NYC, 1969-77, chmn., CEO, 1977-85. Ret. dir. AT&T, GM Corp., Citicorp/Citibank, Met. Life Ins. Co., Bristol-Myers, Dun & Bradstreet, Anaconda Corp. Bd. govs. ARC, 1970-76, nat. fund chmn. 1974-76; hon. trustee, former vice chmn. John F. Kennedy Ctr. for Performing Arts; life trustee Nat. Recreation Found., pres. 1971-75, U. Chgo., Ctr. Coll. Ky., Ctrl. Park Conservancy; founding mem. Citizens Adv. Com. on Environ. Quality, 1966-70. Served to lt. USNR, 1943-46; life gov. N.Y. Presbyn. Hosp. Mem. ABA, Phi Beta Kappa, Omicron Delta Kappa, Delta Kappa Epsilon. Clubs: Racquet and Tennis, Links, Knickerbocker (N.Y.C.); Metropolitan, Alfalfa (Washington); Maidstone (East Hampton). Presbyterian. Office Phone: 212-753-7111.

EVANS, JAMES MIGNON, architect; b. Memphis, May 9, 1938; s. Mignon Kemper and Elizabeth Louise (Fulcher) E.; m. Gayle Jean Dupont, Aug. 21, 1965; children: Matthew Moseby, Benjamin Dupont, Bolin Briscoe. BA, Rice U., 1960; MFA in Architecture, Princeton U., 1962. Registered architect, Tenn., Va., Calif., Ariz., N.Y. Intern architect Perkins & Will Ptnrship., Washington, 1965-66; architect Doxiadis Assocs., Washington, 1966-68, Gassner Nathan & Browne, Memphis, 1969-70, prin., 1970-87, Nathan/Evans/Taylor, Memphis, 1987-95, Nathan/Evans/Taylor/Coleman/Foster, Memphis, 1995—2003, Evans Taylor Foster Childress Archs., Memphis, 2003—. Mem. bldg. code rev. and adv. bd. Memphis and Shelby Counties, 1980-83; mem. Memphis Heritage Adv. Com., 1980-84. Bd. dirs. Dismas Ho., Memphis, 1989—94, pres., 1992, 1993; bd. dirs. Theatre Memphis, 2003—; trustee Grace-St. Luke's Episcopal Sch., Memphis, 1980—86, pres., 1984—85; mem. vestry Grace-St. Luke's Episcopal Ch., 1983—86, 1990—93, 2001—, jr. warden, 1992, 1993, 2004. With US Army, 1963—65. Lowell M. Palmer fellow, 1961-62; recipient Sylvan award Lumberman's Club of Memphis, 1983, 85, Excellence award Masonry Inst. Tenn., 1980, 89, 91, Energy Design Honor award TVA, 1988. Mem. AIA (treas. 1978, peer reviewer 1987—, Honor award 1978, 94, mem. exec. com. Memphis chpt., mem. past pres. coun. 2001-03, chmn. 2004, chmn. awards com. 2001-03), Tenn. Soc. Architects (bd. dirs. 1977-80, Excellence award 1978, 81, 96, , 97, Honor award 1981, 89, 91), Memphis Inst. Architects (v.p. 1980, pres. 1981), Memphis Rotary (chmn. ambassadorial scholarship com. 2003—). Clubs: Univ. of Memphis. Avocations: jogging, gardening, reading. Office: Evans Taylor Foster Childress-Archs 343 N Main St Memphis TN 38103 Home Phone: 901-278-9852; Office Phone: 901-525-5344.

EVANS, JENNIFER G., pharmacist; b. Amsterdam, NY, Aug. 9, 1973; d. Neal C. and Gail A. Evans. BS in Pharmacy, Albany Coll. Pharmacy, NY, 1996. Staff pharmacist CVS Pharmacy, Glens Falls, NY, 1996—97, Express Scripts, Troy, NY, 1997—2001, supr. pharmacy, 2001—05; coord. introductory pharmacy practice experiences Albany Coll. Pharmacy, 2005—. Mem.: Am. Assn. Colls. Pharmacy. Office: Albany Coll Pharmacy 106 New Scotland Ave Albany NY 12208 Office Phone: 518-694-7110. Business E-Mail: evansj@acp.edu.

EVANS, JO BURT, communications executive, rancher; b. Kimble County, Tex., Dec. 18, 1928; d. John Fred and Sadie (Oliver) Burt; m. Charles Wayne Evans II, Apr. 17, 1949; children: Charles Wayne III, John Burt, Elizabeth Wisart. BA, Mary Hardin-Baylor Coll., 1948; MA, Trinity U., 1967. Owner, mgr. Sta. KMBL, Junction, Tex., 1959-61; real estate broker Junction, 1965-74; staff economist, adv. on 21st Congl. Dist., polit. campaign Nelson Wolff, 1974-75; asst. mgr., bookkepper family owned ranches/rental property Junction, 1948—; gen. mgr. TV Translator Corp., Junction, 1968—, sec.-treas., 1980—. Treas., asst. to coord. Citizens for Tex., 1972; historian Kimble Hist. Soc.; mem. Com. of Conservation Soc. to Save the Edwards Aquifer, San Antonio, 1973; homecoming chmn. Sesquicentennial Yr., Junction; treas., asst. coord. New Consitution, San Antonio, 1974; legis. chair Hill Country Women, Kimble County, 1990—; cashier Texan Theatre; campaign chmn. for Challenge U. Mary Hardin, Baylor, 2000; curator Tex. Tech. U. Herbarium, Junction, 2006. Named an outstanding Texan, Tex. Senate, 1973. Mem. AAUW (scholarship named in honor 1973), Nat. Translator Assn., Daus. Republic Tex., Tex. Sheriffs Assn., Nat. Cattlewomens Assn., Internat. Platform Assn., Bus. and Profl. Women (pres. 1981-82), Edwards Plateau Tex. Master Naturalists. Republican. Mem. Unity Ch. Home: PO Box 283 Junction TX 76849-0283 Office: 618 Main St Junction TX 76849-4635 Office Phone: 325-446-3407.

EVANS, JOHN DAVID DANIEL, judge; b. Feb. 5, 1944; children: Reagan, Quentin Cory, Jonathan. BA, U. Western Ont., 1967; LLB, Windsor Law Sch., 1972. Bar: Ont. 1974. Assoc. W.L.S. trivett, Q.C., Orillia, Ont., 1974, Robert J. Carter, Q.C., Toronto, Ont., 1975-76; ptnr. Evans, Kukurin, Timmins, Ont., 1976-77, Perras, Evans, Kukurin & Huot, Timmins, Ont., 1977-80, Riopelle, Evans, Chornyj and Carr, Timmins, 1980-84; apptd. judge Criminal divsn. Provincial Ct., Ont., 1984-90, apptd. regional sr. judge ctrl. east region Ont., 1990-98, sr. judge. Faculty law St. Clair C.C., No. C.C., Laurentian U. Mem. Criminal Lawyers Assn., Can. Bar Assn., Am. Judges Assn. (bd. govs.). Roman Catholic. Avocations: sports, hockey playing. Office: Ont Ct Justice 3 Dominion St Bracebridge ON Canada P1L 2E6

EVANS, JOHN DERBY, telecommunications industry executive; b. Detroit, June 3, 1944; s. Edward Steptoe and Florence (Allington) E.; m. Susan Blair Allan, Apr. 7, 1973 (div. Nov. 1986); children: John Derby, Courtenay Boyd. AB, U. Mich., 1966. Pres. Evans Comm. Sys. Inc., Charlottesville, Va., 1970-72; v.p., gen. mgr. Capitol Cablevision Corp., Charleston, W.Va., 1972-76; regional mgr. Am. TV and Comm. Corp., Denver, 1974-76; exec. v.p., COO Arlington (Va.) TeleCom. Corp., 1976-83; pres. Arlington Cable Ptnrs. Ltd., 1983-94, Suburban Cable Ptnrs., Brooklyn Pk., Minn., 1985-89, Hauser Comm., NYC, 1985-94, Evans Telecomm. Co., 1983—; chmn., CEO Waterford Marine Inc., The Plains, Va., 1996—2001. Staff asst. sec. planning and devel. Dept. HEW, Washington, 1976; co-founder, bd. dirs. Cable Satellite Pub. Affairs Network (C-SPAN), 1979—, exec. com., 1982—93, 1998—, chmn., 1991—93, chmn. fin. com., 1997—; pres. Montgomery Cablevision (LP), Rockville, Md., 1986—94, Washington Metro Cable Club, 1981—; bd. dirs. Falcon Comm. Co., LA, Falcon Cable TV, 1998—2000, GBR Sci., Balt., 1999—2000; v.p. North Ctrl. Cable Comm. Co., Roseville, Minn., 1986—92; mng. gen. ptnr. Waterford Farm Partnership, Middleburg, Va., 1993—; Siciliano forum lectr. U. Utah, 1998; future makers lectr. Emory U., 1999, futurist forum panelist, 2004; bd. dirs. Nelson Cable Co., Lovingston, Va.; lectr. Inst. of the Humanities, U. Mich., 2000; keynote spkr. Exec. Summit on Internat. Health Philanthropy Royal Coll. Physicians, London, 2001; inaugural lectr. Mich. State U. Quello Ctr. for Telecom. Law and Regulation, 2001; spkr. in field; bd. dirs. Alescentor Tech. Holdings, Amman, Israel, 2005—. Trustee C-Span Ednl. Found., 1994—; trustee, vice chmn. bd. trustees Signature Theater, Arlington, 1992—2004; chmn. bd. trustees Evans Found., 1994—; chmn. Cancer/AIDS Rsch. Network, Balt.; mem. steering com. Inst. Human Virology U. Md., Balt., 1996—; bd. dir. Internat. Cancer and AIDS Rsch. Found., 1996—2000, Internat. AIDS Vaccine Initiative, NYC, 2002—, treas., 2003—, chmn. fin. and audit com., 2003—, vice chmn., treas., 2005—; bd. dir. Hollings Cancer Ctr., Charleston, SC, 1998—2004; adv. com. AIDS Rsch. Inst. U. Calif., San Francisco; mem. vis. com. Coll. LS and A, U. Mich., 1994—, mem. pres.'s adv. bd., 1998—, mem. commn. on info. tech., 2000—; chmn. Waterford Project Inc., 2000—03; bd. dir. Eisenhower World Affairs Inst., 1990—2003, chmn. strategic planning com., 1997—2003, vice chmn., 1999—2003; bd. dir. Accerator Tech. Holdings, Amman, Jordan, 2005—. Named to Va. Comm. Hall of Fame, Richmond, Va., 2004; recipient AIDS Achievement award, League African Am. Women, 2000, Lifetime Achievement award, U. Md. Inst. Human Virology, 2007. Mem.: Cable TV Adminstrn., Mktg. Soc. (bd. dir. 1985), Va. Communication Hall of Fame, Va. Commonwealth U., Asia-Pacific Conf. Sci. and Tech. Leaders (U.S. del. 1996), Va. Cable Assn. (bd. dir. 1979—, v.p. 1982, pres. 1983—84, Hall of Fame 2001), Nat. Cable TV Assn. (nat. chmn. awards com. 1981, bd. dir. 1982—, chmn. govt. rels. com. 1985—86, mem. regulatory policy com. 1991—95, chmn. elections, bylaws com. 1991—97, convention com. 1998—, mem. conv. com. 1999—2000, Pres. award 1979, Vanguard award 1984), Sag Harbor Yacht Club, Key West Yacht Club, Boars Head Sports Club (Charlottesville), Farmington Country Club (Inducted Va. Comms. Hall of Fame 2004). Republican. Episcopalian. Avocations: scuba diving, motorcycling, boating.

EVANS, JOHN ROBERT, academic administrator, cardiologist; b. Toronto, Can., Oct. 1, 1929; s. William Watson and Mary Evelyn Lucille (Thompson) E.; m. Jean Gay Glassco, 1954; children: Derek, Mark and Michael (twins), Gillian, Timothy, Willa. MD, U. Toronto, 1952; DPhil (Rhodes scholar), Oxford U., 1955; LLD (hon.), Dalhousie U., McMaster U., McGill U., 1972, Queen's U., 1974, Wilfred Laurier U., 1975, York U., 1977, U. Toronto, 1980, U. Western Ont., 1982, Yale U., 1978, U. Alberta, 2005; DSc (hon.), Meml. U., 1973, U. Montreal, 1977, Royal Mil. Coll., 1989; DHL (hon.), Johns Hopkins U., 1978; D (hon.), U. Ottawa, 1978, U. Limbourg, The Netherlands, 1980. Intern Toronto Gen. Hosp., 1952—53, chief resident physician, 1958—59; practice medicine specializing in cardiology Toronto, 1961—72; assoc. dept. medicine U. Toronto Med. Sch., 1961—65, prof., 1972—, pres. univ., 1972—78, pres. emeritus, 1995—; dir. population, health and nutrition dept. World Bank, Washington, 1979—83; chmn. Allelix Inc., Mississauga, 1983—99; physician Toronto Gen. Hosp., 1961—65; dean Faculty Medicine McMaster U., Hamilton, 1965—72, v.p. health scis., 1967—72; chmn. Torstar Corp., Toronto, 1993—2005, Alcan Aluminium Ltd., Montreal, 1995—2002; vice chmn. NPS-Allelix Inc., 1999—2006; chmn. MaRS Discovery Dist., Toronto, 2000—. Bd. dir. CMA Holdings, Inc., Toronto, Glyco Design, Inc., Alcan Aluminum Ltd., Montreal, MDS health Group, Toronto; hon. fellow London Sch. Hygiene and Tropical Medicine, Univ. Coll., Oxford, England; chmn. Can. Found. Innovation, 1997—2007; trustee Rockefeller Found., NYC, 1982—95, chmn., 1988—95, African Med. Rsch. Found., Canada, 1986—90; trustee Walter and Duncan Gordon Charitable Found., Toronto, 1991—2000, chair, 1998—2000. Decorated Companion Order of Can., Order of Ont.; named, Can. Med. Hall of Fame, 2000, Can. Bus. Hall of Fame, 2005; named an hon. fellow, London Sch. Hygiene and Tropical Medicine, Univ. Coll. Oxford; recipient Gairdner Found. Wightman award,

Gairdner Found., 1992, FNG Starr medal, Can. Med. Assn., 2002, Disting. Leadership medal, Can. Inst. Health Rsch., 2004; Markle scholar, 1960—65. Master: ACP; fellow: Inst. Corp. Dirs., Royal Coll. Physicians (London), Royal Coll. Physicians and Surgeons Can., Royal Soc. Can. Home: 58 Highland Ave Toronto ON Canada M4W 2A3 Office: Mars Discovery Dist Toronto ON Canada M5G 1L7

EVANS, JOHN THOMAS, lawyer; b. N.Y.C., Feb. 28, 1948; s. John Arthur and Dorothy (Reilly) E.; m. Marie Tolnay, June 2, 1979; children—Claire, Grace. B.A., U. Wis., 1970; J.D., Fordham U., 1973. Bar: N.Y. 1974, U.S. Dist. Ct. (so. and ea. dists.) N.Y., U.S. Tax Ct. Asst. dist. atty. N.Y. County, N.Y.C., 1973-79; assoc. Blumenthal & Lynne, N.Y.C., 1979-81; ptnr. Morris & Duffy, N.Y.C., 1982-85, Belair, Klein, Groman & Evans, N.Y.C., 1985—; cons. Vol. Lawyers for Arts, N.Y.C., 1979-84, Hofstra U. Law Sch. Moot Ct. Program, Uniondale, N.Y., 1982; cons., lectr. N.Y.C. Police Dept. Detectives Endowment Assn., 1981—. Author: Arguing Cases Before A Medical Malpractice Law & Strategy; contbr. articles to profl. jours. Recipient Highest award Manhattan Detective Area, N.Y.C., 1979. Mem. N.Y. State Bar Assn., Assn. Bar City of N.Y., N.Y. Criminal Bar Assn. Club: N.Y. Athletic (N.Y.C.). Home: 362 W Broadway New York NY 10013-5303 Office: Belair & Evans 61 Broadway New York NY 10006-2701

EVANS, JONATHAN CHRISTOPHER, social worker; s. Stephen Mike Evans and Pamala Jane Guill. BS in Social Work, U. N.C., Greensboro, 2006; postgrad., N.C. A&T State U., Greensboro, 2006—. Youth/teen dir. J. Smith Young YMCA, Lexington, NC, 1992—98; sales trainer Bass Lake Resort, Salisbury, NC, 1998—2000. With USNR, 2000—02. Decorated Nat. Def. USMC; recipient Sales Person of Yr., Bass Lake Resort/Coast to Coast Resorts, 1998—99, Outstanding Leadership and Svc. award, U. N.C., Greensboro, 2006, Directors award, 2006; scholar, U.S. Marine Corps Found., 2005. Master: YMCA USA (assoc.; staff trainer 1995—2006, Svc. award 1996); fellow: Phi Alpha (hon.); mem.: NASW (assoc.; cert. profl. social worker), DAV (life), Marine Corps League (assoc. Marine Scholar 2005). Democrat. Achievements include research in communication between Adolescents and family and peers. Avocations: golf, tennis, camping, travel. Home: 830 West Market St #257 Greensboro NC 27401 E-mail: evans.jcevans@gmail.com.

EVANS, JOY, foundation administrator; b. Waterbury, Conn., Feb. 15, 1940; 4 children. Student, Hartford Coll. for Women, 1959. Weekly radio personality Young Stars on Parade Sta. WBRY, Waterbury, 1951-58; exec. sec. dir.'s office Discover Am. Travel Orgns., Washington, 1962-71; exec. sec. adminstr.'s office Nat. Ctr. for Housing Mgmt., Washington, 1971-72; exec. sec. mgr.'s office Nat. Visitor's Ctr. Nat. Park Svc. Dept. Interior, 1972-73; staff asst. divsn. pub. programs NEH, Washington, 1973-81, pub. info. officer, office of the chair, 1981—. Founding chair fed. woman's com. NEH, 1980-82, liaison White House task force on the humanities and arts 1981-82; spkr. commencement address Nat. Coll. Bus. and Tech., Charlottesville, Va., 2002, 04. Staff newsletter editor Not Hardcopy Newsletter, 1996-98. Mem. Annandale Homeowner's Assn. (pres. Terrace Townhouses 1989-92, TTA newsletter editor 1988-92), Soc. Govt. Meeting Planners (D.C. chpt. 1991-92). Roman Catholic. Avocations: music, art, dance, photography, theater. Office: Nat Endowment for Humanities Rm 402 1100 Pennsylvania Ave NW Washington DC 20506-0001 Office Phone: 202-606-8446. Business E-Mail: jevans@neh.gov.

EVANS, KAREN ANN, social studies educator; d. Daniel Warren Evans III and Arcola Wandell Evans; m. Michael Barrett Grossi, Dec. 21, 1990. BA, Angelo State U., San Angelo, Tex., 1979; MEd, U. St. Thomas, Houston, 2004. Tchr., team leader Klein Intermediate Sch., Houston, 1984—2002, Alief Taylor HS, 2002—07; lead geogrpahy tchr. Kerr HS, 2007—. Mem. curriculum writing team world geography Alief Ind. Sch. Dist., Houston, 2002—03; mem. various curriculum writing teams Klein Ind. Sch. Dist., 2001. Historical re-enactor (performance) portraying Angel of Goliad in re-enactment of the Massacre of Goliad (made hon. mem. of descendants of Angel of Goliad, 2004). Fellow, Rice U., Nat. Consortium Tchg. Asia, Houston, 2004—05; study tour, Nat. Consortium Tchg. Asia, 2005. Mem.: FOG, AAG, Tex. Assn. Geog. Edn., Tex. State Tchrs. Assn., Asia Soc., Alpha Phi Omega (pres. Univ. Houston chpt. 1982—83). Avocations: historical re-enactment, living history, historical costuming, travel, Asian studies. Office: Kerr HS 8150 Howell-Sugarland Rd Houston TX 77083 Home Phone: 713-729-3207.

EVANS, KENYA, artist; Gallery supr. Contemporary Arts Mus., Houston; mem. Otabenga Jones & Assoc. Exhibited in group shows at Day for Night, Whitney Biennial, 2006. Office: Contemporary Arts Museum Houston 5216 Montrose Blvd Houston TX 77006

EVANS, LANE ALLEN, retired congressman; b. Rock Island, Ill., Aug. 4, 1951; s. Lee Herbert and Joycelene (Saylor) E. BA, Augustana Coll., 1974; JD, Georgetown U., 1978. Bar: Ill. 1978. Mng. atty. Western Ill. Legal Assistance Found., Rock Island, 1978-79; mem. nat. staff Kennedy for Pres., Washington, 1978-80; atty., ptnr. Community Legal Clinic, Rock Island, Ill., 1981-82; mem. U.S. Congress from 17th Ill. Dist., 1983—2007; mem. nat. security com., ranking mem. vets. affairs com., armed svcs. com. Served with USMC, 1969-71. Mem. AmVets, Am. Legion, Marine Corps League, Vietnam Vets Ill. Democrat. Roman Catholic.*

EVANS, LAURIE A., library director; MLS, U. North Tex., Denton, 1973. Mgr. Oak Lawn br. Dallas Pub. Libr., 1980, libr. children's sect., interim dir. librs., 2004—05, dir. librs., 2005—. Mem.: ALA. Office: Director Dallas Pub Libr 1515 Young St Dallas TX 75201-5415 Office Phone: 214-670-1400. Office Fax: 214-670-7839. E-mail: levans@dallaslibrary.org.*

EVANS, LAWRENCE E., lawyer, educator; b. Houston, Mar. 30, 1950; s. Lawrence Edgar and Edith (Kinzy) E.; m. Nancy Campbell, Aug. 20, 1977; children: Christopher, Laura. BA, Washington & Lee U., 1973; JD, South Tex. Coll., 1977. Bar: Tex. 1977, Mo. 1989; registered patent atty. Lawyer Gunn, Lee & Miller, Houston, 1977-88, Herzog, Crebs & McGhee, St. Louis, 1988-2000, Blackwell, Sanders, Peper, Martin LLP, St. Louis, 2000—. Adj. prof. Washington U. Sch. Law, St. Louis, 2000-04 Mem. Metro. Bar Assn. St. Louis (chmn. Patent, Trademark and Copyright sect. 1994), Internat. Trademark Assn., Am. Intellectual Property Law Assn. Office: Blackwell Sanders Peper Martin LLP 720 Olive St Ste 2400 Saint Louis MO 63101 Office Phone: 314-345-6431. Business E-Mail: levans@blackwellsanders.com.

EVANS, LINDA (LINDA EVANSTAD), actress; b. Hartford, Nov. 18, 1942; d. Alba and Arlene Evanstad m. John Derek (div.); m. Stan Herman, 1976 (div.). Owner Linda Evans Fitness Centers. Appearances include (films) Twilight of Honor, 1963, Those Calloways, 1964, Beach Blanket Bingo, 1965, Childish Things, 1969, The Klansman, 1974, Mitchell, 1975, Avalanche Express, 1979, Tom Horn, 1980; (TV series) The Big Valley, 1965-69, Hunter, 1977, Dynasty, 1980-89 (Emmy award nominee 1983); (TV movies) Female Artillery, 1973, Nakia, 1974, The Big Ripoff, 1975, Nowhere to Run, 1978, Standing Tall, 1978, Bare Essence, 1982, I'll Take Romance, 1983 (also exec. prodr.), Dynasty Reunion, 1991, The Gambler Returns: The Luck of the Draw, 1991, Dazzle, 1995, The Stepsister, 1997; (TV mini-series) include Bare Essence, 1982, The Gambler: The Adventure Continues, 1983, North and South Book II, 1986, The Last Frontier, 1986, The Gambler Returns: The Luck of the Draw, 1991, Dazzle, 1995; sr. prodr.: Yanni in Concert: Live at the Acropolis, 1994; author: Linda Evans Beauty and Exercise Book, 1983; guest appearances include Bachelor Father, 1960, The Adventures of Ozzie & Harriet, 1962, My Favorite Martian, 1965, McCloud, 1973, McMillan and Wife, 1975, The Rockford Files, 1975, The Love Boat, 1981, 1982, The Fall Guy, 1981, Dynasty: The Reunion, 1991, Dynasty Reunion: Catfights and Caviar, 2006 and several others. Office: 9696 Culver Blvd Ste 203 Culver City CA 90232-2700

EVANS, LINDA KAY, publishing executive; b. Tipton, Ind., June 16, 1945; d. Walter K. and Helen S. (Fakes) E. BA in English, Purdue U., Lafayette, 1968. Asst. to mng. editor Random House Pubs., NYC, 1969-71; asst. to dir. editorial svcs. Sch. div. McGraw-Hill Book Co., NYC, 1971-75, mgr. state contracts and inventory dept., 1975-88; bookstore owner, pres. The Literary Bookshop, NYC, 1988-93; prodn. mgr. trade div. Simon & Schuster, NYC, 1994—2004, sr. prodn. mgr. trade div., 2004—07; ret., 2007. Pub. cons. for sch. textbooks Prentice-Hall Book Co., Englewood Cliffs, N.J., 1992-93. Recipient Holiday Window Display award to Lit. Bookshop, Greenwich Village C. of C., 1990. Avocations: reading, travel, antiques. Home Phone: 212-534-5306; Office Phone: 212-698-7237.

EVANS, LOUISE, investor, retired psychologist; b. San Antonio; d. Henry Daniel and Adela (Pariser) E.; m. Thomas Ross Gambrell, Feb. 23, 1960. BS, Northwestern U., 1949; MS in Clin. Psychology, Purdue U., 1952, PhD in Clin. Psychology, 1955. Lic. marriage, family and child counselor Calif.; Nat. Register of Health Svc. Providers in Psychology; lic. psychologist, Calif., N.Y. (inactive); diplomate Clin. Psychology, Am. Bd. Profl. Psychology. Intern clin. psychology Menninger Found. Topeka (Kans.) State Hosp., 1952-53; postdoctoral fellow clin. child psychology Menninger Clinic, Topeka, 1955-56; staff psychologist Kankakee (Ill.) State Hosp., 1954-55; head staff psychologist child guidance clinic Kings County Hosp., Bklyn., 1957-58; dir. psychology clinic Barnes-Renard Hosp.; instr. med. psychology Sch. Medicine Washington U., 1959-60; clin. rsch. cons. Episc. City Diocese, St. Louis, 1959-60; pvt. practice Fullerton, Calif., 1960—93; fellow Internat. Coun. Sex Edn. and Parenthood, 1984, Am. U., Washington. Psychol. cons. Fullerton Cmty. Hosp., 1961-81; staff cons. clin. psychology Martin Luther Hosp., Anaheim, Calif., 1963-70; chair, participant psychol. symposiums, 1956—; spkr., lectr. in field. Contbr. articles on clin. psychology to profl. publs. Elected to Hall of Fame Ctrl. H.S., Evansville, Ind., 1966; recipient Svc. award Yuma County (Ariz.) Head Start Program, 1972, Statue of Victory Personality of Yr. award Centro Studi E. Ricerche Delle Nazioni, Italy, 1985, Alumni Merit award Northwestern U. Coll. Arts and Scis., 1997; named Miss Heritage, Heritage Publs., 1965. Fellow AAAS (emeritus), APA (Soc. for the Psychology of Women divsn., psychotherapy divsn., Internat. Psychology Recognition award for lifelong contbns. to advancement of psychology internationally 2002), Soc. Clin. Psychology, Soc. Cons. Psychology (dir. exec. bd. 1976-79), Acad. Clin. Psychology, Am. Assn. Applied and Preventive Psychology (charter), Royal Soc. for the Promotion of Health Eng. (emeritus), Internat. Coun. Psychologists (dir. 1977-79, sec. 1962-64, 73-76, 2 awards 2003, recognition for pioneering leadership in internat. psychology, named amb. for life award 2003), Am. Orthopsychiat. Assn. (life), World Wide Acad. Scholars of N.Z. (life), Assn. Psychol. Sci. (charter), L.A. Soc. Clin. Psychologists (exec. bd. 1966-67), Internat. Coun. Psychologists; mem. AAUP (emeritus), Calif. Psychol. Assn. (life, ins. com. 1961-65), LA County Psychol. Assn. (emeritus), Orange County Psychol. Assn. (charter founder, exec. bd. 1961-62), Am. Pub. Health Assn. (emeritus), Internat. Platform Assn., NY Acad. Scis. (emeritus), Purdue U. Alumni Assn. (life, past pres. coun., mem. dean's club, Citizenship award 1975, Disting. Alumni award 1993, Old Master 1993), Northwestern U. Past 1851 Soc. (Coll. Arts and Scis. Merit award 1997), Ctr. Study Presidency, Soc. Jewelry Historians USA (charter), Alumni Assn. Menninger Sch. Psychiatry, Sigma Xi (emeritus). Achievements include development of innovative theories and techniques of clinical practice; acknowledged pioneer in development of psychology as science and profession both nationally and internationally, and in marital and family therapy, and in consulting to hospitals and clinics. Office: PO Box 6067 Beverly Hills CA 90212-1067 Office Phone: 310-474-1361. Office Fax: 310-474-1361.

EVANS, LYNN LOUISE MORAND, archaeologist; b. Cin., May 21, 1965; d. James M. and Diane L. Morand; m. James V. Evans, May 3, 1997. BA, Beloit Coll., Wis., 1983—87; PhD, U. Pa., Phila., 1987—93. Asst. Beloit Hist. Soc., 1986—87; archaeologist Mackinac State Hist. Parks, Mackinaw City, Mich., 1989—96, curator of archaeology, 1996—. Mem. Mich. State Hist. Preservation Rev. Bd., Lansing, 2001—. Author: (book) Keys to the Past, (monographs) House D of the Southeast Row House, Craft Industries at Fort Michilimackinac. Trainer Girl Scouts Mitten Bay, Saginaw, 1999—2007. Fellow: Conf. Mich. Archaeology; mem.: Coun. NE Hist. Archaeology, Soc. Am. Archaeology, Soc. Hist. Archaeology (midwest current rsch. coord. 2003—), Mich. Archaeological Soc., Phi Beta Kappa. Office: Mackinac State Historic Parks PO Box 873 Mackinaw City MI 49701 Home Phone: 231-436-5347. Business E-Mail: evansll@michigan.gov.

EVANS, MARGARET ANN, human resources administrator, business owner; b. Great Bend, Kans., Dec. 26, 1947; d. Freddy Florence and Peggy (Hawkins) Green; children: Carl André, Christopher Dion. B in Psychology, U. Mo., 1971, MPA, 1972; PhD, Kennedy Western U., 2005. Pers. specialist Met. Jr. Coll., Kansas City, Mo., 1972-73; employee rels. specialist Amoco Oil Co., Kansas City, Mo., 1973-74; classification specialist Richards-Gebaur AFB, Mo., 1974-75; employee rels. officer Govt. Employee Hosp. Assn., Kansas City, 1977-84, mgr. pers., 1984-87, dir. human resources, 1987—. Mem. pers. com. Sta. KKFI, Kansas City, 1989—; mem. cert. bd. Human Resource Certification Inst., exam devel. dir., 1994-95, sec.-treas., 1996-97; pres. Human Resource Mgmt. Assn. Kansas City, 1997-98. Sec., v.p. Booster Club, Hickman Mills HS, Kansas City, 1989—; bd. dirs. Saturday Scholars, 2000-02; mem. adv. bd. CORO, Kansas City, 2002-04, SAVE, Kansas City, 2005-06. Recipient Contbr. of Yr. award Human Resource Mgmt. Assn., 1992, Pres. award 1993, 1995; named One of Kansas City's 100 Most Influential Kansas Citians KC Globe Most Influential African Ams. of Kansas City, 1993, 95, 96, 97; Ford Found. fellow U. Mo., 1971. Mem. NAFE, NAACP, ASTD, Nat. Assn. African Ams. in Human Resources (life), Nat. Forum Black Pub. Adminstrs., Soc. Human Resources Mgmt. (pers. rsch. com. Kansas City chpt. 1989—, mem. nat. rsch. com. 1989-98, nat. com. 1990—, sec.-treas. Mo. state coun. 1992-93, bd. dir., v.p. at large 1999-2000, v.p. Area IV 2001, 02, 03), Pers. Mgmt. Assn. (co-chmn. coll. rels. 1981), Urban League, Links, Inc., Alpha Kappa Alpha (chair midwestern regional conf., 1996, mem. nat. human resource com. 2005-, mem. heritage com. 2005-, Outstanding Grad. Soror). Home: 10216 E 96th St Kansas City MO 64134-2309 Office: Govt Employee Hosp Assn 17306 E US Highway 24 Independence MO 64056-1808 Office Phone: 816-257-3305. Business E-Mail: margaret.evans@geha.com.

EVANS, MARGARET GRIFFIN, music educator; MusB, U. N.C.; MusM, U. Ill.; MusD, Northwestern U., Evanston, Ill. Piano faculty U. Mont., Missoula, Mont., 1982—85; doctoral tchg. fellow Northwestern U., Evanston, 1985—90; piano faculty Meredith Coll., Raleigh, NC, 1994—. Adjudicator numerous competitions, 1982—; judge Bartok-Kabalevsky-Prokofiev Internat. Piano Competition, Music Tchrs. Nat. Assn., 1982—, 57th Hong Kong Schs. of Music Competition, Hong Kong, 2005. Musician: (piano recitalist, concerto soloist) Solo recitals, collaborative performances with orchestra, vocalists and instrumentalists in North Carolina, Illinois, Pennsylvania, Washington, Oregon, Montana, and Switzerland. Recipient Phi Kappa Phi, U. Ill. chpt., Pi Kappa Lambda Cert. of Merit, Meredith Coll., Pi Kappa Lambda, U. Mont., Phi Beta Kappa, U. of NC; Faculty Devel. grants, Meredith Coll., 2000, 2001, 2002, 2003, 2004. Mem.: Raleigh Music Club, Nat. Guild of Piano Tchrs., Raleigh Piano Tchrs. Assn., Music Tchrs. Nat. Assn., Raleigh Chamber Music Guild (bd. of directors 2000—03). Avocations: sailing, horseback riding, travel, cooking, painting. Office: Music Dept Meredith Coll 3800 Hillsborough St Raleigh NC 27607 Home Phone: 919-755-9175; Office Phone: 919-760-8349.

EVANS, MARI, author; b. Toledo; Student, U. Toledo; L.H.D. (hon.), Marian Coll., 1975. Instr. black lit., writer-in-residence Ind. U.-Purdue U. at Indpls., 1969-70; asst. prof. black lit., writer-in-residence Ind. U., Bloomington, 1970-78; asst. prof. Purdue U., 1978-80, Cornell U., 1981-83; assoc. prof. SUNY-Albany, 1985-86. Vis. asst. prof. Washington U., St. Louis, 1980, Northwestern U., 1972-73; disting. writer-in-residence Cornell U., 1983-85; disting. writer-in-residence, assoc. prof. U. Miami, Coral Gables, Fla., 1989; writer-in-residence Spelman Coll., Atlanta, 1989-90; cons. Discovery Grant Program, Nat. Endowment for Arts, 1969-70; cons. ethnic studies Bobbs-Merrill Co., 1970-73. Producer, dir., writer TV program The Black Experience, WTTV, Indpls., 1968-73; author: poems Where Is All the Music, 1968, I Am A Black Woman, 1970, Nightstar, 1980, A Dark and Splendid Mass, 1992; juveniles J.D, 1973, I Look at Me, 1974, Singing Black, 1976, Jim Flying High, 1979; playwright, dir.: River of My Song, 1977, Boochie, 1985, Portrait of a Man, 1985; playwright: stage musical Eyes, 1982, 94, 95; editor: (non-fiction) Black Women Writers 1950-80: A Critical Evaluation, 1984; contbr. poetry, articles and short stories to textbooks, anthologies, periodicals. Chmn. lit. adv. panel Ind. Arts Commn., 1976-77; chmn. Statewide Com. for Penal Reform; mem. bd. mgmt. Fall Creek Pkwy. YMCA; bd. dirs. 1st World Found.; mem. Ind. Corrections Code Commn. Woodrow Wilson Found. grantee, 1968; recipient Ind. U. Writers Conf. award, 1970, 1st Ann. Poetry award Black Acad. Arts and Letters, 1971; John Hay Whitney fellow, 1965-66; MacDowell fellow, 1975; Copeland fellow Amherst Coll., 1980, Nat. Endowment Arts grantee, 1981-82;, Yaddo Writers Colony fellow, 1984; recipient Gwendolyn Brooks award, 1989, 96, Hazel J. Bryant award Bd. dirs., Midwest African Am. Theatre Alliance, 1989, Zora Neal Hurston-Paul Robeson award Nat. Coun. Black Studies, Inc., 1996. Mem. Authors Guild, Authors League Am., African Heritage Studies Assn.

EVANS, MARK IRA, obstetrician, geneticist; b. Bklyn., May 14, 1952; s. Robert Bernard and Sonia Beatrice Evans. BS in Psychology, Tufts U., 1973; MD, SUNY, Bklyn., 1978. Diplomate Am. Bd. Ob-Gyn, Am. Bd. Med. Genetics. Resident in ob-gyn. U. Chgo., 1979—82; med. genetics fellow NIH, Bethesda, Md., 1982—84; dir. reproductive genetics Hutzel Hosp. Wayne State U., Detroit, 1984—2001, Charlotte B. Failing prof. ob-gyn. and human genetics Ctr. Molecular Med./Path., 1991—2001, disting. prof., 2000, dir. Ctr. for Fetal Diagnosis and Therapy, 1985—2001, dir. human genetics program, 1996—2001, chmn., chief, 1998—2001; prof., chmn. ob-gyn, prof. human genetics, dir. fetal therap Hahnemann Hosp., Phila., 2000—02; dir. fetal therapy program MCP Hahnemann U., 2000—02; dir. Inst. Genetics and Fetal Medicine Columbia U. Coll. of Physicians and Surgeons, NYC, 2002—; prof. ob-gyn St. Lukes Roosevelt Hosp. Ctr./Columbia U., 2002—. Mem. adv. bd. Ehlrs Danlos Found., L.A., 1986—, Corning Metpath, Quest Diagnostics, 1988-2000, Lab. Corp., 2003—, Nat. Adv. Bd. on Ethics in Reproduction, Washington; mem. ethics com. Am. Coll. Ob-Gyn., 1987-90, Molecular Medicine and Genetics, Wayne State U. Author: (textbooks) Pretest: Obsterics and Gynecology, 6th rev. edit., 1991, 9th edit., 2000, (with C.C. Lin) Intrauterine Growth Retardation, 1984, (with others) Fetal Diagnosis Therapy: Science, Ethics and the Law, 1989, Reproductive Risks and Prenatal Diagnosis, 1992, The New Reproductive Genetics, 1993, Maternal Genetic Disease, 1996, Invasive Outpatient Procedures in Reproductive Medicine, 1997, Principles and Practice of Medical Therapy in Pregnancy, 1998, Study Guide, 1998, The Unborn Patient, 2001, Contemporary Therapy for Obstetrics & Gynecology, 2002; (with Evans and Rodeck) Ultrasound and Fetal Therapy, 2000; (with Evans, Platt and De La Cruz) Fetal Therapy, 2000; editor: (with others) The Genetic Revolution and Obstetrics and Gynecology, 2002, New Genetics for the Clinician, 2002; contbr. articles to profl. jours. Fellow Am. Coll. Ob-Gyn. (course coordination com. 1996-99), Am. Coll. Med. Genetics (founder); mem. AMA (nat. ultrasound task force 1990-91), Internat. Fetal Medicine Surgery Soc. (pres. 1986-87, 96-97), Am. Soc. Human Genetics, Soc. Gynecol. Investigation, Ctrl. Assn. Ob-Gyn. (bd. dirs. 1998-2000, pres. 2004), Soc. Perinatal Obstetricians, Am. Gynecol. and Obstetrics Soc., Ctrl. Assn. Obstetrics and Gynecologists (v.p. 2004—). Jewish. Office: Inst for Genetics and Fetal Medicine St Lukes Roosevelt Hosp Ctr 1000 10th Ave Ste 11A-11 New York NY 10019 Home Phone: 201-585-0686; Office Phone: 212-523-5895. Business E-Mail: IGFM@chpnet.org.

EVANS, MARSHA JOHNSON, former non-profit association administrator, retired military officer; b. Springfield, Ill., Aug. 12, 1947; d. Walter Edward Johnson and Alice Anne Field; m. Gerard Riendeau Evans, June 30, 1979. AB, Occidental Coll., 1968; MA, Fletcher Sch., 1977, MA in Law & Diplomacy, 1977; postgrad., Nat. War Coll., 1988-89. Commd. ensign USN, 1968, advanced through grades to rear admiral, 1993; mideast policy officer Commander-in-Chief, U.S. Naval Forces, Europe, London, 1977-79; spl. asst. to sec. US Dept. Treasury, Washington, 1979-80; staff analyst Office of Chief Naval Ops., Washington, 1980-81; dep. dir. Pres. Commn. on White House Fellowships, Washington, 1981-82; exec. officer Recruit Tng. Command, San Diego, 1982-84; commanding officer Naval Tech. Tng. Ctr., San Francisco, 1984-86; battalion officer, sr. lectr. polit. sci. U.S. Naval Acad., Annapolis, Md., 1986-88; chief of staff San Francisco Naval Base, 1989-91, U.S. Naval Acad., Annapolis, Md., 1991-92; exec. dir. of the standing com. on mil. and civilian women Dept. Navy, 1992-93; comdr. Navy Recruiting Command, Washington, 1993-95; supt. Naval Postgrad. Sch., Monterey, Calif., 1995-97; CEO, nat. exec. dir. Girl Scouts U.S.A., NYC, 1998—2002; pres. ARC, Washington, 2002—05. Mem. bd. visitors U.S. Mil. Acad. at West Point, 2002-06; interim dir. George C. Marshall European Ctr. Security Studies, Garmisch Partenkirchen, Germany, 1996-97; bd. dirs. Lehman Brothers Holdings, Inc., Weight Watchers Internat., Inc., Huntsman Corp., Office Depot. Advisory bd. Pew Partnership for Civic Change Pew Charitable Trusts; dir. Naval Acad. Found. White House fellow, 1979; Chief Naval Ops. scholar, 1976. Mem. Mortar Bd., Phi Beta Kappa. Home Phone: 703-519-2130; Office Phone: 202-412-2444. E-mail: mevansnps@aol.com.

EVANS, MARTIN FREDERIC, lawyer; b. Nashville, June 12, 1947; s. Robert Clements and Adelaide Hawkins (Roberts) E.; m. Margaret Carroll Kidder, Apr. 17, 1982. BA, U. Va., 1969; JD, Yale U., 1972. Bar: N.Y. 1973, U.S. Dist. Ct. (so. dist.) N.Y. 1973, U.S. Ct. Appeals (2d cir.) 1974, U.S. Ct. Appeals (D.C. cir.) 1981, U.S. Supreme Ct. 1981, D.C. 1982. Assoc. Debevoise & Plimpton, NYC, 1972-80, ptnr. litig. dept., 1981—. Mem. ABA (sect. for antitrust law), Assn. of Bar of City of N.Y., Phi Beta Kappa. Office: Debevoise & Plimpton 919 Third Ave New York NY 10022-6225 Office Phone: 212-909-6293. Business E-Mail: mfevans@debevoise.com.

EVANS, MARY JOHNSTON, corporate director; b. Shawnee, Okla., Feb. 28, 1930; d. Paul Xenophon and Helen Elizabeth (Alford) Johnston; children by previous marriage: Marcy Head Benson, Paul Johnston Head, Eric Talbott Head; m. James H. Evans, 1984. Student, Wellesley Coll., 1947-48, U. Okla., 1949. Dir. Amtrak, 1974-80, vice-chmn., 1975-79. Bd. dirs. Household Internat., Inc., Saint-Gobain Corp., Sunoco, Inc., Delta Air Lines, Inc., Moody's Corp. Pres. Jr. League Oklahoma City, 1968-69; trustee Nat. Coun. Crime and Delinquency, 1971-75, Presbyn. Med. Ctr., Oklahoma City, 1969-75; trustee Brick Presbyn. Ch., 1985-89; bd. dirs. St. Anthony Hosp., 1973-75; bd. visitors U. Pitts. Grad. Sch. Bus., 1978-85; trustee Mary Baldwin Coll., Staunton, Va., 1976-83, Carnegie Hall, 1985-92. Recipient Law Day award-Liberty Bell award Okla. Bar Assn., 1971, Disting. Svc. award U. Okla., 1981; named one of Top 100 Corp.

Women Bus. Week mag., 1976; named to Okla. Hall of Fame, 1978 Mem. Conf. Bd. (Sr.), Colony Club, River Club, Maidstone Club (East Hampton, N.Y.), Pi Beta Phi. Presbyterian (elder). Address: 920 5th Ave New York NY 10021-4160 also: 32 Windmill Ln East Hampton NY 11937-3605

EVANS, MICHAEL D., lawyer; b. Columbia, Mo., Oct. 23, 1946; BA, Okla. State U., 1969; JD, U. Okla., 1973. Bar: Okla. 1973. Asst. dist. atty. Third Jud. Dist. Okla., Tillman County, 1975—82, 1998; city atty. Frederick, Okla., 1982—; with Massad, Evans, & Kent, Frederick, Okla. Fellow: Okla. Bar Found., Am. Bar Found. (life); mem.: ABA, Okla. Bar Assn. (chmn. profl. responsibility commn. 1992, 1995, bd. govs. 1996—98, v.p. 2001, pres.-elect 2004, pres. 2005), Tillman County Bar Assn. (past pres.). Office: Massad Evans & Kent 120 N Ninth St Drawer 606 Frederick OK 73542 Office Phone: 580-335-5531. Office Fax: 508-335-5532. E-mail: meklaw@pldi.net.*

EVANS, NANCY PELTIER, behavioral specialist, educator; d. Frenchy M. and Barbara Anne (Williams) Peltier; m. Geoffery David Evans, Aug. 14, 1983; children: Keith Donald, Laura Anne. BA in Tchg., Sam Houston State U., Huntsville, Tex., 1974. Cert. tchr. Tex., 1974. Tchr., coach Coldspring Ind. Sch. Dist., Tex., 1975—81, Waller Ind. Sch. Dist., Tex., 1981—85, behavioral specialist, 1995—. Named Favorite Tchr. of Yr., Waller Jr. High, 1985. Mem.: Assn. Tex. Profl. Educators (life), Waller Women's Club (social dir. 2002—06). Independent. Roman Catholic. Avocation: travel. Home: 31814 Cypress Cir Waller TX 77484 Office: Waller Ind Sch Dist 2202 Waller Waller TX 77484 Home Phone: 936-931-1353; Office Phone: 936-372-4112. Personal E-mail: nevans46@yahoo.com. Business E-Mail: nevans@waller.isd.esc4.net.

EVANS, NOLLY SEYMOUR, lawyer; b. Augusta, Ga., Sept. 16, 1927; s. Nolly Seymour and Laura (Taylor) E.; m. Judith Anne Leach, Feb. 18, 1965; children: Samantha, Meredydd, Clelia, Nolly. BFA in Music, U. Ga., 1948, MA in English Lit., 1950; LLB, Yale U., 1956; LLD, Yale Law Sch., 1971. Bar: N.Y. 1956. Assoc. firm Milbank, Tweed, Hadley & McCloy, NYC, 1956-64; fin. counsel Amax, Inc., NYC, 1964-70; gen. counsel, sec. Gilman Paper Co., NYC, 1970-74, Crouse-Hinds Co., Syracuse, NY, 1976-82; counsel Hancock & Estabrook, Syracuse, NY, 1982-83; prin. Nolly S. Evans Law Offices, Syracuse, 1983-93. Docent Homewood House Mus., Balt. With US Army, 1947—48. Mem. Federalist Soc., Madison Club (Washington), Balt. Country Club, Confrerie des Chevaliers du Tastevin (grand officer), Sous Commanderie de Etats-Unis (grand officier), Sous Commanderie de Ctrl. N.Y. (grand senechal, grand officier), N.Y., Bordeaux (comdr.), Le Grand Conseil de Bordeaux, Jurade de St. Emilion, Connetable de Guyenne, Royal Over-Seas Club (London), Balt. Country Club, and others. Home: 647 W University Pkwy Baltimore MD 21210-2907 also: Shadowlands Park Luke's Ferry Rd Clarks Hill SC 29821

EVANS, OLIVER H., college administrator; b. Burlington, Vt., June 15, 1944; s. Samuel H. and Louise (Lifsey) E.; m. Eileen Beary, Sept. 10, 1973; children: Rachel, Ethan. BA, Albion Coll., 1966; MA, Purdue U., 1969, PhD, 1972. Asst. prof. Dakota State Coll., Madison, S.D., 1972-74, S.D. State U., Brookings, 1974-78, Creighton U., Omaha, 1978-80, Western Mich. U., Kalamazoo, 1980-84; dir. grad. studies Nazareth Coll., Kalamazoo, 1984-87, v.p. acad. affairs, 1987-90, pres., 1990, Kendall Coll. of Art and Design, Grand Rapids. Cons., evaluator North Cen. Assn., Chgo., 1988—. Author: George Henry Boker, 1984; contbr. articles to profl. jours. Office: Kendall College of Art and Design 17 Fountain St NW Grand Rapids MI 49503-1312*

EVANS, ORINDA D., federal judge; b. Savannah, Ga., Apr. 23, 1943; d. Thomas and Virginia Elizabeth (Grieco) E.; m. Roberts O. Bennett, Apr. 12, 1975; children: Wells Cooper, Elizabeth Thomas. BA, Duke U., 1965; JD with distinction, Emory U., 1968. Bar: Ga. 1968. Assoc. Fisher & Phillips, Atlanta, 1968-69, Alston, Miller & Gaines, Atlanta, 1969-74, ptnr., 1974-79; judge US Dist Ct. (No. Dist.) Ga., Atlanta, 1979—, chief judge. Adj. prof. Emory U. Law Sch., 1974-77; counsel Atlanta Crime Commn., 1970-71 Recipient Disting. award BBB, 1972. Mem. Atlanta Bar Assn. (dir. 1979) Democrat. Episcopalian. Office: US Dist Courthouse 1988 US Courthouse 75 Spring St SW Atlanta GA 30303-3309

EVANS, PAT, mayor; b. Abilene, Tex., Feb. 12, 1943; m. Chuck Evans, 1964; 3 children. BA, U. Tex., Austin, 1964; JD, So. Meth. U., 1991. Atty. Gay & McCall, Inc., 1991—95; family law instr. Southeastern Paralegal Inst., 1996—97; atty., 1991—; dep. mayor pro-tem Plano, Tex., 2000; mayor, 2002—. Tchr. Richardson Ind. Sch. Dist., 1964—70; owner landscape design co. Exec. bd. North Tex. Coun. Govts.; exec. com. Dallas REgional Mobility Coun.; mem. Plano Econ. Devel. Exec. Bd.; past. pres. Jr. League, Plano; mem. Metroplex Mayor's Coun., Collin County Mayor's Coun. Office: City of Plano 1520 Avenue K Plano TX 75074

EVANS, PAUL, osteopath; b. Nutley, NJ, May 23, 1950; m. Roxanne Romack. BS cum laude in Biology, U. Miami, 1972; DO, Phila. Coll. Osteo. Medicine, 1979. Diplomate Am. Bd. Family Medicine, Nat. Bd. Osteo. Examiners; cert. Am. Osteo. Bd. Family Practice. Commd. 2d lt. U.S. Army, 1972, advanced through grades to col., 1995; asst. chief mil. pers. U.S. Army Med. Svc. Corps, Frankfurt, Fed. Republic Germany, 1972-75; intern Letterman Army Med. Ctr., San Francisco, 1979-80; resident in family practice Womack Army Community Hosp., Ft. Bragg, N.C., 1980-82; dir. family practice quality assurance Tripler Army Med. Ctr., Hawaii, 1982-84, dir. residency tng. dept. family practice Hawaii, 1984-86; asst. prof. family practice, physician Uniformed Svcs. U. Health Scis., F. Edward Hebert Sch. Med., Bethesda, Md., 1986-92, clerkship dir., 1986-88, dir. continuing med. edn., 1987-91, asst. prof. mil. and emergency medicine, 1991-92; chief dept. family practice Reynolds Army Community Hosp., Ft. Sill, Okla., 1992-94, chief primary care, 1994-95, chmn. rsch. com., dir. hosp. continuing med. edn., 1992-95, dir. physicians asst. tng. program, dir. quality improvement, 1992-94; tchg. chief dept. family practice Madigan Army Med. Ctr., Tacoma, 1995-97, dir. primary care projects Tricare N.W., 1997-98, dir. primary care, mem. exec. bd. dirs., exec. adv. coun.; clin. assoc. prof. of family medicine U. Wash., 1996-98; ret. U.S. Army, 1998; assoc. dean curricular affairs, dir. ednl. resources/devel. Okla. State U. Ctr. Health Scis., Tulsa, 1998—2003; prof. family med., exec. coun. curriculum com., learning resources com. Okla. State U. Coll. Osteopathic Med., Tulsa, 1998—2003, dir. dept. edn. resources and devel., 1998—2003, prof. family medicine, 2003—04; chief acad. officer, vice dean Ga. campus Phila. Coll. Osteo. Medicine, Suwanee, Ga., 2004—. Presenter, lectr., cons. in field; clin. faculty, family practice residency DeWitt Army Hosp., Ft. Belvoir, Va., 1986-89, 91-92, Malcolm Grow USAF Med. Ctr., Andrews AFB, Md., 1989-91; mem. Nat. Bd. Osteopathic Med. Examiners Competency and Evidence Based Medicine Com., 2005—. Reviewer Am. Family Physician, Patient Care, Military Medicine, Family Medicine, Farmily Practice Mgmt.; mem. editl. bd. Jour. Am. Osteo. Assn., 2003—; contbr. articles to profl. jours. Asst. med. dir. Old Dominion 100 Mile Run, Front Royal, Va., 1990, med. dir., 1991; asst. med. dir. Am. Diabetes Assn. Youth Camp, Honolulu, 1984, med. dir., 1985. USUHS grantee. Fellow Am. Acad. Family Physicians; mem. Am. Osteo. Assn., Am. Coll. Osteo. Family Physicians, Uniformed Svcs. Acad. Family Physicians (chmn. edn. com. 1993-97, sec.-treas. 1997-98), Soc. Tchrs. Family Medicine (genogram rsch. com. 1989-94, managed care com. 1997-2000, faculty devel. com. 1999-2003), Amer. Osteo. Assn., Amer. Coll. Osteo. Family Phys., Ga. Osteo. Assn., Phila. Coll. Osteo. Medicine Alumni Assn. (life), Omicron Delta Kappa, Alpha Epsilon Delta. Avocations: nature art collecting, golf, birdwatching. Home: 3201 St Ives Country Club Pkwy Duluth GA 30097 Office Phone: 678-225-7504. Business E-Mail: paulev@pcom.edu.

EVANS, PAUL VERNON, lawyer; b. Colorado Springs, Colo., June 19, 1926; s. Fred Harrison and Emma Hooper (Austin) Evans; m. Patricia Gwyn Davis, July 27, 1964 (dec. Dec. 2001); children: Paula Jean, Bruce, Mike, Mark, Paul; m. Betty J. Haynes, 2002; m. Frances Irene Pool, Sept. 7, 1947 (div. 1963). BA cum laude, Colo. Coll., 1953; JD, Duke U., 1956. Bar: Colo. 1956, U.S. Dist. Ct. Colo. 1956, U.S. Supreme Ct. 1971, U.S. Ct. Appeals (10th cir.) 1974. Field mgr. Keystone Readers Service, Dallas, 1946-50; sole practice Colorado Springs, 1956-60; ptnr. Goodbar, Evans & Goodbar, 1960-63; sr. ptnr. Evans & Briggs Attys., Colorado Springs, 1963-95; ret., 2001. City atty. City of Fountain, Colo., 1958—62, City of Woodland Park, Colo., 1962—78; atty. Rock Creek Mesa Water Dist., Colorado Springs, 1963—2002. Author instruction materials. Precinct com. man Republican Com., Colorado Springs, 1956-72. Served with USNR, 1944-46, PTO. Recipient Jr. C. of C. Outstanding Achievement award, 1957. Mem. Colo. Mining Assn., Am. Jud. Soc., ABA, Colo. Bar Assn. (com. chmn. 1966-67, 84), El Paso County Bar Assn. (com. chmn. 1956—0, Assn. Trial Lawyers Am., Colo. and Local Trial Lawyers, Tau Kappa Alpha (pres.), Phi Beta Kappa. Clubs: Optimist (pres. 1966-67). Republican. Home and Office: 244 Cobblestone Dr Colorado Springs CO 80906-7624 Office Phone: 719-576-1926. Personal E-mail: paulvevans@msn.com.

EVANS, PETER KENNETH, advertising executive; b. Brighton, Eng., Apr. 18, 1935; s. Percy Edward and Doris (McCoy) E.; m. Juana Santana Ramirez, Mar. 31, 1956; children: Luis Miguel, Linda Rosa Del Rocio, Pilar De Los Angeles. Student, Varndean Sch., Brighton, 1946—50. Asst. art dir. Grant Advt., Toronto, Ont., Canada, 1958—61; creative group head Goodis, Goldberg, Soren, Toronto, 1961—63; v.p., creative dir. Baker/BBDO, Toronto, 1963—65; creative dir. Kenyon & Eckhardt, Toronto, 1965—67, Mexico City, 1967—68; exec. v.p., creative dir. Vladimir & Evans Inc., Miami, Fla., 1968—71; pres., creative dir. Evans & Ciccarone Inc., Miami, 1971—91; mktg. cons., 1991—; propr. Peter Evans Pipes, 1994—2001, Peter Evans Woodcrafting Solutions, 1998—; cartoonist Islander News, Key Biscayne, Fla., 1996—; pres. Peter Evans Response Mktg. & Advt., 1996—, Peter Evans Creative Svcs., 1997—. Instr. advt. Fla. Internat. U., Miami, 1974. Author: Jumpstart Marketing for the New Business Owner, 1993, Treasure Your Teeth, 1998; broadcaster radio reading svc. Sta. WLRN-FM (NPR affiliate), Miami, 1990—; playwright: Ruiz, 1982, Unconscious, 1996, Lost, 1997, Bang, 1998; actor: Scrooge, Social Security, 2000; inventor bed elevator, blind dog head protector, perfect wood carvers bench, sander-expander. Leader Jr. Achievement, Miami, 1968; asst. leader Boy Scouts Am., Miami, 1970; bd. dirs. Key Biscayne Music & Drama Club. Armament technician RAF, Fassberg, Germany, 1953-55, ETO. Recipient awards Can. TV Commls. Festival, N.Y. Art Dirs. Show, Clio awards, Andy awards, 100 Best US TV Commls., Printing Industry Am. awards, Top 24 US New Product Introductions, Miami Big Mike awards, Miami Addy awards, Fla. State Addy awards, 1st pl. Fla. Press Assn. awards, 2006, Best Editl. Cartoons of Yr., 2005, 06, 07; named 100 Top US Creative Men Ad Day/USA, Art Dir. of Yr. Greater Miami Ad Fedn Mem. Nat. Assn. Underwater Instrs., Profl. Assn. Diving Instrs., Dramatists Guild, Nat. Wood Carvers Assn., Am. Birding Assn., Miami Bach Soc., Nat. Audubon Soc., Key Biscayne Beach Club, South Fla. Woodcarvers Club. Anglican. Home and Office: 285 W Mashta Dr Key Biscayne FL 33149-2419

EVANS, PETER YOSHIO, ophthalmologist, educator; b. Tokyo, Dec. 19, 1925; came to the U.S., 1957; s. Paul Yuzuru Kawai and Vicki Wichgraf Evans; m. Helga Kemp, Sept. 19, 1953; children: Johannes, Marina, Michael, André, Thomas, Ursula, Christiane. MD, Innsbruck U., 1951. Resident Innsbruck (Austria) and Frankfurt (Germany) Univs., 1951-55; intern Sisters Charity Hosp., Buffalo, 1957-58; chief dept. ophthalmology D.C. Gen. Hosp., 1958-63; fellow Georgetown U., Washington, 1958-59, program dir. div. ophthalmology, 1963-69, chmn., 1969-83, prof., 1973-92, prof. emeritus, 1992—. Cons. D.C. Columbia Lighthouse for the Blind, 1959-63; sr. cons. D.C. Child and Maternal Welfare Dept., 1961-74; exec. v.p. Joint Commn. Allied Health Pers. in Ophthalmology, St. Paul, 1981-96; bd. dirs. Internat. Eye Found., 1999-2006. Author, producer scientific films; contbr. articles to profl. jours.; editor numerous jours. Recipient Man of Decade award, Joint Commn. on Allied Health Pers. in Ophthalmology, 1997, Promotion of Peace and Vision award, Internat. Eye Found., 2002. Fellow Am. Acad. Ophthalmology (Disting. Svc. award 1982), Austrian Ophthalm. Soc. (First Fuchs Meml. Lectr. 1975), German Ophthalm. Soc., Am.-Austrian Soc. (pres. 1989-91), Cosmos Club D.C. Lutheran. Avocations: skiing, violin, photography, bridge, philately. Home and Office: 3113 Lewis Pl Falls Church VA 22042-2511 Personal E-mail: pye19@cox.net.

EVANS, PHILIP G., former sports association executive; m. Tammy Evans; children: Alex, Logan, Ryan, Henry. B in Hist. and Econs., U. Va., 1984; JD, U. Va. Sch. Law, 1988. Assoc. Latham & Watkins, 1988; with Internat. Family Entertainment, Inc.; positions up to exec. v.p. bus. and legal affairs Continental Basketball Assn.; dir. legal and bus. affairs NBA Devel. League, Greenville, SC, pres., 2002—07; gen. counsel Arena Ventures; cons. Devel. League matters NBA, 2007—. Office Phone: 964-248-1100. Office Fax: 864-248-1102.*

EVANS, R. GREGORY, bioterrorism researcher, educator; b. Columbus, Ohio, Oct. 4, 1946; s. Robert Louis and Almont Evans; m. Rachel Debra Schwartz, Aug. 10, 2005. BA, Hofstra U., 1970; MPH, St. Louis U., 1981, PhD, 1986. Assoc. prof. St. Louis U. Sch. Pub. Health, St. Louis, 1988—2002, prof., 2002—. Dir. divsn. environ. health St. Louis U. Sch. Pub. Health, 1992—2000, assoc. dean, 1994—97, dir., inst. biosecurity, 2000—. Avocations: furniture building, glass bead making, weaving. Office: Saint Louis Univ 3545 Lafayette Ave Saint Louis MO 63104 Office Phone: 314-977-8133. Business E-Mail: evansrg@slu.edu.

EVANS, RICHARD AUSTIN, education educator, consultant; b. Brady, Tex., May 24, 1959; s. Richard Austin Sr. and Dorene Evans; m. Arlene Emma McBee, Aug. 5, 1977; children: Chris, Ray. PhD in ednl. psychology, Tex. A&M, 2005. Rschr. assoc., instr. The Dept. of Ednl. Psychology, Tex. A&M U., College Station, 2000—03; asst. prof., coord. of undergraduate spl. programs U. of Tex. of the Permian Basin, Odessa, Tex., 2003—05; asst. prof. James Madison U., Harrisonburg, Va., 2005—. Consulting White Settlement Sch. Dists., White Settlement, Tex., 2005—. Grant advisor Revival Min. Fellowship Internat., Alvarado, Tex., 2004—06. Grantee Promoting Urban Culturally Diverse Spl. Needs Student Success, U.S. Dept. of Edn., Office of Spl. Edn. Programs, 2004, Tech. at Work, U. of Tex., 2005. Achievements include research in Successful Reading Programs. Home Phone: 540-433-0980; Office Phone: 540-568-6787. Business E-Mail: evansra@jmu.edu.

EVANS, RICHARD W., JR., (DICK), bank executive; b. Uvalde, Tex., 1946; m. Jimmie Ruth Evans. BBA, U. Tex., Austin, 1967. With Frost Bank, 1971—, exec. v.p., 1985, pres., CEO, 1985-93, chmn., 1993-94; chief banking officer Cullen/Frost Bankers, Inc., San Antonio, 1994-98, COO, 1995-98, chmn., 1995—, CEO, 1998—. Mem. adv. coun. FRS, 2003—06; bd. dirs. Fed. Res. Bank Dallas; mem. bus. adv. coun. McCombs Sch. Bus., U. Tex. Gen. campaign chmn. United Way San Antonio, 2003—04, chmn., 2004—05. Recipient Esperanza Hope award, Southwest Mental Health Ctr., 2006. Mem.: World Presidents Orgn., Fin. Svcs. Roundtable, San Antonio Livestock Exposition, Inc. Office: Cullen/Frost Bankers Inc 100 W Houston St PO Box 1600 San Antonio TX 78296 Fax: 210-22-4324.

EVANS, ROBERT, JR., economics professor; b. Sterling, Colo., Mar. 20, 1932; s. Robert and Mary Louise (Paradise) E.; m. Lois Ellen Herr, Nov. 6, 1955 (dec. 1994); children: Karen E., Robert, Janet K., Thomas W., L. Midori, Laura E., Katherine Joan; m. Marian Elizabeth Grotheer, Dec. 26, 1996. SB, MIT, 1954; PhD (Hillman fellow), U. Chgo., 1959. Asst. prof. indsl. relations MIT, 1959-65; assoc. prof. Brandeis U., Waltham, Mass., 1965-71, prof., 1971—, Atran prof. labor econs., 1975-98, chmn. dept. econs., 1970-72, 73-75, 84-87, dean Coll. Arts and Scis., 1975-81; retired, 1998. Vis. prof. Keio U., Tokyo, 1966-67, 72-73, 82-83, 88-89, 94-95; rsch. dir. study on prison industries Can. Corrections Assn., 1968-69. Author: Public Policy Toward Labor, 1965, The Labor Economics of Japan and the United States, 1971, Developing Policies for Public Security and Criminal Justice, 1973. Mem. Acton (Mass.) and Acton Boxborough Regional Sch. Com., 1971-72, 74-82, 84-88, regional chmn., 1972, 79-80, 85-86, town chmn., 1975-77; mem. Acton Fin. Com., 1997—, chair, 2000-2003. With U.S. Army, 1955-57. Fulbright Rsch. scholar, Japan, 1982-83, 88-89; Abe fellow, Japan, 1994-95. Mem. Am. Econ. Assn. Home: 4 Old Meadow Ln Acton MA 01720 E-mail: revans5557@verizon.net.

EVANS, ROBERT L., sports venue executive; married. BA in Econs., MacMurray Coll., Jacksonville, Ill.; MA in Quantitative Econs., Western Ill. U. Econs. analyst Caterpillar Inc., 1975; co-founder, pres. Caterpillar Logistics Svcs. Inc., 1986; v.p. customer support Mazda Motor Am. Inc., 1990—93; mng. ptnr. Ams. Supply Chain Practice Accenture Ltd., 1993—99; pres., COO Aspect Devel. Inc., 0199—2001; co-founder, mng. dir. Symphony Tech. Group, Palo Alto, Calif., 2001—04; pres. Tenlane Farm, LLC, Ky., 2004—; pres., CEO Churchill Downs, Inc., Louisville, 2006—. Bd. mem. Aftermarket Tech. Corp., Tumri Inc. Office: Churchill Downs Inc 700 Central Ave Louisville KY 40208 Office Phone: 502-636-4400.

EVANS, ROBERT SHELDON, manufacturing executive, director; b. Pitts., 1944; BA in History, U. Pa., 1966; MBA in Fin., Columbia U., 1968. V.p. Evans & Co. Inc., 1971-74; v.p. internat. ops. Crane Co., NYC, 1974-78, sr. v.p., 1978-79, exec. v.p., dir., 1979-84, CEO, 1984—2001, pres., chief ops. officer, 1986-91, chmn., 2001—. Chmn., CEO, bd. dirs. Medusa Corp.; bd. dirs. HBD Industries Inc., Fanstel, Inc. Mem. dean's adv. coun. Columbia Grad. Sch. Bus.; trustee Eaglebrook Sch. Office: Crane Co 100 1st Stamford Pl Stamford CT 06902-6740

EVANS, ROBERT WILLIAM, psychologist, theologian; b. Oakland, Calif., Jan. 18, 1958; s. Robert Troy and Gaye Ellen Evans; m. Kamrin Judith Korsmeier, Aug. 3, 1991; children: William Everett, Wade Christian. BA, UCLA, 1981; MA, Western Sem., 1983; PhD, Calif. Profl. Sch. Psychology, 1988, Trinity Div. Sch., 1998; postgrad., Harvard U., 1997—99, Oxford U., Eng., 2000; diploma (hon.), Moscow State U. Med. Sch., 2001. Lic. psychologist Colo., diplomate forensic medicine, forensic psychology, med. psychotherapy, forensic neuropsychology; cert. ordained min. Evangelical Free Ch. Am. Intern depts. psychiatry and neurology Kaiser Hosp. and Med. Ctr., San Francisco, 1987—89; pvt. practice clin. psychologist, 1990—; grad. asst. in systematic theology Trinity Evang. Div. Sch., Deerfield, Ill., 1996—97; tchg. fellow in ethics Harvard U., Cambridge, Mass., 1997—98; pres. Veritas Ministries Internat., Castro Valley, Calif., 1997—; dir. Veritas Inst. for Study of Bioethics and Pub. Values, Castro Valley, 1997—. Adj. prof. Knox Theol. Sem., 1999—, Trinity Evang. Divinity Sch., 2004—; vis. scholar U. Oxford, England, 2001, 02; pastor-theologian Christ Ch., Pleasanton, Calif., 2005—. Author: The Descent of Dignity, 2002; co-author: The Reproduction Revolution, 2000, Aging, Death, and the Quest for Immortality, 2004, Beyond Human Genomics: Exploring Our Post-Human Future, 2004; contbr. articles to profl. jours., mags. Recipient Gold medal for sci. and religion, Ctrl. European Cath. Bishops, 2000, award, Am. Platform Assn. Fellow: Am. Bd. Med. Psychotherapy, Am. Coll. Forensic Psychology, Am. Bd. Forensic Examiners, Ctr. Bioethics and Human Dignity, Am. Bd. Forensic Medicine; mem.: AAAS, Ctr. for Bioethics and Human Dignity, Evang. Philos. Soc., Evang. Theol. Soc., Christian Med. and Dental Assn., Am. Soc. Bioethics and Humanities, Nat. Eagle Scout Assn., UCLA Alumni Assn., Harvard Alumni Club of San Francisco. Mem. Evangelical Free Sh. Am. Address: PO Box 2327 Castro Valley CA 94546-0327 Office Phone: 510-727-1351. Business E-Mail: veritasministries@compuserve.com.

EVANS, ROGER, lawyer; b. Syracuse, NY, Apr. 18, 1951; s. David Longfellow and Louise Maude (Crawford) Evans; children: Jonathan Longfellow, Gillian Crawford, Catherine Leigh, Skylar Elizabeth. AB, Cornell U., 1974; postgrad., Columbia U., 1976-77; JD, Harvard U., 1977. Bar: Ohio 1977, U.S. Dist. Ct. (no. dist.) Ohio 1978, Tex. 1981, U.S. Dist. Ct. (no. dist.) Tex. 1981, U.S. Dist. Ct. (so. dist.) Tex. 1997, U.S. Ct. Appeals (5th, 6th and 11th cirs.) 1981, U.S. Ct. Appeals (10th cir.) 1982, U.S. Tax Ct. 1989, U.S. Dist. Ct. (we. and ea. dists.) Tex. 1998. Assoc. Jones, Day, Reavis & Pogue, Cleve., 1977-81, Dallas, 1981-84; ptnr. Shank, Irwin & Conant, Dallas, 1985, Gardner, Carton & Douglas, Dallas, 1986-88, Vinson & Elkins, Dallas, 1988-91; pvt. practice Dallas, 1991-2001; ptnr. Mathis & Donheiser, Dallas, 2001—. Gen. counsel Equest, Inc., Dallas, 1986—88; instr. trial advocacy, instr. law and econs. So. Meth. U. Sch. Law; instr. labor law Baylor U.; faculty Nat. Inst. Trial Advocacy. Author: Old Buck, 2006. Gen. counsel, bd. dirs. Freedom Ride Found., Dallas, 1985-86; cmty. svcs. bd. mgmt. YMCA, 1990-92; bd. dirs. Legal Svcs. Corp. North Tex., 1991-92; adv. bd. dirs. Providence Christian Sch. Tex., Inc., 1995-2000. Recipient Advocacy award, Dallas Epilepsy Assn., 1995. Mem. Tex. Bar Assn., Dallas Bar Assn., Cornell U. Alumni Assn. (class pres. 1984-89), Harvard U. Law Sch. Alumni Assn. No. Ohio (sec. 1978-81), Harvard Club. Office: 2001 Ross Ave Ste 4600 Dallas TX 75201 Office Phone: 214-661-8921. Business E-Mail: rogerevans@post.harvard.edu.

EVANS, RONALD M., microbiologist, educator; BA in Bacteriology, UCLA, 1970, PhD in Microbiology and Immunology, 1974. Asst. rsch. prof. dept. molecular cell biology Rockefeller U., NYC, 1975—78; from asst. to assoc. prof. tumor virology lab. Salk Inst. Biol. Studies Howard Hughes Med. Inst., La Jolla, Calif., 1978—84, sr. mem. molecular biology and virology lab. Salk Inst. Biol. Studies, 1984—86, prof. gene expression lab Salk Inst. Biol. Studies, 1986—, investigator, 1985—; prof. Salk Institute for Biol. Studies, San Diego. Adj. prof. dept. biology U. Calif., San Francisco, 1985—, adj. prof. dept. biomedical scis. Sch. Medicine, San Diego, 1989—, adj. prof. dept. neurosciences, 1995—; chmn. faculty Salk Inst. Biol. Studies Howard Hughes Med. Inst., La Jolla, 1993—94, La Jolla, 1997—98; mem. sci. adv. bd. SIBIA, 1983—; mem. external sci. adv. com. City of Hope, 1987; mem. molecular biology study sect. NIH, 1983—86, mem. molecular neurobiology study sect., 1984—85; mem. nat. adv. com. Pew Scholars Program in Biomedical Scis., 1987—2000; founder and chair sci. adv. bd. Ligand Pharm., 1988—; mem. program com. Searle Scholars, 1989—91; mem. Alfred P. Sloan Jr. selection com. GM Cancer Rsch. Found., 1991; organizer numerous confs. in field; mem. external sci. adv. bd. Mass. Gen. Hosp., 1996—; mem. sci. adv. bd. Dana Farber Cancer Inst., 1996—, Osaka Bioscience Inst., 1999—; S. Richard Hill, Jr. vis. prof. U. Ala., 1995; Woodward vis. prof. Meml. Sloan-Kettering, 1996; Burroughs Wellcome vis. prof. U. Mass., 1998; spkr. in field, lectr.; March of Dimes chair in Molecular and Developmental Neurobiology Salk Inst., La Jolla, Calif. Editor: Molecular Endocrinology, 1993—97; editor: (assoc. editor) Molecular Brain Rsch., 1985—93, Jour. Neuroscience, 1985—90, Neuron, 1987—93; mem. editl. bd. Receptors and Channels, 1992—93, Genes and Development, 1992—, Hormones and Signalling, 1996—; co-editor: Current Opinion in Cell Biology, 1993. Mem. fellowship screening com. Am. Cancer Soc., 1987—90. Named Calif. Scientist of Yr., Calif. Mus. Sci., 1994; recipient Gregory Pincus medal, Laurentian Soc., 1988, Louis S. Goodman and Alfred Gilman award, Am. Soc. Pharmacology and Exptl. Therapeutics, 1988, Van Meter/Rorer Pharm. prize, Am. Thyroid Assn., 1989, Gregory Pincus

Meml. award, Worcester Found. Exptl. Biology, 1991, Rita Levi Montalcini award, Fidia Rsch. Found. Neuroscience, 1991, Osborne and Mendel award, Am. Inst. Nutrition, 1992, award for cancer rsch., Robert J. and Claire Pasarow Found., 1993, Transatlantic medal, Soc. Endocrinology, 1994, Dickson prize in medicine, U. Pitts., 1994—95, Morton award, U. Liverpool, Biochemical Soc., 1996, Gerald Aurbach Meml. award, Assn. Bone and Mineral Rsch., 1997, Fred Conrad Koch award, Endocrine Soc., 1999, award for disting. achievement in metabolic rsch., Bristol-Myers Squibb, 2000, Alfred P. Sloan Jr. prize, GM Cancer Rsch. Found., 2003, Albert Lasker award for Basic Medical Rsch., 2004, Gairdner award for achievement in med. rsch., Gairdner Found., 2006; fellow, NIH, 1975—78; Rsch. Assoc. fellow, Cancer Rsch. Com. Calif., 1975. Mem.: NAS, Inst. Medicine, 2004, Am. Assn. Cancer Rsch. (chair cancer rsch. com. 2001, Pezcoller Internat. award 2001, Eleventh C.P. Rhoads Meml. award 1990), Am. Acad. Arts and Scis. (fellow), Harvey Soc., Am. Acad. Microbiology, Am. Soc. Microbiology (fellow), Soc. Neuroscience, Soc. Devel. Biology, Endocrine Soc. (Edwin B. Astwood Lectureship award 1993). Office: Salk Inst Biol Studies Howard Hughes Med Inst 10010 N Torrey Pines Rd La Jolla CA 92037 Office Phone: 858-453-4100 ext. 1302. Office Fax: 858-455-1349. Business E-Mail: evans@salk.edu.

EVANS, ROSEMARY HALL, civic worker; b. Lenox, Mass., Mar. 25, 1925; d. Alfred A. and Rosamond (Morse) Hall; m. Richard Morse Colgate, Jan. 1, 1949; children: Jessie Morse, Margaret Auchincloss, Pamela Morse; m. James H. Evans, July 1, 1972 (div. 1984). Trustee Menninger Found., Houston, Princeton, NJ; founding mem., life trustee Nat. Recreation and Park Assn., Washington. Past dir. Nat. Audubon Soc., NYC; former collaborator Nat. Park Svc. Mem.: Colony Club (NYC), Lenox Club (Mass.), Profile Club (Sugar Hill, NH). Avocations: walking, gardening, reading, birdwatching.

EVANS, SARA, country singer, songwriter; b. Mo., Feb. 5, 1971; m. Craig Schelske; children: Avery, Olivia, Audrey. Signed contract with RCA, Nashville, 1996; performer with group Sara Evans & North Santiam. Singer: (albums) Three Clouds and the Truth, 1997, No Place That Far, 1998, Girls' Night Out, 1999, Born to Fly, 2000, Restless, 2003, Real Fine Place, 2005, (singles) True Lies, 1997, Three Clouds and the Truth, 1997, Shame About That, 1997, Cryin' Game, 1998, No Place That Far, 1998, Born to Fly, 2000 (Video Yr., Country Music Assn., 2001); background singer: songs "I Never Really Knew You", Key, 1994; singer "Almost New", Clay Pigeon (Original Soundtrack), 1998, "That's the Beat of a Heart", Where the Heart Is (Original Soundtrack), 2000, "Mary of the Wild Moor", Songcatcher (Original Soundtrack), 2001. Office: RCA Record Group 1400 18th Ave S Nashville TN 37212 Office Phone: 615-301-4300.

EVANS, SEAN, political science professor; s. Sam and Rhonella Evans. BA, David Lipscomb U., Nashville, 1992; MA, U. Ala., Tuscaloosa, 1994; PhD in Polit. Sci., U. Colo., Boulder, 2000. Asst. prof. polit. sci. Union U., Jackson, Tenn., 2000—06, assoc. prof. polit. sci., 2006—, chair dept. polit. sci., 2007—. Mem.: Tenn. Polit. Sci. Assn. (exec. com. mem. 2002—06, sec. 2003—04, treas. 2004—05, v.p. 2005—06, pres.-elect 2006—, pres. 2007—08), So. Polit. Sci. Assn., Am. Polit. Sci. Assn. Mem. Ch. Christ. Office: Union University 1050 Union University Dr Jackson TN 38305 Office Phone: 731-661-5237.

EVANS, SUSAN W., mathematics educator; BA in Math. and Edn., Villa Nova Univ., Phila.; MA in Math. and Edn., Va. Tech. Cert. in young adult math. Nat. Bd. Tchg. Standards. Math. instr., team leader Roanoke Valley Gov.'s Sch. Sci. and Tech.; math. tchr. Rural Retreat (Va.) H.S., 1999—. Named Wytheville-Wythe-Bland C. of C. Tchr. of Yr., Va. Tchr. of Yr., 2007. Office: Rural Retreat High Sch 321 E Buck Ave Rural Retreat VA 24368 Business E-Mail: sevans@wythe.k12.va.us.*

EVANS, TERENCE THOMAS, federal judge; b. Milw., Mar. 25, 1940; s. Robert Hansen and Jeanette (Walters) Evans; m. Joan Marie Witte, July 24, 1965; children: Kelly Elizabeth, Christine Marie, David Rourke. BA, Marquette U., 1962, JD, 1967. Bar: Wis. 1967. Law clk. to justice Wis. Supreme Ct., 1967—68; asst. dist. atty. Milw. County, 1968—70; assoc. Cook & Franke, Wis., 1970—72, ptnr. Wis., 1972—74; county judge Milw. County Ct., 1974—78; cir. judge State of Wis., 1978—80; judge, then chief judge US Dist. Ct. (ea. dist) Wis., Milw., 1979—95; judge US Ct. Appeals (7th cir.), 1995—. Mem.: ABA, Judicial Coun. of Seventh Circuit, Seventh Circuit Bar Assn., Milw. Bar Assn., State Bar Wis. Roman Catholic. Office: US Courthouse & Federal Bldg 517 E Wisconsin Ave Rm 721 Milwaukee WI 53202-4504*

EVANS, THELMA JEAN MATHIS, internist; b. East St. Louis, Ill., Jan. 29, 1944; d. Clemmie and Catherine (Rose) Mathis; m. Timothy Charles Evans, June 29, 1968; children: Cynthia Marie, Catherine Elizabeth (twins). BS in Zoology with honors, U. Ill., 1967; MD, U. Ill., Chgo., 1969. Intern, then resident U. Ill. Hosp., Chgo., 1969-71, fellow in pulmonary medicine, 1971-73; med. dir., acute care unit Presbyn.-St. Luke's Hosp., Chgo., 1973-75, asst. to dir. emergency svcs., 1975-77; staff physician Health Specialists, S.C., Chgo., 1977-80, AT&T (Western Electric), Cicero, Ill., 1980-85, Health First, Inc., Chgo., 1985-89, Michael Reese Health Plan, Chgo., 1989-98; mem. adv. bd. Advocate Profl. Group, Chgo., 1998—; bd. dirs. Advocate Health Care Network, Chgo., 2000—. Instr., Rush Med. Coll., Chgo., 1973-84; tuberculosis control officer, infectious disease sect. Chgo. Dept. Health, 1976-77. V.p., Com. to Elect Timothy C. Evans, Chgo., 1989. Grantee, Chgo. Lung Assn., 1972-73. Fellow: ACP; mem.: AMA, AMWA, NAACP. Democrat. African Methodist Episcopal. Avocations: photography, gardening, collecting thimbles, bells and music boxes. Office: Advocate Health Ctrs 9831 S Western Ave Chicago IL 60643-1791 Office Phone: 777-445-3500. Office Fax: 773-445-3500.

EVANS, THOMAS PASSMORE, management consultant; b. West Grove, Pa., Aug. 19, 1921; s. John and Linda (Zeuner) Evans; m. Lenore Jane Knuth, June 21, 1947; children: Paula S., Christina L., Bruce A., Carol L. BSEE, Swarthmore Coll., Pa., 1942; M in Engring., Yale U., New Haven, Conn., 1948. Registered profl. engr., Pa. Engr. atomic power divsn. Westinghouse Electric Corp., Pitts., 1948-51; dir. R&D AMF, Inc., NYC, 1951-60; dir. rsch. O.M. Scott & Sons Co., Marysville, Ohio, 1960-62; v.p. R&D W. A. Sheaffer Pen Co., Fort Madison, Iowa, 1962-67; dir. rsch. Mich. Tech. U., Houghton, 1967-80; prof. bus. adminstrn. Berry Coll., Mt. Berry, Ga., 1980-86, dir. rsch., mem. faculty, 1980-88. Lt. USN, 1943—46. Mem.: VFW, AAAS, IEEE, Yale Sci. and Engring. Assn., Soc. Plastics Engrs., Am. Phys. Soc., Nat. Def. Indsl. Assn., Am. Forestry Assn., Nat. Trust Hist. Preservation, Air Force Assn., Am. Legion, Tau Beta Pi, Sigma Xi. Achievements include patents in field. Home: 8333 Seminole Blvd Apt 660F Seminole FL 33772-4391

EVANS, TIMOTHY GRANT, international organization administrator; b. Jan. 10, 1961; BSS, U. Ottawa, Can., 1984; PhD in Agrl. Econ., U. Oxford, Eng., 1989; MD, McMaster U., Can., 1992. Intern Brigham and Women's Hosp., Boston, 1992—93, rsch. resident, 1992—96, jr. asst. resident, internal medicine, 1993—94, sr. asst. resident, internal medicine, 1994—96, attending physician, dept. gen. internal medicine and primary care, 1996—97; MacArthur fellow Harvard Ctr. for Population and Devel. Studies, 1992—94; asst. prof., internat. health econ. Harvard U. Sch. Pub. Health, 1995—97; team dir., health equity program The Rockefeller Found., 1997—2003; asst. dir. gen., info., evidence and rsch. WHO, Geneva, 2003—. Fellow, Internat. Exchange of Experts in Rehab., 1994; scholar, Can. Internat. Devel. Agy., 1986—87; Rhodes Scholar, U. Oxford, 1984—88. Office: World Health Orgn Avenue Appia 20 1211 Geneva Switzerland E-mail: evanst@who.int.

EVANS, TOMMY NICHOLAS, obstetrician, gynecologist, educator; b. Batesville, Ark., Apr. 12, 1922; s. James Rufus and Carrye Mae (Goatcher) E.; m. Jessica Ray Osment, June 12, 1945; 1 child, Laura Kathreen AA, Mars Hill Jr. Coll., 1940; student, Duke U., 1940-41; AB, Baylor U., 1942; MD, Vanderbilt U., 1945. Intern U. Mich. Hosp., Ann Arbor, 1945-46, asst. resident ob-gyn, 1948, resident, 1948-49, jr. clin. instr., 1949-50, sr. clin. instr., 1950-51, instr., 1951-54, asst. prof., 1954-56, assoc. prof., 1956-60, prof., 1960-65; prof. ob-gyn Wayne State U., Detroit, 1965-83, dean Sch. Medicine, 1970-72, dir. C.S. Mott Ctr. Human Growth and Devel., 1973-83; sr. attending physician Hutzel Hosp., 1966-83, chief ob-gyn, 1966-82, vice chief of staff, 1967-70, chief of staff, 1970-74, trustee, 1975-78; mem. teaching, surgeon Harper-Grace Hosps., 1965-83, chief gynecology Harper div., 1970-83, chief ob-gyn, 1975-83; chief gynecology, sr. attending physician Detroit Receiving Hosp., 1965-83; chief gynecology U. Colo., Denver, 1983-89, vice chmn. ob-gyn., 1983-89, prof. emeritus ob-gyn., 1989—. Cons. pediatric surgery Children's Hosp.; cons. Sinai Hosp. William Beaumont Hosp., Wayne County Gen. Hosp.; past mem. med. adv. com. Detroit Med. Ctr. Corp. Bd. dirs. Alan Guttmacher Inst. Fellow Am. Assn. Ob-Gyn.; mem. Am. Coll. Obstetricians and Gynecologists (founder, past exec. bd., past pres.), ACS (adv. council ob-gyn credentials com. 1983-85, bd. govs. 1982-86), Am. Fedn. Clin. Research, Am. Fertility Soc., Am. Gynecol. Club (past pres.), Am. Gynecol. Soc. (past pres.), Am. Gynecol. and Obstetrical Soc. (council), AMA, Am. Med. Soc. Vienna, Am. Pub. Health Assn., Am. Soc. Andrology (exec. council), Am. Soc. Study Sterility, Anthony Wayne Soc., Assn. Profs. Ob-Gyn (past chmn. nominating com.), Central Assn. Ob-Gyn (past pres.), Charlie Flowers Ob-Gyn Soc., Chgo. Gynecol. Soc., Continental Gynecol. Soc., Detroit Acad. Medicine, Detroit Cancer Club (past mem. program com.), Engring. Soc. Detroit, Greater Detroit Area Hosp. Council Inc., Internat. Fedn. Ob-Gyn (exec. bd.), Internat. Soc. Advancement Humanistic Studies in Gynecology, Miami Obstet. and Gynecol. Soc., Mich. Assn. Retarded Children, Mich. Cancer Found. (trustee), Mich. Council Study of Abortion, Mich. Soc. Ob-Gyn (past pres.), Mich. State Med. Soc. (past exec. council), Mich. United Cerebral Palsy Assn., Norman Miller Gynecol. Soc. (past pres.), Ob-Gyn Soc. N.Y., Planned Parenthood League, Pan Am. Med. Assn., Royal Soc. Medicine, Soc. Study of Reprodn., Soc. Ob-Gyn of Can., S. Atlantic Assn. Ob-Gyn, numerous others. Republican. Presbyterian. Office: 7501 E Thompson Peak Pkwy Apt 233 Scottsdale AZ 85255-4533 Business E-Mail: tommyevans2000@msn.com.

EVANS, TONY, language educator; s. Connie Evans. AA in Acctg., Franklin U., Columbus, 1990; BS in Fgn. and Second Lang. Edn., Ohio State U., Columbus, 1995, BA in German, 1995, BA in French, 1995, MA in Fgn. and Second Lang. Edn., 1998. Nat. Bd. Cert. Tchr. Nat. Bd. for Profl. Tchg. Stds., 2002. ESL resource tchr. Dublin City Schs., Ohio, 1995—2005, German tchr., 2005—. Writing team Ohio ltd. English proficient stds. Lau Ctr., Ohio Dept. Edn., Columbus, 2002—04; validator English as new lang. Ednl. Testing Svc., 2004—05, Nat. Bd. Profl. Tchg. Stds., 2004—05. Recipient Cert. Appreciation, Ohio Dept. Edn., 2003, 2006. Mem.: TESOL (editor newsletter Ohio chpt. 2002—04, rep. 2004—05), NEA, Ohio Fgn. Lang. Assn., Mensa. Home Phone: 614-436-6433.

EVANS, WALTER REED, retired engineering executive, consultant; b. El Paso, Tex., Oct. 25, 1921; s. Charles Reed and Ruby Estelle (Simpson-Rountree) E.; m. Frances Adelaide Lounsbury, Jan. 15, 1942 (dec. 1975); children: Sandra Frances, Roger Reed, Sharon Adelaide; m. Dorothy May Cuthbertson, 1975; stepchildren: Jack W., William D., Charles T. Rogers. BS in Mech. Engring., U. Tex. Registered profl. engr. La., Tex. Engring. and mech. supr. Celanese and Exxon Corps., Tex. and Venezuela, 1948-57; plant mgr., pres. Falcon Chem. Corp., Lake Charles, La., 1957-59; refining coord., Stanvac divsn. Exxon-Mobil, White Plains, NY, 1959—60; cons. SIP, Inc., Houston, 1960-62; instrument engr. Exxon, Aruba, 1963, mech-.supt. Malaga, Spain, 1964—65, chief engr. Pakistan, 1966—71, divsn. head Sriracha, Thailand, 1972; project mgr. S & B, Inc., Houston, 1973-79; mech. mgr. Arabian Am. Oil Co., Ras Tanura, Saudi Arabia, 1979-81; pvt. practice mech. engring. cons., 1982-88; Tex. state coord., lobbyist ASME, Austin, 1988-94; prof., competency monitor Tex. State Bd. Engring. Registration, 1995-99. Founder, v.p. Structural Metals, Inc. divsn. Comml. Metals, Inc., Seguin, Tex., 1947-48; trustee Teal Petroleum Co. divsn. W.R. Grace Co., 1975-79; apprentice mechanic, aircraft engine, Kelly Field, Tex., 1939; owner's rep. Himont, Inc. divsn. Dupont, 1984-85. Author: Aircraft Engine Overhaul, 1942. Enlisted Tex. N.G., 1938; lt. USAAF, 1942-44, ETO. Fellow ASME (life); mem. NSPE (life), NRA, Squires Bus. Men's Orgn., Austin Amateur Radio, Men's Garden Club, Austin Rifle Club. Republican. Episcopalian. Avocations: hunting, fishing, stamp/coin collecting, gardening, reading. Home and Office: 5055 W Panther Cir #6311 The Woodlands TX 77381

EVANS, WAYNE, obstetrician, perinatologist; b. Cincinnati, Ohio, Apr. 13, 1954; s. Johnnie Kate and Wilbur Evans; m. Jacqueline Evette Brown, Apr. 1, 2001; children: Karoline Odessa, David Wayne;. BS in Biology, Marietta Coll., 1976; AAS Physician Asst., Cin. Tech. Coll., 1978; MD, Med. Coll. of Ohio, Toledo, 1981. Diplomate Am. Bd. Ob-Gyn., Am. Bd. Maternal-Fetal Medicine. Resident, ob-gyn. Good Samaritan Hosp., Cin., 1981—85; gen. obstetrician-gynecologist Milw. Comprehensive Cmty. Health, Milw., 1985—86, MetroHealth of Ind., Indpls., 1986—89, USPHS, Carl Albert Indian Health Facility, Ada, Okla., 1989—91; fellow, critical care medicine U. of Md./RA Crowley Shock Trauma Ctr., Balt., 1991—92; fellow, maternal fetal medicine U. of Pitts./ Magee Womens Hosp., Pitts., 1992—94; dir. of perinatology/clin. asst. prof. U. of Wis. Med. Sch.- Milw. Clin. Campus, 1994—. Dir. of perinatology Aurora Sinai Med. Ctr., Milw., 1995—. Author: (novel) I Seek You, 2001. 0-6 comdr. USPHS, 1989—91, Ada, Okla. Mem.: AMA, State Med. Soc. of Wis., Nat. Perinatal Assn., Soc. of Obstetric Medicine, Milw. Gynecologic Soc. (assoc.). Personal E-mail: docdub@excite.com. E-mail: docdub@hotmail.com.

EVANS, WILLIAM KENDALL, nuclear scientist; b. Malvern, Ark., Aug. 30, 1952; s. William Apperson and Mary Elizabeth Evans; m. Rebecca Ann Davis (dec.). BS in Physics, La. Tech. U., Ruston, 1974, MS in Physics, 1976. Physics instr. U. Ark., Little Rock, 1976—77; health physicist Ark. Dept. Health, Little Rock, 1978—80, TVA, Muscle Shoals, Ala., 1980—82; corp. emergency planning coord. Ark. Power and Light, Little Rock, 1983—84; emergency planner Ill. Power Co., Decatur, 1984—90, supr. emergency exercise and planning, 1991—2002; nuc. safety analyst Ill. Emergency Mmgt. Assn., Springfield, 2002—. Author tng. materials in field. Recipient award, Clinton Power Sta., 1996. Mem.: Health Physics Soc. (25 Yr. Appreciation award 2006), Sigma Pi Sigma. Episcopalian. Avocations: meteorology, coin collecting/numismatics, music, guitar. Home: 2300 Worster Ct Springfield IL 62704 Office Phone: 217-558-6248. Business E-Mail: ken.evans@illinois.gov.

EVANSON, BARBARA JEAN, middle school education educator; b. Grand Forks, ND, Aug. 15, 1944; d. Robert John and Jean Elizabeth (Lommen) Gibbons; m. Bruce Carlyle Evanson, Dec. 27, 1965; children: Tracey, John, Kelly. AA, Bismarck State Coll., 1964; BS in Spl. and Elem. Edn., U. N.D., 1966. Tchr. spl. edn. Winship Sch., Grand Forks, 1966-67, Simle Jr. High, Bismarck, 1967-70; tchr. Northridge Elem. Sch., Bismarck, 1980-86, Wachter Middle Sch., Bismarck, 1986—. Cons. Dept. Pub. Instrn., Bismark, 1988—, Chpt. I, Bismark, 1989—, McRel for Drug Free Schs., Denver, 1990-95. Co-founder The Big People, Bismarck, 1978-95; mem. task force Children's Trust Fund, N.D., 1984; senator N.D. Legislature, Bismarck, 1989-94; mem. N.D. Bridges Adv. Bd., 1991-97, DPI English Adv. Com., 1993—; co-facilitator Lead Mid. Sch. for Carnegie, 1994-97, N.D. Health Adv. Coun., 1993-94, N.D. Tchr.'s Fund for Retirement, State Investment Bd. 1996—; co-founder, bd. dirs. Neighbors Network, 1983—. Recipient Gold Award Bismark Norwest Bank, 1985; named Tchr. of Yr., N.D. Dept. Pub. Instrn., 1989, Legislator of Yr., Children's Caucus, 1991, Outstanding Alumnae, Bismarck State Coll., 1991, Milken Nat. Tchr. of Yr., 1995-96, KX Golden Apple award, 1999. Mem. N.D. Reading Assn., N.D. Coun. of Tchrs. of English., NEA, N.D. Edn. Assn., Bismarck Edn. Assn. Avocations: walking, reading, travel, remodeling. Office: Wachter Middle Sch 1107 S 7th St Bismarck ND 58504-6533

EVANSON, PAUL JOHN, utilities executive; b. NYC, June 16, 1941; s. Edwin F. and Barbara (Marconi) E.; m. Carol Louise Cordaro, Aug. 21, 1965; 1 child, Lisa J. BBA, St. John's U., NYC, 1963; JD, Columbia U., 1966; LLM, NYU, 1970. CPA, N.Y.; Bar: N.Y. 1966. Mgr. Arthur Andersen & Co., NYC, 1966-73; exec. v.p. Moore McCormack Resources, Inc., Stamford, Conn., 1973-88; pres., chief oper. officer Lynch Corp., Greenwich, Conn., 1988-92; sr. v.p., CFO FPL Group, Inc., Juno Beach, Fla., 1992-95; pres. FPL Co., Juno Beach, 1995—2003; pres., CEO, chmn. Allegheny Energy, Inc., Greensburg, Pa., 2003—. Bd. dirs. Lynch Corp. (AMEX), So. Edison Electric Inst., Southeastern Electric Exch.; bd. govs. St. John's U. Chmn., pres. YMCA, Stamford, 1982-88. Mem. Country Club of Darien. Avocations: tennis, reading. Office: Allegheny Energy Inc 800 Cabin Hill Dr Greensburg PA 15601*

EVANS SNOWDEN, AUDRA LYNN, counselor; b. Flint, Mich., July 16, 1976; d. Frances Anne Howard and William Edward Evans; m. Eugene Russell Snowden, Jr., July 21, 2001. BA Comm., Mich. State U., 1997; MEd in Ednl. Leadership, Saginaw Valley State U., 2002; MA in counseling, Oakland U., 2003—05. Nat. bd. cert. counselor, tchr. Mich. 7th grade sci. tchr. Sherman Mid. Sch., Holly, Mich., 2000—04; sch. counselor Richter Intermediate Sch., Holly, Mich., 2004—. Mem. exec. bd. Holly Area Youth Coalition, Mich., 2001—. Named Asset Builder, Holly Area Youth Coalition, 2001; Alpha Gamma Delta scholar, 1997. Mem.: Genessee Area Counseling Assn. (assoc.), Assn. Mich. Sch. Counselors (assoc.), Mich. Counseling Assn. (assoc.), Mich. Sch. Counselor Assn. (assoc.), Phi Beta Delta (assoc.), Golden Key (assoc.), Kappa Delta Pi (assoc.), Chi Sigma Iota (assoc.), Alpha Gamma Delta (life; scholarship chair 1995—96, Scholarship Key 1997). Avocations: scrapbooks, rubber stamping, reading, exercise, travel. Office: Richter Intermediate Sch 920 East Baird St Holly MI 48442 Home Phone: 810-694-4925; Office Phone: 248-328-3037. Office Fax: 248-328-3034. E-mail: audra.snowden@holly.k12.mi.us.

EVARTS, BRIAN, social worker, educator; b. Milford, Conn., July 9, 1949; s. Russell and Rita Evarts; m. Deborah Winchell, Feb. 12, 1988; children: Kaitlin, Benjamin, Jessica Winchell-Evarts. M in Social Svcs., Bryn Mawr Coll., 1981. Acsw NASW, 1988. Sch. social worker Ellington Pub. Schools, Conn., 1985—; instr. Asnuntuck C.C., Enfield, 2003—06. Bd. pres. Ctr. Advancement of Youth, Family and Cmty. Services, Inc., Glastonbury, 1998—, NE Placement Services, Woodstock, 2004—. Home: 155 West Main St #432 Vernon Rockville CT 06066 Office: Ellington HS 37 Maple St Ellington CT 06029 Home Phone: 860-871-6455; Office Phone: 860-896-2352 213. Business E-Mail: bevarts@ellingtonschools.net.

EVARTS, MARY H., mathematics educator; d. Harry J. and Mary V. Brown; children: John C., Suzanne M., Brian M., James B. BA, Immaculata Coll., Pa., 1967; Masters Equivelants Edn., Cabrini Coll., Radnor, Pa., 1988. Cert. secondary sch. tchr. Pa., 1967. Sci. computer programmer GE Missile and Space Vehicle Dept, Valley Forge, Pa., 1967—69; substitute tchr. Haverford Twp. Sch. Dist., Havertown, Pa., 1969—75, tchr. math., 1984—; tchr. St. Norbert Sch., Paoli, Pa., 1981—84. Scheduler Haverford Mid. Sch., 1986—. Mem.: NEA, Haverford Twp. Edn. Assn., Pa. State Edn. Assn. Office: Haverford Twp Sch District 1701 Darby Rd Havertown PA 19083 Home Phone: 610-647-7622.

EVARTS, WILLIAM MAXWELL, JR., lawyer; b. NYC, June 3, 1925; m. Helen Rulison Coleman, Aug. 28, 1948. AB, Harvard U., 1949, LL.B., 1952. Bar: N.Y. 1953, U.S. Ct. Appeals (2d cir.) 1961, U.S. Dist. Ct. (so. and ea. dists.) N.Y. 1974. Assoc. Winthrop, Stimson, Putnam & Roberts, NYC, 1952-62, ptnr., 1962-97, sr. counsel, 1997—. Bd. dirs. United Hosp. Fund, N.Y.C., Scenic Hudson, Poughkeepsie, The Clark Found., N.Y.C.; chmn., 1996-2000, cons. mem., 2001—; chmn. distbn. com. N.Y. Cmty. Trust. Sgt. U.S. Army, 1943-46, ETO. Mem. ABA, Assn. of Bar of City of N.Y. Office: Pillsbury Winthrop Shaw Pittman LLP 1540 Broadway New York NY 10036

EVE, (EVE JIHAN JEFFERS), rap artist, actress; b. Phila., Nov. 10, 1978; Formed female rap duo EDGP; former mem. DMX's Ruff Ryders posse; signed one-yr. deal with DMX's new label Aftermath. Performer: (albums) Let There Be Eve.Ruff Rider's First Lady, 1999, Scorpion, 2001, Eve-Olution, 2002; musician: (songs) "Eve of Destruction", 1998; musician: (with Gwen Stefani) "Let Me Blow Ya Mind", 2001 (Grammy award best rap/sung collaboration, 2001); musician: (with The Roots) "You Got Me"; musician: (with Blackstreet & Janet Jackson) "Girlfriend/Boyfriend"; musician: (with Missy Elliott) "Hot Boyz"; actor: (films) XXX, 2002, Barbershop, 2002, The Woodsman, 2003, Barbershop 2: Back in Business, 2004; (TV series) Eve, 2003; co-exec. prodr. (TV series) Eve, 2003, actor guest appearances Third Watch, 2003, One on One, 2004, actor, voice over (video game) XIII, 2003. Office: Interscope Records 2220 Colorado Ave Santa Monica CA 90404

EVELETH, JANET STIDMAN, law association administrator; b. Balt., Sept. 6, 1950; d. John Charles and Edith Janet (Scales) Stidman; m. Donald P. Eveleth, May 11, 1974. BA, Washington Coll., 1972; MS, Johns Hopkins U., 1973. Counselor Office of Mayor, Balt., 1973-75; asst. dir. Gov. Commn. on Children, Balt., 1975-78; lobbyist Balt., 1978-80; comm. specialist Med. Soc., Balt., 1980-81; dir. pub. affairs Mid-Atlantic Food Dealers, Balt., 1981-84; dir. comm. Home Builders Assn., Balt., 1984-87, Md. Bar Assn., Balt., 1987—. Contbr. articles to profl. jours. Recipient Gov. citation State of Md., 1993, Citizen citation City of Balt., 1993. Mem.: NAFE, Nat. Assn. Bar Execs. (chmn. pub. rels. sect. 1994—95, Achievement award 1995, E.A. Wally Richter award 1997, Luminary award 1999, 2001, 2003), Md. Soc. Assn. Execs. (pres. 1992—93), Am. Soc. Profl. Women, Pi Lambda Theta, Alpha Chi Omega. Office: Md Bar Assn 520 W Fayette St Baltimore MD 21201-1781 Home Phone: 410-821-1008. Business E-Mail: jeveleth@msba.org.

EVELYN, PHYLLIS, minister; d. Aaron K Redcay and Phyllis M Noble, Donald Noble (Stepfather) and Barbara Pfeiffer Redcay (Stepmother); m. Frank C. Templin, Aug. 23, 1963 (div.); children: Charles R Templin, Afton M Templin. BA, Northwestern U., 1960—64; MDiv, Eden Theol. Sem., 1999—2002. Ordination into United Church of Christ Ea. Assn. MO Conf. UCC, 2002. Sales adminstr. for copy products Eastman Kodak Co., Rochester, NY, 1977—84; owner Gulf Island Marine, Cedar Key, Fla., 1984—86; investment exec. Paine Webber, Bakersfield, Calif., 1987—90; fin. advisor Am. Express Fin. Advisors, St. Louis, 1997—99; settled pastor First Congl. Ch. of Shelburne, UCC, Mass., 2002—. Pres. Bd. of Ministerial Aid, MA-UCC, Framingham, Mass., 2005—07; exec. coun. mem. at large Franklin Assn., MA UCC, Greenfield, Mass., 2003—05; ex-officio bd. mem. Hilltown Churches Food Pantry, Ashfield, Mass., 2002—; vol. chaplain Baystate Franklin Med. Ctr., Greenfield, 2004—07; bd. dir. New Eng. Learning Ctr. Women in Transition, Greenfield, 2007—. Publisher (book) American Dream Business Park. Bd. dirs. Pioneer Valley Habitat for Humanity, Florence, Mass., 2003—05, grant writer, liaison to faith cmty. rels. com., 2002—05. Recipient Top Midwest Regional Sales

Rep. 7th Period, Eastman Kodak Co., Copy Products Div., 1980, Blinder President's Club Top Sales Position, Blinder Robinson Inc., 1987. Democrat. United Ch. Of Christ. Achievements include development of copy products market and opening of a new copy products office for Kodak Company in Anchorage, Alaska, 1984. Avocations: travel, flying, sailing. Home: 22 Ch Common Rd Shelburne Falls MA 01370 Office: First Congregational Ch 22 Ch Common Rd Shelburne Falls MA 01370 Home Phone: 413-625-0028.

EVEN, FRANCIS ALPHONSE, lawyer; b. Chgo., Sept. 8, 1920; s. George Martin and Cecilia (Neuman) E.; m. Margaret Hope Herrick, Oct. 16, 1945; children: Janet Beth, Dorothy Elizabeth. BS in Mech. Engring, U. Ill., 1942; JD, George Washington U., 1949. Bar: D.C. 1949, Ill. 1950. Engr. GE, 1945-49; ptnr. Fitch, Even, Tabin & Flannery (patent and trademark law), Chgo., 1952—. Bd. edn., River Forest, Ill., 1963-69; trustee West Suburban Hosp., Oak Park, Ill., 1974-77; mem. bd. Ill. State Hist. Soc., 2000-03. Combat engr., U.S. 3d inf. divsn., 1942-45. Decorated knight French Legion of Honor. Fellow Am. Coll. Trial Lawyers (emeritus); mem. ABA, Am. Intellectual Property Law Assn. (bd. mgrs. 1963-66), Ill. Bar Assn., Chgo. Bar Assn., Intellectual Property Law Assn. Chgo. (bd. mgrs. 1972-73, pres. 1984), No. Ill. Ct. Hist. Assn. (pres. 2000-06), Union League Club (Chgo.), Chgo. Literary Club. Republican. Office: 120 S La Salle St Chicago IL 60603-3403 Home: 134 Windsor Park Dr Apt D-101 Carol Stream IL 60188 Office Phone: 312-577-7000.

EVEN, RANDOLPH M., lawyer; b. 1943; BS, U. Calif.; JD, Calif. Western Sch. Law. Bar: Calif. 1969. Atty. Even, Crandall, Wade, & Lowe and predecessor firm Genson, Even, Crandall & Wade, P.C., Woodland Hills, Calif., Randolph M. Even & Assocs., PLC, 2002—. Mem. legal com. Calif.; lectr. in field. With Calif. Med. Legal Com., 2005—. Mem. Am. Bd. Trial Advocates (diplomate), Assn. So. Calif. Def. Counsel (bd. dirs. 1978-80, 93-98). Office: 5550 Topanga Canyon Blvd STE 280 Woodland Hills CA 91367-7471 Office Phone: 818-226-5444.

EVENS, LUCIE ANN, music educator; b. Pittsfield, Ill., Sept. 28, 1949; d. Mildred Eloise and Walter Orin Cook; m. Mark Evens, Aug. 18, 1974; children: Sarah Rachel, Emily Caroline Moughan, Joshua Adam. BS in music edn., NYU, 1969—74; MS in edn. environ. sci., CUNY, 1989—92. Permanent Music Teacher, Grades PreK-12 NYC & NY State, 1974, Permanent Teacher of Common Branches NYC & NY State, 1987, Certified Reading Specialist NY State, 1987. Kindergarten tchr. P.S. 164Q, Flushing, NY, 1984—86, 4th grade tchr., 1986—89, P.S. 219Q, 1989—90; music tchr. & choral dir. P.S. 164Q, Flushing, NY, 1990—; founding dir. SUNY Maritime Coll. Chorale, Bronx, 2002—; musical dir. Sullivan County Dramatic Workshop, Hurleyville, 2004—. Mem. United U. Professions, Albany, NY, 2003—. Singer: (TV musical documentary) Illinois Sings; actor: (musical) Annie Get Your Gun; musician (also costume designer): (musical) Pippin; dir.: (environmental program) NYC Sanitation Dept. Team Up To Clean Up. Recipient Choral Performance, Pres. of the USA (Bill Clinton), 1993, Dem. Party (Hillary Rodham Clinton), 1992; Molly Parnis award, Molly Parnis, 1990, Bette Midler's Rose award, NYC Dept. of Sanitation, 2001. Mem.: Am. Choral Directors' Assn., Am. Fedn. of Teachers, United Fedn. of Teachers, Music Educators' Assn. of NYC, United U. Professions, Nat. Choral Directors' Assn., Sigma Alpha Iota, Kappa Delta Pi. American Independent. Avocations: gardening, singing, antiques. Home: 147-28 77th Road Flushing NY 11367 Office: PS 164Q Queens Valley School 138-01 77th Avenue Flushing NY 11367 Home Phone: 718-380-7296; Office Phone: 718-544-0630.

EVENS, RONALD GENE, radiologist, educator, health facility administrator; b. St. Louis, Sept. 24, 1939; s. Robert and Dorothy (Lupkey) E.; m. Hanna Blunk, Sept. 3, 1960; children: Ronald Jr., Christine, Amanda. BA, Washington U., 1960, MD, 1964, postgrad. in bus. and edn., 1970-71. Intern Barnes Hosp., St. Louis, 1964-65; resident Mallinckrodt Inst. Radiology, St. Louis, 1965-66, 68-70; rsch. assoc. Nat. Heart Inst., 1966-68; asst. prof. radiology, v.p. Washington U. Med. Sch., 1970-71, prof., head dept. radiology, dir., 1971-72, Elizabeth Mallinckrodt prof., head radiology dept. St. Louis, 1972-99, prof. med. econs., 1988—; pres., sr. exec. ofcr. Barnes-Jewish Hosp., St. Louis, 1999—2005. Radiologist-in-chief Barnes Hosp., St. Louis, 1971-99; radiologist-in-chief Children's Hosp., 1971-99, pres., chief exec. officer, 1985-88; vice chancellor fin. Washington U., St. Louis, 1988-91; mem. adv. com. on splty. and geog. distbn. of physicians Inst. Medicine, Nat. Acad. Scis., 1974-76, Hickey lectr., 1976, Carmen lectr. Calif. U., 1985, Kiewit lectr. Eisenhower Med. Ctr., 1986; Hornick lectr. U. Pitts., 1986; ann. orator Can. Radiol. Soc., 1984; Hodes lectr. Jefferson U., 1991—; Smith lectr. Royal Coll. Physicians, Edinburgh, 1992; Seaman lectr. Columbia Presbyn., 1992; dir. Boatmens Bank Inc., Mallinckrodt Group Inc., Right Choice Inc., Blue Choice, Inc.; chmn. bd. Med. Care Group St. Louis, 1980-86. Contbr. over 210 articles to profl. jours. Active Boy Scouts Am., 1975—; elder Glendale Presbyn. Ch., 1971-74, Kirkwood Presbyn. Ch., 1983-86. Served with USPHS, 1966-68. Advance Acad. fellow James Picker Found, 1970; recipient Disting. Svc. award. St. Louis C. of C., 1972; named Disting. Eagle Scout Nat. Coun., 1983. Fellow Am. Coll. Radiology (chair elect 1995, chair bd. chancellors 1996—); mem. AMA (editl. bd. JAMA), Mo. Radiol. Soc. (pres. 1977-78), Soc. Nuclear Medicine (trustee 1971-75), St. Louis Med. Soc., Mo. State Med. Assn., Soc. Chmn. Acad. Radiology Depts. (pres. 1979), Radiol. Soc. N.Am., Assn. Univ. Radiologists (pres. 1988), Am. Roentgen Ray Soc. (pres. 1989), Phi Beta Kappa, Alpha Omega Alpha (Sheard-Sanford award). Office: Barnes Jewish Hosp Mallinckrodt Inst Radiology Barnes Jewish Plz Saint Louis MO 63110-1016 Address: Barnes-Jewish Hosp One Barnes-Jewish Hospital Plz Saint Louis MO 63110

EVENSON, MERLE ARMIN, chemist, educator; b. LaCrosse, Wis., July 27, 1934; s. Ansel Bernard and Gladys Mabel (Nelson) E.; m. Peggy L. Kovats, Oct. 5, 1957; children— David A., Donna L. BS in Chem. Physics and Math., U. Wis., LaCrosse, 1956; MS in Guidance, Madison, 1960, MS in Sci. Edn., 1960, PhD in Analytical Chemistry, 1966. Diplomate Am. Bd. Clin. Chemists, v.p., 1978-81. Tchr. math. and physics St. Croix Falls (Wis.) High Sch., 1956-57; tchr. chemistry Central High Sch., LaCrosse, 1957-59; instr. dept. medicine U. Wis., Madison, 1965-66, asst. prof., 1966-69, asso. prof., 1971-75, prof., 1975—, prof. dept. pathology, 1979—; asst. dir. clin. lab. Univ. Hosps., 1965-66, dir. clin. chemistry lab., 1966-69, dir. toxicology lab., 1971-87. Chmn. Gordon Rsch. Conf. on Analytical Chemistry, 1978; vis. lectr. Harvard Med. Sch., 1969-71; mem. staff Peter Bent Brigham Hosp., Boston, 1969-71; cons. on analytical and clin. chemistry to AEC, 1968-93, Am. Chem. Soc., Nat. Bur. Standards, FDA, NIH, study sect. mem. 1968-72, ad hoc memberships, 1973-87. Bd. editors: Chemical Instrumentation, 1973-87, Analytical Chemistry, 1974-77, Jour. Analytical Toxicology, 1976-79, Selected Methods in Clin. Chemistry, 1977-81; editor: Contemporary Topics in Analytical and Clincal Chemistry, 1974-83; contbr. numerous chpts. to books, articles to profl. jours.; patentee continuous oil hemoperfusion unit. NIH fellow, 1970-71, NSF, 1959-62; recipient Maurice O. Graff Disting. Alumni award U. Wis., LaCrosse, 1981 Mem. AAAS, Acad. Clin. Lab. Physicians and Scientists, Am. Assn. Clin. Chemists (bd. editors Clin. Chemistry 1970-80, nat. chair pub. rels. com. 1973-78, diplomat 1974, v.p. 1978-81), Am. Chem. Soc. (com. on clin. chemistry 1973-93), Sigma Xi, Kappa Delta Pi. Office: U Wis 1300 University Ave Madison WI 53706-1510 *As a teacher, the fostering of the development of creativity in people who then make contributions to our society is an exciting process. The most significant professional reward I receive is the observation of the successes of others with whom I have interacted and taught.*

EVENSON, ROBERT EUGENE, economist, educator; b. Elmore, Minn., July 25, 1934; s. Edven Herbert and Annie Cecelia (O'Toole) Evenson; m. Judith Joan Ungrodt, June 11, 1967; children: Nancy Lynn, Patsy Ann, Joseph Robert, Sarah Judtih. BA in Bus. Adminstrn., U. Minn., 1961, MS, 1964; PhD, U. Chgo., 1968. Farmer E.H. Evenson & Son, Minnesota Lake, Minn., 1952—60; asst. prof. U. Minn., Mpls. and St. Paul, 1966—68; vis. asst. prof. So. Meth. U., Dallas, 1968—69; assoc. prof. econs. Yale U., New Haven, 1969—74; assoc. vis. prof. Agrl. Devel. Coun., NYC, 1974—77; prof. Yale U., New Haven, 1977—. Cons. World Bank, Washington, 1970—, U.S. AID, 1970—. Author: Agricultural Research and Productivity, 1975, Technology and Income, 1990; editor: Science for Agriculture, 1993. Fellow: AAAS (chair Sect. K), Am. Agrl. Econs. Assn.; mem.: Econometric Soc., Am. Econ. Assn. Home: 322 Audubon Ct New Haven CT 06510

EVERBACH, OTTO GEORGE, lawyer; b. New Albany, Ind., Aug. 27, 1938; s. Otto G. and Zelda Marie (Hilt) E.; m. Nancy Lee Stern, June 3, 1961; children: Tracy Ellen, Stephen George. BS, U.S. Mil. Acad., 1960; LLB, U. Va., 1966. Bar: Va. 1967, Ind. 1967, Calif. 1975, Mass. 1978. Counsel CIA, Langley, Va., 1966-67; corp. counsel Bristol-Meyers Co., Evansville, Ind., 1967-74, Alza Corp., Palo Alto, Calif., 1974-75; sec., gen. counsel Am. Optical Corp., Southbridge, Mass., 1976-81; assoc. gen. counsel Warner-Lambert Co., Morris Plains, N.J., 1981-83; v.p. Kimberly-Clark Corp., Neenah, Wis., 1984-86, sr. v.p., gen. counsel, 1986—, sr. v.p. law & govt. affairs, 1988—2003. Served with U.S. Army, 1960-63. Mem. Am. Bar Assn., Mass. Bar Assn., Ind. Bar Assn., Calif. Bar Assn. Office: Kimberly-Clark Corp DFW Airport Sta PO Box 619100 Dallas TX 75261-9100

EVERDELL, WILLIAM, retired lawyer; b. NYC, May 29, 1915; s. William and Rosalind (Romeyn) E.; m. Eleanore Darling, July 2, 1940; children: William Romeyn, Coburn Darling, Preston. BA, Williams Coll., 1937; LLB, Yale U., 1940. Bar: N.Y. 1941. Assoc. Debevoise & Plimpton, NYC, 1940-49, ptnr., 1949-85, of counsel, 1986-88. Contbr. articles to profl. jours. Trustee Woods Hole Oceanographic Instn., Mass., 1978-86; mem. exec. com., 1981-86, hon. trustee, 1987—; trustee, mem. exec. com. Cold Spring Harbor Lab., N.Y., 1987-93. Served to lt. comdr. USNR, 1942-45, PTO, ATO. Decorated with seven battle stars. Fellow Am. Bar Found.; mem. ABA, Assn. of Bar of City of N.Y. (mem. exec. com. 1960-64), N.Y. State Bar Assn. (chmn. com. corp. law 1971-73). Clubs: The Links (gov. 1959-62) (N.Y.C.). Episcopalian. Avocations: sailing, golf.

EVERETT, C(HARLES) CURTIS, retired lawyer; b. Omaha, Aug. 9, 1930; s. Charles Edgar and Rosalie (Cook) E.; m. Joan Rose Bader, Sept. 7, 1951; children: Jeffrey, Ellen, Amy, Jennifer. BA cum laude, Beloit Coll., 1952; JD, U. Chgo., 1957. Bar: Ill. 1957. Pvt. practice, Chgo., 1957-91; ptnr. Bell, Boyd, Lloyd, Haddad & Burns, 1965-81, successor firm Bell, Boyd & Lloyd, 1981-91; v.p. law, sec., gen. counsel AMRE, Inc., Dallas, 1991-96; v.p. law, sec., gen. counsel, bd. dirs. Am. Remodeling, Inc., Dallas, 1992-96; v.p. Canre Remodelling, Inc., Dallas, 1992-94. V.p., sec. Hans Bader, Cons., Inc., Clearwater, Fla., 1954-99, also bd. dirs.; vis. com. U. Chgo. Law Sch., 1986-89; lectr. Ill. Inst. CLE. Mem. editl. bd. U. Chgo. Law Rev., 1956-57; contbr. articles to profl. jours. Chmn. So. Suburban area Beloit Coll. Ford Found. challange program, 1964-65; pres. The Players, Flossmoor, 1970-71; bd. govs. Lake Shore Dr. Condominium Assn., 1986-91. With AUS, 1952-54. Mem. ABA, Ill. Bar Assn., Chgo. Bar Assn. (mem. securities law com. 1960-91), U. Chgo. Law Sch. Alumni Assn. (dir. 1973-76, pres. Chgo. chpt. 1979-80), Legal Club, Law Club, Monroe Club (bd. govs. 1976-97), Univ. Club Chgo., Order of DeMolay (past master counselor Rock River chpt.), Order of Coif, Sigma Chi, Phi Alpha Delta. Mem. Cmty. Ch. (deacon). Home: 2044 Audubon Ave # 101 Naperville IL 60563 Personal E-mail: curtandje@aol.com.

EVERETT, CLAUDIA KELLAM, retired special education educator; b. Mobile, Ala., Dec. 28, 1933; d. Claude M. and Minnie L. Kellam; m. Thomas Sherwood Everett Sr., June 18, 1953; children: Thomas Sherwood Jr., Sherilisa Ann. BA magna cum laude, Roberts Wesleyan Coll., 1958; MS summa cum laude, Barry U., 1988. Cert. English, spl. edn. tchr. Fla., N.Y. Tchr. Dade County Pub. Schs., Miami, Fla., 1959-67, Carol City Elem. Sch., Miami, 1967-77; pers. mgr., payroll supr. Harrington Cos., Miami, 1977-81; honors English tchr. Citrus Grove Jr. HS, Miami, 1981-87; spl. edn. tchr. Citrus Grove Mid. Sch., Miami, 1987-90; tchr. severely emotionally disturbed children Hilton (N.Y.) HS, 1990-91; tchr. emotionally disturbed and mentally retarded, learning disabled Hill Elem. Sch., Brockport, NY, 1991-92; tchr. emotionally/learning disabled, mentally retarded Oliver Mid. Sch., Brockport, 1991—2001; ret., 2001. Cons. cmty. benevolent agys., Miami, 1969—83; pvt. tutor, 2001—. Author: numerous poems. Youth dir. Ctrl. Alliance Youth, Miami, 1960—80; cmty. advisor youth affairs Carol City, Miami, 1970—87; founder, pres. Tchr.-Parent Study Group, Miami, 1970—80; 1st v.p., sec., treas. PTA Carol City, 1967—77; pres. Teens to S.Am. Christian Missionary Alliance, Miami, 1978—80, cons. tech. action, 1980—90. Recipient Svc. award, Christian Missionary Alliance Cmty., 1980, Youth in Action award, S.Am. Missions, 1978. Mem.: S.E. Edn. Opportunities Handicapped, Coun. Exceptional Children (mem. divsn. learning disabilities 1989—, mem. divsn. mentally retarded 1989—, mem. divsn. emotionally handicapped 1989—). Republican. Avocations: reading, photography, tutoring, writing for children, visiting elderly in nursing homes. Home: 2355 Westside Dr Rochester NY 14624-1933

EVERETT, JAMES JOSEPH, lawyer; b. San Antonio, May 7, 1955; BA, St. Mary's U., San Antonio, 1976; JD, Tex. So. U., 1980. Bar: U.S. Dist. Ct. Ariz. 1987, U.S. Tax Ct. 1980, U.S. Ct. Appeals (9th cir.) 1988. Sr. trial atty. IRS, Phoenix, 1980-87; ptnr. Brnilovich & Everett, Phoenix, 1987-89; owner Law Offices of James J. Everett, Phoenix, 1989—2002; prin., owner James J. Everett & Assocs., P.C., Phoenix, 2002—. Pres. No Nonsense Networking Group, 2004—06; chair Univ. Club Tax Study Group, 2005. Mem. Tex. Bar Assn., Ariz. Bar Assn., State Bar Ariz. (cert. tax specialist), Maricopa County Bar Assn., Ariz. Tax Controversy Group, Valley Estate Planners (Phoenix), Ariz. Soc. Boutiques, St. Thomas Moore Soc., Univ. Club Tax Study Group (chair 2005—). Office: James J Everett & Assocs Paradise Village Office Pk 11811 N Tatum Blvd Ste 4010 Phoenix AZ 85028 Office Phone: 602-230-2212. Business E-Mail: James.Everett@azbar.org.

EVERETT, JAMES W., JR., lawyer; b. Buffalo, Oct. 26, 1957; s. James William and Esther (Kratzer) Everett. BA in Polit. Sci., Coll. Wooster, Ohio, 1979; JD, SUNY, Buffalo, 1984; LLM in Banking Law with honors, Boston U., 1985. Bar: NY 1985, US Dist. Ct. (we. dist.) NY 1989, US Dist. Ct. (no. dist.) NY 1990, US Supreme Ct. 1991. Officer Emil A. Kratzer Co., Inc., Buffalo, 1980—2001; assoc. John C. Peters, P.C., Hartford, Conn., 1986-87; assoc. counsel banks, corps., ins. and small bus. NY State Assembly, Albany, NY, 1987-88; asst. counsel banks, commerce, securities, real property, state and local fin. NY State Senate Majority, 1988-94; v.p., counsel state procs. and taxation Securities Industry Assn., 1995-98; pvt. practice, 1998—. Capital markets counsel NY State Ins. Dept., 2001-; speechwriter chair policy com. Nat. Adv. Counsel Women's Edn. Programs; observer Nat. Conf. Commr. Uniform State Laws Trust Code Drafting Com.; spkr. fin. svcs. Nat. Conf. State Legislators, Exec. Enterprise Inst.; sec. NY State Bar Banking Law Com., 2006-. Author NY Law Revision Commn. Review on Leasing (Art. 2A Remedies), Forward to Bowne Securities Regulation Compilations; contbg. editor Barnert Reports; contbr. to Buffalo News, Bus. Ins., Corp. Fin. Week, The Bank Letter, The Bond Buyer, Compliance Reporter. Mem. judicial nominating com. Erie County (NY) Rep. Com., 1979-2001; deacon N. Presbyn. Ch., Amherst, NY; dir. Friends of Saratoga Battlefield, 2007-. Recipient Cummings-Rumbaugh prize Coll. of Wooster, Ohio, Harmony Heights Sch. Pub. Svc. award. Mem. Assn. Corp. Counsel, Assn. Bar City NY, Nat. Assn. Life Cos., SAR (election com. mem.). Avocations: hiking, bicycling, travel. Office: NYS Insurance Dept One Commerce Plz Albany NY 12224 Office Phone: 518-396-0255. Personal E-mail: everettlaw@juno.com.

EVERETT, JONATHAN JUBAL, lawyer; b. Bellingham, Wash., Sept. 10, 1950; s. John Thomas and Dawn Irene (Speirs) E.; m. Mary Kathryn Penar, May 27, 1973. BA, U. Chgo., 1972; MA in hist., Harvard U., 1975, JD, 1979. Bar: Calif. 1981, Ill. 1982. Law clk. presiding judge U.S. Ct. Appeals (5th cir.), Baton Rouge, 1979-80; assoc. O'Melveny and Myers, LA, 1980-81, Mayer, Brown and Platt, Chgo., 1982-84, Skadden, Arps, Slate, Meagher and Flom, Chgo., 1984-87, ptnr., 1987-96; mng. dir. Dabhol Power Co., 1994, View Group, L.P., Boston, 1996—. Mem.: Securities and Exchange Bd. of India's com. on venture capital reform., Knox Fellow Oxford U. Office: View Grp LP 175 Federal St 14th Fl Boston MA 02110 Office Phone: 617-423-2525. Office Fax: 617-423-3023.

EVERETT, JUDITH, merchandising educator; d. Culbertson; m. Christopher Everett. BS, Kent State U., Ohio, 1972; MA, Kent State U., Kent, Ohio, 1974; MBA, Ariz. State U., Tucson, 1987. Asst. prof. Western Mich. U., 1977—79; prof. No. Ariz. U., Flagstaff, Ariz., 1979—. Author: Guide to Producing a Fashion Show, Promotion in the Merchandising Environment, Writing for Fashion; dir.: (fashion shows) Student productions (NAU's Svc. Learning Awards, 2000). Charter bd. mem. Fashion Group Internat., Phoenix/Scottsdale, Ariz., 1995—2004. Recipient Lifetime Achievement award, Sch. of Comm., 2003. Mem.: Am. Collegiate Retailing Assn., Fashion Group Internat. Office: Northern Arizona University Box 5619 Flagstaff AZ 86011 Office Phone: 928-523-6178.

EVERETT, LATONYA MICHELLE, computer engineer; b. Columbus, Ga., Sept. 23, 1972; d. Franklin Leman and LaMuriel Pierce Everett; 1 child, Indiria Jania. BBA, NC Ctrl. U., 1994, M in Info. Sci., 2005. Software engr. IBM, Rsch. Triangle Pk., NC, 1995—. Author: Earlie E. Thorpe Oral History Collection 1990-1992, 2001. Scholarship, Academic Boosters Club, 1990. Mem.: RTP Black Diversity Networking Group, Phi Beta Lambda, Am. Soc. Info. Sci. and Tech., Alpha Kappa Alpha (scholarship 1990). Achievements include IBM Publish for automation tool. Avocations: cooking, travel, piano, coin collecting/numismatics, music. Home: 217 Glaive Dr Durham NC 27703 Office: IBM 3039 Cornwallis Rd Research Triangle Park NC 27709 Home Phone: 919-957-8826; Office Phone: 919-254-5135. Office Fax: 919-543-7421. Personal E-mail: latonyaeverett@hotmail.com. Business E-Mail: leverett@us.ibm.com.

EVERETT, MARK ALLEN, dermatologist, educator; b. Oklahoma City, May 30, 1928; s. Mark Ruben and Alice (Allen) E.; 1 son, Howard Dean. BA in Polit. Sci., U. Okla., 1947, MD, 1951; USAF intern in pub. health. Intern in pediatrics U. Mich. Med. Sch., 1951, resident in dermatology, 1954-57, instr. dermatology, 1956-57; intern in pub. health Tulane Med. Sch., 1951; mem. faculty U. Okla. Med. Sch., 1959-98, chmn. dept. dermatology, 1964-96, prof. dermatology, head dept., 1967-96, adj. prof. pathology and anatomy, 1975-98, prof., interim head dept. pathology, 1979-84, Regents prof., 1982-98, Regents prof. emeritus, 1998—, chmn. faculty bd., 1974-90; chief staff Okla. Meml. Hosp., 1980-85. Vice chmn. bd. Bone and Joint Hosp., Oklahoma City, 1976-85; chmn. Internat. Com. for Dermatopathology, 1980-86; bd. dirs. Am. Bd. Dermatology, 1985-96, pres. elect, 1994, pres., 1995. Author 200 articles in field, chpts. in books. Pres. Okla. Ballet Soc., 1973, 77-80, Oklahoma City Chamber Orch., 1979-81, Chamber Music Okla., 1989-2001; pres. bd. trustees Everett Found., 1961-; adv. bd. World Lit. Today, 1970-85, Bizzell Libr. Soc., 1982—; bd. visitors Coll. of Fine Arts, U. Okla., 1990-2002, Coll. of Arts and Scis., 1996-99; bd. dirs. Red Earth Inc., 1997-, trustee, 2000, v.p., 2001-04; chair Mus. Com., 1997-2001, Art Com., 2001-03; bd. dirs. Jacobson House, 2002-. With USAF, 1952-54. Recipient Bronze medal U. Okla. Fedn., Mayor's award for Lifetime Contbn. to Arts, Oklahoma City, 1989, Gov.'s Arts award, 1993; grantee Am. Cancer Soc., NIH. Mem. AMA, Am. Acad. Dermatology (chmn. long-range planning coun. 1975-80, dir. 1978-82, chmn. coun. on sci. assembly 1985), Assn. Profs. Dermatology (pres. 1976-78), Am. Soc. Dermatopathology (pres. 1980), Am. Assn. Cancer Rsch., Internat. Acad. Pathology, Am. Dermatol. Assn. (bd. dirs. 1990-95, pres. 1995-96), Am. Soc. Clin. Investigation, Soc. Investigative Dermatology, Radiation Rsch. Soc., Okla. Med. Soc., Coll. Physicians Phila., N.Y. Acad. Scis., N.Mex. Dermatol. Soc., Pacific Dermatol. Assn., South Ctrl. Dermatol. Soc., Austrian Dermatology Soc. (hon.), Polish Dermatology Soc. (hon.), Brit. Assn. Dermatology (hon.), RRC Dermatology RRC Dermatopathology, Gourgerot Soc., Sociètè Française de Dermatologie (hon.), Lotos Club (N.Y.C.), Equestrian Order of the Holy Sepulchre, Phi Beta Kappa. Democrat. Roman Catholic.

EVERETT, PAUL MARVIN, physicist; b. Toledo, Mar. 15, 1940; s. Arthur Marvin and Elizabeth Bernice Everett; m. Sandra Lee McClelland; children: David, Christopher. BS Physics, Case Inst. Tech., Cleve., 1962; PhD, Case Western Res. U., 1968. Rsch. assoc. La. State U., Baton Rouge, 1968—71, adminstrv. asst., 1971—72; asst. prof. physics U. Ky., Lexington, 1972—79; tech. staff Tex. Instruments Ctrl. Rsch. Labs., Dallas, 1979—83; unit mgr., sect. mgr., br. mgr. McDonnell Douglas Microelectronics Ctr., St. Louis, 1983—89; br. mgr. McDonnell Douglas Electronic Sys. Co., St. Louis, 1989—90; chief scientist, product mgr. Magnavox New Eng. Rsch. Ctr., Sudbury, Mass., 1990—91; bus. devel. mgr., program mgr. Litton Electron Devices, Tempe, Ariz., 1992—96; pres., owner Everett Cos. LLC, Phoenix, 1996—; ptnr. Advanced Photonic Techs., Phoenix, 1999—. Apptd. Ahwatukee Foothills Village Planning Com. - City of Phoenix, 1998—. Fellow, NASA, 1965—67; grantee, The Rsch. Corp., 1974—76. Mem.: IEEE, IEEE Phoenix Sect. (mem. exec. com. 2002—04), IEEE Phoenix Area Cons. Network (mem. exec. bd. 2000—, pres. 2002—05), Sigma Xi. Office: Everett Companies LLC 3825 E Mtn Vista Dr Phoenix AZ 85048-7374 Office Phone: 480-706-4753. Personal E-mail: peverett@everettinfrared.com.

EVERETT, RALPH BERNARD, think-tank executive; b. Orangeburg, SC, June 23, 1951; s. Francis G.S. and Alethia (Hilton) E.; m. Gwendolyn Harris, June 22, 1974. BA, Morehouse Coll., 1973; JD, Duke U., 1976. Bar: NC 1977, DC 1979. Adminstrv. asst. NC Dept. Labor, 1976—77; legis. asst. Office of Senator Ernest F. Hollings, Washington, 1977—82; minority chief counsel, staff dir. US Senate Com. on Commerce, Sci., Transp., Washington, 1983—87, chief counsel, staff dir., 1987—89; ptnr. Paul, Hastings, Janofsky & Walker, LLP, Alexandria, Va., 1989—2006; pres., CEO Joint Ctr. for Polit. and Econ. Studies. Bd. dirs. Shenandoah Life Ins. Co., Cumulus Media Inc.; mem. adv. bd. Norfolk So. Corp., Washington, 1991; life mem. bd. visitors Duke U. Sch. Law; former mem. Pres.'s Bd. Advs. on Historically Black Colls. and Univs.; head US Del. to World Telecom. Conf., 1998; US amb. to 1998 Internat. Telecom. Union Plenipotentiary Conf.; bd. trustees Sci. Mus. Va. Former trustee Nat. Urban League, NYC, 1990, 92; senate liaison Clinton/Gore Presdl. Campaign, Washington, 1992; former mem. Congl. Award Found., McLean, Va., 1993—; former mem. Fed. City Coun. Named to The Ebony Power 150, Ebony mag., 2007. Mem.: Econ. Club Washington, Phi Beta Kappa, Alpha Phi Alpha. Office: Joint Ctr for Polit and Econ Studies 1090 Vermont Ave NW Ste 1100 Washington DC 20005-4928 Office Phone: 202-789-3510. Business E-Mail: ralpheverett@jointcenter.org.*

EVERETT, REYNOLDS MELVILLE, JR., lawyer; b. Davenport, Iowa, Jan. 29, 1946; s. Reynolds Melville and Annette (Young) E. BS in Agr., U. Ill., 1968; postgrad., U. Tulsa, 1970-71; JD, Loyola U., Chgo., 1972. Bar: Ill. 1972, U.S. Dist. Ct. (no. dist.) Ill. 1972, U.S. Dist. Ct. (cen. dist.) Ill.

1974. Staff atty. State Nat. Bank, Evanston, Ill., 1972-74; pres. Barash & Everett, LLC, Galva, Ill., 1974—. Panel trustee U.S. Bankruptcy Ct. (cen. dist.) Ill., 1987—; bd. dirs. Peoples Nat. Bank of Kewanee. Bd. dirs. Bishop Hill Heritage Assn., Bishop Hill, Ill., 1976-84, Jet Oil Co., Tulsa, 1978-84; sec. Galva Econ. Devel. Assn., 1983—. With U.S. Army, 1968-70, Vietnam. Mem. ABA (assembly mem. 1976-82, chmn. real estate sec. 1976-82), Am. Coll. Trust and Estate Counsel, Ill. State Bar Assn., Estate Planning, Probate & Trust Coun., Henry County Bar Assn., Midland Country Club (Kewanee, Ill., bd. govs. 1983—), Rotary (local pres. 1978), Shriners, Elks. Office: Everett & Luymes PC Yocum Bank Bldg Galva IL 61434

EVERETT, ROBINSON OSCAR, federal judge, educator; b. Durham, NC, Mar. 18, 1928; s. Reuben Oscar and Kathrine McDiarmid (Robinson) E.; m. Linda Moore McGregor, Aug. 27, 1966; children: Robinson Oscar Jr., James Douglas McGregor, Lewis Moore AB magna cum laude, Harvard U., 1947, JD magna cum laude, 1950; LL.M., Duke U., 1959. Bar: N.C. 1950, D.C. 1954. Prof. law Duke U. Law Sch., Durham, NC, 1950-51, 56—, founder, Ctr. on Law, Ethics and Nat. Security, 1993—; commr. U.S. Ct. Mil. Appeals, Washington, 1953-55; chief judge US Ct. Appeals for the Armed Forces, Washington, 1980-90, judge, 1990—92, sr. judge, 1992; practice law Durham, 1955-80, Councilor N.C. State Bar Council, 1978-83; pres., dir. Triangle Telecasters, Durham, 1966-77. Author: Military Justice, 1956; assoc. editor Law and Contemporary Problems, 1950-51, 56-66; contbr. articles to legal jours. Chair, Durham Redevel. Commn., 1959-75. Served as 1st lt. USAF, 1951-53; to col. Res. (ret.) Named to Assn. Gen. Practice Hall of Fame, 2006; recipient Judge John J. Parker award, NC Bar Assn., 2004. Mem. Am. Law Inst. (life), Conf. Commrs. Uniform State Laws (life), Durham Bar Assn. (pres. 1976-77). Democrat. Presbyterian. Office: Duke U Law Sch Science Drive and Towerview Rd Rm 3002 Durham NC 27708 E-mail: everett@law.duke.edu.

EVERETT, RUPERT, actor; b. Norfolk, Eng., May 29, 1959; Actor: (films) Another Country, 1984, Dance With A Stranger, 1985, Duet For One, 1986, The Right Hand Man, 1987, Hearts of Fire, 1987, Chronicle of a Death Foretold, 1988, The Comfort of Strangers, 1990, The Madness of King George, 1994, Ready to Wear, 1994, Dunston Checks In, 1996, My Best Friend's Wedding, 1997, A Midsummer Night's Dream, 1998, B. Monkey, 1998, Shakespeare in Love, 1998, The Next Best Thing, 1999, An Ideal Husband, 1999, Inspector Gadget, 1999, The Next Best Thing, 2000, South Kensington, 2001, The Importance of Being Earnest, 2002, Unconditional Love, 2002, The Wild Thornberrys Movie (voice), 2002, To Kill a King, 2002, Stage Beauty, 2004, Shrek 2 (voice), 2004, People, 2004, Separate Lies, 2005, (voice) The Chronicles of Narnia: The Lion, the Witch, and the Wardrobe, 2005, Stardust, 2007; (TV movies) The Manhood of Edward Robinson, 1981, Soft Targets, 1982, Princess Daisy, 1983, Arthur the King, 1985, Mr. Ambassador, 2003, Sherlock Holmes and the Case of the Silk Stocking, 2004; (TV series) The Far Pavilions, 1984, Les Liaisons dangereuses, 2003; exec. prodr.: (films) A Different Loyalty, 2004; author: Red Carpets and Other Banana Skins: The Autobiography, 2007*

EVERETT, TERRY, congressman; b. Dothan, Ala., Feb. 15, 1937; m. Barbara Pitts. Owner, pres. The Union Springs Herald; mem. U.S. Congress from 2nd Ala. Dist., Washington, 1993—; nat. security com., agriculture com., veterans' affairs com., and select com. on intelligence. Served in USAF, 1955—59. Republican. Baptist. Office: US Ho of Reps 2312 Rayburn Bldg Washington DC 20515-0102 Office Phone: 202-225-2901. Office Fax: 212-225-8913. E-mail: terry.everett@mail.house.gov.*

EVERETT, TOM, actor; b. Oreg. BA cum laude, Adelphi U.; MFA, NYU Sch of Arts, London Acad. Music/Drama Arts. Actor: (films) Transformers, Curious Case of Benjamin Button, Get Smart, The Alamo, The Island, Beautiful Dreamer, XXX, Intellectual Property, Pearl Harbor, Air Force One, My Fellow Americans, Dances With Wolves, Thirteen Days, Crazy as Hell, Mi Amigo, Vaya Con Dios (aka Hard Time Romance), Best of the Best, The Goodbye Girl, Beverly Hills Cops, Prison, Messenger of Death, Die Hard 2, Earth and the American Dream, Leatherface, Hollywood Vice Squad, others; (Broadway plays) Elizabeth I, Habeas Corpus, Emminent Domain, A Midsummer Night's Dream, (numerous off-broadway and regional theatre plays); (TV films) The Elizabeth Smart Story, McBride, Last Rites, Crash Landing: The Rescue of Flight 232, To Heal a Nation, Gore Vidal's Billy the Kid, Lady Mobster, Double Jeopardy, The Return of Mike Hammer, Thirteen Days to Glory, others; (TV series) C.S.I. Miami, Alias, The Beast, The District, C-16, Pretender, JAG, E.R., West Wing, Ghost Whisperer, Profiler, Picket Fences, Space Above and Beyond, Murder She Wrote, Cheers, LA Law, Hill Street Blues, Birdland, Newhart, Bones, Monk, Medium, 24, Numb3rs, others; songwriter/singer: RCA album Porchlight On In Oregon, ind. album Still Waters (A Collection of Years). Scholar Jacobs Pillow Dance Festival, Perry Mansfield Dance and Drama Sch.; fellow NYU Sch. of Arts, ITT Internat. Fellowship/Fulbright Competition, London Acad. of Music and Dramatic Arts. Mem. The Actors Studio. Roman Catholic. Avocations: cello, guitar, country-western music.

EVERETT, WOODROW WILSON, electrical engineer, educator; b. Newton, Miss., Oct. 11, 1937; s. Woodrow Wilson and Katherine (Thrash) E.; m. Cherry Donna Sarff, Aug. 23, 1958; children: Woodrow W., Leanne Everett Traver. B.E.E., George Washington U., 1959; MS, Cornell U., 1965, PhD, 1968. Project engr. Scott Paper Co., 1959, Ithaca (N.Y.) Rsch. Lab., Atlantic Rsch. Corp., 1962-64; postdoctoral program dir. Rome (N.Y.) Air Devel. Ctr., 1964-75; chmn. bd. N.E. Consortium for Engring. Edn., St. Cloud, Fla., 1975—. Bd. dirs. Device Assos. Corp. N.Y., Masonwood, Inc., Sunoric Corp., ITG, Inc., Thrash Homestead Corp., The Cherwood Corp., SCEEE Svc. Corp. Contbr. articles to profl. jours. Democratic committeeman, Madison County, N.Y., 1976-79; pres. Village of Groton (N.Y.) Appeals Bd., 1966-69; chmn. Groton Planning Bd., 1968-69. Served with USAF, 1959-62. Fellow IEEE (life); mem. Air Force Assn. (life), Res. Officers Assn. (life), Am. Soc. Engring. Edn. Clubs: Rotary. Home: Cherwood Pond King George PO Box 68 Port Royal Sq Port Royal VA 22535-0068 Office: 1101 Massachusetts Ave Saint Cloud FL 34769-3733

EVERETTE, BRUCE L., retail executive; Joined Richmond Divsn. Safeway, Inc., 1968, dist. mgr. Okla. and Va., retail ops. mgr. Phoenix, 1991, divsn. mgr., 1995—98, Calif., 1998—2001, exec. v.p. Pleasanton, Calif., 2001—. Office: Safeway Inc 5918 Stoneridge Mall Rd Pleasanton CA 94588*

EVERHART, GLORIA ELAINE, music educator; d. Thomas and Catherine Rosalie Oland; m. Frederick Everhart, Apr. 13, 1974; 1 child, April. MusB, Peabody Conservatory Music, 1967; postgrad., U. Ill., Towson State U. Tchr. piano, voice, music theory Everhart Piano Studio, Columbia, Md., 1960—; tchr. vocal music Howard County Pub. Schls., 1967—74, tchr. h.s. vocal music, 1984—86; long term substitute music tchr. Glenelg Country Sch., 2002—02. Music dir. The Alleluias, Inc., Columbia, 1987—2004. Dir.: (choral performances) The Alleluias in Concert. Sec., treas. bd. dirs. Everhart Animal Hosp., Inc., 1975—91; music dir. The Alleluias, Inc., Columbia, Md., 1987—2005, Bethany Ln. Bapt. Ch., Ellicott City, Md., 1968—75; min. music and worship Rolling Hills Bapt. ch., Clarksville, 2002—; music min. Bethel Bapt. Ch., Ellicott City, 1997—2002. Mem.: Am. Choral Dirs. Assn. (assoc.). Avocations: reading, internet studies, ethnomusicology, jumble word puzzles, Scrabble. Personal E-mail: geeverhart@verizon.net.

EVERHART, THOMAS EUGENE, retired academic administrator, engineering educator; b. Kansas City, Mo., Feb. 15, 1932; s. William Elliott and Elizabeth Ann (West) E.; m. Doris Arleen Wentz, June 21, 1953; children: Janet Sue, Nancy Jean, David William, John Thomas. AB in Physics magna cum laude, Harvard, 1953; MSc, UCLA, 1955; PhD in Engring., Cambridge U., Eng., 1958. Mem. tech. staff Hughes Research Labs., Culver City, Calif., 1953—55; mem. faculty U. Calif., Berkeley, 1958—78, prof. elec. engring. and computer scis., 1967—78, Miller research prof., 1969—70, chmn. dept., 1972—77; prof. elec. engring., Joseph Silbert dean engring. Cornell U., Ithaca, 1979—84; prof. elec. and computer engring., chancellor U. Ill., Urbana-Champaign, 1984—87; prof. elec. engring. and applied physics, pres. Calif. Inst. Tech., Pasadena, 1987—97, pres. emeritus, 1997—. Fellow scientist Westinghouse Rsch. Labs., Pitts., 1962-63; guest prof. Inst. Applied Physics, U. Tuebingen, Germany, 1966-67, Waseda U., Tokyo, Osaka U., 1974; vis. fellow Clare Hall, Cambridge, U., 1975; chmn. Electron, Ion and Photon Beam Symposium, 1977; cons. in field; sci. and ednl. adv. com. Lawrence Berkeley Lab., 1978-85, chmn., 1980-85; mem. sci. adv. com. GM, 1980-89, chmn., 1984-89; bd. dirs. Saint-Gobain Corp., Acorn Techs., Novelx, Inc.; tech. adv. com. R.R. Donnelly & Sons, 1981-89; sr. sci. advisor W.M. Keck Found., 1997—, dir., 2006-; pro-vice chancellor Cambridge U., 1998; dir. Kevli Found., 2002-. Chmn. Sec. of Energy Adv. Bd., 1990-93; bd. dirs. KCET, 1989-97, Corp. for Nat. Rsch. Initiatives; trustee Calif. Inst. Tech., 1998—; mem. bd. overseers Harvard U., 1999-2005, pres., 2004-05. Marshall scholar Cambridge U., 1955-58, NSF sr. fellow, 1966-67, Guggenheim fellow, 1974-75. Fellow IEEE (Founder's Award medal 2002), AAAS, ASEE, Royal Acad. Engring. (Okawa award 2002); mem. NAE (ednl. adv. bd. 1984-88, mem. com. 1984-89, chmn. 1988, coun. 1988-94, 96-2002), Microbeam Analysis Soc. Am., Electron Microscopy Soc. Am. (coun. 1970-72, pres. 1977), Coun. on Competitiveness (vice-chmn. 1990-96), Assn. Marshall Scholars and Alumni (pres. 1965-68), Athenaeum Club, California Club, Sigma Xi, Eta Kappa Nu. Home: PO Box 1639 Goleta CA 93116 Business E-Mail: everhart@caltech.edu.

EVERHART, VELMA VIZEDOM, retired home economics educator, retired real estate agent; b. Hamilton, Ohio, May 26, 1916; d. Jacob Frederick and Edna (Stewart) Vizedom; m. Herbert Marion Everhart, June 1, 1940 (dec.). BSc in Home Econs., Ohio State U., 1938, MSc in Home Econs., 1954. Cert. tchr. Ohio. Tchr. New Madison Village Sch., Ohio, 1938—41, St. Joseph's Acad., Columbus, Ohio, 1941—43, Columbus City Schs., 1954—56; cafeteria supr. Mt. Carmel Hosp., Columbus, 1943—44; rsch. asst. home econs. Ohio State U., Columbus, 1945—54, assoc. prof. home econs., 1956—78; sales assoc. Heiskell Realtors, Circleville, Ohio, 1979—89. Bd. dirs. Ohio Presbyn. Retirement Ctr., Columbus, 1998—2001, 2005—; pres.-elect. Forum - Thurber Towers, Columbus, 1997—99, bd. dirs., 1999—; mem. Presbyn. life com. Scioto Valley Presbytery, Columbus, 1998—2004; advisor steering com. scholarships Ohio State U., Columbus, 1969—75; mem. Nat. and Ohio Rep. Party; elder, clk. of session Presbyn. Ch., Circleville, 1984—90, trustee, 1993—95. Recipient Alfred J. Wright svc. to students award, Ohio State U., 1964, Student Appreciation award, 1974, Meritorious Svc. award, 2005. Mem.: Coll. Human Ecology Alumni Soc. (sec. 1998—2004), Ohio State U. Alumni Soc., Phi Upsilon Omicron (local chmn. 1964, nat. pres-elect 1972—74, nat. pres. 1974—76, chmn. bd. dirs. ednl. found. 1976—84). Achievements include research in work counter surface finishes. Avocations: golf, football, quilting, collecting Hummel figurines, antiques. Home: 645 Neil Ave # 208 Columbus OH 43215

EVERITT, ALICE LUBIN, labor arbitrator; b. Dec. 13, 1936; d. Isador and Alice (Berliner) Lubin. BA, Columbia U., 1968, JD, 1971. Assoc. Amen, Weisman & Butler, NYC, 1971-78; spl. asst. to dir. Fed. Mediation and Conciliation Svc., Washington, 1978-81; pvt. practice labor arbitration Washington, NYC, 1981-87, Petersburg, Va., 1987—. Mem. various nat. mediation and arbitration panels including Fed. Mediation and Conciliation Svc., U.S. Steel and United Steelworkers, Am. Arbitration Assn. Editor: Dept. Labor publ., 1979. Treas., bd. mem. Petersburg Libr. Found., Inc., 2001—; mem. planning commn. City Petersburg, 1992—2000. Mem. Am. Arbitration Assn., Soc. Profls. Dispute Resolution, Indsl. Rels. Rsch. Assn., Civil War Roundtable of Richmond Office: 541 High St Petersburg VA 23803-3859 Office Phone: 804-733-3200.

EVERITT, ELIZABETH M., school system administrator; d. William Stith; m. Tom Everitt; 1 stepchild, Brian. BS, MA, East Carolina U.; PhD in Spl. Edn., U. N.Mex., 1983. Asst. prin. Mark Twain Elem. Sch., Northeast Heights, prin.; dir. spl. svcs. Albuquerque Pub. Schs., 1995—97, asst. supt. for curriculum and instrn., 1997—98, assoc. supt., 1998—2002, one of 4-person superintendency team, 2002—03, supt., 2003—. Office: Albuquerque Pub Schs 6400 Uptown Blvd, NE Albuquerque NM 87110 Business E-Mail: everitt@aps.edu.*

EVERITT-NEWTON, KATHERINE EVELYN, international management consultant; b. Cleve., Sept. 2, 1957; BS, Bowling Green State U., 1979, MBA, 1981. Sci. systems analyst Eli Lilly & Co., Indpls., 1981-83, systems tng. cons., 1983-84; customer liaison mgr. Ind. U., Bloomington, 1985, prodn. ops. mgr. Indpls., 1985-86; prin. systems cons. Wang Labs., Inc., Carmel, Ind., 1986-93; mgmt. cons. AMT-Sybex (I) Ltd., Dublin, 1994-99; sr. cons. mgr. AMT-Sybex, Ltd., U.K., Letchworth, 1999—2004; ptnr. Cognitus Ltd., Berkshire, England, 2004—. Cons. Ind. Univ., Bloomington, 1984-85, Allied Irish Bank, Dublin, Ireland, 1990-91. Contbr. (book) Introduction to Business, 1980, Introduction to Accounting, 1981, Computers and Data Processing, 1981. Republican. Presbyterian. Avocations: scuba diving, photography, biking, crafts, horseback riding. Home and Office: 2 Beaulieu Close Berkshire RG12 9QL England Office Phone: 44 (0) 7968017403. E-mail: katherine@everitt-newton.com.

EVERLY, JACK, conductor; b. Richmond, Va. Grad., Ind. U. Prin. condr. Am. Ballet Theatre, NYC, 1984—98; mus. dir. & condr. Ameritech's Yuletide Celebration, Indianapolis Symphony Orchestra, 1994—; music advisor Symphonic Pops Consortium, 1998—; prin. pops condr. Indpls. Symphony Orch., 2002—, Balt. Symphony Orch. Conducted shows including Hello, Dolly!, 1978, A Chorus Line, They're Playing Our Song, Showboat, Kismet, Carousel, The Mikado, Hazel Kirk, Everything's Coming Up Roses: The Complete Overtures of Broadway's Jule Styne; conductor Vancouver Symphony, San Diego Symphony, Lake George Opera Festival, Pacific Symphony, Ravinia Festival; music dir., orchestrator In Performance at the White House; conductor world premiers at Am. Ballet Theatre include Sir Kenneth MacMillan's Requiem, Agnes de Mille's The Informer, Mikhail Baryshnikov's Giselle and Swan Lake; conducted music for Disney's The Hunchback of Notre Dame Office: Indianapolis Symphony Orchestra 32 E Washington St Ste 600 Indianapolis IN 46204*

EVERROAD, JOHN DAVID, lawyer; b. Columbus, Ind., Jan. 6, 1940; s. Henry and Margaret L. (Eckleman) E.; m. Patricia Diane Hayworth, June 10, 1967; children: Andrew Quinn, Matthew Oldham. BA, Vanderbilt U., 1962, JD, 1969. Bar: Ariz. 1970, Calif. 1997. Atty. Fennemore Craig PC, Phoenix, 1969—. Mem. panels Nat. Inst. Trial Advocacy programs; lawyer Com. Uniform Jury Standards State of Ariz.; mem. faculty Continuing Edn. Legal Programs. Pres. Parochial Sch. Bd., Phoenix, 1972-78; mem. Christ Luth. Ch., Phoenix, 1969—, sec., 1986, 88-89, pres., 1979-80; bd. dirs. Combined Metro. Phoenix Arts and Scis., 1996-98. With USMC, 1962-66. Fellow ABA, Ariz. Bar Found. (founder), Maricopa County Bar Found. (founder), Am. Coll. Trial Lawyers; mem. Am. Bd. Trial Advocates, Maricopa County Bar Assn. (pres. 1992-93), Ariz. State Bar Assn. (chmn. edit. bd. Jour., com. revisions uniform jury instructions 1984-89, Disciplinary com. 1984-90), Phi Delta Phi. Republican. Lutheran. Avocations: scuba diving, bow hunting. Home: 6615 N 3rd Dr Phoenix AZ 85013-1103 Office: Fennemore Craig PC 3003 N Central Ste 2600 Phoenix AZ 85012-2913 Home Phone: 602-274-3139; Office Phone: 602-916-5302. Business E-Mail: jeverroa@fclaw.com.

EVERS, ALEX STEVEN, anesthesiologist, internist, educator; b. NYC, June 15, 1952; s. Leo and Irma; m. Carol Evers; children: Sam, Jacob, Joseph. MD, NYU, 1978. Intern Michael Reese Hosp., Chgo., 1978-79, resident internal medicine, 1979-81; resident anesthesiology Mass. Gen. Hosp., Boston, 1983; anesthesiologist Barnes Hosp., St. Louis; asst. prof. Washington U. Sch. Medicine, St. Louis, 1983—90, assoc. prof. anesthesiology, pharmacology, & internal medicine, 1990—94, prof., 1994—, chair, dept. anesthesiology, 1994—, Henry E. Mallinckrodt prof. anesthesiology, 1994—. Bd. dirs. Found. Anesthesia Rsch. & Ed.; editorial bd. Anesthesiology, Jour. Clin. Anesthesia, Jour. Anesthesiology, Japan; former chair, bd. dirs. Washington U. Faculty Practice Plan, St. Louis; former pres. Assoc. Univ. Anesthesiologists. Contbr. scientific papers; co-author: (books) Anesthetic Pharmacology: Physiologic Principals & Clinical Practice, 2004. Recipient Established Investigator award, Am. Heart Assoc., Josiah Macy Found. fellowship. Mem. ACP, Am. Soc. Anesthesiologists, Internat. Anesthesia Rsch. Soc., Soc. Critical Care Medicine, Inst. Medicine. Avocations: bicycling, running, swimming, fishing, history. Office: Washington U Sch Medicine Box 8054 216 S Kingshighway Blvd Saint Louis MO 63110-1026

EVERS, GENE, writer; b. NYC, Mar. 26, 1951; s. Lee Evers and Pauline (Leviton) Stein. AA in Liberal Arts, Nassau C.C., Garden City, NY, 1973; BA in Humanities, SUNY, Old Westbury, 1982. Writer L.I. Bus. Rev., Plainview, N.Y., 1978-82; staff Quaker Homecraft, Plainview, 1983-84; ind. writer Bethpage, NY, 1992—. Staff Nassau Ctr. for the Developmentally Disabled, Woodbury, N.Y., 1978-84. Author: (movie script) The Ancient Star of Christmas, 1997, (poems) I Long for the Love of Thee, For That One Moment, My Beloved; songwriter Where My Heart Lies, The Summer Rain A Christmas Song, 1997, Candles of Love, The Northern Wind, We're Flying, Ohio, The Very Last Time, Queen Ann Of The Mountain; author short stories. Named Disting. Poet of the Yr., Internat. Soc. Poets, Owings Mills, Md., 1997; inductee Hall of Fame, Internat. Soc. Poets, 1996. Avocations: model trains, weightlifting, studying history, philosophy and literature. Home: 15 Kensington Circle Apt E Garnerville NY 10923 Office Phone: 516-680-8989.

EVERS, WILLIAMSON MOORE, education policy analyst, political scientist; b. San Francisco, Oct. 18, 1948; s. Henry Kaspar and Emily Stout Evers; m. Leslie Carver Johnson (div.); m. Mary Therese Gingell (div.); children: Daniel Kenneth, Pamela Ruth. BA in Polit. Sci., Stanford U., 1972, MA in Polit. Sci., 1978, PhD in Polit. Sci., 1987. Editor-in-chief Inquiry Mag., San Francisco, 1976—80; vis. asst. prof. Emory U., Atlanta, 1987—88; nat. and vis. fellow Hoover Instn., Stanford (Calif.) U., 1988—94, rsch. fellow, 1995—; sr. advisor edn. to Amb. Paul Bremer Coalition Provisional Authority, Iraq, 2003; sr. advisor US Sec. Edn. Margaret Spellings Washington, 2007—. Adj. assoc. prof. Santa Clara (Calif.) U., 1995—98; commr. State Calif. Commn. for the Establishment Academic Content and Performance Stds., Sacramento, 1996—98; mem. math. content rev. panel State Calif. Standardized Testing and Reporting Program, Sacramento, 1998—2007, mem. history-social sci. content rev. panel, 1999—2007; mem. adv. bd. Calif. History-Social Sci. Project, Davis, 1999—2007; mem. Koret Task Force on K-12 Edn., Hoover Instn., Stanford, 1999—, Nat. Ednl. Rsch. Policy and Priorities Bd., Washington, 2001—02; commr. White House Commn. on Presdl. Scholars, Washington, 2001—07; mem. content rev. panel, history textbook adoption State of Calif., 2005; mem. Math. Sci. Review Panel, Inst. Edn. Sci., US Dept. Edn., Washington, 2005—06; mem. editl. bd. Edn. Next Mag., Stanford, Calif., 2000—07. Author: (public policy research) Victims' Rights, 1996; editor, contbr.: public policy research National Service: Pro & Con, 1990, What's Gone Wrong in America's Classrooms, 1998; co-editor: School Reform: The Critical Issues, 2001, School Accountability, 2002, Teacher Quality, 2002, Testing Student Learning, Evaluating Teaching Effectiveness, 2004. Mem. edn. adv. com. Bush-Cheney Transition, 2000—01; edn. policy advisor Richard Riordan Gubernatorial Campaign, 2001—02, William Simon Gubernatorial Campaign, 2002, George W. Bush Presidential Campaign, 2000, co-chmn. Calif. Edn. Coalition, 2000, co-vice-chmn. Calif. Edn. Coalition, 2004, mem. Nat. Steering Com., Nat. Edn. Coalition, 2004; co-chmn. Gov. Schwarzenegger's Coalition for Edn. Reform, 2005; co-chmn edn. coalition Arnold Schwarzenegger Gubernatorial Campaign, 2006; mem. bd. dirs. East Palo Alto Charter Sch., 1997—2004, pres. Calif., 2003—04; trustee Santa Clara County Bd. Edn., 2004—07. Co-recipient Koret Prize, 2002. Episcopalian. Office: US Dept Edn Office of Secretary 400 Maryland Ave SW Washington DC 20202-0008

EVERSLEY, FREDERICK JOHN, sculptor, engineer; b. Bklyn., Aug. 28, 1941; s. Frederick William and Beatrice Agnes (Syphax) E. BSE.E., Carnegie-Mellon U., 1963. One-man shows include Whitney Mus. Am. Art, N.Y.C., 1970, Nat. Acad. Sci., Washington, 1976, 81, L.A. Inst. Contemporary Art, 1976, Santa Barbara Mus., 1976, Newport Harbor Art Mus., 1976, Oakland Mus. Art, 1977, Palm Springs (Calif.) Desert Mus., 1978, AIA, 1981, Va. Mus., 1981, Bacardi Art Gallery, Miami, 1984, Laband Art Gallery, 1985, Loyola Marymount U., L.A., Hokin Gallery, Palm Beach, Fla., 1988, Juda Gallery, London, 1988, Eva Cohen Gallery, Chgo., 1991, Lorenzelli Arte, Milan, 1992, Pavilion of Saudi Arabia, Expo 92, Seville, Spain, 1992, Capa Gallerie, Brussels, 2003-04, European Space Agy., The Hague, 2004, Osuna Art, Bethesda, 2004; represented in permanent collections Smithsonian Instn., Washington, IRS Nat. Hdqtrs., New Carrollton, Md., Calif. State Coll., L.A., Oakland (Calif.) Art Mus., Milw. Art Center, Whitney Mus. Am. Art, N.Y.C., John Marin Meml. Collection, N.Y.C., U., Kans. Art Gallery, Lawrence, Long Beach (Calif.) Mus. Art, Currier Gallery Art, Manchester, N.H., Taft Mus. Art, Cin., Cranbrook Art Gallery, Bloomfield Hills, Mich., Nat. Acad. Sci., Washington, Nat. Collection Fine Arts, Washington, MIT, Cambridge, Neuberger Mus. Art, Purchase, N.Y., Newport Harbor Art Mus., Newport Beach, Calif., Guggenheim Mus., N.Y.C., Smith Coll. Mus. Art, Northhampton, Mass., Nat. Air and Space Mus., Mus. Contemporary Art, L.A., Palm Springs Desert Mus., Rose Mus. of Art, Brandis U., Boston, Sammlung Goetz, Munich Germany, IRS hdqs., New Carrollton, Md., 1996, Rossini Sculpture Park, Briosco, Italy, 1999, Katzen Art Ctr. Am. U., Washington; artist in residence Nat. Air and Space Mus., Washington, 1977-80. Nat. Endowment Arts grantee, 1972 Mem. L.A. Inst. Contemporary Art, Artworkers Coalition. Address: 1110 Abbot Kinney Blvd Venice CA 90291-3314 Office Phone: 212-431-4222. E-mail: fredever@bigfoot.com.

EVERSOLE, BARBARA LOUISE, administrative assistant; b. Ukiah, Calif., Dec. 25, 1926; d. Clarence and Alta Anita (Eldred) Ballou; m. Walter Robert Eversole, Dec. 16, 1945; children: Ronald Edward, Richard Walter. AA, Armstrong Coll., Berkeley, Calif., 1945. Pvt. sec. Mendocino County Farm Adminstrn., Ukiah, 1945—46, U.S. VA, Ukiah, 1946—48; sec. Eversole Mortuary, Ukiah, 1955—75. Designer, supr. constrn. Hudson-Carpenter Park, Ukiah. Vol. fundraiser, worker Beautification of McGarvey Park, Ukiah; mem. revitalization of downtown com. C. of C., Ukiah; chmn. Cultural Arts Commn., Ukiah; sec. Mendocino County Grand Jury; chmn. bd. trustees Sun House Guild, pres., grant writer. Named Woman of Achievement, Soroptimist Internat., 1981, Outstanding Citizen of Yr., Ukiah C. of C., 1984; recipient award for beautification of McGarvey Park, City of Ukiah, Calif. Parks and Recreation award, 1978, recognition for outstanding hist. preservation, Mendocino County Hist.

Soc. and City of Ukiah, 1981. Mem.: Order Eastern Star (life). Avocations: gardening, writing, travel, landscape design. Home (Winter): 47350 Via Florence La Quinta CA 92253 Home (Summer): 180 Barbara St Ukiah CA 95482 E-mail: beversole@saber.net.

EVERSON, JEAN WATKINS DOLORES, librarian, media consultant, educator; b. Forest City, NC, Feb. 14, 1938; d. J.D. Watkins and Hermie Roberta (Dizard) Watkins; children: Curtis Bryon, Vincent Keith. BS Elem. Edn., U. Cin., 1971, M Secondary Edn., 1973. Cert. X-ray technician. Educator Cin. Pub. Schs., Cin., 1965—2002, classroom tchr., parent/school coord., 1965—2002; work study coord. Butler County Edn. Ctr., Fairfield, Ohio, 1997—98; long term sub. Brown County -Georgetown Sch. Sys., Gerogetown, Ohio, 1993; sr. staff asst., cpc/alcohol substance abuse, inc. Cin. Pub. Schs., Cin., 1992—93; libr. tech. media; libr. media tech. asst. langsam libr. University of Cin.cinnati-Langsam Library, Cincinnati. Dir. and coord. tutoring program So. Baptist Ch., Cincinnati, 1990—91. Author: (booklet) Gospel Music: Copywrite Laws, 1987 (1987). Prodr./dir./coord. city music festival in music hall Cin. Pub. Schs., 1972—77. Mem.: Ohio Assn. Suprs. and Work Study Coords., Music Educator Nat. Conf. Baptist. Avocations: travel, walking. Home: PO Box 8337 West Chester OH 45069 Office: Cin City Pub Schs-Woodward 7001 Reading Rd Cincinnati OH 45237 Home Phone: 513-858-6880. Office Fax: 513-758-1279; Home Fax: 513-858-6880. Business E-Mail: eversoj@cpsboe.k12.oh.us.

EVERSON, MARK WHITTY, international relief organization executive, former federal agency administrator; b. NYC, Sept. 10, 1954; s. Leonard Charles and Marjory (Whitty) Everson; m. Nanette Rutka; 2 children. BA, Yale U., 1976; MS in Acctg., NYU, 1977. Staff acct. Arthur Andersen & Co., NYC, 1976—78, sr. acct., 1978—81, mgr., 1981—82; spl. project officer US Info. Agy. (USIA), 1982—83, spl. asst. to the dir., asst. dir., 1983—85; spl. asst to under sec. US Dept. State, 1985—86; spl. asst. to Atty. Gen. Edwin Meese US Dept. Justice, 1985—86; exec. assoc. commr. Immigration and Naturalization Svc., 1986—87, dep. commr., 1987—88; various fin. & operations positions in the United States, France and Turkey Pechiney Group, 1988—98; group v.p. fin. SC Internat. Svcs., Inc., 1998—2001; contr. fed. fin. mgmt. Office Mgmt. & Budget, Exec. Office of the Pres., Washington, 2001—02, dep. dir. for mgmt., 2002—03; commr. IRS, Washington, 2003—07; pres., CEO Am. Red Cross, Washington, 2007—. Office: American Red Cross National Headquarters 2025 E St NW Washington DC 20006*

EVERSON, STEVEN LEE, lawyer, real estate company executive; b. Philippi, W.Va., June 16, 1950; s. Billie Lee and Mildred Ann (Hill) E.; m. Donna Janine Chmielarz, May 29, 1976; 1 child, Michael. BA in Math. magna cum laude, W. Va. U., 1972; JD, Northwestern U., 1979. Bar: Colo. 1979. Tax sr. acct. Deloitte, Haskins & Sells, Colorado Springs, Colo., 1979-82; v.p., sec., treas. The Schuck Corp., Colorado Springs, 1982—. Instr. real estate U. Colo. Project bus. instr. Jr. Achievement, 1985—87; treas. Steve Schuck for Gov. Com., 1988—98; bd. dirs. Silver Key Sr. Svcs., Inc., 2000—, Boys and Girls Club of Pikes Peak Region, Colorado Springs, 1987—90, UCCS Exec. Club, Colorado Springs, 1988—90; bd. dirs., past chmn. Pikes Peak Found. Mental Health, Colorado Springs, 1986—2001; past chmn. Pikes Peak Mental Health Ctr. Sys., Inc., treas., 2001—03; chmn. bd. dirs. Colorado Springs Christian Schs., 2004—; bd. dirs. Pikes Peak Integrated Svcs., 2003—. Capt. USAF, 1972—76. Named Vol. of Yr., Pikes Peak Mental Health Ctr., 1999, 2002. Mem.: Phi Beta Kappa. Republican. Mem. Ch. of Christ. Avocations: skiing, softball, golf, basketball. Home: 1690 Colgate Dr Colorado Springs CO 80918-8106 Office: The Schuck Corp 2 N Cascade Ave Ste 1280 Colorado Springs CO 80903-1601 Office Phone: 719-327-5803.

EVERS-WILLIAMS, MYRLIE BEASLEY, advocate, cultural organization administrator; b. Vicksburg, Miss., Mar. 17, 1933; m. Medgar Evers (dec. June 11, 1963); 3 children; m. Walter Edward Williams 1975 (dec. 1995). Student, Alcorn State U.; BA in Sociology, Pomona Coll., 1968, Doctorate (hon.); cert., Simmons Coll.; Doctorate (hon.), Medgar Evers Coll., Spelman Coll., Columbia Coll., Chgo., Bennett Coll., Tougaloo Coll., Willamette U. Mem. staff, sec. NAACP; asst. dir. planning Clarmont (Calif.) Colls., 1968—70; v.p. advt. & publicity Seligman & Latz, NYC, 1973-75; dir. consumer affairs Atlantic Richfield Co.; commr. Pub. Works Bd., LA, 1987-95; chairwoman NAACP, 1995-98. Civil rights leader, lectr. Author: For Us the Living, 1967, Watch Me Fly, 1999; co-author (with Steven Kasher) The Civil Rights Movement, 1996, (with Harriet Jacobs) Incidents in the Life of a Slave Girl, 2000, (with Russell J. Rickford) Betty Shabazz, 2003, editor: (with Manning Marable)The Autobiography of Medgar Evers, 2005; contbg. editor Ladies Home Jour. Candidate for Congress in Calif., 1970; candidate for L.A. City Coun., 1987; head So. Calif. Dem. Women's Divsn.; convener Nat. Women's Polit. Caucus; founder, chmn. Medgar Evers Inst.; mem. adv. bd. Boys & Girls Clubs Ams. Youth for Unity and Allstate Found., 2004. Named Woman of Yr., Glamour Mag., 1995, Ms. Mag., 1995, one of Women of Yr., Ladies Home Jour., 1996, one of 200 most influential women, Vanity Fair mag., Jan. 1999; recipient Mary Church Terrell award Delta Sigma Theta, 1996, Althea T.L. Simmons Social Action award, 1998, Spingarn award, NAACP, Atlanta, 1998, Trumpeter's award, Nat. Consumers League, New Orleans, 1998, U.S. Congl. Black Caucus Achievement award, Woman of Honor award LWV, Image award for civil rights NAACP, Woman of the Yr. award State of Calif. Mem.: NAACP (chmn. emeritus, nat. bd. dirs.). Office: MEW Assocs Inc 15 SW Colorado Ave Bend OR 97702-1150

EVERT, CHRIS (CHRISTINE MARIE EVERT), retired professional tennis player; b. Ft. Lauderdale, Fla., Dec. 21, 1954; d. James and Colette Evert; m. John Lloyd, Apr. 17, 1979 (div.); m. Andy Mill, July 30, 1988; children: Alexander James, Nicholas Joseph, Colton Jack. Amateur tennis player, until Dec. 1972; profl. tennis player, 1972-89; ret. from tennis, 1989; owner Evert Enterprises/IMG, Boca Raton, Fla., 1989—; Olympics commentator CBS Sports, 1992. Commentator NBC Sports tennis events; winner numerous tournaments including U.S. Jr. Championship, 1970, 71, U.S. Open, 1975, 76, 77, 78, 80, 82, Wimbledon Singles, 1974, 76, 81, doubles, 1976, Australian Open, 1982, 84, French Open Singles, 1974, 75, 79, 80, 83, 85, 86, Virginia Slims, 1972, 73, 75, 77, 87, European Women's Open, Geneva, 1987, Eckerd Open, 1987; spl. advisor to U.S. Nat. Tennis Team by U.S. Tennis Assn.; bd. dirs. Internat. Tennis Hall of Fame; trustee Womens Sports Found. Corp. spokesperson and rep., appearing in TV commls. and print advertisements; host and organizer Chris Evert Pro-Celebrity Tennis Classic, 1989, 90, 92, 93, 94, 95, 96, 97, 98, 99. Founder Chris Evert Charities, Inc., Healthy Start. Recipient Lebair Sportsmanship trophy, 1971; named Female Athlete of Yr. AP, 1974, 75, 77, 80, Athlete of Yr. Sports Illustrated, 1976, Greatest Woman Athlete of Last 25 Years Women's Sports Found., 1985, Flo Hyman award Women's Sports Found., 1990, Providencia award Palm Beach County Conv. and Visitors Bur., 1991; named one of Top 10 Romantic People of 1989, Korbel; inducted Madison Sq. Garden Walk of Fame, 1993, inductee, Internat. Tennis Hall of Fame, 1995. Mem. U.S. Lawn Tennis Assn. (Top Women's Singles Player award 1974), Nat. Honor Soc., Fla. Sports Found. (bd. dirs.), Women's Tennis Assn. (pres. 1982-91, exec. com., Sportsmanship award 1979, Player Svc. awards 1981, 86, 87).

EVERT, RAY FRANKLIN, botany educator; b. Mt. Carmel, Pa., Feb. 20, 1931; s. Milner Ray and Elsie (Hoffa) I.; m. Mary Margaret Maloney, Jan. 2, 1960; children: Patricia Ann, Paul Franklin. BS, Pa. State U., 1952, MS, 1954; PhD, U. Calif. at Davis, 1958. Mem. faculty Mont. State U., 1958—60, U. Wis.-Madison, 1960—, prof. botany, 1966—77, prof. botany and plant pathology, 1977—88, Katherine Esau prof. botany and plant pathology, 1988—2001, emeritus prof. botany and plant pathology, 2001—, chmn. dept. botany, 1973—74, 1977—79, 1994—98. Vis. prof. U. Natal, Pietermaritzburg, S. Africa, winter, spring 1971, U. Göttingen, W.Ger., summer 1971, 74-75, summer 1988; mem. gen. biology and genetics fellowship rev. panel NIH, 1964-68, NSF Adv. Com. for Biol. Research Ctrs. Program, 1987-88; forensic plant anatomy cons. Author: Esau's Plant Anatomy, Mesistems, Cells and Tissues of the Plant Body: Their Structure, Function and Development, 3d edit., 2006; co-author: Biology of Plants; sci. editor Physiol. Plantarum, 1983-98; mem. editl. bd. Trees, 1991-2000, Internat. Jour. Plant Scis., 1991-98; contbr. articles on food conducting tissue in higher plants and leaf structure-function relationships. Recipient Alexander von Humboldt award, 1974-75, Emil H. Steiger award for excellence in tchg. U. Wis., 1981, Bessey Lectr. award Iowa State U., Ames, 1984, Benjamin Minge Duggar lectureship award Auburn U., 1985, Disting. Svc. citation Wis. Acad. Scis., Arts and Letters, 1985, Hilldale award in biol. sci., 1998; Guggenheim fellow, 1965-66 Fellow Am. Acad. Arts and Scis., AAAS; mem. Bot. Soc. Am. (pres. 1986-87, Merit award 1982, Centennial medal 2006), Am. Inst. Biol. Scis., Wis. Acad. Scis., Arts and Letters, Am. Soc. Plant Physiol., Internat. Assn. Wood Anatomists, Deutschen Botanischen Gesellschaft, Golden Key Nat. Honor Soc., Sigma Xi, Phi Kappa Phi, Phi Sigma, Phi Epsilon Phi., Pi Alpha Xi. Home: 810 Woodward Dr Madison WI 53704-2238 Office Phone: 608-262-2678. Business E-Mail: rfevert@wisc.edu.

EVERT, SANDRA FLORENCE (SANDRA WHEELER), medical/surgical nurse, consultant; b. Saginaw, Mich., Sept. 18, 1949; d. Charles William and Florence Arlene (Babcock) Wheeler; m. Raymond Clyde Evert, Jan. 20, 1968; children: Christine Michelle, Raymond Clyde II. AD cum laude, Lansing C.C., 1986. Consulting nurse Daycare Ctr.; med./surg. staff nurse E.W. Sparrow Hosp., Lansing, Mich., 1986—. Mem. First United Pentecostal, The Liberty Ch. of Grand Ledge, Mich. Mem. Apostolic Ch. Avocations: camping, Bible reading, Christian music, church functions. Home: 10 Willard Ct Grand Ledge MI 48837-1356 Office Phone: 517-230-6981. Personal E-mail: raysan10@aol.com.

EVESQUE, PIERRE HENRI, physics researcher; b. Neuilly, Seine, France, Dec. 26, 1951; s. Jacques François and Nicole Odette (Schulz-Robellaz) E.; m. Claire Françoise Bompaire, Oct. 8, 1981. Grad. in physics, Ecole Superieure Physique et Chimie Industrielles de Paris, Paris, 1976; D degree, U. Paris VI, 1979, D in Physics, 1984. Rschr. ESPCI, Paris, 1976-77, asst. prof., 1977-78; researcher Nat. Ctr. Sci. Rsch., Paris, 1980-93, dir. rsch. Châtenay-Malabry, France, 1993—; postdoctoral fellow UCLA, 1984-85. Cons. European Space Agy., Paris, 1990-93; cons. Pont-à-Mousson, 1990-91. Editor Poudres et Grains, 1993—; contbr. articles to profl. jours. Coun. mem. Fac. Libre de Théologie Réformée, Aix-en-Provence, France, 1987—. With France Air Army, 1978-79. Mem. Am. Phys. Soc., Materials Rsch. Soc., French Assn. Physics, Assn. for Study of Micro-mechanics of Granular Materials (pres. 1997-2005). Presbyterian. Office: Nat Inst Sci Rsch Lab Mécanique/Structures Materiaux Grande Voie des Vignes Ecole Centrale Paris 92295 Chatenay-Malabry France Office Fax: 33141131442. Business E-Mail: pierre.evesque@ecp.fr.

EVIATAR, LYDIA, pediatrician, neurologist; b. Bucharest, Romania, Apr. 7, 1936; came to U.S., 1966; d. Joseph and Ghitea (Scheinberg) Tamir; m. Abraham Eviatar, Oct. 9, 1956; children: Joseph, Daphne. BSc, Faculte des Scis., Strasbourg, 1954; MD, Hadassah Hebrew U., Jerusalem, 1961. Diplomate Am. Bd. Pediatrics, Am. Bd. Neurology with spl. competence in child neurology. Intern and resident Tel Hashoner Hosp., Tel Aviv, 1961-65; U.C.P. fellow UCLA, 1966-67, fellow in pediatric neurology, 1967-69; pediatric neurologist Bronx (N.Y.) Lebanon Hosp., 1970-79; resident in neurology Montefiore Hosp. Med. Ctr., Bronx, 1973-75; pediatric neurologist L.I. Jewish Med. Ctr., 1979-86; chief pediatric neurology Schneider Children's Hosp., New Hyde Park, NY, 1986-99; from assoc. prof. to prof. pediatrics and neurology Albert Einstein Coll. Medicine, Bronx, NY, 1989-99, chief emeritus Pediat. Neurology Sch., 1999—. Co-author: (with others) Pediatric Neurology, 1988, 2004. Grantee Nat. Inst. Neurol. Disease and Blindness, 1970-77, Acad. Cerebral Palsy, 1980-81, Richmond award, 1981; recipient teaching award Am. Acad. Otolaryngology, 1983. Fellow Am. Acad. Pediatrics, Am. Acad. Neurology (cert. neurologist, child neurologist); mem. Epilepsy Soc., Child Neurological Soc. Home Phone: 914-725-5998; Office Phone: 718-470-3450. Business E-Mail: eviatar@lij.edu.

EVINS, DAN W., food products executive; Co-founder Cracker Barrel Old Country Stores, Lebanon, Tenn., 1969, pres., CEO, bd. chmn., 1974—2004, CBRL Group (holding company of Cracker Barrel), 1998—2004, chmn. emeritus Lebanon, Tenn., 2004—. Office: CBRL Group 305 Hartmann Dr Lebanon TN 37087

EVNIN, ANTHONY BASIL, venture capital investor; b. NYC, Mar. 10, 1941; s. Oscar B. Evnin and Nina (Fradkin) Schick; m. Judith P. Ward, June 9, 1962; children: Luke B., Timothy W. BA, Princeton U., 1962; PhD, MIT, 1966. With Union Carbide Corp., 1966-71, Story Chem., 1971-74; gen. ptnr. Venrock Assocs., NYC, 1974—. Bd. dirs. Icagen, Inc., Durham, NC, Memory Pharms. Corp., Montvale, NJ, Renovis, Inc., South San Francisco, Calif., Coley Pharm. Group, Inc., Wellesley, Mass., Sunesis Pharms., Inc., South San Francisco, Pharmos Corp., Iselin, NJ, Infinity Pharms., Inc., Cambridge, Mass. Trustee Princeton U., 1997-2007, Rockefeller U., 1999—. Office: Venrock 30 Rockefeller Plz Fl 35 New York NY 10112-0256

EWALD, LAURA ANNE, school librarian; b. Bryn Mawr, Pa., May 20, 1961; d. Thomas M. and Sharon C. Ewald. BA in Classical Studies, U. Wash., 1985; BA in Drama, Ctrl. Wash. U., 1990; MLS, Ind. U., 1998; MA in Orgnl. Comm., Murray State U., Ky., 2003. Reference libr. Ind. U., Bloomington, Ind., 1998; reference instrn. libr. Murray (Ky.) State U., 1998—2006; asst. libr. pub. svcs. Ruby E. Dare Libr. Greenville Coll., Ill., 2006—. Mem.: ALA, Theatre Libr. Assn., Assn. Christian Librs., Beta Phi Mu. Avocations: community and educational theatre, puppet theatre.

EWALD, ROBERT CHARLES, lawyer; b. Phila., Mar. 8, 1940; s. George R. and Dorothy (Edelen) E. BS, Ind. U., 1962; JD, U. Louisville. 1965. Bar: Ky. 1965, U.S. Ct. Mil. Appeals 1966, U.S. Supreme Ct. 1971. Judge adv. USAF, 1965-68; ptnr. Wyatt, Tarrant & Combs LLP, Louisville, 1968—, chmn. Tort & Ins. Practice Group. Bd. dirs. Legal Aid Soc., Louisville, 1970—, chmn. 1991, 92; pres. Jefferson County Pub. Defenders, Louisville, 1970—; mem. Ky. Atty. Adv. Com., Frankfort, 1980—. Mem. Ky. Commn. on Pub. Advocacy, 1990—, chmn. 1993. Mem.: Ky. Bar Assn. (pres. 2006), Louisville Bar Found. (pres. 1986). Avocations: tennis, scuba diving. Office: Wyatt Tarrant & Combs LLP PNC Plaza 500 W Jefferson St Louisville KY 40202 Office Phone: 502-562-7288. Office Fax: 502-589-0309. E-mail: rewald@wyattfirm.com.

EWALD, ROBERT FREDERICK, insurance company executive, consultant; b. Newark, May 5, 1924; s. Frederick J. and Florence M. (Reiley) E.; m. Jeanine Martinez, Jan. 3, 1976; children: Robert T., Steven A.; children by a previous marriage: William F., John C., George E. BSBA in Econs. with honors, Rutgers U., 1948. Auditor Prudential Ins. Co., Newark, Houston, Chgo., 1948—61; audit mgr. NY Life Ins. Co., NYC, 1962-64; treas. Mass. Gen. Life Ins. Co., Boston, 1965-68; adminstrv. v.p., contr. Res. Life Ins., Dallas, 1969—71; CEO Nat. Ben Franklin Life, Chgo., 1971-77; trustee, CEO, dir. Northcare HMO Rockford Blue Cross Plan, 1979—82; CEO Associated Life Ins. Co., 1979—82; exec. dir. Ill. Life and Health Ins. Guaranty Assoc., Ill., 1983—94, Ill. HMO Guaranty Assn., Chgo., 1987—94; CEO Guaranty Sys. Cons., 1992—; dir., chmn. audit com. Guaranty Reasurance Co., 1993—95. Rep. Ill. Dir. Ins., 1984—. Served with U.S. Army, 1943-46. Fellow Life Mgmt. Inst.; mem. Fin. Execs. Inst., Am. Arbitration Assn., Mensa, VFW. Home: 400 S Northwest Hwy # 403 Park Ridge IL 60068-4907 Personal E-mail: bobewald@comcast.net.

EWALD, ROBERT HANSEN (BO EWALD), computer software company executive; b. 1947; BS, U. Nev., 1969; MS, U. Colo., 1970. With U. Colo., 1970—76, Sperry Univac, 1976—77; at Los Alamos Nat. Lab., 1977-84; with Cray Rsch. Inc., Eagan, Minn., 1984—, v.p. Mendota Heights, Minn., 1985-89, exec. v.p. Chippewa Falls, Wis., 1989—, chief tech. officer, 1992-93, pres., COO, 1994—97, 1994—; exec. v.p., computer systems Silicon Graphics, Inc, 1997, exec. v.p., COO, 1997—98; pres., CEO E-Stamp Corp., 1999—2001; exec. chmn. Learn2 Corp., 2001—02; chmn., CEO Scale Eight, Inc., 2002—03; exec. v.p., pres. Ceridian Human Resources Ceridian Corp., 2003—05; chmn., CEO Linux Network, Inc., 2005—07; CEO Silicon Graphics, Inc. (SGI), Sunnyvale, Calif., 2007—. Mem. Pres. Info. Tech. Adv. Com., 1997—2001; bd. dirs. Ceridian Corp., 1997—2005, Silicon Graphics, Inc. (SGI), 2007—. Office: Silicon Graphics Inc 1140 E Arques Ave Sunnyvale CA 94085*

EWALD, ROBERTA GRANT, artist, writer; b. Mpls., Aug. 25, 1915; d. Oscar and Hanna Theolinda (Johannson) Grant; m. Henry C. Ewald, Sept. 7, 1946; 1 child, Grant Christian. Student, U. Minn., Calif. Sch. Fine Arts, Coll. San Mateo, Golden Gate Coll. Asst. various firms, San Francisco, 1946—64; owner, artist Travers Art Gallery, South San Francisco, 1973—86; owner, adminstr. Ewald Travel Svc., South San Francisco and San Bruno, Calif., 1967—86; founder, pres. Keyboard Prodns., 1990—. Cons. Capuchino Cmty. Theater, 1984; creator, curator WestWing Art Gallery at Sanchez Art Ctr., Pacifica, 1996—2000. Lead role, author: (musical) The Wanderers, 1978; co-producer revision, 1982, 1992; poetry, I'm All I Know, 1983; co-producer: (TV show) Pacifica, 1982; dir.: children's choirs, music events; songwriter, singer, actress, musician (piano and guitar):; writer, illustrator: poetry My View; writer, prodr., lead: (musicals) Madam Bella's Saloon, 1983; Coastside Bowl, 1988; We Meant Well, 1989; prodr.: Moving Matters, 1991, Annual Producer's Showcase, 1993—. Founder Seaside Music Acad., San Francisco State U., 1999. Recipient Merit award, Capuchino Cmty. Theater, 1983, 1984, Lifetime Achievement in Arts, City of Pacifica, 1998, numerous awards for paintings, San Francisco and Calif. art exhibits, Lifetime Achievement award, City of Pacifica. Mem.: Crystal Springs Creative Writers, Citizens Against Waste, Pacific Art Connections, Pacifica Spindrift Players (named Outstanding Mem. 1980), Art Guild, Kiwanis.

EWALD, WENDY TAYLOR, photographer, writer, educator; b. Detroit, June 28, 1951; d. Henry Theodore and Carolyn Davison (Taylor) E.; m. Thomas Joseph McDonough, Oct. 21,1990; 1 child, Michael German. BA, Antioch Coll., 1974. Founder, dir. Camera Work, London, 1971-73, Mountain Photography Workshop, Whitesburg, Ky., 1975-81; tchr. photography Self-Employed Women's Assn., Raquira, Colombia, 1982-84, Gujarat, India, 1988-89; edn. cons. Fotofest, Houston, 1989-91; sr. rsch. assoc. Duke U., Durham, NC, 1991—. Artist-in-residence Ky. Arts Coun., Whitesburg, 1976-80; asst. dir., scriptwriter Cine-Mujer, Bogota, 1986; vis. assoc. prof. photography Bard Coll., Annandale, N.Y., 1996; sr. fellow Vera List Ctr. for Art and Politics New Sch. U., 2001-04. Author, editor: Appalachia: A Self-Portrait, 1978; author: Portraits and Dreams, 1985, Magic Eyes, 1992, I Dreamed I Had A Girl In My Pocket, 1996, Secret Games: Collaborations with Children, 1969-99, 2000, I Wanna Take Me a Picture: Teaching Writing and Photography to Children, 2001; The Best Part of Me: Childen Talk About Their Bodies, 2001. Recipient prize Lyndhurst Found., 1986; Fulbright fellow, fellow Nat. Endowment for Arts, 1988, non-fiction fellow N.Y. Found. for Arts, 1990, MacArthur fellow, 1992. Home: PO Box 582 Rhinebeck NY 12572-0582

EWALD, WILLIAM BRAGG, JR., writer, consultant; b. Chgo., Dec. 8, 1925; s. William Bragg and Mary Ann (Niccolls) E.; m. Mary Cecilia Thedieck, Dec. 6, 1947 (dec. Feb. 1997); children: William Bragg, Charles Ross, Thomas Hart Benton. AB, Washington U., 1946; MA, Harvard U., 1947, PhD, 1951. Instr. English, humanities Harvard U., Cambridge, 1951-54; spl. asst. on White House staff, asst. to Sec. Interior Washington, 1954-61; with IBM, Armonk, 1961-88. Author: The Masks of Jonathan Swift, 1954, The Newsmen of Queen Anne, 1956, Eisenhower the President, 1981, Who Killed Joe McCarthy?, 1984, McCarthyism and Consensus, 1987, Trammell Crow: A Legacy of Real Estate Bus. Innovation, 2005; asst. to former Pres. Eisenhower in preparation of 2-vol. memoirs, White House Years, 1961-64. Pres. Bruce Mus. Assocs., Greenwich, 1972-73; vestry mem. Christ Ch., Greenwich, 1986-89; bd. dirs. Eisenhower World Affairs Inst., 1984-91. Grantee Am. Philos. Soc., 1952, Harvard Found. Advanced Study and Research, 1952-53; Eisenhower Exchange fellow, 1960. Mem. Judson Welliver Soc., Phi Beta Kappa. Clubs: Cosmos (Washington); Round Hill (Greenwich). Republican. Episcopalian. Home and Office: 3 Dewart Rd Greenwich CT 06830-3418

EWALD, WILLIAM BRAGG, III, law educator, philosopher; b. Washington, Sept. 30, 1954; s. William Bragg Ewald Jr. and Mary Thedieck. BA, AM, Harvard U., 1976, JD, 1981; PhD, Oxford U., Eng., 1978. Jr. rsch. fellow Queen's Coll., Oxford, 1982—88; mem. Inst. for Advanced Study, Princeton, NJ, 1988—89; Jean Monnet fellow European U. Inst., Florence, Italy, 1989—91; asst. prof. law and philosphy U. Pa., Phila., 1991—96, prof. law and philosophy, 1996—, William Ewald prof. law. Editor: From Kant to Hilbert, 1996; contbr. articles to law jours. Trustee St. Mark's Sch., Southborough, Mass., 1999—. Grantee, Alexander von Humboldt Stiftung, Göttingen, Germany, 1984—86. Home: 1520 Flat Rock Rd Narberth PA 19072 Office: U Pa Law Sch 3400 Chestnut St Philadelphia PA 19104-6204 Fax: 215-573-2025. E-mail: wewald@law.upenn.edu.

EWALT, HENRY WARD, lawyer; b. Pitts., Pa., July 3, 1940; s. H. Ward and Jane Ewalt; m. Mary Jabsen, June 1, 1968; 2 children. BA in Polit. Sci. cum laude, Allegheny Coll., 1962; MA in Polit. Sci., U. Mich., 1963, JD, 1966. Bar: U.S. Dist. Ct. Pa. 1966, Pa. 1967, U.S. Ct. Appeals (3d cir.) 1975, U.S. Supreme Ct. 1984. Field atty. NLRB, Pitts., 1966-71; ptnr. Reding, Blackstone, Rea & Stewart, Pitts., 1971-75, Tucker Arensberg, P.C., Pitts., 1984-87, Pepper Hamilton, LLP, 1998—2000; chief labor counsel Allegheny County, Pitts., 1971-87; founder, pres. Brooks & Ewalt, Pitts., 1975-84; assoc. gen. counsel labor and employment law Westinghouse Electric Corp., Pitts., 1987-92, assoc., gen. counsel litigation and employment law, 1993-95; v.p., assoc. gen. counsel litigation CBS Corp., 1995—98; founder Balanced Resolutions, Allison Park, Pa., 2007—. Vice-chmn. Allegheny Regional Asset Dist., 1993-96; cons., lectr. in field. Author: Practical Planning - A How to Guide for Solos and Small Law Firms, 1985, Through the Clients Eyes, 1994, 2d edit., 2002. Mem. Pitts. City Planning Commn., 1978-82; trustee Children's Home of Pitts., 1976-85; bd. dirs. Zoar Home, Pitts., 1984-88; pres. Perry Hilltop Citizens Coun., Pitts., 1970-76, pres., Depreciation Lands Mus., 1991-93; mem. Hampton Parks and Recreation Bd., 1991-93, chmn., 2000—2002; mem. Allegheny Land Trust, 1997—2005, pres., 1998-2000; bd. dirs. City Theater, 1997-2003, treas., 2000-03; bd. dirs. Pitts. Garden Place, 1999-2000; bd. dirs. Phipps Conservatory and Botanical Gardens, 2000-03. Decorated Bronze Star, Purple Heart. Fellow Coll. Law Practice Mgmt. (trustee 2000-06); mem. ABA (chmn. practice mgmt. divsn. econs. of law practice sect. 1986), Fed. Bar Assn. (past pres. Pitts. chpt.). Avocations: outdoor sports, gardening, reading. Home: 4436 Mt Royal Blvd Allison Park PA 15101-2669 Office Phone: 412-874-5009.

EWAN, DAVID E., lawyer; b. Camden, NJ, June 23, 1959; s. Eugene H. and Catherine T. (Stannard) E.; m. Lisa J. Draves, Sept. 12, 1998. BA, Dickinson Coll., 1981; JD, Rutgers U., 1991. Bar: N.J. 1991, Pa. 1991, Fla.

1992, Colo. 1994, U.S. Dist. Ct. N.J. 1991, U.S. Ct. Appeals (3d cir.) 1992. Legal intern Camden County Prosecutor, 1989; law clk. U.S. Ct. Appeals (3d cir.), Phila., 1990-91; assoc. Begley, McCloskey & Gaskill, Moorestown, NJ, 1991—2001; pres. Computer Network SOS, Inc., 2002—. Cons. N.J. Land Title Assn., 2000—; sr. adj. prof. paralegal program Burlington County Coll., Pemberton, N.J., 1996—. Contbr. chapters to books. Mem.: Assn. for Info. and Image Mgmt. Internat., Property Records Industry Assn. (bd. dirs. 2003—, co-chair real property law and legal issues com. 2003—), Am. Ednl. Rsch. Assn. Home: 1009 Woodhill Ct Williamstown NJ 08094 Office: PO Box 102 Haddonfield NJ 08033

EWAN, GEORGE THOMSON, physicist, researcher; b. Edinburgh, May 6, 1927; arrived in Can., 1952; s. Alexander Farmer and Jeannie Young (Taylor) E.; m. Maureen Louise Howard, Aug. 7, 1952; children: Elizabeth Louise, Robert Alexander. BS with 1st class honors, Edinburgh U., 1948, PhD, 1952; DSc (hon.), Guelph U., 2001, Laurentian U., 2002, Queen's U., 2005. Asst. lectr. Edinburgh U., 1950-52; rsch. assoc. McGill U., Montreal, Que., Can., 1952-55; asst. to sr. rsch. officer Atomic Energy of Can., Ltd., Chalk River, 1955-70; prof. physics Queen's U., Kingston, Ont., Can., 1970-94; prof. emeritus, 1994—; head dept. Queen's U., Kingston, Ont., Can., 1974-77. Vis. scientist Lawrence Berkeley (Calif.) Lab., 1966. Ford Found. fellow Niels Bohr Inst., Copenhagen, Denmark, 1961-62; Japan Soc. Promotion of Sci. fellow, Tokyo, 1986; recipient Radiation Industry award Am. Nuclear Soc., 1967. Fellow Royal Soc. Can., Royal Soc. Edinburgh, Am. Phys. Soc.; mem. Can. Assn. Physicists (Gold medal Achievement in Physics 1987). Mem. United Ch. Can. Avocations: golf, walking, reading. Office: Queen's U Physics Dept Kingston ON Canada K7L 3N6

EWBANK, THOMAS PETERS, lawyer, retired banker; b. Indpls., Dec. 29, 1943; s. William Curtis and Maxine Stuart (Peters) Ewbank; m. Alice Ann Shelton, June 8, 1968; children: William Curtis, Ann Shelton. Student, Stanford U., 1961—62; AB, Ind. U., 1965, JD, 1969. Bar: Ind. 1969, U.S. Tax Ct. 1969, U.S. Dist. Ct. (so. dist.) Ind. 1969, U.S. Supreme Ct. 1974; cert. trust and fin. advisor. Legis. asst. Ind. Legis. Coun., 1966-67; estate and inheritance tax adminstr. Mchts. Nat. Bank, Indpls., 1967-69; assoc. Hilgedag, Johnson, Secrest and Murphy, Indpls., 1969-71; asst. gen. counsel Everett I. Brown Co., Indpls., 1971-72; with Mchts. Nat. Bank & Trust Co. (now Nat. City Bank), Indpls., 1972-95; from probate adminstr. to sr. v.p. & sr. trust officer, pres. Mechants Capital Mgmt., Inc., Ind., 1990-93; ptnr. Krieg DeVault LLP, Indpls., 1995—. Contbr. articles to profl. jours. Bd. dirs. Noble Found. Ind., 1997—99, Indpls. Art Ctr., 1997—2002, Ruth Lilly Found., 1997—2002, Ctr. Philanthropy, Ind. U., Indpls., 1998—2002, Benjamin Harrison Home Found., 1994—2006, v.p., 1996—98, pres., 1998—2000, sec., 2003—06; bd. dirs. Arthur Jordan Found., 2002—, sec., 2003—04, vice chmn., 2004—06, chmn., 2006—; chmn. adv. com. ARC, 1987—; asst. treas. Ruckelshaus for U.S. Senator Com., 1968; candidate for Ind. Legislature, 1970, 1974. Fellow: Am. Coll. Trust and Estate Counsel, Ind. Bar Found. (life); mem.: ABA, Indpls. Bar Found. (treas. 1976—81), Ind. Bar Assn., Indpls. Bar Assn., Estate Planning Coun. Indpls. (pres. 1982—83), Ind. Soc. Pioneers (bd. dirs. 2004—, pres.-elect 2006—), English Speaking Union Indpls., Kiwanis (Circle K Internat. trustee 1963—64, pres. 1964—65, chmn. internat. com. 1988—90, past treas. Indpls. club, Career Achievement award 2001, Tablet of Hon., Sapphire Cir. Hon., George Hixson Diamond fellow), Meridian Hills Country Club, Blue Key. Republican. Baptist. Office: One Indiana Sq Ste 2800 Indianapolis IN 46204-2017 Office Phone: 317-238-6252. Business E-Mail: tewbank@kdlegal.com.

EWELL, A. BEN, JR., lawyer, small business owner; b. Elyria, Ohio, Sept. 10, 1941; s. Austin Bert and Mary Rebecca (Thompson) Ewell; m. Suzanne E. Ewell; children: Austin Bert III, Brice Ballantyne, Harrison Dale, Jonathan Eli, Tucker Benjamin. BA, Miami U., Oxford, Ohio, 1963; JD, Hasting Coll. Law, U. Calif., San Francisco, 1966. Bar: Calif. 1966, US Dist. Ct. (ea. dist.) Calif. 1967, US Ct. Appeals (9th cir.) 1967, US Supreme Ct. 1982. Pres. A.B. Ewell, Jr., A. Profl. Corp., Fresno, Calif., 1984—, The Clarksfield Co., Inc., Fresno, 1989—; formerly gen. counsel to various water dists. and assn.; gen. counsel and chmn. San Joaquin River Flood Control Assn., 1984—88; CEO Millerton New Town Devel. Co., 1988-94, chmn., 1994-96; pres. Millerton Open Space and Natural Resource Plan, 1999—, Lake Millerton Marinas, LLC. Mem. task force prosecution, cts. and law reform Calif. Coun. Criminal Justice, 1971—74; bd. dirs. Fresno Bulldog Found. Calif. State U. Columnist: Wellington Enterprise, The Wellington Enterprise. Adv. com. St. Agnes Med. Ctr. Found., 1983—89; active San Joaquin Valley Agrl. Water Commn., Fresno County Water Adv. Com., 1989; trustee U. Calif. Med. Edn. Found., 1989—90, Fresno Met. Mus. Art, History and Sci., 1989—90, adv. coun., 1993—94; active Police Activities League; pres. Fresno Conv. and Visitors Bur., 2003—04, bd. dirs., 1997—; active Fresno Bus. Coun., San Joaquin River Pky. Trust, Sierra Foothill Conservancy; chmn. various area polit. campaigns and orgns. including Reagan/Bush, 1984, Deukmejian for Gov., 1986; chmn. min. resources 1st Congrl. Ch., 2006—; bd. dir. Citizens for Cmty. Enrichment, Fresno, 1990—93, Fresno E. Cmty. Ctr., 1971—73; active Fresno Sports Coun., 2004—, Blueprint Regional Advisory Com., 2006—; mem. Fresno COG, Blueprint Roundtable, 2006—. Mem.: SBA, Fresno Coun. Govts., Blueprint Roundtable, Millerton Lake C. of C., Brighton Crest Golf and Country Club (pres. 1989—96), Copper River Country Club, Sigma Nu, Phi Alpha Delta. Office: 466 W Fallbrook Ave Ste 101 Fresno CA 93711-5830 Office Phone: 559-437-1990.

EWELL, GARY L., lawyer; b. Dallas, Nov. 13, 1952; s. Harry L. E. and Nancy (Usher) McKelvy; m. Teresa A. Oppedal, Nov. 14, 1987; children: Madeline, Anna. BA, Brown U., 1975; JD, U. Tex., 1978. Bar: Tex., 1978, D.C., 1980, Calif., 1981. Assoc. Vinson & Elkins LLP, Houston, 1978-81, Morrison & Poerster, San Francisco, 1982-83; pvt. practice San Francisco, 1983-86; ptnr. Seltzer, Ewell & Cravet, San Francisco, 1986-87, Ewell & Levy, San Francisco, 1987-97, Kuenzel & Ewell, San Francisco, 1997; ptnr., co-head Litig. Sect. Vinson & Elkins LLP, Austin, Tex. Bd. trustees Nat. Urban League, N.Y.C., 1980-86. Mem. San Francisco Bar Assn. (bd. dirs. 1983), Barristers Club (bd. dirs. 1983). Office: Vinson & Elkins LLP Ste 100 2801 Via Fortuna Austin TX 78746 Office Phone: 512-542-8526. E-mail: gewell@velaw.com.

EWEN, H. I., physicist; b. Chicopee, Mass., Mar. 5, 1922; s. Arthur and Ruth Frances (Fay) E.; m. Mary Ann Whitney, Feb. 11, 1956; children: Donald, Jim, Bruce, Mark, David, Deborah, Daniel, Rebecca. BA, Amherst Coll., 1943; MA, Harvard U., 1948, PhD, 1951. Mem. faculty Amherst Coll., 1943; co-dir. Harvard Radio Astronomy Program, 1952—58, rsch. assoc. astronomy dept., 1958—80; v.p. Millitech Corp., South Deerfield, Mass., 1989—2000; rsch. prof. Sch. Engring. U. Mass., 2000—. Pres. Ewen Knight Corp., Weston, Mass., 1952-88, Ewen Dae Corp., 1958-88, E.K. Assocs., 1993—; sci. advisor to Cin. Electronics Corp. for USAF Air Weather Svc.; mem. Global Solar Radio Telescope Network, 1977-86. Contbg. author: Advances in Microwaves, vol. 5, 1970, Electromagnetic Sensing of the Earth from Satellites, 1967, Geoscience Instrumentation, 1974, also articles; co-discoverer 21 cm interstellar hydrogen line, 1951; remote sensing of atmospheric ozone distribution (resonant line at 102 GHz), 1966. Served to lt. USNR, 1943-46. NRC fellow, 1946-49; recipient svc. award Harvard Coll., 1977. Fellow AAAS (life), IEEE (Morris E. Leeds award 1970), Am. Acad. Arts and Scis.; mem. Am. Astron. Soc. (Tinsley prize 1988), Phi Beta Kappa, Sigma Xi. Office Phone: 413-665-7435. Personal E-mail: docewen@comcast.net.

EWEN, PAMELA BINNINGS, retired lawyer; b. Mar. 22, 1944; d. Walter James and Barbara (Perkins) Binnings; m. Jerome Francis Ayers, Aug. 22, 1965 (div. July 1974); 1 child, Scott Dylan Ayers; m. John Alexander Ewen, Dec. 13, 1974 (div. Feb. 2003); m. James Craft Lott, Dec. 27, 2003. BA, Tulane U., 1977; JD cum laude, U. Houston, 1979. Bar: Tex. 79, U.S. Dist. Ct. (so. dist.) Tex. 81, U.S. Ct. Appeals (5th cir.) 81. Law clk. Harris, Cook, Browning & Barker, Corpus Christi, Tex., 1977—79; assoc. Kleberg, Dyer, Redford & Weil, Corpus Christi, 1979—80; atty. law dept. Gulf Oil Corp., Houston, 1980—84; assoc. Baker & Botts, L.L.P., Houston, 1980—84, ptnr., 1988—2004; ret. Author: Faith On Trial, 1999, Walk Back the Cat, 2006. La. Legis. scholar, New Orleans, 1976—77. Mem.: ABA (forum com. on franchising 1983—85, law practice mgmt. sect., subcom. Women Rainmakers Assn.), Tex. Assn. Bank Coun., Tex. State Bar (bd. dirs. 1994—97), Am. Petroleum Inst. (com. on product liability 1982—85, spl. subcom. to gen. com. on law), Order of Barons, Jr. Achievement S.E. Tex. (bd. dirs. 1997—2001, bd. dirs. Inprint, Inc. 2002—04). Home: 715 Kiskatom Ln Mandeville LA 70471 Personal E-mail: pamelaewen@bellsouth.net.

EWERSEN, MARY VIRGINIA, retired school system administrator, poet; b. Van Wert County, Ohio, June 7, 1922; m. Herbert Ewersen (dec.); 2 children. BS in Elem. Edn., Bowling Green, 1966, Toledo and Ohio State U. Cert. tchr. K-12, reading, Ohio. Remedial reading tchr. Port Clinton (Ohio) City Schs., 1966-70, reading tchr. chpt. I/coord., 1970-94; ret. Lyrics writer Hilltop Records. Author: Keepsakes and Celebrations!, 1997, (activity card set) From Hyperactive to Happy-Active in Limited Spaces, 1979, The Lures of Pan, 2001, of poems. Mem. Internat. Reading Assn., Sandusky Choral Soc., Acad. Am. Poets, Internat. Soc. Poets, Kappa Delta Pi. Home: 1786 S Hickory Grove Rd Port Clinton OH 43452-9637 Office: 431 Portage Dr Port Clinton OH 43452-1724

EWERT, KEVIN, theater educator; b. Fergus, Ont., Can., May 30, 1965; s. Elmer and Beverley Ewert. BA, U. of Toronto, Can., 1987; MA, PhD, U. of Birmingham, Eng., 1997. Assoc. prof. of theater U. of Pitts., Bradford, Pa., 1999—. Artistic assoc., bd. dirs. Unseam'd Shakespeare Co., Pitts., 1997—2003. Author: (book) Shakespeare Handbooks: Henry V; dir.: (theatrical prodn.) Women Beware Women, The Winter's Tale, The Libertine (One of the Top Ten Theater Prodns. of Yr., Pitts. Post-Gazette, 2000), Coriolanus (Best Prodn. of the Yr., In Pitts. Newsweekly, 1999), Cheapside, The Provoked Wife, The Pelican, Troilus and Cressida, The Pillowman. Gen. mgr. Unseam'd Shakespeare Co., Pitts., 1997—2003. Mem.: Soc. of Am. Fight Dirs., Shakespeare Assn. of Am. Office: U Pitts 300 Campus Dr Bradford PA 16701 Office Phone: 814-362-7583. Business E-Mail: ewert@pitt.edu.

EWIN, DABNEY MINOR, surgeon; b. New Orleans, Dec. 7, 1925; s. James Perkins and Lucille Havard (Scott) E.; m. Ethelyn Alexander Sherrouse, June 6, 1951 (div. 1968); children: Dabney Jr., Constance, Walton, Christopher, Leila; m. Marilyn Allison Abernathy, June 29, 1968. MD, Tulane U., 1951. Intern Jefferson-Hillman Hosp. U. Ala., Birmingham, 1951, resident, 1951-54, Ochsner Found. Hosp., New Orleans, 1954-56; chief resident Huey P. Long Charity Hosp., Pineville, La., 1956-57; pvt. practice, 1957—99; staff physician Concentra Med. Ctrs., 1999—. Cons. staff Touro Infirmary, New Orleans; staff surgeon Charity Hosp. La.; clin. prof. surgery and psychiatry Tulane Med. Sch.; clin. prof. psychiatry La. State U. Contbr. articles to profl. jours. Bd. dirs. Christ Sch., 1979-85; sr. class Sunday sch. tchr. Trinity Episc. Ch., 1960-66. Fellow ACS; mem. AMA (life), Am. Trauma Soc. (dir. 1975-79), Am. Burn Assn., Am. Coll. Occup. and Environ. Medicine (spkr. Ho. of Dels., 1973-75), Am. Bd. Med. Hypnosis (past pres.), Am. Soc. Clin. Hypnosis (past pres.), La. State Med. Soc., Orleans Parish Med. Soc., Surg. Assn. La., New Orleans Surg. Soc., Alton Ochsner Surg. Soc. (past sec.), So. Med. Assn. (chmn. sect. on indsl. medicine and surgery 1966-67), Soc. for Clin. and Exptl. Hypnosis, La. Psychiat. Med. Assn. Republican. Avocations: fishing, tennis. Office: 318 Baronne St New Orleans LA 70112-1606 Home Phone: 504-861-1751; Office Phone: 504-561-1051. Personal E-mail: dabneyewin@aol.com.

EWING, ANNA M., stock exchange executive; Mng. dir., electronic commerce CIBC World Markets; sr. v.p., systems engring. NASDAQ Stock Market, Inc., Conn., 2000—05, exec. v.p. ops., chief information officer, 2005—. Office: NASDAQ Stock Market Inc 80 Merritt Blvd Trumbull CT 06611 also: NASDAQ Stock Market Inc 1 Liberty Plz New York NY 10006

EWING, BENJAMIN BAUGH, environmental engineer, educator, consultant; b. Donna, Tex., Apr. 4, 1924; s. Joshua Fulkerson and Bula Betty (Baugh) E.; m. Elizabeth Malone, Apr. 3, 1947; children: Melissa, Douglas Malone, Frederick Joshua. BS, U. Tex., Austin, 1944, MS, 1949; PhD, U. Calif., Berkeley, 1959. Diplomate: Am. Acad. Environ. Engrs. Instr., asst. prof. U. Tex., Austin, 1947-55; assoc. in civil engring., asst. research engr. U. Calif. at Berkeley, 1955-58; assoc. prof., prof. U. Ill., Urbana, 1958-85, prof. emeritus, 1985—, dir. Water Resource Center, 1966-73, dir. Inst. for Environ. Studies, 1972-85, dir. emeritus, 1985—. Cons. engr., 1959—. Research and publs. in water quality mgmt. and pollution control, water treatment, wastewater treatment, water resources mgmt. Trustee Urbana and Champaign San. Dist., 1974-80; public mem. Ill. Water Resources Commn., 1975-84. Served to lt. (j.g.) CEC, USNR, 1943-46. Recipient Epstein award dept. civil engring. U. Ill., 1961, Harrison Prescott Eddy award for noteworthy research, 1968 Fellow ASCE; mem. Am. Water Works Assn. (life), Water Environment Fedn. (life), Assn. Environ. Engring. Profs. Emeritus. Home: 4374 Cedar Pl Lummi Island WA 98262-8672

EWING, BLAIR GORDON, federal official; b. Kansas City, Mo., Dec. 3, 1933; s. Lynn Moore and Margaret (Blair) E.; m. Barbara F. Thompson, Jan. 3, 1959 (div. Nov. 1991); children: Blair Gordon, Chatham Boyd; m. Martha L. Brockway, Apr. 30, 1994. AB, U. Mo., 1954; postgrad., U. Bonn, Germany, 1957—58; AM, U. Chgo., 1960. Reporter Chgo. City News Bur., 1958-59, UPI, 1959-60, Traffic World Mag., 1960-61; instr. polit. sci. Chgo. City Jr. Coll., 1961-62, SUNY, Binghamton, 1962-67; planning and mgmt. cons. Harold Wise and Assocs., Washington, 1967-69; program analyst Office of Asst. Sec. HEW, Washington, 1969-70; dir. criminal justice planning DC Govt., 1970-72; dir. dept. pub. safety Met. Washington Coun. Govts., 1972-74; dir. planning and evaluation divsn. U.S. Dept. Justice, Washington, 1974—76; dep. dir. Nat. Inst. Law Enforcement and Criminal Justice Dept. Justice, 1976—77, acting dir., 1977—79. U.S. Office Pers. Mgmt., asst. dir., 1979-81, dep. dir., 1981-83; sr. exec. U.S. Office Mgmt. and Budget, 1983-86; dir. Mgmt. Improvement, Dept. Def., 1986-98; adj. prof. Law Ctr., Georgetown U., 1971-74; coll tchr. Montgomery Coll., Md., 2003—. Author: Peace Through Negotiation: The Austrian State Treaty, 1966; contbr. articles to profl. jours. Active Montgomery County Human Rels. Commn., Md., 1975-76, Montgomery County Bd. Edn., 1976-98, pres., 1982-83, 90-91; coun. mem. Montgomery County, 1998-2002 pres., 2000-01; mem. Md. State Bd. Edn., 2007—. With US Army, 1954-56. Recipient Disting. Svc. award Office Pers. Mgmt., 1981, U.S. Dept. Def. Disting. Civil Svc. award, 1990, Presdl. Rank award Meritorious Sr. Exec., 1990; Rotary Found. fellow U. Bonn, 1957-58; Woodrow Wilson fellow, 1956-57. Mem. Md. State Bd. Edn., Phi Beta Kappa. Democrat. Home: 3 Park Valley Rd Silver Spring MD 20910-5424 E-mail: priorities@erols.com.

EWING, BRIAN KIM, retired engineering executive, writer; b. Viroqua, Wis., July 23, 1957; s. Myron Edward and Betty Lavonne (Crook) Ewing; divorced; children: Rebecca, Bradley, Deanna, Amy. AA in Mktg., Blackhawk Tech. Coll., Janesville, Wis., 1997; DDiv (hon.), Progressive Universal Life Ch., 2002, World Christianship Ministries, 2005. Various tech. and cons. positions, 1979—91, 1994—98; maintenance mgr. Panoramic, Inc., Janesville, Wis., 1991—94; lead tech. Tailormade Products, Elroy, Wis., 1998—2001; maintenance coord. U.S. Army Corp. Engrs., Eastman, Wis., 2001—; ret., 2006. Combat sys. planner Royal Saudi Navy, Jubail, Saudi Arabia, 1986—87; freelance writer, 2006—; cons. in field. Author: Surviving the Beast, 1996, numerous poems. Govs. commn. USS Wis., Madison, 1988. With USN, 1975—79. Recipient award, Wis. Sesquicentennial Commn. Mem.: ACLU, So. Poverty Law Ctr., So. Poverty Law Ctr. (Honoree Wall of Tolerance 2004—), Free and Accepted Masons Lodge, Disabled Am. Vets. (life), Wis. Am. Legion, Sons of Union Vets. of Civil War (jr. vice-comdr. 2002—, comdr. 2006). Republican. Methodist. Avocations: gardening, hunting, photography, writing, poetry. Home: 43666 Hounsell Dr Soldiers Grove WI 54655

EWING, CHARLES WILLIAM, JR., healthcare educator; b. Sinton, Tex., Oct. 23, 1954; s. Charles William Ewing and Mona Bohlmann Wendtland. AS, Pensacola Jr. Coll., Fla., 2002; BS in Cardiorespiratory Care, U. South Ala., Mobile, 2005, Accelerated M in Nursing, 2006; MS in Health Edn. and Aging, U. West Fla., Pensacola, 2007. Active USN, 1975—2007, ret., 2007; sr. med. dept. rep. Officer Candidate Sch., USN, Pensacola, 1997—2000; cardiorespiratory therapist Children and Womens Hosp., Mobile, 2002—05; polysomagraphic tech. Pensacola Sleep Ctr., 2003—05; health edn. educator U. West Fla., Pensacola, 2005—; health edn. asst. and advisor Enviromental Health, Pensacola, 2007—. Decorated Humanitarian Svc. medal USN, commendations, Navy Achievement medals. Master: Masons (assoc.; master mason 1988—2007); mem.: Soverign Mil. Order of the Temple of Jerusalum (assoc.; knight 2007), Sigma Phi Omega (assoc.), Gamma Beta Phi (assoc.), Phi Theta Kappa (assoc.; chpt. pres. 2001—02). Avocations: travel, reading. Home: 6810 Saufley Pines Rd Pensacola FL 32526-3709 Home Phone: 850-456-9348.

EWING, DIANE, medical transcriptionist; d. Fred and Kay Zeiger; m. Brad Ewing, Aug. 13, 1982; children: Kevin, Brian, Kristi. Cert. med. transcriptionist Am. Assn. Med. Transcription, 2006. Med. transcriptionist St. Luke's Hosp., Kans. City, 1997—. Home Phone: 660-359-6454; Office Phone: 816-932-2000.

EWING, ELISABETH ANNE ROONEY, priest; b. San Bernardino, Calif. m. James E. Ewing. Student, Mt. San Antonio Coll., 1978. Ordained priest Communion Evang. Episcopal Ch., 1998, ordained to ministry Meth. Ch. Pastor, gen. overseers, CEO St. Matthew's Nationwide Chs., NYC. Mem. Rand Rsch. Corp.; mem. diplomat cir. L.A. World Affairs Coun. Co-editor: (book) Church History, 1996—98, The Church Visible, 1996—98, Life After Death, 1996—98, Bible Lessons, 1996—98; head pub. rels., assoc. editor Pinnacle Today Internat. Mag.; assoc. editor: St. Matthew Tribune. Recipient St. Augustine cross, Archbishop of Canterbury. Mem.: Knights of Malta (dame).

EWING, FRANK MARION, paper company executive, real estate developer; b. Albany, Ga., Apr. 24, 1915; s. Frank Marion and Alpharetta (Tucker) E.; m. Hanna Anderson, June 15, 1935; children: Grace Marit (Mrs. Paul Atherton), Linda Tucker (Mrs. Richard R. Mace), Frances Marion (Mrs. Brian Tennery); m. Jo Anne Bacon Hilley, Mar. 12, 1964; children: Andrew L.; (adopted) Kathleen Melinda, Wayne Edgar; m. Marilyn Hassett Petrie, Mar. 2, 1973; m. Judith H. Viets, July 24, 1999. BA (Sereno Gaylord scholar), Yale U., 1936. Pres., chmn. bd. Frank M. Ewing Co., Inc., Washington, 1937—, Lumber Distbn. Co., Petersburg, Va., 1942-57; Pres., chmn. bd. Ewing Lumber & Millwork Corp., Beltsville, Md., 1958-71; chmn. bd. Kettler Bros. Inc., Gaithersburg, Md., 1965-88; developer Beltsville Indsl. Center, 1950-89. Bd. dirs. Washington Mut. Investors Fund.; industry adv. com. WPB, 1942-46; industry adv. com. to sec. commerce, 1947-50, dep. and later acting asst. sec. def., 1955-56. Gen. campaign chmn. Prince Georges Community Chest, 1955; bd. dirs. Childrens Hosp., Washington. Mem. Prince Georges C. of C. (pres. 1956-57), Kiwanis (bd. dirs. Prince Georges 1948-52), Masons, Chevy Chase Club, Met. Club, Burning Tree Club (Washington), St. Andrew's Royal and Ancient Golf Club (Scotland), Tryall Club (Jamaica). Home (Summer): 5610 Wisconsin Ave PH20C Chevy Chase MD 20815-4415 Home: 4951 Gulf Shore Blvd N Naples FL 34103 Home Phone: 239-261-6464; Office Phone: 301-656-7337.

EWING, GUIN PORTER, historian, art collector; b. Albuquerque, Sept. 20, 1921; s. G. Porter and Rose Betty (Ellersdorfer) Ewing. BA, UCLA, 1943, MEd, 1950, MA, 1954, CPhil, 1963. Tchr. Inglewood H.S., Calif., 1947-50; prof. L.A. City Coll., 1955-2001; instr. UCLA Extension, 1958-70, Calif. State U., Dominguez Hills, 1968-69. Fulbright lectr., Denmark, 1960—61. With US Army, 1942—46. Mem.: Am. Fedn. Tchrs. Home: 7510 Amestoy Ave Van Nuys CA 91406 Personal E-mail: porterewing@msn.com.

EWING, JACK ROBERT, accountant; b. San Francisco, Feb. 14, 1947; s. Robert Maxwell and Blanche Julia (Diak) E.; m. Joan Marie Coughlin Ewing, Nov. 25, 1967; children: Theresa Marie Ewing, Christina Ann Ewing. BS, U. Mo., 1969. CPA. Staff acct. Fox & Co., St. Louis, 1969-70; radio station opr. USAF, Mountain Home, Idaho, 1970-72; internal auditor Air Force Audit Agy., Warren, Wyo., 1972-74; supr. auditor Fox & Co., St. Louis, 1974-79; audit mgr. Erickson, Hunt & Spillman, P.C., Ft. Collins, Colo., 1979-82; stockholder, owner Hunt, Spillman & Ewing, P.C., Ft. Collins, Colo., 1982-93; owner Jack R. Ewing, CPA, 1993—. Lectr. on mental illness and suicide prevention. Mem. Suicide Resource Ctr. of Larimer County, Ft. Collins, 1992—, Leadership Ft. Collins-Class of 1992, State of Colo. Mental Health Planning Coun., 1993—2000; mem. mental health pro bono project, 1996—97; mem. gov.'s citizen panel on suicide prevention, 1998—; mem. indicators and outcomes com.; ptnr. Mental Health and Substance Abuse; mem., pres. Parent Adv. Bd. Beattie Elem. Sch., 1982—83, pres. Parent Adv. Bd., 1986—87; mem. Entrepreneur of Yr. Selection Com., Ft. Collins, Colo., 1989—92; pres. Suicide Resource Ctr. of Larimer County, Ft. Collins, 1998—, bd. dirs.; dir. treas. One West Contemporary Art Ctr., 1989—97, Ctr. for Diversity in Work Place, 1991—96; pres., adv. bd. Larimer County Bd. Mental Health, 1992—99; v.p. Colo. Behavioral Healthcare Coun., 1995—97; mem. steering com. Mental Health and Substance Abuse, 1997—. Mem. Am. Inst. CPAs, Colo. Soc. CPAs (Everyday Heros and Heroines award). Avocations: writing, hiking. Office: 3112 Meadowlark Ave Fort Collins CO 80526-2843

EWING, JAMES E., priest; m. Elisabeth Anne Rooney. DD, ThD. Ordained priest Communion Evang. Episcopal Chs., 1951. Sr. pastor, gen. overseer, pres. bd. govs. and counselors St. Matthew's Nationwide Chs., NYC, 1951—. Mem. Rand Rsch. Corp.; mem. diplomat cir. L.A. World Affairs Coun. Co-author, editor: book Church History, The Church Visible, Life After Death, Bible Lessons, pub., editor, author: Pinnacle Today. With USAF, 1953—57. Recipient St. Augustine cross, Archbishop of Canterbury. Mem.: Sovereign Order St. John of Jerusalem, Knights of Malta.

EWING, JOHN HARWOOD, mathematics professor, department chairman, professional society administrator; b. Bronxville, NY, Nov. 25, 1944; s. Robert Edward and Virginia (Harwood) E.; m. Janice Rusche, May 22, 1965; children: Scott Andrew, Jennifer Beth, Amy Sarah. BS, St. Lawrence U., Canton, NY, 1966; MS, PhD, Brown U., 1971; DS (hon.), St. Lawrence U., 1996. Instr. Dartmouth Coll., Hanover, NH, 1971-73; asst. prof., assoc. prof. math. Ind. U., Bloomington, 1973, prof., chmn. dept., 1986-89, 92-95; exec. dir. Am. Math. Soc., Providence, 1995—. Sci. and Engring. rsch. Coun. fellow U. Newcastle, Eng., 1980-81; Sonderforschungsbereich fellow U. Goettingen, Germany, 1985-86; series editor Springer-Verlag, NYC, 1987-95. Author: Puzzle It Out, 1981; editor: Numbers, 1990, Celebrating 50 Years of Mathematics, 1991, A Century of Mathematics, 1994, Towards Excellence, 1999; editor-in-chief Math. Intelligencer, 1980-

86, Am. Math. Monthly, 1992-96; contbr. articles to profl. jours. Recipient Lester R. Ford award, 1976, George Polya Lectr. award, 1991—92, Polya award, 1996. Fellow: AAAS; mem.: Am. Math. Soc., Math. Assn. Am., Soc. Indsl. and Applied Math., Assn. Women in Math. Episcopalian. Office: Am Math Soc 201 Charles St Providence RI 02904 Office Phone: 401-455-4100. Business E-Mail: jhe@ams.org.

EWING, JOSEPH NEFF, JR., retired lawyer; b. Bryn Mawr, Pa., Nov. 10, 1925; s. Joseph Neff and Anne (Ashton) Ewing; m. Margaret Converse Howe, Dec. 22, 1951; children: Margaret E. Lloyd, Anne A., Elizabeth M. Peifer. AB, Princeton U., NJ, 1947; JD, U. Pa., Phila., 1953. Bar: Pa. 1954, U.S. Supreme Ct. 1978, U.S. Tax Ct. 1992. Assoc. Saul, Ewing, Remick & Saul, Phila., 1953-63, ptnr., 1963-95, of counsel, 1996—. Bd. govs. Main Line Health, Inc., 1988—95; trustee Bryn Mawr Hosp., 1969—96, Bryn Mawr Hosp. Found., 1981—, Hist. Sugartown, Inc., Malvern, Pa., 1990—98, Dunwoody Village, Inc., 1997—, 1st vice chmn., 1999—2004, chmn., 2004—; chancellor Clan Ewing in Am., 1998—2004. Chmn. Willistown Twp. Planning Commn., Malvern, 1960—69, chmn. bd. suprs., 1970—82, chmn. zoning hearing bd., 1985—95, East Goshen Twp., 1996—; chmn. spl. contacts divsn. Phila. United Fund, 1965—66; mem. hosp. coun. southeastern Pa. Mental Health Assn., Phila., 1967—68; elder Paoli (Pa.) Presbyn. Ch., 1970—72; pres. bd. trustees Embreeville (Pa.) State Hosp., 1965—72. Sgt. USMC, 1944—46, sgt. USMC, 1950—51. Mem.: ABA, Pa. Soc. Healthcare Attys. (pres. 1975—77), Nat. Assn. R.R. Trial Counsel, Phila. Assn. Def. Counsel (pres. 1973), Phila. Bar Assn. (med.-legal com. 1962—76, chmn. 1971), Waynesborough Country Club (v.p. 1965—69). Avocations: sailing, photography, gardening, genealogy. Home: 1109 Lincoln Dr West Chester PA 19380-5721 Personal E-mail: joenewing@aol.com.

EWING, KY PEPPER, JR., lawyer; b. Victoria, Tex., Jan. 7, 1935; s. Ky Pepper and Sallie (Dixon) E.; m. Almuth Rott, Apr. 6, 1963; children: Kenneth Patrick, Kevin Andrew, Kathryn Diana. BA cum laude, Baylor U., 1956; LLB cum laude, Harvard U., 1959. Bar: D.C. 1959, U.S. Supreme Ct 1963. Assoc. firm Covington & Burling, Washington, 1959-64; partner firm Prather, Seeger, Doolittle, Farmer & Ewing, Washington, 1964-77; dep. asst. atty. gen. antitrust div. Dept. Justice, Washington, 1978-80; ptnr. Vinson & Elkins, Washington, 1980—2001, of counsel, 2002—03. Mem. Washington Inst. Fgn. Affairs. Author: Competition Rules for the 21st Century: Principles from America's Experience, 2003, 2d edit., 2006; co-editor-in-chief: State Antitrust Practice and Statutes, 3 Vols., 1990; mem. antitrust adv. bd. Antitrust and Trade Regulation Report Bur. Nat. Affairs, 1990—; mem. edit. bd. Antitrust Report Matthew Bender & Co., 1993—. Pres. Potomac Valley League, 1977, Carderock Springs Citizens Assn., 1975-78. Fellow: Am. Bar Found. (life); mem.: ABA (chmn. legis. com. antitrust sect. 1987—91, coun. antitrust sect. 1991—94, fin. officer antitrust sect. 1994—96, chmn. FTC/Dept. Justice working group 1994—97, mem. Ho. of Dels. 1996—98, vice chair antitrust sect. 1998—99, chair-elect antitrust sect. 1999—2000, chair antitrust sect. 2000—01, chmn. nominating com. antitrust sect. 2002—03), D.C. Bar Assn., Internat. Bar Assn. (editl. bd. Bus. Law Internat.), Met. Club. Republican. Episcopalian. Home: 8317 Comanche Ct Bethesda MD 20817-4561 Office: The Willard Office Bldg Rm 719 1455 Pennsylvania Ave NW Washington DC 20004-1013 Office Phone: 202-639-6580. Business E-Mail: kewing@velaw.com.

EWING, PATRICK ALOYSIUS, professional basketball coach; b. Kingston, Jamaica, Aug. 5, 1962; m. Rita Ewing; children: Patrick Aloysius, Randi. BFA, Georgetown U., 1985. Basketball player N.Y. Knickerbockers, NYC, 1985—2000, Seattle SuperSonics, 2000—01, Orlando Magic, Fla., 2001—02; asst. coach Washington Wizards, 2002—03, Houston Rockets, 2003—. Mem. U.S. Olympic Basketball Teams, 1984, 92. Named Divsn. I Most Outstanding Player, NCAA, 1984, Coll. Player of Yr., Sporting News, 1985, 1985, Rookie of Yr., NBA, 1986; named to All-Am. 1st team, Sporting News, 1985, All-Star team, 1986, 1988—93, All-Am. 2d team, 1983—84, NBA All-Star team, 1986—95, All-NBA 2d team, 1988, All-Defensive 2d team, 1988, 1989, All-NBA 2d team, 1989, All-NBA 1st team, 1990, All-NBA 2d team, 1991, All-Defensive 2d team, 1992, All-NBA 2d team, 1992; recipient Naismith award, 1985, Gold medal, U.S. Olympic Basketball Team. Achievements include being a player in NCAA divsn. I championship team, 1984; being a holder of NBA Finals series record for most blocked shots (30), 1994; being co-holder of NBA finals single-game record most block shots (8), 1994. Office: Houston Rockets 1510 Polk St Houston TX 77002-1099

EWING, RAYMOND CHARLES, retired ambassador; b. Cleve., Sept. 7, 1936; s. Thomas Davis and Marion (Andrews) Ewing; m. Jerelyn Patten, Jan. 19, 1962 (dec. May 2006); children: Gregory, Thomas, Joyce, Lillian Patten(dec.). BA, Occidental Coll., 1957; MPA, Harvard U., 1970. Joined Fgn. Svc., Dept. State, 1957; various assignments in Washington, Bern, Switzerland, Rome, Lahore, Pakistan, Vienna, Tokyo, 1957-1977; dir. Office So. European Affairs, Dept. State, Washington, 1977-79; mem. Sr. Seminar, Washington, 1979-80; dep. asst. sec. of state for European affairs 1980-81; amb. to Cyprus Nicosia, 1981-84; dean Sch. Lang. Studies Fgn. Svc. Inst., Washington, 1985-87; dir. Office Career Devel. and Assignments, Dept. State, 1987-89; amb. to Ghana, 1989-92; chargé d'affaires, a.i. to Tanzania Dar es Salaam, 1992; ret., 1993; mng. editor Mediterranean Quarterly, Washington, 1994—. Mem.: Cyprus Am. Archeol. Rsch. Inst. (bd. dirs. 2000—06), Diplomatic and Consular Officers (bd. govs. 2005—), Am. Fgn. Svc. Assn., Sr. Seminar Alumni Assn. (pres. 2004—07). Presbyterian. Avocations: tennis, golf, travel, reading. Office Phone: 202-662-7655. E-mail: medquarterly@aol.com.

EWING, RICHARD EDWARD, mathematics, chemical and petroleum engineering educator; b. Kingsville, Tex., Nov. 24, 1946; s. Floyd Ford and Olivia Clara (Henrichson) E.; m. Rita Louise Williams, Aug. 8, 1970; children: John Edward, Lawrence Alan, Bradley William. BA, U. Tex., 1969, MA, 1972, PhD, 1974; PhD (hon.), U. Bergen, Norway, 1996, Shandong U., China, 1987. Asst. prof. Oakland U., Rochester, Mich., 1974-77, Ohio State U., Columbus, 1977-80, assoc. prof., 1980-81; sr. rsch. mathematician Mobil R & D Corp., Dallas, 1980-82, assoc. mathematician, 1982-83; prof. math., petroleum and chem. engring. U. Wyo., Laramie, 1983-92, J.E. Warren dist. prof. energy and environ., 1984-92, dir. Enhanced Oil Recovery Inst., 1984-92, dir. Inst. for Sci. Computation, 1986-92, dir. Ctr. for Math. Modeling, 1986-92, Wold Centennial chair in energy, 1991-92; dean Coll. Sci. Tex. A&M U., College Station, 1992-2000, prof. math. and engring., 1992—, dir. Inst. for Sci. Computation, 1992—, disting. rsch. chair TEES, 1992, dir. Acad. Advanced Telecom. and Learning Techs., 1996-2000, Dist. prof. math. and engring., 1998—, v.p. for rsch., 2000—; chair in sci. computing Mobil Tech. Co., 1999—, Harrison Endowed chair in Sci., 1999—. Adj. prof. Rice U., Houston, 1980—84, U. Tex., 1998—; steering com. Ctr. for Fluid Dynamics and Geoscis., Columbia, SC, 1987—89; hon. prof. Shandong U., China, 1987; adv. bd. Ctr. Sci. Computing, Jyväskylä, Finland, 1990—, Improved Oil Recovery Ctr., Bergen, Norway, 1990—, Interdisciplinary Ctr. Computational Sci., Heidelberg, Germany, 1992—, Inst. Biosci. Tech., Houston, 1992—; acad. adv. bd. Dow Chem., 1994—; exec. com. Patnership Computational Scis., Oak Ridge Nat. Lab., 1991—98; pres. Environ. Modeling and Analysis Corp., 1991—2000; sci. adv. bd. Inst. for Math. Scis., Alta, Canada, 1996—98; bd. dirs. Nat. Space Biomed. Rsch. Inst., Houston Tech. Ctr., Associated Western U., Southeastern U. Rsch. Assocs., Oak Ridge Assocs. U., Tex. Healthcare and Biosci. Inst., Tex. Soc. Biomed. Rsch., Tex. Inst. for Genomic Medicine, Houston Adv. Rsch. Ctr., Houston Advanced Rsch. Ctr., Tex. Product Devel. and Small Bus. Inc., Bi-Nat. Sustainability Lab.-US-Mex.; adv. coun. NASA, 2001—03, Tex. Coun. on Environ. Tech., 2001—; hon. guest rschr. Wuhan U., China, 1997—; adj. prof. U. Tex., Houston, 1998—; sci. bd. Indsl. Math. Inst., U. SC, 1999—; coun. mem. Harte Rsch. Inst., 2001—04; pres. Tex. GigaPOP, 2002—04; fgn. mem. Acad. Europaea, 2005—; cons. in field. Author: The Mathematics of Reservoir Simulation, 1983, Mathematical Modeling in Energy and Environmental Sciences, 1988; contbr. articles to sci. jours., chpts. to books. Cubmaster Boy Scouts Am., Dallas, 1981, Webelos leader, 1982, asst. scoutleader, Laramie, 1984, asst. scoutmaster, College Station, 1995—. Recipient NASA Pub. Svc. medal, 2003, Innovative Rsch. award Chinese Assn. Sci. and Tech., 2004, Humboldt Rsch. award Sr. US Scientists, 2005, Marin Drinov medal Bulgarian Acad. Scis., 2007, Michael Malone Internat. Leadership award Nat. Assn. State Univs. and Land-Grant Colls., 2007; grantee NSF, Dept. Energy, NRC, US Dept. Def., oil cos., others, 1978—. Fellow AAAS; mem. SIAM (trustee 1986-93), Soc. Petroleum Engrs., Am. Math. Soc., Math. Assn. Am., Internat. Assn. for Math. and Computers in Simulation, Internat. Assn. Computational Mech. (trustee 1991—), Inst. for Advancement Sci. Computing (trustee 1987-93), Geoscis. Inst. (bd. dirs. 1988-92), NY Acad. Scis., Internat. Computer Com. (sci. coun. 1989—). Democrat. Avocations: skiing, tennis, stamp and coin collecting. Home: 2004 Indian Trl College Station TX 77845-5600 Office Phone: 979-845-8585. Business E-Mail: richard-ewing@tamu.edu.

EWING, RUSSELL CHARLES, II, physician; b. Tucson, Aug. 16, 1941; s. Russell Charles and Sue M. (Sawyer) E.; children: John Charles, Susan Lenore. BS, U. Arizona, 1963; MD, George Washington U., 1967. Diplomate Am. Bd. Family Practice. Intern L.A. County-U. So. Calif. Med. Ctr., LA, 1967-68; gen. practice in medicine and surgery Yorba Linda and Placentia, Calif., 1970—96; correctional psychiatrist, 1998—; gen. practice in medicine and surgery Brea, Calif., 1996-97; mem. staff St. Jude's Hosp., Fullerton, Calif., 1970-98, Placentia Linda Cmty. Hosp., 1972-98; vice chief staff, 1977-78; chief staff, 1978-80; bd. dirs., 1974-81; sec., dir. Yorba Linda Med. Group, Inc., 1974-90. Bd. dirs. We. Empire Savs. & Loan Assn., Calif., Ewing Enterprises. Prin. Yorba Linda YMCA, 1973-88, pres., 1973-74, 81. With USN, 1968-70. Fellow Am. Acad. Family Practice; mem. AMA, Am. Coll. Physician Execs., Calif. Med. Assn. (ho. of dels. 1978-90, 92-99, trustee 1990-92), Orange County Med. Assn. (bd. dirs. 1983-90, pres. 1988-89). Republican. Episcopalian. Home and Office: 2300 Iron Pt Rd #1113 Folsom CA 95630-8489

EWING, SCOTT EDWIN, physiatrist, educator; b. Seattle, July 2, 1956; s. Edwin Stanley Jr. and Mary Alice (Castleman) E.; m. Eileen Smith, June 9, 1990; 1 child, Edwin Stanley III. BS, U. Mich., 1980; DO, Midwestern U., 1989. Diplomate Am. Osteo. Bd. Neurology and Psychiatry; MD, Mass. Resident in psychiatry Mass. Gen. Hosp., Boston, 1991-94; clin. fellow in psychiatry Harvard Med. Sch., Boston, 1991-94; chief resident in psychiatry Mass. Gen. Hosp., Boston, 1993-94; fellow in psychopharmacology Harvard Med. Sch., Boston, 1994-95; psychiatrist in charge short term unit McLean Hosp., Belmont, Mass., 1995-96; instr. in psychiatry Harvard Med. Sch., Boston, 1995—; dir. depression and anxiety disorders outpatient clinic McLean Hosp., Belmont, 1996—. Cons. Harvard Pilgrim Health Plan, Boston, 1995-2003. Contbg. author: (book) Challenges in Psychiatric Treatment: Pharmacologic and Psychosocial Strategies, 1996; patentee in field. Mem. Nat. Trust for Hist. Preservation, Washington, 1995—. Recipient Outstanding Resident award NIMH, 1992, Laughlin fellowship Am. Coll. Psychiatrists, 1993, Dupont-Warren fellowship Harvard Med. Sch. Dept. of Psychiatry, 1994-95, Livingston award, 1995. Mem. AMA, Am. Psychiat. Assn., Am. Osteo. Assn., N.Y. Acad. Scis., Am. Coll. Neuropsychiatrists, Harvard Club of Boston, Harvard Faculty Club, Sigma Sigma Phi. Avocations: creative writing, photography, athletics. Office: Harvard U Place Ste 200N 124 Mt Auburn St Cambridge MA 02138

EWING, SIDNEY ALTON, veterinary medical educator, parasitologist; b. Emory Univ., Ga., Dec. 1, 1934; s. Aubrey Coleman and Grace Eliza (Prickett) E.; m. Margaret Jane Steffens, Aug. 16, 1963; children— Holly Annette, Ann Krull, Leah Grace. BSA, DVM, U. Ga., 1958; MS, U. Wis., 1960; PhD, Okla. State U., 1964. Instr. U. Wis., 1960; mem. faculty Okla. State U., Stillwater, 1960—65, 1968—72, prof., head dept. vet. parasitology, microbiology and public health, 1968—72, 1979—84, prof., 1984—91; interim assoc. dean for acad. affairs, 1991—92, 2001—03, Wendell H./Nellie G. Krull endowed prof. vet. parasitology, 1992—2003, Wendell H./Nellie G. Krull prof. emeritus, 2004—; assoc. prof. Kans. State U., 1965—67; prof., head dept. Miss. State U., 1967—68; prof., dean Coll. Vet. Medicine, U. Minn., St. Paul, 1972—78. Adv. bd. Morris Animal Found., Denver, 1967-69, cons., 1969-78; animal health com. NRC, 1971-75; adv. panel U.S. Pharmacopeial Conv., 1980-95 Recipient Outstanding Tchr. of Yr. award Okla. State U. Coll. Vet. Medicine, 1970, SmithKline Beecham award for rsch. excellence Okla. State U., 1991, A.M. Mills award for outstanding contbns. to vet. medicine, 1993, Good Neighbor award Radio Sta. WCCO, Mpls.-St. Paul, 1978; commendation Gov. Minn., 1978; named Veterinarian of Yr., State of Okla., 1997; named to Okla. Higher Edn. Hall of Fame, 2000 Mem. AAUP, AVMA, Am. Assn. Vet. Parasitologists (Disting. Vet. Parasitologist 2002), Am. Soc. Parasitologists, Am. Vet. Med. History Soc., Am. Soc. Rickettsiology, World Assn. Advancement Vet. Parasitology, Conf. Rsch. Workers in Animal Diseases (coun. 1980-85, v.p. 1983-84, pres. 1984-85), Soc. Vector Ecology, Soc. Tropical Vet. Medicine, Minn. Vet. Med. Assn., Okla. Vet. Med. Assn., NY Acad. Sci., Southwestern Assn. of Parasitologists (program officer, pres. elect 2001-02, pres. 2002-2003), Sigma Xi, Phi Kappa Phi, Phi Zeta, Alpha Zeta, Alpha Psi (past nat. pres.), Gamma Sigma Delta, Aghon, Omicron Delta Kappa. Office: Okla State U Dept Vet Pathobiology Stillwater OK 74078-2005 Office Phone: 405-744-8177. Business E-Mail: sidney.ewing@okstate.edu.

EWING, SUSAN R., artist, educator; b. Lawrenceville, Ill., 1955; AA in Music, Stephens Coll., 1974; BA in Jewelry, Metalsmithing, Ind. U., 1976, MFA in Jewelry, Metalsmithing, 1980. Head metals program, disting. prof. Miami U., Ohio, 1981—. One-person shows include Hans Hansen Sølv, Copenhagen, Denmark, Nat. Tech. Mus., Prague, Czech Republic, Phoenix Mus. Art, Ohio Craft Mus., Columbus, Ark. Ctr., Little Rock; group shows include Aspects Gallery, London, Park Ryu Sook Gallery, Seoul, Korea, Schweizerisches Landesmuseum, Zurich, Switzerland, Cercle Mcpl. Galerie Oféo, Luxembourg, Mus. Kunsthandwerk, Frankfurt, Germany, Deutsches Klingenmuseum, Solingen, Germany, Schmuckmuseum, Pforzheim, Germany, Galerie Matter, Cologne, Germany, Galerie Ende, Cologne, Mathildenhohe Mus., Darmstadt, Germany, Galerie Spectrum, Munich, Germany, Galerie Ventil, Munich, Fortunoff's N.Y.C., Urban BobKat Gallery, N.Y.C., Lever House, N.Y.C., Seventh Regiment Armory, N.Y.C., Am. Craft Mus., N.Y.C.; represented in permanent collections White House. Recipient Dolibois Faculty Devel. award, disting. Lifetime Achievement award Ohio Designer Craftsmen; Summer Rsch. fellow Miami U., Ohio Arts Coun. Individual Artist fellow, 1987, 89, 91, Fulbright grantee, 1997, 98; Rsch. Challenge grantee Ohio State Bd. Regents. Home: 45 Hidden Creek Dr Oxford OH 45056 Office: 124 Art Bldg Miami U Oxford OH 45056

EWING, THOMAS WILLIAM, congressman, lawyer; b. Atlanta, Ill., Sept. 19, 1935; m. Connie Lupo, 1981; children: Jane, Kathryn, Sam, Christine Lupo, John Lupo, Stephanie Lupo. BS, Millikin U., 1957; JD, John Marshall Law Sch., Chgo., 1968. Asst. state atty. Livingston County, 1968-73; ptnr. Satter Ewing Beyer & Spires, Pontiac, Ill., 1969-91; mem. Ill. Ho. of Reps., 1974-91, U.S. Congress from 15th Ill. Dist., 1991-2001; mem. sci. com., agr. subcom., transp. and infrastructure coms., house adminstrn. com.; of counsel Davis and Harman L.L.P., Washington. Mem. agr. com. Ill. Ho. Reps., chmn. subcom. on risk mgmt. and specialty crops, subcom. on dept. ops., nutrition and fgn. agr., transp. and infrastructure com., aviation subcom., water resources and environment subcom., joint econ. com., former dep. minority leader, chmn. policy com., house revenue com., 1980, co-chmn. Ill. Econ. and Fiscal Commn., co-chmn. Legis. Space Needs Commn.; mem. biotech adv. coun. Monsanto, chmn. grower adv. coun.; chmn. biomass R&D tech. adv. com. Dept. Agr., Dept. Energy; bd. dirs. Pontiac Nat. Bank Holding Co., Inst. Representative Govt., Washington, D.C. Rep. precinct committeeman; del. Rep. Nat. Conv., 1980, 84, 88, 96, 2000; committeeman 15th Congl. Dist., 1986-93; mem. nat. advocacy com. Am. Diabetes Assn.; bd. dirs. Nat. Futures Assn. With U.S. Army, 1958, USAR, 1957-63. Recipient Best Legislator award Nat. Rep. Legislator of the Yr. award, 1982, Ill. Small Businessmen Assn., 1983, 85, 87, Friend of Agr. award Ill. Agrl. Assn., 1985, 87, 89, 91, Legislator of Yr. award Ill. Assn. Homes for the Aging, 1986. Mem. Livingston County Bar Assn., Pontiac C. of C. (past exec. dir., past pres.), Livingston County Farm Bur., Elks, Moose, Masons. Republican. Methodist. Home: 1647 Mockingbird Ln Pontiac IL 61764-9249 E-mail: TWewing@yahoo.com.

EWING BROWNE, SHEILA, chemistry professor, physical organic chemist; BS, U. Tenn., 1971; PhD, U. Calif., Berkeley, 1974. Joined Mt. Holyoke Coll., S. Hadley, Mass., 1976—, Bertha Phillips Rodger prof. chemistry. Mentors students with independent rsch. projects; mentor New England Bd. of Higher Education's Sci. and Engring. Academic Support Network; co-founder Sistahs in Sci., 1994—. Recipient Presdl. award for Excellence in Sci., Math. and Engring. Mentoring, NSF, 1998, 2005 AAAS Mentor award for Lifetime Achievement, 2006. Achievements include research in biodegradable polymers. Office: Chemistry Dept Mt Holyoke Coll Rm GO2B Carr Lab 50 College St South Hadley MA 01075-6407 Office Phone: 413-538-2020. Business E-Mail: sbrowne@mtholyoke.edu.

EWING-MULLIGAN, MARY, food products executive; Pres. Internat. Wine Ctr., NYC, Inst. Masters of Wine North Am.; exec. dir. Wine & Spirit Edn. Trust, London. Chief judge Critics Challenge, 2004—. Co-author: Wine For Dummies, Red Wine For Dummies, White Wine For Dummies, French Wine For Dummies, Italian Wine For Dummies, Wine Style; contbr. columns in newspapers The Daily News,; featured in Food & Wine mag., NY Times, The Wine Spectator, Newsday, Gourmet mag. Achievements include being the first woman in America to achieve Master of Wine title. Office: International Wine Center 350 7th Ave Ste 1201 New York NY 10001 Office Phone: 212-239-3055. Office Fax: 212-239-3051.

EWY, GORDON ALLEN, cardiologist, researcher, educator; b. Brenham, Kans., Aug. 5, 1933; s. Marvin John and Hazel Miller (Allen) E.; m. Priscilla Ruth Weldon; children: Kim Elizabeth (dec.), Gordon Stuart, Mark Allen. BA, U. Kans., 1955, MD, 1961. Resident, house officer Georgetown U. Hosp., Washington, 1961-64, cardiology fellow, 1964-65; instr. medicine Georgetown U., Washington, 1965-68, asst. prof., 1968-69, U. Ariz., Tucson, 1969-70, assoc. prof., 1970-75, prof. medicine, 1975—, chief cardiology, dir. cardiology fellowship program, 1982—, assoc. head dept. medicine, 1986-94, dir. Sarver Heart Ctr., 1991—, The Gordon A. Ewy MD Disting. Endowed Chair Cardiovasc. Medicine, 2002—. Editor: Cardiovascular Drugs and Management of Heart Disease, 1982, 93, Current Cardiovascular Drug Therapy, 1984, Manual of Cardiovascular Diagnosis and Therapy, 5th edit., 2002; author numerous sci. publs.; contbr. numerous revs. to profl. jours., chpts. to books. Lt. (j.g.) USNR, 1955-57. Fellow ACP, Am. Heart Assn. (mem. clin. coun., nat. faculty advanced cardiac life support 1982-84, chmn. nat. programs subcom. 1982, bd. dirs. Ariz. chpt. 1975-82, 84-89, tchg. fellow 1970-75), Am. Coll. Cardiology (chmn. learning ctr. com. 1988-91, trustee 1992-97), Alpha Omega Alpha. Republican. Avocation: travel. Office: Ariz Health Scis Ctr 1501 N Campbell Ave Tucson AZ 85724-0001 Office Phone: 520-626-2000. Personal E-mail: gaewy@aol.com.

EXNER, FRANK KEPLER, information scientist, indexer; b. Portland, July 8, 1944; s. Theodore Lincoln and Helen Kepler Exner; m. Carol Lee Rosenquist, Apr. 11, 1966; children: David Benjamin, Nina Lee. BS, Bowling Green State U., 1977; M of Info. Sci., N.C. Ctrl. U., 1997; MLS, NC Ctrl. U., 1999; DPhil in Info. Sci., U. Pretoria, 2005. Broadcast engr. WFLD-TV, Chgo., 1968—70, WBGU-TV, Bowling Green, Ohio, 1970—80; tech. writer AT&T Bell Labs., Naperville, Ill., 1980—85, Alcatel, Raleigh, NC, 1985—92, Nortel Networks, Rsch. Triangle Pk., 1992—2001; prof. N.C. Ctrl. U., Durham, 2004—. Editor: Katherine Sharp Rev., 1995—97; contbr. online jour. Mem.: Am. Indian Libr. Assn., Am. Soc. Info. Sci. & Tech., Internat. Soc. Knowledge Orgn. Democrat. Avocation: reading.

EYERMAN, CHARLOTTE, curator, art historian; BA in English, cum laude, Holy Cross Coll., 1987; PhD in History of Art, U. Calif. Berkeley, 1997. Asst. curator paintings J. Paul Getty Mus., LA, 2002—05; curator modern art St. Louis Art Mus., Mo., 2005—. Lectr. impressionism in context So. Meth. U., 1993; tchr. art history U. So. Calif., LA, Art Ctr. Coll. Design, Pasadena; vis. instr. Union Coll., Schenectady, NY, 1994—96, asst. prof. Visual Arts Dept., 1996—2001, John D. and Catherine T. MacArthur asst. prof., 1996—97; Flagship Forum lectr. Smithsonian Associates, 2000; lectr. in field; founder elucidART, Inc. Contbr. articles to profl. jour. Office: Saint Louis Art Mus Forest Park One Fine Arts Drive Saint Louis MO 63110-1380

EYLER, JOHN H., JR., retail toy and game company executive; b. 1948; m. Dolores Eyler; 3 children. Grad., U. Wash.; MBA, Harvard U. With May Dep. Stores Co.; pres., CEO, May D&F, Denver, from 1980; chmn., CEO MainStreet divsn. Fed. Dept. Stores, Inc.; CEO retail subs. Hartmarx, Chgo.; chmn., CEO FAO Schwarz, 1992-2000; pres., CEO Toys 'R' Us, Inc., Paramus, NJ, 2000—05, chmn., 2001—05. Bd. dirs. Donna Karan Internat. Inc.

EYMAN, EARL DUANE, electrical science educator, consultant; b. Canton, Ill., Sept. 24, 1925; s. Arthur Earl and Florence Mabel (Hardin) E.; m. Ruth Margaret Morgan, Apr. 20, 1951; children: Joseph Earl, David James. BS in Engring. Physics, U. Ill., 1949, MS in Math, 1950, postgrad., 1951-64, U. Bradley, 1952-58; PhD in Elec. Engring., U. Colo., 1966. Registered profl. engr., Ill. Scientist Westinghouse Atomic Power Div., Pitts., 1950-51; research engr. Caterpillar Tractor Co., Peoria, Ill., 1951-58, project engr., 1958-66; mem. faculty Bradley U., Peoria, 1952-64; prof. elec. engring. U. Iowa, Iowa City, 1966-92, chmn. elec. engring., 1969-76. Cons. Sundstrand Aviation, Denver, 1966, Gould Simulation Systems Div., Melville, N.Y., 1978-81, U.S. Dept. Commerce, Boulder, 1978-92. Author: Modeling Simulation and Control, 1988; contbr. articles to profl. jours. Chmn., mem. Electricians Examining Bd., Iowa City, 1969-74. Served with USNR, 1944-46 Mem. Eta Kappa Nu (mem., pres. internat. bd. 1972-77), Tau Beta Pi, Theta Tau Avocations: skiing, mountain climbing, hiking.

EYMANN, RICHARD CHARLES, lawyer; b. Hanover, NH, June 6, 1945; BS, U. Oreg., 1968; JD, Gonzaga U., 1976. Bar: Wash. 1976, U.S. Dist. Ct. (ea. dist.) Wash. 1978, U.S. Ct. Appeals (9th cir.) 1987, U.S. Dist. Ct. (we. dist.) Wash. 1989, U.S. Supreme Ct. 1995. Ptnr. Eymann, Allison, Hunter Jones, P.S., Spokane, Wash. Mem. ABA (founder, chmn. nat. appellate advocacy competition 1975-84, bd. advs. 1985-93), ATLA, Wash. State Bar Assn. (bd. govs. 1997-98, pres. elect 1998-99, pres. 1999-2000), Wash. State Trial Lawyers Assn. (bd. govs. 1984-86, 88-95, legis. steering com. 1990-96, membership chair 1984-85, v.p. East 1991-92, fin. com. 1994-95, Trial Lawyer of Yr. 1995, pres. 1996-97), Wash. Trial Lawyers for Pub. Justice (bd. dirs. 1994-98), Am. Bd. Trial Advocates, Spokane County Bar Assn., Am. Inns of Ct. (barrister 1986, master of the bench 1990, Charles L. Powell & Inn pres. 1991-93), Damage Attys. Round Table. Office: Eymann Allison Et Al 2208 W 2nd Ave Spokane WA 99201-5417 E-mail: eymann@eahjlaw.com.

EYNON, RICHARD S., lawyer; b. Des Moines, Iowa, 1943; children: Jeff, Jon, Courtney Perry. BA, Valparaiso U., 1966, JD, 1969. Founding ptnr. Eynon Law Group PC, Columbus, Ind. Mem. Young Mothers Ednl. Devel., Girls Club, Meridian Kiwanis, Family Services & Columbus Ind. Philharmonic; founding mem. Friends of Hidalgo, Inc. Mem.: ABA, Ind. Continuing Legal Edn. Forum (pres. 2005—06), Trial Lawyers Poetic Justice, Am. Judicature Soc., Ind. Bar Found. (bd. dirs. 2004—05), Assn. Trial Lawyers Am., Ind. Trial Lawyers Assn., Bartholomew County Bar Assn. (pres. 1982), Ind. State Bar Assn. (mem. bd. govs. 1988—90, 2000—02, chair Ho. Delegates 2001—02, v.p. 2004—05, pres.-elect 2005—06, pres. 2006—). Office: Eynon Law Group PC 555 First St PO Box 1212 Columbus IN 47201 Office Phone: 812-372-2508. Office Fax: 812-372-4992.

EYRE, CHRIS, film director; b. Portland, Ore., 1968; B. in Media Arts, U. Ariz., 1991; MFA, NYU, 1995. Co-prodr., dir.: (films) Smoke Signals, 1998 (Am. Indian Movie award for Best Film, 1998, Sundance Audience award, Sundance Filmmakers Trophy, 1998, Best Artistic Contbn. award, Tokyo Internat. Film Festival, 1998); prodr.: The Doe Boy, 2001; co-prodr., dir., actor: Skins, 2002; dir.: A Thousand Roads, 2005; dir., actor: (TV films) Skinwalkers, 2002; prodr., dir. Edge of America, 2003 (Dirs. Guild Am. award for Outstanding Directorial Achievement in Children's Programs, 2005); dir.: A Thief of Time, 2004. Address: Creative Artists Agy 9830 Wilshire Blvd Beverly Hills CA 90212-1825 Office Phone: 310-288-4545.

EYRE, IVAN, artist; b. Tullymet, Sask., Can., Apr. 15, 1935; s. Thomas and Kay E.; m. Brenda Fenske, June 14, 1957; children: Keven, Tyrone. Mem. faculty U. N.D., 1958-59; mem. faculty U. Man., Winnipeg, Can., 1959-92, prof. drawing and painting, 1975-92, head drawing dept., 1974-78, prof. emeritus, 1994—; founding mem. Winnipeg Art Gallery, 1996. One-man shows include: Montreal Mus. Fine Arts, 1964, Winnipeg Art Gallery, 1964, 66, 74, 82, 88, 92, 2005, Fleet Galleries, Winnipeg, 1965, 69, 71, Albert White Galleries, Toronto, 1965, Atelier Vincitore Gallery, Brighton, Eng., 1967, Yellow Door Gallery, Winnipeg, 1966, Mount Allison U., 1968, Mendel Art Gallery, Saskatoon, 1968, Jerrold Morris Gallery, Toronto, 1969, 71, 73, Frankfurter Kunst Kabinett, Frankfurt, Ger., 1973, Burnaby Art Gallery, 1973, McIntosh Gallery, U. W. Ont., 1973, Siemens Werk, Erlangen, Germany, 1974, N.B. Mus., St. John, 1976, Gallery I.I.I., U. Man., 1977, 94, Nat. Gallery Can., Ottawa, 1978, Equinox Gallery, Vancouver, 1978, 81, 82, Robert McLaughlin Gallery, Oshawa, 1980, Mira Godard Gallery, Toronto, 1978-80, 90, 92, 94, 96, 99, 2002, Rodman Hall Arts Centre, St. Catherines, Ont., 1980, Art Gallery Windsor, Ont., 1981, Beaverbrook Art Gallery, Fredericton, N.B., 1981, London (Ont.) Regional Art Gallery, 1981, Sir George Williams Galleries, Montreal, 1981, MacDonald Stewart Art Centre, Guelph, Ont., 1981, Brian Melnychenko Gallery, Winnipeg, 1981, 87, The Ctr. for Inter-Am. Rels. NY, 1982, Burlington (Ont.) Art Ctr., 1982, Can. Cultural Centre, Paris, 1982, Can. House Gallery, London, Eng., 1982, Talbot Rice Gallery, Edinburgh, Scotland, 1982, The Art Gallery of Greater Victoria, Can., 1973, 82, 99, Evelyn Aimis Fine Art Gallery, Toronto, 1985, 87, Nat. Gallery of Can., Ottawa, 1988, Ivan Eyre: Personal Mythologies: Images of the Milieu: Figurative Paintings 1957 to 1988 touring Can., Winnipeg Art Gallery, 1989, Nickle Arts Mus., Calgary, 1989, Edmonton Art Gallery, 1989, London (Can.) Regional Art Gallery, 1989; 49th Parallel Gallery, NYC, 1988, Edmonton Art Gallery, 1995, Mackenzie Art Gallery, 1996, Assiniboine Park Pavilion Gallery, Winnipeg, 1998-2004, Art Gallery of Hamilton, 1999, Loch & Mayberry Fine Art, Winnipeg, 2000, Winnipeg Art Gallery, 2005; group shows include: London Regional Art Gallery, 1964, Agnes Lefort Gallery, Montreal, 1964, Nat. Gallery, Ottawa, 1965, 67, 74, Yellow Door Gallery, Winnipeg, 1965, Art Gallery of Ont., Toronto, 1968, Montreal Mus. Fine Arts, 1964, 70, 76, Primera Biennial Americana De Artes Graficas, Cali, Columbia, 1971, Art Gallery Ont., 1970, 76, Winnipeg Art Gallery, 1967, 76, 90, 92, 95, 2002, Glenbow-Alta. Inst., Calgary, 1976, Vancouver Art Gallery, 1977, Mendel Art Gallery, Saskatoon, 1977, 82, 2002, Harbourfront Art Gallery, Toronto, 1977, Edmonton (Alta., Can.) Art Gallery, 1981, 99, 2000, Printworld, US, 1982, Barcelona, Spain, 1982, Seattle Art Fair, 1987, LA Art Fair, 1986-87, Chgo. Art Fair, 1989, Maison de la Culture Cotes-des-Neiges, Montreal, 1992, Galerie de la Ville Dollard-des-Ormeaux, Que., Can. Coun. Art Bank, 1993, Drabinsky Gallery, Toronto, 1993, Hong Kong Art Fair, 1993, Expo '93, Taejon, South Korea, 1993, Loch and Mayberry Fine Art, Winnipeg, 1997, Mira Godard Gallery, Toronto, 1998, 2001, Royal Can. Acad. Arts Prairie Region Exhbn., Winnipeg, 1997, travelling to Regina, 1998, Calgary, 1998, Victoria, 1999, Markham, Ont., 1999, Provinciaal Centrum Voor Kunst En Culture (Patershol) Gent, 2001, Mackenzie Art Gallery, Regina, 2001-02, 04, Gallery I.I.I., U. Manitoba, 2003-04, McMichael Can. Art Collection, Kleinburg, Ont., Can., 2004, Toronto Art Fair, 2005; represented in permanent collections, Assiniboine Pk. Pavilion Gallery Art Collection, Winnipeg, Winnipeg Art Gallery, Nat. Gallery, Ottawa, Vancouver Art Gallery, Edmonton Art Gallery, Montreal Mus. Fine Arts, Art Gallery Ont., Toronto. Decorated Queen's Silver Jubilee medal, Queen's Golden Jubilee medal; nominee Molson prize, 1996; named sr. grantee, Can. Coun., 1966, 1977; recipient Gold medal, Acad. of Italy, 1980, Jubilee award, U. Man. Alumni, 1982, Outstanding Achievement medal, Internat. Biograph.Ctr., 1998. Mem. Royal Can. Acad. Arts, Order Manitoba. Achievements include being subject of books Ivan Eyre (Woodcock), 1981, Ivan Eyre Drawings by Tom Lovatt, 2003, Ivan on Eyre-The Paintings, 2004; subject of various documentary films. Home: 1098 Des Trappistes St Winnipeg MB Canada R3V 1B8

EYRE, PAMELA CATHERINE, retired career officer; b. Chgo., Nov. 3, 1948; d. Francis Thomas and Jane (Burd) E. BA, Ctrl. State U. Okla., 1972; MPA, U. Okla., 1976; postgrad., U. Tex., 1998—. Commd. 2d lt. U.S. Army, 1973, advanced through grades to lt. col., 1991, test and evaluation officer Ft. Gordon, Ga., 1982-85, R&D coord. Ft. Monmouth, N.J., 1985-88, with army gen. staff Pentagon Washington, 1988-91, acquisition policy staff officer Army Secretariat Pentagon, 1991-94, asst. project mgr. Def. Telecom. Svc., 1994-95, test and evaluation officer Army Secretariat Pentagon, 1995-96; ret., 1996; program mgr. unmanned aerial vehicles Mission Techs., Inc., San Antonio, 2000—02. Home: 3103 N Bentsen Palm Dr Mission TX 78574 E-mail: pceyre@gmail.com.

EYRING, HENRY BENNION, bishop; b. Princeton, NJ, May 31, 1933; s. Henry and Mildred (Bennion) E.; m. Kathleen Johnson, July 27, 1962; children: Henry J., Stuart J., Matthew J., John B., Elizabeth, Mary Kathleen. BS, U. Utah, 1955; MBA, Harvard U., 1959, DBA, 1963; DHum (hon.), Brigham Young U., 1985. Asst., then assoc. prof. Stanford U., Palo Alto, Calif., 1962—71; pres. Ricks Coll., Rexburg, Idaho, 1972—77; dep. commr. edn., then commr. LDS Ch., Salt Lake City, 1977—85, presiding bishopric, 1985—92, mem. 1st Quorum of the Seventy, 1992—95, mem. Quorum of the Twelve, 1995—. Author: To Draw Closer to God, 1997, Because He First Loved Us, 2002; co-author: The Organizational World, 1973. With USAF, 1955—57. Recipient Sloan faculty fellowship, MIT, 1963—64. Avocations: painting, woodcarving. Office: LDS Ch Quorum of the Twelve 47 E South Temple Salt Lake City UT 84150-9701

EYRING, MICHAEL BORTH, forensic specialist; m. Donna Mae Andrew, June 15, 1970. BS in Chemistry, Ariz. State U., Tempe, 1971. Forensic scientist Ariz. Dept. Pub. Safety, Phoenix, 1977—2007; cons. forensic sci. Micro Forensics Inst., Ltd., 1986—. Forensic trace analysis instr. Micro Forensics Inst., Ltd, Phoenix, 1986—. Contbr. chapters to books. Recipient Vision award, Internat. Assn. of Forensic Nurses, 1997. Fellow: Am. Coll. Forensic Examiners, Am. Soc. Forensic Scis.; mem.: Internat. Soc. Testing and Materials (sec. com. e-30 1997—98), Sci. Working Group on Materials Analysis. Office: Micro Forensics Inst Ltd PO Box 40048 Phoenix AZ 85067-0048 Home Phone: 602-234-1769; Office Phone: 602-234-1769. Business E-Mail: microfor@fastq.com.

EYSTER, MARY ELAINE, hematologist, educator; m. Robert E. Dye, Jan. 2, 1965; children: Robert E. Dye, Charles Dye. AB, Duke U., 1956, MD, 1960. Intern. N.Y. Hosp.-Cornell Med. Coll., NYC, 1960-61, resident in medicine, 1961-63, fellow in hematology, 1963-66, instr. medicine, 1966-67, asst. prof. medicine, 1967-70; asst. prof. medicine Milton S. Hershey Med. Ctr. Pa. State U., Hershey, 1970-73, assoc. prof. Milton S. Hershey Med. Ctr., 1973-82, prof. Milton S. Hershey Med. Ctr., 1982—, chief hematology divsn., dept. medicine Coll. Medicine, 1973—96; dir. Hemophilia Ctr. Ctrl. Pa., 1973—, Spl. Hematology Lab., Milton S. Hershey Med. Ctr., 1973—96, med. dir., 1997—, Hemostatsis Lab, Milton S. Hershey Med. Ctr., 1997—. Dir. AIDS Clin. Trials Unit Pa. State U., 1987-2000; faculty rsch. assoc. Am. Cancer Soc., 1966-71; mem. State Hemophilia Adv. Com, 1973-90, chmn., 1977-79, 1988-90; mem. policy bd. Coop. F VII inhibitor study Nat. Heart, Lung and Blood Inst., 1975-79; mem. med. and sci. adv. counc. Nat. Hemophilia Found., 1976-77, 83-89, chmn. med. adv. com. Del. Valley chpt., 1979-82; co-investigator, mem. multi-agy. task force on AIDS HHS, 1982-83; mem. blood products adv. com. FDA, 1985-89; mem exec. com. NIH-NIAID Clin. Trials Group, 1987-89; mem. forum on blood safety and availability Inst. of Med., 1993-95; mem. exec. com. second NCI Hemophilia Study Group 2000-2006. USPHS grantee, 1976-95. Fellow ACP; mem. Am. Fedn. Clin. Rsch., World Fedn. Hemophilia, Am. Soc. Hematology, Internat. Soc. Thrombosis and Haemostasis, Insternat. Soc. Hematology, Pa. Soc. Hematology and Oncology (bd. dirs. 1982-85), Am. Assn. for Study Liver Diseases, Hemophilia and Thrombosis Rsch. Soc., Phi Beta Kappa, Alpha Omega Alpha. Office: Milton S Hershey Med Ctr PO Box 850 Hershey PA 17033-0850 Office Phone: 717-531-8399.

EZE, EMMANUEL CHUKWUDI, philosophy professor; b. Agbokete, Akpanya Benue State, Nigeria, Jan. 18, 1963; s. Daniel Madu Eze and Rebecca Uka Udaya. PhD, Fordham U., NYC, 1993. Asst. prof. Mt. Holyoke Coll., South Hardley, Mass., 1999—2000; assoc. prof. DePaul U., Chgo., 2000—. Asst. prof. Bucknell U., Lewisburg, Pa., 1993—98; Diamond disting. visitor in philosophy New Sch. for Social Rsch. Author: (acad. philosophy) Achieving our Humanity: The Idea of the Postracial Future, African Philosophy: An Anthology, Race and the Enlightenment: A Reader, Postcolonial African Philosophy: A Critical Reader. Editor Philosophia Africana, Chgo., 2001—06. Fellow, NEH, 2006. Mem.: Am. Philos. Assn. Office: DePaul U Dept Philosophy 2352 N Clifton Ave Chicago IL 60614 Office Phone: 773-325-7265. Office Fax: 773-325-7268. Business E-Mail: eeze@depaul.edu.

EZEJI, THADDEUS CHUKWUEMEKA, microbiologist, educator; s. Andrew and Theresa Njoku; m. Ifeoma Odaba; children: Jessica, Michael. PhD, U. Rostock, Germany, 2001. Post doctoral rsch. assoc. U. Ill. Urbana-Champaign, Ill., 2001—05, asst. prof., 2005—. Cons. Advanced Biofuels Inc, Chgo., 2005—. Edit. bd. mem. and reviewer (of sci. manuscripts). Expert witness Circuit Ct. Nineteenth Jud. Lake County, Ill., Waukegan, 2006. Recipient award, German Acad. Exchange Svc., 1997; grantee, Ill. Corn Mktg. Bd., 2004, Ill. Ventures, 2006. Mem.: Am. Chem. Soc., Am. Soc. Microbiology. Achievements include patents pending for process for continuous simultaneous butanol production and recovery; first to designed new sparger for efficient simultaneous mixing and mass transfer. Avocations: jogging, ping pong, badminton. Home: 812 East Oakland Ave Urbana IL 61802 Office: Univ Ill Urbana-Champaign 1207 West Gregory Dr Urbana IL 61801 Home Phone: 217-384-6687; Office Phone: 217-244-6354.

EZELL, ELIZABETH ANNE, music educator; b. Knoxville, Tenn., July 14, 1942; d. Thomas Grady and Alma Leona Phelps; m. David Nathan Ezell, Dec. 31, 1984; m. John Bevins Householder (dec.); children: Catherine Householder Grimes, Sarah Householder Smithermann, Amelia Householder Evers. MB, U. Tenn., 1973; MA in Tchg., Citadel, 1983. Cert. tchr. S.C. String tchr. Charleston County Schs., SC, 1978—90, Richland Sch. Dist. I, Columbia, SC, 1990—. Mem.: Music Educators Nat. Conf., S.C. Music Educators. Avocations: reading, swimming, gardening. Home: 2135 Cunningham Rd Columbia SC 29210 Office Phone: 803-256-1695. Office Fax: 803-253-7007. E-mail: dandezell@earthlink.net.

EZELL, MARGARET M., language educator; John Paul Abbott prof. of liberal arts Tex. A&M U., College Sta., 1997—. Author: The Patriarch's Wife: Literary Evidence and the History of the Family, Writing Women's Literary History, Social Authorship and the Advent of Print; editor: (series) Women Writers in English, 1350-1830. Fellow, John Simon Guggenheim Meml. Found., 2003. Office: Tex A&M U Dept English 243D Blocker Bldg (MS 4227) College Station TX 77843

EZELLE, ROBERT EUGENE, diplomat; b. Mattoon, Ill., Dec. 5, 1927; s. Zenner Robert and Nina Leora (Smith) E.; m. Lesly Marion Hopkins, Apr. 30, 1955; children: Robert, Lesley, John, Paul. Student, U. So. Calif., 1947-49, U. Bonn, 1954-56, U. Munich, 1956-57; PhD, U. Vienna, 1960; MS (Sloan fellow), Stanford Grad. Sch. Bus., 1977; Dr.h.c., Nat. U., 1981. Instr. Bonn, Munich and Vienna, 1954-60; dir. lang. sch., San Mateo, Calif., 1960-61; joined U.S. Fgn. Svc., 1961; internat. rels. officer State Dept., Washington, 1961-62, staff asst. Nat. Interdeptl. Seminar, 1962-63; assigned Hong Kong, 1963-65, Bern, Switzerland, 1965-69, Naples, Italy, 1969-72; chief consular affairs sect. Am. Embassy, Bonn, 1972-75; internat. rels. officer State Dept., Washington, 1975-76; dep. consul gen. Am. Embassy, London, 1977-80; consul gen. Am. Consulate Gen., Tijuana, Mex., 1980-84, Am. Embassy, Paris, 1984-88, Haiti, 1988—90; cons., internat. trade, 1990—. Served with USAF, 1949-53. Recipient Gold medal City of Paris, 1988, Superior Honor award Dept. State, 1988. Address: 1608 NE 17th St Battle Ground WA 98604

EZENWA, JOSEPHINE NWABUOKU, social worker; b. Oct. 20, 1959; d. H.M. Eze-Igwe Silas O. and H.R.H. Veronica Ezenwa; children: Bryan, Brenda, Sean. BA in Psychology and Human Svc. (hon.), Fontbonne Coll., St. Louis, 1980; MSW, Washington Univ., St. Louis, 1981; postgrad., St. Louis U., 1991—93. Diplomate Am. Coll. Profl. Mental Health Practitioners, 2002. Rsch. dir. Nat. Benevolent Assn., St. Louis, 1981-89; tchr. U. City Sch. Dist., St. Louis, 1989-94; therapist Presbyn. Children's Home, St. Louis, 1994-95; social worker St. Louis Regional Med. Ctr., 1995-97; founder, chair St. Louis Regional Med. Ctr. Dialysis Support Group, 1995-97; social worker St. Louis U. Hosp., 1997; CEO, pres. BBS Care U.S.A., Inc., St. Louis, 1997—; pres. BBS Charities, Inc., St. Louis, 2000—; chair Bus. Adv. Coun. Nat Rep. Congl. Com., St. Louis, 2002—. Founder and chair St. Louis Regional Med. Ctr. Dialysis Support Group, 1995-97; chair long range planning com. Washington U.; co-chair Bus. Adv. Coun., 2002; presenter in field. Chair bus. adv. coun. Nat. Rep. Congl. Com., 2002—. Named Businesswoman of Yr., Nat. Rep. Congl. Com., 2003; recipient Nat. Leadership award, St. Louis Regional Med. Ctr. Dialysis Support Group, 2002, Gold Medal award, Nat. Rep. Congl. Com., 2003. Mem. NASW, NAFE, Coun. Nephrology Social Workers; Nat. Assn. Forensic Counselors; Nat. Assn. Cognitive Behavioral Therapists, Washington U. Sch. Social Work Alumni Assn. (bd. dir.); Creve Coeur-Olive C. of C.; Lions Club. Avocations: choreography, fashion cons., event coord., design, travel. Office: St Louis U Hosp 3536 Vista Grand Saint Louis MO 63110 also: BBS Care USA Inc 7151-7155 Olive Blvd Saint Louis MO 63130 Office Phone: 314-725-7733.

EZER, MITCHEL J., lawyer; b. Chgo., Jan. 3, 1935; s. Meyer Wolf and Celia Malkeh (nee Goldstein) Ezer; m. Renee Leslie Antman, Feb. 18, 2006; children: Mark Sherman, Renee Ellen, David Andrew. BS, Northwestern U., Evanston, 1956; JD, Yale Law Sch., New Haven, 1959. CPA Calif. Assoc. tchr. U. Calif. LA Sch. Law, 1959—60; assoc. Hastings & Lasker, Beverly Hills, 1960—63; staff counsel U. Studios, Universal City, Calif., 1963—67; atty. Ezer & Williamson Ptnr., LA, 1964—. Office: Ezer and Williamson LLP 1000 Ave of Stars #2100 Los Angeles CA 90067 Business E-Mail: mje@ezerwilliamson.com.

EZGUR, MICHAEL H., real estate company executive; b. 1967; Undergraduate, Univ. Ill. Bar: Ill. Mng. broker Terrapin Realty Co., Chgo. Named one of 40 Under Forty, Crain's Bus. Chgo., 2005. Mem.: Internat. Coun. Shopping Centers, West Loop C. of C., Chgo. Assn. Realtors, Nat. Assn. Homebuilders, West Ctrl. Assn. (pres., mem. bd. dir.). Office: Terrapin Properties 217 N Jefferson St Fl 5 Chicago IL 60661 E-mail: mezgur@terrapingroup.com.*

EZRIN, MYER, retired director; b. Boston, June 23, 1926; s. Joseph and Ida Ezrin; m. Madeline Frager, Aug. 22, 1946; m. Elaine Breker, Dec. 11, 2005; children: Jane Barbara Yourish, Andrea Louise Silverstein, Jonathan Charles. BS Chemistry summa cum laude, Tufts Coll., 1948; PhD Chemistry, Yale U., 1954. Chemist Dupont Coated Fabrics, Fairfield, Conn., 1948—50, Monsanto Chem. Co., Springfield, Mass., 1953—65; project mgr. Springborn Labs., Enfield, Conn., 1965—80; dir. IMS Assocs. Program U. Conn., Inst. Materials Sci., Storrs, 1980—2006; ret., 2006. Expert witness in patent infringement and product liability litig. Springborn Labs., Enfield, 1969—80; expert witness in field, Longmeadow, Mass., 1980—; vis. prof. polymer analysis and characterization U. Conn., Storrs, 1978—79. Co-author: Plastics Analysis Guide - Chemical and Instrumental Methods, 1983; author: Plastics Failure Guide - Cause and Prevention, 1996. Jewish religious sch. tchr., 1955—69; lay rabbi for religious svcs. at coll., 1955—60. Electronic tech mate 2d class USN, 1944—46, Eng. Phi Beta Kappa Undergrad. scholar, Tufts Coll., 1947. Fellow: Soc. Plastics Engrs. (chmn. failure group 1989—91, pres. We. New Eng. sect. 1991—92, new tech. com.); mem.: Am. Chem. Soc. (emeritus), Sigma Xi. Jewish. Achievements include research in electron exchange polymers was the first for synthetic polymers capable of controlled reversible oxidation and reduction; discovery that acid rain contributed to the failure of fiberglass support rod on electrical transmission line; Patent infringement litigation on chemically embossed vinyl flooring, invented an analytical method of analysis that proved infringement resulting in damages of many millions of dollars; aromatic hydrocarbons, including benzene, in air from gasoline vapors are absorbed by plastics; patents for combined electron- and ion-exchange copolymers; biazially oriented crystalline polystyrene; process for the manufacture of biaxially oriented crystalline polystyrene; uniaxially oriented crystalline polymers. Avocation: bible study. Home and Office: 43 Morgan Ridge Longmeadow MA 01106-1757 Home Phone: 413-567-8218. E-mail: mezrin80@comcast.net.

EZZO, DAVID ALBERT, not-for-profit executive, anthropologist, educator; b. Buffalo, June 9, 1963; s. Albert and Ann Ezzo; m. Michelle Martin, Aug. 13, 2005. BA in Anthropology, SUNY, Fredonia, 1985; MA in Anthropology, U. Okla., Norman, 1987; cert. in Personnel Mgmt., SUNY, Buffalo, 1991; student, NYU, NYC, 1996; cert. in Non-Profit Mgmt., U. South Fla., Tampa, 1997; MPA, Hamilton U., 2005; PhD in Anthropology, Richardson U., 2005. Cert. fundraising exec. 1997. From mem. staff to dir. endowment Boy Scouts Am., Buffalo, 1987—2005, dir. endowment, 2005—; dir. devel. and pub. rels. YMCA, St. Petersburg, Fla., 1996—98, dir. cmty. devel. Burbank, Calif., 2002; adj. asst. prof. anthropology Erie C.C. North Campus. Lectr. in field. Contbr. scientific papers. Recipient Vigil Hon. award, Boy Scouts Am., 1981. Avocations: fitness, tennis, music, travel. Home: 52 Kenwood Rd Kenmore NY 14217 Office: GNFC Boy Scouts 401 Mary Vale Dr Buffalo NY 14225 Personal E-mail: daveeagle5@aol.com.

FAATZ, JEANNE RYAN, councilman; b. Cumberland, Md., July 30, 1941; d. Charles Keith and Elizabeth (McIntyre) Ryan; children: Kristin, Susan. BS, U. Ill., 1962; MA, U. Colo., Denver, 1985. Instr. speech dept. Met. State Coll., Denver, 1985-98; sec. to majority leader Colo. Senate, 1976-78; mem. Colo. Ho. Reps. from Dist. 1, 1979-98; dir. Colo. Sch.-to-Career, 1999—2001; councilwoman City of Denver, 2003—. Former ho. asst. majority leader. Past pres. S.W. Denver YWCA Adult Edn. Club; former mem. bd. mgrs. S.W. Denver YMCA; past pres. Harvey Park (Colo.) Homeowners Assn. Gates fellow, Harvard U., 1984. Home: 2903 S Quitman St Denver CO 80236-2208 Home Phone: 303-935-6915; Office Phone: 303-763-8562. E-mail: jeanne.faatz@ci.denver.co.us.

FABBRI, ANNE R., critic, curator; b. Norristown, Pa. d. Remo and Anna Wild (Butterworth) F.; m. Joseph Henry Butera (div.); children: Virginia, Remo, Joseph F. (Jay). AB cum laude, Radcliffe Coll., MA in Art History, Bryn Mawr Coll., 1971. Art lectr. Villanova U., Pa., 1971-73, Drexel U., Phila., 1974-76; art critic, art editor The Drummer, Phila., 1976-79; art critic The Bulletin, Phila., 1978-80; dir. Alfred O. Deshong Mus., Widener U., Chester, Pa., 1980-82, The Noyes Mus., Oceanville, NJ, 1982-91; dir. Paley Design Ctr. Phila. U., 1991-2001; art critic Phila. Daily News, Art in Am., Art Matters, The Art Newspaper, Am. Artist, 1998—, Phila. Style mag., 2002—05, BroadStreetReview.com, 2006—; lectr. arts adminstrn. Rosemont Coll., 2000—03, lectr. humanities, 2001—03. Bd. dirs. Phila. Vol. Lawyers for the arts, 2001-03; mem. adv. com. Main Line Art Ctr.; chair adv. com. Art in City Hall, Phila., 1999-2003; chair New Visions, Phila. Furniture Exhbn., 1998-2004. Chair, mem. adv. com. Art in City Hall, 1999—. Vis. NEH fellow U. Calif.-Berkeley, 1980, Princeton U., 1981; recipient John Cotton Dana award Mus. N.J. Assn. Mus., 1991. Mem. Am. Assn. Museums, Coll. Art Assn., Internat. Assn. Art Critics. Home and Office: 642 Valley View Ln Wayne PA 19087-2024 Office Phone: 610-989-0588. Personal E-mail: arfabbri@aol.com.

FABE, DANA ANDERSON, state supreme court justice; b. Cin., Mar. 29, 1951; d. George and Mary Lawrence (Van Antwerp) F.; m. Randall Gene Simpson, Jan. 1, 1983; 1 child, Amelia Fabe Simpson. BA, Cornell U., 1973; JD, Northeastern U., 1976. Bar: Alaska 1977, U.S. Supreme Ct. 1981. Law clk. to justice Alaska Supreme Ct., 1976-77; staff atty. pub. defenders State of Alaska, 1977-81; dir. Alaska Pub. Defender Agy., Anchorage, 1981—88; judge Superior Ct., Anchorage, 1988—92; deputy presiding judge Third Judicial Dist., 1992—95; justice Alaska Supreme Ct., Anchorage, 1996—, chief justice, 2000—03, 2006—. Chair Alaska Supreme Ct. Civil Rules Com., Alaska Supreme Ct. Judicial Outreach Commn., Alaska Ct. System Law Day Steering Comm., Alaska Teaching Justice Network. Named alumna of yr. Northeastern Sch. Law, 1983; recipient Northeastern Sch. Law Alumni Pub. Svc. award, 1991. Mem.: Am. Judicature Soc. (bd. dirs.), Alaska Bar Assoc. (bd. govs. 1987—88, co-chair Gender Equality Sect.). Office: Alaska Supreme Ct 303 K St Fl 5 Anchorage AK 99501-2013 Office Phone: 907-264-0622.*

FABENS, ANDREW LAWRIE, III, lawyer; b. Washington, Apr. 8, 1942; s. Andrew Lawrie Jr. and Alicia Gordon (Hail) F.; m. Martha Leigh Leingang, June 24, 1966; children: Andrew Lawrie IV, Jennie Leigh. AB, Yale U., 1964; JD, U. Chgo., 1967. Bar: Ohio 1967. Assoc. Thompson, Hine and Flory, Cleve., 1967-74; ptnr. Thompson Hine LLP (formerly Thompson, Hine and Flory), Cleve., 1974—, chmn. estate planning and probate area, 1988-94. Contbr. articles on estate planning and related topics to profl. publs. Pres. Family Health Assn., Cleve., 1978-80, 83-84; trustee A.M. McGregor Home, East Cleveland, Ohio, 1991—, chmn., 2001—; trustee Bascom Little Fund, Cleve., 1985—, Great Lakes Basin Conservancy, 1999—; bd. dirs. Georgian Bay Land Trust, 2006—; vestryman

Christ Episcopal Ch., Shaker Heights, Ohio, 1972-77. Fellow Am. Coll. Trust and Estate Counsel; mem. Ohio State Bar Assn. (coun. estate planning, trust and probate law sect. 1983—, treas. 1997-99, sec. 1999-2001, vice-chmn. 2001-03, chmn. 2003-05), Cleve. Bar Assn. (speaker, com. mem. 1976—), Cleve. Skating Club, Rowfant Club (fellow 2000-03), The Novel Club (sec. 1986-88, pres. 1995-97). Home: 2280 Woodmere Dr Cleveland OH 44106-3604 Office: Thompson Hine LLP 3900 Key Ctr 127 Public Square Cleveland OH 44114-1216 Home Phone: 216-371-5213; Office Phone: 216-566-5736. Business E-Mail: andy.fabens@thompsonhine.com.

FABER, DAVID ALAN, federal judge; b. Charleston, W.Va., Oct. 21, 1942; s. John Smith and Wilda Elaine (Melton) F.; m. Deborah Ellayne Anderson, Aug. 24, 1968; 1 dau., Katherine Peyton. BA, W.Va. U., 1964; JD, Yale U., 1967; LLM, U. Va., 1998. Bar: W.Va. 1967, U.S. Ct. Mil. Appeals 1970, U.S. Supreme Ct. 1974. Assoc. Dayton, Campbell & Love, Charleston, W.Va., 1967-68, Campbell, Love, Woodroe, 1972-74; ptnr. Campbell, Love, Woodroe & Kizer, Charleston, 1974-77, Love, Wise, Robinson & Woodroe, Charleston, 1977-81; US atty. US Dept. Justice, Charleston, 1982-86; ptnr. Spilman, Thomas, Battle & Klostermeyer, Charleston, 1987-91; judge US Dist. Ct. (So. Dist.) W.Va., Bluefield, 1991—, chief judge. Counsel to ethics commn. W.Va. State Bar, Charleston, 1974-76 Served to capt. USAF, 1968-72, to col. W.Va. Air N.G., 1978-92. Nat. law scholar Yale Law Sch. New Haven, 1964-65 Mem.: W.Va. Bar Assn., W.Va. State Bar, Phi Beta Kappa. Republican. Episcopalian. Office: US Dist Ct PO Box 2546 300 Virginia St E Charleston WV 25329 Office Phone: 304-347-3170. Office Fax: 304-347-3171.

FABER, GEORGE DONALD, retired communications executive; b. Mpls., June 17, 1921; s. Morris William and Lowella (Whitman) F.; m. Marjorie Alice Knodel; children: Kathie Diane Goodman, Michael William, Patricia Netzley. Student, Wis. Coll. Music, 1940; BA, Northwestern U., 1941. Writer, announcer, actor Sta. WHBL, Sheboygan, Wis., 1937-39; prodn. mgr. Sta. WMFD, Wilmington, NC, 1939-41; columnist and author Behind the Mike series, Cape Fear Pub. Co., Wilmington, NC, 1940-41; news editor NBC, Chgo., 1943-46; news dir., writer CBS, 1946-56; internat. mgr. CBS films, LA, 1956-71; internat. dir. client rels. Viacom Prodsn. divsn. Paramount TV, 1971—2000. Dir. communications, bd. dir. Callahan and Assocs. L.A. Emmy nomination. Vol. fundraising Childrens Hosp. Mem. Internat. Photo Journalists (hon. life), TV Programs Execs. Com. (publicity), Sigma Delta Chi. Avocations: photography, fundraising for charities. Home: 10760 Cushdon Ave Los Angeles CA 90064-3219 Personal E-mail: georgedfaber@aol.com.

FABER, MICHAEL WARREN, lawyer; b. NYC, June 7, 1943; s. Carl Faber and Harriet Ruth Cohen; m. Adele Zolot, Apr. 16, 1975; children: Evan, Jenna. AB, Hunter Coll., 1964; JD, Fordham U., 1967. Bar: N.Y. 1967, D.C. 1972, U.S. Ct. Claims, 1972, U.S. Supreme Ct. 1972, Colo. 1993. Gen. atty. FCC, Washington, 1967-69, trial atty., 1969-71, atty. advisor to Commr. T.J. Houser, 1971; assoc. Peabody, Rivlin, Lambert & Meyers, Washington, 1971-73; ptnr. Peabody, Lambert & Meyers, Washington, 1973-84, Reid and Priest, Washington, 1984-93, mem. exec. com., 1986-92; prin. The Faber Group, Cascade, Colo., 1993-94; pres. USA Volleyball Ctrs. LLC, Colorado Springs, Colo., 1995-96; owner The Pantry Restaurant, Green Mountain Falls, Colo., 1996—2001; prin. Crossroads Cons., LLC, Cascade, 2001—. Dir. Workforce Partnership study Pikes Peak Workforce Investment Bd., Colorado Springs, 2003; cons. White House Office Telecom. Policy, 1971; chmn. organizing com. Nat. Volleyball League. Bd. dirs. Washington Very Spl. Arts, 1986-93; chair Telecom. Policy Adv. Com., Colo. Springs, 2002—, SAFE Com., Colo. Springs, 2002—; v.p. devel. Pikes Peak United Way, 2003-04, dirs. campaign, 2003. Mem. NY Bar Assn., DC Bar Assn., Fed. Comm. Bar Assn., Colo. Bar Assn., Manitou Springs Edn. Assn. (pres. 2002-04).

FABER, NEIL, advertising executive; b. NYC, May 21, 1938; m. Susan Somer, Jan. 28, 1962; children: Cynthia Farber-Wolf, Amy Farber-Hochberg, Gary Faber. BS, MBA, NYU, 1960. Rsch. analyst Alfred Politz, NYC, 1958-60; eastern sales svc. mgr. ABC, NYC, 1960-63; media supr. Batten, Barton, Durstein & Osborn, NYC, 1964-67; sr. account exec. Wells, Rich, Greene, NYC, 1967-73; v.p., dir. media Della Femina Advt., NYC, 1973-79; founder, pres. Neil Faber Media Inc. Mktg. Media Planning/Buying Co., NYC, 1979—; CEO, chmn. NexGen Media Worldwide Inc. Assoc. prof. mktg. NYU, 1982-2000; lectr. in field. One of the first to develop and introduce new media interactive course at NYU and to utilize web for course exams.; contbr. articles to profl. jours., consumer mags. Recipient Master Communicator award Advt. Agy., Workshop award, Seminar award Mktg. Media. Avocations: music, sports. Office: NexGen Media 54 W 39th St Floor 15 New York NY 10018-2060 Personal E-mail: neil.faber@nexgenmedia.com.

FABER, OLAF ULRICH, structural engineer; b. Dortmund, Germany, Sept. 14, 1964; s. Dieter Wilhelm and Ingrid Faber; m. Minu Tawakol, Mar. 21, 1997; children: Fynn Firouz, Lars Cyrus. Degree in Civil Engring., Ruhr-U. Bochum, Germany, 1994, D in Structural Engring. with distinction, 2001. Cert. Cons. Engr., Chamber of Civil Engrs., Northrhine-Westphalia, Germany, 1996. Project engr. Schürmann, Kindmann & Partners Cons. Engrs., Dortmund, Germany, 1994—95, Dr. Pelle Cons. Engrs., Dortmund, Germany, 1995—96; rsch. engr. Ruhr-U. Bochum, Bochum, Germany, 1996—2001; chief structural engr. Engring. Design Technologies, Inc., Marietta, Ga., 2002—05; sr. structural analyst Uzun & Case Engrs., Atlanta, 2005—. Co-editor: 4th Internat. Conf., Bluff Body Aerodynamics and Applications. Mem.: ASCE. Achievements include research in timevariant reliability for nonlinear problems in structural fatigue, wind engring. and structural dynamics. Office: Uzun & Case Engrs 1180 W Peachtree St Atlanta GA 30309 Home Phone: 678-290-0960; Office Phone: 678-895-9484. Personal E-mail: olaffaber@gmail.com.

FABER, PETER LEWIS, lawyer; b. NYC, Apr. 29, 1938; s. Alexander W. and Anne L. Faber; m. Joan Schuster, June 14, 1959; children: Michael, Julia, Thomas. AB, Swarthmore Coll., 1960; LLB, Harvard U., 1963. Bar: N.Y. 1964. Assoc. Wiser, Shaw, Freeman, Ickes & Williams, Rochester, NY, 1963-65, Parker, Chapin & Flattau, NYC, 1965-66; ptnr. Harter, Secrest & Emery, Rochester, NY, 1966-82, Winthrop, Stimson, Putnam & Roberts, NYC, 1982-84, Kaye, Scholer, Fierman, Hays & Handler, NYC, 1984-95, McDermott, Will & Emery, NYC, 1995—. Mem. adv. com. NYU Ann. Inst. on State & Local Taxation; mem. N.Y. State Coun. on Fiscal and Econ. Priorities, 1991-95. Contbr. articles to profl. jours. Chmn. Rochester Econ. Devel. Com., 1979-82; pres. Rochester Philharm. Orch., Inc., 1980-82; bd. dirs. Met. Rochester Devel. Coun., Harley Sch., 1978-81, Partnership for N.Y.C., 1985-, Boston Early Music Festival, 2007—; mem. fin. com. Monroe County Dem. Party, 1979-82. Fellow Am. Bar Found., Am. Coll. Tax Counsel; mem. ABA (chmn. tax sect. 1991-92, vice chmn. 1986-88, chmn.-elect 1990-91, chmn. com. corp. stockholder relationships tax sect. 1980-82, liaison to IRS for North Atlantic region, vice chmn. spl. com. on integration 1979-81, sec. tax sect. 1984-86), N.Y. State Bar Assn. (chmn. sect. taxation 1976-77, exec. com. sect. taxation 1969—), N.Y. C. of C. (chmn. tax com. 1988—, trustee 1989—, exec. com. 1990—), Monroe County Bar Assn., Am. Law Inst. (tax project adv. group), Rochester Area C. of C. (trustee 1980-82). Home: 300 Central Park W New York NY 10024-1513 Office: McDermott Will & Emery LLP 340 Madison Ave New York NY 10017 Home Phone: 212-873-0850; Office Phone: 212-547-5585. Business E-Mail: pfaber@mwe.com.

FABER, ROBERT CHARLES, lawyer; b. NYC, June 26, 1941; s. Sidney G. and Beatrice (Siebert) F.; m. Carol Z. Zimmerman, Aug. 15, 1965; 1 child, Susan Faber. BA, Cornell U., 1962; JD, Harvard Law Sch., 1965. Bar: N.Y. 1966; U.S. Dist. Ct. (so. dist.) N.Y. 1967; U.S. Ct. Appeals (2nd cir.); U.S. Ct. Appeals (fed. cir.) 1982; U.S. Supreme Ct. 1971; U.S. Patent and trademark Office 1967. Atty., ptnr. Ostrolenk, Faber, Gerb & Soffen, LLP, NYC, 1965—. Lectr. Practicing Law Inst., N.Y.C., 1974—. Author: Landis on Mechanics of Patent Claim Drafting, 3d edit. 1990, 5th edit. 2004. Mem. Am. Intellectual Property Law Assn., N.Y. Intellectual Property Law Assn., Harvard Club of N.Y. Office: Ostrolenk Faber Gerb & Soffen LLP 1180 Ave of Americas New York NY 10036-8401 Office Phone: 212-382-0700. Business E-Mail: rfaber@ostrolenk.com.

FABER, SANDRA MOORE, astronomer, educator; b. Boston, Dec. 28, 1944; d. Donald Edwin and Elizabeth Mackenzie (Borwick) Moore; m. Andrew L. Faber, June 9, 1967; children: Robin, Holly. BA, Swarthmore Coll., 1966, DSc (hon.), 1986; PhD, Harvard U., 1972; DSc (hon.), Williams Coll., 1996. Asst. prof., astronomer Lick Obs., U. Calif., Santa Cruz, 1972-77, assoc. prof., astronomer, 1977-79, prof., astronomer, 1979—; Univ. Prof. U. Calif., Santa Cruz, 1996—. Mem. astronomy adv. panel NSF, 1975-77; vis. prof. Princeton U., 1978, U. Hawaii, 1983, Ariz. State U., 1985; Phillips visitor Haverford Coll., 1982; Feshbach lectr. MIT, Cambridge, Mass., 1990; Darwin lectr. Royal Astron. Soc., 1991; Marker lectr. Pa. State U., 1992; Bunyan lectr. Stanford U., 1992; Tomkins lectr. U. Calif., San Francisco, 1992; Mohler lectr. U. Mich., 1994; mem. Nat. Acad. Astronomy Survey Panel, 1979-81Nfat. Acad. Com. on Astronomy and Astrophysics 1993-1995; chmn. vis. com. Space Telescope Sci. Inst., 1983-84; co-chmn. sci. steering com. Keck Obs., 1987-92, leader DEIMOS spectrograph team, 1993—; mem. Wide Field Camera team Hubble Space Telescope, 1985-97, user's com., 1990-92, mem. advanced radial camera selection team, 1995,co-chmn. TAC review comm., 2002; mem. treas. pgm. advis. comm. 2002-; mem. Calif. Coun. on Sci. and Tech., 1989-94,; Com. on Future Smithsonian Instn., 1994-95; mem. White House Space Sci. Workshop, 1996, Waterman Awards Com., NSF, 1997-99, Nat. Medal of Sci. selection com., 1999-2001; mem. Plumian Prof. selection com. Cambridge U., 1998—. Assoc. editor: Astrophys. Jour. Letters, 1982-87; editorial bd.: Ann. Revs. Astronomy and Astrophysics, 1982-87; contbr. articles to profl. jours. Trustee Carnegie Instn., Washington, 1985—; bd. dirs. Ann. Revs., 1989—, SETI Inst., 1997—; editl. affairs com. Ann. Revs., 1996—; exec. com. Ann. Revs., 1998—; Scripps Instn. Oceanography Coun., 2000--; bd. overseers Fermilab, 2002--. Recipient Bart J. Bok prize Harvard U., 1978, Director's Distinguished Lectr. award Livermore Nat. Lab., 1986; NASA Group Achievement award, 1993, DeVaucouleurs medal U. Tex., 1997; Carnegie Lectr. Carnegie Inst. Washington, 1988, 99; NSF fellow, 1966-71; Woodrow Wilson fellow, 1966-71; Alfred P. Sloan fellow, 1977-81; listed among 100 best Am. scientists under 40, Sci. Digest, 1984, listed among 50 best Am. Women scientists, Discover Mag., 2002; Tetelman fellow, Yale U., 1987. Fellow Calif. Coun. on Sci. and Tech.; mem. NAS (vice chair adv. panel on cosmology 1993, rsch. in astronomy commn. on orgn. and mgmt. astrophysics 2001, co-chmn. TAC rev. commn. 2002, mem. treas. program adv. commn. 2002--), Am. Philos. Soc. Am. Acad. Arts and Scis., Calif. Acad. Scis., 1998—, Am. Astron. Soc. (councilor 1982-84, Dannie Heineman prize 1986), Internat. Astron. Union, Am. Philos. Soc., Phi Beta Kappa, Sigma Xi. Office: U Calif Lick Obs Santa Cruz CA 95064 E-mail: faber@ucolick.org.

FABIAN, LARRY LOUIS, academic administrator; b. Aurora, Ill., May 25, 1940; s. Louis and Emma F.; m. Terese Sulikowski, Dec. 1, 1978; children: Christopher, Laura. BA, Cath. U. Am., 1961, MA, 1963; PhD, Columbia U., 1971. Staff mem. Bur. Intelligence and Research, Dept. State, Washington, 1962; staff mem. Carnegie Endowment for Internat. Peace, NYC, 1964; research staff fgn. policy studies program Brookings Instn., Washington, 1965-71, research asso., co-dir. program on tech. and Am. fgn. policy, 1971-73; sr. assoc., dir. Middle East program Carnegie Endowment for Internat. Peace, Washington, 1974-77, sec., 1977-94; sr. v.p., COO, Coun. on Fgn. Rels., NYC, 1994-95; v.p. Shorebank Corp., Chgo., 1996-98; deputy commr. Chgo. Dept. Housing, 1998; v.p., exec. sec. bd. trustees, exec. dir. N.Y. office Am. U. in Cairo, 1998—. Cons. Hudson Inst., N.Y.C., Rockefeller Found. Author: Soldiers without Enemies, 1971, (with others) Regimes for the Ocean, Outer Space and Weather, 1973, Andrew Carnegie's Peace Endowment, 1985; co-editor: Israelis Speak: About Themselves and the Palestinians, 1976. Mem. Coun. on Fgn. Rels., Century Assn. Roman Catholic. Office: Am U in Cairo NY Office 420 5th Ave Fl 3D New York NY 10018-2729

FABIANO, NICOLA, physicist, researcher; b. Rome, Dec. 9, 1965; s. Savino and Ljerka (Paskovic) F. MSC in Physics, U. Rome, 1991; PhD, U. Perugia, Italy, 1995. Rschr. in physics Nat. Inst. Nuclear Physics, Frascati, Rome, 1992-99, U. Perugia, 1995—. Contbr. articles to profl. jours., including Phys. Jour. Nat. Inst. Nuc. Physics scholar, 1992, Patrick M.S. Blackett scholar, 1994. Business E-Mail: nicola.fabiano@pg.infn.it.

FABING, SUZANNAH, museum director; b. Cin., Oct. 1, 1942; d. Howard Douglas John and Esther Clare (Marting) F.; m. Peter B. Doeringer, June 19, 1965 (div. June 1981); 1 child, Eric Atchley; m. James Alexander Muspratt, Aug. 21, 1993. AB in Art History with hons., Wellesley Coll., 1964; AM, Harvard U., 1965. Asst. to curator of Ancient art to dep. dir. mus. Fogg Art Mus./Harvard U., 1965-83; curator of records Nat. Gallery of Art, Washington, 1983-84, mng. curator of records and loans, 1984-91, head Divsn. of Rsch. on Collections, 1991-92; dir., chief curator Smith Coll. Mus. of Art, Northampton, Mass., 1992—2005. Overview panel NEA, 1993-94; reviewer NEH, 1992-94; surveyor AAM Mus. Assessment Program, 1991—; mem. Art Info. Task Force, Getty Art Info. Program, 1990-94; vis. com. Wellesley Coll. Mus., 1988—, Fitchburg Art Mus., chmn. 1983-88, others; trustee Fitchburg Art Mus., 1975-82, Revels, Inc., 1981-82, 88-92), others. Contbr. articles to profl. jours. Mem. New Eng. Mus. Assn. (panelist), Mus. Computer Network (bd. dirs. 1984-90, sec. 1988, v.p. 1988-89, pres. 1989-90), Phi Beta Kappa. Avocation: languages. Office: Hillyer Hall Smith Coll Northampton MA 01063-0001 E-mail: sfabing@smith.edu.

FABIO, JIM, television producer, film producer, television director, film director, film editor; b. Pitts., Sept. 10, 1971; m. Juliana Mott Fabio, Aug. 18, 2001; 1 child, Isabella Delfina. BS, USAF Acad., Colorado Springs, Colo., 1994; MS, Syracuse U., 1999. Field prodr., dir. project officer 1st Combat Camera Squadron (USAF), Charleston Air Force Base, SC, 1994—2003, sr. prodr., dir. ops., 2003—; prodr., dir., editor tv/film True Blue Creative, NYC, 1999—. Prodr.(editor): (television series) Timeless (Emmy award, 2005), (television special) 58th Annual Tony Awards (Emmy award, 2004), (documentary (short) Bombs Over Baghdad: The Operation Iraqi Freedom Air War (Telly award, 2004). Maj. USAF, 1994—98. Mem.: Am. Mensa (assoc.). Office Phone: 310-927-1492. Business E-Mail: jim.fabio@usa.net.

FA'BOS, JULIUS GYUDA, retired horticulturist, educator; b. Marcali, Hungar, Apr. 15, 1932; s. Istvan Fa'Bos and Gizella Vaida; m. Edith Fa'Bos; children: Anita, Adrian, Bettina. BS, Rutgers U., New Brunswick, NJ, 1961; M in Architecture, Harvard U., Cambridge, Mass., 1964; PhD, U. Mich., Ann Arbor, 1973; D in Horticulture (hon.), U. Horticulture, Budapest, Hungary, 1992. Asst. prof. U. Mass., Amherst, 1964—71, assoc. prof., 1971—76, prof., 1976—98, prof. emeritus, 1998—. Contbr. articles to profl. jours. Founder U. Mass. Fa"Bos Fund, Amherst, 1998. Recipient Disting. Alumni award, Rutgers U., 2000. Avocations: photography, hiking, travel.

FABRICAND, BURTON PAUL, physicist, researcher; b. NYC, Nov. 22, 1923; s. Irving Kermit and Frances (Sobler) F.; m. Heather C. North, Dec. 15, 1972; children by previous marriage: Nicole Diane, Lorraine Stewart. AB, Columbia U., 1947, A.M., 1949, PhD, 1953. Project engr. Philco Corp., Phila., 1952-54; lectr., research asso. U. Pa., 1954-56; sr. research scientist Columbia Hudson Labs., Dobbs Ferry, NY, 1957-69; prof. physics Pratt Inst., Bklyn., 1969-92, prof. emeritus, 1992—; mng. ptnr. Fabricand Assocs., 1970—. Cons. Moore Sch. Elec. Engring., U. Pa., 1954-60, Indsl. Electronic Hardware Corp., N.Y.C., 1960-64; investment mgr. Beating the Street Fund, 1996—; bd. dirs. Murphey, Marseilles, Smith & Nammack, N.Y.C. Author: Horse Sense: A New and Rigorous Application of Mathematical Methods to Successful Betting at the Track, 1965, Beating the Street, 1969, Horse Sense: Updated and Expanded Edition, 1976, The Science of Winning: A Random Walk on the Road to Riches, 1979, Abolish the Income Tax: A New and Rigorous Inquiry into the Wealth of Nations, 1986, Symmetry in Free Markets in Symmetry—Unifying Human Understanding, 1989, The Science of Winning: A Random Walk Along the Road to Investment Riches, 1996, 2002; contbr. numerous articles on atomic and nuclear physics and oceanography. Served U.S. Army, 1942-46. Mem. Am. Phys. Soc., Sigma Xi. Home: PO Box 1107 New Milford CT 06776

FABRICANT, ARTHUR E., lawyer, corporate financial executive; b. NYC, Aug. 8, 1935; s. Henry and Rita (Wilson) F.; m. Sandie Lowry; children: Jill, Mary, John, James, Ann. AB, U. St. Andrews, Scotland, 1954, Union Coll., 1956; JD, Harvard U., 1959. Bar: N.Y. 1960. Atty. spl. group organized crime Office U.S. Atty. Gen., 1959-60; mem. firm Abeles & Clark, NYC, 1960-61; v.p. Seligman & Latz Inc., NYC, 1962-67, pres. internat. divsn. London, 1967-84, COO, pres., 1984-85; chmn. Essanelle Holdings, Ltd., Bermuda, 1985-96, Elizabeth Arden, Inc., 1992-2000. Bd. dirs. Elizabeth Arden Holdings Inc. Fellow Inst. Dirs.; mem. Royal Wimbledon Golf Club; Lyford Cay Club. Home: Old Warren Farm Wimbledon Common England Office: AE Fabricant & Co 39 Camp Rd London SW19 4UR England E-mail: arthurfab@aol.com.

FABRICATORE, CAROL DIANE, artist, educator; d. Sandy and Marilyn Fabricatore; m. David Robert Giroux, May 24, 1986; 1 child, Chloe. AA, Farmingdale U., 1978; BFA, Parsons Sch. Design, 1983; MFA, Sch. Visual Arts, 1992. Asst. dir. art Foote, Cone & Belding/Leber Katz, NYC, 1984—87; freelance illustrator Briarcliff Manor, NY, 1987—. Illustrator The N.Y. Times, NYC, 1992—; prof. Sch. Visual Arts, NYC, 1994—. Contbr. artwork to jours., newspapers and mags.; illustrator: The Black Book, 2004 (Best of Show award, 2004); Exhibited in group shows at 407 Gallery, Chelsea, N.Y., 1996, The San Francisco (Calif.) Show, 2000 (Gold Winner award, 2000), No. Westchester (N.Y.) Ctr. Arts, 2000 (Best of Show award, 2000), SUNY Westchester C.C., 2002, Chung-Cheng Gallery St. John's U., 2004; selected for book and show: Graphis Annual Reports 9, 2005. Avocations: horseback riding, running. Personal E-mail: carol.fabricatore@att.net.

FABRIKANT, CRAIG STEVEN, psychologist; b. Buffalo, Jan. 8, 1952; s. Benjamin and Laurine Miriam (Zucker) F.; m. Carol Diane Golub, Nov. 6, 1977; children: Chad Adam, Carly. BA, Fairleigh Dickinson U., 1974, MA, 1977; PhD, Fla. Inst. Tech., 1983. Intern in psychology N.J. Dept. Human Svcs., Trenton, 1977-78; clin. psychologist North Jersey Devel. Ctr., Totowa, 1978-85, Cedar Grove Residential Ctr.; chief psychologist Hackensack (N.J.) Med. Ctr., 1985-96; pvt. practice, 1984—. Adj. instr. Montclair State Coll., 1980-82; part-time instr. Fairleigh Dickinson U.; lectr. Bergen C.C., 2004—; cons. psychology N.J. Dept. Labor and Industry, Newark, 1980—. Author profl. papers. Mem. APA, Assn. Advancement Behavior Therapy, N.J. Psychol. Assn. Office: 106 Old Hook Rd Westwood NJ 07675-2421 Home: 1512 Palisade Ave Apt 12M Fort Lee NJ 07024 Office Phone: 201-664-7418. Personal E-mail: shrink106@aol.com.

FABRIKANT, GERALDINE, journalist; b. NYC, May 15, 1943; m. Robert T. Metz. Student, Brandeis Univ.; BA, Univ. Wis., 1964. Film editor, 1966—72; freelance writer, 1973—79; reporter Hollywood Reporter, 1976—78, Variety, 1978—81; media editor Bus. Week Mag., 1981—85; reporter to sr. writer, Bus. Day sect. NY Times, 1985—. Recipient Gerald Loeb award for deadline reporting, 1996; Knight-Bagehot Fellow in econ., journalism, Columbia Univ. Grad. Sch. Journalism, 1999. Office: Business Day NY Times 229 W 43rd St New York NY 10036

FABRY, VICTORIA JOAN, biology professor; BA in Biology, U. Calif., Santa Barbara, 1976, MA in Biology, 1983, PhD in Biology, 1988. Postdoctoral investigator chemistry dept. Woods Hole Oceanog. Instn., 1988—90; biogeochemist Marine Environment Lab. IAEA, Monaco, 1990—92; asst. prof. dept. biol. scis. Calif. State U., San Marcos, 1993—97, assoc. prof., 1997—2002, prof., 2002—. Chair dept. biol. scis. Calif. State U., San Marcos, 2000—02. Contbr. articles to profl. jours. Vol. fisheries dept. Peace Corps-Smithsonian Instn. Environ. Prog., Sabah, Malaysia, 1977—79. Recipient President's award, Innovation in Tchg., 2001, President's award, Scholarship and Creative Activity, 2006; grantee Nat. Sea Grant John Knauss Congressional fellowship, US Senate Commerce Com., 1984. Office: Dept Biol Scis Calif State U San Marcos 333 S Twin Oaks Valley Rd San Marcos CA 92096-0001 E-mail: fabry@csusm.edu.

FABUNAN, RUBEN G., physician, research scientist, inventor; b. San Marcelino, Zambales, Philippines, Mar. 15, 1945; arrived in U.S., 1979; s. Roman Battad Fabunan, Sr. and Feliza Pescador Garcia; m. Annie Pilapil Fabunan, Dec. 1973; children: Maritess, Farahnaz, Eileen. BS, U. Philippines, Quezon City, 1966; MD, Southwestern U., Philippines, 1973. Contract med. worker Gov. of Iran, 1976—79; founder Fabunan Med. Clin., San Marcelino, 1975; ind. med. rschr. Gen. Medicine, 1975—; chmn. Fil-Am Tech Inc, 2001—. Named Most Outstanding Southwestern U. Alumnus in Medicine, Cebu City, Philippines, 2002; recipient First Place award in Biotechnology Poison Antidote, Invention Convention, Calif., 1997. Mem.: Nat. Inventors Hall of Fame, Am. Soc. of Patent Holders (life), Philippine Med. Assn. (life). Achievements include patents for Fabunan injection viral treatment for HIV/AIDS, influenza, and dengue fever; envenomation antidote for snake bites, catfish stings, and other poisons; monitor diaper; patents pending in field; invention of driving footguard. Office Phone: 562-496-1479. Office Fax: 213-381-2502. Personal E-mail: farahfabunan@yaahoo.com.

FACCINI, ERNEST CARLO, mechanical engineer; b. Livo, Trento, Italy, May 28, 1949; parents Am. citizens; s. Carlo and Elena Agnes (Pancheri) F.; m. Sharon L. Finisecy; 1 child, Carlo Ernesto. AA, Western Wyo. Community Coll., 1969; BS, U. Wyo., 1972, MS, 1976. Registered profl. engr. Wyo., Md., N.Mex. Engring. technician Laramie (Wyo.) Energy Rsch. Ctr., 1968-71; field engr. Mountain Fuel Supply Co., Rock Springs, Wyo., 1972; research engr. Aberdeen (Md.) Proving Grounds, 1972-73; rsch. asst. mech. engring. U. Wyo., Laramie, 1973-76; engring. asst. Bridger Coal Co., Rock Springs, Wyo., 1973; mech. engr. Naval Explosive Ordnance Disposal Facility, Indian Head, Md., 1976-85; sr. scientist TERA/NMIMT, Socorro, N.Mex., 1986-89; prin. scientist Textron Systems Corp., Wilmington, Mass., 1989—99; rsch. engr. Raytheon Co., Tewksbury, Mass., 1999—. Contbr. articles to profl. jours.; patentee in field. Mem. ASME (chmn. student sect. 1971-72), TMS, Am. Phys. Soc., Internat. Assn. of Bomb Technichians and Investigators. Roman Catholic. Achievements include rsch. in ballistics, shaped charge design, explosively formed projectile and explosive effects; also rschr. in fabrication of Ta metal for warhead liners, application of orbital forging to warhead liners, use of powdered metall. techniques to obtain starting material for forging liners, use of end-game analysis, vulnerability lethality analysis codes in the design of warheads, use of reactive/energetic materials and insensitive explosives applications to warheads; kinetic kill warheads; rod warhead design for missile def. purposes; design of protective plating for ballistic protection of spaces aboard vessels; patentee in field. Home: 9 Spring Rd Londonderry NH 03053-2912 Office: Raytheon Co 50 Apple Hill dr

Tewksbury MA 01876-0901 Office Phone: 978-858-9518. Business E-Mail: Ernest_Faccini@Raytheon.com.

FACCINTO, VICTOR PAUL, artist, gallery administrator; b. Albany, Calif., Oct. 30, 1945; s. Victor A. and Betty Jean (Smith) Pearson; 1 dau., Denise Michelle. BA in Psychology, Calif. State U.-Sacramento, 1969, MA in Art, 1972. Instr. art Calif. State U., 1972-74; asst. to dir. Nancy Hoffman Gallery, NYC, 1974-78; dir. art gallery Wake Forest U., Winston-Salem, NC, 1978—, art faculty, 1983—. Founding mem. multi-media performance group Three People, 1990. One-person shows include Millennium, 1996, 2003, Mus. Modern Art, N.Y.C., 1975, Collective for Living Cinema, N.Y.C., 1976, Phyllis Kind Gallery, N.Y.C., 1980, 82, 87, 2004, N.C. Mus. Art, 1986, Helander Gallery, N.Y.C., 1991, Millennium Film Workshop, N.Y.C., 1996, 2003, Cleve. Performance Art Festival, 1998, Southeastern Ctr. for Contemporary Art, N.C., 1999, Madison (Wis.) Art Ctr., 2000, Louise Ross Gallery, 2007; group shows include Whitney Mus. Am. Art, 1972, 73, 74, Mus. Modern Art, N.Y.C., 1978, Barbara Gladstone Gallery, N.Y.C., 1983, Monique Knowlton Gallery, N.Y.C., 1983, Helander Gallery, Palm Beach, Fla., 1988, 90, Am. Visionary Art Mus., Md., 2002; represented in film study collection Mus. Modern Art, N.Y.C., Philip Morris, Inc.; animated film maker: Shameless, 1974. N.Y. CAPS fellow, 1977; N.C. Arts Coun. fellow, 1982, 86, 2000; recipient 1st prize NYU Small Works Competition, 1983. Home: 1950 Cliffside Dr Pfafftown NC 27040-9507 Office: Wake Forest U PO Box 7232 Winston Salem NC 27109-7232 Home Phone: 336-924-6086; Office Phone: 336-758-5795. Business E-Mail: faccinto@wfu.edu.

FACCIOLA, JOHN MICHAEL, judge; b. Bklyn., Apr. 28, 1945; s. Leo and Antoinette Facciola; m. Gloria J. Carroll, June 27, 1970; children: John, Daniel. BA cum laude in History, Coll. Holy Cross, Worcester, Mass., 1966; JD, Georgetown U., Washington, 1968. Bar: NY 1970, DC 73. Asst. dist. atty., NYC, 1969—73; ptnr. Wikinson, Cagegun & Banker, Washington, 1979—82; asst. atty. US Atty. DC, 1982—97; magistrate judge US Dist Ct. DC, 1997—. Adj. prof. Georgetown U., Washington, 1985—95, Cath. U. Law Sch., Washington, 1995—2006. Editor in chief: Fed. Cts. Law Rev. Sgt. US Army, 1969—75. Recipient Outstanding Alumnus award, Asst. US Attys. Assn., 2003, Caritas award, Cath. Cmty. Svc., Washington, 2007. Mem.: William Bryant Inn of Ct. (pres. 2003—06), John Carrol Soc. (pres. 2004—05), Lawyers Club, Cosmos Club. Roman Catholic. Avocations: sailing, photography. Office: US Courthouse 333 Constitution Ave Washington DC 20001

FACE, E. JOSEPH, JR., state agency administrator; b. Columbia, SC; married; 2 children. Grad., U. Ala., Ctrl. Mich. U. With Va. State Corp. Commn. Bur. Fin. Instns., Richmond, 1979—, dep. commr., 1993—99, commr., 1999—. Rep. state regulators Operation Jump-Start Coalition, Am. Fin. Svcs. Assn. and NACCA; mem. com. computerized loan origination working group US Dept. Housing and Urban Devel.; spkr. in field. Contbr. articles to profl. jours. Office: Bur Fin Instns PO Box 640 Richmond VA 23218-0640 Office Phone: 804-371-9657. Office Fax: 804-371-9416. E-mail: joe.face@scc.virginia.gov.*

FACHNIE, H(UGH) DOUGLAS, film manufacturing company official; b. Windsor, Ont., Can., Sept. 8, 1952; arrived in U.S., 1958; s. Harold Lennox Fachnie and Mary Jane (Schultz) MacKenzie. B Gen. Studies, U. Mich., 1973. Salesman Quarry, Inc., Ann Arbor, Mich., 1974, store mgr. Ann Arbor and Saginaw, Mich., 1974-77; dist. mgr. Fotomat Corp., San Diego, 1977-80, dir. ops. Wilton, Conn., 1980-81, dir. merchandising, 1981-83; mgr. optical products Fuji Photo Film U.S.A., Inc., NYC, 1983-84, product mgr. consumer film Elmsford, NY, 1984-89, sr. product/packaging mgr. film and one-time use cameras, 1989-94, mktg. mgr. consumer photo, 1995-97, 98-00; comml. planning and logistics mgr. profl. and photofinishing Fuji Phot Film USA, Inc., Elmsford, NY, 1998-2000, dir. mktg., color paper and chems., comml. imaging divsn., 2000—. Mem. AAAS, Photog. Mktg. Assn., Digital Imaging Mktg. Assn., Am. Prodn. and Inventory Control Soc., Profl. Photographers Assn. Republican. Avocations: home maintenance, flying, photography, audiophile, curling. Home: 30 Fleetwood Dr Danbury CT 06810-7010 Office: Fujiphoto Film Usa 200 Summit Lake Dr Fl 2 Valhalla NY 10595-1360 E-mail: d.fachnie@att.net.

FACKNER, ROBERT E., protective services official, consultant; b. Bklyn., Feb. 25, 1940; s. Walter Thomas and Maureen Jane Fackner; m. Maureen Jane Levergne, Oct. 13, 1943; children: John, Michael, Jayne. BS in Fire Sci., John Jay Coll., NYC, 1976. Fireman NYC Fire Dept., 1967—83, fire marshal, 1983—86, supervising fire marshal, 1986—91; ret. Self-employed fire investigator, cons., NYC, 1991—, Nassau, NY, 1991—. With USN, 1957—61. Recipient Emily Trevor medal, NYC Fire Dept., 1976, Susan Wagner medal, 1979. Republican. Roman Catholilc.

FACTOR, MAX, III, mediator, arbitrator; b. LA, Sept. 25, 1945; s. Sidney B. and Dorothy F.; BA in Econs. magna cum laude, Harvard U., 1966; JD, Yale U., 1969. Bar: Calif. 1970, US Ct. Appeals (6th cir.) 1971, US Dist. Ct. (ctrl. dist.) Calif. 1971. Law clk. US Ct. Appeals (6th cir.), 1969-71; exec. dir. Calif. Law Ctr., LA, 1973-74; dir. Consumer Protection Sect., Los Angeles City Atty., 1974-77; pvt. practice Factor & Agay, Beverly Hills, Calif, 1978-94; full-time neutral Factor Mediation and Arbitration Svcs., 2000-. Expert witness numerous state and fed. bds., 1974-78; guest lectr. UCLA, U. So. Calif., LA County Bar Assn., Calif. Dept. Consumer Affairs, 1974-76; hearing examiner City of LA, 1975. Contbr. articles to profl. jours. Bd. dirs. Western Law Ctr. for Handicapped, LA, 1977-79, Beverly Hills Unified Sch. Dist., 1979-83; pres. Beverly Hills Bd. Edn., 1983; bd. councilors U. Southern Calif. Law Ctr., LA, 1983—; chmn. Beverly Hills Visitors Bur., 1989-90. Recipient scholarship award Harvard Coll., 1965; Max Factor III Day proclaimed in his honor Beverly Hills City Council, 1979; recipient Disting. Service to Pub. Edn. award Beverly Hills Bd. Edn., 1979; named one of Southern Calif. Top Neutrals, Best Lawyers Am. and Super Lawyers, 2005, 06, 07. Fellow Internat. Acad. Mediators; mem. State Bar Calif. (chair com. on adminstrn. of justice 2006-07), LA County Bar Assn. (chmn. various coms. 1976-78), Southern Calif. Mediation Assn. (pres. 2005-06), Beverly Hills C. of C. (pres. 1987-88), Beverly Hills Edn. Found. (pres. 1977-79). Office: Factor Mediation and Arbitration Svcs 21355 Pacific Coast Hwy Ste 200 Malibu CA 90265 Office Phone: 310-456-3500. Business E-Mail: max@factormediation.com.

FADARE, OLUWOLE, pathologist, researcher, director; s. Adebayo and Ajoke Fadare. BS in Biology magna cum laude, U. DC, Washington, 1995, AASc in Bus. Adminstrn. in summa cum laude, 1996; MD, Howard U., 2000. Cert. in anatomic clin. pathology Am. Bd. Pathology, 2005. Clin. fellow in breast and gynecologic pathology Sch. Medicine Yale U., New Haven, 2004—05; attending pathologist dept. pathology Wilford Hall Med. Ctr., Lackland AFB, Tex., 2005—, assoc. med. dir. transfusion svcs. dept. pathology San Antonio, 2005—. Contbr. over 60 articles to profl. jours. Maj. USAF, 2005, Lackland AFB. Recipient Arthur H. Webb award, U. DC, 1995. Fellow: US and Can. Acad. Pathologists, Am. Soc. Clin. Pathologists, Coll. Am. Pathologists, Internat. Soc. Breast Pathologists, Internal Soc. Gynecol. Pathologists. Office: Wilford Hall Med Ctr Dept Pathology 2200 Bergquist Dr Ste 1 Lackland Afb TX 78236 Home Phone: 203-687-7422. Personal E-mail: oluwolefadare@yahoo.com.

FADDEN, SISTER R. PATRICIA, academic administrator, nun; b. Canonsburg, Pa. d. Gerald and Ruth Fadden. AB in Math., Immaculata Coll.; MA in Edn., Ohio State U.; EdD in Edn., Immaculata Coll. Tchr. elem. sch., 1960—68; tchr. West Cath. H.S. Girls, 1968—77; dir. of studies Cardinal O'Hara H.S., 1977—85; prin. Archbishop Prendergast H.S., Upper Darby, Pa., 1985—90; dir. secondary curriculum and instr. Office of Edn. Archdiocese of Phila., 1991—99; prin. Villa Maria Acad., Malvern, Pa., 1999—2002; pres. Immaculata U., Immaculata, Pa., 2002—. Mem. bd. trustees Immaculata Coll., 1991—2000, adj. faculty, 1991—2000; vice chair exec. com. Commn. on Secondary Schs. Mid. States Assn., mem. strategic planning com., mem. com. on instn.-wide accreditation, mem. com. to restructure; chair IHM Profl. Devel. Com., 1995—2000. Office: Immaculata Coll 1145 King Rd Immaculata PA 19345

FADELL, ANTHONY M. (TONY), computer company executive; BS in Computer Engring., U. Mich., 1991. Software engr., salesman, tech. support engr. Quality Computers, Inc., Grosse Point, Calif., 1986—89; design engr. Ronan, Inc., Woodland Hills, Calif., 1989; founder, sys. dir., rschr. U. Mich., Ann Arbor, Mich., 1988—91; founder, pres., ASIC HW engr. ASIC Enterprises, Inc., Westlake Village, Calif., 1989—92; founder, pres. Constructive Instruments, Inc., Ann Arbor, Mich., 1991—92; diagnostics engr. General Magic, Inc., Sunnyvale, Calif., 1992, hardware & software engr., 1992—94, system architect, 1994—95; contractor, sr. SW engr. Rocket Science, Inc., 1994—95; founder, CTO, dir. engring., dir. bus. develop. Phillips Consumer Electronics, Mobile Computing Group, 1995—98; v.p. bus. develop. Phillips Consumer Electronics, Strategy & Ventures U.S.A., 1998—99; independent mgmt. cons. Beatnik, Inc., 1999; founder, CEO Fuse Systems, Inc., 1999—2000; contractor Apple Computer, Inc., Cupertino, Calif., 2001, sr. dir., iPod & other spl. projects, 2001—04, v.p., iPod engring., 2004—06, sr. v.p., iPod divsn., 2006—. Named one of 50 Who Matter Now, Business 2.0, 2007. Achievements include patents in field. Office: Apple Computer Inc 1 Infinite Loop Cupertino CA 95014 Fax: 650-233-8247. E-mail: tony@fadell.ca.*

FADELY, JAMES PHILIP, writer, educator; b. New Castle, Ind., Jan. 10, 1953; s. Harry Ellison and Viola (Clapp) F.; m. Sally Jane Fehsenfeld, Aug. 16, 1975; children: James Philip Jr., Adele Langsdale. BA, Hanover Coll., 1975; MA, Ind. U., 1977, PhD, 1990. Tchr. Brookstone Sch., Columbus, Ga., 1975-76, Savannah (Ga.) Country Day Sch., 1979-83; lectr. Ind. U., Indpls., 1984—2000; tchr., asst. headmaster St. Richard's Sch., Indpls., 1988-90, tchr., 1990-91, dir. admission and fin. aid, tchr., 1991-2000; dir. mktg. and pub. rels. Univ. H.S., 2000—05, tchr. history, 2000—, dir. coll. counseling, 2000—. V.p. Ind. Libr. and Hist. Bd., 1997—2005, Ind. State Libr. and Hist. Bur. Found., 2004—; lectr. Butler U., 1985, U. Indpls., 1995. Author: A Brief History of St. Richard's School, 1960-1995, 1995, Thomas Taggart: Public Servant, Political Boss, 1856-1929, 1997, The Origins of Woodstock Club, 1997; contbr. articles to profl. jours. Dem. nominee 6th Dist. of Ind. for Congress, 1990; friend Woodrow Wilson House, Conner Prairie living history mus.; mem. Friends of Hist. Deerfield, Mass. Mem.: Ind. Assn. for Coll. Admission Counseling (exec. bd. 2006—), Historic New Harmony, Indpls. Mus. Art, Hist. Madison, Nat. Assn. Coll. Admission Counseling, Ind. Hist. Soc. (mem. com. jrs. 1992—2002, mem. com. bd. resources 2002—, grant 1991—94), Ind. Assn. Historians, Hist. Landmarks Found. Ind., Nat. Coun. for History Edn., Am. Hist. Assn., Leelanau Conservancy, Naples Hist. Soc., Naples Bot. Garden, Ind. U. Alumni Assn., Eng. Speaking Union (chmn. membership Indpls. (Ind.) br. 1994—98, chmn. membership region VI 1996—99, nat. bd. dirs. 1997—2003, exec. com. 1998—2001, pres. Indpls. br. 2002—), Leelanau Hist. Soc., Hanover Coll. Alumni Assn. (bd. dirs. 1985—88), Soc. Ind. Pioneers (bd. govs. 2002—), Marion County Hist. Soc. (treas. 1985—86, bd. dirs. 1985—98), Nat. Trust for Hist. Preservation, Woodstock Club, Hanover Club Indpls. (bd. dirs. 1988—96), Indpls. Lit. Club, Leland (Mich.) Yacht Club, Phi Delta Theta. Democrat. Roman Catholic. Avocation: travel. Home: 9146 N Kenwood Dr Indianapolis IN 46260-1400 Office: Univ HS 2825 W 116th St Carmel IN 46032-8730 Office Phone: 317-733-4475. Personal E-mail: jpfadely@comcast.net.

FADER, BRUCE E., lawyer; b. Bklyn., Nov. 6, 1948; BS in Acctg. cum laude, CUNY, 1970; JD cum laude, Bklyn. Law Sch., 1974. Bar: NY 1975, US Dist Ct, NY Eastern Dist, Southern Dist 1975, US Dist Ct., Calif., Northern Dist. 1982, US Ct Appeals, Second Circuit 1984, US Ct Appeals, Seventh Circuit 1993, US Ct Appeals, Federal Circuit 1993, US Supreme Ct. 2000, US Ct. Appeals, Third Circuit 2002. Law clk. to Hon. Edward R. Neaher U.S. Dist. Ct. (ea. dist.) N.Y., 1974-76; mem. exec. com., atty. litigation & dispute resolution dept. Proskauer Rose LLP, NYC, 1976—. Notes editor Bklyn. Law Rev., 1973-74. Mem.: Am. Judicature Soc., NY Bar Assn. Office: Proskauer Rose LLP 1585 Broadway Fl 27 New York NY 10036-8299

FADER, HENRY CONRAD, lawyer; b. Bronx, NY, Dec. 2, 1946; s. Michael and Ruth (Filler) F.; m. Linda L. Koch, Nov. 23, 1969; children: Melanie, Danielle. AB, U. Rochester, NYC, 1968; MEd, Temple U., 1970; JD, Syracuse U., NY, 1973. Bar: Pa. 1973, U.S. Dist. Ct. (ea. dist.) Pa. 1973, N.J. 1988. Ptnr. Schnader, Harrison, Segal & Lewis, Phila., 1992—2003, chmn. health law dept., 1993—2003; ptnr. Pepper Hamilton LLP, Phila., 2003—. Chmn. bd. dirs. Pa. Chamber Bus. and Industry, 2004—. Vice chmn. Pa. Health Care Cost Containment Coun., 2004—; bd. dirs., solicitor Eagleville (Pa.) Hosp., 1987—; chmn. bd. dirs. Intercultural Family Svcs., Inc., 1998—. Mem. ABA, Pa. Bar Assn., Phila. Bar Assn., Nat. Assn. Bond Lawyers, Am. Health Lawyers Assn. Avocations: tennis, reading, gardening. Office: Pepper Hamilton LLP 3000 Two Logan Sq 18th and Arch Sts Philadelphia PA 19103 Office Phone: 215-981-4640. Business E-Mail: faderh@pepperlaw.com.

FADIMAN, ANNE, writer, educator; b. NYC, Aug. 7, 1953; d. Clifton and Annalee Whitmore (Jacoby) F.; m. George Howe Colt, Mar. 4, 1989; children: Susannah, Henry. BA, Harvard U., 1975. Contbr. editor Harvard Magazine, Cambridge, Mass., 1973-75; instr. Nat. Outdoor Leadership Sch., Lander, Wyo., 1975-76; columnist Country Journal, Manchester, N.H., 1978-79; asst. sci. editor Life, NYC, 1979-81, columnist, 1986-87, staff writer, 1981-88; columnist, editor-at-large Civilization, Washington, 1994—97; editor-in-chief The Am. Scholar, Washington, 1997—2004; Francis writer-in-residence Yale U., New Haven, 2005—. Bd. incorporators Harvard Magazine, Cambridge, Mass., 1985— (bd. dirs., 1985-91), vis. lectr. Smith Coll., 2000-02. Author: The Spirit Catches You and You Fall Down, 1997 (Nat. Book Critics Circle award for nonfiction, 1997, LA Times Book Prize for Current Interest, 1997, Ann Rea Jewell Non-Fiction Prize, Boston Book Rev., 1997), Ex Libris: Confessions of a Common Reader, 1998, At Large and At Small: Familiar Essays, 2007; editor: Best American Essays 2003, 2003, Rereadings, 2005. Recipient Nat. Magazine award for Reporting, Am. Soc. Magazine Editors, 1987, Nat. Mag. award for essays, 2003; named John S. Knight fellow in Journalism Stanford (Calif.) U., 1991-92. Mem. Phi Beta Kappa (hon.).

FADIMBA, KOFFI BAANA, mathematics professor; s. Banena and Ahouda Fadimba; m. Foga Boma Atta, Aug. 25, 1986; children: Bogmsa, Jennifer Wenmi, Marie-Salveria Pehessi. BS (Licence) in Math., U. Bordeaux I, Talence, France, 1980; MS (DEA) in Math. and Applications, U. of Bordeaux I, Talence, France, 1982; PhD in Math., U. SC, Columbia, 1993. Jr. lectr. U. Lome, Togo, 1983—88, tenured asst. prof., 1994—2000; post doctoral fellow Inst. Sci. Computations Tex. A&M, College Station, 1994; vis. scholar, lectr. U. RI, Kingston, 2000—02; asst. prof. math. U. SC, Aiken, 2002—. Contbr. profl. papers to math. jours. Pres. Assn. Sons. and Daus. from Kongah Residing in Lome, Togo, 1995—96. Grantee, U. SC, Aiken, 2004, Rsch. and Productive Scholarship award, U. SC, 2005; Fond d'Aide et de Cooperation fellow, Ministry of Cooperation, France, 1986—88, African Grad. fellow, Africa Am. Inst., NYC, 1988—93, post doctoral fellow, U. SC, Columbia, 1993. Mem.: Reseau Africain de Mathematiques Appliquees pour le Developpement, Math. Assn. Am., Soc. Indsl. and Applied Math., Am. Math. Soc. Home: 30 Early Ct Aiken SC 29803 Office: Univ SC - Aiken 471 University Pky Aiken SC 29801 Home Phone: 803-641-7561; Office Phone: 803-641-3537. Office Fax: 803-641-3726; Home Fax: 803-641-3726. Personal E-mail: koffif@usca.edu.

FAFIAN, JOSEPH, JR., management consultant; b. NYC, 1939; s. Joseph M. and Mary (Alonso) F.; m. Nathalie Coluccio, Oct. 5, 1963; children: John Joseph, Michael Francis. BA, Bklyn. Coll., 1959. Assoc. actuary U.S. Life Ins. Co., NYC, 1967; 2d v.p. USLIFE Corp., 1967-69, v.p., 1969-72, sr. v.p. ops., 1972-76, exec. v.p. life ins., 1976-77, sr. exec. v.p. life ins., 1977-78; pres., chief exec. officer, dir. U.S. Life, 1978-80; pres., dir. Beneficial Nat. Life Ins. Co., NYC, 1980-82, chmn. bd., CEO, 1982-84; founder, pres., CEO, Fafian and Assocs., Inc., SI, NY, 1984—. Dir. Assoc. Madison, pres., COO, 1982-84; acting pres. Maine & Fidelity Life Ins. Co., 1985-86; bd. dirs. Columbia Life. Served with N.G., 1962-67. Fellow Soc. Actuaries; mem. Acad. Actuaries. Home: 74 Mason St Staten Island NY 10304-3106 Office Phone: 718-727-0880. E-mail: jfafian@aol.com. *Guide my actions by three principles: Always be proud of what I am doing; Always seek to improve what I am doing; Always learn more about what I am doing.*

FAGALY, WILLIAM ARTHUR, curator; b. Lawrenceburg, Ind., Mar. 1, 1938; s. William James and Dorothy Rae (Wheeler) F. BA, Ind. U., Bloomington, 1962, MA, 1967. Asst. registrar Art Mus., Ind. U., Bloomington, 1965-66; registrar New Orleans Mus. Art, 1966—67, curator collections, 1967-73, chief curator, 1973-80, asst. dir for art, 1980-2001, Francoise Billion Richardson curator African art, 1997—; curator art U. Art Mus. U. La. Lafayette, 2002—03. Guest curator La. Folk Painting exhibit, Mus. Am. Folk Art, 1973, Exhbn. of Contemporary Painting, Corcoran Gallery of Art, Washington, 1989, Preacher Art, Arthur Roger Gallery, New Orleans, 1990, Geography of the Body: The Art of Mignon Faget, Contemporary Arts Ctr., 1995, Preacher Art, Phyllis Kind Gallery, NYC, 1997, Watercolor U.S.A. 1999, Springfield Art Mus., Mo., 1999, Nat. Works on Paper, McNeese State U., Lake Charles, La., It's a Wonderful World, Contemporary Arts Ctr., New Orleans, 2003, Aristides Logothetis, Cue Art Found., NYC, 2003, Tools of Her Ministry: The Art of Sister Gertrude Morgan, Am. Folk Art Mus., 2004, Resonance from the Past: African Sculpture from the New Orleans Mus. of Art, Mus. for African Art, NYC, 2005; adv. panel visual arts and crafts divsn. arts La. Arts Coun., 1978—81, 1992; guest lectr. S.S. Rotterdam, 1983, H.M.S. Queen Elizabeth II, 1986, Sotheby's, NY, 1996; cons. Liberian Pavilion La. World Expn., 1984, Shapes of Power, Belief and Celebration: African Art from New Orleans Collections, 1989, Fritz Bultman: A Retrospective, 1993, Wyo. Art Mus., Laramie, 1995, Oreg. Biennial, Portland Art Mus., 1995, Roots of Am. Jazz: African Mus. Instruments from New Orleans Collections, 1995, He's the Prettiest: A Tribute to Big Chief Allison "Tootie," Montana's 50 Yrs. of Mardi Gras Indian Suiting, Inside the Congo: An Introduction to the Field Rsch. Archives of Frere Joseph Cornet, New Orleans Mus. Art and Monroe Libr., Loyola U., New Orleans, 2006; selection panelist McKnight Found. Fellowship Program, Minn. Coll. Arts and Design, Mpls., 1986, So. Arts Fedn., NEA Arts Regional Artists Fellowships, 1990; selecton panelist 1984 Visual Arts Fellowships, Wyo. Arts Coun., 1993; selection panelist Adolph and Esther Gottlieb Found. Artist Fellowships, NYC, 1995, Western States Art Fedn./NEA, 1996; bd. dirs. Ctr. for African and African-Am. Studies, So. U., New Orleans, Sac-O-Lait-The Keith Sonnier Found., 2002—, Prospect 1 First Internat. US Biennial, New Orleans, 2007; bd. advisors Wilkinson County Mus., Woodville, Miss.; adj. curator Univ. Art Mus., U. La., Lafayette, 2002—; founder art activities bus. FUN (Fagaly Unltd.), 2001—. Contbr. articles to profl. jours. NEA fellow, 1985, Visual Arts and Media fellow Miss. Arts Commn., 1994, Visual Arts fellow Wyo. Art Coun., 1994; recipient Mayor's Arts award City of New Orleans, 1997, Gov.'s Arts award La. State Arts Coun., 1997, Charles E. Dunbar Jr. Career Svc. award La. Civil Svc. League, 1999, Isaac Delgado Meml. award Fellows of New Orleans Mus. of Art, 2001, Chevalier de l'Ordre des Arts et des Lettres, République Française, 2006. Mem. Am. Assn. Mus. (mem. vis. com. for Tampa Mus. Art accreditation program 1999). Episcopalian. Office: PO Box 19123 New Orleans LA 70179-0123 Business E-Mail: bfagaly@noma.org.

FAGAN, ALANNA, artist, printmaker; b. New Bedford, Mass., 1939; Student, U. Bridgeport, 1963—65, Silvermine Guild Sch. Art, 1965. Painting instr. Silvermine Guild Sch. Art, New Canaan, Conn., 1977—81. Author: (filmstrip) Drawing Animals, 1981, Drawing People, 1981; one-woman shows include Salmagundi Club, NY, 1975, Northeast Harbor Gallery, Maine, 1980, Silvermine Guild Arts Ctr., Conn., 1981, 1986, Fairfield U., 1983, Greene Art Gallery, 1986, Darien Pub. Libr., 1986, Les Castelets, St. Barthelemy, 1988, 1991, La Galerie, 1992, exhibited in group shows at Pastel Soc. Am., NY, 1974—92, Springfield Art Mus., Mass., 1975, Salmagundi Club, NY, 1975—77, Art of the Northeast, Conn., 1977, 1984—85, 1995, 1999—2000, Circle Gallery, NY, 1978, Copley Mus., Mass., 1979, Central Falls Gallery, NY, 1984, Galerie du Mus., Paris, 1985, Nat. Acad. Design, NY, 1986, Greene Art Gallery, Conn., 1986, Westport Arts Ctr., 1988—2007, Allied Artist Am., NY, 1989—91, Craven Gallery, Mass., 1997, Ctr. for Contemporary Printmaking, Conn., 1997—2007, Am. Watercolor Soc., 1997, Stamford Art Assn., Conn., 1998, Brush and Palette Club, 2002, Silvermine Guild, 2003—04, New Haven Paint and Clay Club, 2005—06, Silvermine Guild, 2007, Represented in permanent collections Harvard Club, NY, New Eng. Sch. Law, Mass., Cohen and Wolf PC, Conn., Ctr. for Creative Leadership, NC, Inst. Geografico de Agostini, Italy. Mem.: Ctr. for Contemporary Printmaking, Westport Arts Ctr., Silvermine Guild Artists, Allied Artists Am., New Haven (Conn.) Paint and Clay Club. Home: 73 Housatonic Dr Milford CT 06460 Personal E-mail: alaleo@snet.net.

FAGAN, DREW STEPHEN, language educator; s. Stephen Francis and Diane Marie Fagan. Cert. in Spanish translation, BA, Am. U., Washington, 2001; MA, San Diego State U., 2005; EdD, Columbia U., NYC, 2006. Translator, intern Embassy of Spain, Washington, 1999—2000; translator Vincent Ferrer Found., Madrid, 2000; English tchr., tchr. trainer NOVA Group, Tokyo, 2001—03; grad. tchg. assoc. San Diego State U., 2003—05; Fulbright fellow, lectr. J. William Fulbright Commn., Nitra, Slovakia, 2005—06; lectr. CUNY- LaGuardia CC, Long Island City, NY, 2006—. Guest English lang. lectr. Wuhan U., Wuhan, China, 2005; guest English lang. tchr. trainer Autonomous U. So. Baja Calif., La Paz, Mexico, 2005; presenter in field. Mem.: TESOL, NY State TESOL, Am. Assn. Applied Linguistics, Calif. TESOL, Nat. Italian Am. Found. D-Liberal. Achievements include research in discourse analysis and second language acquisition. Avocations: travel, cooking, languages, hiking. Personal E-mail: dsf2114@columbia.edu.

FAGAN, JOHN ERNEST, lawyer; b. Phila., June 30, 1949; s. George Vincent and Ernestine (Hudak) F. BA with highest honors, U. Notre Dame, 1971; JD, Northwestern U., 1974; LLM, NYU, 1986. Bar: Ill. 1974, Wis. 1977, N.Y. 1979, Va. 1991. Assoc. McDermott Will & Emery, Chgo., 1974-76; internat. tax analyst Allis-Chalmers Corp., Milw., 1976-78; tax counsel Mobil Corp., NYC and Fairfax, Va., 1978-99, Exxon Mobil Corp., Fairfax, 2000—. Author: The Teachings of Pope John Paul II, 2006. Mem. Am. Petroleum Inst. (com. mem.). Office: Exxon Mobil Corp 3225 Gallows Rd Rm 3C2129 Fairfax VA 22037-0002 E-mail: john.e.fagan@exxonmobil.com.

FAGAN, SHAWN FRANCIS, investment company executive; b. Detroit, Apr. 12, 1969; s. Hugh Francis Fagan and Sonja Bruna Dalla Vecchia; m. Laura Glickson, Aug. 5, 1999; children: Hadley Hope, Morgan Ashley. BA, U. Mich., Ann Arbor, 1991; JD, Harvard U., Cambridge, Mass., 1994. Bar: Ill. Clk. Jeoge DH Ginsburg, Washington, 1994—95, Chief Justice William H. Rehnanit, Washington, 1995—96; pntr. Bartlit Beck Herman Palenchar and Scott, Chgo., 1996—2005; mng. dir. Citadel Investment Group, Chgo., 2005—. Named one of Top 15 Litigation in Ill., 2005; named to 40 Attys. under 40 to watch, Ill. Bar Mag., 2004; recipient Seans Prize, Harvard Law Sch., 1992. Office: Citadel Investment Group 131 S Dearborn Chicago IL 60603

FAGEL, BRUCE G., lawyer, former emergency physician; b. Chgo., Oct. 11, 1946; BA with high honors, U. Ill., 1968; MD, U. Ill. Coll. Medicine, 1972; JD with high honors, Whittier Coll. Sch. Law, LA, 1982. Bar: Calif. 1982; lic. to practice medicine Ill., 1973, Calif., 1975. Practiced emergency medicine, 1972—82; atty. Bruce G. Fagel & Associates., Beverly Hills, Calif., 1982—. Seminar spkr. Consumer Attys. Calif., Consumer Attys. Assocs. LA. Author: Liberty on Hold, Families of Victims Need Help Not Lawsuits; guest appearances on CBS, NBC & ABC, featured in LA Times, Sacramento Bee, Oakland Tribune. Mem. Birth Trauma Litigation Group, Inner Circle of Advocates. Capt., medical corps, USAF, 1974—76. Nominee Trial Lawyer of Yr. (6 Times); named one of Top 10 Litigators, Nat. Law Jour., 2003. Fellow: Am. Coll. of Law and Medicine; mem.: LA County Med. Assn., Calif. Med. Assn., Assn. of Trial Lawyers Am., ABA, President's Club of Consumer Attorneys Assn. of LA, Calif., Phi Beta Kappa. Office: Bruce G Fagel Assocs 100 N Cresent Dr Ste 360 Beverly Hills CA 90210 Office Phone: 310-281-8700. Business E-Mail: bgfagel@aol.com.

FAGEN, LESLIE GORDON, lawyer; b. NYC, Apr. 12, 1950; s. Herman and Estelle F. BA, Yale U., 1971; JD, Columbia U., 1974. Bar: N.Y. 1975, D.C. 1985, U.S. Dist. Ct. (so. and ea. dists.) N.Y. 1975, U.S. Ct. Appeals (2d cir.) 1975, U.S. Ct. Appeals (3d cir.) 1991, U.S. Ct. Appeals (7th and fed. cirs.) 1993; U.S. Supreme Ct. 1978. Law clk to judge U.S. Dist. Ct. (ea. dist.) N.Y., Bklyn., 1975; assoc. Milbank, Tweed, Hadley & McCloy, NYC, 1975-76; from assoc. to ptnr. Paul, Weiss, Rifkind, Wharton & Garrison, NYC, 1976—, co-chair litigation dept. Former adj. faculty Cardozo Law Sch., CCNY. Vice-chmn., pres. and trustee The Ednl. Alliance, Inc., 1993-2000; bd. dirs. Maimonides Med. Ctr., 2001-05. Fellow Am. Coll. Trial Lawyers; mem. N.Y. State Bar Assn., Assn. Bar City N.Y. Office: Paul Weiss Rifkind Wharton & Garrison 1285 Avenue Of The Americas New York NY 10019-6028

FAGER, JEFFREY, broadcast executive; b. Wellesley, Mass., Dec. 10, 1954; m. Melinda Fager; 3 children. B in Eng. and polit. sci., Colgate U., 1977. Prodn. asst. Sta. WBZ-TV, Boston, 1977—78; news writer Sta. WEEI Radio, Boston, 1978—79; assignment editor Sta. WGBH-TV, Boston, 1978—79; broadcast prodr. Sta. KPIX-TV, San Francisco, 1979—82; prodr. various broadcasts including weekend edit. CBS Evening News and Nightwatch CBS News, 1982—84; prodr. CBS Evening News, NYC, 1984—85, London, 1985—88, 48 Hours, NYC, 1988—89, 60 Minutes, 1989—94; sr. broadcast prodr. CBS Evening News, 1994—96; exec. prodr. CBS Evening News with Dan Rather, 1996—98, 60 Minutes II, 1998—2004, 60 Minutes, 2004—. Recipient Best TV Series or Spl.: Non-Fiction (60 Minutes), Producers Guild Am., 2006, Prodr. of Yr. award in Non-Fiction TV (60 Minutes), 2007. Office: 60 Minutes 524 W 57th St New York NY 10019 Office Phone: 212-975-3247.*

FAGERBERG, ROGER RICHARD, lawyer; b. Chgo., Dec. 11, 1935; s. Richard Emil and Evelyn (Thor) F.; m. Virginia Fuller Vaughan, June 20, 1959; children: Steven Roger, Susan Vaughan, James Thor, Laura Craft. BS in Bus. Adminstrn., Washington U., St. Louis, 1958, JD, 1961, postgrad., 1961-62. Bar: Mo. 1961. Grad. teaching asst. Washington U., St. Louis, 1961-62; assoc. firm Rassieur, Long & Yawitz, St. Louis, 1962-64; ptnr. Rassieur, Long, Yawitz & Schneider and predecessor firms, St. Louis, 1965-91; pvt. practice St. Louis, 1991—. Mem. exec. com. Citizens' Adv. Council Pkwy. Sch. Dist., 1974—, pres.-elect, 1976-77, pres., 1977-78; bd. dirs. Parkway Residents Orgn., 1969—, v.p., 1970-73, pres., 1973—; scoutmaster Boy Scouts Am., 1979-83; Presbyn. elder, 1976—, pres. three local congs. 1968-70, 77-78, 83-84. Mem. ABA, Mo. Bar Assn., St. Louis Bar Assn., Christian Bus. Men's Com. (bd. dirs. 1975-78, 87-91), Full Gospel Bus. Men's Fellowship, Order of Coif, Omicron Delta Kappa, Beta Gamma Sigma, Pi Sigma Alpha, Phi Eta Sigma, Phi Delta Phi, Kappa Sigma. Lodges: Kiwanis (bd. dirs. 1988-91), Masons, Shriners. Republican. Home and Office: 13812 Clayton Rd Town And Country MO 63017-8407

FAGG, GEORGE GARDNER, federal judge; b. Eldora, Iowa, Apr. 30, 1934; s. Ned and Arleene (Gardner) Fagg; m. Jane E. Wood, Aug. 19, 1956; children: Martha, Thomas, Ned, Susan, George, Sarah. BSBA, Drake U., 1965, JD, 1958. Bar: Iowa 1958. Ptnr. Cartwright, Druker, Ryden & Fagg, Marshalltown, Iowa, 1958—72; judge Iowa Dist. Ct., 1972—82, US Ct. Appeals (8th cir.), 1982—99, sr. judge, 1999—. Faculty Nat. Jud. Coll., 1979. Mem.: Iowa Bar Assn., Order of Coif. Office: US Ct Appeals US Courthouse Annex 110 E Court Ave Ste 455 Des Moines IA 50309-2044*

FAGG, RUSSELL, judge, lawyer; b. Billings, Mont., June 26, 1960; s. Harrison Grover and Darlene (Bohling) F.; m. Karen Barclay, Feb. 15, 1992. BA, Whitman Coll., 1983; JD, U. Mont., 1986; MJS, U. Nev., 1999. Law clk. Mont. Supreme Ct., Helena, 1986-87; atty. Sandall Law Firm, Billings, 1987-89; city prosecutor City of Billings, 1989-91; dep. atty. Yellowstone County, Billings, 1991-94; mem. Mont. State Legislature, Helena, 1991-94; judge State Dist. Ct. (13th dist.) Mont., Billings, 1995—. Dir. Midland Empire Pachyderm Club, 1988-94, pres. 1990-91; chmn. judiciary com. House of Reps., 1993-94. Named Outstanding Young Montanan, Mont. Jaycees, 1994; recipient Young Life Spirit award Billings Young Life, 2002. Avocations: hiking, skiing, reading, tennis. Office: PO Box 35027 Billings MT 59107-5027 Home: 3053 Thousand Oaks St Billings MT 59102 Office Phone: 406-256-2906.

FAGGIN, FEDERICO, electronics executive; b. Vicenza, Italy, Dec. 1, 1941; arrived in U.S., 1968, naturalized, 1978; s. Giuseppe and Emma (Munari) Faggin; m. Elvia Sardei, Sept. 2, 1967; children: Marzia, Marc, Eric. Grad., Perito Industriale Instituto A. Rossi, Vicenza, 1960; D.Physics, U. Padua, Italy, 1965. Sect. head Fairchild Camera & Instrument Co., Palo Alto, Calif., 1968-70; dept. mgr. Intel Corp., Santa Clara, Calif., 1970-74; founder, pres. Zilog Inc., Cupertino, Calif., 1974-80; v.p. computer systems group Exxon Enterprises, NYC, 1981; co-founder, pres. Cygnet Techs., Inc., Sunnyvale, Calif., 1982-86; co-founder, CEO Synaptics, Inc., San Jose, Calif., 1986-99, chmn., 1999—; pres., CEO Foveon, Inc., 2003—. Named to Nat. Inventor's Hall of Fame, 1996; recipient W. Wallace McDowell award, IEEE Computer Soc., 1994, Kyoto prize, 1997, Lifetime Achievement award, European Patent Office, 2006; Marconi Fellowship award, 1988. Achievements include development of silicon gate technology for MOS fabrication, first microprocessor, Intel 4004, Intel8080, Intel4040, Intel8008, Intel 2102A, Zilog Z80 and Z8 microprocessors. Office: Foveon Inc 2820 San Tomas Expwy Santa Clara CA 95051 Business E-Mail: federico.faggin@foveon.com.

FAGIN, ALLEN IAN, lawyer; b. Bronx, NY, Oct. 22, 1949; s. Carl and Frieda (Ehrlich) F.; m. Judith H. Rosenberg, June 29, 1970; children: Robert, Charles. BA summa cum laude, Columbia Coll., NYC, 1971; MPP, Harvard U., 1975, JD cum laude, 1975. Bar: NY 1976, US Dist. Ct., NY Eastern & Southern Dist. 1977, US Ct Appeals, Second Circuit 1984, US Ct Appeals, Eleventh Circuit 1989, US Dist. Ct., NY Northern Dist. 1992, US Ct. Appeals, Sixth Circuit 1997, US Supreme Ct. 1998. Law clk. to Hon. Robert L. Carter U.S. Dist. Ct. (so. dist.) N.Y., 1975-76; assoc. Proskauer Rose LLP, NYC, 1976-83, ptnr., 1983—, former co-chair, labor & employment law dept, 1997—2004, now chmn., 2005—. Fellow: Coll. Labor & Employment Lawyers. Office: Proskauer Rose LLP 1585 Broadway Fl 20 New York NY 10036-8299

FAGIN, BARRY STEVEN, computer science educator, writer; b. Boston, Sept. 2, 1960; s. Arnold D. Fagin and Lois R. Roisman; m. Michele Berdinis Fagin, Aug. 11, 1985; children: Max, Erica. AB magna cum laude, Brown U., 1982; PhD, U. Calif., Berkeley, 1987. Asst. prof. engring. sci. Thayer Sch. of Engring., Dartmouth Coll., Hanover, N.H., 1987-94; prof. computer sci. USAF Acad., Colorado Springs, Colo., 1994—. Program annotator Colo. Springs Symphony, contbr. articles to profl. jours. Co-founder Families Against Internet Censorship, Colorado Springs, 1996—; former info. dir. ACM SIGCAS, N.Y.; mem. Rocky Mountain Skeptics, Colorado Springs. Recipient Civil Liberties award ACLU, 1996; sr. fellow Independence Inst.; Fulbright scholar St. Petersburg (Russia) Tech. State U., 2001. Jewish. Avocations: snowboarding, mountain climbing, scuba, freestyle frisbee, speaking Russian. Office: USAF Acad Dept Computer Sci 2354 Fairchild Dr Colorado Springs CO 80840 Office Phone: 719-333-7377. Fax: 719-333-3338. E-mail: barry.fagin@usafa.mil.

FAGIN, CLAIRE MINTZER, nursing administrator, educator; b. NYC; d. Harry and Mae (Slatin) Mintzer; m. Samuel Fagin, Feb. 17, 1952; children: Joshua, Charles. BS, Wagner Coll., 1948; MA, Tchrs. Coll. Columbia, 1951; PhD, NYU, 1964; DSc (hon.), Lycoming Coll., 1983, Cedar Crest Coll., 1987, U. Rochester, 1987, Med. Coll. Pa., 1989, U. Md., 1993, Wagner Coll., 1993, Loyola U., 1996, Case Western Res. U., 2002; LLD (hon.), U. Pa., 1994, U. Toronto, 2004; DHL (hon.), Hunter Coll., 1993, Rush U., 1996, Johns Hopkins U., 2003. Staff nurse, clin. instr. Sea View Hosp., SI, NY; clin. instr. Bellevue Hosp., NYC; psychiat. nurse cons. Nat. League for Nursing, NYC; asst. chief psychiat. nursing svc. clin. ctr. NIH; rsch. project coord. dept. psychiatry Children's Hosp., Washington; instr., assoc. prof. psychiat.-mental health nursing NYU, NYC, dir. grad. programs in psychiat. mental health nursing, 1965—69; chmn. nursing dept., prof. Herbert H. Lehman Coll., CUNY, NYC, 1969—77; dir. Health Professions Inst., Montefiore Hosp. and Med. Ctr., 1975—77; Margaret Bond Simon dean sch. of nursing U. Pa., Phila., 1977—92, Leadership chair prof., 1992—96, interim pres., 1993—94, dean emeritus, prof. emeritus, 1996—. Bd. dirs. Provident Mut. Ins. Co., 1988—96, chmn. audit com., 1985—96, exec. com., 1986—96, adv. com., 1996—2003; bd. dirs., mem. audit com. Salomon, Inc., 1994—97; bd. dirs., compensation Radian Inc., 1994—2002; bd. dirs. Vis. Nurse Soc., NY, Van Ameringen Found., 1996—2004, Nat. Sr. Citizens Law Ctr.; dir. program bldg. acad. geriatric nursing John A. Hartford Found., 2000—05; spkr., cons. in field. Contbr. articles to profl. jours. Named Disting. Dau. Pa., 1994; recipient Achievement award, Wagner Coll., 1956, Tchrs. Coll., 1975, Disting. Alumna award, NYU, 1979, Founders award, Sigma Theta Tau, 1981, Hon. Recognition award, ANA, 1988, Woman of Courage award, Women's Way, 1990, Alumni Merit award, U. Pa., 1991, First Leadership award, Trustee Coun. Pa. Women, 1991, Caring award, Phila. Vis. Nurses Assn., 1994, Lillian Wald award, N.Y. Vis. Nurses Assn., 1994, Hildegard Peplau award outstanding contbn. psych-nursing, 1994, Pres. medal, NYU, 1998, Nightingale Lamp award, Am. Nurses Found., 2002; disting. scholar, 1984, hon. fellow, Royal Coll. Nursing, 2002, nursing bldg. at U. Pa. named Claire M. Fagin Hall in her honor, 2006. Mem.: Am. Nurses Assn., Nat. League for Nursing (pres. 1991—93), Am. Orthopsychiat. Assn. (bd. dirs. 1972—75, exec. com. bd. dirs. 1973—75, pres. 1985—86), Am. Acad. Nursing (governing coun. 1976—78, Living Legend award 1998, Civitas award 2005), Inst. Medicine of NAS (governing coun. 1981—83, chmn. bd. health promotion and disease prevention 1991—94, mem./chair Lienhard Com. 1999—2004). Address: 200 Central Park S Apt 12E New York NY 10019-1415 Personal E-mail: cfagin@att.net.

FAGIN, DAN, science and environmental writer, reporter; b. Oklahoma City, Feb. 1, 1963; m. Alison Frankel; 2 children. AB, Dartmouth Coll., 1985. Polit. and govt. reporter Sarasota Herald-Tribune, 1985—87, Newsday, 1987—91, environ. writer, 1991—2005. Adj. prof. dept. journalism NYU, 1998—2004, assoc. prof. dept. journalism, 2005—, assoc. dir. sci., health, environ. reporting program. Co-author (with Marianne Lavelle): (books) Toxic Deception (finalist Investigative Reporters & Editors award), 1997. Recipient AAAS Journalism award, 2003. Mem.: Soc. of Environ. Journalists (pres. 2003—04, bd.mem. 2000—04). Office: NYU Dept Journalism Rm 301 10 Washington Pl New York NY 10003 Home Phone: 516-801-2477; Office Phone: 212-998-7971. E-mail: dan.fagin@nyu.edu.

FAGIN, DAVID KYLE, mining executive; s. Kyle Marshall and Frances Margaret (Gaston) F.; m. Margaret Anne Hazlett, Jan. 24, 1959 (dec. July 1999); children: David Kyle, Scott Edward; m. Terry Lee Craig, Dec. 6, 2002. BS in Petroleum Engring., U. Okla., 1960; postgrad., Am. Inst. Banking, So. Meth. U. Grad. Sch. Bus. Adminstrn. Registered profl. engr., La., Okla., Tex. Trainee Exxon-Mobil (formerly Magnolia Petroleum Co.), 1955—56; jr. engr., engr., then ptnr. W.C. Bednar Petroleum Cons., Dallas, 1958—65; petroleum engr. Bank of Am. N.A. (formerly First Nat. Bank Dallas), Dallas, 1965—68; v.p. Rosario Resources Corp. (merged 1980 with AMAX Inc.), NYC, 1968—75; pres. Alamo Petroleum Corp., 1968—82; exec. v.p. Rosario Resources Corp. (now Freeport McMoran Gold), NYC, 1975—77, dir., 1975—80, pres., COO, 1977—82; chmn., dir., pres., CEO Fagin Exploration Co., Denver, 1982—86; pres., COO, bd. dirs. Homestake Mining Co. (now Barrick Gold), Toronto, Ont., Canada, 1986—91; CEO & chmn. Golden Star Resources Ltd., Denver, 1992—96, dir., 1992—; chmn., CEO Western Exploration and Devel. Ltd., Denver, 1997—2000, dir., 1997—2001. Bd. dirs. T. Rowe Price Pub. Mut. Funds, Balt., Canyon Resources Corp., Denver, Golden Star Resources Corp., Denver. Bd. dirs. Denver Area coun. Boy Scouts Am., 1993—, Mineral Info. Inst.; bd. visitors U. Okla. Sch. Engring., 1995-98, 99—, chmn., 2002—04; Nat. Mining Hall of Fame and Mus., 1997—. Mem. AIME (chmn. Dallas sect. of Soc. Petroleum Engrs. 1975, chmn. investment fund 1979-82), Soc. Mining, Metallurgy and Exploration (dir. 1996-97), Soc. Petroleum Engrs., Mining and Metall. Soc. Am., Internat. Mining Profls. Soc. (dir., exec. com., v.p. 1999, pres. 2001-2002). Business E-Mail: dkfagin@aol.com.

FAGIN, STEPHEN ANDREW, historian; b. Dallas, Apr. 9, 1979; s. Stephen David and Debra Ann (Shaw) Fagin; m. Jessica Kimberly King, Oct. 26, 2001. BA, So. Meth. U., Dallas, 2001. Cast mem. Disney Store, Dallas, 1997—2003; oral history coord. Sixth Fl. Mus. at Dealey Plz., 2001—04, oral historian, 2004—. Speaker in field. Contbr. articles to profl. mags. and publs. Hon. bd. dir. Hist. Mesquite, Inc., Tex., 2001—. Mem.: Am. Assn. Mus., Tex. Assn. Mus., Oral Hist. Assn., Golden Key Hon. Soc., Phi Beta Kappa. Avocations: reading, writing, clarinet. Office: Sixth Fl Mus at Dealey Plaza 411 Elm St Ste 120 Dallas TX 75202 Office Phone: 214-747-6660 ext. 6678. Office Fax: 214-747-6662. Personal E-mail: stardeez@hotmail.com. Business E-Mail: stephenf@jfk.org.

FAGLES, ROBERT, classicist, educator, translator; b. Phila., Sept. 11, 1933; s. Charles and Vera Voynow Fagles; m. Marilyn Duchovnay, June 17, 1956; 2 children. BA, Amherst Coll., 1955; MA, Yale U., 1956, PhD in English, 1959. Instr. English Yale U., 1959—60, Princeton U., 1960—62, asst. prof., 1962—65, assoc. prof. English and comparative lit., 1965, dir. comparative lit. program, 1965, prof., 1970, founding dept. chmn. Dept. Comparative Lit., 1975—94, Arthur W. Marks '19 prof. comparative lit., prof. emeritus, 2002—. Translator: Complete Poems by Bacchylides, 1961, The Oresteia by Aeschylus, 1975, The Three Theban Plays by Sophocles, 1982, The Iliad by Homer, 1990 (Harold Morton Landon Translation award Acad. Am. Poets, 1991), The Odyssey by Homer, 1996 (Acad. award lit. Am. Acad. Arts and Letters, 1996), The Aeneid by Virgil, 2006; author: I, Vincent: Poems from the Pictures of Van Gogh, 1978; co-editor: Homer: A Collection of Critical Essays, 1962, Pope's Iliad and Odyssey, 1967. Recipient PEN/Ralph Manheim Medal lifetime achievement in translation, 1997, NJ Humanities Book award, Behrman award disting. achievement in humanities, Princeton U., Nat. Humanities Medal, NEH, 2006. Mem.: Am. Philosophical Soc., Am. Acad. Arts and Sciences, Am. Acad. Arts and Letters. Office Fax: 609-258-1873. E-mail: fagles@princeton.edu.

FAHERTY, DAVID MILES, musical instrument repairman; b. Ft. Worth, Tex., July 8, 1954; s. Frank Patrick and Laura Gene Faherty. Grad., Tarrant County Jr. Coll., 1977. Owner, pres. D.M. Faherty Music Co., Ft. Worth, 1978—. Active US Jaycees, Ft. Worth, 1985-94; pres. Tarrant County Jaycees, 1988-89. Mem. Ft. Worth City Band (v.p. 1984-85), Nat. Assn. of Profl. Band Instrument Repair Technicians (clinician tchr.). Roman Catholic. Avocations: hunting, fishing, musical performance. Office: D M Faherty Music Co PO Box 11102 Fort Worth TX 76110-0102 Office Phone: 817-923-9904. Personal E-mail: milessax@aol.com.

FAHERTY, ROBERT LOUIS, publishing executive; b. St. Louis, Sept. 26, 1939; s. Justin Louis and Elizabeth Veronica (Quigley) F.; m. Claudia C. Hutchison, Jan. 10, 1969; children: Kathleen Marie, Timothy Robert, Mark Robert, Megan Elizabeth, Bridget Justine. BA magna cum laude, Cath. U. Am., Washington, DC, 1961, MA, 1962; STL cum laude, Pontifical Gregorian U., Rome, 1966. Editor St. Louis Rev., 1967—69, Ency. Britannica, Chgo., 1969—72; mng. editor sci./Benefic Press Harcourt Brace Jovanovich, Chgo., 1972—73; mng. editor Scholarly Press, Detroit, 1973—75; co-founder, editor-in-chief Reference Publs., Algonac, Mich., 1975—77; editor-in-chief Congl. Budget Office, Washington, 1977—84; dir. Brookings Instn. Press, Washington, 1984—. Lectr. Howard U. Book Pub. Inst., 1985-89, George Washington U., 2006—; mem. adv. com. on pub. and comm. programs U. Va., 1994-2004, instr., 1995-2004; v.p. Brookings Instn., 2002— Trustee, treas. Ela Area Pub. Libr. Dist., Lake County, Ill., 1973-74; bd. dirs. United Cmty. Ministries, Fairfax County, Va., 1992-99, pres., 1995-99; chmn. Algonac Recreation Commn., 1976-77; mem. bioethics com. for Mid-Atlantic region Kaiser Permanente HMO, 1989-99; mem. Human Svcs. Coun. Fairfax County, 1999— Curators' scholar U. Mo., 1957, Basselin Found.; scholar Cath. U. Am., 1959 Mem. Assn. Am. Univ. Presses (bd. dirs. 1991-94, 97-00, pres. 1998-99), Assn. Am. Pubs. (bd. dirs. 2002-), Internat. Pubs. Assn. (exec. com. 2006-). Home: 4303 Mission Ct Alexandria VA 22310-3353 Office: Brookings Instn 1775 Massachusetts Ave NW Washington DC 20036-2103 Business E-Mail: rfaherty@brookings.edu.

FAHERTY, SANDRA LEE, social worker, psychotherapist; b. Plymouth, Mass., Jan. 13, 1944; d. John Faherty and Pearl Blanch Teto; m. Richard A. Prose, Apr. 7, 1989. BA in Psychology, U. Mass., Dartmouth, 1975; MSW, R.I. Coll., 1983. Cert. clin. hypnotherapist. Psychotherapist, New Smyrna Beach, Fla., 1990—. Social worker Bert Fish Hosp., New Smyrna Beach, 1999—, mem. adv. bd. Named Mental Health Worker of Yr., Volusia Flagler Assn. and Devel. for Counseling, 1992. Mem.: NASW (treas. 1993—, Social Worker of Yr. 1996). Home: 200 N Peninsula Ave New Smyrna Beach FL 32169 Office: 1 Fairgreen Ave New Smyrna Beach FL 32168 Office Phone: 386-426-5060.

FAHEY, JAMES EDWARD, brokerage house executive; b. NYC; s. John Michael and Kathleen Rose Fahey; 2 children. BBA, MBA, Iona Coll., New Rochelle, NY. Registered investment advisor. Territory asst. European Am. Bank, NYC, 1978—80; internat. analyst Texaco, Inc., White Plains, 1981—83; mgr. internat. treasury Am. Standard Inc., NYC, 1984—88; asst. treas. Perkin Elmer Internat., Inc., 1988-91; sr. mgr. internat. treasury Perkin Elmer Corp., Norwalk, Conn., 1988-91; sr. v.p. investments, corp. client group dir. Smith Barney, NYC, 1991—2005; v.p., internat. fin. advisor Merrill Lynch, NYC, 2005—. Active Friends of Am. Cancer Soc., NYC, 1986—2006; leadership com. Tristate Cure Autism Now, 2002—06; mem. leadership com. Austism Speaks, 2007—, NY state advocacy chair. Mem.: Friendly Sons of St. Patrick (NYC). Office: Merrill Lynch 717 Fifth Ave New York NY 10022

FAHEY, JEFF, actor; b. Olean, NY, Nov. 29, 1952; Ptnr. Black Sheep Grips; co-founder Am. Road Prodn. Workshop Series, Raft Theatre, NYC; owner Tyree Productions. TV appearances include: (series) One Life to Live, 1982-85, The Marshall, 1995, Eye of the Wolf, 1995, Serpant's Lair, 1995, (films) The Execution of Raymond Graham, 1985, Curiosity Kills, 1990, Parker Kane, 1990, Iran: Days of Crisis, 1991, Sketch Artist, 1991, In the Company of Darkness, 1993, The Hit List, 1993, Blindsided, 1993, Quick, 1994, Virtual Seduction, 1995, Time Served, 1999, Wolf Lake, 2001, Absolute Zero, 2005, Locusts: The 8th Plague, 2005, The Eden Formula, 2006; film appearances include: Silverado, 1985, Psycho III, 1986, Backfire, 1987, Split Decisions, 1988, Alexander's Treasures, 1989, The Last of the Finest, 1989, Outback, 1989, The Serpent of Death, 1989, True Blood, 1989, Impulse, 1990, White Hunter, Black Heart, 1990, Body Parts, 1991, Iron Maze, 1991, The Lawnmower Man, 1992, Wyatt Earp, 1994, Darkman III: Die Darkman Die, 1996, When Justice Fails, 1997, Lethal Tender, 1997, Catherine's Grove, 1997, Small Time, 1998, No Tomorrow, 1999, Detour, 1999, Spoken in Silence, 1999, Revelation, 1999, Hijack, 1999, The Contract, 1999, The Newcomers, 2000, Spin Cycle, 2000, Epicenter, 2000, The Sculptress, 2000, Choosing Matthias, 2001, Outlaw, 2001, Inferno, 2001, Out There, 2001, Cold Heart, 2001, Maniacts, 2001, Unspeakable, 2002, Blind Heart, 2002, Fallen Angels, 2002, Killing Cupid, 2004, Day of Redemption, 2004, Darkhunters, 2004, Close Call, 2004, Ghost Rock, 2004, Split Second, 2005, Only the Brave, 2005, Scorpius Gigantus, 2006, Messages, 2006, Grindhouse, 2007.*

FAHEY, JOHN M., JR., book publishing executive; b. NYC; m. Heidi Fahey; children: Christopher, Kenneth, Allison. BS in Engring., Manhattan Coll.; MBA, U. Mich. Exec. v.p., COO Time Life Books, 1986—89; pres., CEO, chmn. Time Life Inc., Alexandria, Va., 1989—96; exec. v.p., chair ops. office Nat. Geog. Ventures, Washington, 1996—; pres., CEO Nat. Geog. Soc., Washington, 1998—, Explorers Hall, Washington. Adv. com. mem. Newseum; bd. dir. Jason Found. for Edn., Johnson Outdoors Inc., Exclusive Resorts. Named one of top 100 Irish Americans, Irish Am. mag. Office: Nat Geographic Soc 1145 17th St NW Washington DC 20036-4701*

FAHEY, MIKE, mayor; b. Kansas City, Mo., Dec. 20, 1943; 4 children. BA, Creighton Univ., 1973. Former owner Am. Land Title Co., 1978—90, ret. CEO, 1978—97; mayor City of Omaha, 2001—. Bd. Holy Name Housing, Am. Red Cross Heartland Chpt., Creighton Prep H.S.; chmn. Omaha Planning Bd., 1981. Office: City Hall Ste 300 1819 Farnam St Omaha NE 68183 Business E-Mail: mfahey@ci.omaha.ne.us.*

FAHEY, RICHARD PAUL, lawyer; b. Oakland, Calif., Nov. 2, 1944; s. John Joseph and Helene Goldie (Whetstone) F.; m. Suzanne Dawson, June 8, 1968; children: Eamon, Aaron Chad. AA, Meritt Coll., 1964; BA, San Francisco State U., 1966; JD, Northwestern U., Evanston, Ill., 1971. Bar: N.Mex., 1971, US Dist. Ct. N.Mex., 1972, US Ct. Appeals (10th cir.) 1972, Ohio 1973, US Dist. Ct. (no. and so. dists.), US Supreme Ct. 1975. Atty. in charge Dinebeiina Nahiilna Be Agaditahe, Shiprock, N.Mex., 1971-73; asst. atty. gen. State of Ohio, Columbus, 1973-76; ptnr. Fahey & Schraff, 1976-80; atty. Sanford, Fisher, Fahey, Boyland & Schwarzwalder, 1980-84; of counsel Knepper, White, Arter & Hadden, 1984-85; ptnr. Arter & Hadden, 1985-99; of counsel Vorys Sater Seymour and Pease LLP, 2000—02, ptnr., 2003—; adj. prof. law Capital U., 1976-86, Ohio State U., 1986-87; chmn. Ohio Oil and Gas Regulatory Rev. Commn., 1986-87. Author: Underground Storage Tanks A Primer of the Federal Regulatory Program, 2d edit., 1995; contbr. articles to profl. jours. Vol. Peace Corps.,

Liberia, 1966—68; active Columbus Pub. Schs. Bd. Edn., 1986—93, pres., 1989; trustee Godman Guild Settlement House, 1976—82, Ohio Environ. Coun., 1981—83; adv. bd. WCBE Pub. Radio; Charter rev. com. Columbus City, 1998—99; pres. Audobon Ohio, 1999—2002; mem. sewer and water adv. bd. City of Columbus, 2004—07; mem. Hondo Vol. Fire Dept., Santa Fe, 2006—; exec. com. Dem. Party, Ohio, 1996—2002; trustee Downtown Columbus, Inc., 1989, Pilot Dogs, Inc., 1993—2004, pres., 2001, Cmty. in Sch., 2000—07. Grantee, Russell Sage Found., 1969. Mem. ABA (vice chair Sonreel water quality com. 1993-97), Ohio Bar Assn., N.Mex. Bar Assn., Columbus Bar Assn., Columbus Bar Found. Democrat. Unitarian Universalist. Avocations: travel, fishing, reading, jogging, skiing. Address: 58 Camino Nevoso Santa Fe NM 87505 Office: Vorys Sater Seymour and Pease LLP 52 E Gay St Columbus OH 43215 Home Phone: 614-203-0842; Office Phone: 614-464-5601. Business E-Mail: rpfahey@vssp.com.

FAHEY, WILLIAM THOMAS, II, lawyer; b. Dec. 27, 1949; s. William T. and Mildred K. (Flood) F.; children: William T., Sean E., Erin E. BBA, U. Notre Dame, Ind., 1970; JD, Duke U., Durham, NC, 1973. Bar: W.Va. 1973, US Dist. Ct. (no. dist.) W.Va. 1978, US Ct. Appeals (4th and 6th cirs.) 1981, US Tax Ct. 1985. Spl. counsel W.Va. State Auditor, Charleston, 1973-77; assoc. Pinsky, Barnes, Watson, Cuomo & Hinerman, Weirton, W.Va, 1977-79; ptnr. Barnes, Watson, Cuomo, Hinerman & Fahey, Weirton, W.Va, 1980-84, Hinerman, Fahey & Risovich, Weirton, 1984-85, Hinerman and Fahey, Weirton, 1985-98; counsel Fahey Law Office, Weirton, 1998—2000, 2007—; ptnr. Fahey & Risovich Law Office, Weirton, 2001—07. Asst. pros. atty. Hancock County, Weirton, 1977-78, 1990—; spl. counsel Weirton City mgr., 2001-2003; dist. character com. W.Va. Supreme Ct., 1985—; pres. Hancock County Civil Svc., New Cumberland, W.Va., 1978-81; city solicitor City of New Cumberland, 1978-89; commr. State Delinquent Lands, Charleston, 1977-95; mem. water bd. City of Weirton, 1978-89; bd. dirs. Hancock County Sr. Citizens, Inc., New Cumberland, 1978-89; spl. pros. atty. Brooke County, Ohio County, W.Va., 1998—. Mem. ABA, Am. Assn. Jurists, W.Va. State Bar, W.Va. Trial Lawyers Assn. (bd. govs. 1989—), W.Va. Assn. for Justice, Williams Country Club, Notre Dame Monogram Club, K.C. (adv. 1979—), Am. Quarter Horse Assn. (World Champion Stallion award 1998), Weirton Rotary Club (pres. 2003). Republican. Roman Catholic. Home: 1480 Cove Rd Weirton WV 26062-3820 Office: Fahey Law Office 2116 Pennsylvania Ave Weirton WV 26062-3526 Home Phone: 304-723-1111; Office Phone: 304-723-3220. E-mail: wfahey@prodigy.net.

FAHIEN, LEONARD AUGUST, physician, educator; b. St. Louis, July 26, 1934; s. John Henry and Alice Katherine (Schubkegel) F.; m. Rose Marian Burmeister, June 21, 1958; children: Catherine Fahien Reuter, Lisa Fahien Uldrich, James. AB, Washington U., St Louis, 1956; MD, Washington U., 1960. Intern U. Wis., Madison, 1960-61; surgeon NIH, Bethesda, Md., 1964-66; asst. prof. dept. pharmacology U. Wis. Med. Sch., Madison, 1966-69, asso. prof., 1969-74, prof., 1974—, asso. dean, 1979-83, advisor Children's Diabetes Ctr., 2002—; vis. prof. Inst. Protein Rsch. Osaka U., Japan, 1991; prof. El Julios U. Barcelona (Spain), 1997. Contbr. chapters to books, articles to profl. jours. With USPHS, 1964—66. Numerous NIH grants, 1966—. Mem.: Phi Beta Kappa, Sigma Xi. Lutheran. Home: 3212 Topping Rd Madison WI 53705-1435 Office: 426 S Charter St Madison WI 53715-1626 Business E-Mail: lafahien@facstaff.wisc.edu.

FAHIM, AMR, electrical engineer; s. Mohamed and Perinoor Fahim; m. Sarah Emadeldin Aly, June 23, 2005. PhD, U. Waterloo, Canada, 2000. Sr. engr. Qualcomm, Inc., San Diego, 2000—04; prin. engr. Skyworks Solutions, Irvine, Calif., 2004—05, Newport Media Inc, Lake Forest, Calif., 2005—. Author: Clock Generators for SoC Processors, 2005; assoc. editor: Open Elec. and Electronic Engring. Jour.; contbr. chapters to books, articles to profl. jours., over 25 profl. publs. Recipient Outstanding Achievement cert., Skyworks Solutions, 2005. Mem.: IEEE (assoc. reviewer 2001—, assoc. editor Open Source Elec. and Electronic Engring. Jour. 2007—). Achievements include patents for sigma-delta modulator controlled phase locked loop with noise shaped dither; low-jitter fractional-N All Digital PLL; patents pending for universal mobile TV architecture; DC offset cancellation in cascaded amplifiers; noise shaped order filter design technique; design of one of first commercial all-digital clock generator PLLs; over 40 commercial mixed-signal integrated circuits (ICs) for wireless commerical applications. Office: Newport Media Inc 25371 Commercentre Drive Suite 125 Lake Forest CA 92630 Home Phone: 858-829-4823; Office Phone: 949-340-6169. Personal E-mail: amr.m.fahim@gmail.com.

FAHIM, KAREEM, journalist; Reporter Village Voice, 2004, The New York Times, 2004—. Author: (articles) Last Bus to Baghdad, The Great Arab American Voter Revolt, 2004. Recipient Best Reporting (non-daily newspaper), Deadline Club, the New York City Chapter of the Society of Professional Journalists. Office: The New York Times 229 W 43rd St New York NY 10036

FAHLE, MANFRED, ophthalmology researcher; b. Duesseldorf, Germany, Dec. 10, 1950; s. Fritz and Helma (Westerfeld) F.; m. Sigrid Henke, Aug. 3, 1979; children: Nora Katharina, Till Patrick Jakob; m. Karoline Spang, Aug. 4, 2001. Degree in Biology, U. Goettingen, Fed. Republic Germany, 1972; degree in Medicine, U. Giessen, Fed. Republic Germany, 1973; MA in biology, U. Mainz, Fed. Republic Germany, 1975; MD, U. Tuebingen, Fed. Republic Germany, 1977. Fellow Max-Planck Inst. for Biol. Cybernetics, Tuebingen, 1977-81; head electrophysiol. lab. Univ. Eye Clinic, Tuebingen, 1981-88; vis. scientist U. Calif., Berkeley, 1984, MIT, Cambridge, Mass., 1989-90; fellow German Rsch. Coun., Tuebingen, 1990-93; prof. ophthalmology, head sect. visual sci. Univ. Eye Hosp., Tuebingen, 1994-98; head Inst. Brain Rsch. IV, human-neurobiology U. Bremen, Germany, 2000—, dir. Ctr. Cognitive Sci., 2005—. Wiersma vis. prof. Calif. Inst. Tech., Pasadena, 1996; prof., head dept. optometry and visual sci. City U., London, 1998-99; prof. human neurobiology U. Bremen, Germany, 1999—; dir. Inst. for Brain Rsch., 2003—, Ctr. Cognitive Sci., 2005—; vis. prof. Univ. Coll., London, 1999-2002; part-time prof. Applied Vision Rsch. Ctr., City Univ., 2000—05, Henry Wellcome Labs. of Vision Rsch., London, 2006—. Mem. editl. bd. German Jour. Ophthalmology, 1991-97, Neuroophthalmology, 1993-2003, Vision Rsch., 1994-2004, Pub. Libr. Sci. Biology, 2006—; author: (with T. Poggio) Perceptual Learning, 2002, (with M. Greenlee) Visual Neuropsychology, 2003. Bd. dirs. Grad. Program Neurobiology, Tuebingen, 1986-91, Drug Rsch. Program, Tuebingen, 1996-99. Recipient Heisenberg award German Rsch. Coun., 1989, prize von Humboldt/Max-Planck Soc., 1992. Avocations: music, literature, sailing, windsurfing. Home: Graf-Moltkestr 56 D28211 Bremen Germany Office: Inst Human Neurobiology Argonnenstr 3 D28211 Bremen Germany Fax: 49-421-218-9526. E-mail: mfahle@uni-bremen.de.

FAHMY, IBRAHIM MOUNIR, hotel executive; b. Alexandria, Egypt, July 4, 1943; came to U.S., 1986; s. Ambassador Mounir Ibrahim and Aziza (Kelada) F.; m. Brenda Lee Chenier, Sept. 18, 1970 (div. Jan. 1991); children: Susan Lee, Christine Lynn; m. Ann Marie Jones, Oct. 15, 1995; 1 child, Laila Ann. Certs., St. Mark's Coll., Alexandria, 1949-63; student, U. Alexandria, 1962-63. V.p., gen. mgr. King Edward Hotel, Toronto, Canada, 1982—86; sr. v.p. Can. Forte Hotels Inc., NYC, 1986—95; exec. v.p. Forte Hotels Inc., San Diego, 1986—95; mng. dir. The Carlton, Washington, 1995—99, The Essex House, NY, NY, 1999—2002, Egypt-Starwood Hotels and Resorts Worldwide, Cairo, 2002—. Former dir. Hotel Assn. Met. Toronto, Ont. Hostelry Inst.; mem. ednl. com. Humber Coll. Vol. Kidney Found., Muscular Dystrophy, The Can. Children's Found. Mem. Internat. Wine and Food Soc. Avocations: skiing, english riding, squash, theater, skeet and sporting clay shooting. Home and Office: Sheraton Cairo Hotel Towers and Casino PO Box 11 Cairo 11511 Egypt Office Phone: 202 3369700/800.

FAHMY, NABIL, ambassador; b. NY, Jan. 5, 1951; married; 3 children. BS in Physics and Math., Am. U. Cairo, 1974, MA in Mgmt., 1976. Adv. Cabinet of V.P. of Egypt, 1974—76; mem. Cabinet of the Sec. of the Pres. for External Comm., 1974—76; 2nd sec. Egyptian Mission to UN, Geneva, NYC, 1978—82; mem. Cabinet of the Dep. Prime Min. Fgn. Affairs, Egypt, 1982—84; 1st sec. UN, 1986—; sr. disarmament ofcl. Dept. Internat. Orgns., Min. Fgn. Affairs, 1991—; polit. adv. to fgn. min. Govt. Egypt, 1993—97, amb. to Japan, 1997—99, amb. to US Washington, 1999—. Mem. UN Sec. Gen.'s Adv. Bd. Disarmament Matters, 1999, chmn., 2001; head Egyptian del. to Mid. East Peace Process Steering Com., 1993, Egyptian del. to Multilateral Working Grp. on Regional Security and Arms Control, Madrid Peace Conf., 1991; vice-chmn. 1st com. on disarmament and internat. security affairs 44th session UN Gen. Assembly, 1986. Office: Embassy of the Arab Republic of Egypt 3521 International Ct NW Washington DC 20008

FAHMY HUDOME, RANDA, lawyer; b. Syracuse, NY, Feb. 4, 1964; d. Mahmoud Hussein and Irandukht (Vahidi) F.; m. Michael Hudome; 1 child, Alexandria. BA summa cum laude, Wilkes U., 1986; JD, Georgetown U., 1990. Fin. dir. Holtzman for Congress, Wilkes-Barre, Pa., 1986; lobbyist Citizens for Am., Washington, 1987; legal asst. Hamlin Blaszkow, Washington, 1987; with Koonz, McKenney & Johnson, Washington, 1988, Willkie, Farr & Gallagher, Washington, 1989-90, assoc., 1990—94; fgn. policy counsel to Sen. Spencer Abraham U.S. Senate, 1994—2001; assoc. dep. sec. energy Pres. George W. Bush, 2002—03; pres. Fahmy Hudome Internat., 2004—. Apptd. Md. Comm. for Women; dir. Muslim Women Lawyers for Human Rights. Adminstrv. editor Law and Policy in Internat. Bus., 1989-90. Mem. Rep. Nat. Lawyers Assn., Washington, 1990—. Mem. Internat. Law Soc. Georgetown U. Law Sch. (bd. dirs. Washington chpt. 1988-89), Md. Bar Assn., DC Bar Assn., U.S. Ct. Internat. Trade. Office Phone: 202-429-5566. Office Fax: 202-429-5577. E-mail: randa@fahmyhudome.com.

FAHN, LARRY, former environmental organization administrator; JD, Univ. Calif., 1976. Atty. private practice, San Francisco; exec. dir. As You Sow, San Francisco, 1998—; bd. dirs. Sierra Club, San Francisco, 1999—2005, nat. v.p. conservation, 2002—03, pres., 2003—05.

FAHN, STANLEY, neurologist, educator; b. Sacramento, Nov. 6, 1933; s. Ernest and Sylvia F.; m. Charlotte , June 21, 1958; children: Paul N., James D. BA, U. Calif., Berkeley, 1955, MD, 1958. Diplomate Am. Bd. Neurology. Resident in neurology Neurol. Inst., NY, 1959-62; rsch. assoc. NIH, 1962-65; mem. faculty Columbia U., NYC, 1965-68, prof. neurology, 1973-78, H. Houston Merritt prof., 1978—, dir. Morris K. Udall Parkinson Disease Rsch. Ctr., 1999—2003; mem. faculty U. Pa., Phila., 1968-73. Dir. Dystonia Rsch. Ctr., 1981—97; sci. dir. Parkinson's Disease Found., 1979—; chmn. adv. com. peripheral and nervous sys. drugs FDA, 1987—89, 1991—96; organizer, chmn. World Parkinson Congress, 2006. Editor Movement Disorders, 1985-95; assoc. editor Neurology, 1977-87. With USPHS, 1962-65 Grantee NIH, 1974—77, 1980—82, 1984—91, 1994—. Mem.: Inst. of Medicine, Dystonia Med. Rsch. Found. (hon. life, bd. dirs. 1998—), Movement Disorder Soc. (pres. 1988—91), Am. Neurol. Assn. (v.p. 1987—88, chair jour. oversight com. 1994—96), Am. Acad. Neurology (chair edn. com. 1986—93, v.p. 1993—97, pres.-elect 1999—2001, pres. 2001—03). Home: 155 Edgars Ln Hastings On Hudson NY 10706-1107 Office: 710 W 168th St New York NY 10032-2603 Office Phone: 212-305-5295. Business E-Mail: fahn@neuro.columbia.edu.

FAHNER, HAROLD THOMAS, marketing executive; b. Detroit, Sept. 4, 1940; s. Harold L. and Beatrice H. (Craig) F.; m. Patricia A. (Churchvara), Aug. 25, 1962; children: Michael, Janet, Peter. BS in Econ., U. Detroit, 1962. Sales dept. Dun and Bradstreet, Inc., NYC, 1963-67; mgr. sales tng. Blue Cross Blue Shield, Detroit, 1967-70; mgr. sales, mgmt. tng. A.O. Smith Harvestore Products, Inc., Arlington Heights, Ill., 1970-76, dist. sales mgr., 1976-77, ea. regional mgr., 1977-79, mktg. cons., 1980-82; v.p. mktg. Neuero Corp., West Chgo., Ill., 1982-85; v.p. sales and mktg. Atwater Group, Inc., Mpls., 1985-87; v.p. corp. mktg. Blue Cross Blue Shield of Fla., Inc., Jacksonville, Fla., 1988—2003; prin. Sales and Mktg. Assocs., Jacksonville, Fla., 2003—. Instr. Internat. Sales Mgmt. Inst.; lectr. in mktg., sales field. Author: The Problem Solving Approach to Selling, 1975; The Sales Manager's Model Letter Book, 1976, 2d edit., 1987; Successful Sales Management, 1983. Bd. trustees Grad. Sch. Sales Mgmt. and Mktg., Syracuse Univ. Mem.: Sales and Mktg. Exec. Assn. Internat. (sr. v.p., bd. dirs.). Home: 1601 Ocean Dr S Jacksonville FL 32250-6362 Personal E-mail: halsmktg@att.net.

FAHNER, TYRONE C., lawyer, former state attorney general; b. Detroit, Nov. 18, 1942; s. Warren George and Alma Fahner; BA, U. Mich., 1965; JD, Wayne State U., 1968; LLM, Northwestern U., 1971; m. Anne Beauchamp, July 2, 1966; children— Margaret, Daniel, Molly. Bar: Mich. 1968, Ill. 1969, Tex. 1984, U.S. Dist. Ct. (ea. dist.) Mich. 1968, US Dist. Ct. (no. dist.) Ill. 1969, US Ct. Appeals (7th cir.) 1969, US Ct. Appeals (5th cir.) 1981, US Ct. Appeals (D.C. cir.) 2002, US Supreme Ct. 2002. asst. US atty. for No. Dist. Ill., Chgo., 1971-75, dep. chief consumer fraud and civil rights, 1973-74, chief ofcl. corruption, 1974-75; ptnr. Freeman, Rothe, Freeman & Salzman, Chgo., 1975-77; dir. Ill. Dept. Law Enforcement, Springfield, 1977-79; ptnr. Mayer, Brown, Rowe & Maw, Chgo., 1979-80, 83—, co-chmn. mgmt. com. 1998-2001, chmn. mgmt. com., 2001-; atty. gen. State of Ill., Springfield, 1980-83; instr. John Marshall Law Sch., 1973-76, 78-84; former chmn. Coun. Great Lakes Govs.; chmn. Govs. Adv. Bd. Law Enforcement, 1980-83, Ill. Jud. Inquiry Bd, 1988-92, Chgo., Com. Honest Elections, 1984-92, Com. Internat. Trade and Tourism, Chgo. com. Chgo. Coun. Fgn. Rels. Mem. Toronto sister city com. Chgo. Sister Cities Internat. Program; former bd. dirs. Mex.-Am. Legal Defense and Ednl. Fund; mem. corp. adv. com. U. Mich. Coll. Lit., Sci. & The Arts, mem. major gifts com.; Mex.-Am. Legal Def. and Ednl. Fund; mem. William J. Fulbright bd. fgn. scholarships USIA, 1988-93; active Law Sch.'s Com. Visitors Wayne State U., US Info. Agy., Ill. Racing Bd., 1979-80, United Cerbral Palsy, Chgo., 1981-84, Epilepsy Found. Greater Chgo., Evanston Hist. Soc., Bureau Ednl. and Cultural Affairs, 1988-93. Mem. ABA, Am. Coll. Trial Lawyers, Internat. Assn. Gaming Attys., Mich. Bar Assn., Tex. Bar Assn., Chgo. Bar Assn., Law Club Chgo., Am. Inns of Ct. (Chgo. chpt.), Ill. Ambs. (bd. dirs., past pres.), Northwestern U. Sch. Law Alumni Assn. (bd. dirs. 1990-95, chmn. Class 1967 James B. Haddad professorship fundraising com.), Econ. Club of Chgo., Chgo. Club, Chgo. Commonwealth Club, Legal Club Chgo., Am. Effective Law Enforcement (com. cts. and justice), Commercial Club Chgo., U. Mich. Major Gifts com., Just The Beginning Found. Named, Person of Yr. Chgo. mag., 2002. Republican. Lutheran. Office: Mayer Brown Rowe & Maw LLP 71 S Wacker Dr Chicago IL 60606-4637

FAHNESTOCK, JEAN HOWE, retired civil engineer; b. Pitts., May 22, 1930; d. James Murray and Hazel Margaret (Alberts) F. AA, Stephens, 1950; BS in Civil Engring., Carnegie-Mellon, 1955. Registered profl. engr., Ill., Mich., Iowa. Sr. project mgr. De Leuw, Cather & Co., Chgo., 1955-92; ret. Design mgr. De Leuw, Cather & Co., Kuwait, 1978-81, Abu Dhabi, 1981-85, Kennedy Expy. and Elgin-O'Hare Expy., Chgo., 1985-92. Fellow ASCE (life); mem. NSPE, Ill. Soc. Profl. Engrs. (life). Republican. Presbyterian. Avocations: bridge, travel, politics. Home: 4606 W Bryn Mawr Ave Chicago IL 60646-6632 Personal E-mail: jhf4606@comcast.net.

FAHOUR, AHMED, investment company executive; b. Almoun, Lebanon; B in econ., La Trobe U.; MBA, Grad. Sch. Mgmt. U. Melbourne, 1988. Ptnr. Boston Consulting Group; mng. dir. iFormation Group; sr. v.p. corp. devel. Citigroup, 2000—02; mem. Citigroup Mgmt. com., 2000; CEO Citigroup Alternative Investments Group, NY, 2002, Citigroup Australasia, 2004, Nat. Australia Bank Group, 2004—. Dep. chmn. Australian Bankers' Assn., 2004—. Office: National Australia Bank Group Level 35 500 Bourke St Melbourne Vic 3000 Australia Office Phone: 800-285-3000, 61-2-8225 1000.*

FAHRBACH, RUTH C., state legislator; b. NYC; Grad. high sch., East Meadow, NY. Mem. Dist. 61 Conn. Ho. of Reps., 1981—, minority whip, mem. appropriations com., pub. health com., legis. mgmt. com., select com. of inquiry. Active Windsor Rep. Town Com.; mem. Windsor Bd. Edn., 1977-81, v.p., 1979-80; bd. dirs. Celebrate Windsor, Inc., 2001-04, 05—; local emergency planning com. mem., 2003-. Mem. First Dist. Rep. Womens Club, Fedn. Rep. Women, Civitan Club Windsor (past pres), Nat. Order of Women Legislators, Conn. Order of Women Legislators (sec.), Conn. Fedn. of Rep. Women, Nat. Fedn. of Republican Women, St. Casimir's Lithuanian Club Women's Aux. Home: 592 Poquonock Ave Windsor CT 06095-2204 Office: Legis Office Bldg Rm 4200 Hartford CT 06106-1591 Business E-Mail: ruth.fahrbach@housegop.po.state.ct.us.

FAHRENKROG, EUGENE HENRY, JR., lawyer; b. St. Louis, Jan. 20, 1946; s. Eugene Henry and Julia (Hanpeter) F.; m. Linda L. Stoutenburgh, Aug. 8, 1970; children— Jeffrey, Stacy, Dana. B.A., Ohio U., 1968; J.D., Washington U., St. Louis, 1971. Bar: Mo. 1971. Asst. pros. atty. Pros. Atty.'s Office, St. Louis, 1971-74; assoc. James F. Koester, Inc., St. Louis, 1975-77; ptnr. Eugene H. Fahrenkrog Jr. P.C., St. Louis, 1977—1990, founding ptnr., Walther/Glenn Law Assoc., 1990-; pub. St. Louis Met. Jury Verdict Reporting Service. Mem. Mo. Assn. Trial Attys. (pres. 1983-84), Christian Legal Soc. (pres. 2004-2005). Mem. United Ch. Christ. Office Phone: 314-725-9595.

FAHRINGER, CATHERINE HEWSON, retired savings and loan association executive; b. Phila., Aug. 1, 1922; d. George Francis and Catherine Gertrude (Magee) Hewson; m. Edward F. Fahringer, July 8, 1961 (dec.); 1 child, Francis George Beckett. Grad. diploma, Inst. Fin. Edn., 1965. Notary pub. Fla. With Centrust Bank (formerly Dade Savs. and Loan Assn.), Miami, 1958—85; v.p. Centrust Bank, Miami, 1967—74, sr. v.p., 1974—82, sec., 1975—79, head savs. pers. and mktg. divsn., 1979—83, exec. v.p. office of chmn., 1984, dir., 1984—90, co-chmn. audit com. of bd. dirs., 1990; referral assoc. Referral Network Inc. subs. Coldwell Banker, 1990—. Pub. arbitrator NASD, 1999-2005. Contbr. articles to profl. jours. Trustee United Way of Dade County (Fla.), 1980-87, chmn. audit com. 1982-84, trustee, Pub. Health Trust, Dade County, 1974-84, sec. 1976, vice chmn., 1977-78, chmn. bd., 1978-81; mem. adv. coun. Women's Bus. Devel. Ctr., Fla. Internat. U., 1993-95; mem. spl. steering com. Breast Cancer Task Force, Jackson Meml. Hosp., 1991; hon. bd. govs. U. Miami, Soc. for Rsch. in Med. Edn.; trustee South Fla. Blood Svc., Miami, 1979-84, vice chmn., 1980, chmn., 1981-84; trustee Dade County Vocat. Found., 1977-81; trustee Fla. Internat. U. Found., 1976-90; trustee emeritus, 1990, v.p. bd., 1978-81, pres. 1982-84; bd. dirs. Sta. WPBT-TV, 1984-2002, founding lifetime dir., 1995, chmn. budget and fin. com., 1986, mem. exec. com. 1985-92, sec. 1987, investment com., 1988-90, vice chmn. 1988-92, mem. fin. com., 1992, chmn. audit and control com., 1994, 2000, 2001, mem., 1997-98; bd. dirs., mem. nominating com. Girl Scout Coun., Tropical Fla., 1985-89, chmn. 1988-89, mem. long range planning com., 1986-88; citizens oversight com. Dade County Pub. Sch. System, 1986-90, chmn. 1988-90; bd. dirs. New World Sch. of Arts, 1987-90, chmn. devel. com., 1987-90, chair New World Sch. of Arts Gala, 1990; mem. Disaster Relief Com., chair Hurricane Disaster Relief Distbn. Ctr., 1992; mem. fin. commn., chmn. capital improvement fund com. Coral Gables Congrl. Ch., summer concert series com., chmn. refreshement sub-com.; commd. Stephen min., 1985-1995; mem. grievance com. 11th Jud. Cir. Fla. Bar, 1988-92; bd. trustees United Protestant Appeal, 1994-96; mem. parking adv. bd. City of Coral Gables, 1997-98, bd. of adjustments, 1998—, vice chmn., 2001-2003, chmn.2003—2007, sr. citizens adv. bd., 2007—; mem., 3rd v.p. Bush chpt. Women's Cancer Assn. U. Miami, 1997-99, 2nd v.p., treas. and parliamentarian, 1999-2001, chmn. meml. fund, 1998-2003, 3rd v.p., 2002-03. Named Women of Yr. in fin., Zonta Internat., 1975, amb., Air Def. Arty., 1970, U.S. Army Air Def. Command, 1970, Woman of Yr. in Sports, Links Club, 1986, First Lady of Athletics, Fla. Internat. U., 2003; named one of Notable Women in Miami-Dade County History, Beyond Julia's Daughters 1975-2000, 2007; recipient Trail Blazer award, Women's Coun. of 100, 1977, Cmty. Headliner award, Women in Comm., 1983, Outstanding Citizen of Dade County award, 1984, Honors and Recognition award, Golden Panthers Club of Fla. Internat. U., 1989, Disting. Svc. and Leadership award, Fla. Internat. U., 1991, apprecation, New World Sch. of the Arts, 1990, Meritorious Pub. Svc. award, Fla. Bar, 1991, Outstanding Svc. award, Country Club Coral Gables, 2001, hon. BA, U. Hard Knocks Alderson-Broaddus Coll., 1987, Key to City of Coral Gables for Cmty. Svc., 2000, Dedicated Svc. award, Women's Cancer Assn. of U. Miami, 2001, Outstanding Svc. Award, 2001, Woman's Day Disting. Woman of Svc. Recognition, Coral Gables Congregational Ch., 2006, In The Company of Women Pioneer award, Miami-Dade County, Fla., 2007. Mem.: LWV, Women's Union Russia, Fla. Women's Alliance (bd. dirs. 1983—91, pres. 1987—89), Internat. Women's Alliance, Savs. and Loan Pers. Soc. South Fla., Savs. and Loan Mktg. Soc. South Fla. (past pres.), Inst. Fin. Edn. (life; nat. dir., past pres. Local Greater Miami chpt.), Greater Miami Women's Golf Assn. (social dir. 1999—2001), Greenway Women's Golf Assn. (treas. 1988—89), Balt. Women's Golf Assn., Fla. Internat. U. Athletics Club, Golden Panther Club (bd. dirs. 1988—2007, v.p. 1991, pres. 1992—94), Links Fla. Internat. U. Club (v.p. 1992, bd. dirs., sec.), Country Club Coral Gables (treas. women's golf assn 1988—89, sec., bd. dirs., found. trustee 1993, v.p. bd. dirs. 1994, pres. 1995, chmn. bldg. restoration, capital improvement and maintenance com. 1995—99, bd. advisors 1996—, liaison City of Coral Gables 1997—99, rear commodore, vice commodore, historian, adv., chair The Fleet 1998, commodore 1999, publicity chmn. woman's bd. 2000—01, pres. women's golf assn. 2001—02, mem. adv. bd. dirs. 2002—, golf adv., directory chair 2003), Dade Bus. and Profl. Women's Club (past pres.). Democrat. *Success is putting forth your full effort and loving what you do. Dreams take time, but you can make them happen if you believe in yourself and in your dreams.*

FAIGLEY, JOSEPH RAYMOND, social studies educator; b. Canton, Ohio, July 4, 1948; s. Raymond Charles and Mary Ellen (Gockstetter) Faigley; m. Mary Evelyn Simpson, Nov. 3, 1979. BA, Walsh U., 1972, MA, 1990. Cert. permanent tchr. Ohio, supt. Ohio. Tchr. St. Thomas Aquinas H.S., Louisville, Ohio, 1974—, chair dept. humanities, 1997—99, chair dept. social studies, 1999—; lectr. Walsh U., North Canton, Ohio, 1990—98. Social studies curriculum com. Diocese of Youngstown, Ohio, 1997—98; negotiator Youngstown Diocese Confedn. of Tchrs., 2002. Workshop participant Nat. First Ladies Mus., Canton, Ohio, 2003. Named Tchr. of Week, WHBC Radio, 1992. Mem. Phi Delta Kappa. Office: St Thomas Aquinas HS 2121 Reno Dr NE Louisville OH 44641 E-mail: jfaigley@stahs.org.

FAIGNANT, JOHN PAUL, lawyer, educator; b. Proctor, Vt., Mar. 24, 1953; s. Joseph Paul and Ann (DeBlasio) F.; children: Janelle, Melissa. BA, U. New Haven, 1974; JD, George Mason U., 1978. Bar: Va. 1978, Vt. 1979, U.S. Dist. Ct. Vt. 1979, U.S. Ct. Appeals (4th cir.) 1979, U.S. Supreme Ct. 1992. Assoc. Griffin & Griffin, Rutland, Vt., 1978-79, Miller, Norton & Cleary, Rutland, 1979-84, ptnr., 1984-87, Miller, Cleary and Faignant PC, Rutland, 1988-91, Miller & Faignant, Ltd., Rutland, 1991-97,

Miller Faignant & Whelton PC (now Miller Faignant & Behrens), Rutland, 1997—. Adj. prof. Coll. St. Joseph, Rutland, 1982-90, Castleton State Coll., 2005. Mem. Rutland Town Fire Dept., 1989—; mem., pres. No. New England Def. Counsel, 1995-96. Mem. Va. Bar Assn., Vt. Bar Assn., Assn. Trial Lawyers Am., Def. Rsch. Inst., Am. Bd. Trial Advocates, Internat. Assn. of Def. Counsel. Roman Catholic. Avocation: antique trucks. Home: RR 1 Box 3762 Rutland VT 05701-9214 Office: Miller Faignant & Behrens PC PO Box 6688 1213 Rt 7 N Rutland VT 05702-6688 Office Phone: 802-775-2521 ext. 14. Business E-Mail: jpfutlaw@aol.com.

FAILS, THOMAS GLENN, geologist; b. Unity Twp., Ohio, Feb. 28, 1928; s. T. Glenn and Mary C. (Adams) Fails; m. Mary Ivy Schmid, Mar. 1, 1959; children: Glenn Michael, Nora Anne. Degree geol. engring., Colo. Sch. Mines, 1954; MA Geology, Columbia U., 1955. Cert. petroleum geologist, profl. geologist. Geologist Shell Oil Co., New Orleans, 1956—66; dist. geologist Trend Exploration Ltd., New Orleans, 1967—69, v.p., London, 1970—75; ind. geologist, petroleum prodr. Denver, 1975; pres., owner Raven Exploration Corp., Denver, 1977—; v.p., dir. Pannonian Energy, Inc., Denver, 1998—2000; pres., dir. Pannonian Internat., Ltd., Denver, 2000—. Trustee Bridge Trust, Denver, 1990—93; mem. adv. com. Colo. Geol. Survey, 1991—94. Author: Gulf Coast, U.S.; contbr. articles to profl. jours. Bd. dirs. Belcaro Park Homeowners Assn., Denver, 2004—. With USMC, 1946—48, with Res. USMC, 1950—51. Fellow: Geol. Soc. London; mem.: Rocky Mountain Assn. Geologists (Disting. Pub. Svc. to Earth Sci. award 1993), Petroleum Exploration Soc. Gt. Britain (bd. dirs. 1974—75), Am. Inst. Profl. Geologists (v.p. 1995, pres. 1999, Martin van Couvering Meml. award 2001, Parker medal 2004), Am. Assn. Petroleum Geologists (found. assoc. 2002—). Republican. Lutheran. Home: 965 S Monroe St Denver CO 80209-4939 Office: 4101 E Louisiana Ave Ste 412 Denver CO 80246-3431 Office Phone: 303-759-9733. Personal E-mail: thomgeol@aol.com.

FAIN, JOHN NICHOLAS, biochemistry educator; b. Jefferson City, Tenn., Aug. 18, 1934; s. Samuel Clark and Virginia Manson (Hunt) F.; m. Ann Duff, June 7, 1958; children: Margaret Ann, John Nicholas Jr., James Clark. BS magna cum laude, Carson-Newman Coll., 1956; PhD in Biochemistry, Emory U., 1960. Rsch. assoc. Emory U., Atlanta, 1960-61; NSF fellow NIH, Bethesda, Md., 1961-62, postdoctoral fellow USPHS, 1962-63; biochemist NIH and Nat. Inst. Arthritis and Metabolic Diseases, Bethesda, 1963-65; asst. prof. Brown U., Providence, 1965-68, assoc. prof., 1968-71, prof., 1971-85, chmn. biochemistry, 1975-85; Van Vleet prof., dept. chmn. U. Tenn., Memphis, 1985-2000, Van Vleet prof. of molecular scis., 2000—. Contbr. numerous articles to sci. jours. Del. gen. assembly United Presbyn. Ch., Providence, 1972. Recipient Disting. Alumnus award Carson-Newman Coll., 1986; fellow Cambridge U., 1977-78; NIH Fogarty fellow, 1984-85; Macy Faculty scholar, 1977-78. Mem. Am. Soc. Biol. Chemists. Democrat. Office: U Tenn Health Scis Ctr Coll Medicine Dept Mol Scis 858 Madison Ste GO1 Memphis TN 38163 Office Phone: 901-448-4343. Fax: 901-448-7360. E-mail: jfain@utmem.edu.

FAIN, RICHARD DAVID, cruise line executive; b. Boston, Oct. 9, 1947; s. Morton Edgar and Libby Miriam (Winer) F.; m. Colleen Jo Ferris, July 27, 1969; children: Julie Meredith, Sara Elizabeth, Benjamin Alfred, Jessica Lynn. BS, U. Calif., Berkeley, 1969; MBA, U. Pa., 1972. Mgr. internat. fin. IU Internat. Corp., Phila., 1972-75; joint mng. dir., dir. Gotaas Larsen Shipping Corp., London, 1975-88; chmn., CEO Royal Caribbean Cruise Line, Miami, Fla., 1988—. Chmn. Internat. Coun. Cruise Lines, Washington, 1993-95, Cruise Line Internat. Assn. Chmn. Greater Miami Conf. and Visitors Bur., 1995-97; trustee U. Miami, United Way Miami. Decorated Legion of Honor (France); named ARC Humanitarian of Yr., Dade County, Fla.; inducted South Fla. Bus. Hall Fame, 2004; recipient Ultimate CEO Award, South Fla. Bus. Journ., 2004, Ellis Island Medal Honor, Nat. Ethnic Coalition Org., 2004. Mem. Chaine de Rotisseurs. Office: Royal Caribbean Internat 1050 Caribbean Way Miami FL 33132-2096 Office Phone: 305-539-6603. Business E-Mail: rfain@rccl.com.

FAINARU-WADA, MARK, journalist; Sports staff writer San Francisco Chronicle. Contbr. articles to numerous profl. jours.; author: (Sports Book) Game of Shadows, 2006; numerous appearances on sports radio and television shows. Recipient Dick Schaap Excellence in Sports Journalism award, 2004, George Polk award, 2004, Edgar A. Poe award, White House Correspondent's Assn., 2004. Achievements include being one of original journalists to cover BALCO steroids scandal in baseball. Office: San Francisco Chronicle 901 Mission St San Francisco CA 94103-2988 E-mail: fainaru-wada@sfchronicle.com.

FAINBERG, ANTHONY, physicist; b. London, Jan. 14, 1944; came to U.S., 1947; s. Benjamin and Elizabeth (Martelli) F.; m. Louise Vasvari (div. 1986); m. Diane August, Sept. 7, 1986. AB, NYU, 1964; PhD, U. Calif., Berkeley, 1969. Physicist INFN U. of Turin, Italy, 1970-72; rsch. prof. Syracuse (N.Y.) U., 1973-78; physicist Brookhaven Nat. Lab., Upton, NY, 1978-83; legis. aide Office of Senator Bingaman, Washington, 1983-84; sr. assoc. Office of Tech. Assessment, Washington, 1985-95; dir. Office Policy and Planning for Civil Aviation Security Fed. Aviation Adminstrn., 1996-99; fellow Ctr. for Internat. Security and Arms Control, Stanford, 1991-92; chief advanced concepts divsn. Advanced Sys./Concepts Office Def. Threat Reduction Agy., Dept. of Def., 1999—2002; program mgr. dept. homeland security Sci & Tech. Directorate, Washington, 2002—05; spl. asst. tech. Transp. Security Adminstn., Washington, 2002—; dir. office transformational R&D, Domestic Nuc. Detection Office Dept. Homeland Security, Washington, 2002—05; sr. analyst Inst. for Def. Analysis, Alexandria, Va., 2005—. Editor: (book) The Energy Source Book, 1991. Fellow Am. Phys. Soc. (mem. panel on pub. affairs 1990-92, 95-96, congl. fellow 1983-84); mem. AAAS. Office: SFRD Inst for Def Analyses 4850 Mark Center Dr Alexandria VA Office Phone: 703-845-2545. Personal E-mail: fainberg666@comcast.net.

FAINSTEIN, NORMAN, sociology professor, former academic administrator; m. Susan Fainstein; 2 children. BS with highest honors, MIT, 1966, PhD with highest distinction, 1971. Prof., dep. chair undergrad. programs in gen. studies, dir. summer session dept. sociology Columbia U., NYC, 1971—76; prof., assoc. dean acad. affairs Grad. Sch. Mgmt. and Urban Professions New Sch. for Social Rsch., NYC, 1983—87; prof., dean Sch. Liberal Arts and Scis. Baruch Coll. CUNY, NYC, 1987—95; prof., dean of faculty Vassar Coll., Poughkeepsie, NY, 1996—2001; pres. Conn. Coll., New London, 2001—06. Vis. scholar Harvard U., 2006—. Author: 4 books; contbr. numerous articles to profl. jours. Active Poughkeepsie Inst., Andrew W. Mellon Found. Fellow Woodrow Wilson, NSF, Stouffer, Harvard-MIT Joint Ctr. for Urban Studies. Office: Conn Coll 270 Mohegan Ave New London CT 06320

FAIR, JAMES RUTHERFORD, JR., engineering educator, consultant; b. Charleston, Mo., Oct. 14, 1920; s. James Rutherford and Georgia Irene (Case) Fair; m. Merle Innis, Jan. 14, 1950; children: James Rutherford III, Elizabeth, Richard Innis. Student, The Citadel, 1938-40; BS, Ga. Inst. Tech., 1942; MS, U. Mich., 1949; PhD, U. Tex., 1955; DSc (hon.), Washington U., 1977; HHD (hon.), Clemson U., 1987. Rsch. engr. Shell Devel. Co., Emeryville, Calif., 1954-56; with Monsanto Co., 1942-52, 56-79, engring. dir. corp. engring. dept. St. Louis, 1969-79; McKetta chair chem. engring. U. Tex., Austin, 1979—. Dir., v.p. Fractionation Rsch., Inc., Bartlesville, Okla., 1969—79; pres. James R. Fair, Inc., 1981—2004. Author: North Arkansas Line, 1969, Distillation, 1971, 1998, Louisiana and Arkansas, 1997; contbr. articles to profl. jours. Recipient Profl. Achievement award, Chem. Engring. mag., 1968, King award, U. Tex., 1987. Fellow: AIChE (bd. dirs. 1965—67, inst. lectr. 1979, Walker award 1973, Practice award 1975, Founders award 1977, Separation Tech. award 1994); mem.: NAE, NSPE, Am. Soc. Engring. Edn., Am. Chem. Soc. (Separation Sci. and Tech. award 1993, Acad. Achievement award 2005), Headliners Club (Austin), Faculty Club U. Tex., Sigma Nu. Republican. Presbyterian. Home: 2804 Northwood Rd Austin TX 78703-1603 Office: U Tex Dept Chem Engring Separations Rsch Progr Austin TX 78712 Office Phone: 512-471-0939. Personal E-mail: j.fair@sbcglobal.net. Business E-Mail: fair@che.utexas.edu.

FAIR, JEAN EVERHARD, retired education educator; b. Evanston, Ill., July 21, 1917; d. Drury Hampton and Bess Marion (Everhard) F. BA, U. Ill., 1938; MA, U. Chgo., 1939, PhD, 1953. Tchr. Evanston (Ill.) Twp. High Sch., 1940-48, 1954-58; tchr. U. Minn. High Sch., 1948-49, U. Ill. High Sch., 1951-53; prof. edn. Wayne State U., Detroit, 1958-82, now prof. emeritus. Cons. in edn.; cons. Mich. Ednl. Goals, Objectives and Assessment in Social Studies; reviewer of position statements for teaching and learning, standards, assessment and other manuscripts for Nat. Coun. Social Studies. Contbr. articles to profl. jours. Mem. AAUW, Nat. Council for Social Studies (pres. 1972, dir. 1958-61, 73-75), Assn. for Supervision and Curriculum Devel., Social Sci. Edn. Consortium, LWV, Phi Beta Kappa. Mem. United Ch. Christ.

FAIRBAIRN, JOYCE, Canadian government official; b. Lethbridge, Alta., Can., Nov. 6, 1939; m. Michael Gillan (dec.). BA in English, U. Alta., 1960; B Journalism, Carleton U., 1961. Mem. news staff Ottawa (Ont., Can.) Jour., 1961; mem. staff parliamentary press gallery UPI, Ottawa, 1962-64; mem. staff parliamentary bur. F.P. Publs., 1964-70; legis. asst., sr. legis. advisor Prime Minister of Can. Pierre Elliott Trudeau, 1970-84, comms. coord., 1981-83; mem. Senate for Province of Alta., 1984—, appt. to privy coun., leader govt., 1993-97, minister with spl. responsibility for literacy, 1993-97, spl. advisor for literacy, 1997. Mem. Spl. Senate Com. on Youth, Senate Standing Coms. on Transp. and Comm., Legal and Constl. Affairs, Fgn. Affairs, Agr. and Forestry, mem. senate social affairs com.; founding mem. standing com. on Aboriginal peoples; chair spl. com. on Anti-Terrorism, 2001, 05; vice chair Nat. Liberal Caucus and Western and No. Liberal Caucus, 1984-91; co-chair nat. campaign com. Liberal Party of Can., 1991. Past mem. senate U. Lethbridge; inducted into Kainai Chieftanship, Blood Nation, pres., 2004—; chmn. Friends of Can. Paralympics, 1998-2003; chmn. bd. dirs. Can. Paralympic Found., 2003—. Named hon. col. 18th Air Def. Regt., Royal Can. Army. Office: Can Senate 571-S Centre Block Ottawa ON Canada K1A 0A4 Office Phone: 613-996-4382. E-mail: fairbj@sen.parl.gc.ca.

FAIRBAIRN, URSULA FARRELL, human resources executive; b. Newark, Feb. 5, 1943; d. Henry C. and Clara J. (Ziefle) Otte; m. William Todd Fairbairn III, May 14, 1978; children: W. Todd, Mary, Joyce Sjoberg. BA, Upsala Coll., 1965; MAT in Math., Harvard U., 1966. Instr., numerous mktg. positions IBM, NYC, 1966-78; exec. asst. to sec., White House fellow U.S. Treasury Dept., Washington, 1973-74; exec. asst. to chmn. bd., group dir. IBM, Armonk, N.Y., 1978-79, v.p. mgmt. svcs., then v.p. mktg. ops. west, 1980-84, dir. pers. resources, 1984-87, dir. bus. and mgmt. edn., 1987, dir. edn., 1987-89, dir. edn. and mgmt. devel., 1989-90; sr. v.p. human resources Union Pacific Corp., Bethlehem, Pa., 1990-96; exec. v.p. human resources and quality Am. Express Co., NYC, 1996—2005; pres, CEO Fairbairn Group, LLC, 2005—. Bd. dirs. VF Corp., Greensboro, N.C., Air Products Corp., Allentown, Pa., Sunoco Corp., Phila., Circuit City Stores, Inc., Richmond, Centex Corp., Dallas. Contbg. author: Managing Human Resources in the Information Age, 1991. Mem. Com. of 200, Catalyst, N.Y.C.; vice-chair Nat. Acad.-HR; chair Pers. Round Table. Mem. Bus. Roundtable, Employee Rels. Com., Labor Policy Assn. Avocations: gardening, art, reading, walking, travel. Office: Centex Corp 2728 N Harwood St Dallas TX 75201-1516 Office Phone: 214-981-5000. Office Fax: 214-981-6859.

FAIRBANK, RICHARD D., diversified financial services company executive; b. 1950; BA in Econs., Stanford U., Calif., 1972, MBA, 1981. Cons. Strategic Planning Assocs., 1981—87; chmn., CEO Capital One Fin. Corp., McLean, Va., 1994—2003, chmn., pres., CEO, 2005—; chmn. US region MasterCard Inc., 2002—04. Bd. dirs. MasterCard US Region, 1995—2004, MasterCard Internat. Global Bd., 2004—. Named Best CEO, Instl. Investor mag., Bus. Leader of Yr., Washingtonian Mag. Office: Capital One Fin Corp 1680 Capital One Dr Mc Lean VA 22102-3491 Office Phone: 703-720-1000.*

FAIRBANK, ROBERT HAROLD, lawyer; b. Northampton, Mass., Mar. 4, 1948; s. William Martin and Jane (Davenport) F.; m. Valerie Baker; children: Sarah Julia, David Kivy. AB in Polit. Sci., Stanford U., 1972; MLS, U. Calif.-Berkeley, 1973; JD, NYU, 1977. Bar: Calif. 1977, US Dist. Ct. (cen. and no. dists.) Calif. 1978, US Dist. Ct. (so. dist.) Calif. 1993. Assoc. Gibson, Dunn & Crutcher, LA, 1977-84, ptnr., 1985-96; co-founding ptnr. Fairbank & Vincent, 1996—. Lawyer rep., co-chair 9th cir. Jud. Conf. Ctrl. Dist., 2000—02; bd. dirs. 9th Jud. Cir. Hist. Soc.; lectr. law U. So. Calif. Law Sch., 2004—, Stanford U. Sch. Law, 2007. Author: Effective Pretrial and Trial Motions, 1983, California Practice Guide: Civil Trials and Evidence (The Rutter Group 1993, with yearly updates); mem. editl. bd. NYU Law Rev., 1975-76. Named One of Top 100 Bus. Lawyers in LA, LA Bus. Jour., 1995. Mem. Assn. Bus. Trial Lawyers (co-founder San Francisco and Orange County chpts., bd. govs. 1984-85, treas. 1986-87, sec. 1987-88, v.p. 1988-89, pres. 1989-90), LA County Bar Assn. (fed. cts. com. 1983-85), Jud. Coun. Calif. Adv. Com. on Local Rules (subcom. chair on civil trial rules). Office: Fairbank & Vincent 11755 Wilshire Blvd Ste 2320 Los Angeles CA 90025-1501 Office Phone: 310-996-5520. E-mail: rfairbank@fairbankvincent.com.

FAIRBANKS, RICHARD MONROE, III, lawyer, educator, retired ambassador; b. Indpls., Feb. 10, 1941; s. Richard Monroe, Jr. and Mary Evans (Caperton) F.; m. Ann Shannon O'Connor, June 13, 1962; children: Woods Alexander, Jonathan Barcroft. AB, Yale U., 1962; JD magna cum laude, Columbia U., 1969. Bar: D.C. Assoc. Arnold & Porter, 1969-71; spl. asst. to adminstr. EPA, 1971; staff asst. Domestic Council, Exec. Office of Pres., White House, 1971-72, assoc. dir. energy, environ. and natural resources, 1972-74; founding ptnr. firm Ruckelshaus, Beveridge & Fairbanks, Washington, 1974-81; asst. sec. congressional relations Dept. State, 1981-82, ambassador, spl. negotiator for Middle East peace process, 1982-83, ambassador-at-large, 1984-85; ptnr. Paul, Hastings, Janofsky & Walker, 1986-89, mng. ptnr., 1990-92, sr. counsel, 1992-94, Ctr. for Strategic and Internat. Studies, Washington, 1992-94, mng. dir. for domestic and internat. issues, 1994-99, pres., CEO, 1999-2000, counselor, 2000—. Adj. prof. law Georgetown U., Washington, 1971-72, U. Micme, 2005; chmn. bd. Laydina Prodns.; bd. dirs. SEACOR Holdings Inc., GATX Corp., The Lockhart Cos.; sr. counselor Am. Enterprise Inst., 1985-90; pres. U.S. nat. com. for Pacific Econ. Coop., 1986-92; internat. chair Pacific Econ. Coop. Coun., 1991-92, U.S. vice chair 1992—; mem. Pres.'s Task Force on U.S. Internat. Broadcasting, 1991; vis. prof. U. Miami, 2005, Columbia U. Law Sch., 2007. Founder, 1st pres. Washington chpt. Am. Refugee Com., 1978, mem. nat. bd. dirs., 1977-93; trustee Meridian House Internat., 1978-81; mem. com. natural resources Rep. Nat. Com., 1977-80; mem. Pres.'s Citizens Adv. Com. Environ. Quality, 1974-77; bd. visitors Columbia U. Sch. Law, 1999—. Officer USN, 1962-66. Mem.: ABA, Ctr. for Strategic and Internat. Studies (adv. bd. 1989, bd. trustees 2000—), Coun. Am. Ambassadors, Coun. Fgn. Rels., D.C. Bar Assn., Indian Creek Club, Roaring Fork Club, Chevy Chase Club, Yale Club (N.Y.C.), Met. Club Washington, Burning Tree Club, Anglers Club. Office: Ctr Strategic & Internat Studies 1800 K St NW Washington DC 20006-2202 Business E-Mail: rfairban@csis.org.

FAIRBANKS, ROBERT ALVIN, lawyer; b. Oklahoma City, July 9, 1944; s. Albert Edward and Lucille Imogene (Scherer) F.; m. Linda Gayle Geer, Aug. 26, 1967; children: Chele Lyn, Kimberly Jo, Robert Alvin II, Michael Albert, Richard Alan, Joseph Alexander. BS in Math., U. Okla., 1967, JD, 1973; MBA, Oklahoma City U., 1970, MCJA, 1975; LLM, Columbia U., 1976; MA, Stanford U., 1984; MEd, Harvard U., 1993. Bar: Okla. 1974, U.S. Dist. Ct. (we. dist.) Okla. 1974, U.S. Ct. Customs and Patent Appeals 1974, U.S. Ct. Mil. Appeals, 1974, U.S. Tax Ct. 1974, U.S. Claims Ct. 1975, U.S. Customs Ct. 1975, U.S. Ct. Appeals (10th cir.) 1975, U.S. Supreme Ct. 1977, U.S. Dist. Ct. (ea. dist.) Okla. 1984, Minn. 1993. Commd. 2d lt. USAF, 1967, advanced through grades to capt., 1970, col., 1986; asst. staff judge adv., chief of claims div. Office of Staff Judge Adv., Tinker AFB, Okla., 1974-75; legal asst. to Justice William A. Berry, Okla. Supreme Ct., 1977; pvt. practice Norman, Okla., 1974—; v.p. St. Gregory's U., Shawnee, Okla., 1997—; prof. math. Univ. Ctrl. Okla., 2004—. Instr. bus. adminstrn. U. Md. Far East div., Nha Trang, Viet Nam, 1970-71, Rose State Coll., Midwest City, Okla., 1974; rsch. assoc. in law U. Okla., Norman, 1974, spl. lectr., 1974-75, vis. asst. prof., 1976-77, adj. prof. law, 1984—; vis. asst. prof. law Oklahoma City U., 1977; asst. prof. law U. Ark., Fayetteville, Arks., 1977-81; assoc. prof. law La. State U., Baton Rouge, 1981; rsch. asst. dept. family, community and preventative medicine Stanford (Calif.) Med. Sch., 1981-82; adj. asst. prof. govt. contract law Air Force Inst. Tech., Wright-Patterson AFB, Ohio, 1985—; v.p. St. Gregory's U., Shawnee, Okla.; prof. bus. adminstrn. U. Phoenix; adj. prof. law and mgmt. Okla. Christian U. Coll. Bus.; cons. Cheyenne Tribe, Clinton, Okla., 1977-81, 90, Citizens Band of Pottawatomie Tribe, Shawnee, Okla., 1977-79, Inst. for Devel. of Indian Law, Washington, 1976-81; dir. Native Am. Coll. Prep. Ctr. Bemidji State U., Minn., 1993—; prof. math. U. Cen. Okla., 2004—. Editor-in-chief Am. Indian Law Rev., 1973; editor Okla. Law Rev., 1971-73; producer, dir.: (with Barbara P. Ettinger) "Aa-Niin" film, 1994; author book revs.; contbr. articles to profl. jours. Mem. bd. control Fayetteville (Ark.) City Hosp., 1977-81; cubmaster Boy Scouts Am., Norman, 1982-83, asst. scoutmaster, Stanford, 1981, scoutmaster, Norman, 1990-91, com. mem., den leader, 1988; softball coach Jr. High Girls League, Fayetteville, 1977-81; mem. adv. bd. Native Am. Prep. Sch., Santa Fe; pres., chmn. bd. Native Am. Coll. Prep. Ctr., Bemidji, Minn.; mem. exec. adv. bd. Aerospace Sci. and Tech. Edn. Ctr. of Okla., Okla. City Univ.; mem. legal edn. com., Okla. Bar Assn. U.S. Dept. Edn. fellow Stanford U. Med. Sch.; Charles Evans Hughes fellow Columbia U. Law Sch., 1976; Sequoyah fellow Assn. Am. Indian Affairs, 1975-76; Mellon fellow Harvard U. Sch. Edn., 1993; nominee Pulitzer prize for Disting. Commentary, 1997. Mem. ABA, Okla. Bar Assn., Fed. Bar Assn., Am. Trial Lawyers Assn., Okla. Trial Lawyers Assn., Okla. Indian Bar Assn., Oklahoma County Bar Assn., Assn. Am. Law Schs., N.G. Assn. U.S., Air Force Assn. (life), Res. Officers Assn. (life), Nat. Contract Mgmt. Assn., Soc. Logistics Engrs., Phi Alpha Delta, Phi Delta Epsilon, Phi Delta Kappa. Republican. Roman Catholic. Office: 2212 Westpark Dr Norman OK 73069-4012 Personal E-mail: rafairbanks@sbcglobal.net. Business E-Mail: rfairbanks@ucok.edu.

FAIRCHILD, MORGAN (PATSY MCCLENNY), actress; b. Dallas, Feb. 3, 1950; Actress: (feature films) A Bullet for Pretty Boy, 1970, The Seduction, 1982, The Red-Headed Stranger, 1986, Pee-Wee's Big Adventure, 1985, Campus Man, 1987, Sleeping Beauty, 1987, Deadly Illusion, 1987, Killing Blue, 1988, Phantom of the Mall: Eric's Revenge, 1989, Freaked, 1993, Test Tube Teens from the Year 2000, 1994, Venus Rising, 1995, Criminal Hearts, 1995, Gospa, 1995, Holy Man, 1998, Shattered Illusions, 1998, Nice Guys Sleep Alone, 1999, Unshackled, 2000, Peril, 2000, Held for Ransom, 2000, Jungle Juice, 2001, Teddy Bears' Picnic, 2002, Arizona Summer, 2003, Knuckle Sandwich, 2004, Shock to the System, 2006, (TV movies) The Initiation of Sarah, 1978, Murder in Music City, 1979, Concrete Cowboys, 1979, The Memory of Eva Ryker, 1980, The Dream Merchants, 1980, The Girl, the Gold Watch, and Dynamite, 1981, Honeyboy, 1982, The Zany Adventures of Robin Hood, 1984, Time Bomb, 1984, Our Planet Tonight, 1987, Street of Dreams, 1988, The Haunting fo Sarah Hardy, 1989, How to Murder a Millionaire, 1990, Menu for Murder, 1990, Even Angels Fall, 1991, Writer's Block, 1991, Sherlock Holmes and the Leading Lady, 1992, Perry Mason: The Case of the Skin-Deep Scandal, 1993, Dead Man's Island, 1996, Star Command, 1996, Teenage Confidential, 1996, Into the Arms of Danger, 1997, Bimbo Movie Bash, 1997, Just Deserts, 1999, I was a Teenage Faust, 2002, (TV series) Search for Tomorrow, 1973-77, Flamingo Road, 1981-82, Paper Dolls, 1984, Falcon Crest, 1985-86, Fashion House 2006-, (mini-series) 79 Park Avenue, 1977, North and South, 1985, North and South Book II, 1986, (TV spls.) Bob Hope's Spring Fling of Comedy and Glamour, 1981, Women Who Rate a '10', 1981, Billy Crystal Comedy Hour, 1982, Whatever Became Of.?, 1982, Our Planet Tonight, 1987, (stage prodns.) Night of 100 Stars, 1982, Night of 100 Star II, 1985; guest appearances Kojak, 1976, Rafferty, 1977, Switch, 1977, Happy Days, 1977, The Bob Newhart Show, 1977, Police Women, 1978, Barnaby Jones, 1977, 1978, Mork and Mindy, 1978, 1979, Dallas, 1978, Love Boat, 1981, Magnum, P.I., 1982, Simon & Simon, 1982, My Two Dads, 1989, Murphy Brown, 1989, Rosanne, 1992, Lois & Clark: The New Adventures of Superman, 1993, Murder, She Wrote, 1993, Robin's Hoods, 1993, Burke's Law, 1994, Empty Nest, 1994, Diagnosis Murder, 1994, General Hospital, 1996, Cybill, 1996-97, Head Over Heels, 1997, Touched By An Angel, 1997, The New Addams Family, 1999, Dharma & Greg, 2001, Friends, 1995, 1998, 2001, 7th Heaven, 2001, Roswell, 2002, Providence, 2002, That '80's Show, 2002, Just Shoot Me!, 2003, That '70's Show, 2004. Office: PO Box 46609 Los Angeles CA 90046-0609

FAIRCHILD, PHYLLIS ELAINE, school counselor; b. Franklin, La., Feb. 23, 1927; d. Joseph Virgil and Georgiana (Bourgeois) F. BS in Chemistry and Biology, U. Southwestern La., 1946; postgrad., La. State U., 1949-50, MEd in Guidance, 1966. Cert. chemistry, biology, gen. sci., Spanish and social studies tchr., counselor, La. Tchr. sci. St. Mary Parish Sch. Bd., Franklin, 1952—58, counselor, 1977—82; tchr. sci. Am. Dependent Schs., Yokohama, Japan, 1958—60, London, Lakenheath, England, 1960—61, Ramey AFB, PR, 1961—62, Norfolk City Schs., Va., 1962—63, Iberville Parish Sch. Bd., Plaquemine, La., 1963—66; tchr. sci., counselor East Baton Rouge Parish Sch. Bd., Baton Rouge, 1966—77; counselor Hanson Sch. Bd., Franklin, 1982—94, 1996—98; ret., 1998. Mem. adv. com. La. Dept. Edn., Baton Rouge, 1976, 78. Pres. St. Mary Parish Retired Tchrs. Assn., 2007—. Mem. DAR (regent Attakapas chpt. 2003-05, dir. 6th Dist. 2004-07, La. state chaplain, 2007-), Coun. on Aging Bd., La. Landmarks Soc., Cath. Daus. Am. (co-chmn. religious litergy 1992-94), Fortnightly Lit. Club (pres. 1982-83), Sigma Delta Pi, Pi Gamma Mu, Kappa Kappa Gamma, Delta Kappa Gamma (chmn. membership, scholarship, profl. affairs 1971-77, parliamentarian 1996-98). Avocations: reading, walking, piano, writing. Home: 214 Morris St Franklin LA 70538-6127 Personal E-mail: Phyllis@teche.net.

FAIRCHILD, ROBERT CHARLES, pediatrician; b. Kansas City, Mo., Dec. 22, 1921; s. Charles Clement and Ada Mae (Baker) F.; m. Patricia Louise Russell, May 28, 1964; children— Robert, Nancy, Rex Hartman, Dan Hartman Student, Kansas City Jr. Coll., 1938-40; BA, U. Kans., 1942, MD, 1950. Diplomate Am. Bd. Pediatrics. Intern Kansas City Gen. Hosp., 1950-51; resident in pediatrics U. Kans. Med. Ctr., 1951-53; practice medicine specializing in pediatrics Mission, Kans., 1953-70; dir. area clinics Children's Mercy Hosp., Kansas City, Mo., 1970-74, dir. outpatient services, 1974-88, ret., 1991. Prof. pediatrics emeritus U. Mo.-Kansas City Sch. Medicine; mem. adv. com. Assoc. Degree nursing program Johnson County Community Coll. Contbr. articles to med. jours. Served to maj. U.S. Army, 1942-46 Decorated Bronze Star; recipient Physician's Recognition award AMA, 1990; Porter scholar U. Kans. Sch. Medicine, 1950. Mem. AMA, Am. Acad. Pediatrics, Mo. State Med. Assn., Met. Med. Soc.

of Kansas City, Greater Kansas City Pediatric Soc., Kansas City S.W. Clin. Soc., Alpha Omega Alpha, Nu Sigma Nu, Sigma Nu. Home: Claridge Ct 8101 Mission Rd Apt 233 Prairie Village KS 66208-5247

FAIRCHILD, SAMUEL WILSON, investor, retired federal agency administrator, financial services executive; b. Ft. Eustis, Va., July 16, 1954; s. Henry Howell and Ruby Mae (Love) F.; m. Linda Elizabeth Doremus, May 17, 1986; children: Elizabeth Christine, Samuel Bruce. BS, BA, Coll. William and Mary, 1977. Cons. ITT, Inc., Smithfield, Va., 1977; v.p., gen. mgr. P.A., Inc., Hampton, Va., 1977—83; sr. policy advisor Exec. Office of Pres., Washington, 1983—89; dep. asst. sec. U.S. Dept. Transp., Washington, 1989—91; v.p., sr. fellow Ctr. for Tech. and Pub. Policy Rsch. BDM Internat., Inc., McLean, Va., 1991—94; ptnr. Galland, Kharasch, Morse & Garfinkle, p.c., Washington, 1993—99; v.p. PA Cons. Group, Washington, 1999—2004; pres. Tadpole Group, Morris Plains, NJ, 2004—; mng. dir. Thesus Cap. Ptnrs., Morris Plains, 2004—; CEO Tower Tech. Holdings, Inc., Manitowoc, Wis., 2006—. Chmn. bd. dirs. Schiphol N.Am. Holdings, Amsterdam, 1996—, Loyow.com, Beijing; bd. dirs., CEO Tower Tech Sys., Inc. Manitowoc, Wis., 2005—; bd. dirs., founder, pres. GKMG Cons. Svcs., Washington; ptnr. Innova Aviation Consulting, Chevy Chase, Md., 2005—; bd. dirs. BodyBlue, Inc., Natural Solutions, Toronto; exec. chmn. Dragon Blue, Inc., Morris Plains, NJ; CEO ASP Diversified, Inc., Mpls. Author, editor: Moving America, 1989. Active Boy Scouts Am., Irving, Tex., 1972—, mem. World Scout Bur., Geneva, 1972-80, Coun. for Excellence in Govt.; mem. exec. bd. Las Vegas Internat. Scouting Mus., Nat. Capital Area Coun. Boy Scouts Am., 1990—, Patriots Path coun., 1999—, Scouting Century Found., 1999—; co-chmn. ARC, Alexandria, Va., 1988-90. Recipient Disting. Alumni award Christopher Newport Coll., 1990; Usry Garland scholar Coll. William and Mary/Christopher Newport Coll., 1975. Mem. Nat. Aviation Assn., Coun. for Excellence in Govt., Aero Club. Presbyterian. Avocations: photography, music. Home: PO Box 341 Brookside NJ 07926-0341 Home Phone: 973-543-0102; Office Phone: 973-229-9446. Personal E-mail: samchild7@mac.com. Business E-Mail: sam@tadpolegroup.com.

FAIRCLOTH, LAURIE RICKETSON, critical care nurse; b. Atlanta, May 19, 1957; d. John Fleming Ricketson, Jr and Kathrine Thompson Peters; m. Harry Donald Faircloth, Apr. 4, 1981; children: Theodore Grover Roberts, Todd Hayes, Anna Marie Bass, Brande Jane Shealy. Degree in Nursing, Med. Ctr. Ctrl. Ga., Macon, 1978. RN in advanced trauma care, 2005. Co-coord. clin. Ga. Neurosurgical Inst., Macon, 1979—, instr., 2005—07. Mem.: Soc. Trauma Nurses, Am. Assn. Neurol. Surgeons (membership com. 2005—07). Office: Georgia Neurosurgical Inst 840 Pine St Ste 880 Macon GA 31201 Home Phone: 478-474-5644; Office Phone: 478-743-7092. Office Fax: 478-743-0523; Home Fax: 478-743-0523. Personal E-mail: lauriefaircloth@hotmail.com. Business E-Mail: laurie@ganeurosurg.org.

FAIRES, IAN MATTHEW, music educator; b. Charlotte, NC, Sept. 26, 1977; s. Steven Rossell Faires and Rebecca Lynn Schneider. MusB, Appalachian State U., 1999. Lic. edn. for music grades K-12. Band dir. Charlotte-Mecklenburg Schs., Charlotte, NC, 2000; music dir. Mooresville (N.C.) Intermediate Sch., 2000—; pianist Southside Bapt. Ch., Mooresville, 2001; assoc. music min. Mt. Zion United Meth. Ch., Cornelius, NC, 2002—; pvt. piano tchr. Music & Arts Ctr., Huntersville, NC, 2003—04. Mem., tenor Joyful Hearts, Mooresville, 2003—04, Blessing, Cornelius, 2001—02; asst. dir. Davidson (N.C.) Coll. Pep Band, 2000—. Composer: (recorder method book) Mooresville Intermediate School Recorder Method, 2002. Mem.: N.C. Music Educators Assn., Music Educators Nat. Conf., N.C. Assn. for Educators. Independent. Methodist. Office: Mooresville Intermediate Sch 233 Kistler Farm Rd Mooresville NC 28115 Home: 2625 Moores Park Dr Charlotte NC 28214-2727

FAIRFIELD, BILL L., finance company executive; BS in Engring., Bradley U.; MBA in Bus. Adminstrn., Harvard U. Sr. exec. Eastman Kodak, 1969-73; sr. v.p. Lindsay Mfg. Co., 1975-79; pres. mktg. domestic irrigation divsn. Valmont Industries Inc., 1979-81, pres., gen. mgr. irrigation divsn., 1981-82; pres., CEO, Inacom Corp., Omaha, 1982-99, also bd. dirs.; chmn. Dreamfield Ptnrs. Inc., Dreamfield Capital Ventures, 2000—. Bd. dirs. Fed. Res. Bank Kansas City, Omaha, Sitel Corp., others. Trustee U. Nebr., Lincoln; bd. trustees Boy Scouts Am.; mem. Chancellor's Adv. Coun., U. Nebr., Omaha. Office: The Fairacres Project 206 Fairacres Rd Omaha NE 68132-2706

FAIRFIELD, PAULA KATHLEEN, sound recording engineer; b. Halifax, NS, Can., Sept. 17, 1961; d. Henry Alfred and Sylvia Kathleen Fairfield; life ptnr. Carla Mary Murray. BFA, N.S. Coll. of Art and Design, Halifax, 1984. Freelance sound editor, Toronto, Ont., Canada, 1987—97; freelance picture editor, 1987—96; gen. mgr. Charles St. Video, Toronto, Ont., Canada, 1987—94; sec. treas. Pandora Pictures Inc, Toronto, Ont., Canada, 1987—98; pres. MHz Sound Design Inc, Toronto, Ont., Canada, 1997—2000, LA, 1998—. Cons., design arts Ont. Arts Coun., Toronto, 1992; sr. tech. wirer CTV Networks, Network Relocation and Olympic installation, Toronto, 1994—95; instr., post prodn. sound Ont. Coll. of Art and Design, Toronto, 1997; sound supr., sound designer The Black Dahlia. Dir.: (electronic media installation) MIRAGE, (short film) Screamers, Livewires, Fragments; sound effects editor and sound designer (feature film) Sin City, sound supervisor and sound designer (television series) La femme Nikita, sound effects editor and sound designer Due South; sound supr., sound designer: (TV series) Medium; sound effects editor, sound designer Lost (Golden Reel award, Motion Picture Sound Editors Orgn., 2007); artist (exhibition group) Retrospective of Canadian Film and Video, George Pompidou Centre, Paris, Anteneo Femista De Madrid, Madrid, sound supr. and sound designer (feature film) Assault on Precinct 13, artist (exhibition group) Olympic Musem, Sarajevo, Museum of Modern Art, Zagreb, Croatia, Bienal De La Imagen En Movimento, Madrid, Infermental 10: There-Between-Here, Osnabruck, sound effects editor (feature film) A Love Song for Bobby Long, sound effects editor and sound designer Terminator 3: Rise of the Machines, Spy Kids 3D: Game Over; sound editor, designer: (feature film) The Black Dahlin, 2006; Lucky Number Slevin, 2006. Jury mem. and adjudicator Can. Coun. for the Arts, Ottawa, 1989—97, Toronto Arts Coun., Toronto, 1989—97, Ont. Arts Coun., Toronto, Ontario, 1990—97. Recipient B award, Can. Coun. for the Arts, 1992, Gemini Award for Achievement in Sound Editing: Due South, Acad. of Can. Cinema and TV, 1996, Can. Musicvideo VideoFACT Award, 1994; grantee audio prodn. grantee, Can. Coun. for the Arts, 1990, Explorations grantee, Can. Coun. for the Art, 1990, Video Prodn. grantee, 1989, 1987, Photography grantee, 1986, Film Prodn. grantee, Ont. Arts Coun., 1993, Video Prodn. grantee, 1992, Audio Prodn. grantee, Can. Coun. for the Arts, 1999, 1992, Film Prodn. grantee, 1994. Mem.: Motion Picture Sound Editors Orgn., Acad. TV Arts and Scis., Am. Film Inst., Women in Film, L.A., Am. Working Malinois Assn., United Schutzhund Clubs of Am., Audio Engring. Soc., Soc. of Motion Picture and TV Engrs., Motion Picture Editors Guild, Internat. Alliance of Theatrical Stage Emplyees, Moving Picture Technicians, Artists and Allied Crafts, Profl. Orgn. of Women in Entertainment Reaching Up (founding mem. 2000—03), S.W. Working Dog Assn. Home Phone: 818-907-9906; Office Phone: 818-980-0306.

FAIRFIELD, RICHARD THOMAS, art educator; b. Peoria, Ill., Aug. 7, 1937; s. Bede Joseph and Margaret (Bane) F.; m. Barbara Ann Ropers, Oct. 14, 1961; children: Kimberly Ann, Scott Walter. BFA, Bradley U., 1961; MFA, U. Ill., 1963. Prof. art Eastern Mich. U., Ypsilanti, 1963—. Tchr. print making Santa Rapaqata, Florence, Italy, 1974. One-person shows include Corp. Ctr., Eastern Mich. U., 1990, Albion (Mich.) Coll., 1991; two-person shows Ford Gallery, 1989, River Gallery, Chelsea, Mich., 2005, 06; three-person show Beau Arts Gallery, 1990; exhibited in group shows at Kanagawa Prefectural Gallery, Japan, 1984-90, Art Ctr., Mt. Clemens, Mich., 1988, U. Mus. History of Religion and Atheism, Lviv, USSR, 1990-92, John F. Kennedy Meml. Union Art Gallery, 1990. Bd. dirs. Nat. Kidney Found., Ann Arbor, 1983-89, Mpls. Regional Psychiat. Hosp. Friends, Ypsilanti, 1990-91, Alzheimers Assn. Roman Catholic. Office: Eastern Mich Univ 114 Ford Hall Ypsilanti MI 48197-2251 Business E-Mail: rfairfield@emich.edu.

FAIRFIELD-SONN, JAMES WILLED, management educator, consultant; b. Nashua, NH, Aug. 21, 1948; s. David Alexander and Christine Mary (Fairfield) Sonn; m. Lynn Groark, July 3, 1982; children: Anne Madeline, James Willed, Jr., John Thomas. MS, Cornell U., 1979; MA, Yale U., 1980, MPhil, 1982, PhD, 1985. Mgr. office adminstrn. Hartford Ins. Group, Indpls., 1972-76; asst. prof. mgmt. U. Hartford, West Hartford, Conn., 1982-88, assoc. prof., 1988—2002, prof., 2002—, chmn. mgmt. dept., 1987-90, dir. exec. MBA, 1993-95, interim dean, 2004—05, dean, 2005—. Pres. Fairfield-Sonn Assocs., Centerbrook, Conn., 1981—; v.p. bd. dirs. ENCOMPASS Software. Author: Corporate Culture and the Quality Organization, 2001; contbr. articles and revs. to profl. jours. Named Outstanding Tchr. of Yr., Barney Sch., 1999; Cornell U. indsl. and labor rels. fellow, 1977-78, Yale U. fellow, 1978-82, Olin fellow, 1981. Mem.: Assn. Yale Alumni (chmn. grad. and profl. schs. com. 1982—83), Ea. Acad. Mgmt., Acad. Mgmt. Republican. Congregationalist. Avocations: tennis, travel, gardening. Home and Office: PO Box 1047 Old Lyme CT 06371-0998 E-mail: jimfs@fairfield-sonn.net.

FAIRHURST, MARY E., state supreme court justice; b. 1957; BA in Polit. Sci. cum laude, Gonzaga U., 1979, JD magna cum laude, 1984. Bar: Wash. 1984. Jud. clk. to Hon. William H. Williams Wash. Supreme Ct., 1984, jud. clk. to Hon. William C. Goodloe, 1986; chief revenue, bankruptcy and collections divsn. Wash. Atty. Gen.'s Office, 1986—2002; justice Wash. Supreme Ct., Olympia, 2003—. Mem. Wash. Supreme Ct. Gender and Justice Commn., Access to Justice Bd. Com. Established Lawyers and Students Engaged in Resolution Program; mem. Girl Scouts Bd. of Pacific Peak Council; mem. bd. advisors Gonzaga Law Sch. Recipient Steward of Justice award, 1998, Allies for Justice award, LEGALS, P.S., 1999. Mem.: Wash. Women Lawyers (past pres., Passing the Torch award 1999), Wash. State Bar Assn. (past. pres., mem. bd. govs.). Office: Wash Supreme Ct PO Box 40929 415 12th Ave SW Olympia WA 98504-0929 Business E-Mail: J_M_Fairhurst@courts.wa.gov.*

FAIRMAN, JOEL MARTIN, retired broadcast executive; b. NYC, Mar. 12, 1929; s. Philip A. and Isabelle (Glackman) Feinberg; m. Claire Martin, Oct. 1, 1959; children: Elizabeth, David, Helen. BA, Amherst Coll., 1952; JD, Yale U., 1955. Assoc. Patterson Belknap & Webb, NYC, 1956-61; asst. to pres., v.p. Gianis & Co., Inc., NYC, 1961-65; sr. v.p. and mng. dir. corp. fin. communications group Prudential-Bache Securities and predecessor firms, NYC, 1965-83; chmn. Faircom Inc., 1984-98; vice chmn. Regent Comm., Inc., 1998—2001; chmn. North Shore Strategies Inc., 2001—06. Home: 290 Bayville Rd Locust Valley NY 11560-2003

FAIRMAN, MARC P., lawyer; b. May 25, 1945; BA, U. Calif., Berkeley, 1967; JD cum laude, Harvard U., 1970. Bar: Calif. 1971. Ptnr. McDermott, Will & Emery, Menlo Park; pvt. practice San Francisco. Northern Calif. adv. bd. Entrepreneurship Inst.; bd. trustees Mills Coll. Mem. Am. Inns of Ct., Assn. of Bus. Trial Lawyers. Office: 2 Embarcadero Ctr Ste 1800 San Francisco CA 94111 Office Phone: 415-732-1704. Office Fax: 415-732-1705. Business E-Mail: mfairman@pacbell.net.*

FAIRMAN, RALPH PAUL, physician, medical educator; s. Ralph Charles and Ursula Analisa Fairman; m. LoAnn Christy Fairman, Aug. 16, 1969. BA, Johns Hopkins U., Balt., 1968; MD, U. Mo., Columbia, 1972. Intern W.Va. U. Med. Ctr., 1972—73; field team dir. USPHS, Morgantown, W.Va., 1973—75; med. resident Va. Commonwealth U., Richmond, 1975—77, chief resident, 1977—78, asst. prof. medicine, 1980—86, assoc. prof. medicine, 1986—93, prof. medicine, 1993—. Adj. prof. law U. Richmond, 1994—98. Recipient Disting. Tchg. award, Va. Commonwealth U., 1994, Tchg. Excellence award, 2001, Disting. Svc. award, Richmond Acad. Medicine, 2005. Fellow: ACP, Am. Coll. Chest Physicians; mem.: Am. Thoracic Soc. Office: Va Commonwealth Univ Pulmonary Divsn 1200 E Broad St Richmond VA 23298

FAIRWEATHER, DANIEL EDWARD, music educator; b. Elizabeth, NJ, Oct. 19, 1978; s. Dorothy and Gilbert Fairweather. BMus, Ga. So. U., Statesboro, 1996—2001. Cert. tchr. Ga. Dept. Edn., 2002. Band dir. Atlanta Pub. Schs., 2002—. Pvt. lesson instr. Century Music Ctr., Decatur, Ga., 2003—. Young musicians mentor Salvation Army, Decatur, Ga., 2002—05. Mem.: Ga. Music Educators Assn. (assoc.). Conservative. Achievements include invention of the Fairweather Method - The process of playing rhythm guitar using a small maraca in your hand and foot, in order to simulate the sound of a full rhythm section. Avocations: basketball, art, poetry, travel, disc jockey. Home: 5533 Mountain View Pass Stone Mountain GA 30087 Home Phone: 678-613-4127. Personal E-mail: defairweather@gmail.com.

FAIRWEATHER, ROBERT GORDON LEE, retired lawyer; b. Rothesay, NB, Can., Mar. 27, 1923; s. Jack H.A.L. and Agnes Charlotte (Mackeen) F.; m. Nancy E. Broughall, June 1, 1946 (dec. Aug. 2003); children— Michael, Wendy, Hugh. B.C.L., U. N.B., 1949, LL.D. (hon.), 1973, St. Thomas U., 1977, Queens U., 1978, St. Francis Xavier U., 1980, York U., 1993. Called to bar N.B 1949, created Queen's Counsel 1958. Partner firm McKelvey, MacAulay, Machum & Fairweather, St. John, 1957-77; atty. gen. N.B., 1958-60; chief Can. Human Rights Commn., Ottawa, Ont., 1977-87; chmn. Immigration and Refugee Bd., Ottawa, 1987-92. Mem. Legis. Assembly N.B., 1952-62, M.P., 1962-77. Served with Royal Can. Navy, 1941-45. Decorated officer Order of Can.; recipient Outstanding Achievement award of pub. svc. Govt. Can., 1990, Humanitarian of the Yr. award Can. Red Cross, 1999, New Brunswick Pioneer of Human Rights award, 2002, Order of New Brunswick award, 2005; Ryerson Poly. U. fellow, 1993. Home: 2865 Rothesay Rd Apt 43 Rothesay NB Canada E2E 5VI

FAISON, RALPH E., communications equipment manufacturing executive; b. June 26, 1958; BS in Mktg., Ga. State U., Atlanta; MS in Mgmt., Stanford U., 1992. Various exec. positions AT&T wireless bus. unit; v.p. advt., brand mgmt. Lucent Tech., v.p., new ventures group, 1997—2001; pres., CEO Celiant Corp.(acquired by Andrew), 2001—02; pres., COO Andrew Corp., Westchester, Ill., 2002—03, pres., CEO, 2003—. Bd. dir. WatchMark Corp., NETGEAR, Inc.; bd. adv. New Venture Ptnrs. LLC. Bd. dir. Exec. Club, Chgo. Office: Andrew Corp Ste 900 3 Westbrook Corp Ctr Westchester IL 60154*

FAISON, SETH SHEPARD, retired insurance broker; b. NYC, Jan. 18, 1924; s. John Williams and Caroline Goree (Shepard) F.; m. Susan Tyler, Apr. 14, 1956 (dec. 1978); children: Katharine Faison Spencer, Seth Shepard, Sarah, Ann Faison Muller; m. Sara Williams Rose Chew, Mar. 29, 1980; stepchildren: Sara Holten Chew, Katherine Rose Chew, Arthur Duncan Chew (dec.). BA with honors and distinction, Wesleyan U., 1947. Personnel mgr. NBC, NYC, 1948-53; divsn. mgr. Am. Mgmt. Assn., NYC, 1953-58; asst. v.p. Johnson & Higgins, NYC, 1958-68, v.p., 1968-89; ret., 1989. Chmn. Bklyn. Acad. Music, 1966-72, hon. chmn., 1979—; trustee Bklyn. Inst. Arts and Scis., 1963-81, v.p., 1965-71, exec. v.p., 1971-74, vice-chmn., 1974-79, chmn., 1979-81; trustee/gov. The Bklyn. Mus., 1972-91, vice-chmn. 1976-91, trustee 1993—; trustee Bklyn. Hosp., 1963—, v.p. 1968-82, vice-chmn., 1982-93, chmn., 1993-02, chmn. emeritus, 2003—; bd. govs. Hosp. Trustees of N.Y. State, 1992-97, chmn., 1995-97; trustee Poly Prep., 1962-77, N.Y. Presbyn. Healthcare Sys., 1998-03; bd. dirs. Police Athletic League N.Y., 1957-73, Chelsea Theater Center, 1969-77; regent St. Francis Coll., Bklyn., 1961-70; mem. N.Y.C. Commn. for Cultural Affairs, 1981-91. Lt. (j.g.) USNR, 1943-46. Recipient N.Y. State award for Bklyn. Acad. Music, 1969, BAM award for disting. svc., Bklyn. Acad. Music, 1975, Poly. Prep. Disting. Alumnus award, 1997, Forsythia award, Bklyn. Bot. Garden, 2003, Disting. Trustee award, United Hosp. Fund, 2003, Founders medal, Bklyn. Hosp. Ctr., 2003. Mem. Citizens Union, Huguenot Soc. Am., The Heights Casino Club, Rembrandt Club, Ihpetonga Club (Bklyn.), Bellport Bay Yacht Club (N.Y.). Unitarian (sr. deacon). Home: 1 Pierrepont St Apt 10B Brooklyn NY 11201-3302 E-mail: maisonfaison@verizon.net.

FAISON, W. MACK, lawyer; b. Roanoke Rapids, NC, Oct. 25, 1945; BA, N.C. Ctrl. U., 1966; JD, Harvard U., 1969. Bar: NY 1970, Mich. 1972, US Dist. Ct. (2nd, 5th, 6th and 7th cirs.). Fellow Reginald Heber Smith Cmty. Lawyer, 1969—71; assoc. Miller, Canfield, Paddock and Stone, Detroit, 1972—78, prin., 1978—. Mem. local rules adv. com. Ea. Dist. Mich., U.S. Dist. Ct., civil justice reform act adv. com. Contbr. articles to profl. jours. Mem. NY Cmty. Action for Legal Svs., Inc.; bd. trustees St. Vincent and Sarah Fisher Ctr., 1998—2006. Named Mich. Super Lawyers, 2006, Best Lawyers Am., 2007. Mem. ABA (litig. sect., TIPS sect.), State Bar Mich. (litig. sect., environ. law sect.), Nat. Bar Assn., Detroit Bar Assn., Wolverine Bar Assn., Am. Coll. Trial Lawyers, Assn. Def. Trial Counsel, life mem. 6th cir. jud. Conf.; bd. dir. Wayne County Neighborhood Legal Svs. 1990-92. Office: Miller Canfield Paddock & Stone 150 W Jefferson Ave Ste 2500 Detroit MI 48226-4416 Office Phone: 313-496-7578. Office Fax: 313-496-8453. Business E-Mail: faison@millercanfield.com.

FAISON, WILLIAM FRANKLIN, II, lawyer, retired manufacturing corporation executive; b. Jersey City, Apr. 7, 1933; s. John Butler and Mary Elizabeth (Murphy) F.; m. Susan Preston, June 20, 1959; children: John, Prudence, Dulcie. Student Princeton U., 1951-54; BS, Columbia U., 1958; LLB, U. Va., 1961. Bar: Va. 1961, NY 1963, U.S. dist. ct. (so. dist.) NY 1968, U.S. Ct. Apls. (2d cir.) 1966, U.S. Sup. Ct. 1967. Law clk. to judge U.S. Dist. Ct. NJ, 1961-63; assoc. Haight, Gardner, Poor & Havens, NYC, 1963-68; atty. Commonwealth Oil Refining Co., Inc., NYC, 1968-70; counsel, assoc. gen. counsel Gen. Electric Credit Corp., Stamford, Conn., 1970-78, counsel Gen. Electric Co., Fairfield, Conn., 1978-86; counsel Gen. Electric Co., Schenectady, NY, 1986-97. With AUS, 1954-56. Mem. ABA, Va. State Bar, NY State Bar Assn. Democrat. Unitarian-Universalist. Home: 2555 Tarpon Rd Naples FL 34102-1559

FAISS, ROBERT DEAN, lawyer; b. Centralia, Ill., Sept. 19, 1934; s. Wilbur and Theresa Ella (Watts) F.; m. Linda Louise Chambers, Mar. 30, 1991; children: Michael Dean Faiss, Marcy Faiss Ayres, Robert Mitchell Faiss, Philip Grant Faiss, Justin Cooper. BA in Journalism, Am. U., 1969, JD, 1972. Bar: Nev. 1972, D.C. 1972, U.S. Dist. Ct. Nev. 1973, U.S. Supreme Ct. 1977, U.S. Ct. Appeals (9th cir.) 1978. City editor Las Vegas (Nev.) Sun, 1957-59; pub. info. officer Nev. Dept. Employment Security, 1959-61; asst. exec. sec. Nev. Gaming Commn., Carson City, 1961-63; exec. asst. to gov. State of Nev., Carson City, 1963-67; staff asst. U.S. Pres. Lyndon B. Johnson, White House, Washington, 1968-69; asst. to exec. dir. U.S. Travel Adminstrn., Washington, 1969-72; ptnr., chmn. adminstrv. law dept. Lionel, Sawyer & Collins, Las Vegas, 1973—. Mem. bank secrecy Act Adv. Group U.S. Treasury. Co-author: Legalized Gaming in Nevada, 1961, Nevada Gaming License Guide, 1988, Nevada Gaming Law, 1991, 95, 98. Recipient Bronze medal Dept. Commerce, 1972, Chris Schaller award We Can, Las Vegas, 1995, Lifetime Achievement award Nev. Gaming Attys. Assn., 1997; named One of 100 Most Influential Lawyers in Am. and premier U.S. gaming atty., Nat. Law Jour., 1997. Mem. ABA (chmn. gaming law com. 1985-86), Internat. Assn. Gaming Attys. (founding, pres. 1980), Nev. Gaming Attys. Office: Lionel Sawyer & Collins 300 S 4th St Ste 1700 Las Vegas NV 89101-6053

FAIT, GLENN A., lawyer, educator; BA, Calif. State Univ., Sacramento; JD, Univ. Pacific. Assoc. dean McGeorge Sch. Law, Univ. Pacific, spl. counsel; dir. Inst. for Adminstrv. Justice, Univ. Pacific. Former mayor City of Folsom, Calif. Office: University of the Pacific McGeorge School of Law 3200 Fifth Ave Sacramento CA 95817 Office Phone: 916-739-7049.

FAITH, MARSHALL E., grain company executive; Chmn., dir. The Scoular Co., Omaha. Sect. Bishop Clarkson Mem. Found., Episcopal Diocese Nebr. Office: The Scoular Co Scoular Bldg 2027 Dodge St Ste 300 Omaha NE 68102-1229

FAJANS, STEFAN STANISLAUS, retired internist; b. Munich, Mar. 15, 1918; arrived in U.S., 1936, naturalized, 1942; s. Kasimir M. and Salomea (Kaplan) Fajans; m. Ruth Stine, Sept. 6, 1947; children: Peter S., John S. BS, U. Mich., Ann Arbor, 1938, MD, 1942. Intern Mount Sinai Hosp., NYC, 1942—43; research fellow U. Mich., 1946—47, rsch. fellow, 1949—51, resident, 1947—49; mem. faculty U. Mich. Med. Sch., 1950—, prof., 1961—88, active prof. emeritus, 1988—. Mem. endocrinology study sect. NIH, 1958—62, mem. diabetes and metabolism tng. grants com., 1966—70, mem. nat. diabetes adv. bd., 1987—91; chief divsn. endocrinology and metabolism Mich. Diabetes Rsch. and Tng. Ctr., 1973—87, dir., 1977—86; chmn. Am. zone internat. sci. adv. com. Congresses Internat. Diabetes Fedn., 1977—79; Banting meml. lectr., 1978. Contbr. articles med. publs. Mem. career devel. com. VA Med. Rsch. Svcs., 1987—91. Officer M.C. US Army, 1943—46. Fellow rsch. fellow in medicine, ACP, 1949—50, Life Ins. Med. Inst., 1950—51. Master: ACP; mem.: NAS (sr. mem. inst. med.), Ctrl. Soc. Clin. Rsch., Assn. Am. Physicians, Am. Soc. Clin. Investigation, Am. Fedn. Clin. Rsch., Endocrine Soc. (v.p. 1970—71, coun. 1967—71, 1978—81), Am. Diabetes Assn. (pres. 1971—72, Banting medal 1972, Banting Meml. award 1978), Alpha Omega Alpha, Sigma Xi. Home: 827 Asa Gray Dr # 360 Ann Arbor MI 48105-3520 Office: PO Box 0354 Ann Arbor MI 48109-0354 Home Phone: 734-332-0949; Office Phone: 734-936-5039. Business E-Mail: sfajans@umich.edu.

FAJARDO, GERONCIO CAGIGAS, epidemiologist; b. Cebu City, Cebu, Philippines, May 9, 1957; s. Emilio Caroa and Gorgonia Cagigas Fajardo; m. Amy Marlinda Taylor, June 10, 2000; m. Rita Nyra Arambulo (div.); 1 child, Rosemary Arambulo. BS in Biology, U. San Carlos, Cebu City, 1978; MD, Gullas Coll. Medicine, Cebu, 1984; MBA, NH Coll., Manchester, 1987; MS in Biology, Purdue U., Indpls., 1997; MS in Epidemiology, SUNY, Buffalo, 2004. License Philippine Profl. Regulation Commn./Philippines, 1990; cert. Toxicological Chemist Nat. Registry Cert. Chemists/Wash., DC, 1992. Lab. scientist, dir., cons. NH Dept. Corrections, Med. and Forensic Svcs., Concord, 1988—94; epidemiology grad. asst. Dept. Social and Preventive Medicine, SUNY, Buffalo, 1997—99; cancer epidemiologist Md. Cancer Registry, Balt., 1999; asst. toxicologist Office Chief Med. Examiner, Balt., 1999; pub. health treatment program adminstr. Del. Divsn. Pub. Health, Dover, 1999—2000; health svcs. adminstr. Md. AIDS Adminstrn., Balt., 2000; program dir., environ. health epidemiologist Pa. Dept. Health, Harrisburg, 2001—04, surveillance epidemiologist, 2004—05; med. epidemiologist Ga. Divsn. Pub. Health/Fulton County Med. Examiner's Office, Atlanta, 2005—. Lectr. NH Police Stds. and Tng. Coun., Concord, 1989—93; adj. faculty U. Indpls., Indpls., 1996—97, Ind. U.-Purdue U., Indpls., 1996—97, Ivy Tech Coll., Indpls., 1996—97, NH Coll., Laconia; spkr. in field; presenter in field. Mem.: Am. Soc. for Clin. Pathology, Am. Coll. Epidemiology, Am. Acad.

Forensic Scis. (assoc.). Home: 498 Lantern Wood Dr Scottdale GA 30079 Office: Fulton County Med Examiners Office 430 Pryor St Atlanta GA 30312 Personal E-mail: geronciofajardo@excite.com.

FAJORS, NIQUE, interactive entertainment executive; b. Boston, Nov. 2, 1967; s. Herb and Blanche Christine Fajors; m. Faiza Abdallah Zarroug. BSBA, Suffolk U., 1989; MBA, Harvard U., 1993. Brand mgmt. Procter & Gamble, Cin., 1993-95; exec. v.p. Digital Telemedia, Inc., NYC, 1995-97; pres. Valuecreation.com LLC, NYC, 1997—99; pres. consumer mktg. svcs. Bounty SCA Worldwide, Chgo., 1999—2001; sr. policy adv. Office of the Sec. Dept. Commerce, 2002—04; v.p. brand mgmt. Acclaim Entertainment, Glen Cove, NY, 2004; v.p. sales and mktg. Atari, Inc., NYC, 2005—. Bd. mem. Nat. Childhood Obesity Found. Prodr. (ednl. video) The Invisible Men, 1995; author: Cultural & Economic Revitalization, 1999. Republican. Avocations: travel, photography. Office: Atari Inc 417 5th Ave New York NY 10016 Home: 211 N End Ave 20 B New York NY 10282 Office Phone: 212-726-6553. Office Fax: 212-202-9642. Business E-Mail: nfajors@gmail.com.

FAKAHANY, AHMASS L., investment company executive; b. 1958; BS summa cum laude, Boston U., 1979; MBA, Columbia U., 1981. Fin. staff Exxon Corp.; with Merrill Lynch & Co., Inc., NYC, 1987—, regional contr. Europe, Mid. East and Africa, CFO Japan Region, CFO Pacific Rim Region, chief adminstrv. officer Japan Region, global chief fin. officer, chief adminstrv. officer Corp. and Instl. Client Grp., sr. v.p., fin. dir., COO global mkts. & investment banking, 2001—02, exec. v.p., CFO, head global fin., tech. and svcs., 2002—05, vice chmn., chief adminstrv. officer, 2005—07, co-pres., 2007—. Bd. dirs. Inst. Internat. Fin. Office: Merrill Lynch & Co Inc 4 World Fin Ctr 250 Vesey St New York NY 10080

FAKE, CATERINA, Internet company executive; b. Pitts. m. Stewart Butterfield. BA with honors, Vassar Coll. Lead designer Organic Online; art dir. Salon.com; mem. rsch. staff Interval Rsch.; creative dir. Yellowball; co-founder, v.p. mktg. and cmty. Ludicorp, Vancouver, 2002—05; co-founder Flickr, 2004; with Yahoo!, San Francisco. Co-recipient with Stewart Butterfield, Webby Breakout of Yr. award, 2005; named one of 100 Most Influential People, Time mag., 2006, 50 Who Matter Now, CNNMoney.com Bus. 2.0, 2006.*

FALA, HERMAN CAMILLO, lawyer; b. Phila., Oct. 15, 1949; s. Herman Anthony and Rose Maria (Iannetti) F.; m. Helen E. Perry, June 26, 1971; 1 child, Danielle. BS summa cum laude, U. Notre Dame, 1971; JD cum laude, Harvard U., 1974. Bar: Pa. 1974, U.S. Dist. Ct. (ea. dist.) Pa. 1974. Assoc. Wolf, Block, Schorr & Solis-Cohen, Phila., 1974-82, ptnr., 1982—. Chair real estate dept. Wolf, Block, Schorr & Solis-Cohen. Editor: The Philadelphia Lawyer, 1977—. Bd. dirs. The Wilma Theatre, Phila., 1986—, chmn., 1995-97, Charter H.S. Arch. Design, 2005—. Mem. ABA, Pa. Bar Assn., Phila. Bar Assn. (v.p. 1997, chair exec. com. real property sect. 1998), Am. Coll. Real Estate Lawyers, Phi Beta Kappa. Avocations: photography, amateur astronomy, travel, cooking, writing. Office: Wolf Block Schorr & Solis-Cohen 22d Fl 1650 Arch St Fl 22D Philadelphia PA 19103-2029

FALAI, TACOPO, chef; b. Florence, Italy, 1972; Apprenticeship Pasticceria Marisa; pastry chef Enoteca Pinchiorri, Florence, exec. pastry chef; bread maker for Chef Michel Bras, Laguiole, France; chocolatier Fauchon, Paris; cons. Matsuya, Tokyo; exec. pastry chef Le Cirque 2000, NYC, Osteria del Circo, NYC; exec. chef Bread Tribeca, NYC; owner, exec. chef Falai, NYC, 2005—, Falai Panetteria, NYC, 2005—. Named one of NYC's Rising Stars, StarChefs.com, 2006. Office: Falai Restaurant 68 Clinton St New York NY 10002*

FALB, PETER LAWRENCE, mathematician, educator, investment company executive; b. NYC, July 26, 1936; s. Harry and Bertha (Kirschner) F.; m. Karen Forslund, Oct. 9, 1971; children: Hilary, Alison. AB, Harvard U., 1956, MA, 1957, PhD, 1961. Mem. staff MIT Lincoln Lab., Cambridge, 1960-66; assoc. prof. applied math. U. Mich., Ann Arbor, 1966; prof. Brown U., Providence, 1967—; prin., treas. Dane, Falb, Stone & Co., Inc., Boston, 1977—. Chmn. Barberry Corp., 1968-85; also bd. dirs.; bd. dirs. FES Computing Co., LTCQ, Inc., Toreador Royalty, Infolenz, LTC Media; mng. dir. F-Co. Holdings Co.; vis. prof. Lund (Sweden) Inst. Tech., summers 1971, 72, 74, 76, 78; cons. NASA, Bolt, Beranek & Newman Co. Author: (with M. Athans) Optimal Control: An Introduction to the Theory and its Applications, 1966, (with R. Kalman and M. Arbib) Topics in Mathematical System Theory, 1969, (with J. deJong) Some Successive Approximation Methods in Control and Oscillation Theory, 1969; Methods of Algebraic Geometry in Control Theory, Part I: Scalar Linear Systems and Affine Algebraic Geometry, 1989, Methods of Algebraic Geometry in Control Theory, Part II: Multivariable Linear Systems and Projective Algebraic Geometry, 1999. Home: 245 Brattle St Cambridge MA 02138-4614 Office: Dane Falb Stone & Co Inc 15 Broad St Ste 406 Boston MA 02109-3803 also: Brown U Box F Providence RI 02912 Office Phone: 617-742-0666. Personal E-mail: plf245@aol.com.

FALBER, HAROLD JULIUS, marketing professional; b. Mt. Vernon, NY, Apr. 14, 1946; s. Max William and Cora (Leff) F.; 1 child, Aaron. Student, Hartwick Coll., 1963-65, C.W. Post Coll., 1965-67, MIT, 1981-82. Acct. exec. Scali, McCabe, Sloves, NYC, 1967-71; advt. mgr. Volvo of N. Am., Rockleigh, NJ, 1972; acct. exec. Della Femina, Travisano & Ptnrs., NYC, 1973-75; advt. mgr. Polaroid, Cambridge, Mass., 1976-82; dir. mktg. RJR Nabisco, NYC, 1983-87; pres. Trade Area Restaurant Group, Inc., Stamford, Conn., 1987-96; dir. 1-800-Flowers, 1997—; v.p. sales, mktg. & customer svc./commerce Kiamos & Tosker Inc., 1999—; pres. Trade Area Mktg. Group, Westport, Conn., 2000—04, Hallmark Flowers and Gifts, Kansas City, Mo., 2005—06. Cons. in field. Home: 5 Oak Ln Weston CT 06883-1110

FALCHUK, KENNETH R., gastroenterologist; MD magna cum laude, Ctrl. U. Venezuela, 1967. Cert. Am. Bd. Internal Medicine. Intern U. Pa. Health System in Internal Medicine, 1968; fellow U. Pa. Health System in Cardiology, 1969, Harvard Med. Sch. in Medicine, 1973; resident Brigham and Women's Hospital in Internal Medicine, 1973; fellow Mass. General Hospital in Gastroenterology, 1974; chief resident Brigham and Women's Hospital in Internal Medicine, Boston, 1976; dir. Gastrointestinal Endoscopy Unit New England Deaconess Hospital; dir. network devel. Divsn. of Gastroenteroly, Beth Israel Deaconess Medical Ctr., sr. Gastroenterologist; assoc. prof. medicine Harvard Med. Sch. Mem. Overseers Co. of Crohn's and Colitis Found. of Am., Internat. Bd. Advisors for Planetamedico.com. Contbr. articles, chapters to books, scientific papers. Named Best Intern, Grad. Hospital of U. Pa.; named one of the Top Doctors, Boston Mag.; recipient Humanitarian Award, Crohn's and Colitis Found. of Am., Award of Excellence, Am. Liver Found. Office: Boston Endoscopy Center 175 Worcester Street Wellesley MA 02481 also: Division of Gastroenterology-GI/West 110 Francis Street Suite 8E Boston MA 02215 Home Phone: 617-754-0800; Office Phone: 617-632-8623. Office Fax: 617-754-0820; Home Fax: 617-632-9199.*

FALCK, DAVID PHILLIP, lawyer, utilities executive; b. Hartford, Conn., Mar. 20, 1953; s. Paul M. and Hanna D. (Martin) F.; m. Sally Pruett, Sept. 23, 1979; children: Claire, Sarah, Charles. BA magna cum laude, Colgate U., Hamilton, NY, 1975; JD summa cum laude, Washington & Lee Sch. Law, Lexington, Va., 1978. Bar: NY 1979, US Dist. Ct. (so. dist. NY) 1979. Assoc. Winthrop, Stimson, Putnam & Roberts, NYC, 1978-86; ptnr. Pillsbury Winthrop LLP, NYC, 1987—2007; co-chair corp. and securities practice Pillsbury Winthrop Shaw Pittman LLP (merger), NYC, 2003—05; sr. v.p. law PSEG Svcs. Corp., Newark, 2007—. Trustee Darrow Sch., New Lebanon, NY, 1993-97. Mem. Order of the Coif, Phi Beta Kappa, Edison Elec. Inst. (legal com.). Office: PSEG Svcs Corp PO Box 570 Newark NJ 07101 Office Phone: 973-430-7000.*

FALCO, CHARLES MAURICE, physicist, researcher; b. Ft. Dodge, Iowa, Aug. 17, 1948; s. Joe and Mavis Margaret (Mickelson) F.; m. Dale Wendy Miller, May 5, 1973; children: Lia Denise, Amelia Claire. BA, U. Calif., Irvine, 1970, MA, 1971, PhD, 1974. Trainee NSF, 1970-74; asst. physicist Argonne (Ill.) Nat. Lab., 1974-77, physicist, 1977-82, group leader superconductivity and novel materials, 1978-82; prof. physics and optical scis., research prof. U. Ariz., Tucson, 1982-97, prof. optical scis., chair condensed matter physics, 1998—, dir. lab. x-ray optics, 1986—. Vis. prof. U. Paris Sud, 1979, 86, U. Aachen, 1989; lectr., 1974—; mem. panel on artificially structured materials NRC, 1984-85; co-organizer numerous internat. confs. in field, 1978—; mem. spl. rev. panel on high temperature superconductivity Applied Physics Letters, 1987—; mem. panel on superconductivity Inst. Def. Analysis, 1988—; researcher on artificial metallic superlattices, X-ray optics, auperconductivity, condensed matter physics, electronic materials; curatorial advisor Solomon R. Guggenheim Mus., 1997—, co-curator The Art of the Motorcycle exhbn. Editor: Future Trends in Superconductive Electronics, 1978, Materials for Magneto-Optic Data Storage, 1989; contbr. articles to profl. jours.; patentee in field. Mem. divsn. condensed matter physics Exec. Com. Arts, 1992-94. Alexander von Humboldt Found. sr. disting. grantee, 1989; recipient Art Motorcycle Exbhn. award Internat. Assn. Art Critics, 1999. Fellow IEEE, Optical Soc. Am., Am. Phys. Soc. (counselor 1992-94, exec. com. div. condensed matter physics 1992-94, exec. com. div. internat. physics 1994-98); mem. Materials Rsch. Soc., Coll. Optical Scis., Sigma Xi. Achievements include rsch. on artificial metallic superlattices, X-ray optics, superconductivity, condensed matter physics, electronic materials. Home: 13005 E Cape Horn Dr Tucson AZ 85749-9734 Office: U Ariz Optical Scis Ctr Box 210077 Tucson AZ 85721-0077 Office Phone: 520-621-6771. Business E-Mail: falco@u.arizona.edu.

FALCO, EDIE, actress; b. Northport, NY, July 5, 1963; d. Frank Falco and Judith M. Anderson; 1 adopted child, Anderson. BFA, SUNY, Purchase, NY, 1986. Actress: (films) Sweet Lorraine, 1987, The Unbelievable Truth, 1990, Trust, 1990, Time Expired, 1992, Laws of Gravity, 1992, I Was on Mars, 1992, Bullets Over Broadway, 1994, Backfire!, 1995, The Addiction, 1995, Layin' Low, 1996, The Funeral, 1996, Breathing Room, 1996, Firehouse, 1997, Cost of Living, 1997, Cop Land, 1997, Trouble on the Corner, 1997, A Price Above Rubies, 1998, Hurrican Streets, 1998, Judy Berlin, 1999, Random Hearts, 1999, Overnight Sensation, 2000, Death of a Dog, 2000, Sunshine State, 2002 (Best Supporting Acress award LA Film Critics Assn. 2002, Golden Satellite award best supporting actress 2003), Family of the Year, 2004, The Girl from Monday, 2005, The Great New Wonderful, 2005, The Quiet, 2005, Freedomland, 2006; (TV movies) The Sunshine Boys, 1995, Jenifer, 2001, Fargo, 2003; (TV series) Oz, 1997-99, The Sopranos, 1999-2007 (Golden Globe award best actress in a drama 2000, 03, Emmy for best actress 1999, 2001, 2003, Actor of Yr., Am. Film Inst. 2001, Golden Satellite award 2002, SAG award 2003); TV guest appearances include Homicide: Life on the Street, 1993-94, 97, Law & Order, 1993-94, 97, New York Undercover, 1995; film dir. Rift, 1993; TV prodr. Stringer, 1999; theater appearances include Side Man, 2000, The Vagina Monologues, 2001, Frankie and Johnny in the Clair de Lune, 2002. Office: c/o Sandra Marsh Mgmt 9150 Wilshire Blvd Ste 220 Beverly Hills CA 90212-3429

FALCO, MARIA JOSEPHINE, political scientist; b. Wildwood, NJ, July 7, 1932; d. John J. and Mafalda M. (Barbieri) F. AB, Immaculata Coll., Pa., 1954; student, U. Florence, Italy, 1954-55; MA, Fordham U., 1958; PhD, Bryn Mawr Coll., Pa., 1963; postdoctoral rsch. fellow, Yale, 1965-66; quantitative data analysis, U. Mich., 1968; mgmt. program, Carnegie-Mellon U., 1983. Instr., then asst. prof. history and polit. sci. Immaculata Coll., Pa., 1957-63; asst. prof. polit. sci. Washington Coll., Chestertown, Md., 1963-64; rsch. asst. Genevieve Blatt; candidate for U.S. Senator from Pa., 1964-65; asst. prof., then assoc. prof. polit. sci. Le Moyne Coll., Syracuse, NY, 1966-73, chmn. polit. sci. dept., 1967-73; prof. polit. sci. Stockton State Coll., Pomona, NJ, 1973-76; chmn. social and behavioral scis. faculty U. Tulsa, 1976-79; dean Coll. Arts and Scis., Loyola U., New Orleans, 1979-85; prof. polit. sci. Loyola U., New Orleans, 1985-86; v.p. acad. affairs DePauw U., Greencastle, Ind., 1986-88, prof. polit. sci., 1988-93, prof. emerita, 1993—. Speaker in field; adj. prof. polit. sci. Tulane U., New Orleans, 1996-97. Author: Truth and Meaning in Political Science: An Introduction to Political Inquiry, 1973, Bigotry: Ethnic, Machine and Sexual Politics in a Senatorial Election, 1980; editor: Through the Looking Glass: Epistemology and the Conduct of Political Inquiry: An Anthology, 1979, Feminism and Epistemology: Approaches to Research in Women and Politics, 1987, Feminist Interpretations of Mary Wollstonecraft, 1996, Feminist Interpretations of Niccolo Machiavelli, 2004; cons. editor Political Parties and the Civic Action Groups; contbr. articles and book revs. to profl. jours Mem. Mayor's Task Force on Future of New Orleans, 1983-85, Women's Equity Action League, 1979-81; LWV, 1960-63, 82-84, Country Club Estates Civic Assn.; bd. dirs. Inst. for Human Rels., Loyola U., Inst. Human Understanding, New Orleans, 1985-86; pres. Syracuse chpt. New Dem. Coalition, 1970-71; mem. pres.'s coun. Loyola U., New Orleans, 1997-2000, mem. Ars Dean's coun., 2000-06. Fulbright scholar U. Florence, Italy, 1954-55; faculty fellow in state and local politics Nat. Ctr. for Edn. in Politics, 1964. Mem. AAUP (v.p. LeMoyne chpt. 1971-72), Womens Caucus Polit. Sci. (pres. 1976, named Mentor of Distinction 1989), Am. Polit. Sci. Assn. (Benjamin Evans Lippincott award com. 1976, chmn. sect. program com. 1975, com. acad. freedom and profl. ethics, chair com. for outstanding conv. paper award women and politics rsch. sect. 1990-91), Midwestern Polit. Sci. Assn. (com. status of women), Northeastern Polit. Sci. Assn., S.W. Polit. Sci Assn. (outstanding conv. paper com.), Founds. Polit. Theory Group, Common Cause, Great Lakes Coll. Assn. (dean's coun. 1986-88), Assn. Jesuit Colls. and Univs. (dean's coun. 1979-85), Assn. Am. Colls. (coun. for liberal learning 1985-87), Western Polit. Sci. Assn., Ind. Polit. Sci. Assn. (pres., chair 1992-93), Ind. Social Sci. Assn., So. Polit. Sci. Assn., Jefferson Parish LWV (bd. dirs. 1999—, pres. 2001-02), Jefferson Parish Bus. and Profl. Women (1st v.p. 2002-04, pres. 2004-05), Women Better La., Citizens Safer Jefferson Parish. Roman Catholic. Home: 4709 Tartan Dr Metairie LA 70003 Personal E-mail: msforza2377@yahoo.com. *Despite the fact that it's difficult being a woman in a man's world, I'm glad I'm a woman.*

FALCO, RANDY (RANDEL A.), Internet company executive, former broadcast executive; b. Dec. 26, 1953; m. Susan J. Falco; 3 children. BBA in Fin., Iona Coll., 1975, MBA in Fin., 1979, D (hon.), 2001. Various managerial positions in fin., tech. ops., corp. strategic planning NBC, 1975—86; v.p. fin., adminstrn. NBC Sports, 1986—91; pres., broadcast, network ops. divsn NBC, 1993—98; pres. NBC TV Network, 1998—2003, group pres., 2003—04; pres. NBC Universal TV Networks Group, 2004—05; pres., COO NBC Universal TV, NYC, 2005—06; chmn., CEO AOL LLC, Dulles, Va., 2006—. Broadcast COO Summer Olympics, Barcelona, 1992, Atlanta, 96, Sydney, 2000, Winter Olympics, Salt Lake City, 2002. Bd. dir. Ronald McDonald House. Recipient 6 Emmy awards for work on Olympics. Office: AOL LLC 22000 AOL Way Dulles VA 20166*

FALCO, THOMAS GILBERT, historian, researcher; b. New Haven, Oct. 19, 1940; s. Thomas and Dorothea Gilbert Falco. MPhil in History, Yale U., New Haven, 1994. Asst. hist. libr. Yale Med. Libr., New Haven, 1971—87; rsch. specialist Yale Med. Hist. Libr., New Haven, 1988—. 1st lt. USAR, 1963—69. Lutheran. Avocations: baseball, bowling, contract bridge. Home: 510 Derby Ave West Haven CT 06516 Office: Yale Medical Historical Library 333 Cedar St New Haven CT 06510 Home Phone: 203-387-3367; Office Phone: 203-785-4354. E-mail: thomas.falco@yale.edu.

FALCO-LESHIN, JOANNA M., literature and language professor; b. NYC, Aug. 9, 1953; d. Mary J. Falco; m. Robert I. Leshin. Prof., cons. Miami Dade Coll., Miami. Author (with James Carlos Blake): The Thought of Writing, 1991, Voices of the Heart, 1991; author: Reinventing the Wheel, The Answer to the Post Deconstructionists, Final Fantasy: Diana, The Angel, and the Holy Grail, 2001, The Buddha, The Body The Reason Why: Why Meditate, 2001. Recipient Tchg. Excellence award, Nat. Inst. Staff and Orgnl. Devel., Endowed tchg. chmn., Blockbuster Entertainment Corp. Mem.: MLA, Coll. Composition and Comm., Nat. Coun. Tchrs. English, Fla. Pub. Interest Rsch. Group (founder), Humane Soc., Amnesty Internat. Office: Miami Dade Coll Miami FL 33132 Office Phone: 305-237-3277. Personal E-mail: drjoannafalco@msn.com.

FALCON, ARMANDO, JR., financial consultant, lawyer; b. San Antonio, June 4, 1960; married; 2 children. BA, St. Mary's U., 1983; M in Pub. Policy, Harvard U., 1985; JD, U. Tex., 1988. With San Antonio Econ. Devel. Found.; legis. asst. com. on edn. State Senate, Tex., 1983; law clk. to atty. gen. Tex., 1986—88; pvt. practice; counsel com. on banking and fin. svcs. U.S. Ho. of Reps., 1989—91, dep. gen. counsel, 1991—95, gen. counsel, 1995—97; dir. Office Fed. Housing Enterprise Oversight, 1999—2005; ptnr. The Canonbury Group, London, 2005—. Office Phone: 703-838-9552.

FALCON, RAYMOND JESUS, JR., lawyer; b. NYC, Nov. 17, 1953; s. Raymond J. and Lolin (Lopez) F.; m. Debra Mary Bomeisl, June 4, 1977; children: Victoria Marie, Mark Daniel. BA, Columbia U., NYC, 1975; JD, Yale U., New Haven, Conn., 1978. Bar: NY 1979, US Dist. Ct. (so. and ea. dist.) NY 1979, US Ct. Appeals (DC and 2d cirs.) 1983, Fla. 1987, NJ 1988, US Dist. Ct. NJ 1988, US Ct. Appeals (3rd cir.). Assoc. Webster and Sheffield, NYC, 1978-82; ptnr. Falcon and Hom, NYC, 1982-85; sr. atty. Degussa Corp., Ridgefield Park, N.J., 1985-88, v.p., sec., gen. counsel, 1989-94; pvt. practice Woodcliff Lake, N.J., 1994-95; prin. Falcon & Singer PC, 1995—2006, Montvale, NJ, 2007—. Contbr. articles to profl. jours. Dem. candidate Town Justice, Town of Rye, N.Y., 1983; Dem. jud. del., Westchester, N.Y., 1984-89; mem. planned giving adv. coun. Eastern N.Y. region Am. Cancer Soc., 2001-05. Mem. ABA, N.J. State Bar Assn., Fla. Bar Assn., Bergen County Bar Assn., Nat. Acad. Elder Law Attys., Acad. Spl. Needs Planners, Park Ridge Rotary (bd. dirs. 1997-2001, officer 2001-03, 2006-), Columbia Alumni of Westchester County (v.p., bd. dirs. 1983-90, 1997-2006). Home: 582 Colonial Rd Rivervale NJ 07675-6107 Office: Falcon and Singer PC 221 W Grand Ave Ste 201 Montvale NJ 07645-1729 Office Phone: 201-307-0074, 914-723-3919. Business E-Mail: rfalcon@falconsinger.com.

FALCONE, DAVID J., elementary school educator; BA in Elem. Edn., DeSales U., Ctr. Valley, Pa., 2002; MA in Liberal Studies, SUNY, Stony Brook, 2005, post masters in Sch. Dist. Leadership, 2007. Cert. tchr. pre-K-6 NY. 2d grade tchr. Rocky Point (NY) Sch. Dist., 2002—. Rec. sec. Rocky Point PTA, 2004. Nominee Disney Tchr. of Yr., 2002—03; recipient Jenkins award, Rocky Point PTA, 2006. Mem.: ASCD (assoc.). Office: Rocky Point Sch Dist 90 Rocky Point Yaphank Rd Rocky Point NY 11778 Office Phone: 631-744-1600.

FALCONE, PATRICIA JEANNE LALIM, investor, foundation administrator; b. Montevideo, Minn., Oct. 12; d. Clarence I. and Eva (Corneliusen) Lalim; m. Alfonso Benjamin Falcone, Oct. 22; children: Christopher Lalim Falcone, Steven Lalim Falcone. BS, U. Minn.; MS, PhD, U. Wis. Former libr. asst. U. Minn., St. Paul; former singer/performer Mpls.; former asst. prog. dir. U. Wis. Meml. Union, Madison; former instr. U. Wis., Madison; med. exec. A.B. Falcone, M.D., Ph.D., Fresno, Calif.; pres. Dr. A.B. Falcone Meml. Found. U. Calif. Berkeley. Pvt. investor lectr. in field Patricia Lalim Falcone; spkr., presenter in field. Contbr. articles to profl. jours.;, author various ednl. and profl. pamphlets; former artist/craftsman (textile designs) U. Wis. Traveling exhibit. Bd. dirs. Fresno/Madera Med. Polit. Action Com., Med. Soc., 1985-89, 1990, treas. 1997-2001; bd. dirs. Philip Lorenz Meml. Keyboard Concert, Profl. Exch. Svc. Corp., 2006—; mem. Supts. Roundtable, Fresno Unified Sch. Dist., 1989; chmn. U. Calif., Fresno com. to bring UC campus to Fresno area, 1987—; chmn. Parent Adv. Com. for Gifted and Talented, Fresno Unified Sch. Dist., 1985; citizens adv. coun. U. Calif., San Joaquin, 1991—; mem. Med. Ministries Internat., 2000. Fellow U. Wis.; scholar. Mem.: AAUW, Pacific Legal Found., Edison Computech Assn., Assn. Acad. Excellence (chmn. 1988—91), Med. Alliance of Fresno/Madera County Med. Soc. (exec. bd. 1989—), Med. Ministries Internat., Sharada Sangeet Sadan, Am. Scandinavian Found., U.S. English, Fresno/Verona, Italy Sister City (com. 2001—), St. George Greek Orthodox Ch. Cmty. Luth. Brotherhood, Phi Delta Gamma, Pi Lambda Theta, Kappa Omicron Nu. Avocations: genealogy, swimming, travel, cross country skiing. Office: PO Box 14030 Pinedale CA 93650-4030 also: Riverview Tower # 1707 1920 First St South Minneapolis MN 55454-1055

FALCONE, THOMAS WILLIAM, finance educator; b. Ind., Pa., Oct. 22, 1947; s. Dominick Thomas and Ann Helen Falcone; m. Catherine Lynn McAnulty, Aug. 29, 1971; children: Ryan, Shannon. BS, Penn State Univ., State Coll., Pa., 1967; MBA, Mankato State Univ., Mankato, Minn., 1972; DBA, Kent State Univ., Kent, Ohio, 1985. Mktg. specialist B.F. Goodrich Corp., Independce, Ohio, 1973—77; instr. mktg. Kent State Univ., Kent, Ohio, 1977—79; prof. mgmt. Ind. Univ. of Pa., Ind., Pa., 1979—. Co-dir. mgmt./svcs. Ind. Univ. of Pa., Ind., Pa., 1990—, chmn. mgmt./mktg. dept., 1984—92. Author: Imagining the Entrepreneurial Sys., 2005. Chmn. Ind. County Solid Waste Authority, Ind., Pa., 1989—; bd. mem. Ind. County Redevelopement Authority, Ind., Pa., 1996—, Pa. Resources Coun., Media, Pa., 1982—. SP4 US Army, 1969—71, Panama. Recipient SBA 2003 Rsch. Adv., Small Bus. Adminstrv., 2003, Faculty of the Yr., Eberly Coll. of Bus., 1996, 4 Nat. Runner -ups Case of the Yr., Small Bus. Inst. Dirs. Assn., 1992, 1996, 1999, 2005. Mem.: Acad. Mgmt. Independent. Christian. Achievements include cons. Pa. Dept. of transp. Ind., Regional Med. Ctr., Westmoreland County Girl Scouts, Keystone Carbon Co., Tri-county Workforce Investment Bd. Avocations: golf, landscaping. Home: 2560 Warren Rd Indiana PA 15701 Office: Ind Univ of Pa 308K Ecobit Indiana PA 15705

FALCONE, TOMMASO, reproductive endocrinologist; b. Montreal, Que., Can., Nov. 28, 1953; came to U.S., 1995; s. Michele and Domenica Falcone. Med. degree, McGill U., Montreal, 1981. Bd. cert. in reproductive endocrinology and laparoscopic surgery. Reproductive endocrinologist McGill U., Montreal, 1984-94, Cleve. Clinic Found., 1995—. Editor: Congenital Malformations of Female Genital Tract, 1999; co-author: Atlas of Endoscopic Techniques in Gynecology, 2000, Overcoming Infertility; co-editor: Clinical Reproductive Medicine and Surgery, 2007. Mem. Am. Soc. Reproductive Medicine. Office: Cleve Clinic Found Dept Gyn-A-81 9500 Euclid Ave Dept Gyn-a81 Cleveland OH 44195-0001 Office Phone: 216-444-1758. Business E-Mail: falcont@ccf.org.

FALEOMAVAEGA, ENI FA'AUAA HUNKIN, congressman; b. Vailoatai Village, Am. Samoa, Aug. 15, 1943; s. Eni and Taualai Hunkin; m. Hinanui Bambridge Cave; children: Temanuata Tuilua'ai, Taualai, Nifae, Vaimoana, Leonne. BA in Polit. Sci. and History, Brigham Young U., 1966; JD, U. Houston, 1972; LLM, U. Calif., Berkeley, 1973. Bar: Am.

Samoa, U.S. Supreme Ct. Adminstrv. asst. Am. Samoa del. to Washington, 1973-75; staff counsel to house com. on interior and insular affairs US Congress, Washington, 1975-81; dep. atty. gen. Am. Samoa, 1981-84, lt. gov., 1984-89; territorial del. US Congress from Am. Samoa, 1988, mem., 1989—, mem. internat. rels. com., resources com. Chmn. Gov.'s Task Force for Reorgn. of the Adminstrn., Am. Samoa Adv. Fisheries Council, 1985—, Gov.'s Adv. Com. on Grants Programs, 1985—; mem. nat. lt. gov.'s mission to Egypt, Jordan and Saudi Arabia, South Pacific Leaders Orientation Mission to Paris, 1987; leader Am. Samoa's del. to South Pacific Conf., Noumea New Caledonia, 1987; keynote speaker and leader Am. Samoa's del. to Pacific Trade/Investment Conf., 1986. Author: Navigating the Future: A Samoan Perspective in US-Pacific Relations, 1995. Served with US Army, 1966—69, Vietnam, served with USAR, 1985—. Recipient Alumni Svc. award Brigham Young U., 1979; named Chieftain Faleomavaega, leone Village. Mem. Nat. Conf. of Lt. Govs., Nat. Assn. Secs. of State, Navy League of U.S., VFW, Nat. Am. Indian Prayer Breakfast Group, Lions (charter mem. Pago Pago chpt.), Go for Broke Assn. (life; pres. Samoa chpt.). Democrat. Avocations: crew, golf. Office: US Ho Reps 2422 Rayburn HOB Washington DC 20515 also: PO Box Drawer X Pago Pago AS 96799 Office Phone: 202-225-8577, 684-633-1372. Office Fax: 202-225-8757, 684-633-2680.*

FALES, HALIBURTON, II, lawyer; b. NYC, Aug. 7, 1919; s. DeCoursey and Dorothy Mildred (Mitchell) F.; m. Katharine Ladd, Dec. 27, 1941; children: Nancy, Haliburton, Priscilla, Lucy, William E. Ladd. Student, Harvard U., 1938—41; LLB, Columbia U., 1947. Bar: NY 1948, U.S. Supreme Ct. 1957. Assoc. White & Case, NYC, 1947-58, ptnr., 1959-88, of counsel, 1988-90, ret., 1991. Spl. master Appellate divsn. 1st dept. NY State Supreme Ct., 1983—, chmn. departmental discipline com., 1991—96, spl. counsel, 1997—; nat. ctr. for state cts Warren Burger Assoc., 2002. Author: Trying Cases A Life in the Law, 1997; contbr. articles to profl. jours. Trustee Pierpont Morgan Libr., 1966-99, pres., 1980-88, trustee emeritus, 1999—; trustee St. Barnabas Hosp., 1949-96, trustee emeritus, 1996—; sr. warden St. Luke's Ch., 1967-93; bd. dirs. Union Theol. Sem., 1986-94; bd. visitors Columbia Law Sch., 1993-98, emeritus, 1998—. Lt. comdr. USNR, 1941-45 Recipient Columbia U. medal, 1994. Fellow Am. Bar Found., NY Bar Found., Inst. Jud. Adminstrn., Am. Coll. Trial Lawyers; mem. ABA, Albert Gallatin Assocs., Am. Judicature Soc., Am. Law Inst. (life), Assn. Bar City of NY, NY County Lawyers Assn. (William Nelson Cromwell award 1998), NY State Bar Assn. (pres. 1983-84, chair task force on the prof., 1994-96), Columbia Law Sch. Assn., Inc. (pres. 1991-92), St. Paul's Sch. Alumni Assn. (v.p. 1988-92), Alumni Fedn. Columbia U., The Century Assn. (pres. 1996-99), N.Y. Yacht Club, Union Club (N.Y.). Personal E-mail: hfales@aol.com.

FALES, HENRY MARSHALL, III, chemist; b. NYC, Feb. 12, 1927; s. Henry Marshall and Cecile Marie (Vatet) F.; m. Caroline Eleanor McCullagh, Dec. 20, 1947; children: Marsha Kent Fales Mazz, Suzanne Kent Fales Palmer, Henry Richard. BSc in Chemistry, Rutgers U., 1948, PhD in Organic Chemistry, 1953. Instr. Rutgers U., New Brunswick, N.J., 1953; rsch. chemist, lab. chief Nat. Heart, Lung and Blood Inst., NIH, Bethesda, Md., 1953—2003, mem. sr. biomed. rsch. svc., 2005; adj. prof. anatomy, physiology and genetics Uniformed Svcs. U. Health Scis., 2001—. With USN, 1944-46. Recipient Superior Svc. award U.S. Govt., 1973, 86, Profl. Svc. award Wash. chpt. Alpha Chi Sigma, 50 Yr. Svc. award NIH/Nat. Heart, Lung, and Blood Inst. Mem. Am. Chem. Soc., Am. Soc. Mass Spectrometry (mem.-at-large, sec., v.p. programs, pres., past pres.). Avocations: fishing, stained glass. Home: 3114 Gracefield Rd Apt # 315 Silver Spring MD 20904-7854 Office: NIH NHLBI Bldg 50 Rm 3305 50 South Dr MSC 8014 Bethesda MD 20892-8014 Office Phone: 301-496-2135. E-mail: hmfales@helix.nih.gov.

FALES, LISA JOSE, lawyer; b. Indpls., Apr. 3, 1962; BA, U. Md., 1984; JD, U. Balt., 1990. Bar: Md. 1990, DC 1992, US Dist. Ct., Md. 1992. Legislative specialist, consumer protection div. Md. Atty. Gen. Office, 1983—89; summer assoc. Venable LLP, Balt., 1989; ptnr., govt. antitrust practice group Howrey Simon Arnold & White LLP, Washington; ptnr., regulatory practice group Venable LLP, Washington, 2004—. Co-chair, moderator & presenter Nat. Inst. for Women Corp. Counsel conference, 2003. Bd. dirs. Women's Law Ctr. for Md.; mem. benefits com. NOW Legal Defense and Education Fund. Mem.: ABA (mem. antitrust section), DC Bar Assn. (chair consumer affairs com. 1994—96, mem. steering com. 1996—97, mem. antitrust section), Md. Bar Assn. (mem. antitrust section). Office: Venable LLP 575 7th St NW Washington DC 20004 Office Phone: 202-344-4349. Office Fax: 202-344-8300. Business E-Mail: ljfales@venable.com.

FALESE, ROBERT D., JR., bank executive; m. Mary Falese; 2 children. BS, St. Joseph's Univ., 1969; MBA, Drexel Univ. Mgmt. positions First Pa. Bank, 1966—81; positions through exec. v.p., sr. lending officer Fidelity Bank, 1981—92; exec. v.p., head comml. lending Commerce Bancorp, Cherry Hill, NJ, 1992—2004, pres. comml. & investment banking, 2004—07, pres., CEO, 2007—. Trustee St. Joseph's Univ. Served USMC. Office: Commerce Bancorp 1701 Rt 70 E Cherry Hill NJ 08034*

FALEY, R(ICHARD) SCOTT, lawyer; b. Trenton, NJ, Aug. 18, 1947; s. Henry and Winifred (Goeke) F.; m. Josepha Ann Bartlett, Aug. 29, 1970; children: Scott Joseph, Zachary Lorin, Katherine Winifred. BA, Georgetown U., 1969, JD, 1972; LLM, George Washington U., 1975. Bar: D.C. 1973, U.S. Tax Ct. 1973, U.S. Dist. Ct. D.C. 1973, Mont. 1996. Assoc., ptnr. Danzansky, Dickey, Tydings, Quint & Gordon, Washington, 1972-78; prin. R. Scott Faley, P.C., Washington, 1978—. Bd. dir. Fed. Employees News Digest, Inc., Fairfax, Va., 1980-2004; bd. dir., pres. NCC Trout Unltd., 1985—; del. Mid Atlantic Coun. Trout Unltd., 1985—, v.p., 1992—; bd. dirs. Falling Springs Greenway, Inc., Chambersburg, Pa. Inst. for Safety Analysis, Inc., Rockville, Md., 1980-89. Contbr. articles to profl. jours. Mem. instnl. rev. com. Sibley Meml. Hosp., Washington, 1980—. Capt. USAF, 1974. Mem. ABA, FBA, Univ. Club, Boca Bay Pass Club, The Williams Club, Alpha Phi Omega, Phi Alpha Delta. Roman Catholic. Home: 25 Primrose St Chevy Chase MD 20815-4228 Office: Ste 401 5100 Wisconsin Ave NW Washington DC 20016-4119 Home Phone: 301-652-5875; Office Phone: 202-363-8900. Fax: 202-363-7355. E-mail: faleyfish@aol.com.

FALEY, ROBERT LAWRENCE, retired instruments company executive; b. Bklyn., Oct. 1927; s. Eric Lawrence and Anna F.; m. Mary Virginia Mumme, May 1950; children: Robert Wayne, Nancy Diane. BS in Chemistry cum laude, St. Mary's U., San Antonio, 1956; postgrad., U. Del., Newark, 1958—59. Chemist E.I. Dupont de Nemours & Co., Inc., Wilmington, Del., 1956-60; sales mgr. F&M Sci., Houston, 1960-62; pres. Faley Assocs., Houston, 1962-65; sales mgr. Tech. Inc., Dayton, Ohio, 1965-70; biomed. mktg. mgr. Perkin-Elmer Co., Norwalk, Conn., 1967-69; mktg. dir. Cahn Instruments, LA, 1970-72; pres. Faley Internat., El Toro, Calif., 1972-93, Status Internat., Las Vegas, Nev., 1993-97. Spkr. in field; dir. Whatman Lab. Products Inc., 1981-82, Status Instrument Corp., 1985-87; tech. mktg. cons. Whatman Ltd., Abbott Labs., OCG Tech., Inc., Pacific Biochem., Baker Commodities, Bausch & Lomb Co., Motorola Inc., Whatman Inc., Filtration Scis. Corp., PMC Industries, UVP, Inc., Ericomp, Inc., Data I/O. Contbr. articles to profl. jours. Mem. adv. com. on sci., tech., energy and water U.S. 48th Congl. Dist., 1985-87. With USMS, 1944-47, 1st lt. USAF, 1948-53. Named Charter mem. Aviation Hall of Fame. Fellow AAAS, Am. Inst. Chemists (life); mem. ASTM, Am. Chem. Soc. (life), Instrument Soc. Am. (life), Inst. Environ. Scis., Aircraft Owners and Pilots Assn., U.S. Power Squadrons, VFW (life), Am. Legion, Mil. Officers Assn., Air Force Assn., Silver Wings Fraternity (life, Golden mem.), Masons, Delta Epsilon Sigma (life). Achievements include research in technique of gas chromatography. Home: 27850 Espinoza Mission Viejo CA 92692-2156 Personal E-mail: trebor7231@yahoo.com.

FALGOUST, DEAN THOMAS, lawyer, accountant; b. Vacherie, La., Oct. 21, 1958; s. Joseph Bienvenue and Rose Mary (Landry) F.; m. Janet Marie Dolese, Aug. 7, 1982; children: Luke Bienvenue, Laura Katherine. BS in Acctg., Nicholls State U., 1978; JD, Loyola U., New Orleans, 1982; LLM in Taxation, NYU, 1983. Bar: La. 1982; CPA, La. Auditor A.A. Harmon & Co., New Orleans, 1978-79; pvt. practice acctg. New Orleans, 1980-81; assoc. Chaffe, McCall, Phillips, Toler & Sarpy, New Orleans, 1982-85; dir. tax, v.p. Freeport-McMoRan Inc., New Orleans, 1985-97; v.p., tax and legal Freeport McMoran Copper & Gold, Inc., New Orleans, 1997—, v.p., gen. counsel, 2003—, McMoran Exploration Co., 1997—. Bd. dirs., chmn. First Am. Bank & Trust, One Am. Corp., Vacherie, legal cons., 1984—. Mem. Loyola Law Rev., 1980-82. Mem. ABA, La. Bar Assn. Republican. Roman Catholic. Home: 9631 Garden Oak Ln River Ridge LA 70123-2005 Office: Freeport McMoRan Copper & Gold Inc 1615 Poydras St PO Box 61119 New Orleans LA 70161-1119 E-mail: dean_falgoust@fmi.com.*

FALK, BERNARD HENRY, trade association executive; b. NYC, Sept. 10, 1926; s. Max and Sadie (Orwin) F.; m. Iris G. Tannenbaum, June 13, 1954; children: Cindy, Amy, David. BEE, CCNY, 1950; postgrad., Columbia Sch. Bus., 1954. Field engr. RCA, 1950-52; sales engr. Gen. Precision Corp., 1953-56; exec. sec. Nat. Elec. Mfrs. Assn., 1956-65, v.p. govt. rels., 1966-71, pres., 1972-91, vice chmn., 1991-92; chmn. adv. com. elec. goods Dept. Commerce; pres. elect Internat. Electrotech. Commn., 1994-95, pres., 1995—2000. Mem. exec. adv. com. nat. power survey FPC; mem. Bus. Adv. Coun. on Fed. Reports; chmn. liaison com. White House Trade Assn.; bd. dirs. Underwriters Labs., trustee, 1992-2001; co-chmn. EC 92 com. Dept. Commerce, 1991—. Served with USNR, 1944-46. Mem. Am. Nat. Standards Inst. (dir.), Am. Soc. Assn. Execs. (v.p. 1978, dir., chmn. Key industries assn. Council 1985-86), N.Y. State Soc. Assn. Execs. (pres. 1975), U.S. C. of C. (bd. dirs.). Home: 14 Bermuda Lake Dr Palm Beach Gardens FL 33418-4583

FALK, DIANE M., research information specialist, librarian, writer, editor, director; b. NYC; d. Leon H.E. Falk and J. Constance Moorehead (Lilienthal) Stephenson; m. William Patrick Fitzpatrick, May 9, 2006. BA in English and World Lit., Columbia U., 1973, MLS, 1979. Text editor, bibliog. enhancement N.Y. Times Info. Svc., Inc., NYC, 1980—; rsch. libr., documents analyst Atlantis Energy and Minerals, NYC, 1980-81; project coord. legal dept. GAF Corp., NYC, 1981-82; cataloger Exxon Edn. Found., NYC, 1982; indexer, fact-checker H. W. Wilson & Co., Bronx, N.Y., 1982; bibliog. orgn. The Rockefeller Found., NYC, 1983; rsch. info. specialist Harkavy Info. Svc., NYC, 1983-84, Newsworld Comm., NYC, 1985, features writer, 1977—78, rsch. libr., 1985; dir. rsch., head libr., editl. rsch. specialist, website edn. program assoc. The World & I: The Mag. for Lifelong Learners, Washington, 1986—; program assoc. The World ans I School Com., The World and I mag. Copy editor, rsch. mgr. HSA-UWC, NYC and Washington, 1974-75, 86; reference asst. Lehman Libr., Columbia U., NYC, 1978; rsch. libr., documents analyst UN Ctr. for Transnational Corps., 1979; first membership chair Purestyle, Inc., 2006—; advisor Ultrateen Choice; cons., presenter in field Editor-in-chief FOCUS, 1979-80; contbr. articles to profl. jours. English and comms. prof., vol. United to Serve Am., Washington Saturday Coll., Howard U., Washington, 1992-94; ofcl. lectr., tour guide Washington Times Found. and Corp.; conf. coord. Internat. Acad. Arts, Literary, Bus., Legal and Polit. Groups and Issues, 1991—; vol. Ambs. for Peace Seminars, 2001-03; sponsor Svc. for Peace, 2002. Recipient Corp. award Washington Times Corp., 1997, Lifetime Achievement award Amb. for Peace, 2005, Appt. Cert., 2005, Cert. of Honor, Amb. of Peace award, Interreligious and Internat. Fedn. for World Peace and Interreligous Internat. Peace Coun., 2006. Mem. ALA, World Media Assn. (editor e-jour., conf. coord.), Spl. Librs. Assn., DC Libr. Assn. (cert. of appreciation chair Intellectual Freedom com. 1996-97, 2002-03), Intellectual Freedom Interest Group (chair 1996-97, com. chair 2002-03), Rsch. and Reference Interest Group, Women's Fedn. for World Peace (sec. DC chpt. 1993—, advisor, conf. coord. 2007), Internat. Leadership Seminars (staff vol. 1991—), Internat. Fedn. for World Peace (signature campaign staff 1990-91, vol. 1990—, acting sec. 1993—), Prosperity Coun. (editor newsletter 1991), Inst. Mus. and Libr. Svcs., World Assn. Non-Govtl. Orgns. Avocations: photography, arts, travel, writing. Home: 508 Columbia Rd NW Washington DC 20001-2904 Office Phone: 202-635-4059. Personal E-mail: dianemfalk@yahoo.com. E-mail: dfalk@wmassociation.com.

FALK, EDGAR ALAN, public relations consulting executive, writer; b. Bklyn., Nov. 4, 1932; s. Ralph P. and Lillian (Freud) F. AB, NYU, 1954, postgrad., 1957-59. Pub. rels. asst. Western Electric Co., NYC, 1957-59; dir. pub. rels. Ritter, Sanford, Price & Chalek, NYC, 1959-60; account supr. pub. rels. Batten, Barton, Durstine & Osborn, NYC, 1960-67; group dir. pub. rels. N.W. Ayer & Son, NYC, 1967-73; v.p., dir. pub. rels. div. Cunningham & Walsh, Inc., NYC, 1973-79; dir. communications NBA, 1979-81; pres. Ed Falk Communications, NYC, 1981—. Spkr. nat. convs. retailing orgns. Author: 1,001 Ideas To Create Retail Excitement, 1994; rev.edit. 2003, contbg. editor, writer for several retail publs. Mem. Kings County Rep. County Com., 1958-61. 1st lt. U.S. Army, 1954-56; lt. col. Res. ret. Recipient Freedoms Found. award, 1971 Mem. Pub. Rels. Soc. Am. (recipient Silver Anvil award 1970, 71, 73), The Author's Guild, Res. Officers Assn., Retired Officers Assn. Home and Office: 301 E 78th St New York NY 10021-1322

FALK, HENRY, pediatrician, epidemiologist, researcher; b. NYC, Feb. 7, 1943; m. 1971; 3 children. BA, Yeshiva Coll., 1964; MD, Albert Einstein Coll. Medicine, 1968; MPH, Harvard U., 1976. Intern Children's Hosp., Phila., 1968-69; resident Bronx Mcpl. Hosp. Ctr., NYC, 1969-72; med. epidemiologist Ctr. Disease Control, Atlanta, 1972-75, 1976—; dir. div. of environ. hazards and health effects Nat. Ctr. for Environ. Health, Centers for Disease Control, 1985—99, dir., 2003—; asst. adminstr. Agency for Toxic Substance and Disease Registry (ATSDR), 1999—2003. Mem. Am. Acad. Pediat. (liaison mem. com. environmental health 1978), Am. Coll. Epidemiology Rsch., Am. Pub. Health Assn., Soc. Pediatric Rsch. Epimediologi rsch. on etiology of cancer; environmental and occupational exposures; evaln. vinyl chloride exposed individuals and devel. hepatic tumors. Office: NCEH 1600 Clifton Rd NE Atlanta GA 30333

FALK, JEROME B., JR., lawyer; b. May 25, 1940; AB with honors, Univ. Calif., Berkeley, 1962, JD, 1965. Bar: Calif. 1966, US Supreme Ct. Law clk. Justice William O. Douglas, U.S. Supreme Ct.; sr. dir., civil & appellate litigation Howard Rice Nemerovski Canady Falk & Rabkin, San Francisco. Adj. prof. Univ. Calif. Berkeley, 1968—78; mem. Ninth Cir. Com. Judicial Evaluation, 1980; lawyer rep. Ninth Cir. Judicial Conf., 1983—85; lectr. CLE programs. Bd. chmn. KQED Inc., 1999—2001. Named Order of Coif, U. Calif., Berkeley. Mem.: Calif. Acad. Appellate Lawyers (pres. 1994—95), Assn. Bus. Trial Lawyers No. Calif. (pres. 1993—94), Bar Assn. San Francisco (pres. 1985). Office: Howard Rice Nemerovski Canady Falk & Rabkin 7th Fl 3 Embarcadero Ctr San Francisco CA 94111-4024 Office Phone: 415-434-1600. Office Fax: 415-217-5910. Business E-Mail: jfalk@howardrice.com.

FALK, JOHN H., educational administrator; b. LA, Dec. 6, 1948; s. Ivan and Edith Teresa (Marx) F.; m. Amanda Sue Archerd, Dec. 21, 1969 (div. 1984); children: Joshua, Daniel, Lara; m. Lynn Diane Dierking, July 20, 1990. BA in Zoology, U. Calif., Berkeley, 1970, MA in Zoology, 1972, PhD in Biology and Edn., 1974. Lic. Calif. State tchr. biology. Assoc. dir. Chesapeake Bay Ctr. for Environ. Studies, Edgewater, Md., 1974-83; dir. Smith Office of Ednl. Rsch., Washington, 1983-85; spl. asst., asst. sec. rsch. Smith Instn., Washington, 1986-87; dir. Inst. for Learning Innovation, Annapolis, Md., 1987—, pres. emeritus. Cons. in field; advisor Nat. Mus. Natural History, Washington, Calif. Sci. Ctr., others, prof. Oreg. State U., 2006-. Co-author: Museum Experience, 1992, Learning from Museums, 2000, Free-Choice Sci. Edn., 2001, Lessons Without Limit, 2002, Thriving in the Knowledge Age, 2006; creator learning assessment: Personal Meaning Mapping, 1997; editl. bd. Sci. Edn., Curator. Named to Centennial Honor Roll, Am. Assn. Mus., 2006; NSF grantee, 1991-92, 1993-95, 1993-98, 1998-2001. Mem. AAAS, Visitor Studies Assn., Nat. Assn. for Rsch. in Sci. Tchg., Am. Assn. Mus. Avocations: painting, japanese gardening, volleyball, tennis. Office: Inst for Learning Innovation Ste 280 3168 Braverton St Edgewater MD 21037 Office Phone: 410-956-5144. Office Fax: 410-956-5148. E-mail: falk@ilinet.org.*

FALK, ROBERT HARDY, lawyer; b. Houston, Dec. 27, 1948; s. Arnold Charles and Sara Holmes (Pierce) Falk; m. Donna Kay Watts, Aug. 18, 1973 (div. Apr. 27, 1990); children: Dorian Danielle, Dillon Holmes; m. Patricia K. Stampley, Nov. 5, 1994 (div. Apr. 30, 1999). BS summa cum laude, U. Tex., 1971; BA cum laude highest honors, Austin Coll., 1972; JD, U. Tex., 1975. Bar: Tex. 1975, DC 1977, US Dist. Ct. (so. dist. Tex.) 1975, US Patent Office, US Ct. Appeals (5th cir.) 1976, Ct. Customs and Patent Appeals 1976, NC 1979, US Dist. Ct. (we. dist. NC) 1982, US Dist Ct. (no. dist. Tex.) 1984, US Ct. Appeals (fed. cir.) 1982, US Ct. Appeals (5th cir.) 1983, US Ct. Internat. Trade 1985, US Dist. Ct. (no. dist.) Tex. 1987, US Ct. Appeals (9th Cir.), 2007. Process engr. Exxon Co., USA, Baytown, Tex., 1971-72; atty. Pravel, Wilson & Gambrell, Houston, 1975-77; Patent and Trademark Counsel Organon Inc. div. Akzona, Inc., Asheville, NC, 1977-84; ptnr. Hubbard, Thurman, Tucker & Harris, Dallas, 1984-91; dir. Geary, Glast & Middleton, P.C., Dallas, 1992; mng. ptnr. Falk, Vestal & Fish, LLP, Dallas, 1992—99, Falk & Fish, LLP, Dallas, 1997—; pres. Robert Hardy Falk, P.C., 1983—. Pres. Haw Creek Vol. Fire Dept., Asheville, 1980-84; deacon Cen. Christian Ch., Dallas, 1985-89, St. Michaels of All Angels, 1990-. Fellow, U. Tex., 1972. Mem. ABA, ATLA, Am. Patent Law Assn., Am. Intellectual Property Law Assn. (Bar Register of Preeminent Lawyers 2003-07 for Intellectual Property Law and Patent Lawyers), Tex. Bar Assn., NC Bar Assn., DC Bar Assn., Dallas Bar Assn., Dallas Patent Law Assn., Licensing Exec. Soc., Am. Trial Lawyers Soc., Tex. Trail Lawyers Assn., Univ. Club (Dallas), Gleneagles Country Club (Plano), Plaza of the Ams. Club (Dallas), Champions Golf Club (Houston), Asheville Country Club (NC). Republican. Avocations: golf, fishing, scuba diving, boating, flying, theater. Mailing: PO Box 794748 Dallas TX 75379 Office Phone: 214-954-4400. Business E-Mail: falk@patent.net. E-mail: robertfalk@sbcglobal.net.

FALK, STEVEN B., newspaper publishing executive; Various positions Gannett Newspapers, 1983—87; various positions, including circ. dir. San Francisco (Calif.) Newspaper Agy., 1987—98, pres., CEO, 1998—2000; pres., assoc. pub. & COO San Francisco (Calif.) Chronicle, 2000—03, pres. & pub., 2003—. Office: San Francisco Chronicle 901 Mission St San Francisco CA 94103-2905

FALK, THOMAS J., health products executive; b. Waterloo, Iowa, 1958; m. Karen Falk; 1 child. B in Acctg., U. Wis., 1980; MS in Mgmt., Stanford U., Calif., 1988. With Alexander Grant & Co.; with internal audit staff Kimberly-Clark Corp., Neenah, Wis., 1983, sr. auditor, 1984, sr. fin. analyst, 1986, dir. corp. strategic analysis, 1987, ops. mgr. infant care, diaper plant Beech Island, SC, 1989, v.p. ops. analysis and control, 1990, sr. v.p. analysis and adminstrn., 1991, group pres. infant and child care, 1993, group pres. N.Am. consumer products, 1995, group pres. global tissue, pulp and paper, 1998—99, pres., 1999—2003, COO, 1999—2002, bd. dirs. Tex., 1999—, CEO Tex., 2002—, chmn. Tex., 2003—. Dallas regional advisory bd. JP Morgan Chase; bd. dirs. Centex Corp., Grocery Mfrs. Am., Inc. Bd. govs. Boys and Girls Clubs Am.; bd. dirs. U. Wis. Found. Sloan Fellow, Stanford U. Grad. Sch. Bus., 1988. Office: Kimberly Clark Corp PO Box 619100 Dallas TX 75261-9100 Office Phone: 972-281-1200.*

FALK, WILLIAM JAMES, lawyer; s. Sam and Bertha Falk; m. Laurie Falk; children: Douglas, Andrew, Edward BS, Ill. Inst. Tech., Chgo., 1973; JD cum laude, Suffolk U., Boston, 1977; LLM in Taxation, Washington U., St. Louis, 1982. Bar: Mass. 1977, Mo. 1981. Trial atty. IRS Office of Dist. Counsel, St. Louis, 1977—81; assoc. Thompson & Mitchell, St. Louis, 1982—83, ptnr., 1984—96, Thompson Coburn LLP, St. Louis, 1996—99; mem. Lewis, Rice & Fingersh, LC, St. Louis, 1999—. Contbg. author: Missouri Taxation Law and Practice, 1987, 96; contbr. articles to legal jours. Mem. ABA, Mo. Bar Assn., Bar Assn. Met. St. Louis (chmn. taxation sect. 1992-93, mem. exec. com. 1992-93). Avocations: music, photography. Office: Lewis Rice & Fingersh LC 500 N Broadway Ste 2000 Saint Louis MO 63102-2147

FALKENBERG, MARY ELAINE, small business owner; b. Romeo, Mich., Jan. 10, 1940; d. Paul Emerson and Florence Irene (Joughin) Teal; m. Theodore Henry Falkenberg, June 19, 1965; children: Wendy Elaine, Amy Elizabeth, Theodore Paul. AB in Speech, Geography, Ctrl. Mich. U., 1962. Tchr. West Bloomfield (Mich.) H.S., 1962-63, Coopersville (Mich.) H.S., 1963-65; tchr. forensics Harbor Beach (Mich.) H.S., 1966-69; owner Falkenberg's Screenprinting & Honey, Harbor Beach. Cons. Mary Kay, 2007—. Mem. Thumb Area Reading Coun.; trustee Harbor Beach Sch. Bd., 1991-95; active ch. choir, bible study; chair Zion Luth. Pray Chain, 2005-06, pres. Huron County br. Thrivent Fin. Luth., 2006—. Mem. Mich. Edn. Assn., Mich. Beekeepers Assn. (sec., treas.), Huron County Homemaker Club, Women's Club (program dir.), Luth. Women's Missionary League (pres., sec., treas.), Luth. Brotherhood, Port Hope Sr. Citizens, Altar Guild, Ladies of Zion (pres.), Evangelism (sec. 1994-95, pres. 1995-2000), Bloomer's Garden Club, Jaycettes (pres., v.p., sec., treas., Spark Plug), Ski Club, Thumb Rose Soc. (corr. sec., 2003, 04, 05), Luth. Bible Study, Mom's-in-Touch Prayer Group, Presbyn. Bible Study, Women's Nat. Farm and Garden Assn. (pres. 2005-06), Harbor Beach Cmty. Choir, Cath. Bible Study, Mich. Edn. Assn., Luth. Laymen's League, Aid Assn. for Luth., Harbor Beach Hosp. Aux., Harbor Beach Garden Club. Republican. Avocations: reading, crafts, skiing, gardening, clarinet. Home and Office: 1205 S Klug Rd Harbor Beach MI 48441-9723 Office Phone: 989-479-9075. E-mail: mfalkenbergm@yahoo.com.

FALKENRATH, RICHARD A., protective services official; b. 1969; m. Penelope Wilson; 2 children. Grad., Occidental Coll., 1991; PhD, King's Coll., 1993. Postdoc. rsch. fellow Belfer Ctr. Sci. and Internat. Affairs, John. F. Kennedy Sch. Govt. Harvard U., 1993—95, exec. dir., 1995—98; asst. prof. pub. policy Harvard U., 1998—2003; founder, co-principal investigator exec. session domestic preparedness US Dept. Justice; staff mem. Nat. Security Coun. transition team The White House, 2000, dir. proliferation strategy Nat. Security Coun., 2001; sr. dir. policy and plans, spl. asst. to Pres. Office Homeland Security, 2001—03; dep. asst. to Pres., dep. homeland security advisor The White House, 2003—04; mng. dir. Civitas Group LLC; Stephen and Barbara Friedman sr. fellow Brookings Inst.; dep. commr. for counter terrorism NYC Police Dept., 2006—. Author: (book) Shaping Europe's Military Order: The Origins and Consequences of CFE Treaty, 1995; co-author: Avoiding Nuclear Anarchy: Containing the Threat of Loose Russian Nuclear Weapons and Fissile Material (BSCIA Studies in International Security), 1996, America's Achilles' Heel: Nuclear, Biological, Chemical Terrorism and Covert Attack, 1998. Office: NYC Police Dept One Police Plz New York NY 10038

FALKENSTEIN, SARA ANDRÉ, retired elementary school educator; b. Horicon, Wis., May 24, 1939; d. Edward Marsh and Eunice Mavis; m. Gerald Harvey Falkenstein, June 3, 1961; children: Margaret Sara, Christopher Joel. Student, Dodge County Tchrs. Coll., 1957—59; BS, Oshkosh State U., Wis., 1964; postgrad., Inst. Children's Lit., West Redding, Conn., 2007—. Elem. tchr. Hartford Schs., Wis., 1966, early childhood tchr., 1972—97; sch. sec. Platt Schs., 1968—72; quality control specialist H&R Block, Menomonee Falls, 1998—2000, Waukesha, 2001—02, Milw., 2003—06. Alderman City of Hartford, 1986—95, Hartford Area Devel., Hartford Libr. Bd.; founder, bd. dirs. Schauer Ctr. Named to Outstanding Young Women Am., 1966. Lutheran. Avocations: reading, quilting, camping, handwork. Home: 410 W State St Hartford WI 53027

FALKIE, THOMAS VICTOR, mining engineer, engineering executive; b. Mount Carmel, Pa., Sept. 5, 1934; s. Victor J. and Aldona H. Falkie; m. Jean C. Broscius, Nov. 27, 1957 (dec. Apr. 2001); children: Ann, Thomas, Lawrence, Michael, Christine. BS in Mining Engring., Pa. State U., 1956, MS in Mining Engring., 1958, PhD in Mining Engring., 1961. Fellow, rsch. asst. Pa. State U., University Park, 1956-61, prof., head mineral engring. dept., 1969-73; various staff and managerial positions Internat. Minerals and Chem. Corp., Skokie, Ill., 1961-69, Bartow, Fla., 1961-69; dir. U.S. Bur. Mines Dept. of Interior, Washington, 1974-77; pres., CEO Berwind Natural Resources Corp., Phila., 1977—98, chmn. bd., 1999—2003, bd. dirs., 2004—. Adj. prof. indsl. engring. U. Fla., U. So. Fla., 1966; cons. UN, 1971—73; nat. arbitrator joint industry health and safety com. United Mine Workers and Bituminous Coal Operators Assn., 1973; chmn. coal task force project ind. study US Govt., 1974; chmn. interagy. task force Fed. Coun. Sci. and Tech., 1975—76; mem. bd. mineral and energy resources NRC, 1982—88; mem. adv. com. mining and mineral resources rsch. Dept. of Interior, 1988—94. Contbr. articles to profl. jours. Bd. trustees SME Found., 2003—. Recipient Disting. Alumnus award, Pa. State U., 1995, 2004. Mem.: NAE (councillor 1994—2000), AIME (hon.), Am. Coal Found. (chmn. 1993—2000), Mining and Metall. Soc. Am., Nat. Mining Assn. (bd. dir. 1979—2002, hon. dir. 2002—), Pa. Coal Assn. (bd. dirs. 1980—90), Soc. Mining Engrs. of AIME (bd. dirs. 1971—75, v.p. 1977—79, chmn. Phila. sect. 1980—81, bd. dir. 1984—87, pres. 1988, disting. mem., Erskine Ramsay medal 1991, Disting. Svc. award 2001), Union League Club (Phila.), Tau Beta Pi, Sigma Gamma Epsilon. Republican. Roman Catholic. Home: 347 Echo Valley Ln Newtown Square PA 19073-1619 Office: Berwind Natural Resources Corp 3000 Centre Sq W 1500 Market St Philadelphia PA 19102-2100 Home Phone: 610-356-2639. Personal E-mail: tfalkie@comcast.net.

FALKNER, ELIZABETH, chef; b. San Francisco, Calif; BFA, San Francisco Art Inst., 1989. Chef Café Claude, 1990; pastry chef Masa's, Elka/Miyako Hotel, 1993; head. pastry divsn. Rubicon, 1994; owner, exec. pastry chef Citizen Cake, San Francisco, 1997—. Tchr. prof. pastry courses, Japan, 2001—02; cons. Barilla, Parma, Italy, 2002—03; chef's coun. Chefs for Humanity, 2005—. Featured in Pastry Art and Design mag., Gourmet mag., Food and Wine mag., Travel and Leisure mag., Epica-Japan travel mag., guest appearances (TV series) Iron Chef Am., Tyler's Ultimate, Rachel Ray's $40 a Day, Sugar Rush, Best Of, Bay Café. Named Rising Star Chef, San Francisco Chronicle, 1995, Chef to Look for in the Future, Condé Nast Traveler, 1996; named one of 10 Best Pastry Chefs of Am., Bon Appetit Mag., 2003; recipient Pastry Chef of Yr., San Francisco Mag., 1999, Organic Style Mag. award, 2004. Mem.: Human Rights Campaign (Charles M. Holmes award 2005), Frameline (bd. of dir.), Golden Gate Restaurant Assoc., Les Dames D'Escoffier, Women Chefs and Restaurateurs (Golden Bowl award 2003), James Beard Found. Office: Citizen Cake 399 Grove St San Francisco CA 94102 Office Phone: 415-861-2228. Office Fax: 415-861-0565.*

FALKNER, WILLIAM CARROLL, lawyer; b. Baird, Tex., Mar. 26, 1954; s. Vernon Lee and Eunice Vera (Fore) F.; m. Linda May (Tilley), May 23, 1987; children: Heather Lynn, Holly Ann. BA in Govt., Tarleton State U., Stephenville, Tex., 1976; JD, Stetson U., Gulfport, Fla., 1984. Bar: Fla. 1984, U.S. Dist. Ct. (mid. dist.) Fla. 1985, U.S. Ct. Appeals (11th cir.) 1985. Asst. co. atty., sr. asst. co. atty. Pinellas County Atty.'s Office, Clearwater, Fla., 1985—. Editor Res Ipsa, Clearwater, Fla., 1992-93; contbr. articles to profl. jours. Col. U.S. Army Res. (ret.) Mem. ABA, Fla. Bar Assoc., Clearwater Bar Assoc. Baptist. Avocations: reading, writing, sports, biblical studies. Office: Pinellas County Atty's Office 315 Court St Clearwater FL 33756-5165 Office Phone: 727-464-3354. Business E-Mail: bfalkner@co.pinellas.fl.us.

FALKOW, STANLEY, microbiologist, educator; b. Albany, NY, Jan. 24, 1934; s. Jacob and Mollie (Gingold) F.; children from previous marriage: Lynn Beth, Jill Stuart; m. Lucy Stuart Tompkins, Dec. 3, 1983. BS in Bacteriology cum laude, U. Maine, 1955, DSc (hon), 1979; MS in Biology, Brown U., 1960, PhD, 1961; MD (hon.), U. Umea, Sweden, 1989. Asst. chief dept. bacterial immunity Walter Reed Army Inst. Rsch., Washington, 1963-66; prof. microbiology Med. Sch. Georgetown U., 1966-72; prof. microbiology and medicine U. Wash., Seattle, 1972-81; prof., chmn. dept. med. microbiology Stanford U., Calif., 1981-85, prof. microbiology, immunology & medicine Calif., 1981—, Robert W. and Vivian K. Cahill prof. in cancer rsch. Calif. Karl H. Beyer vis. prof. U. Wis., 1978-79; Sommer lectr. U. Oreg. Sch. Medicine, 1979, Kinyoun lectr. NIH, 1980; Rubbro orator Australian Soc. Microbiology, 1981; Stanhope Bayne-Jones lectr. Johns Hopkins U., 1982; mem. Recombinant DNA Molecule Com, task force on antibiotics in animal feeds FDA, microbiology test com. Nat. Bd. Med. Examiners. Author: Infectious Multiple Drug Resistance, 1975; editor: Jour. Infection and Immunity, Jour. Infectious Agents and Diseases. Recipient Ehrlich prize, 1981, Altemeier medal Surg. Infectious Diseases Soc., 1990, Disting. Achievement in Infectious Disease Rsch. award Bristol-Myers Squibb, 1997; Bristol-Myers Squibb unrestricted infectious disease grantee. Fellow Am. Acad. Microbiology; mem. Inst. Medicine, AAAS, Infectious Disease Soc. Am. (Squibb award 1979), Am. Soc. Microbiology (Becton-Dickinson award in Clin. Microbiology, 1986, Abbott-ASM Lifetime Achievement award, 2003), Genetics Soc. Am., NAS, Royal Soc. UK (fgn.), Sigma Xi. Office: Stanford U Dept Microbiology and Immunology 299 Campus Dr Stanford CA 94305-5402 Office Phone: 650-723-9187, 650-723-2671. Office Fax: 650-725-7282. E-mail: falkow@stanford.edu.*

FALLAT, DALE WILLIAM, lawyer; b. Cleve., Dec. 16, 1944; s. Walter and Susan (Hoshko) F.; m. Sandra Jean Sondgerath, Jan. 31, 1967; children— Amie, Bridget, Colleen, Kathryn. B.A., St. Joseph's Coll., 1966; J.D., U. Toledo, 1970. Bar: Ohio, 1970, U.S. Dist. Ct. (no. dist.) Ohio 1971. Asst. gen. counsel The Andersons, Maumee, Ohio, 1974-79, counsel for govt. affairs, 1979-83, gen. ptnr., mgr. govtl. affairs, 1983-88, mem. mng. com., 1986—, v.p. corp. svcs., 1988—, also bd. dirs. Trustee St. Joseph's Coll., Rensselaer, Ind., 1978-86, McAuley High Sch., Toledo, Ohio, 1982-85; bd. dirs., pres. Toledo Soc. for the Handicapped, 1985-95; bd. dirs. Jr. Achievement Northwest Ohio; trustee Anderson Found., Anderson Fund, 1996—. Named Outstanding alumnus St. Joseph's Coll., 1982; recipient Disting. Alumnus award U. Toledo Law Sch. Mem. Ohio Bar Assn. (chmn. agrl. law com. 1984), Toledo Bar Assn., Ohio C. of C. (bd. dirs. 1987—, chmn.-elect 2007—), Toledo C. of C. (chmn. legis. affairs. com.), Rotary (pres. 1990—91, chmn. bd. dirs. Rotary Service Found., 1986—). Home: 6675 Embassy Ct Maumee OH 43537-9648 Office Phone: 419-891-6474.

FALLCREEK, STEPHANIE JEAN, non-profit organization executive; b. Springfield, Mo., May 6, 1950; d. Martha Jean (Barton) Wertz; m. Jerry R. Tillman, 1987; children: Ernest, Daniel, Christopher, Joseph; stepchildren: Shannon, Tiffanie. AB in History, U. Okla., 1972; MSW in Social Welfare, U. Calif., Berkeley, 1974, DSW in Social Welfare, 1984. Dir. Inst. for Geron. Research and Edn., N.Mex. State U., Las Cruces, 1983-87, N.Mex. State Agy. on Aging, Santa Fe, 1987-91; dir. Office of Planning N.Mex. Dept. of Health, 1991-92; dir. div. long term care N.Mex. Dept. Health, Albuquerque, 1992; exec. dir. Fairhill Ctr. for Aging, Cleve., 1992—2006; pres., CEO Fairhill Ctr. (formerly known as Fairhill Ctr. for Aging), 2006—. Pres. Fallcreek & Assocs., Cleve., 1982—; sr. assoc. Age Wave Inc., Emeryville, Calif., 1985-87; cons., spkr. in field. Author: (with others) A Healthy Old Age: A Sourcebook for Health Promotion with Older Adults, Health Promotion and Aging: Strategies for Action, Health Promotion and Aging: A National Resource of Selected Programs; also articles and book chpts.; mem. editl. bd. Generations, 1999-2002. Bd. dirs. Am. Soc. on Aging, 1992-1995, Nat. Assn. State Units of Aging, 1987-91, S.W. Soc. on Aging, 1992-97, Goodwill Industries Cleve., 1999-2004; moderator First Bapt. Ch. of Greater Cleve., 1997-98; treas., fin. chair Laurel Lake Retirement Cmty., 1999-2004, 06—; bd. dirs. RSVP Greater Cleve., 2002—05, chmn. governance com., 2004—. Danforth fellow, 1972-78; named to Women of Note, Crains Cleve. Bus., 2004. Mem. AAUW, NASW, Nat. Coun. on Aging (policy com. 2004—), Soc. for Values in Higher Edn., Am. Soc. on Aging. Office: Fairhill Ctr 12200 Fairhill Rd Cleveland OH 44120-1013 Office Phone: 216-533-1361. E-mail: sfallcreek@aol.com, sfc@fairhillcenter.org.

FALLDING, HAROLD JOSEPH, sociology educator; b. Cessnock, NSW, Australia, May 3, 1923; s. Frederick and Alice Bessie (Chopping) F.; m. Margaret Hurlstone Hardy, Dec. 18, 1954; children: Marion, Ruth, Helen. Cert. Libr. Sch., Pub. Libr. New South Wales, 1941; BSc, U. Sydney, Australia, 1950, BA, 1951, diploma of edn., 1952, MA with honors, 1955; PhD, Australian Nat. U., 1957. Tchr. h.s. English and history NSW Dept. Edn., 1952—53; sr. rsch. fellow in sociology, dept. agrl. econs. U. Sydney, 1956-58; sr. lectr. sociology U. NSW, 1959—62; vis. assoc. prof. Grad. Sch., Rutgers U., NJ, 1963-65; prof. U. Waterloo, Ont., Canada, 1965-88, disting. prof. emeritus, 1989—. Author: The Sociological Task, 1968, The Sociology of Religion: An Explanation of the Unity and Diversity in Religion, 1974, Drinking, Community and Civilization. The Account of a New Jersey Interview Study, 1974, The Social Process Revisited, 1990; (poetry) Word of the Tangling Fire, 1969, Collected Poetry, 1997, The Complete Poems to 2005, 2005. Mem. Clare Hall, U. Cambridge. Fellow Royal Soc. Can.; mem. Am. Sociol. Assn., Can. Inst. Internat. Affairs, Can. Soc. Sociology and Anthropology, Internat. Sociol. Assn., Soc. Sci. Study of Religion, Assn. Sociology of Religion, Social Sci. Fedn. Can. (dir.) Mem. United Ch. Can. Home: 40 Arbordale Walk Guelph ON Canada N1G 4X7 Office: Sociology Dept U Waterloo Waterloo ON Canada N2L 3G1 *My life has seemed like a series of arrivals at the same crossroads, compelling me to confirm a decision on priorities made very early, that loyalty to truth comes before achievement. Any achievements have consequently seemed surprises—like spin-offs from giving effect to that loyalty.*

FALLEK, ANDREW MICHAEL, lawyer; b. Bklyn., Aug. 15, 1956; m. Elaine Friedman, June 4, 1984. BA, U. Pa., 1978; JD, Vanderbilt U., 1981. Bar: N.Y. 1982, U.S. Dist. Ct. (so. and ea. dists.) N.Y. 1985, U.S. Ct. Appeals (2d cir.) 1991, U.S. Ct. Appeals (D.C. cir.) 1993. Assoc. Belson, Connolly & Belson, NYC, 1981-84; pvt. practice Bklyn., 1984—. Editor in-chief Bklyn. Barrister. Mem. NY State Bar Assn., Bklyn. Bar Assn. (chmn. judiciary com., co-chmn. compensation com., mem. CLE com., trustee, dir. found.), Def. Rsch. Inst., Nathan R. Sobel Am. Inns of Ct. Office: 110 Wall St 19th Fl New York NY 10005 Office Phone: 212-797-4700.

FALLER, DONALD E., marketing and operations executive; b. Jersey City, Mar. 1, 1927; s. Louis John and Gertrude Louise (Hupfield) F.; m. Dolores Adeline Smith, Aug. 28, 1948; children: Mark William, Kyle Lindsay Fernandez, Kimberly Willard, Donald Mark, Krystn Judith, Kelly Bridget Christina Weir. BS, Mich. State U., 1948. Prodn. mgr. Sealtest Foods Kraft, Detroit, 1958-60, dist. mgr., 1960-67, div. mktg. mgr. Cleve., 1967-70; v.p. mktg. Citrus Cen. Inc., Orlando, Fla., 1970-78, exec. v.p. mktg. and adminstrn., mktg. divsn., 1978-83, chief exec. officer, 1980-83; gen. sales mgr. Sunkist Growers Inc., Ontario, Calif., 1984-88, dir. sales, fin. and ops., 1988-90; pres., CEO Trinity Mktg. Cons., Longwood, Fla., 1990—. Bd. dirs. Combank Apopka Freedom Savs. & Loan Assn., Winter Park, Fla., Calif.-Ariz. Citrus League. Bd. dirs. Pace Sch., Alamonte Springs, Fla., 1976-82; mem. Fla. Family Care Coun., 2006—. Mem. Nat. Juice Products Assn. (pres.), Blue Key, Sweetwater Country Club (Longwood, Fla.), Orlando Country Club, Errol Estate Country Club, Alpha Zeta (pres. 1947-48). Republican. Office: Trinity Mktg Cons 732 Riverbend Blvd Longwood FL 32779-2349

FALLER, DOROTHY ANDERSON, training services executive, consultant; b. Chgo., July 6, 1939; d. Albert T. and Lillian G. (Chalbeck) Anderson; m. Adolph Faller, Sept. 5, 1959; children: Carl, Kurt. Student, Ill. Wesleyan U., 1956—59; AB, U. Ill., 1960; MS in Social Adminstrn., CASE Western Res. U., 1975. Lic. ind. social worker. Child welfare worker Klamath County Pub. Welfare Commn., Klamath Falls, Oreg., 1960-67; social svc. cons. Ind. State Dept. Pub. Welfare, 1968-72; adminstrv. asst. Berea (Ohio) Children's Home, 1974; rsch. asst. Case Western Res. U., Sch. Applied Social Scis., 1975, Mandel Sch. Applied Social Scis.; social svcs. supr. Ohio Dept. Pub. Welfare, Cleve., 1975-81; exec. dir. Cleve. Internat. Program, 1981-99; sec. gen., CEO Coun. Internat. Programs USA, 1999—2002; pres. Faller Internat. Tng., 2002—. Cons. Cleve. Found., Am. Sickle Cell Anemia Found., John A. Yankey & Assocs.; field instr. Case Western Reserve U., 1976—77; dir. African Internship Project Substance Abuse Prevention, 1992—95, Ghana Conf., 1995; assisted founding Sch. of Social Work, Addis Abba U., Ethiopia, 2002—06; instr. conflict resolution and fundraising Addis Ababa, NGO Fiscal Mgmt., Ukrainian Women's Group, NGO Issues for Japanese Mcpl. Workers for Cleve. Coun. World Affairs, 2004; mem. adv. coun. Mandel Ctr. Non-Profit Orgns., 1995—96, CASE Western Res. U.; strategic planning Coun. Internat. Fellowship, Goa, India, 2003, Riga, Latvia, 04, Bonn, Germany, 05, Cleve., 07; cons. Ethiopian programs U. Ill., Chgo., 2002—, faculty assoc., 2004; tchr. 1st master social work class Addis Ababa U., 2004; dir. workforce devel. grant Ethopia Coun. of Internat. Programs USA, 2005—06; lectr., cons. in field; trainer Ethiopian workforce grant participants Addis Ababa U. and cmty., Chgo. and Ethiopia, 2005—07; co-chair 50th Anniversary Conf. Coun. Internat. Programs US, 2007, 27th Conf. Coun. Internat. Fellowship, 2007; trainer UNICEF project Setting Up Child Welfare in So. Sudan, 2007. Editor, contbr. Ohio Children's Budget Project: A Public Policy Study, 1975. Bd. dirs. West Shore Unitarian Ch., 1978-81, 2000-03, Volgograd Free Speech Forum, 1995-2001. Grantee Cmty. Criminal Justice Adminstrn., Romania, 1999-2001; hon. by Fulbright Assn., 1999, Cleve. Rotary, 2003. Mem. Acad. Cert. Social Workers (cert.), Nat. Assn. Social Workers (unit chair state bd., exec. com. nat. bd. dirs. 1985-88, chmn. Internat. Activities Com. of Nat. Bd. 1986-89, program com. 1989-91, del. Internat. Fedn. Social Workers, Sweden, 1988, Cleve. unit Social Worker of Yr. 1986, del. from Ohio to del. assembly 1990, conf. chair ann. meeting profession 1993), Nat. Fulbright Assn. (life), CASE Western Res. U. Sch. Applied Social Scis. Alumni Assn., Sigma Kappa (pres. 1959), Alpha Lambda Delta (pres. 1956). Home and Office: 6889 Columbia Rd Olmsted Falls OH 44138-1523 E-mail: dorothyfaller@sbcglobal.net.

FALLER, JAMES ELLIOT, physicist, researcher; b. Mishawaka, Ind., Jan. 17, 1934; s. Elmer Edward and Leona Maxine (Forstbauer) F.; m. Jocelyne T. Bellenger, March 7, 1996; children: William Edward, Peter James. AB summa cum laude, Ind. U., 1955; MA, Princeton U., 1957, PhD, 1963; MA (hon.), Wesleyan U., Middletown, Conn., 1972. Instr. Princeton U., 1959-62; mem. Joint Inst. Lab. Astrophysics, Boulder, Colo., 1963-66, fellow, 1972—; asst. prof. physics Wesleyan U., 1966-68, assoc. prof. physics, 1968-71, prof., 1971-72. Nat. Acad. Sci./NRC postdoctoral fellow, 1963-64; Sloan fellow, 1972-73; recipient Precision Measurement award Nat. Bur. Standards, 1970, Arnold O. Beckman award Instrument Soc. Am., 1970, Exceptional Sci. Achievement medal NASA, 1973, Gold medal Dept. Commerce, 1990, Fed. Lab. Consortium Tech. Transfer award, 1992, Joseph F. Keithley award, 2001, Presdl. Rank award, 2006. Fellow: Am. Phys. Soc.; mem.: AAAS, Internat. Astron. Union, Optical Soc. Am., Am. Geophysical Union, Sigma Xi, Phi Beta Kappa. Home: 303 Hollyberry Ln Boulder CO 80305-5230 Office: JILA Univ Colorado Boulder CO 80309-0001 Office Phone: 303-492-8509. Business E-Mail: fallerj@jila.colorado.edu.

FALLER, KEITH, healthcare insurance company executive; BSBA, MBA, Butler U., Indpls. Cert. CFA. Pres., CEO Anthem Life Ins. Co. Anthem, Inc., pres., CEO Acordia of the South, exec. v.p. Acordia, Inc., exec. v.p. Health Ins., CEO Anthem Health Plans, pres. Blue Cross and Blue Shield's Midwest region; pres., CEO Ctrl. Region SBU WellPoint, Inc. Adv. bd. Union Planters Bank. Bd. trustees Wellness Cmty., Orchard Sch.; bd. advs. Kelley Sch. Bus.; bd. visitors Butler Bus. Sch.

FALLER, SUSAN GROGAN, lawyer; b. Cin., Mar. 1, 1950; d. William M. and Jane (Eagen) Grogan; m. Kenneth R. Faller, June 8, 1973; children: Susan Elisabeth, Maura Christine, Julie Kathleen. BA, U. Cin., 1972; JD, U. Mich., 1975. Bar: Ohio 1975, Ky. 1989, U.S. Dist. Ct. (so. dist.) Ohio 1975, U.S. Ct. Claims 1982, U.S. Ct. Appeals (6th cir.) 1982, U.S. Supreme Ct. 1982, U.S. Tax Ct. 1984, U.S. Dist. Ct. (ea. dist.) Ky., 1991. Assoc. Frost & Jacobs, Cin., 1975-82; ptnr. Frost & Jacobs LLP, Cin., 1982-2000; mem. Frost Brown Todd LLC, Cin., 2000—. Chmn. first amendment, media and advt. practice group Frost Brown Todd LLC, 2001—, co-chmn. India cons. group, 2006—. Assoc. editor Mich. Law Rev., 1974-75; contbg. author: MLRC 50-State Survey of Media Libel and Privacy Law, 1982-93, MLRC 50-State Survey of Media Libel Law, 1999-, MLRC State Survey of Employment Libel and Privacy Law, 1999-. Bd. dirs. Summit Alumni Coun., Cin., 1983-85; trustee Newman Found., Cin., 1980-86, Cath. Social Svc., Cin., 1984-93, nominating com., 1985-88, sec., 1990; mem. Class XVII Leadership Cin., 1993-94; mem. exec. com., def. counsel sect. Media Law Resource Ctr., 1998-2002, chmn. membership com., 2003—; pres., def. counsel sect. Libel Def. Resource Ctr., 2001; mem. parish coun. St. Monica-St. George Ch., 1996-2000. Recipient Career Women of Achievement award YWCA, 1990. Mem. ABA (co-editor newsletter media litig. 1993-97), FBA, Ky. Bar Assn., No. Ky. Bar Assn., No. Ky. Women's Bar Assn., Ohio Bar Assn. (chair media law com. 2001-02), Cin. Bar Assn. (com. mem.), Potter Stewart Inn of Ct., U. Cin. Alumni Assn., Arts & Scis. Alumni Assn. (bd. govs. U. Cin. Coll. 1988-2000), U. Mich. Alumni Assn., Mortar Bd., Leland Yacht Club, Coll. Club, Clifton Meadows Club, Phi Beta Kappa, Theta Phi Alpha. Roman Catholic. Home: 5 Belsaw Pl Cincinnati OH 45220-1104 Office: Frost Brown Todd LLC 2200 PNC Ctr 201 E 5th St Cincinnati OH 45202-4182 Office Phone: 513-651-6941. Business E-Mail: sfaller@fbtlaw.com.

FALLERT, DAVID ORVAL, military officer, military analyst; b. Hastings, Nebr., Oct. 17, 1945; s. Orval Louis and Dora Marie Fallert; m. Mary Elizabeth West, June 3, 1966; children: Andrea Michele Griffith, Audrey Rene Blanks. BS in Biology, Tenn. Technol. U., Cookeville, 1967. Commd. lt. US Army, 1967, advanced through grades to lt. col., 1994, chief orgnl. readiness evaluation team Ft. George G. Meade, Md., 1993—95, sys. analyst emergency preparedness Fort Sam Houston, Tex., 1999—. Decorated Meritorious Svc. medal US Army. Mem.: Mensa (assoc.). Home: PO Box 426 Crandall TX 75114 Office: SRA Intl Inc US Army Med Comd 2050 Worth Rd Fort Sam Houston TX 78234 Home Phone: 972-476-9904; Office Phone: 210-221-8928. Business E-Mail: david.fallert@us.army.mil.

FALLESEN, GARY DAVID, journalist, lay worker; b. Rochester, NY, July 24, 1959; s. Karl David and Mary Lou (Putnam) F.; m. Elaine Gertrude Busse, July 3, 1982; children: Jesse Dane, Hayley Hope BA, St. John Fisher Coll., Rochester, 1981. Sports clk. Democrat & Chronicle, Rochester, 1979-82, sports writer, 1982-88, sports columnist, 1988-92, sports writer, 1992-96; outdoor writer, 1996—. Contbr. articles to Sporting News, Golf World, Golf Jour., CBS Sportsline, Adirondack Explorer, Escape Mag., ESPN.com, Altrec.com, other sports publs; author: Peak Experiences, 2000, (with Kevin Flynn) Mount Everest Confessions of an Amateur Peak Bagger, 2006 Named Sports Writer of Yr., N.Y. State Wrestling Coaches Assn., 1984, Rochester Press-Radio Club, 1986, 2005, Hon. Mention, N.Y. State AP Writers Contest, 1989, 2d pl. column, Profl. Football Writers, 1990, 1st place column Profl. Football Writers, 1991, hon. mention column Profl. Football Writers, 1992, 2d pl. enterprise Football Writers Assn., 1995, hon. mention column Football Writers Assn., 1996, N.Y. Newspaper Pub. Assn. award of excellence, 1996-97, 98, hon. mention N.Y. State AP Writers Contest, 1998 Mem.: Newspaper Guild (exec. com. 1992—, v.p. 1995—2001, officer Local 17), N.Y. State Outdoor Writers Assn., Outdoor Writers Assn. Am. (2d outdoors page 2001, 3d pl. big game hunting, outdoors page 1999, 1st boating, 3d outdoors page 2000), Climbing for Christ Inc. (pres.), Rochester Christian Writers Guild (co-dir.), Am. Alpine Club. Lutheran. Avocations: mountain climbing, photography, drama. Office: Dem & Chronicle 55 Exchange Blvd Rochester NY 14614-2001 Office Phone: 585-957-5489. Business E-Mail: gfallesn@democratandchronicle.com.

FALLETTA, JO ANN, conductor; b. NYC, Feb. 27, 1954; d. John Edward and Mary Lucy (Racioppo) F.; m. Robert Alemany, Aug. 24, 1986. BA in Music, Mannes Coll. Music, NYC, 1976; MA in Music, Juilliard Sch., NYC, 1983, PhD in Musical Arts, 1989; doctorate (hon.), Marian Coll., Wis., 1988, Old Dominion U., 1996, Canisius Coll., 2000. Music dir. Queens Philharmonic, NYC, 1978-91, Den. Chamber Orch., Colo., 1983-92; assoc. condr. Milw. Symphony, Wis., 1985-88; music dir. Women's Philharmonic, San Francisco, 1986-96; music dir., condr. Long Beach Symphony, Calif., 1989-00; music dir. Va. Symphony, Norfolk, 1991—, Buffalo Philharm., 1999—. Over 30 recordings with the London Symphony, the Buffalo Philharmonic, the Virginia Symphony, the English Chamber Orchestra, the New Zealand Symphony, the Long Beach Symphony, the Czech National Symphony and the Women's Philharmonic. Stokowski Conducting Competition, Toscanini Conducting award, John S. Edwards Award, Am. Symphony Orchestra League, Seaver/Nat. Endowment for the Arts Conductors Award, 2002. Office: c/o Genevieve Spielberg Inc 12 Princeton St Summit NJ 07901

FALLETTA, JOHN MATTHEW, pediatrician, educator; b. Arma, Kans., Sept. 3, 1940; s. Matthew John and Norma (Luke) F.; m. Carolyn Ontjes, June 22, 1963; children: Elizabeth, Matthew. AB, U. Kans., 1962, MD, 1966. Diplomate Am. Bd. Pediat., Am. Bd. Hematology-Oncology. Intern in mixed medicine Kans. U. Med. Ctr., Kansas City, 1966-67; surgeon Epidemic Intelligence Svc., Tex. Children's Hosp. USPHS, Houston, 1967-69; asst. instr. pediat. Baylor Coll. Medicine, Houston, 1967-69, resident, 1969-71, chief resident Tex. Children's Hosp., 1971, postdoctoral fellow hematology-oncology, 1971-73, asst. prof. pediat., 1973-76; assoc. prof. Duke U., Durham, NC, 1976-83, prof., 1984—, chief divsn. hematology-oncology, 1976-94, dir. Clin. Pediat. Lab., 1976-95. Chmn. transfusion com. Duke U. Med. Ctr., 1978—, mem. exec. com. med. staff, 1978—, instl. rev. bd. human rsch., 1979—, chmn., 1994—; mem. instl. rev. bd. human rsch. Baylor Coll. Medicine, 1974-76; mem. acad. coun. Duke U., 1982-86, 87-96, 98-2000, exec. com., 1988, faculty compensation com., 1988—, faculty com. on univ. governance, 1988, trustee-faculty com. to rev. pres., 1989, search com. for pres., 1992; cons. pediat. hematologist-oncologist Charlotte Meml. Hosp., NC, 1978-94, mem. Copernicus Independent Rev. Bd., 2002—, vice-chair, 2004—; mem. med.

adv. bd. Children's Cancer Rsch. Fund, 2001—; mem. coun. accreditation Assn. for Accreditation Human Rsch. Protection Programs, Inc., 2005— Contbr. more than 120 articles to Nature, Am. Jour. Ophthalmology, Pediat., New Eng. Jour. Medicine, Clin. Pediat. Oncology, others. Cons. pediat. hematologist-oncologist Project Hope, Pediatric Inst., Krakow, Poland, 1979—; prin. investigator Pediat. Oncology Group, 1981-95, chmn. epidemiology com., mem. prin. investigator's exec. com., new agts. and pharmacology com.; chmn. prophylactic penicillin study I Nat. Heart, Lung and Blood Inst., NIH, 1982-86, chmn. study II, 1987-95; active Cancer Ctr. Support Rev. Com. Nat. Cancer Inst. NIH, 1986-90, NIH Reviewers Res., 1990—, Cancer Clin. Investigation Rev. Com., 1991-96, chmn., 1995-96; trustee Ronald McDonald House Charities, 1986—. Mem. Am. Acad. Pediat., Am. Pediat. Soc., Am. Soc. Clin. Oncology, So. Soc. Pediat. Rsch. (pres. 1981-82), Soc. Pediat. Rsch., NC Pediat. Soc., NC Med. Soc., Phi Beta Kappa, Alpha Omega Alpha. Office: Duke U Med Ctr PO Box 2991 Durham NC 27710-2991

FALLIN, MARY COPELAND, congresswoman, former lieutenant governor; b. Warrensburg, Mo., Dec. 9, 1954; d. Joseph Newton and Mary (Duggan) Copeland; children: Christina, Price. Attended, Oklahoma Baptist U., 1973—75; BS, Okla. State U., 1977; attended, U. Ctrl. Okla., 1979—81. Bus. mgr. Okla. Dept. Securities, Oklahoma City, 1979-81; state travel coord. Okla. Dept. of Tourism, Oklahoma City, 1981-82; sales rep. Associated Petroleum, Oklahoma City, 1982-83; mktg. dir. Brian Head (Utah) Hotel & Ski Resort, 1983-84; dir. sales Residence Inn Hotel, Oklahoma City, 1984-87; dist. mgr. Lexington Hotel Suites, Oklahoma City, 1988-90; real estate assoc. Pippin Properties, Inc., Oklahoma City, 1990-94; mem. Okla. Ho. Reps., Oklahoma City, 1990-94; lt. gov. State of Okla., Oklahoma City, 1995—2007; mem. US Congress from 5th Okla. dist., 2007—, mem. small bus. com., transp. & infrastructure com., vice chmn. Women's Caucus. Chmn. Nat. Conf. Lt. Govs. Mem., del. Okla. Fedn. Rep. Women; mem. Am. Legis. Exch. Coun., Nat. Conf. State Legislatures; former bd. mem. United Way Oklahoma City, YWCA; mem. adv. bd. Trail of Tears; former hon. chair Organ Donor Network; former hon. co-chair Indian Territory Arts and Humanities Coun.; former co-chair Festival of Hope; active Crossings Cmty. Ch. Named Woman of Yr., Ladies in Comm., 1998, Girl Scouts Am., 1998, Nat. Legislator of Yr., Okla. Ladies in the News, Disting. Former Student, U. Ctrl. Okla.; named to The Okla. Women's Hall of Fame, The Okla. Aviation Hall of Fame, 1998; recipient Bi-liner award, 1997, Guardian of Small Bus. award, Small Bus. Adv. award, Nat. Fedn. Ind. Small Bus., Women in the News award, Women in Comm., Clarence E. Page award. Mem.: Aerospace States Assn. (chmn. 2003—05). Republican. Office: 120 N Robinson Ste 100 Oklahoma City OK 73102 also: 1432 Longworth House Office Bldg Washington DC 20515 Office Phone: 405-234-9900. Office Fax: 405-234-9909.*

FALLON, JIMMY, actor; b. Bklyn., Sept. 19, 1974; s. Jim and Gloria Fallon. Attended, Coll. St. Rose. Actor: (TV series) Saturday Night Live, 1998—2004; (TV films) Sex and the Matrix, 2000; (TV miniseries) Band of Brothers, 2001, (guest appearance): (TV series) Spin City, 1998,: (films) Almost Famous, 2000, Anything Else, 2003, The Entrepreneurs, 2003, Taxi, 2004, Fever Pitch, 2005, (voice) Doogal, 2006; co-author (with Gloria Fallon): (book) I Hate This Place: The Pessimist's Guide to Life, 1999; performer: (comedy album) The Bathroom Wall, 2003. Named one of 50 Most Beautiful People in the World, People mag., 2002. Office: Creative Artist Agency 9830 Wilshire Blvd Beverly Hills CA 90212

FALLON, PAT, artist, educator; b. Cartagena, Colombia, Nov. 2, 1939; d. Carlos Fallon and Maureen (Bryne) Fallon Laird; m. Ronald Patrick Conner, Dec. 26, 1960 (div. June 1976); children: Hadley Kathryn Conner, Kenneth Fallon Conner. BA, Antioch Coll., Yellow Springs, Ohio, 1962; BFA, Cleve. Inst. Art, Ohio, 1980; MFA, Kent State U., Ohio, 1982. Prof. Ursuline Coll., Cleve., 1983—. Exhibitions include nat. and internat., U.S., Ireland, Germany. Vol. N.E. Ohio Coalition Homeless, Cleve. Fellow, Ohio Humanities Coun., 1986—94. Mem.: Mus. Contemporary Art Cleve., Amnesty, Cleve. Mus. Art, So. Poverty Ctr. Democrat. Roman Catholic. Home: 3300 Kenmore Rd Shaker Heights OH 44122-3462 Office: Ursuline Coll 2550 Lander Rd Cleveland OH 44124-4318 Business E-Mail: pfallon@ursuline.edu.

FALLON, PATRICK R., advertising executive; b. 1946; With Leo Burnett, Chgo., 1967-69, Stevson & Assocs., Mpls., 1969-76, v.p.; with Martin/Williams Advt., Mpls., 1976-81, v.p.; founder Fallon McElligott Rice (now Fallon Worldwide), Mpls., 1981—; chmn., CEO Fallon Worldwide. Office: Fallon Worldwide Ste 2800 50 S 6th St Minneapolis MN 55402-1550*

FALLON, RICHARD H., JR., law educator; b. Augusta, Maine, Jan. 4, 1952; AB in History, Yale U., 1975, JD, 1980; BA in Philosophy, Politics, and Economics, Oxford U., 1977. Bar: Mass. 1988. Law clk. to Hon. J. Skelly Wright US Ct. Appeals DC Cir., 1980-81; law clk. to Hon. Lewis F. Powell Jr. US Supreme Ct., Washington, 1981-82; asst. prof. law Harvard Law Sch., Cambridge, Mass., 1982-87, prof., 1987—, Ralph S. Tyler, Jr. prof. constl. law, 2004—. Vis. prof. Wash. U., Seattle, spring 1991. Author: Implementing the Constitution, 2001, The Dynamic Constitution - An Introduction to American Constitutional Law, 2004; co-author: Constitutional Law: Cases, Comments, Questions, 2001, Hart & Wechsler's The Federal Courts and The Federal System, 1973, 1988, 1996, 2003. Fellow: Am. Acad. Arts & Sciences. Office: Harvard Law Sch 1563 Massachusetts Ave Cambridge MA 02138 Office Phone: 617-495-3215. Office Fax: 617-496-5156. Business E-Mail: rfallon@law.harvard.edu.

FALLON, WILLIAM JOSEPH, career military officer; b. East Orange, NJ, Dec. 30, 1944; m. Mary Elizabeth Trapp; children: Susan, Barbara, William, Christina. BA, Villanova U., 1967; MA in Internat. Studies, Old Dominion. Advanced through grade to adm. USN, 2005; pilot USS Ranger, 1969; comdr. attack squadron 65 USS Dwight D. Eisenhower, 1984-85; dep. comdr. carrier air wing 8 USS Nimitz; comdr. attack wing 1 Naval Air Sta. Occana, Va., 1989-90, USS Theodore Roosevelt, 1991, comdr. carrier group 8, 1995; comdr. Theodore Roosevelt battle group, comdr. Battle Force 6th Fleet; dep. comdr. in chief, chief staff US Atlantic Fleet, Norfolk, Va., 1996-98, commdr. 2d Fleet, Striking Fleet Atlantic, 1997—2000; vice chief naval ops. USN, Washington, 2000—03; comdr. US Fleet Forces Command & US Atlantic Fleet, Norfolk, Va., 2003—05, US Pacific Command, Honolulu, 2005—07, US Ctrl. Command, MacDill AFB, Fla., 2007—. Office: US Central Command 7115 S Boundary Blvd Tampa FL 33621*

FALLOWS, JAMES MACKENZIE, journalist; b. Phila., Aug. 2, 1949; s. James Albert and Jean (Mackenzie) F.; m. Deborah Jean Zerad, June 22, 1971; children: Thomas Mackenzie, Tad Andrew. BA magna cum laude, Harvard U., 1970; diploma in econ. devel. (Rhodes scholar), Oxford U., 1972. Staff editor Washington Monthly, 1972-74, contbg. editor; freelance mag. writer, 1972-76; assoc. editor Tex. Monthly, 1974-76; chief speechwriter Pres. Jimmy Carter, Washington, 1977-79; Washington editor Atlantic Monthly, 1979-97, nat. corr.; editor US News & World Report, Washington, 1996-98; chief columnist Industry Standard; Techno-Files columnist NY Times, NYC. Nat. commentator Pub. Radio, 1987—. Author: National Defense, 1981, More Like Us, 1989, Looking at the Sun: The Rise of the New East Asia Economic and Political System, 1994, Breaking the News: How the Media Undermine American Democracy, 1996; contbr. articles to numerous mags. and jours. Office: Techno-Files Columnist NY Times 229 W 43rd St New York NY 10036

FALLS, KATHLEENE JOYCE, photographer; b. Detroit, July 3, 1949; d. Edgar John and Acelia Olive (Young) Haley; m. Donald David Falls, June 15, 1974; children: Daniel John, David James. Student, Oakland Community Coll., 1969-73, Winona Sch. Profl. Photography, 1973-80. Lic. amateur radio-technician class, cert. photog. specialist Profl. Photographers Am., 1988, photog. craftsman Profl. Photographers Am., 1990, cert. electronic imaging Profl. Photographers Am., 1990, master artist Profl. Photographers Am., 1990, profl. photographer Profl. Photographers Am., 2004, master electronic imaging Profl. Photographers Am., 2004. Printer Guardian Photo, Novi, Mich., 1967-69; printer, supr. quality control N.Am. Photo, Livonia, 1969—76; free lance photographer, 1969—76; owner, pres. Kathy Falls, Inc., Camden, 1976—2001; ptnr. Taking Better Pictures, 2006—. Instr. continuing edn. Monroe County (Mich.) C.C., 1981—83, instr. digital imaging, 1994—95; instr. Internat. Photography and Art Sch., Indpls., 2004; nat. artisan judge Congl. H.S. Art Competition, 1985—2000; owner Picture Perfect, Carlton, Mich., 1987; co-owner Haleys Gift Shoppe, Dundee, 1989; pub. info. officer Am. Radio Relay League, 1998—2000; pres. Artworks of Hillsdale, 2006—07. Author: (booklet) Emergency Photo-Retouching for Photographers, 1988; photographer (represented in spl. categories) Profl. Photographers Am. Nat. Loan Collection, 1980, 1981, 1983, 1987, 2002, 2004—05, (permanent collections) Monroe County Hist. Mus., Archives Notre Dame; editor: The Hertzian Herald, 1998; contbr. articles to profl. jours. Active Big Bros. and Big Sisters, Monroe, 1986—87; corr. sec. Monroe Women's Ctr., 1986—88; mem. Amateur Radio Emergency Svc.; pres. Our Lady of Knock divsn. Laoh Adrian, Laoh State Bd., 2001—03; pres. Artworks Hillsdale County Arts Coun., 2006; Catechist St. Parick's Ch., Carleton, 1984—87, mem. parish coun., 1998—2000; bd. dirs. Ladies Ancient Order of Hibernians. Mem.: NAFE, Nat. Orgn. Women Bus. Owners, Monroe C. of C. (chmn. council women bus. owners), Monroe County Fine Arts Coun., Am. Photog. Artisans Guild (bd. dir. 1987—, Photog. Artisan degree 1989, Artisan Laurel degree 1991, pres. 1992, editor Palette Page 2001—04, exec. sec. 2001—, exec. dir. 2002, coun. mem., Fuji Masterpiece award 2005), Profl. Photographers Am., Profl. Photographers Mich. (artisan chair 1982—83, bd. dir. 2000—, dir. 2001—02, Best of Show award 1976, Artist of Yr. 1980, Best of Show award 1981, Artist of Yr. 1991, Best of Show award 2001), Detroit Profl. Photographers Assn. (artisan chmn. 1981—82, bd. dir. 1987—, Best of Show award 1981, 1983), Am. Soc. Photographers, Hillsdale Art Guild, Toastmasters, Monroe County Radio Comms. Assn., Ladies Ancient Order of Hibernians (bd. dir. 1998—99), Monroe Camera, Hillsdale County Amateur Radio Club, Scarab Club Detroit, Internat. Club. Republican. Roman Catholic. Avocations: guitar, piano, drawing, travel, camping. Home and Office: 14940 Carpenter Rd Camden MI 49232 Office Phone: 517-368-4995. Personal E-mail: katfalls@tdi.net.

FALLS, ROBERT ARTHUR, artistic director; b. Springfield, Ill., Mar. 2, 1954; s. Joseph and Nancy (Stribling) Falls. BFA, U. Ill., 1976. Artistic dir. Wisdom Bridge Theatre, Chgo., 1977—86, Goodman Theatre, Chgo., 1987—. Dir.: (Broadway plays) Fences, 1987, The Speed of Darkness, 1991, The Rose Tattoo, 1995, The Night of the Iguana, 1996, The Young Man From Atlanta, 1997, Death of a Salesman, 1999 (Tony award, best direction of play, 1999), A Moon for the Misbegotten, 2000, Aida, 2000—04, King Hedley II, 2001, Hollywood Arms, 2002, Long Day's Journey Into Night, 2003 (Drama Desk award, outstanding dir. of play, 2003), Drowning Crow, 2004, The Light in the Piazza, 2005, Shining City, 2006; (plays) Pravada, 1989, The Iceman Cometh, 1990, Abbey Theatre, 1992, Dublin, Griller, A Touch of the Poet, On the Open Road, The Tempest, Three Sisters, Galileo, Landscape of the Body, Book of Night, Pal Joey, Getting Out, In the Belly of the Beast: Letters from Prison, Of Mice and Men, Wings, Mother Courage and Her Children, Hamlet, The Misanthrope, Standing on My Knees, The Food Chain, subUrbia, The Consul and Susannah. Office: Goodman Theatre 170 N Dearborn St Chicago IL 60601-3205

FALOON, WILLIAM WASSELL, physician, educator; b. Pitts., July 6, 1920; s. Joseph Coulter and Martha Louise (Wassell) F.; m. Roberta Jane Emery, Sept. 11, 1948; children: Karen F. Durham, Nancy F. Dodd, William W. BA, Allegheny Coll., 1941; MD, Harvard U., 1944. Diplomate Am. Bd. Internal Medicine; cert. registered arbitrator; ordained as deacon Presbyterian, 1958, elder, 1963. Intern Pa. Hosp., Phila., 1944-45; asst. resident in medicine Albany (N.Y.) Hosp., 1945-46, resident in medicine, 1946-47; rsch. fellow in medicine Harvard Med. Sch., Thorndike Meml. Lab., Boston City Hosp., 1947-48; asst. prof. oncology, instr. medicine Albany Med. Coll., 1948-50; instr. medicine SUNY Coll. Medicine, Syracuse, 1950-51, asst. prof., 1951-56, assoc. prof., 1956-64, prof. medicine, 1964-68; program dir. Adult Clin. Rsch. Ctr., Syracuse, 1965-68; physician-in-chief, dir. clin. rsch. and edn. Santa Barbara (Calif.) Gen.-Cottage Hosps., 1968-69; prof. medicine U. Rochester (N.Y.) Sch. Medicine, 1969-92, emeritus prof. medicine, 1992—; mem. Univ. Senate, 1971-74; mem. staff Strong Meml. Hosp., Rochester, Highland Hosp., 1969-90, chief medicine, 1970-80, dir. gastroenterology and nutrition, 1970-86; sr. attending physician The Genesee Hosp., 1990-91. Mem. editl. bd. Am. Jour. Clin. Nutrition, 1970-76; contbr. articles to profl. jours. Bd. mgrs. Camp Dudley YMCA, 1962-67, 69-74, chmn. bd., 1966-67, 71-73; bd. dirs. Onondaga County Met. Health Coun., Syracuse, 1959-61; mem. adv. com. Onondaga County Health Dept., 1966-68; bd. dirs. Am. Liver Found., 1982-92, pres. we. N.Y. chpt., 1982-83. Fellow ACP, Rochester Acad. Medicine (dir. 1979-82); mem. Am. Fedn. Clin. Rsch. (councillor 1956-59), AAAS, Onondaga County Med. Soc. (exec. com. 1964-66), Am. Assn. for Study Liver Disease, Am. Inst. Nutrition, Am. Soc. Clin. Nutrition, Endocrine Soc., Am. Gastroent. Assn., Western Soc. for Clin. Rsch., Med. Soc. Monroe County, Internat. Assn. for Study Liver, Assn. Program Dirs. Internal Medicine (councillor 1978-80), N.Y. State Dept. Health (bd. profl. med. conduct N.Y. State 1986-97), Island Profl. Rev. Orgn. (cons. 1991-94), Nat. Health Lawyers Assn. (dispute resolver), Gt. Lakes Interurban (sec. 1977-84), Ea. Gut, Oak Hill Country Club (Rochester). Presbyterian. Home: 4 Whitecliff Dr Pittsford NY 14534-2926 Personal E-mail: remfaloon@aol.com.

FALSGRAF, WILLIAM WENDELL, retired lawyer; b. Cleve., Nov. 10, 1933; s. Wendell A. and Catherine J. F.; children: Carl Douglas, Jeffrey Price, Catherine Louise. AB cum laude, Amherst Coll., 1955, LLD (hon.), 1986; JD, Case Western Res. U., 1958. Bar: Ohio 1958, U.S. Supreme Ct. 1972. Ptnr. Baker & Hostetler, Cleve., 1971—2002; ret., 2002. Chmn. vis. com. Case Western Res. U. Law Sch., 1973-76; trustee Case Western Reserve U., 1978-90, chmn. bd. overseers, 1977-78; trustee Cleve. Health Mus., 1975-90, Hiram Coll., 1989—; chmn. bd. trustees Hiram Coll., 1990-99. Recipient Disting. Service award; named Outstanding Young Man of Year Cleve. Jr. C. of C., 1962. Fellow Am. Bar Found., Ohio Bar Found.; mem. ABA (chmn. young lawyers sect. 1966-67, mem. ho. of dels. 1967-68, 70—, bd. govs. 1971-75, pres. 1985-86, bd. dirs. Am. Bar Endowment 1974-84, 87-97), Am. Bar Ins. Plans Cons. (pres. 1991—), Ohio Bar Assn. (mem. coun. of dels. 1968-70), Cleve. Bar Assn. (trustee 1979-82), Amherst Alumni Assn. (pres. N.E. Ohio 1964), The Country Club, LaPaloma Country Club. Office: Baker & Hostetler LLP 3200 National City Ctr Cleveland OH 44114-3485 Home: 268 Twin Creeks Dr Chagrin Falls OH 44023-6702 Home Phone: 440-247-3113; Office Phone: 216-861-7376. Business E-Mail: wfalsgraf@bakerlaw.com.

FALSONE, JACK JOSEPH, physician; b. Queens, NY, Nov. 6, 1923; s. Joseph and Margaret (Cutelli) F.; m. Anna Mandracchia, Dec. 23, 1945; children: Margaret, Catherine. AB, Columbia Coll., 1944; MD, L.I. Coll. Medicine, 1947. Diplomate Am. Bd. Internal Medicine. Intern Bklyn. Hosp., 1947-48, resident in internal medicine, 1948-51; attending physician Norwalk (Conn.) Hosp., 1954—91, assoc. chief chest diseases, 1970-87; instr. coll. medicine Yale U., 1955-61, asst. clin. prof. medicine, 1961-69; sr. rsch. assoc. Beulah Hinds Ctr., Norwalk Hosp., 1991—; vol. physician AmeriCare Free Clinic, Norwalk, 1994—, vol. med. dir., 1999—. Served with AUS, 1943-46, USAF, 1951-53. Fellow ACP; mem. Norwalk Heart Assn. (pres. 1955), Norwalk Med. Soc. (pres. 1975), Am. Coll. Chest Physicians. Roman Catholic. Office: Beulah Hinds Ctr Norwalk Hosp Norwalk CT 06856 Home Phone: 203-227-8165; Office Phone: 203-855-3615. E-mail: jack.falsone@norwalkhealth.org.

FALSTROM, KENNETH EDWARD, lawyer; b. San Luis Obispo, Calif., June 25, 1946; s. William and Irene (Carroll) F.; children: Kenneth Todd, Tricia Karen. BA, UCLA, 1967; JD, U. Calif., Berkeley, 1970. Bar: Calif. 1971, U.S. Dist. Ct. (cen. dist.) Calif. 1977. Rsch. asst. Ctr. Study Dem. Insts., Santa Barbara, Calif., 1971; atty. Law Office Christopher Zajic, Santa Barbara, Calif., 1972; pvt. practice Santa Barbara, Calif., 1973—. Bd. dirs. Hope Sch. Dist. Santa Barbara, 1972-80. Office: 1530 Chapala St Santa Barbara CA 93101-3017

FALTER, ROBERT GARY, real estate broker, educator; b. NYC, Sept. 14, 1945; s. Lawrence Zane and Helen (Smith) F.; m. Kathleen Ann Burrill, July 9, 1982; children: John William Wright III, Jason Michael Wright. AA, St. John's U., 1965, BA, 1967; MA, Kean U., 1973; MBA, Cornell U., 1976; PhD, Walden U., 1993. Lic. real estate broker, cert. real estate instr., notary pub. Adminstrv. resident N.Y. Hosp./Cornell Med. Ctr., NYC, summer 1975; mgr. ophthalmology Hahnemann Med. Coll. & Hosp., Phila., 1976-77; dir. out-patient clinic USPHS Ctr. for Disease Control, Atlanta, 1977—78; project officer ambulatory care data systems USPHS Divsn. Hosps. and Clinics, West Hyattsville, Md., 1978-80; assoc. dir. ambulatory care USPHS Hosp., Boston, 1980-81; adminstr. family medicine Sch. of Medicine U. Tenn., Memphis, 1981-82; asst. v.p. customer svc./instnl. benefits Blue Cross/Blue Shield of N.Y., NYC, 1982-86; assoc. v.p. ops. S.I. Hosp., 1986-87; assoc. dir. adminstrv. svcs. divsn. fed. employee occupl. health USPHS Region II, NYC, 1988-89; health/resources and svcs. adminstr. Rockville, Md., 1989; materiel mgmt. officer, dep. br. chief, 1989; health care adminstr. individual ready rsch. USPHS, Rockville, 1989-90, chief program liaison unit, 1990-91, chief budget officer BOP/HSD, 1991-93, chief br. budget and mgmt. support, 1993-99; chief health svcs. officer Office of the Surgeon Gen./Pub. Health Svc., 1995-99; adminstrv. officer Fed. Med. Ctr., Fed. Bur. Prisons, Devens, Ayer, Mass., 1999-2000, quality risk mgr., 2000; health care adminstr. correctional med. svcs. MCI-Shirley-Medium, Mass., 2000—02; adminstr.-in-tng. Clark Manor Healthcare Ctr., 2002; asst. adminstr. Tower Hill Ctr. for Health and Rehab., Canton, Mass., 2002—03, Harborlights Nursing and Rehab. Ctr., 2002; interim adminstr. Avery Manor Rehab. and Nursing Ctr., Needham, Mass., 2003; adminstr. Linda Manor Extended Care Facility, Leeds, Mass., 2003—04; realtor Coldwell Banker Residential Brokerage Park Ave., Worcester, Mass., 2004—07; regional sales mgr. Weichert Realtors, Home & Land Ptnrs., Auburn, Mass., 2007—. Chmn. hosp. and med. care adminstrs. Health Care Profls. Adv. Com., 1989—91; co-chmn. centennial symposium planning com. Health Svcs. Officers, 1989; lectr. fiscal mgmt. Christian Bros. U., Memphis, 1982; lectr. health econs. grad. program in health svcs. adminstrn. Salve Regina Coll., Newport, RI, 1984; mem. assoc. grad. faculty, acad. advisor Ctrl. Mich. U. Coll. Extended Learning Health Svcs. Adminstrn., 1995—2004; adj. asst. prof. divsn. nursing rsch. Uniformed Svcs. U. Health Scis. Grad. Sch. Nursing, Bethesda, 1996—2001; adj. instr. Vanderbilt U. Sch. Nursing, Nashville, 1999—2005; sr. lectr. Western New Eng. Coll., Springfield, Mass., 2000—; bd. dirs. Nat. Commn. on Correctional Health Care, 1991—94, mem. program com., 1991—92, mem. publs. com., 1991—94, mem. exec. com., 1992—94, mng. editor Jour. Correctional Health Care, 1994—97; adj. asst. prof. preventive medicine and biometrics, Health Svcs. Adminstrn., Uniformed Svcs. U. of Health Scis., Bethesda, 1999—2001; real estate instr., Mass., 2006—. Bd. dirs. Vis. Nurse Assn. Memphis, Inc., 1982; mem. cmty. adv. bd. Primary Health Care for Srs., Allston-Brighton Med. Care Coalition, Boston, 1981; usher coord. St. Michael's Cath. Ch., Poplar Springs, 1989-91; vol. U. Mass. Meml. Med. Ctr., Worchester, 2006-. With US Army, 1968—71, capt., commissioned corps. O-6 US Pub. Health Svc., 1977—2001, ret. US Pub. Health Svc., 2001. Recipient Capt. Stanley J. Kissel, Jr. award USPHS/Health Svcs. Officer, 1994, Surgeon Gen.'s Exemplary Svc. medal USPHS, 1996, 99; named Rookie of Yr., Worcester Rgnl. Assn. Realtors, 2006. Fellow: Am. Acad. Med. Adminstrs. (hon.), Am. Coll. Healthcare Execs. (life; editl. bd. Healthcare Execs. 1986—88, book reviewer Hosp. and Health Svcs. Adminstrn.); mem.: Mil. Officers Assn. Am. (pres. Worcester (Mass.) county chpt. 2002—04), Worcester Regional Assn. Realtors (mem. edn. com. 2005—, Rookie of Yr. 2006), Mass. Assn. Realtors (mem. edn. and events com. 2006—, mem. profl. standards com. 2007—), Nat. Assn. Realtors, Real Estate Educators Assn., D.C.-Md.-Va. Hosp. Assn. (chmn. liaison com. 51st ann. conv. 1991), Commd. Officers Assn. USPHS (sec. Atlanta chpt. 1978), Assn. Mil. Surgeons U.S. (reviewer Mil. Medicine 1989—, cons.), Healthcare Mgmt. Assn. Mass., Assn. Health Care Adminstrs. Nat. Capital Area, Mass. Real Estate Investors and Apt. Owners Assn., Anchor and Caduceus Soc. (charter), Res. Officers Assn. U.S. (newsletter editor Montgomery County chpt. 1989), KC (warden St. Michael's of Poplar Springs coun. 1990—91, chancellor 1991—92, Adelphi Coun. #4181, Shrewsbury, mem. mktg. com. 2005—). Independent. Roman Catholic. Avocations: travel, writing, consulting. Home: 50 Deerfield Rd Shrewsbury MA 01545-1571 Office Phone: 508-407-5154. Personal E-mail: rgf4@cornell.edu. Business E-Mail: bfalter@weichert.com.

FALVEY, W(ILLIAM) PATRICK, judge; b. Penn Yan, NY, Aug. 31, 1946; s. William Jennings and Thelma Rosetta (Hall) F.; m. Suzanne G. Christensen, Sept. 14, 1968; children: Scott P., Jennifer G. BA, Hobart Coll., 1968; JD, John Marshall Law Sch., 1975; postgrad., U. Nev., 1994. Bar: N.Y. 1976, U.S. Dist. Ct. (we. dist.) N.Y. 1979, U.S. Supreme Ct. 1984. Confidential law clerk Hon. Lyman H. Smith Supreme Ct. Yates County, Penn Yan, NY, 1976—77; atty. Dept. Social Svcs. Yates County, Penn Yan, 1976-77, pvt. practice, 1976-88, asst. pub. defender, 1977-80, acting dist. atty., 1980-81, dist. atty., 1981-88; judge Yates County Surrogate and Family Ct., Penn Yan, 1988—; acting justice Supreme Ct. Yates County, Penn Yan, NJ, 1988—; presiding judge Yates County Criminal and Family Drug Treatment Cts., Penn Yan, 2002—. Mem. alternatives to incarceration com. Yates County; chair bd. trustees Yates County Law Libr.; mem. pres.'s adv. coun. Keuka Coll. Mem., adv. bd. Sampson Theatre. 1st lt. U.S. Army, 1969-71, Vietnam. Recipient N.Y. State Conspicuous Svc. Cross, Hon. Hugh R. Carey Gov. N.Y., 1979. Ctr. Dispute Settlement's Disting. Jurist award, 1996. Mem. Ontario/Yates Magistrates Assn., NY Bar Assn., NY State Family and Surrogate Judges Assn., NY State County Judges Assn. (mem. exec. com.), Yates County Bar Assn. (past pres.), VFW, Am. Legion (post comdr. 1981, chair constitution, by-laws com. dept. of NY), Delta Chi (mem. adv. bd. of trustees Hobart chpt., 2004-). Office: Yates County Cts 415 Liberty St Penn Yan NY 14527-1102 Office Phone: 315-536-5128. Business E-Mail: wfalvey@courts.state.ny.us.

FAMIGLIETTI, NANCY ZIMA, computer company executive; b. Hartford, Conn., Nov. 10, 1956; d. Joseph and Angeline (Morello) Zima; m. Arthur R. Famiglietti Jr., May 23, 1981. BA in Math., Computer Sci. cum laude, Ea. Conn. State Coll., 1978. Sr. programmer analyst Hamilton Standard, Windsor Locks, Conn., 1978—82; sys. analyst Cigna Corp., Hartford, 1982—83, sys. designer, 1983—86, lead sys. designer, 1986—89; sys. advisor Aetna Life & Casualty Co., Hartford, 1989—93, sys. adminstr., 1993—94, sr. sys. adminstr., 1994—95, bus. sys. mgr., 1995—98; with Hartford Life, Windsor, Conn., 1998, bus. cons., 1998—2000, team leader, 2000—01, mgr., 2001—04, info. tech. bus.

cons., 2005—. Active Windsor (Conn.) Hist. Soc. Mem. Kappa Mu Epsilon. Avocations: reading, walking, crafts, swimming, bicycling. Home: 81 Mcgrath Rd South Windsor CT 06074-1123

FAN, JIANG, manufacturing executive; arrived in US, 1990; s. Mei-Ying Fan; m. Xi-Yun Yu, July 8, 1989; children: Christine, Derrek. BS, Fuzhou Normal Coll., 1981; MS, Zhejiang U., Hangzhou, China, 1988; PhD, Aiz. State U., Tempe, 1995. Tchr. Fuzhou Normal Coll., 1981—85; engr. China Guangzhou Pharm. Trading Ctr., China, 1988—90; staff scientist Poly Star Corp., Dubline, Calif., 1997—99; engring. mgr. Gold Peak Battery Techs., San Diego, 1999—2006; pres. Am. Lithium Energy, San Marcos, Calif., 2006—. Mem.: Internat. Soc. Electrochemistry, Electrochemical Soc. Achievements include patents for current collector; composite electrolyte; development of lithium ion cell and batteries with the highest specific energy.

FAN, LEE SIU, business executive and vocational training program administrator; b. Hong Kong, Aug. 5, 1948; came to U.S., 1974; s. Kwok-Kam and Po-Hang (Law) F. BSc in Bus. Mgmt. and Mktg., U. Wis., Superior, 1975; MSc in Spl. Edn., Portland State U., 1989; DBA in Bus. Mgmt., Pacific Western U., 1997. Cert. foodsvcs. mgmt. profl. Prodn. and sales mng. coord. Castle Peak Garment Factory Co., Ltd., Hong Kong, 1969-70; mng. exec. Wilson Garment Mfg. Co. Ltd., Hong Kong, 1970-74; ops. mgr. Portland State U., 1975-92; CEO Handily Enterprises (U.S.A.) Inc., Portland, 1991—, Happy Heart Foods Inc., Portland, 1992—, Lok Hop, Inc., Portland, 1996—. Vocat. tng. programs coord. Portland Pub. Schs., Lake Oswego Sch. Dist., Clackamas County Employment Tng. and Bus. Svcs., Oreg. Comm. for the Blind, Westside Youth Ctr., 1986-92; adv. bd. Unicorn Fisheries Ltd., Hong Kong, 1990—. Cmty. svc. provider Loaves & Fishes Sr. Cmty. Ctr., Portland, 1991—; coord. Oreg. Gov.'s Ann. Food Dr., Salem, 1991; mem. diversity commn. Portland State U., 1992; mem. delegation on learning disabilities Citizen Ambassador of People to People Internat., Spokane, Wash., 1994. Recipient Exemplary Svc. award Portland State U., 1985, Extraordinary Svc. award, 1987, various svc. awards, 1972-92. Mem. Coun. for Exceptional Children (Beyond the Call of Duty Svc. award 1992), Nat. Assn. of Coll. and Univ. Food Svcs. (Leadership Program rep. 1986-92, named Food Svc. Mgmt. Profl. 1992), Nike Portland Running Club (2d master runner of yr. 1988, 89), Oreg. Rd. Runners Club (Inspirational Runner of Yr. 1990). Democrat. Avocations: running, community services, coin collecting/numismatics. Office: Handily Enterprises (USA) 6335 SE 82nd Ave Portland OR 97266-5607 Home: 4635 SE 31st Ave Portland OR 97202-3639

FAN, LIANG-SHIH, chemical engineering educator; BS, Nat. Taiwan U., 1970; MS, West Va. Univ., 1973, PhD, 1975; MS in Statistics (with honors), Kansas State Univ., 1978. Disting. Univ. prof. dept. chem. engring., C. John Easton prof. in engring. Ohio State U., Columbus. Recipient Alexander von Humboldt Rsch. award for U.S. Sr. Scientists, 1993, Alpha Chi Sigma award AIChE for Chem. Engring., 1996, Union Carbide Lectureship award Chem. Engring. Divsn. ASEE, 1999, Malcolm E. Pruitt award, Coun. for Chem. Rsch., 2000, E.V. Murphree award in Indsl. Engring. and Chemistry, ACS, 2006, Joseph Sullivant medal Ohio State U., 2006. Mem. NAE, Academia Sinica, Mexican Acad. Scis. Office: Ohio State U Dept Chem Engring 140 W 19th Ave Columbus OH 43210-1110

FAN, SHANHUI, engineering educator; b. 1972; Student, U. Sci. and Tech. China, 1988—92; PhD in Physics, MIT, 1997. Tchg. asst. MIT, 1992—94, rsch. asst., 1994—97, postdoctoral rsch. assoc., physics, 1997—99, rsch. scientist, Rsch. Lab. Electronics, 1999—2001; asst. prof., dept. elec. engring. Stanford U., Calif., 2001—. Cons. Claredon Photonics, 1999—2001, mem. tech. adv. bd., 2001—; invited spkr. in field. Contbr. articles to profl. jours., chapters to books; reviewer for leading scientific jours. in the optics field. Recipient NAS award for Initiatives in Rsch., 2007; David and Lucile Packard Fellowship in Sci. and Engring., 2003. Mem.: NSF (mem. review panels 2001—03), Optical Soc. Am., Am. Phys. Soc. Achievements include patents in field. Office: AP 273 Ginzton Laboratory Stanford CA 94305 Office Phone: 650-724-4759. Office Fax: 650-725-2533. Business E-Mail: shanhui@stanford.edu.*

FAN, SHIRLEY TSUI-YU, music educator; b. Taipei, Taiwan, July 12, 1964; arrived in U.S., 1984; d. David Fan and Mary Tseng Fan; m. Robert Kao, Oct. 29, 1988; children: Amy Kao, Wilson Kao, Kenneth Kao. MusB, Juilliard Sch. Music, 1989; MusM, Rider U., 1996. Cert. music tchr. N.J. Cashier Tangy Fast Food Restaurant, NYC, 1985—88; receptionist, clk. comm. office Juilliard Sch. Music, NYC, 1985—88; tchr. Chinese Zi-Sen Chinese Sch., Queens, NY, 1985—88; piano tchr. Golden Rhythmic Music Sch., Queens, 1989—95; piano artist faculty mem. Westminster Conservatory, Princeton, NJ, 1995—2001; piano chmn. Piano Tchr. Forum of Ctrl. Jersey, 2003—; pvt. piano tchr. Edison, NJ. Tchr. New Sch. Music, Kingston, NJ, 1994—97. Mem.: Am.-Asian Fine Arts Assn. (asst. dir. 2005—), N.J. Chinese Music Tchrs. (publicity events com. 2004—), Piano Tchrs. Soc. Am., N.J. Music Tchrs. Assn. (piano chmn. 2000—), Edison Music Club. Home: 12 Rolling Brook Dr Edison NJ 08820 Office Phone: 732-762-4436. Fax: 908-668-8628. E-mail: shirleyfanty@yahoo.com.

FAN, TAI-SHENG ALLEN, social scientist in computer education and computing, educator; b. Taipei, Taiwan; s. MingShing and LeeYen Fan; m. YiChing Jill Li; 1 child, EnMiao. LLB, Nat. ChungHsin U., Taipei, 1982; MS, Tex. Tech U., 1987; PhD, Oreg. State U., 1996. Lectr. Pingtung Poly. Inst., Neipu, Pingtung, Taiwan, 1987—96; assoc. prof. Nat. Pingtung U. Sci. and Tech., Neipu, 1996—. Editl. reviewer Jour. Info. Mgmt., Taipei, 2003—04, Computers & Education, New York, 2005. Contbr. articles to profl. jours. Deacon Pingtung Bapt. Ch., 1989—2000, 2006—. Recipient Rsch. award, Nat. Sci. Coun., 1997, Ednl. Svc. medal, Ministry Edn., 2000; rsch. grantee, Nat. Sci. Coun., 1997—99, 2000—01, 2002—06. Mem.: Chinese Assn. Info. Mgmt. (life). Achievements include research in computer education, social issues in information technology. Avocations: travel, classical music, gourmet food. Office: Nat Pingtung U Sci Tech Dept MIS No 1 Hsueh-Fu Rd Neipu-Hsiang Pingtung 91207 Taiwan Home Phone: 886-8-7231237; Office Phone: 886-8-7703202 ext. 7905. Office Fax: 886-8-7740306. Business E-Mail: allen@mail.npust.edu.tw.

FAN, XIAOHUI, astrophysicist, educator; b. Beijing; m. Jinyoung Serena Kim, 1995; 1 child. BS, Nanjing U., China, 1992; MS, Chinese Acad. Scis. Beijing Astron. Obs., 1995; PhD, Princeton U., 2000. Mem. Inst. Advanced Study, Princeton, NJ, 2000—02; astronomer Steward Obs. U. Ariz., Tucson, 2002—, asst. prof. dept. astronomy, 2002—05, assoc. prof., 2005—. Contbr. articles to sci. jours. Named one of Brilliant 10, Popular Sci. mag., 2003; recipient Newton Lacy Pierce prize, Am. Astron. Soc., 2003; Alfred P. Sloan Rsch. fellow, 2003, David and Lucile Packard Fellow in Sci. and Engring., 2004. Office: Steward Obs Rm 310 U Ariz 933 N Cherry Ave Tucson AZ 85721-0065 Office Phone: 520-626-7558. E-mail: fan@as.arizona.edu.*

FANCHER, KRISTEN L., lawyer; b. Rochester, Mich., Nov. 30, 1972; d. H. Alan and Joyce M. Knudsen; m. Paul Davis Fancher, June 23, 2001. BA, U. Mich., 1994; JD, Vanderbilt U., 2000. Assoc. Fish & Neave, NYC, 2000—03, Greenberg Traurig, LLP, Atlanta, 2003—. Mem. Entertainment and Sports Sect. State Bar Ga., Atlanta. Contbr. articles to profl. jours. Finalist Best Brief award, Vanderbilt U. Moot Ct. Competition, 1999. Mem.: ABA (mem. forum entertainment and sports industries, mem. intelletual property law sect., co-chair unfair competition-trade identity com. 2006—), Internat. Trademark Assn., Ga. Lawyers for Arts (bd. dirs.). Office: Greenberg Traurig LLP 3290 Northside Parkway Suite 400 Atlanta GA 30327 Office Phone: 678-553-2457. Office Fax: 678-553-2212. Business E-Mail: fancherk@gtlaw.com.

FANCHER, MICHAEL REILLY, editor, publishing executive; b. Long Beach, Calif., July 13, 1946; s. Eugene Arthur and Ruth Leone (Dickson) F.; m. Nancy Helen Edens, Nov. 3, 1967 (div. 1982); children: Jason Michael, Patrick Reilly; m. 2d Carolyn Elaine Bowers, Mar. 25, 1983; Katherine Claire, Elizabeth Lynn. BA, U. Oreg., 1968; MS, Kans. State U., 1971; MBA, U. Wash., 1986. Reporter, asst. city editor Kansas City Star, Mo., 1970-76, city editor Mo., 1976-78; reporter Seattle Times, 1978-79, night city editor, 1979-80, asst. mng. editor, 1980-81, mng. editor, 1981-86, exec. editor, 1987—2006, v.p., 1989—95, sr. v.p., 1995—, editor at large, 2006—. Bd. dirs. Blethen Maine Newspapers, Walla Walla Union-Bulletin, Yakima Herald Rep. Ruhl fellow Hall of Achievement, U. Oreg., 1983 Mem. Am. Soc. Newspaper Editors, Soc. Profl. Journalists, Nat. Press Photographers Assn. (Editor of Yr. 1986). Office: Seattle Times PO Box 70 1120 John St Seattle WA 98111-0070 Business E-Mail: mfancher@seattletimes.com.*

FANCHER, RICK, lawyer; b. Tucson, July 27, 1953; s. James Richard and Margaret Mae (Gum) F.; m. Cecelia Francis Baney, July 12, 1975; children: Jeffery Reed, Ashley Kristin. BA, Trinity U., San Antonio, Tex., 1975; JD, U. Tex., 1978. Bar: Tex. 1979, US Dist. Ct. (we. and so. dists.) Tex. 1981, US Ct. Appeals (5th cir.) 1981. Law clk. U.S. Dist. Ct., Corpus Christi, Tex., 1978-80; asst. atty. City of Corpus Christi, 1980; assoc. Gibbins, Burrow & Bratton, Austin, Tex., 1981, John L. Johnson, Corpus Christi, 1982-85; ptnr. Thornton, Summers, Biechlin, Dunham & Brown, Corpus Christi, 1985-99, Barker, Leon, Fancher & Matthys, Corpus Christi, 2000—05, Barker, Leon & Fancher, Corpus Christi, 2005—. Mem. Tex. Bar Assn., Tex. Bd. Legal Specialization (cert. personal injury trial law). Democrat. Avocations: jogging, bicycling, hunting, golf. Home: 4502 Lake Bistineau Dr Corpus Christi TX 78413-5261 Office: Barker Leon & Fancher 1200 First City Tower II 555 N Carancahua St Corpus Christi TX 78478-0002 Office Phone: 361-881-9217. Business E-Mail: rfancher@blfmlaw.com.

FANCHI, JOHN RICHARD, physicist, educator, consultant; b. Pontiac, Ill., Nov. 17, 1952; s. John Anton and Shirley Mae (Andersen) F.; m. Katherine Frances Goedecke, Aug. 22, 1976; children: Anthony Clifford, Christopher John. BS in Physics, U. Denver, 1974; MS in Physics, U. Miss.; 1975; PhD in Physics, U. Houston, 1977. Rsch. asst. Denver Rsch. Inst., 1970-74; rsch. engr. Getty Oil Co., Houston, 1978-79, Cities Svc. Co., Tulsa, 1979-81; sr. engr. Keplinger & Assocs., Tulsa, 1981-84; advanced sr. engr. Marathon Oil Co., Littleton, Colo., 1984-95, Houston, 1995-98; pres. Access Pubs., Denver, 1990-93; prof. Colo. Sch. Mines, Golden, 1998—2006, dir. undergrad. energy program, 2006; simulation cons. Chevron, 2006—; co-owner Fanchi Enterprises Cons., 1998—. Adj. prof. physics U. Tulsa, 1980-81; vis. scientist Colo. Alliance for Sci., Denver, 1989-95; lectr. Arapahoe C.C., 1992; instr. engring. and math. U. Houston, 1996-97; dir. consortium integrated flow modelling, 2001-05 Author: Parametrized Relativistic Quantum Theory, 1993, Principles of Applied Reservoir Simulation, 3d edit., 2006, Math Refresher for Scientists and Engineers, 3d edit., 2006, Integrated Flow Modeling, 2000, Shared Earth Modeling, 2002, Energy: Technology and Directions for the Future, 2004, Energy in the 21st Century, 2005; co-editor: Gen. Engring. vol. Petroleum Engineering Handbook, 2006; referee: Soc. of Petroleum Engrs., 1981—, Founds. of Physics Jour., 1988—; contbr. over 50 articles to profl. jours. Ctrl. com. Colo. Reps., Denver, 1974; coord. coun. Littleton Pub. Schs., 1989-91, v.p., sch. bd., 1993-95; coach YMCA, Littleton, 1987-92; chmn. accountability com. Runyon Elem. Sch., Littleton, 1990-91. U. Miss. fellow, 1974-75, U. Houston, 1975-77; Colo.-Wyo. Acad. Sci. grantee, 1972. Mem. Am. Phys. Soc., Soc. Petroleum Engrs. (disting.), Internat. Assn. Relativistic Dynamics (co-founder, pres. 1998-2006). Achievements include development of software models of fluid flow in porous media; pioneered development of parametrized relativistic quantum theory; application of high technology to model performance and managed development of world-class size oil and gas fields, geological sequestration of gases, compressed air energy storage for wind energy and geothermal energy; research on the effect of laser radiation on chemical reactions and energy education. Home: 302 Grand View Terr Houston TX 77007 Personal E-mail: goldenjrf@yahoo.com.

FANECA, ALAN, professional football player; b. 1976; s. Alan, Liane; m. Julie Kuchta; 1 child, Annabelle Kathryn. BA in mgmt. entrepreneurship, LSU, 1999. Left guard Pitts. Steelers, 1998—. Named to All-American Team, NCAA, 1997, All-SEC Team, 1997, Pro-Bowl, NFL, 2001—05; recipient All-Rookie Honors, College & Pro Football Weekly, 1998. Office: Pitts Steelers 3400 S Water St Pittsburgh PA 15203

FANELLI, MICHAEL PAUL, musician, educator, writer; b. Evanston, Ill., Feb. 12, 1943; s. George and Gloria (Del Carlo) F.; m. Carla Jean Saiger, May 28, 1978. BMus, U. Ill., 1968, EdD in Music Edn., 2001; MA in Music History, U. Mo., 1981. Cert. tchr. K-12, Webster U. Instr. music U. Ill., 1963—67, U. Mo., Columbia, 1968-74; instr. music, artist-in-residence Stephens Coll., Columbia, 1968-75; profl. double bassist Chgo. Sinfonetta, 1963—65, Mo. Symphony Soc., 1973—78, Gateway Festival Orchestra, 1978—84, St. Louis String Enselble, 1978—87, St. Louis Philharmonic, 1983—87, Champaign-Urbana Symphony Orchestra, 1992—94; instr. instrumental music Sch. Dist. of the City of Ladue, Mo., 1983-87; instr. music U. No. Iowa, Cedar Falls, 1987—2002, asst. prof. distance learning Iown Comms. Network, 1995—, asst. prof. dept. ednl. psychology & foundations, 2002—; instr. of double bass Grinnell (Iowa) Coll., 1996—, U. No. Iowa Skuki Sch., 2001—. Founder, music dir. No. Iowa Jr. Orchestra, Cedar Falls, 1990-92; music dir. No. Iowa Youth Orchestra, 1994—2001; adv. bd. Iowa Alliance for Arts Edn., Des Moines, 1994—2001; presenter in field. Contbr. articles to profl. jours.; contbg. author: American String Teacher, 1997. Double bassist U. Ill., U.S. State Dept. tour of S.Am., 1964. Microcomputer grantee U. No. Iowa, Cedar Falls, 1989, 92, 95-98, 2005. Mem. Iowa String Tchrs. Assn. (editor 1988-92, pres. 1996-98, historian 2004-, Disting. Svc. award 1992, Cert. for Outstanding Contbn. 1996), Iowa Sch. Orchestra Assn. (pres. 1992-96), Am. String Tchrs. Assn. (editl. com. 1997—2005, columns editor, reviewer 2005-, Outstanding Contbr. 1995-97, 99, 2003), Suzuki Assn. of the Americas (column editor 1992-, double base com. 1992-), Mo. String Tchrs. Assn. (sec.-treas. 1983-87), Kappa Delta Pi, Phi Kappa Delta, Phi Kappa Lambda, Phi Mu Alpha. Avocations: American art history, photography, fly fishing, painting. Home: 203 Parkgate Rd Cedar Falls IA 50613-1953 Office: Univ No Iowa Schindler Edn Ctr Cedar Falls IA 50613 Business E-Mail: michael.fanelli@uni.edu.

FANEUIL, EDWARD J., lawyer; b. Boston, July 2, 1952; s. Phillip F. Faneuil and Irene Grass; m. Helene Ostroff, June 18, 1975; children: Ari, Jesse. BA, Trinity Coll., 1974; JD, Suffolk U. Law Sch, 1977. Bar: Mass. 1977. Ptnr. Samek & Faneuil, Boston, 1981-91; gen. counsel Global Petroleum Corp., Waltham, Mass., 1991; gen. counsel, sec. Global Companies LLC, Waltham, Mass., 1998; exec. v.p., gen. counsel, sec. Global Partners LP, Waltham, Mass., 2005—. Office: Global Partners LP Box 9161 800 South St Waltham MA 02453-1478*

FANG, QIANG, history professor; s. Zhenguo Fang and Lanying Zhang. PhD, SUNY, Buffalo, 2006. Editor-in-chief Excellences of Chinese Automotice Industry, Shanghai, 1992—95; asst. prof. Mo. So. State U., Joplin, 2006—. Contbr. articles to profl. jours. Mem.: Am. Chinese Historian Assn. Office: Mo Southern State Univ 3950 E Newman Rd Joplin MO 64801 Home Phone: 417-625-9588; Office Phone: 417-625-9588. Personal E-mail: wancheng99@hotmail.com. Business E-Mail: fang-q@mssu.edu.

FANGER, DONALD LEE, Slavic language and literature educator; b. Cleve., Dec. 6, 1929; s. Max Leon and Rae (Bercu) Fanger; m. Margot Taylor, June 18, 1955; children: Steffen, Ross, Katharine; m. Leonie Jean Gordon, Dec. 6, 2005. BA, U. Calif., Berkeley, 1951, MA, 1954; PhD, Harvard U., 1962. Mem. faculty Brown U., 1960-66, assoc. prof. Slavic langs. and lit., 1964-66; assoc. prof. Slavic langs., dir. div. Stanford U., 1966-68; prof. Slavic and comparative lit. Harvard U., 1968-98, chmn. dept. Slavic langs and lits., 1973-82, Harry Levin rsch. prof. lit., 1998—2003. Mem. bd. syndicators Harvard U. Press, 1968-73. Author: Dostoevsky and Romantic Realism, 1965, The Creation of Nikolai Gogol, 1979; editor: Brown U. Slavic Reprint Series, 1962-66. Mem. program com. Internat. Rsch. and Exchanges Bd., 1968-69, 70-73. With AUS, 1953-55. Guggenheim Found. fellow, 1975-76. Mem. Am. Acad. Arts and Scis., Acad. Lit. Studies, Internat. Comparative Lit. Assn. Office: Harvard U Widener Study L Cambridge MA 02138 Home: 75 Richdale Ave Ste 3 Cambridge MA 02140-2608 Office Phone: 617-495-4092. E-mail: fanger@fas.harvard.edu.

FANGEROW, KAY ELIZABETH, nurse; b. Thomas, Okla., June 27, 1952; d. Byron Frederick and Wilma Jean (Bickford) Mayfield; children: David Andrew, Sarah Elizabeth. Student, Oral Roberts U., 1970-71; BS in Nursing magna cum laude, Calif. State U., Long Beach, 1975; MS in Health Care Adminstrn., U. LaVerne, 1991. RN, Calif.; cert. pub. health nurse. Staff nurse pediatrics service Long Beach Meml. Hosp., 1974-75, Riverside (Calif.) Community Hosp., 1975-76, Parkview Community Hosp., Riverside, 1982—2007; supervising pub. health nurse County Health Dept., San Bernardino, Calif., 1976—, coord. sch. based and sch. linked health care svcs., 1994—2005; dir. Westside Park Sch. Based Health Ctr. FQHC Clinic, 2002—; grant writer County Health Dept., San Bernardino, Calif., 2005—; nursing coord. early intervention program for drug and alcohol exposed infants SART Project, 2005—; program mgr. child and family health svcs., dep. dir. San Bernardino County Dept. Pub. Health, Calif., 2007—. Cons. Am. Home Health, Santa Ana, Calif., 1986—2000; presenter in field. Instr. Inland Counties chpt. Am. Cancer Soc., Riverside, 1977—; mem. cmty. action coun. San Bernardino County Youth Justice Ctr., 1999—; chair child death rev. team San Bernardino County, 2005—06. Recipient Excellence award, San Bernardino County, 2006. Mem. Am. Pub. Health Assn. (co-author abstract 1986, 87, 89, coordinator hypertension worksite project, diabetes control project, pub. health nursing homeless project, presenter ann. meeting 1986, 87, 89), Pub. Health Nurse Group (chmn. 1977-78, vice chmn. profl. performance com. 1978, sec. peer rev. com. 1978), San Bernardino County Asthma Coalition, Sigma Theta Tau (Gamma Alpha chpt., honoree for child abuse prevention supervising pub. health nurse of yr. 2002) San Bernardino County Child Death Review Team (chair, 2005). Democrat. Home: 555 Oak Hill St Ontario CA 91761 Home Phone: 909-988-0288; Office Phone: 909-388-0476. Business E-Mail: kfangerow@dph.sbcounty.gov.

FANI, ROBERT J., gas industry executive; m. Maria Fani; 2 children. BSME, CUNY; MBA, St. John's Univ.; JD, NY Law Sch. With Bklyn. Union Gas Co., 1976—98, v.p., 1992—97, sr. v.p. mktg. & sales, 1997—98, KeySpan Corp. (merger of Bklyn Union Gas. Co. & LILCO), 1998—99; sr. v.p. gas ops. KeySpan Corp., Bklyn., 1999—2000, exec. v.p. strategic svc., 2000—01, pres. energy svc., 2001—03, pres. energy assets & supply group, 2003, pres., COO, 2003—, bd. dir., 2005—. Mem. leadership council Am. Gas Assn.; bd. dir. Gas Tech. Inst. Bd. mem. YMCA, Snug Harbor Cultural Ctr., Staten Island Univ. Hosp., City Coll. NY, Neighborhood Housing Svc. Named to Residential Hall of Honor, Am. Gas Assn., Indsl. & Comml. Hall of Flame. Mem.: Soc. Gas Lighters. Office: KeySpan Corp 1 MetroTech Ctr Brooklyn NY 11201*

FANJUL, ALFIE, JR., (ALFONSO FANJUL), food products executive; b. June 1937; s. Alfonso and Lillian Gomez-Mena Fanjal; m. Tina (div.); children. Grad., Fordham U., NYC. Chmn., CEO Florida Crystals Corp. (Flo-Sun, Inc.), West Palm Beach, Fla., 1960—. Contbr. funds to Dem. Nat. Com. and Dem. Congl. Campaign Com., 1991—; co-chmn. Former President William Clinton's Fla. campaign, 1992; co-sponsored Cuban-Am. fund raiser for Clinton Presdl. Campaign, Miami, 1992. Democrat. Office: Florida Crystals Corp 1 N Clematis St Ste 200 West Palm Beach FL 33401

FANJUL, PEPE (JOSÈ FANJUL), food products executive; s. Alfonso and Lillian (Gomez-Mena) Fanjul; m. Emilia Fanjul. Vice-chmn., pres., COO Florida Crystals Corp. (Flo-Sun, Inc.), West Palm Beach, Fla. Vice-chmn. fin. com. Pres. George H. W. Bush-Dan Quayle presdl. campaign, 1988; mem. Team 100 (group of people giving $100,000 or more to the Rep. Party), 1988, Sen. Bob Dole presdl. campaign; contbr. funds to the Rep. Nat. Com., 1991—. Republican. Office: Florida Crystals Corp 1 N Clemeatis St Ste 200 West Palm Beach FL 33401 Office Phone: 561-366-5100. Office Fax: 561-366-5158.

FANKHAUSER, MARK A., lawyer; b. Wichita, Kans., Dec. 8, 1952; BS, Pitts. State U., 1974; JD cum laude, Harvard U., 1978. Bar: Tex. 1978, bd. cert. (estate planning & probate Law) Tex. Bd. Legal Specialization. Mem. Haynes & Boone, L.L.P., Dallas, 1978-80, Hughes & Luce L.L.P., Dallas, 1980-94; now mem. Little, Pedersen, Fankhauser & Cox, LLP, Dallas, 1994—, ptnr. With USAF, 1971—73, air nat. guard, 1973—77, Mo., NH. Fellow Am. Coll. Trust and Estate Counsel, Tex. Bar Found., chmn. Inheritance Taxes Com. Taxation Sect. State Bar Tex., coun. mem. Probate Sect. Dallas Bar Assn., mem. IRS TE/GE Coun. Gulf States Area, bd. mem. Am. Heart Assn. Tex., mem. adv. bd. Found. NAIFA-Dallas, mem. adv. coun. Communities Found. Tex., mem. Dallas Estate Planning Coun. (bd. govs.) State Bar of Tex. 1994-1996, ABA. Office: Little Pedersen Fankhauser & Cox LLP 901 Main St Ste 4110 Dallas TX 75202-5606 Office Phone: 214-573-2323. Business E-Mail: mfank@lpf-law.com.

FANNIN, DANIEL PAUL CLARK, information systems executive; b. Tallahassee, Dec. 17, 1942; s. Harvey Fayette and Kathryn Alice Fannin; m. Mary La Tourelle, Nov. 13, 2004 children: Tracy Robert, Daniel Paul Clark, Katie Rose. BS in Psychology, Loyola U., Los Angeles, 1965; MBA in Mgmt. with honors, U. N.D., 1974; MS in Computer Sci. with honors, North Tex. State U., 1976. Commd. USAF, 1967, advanced through grades to Lt. Col., 1983; mgr. computer ctr. Strategic Air Command, Beale, Calif., 1970-72, Minot, N.D., 1972-74; program mgr. Dept. of Def. Computer Inst., Washington, 1976-79; edn. with industry Boeing Aerospace Co., Seattle, 1979-80; dir. software and data base mgmt. USAF Data Systems Evaluation Ctr., Montgomery, Ala., 1980-83; comdr. comm and tech. 25th Air Divsn. USAF, Tacoma, 1983-87, ret., 1987; CIO Dept. Social and Health Svcs., State of Wash., Olympia, 1987—91; CEO Shared Client Svcs., 1991—2001; dir. IT World Vision Internat., 2001—. Tech. advisor Space Transp. System, El Segundo, Calif., 1980-83; cons. Computer Security Program Office, Montgomery, 1980-83, Brit. Parliament, England, 1978, N.Y. Police Dept., N.Y.C., 1978, Maritime Adminstrn., Washington, 1978, Comptroller of the Currency, Washington, 1978, FBI, Washington, 1977-79; mem. staff Pres. Carter's Nat. Com. on Electronic Fund, Washington, 1976-79. Editor: Nat. Bur. of Standards Inst. for Computer Sci. and Tech., 1980; contbr. articles to profl. jours. Fellow, Office of Mgmt. Budget. Republican. Roman Catholic. Avocations: tennis, golf, sailing. Home: 48 Hewitt Dr Steilacoom WA 98388-1512 Office: World Vision Internat 800 W Chestnut Ave Monrovia CA 91016 Office Phone: 626-301-7744. Business E-Mail: dan_fannin@wvi.org.

FANNIN, DAVID CECIL, lawyer, consumer products company executive; b. Catlettsburg, Ky., Feb. 5, 1946; s. Cecil and Marie (Conley) F.; m. Lucille Ann Stewart, Jan. 1, 1985; children: Christopher, Brian, Catherine. BA, U. Ky., 1968; MA, U. Ill., 1971; JD, U. Ky., 1973. Bar: Ky. 1974. Assoc. Wyatt, Tarrant & Combs, Louisville, 1974-79, ptnr., 1979—93; authorized house counsel Fla., 1994; exec. v.p., gen. counsel Sunbeam Corp., 1994—98; sr. v.p., gen. counsel Office Depot, Inc., Delray Beach, Fla., 1998—2000, exec. v.p., gen. counsel, 2000—. Bd. advs. VenuLex Corp. Woodrow Wilson fellow, 1968. Mem. ABA, Ky. Bar Assn., Lousville Bar Assn, Am. Corp. Counsel Assn., Am. Soc. Corp. Secs., Phi Beta Kappa, Order of the Coif. Democrat. Baptist. Avocations: music, running. Office: Office Depot Inc 2200 Old Germantown Rd Delray Beach FL 33445-8299 Office Phone: 561-438-4800.*

FANNING, BARRY HEDGES, lawyer; b. Olney, Tex., Dec. 5, 1950; s. Robert Allen and Carolyn (Parker) F.; m. Rebecca Sue Cobbs, May 24, 1975 (dec. Mar. 1997); m. Sherri Winn Perry, Mar. 6, 1999. BBA, Baylor U., 1972, LL.B., 1973. Bar: Tex. 1973, Fla. 1974, U.S. Dist. Ct. (no., ea. we. and so. dists.) Tex. 1974, U.S. Ct. Appeals (5th and 11th cirs.) 1974. Mem. firm Fanning, Harper & Martinson, Dallas, 1974—. Social v.p. Dallas Symphony Orch. Guild, 1975-77; mem. Dallas Regional Young Life Bd., 1977—, fund raising chmn., 1982-84, 86-88, 97—; bd. dirs., exec. fin. com. com., Downtown YMCA, 1997—, chmn. cmty. svcs. fund dr., 2003; mem. Russell Perry Free Enterprise Banquet Com., chmn., 2004; mem. Dallas Bapt. U.; mem. Miss Tex. Pageant Bd., 2003—. Recipient Sam Winstead award, YMCA, 2005. Mem. ABA (vice chmn. young lawyers com. 1980, pub. rels. com. torts sect.), Baylor U. Student Found. (steering com. 1971-72), Baylor Alumni Assn. (bd. dirs. 1978-82, 95), Tryon Coterie (pres. 1971), Highland Park Forensics Found. (pres. 1993-95), Preston Ctr. Legal Assn. (sec. 1993-94, bd. dirs. 1994-95), Dervish Club, Calyx Club, Dallas Baylor Club (bd. dirs. 1976-84, pres. 1981-82), Christian Men's Club, Phi Eta Sigma, Omicron Kappa Delta, Phi Delta Theta. Baptist. Home: 4400 Lorraine Dallas TX 75205 Office: Fanning Harper & Martinson 4849 Greenville Ave Ste 1300 Dallas TX 75206 Office Phone: 972-860-0327. E-mail: bfanning@fhmlaw.com.

FANNING, DAKOTA, actress; b. Conyers, Ga., Feb. 23, 1994; d. Steve and Joy Fanning. Actor: (films) Tomcats, 2001, I Am Sam, 2001 (Best Young Actor/Actress award Broadcast Film Critics Assn.), Father Xmas, 2001, Trapped, 2002, Sweet Home Alabama, 2002, Hansel & Gretel, 2002, Uptown Girls, 2003, The Cat in the Hat, 2003, Man on Fire, 2004, Hide and Seek, 2005, Nine Lives, 2005, War of the Worlds, 2005 (Best Young Actress, Broadcast Film Critics Assn., 2006), Dreamer: Inspired by a True Story, 2005, Charlotte's Web, 2006, (voice): (TV films) Kim Possible: A Stitch in Time, 2003,: (TV miniseries) Taken, 2002, (guest appearances): (TV series) ER, 2000, Ally McBeal, 2000, Strong Medicine, 2000, CSI: Crime Scene Investigation, 2000, The Practice, 2000, Spin City, 2000, Malcolm in the Middle, 2001, The Fighting Fitzgeralds, 2001, The Ellen Show, 2001, Friends, 2004, (guest appearances, voice) Family Guy, 2001. Named one of The 10 Most Fascinating People of 2005, Barbara Walters Special. Office: Osbrink Talent Agy 4343 Lankershim Blvd Ste 100 North Hollywood CA 91602 Office Phone: 818-760-2488.*

FANNING, DELVIN SEYMOUR, soil science educator; b. Copenhagen, NY, July 13, 1931; s. Clarence Roscoe and Faye Theodora (Hays) F.; m. Mary Christine Balluff, Nov. 22, 1958 (dec. Aug. 1994); children: Michael Christopher, Maurine Faye, Christine Kay; m. Emily Louise Wenzel Manning, Nov. 15, 1997. BS, Cornell U., 1954, MS, 1959; PhD, U. Wis., 1964. Cert. profl. soil scientist. Soil scientist Soil Conservation Svc., USDA, 1954, 59-62; grad. rsch. asst. dept. of soils U. Wis., Madison, 1960-64; from asst. prof. to prof. dept. natural resource scis. and landscape arch. U. Md., College Park, 1964-99, emeritus prof., 1999—. Vis. prof. Tech. U. of Munich, Germany, 1971-72, USDA Soil Conservation Svc., Washington, 1986; rsch. assoc. Tex. A&M U., College Station, 1979. Co-author: (with M.C.B. Fanning) Soil: Morphology, Genesis, and Classification, 1989; co-editor Acid Sulfate Weathering, 1982; contbr. entries in Encys., chpts. in books, articles to profl. jours. Bass singer Holy Redeemer Ch. Choir, College Park, Md., 1968—. With U.S. Army, 1954-56. Fellow Am Soc. Agronomy, Soil Sci. Soc. Am. Democrat. Roman Catholic. Achievements include definition, description and naming of processes for sulfide mineral accumulation in soils sulfidization and sulfide mineral oxidation to form sulfuric acid, and reaction of sulfuric acid with soils to form new minerals sulfuricization. Home: 4809 Ravenswood Rd Riverdale MD 20737-1115 Office: Univ Md Dept Environ Sci and Tech College Park MD 20742-5825 Home Phone: 301-864-5561; Office Phone: 301-405-1308. Personal E-mail: delvindel@aol.com. Business E-Mail: dsf@umd.edu. *Know the earth and live in harmony.*

FANNING, ELLEN, biology professor, research scientist; BS in Chemistry, U. Wis.-Madison; PhD in Virology, U. Cologne, Germany, 1977. Asst. prof. Univ. Konstanz, Germany; prof. and acting chair Inst. for Biochemistry Univ. Munich; now Stevenson Prof. Molecular Biology, Dept. Biological Sciences Vanderbilt Univ., Nashville. Vis. prof. Dept. Genetics Harvard Med. Sch.; mem. editl. bd. Jour. of Virology; assoc. dir. Nat. Inst. Health Tng. Grant of Viruses, Nucleic Acids and Cancer; prof. Howard Hughes Med. Inst. Mem.: German Science Found. Peer Review Bd., Milwaukee Found. Corp. (Shaw Scholar Sci. Adv. Bd.), European Molecular Biology Orgn. Office: Vanderbilt U 2325 Stevenson Ctr 1161 21st Ave S Nashville TN 37235 Office Phone: 615-343-5677. Office Fax: 615-343-6707. E-mail: ellen.h.fanning@Vanderbilt.Edu.

FANNING, FRANCIS GERARD, lawyer; b. Chgo., Nov. 20, 1947; s. Francis Joseph and Catherine Beatta (Heatherly) F.; m. Muriel Anne Knoblauch, Aug. 22, 1970; children: Michael G., Christopher J., Patrick D. BA, U. Ill., 1970; MEd, U. Ariz., 1974; JD, Ariz. State U., 1978. Bar: Ariz. 1978, U.S. Dist. Ct. Ariz. 1978, U.S. Ct. Appeals (9th cir.) 1992, U.S. Supreme Ct. 1995, U.S. Ct. Appeals (10th cir.) 1996. Prosecutor intern City Atty., Tempe, Ariz., summer 1977; law clk. Justice William Holohan Ariz. Supreme Ct., Phoenix, 1978-79; assoc. atty. Law Office of Carl Divelbiss, Phoenix, 1979-81; pvt. practice Tempe and Mesa, Ariz., 1981-88, 90—; assoc. Bill Stephens & Assocs., Phoenix, 1988-90. Judge pro tempore Maricopa County Superior Ct., Phoenix, 1991-96, commr. pro tempore, 1982-83; mem. local bd. Supreme Ct. Foster Care Rev. Bd., Phoenix, 1981-85. Vol. Maricopa County Bar Assn. Vol. Lawyers Assn., Phoenix, 1981—; mem. troop com. Troop 7 Boy Scouts Am., Tempe, 1993-98; vol. coach YMCA, Tempe, 1989-93. Named Atty. of Yr., Maricopa County Bar Assn. Vol. Lawyers Program, Phoenix, 1987; named one of Southwest Super Lawyers, 2007. Mem. Ariz. Employment Lawyers Assn. (bd. dirs. 1996-97), Nat. Employment Lawyers Assn. Democrat. Avocations: choral music, music composition. Home: 1941 E Los Arboles Dr Tempe AZ 85284-2586 Office: 500 E Southern Ave Ste B Tempe AZ 85282-5210 Home Phone: 480-839-7096; Office Phone: 480-731-9142. Business E-Mail: fanning@azbar.org.

FANNING, FRED ELDRIDGE, public administrator; b. Valdosta, Ga., Dec. 8, 1956; s. Aden Eldridge and Glenda Jean Fanning; m. Tammy Lu Hanson, Apr. 22, 1978; children: Fred Eldridge Fanning II, Ted Aldridge. AS, Cloud County C.C., 1984; BS, Excelsior Coll., 1993; MEd, Nat. Louis U., 1996; MA, Webster U., 2005. Cert. safety profl. Safety specialist Safety Office, 1st Inf. Divsn., Ft. Riley, Kans., 1986—89, Safety Divsn., 8th Inf. Divsn. (Mech), Bad Kreuznach, Germany, 1989—90; safety mgr. Safety Office, US Army Berlin and Berlin Brigade, 1990—94; safety specialist Safety Divsn., US Army Europe, Heidelberg, Germany, 1994—95; safety dir. G-1, US Army V Corps, Heidelberg, 1995—98, US Army Maneuver Support Ctr., Fort Leonard Wood, Mo., 1999—2004; sr. safety mgr. Office of the Dir. of Army Safety, Arlington, Va., 2004—05; dir. office occupl. safety and health US Dept. Commerce, Washington, 2005—07, dir. for adminstrv svcs., appt. sr. exec. svc., 2007—. Vice chmn. South Ctrl. Mo. Safety Coun., Lebanon, 2000; instr. Pk. Univ., Ft. Leonard Wood, Mo., 2001—04; vice chmn. Greater St. Louis Safety Coun., 2002—04. Author: (technical book) Basic Safety Administration: A Handbook for the New Safety Professional; contbr. articles to jours. Mem. Bd. of Cert. Hazard Control Mgmt., Rockville, Md., 2004—05. Sgt. US Army, 1975—78, Ft. Riley, Kansas. Decorated Good Conduct medal US Army, Achievement medal for Civilian Svc., Armed Forces Civilian Svc. medal, NATO medal for Svc. in the Former Yugoslavia, Commander's Award for Civilian Svc. US Army, Superior Civilian Svc. medal; recipient Bronze medal, US Dept. Commerce. Mem.: Am. Soc. Safety Engrs. (adminstr. pub. sector practice specialty), Sr. Exec. Assn. (assoc.), Missouir Writers Guild (assoc.), Masonic Lodge. R-Conservative. Christian. Avocations: reading, writing, motorcycling. Office: US Dept Commerce 1401 Constitution Ave Rm 6316 Washington DC 20230 Home: 3 Chandler Ct Fredericksburg VA 22405 Office Phone: 202-482-1200. Personal E-mail: fanningf@netscape.com.

FANNING, RONALD HEATH, architect, engineer; b. Evanston, Ill., Oct. 5, 1935; s. Ralph Richard and Leone Agatha (Heath) F.; m. Jenine Vivian Schnelle, Jan. 9, 1960; children: Anthony Lee, Traycee Anne. BArch, Miami U., Oxford, Ohio, 1959. Registered architect in 24 states; registered profl. engr. in 13 states Nat. Coun. of Archtl. Registration Bds., Nat. Coun. of Engrng. Examiners. Pres., CEO, Fanning/Howey Assocs., Inc., Celina, Ohio, 1959—2000, chmn. bd., 2000—. Mng. ptnr. Manning Partnership, Celina 1978-2003, F/H Bldg. Partnership, 1986—; trustee Fanning Family Charitable Remainder Trust, 2003—; guest lectr. San Diego State U., 2007-. Bd. dirs. CEFPI Found. and Charitable Trust, 2001—; chmn. Mercer County Young Reps., Celina, 1962-65. Recipient Fred B. Joyner Profl. Achievement award Delta Gamma chpt. Pi Kappa Alpha, 1997. Mem. NSPE, AIA, Coun. Ednl. Facility Planners Internat. (Great Lakes Midwest regional membership chmn. 1992-97, pres. Great Lakes Midwest region coun. ednl. facility planners internat. 1997-98), Ohio Soc. Profl. Engrs., Ohio Soc. Architects, Soc. Mktg. Profl. Svcs., Fla. Ednl. Facilities Planners Assn., Buckeye Assn. Sch. Adminstrs., Coun. Ednl. Faculty Planners Internat. (membership chmn. 1994-96, dir. 1997-2005, pres.-elect 2002-03, pres. 2003-04, past. pres. 2004-05, cert.). Methodist. Avocations: tennis, bowling, golf. Home: 422 Magnolia St Celina OH 45822-1254 Office: Fanning Howey Assoc Inc PO Box 71 Celina OH 45822-0071 Home Phone: 419-586-3879; Office Phone: 419-586-7771. Business E-Mail: rfanning@fhai.com.

FANNING, SHAWN, information technology executive; b. Harwich, Mass. Student, Northeastern U., 1999. Founder, chief tech. officer Napster, Redwood City, Calif., 1999; founder, CEO Snocap, Inc., 2004—. Actor: (films) The Italian Job, 2003. Named Tech Renegade of Yr., Wired Mag., IT Personality of 2000, IDG News Svc., 2000; recipient Person of Yr. award, PC Mag. Tech. Excellence Awards, 2000. Office: c/o Snocap Inc 128 Spear Street 2nd Fl San Francisco CA 94105

FANNING, THOMAS ANDREW, utilities executive; b. Morristown, NJ, Mar. 12, 1957; s. James E. and Marjorie (Van Morstein) F.; m. Beverly Booher, Mar. 14, 1987; children: Matthew Ryan, Bradley Stephen. BS in Indsl. Mgmt., Ga. Inst. Tech., Atlanta, 1979, MS in Fin., 1980. Fin. analyst Southern Co., Atlanta, 1980, with Southern Co. Svcs., 1983-86, treas. Southern Elec. Internat., 1986, supr. Southern Co. Svcs., 1988, dir. corp. fin. Southern Co. Svcs., 1988, sr. v.p. strategy, v.p., CFO Miss. Power, exec. v.p., CFO Ga. Power, 1999—2002, pres., CEO Gulf Power, 2002—03, exec. v.p., CFO, treas., 2003—. Bd. dirs. St. Joe Co. Ga. Fed. Mgmt. scholar, 1979, Nat. Merit scholar adv. bd. Ga. Inst. Tech., 2003-. Mem. Phi Eta Sigma. Office: Southern Company 30 Ivan Allen Jr Blvd NW Bin SC1505 Atlanta GA 30308 Office Phone: 404-505-0590. E-mail: tafannin@southernco.com.*

FANNING, WILLIAM HENRY, JR., computer specialist; b. NYC, Feb. 12, 1917; s. William Henry and Terese Genevieve (Moloney) F.; m. Mary Major Winter, Sept. 5, 1940; children: Hugh M. (dec.), Helen A. Smith, Mary M., Gerard, William Henry III. BA, Fordham U., Bronx, NY, 1940; postgrad., Cath. U., Washington, DC, 1940-41, Jersey City State Coll., 1977, Pace U., NYC, 1989-91. Exch. clerk NY Times, 1938—40; Greek and German instr. Gonzaga H.S., Washington, 1940—41; reporter, copy editor Nat. Cath. News Svc., Washington, 1941—48, news editor, 1948—55; dir. Rome News Bur., Radio Free Europe, 1955—57, dir. news and info. svcs. Munich, 1957—59, dir. Paris News Bur., 1959—60; editor The Cath. News, NYC, 1960—66; freelance writer CBS-TV, NYC, 1966—68, Harcourt Brace Jovanovich, NYC, 1967—72; v.p. promotion and advt., pop music prodr./agt. Diamond Prodns., Ltd., NYC, 1967—69; analyst CGA Computer Assocs., Holmdel, NJ, 1969—73; programmer/analyst to sr. systems specialist Equitable Life Assurance Soc. US, NYC, 1973—87; computer and network mgr. Mayor's Office of Midtown Enforcement, NYC, 1988—94. Cons. Bill Fanning Productivity Systems, Westport Point, Mass., 1966—; lectr. journalism Good Counsel Coll., White Plains, NY, 1967-69; head US Cath. Bishops Press Rels. Office, Rome-2d Vatican, 1962; mem. pres.'s com. Employment of the Handicapped, 1947-66. Bd. dirs. Westchester Cath. Edn. Coun., NYC, 1963-69; mem. Archdiocese Edn. Coun., N.Y.C., 1961-66. Lt. USNR, 1942-45. Mem. Writers Guild Am., Phi Kappa Theta (hon.). Roman Catholic. Home and Office: Box 234 Westport Point MA 02791-0234

FANNING, WILLIAM JAMES, professional sports team executive, commentator; b. Chgo., Sept. 14, 1927; s. Frank and Gladys Leona (Lighter) F. BA in phys. edn., Buena Vista Coll, 1951; M in Phys. Edn., U. Ill., 1961. Profl. baseball player Chgo. Cubs, 1954, 56, 57; player, mgr. Tulsa Oilers, Tex. League, 1958, Dallas Rangers, Am. Assn., 1959-60, Venezuela, Eau Claire Braves, Wis., 1961-62; spl. assignment scout Milw. Braves, 1963-64, asst. gen. mgr., 1964-66; asst. gen. mgr., farm and scouting dir. Atlanta Braves, 1966-67; 1st dir. Major League Scouting Bur., 1968; gen. mgr. Montreal Expos., 1968-73, v.p., gen. mgr., 1973-77, v.p. player devel., 1977-81, field mgr., 1981-84, v.p. player devel. and scouting, 1982-86, spl. cons. baseball ops., 1989—; radio and TV broadcaster, 1987-88. Spl. cons. baseball ops., 1989-92; major league scout Colo. Rockies, 1993-99; radio baseball show CJAD, Montreal, 1993-2000; spl. asst. to gen. mgr. Toronto Blue Jays, 2001; amb. to amateur baseball Toronto Blue Jays 2002, 03, 04, 05, 06. Served with U.S. Army, 1945-47. Inducted into Can. Baseball Hall of Fame, 2000, Montreal Expos Hall of Fame, 2000. Pentecostal. Home and Office: 154 Tiner Ave Dorchester ON Canada N0L 1G2 Address: One Blue Jays Way Ste 3200 Toronto ON Canada M5V 1J1 E-mail: wordsarepoetry@rogers.com.

FANNJIANG, ALBERT, mathematician, educator; arrived in U.S., 1987; s. W.-C. and W.-Y. Fannjiang; m. Jean Fannjiang; children: Clara, Dominic. PhD, NYU, 1992. Asst. prof. computational and applied math. UCLA, 1992—95; asst. prof. U. Calif., Davis, 1995—99, assoc. prof., 1999—2003, prof. math., 2003—. Contbr. rsch. articles to profl. jours. Recipient U. Calif.-Davis Chancellor fellow, 2001—06; grantee, NSF, 1996—. Mem.: Am. Math. Soc. (Centennial fellow 2002). Achievements include research in transport, propagation, imaging and communication in random media. Office: U Calif Dept Math One Shields Ave Davis CA 95616-8633 Business E-Mail: cafannjiang@ucdavis.edu.

FANONE, JOSEPH ANTHONY, lawyer; b. Sharon, Pa., Apr. 14, 1949; s. Anthony and Nancy Fanone; children: Michael, Kathleen, Peter. AB, Georgetown U., 1971, JD, 1974. Bar: Pa. 1974, D.C. 1980. Asst. atty. gen. Pa. Dept. of Justice, 1974-77; assoc. Squire, Sanders & Dempsey, Washington, 1977-81, Ballard, Spahr, Andrews & Ingersoll, Washington, 1981-83, ptnr., 1983-94, Piper & Marbury, Washington, 1994-95, Ballard, Spahr, Andrews & Ingersoll, Washington, 1996—. Mem. ABA. Office: Ballard Spahr Andrews & Ingersoll 601 13th St NW Ste 1000 Washington DC 20005-3807 Home Phone: 703-360-8454; Office Phone: 202-661-2207.

FANOS, KATHLEEN HILAIRE, osteopathic physician, podiatrist; b. Bremerhaven, Germany, Aug. 18, 1956; came to US, 1957; d. Homer Dantangelo and Ilse Helmar (Ochs) F. AAS in Music, Nassau C.C., Garden City, NY, 1976; BS in Music Edn., Hofstra U., Hempstead, NY, 1978, postgrad., 1978-79; D Podiatric Medicine, Coll. Podiatric Med. and Surgery, Des Moines, 1987, DO, 1994. Diplomate Am. Bd. Internal Medicine. Tchr. music McKenna Jr. HS and Eastlake Elem. Sch., Massapequa, NY, 1978—79; musician numerous profl. orgns., NY, 1979—, Iowa, 1979—; preceptorship in podiatry Bayshore, NY, 1987-88; pvt. practice podiatry Hyde Park, West Roxbury and Brookline, Mass., 1988-91; resident in internal medicine Winthrop U. Hosp., Mineola, NY, 1994-97; internist Cmty. Med. Assocs., Jackson, NJ, 1997-2000, Ocean County Family Care, Jackson, NJ, 2000—03, Hinds Internal Medicine, Jackson, Miss., 2003—. Ins. med. examiner Portamedic, Burlington, Mass., 1988-91. Mem. AMA, ACP, Am. Bd. Internal Medicine, Am. Soc. Internal. Medicine, Am. Osteo. Assn., Am. Coll. Osteo. Family Physicians, NY State Internal Medicine Soc., Phi Theta Kappa, Pi Kappa Lambda, Sigma Sigma Phi, Phi Delta Epsilon. Avocations: music, tennis, bowling, skiing, travel. Office Phone: 601-376-2115. Personal E-mail: kfanos@jam.rr.com.

FANSELOW, MICHAEL SCOTT, psychology professor; b. Bklyn, May 2, 1954; BS magna cum laude with honors, CUNY, Bklyn., 1976; PhD in Behavioral Psychology, U. Wash., 1980. Asst. prof. Rensselaer Poly. Inst., Troy, N.Y., 1980-81, Dartmouth Coll., Hanover, N.H., 1981-86, assoc. prof., 1986-88, UCLA, 1988-89, prof., 1989—. Recipient Troland Rsch. award NAS, 1995. Fellow AAAS, APA (Edwin B. Newman award 1979, D.O. Heb Young Scientist award 1983, Disting. Sci. award 1985). Office: UCLA Dept Psychology PO Box 951563 Los Angeles CA 90095-1563

FANTACI, JAMES MICHAEL, lawyer; b. Rochester, NY, Dec. 23, 1946; s. Anthony and Shirley F.; m. Ellen Louise Steman, Apr. 26, 1969; children: Michael, Matthew. BA, U. Rochester, 1968; JD, U. Va., 1971. Bar: Va. 1971, La. 1972, U.S. Dist. Ct. (ea. dist.) La. Law clk. to Hon. E. Gordon West U.S. Dist. Ct. (ea. and mid. dist.) La., 1971-72; atty. Monroe & Lemann, New Orleans, 1972-84, McGlinchey Stafford, New Orleans, 1984—. Mem. The Chamber/New Orleans and the River Region East Jefferson Coun., 1988-93; chmn. East Jefferson Coun., 1992; chmn. Area Coun. Coord. Com., 1993; chmn. bd. commrs. Jefferson Parish Econ. Devel. Commn., 1999. Contbr. articles to jours. and legal revs. Mem. ABA (bus. law sect., small bus. com., franchising subcom.), La. Bar Assn., Va. Bar Assn., Jefferson C. of C. Home: 114 Sycamore Dr Metairie LA 70005-4025 E-mail: jfantaci@mcglinchey.com.

FANTASIA, (FANTASIA MONIQUE BARRINO), singer; b. High Point, NC, June 30, 1984; 1 child: Zion Quari Barrino. Contestant American Idol, 2004; singer J Records, 2004—. Singer: (songs) I Believe, 2004 (Top Selling Single of Yr., Billboard Music Awards, 2004, Top Selling R&B/Hip-Hop Single of Yr., Billboard Music Awards, 2004), Summertime, 2004, Chain of Fools, 2004, (albums) Free Yourself, 2004, Fantasia, 2006; author: Life Is Not a Fairy Tale, 2005; actor: (TV films) Life Is Not a Fairytale: The Fantasia Barrino Story, 2006; (Broadway plays) The Color Purple, 2007 (Theatre World award, 2007). Recipient Image award for Outstanding Female Artist, NAACP, 2005. Winner, American Idol, 2004. Office: c/o J Records 745 Fifth Ave New York NY 10151*

FANTON, JONATHAN FOSTER, foundation administrator; b. Mobile, Ala., Apr. 29, 1943; s. Dwight F.F. and Marion (Foster) Fanton; m. Cynthia Greenleaf, Aug. 2, 1986. BA, Yale U., 1965, M.Phil., 1977, PhD in Am. History, 1978. Carnegie teaching fellow in history Yale U., 1965-66, lectr. history, 1966-78, spl. asst. to pres., 1970-73, exec. dir. Summer Plans, 1973-76, assoc. provost, 1976-78; v.p. planning U. Chgo., 1978-82; pres., prof. history New Sch. Social Rsch., NYC, 1982—99; pres. John D. and Catherine T. MacArthur Found., Chgo., 1999—. Author: The University and Civil Society, Vol. 1, 1995, Vol. 2, 2002; co-editor: John Brown, The Manhattan Project, 1991. Advisor, trustee Rockefeller Bros. Fund; bd. dirs. Human Rights Watch, Chgo. Hist. Soc.; founding chmn. bd. Security Coun. Report; chair policy and pub. affairs com. Living Cities. Office: MacArthur Found 140 S Dearborn St Chicago IL 60601 E-mail: jfanton@macfound.org.

FANTOZZI, PEGGY RYONE, geologist, environmental planner; b. Providence, Feb. 2, 1948; d. Eugene Baker and Cynthia (Bragg) Ryone; m. Thomas Allen Collins, Jan. 4, 1969 (div. 1985); children: Christin, Cindi; m. Thomas Edward Fantozzi, Mar. 22, 1985 (div. 1989); 1 child, Amy. BA in Earth Scis., Bridgewater State Coll., 1969; MS in Geology, Franklin and Marshall Coll., 1971. Registered sanitarian, Mass.; cert. wastewater treatment operator grade 4-M; cert. soil evaluator. Project mgr. Coastal Zone Mgmt. Grant, Eastham, Mass., 1980—81; geologist, project mgr. BSC Group/Cape Cod, Barnstable Village, Mass., 1982—88; sr. environ. scientist A.M. Wilson Assocs., Osterville, 1988—94, Daylor Consulting Group, Braintree, Mass., 1994—97. Instr. earth scis. and geology Bridgewater (Mass.) State Coll., 1972-74, Cape Cod C.C., West Barnstable, Mass., 1979-82; cons. conservation and health bds. Town of Bourne, Mass., 1984-85; mem., chair State Comm. for the Conservation of Soil, Water and Related Resources, 1996—; mem. Nat. Resources Conservation and Devel. Coun., 1998. Bd. dirs., v.p. Assn. for Preservation of Cape Cod, Orleans, Mass., 1979-85; trustee Cape Cod Mus. Natural History, Brewster, 1982-85; advisor Barnstable County Marine Resources program, 1980-82; chmn. Eastham Conservation Commn., 1978-82, Selectmen's Task Force on Local Pollution, Bourne, 1985-87; del. Barnstable County Water Resources Adv. Coun., 1979-89, Bourne Shore and Harbor Com., 1989-92; rep. Tri-Town Septage treatment Facilities Planning Commn., Eastham, Orleans, citizen's adv. com. groundwater discharge program Mass. Dept. EPA, 1987-88, Surface Water Quality, 1990, 93, Mass. Bays Program Citizen Adv. Steering Com., 1992—; pres. Mass. Assn. Conservation Dists., 1995-98; chair Mass. State Commn. for the Conservation of Soil, Water and Related Resources, 1998—; mem. Cape Cod Water Protection Collaborative, 2006—, mem. steering com., 2006—. Grantee USDA-Natural Resources Conservation Svc., 1997-98. Mem. Nat. Assn. Conservation Dists. (dir.), Mass. Health Officers Assn., Mass. Water Works Assn., Monument Beach Civic Assn. Home: 25 Shore Rd Buzzards Bay MA 02532-5425 Office: Land Use Permitting 25 Shore Rd Bourne MA 02532-5425

FANTZ, JANET NELSEN, school psychologist; b. Chgo., July 29, 1943; d. Harold Frederick and Louise (Maurer) Nelsen; m. Paul Richard Fantz, July 31, 1965; children: Deborah Fantz Clay, Susan Fantz Gibbs, Paul William. BS in Edn., So. Ill. U., Carbondale, 1965, MS in Edn., 1968; post grad. studies, NC State U., Raleigh, 1981—82. Nat. cert. sch. psychologist Nat. Assn. Sch. Psychologists, lic. psychol. assoc. NC State Bd. Examiners Practicing Psychology. Tchr. Mehlville Sch. Dist., Mo., 1965—69, sub. tchr., 1969—71; homebound tchr. Spl. Sch. Dist., St. Louis, 1971—72; sch. psychologist Alachua County Sch. Dist., Gainesville, Fla., 1973—78, Dade County Sch. Dist., Miami, 1979, Wake County Sch. Dist., Raleigh, 1980—. Mentor psychologist Wake County Sch. System, Raleigh, 1990—, mem. assessment com., 1996—2006, chairperson assessment com., 1996—99, learning disabilities com., 2003—05. Vol. March of Dimes Mothers March, 2006; vol. Kids for Christ Woodhaven Baptist Ch., Holly Springs, NC, 2002—03, preschool com. mem., 2005. Mem.: Nat. Assn. Sch. Psychologists, NC Sch. Psychology Assn., Psi Chi, Kappa Delta Pi, Pi Lambda Theta. Baptist. Avocations: travel, bridge, reading. Home: 2002 Ambrose Park Ln Cary NC 27518 Office: Wake County Sch System 3600 Wake Forest Rd Raleigh NC 27611 Office Phone: 919-387-4408. E-mail: jfantz@wcpss.net.

FANUELE, FRANK JOHN, engineering executive, electrical engineer; b. NYC, June 19, 1938; BSEE, Rensselaer Poly. Inst., 1960. Elec. engr. GE, 1960-64; project engr. Fairchild Electrometrics Corp., 1964-69; sys. engring. mgr. Mech. Tech. Inc., 1969-84; tech. sales mgr. Brown & Sharpe Mfg. Co., 1984-86; tech. mktg. mgr. Robotic Vision Sys., 1989; pres. Fanuele Enterprises, Albany, NY, 1986—. Achievements include research in the field of automation. Office: Fanuele Enterprises 256 Partridge St Albany NY 12208-2624 Office Phone: 518-438-0603. Personal E-mail: afanuele@nycap.rr.com.

FANUELE, MICHAEL ANTHONY, retired electronics engineer, research engineer; b. Bronx, NY, Feb. 24, 1938; s. Joseph A. and R. Fanny (Rubino) F.; m. Joyce L. Cassidy, May 23, 1964; children: Gina M., Peter A. BEE, NYU, 1959; MSEE, Rutgers U., 1968. Electronics engr. U.S. Army Combat Surveillance & Target Acquisition Lab., Fort Monmouth, N.J., 1960-72, sr. electronics engr., 1972-80, project officer, 1980-81, dir. ISTA systems div., 1981-85; chief systems and signals analysis div. U.S. Army Electronic Warfare, Reconnaissance Surveillance and Target Acquisition Ctr., Fort Monmouth, N.J., 1985-88; sr. rsch. engr. Ga. Tech. Rsch. Inst., Ga. Inst. Tech., 1988-2001; ret., 2001. Cons. in field; chmn. dept. electomagnetic engring. U.S. Army Internal Tng. Program, Ft. Monmouth, 1968-78, advisor, 1978-88; Army chmn. Tri-Svc. Radar Symposium Steering Group, Ft. Monmouth, 1973-88; Army mem. Internat. Tech. group, 1977-81, Internat. Radar Panel, 1984-88; coord., instr. radar short course Ga. Tech. Patentee in field; contbr. articles to profl. jours. 2d lt. U.S. Army, 1959-60. Mem. IEEE (sr.), Assn. Old Crows, KC (treas. Brickton, NJ 1968-70), Elks Club, Vintage Auto Club Ocean County, Classic Thunderbird Club Internat. Roman Catholic. Avocations: photography, woodworking, collecting records, model building, auto restoration. Home: 244 Enclave Blvd Lakewood NJ 08701 Personal E-mail: mikefanuele@yahoo.com.

FANUS, PAULINE RIFE, librarian; b. New Oxford, Pa., Feb. 14, 1925; d. Maurice Diehl and Bernice Edna (Gable) Rife; m. William Edward Fanus, June 20, 1944; children: Irene Weaver, Larry William, Daniel Diehl. BS, Pa. State U., 1945; MLS, Villanova U., 1961; postgrad., Temple U., 1986—. Periodical libr. Tex. Coll. Arts Industries, Kingville, 1945; tchr. nursery sch. Studio Sch., Wayne, Pa., 1953-55; libr. circulation, reference Franklin Inst., Phila., 1963-66; asst. libr. Ursinus Coll., Collegeville, Pa., 1966; catalog libr., instr. Eastern Coll., St. Davids, Pa., 1967-71; head libr. Agnes Irwin Sch., Rosemont, Pa., 1971-93, head libr. emeritus, 1993—. Book reviewer The Book Report. Mem. AAUP (chpt. sec. Eastern Coll. 1970-71). Home: 78 Holly Dr New Holland PA 17557-9476

FANWICK, ERNEST, lawyer; b. NYC, Feb. 28, 1926; s. Jacob and Jeanette (Lossof) F.; m. Lee Nathan, Sept. 1, 1951; children: Lewis, Leslie, Eric. BS in Elec. Engring., Pa. State U., 1948; JD, Columbia U., 1951. Bar: NY 1952, Conn. 1988, US Patent Office 1952, US Ct. Appeals (2d cir.) 1952, US Supreme Ct. 1958, US Ct. Appeals (fed. cir.) 1982. Sr. patent atty. ITT Fed. Telecom. Labs., Nutley, 1951-55; div. counsel Avion div. ACF, Paramus, NJ, 1955-57; patent counsel Burndy Corp., Norwalk, Conn., 1957-65, dir. legal dept., 1965-75, gen. counsel, 1975-82, v.p., gen. counsel, sec., 1982-89. Faculty Practising Law Inst., NYC, 1964-97; lectr. Conf. Legal Execs., Pa., 1970, 72. Bd. dirs. Aid to Retarded, Stamford, Conn., 1982-87, exec. com., 1997—; bd. dirs. Assn. Jewish Family and Children's Agys., 1992-2000, Jewish Family Svcs., Stamford, 1989-2000; alternate mem. Zoning Bd. Appeals, Stamford, 1990-96; active Am. ARbitration Assn.; arbitration panel NY Stock Exch., Am. Stock Exch., Nat. Assn. Security Dealers. Lt. US Army, 1943-47. Mem. ABA, Conn. Bar Assn., Conn. Patent Law Assn. (pres. 1966), N.Y. Intellectual Property Law Assn., The Corp. Bar Assn., Am. Intellectual Property Assn., Am. Arbitration Assn., Masons. Home Fax: 203-322-4764. Personal E-mail: ernest@fanwick.com.

FANWICK, PHILLIP EDWARD, crystallographer; b. Santa Monica, Calif., May 6, 1947; s. Charles and Dorothy (Lerner) F.; m. Karen Beth Wallick, Apr. 13, 1991; children: Christopher Lee, Micah David, Sarah Brooke. BS, Tulane U., 1969; MS, Iowa State U., 1971, PhD, 1977. Postdoctoral assoc./instr. Tex. A&M, College Station, 1977-79; asst. prof. U. Ky., Lexington, 1979-85; crystallographer Purdue U., West Lafayette, Ind., 1985—. Capt. USAF, 1972-75. Mem. Am. Crystallography Assn. Avocations: music, movies. Home: 3900 N 800 W West Lafayette IN 47906-9405 Office: Dept Chemistry Purdue U West Lafayette IN 47907

FARABOW, FORD FRANKLIN, JR., lawyer; b. Charlotte, NC, Jan. 6, 1938; s. Ford Franklin and Louise (Botts) F.; children— Ford Franklin, III, Amy Kathryn, Andrew Leighton. BS in Chem. Engring., Clemson U., 1959; JD with honors, George Washington U., 1963. Bar: D.C. bar 1965, S.C. bar 1963. With law dept. Swift & Co., Washington, 1959-62; assoc. Nexsen & Pruet, Columbia, SC, 1962-64; with patent dept. Hercules, Inc., Wilmington, Del., 1964-65; ptnr. Finnegan, Henderson, Farabow, Garrett & Dunner, Washington, 1965—. Lectr. to ABA, Am. Patent Law Assn., also others. Contbr. articles to profl. publs. Named one of best lawyers in intellectual property law, Best Lawyers in Am., 2005—06. Mem. ABA, Am. Coll. Trial Lawyers, S.C. Bar Assn., Am. Judicature Soc., Bar Assn. D.C., Am. Patent Law Assn., U.S. Trademark Assn. (chmn. internat. adv. group), Am. Chem. Soc., Clemson U. Alumni Assn., Giles S. Rich Am. Inns of Ct., Tiger Brotherhood, Order of Coif, Phi Eta Sigma, Delta Theta Phi, Bethesda (Md.) Club (bd. dirs. 1987), TPC Club at Avenel, Franklin Sq. Club, Clemson IPTAY. Office: Finnegan Henderson Farabow Garrett & Dunner LLP 901 New York Ave NW Washington DC 20001-4413 Office Phone: 202-408-4000. Office Fax: 202-408-4400. Business E-Mail: ford.farabow@finnegan.com.

FARACI, JOHN VINCENT, JR., paper company executive; b. Summit, NJ, Feb. 16, 1950; s. John V. and Joan (Abbot) F.; m. Heath Holland. BA, Denison U., 1972; MBA, U. Mich., 1974. With Internat. Paper Co., 1974-88; fin. analyst NYC, 1974-75; bus. analyst Statesville, NC, 1975-76; plant contr. Kalamazoo, 1976-77; staff analyst NYC, 1977-78; mgr. mktg. Mobile, Ala., 1978-80; dir. planning NYC, 1980-83; gen. mgr. western ops. Gardiner, Oreg., 1983-85; gen. mgr. wood products group Dallas, 1985-88; v.p., gen. mgr. Masonite div., Chgo., 1988-91; CEO, mng. dir., Carter Holt Harvey Ltd., 1995—99; sr. v.p. finance, CFO International Paper, Purchase, NY, 1999—2000, exec. v.p., CFO, 2000—03, pres., 2003, chmn., CEO, 2003—. Republican. Avocations: mountain climbing, flying, collecting American Antique funiture, tennis, water sports. Office: Internat Paper 400 Atlantic St Stamford CT 06921 Office Phone: 203-541-8000.*

FARACI, PHILIP J., imaging company executive; BA in Applied Mechanics, U. Calif., San Diego, grad. Exec. Program for Scientists and Engrs. Various positions including v.p., gen. mgr. Consumer Bus. Orgn. and sr. v.p., gen. mgr. Injet Imaging Solutions Group Hewlett-Packard; pres., gen. mgr. Telecom bus. unit Gemplus Corp.; COO Phogenix Imaging; dir. Inkjet Systems Program Eastman Kodak Co., Rochester, NY, 2004—05, sr. v.p., 2005—, dir. corp. strategy & bus. devel., 2005, pres. Consumer Digital Imaging Group, 2006—. Office: Eastman Kodak Co 343 State St Rochester NY 14650 Office Phone: 585-724-4000.*

FARAG, SHERIF SHAFIK, physician scientist, educator; b. Alexandria, Egypt, Dec. 6, 1960; s. Shafik and Georgette Farag; m. Sawsan Younan Mansour, Apr. 7, 1991; children: Christian Mark, Kristine Irini. MBBS, U. Melbourne, Victoria, Australia, 1984, PhD, 1995. Intern Royal Melbourne Hosp., 1985, resident in internal medicine, 1986—89; fellow in hematology St. Vincent's Hosp., Melbourne, 1990—95; fellow in bone marrow transplantation Roswell Park Cancer Inst., Buffalo, 1996—97; dir. hematology and bone marrow transplantation Townsville Gen. Hosp., Queensland, Australia, 1997—99; asst. prof. internal medicine Ohio State U., Columbus, 2000—06; dir. hematological malignancies and blood and marrow transplantation Ind. U. Cancer Ctr., Indpls., 2006—; assoc. prof. internal medicine, med. and molecular genetics Ind. U. Sch. Medicine, Indpls., 2006—. Contbr. articles to profl. jours. Bd. deacons St. Mary Coptic Orthodox Ch., Columbus, Ohio, 2002—06. Fellow: Royal Coll. Pathologists Australasia (licentiate), Royal Australasian Coll. Physicians (licentiate); mem.: Internat. Soc. Cellular Therapy, Am. Soc. Blood and Marrow Transplantation, Am. Soc. Clin. Oncology, Am. Soc. Hematology. Achievements include patents pending for use of flow-through immunomagnetic selection to deplete T cells from bone marrow allografts. Avocations: tennis, bicycling. Office: Ind Univ Sch Medicine 635 Barnhill Dr Room 224G Indianapolis IN 46202 Office Phone: 317-278-0460. Business E-Mail: ssfarag@iupui.edu.

FARAGO, JOHN MICHAEL, law educator, consultant; b. NYC, Mar. 8, 1951; s. Ladislas and Liesel (Mroz) F.; m. Sharon Cramer, Nov. 11, 1972 (div.); m. Jeanne Elaine Martin, Dec. 5, 1985; 1 child, Max Farago; stepchildren: Belle Iskowitz, Sarah Iskowitz. BA, MAT, Harvard U., 1972; JD, NYU, 1978, postgrad., 1975-78. Assoc. dean, prof. Valparaiso (Ind.) U. Sch. Law, 1978-82; assoc. prof., assoc. dean for acad. planning CUNY Law Sch., NYC, 1982—86, assoc. prof., dir. systems, 1986—90; assoc. dean for acad. affairs N.Y. Law Sch., NYC, 1990—92; assoc. prof. CUNY Law Sch., NYC, 1992—2004, prof., 2004—. Spl. edn. hearing officer Ind. Edn. Dept., 1979-82, N.Y.C. Bd. Edn., 1982—; hearing officer N.Y. State vocat. Edn., N.Y.C., 1993-98; adj. prof. Tchrs. Coll., 1998; cons. in field Co-author: Junk Food, 1978, Current & Emerging Issues in Special Education, 2002, Special Education Primer; editor: The Family, 1975; editl. bd. Ctr. for Computer-Assisted Legal Instrn., 1997—; contbr. articles to profl. jours. Search coord., chancellor search N.Y.C. Bd. Edn., 1995; v.p. NY State Assn. of Adminstrv. Law Judges, 2005—. Home: 1225 Park Ave New York NY 10128-1758 Office: CUNY Law Sch 65-21 Main St Flushing NY 11367 Office Phone: 212-348-0815. E-mail: Farago@mail.law.cuny.edu.

FARAH, BADIE NAIEM, computer information systems educator, consultant; b. Nazareth, Palestine, Jan. 15, 1946; came to U.S., 1970; naturalized, 1983. s. Naim R. and Afifi F. BS, Damascus U., 1967, MA, 1968; MS, Wayne State U., 1973; MSIE, Ohio State U., 1976, PhD, 1977. Teaching asst. Wayne State U., Detroit, 1971-73; research assoc. Ohio State U., Columbus, 1973-77; sr. systems analyst Gen. Motors Co., Detroit, 1977-78; asst. prof. Oakland U., Rochester, Mich., 1978-82; asst. prof. computer systems Eastern Mich. U., Ypsilanti, 1982-86, assoc. prof., 1986-90, prof., 1990—. Advisor to bd. dirs. S & G Grocer Co., Detroit, 1979-81, vis. gen. mgr., 1980-81. Author: Business Information Systems: Development and Implementation, 1990, 2nd edition, 1995; co-author: Integrated Case Studies in Accounting Information Systems, 1987; contbr. articles to profl. jours. Mem. Am. Inst. Indsl. Engrs., Assn. for Computing Machinery (exec. council Met. Detroit chpt.), Ops. Research Soc. Am., Inst. Mgmt. Scis. (sec. SE Mich. chpt.), Mich. Acad. Sci., Arts and Letters, AAUP, Alpha Pi Mu, Beta Gamma Sigma, Phi Kappa Phi. Syrian Orthodox (pres. local ch. bd.). Research on data communications and networks of computers, e-commerce, management information. Home: 37 Foxboro Dr Rochester Hills MI 48309 Office: Ea Mich U Computer Info Sys Ypsilanti MI 48197 Home Phone: 248-726-0554; Office Phone: 734-487-1098. Business E-Mail: badie.farah@emich.edu.

FARAH, CAESAR ELIE, language educator, historian; b. Portland, Oreg., Mar. 13, 1929; s. Sam Khalil and Lawrice Farah; m. Irmgard Tenkamp, Dec. 13, 1987; 1 child, Elizabeth;children from previous marriage: Ronald, Christopher, Ramsey, Laurence, Raymond, Alexandra. Student, Internat. Coll. Am. U. Beirut, 1941—46; BA, Stanford U., 1952; MA, Princeton U., 1955, PhD, 1957. Pub. affairs asst., cultural affairs officer ednl. exchanges USIS, New Delhi, 1957-58, Karachi, Pakistan, 1958; asst. to chief Bur. Cultural Affairs, Washington, 1959; asst. prof. history and Semitic langs. Portland State U., 1959-63; asst. prof. history Calif. State U., LA, 1963-64; assoc. prof. Near Eastern studies Ind. U., Bloomington, 1964-69; prof. Mid. Eastern and Islamic history U. Minn., Mpls., 1969—, chmn. South Asian and Mid. Eastern studies, 1988-91. Guest lectr. Fgn. Ministry, Spain, Iraq, Iran, Ministry Higher Edn., Saudi Arabia, Yemen, Turkey, Kuwait, Qatar, Tunisia, Morocco, Syrian Acad. Scis., Acad. Scis., Beijing; vis. scholar Cambridge U., 1974; resource person on Middle East media and svc. group, Minn., 1977—; bd. dirs., chmn. Upper Midwest Consortium for Middle East Outreach, 1980—; vis. prof. Harvard U., 1964, 65, Sanaa U., Yemen, 1984, Karl-Franzens U. Austria, 1990, 91, 1997—98, Ludwig-Maximilian U., Munich, 1992—93; vis. Fulbright-Hays scholar U. Damascus, 1994; vis. lectr. Am. U. Beirut, 2001; exec. sec., editor Am. inst. Yemeni Studies, 1982—86; sec.-gen., exec. bd. dirs. Internat. Com. for Pre-Ottoman & Ottoman Studies, 1988—2000, v.p., 2000—; fellow Rsch. Ctr. Islamic History, Istanbul, 1993, Ctr. Lebanese Studies & St. Anthony Coll., Oxford, England, 1994; vis. cons. Sultan Qaboos U., Oman, 2000; mem. exec. bd. Arab Am. Cultural Inst., 2001—. Author: The Addendum in Medieval Arabic Historiography, 1968, Islam: Beliefs and Observances, 7th edit., 2003, Eternal Message of Muhammad, 1964, 3d edit., 1981, Tarikh Baghdad li-Ibn-al-Najjar, 3 vols., 1980—83, 2d edit., 1986, al-Ghazali on Abstinence in Islam, 1992, Decision Making in the Ottoman Empire, 1992, The Road to Intervention: Fiscal Policies in Ottoman Mount Lebanon, 1992, The Politics of Interventionism in Ottoman Lebanon, 2000, The Sultan's Yemen, 2002, Ottomans & Arabs, 2002, First Arab Traveler to Latin America, 2003; contbr. articles to profl. jours.; mem. editl. bd.: Digest of Middle East Studies. Mem. Oreg. Rep. Committeeman, 1960—64. Named Fulbright-Hayes lectr., 1993—94; recipient cert. of merit, Syrian Ministry Higher Edn.; fellow, Am. Coun. Learned Socs., 1953, Am. Rsch. Ctr. Egypt, 1966—67, Fulbright Tgn. and Rsch., Germany, 1992—93, Ford Found., 1966, Am. Philos. Soc., 1970—71; grantee Participants Program, Dept. State Am., 1981, 1984, 1993, Minn. Humanities Commn., 1981, 1985, 1989, 1995, 1998, 2001, Am. Inst. Yemeni Studies, 1999, Coun. Am. Overseas Rsch. Ctrs., 2000, Travel to Collection, NEH, 1989, others; scholar Fulbright Rsch., 1966—67, 1985—86, 1992—93. Mem.: Turkish Studies Assn., Am. Assn. Tchrs. Arabic (exec. bd.), Mid. East Studies Assn. N.Am., Am. Hist. Assn., Royal Asiatic Soc. Gt. Britain, Am. Oriental Soc., Arab Am. Cultural Inst. (co-founder, exec. bd. 2002—), Stanford U. Alumni Assn. (pres. upper Midwest Assn. 1978—79, Leadership Recognition award), Princeton Club, Stanford Club Minn. (dir., pres. 1979), Phi Alpha Theta, Pi Sigma Alpha. Greek Orthodox. Home: 5125 Blake Rd S Edina MN 55436-1125 Office: Univ Minn 839 Soc Sci Towers Minneapolis MN 55455 Office Phone: 612-624-0580. Business E-Mail: farah001@umn.edu.

FARAH, ROGER N., retail company executive; Former chmn., chief exec. officer Rich's, Atlanta, Federated/Allied Merchandising Svcs., NYC; chmn., CEO, Woolworth Corp. (name changed to Venator Group), NYC, 1994-00, also bd. dirs.; pres. & COO Polo Ralph Lauren Corp., NYC, 2000—. Chmn. bd. Venator Group, Inc. Office: Polo Ralph Lauren Corp 650 Madison Ave New York NY 10022-1029*

FARAHAT, MEDHAT S., researcher; arrived in US, 2006, naturalized, 2006; s. Shehata F. Khedr and Samiha A. Badawi; m. Sondos I. ElGazairly, Apr. 29, 1999; children: Deena M., Muhannad M. BS in Gen. Chemistry, Cairo U., Giza, 1988, MS in Organic Chemistry, 1993; PhD in Polymer Chemistry, Ain Shams U., Cairo, 1996. Postdoctoral rsch. fellow polymer chemistry U. Ala., Tuscaloosa, 2000—03; rsch. assoc. Ctr. Materials Info. Tech., 2006—. Quality control mgr. Internat. Co. for Mining and Investment, Sadat City, Menofia, Egypt, 2003—04, Nat. Co. Packaging Materials, ElObour City, Cairo, 2004—05. Contbr. articles to profl. jours. (Top Sci. Papers of Macromolecular Materials and Engring., 2002). Mem.: Am. Chem. Soc. Populist. Moslem. Achievements include research in New UV Curable Acrylated/Methacrylated Oligoesters Derived from PET Waste. Avocations: rowing, swimming, exercise, chess. Office: Ctr for Materials for Info Tech PO Box 870209 Tuscaloosa AL 35487 Personal E-mail: medfarahat@netscape.net.

FARAONE, PHILIP, organist, director, consumer products company executive; b. Providence, June 10, 1957; s. Gaetano and Marie Norma (Tronni) Faraone; m. Deborah Ann Donovan, Aug. 14, 1988; children: Gaetano, Norma Ann. MusB, Barrington Coll., Barrington, RI, 1979; MA in Tchg., R.I. Coll., Providence, RI, 1985. Choir dir, organist Temple Sinai, Cranston, 1984; choir dir., organist St. Sebastian's Ch., Providence, St. Gregory the Great Ch., Warwick, RI, 1980—89; choir dir. Cranston HS West, 1997—; cathedral organist Cathedrals St. Peter & Paul, 1990—; pres. Faraone Coffee Co., LLC, 2000—. Musician: (CD) The Works of C.A. Pelquin. Hon. state chair Rep. Nat. Com., Washington, 2005. Mem.: Am. Guild of Organists, Music Educators Nat. Conf., Consortiums Roman Cath. Cathedral Musicians. Roman Cath. Achievements include dir. 2 European concert tours with Cranston H.S. West choir performance in Vatican City, Florence, Rome, Sorrento, Venice, Palestrina; organist 2 European concert tours with Gregorian Concert Choir, performances in Rome Assisi, Vatican, perfomance in private audience Pope John Paul II. Avocations: reading, walking, ice skating, swimming, travel. Office: Cathedral St Peter & Paul 30 Fenner St Providence RI 02903

FARARO, THOMAS JOHN, sociologist, educator; b. NYC, Feb. 11, 1933; s. Joseph and Anna (Marcello) F.; m. Irene Johanna Fannasch, Dec. 30, 1955; children: Ramona, Raymond. BA, CCNY, 1959; PhD, Syracuse U., 1963. Asst. prof. sociology Syracuse (N.Y.) U., 1963-64; vis. scholar Stanford (Calif.) U., 1964-67; prof. U. Pitts., 1967-99, chmn. dept. sociology, 1980-85, Disting. Svc. prof., 1999—2006, Disting. Svc. prof. emeritus, 2006—. Author: Mathematical Sociology, 1973, Mathematical Sociology, Japanese translation, 1980, The Meaning of General Theoretical Sociology, 1989 (transl. into Japanese 1996), Social Action Systems, 2001; co-author: A Study of a Biased Friendship Net, 1964, Generating Images of Stratification, 2003; editor: Mathematical Ideas and Sociological Theory, 1984; co-editor Rational Choice Theory, 1992, The Problem of Solidarity, 1998, Purpose, Meaning and Action, 2006; assoc. editor Jour. Math. Sociology, 19782006; mem. editl. bd. Am. Jour. Sociology, 1977-79, Am. Sociol. Rev., 1980-82, Social Networks, 1978-82, Sociol. Theory, 1988-90, Sociol. Forum, 1989-92. With USAF, 1952-56. Grantee Social Sci. Rsch. Coun., 1968, NSF, 1969-72. Mem. Am. Sociol. Assn. (chair math. sociol. sect. 1998-99, Disting. Career Math. Social award 2004), Sociol. Rsch. Assn. Office: U Pitts Dept Sociology 230 S Bouquet St Pittsburgh PA 15213-4015 E-mail: tjf2@pitt.edu. *I have devoted my intellectual life to the advancement of theoretical sociology by the use of mathematical methods in presenting theories, clarifying and formalizing concepts, representing social processes and social structures, and explaining social phenomena.*

FARB, THOMAS FOREST, financial executive; b. NYC, Oct. 28, 1956; s. Peter and Oriole (Horch) F.; m. Stacy Siana Valhouli, Apr. 29, 1961; children: Peter Forest Valhouli-Farb, Siana Louisa Valhouli-Farb, Andreas John Valhouli-Farb. AB, Harvard U., 1980. Rsch. assoc. Mass. House Ways and Means Com., Boston, 1976-78; asst v.p. Bank of Boston, 1980-83; v.p., CFO and gen. mgr. ea. ops. Symbolics, Inc., Burlington, Mass., 1983-89; sr. v.p., CFO, contr. Airfund Corp., Lexington, Mass., 1989-92; v.p. corp. devel., CFO, treas. Cytyc Corp., Marborough, Mass., 1992-94; exec. v.p., CFO, treas. Indevus Pharms., Inc., Lexington, Mass., 1994-98; gen. ptnr., CFO Summit Ptnrs., Boston, 1998—2003; mng. dir. New Am. Ptnrs., LLC, Waltham, Mass., 2003—06, Cappello Capital Corp., 2003—06; pres., COO, Indevus Pharm., 2006—. Bd. dir. Fair, Issac and Co., San Rafael, Calif., Redwood Trust, Inc., Mill Valley, Calif., Saf-T-Med. Inc., Barrington, Ill., Symon Comm., Dallas, Veroscan. Dallas, SIV Tech., Worcester, Mass. Mem. Fin. Execs. Inst., Bus. Assocs. Club, Treas. Club Boston, Newcomen Soc. Home: 1228 Lowell Rd Concord MA 01742-5527 Office: Indevus Pharms 33 Hayden Ave Lexington MA 02421 Business E-Mail: tfarb@indevus.com.

FARBER, BERNARD JOHN, lawyer; b. London, Feb. 27, 1948; arrived in US, 1949; s. Solomon and Regina (Wachter) F.; m. Mary Lee Mueller, Feb. 14, 1987; children: Zachary, Anne. BS, U. of State of N.Y., Albany, 1978; JD, Ill. Inst. Tech., 1983. Bar: Ill. 1983, U.S. Dist. Ct. (no. dist.) Ill. 1983, U.S. Ct. Appeals (7th cir.) 1985, U.S. Tax Ct. 1986, U.S. Ct. Mil. Appeals 1986, U.S. Supreme Ct. 1987, U.S. Ct. Appeals (6th cir.) 1988, U.S. Ct. Appeals (4th cir.) 1989, U.S. Ct. Appeals (11th cir.) 1990. Instr. legal writing Chgo.-Kent Law Sch. Ill. Inst. Tech., 1983-85, computer rsch. atty., 1985-86, adj. prof. law, 1987—; legal editor Longman Fin. Svcs., Chgo., 1986-87; rsch. counsel publs. Ams. for Effective Law Enforcement, Chgo., 1987—. Instr. Law Scholastic Aptitude Test; preparation course BAR/BRI, Chgo., 1984-88; v.p. Brickton Montessori Sch., Chgo., 1992-93; sec. bd. dirs., 1993-95. Mng. editor: Chgo.-Kent Law Rev., 1981-82, editor-in-chief, 1982-83; co-author: Protective Security Law, 1996; editor: (with others) Dow Jones-Irwin Handbook of Micro Computer Applications in Law, 1987, Illinois Law of Criminal Investigation, 1986; contbr. articles to profl. jours. Elected mem. Local Sch. Coun., Agassiz Elem. Sch., Chgo., 1996-2004, chmn., 1999-2004, vice-chmn. 2002-2003. Mem. Ill. State Bar Assn., Chgo. Bar Assn., Sci. Fiction Rsch. Assn., Mensa. Avocations: history, computers, science fiction. Home and Office: 1126 W Wolfram St Rear Chicago IL 60657-4330 Business E-Mail: bernfarber@aol.com.

FARBER, DONALD CLIFFORD, lawyer, educator; b. Columbus, Nebr., Oct. 19, 1923; s. Charles and Sarah (Epstein) F.; m. Ann Eis, Dec. 28, 1947; children: Seth, Patricia. BS in Law, U. Nebr., 1948, JD, 1950. Bar: NY 1950. Assoc. Newman, Hauser & Teitler, NYC, 1950-58; pvt. practice, NYC, 1958-80; of counsel Conboy, Hewitt, O'Brien & Boardman, NYC, 1980-84; ptnr. Tanner Propp Fersko & Sterner, NYC, 1984-95, Farber & Rich LLP, NYC, 1995-98; of counsel Hartman & Craven LLP, NYC, 1998—2000, Jacob Medinger & Finnegan LLP, NYC, 2000—. Prof. law York U., Toronto, Ont., Canada, 1970, Toronto, 1972—73; prof. theatre law Hofstra Law Sch., Hempstead, NY, 1974—75; prof. New Sch. for Social Rsch., NYC, 1972—, Hunter Coll., 1978. Author: From Option to Opening, 1968, 5th edit., 2005, 1st Limelight edit., 1988, Producing on Broadway, 1969, Actor's Guide: What You Should Know About the Contracts You Sign, 1971, Producing, Financing and Distributing Film, 1973, 2d edit., 1991, The Amazing Story of the Fantasticks: America's Longest Running Play, 1991, 2d edit., 2005, Producing Theatre: A Comprehensive Legal and Business Guide, 1981, 3d Limelight edit., 1997, Common Sense Negotiation-The Art of Winning Gracefully, 1996; gen. editor (10 vol. series, author theatre vol.) Entertainment Industry Contracts-Negotiating and Drafting Guide. With AUS, 1941—44, ETO. Mem.: Order of Coif. Home: 14 E 75th St New York NY 10021-2657 Office: Jacob Medinger & Finnegan LLP Attn Donald C Farber 1270 Ave of Americas New York NY 10020 Office Phone: 212-524-5035. Personal E-mail: donaldc14@aol.com. Business E-Mail: dcfarber@jmfnylaw.com.

FARBER, EVAN IRA, librarian; b. NYC, June 30, 1922; s. Meyer M. and Estelle H. (Shapiro) F.; m. Hope Wells Nagle, June 13, 1966; children: Cynthia, Amy, Jo Anna, May Beth; stepchildren: David Nagle, Jeffrey Nagle, Lisa Nagle. AB, U. N.C., 1944, MA, BLS, U. N.C., 1953; DHL (hon.), St. Lawrence U., 1980, Susquehanna U., 1989, Ind. U., 1996. Instr. polit. sci. U. Mass., Amherst, 1948-49; librarian State Tchrs. Coll., Livingston, Ala., 1953-55; chief serials and binding div. Emory U. Library, Ga., 1955-62; head librarian Earlham Coll., Richmond, Ind., 1962-94, coll. libr. emeritus, 1994—. Cons. Bates Coll., Eckerd Coll., Colo. Coll., Hartwick Coll., Macalester Coll., Maryville Coll., Knox Coll., Ill. Coll., Messiah Coll., Hiram Coll., Centenary Coll., Colby Coll., Ga. State U., Ripon Coll., Hampshire Coll., Reed Coll., Williams Coll., NEH, Lilly Endowment, North Ctrl. Assn., Assn. Am. Colls., Pew Meml. Trust. Author: (with Andreano and Reynolds) Student Economists Handbook, 1967, Classified List of Periodicals for the College Library, 5th edit., 1972; assoc. editor: Southeastern Librarian, 1959-62; asst. editor: Explorations in Entrepreneurial History, 1964-66; co-editor: Earlham Rev., 1965-72; editor: Combined Retrospective Index to Book Revs. in Scholarly Jours., 1886-1974, 1979-83, Combined Retrospective Index to Revs. in Humanities Jours., 1802-1974, 1983-85, (with Ruth Walling) Essays in Honor of Guy R. Lyle; columnist: Choice Mag., 1974-80, Library Issues, 1982-88; mem. editl. bd. Coll. and Undergrad Librs., Internet and Higher Edn. Recipient Acad./Rsch. Libr. of the Yr., 1980, B.I. Libr. of Yr. award, 1987. Mem. Assn. Coll. and Rsch. Librs. (pres. 1978-79, bd. dirs. 1989-93), ALA (council 1969-71, 79-83). Home: 2030 Chester Blvd Richmond IN 47374 E-mail: evanf@earlham.edu.

FARBER, GEORGE ALLAN, dermatologist, educator; b. Miami, Fla., Jan. 4, 1934; s. Charles R. and Clara M. (Milman) F.; m. Nancy Graves, Dec. 26, 1955; children: George Allan, Michael G., Jeffrey N., Guy C., Scott Q. BS, La. State U., 1955, MD, 1959. Diplomate Am. Bd. Cosmetic Surgery., Am. Bd. Dermatology. Intern So. Bapt. Hosp., New Orleans, 1959-60; resident Charity Hosp. of New Orleans, 1963-66; commd. 2d lt. M.C. USAF, 1955, advanced through grades to lt. col., 1965; chief aviation medicine and mil. pub. health Luke AFB, Phoenix, 1960-63; flight surgeon, chief dermatology and syphilology 12th USAF Hosp., Cam Ranh Bay, Vietnam, 1966-67; chief dermatology svc., cons. to Surgeon Gen. S.E. region USAF Med. Referral Ctr., Keesler AFB, Miss., 1967-70; ret. USAF, 1970; asst. prof. medicine Tulane U. Sch. Medicine, New Orleans, 1970-75, assoc. prof., 1976-84; pvt. practice dermatology, 1970—; clin. assoc. prof. dermatology Tulane U. Sch. Medicine, New Orleans, 1975-84; mem. staff Kenner Regional Ctr. Hosp., 1994-2000. Past mem. staff Charity Hosp. New Orleans, East Jefferson Hosp., So. Bapt. Hosp., Kenner (La.) Regional Med. Ctr.; mem. courtesy staff LifeCare Hosp., Kenner; prof., med. dir. resident and postgrad. accredited tng. program Gulf South Med. and Surgery Inst., Kermer, La.; mem. profl. staff Kenner Dermatology Clinic; ret. dir. Fairground Corp., New Orleans; mem. courtesy staff Northshore Regional Med. Ctr., Slidell, La.; bd. dirs. La. Divsn. Am. Lukemia Soc. Decorated Bronze Star; named Physician of Yr., Nat. Rep. Congl. Com. Physicians' Adv. Bd., 2003, 2004; named one of Ams. Top Physicians, Consumer's Rsch. Coun. Am., 2006. Fellow Am. Acad. Oral and Maxillofacial Surgery; mem. Kenner Med. Soc. (founder, sec./treas. 1998), N.Am. Acad. Cosmetic and Reconstructive Surgery (founder, bd. dirs., pres. 1998-99), Am. Soc. Dermatologic Surgery (co-founder, past officer and dir.), Am. Acad. Cosmetic Surgery (co-founder, past officer and dir.), Am. Bd. Cosmetic Surgery (examiner, rev. course lectr., past officer and dir.), Leukemia and Lymphoma Soc. L.A. (sec. 2005, 06), Am. Acad. Dermatology (life), So. Med. Assn., Internat. Soc. Hair Restoration Surgery, La. State Med. Soc. (mem. pub. health com. and ins. com. 2003-06), St. Bernard Parish Med. Soc. Home: 3705 Florida Ave Kenner LA 70065-2473 Office: Gulf South Med Surg Inst 3705 Florida Ave Kenner LA 70065-2473 Office Phone: 504-471-3100.

FARBER, ISADORE E., psychologist, educator; b. St. Joseph, Mo., May 21, 1917; s. Jacob and Rose (Malkin) F.; m. Billie Frances Gulko, May 5, 1942, (dec.); children: Ronna Ellen (dec.), Deborah. Student, St. Joseph Jr. Coll., 1934-36; BA, U. Mo., 1939, MA, 1940; PhD, U. Iowa, 1946. Instr. psychology U. Rochester, 1946-47; asst. prof. to prof. psychology U. Iowa, 1947-64; vis. prof. U. Wis., 1955, Stanford, 1960; research cons. Med. Sch., U. of Okla., 1956-57; prof. psychology U. Ill., Chgo., 1964-84, prof. emeritus, 1984—, head dept. psychology, 1964-68, 76-81. Vis. prof., sr. Fulbright fellow Hebrew U., Jerusalem, 1971-72. Founding editor Jour. Exptl. Research in Personality, 1965-71; editor Psychology series, Dodd, Mead & Co., 1965-73; cons. editor Jour. Abnormal and Social Psychology, 1955-61, Jour. of Personality, 1955-61, Jour. Abnormal Psychology, 1973-79; contbr. articles to profl. jours. Served with Q.M.C. AUS, 1941-42; to 2d lt. USAAF, 1942-45. Fellow APA, Am. Psychol. Soc.; mem. Midwestern Psychol. Assn. (past pres.), Psychonomic Soc., Midwest Com. for Rational Inquiry, Phi Beta Kappa, Sigma Xi. Jewish. Home: 2601 Chestnut Ave #1303 Glenview IL 60026

FARBER, JEFFREY MARK, diversified financial services company executive; b. Perth Amboy, NJ, Apr. 7, 1964; s. Michael and Diane E. (Ellel) F.; m. Donna Marie Marshall, May 11, 1991; children: Andrew, Jordan. BS in Acctg., Lehigh U., Bethlehem, Pa., 1986; MBA in Fin., NYU, 1992. Staff acct. Deloitte Haskins & Sells, Stamford, Conn., 1986-87, Deloitte Hashm & Sells, NYC, 1987-88; sr. acct. Deloitte & Touche, NYC, 1988-91, mgr., 1991-93, sr. mgr., 1993-96, ptnr., 1996—2000; asst. contr. Bear Stearns, NYC, 2000—04, contr., prin. acctg. officer, 2004—, sr. v.p. fin., 2007—. Mem. AICPA, NY State Soc. CPA (mem. banking com.), SIA, Burning Tree Country Club. Office: Bear Stearns 383 Madison Ave New York NY 10179*

FARBER, JOHN J., chemical company executive; b. Timisoara, Rumania, Aug. 23, 1925; s. Eugene and Magda (Reiter) F.; m. Maya Kleyman, June 28, 1953; children: Sandra, Deborah, Michael, Claudia. MS, U. Cluj, Timisoara, 1948; PhD, Poly. Inst. Bklyn., 1956. Rsch. chemist Sun Chem. Co., NYC, 1951-52; cons. Soc. des Peintures et Vernis Bouvet, Tournus, France, Verneba A.G. Neuallschwill, Basel, Switzerland, Foster Grant Co., Inc., Leominster, Mass., Chemische Fabrik Kalk GmbH, Koln, Kalk, Germany, Asahi Chem. Industry Co., Ltd., Tokyo, 1953-56; chmn. bd., chief exec. officer ICC Industries, Ind., NYC; chmn. Primex Plastics Corp.; pres. Dover Chem. Corp., Ohio. Dir., chmn. Frutarom Ltd., Haifa, Israel. Mem. Am. Chem. Soc., Soc. Plastics Industry, Soc. Plastics Engrs., Nat. Petroleum Refiners Assn., Chem. Mfrs. Assn. Office: ICC Industries Inc 460 Park Ave New York NY 10022-1906

FARBER, PHILLIP ANDREW, retired biological and allied health sciences educator; b. Wilkes-Barre, Pa., Sept. 19, 1934; s. Phillip Henry and Josephine Mary (Penkala) F.; m. Larice M. Krebs; children: Michael, Steven, Phillip, Matthew. BS, King's Coll., Wilkes-Barre, 1956; MS, Boston Coll., 1958; PhD, Cath. U. Am., 1963. Asst. instr. biology dept. Georgetown U., Washington, 1962—63; rschr. biologist perinatal physiology lab. Nat. Inst. Neurol. Diseases and Blindness, NIH, Bethesda, Md., 1963—64; rsch. instr. dept. phys. medicine and rehab. NYU Med. Ctr., NYC, 1964—66; prof., premed. and med. tech. advisor Bloomsburg U., Pa., 1966—2000, prof. emeritus, 2000—. Assoc. cytogenetics dept. lab. medicine and pathology Geisinger Med. Ctr., Danville, Pa., 1967-92; commd. officer USPHS, jr. asst. officer, 1960; mem. Lab. Parasite Chemotherapy Nat. Inst. Allergy and Infectious Diseases, NIH, Bethesda. Contbr. articles to profl. jours., med. guides and encys. Summer rsch. fellow NSF, Cath. U. Am., 1962, Oak Ridge Associated Univs., 1969; USPHS rsch. grantee NYU Med. Ctr., 1965. Mem. AAAS, Am. Soc. Human Genetics, Assn. Pa. State Coll. and Univ. Ret. Faculties, Nat. Geographic Soc., Sigma Xi, Columbia-Montour Torch Club. Roman Catholic. Avocations: reading, fishing, gardening. Home: PO Box 92 Mifflinville PA 18631-0092

FARBER, ROSANN ALEXANDER, geneticist, educator; b. Charlotte, NC, Nov. 21, 1944; d. J. Wilson Jr. and June Adell (Childs) Alexander; m. Gerald Lee Farber, July 28, 1966 (div. Jan. 1969); m. Thomas Douglas Petes, July 20, 1973; children: Laura Elizabeth Petes, Diana Christine Petes. AB in Biology, Oberlin Coll., 1966; postgrad., U. Pitts., 1967-68, Albert Einstein Coll. Medicine, 1969; PhD in Genetics, U. Wash., 1973. Diplomate in clin. cytogenetics and clin. molecular genetics Am. Bd. Med. Genetics. Postdoctoral fellow Nat. Inst. for Med. Rsch., London, 1973-75; rsch. assoc. Children's Hosp. Med. Ctr., Boston, 1975-77; from asst. prof. to assoc. prof. U. Chgo., 1977-88; assoc. prof. dept. pathology and lab. medicine, program molecular biology and biotechnology, curriculum genetics and molecular biology U. N.C., Chapel Hill, 1988-97, prof., 1997—, prof. dept. genetics, 2001—, assoc. chair dept. genetics, 2007—. Mem. U. N.C. Lineberger Comprehensive Cancer Ctr., 1996—. Contbr. articles to profl. jours. NIH grantee, 1978—. Mem. AAAS, Am. Soc. Human Genetics. Achievements include research in human molecular genetics, somatic cell genetics, cancer genetics. Home: 612 Morgan Creek Rd Chapel Hill NC 27517-4928 Office: U NC CB 7525 Brinkhous-Bullitt Bldg Chapel Hill NC 27599 Office Phone: 919-966-6920. E-mail: rfarber@med.nc.edu.

FARBER, SETH C., lawyer; b. San Francisco, Jan. 2, 1964; AB summa cum laude, Harvard Univ., 1986, JD cum laude, 1989. Bar: Mass. 1989, N.Y. 1990, US Dist. Ct. (ea., so. dist. N.Y., ea. dist. Mich., Mass.), US Ct. Appeals (2d, 4th cir.) Law clk. Judge Joseph L. Tauro, US Dist. Ct. Mass.; asst. U.S. atty. so. dist. N.Y.; ptnr. litigation dept. & chmn. Pro Bono com. Dewey Ballantine LLP, NYC. Mem. Criminal Justice Act Panel, So. Dist. N.Y. Editor: Harvard Law Rev.; contbr. articles to profl. jour. Mem.: ABA (chmn. Programming subcom., Criminal Litigation com.). Office: Dewey Ballantine LLP 1301 Ave of the Americas New York NY 10019-6092 Office Phone: 212-259-7227. Office Fax: 212-259-6333. Business E-Mail: sfarber@dbllp.com.

FARBER, STEVEN GLENN, lawyer; b. Phila., July 20, 1946; s. Isadore Irving and Sylvia (Galperin) F.; children: Jamie, Daniel, Zoey, Avi. BBA, Temple U., 1968, JD, 1972. Bar: Pa. 1972, U.S. Dist. Ct. (ea. dist.) Pa. 1972, U.S. Dist. Ct. Appeals (3d cir.) 1972, N.Mex. 1975, U.S. Dist. Ct. N.Mex. 1975, U.S. Ct. Appeals (10th cir.) 1979, U.S. Supreme Ct. 1980. Asst. defender Pub. Defender Assn. Phila., 1972-74; acting dist. pub. defender State of N.Mex., Santa Fe, 1975-76, asst. atty. gen., 1976-78; pvt. practice Santa Fe, 1978—. Mem. N.Mex. Bd. Legal Specialization, 1986-90, chmn., 1991-93. Mem. Santa Fe Mcpl. Home Rule Charter Commn., 1997; bd. dirs. Ptnrs. in Edn., 1997—2002, Santa Fe County United Way, 1998—2002; elected city councilor City of Santa Fe, 1992—96; bd. dirs. Temple Beth Shalom, 1997—, v.p., 2000—01, pres., 2002—03. Mem. Nat. Assn. Criminal Def. Lawyers (vice-chmn. continuing legal edn. com. 1990-91), N.Mex. Lawyers Guild (pres. 1980-81), N.Mex. State Bar Assn. (bd. dirs. criminal law sect. 1980-83, chmn. 1981-82), N.Mex. Criminal Def. Lawyers Assn. (bd. dirs. 1991, treas. 1996), First Jud. Dist. Criminal Def. Lawyers Assn. (sec. 1999), The Hon. Oliver Seth Am. Inn Ct. (master). Democrat. Jewish. Office: PO Box 2473 323 Staab St Santa Fe NM 87504-2473 Home Phone: 505-988-1808; Office Phone: 505-988-9725. Personal E-mail: sgfsaf@aol.com, sfarberlawoffice@aol.com.

FARBER, ZULIMA V., lawyer, former state attorney general; b. El Caney, Oriente, Cuba, Sept. 21, 1944; BA, Montclair State Coll., 1968, MA, 1970; JD, Rutgers U., 1974. Bar: NJ 1974, US Supreme Ct. 1983. Asst. prosecutor Bergen County, NJ, 1975—78; asst. counsel to Gov. Brendan Byrne State of NJ, Trenton, 1978—81, pub. advocate, pub. defender Cabinet of Gov. James J. Florio, 1992—94; assoc. Lowenstein Sandler PC, Roseland, NJ, 1981—85, ptnr. litig., 1986—92, 1994—2006, 2006—; atty. gen. State of NJ, Trenton, 2006; issues mgr. Issues Mgmt., Princeton, NJ, 2007—. Mem. Com. on Criminal Rules, Com. on Evidence Rules, Com. on Character NJ State Supreme Ct., 1986—92, mem. Adv. Com. on Ethics, 1994—; mem. NJ State Adv. Com. US Commn. on Civil Rights, 1987—, chairperson, 1990—94; vis. assoc. Eagleton Inst., Rutgers U., 1994—. Contbr. articles to law jours. Trustee Fairleigh Dickinson U., 1994—; chair bd. trustees Jersey City Med. Ctr., 1982—92, 1994—96. Named one of 25 Women of Influence in NJ, NJBiz Mag., Most Influential Black Americans, Ebony mag., 2006. Fellow: Am. Bar Found.; mem.: Nat. Abortion Rights Action League, NJ Chap. (pres.). Democrat. Office: Lowenstein Sandler PC 65 Livingston Ave Roseland NJ 07068-1791*

FARBERMAN, HAROLD, conductor, composer; b. NYC, Nov. 2, 1930; s. Louis and Lena (Kramer) F.; m. Corinne Curry, June 22, 1958; children: Thea, Lewis. Diploma, Juilliard Sch. Music, 1951; BS, New England Conservatory Music, 1956, MS, 1957. Prin. guest condr. Bournemouth Sinfonietta; founder, dir. Conductors Inst., 1980—. Dir. Stokowski Conducting Competition, 1994; prof. conducting Hartt Sch. Author: The Art of Conducting Technique; percussionist, Boston Symphony Orch., 1951-63, condr., New Arts Orch., Boston, 1955-63, guest condr., Royal Philharm. Orch., London, Denver Symphony Orch., BBC Symphony, Victoria (Can.) Philharm., Miami (Fla.) Philharm., N.Y. Philharm., New Philharmonia Orch., London, Orchestre de Lille, France, Stockholm Philharm., Swedish Radio Orch., Danish Radio Orch., Malmö (Sweden) Symphony Orch., Sydney (Australia) Symphony, Melbourne (Australia) Symphony, Perth (Australia) Symphony, Brisbane (Australia) Symphony, London Smyphony Orch., English Chamber Orch., condr., Colorado Springs (Colo.) Philharm., 1967-68, music dir., condr., Oakland Symphony Orch., 1971-79, rec. artist (condr. or composer) for, Columbia, Capitol, Mercury, Vanguard, Cambridge, Serenus, Boston records, rep. U.S. in, Paris Internat. Composition Competition, 1959; Composer symphonies, string quartet, chamber music, operas, jazz.; pioneered recorded works of Charles E. Ives., Michael Haydn. Scholar Juilliard Sch. Music, 1947-51. Mem. Condrs. Guild (founder, bd. dirs. summer inst.), Nat. Assn. Composers and Condrs. Address: PO Box 543 Germantown NY 12526 Office Phone: 518-537-5955. E-mail: corkycf@aol.com.

FARBISH, ALFRED B., waterproofing materials executive; b. Phila., Sept. 18, 1923; s. Sidney Almeyer and Rachel Bucks Farbish; m. Rita Fayer, Oct. 11, 1951 (dec. July 1995); children: Michael Bucks, Peter Bertram. Student, Oxford U., Eng., 1945; BA, U. Pa., 1948. Civil engr. Corps of Engrs., Phila., 1956-59; quality control Barrett divsn. Allied Chem., NYC, 1959-65; sales mgr. Am. Cyanamid, Wakefield, Mass., 1965-71; pres., owner Rubber & Plastics Corp., Long Island City, NY, 1972-89, Nervastral, Inc., Greenwich, Conn., 1989—. Patentee in field. 1st lt. arty. U.S. Army, 1948-53; lt. col. Corp. Engrs. USAR ret., 1983. Republican. Avocations: rowing, fencing. Home: 351 Pemberwick Rd Apt 916 Greenwich CT 06831 Office: Nervastral Inc 100 Melrose Ave Ste 206 Greenwich CT 06830 E-mail: nrvstrl@aol.com.

FARCI, PATRIZIA, medical educator, researcher; b. Villasimius, Italy, Feb. 2, 1954; came to U.S., 1989; d. Miniato and Eleonora (Scuda) F.; m. Paolo Lusso; 1 child, Emanuele. MD, U. Cagliari, Italy, 1979, cert. infectious diseases, 1983, cert. gastroenterology, 1987. Intern in internal medicine U. Cagliari, 1979-83, asst. prof., 1984-92, head hepatology sect., 1985—, assoc. prof. medicine, 1992—2000, prof. medicine, 2000—. Vis. scientist Free Hosp., London, 1983-85, Lab. of Infectious Diseases/NIAID/NIH, Bethesda, Md., 1989-96; adj. investigator LID/NIAID/NIH, Bethesda, 1997—. Contbr. more than 145 articles to profl. jours. Mem. Am. Assn. for the Study of Liver Diseases. Roman Catholic. Avocations: music, reading, travel. Office: LID NIAID/NIH Bldg 50 Rm 6531 9000 Rockville Pike Bethesda MD 20892-0001 also: Dept Med Scis U Cagliari ss 554 Bivio Sestu 09042 Cagliari Italy Fax: +39-070-510064. E-mail: farcip@pacs.unica.it.

FARDONE, GUY, communications executive; b. 1969; BA, Villanova U. Exec. v.p. & gen. mgr. ATX Comm., Inc., King of Prussia, Pa., 1990—, founder ATX Network Svcs. divsn., 1996, founder ATX Frontline, 2004. Recipient 40 Under 40 award, Phila. Bus. Jour., 2006. Office: ATX Communications Inc 2100 Renaissance Blvd King Of Prussia PA 19406

FARELL, DAN, utilities executive; B in Acctg. and Fin., East Tex. State U.; grad. advanced mgmt. program, Harvard U. CPA Tex. Treas., sec. TU Electric and TU Svcs. subsidiaries Tex. Utilities Co., v.p. TU Electric and TU Svcs. subsidiaries, 1991, chief acctg. officer, 1994, CFO TU Electric subsidiary, 1994, chmn. Ea. Energy, 1995; mng. dir. TXU Australia, 1995, pres. distbn. divsn. Oncor, 2000; pres. TXU Gas, 2002; CFO, exec. v.p. TXU Corp., Dallas, 2003; sr. v.p., PFO TXU Electric Delivery, Dallas, 2004—. Bd. dirs. Victorian Power Exch., Australia, So. Gas Assn., Assn. Tex. Intrastate Natural Gas Pipelines, Energy Reliability Coun. Tex., Leadership Coun. Am. Gas Assn., North Tex. Commn. Dir. North Tex. Commn. United Way; bd. dirs. United Way Met. Dallas; trustee First Bapt. Acad. Mem.: AICPA, Fin. Execs. Inst., Tex. Soc. CPA. Office: TXU Electric Delivery 500 N Akard St Dallas TX 75201-3411 Office Phone: 214-812-4600.

FARENTHOLD, FRANCES TARLTON, lawyer; b. Corpus Christi, Tex., Oct. 2, 1926; d. Benjamin Dudley and Catherine (Bluntzer) Tarlton; children: Dudley Tarlton, George Edward, Emilie, James Dougherty, Vincent Bluntzer (dec.). AB, Vassar Coll., 1946; JD, U. Tex., 1949; LLD, Hood Coll., 1973, Boston U., 1973, Regis Coll., 1976, Lake Erie Coll., 1979, Elmira Coll., 1981, Coll. Santa Fe, 1985. Bar: Tex. 1949. Pvt. practice, 1949-65, 67-76, 80—; mem. Tex. Ho. of Reps., 1968-72; dir. legal aid Nueces County, 1965-67; pres. Wells Coll., Aurora, NY, 1976-80; asst. prof. law Tex. So. U., Houston, Thurgood Marshall disting. vis. prof., 1994-95. Lawyer; b. Corpus Christi, Tex., Oct. 2, 1926; d. Benjamin Dudley and Catherine (Bluntzer) Tarlton; children: Dudley Tarlton, George Edward, Emilie, James Dougherty, Vincent Bluntzer (dec.). AB, Vassar Coll., 1946; JD, U. Tex., 1949; LLD, Hood Coll., 1973, Boston U., 1973, Regis Coll., 1976, Lake Erie Coll., 1979, Elmira Coll., 1981, Coll. of Santa Fe, 1985. Bar: Tex. 1949. Pvt. practice, 1949-65, 67-76, 80—; mem. Tex. Ho. of Reps., 1968-72; dir. legal aide Nueces County, 1965-67; asst. prof. law Tex. So. U., Houston; pres. Wells Coll., Aurora, N.Y., 1976-80; disting. vis. prof. Thurgood Marshall Tex. So. U., Houston, 1994-95. Mem. Human Relations Com., Corpus Christi, 1963-68, Corpus Christi Citizen's Com. Community Improvement, 1966-68; mem. Tex. adv. com. to U.S. Commn. on Civil Rights, 1968-76; mem. nat. adv. council ACLU; mem. Orgn. for Preservation Unblemished Shoreline, 1964—; Dem. candidate for Gov. of Tex., 1972; del. Dem. Nat. Conv., 1972, 1st woman nominated to be candidate v.p. U.S., 1972; nat. co-chmn. Citizens to Elect McGovern-Shriver, 1972; chmn. Nat. Women's Polit. Caucus, 1973-75; mem. Dem. platform com., 1988; trustee Vassar Coll., 1975-83; bd. dirs. Fund for Constl. Govt., Ctr. for Devel. Policy, 1983— , Mexican Am. Legal Def. and Ednl. Fund, 1980-83; chmn. Inst. for Policy Studies, 1986-91; mem. bd. dirs. Rothko Chapel, 1997—. Recipient Lyndon B. Johnson Woman of Year award, 1973. Mem. State Bar Tex. Mem. Human Rels. Com., Corpus Christi, 1963-68, Corpus Christi Citizens Com. Cmty. Improvement, 1966-68; mem. Tex. adv. com. to U.S. Commn. on Civil Rights, 1968-76; mem. nat. adv. coun. ACLU; mem. Orgn. for Preservation Unblemished Shoreline, 1964—; Dem. candidate for Gov. of Tex., 1972; del. Dem. Nat. Conv., 1972, 1st woman nominated to be candidate v.p. U.S., 1972; nat. co-chair Citizens to elect McGovern-Shriver, 1972; chmn. Nat. Women's Polit. Caucus, 1973-75; mem. Dem. Platform Com., 1988; trustee Vassar Coll., 1975-83; bd. dirs. Fund for Constl. Govt., Ctr. for Devel. Policy, 1983—, Mexican Am. Legal Def. and Ednl. Fund, 198--83; chmn. Inst. for Policy Studies, 1986-91; bd. dirs. Rothko Chapel, 1997—, chmn., 2001—. Recipient Lyndon B. Johnson Woman of Yr. award, 1973, Lifetime Svc. award, Dem. Party of Tex., 1998. Mem. State Bar Tex. Home: 2929 Buffalo Speedway Apt 1813 Houston TX 77098-1710

FARGIS, PAUL MCKENNA, publisher, publishing executive, consultant, book developer; b. NYC, Mar. 19, 1939; s. George Bertrand and Elizabeth Harlin (McKenna) F.; m. Elizabeth Hackett, Aug. 22, 1964; children: John Hackett, Alison Katherine; m. Dawn Sangrey, Apr. 23, 1977; 1 child, Christopher Sangrey. Student, Cath. U. Am., 1958; B of Social Sci., Fairfield U., 1961; MA (Publ. Tuition scholar), NYU, 1962. Editorial asst. Prentice-Hall, Inc., Englewood Cliffs, NJ, 1961-62; editor Hawthorn Books, Inc., NYC, 1963-67, v.p., editorial dir., 1967-71; v.p., editor-in-chief Thomas Y. Crowell Co. and Funk & Wagnalls divs. Dun-Donnelley Pub. Corp., NYC, 1971-77; editor-in-chief Apollo Books, NYC, 1972-77; mng. dir. Thomas Y. Crowell divs. Harper and Row, NYC, 1977-78; founder, pres. and pub. The Stonesong Press, Inc., 1978—2003. Dir., sec. Round Stone Press, Inc., 1990-2001; pub. Grand Ctrl. Press, 2001-2003; mem. adv. bd. Grad. Sch. Corp. and Polit. Comm., Fairfield U., 1969-81; pub. arbitrator Am. Arbitration Assn., 1982-2002; pub. seminar lectr. Author: The Consumer's Handbook, 1966, rev. edit., 1974, Company's Coming, 1965; Am. editor: Twentieth Century Ency. Catholicism, 1963-67; editor-in-chief: The New York Public Library Desk Reference, 1989; co-author: Perks and Parachutes, 1997; co-editor: The Big Book of Life's Instructions, 1995; contbr. articles to profl. jour.; patentee in field. Exec. dir. Harrison (NY) Town Recreation Commn., 1970-72; dir. Harrison Town Forum, 1969-73; former bd. dir. US Cath. Hist. Soc.; former trustee Unitarian Universalist Fellowship of No. Westchester; mem. Katonah Bedford Hills Vol. Ambulance Corps. Mem. Am. Book Coun. (bd. dir. 1987-88), Am. Book Producers Assn. (pres. 1986-87, bd. dir. Charitable Book program 1987-89), Book Industry Study Group, Appalachian Mountain Club. Unitarian Universalist. Avocations: carpentry, stonework, travel, hiking, sculpture. Office: 27 W 24th St New York NY 10010

FARGO, HEATHER, mayor; b. Oakland, Ca., Dec. 12, 1952; m. Alan Moll. BS in Environ. Planning and Mgmt., U. Cal. Davis, 1975; attended, Revenue Sources Mgmt. Sch., Boulder, 1981, Kennedy Sch. Govt., Harvard U., 1991. Bd. mem. Environ. Council of Sacramento, 1983—89; mem. Sacramento City Coun., 1989—98; mayor City of Sacramento, Calif., 2001—. Chair bd. dirs. Sacramento Area Flood Control Agy.; bd. dirs. Sacramento Area Council Govt., Sacramento Area Commerce and Trade Org. Office: City Hall 5th Fl 915 I St Sacramento CA 95814 Business E-Mail: hfargo@cityofsacramento.org.*

FARGO, THOMAS BOULTON, retired career military officer; b. San Diego, 1948; Grad., U.S. Naval Acad., 1970. Commd. ensign USN, 1970, advanced through ranks to adm.; various assignments to comd. U.S. Naval Forces, Cen. Command/Comdr., U.S. Fifth Fleet; dep. chief of naval opers., comdr. U.S. Pacific Fleet; comdr. U.S. Pacific Command, Honolulu, 2002—05. Decorated Disting. Svc. medal (4 times), Def. Superior Svc. medal, Legion of Merit (3 times), others; recipient James Bond Stockdale award for Inspirational Leadership, 1989.

FARHA, TODD S., health products executive; b. Wichita, Kans. BA magna cum laude econ., Trinity Univ., 1990; MBA with distinction, Harvard Univ. Bus. Sch., 1995. With Physician Corp. Am.; CEO Oxford Specialty Mgmt., Best Doctors; pres., CEO Wellcare Health Plans Inc., Tampa, Fla., 2002—06, chmn., pres., CEO, 2006—. Mem. mgmt. adv. bd. Towerbrook Capital Partners LP. Trustee Tampa Mus. Art; mem. Fla. Arts Council. Mem.: Phi Beta Kappa.*

FARHADI, ASHKAN, physician, researcher, writer; b. Shiraz, Iran, Mar. 5, 1965; arrived in US, 2000, permanent resident; s. Gholam Ali Farhadi and Sadat Eyni; m. Ziba Ranjbaran, June 20, 1990; children: Arghavan, Nilgoun. Med. Diploma, Shiraz U., Iran, 1989; Internal Medicine Splty., Shiraz U., 1992; Gastroenterology subspeciality, Beheshti (Nat.) U.,

Tehran, Iran, 1994; M in clin. rsch., Rush U., 2001—03; Internal Medicine Splty., Rush U., Ill., 2003—04, Gastroenterology, 2004—06. Lic. MD Ill. Regulation dept., 2002, Iran Med. Assn., 1989. Asst. prof. medicine Beheshti (Nat.) U., Tehran, 1992—94, Mazandaran U., Iran, 1994—99, chmn. dept. medicine, 1998—99; rsch. fellow Rush U., Chgo., 2000—, asst. prof. medicine, physiology and molecular biophysics, 2006—. Author: (book) Irritable Bowel Syndrome, Peptic Ulcer, I Have IBS.Now What?!!!. Recipient Presdl. award, Am. Coll. of Gastroenterology, 2002, Sr. Fellow award, 2002, Third Pl. in the Bd. of Gastroenterology, Mister of Health and Sciences, Iran, 1994, First Pl. in the Bd. of Internal Medicine, 1992, Best Young Investigator, The Iranian Med. Assn., 1990; Award for Rsch., Am. Coll. of Gastroenterology, 2001. Fellow: Am. Coll. Gastroenterology; mem.: Am. Gastroenterological Assn., Sigma Xi. Achievements include invention of creeping colonoscope; automated hot biopsy needle and device; sanitizing container and display; Farhadi's cell culture plate; Farhadi's cell container. Avocation: photography. Office: Rush Medical Coll 1725 W Harrison St Ste 206 Chicago IL 60612 Office Phone: 312-942-5861. Business E-Mail: ashkan_farhadi@rush.edu.

FARHANG, ALI J., lawyer; b. 1971; BA, U. Ariz., 1993; JD, U. Denver, 1997. Tucson atty. rep. US Dist. Ct.; atty. Fennemore Craig Law Firm. Mem., Fed. Bar Tech. Com. Dist. Ariz.; chmn., Fall Employment Seminar Ariz. State Bar, 2005—06. Student mentor U. Ariz. Law Coll.; bd. mem. Metro. YMCA; mem. Fiesta Bowl Com. Named one of 40 Under 40, Tucson Bus. Edge, 2006. Mem.: Iranian Assn. of Tucson (bd. mem.), State Bar of Ariz. (Exec. Coun., Labor and Employment Sect., chair, Employment and Labor Law Continuing Legal Edn. Sect.), Pima County Bar Assn., State Bar of Colo., Young Lawyers Divsn., Ariz. Def. Lawyers Assn., Ariz. Minority Bar Assn., Morris K. Udall Inn of Ct. Office: Fennemore Craig One S Church Ave Ste 1000 Tucson AZ 85707 Office Phone: 520-879-6402. Office Fax: 520-879-6884.

FARHI, JANE-IRIS, cardiologist, internist; b. NYC, May 8, 1953; d. Jean Pierre and Carol F.; m. James Barron. BA summa cum laude, Columbia U., 1977; MD, Harvard U., 1981. Diplomate Am. Bd. Internat. Medicine, Am. Bd. Cardiovascular Disease. Resident in internal medicine Mt. Sinai Med. Ctr., NYC, 1981-84, fellow in cardiology, 1984-86; asst. attending in medicine St. Luke's-Roosevelt Hosp., NYC, 1986-95; clin. asst. in medicine Mt. Sinai Hosp., NYC, 1986-95; pvt. practice intensive cardiology NYC, 1986—; med. dir. Cardiothoracic Surgery Unit, Lenox Hill Hosp., NYC, 1995—. Contbr. articles to med. jours. With Israeli Army, 1971-73. Mem. Am. Coll. Cardiology, Phi Beta Kappa. Office: 1075 Park Ave New York NY 10128-1003

FARIA, ME'SHELL ANITA, special education educator; b. Sanleandro, Calif. d. Frank Faria and Barbara J. Diaz; 1 child, Stephanie Michelle Faria-Jackson. AA in Psychology and Gen. Edn., Coll. Alameda, Calif., 1995. Spl. edn. tchrs. aide Oakland Unified Sch. Dist., Calif., 1992—2007, Berkeley Unified Sch. Dist., Calif., 2006—. Adv. for children with disabilities, Calif., 1987—. Contbr. poetry to lit. publs.; open microphone poet:. Scholar, Coll. Arts and Crafts, 2006—07. Achievements include development of teaching other means of communicating.

FARIAS, BRIAN K., music educator; b. Somerville, NJ, Aug. 19, 1962; s. Arthur E. and Shirley M. Farias. MusB in Edn. cum laude, Boston Conservatory Music, 1984; M in Clarinet Performance, New Eng. Conservatory, 1989; postgrad., Rutgers U., 2002—. Cert. music tchr. N.J., 1984, Pa., 1992, Md., 1998, music tchr.comprehensive grades K-12 Mass., 1984. Music tchr. Sayreville Pub. Schs., Parlin, NJ, 1985—86; band dir. Harvard (Mass.) Pub. Schs., 1989—89, Middlesex (N.J.) H.S., 1990—91, Emmaus (Pa.) H.S., 1991—93, Thomas Pullen Arts Magnet Sch., Landover, Md., 1998—2001; music tchr. Lyndhurst (N.J.) Pub. Schs., 2001—02; band/jazz band dir. Rosa Parks Performing Arts HS, Paterson, NJ, 2002—05. Guest soloist Nutley (N.J.) Symphony Orch., 1983; dir. Best Feet Forward-Holistic Practice, Newton, NJ, 1998—; holistic health practitioner and educator Best Feet Forward, 1999—; healer with music, reflexology, hypnosis and past-life regression, aromatherapy; pvt. lesson instr. Cmty. Conservatory, 1994—97, DeVoe's Music, 1997—98, Calderone Sch. Music, 2000—02, Newton, NJ. Named Competition Winner, Garden State Arts Ctr., 1980, Compeition Winner, Livingston Symphony Orch., 1984, Competiton Winner, Rutgers U., 1990; Performance scholar, Rutgers U. Orch., 2002. Mem.: N.J.-Internat. Assn. for Jazz Edn. (assoc.; pres. N.J. region 1 2002), Nat. Band Assn. (assoc.), Internat. Clarinet Soc. (assoc.), Music Educators Nat. Conf. (assoc.). Achievements include development of Rosa Parks Percussion Ensemble; Louis Armstrong Jazz Award-Rosa Parks HS; John Philip Sousa Band Award-Rosa Parks HS; 1st Place Awards-Music in the Parks for Band-Rosa Parks HS; 1st Place -Music in the Parks for Jazz Band-Rosa Parks HS; Silver Award for Band-NBA Festival, Rosa Parks HS; Best Rhythm, Trombone, soloist-NJ-IAJE Jazz Festival-Rosa Parks HS; NJ State Teen Arts Festival Participant-Rosa Parks HS; 1st Place-Music in the Parks for ELEM Chorus-Lyndhurst Public Schools. Home Phone: 973-383-9658; Office Phone: 973-383-9438. Personal E-mail: healingmusicman@aol.com.

FARIAS-EISNER, ROBIN P., gynecologic oncologist, educator; b. Orleans, France, Nov. 27, 1953; MD, Royal Coll. Physicians and Surgeons Ireland, 1981. Cert. Obstetrics, Gynecology, Emergency Medicine, Gynecologic Oncology. Intern, transitional Mercy Hosp. and Med. Ctr., 1982—83; resident, emergency medicine U. Ill., 1983—85; resident, obstetrics & gynecology David Geffen Sch. Medicine, UCLA, 1986—90, fellow,gynecologic oncology, 1990—92, asst. prof., obstetrics & gynecology, 1992, chief, gynecologic oncology, prof., obstetrics & gynecology, assoc. dir., Jonsson Comprehensive Cancer Ctr. Women's Cancers Program Area; physician, general gynecology practice UCLA Med. Ctr.; asst. prof., obstetrics & gynecology Olive-View Med. Ctr., Sylmar, Calif., 1992. Contbr. articles tp profl. jours. Office: UCLA Jonsson Comprehensive Cancer Ctr 8-864 Factor Bldg Box 951781 Los Angeles CA 90095-1781 Office Phone: 310-206-4619, 310-794-7274. Business E-Mail: rfeisner@obgyn.medsch.ucla.edu.*

FARICY, JOHN HARTNETT, JR., lawyer; b. Augsburg, Germany, Nov. 5, 1955; came to U.S., 1956; s. John Hartnett and Mary Helen Sarah (Bowe) F. BA, Tulane U., 1977; JD, William Mitchell Coll. Law, St. Paul, 1982. Bar: Minn. 1982, U.S. Dist. Ct. Minn. 1983, U.S. Ct. Appeals (2d cir.) 1987, U.S. Supreme Ct. 1988. Ptnr. Faricy & Roen, P.A., Mpls., 1996—. Mem. Univ. Club of St. Paul.

FARINA, DENNIS, actor; b. Chgo., Feb. 29, 1944; m. Patricia Farina (div.); children: Dennis Jr., Michael, Joseph. Former policeman Chgo. Police Dept. Actor: (films) Thief, 1981, Code of Silence, 1985, Jo Jo Dancer, Your Life is Calling, 1986, Manhunter, 1986, Midnight Run, 1988, Open Admissions, 1988, Blind Faith, 1990, People Like Us, 1990, Men of Respect, 1991, We're Talking Serious Money Now, 1991, Street Crimes, 1992, Mac, 1992, Another Stakeout, 1993, Romeon Is Bleeding, 1993, Striking Distance, 1993, Little Big League, 1994, Get Shorty, 1995, Eddie, 1996, That Old Feeling, 1996, Out of Sight, 1998, Saving Private Ryan, 1998, Buddy Faro, 1998, The Mod Squad, 1999, Reindeer Games, 2000, Snatch, 2000, Preston Tylk, 2000, Sidewalks of NY, 2001, Big Trouble, 2002, Stealing Harvard, 2002, Paparazzi, 2004; (TV movies) Through Naked Eyes, 1983, Hard Knox, 1984, The Killing Floor, 1985, Final Jeopardy, 1985, The Birthday Boy, 1986, Triplecross, 1986, Six Against the Rock, 1987, Open Admissions, 1988, The Case of the Hillside Strangler, 1989, Blind Faith, 1990, People Like Us, 1990, Drug Wars: The Cocaine Cartel, 1992, Cruel Doubt, 1992, The Disappearance of Nora, 1993, A Stranger in the Mirror, 1993, One Woman's Courage, 1994, The Corpse Had a Familiar Face, 1994, Out of Annie's Past, 1995, Bonanza: Under Attack, 1995, Perfect Crimes, 1995, Empire Falls, 2004; (TV mini-series) Bella Maffia, 1997; (TV series) Crime Story, 1986-88, In-Laws, 2002-03, Law and Order, 2004-06; (TV appearances) Miami Vice, 1984, 85, 89, Hardcastle and McCormick, 1985, Hunter, 1985, Remington Steele, 1985, Lady Blue, 1986, China Beach, 1989, Tales from the Crypt, 1992, Justice League (voice only), 2005, Law & Order: Trial by Jury, 2005; actor, prodr. (TV series) Buddy Faro, 1998 Office: Geddes Agy 1633 N Halsted St Ste 400 Chicago IL 60614-5517

FARINA, JOHN, lawyer; b. Rockville Center, NY, Oct. 20, 1959; s. Joseph P. Farina and Marilyn A. Echkoff; m. Julia Pressly, May 30, 1987; children: Matthew, Timothy, Nicholas. BA, Villanova U., 1981; JD, Suffolk U., 1985. Bar: Mass. 1985, Fla. 1986. Law clk. U.S. Ct. Appeals (4th dist.), West Palm Beach, Fla., 1985-86; assoc. Winthrop Stimson Putnam & Roberts, Palm Beach, Fla., 1986-90, Edwards & Angell, Palm Beach, 1990-94; ptnr. Boyes & Farina, West Palm Beach, 1994—. Mem. Fla. Probate Rules Com., Fla. Bar Greivance Com., 1998—. Mem. Palm Beach County Bar Assn. Avocations: trap and skeet shooting, running, tennis. Home: 131 Thornton Dr Palm Beach Gardens FL 33418-8089 Office: Boyes & Farina PA 3300 PGA Blvd Ste 900 Palm Beach Gardens FL 33410 Office Phone: 561-694-7979.

FARINELLI, JEAN L., management consultant; b. Phila., July 26, 1946; d. Albert J. and Edith M. (Falini) F. BA, Am. U., Washington, 1968; MA, Ohio State U., Columbus, 1969. Asst. pub. relations dir. Dow Jones & Co., Inc., NYC, 1969-71; account exec. Carl Byoir & Assocs., Inc., NYC, 1972-74, v.p., 1974-80, sr. v.p., 1980-82; pres. Tracy-Locke/BBDO Pub. Relations, Dallas, 1982-87, Creamer Dickson Basford, Inc., NYC, 1987-88, chmn., chief exec. officer, 1988-98; pres., chief exec. officer Eurocom Corp. & PR (U.S.), 1991, Corp. Graphics, Inc., 1992; pres. Farinelli Cons. Group, LLC, 1999—, 20 Sutton Pl. South, Inc., 2003—. Dir. The Cologne Life Reinsurance Co., 1997-99. Recipient PR CaseBook, PR Reporter, N.H., 1984, Silver Spur, Tex. Pub. Rels. Assn., Dallas, 1985, Matrix award Women in Comms., 1993. Mem.: Nat. Found. for Infectious Diseases (former trustee), Arthur W. Page Soc. (treas., v.p. adminstrn. and fin.), Internat. Pub. Rels. Assn. (pub. rels. seminar), Nat. Investor Rels. Inst., The Women's Forum (bd. dirs.), Women in Comms. (chmn. 1995, dir. 1999—, Matrix award 1993), Pub. Rels. Soc. Am. (Silver Anvil awards chmn. 1987, acad. exec. bd. 1990—91, trustee found., Silver Anvil award 1980—81, 1985, Excalibur award Houston chpt. 1985, Best of Show Silver Anvil award 1998). Office: 20 Sutton Pl S New York NY 10022-4165

FARINO, JULIAN, television director, film director, television producer; b. London; m. Branka Katic; children: Louis, Joe. Attended, Cambridge Univ. Dir.: (documentaries) One of the Girls, The Gift, Savage Skies, 1996, 7 Up 2000, 2000; (TV series) In Suspicious Circumstances, 1994, Out of the Blue, 1995, Wokenwell, 1997, Sex and the City, 1998, Bob & Rose, 2000, Flesh and Blood, 2002, Rome, 2005; (TV miniseries) Our Mutual Friend, 1998; (TV films) The Last Yellow, 1999, Byron, 2003; dir., prodr.: (TV series) Entourage, 2004 (Producers Guild award, 2006). Mailing: Home Box Office Entourage 1100 Ave of the Americas New York NY 10036

FARIS, GEORGE N., management consultant; b. Juddaya, Lebanon, Mar. 1, 1941; arrived in U.S., 1958; s. Naim George Faris and Emilie Saadi; m. Claude Moujes, Dec. 12, 1969; children: Ron, Danielle. BSc, Miss. State U., 1961, MSME, 1963; PhD in Mech. Engring., Purdue U., West Lafayette, Ind., 1968. Sr. engr. IBM, 1968—69; chmn., CEO Donbar Devel. Corp., 1969—73, ICAT, Inc., 1973—81; chmn. Am. Internat. Refinery, 1988—2000; mng. dir. Medshipping Estruet Petroleum, Ltd., 1997—2001; chmn., CEO Am. Internat. Petroleum Corp., 1981—2002; chmn. Faris Group, Inc., 2002—. Contbr. articles to profl. jours. Adv. coun. chmn. Georgetown U. Sch. Bus.; adv. coun. Harvard U. Kennedy Sch. Govt.; corp. mem. Coun. on Fgn. Rels.; chmn. internat. adv. bd. Lebanese Am. U., 2004—; chmn. fin. com. Rep. Abroad, 1990—92; pres. Gillian Assn., Greenwich, Conn.; bd. trustees Lebanese Am. U.; pres. bd. 570 Park Ave. Apts., NYC. Recipient Ellis Island Medal of Honor, 2002. Mem.: AAAS, N.Y. Acad. Sci., Palm Beach Yacht Club, Beach Club, Doubles Club, Met. Club, Univ. Club. Republican. Roman Catholic. Achievements include patents for rotary head exchange. Avocations: reading, tennis, swimming, exercise. Home: 570 Park Ave New York NY 10021 Office Phone: 646-660-9614. Business E-Mail: gfaris@farisgroup.com.

FARIS, JAMES VANNOY, cardiologist, educator, health facility administrator; b. Indpls., July 18, 1943; s. Vannoy and Maudeline (Freeman) F.; m. Jacqueline Claire Bexell, July 1, 1978; children: Nathan James, Jamie Lynn, Jenna Claire, Brittany Jean, James Vannoy III, Janessa Marie. AB, Ind. U., 1965, MD, 1968. Diplomate Am. Bd. Internal Medicine, Am. Bd. Cardiology, Am. Bd. Interventional Cardiology. Intern, resident Ind. U. Med. Ctr., Indpls., 1968-71, asst. prof. medicine, 1976-80, assoc. prof. medicine, radiology, 1980-99; chief of staff Richard L. Roudebush VA Med. Ctr., Indpls., 1983-95, chief sect. cardiology, 1995-99; clin. assoc. prof. medicine, med. scis. program Ind. U., Bloomington, 1999—, asst. dean Sch. Medicine, 1983—95; chief med. svc. Bloomington Hosp. and Healthcare Sys., 2005, chief of staff, 2006—. Maj. U.S. Army, 1971-73, Vietnam. Grantee Ind. Heart Assn., VA Cooperative Study, 1999-2000. Fellow Am. Coll. Cardiology; mem. AMA, Ind. State Med. Assn. (parliamentarian), Indpls. Med. Soc. (pres. 1998-99), Monroe Owen County Med. Soc. (pres. 2003), Alpha Omega Alpha, Alpha Epsilon Delta. Republican. Methodist. Avocations: skiing, tennis, water-skiing. Home Phone: 812-334-4185; Office Phone: 812-331-3402. Business E-Mail: jfaris@ima-md.com.

FARISH, WILLIAM S., former ambassador, horse breeder; m. Sarah Farish. Student, U. Va. Stockbroker Underwood, Neuhaus and Co., Houston; pres. Navarro Exploration Co.; founding dir. Eurus, Inc., Capital Nat. Bank, Houston; pres. W.S. Farish and Co., Houston; owner Lane's End Farm, Versailles, Ky., 1980—; U.S. amb. to U.K. U.S. Dept. State, London, 2001—04. Chmn. Churchill Downs Inc., 1992—2001. Past organizing mem. Houston chpt. Nat. Urban League; chmn. Houston Parks Bd. Office: Lane's End Farm PO Box 626 Versailles KY 40383

FARISON, JAMES BLAIR, electrical engineer, biomedical engineer, educator; b. McClure, Ohio, May 26, 1938; s. Blair Albert and Marie Lucille (Ballard) F.; m. Gail Donahue, Mar. 30, 1961; children: Jeffrey James, Mark Donahue. BS summa cum laude in Elec. Engring, U. Toledo, 1960; MS, Stanford U., 1961, PhD, 1964. Registered profl. engr., Tex., Ohio. Asst. prof. elec. engring. U. Toledo, 1964-67, assoc. prof., 1967-74, prof., 1974-95, asst. dean engring., 1969-71, dean engring., 1971-80, prof. elec. engring. and computer sci., 1995-98, prof. bioengring., 1996-98, prof. dean emeritus; prof., chmn. dept. engring. Baylor U., Waco, Tex., 1998—2005, prof., chmn. dept. elec. and computer engring., 2005—07, prof., 2007—. Adj. prof. Med. Coll. Ohio, 1987-98 Contbr. articles to various profl. jours. Recipient Outstanding Young Man of 1971 award Toledo Jr. C. of C., 1972, Boss of Year award Limestone chpt. Am. Bus. Women's Assn., 1973, Toledo's Engr. Yr. award, 1984, Outstanding Tchr. award U. Toledo, 1986; named Disting. Alumnus, U. Toledo, 1983. Fellow Ohio Acad. Sci. (Centennial honoree 1991), Am. Soc. Engring. Edn. (vice chair, program chair, 2002-05, chair 2005-07, multidisciplinary engring. divsn., accreditation activities com. 2005—, Outstanding Campus Rep. 2003); mem. IEEE (sr. mem., Toledo Elec. Engr. of Yr. 1972, 74, 76), NSPE, Ohio Soc. Profl. Engrs. (Young Engr. of Yr. 1973, Citation 1983, Outstanding Engring. Educator 1984), Toledo Soc. Profl. Engrs. (Young Engr. of Yr. 1973), Accreditation Bd. for Engring. and Tech. (program evaluator 1996-2001, 05, engring. accreditation commn. 2006—), Biomed. Engring. Soc., Soc. Mfg. Engrs. (sr.), Internat. Soc. Optical Engring., Tex. Soc. Profl. Engrs., Soc. Woman Engrs. (sr.), Nat. Soc. Black Engrs., Blue Key, Sigma Xi, Tau Beta Pi, Pi Mu Epsilon, Phi Kappa Phi, Eta Kappa Nu (Outstanding Young Elec. Engr. 1971). Home: 9613 Old Farm Rd Waco TX 76712-6402 Office: Baylor U One Bear Pl # 97356 Waco TX 76798-7356 Business E-Mail: Jim_Farison@baylor.edu.

FARISS, BRUCE LINDSAY, endocrinologist, consultant; b. Allisonia, Va., July 22, 1934; s. Alven Pierce and Hetty Jo (Lindsay) Fariss; m. Cheryl Louise Tomasie, Jan. 18, 1975; children: Bruce Lindsay, Melissa, Margaret, Susan, Henry, Sarah Jane, Carline, Adam. BS, Roanoke Coll., 1957; MD, U. Va., 1961. Diplomate Am. Bd. Internal Medicine, Am. Bd. Endocrinology. Med. intern U. Va. Hosp., Charlottesville, 1961-62; commd. capt. M.C. U.S. Army, 1962, advanced through grades to col., 1976; gen. med. officer Ft. Monroe, Va., 1962-63; resident in internal medicine Brooke Gen. Hosp., Ft. Sam Houston, Tex., 1963-66; fellow in endocrinology U. Calif., San Francisco, 1966-68; chief endocrine service Madigan Gen. Hosp., Tacoma, 1968-71, chief clin. rsch. svc., 1968-76, asst. chief dept. medicine, 1972-73, dir. endocrine fellowship program, 1971-76, chief dept. clin. investigation, 1979-85, dir. endocrine-metabolism fellowship tng. program, 1979-85; cons. internal medicine MEDCOM Europe, 1976-79; cons. endocrinology to surgeon gen. U.S. Army, 1979-85; with dept. biology Va. Poly. Inst., Blacksburg, 1987-99; sec., treas. Radford Cmty. Hosp., 1998—2000, vice chmn., 2000—02, chmn., 2002—04, chmn. dept. M & D, 2005—06; clin. assoc. prof. Va. Coll. Osteo. Medicine, Blacksburg, 2006—. Contbr. articles to profl. jours. Mem. bd. suprs. Pulaski County, Va., 1988—2004, mem. recreation com. Va., 1989—93, mem. planning commn. Va., 1992—94, vice chmn. Va., 2000—04. Decorated Legion of Merit with oak leaf cluster; recipient Meritorious Svc. award, Office Surgeon Gen. Army, 1977, Roanoke Coll. medal, 1982. Fellow: ACP, Am. Coll. Endocrinology; mem.: Am. Assn. Clin. Endocrinologists, NY Acad. Sci., So. Med. Assn., Am. Diabetes Assn. (trustee 1986—89), Endocrine Soc. (ednl. com. 1980—83), Am. Fedn. Clin. Rsch., S.W. Va. Med. Soc., Alpha Omega Alpha. Office Phone: 540-674-5900.

FARKAS, CAROL GARNER, nurse, administrator; b. NYC, Apr. 26, 1936; d. Charles Harry and Phyllis (Levine) Schotland; m. Theodore Arthur Garner, 1956 (dec. 1971); children: Charles Hugh Farkas Garner, Judi Beth Garner Farkas, Andrea Lee Garner Farkas Krupen; m. Robin Lewis Farkas, Oct. 17, 1972; adopted children: Bradford Lewis Farkas, Andrew Lawrence Farkas. BSN with distinction, Cornell U., Ithaca, NY, 1976; MPH, Columbia U., NYC, 1980. Nursing dir. Am. Inst. Life Threatening Illness and Loss Columbia Presbyn. Med. Ctr., NYC, 1980—. Del. White House Conf. Aging, NY State Gov.'s Conf. Aging; mem. NY State Hospice Adv. Group, 1979-81; mem. adv. com. office health mgmt. NY State Dept. Health, 1979-81; mem. select com. financing and licensure, com. legis. edn. Nat. Hospice Orgn., 1980—; vol. adminstr., practitioner in symptom control psychiatry dept. Meml. Sloan-Kettering Cancer Ctr., NYC, 1981-96; mem. Choice in Dying, 1991-92, Nat. Coun. Death and Dying, 1990-91, Soc. Right to Die, 1982-90; co-chair med. student conf. nursing com. Columbia Presbyn., NYC, 1992; mem. vis. com. Lank Ctr. for Genitourinary Oncology, Dana Farber Cancer Inst., 2005—; presenter Round Table, Jackson, NY, 2006, presenter in field. Co-editor: Nursing and Thanatology, 1982; contbr. articles to profl. publs., chpts. to books. Bd. mem. NY State Task Force on Life and the Law, 1994-97; presenter in field. Mem. Sigma Theta Tau. Home and Office: PO Box 9223 485 Indian Springs Dr Jackson Hole WY 83002 Office Phone: 307-734-8005. Office Fax: 307-734-8006.

FARKAS, DANIEL FREDERICK, food science and technology educator; b. Boston, June 20, 1933; m. Alice Bridgetta Brady, Jan. 25, 1959; children: Brian Emerson, Douglas Frederick. BS, MIT, 1954, MS, 1955, PhD, 1960. Lic. chem. engr., Calif. Commd. U.S. Army, 1954, advanced through grades to major, 1968, ret., 1974; staff scientist Arthur D. Little, Cambridge, Mass., 1960-62; asst. prof. Cornell U. Agrl Expt. Sta., Geneva, NY, 1962-66; rsch. leader We. regional rsch. ctr. USDA, Albany, Calif., 1967-80; prin. Daniel F. Farkas Assocs., 1976—; prof., chair dept. food sci. U. Del., Newark, 1980-87; v.p. process R & D Campbell Soup Co., Camden, NJ, 1987-90; Jacobs-Root prof., head dept. food sci. and tech. Oreg. State U., Corvalis, 1990-2000, prof. emeritus, 2000—. Contbr. more than 50 articles to peer-reviewed sci. and tech. jours. Fellow Inst. Food Technologists (Nicholas Appert medal 2002); mem. AIChE, Am. Chem. Soc. (profl.), Sigma Xi. Achievements include 5 U.S. patents for centrifugal fluidized bed food drying system, application of ultra-high hydrostatic pressure to food preservation.

FARKAS, GAVRIL, mathematics professor; b. Oradea, Romania, Mar. 19, 1973; s. Gavril and Maria Farkas; m. Lia-Ana Chebeleu, July 27, 1996. PhD, U. Amsterdam, Netherlands, 2000. Asst. prof. math. Princeton U., NJ, 2003—04; assoc. prof math. U. Tex., Austin, 2004—. Rsch. fellow, Alfred Sloan Found., 2005—. Office: Univ Tex Austin Department of Mathematics Austin TX 78712 Office Phone: 512-471-0175. Office Fax: 512-471-9038.

FARKAS, KERRIE R.H., literature and language professor; m. Scott Michael Farkas; children: Dimitry, Kayla. PhD in Rhetoric and Composition, Kent State U., Ohio, 2003. Tchg. fellow dept. English Kent State U., Ohio, 1995—2001; asst. prof. English Millersville U., Pa., 2003—. Internship asst. writing internship program dept. English Kent State U., acting dir. writing internship program dept. English, 2000—01, rsch. asst. to Christina Hass, dept. English; rsch. assoc. Ctr. Rsch. in Workplace Literacy, Ohio; presenter in field. Contbr. papers to profl. confs. Vol. Ohio Reads, 1999—2001, Am. Reads, 1999—2001, Adult Spanish to English Literacy Program, Kennett Square, Pa., 2003—04, Am. Reads Migrant Edn. Program, 2004—05, Spl. Olympics, Phila., 2004—05. Named Academic All Am., Ocean County Coll., 1989—90; recipient Outstanding Female Student Athlete award, 1989—90; fellow, Kent State U., 2002; grantee, Richard A. Toerne Endowment Fund, 1996—2002, Ctr. Rsch. in Workplace Literacy, 1998—99, Writing Program Com. Kent State U., 1999—2002, Faculty Grants Com. Millersville U., 2004, 2005, 2006, Student Engagement Project; scholar, NJ. Natural Gas Co., 1989—90. Mem.: Am. Ednl. Rsch. Assn., Rhetoric Soc. Am., Nat. Coun. Tchrs. of English. Office: Millersville Univ English Dept PO Box 1004 Millersville PA 17551 Home Phone: 717-871-2361; Office Phone: 717-871-2361. Business E-Mail: kerrie.farkas@millersville.edu.

FARKAS, LESLIE GABRIEL, plastic surgeon; b. Ruzomberok, Hungary, Apr. 18, 1915; Can., 1968; s. Charles Samuel and Olga (Kustra) F.; m. Susanna Gál, Oct. 23, 1971; 1 child, Julia. MD, U. Istropolitana, Bratislava, 1941; PhD, Charles U., Prague, 1959; DSc, Charles U., 1968. Resident surgeon Mil. Hosp. and Field Svc., Czechoslovakia, 1941-45; resident in plastic surgery Charles U., Prague, 1945-48, asst. prof., 1948-65, assoc. prof., 1965-68; dir. plastic surgery rsch. lab. Czechoslovak Acad. Scis., 1963-68; dir. divsn. cong. anomalies Hosp. Sick Children, Toronto, Ont., Canada, 1968-69, rsch. fellow divsn. exptl. surgery, 1969-70, asst. scientist Rsch. Inst., 1970-77, sr. scientist, 1977-81, dir. plastic surgery lab. Rsch. Inst., 1970-81, asst. prof., 1970-78, rschr. Ctr. Craniofacial Care and Rsch., 1982—; assoc. prof. U. Toronto, 1978-81, spl. rsch. lectr., 1981-82, assoc. rsch. prof., 1982—. Dir. craniofacial measur. lab., Hosp. for Sick Children, Toronto, 1986—; cons. cleft palate program U. Iowa, 1975-78, dept. neurology Shriver Ctr., Waltham, Mass., 1984-95; with divsn. plastic surgery Royal Victoria Hosp., Montreal, Que.; mem. panel 5th Internat. Congl. Plastic Reconstructive Surgery, Melbourne, Australia, 1971; mem. panel cleft-lip nose Am. Cleft Palate-Craniofacial Assn., Hilton Head, SC, 1991; invited vis. expert med. anthropometry Min. Health Govt. of Singapore, 1987; invited tchr. course med. anthropometry orthodontics Orthodontic and Human Scis. Congress U. Med. Sch., Szeged, Hungary,

1996; session chmn. 8th Internat. Congress on Cleft Palate and Related Craniofacial Abnormalities, Documentation, Anthropometry, Database, Singapore, 1997; cons. in field Author: Hypospadias, 1967, Constructive, Reconstructive and Esthetic Surgery of the Male Urogenital Tract, 1973, Anthropometry of the Head and Face in Medicine, 1981, Anthropometric Facial Proportions in Medicine, 1987, Anthropometry of the Head and Face, 2d edit., 1994; contbr. numerous articles to sci. jours. Recipient Cert. Excellence for rsch. in attractive face Am. Soc. Aesthetic Plastic Surgery, Boston, 1985, Aleš Hrdlička Commemorative medal Czechoslovakia Acad. Scis., Prague, 1992, Vis. Scholar award dept. pediats. faculty medicine U. Calgary, Can., 1992, Salamon Frigyes Commemorative medal Orthodontic Soc. Hungary, 1996, Best Paper of the Yr. award for Surface Anatomy of the Face in Down's Syndrome: Anthropometric Proportion Indices in the Craniofacial Regions in Jour. Craniofacial Surgery, 2002; Med. Rsch. Coun. grantee, 1970-72, Atkinson Charitable Found. grantee, 1973-76, Smythe Found. Can. grantee, 1976-81, Physicians Svcs., Inc. grantee, 1991-99. Fellow Royal Coll. Surgeons; mem. Acad. Medicine Toronto, Am. Soc. Plastic and Reconstructive Surgeons (mem. faculty symposium reconstructive auricle 1972), Can. Soc. Plastic Surgeons, Plastic Surgery Rsch. Coun., Can. Assn. Anatomists, Biomat. Soc. Can., Can. Craniofacial Soc., Internat. Soc. Craniomaxillofacial Surgery, Japanese Soc. Aesthetic Plastic Surgery (hon.). Roman Catholic. Home: 59 Claywood Rd Willowdale ON Canada M2N 2R3 Office: Hosp for Sick Chldn/Pl Surg 555 University Ave Toronto ON Canada M5G 1X8 Office Phone: 416-221-7216. Business E-Mail: lfarkas@interlog.com.

FARKAS, MEREDITH G., librarian; m. Adam Farkas. BA in Am. Hist., with honors, Wesleyan U., 1995—99; MSW, Fla. State U., 1999—2001, M in Info. Studies, 2003—04. Grad. rsch. asst. Fla. State U. Sch. Social Work, 1999—2001; school-based therapist South County Mental Health, Delray Beach, Fla., 2001—02; family therapist Catholic Charities' Bridges to Success Prog., Riviera Beach, Fla., 2002—03; libr. asst. Boca Raton Pub. Libr., Fla., 2003—04; archivist intern Spl. Collections Dept. Fla. Atlantic U., 2004; distance learning libr. Norwich U., Northfield, Vt., 2005—. Adv. com. TechSmith Camtasia, 2005—, PBWiki, 2006—. Author: Social Software in Libraries: Building Collaboration, Communication and Community Online, 2007. Named one of Library Journal's Movers and Shakers, 2006. Mem.: Vt. Libr. Assn., Library and Info. Tech. Assn., Assn. Coll. and Rsch. Libraries, ALA. Office: Norwich Univ Libraries 158 Harmon Dr Northfield VT 05663 Office Phone: 802-485-2168. E-mail: mfarkas@norwich.edu.

FARKAS, PAUL STEPHEN, gastroenterologist; b. NYC, 1952; s. Benjamin J. and Ellen (Tanner) F.; m. Esta Miriam Cantor, June 24, 1973; children: Melanie Sharon, Joshua David. AB magna cum laude with distinction in psychology, Brandeis U., 1972; MD, Tufts U., 1976. Diplomate Am. Bd. Internal Medicine, Am. Bd. Gastroenterology. Intern Baystate Med. Ctr., Sprinfield, Mass., 1976-77, resident in internal medicine, 1977-79; fellow in gastroenterology Albert Einstein Coll. Medicine, Bronx, N.Y., 1979-81; asst. clin. prof. medicine Tufts U., Boston, 1985—; med. advisor Med. Assist Program Springfield Tech. C.C., 1989—. Co-dir. med. edn. Mercy Hosp., Springfield, 1990-95, chmn. dept. gastroenterology, 1995—, dir. libr., 1988-97, mem. exec. com., 1995—, treas. med. staff, 1999—; mem. adv. bd. VNA, Springfield, 1984-88; adj. asst. prof. clin. pharmacology Mass. Coll. Pharmacy, Boston, 1982—. Author: Diagnostic Diagrams Gastroenterology, 1985; contbr. book chpts., articles and revs. in field. Bd. dirs. B'nai Jacob Synagogue, Springfield, 1987-88, Com. for Longmeadow, Mass., 1989, Yeshiva, Longmeadow, 1994-99; trustee Mercy Hosp., 1997-98. Fellow ACP (cmty. based excellence in tchg. award 2000), Am. Gastroent. Assn., Am. Gastro. Assn.; mem. AMA, Am. Coll. Gastroenterology, Am. Soc. Gastrointestinal Endoscopy, New Eng. Soc. Gastrointestinal Endoscopy. Office: 299 Carew St Springfield MA 01104-2301 Office Phone: 413-737-7951. Personal E-mail: docpsf@aol.com.

FARLEY, ANDREW NEWELL, lawyer, consultant; b. Brownsville, Pa., Oct. 31, 1934; s. Andrew Polycarp and Sarah Theresa (Landymore) F.; m. Marta Olha Pisetska, May 5, 1963; children— Andrew Daniel, Mark Landymore. AB, Washington and Jefferson Coll., 1956; MPA, U. Pitts., 1962, JD, 1961; diploma, U.S. Army Command and Gen. Staff Coll., 1972, Indsl. Coll. Armed Forces, 1967; grad., U.S. Army War Coll., 1976. Bar: Pa. 1962, U.S. Supreme Ct. 1965. Assoc. Reed Smith Shaw & McClay, Pitts., 1961-65, ptnr., 1966-91; cons. Pitts., 1992—. Bd. dirs. Corp. Devel. USAM Mid-Atlantic and Ohio; mng. dir. USAM-Nat., 1992—; Am. Arbitration Assn. Nat. Panel Comml. Disputes, 1995—; mediator JAMS-Endispute, 1996—; sec.-treas. Internat. Acad. Mediators, 1996-2000; lectr. in fed. jurisprudence and adminstrv. law U. Pitts.; adminstrv. asst. Pa. Atty. Gen., 1959; counsel to Pa. Constl. Conv., 1968; mem. Pa. Atty. Gen.'s Task Force on Adminstrn., 1970; mem. faculty Pa. Bar Inst. Bus. Lawyer Inst., 1999—. Assoc. editor Pitts Legal Jour., 1963— (mem. exec. com.); contbr. articles to profl. jours. Bd. dirs. Ind. Sch. Chmn. Assn., World Affairs Coun., Pitts., Pitts. Opera, 1986-95; sec., bd. dirs. Found. for Calif. U. Pa.; mem. adv. bd. Western Pa. Advanced Tech. Ctr., Internat. Resuscitation Rsch. Ctr., U. Pitts. Med. Sch., Mon Valley Renaissance; mem. bd. visitors U. Pitts. Grad. Sch. Pub. and Internat. Affairs; trustee Thiel Coll., 1989-95. Brig. gen. U.S. Army. Decorated Meritorious Svc. medals Dept. Def. and US Army, Army Commendation medals; named Mon Valley Renaissance MVP, 1987; recipient Gubernatorial citation, Commonwealth of Pa., 1978, Omicron Delta Kappa award, 1960, Ukrainian award, 2006, Mayoral citation, 2006; Nat. Def. Transp. Assn. fellow, 1956. Mem. Internat. Acad. Mediators, Pa. Bar Assn. (chmn. sect. internat. law, bd. editors, jud. adminstrn. com., statewide computer com. for the cts., alternative dispute resolution com.), In-house Coun. Com., Allegheny County Bar Assn. (fee determination com.), Am. Law Inst., Nat. Health Lawyers Assn., Am. Arbitration Assn., Soc. for Profls. in Dispute Resolution, Assn. U.S. Army (pres. Ft. Pitt chpt., pres. Pa.), Sr. Army Res. Comdrs. Assn. (exec. com.), Pitts. Athletic Assn., Duquesne Club, Pa. State Grange, Masons. Home: 54 N Manorcliff Pl The Woodlands Spring TX 77382

FARLEY, BARBARA SUZANNE, lawyer; b. Salt Lake City, Dec. 13, 1949; d. Ross Edward Farley and Barbara Ann (Edwards) Farley Swanson; m. Arthur Hoffman Ferris, Apr. 9, 1982 (div. 1995); children: Barbara Whitney, Taylor Edwards; m. Michael L. Levine, Aug. 7, 1999. BA with honors, Mills Coll., Oakland, Calif., 1972; JD, U. Calif.-Hastings, San Francisco, 1976. Bar: Calif. 1976. Extern law clk. to justice Calif. Supreme Ct., San Francisco, 1975; assoc. Pillsbury, Madison & Sutro, San Francisco, 1976-78, Bronson, Bronson & McKinnon, San Francisco, 1978-80, Goldstein & Phillips, San Francisco, 1980-84; ptnr., head litigation Rosen, Wachtell & Gilbert, San Francisco, 1984-89; of counsel Lempres & Wulfsberg, Oakland, Calif., 1989—99; pvt. practice, 2000—. Founder, pres. and CEO Fiducety Tech. Inc.; arbitrator U.S. Dist. Ct. (no. dist.) Calif., San Francisco, 1981—, Calif. Superior Ct., San Francisco, 1984—89; judge pro tem San Francisco Mcpl. Ct., 1983—, Alameda County, 2005—; probation monitor Calif. State Bar, 1990—2002; spkr. , author Nat. Bus. Inst. Estate Adminstrn., 2000; spkr. Lorman Edn. Svcs. Tax Exempt Orgns. Contbg. author Calif. Continuing Edn. of the Bar, Nat. Bus. Inst., Lorman Edn. Svcs.; mng. editor Hastings Coll. of Law-U. Calif.-San Francisco Constl. Law Quar., 1975-76; civil litigation reporter. Mills Coll. scholar, 1970-72, U. Calif.-Hastings, San Francisco scholar, 1973-76. Mem. ABA, ATLA, San Francisco Bar Assn., Calif. Trial Lawyers Assn., San Francisco Bar Assn. (del. Calif. State Bar 2003-07), Alameda Bar Assn. Home Phone: 510-652-8391. Personal E-mail: bsuzanne7@aol.com.

FARLEY, CAROLE, soprano; b. Le Mars, Iowa, Nov. 29, 1946; d. Melvin and Irene (Reid) Farley; m. Jose Serebrier, Mar. 29, 1969; 1 child, Lara Adriana Francesca. MusB, Ind. U., 1968. Fulbright scholar Hochschule für Musik, Munich, 1968-69. (Musician of Month, Musical Am./Hi Fidelity 1977), Am. debut at Town Hall, N.Y.C., 1969, Paris debut, Nat. Orch., 1975, London debut, Royal Philharmonic Soc., 1975, S.Am. debut, Teatro Colon, Philharmonic Orch., Buenos Aires, 1975; soloist with, major Am. and European symphony orchs., 1970—, soloist, Welsh Nat. Opera, 1971, 72, Cologne Opera, 1972-75, Phila. Lyric Opera, 1974, Brussels Opera, 1972, Lyon Opera, 1976, 77, Strasbourg Opera, 1975, Linz Opera, 1969, N.Y.C. Opera, 1976, New Orleans Opera, 1977, Cin. Opera, 1977, Met. Opera Co., N.Y.C., 1977—, Zurich Opera, 1979, Chgo. Lyric Opera, 1981, Can. Opera Co., 1980, Düsseldorf Opera, 1980, 81, 84, Palm Beach Opera, 1982, Theatre Mcpl. Paris, 1983, Theatre Royale dela Monnaie Brussels, 1983, Teatro Regio, Turin, Italy, 1983, Nice Opera (France), 1984, 86, 87, 88, Cologne Opera, 1985, Teatro Comunale, Florence, Italy, 1985, BBC Opera, 1987, TeatroColon, Buenos Aires, 1987, 88, 89, Opera de Montpellier (France), 1988, 94, Theatre des Champs Elysees, Paris, 1988, Helsinki Festival, 1989, Tchaikovsky Opera Arias Pickwick/IMP Records, 1993, Met. Opera Premiere Shostakovich Opera Lady Macbeth of Mtzensk, 1994, Theatre Capitole de Toulouse Wozzeck, 1994, internat. tour with Nat. Chamber Orchestra of Toolouse, 2003, San Carlo di Napoli, 2007; on New Zealand Broadcasting Commn. Orchestral Tour, 1986; TV film for ABC Australia La Voix Humaine, also co-producer compact disc and video for BBC, London, 1990; co-producer compact disc and video The Telephone, 1990; recorded compact disc Weill, 1992, Metro. Opera Shostakovich: "Lady Macbeth", 1994, Strausslieder with Czech Philharmonic, 1995, Les Soldats Morts, 1995 (Grand Prix du Disque); recorded for Deutsche Gramophone (Diapason d'or prize 1997), Chandos, CBS, BBC, ASV, RCA, Ricercar and Varese-Sarabande records, London/Decca Records, IMP Masters, Pickwick; new CD Naxos: Selected Songs Ned Rorem, 2001, The Songs of Ernesto Lecuona For Bis Records, 2003; Argentine premier Bomarzo by Alberto Ginastera, Teatro Colón Buenos Aires, 2003, Bolcom Songs for Naxos, 2005. Recipient Abiati prize for her role as Lulu, Italy, 1984, Deutsche Schallplatten award for recording Carole Farley Sings French Songs, 1988, Editor's Choice award, Gramophone Mag., 2005, Editor's Choice award for DVD of Month, Gramophone Mag., 2006; named Alumni of Year, U. Ind., 1976; two-time Grammy nominee, 2004, 2006. Mem.: Am. Guild Mus. Artists. Home: 270 Riverside Dr New York NY 10025-5209 E-mail: caspi123@aol.com. *A young opera singer today has a much greater responsibility than his predecessors 50 years ago. The age of the 200-pound soprano expiring of consumption at the end of La Traviata is a thing of the past. Now we must "look" the part, and be able to act as well as sing.*

FARLEY, GREGORY SCOTT, biology professor; b. Stoughton, Mass., Nov. 24, 1971; m. Ann H. Hartung, July 15, 1995; 1 child, Lauren Grace. BS in Biology, Duke U., Durham, NC, 1994; MS in Biol. Sci., Fla. State U., Tallahassee, 1999. Asst. prof. Chesapeake Coll., Wye Mills, Md., 2003—06, assoc. prof., 2006—. Mem.: Phi Theta Kappa (Paragon award 2007). Office: Chesapeake Coll PO Box 8 1000 Coll Cir Wye Mills MD 21679 Office Phone: 410-822-5400 389.

FARLEY, JAMES NEWTON, retired manufacturing executive, electrical engineer; b. Hutchinson, Kans., Nov. 8, 1928; s. James N. Farley and Elizabeth (Martin) Sanders; m. Nancy J. Hollabaugh, Apr. 30, 1956; children: Sarah Huskey, Timothy, Barbara Carré, James, Stuart. BSEE, Northwestern U., 1950. Registered profl. engr., Ill. Test engr. GE, Schenectady, NY, 1950-51; sales engr. Allen Bradley Co., Milw., 1953-54, Chgo., 1954-60; sales mgr. SpeedFam Corp., Skokie, Ill., 1960-64, pres. Des Plaines, Ill., 1964-87, chmn. bd. dirs., 1987-97; pres., CEO Speedfam-IPEC, Inc., Chandler, Ariz., 1987-92, CEO, chmn. bd. dirs., 1992-97, chmn. bd. dirs., 1997-2001, chmn. emeritus, 2001—02, ret., 2002—. Bd. dirs. Lovejoy, Inc., Downers Grove, Ill., imortgage.com, Scottsdale, Ariz., Ex One Co., Irwin, Pa. Trustee Scottsdale Healthcare Found.; mem. McCormick adv. com. Northwestern U.; mem. adv. bd. Am. Precision Mus., Windsor, Vt. With U.S. Army, 1951-53. Recipient Alumni Merit award Northwestern U., 1996. Mem. Assn. for Mfg. Tech., Oriental Order of Groundhogs, Kappa Sigma. Democrat. Episcopalian. Office: JNF Group 7702 E Doubletree Ranch Rd Ste 300 Scottsdale AZ 85258 Home: 6404 N 52d Pl Paradise Valley AZ 85253

FARLEY, JERRY B., academic administrator; m. Susan Farley. BS in Fin. and Acctg., U. Okla., 1968; MBA, Okla. U., 1972. V.p. bus. and fin. Okla. State U., 1986; CFO Okla. U., Oklahoma City, v.p. adminstrn. and fin., 1994; pres. Washburn U., Topeka, 1997—. Named No. 4 most powerful Topekan, Topeka Capital-Jour., 2000. Office: Washburn U Office of Pres 1700 SW College Ave MO 202 Topeka KS 66621

FARLEY, JOSEPH MCCONNELL, lawyer; b. Birmingham, Ala., Oct. 6, 1927; s. John G. and Lynne (McConnell) F.; m. Sheila Shirley, Oct. 1, 1958 (dec. July 1978); children: Joseph McConnell, Thomas Gager, Mary Lynne. Student, Birmingham-So. Coll., 1944—45; BSME, Princeton U., 1948; postgrad., U. Ala., 1948—49; LLB, Harvard U., 1952; LHD (hon.), Judson Coll., 1974; LLD (hon.), U. Ala. at Birmingham, 1983. Bar: Ala. 1952. Assoc. Martin, Turner, Blakey & Bouldin, Birmingham, 1952-57; ptnr. successor firm Martin, Balch, Bingham & Hawthorne, 1957-65; exec. v.p., dir. Ala. Power Co., 1965-69, pres., dir., 1969-89; v.p. So. Electric Generating Co., 1970-74, pres., dir., 1974-89; exec. v.p., corp. counsel So. Co., 1991-92, exec. v.p. nuclear, bd. dirs., 1989-90; pres., CEO So. Nuclear Oper. Co., Birmingham, 1990-91, chmn., CEO, 1991-92, also bd. dirs.; of counsel Balch & Bingham, LLP, Birmingham, 1993—. Mem. exec. bd. Southeastern Electric Reliability Coun., 1980-2006, chmn., 1974-76; bd. dirs. Edison Electric Inst.; bd. dirs. Southeastern Electric Exch., pres., 1984; adv. dir. So. Co., 1992-97. Mem. Jefferson County Republican Exec. Com., 1953-65; counsel, mem. Ala. Rep. Com., 1962-65; permanent chmn. Ala. Rep. Conv., 1962; alternate del. Rep. Nat. Conv., 1956; bd. dirs. Ala. Bus. Hall of Fame, Birmingham Area YMCA (hon. dir.); chmn. bd. trustees So. Rsch. Inst., 1970-99; trustee Tuskegee U., 1981-2002; trustee Children's Hosp. Birmingham, pres. bd. trustees 1983-85; mem. Pres.'s Cabinet U. Ala.-Tuscaloosa; bd. visitors U. Ala. Sch. Commerce, chmn., 1991-93. Served with USNR, 1948; now lt. ret. Mem. ABA, NAM (bd. dirs. 1987-92), Ala. Bar Assn., Birmingham Bar Assn., Inst. Nuclear Power Ops. (bd. dirs. 1982-89, chmn. 1987-89), U.S. Coun. for Energy Awareness (bd. dirs. 1985-92), Am. Nuclear Energy Coun. (chmn. bd. dirs. 1987-92), Newcomen Soc. N.Am., Birmingham Country Club, Shoal Creek Club, The Club, Mountain Brook Club, Summit Club, Rotary, Phi Beta Kappa, Kappa Alpha, Tau Beta Pi, Beta Gamma Sigma (hon.). Episcopalian. Home: 3333 Dell Rd Birmingham AL 35223-1319 Office: Balch & Bingham LLP PO Box 306 Birmingham AL 35201-0306 Office Phone: 205-226-3464.

FARLEY, KATHERINE G., real estate company executive; b. 1950; m. Jerry I. Speyer, 1991; 1 child. Grad., Brown U., 1971; MA in Architecture, Harvard Grad. Sch. of Design, 1976. Mgr. bus. devel. for E. Asia Turner Construction; sr. mng. dir. Latin Am. and Global Corp. Mktg. Tishman Speyer Properties, NYC, 1984—. Exec. com. mem. Internat. Rescue Com.; chmn. emeritus Women In Need; exec. com. mem. NY Philharmonic, Brearley Sch.; bd. mem. Lincoln Center for the Performing Arts, Lincoln Center Theater, Alvin Ailey Dance Co. Named one of Top 200 Collectors, ARTnews Mag., 2004, 2005, 2006. Avocation: Collector of Contemporary Art. Office: Tishmanspeyer Properties 45 Rockefeller Plz Fl 12 New York NY 10111-1299 Office Phone: 212-715-0300.

FARLEY, MONICA M., medical educator; BA/MD with distinction, U. Mo., Kansas City. Cert. Am. Bd. Internal Medicine, 1983, DEA Certificate 1981, lic. Ga. Med. 1981, diplomate Subspecialty of Infectious Diseases 1986. Intern, internal medicine Emory U. Hosp., 1980—81, resident, internal medicine, 1981—83, fellow, infectious disease, 1983—85; rsch. fellow, pub. health svc. tng. grant, dept. microbiology Emory U. Sch. Medicine, 1985—86, sr. assoc., dept. medicine, 1986—88, asst. prof. medicine, dept. medicine, 1988—93, assoc. prof. medicine, dept. medicine, 1993—99, acting dir., divsn. infectious disease, dept. medicine, 1999—2000, adj. asst. prof. microbiology and immunology, 1994—, prof. medicine, dept. medicine, 1999—, assoc. dir., divsn. infectious diseases, dept. medicine, 2000—; assoc. investigator VA Hosp., Atlanta, 1986—88; rsch. assoc. VA Med. Ctr., Atlanta, 1989—93, staff physician, 1989—; dir. Ga. Emerging Infectious Program, 1996—. Mem., State Med. Adv. Bd. Group B Streptococcus Assn., 1994—99, mem. Nat. Med. Adv. Bd., 1995—99; mem. adv. bd. Pfizer Postdoctoral Fellowship Program in Infectious Diseases, 2002—. Mem. editl. bd. Am. Jour. Med. Sciences, guest editor Am. Jour. Med. Sciences, Emerging Microbial Threats, 1996, reviewer in field; contbr. articles to profl. jours., chapters to books. Recipient Assoc. Investigator award, Med. Rsch. Svc., VA, 1986, Rsch. Assoc. award, Med. Rsch. Svc., 1989, Alumni Achievement award, U. Mo. Kansas City Sch. Medicine, 1994, James H. Nakano Citations for Outstanding Scientific Papers published in 1995, Ctr. for Disease Control, 1996, James H. Nakano Citations for Outstanding Scientific Papers published in 1997, 1998, James H. Nakano Citations for two Outstanding Scientific Papers published in 2000, 2001, Dept. Health and Human Services Secretary's award for Disting. Svc. (FoodNet Surveillance Team), 1998. Fellow: Infectious Diseases Soc. Am. (mem. women's com. 1993—96, mem. program planning com. 2000—03); mem.: Am. Soc. for Microbiology, Infectious Diseases Soc. Ga. (pres. 2003—), Am. Fedn. for Med. Rsch. (AFMR) (pres. elect 1997—98, pres. 1998—99, pres. AFMR Found. 1999—2000), So. Soc. for Clin. Investigation (councilor 1996—2000), Am. Fedn. Clin. Rsch. (AFCR), now Am. Fedn. Med. Rsch. (AFMR) (councilor, So. sect. 1993—94, chair-elect, So. sect. 1994—95, nat. coun. 1994—, chair, So. sect. 1995—96, co-chair, pub. policy com. 1995—, pres. elect 1997—98, pres. 1998—99), Alpha Omega Alpha. Office: VA Med Ctr (Atlanta) Rsch-Infectious Disease 1670 Clairmont Rd Decatur GA 30033 Office Phone: 404-728-7688. Office Fax: 404-329-2210. Business E-Mail: mfarley@emory.edu.

FARLEY, RICHARD JOHN, architect, engineer; b. NYC, June 5, 1948; s. Arthur James and Rita Florence Farley; m. Alice Child Hamilton, July 10, 1976; children: Alexander, Patrick, Elizabeth. BE, Manhattan Coll., 1970; MArch, U. Pa., Phila., 1973, MSE in Urban and Civil Engring., 1973, MArch, 1974. Registered arch., Pa., profl. engr., NJ. Design arch. Environ. Design Collabarative, Phila., 1974—77; assoc. Kling Arch., Engrs., Phila., 1977—91, prin. dir. of projects, 1991—2007; prin. corp. and comml. sector Kling Stubbins Arch., Engrs., 2007—. Adj. assoc. prof. U. Pa., Phila., 1982—, guest lectr. real estate seminars, Wharton Sch. Bus.; prin. project dir. Dow Jones Hdqs., SAP Hdqs. Mem., treas. Urban Land Inst., Phila., 2000—. Recipient G. Holmes Perkins award for excellence in tchg., U. Pa. Fellow: AIA; mem.: Tech. Curriculum Innovations U. Pa., Uran Land Inst. Phila. (exec. com. treas. 2005), Chi Epsilon. Achievements include design of prototypical solar heated and cooled facility for USPS, 1977. Avocation: public speaking. Office: Kling Stubbins Arch Engrs 2301 Chestnut St Philadelphia PA 19103 Office Phone: 215-569-5950. Business E-Mail: rfarley@klingstubbins.com.

FARLEY, TERRENCE MICHAEL, banker; b. NYC, Mar. 6, 1930; s. Terrence M. and Mary A. (Dundon) F.; m. Audrey E. Churchill, June 8, 1952; children: Elizabeth C., Peter, Matthew. BBA, CCNY, 1955. With Brown Bros. Harriman & Co., NYC, 1951—, ptnr., 1972—2004, mng. ptnr., 1983—95, ltd. ptnr., 2005—. Trustee Children's Specialized Hosp., Mountainside, NJ. Mem. Univ. Club, Echo Lake Country Club (Westfield, N.J.), Wianno Club (Osterville, Mass.). Home: 309 Hillside Ave Westfield NJ 07090-2902 Office: Brown Bros Harriman & Co 140 Broadway New York NY 10005-1101

FARLEY, THOMAS T., lawyer; b. Pueblo, Colo., Nov. 10, 1934; s. John Baron and Mary (Tancred) F.; m. Kathleen Maybelle Murphy, May 14, 1960; children: John, Michael, Kelly, Anne. BS, U. Santa Clara, 1956; LLB, U. Colo., 1959. Bar: Colo. 1959, U.S. Dist. Ct. Colo. 1959, U.S. Ct. Appeals (10th cir.) 1988. Dep. dist. atty. County of Pueblo, 1960-62; pvt. practice Pueblo, 1963-69; ptnr. Phelps, Fonda & Hays, Pueblo, 1970-75, Petersen & Fonda, P.C., Pueblo, 1975—. Bd. dirs. Pub. Svc. Co. Colo., Wells Fargo Pueblo, Wells Fargo Sunset, Health Net, Inc., Colo. Pub. Radio. Minority leader Colo. Ho. of Reps., 1967-75; chmn. Colo. Wildlife Commn., 1975-79, Colo. Bd. Govs., 1979-87; bd. regents Santa Clara U., 1987—; commr. Colo. State Fair; trustee cath. found. Diocese of Pueblo, mem. fin. coun.; trustee Great Outdoors Colo. Trust Fund.; pres. Hasan Sch. Bus., Colo. State Univ.-Pueblo, bd. advisors. Recipient Disting. Svc. award U. So. Colo., 1987, 93, Bd. of Regents, U. Colo., 1993, Colo. State U.-Pueblo, Presdl. Seal, 2004; named to Pueblo Hall of Fame, 2005. Mem. ABA, Colo. Bar Assn., Pueblo C. of C. (bd. dirs. 1991-93), Rotary. Democrat. Roman Catholic. Office: Petersen & Fonda PC 215 W 2d St Pueblo CO 81003-3251 Office Phone: 719-545-9330. Business E-Mail: tfarley@petersen-fonda.com.

FARLEY, THOMAS W., stock exchange executive; BA in Polit. Sci., Georgetown U. CFO SunGard Kiodex, NYC, 2000—06, COO, 2003—06, pres. bus. unit, 2006—07; pres., COO, bd. dirs. NY Bd. Trade (NYBOT), NYC, 2007—. Office: The New York Bd of Trade World Fin Ctr One North End Ave 13 th Fl New York NY 10282 Office Phone: 212-748-4000.*

FARMAKIDES, JOHN BASIL, lawyer; b. Symi Island (Dodecanese), Italy; s. Basil John and Anna Maria (Zouroudis) F.; m. Maria T. Kambanis, July 12, 1964; children: Basil J., George S. BS, Case Western Res. U., 1950; JD with honors, George Washington U., 1956; LL.M., Georgetown U., 1958. Bar: D.C. 1957, U.S. Supreme Ct. 1958, Va. 1986. Patent examiner U.S. Patent Office, 1955-59; atty. U.S. Air Force, 1960-61, NASA, 1961-70, mem. bd. contract appeals, 1968-70; asst. gen. counsel NSF, 1970-72; mem. NRC appeals bd. AEC (NRC), 1972-75; chmn. bd. appeals Dept. Energy, Washington, 1975-84; ptnr. Whitney & Dempsey, Washington, 1985-88; arbitrator, 1988—. Adj. prof. in law Am. U. Law Sch., 1964-72; U.S. del. Internat. Conf. on Govt. Computer Experts, Geneva, 1972; chmn. fed. coun. sci. and tech. subcom. Legal Aspects Computerized Info Sys., 1969-72; cons. HEW, NSF; chmn. Nat. Conf. Legal Aspects Computerized Info. Sys., 1969-72; comdg. officer, dir. Joint Army, Navy, Air Force Spl. Analyn Divsn., USAR, 1971-74; mem. U.S. Chinese Workshop on Computerized Info. Sys., NAS, 1972; chief adminstrv. judge City Coun. New Orleans, 1986-89; apptd. mem. first copyright arbitration panel Libr. Congress, 1995. Contbr. articles to profl. jours. Pres. Cosmos Hist. Preservation Found. Recipient letters of appreciation U.S. Army, HEW, NASA, NSF, Achievement award NASA Apollo; Exceptional Svc. medal Dept. Energy. Mem. ABA, Fed. Bar Assn., IEEE, Am. Arbitration Assn., Am. Soc. Pub. Adminstrn., NASA Space League, Phi Delta Phi. Clubs: Cosmos, Washington Golf, Nat. Lawyers.

FARMAKIS, GEORGE LEONARD, retired education educator; b. Clarksburg, W.Va., June 30, 1925; s. Michael and Pipitsa (Roussopoulos) F. BA, Wayne State U., 1949, MEd, 1950, MA, 1966, PhD, 1971; MA, U. Mich., 1978. Tchr. audio-visual aids dir. Roseville (Mich.) Pub. Schs., 1951-57; tchr. Birmingham (Mich.) Pub. Schs., 1957-61, Highland Park (Mich.) Pub. Schs., 1961-90; substitute tchr. Grosse Pointe Pub. Schs., 1990—2003; ret., 2003. Lectr. Oakland County C.C., 1990-92, Lawrence U., 1990-98, Oakland U., 2000—; instr. Highland Park C.C., 1966-68, Wayne County C.C., 1969-70; assoc. mem. grad. faculty Coll. Edn. Wayne State U., 1988-89; founder Ford Sch. Math. High Intensity Tutoring Program, 1971; chairperson Highland Park Sch. Dist. Curriculum Coun. and Profl. Staff Devel. Governing Bd., 1979-82; pres. Mich. Coun. Social Studies, 1985-86; founder, dir. Mich. Social Studies Olympiad, 1987;

founder, editor Mich. Social Studies Jour., 1986; participant ESEA Title I/Nat. Diffusion Network. Author, translator: Letters of Nicholas Gysis, 1842-1901; co-author: Michigan School Finance Curriculum Guide; contbr. poems to books of poetry, articles to Focus jour. Cpl. USNG, 1948-51. Recipient spl. commendation Office of Edn., 1978, Outstanding Svc. award Nat. Coun. Social Studies, 1987, Presdl. award Mich. Coun. Social Studies, 1988, 96. Mem. ASCD (bd. dirs. Mich. chpt. 1983-86), Internat. Reading Assn., Am. History Assn., Nat. Coun. Social Studies (pres. SIG-CASE 1987-88, pres. JESIG 1988-89), Am. Philol. Assn., U. Mich. Alumni Assn., Wayne State U. Coll. Edn. Alumni Assn. (bd. dirs. 1985-86), Mich. Reading Assn., Masons (32 degree), Shriners, Ancient Accepted Scottish Rite, Phi Delta Kappa (Outstanding Educators award 1988). Greek Orthodox. Home: 15215 Windmill Dr Macomb MI 48044-4929

FARMAN, ALLAN GEORGE, radiologist, pathologist, educator; b. Birmingham, Eng., July 26, 1949; came to the U.S., 1980; s. George and Lily (Hewitt) F.; m. Taeko Takemori, May 21, 1996. B Dental Surgery, U. Birmingham, Eng., 1971; PhD, U. Stellenbosch, Cape Town, South Africa, 1977, DSc, 1996; EdS, U. Louisville, 1983, MBA with distinction, 1987. Diplomate Am. Bd. Oral and Maxillofacial Radiology, Japanese Bd. Oral and Maxillofacial Radiology; specialist registration in oral pathology South African Med. and Dental Coun.; lic. specialist Ky. Bd. Dentistry Oral and Maxillofacial Radiology. Sr. lectr. oral pathology U. Stellenbosch, Cape Town, 1974-77; head dept. oral biology U. Riyadh, Saudi Arabia, 1978-79; prof., head divsn. radiology and imaging scis. Dental Sch., U. Louisville, 1980—; clin. prof. dept. diagnostic radiology Med. Sch., U. Louisville, 1990—. Cons. Joint Commn. for Dental Bd. Examination, Chgo., 1984—92, NIH, Bethesda, Md., 1990—; rep. to internat. DICOM com. Am. Dental Assn., 2001—; co-chmn. DICOM Working Group 22, 2003—; adj. prof. anatomical sci. and neurology U. Louisville, 1990—. Author: Oral and Maxillofacial Diagnostic Imaging, 1993, Panoramic Radiology-Seminars on Maxillofacial Imaging and Interpretation, 2007; editor: Advances in Maxillofacial Imaging, 1997, (oral and maxillofacial radiology sect.) Oral Surgery, Oral Medicine, Oral Pathology, Oral Radiology and Endodontics, 1988-95, 2005—; co-editor CARS Procs., Computer-Assisted Radiology and Surgery, 1998-; dep. editor Internat. Jour. Computer Assisted Radiology and Surgery, 2006—; mem. editl. bd. Cranio, Oral Radiology, Acta Stomatologica Croatia, Safundi; deputy editor J. Comput Assisted Radiology and Surgery, 2006—; editor Radiology Seminars on Maxillofacial Imaging and Interpretation, 2007, Panoramic Radiology: Seminars on Maxillofacial Imaging and Interpretation, 2007; contbr. more than 300 articles to profl. jours. Recipient DSM, U. Louisville, 2006. Mem. Am. Dental Assn., Internat. Assn. Dental Rsch., Japanese Soc. Oral and Maxillofacial Radiology, Internat. Assn. Dento Maxillofacial Radiology (pres. 1994-97, trust fund chmn. 1997—, chair tech. and stds. com. 2005—), Internat. Congress and Exposition on Computed Maxillofacial Imaging (initiator, founder, organizer 1995—), Am. Acad. Oral and Maxillofacial Radiology (editor 1988-95, 2006—), Am. Assn. Dental Schs. (chmn. oral radiology sect. 1988-89). Office: U Louisville Sch Dentistry 501 S Preston St Louisville KY 40292-1701 Office Phone: 502-852-1241. Business E-Mail: agfarm01@louisville.edu.

FARMAN, GERRIE P., research scientist; s. George and Donna Farman. PhD, Ill. Inst. Tech., Chgo., 2004. Post-doctoral rsch. fellow U. Ill., Chgo., 2004—. Mem.: Am. Physiol. Soc., Am. Heart Assn., Biophysical Soc. Office: Univ Ill 835 S Wolcott St MSB E-202 Chicago IL 60612 Home Phone: 708-769-3788. Business E-Mail: farman@uic.edu.

FARMAN-FARMAIAN, GHAFFAR, investment company executive; b. Tehran, Iran, Jan. 14, 1930; s. Abdol Hossein Mirza and Massoumeh (Tafreshi) F-F.;m. Jahan Aalam, Aug. 5, 1956; children: Massoumeh, Amir Hossein, Ali Reza, Afsar. D.L.C. with honors, Loughborough Coll., Eng., 1951; MS, U. Ill., 1953; PhD, U. Calif., Berkeley, 1958. Head power div. Karadj Water & Power Orgn., Tehran, 1961—64; mem. Iranian Nat. Com. on Electro-Tech. Standards, Tehran, 1966—79; pres. Armed Forces Communication & Electronic, Tehran, 1970—71; chmn. IEEE, Tehran, 1972—73; mem. Iranian Nat. Com. on Energy Ministry of Water and Power, Tehran, 1972—79; co-founder, chmn. ASEA Iran Co., Tehran, 1973—79; vice chmn. Bank of Tehran, 1973—79; co-founder, bd. dirs. Tehran Ins. Co., 1975—79; pres. Univest Corp., NYC, 1982—, Astle Properties Inc., Houston, 1989—2005. Author tech. papers. Chmn. bd. trustees Cmty. Sch., Tehran, 1975—79. Recipient 1st prize Inst. Elec. Engrs., 1956, 57, Alfred Noble prize Am. Inst. Civil Engrs., 1958. Mem. IEEE (life), Armed Forces Comm. and Electronic Assn. (life). Avocations: financial planning, tennis, hiking. Office: PO Box 3221 CH-1211 Geneva 3 - Rive Switzerland Personal E-mail: gff@ieee.org.

FARMER, CHERYL CHRISTINE, internist, industrial hygienist; b. Detroit, Sept. 15, 1946; d. Donald Richard and Dorothy Ruth Farmer; m. Dennis Michael Mukai, Aug. 3, 1968 (div. Sept. 1977). BA in Edn., Mich. State U., 1968; BS in Biology, Wright State U., 1974; MS in Indsl. Hygiene, U. Mich., 1978; MD, Mich. State U., 1982. Tchr. art Five Points Elem. Sch., Fairborn, Ohio, 1968-70; real estate saleswoman Dawson Realty, 1970; sanitarian trainee Dayton Health Dept., Dayton, 1973; acting chief air pollution control southwest dist. Ohio EPA, 1975, data analyst ctrl. dist. Columbus, 1976; intern St. Joseph Mercy Hosp., Ann Arbor, Mich., 1982-83, resident medicine, 1983-85; internist Winton Hills Med. Ctr., Cin., 1985-87; pvt. practice Ann Arbor, Mich., 1988—. Internist, Elm St. Med. Ctr., Cin., 1987-88; mem. peer rev. com. Magnacare Health Maintenance Orgn., Cin., 1988; mem. membership com. St. Joseph Mercy Hosp., 1990-94; mem. ethics com. Huron Valley Physicians Assn., 1996-2006; mem. bioethics com. Mich. State Med. Soc., 1994—; past com. mem. Washtenaw County Med. Soc., 1992-94; commr. city charter City of Ypsilanti, 1993-94. Co-chmn. Citizens for Clean Air Com., Dayton, 1970-74, Miami Valley Citizens for Transfer, Fairborn, 1974; mayor of Ypsilanti, Mich., 1995-06. Named Woman Physician of the Yr., Mich. State Med. Soc., 2002, one of Washtenaw County's Most Influential Women of 2003, Business Direct Weekly, 2003; recipient Athena award, Ypsilanti area C. of C., 1996, Liberty Bell award, Wash. County Bar Assn., 1998, Bill Steude award for ethics in govt., Mich. Assn. Municipal Atty.'s, 2002, Martin Luther King Jr. Humanitarian award, Eastern Mich. Univ., 2003. Mem. AMA, ACP, LWV, NOW, Sierra Club, Phi Kappa Phi, Kappa Delta Pi, Alpha Kappa Delta (hon.). Democrat. Avocations: sailing, gardening, victorian home restoration. Office: 1950 Manchester Rd Ann Arbor MI 48104-4916 Office Phone: 734-973-4800.

FARMER, CHRISTOPHER J., political scientist, writer; b. Norwich, Conn., Apr. 19, 1965; s. Clifford E. Farmer. BA in Polit. Sci., U. New Haven, 2001, MS in Nat. Security, 2004. Founder, pres. Opord Analytical. Author: (novels) Parr Taken, The Oath of the Necromancer, The Fallen Elves, Stale Donuts, 2005, One Cycle of Darkness, 2005. Sgt. US Army, 1986—95. Decorated Army Commendation medal with four oak leaf clusters, Armed Forces Expeditionary medal with Bronze Star, UN Multinat. Force and Observers Mission UN, Valorous Unit award US Army, Joint Meritorious Unit award, Nat. Def. Svc. medal (2), Army Achievement medal with 4 oak leaf clusters; recipient Rollin G. Osterweis award for Excellence in Polit. Sci., U. New Haven, 2000. Republican. Roman Catholic. Avocations: writing, game theory, travel, skiing. Business E-Mail: president@opordanalytical.com.

FARMER, CORNELIA GRIFFIN, lawyer, consultant, county hearings official; b. NYC, Mar. 3, 1945; d. John Bastin and Elizabeth McCue (Sussman) Griffin; m. William Paul Farmer, Jan. 8, 1972; children: Suzanne Elizabeth, John Paul. BA, Mt. Holyoke Coll., 1967; M in Regional Planning, Cornell U., 1970; JD, Marquette U., 1978. Bar: Wis. 1978, Pa. 1981, Minn. 1996, Oreg. 1999, Ill. 2002. Planner Frederick P. Clark Assoc., Rye, NY, 1970-71, Tri State Regional Planning Com., NYC, 1971-72, State of Wis. and City of Milw., 1973-75; assoc. Friebert & Finerty, Milw., 1978-80, Baskin & Sears, Pitts., 1981-82; cons. County of Allegheny, Pitts., 1983; adj. faculty U. Pitts., 1986-94; jud. law clk. Commonwealth Ct. of Pa., Pitts., 1992-95; pvt. practice Mpls., 1996—99; staff atty., hearings ofcl. Lane Coun. Govts., Eugene, Oreg., 1999—2001. Vic-chmn. loan monitoring com. Pitts. Countywide Corp., 1981—87; child adv. Allegheny County Pro Bono Program, Pitts., 1986—92; mediator Dispute Resolution Ctr., St. Paul, 1998—99; adj. faculty U. Wis., Milw., 1978—79. Book reviewer, referee books and articles. Vol. polit. campaigns Milw., Pitts., Mpls., Chgo., and Eugene, 1972-2004; trustee Falk Sch. Fund; v.p. PTA Falk Lab. Sch. U. Pitts., 1985-89; ct. monitor abuse cases WATCH, Mpls., 1996-99; vol. WITS tutoring and mentoring program, 2002-, Start Making A Reader Today, Eugene, Oreg.; mem. Ill. Adv. Coun. of Midwest Eye-Banks, 2004—; head class agent Mt. Holyoke Coll., 2002—, chair reunion gift com.; mem. classes and reunions com. Mt. Holyoke Coll. Alumnae Assn., 2006—; vol. Cabrini Green Legal Aid Clinic, Chgo., 2005—; lector Holy Name Cathedral, Chgo., 2004—. Mem. ABA, APA, Chgo. Bar Assn., Silver Bay Assn. Coun., Mt. Holyoke Club Pitts. (past pres., treas.).

FARMER, CROFTON BERNARD, atmospheric physicist; b. Cardiff, Wales, May 30, 1931; came to U.S., 1967; s. Francis Herbert and Cicely (Arnott) F.; m. Roberta Josephine Stewart, June 20, 1956; (div); children: Louise Josephine, Joanna Cicely, Philippa Bernice, Christopher Llewellyn; m. Christine Louise Conaway, Feb. 29, 1992. BS, U. London, 1952, PhD, 1968. Research physicist EMI Electronics, Ltd., Eng., 1952-60, head infrared research dept., 1960-62; led sci. expdns. to Bolivian Andes, 1962, 64; sr. research scientist Jet Propulsion Lab., Calif. Inst. Tech., Pasadena, 1967-72, mgr. planetary atmospheres, 1972-75; prin. investigator NASA Viking Mars, 1975-77, Shuttle Spacelab, from 1977. Vis. prof. divsn. geology and planetary sci. Calif. Inst. Tech., 1978-81; disting. vis. scientist Jet Propulsion Lab., 1989—; mem. subcoms. on planetary atmospheres and stratospheric rsch. NASA; chair Mars science adv. group, 2006; cons., lectr. remote sensing of atmospheres. Contbr. articles on solar-terrestrial spectroscopy and composition of planets' atmospheres to sci. jours. Recipient Exceptional Sci. Achievement medal NASA, 1975, 77, 87, Antarctica Svc. medal, 1987, William T. Pecora award NASA and Dept. Interior, 1996.

FARMER, DAN, computer security researcher, computer programmer; BS in Computer Sci., Purdue U. Network security profl. Silicon Graphics, Inc., Calif., Sun Microsystems, Inc.; adminstr. network security Earthlink Network, Inc., 1997—2000; co-founder, chief tech. officer Elemental Security, Inc., San Mateo, Calif., 2003—. With Computer Emergency Response Team; expert witness, cons. for the recording industry in cases against Napster; advisor to US Dept. Def. on protecting networks from cyber-terrorism; testified before Congress regarding cybersecurity. Developed COPS program, Purdue U., 1989, co-creator Security Adminstr. Tool for Analyzing Networks (SATAN), 1995; co-author: The Coroner's Toolkit, Forensic Discovery, Titan. Office: Elemental Security Inc 155 Bovet Rd Ste 100 San Mateo CA 94402 Office Phone: 650-292-1400.

FARMER, EVAN R., dermatologist, researcher; b. Richmond, Va. BS in Biology, Va. Mil. Inst.; MD, John Hopkins U., M in History Ideas. Diplomate Am. Bd. Dermatology, cert. in dermatopathology. Past Kampen-Norins prof., past chmn. dept dermatology Sch. Medicine Ind. U.; formerly with Armed Forces Inst. Pathology, Washington; past resident in dermatology John Hopkins U., past dep. dir. dept. dermatology, dir. depts. dermatopathology, oral pathology, 1977, past rschr. in graft-versus-host disease, prof. dermatology; dean, provost Ea. Va. Med. Sch., Norfolk, 2001—04; prof. pathology and dermatology Va. Commonwealth U., 2004—. Past vol. All Africa Leprosy Rehab. and Tng. Ctr., Addis Ababa, Ethiopia. Address: 580 Mowbery Arch Norfolk VA 23507

FARMER, GUY OTTO, II, lawyer; b. Washington, Jan. 7, 1941; s. Guy Otto and Rose Marie (Smith) F.; m. Drema Houchins, Jan. 27, 1963; children: Caroline E., Guy Otto III. BA in Polit. Sci., W.Va. U., 1963; JD, U. Va., 1966. Bar: Fla. 1966, U.S. Dist. Ct. (mid. dist.) Fla. 1966, U.S. Ct. Appeals (5th cir.) 1967, U.S. Ct. Appeals (11th cir.) 1970, U.S. Supreme Ct. 1970, U.S. Ct. Appeals (6th cir.) 1991, U.S. Ct. Appeals (2d cir.) 1997, cert.: Fla. Bar (specialist in labor and employment law). Assoc. to ptnr. Mahoney, Hadlow & Adams, Jacksonville, Fla., 1966-82; ptnr. Smith & Hulsey, Jacksonville, 1982-88, Foley & Lardner, Jacksonville, 1988—2003, Holland & Knight, Jacksonville, 2003—. Contbr. articles to profl. jours. Bd. dirs. N.E. Fla. Hospice, Jacksonville, 1987-93, Children's Home Soc., Jacksonville, 1988-91, N.E. Fla. Safety Coun., Jacksonville, 1988-2002. Fellow: Am. Bar Found.; mem.: ABA (com. on EEO law and Nat. Labor Rels. Act), Acad. Fla. Mgmt. Attys. (bd. dirs. 2000—02), Jacksonville Bar Assn., Fla. Bar Assn., Epping Forest Yacht Club, Ponte Verda Club, The River Club. Democrat. Methodist. Avocations: reading, gardening, boating, sports. Home: 4244 San Jose Blvd Jacksonville FL 32207-6343 Office: Holland & Knight 50 N laura St Ste 3900 Jacksonville FL 32202 Home Phone: 904-398-1153; Office Phone: 904-798-5419. Business E-Mail: guy.farmer@hklaw.com.

FARMER, KENNETH LLOYD, JR., health facility administrator, retired military officer; b. Leeds, Ala., Apr. 13, 1950; married; 4 children. BS, Auburn U.; MD, U. Ala., 1975; grad., Army Command Gen. Staff Coll., Army War Coll. Diplomate Am. Bd. Family Practice. Commd. 2d lt. U.S. Army, advanced through grades to maj. gen., 2002, ret., 2006; early assignments include Madigan Army Med. Ctr., Ft. Lewis, Wash., 9th Med. Detachment and Health Clinic, Heilbronn, Germany, 1976-79; chief of family practice dept. Keller Army Hosp., West Pt., NY; divsn. surgeon 101st Airborne divsn., Ft. Campbell, Ky.; dep. comdr. clin. svcs. Ft. Campbell Hosp.; comdr. 85th Evacuation Hosp., Dhahran, Saudi Arabia, 1990-91, 22nd Support Group (provisional), 1990—91; dept. chief of family practice residency program Eisenhower Army Med. Ctr., Ft. Gordon, Ga.; comdr. Bayne-Jones Army Cmty. Hosp., Ft. Polk, Darnall Army Cmty. Hosp. and U.S. Army Med. Dept. Activity, Ft. Hood, Tex.; command surgeon U.S. European Command, Stuttgart, Germany, 1994-97; dir. Healthcare Svcs. Ft. Bragg, NC; comdg. gen. 44th Med. Brigade, Ft. Bragg, NC, 1999-2000, Western Regional Med. Command, Tacoma, 2000—02, TRICARE NW Region, Ft. Lewis, 2000—02; surgeon 18th Airborne Corps; dep. surg. gen., chief of staff US Army Commd., 2002—04; commdg. gen. N. Atlantic Regional Med. Command & Walter Reed Army Med. Ctr., Washington, 2004—06; exec. v.p., COO TriWest Healthcare Alliance, Phoenix, 2006—. Decorated Disting. Svc. medal with oak leaf cluster, Def. Superior Svc. medal, Legion of Merit with 3 oak leaf clusters, Bronze Star, Meritorious Svc. medal with 4 oak leaf clusters, Order of Mil. Med. Merit. Fellow Am. Acad. Family Physicians (Robert Graham Physician Exec. award 2001). Office: TriWest Healthcare Alliance 16010 N 28th Ave Phoenix AZ 85053

FARMER, PAUL EDWARD, medical anthropologist; b. Oct. 26, 1959; m. Didi Bertrand; 1 child, Catherine. MD, PhD, Harvard U., 1990. Co-founder, exec. v.p. Partners. in Health, 1987—; Presley prof. med. anthropology dept. social medicine Harvard Med. Sch., Boston, 1995—; attending physician divsn. infectious disease Brigham and Women's Hosp., Boston; med. co-dir. Clinique Bon Sauveur, Haiti. Mem. internat. sci. com. ids; coord. berculosis; mem. DOTS-Plus working group for the global tuberculosis programme WHO; chief advisor tuberculosis programs Open Soc. Inst.; chief med. cons. tuberculosis treatment project in prisons of Tomsk (Siberia) Pub. Health Rsch. Inst.; mem. sci. com. WHO Working Group on DOTS-Plus for MDR-TB; mem. Commonwealth of Mass. Bur. Communicable Disease Control; mem. sci. rev. bd. 10 internat. confs. on AIDS. Author: (book) AIDS and Accusation: Haiti and the Geography of Blame, 1992, The Uses of Haiti, 1994, Infections and Inequalities, 1998, Pathologies of Power, 2003; co-editor: Women, Poverty and AIDS, 1996, The Global Impact of Drug-Resistant Tuberculosis, 1999; contbr. articles to profl. jours. Named a MacArthur fellow, John D. and Catherine T. MacArthur Found., 1993; recipient Margaret Mead award, Am. Anthrop. Assn., 1999, Humanitarian award, Duke U., Heinz Humanitarian award, 2003, Outstanding Internat. Physician award, AMA. Mem.: Inst. of Medicine, 2004 (life). Office: Harvard Med Sch Dept Social Medicine 25 Shattuck St Boston MA 02115

FARMER, PHILIP JOSÉ, writer; b. North Terre Haute, Ind., Jan. 26, 1918; s. George and Lucile Theodora (Jackson) F.; m. Bette V. Andre, May 10, 1941; children: Philip Laird, Kristan. BA, Bradley U., 1950. Laborer, steel mill, Peoria, 1941-52; tech. writer, various cos., 1956-69. Author: 75 books including The Lovers, 1951, Strange Relations, 1960, The Alley God, 1962, Riverworld Series: To Your Scattered Bodies Go, 1971, The Fabulous Riverboat, 1971, The Dark Design, 1977, The Magic Labyrinth, 1980, Riverworld and other Stories, 1979, Tarzan Alive, 1972, The Adventure of the Peerless Peer by John H. Watson, M.D., 1974, The Cache, 1981, A Barnstormer in Oz, 1982, Dayworld, 1983, The Unreasoning Mask, 1983, River of Eternity, 1983, Two Hawks from Earth, 1985, Traitor to the Living, 1985, Fantastic Voyage II, 1985, Dayworld Rebel, 1987, The Grand Adventure, 1987, Venus on the Half-Shell, 1988, Dayworld Breakup, 1990, The World of Tiers, 1993, Naked Came the Farmer, 1998, Nothing Burns in Hell, 1999, The Green Odyssey, 2004, The Best of Philip Jose Farmer, 2005, Tarzan Alive: A Definitive Biography of Lord Greystoke, 2006; short stories Riverworld, 1980. Recipient Hugo award, 1953, 68, 72, Nebula award, 2000, Damon Knight Meml. Grand Master award lifetime achievement, 2000, World Fantasy award Life Achievement, 2001. Mailing: Author Mail Subterranean Press PO Box 190106 Burton MI 48519 *Most of my works are science-fiction. These spring from imaginative speculations-extrapolations on science, technology, psychology, sociology, linguistics, philosophy, and theology. The main emphasis, however, is on the human beings trapped in a bewildering cosmos but fighting to understand it. One of my premises is that if the Creator has not given us physical immortality, then we will make our own. This may be one of the goals of homo sapiens evolution.*

FARMER, RICHARD G., engineering educator; Tchg. assoc., adj. prof. Ariz. State U., 1966—. Contbr. articles to profl. jours. Recipient Ariz. Engr. of Yr., NSPE. Fellow: IEEE (Power Sys. Engring. Disting. Svc. Award, Third Millennium Medal, Power Sys. Dynamic Performance Com. Disting. Svc. Award, Phoenix Section Sr. Engr. of Yr. Award 2004); mem.: NAE. Office: Ariz State U Ira A Fulton Sch Engring Mailcode 5706 Tempe AZ 85287 Office Phone: 480-965-4953. E-mail: aargf@asu.edu.

FARMER, RICHARD GILBERT, academic physician, foundation administrator; b. Kokomo, Ind., Sept. 29, 1931; s. Oscar Irvin and Elizabeth Jane (Gilbert) Farmer; m. Janice Mae Schrank, Nov. 29, 1958; children: Amy Lynn, David Richard. Student, Ind. U., 1949—52; MD, U. Md., 1956; MS in Medicine, U. Minn., 1960. Diplomate Am. Bd. Internal Medicine, Gastroenterology. Fellow in internal medicine Mayo Clinic, Rochester, Minn., 1957—60; mem. staff Cleve. Clinic Found., 1962—91, chmn. dept. gastroenterology, 1972—82, bd. govs., 1974—79, chmn. divsn. medicine, 1975—91, mem. med. exec. com., 1975—91, mem. exec. com. bd. trustees, 1975—77; sr. med. advisor Bur. for Europe Agy. for Internat. Devel. US Dept. State, Washington, 1992—94; cons. health care Ea. Europe and former Soviet Union, 1994—96; med. dir. Quality Health Internat., Boston, 1997—98; cons. Scandinavian Care, 1998—2003; prof. medicine, chief digestive and liver disease unit U. Rochester Med. Ctr., NY, 2004—, prof., chief digestive diseases unit, 2004—; clin. prof. medicine (gastroenterology) Georgetown U. Med. Ctr., Washington, 1992—2004. Mem. nat. sci. adv. bd. Nat. Found. Ileitis and Colitis, 1973—91; mem. nat. adv. bd. Nat. Commn. Digestive Diseases, 1977—79; mem. Coun. Subsplty. Socs. in Internal Medicine, 1978—85; chmn. grants rev. com. Nat. Found. Ileitis and Colitis, 1981—85; mem. com. to assess quality care in Medicare program, GAO and ways and means com. U.S. Ho. of Reps., 1986—89; cons. Am. Medico-Legal Found., Phila., 1996—2003, Inst. for Health Policy Analysis, Washington, 1996—2004; med. dir. Eurasian Med. Edn. Program (Russian Fedn.), 1998—2004. Editor 6 books; contbr. over 275 articles to sci. jours., books. Lt. comdr. USNR, 1960—62. Recipient Jubilee medal, Charles U. Prague, 1998, Mentors Rsch. Scholars award, AGA, 2007. Master: ACP (gov. Ohio 1980—84, health and pub. policy com. 1982—91, chmn. med. tech. assessment com. 1985—86, regent 1985—91, chmn. 1986—88, chmn. clin. practice subcom. 1988—91, del. to AMA 1989—94, Spl. Presdl. citation 1984), Am. Coll. Gastroenterology (trustee, exec. com. 1975—80, pres. 1978—79); mem.: Internat. Orgn. for Study Inflammatory Bowel Disease (dep. chmn. 1982—86), Interstate Postgrad. Med. Assn. (pres. 1983—84), Inst. Medicine of NAS (life), Am. Gastroent. Assn. (commn. on future 1973—74, tng. and edn. com. 1975—78, chmn. subcom. grad. edn. 1975—78), Assn. Program Dirs. in Internal Medicine (founding pres. 1977—79, Founder's award 1993). Democrat. Mem. Soc. Of Friends. Home: 9126 Town Gate Ln Bethesda MD 20817-4111 Office: U Rochester Med Ctr Box 646 Rochester NY 14642 Office Phone: 585-275-7432. Fax: 585-276-1911. Business E-Mail: Richard_Farmer@urmc.rochester.edu.

FARMER, RICHARD T., uniform rental and sales executive; b. Dayton, Ky., Nov. 22, 1934; BBA, Miami U., Ohio, 1956. Founder, chmn. Cintas Corp., Cin., 1968—, CEO, 1968—95. Bd. dir. Fifth Third Bancorp. Trustee Miami Univ., Ohio. Named one of Forbes Richest Americans, 2006. Office: Cintas Corp 6800 Cintas Blvd PO Box 625737 Cincinnati OH 45262-5737*

FARMER, ROBERT LINDSAY, lawyer; b. Portland, Oreg., Sept. 29, 1922; s. Paul C. and Irma (Lindsay) F.; m. Carmen E. Engebretson, Sept. 8, 1943; children: Cort W., Scott L., Eric C. BS, UCLA, 1946; LLB, U. So. Calif., 1949. Bar: Calif. 1949. Since practiced in, LA; mem. Farmer & Ridley, LA, 1949—. Trustee Edward James Found., West Dean Estate, Chichester, Eng. Served with AUS, 1943-46. Mem. ABA, Los Angeles County Bar Assn., Order of Coif, Beta Gamma Sigma, Kappa Sigma, Phi Delta Phi, Annandale Golf Club (Pasadena, Calif.). Home: 251 S Orange Grove Blvd Apt 1 Pasadena CA 91105-1766 Office: 333 S Hope St Los Angeles CA 90071

FARMER, SCOTT D., apparel executive; BA, Miami U., 1981. V.p. mktg. & merchandising, v.p. nat. account div. Cintas Corp., Cin., 1981—94, group v.p. rental div., 1994—97, bd. dir., 1994—, pres., COO, 1997—2003, pres., CEO, 2003—. Office: Cintas Corp 6800 Cintas Blvd Cincinnati OH 45262 Mailing: Cintas Corp PO Box 625737 Cincinnati OH 45262-5737*

FARMER, SUSAN LAWSON, retired broadcast executive, former secretary of state; b. Boston, May 29, 1942; d. Ralph and Margaret (Tyng) Lawson; m. Malcolm Farmer, III, Apr. 6, 1968; children: Heidi Benson, Stephanie Lawson. Student, Garland Jr. Coll., 1960-61, Brown U., 1961-62; LHD, Bryant Coll., 2004. Mem. Providence Home Rule Charter Commn., 1979-80; sec. of state State of R.I., Providence, 1983-87; pres., CEO Sta. WSBE-TV R.I. PBS, Providence, 1987—2004; polit. analyst WJAR-TV NBC, 2006—. Spl. adv. R.I. Family Ct., 1978-83; mem. nat. voting stds. panel Fed. Election Commn. co-chmn. Nat. Voter Edn. Project; mem. electoral coll., 1984; chmn. Gov.'s Com. on Ethics in Govt., 1985-86; mem. tchg. facility and adv. panel Internat. Ctr. on Election Law and Adminstrn.; mem. nat. edn. adv. com. Pub. Broadcasting System,

1987-89; trustee Eastern Ednl. TV Network, 1987-95; mem. R.I. Task Force on Tech., 1995-04, R.I. Info. Mgmt. Commn., 1997; bd. dirs., mem. exec. com. Program Resources Group, 1993-01; mem. Gov.'s Telecom. Task Force, 2000-04; mem. nat. media adv. com. WomenFuture, 2002-04. Bd. dirs. Justice Resources Corp., R.I. Council Alcoholism, R.I. Hist. Soc., Planned Parenthood (R.I. chpt.), R.I. Rape Crisis Ctr., The Newport Inst., Marathon House, Inc., chmn.; mem. Mayor's Task Force on Child Abuse, R.I. Film Commn.; v.p. Miriam Hosp. Found.; mem. adv. com. Women in Polit. and Govtl. Careers Program, U. R.I., 1985-95; mem. adv. bd. Com. for Study of Am. Electorate-Ford Found. Project-Efficacy in State Voting Laws, 1986; mem. Commn. to Study Length of Election Process, 1985-87; steering com. Nat. Fund for America's Future, Project Vote R.I.; bd. dirs. Dawn for Children Tng. Thru Placement; pres. R.I. PBS Found.; bd. dirs. R.I. Anti-Drug Coalition Exec. Com., Nat. Forum for Pub. TV Execs., 1998-2004, chmn., 1999; mem. corp. Butler Hosp. Recipient Nat. Overall Devel. award PBS, 1989, 90, Nat. Advocacy award Assn. Pub. TV Stas., 2004; named Woman of Yr., Nat. Women's Polit. Caucus, 1980, Bus. and Profl. Women, 1983. Mem. NATAS (bd. govs. New Eng. chpt. 1995—), N.E. Assn. Schs. and Colls. (com. on tech. and course instns.), So. Ednl. Comms. Assn. (bd. dirs. 1993-96), R.I. Women's Polit. Caucus (Woman of Yr. 1980), Bus. and Profl. Women (Woman of Yr. 1984), Orgn. State Broadcasting Execs, Agawam Hunt Club, Mill Reef Club (Antigua, West Indies), Nat. Assn. of Ams. Pub. TV Stas. (trustee 1996-2002, Nat. Advocacy award, 2004), Nat. Acad. TV Arts and Scis. (bd. govs. N.E. chpt. 1995-2001), Nat. Ednl. Telecomms. Assn. (bd. dirs. 1997-2004, Nat. Forum Pub. TV Execs. (bd. dirs. 1998-2004, chmn. 1999). Avocations: golf, gardening, art, crossword puzzles, travel. Home: 190 Upton Ave Providence RI 02906-1552 Personal E-mail: sfarmer10@cox.net.

FARMER, TERRY D(WAYNE), lawyer; b. Oklahoma City, May 1, 1949; s. Gayle V. and Allene (Edsall) F.; m. Nicole M. Charlebois; children: Grant L., Tyler M. BA, U. Okla., 1971, JD, 1974. Bar: Okla. 1974, N.Mex. 1975, U.S. Dist. Ct. N.Mex. 1976, U.S. Ct. Claims 1975, U.S. Ct. Appeals (10th cir.) 1977, U.S. Supreme Ct. 1980. Asst. trust officer First Nat. Bank of Albuquerque, 1974-75; assoc. Nordhaus, Moses & Dunn, Albuquerque, 1975-78, ptnr., 1978-80; dir. Moses, Dunn, Farmer & Tuthill, P.C., Albuquerque, 1980—. Pres. Albuquerque Lawyers Club, N. Mex., 1982-83. Named one of Outstanding Lawyers Am. Fellow N.Mex. Bar Found.; mem. N.Mex. Bar Assn. (pres. Young Lawyers div., 1978-79), Okla. Bar Assn., N.Mex. Trial Lawyers, Am. Trial Lawyers Assn. Office: Moses Dunn Farmer & Tuthill PC PO Box 27047 Albuquerque NM 87125-7047 Office Phone: 505-843-9440. Business E-Mail: terry@moseslaw.com.

FARNAM, JAFAR, allergist, immunologist, pediatrician; b. Tabriz, Iran, Dec. 18, 1945; MD, Faculty Medicine Tabriz, 1972. Diplomate Am. Bd. Pediat., Am. Bd. Allergy and Immunology. Intern U. Ill. Hosp., Chgo., 1977-78; resident in pediat. Christ Hosp.- Rush U., Oaklawn, 1978-80; fellow in allergy & immunology U. Tex. Med. Br., Galveston, 1980-82, clin. assoc. prof. internal medicine; with Clear Lake Regional Hosp. Mem. Am. Acad. Pediat., Am. Acad. Allergy, Asthma, and Immunology, Am. Coll. Allergy, Asthma, and Immunology, Tex. Med. Assn., Tex. Allergy Soc. Office: Allergy Asthma Ctr 450 Medical Center Blvd Ste 204 Webster TX 77598-4229 Office Phone: 281-338-2246. Business E-Mail: farnammd@bluegate.com.

FARNAM, THOMAS CAMPBELL, lawyer, educator; b. Indpls., Feb. 13, 1945; s. Frederick Dean Farnam and Isabelle (Campbell) Fearheiley; m. Naomi Maddox Morales, Oct. 6, 2001; children: Rachel Anne Stujenske, Thomas Matthews. BS, Butler U., 1966; JD, Ind. U., Indpls., 1970; LLM in Taxation, Georgetown U., 1973. Bar: Ind. 1970, U.S. Dist. Ct. (so. dist.) Ind. 1970, U.S. Ct. Appeals (7th cir.) 1970, U.S. Tax Ct. 1970, Mo. 1983, U.S. Supreme Ct 1991. Asst. dir. advanced underwriting Indpls. Life Ins. Co., 1970-72; tax atty., employee benefits specialist Emerson Electric Co., St. Louis, 1973-78; benefits cons. Alexander & Alexander, St. Louis, 1978-79; asst. v.p. pension profit sharing Centerre Trust, St. Louis, 1979-82; dir. of pensions St. Louis Home Builders Assn., St. Louis, 1982-83; v.p., gen. counsel, benefits cons. Pension Assocs., Inc., St. Louis, 1983-84; pvt. practice St. Louis, 1984-92, 1993—; adj. prof. Webster U., St. Louis, 1984-93. Bd. dirs. Small Bus. Coun. Am., Washington; exec. com. Employee Benefits Assn. of St. Louis, 1985-99, Art St. Louis, Inc.; steering com. WEB, St. Louis, 1987-90. Contbr. chpt. to book and articles to profl. jours. Trustee Eugene Field Found., St. Louis, 1986—; pres. of trustee Wydown Terr., Clayton, Mo., 1982-93; com. chmn. troop 21 Boy Scouts Am., Clayton, 1989-92, asst. scoutmaster, 1992-98, post advisor Explorer Post 9021, Clayton, 1996-97; mem. parish coun. St. Joseph's Ch., Clayton, 1982-85. Fellow Am. Coll. Tax Counsel, Am. Coll. Employee Benefits Counsel; mem. ABA (taxation, bus. & labor sect., employee benefit coms.), Mo. State Bar Assn., Ind. State Bar Assn., Bar Assn. Met. St. Louis (chair employee benefits com. 1986-93), Noonday Club. Republican. Avocations: restoring 356 porsches, photography, computers, cooking. Office: One Metropolitan Sq 211 N Broadway Ste 2940 Saint Louis MO 63102-2733 Office Phone: 314-241-5848. E-mail: tcf@farnamlaw.com.

FARNER, DARLA A., artist; b. East Chgo., Ind., Mar. 13, 1959; d. Richard Calvin Vickery and Charlene Elizabeth Cornett; m. Randy Dean Farner, Aug. 25, 1988. Degree equivalent in Med. Office, MTI Food C.C., Gresham, Oreg., 1989. Web artist WaterColorInMotion.com, Portland, 1999—. Office: WaterColorInMotion.com 1024 NE 195th Portland OR 97230 Office Phone: 503-666-2804. Business E-Mail: darla.farner@comcast.net.

FARNER, GORDON NOBLE, retired orthopedist, surgeon; b. Norfolk, Nebr., Dec. 30, 1924; s. Floyd Durling and Eth Farner; m. Jeanne Margret Spurgeon; children: Gary, Corrinne. BS, U. Nebr., Omaha, 1946, MD, 1948. Diplomate Am. Bd. Orthop. Surgery. Asst. chief ortohpedic surgery US Army Tripler Army Hosp., Honolulu, 1952—54; chief surgery dept. Marymount Hosp., Cleve., 1970—75, head orthop. surgery; et. With US Army, 1943—44, capt. US Army, 1952—54. Mem.: ACS, Am. Acad. Orthop. Home: 15915 Westerlay Terr Jupiter FL 33477

FARNER, WENDY MINEAU, lawyer; married; 2 children. Grad. summa cum laude, U. Ill., 1985; law degree with honors, U. Chgo. Law Sch., 1988. Cert.: Tex. Bd. Legal Specialization (estate planning and probate law). Ptnr. Farner & Perrin, LLP, Houston. Named one of Top 100 Attys., Worth mag., 2005—06. Office: Farner & Perrin LLP Chase Bldg at Sage Rd 5177 Richmond Ave Houston TX 77056 Office Phone: 713-622-0900. Office Fax: 713-622-8833.*

FARNEY, CHARLOTTE EUGENIA, musician, educator; b. Long Beach, Calif., Jan. 06; d. Charles Thomas and Eugenia Moody (Fisher) Dalton; m. John Nathan Pierce, Aug. 1972 (div. 1978); m. Raymond C. Farney, June 30, 1990; stepchildren: Anna Louise, Paul Jerrod. AA, Orange Coast Coll., Costa Mesa, Calif., 1959; MusB, U. Redlands, 1962; MusM, Yale U., 1966; D of Musical Arts, U. Ariz., 1983. Std. secondary cert. tchg. music K-12 and Spanish Ariz. Cellist Denver Symphony Orch., 1966—69; instr., mem. faculty trio West Tex. State U., Canyon, 1969—71; grad. tchg. asst. cello U. Ariz., Tucson, 1977—81; string orch./gen. music tchr. Tucson Unified Sch. Dist., 1979—90; string orch. tchr. Scottsdale (Ariz.) Unified Sch. Dist., 1995—2001, Washington Elem. Sch. Dist., Phoenix, 2001—; cellist Tucson Symphony Orch., 1977—90, West Valley Symphony, Sun City, Ariz., 1990—2005, String Sounds, Phoenix, 1994—99. Pvt. cello tchr., Denver, 1966—69, Scottsdale, Ariz., 2002—; prin. first chair cellist Amarillo Symphony, Tex., 1969—71; cellist Symphony Orch., Toluca, Mexico, 1974—77; cello soloist Tucson Civic Orch., 1982, Chaparral Christian Ch., 1998—; cons. in field. Author music revs. Asst. Sunday sch. tchr. Scholar, Yale U., 1963—66, Denver Symphony Guild, 1968, Tchrs. Performance Inst./Oberlin Coll., 1969, Blossom Music Sch., 1970. Mem.: Music Educators Nat. Conf., Am. String Tchrs. Assn. with Nat. Sch. Orch. Assn. (coach String Fling Phoenix chpt. 2000—02, coach Cellobration 2001—03), Sigma Alpha Iota (chaplain U. Redlands chpt 1960—61, v.p. mem., program chmn. Phoenix Alumni chpt. 1996—2000, 2004—06, Sword of Honor 1998, Rose of Honor 2000). Avocations: travel, chamber music. Office: Desert View Elem Sch 8621 N 3rd St Phoenix AZ 85020 Personal E-mail: charcello1@cox.net.

FARNGALO, ROSEMARIE MERRITT, school psychologist; d. Ormond StClair and Elaine Louis Merritt; children: Aisha Ferngalo, Zuri Ferngalo. BS in Criminal Justice, CUNY, 1980, MEd in Sch. Psychology, 1993; PhD in Guidance and Counseling, Union Inst. & U., 2004. Cert. sch. psychologist Ga. Instr. Interborn Inst., NYC, 1980—81; health rschr. WHO, Trinidad and Tobago, 1981—84; educator NYC Bd. Edn., Bklyn., 1984—93; sch. psychologist Dekalb County Schs., Decatur, Ga., 1995—. Behavior cons. DPCH, Decatur, 2004—; cons. United Way, Atlanta, 2005—. Named Outstanding Presenter, Peer Helpers Dekalb County, 2004, Unity Cmty. Coalition, Ga., 2004. Mem.: Nat. Assn. Sch. Psychologists, Order Ea. Star (chaplain 2002—04), Zeta Phi Beta (Outstanding Presenter 2003). Democrat. Avocations: travel, music, reading. Office: Deklab County Schs 5839 Meml Dr Stone Mountain GA 30083 Office Phone: 678-676-1930. E-mail: rfarngalo@comcast.net.

FARNHAM, ANTHONY EDWARD, language educator, department chairman; b. Oakland, Calif., July 2, 1930; s. Willard Edward and Frances Fern (Hicks) F.; m. Frances Anne Larkey, Dec. 28, 1957; children: Allen Nicholas, Timothy John. AB, U. Calif.-Berkeley, 1951; MA, Harvard U., 1957, PhD, 1964. Instr. English Mt. Holyoke Coll., South Hadley, Mass., 1961-64, asst. prof., 1964-69, assoc. prof., 1969-72, prof., 1972-99, dept. chmn., 1979-85, prof. emeritus, 1999—. Editor: A Sourcebook in the History of English, 1969; author: Statement and Search in the Confessio Amantis, Mediaevalia 16, 1993. Served with M.I. US Army, 1953—56. Mem. MLA, Am. Cath. Hist. Assn., Medieval Acad. Am., Assn. Literary Scholars and Critics, Dante Soc., New Chaucer Soc., Phi Beta Kappa. Roman Catholic. Home: 23 Atwood Rd South Hadley MA 01075-1601 Office: Mt Holyoke Coll Dept English 50 Coll St South Hadley MA 01075-6421

FARNHAM, CLAYTON HENSON, lawyer; b. New Brunswick, NJ, Aug. 18, 1938; s. Richard Bayles and Naomi Shropshire (Henson) F.; m. Katharine Gross, Sept. 16, 1967; children: Julia Kernan, Richard Bayles II. BA, U. of the South, 1961; LLB, U. Ga., 1967. Bar: Ga. 1968, U.S. Dist. Ct. (no., so. and mid. dists.) Ga. 1968, U.S. Supreme Ct. 1978, U.S. Dist. Ct. (no. dist.) Miss. 1978, U.S. Dist. Ct. (ea. dist.), Tenn. 1997, U.S. Ct. Appeals (5th cir., 11th cir.) 1968, (4th cir.) 1981, U.S. Ct. Appeals (8th cir.) 1992. Law clk. to judge U.S. Dist. Ct., Atlanta, 1967-69; from assoc., to ptnr. Swift, Currie, McGhee & Hiers, Atlanta, 1969-82; ptnr. Drew, Eckl & Farnham, Atlanta, 1983—. Contbr. articles to profl. jours. Lt. (j.g.) USNR, 1961-64. Mem. ABA (coun. TIPS sect. 1989-92), Internat. Assn. Def. Counsel (com. chmn. 1987-89), Ansley Golf Club, Lawyer's Club Atlanta, Old War Horse Lawyer's Club. Home: 30 Inman Cir NE Atlanta GA 30309 Office: Drew Eckl & Farnham 800 W Peachtree St NW PO Box 7600 Atlanta GA 30357 Home Phone: 404-892-2283; Office Phone: 404-885-1400. Business E-Mail: cfarnham@deflaw.com.

FARNSWORTH, ELIZABETH, broadcast journalist; b. Mpls., Dec. 23, 1943; d. H. Bernerd and Jane (Mills) Fink; m. Charles E. Farnsworth, June 20, 1966; children: Jennifer Farnsworth Fellows, Samuel. BA, Middlebury Coll., 1965; MA in History, Stanford U., 1966; LLD (hon.), Colby Coll., 2002. Reporter, panelist PBS World Press, KQED, San Francisco, 1975-77; reporter InterNews, Berkeley, Calif., 1977-80; freelance TV and print reporter, San Francisco, 1980-91; fgn. corr. MacNeil/Lehrer News Hour, San Francisco, 1991-95; chief corr., prin. substitute anchor News Hour with Jim Lehrer, Arlington, Va., 1995-97, San Francisco, 1997-99, sr. corr., 1999—2004, spl. corr., 2005—. Co-author: El Bloqueo Invisible, 1974; prodr., dir. documentary Thanh's War, 1991 (Cine Golden Eagle award); contbr. articles to various publs. Mem. adv. bd. Berkeley Edn. Found., 1990-95, U. Calif. Sch. Journalism, Berkeley; mem. nat. adv. bd. Ctr. Investigative Reporting, 2001-; bd. dirs. Data Ctr., Oakland, Calif., 1993-95. Recipient Golden Gate award San Francisco Film Festival, 1984, Best Investigative Reporting award No. Calif. Radio, TV News Dirs.' Assn., 1986, Blue Ribbon, Am. Film and Video Festival, 1991, Silver World medal N.Y. Film Festivals, 2001; nominee Emmy award, 2002. Mem. AFTRA, NATAS, World Affairs Coun. No. Calif. (bd. dirs. 1998-2004), Nat. Adv. Writers Corps, Phi Beta Kappa. Presbyterian. Avocations: gardening, hiking, poetry.

FARNSWORTH, FRANK ALBERT, retired economics professor; b. Manchester, NH, 1909; s. Frank Adelbert and Lancing Claudine (Miller) F.; m. Ruth Coburn, June 26 1943 (dec. 1970); children: Frank A., Ruth Farnsworth Eldridge, John C.; m. Elizabeth Hoyt Martire, Dec. 26, 1971 (dec. June 1988); children: Elizabeth M. Cutter-Hickman, Amy Martire, John Martire. AB in Econs. with honors, Colgate U., Hamilton, NY, 1939; AM, Harvard U., Cambridge, Mass., 1946, PhD, 1952. With dept. econ. Colgate U., 1941-87, prof., 1957-87, ret., 1987. Dept. chmn., vis. rsch. assoc. Grad. Bus. Sch., Harvard U., 1947-48; Fulbright prof. Norwegian Sch. Econ., Bergen, 1954-55; vis. prof. small bus. Wake Forest U., 1975; vis. fellow Massey Coll.-U. Toronto, Ont., Can., 1968; ex-officio mem. Madison County Indsl. Devel. Agy.; bd. dir. Otter Valley Press, Inc., Am. Tree Farmer, Svc. Corp. of Ret. Execs.; cons. in field. Mem. AAUP, Am. Mgmt. Assn., N.Y. State Econ. Devel. Coun., Masons, Alpha Chi Epsilon, Alpha Delta Phi. Republican. Home: 17 E Kendrick Ave Hamilton NY 13346-1311 Office: 1119 Wheeler Rd Brandon VT 05733-8922 Home Phone: 315-824-1793; Office Phone: 802-247-4128. Personal E-mail: farnsworth@mail.colgate.edu. Business E-Mail: vtotter@together.net.

FARNSWORTH, STEVEN ROBERT, safety engineer; s. Robert Wayne and Ruth Marie Farnsworth; m. Lynette Rae Dass, Sept. 23, 1973; children: Stephanie Lynn Hudson, Shane Robert. AA, Iowa Lakes C.C., 1982. Cert. welding inspector, Am. Welding Soc., 1992, welder, Profl. Svc. Industries, 1998. Shipfitter U.S.S. Basilone U.S. Navy, San Diego, 1973—77, technician hull maintenance U.S.S. White Plaines U.S. Naval Base, Guam, 1984—86, inspector quality assurance USS Hunley Norfolk, Va., 1987—88; welder, heavy equipment operator Spencer (Iowa) Constrn. Co., 1977—79; instr. welding Iowa Lakes C.C., Emmetsburg, Iowa, 1979—84, welding instr., 1988—. With USN, 1973—77. Mem.: Am. Welding Soc. (assoc.), Kiwanis. Democrat. Methodist. Avocations: hunting, golf. Home: 3506 1st Street Emmetsburg IA 50536 Office; Iowa Lakes Community College 3200 College Drive Emmetsburg IA 50536 Home Phone: 712-852-5272; Office Phone: 712-852-3554. Office Fax: 712-852-2152; Home Fax: 712-852-2152. Personal E-mail: sfarnsworth1@iowalakes.edu.

FARNSWORTH, T. BROOKE, lawyer; b. Grand Rapids, Mich., Mar. 16, 1945; s. George Llelwyn and Gladys Fern (Kennedy) Farnsworth; m. Connie D. Hedblom, June 15, 1996; children: Leslie Erin, T. Brooke. BS in Bus., Ind. U., Indpls., 1967, JD, 1971. Bar: Tex. 1971, US Dist. Ct. (so. dist.) Tex. 1972, U.S. Tax Ct. 1972, US Ct. Appeals (5th cir.) 1977, US Ct. Appeals (DC Cir.) 1977, US Supreme Ct. 1978, US Ct. Appeals (11th cir.) 1982, US Dist. Ct. (we. dist.) Tex. 1988, US Dist. Ct. (no. dist.) Tex. 1994, US Ct. Appeals (10th cir.) 2003. Adminstrv. asst. to treas. of State of Ind., Indpls., 1968-71; assoc. Butler, Binion, Rice, Cook & Knapp, Houston, 1971-74; counsel Damson Oil Corp., Houston, 1974-78; prin. Farnsworth & Assocs., Houston, 1978-90, Farnsworth & von Berg, Houston, 1990—. Contbr. articles on law to profl. jours. Law adv. bd. mem. Inst. Energy. Fellow: Tex. Bar Found., Coll. State Bar Tex.; mem.: AAJ, ABA, Inst. for Energy Law (mem. adv. bd.), Houston Bar Assn., State Bar Tex., Champions Golf Club, Olympic Club. Republican. Home: 6038 Pebble Beach Dr Houston TX 77069 Office: Farnsworth and von Berg 333 N Sam Houston Pkwy E Ste 300 Houston TX 77060-2414 Home Phone: 281-444-8000; Office Phone: 281-931-8902. Business E-Mail: tbfarnsworth@farnsworthvonberg.com.

FARON, SALLY ROGERS, performing arts association administrator, consultant; b. Augusta, Maine, Oct. 27, 1931; d. Allan Harvard and Edith Robinson Rogers; m. Louis Charles Faron, Dec. 18, 1974. AB, Wellesley Coll., 1953; MA, Boston U., 1957. Tchr., acad. dean Ho. in the Pines, Norton, Mass., 1953—55, 1959—60; tchr. Beverly (Mass.) HS, 1955—57; asst. to headmaster Mac Duffie Sch., Springfield, Mass., 1960—61; adminstr., tchr., prin., acting head Barnard Sch. for Girls, NYC, 1961—74; adminstrv. asst. Bach Aria Festival, Stony Brook, NY, 1981—86; exec. dir. La Musica di Asolo, Sarasota, Fla., 1989—. Editor: (cookbook) Overtures & Artichokes, 1976; contbr. Ency. Indians of the Ams. Pres., bd. dirs. Suffolk Symphony, Smithtown, NY, 1975—80; founder, pres. Suffolk Music Guild, Stony Brook, 1980—86; mem. adv. coun. Bach Aria Festival, Stony Brook, 1980—90; chmn. Young Artists Competition Suffolk County, Stony Brook, 1979—86; mem. cultural exec. com. Sarasota County Arts Coun., 1992—; bd. dirs. Key Chorale, Sarasota, 2004—. Recipient Founder's medal, Barnard Sch. for Girls, 1973; grantee, NIMH, 1965—66, 1967. Mem.: Chamber Music Am. Office: La Musica PO Box 5442 Sarasota FL 34277 Office Phone: 941-346-2601. Fax: 941-346-2414. E-mail: salfar544@juno.com.

FARQUHAR, DORIS IRENE DAVIS, academic administrator; b. Wharton, Tex., Apr. 4, 1946; d. Charles Roy Davis and Pauline Maxine Tyson Powers; m. 1966 (div. 1981); children: Marcus Lea, Davis Carlton. Student, Southwest Tex. State, 1964-67. Licensed pvt. pilot. Dir. radiology grad. med. edn. M.D. Anderson Cancer Ctr., Houston, 1969-72; dir. grad. med. edn. Baylor Coll. Medicine, Houston, 1972-78; dir. acad. affairs med. sch. U. Tex., Houston, 1978-93; dir. acad. affairs dept. surgery sch. medicine Yale U., New Haven, 1993-99; instr. surgery Va. Commonwealth U. Med. Coll. Va., Richmond, 1999—. Cons. quality assurance improvement WHO, 1997—. Author: Chapter 10 Directory to GME, 1994. Mem. Assn. Am. Med. Colls. (task force GME 1991-95, steering com. GME 1995-97), Assn. Hosp. Med. Educators (bd. dirs. 1993-95, sec.-treas. 1993-95), Houston Livestock Show & Rodeo (life). Avocations: horses, flying, needlepoint. Office: Va Commonwealth U/Med Coll Va Dept Surgery Richmond VA 23298

FARQUHAR, JAMES, geochemist, researcher; b. Chgo., Jan. 6, 1965; s. James Douglas and Sue (Wakeman) F.; m. Lisa Joan Tuit, Dec. 31, 1994; children: James Henry, Anna Ruth. BS, Washington and Lee U., 1987; MSc, U. Chgo., 1990; PhD, U. Alta., Edmonton, Can., 1995. Fellow Carnegie Instn. Washington, 1995-97; NSF fellow U. Calif., San Diego, 1997-99, rsch. chemist, 1999-2001; asst. prof. geochemistry U. Md., College Park, 2000—05, assoc. prof. geochemistry, 2005—. Assoc. prof. Earth Sci. Interdisciplinary Ctr., dept. geology U. Md., 2000-05. Assoc. editor Geochimica et Cosmachanica Acta, 2003—; mem. editl. bd. Geobiology, 2000—. Killam grad. fellow Killam Found., Can., 1993-95; recipient F. W. Clarke medal Geochem. Soc., 2000. Mem. AAAS, Am. Chem. Soc., Am. Geophys. Union. Office: UMCP Dept Geology and ESSIC College Park MD 20742 E-mail: jfarquha@essic.umd.edu.

FARQUHAR, JOHN WILLIAM, physician, educator; b. Winnipeg, Man., Can., June 13, 1927; arrived in U.S., 1934; s. John Giles and Marjorie Victoria (Roberts) Farquhar; m. Christine Louise Johnson, July 14, 1968; children: Margaret F., John C.M.;children from previous marriage: Bruce E., Douglas G. AB, U. Calif., Berkeley, 1949; MD, U. Calif., San Francisco, 1952. Intern U. Calif. Hosp., San Francisco, 1952—53, resident, 1953—54, 1957—58, postdoctoral fellow, 1955—57; resident U. Minn., Mpls., 1954—55; rsch. assoc. Rockefeller U., NYC, 1958—62; asst. prof. medicine Stanford (Calif.) U., 1962—66, assoc. prof., 1966—73, prof., 1978—, C.F. Rehnborg prof. in disease prevention, 1989—2000; dir. Stanford Ctr. Rsch. in Disease Prevention, 1973—98; dir. collaborating ctr. for chronic disease prevention WHO, 1985—99; prof. health rsch. and policy, 1988—. Mem. staff Stanford U. Hosp.; chair Victoria Declaration Implementation com. Author: The American Way of Life Need Not Be Hazardous to Your Health, 1978, 1987; author: (with Gene Spiller) The Last Puff, 1990; author: The Victoria Declaration for Heart Health, 1992, How to Reduce Your Risk of Heart Disease, 1994, The Catalonia Declaration: Investing in Heart Health, 1996, Worldwide Efforts to Improve Heart Disease, 1997; author: (with Spiller) Diagnosis Heart Disease: Answers to Your Questions about Recovery and Lasting Health, 2001; contbr. articles to profl. jours. With US Army, 1944—46. Recipient James D. Bruce award, ACP, 1983, Myrdal prize, 1986, Dana award for Pioneering Achievement in Health, Dana Found., 1990, Nat. Cholesterol award for Pub. Edn., Nat. Cholesterol Edn. Program of NIH, 1991, Rsch. Achievement award, Am. Heart Assn., 1992, Order of St. George for Svc. to Autonomous Govt. of Catalonia, 1996, Joseph Stokes Preventive Cardiology award, Am. Soc. Preventive Cardiology, 1999, Ancel Keys Meml. lectureship, Am. Heart Assn., 2000, Fries prize Improving Health, 2005. Mem.: Internat. Heart Health Soc., Soc. Behavioral Medicine (pres. 1991—92), Am. Heart Assn. (coun. epidemiology and prevention), Am. Soc. Clin. Investigation, Inst. Medicine NAS, Gold Headed Cane Soc., Alpha Omega Alpha, Sigma Xi. Episcopalian. Office: Stanford U Sch of Medicine Stanford Prevention Rsch Ctr 211 Quarry Rd Stanford CA 94305-5705 Business E-Mail: John.Farquhar@stanford.edu.

FARQUHAR, MARILYN GIST, cell biologist, pathologist, educator; b. Tulare, Calif., July 11, 1928; d. Brooks DeWitt and Alta (Green) Gist; m. John W. Farquhar, June 4, 1952; children: Bruce, Douglas (div. 1968); m. George Palade, June 7, 1970. AB, U. Calif., Berkeley, 1949, MA, 1952, PhD, 1955. Asst. rsch. pathologist Sch. Medicine U. Calif., San Francisco, 1956—58, assoc. rsch. pathologist, 1962—64, assoc. prof., 1964—68, prof. pathology, 1968—70; rsch. assoc. Rockefeller U., NYC, 1958—62, prof. cell biology, 1970—73, Sch. Medicine Yale U., New Haven, 1973—87, Sterling prof. cell biology and pathology, 1987—90; prof. pathology cell molecular medicine U. Calif., San Diego, 1990—, chair divsn. cellular and molecular medicine, 1991—99, prof. cellular & molecular medicine, chair dept. cellular & molecular medicine, 1999—. Mem. editorial bd. numerous sci. jours.; contbr. articles to profl. jours. Recipient Career Devel. award NIH, 1968-73, Disting. Sci. medal Electron Microscope Soc., 1987, Gomori medal Histochem. Soc., 1999, A.N. Richards award Internat. Soc. Nephrology, 2003, FASAB Excellence Sci. award, 2006. Mem.: NAS, Internat. Soc. Nephrology (A.N. Richards award 2003), Am. Soc. Nephrology (Homer Smith award 1988, Gottschalk award 2002), Am. Assn. Investigative Pathology (Rous Whipple award 2001), Am. Soc. Cell Biology (pres. 1981—82, E.B. Wilson medal 1987), Am. Acad. Arts and Scis. Home and Office: U Calif San Diego Sch Med 12894 Via Latina Del Mar CA 92014-3730

FARQUHAR, ROBERT MICHAEL, lawyer; b. Chelsea, Mass., Apr. 28, 1954; s. Robert Vociel and Helen Margaret (Stevens) F.; m. Carol Elizabeth Auch, Dec. 16, 1978; children: Stephanie Elizabeth, Andrew Michael. BS, So. Meth. U., 1977, JD, 1980. Bar: Tex. 1980, U.S. Dist. Ct. (no. and ea. dists.) Tex. 1980, U.S. Ct. Appeals (5th and 11th cirs.) 1980, U.S. Supreme Ct. 1990; cert. bus. bankruptcy law Tex. Bd. Legal Specialization. Assoc. Carter Jones MaGee Rudberg Moss & Mayes, Dallas, 1980-82; ptnr. Johnson & Cravens, Dallas, 1982-88; shareholder Winstead Sechrest &

Minick, P.C., Dallas, 1988—. Mem. ABA, Dallas Bar Assn. Republican. Episcopalian. Avocations: bicycling, computers. Office: Winstead Sechrest Minick PC 1201 Elm St Ste 5400 Dallas TX 75270-2199

FARQUHAR, ROBERT NICHOLS, lawyer; b. Dayton, Ohio, Apr. 23, 1936; s. Robert Lawrence and Mary Frances (Nichols) F.; m. Elizabeth Lynn Bryan, Aug. 29, 1959 (div. 1971); children: Robert Nichols, Jensen; m. Carol A. Smith, Dec. 27, 1975. AB, Kenyon Coll., 1958; JD, Cornell U., 1961. Bar: Ohio 1961, Mich. 1993, U.S. Dist. Ct. (so. dist.) Ohio 1962, U.S. Ct. Appeals (6th cir.) 1966, U.S. Supreme Ct. 1978. Assoc. Altick & McDaniel, Dayton, 1961-69; ptnr. Gould, Bailey & Farquhar and predecessor firms, Dayton, 1969-78, Brumbaugh, Corwin & Gould, Dayton, 1978-80, Altick & Corwin, Dayton, 1981—, pres., 1996—2005. Bd. dirs. Ohio Law Abstract Pub., Columbus; city atty., Centerville, Ohio, 1969-2004, Oakwood, Ohio, 1997-2004; sec., gen. counsel Miami Conservancy Dist., 1990-2004; bd. commrs. character and fitness Ohio Supreme Ct., 1987-94, 97-2003, chair, 2000-02. Mem. Montgomery County Rep. Ctrl. Com, 1965-69, exec. com., 1968-69; bd. dirs. Centerville Hist. Soc., 1971-75, 2005—, pres. 1973-74; trustee Montgomery County Legal Aid Soc., 1972-76; trustee Dayton Law Libr. Assn., 1972—, pres., 1980-86; mem. governing bd. Carillon Hist. Park, Dayton, chair, 1999-2001; mem. congressional screening com. U.S. Naval Acad., 1979-83; mem. adv. coun. Bimini Mus., 1994—. Mem. ABA (ho. of dels. 2001-2004), Ohio State Bar Assn. (chmn. legal ethics and profl. conduct com. 1982-86, exec. com. 1988-91, coun. of dels. 1988—), Dayton Bar Assn. Found. (pres. 1984-90), Dayton Bar Assn. (pres. 1984-85), New Eng. Hist. Geneaol. Soc. (coun. mem. 2005—), Dayton Bicycle Club, Dayton Lawyers Club, Delta Phi, Phi Delta Phi. Episcopalian. Home: 1731 Ladera Trl Dayton OH 45459-1403 Office: Altick & Corwin 1700 One Dayton Ctr 1 S Main St Dayton OH 45402-2024 Office Phone: 937-223-1201. Business E-Mail: farquhar@altickcorwin.com.

FARQUHAR, ROBIN HUGH, educational consultant, former university president; b. Victoria, BC, Can., Dec. 1, 1938; s. Hugh Ernest and Jean (MacIntosh) F.; m. Frances Harriet Caswell, July 6, 1963; children: Francine Jean Glandt, Katherine Lynn Buchanan, Susan Ann Storey. BA with honors, U. B.C., 1960, MA, 1964; PhD, U. Chgo., 1967; Hon. Diploma in Adult Edn., Red River C.C., 1989. Tchr., counsellor, coach Edward Milne Secondary Sch., Sooke, B.C., 1962-64; assoc. dir., then dep. dir. Univ. Council Ednl. Adminstrn., Columbus, Ohio, 1966-71; chmn. ednl. adminstrn. dept., asst. dir. Ont. Inst. Studies in Edn., Toronto, 1971-76; prof. U. Toronto, 1974-76; prof., dean Coll. Edn., U. Sask., Saskatoon, 1976-81; prof., pres. U. Winnipeg, 1981-89, Carleton U., Ottawa, Ont., Canada, 1989—96, prof. policy pub. and adminstrn., 1996—2004, prof. emeritus, 2004—; spl. advisor to pres. of Salzburg Seminar, 2002; cons. Assn. Univs. & Colls. of Canada, 2004—, Can. Bureau Internat. Edn., 2004—, European Univ. Assn., 2004—. Author: The Humanities in Preparing Educational Administrators, 1970, Preparing Educational Leaders: A Review of Recent Literature, 1972; editor: Social Science Content for Preparing Educational Leaders, 1973, Educational Administration in Australia and Abroad: Analyses and Challenges, 1975, Canadian and Comparative Educational Administration, 1980, The Canadian School Superintendent, 1989, Advancing Education: School Leadership in Action, 1991, Advancing the Canadian Agenda for International Education, 2001; mem. editl. bd. Jour. Edn. Adminstrn., 1973-86. Campaign chair United Way Winnipeg, corp. sec. Winnipeg Symphony Orchestra, hon. bd. Opera Lyra Ottawa, bd. memb Ottawa-Carleton Econ. Dvpmt. Corp., Prairie Theatre Exchange Fdn., Cdn. Comp. Auditing Fdn. Served with Can. Navy Res., 1956-64. Recipient Edward L. Bernays Found. prize, 1968, Commemorative medal for 125th Anniversary of Confedn. of Can., 1993, Ottawa-Carleton Partnership award of excellence for leadership, 1996, Can. Bur. Internat. Edn. award of Merit, 1998; named Hon. Citizen, City of Winnipeg, 1989; hon. mem. Scouts Can., 1992. Fellow Commonwealth Coun. Ednl. Adminstrn. (former pres.); mem. Can. Bur. Internat. Edn. (former chmn.), Can. Soc. Study Edn. (former pres.), Can. Edn. Assn. (former dir.), InterAm. Soc. for Ednl. Adminstrn. (former dir.), Ottawa-Carleton Econ. Devel. Corp. (former dir.), Ottawa-Carleton Rsch. Inst. (former dir.), Corp. Higher Edn. Forum (former dir.), Nat. Acad. of Sch. Execs. (former dir.). Avocations: music, jogging, reading. Personal E-mail: rfarquha@connect.carleton.ca.

FARQUHARSON, GORDON MACKAY, lawyer, director; b. Charlottetown, PEI, Can., July 12, 1928; s. Percy Alfred and Rachel Lillian (MacKay) F.; m. Judy Lynne Bridges, Oct. 10, 1980; children: Trevor, Jordan; children by previous marriage: Douglas, Tanyss, Rob, Caryn. BA, U. Toronto, 1950; LL.B., Osgoode Hall Law Sch., 1954. Bar: Called to Ont. bar 1954; Queen's Counsel 1965. Pvt. practice, Toronto, 1954—; ptnr. Lang Michener, 1964—. Dir. Doverhold Investments Ltd. Recipient The Queen's Golden Jubilee medal, 2003. Mem. University Club (Toronto), Craigleigh Ski Club, Phi Gamma Delta (pres. 1950). Home: 68-1/2 Walmer Rd Toronto ON Canada M5R2X4 Office: BCE Pl 181 Bay St Ste 2500 Toronto ON Canada M5J 2T7 Home Phone: 416-923-8760; Office Phone: 416-307-4067. Business E-Mail: gfarquharson@langmichener.ca.

FARR, BARRY MILLER, physician, epidemiologist; b. Ft. Leonard Wood, Mo., Nov. 15, 1951; s. Alonza Lewis and Alice Louise (Miller) F.; m. Ann Katherine Henry, Oct. 22, 1977; children: Eric Christopher, Ryan Anthony, Jason Alexander. BA in Chemistry, U. Miss., Oxford, 1975; MD, Washington U., St. Louis, 1978; MSc in Epidemiology, London Sch. Hygiene, 1984. Diplomate Am. Bd. Internal Medicine, Am. Bd. Infectious Diseases. Intern U. Va. Hosp., Charlottesville, 1978-79, resident in internal medicine, 1979-81, fellow in infectious diseases, 1981-83; asst. prof. U. Va., 1983-89, assoc. prof., 1989—, William S. Jordan Jr. prof., 1989, prof. medicine, 1995—. Contbr. articles to profl. jours. Carrier scholar, 1970-74, Culley scholar, 1974-78, Milbank Meml. scholar, 1983-88. Fellow ACP, Infectious Diseases Soc. Am.; mem. Soc. Hosp. Epidemiology of Am., Soc. for Epidemiologic Rsch. Avocations: hunting, fishing, photography, writing.

FARR, CHARLES SIMS, lawyer; b. Hewlett, NY, June 29, 1920; s. John Farr and Hazel (Zealy) Sims; m. Mary Randolph Rue, Dec. 21, 1946 (dec. Dec. 1980); children: Charles Sims, Virginia Farr Ramsey, Randolph Rue, John II; m. Muriel Tobin Byrnes, Oct. 13, 1990. Student, Princeton U., 1938-40; LLB, Columbia U., 1948. Bar: N.Y. 1949, Fla. 1984. Assoc. White & Case, NYC, 1948-58, ptnr., 1959-88, of counsel, 1989-92, ret. Contbr. articles to profl. publs. Chmn. Commonwealth Fund, N.Y.C., 1976-93; trustee St. Luke's-Roosevelt Hosp. Ctr., 1968-92, Gen. Theol. Sem., 1968-77, N.Y. Zool. Soc., Kent Sch.; mem. bd. fgn. parishes Protestant Episcopal Ch., 1954-78, pres. 1977; chancellor to pres. bishop Protestant Episcopal Ch. in U.S.A., 1977-85; vestryman St. James Ch., N.Y.C., 1966-76; sr. warden, 1973-76, jr. warden, 1984-86; mem. coun. Rockefeller U., 1980-92; former mem. bd. visitors Columbia U. Sch. Law. Lt. comdr. USN, 1941—45, ETO, MTO, PTO. Recipient medal Columbia U. Alumni Assn., 1977. Fellow Am. Coll. Probate Counsel (regent 1960-75), Am. Bar Found.; mem. ABA (chmn. tax aspects decendent's estates 1974-76, bd. dirs. real property, probate and trust law sect. 1976-78, chmn. com. application securities laws to fiduciaries 1974-76), N.Y. State Bar Assn. (chmn. trusts and estates com. 1966-68), Assn. of Bar of City of N.Y. (com. profl. responsibility 1972-74), Century Club (trustee 1992-95), Links Club, River Club, Pilgrims Club, Yeamans Hall (S.C.). Independent. Home: PO Box 9455 900 Yeamans Hall Rd Charleston SC 29410: PO Box 835 Flat Rock NC 28731

FARR, DAVID N., electronics executive; married; 2 children. BS in Chemistry, Wake Forest U.; MBA, Vanderbilt U. From mem. staff to CEO Emerson, 1981—2000, CEO, 2000—, chmn., 2004—, pres., 2005—. Mem. The Bus. Coun., Washington; bd. dirs. Delphi Corp. Bd. dirs. Municipal Theatre Assoc., St. Louis; bd. dirs., Greater St. Louis Area Coun. Boy Scouts of Am.; mem. Civic Progress. Office: Emerson 8000 W Florissant Ave PO Box 4100 Saint Louis MO 63136*

FARR, DONALD EUGENE, engineering scientist; b. Clinton, Iowa, July 1, 1933; s. Kenneth Elroy and Nellie Irene (Bailey) F.; m. Sally Joyce Brauer, Mar. 8, 1954; children: Erika Lyn Farr Leventis, Jolene Karyn Farr Walters. BA in Engring. Psychology, San Diego State U., 1961; MT with honors, Nat. U., 1974; postgrad., Calif. Pacific U., 1976-80. Human factors specialist Bunker Ramo Corp., Canoga Park, Calif., Germany, 1964-69; sr. design specialist Gen. Dynamics, San Diego, 1955-63, 69-76; tech. staff Sandia Nat. Labs., Albuquerque, 1977-80; group supr., sr. tech. advisor The Babcock and Wilcox Co., Lynchburg, Va., 1980-82; dir. human factors sys. Sci. Applications, Inc., Lynchburg, 1982-83; human engring. scientist Lockheed Calif. Co., Burbank, 1983-91; MANPRINT mgr. Teledyne Electronic Sys., Northridge, Calif., 1991-94; human engring. scientist, program mgr. Symvionics, Inc., Pasadena, Calif., 1994—. Ergonomics safety cons. govt., industry and academia, 1977—; instr. human factors/design psychology Art Ctr. Coll. of Design, Pasadena, Calif., 2000—; instr./mentor grad. programs Calif. State U., Northridge, 2002—. Contbr. articles to profl. jours. and tech. books. Precinct capt., voter registration vol. Rep. Party, 1963—; lectr., support group Am. Diabetes Assn., LA, 1993—. With USN, 1952—53. Scholarship USN, 1953; recipient Admiral's award NSIA, 1963, River Walk plaque Clinton County, Iowa, 2006. Mem. Human Factors and Ergonomics Soc. (pres. San Diego, L.A. chpt.), Internat. Numismatic Soc. (pres. 1973-75), Am. Nuclear Soc. (human factors chair 1980-82), Am. Legion, NRA Golden Eagles (honor role). Conservative. Lutheran. Achievement include research in human interface design, test, & management aerospace programs including, space shuttle, advanced stealth technology, nuclear weapons, tactical operating systems, commercial nuclear power, computer systems, security systems, human modeling and simulation. Home: 20054 Avenue Of The Oaks Newhall CA 91321-1361 Office: Symvionics Inc 190 Sierra Ct Ste A3 Palmdale CA 93550-7609 Personal E-mail: dfarr@earthlink.net.

FARR, DWAYNE LOUIS, automotive executive; b. Anniston, Ala., Oct. 4, 1973; s. William Lindsey and Martha Ann Farr; m. Kari Christina Parrish, Feb. 3, 1974; children: Kayla Mackenzie, Lindsey-Ann Alexis. BS, U. Ga., Marietta, 1997; D of Theology (hon.), Life U., Sacramento, 2001. Ops. dir. PJ&T Logistics, LLC, West Unity, Ohio, 2003—06; ops. mgr. Exel Automotive Ams., Gadsden, Ala., 2006—. Cons. Gerson Lehrman Transp. Coun., Roanoke, Ala., 2006—07. Author: What must I do to be Saved. Conservative. Baptist. Achievements include research in privatizing Amtrak for express freight. Avocations: reading, bible research, walking, travel. Home: 152 Willow Lane Roanoke AL 36274 Office: Exel Automotive Americas 922 E Meighan Blvd Gadsden AL 35903 Home Phone: 334-863-5724; Office Phone: 256-458-6964. Personal E-mail: dwaynefarr@yahoo.com. E-mail: dwayne.farr@us.exel.com.

FARR, GEORGE FRANK, JR., retired federal official; b. Oak Park, Ill., Aug. 26, 1936; s. George F. and Evelyn Florence (Eigelberner) F.; m. Judith Banzer, June 30, 1962; 1 child, Alec Winfield. BA, Yale U., 1958, PhD in English, 1970. Asst. prof. English U. Calif., Berkeley, 1963-66, Vassar Coll., Poughkeepsie, NY, 1968-76; asst. dir. rsch. programs NEH, Washington, 1976-82, dep. dir. pub. programs, 1982-85, dep. dir. challenge grants, 1985-87, dir. preservation and access programs, 1987—2004, acting dep. chmn., 1999-2000. Mem. task force Nat. Inst. Conservation, Nat. Park Svc. Created fed. grant program for cataloging and preserving U.S. newspapers on a state-by-state basis (U.S. Newspaper Program), 1979—, nat. grant programs for the preservation of brittle books and serials, 1989—, for the preservation of material culture collections in museums and hist. socs., 1990—. Vestry mem. St. Mark's Episcopal Ch., Berkeley, 1965-68, St. Alban's Episcopal Ch., Washington, 1980-83; bd. dirs. English Speaking Union,. Washington. Carnegie Found. Prize Teaching fellow, 1958-59, Wilmarth Lewis Farmington fellow, 1960-61, Jameson award for archival advocacy Soc. of Am. Archivists, 2005. Mem. Sr. Exec. Svc. of U.S. Avocations: history of art, opera, swimming. Home: 5064 Lowell St NW Washington DC 20016-2616 Personal E-mail: questover2@comcast.net.

FARR, IVANNE ESTELLE, small business owner, consultant, artist, sculptor; b. Texarkana, Ark., Feb. 7, 1940; d. Franklin Lynnwood and Leone Faye (Seedig) F.; m. William D. Alsup, Aug. 27, 1960 (div. Aug. 1975); children: Joe Farr (dec.), Mark De Witt, Lara LeAnne. Attended, Tex. State U., San Marcos, 1957—59. Cert. diamonds Gemological Inst. Am., 1980, accredited jewelry profl. 2005, diamond essentials 2005, colored stones essentials 2005, jewelry essentials 2005. Founder, owner Ivanne et Cie, Inc., Corpus Christi, Meridian, Tex., St. Thomas, VI, 1976—; v.p. Internat. Agri-Ventures, Inc., Corpus Christi, 1985—89; owner Bosque River Valley Breeders, Ltd., Emu prodn. facilities, Meridian, Tex., 1990—97. Cons. C.I.C.C., Inc., Montreal, Can., 1985, Mexican Jewelers Assn., Mexico City, 1988, Jireh Resources, Inc., Paris, 1988, CEI, St. Thomas, 2003-04; co-founder, charter pres. Bosque County Tourism Coun., Inc., 1992; co-founder Farr Rsch. Internat., 1997; cons. Bibl. Archaeology Mus., Springfield, Mo., 1997; co-founder, chmn., chair Odyssey of Flight, 1991-94; chmn. John A. Lomax Gathering Trading Post Silent Auction, 1991-94. Active Mus. Oriental Culture, Jr. League, Corpus Christi, 1974-96, Charity League, Inc., 1974-92; bd. dirs. Chem. Dependency Unit South Tex., Coastal Bend Youth City, Palmer Drug Abuse Program; bd. govs., chmn. membership com. Art Mus. South Tex.; chmn. bd. govs., co-founder Alliance for Justice Found., Inc., 1988—; docent Fossil Rim Wildlife Ctr., Glenrose, Tex.; pres. Bosque County Tourism Coun., 1992-96, 99-2003; co-founder Bosque County Chisholm Trail Cowboy Gathering Trail Ride and Rendezvous, 2000-01, Tex. Chisholm Trail Heritage Celebration, 2002-03, co-chmn., 2003; founding pres. Tex. Chisholm Trail Assn., Inc., 2003; founding pres. bd. officers GIA Caribbean Islands Alumni Chpt., 2004; founding sec.-treas. Daus. of the King Assembly Diocese of Virgin Islands, 2005; founding pres. Caribbean Islands Edtl. Found. Inc., 2006; bishop's com. Nazereth By The Sea Espisc. Ch., 2006—. Mem. Gemological Inst. Am. (alumni), Coast Conservation Assn. (mem. internat. com. Corpus Christi Area Econ. Devel. Corp.), Inst. Tex. Cultures (amb.), Jewelers Assn. Am., Marine Mil. Acad. Parents Assn., Navy League (bd. dir.), Norwegian Soc. Tex., PTA, Scandinavian Soc. S. Tex. (co-founder), Tex. Jewelers Assn., Internat. Group (co-founder), Corpus Christi C. of C. (bd. dir.), Am. Emu Assn., Tex. Emu Assn., Emu Coop., Am. Assn. Mus., Ducks Unltd., Mid-Morning Group (co-founder), Tex. State U. Alumni Assn. Republican. Episcopalian. Avocations: water-skiing, snorkeling, travel, sailing, opera. E-mail: farrlands@hotmail.com.

FARR, JUDITH BANZER, retired literature educator, writer, lecturer; b. NYC, Mar. 13, 1936; d. Russell John and Frances Anna (Wissell) Banzer; m. George F. Farr, Jr., June 30, 1962; 1 child, Alec Winfield. BA, Marymount Manhattan Coll., NYC, 1957, LHD, 1992; MA, Yale U., New Haven, Conn., 1959, PhD, 1965. Instr. in English Vassar Coll., Poughkeepsie, NY, 1961-63; asst. prof. St. Mary's Coll., Moraga, Calif., 1964-68; assoc. prof. SUNY, New Paltz, 1968-77, Georgetown U., Washington, 1978-90, prof. of English and Am. Lit., 1990-99, prof. emerita, 1999—. Vis. assoc. prof. Georgetown U., 1977—78; lectr. in field. Author: The Life and Art of Elinor Wylie, 1983, The Passion of Emily Dickinson, 1992, I Never Came to You in White: A Novel, 1996, The Gardens of Emily Dickinson, 2004 (Crawshay award of the Byron, Keats and Shelley Meml. Trust Brit. Acad., 2005); editor: Twentieth Century Interpretations of Sons and Lovers, 1970, New Century Views: Emily Dickinson, 1995; contbr. articles, poems, short stories to profl. and comml. publs. Recipient Alumnae award for Distinction in Arts and Letters, Marymount Manhattan Coll., NYC, 1976, Alpha Sigma Nu Best Book award, 1993, Alumnae award for scholarly distinction, Mary Louis Acad., 2001, Rose Mary Crawshay prize, Byron, Keats and Shelley Meml. Trust, The Brit. Acad., 2005; grantee, NY State Rsch. Found., 1974, Am. Coun. Learned Socs., 1984, 1986, Georgetown U. Ctr. German Studies, 1992; Morgan-Porter fellow, Yale U., 1960—61, Am. Philos. Soc. fellow, 1983. Mem. Authors' Guild, Emily Dickinson Internat. Soc., Cosmos Club. Avocations: antiques, gardening, art. Home: 5064 Lowell St NW Washington DC 20016-2616 Personal E-mail: questover2@comcast.net.

FARR, PAUL A., electric power industry executive; b. Green Bay, Wis. B in acctg., Marquette Univ.; M in mgmt., Purdue Univ. CPA. Acct. Arthur Andersen; internat. tax mgr. Price Waterhouse; internat. fin. mgr. Illinova Generating Co.; dir. internat. tax PPL Global, 1998—99; v.p. fin., CFO PPL Montana, 1999—2001; v.p. ops., COO PPL Global, 2001—03, sr. v.p., 2003—04; v.p., contr. PPL Corp., Allentown, Pa., 2004—05, sr. v.p. fin., 2005—07, exec. v.p., CFO, 2007—. Bd. mem. Allentown Art Mus. Office: PPL Corp 2 N 9th St Allentown PA 18101*

FARR, REETA RAE, special education administrator; b. Edhube, Tex., Jan. 15, 1926; d. Paul Ray and Verna (Biggerstaff) Wright; m. Gerald Edward Self, June 1, 1946 (dec. Dec. 1977); children: Eddie, Lee; m. Barnie B. Farr Jr., Dec. 28, 1978 (wid. Mar. 1997). BS, Southeastern Okla. State U., 1959, MS, 1963. 1st grade tchr. Sherman (Tex.) Pub. Schs., 1959-61, Denison (Tex.) Pub. Schs., 1961-64, spl. edn. tchr., 1964-72, spl. edn. counselor, 1972-76, spl. edn. diagnostician, 1976-85, dir. spl. edn., 1985-94. Named Educator of Yr., Denison Edn. Assn., 1991. Mem. NEA, AAUW (pres. 1981-83), Tex. State Tchrs. Assn. (local pres. 1971), Tex. Ednl. Diagnostician Assn., Tex. Assn. Counseling and Devel., Phi Delta Kappa (sec.-treas. 1983, del. 1978-99), Delta Kappa Gamma. Mem. Ch. Of Christ. Avocation: reading. Home: 23000 2nd Fork Rd Ola ID 83657-5015 E-mail: rfarr@bigskytel.com.

FARR, ROSS, lawyer; b. Eugene, Ore., Feb. 8, 1970; BA, Evergreen State Coll., 1992; JD magna cum laude, Seattle Univ., 2001. Bar: Wash. 2001. Former judicial clerk Wash. State Ct. Appeals; assoc. atty., gen. litig. Ogden Murphy Wallace, P.L.L.C., Seattle. Contbr. articles to numerous profl. jours.; content editor: Wash. Lawyers Practice Manual. Named Wash. Rising Star, SuperLawyer Mag., 2006. Mem.: King Co. Bar Assn. (legal clinician), Wash. State Bar Assn. Office: Ogden Murphy Wallace Ste 2100 1601 Fifth Ave Seattle WA 98101-1686

FARR, SAM, congressman; b. Calif., July 4, 1941; m. Shary Baldwin; 1 child, Jessica. BSc Biology, Willamette U., 1963; student, Monterey Inst. Internat. Studies, U. Santa Clara Law Sch. Vol. Peace Corps, 1963-65; budget analyst, cons. Assembly com. Constl. Amendments; bd. suprs. Monterey (Calif.) County; rep. Calif. State Assembly, 1980-93; mem. U.S. Congress from 17th Calif. dist., 1993—; mem. appropriations com., agr. and military constrn. subcoms. Named Legislator of Yr. Calif. 9 times. Democrat. Avocations: photography, skiing, fly fishing, spanish. Office: Ho of Reps 1221 Longworth Bldg Washington DC 20515-0517*

FARRACE, MELISSA ANNE, language educator, secondary school educator; m. Robert N. Farrace, June 26, 1999. BA, Earlham Coll., Richmond, Ind., 1990; MA, Bowling Green State U., Ohio, 1993. Tchr. french McCord Jr. H.S., Sylvania, Ohio, 1992—96, Elizabeth Seton H.S., Bladensburg, Md., 1996—97; instrnl. tech. specialist Personal Computer Learning Ctrs., Inc., Washington, 1997—98; tchr. french Fairfax County Pub. Schs., Vienna, Va., 1998—. Validator Nat. Bd. Profl. Tchg. Standards, Newark, 2002—03; mentor tchr. Fairfax County Pub. Schs., 2003—, adv. coun. fgn. lang. curriculum, 2005—; chmn. dept. fgn. lang. Kilmer Mid. Sch., Vienna, 2000—. Mem.: Greater Wash. Area Tchrs. Fgn. Langs., Am. Coun.Tchg. Fgn. Langs., Am. Assn. Tchrs. French. Office: Kilmer Middle School 8100 Wolftrap Rd Vienna VA 22182 Home Phone: 703-846-8800; Office Phone: 703-846-8800. Business E-Mail: missie.farrace@fcps.edu.

FARRAKHAN, LOUIS (LOUIS EUGENE WALCOTT), religious organization administrator; b. Bronx, NY, May 11, 1933; changed name from Louis Eugene Wolcott to Louis X, then to Louis Farrakhan; m. Betsy Wolcott; 9 children. Student, Winston-Salem State U., NC. Vocalist, calypso singer, dancer and violinist, Boston; joined Nation of Islam, 1955—, leader of Harlem mosque NYC, 1965—75, nat. spokesman, leader, founder reorganized Nation of Islam, 1977—2006. Founder newspaper The Final Call, 1979—. Author: A Torchlight for America, 1993, Education Is the Key, 2006. Founder Louis Farrakhan Prostate Cancer Found., 2003—. Named one of Most Influential Black Americans, Ebony mag., 2006. Achievements include organizing the Million Man March on Washington, D.C., 1995 and the Million Family March, 2000. Office: Nation of Islam 7351 S Stony Island Ave Chicago IL 60649-3106

FARRALL, HAROLD JOHN, retired accountant; b. Harvard, Nebr., Mar. 25, 1918; s. John William and Olive Almira (Frazell) F. BSBA, Nebr. U., 1940. Clk. teletype ctr. Bur. Aeronautics, Washington, 1946—47; cost acct. Bur. Reclamation Br. Office Region 7, Grand Island, Nebr., 1948—53, fin. officer Ainsworth, Nebr., 1953—54; payroll acct. to supervisory operating acct. Bur. Reclamation Hdqs. Region 7, Denver, 1955—72; supr. accts. payable Dutton-Lainson Co., Hastings, Nebr., 1974—85; ret., 1985. Author: The Rise and Fall of the United States, 1990, 2d edit., 1998, 3rd edit., 2005. With U.S. Army, 1941-45. Regents scholarship U. Nebr., 1936. Mem. DAV, VFW, Am. Legion, Ind. order of Odd Fellows, Fed. Govt. Accts. Assn., Mensa. Avocation: big band music.

FARRAND, JAMES CLINTON, minister, consultant; b. Oklahoma City, Nov. 3, 1947; s. Robert Lee and Gladys Marie Farrand; m. Linda Kay Wilkins, Dec. 24, 1967; children: Carri Danielle, Clinton Robert Vernon. MusB in EDn., Okla. Bapt. U., Shawnee, 1971; MusM, Southwestern Sem., Fort Worth, Tex., 1978; post grad. in Leadership Theory and Devel., post grad. in Exec. and Life Skills Coaching, post grad. in Orgnl. Health and Team Building. Assoc. pastor First Bapt. Ch., McAlester, Okla., 1979—89, Shawnee, 1989—. Adj. prof. Okla. Bapt. U., Shawnee, 1990—93, guest lectr.; condr. Shawnee Choral Soc. Contbg. editor: The Church Musician; contbr. articles to profl. jours. Mem. Shawnee Youth Coalition, Okla., 2002—, Okla. Alliance Liturgy and the Arts, Oklahoma City, 2003—, Shawnee Youth Baseball Assn., 1992—96; pres. The CenturyMen, NYC, 2004—, Faculty Coun. Camerata for Okla. Bapt. U., Shawnee, Okla., 2003—, Gateway to Prevention and Recovery, 2000—, Arts and Humanities Coun., McAlester, 1985—89, Cmty. Concert Series, 1983—88. With US Army, 1969—73. Mem.: Am. Choral Directors Assn. (assoc.), Am. Guild English Handbell Ringers (assoc.). Home: 1 Seneca Shawnee OK 74801 Office: First Baptist Ch 227 N Union Shawnee OK 74801 Home Phone: 405-275-3024; Office Phone: 405-275-6111.

FARRAND, WILLIAM RICHARD, retired geology educator; b. Columbus, Ohio, Apr. 27, 1931; s. Harvey Ashley and Esther Evelyn (Bowman) F.; m. Claudine Brickmann, Aug. 17, 1962 (div. 1983); children: Frederic Hervé, Anne Marie; m. Carola Hill Stearns, Dec. 6, 1988; 1 child, Michelle Diane. BS in Geology, Ohio State U., 1955, MS in Geology, 1956; PhD, U. Mich., 1960. Rsch. assoc. Lamont Geol. Obs. Columbia U., NY, 1960-61, asst. prof. NY, 1961-64; rsch. assoc. in geology U. Mich., Ann Arbor, 1962; postdoctoral rsch. fellow NAS/NRC, Strasbourg, France, 1963-64; asst. prof. geol. scis. U. Mich., Ann Arbor, 1965-67, assoc. prof. geol scis., 1967-74, prof., 1974-2000, prof. emeritus, 2000—, curator analytical collections Mus. Anthropology, 1975-2000, dir. Exhibit Mus., 1993-2000. Vis. prof. U. Strasbourg, France, 1964-65, Hebrew U., Jerusalem, 1971-72,

U. Colo., Boulder, 1983, U. Tex., Austin, 1986; fellow Inst. for Advanced Study, Ind. U., 1985; mem. archaeometry panel NSF, 1989-91; apptd. mem. U.S. Nat. com. Internat. Quaternary Assn., 1989-99, chair, 1995-99; sr. fellow Inst. for Study Earth and Man, So. Meth. U., Dallas, 1991—. Mem. editorial bd. Quaternary Sci. Review, Paleorient, Jour. Archaeological Sci., Review Archaeology, Stratigraphica Archaeologica; contbr. articles and maps to profl jours. With U.S. Army, 1951-53. Fellow AAAS, Geol. Soc. Am. (mem. panel quaternary geology and geomorphology divsn. 1978, vice chmn. archaeological geology divsn, 1979, chmn, 1980, Archaeological Geology award 1986), Ohio Acad. Sci., 1994-96; mem. Am. Quaternary Assn. (sec. 1978-90, program chmn. biennial meeting 1980, pres. 1994-96), Mich. Acad. Sci., Arts and Letters, Internat. Union for Quaternary Rsch. (chmn. working group on Southwest Asia commn. paleoecology early man 1975-83), L'Assn. Francaise pour l'Etude de Quaternaire, Sigma Xi, Phi Beta Kappa. Office: U Mich Mus Anthropology 4009 Ruthven Mus Ann Arbor MI 48109-1079 Business E-Mail: wfarrand@umich.edu.

FARRAR, CONSTANCE MOSHER, marketing executive; b. Cambridge, Mass., Aug. 24, 1925; d. Curtis Howard and Jeannette (Shaw) Mosher; m. Robert Stewart Perkins, Sept. 21, 1946 (div. Oct. 1954); m. Franklin Ernest Farrar, Feb. 4, 1961; 1 child, Bruce Stewart. CLU degree, Am. Coll. Fin. Svc. Profls., 1961; BLS in Interdisciplinary Studies, Boston U., 1981. Chartist Liberty Mut., NYC, 1945-46; asst. cashier, bookkeeper Columbian Nat., Boston, 1946-51; v.p. Baystate Fin. Svcs., Boston, 1951—. Lay Eucharistic min., lay reader, former mem. vestry Episcopalian Ch. Recipient Nat. Quality award, 1970-2000, named Businessman of Yr., Nat. Rep. Congl. Com. Bus. Adv. Coun., 2003. Mem. NAACP (life), New Eng. Leaders Assn. (life), Nat. Assn. Ins. and Fin. Adv. (past bd. dirs., Nat. Quality award for 30 years), Soc. Fin. Svc. Profls., Boston Estate Planning Coun., Golden Key Soc., Zonta (chair status of women com.), Order Ea. Star (past Worthy Matron), Zonta Club of Newton (treas., past pres.). Republican. Avocations: camping, hiking. Home: 1508 Great Plain Ave Needham MA 02492-1237 Office: Baystate Fin Svcs 1 Exeter Plz Ste 1400 Boston MA 02116-2848 Office Phone: 617-585-4550. Business E-Mail: cfarrar@baystatefinancial.com.

FARRAR, DAVID HOLLEMAN, investor; b. Washington, July 8, 1935; s. J. Edward and Charolotte Thompson Farrar; m. Mary Jo Meyers, Aug. 1971. BA, U. Va., Charlottesville, 1957, MBA, 1961. Product mgr. Sterling Drug Co., NYC, 1961—66, Gillette Co., Boston, 1966—69; cons. Comcac Co., Birmingham, Mich., 1969—72; real estate investor Warrenton, Va., 1972—. Mem.: Faquier Springs Coumty Club, Fauquier Club, Colonnade Club, Rotary Club. Avocations: skiing, bicycling, rollerblading, tennis, golf.

FARRAR, DONALD KEITH, retired finance company executive; b. Indio, Calif., May 18, 1938; s. Keith and Sarah S. Farrar; m. Jo Ann Puttler, Dec. 16, 1961; children: Daniel K., Donald S., Douglas S., Kimberly. BSBA, U. So. Calif., 1960; MBA, Harvard U., 1965. With planning div. Paul Revere Life Ins. Co., Worcester, Mass., 1965, budget supr., 1966, asst. to pres., 1967, asst. sec., 1968-73, v.p. investment, 1969-73; v.p. planning Avco Corp., Greenwich, Conn., 1973-74, sr. v.p., chief acct. officer, 1975-77, exec. v.p., 1978-81, pres., 1981-85, also bd. dirs.; sr. exec. v.p., pres. Avco Ops. Textron Inc., Providence, 1985-89, sr. exec. v.p. ops., 1985-89, also bd. dirs.; pres., CEO IMO Industries, Lawrenceville, NJ, 1993-94, chmn., CEO, 1994-97. Pvt. investor 1990-93, 98—, retired. With USNR, 1960-63. Home: 5 Prairie Grass Irvine CA 92603

FARRAR, ELAINE WILLARDSON, artist; b. LA; d. Eldon and Gladys Elsie (Larsen) Willardson; children: Steve, Mark, Gregory, JanLeslie, Monty, Susan. BA, Ariz. State U., 1967, MA, 1969, PhD, 1990. Tchr. Camelback Desert Sch., Paradise Valley, Ariz., 1966-69; mem. faculty Yavapai Coll., Prescott, Ariz., 1970-92, chmn. dept. art, 1973-78, instr. art in watercolor, oil, acrylic painting, intaglio, 1971-92, instr. art relief intaglio and monoprints, 1971-92; grad. advisor Prescott Coll. Master of Arts Program, 1993-97, 2004—. One-woman shows include R.P. Moffat's, Scottsdale, Ariz., 1969, Art Ctr., Battlecreek, Mich., 1969, The Woodpeddler, Costa Mesa, Calif., 1979, exhibited in group shows at Prescott Fine Arts Assn., 1999, 2001—02, Prescott Fine Art Assn., 2006, The Elements, 2001, Prescott Fine Arts Gallery, 2006, others. Mem., curator Prescott Fine Arts Visual Arts com., 1992-97; exec. com., 1996-98; bd. dirs. Prescott Fine Arts Assn., 1995-98, Friends Y.C. Art Gallery Bd., 1992-97. Mem. Northern Ariz. Watercolor Assn., Mountain Artists Guild (past pres.), Women's Nat. Mus. (charter Washington chpt.), mus. of North Ariz. and Phoenix Art Mus., Kappa Delta Pi. *Through the visual arts many ideas and feelings are expressed that would otherwise be lost to the communication of these thoughts to others—a vital link to understanding.and vital to helping release ideas through art therapy when one has been unable to verbalize thoughts and ideas, whether analyzed or not the path is cleared away.universal as is music and dance!.*

FARRAR, FRANK LEROY, lawyer, former governor; b. Britton, SD, Apr. 2, 1929; s. Virgil William and Venetia Soule (Taylor) F.; m. Patricia Jean Henley, June 5, 1953; children— Jeanne Marie, Sally Ann, Robert John, Mary Susan, Ann M. BS, U. S.D., 1951, LL.B., 1953; LL.D., Huron Coll. Bar: SD 1963. Practiced law, Britton, 1957-63; agt. IRS, 1955-57; judge Marshall County, SD, 1958, state's atty. SD, 1959-62; atty. gen. State of S.D., 1963-69, gov., 1969-70; ptnr. Farrar & Spiry, Britton, SD, 1970—. Chmn. Cardinal and Gold Ins. Co., Frank L. Farrar & Assocs., Performance Bankers, Inc., Capital, Fulda, Beresford, Wanbay, Sidney, Uptown, Versailles, Glenrock, Wolf Point Bancorps., Inc., NW Investment Inc., Carlton Agy., Inc., 1st Agy. Hasting, Cairo, First, Inc., Peoples Holding Co.; adv. bd. dirs. Citicorp, Correspondent Resources Inc. Past pres. Pheasant council Boy Scouts Am.; past chmn. S.D. March of Dimes; past fund raising chmn. S.D. Mental Health Assn.; bd. dirs. Rural Coalition Am.; chmn. Marshall County Republican Party, 1959; asst. sgt.-at-arms Rep. Nat. Conv., 1960. Served to capt. U.S. Army Recipient Alumnus Achievement award U. S.D., 1981, named Alumnus of Yr. Sch. Bus., 1979; named Sr. Olympics Athlete of the Yr. for S.D., 4th All Am. for Triathlon, 1999; named to Hall of Fame Sr. Olympics, S.D. Mem. S.D. Bar Assn., Ind. Bar Assn., Wash. Bar Assn., S.D. States Attys. Assn. (asst. pres.), Nat. Dist. Attys. Assn., Alpha Tau Omega, Phi Delta Phi. Lodges: Masons, Shriners, Jesters, Lions, Elks, Odd Fellows, Sportsmen. Address: PO Box 936 Britton SD 57430-0936 Home Phone: 605-448-2171; Office Phone: 605-448-2643. Personal E-mail: ffarrar@wiltonsd.com. E-mail: ffarrar@writtowsd.com.

FARRAR, JOHN EDSON, II, finance company executive, consultant, investment advisor; b. Williamsport, Pa., Oct. 9, 1938; s. John Edson and Ruth (Price) F.; children: John Edson III, Jamie, Ryan. BA in Psychology, Pasadena Coll., 1963; postgrad., Claremont Grad. Sch., 1963-64, U. Calgary, Canada, 1967, U. Calif., Riverside, 1968-71. Cert. in pub. rels. U. Calif., 1972, in mktg. practice U. Calif., 1972, profl. accreditation in pub. rels. practice Pub. Rels. Soc. Am., 1975, registered investment advisor Calif., 1993. Evaluating social svcs. dir. Head Start Dental Rsch. Project Loma Linda Sch. Dentistry, Calif., 1966-67; coord. Head Start Riverside County Econ. Opportunity Bd., Riverside, Calif., 1967; dir. cmty. rels. San Bernardino County Welfare and Probation Depts., Calif., 1968-73; publicity and promotions coord. in charge tourism and indsl. devel. San Bernardino County Econ. Devel. Dept., 1973; dir. pub. rels. Mid. East Boeing Comml. Airplane Co., Seattle, 1973-76, Northwest Hosp., Seattle, 1976-77; owner Craig & Farrar Pub. Rels. and Advt., 1977-80, Aamco Transmissions Ctr. Bremerton, Wash., 1982-86; exec. v.p. Environ. Rsch. and Devel. Corp., Seattle, 1980-82; stockbroker Prudential-Bache Securities, Seattle, 1984-86; ind. fin. and bus. cons. and broker Kent, Wash., 1987-93; pres. Professionally Managed Portfolios, Acton, Calif., 1993—. Lectr. mktg. pub. rels., investment techniques and options strategies Coll. of Canyons, Valencia, Calif.; former chmn. dept. pub. rels. and advt. U. Wash., Sch. Comm., Seattle; instr. pub. rels. City Coll., Seattle; cons. in field. Pres. bd. dirs. Frazee Cmty. Ctr., 1970-71; bd. dirs., pub. relations chmn. Chief Seattle council Boy Scouts Am., promotions chmn. for camping in Southwestern US; exec. bd. Seattle-King County Visitors and Conv. Bur.; mem. Rep. Presdl. Task Force, 1982-84; chmn. March of Dimes WalkAmerica, 1995-96. Recipient Distinction award, San Bernardino County Bd. Suprs., 1973, Outstanding Achievement award, Boeing Co., 1974. Mem. Pub. Rels. Soc. Am. (chpt. pres. 1971, 72, dist. chmn. govt. sect., Recognition of Distinction for Pub. Rels. Excellence 1974), Calif. Social Workers Orgn. (v.p. 1970-71), Soc. for Internat. Devel., Nat. Pub. Rels. Coun. Health and Welfare Svcs., Internat. Pub. Rels. Assn., US-Arab C. of C., Rotary. Lutheran. Avocations: photography, coin collecting/numismatics. Business E-Mail: john@pmpmanagement.com.

FARRAR, JOHN THRUSTON, health facility administrator; b. St. Louis, June 26, 1920; s. Benedict and Ruth Elizabeth (Gregg) F.; m. Joan Hayward Niedringhaus, May 20, 1947 (div. Feb. 1964); children: John Hayward, Leslie Tweedy; m. Pamela Sedgwick Gibson, May 15, 1966 (div. Mar. 1994); children: Elizabeth Gregg, Anne Dandridge; m. Rowena Kay Bryan, Oct. 28, 1995. AB, Princeton U., NJ, 1942; MD, Washington U., St. Louis, 1945. Diplomate Am. Bd. Internal Medicine, Am. Bd. Gastroenterology. Intern St. Louis County Hosp., Clayton, Mo., 1945-46; asst. resident in pathology Boston City Hosp., 1948-49; intern in medicine Mass. Meml. Hosps., Boston, 1949-50, asst. resident in medicine, 1950-51, rsch. assoc. divsn. gastroenterology, 1951-54; instr. medicine Boston U. Sch. Medicine, 1954-55; asst. prof. clin. medicine Cornell U. Coll. Medicine, NYC, 1956-63; assoc. prof. medicine Med. Coll. Va., Richmond, 1963-65, chmn. divsn. gastroenterology, 1963-78, prof. medicine, 1965-92, assoc. dean vets. affairs, 1979-90, prof. emeritus, 1992—. Chief gastroenterology sect. med. svc. Vets. Hosp., N.Y.C., 1955-63; assoc. chief of staff rsch. devel. Vets. Affairs Med. Ctr., N.Y.C., 1956-63; cons. gastroenterology McGuire Vets. Affairs Med. Ctr., Richmond, 1963-78, chief of staff, 1979-90; nat. adv. panel nat. program rev. com. VA, 1965-69; adv. com. gastrointestinal drugs FDA, Washington, 1971-74, 77-82, cons., 1976-77; grants rev. com. Nat. Found. Ileitis Colitis, Inc., 1975-79, nat. scientific adv. com. 1975-79; chmn. long range planning com. Nat. digestive Diseases Edn. Info. Clearinghouse, 1983-85, chmn. scientific Evaluation subcom. 1983-85, chmn. exec. com. advisors, 1983-90; mem. steering com. Internat. Conf. Gastrointestinal Motility, 1975-81, chmn. steering com., 1977-79; chmn. Am. Bd. Gastroenterology, 1979-83; mem. bd. govs. Am. Bd. Internal Medicine, 1979-85; first vice-chmn. Coalition Digestive Desease Orgns., 1983-85; pres. Digestive Disease Nat. Coalition (formerly Coalition Digestive Disease Orgns.), 1986-91; rsch. com. Am. Fedn. Aging Rsch., 1983-89; assoc. dep. chief med. dir. Dept. Vets. Affairs, Vets. Affairs Ctrl. Office, Washington, 1990-91, dep. chief med. dir., 1991-93, acting under sec. health, 1993-94, dep. under sec. health, 1994-95; assoc. chief of staff extended care Vets. Affairs med. Ctr., Martinsburg, W.Va., 1995—. Author: (chpts.) Miniaturization, 1961, Modern Trends in Gastroenterology, 1961, Medicine, Essentials of Clinical Practice, 1970, Medical Engineering, 1974, Gastrointestinal Motility, 1971, Scientific Foundations of Gastroenterology, 1980, Tratado De Gastroenterologia Y Hepatologia, 1982, Clinics in Gastroenterology, 1982, Clinical Medicine, 1983, Social Security Practice Guide, 1986, Surgical Management of the Elderly Patient, 1992; editor: Practice of Medicine, Vol. Gastroenterology, 1973-78; mem. editl. bd. Am. Jour. Digestive Diseases, 1959-64, 88—, editor, 1968-76, Gastroenterology, 1964-68, Am. Jour. Med. Electronics, 1962-82; mem. editl. coun. Rendiconti Romani di Gastro-enterologia, 1969-89; contbr. over 55 articles to profl. jours. Bd. trustees Elk Hill Farm for Boys, 1974-80; pres. Goochland Family Svc. Soc., 1975-76, 79-81. Capt. U.S. Army Med. Corps., 1946-48. Mem.: ACP (coun.subspecialty socs. 1985—88, chmn. gastroenterology com. 1985—88, chair Washington 1986, chair San Francisco 1987), Am. Liver Found. (bd. dirs. 1986—, chmn. 1990—94), Am. Clin. Climatol. Assn., Am. Gastroent. Assn. (rssch. com. 1968—71, nat. liaison com. 1971—73, 1977—80, treas. 1972—77, chmn. publs. com. 1977—80, gov. bd. 1972—77, 1980—89, v.p 1980—81, pres.-elect 1981—82, pres. 1982—83, chmn. com. pub. policy and govt. rels. 1986—89, historian, archivist 1989—98), Am. Fedn. Clin. Rsch. Home: 431 Dogleg DR Williamsburg VA 23188-7411 Personal E-mail: farrar8@cox.net.

FARRAR, STANLEY F., lawyer; b. Santa Ana, Calif., Mar. 24, 1943; BS, U. Calif., Berkeley, 1964, JD, 1967. Bar: Calif. 1968, NY 1969. Ptnr. Sullivan & Cromwell LLP, Tokyo. Mem. ABA (chmn. subcom. on bank holding cos. and nonbank activities banking law com. 1980-85, chmn. letters credit subcom. uniform comml. code com. 1982-88, sect. bus. law), State Bar Calif. (chmn. fin. instns. com. 1981-82). Office: Sullivan & Cromwell LLP Otemachi First Sq 5-1 Otemachi 1-chome Tokyo 100-0004 Japan Business E-Mail: farrars@sullcrom.com.

FARRAR, STEPHEN PRESCOTT, glass products manufacturing executive; b. Concord, NH, Jan. 27, 1944; s. Prescott Samuel and Katherine (Hitchcock) F.; m. Kathleen D. Clark, Dec. 28, 1968 (dec.); children: Sheila E. Bermudez, Stephen Prescott Jr.; m. Rose Marie Bucar, July 4, 1998. BA, Bowdoin Coll., 1965; MSFS, Georgetown U., 1967. Internat. economist U.S. Dept. Commerce, Washington, 1966-72, Office of Mngt. and Budget, Washington, 1972-80, chief econ. affairs br. IAD, 1980-86; dir. internat. econ. affairs NSC, Washington, 1986-88, spl. asst. to Pres. and sr. dir. internat. econ. affairs, 1988-89; dep. exec. sec. Econ. Policy Coun., The White House, Washington, 1989-92; spl. asst. to Pres. for Policy Devel. Office of Policy Devel., the White House, Washington, 1989-92; chief of staff Office of the U.S. Trade Rep., Washington, 1992-93; dir. internat. bus. Guardian Industries Corp., Auburn Hills, Mich., 1993—. Mem. Coun. on Fgn. Rels. Republican. Avocations: tennis, running. Office: Guardian Industries Corp 2300 Harmon Rd Auburn Hills MI 48326-1714 Office Phone: 248-340-2104. Business E-Mail: sfarrar@guardian.com.

FARRAR, THOMAS C., chemist, educator; b. Independence, Kans., Jan. 14, 1933; s. Otis C. and Agnes K. F.; m. Friedemarie L. Farrar, June 22, 1963; children: Michael, Christian, Gisela. BS in Math., Chemistry, Wichita State U., 1954; PhD in Chemistry, U. Ill., 1959. NSF fellow Cambridge U., Eng., 1959-61; prof. chemistry U. Oregon, Eugene, 1961-63; chief, magnetism sect. Nat. Bur. Standards, Washington, 1963-71; dir. R & D Japan Electron Optics Lab., Cranford, N.J., 1971-75; dir. instr. NSF, Washington, 1975-79; prof. chemistry U. Wis., Madison, 1979—. Chmn. adv. com. MIT Nat. Magnetics Lab., Cambridge, Mass., 1979-84. Author: Introduction to Pulse NMR Spectros, 1989, Density Matrix Theory, 1995; contbr. over 150 articles to profl. jours. Recipient Silver medal Dept. Commerce, Washington, 1971, Silver medal Nat. Science Found., Washington, 1979. Fellow Wash. Acad. Science; mem. Am. Chem. Soc. (sec.-treas. Wis. sect. 1986-89), Am. Physical Soc. Office: Univ Wis Dept Chemistry 1101 University Ave Madison WI 53706-1322 Home Phone: 608-238-2939; Office Phone: 608-262-6158. Personal E-mail: tcfarrar@sbcglobal.net. E-mail: tfarrar@chem.wisc.edu, farrartcf@yahoo.com.

FARRELL, EDMUND JAMES, retired English language educator, writer; b. Butte, Mont., May 17, 1927; s. Bartholomew J. and Lavinia H. (Collins) F.; m. Jo Ann Hayes, Dec. 19, 1964; children: David (dec.), Kevin, Sean. AB, Stanford U., 1950, MA, 1951; PhD, U. Calif., Berkeley, 1969. Chmn. English dept. James Lick HS, San Jose, Calif., 1954-59; supr. secondary English U. Calif., Berkeley, 1959-70; adj. prof. English U. Ill., Urbana, 1973-78; prof. English edn. U. Tex., Austin, 1978—92, prof. emeritus, 1992—; pres. Farrell Ednl. Svcs., Inc., Austin, 1981-97; ret., 1997. Participant revision lit. objectives Nat. Assessment of Ednl. Progress, Denver, 1972-73, 78; adv. com. Ctr. for the Book, Libr. of Congress, 1980-86; chmn. adv. com. on English, Coll. Bd., NYC, 1974-79, council acad. affairs, 1978-79; guest lectr. local, state and nat. confs. of English tchrs., 1954—; reader compositions for advanced placement program Rider Coll., Princeton, NJ, 1969, 72-77; pres. Calif. Assn. Tchrs. English, 1962-63; sr. editl. cons. EMC Masterpiece Series, 1999-2006. Author: (with others) Exploring Life Through Literature, 1964, Counterpoint in Literature, 1967, Projection in Literature, 1973, Outlooks Through Literature, 1973, Fantasy: Forms of Things Unknown, 1974, Science Fact/Fiction, 1974, Comment, 1976, Myth, Mind and Moment, 1976, I/You, We/They, 1976, Traits and Topics, 1976, Reality in Conflict, 1976, To Be, 1976, Arrangement in Literature, 1979, Purpose in Literature, 1979, Album U.S.A., 1983, Discoveries in Literature, 1985, classic edit., 1989, Patterns in Literature, 1985, classic edit., 1989, Transactions with Literature, 1990, The Perceptive I, 1997. With USN, 1945-46. Fellow Nat. Conf. Rsch. on Lang. and Literacy; mem. Nat. Coun. Tchrs. English (field rep. 1970-71, asst. exec. sec. 1971-73, assoc. exec. dir. 1973-78, chmn. commn. lit. 1979-83; trustees rsch. found. 1983-85; fund for tchg. of English 1993-96, Disting. Svc. award 1982, James R. Squire award 1999), Tex. Joint Coun. Tchrs. of English (pres. 1986-87, Disting. English Educator award 1989-90, Disting. Lifetime Svc. award 1999). Unitarian Universalist. Home: 6500 Sumac Dr Austin TX 78731-4117 Office: U Tex Dept Curriculum and Instrn Austin TX 78712 Business E-Mail: farrell@mail.utexas.edu.

FARRELL, GREGORY ALAN, biomedical engineer; b. Bklyn., May 12, 1942; s. Edmond William and Edna Florence (Williams) F.; m. Mary Louise Lupiani, Sept. 3, 1966; children: Juliana Eden, Cristina Elizabeth. BSME, Cooper Union, 1964; MS in Biomed. Engring., Columbia U., 1972, postgrad., 1972—. Mech. engr. Gen. Dynamics, San Diego, 1964-65, Rochester, NY, 1965-67; rsch. asst. Columbia U. Med. Sch., NYC, 1968-69; instr. pathology N.Y. Med. Coll., 1969-72; rsch. engr. Technicon Instruments Corp., Tarrytown, NY, 1972-82; mgr. mech. engring. Baker Instruments Corp., Allentown, Pa., 1982-84, prin. mech. engr., 1984-86; prin. engr. Nat. Patent Devel. Corp., NYC, 1986-87; project engr. Bayer Diagnostics (divsn. Bayer Healthcare), Tarrytown, 1987—90, new product devel. mgr., 1990—99, prin. staff engr., 2000—, mgr. mech. engring., 2001—05; pres. Gregory A. Farrell & Assocs., LLC, 2006—. Patentee in field; contbr. articles to profl. jours. Winner med. design excellence award, Indsl. Designers Soc. Am., 1998. Democrat. Roman Catholic. Achievements include development of several automated clinical hematology, chemistry and immunology instruments. Home: 447 Hillcrest Rd Ridgewood NJ 07450-1520 Home Phone: 201-652-2873. Personal E-mail: gfarrell@gregoryafarrell.com.

FARRELL, HERMAN D., JR., (DENNY FARRELL), state legislator, former political organization administrator; b. White Plains, NY, Feb. 4, 1932; s. Herman and Gladys Farrell; m. Theresa Farrell, 1958; children: Monique Farrell-Guidry, Herman III, Sopia Llene. Confidential aide Supreme Ct. Justice, 1966—72; asst. dir. Mayor's Office NYC, Washington Heights, NY, 1972—74; mem. NY State Assembly, 1975—, mem. rule com., chmn. ways & means com. Chmn. Subcommittee on Fin. Institutions of Nat. Conf. State Legislators, 1981-82; Dem. County Leader, NYC, 1981-; vice chmn. NY State Dem. Party, 1983-93, chmn., 2001-06 Sgt. US Army, 1952—54. Named Man of Yr., NY State Supreme Ct. Officer's Assn.; recipient Muriel Silberberg award, NY Affirmative Action Coun. award, Appreciation award, Boricua Coll., Childs Meml. Ch. award, NY State Ct. Clerks Assn. award, Cert. of Appreciation, Am. Legion. Mem.: Tioga Carver Com. Found. Office: NY State Assembly 2541-55 Adam Clayton Powell Jr Blvd New York NY 10039*

FARRELL, JEFFREY MICHAEL, electrical engineer, consultant; s. Michael and Paula Farrell. MS, SUNY, Buffalo, 2003. Radar systems engr. Tech. Svc. Corp., Silver Spring, Md., 2002—05; sr. cons. Booz Allen Hamilton, Arlington, Va., 2005. Mem.: IEEE. Home Phone: 202-309-0700. Personal E-mail: farrell2005@hotmail.com.

FARRELL, JOHN L., JR., lawyer, consultant, corporate financial executive; b. NYC, Jan. 24, 1929; s. John Lawrence and Edna (Ziegler) F.; m. Beverly H. Farrell; children: John Lawrence III, Maureen, Jayne, Dianne, Michael. BA, St. Peters Coll., NJ, 1950; LL.B., St. John's U., 1955; MBA, NYU, 1960. Bar: N.Y. 1956. Asst. counsel ACF Industries, Inc., NYC, 1955-61; counsel, sec., asst. to chmn. Knox Glass, Inc., NYC, 1961-68; adminstrv. liaison Williams Cos., Tulsa, 1968-69; cons. on mergers and acquisitions, 1969-71; sr. v.p. law and adminstrn., sec. U.S. Filter Corp., NYC, 1971-82; pres., chief operating officer FRACORP, Tulsa, 1983-84; cons. on mergers, acquisitions and fin. Frates Enterprises, Tulsa, 1984-87; prin. The Morgan Investment Group, Tulsa, 1988—; chmn. exec. com. Diagnostics, Inc., Tulsa, 1989-96. Mem. Ardsley (N.Y.) Sch. Bd., 1965-68. Served to 1st lt. U.S. Army, 1951-53. Republican. Roman Catholic. Home: 2128 E 60th Pl Tulsa OK 74105-7021

FARRELL, JOHN MARSHALL, architect; b. Poplar Bluff, Mo., Nov. 2, 1942; s. Marshall Dee and Frieda Mae (Burk) F.; m. Susan Martha Garbett, Dec. 7, 1968; children— Kevin, Elizabeth. B.Arch., Tex. Tech U., 1965. Registered architect Tex., N.Mex., Calif., Fla. Designer Skidmore Owings & Merrill, Chgo., 1968-70; project architect Bernard Johnson Inc., Houston, 1970-72; project architect NSHD Inc., Houston, 1972-73; prin., corp. dir., project mgr. Golemon & Rolfe Assocs. Inc., Houston, 1973-83; former pres. Farrell-Robson Architects Inc.; prin. FKP Architects, Tex., 1998-.Mem. zoning and planning commn. City of West University Place (Tex.), 1980-82; v.p. West University Little League, 1981-83; mem. adminstrv. bd. St. Luke's United Methodist Ch., Houston, 1982-84. Served as officer USNR, 1965-68; Vietnam. Mem. AIA (past dir. Houston chpt.), Tex. Soc. Architects, NCARB (cert.), Council Ednl. Facility Planners. Club: Briar. Archtl. works: U. Houston at Clear Lake City, 1975; Riverwalk Marriott Hotel, San Antonio, 1978; Oak Ridge High Sch., Conroe, Tex., 1981; Saida Hilton Condominium, South Padre Island, 1982; Crowne Plaza West Loop Hotel, Houston, 1983. Office: FKP Architects 8 Greenway Plaza, Ste 300 Houston TX 77046-6501

FARRELL, JOSEPH, film producer and company executive, financial analyst, writer, sculptor; b. NYC, Sept. 11, 1935; s. John Joseph and Mildred Veronica (Dwyer) F. AB summa cum laude, St. John's Coll., 1958; A.M., U. Notre Dame, 1959; JD, Harvard U., 1965. Bar: N.Y. 1965. With firm Milbank, Tweed, Hadley & McCloy, NYC, 1964-65; exec. assoc. Carnegie Corp. N.Y., 1965-66; exec. v.p., chief oper. officer Am. Council of Arts, 1966-71; cons. Rockefeller Bros. Fund, Spl. Projects, 1966-74, exec. v.p., 1974-77; vice chmn. Louis Harris & Assocs. (Harris Poll), NYC, 1978; chmn., CEO, Nat. Rsch. Group, Inc., subs. VNU, L.A., London and Tokyo, 1978—. Movie market analyst and cons., 1978—; movie exec. producer, 1986—; sculptor, 1958—; designer Farbino Furniture, 1982—. Author, editor: Americans and the Arts, 1973, 75, Museums: USA, 1973, The Cultural Consumer, 1973, The U.S. Arts and Cultural Trend Data System, 1977; author: (novel) Birds of Prey, 1998; screenwriter The Foundation, Second Son, 1990—. Mem. Gov. N.Y. Task Force on Arts, 1975; founder, bd. dirs. Vol. Lawyers for Arts, 1968-76; bd. dirs. Arts and Bus. Coun. N.Y., 1973-76; bd. advisors Actors Studio, 1983-90. Woodrow Wilson fellow, 1958; named among Top 100 Influential People in Hollywood, Premiere mag., 1998, 99. Office: 6255 W Sunset BLVD #19TH-FLR Los Angeles CA 90028-7403

FARRELL, MARGARET DAWSON, lawyer; b. Bellingham, Wash., July 23, 1949; d. Sterling Jacob and Irene Hegg; m. David S. Farrell, June 10, 1972; children: Lindsay S., Charles D. BA cum laude, Smith Coll., 1971; postgrad., Georgetown U., 1971-72; JD, U. Cin., 1974. Bar: Ohio

1974, U.S. Dist. Ct. (so. dist.) Ohio 1974, R.I. 1976, U.S. Dist. Ct. R.I. 1976. Assoc. Frost & Jacobs, Cin., 1974-76; from assoc. to ptnr. Tillinghast, Collins & Graham, Providence, 1976—81; ptnr. Hinckley, Allen & Snyder LLP, Providence, 1981—. Lectr. Bryant Coll., 1979-80; dir., Bank R.I., 1996-2006, sec. 1996—, dir. Bancorp R.I., Inc., 2000-2006, sec. 2000—. Trustee Women and Infants Hosp., Providence, 1981—, sec., 1982-96, vice chair, 1996-2003, chair 2004-2007; bd. dirs. Women and Infants Corp., Providence, 1989—2003, chair 2004-2007, sec., 1989-96, vice chair, 1996-2003, chair, 2004—; trustee, sec. Providence Preservation Soc. Revolving Fund, 1982-88; trustee Butler Hosp., 1995—; Care New England Health Sys., 1996—, R.I. Hist. Soc., 1980-85, Gordon Sch., East Providence, R.I., 1990-95; trustee Hosp. Assn. R.I., 1989-2003, mem. exec. coun., 1998-2003; trustee, sec., pres. Found. for Repertory Theatre, R.I., 1978-84; R.I. del. Am. Hosp. Assn. Congress Hosp. Trustees, 1993-98; mem. R.I. Bd. Regents for Elem. and Secondary Edn., 1987-90. Mem. ABA, R.I. Bar Assn. Avocations: golf, sailing, skiing, horseback riding. Office: Hinckley Allen & Snyder LLP 50 Kennedy Plz Ste 1500 Providence RI 02903 Office Phone: 401-274-2000.

FARRELL, MARY M(AGGIE), Dean of Libraries; BA in Am. Studies, U. Mo., Kansas City, 1984; MLS, U. Ariz., 1988; MPA, Ariz. State U., 1992. Acting head, govt. documents svc. Ariz. State U., 1991—92, Ariz. State documents libr., 1989—93; libr. book fellow Am. Libr. Assn./US Info. Agy., Dalhousie U., Halifax, Nova Scotia, Canada, 1993; head, govt. publications U. Nev., Las Vegas, 1993—95; libr./internet cons., electronic transition staff Libr. Programs Svc. Govt. Printing Office, 1995—96; assoc. dean libraries Mont. State U., 1996—2002; dean libraries U. Wyo., 2002—. Del. Online Computer Libr. Ctr., Dublin, 2000—, mem. exec. com., 2002—03, preservation and electronic collections interest group chair, 2003—04, v.p., 2004—05, users' coun. ,BCR rep., 2000—06, bd. trustee, 2007—; chair Colo. Alliance Librs. Mems. Coun., 2003—04; mentor Mountain Plains Libr. Assn. Leadership Inst., 2004. Contbr. articles to profl. jours. Mem.: ALA (mem. conf. contributed papers com. 2003—05, coun. mem. 2004—07). Office: Dean Libraries U Wyo Coe Libr PO Box 3334 Laramie WY 82071-3334 Address: Online Computer Libr Ctr Inc 6565 Kilgour Pl Dublin OH 43017-3395 Office Phone: 307-766-3279. Office Fax: 307-766-2510. Business E-Mail: farrell@uwyo.edu.*

FARRELL, MICHAEL LYNN, medical educator; b. Sioux Falls, SD, May 30, 1953; s. Robert Leo and Elizabeth M. Farrell; m. Mirna Celeste Farrell, July 5, 1980; children: Nicole, Jennifer, Evan. MD, U. Minn., Mpls., 1979; MPH, Tulane U., New Orleans, 1990. Commd. 2d lt. USAF, 1980, advanced through grades to col. Tchr. Cmty. Bible Sch., San Antonio, 2001—. Mem.: Soc. US Air Force Bapt. Surgeons, Aerospace Med. Assn. Republican. Avocations: fly fishing, tennis, hiking. Home: 530 Stonewood St San Antonio TX 78216 Office: USAF 2601 Louis Bauer Rd San Antonio TX 78235

FARRELL, MICHAEL W., judge; b. 1938; Grad., U. Notre Dame; MA, Columbia U.; JD, Am. U. Law clerk to Assoc. Judge John P. Moore Md. Ct. Spl. Appeals, 1973; atty. criminal divsn. U.S. Dept. Justice; chief appellate divsn. Office U.S. Atty. D.C., 1982-89; assoc. judge D.C. Ct. Appeals, 1989—. Chmn. Eng. dept. Georgetown Prep. Sch. Office: Ct Appeals 500 Indiana Ave NW Rm 6000 Washington DC 20001-2131*

FARRELL, MIKE, actor; b. St. Paul, Feb. 6, 1939; s. Michael and Agnes Farrell; m. Judy Hayden, 1963 (div.); children: Michael, Erin; m. Shelley Fabares, 1984. Student, UCLA, Jeff Corey Workshop, Hollywood. Profl. debut in little theatre prodn. Rain, 1961; motion pictures include: Captain Newman, M.D, 1964, The Americanization of Emily, 1964, The Graduate, 1967, Targets, 1968; numerous TV appearances; regular on TV series Days of Our Lives, NBC-TV, The Interns, CBS-TV, 1970-71, The Man and the City, ABC-TV, 1971-72, M*A*S*H, CBS-TV, 1975-83, The Killers Within, 1995, Superman, 1996, Providence, 1999—; TV spls. include Ladies of the Corridor, PBS, 1975, Child Sexual Abuse, PBS, 1984, JFK, A One-Man Show; TV movies include: The Questor Tapes, The Longest Night, Battered, Sex and the Single Parent, Damien, The Leper Priest, Prime Suspect, 1982, Choices of the Heart, 1983, Memorial Day, 1984, Private Sessions, 1985, Vanishing Act, 1986, A Deadly Silence, 1989, (also co-author) Incident at Dark River, 1990, The Whereabouts of Jenny, 1991, Silent Motive, 1991, Hart to Hart: Old Friends Never Die, 1994, Vows of Deception, 1996, Tangled Web, 1996, Behind the Laughs, 1997, Sins of the Mind, 1997, The Crooked E: The Unshredded Truth About Enron, 2003, Miracle Dogs, 2003, The Clinic, 2004; co-producer motion picture Dominick and Eugene, 1988; dir. M*A*S*H episodes, (TV movie) Run Till You Fall, CBS-TV, 1988; prodr. (films) Memorial Day, 1983, Dominick and Eugene, 1988, Incident at Dark River, 1989, Silent Motive, 1991, Patch Adams, others; dir. M*A*S*H, 1972, Run Till You Fall, 1988; TV guest appearances include Bonanza, 1959, I Dream of Jeannie, 1965, The Monkees, 1966, Ghost Story, 1972, The Six Million Dollar Man, 1974, Murder, She Wrote, 1984, Matlock, 1986, others. Involved in polit. and social causes; active Human Rights Watch, CONCERN/Am., Calif. State Commn. on Jud. Performance; pres. Death Penalty Focus. Served USMC. Recipient Valentine Davies award, Writers Guild Am., 1996. Mem. AFTRA, Screen Actors Guild.

FARRELL, PAMELA CHRISTINE, secondary school educator; b. Cin., Jan. 5, 1965; d. Thomas Harry and Barbara Jane Farrell; children: Thomas Patrick Farrell-Turner, Ronald Bryan Farrell-Creed. M, U. Dayton, Ohio, 1998. Cert. Comprehensive Math. and Sci. Tchr. State of Ohio, 1985. Tchr. Ripley-Union-Lewis-Huntington H.S., Ohio, 1985—94, Milford Exempted Village Schs., Ohio, 1994—97, Princeton City Schs., Cin., 1997—. Tchr. Brown County Schs., Georgetown, Ohio, 1987—93, So. State C.C., Fincastle, Ohio, 1988—90. Tchr. catechism St. Michael Ch., Sharonville, Ohio, 2003—. Named Tchr. of Yr., Radio Shack, 2000; recipient Tchr. Achievement award, Ashland, 1996, Commendation award, Sci. Edn. Coun. Ohio, 2000; Martha Holden Jennings scholar, U. Dayton, 1989. R-Consevative. Roman Catholic. Achievements include patents pending for Static Magic or PONAM. Avocations: travel, bicycling, hiking, sports, Special Olympics. Home: 11004 Main Street Cincinnati OH 45241 Office: Princeton High School 11080 Chester Road Cincinnati OH 45246 Home Phone: 513-563-2856; Office Phone: 513-552-8410. Personal E-mail: suavenus@aol.com. E-mail: pfarrell@princeton.k12.oh.us.

FARRELL, PATRICIA ANN, psychologist, educator, writer; b. NYC; d. Joseph and Pauline Farrell. BA, Queens Coll.; MA, PhD, NYU. Lic. psychologist, NJ, Fla.; cert. online computer instr. Assoc. editor Pubs. Weekly Mag., NYC; editor Bestsellers Mag., NYC; assoc. editor King Features Syndicate, NYC; staff psychologist, intake coord. Mid-Bergen Cmty. Mental Health Ctr., Paramus, NJ; instr. Bergen C.C., Paramus, 1978-94; prof. clin. psychology Walden U., 1995—2001. Resident clin. psychology Am. Inst. for Counseling, NJ, 1990-91; cons. Family Counseling Svc. of Ridgewood, NJ, 1984; clin. psychology intern Marlboro (NJ) Psychiat. Hosp., 1984-85, staff psychologist, 1985-87; rsch. analyst Mt. Sinai Sch. Medicine, 1987-88; account exec., sr. med. writer Manning, Selvage and Lee, NYC, 1988-90; sr. clin. psychologist, mem. med. staff Greystone Pk. (NJ) Psychiat. Hosp., 1990-96; pvt. practice psychology, Englewood Cliffs, NJ; health sci. editor Time Warner Cable, Channel 10 News, 1995-2000; med. specialist NJ Divsn. Disability Determination, 1997—; police surgeon Boro Ft. Lee, NJ, 1998-2005; psychiatry preceptor U. Medicine and Dentistry NJ Med. Sch.; cons. pharm. clin. protocols; psychologist, expert moderator on anxiety and panic WebMD, 2000—. Guest radio and TV shows including The Today Show, Good Morning Am., Crier Live, Anderson Cooper 360, Nat. Geog. TV, MSNBC, Fuji TV, The Abrams Report, The Big Idea, Ron Reagan's Connections, Hollywood at Large, The View, The O'Reilly Factor, ABC Sports Spl., VH1, E!, ABC World News with Anderson Cooper AC 360, Court TV, Rapid Fire, CNN Radio, Geraldo Rivera Show, Newsweek-on-Air, Voice of Am., Family Talk, Up Front Tonight, Buchanon & Press, Pros and Cons, Local Live, USA Radio Network, Ken Hamblin Show, KNU Radio, Fox Beyond the News, Real Talk, Jay Thomas Radio Show, Sally Jessy Raphael, Montel Williams, Gordon Elliott Show, Inside Edit., Am. Jour., Joan Rivers Show, Fox Cable News, Good Day NY, Mark Walberg, Am. After Hours, Dini, The Shirley Show, Camilla Scott, USA Live, Alive and Wellness with Carol Martin, News Talk, Maury Povich, Caucus NJ, It's Your Call, One-on-One, The Carnie Wilson Show, AP Newswire, Judge for Yourself TV Show, NYC 10 O'Clock News, Cosmo, Redbook, Self, Shape, Fitness, Latina, Maxim, Good Housekeeping, AARP, Cooking Light, Smart Money, Ct. TV Investigative Reports, In Touch, Woman's World, Achieve Solutions, All You, First for Women, Washington Post, Fox & Friends, Eyewitness News, Reuters TV, Timeout NY, Detroit News, Knight-Ridder News, Chgo. Tribune, Home Office Computing, Working Woman, NY Post, Boston Globe, NY Daily News, NY Times, Chateleine, New Woman, Phila. Enquirer, WPIX-TV, NY, UPN 9 News, WWOR-TV News, WNRR-TV, In Your Interest, LTV, Channel 10 News, On Campus, Sta WTTM, WSNJ, WHSI-TV, Bloomberg News, UPI News, KGAB, WSAR, Don Weeks Show, Common Concerns, WHSE-TV, Alan Nathan's Battle Lines, Dirk Van NBC radio, Ruth Koscielak Show, Voice of Am., WTOP, Redbook, Ramp, Eyewitness News, Cork Talks Back, TalkSport, The Week, Pink, Life & Style, Ladies Home Jour., Reuters TV, Bev Smith Show, Fitness, Shape, Prevention, In Touch, More, The Oregonian, Arnie Arneson Show, Talk Am., Real Simple, Quick and Simple, Marie Claire, Seventeen, Parents, Shape, Prevention, AARP Bull., Women's Health, Inside TV, Baby Talk, Family Circle, Women's Day, Metro NY, Physical, Wall St. Jour. Radio, Christian Single, Mental Health Law Report; author: (manual) Alzheimer's Disease Assessment Scale test, How To Be Your Own Therapist, 2004, 07; contbr. chpts. Fifty Things to Do When You Turn Fifty, 2005; contbr. articles to Writer's Digest, Real World, Postgrad. Medicine, newspapers. Bd. dirs., chmn. med. liaison com. liaison to dept. psychiatry Bergen Pines County Hosp., Paramus, 1994-95. McDonald's rsch. grantee, 1994-95; recipient Sci. award Rotary Club. Avocations: exercise, racquetball, kite-flying, film making. Office: PO Box 1525 Englewood Cliffs NJ 07632-0283

FARRELL, PATRICK, artist; s. Ira Patrick Farrell and Carmen Marie Greenless. Co-founder, dir., art dir. River Edge Galleries, Mishicot, Wis., 1984—89. Exhibitions include Wis. Acad. Scis., Arts and Letters, Madison, 1992, Anderson Arts Ctr., Kenosha, Wis., 1996, Charles Allis Art Mus., Milw., 1998. Recipient Benedictine Mert award, Am. Fedn. Arts, 1972, Spl. Purchase award, Milw. Art Ctr., 1974, award of Excellence, Milw. Art Commn., 1984. Mem.: Allied Artists Am. (hon. meml. award 1994, 1997). Independent. Avocations: antiques, collector of recorded music. Office: PO Box 1297 Milwaukee WI 53201 Office Phone: 414-964-0524.

FARRELL, PATRICK V., academic administrator; BS, U. Mich., PhD in Mech. Engring.; MS, U. Calif., Berkeley. Mem. mech. engring. faculty U. Wis.-Madison, 1982—, dir. Engine Rsch. Ctr., 1999—2001, assoc. dean academic affairs, 2001—05, exec. assoc. dean, 2005—06, provost, vice chancellor academic affairs, 2006—. Office: U Wis-Madison / Office of Provost 150 Bascom Hall 500 Lincoln Dr Madison WI 53706 Office Phone: 608-262-1304. Office Fax: 606-265-3324. E-mail: pfarrell@provost.wisc.edu.*

FARRELL, PHILIP M., physician, dean, educator, researcher; b. St. Louis, Nov. 26, 1943; m. Alice Yeakle; children: Michael Henry, David Sean, Bridget Mary. AB, St. Louis U., 1964, MD, PhD, St. Louis U., 1970. Diplomate Am. Bd. Pediatrics. Intern U. Wis. Hosps., 1970—71, resident in pediatrics, 1971—72; fellow pediatric metabolism br. Nat. Inst. Arthritis, Metabolism and Digestive Diseases, NIH, Bethesda, Md., 1972—74, sr. investigator pediatric metabolism br., 1974—75; chief Neonatal and Pediatric Medicine Br., Nat. Inst. Child Health and Human Devel., NIH, Bethesda, Md., 1975—77, Chief, Sect. Devel. Biology and Clin. Nutrition, 1975—77; Asst. prof. dept. child health George Washington U., Washington, 1975; asst. prof. pediatrics U. Wis., Madison, 1977-78, dir. Cystic Fibrosis Ctr., 1977—83, co-dir., 1983—88, affiliate scientist Wis. Regional Primate Research Ctr., 1978, affiliate faculty dept. nutrition scis., 1978, assoc. prof. pediatrics, 1978-82, dir. Pediatric Pulmonary Specialized Ctr. of Research, 1981-85, prof. pediatrics, 1982—, chmn. dept. pediatrics, 1985-95, med. dir. Children's Hosp., 1988—95, Alfred Dorrance Daniels Prof. on Diseases of Children, 1990—, interim dean Med. Sch., 1994—95, dean Med. Sch., 1995—, vice-chancellor med. affairs, 2001—. Editor: Lung Development: Biological and Clinical Perspectives, 1982. Avalon Found. scholar, 1965-67, Thurston Meml. scholar, 1966-70; Fogarty Internat. fellow, 1985. Mem. Am. Chem. Soc., Am. Acad. Pediatrics, Soc. Pediatric Rsch., Am. Thoracic Soc., Soc. Exptl. Biology and Medicine, Am. Inst. Nutrition, Am. Soc. Clin. Nutrition, Wis. Assn. Perinatal Care, Sigma Xi, Phi Beta Kappa, Alpha Omega Alpha. Office: Univ Wis School of Med 4129 Health Sciences Learning Ctr 75 Highland Ave Madison WI 53705-2221 Office Phone: 608-263-4900.

FARRELL, SUZANNE (ROBERTA SUE FICKER), ballerina; b. Cin., Aug. 16, 1945; d. Robert Ficker and Donna (Von Holle) Holly; m. Paul Mejia, Feb. 21, 1969 (div. 1997). Studies with Marian LaCour, Cin. Conservatory Music; student, Sch. Am. Ballet, 1960—61; LHD (hon.), Georgetown U., 1984, Fordham U., 1987; DFA (hon.), Yale U., 1988; LLD (hon.), U. Notre Dame, 1990; D of Performing Arts (hon.), U. Cin., 1990; ArtsD (hon.), Middlebury Coll., 1992; LHD (hon.), Coll. Mt. St. Vincent, 1995; Doctorate (hon.), Harvard U., 2004. With Maurice Bejart's Ballet of the 20th Century, Brussels, 1969, NYC Ballet, 1961—69, 1975—89, became featured dancer, 1962, prin. dancer, 1965—69, 1975—89; program creator, Exploring Ballet with Suzanne Farrell Kennedy Ctr., Washington, 1993—; artistic dir. The Suzanne Farrell Ballet, 2000—. Hon. lectr. dance U. Cin.; guest tchr. Sch. Am. Ballet, Kennedy Ctr. for Performing Arts; prof. dance Fla. State U., 2000—, Francis Eppes Chair in Arts. Appeared in film version Midsummer Night's Dream, Bejart Ballet of 20th Century, Brussels, 1971—75, appeared as Juliet in Romeo and Juliet, appeared with NYC Ballet in New Ravel Festival, Tzigane, in G Major, 1976, (documentary) Elusive Muse, 1996, created roles in other ballets Ah, Vous Dirais Je, Maman?, the young girl in Rose in Nijinsky, Clown of God, 1971, Laura in I Trionfi, (NYC Ballet) Chaconne, Mozartiana, Diamonds, featured in TV show Balanchine Dance in Am., Parts I-IV, featured in Exploring Ballet with Suzanne Farrell at the Kennedy Ctr., 1993—; author: (autobiography) Holding on to the Air, 1990; repetiteur George Balanchine Trust. Mem. sr. adv. bd. NY chpt. Arthritis Found.; mem. arts adv. bd. Princess Grace Found.-USA; mem. NY State Coun. on Arts; pres. bd. Profl. Children's Sch. Recipient Merit award, Mademoiselle mag., 1965, Dance mag. award, 1976, Award of Honor for Arts and Culture, NYC, 1979, Spirit Achievement award, Albert Einstein Coll. Medicine, 1980, Merit award, Brandeis U., Emmy award, 1985, Golden Plate award, Am. Acad. of Achievement, 1987, Arts award, Gov. of NY State, 1988, Nat. Medal of Arts, 2003, Capezio Dance Award, 2005, Kennedy Ctr. Honor, John F. Kennedy Ctr. for Performing Arts, 2005.

FARRELL, THOMAS FRANCIS, II, energy executive; b. Ft. Buckner, Okinawa, Japan, 1954; m. Anne Garland Tullidge; 2 children. BA in Econs., U. Va., 1976, JD, 1979. Ptnr. McGuire, Woods, Beatle & Booth, 1981-95; v.p., gen. counsel Dominion Resources Inc., Richmond, Va., 1995-97, sr. v.p. corp. affairs, 1997-99, exec. v.p., gen. counsel, corp. sec. Va. Power, exec. v.p., 1999—2003, CEO Dominion Generation, CEO Dominion Energy, 2000—04, COO, 2004—06; pres. Dominion (formerly Dominion Resources), Richmond, 2004—, bd. dirs., 2005—, CEO, 2006—, chmn., 2007—. Chmn. nominations to the appellate ct. com. State of Va. Mem. Va. Bar Assn. (exec. com., chmn. young lawyers sect.), Va. Law Found. (mem. continuing legal edn. com.). Office: Dominion PO Box 26532 Richmond VA 23261-6532 Office Phone: 804-819-2400.*

FARRELL, W. JAMES, metal products manufacturing company executive; b. NYC, 1942; married; 5 children. BA in Electrical Engring., U. Detroit, 1965. Joined Ill. Tool Works., Inc., Glenview, Ill., 1965, sales corr., Shakeproof div., 1965—68, sales engr., 1968—70, automotive acct. mgr., 1972—77, v.p., group pres. Fastener Group, 1977—83, exec. v.p. Glenview, Ill., 1983—94, pres., 1995—96, CEO, 1995—2005, chmn. bd., 1996—2006. Bd. dirs. Allstate Ins. Co., Sears, Roebuck and Co., 1999—, Kraft Foods, 2001—, United Airlines; bd. dir. 3M Co., 2006—; bd. dirs. Fed. Reserve Bank Chgo., chmn., 2001—03, 2004—. Dir. Big Shoulders Fund, Chgo. Public Library Found.; chmn. Jr. Achievement Chgo.; trustee Northwestern U.; advisory bd. mem. J.L. Kellogg Grad. Sch. Mgmt.; trustee Rush Presbyterian-St. Luke's Medical Ctr.; chmn. bd. trustees Mus. Sci. and Industry; dir. Lyric Opera Chgo.; vice chmn. United Way Crusade of Mercy. Served criminal investigation div. US Army, 1965—67, Alaska. Mem.: Econ. Club Chgo. (chmn.), Chgo. Club (pres.), Comml. Club Chgo. (civic com.), Executives Club Chgo., Mid-Am. Com., Ill. Bus. Roundtable, Bus. Coun.

FARRELL, WARREN THOMAS, author; b. NYC, June 26, 1943; s. Thomas Edward and Muriel (Levy) F.; m. Ursie Otte Fairbairn, June 19, 1966 (div. 1977); m. Liz Dowling, Aug. 4, 2002. BA in Social Sci., Montclair State U., NJ, 1965; MA in Political Sci., U. Calif., LA, 1966; PhD in Political Sci., NYU, 1974; D. of Humane Letters, Profl. Sch. Psychology, San Diego, 1985. Diplomate Am. Bd. Sexology; cert. tchr. NJ. Adj. asst. prof. Sch. of Medicine U. Calif., San Diego, 1986—88; candidate for Gov. Calif. 2003 Recall Election, First Candidate in US History on ballot as "Fathers' Issues" Candidate; cons. & spkr. Young Presidents' Orgn., 2003; cons. in field. Author: The Liberated Man, 1975, Why Men Are The Way They Are, 1986, 1987, 1988, The Myth of Male Power, 1993, 1994, Women Can't Hear What Men Don't Say, 1999 (Book-of-the-Month Club, 1999), Father and Child Reunion, 2001, Why Men Earn More, 2005 (1 of 5 Best Career Books, US News & World Report, 2005); contbr. articles to profl. jours.; TV appearances include Oprah, Donahue, The Today Show, Larry King Live, ABC World News with Peter Jennings, NBC Nightly News, CBS News Sunday Morning, Crossfire, CBC's Newsworld, CNN Spl. on Candidacy, 2003, TV spls. ABC's 20/20, ABC (Australia), BBC (Britain), CBC (Can.), People Mag., Parade Mag., Japan Times, NY Times, Wall St. Jour., Time, US News & World Report, USA Today, Forbes, Der Speigel, Mac Leans, London Times, So. China Morning Post, others. Recipient Outstanding Contribution award Calif. Assn. Marriage Family Therapists, 1988, Pioneer in the Psychology of Fatherhood award Onstep Inst. Mental Rsch., 2000; named Top 100 Thought Leaders worldwide Fin. Times, 2000. Mem. Nat. Coalition Free Men (adv. bd. 1996—2002, best book 1986), Nat. Congress Fathers & Children (bd. dirs. 1992—, best book 1993), Nat. Org. Women (N.Y.C Chpt. bd. dirs. 1970-73), Children's Rights Council (adv. bd. 1985—), Am. Coalition of Fathers and Children (bd. dirs. 96-98). Unitarian Universalist. Achievements include books published in more than 50 countries and more than 10 languages. Home and Office: 2982 Las Olas Ct Carlsbad CA 92009 Office Phone: 760-753-5000. Personal E-mail: warren@warrenfarrell.com.

FARRELL, WILLIAM EDGAR, sales executive, management consultant; b. Jeanette, Pa., Mar. 13, 1937; s. Arthur Richard and Lelia (Ryder) F.; m. Sara Lynnette Swing, Aug. 20, 1960; children: Wendy J., Tracy L., Rebecca J. BS in Edn., Pa. State U., 1959. Location mgr. IBM Corp., Dover, Del., 1969-72, corp. lobbyist Washington, 1972-74, planning cons., 1974-78, nat. mktg. mgr., 1978-80, exec. asst., 1980-81, account exec. Denver, 1981-87, policy exec., 1987-91; pres., CEO Weatherall Co., Inc., Englewood, Colo., 1993-97; chief info. officer, v.p. info. tech. & purchasing Wild West, Inc., Kearney, Nebr., 1998—2001; v.p. sales SKYDEX Tech., Inc., Centennial, Colo., 2001—05; CFO Shore Entertainment, 2005—, Shore Mgmt. Svcs., 2005—. CFO Wide Horizon, Inc., Denver, 1987-92, chmn. bd. trustees, 1989-92; pres. Exec. Mgmt. Cons., 1987—; sec.-treas. Electronic Shoe Enterprises Inc., 1991-94; mem. Colo. Info. Mgmt. Commn., 1992-95; sec.-treas. Energaire Corp., 2003—, G.S. Cole & Assocs., Inc., 2003—; ptnr. Hand Pillows Dot Com.; CFO Swing Family and Cosmetic Dentistry, 2006—. Founding mem. River Falls Cmty. Assn., Potomac, Md., 1975; first reader First Ch. of Christ Scientist, Chevy Chase, Md., 1976-80; chmn. Amigo's De Ser; bd. dirs. Rocky Mountain Ser, 1991-92; trustee Cole Family Trust, 2003—. Recipient Outstanding Contbn. award IBM Corp., 1968. Republican. Achievements include patents pending for pole vaulting soft box. Avocation: flying instrument SEL airplanes. Office Phone: 303-796-8609. Personal E-mail: wefar007@aol.com.

FARRELL, WILLIAM JOSEPH, university chancellor; b. Milw., Aug. 17, 1936; s. William John and Rita (Taggart) F.; m. Carol Mary Leeming, Aug. 1, 1959; children: William Jr., Charles, Elizabeth. BS summa cum laude, Marquette U., 1958, MBA, 1976; MA, U. Wis., 1959, PhD, 1961; DHL (hon.), St. Anselm's Coll., 1998. Instr. U. Chgo., 1961-63, asst. prof., 1963-68; assoc. prof. Marquette U., Milw., 1968-75, dir. of Found. Support, 1970-75; assoc. v.p. of research U. Iowa, Iowa City, 1975-84; pres. Plymouth (N.H.) State Coll., 1984-92; chancellor Univ. System of N.H., 1992—2000. Vis. prof. U. Calif., Berkeley, 1967-68; trustee Univ. Sys. N.H., 1984—, St. Anselm's Coll., 1992—, chair ednl. policy com., 1995—, mem. exec. com., 1995—, state del. New Eng. Bd. Higher Edn., 1984—, chair N.H. del., 1995—. Co-editor English Literature 1600-1800: A Bibliography of Modern Studies, 1972; editor: (jour.) Renascence: Essays on Values in Literature, 1969-72; contbr. numerous articles to profl. jours. Bd. dirs. N.H. Music Festival, Center Harbor, 1984-93, Bus. and Industry Assn. of N.H., 1998—; mem. N.H. Postsecondary Edn. Commn., 1984—, mem. exec. com., 1988-93, chmn., 1990-92. Woodrow Wilson fellow, 1958, Danforth fellow, 1958. Mem. N.H. Coll. and Univ. Coun. (chmn. 1989-91), Am. Assn. State Colls. and Univs., Am. Coun. on Edn., Nat. Assn. Sys. Heads, Nat. Assn. State Univs. & Land Grant Colls., State Higher Edn. Exec. Officers, N.H. Bus. and Industry Assn. (bd. dirs. 1998—). Roman Catholic. Office: Univ System NH Dunlap Ctr 25 Concord Rd Durham NH 03824-6624 Home: 10 Taft St Nashua NH 03060-5019

FARRELLY, BOBBY (ROBERT LEO RARRELLY JR.), scriptwriter, film director and producer; b. Cumberland, RI, 1958; m. Nancy Farrelly; 2 children. Student, Rensselaer Poly. Inst. Writer, prodr. Outside Providence, 1999; writer, co-prodr., dir. Dumb and Dumber, 1994; exec. prodr., writer, dir. There's Something About Mary, 1998; writer, prodr., dir. Me, Myself and Irene, 2000, Shallow Hall, 2001. Stuck on You, 2003; writer Bushwacked, 1995; dir. Kingpin, 1996; dir., prodr. Osmosis Jones, 2001; prodr. Say It Isn't So, 2001; exec. prodr. The Ringer, 2005, (TV series) Ozzy & Drix, 2002; dir. Fever Pitch, 2005. Recipient Screenwriter of Yr. ShoWest Conv., 1999. Office: Creative Artists Agy c/o Adam Kantor 9830 Wilshire Blvd Beverly Hills CA 90212-1825

FARRELLY, PETER JOHN, screenwriter; b. Phoenixville, Pa., Dec. 17, 1956; s. Robert Leo and Mariann (Neary) F. BA, Providence Coll., 1979; MFA, Columbia U., 1987. Salesman U.S. Lines, Inc., Boston, 1979-81; bartender various libationary locales, Boston, 1981-85; screenwriter Paramount Columbia and Disney Studios, Los Angeles, 1985—. Author Outside Providence, 1988; co-writer (TV spls.) Our Planet Tonight, 1987, Paul Reiser: Out on a Whim, 1987; writer (film) Dumb & Dumber, 1994, Bushwhacked, 1995, There's Something About Mary, 1998; dir. (film) Dumb & Dumber, 1994, Kingpin, 1996, There's Something About Mary, 1998, Fever Pitch, 2005; prodr. There's Something About Mary, 1998,

Outside Providence, 1999; writer, co-dir, prodr.: Me, Myself & Irene, 2000, Shallow Hal, 2002; exec. prodr. (TV series) Oxxy & Drix, 2002; writer, dir., prodr. Stuck on You, 2003. Mem. Writers Guild Am. West. Roman Catholic.

FARRER, CLAIRE ANNE RAFFERTY, anthropologist, educator; b. NYC, Dec. 26, 1936; d. Francis Michael and Clara Anna (Guerra) Rafferty; 1 child, Suzanne Claire. BA in Anthropology, U. Calif., Berkeley, 1970; MA in Anthropology and Folklore, U. Tex., 1974, PhD in Anthropology and Folklore, 1977. Various positions, 1953-73; fellow Whitney M. Young Jr. Meml. Found., NYC, 1974-75; arts specialist, grant adminstr. Nat. Endowment for Arts, Washington, 1976-77; Weatherhead resident fellow Sch. Am. Rsch., Santa Fe, 1977-78; asst. prof. anthropology U. Ill., Urbana, 1978-85; assoc. prof., coord. applied anthropology Calif. State U., Chico, 1985-89, prof., 1989—2001, prof. emerita, 2002—, dir. Multicultural and Gender Studies, 1994. Cons. in field, 1974—; mem. film and video adv. panel Ill. Arts Coun., 1980-82; mem. Ill. Humanities Coun., 1980-82; vis. prof. U. Ghent, Belgium, 1990; vis. prof. Southwestern studies Colo. Coll., Colorado Springs, 2002-06, Hulbert chair in Southwestern studies, 1997; bus. mgr. Calif. Folklore Soc., 1994-99; NEH and Harry J. Gray disting. vis. prof. in humanities U. Hartford, Conn., 2002-03. Author: Play and Inter-Ethnic Communication, 1990, Living Life's Circle: Mescalero Apache Cosmovision, 1991, Thunder Rides a Black Horse: Mescalero Apaches and the Mythic Present, 1994, 96, others; co-founder, co-editor Folklore Women's Commn., 1972; editor spl. issue Jour. Am. Folklore, 1975, 1st rev. edit., 1986; co-editor: Forms of Play of Native North Americans, 1979, Earth and Sky: Visions of the Cosmos in Native North American Folklore, 1992; contbr. numerous articles to profl. jours., mags. and newspapers, chpts. to books. Recipient J. Gordon prize in S.W. Studies, Colo.Coll.; numerous fellowships and grants. Fellow Am. Anthrop. Assn.; mem. Authors Guild, Am. Ethnol. Soc., Am. Folklore Soc., Am. Soc. Ethnohistory, Astronomy in Culture. Home: PO Box 50293 Colorado Springs CO 80949-0293 Personal E-mail: crfarrer@earthlink.net.

FARRIA, DIONE MARIE, radiologist, educator; d. Guy Villa and Betty Session Farria; children: Ethan Wondemu, Eva Almaz. BS, Xavier U., New Orleans, 1985; MPH, UCLA, 1997; MD, Harvard Med. Sch., Boston, 1989. Asst. prof. Thomas Jefferson U. Hosp., Phila., 1998—99; asst. prof. radiology Wash. U. Sch. Medicine, St. Louis, 1999—. Co-dir. program elimination cancer disparities Siteman Cancer Ctr., St. Louis, 2003—; adj. asst. prof. St. Louis U. Sch. Pub. Health, 2002—. Author: (educational cd-rom) Interpretive Skills Assessment, Versions 1 and 2, (video) Between Friends: Dealing with the Diagnosis of Breast Cancer, (patient handbook) One Step at a Time: Dealing with the Diagnosis of Breast Cancer; contbr. articles to profl. jours. Recipient Career Devel. award, Dept. Def., 2000—03, Salute to Excellence in Health Care award, Mound City Med. Forum/St. Louis Am. Found., 2004, Clin. Trials Participation award, Am. Soc. Clin. Oncology, 2005, Disting. Com. Svc. award, Am. Coll. Radiology, 2005; fellow, Am. Roentgen Ray Soc., 1997—98, Cancer, Culture and Literacy Inst., Tampa, Fla., 2005; grantee, Nat. Cancer Inst., 2005—, Avon Found., 2005—06; scholar Robert Wood Johnson scholar, UCLA, 1995—97. Fellow: Am. Coll. Preventive Medicine (mem. com. 2004), Soc. Breast Imaging (breast imaging patterns ad hoc com. 2003); mem.: Am. Coll. Radiology (edn. com. appropriateness criteria expert panel 2002). Avocations: gardening, reading. Office: Washington U Sch Medicine 510 S Kingshighway Blvd Box 8131 Saint Louis MO 63110 Home Phone: 314-569-9063; Office Phone: 314-454-7696.

FARRINGTON, GREGORY C., former academic administrator; b. Bronxville, NY, Aug. 4, 1946; B in Chemistry, Clarkson U., 1968; AM in Chemistry, Harvard U., 1970, PhD in Chemistry, 1972; degree (hon.), U. Uppsala, Sweden, 1984. Staff sci. GE, Schenectady, NY, 1972-79; assoc. prof. materials sci. and engring. U. Pa., 1979-84, prof., 1984, chair dept. materials sci. and engring., 1984-87, dir. Lab. for Rsch. on Structure of Matter, 1987-90, dean Sch. Engring. and Applied Sci., 1990-98; pres. Lehigh U., Bethlehem, 1998—2006, pres. emeritus, prof., 2006—. Bd. trustees St. Luke Hosp. & Health Network, Nat. Mus. of Indsl. History, Lehigh Valley Partnership, Lehigh Valley Econ. Devel. Corp. Contbr. chapters to books, articles 100 articles to tech. jours. Achievements include holding or sharing more than two dozen patents. Office Phone: 610-758-6636.

FARRINGTON, HELEN AGNES, personnel director; b. Queens, NY, Dec. 1, 1945; d. Joseph Christopher and Therese Marie (Breazzano) F AS, Interboro Inst., NYC, 1965; AA, Ohio State U., 1983, BS Human Resource Mgmt., 1987; Mgmt. cert., U. Mich., 1980. Pers. adminstr. Am. Electric Power Co., NYC, 1974—79, supr. human resources Ohio Power divsn. Newark, 1979—87; dir. human resources Citizens Utilities Co., Stamford, Conn., 1987—88; mgr., exec. search firm Arthur Lyle Assocs., Norwalk, Conn., 1988—89; dir. human resources CaroLee Designs, Inc., Greenwich, Conn., 1990—92, ind. human resources cons., 1992—94; dir. human resources Gartner Group, Stamford, 1993—; prin., CPO HFA Resources LLC, Niwot, Colo., 1996—; pres. Helen Farrington Group, Niwot, 2005—. Bd. dirs. emeritus Boulder Cmty. Hosp.; former bd. dirs.-at-large MARC, Lakewood, Colo. Mem.: Consultants Forum, Boulder Area Human Resources Assn., Colo. Human Resources Assn., Soc. Human Resources Mgmt. (cons. forum), Boulder C. of C. Office: PO Box 438 Niwot CO 80544-0438 Office Phone: 303-417-9025. Personal E-mail: helenfarrington@msn.com.

FARRINGTON, JOHN WILLIAM, academic administrator, dean, research scientist; b. New Bedford, Mass., Sept. 25, 1944; s. John James Grace and Hazel Evelyn F.; m. Shirley Gale Hutchinson, May 28, 1966; children: Karen Lee Sabetta, Jeffrey William. BS in Chemistry, U. Mass. Dartmouth, 1966, MS in Chemistry, 1968; PhD in Oceanography, U. R.I., 1972. Grad. tchg. asst. U. Mass. Dartmouth, New Bedford, 1966—68; summer rsch. fellow Biochem. Rsch. Labs. Dow Chem. Co., Midland, Mich., 1968; grad. rsch. asst. Grad. Sch. Oceanography U. R.I., Kingston, 1968—69, fed. water quality adminstrn. fellow Grad. Sch. Oceanography, 1968—71; postdoctoral investigator, asst., assoc., sr. scientist Chemistry dept. Woods Hole Oceanographic Inst., Mass., 1971—88, dir. coastal rsch. ctr., 1982—87; Michael P. Walsh prof., dir. Environ. Scis. Program U. Mass., Boston, 1988—90; assoc. dir. edn., dean, sr. scientist Woods Hole Oceanographic Inst., 1990—2002, v.p. acad. programs, dean, 2002—05, sr. scientist emeritus, 2006—. Cons. several cos., adv. nat., internat. orgns. with respect to oceanography; vis. prof. Dixie State Coll. Utah, 2007. Contbr. over 120 sci. jour. articles and book chpts. Trustee Bermuda Biological Station for Rsch, Bermuda, N.Y., 1990—, New Bedford Aquarium, 1998—, Big Brother/Big Sisters, Cape Cod and the Islands, Mass., 1998-2002; asst. cub master, Weblos leader Falmouth Pack, St. Barnabas Ch., Falmouth, Mass., 1978-79; overseer Sea Edn. Assn.,2005—. Recipient Best Paper award Organic Geochemistry Divsn./Geochemical Soc., Marine Educator award Mass. Marine Educators Assn., 1996, Excellence in Rsch. award U. R.I. Alumni/ae Assn., Kingston, 1998, USGS Amb. of Sci. award, 2001, David B. Stone award N.E. Aquarium, 2001, Bostwick H. Ketchum award WHOI, 2003. Mem. AAAS, Am. Chem. Soc., Am. Geophysical Union, Oceanography Soc., Estuarine Rsch. Fedn., Sigma Xi (pres. Woods Hole chpt. 1995-96), Nat. Assoc. of the Nat. Academies. Protestant. Office: Woods Hole Oceanographic Inst MS #25 360 Woods Hole Rd Woods Hole MA 02543-1536 Office Phone: 508-289-3911. Business E-Mail: jfarrington@whoi.edu.

FARRIOR, EVAN BELL, special education educator, writer; b. Jersey City, June 2, 1952; BA, N.J. City U., 1977. Cert. tchr. of the handicapped. Supr. Hudson County Enterprise, Jersey City, 1978—83; tchr. spl. edn. Jersey City Pub. Sch., 1983—. Advocate for spl. needs Farrior Advocacy Svc., Jersey City, 1983—. Author: (book) Enoch: A Faith Tale, 1995, Love Is a Strange Thing, 2003. Notary pub., signing agt. Farrior Notary & Fax Svcs., Jersey City, 1995—; pres., owner Farrior Enterprise, Jersey City, 2002—; bus. adv. coun. Nat. Rep. Congl. Com., 2003—05; pres. Evan B. Farrior Ministries, Jersey City, 1995—. Named Golden Poet, World of Poetry, 1986, 1987, 1988, 1989, 1990, 1991, 1992; recipient citation, County of Hudson, 1991, Svc. award, Afro Am. Indsl. Women's Club, 1988, citation, County of Hudson, 1999, Businessman Yr., Nat. Rep. Congl. Com., 2003, 2004, 2005, 2006, Leadership award, 2003, 2004, 2005, Ronald Reagan Gold medal, 2004, 2005. Mem.: CEC, Nat. Edn. Assn., Nat. Rep. Congressional Com., Internat. Soc. Poet (Poet Yr. 1999, 2000, 2001, 2002, 2003, 2004, 2005), Flagship Interval Assn. Inc., Interval Internat., Spl. Olympics, N.J. State Coun. on Arts, Hudson County Coun. on Arts, Nat. Notary Assn., Famous Poet Soc. (Famous poet 1998, 1999, 2000, Famous Poet 2001, 2002, 2003), Internat. Soc. Poets (Editor's Choice 2000, 2001, 2002, US Amb. Poetry, Man of Yr. 2006), Authors League of Am., Inc., Author's Guild, Am. Christian Writers, Feed the Children, N.J. Performing Arts Ctr., N.J. Edn. Assn., Hudson County Edn. Assn., Jersey City Edn. Assn. Avocations: travel, writing, cooking, singing, listening to music. Home: 79 Charles St Jersey City NJ 07307 Office Phone: 201-656-0177.

FARRIS, G. STEVEN, energy executive; Grad. in history and acctg., Okla. State U. Exec. v.p. Robert W. Berry Inc., 1978—83; v.p. & treas. Terra Resources, 1983—88; v.p. exploration and prodn. Apache Corp., Houston, 1988-91, sr. v.p., 1991-94, pres., COO, 1994—2002, pres., CEO, COO, 2002—. Mem. Nat. Petroleum Coun. Mem. steering com. Energy Tchrs.; trustee Ucross Found. Office: Apache Corp 2000 Post Oak Blvd Ste 100 Houston TX 77056-4400*

FARRIS, JEFFERSON DAVIS, university administrator; b. Springdale, Ark., Sept. 30, 1927; s. Jeff D. and Loretta J. (Grunder) F.; m. Patricia Ann Camp, July 31, 1948; children— Rebecca, Elizabeth, Jefferson Davis III. BS in Engring, U. Central Ark., 1949; MA, Peabody Coll., 1950; M.P.H. (USPHS fellow), U. Mich., 1957; Ed.D., U. Ark., 1963; DHL, Sch. of Ozarks, 1981. Tchr. public high sch., Pine Bluff, Ark., 1950-57; dir. public health edn. Ark. Dept. Health, Little Rock, 1957-61; prof. health edn. U. Central Ark., Conway, 1961-86, chmn. dept. health and phys. edn., 1961-68, dean, 1968-75, univ. pres., 1975-86; nat. exec. dir. Nat. Assn. Intercollegiate Athletics, Kansas City, Mo., 1986-91. Mem. adv. com. Nat. Endowment Humanities; chair U.S. Collegiate Sports Coun., 1988-91. Editor: A Guide for School Health Education, 1956, Handbook for Elementary Physical Education, 1964. Mem. Ark. Gov.'s Council on Youth Fitness; bd. dirs. Conway (Ark.) Meml. Hosp., 1971-86, civilian aide for Ark. to sec. of army, 1979-81. Served with USN, 1946-48. Named Layman of Yr. Ark. Assn. Dentistry for Children, 1970 Mem. Ark. Assn. Deans (pres. 1968-75), Nat. Assn. Intercollegiate Athletics. Clubs: Rotary (pres. local, Paul Harris fellow 1986). Methodist. Home: 106 Covington Right Ct Hot Springs AR 71901 Personal E-mail: jefffarris@ccblelynx.com.

FARRIS, JEROME, federal judge; b. Birmingham, Ala., Mar. 4, 1930; s. William J. and Elizabeth Farris; 2 children. BS, Morehouse Coll., 1951, LLD, 1978; MSW, Atlanta U., 1955; JD, U. Wash., 1958. Bar: Wash. 1958. Mem. Weyer, Roderick, Schroeter and Sterne, Seattle, 1958—59; ptnr. Weyer, Schroeter, Sterne & Farris and successor firms, Seattle, 1959—61, Schroeter & Farris, Seattle, 1961—63, Schroeter, Farris, Bangs & Horowitz, Seattle, 1963—65, Farris, Bangs & Horowitz, Seattle, 1965—69; judge Wash. State Ct. of Appeals, Seattle, 1969—79, US Ct. Appeals (9th cir.), Seattle, 1979—95, sr. judge, 1995—. Lectr. U. Wash. Law Sch. and Sch. Social Work, 1976—; mem. faculty Nat. Coll. State Judiciary, U. Nev., 1973; adv. bd. Nat. Ctr. for State Cts. Appellate Justice Project, 1978—81; founder First Union Nat. Bank, Seattle, 1965, dir., 1965—69; mem. Jud. Wellness III Com., 2005—, US Supreme Ct. Jud. Fellows Commn., 1996—2002, Jud. Conf. Com. on Internat. Jud. Rels., 1997—2000; chmn. Ninth Circuit Judicial Conf. Com., Ninth Circuit Standing Com. on Fed. Pub. Defenders. Del. The White House Conf. on Children and Youth, 1970; mem. King County (Wash.) Youth Commn., 1969—70; vis. com. U. Wash. Sch. Social Work, 1977—90; mem. King County Mental Health-Mental Retardation Bd., 1967—69; past bd. dirs. Seattle United Way; mem. Tyee Bd. Advisers, U. Wash., 1984—88, bd. regents, 1985—97, pres., 1990—91; trustee U. Law Sch. Found., 1978—84, Morehouse Coll., 1999—; mem. vis. com. Harvard Law Sch., 1996—2005. With Signal Corps US Army, 1952—53. Recipient Disting. Svc. award, Seattle Jaycees, 1965, Clayton Frost award, 1966. Fellow: Am. Bar Found. (chair of fellows 2000, bd. dirs. 1987, exec. com. 1989—97); mem.: ABA (exec. com. appellate judges conf. 1978—84, chmn. conf. 1982—83, exec. com. appellate judges conf. 1987—88, del. jud. adminstrn. coun. 1987—88, sr. lawyers divsn. coun. 1998—), State-Fed. Jud. Coun. State Wash. (vice-chmn. 1977—78, chmn. 1983—87), Wash. Coun. on Crime and Delinquency (chmn. 1970—72), U. Wash. Law Sch., Order of Coif (mem. law rev.). Office: US Ct Appeals 1010 5th Ave Seattle WA 98104*

FARRIS, PAUL LEONARD, agricultural economist; b. Vincennes, Ind., Nov. 10, 1919; s. James David and Fairy Julia (Kahre) F.; m. Rachel Joyce Rutherford, Aug. 16, 1953; children: Nancy, Paul, John, Carl. BS, Purdue U., 1949; MS, U. Ill., 1950; PhD, Harvard U., 1954. Asst. prof. agrl. econs. Purdue U., West Lafayette, Ind., 1952-56, assoc. prof., 1956-59, prof., 1959-90, prof. emeritus, 1990—, head dept. agrl. econs., 1973-82; agrl. economist Dept. Agr., Washington, 1962; project leader for meat and poultry Nat. Commn. Food Mktg., Washington, 1965-66. Editor: Market Structure Research, 1964, Future Frontiers in Agricultural Marketing Research, 1983; contbr. articles to profl. jours. Served with AUS and USAAF, 1941-46. Fellow Am. Agrl. Econs. Assn.; mem. Am. Econ. Assn. Home: 1510 Woodland Ave West Lafayette IN 47906-2376 Office: Purdue U Dept Agrl Econs West Lafayette IN 47907

FARRIS, RONALD M., retired intelligence officer; b. Plainview, Tex., Dec. 17, 1938; s. Harvy Ozean Farris and Lockie Myrtle Crawford; m. Helen M. Irvine, Nov. 25, 1964; children: Ronald M. Jr., Christopher A., Jeffrey T. BA, U. Tex., Austin, 1961; MBA, U New Orlean, La., 1984. Intelligence officer CIA, Washington, 1968—72, 1987—93, Denver, 1972—77, New Orleans, 1977—82, Miami, Fla., 1982—87, Houston, 1993—98; ret. Lt. USN, 1961—68, Pacific Fleet, lt. comdr. USN, 1968—98. Recipient Distinction cert., CIA, 1998. Mem.: Phi Eta Sigma, Phi Beta Kappa. Avocations: golf, genealogy, reading. Personal E-mail: ronmfarris@hotmail.com.

FARRIS, TRUEMAN EARL, JR., retired newspaper editor; b. Sedalia, Mo., June 2, 1926; PhB in Journalism, Marquette U., Milw., 1948; MA in Polit. Sci., U. Wis.-Milw., 1989. Reporter Milw. Sentinel, 1945-62, asst. city editor, 1962-75, city editor, 1975-77, mng. editor, 1977-89. Juror Pulitzer Prizes, 1985-86; dean's coun. Student Publs. Bd., Coll. of Comm., Journalism and Performing Arts, Marquette U., 1987-92; bd. visitors U. Wis., Milw., 1991-2000; commitment adv. panel, U. Wis., Milw., 2000; bd. dirs. Wis. Masonic Jour., Newspaper of State Grand Lodge, 1993—, pres. 2004—. Author series of stories: Japan, 1980. Served with U.S. Army, 1955 Recipient By-Line award Marquette U., 1987; named to Milw. Press Club Media Hall of Fame, 1989. Mem. AP Mng. Editors Assn. (dir. 1980-87, editor ann. reports 1979-85), Milw. Soc. Profl. Journalists (pres. 1982-83), Milw. Press Club (pres. 1968, several reporting awards, editorial writing award 1957, included Media Hall of Fame 1989), Civil War Round Table (sec.), Mil. Order Loyal Legion of U.S. (recorder). Methodist. Avocations: reading, genealogy, civil war history. Home: 3192 S 80th St Milwaukee WI 53219-3501 Office: Milwaukee Sentinel PO Box 371 Milwaukee WI 53201-0371

FARRIS, VERA KING, former college president; b. Atlantic City, July 18, 1940; BA in Biology magna cum laude, Tuskegee Inst., 1959; MS in Zoology, U. Mass., 1962, PhD in Zoology/Parasitology, 1965; LHD (hon.), Marymount Manhattan Coll., 1985; LLD (hon.), Monmouth Coll., West Long Branch, NJ, 1987; DSc honoris causa, Johnson and Wales Coll., 1988. Dean spl. programs, assoc. prof. pathology and biology SUNY, Stony Brook, 1968-72, vice provost acad. affairs, prof. biological sci. Brockport, 1973-80; v.p. acad affairs, prof. biological sci. Kean Coll. N.J., Union, 1980-83; pres. Stockton State Coll., Pomona, NJ, 1983—2003. Contbr. articles to profl. jours. Founding mem. Gov.'s Pride award acad., 1986—, Gov.'s adv. coun. Holocaust Edn. in N.J., 1982—. Recipient Golden Trefoil award, Delaware Valley Coun. Girl Scouts Am., 1987,Chancellors Medal for Exemplary and Extraordinary Svc., U. Mass., 1986, Honor Roll Ednl award Wash. Ctr. for Internships and Acad. Seminars, Commendation for Outstanding Achievement in Edn., N.J. Assembly, 1993, others; named Lifetime Honorary citizen of Atlanta, 1984, N.J. Woman or Yr. N.J. Woman's Mag. Mem. Am. Coun. Edn. (bd. dirs. 1988-91), Coun. Post-Secondary Accreditation (bd. dirs. 1988—), Middle States Assn. Colls. and Secondary Schs. (pres. bd. trustees), Am. Assn. State Colls. and Univs. (nominating com.), N.J. State Bd. Examiners, N.J. State Coll. Pres. (chair 1987-89), B'naiB'rith (life hon.), Cosmos Club (Washington). Home: 689 St Andrews Dr Egg Harbor City NJ 08215-5119

FARROW, MARGARET ANN, former lieutenant governor; b. Kenosha, Wis., Nov. 28, 1934; d. William Charles and Margaret Ann (Horan) Nemitz; m. John Harvey Farrow, Dec. 29, 1956; children: John, William, Peter, Paul, Mark. Student, Rosary Coll., 1952-53; BS in Polit. Sci. and Edn., Marquette U., 1956, postgrad., 1975-77. Tchr. Archdiocese of Milw., 1956-57; trustee Elm Grove Village, Wis., 1976-81, pres. Wis., 1981-86; mem. Wis. Assembly, Madison, 1986-89, Wis. Senate from 33rd dist., Madison, 1989—2001; lt. gov. State of Wis., 2001—03; dir. local govt. affairs Whyte Hirshboeck Dudek Govt. Affairs, 2003—. Chair govt. effectiveness, 1998-2001, asst. majority leader, 1998; mem. joint com. on audit, 1993-97, mem. joint survey com. on tax exemptions, 1993-97, chair Wis. women's coun., 1991—, Rep. caucus chair, 1996, 99, mem. coun. on workforce excellence, 1995—, mem. Wis. glass ceiling commn., 1993—; mem. Senate Com. on edn., 1999, Senate com. on labor, 1999. Republican. Home: W 262 # 2402 Deer Haven Dr Pewaukee WI 53072-4572

FARRUG, EUGENE JOSEPH, SR., retired lawyer; b. Detroit, May 22, 1928; s. Michael and Bridget Mary (Foley) F.; children: Elizabeth Marie Streit, Eugene Joseph Jr., Pamela Ann, Bridget Louise, Donna Michele. BBA, U. Mich., 1950, JD, 1958. Bar: Ill. 1958, U.S. Dist. Ct. (no. dist.) Ill. 1958; U.S. Supreme Ct. 1980. With Lincoln-Mercury divsn. Ford Motor Co., Dearborn, Mich., 1950, with Aircraft Engine divsn., 1951; assoc. McKenna, Storer, Rowe White & Farrug, Dearborn, 1958-62, ptnr., 1962-92, of counsel, 1992—. Mem. vis. com. U. Mich. Law Sch. Mem. Citizens of Greater Chgo., 1970-80, pres., 1976-79. Served with US Merchant Marines, 1944-45, USN, 1951-55. McGreggor Fund scholar, 1946; Mich. Bd. Realtors scholar, 1949. Mem. Ill. Bar Assn., Chgo. Bar Assn., DuPage County Bar Assn., Soc. Trial Lawyers, Am. Judicature Soc., Cath. Lawyers Guild, Phi Alpha Delta. Lodges: Kiwanis (pres. 1964). Home: 6602 Westmore Land Dr Woodridge IL 60517-1659 Home Fax: 630-323-1162. Personal E-mail: gene@farrug.com.

FARSHIDI, ARDESHIR B., cardiologist, educator; b. Kerman, Iran, June 13, 1945; arrived in U.S., 1972, naturalized, 1977; s. Jamshid and Farangis Farshidi; m. Katayoon Kavoussi, Jan. 2, 1982. MD, Tehran U., 1969. Diplomate Am. Bd. Internal Medicine, Am. Bd. Cardiovasc. Disease, Am. Bd. Cardiac Electrophysiology. Intern, Washington, 1972—73; resident U. Pa., Phila., 1973—75, resident in cardiology, 1975—77, electrophysiologist, 1977—78; asst. prof., assoc. prof. medicine U. Conn., Farmington, 1978—84; dir. electrophysiology LA Heart Inst., 1984—90; dir. arrhythmia ctr. Los Robles Regional Med. Ctr., 1990—. Dir. electrophysiologist U. Conn., Farmington, 1982—84, attending cardiologist, 1982—84; co-dir. electrophysiology, asst. prof. medicine Yale U., 1979—82; attending cardiologist Yale U. Hosp., 1979—82; chief cardiology sect. VA Hosp., Newington, Conn., 1982—84. Rschr. Am. Heart Assn., 1981. Lt. Iranian Army, 1969—72. Fellow: ACP, Am. Heart Assn., Am. Coll. Cardiology; mem.: Am. Electrophysiologic Soc., Am. Fedn. Clin. Rsch. Achievements include research in clin. cardiac electrophysiology and arrhythmia. Home: 3011 Grandoaks Dr Westlake Village CA 91361-5563 Office: 2100 Lynn Rd Ste 220 Thousand Oaks CA 91360-8036 Home Phone: 818-865-1286; Office Phone: 805-449-9990.

FARSON, RICHARD EVANS, psychologist; b. Chgo., Nov. 16, 1926; s. Duke Mendenhall and Mary Gladys (Clark) F.; m. Elizabeth Lee Grimes, May 21, 1954 (div. 1962); children: Lisa Page, Clark Douglas; m. 2d Dawn Jackson Cooper, Jan. 4, 1964 (div. 1990); children: Joel Andrew, Ashley Dawn, Jeremy Richard. BA, Occidental Coll., LA, 1947, MA, 1951; postgrad., UCLA, 1948-50; PhD, U. Chgo., 1955. Dean Sch. Design Calif. Inst. Arts, Valencia, 1969-73; pres. Esalen Inst., Big Sur and San Francisco, 1973-75; faculty Saybrook Inst., San Francisco, 1975-79; pres. Western Behavioral Scis. Inst., La Jolla, Calif., 1958-68; chmn. bd. Western Behavior Scis. Inst., La Jolla, Calif., 1968-79, pres., 1979—. Dir. Internat. Design Conf. in Aspen, Colo., 1971-2001, pres. 1976-80, 94-97; pub. dir. AIA, 1999-2001. Editor: Science and Human Affairs, 1967; author: Birthrights: A Bill of Rights for Children, 1974, Management of the Absurd: Paradoxes in Leadership, 1996; (with others) The Future of the Family, 1969; (with Ralph Keyes) Whoever Makes the Most Mistakes Wins: The Paradox of Innovation, 2002. Served to lt. j.g. USNR, 1955-57. Fellow, Ford Found., 1953—54, World Acad. Art and Sci., Design Futures Coun. Mem.: APA. Home: 252 Prospect St La Jolla CA 92037-4225 Office Phone: 858-454-2048. Personal E-mail: rfarson@wbsi.org.

FARSTRUP, ALAN E., educational association administrator; Student, Grand View Coll., Des Moines, 1959—61; BA, U. Iowa, Iowa City; tchg. cert., U. Calif., Berkeley; PhD in Reading Curriculum and Instrn., U. Minn., 1977. Tchr. classroom remedial reading and English Jr. HS level; faculty mem. reading edn. U. Tex., San Antonio, U. RI; reading specialist, cons., project adminstr.; supr., dir. rsch. activities Internat. Reading Assn., Newark, Del., 1985—91, acting exec. dir., 1991—92, exec. dir., 1992—. Mem. adv. bd. Children's Literacy Initiative. Co-editor (with S. Jay Samuels): What Research Has to Say About Reading Instruction, 3rd ed., 2002. Mem. US Peace Corps, Afghanistan. Office: Internat Reading Assn 800 Barksdale Rd Newark DE 19714 Office Phone: 302-731-1600.*

FARUKI, CHARLES JOSEPH, lawyer; b. Bay Shore, NY, July 3, 1949; s. Mahmud Taji and Rita Trownsell Faruki; m. Nancy Louise Glock, June 15, 1976 (div. Oct. 1995); m. Michelle F. Zalar, June 15, 1996; children: Brian Andrew, Jason Allen, Charles Joseph Jr. BA summa cum laude, U. Cin., 1971; JD cum laude, Ohio State U., Columbus, 1973. Bar: Ohio 1974, US Dist. Ct. (no. and so. dists.) Ohio 1975, US Ct. Appeals (9th cir.) 1977, US Tax Ct. 1977, U.S. Supreme Ct. 1977, US Ct. Appeals (6th cir.) 1978, US Dist. Ct. (no. dist.) Tex. 1979, US Dist. Ct. (ea. dist.) Ky. 1982, US Ct. Appeals (D.C. cir.) 1982, US Ct. Customs and Patent Appeals 1982, US Ct. Appeals (4th cir.) 1986, US Ct. Appeals (2d cir.) 1989, US Ct. Appeals (fed. cir.), 1991, US Ct. Appeals (8th cir.) 1997. Assoc. Smith & Schnacke, Dayton, Ohio, 1974—78, ptnr., 1979—89; founder, mng. ptnr., complex litig. practice Faruki Ireland & Cox PLL, Dayton, 1989—. Mem. local rules adv. com. US Dist. Ct. (so. dist.) Ohio, 1992—2003, mem. civil justice reform act adv. com., 1995—98, chair fed. bar examination com., 1997—, mem. outside automation evaluation com., 2000—; mem. exec. com. U. Dayton Sch. Law Adv. Com., 2001—; adj. prof. U. Dayton Sch. Law; lectr. in field. Contbr. articles in field. Trustee Dayton Bar Assn. Found., 1997—2003, pres., 2002—03; mem. bd. mgr., sec. Mus. of USAF

Found., 2006—; mem. bd. trustees Dayton Philharmonic Orch. Capt. USAR, 1971—79. Named Outstanding Lawyer, Greater Dayton Vol. Project; named one of Ohio's Top Ten Super Lawyers, Dayton's Most Powerful, Dayton Bus. Jour.; named to Best of Bar; recipient Spl. Svc. award, U. Dayton Sch. Law, Peacekeeper award, Artemis Ctr. for Alternatives for Domestic Violence. Fellow: Am. Coll. Trial Lawyers (complex litig. com. 1993—98, Ohio state com. 1998—2006, chmn. 2004—05), Ohio State Bar Found., Am. Bar Found. (life); mem.: FBA (officer and exec. com. Dayton chpt. 1988—93, pres. 1991—92), ABA, Dayton Intellectual Property Law Assn., Fed. Cir. Bar Assn., Dayton Bar Assn. (officer 1992—94, pres. 1994—95, trustee 1997—2004, pres. 2002—03), Ohio State Bar Assn. (bd. govs. antitrust sect. 1992—, vice-chair antitrust sect. 2006—, chair fed. cts. and practice com. 2007—), Am. Bd. Trial Advocates. Avocations: coin collecting/numismatics, art. Office: Faruki Ireland & Cox PLL 500 Courthouse Plz SW Dayton OH 45402 Home: 138 Rue Marseille Dayton OH 45429 Home Phone: 937-298-5649; Office Phone: 937-227-3705. Business E-Mail: cfaruki@ficlaw.com.

FARVARDIN, NARIMAN, engineering educator; b. Tehran, Iran, July 15, 1956; m. Hoveida Farvardin. BS in elec. engring., Rensselaer Poly. Inst., Troy, NY, 1979, MS in elec. engring., 1980, PhD in elec. engring., 1983. Vis. prof. Ecole Nationale Superieure des Telecommunications, Paris, 1990—91; asst. prof. elec. and computer engring. U. Md., 1984—88, assoc. prof., 1988—93, prof., 1993—, joint appt. Inst. Sys. Rsch., chair dept. elec. and computer engring., 1995—2000, dean A. James Clark Sch. Engring., 2001—. Co-recipient Award of Excellence, Md. Indsl. Partnerships Program, 1992, Invention of Yr. Award, U. Md., 1999; recipient George Corcoran Award, Dept. Elec. Engring., U. Md., 1987, Presdl. Young Investigator Award, NSF, 1987, Outstanding Systems Engring. Faculty Award, Inst. for Systems Rsch., U. Md., 1993. Fellow: IEEE; mem.: Am. Soc. Engring. Edn. Avocations: racquetball, reading, music. Office: Clark Sch Engring U Md 3110 Kim Enring Bldg College Park MD 20742 Business E-Mail: farvardin@umd.edu.

FARWELL, ELWIN D., minister, consultant; b. Branch County, Mich., May 1, 1919; s. Don J. and Dessa (Clingan) F.; m. Helen Irene Hill, Aug. 23, 1942; children: Don Lucian, Helen Kay, James Lyman, Judith Anne. BS, Mich. State U, 1943, MS, 1947; EdD, U. Calif., Berkeley, 1959; BD, Pacific Lutheran Theol. Sem., Berkeley, 1959; LLD (hon.), Loras Coll., 1969, Valparaiso U., 1980, Luther Coll., 1986, Dana Coll., 1992, Calif. Luth. U., 1994; LHD (hon.), St. John's U., 1981, St. Olaf Coll., 1982. Instr. animal husbandry Mich. State U., 1947-49, asst. prof., 1949-55; cons. point 4 program State Dept. U. Nacional, Colombia, 1952; adminstrv. asst. to chmn. Center Study Higher Edn., U. Calif. at Berkeley, 1956-59; ordained to ministry Luth. Ch., 1958; pastor in Andrew, Iowa, 1959-61; academic dean Calif. Luth. Coll., Thousand Oaks, Calif., 1961-63; pres. Luther Coll., Decorah, Iowa, 1963-82; vis. scholar U. Calif.-Berkeley, 1982; profl. cons., 1983—; pres. Dana Coll., Blair, Nebr., 1985-86; dir. study theol. edn. Luth. Ch. U.S.A., 1984-86; adminstrv. cons. Pacific Luth. Theol. Sem., 1987-88; interim bishop Nebr. Synod Evan. Luth. Ch. in Am., 1990; interim pastor St. Paul Luth. Ch., Monona, Iowa, 1990-91, 97; interim bishop Rocky Mountain Synod Evangel. Luth. Ch. in Am., 1993-94. Author: Livestock Development and Selection, 1951, (with others) Stability of Change, 1964; contbr. articles to profl. jours., encys. Mem. Iowa Gov.'s Com. Conservation Natural Resources, 1964-68, Iowa Gov.'s Commn. Coop. State and Local Govt., 1964-66; mem. Iowa Coordinating Coun. Higher Edn., 1967-70, pres., 1968-69; chmn. Com. Intergovtl. Coop. and Comm., 1964-65, Gov.'s Com. on Govt. Reorgn., 1966, State Adv. Com. on Cmty. and Jr. Coll., 1965-69; mem. exec. com. Iowa Assn. Pvt. Colls. and Univs., 1964-73, 76-78, chmn., 1971-72; chmn. Coun. Coll. Pres.'s Am. Luth. Ch., 1976-77; mem. exec. com. Norwegian-Am. Mus. Assn., 1965-71; chmn. World Brotherhood Found., 1962-77; chmn. Iowa Coll. Found., 1968-69; mem. Iowa Campaign Fin. Disclosure Commn., 1977-91, chmn., 1980-81, 87-89; mem. Iowa Mental Health Adv. Coun., 1978-81, Am. Scandinavian Found.; bd. govs. Calif. Luth. Ednl. Found., 1957-59; bd. dirs. Inst. European Studies, 1977-81; bd. Nat. Luth. Campus Ministry, 1966-69; pres. Luth. Ednl. Conf. N.Am., 1973-74, mem. legis. policy com., 1978-81; counselor Luth. Coun. U.S.A., 1975-79; bd. dirs. Gundersen Med. Found., La Crosse, Wis., 1976-81; bd. regents Dana Coll., 1986-95; trustee Iowa Natural Heritage Found., 1983-92, Iowa Humanities Found., 1992-2002; bd. dirs. Luth. Social Svc. of Iowa, 1992-95, Winneshiek County Hosp. Found., 1992-97. Capt. U.S. Army, 1943-46, PTO. Decorated Knight's Cross 1st class Order St. Olav, 1975, Knight's Cross 1st class Order No. Star, 1977 (Sweden); recipient Disting. Patriarchs award Mich. State U., 1993. Mem. Ctrl. State Coll. Assn. (dir. 1964-76, chmn. 1967), Nat. Assn. Ind. Colls. and Univs. (bd. dirs. 1977-78), Oneota Golf and Country Club (pres. 1987-89), Rotary, Phi Beta Kappa, Phi Delta Kappa, Alpha Gamma Rho, Alpha Zeta. Lutheran. Home: 504 Locust Rd # 3 Decorah IA 52101-1002 Personal E-mail: farwelle@luther.edu.

FARWELL, NANCY LARRAINE, public relations executive; b. Sellersville, Pa., May 2, 1944; d. Warren Gregory and Mary Rita (Zaniboni) F. BA, Pa. State U., 1966. Asst. TV rep. H.R. TV Reps., Phila., 1966-68; various positions Hawthorne Advt. Inc., Phila., 1968-73; dir. employee rels. Colonial Penn Group, Inc., Phila., 1973-75, mgr. press rels., 1976-78, mgr. pub. rels., 1978-82; dir. comm. Provident Mut. Life Ins. Co., Phila., 1982-83, asst. v.p., comm., 1983-87; pres. Nancy Farwell Assocs., Phila., 1987-90; v.p. Anne Klein & Assocs., Inc., Mt. Laurel, NJ, 1990-92, sr. v.p., 1992-97, sr. v.p., COO, 1998-2001, sr. v.p. strategic planning, 2001—03, sr. councilor, 2003—. Adv. bd. City of Phila. Century IV Tall Ships, 1982. Author: (photo essay) Philadelphia, 1976; contbr. chpt. to home health care mktg. book. Founder, co-chair Portico Row Neighborhood Assn., Phila., 1989-92; bd. dirs. Washington Sq. West Project Area Com., Phila., 1990-92, Boys and Girls Clubs of Metro Phila. Adv. Coun., 1991—; adv. com. Phila. 6th Police Dist., 1990-92. Mem. Pub. Rels. Soc. Am. (12 Pepperpot awards, 2 Awards of Excellence, Silver Anvil award of Excellence), Phila. Pub. Rels. Assn. Office: Anne Klein and Assoc Inc 401 Route 73 N Ste 108 Marlton NJ 08053-3429 Office Phone: 856-988-6560.

FARWELL, WALTER MAURICE, vocalist, educator; b. Sidney, Iowa, Mar. 29, 1928; s. Clyde Ross and Erma Leona (Liggett) F. B.Mus.Edn., U. Mo., Kansas City, 1950; MA, U. Iowa, 1953. Vocal music tchr. pub. schs., Fayette, Iowa, 1953-59; head voice tchr. Wartburg Coll., Waverly, Iowa, 1960-61; vocal music tchr. pub. schs., Tipton, Iowa, 1961-67, music educator Davenport, Iowa, 1967-90. Choir dir. Meth. Ch., Fayette, Tipton, 1953—; vocal soloist, 1953—; organist Replacement Tng. Ctr., Ft. Bragg, N.C., 1951-52. Author: (4 vols.) History of Fremont County, Iowa, 1968-91; contbr.: Bells of Stony Creek, 1994; editor: Court Records Atchison County, Mo. (pamphlet), 1985; cons. (county history) Thumbprints in time, 1996; contbr. historical articles to profl. pubs. Cpl. U.S. Army, 1950-52. Recipient Am. Legion award, 1941. Mem. NEA, Davenport Area Ret. Tchrs. Assn., Fremont County Hist. Soc. (charter). Methodist. Avocation: historical and genealogical research. Home: 549 E 4th St Tipton IA 52772-1933 E-mail: farwellwalter@hotmail.com.

FASH, VICTORIA R., business executive; Sr. v.p. bus. strategy Dun & Bradstreet Corp., 1995-96; exec. v.p., CFO Cognizant, 1996—; exec. v.p., chmn., CEO IMS Internat., Westport, Conn., 1999—. Bd. dirs. Orion Capital Corp. Office: IMS Health Inc 1499 Post Rd Fairfield CT 06430-5940

FASHING, EDWARD MICHAEL, ranch owner, physical science educator; b. Chgo., Jan. 27, 1936; s. Michael George and Leontine (LeClercq) F.; m. Annette Louise Lubker, Jan. 29, 1959; children: Anita Fashing Kiska, Mary Fashing Schillig, Edward Jr., James, John. BS in Chemistry, Loyola U., Chgo., 1960; MS in Chemistry, DePaul U., 1968; postgrad., U. Mo., 1982-84. Cert. jr. coll. chemistry tchr., Ill. Instr. geology, phys. sci., chemistry of hazardous materials Triton Coll., River Grove, Ill., 1969-81; Simmental cattle rancher and vinologist Cedar Ln. Farm, Sturgeon, Mo., 1973—; asst. prof. N.E. Mo. State U. (Truman State), Kirksville, Mo., 1981-82; chemistry asst. U. Mo., Columbia, 1982-84; instr. physics Columbia (Mo.) Coll., 1986; summerreading tchr. Centralia Elem. Sch., 1998—. Spkr. in field. Writer, news commentator, show moderator, producer Farm Forum Sta. KOPN-Radio, 1985-89; freelance reporter, columnist, proofreader Am. Agr. Reporter; editor Mo. Am. Agr. Newsletter, 1990—; contbr. KBHK Plains Radio Network Talk Show, Wellington, Tex., 2006—; mem. editl. bd., writer religious and cultural cyber jour. Just Good Company, 2002-07. Mem. N.Am. Farm Alliance; leader 4H, Sturgeon, 1974—84, 1988; creator posters Mo. Rural Crisis Ctr., Columbia, 1986—93; publicity dir. Am. Agrl. Movement Grassroots, 1985, demonstrator, 1985, spokesman Chgo. demonstrations, 1984, 1985, 1986; v.p. comm. Am. Agr. Movement, Inc., Mo., 1991—, nat. v.p. comm., 2003—; mem. Nat. Farm Org.; pres. Farm Alliance of Rural Mo., 1997—99, v.p., 1999—2001; mem. Orgn. Competitive Markets; lobbyist Nat. Farmers Union, 1990; Dem. rep. Mo. State Conv., 1988, 1990, 2003; lobbyist R-Calf, 1999—; Roman Cath. cantor, lector and extraordinary min.; bd. dir. Mo. Rural Crisis Ctr., Columbia, 1989—92, Farm Alliance of Rural Mo., 1986—89, 1995—. NSF grantee, 1966, 76; 2d place winner steer carcass judging contest Mo. State Fair, 1995; breeder of 10 winning steer carcasses, 1973-99, Boone County, Mo. and Mo. State Fair, 1995, 2000. Mem.: AAAS, Am. Chem. Soc., Am. Corn Growers Assocs., Mo. Stockmans Assn., Am. Chem. Soc. Democrat. Avocations: rockhounding, gardening, writing, entomology. Address: Cedar Ln Farm 2898 Audrain Road 114 Sturgeon MO 65284-2023 Personal E-mail: emfashing@socket.net.

FASICK, ADELE MONGAN, library and information scientist, educator; b. NYC, Mar. 18, 1930; d. Stephen Leo and Florence (Geary) Mongan; m. Frank Fasick, Aug. 14, 1955 (div. 1986); children: Pamela, Laura, Julia. BA, Cornell U., 1951; MA, Columbia U., 1954, MSLS, 1956; PhD, Case Western Reserve U., 1970. Libr. N.Y. Pub. Libr., 1955-56, L.I.U., Bklyn., 1956-58; asst. prof. Rosary Coll., River Forest, Ill., 1970-71; prof. U. Toronto, 1971-96, dean Faculty of Libr. and Info. Sci., 1990-95. Adj. prof. San Jose State U., 1999—, U. .C., 2002—. Author: Managing Children Services in Public Libraries, 1991, 2d edit., 1998, Beauty Who Would Not Spin, 1987, Opening Doors to Children, 2005; co-author: ChildView, 1987; editor: Lands of Pleasure, 1990; editor International Research Abstracts: Youth Library Services, 1993-98. Mem.: ALA (com. on accreditation 1990—92), Assn. Librs. and Info. Sci. Edn. (pres. 1992), Internat. Fedn. Libr. Assn. (sec./treas. sect. on reading 1997—2003), Assn. Libr. Svc. to Children (exec. bd. 1980—84). Personal E-mail: adele1810@yahoo.com.

FASKE, DONNA See KARAN, DONNA

FASMAN, MARJORIE LESSER, artist, writer; b. San Francisco, Dec. 1, 1916; d. Sol Leonard and Fay (Grunauer) Lesser; m. Morris Pfaelzer II, Apr. 12, 1938 (div. 1959); children: Fay Ellen Pfaelzer Abrams, Betty Pfaelzer Rauch; m. Michael J. Fasman, Mar. 30, 1961. Student, Wellesley Coll., 1934-37; BA in English Lit., U. Pa., Phila. Designer for Mercado and cmty. events L.A. Music Ctr., 1946-48. Author: The Diary of Henry Fitzwilliam Darcy, 1998. Vol. Physicians for Social Responsibility, L.A.; founder (with others) Venice Family Clinic, 1985, UCLA Med. Ctr. Auxiliary (bd. dirs.). Recipient Corit Kent Peace award Immaculate Heart Coll., 1992, Golden Bruin award UCLA. Mem. Women of L.A. (Hope is a Woman award 1998). Democrat. Jewish. Avocation: writing.

FASMAN, ZACHARY DEAN, lawyer; b. Chgo., Oct. 27, 1948; s. Irving D. and Lillian V. (Vilatzer) F.;m. Andrea L. Udoff; children: Jonathan, Benjamin, Rebecca. BA, Northwestern U., 1969; JD, U. Mich., 1972. Bar: Ill. 1972, D.C. 1977, N.Y. 2001, U.S. Supreme Ct. 1977. Assoc., then ptnr. Seyfarth, Shaw et al, Chgo. and Washington, 1972-81; ptnr. Wald, Harkrader et al, Washington, 1981-83, Crowell & Moring, Washington, 1983-88, Paul, Hastings, Janofsky & Walker, Washington, 1988—2000, NYC, 2000—. Author: Equal Employment Audit Handbook, 1983, Employment Law Compliance Manual, 1988, What Business Must Know About The ADA, 1992. Mem. ABA (labor law sect., litig. sect.), Coll. Labor and Employment Lawyers, Order of Coif. Office: Paul Hastings Janofsky & Walker 75 E 55th St New York NY 10022 Home: 11 Riverside Dr Apt 12J-E New York NY 10023 Office Phone: 212-318-6315. Office Fax: 212-318-6837. Business E-Mail: zacharyfasman@paulhastings.com.

FASNACHT, HEIDE ANN, artist, educator; b. Cleve., Jan. 12, 1951; BFA, R.I. Sch. Design, 1973; MA in Studio Art, NYU, 1981. Vis. artist Bennington Coll., Vt., 1980, 1983, Cranbrook Acad., Bloomfield Hills, Mich., 1984, Cleve. Art Inst., 1981; asst. prof. art SUNY-Purchase, 1981—87; art instr. Parson's Sch. Design; vis. artist R.I. Sch. Design, 1985, Md. Inst. Coll. Art, 1985; asst. prof. dept. visual and environ. studies Harvard U., Cambridge, Mass., 1993—94, Pilchuck artist-in-residence, 2004, Montalvo artist-in-residence, 2006. One-woman shows include New Gallery of Contemporary Art, Cleve., 1981, Vanderwoude/Tananbaum Gallery, N.Y.C., 1983, 1985, Hill Gallery, Birmingham, Mich., 1984, 1986, Germans van Eck Gallery, N.Y.C., 1988, Yale U. Art Gallery, 2002, Kent Gallery, N.Y.C., 2003, 2005, 2007, Galeria Trama, Barcelona, 2003, Galerie les Filles du Calvaire, Paris and Brussels, 2005, Bernard Toale Gallery, Boston, 2005, 2007, one-man shows include Pan-Am. Gallery, Dallas, 2006, Represented in permanent collections Bklyn. Mus. Art, Dallas Mus. Art, Columbus Mus. Art, Norton Gallery of Art, Santa Barbara Mus. Art, Yale Art Gallery, Phila. Mus. Art, Mus. Fine Arts, Boston, Hammer Mus., UCLA, Yale Art Gallery, Fogg Mus.; contbr. articles to profl. jours. Fellow, MacDowell Colony, 1981, 1983, 2005, Yaddo, 1980, 1985, Hand Hollow Found., 1983, Rockefeller Found., 2003, Lucas Vusual Arts Program, Montalvo; grantee, NEA, 1979, 1994, Athena Found., 1983, Louis Comfort Tiffany Found., 1986, Guggenheim Mus., 1991, Adolph and Esther Gottlieb Found. Home: 4 White St Apt 4A New York NY 10013-2469 Home Phone: 212-966-3061.

FASO, JOHN J., lawyer, former state legislator; b. Massapequa, NY, Aug. 25, 1952; m. Mary Frances Faso; children: Nicholas, Margaret. BA, SUNY, Brockport, 1974; JD, Georgetown U., 1979. Mem. staff house govt. ops. com. U.S. Ho. of Reps., Washington, 1979-81; exec. dir. N.Y. State Senate Office, Washington, 1981-83; counselor Rapport, Meyers, Griffen & Whitbeck, Hudson, N.Y.; mem. N.Y. State Assembly, Albany, 1987—2002, minority leader, 1998—2002; ptnr. Manatt, Phelps & Phillips LLP, Albany, 2003—. Bd. mem. Buffalo Fiscal Stability Authority, 2003—06. Formerly mem. N.Y. State Legis. Bill. Drafting Commn., Albany; mem. Columbia County Rep. Com.; chmn. Kinderhood Town Rep. Com. Recipient Guardian of Small Bus. award, Nat. Fedn. Ind. Businesses, 1996, Disting. Pub. Svc. award, Nelson A. Rockefeller Coll. Pub. Affairs & Policy, 1997. Mem. KC, Lions, Elks. Republican. Roman Catholic.

FASS, PETER MICHAEL, lawyer, educator; b. Bklyn., Apr. 11, 1937; s. Irving and Bess (Fordin) F.; m. Deborah K. Orshan, May 6, 1989; 1 child, Olivia Jae; children from previous marriage: Brian Samuel, Lyle Williams. BS in Econs. with honors, U. Pa., 1958; JD cum laude, Harvard U., 1961; LLM, NYU, 1964. Bar: N.Y. 1965; CPA. From assoc. to ptnr. Carro, Spanbock, Fass, Geller, Kaster & Cuiffo, NYC, 1968-86; ptnr. Kaye, Scholer, Fierman, Hayes & Handler, NYC, 1988-95, Battle Fowler LLP, NYC, 1995-2000, Proskauer Rose LLP, NYC, 2000—. Adj. asst. prof. real estate NYU; lectr. Practicing Law Inst., N.Y. Law Jour., Instl. mag., Ill. Inst. Continuing Legal Edn.; spl. cons. Calif. Commr. of Corps Real Estate Adv. Com.; mem. ad hoc com. Real Estate Securities and Syndication Inst., chmn. regulatory legis. and taxation com., 1975-76; mem., dir. participant/real estate com. NASD, 1991-94. Co-author: Tax Advantaged Securities, 1977—, Real Estate Syndication Handbook, 1985-87, Tax Aspects of Real Estate Investments, 1988—, Blue Sky Practice Handbook, 1987—, Real Estate Investment Trusts Handbook, 1987—, S Corporation Handbook, 1985—, Tax Advantaged Securities Handbook, 1979—; contbr. articles to profl. jours. Recipient Haskins award for outstanding achievement in N.Y. State CPA's exam., 1964. Mem. ABA (chmn. real estate investment com., real property, probate and trust sect.), N.Y. State Bar Assn., Am. Inst. CPA's, N.Y. State Soc. CPA's, Pi Lambda Phi, Beta Gamma Sigma, Beta Alpha Psi. Home: 115 Central Park W New York NY 10023-4153 Office: Proskauer Rose LLP 1585 Broadway New York NY 10036-8299 Home Phone: 212-721-6697; Office Phone: 212-969-3445. Personal E-mail: reitman411@aol.com. Business E-Mail: pfass@proskauer.com.

FASSEL, JIM (JAMES E. FASSEL), former professional football coach; b. Anaheim, Calif., Aug. 31, 1949; m. Kitty Fassel; children: John, Brian, Jana, Mike. Coach Fullerton Coll., 1973; player, coach Hawaii Hawaiians, WLF, 1974; coach U. Utah, 1976, head coach, 1985—89; coach Weber St., 1977—78, Stanford U., 1979—83; asst. coach New Orleans Breakers, USFL, 1984; asst. head coach/offensive coord. Denver Broncos, 1993—94; quarterback coach Oakland Raiders, 1995; offensive coord., quarterback coach Ariz. Cardinals, 1996; asst. coach NY Giants, 1991-92, head coach, 1997—2003; sr. cons. Baltimore Ravens, 2004—05, offensive cord., 2005—06. Named NFL Coach of the Yr., 1997.

FASSLER, KERIN IRENE, accountant; b. Vallejo, Calif., Jan. 4, 1948; d. Robert Wayne and Leila Jean Hall; m. Micheal Joseph Fassler, June 2, 1993; children: Michelle Ann Garcia, Preston Daniel; m. David Michael Mayugba, Oct. 24, 1966 (div.); children: Christina Denise Mayugba, Jennifer Irene Mayugba. AA, Am. River Jr Coll., Sacramento, Calif., 1989; BS, Regents Coll., Albany, NY, 1995; MA, Webster U., St. Louis, 1999. Farm laborer, Dixon, Calif., 1968—71; various govt. positions Sacramento, 1972—78; realtor assoc. Red Carpet, Sacramento, 1978—82; bus. owner Kerin's RV Rentals, Sacramento, 1986—90; budget analyst Various Govn't Agencies, 1986—97; mgmt./program analyst DOD, 1997—2005; sys. acct. US Army Corps Engrs., Anchorage, 2002—. Chmn. Red Carpet Realtors Associate's Com., Sacramento, 1980—80; bd. dirs. Info. and Referral Program United Way, Sacramento, 1988—91; pres. Internat. Tng. in Comm., Sacramento, 1989—89. Decorated Achievement Medal for Civilian Svc. US Army, Commander's Award for Civilian Svc.; recipient Presdl. Recognition, Pres. Ronald Reagan, 1988. Mem.: Am. Soc. of Mil. Comptrollers (assoc.; v.p. Denali chpt. 1996), Intertel (assoc.), Mensa (assoc.). Republican. Roman Catholic. Avocations: crocheting, scuba diving, skiing, sewing, crafts. Office: US Army Corps of Engrs 2204 3rd St Elmendorf Afb AK 99506 Home Phone: 907-622-4850; Office Phone: 907-753-2894. Personal E-mail: kifmjf@earthlink.net.

FASSLER, MARGOT ELSBETH, music educator, religious studies educator; b. Oswego, NY; d. Frank B. Fassler and Susan Cooper Fassler Babcock; m. Peter Jeffery; children: Joseph Fassler, Frank Jeffery. MA, Syracuse U., 1976; MPhil, Cornell U., 1980, PhD, 1983. Asst. prof. Mills Coll., Oakland, Calif., 1982-83, Yale U., New Haven, 1983-89, prof., 1994—; dir. Yale Inst. Sacred Music, New Haven, 1994—; assoc. prof. Brandeis U., Waltham, Mass., 1989-94. Author: Gothic Song, 1993; contbr. articles to profl. jours. Recipient Elliott prize Medieval Acad. Am., 1985, Kinkeldey award Am. Musicological Soc., 1994. Fellow Am. Acad. Arts & Scis.; mem. Am. Musicological Soc. (bd. dirs. 1989-92), Med. Acad. Am. Office: Yale Inst Sacred Music 409 Prospect St New Haven CT 06511-2167*

FASSOULIS, SATIRIS GALAHAD, communications executive, director; b. Syracuse, Aug. 19, 1922; s. Peter George and Anastasia P. (Limpert) Fassoulis. BA, Syracuse U., NY, 1945. V.p. Commerce Internat. Corp., 1949—75; chmn. Global Comm. Co., NYC, 1976—, Global Def. Products Inc., NYC, 1976—; pres. CIC Internat. Ltd., 2000—, Columbia Def. Corp., 2000—; chmn. CIC Aerospace Corp. Bd. dirs. Comml. Exports Ltd., UK, CIC Internat. Ltd., NYC, Colombia Tech. Corp., Colombia Energy Corp., Africa One Ltd. Mem. US Congl. Adv. Bd.; bd. dirs. Better Life Enterprises for Blind, Inc.; chmn. Internat. Cultural Exch. 1st lt. USAAF, 1941—45. Decorated Purple Heart, Air medal with 3 oak leaf clusters, Prisoner of War medal. Mem.: Am. Def. Preparedness Assn., Internat. Platform Assn., Assn. US Army, Air Force Assn., Armed Forces Comm. and Electronics Assn., NY C. of C., Navy League US, US Naval Inst., NY Athletic Club, Order Ahepa. Republican. Episcopalian. Home: 20 Waterside Plz New York NY 10010-2612 Office: 5 Marine View Plz Apt 310 Hoboken NJ 07030 Office Phone: 201-792-1800. Personal E-mail: sgfcic@compuserve.com. Business E-Mail: fassoulis@cic-international.com.

FAST, ERIC CARSON, manufacturing executive; b. Boston, July 10, 1949; s. Robert Eberle and Carol (Waters) F.; m. Patricia Nelson, May 31, 1980; children: Allison, Christina, Lillian. BA, U. N.C., 1971; MBA, NYU, 1978. Asst. treas. U.S. Industries Inc., NYC, 1975—77; treas. Macmillan Inc., NYC, 1979—84; v.p. Salomon Bros. Inc., NYC, 1984-88, mng. dir., 1989-91, co-head of global investment banking; bd. dir. Crane Co., 1999—, pres., COO, 1999—2001, pres. CEO, 2001—. Office: c/o Crane Co 100 First Stamford Place Stamford CT 06902*

FAST, HENRYK, mathematician, educator; s. Leon and Regina (Stiel) Fast; m. Nora Elisabeth Vazquez, Apr. 1990 (div. Aug. 2003); children: Monica, Tamara, Maximiuk, Simon, Sheila, Jessica. MS, U. Wroclaw, Poland, 1951; PhD in Math., Polish Acad. Sci., Warsaw, 1958. Adj. instr. U. Wroclaw, Poland, 1956—60; asst. prof., math. U. Notre Dame, Ind., 1962—66; prof., math. Wayne State U., Detroit, 1966—94. Contbr. articles to profl. jours. Avocation: painting. Home: 13751 Rustic Dr North Royalton OH 44133 E-mail: hfast@earthlink.net.

FAST, JULIUS, writer, editor; b. NYC, Apr. 17, 1919; s. Barnett Arthur and Ida (Miller) F.; m. Barbara Hewitt Sher, June 8, 1946; children: Jennifer, Melissa, Timothy Hewitt. BA, NYU, 1941. Sr. writer Smith, Kline & French Pharms., Phila., 1955-57; chief dept. med. communications Purdue Fredericks, NYC, 1957-62; feature editor Med. News, 1962-63; sr. editor Med. World News, 1963-64; editor Ob-Gyn Observer, NYC, 1965-75. Author: (mystery novels) Watchful at Night, 1945, Bright Face of Danger, 1946, Walk in Shadow, 1948, Model for Murder, 1956, Street of Fear, 1959, A Trunkfull of Trouble, 2002, (fiction) What Should We Do About Davey?, 1987, (sci. fiction) League of Grey-Eyed Women, 1970, (nonfiction) Blueprint for Life, 1963, Beatles, 1968, What You Should Know About Sexual Response, 1966, Body Language, 1970, Incompatibility of Men and Women, 1971, You and Your Feet, 1971, The New Sexual Fulfillment, 1972, Bisexual Living, 1974, The Pleasure Book, 1975, Creative Coping, 1976, The Body Language of Sex Power and Aggression, 1977, Psyching Up, 1978, Weather Language, 1979, Talking Between the Lines, 1979, Body Politics, 1980, The Body Book, 1981, Sexual Chemistry, 1983, Ladies Man, 1983, The Omega-3 Breakthrough, 1987, Subtext, 1990, Legal Atlas of the United States, 1996, Courtroom Communication Skills, 1994. Served with AUS, 1942-46. Recipient Mystery Writers Am. award, 1944 Home: 720 West End Ave Apt 1608 New York NY 10025-6299

FAST, KENNETH H., lawyer; b. Newark, Apr. 1929; s. Moe M. and Eva H. Fast; m. Judith Nicholson, Nov. 23, 1969; children: Jonathan Nicholson, Madelaine M. BA, Lafayette Coll., 1951; LLB, Yale U., 1954. Bar: N.J. 1954, D.C. 1954, U.S. Ct. Appeals (3d cir.) 1958, U.S. Supreme Ct. 1960. Ptnr. Fast & Fast, East Orange, N.J., 1957-86, Fox and Fox, LLP, Livingston, NJ, 1987—2007, of counsel, 2007—. Trustee Weisberger Fund for Aged, Poor and Needy, Livingston, N.J., 1969—. 1st lt. USAF, 1955-57. Mem. N.J. State Bar Assn., Essex County Bar Assn. Home: 91 Fairfield Dr Short Hills NJ 07078-1718 Office Phone: 973-597-0777.

FASTOVSKY, DAVID E., geoscientist, educator; BA in Biology, Reed Coll.; MA in Paleontology, U. Calif., Berkeley; PhD, U. Wis., Madison, 1986. Prof. geosciences U. RI. Contbr. articles to sci. jours.; co-author: The Evolution and Extinction of the Dinosaurs, 2004. Mem.: Soc. Vertebrate Paleontology, Soc. Sedimentary Geology (SEPM), Paleontol. Soc., Geol. Soc. Am. (Disting. Svc. award 2006). Office: U RI Dept Geosciences 317 Woodward Hall 9 E Alumni Ave Kingston RI 02881-2019 E-mail: defastov@uri.edu.

FASTOW, JAY N., lawyer; b. Newark, Feb. 6, 1953; BA magna cum laude, Brandeis U., 1974; JD, Yale U., 1977. Bar: NY 1978, US Dist. Ct. (so. & ea. dists.) NY 1980, US Dist. Ct. (no. dist.) Calif. 1982, US Ct. of Appeals (9th cir.) 1984, US Ct. of Appeals (3d cir.) 1985, US Supreme Ct. 1985, US Dist. Ct. Ariz. 1990, US Ct.of Appeals (2nd, 5th, & 6th cirs.). Mem. Weil, Gotshal & Manges, NYC, ptnr. Spkr. in feilds; fin. svcs. adv. Consumer Fin. Svcs. Law Report. Contbr. articles to profl. jours. Recipient Best Lawyers in Am., NY Super Lawyers., 2006. Mem. ABA, NY State Bar Assn., Assn. Bar NYC (mem. antitrust com.), mem. (bd. editors) Jour. Payment Systems Law , mem. (bd. adv.) Antitrust Counselor. Office: Weil Gotshal & Manges 767 5th Ave New York NY 10153-0119 Office Phone: 212-310-8644. Office Fax: 212-310-8007. Business E-Mail: jay.fastow@weil.com.

FASUSI, JIMMY ADEBAYO, small business owner; arrived in U.S., 1997; s. John Olawole Fasusi and Harold Harford; m. Patricia Elizabeth Harford, Feb. 15, 2002. BSc, U. Ibadan, Nigeria, 1995. Cert. engr., Nat. Inst. Sci. and Tech., Nigeria. Mgr. Circuit City, Frederick, Md., 1998—2002; pres., CEO X-Class Corp., Kensington, Md. Mem.: IEEE, Soc. for Human Resource Mgmt. Home: 5630 Duchaine Dr Lanham MD 20706 Office: X-Class Corp 3827 Plyers Mill Rd Kensington MD 20895 Home Phone: 301-306-5488; Office Phone: 301-946-0800. Office Fax: 301-946-0801. Personal E-mail: jfa820@aol.com. E-mail: jimmy@kensingtonofficemachines.com.

FATEMI, FARAMARZ SAIFPOUR, history and political science professor, consultant; b. Isfahan, Iran, Aug. 6, 1935; arrived in US, 1949; s. Nasrollah Saifpour and Shayesteh (Ostovar) Fatemi; m. Afsar Nouri-Esfandiary, Dec. 15, 1962; children: Faranak, Roshanak. BA, Earlham Coll., Richmond, Ind., 1955; MA, Columbia U., 1958; PhD, New Sch. for Social Rsch., 1976. Prof. Fairleigh Dickinson U., Teaneck, NJ, 1961—, chair dept. history, polit. sci. and internat. studies, 1984-95, dir. Sch. Polit. and Internat. Studies, 1996-99, dir. Sch. History, Polit. and Internat. Studies, 2000—; CEO Nouri Enterprises, Ho-Ho-Kus, NJ, 1991—; pres. acad. senate Fairleigh Dickinson U., Teaneck, NJ, 1994-96, participant bd. trustees. Vis. prof. Shippensburg State Coll., Pa., 1964—65, 1969; mem. Ctr. Internat. Studies Bergen CC, Paramus, NJ, 1980—95, chmn., 1992—93; dir., CFO Fairleigh Dickinson Credit Union, Madison, NJ, 1987—; pres. Lakeland chpt. NJ Credit Union League, 1998—99; fellow Peace Inst. Kyung Hee U., Seoul, 1985—. Co-author: Sufism: Message of Brotherhood, Harmony and Hope, 1976 (UNESCO Internat. Book award, 1977), Love, Beauty and Harmony in Sufism, 1978; author: USSR in Iran, 1980; editor: Reflections on the Time of Illusion, Vol. II, 1991, Vol. III, 2002. Mem. adv. bd. Internat. Awareness Network, NYC, 1991—; mem. NJ World Trade Coun., Trenton, 1992—, bd. dirs., 1996—, vice chmn., 2001—04; advisor Persian Humanitarian and Cultural Soc., Passaic, NJ, 1988—; dir. Sch. Bd. Overseers, NJ, 2005—. Recipient Kurt Riezler Meml. award, New Sch. Social Rsch., 1976, Disting. Faculty Svc. award, Fairleigh Dickinson U., 1993, Meritorious Svc. award, Credit Union Affilliattes NJ, 1999; vis. scholar, Cambridge U., Eng., 1984, Consotium Global Interdependence, Princeton, 1985. Mem.: Pi Sigma Alpha, Phi Alpha Theta. Home Phone: 201-652-1457; Office Phone: 201-692-2272. Business E-Mail: fatemi@fdu.edu.

FATEMI, KHUSROW, academic administrator, economics educator; BA, Abadan Inst. Tech., Iran; MBA, Univ. So. Calif., PhD in internat. rels. Sr. economist Nat. Iranian Oil Co., 1972—79; asst. prof. Middle Tenn. State Univ., 1979—82; prof. internat. bus. Tex. A&M Univ., 1982—90, dean coll. bus., grad. sch. internat. trade & bus. adminstrn., 1990—98; dean, prof. internat. bus. San Diego State Univ., Imperial Valley, 1998—2004; pres. Ea. Oreg. Univ., La Grande, 2004—. Editor (founding): Global Economy Quarterly, The Internat. Trade Jour.; contbr. articles to profl. jours. Bd. dir. U.S.-Mex. C. of C. Mem.: Internat. Mgmt. Develop. Assn. (past pres., Internat. Dean of the Year 1999). Office: Eastern Oregon Univ Office of the President 1 University Blvd La Grande OR 97850-2899*

FATHALLAH, HASSANA, research scientist; d. Hassan Fathallah and Leila Saad. BS in Biochemistry and Molecular Sci., U. Paris XI, 1990, MS in Biology, 1993, PhD (hon.) in Biochemistry, 1997. Rsch. assoc. Mt. Sinai Med. Ctr., NYC, 1998—2003, instr., 2004—05, asst. prof., 2005—. Author: (edn. book) Hemoglobinopathies, 2003, Induction of Fetal Hemoglobin in the Treatment of Sickle Cell Disease, 2006. Mem.: Internat. Soc. Exptl. Hematology, Nat. Geog. Soc., NY Acad. Scis., Am. Soc. Hematology. Achievements include research in inhibition of deoxygenation-induced membrane protein dephosphorylation and cell dehydration by phorbol esters and okadaic acid in sickle cells; effects of PKC alpha activation on Ca2+ pump and K (Ca) channel in deoxygenated sickle cells; deoxygenation of sickle red blood cells stimulates KCl cotransport without affecting Na/H exchange; insulin stimulates NHE1 activity by sequential activation of phosphatidylinositol 3-kinase and protein kinase C zeta in human erythrocytes; role of epigenetic modifications in normal globin gene regulation and butyrate-mediated induction of fetal hemoglobin. Office: Mt Sinai Med Ctr One Gustave L Levy Pl Box 1079 New York NY 10029 Office Phone: 212-241-7931. Business E-Mail: hassana.fathallah@mssm.edu.

FATHAUER, THEODORE FREDERICK, meteorologist; b. Oak Park, Ill., June 5, 1946; s. Arthur Theodore and Helen Ann (Mashek) Fathauer; m. Mary Ann Neesan, Aug. 8, 1981. BA, U. Chgo., 1968. Cert. cons. meteorologist. Rsch. aide USDA No. Devel. Labs., Peoria, Ill., 1966, Cloud Physics Lab., Chgo., 1967; meteorologist Sta. WLW Radio/TV, Cin., 1967-68, Nat. Meteorol. Ctr., Washington, 1968-70, Nat. Weather Svc., Anchorage, 1970-80, meteorologist-in-charge Fairbanks, Alaska, 1980-98, lead forecaster, 1998—. Instr. USCG Aux., Fairbanks, Anchorage, 1974—97, U. Alaska, Fairbanks, 1975—76; specialist in Alaska meteorology. Co-author: Denali's West Buttress, 1997, Living with the Coast of Alaska, 1997, (column) Weatherwatch, Weatherwise Mag., 2004—; contbr. articles to mags. and jours. Bd. dirs. Fairbanks Concert Assn., 1988—, Friends U. Alaska Mus., 1993—, pres., 1993—95, sec., 1997—98; bd. dirs. Fairbanks Symphony Assn., 1994—, sec., 1994—2001, treas., 2001—; trustee U. Alaska Found., 1997—, mem. coll. fellows, 1993—, mem. exec. com., 1997—, vice chair, 1998—99, chair, 2000—01; mem. adv. bd. Salvation Army, Fairbanks, 1997—; bd. dirs. No. Alaska Combined Fed. Campaign, 1996—, campaign chmn., 1996—97; bd. visitors U. Alaska, Fairbanks, 1995—; mem. KUAC Pub. Radio Leadership Coun., 2006—. Recipient Fed. Employee of the Yr. award, Fed. Exec. Assn., Anchorage, 1978. Fellow: Royal Meteorol. Soc., Am. Meteorol. Soc. (mem. sci. and tech. adv. com. coastal environments 1998—2004, co-chmn. Conf. Coastal Environment 2003, TV and radio seals approval); mem.: AAAS, Oceanography Soc. (charter mem.), Nat. Weather Assn. (charter mem.), Am. Sailing Assn., Can. Meteorol. and Oceanog. Soc., Arctic Inst. N.Am. (exec. sec. U.S. Corp. 1998—2003, bd. govs. U.S. Corp. 2003—), Western Snow Conf., Am. Geophys. Union, Am. Polar Soc., Greater Fairbanks C. of C. Catholic. Achievements include being a member of the science team on the voyage of the CCGS "Sir Wilfrid Laurier" from Victoria, BC to Barrow, Alaska, July 2006. Avocations: reading, music, skiing, canoeing. Home: 1738 Chena Ridge Rd PO Box 80210 Fairbanks AK 99708-0210 Office: Nat Weather Svc Forecast Office Internat Arctic Rsch Ctr U Alaska PO Box 757345 Fairbanks AK 99775-7345 Office Phone: 907-474-5606. Business E-Mail: ted.fathauer@gi.alaska.edu.

FATHEREE, JOSEPH G., informaation technology educator; BA in History, Ea. Ill. Univ., MEd in Ednl. Adminstrn. English tchr. Effingham (Ill.) H.S., 1990—94, history tchr., 1994—2000, tech. instr., 2000—. Named Ill. Tchr. of Yr., 2007; recipient Mid-Am. Emmy award (three), Telly award. Office: Effingham High Sch 1301 W Grove Effingham IL 62401 Office Phone: 217-540-1100. Business E-Mail: fatheree@u40gw.effingham.k12.il.us.*

FATHPOUR, SASAN, optical engineer, researcher; s. Hossein Fathpour and Roohangiz Zamanifar. BS, Isfahan U. Tech., Iran, 1995; MS, U. BC, Vancouver, Can., 2000; PhD, U. Mich., Ann Arbor, 2005. Quality control engr. Isfahan Optical Industry, Iran, 1995—97; R & D engr. Pardian Inc., Isfahan, 1997—98; postdoctoral rsch. fellow UCLA, 2005—. Recipient Chancellor's award for Postdoctoral Rsch., UCLA, 2007; fellow, Isfahan U. Tech., 1991—95, Internat. Student fellow, U. Mich., 2000. Mem.: IEEE, Optical Soc. Am. Achievements include discovery of two-photon photovoltaic effect; patents pending for negative dissipation optical modulator; first to demonstration of temperature invariant operation in any semiconductor laser; demonstration the fastest quantum dot lasers to date (by tunnel injection and acceptor doping); demonstration of zero linewidth enhancement factor and zero dynamic chirp for the first time in any semiconductor laser; demostration of energy harvesting in silicon photonics with worldwide press coverage (more than 30 occurences); research in record high-temeparture operation of spin-polarized light sources. Office: UCLA Elec Engring Dept 420 Westwood Plz Los Angeles CA 90095-1594 Office Phone: 310-206-4554.

FATIADI, ALEXANDER JOHN, retired chemist; b. Kharkov, Ukraine, Oct. 22, 1922; s. Evan George and Maria Ivan Fatiadi; m. Irina Ivan Matusevich, July 20, 1952; children: Elena, Irene, Tamara, Julia. PhD in Organic Chemistry, U. Mainz, Germany, 1950; MSc in Phys. Chemistry, George Washington U., 1959; DSc (hon.), World U. of Ariz., 1985. Rsch. assoc. George Washington U., Washington, 1952—59; rschr. Nat. Inst. Stds. and Tech., Gaithersburg, Md., 1959—91. Contbr. articles to profl. jours. Recipient Internat. Scholars award, U. Strasbourg, France, 1973, Hillebrand award, Washington Chem. Soc., 1982. Mem.: N.Y. Acad. Scis., Royal Chem. Soc., Am. Chem Soc. Avocations: history of civilization, classical music. Home: 7516 Carroll Ave Takoma Park MD 20912-5716

FATIĆ, VUK MARKO, electrical engineer, educator, researcher; b. Pancevo, Serbia, Yugoslavia, Mar. 22, 1932; came to U.S., 1970; s. Marko V. and Nelka (Vuletic) F.; m. Nada A. Dragic, Aug. 10, 1970. Diploma in electrical engring., Belgrade U., 1960; MS, Va. Poly. Inst. and State U., 1973, PhD, 1976. Rsch. engr. Vojno Tehnicki Inst., Beograd, Yugoslavia, 1961-68; asst. Novi Sad (Yugoslavia) U., 1968-70; instr. Va. Poly. Inst. and State U., 1973-75; asst. prof. Union Coll., Schenectady, NY, 1975-76, assoc. prof., 1985—95, prof., 1995—; from asst. prof. to assoc. prof. Tri-State U., Angola, Ind., 1976-85; assoc. prof. Rose Hulman Inst. Tech., Terre Haute, Ind., 1985. Contbr. over 70 articles in variational principles for dissipative systems of profl jours. Rsch. grantee Internat. Rsch. & Exch. Bd., N.Y.C., 1970-71, NSF & NEH, Washington, 1980. Mem. IEEE (sr.), Sigma Xi, Phi Kappa Phi, Eta Kappa Nu, Tau Beta Pi. Avocations: jazz music, literature. Home: 1377 Tracy Ave Niskayuna NY 12309-3712 Office Phone: 518-388-6320. Business E-Mail: faticv@union.edu.

FATOVIC, ROBERT DEAN, lawyer; b. Englewood, NJ, Mar. 1965; m. Leeanna D. Black. BS magna cum laude in Fin., Boston Coll., 1987, JD, 1990. Bar: NJ 1991, Fla. 1997. Assoc. Hannoch Weisman, P.C., NJ, 1990—94; asst. divsn. counsel Ryder Sys. Inc., Miami, 1994—96, assoc. divsn. counsel, 1996, assoc. div. counsel through sr. v.p. & dep. gen. counsel, 1996—2002, sr. v.p. US Supply Chain Operation, High-Tech and Consumer Industries, 2002—04, exec. v.p., chief legal officer, sec., 2004—. Mem.: ABA. Office: Ryder System Inc 11690 NW 105th St Miami FL 33178

FATT, WILLIAM ROBERT, hotel executive; b. Toronto, Ont., Can., Mar. 11, 1951; BA in Econs., York U., Toronto. Auditor Thorne Riddell, Toronto, 1973-75; asst. contr. Revenue Properties Co. Ltd., Toronto, 1975-77; acctg. analyst The Consumers Gas Co., Toronto, 1977-78; asst. treas. Hiram Walker Resources, Toronto, 1978-82, treas., 1982-84, v.p., treas., 1984-86; v.p. Morgan Bank of Can., Toronto, 1986-88; treas. Can. Pacific Ltd., Toronto, 1988, v.p., treas., 1988-90, v.p. fin. and acctg., CFO, 1990-94, exec. v.p. and CFO Toronto and Calgary, 1994; CEO Fairmont Raffles Hotels Internat., Toronto, 1998—; also bd. dirs. Vice chmn., trustee Legacy Hotels Real Estate Investment Trust. Office: Fairmont Raffles Hotels Internat 100 Wellington St W # 1600 Toronto ON Canada M5K 1B7

FATTAH, CHAKA, congressman, former state legislator; b. Phila., Nov. 21, 1956; m. Reneé Chenault-Fattah; 4 children. Student, Phila. CC, 1976; grad. sr. exec. prog. for state ofcls., Harvard U. John F. Kennedy Sch. Govt., 1984; M in Govt. Adminstrn., U. Pa. Fels Sch. of State and Local Govt., 1986. Spl. asst. to dir. housing and cmty. devel., Phila., 1980; spl. asst. to mng. dir. housing and cmty. devel., 1981; policy asst. Greater Phila. Partnership; mem. Pa. Ho. Reps., 1982-88, Pa. State Senate, 1988-94, US Congress from 2nd Pa. dist., 1995—. Mem. appropriations com., US Congress. Founder Am. Cities Conf. and Found.; leader task force Child Devel. Initiative, Phila.; founder, convenor Grad. Opportunities Conf., Pa.; chmn. exec. com. Pa. Higher Edn. Assistance Agy.; creator Jobs Project. Named to Time Mag.'s roster of America's most promising leaders, 1994; named one of Ebony Mag.'s 50 Future Leaders, 1984, Most Influential Black Americans, Ebony mag., 2006; recipient Pa. Pub. Interest Coalition's State Legislator of Yr. award Democrat. Baptist. Office: US House Reps 2301 Rayburn House Office Bldg Washington DC 20515-0001 Office Phone: 202-225-4001. Office Fax: 202-225-5392.*

FATTORI, RUTH A., human resources specialist, electronics executive; BS, Cornell U. Advanced mfg. engr., various human resources positions Xerox Corp.; mng. dir. European ops., v.p., chief quality officer GE Capital, London; sr. v.p. human resources Siemans Corp., Siemans AG, Asea Brown Boveri; exec. v.p. process and productivity Conseco, Inc.; sr. v.p. human resources, comm. productivity and quality global tech. infrastructure group JPMorgan Chase & Co.; exec. v.p. human resources Motorola, Inc., Schaumburg, Ill., 2004—. Bd. trustees Polytechnic U., Trinity Pawling Sch. Office: Motorola Inc 1303 E Algonquin Rd Schaumburg IL 60196 Office Phone: 847-576-5000. Office Fax: 847-576-5372.*

FAUCETTE, GLORIA MARIE, accountant, educator; b. Burlington, NC, Aug. 29, 1948; d. Jesse Graham and Mildred Kathryn Faucette. BA in Social Scis., Elon Coll., 1982; BS in Acctg., N.C. A&T State U., 1991; MBA, Elon Coll., 1993. Social worker Alamance County Dept. Social Svcs., Burlington, NC, 1974-89; instr. acctg. and bus. N.C. A&T State U., Greensboro, NC, 1991-99, N.C. AT&T State, Greensboro, NC, 2000—01; acct. Cobb Ezekiel Brown and Co., Graham, NC, 1999—2000; bus. tchr. Hawfields Mid. Sch., 2001—06, A.L. Stanback Mid. Sch., 2006—. Mem. acad. rels. com. Inst. Internal Auditors, Greensboro, 1996-97; cons. bus. ednl. career decisions mid/secondary sch. students; small bus. cons. Contbr. articles to profl. jours. Mem. AICPA, N.C. Assn. CPA (mem. acctg. edn. com. 1995-97; chair careers in acctg. com. 1999), Beta Alpha Psi, Beta Gamma Sigma Democrat. Methodist.

FAUCI, ANTHONY STEPHEN, federal agency administrator, allergist, immunologist; b. Bklyn., Dec. 24, 1940; s. Stephen A. and Eugenia A. Fauci. AB, Coll. of Holy Cross, 1962; MD, Cornell U., 1966; DSc (hon.), Coll. Holy Cross, 1987, Georgetown U., 1990, Hahnemann U., 1990, Mt. Sinai Sch. Medicine, 1990, Universita di Roma, 1990, St. John's U., 1991, LI U., 1992, Med. Coll. Wis., 1993, Bard Coll., 1993, Bates Coll., 1993, SUNY, Farmingdale, 1994, U. Conn. Health Ctr, 1994; DSc, Duke U., 1995; doctorate (hon.). Diplomate Am. Bd. Internal Medicine, Am. Bd. Allergy and Immunology (bd. dirs. 1984 to date), Am. Bd. Infectious Diseases. Intern N.Y. Hosp.-Cornell Med. Ctr., 1966—67, asst. resident in medicine, 1967—68, chief resident dept. medicine, 1971—72; clin. assoc. Nat. Inst. Allergy and Infectious Diseases-NIH, Bethesda, Md., 1968—70, sr. staff fellow, 1970—71, sr. investigator, 1972—74, head, clin. physiology sect., 1974—80, dep. clin. dir., 1977—80, chief Lab. Immunoregulation, divsn. intramural rsch., 1980—, sect. head, immunopathenogenesis sect., dir. Bethesda, Md., 1984—; dir. Office of AIDS Rsch., NIH, assoc. dir. NIH for AIDS Rsch., 1988—94. Cons. Naval Med. Ctr., Bethesda, 1972—; lectr. in field. Editor: Harrison's Principles of Internal Medicine; contbr. numerous articles to profl. jours. Trustee Doris Duke Charitable Found. With USPHS, 1968—96. Named One of the Top 50 Scientific Leaders, Scientific Am., 2003, 13th Most Cited Scientists, Inst. for Scientific Information, 1983—2002, 9th Most Cited Scientist in Immunology, 1993—2003, America's Best in Sci. and Medicine, CNN/Time Mag., 2001, Scientist of Yr., R&D Mag., 2005; recipient meritorious svcs. award, USPHS, 1979, Arthur S. Fleming award, 1983, Squibb award, Infectious Diseases Soc., 1983, Commrs. Spl. Citation, FDA, 1984, Clemons von Pirquet award, Georgetown U. Med. Ctr., 1986, Disting Clin. Educator award, NIH Clin. Ctr., 1988, Leadership award, Columbus Citizens Found., Inc., 1988, spl. award for rsch. in AIDS, Nat. Hemophilia Fedn., 1989, Lee P. Brown Nat. Pub. Svc. award, Nat. Acad. Pub. Adminstrn. and Nat. Soc. for Pub. Adminstrn., 1989, numerous awards, Duke U., AMA, Children's Hosp., Nat. Med. Ctr., Surgeon Gen., Am. Assn. Physicians for Human Rights, Nat. Health Coun., Nat. Found. Infectious Disease, Helen Hayes award for med. rsch., 1989, Excellence in Pub. Svc. award, Com. for Support of Pub. Svc., 1990, Lifetime Sci. award, Inst. Advanced Studies in Immunology and Aging, 1990, Internat. Chiron prize, 1990, Pres. award, N.Y. Acad. Sci., 1990, Thomas H. Ham-Louis R. Wasserman award, Am. Soc. Hematology, 1992, Dr. Nathan Davis award, AMA, 1992, Outstanding Achievement award, Howard U., 1992, Humanitarian award, Tiro a Segno Fedn., 1993, Cartwright prize, Columbia U. Coll. Physicians and Surgeons, 1993, Commr. of Honor award, SUNY-Farmingdale, 1994, Theobald Smith award, Albany Med. Coll., 1995, Coord. Com. award, ABA, 1996, David Rumbough Sci. award, Juvenile Diabetes Fedn. Internat., 1996, award, Nat. Coun. Internat. Health, 1996, March of Dimes Fedn., 1996, Ellen Browning Scripps medal, Scripps Fedn. Medicine and Rsch., 1996, Md. Gov.'s Citation, 1997, Thomas J. D'Alesandro Jr. award, Assoc. Italian Am. Charities, 1997, San Marino prize for medicine, 1997, John P. McGovern award, Am. Med. Writers Assn., 1997, Frank Brown Berry prize in fed. med., US Med. and Delta Dental Plan Calif., 1999, Frank Annunzio award in Humanitarian Field, Christopher Columbus Fellowship Found., 2001, Albany Med. Center prize in Medicine and Biomedical Rsch., 2002, Ellis Island Family Heritage award, Statue of Liberty-Ellis Island Found., 2003, 2005 Nat. Medal Sci., NSF, 2007. Master: AAAS (Westinghouse award 1988); fellow: Am. Acad. Microbiology, Am. Acad. Arts and Scis., N.Y. Acad. Medicine (hon. Extraordinary Accomplishments award 2004), Am. Acad. Allergy, ACP (Richard and Hinda Rosenthal award 1995, John Phillips Meml. award 1997), Am. Acad. Allergy Asthma and Immunology (hon.), Am. Med. Writers Assn. (hon.); mem.: Am. Philos. Soc., NAS, Royal Acad. Medicine (Spain), Royal Danish Acad. Sci. and Letters (fgn.), Inst. Medicine of NAS (coun. mem.), Assn. Am. Physicians (recorder 1988—93, councillor 1993—), Am. Soc. for Clin. Investigation, Infectious Diseases Soc. Am., Commd. Officers Assn. USPHS (Pub. Health Leader of Yr. award), Internat. AIDS Soc., Am. Fedn. Clin. Rsch. (pres. 1980—81), Am. Soc. Cell Biology, Am. Soc. Virology, Am. Assn. Immunologists (program chmn. 1982—85, Kober lectr. 1988, Lifetime Achievement award 2005). Roman Catholic. Avocations: running, tennis. Office: Nat Inst Allergy & Infectious Diseases MSC 6612 6610 Rockledge Dr Bethesda MD 20892-6612 Office Phone: 301-496-2263. Office Fax: 301-496-4409. E-mail: af10r@nih.gov.*

FAUDE, WILSON HINSDALE, museum director, consultant; b. Hartford, Conn., Feb. 20, 1946; s. John Paul and Helen (Hinsdale) Faude; m. Janet Bailey, 1985; children: Sarah Hinsdale, Paul Bailey. BA, Hobart Coll., 1969; MA, Trinity Coll., 1975. Curator Mark Twain Meml., Hartford, 1971—78; exec. assoc. to v.p. for devel. U. Hartford, West Hartford, Conn., 1981—85; exec. dir. Old State House, Hartford, 1978—81, 1985—2001, exec. dir. emeritus, 2002—. Commr. Conn. Arts Commn., 1975—83, Conn. Hist. Commn., 1980; hon. mem. 350th commn. Conn. Arts Commn., 1984—86; chmn. Conn. Hist. Commn., 1984—96; guest curator Wadsworth Atheneum, 2004; archivist City of Hartford, Conn., 2006—. Author: (book) Renaissance of Mark Twain's House, 1977, The Great Hartford Picture Book, 1985, The Old Photograph Series: Hartford, 1994, The Old Photograph Series: Hartford, vol. II, 1995, The Old Photograph Series: Hartford, vol. III, 1997, Lost Hartford, 2000, The Old Photograph Series: West Hartford, 2004; author: (with others) Connecticut Firsts, 1978, 1985, 1996, 2000, Birthplace of Democracy, 1979; contbr. articles to profl. jours.; Cow Parade, 2004, 2007. Reader Talking Books for the Blind and Handicapped Conn. Vols. Svcs., 1986—; mem. faculty Cooperstown Seminars, 1979—80, 1984—88; corporator Hartford Art Sch., West Hartford, 1980—98; mem. Conn. Heritage Task Force, 1980—82; corporator Hartford Hosp., 1992—; bd. dir. Conn. Equestrian Ctr., 1996, Stowe Ctr., 1996—97, Conn. Women's Hall of Fame, 1996—2004, Conn. Valley Girl Scout Coun., 2006—; trustee Renbrook Sch., West Hartford, 1984—85; hon. trustee Mark Twain Ho., 1997—. With US Army, 1969—71. Named Capt., 1st Co. Gov. Foot Guard, 1979—, Civitan Man of the Yr., 1997; recipient 1st prize needlepoint, Ea. State Expn., 1997, Disting. Adv. for the Arts award, State of Conn., 1998, Thomas Hooker award for disting. cmty. svc., Ancient Burying Ground Assn., 1999. Mem.: Pub. Rels. Soc. Am. (Pub. Svc. Merit award 2001), Mark Twain Meml., Century Assn., Nat. Arts Club, Druid Soc. Episcopalian. Home and Office: 42 Fulton Pl West Hartford CT 06107-1128 Office Phone: 860-523-8226. Personal E-mail: wilsonfaude@comcast.net.

FAUGHN, DALE, biology educator; b. Lamasco, Ky., Nov. 8, 1925; s. Arthur Wayne and Nancy Dora Faughn; m. Virginia Ray Chandler, Oct. 9, 1949; children: Phillip, Timothy, Stephen, Nathan, Mark, Ruth, Paul. BS, Murray State U., Ky., 1949; MA, Murray State U., 1958. Cert. biology tchr. Ky. Dept. Edn. Tchr. Caldwell County Bd. Edn., Princeton, Ky., 1949—. Mem. evaluation team Nat. Coun. Accreditation Tchr. Edn. Author poetry. Tchr. Civil Def., Princeton; scoutmaster Boy Scouts Am., Fredonia, Ky., 1949—53. Corp. USMC, 1944—46, WW II. Named HS Tchr. of Yr., Ky. Dept. Edn., 1996, Citizen of Yr., Kiwanis, 1996, Outstanding Tchr., Murray State U., 1999, HS Sci. Tchr. of Yr., Ky. Sci. Tchr. Assn., 2002; named to, Nat. Tchrs. Hall of Fame, 1998, Baxter Blood Donor Hall of Fame, 2004; recipient Valley Forge Tchrs. medal, Freedom Found., 1965, William F. Brown Outstanding Tchr. award, 1986, Poet Loreate, Ky. House of Rep., 1986, Tchr. Achievement award, Ashland Oil, 1990, Tchr. award, Optimists, 2000; scholar, Tandy Tech., 1989—90. Mem.: Caldwell County Classroom Tchrs. Assn., Nat. Assn. Biology Tchrs., Ky. Acad. Sci., Nat.

Sci. Tchr. Assn. Baptist. Home: 7099 Goodsprings Rd Fredonia KY 42411 Office: Caldwell County High Sch 350 Beckner Ln Princeton KY 42445 Office Phone: 270-365-8010. Office Fax: 270-365-9742. Business E-Mail: dale.faughn@caldwell.kyschools.us.

FAUL, JUNE PATRICIA, education specialist; b. Detroit; d. John William and Shirley Olive (Block) Lynch; m. George Johnson Faul, EdD, Dec. 22, 1949; children: Robert M., Alison. BA, U. Calif., Berkeley, 1952. Cert. elem. tchr., Calif. Tchr. Tulare County (Calif.) Schs., 1945-46, Tulare City Schs., 1946-48, Visalia (Calif.) City Schs., 1948-49, Richmond (Calif.) City Schs., 1951-52, Pacific Grove (Calif.) Sch. Dist., 1965-85; designated English tchg. specialist State of Calif., 1969—; edn. cons. Leo A. Meyer Assocs., Inc., Hayward, Calif., 1993—. Prin. Group Four Assocs.; lectr. Calif. State U., Fresno, 1969, U. Calif., Santa Cruz, 1970. Co-author: The New Older Woman, 1996. Apprd. mem. first human rels. commn. City of Richmond, 1962-64; adv. bd. Family Resource Ctr.; founding mem., 1st pres. Monterey (Calif.) Peninsula Child Abuse Prevention Coun., 1974; hon. life mem. Calif. PTA; bd. dirs. Carmel Cultural Commn., 1964-67, Harrison Meml. Libr. Bd., Carmel, Calif., 1978-84; bd. dirs. Monterey Peninsula Airport Dist., 1980-2004; co-founder 100 Women Supporting Women, Monterey Peninsula Coll., 1997; vol. chair Women Mentoring Women, 2004. Named Woman of Yr., Monterey County Bd. Suprs. Com., 2005. Mem. Friends of Hopkins Marine Sta. (founder, bd. dirs.), Carmel Heritage (founder, bd. dirs.), Monterey NAACP (life), Monterey Mus. Art (life), Monterey Symphony Guild (life). Democrat. Avocation: writing. Home: PO Box 4365 Carmel CA 93921-4365

FAULCONER, ROBERT JAMIESON, pathologist, educator; b. Sedlescombe, Sussex, Eng., July 11, 1923; came to U.S., 1925, naturalized, 1932; s. Robert Hoffman and Gladys Alice (Jamieson) F.; m. Virginia Myrl Davis, Aug. 11, 1945; children: Anne Faulconer Hurley, Elizabeth Myrl, Mary Waite, John Edmund. BS, Coll. William and Mary, 1943; MD, Johns Hopkins U., 1947; DSc (hon.), Ea. Va. Med. Sch., 1998. Diplomate Am. Bd. Pathology. Intern Johns Hopkins Hosp., 1948, fellow, 1948-49; resident Presbyn.-U. Pa. Med. Ctr., Phila., 1949-52; pathologist DePaul Hosp., Norfolk, Va., 1954-78, pathologist, dir. labs., 1965-78; clin. prof. pathology Med. Coll. Va., 1972-79; prof. pathology Ea. Va. Med. Sch., 1974-94, chmn., 1978-93, prof. emeritus, 1994—. Cons. pathologist U.S. Naval Hosp., Portsmouth, Va., VA Hosp., Hampton, Va., Children;s Hosp., Norfolk, Va. Beach Gen. Hosp.; chmn. Health Svcs. Adv. Bd., Norfolk; mem. adv. com. Va. Cancer Registry. Med. editorial bd. Histology and Histopathology Jour.; contbr. articles on pathology to profl. publs. Pres. Va. div. Am. Cancer Soc., 1963-66, mem. nat. bd. dirs., exec. and sci. rev. coms.; bd. visitors Coll. William and Mary, 1972-76, 79-87, chmn. William and Mary Olde Guarde, 1997-98. With USNR, 1943-46, M.C., U.S. Army, 1952-54. Recipient J. Shelton Horsley award merit, Va. div. Am. Cancer Soc., 1966, Alumni medallion, Coll. William and Mary, 1985. Fellow AAAS; mem. AMA, Internat. Acad. Pathology, Am. Soc. Clin. Pathologists, Coll. Am. Pathologists, Am. Assn. Anatomists, Am. Soc. Clin. Oncology, Am. Assn. Phys. Anthropologists, Va. Soc. Pathology (pres. 1958-59), Norfolk Acad. Medicine (pres. 1964-65), Am. Assn. History of Medicine, Am. Assn. Pathologists, Assn. Pathology Chmn., Cypher Soc. (Coll. William and Mary), Norfolk Yacht and Country Club, Town Point Club (bd. govs.), Commonwealth Club (Richmond), Sigma Xi. Episcopalian. Home: 1507 Buckingham Ave Norfolk VA 23508-1354 Office: Ea Va Med Sch Med Coll of Hampton Roads PO Box 1980 Norfolk VA 23501-1980 Business E-Mail: crd@borg.evms.edu.

FAULES, BARBARA RUTH, retired elementary school educator; b. Austin, Tex., Mar. 10, 1940; d. Milton Friedrich Hausmann and Ruth Elizabeth Hornbuckle; m. John Wilson Faules, May 30, 1967. BA cum laude, Harding U., 1962; MA in Curriculum and Instrn., U. Mo., Kansas City, 1995. Cert. elem. tchr., Mo. Tchr. 4th grade Searcy Grammar Sch., Ark., 1962—64, Pulaski County Spl. Sch., Little Rock AFB Elem., Jacksonville, Ark., 1964—67; tchr. grades 3, 4, and 6 Butcher Greene Elem. Consol. Sch. Dist. #4, Grandview, Mo., 1967—98, ret., 1998. Contbr. (poetry) Sunrise and Soft Mist, 1999 (Editor's Choice 1999). Mem. Nat. Congress Parents and Tchr. (hon. life mem.). Mem. Ch. of Christ. Avocations: freelance photography, writing, gardening, reading, travel. Home: 9131 Big Bethel Dr San Antonio TX 78240-2852 Personal E-mail: tchow1101@sbcglobal.net.

FAULK, MARSHALL WILLIAMS, retired professional football player; b. New Orleans, Feb. 26, 1973; s. Roosevelt and Cecile Faulk; married; 3 children. Student, San Diego State U., 1991—93. Running back Indpls. Colts., 1994-99, St. Louis Rams, 1999—2007; analyst, NFL Total Access NFL Network, 2005—. Founder The Marshall Faulk Found., 1994—. Named Am. Football Conf. (AFC) Rookie of Yr., 1994, NFL Pro Bowl MVP, 1994, NFL MVP, 2000, 2001, NFL Offensive Player of the Yr., AP, 1994, 1999—2001; named to Am. Football Conf. (AFC) Pro-Bowl, 1995—96, Nat. Football Conf. (NFC) Pro-Bowl, 1999—2003; recipient Espy Award for Best Football Player, ESPN, 2001, 2002, Bert Bell award, 2001. Achievements include being a member of Super Bowl XXXIV Champion St. Louis Rams, 2000; being the first player in NFL history to gain 2,000 yards from scrimmage in four consecutive seasons. Office: The Marshall Faulk Found 1116 E Market St Indianapolis IN 46202*

FAULKNER, FRANCES MAYHEW, retired federal agency administrator; b. Englewood, NJ, Feb. 21, 1930; d. Benjamin Alan and Laura Sanford Mayhew; m. Douglas Albert Faulkner, Sept. 1949 (dec.); children: June E., Lee A., Glen A. Student, Brown U., Providence, 1947—48. Postmaster US Postal Svc., New Kingston, NY, 1987—2005; ret. Mem.: NY State Hist. Assn., Del. County Hist. Assn. (Merit award 2005), Nat. Assn. Postmasters US, Hist. Soc. Middletown, New Kingston Valley Assn. Democrat. Avocations: travel, reading, gardening, antiques.

FAULKNER, JAMES VINCENT, JR., lawyer; b. NYC, Mar. 25, 1944; s. James Vincent and Josephine Rita (Fitzsimmons) F.; m. Bettina Van Der Plas, Aug. 10, 1968; children: Aylsia, Martina, James III. BA, Georgetown U., 1966, MS, 1968, JD, 1970. Assoc. Appleton, Rich & Perrin, NYC, 1970-72, Lord, Day & Lord, NYC, 1972-75; sr. corp. atty. Union Pacific Corp., NYC, 1975-77, asst. gen. counsel, 1977-80, assoc. gen. counsel, 1980-83, dep. gen. counsel, 1983-88; sr. v.p., gen. counsel USPCI Inc. subs. Union Pacific Corp., Houston, 1988-93; v.p., law atty. Tenneco Inc., Houston, 1993—95; v.p., gen. counsel Tenneco Packaging, 1995—99; v.p., gen. counsel, sec. Pactiv Corp., 2000—06. Mem. Sch. bd. St. Patrick's Ch., Bedford, N.Y., 1979-81, parish council, 1981-84. Mem. ABA, Am. Corp. Counsel Assn. (dir. 1985-88), Assn. Bar City N.Y. (com. on uniform state laws 1971-72). Clubs: Bedford Golf and Tennis. Republican. Roman Catholic. Avocations: squash, riding.*

FAULKNER, JULIA ELLEN, opera singer; b. St. Louis, Nov. 1, 1957; d. Seldon and Dona Leah (Clark) F. MusB cum laude, Ind. U., 1980, MusM, 1983. Instr. voice No. Ariz. U., Flagstaff, 1984, Iowa State U., 1984-85; studio voice tchr., 1998—; asst. prof. U. Wis. Sch. Music, 2003—. Master tchr. young artist program Lamusica Lirica, 2004—; master tchr. Top Opera, 2005—. Solo performances with opera cos. and theaters at La Scala, Carnegie Hall, NYC, San Francisco Opera Ctr., 1985-86, Woldftrap Opera Co., Vienna, Va., 1986, Bavarian State Opera, Munich, 1987-91, Vienna State Opera, Austria, 1991-97, Met. Opera, NYC, LA Philharm., San Francisco Philharm., also in Miami Fla., Berlin, Hamburg, Germany, Lyon, Jerusalem, Bordeau, Stockholm, Amsterdam and Genoa; dir. Oklahoma and Old Maid and the Thief, Flagstaff, 1984; rec. artist Elektra, 1990, Der Rosenkavalier, 1991, Rossini, Semiramide, Schumann, Genoveva; recorded Pergolesi Stabat Mater Deutsche Grammophone Das Paradis und die Peri, Verdi's Falstaff. Recipient award Met. Opera, N.Y.C., 1985, 3d prize Whitaker Internat. Voice Competition, 1985, Festspiel prize Bavarian State Opera, 1988. Democrat. Office: Sch of Music Univ Wis Madison WI 53703 Office Phone: 608-263-1922. Business E-Mail: jfaulkner2@wisc.edu.

FAULKNER, KRISTINE, communications executive; b. 1968; Bus. devel. mgr. Digital City Hampton Roads, gen. mgr.; dir., internet pub. Daily Press, Va.; sr. product mgr., Web Hosting Services Cox Comm., Atlanta, 2000—04, v.p., Product Devel. and Mgmt., 2004—. Named one of 40 Executives Under 40, Multichannel News, 2006. Office: Cox Communications 1400 Lake Hearn Dr Atlanta GA 30319 Office Phone: 404-843-5000. Office Fax: 404-843-5975.

FAULKNER, LARRY RAY, foundation and former academic administrator; b. Shreveport, La., Nov. 26, 1944; s. James Clifford and Doris Louise (Koch) Faulkner; m. Mary Ann Jordan, Aug. 14, 1965; children: Brian Jordan, Susan Louise. BS, So. Meth. U., 1966; PhD, U. Tex., Austin, 1969; DSc (hon.), So. Meth. U., 2000. Asst. prof. chemistry Harvard U., Cambridge, Mass., 1969—73; asst. prof. U. Ill., Urbana-Champaign, 1973—75, assoc. prof., 1975—79, mem. materials rsch. lab., 1978—90, prof., 1979—83, prof. chemistry, dept. head, 1984—89, dean Coll. Liberal Arts and Sci., 1989—94, provost and vice chancellor acad. affairs, 1994—98; prof. chemistry U. Tex., Austin, Tex., 1983—84, pres., 1998—2006, Houston Endowment Inc., 2006—. Author (with A.J. Bard): Electrochemical Methods, 1980, 2d edit., 2001; editor: Jour. Electroanalytical Chemistry, 1980—85; mem. edit. bd.: Jour. Electrochem. Soc., 1975—80. Recipient U.S. Dept. Energy award, 1986. Fellow: Electrochem. Soc. (v.p. 1988—91, pres. 1991—92, Edward Weston fellow 1969, Young Author's prize 1976, Edward Goodrich Acheson medal 2000), Am. Acad. Arts and Scis.; mem.: AAAS, Soc. Electroanalytical Chemistry (Charles N. Reilly award 1998), Am. Chem. Soc. (award in analytical chemistry 1992), Phi Kappa Phi, Phi Beta Kappa (Grad. Rsch. award Tex. Gamma chpt. 1969—70). Office: Houston Endowment Inc 600 Travis, Ste 6400 Houston TX 77002-3000 Home: 2306 Mimosa Dr Houston TX 77019 Home Phone: 713-533-0994; Office Phone: 713-238-8110. Office Fax: 713-238-8101.

FAULKNER, LAURA R., lawyer; b. Columbus, Ohio, Aug. 18, 1974; BA in Polit. Sci., Miami U., 1996, BA in Eng. Lit., 1996; JD, U. Dayton, 1999. Bar: Ohio 1999, US Dist. Ct. Southern Dist. Ohio 2000, US Dist. Ct. Northern Dist. Ohio 2001. Assoc. Weltman, Weinberg & Reis Co., L.P.A., Cin. Named one of Ohio's Rising Stars, Super Lawyers, 2006. Mem.: Am. Bankruptcy Law Forum, Cin. Bar Assn., Ohio State Bar Assn. Office: Weltman, Weinberg & Reis Co LPA 525 Vine St Ste 800 Cincinnati OH 45202 Office Phone: 513-723-2200. Office Fax: 513-723-2239.

FAULKNER, ROBERT LLOYD, advertising executive, graphics designer; b. Chgo., Nov. 8, 1934; s. L. Lester and Agnes Elizabeth (Irons) F.; m. Elizabeth Alice Thomas, June 14, 1958; children: Anne Elizabeth, Lynn Marie, Thomas Robert. BFA in Advt. Design, U. Ill., 1958. Account exec. Brad Sebstad Advt., Chgo., 1966—67; sr. account exec. D'Arcy Advt. Co., Chgo., 1967—70; v.p. Wm. A. Robinson Inc., Northbrook, Ill., 1970—71; nat. mdse. and promotion mgr. James B. Beam Distilling Co., Chgo., 1971—73; v.p. Coord. Advt., Chgo., 1973—77, Grant/Jacoby Inc., Chgo., 1977—79, Kennedy Advt., Chgo., 1979—86; exec. v.p. Kamen/Faulkner Inc., Chgo., 1986—89; pres., owner Bob Faulkner Corporation, Westchester, Ill., 1989—. Course coord., advt. lectr. grad. level advt. courses Northwestern U. and Roosevelt U., Chgo., 1980-85; computer instr. SeniorNet. Author: Learn to Cross Country Ski, 1976; co-author: Cross-Country Skiing for Everybody, 1975. Dir. Western Springs Hist. Soc., 1992-95; mem. Illegitimate Theatre of Western Springs; pres. Indian Prarie Computer Club, 2007—. Recipient numerous advt. awards. Mem. Bus. Mktg. Assn. (Cert. Bus. Communicator), Nat. Ski Patrol (life), Model T Ford Owners Assn., Sports Car Club Am., Portage Lake Yacht Club. Episcopalian. Avocation: fine art painting. Home and Office: 11523 Burton Court Westchester IL 60154 Home Phone: 708-492-1330; Office Phone: 708-492-1330. E-mail: bofaulk@hotmail.com.

FAULKNER, WALTER THOMAS, lawyer, director; b. New Haven, Sept. 17, 1928; s. Walter Thomas and Alice Marion (McGushin) F.; m. Joan Lee Hills, Mar. 17, 1956; children: John, Andrew, George, Susan. AB, Providence Coll., 1952; LL.B., Columbia U., 1955. Bar: N.Y. State 1956. Since practiced in, NYC; assoc. firm Rogers, Hoge & Hills, 1959-65, ptnr., 1965-86, Kelley Drye & Warren, 1987—. Sec. Sterling Drug Inc., 1973-78, Bacardi Corp., 1975-96. Bd. govs. Sound Shore Med. Ctr. Westchester. Served with AUS, 1946-48. Mem. Assn. of Bar of City of N.Y., ABA, N.Y. State Bar Assn., Am. Soc. Corp. Secs. Home: 64 Woodbine Ave Larchmont NY 10538-3525 Office: Kelley Drye & Warren 101 Park Ave New York NY 10178-0062

FAULMANN, ROGER RAY, retired music educator; b. Mt. Clemens, Mich., Jan. 27, 1938; m. Jo E. Dunbar, Dec. 27, 1964; 1 child, Bryan A. BME, Baldwin-Wallace Coll., 1960; MusM, U. of Mich., 1967. Cert. tchr. Fla., 1985. Instrumental gen. music dir. Fraser (Mich.) Pub. Schs., 1960—63; instrument/gen. music tchr. Port Huron (Mich.) Pub. Schs., 1963—64; dir. of bands Lake Orion (Mich.) Cmty. Schs., 1963—67; percussion prof. and band dir. Ill. State U., Normal, Ill., 1967—80; dir. of bands and percussion S.Dak. State U., Brookings, SD, 1980—83; dir. of bands Miami-Dade (Fla.) County Schs., 1985—2000; ret., 2000. Faculty Interlochen Arts Ctr., Mich., 1963—76; prof. and band dir. Ill. State U., 1967—80; cons. Fleisher-Hinton Music, Denver, 1983—85; guest condr. in field. Contbr. articles to profl. jours.; percussionist: numerous internat. venues. Mem.: Music Educators Nat. Coll., Am. Sch. Bandmasters Assn., Fla. Bandmaster Assn. Liberal. Episcopalian. Avocations: model trains, holocaust research, political activist. Home: 10386 West Marion Dr Traverse City MI 49686 Office Phone: 231-357-5965. Personal E-mail: rfaulmann@aol.com.

FAULS, THOMAS E. (TED FAULS), lawyer; b. Fredericksburg, Va., 1961; AB, Coll. William & Mary, 1983, JD, 1986. Bar: Va. 1986. Assoc. Troutman Sanders LLP, Richmond, Va., 1986—94, ptnr., 1995—, practice group leader, 1998—2007, mng. ptnr. Richmond office, 2006—. Mem.: ABA, Va. Bar Assn. Office: Troutman Sanders LLP Riverside on the James 1001 Haxall Point 14th Fl PO Box 1122 Richmond VA 23219 Office Phone: 804-697-1200. Office Fax: 804-697-1339. Business E-Mail: ted.fauls@troutmansanders.com.

FAUNCE, SARAH CUSHING, retired curator; b. Tulsa, Aug. 19, 1929; d. George Jr. and Helen Pauline (Colwell) F. BA, Wellesley Coll., 1951; MA, Washington U., St. Louis, 1959; postgrad., Columbia U., 1960-63. Tchr. history Hartridge Sch., Plainfield, NJ, 1954-56; tchr. art Mary C. Wheeler Sch., Providence, 1958-59; instr. art history Barnard Coll., NYC, 1962-64; sec. adv. council art history Columbia U., 1963-70, registrar, curator, 1965-70; exhbn. cons. Jewish Mus., NYC, 1968-70; curator paintings and sculpture Bklyn. Mus. Art, 1970-98, curator emeritus, project dir. Courbet Catalogue Raisonné project, 1998—. Author: Courbet, 1993; exhbn. catalog author: Anne Ryan Collages, 1974, Carl Larsson, 1982; author, editor: Belgian Art 1880-1914, 1980, Courbet Reconsidered, 1988, In the Light of Italy: Corot and Early Plein Air Painting, 1996; editor: Northern Light: Realism and Symbolism in Scandinavian Painting 1880-1910, 1982. Travel grantee Columbia U., 1963 Mem. AAM-ICOM, Coll. Art Assn., Phi Beta Kappa. Democrat. Office Phone: 646-878-2707. E-mail: faunce.courbet@mindspring.com.

FAURE, GUNTER, geology educator; b. Tallinn, Estonia, May 11, 1934; s. Arnulf and Stella (von Harpe) F.; m. Barbara L.L. Goodell, Sept. 5, 1959 (div. Feb. 1985); children: Mary Jennifer, John Eric, Pamela Anne, David Christopher; m. Teresa M. Mensing, June 4, 1988. B.Sc., U. Western Ont., 1957; PhD, MIT, 1961; fellow, Sch. Advanced Studies, 1961-62. Asst. prof. geology Ohio State U., 1962-65, assoc. prof., 1965-68, prof., 1968—2002, prof. emeritus, 2002—; field work Antarctica. Author: (with J.L. Powell) Strontium Isotope Geology, 1972, Principles of Isotope Geology, 1977, 2d edit., 1986, Principles and Applications of Geochemistry, 1991, 2d edit., 1998, Origin of Igneous Rocks, 2001, (with T.M. Mensing) Isotopes: Principles and Applications, 2005, (with T.M. Mensing) Introduction to Planetary Science, 2007; editor-in-chief Jour. Isotope Geoscience, 1983-88; exec. editor Geochimica et Cosmochimica Acta, 1989-97; assoc. editor Geochimica et Cosmochimica Acta, 1989-99; contbr. articles to profl. jours. Named an Honoree, Applied Geochemistry, 2004; recipient Gold medal in honours geology, U. Western Ont., 1957, Disting. Tchg. award, Ohio State U., 1970, 1983, 1999, Antarctic Svc. medal, 1976. Fellow Geol. Soc. Am. (sr.), Geochem. Soc. (Disting. Svc. award 2005), European Assn. Geochemistry; mem. Planetary Soc., Meteoritical Soc., Internat. Assn. Geochemistry and Cosmochemistry (v.p. 1992-96, pres. 1996-2000, treas. 2005—, newsletter editor 1999-2002), Ohio Acad. Scis., Geol. Assn. Can., Byrd Polar Rsch. Ctr. Ohio State U. Office: 125 S Oval Mall Columbus OH 43210-1308 Office Phone: 614-292-3454.

FAURI, ERIC JOSEPH, lawyer; b. Lansing, Mich., Feb. 16, 1942; s. Fedele Fauri and Iris M. Petersen; m. Sherrill Lynn Nurenberg, July 15, 1969; children— Lauren, Nadia, Kirk. B.A., U. Del., 1963; J.D. with distinction, U. Mich., 1966. Bar: Mich. 1967, U.S. Dist. Ct. (ea. dist.) Mich. 1967, U.S. Dist. Ct. (we. dist.) Mich. 1972, U.S. Ct. Appeals (6th cir.) 1974. Assoc. Dykema, Gossett, Spencer, Goodnow & Trigg, Detroit, 1966-71; Parmenter Forsythe, Rude et al, Muskegon, Mich., 1971-73; ptnr. Parmenter, Forsythe, Rude et al, Muskegon, 1973—; Parmenter O'Toole, 1992—. Served to capt. U.S. Army, 1967-68. Mem. ABA, State Bar Mich. Office: Parmenter O'Toole 601 Terrace St PO Box 786 Muskegon MI 49443

FAUSEL, ALAN, art appraiser; BA in Art Hist., UCLA; MA in Art Hist., Stanford Univ. Asst. curator, European sculpture, decorative arts Fine Arts Mus., San Francisco, 1986—89; curator Frick Art Mus., Pittsburgh, 1989—91; dir., European painting dept. and mus. svcs. dept. Butterfield & Butterfield, San Francisco, 1991—94; sr. v.p., dir., painting, drawing dept. Doyle New York, 1994. Adj. lectr. NYU Grad. Sch. Edn.; lectr. Appraisal Assn. Am.; appraiser Antiques Roadshow, WGBH-PBS. Office: Doyle New York 175 E 87th St New York NY 10128 Office Phone: 212-427-4141 ext. 238. Office Fax: 212-369-0892. Business E-Mail: alan@doylenewyork.com.

FAUSOLD, MARTIN LUTHER, history professor; b. Irwin, Pa., Nov. 11, 1921; s. Samuel and Edna (Breegle) F.; m. Daryl Ethel Clement, June 18, 1949 (dec. May 1995); children: Sharon Ann, Cynthia Lynn, Marti Clement, Martin Samuel; m. Marjorie F. Dimpfl, June 22, 1996 (div. Apr. 2005). BA, Gettysburg Coll., 1944; PhD, Syracuse U., 1953. Ptnr. Fausold Dairy Co., Blairsville, Pa., 1946-49; from asst. prof. to prof. history and govt. State U. N.Y., Cortland, 1952-58; prof. history and govt., chmn. social sci. divsn. SUNY, Geneseo, 1959-69, prof. Am. history, 1969-85, disting. svc. prof. Am. history, 1985-92, prof. emeritus, 1992—. Univ. awards com. SUNY, chmn., 1970-78, joint awards coun., 1970-82, dir. oral history project, 1983—; co-dir. permanent exhibit Valley Village Collage SUNY Geneseo. Author: Gifford Pinchot: Bull Moose Progressive, 1961, James W. Wadsworth Jr.: The Gentleman from New York, 1975, The Presidency of Herbert Hoover, 1985, also articles, book reviews to profl. jours.; editor: The Hoover Presidency: A Reappraisal, 1974; co-editor: The Constitution and the American Presidency: A Reappraisal, 1991. Chmn. Cortland Bd. Pub. Works, 1956; trustee Wadsworth Library, 1976-87. Served to lt. (j.g.) USNR, 1942-46. SUNY Faculty Exch. scholar, 1978-92, recipient Disting. Alumni award Gettysburg Coll., 2004. Mem. Faculty Assn. State U. N.Y. (pres. 1964- 67). Democrat. Presbyterian (elder 1968-70, 84-86). Home: Valley Manor 1570 East Ave Apt 315 Rochester NY 14692 Personal E-mail: mlfausold@aol.com.

FAUST, CARRISSIMA WASHINGTON, educational consultant; b. Phila., Feb. 29, 1948; d. Richard Vanderlippe and Carrissíma Hemena Washington; m. Gerald André Faust, June 25, 1995; 1 child, Shanel René. BS in Elem. Edn., Cheyney U., Pa., 1972; MSEd in Urban Edn., Temple U., Phila., 1982; EdD in Ednl. Leadership, Nova Southeastern U., Miami, Fla., 2003. Tchr. adults CITA, Phila., 1973—74; reading tchr. Sch. Dist. Phila., 1975—99, asst. prin., 1999—2003; pvt. practice ednl. cons., 2004—. Named to Gov.'s Inst. Sch. Leadership, Gov. Casy, 1999; recipient Prin.'s award, Jones Mid. Sch., Phila., 1996. Mem.: ASCD, Phi Gamma Sigma. Avocations: reading, needlepoint. Home: 863 Timber Ln Dresher PA 19025-1811 Personal E-mail: faustcg@aol.com.

FAUST, DREW GILPIN (CATHARINE), academic administrator, historian; b. NYC, Sept. 18, 1947; d. McGhee Tyson and Catharine (Mellick) G.; m. Stephen Faust, Dec. 28, 1968 (div. 1976); m. Charles E. Rosenberg, June 7, 1980; 1 child, Jessica Rosenberg, 1 stepdaughter, Leah BA magna cum laude, Bryn Mawr Coll., 1968; MA, U. Pa., Phila., 1971, PhD, 1975; LHD (hon.), Bowdoin Coll., 2007. Asst. prof. Am. civilization U. Pa., Phila., 1976—80, assoc. prof., 1980—84, prof., 1984—89, Stanley I. Sheerr prof. history, 1988—89, Annenberg prof. history, 1989—2000; Lincoln prof. history Harvard U., Cambridge, Md., 2001—, dean Radcliffe Inst. for Advanced Study, 2000—07, pres., 2007—. Walter Lynwood Fleming lectr. La. State U., 1987; mem. ednl. adv. bd. Guggenheim Found., 1988—; cons. Before Freedom Came: African American Life in the Antebellum South, exhbn. at Mus. Confederacy, 1988-91; NEH panel Interpretive Rsch. Program, 1987; mem. Pulitzer Prize History Jury, 1986, 90; lectr. various colls. and univs. Author: A Sacred Circle: The Dilemma of the Intellectual inthe Old South, 1977, paperback edit., 1986, James Henry Hammond and the Old South: A Design for Mastery (Jules F. Landry award, 1982), 1982, The Creation of Confederate Nationalism: Ideology and Identity in the Civil War South, 1988, Southern Stories: Slaveholders in Peace and War, 1992, Mothers of Invention: Women of the Slaveholding South in the American Civil War, 1996 (Avery Craven prize 1996, Honorable metion annual awards, Asn. Am. Pub., 1997, Francis Parkman prize Soc. Am. Hisorians, 1997); mem. editl. bd. Jour. Am. History, 1991—, Pa. Mag. History and Biography, 1986-89, Jour. So. History, 1981-86; contbr. articles to profl. jours. Trustee Andrew Mellon Found. Recipient: Charles Sydnor award, Prize Soc. Historians of Early Am. Republic, 1983, article prize Berkshire Conf. Women's Historians, 1991; U. Pa. Rsch. Found. grantee, 1982; assoc. fellow Stanford Humanities Ctr., Stanford U., 1983-84, Am. Coun. Learned Socs. fellow, 1986, Guggenheim fellow, 1987, Mass. Hist. Soc. fellow, 2002, Elizabeth Hall fellow Concord Acad., 2003; named one of The World's Most Influential People, TIME mag., 2007 Mem. So. Hist. Assn. (chair nominating com. 1993, exec. coun. 1987-90, Frank L. Owsley prize com. 1987, pres. 1999-2000), Am. Hist. Assn. (v.p. profl. divsn. 1992-95, coun. mem. 1992—), Orgn. Am. Historians (chair Avery Craven Prize Com. 1991, 97, chair program com. 1987, mem. coun. 1999-2002), Am. Studies Assn. (mem. coun. 1988-90, Honorable metion Hope Franklin award, 1997), Hist. Soc. Pa. (mem. bd. 1988-91), So. Assn. Women Historians (membership com. 1988-, pres. 1998-99), Am. Acad. Arts & Scis., Am. Philosophical Soc. Office: Office of Pres Harvard U Massachusetts Hall Cambridge MA 02138 E-mail: drew_faust@harvard.edu.

FAUST, EMANUEL, JR., lawyer; b. Columbia, SC, May 1, 1958; BA, U. SC, 1980; JD, Duke U., 1983. Bar: DC 1983, US Dist. Ct. DC 1984. Assoc. Davis Polk & Wardwell, 1983—87, Dickstein Hapiro Morin & Oshinsky LLP, Washington, 1987—92, ptnr., 1992—, co-chmn. diversity com./ quality of life com. Mem.: DC Bar. Office: Dickstein Shapiro Morin & Oshinsky LLP 2101 L St NW Washington DC 20037-1526 Office Phone: 202-861-9127. Office Fax: 202-887-0689. E-mail: fauste@dsmo.com.

FAUST, NAOMI FLOWE, education educator; b. Salisbury, NC; d. Christopher Leroy and Ada Luella (Graham) Flowe; m. Roy Malcolm Faust, Aug. 16, 1948. AB, Bennett Coll., Greensboro, NC; MA, U. Mich., 1945; PhD, NYU, 1963. Tchr. elem. Pub. Schs. Gaffney, SC; tchr. English, French, phys. edn. Atkins HS, Winston-Salem; instr. English Bennett Coll. and So. U., Scotlandville, La., 1944—46; prof. English Morgan State Coll., Balt., 1946—48; tchr. English Greensboro Pub. Schs., NC, 1948—51, NYC Pub. Schs., 1954—63; prof. edn. Queens Coll. of CUNY, Flushing, 1964—82; writer, lectr., poetry readings, 1982—. Lectr. in field. Author: Discipline and the Classroom Teacher, 1977; (poetry) Speaking in Verse, 1974, All Beautiful Things, 1983, And I Travel by Rhythms and Words, 1990, Visions for the 21st Century, 2007; contbr. poetry to jours. Named Tchr.-Author of 1979, Tchr.-Writer; recipient Cert. of Merit for Poem Cooper Hill Writers Conf., 1970, Achievement award LI br. AAUW, 1985, Poet of the Millennium award Internat. Poets Acad., Excellence in World Poetry award Internat. Poets Acad., 2002; named Internat. Eminent Poet, Internat. Poets Acad. Mem. AAUP, AAUW, Acad. Am. Poets, Nat. Coun. Tchrs. English, Nat. Women's Book Assn., Nat. Assn. Univ. Women (LI br.), World Poetry Soc. Intercontinental, NY Poetry Forum, Poetry Soc. Am., NAACP, United Negro Coll. Fund, Alpha Kappa Alpha, Alpha Kappa Mu., Alpha Epsilon. Home: 11201 175th St Jamaica NY 11433-4135

FAUTH, JOHN J., venture capitalist; BS, Georgetown Univ. Vp, sr. credit off. Citicorp U.S.A.; pres., CEO Churchill Industries, Mpls., 1982—; chmn., dir., pres., CEO Churchill Capital, Inc., Mpls., 1987—. Chmn., bd adv, Georgetown Univ. Grad. Sch. Bus. Adminstrn.; bd. dir. Georgetown Univ. Office: Churchill Capital Inc 333 S 7th St Ste 2400 Minneapolis MN 55402-2435

FAVALO, JOHN FRANK, marketing executive; b. Syracuse, NY, July 6, 1946; s. John B. and Alberta C. (Maxon) F.; m. Donna JoAnne Ainslie, Dec. 21, 1968; children: Christina Helene, Jeffrey John. BA, Syracuse U., 1968. Acct. exec. Fred Riger Advt., inc., Binghamton, NY, 1968-69; copywriter V.C. Graphics, Inc., Syracuse, 1969-70; mgmt. supr. Sage Advt., Inc., Syracuse, 1970-80, exec. v.p., 1984-86, pres., 1986; now mng. ptnr. Group B2B Eric Mower & Assoc., Syracuse. Mem. Mayor's Advt. Coun., Syracuse, 1988; adj. prof. S.I. Newhouse Sch. Pub. Comms., Syracuse U. Mem. mktg. com. United Way Central NY, Syracuse, 1987—; mem. Hamilton White Soc., Syracuse, 1988—. Recipient Effie award Am. Mktg. Assn. NY, 1984. Mem.: Inst. for Study of Bus. Markets, Bus. Profl. Advt. Assn., Bus. Mktg. Assn. (chmn. internat. bd. dirs. 2006—07), Bellevue Country Club, Syracuse Ad Club. Republican. Roman Catholic. Avocations: golf, bowling, jogging. Office: EMA Syracuse 500 Plum St Syracuse NY 13204 Office Phone: 315-466-1000. Office Fax: 315-466-2000.*

FAVALORA, JOHN CLEMENT, archbishop; b. New Orleans, Dec. 5, 1935; s. Felix J. and Leona M. (Stevens) F. BA in Philosophy and History, Notre Dame Sem., New Orleans, 1958; STL, Pontifical Gregorian U., Rome, 1962; MEd, Tulane U., 1969. Ordained priest Roman Cath. Ch., 1962. Asst. pastor St. Theresa of the Child Jesus Ch., New Orleans, 1962—70; sec. to archbishop Archdiocese of New Orleans, 1963—65, vice chancellor, 1963—65; vice rector St. John Prep., New Orleans, 1964—67, 1968—71; dir. Office of Permanent Diaconate, New Orleans, 1971—74; adminstrv. asst. Notre Dame Sem., New Orleans, 1971—73, rector-pres., 1981—86; pastor St. Angela Merici Ch., Metairie, La., 1973—79; dir. Office of Vocations, New Orleans, 1979—81; bishop Diocese of Alexandria, La., 1986—89, Diocese of St. Petersburg, Fla., 1989—94; archbishop Diocese of Miami, 1994—. Ecclesiastical notary Archdiocese of New Orleans, 1962—64, pro-synodal judge, 1973—79; dean East Jefferson Deanery, New Orleans, 1974—77; vicar Pastoral Planning, New Orleans, 1976—81; chmn. Permanent Diaconate Adv. Com., New Orleans, 1984; consultor Archdiocese of New Orleans, 1984—86. Office: Archdiocese of Miami Pastoral Ctr 9401 Biscayne Blvd Miami Shores FL 33138

FAVARD, KRISTI, lawyer; b. Glendive, Mont., June 28, 1976; d. Lana Hovland; m. Saurel Favard, Apr. 26, 2002; children: Jasmyn, Tristan. Student, U. Mont., Missoula, 1994—97; BA, Heritage Coll., Toppenish, Wash., 2000; JD, U. Wash., Seattle, 2003. Atty. Bullivant Houser Bailey, Seattle, 2004—06, Groff Murphy, Seattle, 2006—. Office: Groff Murphy 300 E Pine Seattle WA 98122 Home Phone: 206-920-9977; Office Phone: 206-628-9500. Office Fax: 206-628-9506. Business E-Mail: kfavard@groffmurphy.com.

FAVARO, MARY KAYE ASPERHEIM, pediatrician, writer; b. Edgerton, Wis., Sept. 30, 1934; d. Harold Wilbur and Genevieve Catherine (Hyland) Asperheim; m. Biagio Philip Favaro, May 31, 1969; children: Justin Peter, Gina Sue. BS, U. Wis., 1956; MS, St. Louis Coll. Pharmacy, 1965; MD, U. Wis., 1969. Instr. pharmacology St. Louis U. and St. Mary's Hosp. Sch. Practical Nurses, 1959-64; staff pharmacist U. Hosps., Madison, Wis., 1964-65; intern Albany (N.Y.) Med. Center, 1969-70; resident, 1970-71; resident in pediatrics U. S.C., Charleston, 1971-72, asst. prof. pediatrics, 1973-75; pvt. practice pediatrics, 1974-99; ret. Author: Pharmacology, an Introductory Text, 2005; The Pharmacologic Basis of Patient Care, 1985. Mem.: AMA. Roman Catholic. Home: 1407 Southwood Dr Surfside Beach SC 29575 Office Phone: 843-267-6879. Personal E-mail: maryfav@aol.com.

FAVINI, PAUL FUREY, costume designer, educator; b. Scranton, Pa., June 14, 1960; s. Marcel Peter Favini and Elizabeth Jane Furey Favini; life ptnr. John William Reger. AAS, Fashion Inst. Tech., NYC, 1982; BS, U. Scranton, 1987; MFA, Ind. U., Bloomington, 1997. Resident designer Costume World, Deerfield Beach, Fla., 1998—2000; assoc. prof. U. Fla., Gainesville, 2000—. Costume designer: (plays) Man of La Mancha/Phoenix Entertainment; (theatre design) Moonlight and Magnolias/ Cape Playhouse; Tosca- Tri-Cities Opera. Bd. mem. Gainesville Cmty. Alliance, Fla., 2003—05. Named Grad. Mentor of Yr., Coll. Fine Arts, U. Fla., 2004. Mem.: United Scenic Artists, Local 829 (assoc.). Home: 3809 NW 48th Terrace Gainesville FL 32606 Office: University of Florida McGuire Pavilion #204 Gainesville FL 32611-5900 Home Phone: 352-371-6774; Office Phone: 352-273-0525. Office Fax: 352-392-5114. Personal E-mail: paulffavini@aol.com. Business E-Mail: favinip@ufl.edu.

FAVORULE, DENISE, publishing executive; With Ogilvy & Mather Worldwide, 1978—90, v.p., account dir., 1985—90; advt. dir. Stagebill Mag. Primedia, 1993—96; ea. advt. dir. Prevention mag. Rodale Inc., 1996—98, nat. advt. dir. Prevention mag., 1998—99, assoc. pub. Prevention mag., 1999—2000, v.p., pub. Prevention Mag., 2000—04, v.p., group pub. Women's Pub. Group, 2004—05, sr. v.p., mng. dir. Mktg. Solutions Group, 2005; sr. v.p., group pub. dir. Reader's Digest, 2006—07, The Knot, 2007—. Office: The Knot 462 Broadway 6th Fl New York NY 10013*

FAVRE, BRETT LORENZO, professional football player; b. Pass Christian (Gulfport), Miss., Oct. 10, 1969; s. Irvin and Bonita Favre; m. Deanna Tynes, July 14, 1996; children: Brittany, Breleigh. BS in Spl. Edn., So. Miss. U., 1991. Quarterback Atlanta Falcons, 1991—92, Green Bay Packers, 1992—; owner Brett Favre's Steakhouse, Brett Favre's Two Minute Grill. Co-author (with Chris Havel): Favre: For the Record, 1997; co-author: (with Bonita Favre and Chris Havel) Favre, 2004; actor: (films) There's Something About Mary, 1998. Founder Brett Favre Found., 1996. Named to Nat. Football Conf. Pro Bowl Team, 1992, 1993, 1995—97, 2001—03; recipient NFL MVP award, AP, 1995, 1996, 1997, Espy Award for Best Football Player, ESPN, 1996, 1997, Espy Award for Best Moment, 2004. Achievements include the only player in pro fooball history to win the MYP award 3 times, 1995, 1996, 1997; being a member of Super Bowl XXXI Champion Green Bay Packers, 1997; holds the NFL record for career completions, 2006. Office: Green Bay Packers PO Box 10628 Green Bay WI 54307-0628

FAVRE, KELLY ANN, surgeon; b. Milw., Dec. 11, 1970; d. Allen Brian and Connie Ann Cimbalnik; m. Jonathan Keene Favre, Oct. 28, 2000; children: Dean, Derek. BS distinction, U. Wis., Madison, 1993; MD, U. Wis. Med. Sch., Madison, 1997. Diplomate Am. Bd. Gen. Surgery. Gen. surgeon Southwest Surg. Assocs., Tucson, 2002—. Mem.: ACS. Office: Southwest Surg Assocs 1951 N Wilmot Bldg 2 Tucson AZ 85712

FAVREAU, JON, actor, film director, film producer; b. Queens, NY, Oct. 19, 1966; m. Joya Tillem, Nov. 24, 2000; children: Max, Madelaine, Brighton Rose. Actor: (films) Folks!, 1992, Hoffa, 1992, Rudy, 1993, PCU, 1994, Mrs. Parker and the Vicious Circle, 1994, Batman Forever, 1995, Notes From Underground, 1995, Just Your Luck, 1996, Persons Unknown, 1996, Dogtown, 1996, Deep Impact, 1998, Very Bad Things, 1998, Love & Sex, 2000, The Replacements, 2000, Daredevil, 2003, Something's Gotta Give, 2003, Wimbledon, 2004, The Break-Up, 2006, (voice) Open Season, 2006,: (TV films) Grandpa's Funeral, 1994, Rocky Marciano, 1999; (TV series) Ain't It Cool News, 2001, (TV appearances) Seinfeld, 1994, Chicago Hope, 1994, The Larry Sanders Show, 1995, Tracey Takes On., 1996, Friends, 1997, Hercules, 1999, Dilbert, 2000, The Sopranos, 2000, (voice only) Buzz Lightyear of Star Command, 2000, The King of Queens, 2004, My Names Is Earl, 2006; actor, prodr., writer: (films) Swingers, 1996; actor, prodr., writer, dir. Made, 2001; actor, prodr. The Big Empty, 2003; actor, dir. Elf, 2003; dir.: Zathura, 2005; writer, dir., prodr.: (TV films) Smog, 1999; dir.: Life on Parole, 2003; prodr.: (TV series) Undeclared, 2001; exec. prodr., host (TV series) Dinner for Five, 2001—; exec. prodr.: (TV films) Hooligans, 2005; writer: (films) The First $20 Million Is Always the Hardest, 2002. Office: c/o Creative Artists Agy Inc 9830 Wilshire Blvd Beverly Hills CA 90212*

FAWBUSH, ANDREW JACKSON, lawyer; b. Miami, Fla., Oct. 7, 1946; s. Andrew T. Fawbush; m. Melinda Wheeley, Dec. 18, 1982; children: Andrew J. Jr., Tyler S., Karin J., Michelle L. BSBA in Acctg., with high honors, U. Fla., 1972, JD, 1974. Bar: Fla. 1975, DC 1994, NY 1995. Assoc. Smith & Hulsey, Jacksonville, Fla., 1975-80, ptnr., 1980-88, LeBoeuf, Lamb, Greene & MacRae LLP, Jacksonville, 1988—, chmn. employee benefits dept., 1993-95, mng. ptnr. Fla. office. Contbg. author The Tax Lawyer. Bd. dirs. YMCA, Jacksonville, 1981-83; bd. dirs., past pres. Employee Benefits Coun. N.E. Fla.; bd. dirs., exec. com. Gator Boosters, Inc.; trustee, tchr. Cert. Employee Benefits Specialists, U. North Fla., 1982-88, Southside United Methodist Church; bd. dirs. U. Fla. Found., 1993. With U.S. Army, 1968-70. Mem. ABA - Tax Sect. (employee benefits com.), Fla. Bar Assn. (spkr. employee benefit sect. 1983-88), D.C. Bar Assn., N.Y. Bar Assn., U. Fla. Alumni Assn. (bd. dirs. 1987-98, pres. 1994), Jacksonville C. of C. (gen. counsel, sports coun., mem. exec. com.), U. Fla. Athletic Assn. (v.p., bd. dirs.). Office: LeBoeuf Lamb Greene MacRae 50 N Laura St Ste 2800 Jacksonville FL 32202-3634 Office Phone: 904-630-5340. Office Fax: 904-353-1673. Business E-Mail: afawbush@llgm.com.

FAWCETT, CHARLES WINTON, lawyer; b. Long Beach, Calif., May 26, 1946; s. Phillip Nimmons and Beatrice Stricker (Winton) F.; m. Kathleen Gloria Mayes, Dec. 15, 1975; children: Reid Charles, Tracie Diane, Ryan Mayes, Marni Taylor. BA, U. Calif., Santa Barbara, 1968; JD, U. Calif., Berkeley, 1971. Bar: Idaho 1971, Wash. 1975, U.S. Tax Ct. 1982. Staff atty. Idaho Legal Aid Services, Lewiston, 1971-73, Caldwell, 1973-74; adminstrv. law judge State of Wash., Seattle, 1974-76; asst. atty. gen. State of Idaho, Boise, 1976-77; sr. ptnr. Skinner Fawcett, Boise, 1977—. Contbr. articles to law jour. Mem. Idaho Bar Assn., Boise Bar Assn., Nat. Assn. Bond Lawyers, Comml. Law League Am. Office: Skinner Fawcett PO Box 700 Boise ID 83701-0700

FAWCETT, CHRISTOPHER BABCOCK, civil engineer, construction and water resources company executive; b. NYC, Dec. 17, 1951; s. George Gifford Fawcett Jr. and Andi Adams Emerson; m. Nina Beth Williamson, June 20, 1986 (div. Aug. 1993); 1 child, Kyle Christopher Adams. Student, U. Okla., 1969—72, Concordia U., Montreal, Que., Can., 1979—81; BS, Clarkson U., 1984. Lic. civil engr.; registered civil engr., NY. Owner C.B.F. Handyman Co., NYC, 1974-77; v.p., gen. mgr. Fawcett & Fawcett, Inc., NYC, 1977-84; project mgr. U.S. Army Corps Engrs., NYC, 1985-86; asst. project mgr. N. Kruger Constrn., Inc., Locust Valley, NY, 1986-87; project mgr., engr. Finch, Pruyn & Co., Inc., Glens Falls, NY, 1987-98; propr. Caton Hill Enterprises, 1992—; sr. project mgr. and project exec. Santa Fe Constrn., Inc., NYC, 2002—04; sr. project mgr. J.H. Mack, LLC, Teaneck, NJ, 2004—05; sr. project mgr. preconstrn. svcs. Plaza Constrn. Corp., NYC, 2005—06. Judge HS sci. and engring. event NY Acad. Scis., NYC, 2003-07; founder, past chmn. Tri-County Nat. Engrs. Week and Nat. Jr. HS Mathcounts Competition programs, Glens Falls, 1987-98; founding sponsor Challenger Ctr. Space Sci. Edn.; bd. dirs., treas. 16 E 96th St. Corp., 2003-05. Mem. NSPE, ASCE, NY Acad. Scis., Nat. Space Soc. (charter), Engrs. for Edn., Order of Engr., Cousteau Soc., Masons. Avocation: scuba diving. Office: Caton Hill Enterprises 16 E 96th St Ste 2A New York NY 10128-

FAWCETT, DAVID B., III, lawyer; b. Pitts., Aug. 5, 1958; BA, Carnegie Mellon Univ., 1980; JD, Univ. Pitts., 1985. Bar: Pa. 1985. Shareholder, litig. sect. Buchanan Ingersoll PC, Pitts. Trustee Carnegie Mus., Pitts., Carnegie Libr., Pitts.; mem. Allegheny County Council, Allegheny County Bd. Elections. Mem.: ABA, Pa. Bar Assn., Allegheny County Bar Assn. Office: Buchanan Ingersoll PC 20th Fl One Oxford Ctr 301 Grant St Pittsburgh PA 15219-1410 Office Phone: 412-562-3931. Office Fax: 412-562-1041. Business E-Mail: fawcettdb@bipc.com.

FAWCETT, DON WAYNE, retired anatomist; b. Springdale, Iowa, Mar. 14, 1917; s. Carlos J. and Mabel (Kennedy) F.; m. Dorothy Marie Secrest, 1941; children: Robert S., Mary Elaine, Donna, Joseph. AB cum laude, Harvard, 1938, MD, 1942; DSc (hon.), U. Siena, Italy, 1974, NY Med. Coll., 1975, U. Chgo., 1977, U. Cordoba, Argentina, 1978; MD (hon.), U. Heidelberg, Germany, 1977; DVM (hon.), Justus Liebig U., Giessen-Lahn, Germany, 1977; DSc (hon.), Georgetown U., 1987, U. Rome, 1997. Intern surgery Mass. Gen Hosp., Boston, 1942-43; instr. anatomy Harvard Med. Sch., 1946-48, asso. anatomy, 1948-51, asst. prof. anatomy, 1951-55, Hersey prof. anatomy, 1958-80, James Stillman prof. comparative anatomy, 1962-80, sr. asso. dean preclin. affairs, 1975-77; prof. anatomy Cornell Med. Coll., 1955-58; scientist Internat. Lab. Research on Animal Diseases, Nairobi, Kenya, 1980-85. Author: The Cell, 1966, 2d edit., 1981, Textbook of Histology, 1968, 10th edit., 1975, 11th edit., 1986, 12th edit., 1993. Served as capt. M.C. AUS, 1943-46; bn. surgeon A.A.A. John and Mary Markle scholar med. sci., 1949-54; recipient Lederle Med. Faculty award, 1954 Fellow Am. Acad. Arts and Sci., Nat. Acad. Sci. US, Royal Microscopical Soc. (hon.); mem. AAAS, NY Acad. Sci., Am. Assn. Anatomists (pres. 1964- 65, Henry Gray award 1983, Centennial medal 1987), NY Soc. Electron Microscopists (pres. 1957-58), Histochem. Soc., Tissue Culture Assn. (v.p. 1954-55), Soc. Exptl. Biology and Medicine, Assn. Anatomy Chairmen (pres. 1973-74), Am. Soc. Zoologists, Am. Soc. Mammalogists, Electron Microscope Soc. Am. (Disting. Scientist award in Life Scis. 1989), Soc. Study Devel. and Growth, Harvey Soc., Am. Soc. Cell Biology (pres. 1961-62), Argentine Nat. Acad. Sci., Anat. Soc. So. Africa (hon.), Japanese Anat. Soc. (hon.), Anat. Soc. Australia and N.Z. (hon.), Japanese Electron Microscope Soc., Internat. Fedn. Soc. Electron Microscopy (pres. 1976-78), Am. Soc. Andrology (pres. 1977-78), Soc. Study Reprodn. (Carl Hartman award 1985), Mexican (hon.), Canadian (hon.) Assn. Anatomists. Home: 3710 American Way Apt 325 Missoula MT 59808-1927 Business E-Mail: dfawcett11@bresnan.net.

FAWCETT, JOHN SCOTT, real estate developer; b. Pitts., Nov. 5, 1937; s. William Hagen and Mary Jane (Wise) F.; m. Anne Elizabeth Mitchell, Dec. 30, 1960; children: Holly Anne, John Scott II (dec.). BS, Ohio State U., 1959. Dist. dealer rep. Shell Oil Co., San Diego, 1962-66; dist. real estate rep. Shell Oil, Phoenix, 1967-69, region real estate rep. San Francisco, 1970-71, head office land investments rep. Houston, 1972-75; pres., CEO Marinita Devel. Co., Newport Beach, Calif., 1976—. Lectr. in land devel. related fields. With U.S. Army, 1960-61. Named Ky. Col., Gov. Ky., 1996; named to Hall of Fame, Assn. Corp. Real Estate Exec., 2005. Mem. Internat. Coun. Shopping Ctrs., Internat. Right of Way Assn., Internat. Inst. Valuers, Inst. Bus. Appraisers, Nat. Assn. Rev. Appraisers and Mortgage Underwriters, Am. Assn. Cert. Appraisers, Urban Land Inst., Nat. Assn. Real Estate Execs. (pres. LA chpt. 1975), Calif. Lic. Contractors Assn., Bldg. Industry Assn., U.S. C. of C., Town Hall of Calif., Ohio State U. Alumni Assn., Toastmasters (pres. Scottsdale Ariz. club 1968, pres. Hospitality T club 1964), U. Athletic Club, Phi Kappa Tau. Republican. Roman Catholic. Avocations: antiques, tennis, skiing. Home: 8739 Hudson River Cir Fountain Valley CA 92708-5503 Office: Marinita Devel Co 3835 Birch St Newport Beach CA 92660-2600 Office Phone: 949-756-8677. Business E-Mail: scott@marinita.com.

FAWCETT, JOHN THOMAS, archivist; b. West Branch, Iowa, Nov. 27, 1943; s. Floyd Thomas and Mary Helen (Miller) F.; m. Sharon Atchison, July 25, 1971 (div. 1993); children: Allen, Katherine BA, U. Iowa, 1966; MA, U. Tex., 1978. Archivist, mus. tech. Herbert Hoover Libr., West Branch, Iowa, 1962-67; asst. acting dir., exec. dir. Herbert Hoover Libr. and Assn., West Branch, Iowa, 1983-87; archivist Office Presdl. Librs., Washington, 1967-68, supervisory and acting dir., 1978-83, asst. archivist, 1987-95; mil. aide to President of U.S. Exec. Office, Austin, Tex., 1968-70; supervisory archivist Lyndon B. Johnson Libr., Austin, 1970-78; pres. John T. Fawcett and Assocs., Inc., Washington, 1995—. Trustee Woodrow Wilson Presdl. Libr., 2002—. Mem. exec. bd. Boy Scouts Am., 1984-87; archives cons. Baylor U., 2004- Mem. Masons, Kiwanis (pres. 1985) Personal E-mail: jtfawcett@gmail.com.

FAWCETT, JOY LYNN, retired professional soccer player; b. Inglewood, Calif., Feb. 8, 1968; m. Walter Fawcett; children: Katelyn Rose, Carli, Madilyn Rae. Degree in phys. edn., U. Calif., Berkeley, 1990. Women's soccer coach UCLA, 1993-97, 1993—97; mem. U.S. Nat. Women's Soccer Team, 1987—2004; profl. soccer player San Diego Spirit, 2001—03. Named 3-time All-Am., 1987—89, Most Valuable Player, So. Calif., L.A. Times, 1987, World Cup Champion, 1991, 1999, MVP, WUSA, 2002, Defender of Yr., 2002; named to, U. Calif. Berkeley Hall of Fame, 1997; recipient Silver medal, Sydney Olympics, 2000. Achievements include 1995 FIFA World Cup, Sweden; 1994 CONCACAF Qualifying Championship, Montreal; U.S. Olympic Festival, Denver, 1995; FIFA Women's World Cup, Sweden, 1995; gold medal U.S. Women's Soccer Team, Atlanta Olympic Games, 1996, Athens Olympic Games, 2004; mem. Ajax of Manhattan Beach Club Soccer Team (champions U.S. Women's Amateur Nat. Cup, 1992, 93). Office: US Soccer Fedn 1801-1811 S Prairie Ave Chicago IL 60616

FAWCETT, MATTHEW KNOWLTON, lawyer; b. NYC; m. Christine Anderson; children: Paxton, Ainsley. B in rhetoric, U. Calif. Berkeley, 1989; LLD, UCLA, 1992. With Proskauer Rose, San Francisco, 1992—94, Morrison & Foerster, 1994—97, Fujitsu Am. Inc., 1997—99, E-Tech Dynamics, 1999—2000, JDS Uniphase Corp., San Francisco, 2000—, v.p., gen. counsel. Office: JDS Uniphase Corp 1768 Automation Pkwy San Jose CA 95131*

FAWCETT, SHARON KAY ATCHISON, archivist; b. Abilene, Kans., May 13, 1946; d. Marvin Eugene and Janelda Rae (Durand) Atchison; m. John T. Fawcett, July 25, 1970 (div. Nov. 1993); children: Allen Atchison, Katherine Durand. BA, U. Tex., 1967, MLS, 1969. Archivist Lyndon B. Johnson Libr., Austin, Tex., 1969-77; cons., West Branch, Iowa, 1983-88; asst. br. chief gen. reference dept. The Nat. Archives & Records Adminstrn., Washington, 1977-79, chief reference svcs. br., 1988—93, dir. user svcs. divsn., 1993—96, dep. asst. archivist for presdl. libraries, 1997—2004, asst. archivist for presdl. libraries, 2004—. Lectr. Modern Archives Inst., Washington, 1991-94. Pres. sch. bd. Montessori Sch. No. Va., Annandale, 1981-82; mem. sch. bd. West Branch Ind. Sch. Dist., 1987-88. Recipient Disting. Svc. award Nat. Inst. Geneal. Rsch., 1992. Office: The Nat Archives & Records Adminstrn 8601 Adelphi Rd College Park MD 20740-6002

FAWCETT, SHERWOOD LUTHER, lab administrator; b. Youngstown, Ohio, Dec. 25, 1919; s. Luther T. and Clara (Sherwood) F.; m. Martha L. Simcox, Feb. 28, 1953; children: Paul, Judith, Tom. BS, Ohio State U., 1941, PhD (hon.); MS, Case Inst. Tech., 1948, PhD, 1950; PhD (hon.), Gonzaga U., Whitman Coll., Otterbein Coll., Detroit Inst. Tech., Ohio Dominican Coll. Registered profl. engr., Ohio. Mem. staff Columbus (Ohio) Labs. Battelle Meml. Inst., 1950-64, mgr. physics dept., 1959-64; dir. Pacific Northwest Labs., Richland, Wash., 1964-67; trustee Battelle Meml. Inst., Columbus, 1968-92, exec. v.p., 1967-68, CEO, 1968-84, pres., 1968-80, chmn., 1981-84, chmn. bd. trustees, 1985-87, assoc. trustee, 1987-94. Chmn. bd. dirs. Transmet Corp. With USNR, 1941-46. Decorated Bronze Star; recipient Washington award Western Soc. Engrs., 1989. Mem. AIME, NSPE, Am. Phys. Soc., Am. Nuc. Soc., Am. Phys. Soc., Sigma Xi, Tau Beta Pi, Delta Chi, Sigma Pi Sigma. Home: 1852A Riverside Dr Columbus OH 43212-1875 Office: Transmet Corp 4290 Perimeter Dr Columbus OH 43228-1036 Business E-Mail: tmc@transmet.com.

FAWCETT-YESKE, MAXINE ANN, music educator; m. Robert Yeske. BS in Music, U. Colo., Denver, 1983; MusM, U. Nebr., Omaha, 1987; PhD in Music, U. Colo., Boulder, 1997. Tchr. U. Colo., Boulder, Met. State Coll., Denver; asst. prof. music Truman State U., Kirksville, Mo., 1997—99; assoc. prof. music Nebr. Wesleyan U., Lincoln, 1999—. Contbr. articles to profl. jours.; contbg. author: Women and Music in America Since 1900: An Encyclopedia. Recipient US Prof. of Yr. award for State of Nebr., Carnegie Found. for Advancement of Tchg. and Coun. for Advancement and Support of Edn., 2006. Mem.: Soc. for Am. Music, Am. Musicological Soc., Nebr. Music Educators Assn., Nat. Assn. Music Educators, Delta Kappa Gamma, Pi Kappa Lambda. Office: Nebr Wesleyan U 5000 Saint Paul Ave Lincoln NE 68504 Office Phone: 402-465-2291. E-mail: mfy@nebrwesleyan.edu.

FAWLEY, JOHN JONES, retired banker; b. Phila., Oct. 1, 1921; s. James L. and Edna (Jones) F.; m. Ann Kemp, Jan. 8, 1944; children: Jo Ann (Mrs. Richard High), Christine, James K. BS in Econs, U. Pa., 1948; grad., Rutgers U., 1957. With First Pa. Bank, Phila., 1948-69, sr. v.p., 1968-69; pres., dir. United Va. Bank/First & Citizens Nat. Bank, Alexandria, Va., 1969-72; exec. v.p. Indsl. Valley Bank, Phila., 1973-83, Dauphin Deposit Bank, Harrisburg, Pa., 1983-87. Lectr. Comml. Lending Sch., U. Okla.,

1969 Former trustee Hahnemann U. With AUS, 1942-45. Mem. Robert Morris Assocs. (nat. pres. 1972-73), Masons. Home: Brittany Pointe Estates #2214 1001 Valley Ford Rd Lansdale PA 19446 also: Pinecrest Lake Pocono Pines PA 18350

FAWSETT, PATRICIA COMBS, federal judge; b. 1943; BA, U. Fla., 1965, MAT, 1966, JD, 1973. Pvt. practice law Akerman, Senterfitt & Edison, Orlando, Fla., 1973-86; commr. 9th Cir. Jud. Nominating Commn, 1973-75, Greater Orlando Crime Prevention Assn., 1983-86; judge US Dist. Ct. (Mid. Dist.) Fla., Orlando, 1986—, chief judge. Trustee Legal Aid Soc., 1977-81, Loch Haven Art Ctr., Inc., Orlando, 1980-84, U. Fla. Law Sch., 2001—; hon. trustee Reago Spiritual Scholarship Found., 1999—; commr. Orlando Housing Authority, 1976-80, Winter Park (Fla.) Sidewalk Festival, 1973-75; bd. dirs. Greater Orlando Area C. of C., 1982-85. Mem. ABA (trial lawyers sect., real estate probate sect.), Am. Judicaturs Soc., Assn. Trial Lawyers Am., Fla. Bar Found. (bd. dirs. grants com.), Commn. on Access to Cts., Fla. Coun. Bar Assn. Pres.'s (pres., bd. dirs. 9th cir. grievance com.) Osceola County Bar Assn., Fla. Bar (bd. govs. 1983-86, budget com., disciplinary rev. com., integration rule and bylaws com., com. on access to legal system, bd. of cert., designation and advt., jud. adminstrn., selection and tenure com., jud. nominating procedures com., pub. rels. com., ann. meeting com., appellate rules com., spl. com. on judiciary-trial lawyer rels., chairperson midyr. conv. com., bd. dirs. trial lawyers sect.), Orange County Bar Assn. (exec. coun. 1977-83, pres. 1981-82), Order of Coif, Phi Beta Kappa. Office: US Dist Ct Federal Bldg 80 N Hughey Ave Ste 611 Orlando FL 32801-2231

FAX, CHARLES SAMUEL, lawyer; b. Balt., Sept. 12, 1948; s. David Hirsch and Eleanor Shirley (Lobe) F.; m. Nancy Lee Gruenberg, 1980 (div. 1995); children: Joanna May, Benjamin Zachary; m. Michele Weil, 1996. BA, Johns Hopkins U., Balt., 1970; JD with honors, George Wash. U., Washington, DC, 1973. Bar: DC 1974, NY 1974, Md. 1990. Office of dist. atty., NYC (Bronx county), 1973-74; assoc. Chapman, Duff & Paul, Washington, 1975-79, ptnr., 1979-84, Porter, Wright, Morris & Arthur, Washington, 1985-89; sr. ptnr., co-chmn. lit. dept. Shapiro Sher Guinot & Sandler (formerly Shapiro and Olander), Balt., 1989—2006; mem. exec. com. Shapiro Sher Guinot & Sandler, Balt., 1999—2005; counsel Rifkin, Livingston Levitan & Silver, Greenbelt, Md., 2006—; gen. counsel Parents and Children Together, Inc., 1992-98; apptd. mediator Cir. Ct. for Balt. City, 1994-98; spl. outside litigation counsel Commonwealth P.R. Dept. Justice, 1998-2001, Balt. City Mayor, 1994—95. Mem. faculty Exec. Enterprises, Inc., NYC, Chgo., 1985-86; lectr. fed. personnel litigation Adminstrv. Law Inst., Washington, Chgo., San Francisco, 1982-83; lectr. Md. Mcpl. League, 1990-98; book rev. Cleve. Plain Dealer. Co-author: Discovery Problems and Their Solutions, 2005; online editor: Litig. News online, 2006—; contbr. articles to newspapers and mags. Mem. Washington com. Sch. Arts and Scis., Johns Hopkins U., 1987—89; class of '70 agt. Johns Hopkins U., 1995—; chmn. Jewish Nat. Fund Nat. Makor Leadership Group, 2004—; nat. bd. trustees Jewish Nat. Fund, 2004—, bd. dirs. Md. region, 2002—, chmn. exec. com., 2002—03, chmn. Md. region ann. campaign, 2002, pres., 2003—05, pres. Mid-Atlantic zone, 2005—; bd. dirs. Am. Friends of Haifa Music Festival, 2002—03. Mem. Johns Hopkins U. Soc. for 2d Decade, Tudor and Stuart Club, Johns Hopkins Club, Alpha Delta Phi. Democrat. Jewish. Home: 10720 Gloxinia Dr North Bethesda MD 20852-3404 Office: Rifkin Livningston Levitan & Silver 6305 Ivy Ln Ste 500 Greenbelt MD 20770 Home Phone: 301-468-1053; Office Phone: 301-345-7700.

FAXON, ALICIA CRAIG, art educator, department chairman; b. NYC, July 27, 1931; d. William Donald and Clara Alicia (Harnecker) Craig; m. Richard Bremer Faxon, Feb. 21, 1953; children: Richard Paul, Thomas Hardwick. AB, Vassar Coll., 1952; MA, Radcliffe Coll., 1953, Boston U., 1971, PhD, 1979; DHL (hon.), Simmons Coll., 1998. Lectr. New Eng. Sch. Art and Design, Boston, 1974-77; acting dir. Danforth Mus., Framingham, Mass., 1977; teaching assoc. Boston U. Sch. for Art, 1978-79; vis. lectr. Simmons Coll., Boston, 1979-80, asst. prof. art, 1980-86, assoc. prof., 1986-91, chmn. dept. art and music, 1987-93, prof. art, 1991-93, alumnae endowed chair, 1992-93. Lectr. Sch. for Lifelong Learning, Harvard U., Cambridge, Mass., 1978-80; program chmnn. Women's Studies Adv. Bd., 1982-84; R.I. editor Art New Eng., 1994-99. Author: Catalog Raisonnè of Prints of J.-L. Forain, 1982, Pilgrims and Pioneers, 1987, Dante Gabriel Rossetti, 1989; co-author: (with Liana Cheney and Kathleen Russo) Self-Portraits of Woman Painters, 2000; co-editor (with Susan Casteras) Pre-Raphaelite Art in its European Context, 1995; mem. editl. bd. Woman's Art Jour., 1989—. Mem. acquisitions com. Danforth Mus., 1974—89, trustee, 1975—77. Recipient Nan award for art criticism Art New Eng., 1987; grantee Nat. Endowment for Arts, 1982, Simmons Coll., 1984, NEH, 1989, 92. Mem. Coll. Art Assn. (chmn. pre-Raphaelite session 1990), Pre-Raphaelites and the Myth Image (chmn. 2005, chmn. creating culture in 19th century Boston session 2007), Women's Caucus for Art (program co-chmn. 1986-88), Victorian Soc., 19th Century Art Historians Group, Vassar Coll. Alumnae Assn. Democrat. Episcopalian. Avocations: travel, writing.

FAXON, ROGER, music company executive; BA, Johns Hopkins U. Exec. v.p./COO Lucasfilm Ltd., Calif., 1980—84; founding ptnr. Mount Co., Calif., 1984—86; sr. exec. v.p. Columbia Pictures, Calif., 1986—90; COO N.Am. & South Am. ops. Sotheby's, NYC; CEO Sotheby's Europe, London; sr. v.p. worldwide bus. devel. & strategy EMI, 1994—99; exec. v.p. & CFO EMI Music Pub., 1999—2002, pres. & COO, 2005—06, pres. & co-CEO, 2006—07, chmn. & CEO, 2007—; CFO & exec. dir. EMI Group plc, London, 2002—05. Bd. dirs. EMI Group plc, London. Mem.: Nat. Music Publishers' Assn. (bd. dirs. 2007—), ASCAP (bd. dirs. 2005—). Office: EMI Music Publishing 42nd Fl 1290 Ave of the Americas New York NY 10104 Office Phone: 212-492-1200. Office Fax: 212-492-1865.*

FAY, ABBOTT EASTMAN, history professor; b. Scottsbluff, Nebr., July 19, 1926; s. Abbott Eastman and Ethel (Lambert) F.; m. Joan D. Richardson, Nov. 26, 1953; children: Rand, Diana, Collin. Grad., Scottsbluff Jr. Coll., Nebr.; BA, Colo. State Coll. Edn., 1949, MA, 1953; postgrad., U. Denver, 1961-63; cert. advanced study, Western State U., 1963. Tchr. Leadville (Colo.) Pub. Schs., 1950-52, elem. prin., 1952-54; prin. Leadville Jr. H.S., 1954-55; pub. info. dir., instr. history Mesa Coll., Grand Junction, Colo., 1955-64; asst. prof. history Western State Coll., Gunnison, Colo., 1964-76, assoc. prof. history, 1976-82, assoc. prof. emeritus, 1982—. Adj. faculty Adams State Coll., Alamosa, Colo., Mesa State Coll., Grand Junction, Colo., 1989—; propr. Mountaintop Books, Paonia, Colo.; bd. dirs. Colo. Assoc. Univ. Press; dir. hist. tours; columnist Valley Chronicle, Paonia, Beacon, Grand Junction, Free Press, Grand Junction, The Historian, Fruita, Colo., Grand Mesa Byway News, Delta, Colo.; profl. speaker in field; cons. Colo. Welcome Ctr., 1997—. Author: Mountain Academia, 1968, Writing Good History Research Papers, 1980, Ski Tracks in the Rockies, 1984, Famous Coloradans, 1990, I Never Knew That About Colorado, 1993, Beyond The Great Divide, 1999, To Think That This Happened in Grand County!, 1999, A History of Skiing in Colorado, 2000, More That I Never Knew About Colorado, 2000, The Story of Colorado Wines, 2002, Grand Mesa Country, 2005; playwright: Thunder Mountain Lives Tonight!; contbr. articles to profl. jours.; freelance writer popular mags. Founder, coord. Nat. Energy Conservation Challenge; travel cons. Colo. State Welcome Ctr., 1997-99; project reviewer NEH, Colo. Hist. Soc.; steering com. West Elk Scenic & Historic Byway, Colo., 1994—; founder Leadville (Colo.) Assembly, pres., 1953-54; mem. Advs. of Lifelong Learning, 1994—. Named Top Prof. Western State Coll., 1969, 70, 71; fellow Hamline U. Inst. Asian Studies, 1975, 79; recipient Colo. Ind. Pubs. award, 1998. Mem. Western Writers Am., Rocky Mountain Social Sci. Assn. (sec. 1961-63), Am. Hist. Assn., Assn. Asian Studies, Western History Assn., Western State Coll. Alumni Assn. (pres. 1971-73), Internat. Platform Assn. Profl. Guides Assn. Am. (cert.), Rocky Mountain Guides Assn., Colo. Antiquarian Booksellers Assn., Am. Legion (Outstanding Historian award 1981), Phi Alpha Theta, Phi Kappa Delta, Delta Kappa Pi. Home: 679 Brentwood Dr 11A Palisade CO 81526

FAY, CONNER MARTINDALE, retired marketing executive; b. Chillicothe, Mo., May 9, 1929; s. Vernon Martindale and Corinne (Conner) F.; m. Evelyn Caffey Buford, Dec. 2, 1961; children: Leslie Conner Francesca, Buford Martindale Edoardo, David Curtis Anselmo. BA, Yale U., 1951; MBA cum laude, Harvard U., 1953. Brand mgr. Procter & Gamble Co., Cin., 1956-62; mktg. mgr. Procter & Gamble Co. Italia, Rome, 1962-69; sr. v.p. Clairol Inc., NYC, 1970-89; mgmt. cons., 1989-93; ret., 1993. Mem. bd. fgn. parishes Am. Episcopal Ch., N.Y., 1977-2005, pres., 1989-2005; bd. dirs. St. Paul's Ch., Rome, 1977-2005, pres., 1989-2001; bd. dirs. St. James Ch., Florence, Italy, 1977-2005, pres., 1989-2000; vice chmn. St. Stephen's Sch., Rome, 1980-94; trustee Samuel and Lois Silberman Fund of N.Y. Cmty. Trust, 1993—; sr. warden St. Mary the Virgin Episcopal Ch., Chappaqua, N.Y., 1982-83, 91-93; chmn. coun. of advisors Hunter Sch. Social Work, CUNY, 1985-97; various offices Yale Alumni Fund, including chmn., 1996-98, agt., 1996—, 50th and 55th reunion spl. gifts co-chair Class of 1951; bd. dirs. Yale Alumni Chorus Found., 2003—, v.p., 2004—; bd. dirs. Katonah Mus. Art, 1995—, treas., 2001-03. Recipient Yale medal, 2000. Mem. Am. Indsl. Health Coun. (bd. dirs. 1979-91, chmn. 1988-89), Yale Glee Club Assocs. (pres. 1979-81, treas. 1996-2001, medal 2007), Yale Club NYC. Democrat. Avocation: music. Business E-Mail: conner.fay@aya.yale.edu.

FAY, CRAIG ALAN, engineering executive; b. Rochester, NY, Dec. 13, 1949; s. Robert E. Fay and Dorothy Mae Lynch; m. Pauline Anne Stoddart, Aug. 26, 1972; 1 child, James Robert. BA in Polit. Sci. and History, U. Rochester, 1983. Nat. security agy. Govt., Washington, 1976—79; mgr. software sys. Structured Broker Support, Albuquerque, 2005—06; mgr. QA engring. Thornburg Mortgage, Santa Fe, 2006—. Vol. LA Sheriff's Dept., Monrovia, 1995—2002. Staff sgt. USAF, 1969—76. Mem.: MENSA. Independent. Home Phone: 505-280-0253. Business E-Mail: cfay@thornburgmortgage.com.

FAY, DONALD P., lawyer; m. Patricia W. Fay; children: Carolyn J., Catherine A. BSME, MME, JD, So. Meth. U. Atty. comml. law dept. Johnson & Wortley PC; sr. counsel HCA Inc., 1993—94, v.p. legal, 1994—97, sr. v.p. Pacific Group, 1998—99; exec. v.p., gen. counsel, corp. sec. Triad Hospitals Inc., Plano, Tex., 1999—2005; atty. Johnson & Gibbs, Dallas, 2005—.*

FAY, GLENN MILLS, JR., science educator; b. Middlebury, Vt., July 3, 1954; s. Glenn Mills Sr. and Virginia Field (Powers) F.; m. Donna Sutton, Jul. 11, 1987; children: Addison, Lillian. BS, U. Vt., 1976, EdD, 1995; MEd, Colo. State U., 1981. Sci. tchr. Lake Region Union H.S., Orleans, Vt., 1976—79, Shelburne (Vt.) Mid. Sch., 1982—83, Champlain Valley H.S., Hinesbury, Vt., 1983—. Adj. prof. U. Vt. Burlington, Trinity Coll. Vt. Author: Science in the Service of Reform, 1992; contbr. articles to profl. jours. Recipient Gustav Ohaus award NSTA Ohaus, 1990, Scimat fellowship NSF, 1993, Presdl. award in Excellence in Teaching NSF, 1993. Mem. Vt. Sci. Tchrs. Assn. (bd. dirs. 1991—), Vt. Profl. Standards Bd (bd. dirs. 1995-2001), Nat. Sci. Tchrs. Assn. Avocations: running, hiking. Home: PO Box 177 South Hero VT 05486-0177 Office: Champlain Valley Union HS 369 CVU Rd Hinesburg VT 05461-9403

FAY, JAMES ALAN, mechanical engineering educator; b. Southold, NY, Nov. 1, 1923; s. William Joseph, Jr. and Margaret (Keenan) F.; m. Agatha Marie Kelly, Jan. 12, 1946; children: David Anthony, Mark Bernard, Colin Michael, Jamie Martin, Peter Robert, Michele Marie. BS, Webb Inst. Naval Architecture, 1944; MS, MIT, 1947; PhD, Cornell U., 1951. Research engr. Lima-Hamilton Corp., 1947-49; asst. prof. engring. mechanics Cornell U., 1951-55; mem. faculty MIT, 1955-89, prof. mech. engring., 1960-89, prof. emeritus, 1989—. Cons. to govt. and industry; mem. NRC Environ. Studies Bd., 1973-78, 80-83 Author: (Text books) Molecular Thermodynamics, 1965, Introduction to Fluid Mechanics, 1994, Energy and the Environment, 2002; contbr. articles to profl. jours. Chmn. Boston Air Pollution Commn., 1969-72, Mass. Port Authority, 1972-77; bd. dirs. Union Concerned Scientists, 1978—, Conservation Law Found., 1984-94. Served with USNR, 1942-46. Overseas fellow Churchill Coll., Cambridge U., 1980; Fulbright lectr., India, 1990. Fellow Am. Acad. Arts and Scis., Am. Phys. Soc. (exec. com. div. fluid dynamics 1964-67), AAAS, AIAA (chmn. plasmadynamics com. 1966-68); mem. NAE, ASME, Air and Waste Mgmt. Assn., Sigma Xi. Home: 36 Spruce Hill Rd Weston MA 02493-2134 Office: MIT Rm 3-258 Cambridge MA 02139-4307 Office Phone: 617-253-2236. Business E-Mail: jfay@mit.edu.

FAY, KEVIN J., public relations executive; Grad., U. Va.; JD, Am. U. Bar: Va. With Alcalde & Fay, Arlington, Va., 1982—; pres. Exec. dir. Internat. Climate Change Partnership; counsel Alliance for Responsible Atmosphere Policy. Mem. bd. govs. Bishop Denis J. O'Connell HS; bd. dirs. World Children's Choir; mem. exec. com. Leukemia Soc. Ball; mem. Fairfax County Pk. Authority Bd. Named Citizen of Yr., McLean Times and Providence Jour.; recipient Lord Fairfax award, Fairfax County Bd. Supervisors, 2000, Cath. Schools Bus. Partnership award, Cath. Bus. Network No. Va., 1999, 2000. Office: Alcalde & Fay 2111 Wilson Blvd 8th Fl Arlington VA 22201 Office Phone: 703-841-0626. Business E-Mail: fay@alcalde-fay.com.

FAY, MARY ANNE, retail executive; m. Mark A. Fay. Jr. exec. program, Allied Dept. Stores, 1955; exec. program, Federated Dept. Stores, 1970; grad. in retail, U. Minn. V.p. gen. mdse. mgr. Levy's, Federated Dept. Stores, Tucson, 1974—83, regional v.p. stores, 1981—83; v.p. divsnl. mdse. mgr. Mainstreet, Federated Dept. Stores, Chgo., 1983—86, Alexander's Inc., NYC, 1986—92. Pvt. practice retail cons., Tucson, 1992—. Lifetime trustee Carondelet, Tucson, 1994—2005; chair Ariz. Cancer Ctr., Tucson, 1998—2002; bd. dirs. Tucson Symphony Women's Assn., 2001—05, ARC. Achievements include one of the first vice presidents in my field at Federated Dept. Stores. Home: 5421 N Paseo Soria Tucson AZ 85718 Home Phone: 520-529-3699.

FAY, SISTER MAUREEN A., university president; BA in English magna cum laude, Siena Heights Coll., 1960; MA in English, U. Detroit, 1966; PhD, U. Chgo., 1976. Tchr. English, speech, moderator student newspaper, student council St. Paul High Sch., Grosse Pointe, Mich., 1960-64; chairperson English dept., dir. student dramatics, moderator student publs. Dominican High Sch., Detroit, 1964-69; co-dir. Cath. student ctr. Adrian (Mich.) Coll., 1969-71; instr. English Siena Heights Coll., Adrian, 1969-71; evaluators inst. criminal justice execs. U. Chgo., 1971-73; instr. English U. Ill., Chgo., 1971-74; dir. evaluation sch. new learning DePaul U., Chgo., 1974-75; fellow in acad. adminstrn. Saint Xavier Coll., Chgo., 1975-76, dean. grad. studies, 1979-83, dean continuing edn., 1976-83; asst. prof. No. Ill. U., Dekalb, 1980-83; pres. Mercy Coll. Detroit, 1983-90, U. Detroit Mercy, 1990—. V.p. VAUT Corp, bd. dirs. four inner city high schs., Archdiocese Chgo.; mem. exec. com. Assn. Mercy Colls.; adv. com. Adult Learning Svcs., The Coll. Bd., Met. Affairs Corp. of Detroit and S.E. Mich., cons. Nat. Assn. for Religious Women, 1974-75, North Cen. Assn. Colls. and Schs., evaluator commn. on higher edn.; trustee Rosary Coll., River Forest, Ill., New Detroit, Inc., 1993; emeritus mem. div. bd. Mercy Hosps. and Health Svcs. of Detroit; bd. dirs. Nat. Bank of Detroit, S.E. Econ. Growth Corp., 1992; mem. Nat. Commn. Ind. Higher Edn.; commr. North Centrl Assocs., Commn. on Instns. of Higher Edn., 1993. Asst. editor: (book rev.): Adult Education, A Journal of Research and Theory, 1971-74. Bd. dirs. United Way SE Mich., 1991, Assn. Catholic Colls. and Univs., 1992; Steering com. Metro Detroit GIVES; exec. com., edn. task force Detroit Strategic Planning com., 1987; trustee Mich. Opera Theatre; bd. dirs. Greater Detroit Interfaith Round Table Nat. Conf. Christians and Jews, Inc., The Detroit Symphony; mem. Nat. Bipartisan Commn. on Ind. Higher Edn. in U.S., 1993. Mem. Am. Assn. Higher Edn., North Cen. Assn. (cons., evaluator commn. on higher edn.), Nat. Assn. Ind. Colls. and Univs. (bd. dirs.), Assn. Ind. Colls. and Univs. of Mich. (exec. com., chairperson), Am. Assn. Cath. Colls. and Univs., AAUW, Pi Lambda Theta. Office: U Detroit Mercy Office Pres PO Box 19900 4001 W McNichols Rd Detroit MI 48219-0900

FAY, MICHAEL LEO, lawyer; b. Springfield, Mass., Oct. 3, 1949; s. Joseph L. and Marie A. (Wilson) Fay; children: Matthew, Kathryn, Christopher. BA summa cum laude, Dartmouth Coll., 1971; postgrad., Oxford U., Eng., 1972; JD, Harvard U., 1975. Bar: Mass. 1975, US Tax Ct. 1992. Assoc. Wilmer, Cutler Pickering, Hale & Dorr, Boston, 1975-80, jr. ptnr., 1980-85, sr. ptnr., 1985—, former chmn. pvt. client dept. Bd. dir. Family Firm Inst., 1993—99; lectr. Mass. Continuing Legal Edn., Boston, 1984—. Mem. corp. Tenacre Country Day Sch., Wellesley Hills, Mass., 1992—, Ptnrs. Healthcare, 1994—; bd. profl. adv. Boston Found., 2002—; mem. Dartmouth Alumni Coun., 2000—; overseer Aquinas House/Cath. Students Ctr. Dartmouth Coll., Hanover, NH, 1984—; sec. Dartmouth Ednl. Assn., Boston, 1984—. Named one of Top 100 Lawyers, Worth Mag., 2005—07. Fellow: Am. Coll. Trust and Estate Counsel; mem.: ABA, Boston Bar Assn., Mass. Bar Assn. (sec.), Dartmouth Club Greater Boston (sec. 1984—2000). Republican. Roman Catholic. Office: Wilmer Cutler Pickering Hale and Dorr 60 State St Boston MA 02109-1816 Office Phone: 617-526-6320. Business E-Mail: michael.fay@wilmerhale.com.

FAY, MIRIAM SOLER, school counselor, educator; d. Jose Hugo and Maria Carmen Soler; m. Jack Revelle Fay, Jan. 12, 1984; children: Jessica, Eric. JD, St. Thomas U., 1969; MEd in Guidance & Counseling, Stetson U., 1992; EdD in Ednl. Leadership, U. Mo., 2004. Cert. K-12 Sch. Guidance Counselor Fla., 1995, State Lic. K-12 Sch. Guidance Counselor Kans., 1997, State Cert. K-12 Sch. Guidance Counselor Okla., 1999, Mo., 2000. Govt. mediator for labor unions Ministry of Labor and Social Security, Bogotá, Colombia, 1970—83, labor law counsel for women and minors, 1983—93; sch. counselor Volusia County Schs., Deland, Fla., 1993—96, co-sponsor of tchrs. as mentors, 1994—95; sch. counselor Tulsa Pub. Schs., Tulsa, Okla., 1997—98; guidance counselor Lewis & Clark Mid. Sch., Tulsa, 1997—98, Neosho R-5 Sch. Dist., Mo., 2001—; rsch. assoc. Mo. So. State U., Joplin, 1998—2001. Career fairs sponsor Osteen Elem., 1994—95, DeLeon Springs Elem., 1994—95; chair students reach-out program; coord. career fairs, testing and parenting groups Benton Elem., Neosho R-5 Sch. Dist.; co-sponsor secondary migrant summer inst. for minorities at risk. Creator labor counsel Women and Minors Task Force; career and employability edn. counselor HS Summer Migrant Inst., Fla., 1996. Mem.: Am. Ednl. Rsch. Assn., Am. Sch. Counselors Assn., Phi Delta Kappa Internat. Avocations: home improvement projects, volunteering. Home Phone: 417-627-9585; Office Phone: 417-437-1670. Personal E-mail: m_fay@sbcglobal.net.

FAY, PETER THORP, federal judge; b. Rochester, NY, Jan. 18, 1929; s. Lester Thorp and Jane (Baumler) Fay; m. Claudia Pat Zimmerman, Oct. 1, 1958; children: Michael Thorp, William, Darcy. BA, Rollins Coll., 1951, LLD, 1971; JD, U. Fla., 1956; LLD, Biscayne Coll., 1975. Bar: Fla. 1956, U.S. Supreme Ct. 1961. Ptnr. firm Nichols, Gaither Green, Frates & Beckham, Miami, Fla., 1956—61, Frates, Fay, Floyd & Pearson (and predecessors), Miami, 1961—70; prof. Fla. Jr. Bar Practical Legal Inst., 1959—65; judge US Dist. Ct. for So. Fla., Miami, 1970—76, US Ct. Appeals (5th cir.), 1976—81, US Ct. Appeals (11th cir.), 1981—94, sr. judge, 1994—; lectr. Fla. Bar Legal Inst., 1959—; faculty Fed. Jud. Center, Washington, 1974—94. Mem. Jud. Conf. Com. for Implementation Criminal Justice Act, 1974—82, Adv. Com. on Codes of Conduct, 1980—87, Ad Hoc Com. on Cameras in the Courtroom, 1983—84, Adv. Com. on Appellate Rules, 1987—90, Eleventh Circuit Standing Edn. Com.; mem. exec. com. Eleventh Circuit Judicial Coun.; co-chmn. Nat. Jud. Coun. for State and Fed. Cts., 1990—. Mem. Orange Bowl Com., 1974—; dist. collector United Fund, 1957—70; mem. adminstrv. bd. St. Thomas U., 1970—; trustee U. Miami, Fla., 1989—; mem., supr. Ind. Counsel, 1994—. Lieutenant USAF, 1951—53. Mem.: ABA, Medico Legal Inst., John Marshall Bar Assn. (past pres.), Dade County Bar Assn., Fla. Bar Assn., Fla. Acad. Trial Attys., Law Sci. Acad., Miami C. of C., U. Fla. Alumni Assn. (dir.), Fla. Coun. of 100, Miami Club, Coral Oaks Club (Miami), Wildcat Cliffs Club (N.C.), Snapper Creek Lakes Club (Miami), Phi Delta Theta (past sec.), Phi Kappa Phi, Pi Gamma Mu (past pres.), Omicron Delta Kappa (past pres.), Phi Delta Phi (past pres.), Order of Coif. Republican. Roman Catholic.*

FAY, REGAN JOSEPH, lawyer; b. Cleve., Sept. 19, 1948; s. Robert J. and Loretta Ann (Regan) F.; m. Michelle P. Fay; children: John, Mary, Matthew, Jessica, Samantha. BS in Chem. Engring., MIT, 1970; JD with honors, George Washington U., 1974. Bar: Ohio 1974, U.S. Dist. Ct. (no. dist.) Ohio 1974, U.S. Patent Office 1973, U.S. Ct. Appeals (fed. cir.) 1974, U.S. Ct. Appeals (9th cir.) 1975, U.S. Dist. Ct. (ea. dist.) Wis. 1976, U.S. Dist. Ct. (no. dist.) Tex. 1986, U.S. Supreme Ct. 1988. Patent examiner U.S. Patent and Trademark Office, Washington, 1970-72; law clk. to presiding justice U.S. Ct. Customs and Patent Appeals, Washington, 1973-75; assoc. Yount & Tarolli, Cleve., 1975-79; assoc., then ptnr. Jones, Day, Reavis & Pogue, Cleve., 1979—. Lectr. patent and trademark law Case Western Res. U., Cleve., 1976-86. Mem. Cleve. Intellectual Property Law Assn (pres. 1996-97). Republican. Roman Catholic. Avocation: skiing. Office: Jones Day Reavis & Pogue 901 Lakeside Ave E Cleveland OH 44114-1190 Office Phone: 216-586-7327. E-mail: rjfay@jonesday.com.

FAY, RICHARD JAMES, mechanical engineer, engineering executive, educator; b. St. Joseph, Mo., Apr. 26, 1935; s. Frank James and Marie Jewell (Senger) Fay; m. Marilyn Louise Kelsey, Dec. 22, 1962. BSME, U. Denver, 1959, MSME, 1970. Registered profl. engr., Colo., Nebr. Design engr. Denver Fire Clay Co., 1957—60; design, project engr. Silver Engring. Works, 1960—63; rsch. engr., lectr. mech. engring. U. Denver, 1963—74; asst. prof. Colo. Sch. of Mines, 1974—75; founder, pres. Fay Engring. Corp., Denver, 1971—. Contbr. articles to profl. jours.; patentee in field. With Colo. N.G., 1962. Mem.: La Societe des Ingenieurs L'Automobile (France), ASME (past chmn. Colo. sect., past regional v.p.), Soc. Automotive Engrs. (past chmn. Colo. sect.). Office: 5201 E 48th Ave Denver CO 80216-5316

FAY, TERRENCE MICHAEL, lawyer; b. Cleve., Feb. 25, 1953; s. J. Francis and Alice Wilsona (Porter) F.; m. Beverly Ann Luciow, Feb. 25, 1983; children: Robert Michael, Katherine Elizabeth. BA cum laude, Baldwin Wallace Coll., 1974, BS cum laude, 1975; JD, Ohio State U., 1978. Bar: Ohio 1978, US Dist. Ct. (no. dist.) Ohio 1983, US Dist. Ct. (so. dist.) Ohio 1987, US Ct. Appeals (6th cir.) 1987, US Dist. Ct. (no. dist.) Ind. 1992, US Dist. Ct. (ea. dist.) Mich. 1993. Law clk. for chief adminstrv. law judge Ohio Power Siting Commn., Columbus, 1977-78; asst. atty. gen. environ. sect. Ohio Atty. Gen.'s Office, Columbus, 1978—88, chief civil atty., 1987-88; sr. assoc. Smith & Schnacke, L.P.A., Columbus, 1988-89, Benesch, Friedlander, Coplan & Aronoff, Columbus, 1989-90, ptnr., 1992—2001, chair hiring com., 1995—97; of counsel Frost, Brown, Todd LLC, Columbus, 2002—04, ptnr., 2005—. Bd. dirs. Hucksters, Inc., Columbus, 1990. Abrahms scholar, 1975; recipient Book award Lawyers Coop., Inc., 1978, Ohio Gov.'s Spl. Recognition award, 1988; named Ohio

Super Lawyer, 2006. Mem. Phi Alpha Theta, Omicron Delta Kappa, Pi Kappa Delta, Psi Chi. Office: Frost Brown Todd LLC One Columbus Ste 2300 10 W Broad St Columbus OH 43215-3467 Home Phone: 216-346-7793; Office Phone: 614-559-7213. Business E-Mail: tfay@fbtlaw.com.

FAY, THOMAS A., philosopher, educator; b. Utica, NY, July 18, 1927; s. Thomas A. and Theresa A. (Miller) F.; m. Evelyn C. DaCorta, Apr. 6, 1984 BA, Cath. U. Am., 1952; MA, U. Laval, Quebec, 1963; PhD, Fordham U., 1970. Asst. prof. philosophy St. Bernard Coll., 1963-64; mem. faculty St. John's U., Jamaica, N.Y., 1967—, prof. philosophy, 1977—; chmn. dept. philosophy St John's U., Jamaica, N.Y., 1974-80. Vis. prof. Drew U., 1969 Author: Heidegger: The Critique of Logic, 1977, And Smoking Flax Shall He Not Quench: Reflections on New Testament Themes, 1979; mem. editorial bd. Guidebook for Publishing Philosophy, 1977, 2d edit., 1986; contbr. articles to profl. jours. Served with U.S. Army, 1945-46. Mem. Am. Cath. Philos. Assn. (pres. Met. chpt. 1975-81, exec. council 1976-79), Internat. Thomistic Soc. (v.p.), Internat. Soc. Metaphysics, Am. Philos. Assn., Medieval Acad. Am. Home: 20 Melody Ln Kings Park NY 11754-5026 Personal E-mail: tafay@aol.com.

FAY, THOMAS F., library director; BA in Fine Arts, U. Nev., Las Vegas. Page Overton Libr., 1983; various positions including computer technician, network specialist and network mgr. Las Vegas-Clark County Libr. Dist.; computer network specialist Cooperative Librs. Automated Network; info. tech. mgr. Henderson Dist. Pub. Librs., Nev., dir. Nev., 2004—. Mem.: Nev. Libr. Assn. (Scholarship 2000). Office: Henderson Dist Pub Librs Adminstrn 280 S Green Valley Pky Henderson NV 89012 Office Phone: 702-492-6595. Office Fax: 702-492-1711. E-mail: tffay@hdpl.org.

FAY, TONI GEORGETTE, communications executive; b. NYC, Apr. 25, 1947; d. George E. and Allie C. (Smith) Fay. BA, Duquesne U., Pitts., 1968; MSW, U. Pitts., 1972, MEd, 1973. Caseworker N.Y.C. Dept. Welfare, 1968-70; regional commr. Gov. Pa. Coun. Drugs and Alcohol, 1973-76; dir. social svcs. Pitts. Drug Abuse Ctr., 1972-73; dir. planning and devel. Nat. Coun. Negro Women, 1977-79; exec. v.p. D. Parke Gibson Assocs., 1979-82; mgr. cmty. rels. Time Inc. (now Time-Warner Inc.), NYC, 1982-83, dir. corp. cmty. rels. and affirmative action, 1983-93, v.p., corp. officer, 1993-2001; pres. TGF Assocs., Englewood, NJ, 2001—. Bd. dirs. UNICEF, Congl. Black Caucus Found., NAACP Legal Def. Fund Bd., Franklin and Eleanor Inst., Apollo Theatre Found.; apptd. bd. advs. Nat. Inst. Literacy, 1996—, Nat. and Cmty. Svc., 2000. Named Woman of the Yr., Pitts. YWCA, 1975, N.Y. Women's Forum; named one of 100 Top Women in Bus., Dollars and Sense Mag., 1986; recipient Twin award, YWCA U.S.A., 1987. Office: TGF Assocs 233 W Hudson Ave Englewood NJ 07631 Personal E-mail: tonigfay@aol.com.

FAY, WILLIAM FREDERICK, film producer; b. Redmond, Wash., July 25, 1956; s. James Russell and Patricia Jean Fay; m. Jody Beth Silverman, June 14, 1987; children: Caitlin Emily, Natasha Anne, Megan Elizabeth. Student, Stanford U., 1974-76; BA, UCLA, 1978. Prodn. exec. Film Finances Ltd., London, 1988-90, New World Entertainment, LA, 1990; pres. Boy Meets Girl Prodns., Beverly Hills, Calif., 1991—2005; CEO, Centropolis Effects, L.L.C., Santa Monica, Calif., 1996-2001; pres. Centropolis Entertainment, LA, 1996-2001; pres. prodn. Legendary Pictures, 2005—. Exec. prodr.: (films) The Hunted, 1995, Independence Day, 1996, Godzilla, 1998, The Patriot, 2000, The Ant Bully, 2006, We Are Marshall, 2006, Superman Returns, 2006, 300, 2007. Avocation: tennis. E-mail: wfay@legendarypictures.com.

FAYARD, GARY P., beverage company executive; BS, U.of Ala., 1975. CPA Ga., Ala. Ptnr., area dir. audit svcs., manfacturing svcs. Ernst & Young; dep. controller, v.p. Coca-Cola Co., 1994—99, sr. v.p., CFO, 1999—2003, exec. v.p., CFO, 2003—. Bd. dirs. Coca-Cola SABCO, Coca-Cola Enterprises, Panamco, 2001—. Bd. dirs. Fin. Acctg. Standards Advisory Bd.; Atlanta Area Coun. Boy Scouts Am.; bd. visitors U. of Ala. Mem.: Fin. Exec. Inst., Am. Inst. CPAs. Office: Coca Cola Co PO Box 1734 Atlanta GA 30313*

FAYER, MICHAEL DAVID, chemist, educator; b. LA, Sept. 12, 1947; s. William and Frieda Fayer; m. Terry Wolfe, Dec. 21, 1968; children: Victoria, William. BS, U. Calif., Berkeley, 1969, PhD, 1974. Asst. prof. chemistry Stanford U., 1974—80, assoc. prof. chemistry, 1980—84, prof. chemistry, 1984—2000, David Mulvane Ehrsam and Edward Curtis Franklin prof. of chemistry, 2000—. Prof. physics U. Grenoble, France, 1982; invited lectr. in field. Author: (book) Elements of Quantum Mechanics, 2001; contbr. articles to sci. jours.; mem. editl. bd. Jour. Chem. Physics, 1987—90, mem. adv. bd. Jour. Phys. Chemistry, 1986—89, adv. editor Chem. Physics Letters, 1984—, Chem. Physics, 1985—, assoc. editor Jour. Luminescence, 1988—. Recipient E. Bright Wilson award in Spectroscopy, Am. Chem. Soc., 2007; fellow Alfred P. Sloan fellow, Sloan Found., 1977, Camille & Henry Dreyfus Found. fellow, Dreyfus Found., 1977, Guggenheim Found. Fellow, 1983—84. Fellow: Am. Acad. Arts and Sciences, Am. Phys. Soc. (Earl K. Plyer prize for molecular spectroscopy 2000); mem.: NAS, Phi Beta Kappa, Sigma Xi. Office: Dept Chemistry KECK 113 Stanford University Stanford CA 94305-5080 Office Phone: 650-723-4446. Office Fax: 650-723-4817. E-mail: fayer@stanford.edu.*

FAYSSOUX, PATRICIA ANN PAYSOUR, music educator; b. Gastonia, NC, Sept. 29, 1953; d. Earl McFalls and Patsy Marlene (Sills) Paysour; m. John Oliver Fayssoux, Oct. 13, 1973; children: Johnathan Lee, Lauren Patricia, Christopher Lane Paysour. B in Music Edn., Greensboro Coll., 1975. Music dir., art tchr. Oak Ridge Mil. Acad., NC, 1975—82; tchr. music and mentally handicapped and emotionally-handicapped and gifted and talented Belton Elem. and Middle Schs., SC, 1982—87; music tchr. Cramerton Middle and Bess Elem. Schs., Gastonia, NC, 1988—90; music tchr. and handbell dir. Cramerton Middle Sch., 1999—. Mem. cmty. rels. bd. Gaston Gazette Newspaper, 1995—97; mem. coun. ministries Myers Meml. United Meth. Ch., Gastonia, 1992—96, coord. nursery, 1992—96, children and youth handbell dir., 1988—2004; bd. dirs. Am. Red Cross, Gastonia, 1998—2002. Recipient Vol. Svc. award, Boy Scouts Am. Troop #4, Vol. of Yr., Am. Red Cross, 1999, Tchr. of Yr., Cramerton Middle Sch., 2004—05. Mem.: Am. Guild of English Handbell Ringers, Nat. Educators Assn., Am. Choral Dirs. Assn., Music Educators Am., Music Educators N.C. Achievements include school handbell choirs achieving Superior Ratings, have performed at the American Pavillon, Epcot Center, Open House at Christmas in the N.C. State Captiol Building, Gaston County Museum; opening act for Russian ballets Nutcracker in Charlotte, N.C., and annually for Charlotte Philharmonic Orch. Avocations: solo handbell ringing, travel, reading. Home: 3530 Country Club Dr Gastonia NC 28056 Business E-Mail: pfayssoux@gaston.k12.nc.us.

FAZIO, ANTHONY LEE, investment company executive; b. Wheeling, W.Va., Jan. 27, 1937; s. Frank G. and Julia Louise (DeFillipo) F.; m. Faye Elizabeth Kelly, Sept. 3, 1964; children: Tracey Lee, Kelly Ann. BSEE, W.Va. U., 1959. Registered investment advisor, investment mgmt. cons., bus. mgmt. cons.; cert. fin. planner. With computer div. RCA, 1964-72, mgr. product mktg., 1970-71, mgr. systems planning, 1971-72; dir. bus. and product planning Univac, 1972-73, dir. product mktg. and bus./product planning N.Am., 1973-75, regional mgr., 1975-77; v.p. sales Sycor, Inc., Ann Arbor, Mich., 1977-78, No. Telecom Systems Corp., 1978-79, v.p. mktg., 1979-80; pres. Gibbs Irwin Investments Co., 1981-83; product procurement and due diligence officer Midland Mgmt. Corp., 1983-86; pres. Fazio Investments, Inc., 1986—. With U.S. Army, 1959-61. Mem. Inst. Cert. Fin. Planners, Minn. Soc. Inst. Cert. Fin. Planners (pres.-elect, bd. dirs.), Tau Beta Pi, Eta Kappa Nu. Republican. Home and Office: 4770 Regents Walk Ste 100 Excelsior MN 55331-9209

FAZIO, EVELYN M., publisher, writer, agent, editor; b. Hackensack, NJ; BA in History, U. Bridgeport, 1975; MA in History, U. Conn., 1977. Cert. social studies tchr. NJ. Tchr. social studies Cedar Grove (N.J.) High Sch., 1977-79; prodn. editor Prentice-Hall, Inc., Englewood Cliffs, NJ, 1980-82, devel. editor, 1982-83, acquisitions editor, 1983-85; sr. acquisitions editor P-H/Simon & Schuster, Inc., Englewood Cliffs, 1985-88; mng. editor Random House, Inc., NYC, 1988—; exec. editor polit. sci., internat. rels. and policy studies Paragon House Pubs., Inc., NYC, 1989-91; editorial dir. Marshall Cavendish Pubs., N. Bellmore, NY, 1992-95; v.p., pub. M.E. Sharpe, Armonk, NY, 1995—2001; v.p. e-content acquisition Baker & Taylor, Bridgewater, NJ, 2001—03; dir. EMF Agy., Hackensack, 2003—; agt. Internat. Lit. Arts, LLC, Hackensack, 2004—07, ptnr. Moscow, Pa., 2004—06; pub. Westside Books, Lodi, NJ, 2006—. Co-author: (series) Staying Sane When Your Family Comes to Visit, Staying Sane When You're Dieting, Staying Sane When You Quit Smoking, 2005, Staying Sane When You're Planning Your Wedding, Staying Sane When You're Buying or Selling Your Home, Staying Sane When You're Going Through Menopause, Poker with the Girls, 2007. Mem.: Soc. Children's Book Writers and Illustrators.

FAZIO, PETER VICTOR, JR., lawyer; b. Chgo., Jan. 22, 1940; s. Peter Victor and Marie Rose (LaMantia) F.; m. Patti Ann Campbell, Jan. 3, 1966; children: Patti-Marie, Catherine, Peter. AB, Coll. of Holy Cross, Worcester, Mass., 1961; JD, U. Mich., 1964. Bar: Ill. 1964, US Dist. Ct. (no. dist.) Ill. 1965, US Ct. Appeals (7th cir.) 1972, US Supreme Ct. 1977, DC 1981, US Ct. Appeals (DC cir.) 1988, Ind. 1993. Assoc. Schiff, Hardin & Waite, Chgo., 1964-70, ptnr., 1970-82, 84-95, mng. ptnr., 1995—2000, 2006, chmn., 2001—06; exec. v.p. Internat. Capital Equipment, Chgo., 1982-83, also bd. dirs., 1982-85, sec., 1982-87; exec. v.p., gen. counsel NiSource Inc., 2000—06. Bd. dirs. Planmetrics Inc., Chgo., 1984-92, Chgo. Lawyers Commn. for Civil Rights Under Law, 1976-82, co-chmn., 1978-80; bd. dirs. Seton Health Corp. No. Ill., Chgo. 1987-90, vice chmn., 1989-90. Trustee Barat Coll., Lake Forest, Ill., 1977-82; bd. dirs. St. Joseph Hosp., Chgo., 1990-95, mem. exec. adv. bd., 1984-89, chmn., 1986-89; vice chmn. bd. dirs. Cath. Health Ptnrs., 1995-99, chmn., 1999—; dir. exec. com. Ill. Coalition, 1994-2005, NW Ind. Forum, 1994-98. Mem. ABA (coun. 1991-94, chmn. sect. pub. utility, transp. and comm. law 2000-01), FBA, Ill. Bar Assn., Chgo. Bar Assn., Fed. Energy Bar Assn., Edison Electric Inst. (chmn. legal com. 1999-2001), Am. Gas Assn. (legal com.), Corp. Secretaries and Governance Profls. (sec.)., Met. Club, Econ. Club Chgo., Comml. Club Chgo. Office: Schiff Hardin LLP 6600 Sears Tower 233 S Wacker Dr Chicago IL 60606-6473 Home Phone: 312-664-6282; Office Phone: 312-258-5634. Business E-Mail: pfazio@schifhardin.com.

FAZIO, VIC (VICTOR HERBERT FAZIO JR.), lawyer, former congressman; b. Winchester, Mass., Oct. 11, 1942; m. Judy Kern; children: Dana Fazio, Anne Fazio (dec.), Kevin Kern, Kristie Kern. BA, Union Coll., Schenectady, 1965; postgrad., Calif. State U., Sacramento. Journalist, founder Calif. Jour.; congl. and legis. cons., 1966-75; mem. Calif. State Assembly, 1975-78; mem. US Congress from Calif. 3rd Dist., 1979-98; former chmn. Dem. Congl. Campaign Com.; chmn. Dem. caucus, house steering policy com.; mem. legis. br. appropriations subcom.; ranking mem. appropriations subcom. energy and water; sr. ptnr. Clark & Weinstock, Washington, 1999—; sr. adv. Akin Gump Strauss Hauer & Feld LLP, Washington, 2005—. Former mem. Sacramento County Charter and Planning Commns. Bd. dirs. Asthma Allergy Found., Jr. Statesman, Nat. Italian-Am. Found. Coro Found. fellow; named Solar Congressman of Yr. Mem. Air Force Assn. Office: Clark & Weinstock Inc 52 Vanderbilt Ave New York NY 10017-3808

FAZIO, VICTOR WARREN, physician, colon and rectal surgeon; b. Sydney, Feb. 2, 1940; came to U.S., 1971; s. Victor Warren and Kathleen Eleanor (Hills) F.; m. Carolyn Kisandra Sawyer, Dec. 2, 1961; children: Victor, Jane, David. MB, BS, U. Sydney, 1965, MS with honors, 1997; MD with honors, U. Lodz, 2003. Diplomate Am. Bd. Colon and Rectal Surgery; cert. FRACS, 1971. Intern and resident St. Vincent's Hosp., Sydney, 1965-67, surgical registrar, 1969-71; lectr. anatomy U. NSW Med. Sch., Sydney, 1967; surg. registrar Repatriation Gen. Hosp., Concord, Australia, 1968; gen. surgeon Australian Surg. Team, Bien Hoa, Vietnam, 1971; fellow gen. surgery Lahey Clinic, Boston, 1972; fellow colorectal surgery Cleve. Clinic, 1973, staff surgeon colorectal surgery, 1974, chmn. dept. colon and rectal surgery, vice chmn. divsn. surgery, 1975—. Bd. govs. Cleve. Clinic Found., 1990-95, 98-99, exec. mem. bd. trustees, 1994-95. Author 520 manuscripts and book chpts.; editor: Current Therapy in Colon and Rectal Surgery, 1989, 2d edit., 2004; editor-in-chief Diseases of Colon and Rectum, 1997—. Decorated Order of Australia. Fellow ACS, Royal Australian Coll. Surgeons (hon.), Royal Australasian Coll. Surgeons, Am. Soc. Colon and Rectal Surgery (pres. 1995-96), Royal Coll. Surgeons (Eng., hon.), Royal Coll. Surgeons (Edinburgh, hon.); mem. Soc. Pelvic Surgeons (exec. com. 1980, pres. 2003), Soc. for Surgery Alimentary Tract, Ctrl. Surg. Assn., James IV Assn. Surgeons, Ohio Valley Soc. Colon and Rectal Surgeons (past pres.), Am. Surg. Assn. Roman Catholic. Avocations: naval history, sailing. Office: Cleve Clinic Desk A-111 9500 Euclid Ave Cleveland OH 44195-0001

FAZZOLARI, SALVATORE D., mining products executive; BBA in Acctg., Pa. State U. CPA, Pa.; cert. info. sys. auditor. With Pa. Auditor Gens. Bur. Spl. Audits; sr. auditor Harsco Corp., Camp Hill, Pa., 1980-85, dir. internal audit, 1985-93, sr. v.p., COO, 1993—99, CFO, treas., 1999—, and pres., 2006—. Office: Harsco Corp PO Box 8888 350 Poplar Church Rd Camp Hill PA 17011

FEAGLEY, MICHAEL ROWE, lawyer; b. Exeter, NH, Feb. 1, 1945; s. Walter Charles and Laura (Rowe) F. AB cum laude, Wesleyan U., 1967; JD, Harvard U., 1973. Bar: Mass. 1974, Ill. 1973, US Dist. Ct. (no. dist. Ill.) 1973, US Dist. Ct. (ctrl. dist. Ill.) 1992, US Ct. Appeals (3rd cir. 1997, 6th cir. 1994, 7th cir. 1982, 8th cir. 1992, 10th cir. 1986), US Supreme Ct 1996. Assoc. Mayer, Brown, & Platt, Chgo., 1973-79; ptnr. Mayer, Brown, Rowe & Maw, Chgo., 1980—. Instr. Nat. Inst. Trial Advocacy, Chgo., 1978-96, John Marshall Law Sch., Chgo., 1982-86. Served to 1st lt. US Army, 1968—71, Vietnam. Fellow Am. Coll. Trial Lawyers; mem. ABA, Chgo. Coun. Lawyers, Chgo. Bar Assn., Union League Club (Chgo.). Office: Mayer Brown Rowe & Maw 71 S Wacker Dr Chicago IL 60606 Office Phone: 312-701-7065. Office Fax: 312-706-8623. E-mail: mfeagley@mayerbrownrowe.com.*

FEARING, WILLIAM KELLY, art educator, artist; b. Fordyce, Ark., Oct. 18, 1918; s. George David and Frankie (Kelly) F. BA, La. Tech. U., 1941; MA, Columbia U., 1950. Classroom tchr. Windfield Pub. Schs., La., La., 1942-43; prodn. illustrator Consolidated Vultee Aircraft, Fort Worth, 1943-45; prof. art Tex. Wesleyan Coll., Fort Worth, 1945-47, U. Tex., Austin, 1947-87, Ashbel Smith prof., 1983—, Ashbel Smith prof. emeritus, 1987—. Author: (with C.I. Martin and E. Beard) Our Expanding Vision, 1960, The Creative Eye, 1969, 2d edit., 1979, (with E. Beard, N. Krevitsky, C.I. Martin) Art and the Creative Teacher, 1971, (with E.L. Mayton, B. Francis, E. Beard) Helping Children See Art and Make Art, 1982, (with E.L. Mayton and R. Brooks) The Way or Art Inner Vision Outer Expression, 1986; guest editor Tex. Quar., Creativity and the Human Spirit, vol. XVI, 1978; one man shows include El Paso Mus. Art, Esther Bear Gallery, Santa Barbara, 1964, Gallery Visual Arts, La. Tech. U., Ruston, 1966, U. Tex. Art Mus., Austin, 1967, Ft. Worth Art Ctr., 1969, Witte Meml. Mus., San Antonio, 1969, U. Tex. Art Mus., Austin, 1974, Mary Moore Gallery, LaJolla, 1975, Mary Moffett Gallery, La. Tech. U., 1976, DuBose Gallery, Houston, 1977, L and L Gallery, Longview, 1975, 78, Retrospective Spencer Gallery, Fine Arts Ctr., U. Ark., Monticello, 1981, Mary Moffett Gallery, Sch. Art and Arch., La. Tech. U., 1981, Old Jail Art Ctr., Albany, Tex., 1985, Retrospective Marion Koogler McNay Art Mus., San Antonio, 1986, Valley House Gallery, Dallas, 1992, 96, Robinson Galleries, Houston, 1995, Flatbed Press and Gallery, Austin, 1995, 97, Pascal/Robinson Galleries, Houston, 1999, U. Tex., Austin, 2002, Creative Rsch. Labs., 2002, Sixty Year Retrospective Flatbed Internat. Press Galleries, Austin, 2002, Sixty Year Retrospective Old Jail Art Ctr., 2003, Sixty Year Retrospective Arlington Mus. of Art, 2003, Lotus Gallery, Austin, 2007; exhibited in group shows at Carnegie Inst., Pitts., 1955-57, Pa. Acad. Art, Phila., 1954-56, Mus. Fine Arts, Houston, 1956-57, Dallas Mus. Fine Art, 1956-57, Munson-Williams-Proctor Inst., Utica, 1956-57, Edwin Hewitt Gallery, NYC, 1957, Dallas Mus. Fine Art, 1958, Am. Fedn. Art, 1958, Mus. Fine Art of Little Rock, 1961, Colorado Springs Art Ctr., 1961, 63, Philbrook Art Ctr., Tulsa, 1963, Ft. Worth Art Ctr., 1963, U. Ill., Urbana, 1955, 59, 63, Denver Art Mus., 1963, U. Ariz. and Ark Art Ctr., 1964-65, NY World's Fair, Tex. Pavillion, 1964, Tex. Pavillion Hemistair, San Antonio, 1968, Tex. Tech U. Mus. Art, Lubbock, 1978, Art Gallery Sch. Art and Architecture, La. Tech. U. Ruston, 1984, Jack S. Blanton Mus. Art (formerly Archer M. Huntington Art Gallery), U. Tex., Austin, 1963-82, 83-2001, Longview Mus. and Arts Ctr., Tex., 1962-63, 75, 85, 90-91, Amarillo Art Ctr., Tex., 1988, Dallas Mus. Fine Arts, 1991, 2003, Robinson Gelleries, Houston, 1993, 94, 96-99, Valley House gallery, Dallas, 1994-99, 2001, 04, Flatbed Press and Gallery, Austin, 1996-2001, 04, Ga. Art Mus., U. Ga., Athens, 1997, Marion Koogler McNay Art Mus., San Antonio, 1997-2001, Mus. of Big Bend, Sul Ross State U., Alpine, Tex., 1998, Nancy Wilson Scanlon Gallery, Helms Fine Art Ctr., Austin, 1999, Austin Mus. Art, 2000, Pascal Robinson Galleries, 2000-01, McKinney Contemporary Art Ctr., Dallas, 2000, Tex. Roots: Arlington Mus. Art, 2000, Ctr. for Visual Arts, Denton, Tex., 2000, Old Jail Art Ctr., Albany, Tex., 2001, 06, San Angelo Art Mus., Tex., 2002, San Angelo Mus. Fine Art, 2002, Tex., Modern Art Mus Ft. Worth, 2003, David Dike Gallery, Tex, 2004, Ft. Worth Cmty. Art Ctr., 2005, Morticello Art Gallery, Ft. Worth, 2005-06, Valley House Gallery, Dallas, 2005, Adler Print Collection, Princeton U., NJ, 2005, Austin Mus. Art, 2005, Heritage Galleries Tex. Art, Dallas, 2005-07. Recipient E. William Doty award, U. Tex. Coll Fine Arts, Austin, 2007. Mem. Nat. Soc. Lit. and Arts, Austin Mus. of Art, Tex. Fine Arts Assn. Home: 914 Calithea Rd Austin TX 78746-2716

FEARON, CHARLENE O'BRIEN, special education educator; b. Worcester, Mass., Feb. 17, 1952; d. Robert Joseph and Christine Rita O'Brien; m. Laurence William Fearon, July 6, 1990; 1 child, Caitlin. BA in Edn., St. Joseph Coll., West Hartford, Conn., 1974, MA in Edn., 1977; postgrad., Fairfield U., Conn., 1985—89. Spl. edn. tchr. Worcester Pub. Schs., 1974—75, Regional Dist. # 4, Deep River, Conn., 1975—. Adj. faculty mem. Ctrl. Conn. State Coll., New Britain, Conn., 1979, St. Joseph Coll., West Hartford, Conn., 1979—86; cons. adv. com. Conn. State Dept. Edn., Hartford, 1986—99. Trustee United Ch. of Chester, Conn., 2004—. Avocations: photography, reading, drawing, walking. Personal E-mail: Fearun@aol.com.

FEARON, LEE CHARLES, chemist; b. Tulsa, Nov. 22, 1938; s. Robert Earl and Ruth Belle (Strothers) F.; m. Wanda Sue Williams, Nov. 30, 1971 (div. June 1998); m. Shirlene Olsen, Dec. 9, 2000. Student, Rensselaer Polytech. Inst., 1957-59; BS in Physics, Okla. State U., Stillwater, 1961, BA in Chemistry, 1962, MS in Analytical Chemistry, 1969. Rsch. chemist Houston process lab. Shell Oil Co., Deer Park, Tex., 1968-70; chief chemist Pollution Engring. Internat., Inc., Houston, 1970-76; rsch. chemist M-I Drilling Fluids Co., Houston, 1976-83; cons. chemist Profl. Engr. Assocs., Inc., Tulsa, 1983-84; chemist Anacon, Inc., Houston, 1984-85; scientist III Bionetics Corp., Rockville, Md., 1985-86; sr. chemist L.A. County Sanitation Dist., Whittier, Calif., 1986; chemist Test Am., West Sacramento, Calif., 1986-87; cons. chemist Branham Industries, Inc., Conroe, Tex., 1987-89; chemist 4, Lab Accreditation unit EAP, Wash. State Dept. Ecology, Manchester, 1989—. Cons. chemist Terra-Kleen, Okmulgee, Okla., 1988—94, Excel Pacific, Inc. & Precision Works, Inc., Camarillo, Calif., 1993—96, 2002—, Precision Works, Inc., 2002—. With US Army, 1962—65. Fellow: Am. Inst. Chemists; mem.: AAAS, Am. Chem. Soc. Achievements include patents for environ. soil remediation tech. Avocations: photography, travel. Home: PO Box 514 Manchester WA 98353-0514 Office: PO Box 488 Manchester WA 98353-0488 Personal E-mail: limafox@wavecable.com. Business E-Mail: lfea461@ecy.wa.gov.

FEARON, RICHARD H., manufacturing executive; BA with distinction, Stanford U., Calif.; MBA, Harvard U., JD cum laude. Dir. strategic planning Walt Disney Corp.; cons. Boston Consulting Group, LA, Booz Allen Hamilton, Singapore; gen. mgr. corp. devel., vice-chmn. chems. NatSteel Ltd., Singapore, 1990—95; sr. v.p. corp. devel. Transamerica Corp., 1995—2000; co-founder Willow Place Ptnrs., Menlo Park, Calif., 2001—02; exec. v.p., CFO, chief planning officer Eaton Corp., Cleve., 2002—. Bd. dirs. PolyOne Corp.; chmn. CFO Coun. Mfrs. Alliance. Bd. mem. Playhouse Sq. Found. Baker Scholar. Mem.: Phi Beta Kappa. Office: Eaton Corp Eaton Ctr 1111 Superior Ave Cleveland OH 44114-2584 Office Phone: 216-523-5000.*

FEARRINGTON, ANN PEYTON, writer, illustrator, news correspondent; b. Winston-Salem, NC, Aug. 25, 1945; d. James Cornelius Pass Fearrington and Florence Moore (McCanless-Fearrington) Blackwood; m. Hege Hill Russ, Sept. 1967 (div. 1984); children: James Pass Fearrington Russ, Joseph Peyton Fearrington Russ; m. Vance Edwin Cox, Jr., June 17, 1985; 1 stepson, Charles Jonathan Cox. BA in Secondary Edn. and English, U. N.C., 1967; MS in Life Scis., Botany & Horticulture, N.C. State U., 1972. Mid. sch. tchr. Wake County Sch. Sys., Raleigh, 1967-71; landscape designer pvt. practice NYC, Winston-Salem, N.C., 1972-83; corr. Raleigh News & Observer, 1993—. Writer/artist-in-residence Raleigh-Wake County Pub. Schs., 1997-2000. Author, illustrator: Christmas Lights, 1996, Little Green Book-18 Keys to Your Child's Reading Success, 1998 (Southeastern Newspaper Assn. Literacy award 1999), Teacher and Librarian Guide for the Little Green Book, 2000, Pequeño Libro Verde, 2000, Who Sees the Lighthouse?, 2004. Sch. libr. vol. Wake County Sch. Sys., Raleigh, 1985—; Sunday Sch. tchr. Highland United Meth. Ch., Raleigh, 1986-90. Recipient Literacy award, Southeastern Newspaper Assn., 1999. Mem.: N.C. Reading Assn. (James B. Hunt Literacy award 2001), Internat. Reading Assn., Soc. Children's Book Writers and Illustrators, Beatrix Potter Soc., N.C. State Univ. Club. Avocations: gardening, reading, sketching.

FEARS, JESSE RUFUS, historian, educator, academic dean; BA summa cum laude, Emory U., 1966; MA, Harvard U., 1967, PhD, 1971. Asst. prof. classical langs. Tulane U., New Orleans, 1971-72; asst. prof. history Indiana U., Bloomington, 1972-75, assoc. prof. history, 1975-80, prof. history, 1980-86, dist. faculty rsch. lectr., 1981; prof., chair classical studies Boston U., 1986-90, assoc. dean Coll. Liberal Arts, 1987-89; fellow Ctr. Human Freedom Wash. U., 1989—90; dir. humanities found. Boston U., 1988-90; dir. div. rsch. NEH, 1992—93; dean Coll. Arts and Scis. U. Okla., Norman, 1990-92, prof. Classics, 1990—2004, David Ross Boyd Prof., 2004—, G.T. and Libby Blankenship prof. history of liberty, 1992—, dir. Ctr. for History of Liberty, 1992—; Sigma Chi scholar in residence Miami U., 2003; dist. vis. prof. Washington & Lee U., 2005; fellow Okla. Coun. Pub. Affairs, 2006. Adj. scholar Okla. Coun. Pub. Affairs, 1996—. Author: Princeps A Diis Electus, 1977, (monographs) The Cult of Jupiter, 1981, The Theology of Victory, 1981, The Cult of Virtues, 1981; books on audio and video tape: A History of Freedom, 2001, Famous Greeks, 2001, Famous Romans, 2001, Winston Churchill, 2001, Books That Have Made History,

2005; editor: (3 vols.) Selected Writings/Lord Acton, 1985-88; contbr. chpts. to books, numerous articles to profl. jours. Bd. dirs. Okla. Sch. Sci./Math. Found., Oklahoma City, 1990—; pres. Vergilian Soc., 2002-04. Recipient Judah P. Benjamin award, Military Order of Stars and Bars, 1996, Great Plains Region Excellence in Tchg. award, U. Continuing Edn. Assn., 2003, CAMWS award for Excellence in College Tchg, 2005, Nat. award for Teaching Excellence, U. Continuing Edn. Assn., 2005, Medal for Excellence in Coll. and Univ. Tchg., Okla. Found. Excellence, 2006; Danforth fellow, Danforth Found., 1966-71, Woodrow Wilson fellow, Woodrow Wilson Found., 1966-67, Harvard Prize fellow, 1966-71, Sheldon Travelling fellow, 1969-71, fellow Am. Acad. in Rome, 1969-71, Guggenheim Found., 1976-77, Howard Found., 1977-78, Alexander Von Humboldt, 1977-78, 80-81; grantee Am. Philos. Soc., 1972, 79, NEH, 1974, Am. Coun. Learned Soc., 1979, Woodrow Wilson, 1983, Kerr Found., 1994, 1999, 2003, 2005, Zarrow Found., 2000, 2001, 2002. Mem. Classical Assn. Middle West and South, Phi Beta Kappa, Golden Key Nat. Honor Soc. Office: U Okla Blakeship Chair 640 Parrington Oval Old Sci Hall Rm 102 Norman OK 73019-3065 Home Phone: 405-364-9787. Business E-Mail: jrfears@ou.edu.

FEARS, LINDA, editor-in-chief; Grad., Cornell Univ. Lifestyle dir. Am. Health for Women; sr. editor, lifestyle dir. Ladies' Home Jour.; editor articles Parents Mag., 1999—2000, dep. editor, 2000—04; editor-in-chief YM Mag., NY, 2004, Family Circle, 2005—. Office: Meredith Corp Family Circle Mag 375 Lexington Ave 9th Fl New York NY 10017-5514 Office Fax: 212-499-2000.*

FEASER, DEBORAH ELLEN, mathematics educator; b. Harrisburg, Pa., Mar. 15, 1950; d. Donald Leroy and Barbara Ellen Feaser. A in Acctg., Harrisburg Area C.C., Pa., 1974, A in Computer Networking, 2004—04; BS in Edn., Shippensburg U., Pa., 1988. Cert. Network+ CompTIA, 2004. Savs./comml. teller Dauphin Deposit Bank and Trust Co., Harrisburg, Pa., 1968—73; elem. tchr. Faith Tabernacle Sch., Harrisburg, 1973—81, tchr. math. and bus. edn. Mechanicsburg, Pa., 1981—. Yearbook advisor Faith Tabernacle Sch., 1983—, fund raiser advisor, 1988—. Recipient Academic Achievement award, US Achievement Acad., 1987, 1988, Merit award, Nat. Bus. Edn. Assn., 1988, Academic Achievement award, Shippensburg U., 1987, 1988, 1989. Avocations: walking, bicycling, gardening, reading. Home: 432 Cockley Rd Boiling Springs PA 17007-9686 Office: Faith Tabernacle Sch 1410 Good Hope Rd Mechanicsburg PA 17050 Home Phone: 717-258-4398; Office Phone: 717-975-0641. Office Fax: 717-975-9920; Home Fax: 717-258-4398. Personal E-mail: debfeaser@juno.com. Business E-Mail: deborah.feaser@ftcschool.org.

FEASTER, JAY, professional sports team executive; m. Anne Feaster; children: Theresa, Bobby, Libby, Ryan, Kevin. Grad. summa cum laude, Susquehanna U.; JD cum laude, Georgetown U. Atty. McNees, Wallace & Nurick, Harrisburg, Pa.; asst. to pres. Hershey Bears (AHL), 1989, gen. mgr., 1990, pres.; v.p. Hershey Sports and Entertainment; asst. gen. mgr. Tampa Bay Lightning, 1998—2002, exec. v.p., gen. mgr., alt. gov., 2002—. Mem. USA Hockey Internat. Coun. Named NHL Exec. of Yr., The Sporting News, 2004. Achievements include being the general manager of Stanley Cup Champion Tampa Bay Lightning, 2004. Office: Tampa Bay Lightning Hockey Club 401 Channelside Dr Tampa FL 33602

FEATHER, GLORIA ANNE, language educator; BA, U. Pitts., 1973, MEd, 1977. Tchr. Bethel Park Sch. Dist., Pa., 1974—. Mem.: Nat. Coun. Tchrs. English.

FEATHERMAN, BERNARD, steel company executive; b. May 3, 1929; m. Sandra Green; children: Andrew C., John James. BS, Temple U., Phila., 1951; postgrad., Grad. Bus. Sch., 1951—52, Law Sch., 1952—54, Wharton Sch., U. Pa., 1965—66. Chmn. bd. dirs. Western Metal Bed Co., Phila., 1978-86; with CIATEQ USA, Inc., 1995-98; dir. Pa. Steel and Aluminum Corp. (now Pa. Steel Corp.), Bensalem, 1972—, Wardwell Retirement Complex, Saco, Maine, 1998—, Counselling Svcs., Inc., Saco, 1998-2000, Newsletter Pub. Co., Phila., Am. Red Cross So. Maine, 2000—. Contbr. articles to profl. jours.; inventor electronics locking locker. Mem. exec. bd. Southeast chpt. Nat. Found. March of Dimes, 1969-82, vice-chmn., 1978-80; pres. Phila. Assn. for Retarded Citizens, 1975-77, trustee, 1983-96; trustee Phila. Devel. Disabilities Corp., 1991-96, Equity 591 F8AM, 1990-92; chmn. Mayor's Adv. Com. on Mental Health-Mental Retardation, Phila., 1979-92, bd. dirs. 1993; mem. tax policy and budget rev. com. City of Phila., fiscal adv. com., 1990; bd. dirs. Costar, Inc., 1989-92; co-chmn. Mayor's Small Bus. Adv. Com., Phila., 1979-92, mem., 1979-95; del. White House Conf. on Small Bus., 1980, Pa. del., 1995, vice-chmn., 1986; chmn. small bus. coun. Dem. Nat. Com., 1982-84; fin. chmn. Pa. Dem. Orgn., 1985-86; mem. adv. bd. Coll. Liberal Arts and Scis., Temple U., 1982-91, chmn. incubator program, 1989-91, chmn. Entrepreneurial Inst., 1990; co-dir. Enterpreneurial Inst. U. New Eng., 1996-98; adv. bd. West Chester State U. Bus. Sch., Pa., 1986-87, Frankford Hosp., 1983—; steering com. entrepreneurial forum Drexel U. Bus. Sch., 1988-91; chmn. 3d Congl. Small Bus. Coun., Phila., 1984-88; bd. dirs. Phila. Citywide Devel. Corp., 1984-96; bd. dirs. Phila. Loan Fund, Inc., 1987-88, ARC, York County, Sanford, Maine. 2004—, corporator So. Maine Med. Ctr., 2005—, York County Econ. Devel.Summit Steering Com., 2004; bd. dirs. Coastal Counties Workforce Bd., Topshawn, Maine, 2006-, Maine Merchants Assn., Augusta, 2006-; regulatory fairness bd. US Small Bus. Adminstrn., Region 1, 2007—. Recipient award of appreciation Small Bus. Coun., Dem. Nat. Com., 1983; Gold medal of Honor Adult Trainees Found., Phila., 1976; citation White House Conf. on Small Bus., 1980; named Entrepreneur of Yr. Mid Atlantic Region Supporter of Entrepreneurship, 1990, Ea. Pa. Small Bus. Adv. of Yr. SBA, 1991. Mem. Assn. of Steel Distbrs. (nat. pres. 1975-76, 86-87, named Steel Distbr. of Yr. 1976), Inst. Am. Entrepreneurs (life), Shelving Mfrs. Assn. (nat. chmn. 1977-78), Pa. Soc., Assn. Steel Distbrs. (nat. pres. 1975-76, 86-87, Hunting Park-Germantown Bus. Assn. (pres. 1986-96), Biddeford/Saco C. of C. (bd. dirs. 2002—, pres., CEO, 2005—), Rotary, Masons (trustee), B'nai Brith (pres. 1980-82, Nat. Youth Svcs. award Quaker City lodge 1985). Home: PO Box 428A Kennebunkport ME 04046-1728 Office Phone: 207-282-1567. Personal E-mail: bernard@biddefordsacochamber.org.

FEATHERMAN, SANDRA, retired academic administrator, political science professor; b. Phila., Apr. 14, 1934; d. Albert N. and Rebe (Burd) Green; m. Bernard Featherman, Mar. 29, 1958; children: Andrew Charles, John James. BA, U. Pa., 1955, MA, PhD, U. Pa., 1978. Asst. prof. dept. polit. sci. Temple U., Phila., 1978-84, assoc. prof., 1984-91, asst. to pres., 1986-89, pres. faculty senate, 1985-86, dir. Ctr. Pub. Policy, 1986-91; vice chancellor acad. adminstrn., prof. polit. sci. U. Minn., Duluth, 1991-95; pres. U. New Eng., Biddeford, Maine, 1995—2006, pres. emeritus, 2006—. Mem. New Eng. Assn. Schs. and Coll. Higher Edn. Commn., 2002—06; mem. commn. women in higher edn. Am. Coun. Edn., 2005—; commr. commn. on accreditation Am. Osteopathic Assn., 2007—. Author: Jews, Black and Ethnics, 1979, Race and Politics at the Millenium, 2000; contbr. articles to profl. jours. Nat. bd. Girls Inc., 1971—74; pres. Pa. Fedn. C.C., Girls Inc.; sec. Maine Women's Forum, 2002—, pres., 2005—; bd. Maine Compact Higher Edn., 2003—06, exec. bd., 2003—06; commr. Am. Coun. on Edn. Commn. on Women in Higher Edn., 2005—07; chair Maine Commn. on Jud. Compensation, 2005—; chair ethics commn. State of Maine, 2006—07; chair Gov.'s Blue Ribbon Commn. on Health Care, Maine, 2006—07, Maine, 2006; bur. osteo. edn. Am. Osteo. Assn., 2004—06; nat. bd. dirs. Women and Founds.-Corp. Philanthropy, 1986—91; bd. dirs. Citizens Com. Pub. Edn. Phila., 1977—89, pres., 1979—81; trustee C.C. Phila., 1970—92, chmn. bd. trustees, 1984—86; bd. mem. Samuel Fels Found., 1978—, pres., 2007—; bd. dirs. United Way SE Pa., 1977—89, United Way Pa., 1981—84, U. New Eng., Gulf of Maine Aquarium, Kennebec Girl Scout Coun., Virginia Gildersleeve Internat. Fund., 2003—, Vis. Nurse Assn., 2002—03; chair Assembly Pres. Am. Assoc. Coll. Osteopathic Medicine; chmn. Maine Commn. on the State Ceiling on Tax-exempt Bonds, 1999—2000; bd. dirs. Maine Cmty. Found., 2006—, mem. exec. com., 2007—. Named Disting. Daughter Pa., State Pa., 2004; recipient Brooks Graves award, Pa. Polit. Sci. Assn., 1982, Cmty. Svc. award, City of Phila., 1984, Women's Achievement award, YWCA, 1989, Adminstr. of Yr. award, Minn. Women in Higher Edn., 1994, Champion of Econ. Growth award, Maine Devel. Found., 2002, Women Who Make a Difference award, Internat. Women's Forum, 2004, Women of Distinction award, 2004, Woman of Distinction award, Kennebec Coun. Girl Scouts USA, 2006. Mem.: AAUW (bd. dirs. Phila. chpt. 1975—78, 1980—91, pres. 1984—86, nat. chair internat. fellowships panel 1987—91, nat bd. dirs. 1993—, Outstanding Woman award 1986), Am. Coun. Edn. (commn. on advancement racial and ethnic equality 2001—04, commn. women higher edn. 2005—06), Maine Ind. Colls. Assn. (pres. 1998—2000), Greater Portland Alliance Colls. and Univs. (pres. 1997—98), Nat. Assn. Ind. Colls and Univs. (com. policy analysis & pub. rels. 2001—), Am. Polit. Sci. Assn. Office: U New Eng PO Box 428A Kennebunkport ME 04046 Office Phone: 207-602-2306. Business E-Mail: sfeatherman@une.edu.

FEATHERSTONE, DIANE L., utilities executive; B in Econs. and History, Towson U., Md.; M in Econs., U. Va., Charlottesville. CPA; cert. fraud examiner. Various positions in human resources, fin. and acctg. Balt. Gas and Electric Co.; with Constellation, 1976; mng. dir. strategic planning Constellation Power Source; pres., CEO Constellation Energy Source; v.p. mgmt. consulting and auditing Constellation Energy Group, Balt.; v.p., gen. auditor Edison Internat., Rosemead, Calif., 2002, v.p., gen. auditor So. Calif. Edison subs., 2002, sr. v.p. human resources, sr. v.p. human resources So. Calif. Edison subs. Office: Edison Internat 2244 Walnut Grove Ave Rosemead CA 91770-3714 Office Phone: 626-302-1212.*

FEATHERSTONE, JOHN DOUGLAS BERNARD, dean, biochemistry educator; b. Stratford, New Zealand, Apr. 26, 1944; arrived in U.S., 1980. s. Alfred Douglas and Yvonne May (Richmond) F.; children: Michelle, Mark. BS chemistry and math., Victoria U., Wellington, New Zealand, 1962-64; MS phys. chemistry, U. Manchester, 1975; PhD chemistry, Victoria U., Wellington, New Zealand, 1977. Quality control chemist Unilever, New Zealand, 1965-66; tech. mgr. chem. Industries, Wellington, New Zealand, 1966-72; prodn. mgr. Quinoderm Pharms., Oldham, England, 1972-74; lect.r pharm. chemistry Ctrl. Inst. Tech., New Zealand, 1977-78; sr. rsch. fellow Med. Rsch. Coun., New Zealand, 1979-80; cons., dental chemistry and dental products, 1980—; asst. prof., part-time U. Rochester, NY, 1980-83; sr. rsch. assoc. Eastman Dental Ctr., Rochester, NY, 1980-88, chmn. dept. oral scis., 1983-95; assoc. prof. U. Rochester, NY, 1983-95; prof. Eastman Dental Ctr., Rochester, NY, 1988-95; prof. dept. of restorative dentistry U. Rochester, NY, 1995; prof. U. Calif., San Franscisco, 1995—99, prof, San Francisco, 1995—99, prof., chmn. dept. of preventive and restorative dental sci., 1999—; interim dean U. Calif. Sch. Dentistry, San Francisco, 2007—. Contbg. articles to profl. jour. Leader scouts, New Zealand, 1962-71; mem. New Zealand Nat. Tchg. Team, 1968-71; asst. nat. commr. Venturer Scouts New Zealand, 1968-70; mem. New Zeland Outdoor Tchg. Adv. Bd., 1978-79; New Zealand Mountain Rescue, 1976-80. Named Rsch. Lctr. of the Yr., Sch. of Dentistry, U. Calif., San Francisco, 2003; recipient Colgate Rsch. prize, New Zeland Internat. Assn. Dental Rsch., 1976, Colgate Travel Award, Internat. Assn. Dental Rsch., 1976, Edward Hatton Award, World Internat. Assn. Dental Rsch. Meeting, 1977, Hamilton Award, Royal Soc. New Zeland, 1979, Disting. Scientist Award, Internat. Assn. Dental Rsch., 2000, Zsolnai Rsch. Award, European Orgn. for Caries Rsch., 2002, Norton M. Ross Award, 2007. Fellow New Zeland Inst. Chemistry; mem. AAAS; Am. Chem. Soc.; European Orgn. Caries Rsch. (sr.); Internat. Assn. Dental Rsch. Office: U Calif San Francisco Dental Sch Dept Preventive Restorative Dental Sci 707 Parnassus Ave San Francisco CA 94143-0001 also: PO Box 371072 Montara CA 94037-1072 E-mail: jdbf@itsa.ucsf.edu.*

FEAVER, GEORGE ARTHUR, political science professor; b. Hamilton, Ont., Canada, May 12, 1937; arrived in U.S., 1967; s. Harold Lorne and Doris Davies (Senior) F.; m. Nancy Alice Poynter, June 12, 1963 (div. 1978); m. Ruth Helene Tubbesing, Mar. 8, 1986 (div. 1991); children: Catherine Fergusson, Noah George, Anthea Jane, Elysia Beatta. BA with honors, U. B.C., 1959; PhD, London Sch. Econs., 1962. Asst. prof. Mt. Holyoke Coll., South Hadley, Mass., 1962-65; lectr., rsch. assoc. London Sch. Econs. and Univ. Coll., London, 1965-67; assoc. prof. Georgetown U., Washington, 1967-68, Emory U., Atlanta, 1968-71, U. B.C., Vancouver, Canada, 1971-74, prof., 1974—2002, prof. emeritus, 2002—. Vis. fellow Australian Nat. U., Canberra, 1987, London Sch. Econs., 1991-92. Author: From Status to Contract, 1969; editor: Beatrice Webb's Our Partnership, 1975; editor: The Webbs in Asia: The 1911-12 Travel Diary, 1992; co-editor: Lives, Liberties and the Public Good, 1987; contbr. articles to profl. and gen. jours., chpts. to books. Fellow Can. Coun., 1970-71, 74-75, Am. Coun. Learned Socs., 1974-75, Social Scis. and Humanities Rsch. Coun. of Can., 1981-82, 86-91, Andrew Mellon fellow Harry Ransom Humanities Rsch. Ctr., U. Tex., Austin, 2006-07. Mem. Can. Polit. Sci. Assn., Am. Polit. Sci. Assn., Am. Soc. Polit. and Legal Philosophy, Conf. Study Polit. Thought, Inst. Internat. Philosophie Politique, The Traveller's Club (London). Avocations: rambling, wine appreciation. Home: 4776 W 7th Ave Vancouver BC Canada V6T 1C6 Office: Univ BC Dept Polit Sci Vancouver BC Canada V6T 1Z1 Home Phone: 604-228-9978; Office Phone: 604-822-2832. Business E-Mail: feaver@politics.ubc.ca.

FEAZELL, VIC, lawyer; b. Monroe, La., June 8, 1951; 1 child, Gregory Victor. BA, Mary Hardin Baylor Coll., 1972; JD, Baylor U., 1979. Bar: Tex. 1979, U.S. Dist. Ct. (5th cir.) 1988, U.S. Dist. Ct. (no. dist) 1988, U.S. Dist. Ct. (so. dist), 1989. Dir. drug abuse treatment program Mental Health-Mental Retardation, Waco, Tex., 1975-79; pvt. practice, 1979-82, Austin, 1989-94, 2004—; dist. atty. McLennan County, 1983-88; of counsel Rosenthal and Watson, 1995-2000; shareholder Feazell, Rosenthal and Watson, 2001—04; ptnr. Feazell & Tighe, 2004—. Pres. McLennan County Peace Officers Assn., Waco, 1984-87; pro bono def. counsel Henry Lee Lucas, 1989-94; expert legal corr. O.J. Simpson Trial, KTBC TV. Primary character: Careless Whispers, 1986 (Edgar award 1986); exec. prodr. Rhinos the Movie, Natural Selection, Final Redemption, Blood Sweat and Teeth, Rage in the Cage; pres. One Horn Prodns.; contbr. articles to profl. jours. Del. State Dem. Conv., Houston, 1988. Named Outstanding Young Alumni, U. Mary Hardin Baylor, Belton, Tex., 1985, Peace Officer of Yr., Waco JC's, 1986. Fellow Tex. Bar Found. (life); mem. ABA (chmn. jud. affairs com.), ATLA, Nat. Assn. Criminal Def. Lawyers (life), Tex. Trial Laywers Assn., Coll. of State Bar of Tex., Tex. Criminal Def. Lawyers Assn., State Bar Tex., Bar of U.S. Fifth Cir., Austin Bar Assn. (chmn. jud. affairs com.). Avocation: flim making. Office: Bldg 2 6300 Bridgeport Pky Ste 220 Austin TX 78730 Office Phone: 512-372-8100. Business E-Mail: vic@vicfeazell.com.

FECHTEL, VINCENT JOHN, legal administrator; b. Leesburg, Fla., Aug. 10, 1936; s. Vincent John and Annie Jo (Hayman) F.; m. Dixie Davenport, Feb. 1992; children: John, Katherine, Elizabeth D., MaryKatherine. BSBA, U. Fla., 1959. Mem. Fla. Ho. of Reps., 1972-78, Fla. Senate, 1978-80; parole commr. U.S. Dept. Justice, Chevy Chase, Md., 1983-96. Served with USNR and Fla. Nat. Guard. Mem. Alpha Tau Omega. Republican. Methodist. Home: 1414 Park Dr Leesburg FL 34748-6736

FECK, ASMUS WILHELM, retired mechanical engineer; b. Hamburg, Germany, July 11, 1920; arrived in US, 1965; s. Wilhelm A. and Frieda (Hafel) Feck; m. Elisabeth M. Feck-Unruh, Nov. 5, 1947; children: Axel, Jens. BS in Internat. Bus. Adminstrn., Comml. Coll., Hamburg, Germany, 1939; grad., Technische U., Hannover, Germany, 1951; MS in Mech. Engring., Engring. Coll., Hamburg, 1952. Lic. mech. and marine engr., Germany, UK. Engring. apprentice AERO airplane mfg. co., 1936—39; marine design, application and patent engr. Kort Propulsion Co., 1947—51; mgr. marine engring. sales Worthington Corp., Germany, 1951, mkgr. engineered products, 1953, gen. sales dir., 1957—59, European mgr. marine and nuc. energy Paris, 1960—65, mgr. internat. marine divsn. NJ, 1965—70; mgr. internat. marine and govt. dept. Studebaker-Worthington, Harrison, NJ, 1970—72; mem. staff internat. tanker design dept. ESSO/EXXON Co., NYC and Florham Park, NJ, 1972—87; ret., 1987. Instr. in field. Lt. German Air Force, 1941—47. Recipient Internat. Marine Engring. Merit award, Worthington Corp., 1967. Mem.: Soc. Naval Archs. and Marine Engrs., Soc. Naval Archs. and Marine Engrs. Germany, Soc. Mech. Engrs. Germany, Inst. Marine Engrs London (past chmn., vice chmn.), Propeller Club Port NY. Home: 5001 Little River Rd Apt W505 Myrtle Beach SC 29577-2461

FECTEAU, ROSEMARY LOUISE, educational administrator, educator, consultant; b. Niagara, Wis., Aug. 7, 1930; d. Andrew Raymond and Julianna Agnes (Wodenka) Waitrovich; m. Jack Richard Fecteau Sr. (dec. Dec. 1994), June 12, 1954; children: Michele, Julienne, Gervaise, Jack Jr., Andrew, Anne-Marie. BA with high distinction, U. R.I., Kingston, 1974; MS in Edn., U. Maine, Portland-Gorham, 1976; MS in Ednl. Adminstrn., U. So. Maine, Gorham, 1979; PhD, Columbia Pacific U., Novato, Calif., 1999, Columbia Commonwealth U., 2003. Cert. supt. schs. K-12. Sec. A.O. Smith Corp., Milw., 1949-54; sec. to Judge Irving W. Smith, Niagara, 1954-55; asst. tchr. Regional Resource Rm., Yarmouth, Maine, 1974-75; prin. Breakwater Sch., Cape Elizabeth, Maine, 1975-78; tchr. grades 6-8 Wells (Maine) Jr. H.S., 1978-79; dir. spl. svcs. Maine Sch. Adminstrv. Dist. 75, Bowdoin, Bowdoinham, Harpswell, Topsham, Maine, 1979-84; ednl. cons. various states, 1984—; mem. policy adv. group for Maine Gov. John Baldacci, 2002. Owner Serendipity Acres Sheep Farm; secondary handicapped task force State Dept. Edn., Augusta, 1980-81; chairperson nat. insvc. network U. Ind., Topsham, Maine, 1981-84. Author: Discover the Key to Equal Educational Opportunity: Follow the Path of Education Legislation, 2004. Mem. Maine Spl. Edn. Rev. Team; founder Project Co-Step and Project S.E.A.R.C.H.; mem. focus group Casco Bay Estuary Project Maine; brownie leader, girl scout cons. Girl Scouts Am., Erie, Pa., 1965-66; dir. women's Cursillo Movement, Erie, 1967; co-chair publicity St. Vincent Hosp., Erie, 1966-67; chair conservation commn. Town of North Yarmouth, 1987; del. Maine Dem. Conv., 1986; bd. dirs. Columbia Pacific U., 2004—. Mem.: Maine Real Estate Assn., Maine Children's Alliance, Physicians for Social Responsibility, Union of Concerned Scientists, Maine Organic Farmer and Gardener Assn., North Yarmouth Hist. Soc., U. So. Maine Alumni Assn. Avocations: music, arts, exercise. Home: Serendipity Acres 140 W Pownal Rd North Yarmouth ME 04097-6819 Home Phone: 207-829-5859; Office Phone: 207-756-5743. Personal E-mail: SAEBOOK@aol.com.

FECZKO, JOE, cosmetics executive; b. NJ; married; 1 child. Various positions Bloomingdale's, Neiman Marcus; exec. v.p., chief creative officer Federated Dept. Stores Inc.; group v.p. global design Avon Products Inc., 2006—. Office: Avon Products Inc 1345 Avenue of the Americas New York NY 10105-0196 Office Phone: 212-282-5000. Office Fax: 212-282-6049.*

FECZKO, JOSEPH M., pharmaceutical executive; BSc, Loyola U.; MD, U. Ill. Chgo. Coll. Medicine. With internat. med. mktg. Pfizer, Inc., NYC, 1982—86, mem. staff to grp. dir. European clin. devel. and ops. Pfizer Ctrl. Rsch. England, 1986—92, sr. v.p. med. and regulatory ops. Global Pharms., 1996—2002, chief med. officer, 2002—; med. dir. rsch. and devel. hdqs. Glaxo, London, 1992—96. Mem. tech. strategy bd. Dept. Trade and Industry, England; mem. adv. bd. U. Miami Ctr. Aging Rsch.; mem. Internat. Trachoma Initiative, Nat. Found. Infectious Diseases. Mem.: NY Acad. Medicine, Am. Fedn. Aging Rsch. Office: Pfizer Inc 235 E 42nd St New York NY 10017

FEDDERS, JOHN MICHAEL, lawyer; b. Covington, Ky., Oct. 21, 1941; s. Aloysius Henry and Mary Margaret (Schmidt) F.; children: Luke D., Mark A., Matthew C., Andrew M., Peter J. BA in Journalism, Marquette U., 1963; LL.B., Cath. U. Am., 1966. Bar: N.Y. 1967, D.C. 1967. Assoc. Cadwalader, Wickersham & Taft, NYC, 1966-71; exec. v.p. Gulf Life Holding Co., Dallas, 1971-73; with firm Arnold & Porter, Washington, 1973-81; ptnr., 1975-81; dir. Div. of Enforcement, SEC, 1981-85; ptnr. Miller, Cassidy, Larroca & Lewin, 1985-87; sole practice Washington, 1987—. Lectr. in field. Contbr. articles to legal jours. Recipient Service award Marquette U., 1977, Achievement award Cath. U. Am. Alumni Assn., 1982, Chmn.'s award for excellence SEC, 1982, Supervisory Excellence award, SEC, 1983 Mem. ABA, Assn. Bar City N.Y., Sigma Delta Chi, Phi Alpha Delta. Republican. Roman Catholic. Office: 1914 Sunderland Pl NW Washington DC 20036-1608 Office Phone: 202-659-2424. Business E-Mail: jfedders@erols.com.

FEDELE, MICHAEL CHRISTIAN, lieutenant governor, computer company executive; b. Minturno, Italy, Mar. 30, 1955; came to US, 1957, naturalized, 1965; s. Antonio and Filomenia (Corrente) F.; A.S., Norwalk State Tech. Coll., 1975; B.S., Fairfield U., 1977; m. Carol Ann Zezima, Oct. 17, 1976; children— Michael Christian, Briana Lyn, Alesandra. Computer operator Bristol Myers Co., Stamford, Conn., 1973-75, systems programmer, 1975-79; sr. systems programmer Duracell Internat., Bethel, Conn., 1979-80, mgr. systems and ops., 1980-81, asst. dir. info. systems, 1981-86, dir. info. systems, 1986-88; pres. Dana Mktg. Inc., Stamford, 1988-91; pres., owner Pinnacle Grp., 1991—, lt.gov., State of Conn., 2007-. Constable, Stamford, Conn., 1983-83, town bd. reps., 1987-91; mem. Stamford Republican Town Com., 1985, state rep., 1993-2002. Mem. Data Processing Mgrs. Assn., Am. Mgmt. Assn. Republican. Roman Catholic. Office: State Capitol Rm 304 Hartford CT 06106 Office Phone: 860-524-7384. Office Fax: 860-524-7304.*

FEDER, ARTHUR A., lawyer, association administrator; b. NYC, Mar. 23, 1927; s. Leo and Bertha (Franklin) F.; m. Ruth Musicant, Sept. 4, 1949; children: Gwen Lisabeth, Leslie Margaret, Andrew Michael. BA, Columbia Coll., 1949; LLB, Columbia U., 1951. Bar: N.Y. 1951. Assoc. Fulton Walter & Halley, 1951-53; rsch. asst. Am. Law Inst. Fed. Income, Estate and Gift Tax Project, 1953-54; assoc., ptnr. Roberts & Holland, NYC, 1954-66; ptnr. Willkie, Farr & Gallagher, NYC, 1966-69, Fried, Frank, Harris, Shriver & Jacobson, NYC, 1970-94, of counsel, 1994—; sr. adv. to exec. com. Herzog, Heine, Geduld Inc., NYC, 1996—2001; counsel Geduld & Co., LLC, NYC, 2002—, Cougar Trading, 2002—. Lectr. in law Columbia U., 1961-63; lectr. Am. Law Inst., NYU Inst. on Fed. Taxation, Practicing Law Inst., various profl. groups. Editor Columbia Law Rev., 1949-51; contbr. articles to profl. jours. With USN, 1945-46. Fellow Am. Coll. Tax Counsel; mem. ABA (taxation sect., chmn. com. on real property tax problems 1964-66, com. on legis. drafting 1968-84), Assn. of Bar of City of N.Y. (various coms.), N.Y. State Bar Assn. (taxation sect., co-chmn. various coms. 1982-86, sec. 1987-88, 2d vice chmn. 1988-89, vice chmn. 1989-90, chmn. 1990-91), Internat. Fiscal Assn. (coun. U.S.A. br. 1984-91), Am. Law Inst. (tax adv. group fed. income tax project), Univ. Club, Phi Beta Kappa. Democrat. Home: 25 W 81st St New York NY 10024-6023 Office: Cougar Trading 375 Park Ave New York NY 10152 Home Phone: 212-877-2464; Office Phone: 212-702-0690. Personal E-mail: afeder@nyc.rr.com. E-mail: afeder@cougartrading.com.

FEDER, BARNABY, reporter; BA, Williams Coll., 1972; JD, Univ. Calif., Berkeley. Writer World Bus. Weekly, Energy User News; tech. & med. device reporter New York Times, NYC, Chgo., London, 1980—. Office:

New York Times 229 W 43d St New York NY 10036 Office Phone: 212-556-7728. Office Fax: 212-556-1448. Business E-Mail: barnaby@nytimes.com.

FEDER, BENJAMIN, computer game company executive; BA, Columbia U., 1986; MBA, Harvard U., 1991. Corp. develop. mgr., Fox News Corp., sr. exec. to exec. v.p., News MCI Internet Ventures; founder, CEO MessageClick, Inc. (sold to Verso Technologies in 2000); co-founder, ptnr. ZelnickMedia, NYC, 2001—; interim CEO Take2 Interactive Software, Inc, NY, 2007—. Bd. dir. Columbia Music Entertainment, Take2 Interactive Software, Inc., NY, 2007—. Bd. dir. Nat. Family Caregivers Assn. Office: Take2 Interactive Software Inc 622 Broadway New York NY 10012 also: ZelnickMedia 650 5th Ave New York NY 10019*

FEDER, HARRY SIMON, bank executive; b. NYC, Aug. 20, 1953; s. Morris Louis and Lucy (Kraus) F.; m. Gilli Bortman, Mar. 1, 1977; children: Jean Ella, Laura Ann. BA in Econs., NYU, 1974; MBA in Internat. Fin., Syracuse U., 1976. Credit analyst Israel Discount Bank of N.Y., NYC, 1977-78, with domestic lending, 1978-79, with internat. lending, 1979-81, asst. v.p. corr. banking, 1981-85, v.p. treasury, 1986-94, 1st v.p. treasury, 1995-96, mgr. corr. banking and treasury, 1996-2000, sr. v.p. treasury and non-bank product devel., 2001—. Avocations: collecting stamps and coins, travel. Home: 66 Dora Ln New Rochelle NY 10804-1006 Office: Israel Discount Bank NY 511 5th Ave Rm 1003 New York NY 10017-4997

FEDER, JUDITH, dean; BA in Polit. sci., Brandeis U., 1968; MA in Polit. sci., Harvard U., 1970, PhD in Polit. sci., 1977. Rsch. fellow Brookings Inst., Washington, 1972—73; rsch. assoc. Spectrum Rsch., Inc., Denver, 1974—75; health policy analyst Govt. Rsch. Corp., Washington, 1975—76; svc. fellow Nat. Ctr. Health Svcs. Rsch., Dept. Health, Ed. & Welfare, 1976—77; sr. rsch. assoc. The Urban Inst., 1977—84; co-dir. Ctr. Health Policy Studies Georgetown U. Sch. Medicine, 1984—92; acting asst. sec. planning & evaluation US Dept. HHS, 1993—95; rsch. prof. pub. policy Georgetown U., 1995—98, prof., dean policy studies, 1999—. Author: Medicare: The Politics of Federal Hospital Insurance, 1977; co-author: Financing Health Care for the Elderly: Medicare, Medicaid and Private Health Insurance, 1979, Insuring the Nation's Health: Market Competition, Catastrophic and Comprehensive Approaches, 1981; editor (with John Holahan and Theodore Marmor): National Health Insurance: Conflicting Goals and Policy Choices, 1980; editor: (with Diane Rowland and Anita Salganicoff) Medicaid Financing Crisis: Balancing Responsibilities, Priorities and Dollars, 1993; contbr. articles to profl. jours., chapters to books. Sr. advisor Kaiser Family Found. commn. on Medicaid & the Uninsured; staff dir. US Congress Pepper Commn., 1989—91. Mem.: Nat. Acad. Soc. Ins., Nat. Acad. Pub. Adminstrn., Inst. Medicine. Office: Georgetown Pub Policy Inst 3600 N St NW Ste 200 Washington DC 20007

FEDER, ROBERT, lawyer; b. NYC, Nov. 29, 1930; BA cum laude, CCNY, 1953; LLB, Columbia U., 1953. Bar: N.Y. 1953, U.S. Tax Ct. 1956, U.S. Dist. Ct. (so. dist.) N.Y. 1974. V.p., gen. counsel Presdl. Realty Corp., White Plains, N.Y., 1953-71; ptnr. Cuddy & Feder LLP, White Plains, 1971—. Bd. dirs. Westchester County (N.Y.) Legal Aid Soc., 1972—, pres., 1974—78; adj. prof. sch. bus. Columbia U., NYC, 1988—89; bd. dirs. Presdl. Realty Corp. (Amex), Interplex Industries, Inc., Stellaris Health Network, Inc., vice chmn., 2001—04; adj. prof. Pace U. Law Sch., 1985—87. Pres. White Plains Cmty. Action Program, 1967—69; bd. dir. White Plains Hosp. Ctr., 1978—, also sec., treas., chmn., 1992—97, 2002—05; commr. White Plains Housing Authority, 1984—2002; chmn. White Plains Jud. Rev. Com., 2003, 2007, 2007; trustee SUNY-Purchase Coll. Found., 1988—, vice-chmn., 1995—. Mem.: ABA, Westchester County Bar Assn., Am. Coll. Real Estate Lawyers, White Plains Bar Assn., N.Y. State Bar Assn. Home: 9 Oxford Rd White Plains NY 10605-3602 Office: 445 Hamilton Ave 14th Fl White Plains NY 10601 Home Phone: 914-946-6342; Office Phone: 914-761-1300. Business E-Mail: rfeder@cuddyfeder.com. E-mail: rfeder@pipeline.com, RobertFeder@optonline.net.

FEDER, ROBERT, columnist; b. Chgo., May 17, 1956; s. Harold J. and Selma (Reisberg) F.; m. Janet Gail Elkins, June 16, 1985; 1 child, Emily Jacklyn. BS in Journalism, Northwestern U., 1978. Reporter, news editor Lerner Newspapers, Chgo., 1974-78, mng. editor, 1978-80; reporter Chgo. Sun-Times, 1980-83, TV/radio columnist, 1983—. Project cons. (TV documentary) Radio Faces, 1989; contbr. (spl. report) Ency. Brittanica, 1983, World Book Ency., 1996. Recipient Page One award Chgo. Newspaper Guild, 1976; named Best Daily Newspaper Columnist, New City, 1997. Mem. Soc. Profl. Journalists, Chgo. Headline Club, Chgo. Newspaper Guild, Northwestern Club of Chgo., Skokie Hist. Soc. Office: Chgo Sun-Times 350 N Orleans St Chicago IL 60654-1502 Business E-Mail: feder@suntimes.com.

FEDER, SAMUEL L., lawyer; b. 1971; AB, Coll. William and Mary; JD summa cum laude, U. Mich. Bar: 1996. Law clk. to Hon. Edward R. Becker US Ct. Appeals (3rd Cir.); atty. Harris, Wiltshire & Grannis, Kellogg, Huber, Hansen, Todd & Evans; trial atty. Fed. Programs Br. US Dept. Justice; legal adv. to Commr. Furchtgott-Roth FCC, Washington, legal adv. on common carrier matters to Commr. Martin, legal adv. to chmn., gen. counsel. Office: Office of General Counsel FCC 445 12 St SW Washington DC 20554

FEDER, SAUL E., lawyer; b. Bklyn., Oct. 8, 1943; s. Joseph Robert and Toby Feder; m. Marcia Carrie Weinblatt, Feb. 25, 1968; children: Howard Avram, Fayge Miriam, Tamar Miriam, Michael Elon, David Ben-Zion Aaron, Alexandra Rachel, Evan Daniel, Sarah Lily, Maya Malka, Batsheva, David E., Natan, Tehilla, Jamie. BS, NYU, 1965; JD, Bklyn. Law Sch., 1968. Bar: NY 1969, US Ct. Appeals (2d cir.) 1969, US Ct. Claims 1970, US Customs Ct. 1972, US Supreme Ct. 1972, US Ct. Customs and Patent Appeals 1974. Mng. lawyer Queens Legal Svcs., Jamaica, NY, 1970-71; ptnr. Previte-Glasser-Feder & Farber, Jackson Heights, NY, 1972-73, Hein-Waters-Klein & Feder, Far Rockaway, NY, 1973-78, Regosin-Edwards-Stone & Feder, NYC, 1979—. Spl. investigator Bur. Election Frauds, Atty. Gen.'s Office, NYC, 1976—77, spl. dep. atty. gen., 1969—70; arbitrator, consumer counsel small claims divsn. Civil Ct. City of NY, 1974—. Pres. Young Israel Briarwood, Queens, NY, 1978; chmn. polit. affairs com. Young Israel Staten Island, 1985—; rep. candidate State of NY Assembly, Queens, 1976; chmn. Stat Pac Polit. Action Com. Mem.: Com. on Law and Pub. Affairs, Internat. Acad. Law & Sci., Am. Jud. Soc., Soc. Med. Jurisprudence, Am. Arbitration Assn., NY Bar Assn., Queens County Bar Assn., Nassau County Bar Assn., Am. Judges Assn., NY Trial Lawyers Assn., Richmond County Bar Assn. Republican. Home: 259 Ardmore Ave Staten Island NY 10314-4349 Office: Regosin Edwards Stone & Feder 225 Broadway Ste 613 New York NY 10007-3059 Office Phone: 212-619-1990. Business E-Mail: sfeder@resflaw.com.

FEDERER, ROGER, professional tennis player; b. Basel, Switzerland, Aug. 8, 1981; s. Robert and Lynette Federer. Prof. tennis player Assn. Tennis Profls., 1998—; founder RF- RogerFederer Fragrance Line, 2003—. Mem. Swiss Davis Cup Team, 1999—. Goodwill amb. UNICEF, 2006—. Named Swiss of Yr., 2003, ATP Player of Yr., 2004, 2006, ATPtennis.com Fans' Favorite, 2004—06, Player of Yr., Internat. Tennis Writers Assn., 2004—06, Amb. for Tennis, 2004—06, Acad. Outstanding Athlete of Yr., US Sports Acad., 2005, 2006; named one of The World's Most Influential People, Time Mag., 2007; recipient Stefan Edberg Sportsmanship award, ATP, 2004, 2006, Arthur Ashe Humanitarian of Yr. award, 2006, Best Male Tennis Player, ESPY awards, 2005—07, Sportsman of the Yr., Laureus World Sports Awards, 2006. Achievements include winner, Wimbledon, 2003-07, Australian Open, 2004, 2006-07, US Open, 2004-06; winner, Qatar Open, 2006, Pacific Life Open, 2006, NASDAQ-100 Open, 2006, Gerry Weber Open, 2006, Rogers Cup, 2006, Japan Open, 2006, Masters Series, Madrid, 2006, Basel, 2006, Masters Cup, 2006; winner, Hamburg Masters, 2002, 2004-05, 2007, Western & Southern Grp. Fin. Masters, 2007; 50 Career Singles titles, 11 Grand Slam titles, 7 Doubles titles; became first player since 1988 to win three legs of the Grand Slam in the same year, 2004; holding record for consecutive wins (42) on grass-court, 2006; tied record of 160 consecutive weeks as the top-ranked player in men's tennis in 2007; runner-up, French Open, 2006; runner-up, Shanghai Cup, 2005, winner, Shanghai Cup, 2006. Avocations: golf, soccer, skiing, music, video games, playing cards.*

FEDERICO, JOSEPHINE A.M., music educator; b. Syracuse, NY, June 14, 1942; d. Matthew Frank and Mary Jane (Calcagno) Sindoni; m. Carmine Federico, June 20, 1964; children: Carmen J., Joanna M. Federico Cox. MusB in Music Edn., Marywood U., Scranton, 1964; MusM in Music Edn., Syracuse U., 1970; postgrad., Eastman Sch. Music, Rochester, NY, 1987, U. Buffalo, E. Stroudsburg U., Pa. Vocal music tchr. North Syracuse Ctrl. Schs., NY, 1964—68; pvt. music tchr. Liverpool, NY, 1964—; music dir. St. Margarets Ch., Mattydale, NY, 1979—84; choir dir. St. Rose Lima Ch., North Syracuse, 1983—84; music tchr. Solvay Sch. Dist., NY, 1986—89, Diocese of Syracuse/St. Rose Lima Sch., North Syracuse, 1989—2007. Dir. Italian Choraliers of Syracuse, 1980—; accompanist N.Y. State convs. of Order Sons of Italy in Am., 1980—; adjudicator N.Y. State Sch. Music Assn., 1984—; diocesan rep. Onondaga County Music Educators Assn., 1989—. Com. mem. Onondaga County Columbus Quincentennial Commn., 1990—92. Recipient Outstanding Music Educator award, Syracuse Symphony Orch., 2000. Mem.: Onondaga County Music Edn. Assn. (bd. dirs.), Onondaga County Music Educators Assn., Pastoral Musicians Assn., Ctrl. N.Y. Assn. Music Tchrs., N.Y. State Sch. Music Assn., Music Educators Nat. Conf., Marywood Coll. Alumni Assn. (pres. 1980—81), Order Sons of Italy in Am. (mem. state scholarship commn. 1980—, state trustee 1984—88, Progresso lodge pres. 1998—, state trustee 2006—). Roman Catholic. Home and Office: 4966 Driftwood Dr Liverpool NY 13088 Office Phone: 315-457-5010.

FEDERING, ERIC K., legislative staff member, public information officer; b. Bronx, NY, Feb. 10, 1960; s. Abe and Eileen Federing; m. Daphne V. Clones, May 2000. BA with distinction, George Washington U., 1982. Aide U.S. Dept. State, Washington, 1979-81; founder, dir. motion picture restoration effort MAD WORLD Campaign, Washington, 1982-91; press sec., speechwriter for mem. of congress Rep. Norman Y. Mineta, Washington, 1987-93; supr. press info. ctr. Dem. Nat. Conv., NYC, 1992, dir. press info. ctr. ops. Chgo., 1996, LA, Calif., 2000, Boston, 2004; dir. comm. Pub. Works and Transp. Com. U.S. Ho. of Reps., Washington, 1993-94, Dem. dir. comm. Transp. and Infrastructure Com., 1994-97; press sec. Senator Joseph I. Lieberman, Washington, 1997-99; dir. bus. pub. policy, govt. affairs KPMG LLP, 1999—; mem. transition team Sec.-Designate Norman Y. Mineta U.S. Dept. Commerce, 2000. Congl. liaison to Smithsonian Instn. Bd. Regents, 1995; U.S. dir., founder Washington internship program The Flinders U. Australia, 1999-2003; founder, dir. Uni-Capitol Washington Internship Programme, 2003—; lectr. in field. Press sec. to nat. co-chair Dukakis-Bentsen Presdl. Campaign, Washington, 1988; prin. Coun. for Excellence in Govt., 2002—; bd. dirs. Nat. Japanese Am. Meml. Found., 2003—; bd. dirs. Nat. Conf. on Citizenship, 2004—. Recipient Outstanding Achievement commendation Sec. of State, 1981, Chmns. Excellence in Volunteerism award KPMG LLP, Washington, 2004. Mem. Phi Beta Kappa. Democrat. Avocations: sound recordings, motion pictures, theater restoration, photography. E-mail: efedering@kpmg.com.

FEDERLE, MICHAEL, publishing executive; married; 2 children. B, Colby Coll., 1981. With New Eng. Publs., Camden, Maine, Color Computer mag. (bought by Ziff Davis); sales devel. mgr. People Mag., 1985; assoc. advt. dir. Life Mag., NY, 1992; NY advt. dir. Fortune Mag., 1995, assoc. pub. NYC, 1997—99, pub., 1999—. Office: Time Inc Time Life Bldg Rockefeller Ctr New York NY 10020-1393*

FEDERMAN, DANIEL DAVID, academic administrator, endocrinologist, educator; b. NYC, Apr. 16, 1928; m. Elizabeth Buckley; children: Lise, Carolyn. BA, Harvard U., 1949, MD, 1953. Diplomate Am. Bd. Internal Medicine. Intern Mass. Gen. Hosp., Boston, 1953—54, resident in medicine, 1954—55, fellow in medicine, 1958—60; instr. to prof. Harvard Med. Sch., Boston, 1961—72, dean students and alumni, 1977—89, prof. medicine, 1977—92, dean med. edn., 1989—2000, Carl W. Walter prof. medicine and med. edn., 1992—, sr. dean alumni rels. and clin. tchg., 2000—; chmn. medicine Stanford Med. Sch., Palo Alto, Calif., 1972—77. Author: (med. textbook) Abnormal Sexual Development, 1967; editor: Scientific American Medicine. Recipient Disting. Educator Award, Endocrine Soc., 1999, Abraham Flexner Award for Disting. Svc. to Med. Edn., Assn. Am. Med. Colleges, 2001. Master: ACP (pres. Phila. 1982—83, named Mass. Physician of Yr. 1994, Disting. Tchr. Award 1995); mem.: Inst. Medicine. Office: Harvard Med Sch Office of Dean Bldg A-101 25 Shattuck St Boston MA 02115-6027

FEDERSPIEL, HOWARD M., political science professor; b. Springville, NY, Mar. 10, 1932; s. Velma V. Martindill and Manley M. Federspiel; m. Johanna H. Hirsch, July 9, 1957 (dec.); children: Karen A., Karl J. BA, Capital U., Bexley, Ohio, 1954; MA, McGill U., Montreal, Quebec, Can., 1962, PhD, 1966. Fgn. affairs analyst US Dept. State, Washington, 1962—66; internat. affairs analyst Rsch. Analysis Corp., McLean, Va., 1966—68; fgn. affairs analyst Advanced Studies Group of Westinghouse Corp., Arlington, Va., 1968—68; asst. prof. polit. sci. and history Lenoir-Rhyne Coll., Hickory, NC, 1968—70; prof., dept. chair polit. sci. Winthrop U., Rock Hill, SC, 1970—79; assoc. dean Ohio State U., Newark, Ohio, 1979—84; field dir. and team leader Asian Devel. Bank, U. North Sumatra Devel. Project, Medan, North Sumatra, Indonesia, 1984—86; assoc. dir. World Bank, Third Indonesian Higher Edn. Project, Jakarta, Indonesia, 1987—88; vis. prof. McGill U. Inst. Islamic Studies, Montreal, 1992—93; dir. Can.-Indonesia Muslim Higher Edn. Project, Montreal, 1995—96; prof. polit. sci. Ohio State U., Newark, Ohio, 1979—. Cons. Asian Devel. Bank, U. North Sumatra Higher Edn. Project, Medan, North Sumatra, Indonesia, 1989, Asian Devel. Bank, Manila, 1990; project dir. tng. Sr. Indonesian Dept. Religion Adminstrs., Montreal, 1993; program dir. seminar contemporary Islam Ohio U., Athens, 2003. Author: (scholarly book) Persatuan Islam: Islamic Reform in Twentieth Century Indonesia, 1979, Muslim Intellectuals and National Development in Indonesia, 1992, The Usage of Traditions of the Prophet in Contemporary Indonesia, 1993, Popular Indonesian Literature of the Qur'an, 1994, A Dictionary of Indonesian Islam, 1995, Islam and Ideology in the Emeging Indonesian State, 2001, Indonesian Muslim Intellectuals of the 20th Century, 2007, Sultans, Shamans and Scholars: Islam and Muslims in Southeast Asia, 2007. Vice chair Mcpl. Planning Coun., Rock Hill, 1966—69; precinct chair Dem. Party, Rock HIll, 1960—69; co-author ch. history St Paul's Luth. Ch., Newark, 1984; mem. adv. coun. US Info. Svc. Office, Medan, 1955—56. Specialist third class and German translator US Army, 1955—58, German Federal Republic. Fellow, US Endowment Humanities, 1979; scholar, Conf. Group on German Politics, 1974, Fulbright Commn., 1994. Mem.: Mid. East Assn. Am., Assn. Asian Studies (S.E. regional pres. 1976—77). Independent. Lutheran. Avocations: gardening, woodworking, carpentry. Office: Ohio State Univ 1179 University Dr Newark OH 53055-1797 Office Phone: 740-366-9297. Office Fax: 740-366-5047. Business E-Mail: federspiel.1@osu.edu.

FEDEWA, MICHAEL JOSEPH, school system administrator; b. Mt. Pleasant, Mich., Nov. 16, 1958; s. Frank Arnold and Barbara Kay Fedewa; m. Beverly Bernard Fedewa, Nov. 24, 1982; children: Michael Joseph Jr., Doranna Margaret. BA, Alma Coll., 1981; MEd, N.C. State U., 1987, DEd, 2005. Tchr., coach South Granville HS, Creedmoor, NC, 1981—83, asst. prin., 1983—85, prin., 1991, 1994, Mary Potter Mid. Sch., 1986—89; tchr. evaluator Granville County Schs., Oxford, NC, 1986; prin. No. Granville Mid. Sch., Oxford, NC, 1989—91, South Granville Mid. Sch., Creedmoor, NC, 1991—94; supt. schs. Diocese of Raleigh, NC, 1994—. Chmn. adv. com. N.C. Charter Schs., Raleigh, 1997—2005, Pks. and Recreation, Ocford, NC, 2001—. Mem. Lions Club, Oxford, NC, 1990, South Granville Exch. Club, Creedmoor, NC, 1991—94. Named Outstanding Young Educator, Jaycees, 1987, Prin. of Yr., Granville County Schs., 1993; recipient Disting. Alumnus award, N.C. State U., 1989. Mem.: NEA, ASCD, Chief Adminstrs. Cath. Edn., N.C. ASCD, K.C. (Grand Knight 1997—99). Roman Catholic. Avocations: golf, basketball, running, attending sporting events. Home: 108 Planters Pl Oxford NC 27565 Office: Diocese of Raleigh 715 Nazareth St Raleigh NC 27606 E-mail: fedewa@raldior.org.

FEDOROCHKO, WILLIAM, JR., retired military officer, military analyst; b. Bayonne, NJ, Sept. 6, 1940; s. William and Helen (Dinis) F.; m. Sandra L. Clements, Dec. 10, 1966; 1 child, Sharon. BA in Econs., Washington and Jefferson Coll., 1962; MA in Econs., U. Pitts., 1971. Commd. 2d lt. U.S. Army, 1962, advanced through grades to brig. gen., 1989; platoon leader, staff officer 14th Armored Cav. Rgt., Fed. Republic Germany, 1962-64; staff officer Dept. Army, Washington, 1973-76; comdr. 1st Armored Div. Materiel Mgmt. Ctr., 501st Supply and Transport Bn., Fed. Republic Germany, 1976-80; student Def. Systems Mgmt. Coll., 1980, Indsl. Coll. Armed Forces, 1981; spl. asst. for joint activities Office of Comdr., Army Materiel Command, Alexandria, Va., 1981-83; chief acquisition and support program analysis div. Office Chief of Staff Army, Washington, 1983-84; comdr. 13th Support Command, Ft. Hood, Tex., 1984-87; spl. asst. Office Under Sec. Def. for Acquisition, Washington, 1987-88, dep. dir. program integration, 1988-90; dep. dir. force structure and resources Joint Staff, J-8, Washington, 1990-93; ret., 1993; sr. policy analyst RAND, Washington, 1993-94; sr. fellow Logistics Mgmt. Inst., McLean, Va., 1994-98; policy analyst strategy, forces and resources divsn. Inst. for Defense Analyses, Alexandria, Va., 1998—. Decorated Legion of Merit with 4 oak leaf clusters, Def. D.S.M. with oak leaf cluster. Mem. Assn. Quartermasters. Baptist. Avocations: golf, tennis. Home: 11404 Stonewall Jackson Dr Spotsylvania VA 22553-4607 Office: Inst for Def Analyses 4850 Mark Center Dr Alexandria VA 22311-1882 Business E-Mail: wfedoroc@ida.org.

FEDOROFF, NINA VSEVOLOD, research scientist, consultant, educator; b. Cleve., Apr. 9, 1942; d. Vsevolod N. Fedoroff and Olga S. (Snegireff) Stacy; children: Natasha, Kyr, James. BS, Syracuse U., NY, 1966; PhD, Rockefeller U., N.Y.C., 1972. Asst. mgr. transl. bur. Biol. Abstracts, Phila., 1962-63; flutist Syracuse Symphony Orch., 1964-66; acting asst. prof. UCLA, 1972-74; postdoctoral fellow UCLA and Carnegie Inst. Washington, Los Angeles and Balt., 1974-78; staff scientist Carnegie Inst. Washington, Balt., 1978-95; dir. Biotechnol. Inst., Pa. State U., 1995—, Willaman prof. of life scis., 1995—, Evan Pugh prof., 2002—; external prof. Santa Fe Inst., 2003—. Dir. Life Scis. Consortium, Pa. State U., 1996—2002; prof. dept. biology John Hopkins U., 1979-95; mem. devel. biology panel NSF, Washington, 1979-80; sci. adv. panel Office of Tech. Assessment, Congress, Washington, 1979-80; recombinant DNA adv. com. NIH, Bethesda, Md., 1980-84; sci. adv. com. Japanese Human Frontier Sci., 1988; sci adv. com. Competitive Rsch. Grants Office, USDA; mem. commn. on life scis., basic biology bd. NRC, NAS, 1984-90; bd. dirs. Genetics Soc. Am.; mem. bd. overseers Harvard U., 1988-91; trustee BIOSIS, Phila., 1990-96; mem. NAS Coun., 1991-94; dir. Internat. Sci. Found., 1992-93; mem. adv. com. Directorate for Biol. Scis., 1994-97; bd. dirs. Sigma-Aldrich Corp.; mem. nat. sci. bd. NSF, 2000-06; sci. and tech. advisor to US Sec. of State Condoleezza Rice, 2007-. Editor: Gene, 1981—84, Perspectives in Biology and Medicine, 1991—2001, Procs. Nat. Acad. Sci., 1996—2000; editor, bd. rev. editors: Sci., 1985, mem. sci. adv. bd.: The Plant Jour., 1991—98, book editor: various publs.; contbr. chapters to books articles to profl. jours. Named 2006 Nat. Medal Sci. Laureate, NSF, 2007; recipient Merit award, NIH, 1990, Howard Taylor Ricketts award, U. Chgo., 1990, Arents Pioneer award, Syracuse U., 2003; grantee, NSF and USDA, 1979—84, NIH, 1984—99, NSF, 1992—, NASA, 1997—2000. Mem.: AAAS, NAS (editor procs. 1995—2000), AAAS (bd. dirs. 2000—03), European Acad. Scis., Am. Acad. Arts and Scis., Nat. Sci. Bd., Sigma Xi (McGovern Sci. and Soc. medal 1997), Phi Beta Kappa (vis. scholar 1984—85, vis. scholar 1984—85). Avocations: choral music, gardening, tango. Home: 2398 Shagbark Ct State College PA 16803-3367 Office: Huck Insts Life Scis Pa State U University Park PA 16802

FEDOROV, SERGEI, professional hockey player; b. Pskov, Russia, Dec. 13, 1969; Mem. Detroit Red Wings, 1990—2003, Anaheim Mighty Ducks, 2003—05, Columbus Blue Jackets, 2005—. Founder Sergei Fedorov Found., 1998—. Named to NHL All-Star Game, 1992, 1994, 1996, 2001—03; recipient Hart Trophy, 1994, Selke Trophy, 1994, 1996, Lester B. Pearson award, 1994, Player of Yr. award, Hockey News, 1994, Sporting News, 1999, Hockey Digest, 1994, Silver medal, Olympic Games, Nagano, Japan, 1998. Achievements include being a member of Stanley Cup Champion Detroit Red Wings, 1997, 1998, 2002. Avocations: golf, boating, travel. Office: c/o Columbus Blue Jackets 200 W Nationwide Blvd Columbus OH 43215

FEE, ELIZABETH, medical historian, administrator; b. Belfast, Northern Ireland, Dec. 11, 1946; d. John Alexander and Deirdre (Carson) F. BA, Cambridge U., Eng., 1968, MA, 1972; PhD, Princeton U., 1978. came to U.S., 1968. Prof. history and health policy Johns Hopkins U., Balt., 1978—; chief history of medicine divsn. Nat. Libr. of Medicine, Bethesda, Md., 1995—. Author: Women and Health: The Politics of Sex in Medicine, 1983, Disease and Discovery: A History of the Johns Hopkins School of Hygiene and Public Health, 1916-1939, 1987, (with Daniel M. Fox) AIDS: The Burdens of History, 1988 (with Linda Shopes and Linda Zeidman) The Baltimore Book: New Views of Local History, 1991, (with Roy M. Acheson) A History of Education in Public Health: Health That Mocks the Doctors' Rules, 1991, (with Daniel M. Fox) AIDS: The Making of a Chronic Disease, 1992, (with Nancy Krieger) Women's Health, Politcs, and Power: Essays on Sex/Gender, Medicine, and Public Health, 1994, (with Steven H. Corey) Garbage! The History and Politics of Trash in New York City, 1994, (with Esther M. Sternberg, Anne Harrington, Thedore Brown) Emotions and Disease: An Exhibition at the National Library of Medicine, 1997, (with Theodore M. Brown) Making Medical History: The Life and Times of Henry E. Sigerist, 1997, (with Theodore M. Brown) The APHA: 125 Years Old--and Approaching the Millennium, 1997, (with Theodore M. Brown) American Public Health Association. Conflict and Controversy: From Medical Care Policy to the Politics of Environmental Health, 1998, (with Charles S. Marwick) Breath of Life: An Exhibition That Examines the History of Asthma, the Experiences of People with Asthma, and Contemporary Efforts to Understand and Manage the Disease, 2001, (with Susan E. Lederer and Patricia Tuohy) Frankenstein: Penetrating the Secrets of Nature: An Exhibition by the National Library of Medicine, 2002; contbr. monographs to profl. jours. Recipient Kellogg Nat. fellowship, Kellogg Found., 1984-87, Golden Apple award, Johns Hopkins U., 1991, NCM Regents award for scholarship, 2000. Mem. Am. Pub. Health Assn. (Viseltear award 1997), Sigerist Circle (chair), Am. Assn.

History of Medicine. Avocations: gardening, hiking, theater. Office: Nat Libr Medicine 8600 Rockville Pike Bethesda MD 20894-0001 Home Phone: 301-571-4324; Office Phone: 301-496-5406. E-mail: elizabeth_fee@nlm.nih.gov.

FEE, WILLARD EDWARD, JR., otolaryngologist; b. Portchester, June 10, 1943; s. Willard E. and Jane Frances (Cromwell) F.; m. Caroline Fee, June 13, 1965; children: Heather, Adam. BS cum laude, U. San Francisco, 1965; MD magna cum laude, U. Colo., 1969. Cert. Am. Bd. Otolaryngology, 1974. Intern Harbor Gen. Hosp., Torrance, Calif., 1969-70; resident in gen. surgery Wadsworth VA Hosp., LA, 1970-71; resident in head and neck surgery UCLA Sch. Medicine, 1971-74; asst. prof. Stanford (Calif.) U. Med. Ctr., 1974-80, assoc. prof. otolaryngology, 1980-86, prof., 1986—, Edward C. & Amy H. Sewall prof., 1995—, chmn. dept., 1980-00. Dir. Am. Bd. of Otolaryngology, Houston, 1985-2003; chmn. med. sch. faculty senate Stanford U., 1992-94. Editl. bd. Archives in Otolaryngology, Chgo., 1984-95; contbr. numerous articles to profl. jours. Mem. Collegium ORLAS-US (chmn. 1995-2001), Paul H. Ward Soc., Inc. (pres. 1988-89), Am. Soc. Head and Neck Surgery (pres. 1989-90), Am. Acad. Otolaryngology and Head and Neck Surgery, Calif. Soc. Otolaryngology (pres. 1995-99), Alpha Omega Alpha. Home: 907 Clark Way Palo Alto CA 94304 Office: 875 Blake Wilbur Dr Cancer Ctr Rm 2227 Stanford CA 94305-5826 Office Phone: 650-725-6500.

FEEHERRY, ANTHONY M., lawyer; b. Worcester, Mass., July 27, 1947; AB magna cum laude, Coll. of Holy Cross, 1969; JD cum laude, Boston U., 1974. Bar: Mass. 1974. Law clk. to Hon. James L. Oakes U.S. Ct. Appeals, 2d cir., 1974-75; ptnr., litig. dept. Goodwin Procter LLP (formerly Goodwin, Procter & Hoar), Boston; co-chair, litig. dept. Goodwin Procter LLP, Boston, 1995—2004. Mem. Zoning Appeals Bd., Wenham, Mass. Mem.: ABA, Boston Bar Assn. Address: Goodwin Procter LLP Exchange Pl 53 State St Boston MA 02109-2803 Office Phone: 617-570-1390. Office Fax: 617-523-1231. Business E-Mail: afeeherry@goodwinprocter.com.

FEEKS, J. MICHAEL, bank executive; b. Grand Rapids, Mich., July 19, 1942; s. John O'D. and Evelyn R.F. BBA, Manhattan Coll., 1964; MBA, NYU, 1970. Sr. v.p. Mfrs. Hanover Trust Co., NYC, 1980-87; pres., COO Poughkeepsie Savs. Bank, FSB, 1987-91; exec. v.p. Citizens First Nat. Bank of N.J., 1982-94; regional pres. Summit Bank, Princeton, NJ, 1994—2000; mng. dir. Concurrent Technologies Corp., Liberty Corner, NJ, 2000—; prin. Bank Experts Group, Liberty Corner, NJ, 2000—. Office: Concurrent Technologies Corp 150 Allen Rd Liberty Corner NJ 07938 Office Phone: 908-696-7973.

FEELISCH, MARTIN, research scientist, consultant; b. Remscheid, Northrhine Westfalia, Germany, June 18, 1959; s. Guenter Max and Hildegard Feelisch; m. Lucia del Pilar Revelo Silva, Jan. 28, 1999; children: Nicolas Constantin, Lucia Gabriela Revelo, Marco Laurenz, Nicole Martina. Pharmacy Technician, Pharmazeutisch-Technische Lehranstalt, Solingen, Germany, 1979—81; BSc, Heinrich-Heine-U., Dusseldorf, Germany, 1985; PhD summa cum laude, Heinrich-Heine-University, Dusseldorf, Germany, 1988. Venia legendi for Pharmacology & Toxicology U. Cologne, Germany, 1997, lic. pharmacist Head Provincial Govt. Dusseldorf, Germany, 1986, cert. specialist for drug info. Apothekerkammer Nordrhein, Germany, 1992, Expert Degree in Pharmacology German Pharmacological Soc., 1992. Vis. rsch. scientist The Wellcome Rsch. Labs., Beckenham, Kent, England, 1989—90; head dept. pharmacology Schwarz Pharma AG, Monheim, Northrhine-Westfalia (NRW), Germany, 1990—97, dir. pharmacology and internat. project coord., 1991—97; sr. lectr. , sci. coord. Wolfson Inst., U. Coll. London, 1997—99; prof. molecular and cellular physiology La. State U. Health Scis. Ctr., Shreveport, 1999—2003; prof. medicine, prof. biochemistry Boston U. Sch. Medicine, 2003—07; prof. exptl. medicine & integrative biology U. Warwick, Coventry, England, 2007—. Co-founder, dir. The Nitric Oxide Soc., 1996—; cons. Lacer S.A., Barcelona, 1997—99; vis. prof. pharmacology U. Florence, Italy, 1999—99; sci. adv. bd. mem. Vasopharm Biotech GmbH, Giessen, Germany, 2000—, NitroMed Inc., Bedford, Mass., 2003—. Author, editor: reference book Method in Nitric Oxide Research, 1996, mem. editl. bd.: Nitric Oxide Chemistry & Biology, 1993—, Endothelium, 1993—, Brit. Jour. Pharm., 2005—; contbr. articles to profl. jours. Named Hon. Sr. Lectureship in Pharmacology, U. Coll. London, 1998—99; fellow, Smith Kline Dauelsberg, 1987—88; grantee, Nat. Heart, Blood and Lung Inst., 2002—. Mem.: Nitric Oxide Soc. (dir. 1996—2003), Soc. for Free Radical Biology and Medicine, German Pharm. Soc., German Soc. for Cardiology, Heart and Circulation Rsch., German Soc. for Exptl. and Clin. Pharmacology and Toxicology (Fritz-Kulz prize 1990), Am. Physiol. Soc., Am. Heart Assn., Am. Chem. Soc. Achievements include patents in field. Office: U Warwick MEd Sch Gibbet Hill Campus Coventry CV4 7AL England Home Phone: 617-838-3553; Office Phone: 617-414-8150. Business E-Mail: feelisch@bu.edu.

FEENEY, DON JOSEPH, JR., psychologist; b. Greenville, NC, Jan. 17, 1948; s. Don Joseph Sr. and Louise (Saieed) Feeney; 1 child, Kelly Lynn. BA, Colgate U., 1971; MA, Gov.'s State U., 1973; PhD, Loyola U., Chgo., 1979. Registered psychologist Ill., Ind., diplomate Am. Bd. Psychol. Specialties, Am. Bd. Psychology, cert. addictions counselor; profl. coach Grow Tng. Inst., Inc. Clin. dir. Champaign (Ill.) Coun. on Alcoholism, 1976-79; pvt. practice psychology, hypnotherapy, family svcs. Downers Grove, Ill., 1979—, Dangerous Drugs Com., Chgo., 1979-80; psychologist Tri-City Mental Health Ctr., East Chicago, Ind., 1980-82; psychologist alcohol treatment program Christ Hosp., Oak Lawn, Ill., 1982—; cons. Cons. Psychol. Svcs. PC, Downers Grove, 1985—, ceo, 1998—. Chmn. adv. coun. alcoholism Govs. State U., University Park, Ill., 1979—82; devel., presenter self-hypnosis and wellness programs on smoking, weight control and chem. abuse. Author: Entrancing Relationships: Exploring the Hypnotic Framework of Addictive Relationships, 1999, Motif: The Transformative Creation of Self, 2001, Creating Cultural Motifs in the War Against Terrorism, 2003; contbr. articles to profl. jours.; guest cons. (TV series) Oprah Winfrey, Jerry Springer, Jenny Jones, others. Loyola U. fellow, 1976. Fellow: Am. Coll. Forensic Examiners (diplomate); mem.: APA, Chgo. Coun. Fgn. Rels., Ill. Psychol. Assn. Roman Catholic. Avocations: chess, tennis, weightlifting, jogging, reading. Office: Cons Psychol Svcs PC 6900 Main St Ste 160 Downers Grove IL 60516-3455 Office Phone: 708-921-3827. Personal E-mail: drtc11@hotmail.com.

FEENEY, JOAN N., judge; BA in French and Govt., Conn. Coll., 1975; MA, Amherst Coll.; JD, Suffolk Univ. Law Sch., 1978. Law clk. to Judge Harold Lavien U.S. Bankruptcy Ct. Mass., 1978-79, law clk. to Judge James N. Gabriel, 1978-79, 82-86; assoc. Feeney & Freeley, Boston, 1979-82; assoc., then ptnr. Hanify & King P.C., Boston, 1986-92; bankruptcy judge U.S. Bankruptcy Ct. Mass., Boston, 1992—. Mem. Suffolk Univ. Law Review, 1976-78; editor Suffolk Transnational Journal, 1977-78, Suffolk Voluntary Defenders, 1977-78, Volunteer Lawyer's Project. Mem. Mass. Assn. of Women Lawyers, Am. Bankruptcy Inst. Office: Thomas O'Neill Federal Bldg 10 Causeway St Rm 1101 Boston MA 02222-1009

FEENEY, JOHN ROBERT, banker; b. Newark, Feb. 26, 1950; s. P. John and Elizabeth (Podda) F.; m. Judi Tomkowit, June 22, 1974; children: Michael, Ryan, Mark. BS, U. Del., 1972; MBA, Seton Hall U., 1977. Asst. sec., also various other positions Irving Trust Co., NYC, 1972-76; asst. sec., mgr. profit planning Irving Bank Corp., NYC, 1976-78; controller, v.p. Ocean County Nat. Bank, Point Pleasant, NJ, 1978-81, controller, sr. v.p., 1981-83; sr. v.p., CFO, The Summit Bancorporation, NJ, 1983-85, exec. v.p., CFO NJ, 1985-93, sr. exec. v.p., CFO NJ, 1994-96; exec. v.p. Summit Bancorp, NJ, 1996—2001; exec. v.p., CFO Shrewsbury State Bank, 2001—05; sr. v.p. First Atlantic Fed. Credit Union, 2005—. Republican. Roman Catholic. Avocations: surfing, basketball, golf. Home: 249 Williamsburg Dr Shrewsbury NJ 07702-4564

FEENEY, MARK, journalist; b. Winchester, Mass., July 28, 1957; s. Henry Patrick and Agnes Patricia (Carney) F.; m. Claire Silvers; 1 child, William. BA, Harvard U., 1979. Rschr. The Boston Globe, 1979, data base mgr., 1980, asst. book editor, 1982, book editor, 1993-94; staff writer Boston Globe Mag., 1993-94; editor Focus sect. The Boston Globe, 1991—95; staff reporter Boston Globe Mag., 1995—; lectr. Am. studies Brandeis U., 2004—; Robbins prof. writing Princeton U., 2007. Author: Nixon at the Movies, 2004; contbr. articles to The New Republic, Commonweal, Washington Monthly, L.A. Times, other publs. Mem. Nat. Book Critics Circle (v.p. 1986-89). Democrat. Roman Catholic. Home: 26 Mead St Cambridge MA 02140-2014 Office: The Boston Globe 135 Morrissey Blvd Boston MA 02125-3338

FEENEY, MARYANN MCHUGH, not-for profit professional; b. Bklyn., July 9, 1948; d. Michael Daniel and Mary Bridget (Hourican) McH.; m. Brian Francis Feeney, Sept. 21, 1974 (dec. Mar. 1992); 1 child, Michael. BA, Marymount Manhattan Coll., 1980; MA, Bklyn. Coll., 2002. Human resources mgr. Muir Cornelius Moore, Inc., NYC, 1977-84; human resources dir. Statue of Liberty-Ellis Island Found., NYC, 1984—88; pres. The Taft Inst., NYC, 1988—97; dir. nat. fundraising Girls Scouts U.S.A., NYC, 1997—99; exec. dir. Bklyn. Tech. H.S. Alumni Assn., 2003—05; dir. instnl. advancement Bishop Loughlin Meml. H.S., 2005—. Exec. prodr. Your Vote Video, 1991 (nominated ACE and Emmy awards 1991). Bd. dirs. Bklyn. Conservatory of Music, 1992-94, SFX-Prospect Park Baseball, Bklyn., 1986-2006; pres. emeritus, trustee The Taft Inst. at Queens Coll., 1997—. Recipient Cmty. Svc. award SFX-Prospect Park Baseball, 1992, 95, 97. Mem. Ireland House at NYU, Park Slope Civic Coun. (trustee). Democrat. Roman Catholic. Avocations: reading, history, gardening. Office Phone: 718-857-2700. Personal E-mail: mfeeney3@aol.com.

FEENEY, MATTHEW EDWARD, linguist, educator; b. Livermore, Calif., Dec. 24, 1955; s. Martin Edward and Dorothy Ann Feeney. BA, U. Wyo., 1980; MA, SUNY, Albany, 1988; Cert. Advanced Study, 1994; PhD, U. Kans., 2003. Lang. lab. asst. U. Wyo., Laramie, 1989—91, editor English transls. Russian articles, 2004—; grad. asst. SUNY, Albany, 1991—93, dir. study abroad program in Moscow, Russia, 1992—93; tchg. asst. dept. Slavic lang. and lit. U. Kans., Lawrence, 1998—2003, dir. summer study abroad program in Croatia, 2002—03; asst. prof. Russian lang. and Slavic studies Our Lady of Corpus Christi, Tex., 2006—. Presenter in field. Contbr. articles and scholarly papers to profl. jours. and confs.; editor: (English transls. Russian articles in lit. criticism) U. Wyoming, 2004—. Mem.: MLA, Ctrl. Assn. Russian Tchrs. Am., Am. Assn. Tchrs. Slavic and East European Langs., Profl. Assn. Edn., Pi Lambda Theta Internat. Honor Soc. Office Phone: 361-289-9095. Personal E-mail: mef2@hotmail.com.

FEENEY, TOM, congressman; b. Phila., May 21, 1958; m. Ellen Stewart. BA in Polit. Sci., Pa. State U., 1980; JD, U. Pitts., 1983. Mem. Fla. Ho. of Reps., 1990—94, 1996—2002, speaker, 2000—02; majority coun. liaison; mem. procedural coun. chair reapportionment com.; mem. econ. impact, govt. responsibility, justice couns.; mem. US Congress from 24th Fla. dist., 2003—; mem. Ho. Judiciary com., Fin. Svcs. com., Sci. com. Rep. nominee lt. gov., 1994; legis. del. chmn. Orange County, 1993, Seminole County, 1996; ambassador to Macedonian Govt., Internat. Rep. Inst., 1995; bd. dir. U. Activity Ctr. Transp. Authority, Mosley's High-Tech Tutoring, Cornerstone Inc. Distbn. Ctr., OIA Kidsway Inc., James Madison Inst., former dir.; mem. bus. leadership coun. City of Light; mem. rep. exec. com. Orange and Seminole County; former Fla. chmn. Empowerment Network; former chmn. edn. task force Am. Legis. Exchang Coun., 1992-94. Recipient Outstanding Legislator of Yr. award Ctrl. Fla. Young Rep., 1991, 92, Am. Legis. Exchange Coun., 1992, So. Coll. Cmty. Svc. award, 1992, Orlando Leadership award, 1993, 40 Under 40 award Orlando Bus. Jour., 1996. Mem. East Orange C. of C., S.W. Volusia, C. of C., Sandord C. of C., Oviedo C. of C. Republican. Presbyterian. Avocations: history, politics, philosophy, reading. Address: 12424 Research Pksy Orlando FL 32826-2109 Office: 323 Cannon House Off Bldg Washington DC 20515*

FEERICK, JOHN PAUL, neurologist, researcher, military officer; b. NYC, Aug. 15, 1950; s. James Paul and Frances Teresa (Ugis) Feerick; children from previous marriage: John Paul, Meaghan Ann, Catherine Marie, Thomas Patrick. Diploma, U. Vienna, Austria, 1967; BS in Biology, Georgetown U., Washington, 1972, MD, 1978. Diplomate Am. Bd. Pain Mgmt., cert. neurorehabilitation Am. Soc. Neurorehabilitation. Intern dept. neurology med. ctr. Georgetown U., Washington, 1978—79, resident dept. neurosurgery med. ctr., 1980—81, chief resident dept. neurosurgery med. ctr., 1982; commd. ensign USN, advanced through grades to capt., 1979; neurologist Geisinger Med. Group, Wilkes-Barre, Pa., 1982—87; neurologist, rschr. Zamesville, Ohio, 1987—2004; force surgeon II Marine Expeditionary Force, Camp Lejeune, NC, 2005; dir. field study team 1st marine divsn USMC, Iraq, 2006—. Dir. stroke & neurpharmacologic rsch. Pharmacotherapy Rsch. Assocs., Inc., Ohio, 1987—2004; dir. combat traumatic brain injury rsch. USMC, Iraq, 2006. Editor-in-chief: Neurorehabilitation News, 1992—2004, spl. issues editor: Neurorehabilitation and Neural Repair, 1997—2004. Recipient DSM, Ohio State Legis., 2002. Fellow: Am. Heart Assn.; mem.: AMA, VFW, Am. Soc. Neurorehabilitation, Am. Acad. Neurology, Am. Legion. Avocation: archaeology. Home: 829 S Quincy St Arlington VA 22204

FEESER, LARRY JAMES, retired civil engineering educator, researcher; b. Hanover, Pa., Feb. 23, 1937; s. Cyrus Myers and Arelia Cecilia (Stonesifer) F.; m. Patricia Marianne Reinhold, Aug. 19, 1961; children—Anne Elizabeth, David John BS in Civil Engring., Lehigh U., 1958; MS, U. Colo., 1961; PhD, Carnegie-Mellon U., 1965. Registered profl. engr., Colo., 1963, N.Y., 1974. From instr. to prof. civil engring. U. Colo., Boulder, 1958-74; prof., chmn. dept. civil engring. Rensselaer Poly. Inst., Troy, NY, 1974-82, assoc. dean engring., 1982-85, vice provost for computing and info. tech., 1985-90, prof. civil engring., 1990—2004, prof. emeritus, 2005—, dir. ctr. for infrastructure and transp. studies, 1993-95. Cons. Jorgensen & Hendrickson Engrs., Denver Contbr. articles to profl. jour. Named one of Those Who Made Marks in 1981, Engring. News Record, 1982; Ford Found. fellow, 1961-63; NSF Sci. Faculty fellow, 1971-72 Fellow Am. Concrete Inst., ASCE (hon., nat. dir. 1979-82), fellow, Nat. Soc. Profl. Engrs. (nat. v.p. 1998-99); mem. Am. Soc. Engring. Edn.

FEFFER, GERALD ALAN, lawyer; b. Washington, Apr. 24, 1942; s. Louis Charles and Elsie (Glick) F.; children: Andrew, John, Keith. BA with honors, Lehigh U., 1964; JD, U. Va., 1967. Bar: N.Y. 1968, D.C. 1980. Assoc. Mudge, Rose, Guthrie & Alexander, NYC, 1967-71; asst. U.S. atty. (so. dist.) NY US Dept. Justice, 1971-76, asst. chief criminal divsn., 1975-76; ptnr. Kostelanetz & Ritholz, NYC, 1976-79; dep. asst. atty. gen. tax divsn. US Dept. Justice, Washington, 1979-81; ptnr. Steptoe & Johnson LLP, Washington, 1981-86, Williams & Connolly LLP, Washington, 1986—. Mem. editl. bd. Busniess Crimes Bulletin: Compliance and Litigation; contbr. articles to profl. jours. Fellow Am. Coll. Tax Counsel, Am. Coll. Trial Lawyers; mem. ABA (criminal justice litigation and taxation sects.), Nat. Assn. Criminal Def. Lawyers, Nat. Inst. on Criminal Tax Fraud (chmn.). Office: Williams & Connolly LLP 725 12th St NW Washington DC 20005-5901 Office Phone: 202-434-5007.

FEFFERMAN, CHARLES LOUIS, mathematics professor; b. Washington, Apr. 18, 1949; s. Arthur Stanley and Liselott Ruth (Stern) Fefferman; m. Julie Anne Albert, Feb. 1975; children: Nina Heidi, Elaine Marie. BS, U. Md., 1966, Doctorate (hon.), 1979; PhD, Princeton U., 1969; Doctorate (hon.), Knox Coll., 1981, Bar-Ilan U., Israel, 1985, U. Madrid, 1990. Asst. prof. U. Chgo., 1970—71, prof. math., 1971—73; lectr. math. Princeton (N.J.) U., 1969—70, prof. math., 1973—84, Herbert Jones U. prof., 1984—, grad. dir. dept. math., 1997—99, dept. chmn., 1999—2002. Vis. prof. U. Md., Calif. Inst. Tech., Courant Inst. Math. Scis., NYU, U. Paris, Mittag-Leffler Inst., Djursholm, Sweden, Weitzmann Inst., Rehovot, Israel, Bar-Ilan U., Ramat-Gen, Israel, U. Madrid (Aútonoma). Author: Reviewing U.S. Mathematics - A Plan for the Nineties, research papers. Recipient Salem prize for outstanding work in fourier analysis by young mathematician, 1978, Alan T. Waterman award, 1978, Fields medal, Internat. Cong. Mathematicians, 1978, 1984; grantee Nat. Sci. Found. Fellowship, 1966—69, Alfred P. Sloan Fellowship, 1970, NATO Postdoctoral Fellowship, 1971. Mem.: Am. Philos. Soc., Am. Acad. Arts and Scis., Am. Math. Soc., Nat. Acad. Scis. Home: 234 Clover Ln Princeton NJ 08540-4051 Office: Princeton U Math Dept 1102 Fine Hall Washington Rd Princeton NJ 08544-1000

FEFFERMAN, HILBERT, government official, lawyer; b. NYC, June 5, 1913; s. Jacob and Sarah F.; m. Helen Libby Relkin, June 16, 1940. BS magna cum laude in philosophy (hon.), NYU, 1934; JD, Harvard U., 1937. Bar: NY 1938, U.S. Supreme Ct. 1953. Pvt. practice, NYC, 1938-41; atty. U.S. Housing and Home Fin. Agy., Washington, 1941-59, asst. gen. counsel for legislation, 1960-62, assoc. gen. counsel for ops., 1962-67; chief legislative counsel HUD, Washington, 1967-72; cons. Housing and Devel. Legislation, Bethesda, Md., 1973—. Lectr., vis. prof. city planning MIT, Cambridge, Mass., 1973-76. Contbr. articles to profl. jours. Recipient Disting. Svc. award, HUD, 1968. Mem.: Phi Beta Kappa. Home and Office: 5661 Bent Branch Rd Bethesda MD 20816-1049 Personal E-mail: helenfefferman@aol.com.

FEGAN, JEFFREY P., airport executive; BS in Geography, Frostburg U.; M in City Planning, Ga. Inst. Tech.; advanced airport mgmt. course, Internat. Aviation Mgmt. Tng. Inst., Montreal. Aviation cons., 1978-83; noise abatement officer Westchester County Airport, N.Y., 1983-84; chief planner Dallas/Ft. Worth Internat. Airport Bd., 1984, asst. dir., dir. planning and engring., 1989-93, dep. exec. dir. fin. and adminstrn., 1993-94, exec. dir., chief adminstr., exec. officer, 1994—. Mem. Airports Coun. Internat.-NA Environ. Affairs Com., Internat. Civil Airports Assn.-Passenger Facilitation World Com., Am. Assn. Airport Execs., Am. Planning Assn., Am. Inst. Cert. Planners. Office: DFW Int'l Airport Adminstrn PO Box 619428 Dallas TX 75261-9428

FEGLEY, KENNETH ALLEN, systems engineering educator; b. Mont Clare, Pa., Feb. 14, 1923; s. Henry Stanley and Bertha (Malone) F.; m. Virginia Ruth Weaver, Sept. 1, 1951; children: Alan Donald, John David, Paul Andrew. BSEE, U. Pa., 1947, MSEE, 1950, PhD, 1955. Instr. Moore Sch. Elec. Engring., U. Pa., Phila., 1947-53, assoc., 1953-55, asst. prof., 1955-58, assoc. prof., 1958-66, prof. elec. engring., 1966-72; prof. sys. engring. U. Pa., Phila., 1972-90, chmn. dept. sys. engring., 1972-75, chmn. dept. sys., 1986-93, Joseph Moore prof. sys., 1990-93, Joseph Moore prof. emeritus sys., 1993—. Cons. U.S. Army, Phila., Dover, N.J., 1955-85, USN, Phila., 1970-86. Contbr. numerous articles to tech. jours. and chpts. to books. With USN, 1944-46. Fellow IEEE, AAAS; mem. Am. Soc. Engring. Edn., Masons, AAUP, Sigma Xi, Eta Kappa Nu, Tau Beta Pi, Sigma Tau. Democrat. Presbyterian. Office: U Pa Dept Electrical and Systems Engring Philadelphia PA 19104-6315 Personal E-mail: kfegley@arclp.net.

FEHER, GEORGE, biophysicist, educator; b. Czechoslovakia, May 29, 1924; s. Ferdinand and Sylvia (Schwartz) Feher; m. Elsa Rosenvasser, June 18, 1961; children: Laurie, Shoshanah, Paoli. BS in Engring. Physics, U. Calif., Berkeley, 1950, MSEE, 1951. PhD in Physics, 1954; PhD (hon.), Hebrew U. Jerusalem, 1994. Rsch. physicist Bell Tel. Labs., Murray Hill, NJ, 1954-60; vis. assoc. prof. Columbia U., NYC, 1959-60; prof. physics U. Calif., San Diego, 1960—92, rsch. prof. physics, 1993—. Vis. prof. biology MIT, Cambridge, 1967-68; William Draper Hawkins lectr. U Chgo., May 1986; Raymond and Beverly Sackler disting. lectr. U. Tel-Aviv, June 1986; vis. prof. Hebrew U. Jerusalem, Israel, spring 1989, 93; bd. govs. Weizmann Inst. Sci., Rehovot, Israel, 1988-, Technion-Israel Inst. Tech., Haifa, 1968-. Author: Electron Paramagnetic Resonance with Applications to Selected Problems in Biology, 1970; contbr. articles to profl. jous., chpts. to books. Recipient Oliver E. Buckley Solid State Physics prize, 1976, Inaugural Ann. award Internat. Electron Spin Resonance Soc., 1991; co-recipient 2006/2007 Wolf Found. Prize in Chemistry, Israel; NSF fellow, 1967-68. Fellow AAAS, Internat. EPR/ESR Soc. (Zavoisky award 1996), Biophysical Soc.; mem. Am. Phys. Soc. (prize 1960, biophysics prize, 1982), Biophys. Soc. (nat. lectr. 1983), NAS, Am. Acad. Arts & Scis. (Rumford medal 1992), Sigma Xi. Office: Dept Physics U Calif 9500 Gilman Dr Dept 319 La Jolla CA 92093-0319 E-mail: gfeher@physics.ucsd.edu.

FEHNER, MICHAEL RICHARD, lawyer; s. Richard Edwin and Eileen Allice Fehner; m. Jeannie Su, Aug. 9, 1997; children: Nicole Sue, Zachary Michael. BA in Polit. Sci., English, and Am. Studies, St. Olaf Coll., 1992; JD, Yale U., 1995. Bar: Minn. 1995, D.C. 1997, Calif. 2000, U.S. Dist. Ct. (ctrl. dist.) Calif. 2000, U.S. Dist. Ct. (no. dist.) Calif. 2004. Jud. law clk. Hon. Richard H. Kyle, U.S. Dist. Judge, St. Paul, 1995—96; assoc. Sidley & Austin, Washington, 1996—98, Dorsey & Whitney LLP, Mpls., 1998—2000; assoc., sr. counsel Irell & Manella LLP, Newport Beach, Calif., 2000—. Adj. prof. Law Sch. George Wash. U., Washington, 1997—98; tchg. asst. Law Sch. Yale U., New Haven, 1994—95. Editor: Yale Law Jour., Yale Jour. Law & the Humanities. Recipient Tosdal award, St. Olaf Coll., 1992; scholar, Nat. Merit Scholarship Orgn., 1988—92; Coker fellow, Yale U. Law Sch., 1994—95. Mem.: ABA, DC Bar Assn., Orange County Bar Assn., Calif. Bar Assn., Minn. State Bar Assn., Phi Beta Kappa. Office: Irell & Manella LLP 840 Newport Center Drive Suite 400 Newport Beach CA 92660-6324 Office Phone: 949-760-0991.

FEHR, GREGORY PARIS, marketing and distribution company executive; b. Urbana, Ill., Nov. 10, 1943; s. Orval Joachim and Cuba Lucile (Paris) F.; m. Sharon Louise Burba, Jan. 21, 1965 (div. Jan. 1975); children: Kristina K., Gregory Tyson Howard; m. Kathleen Lorretta Meyers, Aug. 10, 1990. BS in Indsl. Engring., Okla. U., 1967; MBA, Drake U., 1977. Registered profl. mech. engr. Iowa, Okla., Ala.; cert. corrosion technologist, cathodic protection specialist. From engr. to sr. project engr. Fisher Controls Co., Marshalltown, Iowa, 1967-77; fgn. liaison GE, Portland, Maine, 1977-79; gen. mgr. Arabian Am. Oil Co., Dhahran, Saudi Arabia, 1979-81; v.p. Oil Tech. Svcs., Houston, 1981-85; mgr. materials engring. Std. Oil Prodn. Co., Houston, 1985-86; mgr. nuc. products Wyle Labs., Huntsville, Ala., 1986-88; sr. materials engr. Sci. Applications Internat., Las Vegas, Nev., 1988-96; v.p. GPF Mktg. and Distbn., Las Vegas, 1988—; sr. project mgr. Converse Cons. S.W., Inc., Las Vegas, 1996—2002, Terracon Cons. Engrs. and Scientists, 2002—. Cons. task groups Am. Petroleum Inst., 1983-86, Electric Power Rsch. Inst., San Mateo, Calif., 1986-89; chmn. employee adv. coun. Sci. Applications Internat., Las Vegas, 1992. Contbr. articles and tech. papers to profl. jours. Pres. Marshalltown Tennis Assn., 1972-73; head swim coach YMCA/YWCA, Marshalltown, 1973-74; mem. adv. bd. Marshalltown C.C., 1975. Mem. NSPE, ASME, Nat. Assn. Corrosion Engrs., Am. Petroleum Inst., Am. Soc. Nondestructive Testing. Avocations: skiing, scuba diving, sailing, photography. Office: GPF Marketing and Distribution Ste 212 4600 E Sunset Rd Henderson NV 89014

FEHR, JOHN WILLIAM, newspaper editor; b. Long Beach, Calif., Mar. 8, 1926; s. John and Evelyn (James) F.; m. Cynthia Moore, Sept. 4, 1951; children— Michael John, Martha Ann BA in English, U. Utah, 1951. City editor Salt Lake City Tribune, 1964-80, mng. editor, 1980-81, editor, 1981-91. Served to 1st lt. USAF, 1951-53 Mem. Am. Soc. Newspaper Editors, Sigma Chi Home: 468 13th Ave Salt Lake City UT 84103-3229

FEHR, KENNETH MANBECK, retired computer company executive; b. Schuylkill Haven, Pa., Feb. 21, 1927; s. Theodore E. and Eva (Manbeck) F.; m. Jean Alice Greenawalt, June 28, 1952; children: K. Craig, Karen Jean, K. Todd. BS, Pa. State U., State College, 1951; MBA, U. Pitts., 1953. With U.S. Steel Corp., 1951-62, div. controller, 1962; controller Interlake Steel Corp., Chgo., 1962-68; v.p. fin. Hallicrafters Co., 1968-71, E.W. Bliss Co., Salem, Ohio, 1971-74; treas. Alliance Machine Co., Ohio, 1974-86; pres. I.M.S. Corp., Hudson, Ohio, 1986-90, Fehr & Greenawalt Investments, Salem, Ohio, 1990—, Salem Security Storage, LLC, 2002—. Bd. dirs. Fegreen Inc.; night sch. tchr. U. Pitts., 1956—57. Treas. Salem Renaissance. With USNR, 1945—46. Mem.: Nat. Assn. Accts., Fin. Execs. Inst., Salem Hist. Soc., Salem Preservation Soc., Salem-Golf Club, Kiwanis (chpt. pres.), Masons. Home: 725 S Lincoln Ave Salem OH 44460-3709 Office: 1210 So Ellsworth Ave Salem OH 44460 Personal E-mail: fehrken@hotmail.com.

FEHRENBACH, T.R. (THEODORE REED FEHRENBACH), writer; b. San Benito, Tex., Jan. 12, 1925; s. T.R. and Rose Mardel (Wentz) F.; m. Lillian Breetz, Aug. 22, 1951. BA magna cum laude, Princeton U., 1947. Field supr. Travelers Ins. Co., San Antonio, 1954-56; owner ind. ins. agy. San Antonio, 1956-69; mng. trustee Fehrenbach Trusts, 1970—; pres. Royal Poinciana Corp., San Antonio, 1971-92. Author: This Kind of War, 1963, This Kind of Peace, 1966, Lone Star (PBS TV Series 1985-86), 1968, Fire and Blood, 1973, Comanches, 1974, Seven Keys to Texas, 1983, Texas: A Salute From Above, 1985, others; contbr. numerous articles, stories to mags., U.S. fgn. periodicals. Mem. Tex. 2000 Commn., 1981-82; chmn. Tex. Hist. Commn., 1987-91; mem. design adv. com. Tex. Quarter Dollar, 2001-03. 1st lt. AUS, 1943-46, lt. col., 1950-53, Korea. Recipient Disting. Civilian Svc. medal, Freedoms Found. award, 1965, Evelyn Oppenheimer award, 1968, Lon Tinkle award from Tex. Inst. Letters for excellence sustained throughout a career, 2005, citations Tex. Ho. of Reps., 1969, 73, Tex. Legislature, 1977, 2003 Bookend award Tex. Book Festival, 2005; T.R. Fehrenbach Book awards created in his honor Tex. Hist. Commn., 1986; named Disting. Citizen, San Antonio, 1973, Knight of San Jacinto, Primicerius Order of St. Maurice. Fellow Am. Numismatic Soc., Tex. State Hist. Assn.; mem. Philos. Soc. Tex., Authors Guild, Sci. Fiction Writers Am., Conopus Club, Argyle Club, Torch Club, Princeton Club of N.Y.C., Garden of the Gods Club (Colo.). Republican. Episcopalian. Home: 131 Mary D Ave San Antonio TX 78209-5667 Office: 5108 Broadway St San Antonio TX 78209-5746 Office Phone: 210-824-5511.

FEHRENBACHER, JOHN W., surgeon; s. Gilbert and Alberta Fehrenbacher; m. Cindy Funke, Aug. 11, 1973; children: Noah, Ike, Victor. BS, U. So. Ind., Evansville, 1972, PhD (hon.), 1986; MD, Ind. U., Indpls., 1976. Diplomate Am. Bd. Gen. Surgery, Am. Bd. Thoracic Surgery. Cardiothoracic surgeon Meth. Hosp., Indpls., intern, surg. resident, 1976—81; resident in thoracic and cardiovascular surgery Ind. U. Med. Ctr., Indpls., 1981—83; mem. Cardiovascular Surg. Svcs., PC, Indpls., 1983—2000; pres. CorVasc MD's PC, Indpls., 2000—. Surg. dir. lung transplant Meth. Hosp., Indpls., bd. dirs. Midwest Heart Inst.; surg. dir. lung transplantation Clarian Health, Indpls., dir. oper. rm. cardiovascular core; mem. staff Meml. Hosp., Indpls., 1983—, Riverview Hosp., Noblesville, Ind., 1983—, St. Vincent Hosp., Indpls., 2001—, Ball Meml. Hosp., Muncie, Ind., 2001—, Heart Ctr. Ind., Indpls., 2002—; presenter in field. Contbr. articles to med. jours. Named Tchr. of Yr. in Surgery, Meth. Hosp. Ind., 1987, Ind. U., 2003; recipient J.K. Berman award, 1980, USUE Alumni of Yr. award, 1981. Mem.: AMA, ACS, Soc. Thoracic Surgeons, Internat. Soc. Heart and Lung Transplantation, Marion County Med. Assn., Ind. Med. Assn. Office: 1801 N Senate Blvd Ste 755 Indianapolis IN 46202

FEI, JAMES ROBERT, engineering executive, consultant; b. Tucson, May 24, 1947; s. Robert Fleming and Barbara Jean (Dukes) F.; m. Patricia Christine Wilson, Aug. 24, 1968; children: Robert Fleming, Christina Kalani. BSME, U. So. Calif., 1969; MS in Ocean Engring., U. Hawaii, 1973. Registered profl. engr., S.C., La., Tex., Ga., Va., N.H., N.C. Design engr. USN, Mare Island, Calif., 1969-70; project mgr. Pearl Harbor (Hawaii) Shipyard, 1970-73; mech. systems engr. Submarine Maintenance Monitoring Systems Office Dept. of the Navy, Washington, 1973-76; chmn., chief exec. officer Life Cycle Engring., Inc., Charleston, SC, 1977—. Bd. dirs., adv. bd. Nat. Bank of S.C., 1985-92; mem. adv. coun. St. Francis Hosp., 1992-95; mem. pres.'s adv. coun. Med. U. S.C., Charleston, 1995-96; mem. Cold War Submarine Meml. Found., exec. com., bd. Mem. SCSPE, NSPE, ASME, Navy League. Republican. Avocations: golf, boating. Office: Life Cycle Engring Inc 4360 Corporate Rd Charleston SC 29405-7445 Home Phone: 843-571-3181; Office Phone: 843-744-7110. Business E-Mail: jfei@lce.com.

FEI, JUN, art educator, graphics designer; b. Jingzhou, Hubei, China, Jan. 20, 1970; arrived in U.S., 2003; m. Wei Yang, Oct. 11, 1994. BA, Ctrl. Acad. of Fine Arts, Beijing, 2002; MFA, Alfred U., NY, 2005. Art editor China Film Press, Beijing, 1992—96; founder & art dir. Beijing Rule Art Svc. Co., LTD., 1996—2002; art dir. Beijing Jianya Advt. Co., 1999—2001, Pooga - Chinese Aviation Tourism Guide Mag., Beijing, 2001—03; vis. prof. Ctrl. Acad. of Fine Arts, Beijing, 2002—03; vis. prof. Sch. of Art and Design Alfred U., 2005—06. Interactive installation, Jijizhazha, Transformation, Play you, back; prodr.: (book) New year papers; author: (journal) Art and Design Magazine; art editor, book designer (book) Outstanding folk paper-cuts in China (Golden Prize, The 1st Chinese Design Art Exhbn., 1998); video installation, "init". Recipient First Prize, 4th Nat. Book Design Art Exhbn., Beijing, 1994, 11th Chinese Book Competition, Beijing, 1997, Excellent Prize, 1st Chinese Design Art Exhbn., Chengdu, 1998, 2nd Prize, The 13th No. China Book Design Art Competition and Seminar, Haerbin, 2000, Excellent Prize, The Digital Media Art Competition of Students from Art Academies of China, 2002; scholar, Alfred U., 2003—05. Mem.: Chinese Assn. Book Design (assoc.; beijing, china 1994—2005). Home: Apt 2102 Wangjinghuayuan Chaoyang District, Beijing 100102 China Office: Sch Art & Design NYSCC Alfred Univ 2 Pine St Alfred NY 14802 Home Phone: 416-299-1868; Office Phone: 607-871-2610. Personal E-mail: feijun70@yahoo.ca.

FEIBEL, FREDERICK ARTHUR, financial consultant; b. Chgo., Oct. 27, 1942; s. Fred and Emma Feibel; m. Marlene Ruth Edwards, Aug. 7, 1965; 1 son, Frederick Curtis. BSEE, Purdue U., 1964; MBA, Northwestern U., 1970. Project engr. Johnson Controls Corp., Milw., 1964-69; sr. mgmt. cons. Arthur Andersen & Co., Chgo., 1970-76; rep. pension fund evaluation A.G. Becker Securities Co., Chgo., 1976-77; spl. agt. Northwestern Mut. Life Ins. Co., Milw., 1977-82; pres. F.A. Feibel Fin. Assocs., Northbrook, Ill., 1982—. Chmn. Village of Northbrook Bicentennial Commn., 1975-76, Boy Scouts Am. Troop 67, 1990—; v.p. Northbrook Civic Found., 1977, pres., 1978, also bd. dirs.; deacon Northfield Cmty. Ch., 1978-81, 95-98, asst. treas., 1986—; trustee Northfield Rural Fire Dist., 2000—. Recipient Disting. Svc. award State of Ill., 1976, Northbrook Civic Found., 1983, 89, Civic Svc. award Northbrook B'nai B'rith, 1981-82, Vol Initiative of Pvt. Sector Recognition award Northbrook C. of C. and Industry, 1985, Vol. Appreciation award Northbrook Park Dist, 1987; named Northbrook Rotary Man of Yr, 1978-79, Hall of Fame Ill Festival Assn., 1992. Mem. Greater North Shore Estate Planning Coun., Eta Kappa Nu, Tau Beta Pi. Home: 1841 Western Ave Northbrook IL 60062-5041 Office: FA Feibel Fin Assocs PO Box 355 Northbrook IL 60065-0355 Office Phone: 847-272-8152. Personal E-mail: fafmoneyman@comcast.net.

FEICHTNER, DOUGLAS J., lawyer; b. Cin., July 15, 1977; BA, Miami U., 1999; JD, U. Cin. Coll. Law, 2002. Bar: Ohio 2002, US Dist. Ct. Southern Dist. Ohio. Assoc. Dinsmore & Shohl LLP, Cin. Tutor Cin. Youth Collaborative; leadership coun. mem. Hamilton County Rep. Party. Named one of Ohio's Rising Stars, Super Lawyers, 2006. Mem.: Def. Rsch. Inst., Cin. Bar Assn., Ohio State Bar Assn., Par Club, Evans Scholar. Office: Dinsmore & Shohl LLP 255 E Fifth St Ste 1900 Cincinnati OH 45202-4700 Office Phone: 513-977-8200. Office Fax: 513-977-8141.

FEIDLER, MARK L., telecommunications industry executive; BA, Duke Univ.; JD, Vanderbilt Univ. Atty. King & Spalding, Atlanta, 1981—86; with Robinson-Humphrey Co., 1986—90; principal Breckenridge Group, 1990—91; dir. strategic transactions BellSouth Corp., Atlanta, 1991—93, v.p. corp. develop., 1993—96, pres. interconnection svc., 1996—98, pres. Bell South Mobility, 1998—2000; COO Cingular Wireless, 2000—04; chief staff officer BellSouth Corp., Atlanta, 2004—05, pres., COO, 2005—. Bd. dir. Cingular Wireless. Bd. mem. Great Schools Atlanta, Ctr. for Puppetry Arts, Schenck Sch.

FEIG, STEPHEN ARTHUR, pediatrician, preventive medicine physician, hematologist, oncologist, educator; b. NYC, Dec. 24, 1937; s. Irving L. and Janet (Oppenheimer) F.; m. Judith Bergman, Aug. 28, 1960; children: Laura, Daniel, Andrew. AB in Biology, Princeton U., NJ, 1959; MD, Columbia U., NYC, 1963. Diplomate Am. Bd. Pediat., Am. Bd. Hematology-Oncology. Intern Mt. Sinai Hosp., NYC, 1963-64, resident in pediat., 1964-66; hematology fellow Children's Hosp. Med. Ctr., Boston, 1968-71, assoc. in medicine, 1971-72; asst. prof. pediat. UCLA, 1972-77, chief divsn. hematology and oncology Sch. Medicine, 1977—2005, assoc. prof., 1977-82, prof., 1982—2005, exec. vice chmn. dept. pediat. Sch. Medicine, 1994—2004, prof. emeritus, 2005—. Trustee LA chpt. Leukemia Soc. Am., 1978—2004, trustee, 1984—2004; chair exec. com. subsect. hemotology/oncology Am. Acad. Pediat.; mem. Coun. Pediat. Subspltys., 2006—; bd. dirs. Camp Ronald McDonald for Good Times; active numerous other pediatric hosp. and med. sch. coms Reviewer Am. Jour. Pediatric Hematology/Oncology, Blood, Pediat., Pediatric Rsch., Jour. Pediat.; contbr. articles to profl. jours.; editl. bd. Jour. Pediat. Hematology & Oncology. Served with USNR, 1966-68. Mem. Am. Soc. Hematology, Soc. Pediatric Rsch., Am. Pediatric Soc., Internat. Soc. Exptl. Hematology, Am. Assn. Cancer Rsch. Jewish. Avocation: native arts. Office: UCLA Sch Medicine Dept Pediatrics 10833 Le Conte Ave Los Angeles CA 90095-3075 Office Phone: 310-825-6708. Business E-Mail: sfeig@mednet.ucla.edu.

FEIGEN, BRENDA S., lawyer, film producer, writer; b. Chgo., July 7, 1944; d. Arthur Paul Feigen and Shirley (Bierman) Feigen Kadison; 1 child, Alexis Feigen Fasteau. BA in Math. cum laude, Vassar Coll., Poughkeepsie, NY, 1966; JD, Harvard U., 1969. Bar: Mass. 1970, N.Y. 1971, Calif. 2001. Chief analyst Boston Redevel. Authority, 1969; assoc. firm Rosenman, Colin, Kaye, Petschek, Freund & Emil, NYC, 1970; pvt. practice NYC, 1974—, LA, 2001—. Founder, coordinating dir. Women's Action Alliance, NYC, 1970—72; co-founder Ms. Mag., 1971; dir. Nat. Women's Rights project ACLU, NYC, 1972—74; ptnr. Fasteau and Feigen, NYC, 1974—80; assoc. Hess, Segall, Guterman, Pelz & Steiner, NYC, 1980—81; atty., motion picture agt. William Morris Agy., NYC, 1982—87; pres. Brenda Feigen Prodns., NYC and LA, 1987—97; ptnr. Baxter/Feigen Prodns., 1991—92, Berton & Feigen, Beverly Hills, 1992—94; of counsel Berton & Donaldson, Beverly Hills, 1994—96, Kenoff and Machtinger LLP, 2004—; gen. counsel Feigen/Parrent Lit. Mgmt., Bel Air, Calif., 1995—2004, Reel Life Women Prodn. Co., Bel Air, 1996—2004; chair Nat. Breast Cancer Edn. and Legal Ctr., Bel Air, 2001—04; prof. UCLA Ext., 1990; adv. com. Am. Friends of Israel Mus., 2002—04; moderator panels and seminar Harvard Law Sch., Vassar Coll., 2001, Calif. Lawyers Arts, 2003, Lavender Law Conf., 2004, Tex. Entertainment Law Inst., 2004, Austin Film Festival and Writing Conf., 2004; bd. advisors Am. Screenwriters Assn., 2004—; co-chair and panelist confs. and seminars in field of entertainment law; spkr. in field. Prodr.: (films) NAVY SEALS, 1990; author: Not One of the Boys: Living Life as a Feminist (Knopf), 2000; contbr. articles to profl. jours., chapters to books, book reviews. Bd. dirs. Film Forum, 1986-90, N.Y. Women in Film, 1985-86, Calif. Lawyers for the Arts, 1996—, Population Media Ctr., 2003—; mem. PEN Ctr. USA West, 1996—2005, Authors' Guild, 1996—2005, Harvard Com. Entertainment, Sports and Cyberspace Law, 1997—2004; candidate for N.Y. State Senate, 1978; panelist L.A. Times Book Festival, 2001. Hon. Pres.'s fellow Columbia U., 1977, 78; participant Exec. Seminar, Aspen Inst., 1979. Mem. ABA (panelist film divsn.), ATLA, LGLA, NOW (nat. legis. v.p., bd. dirs. 1970-71), Show Coalition (bd. govs. 1990-92), Calif. State Bar Assn., Los Angeles County Bar Assn., NY Civil and Criminal Cts. Bar Assn., Beverly Hills Bar Assn., Women Lawyers Assn. LA, Women's Action Alliance (co-founder, dir.), Nat. Women's Polit. Caucus (co-founder, nat. adv. com.). Democrat. Office: Kenoff & Machtinger LLP 1901 Ave of Stars Ste 1775 Los Angeles CA 90067 Home Phone: 310-271-0606; Office Phone: 310-552-0808. Business E-Mail: bfeigen@feigenlaw.com, bfeigen@entertainmentlawla.com.

FEIGEN, RICHARD L., art dealer, collector, writer; b. Chgo., Aug. 8, 1930; s. Arthur P. and Shirley (Bierman) F.; m. Sandra Elizabeth Canning Walker, Feb. 23, 1966 (div. 1978); children: Philippa Canning, Richard Wood Bliss; m. Margaret Langan Culver, Sept. 12, 1998 (div. 2002); m. Countess Isabelle Harnoncourt, May 5, 2007. BA, Yale U., New Haven, Conn., 1952; MBA, Harvard U., Cambridge, Mass., 1954. Asst. treas. Beneficial Standard Life Ins. Co., LA, 1955—56; mem. NY Stock Exchange, 1956—57; pres., dir. Richard L. Feigen & Co., Inc., NYC, 1957—. Mem. com. works fine art NY State Office Bldg., Harlem; lectr. in field. Author: Tales from the Art Crypt, 2000; contbr. articles to profl. jours. Candidate, del. Dem. Nat. Conv., 1972; trustee John Jay Homestead Assn., Katonah, NY, 1979-90, Lincoln U., Pa., 1988-92; mem. pres.'s coun. U. South Fla. Fellow Mpls. Soc. Fine Arts, Met. Mus. Art, Art Inst. Chgo.; mem. Art Dealers Assn. Am. (bd. dirs. 1972-76, 97-99, 2001-05), Harvard Bus. Sch. Assn., Century Assn., Arts Club, Casino Club. Home: Cantitoe House Cantitoe Rd Katonah NY 10536-9718 also: 1 rue Allent 75007 Paris France also: 960 Fifth Ave New York NY 10021-1708 Office: 34 E 69th St New York NY 10021-5016 Home Phone: 914-232-8476; Office Phone: 212-628-0700. Business E-Mail: rfeigen@rlfeigen.com.

FEIGENBAUM, ARMAND VALLIN, systems engineer, information technology executive; b. NYC, Apr. 6, 1920; s. S. Frederick and Hilda (Vallin) F. BS, Union Coll., 1942, DSc (hon.), 1992; MS, MIT, 1948, PhD, 1951; LHD (hon.), U. Mass., 1996; DSc (hon.), Mass. Coll. Liberal Arts, 2003. Engr. test program GE, Schenectady, 1942-45, factory tng. course, 1945-47, sales engr., 1947-48, supr. tng. mfg. personnel Lynn, Mass., 1948-50, asst. to gen. mgr. aircraft gas turbine divsn. Cin., 1950-52, mgr. aircraft nuclear propulsion dept. NYC, 1952, co. mgr. quality control, 1956, co.-wide mgr. mfg. ops. and quality control, 1958-68; pres., CEO Gen. Systems Co., Inc., Pittsfield, Mass., 1968—; Nat. Acad. Engring. U.S., 1992—. Bd. overseers Malcolm Baldrige Nat. Quality Program, Washington, 1988-91; founding chmn. global quality body Internat. Acad. Quality, pres., 1966-79, chmn. bd. dirs., 1979—; adv. group US Army, 1966—; lectr. MIT, U. Cin., Union Coll., U. Pa.; spkr. in field. Author: Quality Control-Principles and Practice, 1951, Total Quality Control-Engineering and Management, 1961, Management Programming, 1980, The Organization Process, 1980, Total Quality Control, 3d edit., 1983, Total Quality Control, 40th Anniversary edit., 1991, The Power of Management Capital (translation in Japanese, Chinese, Brazilian Portuguese, Taiwanese, Arabic, others), 2003; contbr. articles to profl. jours. Chmn. inst. adminstrn., mgmt. coun. Union Coll., 1963—. Recipient Founders medal, 1977, medaille Georges Borel, Republic of France, 1988, Disting. Svc. award Nat. Inst. for Engring., Mgmt. and Sys., 1991, Disting. Leadership award Quality and Productivity Mgmt. Assn., 1993, Ishikawa/Harrington medal Asia-Pacific Quality Orgn., 1996; Armand V. Feigenbaum Mass. Quality award established by Gov. Mass., 1992, Singapore's Ngee Ann Polytechnic inaugurated the ann. Dr. A.V. Feigenbaum Gold medal award for outstanding quality assurance engring. grad., 1994, Mass. Gov.'s proclamation on 50th anniversary of book, 2001, Feigenbaum Leadership Excellence award, Dubai, UAE, 2005, Six Sigma Grand Master medal Walter L. Hurd Found., 2006; fellow World Acad. Productivity Sci., 1993; Armand V. and Donald S. Feigenbaum Hall named in his honor Union Coll., 1996, Armand and Donald Feigenbaum Disting. Professorship named in his honor U. Mass. Med. Sch., 1998; recognized with the Outstanding Engring. Alumnus award, 2003. Fellow Am. Soc. Quality Control (pres. 1961-63, chmn. bd. 1963-64, Edwards medal 1966, Lancaster medal 1982, hon. mem. 1986, Feigenbaum award established 1999), World Acad. Productivity Sci.; mem. IEEE (life), NSPE (Disting. Svc. award 1991), ASME (life), AAAS (hon.), Nat. Security Indsl. Assn. (nat. award merit 1965), Inst. Math. Stats., Acad. Polit. and Social Scis., Am. Econ. Assn., Soc. Advancement Mgmt., Indsl. Rels. Rsch. Soc., Coun. Internat. Progress in Mgmt. (chmn. bd. 1968-70), China Assn. Quality Control (hon. advisor), Argentine Inst. Quality (hon.), Philippines Soc. for Quality Control (hon.), NAE. Home: 123 Ann Dr Pittsfield MA 01201-8405 Office: Berkshire Common South St Pittsfield MA 01201-6123 Office Phone: 413-499-2880.

FEIGENBAUM, DAVID LOUIS, lawyer; b. Pitts., Sept. 5, 1947; s. Simon and Pauline (Simon) Feigenbaum; m. Maureen I. Meister, Apr. 28, 1979. BS, Yale Coll., 1969; JD, Harvard U., 1972. Bar: Pa. 1972, Mass. 1982. Assoc. Kirkpatrick & Lockhart, Pitts., 1972—79, ptnr., 1979—80; assoc. Fish & Richardson, Boston, 1980—84, ptnr., 1985—.

FEIGENBAUM, EDWARD ALBERT, retired computer science educator; b. Weehawken, NJ, Jan. 20, 1936; s. Fred J. and Sara Rachman; m. H. Penny Nii, 1975. BEE, Carnegie Inst. Tech., 1956, PhD in Indsl. Adminstrn., 1960; DSc (hon.), Aston U., UK, 1989. From asst. prof. to assoc. prof. bus. adminstrn. U. Calif., Berkeley, 1960—65; from assoc. prof. computer sci. to prof. Stanford U., 1965—95, prin. investigator heuristic programming project and knowledge sys. lab., 1965—2001, chmn. dept. computer sci., 1976-81, dir. Computation Ctr., 1965-68, Kumagai prof. computer sci., 1995—2001, emeritus, 2001—; pres. Intelli Genetics Inc., 1980—82, mem. tech. adv. bd., 1983-86; chmn., dir. Teknowledge, Inc., 1981-82; dir. IntelliCorp, 1984-90; chief scientist USAF, 1994-97. Mem. computer and biomath. scis. study sect. NIH, 1968-72, adv. com. on artificial intelligence in medicine, 1974-92; mem. Math. Social Sci. Bd., 1975-78, Internat. Joint Coun. on Artificial Intellignece, 1973-83; computer sci. adv. com. NSF, 1977-80; chief scientist, USAF, 1994-97; sci. adv. bd. USAF, 1997-2000; sci. advisor Air Force Office Sci. Rsch., 2000-07; trustee Computer History Mus., 2005-; cons. in field. Author: (with others) Information Processing Language V Manual, 1961, (with P. McCorduck) The Fifth Generation, 1983; author: (with R. Lindsay, B. Buchanan, J. Lederberg) Applications of Artificial Intelligence to Organic Chemistry: the Dendral Project, 1980; Editor: (with J. Feldman) Computers and Thought, 1963, (with A. Barr and P. Cohen) Handbook of Artificial Intelligence, 1981, 82, 89, (with Pamela McCorduck and H. Penny Nii) The Rise of the Expert Company: How Visionary Companies are using Artificial Intelligence to Achieve Higher Productivity and Profits, 1988, The Japanese Entrepreneur: Making the Desert Bloom, 2002; mem. editorial bd.: Jour. Artificial Intelligence, 1970-88. Trustee Charles Babbage Found. History of Info. Processing, U. Minn., 2000-03, 2004-; mem. Feigenbaum-Nii Found., 2000—. Feigenbaum medal named in his honor World Congress on Expert Systems, 1991. Fellow AAAI, AAAS, Am. Coll. Med. Informatics, Am. Inst. Med. and Biol. Engring.; mem. NAE, Assn. Computing Machinery (nat. coun. 1966-68, chmn. spl. interest group on biol. applications 1973-76, A.M. Turing award 1994), Am. Assn. Artificial Intelligence (pres. 1980-81, Robert S. Engelmore Meml. award 2004), Am. Acad. Arts and Scis., Cognitive Sci. Soc. (coun. 1979-82), Sigma Xi, Tau Beta Pi, Eta Kappa Nu, Pi Delta Epsilon. Home: 1017 Cathcart Way Palo Alto CA 94305-1048 Office: Stanford U Knowledge Systems Lab Gates Computer Sci Rm 220 Stanford CA 94305-9020 Business E-Mail: feigenbaum@cs.stanford.edu.

FEIGENBAUM, JOAN, computer scientist, mathematician; b. Bklyn., Sept. 19, 1958; d. Harry and Joyce Leslie (Gildersleeve) F.; m. Jeffrey Nussbaum. BA in Math. magna cum laude, Harvard U., 1981; PhD in Computer Sci., Stanford U., 1986; MA (Privatum), Yale U., 2001. Prin. mem. tech. staff AT&T Bell Labs., Murray Hill, NJ, 1986—95; head, algorithms and distributed data AT&T Labs-Rsch., Florham Park, NJ, 1998—99, mem. rsch. staff, 1996—2000; prof. computers sci. dept. Yale U., New Haven, 2000—05, Henry Ford II prof. computer sci., 2006—. Program chair CRYPTO-91, Santa Barbara, Calif., 1991; mem. program com. STOC-91, New Orleans, 1991, STOC-94, Montreal, Can., STOC-99, Atlanta; panel mem., Grace Hopper Celebration of Women in Computing, Sci. Policy, 1994; co-chair DIMACS Workshops, 1989, 90, 96; program com. chair Crypto, 1991, IEEE Conf. on Computational Complexity, 1998; program com. mem. Crypto, 1989, 1993, 1996, Eurocrypt, 1992, 1999, IEEE Conf. on Computation Complexity, 1993, Internat. Computing and Combinators Conf., 1998, Financial Cryptography, 1999, 2000, workshop on Internet and Network Economics, 2005; NSF, mem. eight proposal-evaluation panel, 1993-2005; steering-com. mem., DIMACS Special Focus on Computation and the Socio-Economic Sciences, 2004-; session organizer, chair, Info. Security: Principles and Pub. Policy, AAAS, 1995, Incentive Compatibility in Internet Computation, AAAS, 2003; mem., NAS Computer Sci. and Telecommunications Bd., 2002-; bd. dir. Inst. Math. and Its Applications, 1999-2002; adv. bd. mem., John Hopkins U. Computer Sci., 1999-2002; steering com. mem., DIMACS spl. year on massive data sets, 1997-98; co-chair DIMACS spl. focus on Next Generation networks, 2000-2003; NRC panel mem., Intellectual Property Protection in the Emerging Information Infrastructure, 1998-99; steering com. mem., conf. on computational complexity, 1994-97, DIMACS spl. yr. on logic and algorithms, 1995-96; project com. chair, DIMACS, 1994-96; participant, NAS Frontiers of Sci. Symposium, 1995; session organizer, chair, Security and Privacy in the Information Economy, NAS Frontiers in Sci. Symposium, 1996; panel mem., Past, Present, and Future Challenges, NSF Conf. on Women in Sci., 1995; speaker various colls., univs. and confs. Mem. editl. bd. Jour. Algorithms, 1992-96, SIAM Jour. on Computing, 1993-2002; guest editor, 1989-90, Jour. Cryptology, mem. editl. bd. 1990-96, editor-in-chief, 1997-2002; area editor Comm. of Assn. for Computing Machinery, 1988-89; guest editor Jour. Computer and Sys. Scis., 1991, 1998, IEEE Trans. on Information Theory, 1996; adv. bd. mem. Jour. Privacy Tech., 2004-;contbr. articles to profl. jours. Invited spkr. Internat. Congress of Mathematicians, Berlin, 1998. Math. Scis. Postdoctoral fellow NSF, 1986, Xerox Corp. Grad. fellow, 1984. Fellow Assn. Computing Machinery (guest editor, Communication of the ACM, 1988-89; program com. mem. symposium on theory of computing, 1991, 1994, 1999, 2001, conf. on computer and communications security, 1993, 1994, 2005, ACM/SIAM symposium on discrete algorithms, 1999, workshop on security and privacy in digital rights mgmt., 2001, symposium on principals of distrubuted computing, 2004; Sigecom vice-chair, 2005-2007, Sigact exec. com. mem., 2005-2007; program com. chair, workshop on digital rights mgmt., 2002; co-chair conf. on electric commerce, 2004; gen. chair conf. on electronic commerce, 2006); charter mem., Computing Rsch. Assn. Com. on the Status of Women, 1991-96; mem. Am. Math. Soc., Assn. for Women in Math.(mem.-at-large, 2000-04; tutorial co-chair, conf. on electronics commerce, 2003; gen. co-chair, workshop on digital rights mgmt., 2003; selection com. mem., Grace Murray Hopper award, 2001-), Internat. Assn. Cryptologic Rsch. (program com. CRYPT089 conf. 1989, CRYPTO93 conf. 1993, Eurocrypt92 conf. 1992, Eurocrypt 99 conf. 1999, COCCS93 conf. 1993, COCCS94 conf. 1994, fellows selection com., 2003-), Phi Beta Kappa. Democrat. Jewish. Home: 148 W 23rd St Apt 2A New York NY 10011-2447 Office: Yale U Dept Computer Sci PO Box 208285 New Haven CT 06520-8285 Office Phone: 203-432-6432. Office Fax: 203-432-6373. Business E-Mail: jf@cs.yale.edu.

FEIGENSON, MARK DANIEL, geologist, educator; m. Ann B. Summer, Aug. 3, 1975; children: Keith, Steven(dec.) , Kalie. BS, U. Md., College Park, 1974; MS, George Washington U., Washington, 1978; PhD, Princeton U., NJ, 1982. Prof. Rutgers U., New Brunswick, NJ, 1982—. Fellow: Geol. Soc. Am.; mem.: Am. Geophys. Union. Office: Rutgers U Dept Geol Scis New Brunswick NJ 08903 Home Phone: 609-439-8271; Office Phone: 732-445-3149. Office Fax: 732-445-3374. E-mail: feigy@rci.rutgers.edu.

FEIGHT, THEODORE J., financial planner; b. Alma, Mich., Oct. 18, 1946; s. William T. Feight and Wilma (Richardson) Recker; m. Kathleen Lischkge, June 13, 1969; children: Jay David, Richard Thomas, James Daryl, Brian Lynn BS, We. Mich. U., Kalamazoo, 1972. Cert. divorce specialist, fin. planner. Dist. mgr. Clark Oil, Milw., 1972—73; fin. planner Mut. Benefit Life Ins. Co., Lansing, Mich., 1973—78, Creative Fin. Design, Lansing, 1978—. Mem. Inst. CFP Registry, Denver, 1991—; bd. dirs., treas. Commemorative Bucks of Mich., Inc.; webmaster Michigancdp.com., Buckfax.com Ghost writer book on fin. planning, 1984. Bd. dirs. The Adoption Cradle, Battle Creek, Mich., 1993-98. With U.S. Army, 1967-68, Viet Nam Decorated DSM, Air medal with 2 bronze stars; winner nat. championship USAPL Powerlifting, 2001, 2002, 2004, Powerlifting Nat. Championship, Am. Amateur Powerlifting Fedn., 2001, 2004, WABDL, 2001, 2002, 2003, 2004, Amateur World Powerlifting Congress, 2002, World Championships, 2002, 2003, 2004. Mem. NAPFA (bd. dirs.), Fin. Planning Assn. (bd. dirs., past pres.), Inst. CFP, Mich. State Assn. Life Underwriters (Nat. Pub. Svc. award 1980), Lansing Assn. Life Underwriters (bd. dirs. 1978-79), Mich. Cert. Divorce Planners (pres.), Mich. Fin. Planning Assn. (bd. dirs., pres. 2004—, past pres.), Rotary Internat. (bd. dirs. 1979-81) Avocations: hunting, golf, Karate, cars, power lifting. Home and Office: Creative Fin Design 2112 Tulane Dr Lansing MI 48912-3546 Office Phone: 517-371-5100. Personal E-mail: ted-feight@comcast.net. Business E-Mail: ted-feight@creativefinancialdesign.com.

FEIGIN, BARBARA SOMMER, marketing consultant; b. Berlin, Nov. 16, 1937; arrived in US, 1940, naturalized, 1949; d. Eric Daniel and Charlotte Martha (Demmer) Sommer; m. James Feigin, Sept. 17, 1961; children: Michael, Peter, Daniel. BA in Polit. Sci., Whitman Coll., 1959; cert. of Bus. Adminstrn., Harvard-Radcliffe Program Bus. Adminstrn., 1960. Mktg. rsch. asst. Richardson-Vick Co., Wilton, Conn., 1960-61; market rsch. analyst SCM Corp., NYC, 1961-62; group rsch. supr. Benton & Bowles, Inc., NYC, 1963-67; assoc. rsch. dir. Marplan Rsch. Co., NYC, 1968-69; exec. v.p. worldwide strategic svcs., mem. agy. policy coun. Grey Advt. Inc., NYC, 1969-99. Bd. dirs. VF Corp., Circuit City Stores, Inc.; past chmn. Advert Rsch. Found. Contbr. articles to profl jours. Overseer emeritus Whitman Col; past bd advisors Catalyst. Recipient Women Achievers Award, YWCA, 1987. Mem.: Mkt. Rsch. Hall of Fame.

FEIGIN, JOEL, composer, educator; b. NYC, May 23, 1951; s. Irwin and Mollie Kanowitz Feigin; m. Severine Neff, 1986. BA, Columbia U., 1968—72; MA, Juilliard Sch., 1977; DMA, 1982. Mellon post doctoral fellowship Cornell U., 1983—85; asst. prof. U. Ut., 1985—87; faculty Manhattan Sch., 1988—92; asst. prof. U. Calif., 1992—97, assoc. prof., 1997—2002, prof., 2002—. Composer: (Operas) Mysteries of Eleusis, 1986, The Ferryman, 1997, Twelfth Night, 2004, (chamber music) variations of violin, piano and string quartet (speculum musicae and auros group for new music composition competitions, 1998), Veränderungen, 1995, Transcience, 1996 (third place internat. chamber music competition, 1997), vocal and choral music, (video soundtrack) Music for Mountains and Rivers, 1996. Andrew D. Mellon post-doctoral fellow, Cornell U., 1983—85, Guggenheim fellow, 1985—86, Sr. Fulbright fellow, Moscow State Conservatory, 1998—99, winner, NYCO Vox Competition, 2004, Opera Am. Showcase, 2006. Avocations: reading, sitting zaren. Office: U Calif Music Dept Rm 1121 Santa Barbara CA 93105

FEIGON, JUDITH TOVA, ophthalmologist, educator, surgeon; b. Galveston, Tex., Dec. 2, 1947; d. Louis and Ethel Feigon; m. Nathan C. Goldman; children: Michael G., Miriam G. AB, Barnard Coll., Columbia U., 1970; postgrad., Rice U., U. Houston, 1970-71; MD, U. Tex., San Antonio, 1976. Diplomate Am. Bd. Ophthalmology. Intern Mt. Auburn Hosp., Cambridge, Mass.; intern, clin. tchg. fellow Harvard U. Med. Sch., 1976-77; resident in ophthalmology Baylor Coll. Medicine, Houston, 1977-80, fellow in retina, 1980-82, clin. faculty, 1982-95; asst. prof. ophthalmology U. Tex. Med. Br., Galveston, 1982-85, clin. asst. prof., 1985-91, clin. assoc. prof., 1992—; pvt. practice medicine specializing ophthalmology, vitreoretinal diseases, surgery, Houston, 1983—. Physician advisor to Houston br. Tex. Soc. to Prevent Blindness, 1987-89, also bd. dirs., mem. staff Meth., St. Lukes, Tex. Children's Hosp. Contbr. articles to profl. publs. Mem. Assn. Am. Physicians and Surgeons, Am. Acad. Ophthalmology, Tex. Med. Assn. Houston Ophthal. Soc., Harris County Med. Soc., U. Tex. San Antonio Alumni Assn., Am. Soc. Retina Specialists, Tex. Ophthalmol. Assn., Houston Ophthal. Soc. (exec. bd. 2000-03). Office: 7515 Main St Ste 650 Houston TX 77030-4599 Office Phone: 713-799-1737.

FEIKENS, JOHN, federal judge; b. Clifton, NJ, Dec. 3, 1917; s. Sipke and Corine (Wisse) F.; m. Henriette Dorothy Schulthouse, Nov. 4, 1939; children: Jon, Susan Corine, Barbara Edith, Julie Anne, Robert H. AB, Calvin Coll., Grand Rapids, Mich., 1938; JD, U. Mich., 1941; LLD (hon.), U. Detroit, 1979, Detroit Coll. Law, 1981. Bar: Mich. 1942. Gen. practice law, Detroit; dist. judge Ea. Dist. Mich., Detroit, 1960-61, 70-79, chief judge, 1979-86, sr. judge, 1986—. Past co-chmn. Mich. Civil Rights Commn.; past chmn. Rep. State Central Com.; past mem. Rep. Nat. Com.; mem. com. visitors U. Mich. Law Sch. Past bd. trustees Calvin Coll. Fellow Am. Coll. Trial Lawyers; mem. ABA, Detroit Bar Assn. (dir. 1962, past pres.), State Bar Mich. (commr. 1965-71), U. Mich. Club (com. visitors). Office: US Dist Ct 851 Theodore Levin US Ct 231 W Lafayette Blvd Detroit MI 48226-2700

FEIL, MICHAEL BRUCE, statistician; b. Urbana, Ill., Apr. 30, 1949; s. Richard Anthony and Barbara June Feil; m. Dana Marie Strack, Sept. 6, 1975; children: Margaret Anne, Robert Bruce. BS in Med. Tech., Rutgers U., 1974, MBA, 1979; MS, Georgetown U., 1985; DSc, Canterbury U., 2002. Cert. medical technologist Am. Soc. Clin. Pathologists. Staff technologist North Jersey Blood Ctr., East Orange, NJ, 1974—78, systems analyst, 1979—80; market analyst Am. Blood Commn., Arlington, Va., 1980—81; staff technologist quality control Georgetown U. Hosp., Washington, 1982—86; statistician Dept. Veterans Affairs, Washington, 1986; sr. assoc. Moshman Assoc., Inc., Bethesda, Md., 1986—90; statistician NIMH, Bethesda, 1991—2000; chief statistician Agrl. Mktg. Svc., Washington, 2000—. Contbr. articles to profl. jours. Recipient Pub. Health Spl. Recognition award, US Govt., HHS, 1995, Staff Recognition award, US Govt., HHS, Pub. Health Svc., NIH, 1997. Mem.: Wash. Statis. Soc. (bd. dirs., editor 1995—, Pres. award 1997, 2002), Am. Statis. Soc. Lutheran. Avocations: target shooting, travel. Home: 2361 Emerald Heights Ct Reston VA 20191-1750 Office: Agrl Mktg Svc 1400 Independence Ave SW MS-0223 Washington DC 22050-0223 Office Phone: 202-690-3130. Personal E-mail: pdrule@comcast.net. Business E-Mail: michael.feil@usda.gov.

FEILER, WILLIAM S., lawyer; b. NYC, Oct. 1, 1946; s. John E. and Monica M. (Mealy) F.; m. Louise A. Brizzolara, May 30, 1970; children: Michael, Christine, Thomas, Stephen. BE, Manhattan Coll., 1968; JD, Fordham U., 1972; postgrad., U. Chgo., 1974; LLM in Trade Regulation, NYU, 1978. Bar: Ill. 1972, U.S. Dist. Ct. (no. dist.) Ill. 1972, U.S. Patent Office 1973, U.S. Ct. Appeals (7th cir.) 1973, N.Y. 1975, U.S. Dist. Ct. (so. and ea. dists.) N.Y. 1975, U.S. Ct. Appeals (2nd cir.) 1975, U.S. Supreme Ct. 1976, N.J. 1977, U.S. Ct. Appeals (3d cir.) 1977, U.S. Dist. Ct. N.J. 1979, U.S. Ct. Appeals (6th cir.) 1979., U.S. Dist. Ct. (we. dist.) N.Y. 1980, U.S. Ct. Appeals (fed. cir.) 1982, D.C. 1991, U.S. Dist. Ct. (no. dist.) N.Y. 1991, U.S. Dist. Ct. (ctrl. dist.) Ill. 2005. Staff engr. Con Edison, NYC, 1968-69; assoc. Dressler, Goldsmith et al., Chgo., 1972-74; adj. asst. prof. Manhattan Coll., Riverdale, N.Y., 1975-78; ptnr. Morgan & Finnegan, NYC, 1976—. Arbitrator U.S. Dist. Ct. N.J., 1985—, Am. Arbitration Assn., CPR Inst., World Intellectual Property Orgn.; mem. NASD Dispute Panel. Contbr. articles to profl. jours. Pres. St. Cassian Sch. Bd., Upper Montclair, N.Y., 1980-82. Mem. ABA, Assn. of Bar of City of N.Y., N.Y. Patent Law Assn., N.Y. Patent Trademark Law Assn., Phi Alpha Delta. Roman Catholic. Achievements include patents for baby cradle; litigation support system and method. Avocations: golf, fishing, photography. Office: Morgan Finnegan Llp 3 World Financial Ctr Fl 21 New York NY 10281-2101 Home Phone: 973-744-0505; Office Phone: 212-415-8700. Business E-Mail: wsfeiler@morganfinnegan.com.

FEILMEIER, STEVE, corporate financial executive; M in Acctg., Wichita State U. Joined Koch Industries, Wichita, Kans., 1997, v.p. tax, fin. and acctg., sr. v.p., CFO, 2002—, also bd. dirs. Bd. dirs. Big Bros. Big Sisters Sedgwick County, former chmn., treas., 2003. Office: Koch Industries 4111 E 37th St Wichita KS 67220*

FEIMAN, THOMAS E., investment company executive; b. Canton, Ohio, Dec. 21, 1940; s. Daniel Thaviu and Adrienne (Silver) F.; m. Marilyn Judith Miller, June 26, 1966; children: Sheri, Michael. BS in Econs., U. Pa., 1962; MBA, Northwestern U., 1963. CPA, Calif. Staff acct. Arthur Young & Co., LA, 1963-66; field auditor IRS, LA, 1966-68; pvt. practice acctg. Thomas Feiman, C.P.A., LA, 1968-69; ptnr. Wideman & Feiman, C.P.A.s, LA, 1969-74; pres. Wideman, Feiman, Levy, Sapin & Ko, LA, 1974-93; investment mgr., v.p. Schroder Wertheim & Co., Inc., 1993-96; CFO Spinal Home Health Systems, Inc., LA, 1983-85; fin. cons., v.p. Merrill Lynch, 1996—2004, UBS, 2004—; pres., dir. Urol. Scis. Rsch. Found., 1993—. Sr. instr. UCLA Extension, 1967-84. Trustee Temple Israel of Hollywood, Calif., 1981-83, treas., 1983-84. Recipient cert. of award IRS, 1967. Mem. AICPA, Calif. Soc. CPAs, Northwestern Bus. So. Calif. Club (pres. 1977-80), Northwestern Alumni of So. Calif. Club (trustee 1977-92, treas. 1977-90 L.A.). Republican. Jewish. Office: UBS Financial Svcs 21650 Oxnard St Woodland Hills CA 91367-4907 Personal E-mail: thomasfeiman@yahoo.com. Business E-Mail: thomasfeiman@ubs.com.

FEIN, IRVING ASHLEY, television and motion picture executive; b. Bklyn., June 21, 1911; s. Harry and Fannie (Milstein) F.; m. Florence Kohn, Dec. 25, 1941 (dec.); children: Michael Anthony, Patricia Ann; m. Marion Shepard Schechter, June 21, 1969. Student, U. Balt., 1928-29, U. Wis., 1930-32; LLB, St. Lawrence U., 1936. Publicity and advt. dept. Warner Bros., NYC, 1933-36; dir. exploitation and radio West Coast studios, 1936; asst. publicity dir. Samuel Goldwyn, 1941; dir. exploitation and radio Columbia Pictures, Hollywood, 1942; publicity, advt. dir. Amusement Enterprises, Inc., 1947; with CBS, Inc., 1948-56, dir. exploitation Hollywood, 1950; dir. publicity and exploitation CBS Radio, Hollywood, 1951-53, dir. pub. relations, 1953-55, v.p. sales promotion, advt. and press info. NYC, 1955-56; pres. J & M Prodns., Inc., Beverly Hills, Calif., 1956-65; exec. v.p. J.B. Prodns., 1965-75; producer Jack Benny Programs, 1958-74; pres. TV Prodn. Co. Producer: George Burns TV spls., 1975-96, (films) Just You and Me Kid, Oh God! You Devil, Eighteen Again; author: Jack Benny: An Intimate Biography, 1976. Recipient Emmy award, 1961. Home: 1100 Alta Loma Rd Los Angeles CA 90069-2455 Office Phone: 310-657-5000.

FEIN, RASHI, health sciences educator; b. NYC, Feb. 6, 1926; s. Isaac M. and Clara(Wertheim) F.; m. Ruth Judith Breslau, June 19, 1949; children: Alan, Michael, Karen, Bena (dec.). Student, Bridgeport Jr. Coll., 1942—43; BA, Johns Hopkins U., 1948, PhD, 1956; LittD (hon.), SUNY, 1996. Mem. staff Pres.'s Commn. on Health Needs, 1952; from lectr. to assoc. prof. U. N.C., 1952-61; statistician Bur. of Census, 1958-59; sr. staff Pres.'s Coun. Econ. Advisers, 1961-63; sr. fellow Brookings Inst., 1963-68; prof. Harvard U., 1968-99, prof. emeritus, 1999—; Heath Clark lectr. London Sch. Hygiene and Tropical Medicine, 1980; chmn. med. assistance adv. coun. to sec. HEW, 1967-69; mem. adv. com. research and devel. Social Security Adminstrn., 1968-71; mem. Nat. Manpower Policy Task Force, 1967-79, Office Tech. Assessment, Health Adv. Panel, 1981-86. Mem. spl. med. adv. group VA, 1987-91; mem. nat. adv. rsch. resources coun. NIH, 1995-99, emeritus; chair nat. adv. com. Robert Wood Johnson Found. Scholars in Health Policy Rsch. Program; bd. dirs. Ctr. for Child Health Rsch., Am. Acad. Pediat. Author: Economics of Mental Illness, 1958, The Doctor Shortage: An Economic Diagnosis, 1967, (with Gerald Weber) Financing Medical Education: An Analysis of Alternative Policies and Mechanisms, 1971, (with Charles Lewis and David Mechanic) A Right to Health: The Problem of Access to Primary Medical Care, 1976, Alcohol in America: The Price We Pay, 1984, Medical Care, Medical Costs: The Search for a Health Insurance Policy, 1986, 89, (with Julius Richmond) The Health Care Mess: How We Got Into It and What It Will Take To Get Out, 2005. Mem. bd. overseers Beth Israel Deaconess Med. Ctr., Boston, 1972—; trustee Hebrew Sr. Life, Boston, 1976—; mem. com. of visitors Goucher Coll., 1999—; bd. dirs. Harvard Cmty. Health Plan Found., 1980—87; mem. tech. bd. Millbank Meml. Fund, 1975—78, 1986—90, bd. dirs., 1987—90. Recipient John M. Russell award for advancement knowledge in medicine, 1971; fellow Inst. History Medicine Johns Hopkins U., 1951-52; traveling fellow WHO, 1971. Mem. APHA, AAUP, Inst. Medicine of NAS (Adam Yarmolinsky medal for contbns.), Nat. Acad. Social Ins., Am. Econ. Assn., Am. Adv. Coun. World Orgn. for Ednl. Resources and Tech. Tng. Union. Jewish. Office: Harvard U Sch Medicine Dept Social Medicine 641 Huntington Ave 2d Fl Boston MA 02115-6019 Business E-Mail: rashi_fein@hms.harvard.edu.

FEIN, ROGER GARY, judge; b. St. Louis, Mar. 12, 1940; s. Albert and Fanny (Levinson) F.; m. Susanne M. Cohen, Dec. 18, 1965; children: David L., Lisa J. Student, Washington U., St. Louis, 1959, NYU, 1960; BS, UCLA, 1962; JD, Northwestern U., 1965; MBA, Am. U., 1967. Bar: Ill. 1965, US Dist. Ct. (no. dist.) Ill. 1968, US Ct. Appeals (7th cir.) 1968, US Supreme Ct. 1970. Atty. divsn. corp. fin. SEC, Washington, 1965—67; ptnr. Arvey, Hodes, Costello & Burman, Chgo., 1967—91, chmn. adminstrn. and dissolution com., 1992—2003; ptnr. Wildman, Harrold, Allen and Dixon, Chgo., 1992—2003, co-chair corp., securities and tax practice group, 1992—99; judge Cir. Ct. Cook County, 2003—. Mem. Securities Adv. Com. to Sec. State Ill., 1973—, chmn., 1973-79, 87-93, vice-chmn., 1983-87, chmn. emeritus, 1994—; spl. asst. atty. gen. State of Ill., 1974-83, 85-99; spl. asst. state's atty. Cook County, Ill., 1989-90; mem. Appeal Bd., Ill. Law Enforcement Commn., 1980-83; mem. lawyer's adv. bd. So. Ill. Law Jour., 1980-83; mem. adv. bd. securities regulation and law report Bur. Nat. Affairs Inc., 1985-02; lectr., author on land trust financing, consumer credit and securities law. Mem. Bd. Edn., Sch. Dist. No. 29, Northfield, Ill., 1977-83, pres., 1981-83; mem. Pub. Vehicle Ops. Citizens Adv. coun. City Chgo., 1985-86; mem. Anti-Defamation League Greater Chgo./Upper Midwest Region, Chgo. regional bd., 1975-91, vice chmn., 1980-88, exec. com., 1996—, co-chair pub. affairs com., 1999-2003, assoc. nat. commr., 2000—; chmn. lawyers' com. for ann. telethon Muscular Dystrophy Assn., 1983; past bd. dirs. Jewish Nat. Fund, Am. Friends Hebrew U., Northfield Cmty. Fund. Recipient Pub. Svc. award Sec. State Ill., 1976, Citation of Merit, WAIT Radio, 1976, Sunset Ridge Sch. Cmty. Svc. award, 1984, City of Chgo. Citizen's award, 1986; named one of Leading Ill. Attys., Am. Rsch. Corp., 1997. Fellow Am. Bar Found., Ill. Bar Found. (charter fellow, bd. dirs. 1978-88, v.p. 1982-84, pres. 1984-86, chmn. Fellows 1983-84, chmn., past pres. adv. com. 1988-90, Cert. of Appreciation 1985, 86, Silver fellow 1997), Chgo. Bar Found; mem. ABA (ho. of dels. 1981-85, state regulation of securities com. 1982-2003, Ill. liaison of com., chmn. subcom. liaison with securities adminstrs. and NASD 1998-2003), Ill. State Bar Assn. (bd. govs. 1976-80, del. assembly 1976-88, sec. 1977-78, cert. of appreciation 1980, 88, chmn. Bench and Bar com. 1982-83, chmn. Bench and Bar sect. coun., 1983-84, chmn. bar elections supervision com. 1986-87, chmn. assembly com. on hearings 1987-88, mem. com. on jud. appointments 1987-90), Chgo. Bar Assn. (mem. task force delivery legal svcs. 1978-80, cert. of appreciation 1976, chmn. land trusts com. 1978-79, chmn. consumer credit com. 1977-78, chmn. state securities law subcom. 1977-79), Ill. Judges Assn., Decalogue Soc. Lawyers, Northwestern U. Sch. of Law Alumni Assn. (past dir.), Standard Club, The Law Club of the City of Chgo., Tau Epsilon Phi, Alpha Kappa Psi, Phi Delta Phi. Office: Circuit Court Cook County Ill Second Mcpl Dist 5600 Old Orchard Rd Skokie IL 60077 Office Phone: 847-470-7200.

FEIN, RONALD LAWRENCE, lawyer; b. Detroit, Aug. 26, 1943; s. Lee Allen and Billie Doreen (Thomas) F.; m. Sandra Siegel, March 21, 2006; children: Samantha, Mark. AB with honors, UCLA, 1966; JD with honors, U. San Diego, 1969. Bar: Calif. 1970, U.S. Dist. Ct. (cen. dist.) Calif. 1970. Assoc. Gibson, Dunn & Crutcher, Los Angeles, 1969-75; chief dep. commr. of corps. State of Calif., Los Angeles, 1975-78; ptnr., mem. firmwide adv. com., chmn. corp. fin./mergers and acquisitions sect., chmn. corp. dept. Jones, Day, Reavis & Pogue, Los Angeles, 1978-87; ptnr., mem. exec. com., chmn. gen. bus. dept. Wyman, Bautzer, Kuchel & Silbert, LA, 1987-91; sr. ptnr. Stutman, Treister & Glatt, 1991—. Bd. dirs. Executours, Inc., Los Angeles, Lottery Info., North Hollywood, Calif., Malibu Grand Prix, Woodland Hills, Calif.; adj. prof. law Loyola U., Los Angeles, 1976; mem. Commr.'s Circle Adv. Com. to the Calif. Commr. of Corps., Fin. Lawyers Conf.; mem. adv. bd. Inst. Corp. Counsel U. S.C Articles editor San Diego Law Rev., 1969; contbr. articles to profl. jours. Co-dir. protocol for boxing Los Angeles Olympic Organizing Com., 1984. Lt. USAF, to 1966-69. Mem. ABA (corp., banking and bus. law sect., mem. ad hoc com. on merit regulation, mem. fed. regulation of securities com., mem. ad hoc com. on the Uniform Limited Offering Exemption, com. on Counsel Responsibility, mem. ad hoc com. on Regulation D, mem. subcom. on Registration Statements—1933 Act, vice chmn. state regulation securities com., chmn. pvt. offering exemption and simplification of capital formation subcom., chmn. NASAA Omnibus guideline subcom.), Calif. Bar Assn. (bus. law sect.), Los Angeles County Bar Assn. (mem. exec. com. bus. and corps. law sect.), Nat. Assn. Securities Dealers, Inc. (mem. subcom. on indemnification, mem. arbitration panel, mem. adv. bd. Prentice-Hall West coast mergers and acquisitions panels), Mountaingate Country Club. Avocations: sports, reading, theater. Home: 455 N Oakhurst Dr Beverly Hills CA 90210-3911 Office: FL 12 1901 Avenue of the Stars Los Angeles CA 90067-6013 Home Phone: 310-274-5206; Office Phone: 310-228-5780. Business E-Mail: rfein@stutman.com.

FEIN, RONNIE, journalist, writer; b. NYC, June 5, 1943; d. William and Lily (Hoffman) Vail; m. Edward Fein, Nov. 15, 1969; children: Meredith, Gillian. BA, Northwestern U., 1964; LLB, NYU, 1967. Atty. Chadbourne, Parke, Whiteside & Wolff, NYC, 1967-70, Rosenman, Colin, NYC, 1970-71; dir. Ronnie Fein Sch. Creative Cooking, Stamford, Conn., 1971—; freelance demonstrator cooking, dept. stores various locations, 1971—; journalist Stamford Trader, 1980-81, The Advertiser, New Canaan, 1981-98, Times-Mirror/Tribune newspapers, 1984—, Consumer's Digest Mag., 1989—, Darien Times, 1993—98, Newsday, 1995—, Hersam-Acorn newspapers, 1997—98, LA Times Syndicate, 1999—, Westport Mag., 1999—, Greenwich Mag., 1999—, Conn. Mag., 2006, Wild Catch Mag., 2006—; editor East Coast, 2007. Talk show host The New WNLK, Norwalk, Conn., 1984; contbg. editor The New Cook's Catalogue, 2000, Tribune Newspapers, 2001—, Conn. Mag., 2005—. Author: The Complete Idiot's Guide to Cooking Basics, 1995, 3d edit., 2000, The Complete Idiot's Guide to American Cooking, 2002. Alumni admissions dir. Fairfield County, Northwestern U., Evanston, Ill., 1985-98. Fellow Conn. Women's Culinary Alliance (charter, newsletter co-chmn. 1988-89, pres. 1996-97). Home: 32 Heming Way Stamford CT 06903 Personal E-mail: ronnievfein@optonline.net.

FEIN, SEYMOUR HOWARD, pharmaceutical executive; b. NYC, Oct. 28, 1948; s. Abner and Beatrice (Wolkoff) Fein; m. Mary Louise Orizzonto, Apr. 1, 1979; children: Jessica Ann, David Thomas, Renee Elizabeth, Jonathan Parker. BA, U. Pa., 1970; MD, N.Y. Med. Coll., 1974. Intern Dartmouth-Hitchcock Med. Ctr., Hanover, NH, 1974-75, resident in internal medicine, 1975-77; fellow in hematology, oncology Beth Israel Hosp., Harvard Med. Sch., Boston, 1977-80; instr. medicine Harvard Med. Sch., Boston, 1979-80; sr. rsch. physician Hoffmann-LaRoche, Nutley, NJ, 1980-83; dir. med. rsch. Miles Pharmaceuticals, West Haven, Conn., 1983-86, Rorer Pharms., Ft. Washington, Pa., 1986-87; v.p. med. rsch. Greenwich Pharms., Ft. Washington, 1987-88; dir. clin. rsch. and devel. Anaquest, Murray Hill, NJ, 1988-92; v.p. clin. rsch. and biostats. Oxford Rsch. Internat. Corp., Clifton, NJ, 1992-94; pres. Fein Consulting and Rsch. Svcs., New Canaan, Conn., 1994—. Mng. ptnr. CNF Pharma LLC, New City, NY, 2002—; chmn. ChiRhoClin Inc., Burtonsville, Md., 1997—2005; chief med. officer Serenity Pharms., Inc., New City, 2007—. Mem.: AAAS, N.Y. Acad. Scis., Am. Soc. Clin. Oncology. Republican. Jewish. Avocations: reading, cooking, tennis, gardening, travel. Office Phone: 845-639-1820. Personal E-mail: seymour.fein@markusresearch.com.

FEIN, STEPHANIE LYNNE, language educator; b. Bklyn., July 4, 1950; d. Marvin Julian Forray and Muriel Lee Gordon; m. Henry George Fein, Apr. 30, 1972; children: Sondra, Joshua, Arielle. BA, Vassar Coll., Poughkeepsie, NY, 1972; MA, NYU, 1974, PhD, 1977. Tchr. bilingual PS 45, Bklyn., 1972—76, PS 15 187, NYC, 1976—77; tchr. Spanish Green Acres Sch., Rockville, Md., 1977—. Former faculty liaison Green Acres Sch., dir. Peruvian exch. program. Mem.: ACTFL, Phi Beta Kappa. Democrat. Jewish. Avocations: travel, art, opera, cooking, music. Office: Green Acres Sch 11701 Danville Dr Rockville MD 20852

FEIN, WILLIAM, ophthalmologist; b. NYC, Nov. 27, 1933; s. Samuel and Beatrice (Lipschitz) F.; m. Bonnie Fern Aaronson, Dec. 15, 1963; children: Stephanie Paula, Adam Irving, Gregory Andrew. BS, CCNY, 1954; MD, U. Calif., Irvine, 1962. Diplomate Am. Bd. Ophthalmology. Intern L.A. County Gen. Hosp., 1962-63, resident in ophthalmology, 1963-66; instr. U. Calif. Med. Sch., Irvine, 1966-69; faculty U. So. Calif. Med. Sch., 1969—, assoc. clin. prof. ophthalmology, 1979—; attending physician Cedars-Sinai Med. Ctr., LA, 1966—, chief ophthalmology clinic svc., 1979-81, chmn. divsn. ophthalmology, 1981-85; attending physician L.A. County-U. So. Calif. Med. Ctr., 1969—; chmn. dept. ophthalmology Midway Hosp., 1975-78; dir. Ellis Eye Ctr., LA, 1984—. Mem. editorial bd. CATARACT, Internat. Jour. of Cataract and Ocular Surgery, 1992—; contbr. articles to profl. jours. Chmn. ophthalmology adv. com. Jewish Home for Aging of Greater L.A., 1993—. Fellow Internat. Coll. Surgeons, Am. Coll. Surgeons; mem. Am. Acad. Ophthalmology, Am. Soc. Ophthalmic Plastic and Reconstructive Surgery, Royal Soc. Medicine, AMA, Calif. Med. Assn., L.A. Med. Assn. Home: 718 N Camden Dr Beverly Hills CA 90210-3205 Office Phone: 310-859-0760.

FEINBERG, DAVID ERWIN, retired publishing executive; b. Mpls., 1922; Grad., U. Minn., 1948. Chmn., chief exec. officer EMC Corp., St. Paul. Sec. bd. dirs., v.p. Paradigm Pub., Inc. Home: 111 Kellogg Blvd E Saint Paul MN 55101-1237 Office: EMC Corp 875 Montreal Way Saint Paul MN 55102-4245

FEINBERG, DAVID M., energy executive, lawyer; b. 1969; m. Felicia Feinberg; children: Sofia, Ella. BME, U. Pa., B in Psych.; JD, Harvard Law Sch., 1995. Law clk. to Hon. Joel Flaum US Ct. Appeals (7th Cir.); ptnr. Jenner & Block LLP, Chgo., 1996—2004; dep. gen. counsel Allegheny Energy Inc., Beach Haven, Pa., 2004—06, v.p., gen. counsel, sec., 2006—. Avocation: golf.*

FEINBERG, DENNIS LOWELL, dermatologist; b. Bridgeport, Conn., June 10, 1951; AB, Cornell U., 1973; MD, SUNY, Syracuse, 1976. Diplomat Nat. Bd. Med. Examiners, Am. Bd. Internal Medicine, Am. Bd. Dermatology. Intern U. Miami (Fla.) Affiliated Hosps., 1976-77, resident, 1977-78, Johns Hopkins Med. Inst., Balt., 1978-80; dermatologist pvt. practice, Washington, 1981, Stratford, Conn., 1981—. Sr. attending Bridgeport Hosp., 1981—; attending St. Vincent's Med. Ctr., Bridgeport, 1981—; cons. Milford (Conn.) Hosp., 1982-2000; asst. clin. prof. Yale U. Sch. Medicine, New Haven, 1985—. Fellow Am. Acad. Dermatology; mem. AMA, ACP, Atlantic Dermatol. Soc., New Eng. Dermatol. Soc., Conn. Dermatology and Dermatologic Surgery Soc. (pres.), Conn. State Med. Soc., Fairfield County Med. Assn., Greater Bridgeport Med. Assn., Syracuse Med. Alumni Assn. Office: 2875 Main St Stratford CT 06614-4937

FEINBERG, HERBERT, apparel executive, real estate company executive; b. NYC, June 20, 1926; s. Harry Feinberg and Dorothy (Hurwitz) Goldstein; m. Audrey Frank, Sept. 15, 1948 (div. Mar. 1972); children: Michael(dec.) , Mark, Harry; m. Barbara Mays Jones, May 25, 1972 (div. June 1989); 1 child, Candice; m. Sandi Ann Gold, June 1989; 1 child, Tara. BS, U. Ill., 1949. Owner, v.p. Monsieur Henri Wines Ltd., NYC, 1949-72; owner, pres. Hudson Valley Wine Village, Highland, NY, 1972—, Renet Champagne Cellars, Highland, NY, 1988. With USAF, 1944-46. Republican. Jewish. Avocations: tennis, boating. Home: 472 Mariner Dr Jupiter FL 33477

FEINBERG, JEFFREY ENOCH, religious studies educator, writer; b. Chgo., Mar. 10, 1951; s. Sidney Theodore and Sher Lee F.; m. Patricia Elaine Feinberg, June 15, 1979; children: Avraham David, Zechariah Daniel, Shoshannah Tirzah. BA, Univ. Calif., Berkeley, 1972; MBA, MA, U. Chgo., 1976; MDiv, Trinity Internat. Univ., 1985, PhD, 1988. Instr. Trinity Coll., Deerfield, Ill., 1978-79,82-85; chair of econ./mgmt. Trinity Coll. Sch. of Econ./Mgmt., Deerfield, 1985; educator Adat Hatikvah Congregation, Chgo., 1988-91, interim leader, 1991; rabbi Etz Chaim Congregation, Buffalo Grove, Ill., 1994—; pres. Peniel Cmty. Ctr., Lake Forest, Ill., 1991—, Found. for Leadership and Messianic Edn., Lake Forest, 1988—. Steering com. Union Messianic Jewish Congregations, Albuquerque, 1994—, mem. exec. com.; founder Dayeinu, Lake Forest, 2006—. Recipient Internat. Writer of the Year, Internat. Biog. Ctr., Cambridge, England, 2003. Office: Flame Foundation 234 Surrey Ln Lake Forest IL 60045-3474 E-mail: enoch@flamefoundation.org.

FEINBERG, KENNETH ROY, lawyer, educator; b. Brockton, Mass., Oct. 23, 1945; s. Martin B. and Dorothy (Rubenstein) F.; m. Diane Shaff, June 29, 1975; children: Michael, Leslie, Andrew. BA cum laude, U. Mass., 1967; JD, NYU, 1970. Bar: NY 1971, DC 1977, Mass. 1980. Law clerk to Chief Judge Stanley H. Fuld NY State Ct. of Appeals, 1970—72; asst. U.S. atty. So. Dist. NY, 1972-75; gen. csl. subcom. on adminstrv. practice and procedure Com. on Judiciary, U.S. Senate, 1975-77; spl. counsel Com. on Judiciary, US Senate, 1979-80; adminstrv. asst. Senator Edward M. Kennedy, 1977-79; mng. ptnr. Kaye, Scholer, Fierman, Hays & Handler, Washington, 1980-92; ptnr., founder The Feinberg Group, Washington, 1993—. Adj. prof. law Georgetown U. Law Ctr., 1979-. Author: What Is Life Worth?: The Unprecedented Effort to Compensate the Victims of 9/11, 2005. Trustee Dalkon Shield Claimants Trust; active Presdl. Adv. Commn. Human Radiation Experiments, Presdl. Commn. Catastrophic Nuclear Accidents, 1989-90, Carnegie Commn. Task Force Sci. and Tech. in Judicial and Regulatory Decision Making, 1989-93, Nat. Judicial Panel, Ctr. Pub. Resources, Marine Spill Response Corp., Spl. Master, Fed. Sept. 11th Victim Compensation Fund, 2001-2005. Named one of 27 Future Leaders of Am. Major Firms, The Am. Lawyer, 1986, one of 100 Most Influential Lawyers in Am., Nat. Law Jour. Mem. Am. Arbitration Assn., Bar Assn. City N.Y., Bar Assn. D.C., Mass. Bar Assn. Office: The Feinberg Group Ste 390 Willard Office Bldg 1455 Pennsylvania Ave NW Washington DC 20004-1008 Office Phone: 202-371-1110. Office Fax: 202-962-9290.*

FEINBERG, LAWRENCE EDWARD, language educator, researcher; b. NY, Nov. 13, 1941; s. Samuel and Nettie (Weissman) Feinberg; m. Nana Nikolaishvili, Nov. 24, 1994. BA cum laude, Middlebury Coll., 1962; MA, Harvard U., 1964, PhD, 1969. Asst. prof. U. Colo., Boulder, 1967—70; from asst. prof. to assoc. prof. U. N.C., Chapel Hill, 1970—. Contbr. articles to profl. jour. Mem.: Linguistic Soc. Am., Am. Assn. Tchrs. Slavic and East European Langs., Am. Assn. for Advancement of Slavic Studies. Home: 1506 Halifax Rd Chapel Hill NC 27514 Office: Univ NC Dey Hall 418 CB 3165 Chapel Hill NC 27599-3165 Business E-Mail: lfeinberg@email.unc.edu.

FEINBERG, NORMAN MAURICE, real estate company executive; b. Bklyn., Nov. 28, 1934; s. Harry and Beatrice (Soroca) F.; m. Arline S. Itzkoff, Nov. 26, 1960; children: Mitchell, David. BS, NYU, 1956. Exec. Columbia Pictures Corp., NYC, 1956-62; pres. Gateside Corp., Rye, NY, 1965—. Owner, gen. ptnr. 27 cos., Rye. Arbitrator Am. Arbitration Assn., NYC; trustee, chmn. bd. Bklyn. Mus.; bd. dirs. Assn. for Mentally Ill Children, Scarborough, NY; former chmn. bd. St. Mary's Health Sys., trustee; mem. adv. bd. Steven L. Newman Real Estate Inst. of Baruch Coll., CUNY. Mem. World Pres. Orgn., Young Pres. Orgn. (chmn.), Chief Exec. Officers Assn. Avocations: art collecting, skiing, tennis, travel, languages. Home: 15 E 69th St New York NY 10021-4905 Office: Gateside Corp 555 Theodore Fremd Ave Rye NY 10580-1451 Office Phone: 914-967-7500.

FEINBERG, PAUL H., retired lawyer; b. Yonkers, NY, Nov. 24, 1938; AB, U. Pa., 1960; LLB cum laude, Harvard U., 1963; LLM, NYU, 1970. Bar: N.Y. 1965, Ohio 1979. Asst. gen. counsel The Ford Found., 1971-77; ptnr. Baker & Hostetler LLP, Cleve., ret. Speaker in field. Contbr. articles to profl. jours. Mem. ABA (mem. sect. taxation, mem. tax exempt orgns. com., co-chair subcom. non C3 organs. 1993-94, co-chair subcom. pvt. founds. 1995—), Ohio State Bar Assn., Cleve. Bar Assn. (treas. 1996-99). Home: 3200 Nat City Ctr 1900 E 9th St Cleveland OH 44114-3475 Office Phone: 216-861-7498.

FEINBERG, RICHARD, anthropologist, educator; b. Norfolk, Va., Nov. 4, 1947; s. Isadore and Rose Selma (Hartmann) F.; m. Nancy Ellen Grim, Apr. 15, 1978; children: Joseph Grim Feinberg, Kate Grim-Feinberg. AB, U. Calif., Berkeley, 1969; MA, U. Chgo., 1971, PhD, 1974. Asst. prof. anthropology Kent (Ohio) State U., 1974-80, assoc. prof., 1980-86, prof., 1986—. Mem. editorial bd. Kent State U. Press, 1990-93; chair Kent State U. Faculty Senate, 1997-98; pres. Kent Rsch. Group, 1997-98. Author: Anuta: Social Structure of a Polynesian Island, 1981, Polynesian Seafaring and Navigation, 1988; editor: Politics of Culture in the Pacific Islands, 1995, Seafaring in the Contemporary Pacific Islands, 1995, Leadership and Change in the Western Pacific, 1996, Oral Traditions of Anuta, 1998, The Cultural Analysis of Kinship: The Legacy of David M. Schneider, 2001, (with others) Oceania: An Introduction to the Cultures and Identities of Pacific Islanders, 2002, Anuta: Polynesian Lifeways for the Twenty-first Century, 2004. Kent State Rsch. Coun. grantee, 1983, 88, 00; Wenner-Gren Found. grantee, 1991. Fellow: Assn. for Social Anthropology in Oceania (newsletter editor 1986—90, program coord. 2000—03, exec. bd. mem. 2003—06, chair 2005—06), Am. Anthrop. Assn.; mem.: Ctrl. States Anthrop. Soc. (bull. editor 1994—98, 2d v.p. 2002—03, 1st v.p. 2003—04, pres. 2004—05), Am. Ethnological Soc., Polynesian Soc. Avocations: camping, white water kayaking, scuba diving, folk music, bicycling. Office: Kent State U Dept Anthropology Kent OH 44242-0001 Office Phone: 330-672-2722. Business E-Mail: rfeinber@kent.edu.

FEINBERG, RICHARD ALAN, psychologist; b. Oakland, Calif., Aug. 12, 1947; s. Jack and Raechel Sacks (Hoff) F. BA, Calif. State U., Hayward, 1969; MA in Clin. Psychology, Mich. State U., 1972, PhD, 1979. Cert. Nat. Register Health Svc. Providers in Psychology. Instr. Merritt Coll., Oakland, 1975-76; clin. psychology Highland Gen. Hosp., Oakland, 1976-79; assoc. Lafayette Ctr. Counseling and Edn., 1978-79; clin. psychology Tri-City Mental Health Ctr., Fremont, Calif., 1979-81, dir., 1981-86; pvt. practice, Fremont, 1976—. Participant profl. conf. USPHS fellow, 1969-71. Mem. APA, Calif. Psychol. Assn. Home: 1684 Decoto Rd #256 Union City CA 94587

FEINBERG, ROBERT S., plastics company executive, marketing professional; b. Newark, May 14, 1934; s. Clarence Jacob and Sabina (Zorn) Feinberg. BA in English, BS in Chemistry, Trinity Coll., Hartford, Conn., 1955; MBA in Mktg., Fairleigh Dickinson U., 1966; diploma in advt., Assn. Indsl. Advt., 1967, NY Inst. Advt., 1967. Pres. Trebor Assocs. and Trebor Plastics Co., Teaneck, NJ, 1961—; mktg. cons. computer software Zettler Softwear Co., Burroughs Corp.; sr. coun. Yankelovich, Skelly and White, Inc.; cons. Greenwich Assocs.; co-chmn., ptnr. Edgeroy Co., Inc., Ridgefield and Palisades Park, NJ, 1973—, LeMont Sales Co., Teaneck, NJ, 1973—. Cons. plastics formulations W. R. Grace, Endicott Johnson, Brown Shoe Co., U.S. Shoe Co., Ciba, Uniroyal. Author: Olympia Shoe Co. (Harvard Case Book Series). Mem.: U.S. Profl. Tennis Assn., Sell Overseas Am., Sporting Goods Mfrs. Assn., Soc. Plastics Engrs. (sr.), Bergen County Tennis League (v.p.), Ahdeek Tennis Club. Achievements include patents in polymer and mechanical engineering fields; co-inventor Edgeroy Ball Press (Internat. Tennis Hall of Fame). Home: PO Box 273 Teaneck NJ 07666-0273

FEINBERG, SANDRA LEE, library director; b. Saginaw, Mich., July 31, 1946; d. Langeneker Frank and Elisabeth Ann (Ackerman) Langeneker; m. Richard Philip Feinberg, June 12, 1969; children: Jacob, Theodore. BA, Western Mich. U., 1968; AMLS, U. Mich., 1971. Lic. pub. libr., NY tchr. Spl. edn. Romulus Cmty. Schs., Mich., 1968—70; asst. dir. Middle Country Pub. Libr., Centereach, NY, 1971—91, dir., 1991—; founding bd. mem. Middle Country Libr. Found., Centereach, NY, 1997—. Adj. prof. LI U. Post Libr. Sch., 1986, 87, SUNY Stony Brook, 1990. Author: Menu for Mealtimes, Family Resource Book, Welcome to Parenthood: A Listing of Suffolk County Resources for New Parents; co-author: Running a Parent/Child Workshop: A How-To-Do-It Manual for Librarians, 1995, Serving Families & Children Through Partnerships: A How-To-Do-It Manual for Librarians, 1996, Learning Environments for Young Children: Rethinking Library Spaces & Services, 1998, Including Families of Children with Special Needs: A How-To-Do-It Manual for Librarians, 1999, The Family-Centered Library Handbook, 2006. Bd. dirs. Suffolk Coalition for Parents & Children, Suffolk County, NY, 1981—; v.p., bd. dirs. Child Care Coun. of Suffolk Inc., Huntington, 1986—; com. mem., interviewer Child Watch Project of Children's Def. Fund, SUNY Stony Brook, 1982; com. on pre-sch. activities handbook Youth Svcs., NY Libr. Assn., NYC, 1985; coord. Early Childhood Resource Ctr., NY Pub. Libr., NYC, 1985; mem. citizens' task force on Child Abuse & Neglect State of NY, 1987—; mem. Suffolk County Task Force on Domestic Violence, 1990. Named Woman of Yr., Times of Middle Country, 2005, LI Woman of Yr., Suffolk Cmty. Coun., 2006; recipient Charlie Robinson award, Pub. Libr. Assn./Baker & Taylor, 2007. Mem.: ALA, Librs. Alliance for Parents & Children, Children's Libr. Assn. of Suffolk County (exec. bd. 1971—80, pres. 1976—78), Libr. Dirs. Assn. Avocations: walking, golf. Office: Middle Country Pub Libr 101 Eastwood Blvd Centereach NY 11720-2733 Office Phone: 631-585-9393 ext. 200. E-mail: feinbergsandra@mcpl.lib.ny.us.

FEINBERG, SHELDON NORMAN, pediatrician, educator; b. NYC, Mar. 16, 1930; m. MaryEllen Wisker, Jan. 2, 1988; children: Lynn Ann, Bette Joan, Barbara Ellen, Paul Howard, John Joseph. MD, N.Y. Med. Coll., 1955. Diplomate Am. Bd. Pediat. Intern Bronx Mcpl. Hosp. Ctr., NYC, 1955-56; resident Met. Hosp., NYC, 1956-57; fellow pediatrics N.Y. Med. Coll., 1959-60; pediat. staff Passack Valley Hosp., Westwood, NJ, 1960-82; emergency physician various hosps., 1982-85; pediat. staff Hackensack (N.J.) U. Med. Ctr., 1985—; clin. asst. prof. pediat. U. Med. & Dentistry N.J., Newark, 1985—. Inventor infant scale guard, simple stool stain. Maj. USAF med. corps., 1957-59. Honor award Bergen County Med. Soc., 1965. Fellow Am. Acad. Pediat.; mem. AMA, N.J. Pediat. Soc. (pres. 1989-91, Honor award 1991). Home: 125 N Country Rd Mount Sinai NY 11766-1503

FEINBERG, WENDIE, television producer; BS in Journalism, U. Fla.; MS in Journalism, Boston U. Sr. prodr. Nightly Bus. Report, Miami, Fla. Recipient of three local Emmy Awards for Best Newscast, Best Investigative Reporting, and Best Pub. Affairs Programming, Best News Series/Documentary, Radio & TV News Directors Assn., 1990. Office: NBR Enterprises 14901 NE 20th Ave Miami FL 33181-1121

FEINBERG, WILFRED, federal judge; b. NYC, June 22, 1920; s. Jac and Eva (Wolin) Feinberg; m. Shirley Marcus, June 23, 1946; children: Susan Stelk, Jack, Jessica Twedt. BA, Columbia U., 1940, LLB, 1946, LLD (hon.), 1985, Syracuse U., 1985; LLD (hon.), Bklyn. Law Sch., 1998. Bar: N.Y. 1947. Law clk. Hon. James P. McGranery US Dist. Ct. (ea. dist.) Pa., 1947—49; assoc. Kaye, Scholer, Fierman & Hays, NYC, 1949—53; ptnr. McGoldrick, Dannett, Horowitz & Golub, NYC, 1953—61; dep. supt. NY State Banking Dept., NYC, 1958; judge US Dist. Ct. (so. dist.), NYC, 1961—66, US Ct. Appeals (2nd cir.), NYC, 1966—, chief judge, 1980—88, sr. judge, 1991—. Mem. US Jud. Conf. US, 1980—88, chmn. exec. com., 1987—88, mem. Devitt award com., 1989, 90, mem. long-range planning com., 1991—96; Madison lectr. NYU Law Sch., 1983; Sonnett lectr. Fordham U. Law Sch., 1984; Inaugural Howard Kaplan Meml. lectr. Hofstra U. Law Sch., 1986; The Future of Justice lectr. Inst. of Comparative Law, Chuo U., Japan, 1991. Editor-in-chief: Columbia Law Rev., 1946; contbr. to profl. jours. and mags. With US Army, 1942—45. Recipient Learned Hand medal for excellence in fed. jurisprudence, 1982, Gold medal, award for disting. svc. in the law, NY State Bar Assn., 1990, medal for excellence, Columbia Law Alumni Assn., 1990, Pursuit of Justice award, Internat. Assn. Jewish Lawyers and Jurists, 1993, Disting. Pub. Svc. award, NY County Lawyers Assn., 1994, Edward Weinfeld award, 1995, Ann. Wilfred Feinberg prize named in his honor for best student work at Columbia Law Sch. related to fed. cts., 1998, Edward J. Devitt Disting. Svc. to Justice award, 2003. Mem.: ABA, Am. Law Inst., Am. Judicature Soc., N.Y. County Lawyers Assn., Assn. of Bar of City of N.Y., Phi Beta Kappa. Office: US Ct Appeals 2nd Cir Room 2004 US Court House Foley Sq New York NY 10007-1501*

FEINER, AVA SOPHIA, public affairs consultant, management consultant, economist; b. Bklyn., Feb. 13, 1950; d. Ignace and Lola (Pasternak) F.; m. Clifford Douglas Stromberg, June 25, 1972; children: Kimberly Greta, Eric George. BA summa cum laude, Yale U., New Haven, Conn., 1971; MA, Harvard U., Cambridge, Mass., 1974, PhD in Govt., 1978. Legis. asst. to U.S. Senator Bill Bradley, Washington, 1979-82; dir. internat. trade policy U.S. C. of C., Washington, 1982-83, mgr. internat. policy dept., 1983-85; corp. program dir. IBM, Washington, 1985-87, corp. dir. pub. affairs, trade and investment, 1987; pres. Feiner Pub. Affairs Cons., Washington, 1988—; co-founder, dir. Washington Alive! Inc., 1989-90; pres. Washington Networks, 1990—; mem. campaign and transition team Ehrlich for Gov., 2002; mem. Md. State Ethics Commn., 2003—06. Tchg. fellow Harvard U., Cambridge, Mass., 1972-74; lectr. nat. and internat. politics and econs., 1978—; bd. dirs. World Trade Forum, Washington, 1987-89. Co-author: American Excellence in A World Economy, 1987; contbr. articles on econs., trade, fgn. policy to various publs. Del. to Atlantic Coun. Young Leadership Program, Wis. and Can., 1978, 80, Aspen Inst. Exec. Seminar, 1982, Germany-U.S. Young Leadership Conf., San Francisco, 1982, Harbor Sch. Bd., 1992-93; co-chair Holton-Arms Sch. Silent Auction, 1995-96; mem. adv. com. Cmty. Homeowners, 1999—04, chmn., 2001—04; 1st v.p. Potomac Women's Rep. Club., 2002-03. Fgn. Policy fellow Brookings Instn., 1975-76, guest scholar, 1976-77; Carnegie Endowment for Internat. Peace fellow, 1975-76; finalist Photographer's Forum Mag. Mem.: Trade Policy Forum, Coun. Fgn. Rels. (task force on women 1988—91, term membership com. 1988—91, internat. affairs fellows com. 1991—95, Washington program adv. com. 1995—98), Phi Beta Kappa. Avocations: photography, Karate, swimming, bicycling, tennis.

FEINGOLD, DANIEL LEON, anesthesiologist, consultant; b. Boston, May 19, 1958; s. Macey Gerson and Hélène Sultana (Benlolo) F. BS with distinction, U. Ill., Chgo., 1980; MD, U. Health Scis., Chgo. Med. Sch., 1984. Intern Weiss Meml. Hosp., Chgo., 1984-85; resident in anesthesiology U. Ill. Hosps. and Clinics, Chgo., 1986-89; anesthesiologist Hosp. Anesthesia Group, Chgo., 1989—. Contbr. articles to profl. publs. Mem. AMA, AAAS, Am. Soc. Anesthesiologists, Ill. State Med. Soc. Home: PO Box 577429 Chicago IL 60657-7429 Office: PO Box 25678 Chicago IL 60625-0678

FEINGOLD, DAVID SIDNEY, microbiology and biochemistry educator, researcher; b. Chelsea, Mass., Nov. 15, 1922; s. Louis Edward and Miriam F.; m. Batia Babette Haber, Nov. 15, 1949; children: Oded, Anat, Michele. BS, MIT, 1944; PhD, Hebrew U., Jerusalem, Israel, 1956. Chemist Lucidol Corp., Buffalo, 1944; jr. research biochemist U. Calif. at Berkeley, 1957-60; asst. prof. biology U. Pitts., 1960-62, asso. prof., 1962-65, prof., 1965—; prof. microbiology Sch. Medicine, 1966-93, prof. emeritus molecular genetics and biochemistry, 1993—. Contbr. articles to profl. jours. With USNR, 1944—46. Recipient State of Israel prize in natural sci., 1957, Career Devel. award NIH, 1965-75 Fellow Infectious Disease Soc. Am.; mem. Internat. Endotoxin Soc., Am. Soc. for Biochemistry and Molecular Biology. Home: 6420 Bartlett St Pittsburgh PA 15217-1832 Personal E-mail: udpglcdh@juno.com.

FEINGOLD, RUSSELL DANA, senator, lawyer; b. Janesville, Wis., Jan. 2, 1953; m. Mary Erpenbach; 2 children. BA in Polit. Sci., with honors, U. Wis., Madison, 1975; postgrad., Magdalen Coll., Oxford U., Eng., 1975—77; JD with honors, Harvard U., 1979. Bar: Wis. 1979. Assoc. Foley & Lardner, Madison, 1979—82, LaFollette, Sinykin, Anderson & Munson, Madison, 1983—85, Goldman & Feingold, 1985—88; mem. Wis. State Senate, 1983—92; US Senator from Wis., 1993—. Mem. com. budget US Senate, com. fgn. relations, com. judiciary, com. intelligence, commn. security and cooperation in Europe. Recipient Senator of Yr. award, Nat. Assn. Police Orgn., 1997, Profile in Courage award, John F. Kennedy Libr. Found., 1999, Mr. Smith Goes to Washington award, Taxpayers for Common Sense, 2000, Paul H. Douglas Ethics in Govt. award, Inst. Govt. and Public Affairs, U. Ill., 2000; scholar, Wis. Honors scholar, 1971, Rhodes scholar, 1975. Mem.: Dane County Bar Assn., Wis. Bar Assn., ABA, Phi Beta Kappa. Democrat. Jewish. Office: US Senate 506 Hart Senate Office Bldg Washington DC 20510-0001 also: District Office Rm 100 1600 Aspen Commons Middleton WI 53562-4626 Office Phone: 202-224-5323, 608-828-1200. Office Fax: 202-224-2725.

FEINHANDLER, EDWARD SANFORD, writer, photographer, art dealer; b. Elko, Nev., Jan. 13, 1948; s. Samuel and Sylvia (Manus) F. BA, U. Nev., 1972; BS Elem. Edn., Sierra Nevada Coll., 1997. Supr. underprivileged Washoe County Extension Program, Reno, 1970—71; sports editor, writer Sagebrush Campus newspaper, Reno, 1971—72; internal salesman and mgr. Trigon Corp., Sparks, Nev., 1975—88; owner and operator Art Internat. Gallery Extraordinaire, Reno, 1981—2005; tennis dir. City of Sparks, 1991—93, 2004—05, Cmty. Edn. Program, Sparks, 1994, Sparks YMCA, 1995—96; phys. edn. dir., coach 8th grade B boys basketball Clayton Mid. Sch., 2000—01, advisor boys and girls wrestling, 2001; coach freshmen boys basketball Sparks H.S., 2003—05. With nat. news Top Ten radio interviews, U.S., Can. and Eng.; freelance writer and photographer newspapers U.S. and Can.; pres. No. Nev. H.S. Tennis Assn., 1996; coach 2005 AAA Freshmen Boys Basketball League Champions, Sparks, Nev. Contbr. articles to newspapers and mags.; extra in various movies; TV interviews AM Chgo., AM L.A., 1979, Afternoon Exchange, Cleve., 1979, To Tell the Truth, 1975, Reno Tonight, 1989, Fox Across America, 1989, Wheel of Fortune, 1995; radio interviews include Nat. Enquirer TV show, 1999-2000, London and New Zealand radio, 2000, Bogota, Colombia, 2001, Sydney, Australia, Durban, South Africa, Dublin, Ireland, North Adelaine, Australia, WGN, Chgo., 2005; contbr. articles to profl. jours., local newspapers. Player, coach Summer Volleyball League, Reno, 1982-85; tennis coach Cmty. Svc. Ctr., Reno, 1986-88, 94; founder Joell Vowell softball event Make-A-Wish Found., Reno, 1985-04; active journalism dept. U. Nev., 1985-01, UNR Children's Svcs., Reno, 1986-88; basketball coach Little Flower Cath. Sch., 1987-89; head coach girls varsity tennis team Bishop Manogue H.S., 1989-91; coach boys varsity tennis Sparks HS, 1993-97, 00-04, girls varsity tennis, 2001-04, spl. olympics, 1989, Bishop Monogue girls jr. varsity basketball, 1989-90; head coach freshman boys Sparks HS, 2003-05; active Ptnrs. in Edn., 1988-00, Jr. Achievement, 1989-94, Animal Welfare Inst., Statue of Liberty Found., 1984-01, No. Nev. Cancer Coun., United Blood Svcs., Arthritis Found., Cancer Soc., Sta. KNPB, Ret. Sr. Citizens, Reno Fire Dept. Christmas Basket Delivery, 1991—, Sierra Arts Found.; vol. free tennis lessons, 1993-; fundraiser H.L.A. Testing United Blood Svcs., 1991-00; founder, pres. No. Nev. Youth Opportunistic Tennis program, 1997—, Huey Feinhandler Found., 2001-; guest spkr. Rotary Internat., Nev., 1999, Reno Sertoma Club, 2003—, Lions Club, 2003—; blood donor United Blood Svc., 1993— (1st donor Washoe County to reach 500+ platelet donations); vol. other cmty. activities; leader donations Sparks HS Athletic Auction, 2001-07. Sgt. US Army, 1968-69, Vietnam. Winner Ugly Man contest Make-A-Wish Found., 1999, 01, 03-07, No. Nev. Bone Marrow Program, 1991-98, 00, Ugly Bartender contest Multiple Sclerosis and Make-A-Wish Found., 1989-07, Ugly Man contest U. Nev., Reno, 1967, 70-72, Ugly Necktie contest Krispy Kreme, 2004; Sparks Tennis Club singles, doubles, and mixed doubles champion B/C divsn., 1994, Singles B champion, Mixed B Doubles champion, 1995, 2001, Ladder B Singles Men's champion, 1996, 97, 3d Ann. B Doubles champion, 1996; recipient numerous tennis, billiards, volleyball and bowling awards including 1st pl. C divsn. NNCC Tennis Tournament, 1991, RTC C Mixed Doubles champion, 1992, Open Doubles champion Sparks Recreation Dept., 1993, finalist Over 50 Singles Open, Sparks Recreation Dept., 2005; recipient Cmty. Svc. award United Blood Svcs., 1995, Svc. Above Self award Rotary Internat., 1995, Joeil Vowell Charity Softball award Make-A-Wish Found.,

1997-98, Cmty. Safety award Associated Builders and Contractors, 1997, Spl. Thank You award Pine Mid. Sch. Students Concerned with Quick Thinking and Great Effort, 1997, Warren Brown award US Tennis Assn., 2003, Angel award, nominee Reno Hero award, 2006, Gov.'s Points of Light award, Nev., 2005-06. Mem. DAV, Orthodox Jewish Union, Elks (Vol. of Yr. award 2004-05), Am. Legion. Democrat. Avocations: bowling, tennis, basketball, baseball, volleyball. Office: Huey Feinhandler Found PO Box 13405 Reno NV 89507-3405 Office Phone: 775-358-7033. Personal E-mail: mruglyed@yahoo.com, hueyfein@msn.com.

FEININGER, THEODORE LUX, artist; b. Berlin, June 11, 1910; s. Charles Lyonel and Julia (Lilienfeld) F.; m. Patricia Randall, Dec. 17, 1954; children: Lucas, Conrad, Charles. Grad., Bauhaus, Dessau, Germany, 1929. Instr. Sarah Lawrence Coll., 1950-52; lectr. drawing and painting Harvard U., 1953-62; instr. drawing and painting Boston Fine Arts Mus. Sch., 1962-75. Author: Lyonel Feininger: City at the Edge of the World, 1965, Photographs of the 20s and 30s (illustrated catalogue), 1980, (autobiography) Zwei Welten, 2006; exhbns. include Am. Realists and Magic Realists, Mus. Modern Art, N.Y.C., 1943, Revolution and Tradition in Modern Am. Art, Bklyn. Mus., 1951, Whitney Mus. Am. Art Ann., N.Y.C., 1951, Am. Painters, MIT, 1954, Retrospective, Busch-Reisinger Mus., 1962, Wheaton Coll., 1973, Wamsutta Club, New Bedford, Mass., 1974, Prakapas Gallery, N.Y.C., 1980, Sacramento St. Gallery, Cambridge, Mass., 1982, Gallery on the Green, Lexington, Mass., 1986, 88, 90, 92, Achim Moeller Fine Art, N.Y.C., 1954-94, Staatliche Galerie Moritzburg Halle, Saale, Germany, 1998, Städtisches Mus. Karlsruhe, Germany, 2001; represented in permanent collections Mus. Modern Art, N.Y.C., Busch-Reisinger Mus. and Fogg Art Mus., Harvard U., Altonaer Mus., Hamburg, Germany, Schleswig-Holstein Landes Mus., Mus. Folkwang, Essen, Germany, Bauhaus Mus., Weimar, Germany, Getty Mus., Calif., Met. Mus., N.Y., L.A. County Mus., Stedelijk Mus., Amsterdam, Guggenheim Mus., N.Y., Staatliche Galerie Moritzburg, Germany. With US Army, 1942—45. Mem. Westport Art Group. Democrat. Address: 22 Arlington St Cambridge MA 02140-2713 *The practice and teaching of art has shown me that I must seek progress on the basis of understanding and assimilating tradition; that every individual incorporates both revolutionary and conservative tendencies; and that the task of the individual lies in assessing and acting upon his findings, his own proportionate share of these two conflicting trends. I am Society, and Society cannot do without me.*

FEINSILVER, DONALD LEE, psychiatry professor; b. Bklyn., July 24, 1947; s. Albert and Mildred (Weissman) Feinsilver. BA, Alfred U., 1968; MD, Autonomous U., Guadalajara, Mexico, 1974. Diplomate Am. Bd. Psychiatry and Neurology, Am. Bd. Forensic Psychiatry. Intern in medicine L.I. Coll. Hosp., Bklyn., 1975—76; resident in psychiatry SUNY-Bklyn., 1977—78, chief resident, 1979; asst. prof. psychiatry and surgery Med. Coll. Wis., Milw., 1980—85, assoc. prof., 1985—; dir. psychiat. emergency svc. Milw. County Mental Health and Med. Complexes, 1980—88; dir. med.-psychiat. unit Milw. Psychiat. Hosp./West Allis Meml. Hosp., 1988—. Contbr. articles to profl. jours.; editor: Crisis Psychiatry: Pros and Cons, 1982; mem. editl. bd.: Psychiat. Medicine Jour., 1983—. Mem.: AAAS, AMA, Acad. Psychosomatic Medicine, Am. Acad. Psychiatry and the Law, Am. Psychiat. Assn. Office: West Allis Psychiat Assocs 2424 S 90th St Milwaukee WI 53227-2455 Home Phone: 414-961-2670; Office Phone: 414-328-8690. Personal E-mail: DFeinsilver@prodigy.net.

FEINSTEIN, ALLEN LEWIS, lawyer; b. NYC, Apr. 18, 1929; s. Jacob and Kate (Goldberg) F.; m. Charlesa Joan Wolfe, Dec. 14, 1957. AB, CCNY, 1949; LLB, Columbia U., 1952. Bar: N.Y. 1952, U.S. Supreme Ct. 1958, Ariz. 1960, U.S. Dist. Ct. Ariz. 1960, U.S. Ct. Appeals (9th cir.) 1960. Assoc. Proskauer Rose Goetz & Mendelsohn, NYC, 1955-59; law clk. to justice Supreme Ct. Ariz., Phoenix, 1959-61, 1st adminstrv. dir., 1961-64; pvt. practice law Phoenix, 1964-72, 1995—; ptnr. Daughton Feinstein & Wilson, Phoenix, 1972-86; sr. ptnr. Rawlins, Burrus, Lewkowitz & Feinstein, P.C., Phoenix, 1986-95. Mem. Phoenix Housing Code Com., 1968; vice-chmn. adv. com. State Legislative com. on Medicaid; mem. Phoenix Charter Review Com., 1969; mem. exec. com. Phoenix Sister City Commn., 1973-75 Author: First, Second and Third Reports of Courts of Arizona, 1962, 63, 64. Bd. dirs. Meml. Hosp. Phoenix, chmn., 1973-76, Community Coun., 1970-76, Ariz. Jewish Hist. Soc.; chmn. Meml. Hosp. Found., 1980-82; bd. dirs., chmn. coun. trustees, mem. exec. com. Ariz. Hosp. Assn., 1981-87, chmn. 1986-87, Ariz. del. to nat. conf. governing bds.; chmn. PMH Health Resources, Inc., 1983-89, Ariz. Voluntary Hosp. Fedn., 1984-88; chmn. Phoenix chpt. Am. Jewish Com., 1989-91; legal advisor Salt River Pima-Maricopa INdian Cmty. Police Commn., 1997-2002. 2d lt. USAF, 1952-53. Mem. Ariz. Bar Assn., Maricopa County Bar Assn., State Bar Ariz. (chmn. com. civil practice and procedure 1971-74, chmn. long-range com. 1980, peer rev. com., sole practitioner com. sect., alternate dispute resolution sects., mentor-mentee com.), Univ. Club Phoenix (pres. 1971-72), Phi Beta Kappa, Phi Delta Phi. Democrat. Jewish. Address: 2110 Encanto Dr SW Phoenix AZ 85007-1526 Personal E-mail: alfeinstein@cox.net.

FEINSTEIN, BRETT, political scientist, consultant; s. Janet Feinstein. BA, Conn. Coll., New London, 1991. Dir. politics and finance Rep. Party of Va., Richmond, Va., 1996—97; ptnr. Pound, Feinstein & Assocs., Inc., Richmond, 1997—. Mem.: Bull and Bear Club. Republican. Avocations: travel, poker, backgammon, reading, films. Office: Pound Feinstein & Assocs Inc 700 East Main St Ste 1508 Richmond VA 23219 Home Phone: 804-301-4901; Office Phone: 804-644-6901.

FEINSTEIN, DEBORAH, lawyer; b. Champaign, Ill., Dec. 30, 1960; BA with honors, U. Calif., Berkeley, 1983; JD cum laude, Harvard U., 1987. Bar: D.C. 1987. Asst. to dir. Bur. of Competition, FTC, 1989-91; atty. adv. to commr. FTC; ptnr. Arnold & Porter LLP, Washington. Contbr. articles to profl. jours. Named one of The 50 Most Influential Women Lawyers in Am., Nat. Law Jour., 2007; recipient Am. Leading Bus. Lawyers, by Chambers USA, 2003—06, leading lawyer, by Lawdragon mag., 2006, Best Lawyers Am., 2007. Office: Arnold & Porter 555 12th St NW Washington DC 20004-1206 Office Phone: 202-942-5015. Office Fax: 202-942-5999. Business E-Mail: Deborah.Feinstein@aporter.com.*

FEINSTEIN, DIANNE, senator; b. San Francisco, June 22, 1933; d. Leon and Betty (Rosenburg) Goldman; m. Bertram Feinstein, Nov. 11, 1962 (dec.); 1 child, Katherine Anne; m. Richard C. Blum, Jan. 20, 1980. BA History, Stanford U., 1955; LLB (hon.), Golden Gate U., 1977; D Pub. Adminstrn. (hon.), U. Manila, 1981; D Pub. Service (hon.), U. Santa Clara, 1981; JD (hon.), Antioch U., 1983, Mills Coll., 1985; LHD (hon.), U. San Francisco, 1988. Fellow Coro Found., San Francisco, 1955-56; with Calif. Women's Bd. Terms and Parole, 1960-66; mem. Mayor's com. on crime, chmn. adv. com. Adult Detention, 1967-69; mem. Bd. Suprs., San Francisco, 1970-78, pres., 1970-71, 74-75, 78; mayor City of San Francisco, 1978-88; US Senator from Calif., 1992—. Mem. exec. com. U.S. Conf. of Mayors, 1983-88; Dem. nominee for Gov. of Calif., 1990; mem. Nat. Com. on U.S.-China Rels.; mem. judiciary com., appropriations com., rules and adminstrn. Com., energy and natural resources com; mem. Coun. Foreign Rels. Mem. Bay Area Conservation and Devel. Commn., 1973-78; mem. Senate Fgn. Rels. Com. Recipient Woman of Achievement award Bus. and Profl. Women's Clubs San Francisco, 1970, Disting. Woman award San Francisco Examiner, 1970, Coro Found. award, 1979, Scopus award Am. Friends Hebrew U., 1981, French Legion of Honor, 1984, Brotherhood/Sisterhood award NCCJ, 1986, Comdr.'s award U.S. Army, 1986, Disting. Civilian award USN, 1987, Coro Leadership award, 1988, Pres. medal U. Calif., San Francisco, 1988, Lifetime Achievement award, Nat. AIDS Found., 1993, Awareness Achievement award, Bd. of Sponsors Breast Cancer Awareness, 1995, Donald Santarelli award, Nat. Orgn. for Victims Assistance, 1996, Congl. Excellence award, MADD, 1997, Paul E. Tsongas award, Lymphoma Rsch. Assn. of Am., 1997, Abraham Lincoln award, Ill. Coun. Against Handgun Violence, 1998, Congl. award, Nat. Assn. Police Orgn., 1999, Celebration of Courage award, Handgun Control, Inc., 1999, Congl. Champion award, Coalition Cancer Rsch., 1999, Winning Spirit award, Women's Info. Network Against Breast Cancer, 2000, Recognition award, Susan G. Komen Breast Cancer Found., 2000, Woodrow Wilson award, Woodrow Wilson Internat. Ctr. Scholars, 2001, Torch of Liberty award, Anti-Defamation League, 2002, Dr. Nathan Davis award, AMA, 2002, Pub. Svc. award, Am. Soc. Hematology, 2003, Leadership award, Alta Med Health Svcs. Corp., 2004, Pat Brown Legacy award, 2004, Lifetime of Idealism award, City Yr., 2004, Legislator of Yr. award, Calif. Sch. Resource Officer's Assn., 2004, Nat. Disting. Advocacy award, Am. Cancer Soc., 2004, Women of Achievement award, Century City Chamber of Commerce, 2004, Friend of Watershed award, Ventura County Assn. of Water Agencies, 2004, Outstanding Mem. US Senate award, Nat. Narcotic Officers Assn. Coalition, 2005; named Number One Mayor All-Pro City Mgmt. Team City and State Mag., 1987, Person of Yr., Nat. Guard Assn. Calif., 1995, Funding Hero, Breast Cancer Rsch. Found., 2004; named one of Congl. Quarterly's Top 50 Mem. of Congress, 2000, Most Powerful Women, Forbes mag., 2005. Mem. Trilateral Commn., Japan Soc. of No. Calif. (pres. 1988-89), Inter-Am. Dialogue, Nat. Com. on U.S.-China Rels. Democrat. Jewish. Office: US Senate 331 Hart Senate Office Bldg Washington DC 20510-0001 also: District Office Ste 2450 One Post Street San Francisco CA 94104 Office Phone: 202-224-3841, 415-393-0707. Office Fax: 202-228-3954, 415-393-0710.*

FEINSTEIN, FRED IRA, lawyer; b. Chgo., Apr. 6, 1945; s. Bernard and Beatrice (Mines) Feinstein; m. Judy Cutler, Aug. 25, 1968; children: Karen, Donald. BSc, DePaul U., 1967, JD, 1970. Bar: Ill. 1970, U.S. Supreme Ct. 1977. Ptnr. McDermott, Will & Emery LLP, Chgo., 1976—. Lectr. in field. Contbr. articles to profl. jours. Pres. Skokie/Evanston (Ill.) Action Coun., 1981—84; bd. dirs. Temple Judea Mizpah, Skokie, 1982—84, Deborah Goldfine Meml. Cancer Rsch., 1968—, YMCA of Chgo.1985, 1985—. Mem.: Am. Coll. Real Estate Lawyers, Ill. Bar Assn., Blue Key, Union League, Beta Alpha Psi, Beta Gamma Sigma, Lambda Alpha, Pi Gamma Mu. Office: McDermott Will & Emery LLP 227 W Monroe St Ste 4700 Chicago IL 60606-5096 Office Phone: 312-984-7665. E-mail: ffeinstein@mwe.com.

FEINSTEIN, LEONARD, retail executive; Co-founder Bed Bath & Beyond, Union, NJ, 1971, co-CEO, 1971—2003, pres., 1992—99, co-chmn., 1999—. Bd. dir. Bed Bath & Beyond, Union, NJ, 1971—. Office: Bed Bath & Beyond 650 Liberty Ave Union NJ 07083*

FEINSTEIN, MICHAEL JAY, singer, pianist, musicologist, actor; b. Columbus, Ohio, Sept. 7, 1956; s. Edward and Florence Mazie (Cohen) F. Grad. high sch., Columbus, 1974. Personal archivist Ira Gershwin, LA, 1977-83; asst. Harry Warren, LA, 1979-81; recorded with Elektra, Angel. Accompanist Liza Minnelli, Rosemary Clooney, John Bubbles, Rose Marie, Jessie Matthews, Estelle Reiner, Leona Mitchell, 1980-84; singer, pianist Le Mondrian Hotel, West Hollywood, 1984-85, 87, York Hotel, San Francisco, 1985-87, Algonquin Hotel, N.Y.C., 1986, 87, The White House, Washington, 1986, 88, 89, Ritz Hotel, 1986, Mondavi Festival, 1986, Singers Salute to the Songwriter, L.A., 1986, 87, 88, 50th Anniversary George Gershwin Celebration, Hollywood Bowl, L.A., 1987, 100th Birthday Celebration for Irving Berlin, Hollywood Bowl, L.A., 1988 and Carnegie Hall, N.Y., 1988, Royal Command Performance, Palace Theatre, London, 1988, Dominion Theatre, London, 1989; Libr. of Congress Gerswhin Concert, 1989; performed with Houston Pops Orch., 1987, San Francisco Symphony & Pops Orch., 1987, 88, Liza Minnelli in European tour, 1987, Atlanta Symphony, 1988, Aspen Music Festival, Colo., 1988; appeared on Broadway and across country in show Michael Feinstein in Concert: Isn't it Romantic, 1988-89, Piano and Voice, 1990, Cole Porter 100th Birthday Concert Carnegie Hall, 1991; toured with Rosemary Clooney, 1991—; TV appearances include A Musical Toast: The Stars Shine for Pub. TV, 1986, Broadway Sings: The Music of Jule Styne, 1987, George Gershwin Remembered, 1987, Celebrating Gershwin: 'SWonderful, 1987, thirtysomething, 1987, The Two Mrs. Grenvilles, 1987, Nightline, 1988, A Grand Night: The Performing Arts Salute Pub. TV, 1988, Omnibus, 1989, An All-Star Salute to the Pres., 1989, Pat Sajak Show, 1989, Nightwatch, 1989, Royal Command Performance, BBS-TV, 1988, London TV Michael Feinstein in Concert BBC-TV, 1989, PBS-TV, Michael Feinstein in Concert, 1991, Wolf Trap 20th Anniversary Concert, 1991, PBS, Am. Masters-Cole Porter, 1990, others; film, Scenes from the Class Struggle in Beverly Hills; albums include Pure Gershwin, 1985, Live at the Algonquin, 1986, Remember: Michael Feinstein Sings Irving Berlin, 1987, Isn't it Romantic, 1987, Over There: Songs of War and Peace c. 1900-1920, 1989, The M-G-M Album, 1989, Michael Feinstein Sings the Burton Lane Songbook Vol. One, 1990, Michael Feinstein Sings the Jule Styne Songbook, 1991, Pure Imagination, 1991, Michael & George, 1998, Big City Rhythms, 1999, Hopeless Romantics, 2005; editor: Ira Gershwin Songbook; contbr. articles to Washington Post, N.Y. Times. Recipient Golden Laurel award San Francisco Coun. on Entertainment, 1985, 87, 88, N.Y.C. Seal of Recognition, 1987, Drama Desk award, 1988, Outer Critics Circle award, 1988; scholarships in his honor were established at Calif. State, Los Angeles and Queens Coll., N.Y.C. Mem. ASCAP, AFTRA, SAG, Am. Fedn. Musicians, Actor's Equity, Players Club. Office: c/o Buddy Morra Morra Brezner & Steinberg Los Angeles CA 90028

FEINSTEIN, MILES ROGER, lawyer; b. Camden, NJ, June 25, 1941; s. Louis Emory and Sylvia K. (Jacobs) F.; m. Margaret Bott, Oct. 3, 2000; children: Bari, Matthew, Elizabeth. BA, Rutgers U., 1963; JD, Duke U., 1966. Bar: NJ 1966, US Dist. Ct. NJ 1966, US Ct. Appeals (3d cir.) 1967, US Ct. Appeals (2d cir.) 1971. Pvt. practice, Clifton, NJ, 1967—. Mem. Passaic Criminal Justice commn.; mem. com. on drugs and cts. NJ Supreme Ct.; mem. speedy trial com. NJ Supreme Ct.; expert commentator Nat. Courtroom TV; lectr. NJ Inst. of Continuing Legal Edn., Trial Lawyers Assn., and other bar groups and civic assns.; appeared on numerous TV and radio shows. Author: Historical Development of Pineys of Southern New Jersey. Trustee Passaic County Heart Fund, 1970-93, Passaic County Cancer Soc.; chmn. Passaic County March of Dimes, 1989. Named Man of Yr., Passaic County Heart Fund, 1976, Passaic County Cancer Soc., 1978, Passaic County coun. Boy Scouts Am., 1978, Passaic County Bad Guys Charitable Orgn., 1974; named one of NJ's Super Lawyers NJ Monthly Mag., NJ Super-Lawyers Mag., Living Legend in field of Law Book of Living Legends, Best Lawyers in Am.; recipient award Passaic Civic Orgn., Humanitarian award Unico, 1976, Nationwide Bail Bonds award Policeman's Benevolent Assn., Disting. Svc. award, 1980, 84, 85, History prize Soc. Colonial Wars, PBA Silver Shield, Martindale-Hubbel A/V rating; subject of numerous legal and newspaper articles. Mem. ABA, Assn. Trial Lawyers Am., Nat. Assn. Criminal Def. Lawyers, Fed. Bar Assn., NJ Bar Assn. (criminal law com. 2000-2002), NJ Assn. Criminal Def. Lawyers (former trustee, treas., v.p., pres. 1990-91; lectr.), NJ Assn. of Trial Lawyers (bd. govs. 1992-93), Passaic County Bar Assn. (chmn. criminal law com. 1990-93), Phi Beta Kappa, Phi Delta Phi, Phi Alpha Theta (Henry Rutgers scholar). Avocations: sports, theater, stamp collecting/philately. Office: 1135 Clifton Ave Clifton NJ 07013-3642 Office Phone: 973-779-1124. Personal E-mail: mrfeinsteinesq@aol.com.

FEINSTEIN, ROBERT P., dermatologist; b. NYC, July 31, 1941; s. Jerome and May (Wolpin) F.; m. Diane Marla Gutstein, Oct. 25, 1969; children: Steven, Michelle, Suzanne, Gary, Lori. AB in Biology, NYU, 1963, MD, 1967. Diplomate Am. Bd. Dermatology. Intern Kings County Hosp. Ctr., Bklyn., 1967-68; resident in dermatology Columbia U., NYC, 1968-71, assoc. clin. prof. dept. dermatology; chief of dermatology, innoculations and phys. exams. Navy Regional Med. Clinic, Washington, 1971-73; pvt. practice in dermatology Mineola, NY, 1973-99, Smithtown, NY, 1983-2000. Author: (book) Dermatology, 1975, (monograph) Rosacea, 1998; contbr. articles to profl. jours. Lt comdr. USNR, 1971-73. Fellow Am. Acad. Dermatology (mem. managed care com., 1995-99, mem. com. physician practice, professionalism study group program for dermatology in 21st cent., vice chmn. adv. bd. 2001-04), Am. Soc. for Dermatologic Surgery, Noah Worcester Dermatology Soc.; mem. AMA, NY State Soc. of Dermatology (pres. 1997-99), L.I. Dermatology Soc. (pres. 1996-98), Suffolk County Dermatology Soc. (pres. 1982-84), Atlantic Dermatology Soc. (bd. dirs. 1995), NY State Med. Soc. (health care delivery sys.). Avocation: golf. Office Fax: 631-824-9393.

FEINSTEIN, ROCHELLE, artist, educator; BFA, Pratt Inst., 1975; MFA, U. Minn., 1978. Represented by Max Protetch Gallery, NYC; tchr. Bonnington Coll., 1979—94; assoc. prof. painting, printmaking Yale U., 1994—98, prof. painting and printmaking, 1998—. Participant pub. arts project CETA/NY Artists Program, 1978—79. Represented in permanent collections Mus. Modern Art, one-woman shows include, Emily Sorkin Gallery, 1987, 1989, David Beitzel Gallery, 1993, Max Protetch Gallery, NY, 1994, Paintings, Halsey Gallery, Charleston, NC, 1995, Copycats, Bill Maynes Gallery, NY, 1996, The Wonderfuls, Jersey City Mus., NJ, 1996, Men, Women, and Children, Max Protetch Gallery, 1996, Pictures, Ten in One Gallery, NY, 2002, exhibited in group shows, Exit Art, NY, 1986, To Make the Visible Seen, Studio Sch., NY, 1987, The Debate on Abstraction: The Persistence of Painting, Hunter Coll., NY, 1989, The Painting Project, 1991, Abstraction, Schmidt Contemporary, St. Louis, 1992, Works on Paper/Faculty, Yale U. Sch. Art, 1995, Just What do You Think You're Doing, Dave?, Williamsburg Art & Historical Soc., NY, 1997, The Drawing File, Pierogi 2000, The Gasworks, London, 1997, Conversation, Art Resources Transfer, NY, 1999, Liste Art Fair, Basel, Switzerland, 2002, A More Perfect Union, Max Fish, NY, 2004, Nat. Acad. Mus., NY, 2006. Grantee Louis Comfort Tiffany Found., 1997, Found. Contemporary Performance ARts, 1999, Teseque Found., 2000, Pollock-Krasner Found., 2000, Civitella Raineri Residency, 2001, Marie Walsh Sharpe Found., 2002, Giverny Artists Residency, 2003; Nat. Endowment for the Arts grantee, 1990, Joan Mitchell Found. grantee, 1994, John Simon Guggenheim Meml. Found. fellow, 1996. Office: Yale U Sch Art PO Box 208339 New Haven CT 06520-8339

FEINTUCH, HENRY PHILIP, public relations executive; b. Bklyn. BA, Bklyn. Coll. TV and Radio, 1976. Anchorperson, reporter Stas. WMTR and WDHA-FM, N.J.; news editor Sta. WCBS-TV, NYC; pub. rels. sr. acct. exec. Paul Kaufman Assocs., NYC, Booke and Co., NYC; dir. corp. comm. Ring Group N.Am., NYC, 1985-86; mng. ptnr. KCSA Pub. Rels., NYC, 1987—. Office: KCSA Pub Rels 800 2nd Ave New York NY 10017-4709 E-mail: hfeintuch@kcsa.com.

FEIR, DOROTHY JEAN, entomologist, educator, physiologist; b. St. Louis, Jan. 29, 1929; d. Alex R. and Lillian (Smith) F. BS, U. Mich., 1950; MS, U. Wyo., 1956; PhD, U. Wis., 1960. Instr. biology U. Buffalo, 1960-61; mem. faculty St. Louis U., 1961—, prof. biology, 1967-99, prof. biology emeritus, 1999—. Mem. tropical medicine and parasitology study sect. NIH, 1980-84 Editor Environ. Entomology, 1977-84; mem. editl. bd. Jour. Med. Entomology, 1995-99, chair editl. bd., 1999. Named Woman of Yr., St. Louis U., 1998. Fellow Entomol. Soc. Am. (hon., pres.-elect 1987-88, pres. 1988-89, Riley Achievement award north ctrl. br. 1993), Mo. Acad. Sci. (v.p. 1987-88, pres.-elect 1988-89, pres. 1989-90, Most Disting. Scientist award 1995); mem. AAAS, Am. Physiol. Soc., N.Y. Acad. Sci., Phi Beta Kappa, Sigma Xi. E-mail: feirdj@slu.edu.

FEIRSON, STEVEN B., lawyer; b. Bklyn., June 6, 1950; s. Aaron M. and Gertrude Feirson. BA, U. Pa., 1972; JD, U. Chgo., 1975. Bar: Pa. 1975, US Dist. Ct. (ea. dist. Pa.) 1975, US Dist. Ct. (ea. dist. Mich.) 1996, US Ct. Appeals (3rd cir.) 1976, US Ct. Appeals (2nd and 9th cirs.) 1990, US Ct. Appeals (8th cir.) 1992, US Ct. Appeals (6th cir.) 1994, US Ct. Appeals (5th cir.) 2003, US Supreme Ct. 1980. Assoc. Dechert LLP, Phila., 1975-83, ptnr., 1983—. Mem.: Phila. Bar Assn. Office: Dechert LLP Cira Ctr 2929 Arch St Philadelphia PA 19104-2808 Office Phone: 215-994-2489. Office Fax: 215-994-2222. E-mail: steven.feirson@dechert.com.*

FEISEL, LYLE DEAN, retired dean, electrical engineer, educator; b. Tama, Iowa, Oct. 16, 1935; s. Clyde Edward and Clara Maria (Ehlers) F.; m. Dorothy Evelyn Stadsvold, June 15, 1957; children: Patricia, Margaret, Kenneth. BSEE, Iowa State U., 1961, MSEE, 1963, PhD in Elec. Engring., 1964. Registered profl. engr., S.D. Engr. Honeywell, Mpls., 1961-62; staff engr. IBM Corp., Poughkeepsie, NY, 1963, Burlington, Vt., 1967; mem. faculty of elec. engring. S.D. Sch. of Mines, Rapid City, 1964-83, head elec. engring. dept., 1975-83; dean Watson Sch. SUNY, Binghamton, 1983—2001. Vis. prof. Cheng Kung U., Tainan, Taiwan, 1969-70; rsch. engr. Northrop Corp., L.A., 1974; Wachmeister prof. engring. Va. Mil. Inst., 1982; mem. engring. accreditation commn. Accreditation Bd. Engring. and Tech., 1987-92, bd. dirs., 1992-97. Nat. Def. fellow, 1961-64; recipient profl. achievement citation Iowa State U., 1984, Ednl. Achievement award N.Y. State Soc. Profl. Engrs., 1989. Fellow IEEE (pres. edn. soc. 1978-79, v.p. ednl. activities 2000-02, Meritorious Svc. award, Ben Dasher award 1983, Centennial medal 1984, Ronald J. Schmitz award 1989, achievement award Edn. Soc. 1999, Third Millennium medal 2000), NSPE (Achievement award 2002) Am. Soc. Engring. Edn. (bd. dirs. 1982-83, 94-99, pres. 1997-98); mem. S.D. Renewable Energy Assn. (pres. 1979-81, N.Y. State Engr. of Yr. 2000), Tau Beta Pi (Disting. Alumnus award 2002), Eta Kappa Nu Assn. (bd. govs. 2004-06). Democrat. Lutheran. Address: PO Box 839 Saint Michaels MD 21663 Home Phone: 410-745-4266. E-mail: l.feisel@ieee.org.

FEIT, BARBERI PAULL, composer, lyricist, psychotherapist, writer; b. NYC, July 27, 1949; d. S. Paull and Alyce (Togniere) Platt; m. Glenn M. Feit, May 24, 1975. Diploma, Juilliard Sch. Music, NYC, 1972; BS, NYU, 1979, MS, 1980. Dir. Barberi Paull Musical Theatre, 1969-75; pvt. practice psychotherapy NYC, 1980—. Studied with Pulitzer prize winning composers Charles Wuorinen and Jacob Druckman; gen. asst. to Mme. Koussevitzky at Tanglewood and asst. condr. to Leonard Bernstein, 1972—74; founder Illumina, Inc.; creator Illumina, Inc. Imprint; co-founder Barberi Paull Feit and Glenn Martin Feit Charitable Trust; spkr. in field. Composer: The American Dream, I Have a Dream, Believe, Celebration, Angel Music, electronic ballets, music for films, A Christmas Carol and Close to the Sky, others; author: Le Petit Foret, 1999, The Angel Chronicles, 2002, Love and Dreams, 2005; pub.: newsletter The Loveletter, 1990—, eNewsletter, 1998—. Named honoree tours, Meet the Composer, 1972—80; recipient Lehman Engles BMI Musical Theatre Workshop fellow, 1972—73, Dellus award, 1979, Emmy award, 2000, 2001, Am. Cancer Soc., 2001; fellow, NEA, 1982. Mem.: ASCAP (awards 1980—), Internat. League Women Composers (bd. dir.), The Century Assn., Hort. Soc. N.Y. (vice-chmn.), The Met. Opera Club, Mus. City of N.Y. (vice-chmn.), The Doubles Club. Avocations: interior decorating, yachting, French, landscape and floral design. Home: PO Box 1906 Bridgehampton NY 11932-1906 Office: One Lincoln Plz # 33K New York NY 10023 Personal E-mail: barberi27@aol.com.

FEIT, GLENN MARTIN, lawyer; b. Elizabeth, NJ, Oct. 16, 1929; s. Charles Theodore and Beatrice (Esther) F.; m. Rona F. Gottlieb, June 14, 1953 (div. 1974); children: Glenn M., John Paul, Adam Gibbs (dec.); m. Barberi Platt Paull. BS in Econ., U. Pa., 1951; JD magna cum laude, Harvard U., 1957. Bar: N.Y. 1958, U.S. Dist. Ct. (2d dist.) 1959). Assoc. Cravath, Swaine & Moore, NYC, 1957-64; ptnr. London, Buttenwieser & Chalif, NYC, 1965-70, Feit & Ahrens, NYC, 1970-88, Feit & Shor, NYC,

1988-89, Proskauer Rose LLP, NYC, 1989—. Bd. dirs. Blair Industries, Inc., Scott City, Mo.; sec. Charterhouse Group Internat., Inc., N.Y.C. Mem. editl. bd. Harvard Law Rev., 1955-57. Lt. USN, 1951-54. Mem. ABA, Assn. Bar City NY, Aircraft Owners and Pilots Assn., Exptl. Aircraft Assn., Tailhook Assn., Seaplane Pilots Assn., Navy League, New Eng. Soc. City N.Y., N.Y. Yacht Club, Harvard Club, Doubles Office: Proskauer Rose LLP 1585 Broadway New York NY 10036-8299 Home Phone: 212-873-8110. Business E-Mail: gfeit@proskauer.com.

FEITH, DOUGLAS JAY, former federal agency administrator; b. Phila., July 16, 1953; s. Dalck and Rose (Bankel) F.; m. Tatyana Belenky, July 8, 1979 (separated). AB magna cum laude, Harvard Coll., 1975; JD magna cum laude, Georgetown U., 1978. Bar: D.C. 1978. Assoc. Fried, Frank, Harris, Shriver and Kampelman, Washington, 1978-81; Mid. East specialist NSC, Washington, 1981-82; spl. counsel to asst. sec. for internat. security US Dept. Def., Washington, 1982-84, dep. asst. sec. def. for negotiations policy, 1984-86, under sec. def. for policy, 2001—05; mng. atty. Feith and Zell, P.C., Washington, 1986—2001. Vis. prof., Disting. Practitioner in Nat. Security Policy, Edmund A. Walsh Sch. Fgn. Svc. Georgetown U., 2006—. Author: War and Decision: Inside the Pentagon at the Dawn of the War on Terrorism, 2007. Recipient Disting. Pub. Svc. medal, US Dept. Def., 1986, 2005. Mem. Coun. Fgn. Rels. Office: Edmund A Walsh Sch Fgn Svc InterCultural Ctr Rm 805 37th & O St NW Washington DC 20057 E-mail: djf35@georgetown.edu.

FEITLER, ROBERT, shoe company executive; b. Chgo., Nov. 19, 1930; s. Irwin and Bernice (Gombrig) F.; m. Joan Elden, May 30, 1957; children: Pamela, Robert, Richard, Dana (dec.). BS, U. Pa., 1951; JD, Harvard U., 1954. Pres. Weyco Group, Inc., Milw., 1968-96, chmn. exec. com., 1996—. Bd. dirs. Assoc. Bank, Milw., Assoc. Banc-Corp., Strattec Security Corp., TC Mfg. Co. Chmn. Smart Family Foun.; past pres. Milw. Art Mus., Nat. Forest Found.; trustee U. Chgo. Newberry Libr., U. Chgo. Hosps.; chmn. bd. govs. Smart Mus. at U. Chgo. With U.S. Army, 1954-56. Mem. U. Club Milw. (bd. dirs.), Harvard Club (N.Y.C.). Home: 179 E Lake Shore Dr # 16E Chicago IL 60611-1340 Office: Weyco Group Inc 333 W Estabrook Blvd Glendale WI 53212 Personal E-mail: bobf1712@aol.com.

FEITO, JOSE, architect; b. Havana, Cuba, Jan. 30, 1929; arrived in U.S., 1961; s. Jose and Hermina (Mayo) F.; m. Bertha A. Abascal, Oct. 7, 1995; children: Patricia Maria, Maria Esther, Jose Alfonso, Sergio P. (dec.). MArch, U. Havana, 1954. Registered arch., Fla. Prin. J. Feito Archs., Havana, 1954-60; assoc. J. DeHaro Archs., Madrid, 1960-61; ptnr. Ferendino et al, Miami, Fla., 1966-79; prin. F&F Archs. and Planners, Miami, 1979-80, F&F Fraga and Feito Archs., Miami, 1980—. Pres. Professio Inc., Miami, 1983-84. Bd. dirs. Dade Co. Shoreline Com., 1986—; chmn. Gov.'s com. for Handicapped, Miami, 1973-75; trustee United Way, Miami, 1979-84. Recipient Meritorious Svcs. citation Gov.'s Com. for Handicapped, 1975. Fellow AIA (pres. Miami South chpt. 1977, Honor award 1985); mem. Fla. Assn. AIA (bd. dirs. 1978, Excellence award 1985), Interam. Businessmen's Assn. (pres. 1978-80), Cuba Soc. Archs. (Gold medal 1957), Cuban Mus. Arts and Culture (founder), Greater Miami C. of C. (mem. bd. govs. 1978-83). Republican. Roman Catholic. Avocations: history, tennis, sailing. Office: F&F Fraga & Feito Archs 2151 NW 93rd Ave Miami FL 33172-4804 Home Phone: 305-594-7834; Office Phone: 305-591-8006. E-mail: ffarchit@bellsouth.net.

FEJER, T. WILLIAM, musician, composer, architect, furniture designer; b. LA, Sept. 18, 1940; s. Andrew A. and Edith (Behal) F.; divorced; children: Tony (Stephen), Andrew. BS in Architecture, Ill. Inst. Tech., 1964, MS, 1967. Exhibit designer 20th century Art Inst. Chgo., 1962-67; archtl. draftsman Mies Van de Rohe, Chgo., 1964-66; design architect Skidmore, Owings & Merrill, Chgo., 1966-68; mng. dir. Evanston (Ill.) Art Ctr., 1970-72; instr. architecture Ill. Inst. Tech., Chgo., 1967-74; nat. designer, advt. mgr. Plastofilm, Chgo., 1974-84; creative dir. Design Prodns., Chgo., 1984-87; staff pianist Nordstrom, Schaumburg, Ill., 1993—97; CEO Live From Chgo., 1968—. Co-dir., chief composer Anderson/Fejer Musicals, Round Lake, Ill., 1996—; ofcl. pianist Boy Scouts Am., Chgo., 1990—; entertainment coord. Internat. Press Club Chgo., 1992-96; theme composer Little City Found., Chgo., 1992; founder No One You Know Found., 2005— Designer contemporary furniture; composer: (musical comedy) Menage A Trois, 1997. Spl. occasion pianist Unitarian Ch., Chgo., 1987—97; vol. entertainment chair Woodfield Area Charitable Orgn., Schaumburg, 1994—97; founder No One You Know Found., 2005. Recipient Outstanding Archtl. Design award Women's Archtl. League, 1963. Mem. Internat. Press Club Chgo. (cartoonist), Gulf Jazz Soc., Phi Gamma Delta. Avocations: art collecting, photography, skiing, sailing, golf. Home: 1836 N East Ave Lot 24 Panama City FL 32405-6258 Office Phone: 850-215-3409. Personal E-mail: ruthswritings@aol.com.

FEJES, ROBERT R., minister; b. Meadville, Pa., Sept. 12, 1946; s. John Jospeh and Helen Bean Fejes; m. Patricia Ann Hayden, May 11, 1974; children: Lara Elizabeth, Jon Hayden. B Music Edn., Fla. State U., 1968, MusM, 1973. Consecrated lay worker United Meth. Ch., 1974, ordained diaconal minister United Meth. Ch., 1977, ordained United Meth. Ch., 97. Music and edn. dir. First United Meth. Ch., Sebring, Fla., 1968—69; music and youth dir. Centenary United Meth. Ch., Quincy, Fla., 1971—73; dir. music and youth First United Meth. Ch., Ft. Meade, Fla., 1973—75, dir. music St. Petersburg, Fla., 1975—91; min. music Broadway United Meth. Ch., Paducah, Ky., 1991—. Dir. Paducah Symphony Chorus, 1991—97. With US Army, 1969—71. Mem.: Am. Guild English Handbell Ringers, Choristers Guild, Am. Choral Dirs. Assn., Fellowship of United Methodists in Music and Worship Arts (v.p. 1981—83, pres. 1991—93, pres. Fla. chpt., v.p. Fla. chpt.). Home: 4075 Cleary Dr Paducah KY 42001 Office: Broadway United Meth Ch 701 Broadway Paducah KY 42001 Office Phone: 270-443-2401. Office Fax: 270-443-8701. Personal E-mail: rrfejesbumc@comcast.net.

FELCH, WILLIAM CAMPBELL, internist, editor; b. Lakewood, Ohio, Nov. 14, 1920; s. Don Harold Willison and Beth (Campbell) Felch; m. Nancy Cook Dean, Aug. 4, 1945; children: William Campbell, Robert Dean. BA, Princeton U., 1942; MD, Columbia U., 1945. Diplomate Nat. Bd. Med. Examiners, Am. Bd. Internal Medicine. Intern St. Luke's Hosp., NYC, 1945—46, resident in internal medicine, 1948—51; pvt. practice specializing in internal medicine Rye, NY, 1951—88; chief staff United Hosp., Port Chester, NY, 1975—77; med. dir. Osborn Home, Rye, NY, 1979—88; exec. v.p. Alliance for Continuing Med. Edn., 1978—91. Author: Aspiration and Achievement, 1981, Decade of Decision, 1989, Vision for the Future, 1992, The Secrets of Good Patient Care, Thoughts on Medicine for the 21st Century, 1996, Alliance for Continuing Medical Education: The First 20 Years, 1996; editor: The Internist, 1975—86, ACME Almanac, 1978—91, Jour. of Continuing Edn. in Health Professions, 1992—95; co-editor: Continuing Med. Edn.: A Primer, 2d edit., 1991. Trustee N.Y. Med. Coll. , Valhalla, 1971—73. Capt. US Army, 1946—48. Named Internist of Distinction, Internal Medicine Soc. N.Y. County, 1973; recipient award of merit, N.Y. State Soc. Internal Medicine, 1976, Disting. Svc. award, Alliance for Continuing Med. Edn., Founder's medal, 1995. Mem.: AMA (chmn. coun. on legislation 1977—79), ACP, Inst. of Medicine NAS, Am. Soc. Internal Medicine (pres. 1973—74), Alliance for Continuing Med. Edn. (exec. v.p. 1978—91). Home: 8545 Carmel Valley Rd Carmel CA 93923 Personal E-mail: srfelch@comcast.net.

FELCYN, DIANE ANNETTE, art association administrator; b. East Norriton Twp, Pa., Aug. 25, 1978; d. Zdzislaw J. and Anna Felcyn; m. Mark Allen Natale, Oct. 17, 2003. BA, Chestnut Hill Coll., Phila., 2000; MA, U. of the Arts, Phila., 2001. Curator of edn. Telfair Mus. of Art, Savannah, Ga., 2001—06; asst. dir. Perkins Ctr. for Arts, Moorestown and Collingswood, NJ, 2006—. Contbr. mus. catalog. Bd.-elect rep. mus. divsn. Ga. Art Edn. Assn., 2006—. Named Ga. Mus. Educator of Yr., Ga. Art Edn. Assn., 2006, S.E. Region Mus. Educator of Yr., Nat. Art Edn. Assn., 2006; recipient Youth Art Month Excellence award, Ga. Art Edn. Assn., 2003, 2005. Office: Perkins Ctr for Arts 395 Kings Hwy Moorestown NJ 08057 Business E-Mail: dfelcyn@perkinscenter.org.

FELD, ALAN DAVID, lawyer; b. Dallas, Nov. 13, 1936; s. Henry R. and Rose (Scissors) F.; m. Anne Sanger, June 1, 1957; children: Alan David, Elizabeth S., John L. BA, So. Methodist U., 1957, LL.B., 1960. Bar: Tex. 1960. Since practiced in Dallas; from ptnr. to chmn. bd. Akin, Gump, Hauer, Strauss & Feld, Dallas, 1960-96, sr. exec. ptnr., 1996—. Lectr. Southwestern U. Med. Sch.; chmn. Tex. State Securities Bd. 1985-1991; bd. dirs. Clear Channel Comms., Inc. Contbr. articles to legal jours. Trustee AMR Advaantage Funds, So. Meth. U.; bd. dirs. Dallas Day Nursery Assn., Timberlawn Found., Dallas Symphony Orch. Mem.: ABA, Dallas Bar Assn., D.C. Bar Assn., Tex. Bar Assn., Dallas Country Club, Royal Oaks Country Club (corr.), Salesmanship Club, Phi Delta Phi. Office: Akin Gump Strauss Hauer & Feld 1700 Pacific Ave Ste 4100 Dallas TX 75201-4675 Office Phone: 214-969-2712. Business E-Mail: afeld@akingump.com.

FELD, CAROLE LESLIE, marketing executive; b. LA, Nov. 12, 1955; d. Harold Brenman and Phyllis Pearl (Fishman) F.; m. David C. Levy; 1 child, Alexander Wolf Levy. BA, U. Calif., Berkeley, 1979; MBA, U. So. Calif., 1982. Mgr. rsch. Columbia Pictures, LA, 1982—83; dir. promotion and field pub. Tri-Star Pictures, NYC, 1983—86; dir. promotion and retention mktg. Home Box Office, NYC, 1987—92; v.p. promotion and advt. Pub. Broadcasting Svc., Washington, 1992—97, sr. v.p. advt., promotion and corp. comm., 1995—99, sr. v.p. comm. and brand mgmt., 1999—2000; v.p. brand mktg. The Motley Fool, Washington, 2000—01, mktg. cons., 2002—03; prin. Giving Tree Group, Washington, 2003—. Pres. CINE; cons. New Sch. Beacons in Jazz Program, N.Y.C., 1990—. Named one of Mktgs. Top 100 Advertising Age, 1995. Achievements include creator "PBS Kids" brand. Avocations: skiing, travel, art, films. Office Phone: 202-415-2669. Business E-Mail: carole@givingtreegroup.com.

FELD, ELIOT, dancer, choreographer, performing company executive; b. Bklyn., July 5, 1942; s. Benjamin Noah and Alice (Posner) Feld. Student, High Sch. Performing Arts, NYC, 1954-58; DFA (hon.), Juilliard Sch., 1991. Artistic dir. Ballet Tech, NYC. Dancer child prince The Nutcracker, NYC Ballet, 1954, West Side Story, 1958, Donald McKayle Co., Sophie Maslow Co., Pearl Lang Co., Mary Anthony Co., I Can Get It for You Wholesale, 1962, Fiddler on the Roof, Am. Ballet Theatre, 1963, Les Noces, Wind in the Mountains, Dark Elegies, Fancy Free, Billy the Kid, Helen of Troy, Giselle; founder Am. Ballet Co., 1968, dancer, mgr., chief choreographer, 1969—71, Bklyn. Acad. Music; choreographer Am. Ballet Theatre, Royal Danish Ballet, Nat. Ballet of Can., NYC Ballet; founder, artistic dir., chief choreographer Feld Ballets, NY, 1974, founder New Ballet Sch., 1978, Kids Dance, 1994, Ballet Tech, 1996, prin. founder The Joyce Theatre, 1982, The Lawrence A. Wien Ctr. Dance and Theater, 1986; choreographer Harbinger, 1967, At Midnight, 1967, Meadowlark, 1968, Intermezzo, 1969, Cortege Burlesque, 1969, Pagan Spring, 1969, Early Songs, 1970, Cortege Parisien, 1970, Consort, 1970, A Poem Forgotten, 1970, Romance, 1971, Theatre, 1971, The Gods Amused, 1971, A Soldier's Tale, 1971, Eccentrique, 1971, Winters Court, 1972, Jive, 1973, Sephardic Song, 1974, Tzaddik, 1974, The Real McCoy, 1974, Mazurka, 1975, Excursions, 1975, Impromptu, 1976, Variations on 'America', 1977, A Footstep of Air, 1977, Santa Fe Saga, 1978, La Vida, 1978, Danzon Cubano, 1978, Half-Time, 1978, Papillon, 1979, Circa, 1980, Anatomic Balm, 1980, Scenes, 1980, Play Bach, 1981, Song of Norway, 1981, Over the Pavement, 1982, Straw Hearts, 1983, Summer's Lease, 1983, Three Dances, 1983, Adieu, 1984, The Jig Is Up, 1984, Moon Skate, 1984, Intermezzo No. 2, 1985, Against the Sky, 1985, The Grand Canyon, 1985, Aurora I, 1985, Aurora II, 1985, Medium: Rare, 1985, Echo, 1986, Bent Planes, 1986, Skara Brae, 1986, Embraced Waltzes, 1987, A Dance for Two, 1987, Shadow's Breath, 1987, Petipa Notwithstanding, 1988, Kore, 1988, The Unanswered Question, 1988, Asia, 1988, Love Song Waltzes, 1988, Ah Scarlatti, 1989, Mother Nature, 1989, Contra Pose, 1990, Charmed Lives, 1990, Ion, 1990, Fauna, 1990, Common Ground, 1991, Savage Glance, 1991, Clave, 1991, Evoe, 1991, Endsong, 1991, Wolfgang Strategies, 1992, To the Naked Eye, 1992, Hello Fancy, 1992, Frets and Women, 1992, Hadji, 1992, Blooms Wake, 1993, The Relative Disposition of the Parts, 1993, Doo Dah Day, 1993, MRI, 1993, Doghead & Godcatchers, 1994, 23 Skidoo, 1994, Gnossiennes, 1994, Ogive, 1994, Chi, 1994, Ludwig Gambits, 1995, Tongue and Groove, 1995, Meshugana Dance, 1996, Paean, 1996, Paper Tiger, 1996, Shuffle, 1996, Industry, 1996, Evening Chant, 1996, Jukebox, 1997, Re:X, 1997, Yo Shakespeare, 1997, Joggers, 1997, Umbra Rumba, 1997, Yo Johann, 1997, The Last Sonata, 1997, Simon Sez, 1998, Cherokee Rose, 1999, Mending, 1999, Felix: the ballet, 1999, Apple Pie, 1999, Nodrog Doggo, 2000, Coup de Couperin, 2000, Organon, 2001, Pacific Dances, 2001, Skandia, 2002, Pianola: Raven, 2002, Lincoln Portrait, 2002, Behold the Man, 2002, (ballets) Pianola: Indigo, 2002, Mr. XY2, 2003, French Overtures, 2003. Recipient Dance Mag. award, 1990, Guggenheim Fell., 1969. Achievements include coreographic over 180 ballets since 1967. Office: Ballet Tech 890 Broadway Fl 8 New York NY 10003-1211 Office Fax: 212-353-0936. E-mail: staff@ballettech.org.*

FELD, JOSEPH, construction executive; b. NYC, June 25, 1919; s. Morris David and Golda (London) F.; m. Doris Rabinor (dec.); 1 child, Elaine Susan; m. Mairuth Hirsch Maloney, July 25, 1999. Student, CCNY, 1946—47. Builder housing, apt. projects, L.I., NYC, N.J., 1948-54; pres. Kohl and Feld, Inc., builder housing devels., Rockland County, N.Y., 1955-57, Feld Constrn. Corp., New City, N.Y., 1957—, Birchland Constrn. Corp., 1957-70, Ramapo Towers, Inc., 1963-83. Vice-chmn. People's Nat. Bank Rockland County, Monsey, N.Y., 1974-85. Mem. Clarkstown Bldg. Code Com., 1959; mem. indsl. devel. adv. com. Rockland County Bd. Suprs., 1969-71; chmn. housing adv. coun. Rockland County Legislature, 1976-86; chmn. Housing Task Force, 1979-80; mem., past pres. Men's Club; mem. Rockland County coun. Jewish War Vets., past commdr. New City post. Staff sgt. AUS, 1941-45. Mem. Rockland County Assn., Inc. (former bd. dir.), Rockland County Home Builders Assn. (past pres., bd. dirs., chmn. rental housing com.), Nat. Assn. Home Builders (past bd. dirs., mem. rental housing com.), N.Y. State Assn. Home Builders (past dir., mem. rental housing com.), Rockland County Apt. Owners Assn. (pres., bd. dirs. 1971-94), Rockland County Bd. Realtors, N.Y. State Assn. Realtors (past dirs.), Masons, Lions (local pres. 1959-60, zone chmn. 1961-62). Home: 901 E Camino Real Apt 6C Boca Raton FL 33432-6344 Personal E-mail: bocamanj@aol.com.

FELD, KAREN IRMA, columnist, journalist, commentator, speech professional; b. Washington, Aug. 23; d. Irvin and Adele Ruth (Schwartz) F. BA, Am. U., 1969. Columnist, reporter Roll Call Newspaper, Washington; coord. nat. pub. rels. Ringling Bros./Barnum & Bailey Circus, Washington; publicist Twentieth Century Fox, LA; pub. rels. account exec. Harshe, Rotman & Druck, LA; freelance writer, broadcaster; corr. People mag., Washington, 1980—85; adj. instr. Polit. Campaign Mgmt. Inst. Kent State U., 1981; broadcaster Voice Am., 1984; columnist, contbg. editor Capitol Hill mag., Washington, 1980—89; columnist Washington Times, 1986—87, Universal Press Syndicate, 1988—89, Creators Syndicate, 1989—90; syndicated columnist Capital Connections, 1990—; Prodigy polit. columnist, 1990—93. Radio/TV commentator syndicated radio segment Radio America, 1993-04; syndicated columnist Nat. Post, 1998-99; Washington editor Delta Shuttle Sheet, 2000-05; columnist Washington Examiner, 2005-06; feature writer, theater critic Times Cmty. Newspaper, 2006—; fellow, website columnist Politiclmavens; lectr. in field. Contbr. articles to Parade mag., People mag., Money mag., Time mag., Vogue mag., George, USA Weekend, Family Circle, others. Recipient Health Journalism award Am. Chiropractic Assn., 1991. Mem. AFTRA/SAG, Nat. Fedn. Press Women (Excellence in Journalism award 1984-07), Capital Press Women (v.p. 1985-91, Excellence in Journalism award 1984-06), Am. Soc. Journalists and Authors (award), N.Am. Travel Journalists Assn. (Best Mag. Feature award 2003), Nat. Press Club, Capitol Hill Club, Woodmont Country Club (Rockville, Md.), U.S. Senate Press Gallery, White House Corr. Assn., Soc. Profl. Journalists (bd. dirs., v.p. chpt., Editl. Writing award 2004), SDX Found. (bd. dirs.) Jewish. Office: 1698 32nd St NW Washington DC 20007-2969 Office Phone: 202-337-2044. Business E-Mail: news@karenfeld.com.

FELD, MICHAEL STEPHEN, physics professor; b. NYC, Nov. 11, 1940; s. Albert and Lillian R. Norwalk; m. Alison M. Hearn; children: David A., Jonathan R., Alexandra A. SB in Humanities and Sci., MIT, 1963, SM in Physics, 1963; PhD in Physics, M.I.T., 1967. Postdoctoral fellow MIT, Cambridge, 1967-68, asst. prof., 1968-73, assoc. prof., 1973-79, prof. physics, 1979—, dir. George R. Harrison Spectroscopy Lab., 1976—, dir. Laser Research Ctr., 1979—; dir. Laser Biomed. Research Ctr., 1985—. Co-editor: Fundamental and Applied Laser Physics, 1973, Coherent Nonlinear Optics, 1980. Alfred P. Sloan rsch. fellow, 1973; recipient Disting. Svc. award MIT Minority Cmty., 1980, Gordon Y. Billard award, 1982, Thompson award Spectrochimica Acta, 1991, Vinci d'Excellence, France, 1995, Disting. Baltzer Colloquim spkr. Princeton U., 1996, Lamb medal Physics of Quantum Electronics Soc., 2003. Fellow: AAAS, Am. Optical Soc., Am. Phys. Soc., Am. Soc. Laser Medicine and Surgery (bd. dirs.), Sigma Xi. Office: MIT G R Harrison Spectroscopy Lab 77 Massachusetts Ave 6-014 Cambridge MA 02139 Business E-Mail: msfeld@mit.edu.

FELDBERG, MEYER, investment advisor, university dean emeritus; b. Johannesburg, Mar. 17, 1942; s. Leon and Sarah (Kretzmer) F.; m. Barbara Erlick, Aug. 9, 1965; children: Lewis Robert, Ilana. BA, Witwatersrand U., Johannesburg, 1962; MBA, Columbia U., 1965; PhD, Cape Town U., S. Africa, 1969. Product mgr. B.F. Goodrich Co., Akron, Ohio, 1965-67; dean Grad. Sch. Bus., U. Cape Town, 1968-79; assoc. dean J.L. Kellogg Sch. Mgmt., Northwestern U., Evanston, Ill., 1979-81; prof., dean Sch. Bus., Tulane U., New Orleans, 1981-86; pres. Ill. Inst. Tech., Chgo., 1986-89, chmn. bd. govs. Rsch. Inst.; dean Grad. Sch. Bus. Columbia U., NYC, 1989—2004, Sanford C. Bernstein prof. leadership and ethics, 2003—04; sr. advisor Morgan Stanley, 2004—. Bd. dirs. Federated Dept. Stores, UBS Funds, Revlon, Inc., Primedia Inc., Sappi Ltd.; vis. prof. MIT, 1974, Cranfield Inst. Tech., 1970, 76. Author: Organizational Behaviour: Text and Cases, 1975; contbr. articles to profl. jours. Named Jaycee Young Man of Yr., 1972 Mem. Univ. Club (N.Y.C. and Chgo.), Econ. Club (N.Y.C. and Chgo.). Home: 1585 Broadway # 33 New York NY 10036-8200 Home Phone: 212-724-2425; Office Phone: 212-761-7400. Business E-Mail: meyer.feldberg@morganstanley.com.

FELDBERG, MICHAEL SVETKEY, lawyer; b. Boston, May 21, 1951; s. Sumner Lee Feldberg and Eunice (Svetkey) Cohen; m. Ruth Lazarus, Sept. 23, 1978; children: Rachel, Jesse, Ben. BA, Harvard U., 1973, JD, 1977. Bar: N.Y. 1978, U.S. Dist. Ct. (ea. and so. dists.) N.Y. 1978, U.S. Ct. Appeals (2d cir.) 1983, U.S. Supreme Ct. 1994. Assoc. Orans, Elsen, Polstein & Naftalis, NYC, 1977—80; asst. U.S. atty. So. Dist. of N.Y., NYC, 1981—84; ptnr. Shea & Gould, NYC, 1985—91, Schulte Roth & Zabel, NYC, 1991—2003; ptnr., head U.S. Litig. Allen & Overy, NYC, 2003—. Dir. Facing History and Ourselves. Bd. dirs. 92d St. YMCA, NYC; mem. Facing History and Ourselves. Mem. Assn. Bar City N.Y. (criminal law com., com. on the judiciary, com. on profl. responsibility). Office: Allen & Overy 1221 Avenue of the Americas New York NY 10020 Home Phone: 212-996-4384; Office Phone: 212-610-6360. Business E-Mail: michael.feldberg@allenovery.com.

FELDBERG, SUMNER LEE, retired retail executive; b. Boston, June 19, 1924; s. Morris and Anna (Marnoy) F.; married; children: Michael S., Ellen R.; stepchildren: Mollye S., Beth, James. BA, Harvard, 1947, MBA, 1949. With New England Trading Corp., 1949-56; treas. Zayre Corp., 1956-73, sr. v.p., 1965-68, exec. v.p., 1969-73, chmn. bd., 1973-87; chmn. exec. com. Zayre Corp. (name now TJX Cos., Inc.), 1987-89; chmn. bd. B.J.'s Wholesale Club, 1989-96, TJX Cos., Inc., Framingham, Mass., 1989-95. Trustee Beth Israel Hosp., Combined Jewish Philanthropies of Greater Boston. Served to 1st lt. USAAF, 1943-46. Office: 770 Cochituate Rd Framingham MA 01701-9175 also: PO Box 9175 Framingham MA 01701-9175

FELDER, MIRA B., dean, academic administrator; BA in English, French, Bklyn. Coll.; post grad, Hostra U., Hempstead, NY; MA in Applied Linguistics, English, Temple U., Phila.; post grad. in Ednl. Adminstrn. and Supervision, Bklyn. Coll. Instr. reading, grammar, composition Toras Emes, Bklyn., 1961—63; instr. secondary English, French Phila. Sch. Sys., 1964—67; instr. English, ESL Phila. CC, 1970—72; instr. English Phila. Coll. Art, 1972—73; instr. English, ESL Hunter Coll., NYC, 1974—75; instr. ESL Borough of Manhattan CC, NYC, 1976—78; asst. prof. Touro Coll., NYC, 1978—91, assoc. dean sch. career and applied studies, 1991—. Editorial asst. Jewish Pub. Soc., Phila., 1968; coord. devel. English Phila. Coll. Art, 1972—73; coord. computer programming Borough of Manhattan CC, 1976—78; reviewer Harcourt Brace Jovanovich, NYC, 1976—78; ESL divisional officer Touro Coll., 1978—. Co-author: Light and Lively, 1979, Laugh and Learn, 1987; author: ESL Textbook I, 1996, ESL Textbook II, 1996. Mem.: TESOL, MLA. Office: Touro Coll 1602 Ave J Brooklyn NY 11230

FELDER, RAOUL LIONEL, lawyer; b. Bklyn., May 13, 1934; s. Morris and Millie (Goldstein) F.; m. Myrna Felder, May 26, 1963; children: Rachel, James. BA, NYU, 1955, JD, 1959; postgrad., U. Bern, Switzerland, 1955-56; Fellow in Jurisprudence (hon.), Oxford U., 1995. Bar: NY 1959, US Dist. Ct. (so. and ea. dists.) NY 1962, US Ct. Appeals (2d cir.) 1962, US Supreme Ct. 1970. Pvt. practice, NYC, 1959-61, 64—; asst. US atty., 1961-64; of counsel Weiss & Handler, P.A., Boca Raton, Fla. Faculty Practicing Law Inst., 1979, Marymount Coll., 1982-85, Ethical Culture Sch., 1981-82; moderator Nat. Conf. on Child Abuse, 1989; apptd. to NYC Cultural Affairs Adv. Commn., 1995-2001, State Commn. on Child Abuse, 1996, Com. on Character and Fitness; bd. dirs. Kidney and Urology; mem. NY State Commn. Judicial Conduct, 2003-07, chmn., 2006—. Author: Divorce: The Way Things Are, Not the Way Things Should Be, 1971, Lawyers Practical Handbook to the New Divorce Law, 1981, Lawyer's Guide to Equitable Distribution, 1988, Raoul Felder's Encyclopedia of Matrimonial Clauses, 1990, Bare Knuckle Negotiation: Savvy Tips and True Stories From the Master of Give and Take, 2004; co-author: (with Barbara Victor) Getting Away with Murder: Weapons for the War Against Domestic Violence, 1996; (with Jackie Mason) Jackie Mason and Raoul Felders' Guide to New York and Los Angeles Restaurants, 1996, Jackie Mason and Raoul Felder's Guide to New York City, 1997, Schmucks: Our Favorite Fakes, Frauds, Lowlifes, Liars, the Armed and Dangerous, and Good Guys Gone Bad, 2007; columnist Fame mag., 1988-92, Am. Women Mag., 1994, NY Daily News Sundays, 1995, Am. Spectator Mag, 1999-2001, Washington Times, 1999-2002, Gotham Mag., 2003-04; commentator Cable News Network, 1989, BBC World Wide, 1994-95, 97, Crossing the Line (TV series), 1997-99, The Felder Report (TV series), 1998-99, guest commentator Court TV, 1992, bd. advisors, 1992-95, editl. contbr.; (documentary) Survival Guide to New York, 1998; host (TV series) Metrolaw, 1995-97; host (radio) Felder Report, 1997-2002, TalkAmerica

Mem. Gov.'s Commn. on Child Abuse, 1989; chmn. Nat. Kidney Found. Auction, NY Fund; chmn. dinner Jerusalem Reclamation Project; bd. dirs. Big Apple Greeters, 1997—99, Cop Care, Hosp. Audiences Inc., Nat. Kidney Found., NYC Econ. Devel. Corp., 2000—01, Kidney and Urology Found. Am., NY Cops Found.; hon. police commr. NY City Police Comms., 2000—; grand marshall USA Day Washington, Israel Day Parade, NYC; apptd. Cultural Adv. Commn., NYC, 1994—2001, 2001—02. Named Man of Yr. Bklyn. Sch. for Spl. Children, Met. Geriatric Ctr., Shield Inst., 1997; recipient Defender of Jerusalem medal, 1990, Crimebusters award Take Back NY, 1996, Child Abuse Prevention Svc. award, Child Safety Inst. 1998. Mem. ABA (judge nat. finals client counseling competition), Assn. of Bar of City of NY (spl. com. matrimonial law 1975-77, character and fitness com. 2006—), NY State Trial Lawyers Assn. (matrimonial law com. 1971-76, chmn. 1974-75), Am. Arbitration Assn., Minion of the Stars (chmn. bd. 1993) Office: Raoul Lionel Felder PC 437 Madison Ave New York NY 10022-7001 Office Phone: 212-832-3939. Business E-Mail: raoulfelder@raoulfelder.com.

FELDER, WILSON NORFLEET, II, engineering executive; b. NYC, July 20, 1946; s. Thomas Brailsford and Betty (Rice) Felder; m. Laura Lee Stottemyer, Oct. 28, 1978; children: William, Julia. BA in Geology, U. Va., 1968, MA in Environ. Sci., 1973, PhD in Environ. Sci., 1978. Rsch. assoc. U. Va., Charlottesville, 1976-78; with TRW Corp., McLean, Va., 1978—2001, staff engr. command and control dept., 1978-81, mgr. intelligence project, 1981-83, mgr. electronics dept., 1983-85, mgr. nat. weather svc. project Silver Spring, Md., 1985, pres. aviation svcs.; spl. asst. to dir. Terminal Bus. Svc. FAA, transition exec., dir. tech. devel. Air Traffic Orgn., 2003—06, exec. sponsor Nat. Ctr. of Excellence in Ops. Rsch., dir. William J. Hughes Tech. Ctr., 2006—. Contbr. articles to profl. jours. Served to lt. comdr. USNR, 1969-76. Fellow AIAA; mem. Am. Geophys. Union, Geol. Soc. Am., IEEE, Armed Forces Comm. and Electronics Assn., Oceanic Engring. Soc., Air Traffic Control Assn., Govt. Electronics Industries Assn., US Naval Inst., Am. Oceanic Orgn. Clubs: Army and Navy (Washington). Republican. Episcopalian. Office: William J Hughes Tech Ctr FAA Atlantic City Internat Airport Atlantic City NJ 08405*

FELDER-HOEHNE, FELICIA HARRIS, librarian, researcher; b. Knoxville, Tenn. d. Henry Thomas and Luvilla Tate Harris. BS in English, Knoxville Coll., 1958; MS in Libr. Sci., Atlanta U., 1966; postgrad., U. Tenn., 1972—78. English tchr. McMinn County Schs., J.L. Cook Sch., Athens, Tenn., 1958—60; adminstrv. asst. Knoxville (Tenn.) Coll., 1960—63, adminstrv. asst. to the dir. pub. rels., 1963—65; grad. libr. asst. Trevor Arnett Libr., Atlanta U., 1965—66; head circulation and reserve svcs. Alumni Libr. Knoxville Coll., 1966—69; tchr., libr. summer study skills program United Presbyn. Ch., Bd. Nat. Missions, Knoxville Coll., 1967—68; prof., reference libr. John C. Hodges Libr. U. Tenn., Knoxville, 1969—. Founder, dir. LARKS: Librs. Linking with At-Risk Students, Knoxville, 1997—; prin. rschr. The George Washington Carver DVD Project, 2003. Author: A Subject Guide to Basic Reference Books in Black Studies; co-author: (online ency.) Project TAPP: Tennesse Authors Past and Present, 1999—; contbr. Notable Black American Women, Book I, Notable Black American Women, Book II, Behavioral & Social Sciences Librarian;, author poems; contbr. articles to profl. jours. Adv. bd. Mentoring Acad. for Boys, Knoxville, 1997—; sec. to bd. Ctr. for Neighborhood Devel., Knoxville, 2000—02; dir. pub. rels. Concerned Assn. Residents East, Knoxville, 1988—90; active Tenn. Valley Energy Coalition, Knoxville, 1988—90, Town Hall East, Knoxville, 1988—, Save Our Cumberland Mountains, Tenn., 1988—; religious task force World's Fair, Knoxville Internat. Energy Exposition, 1982; pres. Spring Place Neighborhood Assn., Knoxville, 1980—; pk. vol. Knox County Pk. Vol. Corps., 2003—; land devel. com. Knoxville Farmer's Mkt., 2004—05; cmty. action com. Leadership Class 2005; active West End Acad. Outreach, 1989—, Solutions to Issues of Concern to Knoxvillians, 1999—, Tribe One, 2000—, Safety City Outreach of Knoxville PD, 2004—, Cmty. Action Com. Leadership Class, 2005, Teen Challenge, 1985—; bd. dirs. Knoxville-Knox County Libr., 1971—77, sec. to bd., 1972—77; bd. dirs. Knox County Libr. Legacy Found., 2007—; apptd. bd. Knox County Pub. Libr. Found., Tenn., 2007; guest Be Pretty Proud program Keep Knoxville Beautiful Bd., 2007; bd. dirs. Ctr. for Neighborhood Devel., Knoxville, 1998—2002, UT Fed. Credit Union, Knoxville, 1984—89; adv. bd. dirs. Knox County Parks and Recreation, 2004—; adv. bd. dirs. Bd. Probation and Parole State of Tenn., Knoxville, 2003—; mem. YWCA, YMCA. Named Citizen of Yr., Order of Ea. Star, 2004, in her honor Dedicated Svc. Meml. Pk. Bench, Knox County Pks. and Recreation Dept., Mayor Mike Ragsdale, 2006; named one of Outstanding Young Women of Am., 1967; named to U. Tenn. African Am. Hall Fame, 1994; recipient Cert. of Merit for Contbns. to Edn., Jack and Jill, Inc., 1976, Plaque of Appreciation, Interdenominational Concert Choir, 1976, Religious Svc. award, NCCJ, 1976, Citizen of the Yr. award, Order of the Ea. Star Prince Hall Masons, 1979, Cert. of Appreciation, Knoxville's Internat. Energy Exposition, 1982, Pub. Svc. award, U. Tenn. Nat. Alumni Assn., 1984, Habitat for Humanity award, 1992, Merit award for outstanding achievement, City of Knoxville, Mayor Ashe, 1994, The Humanitarian Libr. Spirit award, 1994, Spl. Svc. commendation, Mayor Victor Ashe, 1994, Spirit award, The Miles 500 Libr., 1994, 1999, 2005, Citation for Svc., Knoxville Police Dept., 1998, Cmty. Cornerstone award, Knoxville News-Sentinel, 1998, Harold B. Love Outstanding Cmty. Involvement award, Tenn. Higher Edn. Commn., 2003, The Vol. Spirit award, U. Tenn., 2003, Plaque of Appreciation, U. Tenn. Fed. Credit Union, 2004, Sincerity Disting. Libr. award, Daily Beacon, 2004, Hardy Liston Symbol of Hope award, U. Tenn., 2006. Mem.: LWV, NAACP, ALA, Nat. Mus. Women in the Arts (charter), East Tenn. Libr. Assn., Tenn. Libr. Assn., Knoxville Opera Guild, Met. Opera Guild, Knoxville Opera Co. (bd. dirs. 1999—2005), Character Counts Orgn., Dogwood Arts Festival (charter), Beck Cultural Exch. Ctr. (charter), Citizens Police Acad. Alumni Assn., Alpha Kappa Alpha (Orchid award Keep Knoxville Beautiful 2006, A Living Legacy award Bronze Pk. Bench 2006). Achievements include first to first African American librarian hired at the University of Tennesse campus and faculty. Avocations: community service, music, poetry, theater. Office: 152M John C Hodges Libr 1015 Volunteer Blvd Knoxville TN 37996-1000 Business E-Mail: ffelder@utk.edu.

FELDERSTEIN, STEVEN HOWARD, lawyer; b. Rochester, NY, Oct. 28, 1946; s. Lester and Ruth (Tatelbaum) Felderstein; m. Sandra Lynn Goldman, Aug. 24, 1969; 1 child, Janis. BA, SUNY, 1968; JD, U. Calif., San Francisco, 1973. Bar: Calif. 1973. Law clk. U.S. Dist. Ct., Sacramento, 1973—75; ptnr. Felderstein Rosenberg & McManus, Sacramento, 1978-86, Diepenbrock, Wulff, Plant & Hanmegan, LLP, Sacramento, 1986-98, Felderstein Fitzgerald Willoughby & Pascuzzi LLP, Sacramento, 1999—. Adj. prof., U. the Pacific McGeorge Sch. Law, 2003—; Ea. dist. Calif. lawyer rep. 9th Cir. Ct. Appeals, 2004—. Contbr. articles to profl. jours. Bd. trustees Jewish Fedn. Sacramento Region, 1990—95. Named one of Best Lawyers in Am., Woodland White, Inc., 1987—, Super Lawyers of No. Calif., Law and Politics Mag., 2003—. Mem.: Anthony M. Kennedy Inn of Ct. (master of the Bar 1999—2001), Calif. Bankruptcy Forum (v.p. 1998, pres. 1998—99), Am. Coll. Bankruptcy, Practicing Law Inst. (lectr. 1995—), Calif. Continuing Edn. of Bar (lectr. 1987—), Calif. Bar Assn. (uniform comml.code com. bus. sect. 1983—85, insolvency com. bus. sect. 1999—2003). Office: Felderstein Fitzgerald Willoughby & Pascuzzi LLP 400 Capitol Mall Ste 1450 Sacramento CA 95814-4434 Home Phone: 916-485-7816; Office Phone: 916-329-7400. Office Fax: 916-329-7435. Business E-Mail: sfelderstein@ffwplaw.com.

FELDKAMP, JOHN CALVIN, retired lawyer, educator; b. Milw., Sept. 5, 1939; s. Leroy Lyle and Dorothea Arpke (Reineking) F.; m. Barbara Joan Condon, June 30, 1962; children: John Calvin Jr. (dec. 2004), Stephen Patrick, Amy Genevieve. BA, U. Mich., 1961, JD, 1965. Bar: Mich. 1970, NJ 1980, DC 1983. Asst. to v.p. U. Mich., Ann Arbor, 1964-66, dir. housing, 1966-77; gen. mgr. svcs. Princeton U., NJ, 1977-82; pvt. practice law Ann Arbor, 1970-77, Princeton, NJ, 1977-82; assoc. Caplin & Drysdale, Washington, 1982-85; exec. dir. Brown & Wood, NYC, 1985—2001; exec. dir. NYC office Sidley, Austin, Brown & Wood, 2001—05; NY exec. dir. Sidley Austin LLP, NYC, 2006; ret., 2006. Councilman, City of Ann Arbor, 1967-69; hearing referee Mich. Civil Rights Commn., Lansing, 1975-77. Mem. Rotary (bd. dirs. Ann Arbor 1970-77, Princeton 1978-82). Home Phone: 732-892-3251; Office Phone: 212-839-5560. Office Fax: 212-839-5599. Business E-Mail: jfeldkamp@sidley.com.

FELDMAN, ALLAN MAURICE, economist; b. Paterson, NJ, Jan. 9, 1943; s. Jacob and Rachel (Eisen) F.; m. Barbara Ellen Moses, June 19, 1965; children: Paula, Elizabeth, Jacob. BS in Math., U. Chgo., 1965, MA in Anthropology, 1967; PhD in Econs., Johns Hopkins U., 1972. Asst. prof. econs. Brown U., Providence, 1971—, assoc. prof. econs., 1978—. Cons., expert witness, Providence, 1975—. Author: Welfare Economics and Social Choice Theory, 1980, 2d edit. (with Roberto Serrano), 2006. Treas. Common Sense, Providence, 1983-84. Recipient fellowship, Johns Hopkins U., 1970, Richard D. Irwin fellowship, Richard D. Irwin Found., 1971. Mem. Nat. Assn. Forensic Economists, Am. Law and Economic Assn., Phi Beta Kappa (treas. R.I. Alpha chpt. 1999-2006). Avocations: antique clocks, hiking, nature study. Office: Brown U Dept Econs Providence RI 02912-0001 Home Phone: 401-751-1281; Office Phone: 401-863-2415. E-mail: allan_feldman@brown.edu.

FELDMAN, ALLAN ROY, corporate development and marketing executive; b. Chgo., June 2, 1945; s. Michael and Sophie (Grossman) F.; m. Micki McCabe, Sept. 21, 1984. BS, Roosevelt U., 1968; postgrad., U. Louvain, Belgium, 1969-71; MBA, U. Chgo. Asst. to dir. gen. Rank-Xerox, S.A., Brussels, 1969-71; dir. new bus. ventures graphic sys. group Rockwell Internat. Corp., Chgo., 1971-73, dir. mktg., consumer ops., 1973—78; group v.p. Chromalloy Am. Corp., NYC, 1978-80; mng. ptnr. Mktg. Trademark Cons., NYC, 1980-85; CEO Leveraged Mktg. Corp. Am., NYC, St. Louis, San Diego and Shanghai, 1986—; founder, chmn. Mensa Process, NYC, London and Atlanta, 2006—; chmn. LMCA Brand Licensing & Cons. Co., Ltr., Shanghai, 2007—. Bd. dirs. Alimansky Venture Group, Inc., N.Y.C., Growthtech Corp., N.Y.C., Intellectual Property Mgmt. Inst., Lic. Industry Merchants Assn.; guest lectr. Columbia U.; invited mem. U.S. del. to discuss brand licensing with Chinese govt., Shanghai; spkr. trademark licensing and brand bldg., orgns. including Internat. Trademark Assn. and Licensing Execs. Soc., various U.S., European and Asian confs. Bd. dirs. 329108 Owners Corp., N.Y.C., 1993, bd. adv., Intellecutal Property Mgmt. Inst., 2000-. Mem. Licensing Industry Merchants Assn. (officer bd. dirs. 2001—), Licensing Execs. Soc., Internat. Trademark Assn., Univ. Club. Avocations: master carpenter, photography, motorcycle riding, wine tasting. Office: Leveraged Mktg Corp of Am 156 W 56th St New York NY 10019-3800 Office Phone: 212-265-7474. E-mail: allanf@lmca.net.

FELDMAN, ARLENE KARP, special education educator, director; b. Bklyn, Dec. 17, 1946; d. Jack and Estelle Karp; m. Harvey Owen Feldman, Jan. 28, 1968; children: Jaclyn Feldman Gollinger, Matthew Todd, Melissa Lauren, Andrew Jason. BA, Bklyn Coll., 1967; MA, Fairleigh Dickinson U., Teaneck, NJ, 1979; diploma, Fordham U., Tarrytown, NY, 1990. Cert. sch. dist. adminstr. NY State Edn. Dept., 1990, pub. sch. tchr. NY State Edn. Dept., 1979, learning disabilities tchr./cons. NJ Edn. Dept., 1979, elem. sch. tchr. NJ Edn. Dept., 1979. Pub. sch. tchr. NYC Pub. Schs., Bklyn., 1967—68; elem. sch. tchr. Abington Sch. Dist., Rockledge, Pa., 1968—70; resource rm. tchr. Goshen Sch. Dist., NY, 1981—82; spl. edn. tchr. Chester Union Free Sch. Dist., NY, 1985—89, asst. supt. spl. edn. and instrn., 1990—91; edn. dir. Janet Lockwood Sch. UCP, Goshen, 1989—90; dir. spl. programs Fla. Union Free Sch. Dist., Florida, NY, 1991—95; dir. spl. edn. Valley Ctrl. Sch. Dist., Montgomery, NY, 1995—; adj. prof. SUNY, New Paltz, 2002—. Mem. adv. bd. Orange County CC. Chairperson religious sch. com. Monroe Temple of Liberal Judaism, Monroe, NY, 1988—98; vp, sec., bd. mem. Women's Am. ORT, Monroe, NY, 1975—85. Recipient Excellence in Adminstrn. award, NY State Coun. for Exceptional Children, 1994. Mem.: Valley Ctrl. Adminstrs. Assn., Sch. Adminstrs. Assn. NY, Coun. Exceptional Children, Orange Ulster Chairpersons, Phi Delta Kappa. Achievements include development of collaborative teaching model at valley central school district. Avocations: travel, skiing, reading, cooking, music, Broadway shows. Home: 8 West End Dr Highland Mills NY 10930 Office: Valley Ctrl Sch Dist 944State Rte17K Montgomery NY 12549 Home Phone: 845-928-9535; Office Phone: 845-457-2400 8116. Office Fax: 845-457-4254. Business E-Mail: afeldman@vcsd.ouboces.org.

FELDMAN, ARTHUR M., cardiologist; m. Susan Boochever; children: Emily Kate, Elizabeth Willa. BA, Gettysburg Coll., Pa., 1970; MS, U. Md., 1973, PhD, 1974; MD, La. State U., 1981. Diplomate Nat. Bd. Med. Examiners; diplomate in internal medicine and in cardiovasc. disease Am. Bd. Internal Medicine. Intern, resident, fellow in cardiology Johns Hopkins Hosp., Balt., 1981-86, from asst. prof. to assoc. prof. medicine, 1986-94; Harry S. Tack prof. medicine, prof. cell biology/physiology U. Pitts., 1994—2002, chief divsn. cardiology, dir. Cardiovasc. Inst., 1998—2002; Magee prof., chmn. dept. medicine Jefferson Med. Coll., Phila., 2002—. Chief sci. advisor, bd. dirs., co-founder Cardioline, Inc. Editor-in-chief Clin. and Transkeletal Sci.; mem. editl. bd. Heart Failure, Jour. Cardivasc. Pharmacology and Therapeutics, Jour. Cardiovasc. Pharmacology, Clin. Cardiology, Cardiac Failure, others. Trustee Gettysburg Coll., 1996-2002. Grantee, NIH, 1989—94, 1999—. Fellow: Am. Coll. Cardiology, Coun. Clin. Cardiology (exec. com. 1996—2000, basic rsch. coun.), Am. Heart Assn. (heart failure com.); mem.: Assn. Univ. Cardiologists (councilor 1999—2001), Heart Failure Soc. Am. (founding mem. 1995, sec. 1996—98, pres. 1998—2000), Assn. Profs. Cardiology (treas. 2000—01, pres. 2002—03), Assn. Subsplty. Profs., Internat. Soc. Heart Rsch., Assn. Am. Physicians, Am. Soc. Clin. Investigation. Home: 136 Knightsbridge Wynnewood PA 19096 Office: Jefferson Med Coll Coll Bldg Rm 822 1025 Walnut St Philadelphia PA 19096 Office Phone: 215-955-6946. Business E-Mail: arthur.feldman@jefferson.edu.

FELDMAN, BORIS, lawyer; b. South Bend, Ind., 1955; BA in history summa cum laude, Yale U., 1977; JD, Yale Law Sch., 1980. Law clk. to Judge Abraham D. Sofaer, US Dist. Ct. for So. Dist. NY, 1980—81; assoc. Arnold & Porter, Washington, 1981—85; spl. asst. to legal adviser US Dept. State, 1985—86; atty. Wilson Sonsini Goodrich & Rosati, Palo Alto, Calif., 1986—, mem. exec. mgmt. com., chair policy com. Note & topics editor Yale Law Jour., Vol. 89; mem. Ninth Circuit Lawyer Rep. Coordinating Com.; co-chair lawyer rep. to No. Dist. Calif.; bd. dirs. Silicon Valley Campaign for Legal Svcs.; mem. Santa Clara County Superior Ct. Task Force on Complex Lit.; mem. adv. bd. Securities Regulation Inst. Author: 20 articles on various disclosure topics. Named one of Top 45 Lawyers in Country Under Age of 45, Am. Lawyer, 1995, 100 Most Influential Lawyers in Calif., LA Daily Jour., 2002, Top Ten Lawyers in Bay Area, San Francisco Chronicle. Mem.: Phi Beta Kappa. Office: 650 Page Mill Rd Palo Alto CA 94304 Office Fax: 650-493-6811.*

FELDMAN, BRUCE ALLEN, otolaryngologist; b. Washington, Mar. 22, 1941; s. Irvin and Miriam Thelma (Rothstein) F.; m. Sharon Lee Pearlman, Dec. 25, 1966; children: Kathryn Ellen, Michael Aaron. AB, Dartmouth Coll., 1962, B Med. Sci., 1963; MD, Harvard U., 1965. Diplomate Am. Bd. Otolaryngology. Intern Hosp. of U. Pa., Phila., 1965-66, resident in surgery, 1966-67; resident in otolaryngology Mass. Eye and Ear Infirmary-Harvard U., Boston, 1967-70; pvt. practice Washington, 1972—; clin. prof. surgery (otolaryngology), pediatrics George Washington U., Washington, 1990—; clin. prof. otolaryngology Georgetown U. Sch. Medicine, Washington, 1995—. Pres. med. staff Children's Hosp. DC Nat. Med. Ctr., Washington, 1994-96; vice chmn. bd. Children's Hosp. DC, Washington, 1994-1996, bd. dirs., 1994-2004; pres. Feldman ENT Group, PC. Contbr. articles to med. jours., chpt. to book. Bd. dirs. Childrens Hosp. of D.C., 1994-2004, vice chmn. bd., 1996-98. Lt. comdr. M.C., USNR, 1970-72. Mosby scholar, 1963; recipient Physician's Recognition award Children's Hosp. Washington, 1991. Fellow ACS, Am. Laryngol., Rhinol. and Otol. Soc. (Mosher award 1981), Am. Acad. Pediatrics, Am. Acad. Otolaryngology; mem. AMA, Acad. Medicine Washington, Med. Soc. D.C., Jacobi Med. Soc. (pres. 1986-87), Washington Met. Ear, Nose and Throat Soc. (pres. 1978-79), Woodmont Country Club (Rockville, Md.), Phi Beta Kappa, Alpha Omega Alpha, Phi Delta Epsilon (pres. grad. club 1979-80). Jewish. Office: 5454 Wisconsin Ave Chevy Chase MD 20815 Office Phone: 301-652-8847. E-mail: fodm.physician@verizon.net.

FELDMAN, CECILE ARLENE, dean, dental educator; b. NYC, Oct. 8, 1959; d. Melvin and Claire (Halpern) F.; m. Harry Kenneth Zohn, Aug. 19, 1984. BA, U. Pa., 1980, DMD, 1984, MBA, 1985. Asst. prof. U. Pa. Sch. Medicine, 1985—88, NJ Dental School, U. Medicine & Dentistry NJ, Newark, 1988—98, prof. dept. gen. dentistry and cmty. health, 1998—, acting to interim dean, 1999—2001, dean, 2001—. Cons., author in field; leadership inst. fellow Am. Dental Edn. Assn., 1988; adj. prof. dept. dental care systems U. Pa., sr. adj. fellow Leonard Davis Inst. Health Econs., Wharton Sch. Fellow Acad. Gen. Dentistry, Internat. Coll. Dentists, Am. Coll. Dentists; mem. ADA, Am. Assn. Dental Schs., Internat. Assn. Dental Rsch., Am. Assn. Pub. Health Dentistry, Am. Med. Informatics Assn., N.J. Dental Assn. Office: NJ Dental Sch 110 Bergen St Newark NJ 07103-2400 Office Phone: 973-972-4634. Office Fax: 973-972-3689. Business E-Mail: feldman@umdnj.edu.

FELDMAN, CLARICE ROCHELLE, lawyer; b. Milw., Dec. 2, 1941; d. Harry and Beatrice (Hiken) Wagan; m. Howard J. Feldman, July 11, 1965; 1 child, David Lewis. BS, U. Wis., 1963, LL.B., 1965. Bar: Wis. 1965, D.C. 1969, Md. 1984. Appellate atty. NLRB, Washington, 1965—69; co-counsel to Joseph A. Yablonski, Washington, 1969; atty. Washington research project Clark Coll., 1970-72; asso. gen. counsel United Mine Workers Am., Washington, 1972-74; partner Becker, Channell, Becker & Feldman, Washington, 1974-76, Becker & Feldman, 1976-77; gen. counsel Ams. for Energy Independence, Washington, 1978-80; atty. Office of Spl. Investigations, Dept. Justice, 1980-84; pvt. practice law Washington, 1984-98; atty. pro bono, 1999—. Trustee Washington Internat. Sch., 1987-98; advisor Assn. Union Democracy. Mem. Wis., D.C., Md. bar assns. Republican. Jewish. Home: 4455 29th St NW Washington DC 20008-2307

FELDMAN, DANIEL LEE, former state official; b. NYC, June 22, 1949; s. Henry Asher and Rennie (Rock) F.; m. Cecilia Gardner; 2 children, Asher & Leah. AB, Columbia Coll., 1970; JD, Harvard U., 1973. Bar: NY 1975, US Ct. (so. & ea. dist.) NY, US Ct. (2nd cir.), US Supreme Ct. 1996. Assoc. law firm Olwine, Connelly, Chase, O'Donnell & Weyher, NYC, 1973-74; adj. prof. Bklyn. Law Sch., 1990-94; mem. N.Y. State Assembly, 1981-99, counsel to com. ans subcom., and to full Assembly; asst. dep. atty. gen. program devel. Atty. Gen. State of N.Y., 1999—2005; exec. dir. & gen. counsel NY State Trial Lawyers Assn., NYC. Adj. prof. of law Fordham U. Sch. of Law. Author: Reforming Government, 1981; contbr. articles to profl. jours. Recipient Williston prize Harvard U., 1971; Alfred P. Sloan Found. N.Y. Urban fellow, 1969. Mem. APSA, Am. Soc. Pub. Adminstrn., KP, Assn. Bar City NY (com. alternative dispute resolution 2000-2003; State Affairs com. 2003-; adv. Grp. State Fed. jud. coun. 2004-), Am. Polit. Sci. Assn. Office: NY State Trial Lawyers Assn 132 Nassau St New York NY 10038 Office Phone: 212-349-5890. Office Fax: 212-608-2310. Business E-Mail: dfeldman@nystla.org.

FELDMAN, EDMUND BURKE, art critic; b. Bayonne, NJ, May 6, 1924; s. Lucian Theodore and Bertha (Seldin) F.; m. Lailah G. Link, Mar. 15, 1953; children: Eva Jeanne, Jessica Marion. B.F.A., Syracuse U., 1949; MA, UCLA, 1951; Ed.D., Columbia U., 1953. Curator painting and sculpture Newark Mus., 1953; assoc. prof. art Livingston (Ala.) State U., 1953-56, Carnegie Inst. Tech., 1956-60; head art div. State U. Coll., New Paltz, NY, 1960-66; vis. prof. art Ohio State U., 1966; prof. art U. Ga., Athens, 1966-91, Alumni Found. disting. prof. art, 1973-91, prof. emeritus, 1991—. Vis. prof. aesthetic edn. U. Calif., Berkeley, 1974; bd. govs. Pitts. Plan for Art, 1964-66; mem. U.S. Office Edn., Art TV Project, Whitney Mus., 1967, Ednl. Testing Svc., N.Y.C., 1969-70, Coll. Entrance Exam Bd., Princeton, N.J., 1969-70, Nat. Instructional TV Ctr., Bloomington, Ind., 1969-71; editorial cons. art Prentice-Hall, Inc. (arts and humanities Canfield Press subs. Harper & Row); advisor Ga. Coun. for arts, 1973-74, Nat. Faculty for Arts and Humanities, 1986; cons. J. Paul Getty Trust, 1981-85. Author: Art as Image and Idea, 1967, Varieties of Visual Experience, 1971, 4th edit., 1992, The Artist, 1982, 2d edit., 1994, Thinking About Art, 1985, Practical Art Criticism, 1993, Philosophy of Art Education, 1995; editor Art Bull., Ea. Arts Assn., 1957-60, Art in American Institutions, 1970; mem. editorial bd. Rev. Rsch. in Visual Arts Edn., 1975-77; mem. editorial adv. bd. Jour. Aesthetic Edn., 1976-80; chmn. editorial bd. Ga. Rev., 1977. Served with USAAF, 1942-46. Recipient Roswell Hill prize in painting Syracuse U., 1948 Fellow Nat. Art Edn. Assn. (pres. 1981-83, Disting. 1984), Royal Soc. Arts; mem. Coll. Art Assn., U.S. Soc. for Edn. Through Art, Tau Sigma Delta, Kappa Delta Pi, Kappa Pi, Phi Kappa Phi. Jewish. Home: 140 Chinquapin Pl Athens GA 30605-3314 Office: U Ga Sch Art Athens GA 30602

FELDMAN, ELAINE BOSSAK, medical nutritionist, educator; b. NYC, Dec. 9, 1926; d. Solomon and Frances Helen (Fania) Nevler Bossak; m. Herman Black, Dec. 23, 1951 (div. 1957); 1 child, Mitchell Evan; m. Daniel S. Feldman, July 19, 1957 (dec. June 2005); children: Susan, Daniel S. Jr. AB magna cum laude, NYU, 1945, MS, 1948, MD, 1951. Diplomate Am. Bd. Internal Medicine, Nat. Bd. Med. Examiners; cert. in Clin. Nutrition. Rotating intern Mt. Sinai Hosp., NYC, 1951-52, resident in pathology, 1952, asst. resident, 1953, fellow in medicine, resident in metabolism, 1954-55, rsch. asst. in medicine, 1955-58, clin. asst. physician Diabetes Clinic, 1957; asst. vis. physician Kings County Hosp., Bklyn., 1958-66, assoc. vis. physician, 1966-72; asst. attending physician Maimonides Hosp., Bklyn., 1960-68; spl. fellow USPHS Dept. of Physiol. Chemistry U. of Lund, Sweden, 1964-65; attending physician Eugene Talmadge Meml. Hosp., Augusta, Ga., 1972-92, Univ. Hosp., Augusta, 1972-92, cons., 1973; prof. medicine Med. Coll. Ga., Augusta, 1972-92, prof. emeritus, 1992—, chief sect. of nutrition, 1977-92, chief emeritus, 1992—, acting chief sect. of metabolic/endocrine disease, 1980-81, prof. physiology and endocrinology, 1988-92, prof. emeritus physiology and endocrinology, 1992—; instr. medicine SUNY Downstate Med. Ctr., 1957-59, asst. prof. medicine, 1959-68, assoc. prof. medicine, 1968-72. Tchg. fellow dept. zoology U. Wis. Grad. Sch., 1945-46, dept. biology NYU Grad. Sch., 1946-47; cons. N.Y.-N.J. Regional Ctr. for Clin. Nutrition Edn., 1983-92; vis. prof. and Harvey lectr. Northeastern Ohio Sch. Medicine, Youngstown, 1985; cons., vis. prof. U. Nev. Sch. Medicine (NCI grant), 1989-94; mem. nat. adv. com. nutrition fellowship program Nat. Med. Fellowship Inc., 1988-95; dir. Ga. Inst. Human Nutrition, 1978-92, dir. emeritus, 1992—; dir. Clin. Nutrition Rsch. Unit, 1980-86; mem. med. nutrition curriculum initiative adv. bd. U. N.C., Chapel Hill, 1992-2001; advisor ednl. materials Am. Inst. Cancer Rsch., 1997—. Author: Essentials of Clinical Nutrition, 1988; (with others) Conference on Biological Activities of Steroids in Relation to Cancer, 1969, Nicotinic Acid, 1964, The Menopausal Syndrome, 1974, Hyperlipidemia, Medcom Special Studies, 1974, Medcom Famous Teaching in Modern Medicine, 1979,

Harrison's Principles of Internal Medicine, 1980, Health Promotion: Principles and Clinical Applications, 1982, The Encyclopedic Handbook of Alcoholism, 1982, The Climacteric in Perspective, 1986, Selenium in Biology and Medicine, Part A., 1987, Medicine for the Practicing Physician, 1988, Clinical Chemistry of Laboratory Animals, 1989, Ency. Human Biology, 1991, Laboratory Medicine: The Selection and Interpretation of Clinical Laboratory Studies, 1993, Modern Nutrition in Health and Diseases, 1994, Nutrition Assessment-A Comprehensive Guide for Planning Intervention, 1995, The Women's Complete Healthbook, 1995, The American Medical Women's Association's Guide to Nutrition and Wellness, 1996, Normal Nutrition and Therapeutics, 1996, Handbook of Nutrition and Food, 2001; editor: Nutrition and Cardiovascular Disease, 1976, Nutrition in the Middle and Later Years, 1983 (paperback edit. 1986), Nutrition and Heart Disease, 1983, Handbook of Nutrition and Food, 2001, 2d edit., 2007, Human Nutrient Needs in the Life Cycle, 2001; mem. editl. adv. bd. Contemporary Issues in Clin. Nutrition, 1980-92; mem. edit. bd. Am. Jour. Clin. Nutrition, 1983-91, 92-98, Jour. Clin. Endocrinology and Metabolism, 1984-88, MidPoint: Counseling Women through Menopause, 1984-85, Jour. Nutrition, 1985-89; cons. editor Jour. Am. Coll. Nutrition, 1982-94; mem. edit. bd. Complementary Med. for the Physician, 1996-2000; contbg. editor Nutrition Rev., 1997-2002; mem. editl. bd. Nutrition Today, 1999—; reviewer Jour. Lipid Rsch., Biochm. Pharmacology, Sci., The Physiologist, Jour. Am. Acad. Dermatology, Israel Jour. Med. Scis., N.Y. State Jour. Medicine, Jour. of Nutrition Edn., Jour. Am. Dietetic Assn., Am. Jour. Medicine, Am. Jour. Med. Sci., So. Med. Jour., Jour. AMA, Jour. NCI; contbr. more than 175 articles to profl. jours; presenter in field. Mem. tech. adv. com. for sci. and edn. Rsch. Grants Program, Human Nutrition Grants Peer Panel, USDA, 1982, mem. bd. sci. counselors human nutrition; Community Svc. Block Grant Discretionary Program Panel; vice chmn. Urban and Rural Econ. Devel. Panel, Dept. HHS, 1982, grant reviewer, 1983; mem ad hoc and spl. rev. coms. and groups NIH, 1979-93, mem. nutrition study sect., 1976-80; mem. Rev. Panel Nat. Nutrition Objectives, Life Scis. Rev. Office, Fed. Am. Socs. Exptl. Biology, 1985-86; mem. subcom. Women's Health Trial Nat. Cancer Inst., 1987, mem. bd. sci. counselors cancer prevention and control program, 1990-94; mem. adv. com. Clin. Nutrition Rsch. Unit, U. Ala., 1986-94, Ga. Nutrition Steering Com., 1974-75, Ctrl. Savannah River Area Nutrition Project Coun. 1974-75, ednl. adv. com. Health Central, 1980; mem. geriatrics and gerontology rev. com. Nat. Inst. on Aging, 1986-90; breast cancer initiative peer rev. Dept. of Def., 1997, 98. N.Y. Heart Assn. rsch. fellow, 1955—57. Fellow Am. Heart Assn. Coun. on Atherosclerosis (nominating com. 1978, chmn. nominating com., mem. exec. com. 1979-80, Spl. Recognition award 1995), Am. Inst. Nutrition (grad. nutrition edn. com. 1980-83, 89-93); mem. Am. Coll. Nutrition (chmn. com. pub. affairs), Am. Soc. for Clin. Nutrition (com. on nutrition edn. 1982, chmn. subcom. on nutrition edn. in med. schs. 1983-84, chmn. com. on med./dental residency edn., 1985-87, com. on subsplty. tng. 1988-92, nominating com. 1982, 90, chair nominating com. 1994, com. on clin. practice issues in health and disease 1989-92, Nat. Dairy Coun. award 1991, rep. coun. acad. socs. 1990-96, membership com. 1996-2005, chair 1999, 2000), Fedn. Am. Socs. Exptl. Biology. Am. Oil Chemists Soc., Am. Physiol. Soc., Endocrine Soc., Soc. Exptl. Biology and Medicine, So. Soc. Clin. Investigation, Am. Diabetes Assn., Am. Fedn. Clin. Rsch., Am. Gastroent. Assn., AMA (Joseph B. Goldberger award 1990), Am. Med. Women's Assn. (profl. resources com. 1975-76, med. edn. and rsch. fund com. 1976-79, chmn. 1978-90, chmn. student liaison subcom. of membership com. 1981-84, pres. Br. 51, Augusta 1977-80, treas. 1980-97, Calcium Nutrition Edn. award 1991, CSRA Girl Scout Women of Excellence award 1994), Am. Soc. Parenteral and Enteral Nutrition, Am. Heart Assn. (Ga. affiliate, nutrition com., chmn. sci. session for nutritionists, 1978, chmn. nutrition com. 1979-90, mem. long range planning com. 1980-81, rsch. com. 1980-83, bd. dirs. 1987-90, profl. edn. task force, 1988-89), Richmond Country Med. Assn., Augusta Opera Assn. (bd. dirs. 1973-2002, 06—, rec. sec. 1973-74, pres. 1974-75, coord. audience devel. 1975-77, at-large exec. com. 2006—, chair nominating com. 1994-96, 07—, corr. sec. 1998-99, 1st v.p. 1999-2000, chair search com., gen. dir. 2002), Augusta Symphony League, 2005—, Augusta Sailing Club (women's com. 1973), Greater Augusta Arts Coun. (Arts Festival Collage 1982 chmn. promotion and publicity com., Festival coms. 1983-86, 89-93, 95, 96, 98, 99, bd. dirs. 1984-94, Vol. of the Yr., 2001), Gertrude Herbert Inst. Art (bd. dirs. 1987-92), Authors Club Augusta, Philomathic Club (sec. 1999-2001), Phi Beta Kappa, Sigma Xi (chpt. sec. 1982-83, pres. elect 1983-84, pres. 1984-85), Alpha Omega Alpha. Avocations: opera, wine tasting, travel. Home: 4275 Owens Rd Apt 1222 Evans GA 30809 Personal E-mail: efeldman17@comcast.net.

FELDMAN, ERIC ADAM, law educator, academic administrator; b. NYC, Oct. 18, 1959; s. Saul and Gloria F.; m. Stephanie Cecile Cridelose, June 20, 1997. Student, U. Leeds, 1979-80; BA in History and Philosophy of Sci. cum laude, Vassar Coll., 1982; JD, U. Calif., Berkeley, 1989, PhD in Jurisprudence and Social Policy, 1994; student, Nichibei Kaiwa Gakkuen, Tokyo, 1990-91. Bar: Calif. 1989. Rsch. asst. Hastings Ctr., NYC, 1982-84; tchg. asst. Sch. Journalism Columbia U., NYC, 1984; vis. fellow biomed. ethics Mitsubishi-Kasei Inst. Life Scis., Japan, 1984-85; assoc. LeBoeuf, Lamb, Leiby & MacRae, San Francisco, 1989; fgn. rsch. scholar Inst. Social Scis. U. Tokyo, 1990-91, rsch. scholar faculty law internat. ctr. comparative law and politics, 1991-93; health policy rsch. scholar Instn. Social and Policy Studies Yale U., vis. fellow Sch. Law, 1994-96; assoc. dir. Inst. Law and Soc. NYU, 1996—2001; mem. Ctr. for Asian Studies U. Pa., Phila., 2002—, sr. fellow Ctr. for Bioethics, 2001—, asst. prof. law, 2001—. Cons. Toyota Found., Tokyo, 1993-95, World Health Orgn., 1995-96; vis. prof. Inst. D'Etudes Politiques de Paris, 1999; mem. organizing com. 1999 Law and Soc. Assn. Grad. Student Workshop; prin. investigator various profl. projects; organizer, cons., participant AIDS prevention: bldg. U.S./Japan cooperation and exchange project, 1994-96; chair various profl. meetings; presenter in field. Co-author: AIDS in the Industrial Democracies: Passion, Politics, and Policies, 1992, German transl., 1993, Containing Health Care Costs in Japan, 1996, Comparing Legal Cultures, 1997; guest editor Jour. AIDS and Human Retrovirology, 1997; mem. editl. bd. Law and Soc. Rev., 1998—; contbr. articles to profl. jours.; book reviewer in field; reviewer numerous manuscripts. Vol. Tenderloin Housing Clinic, San Francisco, 1987; bd. dirs. Village Acad. Charter Sch., New Haven, 1997-98. Recipient award U.S.-Japan Culture Ctr. Essay Contest, 1988; Fulbright Grad. Rsch. fellow Japan-U.S. Ednl. Commn./IIE, 1989-93; Toyota Found. Rsch. fellow, 1990; Dissertation grantee Social Sci. Rsch. Coun., Joint Com. Japanese Studies, 1991; Rsch. fellow Japan Soc. Promotion Sci., 1992; Doctoral Dissertation Improvement grantee NSF, 1993; Robert Wood Johnson Found. scholar, 1994-96; Abe fellow Social Sci. Rsch. Coun., Am. Coun. Learned Socs. and Ctr. Global Partnership, 1998—; Stephen Charney Vladeck Jr. Faculty fellow NYU, 1999. Mem. Law and Soc. Assn., Assn. Asian Studies, Japan Policy Rsch. Inst., The Hastings Ctr. Office: U Pa Law Sch 3400 Chestnut St Philadelphia PA 19104 Home: 1737 Chestnut St # 1 Philadelphia PA 19103-4107 Office Phone: 215-573-6400. Fax: 215-573-2025. E-mail: efeldman@law.upenn.edu.

FELDMAN, EVA LUCILLE, neurology educator; b. NYC, Mar. 30, 1952; d. George Franklin and Margherita Enriceta (Cafiero) F.; children: Laurel, Scott, John Jr. BA in Biology and Chemistry, Earlham Coll., 1973; MS in Zoology, U. Notre Dame, 1975; PhD in Neurosci., U. Mich., 1979, MD, 1983. Diplomate Am. Bd. Neurology; lic. med. practitioner, Mich. Instr. dept. neurology U. Mich., Ann Arbor, 1987-88, asst. prof. neurology, 1988-94, mem. faculty Cancer Ctr., 1992-2000, assoc. prof. neurology, 1994-2000, prof., 2000—, Russell N. DeJong prof. neurology, 2004—. Mem. faculty neurosci. program U. Mich., Mich. Diabetes Rsch. and Tng., Ann Arbor, 1988—; dir. JDRF Ctr. for the Study of Complications in Diabetes. Contbr. chpts. to books, articles to profl. jours. Grantee, NIH, 1989, 1994, 1997, 1998, 2001, 2003, 2006, Juvenile Diabetes Rsch. Found., 1994, 1997, 1999, 2001, 2006, Am. Diabetes Assn., 2005. Achievements include research on the elucidation of the role of growth factors in the pathogenesis of human disease.

FELDMAN, FRANKLIN, retired lawyer, printmaker; b. NYC, Nov. 12, 1927; s. Reuben and Anne (Schulman) F.; m. Naomi Goldstein, June 3, 1956; children: Sarah, Eve, Jacob. BA, NYU, 1948; LLB, Columbia U., 1951. Bar: N.Y. 1952. Mem. office Gen. Counsel, USAF, Dept. Def., Washington, 1951-53; atty. office gen. counsel to gov. State of N.Y., Albany, 1954; assoc. Stroock & Stroock & Lavan, NYC, 1955-64, ptnr., 1965-88, counsel, 1989—2004; ret., 2004. Cons. Temp. N.Y. Commn. on Constl. Conv., 1967; lectr. in law Columbia Law Sch., 1979-2001. Editor-in-chief Columbia U. Law Rev., 1950-51; author: (with Stephen E. Weil) Art Works: Law, Policy and Practice, 1974, Art Law, 1986 (Best Law Book Published in 1986, Scribes); contbr. articles to profl. jours. Trustee Am. Jewish Hist. Soc., Waltham, Mass., 1987-96. 1st lt., USAF, 1951-53. Yaddo Fellow, Saratoga Springs, 1983. Fellow Am. Bar Found. (life); mem. Assn. Bar City of N.Y. (chmn. art com. 1968-71), Internat. Found. Art Rsch. (pres. 1971-76, bd. dirs. 1976-96), Ltd., Soc. Am. Graphic Artists, Century Assn., Pvt. Art Dealers Assn., Inc. (counsel, dir. 1993-2006), Grolier Club. Jewish. Home: 15 W 81st St New York NY 10024-6022 Personal E-mail: ffeldman1@nyc.rr.com.

FELDMAN, GARY JAY, physicist, researcher; b. Cheyenne, Wyo., Mar. 22, 1942; married; 2 children. BS, U. Chgo., 1964; AM, Harvard U., 1965, PhD in Physics, 1971. Research assoc. in physics Stanford Linear Accelerator Ctr., Stanford U., Calif., 1971-74, staff physicist Calif., 1974-79, assoc. prof. Calif., 1979-83, prof. Calif., 1983-90; prof. physics Harvard U., Cambridge, Mass., 1990-92, Frank B. Baird, Jr. prof. sci., 1992—, chmn. dept. physics, 1994-97. Sci assoc. CERN, Switzerland, 1982-83. Fellow Am. Phys. Soc. (chmn. divsn. particles and fields 1992), Am. Acad. Arts and Scis. Office: Harvard U Lyman Lab Cambridge MA 02138 Office Phone: 617-496-1044. E-mail: feldman@physics.harvard.edu.

FELDMAN, GARY MARC, nutritionist, consultant; m. Debra Lynn. Diploma in Sci. of Nutritional Cons., Am. Nutrition Cons. Assn., 1986. Pres. Steps In Health, Ltd., Douglaston, NY, 1986-88, Margate, Fla., 1988-90, Lake Grove, NY, 1990—. Freelance health/nutrition writer; educator in sci. of food and nutritional supplementation; spkr., writer on genetically modified organisms related to food; instr. adult program Great Neck Pub. Schs., 2007. Developer: Steps in Health Ltd.'s Catalogue of Vegetarian Name-Brand Nutritional Supplements and Health Products; author nutrition newsletter; contbr. health/nutrition articles to jour. Vol. listen to children program Mental Health Assn. and Vol. Program Broward County (Fla.) Pub. Schs., 1989; arbitration participant Better Bus. Bur. South Fla., 1989-90. Mem. Life Extension Found., Pub. Citizen Health Rsch. Group, People for Ethical Treatment of Animals, Doris Day Animal League, Humane Soc. Broward County, Ctr. for Sci. in the Pub. Interest, Internat. Platform Assn., N.Y. State Sheriffs Assn., L.I. Assn. Inc., Herb Rsch. Found., Vegetarian Resource Group, N.Am. Vegetarian Soc., Nutritionists Health Am. (nutrition edn. program com.), Ctr. Sci. Pub. Interest (edn. com.), Feingold Assn., U.S. Co-op Am. Bus. Network, N.Y. Acad. Scis. Avocations: reading and data collection in health field, bodybuilding. Office: PO Box 220123 Great Neck NY 11022-0123

FELDMAN, GRACE A., music educator; b. Bklyn., Mar. 17, 1940; d. Ben Feldman and Sadie Goldberg. BA, Bklyn. Coll., 1960; MMus, Yale U., 1963. Asst. dir. viol studies N.Y. Pro Musica, 1959—60; dir. viol studies Boston Mus. Fine Arts, 1964—71; instr. viola da gamba Wellesley Coll., Mass., 1964—70; instr. viola da gamba, violin, viola, recorder and ensemble coach Neighborhood Music Sch., New Haven, 1964—, chair ensemble dept., 1966—, chair early music dept., 1980—, chair string dept., 1982—; instr. viola da gamba New Eng. Conservatory, Boston, 1971—85. Tchr. viol Viola da Gamba Soc., 1991—; dir. ensemble program Ednl. Ctr. for the Arts, New Haven, 1973—75; instr. viola da gamba Hartt Sch. Music, West Hartford, Conn., 1978—81; dir. New Eng. Consort of Viols, 1973—90; performer various venues including Manhattan Consort, N.Y. Pro Musica Viol Consort, Stanley Buetens Lute Trio, N.Y. Consort of Viols, Lyric Hexachord, others; condr. workshops in field; performances include Clarion Concerts, 1969—71, Richard Lalli, 1995; many others. Author: The Golden Viol, 1994—2004, Baroque Ensemble Books, 1989—93, Baroque Duos, 1990—93, Stepping Stones, 2005—07; musician: (CDs) Classic Editions: Manhattan Consort, N.Y. Pro Musica, Vanguard: Joan Baez, The Playford Consort, many others. Recipient Women in Leadership award, New Haven YMCA, 1984, Cert. of Merit, Yale Sch. Music, 1989, Arts award, Arts Coun. Greater New Haven, 1996, Elm and Ivy award, Cmty. Found., 1999, Excellence in Music Tchg., N.H. Symphony, 2004; grantee Walter Braun Meml. prize, Bklyn. Coll., 1960; scholar Selma Stein Music scholar, 1960. Mem.: Viola da Gamba Soc. (bd. dirs. 1984—89, edn. com. 1988—), Playford Consort, New Eng. Viol Consort (dir. 1973—90), N.Y. Viol Consort. Home: 100 York St 15E New Haven CT 06511-5623

FELDMAN, H. LARRY, lawyer; b. Tyler, Tex., Apr. 18, 1941; s. Henry and Bess (Booken) F.; m. Janice Kay Asner, June 26, 1960; children: Joseph, Katherine. BA, U. Okla., 1963; JD, So. Meth. U., 1966. Bar: Tex. 1966, US Dist. Ct. (no. dist.) Tex. 1969, US Supreme Ct. 1976. Adj. prof. law U. Dallas, 1967-68; mem. dept. tax Peat, Marwick & Mitchell, 1968-69; atty. Marks, Time & Aranson, 1970; ptnr. Feldman, O'Donnell & Neil, Dallas, 1971; sole practice Dallas, 1971—. Mem. ATLA, Tex. Trial Lawyers Assn., Phi Alpha Delta. Jewish. Personal E-mail: janicedallas@hotmail.com.

FELDMAN, HARRIET RUTH, dean; b. Bklyn., May 5, 1945; d. Mickey and Florence (Gordon) Martin; m. Ronald M. Feldman, Dec. 22, 1973; children: Craig, Jaime. Diploma in nursing, L.I. Coll. Hosp., 1965; BS, Adelphi U., 1968, MS, 1971; PhD, NYU, 1984. Asst. dean Adelphi U., Garden City, N.Y., 1984-87; prof., chairperson dept. nursing Fairleigh Dickinson U., Teaneck, N.J., 1987-93; dean Lienhard Sch. Nursing Pace U., 1993—. Pres. Deans and Dirs. of Nursing Greater NY, 2001—, Strategies for Nursing Leadership, 2001; accreditation site visitor Commn. on Collegiate Nursing Edn., 1999—. Editor: Nursing Leadership Forum, 1998—, Nursing Leaders Speak Out: Issues and Opinions, 2001; co-author: Nurses in the Political Arena: The Public Face of Nursing, 2000; contbr. articles to profl. jours. Fellow: Am. Acad. Nursing; mem.: Am. Assn. Colls. Nursing (mentor Leadership for Acad. Nursing program 1999—2002). Home: 2243 Brody Ln Bellmore NY 11710-5101 E-mail: hfeldman@pace.edu.

FELDMAN, HELAINE, editor, public relations associate; b. Bklyn., June 22, 1937; d. Joseph H. and Ruth Levine; m. Chester Feldman, Aug. 6, 1961; children: Jeffrey, David. BS, Syracuse Univ., Syracuse, NY, 1958. Assoc. editor Dick Moore & Assoc., Inc., New York, NY, 1966—, sr. assoc., 1966—. Contbg. editor: (newsletter) Equity News, 1975, Aftra Mag., 1990. Mem.: Drama Desk, Coalition of Profl. Women in the Arts & Media, League of Profl. Theatre Women. Home: 144-09 Coolidge Ave Briarwood NY 11435 Office: Dick Moore & Assoc 165 W 46th St New York NY 10036 Office Phone: 212-719-9570. E-mail: helfel22@aol.com.

FELDMAN, IRVING, poet; b. Bklyn., Sept. 22, 1928; m. Carmen Alvarez del Olmo, 1955; 1 son, Fernando R. Student, CCNY, Columbia U. Formerly prof. English U. PR, Rio Piedras, Kenyon Coll., Gambier; disting. prof. English SUNY, Buffalo, 1964—2005, disting. prof. emeritus, 2005—. Author: Works and Days, 1961, The Pripet Marshes, 1965, Magic Papers, 1970, Lost Originals, 1972, Leaping Clear, 1976, New and Selected Poems, 1979, Teach Me, Dear ister, 1983, All of Us Here, 1986, The Life and Letters, 1994, Beautiful False Things, 2000, Collected Poems, 1954-2004; contbr. to periodicals. Recipient poetry prize Jewish Book Coun. Am., 1962, award Nat. Inst. and AAAL, 1973; Ingram Merrill Found. grantee, 1963, N.Y. State Creative Artists Pub. Svc. grantee, 1980; Guggenheim fellow, 1973, Acad. Am. Poets fellow, 1986, MacArthur fellow, 1992; grantee Nat. Endowment for the Arts, 1987. Office: SUNY Dept English Buffalo NY 14260-0001 E-mail: leftyfeldman@hotmail.com.

FELDMAN, JACQUELINE, retired small business owner; b. Bklyn., May 21, 1936; d. Emanuel L. and Tillie Rappon; m. Gerald D. Feldman (dec.); children: Bruce G., Lee A. Owner Sweet Stop Inc., Staten Is., NY, 1978—86; purchasing agent Va. Med. Ctr., Bklyn., 1971—78. Mem. arts and culture bd. City of Pembrooke Pines, Fla., 1990—94; vol., bd. mem. Deborah Heart, Pembrooke Pines, 1999—2006. Mem.: Half Century Club (pres., founder 1993—2000). Democrat. Jewish. Home: 1151 SW 128 Ter #D405 Pembroke Pines FL 33027

FELDMAN, JEFFREY MARK, anesthesiologist; b. Phila., Sept. 30, 1956; m. Debra Feldman. BA in Physics, Franklin and Marshall Coll., Lancaster, PA, 1978; MS in Bioengineering, U. Pa., Phila., 1980; MD, Albany Med. Coll., NY, 1983. Cert. Am. Bd. Anesthesiology, 1987. Divsn. chief gen. anesthesia Children's Hosp. Phila., 2006—. Tech. sect. editor: jour. Anesthesia and Analgesia, 2006—07. Achievements include patents for system and method of multi-sensor fusion of physiological measurements. Office: Children's Hospital Phila 34th and Civic Ctr Blvd 9th Fl Main Philadelphia PA 19129 Office Phone: 215-590-1858.

FELDMAN, JOEL MARTIN, retired judge; b. Atlanta, Jan. 2, 1941; s. Louis Aaron and Rosalie (Bach) F.; m. Debora A. Kirkpatrick; children: Lawrence A., Allison R. AB in Law, Emory U., 1962, JD, 1964. Bar: Ga. 1963, U.S. Dist. Ct. (no. dist.) Ga. 1963, U.S. Ct. Mil. Appeals 1964, U.S. Ct. Appeals (5th cir.) 1963, U.S. Ct. Appeals (11th cir.) 1981, U.S. Supreme Ct. 1967. Asst. legis. counsel Gen. Assembly Ga., Atlanta, 1964-66; asst. atty. gen. State of Ga., Atlanta, 1966-68; asst. dist. atty. Atlanta Jud. Cir., 1968-72, 74; legis. asst., legal counsel Sen. Sam Nunn of Ga., 1973-74; magistrate U.S. Dist. Ct. (no. dist.) Ga., Atlanta, 1974—2006; cert. mil. judge Naval-Marine Corps Trial Judiciary, 1982-92; ret., 2006. Former chmn. North Fulton Citizens Mental Health Adv. Coun.; pres. Temple Sinai Synagogue, Atlanta, 1994-96; chmn. Met. Atlanta 50th Ann. WWII Commemorative Cmty. With USAFR, 1964, capt. USNR, 1964-92. Mem. Fed. Bar Assn., State Bar Ga., Atlanta Bar Assn., Naval League U.S. (pres. Atlanta coun. 1985-86), Naval Res. Assn. (pres. 6th Dist. 1982-83), Fed. Magistrate Judges Assn. (dir. 11th cir. 1982-83), Atlanta Lawyers Club, Navy League (Atlanta dir., pres.), Naval Order (Atlanta pres., dir.). Home: 9785 LaView Cir Roswell GA 30075 Personal E-mail: heldman9785@charter.net.

FELDMAN, JOEL SHALOM, mathematician; b. Ottawa, Ont., Can., June 14, 1949; s. Keiva and Anna (Ain) F. BS, U. Toronto, Ont., 1970; AM, Harvard U., 1971, PhD, 1974. Rsch. fellow Harvard U., Cambridge, Mass., 1974-75; Moore instr. MIT, Cambridge, 1975-77; prof. U. B.C., Vancouver, Can., 1977—; Aisenstadt chair lectr., Ctr. Rsch. Math. U. Montréal, 1999—2000. Assoc. editor Revs. Math. Physics, 1988—, Can. Jour. Math., 1994-98, Can. Math. Bull., 1994-98, Math Phys. EJ, 1995—, Ann. Henri Poincaré, 2000—, Jour. Math. Physics, 2005—; contbr. articles to profl. jours. Recipient Killam Rsch. prize U. B.C., 1988, Jeffery-Williams prize CMS, 2004, Faculty of Sci. Achievement award for Tchg., U. B.C., 2004, Killan Tchg. prize Faculty of Sci., 2006-07, prize in theoretical and math. physics Can. Assn. Physicists-Ctr. Rsch. Math., Ctr. Rsch. Math.-Fields-Pacific Inst. for Math. Scis. prize, 2007; Woodrow Wilson fellow, 1970. Fellow: Royal Soc. Can. (John L. Synge award). Office: U BC Dept Math Vancouver BC Canada V6T 1Z2

FELDMAN, LARRY ROBERT, lawyer; BS, San Fernando Valley State Coll., 1966; JD, Loyola U., 1969. Ptnr. Kaye Scholler LLP. Fellow: Am. Coll. of Trial Lawyers; mem.: Assn. of Bus. Trial Lawyers (bd. of govs.), Am. Bd. of Trial Advocates (v.p.), Internat. Acad. of Trial Lawyers, Calif. Trial Lawyers Assn. (bd. of govs. 1981), LA County Bar Assn. (pres. 1987—88), LA Trial Lawyers Assn. (pres. 1984). Office: Kaye Scholler LLP 1999 Ave of the Stars Ste 1700 Los Angeles CA 90067 Office Phone: 310-788-1090. Office Fax: 310-788-1200. E-mail: larryfeldman@kayescholer.com.*

FELDMAN, LEONARD CECIL, physicist; b. NYC, June 8, 1939; s. Milton and Minnie (Schulman) F.; m. Elizabeth Gecsey, July 5, 1964; children: Gregory, Dana. MS, Rutgers U., 1963, PhD, 1967. Mem. tech. staff radiation physics rsch. dept. AT&T Bell Labs., Murray Hill, NJ, 1967-83, supr. materials interfaces, 1983-84, dept. head materials interfaces and ceramics, 1984-87, dept. head thin film semicondr. rsch., 1987-90, dept. head silicon device rsch., 1990-92, dept. head silicon materials rsch., 1992-96; Stevenson prof. Vanderbilt U., Nashville, 1996—. Guest scientist Aarhus (Denmark) U., 1970-71; vis. prof. Cornell U., Ithaca, N.Y., 1981, 82, 88; cons. Livermore (Calif.) Nat. Lab., 1989—; chmn. Gordon Conf. on Particle Solid Interactions, 1978, Gordon Conf. on Defects in Semicondrs., 1994; chmn. internal sci. coun. Danish Microelectronics Ctr.; mem. adv. com. N.J. Inst. Tech., Colo. Sch. Mines, Livermore Nat. Labs.; disting. vis. scientist Oak Ridge Nat. Lab., 1996—. Co-author: Materials Analysis by Ion Channeling, 1982, Fundamentals of Surface and Thin Film Analysis, 1986 (transl. into Japanese 1988, Russian, 1989), Electronic Thin Film Science, 1992; editor Applied Surface Sci., 1985-96; contbr. over 360 articles on semiconductor interface sci. to sci. jours. Recipient Disting. Merit award in material sci. and engring. U. Ill., 1989, sci. alumni award Drew U., 1995. Fellow AAAS, Am. Phys. Soc. (David Aller award 1999), Am. Vacuum Soc.; mem. IEEE, Materials Rsch. Soc., Am. Ceramic Soc., Danish Acad. Arts and Scis. Achievements include patent on semiconductor heterostructures having GexSi1-x layers, 20 others in thin films; discovery of structure of clean silicon surfaces; first demonstration of preservation of surface structures at buried interfaces; developement of technique of Rutherford Scattering for surface and interface analysis. Home: 510 Belgrave Park Nashville TN 37215-2450 Office: Vanderbilt Univ Dept Physics and Astronomy Nashville TN 37235 Business E-Mail: l.c.feldman@vanderbilt.edu.

FELDMAN, LEWIS G., lawyer; b. NYC, Feb. 13, 1956; BA with highest honors, U. Calif., Santa Cruz, 1978; JD, U. Calif., Davis, 1982. Bar: Calif. 1982. Ptnr. Goodwin Procter LLP, LA. Chair Goodwin Proctor LLP, chair pub.pvt. devel. practice; bd. mem. City of Hope Real Estate Industry Council, Univ. So. Calif. Lusk Ctr. for Real Estate Devel. Editor (exec.): UC Davis Law Rev.; contbr. articles to newspapers & profl. jours.; mem. editl. adv. bd. Real Estate So. Calif. Bd. mem. United Way of Greater LA. Mem.: ABA, Nat. Assn. Bond Lawyers, Nat. Assn. Real Estate Investment Trusts, Urban Land Inst., LA Bar Assn., Beverly Hills Bar Assn. Office: Goodwin Procter LLP 21st Fl MGM Tower 10250 Constellation Blvd Los Angeles CA 90067-6221 Office Phone: 310-788-5188. Business E-Mail: lfeldman@goodwinprocter.com.

FELDMAN, MARC DAVID, psychiatrist; b. Kingston, NY, Sept. 9, 1958; AB, Dartmouth Coll., 1980, MD, 1984. Diplomate Am. Bd. Psychiatry and Neurology, Am. Acad. Pain Mgmt, Nat. Bd. Med. Examiners. Resident in psychiatry Duke U. Med. Ctr., Durham, NC, 1984-88, asst. prof., 1988-90; chief resident in psychiatry Durham VA Med. Ctr., NC, 1987-88; med. dir. Hill Crest Hosp., Birmingham, Ala., 1990-93; vice chair dept. psychiatry U. Ala., 1993—2002, med. dir. Ctr. for Psychiat. Medicine, 1993—2002, dir. divsn. adult psychiatry, 1994—2002, clinical prof. psychiatry, 2002—. Acting dir. psychosocial support program Duke Comprehensive Cancer Ctr., 1989-90; pvt. practice, 1990-93; med. dir. United Behavioral Sys., 1996—1999. Contbr. articles to profl. jours. Laughlin fellow Am. Coll. Psychiatrists, 1988; Rufus Choate scholar Dartmouth Coll., 1977-79, others. Mem.: Birmingham Psychiat. Soc., Ala. Psychiat. Assn., Am. Psychiat. Assn., Phi Beta Kappa. Avocations: movies, computing, collecting contemporary art. Office Phone: 205-529-1500. Personal E-mail: mdf@myself.com.

FELDMAN, MARK I., lawyer; b. Mar. 15, 1950; BSIE with honors, Univ. Ill., 1971; JD, Georgetown Univ., 1974. Bar: Ill. 1974, US Dist. Ct. (no. dist.) Ill., US Ct. Appeals (7th and Fed. cir.), US Patent and Trademark Off. Sr. trademark counsel G.D. Searle & Co.; ptnr. DLA Piper Rudnick Gray Cary US LLP, Chgo. Mem.: ABA, Am. Intellectual Property Assn. (chair, franchising com. 1997—2000), Intellectual Property Law Assn. Chgo. (bd. mgrs. 1996—97, v.p. 2002—03, pres.-elect 2004, pres. 2005), Internat. Trademark Assn., Brand Names Edn. Found. Office: DLA Piper Rudnick Gray Cary US LLP Ste 1900 203 N LaSalle St Chicago IL 60601-1293 Office Phone: 312-368-7084. Office Fax: 312-236-7516. Business E-Mail: mark.feldman@dlapiper.com.

FELDMAN, MARTHA SUE, political scientist, educator; b. Oak Ridge, Tenn., Mar. 31, 1953; d. Melvin J. and Nancy Ann (McCarty) Feldman; m. Hobart Taylor, III, Oct. 30, 1993; 1 child, Bruce Alexander Feldman Taylor. BA in Polit. Sci., U. Wash., 1976; MA in Polit. Sci., Stanford U., 1980, PhD in Polit. Sci., 1983. Asst. prof. dept. polit. sci., asst. rsch. sci. Inst. Pub. Policy Studies U. Mich., Ann Arbor, 1983—89, assoc. prof. dept. polit. sci., 1989—2001, assoc. prof. Sch. Pub. Policy, 1995—2001, prof. polit. sci. and pub. policy, 2001—03, assoc. dean Ford Sch. Pub. Policy, 2001—03; prof., Johnson chair for civic governance and pub. mgmt., dept. policy, planning and design Sch. Social Ecology, U. Calif. Irvine, 2003—. Health svcs. rschr. U. Wash., Seattle, 1975—76; cons. to Com. on Ability Testing NAS, Washington, 1980; regulatory impact analyst for fossil fuels Dept. Energy, Washington, 1980—81; vis. scholar Stanford U. Ctr. Orgns. Rsch., Calif., 1990—91; vis. prof. Luigi Bocconi U., Milan, 1991, Swedish Sch. Econs., Helsinki, Finland, 1992, U. Bergen, Norway, 2002. Author: Order Without Design: Information Production and Policy Making, 1989, Strategies for Interpreting Qualitative Data, 1994; co-author: Reconstructing Reality in the Courtroom, 1981, Gaining Access, 2003; editor: Orgn. Sci., 2006—; contbr. articles to profl. jours. NIMH fellow, 1978—79, Brookings Instn. Rsch. fellow, 1979—80, Ameritech fellow, 1986, Rackham Faculty Rsch. grantee, 1984—85. Office: U Calif Irvine Dept Policy Planning and Design 226G Social Ecology I Irvine CA 92697-7075 E-mail: feldmanm@uci.edu.

FELDMAN, MARVIN HERSCHEL, financial consultant; b. East Liverpool, Ohio, Dec. 1, 1945; s. Ben and Freda (Zaremberg) F.; m. Vicki Jo Smith, Mar. 18, 1967; children: Terri Nicole, Barbi Lynn. BS, Ohio State U., 1967. CLU, chartered fin. cons. Agt. N.Y. Life Ins. Co., Columbus, Ohio, 1967-69, 74—, asst. mgr., 1969-74; ptnr. Feldman Agy., East Liverpool, 1974—; corp. sec., v.p. Fremar Corp., East Liverpool, 1974—; pres. Fremar Mgmt. Co., Youngstown, 1975-89, Fremar Fin. Group, East Liverpool, 1983—2004; mng. exec. Royal Alliance Assocs., Inc., East Liverpool, 1983—2003; reg. rep. Valmark Securities, Inc., 2003—; prin. Feldman Fin. Group, 2003—. Founding dirs. 1st Nat. Cmty. Bank, East Liverpool, Ohio, 1987—; mem., sec. agt. adv. coun. NY Life, NYC, 1985-86; spkr. in field. Contbr. articles to profl. jours. Mem. Econ. Devel. Com., East Liverpool; chmn. United Jewish Appeal, East Liverpool, Ohio, 1976—2002; v.p., sec. Temple Beth Shalom, East Liverpool; bd. dirs. East Liverpool City Hosp., 1992—2001, chmn., 1998—99. Mem. Nat. Assn. Ins. and Fin. Advisors, Am. Soc. Fin. Svc. Profls., Fin. Planners Assn., Assn. Advanced Life Underwriters, Million Dollar Round Table (life, v.p. divsn. 1985-86, ann. meeting chmn. 1998, exec. com. 1998-2003, pres. 2002), Top of the Table (bd. dirs. 1982-87, chmn. 1985-86, Million Dollar Round. Table Found. Cir of Life award 2004). Republican. Avocations: golf, reading, sports car racing, boating. Office: Feldman Fin Group 28870 US 19N Ste 337 Clearwater FL 33761 Office Phone: 727-723-9020. Business E-Mail: tfa@financialprtnr.com.

FELDMAN, NANCY JANE, insurance company executive; b. Green Bay, Wis., July 6, 1946; d. Benjamin J. and Ellen M. Naze; m. Robert P. Feldman, Aug. 24, 1968 (dec. May 2006); 1 child, Sara J. BA, U. Wis., 1969, MS, 1974. Supr. EPSDT program Minn. Dept. Human Svcs., St. Paul, 1974-80, supr. healthcare programs, 1980-84; team leader human resources budget Minn. Dept. Fin., St. Paul, 1984-87; asst. commr. Minn. Dept. Health, St. Paul, 1987-91; team leader CORE program Minn. Dept. Adminstrn., St. Paul, 1991-93; dir. state pub. programs Medica, Allina Health Sys., Mpls., 1993-95; CEO UCare Minn., St. Paul, 1995—. Bd. mem. Minn. Coun. Health Plans, Mpls., 1995-, Ctr. for Victims of Torture, 1997- (chair 2004-06, vice-chair 2007-), Stratis Health, 2000-, Nat. Inst. Health Policy, 2002-, Assn. Cmty. Health Plans, 2003-; chair Health Care Devel. Com., Vols. Am. Nat. Svc., 2005-. Mem. Women's Health Leadership Trust. Avocations: distance swimming, bicycling, travel. Office: UCare Minn PO Box 52 Minneapolis MN 55440-0052 Home: 4822 Folwell Dr Minneapolis MN 55406 Business E-Mail: nfeldman@ucare.org.

FELDMAN, NOAH, law educator; b. 1970; m. Jeannie Suk. AB summa cum laude, Harvard U., 1992; DPhil in Islamic Thought, Oxford U., 1994; JD, Yale U., 1997. Bar: NY 1998. Law clk. to Hon. Harry T. Edwards US Ct. Appeals DC Cir., 1997—98; law clk. to Hon. David H. Souter US Supreme Ct., 1998—99; jr. fellow Soc. Fellows Harvard U., Cambridge, Mass., 1999—2001; asst. prof. law NYU Sch. Law, 2001—04, assoc. prof., 2004—05, prof., 2005—, Cecelia Goetz prof. law, 2006—. Adj. fellow New Am. Found., Washington; vis. prof. Yale U., 2004, Harvard U., 2005. Author: After Jihad: America and the Struggle for Islamic Democracy, 2003, What We Owe Iraq: War and the Ethics of Nation Building, 2004, Divided by God: America's Church-State Problem and What We Should Do About It, 2005. Named one of NY Influentials, NY Mag., 2006; Rhodes scholar. Office: NYU Sch Law Vanderbilt HallRm 411C 40 Washington Sq S New York NY 10012-1099 Office Phone: 212-998-6711. E-mail: noah.feldman@nyu.edu.

FELDMAN, RACHEL BETH, psychologist; d. Sidney and Frieda Feldman. BA magna cum laude, Wesleyan U., 1977; MSc, Columbia U., 1986, MPhil, 1987, PhD, 1990. Lic. psychologist NY, 1991. Spl. edn. therapist Soundview Throggs Neck Cmty. Mental Health Ctr., Albert Einstein, Bronx, NY, 1980—83; psychology intern St. Luke's Hosp., NYC, 1986—87; rsch. interviewer, dept. genetic epidemiology NY State Psychiat. Inst., NYC, 1988—92; psychologist Our Lady Mercy Med. Ctr., Bronx, 1990—93, Beth Israel Med. Ctr., NYC, 1993—94, Health Ins. Plan Greater N.Y./Queens Mental Health Svc., Rego Park, NY, 1993—. Program designer, tchr. Ramah Day Camp, Nyack, NY, 1975, Oddfellows Children's Theatre, Middletown, Conn., 1975—76, Youth Svcs. Dept., Middletown, Conn., 1977; conf. co-coord. Clin. Psychology Students' Assn., NYC, 1986. Fellowship, Thomas J. Watson Found., 1978-1979. Mem.: APA, Greek Am. Behavioral Sci. Inst. Office: HIP Queens Mental Health 97 45 Queens Blvd Rego Park NY 11374 Office Phone: 718-459-0500 1224. Personal E-mail: rfeldman1@earthlink.net.

FELDMAN, ROBERT C. (BOB), public relations executive; b. NYC, Oct. 22, 1956; BA, Syracuse U., 1978. Gen. mgr. Sta. WPNR-FM Utica Coll. Syracuse U., 1976-78; from asst. acct. exec. to sr. v.p., group mgr. Burson-Marsteller, 1978-88; sr. v.p. Ketchum Pub. Rels., NYC, 1988-97; pres., CEO GCI Group, Inc., 1997—2005; head corp. comms. DreamWorks Animation SKG, Glendale, Calif., 2005—07; founder, mng. ptnr., CEO Feldman & Ptnrs., LA, 2007—. Adj. prof. corp. reputation U. So. Calif.; lectr. in field. Contbr. articles to profl. jours. Bd. dirs. Thurgood Marshall Scholarship Fund; bd. trustees Pub. Rels. Inst. Mem.: Arthur Page Soc., Coun. Pub. Rels. Firms (bd. dirs.), Pub. Rels. Seminar, Pub. Rels. Soc. Am. Office: Feldman & Ptnrs Ste 2000 8491 Sunset Blvd Los Angeles CA 90069 Office Phone: 310-360-0211. Office Fax: 310-360-0250. E-mail: bob@feldmanandpartners.com.*

FELDMAN, ROGER DAVID, lawyer; b. NYC, Apr. 7, 1943; s. Louis and Dora (Goldsmith) Feldman; m. Gail Steg, May 31, 1969; children: Rebecca, Seth. AB, Brown U., 1962; LLB, Yale U.; MBA, Harvard U. Bar: N.Y. 1966, DC 1977. Ops. rsch. analyst Office Asst. Sec. Def., Washington, 1967—68; staff asst. Office US Pres., Washington, 1968—69; assoc. LeBoeuf, Lamb, Leiby, and MacRae, 1969—75; ptnr. Le Boeuf, Lamb, Leiby; and MacRae, 1977—83; dep. asst. adminstr. FEA, Washington, 1975—77; mng. ptnr. project fin. group Nixon, Hargrave, Devans, and Doyle, Washington, 1983—89; head ptnr. project fin. group McDermott, Will, and Emery, Washington, 1989—97; co-chair project fin. group Bingham McCutchen, LLP, 1997—2006, Andrews Kurth LLP, 2006—. Mem. fin. adv. bd. EPA, 1989—92; bd. dir. R. J. Rudden and Assocs., Inc., Cogeneration Inst., Am. Coun. Renewable Energy, chair environ. credits com.; bd. dir. Water Industry Coun., N.E. Energy and Commerce Assn., chair fin. com.; pres. Nat. Coun. Pub. Pvt. Partnerships, 1983—98, chair, 1998—. Author (with others): Infrastructure Finance: Tools for the Future, 1988, Public-Private Ventures in Transportation, 1990; author: Comprehensive Guide to Water and Wastewater Finance, 1991, Privatization of Public Utilities, 1995, Privatization, 1995; mem. bd. editors Yale Law Jour., 1964—65, Jour. Structured and Project Fin., 1995—, Constrn. Bus. Rev., 1992—; Wash. editor: Cogeneration Monthly Letter, 1987—98, Merchant Power Monthly, 1998—; editor: Strategic Planning for Energy and the Environment, 1992— (Author of the Yr., 1998), Power Marketers Assn. On Line Mag., 1999—, Power Exec., 2002—; contbr. articles to profl. jours. Mem.: ABA (chmn. energy law com. 1980—83, alt. energy sources com. 1981—84, chmn. environ. values com. 1983—89, chair privatization 1985—90, chair energy sources com. 1986—90, chmn. energy fin. 1990—91, chair renewable energy resources 2003—06, chair spl. com. energy & environ. fin. 2006—), Assn. Energy Engr. (Cogeneration Profl. of the Yr. 1990), DC Bar Assn. (chair internat. fin. and investment com. 1998—), NY Bar Assn., Nat. Coun. Pub. and Pvt. Partnerships (Outstanding Contbn. to Privatization award), Fed. Energy Bar Assn. (chmn. cogeneration com. 1981—82), Internat. Pct. Infrastructure Assn. (v.p.), Internat. Pvt. Water Assn. (v.p.), N.E. Energy and Commerce Assn. (bd. dirs., chair reliability and security com.), Phi Beta Kappa. Office Phone: 202-662-3048. Business E-Mail: rogerfeldman@andrewskurth.com.

FELDMAN, ROGER LAWRENCE, artist, educator; b. Spokane, Wash., Nov. 19, 1949; s. Marvin Lawrence and Mary Elizabeth (Shafer) Feldman; m. Astrid Lunde, Dec. 16, 1972; children: Kirsten B., Kyle Lawrence. BA in Art Edn., U. Wash., 1972; postgrad., Fuller Theol. Sem., Pasadena, Calif., 1972—73, Regent Coll., Vancouver, B.C., 1974; MFA in Sculpture, Claremont Grad. U., Calif., 1977. Tchg. asst. Claremont Grad. U.; prof. art Biola U., La Mirada, Calif., 1989-2000, Seattle Pacific U., 2000—. Adj. instr. Seattle Pacific U., 1979-80, 82-83, Linfield Coll., 1978, Edmonds C.C., 1978-80, Shoreline C.C., 1978; guest artist and lectr. One-man shows include Art Ctr. Gallery, Seattle Pacific U., 1977, 83, 84, Linfield Coll., McMinnville, Oreg., 1979, Blackfish Gallery, Portland, 1982, Lynn McAllister Gallery, Seattle, 1986, Biola U., 1989, 93, Coll. Gallery, La. Coll., Pineville, 1990, Gallery W, Sacramento, 1991, 96, Aughinbaugh Gallery, Grantham, Pa., 1992, Riverside Art Mus., 1994, Azusa Pacific U., 1995, Cornerstone '96, Bushnell, Ill., 1996, Barnsdall Art Park, LA, 1996, Davison Gallery Roberts Wesleyan Coll., Rochester, NY, 1997, Concordia U., Irvine, Calif., 1999, Northwestern Coll., St. Paul, 2000, Union U., Jackson, Tenn., 2001, F. Schaeffer Inst., St. Louis, 2001, G. Fox U., Newberg, Oreg., 2001, Seattle Pacific U., 2002, Suyama Space, Seattle, 2005, Schloss Mittersill, Austria, 2005, Beyond Malibu, Princess Louisa Inlet, BC, Can., 2007; numerous group shows including most recently Weaver Art Gallery, Bethel Coll., Mishawaka, Ind., 1998-, Concordia U. Art Gallery, Mequon, Wis., 1999, Palos Verdes Art Ctr., Calif., 1999, Grand Canyon U., Phoenix, 2000, Tryon Ctr. Visual Arts, Charlotte, NC, 2001, U. Dallas, 2001, Weaver Gallery, 2001, John Brown U., Siloam Springs, Ark., 2001, Sweetwater Ctr. for the Arts, Sewickley, Pa., 2002, Ind. Wesleyan U., Marion, 2002, Tacoma Art Mus., 2004, Mus. Bibl. Art, NYC, 2005, Gordon Coll., Wenham, Mass., 2006, Schloss Mittersill, Austria, 2007; comms. Wheaton, Pasadena, Calif., 1999, Renton Vocat. Tech Inst., 1987-89. Recipient King County Arts Commn. Individual Artist Project award, Seattle, 1988, Natl. Endowment for the Arts Individual Artist fellowship in Sculpture, 1986, David Gaiser award for sculpture Cheney Cowles Mus., 1980, Disting. award for Harborview Med. Ctr. "Viewpoint", Soc. for Tech. Comm., 1987, Design award for "Seafirst News", Internat. Assn. Bus. Comm., 1987, Pace Setter award, 1987, Prescott Sculpture award Christians in the Visual Arts, 2005, others; Connemara Sculpture grant, 1990, Biola U., 1991; Faculty Rsch. grantee Seattle Pacific U., 2001-02, Sr. Faculty Rsch. grantee, 2005-06, Faculty Rsch. grantee, 2007. Office: Seattle Pacific U 3307 Third Ave West Seattle WA 98119 Home Phone: 206-282-4634; Office Phone: 206-281-3442. Business E-Mail: rfeldman@spu.edu. E-mail: rakfeldman2@comcast.net.

FELDMAN, RONALD ARTHUR, sociologist, educator, social worker; b. Buffalo, Jan. 17, 1938; s. David Jacob and Clara (Spector) F.; m. Dina Cohen Feinstein, Dec. 23, 1962; children: Daniel, Deborah, Darrah. BA, U. Buffalo, 1960; MSW, U. Mich., 1963, PhD, 1966. Cert., Acad. Cert. Social Workers. Asst. prof. U. Calif., Berkeley, 1966-68; Fulbright lectr. Social Services Acad., Ankara, Turkey, 1968-69; assoc. prof. Washington U. Sch. Social Work, St. Louis, 1969-72, prof., 1972-86, acting dean, 1973-74; dir. Ctr. for Study of Youth Devel., Boys Town, Nebr., 1974-78, Ctr. for Adolescent Mental Health, St. Louis, 1983-87; assoc. dean Columbia U. Sch. Social Work, NYC, 1985-86, prof., dean, 1986—2001, Ruth Harris Ottman Centennial prof., 1995—, dir. Ctr. for Study of Social Work Practice, 2002—, dean emeritus, 2001—. Cons. NIMH, Rockville, Md., 1980-91; bd. dirs. Ednl. Inst., Jewish Bd. Family and Children's Svcs., N.Y.C., 1986-2004, William T. Grant Found., Bd. Behavior and Mental Disorders, Inst. Medicine. Sr. author: Contemporary Approaches to Group Treatment, 1975, The St. Louis Conundrum: The Effective Treatment of Antisocial Youths, 1983, Children at Risk: In the Web of Parental Mental Illness, 1987; sr. editor: Advances in Adolescent Mental Health, vols. 1-4, 1986—. Citizen leader Clayton (Mo.) Bd. Edn., 1981-82; mem. profl. rev. bd. Mo. Dept. Mental Health, Jefferson City, 1981-86; trustee Wm. T. Grant Found., 1993-2004 Recipient Disting. Faculty award Washington U., St. Louis, 1984; research grantee NIMH, Rockville, Md., 1970-75, 80-84, Office of Human Devel. Services, Washington, 1983-87. Fellow NASW, Soc. for Rsch. in Child Devel.; mem. Coun. on Social Work Edn. (bd. dirs. 1992-95), Am. Sociol. Assn., Internat. Assn. Child and Adolescent Psychiatry and Allied Professions (v.p. 1995-2005). Avocations: swimming, tennis. Office: Columbia U Sch Social Work 1255 Amsterdam Ave New York NY 10027 Office Phone: 212-851-2265. Business E-Mail: rafi@columbia.edu.

FELDMAN, SAMUEL MITCHELL, neuroscientist, educator; b. Phila., Sept. 26, 1933; s. Boris and Fanya B. (Shrager) F.; children— Lee Stephen, David Saul. BA, U. Pa., 1954; MA, Northwestern U., 1955; PhD, McGill U., 1959. Fellow in physiology U. Wash., Seattle, 1958-60; from instr. to asso. prof. physiology Albert Einstein Coll. Medicine, 1960-71; prof. psychology N.Y. U., 1971—, head dept., 1972-76, prof. neuroscience, 1988—, dir. grad. studies neural sci., 1989—; mem. psychol. sci. study sect. NIMH, 1968-72, chmn., 1970-72, mem. biol. sci. tng. grant rev. com., 1977-83. Cons. in field. Contbr. articles to profl. jours. Fellow USPHS, 1958-60; recipient Career award, 1969-71, research grantee, 1963— Mem. Am. Physiol. Soc., Soc. Neurosci., Sigma Xi. Home: 336 Ctrl Pk W New York NY 10025 Office: New York Univ Ctr for Neural Science New York NY 10003

FELDMAN, SARI, library director; b. May 29, 1953; With Onondaga County Pub. Libr.; head cmty. svcs. Cleve. Pub. Libr., 1997, dep. dir.; exec. dir. Cuyahoga County Pub. Libr., Ohio, 2003—. Adj. faculty mem. Syracuse U. Sch. Info. Studies; mem. WebJunction E-Learning Adv. Com. Co-author (with Sandra Feinberg and Joan Kuchner): Learning Environments for Young Children: Rethinking Library Space and Services, 1998. Pres. Cuyahoga County Pub. Libr. Found. Bd. Office: Cuyahoga County Pub Libr 2111 Snow Rd Parma OH 44134 Office Phone: 216-749-9490.*

FELDMAN, SHANA MADIGAN, legal assistant; b. Washington, Feb. 20, 1977; d. Michael James Madigan and Donna Tolli Bartlett, George Lewis Bartlett (B. General USMC, Retired) (Stepfather); m. Juan Pablo Feldman, Nov. 19, 2005; 1 child, Joaquin Patrick. BA, U. Pa., Phila., 1999; JD, Georgetown U., Washington, 2004. Bar: Md. 2004. Jud. law clk. to chief judge Thomas F. Hogan US Dist. Ct., Washington, 2004—06; legal asst. O'Sullivan, Graev & Karabell (now O'Melveny), NYC, 1999—2000. Liberal. Avocations: travel, skiing, tennis. Home Phone: 202-518-2520.

FELDMAN, STANLEY GEORGE, lawyer; b. NYC, Mar. 9, 1933; s. Meyer and Esther Betty (Golden) F.; m. Norma Arambula; 1 dau., Elizabeth L. Student, UCLA, 1950—51; LLB, U. Ariz., 1956. Bar: Ariz. 1956. Practiced in, Tucson, 1956-81; ptnr. Miller, Pitt & Feldman, 1968-81; justice Ariz. Supreme Ct., Phoenix, 1982—2002, chief justice, 1992-97; of counsel Haralson, Miller, Pitt Feldman & McAnally. Lectr. Coll. Law, U. Ariz., 1965-76, adj. prof., 1976-81, 2000, 03, 05, 06. Bd. dirs. Tucson Jewish Community Council, U. Ariz. Found., 1999-2005. Mem. ABA, Am. Bd. Trial Advocates (past pres. So. Ariz. chpt.), Ariz. Bar Assn. (pres. 1974-75, bd. govs. 1967-76), Pima County Bar Assn. (past pres.), Am. Trial Lawyers Assn. (dir. chpt. 1967-76), U. Ariz. Law Coll. Assn., Ariz. Trial Lawyers Assn. (bd. dirs. 2006-). Democrat. Jewish. Office: 1 S Church Ave Ste 900 Tucson AZ 85701-1620 Office Phone: 520-792-3836. E-mail: sfeldman@hmpmlaw.com.

FELDMAN, STEPHEN, academic administrator; b. NYC, Sept. 11, 1944; s. Harry and Mae (Morris) F.; m. Constance M. Lerudis, June 1, 1969; children— Jennifer Dawn, Timothy Richard. BBA, CCNY, 1966, MBA, 1968, PhD (fellow), 1971. Chmn. dept. banking, fin. and investments Hofstra U., Hempstead, NY, 1969-77, assoc. prof., 1974-77; dean Ancell Sch. of bus. Western Conn. State U., Danbury, 1977-81, pres., 1981-92, Nova Southeastern U., Ft. Lauderdale, Fla., 1992-94; v.p. real estate Ethan Allen Inc., Danbury, 1995-96; v.p. univ. rels., devel. Calif. State U., Long Beach, 1996-99; pres. Astronaut Meml. Found., Kennedy Space Ctr., Fla., 1999—. Bd. dirs. Ethan Allen Inc., Sci. Horizons Inc.; cons. IBM, N.Y. Telephone Co. Editor: Credit Unions, 1974, Handbook of Wealth Management, 1977, Smarter Money, 1985; contbr. articles to profl. jours. Trustee Danbury Hosp., United Way. Mem. Am. Assn. State Colls. and Univs. (chmn. corp. coll. rels.), Greater Ft. Lauderdale C. of C. Office: Astronaut Meml Found Ctr Space Mail Code Amf Kennedy Space Center FL 32899-0001 E-mail: sfeldman@amfcse.org.

FELDMAN, TED, cardiologist; b. Lincoln, Nebr., Nov. 3, 1952; BA, Ind. U., 1974, MD, 1978. Diplomate Am. Bd. Internal Medicine, Am. Bd. Cardiology. Intern medicine Rush Med. Coll., 1978-79, resident, 1979-81, chief resident, 1981-82; fellow cardiology U. Chgo., 1982-85, asst. prof. medicine, 1985-92, assoc. prof., 1992-97, prof., 1997—, dir. interventional cardiology, 1988—, dir. cardiac catheterization lab., 1997—. Contbr. articles to profl. jours. Fellow Am. Coll. Cardiology, Soc. for Coronary Angiography and Intervention. Office: U Chgo Hosps 5841 S Maryland Ave Rm 5076 Chicago IL 60637-1463

FELDMAN, VITALY, entrepreneur; b. Belarus, 1981; Grad., Pace U., NYC. Fin. advisor, NYC; co-founder & co-pres. MetroHorse.com, Hackensack, NJ, 2006—. Named one of Best Entrepreneurs Under 25, Bus. Week, 2006. Office: MetroHorse 1 University Plz Dr Hackensack NJ 07601 Office Phone: 201-441-9696.

FELDMAN, WALTER SIDNEY, artist, educator; b. Lynn, Mass., Mar. 23, 1925; s. Hyman and Fradel (Gordon) F.; m. Barbara Rose, June 4, 1950; children— Steven, Mark. BFA, Yale U., New Haven, Conn., 1950, MFA, 1951; studied with, Willem de Kooning, 1950—51; MA (hon.), Brown U., Providence, 1953. Instr. painting Yale U., 1951—53; mem. faculty dept. art Brown U., 1953—, prof., 1961—, John Hay prof. bibliography, 1993—, chmn. studio divsn., 1973—; founder Ziggurat Press, 1985—; dir. Brown/Ziggurat Press, 1990—. Vis. prof. Harvard U., 1968, U. Calif., Riverside; artist-in-residence Dartmouth Coll., 1978; cons. Providence Lithography Co.; artist-in-residence Rutgers Ctr. for Innovative Printmaking, 1993. One-man shows include Kruaushaar Galleries, NYC, 1958, 61, 63, Obelisk Gallery, Boston, 1965-66, 67, Inst. Contemporary Arts, London, 1967-68, Bristol Mus., 1975, Hopkins Ctr., Dartmouth Coll., 1978; group shows include Mus. Modern Art, 1954, 55, Bklyn. Mus., 1957-58, 60, Corcoran Gallery, Washington, 1959, Butler Inst. Am. Art, Youngstown, Ohio, 1960, Harvard U. Carpenter Ctr. for Visual Arts, 1963, Lowe Art Ctr., Syracuse, 1964, Inst. Contemporary Art, Boston, 1961, 66; represented in permanent collections at Brown U., Fogg Mus., LA County Mus., Met. Mus. Art, Mus. Modern Art, Phoenix Art Mus., Princeton U., Yale U. Art Gallery, Lehigh U. Art Collection, U. Mass., Mex.-Am. Inst., U. Florence, Italy, Folger Shakespeare Libr., Washington, Fuller Mus., Brockton, Mass., Victoria and Albert Mus., London and others. Served with US Army, 1943-46. Decorated Purple Heart, Combat Inf. Badge; Alice Kimball English fellow Yale U., 1950, Fulbright fellow, Italy, 1956-57; Eliza Howard fellow Mex., 1961; recipient Gov.'s award for arts, 1980. Home: 107 Benevolent St Providence RI 02906-3154 Office: Brown U 64 College St Providence RI 02912-9021 Home Phone: 401-751-6645; Office Phone: 401-863-3365. Business E-Mail: walter_feldman@brown.edu.

FELDMANN, EDWARD GEORGE, pharmaceutical chemist, pharmacologist; b. Chgo., Oct. 13, 1930; s. Edward Louis and Vera (Arnesen) F.; stepmother Helen E. Whitney; m. Mary J. Evans, Aug. 30, 1952; children: Ann Marie Whittington, Edward William, Robert George, Karen Lynn Zaragoza. BS in Chemistry, Loyola U., Chgo., 1952; MS in Pharmacy (research fellow Am. Found. Pharm. Edn. 1953-55), U. Wis., 1954, PhD in Pharm. Chemistry-Biochemistry, 1955; postgrad., Northwestern U., 1956, U. Chgo., 1958. Tchg. asst. Loyola U., Chgo., 1951—52; rsch. asst. U. Wis., 1952—53; sr. chemist Am. Dental Assn., 1955—58, dir. divsn. chemistry, 1958—59; assoc. dir. sci. divsn. Am. Pharm. Assn., 1959—60, dir., 1960—85, assoc. editor sci. edit. assn. jour., 1959—60, editor, 1960—97, assoc. exec. dir. sci. affairs, 1970—83, v.p. sci. affairs, 1983—85, project dir. Handbook of Non-Prescription Drugs, 1985—89, mng. editor, 1989—90, project cons. Handbook on Non-Prescription Drugs, 1991—93, mem. adv. panel, 1994—95; exec. sec. Acad. Pharm. Scis., 1983—85; mem. adv. panel Am. Pharm. Assn., 1994—99; pvt. pharm. cons., 1985—; assoc. dir. revision Nat. Formulary, 1959—60; dir. revision Nat. Fomulary, 1960—70. Adv. panel drugs Nat. Formulary, 1955-60, Am. Pharm. Assn. Handbook of Non-Prescription Drugs, 1994-95; reviewer Internat. Pharmacopeia, WHO, 1958; spl. lectr. drug standards George Washington U., 1960-64; del. conf. on fellowships Nat. Health Council, 1960; mem. coordinating com. Nat. Conf. Antimicrobial Agts., Soc. Indsl. Microbiology, 1960-63; adv. panel pharm. nomenclature A.M.A.-Am. Pharm. Assn.-U.S. Pharmacopeia, 1961-66, nomenclature com., 1962-66; sec. U.S. Com. Internat. Drug Standards, 1964-65; adv. panel food chems. codex Nat. Acad. Scis.-NRC, 1961-71, liaison rep. to drug research bd., 1968-76; spl. liaison rep. to Commn. of Life Scis., NAS-NRC, 1973-85; lab. com. Am. Pharm. Assn. Found., 1961-75; mem. com. Ebert prize, 1961-75; judge Lunsford-Richardson Pharmacy Awards, 1962-69; cons. Council on Drugs, A.M.A., 1962; vis. scientist Am. Assn. Colls. of Pharmacy, NSF, 1963-66; expert adv. panel on internat. pharmacopeia and pharm. preparation World Health Orgn., 1963-75; mem. US President's Task Force on Hosp. Drug Coverage Under Medicare, 1963-64; drug abuse cons. to Office of US Pres., Lyndon B. Johnson, 1965, drug cons. Office Sec., U.S. Dept. Health, Edn. and Welfare, 1967-70; nomenclature cons. to Commr., U.S. Food and Drug Adminstrn., 1968-71; mem. expert working group Indsl. Devel. Orgn., UN, 1969; organizing com. 31st Internat. Congress Pharm. Scis., 1970-71; mem. NRC, 1971-85; del. U.S. Pharmacopeia, 1970-85, 90-95; mem. Nat. Council on Drugs, 1976-83; scientific adv. bd. Biodecision Labs., Inc., 1987-90; scientific cons. Am. Assn. Pharmaceutical Scientists, 1986-93; pharm. scis. cons. ERGO Sci. Inc., 1992—; steering com. Japan-U.S. Pharmaceutical Scis. Congress, 1987; expert witness congressional drug legis. hearings and civil litigation cases, Drug quality specifications, Fed. legal requirements, Clinical pharmacology and Toxicology, 1965-; lectr. in field. *Dr. Feldmann's professional achievements encompassed four broad areas: conducted laboratory research, most notably to experimentally determine relative duration of action of dental local anesthetic agents; subsequently, coordinated and directed development and adoption of official standards of quality for numerous pharmaceutical products; concurrently, edited leading pharmaceutical research journals broadly fostering major advances in medicinal research, while editing numerous drug reference books thereby facilitating transfer of new pharmaceutical information from research laboratories into clinical practice; lastly, served as frequent consultant to government agencies and Congressional committees, helping to shape public policy, regulations, and legislation on various pharmaceutical issues, e.g., generic drug equivalency.* Assoc. editor Drug Standards, 1959-60, editor, 1960; chmn. (1960-70) Nat. Formulary Bd.; editor Jour. Pharm. Scis., 1961-75, cons. editor, 1975-85, 87-89, interim editor, 1991, editor in chief, 1991-94, emeritus editor 1994-95; editor APS Accd. Reporter, 1983-85; author more than 420 articles in field, editor or co-editor 24 ref. books; mem. editorial adv. bd. Index Chemicus, 1968-71; med. contbr. World Book Ency., 1986-88. Mem. membership com. Ravenwood Park Citizens Assn., Falls Church, Va., 1962, mem. nominating com., 1971-72; mem. Lake Barcroft Community Assn., 1975-97. Recipient Spl. Recognition award U.S. Pres. Lyndon Johnson, 1965, Man of Yr. award Nat. Assn. Pharm. Mfrs., 1970, Disting. citation U. Wis., 1971, Commr.'s citation FDA, 1975, G.A. Bergy Lectr. award U. W.Va., 1975, Pres. award Am. Assn. Pharm. Scis., 1993. Fellow Acad. Pharm. Scis.; mem. Am. Pharm. Assn. (life, Hon. Mem. award 2005), Am. Chem. Soc. (emeritus), Am. Assn. Pharm. Scis. (charter mem., fellow, fellows selection com. 1989, Pres.'s award 1993), N.Y. Acad. Scis., Nat. Soc. Med. Rsch. (coun. 1961-69), Am. Testing Materials, Coun. Biology Editors, AMA (affiliate), Fedn. Internat. Pharm., US Tennis Assn., Mid-Atlantic Tennis Assn., Fla. Tennis Assn., Sarasota County Sr. Men's Tennis Assn. (team capt. 2003-), Sleepy Hollow Bath and Racquet Club (Falls Church, Va.), Arlington Tennis and Squash Club, 4-Seasons Tennis Club, Fairfax Golden Racquets Club, Venice (Fla.) Golf and Country Club (bd. mem. tennis assn. 1998-05, pres. 2002-05, mem. sports and health com. 2002-05), K.C., Sigma Xi, Rho Chi, Lambda Chi Sigma. Roman Catholic. Home and Office: 316 Wild Pine Way Venice FL 34292-4624 Office Phone: 941-497-7833. Office Fax: 941-408-0057.

FELDMANN, JUDITH GAIL, language professional, educator; b. Grenora, ND, Jan. 10, 1938; d. Jule and Evelyn (Hagen) F.; children: Robert, Carole Elizabeth. BA magna cum laude, Minot State Tchrs. Coll., 1962; MA, Mich. State U., 1971; postgrad, U. Oslo, 1980, U. London, 1982-85; postgrad., Western Mich. U., 1987, Eastern Mich. U., 1992-93, Harvard U., 1994. Cert. tchr., secondary adminstrn., Mich. English tchr. Minot Pub. Schs., ND, 1961, Charlotte Pub. Schs., Mich., 1962; grad. asst. instr. Mich. State U., East Lansing, 1996; reading specialist, English educator Jackson (Mich.) Pub. Schs., 1964—2005, English educator, 1964—2005. Mem. ASCD, Internat. Reading Assn., Mich. Reading Assn. (presenter Grand Rapids 1995), Jackson Edn. Assn. (v.p.). Home and Office: 2791 Brookside Blvd Jackson MI 49203-5532 Personal E-mail: judithfeldmann@comcast.net.

FELDMAN NEBENZAHL, BERNARDO, composer, educator; b. Mexico City, Sept. 28, 1955; s. Jaime Feldman Shtiglick and Felicie Nebenzahl de Feldman; children: Kendahl May Goldwater-Feldman, Gisèle Aliyah Goldwater-Feldman. Advanced Musical Studies, Nat. Conservatory of Music, Mexico City, 1969—78; BA, BS Sci. and Humanities, Mex. Nat. U., Mexico City, 1979; BFA, Calif. Inst. of the Arts, Valencia, 1983; MFA, Calif. Inst. Arts, Valencia, 1985; PhD, UCLA, 1992—2000. Pres. Soc. for Electro-Acoustic Music in the U.S., Los Angeles Chapter, Calif., 1987—90; music faculty Calif. Inst. of the Arts, Valencia, Calif., 1988—99; chmn., dept. of music Coll. of the Canyons, Santa Clarita, Calif., 1989—. Faculty mem. Calif. Inst. of the Arts, Valencia, Calif., 1988—99. Composer (libretist): (electro-rock opera) Fractured Stories (Am. Soc. for Composers, Authors, and Publishers, 2005); composer: (sound designer) (film) Paris is a Woman (Best Short Film at the NY Internat. Ind. Film Festival, 2003); composer: (music producer) (multimedia) Creatures of Habit (Pew Charitable Trust & Lila Wallace-Reader's Digest Award, 1994); composer: (symphonic score) In Red and Black (Am. Soc. for Composers, Authors and Publishers, 1986). Panelist Cultural Affairs Dept., LA, Calif., 2002—03. Recipient Meet the Composer, Meet the Composer, Inc., 1986, 1988, 1992, 1996. Achievements include Innovative performances involving live musicians interacting with electronics. Avocations: outdoors activities, films, soccer. Home: 121 Strand St Ste #9 Santa Monica CA 90405 Office: Santa Clarita Cmty Coll Dist 26455 Rockwell Canyon Rd Santa Clarita CA 91355 Office Phone: 310-663-9322. Office Fax: 661-259-8302; Home Fax: 661-259-8302. Personal E-mail: feldman_b@canyons.edu.

FELDSTEIN, JOSHUA, educational administrator; b. Russia, Apr. 12, 1921; arrived in U.S., 1939, naturalized, 1944; s. Cemach and Fania B. Feldstein; m. Miriam Myzel, Dec. 24, 1944; children: Theodore Lee, Daniel Ethan. BS, Delaware Valley Coll., 1952; MS, Rutgers U., 1956, PhD, 1962. Instr. horticulture Delaware Valley Coll., Doylestown, Pa., 1952—56, asst. prof. horticulture, 1956—60, assoc. prof. horticulture, 1960—65, prof. horticulture, 1965—, chmn. dept., 1959—69, chmn. plant sci. divsn., 1966—73, assoc. dean, 1969—73, dean, 1973—75; pres. Delaware Valley Coll. Sci. and Agr., Doylestown, Pa., 1975—87, pres. emeritus, 1987—, interim pres., 1995—97. Coord. nat. tchg. fellowships, student fin. aid, chmn. admissions, curriculum, athletics, student affairs, acad. std. coms. Delaware Valley Coll. Sci. and Agr. Author (with N.F. Childers): Effect of Irrigation on Fruit Size and Yield of Peaches in Pennsylvania, 1957; author: Peach Irrigation in a Humid Region, 1964, Effects of Irrigation on Peaches in Pennsylvania, 1965. Recipient Legion of Honor, Chapel of Four Chaplains, Phila., 1974, award, Pa. Future Farmers Am., 1980. Mem.: Commn. of Ind. Colls. and Univs., Pa. Assn. Colls. and Univs., Soil Conservation Soc. Am., Ea. Assn. Coll. Deans and Advs. to Students, Am. Inst. Biol. Scis., Am. Soc. Hort. Sci. Jewish. Office Phone: 215-345-1863. Office Fax: 215-340-9519.

FELDSTEIN, MARTIN STUART, economist, educator; b. NYC, Nov. 25, 1939; s. Meyer and Esther (Gevarter) Feldstein; m. Kathleen Foley, June 19, 1965; children: Margaret, Janet. AB summa cum laude, Harvard U., Cambridge, Mass., 1961; MA, Oxford U., 1964, DPhil, 1967; LLD (hon.), Rochester U., 1984, Marquette U., Milw., 1985. Rsch. fellow Nuffield Coll., Oxford U., 1964—65, ofcl. fellow, 1965—67, lectr. pub. fin., 1965—67; asst. prof. econs. Harvard U., 1967—68, assoc. prof., 1968—69, prof., 1969—, George F. Baker prof., 1984—; pres. Nat. Bur. Econ. Rsch., 1977—82, 1984—; chmn. Coun. Econ. Advisers, 1982—84, mem. pres.'s fgn. intelligence adv. bd., 2006—, mem. pres. fgn intelligence adv. bd., 2006—. Bd. dirs. AIG, Eli Lilly; mem. internat. adv. coun. J.P. Morgan. Bd. contbrs.: Wall St. Jour. Hon. fellow, Nuffield Coll. Fellow: Am. Philos. Soc., Nat. Assn. Bus. Economists, Econometric Soc. (coun. 1977—82), Brit. Acad. (corr.), Am. Acad. Arts and Scis.; mem.: European Econ. Assn., Nat. Tax Assn. (Daniel Holland medal 2003), Trilateral Commn. (exec. com. 1987—), Coun. on Fgn. Rels. (bd. dirs. 1998—), Inst. Medicine of NAS, Austrian Acad. Scis. (fgn.), Am. Econ. Assn. (exec. com. 1980 2005—, v.p. 1988, pres. 2004, John Bates Clark medal 1977), Phi Beta Kappa. Home: 147 Clifton St Belmont MA 02478-2603 Office: Nat Bur Econ Rsch Inc 1050 Massachusetts Ave Cambridge MA 02138-5317 Office Phone: 617-868-3905. Business E-Mail: mfeldstein@nber.org, mfeldstein@harvard.edu.

FELDSTEIN, PAUL JOSEPH, management educator; b. NYC, Oct. 4, 1933; s. Nathan and Sarah Feldstein; m. Anna Martha Lee, Dec. 24, 1968; children: Julie, Jennifer. BA in Econs., CCNY, 1955; MBA in Fin., U. Chgo., 1957, PhD in Econs., 1961. Dir. divsn. rsch. Am. Hosp. Assn., Chgo., 1961-64; prof. Sch. Pub. Health U. Mich., Ann Arbor, 1964-87; prof. Paul Merage Sch. Bus. U. Calif., Irvine, 1987—. Author: Health Policy Issues: An Economic Perspective on Health Reform, 4th edit., 2007, Health Care Economics, 6th edit., 2005, The Politics of Health Legislation, 3d edit., 2006; contbr. articles to profl. jours. 1st lt. inf. US Army. Mem. Am. Econs. Assn. Office: Univ Calif Paul Merage Sch Business Irvine CA 92697-0001 Office Phone: 949-824-8157. Business E-Mail: pfeldste@uci.edu.

FELDT, GLORIA A., social services administrator; b. Temple, Tex., Apr. 13, 1942; m. Alex Barbanell; 3 children; 3 stepchildren. BA in Sociology and Speech with honors, U. Tex. Permian Basin, 1974; postgrad., Ariz. State U., Western Behavioral Scis. Inst., La Jolla, Calif. Broadcast operator Sta. KOIP-FM, Odessa, Tex., 1965-67; substitute tchr. Ector County Ind. Sch. Dist., Odessa, Tex., 1967-68; tchr., spl. projects dir. head start Greater Opportunities of the Permian Basin, Odessa, Tex., 1968-73; exec. dir. Planned Parenthood of West Tex., Odessa, 1974-78; exec. dir., CEO Planned Parenthood Ctrl. and Northern Ariz., Phoenix, 1978-96; pres. Planned Parenthood Fedn. Am., Planned Parenthood Action Fund, NYC, 1996—2005; also bd. dirs. Planned Parenthood Fedn. Am. Mem. steering com. Pro-Choice Ariz.; founder Planned Parenthood Fedn. Am. Leadership Inst.; cons. in leadership and strategic planning for non-profit orgns. Spkr. in field; Author: Behind Every Choice Is a Story, 2003, The War on Choice:The Right-Wing Attack on Women's Rights and How to Fight Back, 2004. Mem. exec. bd. Ariz. Affordable Health Care Found.; bd. dirs. Pro-Choice Resource Ctr., Hospice of the Valley; mem. cmty. adv. bd. Jr. League of Phoenix; mem. adv. bd. UN Assn.; charter mem. Ariz. Women's Town Hall; active Charter 100, World Affairs Coun., Ariz. Acad. Town Halls. Recipient Women of Achievement award, 1987, Ruth Green award Nat. Exec. Dirs. Coun., 1990, award Women Helping Women, 1989, 94, Golden Apple award Sun City chpt. NOW, 1995, City of Phoenix Martin Luther King, Jr. Living the Dream award City of Phoenix Human Rels. Commn., 1996. Mem. APHA, Nat. Family Planning and Reproductive Health Assn., Ariz. Pub. Health Assn.

FELDT, LEONARD SAMUEL, academic administrator, educator; b. Long Branch, NJ, Nov. 2, 1925; s. Harry and Bessie (Doris) F.; m. Natalie Ruth (Fischer), Aug. 29, 1954; children: Sarah Feldt Roach, Daniel C. BS in Edn., Rutgers U., 1950, EdM, 1951; PhD, U. Iowa, 1954. Asst. prof. to prof. U. Iowa, Iowa City, 1954-94, dir. testing programs, 1981-94, Lindquist prof. ednl. measurement, 1981-94, prof. emeritus, 1994. Pres. Iowa Measurment Rsch. Found., Iowa City, 1978-2004, v.p., 2004—; editor standardized tests, Iowa Tests Ednl. Devel., 1960—. With US Army, 1943—46. Recipient Disting. Svc. Award Rutgers U., 1999; Disting. Achievement Award, Nat. Ctr. for Rsch. on Evaluation Stds. and Student Testing, 1999. Mem.: Am. Stats. Assn., Psychometric Soc., Nat. Coun. on Measurement in Edn. (Career Contbns. award 1994), Am. Ednl. Rsch. Assn. (E.F. Lindquist award 1995), Sigma Xi, Phi Beta Kappa. Avocations: golf, stock market. Home: 810 Willow St Iowa City IA 52245-5438 Office: Univ Iowa Lindquist Ctr Iowa City IA 52242 Home Phone: 319-338-3749. Business E-Mail: leonard-feldt@uiowa.edu.

FELDT, MARY, elementary school educator; B in Wellness and Health promotion, Univ. Wis., Stevens Point; M in Phys. Edn., Univ. Wis. Phys. edn. tchr. Waupaca (Wis.) Learning Ctr. Vol. Waupaca County Nutrition and Activity Coalition; mem. Gov. Coun. Phys. Fitness and Health, 2006—. Named Wis. Elem. Sch. Tchr. of Yr., 2005, Wis. Tchr. of Yr., 2006. Office: Waupaca Learning Ctr 1515 Shoemaker Rd Waupaca WI 54981 Business E-Mail: mfeldt@wsd.waupaca.k12.wi.us.*

FELDTMAN, ROBERT, surgeon; s. Earnest Feldtman and Mary Wright; m. Susan Feldtman, Aug. 18, 1969. MD, UTMB, Galveston, 1972. Lic. thoracic & cardiovascular surgeon ABTS, 1984, vascular surgeon ABS, 1984. Cardiovascular surgeon Ctrl. Tex. Va. Med Ctr., Temple, 2000—, Scott & White Med. Ctr., Temple, Tex., 2003—. Col. USAFR, 1969—99, Lackland AFB, Tex. Decorated Legion of Merit USAF. Fellow: ACS. Conservative-R. Avocations: aviation, amateur radio, hunting, fishing. Office: Scott& White Med Ctr 2401 So 31st St Temple TX 76508 Business E-Mail: rfeldtman@swmail.sw.org.

FELGAR, RAYMOND EUGENE, pathologist, educator; b. Mt. Pleasant, Pa., Mar. 2, 1963; s. Samuel Hurst and Anna June (Stull) Felgar. BS in Microbiology with honors, Pa. State U., University Park, 1985; PhD in Pathology, U. Pitts., 1990, MD, 1992. Diplomate Am. Bd. Pathology in Anatomic and Clin. Pathology, Am. Bd. Pathology, cert. subspecialty in Hemotology Am. Bd. Pathology. Resident in anatomic and clin. pathology U. Pa. Med. Ctr., Phila., 1992—96; fellow in hematopathology dept. pathology Vanderbilt U., Nashville, 1996—98; dir. hematopathology and clin. flow cytometry Hahnemann Hosp., Phila., 1998; asst. prof. dept. pathology and lab medicine MCP-Hahnemann Sch. Medicine, Phila., 1998; dir. clin. flow cytometry lab., hematopathologist, dir. hematopathology Strong Meml. Hosp., Rochester, NY, 1998—2007; asst. prof. Dept. Pathology & Lab. Medicine U. Rochester Sch. Medicine & Dentistry, 1998—2004, assoc. prof. Dept. Pathology & Lab Medicine, 2004—06; assoc. dir. hematopathology fellowship program U. Pitts. Med. Ctr., 2007—; assoc. prof. dept. pathology U. Pitts. Sch. Medicine, 2007—. Co-dir. Course on T-cell lymphomas, ASCP Nat. Meeting; mem. sci. adv. bd. Bioreference Labs. Inc., Elmwood Park, N.J. Contbr. articles to profl. jours., chapters to books. NIH med. scientist tng. fellow, 1987-92. Fellow Coll. Am. Pathologists, Am. Soc. Clin. Pathologists (co-dir. course t-cell lymphomas nat. mtg.); mem. AMA, Am. Soc. Hematology, U.S. and Can. Acad. Pathology, Soc. for Hematopathology, European Assn. for Hematopathology, Eastern Coop. Oncology Group (pathology com.), Southwestern Oncology Group, Children's Oncology Group, Pa. State U. Alumni Assn., Phi Beta Kappa. Business E-Mail: felgarre@upmc.edu.

FELGER, RALPH WILLIAM, education educator, retired military officer; b. Hamilton, Ohio, Oct. 14, 1919; s. Edward Lewis and Blanche Esther (House) F.; m. Bernice Regina Moeller, Dec. 28, 1944 (dec.); 1 child, Mary Karen. BA, Whitworth Coll., Spokane, Wash., 1950; MBA, U. Denver, 1952; MS, Trinity U., San Antonio, 1954. Cert. instr. bus. and psychology Calif. Commd. 2d lt. U.S. Army, advanced through grades to 1st lt., pers. tng. officer, 1942—46, relieved from active duty, 1946; commd. 1st lt. USAF, 1951, advanced through grades to col., edn. and pers. officer, 1951—67, ret., 1967; asst. prof. Bakersfield Coll., Calif., 1967—68; dean continuing edn. Lincoln Land C.C., Springfield, Ill., 1968—72; dir. corp. tng. Sangamo Electric Co., West Union, SC, 1972—74; asst. campus dir. Ohio State U., Marion, 1974—79, asst. to v.p. Columbus, 1979—83; exec. v.p. Internat. Mgmt. Inst., Westerville, Ohio, 1983—84; dir. continuing edn. N.Mex. Inst. Mining and Tech., Socorro, 1984—85; part-time cons. edn. and mktg. Midwest Human Resource Sys., Columbus, 1985—89; acad. counselor Franklin U., Columbus, 1990—91; mgr. edn. program Jr. Achievement of Ctrl. Ohio, Columbus, 1991—92; v.p. Career Mgmt. Ctrs., Inc., Columbus, 1991—92; ret., 1992. Chmn. Ill. divsn. United Way, Springfield, 1972; active Police Human Rels. Com., Springfield, 1970-72; bd. dirs. ARC, Oconee, SC, 1973; edn. chmn. Marion Econ. Coun., Ohio, 1975-79, Marion County chpt. Am. Heart Assn., 1975-79. Decorated Legion of Merit, U.S. Joint Chiefs of Staff Badge, 3 USAF Commendation medals; recipient 2 commendations United Way Cmty. Svc. Mem.: U.S. Ret. Mil. Officers Assn., Pers. Mgrs. Club (v.p. 1972—74), Delta Sigma Pi (life). Avocations: fishing, camping, travel, cooking, reading. Home and Office: 1300 O Ave Apt 106 Anacortes WA 98221 Office Phone: 360-588-9778.

FELICE, WILLIAM F., political science professor; PhD in Polit. Sci., NYU. Prof., dept. Polit. Sci. Eckerd Coll., Fla. Author: The Global New Deal, Taking Suffering Seriously. Recipient US Prof. Yr. State of Fla., Carnegie Found. Advancement Tchg., 2006. Office: Eckerd Coll 4200 54Tth Ave S Saint Petersburg FL 33711

FELICETTI, DANIEL A., academic administrator; b. NYC, Apr. 25, 1942; s. Ernest and Rose (DiAdamo) F.; m. Barbara D'Antonio, July 13, 1969. BA in Polit. Sci., Hunter Coll., 1963; MA in Polit. Sci., NYU, 1966, PhD in Polit. Sci., 1971. From asst. to assoc. prof. Fairfield (Conn.) U., 1967-77, chmn. dept. politics, 1973-76, spl. asst. to pres., 1977; acad. v.p., acad. dean Wheeling (W.Va.) Coll., 1977-80; sr. v.p. for acad. affairs Coll. New Rochelle, NY, 1980-81, Southeastern U., Washington, 1982-84; v.p. acad. affairs U. Detroit, 1984-89; pres. Marian Coll., Indpls., 1989-99, Capital U., Columbus, Ohio, 1999-2001; founder Higher Edn. Leadership Projects Consulting Svc., 2001—. Participant Am. Coun. on Edn., Washington, 1976-77, vis. assoc., 1984-85; intern Inst. for Ednl. Mgmt. program Harvard U., 1981; cons. Coun. for Ind. Colls., Washington, 1986. Trustee Am. Heart Assn., Mich.; bd. dirs. Am. Heart Assn., Ind., Mental Health Assn. Marion County, Econ. Club Indpls., Coun. Ind. Colls.; mem. health and substance abuse com. New Detroit, Inc., 1986-89; mem. Greater Indpls. Progress Com.; mem. Pub. Safety Task Force Ind.; mem. Colls. Ind. Found.; mem. Indpls. delegation to Pres.'s Summit for Am.'s Future, 1997. Trustee Am. Heart Assn., Mich.; bd. dirs. Am. Heart Assn., Ind., Mental Health Assn. Marion County, Econ. Club Indpls., Coun. Ind. Colls.; mem. health and substance abuse com. New Detroit, Inc., 1986-89; mem. Greater Indpls. Progress Coml; mem. Pub. Safety Task Force Ind.; mem. Colls. Ind. Found.; mem. safety vision coun. United Way Columbus. Named to Hunter Coll. Hall of Fame, Hunter Coll. Alumni Assn., 1986; recipient Cert. of Recognition Sen. Lugar, 1994; Lilly Found. vis. faculty fellow Yale U., 1975; named Sagamore of the Wabash Gov. of Ind., 1990. Mem. Indpls. Athletic Club, received hon. doctoral degree from Marian Coll., 1999, Columbus C. of C. (pub. rels. com.), Rotary, Alpha Sigma Nu (hon.), Beta Gamma Sigma (hon.). Democrat. Roman Catholic. Avocations: baseball, reading, antiques.

FELICIANO, JOSÉ, entertainer; b. Larez, P.R., Sept. 10, 1945; s. Jose and Hortencia (Garcia) F.; m. Susan Feliciano; children: Melissa, Jonathan, Michael. DHL (hon.), 2001. Pres. Feliciano Enterprises. Folk singer in Greenwich Village, N.Y.C., 1962, rec. artist for Universal Records; TV appearances Feliciano—Very Special, 1969, Monsanto Night Presents Jose Feliciano, 1972, Statue of Liberty Celebration, 1984, Absolutely the Best, 2000, Feliciano, A Legend in Concert, 2000, over 100 others; has performed with major symphonies worldwide; composer some of own material including: Affirmation, Rain, Chico and the Man, Feliz Navidad, Ay Carino, Como tu Quieres; composer: guitar concerto Concerto de Paulinho, Mozartean Influence. Recipient 6 Grammy awards, including award in 1990, 16 Grammy nominations, Best Folk Guitarist award Guitar Player Mag. 1973, Best Pop Guitarist award 1973-77; more than 40 Gold and Platinum recotds; star in his name implanted on Hollywood Blvd., 1987. Achievements include having José Feliciano Sch. Performing Arts, East Harlem, N.Y., dedicated in his honor, 1987; being Amb. before the UN for Internat. Immigrants Found., 2003. Address: Feliciano Enterprises 606 Post Rd # Ste 880 Westport CT 06880 *The greatest tragedy for many so-called handicapped people is that they let others convince them that there are limits to what they can accomplish. It's just not so.*

FELIX, ARTHUR MARTIN, chemistry educator, researcher; b. NYC, June 15, 1938; s. Barney and Beatrice (Thaler) F.; m. Maureen A. Kopelson, Oct. 28, 1967; children: Alison, Stephan. BA, NYU, 1959; PhD, Poly. U. N.Y., 1964. Rsch. assoc. Harvard U., Cambridge, Mass., 1964-66; sr. scientist Hoffmann-La Roche Inc., Nutley, NJ, 1966-75, rsch. fellow, 1976-80, rsch. group chief, 1980-83, asst. dir., 1983-85, dept. head, 1985-95; asst. prof. chemistry William Paterson Coll., Wayne, NJ, 1995-97, Ramapo Coll., Mahwah, NJ, 1998—2003, assoc. prof. chemistry, 2003—. Adj. asst. prof. Fairleigh Dickinson U., Teaneck, N.J., 1967-79, Hunter Coll., CUNY, 1974-75; adj. prof. U. of Medicine and Dentistry of N.J., 1992—; guest investigator Rockefeller U., N.Y.C., 1968-69. Contbr. more than 180 articles mainly on peptide synthesis to sci. jours. Bd. dirs. Big Bros.-Big Sisters Bergen-Passaic, N.J., 1980-82; pres. Washington Sch. Home Sch. Assn., West Caldwell, N.J., 1980-82. Mem. Am. Chem. Soc., Am. Peptide Soc. (sec. 1990-93), N.J. Inst. Chemists (coun. 1983-84), Sigma Xi (chpt. pres. 1980-81, 2000-01). Achievements include 30 patents related to drug discovery; synthesis of biologically important peptides including immunotropics, vaccines and growth factors. Office Phone: 201-684-7793. Personal E-mail: artfelix@verizon.net. Business E-Mail: afelix@ramapo.edu.

FELIX, CHERYL A., air transportation executive; b. St. Paul, Aug. 31; d. Lawrence J. and Beverly J. McGuinn; m. Guy J. Felix, May 20, 2000; children: Tyler B., Logan C. AA, Normandale C.C., Bloomington, Minn.; AAS in Exec. Secretarial, Inver Hills C.C., Inver Grove Heights, MN; BA in Polit. Sci., St. Cloud State U., 2000, BA in Pub. Adminstrn., 2000; MBA, Embry-Riddle Aero. U., 2003. Customer svc., tech. support adminstr. Shadin Co., Inc., St. Louis Park, Minn., 1995—98; materials mgr. Dallas Airmotive, Mpls., 2000—01; engring. adminstr., master planner/scheduler Shadin Co., Inc., St. Louis Park, Minn., 2001—03; purchasing, inventory analyst Wipaire, Inc., South St. Paul, Minn., 2004—06; sr. analyst domestic revenue mgmt. Continental Airlines, Houston, 2006—. Grad. rsch. asst. Embry-Riddle Aero. U. Mem.: Am. Soc. Pub. Adminstrn., Women Aviation, Internat., Exptl. Aircraft Assn., Aircraft Owners and Pilots Assn., Internat. Aerobatic Club. Avocations: aerobatics, politics, pool. Office Phone: 713-324-5572. Business E-Mail: cheryl.felix@coair.com.

FELIX, LARRY R., federal agency administrator; b. Port of Spain, Trinidad; married; 2 children. Grad., CUNY, 1980; postgrad., Columbia U. Fin. investigator Irving Trust; with U.S. Bond Divsn.; various positions including mgr. mktg., chief external affairs, assoc. dir. tech., chair inter-agy. currency design taskforce Bur. Engraving and Printing, US Dept. Treasury, Washington, 1992—2004, dep. dir., 2004—06, dir., 2006—. Office: Bur Engraving and Printing US Dept Treasury 14th and C Streets SW Washington DC 20228 Office Phone: 202-874-3019.

FELIX-GETZIK, ERIKA MICHELE, pharmacist; b. DuBois, Pa., May 20, 1978; d. Edward Francis Felix Jr. and Malinda (Boyles) Felix; m. Kristopher David Getzik, May 18, 2002. PharmD, U. Pitts., 2002. Lic. pharmacist Mass., 2002, Pa., 2002. Pharmacy practice resident Tufts-New

Eng. Med. Ctr., Boston, 2002—03; cardiology splty. resident U. Pitts. Med. Ctr., Pitts., 2003—04; asst. prof. pharmacy practice Mass. Coll. Pharmacy and Health Scis., Boston, 2004—. Contbr. articles to profl. jours. Recipient Comm. award, U. Pitts., Roche Pharms., 2002, Pharmacy Faculty Preceptor of the Yr., Roche Pharms., 2005—06. Mem.: Am. Acad. Colls. Pharmacy, Am. Soc. Health Sys. Pharmacists, Am. Coll. Clin. Pharmacists, Am. Heart Assn. Independent: Roman Catholic. Avocations: travel, cooking, yoga, reading, exercise. Office: Mcphs 179 Longwood Ave Boston MA 02115 Home Phone: 617-266-3708; Office Phone: 617-732-2182. Business E-Mail: erika.felix-getzik@mcphs.edu.

FELKER, OUIDA JEANETTE WEISSINGER, special education educator; b. Vicksburg, Miss., Oct. 31, 1931; d. Eugene Liddell and Alice Byron (Cato) Weissinger; m. George Hugh Boyd Jr., Feb. 5, 1958 (div. 1968); children: James Eugene, Ouida Ann Boyd Baldwin, Alice Emelyn Boyd Dewey, Rosalie Jeanette, George Hugh III; m. Paul Henry Felker Jr., Mar. 4, 1983 (dec.). BS, U. Tenn., 1952; MA, U. South Fla., 1974, EdS, 1985; EdD, U. Sarasota, 1987; grad. gemologist, Gemological Inst. Am., 1993. Cert. ins. appraiser. Tchr. health, phys. edn. South HS, Knoxville, Tenn., 1953; founder, exec. dir. Happyland Kindergarten, Clayton, Ga., 1955-56; tchr. spl. edn. Laurel Student Ctr., Fla., 1968-72; tchr. spl. edn., vocat. coord. Sarasota County Student Ctr., Fla., 1972-78, tchr., 1985-88; founder, exec. dir. Exceptional Industries, Venice, Fla., 1979-82; staffing specialist Nokomis Elem. Sch., Fla., 1988-90, Englewood Elem. Sch., Fla., 1990—97, Taylor Ranch Elem. Sch., Venice, Fla., 1990—97; ret. Tchr. of handicapped Venice Area Rotary Clubs, Fla., Rio de Janeiro, 1982; liaison for exception student edn. Ideal Alternative HS and Life Program, 1990-97; owner Jewelery by Appointment, 1989-, Weddings by Ouida in a Tropical Setting. Bd. dirs. St. Mark's Day Sch., Venice, 1986-89; mem. St. Mark's Choir; past pres. Episcopal Ch. Women, Venice Area Coll. Club. Mem. Fla. Rehab. Assn. (past chpt. treas. and pres.), Suncoast Gesneriad Soc. (v.p. 1987-91), Accredited Gemologist Assn. (cert. 1992—), Nat. Assn. Jewelry Appraisers, Nat. Jewelry Appraisal Registry, Phi Mu Alumnae Assn. (treas. 1992-93, v.p. 1994-95, pres. 1995—). Republican. Episcopalian. Avocations: gemology, gardening, ethnic cooking. Home: 729 Apalachicola Rd Venice FL 34285-1605 Personal E-mail: ouida.jba@verizon.net.

FELKNOR, BRUCE LESTER, publishing executive, consultant, writer; b. Oak Park, Ill., Aug. 18, 1921; s. Audley Rhea and Harriet (Lester) F.; m. Joanne Sweeney, Feb. 8, 1942 (div. Jan. 1952); 1 child, Susan Harriet Felknor Pickard; m. Edith G. Johnson, Mar. 1, 1952; children: Sarah Anne Felknor Ragland, Bruce Lester II. Student, U. Wis., 1939—41. Reporter Dunn County News, Menomonie, Wis., 1937—39; freight brakeman Pa. R.R., NYC, 1941, asst. yardmaster, 1942; prodn. coord. Hwy. Trailer Co., Edgerton, Wis., 1943; radio officer U.S. Maritime Svc., 1944—45; flight radio officer Air Transport Command, 1945; mem. pub. rels. dept. Am. Airlines, 1945; writer pub. rels. dept. ITT, 1946; Southeast regional pub. rels. dir. Ford Motor Co., Chester, Pa., 1946—48; free lance pub. res. NYC, 1948—49; pub. rels. exec. Foote, Cone & Belding, Inc., NYC, 1950—53; v.p. Market Rels. Network, NYC, 1954—55; exec. dir. Fair Campaign Practices Com., Inc., NYC, 1956—66; asst. to chmn. and pub. William Benton Ency. Brit., 1966—70, dir. mktg. info. internat. divsn., 1970—73, dir. advt. and promotion, 1973, dir. pub. info., 1974—76, exec. editor, 1977—83, dir. yearbooks, 1983—85; editl. cons., 1985—. Vis. lectr. Hamilton Coll., 1966, 75, 82; history editor Mcht. Marine internet web site www.usmm.org, 1999—. Author: Fair Play in Politics, 1960, State-by-State Smear Study, 1956, You Are They, 1964, (with C.P. Taft) Prejudice & Politics, 1960, Dirty Politics, 1966, reprinted, 1975, 2001, (with Frank Jonas et al) Political Dynamiting, 1970, How to Look Things Up and Find Things Out, 1988, Political Mischief: Smear, Sabotage, and Reform in U.S. Elections, 1992, The Highland Park Presbyterian Church: A History 1871-1996, 1996 (Robert Lee Stowe award 1997), The U.S. Merchant Marine at War 1775-1945, 1998, The Great Witch Hunt of the Presbyterian Left, 2001, Of Clubbable Nature: Chicago's Tavern Club at 75, 2005; editor: The U.S. Government: How and Why it Works, 1978; also various newspaper, jour. and yearbook articles on politics; contbg. editor (with Clifton Fadiman) The Treasury of the Encyclopaedia Britannica, 1992; contbr. Encyclopedia of the American Presidency, 1993. Chmn. Citizens Com. for Sch. Centralization in Armonk, N.Y., 1957-61; ruling elder, chmn. com. religion and race Presbytery Hudson River, 1963-67, mem. nat. coun. on ch. and soc., 1966-72; bd. dirs., mem. exec. com. Fair Campaign Practices Com.; mem. nat. adv. bd. Amigos de las Americas, 1982-89, Am. U., Washington, 1982—; mem. Ill. Literacy Coun., 1984-86; mem. bd. advisors, acad. adv. coun. Nat. Strategy Forum, 1987—; mem. bd. edn. Lake Forest (Ill.) H.S. Dist., 1989-93. Republican. Presbyterian. Home and Office: 509 Trinity Ct Evanston IL 60201-1908 Home Phone: 843-570-3469. E-mail: bruce_felknor@yahoo.com. *Man's greatest gifts are empathy and the ability to penetrate balderdash.*

FELL, ELIZABETH P., education educator; d. Alvin Curtis and Annie Mae Paul; m. Ray Fell, Dec. 18, 1965; children: Ashley, Allison, Kirk. BS in Edn., Livingston U, 1964, ME, 1968; EdD in Elem. Edn., U. Ala. Birmingham, 1985. Cert. Elem. Edn. 1975. Elem tchr. elem. sch., Ga., Fla., Ala., 1964—81; asst. prof. Mobile Coll., Ala., 1981—89; prof., chair, Curriculum and Instrn. Troy U., Dothan, Ala., 1989—2005; ret. Nat. Scholastic Judge Am. Jr. Miss, Mobile, 1986—89; SACS Facilitator and Review Chmn. So. Assn. of Coll. and Sch. Ala. Elem. and Middle Sch. Vol. Ret. Seniors Vol. Program, Grandparents Raising Grandchildren, Vols. in Police Svc., Habitat for Humanity Assessment. Named Ms. Flaming Glow/Ms. Congeniality, Ms. Sr. Sweetheart of Am., 2004. Mem.: AACTE, Nat. Council for the Social Studies, Nat. Council for Tchr. of English, Alpha Delta Kappa (state bd., state corr. sec.), Phi Delta Kappa (hon.), Kappa Delta Pi (Counselor). E-mail: gfell@ala.net.

FELL, SAMUEL KENNEDY (KEN), infosystems executive; b. Wilmington, Del., Oct. 6, 1944; s. S. Kennedy and Anna Elizabeth (Alford) F.; m. Diana Marie Dickson, May 8, 1965; children: Melissa Ann, Michael Kennedy. BSBA, Oklahoma City U., 1983; postgrad. in bus., John F. Kennedy U.; grad. exec. mgmt. program, Duke U., 1991. Mgmt./data processing sys. designer/implementor Gen. Motors Corp., Detroit and Oklahoma City, 1967-81; v.p. info. systems Totco Divsn. Baker Internat., Norman, Okla., 1981-85; v.p. computer info. Cleve. Pneumatic subs. Pneumo Abex Corp. div. IC Industries, 1985-88; sr. dir. systems devel. Sprint, Kansas City, Mo., 1988-95; exec. v.p. product devel., exec. bd. mem. SynQuest, Inc., A Warburg Pincus Co., 1995-2000; CIO NYISO, Schenectady, N.Y., 2000—. Mem.: Data Processing Mgrs. Assn., Soc. Info. Mgrs., Oracle Users Group. Office: NY ISO 3890 Carman Rd Schenectady NY 12303

FELLEGI, IVAN PETER, statistician; b. Szeged, Hungary, June 22, 1935; immigrated to Can., 1957. s. Andor and Barbara (Partos) F.; m. Marika Gulyas, Dec. 27, 1958; children— Nicolette, Vivien. BSc, U. Budapest, Hungary, 1956; MSc, Carleton U., Ont., Can., 1958, PhD, 1961; PhD (hon.), Simon Fraser U., 1995; LLD (hon.), McMaster U., 1997; PhD (hon.), Carleton U., 1999; D (hon.), U. Que., 2001, U. Montreal, 2002. With Statistics Can., Ottawa, Ont., 1957—, asst. chief statistician, 1973-84, dep. chief statistician, 1984-85, chief statistician of Can., 1985—. Contbr. articles to profl. jours. Bd. govs. Carleton U., 1989—, chmn. bd. govs., 1995-97; chair Conf. European Statisticians, 1993-97. Decorated officer Order of Can., Order of Merit of the Hungarian Republic; recipient Robert Schuman medal, European Cmty., 1997, Outstanding Achievement award, Pub. Svc. Can., 2002. Fellow AAAS, Am. Statis. Assn., Royal Statis. Soc. (hon.); mem. Internat. Statis. Inst. (hon., pres. 1987-89), Statis. Soc. Can. (pres. 1982), Internat. Assn. Survey Statisticians (pres. 1985-87). Home: 16 Larchwood Ave Ottawa ON Canada K1Y 2E3 Office: Statistics Canada RH Coats Bldg Tunney's Pasture Ottawa ON Canada K1A 0T6

FELLER, AVI, political science scholar; s. Daniel D. and Sharona F. BA in Polit. Sci., Applied Math., Yale Univ., 2007; MSc. student in Applied Statistics, Oxford Univ., 2007—. Rhodes Scholar. Jewish. Achievements include conducting rsch. and interning at US Dept. of State, Bur. of Oceans and Internat. Environ. and Scientific Affairs, Off. of Policy Coordination and Initiatives. Avocations: sailing, opera, guitar.*

FELLER, BENJAMIN E., actuary; b. Bronx, NY, Mar. 4, 1947; s. Morris and Beatrice (Wolff) F.; m. Debra May Morane, June 1973 (div. 1983); children: Amy; m. Sue Ann Kaufman, Sept. 23, 1984; children: Meredith; stepchildren: Stefanie McCoy, Alison McCoy. BS in Math., Clarkson U., Potsdam, NY, 1968; MA in Math., Ind. U., 1971. Enrolled actuary. Actuarial asst. U.S. Life Ins. Co., NYC, 1971-75; assoc. actuary The Wyatt Co., Washington, 1975-76; cons. actuary Buck Cons., NYC, 1976-85; ptnr. Chernoff Diamond & Co., Williston Park, N.Y., 1985-92; pres. Pension Rev. Svcs., Melville, NY, 1992—. Contbr. articles to profl. jours. Fellow Soc. Actuaries; mem. Am. Soc. Pension Actuaries, Am. Acad. Actuaries, Bklyn. Tech. H.S. Alumni Assn. (dir.). Republican. Jewish. Home: 10 Allison Dr Old Bethpage NY 11804-1602 Office: Pension Rev Svcs 445 Broad Hollow Rd Ste 8 Melville NY 11747 Office Phone: 516-694-5500. Business E-Mail: bfeller@pensionreviewservices.com.

FELLER, ROBERT LIVINGSTON, chemist, art conservation scientist; b. Newark, Dec. 27, 1919; s. William Henry and Edna (Buckelew) F.; m. Ruth M. Johnston, Mar. 31, 1975 (dec. 2000). AB, Dartmouth Coll., 1941; MS, Rutgers U., 1943, PhD, 1950. Sr. fellow Nat. Gallery Art Research Project, Mellon Inst., Pitts., 1950-76; dir. Research Ctr. on Materials of Artist and Conservator, Carnegie-Mellon Rsch. Inst., Pitts., 1976-88, dir. emeritus, 1988—. Vis. scientist Conservation Ctr., Inst. Fine Arts, NYU, 1961; pres. Nat. Conservation Adv. Council, 1975-79 Co-author: On Picture Varnishes and their Solvents, 2d rev. edit., 1985, Evaluation of Cellulose Ethers for Conservation, 1990; author: Accelerated Aging: Photochemical and Thermal Aspects, 1994; editor: Artists' Pigments: A Handbook of Their History and Characteristics, Vol. I, 1986. Served with USN, 1944-46. Recipient Coll. Art Assn.-Nat. Inst. for Conservation Joint award, 1992, Univ. Products award for disting. achievement in conservation of cultural property, 2000. Fellow Internat. Inst. Conservation Hist. and Artistic Works (hon.), Am. Inst. Conservation Hist. and Artistic Works (hon.), Illuminating Engring. Soc.; mem. AAAS, Am. Chem. Soc. (Pittsburgh award 1983), Internat. Coun. Museums (pres. conservation com. 1969-78), Fedn. Socs. Coatings Tech., Inter-Soc. Color Coun., Am. Inst. Conservation. Clubs: Cosmos (Washington). Achievements include research on deterioration of varnishes, paper, pigments and dyes used by artists. Office: Carnegie Mellon U Artists Materials Rsch Ctr 700 Technology Dr Pittsburgh PA 15219-3124

FELLER, ROBERT WILLIAM ANDREW, public relations executive, retired professional baseball player; b. Van Meter, Iowa, Nov. 3, 1918; s. William and Lena (Forrett) F.; m. Anne Morris Gilliland, Oct. 1, 1974. Pub. rels. exec. Cleveland Indians Baseball Team, 1936-56. Played first major league game Cleve. vs. St. Louis Browns, 1936; pitched 3 no-hitters Cleve. vs. Chgo., 1940, Cleve. vs. N.Y., 1946, Cleve. vs. Detroit, 1951; member 9 all-star teams. Author: Strikeout Story, 1947, How to Pitch, 1948, Now Pitching Bob Feller, 1990, Bob Feller's Little Black Book of Baseball Wisdom, 2000. CPO USNavy, 1941-45, PTO. Recognition for mil. svc. and baseball contbn. US Congress, Washington, 2006; inducted to Baseball Hall of Fame, Cooperstown, NY, 1962; named Greatest Living Right-Hand Pitcher Profl. Baseball Centennial Celebration, 1969. Mem. Green Berets (hon.). Republican. Episcopalian. Avocation: restoring tractors. Home Fax: 440-423-3248.

FELLERS, RHONDA GAY, lawyer; b. Gainesville, Tex., July 20, 1955; d. James Norman and Gaytha Ann (Sanders) F.; m. Bruce C. Hinton, Oct. 15, 1981 (div. Oct. 1985). BA, U. Tex., 1977, JD, 1980; LLM in Taxation, U. Denver, 1987. Bar: Tex. 1981, Colo. 1981, U.S. Dist. Ct. (no. dist.) Tex. 1982, U.S. Dist. Ct. Colo. 1985, U.S. Tax Ct. 1985, U.S. Ct. Appeals (5th cir.) 1986, U.S. Ct. Appeals (10th cir.) 1989, U.S. Supreme Ct. 1993, U.S. Ct. Claims 1993. Assoc. Walters & Assocs., Lubbock, Tex., 1981-83; gen. counsel Security Nat. Bank, Lubbock, 1983; sole practice Lubbock, 1983-87; assoc. Melvin Coffee & Assocs., P.C., Denver, 1984-85, 87-90; atty. adviser U.S. Tax Ct., Washington, 1990-94; pvt. practice Pinehurst, Tex., 1994-98; with Arthur Andersen LLP, Houston, 1998—2002; sole practice, 2002—. Mem. ABA, State Bar Tex., Colo. Bar Assn., Houston Bar Assn. Avocations: golf, tennis, photography. E-mail: rgfellers@sbcglobal.net.

FELLHAUER, DAVID E., bishop; b. Kansas City, Mo., Aug. 19, 1939; Student, Pontifical Coll. Josephinum; D in Canon Law, PhD, St. Paul U., Ottawa, Can. Ordained priest Roman Cath. Ch., 1965. Former prof. Holy Trinity Sem., Dallas; judicial vicar Diocese of Dallas, 1990; bishop of Victoria Tex., 1990—. Bd. govs. Canon Law Soc. Am. Recipient Role of Law award, Canon Law Soc., 1998. Office: PO Box 4070 Victoria TX 77903-4070

FELLMAN, RICHARD MAYER, retired lawyer; b. Omaha, May 30, 1935; s. Leon E. and Frances (Green) F.; m. Beverly Bloom, Jan. 12, 1964; children: Susan, Deborah, Jonathan, Daniel. BA in Polit. Sci., U. Nebr., 1957, JD, 1959; Grad., Infantry Sch., Ft. Benning, Ga., 1959. Bar: Nebr. 1959, U.S. Dist. Ct. Nebr. 1959. Farm editor, reporter Lincoln (Nebr.) Star, 1956-58; state capitol reporter AP, Lincoln, 1958; assoc. Marks, Clare, Hopkins & Rauth, Omaha, 1960-64; ptnr. Fellman & Stern, Omaha, 1965-73, Fellman Law Offices, Omaha, 1973-86, Fellman, Moylan, Natvig, Wilke & Wik, Omaha, 1987—2004; ret., 2004. Lectr., dept. polit. sci. U. Nebr., Omaha, 2004—. Chair jud. subcom. Nebr. State Legis. on No Fault Divorce, 1973-74; bd. dirs. Vol. Bur., 1965-67; bd. dirs. NCCJ, 1968-72, Omaha-Douglas County Health Dept., 1977-80; mem. Omaha-Douglas Bldg. Commn., 1977-80; bd. dirs. Metro Area Planning Agy., Omaha, 1979; founding bd. dirs. Omaha Coun. on Domestic Violence, mem. 1996-2003; hon. bd. dirs. Alzheimer's Assn., Omaha, 1997-98; governing authority Omaha Symphony Assn.; pres. Beth El Synagogue, 2003-05, bd. dirs. 1995-2006, Omaha; chmn. Omaha com. Anti-Defamation League, 1967-70; mem. Nat. Civil Rights Com. and Law Com., 1965—; bd. dirs. Jewish Fedn. Omaha, 1969-72; founding pres. Omaha Jewish Day Sch. (now Friedel Acad.), 1970; gen. men's chair United Jewish Appeal, 1968; bd. dirs. Omaha Jewish Press, J.C.C. Libr. Br., Nebr. Jewish Hist. Soc., Jewish Coll. Learning; organizer, chair Nebr. Dem. State Reform Commn., 1971; mem. Douglas County Bd. Commrs., 1977-80, chair of bd., 1980; senator State of Nebr., 1973-74, mem. jud. com. and govt., mil. and vets. affairs com.; mem. Mid-Am. coun. adv. bd. Boy Scouts Am., 1983—, cub and scout troop committeeman, 1980-87, former chair coun. Jewish cmty. relationships com., 1985-96. Capt. USAR, 1959-66. Recipient Humanitarian of the Yr. award, Sons of Italy, 1977, Silver Beaver award, 2003, Shofar Scout award, 1999. Mem. Nebr. Trial Lawyers Assn. (bd. dirs. 1971-72, legis. com. 1992-95), Nebr. Bar Assn. (chmn. family law com. 1971-72, 75-76), Omaha Bar Assn. (chair com. on domestic violence 1996, Pro Bono Publico award 1972), Nebr. Constiutional Rev. Commn., Rotary, Delta Sigma Rho, Zeta Beta Tau. Democrat. Jewish. Home: 14101 Eagle Run Rd Omaha NE 68164-5422 Office Phone: 402-578-5893. Personal E-mail: fellmanrm@aol.com.

FELLOWS, ALICE COMBS, artist; b. Atlanta, Sept. 14, 1935; d. Andrew Grafton III and Wilhelmina Drummond (Jackson) Combs; m. Robert Ellis Fellows Jr., Aug. 20, 1957 (div. 1978); children: Ariadne Elisabeth Fellows-Mannion, Kara Suzanne Fellows. BFA, Syracuse U., 1957; M in Clin. Psychology, Antioch U., 1992. Guest artist Yaddo, Saratoga Springs, N.Y., 1991; artist-in-residence Dorland Colony, Temecula, Calif., 1983; guest lectr. psychology seminar UCLA, 1990. Exhibited works in numerous group and one-woman shows including The True Artist, di Rosa Preserve, Napa, 2004, Shakespeare As Muse, Schneider Mus., Ashland, Oreg., 2004, di Rosa Preserve, Napa, 2003, 04, Hiromi Gallery, Santa Monica, Otis Gallery, Otis Coll. Art and Design, L.A., 2000, L.A. Mcpl. Art Gallery, C.O.L.A. Fellows Exhbn., 1998, El Camino Coll., 1997, Hunsaker-Schlesinger Gallery, 1996, The Armory Ctr. at Pasadena, 1996, Barnsdall Mcpl. Gallery, 1995, Claremont Grad. Sch. Gallery, 1991, Saxon-Lee Gallery, L.A., 1989, Santa Monica Coll. Gallery Art, 1988, J. Rosenthal Gallery, Chgo., 1986, The Biennial at the Hirshhorn Mus. and Sculpture Garden, Washington, 1986, Kirk de Gooyer Gallery, L.A., 1984, 85, many others; works represented in numerous collections including The Norton Collection, Santa Monica, Broad Found., Santa Monica, Mint Mus., Charlotte, N.C., N.C. Mus. Raleigh, N.C., Security Pacific Corp., L.A., Ft. Lauderdale Mus.; others. Arts commr. City of Santa Monica Arts Commn., 1995—99; mem. Pub. Art Com., Santa Monica, 1996—2000; mem. artists adv. bd. L.A. Mcpl. Art Gallery at Bransdall, 1998—2001. Recipient Durfee Found. award; grantee Dale Chihuly grant for Srs. Making Art Workshops, 1996; painting fellow Western States Arts Fedn./NEA, 1990, painting fellow Getty Trust, 1990, NEA fellow in painting, 1991, City of L.A. Individual Artist's fellow, 1998. Home: 18880 Melvin Ave Sonoma CA 95476 E-mail: alice@alicefellows.com.

FELLOWS, ESTHER ELIZABETH, musician, educator; b. Miami, Ariz., Nov. 5, 1952; d. John Wilmont and Flora Elizabeth (Eyestone) Walker; m. James Michael Fellows, Aug. 20, 1976; children: Joy Christine, Rachel Lindsay, Daniel Matthew, Jessica Grace. B in Music Edn., U. Colo., 1975. Co-dir. Children's Piano Lab. U. Colo., Boulder, 1975-76; instr. So. Calif. Conservatory Music, Sun City, 1976-78; pvt. instr. Ft. Lauderdale, 1978-84; instr. Ft. Lauderdale Christian Sch., 1981-83; sect. violinist Signature Symphony Tulsa Ballet Orch., 1984—2006, Bartlesville Symphony, Okla., 1990—; pvt. instr. Broken Arrow, Okla., 1984—, Mounds, Okla. Pvt. instr. Ft. Lauderdale, 1978-84. Mem. Music Tchrs. Nat. Assn. (cert. piano, violin and viola), Am. String Tchrs. Assn., Am. Viola Soc., Okla. Music Tchr. Assn. (chmn. dist. achievement auditions), Suzuki Assn. Am., Hyechka Music Club Tulsa, Tulsa Accredited Music Tchrs. Assn. (past pres., now parliamentarian). Avocation: biking. Home: 19821 S Harvard Ave Mounds OK 74047-5049 E-mail: jefellows@juno.com.

FELLOWS, GERALD LEE, lawyer; b. Joliet, Ill., Mar. 21, 1962; s. Barbara Ann Gast; m. Lee Ann Hankowitz, July 27, 1963; children: Christopher Lee, Anna Elisabeth. BS, U. Ill., 1984; MS, Pa. State U., 1989; JD, Marquette U., 1992. Bar: U.S. Patent & Trademark Office 1992. Engr., foundry supr. GM, Saginaw, Mich., 1985—87; assoc. Reinhart Boerner Van Deuren, Milw., 1991—98; ptnr. Michael Best & Friedrich LLP, 1998—, Milw. office mng. ptnr., 2005—07; ptnr. Greenberg Traurig LLP, Phoenix, 2007—. Adj. asst. prof. Marquette U. Law Sch., Milw., 1993—98. Chair Flood Remediation Task Force, Elm Grove, Wis., 2000—01; commr. Police and Fire Commn., Elm Grove, 2003—06. Named one of Best Lawyers in Am., 2005—; recipient AV rating, Martindale-Hubbel, 2002—. Mem.: State Bar Wis. (chair intellectual property sect.), Soc. Automotive Engrs. (chair Milw. chpt. 1999—2000). Office: Greenberg Traurig LLP 2375 E Camelback Rd Ste 700 Phoenix AZ 85016 Home Phone: 480-659-3659; Office Phone: 602-445-8383. Office Fax: 602-445-8100. Business E-Mail: fellowsj@gtlaw.com.

FELLOWS, JERRY KENNETH, lawyer; b. Madison, Wis., Mar. 19, 1946; s. Forrest Garner and Virginia (Witte) F.; m. Patricia Lynn Graves, June 28, 1969; children: Jonathon, Aaron, Daniel. BA in Econs., U. Wis., 1968; JD, U. Minn., 1971. Bar: U.S. Dist. Ct. (no. dist.) Ill. 1971. Ptnr. McDermott, Will & Emery, Chgo., 1971—2002; with Bell, Boyd & Lloyd LLC, Chgo., 2002—. Speaker Bur. Nat. Affairs, Washington, 1985—. Contbr. articles to profl. jours. Bd. dirs. Midwest Benefits Coun., 1998. Mem. U. Minn. Law Alumni Assn. (bd. visitors), Gamma Eta Gamma. Avocations: coaching track, basketball, baseball. Home: 4541 Middaugh Ave Downers Grove IL 60515-2761 Office: Bell Boyd & Lloyd LLC 70 West Madison St Ste 3100 Chicago IL 60602-4207 Office Phone: 312-807-4358. Business E-Mail: jfellows@bellboyd.com.

FELLOWS, JOHN, delivery service executive; Grad. in engring., Dalhousie U., Nova Scotia Tech. Coll. With Canadian Nat. Railways; v.p., corp. strategy and devel. Canada Post Corp., Ottawa, Canada; chmn., CEO DHL Holdings Inc., Plantation, Fla., 2001—. Office: DHL Holdings 1200 S Pine Island Rd Ste 600 Plantation FL 33324

FELLOWS, ROBERT ELLIS, medical educator, researcher; b. Syracuse, NY, Aug. 4, 1933; s. Robert Ellis and Clara F.; m. Karlen Kiger, July 2, 1983; children: Kara, Ari, Thomas, Gregory, Jamey. AB, Hamilton Coll., 1955; MD, CM, McGill U., 1959; PhD, Duke U., 1969. Intern NY Hosp., NYC, 1959—60, asst. resident, 1960—61, Royal Victoria Hosp., Montreal, Que., Canada, 1961—62; asst. prof. dept. medicine Duke U., Durham, NC, 1966—76, asst. prof. dept. physiology and pharmacology, 1966—70, assoc. prof. dept. physiology and pharmacology, assoc. dir. med. scientist tng. program, 1970—76; prof. & chmn., dept. physiology and biophysics U. Iowa Coll. Medicine, 1976—2002, prof. dept. physiology and biophysics, 1976—, dir. med. sci. tng. program, 1976—97, dir. physician sci. program, 1984—88, dir. neurosci. program, 1984—88. Mem. Nat. Pituitary Agy. Adv. Bd.; mem. NIH Population Rsch. Com., 1981-86, VA Career Devel. Rev. Com., 1985-88; cons. NIH, NSF, March of Dimes. Mem. editl. bd. Endocrinology, Am. Jour. Physiology. Mem. AAAS, Am. Chem. Soc., Am. Fedn. Clin. Rsch., Am. Physiol. Soc., Am. Soc. Biol. Chemists, Am. Soc. Cell Biology, Assn. Chmn. Depts. Physiology, Biochem. Soc., Biophys. Soc., Endocrine Soc., Internat. Soc. Neuroendocrinology, NY Acad. Scis., Soc. for Neurosci., Assn. Neurosci. Depts. and Programs (pres. 1995-96), Sigma Xi, Alpha Omega Alpha. Home: 135 Pentire Cir Iowa City IA 52245-1575 Office: 5-472 Bowen Sci Bldg Iowa City IA 52242 Office Phone: 319-335-7804. Business E-Mail: robert-fellows@uiowa.edu.

FELLS, CHARLES DAYTON, civil engineer, educator; b. Everett, Wash., June 29, 1933; s. Everett Orrin and Isabel Helen Fells; m. Patricia Anne Campbell, Jan. 9, 1993; 1 child, Donald Kevin; m. Audrey Carol Morgan, Sept. 29, 1962 (div. Mar. 1992). BS, Mont. State U., Bozeman, 1983. Gen. mgr. Constrn. Assist, Bothell, Wash., 1984—89; quality evaluator USN, Pearl Harbor, Hawaii, 1989—90; quality control engr. Kiewit Constrn. Co., Princeville, Hawaii, 1990—91; project engr. Engrs., Surveyors, Hawaii, Honolulu, 1991—93; compliance inspector cons. Honolulu, 1994—96; project engr. G.W. Murphy Constrn., Honolulu, 1995—96; mem. faculty U. N.Mex., Los Alamos, 1996—2000; ret., 2000. Continuing edn. lectr. C.C. Beaver County, Monaca, Pa., 2002—03. Contbr. articles and papers to profl. jours. Mem.: VFW (master of ceremonies for Vets. Day, Los Alamos 1997), U.S. Naval Inst., Am. Legion. Avocations: historical writing and research, public speaking, long distance running, military history. Home: 216 Pine Rd Sewickley PA 15143 Personal E-mail: chuckfells@aol.com.

FELLS, ROBERT MARSHALL, lawyer; b. NYC, Sept. 27, 1950; s. Marshall Raymond and Theresa Katherine (Madigan) F.; m. Maureen Ellen Tierney, Aug. 3, 1974; children: Veronica, Robert, Patrick. BA in History, Iona Coll., 1972; JD, George Mason U., 1976. Bar: Va. 1979, U.S. Dist. Ct. (ea. dist.) Va. 1980, U.S. Ct. Appeals (4th cir.) 1979, U.S. Supreme Ct. 1989. Legal asst. Howrey & Simon, Washington, 1977-83; legal advisor Cemetery Consumer Svc. Coun., Washington, 1983—. External COO, gen. counsel Internat. Cemetery, Cremation and Funeral Assn., Sterling, Va., 1983—, pres. gen. counsel, 1983—; instr. Inst. for Legal Studies, Alexandria, 1988. Author: George Arliss: The Man Who Played God, 2004; editor Cemetery Legal Compass, 1991-2000; contbg. editor (newsletter) ICCFA

Wireless, 2000-; contbr. articles to numerous jours. Organizer Arlington (Va.) Film Workshop, 1975-82, Alexandria Coun. on the Arts, 1979-81; pres. The Cinevox Soc., Annandale, Va., 1983; Eucharistic minister St. Andrew Ch., Clifton, Va., 1990-01; religious edn. tchr., 1993-; mem. bd. regents Nat. Mus. Funeral History, 2005-; bd. dirs. ICCFA Ednl. Found., 2005-. Mem. KC. Republican. Roman Catholic. Avocations: jogging, pianist, silent film historian, musicologist. Home: 15429 Martins Hundred Dr Centreville VA 20120-1169 Home Phone: 703-830-7716; Office Phone: 703-391-8400. Business E-Mail: rfells@iccfa.com.

FELMAN, MARC DAVID, air force officer; b. Biloxi, Miss., June 19, 1954; s. Harold Arnold and Vivian Kathryn (Knox) F.; m. Pamela Adams, Feb. 29, 1992; 1 child, Marc David. BS in History, USAF Acad., 1976; MS in Systems Mgmt., U. So. Calif., 1982; postgrad., U. Ala., 1990-91; MS in Air Power Art and Sci., USAF Sch. Adv. Airpower Study. Commd. 2d lt. USAF, 1976, advanced through grades to col., 1996; pilot 909th Air Refueling Squadron, Kadena Air Base, Japan, 1978-80, aircraft commander, 1980-82; flight comdr. 9llth Air Refueling Squadron, Goldsboro, NC, 1983-85; current ops. planner 68th Air Refueling Wing, Goldsboro, 1985-88, flight examiner, 1988-89; assigned to Air U. faculty Air Command Staff Coll., Montgomery, Ala., 1989-91; 1st class Air Force Sch. for Advanced Airpower Studies, Maxwell AFB, Ala., 1991-92; comdr. 911th Air Refueling Squadron, Goldsboro, NC, 1992-94; squadron comdr. 711th Air Refueling Squadron, Goldsboro, 1994; strategic planner, strategy divsn. Office Joint Chiefs of Staff, Washington, 1995-97; comdr. 34th Ops. Group, USAF Acad., Colo., 1997-98; Harvard Internat. fellow Weatherhead Ctr. for Internat. Affairs, Harvard U., Cambridge, Mass., 1998-99; from asst. dep. chief of staff for plans and policy to dir. staff NATO AirSouth, 1999—2001; comdr. 39th Wing, 2002—03; dep. dir. operational plans and joint matters HQ Air Force, Pentagon, 2003—05; assoc. Booz Allen Hamilton, McLean, Va., 2005—. Decorated DFC, DSM, Legion of Merit; Eaker fellow, 1999; recipient Mackay trophy USAF and Nat. Aeros. Assn., 1986, Kalberer trophy SAC, 1986, Jabara trophy USAF Acad., 1988; named Lifetime Harvard Internat. fellow, Ira C. Eaker fellow. Mem. Air Force Assn., Daedalians, Am. Legion, USAF Acad. Assn. of Grads., Phi Kappa Sigma. Avocations: music, reading, soccer, golf. Home: 3503 Beaver Ford Rd Woodbridge VA 22192 Office: Booz Allen Hamilton Tysons Corners Mc Lean VA 22102 E-mail: fenix76@aol.com.

FELS, GERALD, insurance company executive; Grad., Nichols Coll., 1966. CPA. Exec. v.p., CFO Commerce Group Inc., Webster, Mass., 1975—2006; pres. Commerce Ins. Co., 2001—06; chmn., pres., CEO Commerce Group Inc., 2006—. Trustee emeritus, past chmn. Nichols Coll. Office: Commerce Group Inc 211 Main St Webster MA 01570*

FELS, JAMES ALEXANDER, lawyer, mediator; b. Chgo., Nov. 13, 1944; s. William Frederick and Rosemary (Budasi) Fels; m. Nancy Ann Dugan, July 15, 1967; children: Jeffery Scott, Scott Thomas, Thomas Jeffery. BS, Butler U., 1970; JD magna cum laude, Ind. U., 1974. Bar: Ind. 1974, U.S. Dist. Ct. (so. dist.) Ind. 1974. Assoc. atty. Wilson & Tabor, Indpls., 1974-76, Wilson, Tabor & Holland, Indpls., 1976-81; mng. atty. Holland & Tabor, Indpls., 1981-87; ptnr. Tabor, Fels & Tabor, Indpls., 1987-2000, Mediation Group LLC, Indpls., 2000—. With US Army, 1967—72. Mem.: ABA, Assn. Conflict Resolution, Indpls. Bar Assn., Ind. Trial Lawyers Assn., Ind. Bar Assn., Am. Coll. Civil Trial Mediators. Democrat. Roman Catholic. Home: 8136 Rush Pl Indianapolis IN 46250-4266 Office: 8888 Keystone Xing Ste 1500 Indianapolis IN 46240-4614 Home Phone: 317-845-5294; Office Phone: 317-569-3000. Personal E-mail: jfels@comcast.net. Business E-Mail: jfels@mede8.com.

FELS, NICHOLAS WOLFF, lawyer; b. White Plains, NY, Mar. 19, 1943; s. Lawrence P. and Fredricka (Gaines) F.; m. Susan T. McEwan, Dec. 28, 1968; 1 child, Sarah. BA magna cum laude, Harvard U., 1964; MA, U. Calif., Berkeley, 1965; LLB cum laude, Harvard U., 1968. Bar: NY 1968, Calif. 1970, US Dist. Ct. (cen. dist.) Calif. 1970, DC 1971, US Dist. Ct. DC 1971, US Ct. Appeals (10th cir.) 1976, US Ct. Appeals (DC cir.) 1977, US Supreme Ct. 1978, US Ct. Appeals (4th cir.) 1979, US Ct. Appeals (8th cir.) 1981, US Ct. Appeals (5th cir.) 1982. Law clk. to Hon. John Minor Wisdom U.S. Ct. Appeals, New Orleans, 1968-69; atty. OEO Legal Svcs., LA, 1969—70; assoc. Covington & Burling, Washington, 1970-76, ptnr., energy practice group, 1976—2006, sr. counsel, 2006—. Mem. Nat. Com. on US-China Relations, NYC, 1982—. Contbr. articles to profl. jours. Bd. dirs. DC Edn. Compact, 2005—. Mem. Energy Bar Assn., DC Appleseed Ctr. (bd. dirs. 1994—, pres. 1996-2000). Office: Covington & Burling 1201 Pennsylvania Ave NW Washington DC 20004-2401 Office Phone: 202-662-5648. Office Fax: 202-662-6291. Business E-Mail: nfels@cov.com.

FELS, RENDIGS, economist, educator; b. Cin., June 11, 1917; s. Clifford George and Estella Luella (Rendigs) F.; m. Beatrice Carmichael Baker, Dec. 27, 1941, (dec.); children: Charles Wentworth Baker, Carmichael (dec.); m. Marilyn W. Whiteman, July 15, 2001. AB, Harvard U., 1939, PhD, 1948; AM, Columbia U., 1940. Mem. faculty Vanderbilt U., 1948—, prof. econs., 1956-82, prof. emeritus, 1982—, dir. grad. program econ. devel., 1956- 57, chmn. dept. econs. and bus. adminstrn., 1962-65, 77-79. Chmn. Univs.-Nat. Bur. Com., 1962-67. Author: American Business Cycles, 1865-1897, 1959, Challenge to the American Economy, an Introduction to Economics, 1961, 2d edit, 1966, (with C. Elton Hinshaw) Forecasting and Recognizing Business Cycle Turning Points, 1968; Editor: (with Stephen Buckles) Casebook of Economic Problems and Policies, 5th edit, 1981. Served with USAAF, 1942-46. Mem. Am. Econ. Assn. (sec.-treas. 1970-75, treas. 1976-87), Midwest Econ. Assn. (pres. 1984-85), So. Econ. Assn. (pres. 1967-68) Personal E-mail: rendigsf@aol.com.

FELSBURG, DAVID F., engineering executive, educator; b. Wilmington, Del., July 3, 1946; s. Francis Edward and Alice Jenny (Biscoe) F.; children: Michelle A., David W., Daniel E., Darrell B., Darren T. BS in Electronics Engrng., N.Mex. State U., Las Cruces, 1975; M in Engrng., U. Utah, 1980; grad., So. Bapt. Sem. Ext., Colorado Springs, 1985; postgrad. in Ministry, Luther Rice Sem., 2002—05; postgrad., Capella U., 2005—. Ordained pastor So. Bapt. Ch., 1981. Chief technician, sys. trainer 1961 Comm. Squadron, Clark AFB, The Philippines, 1969-73; dir. plans and programs 4754 Radar Evaluation Squadron, Hill AFB, Utah, 1976-79; dir. USAF/FAA Joint Ops. for Atmospheric Def. Hdqs. N.Am. Aerospace Def. Command, Colorado Springs, 1979; comdr., dir. comms. sys. 47 Comms. Group, Cheyenne Mountain AFB, Colo., 1979-81; dept. head math., football defensive line coach USAF Acad., Colorado Springs, 1981-85; sr. program mgr., dir. ops. CTA Inc., Boston, 1985-89; v.p., dir. ops. CTA Inc. Northeastern Region, Boston, 1989-97; pres., co-founder Paloma Sys., Inc., Alexandria, Va., 1997—; founder, pres. CEO US Vets Technologies, Inc., 2006—. Author: New Christians Everyday, 1987; author, editor 24 tech. bus. proposals, 1985—; lectr. in field. Interim pastor Faith Evangelical Ch., Melrose, Mass., 1996-97; pastor, tchr., evangelist, seminar leader Bapt. Chs., N.Mex., Tex., Miss., Utah, Colo., Mass., NH, Maine, Conn., RI, Vt., Va., 1973—; pastor Bon Air Bapt. Ch., Arlington, Va, 2003-; founder Eton Park Home Owners Assn., Alexandria, 1998; founder, pastor Alexandria Bible Chapel, 1997, Wilmington Bible Chapel, Mass., 1990; platinum mem. Rep. Nat. Com., Washington, 1993—. Mem. IEEE, Nat. Def. Indsl. Assn. (chpt. pres. 1995-98, Pres. award 1996-97, bd. dirs. 1998-), Air Force Comms. Electronics Assn. and Air Force Assn., Assn. of Old Crows. Republican. Southern Baptist. Avocations: preaching and teaching bible, golf. Office: 11250 Waples Mill Rd Ste 300 S Fairfax VA 22030 Home: PO Box 3740 Oakton VA 22124-3740 Fax: 703-591-0987.

FELSENTHAL, STEVEN ALTUS, lawyer; b. Chgo., May 21, 1949; s. Jerome and Eve (Altus) F.; m. Carol Judith Greenberg, June 14, 1970; children: Rebecca Elizabeth, Julia Alison, Daniel Louis Altus. AB, U. Ill., 1971; JD, Harvard U., 1974. Bar: Ill. 1974, U.S. Dist. Ct. (no. dist.) Ill. 1974, U.S. Ct. Claims 1975, U.S. Tax Ct. 1975, U.S. Ct. Appeals (7th cir.) 1981. Assoc. Levenfeld, Kanter, Baskes & Lippitz, Chgo., 1974-78; ptnr. Levenfeld & Kanter, Chgo., 1978-80, Levenfeld, Eisenberg, Janger, Glassberg & Lippitz, Chgo., 1980-84; sr. ptnr. Sugar, Friedberg & Felsenthal, Chgo., 1984—. Lectr. Kent Coll. Law, Ill. Inst. Tech., Chgo., 1978-80. Mem. ABA, Ill. Bar Assn., Chgo. Bar Assn., Chgo. Coun. Lawyers, Harvard Law Soc. Ill., Standard Club, Harvard Club, Phi Beta Kappa. Office: Sugar Friedberg & Felsenthal 30 N La Salle St Ste 3000 Chicago IL 60602-3327 Office Phone: 312-704-9400. Business E-Mail: saf@sff-law.com.

FELSHER, STEVEN G., advertising executive, lawyer; b. 1949; BA in classical Greek, Dickinson Coll., 1969; JD, Yale Law Sch., 1973. With Marshall, Bratter, Greene, Allison & Tucker, 1973-79; v.p. Gray Advt., Inc., NYC, 1979-86, sr. v.p., 1986-89, exec. v.p. fin. worldwide, sec., treas., 1989—. Fellow Thomas Watson. Office: Grey Advt Inc 777 3rd Ave New York NY 10017-1401 Office Phone: 212-546-2000.

FELSINGER, DONALD E., utilities corporation executive; BSME, U. Ariz. Exec. v.p. SDG&E (subs. Enova Corp.), 1993-96, pres., CEO, 1996-98, Enova Corp., 1998; group pres., unregulated affils. Sempra Energy (merger of Pacific Enterprises/Enova Corp.), San Diego, 1998—2004; pres., COO Sempra Energy, 2004—06, chmn., CEO, 2006—. Bd. dirs. Edison Electric Inst. Bd. dirs. U.S.-Mexico C. of C., Greater San Diego C. of C., Inst. of the Americas, San Diego Holiday Bowl. Office: Sempra Energy 101 Ash St San Diego CA 92101-3017*

FELSTED, CARLA MARTINDELL, librarian, writer, editor; b. Barksdale Field, La., June 21, 1947; d. David Aldenderfer Martindell and Dorthe (Hetland) Horton; m. Robert Earl Luna, Aug. 24, 1968, (div. 1972); m. Hugh Herbert Felsted, Nov. 2, 1974. BA in English, So. Meth. U., 1968, MA in History, 1974; MLS, Tex. Woman's U., 1978. Cert. secondary tchr., Tex.; cert. learning resources specialist, Tex. Tchr. Bishop Lynch High Sch., Dallas, 1968-72, Lake Highlands Jr. High Sch., Richardson, Tex., 1973-75; instr. Richland Coll., Richardson, Tex., 1973-76; library asst. So. Meth. U., Dallas, 1977-78; librarian Tracy-Locke Advt., Dallas, 1978-79; corp. librarian Am. Airlines, Inc., Ft. Worth, 1979-84; research librarian McKinsey & Co., Dallas, 1984-85; reference librarian St. Edward's U., Austin, Tex., 1985—2002, assoc. prof., 1994—2002; libr. Sedona (Ariz.) Pub. Libr., 2003—. Ptnr. Southwind Info. Svcs. and Southwind Bed-Breakfast, Wimberley, Tex., 1985-92. Editor, compiler: Youth and Alcohol Abuse, 1986; co-editor Mexican Meanderings, 1991-99; contbr. Frommer's travel guides, 1991-96. Mem. adv. bd. Sch. Libr. and Info. Scis., Tex. Women's U., Denton, 1982-84; mem. curriculum com. Wimberley Ind. Sch. Dist., 1986; bd. dirs. Hays-Caldwell Coun. on Alcohol and Drug Abuse, San Marcos, Tex., 1986-88, Inst. Cultures for Wimberley Valley, 1989-91, Tex. Alliance Human Needs, 1992-96; Tex. Team Survivor, Danskin Triathlon, 1995-2002, co-capt. 1997-99; vol. Breast Cancer Resource Ctr., 1998-2000, Sedona Cultural Pk., 2003-04, Sedona Pub. Libr., 2003, Sedona Gt Decisions, 2003-; dem. party precinct comm., 2004-06 Grantee St. Edward's U., 1986-89, 96. Mem. ALA, Tex. Libr. Assn. (dist. program com., membership com. 1986-88, Tex.-Mex. rels. com. 1992-2002), REFORMA, Wimberley C. of C. (bd. dirs. 1987-88). Unitarian Universalist. Avocations: health issues research and advocacy, regional and ethnic cooking, physical fitness, art history, travel.

FELSTINER, JOHN, literature educator, translator; b. Mt. Vernon, NY, July 5, 1936; s. Louis John Felstiner and Gertrude Robison Shiman; m. Mary Lowenthal, Feb. 19, 1966; children: Sarah Alexandra, Aleksandr Lowenthal. BA, Harvard Coll., 1958; PhD, Harvard U., 1965. Vis. prof. of English The Hebrew U., Jerusalem, 1974—75; vis. prof. of comparative lit. Yale U., New Haven, 1990—90; vis. faculty Ny State Summer Writers Inst., Saratoga Springs, NY, 1997—99; vis. prof. of English Yale U., New Haven, 2002—02; fulbright-Hays prof. in Am. lit. U. Chile, Santiago, Chile, 1967—68; prof. of English Stanford U., Stanford, Calif., 1965—. Cons./evaluator publs., jours., univ. depts., founds., 1965—; judge Am. PEN, MLA, Helen and Kurt Wolff Lit. Prize, 1980—2003; v.p. Ctr. Art Transl., San Francisco, 2000—. Author: (book) The Lies of Art: Max Beerbohm's Parody and Caricature, Paul Celan: Poet, Survivor, Jew (Truman Capote award for lit. criticism, 1997), (poetry) Twenty Questions I Wish I'd Asked My Father (Mass. rev.), The Runners in the Luxembourg Gardens (Paris rev.), (scholarly study) Translating Neruda: The Way to Macchu Picchu (Calif. commonwealth club gold medal, 1981); translator: (literary translation) The Dark Room and Other Poems by Enrique Lihn, (anthology) Selected Poems and Prose of Paul Celan, 2001, (bibliophile edition) Heights of Macchu Picchu/Alturas De Macchu Picchu, Deathfugue/Todesfuge; co-editor: (book) Jewish American Literature: A Norton Anthology, 2000; contbr. articles to profl. jours. Bd. dirs. Holocaust Ctr. No. Calif., San Francisco, 1979—2003. Lt. USN, 1958—61. Finalist James Russell Lowell prize, MLA, 1997, Nat. Book Critics Cir., 1996; named resident in Yaddo, Macdowell, Djerassi, Rockefeller, Bellagio, Millay, Mesa Refuge and Jentel Artist colonies, 1993—2002; recipient Kenyon Rev. prize for Lit. Criticism, 1967, publ., Brit. Comparative Lit. Assn., Gold medal, Coun. Advancement and Support Edn., 1991, Translation prize, Brit. Comparative Lit. Assn., Lois Roth prize, MLA, 2001, transl. prize, 2001, ATA, 2001, Pen West Transl., 2001, citation, Nat. Book Critics Cir., 1995; Guggenheim fellow, Rockefeller fellow, NEH fellow, NEA fellow, Stanford Humanities Ctr. fellow, 1983—2005. Mem.: Am. Acad. Arts and Scis., Paul Celan Soc. Democrat. Jewish. Avocations: book and map collecting, acappella singing, hiking, running. Office: English Dept Stanford U Building 460 Stanford CA 94305-2087 Office Phone: 650-723-4722. Business E-Mail: felstiner@stanford.edu.

FELSTINER, MARY LOWENTHAL, retired history professor; b. Pitts., Feb. 19, 1941; d. Alexander and Anne Lowenthal; m. John Felstiner, Feb. 19, 1966; children: Sarah Alexandra, Aleksandr. BA, Harvard U., 1963; MA, Columbia U., 1966; PhD, Stanford U., 1971. Prof. history San Francisco State U., 1972—2006, prof. emeritus, 2006—. Author: To Paint Her Life, 1994, Out of Joint, 2005. Recipient prize in women's history, Am. Hist. Assn., 1995. Mem.: Phi Beta Kappa. Office: San Francisco State Univ History Dept 1600 Holloway Ave San Francisco CA 94132-1722

FELT, MARK (DEEP THROAT, WILLIAM MARK FELT SR.), former federal agency administrator; b. Twin Falls, Idaho, Aug. 17, 1913; s. Mark Earl and Rose (Dygert) Felt; m. Audrey Isabelle Robinson, June 15, 1938; children: Audrey Joan, William Mark Jr. BA, U. Idaho, 1935; LLB, George Washington U., 1940, JD, 1968. Bar: DC 1941, US Supreme Ct. 1955. Adminstrv. asst. to Senator D. Worth Clark US Senate, Washington, 1938—41; atty. FTC, Washington, 1941; spl. agt. FBI, Washington, 1942—73, supr. counterintelligence ops., 1942—45, agt. charge Salt Lake City, 1956—58, Kansas City, Mo., 1958—62, asst. dir. insp. divsn. Washington, 1962—71, dep. assoc. dir., 1971—72, assoc. dir., 1972—73, ret., 1973; revealed as Deep Throat, insider source that led to Watergate scandal, 2005. Author: (memoir) The FBI Pyramid from the Inside, 1979; co-author (with John O'Connor): A G-Man's Life: The FBI, Being Deep Throat, and the Struggle for Honor in Washington, 2006.

FELTENSTEIN, HARRY DAVID, JR., chemicals executive; b. St. Joseph, Mo., Nov. 6, 1920; s. Harry David and Isabel (Rosenbaum) F.; m. Rosalie Goldstein, Jan. 18, 1945 (dec. Sept. 1977); children: Andrew, Martha; m. Carmen Arechabala Fernandez, Aug. 24, 1979; 1 son, Henry. BS, Harvard U., 1942. Engaged in book pub., 1946-50; with Merrill Lynch, Pierce, Fenner & Smith, 1951-57, Lithium Corp., Am. Inc., NYC, 1957-69, fin. v.p., treas., 1957-58, exec. v.p., treas., 1958-60, pres., treas., 1960-69; pres., dir. Beryllium Metals & Chems. Corp., 1962-69, Gt. Salt Lake Minerals and Chems. Corp., 1967-69; exec. v.p., dir. Gulf Resources & Chem. Corp., 1967-69; pres., bd. dirs. Fuel Mgmt. Corp., Washington, 1970-94, chmn., 1995—; pres., bd. dirs. Internat. Wine Investors, Ltd., 1972-86, Wildenstein & Co., 1972-74; European rep. C & K Coal Co. divsn. Gulf Resources & Chem. Corp., 1981-82; cons. to Spanish govt. cos., 1990—97. Author: Dreamworlds, 2004. Served with USNR, 1942-46. Address: Calle Lerez 4 Madrid 2002 Spain Home Phone: (3491) 563-7621. Personal E-mail: harry.feltenstein@gmail.com.

FELTER, EDWIN LESTER, JR., judge; b. Washington, Aug. 11, 1941; s. Edwin L. Felter and Bertha (Peters) Brekke; m. Yoko Yamauchi-Koito, Dec. 26, 1969. BA, U. Tex., 1964; JD, Cath. U. of Am., 1967. Bar: Colo. 1970, U.S. Dist. Ct. Colo. 1970, U.S. Ct. Appeals (10th cir.) 1971, U.S. Supreme Ct. 1973, U.S. Tax Ct. 1979, U.S. Ct. Claims 1979, U.S. Ct. Internat. Trade 1979. Dep. pub. defender State of Colo., Ft. Collins, 1971-75; asst. atty. gen. Office of the Atty. Gen., Denver, 1975-80; state adminstrv. law judge Colo. Office Adminstrv. Cts., Denver, 1980-83, chief adminstrv. law judge, 1983-98, sr. adminstr., law judge, 1998—. Disciplinary prosecutor Supreme Ct. Grievance Com., 1975-78; mem. faculty Nat. Jud. Coll., 1999—; cons. Star Viet Nam, Hanoi, 2003; adj. prof. law U. Denver Coll. Law. Contbg. editor Internat. Franchising, 1970. Mem. Colo. State Mgmt. Cert. Steering Com., 1983-86; No. Colo. Criminal Justice Planning Coun., Ft. Collins, 1973-75; bd. dirs., vice chmn. The Point Cmty. Crisis Ctr., Ft. Collins, 1971-73; mem. Denver County Dem. Party Steering Com., 1978-79, chmn. 12th legis. dist., 1978-79; bd. dirs., pres. Denver Internat. Program, 1989-90. Fellow: ABA (advisor to nat. com. on state laws 2004—, mem. standing com. ethics and profl. responsibility 2006—), Am. Inns Ct. (pres.-elect 2007—); mem.: Rhone Brackett Inn (pres.-elect), Canadian Coun. and Adminstrn. Tribunals, Internat. Bar Assn., Colo. Bar Assn. (chmn. grievance policy com. 1991—94, interprofl. com. 1995—), Nat. Assn. Adminstrv. Law Judges (pres. Colo. chpt. 1982—84, chair fellowship com. 1996—2006, Fellowship winner 1994), Denver Bar Assn., Arapahoe County Bar Assn., Nat. Conf. Adminstrv. Law Judiciary (chair 2000—01). Office: Colo Office Adminstrv Cts Ste 1300 633 17th St Denver CO 80202 Office Phone: 303-866-5676. Business E-Mail: ed.felter@state.co.us.

FELTER, JOHN KENNETH, lawyer; b. Monmouth, NJ, May 9, 1950; s. Joseph Harold and Rosanne (Bautz) F. BA magna cum laude, MA in Econs., Boston Coll., 1972; JD cum laude, Harvard U., 1975. Bar: Mass. 1975, D.C. 2002, N.Y. 2003, U.S. Dist. Ct. Mass. 1976, U.S. Dist. Ct. (so. dist.) N.Y. 2006, U.S. Dist. Ct. (no. dist.) NY 2007, U.S. Dist. Ct. (ea. dist.) Tex. 2007, U.S. Ct. Appeals (1st cir.) 1977, U.S. Ct. Appeals (2d cir.) 2002, U.S. Ct. Appeals (fed. cir.) 2005, U.S. Ct. Appeals (9th cir.) 2006, U.S. Tax Ct. 1993, U.S. Supreme Ct. 1982. Assoc. Goodwin Procter LLP, Boston, 1975-83, ptnr., 1983—. Spl. asst. gen. Commonwealth of Mass., 1982-84, 94-95; spl. counsel Town of Plymouth, Mass., Town of Salisbury, Mass., Town of Edgartown, Mass.; spl. outside counsel City of Boston, 1990-92; mem. devel. com. Greater Boston Legal Svcs., 1980-99, bd. dirs., 1982—, mem. exec. com., 1989-93; mem. faculty Mass. Continuing Legal Edn., Inc., Boston. Mem. adv. com. The Boston Plan for Excellence in Pub. Schs.; mem. elem. edn. com. Blue Ribbon Commn. on Cmty. Learning Ctrs.; VIP panelist Easter Seals Telethon, Boston, 1978-79. Named one of Am.'s Leading Lawyers for Bus., Chamber's USA, Best Lawyers in Am. Fellow: Am. Coll. Trial Lawyers; mem.: ABA (litigation sect., mem. personal rights litigation com., mem. ABA-Am. Law Inst. com. on cont. edn.), Greater Boston C. of C. (mem. edn. com., mem. health care com.), Boston Bar Assn. (bd. dirs. law firm resources project 1985—, mem. coll. and univ. law com. 1986—, chmn. fed. rules com. litigation sect. 1994), Mass. Bar Assn., Am. Arbitration Assn. (comml. arbitrator). Office: Goodwin Procter LLP Exchange Pl 53 State St Ste 17 Boston MA 02109-2881 Office Phone: 617-570-1211. Business E-Mail: kahuna@goodwinprocter.com.

FELTHEIMER, JON, entertainment company executive; B in Economics, Washington Un. Pres., CEO New World Entertainment, 1989—97; exec. v.p. Sony Pictures Entertainment Inc., 1997—99; pres. Columbia Tristar TV; CEO Lions Gate Entertainment, 2000—, co-chmn. bd. dirs. Named one of 50 Most Powerful People in Hollywood, Premiere mag., 2006. Office: Lions Gate Entertainment Inc 2700 Colorado Blvd Santa Monica CA 90404

FELTHOUS, ALAN ROBERT, psychiatrist; b. San Francisco, Oct. 16, 1944; s. Robert Alan and Agnetta Wilhelmena (Blindheim) F.; m. Mary Louise Wilkins, Aug. 6, 1971; children: Erik Alan, Emily Anna, Elizabeth Ashley. BS, U. Wash., 1967; MD, U. Louisville, 1971. Diplomate Nat. Bd. Med. Examiners, Am. Bd. Psychiatry and Neurology added qualifications in forensic psychiatry, Am. Bd. Forensic Psychiatry (v.p. 1992-93, pres. 1993-94). Intern Roosevelt Hosp., NYC, 1971-72; resident in psychiatry McLean Hosp./Harvard Med. Sch., Belmont, Mass., 1972-75; staff psychiatrist Naval Regional Med. Ctr., Oakland, Calif., 1975-77; psychiatrist, sect. chief Menninger Found., Topeka, 1977-83, dir. adult divsn., 1993—; chief forensic svc. dept. psychiatry and behavioral scis. U. Tex. Med. Br., Galveston, 1984—, assoc. prof. dept. psychiatry and behavioral scis., 1984-89, prof. dept psychiatry and behavioral scis., 1989-98, Marie B. Gale centennial prof. psychiatry, 1994-98; prof. dept. psychiatry So. Ill. U. Sch. Medicine, Springfield, 1998—2006, dir. forensic psychiatry, 1998—2006; med. dir. Chester Mental Health Ctr., Ill., 1998—2006; prof. sch. law Carbondale, 2001—06; prof. psychiatry, dir. forensic psychiatry St. Louis U. Sch. Medicine, 2006—. Cons., mem. expert panel on psychiat. disorders and comml. drivers U.S. Dept. Transp., Fed. Hwy. Adminstrn., Washington, 1990; assn. dirs. Forensic Psychiatry Fellowship Programs, 2006—, sec., 2006—. Author: The Psychotherapist's Duty to Warn or Protect, 1989; newsletter editor: Am. Acad. Psychiatry and the Law, 1988-93; co-editor (forensic sect.) Current Opinion in Psychiatry, 1993-2001, Behavioral Sciences and the Law, 1997-2001, sr. editor, 2002-; contbr. articles to profl. jours. Capt. USNR, 1969—99. Recipient Wood-Prince awards for sci. pubs., The Menninger Found., 1978—82, Outstanding Achievement award, Gulf Coast Mental Health and Mental Retardation, Galveston, 1991, Exemplary Psychiatrist award, Nat. Alliance for the Mentally Ill, 1993. Fellow Am. Acad. Forensic Scis. (sect. sec. psychiatry and behavioral sci., chmn. 1997-2000, dir. 2000-03, mem.-at-large exec. com. 2002-03, Maier I. Tuchler award 2000), Am. Psychiat. Assn. (disting.); mem. Am. Acad. Psychiatry and the Law (pres.-elect 2005-06, pres. 2006-, Outstanding Svc. award 1994), German Soc. for Psychiatry, Psychotherapy and Neurology, Naval Res. Assn. (life). Achievements include research in abnormal aggressive behaviors. Office: St Louis U Sch Medicine Dept Neurol Psychiatry 1438 S Grand Blvd Saint Louis MO 63104 Personal E-mail: arfelt@aol.com. Business E-Mail: felthous@slu.edu.

FELTON, EDWARD WILLIAM, computer scientist, educator; b. Mar. 25, 1963; BS with honors, Calif. Inst. Tech., 1985; MS in Computer Sci. and Engring., U. Wash., 1991, PhD in Computer Sci. and Engring., 1993. Sr. computing analyst Concurrent Computing Project, Calif. Inst. Tech., 1986—89; asst. prof. computer sci. Princeton U., 1993—99, assoc. prof., 1993—2003, dir. Secure Internet Programming Lab., Dept. Computer Sci., 1996—, prof., 2003—05, prof. computer sci. and pub. affairs, 2005—. Cons. US Dept. Justice, 1998—2002, Robins, Kaplan, Miller & Ciresi, 1998—, Certus Ltd., 2000—02, Electronic Frontier Found., 2001—, Keker & Van Nest, 2002, US Fed. Trade Commn., 2004; Java security adv. bd. mem. Sun Microsystems, 1997—; tech. adv. bd. mem. NetCertainty.com, 1999—2002, Cigital Inc., 2000—, Cloakware Ltd., 2000—, Propel.com, 2000—02; founder Freedom to Tinker weblog. Contbr. Dynamic Tree Searching, 1995, Java Security: Hostile Applets, Holes and Antidotes, 1996, Java Security: Web Browsers and Beyond, 1997, Securing Java:

Getting Down to Business with Mobile Code, 1999; contbr. articles to profl. jours. Recipient Sci. Am. Fifty Award, 2004, EFF Pioneer Award, 2005; grantee Alfred P. Sloan Fellowship, 1997. Office: Princeton U 35 Olden St Princeton NJ 08540 Office Phone: 609-258-5906. Office Fax: 609-258-1771. E-mail: felten@cs.princeton.edu.

FELTON, HELEN MARTIN, retired adult education educator, writer; d. George Burnie Martin, Sr. and Mabel Benjamin Martin; m. Samuel Page Felton, Dec. 31, 1955; 1 child, Samuel Page Jr. BA in Speech and Drama, Miami U., Oxford, Ohio, 1949; MA in Drama, U. Wash., 1952. Instr. and cons. Adult Edn. Supervision and Mgmt. Program's Interpersonal Comm. for Suprs. South Seattle CC, 1971—90; team tchr. interpersonal comm. ext. program U. Wash., Seattle, 1973—80; adj. instr. speech comm., drama and creative dramatics Shoreline CC, Wash., 1974—84; mem. grad. com. Antioch U., Seattle, 1995—98; ret., 1998. Box office staff Penthouse Theatre Drama Dept. U. Wash., Seattle, 1951—51, sec. creative drama office, 1951—52; camp councilor Girl Scouts, LA, 1952—52; asst. field exec. Girl Scout Coun., LA, 1953—53, dist. dir. and program tng. advisor, Seattle, 1955—60; customer contact rep. Gas Co., Seattle, 1954—55; presenter in field. Dir.(writer): (plays) Alaska Hawaii and Japan, (asst. dir.) Thurber Carnival, (music dir.): (Operas) Threepenny Opera; contbr. Together: Communicating Interpersonally, 1st edit., 1975, 2nd edit., 1980. Mem.: Internat. Assn. Theatre for Children and Young People U.S. Ctr., Am. Assn. Theatre Educators, Theatre Comm. Group. Avocations: drama, music, international relations.

FELTON, JULE WIMBERLY, JR., lawyer; b. Macon, Ga., July 22, 1932; s. Jule Wimberly and Mary Julia (Sasnett) F.; m. Kate Gillis, May 15, 1965; children— Jule Wimberly III, Mary Katherine, Laura Borden Student, Emory U., Atlanta, 1949-50; AB, U. Ga., Athens, 1954, LL.B, 1955. Bar: Ga. 1954. Assoc. Hansell & Post, Atlanta, 1955-59, mng. ptnr., 1959-89; sr. of counsel Jones Day Reavis & Pogue, Atlanta, 1989-92; ptnr. Ford & Felton, 1993-95, Proctor, Felton & Atkinson, Atlanta, 1995-96, Proctor, Felton & Chambers, Atlanta, 1996-99. Bd. dirs. dept. cmty. affairs Ga. State, chair, 2003—. Mem. Ga. Gen. Assembly, Atlanta, 1969-72; mem. ofcl. bd. dirs. Northside United Meth. Ch., Atlanta, 1974-85, 88; mem. U. Ga. Bd. Visitors, 1986, 87, 91, chmn., 1987-88, 93-94; bd. dirs. Ga. Dept. Cmty. Affairs Bd., 1999-2003, chair, 2002-03. 1st lt. JAGC, U.S. Army, 1955-56. Recipient Disting. Svc. award, U. Ga. Law Sch. Fellow Am. Bar Found.; mem. ABA, Ga. Bar Assn. (pres. 1973-74), Nat. Conf. Bar Pres., Am. Coll. Trial Lawyers, Ga. Bar Found., Am. Judicature Soc., U. Ga. Law Sch. Assn. (pres. 1984-85), Lawyers Club Atlanta, Old War Horse Lawyers Club (pres. Atlanta chpt. 1983), Piedmont Driving Club, Capital City Club. Avocations: piano, golf, boating. Home: 1061 Arbor Trce NE # 34 Atlanta GA 30319-5381 Office Phone: 404-239-0750. Business E-Mail: jwf@petersonharris.com.

FELTS, MARGARET JEAN, secondary school educator; b. Richmond, Va., Aug. 7, 1965; d. Benjamin R. and Jean Felts. BA, Mary Wash. Coll., 1987. Cert. tchr. secondary social studies Va. Admissions counselor Mary Wash. Coll., 1987—88; tchr. Va. Beach City Pub. Schs., Va. Beach, Va., 1988—. Cheerleading coach Kempsville HS, 1990—95, asst. student activities coord., 1997—2001; chmn. Safe Schs. Action Team, Kempsville HS, 2003—; scholarship com. mem. Kempsville HS, 2003—. Stage mgr.: Arts Guild of Christ and St. Lukes Espisc. Ch., 1997—2000. Tchr. coord. CEL Voting Precinct, Va. Beach, Va., 2004; vol. Boardwalk Art Show, Va. Beach Art Ctr., Va. Beach, Va., 1995—; usher Bayside Presbyn. Ch., Va. Beach, Va., 1999—. Mem.: Parent Tchr. Student Assn. Avocations: travel, theater, reading, movies, Nascar. Office: Kempsville HS 5194 Chief Trail Virginia Beach VA 23464 Office Phone: 757-474-8400. Office Fax: 757-474-8404. E-mail: margaret.felts@vbschools.com.

FELTUS, ALAN EVAN, artist; b. Washington, May 1, 1943; s. John Randolph Feltus and Anne Eve Winter; m. Toni Travis, May 1968 (div. 1974); m. Lani Helena Irwin, Dec. 10, 1978; children: Tobias, Joseph. Student, Tyler Sch. Fine Arts, Phila., 1961-62; BFA, Cooper Union, 1966; MFA, Yale U., 1968. Instr. painting and drawing Sch. of Dayton Art Inst., 1968-70; asst. prof. art dept. Am. U., Washington, 1972-84; artist, 1984—. One-person shows include Forum Gallery, NYC, 1976, 80, 83, 85, 87, 91, 94, 96, 98, 2002-03, 05, Ann Nathan Gallery, Chgo., 1994, 98, 2000, 03, Huntington (W.Va.) Mus. Art, 2000, Wichita (Kans.) Art Mus., 1987, Hemphill Fine Arts, Washington, DC, 2001, Boulder Mus. Contemporary Art, 2007. Mem.: NAD (nat academician 1994—). Avocations: lectures, workshops. Office: Forum Gallery 745 Fifth Ave New York NY 10151 Office Phone: 212-355-4545. Fax: 212-355-4547. E-mail: alan@alanfeltus.com.

FELTY, KRISS DELBERT, lawyer; b. Cleve., May 5, 1954; s. John Gilbert and Stephanie (Kriss) F. BA in Psychology, Case Western Res. U., 1976; postgrad., Cleve. State U., 1977-79; JD, U. Akron, Ohio, 1983. Bar: Ohio 1983, Tex. 1988, Wis. 1989, U.S. Dist. Ct. Ohio 1983, U.S. Ct. Appeals (6th cir.) 1984, Fla. 1985, U.S. Supreme Ct. 1986. Assoc. Dennis Reimer Co., LPA, Twinsburg, Ohio, 1983-87; mng. ptnr. Shapiro & Felty, Independence, Ohio, 1987--. Mem. ABA, Fla. Bar Assn., Ohio Bar Assn., Greater Cleve. Bar Assn., Cuyahoga County Bar Assn., Mortgage Bankers Assn. Am., Ohio Mortgage Bankers Assn., Mortgage Bankers Assn. Met. Cleve., Phi Kappa Theta (trustee 1973-74). Avocations: golf, swimming, reading, music, leaded glass lamps. Office: Shapiro & Felty 1500 W 3d St Ste 400 Cleveland OH 44113

FELZER, BENJAMIN SETH, ecologist, researcher; s. Lionel and Doris Felzer. BA, Swarthmore Coll., 1987; MS, U. Colo., Boulder, 1991; PhD, Brown U., 1996. Postdoctoral fellow Nat. Ctr. Atmospheric Rsch., Boulder, Colo., 1995—98; project scientist U.S. Nat. Assessment, Boulder, 1998—2000; program specialist NOAA OGP, Silver Spring, Md., 2000—01; rsch. assoc. Ecosystems Ctr., Marine Biological Lab., Woods Hole, Mass., 2001—. Contbr. articles various profl. jours. Guest lectr., mentor studies various locations. Mem.: Ecol. Soc. Am., Am. Meteorol. Soc., Am. Geophys. Union, Sigma Xi (Outstanding Rsch. award 1995). Avocations: hiking, backpacking. Office: Ecosystems Ctr Marine Biol Lab 7 MBL St Woods Hole MA 02543 Office Phone: 508-289-7748. Business E-Mail: bfelzer@mbl.edu.

FENDER, KIMBER L., library director, educator; m. Robert C. Fender, Jan. 16, 1982; children: Geoffrey, Allison. BS in Anthropology, No. Ky. U., Highland Heights, 1981; MLS, U. Ky., Lexington, 1983. Circulation supr. Xavier U., Cin., 1982—83; reference libr. Boone County Pub. Libr., Florence, Ky., 1983—85; head pub. svcs. Campbell County Pub. Libr., Cold Spring, Ky., 1985—86; mgr. info. svcs. ATE Mgmt. and Svcs. Co., Cin., 1986—88; libr. Instns./Books-by-Mail Dept. Pub. Libr. Cin. & Hamilton County, 1988—93, asst. to dep. libr. main libr. svcs., 1993—95, asst. to dir./clk.-treas., 1995—98, head info. systems, 1998, exec. dir., 1999—. Co-convener libr. svcs. Greater Cin. Libr. Consortium, 1990—93, direct lend and interlibrary loan contact person, 1993—98, mem. exec. bd., 1998—2002, v.p., 2004—05, pres., 2005—06; mem. tech. adv. com. Ohio Pub. Libr. Info. Network, 1997—98, bd. trustees, 2000—06, chair, 2005—06; adj. prof. U. Ky. Sch. Libr. and Info. Sci., 2000—. Mem. govt. rels. com. Ohio Libr. Coun., 1998—2004, 2006—, chair Ready to Read Initiative, 2006—; libr. svcs. and tech. act adv. coun. State Libr. of Ohio, 2000—; trustee SW Ohio Workforce Investment Bd., 2004—; mem. Success by 6 Steering Coun., 2006—; sec. St. John Evang. Luth. Ch. Coun., 2005—06, pres., 2007. Recipient Profl. Achievement award, No. Ky. U., 1999, Outstanding Alumni award, U. Ky. Sch. Libr. and Info. Sci. Alumni Assn., 2001. Mem.: Lambda Alpha. Office: Pub Libr Cin and Hamilton County 800 Vine St Cincinnati OH 45202-2009 Office Phone: 513-369-6972. Office Fax: 513-369-6993. E-mail: kim.fender@cincinnatilibrary.org.*

FENDLER, JANOS HUGO, chemistry professor; b. Budapest, Hungary, Aug. 12, 1937; came to U.S., 1964; s. Janos and Vilma (Csiky) F.; m. Eleanor Johnson, june 15, 1965 (div. 1975); children: Michael, Lisa; m. Ann Fendler, Feb. 15, 1976 (div. 1997); children: Peter, Monika; m. Eliza Hutter, Sept. 15, 1997; children: Veronika Isabelle, David Viktor. BSc, U. Leicester, Eng., 1960; Diploma in Radiochemistry, Leicester Coll. Tech., 1961; PhD, U. London, 1964, DSc, 1978; DSc (hon.), U. Szeged, Hungary, 1999. Postdoctoral fellow U. Calif., Santa Barbara, 1965-66; fellow Mellon Inst., Pitts., 1966-70; assoc. prof. chemistry Tex. A&M U., College Station, 1970-75, prof., 1975-81; prof. chemistry Clarkson Coll., Potsdam, NY, 1982-85; disting. prof. chemistry, dir. Ctr. Membrane Engring. & Sci. Syracuse U., 1985-97; disting. Camp prof. chemistry Clarkson U., 1997—. Adj. prof. U. Montreal, 1967—94; indsl. cons., vis. prof., Japan, 1975, Switzerland, 79, Sweden, 81, France, 85, Germany, 92, Israel, 97, Paris, 2001—. Author: Catalysts in Micellar and Macromolecular Systems, 1975, Membrane Mimetic Chemistry, 1982, Membrane Mimetic Approach to Advanced Materials, 1994; rsch., numerous publs. in field; N.Am. editor Colloid and Polymer Sci.; mem. editl. bd. Jour. Organic Chemistry, 1978-82, jour. Colloid and Interface Sci., 1981-87, Langmuir, 1985-87, Bull. Chem. Soc. France, 1986-92, Magyar Kèmiai Folyoirat, 1992—, Advanced Materials, 1994—, Chemistry of Materials, 1997—. Recipient Sr. Humboldt Rsch. award, 1992. Mem. Am. Chem. Soc. (Kendall award 1982), Royal Chem. Soc., Internat. Assn. Colloid and Interface Scientists. Home: 608 Swan St Potsdam NY 13676-1147 Office: Clarkson U Ctr Adv Material Processing PO Box 5814 Potsdam NY 13699-0001 E-mail: fendler@clarkson.edu.

FENDRICK, ALAN BURTON, retired advertising executive; b. Bronx, NY, Mar. 22, 1933; s. Louis and Esther (Silberberg) F.; m. Beverly R. Schoenfeld, June 12, 1960; children: Sarah Fendrick, Lisa Rubinstein. AB with honors in Econs, Columbia U., 1954; MBA, Harvard U., 1958. Asst. sales mgr. splty. divsn. Hankins Container Co., 1958-60; mgr. bus. adminstrn., ops. and engring. NBC, 1960-67; exec. v.p., sec., treas. Grey Advt. Inc., NYC, 1967-89, exec. v.p., chmn. fin. com., 1990-93. Trustee Woodlands H.S. Scholarship Fund, Greenburgh, N.Y., pres., 1977-78; trustee Jewish Child Care Assn. N.Y., 1985-97, hon. trustee, 1997—; trustee SAG Producers Pension and Health Plans, 1993-2007; mem. sch. bd. Mt. Plesant Cottage Sch., 1985-99; bd. dirs. Columbia Coll. Alumni Assn., 1989-96. With AUS, 1954-56. Mem. Am. Assn. Advt. Agys. (chmn. com. on fiscal control 1979-81), Advt. Agy. Fin. Mgmt. Group (chmn. exec. com. 1980-82, pres. 1982-84), Winden Hill Condominium Assn. (bd. mgrs. 2001—), Otis Woodlands Club Inc. (bd. dirs. 1985-89, treas. 1984-88), Columbia U. Alumni Club of Sarasota (pres. 1997-2006). Jewish (trustee temple). Home: 5880 Midnight Pass Rd Sarasota FL 34242-4106 Personal E-mail: bevalan711@verizon.net.

FENECH, DANIEL THOMAS, cartoonist; b. Garden City, Mich., 1957; s. Carmel John and Elizabeth Frances (Borg) Fenech; m. Linda M. Speegle, Dec. 7, 1992. BA, U. Mich., 1979. Coll. intern WXYZ-TV, ABC, Southfield, Mich., 1978—79; tech. on-air dir. WEYI-TV, Flint, Mich., 1979—80; cartoonist Daniel Fenech Prodns., Saline, Mich., 1980—. Contbr. to over 90 newspapers including USA Today, Best Editorial Cartoons of the Year, 2001-07. Pres. bd. of trustees Saline Dist. Libr., 1998—2001. Mem.: Assn. Am. Editl. Cartoonists. Avocations: reading, swimming, running, travel, reading.

FENECH, JOSEPH CHARLES, lawyer; b. London, May 28, 1950; came to U.S., 1953; s. Carmel John and Elizabeth Frances (Borg) F.; m. Cynthia A. Rennie, June 14, 1980 (div. 1998); children: Paul C., Peter J., Elizabeth F. BA with high hons., Honors Coll. Mich. State U., 1972; JD, U. Mich., 1975. Bar: Mich. 1975, U.S. Dist. Ct. (ea. dist.) Mich. 1975, U.S. Ct. Appeals (6th cir.) 1977, Ill. 1980, U.S. Dist. Ct. (no. dist.) Ill. 1980, U.S. Dist. Ct. (ctrl. dist.) Ill. 1993, U.S. Dist. Ct. (ea. dist.) Wis. 1993, U.S. Ct. Appeals (7th cir.) 1980, U.S. Supreme Ct. 1993, U.S. Tax Ct. 1993. Law clk. Washtenaw Cir. Ct., Ann Arbor, Mich., 1975-76; asst. atty. gen. State of Mich., Detroit, 1976-80; labor rels. counsel McDonald's Corp., Oak Brook, Ill., 1980-82, sr. internat. atty., 1982-84; sr. mem. Fenech, Pachulski & Welgat, P.C., Oak Brook, Ill., 1985—2006; pvt. practice Naperville, Ill., 2006—. Contbr. articles to profl. jours. Bd. dirs. Cath. Charities Diocese of Joliet, Ill.; active Family Focus, Mich., 1979-80, Internat. Found. Employee Benefit Plans, Brookfield, Wis., 1980-83, Chmns. Club Ctrl.; mem. bd. govs. DuPage Hosp., Ctrl. DuPage Hosp. Tree Life, Ctrl., Glen Oaks Med. Ctr., Tree of Life, Rep. Campaign Coun., 1995; supt. adv. com. Naperville Cmty. Sch. Dist. 203; improvement com. Mill St. Sch., Naperville; charter mem. Marklund Children's Home Endowment; bd. govs. Ctrl. DuPage Hosp. Named Regents scholar U. Mich., 1973, 74, 75, Trustees scholar Mich. State U., 1969-72. Mem. ABA, Ill. State Bar Assn., Mich. Bar Assn., DuPage Estate Planning Coun., U. Mich. Lawyers Club, Ill. Bankers Assn., Ill. Mortgage Bankers Assn., Internat. Platform Assn., Am. Hosp. Assn. (sr. mem.), Am. Acad. Healthcare Attys. (sr. mem.), Mich. State U. Pres. Club. Office Phone: 630-357-8079.

FENG, CHENGDE, mathematician, educator; b. Shanghai, Dec. 12, 1942; arrived in U.S., 1990; s. Xianfu and Huaiyu Jiang Feng; m. Yunhua Xu Feng, Jan. 25, 1969; 1 child, Zuming. BS in Math., East China Normal U., Shanghai, 1964. Co-founder, chief instr. Tianjiu Math Spare-Time Sch., 1980; head coach math team Tianjiu H.S., 1980—90; tchr. math Liao Yuan H.S., Tianjiu, 1984—85; sr. lectr. Hong Qiao Tchrs. Inst., Tianjiu, 1985—90; vis. scholar Johns Hopkins U., Balt., 1990—91; prof. math. Okla. Sch. Sci. and Math, Oklahoma City, 1991—. Dir. Study of Mathematically Precocious Youth, Tianjin, 1988—90; mem. Math Counts Question Writing Com., Washington, 2000—; AP reader Ednl. Testing Svc., 2000—; lectr. in field; faculty Math Olympiad summer programs, 2002; tchr. AMC programs, 2002—06. Co-author: Math Counts Handbook/Questions, 2006; editor: Coach's Corner Imagine, 1994—98; contbr. articles to profl. jours. Recipient Sci. and Tech. Nurturer award, Sci. and Tech. Soc., China, 1986, Ann Simmons Alspangh Faculty award, OSSM Found., 2005. Mem.: Nat. Coun. Tchrs. Math., Math Assn. Am. (Edyth May Sliffa award 1992). Avocations: reading, cooking, baseball, basketball, volleyball. Home: 1141 N Lincoln Blvd Oklahoma City OK 73104 Office: Oklahoma Sch of Science and Math 1141 N Lincoln Blvd Oklahoma City OK 73104

FENG, JIANHUA, education educator; m. Connie Wang, Aug. 28, 1995; children: Lulu W., Sengseng W. EdD, Memphis State U., 1988—92. Cert. InTech Ga., 2002. Assoc. prof. Mercer U., Macon, Ga., 1999—. Exec. dir. Am. Scholarship Found. Internat. Edn., Atlanta. Mem.: Nat. Assn. Multicultural Edn. Independent. Avocations: writing, tennis, travel.

FENG, JINJUAN, information scientist, educator; BA, Huazhong U. Sci., China, 1996; MA, Ctrl. U. Fin. and Econs., China, 1999; PhD in Info. Sys., U. Md., Balt. County, 2000—05. Rsch. asst. U. Md., 2000—05; asst. prof. info. sci. Towson U., Md., 2005—. Recipient Best paper award, Hawaii Internat. Conf. Sys. Scis., 2005; Rsch. grants to develop speech interface for users with disabilities, US Dept. Edn., Nat. Inst. Disability & Rehab. Rsch., 2005—. Achievements include research in effective speech interface for users with disabilities. Office: Towson Univ CIS Dept 7800 York Rd Towson MD 21252 Business E-Mail: jfeng@towson.edu.

FENG, LEI, medical researcher; arrived in U.S., 1989; s. Liesun Feng; m. Chen Zheng, Aug. 17, 1999. BS, Peking Union Med. Coll., 1989; MD, Columbia U., 1998; PhD, The Rockefeller U. Lic. NY, 1999, Calif., 2004, diplomate Am. Bd. Radiology, 2003. Assoc. rsch. scientist Columbia U., NYC, 1998—2003; clin. instr. UCLA, LA, 2004—05; asst. prof. Columbia U., 2004—05; dir. interventional neuroradiology Kaiser L.A. Med. Ctr., 2005—; asst. prof. UCLA, 2005—. Prin. investigator Am. Diabetes Assn., Alexandria, Va., 2004—, Juvenile Diabetes Rsch. Found., NYC, 2004—05; holman pathway rsch. resident Radiology Soc. N.Am., Chgo., 1999—2003. Contbr. articles to profl. jours., chpts. to books. Recipient Holman Rsch. Resident Seed award, Radiol. Soc. N.Am., 2000; fellow, Columbia U., 2003—04; grantee, Am. Diabetes Assn., 2004, Juvenile Diabetes Rsch. Found., 2004. Mem.: AMA, Am. Coll. Radiologist. Achievements include invention of Endothelial biopsy; research in MRI guided neurovascular intervention. Office: South Calif Permanente Med Gourp 4867 Sunset Blvd Los Angeles CA 90027 Home Phone: 310-429-4397; Office Phone: 323-783-5376.

FENG, MARK I., urologist, surgeon; arrived in U.S., 1979; s. Hsien and Anne Feng; m. Lisa Hong; children: Matthew, Luke, John Thomas. BS magna cum laude, U. Mich., 1991, MD, 1995. Resident Kaiser Permanente Med. Ctr., LA, 1995—2001; staff urologic surgeon Kaiser Permanente, Baldwin Park, 2002—. Recipient award, Outstanding Coll. Students Am., 1987—89, Outstanding Laproendoscopic Surgeon award, Laparoendoscopic Soc., 2000, Outstanding Rsch. award, Kaiser Permanente, 2000, 2001. Mem.: Endourology Soc., Laparoendoscopic Surgeons, Am. Urol. Assn. (bd. cert., Western Sect. scholar 1999). Office: Kaiser Permanente 1011 Baldwin Park Blvd Baldwin Park CA 91706 Office Phone: 626-851-6381. Office Fax: 626-851-6397; Home Fax: 626-851-6397.

FENG, WENDY LAI, lawyer; AB, Harvard U., Cambridge, Mass., 1991, JD, 1994. Law clk. to Hon. Edward E. Carres, US Ct. Appeals (11th cir.), 1994—95; assoc. Covington & Burling LLP, San Francisco, 1995—2002, spl. counsel, 2002—. Office: Covington & Burling LLP One Front St San Francisco CA 94111 Office Phone: 415-591-6000. Office Fax: 415-591-6091. Business E-Mail: wfeng@cov.com.

FENG, YING, painter, art educator; b. Chengdu, China, Mar. 16, 1951; arrived in US, 1999; d. Pu-Zhao Feng and ChengHua Zhou; divorced; 1 child, Xiao Qin. BFA, Si-Chuan Norman U., China, 1994. Pres. Jingzi Art Co., Chengdu, 1985—99; dir. North Am. Pastel Artists Assn., NY, 2002—, mem. jury selection, 2005—. Art instr. Golden Eagle Inst., NY, 2004—; vis. prof. Si-Chuan U., Chengdu, 2004—. Pastel paintings, A Tibetant Old Man, 2002 (Silver medal, 2002), A Happy Farmer, 2003 (Gold medal, 2003), A Happy Girl, 2005 (Gold medal, 2005). Fellow: Am. Artists Profl. League (Vera Sickinger, Best in Portrait, award 2006); mem.: Audobon Arts Inc., Pastel Soc. Am. (signature). Home: 141 25 Northern Blvd Apt C11 Flushing NY 11354 Personal E-mail: yingpastel@yahoo.com.

FENIGER, JEROME ROLAND, JR., broadcast executive; b. Peoria, Ill., June 16, 1927; s. Jerome Rol and Marie Dorothy (Miller) F.; m. Marian Laura Schwartz, June 24, 1951; children: Robin Jean, Bruce David. BA, U. Iowa, 1948; postgrad., Columbia U., 1948, N.Y. U., 1949-50; D.Bus. in Sci. (hon.), St. John's U., 1984. Advt. account exec. Biow Co., NYC, 1949-50; chief advt. time buyer Cunningham & Walsh, NYC, 1950-51, v.p., 1954-60; sales exec. CBS, NYC, 1952-54; exec. Cowles Comm. Co., NYC, 1960-65; v.p. Grey Advt. Inc., NYC, 1965-70; pres. Horizons Comm. Corp., NYC, 1970-83; mng. dir. Sta. Reps. Assn., Inc., NYC, 1983—2002; life bd. dirs. Advt. Coun., 1984—2002. Pres. Louise Wise Svcs., 1986-89; mem. pvt. sector commn. USIA/Voice of Am. Trustee Columbia Grammar and Prep Sch., 1965-77, treas., 1970-77; bd. dirs. UJA Fedn. on Domestic Affairs. Sgt. USAF, 1946—47. Recipient Disting. Alumnus award, U. Iowa, 2002. Mem. Internat. Radio and TV Soc. (pres. 1975-77), Friars Club, Dutch Treat Club, Yale Club of N.Y.C. Democrat. Home: 16 W 77th St New York NY 10024-5126 Personal E-mail: srajerry@aol.com.

FENIGER, SUSAN, chef, television personality, writer; Former mem. staff Le Perroquet, Chgo., Ma Maison, LA, L'Oasis, France; formerly chef, co-owner City Cafe, LA; chef, co-owner CITY, LA, 1985—94, Border Grill, LA, 1985—91, Santa Monica, 1990—, Las Vegas, 1998—, Ciudad, LA, 1998—. Co-host (TV series) Too Hot Tamales, 1995—, Tamales' World Tour, (radio show) Good Food; co-author: City Cuisine, 1989, Mesa Mexicana, 1994, Cantina, 1996, Cooking with Too Hot Tamales, 1997, Mexican Cooking for Dummies; guest appearances (TV series) Oprah Winfrey Show, Maury Povich, Today Show, Sabrina the Teenage Witch, featured in USA Today, People Mag., Entertainment Weekly. Active Scleroderma Rsch. Found. Named Chef of Yr., Calif. Restaurant Writers, 1993. Mem.: Chef's Collaborative 2000, Women Chefs and Restaurateurs. Office: Border Grill 1445 4th St Santa Monica CA 90401*

FENIMORE, GEORGE WILEY, management consultant; b. Bertrand, Mo., 1921; BBA in Fin., Northwestern U., 1941; LLB, Harvard U., 1947; postgrad., UCLA, 1955; LLD (hon.), Southwestern U., 1992. Bar: Mich. 1948. Asst. to dir. planning Ford Motor Co., Dearborn, Mich., 1947-48; exec. to v.p. and gen. mgr. Hughes Aircraft Co., Culver City, Calif., 1948-53; adminstrv. mgr. tech. products Packard Bell Electronics Co., 1954-55; with TRW, Inc., LA, 1955-64; v.p., gen. mgr. TRW Internat., LA, 1959-64; v.p. internat. ops. Bunker Ramo Corp., LA, 1964-65; dir. pub. rels., then corp. sec. Litton Industries, Inc., Beverly Hills, Calif., 1965-73, v.p., corp. sec., 1973-81, sr. v.p., corp. sec., 1981-86, mgmt. cons., 1986—. Past chmn. bd. Southwestern U. Sch. Law; mem. Calif. Tchrs. Retirement Bd.; cons. JCM Group. Bd. dirs. Children's Bur. L.A., Child Shelter Homes a Rescue Effort; sec. French Found. for Alzheimer's Rsch.; past mem. Calif. Fair Polit. Practices Commn., 1986-91; mem. United Way Emergency Food Sys. Study Task Force; elder, chmn. fin. com. Westwood Presbyn. Ch.; past trustee Sheldon Jackson Coll., Sitka, Alaska; mem. Beverly Hills Mayor's Econ. Adv. Com. and MOVE com., Calif. Fraud Assessment Commn. Maj. USAAF, WW II. Recipient Citizen of Yr. award, Beverly Hills Lions Club, 1976, Spirit Honoree, Beverly Hills Edn. Found., 1986, Beverly Hills YMCA, 1988, Brentwood/San Vicente C. of C., 1987, Hon. Citizen award, Beverly Hills City Coun., 1986, Guardian Angel award, Child S.H.A.R.E., 1989, Lifetime Achievement award, 2001, Highest award for Lifetime Svc. to Cmty., Key to City of Beverly Hills, 1990, State Gold award, Calif. Tchrs. Assn., 1993. Mem. Am. Soc. Corp. Secs. (dir., past nat. dir., past pres. L.A. Group), Beverly Hills C. of C. (past pres., Citizen of Yr. award 1979, chmn. edn. com., bd. dirs., David Orgell Meml. award 1990), Mandeville Canyon Assn. (past pres.), Bar Assn. Mich., L.A. Country Club, Rotary (past pres. Beverly Hills, Paul Harris fellow, William C. Ackerman trophy 1986), Shriners, Presbyterian. Office Phone: 310-472-9264. Personal E-mail: fenimore98@aol.com.

FENINGER, CLAUDE, retired hotel executive; b. Cairo, Jan. 15, 1926; arrived in US, 1960; s. Paul and Therese (De Rogatis) Feninger; m. Jill Ellis, Nov. 26, 1986; 1 child, Eric. Student, Lycee Francais, Cairo, 1935, Lincoln Coll., 1943, Am. U., 1945; MA, Lausanne Sch. Hotel Mgmt., Switzerland, 1948. Mgr. Shepheards Hotel, 1952, Dhahran Airport Hotel, 1954, Hilton Hotels Internat., 1955—67; pres. Sheraton Internat., 1968—74; chmn. bd., CEO Omni Hotels, Atlanta, 1974—80; pres. Aramark Internat., Phila., 1980—. Author: (book) Sang Froid, 2006. Home: 2045 Yellow Springs Rd Malvern PA 19355-8702 Office: Aramark Corp ARA Svcs Inc 1101 Market St Ste 45 Philadelphia PA 19107-2988 Personal E-mail: cfeninger@aol.com.

FENN, DANIEL JONATHAN, organist; b. McComb, Miss., Apr. 21, 1979; s. David James and Carolyn Bowlin Fenn. MusB, Miss. Coll., Clinton, 2002; MusM, U. Houston, 2004. Organist Thompson Bapt. Ch., Smithdale, Miss., 1992—97, St. Luke's United Meth. Ch., Jackson, Miss., 1997—2000, Alta Woods Bapt. Ch., Jackson, 2000—02; organist, music assoc. Grace Presbyn. Ch., Houston, 2002—06. Mem.: The Am. Choral Dirs. Assn., The Am. Guild Organists (chpt. exec. bd. mem. 2006—). Home Phone: 713-416-4279; Office Phone: 713-267-5061. Personal E-mail: danieljfenn@yahoo.com. Business E-Mail: dfenn@gpch.org.

FENN, JOHN BENNETT, chemist, educator; b. NYC, June 15, 1917; s. Herbert Bennett and Jeanette Clyde (Dingman) F.; m. Margaret Elizabeth Wilson, June 6, 1939; children: Margaret Marianne, Barbara Leigh, John Bennett. AB, Berea Coll., 1937; PhD, Yale U., 1940. Research chemist (Monsanto Chem. Co.), Anniston, Ala., 1940-43, Sharples Chems., Inc., Wyandotte, Mich., 1943-45; v.p. Experiment, Inc., Richmond, Va., 1945-52; dir. Project SQUID, Princeton, 1952-62, prof. mech. engring., 1959-63, prof. aerospace scis., 1963-66; prof. applied sci. and chemistry Yale U., 1967—80; pres. Relay Devel. Corp., 1975—; prof. of engineering Yale U., 1980—87, prof. emeritus, 1987—93; prof. of analytical chem. Virginia Commonwealth U., 1993—. Vis. scientist N.Am. Aviation Sci. Center, 1965-66; vis. prof. U. Trento, Italy, 1976, U. Tokyo, 1979, U. of China, 1987; dir. Thermal Research & Engring. Corp., 1952-59; sci. liaison officer Office Naval Research, London, 1955; dir. Aero Chem. Research Labs., 1956-60; cons. UN; vis. prof. Indian Inst. Sci., Bangalore. Author: Engines, Energy and Entropy, 1982; editor: (with A.B. Cambel) Transport Properties in Gases, 1958, Dynamics of Conducting Gases, 1960. Recipient Sr. Scientist award Alexander von Humboldt Found., 1983-84, Disting. Alumnus award Berea Coll., 1987, Nobel Prize in Chemistry, 2002. Mem. Am. Chem. Soc., AAAS, Am. Inst. Chem. Engrs., Internat. Soc. Mass Spectrometry (sec. 2000), Sigma Xi. Office: VCU Dept of Chemistry 1001 W Main St PO Box 842006 Richmond VA 23284-2006

FENN, ORMON WILLIAM, JR., furniture company executive; b. Tyler, Tex., Mar. 13, 1927; s. Ormon William and Madonna (Muphree) Fenn; m. Lucille Adrianne Kelley (dec.); children: Andrea Lee, Miles Linton, Kelly Sue, Michael Thomas; m. Candace P. Wilkinson, 2005. Student, U. Minn., 1945, Okla. U., 1945, Imperial U., Tokyo, 1946; BS in Applied Econs., Yale U., 1949. Asst. dist. mgr. Armsrong Cork Co., Lancaster, Pa., 1949-59, asst. gen. sales mgr., 1959-70; v.p., gen. sales mgr. Thomasville (N.C.) Furniture Industries, Inc., 1970-74, sr. v.p., gen. sales mgr., 1974-77; exec. v.p. sales and mktg. Stanley Furniture Co. Mead Corp., Stanleytown, Va., 1977-78, pres., vice chmn., 1978-79; pres. CEO Stanley Furniture Co., 1979-82; vice chmn. LADD Furniture Co., High Point, NC, 1982-92, dir., 1982-98. Chmn. emeritus N.C. furnishings export coun. N.C. Dept. Commerce, High Point, 1993—; chmn. N.C. Home Furnishing Coun., 1995-97; past chmn. bd. govs. Western Mdse. Mart, San Francisco; past chmn. market adv. bd. High Point So. Furniture Market Center; past dir. N.C. Furniture Export Office; past chmn. Internat. Home Furnishings Mktg. Assn.; past bd. dirs. Furniture Info. Coun.; past bd. dirs./exec. com. Home Furnishing Coun.; bd. dirs. Am. Furniture Mfrs. Hall of Fame; apptd. by Gov. of N.C. to nat. adv. bd. HandMade in Am.; bd. dirs. Vaughn Bassett Funriture Co., Galax, Va. Past adv. bd. Bryan Sch. Bus. and Econs., U. NC, Greensboro; appt. hon. consul gen. Japan, 1999-2004; bd. dirs. High Point Cmty. Found., bd. trustees. 1st lt. US Army, 1944—52, PTO. Recipient The Order of the Long Leaf Pine award (NC) Gov. Hunt (N.C. highest civilian honor), 1995. Mem. String and Splinter Club (bd. dirs.), High Point Country Club (mem. sr. bd. dirs.). Episcopalian. Avocations: golf, hunting, physical fitness. Home: 510 Emerywood Dr High Point NC 27262-2812 Personal E-mail: billfenoo@hotmail.com.

FENN, PATRICK B., lawyer; b. Atlanta; BA with honors, Univ. Va., 1977, JD, 1982. Bar: NY 1983. Ptnr., head tax practice group and mem. mgmt. com. Akin Gump Strauss Hauer & Feld LLP, NYC. Articles editor Va. Tax Rev., 1981—82. Named one of World's Leading Tax Advisers, Euromoney, 2003. Mem.: ABA. Office: Akin Gump Strauss Hauer & Feld LLP 590 Madison Ave New York NY 10022-2524 Office Phone: 212-872-1040. Office Fax: 212-872-1002. Business E-Mail: pfenn@akingump.com.

FENNEBRESQUE, JOHN C., lawyer; b. Oyster Bay, NY, Apr. 25, 1947; s. John Drouet and Frances (Campbell) Fennebresque; m. Frances Woltz, June 6, 1970; children: John C. Jr., Amy W., Frances C., William T. BA, U. NC, 1970; JD, Vanderbilt U., 1973. Bar: NC 1973. From assoc. to ptnr. Moore & Van Allen, Charlotte, NC, 1973—93; ptnr. Fennebresque, Clark, Swindell & Hay, Charlotte, 1993—98; mng. ptnr. Charlotte office McGuireWoods LLP, 1998—. Bd. governors, U. NC, 1995-2003; bd. dirs. New Arena Com., Charlotte, Mint Mus. Art. Republican. Presbyterian. Avocations: golf, reading. Office: McGuireWoods LLP Bank of Am Corp Ctr 100 N Tryon St Ste 2900 Charlotte NC 28202-4011 Office Phone: 704-373-8989. Office Fax: 704-353-6180. Business E-Mail: jfennebresque@mcguirewoods.com.

FENNELL, DIANE MARIE, marketing professional, process engineer; b. Panama, Iowa, Dec. 11, 1944; d. Urban William and Marcella Mae (Leytham) Schechinger; m. Leonard E. Fennell, Aug. 19, 1967; children: David, Denise, Mark. BS, Creighton U., Omaha, 1966. Process engr. Tex. Instruments, Richardson, 1974-79; sr. process engr. Signetics Corp., Santa Clara, Calif., 1979-82; demo lab. mgr. Airco Temescal, Berkeley, Calif., 1982-84; field process engr. Applied Materials, Santa Clara, 1984-87; mgr. product mktg. Lam Rsch., Fremont, Calif., 1987-90; dir. sales and mktg. Ion & Plasma Equipment, Fremont, Calif., 1990-91; pres. FAI, Half Moon Bay, Calif., 1990-96; v.p. mktg. Tegal Corp., Petaluma, Calif., 1997-99; v.p. mktg. and sales Semicaps, Inc., Santa Clara, Calif., 1999—2001; exec. dir. Ctr. for Internat. Devel., Santa Clara, 2001—03; pres. World Info., Menlo Park, Calif., 2003—. Founder, coord. chmn. Plasma Etch User's Group, Santa Clara, 1984-87; tchr. computer course Adult Edn., Half Moon Bay, Calif., 1982-83. Founder, bd. dirs. Birth to Three program Mental Retardation Ctr., Denison, Tex., 1974-75; fund raiser local sch. band, Half Moon Bay, 1981-89; community rep. local sch. bd., Half Moon Bay, 1982-83. Mem. Am. Vacuum Soc., Soc. Photo Instrumentation Engrs., Soc. Women Engrs., Material Rsch. Soc., Commonwealth Club. Avocations: hiking, reading, gardening. Home: 441 Alameda Ave Half Moon Bay CA 94019-5337

FENNELL, LAURA A., lawyer; BA, Calif. State U.; JD, Santa Clara U. Assoc. Wilson Sonsini, Goodrich and Rosati; v.p. corp. legal recourses, acting gen. counsel Sun Microsystems; v.p., gen. counsel, sec. Intuit Inc., Mountain View, Calif., 2004—. Office: Intuit 2700 Coast Ave Mountain View CA 94043*

FENNELL, MADALINE, elementary school educator; BA in Elem. Edn, Creighton Univ., Nebr.; MA in Elem. Edn., Univ. Nebr., Omaha. Tchr. Omaha Pub. Schs., 1989—; now tchr. Franklin Elem. Sch., Omaha. Named Nebr. Tchr. of Yr., 2007; named an Outstanding American Tchr., Nat. Honor Roll; recipient Carol Stowe Humanitarian award, NEA student program, Ruth E. Pyrtle Leadership award, Nebr. State Edn. Assn. Office: Franklin Elem Sch 3506 Franklin St Omaha NE 68111 E-mail: mfennell1@cox.net.*

FENNELL, STEPHEN A., lawyer; BA magna cum laude, U. Md., 1974; JD magna cum laude, Georgetown U., 1978. Bar: DC 1980, Md. 1987. Law clk. for Judge Edward S. Northrop US Dist. Ct. (Dist. Md.), 1978—79; ptnr., litig. dept. Steptoe & Johnson LLP, Washington, mem. exec. & profl. advancement com., chmn. hiring & pro bono com. Editor: Georgetown Law Jour.; contbr. articles to profl. jour.; spkr. in field. Mem.: Phi Beta Kappa. Office: Steptoe & Johnson LLP 1330 Connecticut Ave NW Washington DC 20036 Office Phone: 202-429-8082. Office Fax: 202-429-3902. Business E-Mail: sfennell@steptoe.com.

FENNELLY, JANE COREY, lawyer; b. NYC, Dec. 12, 1942; d. Joseph and Josephine (Corey) F. BA, Cornell U., 1964; MLS, UCLA, 1968; JD, Loyola U., LA, 1974. Bar: Calif. 1974, U.S. Dist. Ct. (ctrl. and so. dists.) Calif. 1974, U.S. Dist. Ct. (ea. dist.) Calif. 1977, U.S. Dist. Ct. (no. dist.) Calif. 1980, N.Y. 1982, Colo. 1993, Ariz. 1995. Ptnr. Graham & James, 1976-83; with legal dept. Bank of Am., LA, 1973-76, Wyman, Bautzer, Kuchel & Silbert, LA, 1983-87, Dennis, Shafer, Fennelly & Creim (merged with Bronson & McKinnon), LA, 1987-96; with Squire, Sanders & Dempsey, Phoenix, 1996—98; prin. Jane C. Fennelly, P.C., Phoenix, 1998—; of counsel Creim, Macias & Koenig LLP, LA, 1999—. Mem. L.A. County Bar Assn. (bd. dirs., mem. exec. com. comml. law and bankruptcy sect. 1989-92). Home: 15356 W Pasadena Dr Surprise AZ 85374 Office: #610 Ste 101 15508 W Bell Rd Surprise AZ 85374 Office Phone: 602-909-1855. Personal E-mail: jane.fennelly@azbar.org.

FENNER, CHRIS, pastor; b. Kalamazoo, Feb. 28, 1981; s. Richard G. and Gerri Fenner; m. Desiree Hill, Aug. 6, 2005. BS in Music Edn., Western Mich. U., 2003. Cert. pastor of worship Bapt. State Conv. of Mich., 2001; tchr. State of Mich., 2003. Dir. of choirs Covert Pub. Schs., Covert, Mich., 2004—06; pastor of worship Covert Cmty. Ch., Covert, Mich., 2004—05, New Hope Baptist Ch., Versailles, Ky., 2006—07. Music tchr. Lessons in Voice, Piano, and Guitar, Kalamazoo, 2003—06, Versailles, Ky., 2007; worship cons. First Bapt. Ch. of Portage, Portage, Mich., 2005—06; guest performer Reformed Ecumenical Coun. World Assembly, Utrecht, Netherlands, 2005; hymnology rsch. asst. So. Baptist Theol. Sem., Louisville, 2007. Author (webmaster): (website) acdami.org; author: (director) (musical) Love: Lost & Found, (musical comedy) How to Lose a Girl in 10 Days; author: (editor and webmaster) (website) fennerfamily.com; prodr.(conductor): The Road We've Traveled, Nativity Suite; dir.: Come to the Table; author: FYI: Worship History and Theology. Music dir. Mall City Chorus, Kalamazoo, Mich., 2003—06. Recipient Mem. of the Yr., Mall City Chorus, 2000—01. Mem.: Hymn Soc. US and Can., Am. Choral Dirs. Assn. of Mich. (chair of music tech. 2004—07). Achievements include development of the first ACDA websites in the nation to offer online registration for its conventions; creation of music notation projection resources for church worship. Home: 107 Fenley Ave Apt Y3 Louisville KY 40207-2552 Home Phone: 502-544-6280. Personal E-mail: fennertree@aol.com.

FENNER, SUZAN ELLEN, lawyer; b. Grand Junction, Colo., Dec. 5, 1947; d. Harry J. and Louise (Bain) Shaw; m. Michael Lee Riddle, Apr. 24, 1969 (div. Feb. 1976); m. Peter R. Fenner, Nov. 24, 1978; children: Laura Elizabeth, Adam Kyle. BA, Tex. Tech U., 1969, JD, 1971. Bar: Tex. 1972, U.S. Dist. Ct. (no. dist.) Tex. 1972. Assoc. Smith & Baker, Lubbock, Tex., 1971-72; law clk. to presiding judge US Dist. Ct., Dallas, 1972-73; assoc. Gardere Wynne Sewell LLP, Dallas, 1973-78, ptnr., 1978—. Chair retirement com. Gardere Wynne Sewell LLP, 1973—2006, chair employee benefits practice, 1978—, mem. ptnrs. bd., 1991—94, chair tax practice, 2001—06, chair diversity com., 2006—; bd. dirs. Tex. Lawyers Ins. Exch., 1983—, S.W. Benefits Assn. (formerly S.W. Pension Conf.), 1987—92, pres., 1990—91. Bd. dirs. East Dallas Devel. Ctr., 1982—91; Lone Star coun. Camp Fire USA, 1995—2001, v.p. outdoor programs, 1996—98, pres.-elect, 1997, pres., 1998—2000; bd. dir. Episcopal Ch. Women of the Diocese of Dallas, 1992—2002, pres., 1996—2000; del. to triennial nat. conv. Episcopal Diocese of Dallas, 1994, 1997, 2000, asst. chancellor, 1994—2004, exec. coun., 1995—2000, standing com., 2001—04; pres. Episcopal Ch. Women for Episcopal Ch. of Ascension, 1992, bd. dir., 1992—94; pres. Province VII Episcopal Ch. Women, bd. dir., 1999—2002; exec. coun. Province VII of the Episcopal Ch., 1999—2002; mem. vestry Episcopal Ch. of the Ascension, 1996—99, 2005—, sr. warden, 2007; bd. dir. High Adventure Treks for Dads and Daus., 2005—. Recipient Outstanding Vol. award, Camp Fire USA, Lone Star Coun., 2003. Mem. ABA, Tex. Bar Assn. (chmn. bar. jour. com. 1982-88), Dallas Bar Assn. (treas. employee benefits com. 1998, sec. 1999, v.p. 2000, pres. 2001), Dallas Bus. League (pres. 1986). Avocation: sailing. Home: 600 Goodwin Dr Richardson TX 75081-5603 Office: Gardere Wynne Sewell LLP 1601 Elm St Ste 3000 Dallas TX 75201-4761 Office Phone: 214-999-4576. Business E-Mail: sfenner@gardere.com.

FENNESSEY, PAUL VINCENT, pediatrics and pharmacology educator, researcher; b. Oct. 3, 1942; m. Susan Blackwell; children: Shirley, Karl, Shaun. BS in Chemistry, U. Okla., 1964; PhD of Organic Analytical Chemistry, MIT, 1968. Rsch. asst. U. Okla., Norman, 1963-64; predoctoral fellow MIT, Cambridge, 1964-69; asst. prof. pediat. and pharmacology U. Colo. Health Sci. Ctr., Denver, 1975-81, co-dir. mass spectral ctr., 1980, assoc. prof. pediat. and pharmacology, 1981-90, prof. pediat. and pharmacology, 1990—, vice chair pediat., 1991—. Contbr. articles to profl. jours. Asst. program scientist Viking Project, Martin Marietta Corp., Denver, 1969-72, program scientist, 1972-74. Recipient NSF Undergrad. Rsch. award, 1963-64, Merck award in Organic Chemistry, 1963; fellow Woodrow Wilson, 1964-65, NIH, 1964-68. Mem. Am. Chem. Soc., Am. Soc. Mass Spectrometry, Nat. Acad. Clin. Biochemists, Soc. Inherited Metabolic Diseases, Am. Soc. Pharmacology and Exptl. Therapeutics, Internat. Soc. Study Xenobiotics, Sigma Xi. Home: 13009 S Parker Ave Pine CO 80470-9617 Office: U Colo Health Sci Ctr 4200 E 9th Ave # C232 Denver CO 80220-3706 Home Phone: 303-838-4359; Office Phone: 303-315-7286. Business E-Mail: paul.fennessey@uchsc.edu.

FENNESSY, RICHARD A., information technology executive; BS, Mich. State Univ. Mgmt. positions IBM, 1987—2004, gen. mgr. worldwide PC direct, v.p. worldwide mktg. PC div., gen. mgr. worldwide ibm.com; pres., CEO Insight Enterprises, Inc., Tempe, Ariz., 2004—, bd. dir., 2005—. Office: Insight Enterprises Inc 1305 W Auto Dr Tempe AZ 85284 Office Phone: 480-902-1001. Office Fax: 480-902-1157.*

FENNING, LISA HILL, lawyer, mediator, retired judge; b. Chgo., Feb. 22, 1952; d. Ivan Byron and Joan Hill; m. Alan Mark Fenning, Apr. 3, 1977; 4 children. BA with honors, Wellesley Coll., 1971; JD, Yale U., 1974. Bar: Ill. 1975, Calif. 1979, U.S. Dist. Ct. (no. dist.) Ill., U.S. Dist. Ct. (no., ea., so. & cen. dists.) Calif., U.S. Ct. Appeals (6th, 7th & 9th cirs.), U.S. Supreme Ct. 1989. Law clk. U.S. Ct. Appeals 7th cir., Chgo., 1974-75; assoc. Jenner and Block, Chgo., 1975-77, O'Melveny and Myers, LA, 1977-85; judge U.S. Bankruptcy Ct. Cen. Dist. Calif., LA, 1985-2000; mediator JAMS, Orange, Calif., 2000-01; ptnr. Dewey Ballantine LLP, LA, 2001—. Bd. govs. Nat. Conf. Bankruptcy Judges, 1989-92; pres. Nat. Conf. of Women's Bar Assns., N.C., 1987-88, pres.-elect, 1986-87, v.p., 1985-86, bd. dirs.; lectr., program coord. in field; bd. govs. Nat. Conf. Bankruptcy Judges Endowment for Edn., 1992-97, Am. Bankruptcy Inst., 1994-2000; mem., bd. advisors Nat. Jud. Edn. Program to Promote Equality for Women and Men in the Cts., 1994—. Mem., bd. advisors: Lawyer Hiring & Training Report, 1985-87; contbr. articles to profl. jours. Durant scholar Wellesley Coll., 1971; named one of Am's. 100 Most Important Women Ladies Home Jour., 1988, LA's 50 Most Powerful Women Lawyers LA Bus. Jour., 1998, So. Calif. Superlawyers LA Mag., 2005, 06. Fellow Am. Bar Found., Am. Coll. Bankruptcy (bd. regents 1995-98); mem. ABA (standing com. on fed. jud. improvements 1995-98, mem. commn. on women in the profession 1987-91), Individual Rights and Responsibilities sect. 1984—, bus. law sect. 1986—, bus. bankruptcy com.), Nat. Assn. Women Judges (nat. task force gender bias in the cts. 1986-87, 93-94), Nat. Conf. Bankruptcy Judges (chair endowment edn. bd. 1994-95), Am. Bankruptcy Inst. (nominating com. 1994-95, bd. steering com. stats. project 1994-96), Calif. State Bar Assn. (chair com. on women in law 1986-87), Women Lawyers' Assn. L.A. (ex officio mem., bd. dirs., chmn., founder com. on status of women lawyers 1984-85, officer nominating com. 1986, founder, mem. Do-It-Yourself Mentor Network 1986-96), Phi Beta Kappa. Democrat. Office: Dewey Ballantine LLP 333 S Grand Ave 26th Fl Los Angeles CA 90071 Office Phone: 213-621-6000. Business E-Mail: Lfenning@deweyballantine.com, lfenning@dbllp.com.

FENNO, EDWARD THORNDIKE, lawyer; b. Detroit, May 25, 1966; s. John Brooks and Judith Fenno; m. Rebecca Patton, Aug. 15, 1992; children: Brant A., Eric P. BA, Princeton U., NJ, 1988; JD, U. So. Calif., 1994. Bar: Calif. 1994, SC 2000. Profl. tennis player Internat. Tennis Fedn., London, 1989—90; assoc. Musick, Peeler & Garrett, LA, 1994—98, Bostwick & Hoffman, Santa Monica, Calif., 1998—99, Moore & Van Allen, Charleston, SC, 2000—06; atty., mng. mem. Fenno Law Firm, LLC, Charleston, SC, 2006—. Vice chmn. ThinkTEC, Charleston, 2004—. Contbr. articles to profl. jours. Mem. steering com. Charleston Metro Sports Coun., 2001—03. Mem.: ABA (mem. forum on comm. law, IP law sect.), SC. Broadcasters Assn. (assoc.), SC. Press Assn. (assoc.). Avocation: tennis. Office: Fenno Law Firm LLC 171 Church St Ste 160 Charleston SC 29401 Office Phone: 843-720-3747. Office Fax: 843-577-0460.

FENNO, RICHARD FRANCIS, JR., political scientist, educator; b. Winchester, Mass., Dec. 12, 1926; s. Richard Francis and Mary Brooks (Tredennick) Fenno; m. Nancy Davidson, Sept. 10, 1948; children: Mark Richard, Craig Pierce. Student, Williams Coll., 1944-46; AB, Amherst Coll., 1948, LLD (hon.), 1986; PhD, Harvard U., 1956; LHD (hon.), Union Coll., 1989. Instr. govt. Wheaton (Mass.) Coll., 1951-53; instr. polit. sci. Amherst Coll., 1953-56, asst. prof., 1956-57; mem. faculty U. Rochester, NY, 1957—, prof., 1964—, Don Alonzo Watson prof. polit. sci., 1971-78, William R. Kenan prof. polit. sci., 1978—, Disting. Univ. prof., 1985—. Author: (book) The President's Cabinet, 1959, The Power of the Purse, 1966, Congressmen in Committees, 1973, Home Style: U.S. House Members in Their Districts, 1978 (Woodrow Wilson Found. award, 1979, D. B. Hardeman prize, 1980); author: (with F. Munger) National Politics and Federal Aid to Education, 1962; author: The Making of a Senator: Dan Quayle, 1989, The Presidential Odyssey of John Glenn, 1990, Watching Politicians, 1990, The Emergence of a Senate Leader: Pete Domenici and the Reagan Budget, 1991, Learning to Legislate: The Senate Education of Arlen Specter, 1991, When Incumbency Fails: The Senate Career of Mark Andrews, 1992; editor: The Yalta Conf., 1956, 1973, (book) Senators on the Campaign Trail: The Politics of Representation, 1996, Learning to Govern: An Institutional View of the 104th Congress, 1997, Congress at the Grassroots: Represntational Change in the South, 1970-1998, 2000, Going Home: Black Representatives and Their Constituents, 2003, Congressional Travels, 2007. With USNR, 1944—46. Rockefeller Found. fellow, 1963—64, Ford fellow, 1971—72, Guggenheim fellow, 1976—77, Russell Sage Found. grantee, 1978, 1980—85. Mem.: Am. Philos. Soc., Am. Acad. Arts and Scis., Social Sci. Rsch. Coun. (dir. 1973—75, fellow 1960—61), Nat. Acad. Scis., Am. Polit. Sci. Assn. (coun. 1971—73, v.p. 1975—76, pres. 1984—85), Phi Beta Kappa. Home: 108 Farm Brook Dr Rochester NY 14625-1519

FENSELAU, CATHERINE CLARKE, chemistry professor; b. York, Nebr., Apr. 15, 1939; d. Lee Keckley and Muriel (Thomas) Clarke; m. Allan Herman Fenselau, 1962 (div. 1980); children: Andrew Clarke, Thomas Stewart; m. Robert James Cotter, 1984. AB, Bryn Mawr Coll., 1961; PhD, Stanford U., 1965. Research scientist U. Calif.-Berkeley, 1965-67; instr. to prof. Johns Hopkins U., Balt., 1967-87; chmn. chemistry, biochemistry U. Md., Balt. County, 1987-98, prof. dept. chemistry and biochemistry College Park, 1998—; chmn. dept. chemistry and biochemistry, 1998-2000. Cons. NIH, NSF, USDA, U.S. Army, FDA, others. Editor: Biomed. Environ. Mass Spectrometry, 1973—89; editor: (assoc. editor) Analytical Chemistry, 1990—; contbr. articles to profl. jours. Recipient Hillebrand prize, Chem. Soc. Washington, 2005. Fellow: AAAS; mem.: Internat. Human Proteomic Orgn. (v.p. 2007—), U.S. Human Proteomic Orgn. (pres. 2004—06), Am. Soc. Pharmacology and Exptl. Therapeutics, Am. Chem. Soc. (Garvan medal 1985, Md. Chemist award Md. sect. 1989), Am. Soc. Mass Spectrometry (pres. 1980—82). Office: U Md Dept Chemistry Biochemistry College Park MD 20742-0001 Business E-Mail: fenselau@umd.edu.

FENSKE, JERALD ALLAN, minister; b. Wausau, Wis., Sept. 29, 1960; s. Martin W. and Whynona B. (Ramthun) F.; m. Kay A. Lang, Aug. 17, 1985; children: Kiersten, Deena. BA, Lakeland Coll., 1983; MDiv, United Theol. Sem. of the Twin Cities, 1988. Ordained to ministry United Ch. of Christ, 1991. Pastor Congl. Ch. of Excelsior United Ch. of Christ, Excelsior, Minn., 1998—. Mem. Excelsior Masons, Western Clergy Cluster United Ch. of Christ, Excelsior Ministerial Assoc. Mem. Lakeland Coll. Alumni Assn. (Zeta Chi chpt.). Home: 17411 Creek Ridge Pass Minnetonka MN 55345-6230 Office: Congl Ch Excelsior United Ch Christ 471 3rd St Excelsior MN 55331-1945 Office Phone: 952-474-5919.

FENSTER, ALBERT M., lawyer; b. 1952; AB with distinction, U. Mich., 1973; JD cum laude, Harvard U., 1976. Bar: NY 1977, US Dist. Ct. (so. and ea. dists.) NY 1977. Ptnr. Corp. & Fin. Dept. Kay, Scholer LLP, NYC. Office: Kaye Scholer LLP 425 Park Ave New York NY 10022 Office Phone: 212-836-8205. E-mail: afenster@kayescholer.com.

FENSTER, HERBERT LAWRENCE, lawyer; b. NYC, Mar. 29, 1935; s. Oscar Samuel and Bessie Estelle (Schafran) Fenster; m. Gail Frances Meier, Apr. 18, 1964; children: Christopher Lawrence, Jennifer Gail, Jonathan Adam; m. Jane Porter Elam Allen, Dec. 31, 1993. AB, U. Pa., 1957, MA, 1958; JD, U. Va., 1961. Bar: Va. 1961, D.C. 1962, U.S. Supreme Ct. 1967, Colo. 1993. Assoc. Sellers, Conner & Cuneo, Washington, 1961—66, prin., 1967—78, sr. ptnr., 1978—80, McKenna, Conner & Cuneo, Washington, 1980—90, McKenna & Cuneo, Washington, 1990—2002, McKenna, Long & Aldridge, Washington, 2002—. Bd. dirs. Nat. Chamber Litig. Ctr., Washington, Keewaydin Found., Middlebury, Vt., trustee, corp. dir.; legal adviser Reagan-Bush Campaign Com., Washington, 1980—83; mem. pres.'s pvt. sector survey Grace Commn., Washington, 1982—. Fellow: ATLA; mem.: ABA (treatise Anti Deficiency Act 1979), Am. Law Inst., D.C. Bar Assn., Fed. Bar Assn., Univ. Club, Met. Club. Republican. Episcopalian. Home: 845 6th St Boulder CO 80302-7418 Address: 1875 Lawrence St Denver CO 80202-1370

FENSTER, ROBERT DAVID, lawyer; b. NYC, Sept. 25, 1946; BA, Queen's Coll., 1968; JD, Bklyn. Law Sch., 1973. Bar: N.Y. 1974, U.S. Dist. Ct. (so. and ea. dists.) N.Y. 1974, U.S. Supreme Ct. 1977. Investigator, prosecutor N.Y. Stock Exch., NYC, 1972-73; ptnr. law firms Rockland County, 1974—80; prin. Robert D. Fenster, Atty. at Law, P.C., 1980—2001; ptnr. Fenster & Kurland LLP, New City, 2002—. Bd. dirs. Brit. Pub. Corp., various other corps. Advisor Clarkstown Youth Ct., New City, NY, 1982; bd. dirs. Legal Aid Soc., Rockland County, 1974—78, Nyack Hosp. Found., 1995—2000, Good Samaritan Hosp. Found. Mem. ABA, NY State Bar Assn., Rockland County Bar Assn., Am. Arbitration Assn. (arbitrator). Office: Fenster & Kurland LLP Attys at Law 337 N Main St Ste 11 New City NY 10956-4310 Office Phone: 845-638-4700. Fax: 845-638-4767. Business E-Mail: mail@fkllp.com.

FENSTER, SAUL K., retired academic administrator; b. NYC, Mar. 22, 1933; s. Samuel and Rose (Glass) F.; m. Roberta Schamis, Jan. 11, 1959; children: Deborah, Lisa, Jonathan. Student, Bklyn. Coll., 1949-51; B of Mech. Engring., CUNY, 1953; MS, Columbia U., 1955; postgrad., NYU, 1955-56; PhD, U. Mich., 1959; LLD, Rutgers U., 2002, William Paterson U., 2002; DHL (hon.), N.J. Inst. Tech., 2002. Lectr. mech. engring. CUNY,

1953-56; teaching fellow engring. mechanics U. Mich., 1956-57, with univ. Rsch. Inst., 1957-58; rsch. engr. Sperry-Rand Corp., 1959-62; prof. engring. Fairleigh Dickinson U., Teaneck, NJ, 1962-78, chmn. dept. physics, 1962-63, chmn. dept. mech. engring., 1963-70, grad. adminstrv. asst. to dean, 1965-70, assoc. dean, 1970-71, exec. asst. to pres., 1971-72, provost Rutherford campus, 1972-78; pres. N.J. Inst. Tech., Newark, 1978—2002, N.J. Inst. Tech. (Found.), 1978—2002. Bd. dirs. Prudential Mut. Funds, 1983—; vice-chmn. Bus.-Higher Edn. Forum, 1992; cons. in field. Author: (with Wallace Arthur) Mechanics, 1969, (with A. Cahit Ugural) Advanced Strength and Applied Elasticity, 1975, 87, 94; contbr. chpts. to books, tech. papers. Active Hudson River Waterfront Study and Planning Commn., 1979-80; bd. dirs. NJ Assn. Colls. and Univs., 1980-2002, NJ Alliance for Action, 1982-2002, R&D Coun. NJ, 1994-2002, Regional Bus. Partnership, 1994-95, Prosperity NJ, Inc., Soc. Mfg. Engrs. Edn. Found., 1998-2002; trustee Newark Boys Chorus Sch., 1980-84, Newark Acad., 1984-86; mem., vice chmn. NJ Water Supply Authority, 1981-88; mem. NJ Commn. on Sci. and Tech., 1985—; bd. govs. Union County Coll.; mem. Commn. Def. Conversion and Cmty. Assistance, 1993; mem. Commn. on Jobs, Growth and Econ. Devel., 2003—; mem. NJ Coun. on Job Opportunities; bd. visitors Air U., 1993-98; bd. trustees Leir Charitable Found., 2006—, Ridgefield Found. Shell fellow U. Mich., 1957-58. Fellow ASME, Am. Soc. Engring. Edn., Soc. Mfg. Engrs.; mem. AAAS, Assn. Ind. Colls. and Univs. N.J. (chmn. bd. 1978-80, bd. dirs. 1980-96), Greater Newark C. of C. (bd. dirs. 1980-91), N.J. State C. of C. (bd. dirs. 1987-2002), Coun. on Competitiveness, Sigma Xi, Tau Beta Pi, Omicron Delta Kappa, Pi Tau Sigma. Office: NJ Inst Tech Office of Pres Emeritus University Heights Newark NJ 07102 Home: 477 Ocean Ave N Long Branch NJ 07740 Home Phone: 732-571-2990. Personal E-mail: sfenster477@comcast.net. Business E-Mail: fenster@njit.edu.

FENSTERMACHER, JOYCE DORIS, real estate agent, real estate appraiser; b. Scranton, Pa., Feb. 25, 1932; d. Brenton Luellen and Doris Baer; m. J. Gordon Fenstermacher, Dec. 10, 1955; children: Karen, Peter, Christopher. BA, U. Miami, 1953. Lic. real estate broker Pa., cert. residential appraiser. Real estate agt. Fried Realty, Harrisburg, Pa., 1972, Doucherty & Twigg, Harrisburg, Pa., 1973—77, Jack Gerghen Realty, Harrisburg, Pa., 1977—82, Coldwell Banker Realty, Harrisburg, Pa., 1982—91, Re/Max Realty Profls., Harrisburg, Pa., 2001—05; appraiser Robert Jones Appraisers, Harrisburg, Pa., 1991—2001. Singer, actress Harrisburg Cmty. Theater; lead singer York (Pa.) Cmty. Theater; founder Harrisburg Opera Soc.; elder Faith Presbyn. Ch., 1989—91, pres. corp., 1991. Named one of Business Women of Yr., Patriot News, Harrisburg, 1990. Mem.: Harrisburg Bd. Realtors (mem. ethics com. 1985—91, mem. legis. com. 2003—05). Republican. Avocations: golf, singing. Home: 4427 Avon Dr Harrisburg PA 17112 Office: Re/Max Realty Profls Inc 1250 N Mountain Rd Harrisburg PA 17112

FENSTERSTOCK, BLAIR COURTNEY, lawyer; b. NYC, Aug. 20, 1950; s. Nathaniel and Gertrude (Isaacson) Fensterstock; children: Michael Bayard, Evan Steele, Laurel Sage. AB summa cum laude, Bowdoin Coll., 1972; JD, Columbia U., 1975. Bar: Ind. 1976, N.Y. 1976, U.S. Dist. Ct. (so., ea. and no. dists.) 1976, U.S. Ct. Appeals (2d cir.) 1976, U.S. Customs Ct. 1976, U.S. Ct. Internat. Trade 1976, U.S. Supreme Ct. 1980, U.S. Ct. Appeals (5th cir.) 2004. Assoc. Simpson, Thacher & Bartlett, NYC, 1975-79, Dewey, Ballantine, Bushby, Palmer & Wood, NYC, 1979-83; v.p., assoc. gen. counsel, asst. sec. Reliance Group Holdings, Inc., NYC, 1983-91; sr. v.p., gen. counsel, sec. Frank B. Hall & Co., Inc., 1987-92; ptnr. Sutherland, Asbill & Brennan, 1993-95, Brock, Fensterstock, Silverstein & McAuliffe, LLC, NYC, 1995-98, Fensterstock & Ptnrs., LLP, NYC, 1998—. Mem. bd. visitors Columbia U. Sch. Law, 1988—; mem. bd. dirs. Worthpoint Corp., 2007. Bd. dirs. Safety Nat. Casualty Corp., 1990—93; vice chmn. regents Ctr. Security Policy, 2003—04. Harlan Fiske Stone scholar, Columbia U., 1975. Master: NY Inn of Ct. (pres. 2006—07); fellow: Am. Acad. Trial Counsel (charter), NY Bar Found.; mem.: ABA, Am. Arbitration Assn. (panel arbitrators), Coun. NY Law Assocs. (bd. dirs. 1979—82), Assn. Bar City of NY, NY State Bar Assn., Internat. Peace Acad. (sec. 1977—79), Lawyers Com. Internat. Human Rights (bd. dirs. 1979—80), The Carnegie Club at Skibo Castle (Dornoch, Scotland), Eden Club (St. Andrews, Scotland), Pinehurst Country Club (NC), Palmas del Mar Country Club (P.R.), Univ. Club. (NYC), Bayonne Golf Club (NJ), Phi Beta Kappa. Republican. Jewish. Home: 10 West St New York NY 10004-Office: Fensterstock & Ptnrs LLP 30 Wall St New York NY 10005-2201 Home Phone: 212-566-1331; Office Phone: 212-785-4100. Business E-Mail: bfensterstock@fensterstock.com.

FENTON, CHARLES E., lawyer; BS, Johns Hopkins U., Balt.; JD, Georgetown U. Law Sch. Bar: Md. 1973. Atty. Miles & Stockbridge, 1974—80, ptnr., 1980—89; gen. counsel Black & Decker Corp., Balt., 1989—, v.p, 1989—96, sr. v.p., 1996—. Mem.: Md. State Bar Assn., ABA. Office: Black & Decker Corp 701 E Joppa Rd Towson MD 21286 Office Phone: 410-716-3900. Office Fax: 410-716-2933.*

FENTON, CLIFTON LUCIEN, investment banker; b. Bryan, Ohio, May 11, 1943; s. Gibson Lucien and Elizabeth (Newcomer) F.; m. Judith Todd Wallis, June 23, 1973; children: Gregory, Eric, Alyssa. AB, Princeton U., 1965; JD, Ohio State U., 1968; MBA, Columbia U., 1970; grad., Kellog Grad. Sch. Mgmt., 2001. Bar: Ohio 1968. Assoc. Bank N.Y., NYC, 1970-72, Morgan Guaranty Trust Co., NYC, 1972; v.p. Kidder, Peabody, NYC, 1972-84; mng. dir. Prudential-Bache Securities, NYC, 1984-89; v.p., nat. mgr. John Nuveen & Co., Chgo., 1989-95, v.p. and mgr. Investment Banking Divsn., 1995-99; mng. dir. and co-head pub. fin. U.S. Bancorp Piper Jaffray, Chgo., 1999-2000. Bd. dirs. Associated Colls. Ill. Pinnacle Forum Chgo. and Good City, Heritage at Millenium Park. Mem. Met. Club (N.Y.C.), Univ. Club Chgo. Avocations: water-skiing, sailing, piano, skiing. Home: 130 N Garland Ct Chicago IL 60602 E-mail: cliffenton@comcast.net.

FENTON, DENNIS MICHAEL, medical products executive; b. Roslyn, NY, Nov. 2, 1951; s. Robert Edward and Catherine (O'Dwyer) F.; m. Linda Marie Owens, June 30, 1974. BS in Biology, Manhattan Coll., 1973; PhD in Microbiology, Rutgers U., NJ, 1977. Rsch. scientist Pfizer Co., Groton, Conn., 1977-81, AmGen, Inc., Thousand Oaks, Calif., 1982-84, head lab., 1984—85, dir. pilot plant ops., 1985—88, v.p. pilot plant ops. and clin. mfg., 1988—91, v.p. process devel., facilities and mfg. svcs., 1991—92, sr. v.p. sales and mktg., 1992—95, sr. v.p. ops., 1995—2000, exec. v.p. ops., 2000—. Bd. dirs. Biotechnology Industry Orgn. Contbr. articles to profl. jours.; patentee in field. Bd. trustees Keck Grad. Inst., Rutgers U.; bd. regents Calif. Luth. U. Mem. Am. Chem. Soc., Soc. Indsl. Microbiology, Am. Soc. Microbiology, Parenteral Drug Assn. Avocations: sports, music, hiking, camping. Office: Amgen Inc One Amgen Center Dr Thousand Oaks CA 91320-1799 Office Phone: 805-447-1000. Office Fax: 805-447-1010.*

FENTON, ELLIOTT CLAYTON, lawyer; b. Oklahoma City, Nov. 26, 1914; s. Edgar R. and Mary (Gaddo) F.; m. LeNoir Massey, July 6, 1939; children: Mike, Ann Wallis; m. Ruby L. Simpson, Aug. 21, 2002. BA, U. Okla., Norman, 1935, LLB, 1937. Bar: Okla. 1937, US Dist. Ct. (no., ea. and we. dists.) Okla., US Ct. Appeals (10th cir.), US Supreme Ct., US Ct. Mil. Appeals. Atty. Looney & Fenton, Oklahoma City, 1937—38; atty., claims rep. Nat. Mut. Casualty Co., Tulsa, 1938-40, Hartford Ins. Group, Oklahoma City, 1940-47; atty. Fenton & Fenton, Oklahoma City, 1947—. Chmn. bd. trustees United Meth. Found., Okla., 1973-83; chancellor United Meth. Found., Okla., 1983-89; bd. dirs. Ctrl. Okla. United Meth. Retirement Facility, Inc. Ret. comdr. USNR. Fellow Am. Bar Found; mem. Internat. Assn. Def. Counsel, Def. Rsch. Inst. (state chmn. 1978-83), Okla. Assn. Def. Counsel (pres. 1972), Okla. County Bar Assn. (bd. dirs.). Republican. United Methodist. Avocation: golf. Home: 14901 N Penn Ave Duplex 4A Oklahoma City OK 73134-6079 Office: Fenton Fenton Smith et al 1 Leadership Sq Ste 800 Oklahoma City OK 73102 Home Phone: 405-749-1444; Office Phone: 405-235-4671. Personal E-mail: elbeau88@cox.net. Business E-Mail: ecfenton@fentonlaw.com.

FENTON, HOWARD NATHAN, III, lawyer, educator; b. Toledo, May 6, 1950; s. Howard Nathan, Jr. and Maxine Claire (LaFountaine) F.; children: William Carl, Margaret Claire, Andrew Scimeca, Julie Marie, Christopher Howard; m. Beth Anne Kostic, Mar. 9, 2001. BS with honors, U. Tex., 1971, JD with honors, 1975. Bar: Tex. 1975, D.C. 1976, Ohio 1990, U.S. Dist. Ct. D.C. 1976, U.S. Ct. Appeals (D.C. cir.) 1976. Assoc. Williams & Jensen PC, Washington, 1975-77; ptnr. Swift & Swift PC, Washington, 1978; supervisory compliance officer office antiboycott compliance Internat. Trade Adminstrn./U.S. Dept. Commerce, Washington, 1979-80, dir. compliance policy, 1981-84; assoc. prof. Miss. Coll. Sch. Law, Jackson, 1984-87, prof., 1987-88, Ohio No. U. Coll. Law, Ada, 1988—, assoc. dean, 1988-93, interim dean, 1995—96, dir. internat. law program, 2006—. Cons. adminstrv. law reform to govts. of Bosnia Herzegovina, Ukraine, Georgia, Armenia, Uzbekistan, 1996—; chief of party US AID Rule of Law Project, Tbilisi, Georgia, 2001-02; cons. Adminstrv. Conf. U.S., 1989-91, 93-94; fellow Nat. Ctr. for Export/Import Studies, Georgetown U., Washington, 1983-86; adj. faculty Cath. U. Law Sch., Washington, spring 1984; mem. U.S.-Can. Free Trade Agreement Dispute Panel, 1993-94, N.Am. Free Trade Agreement Dispute Panel, 1994—. Contbg. editor: Boycott Law Bull, 1984—92. Fellow Ohio State Bar Found.; mem. ABA, Ohio State Bar Assn. (chmn. internat. law com. 2002-06), Am. Soc. Internat. Law. Democrat. Office: Pettit Coll of Law Ohio Northern U Ada OH 45810 Office Phone: 419-772-2233. Personal E-mail: fentonhoward@hotmail.com. Business E-Mail: h-fenton@onu.edu.

FENTON, JEFFREY J., management consultant, wholesale distribution executive; BS mech. engring., Northeastern Univ.; MS (Sloan Fellow), MIT. Mgmt. positions with GE, 1980—98; CEO GE Capital Modular Space, 1998—99, Maxim Crane Works, 2000—02, Devonshire Advisors LLC; chmn. BlueLinx Holdings, Atlanta, 2004—. Bd. dir. IAP Worldwide Services; advisor, sr. mem. ops. team Cerberus Capital Mgmt. Mailing: BlueLinx Holdings 4300 Wildwood Pkwy Atlanta GA 30339*

FENTON, LAWRENCE JULES, medical educator; b. Chgo., June 1, 1940; s. Arthur S. Fenton and Dorothy (Schochet) Wade; m. Gayle Ann Yeager, Apr. 10, 1965; children: Lori Ann Novak, Scott L. BS, U. Mich., 1962; MD, U. Cin., 1966. Diplomate Am. Bd. Pediatrics, Sub-bd. Neonatal and Perinatal Medicine. Intern U. Cin. Med. Ctr., 1966-67, jr. and sr. resident, 1967-69, chief pediatric resident, 1969-70, fellow neonatal, perinatal medicine, 1972-74; asst. prof. pediatrics U. Ariz. Health Scis. Ctr., Tucson, 1974-78; assoc. prof. pediatrics U. S.D. Sch. Medicine, Sioux Falls, 1978-84, head sect. of neonatal, perinatal medicine, 1979-88, prof. pediatrics, 1984—, chmn. dept. pediatrics, 1988—. Dir. newborn intensive care unit Sioux Valley Hosp., 1980-88; chmn. pharmacy and therapeutics com. Sioux Valley Hosp., 1982-97, bd. dirs., 1997—2002; v.p. children's med. svcs. Sioux Valley Hosp. and U. S.D. Med. Ctr., 2000-02. Author: (with others) Current Therapy in Neonatal and Perinatal Medicine, 1989, Conn's Current Therapy, 1989, 90; contbr. articles to profl. jours. Chmn. rsch. funding group Am. Heart Assn., Dakota Affiliate, 1986-88; mem. allocations com. Childrn's Miracle Network Telethon, Sioux Falls, 1986-87; bd. dirs. Childrens Miracle Network, 1996-99; chmn. Health Svcs. Adv. Com., State of S.D., 1991-93. Maj. U.S. Army, 1970-72. Rsch. grantee Nat. Inst. Child Health and Human Devel., Tucson, Sioux Falls, 1976-79, Am. Heart Assn., Sioux Falls, 1984; recipient Army Commendation medal, 1991-93, Pioneer award S.D. Perinatal Assn., 1993; inductee Hall of Honor Children's Hosp. U. Cin. MEd. Ctr., 1993. Fellow Am. Acad. Pediatrics; mem. Society for Pediatric Rsch., Midwest Soc. for Pediatric Rsch., Assn. Med. Sch. Pediatric Dept. Chmn., S.D. States Med. Assn. Avocations: water-skiing, boating, hiking, scuba diving, classical music. Office: 1305 W 18th St Sioux Falls SD 57117-5039 Home Phone: 605-335-8815; Office Phone: 605-333-7197. Business E-Mail: ijfenton@usd.edu.

FENTON, NOEL JOHN, venture capitalist; b. New Haven, May 24, 1938; s. Arnold Alexander and Carla (Mathiasen) F.; m. Sarah Jane Hamilton, Aug. 14, 1965; children: Wendy, Devon, Peter, Lance. BS, Cornell U., 1959; MBA, Stanford U., 1963. Research asst. Stanford (Calif.) U., 1963-64; v.p. Mail Systems Corp., Redwood City, Calif., 1964-66; v.p., gen. mgr. products div. Acurex Corp., Mountain View, Calif., 1966-72, pres., chief exec. officer, dir., 1972-83, Covalent Systems Corp., Sunnyvale, Calif., 1983-86; mng. gen. ptnr. Trinity Ventures Ltd., 1986—. Bd. dirs. Multifamily Tech. Solutions, Inc., LoopNet, Inc., SciQuest, Inc., ID Analytics, Inc., Blue Tarp Fin., Inc. Mem. adv. coun. resource Ctr. for Women, chmn. bd. dirs. 1987-88; mem. San Jose Econ. Devel. Task Force, 1983, Young Pres.'s Orgn., 1976-88, Pres. Reagan's Bus. Adv. Panel; mem. World Pres.'s Orgn., 1988—, dir., 1994-2000; mem. athletic bd. Stanford U., 2003—. Lt. (j.g.) USN, 1959-61. Mem. Am. Electronics Assn. (chmn. 1978-79, dir. 1976-80), Santa Clara County Mfrs. Group (dir. 1980-83), Chief Execs. Orgn., Stanford Bus. Sch. Alumni Assn. (pres. 1976-77, dir. 1971-76), Stanford Alumni Assn. (exec. bd. 1985-89). Republican. Episcopalian. Home: 247 Mapache Dr Portola Valley CA 94028-7354 Office: Trinity Ventures Bldg 4 3000 Sand Hill Rd Ste 160 Menlo Park CA 94025-7113 Business E-Mail: noel@trinityventures.com.

FENTON, ROBERT EARL, electrical engineering educator; b. Bklyn., Sept. 30, 1933; s. Theodore Andrew and Evelyn Virginia (Brent) F.; m. Alice Earlyn Gray, Dec. 13, 1934; children: Douglas Earl, Andrea Leigh. BEE, Ohio State U., 1957, MEE, 1960, PhD in Electrical Engring., 1965. Registered profl. engr., Ohio. Engr. rsch. N. Am. Aviation, Columbus, Ohio, 1957; instr. electric engring. Ohio State U., Columbus, 1960-65, prof., 1965-95, prof. emeritus, 1995—. Cons. transp. sys. divsn. GM, Warren, Mich., 1974-80, Battelle Meml. Inst., Columbus, Ohio, 1991-93. Inventor kinesthetic-tactile display; contbr. articles to profl. jours. Capt. USAF, 1957-60. Recipient Outstanding Tchr. award Eta Kappa Nu, 1963, Neil Armstrong award Ohio Soc. Profl. Engrs., 1971, Pioneering Rsch. award Nat. Automated Hwy. Systems Consortium, 1997, Significant Achievement award Intelligent Vehicle Hwy. Sys. Ohio, 1993. Fellow IEEE (IEEE Millennium medal 2000), Radio Club Am., IEEE Vehicular Tech. Soc. (pres. 1985-87, v.p. 1983-85, treas. 1981-83, prize paper 1980, Avant Garde award, 1982, Stuart F. Meyer Meml. award 1998), NAE. Avocations: bicycling, swimming, classical music. Home: 2177 Oakmount Rd Columbus OH 43221-1229 Office: Ohio State Univ Dept Elec Engring 2015 Neil Ave Dept Elec Columbus OH 43210-1210 Home Phone: 614-457-0479. Business E-Mail: fenton.2@osu.edu.

FENTON, ROBERT LEONARD, lawyer, writer, film producer; b. Detroit, Sept. 14, 1929; s. Ben B. and Stella Frances (Saffir) F.; children: Robert L. Jr., Cynthia R. AB, Syracuse U., 1952; LLB, U. Mich., 1955. Bar: Mich. 1955. Asso. Marks, Levi, Thill & Wiseman, Detroit, 1955-60; ptnr. Fenton, Nederlander, Tracy & Dodge, Detroit, 1960-85; pvt. practice Detroit, 1985—. Adj. prof. U. Mich. Law Sch., Marygrove Coll., Detroit, 2002-03; lectr. Flint and Lansing Real Estate Bds., 1966-68; spl. counsel Detroit Fire Dept., 1975—, Mich. Motion Picture and TV Commn., 1978-82; producer Universal Studios, Calif., 1983-86, 20th Century Fox, 1986-87; guest lectr. U. Mich. Law Sch., 1998; presenter entertainment law seminar, U. Mich., Apr. 1998, writers workshop Holland Am. Cruise Lines, Feb. 1999; condr writers workshops. Author: (novels) Black Tie Only, 1990, Blue Orchids, 1992, Royal Invitation, 1995; producer NBC movie of week Double Standard, 1988, Woman on the Ledge, 1993. Treas. Oakland County Dem. Com., 1960-64; mem. Dem. State Fin. Com., 1966-69, Nat. Fin. Com., 1962-74, Dem. Pres.'s Club, 1962-74; fin. adviser to Mayor Roman S. Gribbs, 1969-73, Mayor Coleman A. Young, 1974-94; chmn. State of Mich. Film and TV Commn.; bd. dirs. Detroit Bicentennial Commn., Rivers and Harbour Congress of U.S.; mem. adv. bd. NAACP, U. Mich. Pres.'s Club. Served with USAF, 1950-52. Recipient Distinguished Pub. Service medal City of Detroit, 1973, Letter of Commendation USAF, 1953; named Man of the 60's City of Detroit, 1964; decorated Order of St. Johns of Jerusalem, 1980. Mem. ABA, Mich., Detroit bar assns., Econs. Club, Acad. Magical Arts, Soc. Preservation Variety Arts, Franklin Hills Country Club, Variety Club of Detroit (bd. dirs.), Variety Clubs Internat., Recess Club (Detroit), St. James Club (L.A., N.Y.C., London, Paris), Mt. Kenya Safari Club (Nairobi), Masons, Shriners. Office: Village Park Bldg 31800 Northwestern Hwy Ste 204 Farmington Hills MI 48334-1604 Home Phone: 248-474-8709; Office Phone: 248-855-8780. Personal E-mail: fenent@msn.com.

FENTON, THOMAS CONNER, lawyer; b. Cin., Feb. 9, 1954; S. William Conner and Virginia (Rawnsley) F.; m. Karen Lois Haswell, Oct. 20, 1979; children: Margaret Lois, Rebecca Conner, Robert Ellis. BA, Centre Coll., 1976; JD, Ohio State U., 1979. Bar: Ky. 1979, U.S. Dist. Ct. (we. dist.) Ky. 1979, U.S. Ct. Appeals (DC cir.) 1981, U.S. Dist. Ct. (ea. dist.) Ky. 1985, U.S. Ct. Appeals (6th cir.) 1986. Assoc. Greenebaum, Treitz, Brown & Marshall, Louisville, 1979-85, ptnr., 1985-88; v.p., counsel Nat. City Bank Ky., Louisville, 1989-93; counsel Nat. City Corp., Cleve., 1989-93; v.p. human resources Nat. City Processing Co., Louisville, 1993-95; of counsel Morgan & Pottinger PSC, Louisville, 1996-2001, mem., 2001—. Lectr. Ohio Bankers Assn. Sch. of Human Resources Adminstrn., 1989-91. Author: Affirmative Action Relevant to Bankers, 1996, Leadership Kentucky, 2004. Bd. trustees St. Matthews United Meth. Ch., 2001—03, chmn., 2002—03; bd. dirs. ElderServe Inc., Louisville, 1983—91, 1995—2001, 2003—, sec., 1984—86, v.p., 1986—87, pres., 1987—90; bd. dirs. Louisville Youth Choir, Inc., 1996—, chmn., 1997—2002, 2005—. Mem. Ky. Bar Assn. (chmn. labor rels. law sect. 1981-83), Louisville Bar Assn. Methodist. Home: 11003 Fox Moore Ct Louisville KY 40223-5531 Office: Morgan & Pottinger PSC 601 W Main St Louisville KY 40202-2976 Office Phone: 502-560-6754. Business E-Mail: tcf@morganandpottinger.com.

FENTON, THOMAS TRAIL, journalist; b. Balt., Apr. 8, 1930; s. Matthew Clark and Beatrice (Trail) F.; m. Simone France Marie Lopes-Curval, Jan. 10, 1959; children: Ariane France, Thomas Trail. AB, Dartmouth Coll., 1952; PhD (hon.), U. Balt., 1999. Mem. staff Balt. Sun, 1961-70, chief Rome bur., 1966-68, chief Paris bur., 1968-70; reporter-producer Rome bur. CBS News, 1970-73, corr. Tel Aviv bur., 1973-77, corr. Paris bur., 1977-79, chief European corr. London, 1979-94, Moscow, 1994-96, London, 1996—2004; corr. Public Radio Internat., 2006—. Assignments include Middle East War, 1967, Paris Peace Talks, 1968, Paris Riots, 1968, Indo-Pakistan War, 1971, Middle East War, 1973, Islamic Revolution and takeover of the Am. Embassy in Tehran, 1979, Revjavik Summit, 1985, Revolution in Ea. Europe, 1989-90, Desert Storm, 1991, Moscow Coup, 1991, Collapse of Communism and the Soviet Union, 1992, War in Former Yugoslavia, 1992, War in Chechnya, 1995, Kosovo War, 1999, Death of Princess Diana, 1997, War Against Terrorism Pakistan, 2001, Afghanistan, 2002, War in Iraq, 2003, American mid-term elections, 2006; author: Bad News: the Decline of Reporting, the Business of News and the Danger to Us All, 2005. Served with USN, 1952-61. Recipient Overseas Press Club awards for articles from Paris, 1968, for coverage Indo-Pakistan War, 1971, Mid. East War, 1973, Sadat visit to Jerusalem, 1977, Mountbatten funeral, 1980, hunger in Africa, 1981, radio documentary series, 1992, Emmy awards NATAS for bombing of Marines in Beirut, 1983, for assassination in Indira Gandhi, 1984, 2 Emmy awards for death of Princess Diana, 1998, DuPont award, 1990, Weintal award Georgetown U., 1999. Mem. Soc. the Cin., Internat. Inst. Strategic Studies, Chatham House, Royal United Svcs. Inst., Assn. Am. Corrs. London, Assn. de la Presse Presdl. Paris, Fgn. Press Assn. in London, Soc. Profl. Journalists, Frontline Club, Media Soc., Ends of the Earth Club, Monday Lunch Club. Avocations: drawing, photography. Personal E-mail: ttfenton@yahoo.com.

FENTON, TIM, food service executive; LLB, U. Western Ont., Can., 1986. With McDonald's Corp., 1973—, various restaurant and ops. pos., including ops. mgr. South Fla. region, field svc. mgr. Kansas City region, others, dir. Asia Pacific, 1990—92, mng. dir. McDonald's Poland, v.p. McDonald's Ctrl. Europe North, 1992—95, v.p., mng. dir. Middle East Devel. Co., sr. v.p., Southeast Asia/Middle East/Africa, pres., East Divsn., McDonald's USA Oak Brook, Ill., pres., McDonald's Asia, Pacific, Middle East and Africa, 2005—. V.p. Am. C. of C., Warsaw, 1992—95; bd. dirs. Friends of Luetefska Children's Hosp., Warsaw, 1994—95. Office: McDonald's Corp McDonald's Plz Oak Brook IL 60523

FENTY, ADRIAN M., mayor; b. Washington, Dec. 7, 1970; s. Philip and Jan Fenty; m. Michelle Cross Fenty; children: Matthew, Andrew. BA, Oberlin Coll., 1992; JD, Howard U., 1996. Intern Senator Howard Metzenbaum, Senator Eleanor Holmes-Norton, Senator Joseph P. Kennedy; lead atty., counsel Coun.'s Com. on Edn., Libraries and Recreation; counsel mem. Ward 4, Washington, DC City Coun., 2001—07, former co-chair Spl. Com. on Comprehensive Housing Strategy for DC, chairperson Com. on Human Svcs.; mayor Washington, DC, 2007—. Bd. mem. Lamond-Riggs Recreation Ctr., Friends of Upshur Recreation Ctr. Recipient Commitment to Social Justice award, DC Acorn, Courageous Cmty. Svc. award, Fedn. of Citizens. Mem.: 16th St. Neighborhood Civic Assn. (former pres.), Kappa Alpha Psi Fraternity. Democrat. Office: John A Wilson Bldg 1350 Pennsylvania Ave NW Ste 600 Washington DC 20004 E-mail: mayor@dc.gov.*

FENVES, GREGORY L., engineering educator; PhD, U. Calif. Berkeley. Prof. civil engring. U. Calif. Berkeley, T.Y. and Margaret Lin Prof. Engring., chair, dept. civil and environmental engring. Asst. dir. industry programs Pacific Earthquake Engring. Rsch. Ctr. U. of Calif. Berkeley; mem. Ctr. for Information Technol. Rsch. in the Interest of Society. Recipient Walter L. Huber Civil Engring. Rsch. prize ASCE, 1995. Office: U Calif Berkeley Dept Civil Engring MC 1710 Berkeley CA 94720-1710

FENWICK, JAMES HENRY, editor, writer, columnist; b. South Shields, Eng., Mar. 17, 1937; came to U.S., 1965; s. James Henry and Ellen (Tinmouth) F.; m. Suzanne Helene Hatch, Jan. 27, 1968. BA, Oxford U., Eng., 1960. Freelance lectr., writer, 1960-65; assoc. editor Playboy mag., Chgo., 1965-71; planning and features editor Radio Times, BBC, London, 1971-77, U.S. rep. NYC, 1978-87; sr. editor Modern Maturity mag., Lakewood, Calif., 1987-90, exec. editor, 1990-91, editor, 1991-98; contbg. editor Get Up and Go!, Age Wave Comm., Lakewood, Calif., 1998-99; editor Next Mag., Palm Springs, Calif., 2000—01, Desert Mag., Palm Springs, 2002—04, food columnist, 2004—, The Desert Sun, Calif., 2004—. Author (with Eric Wadlund): Palm Springs Flavors, 2007. Business E-Mail: fenwickfood@aol.com.

FENWICK, SHERIDAN MELLON, psychologist, director; d. Robert Thomas and Janet Mellon Fenwick; m. Worth V. Bruntjen, May 26 (dec.); 1 child, Ashley Fenwick Naditch stepchildren: Warner Bruntjen, Eric Bruntjen. BA, Goucher Coll., 1963; attended, Yale Law Sch., 1963—64; D in psychology, Cornell U., 1975. Dir. social policy planning City Chgo., 1965—70; asst. prof. Columbia U., NYC, 1975—77; dir. behavioral med. clinic Abbott-N.W. Hosp., Mpls., 1981—94; exec. officer Psy Bar, LLC, Edina, Minn., 1995—. Trustee, chmn. academic affairs com. Mpls. Coll. Art and Design, 1992—99; chmn. Ripley Meml. Fdn., 1993—95. Author: Getting It, 1976. Trustee Illusion Theater, 1990—96. Mem.: Jane Austin Soc. Avocations: tennis, bicycling. Office: Psy Bar LLC 5150 Edina Ind Blvd Edina MN

FENZL, TERRY EARLE, lawyer; b. Milw., Mar. 19, 1945; s. Earle A. and Elaine A. (Chandler) F.; m. Barbara Louise Pool, June 24, 1967; children: Allison, Andrew, Ashley. BBA, U. Wis., 1966; JD, U. Mich., 1969. Bar: Ariz. 1970, U.S. Dist. Ct. Ariz. 1970, U.S. Ct. Claims 1970, U.S. Ct. Appeals (9th cir.) 1973, U.S. Supreme Ct. 1973, U.S. Dist. Ct. (no. dist.) Calif. 1983. Assoc. Brown & Bain, P.A. and predecessor firms, Phoenix, 1969-74; ptnr. Perkins Coie Brown & Bain, P.A. and predecessor firms, Phoenix, 1975—. Mem. ABA, Ariz. State Bar Assn., Maricopa County Bar Assn., Ariz. Town Hall. Democrat. Mem. United Ch. of Christ. Home: 6610 N Central Ave Phoenix AZ 85012-1014 Office: Ariz Atty Gen Office Chief of Staff 1275 W Washington Phoenix AZ 85007 Office Phone: 602-542-5025. Business E-Mail: terry.fenzl@azag.gov.

FEODOROV, JOHN, artist; b. LA, 1960; BFA in Drawing and Painting, Calif. State U., Long Beach; MFA, Vt. Coll., Montpelier. Arts commr., Seattle, 2000—03; art tchr. Western Wash. U. Fairhaven Coll. Interdisciplinary Studies, Bellingham. Arts educator Arts Corps, Seattle, 2001—. Musician: (band) Fishmagic, Skinwalkers, Ecce Hobo; exhibitions include What Makes the Red Man Red?, King County Art Commn., 1995, Here/After, SOIL, Seattle, 1999, Office Shamans and Other Mythologies, Sacred Circle Gallery, Seattle, 2001, Myths and Prophesies, Howard House, Seattle, 2002, Four Sacred Spaces, 911 Media Arts Ctr., Seattle, 2005, prin. works include Road to Heaven, 2004, Heaven, 2004, Origin of Religion, 2005, Chosen One, 2005, Breath of Life, 2005, Myth Today, 2005, Office Shaman, 2005, Gods Feeding, 2005, Sucrement, 2006, Temple, 2006, Alphabet, 2006. Recipient Sheldon Bergh award, Basil H. Alkazzi Found., NYC, 1995, Artist Assistance award, Jack Straw Found., Seattle, 2002; grantee GAP grant, Artist Trust, Seattle, 2000. Office: Fairhaven Coll Western Wash U 516 High St Bellingham WA 98225-9118 E-mail: john@johnfeodorov.com.

FEOLA, MARIO, researcher; b. Campora, Italy, Mar. 20, 1927; US, 1956; s. Giosue and Alfonsina Feola; m. Arleen Sabo Feola; children: Terri, Susi, Peter, Helen. MD, U. Naples, 1950. Internship Christ Hosp., Jersey City, 1956—57; residence in surgery St. Vincent Hosp., Cleveland, Ohio, 1957—61; residency in thoracic surgery Bayor Coll. Medicine, Houston, 1969—71; assoc. prof. surgery Jefferson Coll. Medicine, Phila., 1974—77; prof. surgery Tex. Tech. U., Lubbock, Tex., 1977—. Chief med. officer Hemobiotech, Dallas, 2004—. Recipient Best Tchr. award, Tex. Tech. U., 1992, 1995, 2002; grant, Nat. Inst. Health, 1997—2000. Achievements include patents in field of blood substitutes. Avocations: music, accordion. Home: 131 N Utica Ave Lubbock TX 79416

FERBEL, THOMAS, physicist, educator; b. Radom, Poland, Dec. 12, 1937; arrived in U.S., 1949, naturalized, 1955; s. Joseph and Natalie (Gotfryd) F.; m. Barbara G. Goolnick, Apr. 20, 1963; children: Natalie, Peter Jordan. BS, Queens Coll., 1959; MS, Yale U., 1960, PhD, 1963. Research staff physicist Yale U., New Haven, 1963-65; asst. prof. physics U. Rochester, NY, 1965-69, assoc. prof. NY, 1969-73, prof. NY, 1973—, assoc. dean grad. studies NY, 1989-91; sci. assoc. CERN, Geneva, 1980-81. Vis. scientist cen. design group Superconducting Supercollider, Lawrence-Berkeley Lab., U. Calif., 1988-89; vis. prof. LAL, Orsay, France, 1995, U. Mainz, Germany, 2001, U. Freiburg, Germany, 2002; mem. program adv. com. Stanford Linear Accelerator Ctr., Calif., 1974-76, Brookhaven Lab., Upton, N.Y., 1981-84; exec. com. Users' Orgn. of Brookhaven Lab., 1972-74; exec. com. Fermi Nat. Accelerator Lab., 1973-75, chmn., 1986-87; sci. dir. Biennial Advanced Study Inst. on High Energy Physics, St. Croix, 1980-2000; mgr. U.S. LHC rsch. program CERN, 2004—. Author: (with A. Das) Introduction to Nuclear and Particle Physics, 1993, second edit., 2004; editor: Techniques and Concepts of High Energy Physics, Vol. 1-X, Silicon Detectors in High Energy Physics, 1982, Experimental Techniques in High Energy and Nuclear Physics, 1991; mem. editl. bd. Phys. Rev., 1978-80, Zeitschrift fur Physik, 1981-85, Internat. Jour. Modern Physics, 1995—. Recipient Alexander von Humboldt prize, 1995; Alfred P. Sloan fellow, 1970, John S. Guggenheim fellow, 1971; Particle Physics and Astronomy Rsch. Coun. sr. fellow Imperial Coll., London, 2002-03. Fellow Am. Phys. Soc. (sec.-treas. divsn. particles and fields 1983-85, chmn. com. on internat. freedom of scientists 1990-92, mem. com. on internat. sci. affairs 1999-2001). Office: U Rochester Dept Physics Rochester NY 14627

FERBER, LEONARD, lawyer; b. Albany, NY, July 19, 1957; AB with high distinction, U. Mich., 1979; JD, U. Pa., 1983. Bar: Ill. 1983. Ptnr., co-char Tech. Practice Katten Muchin Zavis Rosenman, Chgo. Mem.: ABA, Internet Exec. Club, Chgo. Software Assn., Chgo. Bar Assn., Phi Beta Kappa. Office: Katten Muchin Zavis Rosenman 525 W Monroe St, Ste 1600 Chicago IL 60661 Office Phone: 312-902-5679. Office Fax: 312-577-8806. E-mail: leonard.ferber@kmzr.com.

FERBER, LINDA S., museum director; BA cum laude, Barnard Coll., NYC, 1966; MA, Columbia U., NYC, 1968, PhD in Art History, 1980. Curator Am. Painting and Sculpture The Bklyn. Mus., 1970-97, chief curator, 1985-99, Andrew W. Mellon curator Am. Art, 1997—2005; v.p., dir. NY Hist. Soc. Mus., 2005—. Author: William Trost Richards (1833-1905): American Landscape and Marine Painter, 1980, Tokens of a Friendship: Miniature Watercolors by William T. Richards, 1982, (with others) The New Path: Ruskin and the American Pre-Raphaelites, 1985, Never at Fault: The Drawings of William T. Richards, 1986, (with others) Albert Bierstadt: Art and Enterprise, 1991, (with others) Masters of Color and Light: Homer, Sargent and the American Watercolor Movement, 1998, Pastoral Interlude: William T. Richards in Chester County, 2001, (with others) In Search of a National Landscape: William T. Richards in the Adirondacks, 2002, (with others) Kindred Spirits: Asher B. Durand and the American Landscape, 2007; contbr. articles on 19th and 20th century Am. art history. Wyeth Endowment for Am. Art fellow, 1976-77; recipient Disting. Alumna award Barnard Coll., 2001, Fleischman award Smithsonian Archives of Am. Art, 2002. Mem. Coll. Art Assn., Am. Assn. Mus., Am. Studies Assn., Assn. Art Mus. Curators, Century Assn., Orgn. Am. Historians, Assn. for State and Local History, Cosmopolitan Club, Phi Beta Kappa. Office: NY Hist Soc 170 Ctrl Pk W New York NY 10024 Office Phone: 212-485-9259. Business E-Mail: lferber@nyhistory.org.

FERBER, NORMAN ALAN, retail executive; b. NYC, Aug. 25, 1948; m. Rosine Abergel; children: Robert, Lauren, Richard. Student, Bklyn. Coll., 1965-68, L.I.U., 1968-70. Buyer, mdse. mgr. Atherton Industries, NYC, 1976-79; v.p., mdse. mgr. Raxton Corp., NYC, 1979-82; v.p. Fashion World, NYC, 1982; v.p merchandising, mktg. and distbn. Ross Stores Inc., Newark, Calif., 1984-87, pres., COO, 1987-88, pres., CEO, 1988-93, chmn., CEO, 1993-96, chmn., 1996—. Office: Ross Stores Inc 4440 Rosewood Dr Pleasanton CA 94588*

FERBER, ROBERT RUDOLF, retired physics researcher, educator, science administrator; b. June 11, 1935; s. Rudolf F. and Elizabeth J. (Robertson) F.; m. Eileen Merhaut, July 25, 1964; children: Robert Rudolf, Lynne C. BSEE, U. Pitts., 1958; MSEE, Carnegie-Mellon U., 1966, PhD in Semiconductor Physics, 1967. Registered profl. engr., Pa. Mgr. engring. dept. WRS Motion Picture Labs., Pitts., 1954-58, sec., 1959-76, v.p., 1976-79; sr. engr. Westinghouse Rsch. Labs., Pitts., 1956-67; mgr. nuclear effects group Westinghouse Elec. Corp., Pitts., 1967-71, mgr. adv. engr. energy projects East Pittsburgh, 1971-77; photovoltaic materials and collector rsch. mgr. Jet Propulsion Lab., Pasadena, Calif., 1977-85, SP100 Project contract tech. mgr., 1985-90, asst. project mgr. Spaceborne Imaging Radar, 1990-96, Earth Observing Sys. microwave limb sounder radiometer, 1995-99, mgr. Herschel HIFI project amplifier devel. task mgr., 2000—04, ret., 2004. V.p. Executaire Inc., Pitts., 1960-64; pres. Tele-Cam Inc., Pitts., 1960-78. Editor: Transactions of the 9th World Energy Conf. 1974, Digest of the 9th World Energy Conf., 1974. Contbr. articles to profl. jours.; patentee in field. Mem. Franklin Regional Sch. Dist. Bd., Murrysville, Pa., 1975-77. Fellow Buhl Found., 1965-66, NDEA, 1976-77. Mem. IEEE (sr.), ASME (chmn. 1986 Solar Energy divsn. conf.). Republican. Lutheran. Home: 12865 Moss Rock Dr Auburn CA 95602 Personal E-mail: rrferber@sbcglobal.net.

FERBER, SAMUEL, publishing executive; b. NYC, June 6, 1920; s. Isidore and Sadie (Irgang) F.; m. Beatrice Ruth Ziman, June 18, 1944; children: Bruce Joseph, Joel David. BBA, CCNY, 1941; postgrad., Columbia U., 1946-48. Promotion dir. Nat. Advt. Service, Inc., NYC, 1946-50, Boys' Life mag., NYC, 1950-52; promotion dir. Esquire mag., NYC, 1952-58, advt. mgr., 1959-65, sr. v.p., assoc. pub., 1965-70, advt. dir., 1970-74, pub., 1974-76; co-dir. Esquire mag. (Bus. and the Arts awards program), 1966-74; dir. Esquire mag. (Corp. Social Responsibility awards program), 1972-75; sr. v.p., prin. Altman, Stoller, Weiss Advt., 1976-80, exec. v.p., 1980-82; v.p. Nadler & Larimer Advt., 1982-84; owner Sam Ferber, Pub. Cons., 1984—. Faculty econs. and advt. Latin Am. Inst., NYC, 1946-49; bd. advisors Alliance Resident Theatres, NYC, 1987—; lectr. in fied. Mem. Leader Gt. Books Discussion Group, Bd. Art/N.Y. Served with Adj. Gen.'s Dept. AUS, 1942-46. Personal E-mail: sambeaf@cs.com. *I have always subscribed to the philosophy of my former colleague, Arnold Gingrich, that one should "never leave well enough alone"... When things are progressing smoothly is the precise moment to plan the evolutionary change that insures progress and vitality. In my time, I have seen pillars of industry and publishing fall by the wayside because their emphasis has been on self-preservation rather than innovation.*

FERDINANDI, V. MICHAEL, retail executive; B in Indsl. Edn., M in Indsl. Edn., Rhode Island Coll.; PhD, Boston U. Various positions Ford Motor Co.; dir. human resources PepsiCo, Inc., 1994—96, v.p. ops. Can., 1996—99; v.p. human resources and orgnl. devel. CVS Pharmacy, Inc., Woonsocket, RI, 1999—2002, sr. v.p. human resources and corp. comm., 2002—07; sr. v.p. HR & Corp. Comm. CVS Caremark Corp., 2007—. Bd. trustees William M. Davies, Jr. Career & Tech. H.S. Office: CVS Caremark Corporation Corporate HQs One CVS Drive Woonsocket RI 02895*

FEREBEE, STEPHEN SCOTT, JR., retired architect; b. Detroit, July 30, 1921; s. Stephen Scott and Caroline (Cheatham) F.; m. Mary Elizabeth Cooper, July 7, 1945 (dec. Dec. 2006); children: Scott III, John, Caroline. BArch in Engring., N.C. State U., 1948; DFA (hon.), U. N.C., Charlotte, 1992. Job capt. A.G. Odell, Jr. & Assocs., Charlotte, NC, 1948—53; ptnr. Higgins & Ferebee, Charlotte, 1953—59, Ferebee & Walters, 1959—64; pres. Ferebee, Walters & Assos., Charlotte, 1964—86; chmn., CEO FWA Group, Charlotte, 1987—90, project exec., 1991—95; planning, design and devel. cons., 1996—2003; ret., 2003. Dir. AIA Found., Washington, 1986-87, Prodn. Systems for Architects and Engrs., Inc., Washington, 1969-71, 77-78, Republic Bank & Trust Co., Charlotte, 1971-91, John Crosland Co., Charlotte, 1973-83. Prin. projects include Southpark Mall, Colonial Heights, Va., 1989, Tech. Ctr. for Union Carbide Agrl. Products Co., Inc, Research Triangle Park, N.C., 1982, Coll. Vet. Medicine, N.C. State U., Raleigh, 1983, Charlotte Conv. Ctr., 1994, Coll. Architecture bldg., U. N.C., Charlotte, 1990. Bd. dirs. United Cmty. Svcs., Charlotte, 1977—82, Opera Carolina, Charlotte, 1988—91, Aldersgate, Charlotte, 1995—2004, 2005—06, Habitat for Humanity, Charlotte, 1999—2002; pres. N.C. Design Found., 1966—68, 1978—79. Capt. 101st Airborne Divsn. AUS, 1942—46, maj. gen. Res. (ret.). Decorated D.S.M., Bronze Star, Purple Heart, Croix de Guerre France and Belgium, Order of the Long Leaf Pine State of N.C.; recipient Watauga medal, N.C. State U., 2001. Fellow: AIA (pres. N.C. 1964, chmn. commn. profl. practice 1971, nat. pres. 1973, chancellor Coll. of Fellows 1987, Deitrick medal N.C. chpt. 1995, F. Carter Williams Gold medal N.C. chpt. 2004), Internat. Union Architects (coun. 1975—81), Royal Archtl. Inst. Can. (hon.); mem.: Mex. Soc. Architects (hon.), N.C. State U. Alumni Assn. (pres. 1980—81), Charlotte C. of C. (v.p. 1975—76, bd. dirs. 1989—91), Rotary (pres. Charlotte East 1997—98), Phi Kappa Phi. Methodist. Home: 3800 Shamrock Dr Charlotte NC 28215-3220 Personal E-mail: sferebee@carolina.rr.com.

FERENCE, EDWARD W., engineering executive, structural engineer; b. Central City, Pa., Nov. 7, 1927; s. Andrew and Elizabeth C. Ference; m. Virginia J. Dedik, 1960; children: Edward, John, Mary-Jean. BSCE, U. Pitts., 1951; postgrad., Columbia U., NYC, 1952—53. Stress analyst N.Am. Aviation, Inglewood, Calif., 1951-52, Kaiser Metal Products, Bristol, Pa., 1952-54; structural engr. Avro Aircraft, Toronto, Ont., Can., 1954-59, Grumman Aircraft Co., Bethpage, L.I., N.Y., 1959-62, Cleve. Pneumatic, 1961-62, Vertol Divisn. Boeing, Morton, Pa., 1962-68; owner, sales engr. United Tech. Svcs., Allentown, Pa., 1968-70; structural engr. Boeing Vertol Co., Ridley Park, Pa., 1970-71; prin. engr. GE, Erie, Pa., 1971-74, Westinghouse Electric Corp., Pitts., 1974-90. Staff sgt. U.S. Army, 1944-46, ETO. Mem. VFW (life), NRA (life), Am. Legion (life), U.S. Constabulary Assn. (life), Tau Beta Pi (life). Achievements include patents in field. Avocations: antique cars, woodworking, shooting. Home: 1415 Clearview Dr Greensburg PA 15601-3703 Personal E-mail: geference1@aol.com.

FERENCZ, BENJAMIN BERELL, lawyer; b. Soncuta Mare, Romania, Mar. 11, 1920; arrived in U.S., 1921, naturalized, 1933; s. Joseph Ferencz and Sarah (Legman) Ferencz Schwartz; m. Gertrude Fried, Mar. 29, 1946; children: Carol, Robin Eve, Donald Martin, Nina Dale. BSS, CCNY, 1940; JD, Harvard U., 1943. Bar: N.Y. 1943, U.S. Supreme Ct. 1943, U.S. Dist. Ct. (so. and ea. dists.) N.Y. 1958. Exec. counsel U.S. Chief Counsel War Crimes, Nuremberg, Germany, 1946—48; dir. gen. Jewish Restitution Orgn., Franfurt, Germany, 1948—56; ptnr. Taylor, Ferencz & Simon, NYC, 1956—. Adj. prof. Pace U. Sch. Law, NYC; dir. United Restitution Orgn., London, Frankfurt, NYC, 1948—. Author: Less than Slaves, 1979 (Nat. and Present Tense Lit. awards, 1980), Defining International Aggression, 2 vols., 1975, An International Criminal Court, 2 vols., 1980, Enforcing International Law, 2 vols., 1983, Common Sense Guide to World Peace, 1985, New Legal Foundations for Global Survival, 1994. Mem. Human Rights Commn., New Rochelle, NY, 1975—. With inf. US Army, 1943—45, ETO. Mem.: Internat. Law Assn., Am. Soc. Internat. Law (v.p. 1979—80), World Peace Through Law Ctr., Amnesty Internat., Internat. League Human Rights, Harvard Club (N.Y.C.), B'nai B'rith (local pres. 1960, counsel supreme lodge 1966—70). Democrat. Jewish. Home: 14 Bayberry Ln New Rochelle NY 10804-3402 Personal E-mail: benferen@aol.com.

FERENCZ, CHARLOTTE, pediatrician, epidemiologist, preventive medicine physician, educator; b. Budapest, Hungary, Oct. 28, 1921; came to U.S., 1954; d. Paul Ferencz and Livia deFekete. BSc, McGill U., 1944, MD, CM, 1945; MPH, Johns Hopkins U., 1970. Cert. pediatrics Royal Coll. Physicians and Surgeons, Can., pediatric cardiology Am. Bd. Pediatrics. Demonstrator McGill U., Montreal, 1952-54; asst. prof. pediatrics Johns Hopkins U., Balt., 1954-58, U. Cin., 1959-60; asst. prof. SUNY, Buffalo, 1960-66, assoc. prof., 1966-73; assoc. prof. epidemiology and preventive medicine U. Md. Sch. Medicine, Balt., 1973-74, prof., 1974-98, prof. pediatrics, 1985—, prof. emeritus, 1998—. Prin. investigator population based study Etiology of Congenital Heart Disease, 1981-89; mem. epidemiology and disease control study sect. NIH, 1984-88; pres. Delta Omage Alpha chpt. Pub. Health Soc., 1990-92. Recipient M.E.S. Abbott scholarship McGill U., 1943-45, M.E.R.I.T. award Nat. Heart, Lung & Blood Inst., 1987, Fogarty Internat. Ctr. Health Sci. Exchange award NIH, 1988, Helen B. Taussig award Am. Heart Assn. Md. Affiliate, 1991, Achievement award Univ. Ctr. Life Scis., Balt., 1993, Johns Hopkins U. Disting. Alumnus award, 2001. Fellow Am. Acad. Pediatrics (Spl. Achievement award Md. chpt. 1994), Am. Coll. Cardiology; mem. Teratology Soc. Democrat.

FERENCZ, GARRETT R., lawyer; BA cum laude, Univ. Wash., 1999; JD magna cum laude, Seattle Univ., 2002. Bar: Wash. 2002. Assoc. atty., personal injury, employment law The Blankenship Law Firm, P.S., Seattle, 2002—. Contbr. articles to numerous profl. jours. Named Wash. Rising Star, SuperLawyer Mag., 2006. Mem.: ABA, Wash. State Bar Assn. Office: The Blankenship Law Firm PS Washington Mutual Tower 1201 Third Ave 29th Fl Seattle WA 98101

FERENS, DANIEL VINCENT, retired civilian military employee; b. Oswego, NY, Feb. 26, 1948; s. Walter Frank and Sophie (Longeski) F.; m. Marcella Jean Spinner, Apr. 28, 2001. BS, Rensselaer Poly. Inst., 1969, MSEE, 1970; MBA, U. No. Colo., 1976. Satellite sys. engr. air def. co. USAF, Denver, 1971-75, computer software engr. Aeronaut. Sys. Ctr. Dayton, Ohio, 1976-77, program mgr. Aeronaut. Sys. Ctr., 1977-78; engring. cost analyst civil svc. USAF Avionics Lab., Dayton, 1978-83; assoc. prof. civil svc. USAF Inst. Tech., Dayton, 1984-97; program dir., 1995-97; adj. assoc. prof. civil svc. USAF Inst. Tech., Dayton, 1998-2000; corp. affordability officer civil svc. USAF Rsch. Lab., Dayton, 1998-00, directorate rep. Corp. Affordability Coun., 1999—2001; tchr. software mgmt. NATO Officers, Belgium, 2000; program mgr. USAF Rsch. Lab., Rome, NY, 2001—07. Software estimating cons. Aeronautics Sys. Ctr., Dayton, 1984—2000, Electronic Sys. Ctr., Boston, 2000—02; adj. instr. SUNY Inst. Tech., Utica, 2003—; analyst ITT Industries, Rome, 2007—. Author: Mission Critical Computer Software Management, 1987, Defense System Software Project Management, 1990; guest editor: Engineering Cost and Production Economics, 1988; contbr. 35 articles to profl. jours. Tchr. adult Sunday sch. Kirkmont Presbyn. Ch., Beaver Creek, Ohio, 1987—2000, chmn. edn. com., 1992; adult Sunday sch. tchr. Abiding Christ Luth. Ch., Fairborn, Ohio, 2000—01; mem. Christian edn. com. First Presbyn. Ch., Rome, NY, 2002—, adult Sunday Sch. tchr. Capt. USAF, 1969—78. Decorated USAF Commendation medal. Mem. Internat. Soc. Parametric Analysts (bd. dirs. 1979-80, 2004-06, pres. Midwest chpt. 1993-94, Internat. Parametrician of the Yr. award 1990, Freiman Lifetime Achievement award 1999, keynote spkr. European Symposium, 1999, life), Internat. Function Point Users Group (univ. mem., edn. com. 1999-2000), Soc. Cost Estimating and Analysis (edn. com. 1992-2007), Soc. Logistics Engrs. (assoc. editor newsletter 1993), Toastmasters Internat. (pres. 2003-04, area gov. 2003-05, dist. 65 sec. 2006-07, dist. lt. gov. mktg., 2007-, Area Gov. of Yr. 1987, Disting. Toastmaster 2004), Polish Legion Am Vets. Avocations: model railroading, church activities, travel, games, reading. Mailing: PO Box 96 Oswego NY 13126 Office: ITT AES 775 Vaedalian Dr Rome NY 13441 Personal E-mail: marfdanf@aol.com.

FERENSOWICZ, MICHAEL JAY, real estate company executive; b. Detroit, July 19, 1952; s. Anthony John and Margaret Mary (Denny) F.; children: Claire, Rachel. BA, Harvard U., 1975; MBA, Northeastern U., 1983. Adminstrv. asst. Boston Mayor's Office Community Devel., 1975-78; fin. intern Fin. Group/Northeastern U., Boston, 1981-82; project dir./gen. ptnr. Real Property Resources, Inc., Torrance, Calif., 1983-88; ptnr. F.T. Von Der Ahe Co., Newport Beach, Calif., 1988-90; exec. v.p. Access Realty Advisors, Inc., Olympic Valley, Calif., 1990—; comml. devel. dir. The Village Squaw Valley USA, Olympic Valley, Calif.; v.p. village devel. and strategic partnerships Tamarack Resort LLC, Idaho, 2004—. Walker-Beale Fund scholar Harvard U., 1971-72, Edwin S. George Fund scholar, 1973-74. Mem. Mus. Contemporary Art L.A. (charter), Harvard Club So. Calif. Roman Catholic. Avocations: modern art, travel, golf. Home: PO Box 2301 Mccall ID 83638-2301 Office: Tamarack Resort LLC Village Devel 311 Village Dr PMB 3026 Donnelly ID 83615 Office Phone: 208-325-1075. Business E-Mail: mferensowicz@tamarackidaho.com.

FERENTINO, SHEILA CONNOLLY, psychologist, consultant; d. John Francis Connolly and Mabel Rose McCabe; 1 child, James. BA, Hunter Coll. CUNY; MS in Spl. Edn., CUNY, 1963; profl. diploma in Psychology, St. John's U., 1973; PhD in Psychology, Hofstra U., 1991. Cert. tchr. blind and partially sighted NYS, 1962, braillist Libr. Congress, 1964, sch. psychologist NY, 1972, lic. psychologist NY, 1993. Tchr. elem. sch. Nassau County Sch. Dist., 1960—61; tchr. blind Nassau Bd. Cooperative Edn. Svcs. Spl. Edn., NY, 1961—72, psychologist, 1972—2004; child psychologist, children with disabilities pvt. practice, Freeport, NY, 2005—. Tchr. Summer Headstart, Hollis, NY, 1968—69, dir., 1970; adj. prof. Hunter Coll. CUNY, NYC, 1963—65; asst. dir. after sch. activities for blind Bd. Cooperative Edn. Svcs., 1965—70. Contbr. articles to profl. jours. Chmn. mus. trips com. Helen Keller Svcs. for Blind, Nassau County, 1961—70; contbr. Evaluation Measures for Handicapped Pre-Schoolers. Grantee, NY State Dept. Edn., 1980, 1989, Vanderbilt U., 1988. Mem.: APA, Nat. Assn. Prevention Blindness, Nassau Couny Psychol. Assn., NY State Psychol. Assn., Sigmund Freud Soc., Orton Soc. Avocations: classical music, opera, travel, wildlife conservation, maritime museums. Home: 18-05 215 St Apt 2B Bayside NY 11360 Office: 110 Garfield St Freeport NY 11520 Office Phone: 917-655-5691. Personal E-mail: posone@verizon.net.

FERENTZ, KEVIN SCOTT, physician; b. New York, NY, Apr. 26, 1958; s. Leslie Benjamin and Sylvia F.; m. Lisa Roslyn Ettinger, Nov. 13, 1983; children: Jacob Avi, Zachary Daniel, Noah Samuel. MD, SUNY, Buffalo, 1983. Diplomate Nat. Bd. Med. Examiners, cert. Am. Bd. Family Practice. Assoc. prof. dept. family medicine U. Md. Sch. of Medicine, Balt., 1993—2005, dir. clin. ops., dept. family medicine, 2005—. Residency dir. Dept of Family Medicine, Balt., 1993—. Contbr. articles; host (weekly nat. radio show) Sunday Rounds. Mem. adv. bd. Tova Ho., Balt., 2002. Recipient Resident rsch. award, North Am. Primary Care Rsch. Group Nat. Meeting, 1986. Mem.: Assn. Family Practice Residency Dirs., Soc. Tchrs. Family Medicine, Md. Acad. Family Physicians (pres. 1997—98), Am. Acad. Family Physicians (chair, com. on pub. rels. and mktg. 1995—96, Exemplary Tchr. of Yr. 1999, Pub. Rels. award 1991, Outstanding Program Dir. 2004). Democrat. Jewish. Achievements include organized smoking cessation program for Baltimore County High Schools, using medical students and residents as group leaders. Avocations: theater, music. Office: U Md Sch Medicine 29 South Paca St Baltimore MD 21201 Office Fax: 410-328-2555. Personal E-mail: kev107@aol.com. Business E-Mail: kferentz@som.umaryland.edu.

FERENTZ, KIRK, college football coach; b. Royal Oak, MI, Aug. 1, 1955; m. Mary Ferentz; 5 children. Grad. in English Edn., U. Conn., 1978. Student asst. U. Conn., 1977; English lit. teacher Worcester Academy, 1978—79; grad. asst. offensive line coach U. Pitts., 1980; offensive line coach Iowa U. Hawkeyes, 1981—89; head coach U. Maine, 1990—92; asst. head coach & offensive line coach Cleve. Browns (later became the Baltimore Ravens, NFL), 1992—98; head coach Iowa U. Hawkeyes, 1998—. Recipient Assoc. Press and The Walter Camp Football Founds. Coach of the Year, 2002, Nat. Coach of the Year, 2002, Dave McClain Big Ten Coach of the Year honor, 2002, 2004. Achievements include winning the Alamo Bowl (2001), Outback Bowl (2004), Capital One Bowl (2004), and two Big Ten championships (2002, 2004); being just one of seven Big Ten coaches ever to guide a team to 10 wins or more in three straight seasons; over the past seven seasons, 46 of 54 senior starters under Coach Ferentz, have been selected in the NFL Draft or signed to an NFL free agent contract. Office: Iowa Hawkeyes Hayden Fry Football Complex Iowa City IA 52242 Office Phone: 319-335-8943.

FERETIC, EILEEN SUSAN, editor; d. Joseph Anthony and Eileen Helen (Sohl) F.; m. William Kulakoski; 1 child, Shannon. BA, Fordham U. Editor Hearst Bus. Comms., LI, NY, 1972—90; editorial dir. FM Bus. Pub., Garden City, 1990—92; editor Corporate Sys. mag., 1975—80, Office Products News, 1972-82, Today's Office, 1982-92; also editorial dir. Office Group, 1978-92; editor in chief Beyond Computing mag., NYC, 1992—2003; exec. editor Ziff Davis Media, NYC, 2003—. Industry rep. U.S. Dept. Commerce, 1980, 83; mem. Pres.'s Pvt. Sector Survey on Cost Control/Office Automation Task Force, 1982 Co-author textbook on adminstrv. procedures in electronic office, 1979; co-producer, host (TV series) Office Automation; contbr. World Book Ency. Recipient N.Y. Daily News award journalism; Long Island Press Club Writing award. Home: 115 Rita Dr East Meadow NY 11554-1326 Office: Ziff Davis Media 28 E 28th St New York NY 10016 Office Phone: 212-503-5625. Personal E-mail: efreretic@aol.com.

FERGENSON, ARTHUR FRIEND, lawyer; b. NYC, Dec. 9, 1947; s. A. Leon and Constance Elinor (Friend) F.; children: Leah F., Nina E. Festa, Micah F. AB, Dartmouth Coll., 1969; JD, Yale U., 1972. Bar: N.Y. 1973, U.S. Dist. Ct. (so. dist.) N.Y. 1973, D.C. 1975, U.S. Ct. Appeals (2d cir.) 1975, U.S. Dist. Ct. Md. 1984, U.S. Ct. Appeals (4th cir.) 1984, Md. 1985, U.S. Supreme Ct. 1986. Law clk to Hon. Thomas P. Griesa U.S. Dist. Ct., NYC, 1972-73; law clk. to U.S. Chief Justice Warren E. Burger U.S. Supreme Ct., Washington, 1973-74; atty. Covington & Burling, Washington, 1974-76; asst. prof. Ind. U. Sch. Law, Bloomington, 1976-79; assoc. prof. U. Md. Sch. Law, Balt., 1979-81; gen. counsel Action Agency, Washington, 1981-82; cons. Nat. Inst. Justice, Washington, 1982-83; asst. U.S. atty. U.S. Atty.'s Office, Balt., 1983-85; ptnr., of counsel Weinberg and Green, Balt., 1985-95; of counsel Ballard Spahr Andrews & Ingersoll, Balt., 1995—2001; ptnr. DLA Piper, 2001—. Mem. adv. coun. Atlantic Legal Found., Inc., 1997—. Editl. bd. mem. Bus. Law Today, 2001—, Trustee Ctr. Stage, Balt., 1987-06. Republican. Jewish. Avocations: theater, films, politics, political theory. Office: 6225 Smith Ave Baltimore MD 21209 Office Phone: 410-580-4438. Business E-Mail: arthur.fergenson@dlapiper.com.

FERGIE, (STACY ANN FERGUSON), singer; b. Whittier, Calif., Mar. 27, 1975; d. Terri and Pat Ferguson. Band mem. Wild Orchid, 1996—2002, Black Eyed Peas, 2003—. Singer: (albums with Wild Orchid) Wild Orchid, 1997, Oxygen, 1998, Fire, 2001, (albums with Black Eyed Peas) Elephunk, 2003, Monkey Business, 2005 (Favorite Rap/Hip-Hop Album, Am. Music Awards, 2006), (solo albums) The Dutchess, 2006, (songs) (with Wild Orchid) At Night I Pray, 1996, Talk to Me, 1997, Supernatural, 1997, Be Mine, 1998, Stuttering (Don't Say), 2001, (with Black Eyed Peas) Where is the Love?, 2003, Shut Up, 2003, Let's Get It Started, 2004 (Grammy, Best Rap Performance, 2005), Hey Mama, 2004 (MTV Music Video Award), Don't Phunk with My Heart, 2005 (Grammy award, Best Rap Group Performance, 2006), Don't Lie, 2005 (Grammy award for Best Group Pop Vocal Performance, 2007), My Humps, 2005 (MTV Video Music award for Best Hip-Hop Video, 2006), (as solo artist) London Bridge, 2006; actor: (films) Be Cool, 2005, Poseidon, 2006, Grindhouse (Planet Terror segment), 2007; (TV series) Kids Incorporated, 1984—89, The Charlie Brown & Snoopy Show, 1984—85, Great Pretenders, 1999. Named one of 50 Most Beautiful People in the World, People mag., 2004; recipient MTV Europe award for Best Pop Act (with Black Eyed Peas), 2004, 2005, Favorite Pop Group & Rap Group, Am. Music Awards, 2005, Favorite Soul/Rhythm & Blues Grp., 2006, Favorite Rap/Hip-Hop Grp., 2006.*

FERGUS, GARY SCOTT, lawyer; b. Racine, Wis., Apr. 20, 1954; s. Russell Malcolm and Phyl Rose (Muratore) F.; m. Isabelle Sabina Beekman, Sept. 28, 1985; children: Mary Marckwald Beekman Fergus, Kirkpatrick Russell Beekman Fergus. AB, Stanford U., 1976; JD, U. Wis., 1979; LLM, NYU, 1981. Bar: Wis. 1979, Calif. 1980. Assoc. Brobeck, Phleger & Harrison, San Francisco, 1980-86, ptnr., 1986—2001, mng. ptnr. products liability, ins. coverage, environ. and antitrust/appellate practices, 1996-2000, sr. ptnr. e-commerce anti-trust group, 2000—01; founder law firm Fergus, San Francisco, 2002—. Mem. ABA. Home: 3024 Washington St San Francisco CA 94115-1618 Office: Fergus a law firm 595 Market St Ste 2430 San Francisco CA 94105 Home Phone: 415-567-3129; Office Phone: 415-537-9032. Business E-Mail: gfergus@ferguslegal.com.

FERGUS, PATRICIA MARGUERITA, language educator, writer, editor; b. Mpls., Oct. 26, 1918; d. Golden Maughan and Mary Adella (Smith) Fergus. BS, U. Minn., 1939, MA, 1941, PhD, 1960. Various pers. and editing positions US Govt., 1943-59; mem. faculty U. Minn., Mpls., 1964-79, asst. prof. English, 1972-79, coord. writing program conf. on writing, 1975, dir. writing centre, 1975-77; prof. English and writing, dir. writing ctr., assoc. dean Coll. Mt. St. Mary's Coll., Emmitsburg, Md., 1979-81; dir. writing seminars Mack Truck, Inc., Hagerstown, Md., 1979-81; writer, 1964—. Editor, 1997—; vocal soloist, 1997—; editl. asst. to pres. Met. State U., St. Paul, 1984—85; coord. creative writing, writer program notes for Coffee Concerts The Kenwood, 1992—94; dir. Kenwood Scribes Presentation, 1994; spkr., cons. in field; dir. 510 Groveland Assocs.; bus. mgr. Eitel Hosp. Gift Shop; freelance manuscript editor, 1997—99; writer, reviewer Whittier Pubs., Long Beach, NY, 1997; instr. Elderlearning Inst., 1999—2000, Univ. Coll., U. Minn., 1999—2000; poetry and prose reading, retirement cmtys., 2002—06; pres., resident coun. Walker Tree Tops, Mpls., 2003—04, spl. events dir., master of ceremonies, dir., spkr., 2003—06. Author: Spelling Improvement, 5th edit., 1991; contbr. to Downtown Cath. Voice, Mpls., Mountaineer Briefing, ABI Digest, Women in the Arts The Penletter; contbr. poems to Minn. English Jour., Women in the Arts, Decatur Area Arts Coun. Newsletter, Mpls. Muse, The Moccasin, Heartsong and Northstar Gold, The Pen Woman, Midwest Chaparral, Rhyme Time, The Best of Rhyme Time, 1998, Fantasy, 1998; contbr. short stories to anthologies, including Seeking the Muses, Inspired Works of Creativity, 2000; musical works performed at St. Olaf Ch., 1997, Nat. League Am. Pen Women, 1998. Mem. spl. vocal octet St. Olaf Ch. Choir, 1977-79, 81-92, St. Olaf Parish Adv. Bd., 1982-84, Windmore Found. for the Arts., 1996. Recipient Outstanding Contbn. award U. Minn. Twin Cities Student Assembly, 1975, Horace T. Morse-Amoco Found. award, 1976; Golden Poet award World of Poetry, 1992; Ednl. Devel. grant U. Minn., 1975-76, Mt. St. Mary's Coll. grant, 1980; 3d prize vocal-choral category Nat. Music Composition Contest, Nat. League Am. Pen Women, poetry prize No. Dist. Women's Club, Va., 1996. Mem.: Midwest Fedn. Chaparral Poets (poetry judge, 1st prize 1998, 1999, 2001, 2003, 2d prize 2006), Mpls. Poetry Soc. (pres. 2000—02, numerous poetry prizes including 1st prize 1999, 2d prize 2003, 1st prize 2006, 2007), World Lit. Acad., Nat. League Am. Pen Women (Minn. br. and state past pres., 1st pl. Haiku nat. poetry contest 1992), Minn. Coun. Tchrs. English (chmn. career and job opportunities comm., spl. com. tchr. licensure, sec. legis. com.), Nat. Coun. Tchrs. English (regional judge 1974, 1976—77, state coord. 1977—79), Mpls. Woman's Club (critic writers group). Roman Catholic. Home and Office: 1509 10th Ave S 319 Minneapolis MN 55404-1752 Office Phone: 612-827-4867.

FERGUSON, BRADFORD LEE, lawyer; b. Ottumwa, Iowa, May 29, 1947; s. G. Wendell and Virginia Sue (Baker) Ferguson. BA, Drake U., 1969; JD, Harvard U., 1972. Bar: Minn. 1972, Ill. 1980. Assoc. Dorsey, Marquart, Windhorst, West & Halladay, Mpls., 1972-75; legis. asst. Senator Walter F. Mondale, Washington, 1975-77; spl. asst. to asst. sec. tax policy U.S. Treasury Dept., Washington, 1977-78, assoc. tax legis. counsel, 1978-80; ptnr. Hopkins & Sutter, Chgo., 1980-96, Sidley & Austin, Chgo., 1996-2001. Fellow Am. Coll. Tax Counsel; mem. Chgo. Bar Assn.

FERGUSON, CHARLES AUSTIN, retired newspaper editor; b. New Orleans, Mar. 16, 1937; s. Austin and Josephine Hayes (Gessner) F.; m. Jane Pugh, Dec. 21, 1961; children: Elizabeth Hayes, Caroline Pugh. BA, Tulane U., 1958, LL.B., 1961; DLitt (hon.), Dillard U., New Orleans, 1996. Bar: La. bar 1961. From reporter to editor States-Item, New Orleans, 1961-80; editor Times-Picayune/States-Item, New Orleans, 1980-90. Anchor TV program City Desk, New Orleans, 1971-78 Trustee Dillard U., New Orleans, 1972—2005, chmn. exec. com., 1978—2005, chmn. bd. trustees, 1992—2005, emeritus, 2005—; mem. adv. bd. Nieman Found., Harvard U., 2004—; co-chmn. Louis Armstrong Meml. Park Com., New Orleans, 1971-79. Recipient Torch of Liberty award Anti-Defamation League of B'nai B'rith, 1981; Nieman fellow, 1965-66 Mem. La. Bar Assn., Internat. Lawn Tennis Club U.S.A., New Orleans Lawn Tennis Club, Harvard Club (N.Y.C.). Home: 1448 Joseph St New Orleans LA 70115-4263

FERGUSON, CHRISTOPHER J., astronaut; b. Phila., Pa., Sept. 1, 1961; s. Norman (Stepfather) and Mary Ann Pietras; m. Sandra A. Cabot; 3 children. BS in Mech. Engring., Drexel U., 1984; MS in Aeronautical Engring., Naval Postgraduate Sch., 1991. Temporary assignment Naval Test Pilot Sch., Naval Air Station, Patuxent River, Md.; flight tng. Fla., Tex.; ordered to F-14 replacement tng. squadron Virginia Beach, Va.; joined Red Rippers of VF-11; assigned to as the project officer for F-14D weapon separation program Ordinance Branch, Strike Aircraft Test Directorate, NAS Patuxent River, 1992—94; instructor Naval Test Pilot Sch., 1994—95; joined Checkmates of VF-211; served as F-14 Class Deck officer Comdr. Naval Air Force, Atlantic Fleet; astronaut, pilot NASA Johnson Space Ctr., 1998—. Pilot Space Shuttle Atlantis (STS-115), 2006. Recipient Navy Strike/Flight Air medal, Navy Commendation medal (3), Navy Achievement medal. Mem.: Soc. Exptl. Test Pilots. Avocations: golf, woodworking, running, drums. Office: Astronaut Office CB NASA Lyndon B Johnson Space Ctr Houston TX 77058

FERGUSON, CLEVE ROBERT, lawyer, educator; b. Long Beach, Calif., Dec. 31, 1938; s. Frank H and Ruth S Ferguson; m. Kathryn Jane Weaver, Apr. 10, 1965 (div. June 25, 1995); children: Sharon Anne, Robert Timothy; m. Peggy Burke Daniell, Nov. 19, 1995. Attended, U. Vienna, 1960—61; AB in Econs., U. So. Calif., 1961, JD, 1965. Bar: Calif 1966, U.S. Dist. Ct. (cen. dist.) Calif. 1966, U.S. Ct. Appeals (9th cir.) 1987, U.S. Supreme Ct. 1975. Assoc. Musick, Peeler & Garrett, LA, 1965—69, Hayes & Hume, Beverly Hills, Calif., 1969—74; pvt. practice Claremont, Calif., 1974—; adj. prof. physics and astronomy U. La Verne, Calif., 1993—2005; pres., CEO Mars Manned Mission Corp.; pres. Hyde Mountain Mktg. Co., 2004—; adj. prof. Coll. Law U. La Verne, 1994—2001. Alcohol and drug abuse com. Calif. State Bar, 1990—91; instr. astronomy and bus. law Chapman U., 1992—93; instr. telescope use and telescope optics UCLA, U. Calif., Irvine; lectr. in field. Editor (rschr.): Quarter Circle 81, Prescott and Camp Wood, Arizona, 1883-1912, 2004; columnist Claremont Inst. Active Stony Ridge Obs., 1985—, pres., 1994—97; co-founder, bd. trustees Mt. Wilson Inst., Calif., 1987—; lectr., cons. Mcpl. Officers for Redevel. Reform, Calif., 1996—; trustee Pilgrim Congl. Ch., Pomona, Calif.; bd. dirs. Clan Fergusson Soc. N.Am., 1987—2000; chmn., bd. dirs. Pasadena Area Opera Trust. With US Army, 1961—62. Named to, Knights Templar of Jerusalem, Grand Priory of the Scots, 1998—. Fellow: Soc. Antiquaries Scotland; mem.: LA Opera Leagues, Sons of the Revolution, Univ. Club Pasadena, Beta Theta Pi. Avocations: astronomy, dry fly fishing, skiing, mountaineering. Office: C Robert Ferguson Atty at Law 237 W 4th St Claremont CA 91711-4710 Home Phone: 909-392-7773; Office Phone: 909-482-0782. Personal E-mail: crflawyer@earthlink.net. Business E-Mail: crf@marsmannedmission.org.

FERGUSON, CRAIG, actor; b. Glasgow, Scotland, May 17, 1962; m. Sascha Ferguson, July 18, 1998 (div.); 1 child, Milo. Actor (tv series) The Ferguson Theory, 1994, Freakazoid!, 1995, Maybe This Time, 1995, The Drew Carey Show, 1996—2003, (film) Modern Vampyres, 1999, The Big Tease, 1999, Born Romantic, 2000, Saving Grace, 2000, Chain of Fools, 2000; writer (film): The Tease, 1999; tv guest appearances include: Red Dwarf, 1988, Chelmsford 123, 1988, Have I Got News for You, 1991, The Brain Drain, 1993, Almost Perfect, 1995; co-writer, co-prodr., actor: Je M'Appelle Crawford; comedian, comic actor in one-man shows, U.K.; writer (screenplay): All American Man, (with others) Saving Grace, The Ferguson Theory; host: The Late Late Show with Craig Ferguson, 2005-; author: (novels) Between the Bridge and the River, 2006. Office: William Morris Agency 151 S El Camino Dr Beverly Hills CA 90212-2775

FERGUSON, D'BRICKASHAW, professional football player; b. NYC, Dec. 10, 1983; s. Edwin and Rhunette. BA in Religious Studies, Univ. Va., 2006. Offensive lineman New York Jets, 2006—. Named First-team All-ACC, 2004, First Team All-American, 2005—06; named to Freshman All-American Team, 2002. Achievements include 4th overall selection in NFL Draft by New York Jets, 2006. Office: New York Jets 1000 Fulton Ave Hempstead NY 11550

FERGUSON, DIANA S., food products executive; b. 1963; BA in Psychology, Yale U.; MA in Mgmt., Northwestern U. With Eaton, Fannie Mae, First Nat. Bank Chgo., IBM; v.p., treas. US Fort James Corp., Sara Lee Corp., 2001—04, sr. v.p. strategy & corp. devel., 2004—07, CFO, Sara Lee Foodservice, 2006—07; exec. v.p. fin., CFO Merisant Worldwide, Inc., 2007—. Named to The 40 Under 40, Crain's Chgo. Bus., 2002. Fellow; Leadership Greater Chgo. Office: Merisant Worldwide Inc 10 S Riverside Plz Ste 850 Chicago IL 60606*

FERGUSON, DONALD LITTLEFIELD, retired lawyer; b. Greenville, SC, June 10, 1930; s. H. L. and Anne (Littlefield) F.; m. Barbara Wilson, May 20, 1961; children: Donald L. Jr., David Wilson, Robert Neil. BA, Furman U., 1951; LLB, Tulane U., 1954. Bar: S.C. 1954, U.S. Ct. Mil. Appeals 1955, U.S. Dist. Ct. S.C. 1957, U.S. Ct. Appeals (4th cir.) 1974. Assoc. Haynsworth, Marion, McKay & Guerard, Greenville, 1954-61, ptnr., 1961—, sr. ptnr., 1961—2004; ret. Capt. USAF, 1954-57. Mem. ABA, Am. Judicature Soc., S.c. Bar Assn., Poinsett Club, Phi Kappa Phi, Phi Delta Phi. Baptist. Home: 612 Roper Mountain Rd Greenville SC 29615-4227 Office: Haynsworth Sinkler & Boyd 75 Beattie Pl Greenville SC 29601-2130

FERGUSON, EARL WILSON, cardiologist, medical executive, telemedicine consultant; b. Lebanon, Pa., Aug. 29, 1943; s. Warren Earl and Norma Laura (Wilson) F.; m. Sun Hye Paik, May 1, 1998; children: Steven Mark, Matthew Earl, Erin Lee. BA in Chemistry, Baylor U., 1965; MD, PhD in Physiology, U. Tex., Galveston, 1970. Diplomate Am. Bd. Internal Medicine, Cardiovasc. Disease, Am. Bd. Preventive Medicine. Grad. tchg. asst. dept. physiology U. Tex. Med. Br., Galveston, 1967-70, intern medicine, 1970-71; resident medicine, then fellow cardiology Duke U. Med. Ctr., Durham, NC, 1971-75, mem. assoc. faculty dept. medicine, 1974-75; research assoc. cardiology VA Hosp., Durham, 1974-75; commd. lt. USAF, 1966, advanced through grades to col., 1984-95; staff cardiologist, dir. coronary care Wilford Hall USAF Med. Ctr., Lackland AFB, Tex., 1975-76, chief cardiology, dir. cardiology tng. program, 1983-84; asst. prof. biochemistry, medicine and mil. medicine Uniformed Svcs. U. Health Scis., Bethesda, Md., 1976-80, assoc. prof. physiology, medicine and mil. medicine, 1980-84, asst. comdt., 1977-82, mem. faculty senate, 1979-80, adj. prof. physiology, 1984-93; dir. hosp. svcs. USAF Med. Ctr., Scott AFB, Ill., 1984-86; comdr. USAF Hosp., Little Rock AFB, Ark., 1986-88; dep. command surgeon Mil. Airlift Command, Scott AFB, 1988-90; dir. Aerospace Medicine and Occupl. Health NASA, Washington, 1993-96; comdr. USAF Med. Ctr., Wiesbaden, Germany, 1990-93; CEO Sun Biomed. Techs., 2000—. Cons. to surgeon gen. for cardiology, medicine and physiology USAF, 1980—95; cons. N.J. State Police and N.J. Atty. Gen.'s Office, 1984—90, Ind. Atty. Gen's Office, 1985—87, NASA, 1997—, life scis. subcom., 1989—93, interagency working group on telemedicine, 1994—96; adj. assoc. prof. preventive medicine Uniformed Svcs. U. Health Scis., Bethesda, Md., 1993—96; physician So. Sierra Med. Clinic, Ridgecrest, Calif., 1996—2007; advisor House/Senate Com. on telemedicine and health care, 1994—96; corp. bd. Ridgecrest Regional Hosp., 1997—; chair bd. dir. Calif. Telemedicine and eHealth Ctr., 2002—04, adv. com., 2004—05; chief of medicine Ridgecrest Regional Hosp., 2001—04, chief of staff, 2005—06, spl. asst. telemedicine outreach and rural health care devel., 2007—; clin. prof., clin. dir. telehealth initiative Health Sci. Ctr. Loma Linda U., 2005—07; external adv. com. Nat. Space Biomed. Rsch. Inst., Houston, 2006—. Mem. editl. bd.: Telemedicine and e-Health Jour., 1996—2003, 2007—; contbr. articles to profl. jours. Rsch. grantee VA, 1974-75, Dept. Def., 1976-82, NASA, 1982-84, Coop. R&D Agreements, Naval Air Warfare Ctr., China Lake, Calif., 2000—, Dept. Def. SBIRS, 2002—, NSF, 2004-05, Ctr. Disease Control, 2006—, Coop. R&D Agreement VA, 2007—; Cardiovasc. Health fellow Health Forum/Am. Hosp. Assn., 1999-00; Ashbel Smith Disting. Grad., 1993. Fellow ACP, Am. Coll. Cardiology (bd. govs. 1985-88), Am. Coll. Preventive Medicine, Calif. State Rural Healthcare Assn. (bd. dirs. 2006—). Unitarian Universalist. Avocations: physical fitness activities, flying. Office: Ridgecrest Regional Hosp 1081 N China Lake Blvd Ridgecrest CA 93555 Office Phone: 760-499-3454. Business E-Mail: e.ferguson@rrh.org.

FERGUSON, EMMET FEWELL, JR., retired surgeon; b. DeSoto, Ga., Mar. 28, 1921; s. Emmet Fewell Sr. and Emma Ruth (Smith) F.; Edith Geraldine Strozier, Nov. 26, 1954; children: Berrylin, Joann, Virginia, Fran, Emmet III. Student, U. Ga., 1938-40; BS in Elec. Engring., US Naval Acad., 1943; MD, Med. Coll. Ga., 1950. Diplomate Am. Bd. Surgery, Am. Bd. Colon-Rectal Surgery. Rsch. assoc. U.S. Naval Hosp., St. Albans, NY, 1950-51; surg. resident U. Fla., Jacksonville, 1951-53, 54-55, U. Ala., Brimingham, 1953-54; pvt. practice Jacksonville, 1955-93; pres. staff Meth. Hosp., Jacksonville, 1958-60, U. Hosp., Jacksonville, 1972-73; chief colon rectal surgery Bapt., Meth., and St. Vincents Hosps. Clin. prof. surgery coll. medicine U. Fla., 1960-93; mem. med. missions to Honduras, Costa Rica, Nicaragua, Ecuador; del., speaker Pan Am. Med. Meeting, Buenos Aires, 1967; mem. adv. com. coll. medicine U. Fla., Gainesville, 1976-82; chmn. bd. dirs. N.E. Fla. Health Svc. Agy., 1980-2000; mem. Statewide Health Coun., 1980-89, chair, 1980-82. Author: Commonly Memorized Verse, 1991, The Five Most Important Numbers in our World, 1995, Guide to the Major and Minor Springs of Florida, 1997; contbr. articles to profl. jours. Del., speaker from Jax C. of C. to Internat. Exhbn., Moscow, 1959; tchr. Sunday sch. Riverside Bapt. Ch., 1955—, deacon, 1960, 90; del. from Am. Cancer Soc. to Internat. Cancer Soc., Tokyo, 1966; mem. United Way Bd., Jacksonville, 1970-80, chmn. profl. divsn., 1980; chmn. Fla. host com. Pres. Carter's Inauguration, Washington, 1977; life mem. Jacksonville Hist. Soc., pres., 1986-88; mem. Jacksonville Indigent Care Com.; bd. regents Nat. Libr. Medicine, Washington, 1977-81; founder bd. dirs. Bapt. Towers, 1970—; trustee, pres. bd. trustees Riverside Bapt. Day Sch., 1971-75; trustee health sci. ctr. libr. U. Fla., 1972-93; trustee Bartram Sch., 1974-84, pres., 1976-77; mem. exec. com., mem. office state commn. rsch., profl. svc. Am. Cancer Soc. With USN, 1940-46, 50-51, capt. M.C. res. Decorated Am. Def. medal, Naval Res. medal; recipient Disting. Svc. award Fla. divsn. Am. Cancer Soc., Tampa, 1972, 75, Silver Beaver award Boy Scouts Am., 1986, Emmet Ferguson award U. Fla. Health Sci. Ctr. Fellow ACS (pres. Fla. chpt. 1968), Am. Soc. Surgery Alimentary Tract, Am. Soc. Colon Rectal Surgeons, Piedmont Soc. Colon Rectal Surgeons (pres. 1996-97), Fla. Soc. Colon Rectal Surgeons (pres. 1972-74, 76-78); mem. AMA, Fla. Med. Assn. (life), So. Med. Assn., Southeastern Surg. Congress (Best Motion Picture award 1975), Duval County Med. Soc. (life, editor bull. 1970-73, pres. 1975-76), Navy League (life, pres. Jacksonville coun. 1983-84, Commendation award 1984), Sons Confederate Vets., Rotary (bd. dirs. 1978-80, chmn. com. polio plus 1987-88, Commendation award 1989, Adm. Kaufman award 2004, Paul Harris fellow, 2007), St. John's Dinner Club (pres. 1975-78, Commendation award 1978), Fla. Yacht Club (life), River Club, Kappa Sigma. Democrat. Avocations: hunting, fishing, tennis, sailing, sculpting. Personal E-mail: effjr@aol.com.

FERGUSON, GARY LEE, public relations and security management executive; b. Okarche, Okla., Sept. 17, 1949; s. Jack J. Ferguson and Joan C. (Hauser) Long; m. Georgia A. Keller, Jan. 20, 1975 (div. Nov. 1994); 1 child, Laura J. BA in English, Met. State Coll., Denver, 1980; MA in Comm., U. No. Colo., 1992. Dir. pub. rels. Assoc. Builders and Contrs., Denver, 1981-83; pres. Ferguson Comm., Inc., Littleton, Colo., 1983-88; mng. editor MacGuide Mag., Lakewood, Colo., 1988-89; sr. adminstr. pub. affairs Ball Aerospace and Technologies, Broomfield, Colo., 1989-94; journalism instr. Colo. State U., Ft. Collins, 1994-95; sr. rep., pub. rels. Storage Tech. Corp., Louisville, Colo., 1995-2000; prin. Ferguson Assocs., Lakewood, 2000—02; transp. security mgr., transp. security adminstrn. U.S. Dept. Homeland Security, 2002—. Author: (book of poetry) Excavating Camelot, 1979. Mem. Pub. Rels. Soc. Am. (chair employee comm. sect. 1999, immediate past chair employee com. sect. 2000, Gold Pick for feature/news writing 1991, Gold Pick Award of Merit for feature writing 1992, Silver Pick award for feature writing 1993, Silver Pick award for mag./periodicals 1994), Soc. Profl. Journalists (pres. Colo. chpt. 1992-93, 94-95, dir.-at-large 1993-94, 96-97, v.p. membership 1991-92, sec. 1990-91, Circle of Excellence award).

FERGUSON, GARY WARREN, retired public relations executive; b. Stockton, Kans., May 5, 1925; s. Richard and Nelle (McBee) F.; m. Doris Drisler, Oct. 2, 1948; children: Arthur Richard, Frances (Mrs. Gregory H. Gebhart), Robert Warren, Scott William. AB, Yale U., 1946; MS in Journalism, Columbia U., 1948. Reporter Providence Jour. Bull., 1948-49, Richmond (Va.) News Leader, 1949-52, St. Louis Post-Dispatch, 1954-55, spl. writer, 1955-60; counselor Fleishman-Hillard, Inc., St. Louis, 1961-62, sr. ptnr., 1962-71; pres. Gary Ferguson Assocs., Inc., 1971-93. Vice-chmn. Dorf and Stanton Comm., Inc., 1988-93; editorial cons., 1993-99. Mem. founding bd. Greater St. Louis Coun. Alcoholism, 1965, pres., 1966-69; pres. mental Health Assn., St. Louis, 1980-81; trustee World Affairs Coun. St. Louis, 1990-95. Recipient Bishop's award Episcopal Diocese Mo., 1965. Mem.: Press Club Met. St. Louis. Home: 55 S Gore Ave Apt 1j Saint Louis MO 63119-2938

FERGUSON, GERALD PAUL, lawyer; b. Teaneck, NJ, Oct. 17, 1951; s. James Richard and Ilene Veronica (Meyer) F.; m. Nancy Ivers, Aug. 20, 1977; 1 child, James Ralph. BA, Fairleigh Dickinson U., 1974; JD, Capital U., 1979. Bar: Ohio 1979, U.S. Dist. Ct. (so. dist.) Ohio 1980, U.S. Ct. Appeals (6th cir.) 1986, U.S. Supreme Ct. 1990. Ptnr. Vorys, Sater, Seymour and Pease, Columbus, 1979—; mem. rules adv. com. Ohio Supreme Ct., Columbus, 1993. Mem. ABA (litigation sect., mem. trial evidence subcom. 1985-86), Ohio State Bar Assn. (mem. jud. adv. and legal reform com., unauthorized practice law com. 1985-90), Columbus Bar Assn. (chmn. juror subcom. 1979-86). Roman Catholic. Avocations: tennis, golf, fishing. Office: Vorys Sater Seymour & Pease 52 E Gay St Columbus OH 43215-3161 Office Phone: 614-464-6484. Business E-Mail: gpferguson@vssp.com.

FERGUSON, GLENN WALKER, writer, educator, retired ambassador; b. Syracuse, NY, Jan. 28, 1929; s. Forrest Erwin and Mabel Gertrude (Walker) F.; m. Patricia Lou Head, June 22, 1950; children: Bruce Walker, Sherry Lynn, Scott Sherwood. BA, Cornell U., 1950, MBA, 1951; grad., U. Santo Tomas, Manila, 1953; student, U. Chgo. Law Sch., 1955-56; JD, U. Pitts., 1957; D.S. (hon.), Worcester Poly. Inst., 1973; LL.D. (hon.), Sacred

Heart U., 1974; DHL (hon.), Am. U. Paris, 1995. Staff assoc. Govtl. Affairs Inst., Washington, 1954—55; asst. editor, asst. sec.-treas. Am. Judicature Soc., Chgo., 1955—56; asst. to chancellor and asst. dean Grad. Sch. Pub. Affairs, U. Pitts., 1956—60; with McKinsey & Co. (mgmt. cons.), Washington, 1960—61, Peace Corps, 1961—64, rep. Thailand, 1961—63, assoc. dir. Washington, 1963—64; dir. Vols. in Svc. to Am., Washington, 1964—66; U.S. ambassador to Kenya, 1966—69; chancellor L.I. U., 1969—70; pres. Clark U., 1970—73, U. Conn., 1973—78, Radio Free Europe/Radio Liberty, Munich, 1978—82, Lincoln Ctr. Performing Arts, NYC, 1983—84, Equity for Africa, 1985—92, Am. U. Paris, 1992—95. Cons. govt. agys., 1959-64, TV moderator fgn. affairs, Pitts., 1957-60; USIS lectr. India, Sudan, Uruguay, Argentina, 1984-92; vis. prof. fgn. policy Conn. Coll., 1990, U. R.I., 1991; cons. Internat. Exec. Svc. Corps., Uruguay, 1992—. Author: (aphorisms) Unconventional Wisdom, 1999, (essays) Americana Against the Grain, 1999, Tilting at Religion, 2003, Sports in America, 2004, Traveling the Exotic, 2005; contbr. articles to profl. jours. Human rights commr. City of Worcester, Mass., 1971-72; trustee Cornell U., 1972-76, former mem. corp. bds.; mem. French-Am. Commn. for Ednl. Exch., 1992-95. 1st lt. USAF, 1951-53, Korea. Recipient Arthur S. Flemming award, 1968; Asso. fellow Timothy Dwight Coll., Yale U. Mem.: Am. Birding Assn., ABA, Coun. Am. Ambs. (bd. dirs. 1996—2003), Fgn. Policy Assn. (bd. dirs. 1974—83), Coun. Fgn. Rels., Fed. Bar Assn., Nat. Press Club, Phi Delta Phi, Psi Upsilon, Phi Beta Kappa. Address: 1060 Governor Dempsey Dr Santa Fe NM 87501-1078

FERGUSON, J. BRIAN, chemicals executive; b. Lubbock, Tex., June 16, 1954; B in Chem. Engring., Ariz. State U., 1977. Rsch. and devel. staff Eastman Kodak Co., Longview, Tex., 1977, various mfg. and staff pos., various bus. and strategic planning pos. Kingsport, Tenn., 1989, Washington, 1992—94; v.p. industry and fed. affairs Eastman Co., Washington, 1994, mng. dir. for Gtr. China Hong Kong; mng. dir. Eastman Chem. Asia Pacific Pte., Ltd., Singapore; pres. Eastman Co. Polymers Group, 1999, Eastman Co. Chems. Group, 2001; chmn., CEO Eastman Chem. Co., Kingsport, Tenn., 2002—. Office: Eastman Chem Co PO Box 511 100 N Eastman Rd Kingsport TN 37662-5075*

FERGUSON, JAMES CLARKE, mathematician, algorithmist; b. Spokane, Wash., June 23, 1938; s. James Forsythe and Dorothy Eileen (Dillon) F. MS in Math., U. Wash., 1963; PhD in Math., U. N.Mex., 1984. Sci. programmer Boeing, Seattle, 1960-64; staff mem. GE Tech. Mil. Planning Office, Santa Barbara, Calif., 1964-66; mathematician TRW, Inc., Redondo Beach, Calif., 1966-71, Teledyne-Ryan Aero., San Diego, 1971-77; staff mem. Los Alamos (N.Mex.) Nat. Lab., 1977-85; sr. scientist Tektronix, Beaverton, Oreg., 1985-87, BBN Systems and Techs. Corp., Bellevue, Wash., 1987-92; with Point Control, Eugene, 1993-94, Camax Mfg. Technologies, Eugene, 1994-95, mathematician SDRC/Camax, Eugene, 1995-2000, consulting mathematician, 2001—. Cons. in field, 1975-87. Co-author: Key Works in Geometric Modeling, 1991, Fundamental Developments of Computer Aided Geometric Modeling, 1992; contbr. articles to profl. jours. Recipient advanced study fellowship, Los Alamos Nat. Lab., 1981. Mem. Assn. Computing Machinery, Soc. Indsl. and Applied Math. Achievements include introduction of parametric curve and surface techniques into computer aided geometric design field; complete classification of parametric planar cubics; application of parametric curve techniques to problem of shape preservation. Home: PO Box 1783 Hillsboro OR 97123-1783 E-mail: dddjim@earthlink.net.

FERGUSON, JOHN, JR., professional sports team executive; b. Montreal, July 7, 1969; m. Stephanie Ferguson; children: Emily, John, Grace. BA magna cum laude, Providence Coll.; JD, Suffolk U. Bar: Mass. 1989. Player agent NHL, with hockey ops. and legal depts., 1994, 1995; mem. scouting staff Ottawa Senators, 1993—96; asst. gen. mgr. St. Louis Blues, 1997—2001, v.p. hockey ops., 2001—03; pres., gen. mgr. Worcester IceCats; v.p., gen. mgr. Toronto Maple Leafs, 2003—. Former chmn. Am. Hockey League's Competition Com. Office: Toronto Maple Leafs Air Canada Ctr 40 Bay St Ste 300 Toronto ON Canada

FERGUSON, JOHN D., cardiovascular surgeon, researcher, retired military officer; b. Aug. 25, 1947; BS in Biology, Okla. Christian Coll., Oklahoma City; MD, U. Okla., Oklahoma City, PhD in Parasitology. Diplomate Am. Bd. Surgery. Surg. resident U. Okla., Oklahoma City, 1977—79, St. Anthony Hosp., 1979—81; cardiothoracic surg. fellow St. Louis U., 1981—83; ret. col. Army Nat. Guard, Ala., chmn. med. adv. coun., 1998—2002. Postdoctoral fellow, NIH U. Okla. Coll. Health, 1969. Mem.: Internat. Soc. Heart and Lung Transplantation.

FERGUSON, JOHN DUNCAN, medical research educator; b. Saskatoon, Sask., Can., Aug. 20, 1929; s. George Alexander and Urdine (LeValley) F.; m. Tamara van den Bergh, Sept. 12, 1958. MA, U. Toronto, Ont., Can., 1956; PhD, Columbia U., 1966. Project dir. Bur. Applied Social Rsch., Columbia U., NYC, 1958-64; asst. prof. Northeastern U., Boston, 1966-68; from assoc. prof. to prof. U. Windsor, Ont., 1968—; mem. assoc. med. staff Harper Hosp., Detroit, 1982-2000, rsch. cons., 2000—. Author reports in field. Grantee Ont. Cmty. and Social Svcs. Ministry, 1991-93. Presbyterian. Home: 1516 Iroquois Ave Detroit MI 48214-2747 Office: U Windsor Windsor ON Canada N9B 3P4 E-mail: tamjackferg@worldnet.att.net.

FERGUSON, JOHN PATRICK, health facility administrator; b. Weehawken, NJ, Jan. 22, 1949; s. Donald George and Margaret (Rienzo) F.; m. Gene Marie Promersperger, Jan. 16, 1971; children: Adam, David, Kate. BS in Econs., St. Peter's Coll., 1970; MBA in Hosp. Adminstrn., George Washington U., 1973; LHD (hon.), Felician Coll., 2005. Sr. v.p. St. Vincent's Hosp., NYC, 1972-81; v.p. ops. Hackensack U. Med. Ctr., NJ, 1981—85, sr. v.p., 1985, acting pres., chief exec. officer, 1985—86, pres., chief exec. officer, 1986—. Pres. Met. Health Adminstrs., NYC, 1977—78; adj. faculty New Sch. for Social Rsch. Grad. Sch. Mgmt. and Urban Professions, NYC, 1978—84; chmn. bd. trustees Univ. Health Sys. (now NJ Coun. Tchg. Hosps.), Trenton, 1999—2001, vice chmn., 2002—03; trustee UMDNJ, 2002—05, sec. bd. trustees, 2003—05. Trustee Garden State Arts Found., 2004—07; mem. jobs growth and econ. devel. commn. State of NJ, 2002; co-chmn. health transition team Gov.-elect Jim McGreevey, 2001; trustee Molly Found. for Diabetes Rsch., 1995—; commr. Econ. Devel. Commn. of City of Hackensack, 1996—2002; founding commr. Bergen County Econ. Devel. Corp., 1996—2007; mem., bd. govs. Greater NY Hosp. Assn., 2000—; trustee St. Peter's Coll., 2000—06; mem. bd. dirs. Martha's Vineyard Hosp., Inc., 2000—; chmn. bd. dirs. Martha's Vineyard Hosp., 2002—; mem. exec adv. com. State of NJ Commn. on Cancer Rsch., 2000. Named One of Top 12 Up and Coming Healthcare Execs., Modern Healthcare mag., 1988, One of 50 Bus. People to Watch for the 1990's, NJ Bus. Jour., 1990, Citizen of Yr., Meadowlands Regional C. of C., 1993, Man of Yr., Nat. Burn Victim Found., 1994, Humanitarian of Yr., Make A Wish Found., 1996, Disting. Citizen of NJ, Ramapo Coll. Found., 1998, Humanitarian of Yr., Boys' Towns of Italy, 1999; named one of 100 Most Powerful People in Healthcare in US, Modern Healthcare Mag., 2004, 2005, 2006, NJ 50 Most Influential Players in Polit. Healthcare Arena, Healthsense, Inc., 2005, 400 People Who Make a Difference, Cape Cod Life Mag., 2007; named to, Found. for Free Enterprise Hall of Fame, 2002; recipient Man of Yr. award, Tomorrow's Children's Fund, 1989, Medallion award, Bergen CC, 1993, Disting. Cmty. Svc. award, Anti-Defamation League, 1995, Disting. Citizen award, Hackensack C. of C., 1995, Disting. Cmty. Health Svc. award, Bergen County Bd. of Chosen Freeholders, 1996, Pres.'s award, NJ State Nurses Assn., 1999, Med. Exec. award, Acad. Medicine NJ, 2000, Good Scout award, No. NJ Coun. Boy Scouts Am., 2000, Ellis Island medal of honor, 2002, Disting. Alumni award for profl. achievement, St. Peter's Coll., 2002, Humanitarian award, Nat. Conf. for Cmty. and Justice, 2003, Disting. Alumni award, George Washington U. Health Sci. Mgmt. and Policy, 2004, County of Bergen Significant Contbr. honor, Bergen Cath. HS, 2006. Fellow: Am. Coll. Healthcare Execs. (regent, gov. dist. II 1994—99, Regents Recognition award 2004); mem.: Met. Health Adminstrn. Assn. (Distinction award 1997), Am. Fedn. for Aging Rsch. (bd. dirs. 1997—2000), Commerce and Industry Assn. NJ (bd. dirs. 1996—, chmn.'s award for Outstanding Leadership 1997), Am. Heart Assn. (pres. Mid-Bergen divsn. 1992—93, bd. dirs. 1993—94), Cath. Hosp. Assn., Am. Hosp. Assn. Office: Hackensack U Med Ctr 30 Prospect Ave Hackensack NJ 07601-1912 Office Phone: 201-996-2002. Business E-Mail: lgiani@humed.com.

FERGUSON, KINGSLEY GEORGE, retired psychologist; b. Newcastle-on-Tyne, Eng., Apr. 13, 1921; emigrated to Can., 1927; s. William George and Isobel (Finnegan) F. BA in English and French, U. Western Ont., 1943; MA in Psychology, U. Toronto, 1951, PhD, 1956. Diplomate Am. Bd. Profl. Psychology. Staff psychologist Sunnybrook Vets. Hosp., Toronto, Ont., Canada, 1949-50; chief psychologist Westminster Vets. Hosp., London, Ont., Canada, 1950-61, Montreal Gen. Hosp., Ont., Canada, 1961-68; psychologist-in-chief Clarke Inst. Psychiatry, Toronto, 1968-86. Chmn. Ont. Bd. Examiners in Psychology, Toronto, 1972-77. Served to lt. Can. Navy, 1942-45 Fellow Can. Psychol. Assn.; mem. Am. Psychol. Assn., Ont. Psychol. Assn. (pres. 1959-60; Lifetime Achievement award 1994-97). Address: 694 Sammon Ave Toronto ON Canada M4C 2E4 Personal E-mail: geordie614@sympatico.ca.

FERGUSON, KITTY GAIL, writer, educator; b. San Antonio, Tex., Dec. 16, 1941; d. Herman Alvin and Prestyne Norma (Hocker) Vetter; m. Yale Hicks Ferguson, Aug. 26, 1961; children: Colin Yale, Duff Christopher, Caitlin Christiana. BA, Juilliard Sch. of Music, 1965, MS, 1966. Freelance singer, NYC, 1965-72; music dir. Cmty. Presbyn. Ch., Chester, N.J., 1974-77; music dir./founder Chester Ensemble, 1975-80; music dir. Brookside (N.J.) Cmty. Ch., 1977-82, Liberty Corner Presbyn. Ch., Liberty Corner, N.J., 1982-86. John Elbridge Hines lectr. sci. and religion Episcopal Diocese of Newark, 1994; bd. advisors John Templeton Found., 2001—; coord. St. Peter's-Kothapallimitta Companionship St. Peter's Episcopal Ch., Morristown, NJ, 2000—. Author: Black Holes in Spacetime, 1991, Stephen Hawking: Quest for a Theory of Everything, 1992, 1993, The Fire in the Equations: Science, Religion, and the Search for God, 1994, rev. edit., 2004, Prisons of Light: Black Holes, 1996, 1998, Measuring the Universe: Our Historic Quest to Chart the Horizons of Space and Time, 1999, 2000, Tycho and Kepler: The Unlikely Partnership That Changed Forever Our Understanding of the Heavens, 2002, 2003. Office: Rita Rosenkranz Lit Agy 440 W End Ave #15D New York NY 10024

FERGUSON, LEWIS HAMILTON, III, lawyer; b. Abilene, Tex., Oct. 22, 1944; s. Lewis H. Jr. and Helen Frances (Kircher) Knoepp; m. Lauralee A. Matthews, Jan. 1, 1976. BA, Yale U., 1966, King's Coll., 1968, MA, 1972; JD, Harvard U., 1971. Bar: Mass. 1971, D.C. 1972, U.S. Tax Ct. 1972, U.S. Claims Ct. 1972. Law clk. to Hon. Frank Murray US Dist. Ct. Dist. Mass, 1971—72; assoc. Covington & Burling LLP, Washington, 1972-75, Williams & Connolly LLP, Washington, 1975-79, ptnr., 1979—93, 1998—2004; sr. v.p., gen. counsel Wright Med. Tech., Inc., Arlington, Tenn., 1994—97; gen. counsel Pub. Co. Acctg. Oversight Bd., Washington, 2004—07; ptnr. Gibson, Dunn & Crutcher LLP, Washington, 2007—. Adj. prof. Georgetown U. Law Ctr., Washington, 1980-88. Bd. dirs., treas. Am. Friends of Cambridge (Eng.) U., 1975-88. Office: Gibson Dunn & Crutcher LLP 1050 Connecticut Ave Washington DC 20036*

FERGUSON, LISA BERYL, accountant; b. LA, Apr. 17, 1958; d. Harry Alfred Abramson and Dolores Gloria Cohen; m. Jeffrey Monroe Ferguson, June 23, 1984 (div. Oct. 1992); children: Kate Emily, Colin James; m. Michael Jonathan Miqdadi, May 17, 2003. BSBA, U. Phoenix, 1997. CPA Calif., 2000; notary pub. Calif., 1979. Acct. Neal Levin and Co., Beverly Hills, Calif., 1978—2002; acct., mng. ptnr. Premier Bus. Mgmt. Group, 2003—. Democrat. Office: Premier Bus Mgmt Group 15260 Ventura Blvd # 1700 Sherman Oaks CA 91403 Office Phone: 818-933-2600.

FERGUSON, LLOYD ELBERT, retired manufacturing engineer; b. Denver, Mar. 5, 1942; s. Lloyd Elbert Ferguson and Ellen Jane (Schneider) Romero; m. Patricia Valine Hughes, May 25, 1963; children: Theresa Renee, Edwin Bateman. BS in Engring., Nova Internat. Coll., 1983. Cert. hypnotherapist, geometric tolerance instr. Crew leader FTS Corp., Denver, 1968-72; program engr. Sundstrand Corp., Denver, 1972-87, sr. assoc. project engr., 1987-90, sr. liaison engr., 1990-93; sr. planning engr. Hamilton Sundstrand Corp., Denver, 1990-2000; ret., 2000. V.p. Valine Corp. Lic. practitioner of religious sci. United Ch. of Religious Sci., L.A.; team capt. March of Dimes Team Walk, Danver, 1987; mem. AT&T Telephone Pioneer Clowns for Charity. Recipient recognition award AT&T Telephone Pioneers, 1990 Mem. Soc. Mfg. Engrs. (chmn. local chpt. 1988, zone chmn. 1989, achievement award 1984, 86, recognition award 1986, 90, appreciation award 1988), Nat. Mgmt. Assn. (cert., program instr. 1982—, honor award 1987, 90), Am. Indian Sci. and Engring. Soc., Colo. Clowns, Elks, North Jeffco Gen and Mineral Club. Mem. United Ch. of Religious Sci.

FERGUSON, MARGARET ANN, tax specialist, consultant; b. Steuben County, Ind., Mar. 24, 1933; d. Leo C. and Ruth Virginia (Engle) Wolf; m. Billy Hugh Ferguson, Feb. 15, 1955 (dec. Oct. 1971); children: Theresa Ruth, Scott Earl, Wade Leo, Luke, Angela, Cynthia, Brenda. AA in Psychology/Social Svs., Palomar Coll., San Marcos, Calif., 1977; BA in Behavioral Sci., Nat. U., Vista, Calif., 1980. Enrolled agt. Office mgr., adminstr. asst. Better Bus. Bur., San Diego, 1979-82; tax technician IRS, Oceanside, Calif., 1982-84, problem resolution tax specialist, 1985-87, revenue agt., 1987-90; pvt. cons. Vista, Calif., 1991—. Instr. adult edn. Vista Unified Sch. Dist., 1990-99; mem. adv. com. of nat. cemetery sys. Dept. Vet. Affairs, 1991-98; adv. coun. IRS, 1999-2001, mem. taxpayer advocate panel, 2005—. Mem. AAUW (treas.), Calif. Assn. Ind. Accts., Calif. Soc. Enrolled Agts. (dir. Palomar chpt. 1993-95, 2000-01, 1st v.p. 1998-2000), Inland Soc. Tax Cons., Assn. Homebased Bus., Gold Star Wives Am., Inc. (regional pres. 1989-90, chpt. pres. 1992-93, 96-97, nat. pres. 1993-95, chmn. nat. bd. dirs. 2004-06). Avocations: lace making, needle work, gardening, writing. Home and Office: 1161 Tower Dr Vista CA 92083-7144 Personal E-mail: gswtax@sbcglobal.net.

FERGUSON, MARK KENDRIC, surgeon, educator; b. Mpls., Jan. 10, 1951; s. David Lee and Shirley (Mark) F.; m. Phyllis Marie Young, July 8, 1989; 1 child, Benjamin. AB, Harvard U., 1973; MD, U. Chgo., 1977. Diplomate Am. Bd. Surgery, Am. Bd. Thoracic Surgery. Resident U. Chgo., 1977-81, chief resident gen. surgery, 1981-82, fellow cardiothoracic surgery, 1982-84, asst. prof., 1984-88, assoc. prof., 1988—97, prof., 1998—; chief thoracic surgery U. Chgo. Med. Ctr. Fellow ACS, Am. Assn. Thoracic Surgery, Soc. Thoracic Surgeons, Soc. Surg. Oncology, Am. Surg. Assn. Office: U Chgo Med Ctr MC 5040 5841 S Maryland Ave Chicago IL 60637-1463 Office Phone: 773-702-3551.

FERGUSON, MICHAEL A. (MIKE), congressman; b. Ridgewood, NJ, July 22, 1970; s. Thomas G. and Roberta (Chiaviello) Ferguson; m. Maureen Ferguson; 4 children. BA in Govt., U. Notre Dame, Ind., 1992; M in Pub. Policy, Georgetown U., Washington, 1994. History teacher, coach, faculty coord. Mt. St. Michael Acad., Bronx, NY, 1992—93; mem. US Congress from 7th NJ dist., 2001—, mem. energy and commerce com., subcom. on health, subcom. on oversight and investigations, subcom. on telecommunications and the Internet, subcom. on commerce, trade and consumer protection. Founder, Strategic Edn. Initiatives, Inc.; exec. dir. Better Schs. Found., 1994, dir. Save Our Schoolchildren, 1994, exec. dir. Cath. Campaign for Am., 1995-97; adj. prof. polit. sci., Brookdale Cmty. Coll., Lincroft, NJ, 1997-2000 Recipient Hero of the Taxpayer award, Americans for Tax Reform, 2004, Outstanding Legis. of the Yr., NJ Veterans of Fgn. Wars, 2005, Legis. of the Year award, Nat. Visiting Nurses Assn., 2006. Mem. Nat. Fedn. Ind. Bus., NJ C. of C., Epilepsy Found. NJ, Delbarton Sch., Friendly Sons of St. Patrick, Italian-Am. Found., Sierra Club, KC, Warren Profl. and Bus. Assn. Republican. Roman Catholic. Office: US Ho Reps 214 Cannon House Office Bldg Washington DC 20515-3007 also: Dist Office 45 Mountain Blvd Warren NJ 07059 Office Phone: 202-225-5361, 908-757-7835. Fax: 202-225-9460; Office Fax: 908-757-7841.*

FERGUSON, MILTON CARR, JR., lawyer; b. Washington, Feb. 10, 1931; s. Milton Carr and Gladys Ferguson; m. Marian Evelyn Nelson; children: Laura, Sharon, Marcia, Sandra. BA, Cornell U., 1952; LL.B., 1954; LL.M., N.Y. U., 1960. Bar: N.Y. 1954. Trial atty. tax div. Dept. Justice, Washington, 1954-60, asst. atty. gen., 1977-81; asst. prof. law U. Iowa, 1960-62; assoc. prof. NYU, NYC, 1962-65, prof., 1965-77; of counsel Wachtell, Lipton, Rosen & Katz, NYC, 1969-76; ptnr. Davis Polk & Wardwell, NYC, 1981—2001, sr. counsel, 2002—. Vis. prof. Stanford (Calif.) U., 1972—73; spl. cons. Dept. Treasury, PR, 1974; adj. prof. NYU, NYC, 1981—2002, trustee, Lewis & Clark Coll., Portland, Oreg., mem. bd. visitors Law Sch.; mem. adv. coun. Cornell U., Ithaca, NY. Author (with others): Tax Legislation in Perspective, 1965, Federal Income Taxation of Estates and Beneficiaries, 1970, 1994. Trustee NYU Law Ctr. Found. Mem.: ABA (chmn. tax sect. 1993—94), Soc. Illustrators, N.Y. State Bar Assn. Home: 32 Washington Sq W New York NY 10011-9156 Office: Davis Polk & Wardwell 450 Lexington Ave New York NY 10017-3982 Office Phone: 212-450-4840. Business E-Mail: carr@dpw.com.

FERGUSON, NIALL CAMPBELL DOUGLAS, history professor, writer; b. Glasgow, Scotland, Apr. 18, 1964; s. James Campbell Campbell and Molly Archibald Ferguson; m. Susan Margaret Douglas, 1994; 3 children. BA, PhD, Magdalen Coll., Oxford U., 1981—89; Hanseatic Scholar, U. Hamburg, 1986—88. Rsch. fellow Christ's Coll., Cambridge U., 1989—90; official fellow and lectr. Peterhouse, Cambridge, 1990—92; fellow & tutor modern history Jesus Coll., Oxford U., 1992—2000, sr. rsch. fellow, 2003—; prof. polit. & fin. history Oxford U., 2000—02; John E. Herzog prof. fin. history Leonard N. Stern Sch. Bus. NYU, NYC, 2002—04; Laurence A. Tisch prof. history Harvard U., 2004—, William Ziegler prof. bus. adminstrn. bus. sch., 2006—. Judge Samuel Johnson Prize for Non-Fiction, 2001; writer & presenter TV documentaries on modern history; vis. prof. modern European history Oxford U., 2003—. Contbr. articles to newspapers; author: Paper and Iron: Hamburg Business and German Politics in the Era of Inflation 1897-1927, 1995, The World's Banker: A History of the House of Rothschild, 1998, The Pity of War: Explaining World War I, 1998, The Cash Nexus: Money and Power in the Modern World 1700-2000, 2001, Empire: The Rise and Demise of the British World Order and the Lessons for Global Power, 2002, Colossus: The Price of America's Empire, 2004, The War of the World: Twentieth-Century Conflict and the Descent of the West, 2006; editor: Jour. Contemporary History, 2004—. Recipient Wadsworth Prize for Bus. History, 1998; Houblon-Norman fellowship, Bank of England, 1998—99. Mem.: German Hist. Soc. (sec. 1991—97). Office: Harvard U Ctr European Studies 27 Kirkland St Cambridge MA 02138

FERGUSON, R. NEIL, computer scientist, consultant; b. Dallas, June 22, 1952; s. Roy and Hellon Ferguson; m. L. Jean Ferguson, Aug. 12, 1977; 1 child, Rheachel Claire. BA in Psychology, U. Tex., 1976; grad., Winfield Sch. Race Driving, 1984. Systems engr. EDS, Dallas, 1976-77; systems programmer Collins Radio/Rockwell Internat., Richardson, Tex., 1977-78; systems programmer/analyst Moore Bus. Systems, Denton, Tex., 1978-79; supr., computer graphics Atlantic Richfield Co., Dallas, 1979-85; software engring. specialist E-Systems, Inc., Garland, Tex., 1986-90; dir. product mgmt., graphics and database systems MPSI, Inc., Irving, Tex., 1990-92; pvt. practice computer cons. Lewisville, Tex., 1990—; owner Computer Sys. Svc. & Cons. Co. Tech. program dir. Internat. Microcomputer Exposition, Dallas, 1978. Vol. computer sys. adminstr. Trinity Presbyn. Ch., 1997-2000. Recipient Golden Eagle award Am. Acad. Achievement, Tymshare award Tymshare Corp., Panasonic Sci. Achievement award Matsushita Electric Corp. of Am. and Jr. Engring. Tech. Soc., NASA award, Dallas County Med. Soc. award, 1st Place award in math. and computers 21st Internat. Sci. Fair; featured in Grolier's Sci. Ency. supplement, 1967; named Regional Class Champion, Sports Car Club of Am. Mem. Assn. for Computing Machinery, Spl. Interest Group on Computer Graphics, Am. Congress Surveying and Mapping, Am. Soc. Photogrammetry and Remote Sensing. Avocations: exotic sportscar restoration, stamp collecting/philately, scale model car construction, wrist and pocket watch collecting and restoration, jewelry design. Home and Office: 1097 Holly Ln Lewisville TX 75067-5711

FERGUSON, RICHARD L., educational association administrator; BS in Math., Ind. U. Pa.; D in Ednl. Rsch., U. Pitts., 1969; MA in Math., Western Mich. U. Tchr. math. Wilkinsburg Sch. Dist., Pa., Mt. Lebanon Sch. Dist., Pa.; rsch. assoc., faculty mem. U. Pitts.; with Am. Coll. Testing Program, Iowa City, 1972—, dir. test devel., v.p. rsch. devel., exec. v.p., CEO, chmn., 1988—; adj. prof. Dept. Psych. and Quantitative Founds. U. Iowa. Office: Am Coll Testing Prog 500 ACT Dr PO Box 168 Iowa City IA 52243-0168*

FERGUSON, ROGER WALTER, JR., reinsurance company executive, former federal official; b. Washington, Oct. 28, 1951; m. Annette L. Nazareth; two children. BA in Econs. magna cum laude, Harvard U., 1973, JD cum laude, 1979, PhD in Econs., 1981; PhD (hon.), Lincoln Coll., Webster U. Bar: N.Y. 1983. Atty. Davis Polk & Wardwell, NYC, 1981-84; assoc. and ptnr. McKinsey & Co., Inc., NYC, 1984-97; mem. bd. govs. Fed. Res. Sys., Washington, 1997—2006, vice chmn., 1999—2006; chmn. Swiss Re Am. Holdings Corp., Armonk, NY, 2006—; mem. exec. bd. Swiss Reinsurance Co., Zurich, 2006—, group fin. market strategist, 2006—. Chmn. Joint Yr. 2000 Council, 1998—2000, Group of Ten Working Party on Financial Sector Consolidation, 1999—2001, Comm. on the Global Financial System, 2003—, Financial Stability Forum, 2003—; bd. trustees Inst. Advanced Study, 2004—. Past treas. Friends of Edn.; trustees' com. Mus. Modern Art, N.Y.C.; bd. overseers Harvard U., 2003—. Hon.fellow Pembroke Coll., Cambridge U., 1973-74, 2004-; recipient Bond Market Assn. Disting. Svc. award. Office: Swiss Re Am Holdings Corp 175 King St Armonk NY 10504

FERGUSON, SARAH, The Duchess of York; b. London, Oct. 15, 1959; d. Ronald Ivor Ferguson and Susan Mary (Fitzherbert Wright) Barrantes; m. Andrew, Duke of York, July 23, 1986 (div. 1996); children: Beatrice Elizabeth Mary, Eugenie Victoria Helena. Student, Hurst Lodge, Sunningdale, Eng., Queen's Secretarial Coll., London. Spokeswoman Weight Watchers Internat., 1997—. Author: Budgie the Little Helicopter, 1989, Budgie at Bendick's Point, 1989, Budgie Goes to Sea, 1991, Budgie and the Blizzard, 1991, Victoria and Albert-Life at Osborne House, 1991, Travels with Queen Victoria, 1993, My Story, 1996, Dining with the Duchess, 1998, Winning the Weight Game, 2000, Dieting With the Duchess, 2000, What I Know Now, 2003, Little Red, 2003, Little Red's Christmas, 2004. Recipient Mother Hale award, 1996. Address: Simon & Schuster Publicity Dept Ste C3A 1230 Avenue Of The Americas Fl Concl New York NY 10020-1586

FERGUSON, STACY ANN See FERGIE

FERGUSON, STANLEY LEWIS, lawyer; b. Evanston, Ill., Aug. 2, 1952; m. Mary M. Pyle, Aug. 16, 1980; children: Kate, Brooke. BA, Northwestern U., Evanston, Ill., 1975; JD cum laude, Boston U., 1978. Bar: Ill. 1978, US Dist. Ct. No. Dist. Ill. 1978, US Ct. Appeals 6th and 7th circuits. Assoc. Kirkland & Ellis, Chgo., 1978-85, ptnr., 1985-87; named asst. gen. counsel USG Corp., Chgo., 1987, assoc. gen. counsel litig., v.p., assoc. gen. counsel, 1999—2000, v.p., gen. counsel, 2000—01, sr. v.p., gen. counsel, 2001—04, exec. v.p., gen. counsel, 2004—. Mem. ABA, Ill. Bar Assn., Legal Club Chgo. Office: USG Corp 550 W Adams St Chicago IL 60661 Office Phone: 312-436-5387. Business E-Mail: sferguson@usg.com.

FERGUSON, THOMAS GEORGE, retired healthcare advertising agency executive; b. Newark, Oct. 14, 1941; s. George Francis and Dorothy Marie (Stinson) F.; m. Roberta Chiaviello, Jan. 27, 1967; children: Thomas, Jr., Michael, Cathleen, Margaret. BS in Bus. Mgmt., Fairleigh Dickinson U., 1965. Product mgr. Bard-Parker div. Becton Dickinson & Co., Lincoln Park, N.J., 1965-70; acct. exec. L.W. Frolich, Inc., 1970-71; v.p., acct. group supr. Sudler & Hennessey, Inc., N.Y.C., 1971-74; chmn., pres. Thomas G. Ferguson Assocs., Inc., Parsippany, N.J., 1974—; chmn. Ferguson Common Health USA. Mem. Hemophilia Assn. N.J., 1981-98, ret., 1998; bd. dirs. Tri-County Scholarship Fund, Paterson, N.J., 1982—; pres., bd. trustees Epilepsy Found. N.J., Trenton, 1982—; past pres., bd. mem. Delbarton Sch. Fathers & Friends, Morristown, N.J. Served with USNG, 1971. Recipient Humanitarian award Hemophilia Assn. N.J., 1985, Disting. Svc. award Epilepsy Found. N.J., 1987. Mem. Pharm. Advt. Club, Pharm. Mfrs. Assn., Midwest Pharm. Advt. Club, Nat. Wholesale Druggists' Assn., Bus. Publication Audits, Fairleigh Dickinson U. Alumni Assn. Republican. Roman Catholic. Clubs: Morris County Golf (bd. dirs. 1975—), Baltusrol Golf. Avocation: golf. Office: Ferguson Common Health USA 30 Lanidex Plz W Parsippany NJ 07054-2717

FERGUSON, WARREN JOHN, federal judge; b. Eureka, Nev., Oct. 31, 1920; s. Ralph and Marian (Damele) Ferguson; m. E. Laura Keyes, June 5, 1948; children: Faye F., Warren John, Teresa M., Peter J. BA, U. Nev., 1942; LLB, U. So. Calif., 1949; LLD (hon.), Western State U., San Fernando Valley Coll. Law. Bar: Calif. 1950. Mem. firm Ferguson & Judge, Fullerton, Calif., 1950—59; city atty. for cities of Buena Park, Placentia, La Puente, Baldwin Park, Santa Fe Springs, Walnut and Rosemead, Calif., 1953—59; mcpl. ct. judge Anaheim, Calif., 1959—60; judge Superior Ct., Santa Ana, Calif., 1961—66, Juvenile Ct., 1963—64, Appellate Dept., 1965—66; U.S. dist. judge Los Angeles, 1966—79; judge US Cir. Ct. (9th cir.), Los Angeles, 1979—86; sr. judge US Ct. Appeals (9th cir.), Santa Ana, 1986—; faculty Fed. Jud. Ctr., Practising Law Inst., U. Iowa Coll. Law, NY Law Jour. Assoc. prof. psychiatry (law) Sch. Medicine, U. So. Calif.; assoc. prof. Loyola Law Sch. With US Army, 1942—46. Decorated Bronze Star. Mem.: Orange County Bar Assn., Calif. Bar Assn., ABA, Theta Chi, Phi Kappa Phi. Democrat. Roman Catholic. Office: US Courthouse 411 W 4th St Ste 10080 Santa Ana CA 92701-4500 E-mail: judge_ferguson@ca9.uscourts.gov.*

FERGUSON, YALE HICKS, political scientist, educator; b. Austin, Tex., May 28, 1940; s. Phil Moss and Marion (Hicks) Ferguson; m. Kitty Gail Vetter, Aug. 26, 1961; children: Colin Yale, Duff Christopher, Caitlin Christiana. BA magna cum laude, Trinity U., 1960; PhD, Columbia U., 1967. Lectr. CUNY, Bklyn., 1965; instr. Rutgers U., Newark, 1966-67, from asst. prof. to assoc. prof. polit. sci., 1967—77, prof., 1977-98, prof. II, 1998—, chmn. dept. polit. sci., 1985-90, 96-01, co-dir. Ctr. for Global Change and Governance, 2002—05, co-dir. Grad. Divsn. Global Affairs, 2005—. Hon. prof. U. Salzburg, Austria, 2002—; rschr. Fgn. Svc. Inst. U.S. Dept. State, Washington, 1979. Author (with R.W. Mansbach): The Web of World Politics: Nonstate Actors in the Global System, 1976, The Elusive Quest: Theory and International Politics, 1988, The State Conceptual Chaos and the Future of International Relations Theory, 1989, Polities: Authority, Identities and Change, 1996, The Elusive Quest Continues: Theory and Global Politics, 2003, Remapping Global Politics: History's Revenge and Future Shock, 2004; author: (with J.N. Rosenau et. al.) On the Cutting Edge of Globalization: An Inquiry into American Elites, 2006; contbg. editor: Handbook L.A. Studies, 1979—86; co-editor: Continuing Issues in International Politics, 1973, Political Space: Frontiers of Change and Governance in a Globalizing World, 2002; editor: Contemporary Inter-American Relations, 1972; contbr. articles to profl. jours., chpts. to books; mem. adv. bd. European Jour. Internat. Rels., 1995—2000, Internat. Studies Quar., 1998—2003, Internat. Studies Rev., 2003—, Global Governance, 2005—. Named Fulbright prof., U. Salzburg, 1992—93; recipient Bd. Trustees award Excellence in Rsch., Rutgers U., 1999; fellow, Norwegian Nobel Inst., 1996; scholar, U. Padova, 2001—02; Ctr. Internat. Studies fellow, Cambridge U., 1986—87, 1991. Mem.: AAUP, European Acad. Scis. and Arts, Commn. of History Internat. Rels., Mid Atlantic Coun. L.Am. Studies (exec. com. 1988—90), Brit. Internat. Studies Assn., Internat. Studies Assn. (NE bd. dirs. 1996—2000), Clare Hall (life). Episcopalian. Avocations: tennis, swimming, photography. Office: Rutgers U Grad Divsn Global Affairs 123 Washington St Ste 510 Newark NJ 07102 Office Phone: 973-353-5585.

FERGUSSON, FRANCES DALY, former academic administrator; b. Boston, Oct. 3, 1944; d. Francis Joseph and Alice (Storrow) Daly. BA in Art History, Wellesley Coll., 1965; MA in Art History, Harvard U., 1966, PhD in Art History, 1973; DLitt, U. Hartford, 2000, U. London, 2001, Bard Coll., 2006. Asst. prof. art Newton Coll., Mass., 1969—75; assoc. prof. art U. Mass., Boston, 1974—82, asst. chancellor, 1980—82; provost, v.p. acad. affairs, prof. art Bucknell U., Lewisburg, Pa., 1982—86; pres. Vassar Coll., Poughkeepsie, NY, 1986—2006. Bd. dirs. HSBC Bank USA, Wyeth Pharms., 2005—, Mattel, Inc., 2006—; trustee Mayo Found., 1988—2002, chmn., 1998—2002; trustee Ford Found., 1989—2001, Hist. Hudson, 1990—99. Bd. overseers Harvard U., 2002—; bd. dirs. Noguchi Found., 2004—, Fgn. Policy Assn., 2003—, Found. Contemporary Arts, 2006—, Nat. Humanities Ctr., 2006—, Second Stage Theater, 2006—; trustee J. Paul Getty Trust, 2007—. Recipient Founder's award, Soc. Archtl. Historians, 1973, Eleanor Roosevelt at Val-Kill medal, 1998, Centennial medal, Harvard Grad. Sch. of Arts and Scis., 1999, Alumni award, Wellesley Coll., 2001; fellow Am. Acad. Arts & Sciences, 2002. Avocation: piano.

FERHOLT, J. DEBORAH LOTT, pediatrician; b. New Rochelle, NY, Aug. 27, 1942; d. Sidney and Rose Lott; m. Julian Ferholt, June 19, 1963; children: Beth, Sarah. BS in Biology, U. Rochester, 1963, MD, 1967. Diplomate Am. Bd. Pediat. From instr. to assoc. prof. Yale Sch. Nursing, New Haven, 1969-90, lectr., 1990—2001, clin. assoc. prof. pediatrics, 1987—2003; pvt. practice pediatrics New Haven, 1982—. Author: (book) Health Assessment of Children, 1980 (Best Pediatric Book award 1981). Fellow Am. Acad. Pediatrics. Office: 303 Whitney Ave New Haven CT 06511-7204 Home Phone: 203-281-7273; Office Phone: 203-776-1243.

FERLAND, BRENDA L., state representative; b. Lebanon, NH, Oct. 23, 1949; d. Wilbur Fred Snelling and Lorraine Latouche; m. Daniel Edward Ferland; children: Lisa Marie, James Daniel. State rep. N.H. Ho. of Reps., Concord, 1997-98, 2001—. Treas. Charlestown (N.H.) Econ. Assn. Tourism, 1996-, Jesse Farwell Sch. Trust, 1990-95; mem. Charlestown Bd. of Select, 2000—, N.H. Traffic Safety Commn., 1998-, VFW Ladies Aux., 1999. Office: NH State Legis State House Concord NH 03301

FERLINGHETTI, LAWRENCE, poet; b. Yonkers, NY, 1919; s. Charles and Clemence (Mendes-Monsanto) F.; children: Julie, Lorenzo. AB, U. N.C.; MA, Columbia U., Doctorat de l'Université, mention très honorable, Sorbonne, 1950. Founder (with Peter D. Martin) first all paperbound bookstore in U.S., City Lights Books, San Francisco, 1955-, City Lights Rev., firm also publishes works of modern poets and writers; widely traveled poetry reader, also painter; participant (with Allen Ginsberg), Pan Am. cultural conf., U. Concepcion, Chile, 1960; participant, One World Poetry Festival, Amsterdam, 1981, Internat. Poetry Festival of Rome, 1979-85, World Congress of Poets, Florence, Italy, 1986, U.N. World Poetry Day, Delphi, Greece, 2000; author: poetry Pictures of the Gone World, 1955, A Coney Island of the Mind, 1958, Starting from San Francisco, 1961, The Secret Meaning of Things, Open Eye, Open Heart, 1973, Who Are We Now?, 1976, Landscapes of Living and Dying, 1979, Endless Life: Selected Poems, 1981, Over All the Obscene Boundaries, 1984, These Are My Rivers: New and Selected Poems, 1955-1993, 1993; novel Her, 1960, Routines; plays Back Roads to Far Places; (poetry) A Far Rockaway of the Heart, 1997; poetry and prose jour. Northwest Ecolog, 1978, (with Nancy J. Peters) Literary San Francisco: A Pictorial History, 1980; Seven Days in Nicaragua Libre, 1984, novel Love in the Days of Rage, 1988, How to Print Sunlight, 2001, Americus: Book One, 2004; performed in literary events Winter Olympic Games, Calgary, 1988; one-man exhbns., paintings: Butler Inst. Am. Art, Youngstown, Ohio, 1993, Retrospective Painting Exhbn. Palazzo delle Esposizioni, Rome, 1996. Lt. comdr. USNR, World War II, Normandy. A San Francisco street named in his honor, 1994; recipient poetry prize City of Rome, 1993; Premio Internazionale Flaiano, Italy, 1999, di Ostia, Italy, 99, Premio Internazionale di Camaiore, Italy, 1999, Premio Cavour, Italy, 2000, Poet Laureate of San Francisco, 1998-2000, L.A. Times Book Festival Lifetime Achievement award, 2001, ACLU award, 2001, elected to the Am. Acad. Arts and Letters, 2003, Authors Guild Lifetime Achievement award, 2003, Robert Frost medal Poetry Soc Am, 2003, Curtis Benjamin award for creative publishing, 2005, Literarian awrd Nat. Book Award Found., 2005. Address: City Lights Booksellers and Pubs 261 Columbus Ave San Francisco CA 94133-4519 Office Phone: 415-362-8193 x13.*

FERLINZ, JACK, cardiologist, educator; b. Marburg, Austria, Feb. 18, 1942; came to U.S., 1957. s. Anthony and Maria (Nachtigall) F. AB, Harvard U.; MBA, Northeastern U., 1965; MD, Boston U., 1969; doctorate (hon.), U. Maribor, Slovenia, 1990. Diplomate Am. Bd. Internal Medicine, Am. Bd. Cardiovascular Diseases. Intern. U. Hosp. Boston U., 1969-70; jr. resident M. Hitchcock Hosp. Dartmouth Med. Sch., Hanover, NH, 1970-71; sr. resident Jackson Meml. Hosp., U. Miami, 1971-72; NIH rsch. fellow cardiology P.B. Brigham Hosp., Harvard U., Boston, 1972-74; dir. cardiac cath. lab., asst. chief cardiology V.A.M.C., Long Beach, Calif., 1974-82; asst. prof. medicine U. Calif., Irvine, 1975-81, assoc. prof. medicine, 1981-82; chmn. adult cardiology Cook County Hosp., Chgo., 1982-88; prof. medicine Chgo. Med. Sch., North Chicago, Ill., 1984-88; chmn. dept. of internal medicine Providence Hosp., Southfield, Mich., 1988-92; clin. prof. medicine Wayne State U. Sch. Medicine, Detroit, 1989-92; dir. med. edn. & rsch., prof. medicine & cardiology Hamad Med. Ctr., Doha, Qatar, 1992-94; chief dept. medicine Aleda E. Lutz VA Med. Ctr., Saginaw, Mich., 1994—; clin. prof. medicine Mich. State U. Coll. Human Medicine, 1994—. Vis. prof. numerous U.S., Canadian and European med. schs., 1980—. Mem. editl. bds. Am. Jour. Cardiology, 1989—, Am. Jour. Noninvas Cardiology, 1987—, Jour. Am. Coll. Cardiology, 1984-88, 89-93; contbr. over 300 book chpts. and sci. papers. Named to Begg's Soc. Boston U. Sch. Medicine, 1969. Fellow Am. Coll. Cardiology, Am. Coll. Chest Physicians (chmn. coronary sect. 1983-85), Am. Heart Assn., Am. Coll. Physicians, Am. Coll. Angiology; mem. Am. Fedn. Clin. Rsch., Am. Soc. Clin. Pharm. Therapy. Avocations: mountain climbing, skiing, tennis, scuba diving. Office: VA Med Ctr 1500 Weiss St Saginaw MI 48602-5251 Home Phone: 989-792-6244; Office Phone: 989-497-2500 x3523. Business E-Mail: jack.ferlinz@med.va.gov.

FERM, ROBERT LIVINGSTON, religion educator; b. Wooster, Ohio, Jan. 2, 1931; s. Vergilius Ture Anselm and Nellie Agnette (Nelson) F.; m. Fleur Kinney, June 28, 1952 (div. 1968), children: Eric, Alison; m. Sonja Olson. BA, Coll. Wooster, 1952; BD, Yale U., 1955, MA, 1956, PhD, 1958. From instr. to assoc. prof. religion Pomona Coll., Claremont, Calif., 1958-67, prof., 1967-69, acting chmn. dept. religion, 1960-63, chmn. dept. religion, 1963-69; prof., chmn. dept. religion Middlebury (Vt.) Coll., 1969-94, Pardon E. Tillinghast prof. religion, 1988-2000, Tillinghast prof. religion emeritus, 2000. Author: Jonathan Edwards The Younger 1745-1801: A Colonial Pastor, 1976, Piety, Purity Plenty: Images of Protestantism in America, 1991; editor Readings in the History of Christian Thought, 1964, Issues in American Protestantism, 1969. Mem. Am. Acad. Religion. Presbyterian. Home: PO Box 752 Middlebury VT 05753-0052

FERN, ALAN MAXWELL, art historian, retired museum director; b. Detroit, Oct. 19, 1930; s. Martin and Rose F.; m. Lois Ann Karbel, Mar. 17, 1957. AB, U. Chgo., 1950, MA, 1954, PhD, 1960. Asst., instr., asst. prof. humanities The Coll., U. Chgo., 1952-61; asst. curator prints and photographs divsn. Libr. of Congress, Washington, 1961, curator fine prints, 1962-64, asst. chief, 1964-73, chief, 1973-76, dir. rsch. dept., 1976-78, dir. spl. collections, 1978-82; dir. Nat. Portrait Gallery, 1982-2000; ret., 2000. Author: A Note on the Eragny Press, 1957, (with others) Art Nouveau, 1960, (with M. Constantine) Word and Image, 1968, Leonard Baskin, 1970, (with M. Constantine) Revolutionary Soviet Film Posters, 1974; introductory essay Lasansky: Printmaker, 1975, Eichenberg, The Wood and the Graver, 1977, People and Power, 1985, Arnold Newman's Americans, 1992, (with H. Wright) Prints at the Smithsonian, 1996; contbr. articles to profl. jours. Bd. dirs. Smart Mus. Art, Chgo., Washington; active U.S Senate Curatorial Adv. Bd., State Md. Commn. on Artistic Property. Decorated chevalier Ordre de la Couronne (Belgium), Ordre des Arts et Lettres (France), comdr. Royal Order of Polar Star (Sweden); Fulbright scholar Courtauld Inst., U. London, 1954-55. Mem. Print Coun. Am. (past pres.), Coll. Art Assn., Am. Antiquarian Soc., AIA (hon.), Double Crown Club (hon.), Cosmos Club (pres. 2006-07), Grolier Club (NYC). Home: 3605 Raymond St Chevy Chase MD 20815-4151

FERNALD, HAROLD ALLEN, publishing executive; b. Haverhill, Mass., June 1, 1932; s. Harold Allen and Leona Swan (Horton) F.; m. Sally Camilla Carroll, June 23, 1956; children: Robert Arthur, Melissa Anne, Thomas Allen. BA in Psychology, U. Maine, 1954; MBA, NYU, 1964; PhD, U. Maine, 2002. Trainee Nat. Shawmut Bank, Boston, 1954—55; sales Carter's Ink Co., Cambridge, Mass., 1955—56; sect. chief Western Electric Co., Andover, Mass., 1956—60, buyer NYC, 1960—64; corp. devel. Holt Rinehart & Winston, NYC, 1964—66, pers. dir., 1966—68, mgr. adminstrn., 1968—70; v.p. adminstrn. CBS, Inc. Pub. Group, 1970—77, v.p., gen. mgr. coll. pub. divsn., 1971—77; pub. Down East mag., Fly Rod and Reel mag., Fly Tackle Dealer Mag., Shooting Sportsman Mag., Fishing Tackle Trade News; pres. Down East Enterprise, Inc., Camden, Maine, 1977—2002, chmn., 2002—; pres. Twin City Printery, Inc., Lewiston, Maine, 1978—80, Fernald-Spahn Enterprise, Inc., Rockport, Maine, 1978—80; pres., treas. Hanson Energy Products, Inc., Newcastle, Maine, 1981—85; co-chmn., treas. Global Info. Inc., NYC, 1987—95; pub., CEO Fishing Tackle Trade News, 1995—99. Bd. dirs. John Wiley & Sons., Inc., N.Y.C., 1978-2003, United Publs., Inc., Foreside Co., Inc., Sun Jour., Inc., U. Maine Press; chmn. Performance Media, LLP, 2000—. Vice chmn. Maine Gov.'s Coun. Vacation Travel, 1979-81; bd. dirs. N.E. Health Found., 1982-89, 91-99; bd. dirs. U. Maine-Orono Devel. Found., 1982—, vice chair, 1991, chmn., 1992-93; mem. U. Maine Pres.'s Coun., 1995-97, bd. visitors, vice chmn., 2000-2002, chmn., 2003-05; bd. dirs. Maine Cmty. Found., 1989-99, Bay Chamber Concerts, Inc., 1981-85, U. Maine Alumni Coun.; v.p. Farnsworth Mus., 1985-88, pres., 1988-93; chair Knox County Fund, 1996-99, Expansion Arts Fund, 1995-99; mem. Maine Gov.'s Bus. Adv. Com., 1985-86; v.p. Maine Tourism Commn., 1981-89; pres. 1st Congl. Ch., Camden, 1985-86; dir. The Camden Conf., 1987-92. Mem. Assn. Am. Pubs., Internat. Regional Mag. Assn. (dir., pres. 1988-89), Camden-Rockport C. of C. (dir. 1977-85), Alpha Tau Omega, Sigma Mu Sigma. Clubs: Camden Outing (dir. 1979). Lodges: Masons, Rotary (Camden pres. 1986).

FERNANDES, EDWARD F., lawyer; b. Carver, Mass. BA, Dartmouth Coll., 1980; JD, Columbia U., 1983. Bar: Mass., Tex., US Dist. Ct. (all dists. Tex., Mass. and Ariz.), US Ct. Appeals (1st and 5th cirs.). Ptnr. Weil, Gotshal & Manges, LLP, Houston, Solar & Fernandes, LLP; mng. ptnr. Brobeck, Phleger & Harrison, LLP, Austin, Tex., 2000—03; ptnr. litig. and energy Akin, Gump, Strauss, Hauer & Feld, LLP, Austin, 2003—. Former dir. Houston Bar Assn.; former pres. Houston Referral Svc.; former adj. prof. U. Houston Sch. Law; mem. steering com. State Bar Tex. Minority Counsel Prog. Mem Econ. Devel. Coun. Greater Austin C. of C. Named a Tex. Super Lawyer, Tex. Lawyers, 2004, 2005, 2006; named one of Top 10 Trial Lawyers in Am., Nat. Law Jour., 2004, Top Comml. Litigators in Austin, Austin Bus. Jour., 2004. Office: Akin Gump Strauss Hauer & Feld LLP Ste 2100 300 W 6th St Austin TX 78701-3911 Office Phone: 512-499-6265. Office Fax: 512-499-6290. E-mail: efernandes@akingump.com.*

FERNANDES, JANE K., former academic administrator, sign language professional; b. Worcester, MA, Aug. 21, 1956; d. Richard Paul and Mary Kathleen (Cosgrove) Kelleher; m. James John Fernandes; children: Sean William, Erin Frances. BA comparative lit., Trinity Coll., Hartford, CT, 1978; MA comparative lit., U of Iowa, Iowa City, IA, 1980, PhD comparative lit., 1986. Acting dir. (ASL prog.) Northeastern U., Boston, 1986—87; chmn. (sign comm.) Gallaudet U., Wash., DC, 1987; coord. (interp. tng.) Kapiolani C.C., Honolulu, 1988—90; dir. Statewide Ctr., Dept. of Ed., Honolulu, 1990—95; v.p. Gallaudet U, Wash., DC, 1995—2000, provost, 2000—06. Edit. rev. bd. Perspectives in Ed. & Deafness, Wash., DC, 1994—97. Co-author: (novels) Signs of Eloquence, 2003. Chair State Commn. Persons with Disabilities, Honolulu, 1993—95, mem., 1988—95; mem. (bd. of dir.) Goodwill Indust. of Honolulu, Honolulu, 1992—95; joint com. Am. Annuls of the Deaf, 2005—. Recipient Alice Cogswell, Gallaudet U, 1993; fellow alumni, U. Iowa, 2001. Mem.: Nat. Assoc. of the Deaf.

FERNANDES, JEANNE MARY, retired human resources specialist; b. Nairobi, Kenya, May 21, 1948; came to U.S., 1984; d. John Joseph and Joan Bertha (Correya) Athaide; m. Leonard Maurice Fernandes, Oct. 17, 1970; children: Donna Michelle, Nigel Leonard. Royal Soc. arts Diploma, Kenya Poly., 1965. Sec. East African Community, Nairobi, Kenya, 1966-67; exec. sec. East African Airways, Nairobi, 1968-69; adminstrv. asst. to M.D. Cadbury Schweppes, Nairobi, 1969-73; exec. sec. Pfizer Africa Middle East M.C., Nairobi, 1973-79, pers. adminstr., 1979-84; internat. pers. specialist Pfizer, Inc., NYC, 1984-87, sr. pers. assoc., 1987-91, assoc. pers. mgr., 1991-92, pers. mgr., 1992-98, dir. employee resources and comms., 1999-2001, dir. human resources, values and global diversity, 2001—02, dir., team leader global comms. and measurement, 2002—06; ret., 2007. Mem. NAFE, Am. Fedn. Police, Am. Mgmt. Assn., N.Y. Personnel Mgmt. Assn., Nat. Fgn. Trade Coun. (immigration com.), Roman Catholic. Avocations: music, dance, reading. Home: 27 Ballaro Dr Huntington CT 06484-2424 Office: Pfizer Inc 42nd St New York NY 10017 E-mail: kenyajeanne@aol.com.

FERNANDES, VERÔNICA ROLIM S., cardiologist, researcher; b. Fortaleza, Ceará, Brazil, May 24, 1974; d. Francisco Omar and Gleide Rolim Fernandes. MD, Fed. U. São Paulo, Brazil, 1997; Master's in Cardiology, Fed. U. São Paulo, 2003; PhD, Fed U. São Paulo with Johns Hopkins U., 2006. Resident in cardiology U. São Paulo, Ribeirão Preto, Brazil, 2001; resident in echocardiography Beneficencia Portuguesa Hosp., São Paulo, 2002; postdoctoral rsch. fellow in cardiovasc. imaging Johns Hopkins U., Balt., 2003—. Contbr. articles to profl. jours. Mem.: European Soc. Cardiology Radiology (Best Abstract prize 2005), Am. Heart Assn. (Stanley L. Blumenthal, MD, Cardiology Rsch. award 2002), Soc. Cardiovasc. Magnetic Resonance (assoc.). Roman Catholic. Achievements include research in detailed evaluation of regional cardiac function by tagging magnetic resonance in 1100 participants from multi ethnic study of Atherosclerosis with no symptoms to cardiovascular disease. Avocations: painting, travel, music, movies, reading. Office Fax: 410-614-8222. Business E-Mail: vfernan2@jhmi.edu.

FERNANDEZ, ALBERTO DE DIOS, physician; b. Miami, Feb. 24, 1966; s. Alberto Fermin and Gloria Victoria Fernandez; m. Bianca R. Fernandez, June 23, 1990; children: Nicolas, Cristina. BS, U. Miami, 1988; MD, U. Pa., Phila., 1992. Diplomate Am. Acad. Otorhinolanyngology Head and Neck Surgery. Resident Baylor Coll. Medicine, Houston, 1992—98; ptnr. South Fla. ENT Assn., Miami, 1998—. Fellow, ACS. Fellow: ACS; mem.: Am. Acad. Otorhinolanyngology Head and Neck Surgery, South Fla. ENT Assn. (bd. mem. 2001—). Office: South Fla ENT Assn 8940 N Kenneth Dr #504E Miami FL 33176

FERNANDEZ, ALFREDO TUMBAGA, JR., military officer; b. Andrews AFB, Md., Nov. 19, 1970; s. Alfredo Gangano and Resenda (Tumbaga) Fernandez; m. Rebecca Isedro Fernandez, Apr. 10, 2007; children: Alistair, Alexie, Isabelle. BS, San Diego State U., 1993; MA, U. Phoenix, 2000; MPH, U. Wash., Seattle, 2006. Cert. Calif. Dept. Health Svcs. Environ. health officer, naval hosp. Camp Legune USN, Jacksonville, NC, 1994—96, environ. health officer, med. rsch. unit 43 Cairo, 1996—98, environ. health officer marine aircraft San Diego, 1998—2000, dept. head naval hosp. Yokusuka, Japan, 2001—04, asst. dept. head, naval med. ctr. San Diego, 2006—. Decorated Achievement medal USN, Commendation medal. Mem.: Nat. Environ. Health Assn. Avocations: exercise, reading, gardening. Office: Naval Med Ctr San Diego 34800 Bob Wilson Dr San Diego CA 92134

FERNANDEZ, ANTONIO S., investment company executive; BBA, Pace U., NY. Sys. engring. mgr. Electronic Data Sys.; v.p. duPont Glore Forgan; dir. ops., treas. Thompson McKinnon; founder, former head, internat. investment banking dept. Oppenheimer & Co., Inc., several positions including: exec. v.p., dir. ops., treas., CFO, dir., 1979—99. Bd. dir. Banco Latinoamericano de Exportaciones, 1992—99, Terremark Worldwide, Inc., 2003—, Spanish Broadcasting Sys. CL A, 2004—. Trustee Mulenberg Coll.

FERNANDEZ, FERDINAND FRANCIS, federal judge; b. 1937; BS, U. So. Calif., 1958, JD, 1963; LLM, Harvard U., 1963. Bar: Calif. 1963, US Dist. Ct. (cen. dist.) Calif. 1963, US Ct. Appeals (9th cir.) 1963, US Supreme Ct. 1967. Elec. engr. Hughes Aircraft Co., Culver City, Calif., 1958-62; law clk. to dist. judge US Dist. Ct. (ctrl. dist.) Calif., 1963-64; pvt. practice law Allard, Shelton & O'Connor, Pomona, Calif., 1964-80; judge Calif. Superior Ct. San Bernardino County, Calif., 1980-85, US Dist. Ct. (ctrl. dist.) Calif., LA, 1985-89, US Ct. Appeals (9th cir.), LA, 1989—2002, sr. judge, 2002—. Lester Roth lectr. U. So. Calif. Law Sch., 1992. Contbr. articles to profl. jours. Vice chmn. City of La Verne Commn. on Environ. Quality, 1971-73; chmn. City of Claremont Environ. Quality Bd., 1972-73; bd. trustees Pomona Coll., 1990-05. Fellow Am. Coll. Trust and Estate Counsel; mem. ABA, State Bar of Calif. (fed. cts. com. 1966-69, ad hoc com. on attachments 1971-85, chmn. com. on adminstrn. of justice 1976-77, exec. com. taxation sect. 1977-80, spl. com. on mandatory fee arbitration 1978-79), Calif. Judges Assn. (chmn. juvenile cts. com. 1983-84, faculty mem. Calif. Jud. Coll. 1982-83, faculty mem. jurisprudence and humanities course 1983-85), L.A. County Bar Assn. (bull. com. 1974-75), San Bernardino County Bar Assn., Pomona Valley Bar Assn. (co-editor

Newsletter 1970-72, trustee 1971-78, sec.-treas. 1973-74, 2d v.p. 1974-75, 1st v.p. 1975-76, pres. 1976-77), Estate Planning Coun. Pomona Valley (sec. 1966-76), Order of Coif, Phi Kappa Phi, Tau Beta Pi, Eta Kappa Nu. Office: US Ct Appeals 9th Cir 125 S Grand Ave Ste 602 Pasadena CA 91105-1621*

FERNANDEZ, FERNANDO LAWRENCE, aeronautical engineer, research and development company executive; b. NYC, Dec. 31, 1938; s. Fernando and Luz Esther (Fortuno) F.; m. Carmen Dorothy Mays, Aug. 26, 1962; children: Lisa Marie, Christopher John (dec.). ME, Stevens Inst. Tech., 1960, MS in Applied Mechanics, 1961; PhD in Aeronautics, Calif. Inst. Tech., 1969. Engr. Lockheed Missiles & Space Co., Sunnyvale, Calif., 1961-63; div. mgr. The Aerospace Corp., El Segundo, Calif., 1963-72; program mgr. R & D Assocs., Santa Monica, Calif., 1972-75; v.p. Phys. Dynamics, Inc., San Diego, 1975-76; pres. Arete Assocs., San Diego, 1976-93, AETC Inc., San Diego, 1994-98; dir. Def. Advanced Rsch. Projects Agy., Arlington, Va., 1998-2001; disting. rsch. prof., dir. inst. tech. initiatives Stevens Inst. Tech., Hoboken, NJ, 2001—05; pvt. cons., 2005—. Mem. Chief Naval Ops. Exec. Panel, Washington, 1983-98; chair Def. Sci. Bd. Tech. Panel on Role of DOD in Homeland Security, 2003; chair naval rsch. com. Merrimac Industries, 2007-; mem. security sci. and tech. adv. com. Dept. Homeland Security, 2007-. Mem. Naval Rsch. Adv. Coun., 2004—. Office Phone: 858-922-2546. Personal E-mail: frankdarpa@yahoo.com.

FERNANDEZ, GENO, insurance company executive; b. 1976; Student in sem. edn., Notre Dame Sem.; BA in Theology, Classics, and Philosophy summa cum laude, U. Notre Dame, 1996; MA in Classics, Oxford U., 1999, PhD, 2000; JD, Harvard Law Sch., 2000. With McKinsey & Co., Chgo., 2000—, ptnr. Lectr. in field; spl. attaché for econ. affairs to Sec. of State diplomatic staff at Vatican. Contbr. articles on bus. ins., knowledge mgmt. in fin. instns., and ins. regulation. Pro-bono work on strategy, ops., and portfolio mgmt. Vatican, Archdiocese of Chgo., U. Notre Dame; counselor women's shelter, Ind. Named one of 40 Under 40, Crain's Chgo. Bus., 2005. Office: McKinsey & Co Ste 2900 21 S Clark St Chicago IL 60603-2900 Office Phone: 312-551-3970. Office Fax: 312-551-4200. Business E-Mail: geno_fernandez@mckinsey.com.

FERNANDEZ, HAPPY CRAVEN (GLADYS), academic administrator; b. Scranton, Pa., Mar. 3, 1939; d. Orvin William and Florence (Waite) Craven; m. Richard Ritter Fernandez, June 10, 1961; children: John Ritter, David Craven, Richard William. BA, Wellesley Coll., 1961; MA in Teaching, Harvard U., 1962; MA, U. Pa., Phila., 1970; EdD, Temple U., 1984. Social studies tchr. various pub. schs., 1961-64; from vis. asst. prof. to prof. Sch. Social Adminstrn. Temple U., Phila., 1974—92; exec. dir. Parents Union for Pub. Sch., Phila., 1980-82; dir. The Child Care and Family Policy Inst., Phila., 1988-92; city councilwoman Phila., 1992-98; candidate for mayor City Phila., 1998-99; pres. Moore Coll. of Art and Design, Phila., 1999—. Cons. Nat. Com. for Citizens in Edn., Columbia, Md., 1982—87, Phila. Youth Study Ctr., 1988—90; commr. Phila. Gas Commn, 1992—97; trustee Edn. Law Ctr., Phila., 1983—2005; bd. dirs. Cultural Fund, 1996—98; chair Select Com. on Bus. Taxes, 1992—98, Select com. on Land Reuse, 1997—98; pres. Delaware Valley Child Care Coun., 1988—90. Author: Parents Organizing to Improve Schools, 1976, The Child Advocacy Handbook, 1980, Elder Care and Child Care Policies of Philadelphia Area Businesses, 1991. Chair bd. dirs. Am. for Dem. Action, Phila., 1984—86; chair Children's Coalition, 1982—86; bd. dirs. Phila. Citizens for Children and Youth, 1986—93; founder Parents Union for Pub. Schs., 1972—, chair Phila., 1972—75, 1978—80; trustee Phila. Award, 2003—; chair Phila. award, 2006—; pres. bd. Parkway Coun. Found., Phila., 2006—; del. Dem. Nat. Conv., 1988, 1992, 1996; bd. dirs. Greater Phila. Cultural Alliance, 2000—, chmn. bd., 2004—06, Pa. Women's Forum, 2000—. Recipient Women in Edn. award Women's Way, 1989, Pub. Citizen of Yr. award NASW, 1991, Local Elected Ofcl. award Pa. Citizens for Better Librs., 1993, Pub. Svc. award Homeowners Assn. Phila., 1994 Phila. Op. Smile award, 1999, Woman of Yr.-Ivy Willis award, 2000, Fleisher Art Meml. Founders award 2001, Woman of Achievement award AAUW, 2005; named Outstanding Advisor, Health Promotions Coun., 1994, 2002, Disting. Dau. of Pa., 2002—; Wellesley Coll. scholar, 1961. Mem.: Nat. Assn. Ind. Colls. and Univs. (bd. dirs. 2003—06), Assn. Ind. Schs. of Art and Design (nat. sec. 2001—04, vice chmn. nat. bd. dirs. 2004—). Mem. United Church Of Christ. Avocation: tennis. Home: 3400 Baring St Philadelphia PA 19104-2076 Office: Moore College 20th & Parkway 4 Philadelphia PA 19103 Office Phone: 215-568-4515 x1100. Business E-Mail: hfernandez@moore.edu.

FERNANDEZ, (I)DALIA P., educational association administrator; b. Tegucigalpa, Honduras; arrived in US, 1976; m. Antonio Fernandez. BS, Boston U.; MBA, Averett U. Mgr. fin. sys. Gen. Dynamics, 1991—98; program mgr. Hispanic Coll. Fund, Washington, 1999—2001, v.p., COO, 2001—07, pres., 2007—. Co-founder, pres. Latinas Investing Power; nat. panelist Ptnrs. in Edn., White House Initiative on Excellence in Edn. Nat. Hispana Leadership Inst. Fellow, 2007. Office: Hispanic Coll Fund, Inc Ste 450-A W 1301 K St NW Washington DC 20005 Office Phone: 202-296-5400. Office Fax: 202-296-3774.*

FERNANDEZ, JAMES, anthropology educator; b. Chgo., Nov. 27, 1930; m. Renate Helene Lellep, Oct. 18, 1958; children: Lisa Oyana, Luke Oliver, Andrew McClintock. BA, Amherst Coll., 1952; postgrad. in cultural anthropology, Northwestern U., 1953—54; postgrad., U. Madrid, 1954—55, Museo Etnologico Barcelona, 1955; PhD, Northwestern U., 1962. Tchg. asst. Northwestern U., 1955—57, grad. rsch. fellow in program of African studies, 1956—57; instr. sociology and anthropology Smith Coll., 1961—62, asst. prof. anthropology, 1962—64; area program dir. Gabon Peace Corps trainees, St. Thomas, 1962—63; cons., lectr. Fgn. Svc. Inst., Washington, 1964—70; prof. anthropology Dartmouth Coll., 1969—75, chmn. dept. anthropology, 1971—75; prof. anthropology Princeton U., 1975—86, chmn. dept. anthropology, 1978—82; prof. anthropology U. Chgo., 1982—. Lectr. and cons. in field. Recipient Guggenheim fellowship, 2003, Carnegie Fund Grant for African Rsch., 1955, Ford Found. fellowship, 1957, Ford Found. Ext. fellowship, 1959, Social Sci. Rsch. Coun.-Am. Coun. Learned Socs. African Rsch. fellowship, 1965, NSF grant, 1970, 1971, Spanish-N.Am. Joint Com. fellowship, 1977, NEH grant, 1988—89. Fellow: African Studies Assn., Am. Anthropol. Assn., Am. Acad. Religion, Am. Acad. Arts and Scis.; mem.: Northeastern Anthropol. Assn. (pres. 1973), Sigma Xi. Office: U Chgo Dept Anthropology 1126 E 59th St Chicago IL 60637 E-mail: jwf1@uchicago.edu.

FERNANDEZ, JAMES, retail products executive; m. Dolores Fernandez; 2 children. MBA, Fordham, 1982. CPA. Mem. fin. staff Avon; various positions in fin. planning and mgmt. Tiffany, 1983—89, sr. v.p., CFO, 1989—97; exec. v.p., CFO, 1998—. Bd. dir. Dun & Bradstreet Corp. Office: Tiffany & Co 727 5th Ave New York NY 10022

FERNANDEZ, JORGE LUIS, lawyer; b. Pinar del Rio, Cuba, 1949; BA, Calvin Coll., Grand Rapids, Mich., 1970; M in adminstrn. and supervision, Fla. Internat. Univ., 1975; JD, Wayne State U. Sch. Law, Detroit, 1979. Mem. city atty.'s office Law Dept., Miami, Fla., 1982—91, city atty., 1988—91, 2004—; county atty. Sarasota County, Fla., 1991—2004. Recipient Govt. Hispanic Bus. Adv. of the Yr. Award, US Hispanic C. of C., President's Excellence Award for Outstanding & Disting. Cmty. Svc., Gulf Coast Latin C. of C., 1997—98, Claude Pepper Outstanding Govt. Lawyer Award, Fla. Bar, 1998. Mem.: Nat. Cmty. Devel. Assn. (coun.), Internat. Mcpl. Lawyer's Assn. (coun.), Fla. Bar Assn., ABA (coun. Govt. & Pub. Sector Lawyer's Divsn.). Office: 444 SW 2nd Ave Suite 945 Miami FL 33130 Office Phone: 305-416-1800. Office Fax: 305-416-1801. E-mail: law@ci.miami.fl.us.

FERNANDEZ, JOSE WALFREDO, lawyer, department chairman; b. Cienfuegos, Cuba, Sept. 19, 1955; arrived in U.S., 1967; s. Jose Rigoberto and Flora (Gomez) Fernandez; m. Andrea Gabor, June 22, 1985. BA, Dartmouth Coll., 1977; JD, Columbia U., 1980; MA, Dartmouth Coll., 2002. Bar: NY 1981, NJ 1981, US Dist. Ct. NJ 1981, US Dist. Ct. (So. dist.) NY 1984. Assoc. Curtis, Mallet, Prevost, Colt & Mosle, NYC, 1981-84, Baker & McKenzie, NYC, 1984-89, ptnr., 1989-96, O'Melveny & Myers LLP, NYC, 1996—2006, mng. ptnr. NY office, 2002—03, mem. policy com., head internat. practice, chair L.Am. practice, 2006; co-chair L.Am. practice Latham & Watkins LLP, NYC, 2006—. Adj. prof. NY Law Sch., 1984—88; mem. Council on Fgn. Rels. Contbr. Mem. adv. bd. Coun. of Ams., 2001—; bd. trustees Dartmouth Coll., 2002—, Mid.East Inst., 2004—; dir. Ballet Hispanico, 1994—, WBGO-FM Newark Pub. Radio, 1997—, Accion Internat., 2006—; bd. dirs. Columbia Law Sch. Alumni Assn., 1991—94. Mem.: ABA (chmn. Inter-Am. law com. 1985—88, Ctrl. Am. task force 1985—89, presdl. L.Am. adv. commn. 1986—91, chmn. Inter-Am. law com. 1991—94), Assn. of the Bar of the City of NY (mem. com on fgn. and comparative law 1984—87, chmn. Inter-Am. affairs com. 1996—98, dir. city bar fund 1999—), Brazilian-US C. of C. (dir. 1995—, sec. 2005—). Avocations: sports, non-fiction writing, travel. Home: 508 E 87th St New York NY 10128-7602 Office: Latham & Watkins LLP 885 Third Ave New York NY 10022 Office Phone: 212-906-1608. Office Fax: 212-751-4864.

FERNANDEZ, KATHLEEN M., cultural organization administrator; b. Dayton, Ohio, Oct. 8, 1949; d. Norbert Katzen and Yenema Vermeda (Bermingham) F.; m. James Robert Hillibish, Oct. 1, 1977. BA, Otterbein Coll., 1971. Edn. asst. Ohio Hist. Soc., Columbus, 1971, vol. coord., 1971-74, interpretive specialist Zoar, 1975-88; site mgr. Village State Meml., Zoar, 1988—2004; freelance mus. cons. Canton, Ohio, 2004—05; exec. dir. North Canton Heritage Soc., 2006—. Author: A Singular People: Images of Zoar, 2003. Bd. dirs., newsletter editor Ohio & Erie Canal Corridor Coalition, Akron, 1989—. Mem. Am. Assn. State and Local History, Nat. Trust Hist. Preservation, Zoar Cmty. Assn., Communal Studies Assn. (pres. 1981, editor newsletter 1981-86, 1997-2004, bd. dirs. 1995—, exec. dir. 2004—), Am. Assn. Mus. (surveyor mus. assistance program 1999—). Office: 200 Charlotte St NW North Canton OH 44720

FERNÁNDEZ, LIANNE, elementary school educator, consultant; b. Havana, Cuba, Mar. 26, 1961; d. Otto José and Maria Delgado Fernández; m. Wendell H. Christensen III, July 4, 2006. AA with hons., Daytona Beach CC, Fla., 1985; BSc cum laude, U. Ctrl. Fla., 1988. Cert. educator Fla. Dept. Edn., 1988. Tchr. Pine Trail Elem. Sch., Ormond Beach, Fla., 1988—98; tchr. reading lang. arts Volusia County Sch. Bd., Daytona Beach, Fla., 1998—2000; literacy coach, academic support Westside Elem. Sch., Daytona Beach, Fla., 2000—04; reading coach, academic support South Daytona (Fla.) Elem. Sch., 2004—. Cons. in field. Author: Reading and Writing Strategically: Raising the Bar of Expectations, 2001. Mem. Cmty. Leadership Com. Closing the Achievement Gap. Named Tchr. of Yr., Pine Trail Elem. Sch., 1998, Westside Elem. Sch., 2004; recipient citation, U.S. Army, 1991; grantee, Futures Volusia County Sch. Bd., 2002. Mem.: So. Assn. Colls. and Schs. (mem. latin american team 2004, leader accreditation and sch. improvement team 2004—), Internat. Reading Assn. (none). Avocations: sewing, reading, computers, writing. Home: 2913 Windle Lane South Daytona FL 32119-8534 Office: South Daytona Elementary School 600 Elizabeth Place South Daytona FL 32119 Home Phone: 386-760-6989; Office Phone: 386-322-6180. Personal E-mail: lianne331@aol.com.

FERNANDEZ, LISA, softball player; b. Long Beach, Calif., Feb. 27, 1971; m. Mike Lujan. Grad., UCLA, 1995. Mem. Calif. Commotion Amateur Softball Assn.; pitching and hitting coach UCLA Softball Team, 1995—. Pitcher U.S. Olympic Softball Team, Atlanta, 1996, Sydney, 2000, Athens, 04. Recipient Gold medal Pan Am. Games, 1991, 1999, ISF Women's World Championship, 1990, 94, 1998, 2002, Women's World Challenger Cup, 1992, Intercontinental Cup, 1993, South Pacific Classic, 1994, Superball Classic, 1995, Atlanta Olympics, 1996, Sydney Olympic Games, 2000, Athens Olympic Games, 2004, Honda award, 1991-93; named All-Am. Amateur Softball Assn., 1990-1993, 1995-1999, Sports Woman of Yr., 1991-92, MVP ASA Women's Major National, 1992, 1996-1999, mem. ASA Women's Major National Championship teams, 1990-92, 1996-99, NCAA Championship teams, 1990, 1992 Office: USA Softball 2801 NE 50th St Oklahoma City OK 73111-7203 also: TPS Hdqs care Lisa Fernandez PO Box 35700 Louisville KY 40232-5700

FERNANDEZ, MANNY (EMMANUEL FERNANDEZ-LEMAIRE), professional hockey player; b. Etobicoke, Ont., Can., Aug. 27, 1974; m. Karine Fernandez; 1 child, Mattyas. Goalie Dallas Stars, 1999—2000, Minn. Wild, 2000—07, Boston Bruins, 2007—. Co-recipient William M. Jennings Trophy, 2007. Office: Boston Bruins TD Banknorth Garden 100 Legends Way Boston MA 02114*

FERNANDEZ, MARGARET J., pharmacist; b. Miami, Fla., Sept. 5, 1978; d. Manuel Arthur and Margarita Fernandez. BS in Biol. Scis., Fla. Internat. U., Miami, 2001; PharmD, Nova Southeastern U., Ft. Lauderdale, Fla., 2005. Bd. cert. pharmacotherapy 2006. Pharmacy practice resident Jackson Meml. Hosp., Miami, 2005—06, clin. hosp. pharmacist, 2006—. Recipient Clin. Skills award, Facts & Comparisons, 2005. Mem.: Dade County Pharmacy Assn., Am. Soc. Health-Systems Pharmacy, Am. Coll. Clin. Pharmacy, Ro Chi.

FERNANDEZ, RAUL J., data processing executive; m. Jean Marie Fernandez; 1 child, Sofia. BA in Economics, U. Md. Dir. emerging techs. govt. contracting firm, Bethesda, Md.; founder, pres., CEO, chmn. bd. Proxicom, 1991-2000; founder, CEO, chmn. bd. Proxicom (acquired by Dimension Data North America), 2000—01; CEO Dimension Data North America, 2001—02, chmn. emeritus, 2002; chmn. ObjectVideo, 2002—, CEO, 2004—. Bd. dirs. No. Va. Tech. Coun, Liz Claiborne, Critical Path, Internosis; mem. President's Coun. of Advisors on Sci. and Tech.; special advisor Gen. Atlantic Partners; co-owner Wash. Capitals, 2000—, Wash. Wizards, 2000—, Wash. Mystics, 2000—, MCI Ctr., 2000—. Office: ObjectVideo 11600 Sunrise Valley Dr Ste 290 Reston VA 20191 Office Phone: 703-654-9300. Office Fax: 703-654-9399.

FERNÁNDEZ, TERESITA, sculptor; b. Miami, 1968; BFA, Fla. Internat. U., 1990; MFA, Va. Commonwealth U., 1992. Artist-in-residence ArtPace, San Antonio, 1998; fellow Am. Acad. in Rome, 1999; artist-in-residence The Fabric Workshop and Mus., Phila., 2005. Represented by Lehmann Maupin Gallery, NYC. Exhibitions include Real/More Real, Mus. Contemporary Art, Miami, 1995, South Fla. Cultural Consortium, Boca Raton Mus. Art, 1995, Defining the Nineties, Mus. Contemporary Art, Miami, 1996, Container 96, Copenhagen Cultural Capital, 1996, Enclosures, New Mus. Contemporary Art, NYC, 1996, Corcoran Gallery Art, Washington, DC, 1997, X-Site, Contemporary Mus., Balt., 1997, The Crystal Stopper, Lehmann Maupin Gallery, 1997, Seamless, De Appel, Amsterdam, 1998, Threshold, The Power Plant, Toronto, 1998, Borrowed Landscape, Deitch Projects, NYC, 1999, Luminous Mischief, Yokohama Portside Gallery, Japan, 1999, Deja-vu, Miami Art Fair, 2000, not seeing, Doug Lawing Gallery, Houstin, 2000, Reading the Museum, Nat. Mus. Modern Art, Tokyo, 2001, Off the Grid, Lehmann Maupin Gallery, 2002, Marie Walsh Sharpe Art Found. Show, Ace Gallery, NYC, 2002, The Young Latins, Nassau County Mus. Art, NY, 2002, Helga de Alvear, Madrid, 2003, In Situ: Installations and Large-Scale Works, 2004, Lehmann Maupin Gallery, 2005. Named a MacArthur Fellow, John D. and Catherine T. MacArthur Found., 2005; recipient Louis Comfort Tiffany Biennial award, 1999; Individual Artist's Grant, Visual Arts, NEA, 1994, Cintas Fellow, 1994, CAVA Fellow, Nat. Found. Advancement in Arts, 1995, Metro-Dade Cultural Consortium Grant, 1995. Mailing: c/o Lehmann Maupin Gallery 540 West 26th St New York NY 10001-5504

FERNANDEZ DE CORDOVA, SERGIO ALONSO, advertising executive, publishing executive; b. Miraflores, Peru, Jan. 28, 1975; s. Gonzalo Fernandez de Cordova and Maria Estela De Veyga. BS in Sociology, Rutgers U., New Brunswick, NJ, 1999. Owner/pub. The Edgewater Residential, NJ, 1987—; founder Fuel Outdoor, NYC, 2002—. Admission com. bd. mem. The Friars Club, NYC, 2005; chmn. polit. affairs com. Entrepreneurs' Orgn., NYC, 2005—. Independent. Roman Catholic. Avocation: swimming. Office: Fuel Outdoor 149 5th Ave 11th Fl New York NY 10010 Home Phone: 646-239-6370; Office Phone: 212-796-4190. Business E-Mail: sfdecordova@fueloutdoor.com.

FERNÁNDEZ-VELAZQUEZ, JUAN RAMON, university chancellor; b. San Juan, Aug. 9, 1936; s. Ramon Fernández-Serrano and Elena Velazquez; m. Norah Moran, 1960 (div. 1967); children: Lynnette, Yasmin; m. Sonia M. Ramirez, Aug. 12, 1971 (div. 1992); 1 child, Juan Ernesto. BS, U. P.R., 1957, M in Pub. Adminstrn., 1963; PhD, CUNY, 1978; D honoris causa, U. Nacional, Piura, Peru, 1987. Adminstrv. tech. II Dept. Labor, San Juan, 1960; asst. to dir., lectr. Sch. Pub. Adminstrn., U. P.R., Río Piedras Campus, 1961-64, asst. prof., 1969-72, 79-80, assoc. prof., 1980-85, prof., 1984—, also chancellor, 1985-92; acad. senator faculty of social scis. U. P.R., 1983-85, mem. univ. bd., rep. Río Piedras Campus Acad. Senate, 1984-85; spl. asst. to Gov. of P.R., 1965-68; prof. Bklyn. Coll., CUNY, 1973-76; prof. sch. of pub. affairs Baruch Coll., CUNY, 1994—. Vis. assoc. rschr. Bildner Ctr. CUNY Grad. Sch., 1993-95; participant Fifth Ann. Conf. Caribbean Studies Assn., Curacao, 1980 and ann. meeting, 1981, seminar P.R. Planning Bd., 1979, symposium P.R. Found. for the Humanities, 1979, panel discussion Inst. Policy Scis. Ctr. for Study of State Policy, Duke U., 1981, seminar for grad. students Grad. Sch. Edn., Harvard U., 1981, Fifth Hispanic-Am. Conf., U. Mich., Ann Arbor, 1983, other confs., seminars; lectr. in field, 1975—; cons. Tchr.'s Assn., Hato Rey, P.R., 1984; hon. prof. U. Iberoamericana Sto. Do., Dominican Republic; lectr., bd. dirs. Ralph Bunche Inst. on the UN, 1986; vis. scholar, Bildner Ctr. for Western Hemisphere Studies, CUNY, 1993, adv. to the pres., Interam. U. P.R., 1996-97; founder Consenso Nacional Puertorriqueno, 1999; coodr. Com. for Devel. of Vieques Island, P.R., 1999; spl. commr. for Vieques and Culebra, Gov. P.R., 2001-04; P.R. state pres. AARP, 2006—. Contbr. chpts. to books and articles to profl. jours. Mem. Puerto Rico's delegation to UNESCO World Conf. on Higher Edn., Paris, 1998; del. to Internat. Sem. on Evaluation and Accreditation Models for Higher Edn. Instns. in Latin Am. and the Caribbean/sponsored by IESALC-UNESCO, San Juan, 1999 Named Most Disting. Grad. Class 1953, Ctrl. High Sch. P.R.; Ford Found. grantee, 1981; recipient Disting. Alumni award CUNY, 1988. Mem. Acad. Arts, History and Archeology of P.R., Acad. for the Humanities and Scis., Caribbean Studies Assn.

FERNBERGER, MARILYN FRIEDMAN, not-for-profit developer, consultant, volunteer; b. Phila., Aug. 13, 1927; d. David and Edith (Rosen) Friedman; m. Edward Fernberger, June 21, 1947; children: Edward Jr., Ellen, James. BA, U. Pa., 1948. Promoter, developer, executor major events for cmty. orgns. and instns. on local, nat. and internat. basis. Co-chmn. US Pro Indoor Tennis Championships, 1967-92; co-chmn. Phila. Women's Tennis Championships, 1970-79; cons. tennis promoters throughout US, creates new events and expands markets for existing events; staged profl. women's tennis tournament, Phila., 1970-79; cons. Internat. Mgmt. Group for Advanta Women's Tennis Championships; cons. on fundraising and art adminstrn.; former event coord. U. Pa. Inaugural Centenary Tennis Hall of Fame dinner; bd. dirs. Phila. Internat. Indoor Tennis Corp., Nat. Jr. Tennis League, Am. Tennis Assn., Phila. Tennis Patrons Assn., Phila. Youth Tennis & Edn. Benefit, Arthur Ashe Youth Tennis and Edn. Bd.; bd. dirs. Group of Four representing Wimbledon Mus., London, Roland Garros Mus., Paris, Tennis Australia Mus., Melbourne, and Internat. Tennis Hall of Fame, Newport, RI; lifetime trustee Internat. Tennis Hall of Fame; v.p. Middle States Patrons Assn.; chmn. Middle States Devel. Com., chmn. membership com.; chmn. Nat. Arthur Ashe Day; publ. com. U.S. Tennis Assn.; mem. Phila. Women's Interclub Bd.; founder, mgr. Ea. Pa. Boy's Championships; active Phila. Gold Cup; founder, chmn. People to People Sports Jr. Exhbns. Contbr. to nat. and internat. publs., including World Tennis mag., Tennis South Africa, Tennis Italiano, Tenis Espanol, Algeman Dagblad, Royal Tennis, Japan, Tennis Australia, Tennis de France, Brit. Lawn Tennis Jour. of Lawn Tennis Assn., Eng. Trustee Phila. Mus. Art; lifetime bd. mem., mem. adv. com. Phila. Mus. Art Assocs.; past pres. Rodin Mus., mem. bd. or officer United Way, Nat. Coun. Jewish Women, Fairmount Park Assn. for Hist. Sites, Phila. Sports Congress, Nat. Art Mus. Sport, Internat. Tennis Hall of Fame and Mus.; sec. treas. Tennis N.Am., Internat. Tennis Tournamet Dirs. Assn.; pres., Women's Tournament Dirs. Assn.; active Pa. Ballet, Emergency Aid, Albert Einstein Med. Ctr., Drama Guild, Ctr. for Internat. Visitors, Festival Theatre New Plays, U. Arts, Inst. Contemporary Art; mem. assocs. com., past chmn., life mem., pres. Rodin Mus.; bd. dirs. Phila. Mus. Art; life trustee Internat. Tennis Hall of Fame and Mus.; mem. mus. devel. gala 2004 50th anniversary celebration, mus. com. dir., long range planning com., accreditation com., ann. fund com.; chmn. Phila. City of Yr. 1996 Dinner, Internat. Tennis Hall of Fame, mem. gala com. 1980-, lifetime trustee 2005. Recipient Marlboro award, Humanitarian Svc. award Phila. Bd. Edn., Kelly award Pa. Parks and Recreation Commn., Cmty. Svc. award Big Bros.-Big Sisters, Police Athletic League, Coren award Nat. Jr. Tennis League Phila., YWCA, Phila., Mangan Svc. award USTA/Mid. States, Pub. Svc. award City of Phila., 8 times, Appreciation award Orange Bowl Com. Rotary Club, Phila., Phila. Bd. Edn., Chmn.'s award Internat. Tennis Hall of Fame and Mus., Pres.'s award Internat. Tennis Hall of Fame, 2002; named to USTA/Mid. States Hall of Fame, 1999; enshrined in Phila. Jewish Sports Hall of Fame, 2005, Major Wingfield Soc. of USTA, 2006. Mem. US Tennis Writers Assn. (bd., officer), Internat. Tennis Tournament Dirs. Assn. (bd., officer), Assn. Tournament Dirs. (bd., officer), U. Pa. Alumni Assn. (bd., officer), Internat. Tennis Club USA (hon., Olympic planning com.). Home and Office: 1112 Penmore Pl Rydal PA 19046-1239 Office Phone: 215-886-4222. Home Fax: 215-886-4230.

FERNELIUS, NILS CONARD, physicist; b. Columbus, Ohio, Nov. 10, 1934; s. Willis Conard and Anna Naomi (Baker) F. AB, Harvard U., 1956; student, Oxford U., 1956—57; MS, U. Ill., 1959, PhD, 1966. Rsch. assoc. dept. physics U. Ill., Urbana, 1966—67; asst. physicist Materials Sci. Divsn., Argonne, Ill., 1968—71; v.p. Rsch. Cons., Oak Ridge, Tenn., 1971—72; sr. fellow Nat. Rsch. Coun. Aerospace Rsch. Lab., Wright-Patterson AFB, Ohio, 1973—75; vis. scientist Universal Energy Sys., Dayton, Ohio, 1975—76; physicist U. Dayton Rsch. Inst., 1977—82; sr. rsch. assoc. Nat. Rsch. Coun. Materials Lab., Wright-Patterson AFB, 1982—85; vis. scientist Systran Corp., Dayton, 1985, 1987—88; physicist Stolle Corp., Sidney, Ohio, 1985—86, Materials Directorate Air Force Rsch. Lab., Wright-Patterson AFB, 1988—. Contbr. articles to profl. jours. NSF fellow, 1959-62. Mem. IEEE (sr.), SPIE, Optical Soc. Am., Am. Phys. Soc. (life), Am. Assn. Physics Tchrs., Lasers and Electro-Optics Soc., Soc. Applied Spectroscopy (George Rappoport Meml. award 1995), Materials

Rsch. Soc., Sigma Xi. Avocations: genealogy, stamp collecting/philately, travel, photography. Home: 1528 Sussex Rd Troy OH 45373-2446 Office: AFRL/MLPSO Materials Directorate Air Force Rsch Lab Wright Patterson Afb OH 45433

FERNHOLZ, ERHARD ROBERT, investment executive; b. Princeton, NJ, Mar. 27, 1941; s. Erhard and Mary (Briganti) F.; m. Luisa Turrin, June 4, 1970; children: Daniel, Ricardo. AB, Princeton U., 1962; PhD, Columbia U., 1967. Rsch. dir. Met. Securities, NYC, 1980-87; chief investment officer, founder Enhanced Investment Techs., Princeton, 1987—; founder, trustee Minerva Rsch. Found., 1993—. Author: Stochastic Portfolio Theory, 2002; contbr. articles to profl. jours.; patentee in field. NSF grantee, 1963-69. Home: 12 Dogwood Ln Princeton NJ 08540-5629 Office: Enhanced Investment Techs One Palmer Sq Princeton NJ 08542 Business E-Mail: bob@enhanced.com.

FERNSLER, JOHN PAUL, lawyer; b. Lebanon, Pa., Dec. 24, 1940; s. K. Paul and Elizabeth M. (Snyder) F.; m. Christine Joan Chester, July 31, 1965; children: Euan, Scott. AB, Dickinson Coll., 1962; JD, U. Mich., 1965. Bar: Pa. 1965, U.S. Dist. Ct. (ea. and we. dists.) Pa., U.S. Ct. Appeals (3d cir.). Assoc. Snyder, Balmer & Kershner, Reading, Pa., 1965-66; dep. atty. gen. Commonweatlh of Pa., Harrisburg, 1968-70; chief counsel HUD, Pitts., 1970-81; ptnr. Reed Smith Shaw & McClay, Pitts., 1981-97; corp. counsel Weis Markets, Inc., Sunbury, Pa., 1997—2002; prof. bus. law Bucknell U., Lewisburg, Pa., 2003—, pre-law advisor, 2007—. Lectr., spl. cons. Mortgage Bankers Assn., 1985-92; solicitor Mt. Lebanon Parking Authority, 1990-91; mem. Mt. Lebanon Commn., 1992-96, pres. 1993; bd. dirs., treas. Med./Rescue Team South Authority, 1995-97; bd. dirs. Rail Authority, 2004—; chair land preservation subcom. of real property adv. com. Pa. Joint State Govt. Commn., 2004—. Contbr. articles to profl. jours. Active Mt. Lebanon Zoning Hearing Bd., 1981—88, sec., 1982, chmn., 1983—88; bd. dirs. or pres. Linn Conservancy, 2001—05; pres. Lewisburg Neighborhoods Corp., 2006—; chmn. Mt. Lebanon Rep. Com., 1990—92; bd. dirs., counsel Coun. for Luth. Campus Ministry in Gt. Pitts., 1979—82. Decorated Commendation medal; recipient Spl. Cert. Pa. Dept Community Affairs, 1970. Mem. ABA (urban state and local law sect. coun. 1984-87), Pa. Bar Assn., Allegheny County Bar Assn. (real property sect., chmn., 1988), Am. Coll. Real Estate Lawyers (elected). Republican. Episcopalian. Avocations: bicycling, walking, photography. Home: 20 Brown St Lewisburg PA 17837-2104 Office: Bucknell Univ Career Devel Ctr Lewisburg PA 17837 Office Phone: 570-577-1370. E-mail: jfernsle@bucknell.edu.

FERNSTROM, JOHN DICKSON, pharmacology and nutrition researcher, educator; b. NYC, July 9, 1947; s. Karl Dickson and Dorothy Weston (Bond) F.; m. Madelyn Jill Hirsch; children: Aaron, Lauren. SB, MIT, 1969, PhD, 1972. Research fellow Roche Inst. of Molecular Biology, Nutley, N.J., 1972-73; asst. prof. MIT, Cambridge, Mass., 1973-77, assoc. prof., 1977-82, U. Pitts. Sch. of Medicine, 1982-87, prof. psychiatry, behavioral neurosci., 1987—; prof. pharmacology U. Pitts. Sch. Medicine, 1992—. Mem. Nat. Inst. Neurol. and Communicative Disorders and Stroke/NIH Program Project Rev., Bethesda, Md., 1978-82, chmn., 1981-82; mem. NASA Life Scis. Adv. Commn., Washington, 1980-86, NIMH Neurosci. Br. Evaluation Panel, Rockville, Md., 1983, Nat. Adv. Coun., Monell Chem. Senses Ctr., Phila., 1987—; mem. nutrition program rsch. evaluation panel Nat. Inst. Childhood Diseases, 1989; Burroughs-Wellcome vis. prof. basic med. scis., 1993; mem. com. on mil. nutrition rsch., food and nutrition bd. NAS, 1994-2001, com. dietary ref. intake, 1997-2003. Contbr. articles to profl. jours. Recipient Rsch. Scientist Devel. award NIMH, Rockville, 1979-88, Alfred P. Sloan fellowship in neurochemistry A.P. Sloan Found., N.Y.C., 1974-76, Predoctoral fellowship NIH, Bethesda, 1970-72, Rsch. Scientist award NIMH, Rockville, 1989-94. Mem. Am. Soc. for Neurochemistry, Am. Soc. for Pharmacology and Exptl. Therapeutics, Am. Physiol. Soc., Am. Inst. Nutrition (chmn. nervous system sect., mem. publ info. com., mem. coun., Mead-Johnson award 1980), Endocrine Soc. Office: U Pitts Dept Psychiatry 3811 Ohara St Pittsburgh PA 15213-2593 Office Phone: 412-246-5297.

FEROLETO, JOHN, lawyer; b. Aug. 4, 1953; s. John and Antoinette Feroleto; m. Paula Feroleto, June 23, 1981; children: John, Joel, Kathleen. BA, SUNY, Buffalo, 1975; JD, U. Buffalo, 1983. Atty. Lewis & Lewis, PC, Buffalo, 1987—95; pvt. practice Buffalo, 1995—. Co-chair PAC task force ATLA, Washington, 2002—05, chair small practice sect., 2004, officer interstate trucking litigation sect., 06, chair PAC task force, 06. Mem.: NY State Bar Assn., Erie County Bar Assn., Western NY Trial Lawyers Assn. (past pres., bd. dir.), Am. Assn. of Justice. Office: John Feroleto Attys at Law 1220 Liberty Bldg 424 Main St Buffalo NY 14202 Office Phone: 716-854-0700. Office Fax: 716-854-0265.

FEROZ, EHSAN HABIB, accounting educator, researcher, writer; came to US, 1979, permanent resident, 1983, naturalized, 1990; s. Mohammad Obaidul and Sabera Hakim; m. Kishwar Sultana; children: Rubens, Jonas, Amran. BA with honors, U. Dacca, 1972, MA with first class honors, 1974; MA, Carleton U., 1978; PhD, U. Chgo., 1982. Cert. fraud examiner; cert. govt. fin. mgr. Asst. prof. acctg. SUNY, Buffalo, 1983-86, CUNY, Baruch, 1986-89; vis. asst. prof. acctg. Carlson Sch. of Mgmt. U. Minn., 1989-91, assoc. prof. acctg., assoc. mem. grad. faculty, 1991-93, prof. acctg., assoc. mem. grad. faculty, 1993—2005; prof. acctg. Milgard Sch. Bus. U. Wash., Tacoma, 2005—. Invited guest Ctr. For Internat. Studies MIT, 1979; disting. faculty mentor U. Minn., 1990—91, spl. project assoc. of vice-chancellor for acad. adminstrn, 1995, mem. govt. accountability office's adv. coun. on govt. auditing standards, 2002—, faculty mentor sch. bus. and econs., mem. honors and awards com., dean search com., outcome measures com., student behavior judiciary com., libr. policy com.; presenter in field. Mem. editl. bd. Internat. Jour. Acctg., Internat. Jour. Acctg. & Bus. Soc., Rsch. in Govtl. & Non Profit Acctg.; contbr. articles to profl. jours. Bd. dirs. Duluth Children's Mus., 1996—2002; mem. Arrowhead Interfaith Coun., 2002—04. Named one of One Thousand Great Ams., 2005; recipient Highly Commended award, Emerald Lit. Network, 2006. Mem.: Am. Acctg. Assn. (mem. fin. mem. com. 1992—93, mem. FASAB subcom. of govt. & non-profit sect. 1995—98, mem. fin. com. 2000—02, govt. & non-profit edn. chair 2005, mem. sec. liaison com. 2005, edn. chair, govt. & non-profit sect. 2005), Assn. Cert. Fraud Examiners, Assn. Govt. Accts. Avocations: walking, swimming. Office: Univ Wash Milgard Sch Bus 1900 Commerce St Box 358420 Tacoma WA 98402 Business E-Mail: ehf2@u.washington.edu.

FERRAND, LOUIS GEORGE, lawyer; b. East Grand Rapids, Mich., Apr. 12, 1942; s. Louis George and Margaret Louise (LaBour) F.; m. Mary Eleanore Braseth, Oct. 25, 1969; children: Anne Elizabeth, Gregory Louis, Jacqueline Louise. BA, Alma Coll., 1964; JD, U. Mich., 1971. Bar: Mich. 1971, D.C. 1974, U.S. Supreme Ct. Pres., co-founder Cornerstone Project, Inc., Bklyn., 1966; vol. Peace Corps., Dominican Republic, 1966-68, trainer, 1968; dir. manpower programs Grand Rapids CAP, Mich., 1969-70; trial atty. Dept. Justice, Washington, 1971-76; counsel for civil rights Dept. Labor, Washington, 1976-81, dep. assoc. solicitor for civil rights, 1981-87, dep. assoc. solicitor for mine safety and health, 1987-88; of counsel Newman & Newell, 1988-89; sr. atty. OAS, 1990-94, prin. atty., 1994—2004, dir. Office of Gen. Legal Svcs., dep. gen. counsel, 2004—05, legal advisor to the OAS sec. gen., 2005—, dir. dept. legal svcs., 2005—. Bd. dirs. Ayuda, Inc., 1988—2003, hon. trustee, 2003—05, chair legal affairs and pers. coms., exec. com.; officer at large, bd. dirs. Parklawn Recreation Assn., Alexandria, Va., 1982—84, No. Va. Meml. Soc., 1991—95, Arlington Retirement Housing Corp., 1988—93; co-founder, bd. dirs. Fondo Quisqueya Found., Inc., 1993—, treas., 1993—2005, pres., 2005—; co-founder, bd. dirs. Friends of Williamsburg Rowing, Inc., 1993—97, treas., 1993—95; leader cub scout pack George Washington dist. Boy Scouts Am., 1984—86; basketball coach Recreational League, 1983—89; bd. dirs. T.C. Williams H.S. Track Boosters, 1992—97, treas., 1992—95, co-pres., 1995—96; chmn. social responsibilities com. Unitarian Ch., Arlington, Va., 1981, co-chmn. capital fund dr., 1993—94; trustee Unitarian Ch. of Arlington, 1984—87, chmn. bd. trustees, 1986—87; bd. dirs. MOAS Found., 1997—2006, treas., 1999—2006; bd. dirs. I-A Bar Found., 1995—2005; incorporator, bd. dirs. Young Americas Bus. Trust, Inc., 1999—, vice chair, 1999—2005; incorporator, bd. dirs. The Am.'s Endowment, Inc., 2003—06. Mem.: Am. Law Inst., Fed. Am. Inns of Ct. (co-founder, charter mem., master 1989—, program chmn. and counselor 1998—99, pres. 1999—2000), Inter-Am. Bar Assn. (co-chmn. labor law sect. 1986—91, asst. sec. 1989—91, asst. treas. 1993—94, sec. gen. 1995—2004, mem. exec. com. 1995—2004, coun. mem. 1995—, mag. editor 1999—2004), Mich. Bar Assn., D.C. Bar Assn., Fed. Bar Assn. (bd. dirs. D.C. chpt. 1986—, officer 1988—94, co-chmn. nat. conv. com. 1989, pres. 1993—94, nat. cir. officer 1993—97, nat. coun. mem. 1993—99, chair fed. career svc. divsn. 1996—99, nat. coun. mem. 2003—05), Fed. Bar Found. (adv. 1994—99). Avocations: reading, hiking, swimming, bicycling, travel. Office: Dept Legal Svcs Gen Secretariat Orgn Am States Washington DC 20006 Office Phone: 202-458-3903. Business E-Mail: lferrand@oas.org.

FERRANDO, JONATHAN P., lawyer, automotive executive; b. Kalamazoo, 1966; BA in Econs., U. Mich., 1988; JD, Harvard U., 1991. Atty. Skadden, Arps, Slate, Meagher & Flom, Chgo.; sr. v.p., gen. counsel automotive retail group AutoNation, Inc., Fort Lauderdale, Fla., 1996—2000, sr. v.p., gen. counsel, corp. sec., 2000—. Office: AutoNation Inc 110 SE 6th St Fort Lauderdale FL 33301*

FERRANTE, JOAN MARGUERITE, language and literature educator, writer; b. NYC, Nov. 11, 1936; d. Nicholas Henry and Josephine (Pisacane) Ferrante; m. R. Carey McIntosh. Student, Brearley Sch., 1950-54, Radcliffe Coll., 1954-55; BA, Barnard Coll., 1958; MA, Columbia U., 1959, PhD, 1963. Asst. prof. English and comparative lit. Columbia U., NYC, 1966-70, assoc. prof., 1970-74, prof., 1974—2007, chmn. English and comparative lit., 1988-91, dir. Ctr. Italian Studies, 1977-80, prof. emerita, 2007—. Lectr. modern langs. Swarthmore (Pa.) Coll., 1968; lectr. medieval studies Fordham U., NYC, 1976; Andrew Mellon prof. humanities Tulane U., 1984. Author: (book) The Conflict of Love and Honor, 1973, Guillaume d'Orange, Four Twelfth Century Epics, 1974, Woman as Image in Medieval Literature from the Twelfth Century to Dante, 1975; author: (with Robert Hanning) The Lais of Marie de France, 1978; author: The Political Vision of the Divine Comedy, 1984, To the Glory of Her Sex: Women's Roles in the Composition of Medieval Texts, 1997; editor (with George Economou): In Pursuit of Perfection, Courtly Love in Medieval Literature, 1975; editor: (with Robert hanning) The Challenge of the Medieval Text, 1985; editor: Database: Epistolae, Correspondence of Medieval Women, Texts and Translations; mem. adv. bd. Speculum, 1975—78, cons. editor Records of Civilization, 1975—. Am. Coun. Learned Socs. fellow, 1969—70, NEH fellow, 1980—81. Fellow: Medieval Acad. Am. (councillor, 2d v.p. 1998—99, 1st v.p. 1999—2000, pres. 2000—01); mem.: MLA (exec. coun. 1986—90), Dante Soc. Am. (councillor, v.p. 1978—83, pres. 1985—91), Phi Beta Kappa (senator 1979—97, v.p. 1988—91, pres. 1991—94). Office: Columbia U 614 Philosophy Hall New York NY 10027 Business E-Mail: jmf2@columbia.edu.

FERRANTE, JON VISCONTI, leadership and technology transfer executive, consultant; s. Leonard and Rose Ellen Ferrante. BS in Fgn. Svc., Georgetown U.; PhD, Union Inst. and U., Cin., 1994. Cert. clin. hypnotherapy Calif., 1997. Instr. Case Western Res. U. Grad. Sch. Edn.; cons., civil servant Naval Sea Sys. Command, Washington, 1981—96; cons. US Dept. Army; cons., coach Dept. Def., Washington, 1997—; exec., cons., coach Unified Industries Inc., Springfield, Va., 1999—. Singer: (Operas) Carnegie Hall, Lincoln Ctr., Kennedy Ctr., Cleve. Orch.; author: The Shih Tzu Heritage, Reflections of Human Leadership. Dir. nat. art contest children and teens Kennedy Ctr. Performing Arts, Washington, 1971—72; chair Navy Leadership Advocates Group. Scholar, US Dept. of Navy, 1983—92, US Pres., 1992—93, Chief of Naval Ops., 1993—95. Mem.: APA (assoc.), Woodrow Wilson Inst. Scholars (assoc.). Independent. Avocations: singing, dog breeding and judging, Am. Kennel Club. Home: 1130 S 17th St Arlington VA 22150 Office: Unified Industries Inc 6551 Loisdale Ct Springfield VA 22150 Home Phone: 703-922-9800. Office Fax: 703-971-5892. Business E-Mail: ferrante@uii.com.

FERRANTI, THOMAS, JR., lawyer; b. SI, NY, Mar. 14, 1969; s. Thomas and Janet Rose (Giordano) F.; m. Renée Esposito, July 11, 1998; children: Olivia Nicole, Christian Peter Thomas. BA, St. John's U., NYC, 1991, JD, 1994. Bar: NY 1995, NJ 1995, DC 1995. Dietary aide SI U. Hosp., 1987—93; intern Dept. of Investigation, NYC, 1990, Justice Finnegan, NY State Supreme Ct., Queens, 1990; legal intern Macy's Northeast, NYC, 1991, NYC Coun., SI, 1992; intern Supreme Ct. trial divsn. Richmond County Dist. Atty., SI, 1993-94; tchr. law Monsignor Farrell HS, SI, 1994-95; pvt. practice, SI, 1995—. Lawyer, witness Criminal Trial Inst., St. John's U., 1991-94, Civil Trial Inst., 1991-94; tutor, counselor Student Network Accessing Counselor Program, 1991-94; fire fighter NYC Fire Dept., 1993—. Gen. mgr., pres. Sta. WMOC, SI, 1989-91; mem. adv. bd. Cmty. Resources SI, 2002-03. St. John's U. scholar, 1988-91. Mem. ABA, NY State Bar Assn., Nat. Italian-Am. Bar Assn., Golden Key, Lambda Kappa Phi, Kappa Gamma Pi, Iota Alpha Sigma (pres. 1990-91). Roman Catholic. Avocations: aquarium hobbyist, weight training, science fiction, coin collecting/numismatics, travel. Home and Office: 99 Pitney Ave Staten Island NY 10309-1918 Fax: 718-317-5294. E-mail: tofesq@aol.com, tofesq@verizon.net.

FERRARA, ALBERT E., corporate executive; m. Rita Bobola; three children. BS, JD, U. Va. Tax atty. to various profl./mgr. positions USX Corp., Pitts., 1973-83; with Marathon Oil, Findlay, Ohio, 1983; tax mgr. Marathon Oil U.K., Ltd., London, 1983-89; dir. taxes USX Corp., Pitts., 1989-90, asst. treas. corp. fin., 1990-94, sr. fin. mgmt. positions, 1994—2002; v.p. corp. develop. NS Group Inc., 2002—03; dir. strategic planning AK Steel Holding Corp., Middletown, Ohio, 2003, v.p. fin., CFO, 2003—. Office: USX Corp 600 Grant St Pittsburgh PA 15219-2702*

FERRARA, ANNETTE, editor, educator; MA in Modern Art History, Theory and Criticism, Sch. of the Art Inst. Chgo. Rsch. asst. The Andy Warhol Catalogue Raisonné Project; dir. Alan Koppel Gallery, Chgo.; asst. dir. The Arts Club Chgo.; founding editor, writer TENbyTEN, Chgo., 1999—. Guest lectr. Columbia Coll., DePaul, SAIC; tchr. contemporary art history Mus. of Contemporary Art, Chgo. Co-author: Xtreme Interiors, 2003; contbr. writings to Artforum, Book Forum, Zingmagazine, Provincecton Arts. Mem.: Chgo. Art Critics Assn. Office: TENbyTEN 222 S Morgan 3E Chicago IL 60607 Office Phone: 312-421-0480. Office Fax: 312-421-0491. Business E-Mail: contact@tenbyten.net.

FERRARA, LEE, graphics designer, artist, educator; b. Somerville, Mass. d. Joseph Charles and Mary Rose (Macalini) F BFA, Mass. Coll. Art, 1951; postgrad., Yale U., 1951; MFA Visual Comm., Syracuse U., 1976. Sr. designer Montgomery Ward, Chgo., 1956—61; graphic designer Raymond Loew and Assocs., Chgo., Chapman, Goldsmith, and Yamasaki, Chgo., 1961—63; dir. design Family Products, Inc., Tyngsboro, Mass., 1972—82; founder, graphic designer Lee-Graphics, Santa Monica, Calif. Sr. designer Container Corp. Am., Boston, Walter Dorwin Teague, N.Y.C., 1971-72; mem. Winc Arts Coun., 1997-2000; freelance designer cos. including Max Factor Hollywood, Pacific Air Inc., Metric Sys., Pacific Game Co., Chicken Delight, Joyce Chen, Sunbeam Corp., Teledyne, numerous others Exhibns. include New Eng. Watercolor Soc., 1994, 95, 2002, 2003, Plymouth Art Assn., 1996, Dedham Art, 1996, Haverhill Art, 1997, Andover Art, 1997, 1998, Sharon Art Ctr., N.H., Copley Soc., Boston, 1996, Concord Art Assn., 1997, 2006, Lexington Arts and Crafts, Springfield (Mass.) Art League, 1998, Captured Wildlife 5th Annual, 1998, Internat. Nature Fine Arts Competition Bennington Art Complex, 1998, Arts Coun. S.E. Mo., Faulkner Centennial U. Mus., Acad. Artists Assn., 1998, Nat. Park Acad. Arts Top 200, 1998, Catharine Lorillard Wolfe Nat. Arts Club, 1998, 2001, Cambridge Art Assn., numerous others; author poems; contbr. articles to mags. publication, Art Of Color Printing On Pressure-Sensitve Labels Participant advanced project mentor program Lincoln Sch., 1993, mem. arts lottery coun., 1998-2000; bd. dirs. Civic Symphony, 1982-88 Recipient Cert. of Appreciation, Lincoln Sch., 1993, Editor's Choice award Nat. Libr. Poetry, 1994, awards 3 categories Dedham Art, 1996, 2d Pl. award Haverhill Art, 1997, 2d Pl. award Andover Art, 1997, 1st prize mixed media Andover Art in Park, 1998, Wilkins Art Cons. award Acad. Artists Assn. Nat. 1998, 2d Pl. 25th Annual Winter Show Duxbury Art Assn., Lex, Beford, Concord Art, 2005 Mem. Am. Inst. Graphic Arts, Am. Artists Profl. League (signature), New Eng. Watercolor Soc. (signature), Soc. Typographic Art (exhbn. chmn.), Artists Guild (Chgo.), Art Dirs. Club L.A., Concord Art Assn. (Mixed Media Collage award, Watercolor award 1999, 2002, Disting. Artist 2002), Copley Soc. (past bd. dirs.), North Shore Art Assn. (bd. dirs.), Allied Artists Am., Lexington Arts and Crafts (Rogowitz award, Most Creative award 2001, 02, 05, 06). Achievements include pioneer design of fabric overlay for plastic cap. Avocations: acting, writing, tennis, folk music, mycology. Home: 41 Franklin Rd Winchester MA 01890 Personal E-mail: leeferraradesigns@yahoo.com.

FERRARA, NAPOLEONE M.A., molecular oncologist; b. Catania, Italy, July 26, 1956; arrived in US, 1983; MD cum laude, U. Catania Med. Sch., Italy, 1981. Resident dept. ob-gyn. U. Catania Med. Sch., 1981—85; rsch. fellow gynecology and reproductive scis. U. Calif. Reproductive Endocrinology Ctr., San Francisco, 1983—85; intern dept. ob-gyn. Oreg. Health Scis. U., Portland, 1985—86; rsch. fellow U. Calif. Cancer Rsch. Inst., San Francisco, 1986—88; scientist Genentech, South San Francisco, 1988—93, sr. scientist, 1993—97, staff scientist, 1997—2002, fellow dept. molecular oncology, 2002—. Mem. sci. adv. com. Student Vision, Boston. Mem. editl. bd.: Angiogenesis, Cardiac and Vascular Regneration, Endothelium, Jour. Cardiovasc. Pathobiology, Jour. Clin. Investigation, Vascular Pharmacology; contbr. articles to sci. jours. Recipient Prize for rsch. in opthalmic disorders, Italian Assn. for the Search and Cure of Diseases of the Eyes, 2004, Prize for sci. excellence in medicine, Am.-Italian Cancer Found., 2004, Award for medicine, Discover Mag., 2004, Bruce F. Cain Meml. award, Am. Assn. Cancer Rsch., 2005, Grand Prix Lefoulon-Delalande-Institut de France award, 2005, GM Cancer Rsch. award, 2006. Mem.: NAS. Achievements include research leading to the creation of Avastin, an FDA-approved targeted therapy indicated for first-line treatment of patients with certain types of metastatic carcinoma. Office: Genentech 1 DNA Way Mailstop 40 South San Francisco CA 94080-4990

FERRARA, PETER JOSEPH, federal official, lawyer, author, educator; b. NYC, Apr. 26, 1955; s. Joseph B. and Betty (San Filippo) F.; 1 child, Peter Joseph Jr. BA, Harvard U., 1976, JD, 1979. Bar: NY 1980, DC 1984. Assoc. firm Cravath, Swaine & Moore, NYC, 1979-81; spl. asst. to asst. sec. for policy devel. and research HUD, Washington, 1981-82; mem. sr. staff White House Office Policy Devel., Washington, 1982-83; of counsel Shaw Pittman, Potts & Trowbridge, 1983-92; assoc. prof. George Mason Sch. Law, 1987-91, 2000—; assoc. dep. atty. gen. U.S. Justice Dept., Washington, 1992-93; sr. fellow Heritage Found., 1993-94, Nat. Ctr. for Policy Analysis, Washington, 1994-95; gen. counsel and chief economist American for Tax Reform, Washington, 1995-2000; pres. Virginia Inst. Pub. Policy, Gainesville. Sr. fellow CATO Inst., Washington, 1988-91, 95—; dir. Legal Svcs. Corp., 1984; assoc. prof. law George Mason U. Sch. Law, 2000—. Author: Social Security: The Inherent Contradiction, 1980, (with others) Enterprise Zones Sourcebook, 1981, Social Security: The Family Security Plan, 1982, Social Security: Averting the Crisis, 1982, Religion and the Constitution, 1983, (with others) Mandate for Leadership II, 1984, (with others) Beyond the Status Quo: Policy Proposals for America, 1985, Social Security: Prospects for Real Reform, 1985, (with others) The Political Economy of Privatization, 1987, (with others) The Third Generation, 1987, (with others) The Judges' War, 1987, (with others) Mandate for Leadership III, 1988, (with others) An American Vision, 1988, (with others) A New Deal for Social Security, 1998; editor and co-author: Free the Mail: Ending the Postal Monopoly, 1990, issues 94 1994, The Choctaw Revolution: Lessons for Federal Indian Policy, 1998; contbr. articles to profl. jours. John M. Olin Disting. fellow Heritage Found., 1987-88. Republican. Office: Virginia Inst Pub Policy 7326 Early Marker Ct Gainesville VA 20155 Office Fax: 703-753-5900.

FERRARA, RALPH C., lawyer; b. Gloversville, NY, June 16, 1945; s. Rufus Ferrara and Clara F. Riccitiello. BSBA, Georgetown U., 1967; JD, U. Cin., 1970; LLM in Corp. Law, George Washington U., 1972. Bar: DC 1970, NY, 1982, Fla., 1990, Colo., 1993, US Ct. Appeals, US Supreme Ct. Profl. asst. to law libr. Nat. Law Ctr., Washington, 1970-72; mem. faculty George Washington U. Nat. Law Ctr., Washington; atty. divsn. enforcement SEC, Washington, 1971-72, trial atty. divsn. trading and markets, 1972-73, spl. counsel to chief enforcement atty., 1973-74, supervisory trial atty., 1974-75, spl. counsel to chmn., 1975, asst. gen. counsel, 1975-76, exec. asst. to legal counsel, 1976-77, exec. asst., 1977-78, gen. counsel, 1978-81; mng. ptnr. Debevoise & Plimpton LLP, Washington, 1981—2004; ptnr., litig. dept. LeBoeuf, Lamb, Greene & MacRae LLP, Washington, 2005—. Faculty, Nat. Law Ctr., George Wash. U., 1970-1972; gen. counsel, bd. of visitors, U. Cin. Coll. Law; bd. advisors, Ctr. Corp. Law, U. Cin. Coll. Law, 1987-; mem. adv. bd. Securities Regulation & Law Report and Rev. Fin. Svcs. Regulation, 1987-; mem. e-Securities bd. advisors, 1998-; mem. Washington, DC Panel of Distinguished Neutrals, CPR Inst. Dispute Resolution, 1996-, Administrv. Conf. US, 1982-85, Ray Garrett Inst. adv. com., 1982-84, Securities Law adv. com., Practising Law Inst., 1981-; co-chair, Ann. Inst. Securities Regulation, 1994-98, Sweeping Reform: Litigating & Bespeaking Caution Under the New Securities Law, 1996; mem. Legal Adv. com., NY Stock Exch. bd. dirs.; Chmn. Ctr. Pub. Resources, Inc., 1992-94, Securities Dispute Com., 1988-1989; bd. advisors, D & O Advisor, 2003—; dir. Park Pl. Entertainment. Author: Takeovers II: A Strategists' Manual for Business Combinations in the 1990s, 1993, Shareholder Derivative Litigation: Beseiging the Board, 1995, Ferrara on Insider Trading the Wall, 1995, Managing Marketeers: Supervisory Responsibilities of Broker-Dealers and Investment Advisors, 2000, Takeovers: A Strategic Guide to Mergers and Acquisitions, 2001; contbr. articles on topics related to fed. securities law to profl. jours. With USAR. Named one of 75 Best Lawyers, Washingtonian mag., 2002; recipient John L. Sayler award, Am. Jurisprudence award, Judge Alfred Mack award. Mem. ABA (mem. sect. on corp., banking & bus. law, fed. regulation of securities com., task force on insider trading controls, 1985—, task force SEC settlements, 1987-1989, task force on sect. 15 (c) (4) Proceedings, 1987-, task force on securities arbitration, 1987-, sect. planning & rev., 1986-, vice-chmn. civil liabilities & litig. subcommittee, 1981-, chmn. task force on broker-dealer compliance, 1988-, chmn., market structures working group of the task force on rev. of fed. securities laws), FBA (exe. coun. securities law com. 1978-, nat. coun., gen. counsels' com. 1978-81), Southwestern Legal Found. (adv. com.), Insurance Marketplace Standards Assn. (Independent Assessor Certification Market Conduct Program, 1997), Am. Law Inst. Office: LeBoeuf Lamb Greene & MacRae LLP 1875 Connecticut Ave NW Ste 1200 Washington DC 20009-5728*

FERRARI, GIANNANTONIO, electronics executive; Diploma in Acctg., U. Milan. With Gavazzi SpA, 1960, Honeywell Italia, 1965; gen. mgr. Honeywell Iran, Honeywell Greece; dir. fin., administrn., and human resources Honeywell Mid. E.; controller Honeywell Europe, 1981-85, v.p. fin. and adminstrn., 1985-88, pres., 1992-97; v.p. Western Europe, Mid. E., Africa Honeywell, Inc., Italy, 1988-92, pres., COO, 1997—. Bd. dirs. No. State Power Co., Nat. Assn. Mfrs.; bd. govs. Nat. Elec. Mfrs. Assn. Office: 1985 Douglas Dr N Minneapolis MN 55422-3992

FERRARI, RAFFAELE, oceanographer, educator; s. Attilio Ferrari and Gabriella Mortara; m. Anna Leonova, Apr. 15, 1999; 1 child, Elena. Diploma, Med. Sch. San Govannino, Turin, Italy, 1981; grad. in classics, Liceo Classico Val Salice, Turin, 1986; MS in Physics, U. Turin, 1994; PhD in Fluid Dynamics, Poly. Turin, 1999; PhD in Oceanography, Scripps Inst. Oceanography, 2000. Rsch. asst. Politecnico di Torino, Torino, Italy, 1994—97, Scripps Instn. of Oceanography, La Jolla, 1995—2000; postdoctoral scholar Woods Hole Oceanog. Instn., Mass., 2000—01; assoc. prof. MIT, Cambridge, Mass., 2002—. Recipient Victor P. Starr Career devel. Chair, MIT, 2003, Fofonoff award, Am. Meteorology Soc., 2007; grantee Climate Process Team Leader, NSF, 2004; Killian and Lee scholar, MIT, 2004. Mem.: Am. Meteorol. Soc. Office: 54 1420 MIT 77 Massachusetts Ave Cambridge MA 02139 Office Phone: 617-253-7762. Office Fax: 617-253-4464.

FERRARI, ROBERT JOSEPH, finance educator, retired bank executive; b. Bklyn., Dec. 3, 1936; m. Patricia A. Cantalupo, Sept. 6, 1958 (dec. Jan. 1991); children: Robert Joseph, James G., Judith A., Thomas A. BS in Econs., Villanova U., Pa., 1958; MBA, NYU, 1962; grad. certificate, Brown U., Providence, RI, 1969, Henry George Sch. Social Sci., NYC, 1961; DSc, London Inst., 1973. With arbitrage dept. Goodbody & Co., 1957-60; bank auditor Fed. Res. Bank, NYC, 1960-65; v.p. fin. Am. Savs. Bank, NYC, 1965-81; prof., chair dept. econs. and bus. Marymount Coll. of Fordham U., Tarrytown, 1981—. Cons. LaCorte Agy., Inc., 1963—65. Office: Marymount Coll of Fordham Univ 100 Marymount Ave Tarrytown NY 10591-3704 Home: 425 River Rd Pipersville PA 18947 Office Phone: 914-332-7461. Business E-Mail: rferrari@fordham.edu.

FERRARO, BETTY ANN, retired state senator; b. Newport, Vt., Mar. 3, 1925; d. Clarence John and Mauretta Rowena (Potter) Morse; m. Dominic Thomas Ferraro, Oct. 8, 1964; children: Deborah, David, Susan, Barbara. Student, Mary Hitchcock Hosp. Sch. Nursing, Coll. St. Joseph, Rutland, Vt. Exec. sec. to asst. treas. Ctrl. Vt. Pub. Svc. Corp., Rutland, 1943-44; sec. to dean N.Y. Med. Coll., NYC, 1944-46; model G. Fox Co., Hartford, Conn., 1947; corp. sec., office mgr. John Russell Corp., Rutland, 1970-80; exec. dir. Rutland Area Coordinated Child Care Com., Washington, 1977-79; adminstrv. asst. Hilinex of Vt., Rutland, 1981-83; owner Classic Connection Gift Shop, Rutland, 1983-87; adminstr. Vicon Recovery Sys., Inc., Rutland, 1987-90. Owner, operator nursery sch., 1973—77; mgr. Day Care Ctr., 1978—80; mem. Rutland City Bd. Aldermen, 1984—86, 2001—03; resource dir. Rutland City Emergency Mgmt. Team for State of Vt., 1984—90; mem. Vt. State Cmty. Devel. Commn., 1986. Chmn. Rutland City Rep. Com., 1991-93; county committeewoman State Rep. Com., 1984-86, rep.; rep. Rutland County Rep. Com.; state del. Rep. Nat. Conv., 1992; Rep. campaign coord. State of Vt., 1997-98; county co-chair Jim Douglas for Gov., 2001-02; mem. Vt. Ho. Reps., 1990-92; mem. Vt. Senate, 1992-94, 95-97; mem. jud. nominating bd. Human Resource Investment Com., 1995-96, Vt. Student Assistance Corp. Bd.; mem. Amtrak Study Commn., 1995-96; bd. dirs. Vt. Physicians Coun., 1997—, Coll. St. Joseph, 1996-2000, Marble Valley Transit, 1996—, sec. bd. dirs.; mem. adv. bd. Paramount Theatre, 1997-2000; sec., receptionist Orton Family Found., 1999-2000; sec., receptionist Eddy Enterprises, Inc., 2000-01; county co-chair Jim Douglas for Gov., 2002; hon. chair Kevin Mullin for Sen. Campaign, 2004—; mem. Vt. State Transp. Bd, 2003-05; devel. coord. Neighbor Works We. Vt., 2002-2005. Fleming Inst. fellow, 1995; named Woman of Yr. Green Mt. Coun. of Boy Scouts Am. Mem. Nat. Assn. Women in Constrn. (chartered, past pres.), Rutland County Rep. Women. Republican. Roman Catholic. Avocation: flower arranging. Home and Office: Condo 17 155 Dorr Dr Rutland VT 05701-3853 Home Phone: 802-773-8798. Personal E-mail: bettymferraro@verizon.net.

FERRARO, GERALDINE ANNE, lobbyist, former congresswoman; b. Newburgh, NY, Aug. 26, 1935; d. Dominick and Antonetta L. (Corrieri) F.; m. John Zaccaro, 1960; children: Donna, John, Laura. BA, Marymount Manhattan Coll., 1956; JD, Fordham U., 1960; postgrad., NYU Law Sch., 1978; degree (hon.), Marymount Manhattan Coll., 1982, NYU Law Sch., 1984, Hunter Coll., 1985, Plattsburgh Coll., 1985, Coll. Boca Raton, 1989, Va. State U., 1989, Muhlenberg Coll., 1990, Briarcliffe Coll. for Bus., 1990, Potsdam Coll., 1991. Bar: N.Y. 1961, U.S. Supreme Ct. 1978. Atty. pvt. practice, NYC, 1961-74; asst. dist. atty. Queens County, NY, 1974-78; chief spl. victims bur., 1977-78; mem. US Congress from 9th NY Dist., 1979—85; sec. House Democratic Caucus; 1st woman vice presdl. nominee on Democratic ticket, 1984; fellow Harvard Inst. Politics, Cambridge, Mass., 1988—92; mng. ptnr. Keck Mahin Cate & Koether, NYC, 1993-94; pres. G&L Strategies Golin Harris Internat., NYC, 1999—2003; exec. v.p., head pub. affairs The Global Consulting Group, NYC, 2003—07; prin. Blank Rome Govt. Rels. LLC, NYC, 2007—. US amb. to UN Human Rights Commn., 1994-95; co-host Crossfire, CNN, 1996-97, Fox News Nightly, 1999—. Author: Changing History: Women, Power, and Politics, 1993, Framing a Life: A Family Memoir, 1998; co-author (with Linda Bird Francke) Ferraro, My Story, 1985 Chair Dem. Platform Com., Bertarelli Found.; Dem. candidate U.S. Senate, 1992, 98; U.S. President Clinton's appointee to UN Human Rights Commn. Conf., Geneva, 1993, World Conf., Vienna, Austria, 1993, World Conf. on Women, 1995; bd. dirs. Fordham Law Sch. Bd. Visitors; bd. advocates Planned Parenthood Fedn. Am.; bd. dir. Nat. Women's Health Rsch. Ctr., Nat. Dem. Inst. Mem. Queens County Women's Bar Assn. (past pres.), Coun. Fgn. Rels., Internat. Inst. Women's Polit. Leadership (former pres.). Roman Catholic. Office: Blank Rome Govt Rels LLC The Chrysler Bldg 405 Lexington Ave New York NY 10174

FERRARO, JOHN FRANCIS, corporate financial executive; b. NYC, Jan. 3, 1934; s. John Anthony and Angelina (Figliola) F.; children: Elizabeth Ann, John Robert, Laura Marie, Rosemary. BS in Indsl. Engring. with honors and distinction, NYU, 1962. With United Technologies Corp., Windsor Locks, Conn., 1962-66; sr. project engr. United Techs. Corp., Windsor Locks, Conn., 1962-64, chief research and devel. promotion, 1964-66; founding ptnr. P.M.C. Corp., 1966-78; chmn. bd., chief exec. officer Thermodynetics, Inc., 1978—; pres. Pioneer Capital Corp.; mng. dir. Capital Mgmt. Ptnrs. LLC. Contbr. numerous articles on bus., fin. and stock market to fin. publs., 1966-81; contbg. editor: Handbook of Wealth Management, 1977. Trustee Birth Right, Conn., 1970—80; chmn. Congl. Com. for Apointees USAF Acad., 1980; commr. Develop Agy., Enfield, Conn., 1981; mem. Gov.'s task force for mfg. State of Conn., 1989—91; mem. exec. com. Holy Family Retreat League, 1984—88; mem. bd. advisors St. Joseph's Residence, Conn., 1991—2001; trustee Suffield Acad., Conn., 1980—93, chair budget and fin. com., 1987—92; trustee Western New Eng. Coll., 1997—2003. 1st lt. USAF, 1954—58. Decorated Meritorious Service medal. Mem.: Psi Upsilon. Home: 86 Berkshire Ave Southwick MA 01077-9642 Office: 651 Day Hill Rd Windsor CT 06095-1719 Personal E-mail: jigfox@comcast.net.

FERRARO, MARGARET LOUISE (PEG), secondary school educator; b. Apr. 9, 1939; BS in Edn., Kutztown State U., 1961. Tchr. Abington Sch. Dist., Pa., 1961—64; tchr. secondary sch. Nazareth Area Sch. Dist., Pa., 1978—2001. Chmn. zoning bd. Upper Nazareth Twp., 1970, sec. planning commn., 1968, treas., 1986, 1st woman elected to bd. suprs., 1986; bd. dirs., chair edn. com. Lehigh Valley Chamber Orch., 1982-2001; 1st Rep. woman elected countywide Northampton County Coun., 1989-97, 3d term, 2001-05, v.p., 2002-05; chmn. Northampton County Rep. Com., 1998-2002; active Northampton County Indsl. Devel. Authority, 2003-06, Northampton County Housing Authority, 2003—, Northampton County Gen. Purpose Authority, 2006—,; adv. bd. Excellence In Pub. Svc., Inc., 2006—; active Rep. State Com., Pa., 1984—, asst. sec. leadership com., 1994—. Recipient Nazareth Area H.S. Disting. Alumni award, 1994 Republican. Home: 339 Schoeneck Ave Nazareth PA 18064-1224

FERRAZ, FRANCISCO MARCONI, neurological surgeon; b. Floresta, Pernambuco, Brazil, Aug. 14, 1951; arrived in U.S., 1976; Student, Colegio Nobrega, Recife-Brazil, 1967—69; MD, Faculdade de Medicine da Universidade Federal de Pernambuco-Brazil, 1975. Diplomate Am. Bd. Neurol. Surgery. Intern Jamaica Hosp., NYC, 1976—77; resident Georgetown U. Med. Ctr. and Affiliated Hosps., Washington, 1977—82; pvt. practice medicine specializing in neurol. surgery Washington, 1982—; mem. staff Georgetown U. Hosp., 1982—, Arlington Hosp., 1982—; chief divsn. neurosurgery, faculty clin. instr. Georgetown U. Sch. Medicine, 1982—; faculty clin. assoc. prof. George Washington Sch. Medicine, 1994—. Cons. in health care fin., internat. health care. Contbr. articles to profl. jours. Fellow: ACS, Internat. Coll. Surgeons; mem.: AMA, Congress of Neurol. Surgery, Washington Acad. Neurosurgery, Neurosurg. Soc. of D.C., Arlington Med. Soc., Am. Assn. Neurol. Surgeons. Office: 611 S Carlin Springs Rd Ste 105 Arlington VA 22204-1061 Office Phone: 703-845-1552. Business E-Mail: fferraz@cox.net.

FERRE, ANTONIO LUIS, newspaper publisher; b. Ponce, P.R., Feb. 6, 1934; s. Luis A. and Lorenza (Ramirez de Arellano) F.; m. Luisa Rangel, Feb. 23, 1963; children: Maria Luisa, Antonio Luis, Luis Alberto, Maria Eugenia, Maria Lorenza. AB magna cum laude, Amherst Coll., Mass., 1955, PhD (hon.) in Humanities, 1995, HHD (hon.), 1994; MBA, Harvard U., Cambridge, Mass., 1957; student Inst. for Sr. Mgmt. and Govt. Execs., Dartmouth Coll., Hanover, NH, 1958; PhD in Comm. Sci. (hon.), U. Turabo, 1992. Vice chmn. Banco Popular, 1994—2000; pres., editor El Nuevo Dia, 1968—2006. Chmn. P.R. Conservation Trust, 1993-97. Author: (essays) Un Alto en el Camino; Pan, Paz y Palabra; also numerous newspaper editorials. Pres. P.R. Coun. on Higher Edn., 1966-68, Gov.'s Adv. Coun., 1968-72; mem. Gov.'s Labor Adv. Coun., 1975; pres. Com. for Econ Devel. P.R., 1984-90; vice chmn. Ponce Mus. Art, 1985-2000. With US Army, 1958. Recipient Presdl. citation, 1976. Mem. P.R. Mfrs. Assn. (pres. 1965-66), Am. Mgmt. Assn. (President's Assn. 1963-70), Coun. of Fgn. Rels., Inter-Am. Dialogue, P.R. C. of C., Dorado Beach and Golf Club, Bankers Club P.R., Club Deportivo de Ponce, Phi Beta Kappa. Roman Catholic. Office: Grupo Ferre Rangel PO Box 9066590 San Juan PR 00960-6590 Office Phone: 787-641-8070. E-mail: alferre@gfrpr.com.

FERREE, CAROLYN RUTH, retired radiation oncologist, educator; b. Liberty, NC, Jan. 29, 1944; d. Numer Floyd and Mary Isabel (Glass) Black; m. Richard C. Sanders, June 5, 1999. BA, U. N.C., Greensboro, 1966, DSc (hon.), 1998; MD, Bowman Gray Coll., Winston-Salem, NC, 1970. Diplomate Am. Bd. Radiation Oncology. Intern medicine N.C. Bapt. Hosp., Winston-Salem, 1970-71, resident in radiation oncology, 1971-74; instr. radiation oncology Bowman Gray Sch. Medicine, Winston-Salem, 1974-75, asst. prof., 1975-80, assoc. prof., 1980-87, prof., 1987—2007; ret., 2007. Contbr. articles to profl. jours. Mem., v.p. County Bd. of Pub. Health, Winston-Salem, 1985-92; bd. dirs. U. N.C.-Greensboro Excellence Found., 1988-94; med. dir. Forsyth County chpt. Am. Cancer Soc., 1975-90; bd. dirs. Hospice, 1998—; trustee U. N.C.-Greensboro, 2005—. Recipient Disting. Svc. award U. N.C.-G Alumni, 1997, Disting. Achievement award Wake Forest U. Sch. Medicine, 1999; named Disting. Woman of N.C. in Professions, Gov.'s award, 1998, Patient Advocate award Cancer Svcs., 2002, Outstanding Oncologist award So. Assn. Oncology, 2005; voted Top Dr. by peers, 2000-05. Fellow Am. Coll. Radiology; mem. AMA (N.C. del. to AMA), Pediat. Oncology Group (radiotherapy coord.), N.C. Med. Soc. (2d v.p. 1990-91, sec.-treas. 1991-95, pres.-elect 1996, pres. 1997), Am. Soc. Therapeutic Radiologists Orgn. Office: Wake Forest U Sch Medicine Med Center Blvd Winston Salem NC 27157-0001 Home Phone: 336-765-5515; Office Phone: 336-713-3600. Business E-Mail: cferree@wfubmc.edu.

FERREE, JOHN NEWTON, JR., fundraising specialist, consultant; b. Wadesboro, NC, Nov. 21, 1946; s. John Newton and Mary Cleo Ferree. AA, Bluefield Coll., Va., 1966; BA, Baylor U., 1968; JD, Cumberland Sch. Law, Samford U., 1975. Bar: Ala. Contr. Aetna Life Ins. Co., Seattle, 1972; atty. Ferree & Armstrong, Alabaster, Ala., 1975-82; exec. dir. Northwest Bapt. Found., Portland, Oreg., 1982-84; asst. v.p. Harris Trust Co. of Ariz., Scottsdale, 1984; v.p. Bapt. Found. of Ariz., Phoenix, 1985-89; dir. planned giving Phoenix Children's Hosp., 1989-91; pres. Scottsdale (Ariz.) Healthcare Found., 1991—; bd. dir. Nat. Com. Planned Giving, 1994-96. Bd. dirs. FBI Citizen's Acad. Found., 1994-2005, v.p. 1994-96, 98-99, Charitable Accord, v.p., 1996-1998; instr. Cannon Sch. Found. Mgmt., 1995-2000; adj. prof. Ariz. State U., 1998-2000; cons. in field. Named Ariz. Profl. Fundraiser of Yr., 1996. Mem. Assn. Fundraising Profls. (pres. greater Ariz. chpt. 1991), Planned Giving Roundtable of Ariz. (pres. 1992, 97), Assn. for Healthcare Philanthropy. Republican. Baptist. Office: Scottsdale Healthcare Found 10001 N 92d St Ste 121 Scottsdale AZ 85258-4530 Home Phone: 480-314-4616; Office Phone: 480-882-4516. Business E-Mail: jferree@shc.org.

FERREIRA, ARMANDO THOMAS, sculptor, educator; b. Charleston, W.Va., Jan. 8, 1932; s. Maximiliano and Placeres (Sanchez) F.; children: Lisa, Teresa. Student, Chouinard Art Inst., 1949—50, Long Beach City Coll., 1950—53; BA, UCLA, 1954, MA, 1956. Asst. prof. art Mt. St. Mary's Coll., 1956-57; mem. faculty dept. art Calif. State U., Long Beach, 1957—, prof., 1967—, chmn. dept. art, 1971-77, assoc. dean Sch. Fine Arts, acting dean Coll. Arts. Lectr., cons. on art adminstrn. to art schs. and univs., Brazilian Ministry Edn. One-man shows include, Pasadena Mus., 1959, Long Beach Mus., 1959, 69, Eccles Mus., 1967, Clay and Fiber Gallery, Taos, 1972; exhibited in group shows at L.A. County Art Mus., 1958, 66, Wichita Art Mus., 1959, Everson Mus., 1960, 66, San Diego Mus. Fine Arts, 1969, 73, Fairtree Gallery, N.Y.C., 1971, 74, L.A. Inst. Contemporary Art, 1977, Utah Art Mus., 1978, Bowers Mus., Santa Ana, Calif., 1980, No. Ill. U., 1986, Beckstrand Gallery, Palos Verdes (Calif.) Art Ctr., 1987, U. Madrid, 1993; permanent collections include Utah Mus. Art, Wichita Art Mus., Long Beach (Calif.) Mus. Art, State of Calif. Collection, Fred Jones Jr. Mus. Art U. Okla., U. Okla. Art Mus.; vis. artist, U. N.D., 1974. Fulbright lectr. Brazil, 1981. Fellow: Nat. Assn. Schs. Art and Design (bd. dirs.). Personal E-mail: atferreira@msn.com. *I suppose much of my own life has been shaped by my experience as a first generation American. What modest success I may have had in my work is considerably due to that sense of ambition with which immigrant parents imbue their children. My vision as an artist is also shaped by the strong sense of Spanish culture that was part of my upbringing.*

FERREIRA, JO ANN JEANETTE CHANOUX, management consultant, delivery service executive; b. Dec. 3, 1943; d. John W. and June B. Chanoux; m. G. Dodge Ferreira, Apr. 21, 1979 (div. Dec. 1993). BS, Purdue U., 1965, MS, 1969. With sys. devel. rsch. IBM, San Jose, Calif., 1965-67; asst. dir. mgmt. info. sys. edn. Union Carbide Corp., NYC, 1969; mgmt. cons. Touche Ross & Co., NYC, 1974-75; dir. corp. devel. strategy cons. A.T. Kearney-Mgmt. Cons., Chgo., 1975-83; dir. Computer Devel. Ctr. United Airlines, 1983-88; pres. WSG Designs Inc., Northbrook, Ill., 1988-92; gen. mgr. acoustic rsch. divsn. Internat. Jensen, Inc., Lincolnshire, Ill., 1993—, v.p. bus. plans and export ops., 1994—, v.p. emerging markets, 1994-97; mng. dir. market planning and analysis Fed Express, 1998, mng. dir., hub area bus. devel., 1997—. Lectr. Purdue U., 1969, 73-74; guest lectr. Northwestern U., 1981; mem. adv. bd. Grad. Sch. Bus. U. Alaska; spkr. in field. Contbr. articles to profl. publs. NSF fellow, 1969. Mem. Inst. Mgmt. Cons. (cert. mgmt. cons.), am. Arbitration Assn., Japan Am. soc., Phi Kappa Phi.

FERRELL, CATHERINE K., sculptor, painter; b. Detroit, Apr. 27, 1947; d. Robert Byron and Elizabeth (Crapo) Klemann; m. William Barksdale Ferrell Jr., Nov. 4, 1987; children: Adrienne Elizabeth, Peter Klemann. Student, U. Mich., 1966-67; BA in Sculpture, Fla. Atlantic U., 1969; MA in Sculpture, U. Miami, Fla., 1972. Asst. to sculptor Luis Montoya Montoya Art Studios, West Palm Beach, Fla., 1983; pres., sculptor Art Equities, Inc., Vero Beach, Fla., 1986—. One-woman shows include Musee Universale, Montreal, Can., 1985, Elliott Mus., Stuart, Fla., 1985, Lighthouse Gallery Inc., 1991, J. Sexton Gallery, Vero Beach, Fla., 1996, McCreeless Fine Arts Gallery, Asbury Coll., Lexington, Ky., 1996, U. Mich., Flint, 1996, Cornell Mus., Delray Beach, Fla., 1999, Pen Brush, Inc., NY, 2002, Pen and Brush Inc., NYC, 2002, Cheryl Newby Gallery, SC, 2003, Gallery of the Masters, Loveland, Colo., 2007; represented in permanent collections: Norton Mus. Art, West Palm Beach, Fla., Bennex Internat., Oslo, Norway, Brevard Mus. Art, Melbourne, Fla., Gunter Schultz-Franke, Arch., Osnabruch, West Germany, dr. Paul Gingras, Palm Beach, Fla.; numerous pvt. collections Recipient Silver medal, Audubon Artists Am. Fellow Am. Artists Profl. League; mem. Am. Soc. Marine Artists, Am. Acad. Women Artists, Knickerbocker Artists, Allied Artists (assoc.), Profl. Artists Guild, Artists Forum, Pen and Brush, Inc., Catherine Lorillard Wolfe Art Club, Salmagundi Club (Cert. of Merit, Elliot Liskin Meml. award 1993, Pres. award 1994) Home: 12546 Highway A1A Vero Beach FL 32963-9411 Home Phone: 772-589-1552. Personal E-mail: tcferrell@aol.com.

FERRELL, CHARLES MADISON, nuclear engineer, physicist; b. Clarksburg, W.Va., Apr. 30, 1928; s. Benjamin Franklin and Mary Ethlyn (Selby) F.; m. Donnie Sue Thompson, Aug. 30, 1957; children: Donald Franklin, Jeffrey Madison, Kimberly Marilyn. BS, Salem Coll., W.Va., 1950; postgrad., Vanderbilt U., 1954-55, W.Va. U., 1955-56, U. Md., 1959-61. Phys. scientist U.S. Army Chem. Corps, Edgewood, Md., 1951-52, physicist Frederick, Md., 1953-54; radiol. physicist U.S. AEC, Oak Ridge, 1956-57, Germantown, Md., 1957-74; nuc. engr. U.S. NRC, Bethesda and Rockville, Md., 1974-95; cons., 1995—. Co-author 5 U.S. Nuc. Regulatory publs. Dist. advancement chmn., unit commr. Seneca Dist. and Forest Oak coun. Boy Scouts Am., 1993-2006; grand marshal Gaithersburg Labor Day Parade, 2005. With U.S. Army, 1950-52. U.S. AEC radiol. physics fellow, 1954-55; recipient Silver Beaver award Boy Scouts Am., 1998, numerous vol. svc. awards including Nat. Assn. of Ret. Fed. Employees State of Md. award, 1997, City of Gaithersburg, Md. People of Character award, 1997,City of Gaithersburg Disting. Citizen Outstanding Cmty. Svc. award, 2004, James E. West Fellow award Boy Scouts, 2007; named to Md. Sr. Citizens Hall of Fame, 2001. Mem. Health Physics Soc. (emeritus), Shriners. Methodist. Achievements include design of instrumentation to measure thermal radiation from nuclear tests; gamma radiation shielding studies; evaluation of radioactive sealed sources and devices for AEC licenses; evaluation of shipping casks for spent reactor fuel; tech. asst. to AEC office of Hearing Examiner on Contract Appeal cases and nuclear power reactor licensing; evaluation of power reactor site safety and design basis accidents. Home: 227 Rolling Rd Gaithersburg MD 20877-2041

FERRELL, CONCHATA GALEN, actress, performing arts educator; b. Charleston, W.Va., Mar. 28, 1943; d. Luther Martin and Mescal Loraine (George) F.; m. Arnold A. Anderson; 1 dau., Samantha. Student, W.Va. U., 1961-64, Marshall U., 1967-68. Actor: (NY theater appearances) The Hot L Baltimore, 1973, The Sea Horse, 1973—74 (OBIE award and Drama Desk award, 1974), Battle of Angels, 1975; (plays) Getting Out, 1978, Here Wait, 1980, Picnic, 1986; (TV series) The Hot L Baltimore, 1975, B.J. and the Bear, 1979, McClain's Law, 1981, E.R., 1984, A Peaceable Kingdom, 1989, L.A. Law, 1991, Hearts Afire, 1993—94, Townies, 1996, Teen Angel, 1997, Push, Nevada, 2002, Two & 1/2 Men, 2003—, (movies) Network, 1975, Dangerous Hero, 1975, Heartland, 1981, Where the River Runs Black, 1986, For Keeps, 1987, Mystic Pizza, 1987, Witches of Eastwick, 1987, Chains of Gold, 1990, Edward Scissorhands, 1990, Family Prayers, 1993, True Romance, 1993, Samurai Cowboy, 1993, Heaven and Earth, 1993, Freeway, 1995, Touch, 1996, My Fellow Americans, 1996, Erin Brokovich, 2000, Crime and Punishment-High School, 2000, Stranger Inside, 2001, K-Pax, 2001, Mr. Deeds, 2002, Kabluey, 2007, (TV movies) A Girl Called Hatter Fox, 1977, A Death in Canaan, 1977, The Orchard Children, 1978, Before and After, 1979, Bliss, 1979, Reunion, 1980, The Rideout Case, 1980, The Great Gilley Hopkins, 1981, Life of the Party, 1982, Emergency Room, 1983, Nadia, 1984, Miss Lonely Hearts, 1985, Samaritan, 1986, Northbeach and Rawhide, 1986, Picnic, 1986, Eye on the Sparrow, 1987, Runaway Ralph, 1987, Goodbye Miss Liberty (Disney Channel), 1988, Running Mates, 1990, Deadly Intentions, Again, 1990, Back Field in Motion, 1991, 120 Volt Miracle, 1992, Forget Me Not, 1996, Sweetdreams, 1996, Amy and Isabelle, 2001. Recipient Wrangler award Nat. Cowboy Hall of Fame, 1981, Most Promising Newcomer award Theatre World, 1974, Emmy award nomination, 1991-92, 2004-2005. Mem. AFTRA, ACLU, NOW, SAG, Actors Equity Assn., Women in Films, Circle West. Democrat. Office: 360 N Crescent Pl North Bldg Beverly Hills CA 90210 Personal E-mail: chattagail@hotmail.com.

FERRELL, ELIZABETH ANN, lawyer; b. Morgantown, W.Va., Feb. 10, 1957; BA magna cum laude, U. SC, 1979, JD, 1982. Bar: SC 1982, DC 1985. Law clk. to Hon. Sol Blatt, Jr. US Dist. Ct. Dist. SC, 1982—84; assoc. Pierson Ball & Dowd, Washington, Piper & Marbury, Washington, 1988—91, ptnr., 1991; ptnr., govt. contracts group Sonnenschein Nath & Rosenthal LLP, Washington, 1991—. Office: Sonnenschein Nath & Rosenthal LLP Ste 600, E Tower 1301 K St NW Washington DC 20005 Office Phone: 202-408-6420. Office Fax: 202-408-6399. Business E-Mail: eferrell@sonnenschein.com.

FERRELL, JAMES EDWIN, nuclear energy industry executive; b. Atchison, Kans., Oct. 17, 1939; s. Alfred C. and Mabel A. (Samson) F.; m. Elizabeth J. Gillespie, May 10, 1959; children: Kathryn E., Sarah A. BS in Bus. Adminstrn., U. Kans., 1963. Chmn., CEO Ferrellgas Partners, Overland Park, Kans., 1965—. Bd. dirs. United Mo. Bancshares, Kansas City; past pres. World LP Gas Assn.; past chmn. Propane Vehicle Council. Bd. dirs. Coun. Ind. Colls., 1988-91; trustee Kansas City Symphony, 1987—. Served to 1st lt. U.S. Army, 1963-65. Republican. Lutheran. Office: Ferrellgas Partners 7500 College Blvd Overland Park KS 66210 Office Fax: 816-792-7985.*

FERRELL, MICHAEL J., lawyer; b. Detroit, Mar. 27, 1951; BS in History & Polit. Sci., Mercy Coll. of Detroit, 1973; JD, George Mason U., 1979. Bar: DC, Va. Various legislative positions US Ho. of Reps. & US Senate, Washington; gen. ptnr. O'Connor & Hannon, Washington; sr. staff v.p., legislative counsel Mortgage Bankers Assn. of Am.; founder Potomac Partners; ptnr., legislative & govt. affairs, trade & professional assn. Venable LLP, Washington, 2002—, former co-chair, homeland security practice group, former chair, legislative practice. Office: Venable LLP 575 7th St NW Washington DC 20004 Office Phone: 202-344-8588. Office Fax: 202-344-8300. Business E-Mail: mjferrell@venable.com.

FERRELL, MILTON MORGAN, JR., lawyer; b. Coral Gables, Fla., Nov. 6, 1951; s. Milton M. and Annie (Blanche) Bradley; m. Lori R. Sanders, May 22, 1982; children: Milton Morgan III, Whitney Connolly. BA, Mercer U., 1973, JD, 1975. Bar: Fla. 1975, Ga. 1975, NY 2005, DC 2005, US Dist. Ct. (mid. dist. Ga.), US Dist. Ct. (mid. and so. dists. Fla.),

US Dist. Ct. (so. and ea. dists. NY), US Supreme Ct., US Ct. Fed. Claims, US Ct. Appeals (2nd, 3rd, 5th, 9th and 11th cirs.), US Ct. Appeals (dist. DC). Asst. state's atty. State's Atty.'s Office, Miami, 1975—77; ptnr. Ferrell & Ferrell, 1977—84, Ferrell Williams, P.A., 1987—90; pvt. practice Ferrell Law, P.A., 1990—2006, CEO. Bd. dirs. Authentix, Inc., 2000—05, Stone Technologies, 2000—01. Trustee Mus. Sci. and Space Transit Planetarium, 1977—82; trustee, mem. legal. com., chair com. Project to Cure Paralysis U. Miami, 1985—94; mem. Ambs. of Mercy, Mercy Hosp. Found., Inc., 1985—94; trustee Greater Miami and the Keys chpt. ARC, mem., 2001—, bd. dirs., 2001—, Robinson Charitable Found., 1993—, Performing Arts Ctr. Found., 1998—, Jackson Meml. Found., 1999—2004; bd. trustees Eaglebrook Sch., 1995—98, Mercer U., 2004—; trustee United Way of Miami-Dade, 2000—; bd. dirs. The Founders Mount Sinai Med. Ctr. Found., 2002—; chmn. Jackson Meml. Found., 2004—. Named one of Top 100 Attys., Worth mag., 2006. Mem. ABA (grantee 1975), Am. Bd. Criminal Lawyers (bd. dirs. 1982-83, sec. 1983-85, v.p. 1985-86, pres. 1986-87), Nat. Assn. Criminal Def. Lawyers, Am. Bar Found., Fla. Bar Assn. (jury instrns. com. 1987-89, chmn. grievance com. L 1987-90), Dade County Bar Assn. (bd. dir. 1977-80), Assn. Trial Lawyers Am., Bath Club (bd. gov. 1992-95), Miami City Club, Univ. Club, Banker's Club, Cat Cay Yacht Club, Inc. (bd. dir. 1997-2000, treas. 1998-99, pres. 1999-2000), Indian Creek Country Club, LaGorce Country Club, Fisher Island Club, GlenArbor Golf Club, Farmington Country Club Office: Ferrell Law PA Miami Ctr 201 S Biscayne Blvd Fl 34 Miami FL 33131-4325 Office Phone: 305-371-8585. E-mail: mmf@ferrellworldwide.com.

FERRELL, PAUL CLEVELAND, writer; b. Morehouse, Mo., Aug. 17, 1943; s. Sherman Gentry and Virginia Irene (Brawley) F.; m. Wanda Darlene Jones, Nov. 27, 1963. Student, Mineral Area Jr. Coll., Flat River, Mo., 1965—66, U. Mo., S.E. Mo. State U. Registered technologist Am. Radiol. Soc. Head radiology dept. Madison Meml. Hosp., Fredericktown, Mo., 1965-66; ambulance attendant Pub. Emergency Svc., Sikeston, Mo., 1970-73; tchr. math. Sikeston Pub. Schs., 1978-80, vocat. instr., 1980-85; ghost writer Sikeston, 1981-84; author Bloomfield, Mo., 1985—. Mem. adv. bd. Vocat. Edn., Sikeston, 1980—85; lectr. in math., health and philosophy. Author: Diet and the Cardiovascular Condition, 1995, The Utopian Cause, 1996, Night Reader I, 1997, Night Reader II, 1997, Morehouse Missouri, 1997, vol. 3, 2001, Night Reader III, 1998, Good Son/Bad Son, 1999, The Songs and Dreams of the Iconoclast and the Misanthrope, 2000, others; ghost writer, editor: The Headlee Anthology, 1984; author (cultural newsletter) The Plow and the Stars, 1992-93; inventor game Choice and Chance, 1992. With USN, 1966—70, Vietnam. Mem.: Am. Registry Radiol. Technologists. Avocations: history, performing arts. Office: The Plow and the Stars 21212 County Road 510 Bloomfield MO 63825-8500 Personal E-mail: starplow@hotmail.com.

FERRELL, RICHARD BRADLEY, neuropsychiatrist; b. South Bend, Ind., Aug. 13, 1943; s. Rupert Tyler and Beatrice Bradley Ferrell; m. Melanie A. Ferrell; children: Catherine Lynn Ferrell de Correa, Elisabeth Jane Ferrell Horan, Anne Christine. AB, DePauw U., 1961—65; MD, Ind. U., 1965—69. Diplomate Am. Bd. of Psychiatry and Neurology, Inc., 1975, Am. Bd. of Psychiatry and Neurology, Inc., 2001, cert. in Behavioral Neurology and Neuropsychiatry United Coun. Neurologic Subspecialties, 2006. Asst. prof. psychiatry Dartmouth Med. Sch., 1975—81, assoc. prof. psychiatry, 1975—. Contbr. articles to profl. jours. Girls basketball coach Hanover Recreation Dept., Hanover, NH, 1982—2005; bd. mem. Opera North, Lebanon, NH, 1991—97. Recipient Alpha Omega Alpha Mem., Alpha Omega Alpha, 1969. Fellow: Am. Psychiatric Assn. (disting. life fellow); mem.: Am. Neuropsychiatric Assn. Office: Dartmouth-Hitchcock Med Ctr One Medical Ctr Dr Lebanon NH 03756 Home Phone: 802-649-2728; Office Phone: 603-271-5804. Business E-Mail: richard.ferrell@dartmouth.edu.

FERRELL, ROBERT HUGH, historian, educator; b. Cleve., May 8, 1921; s. Ernest Henry and Edna Lulu (Rentsch) F.; m. Lila Esther Sprout, Sept. 8, 1956 (dec. Jan. 2002); 1 dau., Carolyn Irene. BS in Edn., Bowling Green State U., 1946, BA, 1947, LLD (hon.), 1971; MA, Yale U., 1948, PhD, 1951. Intelligence analyst U.S. Air Force, 1951-52; lectr. in history Mich. State U., 1952-53; asst. prof. history Ind. U., 1953-58, asso. prof., 1958-61, prof., 1961-74, Disting. prof., 1974-88, emeritus, 1988—. Vis. prof. Yale U., 1955-56, Am. U. at Cairo, 1958-59, U. Conn., 1964-65, Cath. U. Louvain, Belgium, 1969-70, Naval War Coll., 1974-75, U.S. Mil. Acad., 1987-88. Author: Peace in Their Time, 1952, American Diplomacy in the Great Depression, 1957, American Diplomacy: A History, 1959, 4th edit., 1987, Frank B. Kellogg and Henry L. Stimson, 1963, (with M.G. Baxter and J.E. Wiltz) Teaching of American History in High Schools, 1964, George C. Marshall, 1966, (with R.B. Morris and W. Greenleaf) America: A History of the People, 1971, (with others) Unfinished Century, 1973, Harry S. Truman and the Modern American Presidency, 1983, Truman: A Centenary Remembrance, 1984, Woodrow Wilson and World War I, 1985, Harry S. Truman: His Life on the Family Farms, 1991, Ill-Advised, 1992, Choosing Truman: The Democratic Convention of 1944, 1994, Harry S. Truman: A Life, 1994, The Strange Deaths of President Harding, 1996, The Dying President: Franklin D. Roosevelt, 1998, The Presidency of Calvin Coolidge, 1998, Truman and Pendergast, 1999, Harry S. Truman, 2003, Collapse at Meuse-Argonne, 2004, Five Days in October: The Lost Battalion of World War I, 2005, Presidential Leadership: From Woodrow Wilson to Harry S. Truman, 2006, Harry S. Truman and the Cold War Revisionists, 2006, America's Deadliest Battle: Meuse-Argonne, 1918, 2007; editor: (with H.H. Quint) The Talkative President: The Off-the-Record Press Confreneces of Calvin Coolidge, 1964, Off the Record: The Private Papers of Harry S. Truman, 1980, The Autobiography of Harry S. Truman, 1980, The Eisenhower Diaries, 1981, Dear Bess: The Letters from Harry to Bess Truman, 1983, (with Samuel Flagg Bemis) American Secretaries of State and Their Diplomacy, 10 vols., 1963-85, Banners in the Air: The Eighth Ohio Volunteers and the Spanish-American War, 1988, Monterrey is Ours!, 1990, Truman in the White House: The Diary of Eben Ayers, 1991, (with L.E. Wikander) Grace Coolidge: An Autobiography, 1992, Holding the Line: The Third Tennessee Infantry 1861-64, 1994, Truman and the Bomb, 1996, (with Joan Hoff) Dictionary of American History Supplement, 2 vols., 1996, FDR's Quiet Confidant: The Autobiography of Frank C. Walker, 1997, The Kansas City Investigation, 1999, A Youth in the Meuse-Argonne: A Memoir of World War I, 1917-1918, 2000, A Colonel in the Armored Divisions: A Memoir 1941-1945, 2001, In the Philippines and Okinawa: A Memoir 1945-1948, 2001, Meuse-Argonne Diary, 2004, Trench Knives and Mustard Gas, 2004, A Soldier in World War I, 2004, Argonne Days in World War I, 2007. Served with USAAF, 1942-45. Mem. Soc. Historians, Am. Fgn. Rels. Orgn. Am. Historians, Am. Hist. Assn. Home: 3496 Daleview Ann Arbor MI 48105

FERRELL, WILL (JOHN WILLIAM FERRELL), actor; b. Irvine, Calif., July 16, 1967; s. Lee and Kay Ferrell; m. Viveca Paulin, Aug. 12, 2000; children: Magnus Paulin, Mattias. Degree in Sports Info., U. So. Calif. Comedian with group The Groundlings. Actor: (films) Men Seeking Women, 1997, Austin Powers-International Man of Mystery, 1997, The Thin Pink Line, 1998, The Suburbans, 1999, Austin Powers: The Spy Who Shagged Me, 1999, Dick, 1999, Superstar, 1999, Drowning Mona, 2000, The Ladies Man, 2000, Jay and Silent Bob Strike Back, 2001, Zoolander, 2001, Old School, 2003, Elf, 2003, Melinda and Melinda, 2004, The Wendell Baker Story, 2005, Kicking & Screaming, 2005, Bewitched, 2005, Wedding Crashers, 2005, The Producers, 2005 (Best Performance by an Actor in a Supporting Role in a Motion Picture, Hollywood Fgn. Press Assn. (Golden Globe award), 2006), Winter Passing, 2005, Stranger Than Fiction, 2006, Blades of Glory, 2007, (voice only) Curious George, 2006,: (TV films) Bucket of Blood, 1995; actor, writer (films) A Night at the Roxbury, 1998, Anchorman: The Legend of Ron Burgundy, 2004, prodr., actor, writer Talladega Nights: The Ballad of Ricky Bobby, 2006 (Choice Movie Actor: Comedy, Teen Choice Awards, 2007), actor, writer (video) Wake Up, Ron Burgundy: The Lost Movie, 2004; actor: (TV series) Saturday Night Live, 1995—2006; voice (TV series) Cow and Chicken, The Oblongs, King of the Hill, 1999, Family Guy, 2000, 2001, guest appearances Grace Under Fire, 1995, Living Single, 1995. Named one of 50 Most Powerful People in Hollywood, Premiere mag., 2005—06. Office: c/o Jason Heyman Creative Artists Agy 9830 Wilshire Blvd Beverly Hills CA 90212*

FERREN, JOHN MAXWELL, judge; b. Kansas City, Mo., July 21, 1937; s. Jack Maxwell and Elizabeth Anne (Hansen) Ferren; m. Ann Elizabeth Speidel, Sept. 4, 1961 (div.); children: Andrew John, Peter Maxwell; m. Linda Jane Finkelstein, June 17, 1994. AB magna cum laude, Harvard U., 1959, LLB, 1962; LLD, Maryville Coll., Tenn., 2007. Bar: Ill. 1962, Mass. 1967, D.C. 1970. Assoc. Kirkland, Ellis, Hodson, Chaffetz & Masters, Chgo., 1962—66; dir. Neighborhood Law Office Program Harvard U. Law Sch., Cambridge, Mass., 1966—68; tchg. fellow, dir. Legal Svcs. Program Harvard Law Sch., Cambridge, 1968—69, lectr. law, dir. Legal Svcs Program, 1969—70; ptnr. Hogan & Hartson, Washington, 1970—77; assoc. judge D.C. Ct. Appeals, 1977—97; corp. counsel D.C., 1997—99; sr. judge D.C. Ct. Appeals, 1999—, disciplinary bd., 1972—76; fellow Woodrow Wilson Internat. Ctr. for Scholars, 2000—01; exec. com., bd. dirs. Council on Legal Edn. for Profl. Responsibility, 1970—80. Exec. com. Washington Lawyers Com. for Civil Rights Under Law, 1970—77; adj. lectr. U. Iowa Coll. Law, 2006—. Author: Salt of the Earth, Conscience of the Court: The Story of Justice Wiley Rutledge, 2004; contbr. articles to profl. jours. Exec. com. of legal adv. com. Nat. Com. Against Discrimination in Housing, 1974—77; steering com. Nat. Prison Project ACLU Found., 1975—77; legis. subcom. on consumer credit Chgo. Commn. on Human Rels. Com. on New Residents, 1964—66; originator, chmn. Neighborhood Legal Advice Clinics, Ch. Fedn. Greater Chgo., 1964—66; treas., bd. dirs. Firman Neighborhood House, Chgo., 1964—66; bd. dirs. Frederick B. Abramson Meml. Found., 1991—97, People's Devel. Corp., Washington, 1970—74, George A. Wiley Meml. Fund, 1974—84, Nat. Resource Ctr. for Consumers of Legal Svcs., 1973—77, Ctr. for Law and Edn., Cambridge, Mass., 1989—94. Fellow: Am. Bar Found.; mem.: ABA (commn. on nat. inst. justice 1972—80, consortium on legal svcs. and pub. 1972—73, 1976—79, chmn. 1979—82, chmn. spl. com. on pub. interest practice 1976—78), Am. Law Inst., Phi Beta Kappa. Presbyterian. Office: Dist Columbia Ct Appeals 500 Indiana Ave NW Washington DC 20001-2131 Office Phone: 202-879-2772. E-mail: jferren@dcca.state.dc.us.

FERRER, MIGUEL ANTONIO, brokerage house executive; b. Ithaca, NY, May 18, 1938; s. Miguel and Conchita (Bolivar) F.; m. Suzan Nudelman, Aug. 1962 (div. 1973); children: Miguel Antonio, Ilena Christine; m. Lizette Gratacos, Sept. 4, 1980 (div. 2000); children: Alejandro Miguel, Augusto Miguel BA, Cornell U., 1959, MBA, 1961. Account exec. Merrill Lynch Pierce Fenner Smith, San Juan, P.R., 1961-65; br. mgr. Eastman Dillon Union Securities, San Juan, 1965-71, ptnr., 1971-73; sr. v.p. Blyth Eastman Dillon & Co., Inc., San Juan, 1973-80, PaineWebber Inc., San Juan, 1980—; CEO UBS Fin. Svcs., Inc. of P.R., Hato Rey, 1983—; chmn. PaineWebber Latin Am., 1993-98; CEO, chmn. UBS Trust Co. of P.R., 1997—. Bd. dirs. P.R. Investors Tax Free Fund, Alianza para el Desarrollo de Puerto Rico, Comision Pro Sede ALCA; dir. consultive bd. U. P.R., Rio Piedras, 1989-92; mem. governing bd. P.R. Strategy Project Bd. dirs. PR Aqueducts and Sewer Authority, San Juan, 1986-88, PR Pub. Broadcasting Corp., 1990-92, PR Mus. Arch. San Juan, Mus. of Art PR, San Juan, 2007; Rafael Hernández Colon Found., 1993-2000, U. PR Found., 1995, 2001; pres. fund raising ARC, Rio Piedras, 1990-91; bd. dirs., treas. Casa del Libro, San Juan; founding dir. Found. Friends of PR Acad. of Spanish Lang., 1996—; trustee Cornell U. Recipient Top Mgmt. award in fin. Sales and Mktg. Execs. Assn., 1980 Mem. Securities Industry Assn. (founding mem., bd. dirs., past pres.), P.R. Fin. Analysts Assn. (founding mem., past pres.), Alianza el Desarrollo PR (founder, bd. dirs.), Com. Pro Sede ALCA (founder, bd. dirs.), Banker's Club Avocations: gymnasiums, art collecting, philanthropy. Home: Cond Millenium PH 8 San Juan PR 00901-2316 Office: UBS Financial Svcs Inc of PR American International Plz Penthouse Fl Hato Rey PR 00918

FERRERA, AMERICA GEORGINE, actress; b. LA, Apr. 18, 1984; Student in Internat. Rels. and Theater, U. So. Calif. Actor: (films) Real Women Have Curves, 2002 (Best Actress, Sundance Jury award), The Sisterhood of the Traveling Pants, 2005, Lords of Dogtown, 2005, How the Garcia Girls Spent Their Summer, 2005, 3:52, 2005, Steel City, 2006; (TV films) Gotta Kick It Up!, 2002, $5.15/Hr., 2004, Plainsong, 2004; (TV series, 1 episode) Touched by an Angel, 2002, CSI: Crime Scene Investigation, 2004; (TV series) Ugly Betty, 2006— (Best Performance by an Actress in a TV Series, Comedy, Golden Globe award, Hollywood Fgn. Press Assn., 2007, Outstanding Performance by a Female Actor in a Comedy Series, SAG, 2007, Choice TV: Breakout, Teen Choice Awards, 2007); (plays, off-Broadway) Dog Sees God: Confessions of a Teenage Blockhead, 2005. Named one of The World's Most Influential People, Time mag., 2007; recipient Movieline Breakthrough award, 2005. Mailing: Ugly Betty Raleigh Studios 5300 Melrose Ave Los Angeles CA 90038*

FERRERA, ARTHUR ROCCO, food distribution company executive; b. Boston, Feb. 1, 1916; s. James F. and Mary (Mangini) F.; m. Mildred Grace Rugg, Sept. 9, 1944; children: Kenneth Grant, James Howard. AB, Harvard U., 1938. Co-founder James Ferrera & Sons, Inc., 1945—, pres., 1945-57, chmn. bd., 1957-89, chmn. emeritus, cons., 1989-91, ret., 1991. Chmn. emeritus, cons. James Ferrera & Sons, Inc.; dir. Commonwealth Bank of Boston, 1966-70; past dir. Romi Foods, Toronto; chmn. food divsn. CD, Mass., 1966. Served with AUS, 1942-46; to lt. col. USAFR (ret.) Name to Mass. Food Assn. Hall of Fame, 1993; recipient Cert. of Recognition, U.S. Dept. Def., 2000. Mem. New Eng. Wholesale Food Distbrs. Assn. (dir., past pres.), Nazareth Food Assn. (dir.), Mass. Food Assn. (Hall of Fame 1993), DAV (life). Clubs: Officers (Bedford, Mass.). Republican. Roman Catholic. Home: 4425 Linthicum Rd Dayton MD 21036-1033 Personal E-mail: murugg@att.net.

FERRERI, MICHAEL VICTOR, optometrist; b. Park Ridge, Ill., May 15, 1967; s. Samuel Joseph and Dolores Jean (Liebich) F.; m. Heather Elaine (Katz) F.; children: Christopher, Anthony. BS in Biol. Scis., U. Calif., Irvine, 1989; OD, So. Calif. Coll. Optometry, 1993. Cert. therapeutic optometrist, Calif., Tex. Extern Ctr. for Partially Sighted, Santa Monica, Calif., 1992—93; pvt. practice Long Beach, Calif., 1993—2000; assoc. optometrist Antelope Mall Vision Ctr., Palmdale, Calif., 1995—99, So. Calif. Permanente Med. Group, Fontana, 2000—. Color vision analysis cons. Dept. Health and Human Svcs., Long Beach, 1994-97; participating doctor Vision USA, Long Beach, 1995-2000. Contbr. articles to profl. jours. Mem. Rep. Nat. Com., 1991—; v.p. congregation Grace Luth. Ch., Long Beach, 1996-99, also elder. Recipient Corning Low Vision award Corning Optics, Anaheim, Calif., 1993, Vision Therapy Enhancement cert. So. Calif. Coll. Optometry, Fullerton, 1993, appreciation cert. for outstanding contbns. to Save Your Vision Week, U.S. Senate, 1997, gov.'s letter of commendation for organizing coloring and essay contest for sch. children State of Calif., 1997, appreciation certificate Calif. Optometric Assn., 1998, Svc. award Kaiser Permanente Optometry Dept., 2003, Cert. of Recognition, Nat. Campaign for Tolerance, 2004, Eisenhower Commn. Rep. Nat. Com., 2005. Mem. Am. Optometric Assn. (contact lens sect.), Calif. Optometric Assn., Fellowship of Christian Optometrists, Optometric Ext. Program (clin. assoc.), Rio Hondo Optometric Soc. (treas. 1997-99). Avocations: camping, golf, watersports. Home: PO Box 217 Corona CA 92878-0217 Office: So Calif Permanente Med Group Bldg 4 Mod 1 9985 Sierra Ave Fontana CA 92335 Personal E-mail: eyedocmf@usa.com.

FERREYRA, RAFAEL ANDRES, agricultural and biological engineer, consultant, researcher; b. Cordoba, Argentina; m. Liliana Ferrer; children: Nicolas, Tomas. Elec. and Electronic Engr., Nat. U. Cordoba, MS in Agrometeorology; PhD in Agrl and Biol. Engring., U. Fla. Rsch. fellow Assn. for Technol. Rsch., Cordoba, 1990—91, Secretariat of Sci. and Tech., Cordoba, 1992—94; mng. ptnr. Dexar, Cordoba, 1993—99; rsch. fellow CEPROCOR-Remote Sensing Group, Cordoba, 1994—99; asst. prof. Sch. Electronic Engring., Cath. U. Cordoba, 1997—99; grad. assoc. dept. agrl. and biol. engring. U. Fla., Gainesville, 1999—2003; cons. Ag Connections, Inc., Murray, Ky., 2003—04, mgr. biol. applications, 2004—. Advisor to the min. of edn. Province of Cordoba, Argentina, 1995—96. Contbr. articles to jours. Vol. Boy Scouts Am. Alumni Grad. fellow, U. Fla., 1999—2003, Brazilian-Argentine Sch. of Informatics scholar, 1989, Karplus Summer Rsch. grantee, IEEE Neural Networks Soc., 2002, Sigma Xi grantee, 2001, Phi Kappa Phi grad. scholar, 2001. Mem.: IEEE, AAAS, Soc. Conservation Biology, Crop Sci. Soc. Am., Am. Soc. Agronomy, Am. Soc. Agrl. Biol. Engrs., Am. Peanut Rsch. and Edn. Soc., Am. Geophys. Union, Assn. for Computing Machinery, Soil Sci. Soc. Am., Internat. Soc. for Ecol. Modelling, IEEE Neural Networks Soc., Sigma Xi, Phi Kappa Phi, Alpha Epsilon (pres., UF chpt. 2001—03), Alpha Zeta. Office: Ag Connections Inc 1576 Killdeer Trail Murray KY 42071 Home: PO Box 978 Murray KY 42071-0016 Office Phone: 270-435-4369. Office Fax: 270-435-4363. Personal E-mail: aferreyra@ieee.org. Business E-Mail: andres.ferreyra@agconnections.com.

FERRI, KAREN LYNN, lawyer; b. McKeesport, Pa., Aug. 15, 1956; d. Edward James and Carole Elizabeth (Petterson) Ferri. BA, Duquesne U., 1977, JD, 1981. Bar: Pa. 1981, U.S. Dist. Ct. (we. dist.) Pa. 1981, U.S. Supreme Ct. 1986. Law clk. Weiler & Dolfi, Pitts., 1980-81, assoc., 1981-84; of counsel Stokes, Lurie & Cole, Pitts., 1984-90; sole practice Murrysville and Pitts., 1984—. Weekend mgr. Ferri Supermarkets Inc., Murrysville, Pa., 1977-90; atty. Ferri Enterprises, 1981-96. Bd. dirs. Crisis Ctr. North, Pitts., 1986-89, vol., 1986-2001; bd. dirs. Planned Parenthood, 1998-2005, Action Fund, 2005-. Recipient Sr. Leaders award Duquesne U., 1977, Am. Jurisprudence award Joint Pubs. Total Client-Service Library Pitts., 1978-79. Mem.: ABA (family law sect. 2003—), Allegheny County Bar Assn. (mem. family law sect.), Pa. Bar Found., Pa. Bar Assn. (family law sect.), Duquesne U. Alumni Assn., Am. Inns of Ct. (Pitts. chpt. 1992—95), Westmoreland County Bar Assn. (family law com., fee dispute com.), Women's Bar Assn. Roman Catholic. Home: 3319 Carriage Cir Export PA 15632-9214 Office: 3950 William Penn Hwy Ste 2 Murrysville PA 15668 Office Phone: 724-733-4666.

FERRIER, RICHARD BROOKS, architect, educator; b. Ft. Worth, Mar. 29, 1944; s. Samuel Foster and Opal Birtha (Brooks) F.; m. Lynna Gail Elmore Mindlin; 1 child, Sean Brooks. BA, Tex. Tech U., 1968; MA in Art, U. Dallas, Irving, Tex., 1973. With planning dept. City of Lubbock, Tex., 1962-63; with Atcheson, Atkinson and Cartwright: Architects, Lubbock, 1963-65, Engring. Assocs., Lubbock, 1966-68; mem. faculty U. Tex., Arlington, 1968—, prof. architecture, assoc. dean, 1980-95; prin. Richard B. Ferrier, AIA, architect, Arlington, 1982-91, Firm X Richard B. Ferrier, FAIA, architect, Arlington, 1991—. With Ralph Kelman, architects, Dallas, 1969-70; assoc. William S. Austin, Architect, Arlington, 1976-80; with Comm. Cons., Arlington, 1970-82; mem. architecture adv. bd. Dallas County C.C., 1983-88; architecture critic Ft. Worth Star Telegram, 1989; lectr., juror in field. Contbr. articles and revs. to profl. jours.; prin. works includeNat. Compact House Design Competition, 1990 (First Place), EML House, 1991, Nat. Cowboy Hall of Fame Addition, 1992, DMA Tower, 1993, Nara Toto, 1994, Bar K R Ranch, 1994, Compact House III, 1996, New Lighthouse Ch., 1997; exhibited in numerous group shows, 1968—, including Dallas Mus. Art, 1991-99, Arlington Mus. Art, 1992-2002, Tex. Fine Arts Assn., Austin, 1992-98, Archtl. Gallery, Chgo., 1994. Named Alumni of Yr., Tex. Tech U. Coll. Architecture, 1993; recipient numerous awards Am. Soc. Archtl. Illustrators, 1986—, 12 awards Tex. Architect Graphics Competition, 1988—, amateur animated film award Cannes Internat. Film Festival, 1973, Romieniec award Tex. Soc. Archs., 1997. Mem. AIA (elected to Coll. Fellows 1993, recipient 12 Dallas design awards 1991-2005, 50 Dallas graphic awards 1980—, including 17 honor awards). Democrat. Episcopalian. Home: Firm X 1628 Connally Ter Arlington TX 76010-4516 Office: U Tex Sch Arch PO Box 19108 Arlington TX 76019-0001 Office Phone: 817-469-8605. Fax: 817-469-1856. Personal E-mail: firmx@aol.com.

FERRIERO, DAVID S., library director; m. Gail Zimmerman. BA, Northeastern Univ., 1972, MA, 1976; MS, Simmons Grad. Sch. Libr. & Info. Sci., Boston. Positions through assoc. dir. pub. services & acting dir. libraries MIT Libraries, Cambridge, Mass., 1965—96; Rita Diallonardo Holloway Univ. Libr., vice provost for libr. affairs Duke Univ., 1996—2004; Andrew W. Mellon dir. & chief exec. Rsch. Libraries NY Pub. Libr., NYC, 2004—. Bd. dir. Ctr. for Rsch. Libraries, Rsch. Libraries Group; mem. Council on Libr. & Info. Resources/Am. Assn. of Publishers Joint Working Group on Scholarly Comm. Mem. editl. bd. Early English Books Online. Hosp. corpsman USN, Vietnam. Office: NY Pub Library 5th Ave and 42d St New York NY 10018 Office Phone: 212-930-0674.

FERRIERO, DONNA M., pediatric neurologist; B., M., Rutgers U.; MD, U. Calif. San Francisco, 1979. Prof. neurology & pediatrics U. Calif. San Francisco, 1987—, chief of Child Neurology; vice dean U. Calif. San Francisco Sch. Medicine, 2005—; dir. Neonatal Brain Disorders Ctr., U. Calif. San Francisco. Chmn. Chancellor's Comm. on Status of Women U. Calif. San Francisco, mem. Chancellor's Coun. on Faculty Life; editorial bd. Jour. Cerebral Blood Flow & Metabolism; adv. bd. Neurophyxia. Contbr. scientific papers; editor: (books) Developmental Neuroscience: Developmental Brain Injury, 2005, Pediatric Neurology: Principles & Practice, 2006. Mem. Soc. Pediat. Rsch. Coun.; bd. dirs. Child Neurology Found., 2000—05, Child Neurology Soc., 2005—. Recipient Disting. Teaching award, Academic Senate, Chancellor's award for the Advancement of Women, U. Calif. San Francisco, 2000, Sidney Carter award, Am. Acad. Neurology. Mem.: Am. Neurol. Assoc., Inst. Medicine (award 2005). Office: UCSF Depts of Neurology & Pediatrics 521 Parnassus Ave San Francisco CA 94143 Office Phone: 415-502-1099. Office Fax: 415-502-5821. E-mail: ferrierod@neuropeds.ucsf.edu.

FERRILLO, PATRICK J., JR., dean, endodontist; b. St. Louis, Mar. 4, 1941; s. Patrick J. Ferrillo Sr. BS in biology, Georgetown U., 1973; DDS, Baylor U., 1976, cert., 1978. Instr. Baylor Coll. of Dentistry, Dallas, 1976-78; clin. asst. prof. So. Ill. U. Sch. Dental Medicine, Alton, 1978-79, asst. prof., 1979-84, sect. head, 1979-87, dir. current affairs, 1982-87, acting chmn., 1984-85, chairperson, 1985-87, acting dean, 1986-87, dean, assoc. prof., 1987—2002; dean Sch. Dental Medicine Univ. of Nevada, Las Vegas, 2002—, vice provost divsn. health sciences, 2002—. Pres. Am. Assn. Dental Schs., Washington, DC, 1999—2000. Fellow Am. Coll. Dentists, Internat. Coll. Dentists; mem. Omicron Kappa Upsilon (v.p. 1988-89, pres. 1989-91), Phi Kappa Phi. Office: Univ Nevada Sch Dentistry 4505 Maryland Pkwy Box 453055 Las Vegas NV 89154 Office Phone: 702-895-2952. Business E-Mail: pat.ferrillo@ccmail.nevada.edu.

FERRINI, JAMES THOMAS, lawyer; b. Chgo., Jan. 14, 1938; s. John B. and Julia (Marre) F.; m. Jeanne Marie Fontana, June 8, 1963; children: Anthony, Mary Caren, Emily, Joseph, Danielle. JD, Loyola U., 1963. Bar: U.S. Supreme Ct. 1963, U.S. Ct. Appeals (7th cir.) 1967, U.S. Ct. Appeals (8th cir.) 1969, U.S. Ct. Appeals (3d cir.) 1975, U.S. Ct. Appeals (6th cir.) 1982, U.S. Ct. Appeals (10th cir.) 1984, U.S. Ct. Appeals (4th cir.) 1987, U.S. Ct. Appeals (9th cir.) 1989. Sr. ptnr. Clausen Miller Gorman Caffrey & Witous, P.C., Chgo., 1963—. Mem. pattern jury instructions Ill. Supreme Ct. Commn., Chgo., 1978-94. Contbr. articles to profl. jours. Mem. Mary

Seat of Wisdom Parish, Park Ridge. Fellow Am. Acad. Appellate Lawyers; mem. ABA, Ill. Bar Assn., Chgo. Bar Assn. (chmn. civil practice com.), Ill. Assn. Def. Trial Counsel, Appellate Lawyers Assn. (pres. Chgo. chpt. 1978, 79), Justinian Soc. Roman Catholic. Avocations: handball, sailing, skiing, cooking. Office: Clausen Miller PC 10 S La Salle St Ste 1600 Chicago IL 60603-1098 Office Phone: 312-606-7597. Business E-Mail: jferrini@clausen.com.

FERRIOLA, JOHN J., manufacturing executive; Mgr. maintenance and engring. Nucor Steel, Jewett, Tex., 1992—95, gen. mgr. Norfolk, Nebr., 1995—98, Crawfordsville, Ind., 1998—2001, Vulcraft, Grapeland, Tex., 1995; v.p. Nucor Corp., Charlotte, NC, 1996—2001, exec. v.p., 2002—. Office: Nucor Corp 1915 Rexford Rd Charlotte NC 28211 Office Phone: 704-366-7000. Office Fax: 704-362-4208.*

FERRIS, CARLISLE KEITH, artist; b. Honolulu, May 14, 1929; s. Carlisle Iverson and Virginia Brecht Ferris; m. Margaret Jo Todd, June 13, 1953; children: Nancy Dean Ferris Huggins, Carlisle Todd. Student, Tex. A&M U., College Station, 1946—48, George Washington U., Washington, 1949, Corcoran Sch. Art, 1948—49; DHL (hon.), Daniel Webster Coll., Nashua, NH, 1995. Apprentice artist Civil Svc., AF Publs., Randolph AFB, Tex., 1947; stripper, opaquer Universal Printing Co., St. Louis, 1951—52; prodn. mgr. Cassel Watkins Paul Art Studio, St. Louis, 1952—56; freelance illustrator Aerospace Corp. Accts., NYC, 1956—58, Morris Plains, NJ, 1958—83; pres., artist Keith Ferris Inc., Morris Plains, 1983—. Lectr., spkr. in field. Mural, Smithsonian Nat. Air and Space Mus., 1976, 1980, Represented in permanent collections USAF, Washington, one-man shows include George Bush Presdl. Libr., College Station, 2003; author: Aviation Art of Keith Ferris, 1978. Trustee Mighty Eighth AF Mus., Savannah, Ga., 2002—. Recipient Laureate award for lifetime achievement, Aviation Week and Space Tech., NYC, 2004, Lifetime Achievement award, AF Art Program, Washington, 2006. Mem.: Am. Soc. Aviation Artists (past pres., founder), Soc. Illustrators (life; AF art chmn. 1967—70, 1979—91, hon. art chmn. 1991—, named to Illustrators Hall of Fame 2006), USAF Thunderbirds Flight Demonstration Team (hon.). Achievements include invention of deceptive air combat camouflage. Avocations: wood and metalwork, photography, collection military and aviation books. Home and Office: Keith Ferris Inc 50 Moraine Rd Morris Plains NJ 07950

FERRIS, CHARLES DANIEL, lawyer, former government official; b. Boston, Apr. 9, 1933; s. Henry Joseph and Mildred Mary (MacDonald) F.; children: Caroline, Sabrina. AB, Boston Coll., 1954, JD, 1961, LL.D. (hon.), 1978; grad. Advanced Mgmt. Program, Harvard U., 1971. Bar: Mass. Supreme Jud. Ct. bar 1961, D.C. bar 1969. Research physicist Sperry Gyroscope Co., Gt. Neck, N.Y.C., 1954-55; asst. prof. naval sci. Harvard U., 1958-60; trial atty. Dept. Justice, Washington, 1961-63; gen. counsel U.S. Senate Democratic Policy Com., U.S. Senate Majority Counselor; also chief counsel to U.S. Senate Majority Leader Mansfield, 1963-76; gen. counsel U.S. Ho. of Reps. Speaker Thomas P. O'Neil, 1977; chmn. FCC, Washington, 1977-81; sr. ptnr. Mintz, Levin, Cohn, Ferris, Glovsky & Popeo, Washington and Boston, 1981—, chmn., Fed. Law Sect. Bd. dirs. Cablevision, Bethpage, NY, KIDSNET, Washington. Author: Cable Television Law-A Video Communications Practice Guide, 3 vols., 1983, rev., 1984-2006. Mem. steering com. Clearinghouse for Children's TV, Washington, 1982-86; trustee Boston Coll., Chestnut Hill, Mass., 1987—; vice chmn. bd. trustees Maureen and Mike Mansfield Found., 1993—. Lt. USN, 1955-60. Mem. Mass. Bar Assn., D.C. Bar Assn. Democrat. Roman Catholic. Office: Mintz Levin Cohn Ferris Glovsky & Popeo PC Ste 900 701 Pennsylvania Ave NW Washington DC 20004 Home: 5610 Wisconsin Ave Apt 1402 Chevy Chase MD 20815 Home Phone: 301-657-8865; Office Phone: 202-434-7301. Office Fax: 202-434-7400. Business E-Mail: cdferris@mintz.com.

FERRIS, JAMES LEONARD, academic administrator; b. Bellingham, Wash., Jan. 15, 1944; s. Gerald Durward and Esther Evelyn (Larson) F.; m. Virginia Marie Dowde, June 23, 1972; children: Eric, Heidi. BSChemE, U. Wash., 1966; MS in Pulp and Paper Sci., Lawrence U., Appleton, Wis., 1969, PhD in Pulp and Paper Sci., 1974; Advanced Mgmt. Program, Harvard Bus. Sch., 1992. Mill engr. Weyerhaeuser Paper Co., Everett, Wash., 1966-67, scientist R & D dept., 1974-75, mgr. tech. svcs. pulp div. Tacoma, 1975-80, dir. R & D, 1980-85, mgr. mfg. pulp div., 1985-88, v.p. rsch., 1988-96; pres. Inst. Paper Sci. and Tech., Atlanta, 1996—. Pres. Inst. Paper Sci. and Tech., Atlanta, 1996-2004; dir. Atlanta Consortium Higher Edn., 1998—; bd. dirs. World Waste Techs., Inc. Bd. dirs. Albany Internat. Corp. Lt. (j.g.) USN, 1970-72, Vietnam. Mem. TAPPI. Office: Inst Paper Sci and Tech 500 10th St NW Atlanta GA 30318-5794

FERRIS, JAMES PETER, chemist, educator; b. Nyack, NY, July 25, 1932; s. Richard B. and Mabel G. (Collier) F.; m. Joan E. Herrlich, Sept. 3, 1955 (div. 1985); children: Alison R., Laura J.; m. Susan Shipherd, Mar. 7, 1992. BS, U. Pa., 1954; PhD, Ind. U., 1958. Postdoctoral researcher MIT, 1958-59; asst. prof. Fla. State U., 1959-64; research assoc. Salk Inst., 1964-67; assoc. prof. chemistry Rensselaer Poly. Inst., Troy, NY, 1967-73, prof., 1973-97, chmn. dept. chemistry, 1980-83, rsch. prof., 1997—. Dir. N.Y. Ctr. for the Study of the Origins of Life, a NASA NSCORT, 1998—; vis. prof. Lab. Organic Chemistry, Swiss Fed. Inst. Tech., Zurich, 1985-86, Salk Inst., 1995; mem. life scis. adv. com. NASA, 1987-88, chair adv. panel on exobiology, 1995—; mem. task force on life scis. of space sci. bd. NRC, 1984-86, past vice chair subcomm. F3 com. space rsch., sci. com. oceanic rsch. working group on hydrothermal sys., 1989-92, mem. space studies bd., 1990-94, com. planetary and lunar exploration, 1998; mem. panel on exobiology Am. Inst. Biol. Scis., 1984-90. Mem. editl. bd. Biosystems. Recipient Career Devel. award USPHS, 1969-74; NRC fellow, 1976 Fellow AAAS, Internat. Soc. for Study Origins of Life (treas. 1980-89, editor Origins Life and Evolution of Biosphere 1982-99, pres. 1993-96, Oparin medal 1996, exec. coun. 2005—); mem. Am. Chem. Soc., Univ. Space Rsch. Assn. (bd. trustees 1999-2005), Clay Minerals Soc., Inter-Am. Photochem. Soc Home: 10 Saddle Hill Rd Wynantskill NY 12198-7616 Office: Rensselaer Poly Inst Dept Chemistry Troy NY 12180 Office Phone: 518-276-8493. Business E-Mail: ferrij@rpi.edu.

FERRIS, ROBERT ALBERT, lawyer, venture capitalist; b. NYC, May 11, 1942; s. Albert Gerard and Helen Elizabeth (Jones) F.; m. Evelyn T. Jarvis; children: Robert C., Kathleen J. AB, Boston Coll., 1963; JD, Fordham U., 1966; grad. Advanced Mgmt. Program, Harvard U., 1974. Bar: NY 1967, Calif. 1973. Assoc. Carter Ledyard & Milburn, NYC, 1966-71; v.p., sec. Arcata Corp., Menlo Park, Calif., 1972-82; ptnr. Sequoia Assocs., Menlo Park, 1982-98; mng. dir. Caxton-Iseman Capital Inc., NYC, 1998—. Bd. dirs. Buffets, Inc., Ply Gem Industries, Inc., Prodigy Health Group, Covant Techs., Inc., Electrograph Holdings Inc.; bd. overseers Hooven Instn., Stanford U.; trustee Fordham U. Served with AUS, 1966-67. Home: 77 Elena Ave Atherton CA 94027-4025 E-mail: raferris@comcast.net.

FERRIS, ROGER PATRICK, architect; b. Buffalo, Jan. 3, 1952; s. Herbert Parkhill and Dolores (Murphy) F.; m. Yvonne DeHaas, May 20, 1995; children: Wren, Georgia. BA, La Salle Coll., 1974; postgrad., Columbia U., 1977-78; M in Design, Harvard U., 1982. Registered arch., Conn., N.Y., Mass., Vt., Maine, N.H., Ill., Tex., N.Mex., Washington, Va., N.C., Pa., R.I., N.J., Fla., S.C., N.C.; cert. Nat. Coun. archtl. Registration Bds. Arch. Victor Christ-Janer & Assocs., new Canaan, Conn., 1974-78; prin. Landworks Assocs., Southport, Conn., 1978-80, Ferris Franzen Assoc., Southport, 1980-82, Ferris Architects, Westport, Conn., 1982-98, Roger Ferris & Ptnrs., Westport, Conn., 1998—. Co-editor: Architectural Practices in the Nineties, 1996. Recipient Progressive Architecture Citation award, 1991, Outstanding Design award James Beard Found., 1997; Loeb fellow in advanced environ. design Grad. Sch. Design Harvard U., 1991, 92. Recipient Smart Growth Masterplanning award, U.S. EPA, 2005. Mem.: AIA (New Eng. regional award excellence in arch. 1985, Design award Conn. 1985—86, Builders Nat. Design and Planning award 1988, 1988—92, Design award Conn. 1989, 1993—94, New Eng. regional award excellence in arch. 1994, Builders Nat. Design and Planning award 1994, Design award Conn. 1996—98, New Eng. regional award excellence in arch. 1997, Builders Nat. Design and Planning award 1998, New Eng. regional award excellence in arch. 1999, 2000, 2001, Design award Conn. chpt. 2002, 2003, Residential Architect Design award 2004, New Eng. regional award excellence in arch. (2) 2005, Design award Conn. chpt. 2005, Honor awards for Design Excellence N.Y. chpt. (2) 2005, cert., Design award Conn. 2006), Conn. Trust Hist. Preservation (Conn. Preservation Design award 1994), Royal Inst. Brit. Archs., Am. Planning Assn. Business E-Mail: ferris@ferrisarch.com.

FERRIS, RONALD CURRY, bishop; b. Toronto, Ont., Can., July 2, 1945; s. Herald Bland and Marjorie May (Curry) F.; m. Janet Agnes Waller, Aug. 14, 1965; children: Elisa, Jill, Matthew, Jenny, Rani, Ramesh. Grad., Toronto Tchrs. Coll., 1965; BA, U. Western Ont., London, 1970; MDiv, Huron Coll., London, 1973, DD (hon.), 1982; DMin, Pacific Sch. of Religion, Calif., 1995; STD (hon.), Thorneloe U., 1995. Ordained to ministry Anglican Ch., 1970. Tchr. Pape Ave. Sch., Toronto, 1965-66; prin. Carcross Elem. Sch., Y.T., 1966-68; incumbent St. Luke's Ch., Old Crow, Y.T., 1970-72; rector St. Stephen's Ch., London, Ont., 1973-81; bishop Diocese of Yukon, Whitehorse, 1981-95, Diocese of Algoma, Sault Sainte Marie, Canada, 1995—. Author: (poems) A Wing and a Prayer, 1990. Home: 134 Simpson St Sault Sainte Marie ON Canada P6A 3V4 Office: Diocese of Algoma Box 1168 Sault Sainte Marie ON Canada P6A 5N7 Office Phone: 705-256-5061. Business E-Mail: bishop@dioceseofalgoma.com.

FERRIS, RUSSELL JAMES, II, writer; b. Rochester, NY, June 11, 1938; s. Russell James and Phyllis Helen (Breheny) F.; m. Ilma Maria dos Santos, June 29, 1968. Student, St. Bonaventure U., NY, 1956-59; BS, U. Rochester, NY, 1967; MS, Emerson Coll., Boston, 1989; PhD, Universal Life Ch., 1983. Cert. social worker. Film inspector City of Rochester, 1962-67; social worker Tulare County, Visalia, Calif., 1967-69, Alameda County, Oakland, Calif., 1969-71. Author: The Unholy Ghost, 1955, They Learn Too Late, 1956, Walk the Slab, 1958, Indian Sign, 1959, The Scream that Toppled Hades, 1960, Crescendo, 1972, numerous short stories and speeches. With USAR, 1956-68. Botany fellow, Emerson Coll., 1989. Mem.: Blue Army, KQED-TV Pub. Broadcasting System, United Macanese Assn., Air Force Assn., Assn. U.S. Army, Res. Officers Assn. (life), Mil. Officers Assn. Am. (life). Libertarian. Roman Catholic. Avocation: aviculture. Home and Office: 202 Font Blvd San Francisco CA 94132-2404

FERRIS, WILLIAM MICHAEL, lawyer; b. Jackson, Mich., May 1, 1948; s. Franklyn C. and Betty J. (Dickerson) F.; m. Cynthia L. Muffitt, June 26, 1970 (div.); 1 child, Christina M.; m. Kathleen S. Santacroce, Mar. 21, 1987; stepchildren: Michael W. Santacroce, Megan D. Santacroce. BS with distinction, U.S. Naval Acad., 1970; JD summa cum laude, U. Balt., 1978, LLM in Taxation, 1994. Commd. ensign USN, 1970, advanced through grades to lt., 1974, resigned active duty, 1977; staff atty. Md. Legis., Annapolis, 1977-78, 80-81; assoc. Semmes, Bowen & Semmes, Balt., 1978-80; ptnr. Ferris & Robin, Annapolis, 1981-83, Krause & Ferris, Annapolis, 1983-87, Michaelson, Krause & Ferris, PA, Annapolis, 1987-91, Krause & Ferris, Annapolis, 1991—. Adj. faculty Anne Arundel CC, 1988—, U. Balt. Sch. Law, 1997-2004 Author: Maryland Style Manual for Statutory Law, 1985; article supr. Md. Annotated Code, 1981-84. Elder Woods Meml. Presbyn. Ch., Severna Park, Md., 1980—; temporary zoning hearing officer Anne Arundel County, Annapolis, 1984—87; hearing officer Anne Arundel County Bd. Edn., Annapolis, 1990—98; pres. Md. Bd. Dental Examiners, Balt., 1987—88; mem. inquiry com. Md. Atty. Grievance Commn., 1987—2001; mem. Md. Commn. on Jud. Disabilities, 1995—2005; treas. Bay Hills Cmty. Assn., 1990—96. Comdr. USNR, 1984—91. Mem. ABA, Md. State Bar Assn., Maritime Law Assn., Anne Arundel County Bar Assn. Republican. Avocations: golf, running, tennis, Bocce. Home: 115 Terrapin Ln Stevensville MD 21666 Office: Krause & Ferris 196 Duke of Gloucester St Annapolis MD 21401-2515 Office Phone: 410-263-0220. Business E-Mail: wferris@krauseferris.com.

FERRITOR, DANIEL E., retired chancellor; b. Kansas City, Mo., Nov. 8, 1939; m. Patricia Jean Ferritor; children: Kimberly Ann, Kristin Marie, Sean Patrick. BA, Rockhurst Coll., 1962; MA, Washington U., St. Louis, 1967, PhD, 1969. Tchr. grade sch., Raytown, Mo., 1962-64; program assoc., asst. dir. Nat. Program on Early Childhood Edn., 1970-71; asst. program dir. CEMREL Inc., St. Ann, Mo., 1969-70, assoc. dir. instrnl. systems program, 1970-71; asst. prof. sociology U. Ark., Fayetteville, 1967-68, assoc. prof., 1973-79, prof., 1979-85, chmn. dept., 1973-85, vice chancellor for acad. affairs, provost, 1985-86, chancellor, 1986-97, prof., 1997—, chancellor emeritus, 1998—. Author: (with Robert L. Hamblin, D. Buckholdt, M. Kozloff and L. Blackwell) The Humanization Processes, 1971; contbr. articles to profl. jours. Office: Dept Sociology Social Work Criminal Justice U Ark Fayetteville AR 72701 E-mail: def@uark.edu.

FERRO, ELIZABETH KRAMS, lawyer; b. Cheverly, Md., Oct. 14, 1948; d. Harry Francis and Jeanne Elizabeth (Edwards) Krams; children: Stephen Christopher, Elizabeth Juliet, Alexander Eli; m. Jose M. Ferro, Oct. 7, 1994. BS magna cum laude, U. Md., 1977; JD, George Washington U., 1982. Bar: D.C. 1983. Adminstr. Raleigh Stores Corp., Washington, 1973-83; atty. Lansfam Mgmt. Corp., Balt., 1983-2000, corp. sec., 1986-2000. V.p., dir. Sidney Lansburgh III Found., 1989—; bd. dirs. Debel Foods Corp., Elizabeth, N.J., 1986. Mem.: D.C. Bar Assn., Phi Kappa Phi, Alpha Sigma Lamda. Roman Catholic. Office: Elizabeth K Ferro Esq 300 E Lombard St Ste 1800 Baltimore MD 21202-6739 Home: 12801 Old Columbia Pike # 126 Silver Spring MD 20904 Home Phone: 301-935-5508. Personal E-mail: eferro1048@aol.com.

FERRO, GUY (GAETANO FERRO), lawyer; b. July 6, 1952; With Marvin, Ferro & Barndollar, LLC, New Canaan, Conn. Contbr. articles to profl. jours.; sr. topical editor: Conn. Bar Jour., exec. editor: Conn. Law Rev. Named one of 100 Top Attys., Worth mag., 2006, Conn.'s Top 10 Lawyers, SuperLawyers mag., 2006. Mem.: Conn. Bar Assn. (past chair family law sect., editor-in-chief of family law sect. newsletter), Am. Acad. Matrimonial Lawyers (editor-in-chief of jour, treas., v.p., first v.p., pres.-elect, pres. 2006—). Office: Marvin Ferro & Gaetano 220 Elm St Ste 100 New Canaan CT 06840 Office Phone: 203-966-9655. Office Fax: 203-966-7006. E-mail: gferro@marvinandferro.com.

FERRON, JENNIFER, marketing executive; BA in Communications, Boston Coll. Acct. exec. Arnold Publ. Relations, Boston; with Kraft Sports Mgmt. Group (New England Patriots and Foxboro Stadium), 1997—, v.p. mktg. ops., 2006—. Media planner FIFA Women's World Cup. Named one of 40 Under 40, Boston Bus. Jour., 2006. Office: New England Patriots Kraft Sports Mgmt One Patriot Pl Foxboro MA 02035-1388

FERRUOLO, STEPHEN CARL, lawyer, historian; b. Providence, July 26, 1949; s. Anthony Frank and Virginia (DePetrillo) F.; m. Karen McLaughlin, Feb. 23, 1974 (div. 1981); m. Carolyn Elisabeth Springer, Aug. 27, 1988. BA magna cum laude, Wesleyan U., Middletown, Conn., 1971; MPhil, Oxford U., Eng., 1973; MA, Princeton U., 1975, PhD, 1979; JD with distinction, Stanford U., 1990. Bar: Calif. Lectr. Bennington (Vt.) Coll., 1977-79; asst. prof. Stanford (Calif.) U., 1979-87; judicial clk. to Hon. Bruce M. Selya U.S. Ct. Appeals (1st cir.), Providence; atty. Heller, Ehrman, White, & McAuliffe, LLP, San Francisco, 1993—. Author: Origins of the University, 1985; co-author: University and the City, 1988; contrbr. articles to profl. jours. Rhodes scholar, 1971; Danforth fellow, 1971. Mem. Order of the Coif. Home: 85 Cavalcade Blvd Warwick RI 02889-1604 Office: U S Courthouse 311 Federal Providence RI 02903-1454

FERRY, DANNY, professional sports team executive, retired professional basketball player; b. Hyattsville, Md., Oct. 17, 1966; s. Bob Ferry; m. Tiffany Ferry; children: Hannah, Grace, Sophia, Lucy, Jackson. Grad., Duke U., 1989. Draft pick LA Clippers, 1989; player Italian League, 1989—90, Cleve. Cavaliers, 1990—2000, gen. mgr., 2005—; player San Antonio Spurs, 2000—03, dir. basketball ops., 2003—05. Bd. mem. Hathaway Brown Sch., Shaker Heights, Ohio, Playing for Peace. Named to Duke U. Sports Hall of Fame, 2004. Achievements include winning the 2003 NBA Championship as a member of the Spurs. Office: Cleve Cavaliers One Center Ct Cleveland OH 44115-4001*

FERRY, DAVID KEANE, electrical engineering educator; b. San Antonio, Oct. 25, 1940; s. Joseph Jules and Elizabeth (Keane) F. m. Darleen Heitkamp; Aug. 25, 1962; children: Lara Annette, Linda Renee. BSEE, Tex. Tech U., 1962, MSEE, 1963; PhD, U. Tex., 1966. Lectr. U. Tex., Austin, 1966; postdoctoral fellow U. Vienna, 1966-67; asst. prof., then assoc. prof. Tex. Tech. U., Lubbock, 1967-73; sci. officer Office Naval Rsch., Arlington, Va., 1973-77; prof., head elec. engring. Colo. State U., Ft. Collins, 1977-83; Regent's prof., dir. Ctr. for Solid State Electronics Rsch. Ariz. State U., Tempe, 1983-89, Regent's prof., chair elec. computing engring., 1989-92, Regent's prof., 1992—. Mem. microelectronics panel NRC, Washington, 1977-79; mem. materials rsch. coun. Def. Advanced Rsch. Projects Agy., Arlington, 1982-98; mem. supercomputer adv. group NSF, Washington, 1984-87. Author (with D.R. Fannin): Physical Electronics, 1971; author: (with L.A. Akers and E.W. Greeneich) Ultra Large Scale Integrated Microelectronics, 1988, Semiconductors, 1991; author: (with R.O. Grondin) Physics of Submicron Devices, 1991, Quantum Mechanics, 1995, 2d edit., 2000; author: (with S.M. Goodnick) Transport in Nanostructures, 1997, Semiconductor Transport, 2000; author: (with J.P. Bird) Electronic Materials and Devices, 2001, Semiconductor Transport, 2001; numerous pub. sci. articles; editor: GaAs Technology, 1985, GaAs Technology II, 1989; editor: (with J.R. Barker and C. Jacoboni) Physics of Nonlinear Transport in Semiconductors, 1979, Granular Nonelectronics, 1991; editor: (with C. Jacoboni) Quantum Transport in Semiconductors, 1992; editor: (with C. Jacoboni, A.P. Jauho, H.L. Grubin) Quantum Transport in Ultrasmall Devices, 1995; editor: (with S. Odd) Silicon Nanoelectronics, 2005; patentee in field. Fellow IEEE (Cledo Brunetti prize for advancements in nanoelectronics 1999), Am. Phys. Soc.; mem. Sigma Xi. Avocations: photography, skiing. Office: Ariz State U Elec Dept Tempe AZ 85287

FERRY, JOAN EVANS, school counselor; b. Summit, NJ, Aug. 20, 1941; d. John Stiger and Margaret Darling (Evans) F. Attended, Lansdale Sch. Bus., Pa., 1962, Lehigh U., 1965; BS, U. Pa., 1964; EdM, Temple U., 1967; postgrad., U. Hawaii, 1968, U. Pitts., 1970, Villanova U., 1981. Cert. cash flow cons. Am. Cash Flow Inst., Orlando, Fla., 2004, sch. counselor, play therapist, youth effectiveness therapist, parent effectiveness therapist. Indsl. photographer Bucksco Mfg. Co., Inc., Quakertown, Pa., 1958-59; math. and German tutor St. Lawrence U., Canton, NY, 1959-61; research asst. U. Pa., Phila., 1963; tchr. elem. sch. Pennridge Schs., Perkasie, Pa., 1964—77, elem. sch. counselor, 1979—2001; pvt. practice counselor, real estate partnership Perkasie, 1981—; asst. mgr. Holiday House Pool & Recreation Ctr., 1981—87; chair child study team Perkasie Elem. Sch., 1988-94; editor Princeton Pub. Group, NJ, 2000—; owner Capitial Funding Solutions, 2003—; self-employed as cash flow cons., 2004—. Tutor math., German, St. Lawrence U., Canton, N.Y., 1959-61; dir. first aid, tennis instr. Harry Hopman Internat. Tennis Camp, Amherst, Mass., 1970-74; supervisory tchr. East Stroudsburg U., Pennridge Schs., 1971-74; research asst. U. Pa., Phila., 1963; mem. acad. coms. for Pennridge Schs.; adj. faculty Bucks County Community Coll., 1983—; instr. Am. Inst. Banking, 1982—; notary pub., 1986—; mcpl. auditor, sec. bd. auditors, 1984-90, mcpl. auditor 1990—, chmn. bd. auditors 1990—; cons. in field. Author Learning Styles of Elementary School Children, 1963; Angola: A Nation in Ferment, 1963; Relationships of Selected Variables in a Fifth Grade Classroom, 1966; author (with others) Life-Time Sports for the College Student: A Behavioral Objective Approach, 1971, 3d rev. edit. 1978; Elementary Social Studies as a Learning System, 1976; Studies in the Care of the Chronically Ill and Disabled, 1978; Studies in the Care of the Chronically Ill and Disabled, 1978 Vol. elem. sch. counselor Perkasie, 1979-81; life saving and tennis instr., 1981-87; mem. Hilltown Civic Assn., 1965-70, 92—; vol. Mennonite Disaster Svcs., 1966-69; chair exec. com. Hilltown PTO, 1965-73; soloist Good Shepherd Episcopal Ch. Choir, Hilltown, 1964-77, mem. choir, 2000—; mem. steering com. Perkasie Sch., 1989-95; poll watcher, 1993; med. vol. Olympics, Atlanta, 1996; vol. Dublin Ambulance Squad, 1996-2000, House Rabbit Soc., Chadds Ford, Pa., 1998—, Spl. Olympics World Games, Summer, N.C., 1999, Silverdale Quick Response Med. Svc., 1999-2001, Chalfont Ambulance Squad, 2000—; mem. Dublin Vol. Fire and Ambulance Co., Silverdale (Pa.) Fire Co.; mem. prin.'s round table Perkasie (Pa.) Sch., 1997; vol. House Rabbit Soc. Southeastern Pa./Del. Foster Home and Sanctuary, Chadds Ford, Pa., 1998—; vol. marshal Wachovia US Pro Championship Cycling Race, Phila., 1999-2006; vol. spl. driver Bush Family and Friends at Rep. Nat. Conv., Phila., 2000, Bucks County Crisis Response Team, 2001—; mem. Chalfont Chem. Fire Engine Co. No. 1; mem. Nat. Arbor Day Found., Best Friends Animal Sanctuary; mem. Pres. task force on small bus. issues, Nat. Fed. Bus. Issues, 2005—. NSF grantee, Washington, 1972-73, Philanthropic Edn. Orgn. grantee, Doylestown, Pa., 1982; recipient Judith Netzky Meml. Fellowship award B'nai B'rith, Phila., 1979, awards Am. Cancer Soc., 1984-86, Internat. Honor Soc. In Edn., 1986, Achievement award Women's Inner Circle, 1990, Golden Acad. award for lifetime achievement, 1991, World Biography Hall Fame, 1991, Hon. Educator cert. St. Joseph's Indian Sch., 1984-86, ARC, Cert. Achievement in Recognition of Contbn. as Med. Svcs. Vol. at Centennial Olympic Games, 1996, Honor Award for Svc. to Edn. and Tchg. Profession, 1996, 99, Cert. of recognition. Internat. Olympic Com., 1997, Cert. of appreciation Atlanta Olympics Med. Team, 1997; Durning scholar Delta Delta Delta, Arlington, Tex., 1981, Am. Mgmt. Assns. scholar, NYC, 1983; named to Internat. Tennis Hall of Fame, 1972, Cmty. Leaders of Am. Hall of Fame, 1990, Internat. Bus. and Profl. Women's Hall of Fame, 1994, Cert. of Appreciation , Nat. Ski Patrol Sys., 1997, Millennium Hall of Fame, 1999; World Whos' Who Hall of Fame, 2001, Women's Internat. Hall of Fame, 2003, recipient Lifetime Achievement Acad. Humane Soc. US, award for Outstanding Svc. to Edn. Pennridge Schs., 1999, Cert. of appreciation Spl. Olympics World Summer Games, 1999, Nancy Sugalski Outstanding Dedication award, 1999, Disting. Hall Fame, Internat. Directory, 2000, Internat. Educator of Yr. award, Biog. Assn. Ely, World Lifetime Achievement award, Raleigh, 2003, 07, Decree of Excellence, St. Thomas' Pl., Great Britain, 2006. Mem. AAUW, NEA, NAFE, Humane Soc. U.S., Pa. State Edn. Assn. (polit. action com. for edn., chair Pennridge Schs. 1986—, del. leadership conf. 1987, 89, Honor award for svc. to edn. and tchg. profession, 1996, 99), Pennridge Edn. Assn. (faculty rep. 1986-88, exec. coun. 1986—, negotiations resource com. 1987-89, 1990-93, steering com. Perkasie Sch. 1989-95, chair Child Study Team, 1988-94, Instructional Support Team, 1992—), Am. Inst. Banking (chair 1987), U.S. Tennis Assn. (hon. life), Pa. and Mid. States Tennis Assn. (hon. life), U.S. Profl. Tennis Registry, Mid. States Profl. Tennis Registry, Women's Internat. Tennis Assn., Nat. Ski Patrol (Svc. Recognition award 1994, 2004), Spring Mountain Ski Patrol (Outstanding Aux., 1993, 1999, Dedication award, 1995, Svc. award, 1996,

2004), Pa. Elected Women's Assn., Bucks County Assn. Twp. Ofcls., Bucks County Sch. Counselors Assn., Pa. Sch. Counselors Assn., Pa. Assn. Notaries, Am. Soc. Notaries, Am. Cash Flow Assn., Phila. Area Cash Flow Assn., Internat. Fedn. Univ. Women, Internat. Platform Assn., Rails-to-Trails Conservancy, World Wildlife Fund, Bucks County Sch. Counselors Assn., Pa. Assn. Sch. Retirees, Highpoint Athletic Club, Pennridge Cmty. Rep. Club. (rec. sec. 1986-91, publicity chmn. 1991-92, Pen care chmn. 1992—), Assn. Tennis Profls. Tour Tennis Ptnrs., Sierra Club, The Nature Conservancy, Nat. Parks Conservation Assn., Ocean Conservancy, Nat. Wildlife Fedn., John Wayne Found., Nat. Fedn. Indep. Bus., Mediterranean Club, Phila. Sports Club, Delaware Valley Jaguar Club, Jaguar Clubs N.Am., Internat. Yacht Racing Assn., Peace Valley Yacht Club, Kappa Delta Pi, U. Pa. Alumni Club of Bucks County. Episcopalian. Avocations: land and water sports, flying, music, photography, travel. Office Phone: 215-738-3600. Personal E-mail: joanferry@comcast.net. Business E-Mail: capitalfundingsolutions@comcast.net.

FERRY, MARTHA MORTON, non-profit executive; b. Amherst, Mass., Apr. 5, 1945; d. Edward Morrison and Dorothy Mae (Beck) F. AB, Mt. Holyoke Coll., 1966; MBA, Harvard U., 1968. Asst. mgmt. sci. officer Bankers Trust Co., NYC, 1968-71; v.p. Am. Express Internat. Bank Corp., NYC, 1971-82; sr. v.p. Nat. Westminster Bank USA, NYC, 1982-88; CFO Cmty. Svc. Soc. of N.Y., 1989—2002, Assn. Jr. Leagues Internat., 2002—; Bd. dirs. NY Women's Found., 2001—07, treas., 2002—04, bd. dirs., NYC YWCA, 1987-99, bd. trustees, 1st Presbyn. Ch., NYC, 1997-2000, session, 2000-02, 04-05. Mem. Fin. Womens Assn. N.Y., Alumnae Assn. Mt. Holyoke Coll. (treas. 1983-86), Harvard Club, Mt. Holyoke Club (pres. 1974-75, bd. dirs. 1988-98). Democrat. Presbyterian. Avocations: travel, reading, performing arts. Office Phone: 212-951-8364.

FERRY, MILES YEOMAN, state legislator; b. Brigham City, Utah, Sept. 22, 1932; s. John Yeoman and Alda (Cheney) F.; m. Suzanne Call, May 19, 1952; children: John, Jane Ferry Stewart, Ben, Sue Ferry Thorpe; foster children: Helen and Nora Buck. BS, Utah State U., 1954. Rancher, Corinne, Utah, 1952; pres. J.Y. Ferry & Son, Inc.; mem. Utah Ho. of Reps., 1965-66, Utah Senate, 1967-84, minority whip, 1975-76, minority leader, 1977-78, pres. senate, 1979-84; mem. presdl. advisor commn. on intergovtl. affairs, 1984; mem. governing bd. Council State Govts., 1983-84. V.p. Legis./Exec. Consulting Firm, 1994—; chmn. Corinne Cemetery Dist., 1989—. Pres. Brigham Jr. C. of C., 1956-61, Nat. Conf. of State Legislators, 1984, v.p., 1982, pres.-elect, 1983, pres., 1984; v.p. Utah Jr. C. of C., 1960-61; nat. dir. Utah Jaycees, 1961-62; pres. Farm Bur. Box Elder County, 1958-59; food and agr. commr. USDA, commr. agr. State of Utah, 1985-93. Recipient award of merit Boy Scouts Am., 1976, Alumnusi of Yr. award Utah State U., 1981, award of merit Utah Vocat. Assn., 1981, Friend of Agr. award Utah Farm Bur., 1988, Cert. Appreciation USDA, 1988, Contbn. to Agr. award Utah-Idaho Farmers Union, 1989, Disting. Svc. award Utah State U., 1993, 94; named Outstanding Young Man of Yr., Brigham City Jr. C. of C., 1957, Outstanding Nat. Dir. U.S. Jaycees, 1963, Outstanding Young Man in Utah, Utah Jr. C. of C., 1961, Outstanding Young Farmer, 1958, One of 3 Outstanding Young Men of Utah, 1962, Rep. Legislator of Yr., 1984, One of 10 Outstanding Legislators of Yr., 1984. Mem. SAR, Sons Utah Pioneers, Gov.'s Cabinet, Utah Commn. Agr., Fed. Rsch. Com., Nat. Assn. State Depts. Agr. (bd. dirs. 1989), Western Assn. of State Depts. of Agr. (v.p. 1990-91, pres. 1991-92), Western U.S. Agr. Trade Assn. (sec. treas- elect 1987-88, pres. 1989-90), Utah Cattlemen's Assn., Nat. Golden Spike Assn. (dir. 1958—), Phi Kappa Phi, Pi Kappa Alpha. Republican. Address: 815 N 6800 W Corinne UT 84307-9737 Office Phone: 435-744-2258. Personal E-mail: lec23@comcast.net.

FERSHTMAN, JULIE ILENE, lawyer; b. Detroit, Apr. 3, 1961; d. Sidney and Judith Joyce (Stoll) F.; m. Robert S. Bick, Mar. 4, 1990. Student, Mich. State U., 1979-81, James Madison Coll., 1979-81; BA in Philosophy and Polit. Sci., Emory U., 1983, JD, 1986. Bar: Mich. 1986, U.S. Dist. Ct. (ea. dist.) Mich. 1986, U.S. Ct. Appeals (6th cir.) 1987, U.S. Dist. Ct. (we. dist.) Mich. 1993. Assoc. Miller, Canfield, Paddock and Stone, Detroit, 1986-89; assoc. Miro, Miro & Weiner P.C., Bloomfield Hills, Mich., 1989-92; pvt. practice, Bingham Farms, Mich., 1992—; of counsel Zausmer, Kaufman August & Caldwell, P.C., Farmington Hills, Mich., 2002—. Adj. prof. Schoolcraft Coll., Livonia, Mich., 1994—; lectr. in field. Author: Equine Law & Horse Sense, 1996, More Equine Law and Horse Sense, 2000 Bd. dirs. Franklin Cmty. Assn., 1989-92, sec., 1991-92; mem. Franklin Planning Commn., 1993-94; bd. dirs. Am. Youth Horse Coun., 2003—. Recipient Nat. Ptnr. in Safety award Assn. for Horsemanship Safety and Edn., 1997, Outstanding Achievement award Am. Riding Instrs. Assn., 1998, Catalyst award, 2002; named one of 40 Bus. Leaders Under 40, Crain's Detroit Bus., 1996. Mem. ABA (planning bd. litigation sect. young lawyers divsn., vice chair ABA/TIPS animal ins. law 2005—), FBA (courthouse tours com. Detroit chpt., featured in Barrister mag. in 21 Young Lawyers Leading US into 21st Century 1995), State Bar Mich. (exec. coun. young lawyers sect. 1989-96, chmn. 1995-96, bd. commrs. 1994-96, 99—, grievance com. 1997-99, structure and governance com. 1997-98, strategic planning action group 2001, rep. assn. 1997-2002, chmn. rep. assembly 2001-02, exec. com. 2006—), Oakland County Bar Assn. (profl. com. 1995—, chmn. 1998-99 Inns of Ct. com. 1995—, chair 1998-99, bd. dirs. 2001—, sec. 2007—, Professionalism award 2000), Mich. State Bar Found. (trustee 2003—), Markel Equestrian Safety Bd., Women Lawyers Assn., Soc. Coll. Journalists, Phi Alpha Delta, Omicron Delta Kappa, Phi Sigma Tau, Pi Sigma Alpha. Avocations: horse showing, writing, music, art. Office: 31700 Middlebelt Rd Ste 150 Farmington Hills MI 48334 Home: 31700 Briarcliff Franklin MI 48025 Office Phone: 248-851-4111. Personal E-mail: fershtman@aol.com.

FERSTANDIG ARNOLD, GAIL, research scientist, educator; m. Edward Arnold, 1981; children: Elizabeth, Emily. PhD, Purdue U., 1987. Sr. rsch. scientist Rutgers U., Ctr. of Advanced Biotechnology and Medicine, Piscataway, NJ, 1987—. Partnered (with husband Edward Arnold) in 1987 to form laboratory at Rutgers University, Center of Advanced Biotechnology and Medicine that is working with a 20 member research team to develop and apply structure-based drug and vaccine designs for the treatment and prevention of serious human diseases, most notably AIDS. Co-directs (with husband Edward Arnold) an effort to develop chimeric human rhinoviruses as potential vaccines for HIV/AIDS. Office: Rutgers U Ctr Advanced Biotechnology & Medicine 679 Hoes Ln Rm 020 Piscataway NJ 08854 Office Phone: 732-235-4343. Office Fax: 732-235-5788. Business E-Mail: gfarnold@cabm.rutgers.edu.

FERTIG, HOWARD, publishing executive; b. NYC; s. Benjamin and Rose (Mallman) F.; children: Paul, Daniel; m. Ana-Maria Daranga, 2004. BA, NYU. Asst. editor Commentary mag., NYC, 1960; editor Alfred A. Knopf, Inc., NYC, 1961-62; chief editor Univ. Library Paperbacks, Grosset & Dunlap, Inc., NYC, 1962-65; pres., editor-in-chief Howard Fertig, Pub., NYC, 1966—. Mem. MLA, P.E.N., Am. Hist. Assn., Friends of Columbia Library. Office: Howard Fertig Pub 80 E 11th St New York NY 10003-6000 Home: 235 Garth Rd Scarsdale NY 10583 Office Phone: 212-982-7922.

FERTITTA, GEORGE A., marketing executive; b. June 16, 1946; m. Naomi G. Fertitta; 2 children. BA, Tulane U. Founding ptnr., pres., CEO Margeotes Fertitta Powell (previously Margeotes Fertitta & Ptnrs.), NYC, 1973, chmn., 2006; CEO mktg. ops. NYC, 2006—. Bd. dirs. PowerOne Media Inc. Office: NYC & Co 810 Seventh Ave New York NY 10019

FERVENZA, FERNANDO C., nephrologist, educator; b. Livramento, R.S., Brazil, Nov. 21, 1958; s. Fernando E. and Lorena C. Fervenza; 1 child, Sophia. MD, PUCRS, 1982; PhD, Oxford U., 1991. Diplomate Am. Bd. Internal Medicine and Nephrology. Sr. house officer, sr. registrar Renal Unit Oxford U., England, 1986—91; asst. prof. Medicine PUCRS, Porto Alegre, Brazil, 1991—93; fellow Nephrology divsn. Stanford U., Calif., 1993—97; resident Internal Medicine Mayo Clinic, Rochester, Minn., 1997—99; asst. prof. Mayo Med. Sch., Rochester, Minn., 1999—2004; assoc. prof. Mayo Clinic Coll. Medicine, Rochester, Minn., 2004—. Cons. nephrology, hypertension Mayo Clinic, Rochester, 1999—. Fellow: ACP, Am. Soc. Nephrology. Office: Mayo Clinic 200 First St SW Rochester MN 55905 Office Phone: 507-266-7961. Office Fax: 507-266-7891. Business E-Mail: fervenza.fernando@mayo.edu.

FERZLI, GEORGE SALEM, surgeon; b. Lebanon, Jan. 10, 1955; came to U.S., 1979; s. Salem and Milia Ferzli; m. Berthe Ferzli, Aug. 25, 1983; children: Georgina, Christina, George Jr., Christopher. MD, St. Joseph U., Beirut, 1979. Lic. physician, France, N.J., N.Y.; diplomate Am. Bd. Gen. Surgery, Am. Bd. Surg. Critical Care. Resident gen. surgery S.I. (N.Y.) U. Hosp., 1979-84, dir. surg. ICU, assoc. dir. surgery, 1984—90, dir. laparoendoscopic surgery, 1991—2003; prof. surgery SUNY Health Sci. Ctr., Bklyn., 1999—; dir. laparoendoscopic surgery Luth. Med. Ctr., Bklyn., 2004—, chmn. dept. surgery, 2005—. Vis. and oper. surgeon NYU, Cornell U., Columbia Presbyn. Hosp., Beth Israel Hosp., Maimonides Med. Ctr., Montefiore Hosp., L.I. Coll. Hosp., St. Mary's Hosp., Valley Hosp., St. Peter's Hosp., U. Medicine and Dentistry N.J. Children's Hosp., Newark, Overlook Hosp., L.I. Coll. Hosp., China, South Africa, France, Russia, Bahrain, Kuwait, Kazakhstan, Greece, Egypt, Lebanon, Uzbekistan Portugal, Belgium, Can., Japan, Singapore, Italy, Dominican Republic; vis. prof. Spain, Portugal, Norway, Singapore, Italy, Belgium, Turkey, Japan, France, Can., Scotland, Poland, Switzerland. Reviewer Jour. ACS, Surg. Endoscopy, Am. Jour. Surgery, Archives of Surgery, Jour. Laparoendoscopic Surgery, contbr. over 100 articles to profl. jours., chpts. to books; patentee in field. Fellow ACS, Am. Coll. Gastroenterologists; mem. Soc. for Surgery Alimentary Tract, Am. Soc. Bariatric Surgery, N.Y. Surg. Soc., Soc. Internat. de Chirurgie, Soc. Am. Gastrointestinal Endoscopic Surgeons, Assn. Francaise de Chirurgie, Soc. Critical Care Medicine, Am. Soc. Parenteral and Enteral Nutrition, Richmond County Med. Soc., Med. Soc. State N.Y., European Assn. Endoscopic Surgery, Internat. Fedn. Surg. Colls. Office: 65 Cromwell Ave Staten Island NY 10304-3933 Office Phone: 718-667-8100. Business E-Mail: info@drferzli.com.

FERZOCO, STEPHEN JOHN, surgeon; BA, Tufts U., 1988; MD, Yale U. Sch. Med., 1993. Intern Brigham and Women's Hospital, Boston, 1993—94, resident in gen. surgery, 1994—2000, assoc. program dir. of residency training program, Dept. of Surgery, chief of emergency surgery, assoc. dir. of Level 1 Trauma Ctr.; assoc. prof. of surgery Harvard Med. Sch. Med. adv. Emmi Solutions, LLC. Office: Brigham and Women's Hospital Divsn General & Gastrointestinal Surgery 75 Francis Street ASBII- 3rd Floor Boston MA 02115 Office Phone: 617-732-6819. Office Fax: 617-739-1728. E-mail: sferzoco@partners.org.*

FESEN, ROBERT A., astronomer, educator; BS, Villanova U., 1971; MS, U. Hawaii, 1973; PhD, U. Mich., 1981. Computer programmer AT&T Comptrollers Dept., New Brunswick, NJ, 1973—76; tchg. asst. dept. astronomy, rsch. asst. Mich. Spectral Catalogue Project U. Mich., 1976—81; NAS-NRC rsch. assoc. Goddard Space Flight Ctr., Greenbelt, Md., 1981—83; rsch. assoc., lectr. dept. astrophysics, planetary and atmospheric scis. and honors dept. U. Colo., 1983—86, fellow Ctr. Astrophysics and Space Astronomy, 1986—89; asst. prof. dept. physics and astronomy Dartmouth Coll., 1989—92, assoc. prof., 1992—98, prof., 1998—. Acting dir. MDM Obs., Ariz., 1992—94. Contbr. articles to sci. jours. Office: Dept Physics and Astonomy Dartmouth Coll 6127 Wilder Lab Hanover NH 03755-3528 E-mail: fesen@snr.dartmouth.edu.

FESHBACH, MURRAY, demographer, educator; b. NYC, Aug. 8, 1929; s. Benjamin and Lilly (Harfenist) F.; m. Muriel Joan Schreiner, Dec. 30, 1956; children: Michael Lee, David Steven. AB in History, Syracuse U., 1950; MA in History, Columbia U., 1951; PhD in Econs., Am.U., 1974. Rsch. asst. Nat. Bur. Econ. Rsch., NYC, 1955-56; economist U.S. Bur. Census, Washington, 1957-67; chief USSR population, employment, rsch. and devel. br., 1967-81; sr. rsch. scholar Georgetown U., Washington, 1981-84, rsch. prof. demography, 1984-2000; sr. scholar Woodrow Wilson Internat. Ctr. for Scholar, Smithsonian Instn., Washington, 2000—. Rsch. emeritus prof., 2000—; bd. dirs. Internat. Rsch. and Exch. Bd., program com., 1975-94; cons. Rand Corp., Santa Monica, Calif., 1981-90, U.S. Dept. Def., 1981-90, U.S. Dept. State, 1982-83, NSF, 1987, World Bank, 1992-93, Health Found. of Russia, 1992, Russian Winter Campaign, 1992; sr. advisor CH2M Hill on Environ. Policy and Tech. in Russia; vis. prof. Columbia U., N.Y.C., 1983-84; Sovietologist-in-residence Office of Sce. Gen., NATO, Brussels, 1986-87; internat. adv. bd. Fernand Braudel Inst. World Econs., Sao Paulo, Brazil; disting. vis. lectr. U.S. Dept. State. Author: Ecological Disaster: Cleaning Up the Hidden Legacy of the Soviet Regime, 1995, Russian Population Meltdown, 2001; (with Alfred Friendly Jr.) Ecocide in the USSR: Health and Nature Under Siege, 1992; editor-in-chief Environmental and Health Atlas of Russia, 1995; editor National Security Issues in the USSR, workship held at NATO, Nov. 6-7, 1986, Brussels, Dordrecht, Nijhoff, 1987; contbr. articles to profl. jours. Mem. Coun. on Fgn. Rels. Served to sgt. U.S. Army, 1951-55. Recipient Silver medal Dept. Commerce, Washington, 1979; Woodrow Wilson Internat. Ctr. for Scholars fellow Smithsonian Instn., 1979. Mem. Assn. Comparative Econ. Studies (pres. 1985), Am. Assn. for Advancement of Slavic Studies (pres. Washington chpt. 1974-78, bd. dirs. 1979-82, v.p. 1984-85, nat. pres. 1985-86), Internat. Union for Sci. Study of Population, Internat. Instn. Strategic Studies, Ctr. for Strategic and Internat. Studies (adv. coun.), Cosmos Club. Democrat. Jewish. Home: 11403 Fairoak Dr Silver Spring MD 20902-3136 Office: Woodrow Wilson Internat Ctr for Scholar Smithsonian Instn 1300 Pennsylvania Ave NW Washington DC 20004-3027

FESKO, COLLEENE, art appraiser; B, Bucknell Univ. Tchr., art hist. Mount Ida Coll.; appraiser Childs Gallery, Boston; cons. Vespi Corp.; joined Skinner, Inc., Boston, 1987, now v.p., and dir., Am., European paintings & prints dept. Appraiser Antiques Roadshow, WGBH-PBS; founder, Firewall Gallery Skinner, Inc. Lectr., writer in field. Mem.: Art Table women in arts orgn. Office: Skinner Inc 63 Park Plz Boston MA 02116 Office Phone: 617-350-5400. Office Fax: 617-350-5429. Business E-Mail: tvappraisers@skinnerinc.com.

FESKOE, GAFFNEY JON, management consultant; b. NYC, Feb. 21, 1949; s. George Jon and Mary Margaret (Gaffney) F.; children: Gregory, Alexandra, Julia, Elizabeth. BS, Boston Coll., 1971; MBA, Fordham U., 1976. With Mfrs. Hanover Trust, NYC, 1971-75; asst. treas. European-Am. Bank, NYC, 1975-77; asst. v.p. Citibank, N.A., NYC, 1977-80; asst treas. US Filter Corp., NYC, 1980-82, Maine Ctrl. R.R. Corp.; v.p. Bank of NY, NYC, 1982-84; cons. Arthur D. Little, Inc., NYC, 1986-88; exec. v.p. Madison One Group, NYC, 1988-93; mng. ptnr. Horton Group Internat., NYC, 1994-95; pres. Halifax Assocs., LLC, Westport, Conn., Navigator Assocs. LLC; ptnr. Handy Assocs. Corp., NYC, 1998—2006. Advisor Halifax Ship Yard, 1997-99. Trustee Yale Libr. Assocs., 1983—; mem. Darien Cable TV and Comm. Commn., Conn., 1985-87; mem. steering com. Friends of Yale Ctr. for Brit. Art, 1989-95; mem. London Libr. Mem. Bibliog. Soc. (London), Bibliog. Soc. Am., Boston Athenaeum (propr.), Can. Soc. NY, Club of Odd Vols. (Boston), Mass. Hist. Soc., Conn. Acad. Arts and Scis., Union Club Boston. Roman Catholic. Office: 191 Post Rd West Westport CT 06880 Office Phone: 203-221-2708. Business E-Mail: gfeskoe@halifaxassoc.com.

FESSEL, WALFORD JEFFREY, rheumatologist; b. London, June 20, 1932; came to U.S., 1957; s. Jack Isaac and Alma (Yarmolinski) F.; m. Nicole J. Noble, Sept. 11, 1957; 1 child, Jason N. MB, BS, U. London, 1955. Diplomate Am. Bd. Internal Medicine. Intern U. Coll. Hosp., London, 1955; resident Can. Red Cross Hosp., Taplow, England, 1956, U. Calif., San Francisco, 1963, 64; rheumatologist Kaiser-Permanente, San Francisco, 1965—, chief of medicine, 1979-89, dir. internal medicine residency tng. program, 1979-89, dir. HIV rsch. unit, 1989—; clin. prof. medicine U. Calif., San Francisco, 1983-97, mem. clin. faculty promotion com., 1986—, emeritus clin. prof. medicine, 1997—. Chmn. regional chiefs of medicine No. Calif. Permanente Med. Group, 1980-89. Contbr. articles to profl. jours. Fellow ACP, Royal Coll. Physicians, Am. Coll. Rheumatology (founder). Jewish. Avocations: gardening, art, music, travel, languages. Office: Kaiser Permanente 2238 Geary Blvd San Francisco CA 94115-3394 Office Phone: 415-833-2854. Business E-Mail: jeffrey.fessel@kp.org.

FESSENDEN, ANN T., law librarian; b. Norman, Okla., Oct. 4, 1951; d. Wayne B. and Tula D. (McCarty) F.; m. Ronald F. Bock, June 6, 1992; 1 child, Michael F. Bunnell. BA in Jour., U. Okla., 1974, MLS, 1977; JD magna cum laude, U. Miss., 1984. Acquisitions asst. U. Okla., Norman, 1974-77; tech. svcs. libr. U. Miss., University, 1978-84, co-acting law libr., 1982; cir. libr. U.S. Ct. Appeals (8th cir.), St. Louis, 1984—. Contbg. author (book) Judicial Opinion Writing Manual, 1991; contbr. articles to profl. jours. Mem. Am. Assn. Law Librs. (exec. bd. 2002-05, v.p., pres.-elect 2006-07, pres. 2007—), Mid-Am. Assn. Law Librs. (v.p., pres. 1992-94), Beta Phi Mu. Office: US Ct Appeals Libr 111 S 10th St Rm 22300 Saint Louis MO 63102

FESSLER, ANN HELENE, artist, photography educator; b. Toledo, Oct. 2, 1949; d. Clifford Manum and Hazel Rose (Grove) F. BA in Art, Ohio State U., 1971; MA in Media Studies, Webster Coll., 1975; MFA in Photography, U. Ariz., 1981. Faculty Webster Coll., St. Louis, 1975-79; vis. artist Tyler Sch. Art, Phila., 1981-82; prof. Md. Inst., Coll. Art, Balt., 1982-93; head photography dept. R.I. Sch. of Design, 1993—. Artist in residence Derbyshire (Eng.) Coll. Higher Edn., 1987, Visual Studies Workshop, Rochester, N.Y., 1989, Glasgow (Scotland) Sch. Art, 1990, 91; bd. dirs. Mus. for Contemporary Arts, 1990—; artist, bd. dirs. Md. Art Place, Balt., 1985-87, artist adv. com., 1983-85; panelist, site visitor Md. State Arts Coun., 1989—. Author: (artists' book) Guide to Coloring Hair, 1982, First Aid for the Wounded, 1987, Water Safety, 1989, Art History Lesson, 1991, Genetics Lesson, 1992. Md. State Arts Coun. fellow, 1985, 88, 92, Nat. Endowment for the Arts fellow, 1989; Art Matters, Inc. grantee, 1990. Office: RI Sch Design Coll Art 2 College St Providence RI 02903-2784

FESSLER, RAYMOND R., metallurgical engineering consultant; b. St. Nazianz, Wis., May 6, 1939; BS, Carnegie Inst. Tech., 1961; PhD in Metallurgy, MIT, 1965. Staff mem. Battelle Columbus Divsn., 1965-68, assoc. mgr. ferrous metallurgy sect., 1968-77, mgr. phys. metallurgy sect., 1977-82, assoc. dir. programs corp. tech. devel., 1982-83, mgr. transp. and structure dept., 1983-85, mgr. advanced materials dept., 1985-86; dir. basic indsl. rsch. lab. Northwestern U., Evanston, Ill., 1987-96; prin. cons. BIZTEK Cons., Inc., Evanston, Ill., 1997—. Fellow Am. Soc. Metals Internat. Achievements include research in physical metallurgy of steels, high temperature alloys and nonferrous metals; fracture toughness; metal physics; optical and electron metallography; advanced ceramics; process and physical metallurgy; polymers; corrosion; electrochemistry; mechanics. Address: 820 Roslyn Ter Evanston IL 60201-1724 Personal E-mail: BIZTEKrrf@aol.com.

FESTA, (AL)FRED E., chemicals executive; BS magna cum laude, SUNY, Oswego. With General Electric, 1981—93; fin. & mgmt. positions through v.p., gen. mgr. Allied Signal, 1993—2000; pres., CEO ICG Commerce, 2000—02; ptnr. Morgenthaler Private Equity, 2002—03; pres., COO W.R. Grace & Co., Columbia, Md., 2003—05, pres., CEO, 2005—. Office: WR Grace & Co 7500 Grace Dr Columbia MD 21044*

FESTA, CONRAD, academic administrator; AB, Wheaton Coll., 1952; MA in Lit., Cornell U., 1960; PhD in Lit., U. SC, 1968; PhD (hon.), Coll. Charleston, 2001. Prof. English Old Dominion U., Va., 1961—87, chair Dept. English Va., 1980—85, assoc. dean Coll. Arts and Letters Va., 1985—87; prof. English Coll. Charleston, SC, 1987—2001, sr. v.p. academic affairs, provost SC, 1987—2002, exec. asst. to pres. SC, 2001—03, pres. SC, 2006—; exec. dir. SC Commn. on Higher Edn., 2003—06. Founder, dir. Inst. for Tchg. and Learning in Higher Edn., Coll. of William and Mary, 1978—; mem. founding team Consortium for Pub. Liberal Arts Colls.; mem. accreditation team So. Assn. for Colls. and Sch., Middle States Assn. of Colls. and Schs. Contbr. articles to profl. jours. Mem. USN, 1952—57. Recipient Award for Tchg. Excellence, Modern Language Assn., 1972, Delta Phi Omega Disting. Faculty Award, 1974, Order of the Palmetto, 2006; Danforth Fellow, 1980. Office: Coll of Charleston Randolph Hall 66 George St Charleston SC 29424 Office Phone: 843-953-5500. Office Fax: 843-953-5811.

FESTA, ROGER REGINALD, chemist, educator; b. Norwalk, Conn., Sept. 6, 1950; s. Reginald and Rosemary (Chappa) F. BA in Biology and Chemistry magna cum laude, St. Michael's Coll., 1972; MA in Agr., U. Vt., 1979; cert. in Adminstrn., Fairfield U., 1981; PhD in Edn., U. Conn., 1982. Tchr. Cen. Cath. High Sch., Norwalk, 1975-79, Brien McMahon High Sch., Norwalk, 1979-82; asst. prof. chemistry Truman State U. (formerly N.E. Mo. State U.), Kirksville, 1983-89, dir. Chem. Comm. Devel. Ctr., 1983-90, assoc. prof., 1989-97, prof., 1997—, coach men's volleyball, 1991-2000, dean frats., 1991-92. Adj. prof. U. Conn., 1983. Author: National Curriculum Development Programming for Teachers of High School Chemistry, 1981, Fairfield County High School Chemistry Curriculum Handbook, 1982. Sec. Diocese Bridgeport (Conn.) Edn. Assn., 1978-79, sci. cons. schs. office, 1979, exec. adminstr., 1979; bd. dirs. Norwalk Community Services Agy., 1980-81. Named one of Ten Outstanding Young Men of Mo., Mo. Jaycees, 1986. Fellow Am. Inst. Chemists (pub. edn. com. 1980-83, edn. editor The Chemist Jour. 1981-95, mem. editl. bd. The Chemist 1986-91, bd. dirs. 1982-99, chmn. nat. meetings com. 1982-91, 94-95, history com. 1982-99, archivist 1983-2002, sec. 1991-93, pres.-elect 1994-95, pres. 1996-97), Am Inst. Chemists Found. (trustee 1992-); mem. Am. Chem. Soc. (founding editor The Fairfield Chemist 1978-79, assoc. editor Jour. Chem. Edn. 1980-89, vice chmn. edn. com. Western Conn. sect. 1979-81, chmn. elect Mark Twain sect. 1985, chmn. 1986, exec. bd. 1984-95, program chair 1984-95), St. Louis Inst. Chemists (founder 1984, pres. 1985-87, sec.-treas. 1987—), Coun. Scientific Soc. Pres. (mem. 1996-97, emeritus 1998-), Acad. Sci. St. Louis, Assn. Frat. Advisors, Coll. Frat. Editors' Assn., Kirksville Jaycees (bd. dirs. 1983-86, sec. 1984-85, chair ret. sr. vols. com. 1985-87), Order of Omega, Delta Epsilon Sigma, Alpha Chi Sigma (assoc. editor The Hexagon 1984-99), Sigma Phi Epsilon (advisor Truman State U. chpt. 1991—, bd. govs. ednl. found. 1993—). Democrat. Roman Catholic. Home: 114 E McPherson St Kirksville MO 63501-3570 Office: Truman State U 100 E Normal Ave Kirksville MO 63501-4200 Home Phone: 660-665-3667; Office Phone: 660-785-4524. Business E-Mail: rrf@truman.edu.

FETCHERO, JOHN ANTHONY, JR., otolaryngologist; b. Jeannette, Pa., June 4, 1951; s. John Anthony Sr. and Cleda (Byerly) F.; m. Wynona Ann Kestler, Feb. 26, 1982; children: John Anthony III, Christopher Jason, Dominic Vincent, Victor Thomas. BS in Biology, St. Vincent Coll., 1973; DO, Coll. Osteo. Medicine, Des Moines, 1976. Intern Des Moines Gen. Hosp., 1976-77; Flight surgeon Naval Aero. Med. Inst., Pensacola, Fla., 1977-78; resident Nat. Naval Med. Ctr., Bethesda, Md., 1980-84; otorhinolaryngologist, oro-facial plastic surgeon Am. Co. Osteo. Opthalmology and Otorhinolaryngology, 1987; otolaryngologist Am. Coll. Otolaryngology, 1988; pvt. practice, Orange Park, Fla., 1988—. Capt. USNR,

1973—2001, ret. Med. Sch. scholar USN, 1973-76. Mem. Fla. Osteo. Assn., Osteo. Acad. Otorhinolaryngology, Am. Acad. Otolaryngology, Am. Osteo. Assn., Fla. Med. Assn., Clay County Med. Soc. Republican. Roman Catholic. Avocations: running, photography, boating, bowling. Home: 2862 Country Club Blvd Orange Park FL 32073-5728 Office Phone: 904-278-3820. Personal E-mail: johnjr@dnamail.com.

FETHKE, GARY C., economics professor, former dean; m. Carol Fethke; 2 children. BA in economics, U. Iowa, 1964, PhD in economics, 1968. Faculty mem. U. Iowa, 1974—, interim pres., 2006—07; prof. mgmt. scis. and econs. Henry B. Tippie Coll. Bus., U. Iowa, 1994—, dean, 1994—2006, Leonard A. Hadley prof. leadership, 2003—. Office: Henry B Tippie Coll Bus Pappajohn Bus Bldg 21 E Market St Iowa City IA 52242-1994 also: Office of Pres U Iowa 101 Jessup Hall Iowa City IA 52242-1316 Home Phone: 319-337-3709; Office Phone: 319-335-3549. Personal E-mail: president@uiowa.edu. Business E-mail: gary-fethke@uiowa.edu.*

FETKOVICH, MICHAEL J., retired petroleum engineer; Retired sr. prin. reservoir engr. Phillips Petroleum Co., Bartlesville, Okla. Recipient Anthony F. Lucas Gold Medal, Am. Inst. of Mining, Metallurgical, and Petroleum Engrs., 1999. Mem.: NAE.

FETLER, ANDREW, author, educator; b. Riga, Latvia, July 24, 1925; came to U.S., 1939, naturalized, 1944; s. Basil Andreyevitch and Barbara (Kovalevski) Fetler-Malof; 1 son, Jonathan. Student, U. Chgo., 1946-48; BA, Loyola U., Chgo., 1959; M.F.A., U. Iowa, 1964. Tchr. Master Fine Arts Program in English, U. Mass., Amherst, 1964-89. Author: The Travelers, 1965, To Byzantium, 1976, Norton Anthology of Short Fiction, 5th edit., 1994; contbr. fiction to lit. quars. Served with AUS, 1944-46. Recipient grants for fiction writing Iowa Industries, 1962-63; grantee Mass. Arts and Humanities Found., 1976, Nat. Endowment for Arts, 1976-77, 83-84, Guggenheim Found., 1978-79; recipient O. Henry awards, 1977, 84 Home: 46 Arnold Rd Pelham MA 01002-9789

FETLER, PAUL, retired composer; b. Phila., Feb. 17, 1920; s. William Basil and Barbara (Kovalevski) Fetler-Malof; m. Ruth Regina Pahl, Aug. 13, 1947; children: Sylvia, Daniel, Beatrix. MusB, Northwestern U., 1943; MusM, Yale U., 1948; PhD, U. Minn., 1956. From instr. to prof. music theory and composition U. Minn., Mpls., 1948—91, ret., 1992. Vis. composer, condr. and lectr. various colls. and univs. Composer: Symphonic Fantasia, 1941, Passacaglia for orch., 1942, Sextet for string quartet, clarinet and horn, 1942, Dramatic Overture, 1943, Prelude for orch., 1946, Orchestral Sketch, 1949, A Comedy Overture for Orchestra, 1952, Gothic Variations for Orchestra, 1953, Impromptu for piano, 1953, Contrasts for orch., 1958, Sing Unto God for mixed voices, 1958, Nothing but Nature for mixed voices and orchestra, 1961, Soundings for orch., 1962, Jubilate Deo for voices and brass, 1963, Te Deum for mixed voices, 1963, Four Symphonies, 1948-67, Cantus Tristis for orch., 1964, Five Pieces for guitar, 1964; opera Sturge Maclean, 1965, A Contemporary Psalm for chorus, organ and percussion, 1968, Prayer for Peace for mixed voices, 1969, Hosanna for mixed voices, 1970, Cycles for percussion and piano, 1970, The Words From the Cross for mixed voices, 1971, First Violin Concerto, 1971, Four Movements for guitar, 1972, Dialogue for flute and guitar, 1973, Six Pastoral Sketches for guitar, 1974, Lamentations for chorus, narrator, percussion and flute, 1974, Three Venetian Scenes for guitar, 1974, Dream of Shalom for mixed voices, 1975, Songs of the Night for voices, narrator and flute, 1976, Three Poems by Walt Whitman for narrator and orch., 1975, Pastoral Suite for piano trio, 1976, Celebration for orch., 1976, Three Impressions for guitar and orch., 1977, Five Piano Games, 1977, Sing Alleluia, 1978, Song of the Forest Bird for voices and chamber orch., 1978, Six Songs of Autumn for guitar, 1979, Second Violin Concerto, 1980, Missa de Angelis for three choirs, orch., organ and handbells, 1980, Serenade for chamber orch., 1981, Rhapsody for violin and piano, 1982; song cycle The Garden of Love for voice and orch., 1983, Piano Concerto, 1984; Capriccio for chamber orch., 1985; Frolic for Flute, Winds and Strings, 1986, Three Excursions, A Concerto for Percussion, Piano and Orchestra, 1987, String Quartet, 1989, Toccata for Organ, 1990, numerous sacred and secular choral works, 1949-93, Twelve Sacred Hymn Settings, 1993, Divertimento for Flute and Strings, 1994, December Stillness for Flute, Harp and Voices, 1994, Suite for Woodwind Trio, 1995, Up the Dome of Heaven, Three Pieces for Mixed Voices and Flute, 1996; Toccata for Organ, 1997, The Raven for basso, clarinet, percussion and string, 1998, Saraband variations for guitar, Folia Lirica, 1999, Lyric Dialogue for Piano and chamber orchestra, 2004. Served with AUS, 1943-45. Recipient Guggenheim award, 1953, 60, Soc. for Publ. Am. Music award, 1953, cert. of merit Yale U. Alumni Assn., 1975, NEA award, 1975, 77, 87; Ford Found. grantee, 1958. Mem. ASCAP (ann. award 1962—), Sigma Alpha Iota (nat. arts assoc.) Home: 174 Golden Gate Pt Apt 32 Sarasota FL 34236-6602 Office: U Minn 100 Ferguson Hall Minneapolis MN 55455 Personal E-mail: paulfetler@webtv.net. *Ultimately there is no way to explain a new work of art if it does not explain itself.*

FETNER, ROBERT HENRY, radiobiologist; b. Savannah, Ga., Feb. 22, 1922; s. William Westcott and Lucille Fedora (Goodrich) F.; m. Mary Carolyn Guiney, July 8, 1972; 1 dau., Amber. BS, U. Miami, Fla., 1950, MS, 1952; PhD, Emory U., 1955. Mem. faculty Ga. Inst. Tech., Atlanta, 1955—, prof. radiation biology, 1963—, dir. Sch. Biology, 1964-70. Cons. in field. Contbr. articles in field to profl. jours.; patentee computer digitizer. Served with AUS, 1942-45. Decorated Combat Inf. badge. Mem. Ga. Acad. Sci. (editor bull. 1960-64), Sigma Xi, Phi Kappa Phi. Presbyterian. Address: 2219 Walker Dr Lawrenceville GA 30043-2473 Office Phone: 770-963-6118. Personal E-mail: roberthfetner@bellsouth.net. *My most rewarding career experience has been as a participant in the search for knowledge in science.*

FETRIDGE, CLARK WORTHINGTON, publishing executive; b. Chgo., Nov. 6, 1946; s. William Harrison and Bonnie-Jean (Clark) F.; m. Jean Hamilton Huebner, Apr. 19, 1980; children: Clark Worthington II, William Hamilton. BA, Lake Forest Coll., 1969; MBA, Boston Coll., 1971. Money market specialist Continental Ill. Nat. Bank, Chgo., 1971-73; with Dartnell Corp., Chgo., 1973-98, sr. v.p., 1977-78, pres., CEO Chgo., 1978-98, chmn. bd., CEO, 1995-98; pres. The Ravenswood Corp., Chgo., 1998—2002; mng. ptnr. Michigan Ave. Ventures, Chgo., 2002—07, Ravenswood Advisors, Chgo., 2007—. Bd. dirs. Clin. Resources Internat., Inc., M.R. Mead & Co. LLC., Old People's Home of Chgo. Author: Office Administration Handbook, 1975. Trustee Lake Forest Coll., 1977-85, 91-95, Jacques Holinger Meml. Found., 1983-95; pres. Dartnell Found., 1989—; trustee Latin Sch. Chgo., 1990-94; bd. dirs. Newcomen Soc. U.S.; internat. commr. Boy Scouts Am., 1992-95, mem. nat. exec. bd., 1986-96, mem. internat. com., mem. Chgo. coun.; pres. U.S. Found. Internat. Scouting 1991-95; chmn. 1200 Club Ill., 1975-84; Rep. candidate for Congress, 1972; del. Rep. Nat. Conv., 1976; bd. dirs. Rep. Fund of Ill., 1980-2006; mem. pres.'s coun. Mus. Sci. and Industry, Chgo., 1986-94. Mem. Ill. Mfrs. Assn. (bd. dirs. 1990-96), Latin Sch. Chgo. Alumni Assn., St. Andrews Soc. (bd. dirs. 1994-97, 98—), Nat. Eagle Scout Assn. (chmn. 1985-88), Chgo. Pres. Orgn. (bd. dirs. 1998-2001), Tau Kappa Epsilon. Republican. Episcopalian. Office: Monroe Advisors 79 W Monroe Ste 920 Chicago IL 60603 Home Phone: 312-664-1988; Office Phone: 312-236-1332. Office Fax: 312-236-1343.

FETSCH, SUSAN HACKLER, nursing administrator, educator; d. Eugene Theodore and Ruth Ann Hackler; m. Robert Allen Fetsch, Oct. 10, 1981; children: Emily Lydon, Elizabeth Ruth. BSN, U. of Kans., Lawrence, 1979; MS, U. of Minn., Mpls., 1983; PhD, U. of Kans., Lawrence, 1991. RN Kans. State Bd. of Nursing, Mo. State Bd. of Nursing. Instr. pediat. nursing U. of Kans., Kansas City, 1983—86, rsch./tchg. asst., 1988—91; asst. prof. of nursing William Jewell Coll., Liberty, Mo., 1991—93; dean of nursing Avila U., Kansas City, 1994—, Robert Wood Johnson exec. nurse leader program, 2006. Mem. task force on minimum stds. Mo. State Bd. of Nursing, Jefferson City, 2004—; site visit evaluator, team leader Commn. on Collegiate Nursing Edn., Washington, 1998—, budget com. mem., 2007—. V.p. bd. ops. Kans. Action for Children, Topeka, 2000—02; adv. bd. Statewide Report Card on the Status of the Health of Kans. Children, Topeka, 1998—2004; mem. steering com. Kansans Connect for Kids, Topeka, 1997—98. Recipient Nursing Rsch. Svc. sward, Nat. Ctr. for Nursing Rsch., 1989—91, Nurse in Wash. Internship Scholarship award, Nurse in Wash. Internship Sponsor, 2003, Kennedy Inst. of Ethics scholarship, Kennedy Found., 1990, Nurse Traineeship award, Dept. of Health , Edn., and Welfare, 1987—88, PhD Award for Outstanding Scholarship and Leadership Performance, U. of Kans. Sch. of Nursing, 1991, Ada Sue Hinshaw Rsch. award, 1990. Mem.: Greater Kans. City Area Nurse Educators (chair 2004—06), Mo. Assn. of Colleges of Nursing, Am. Assn. of Nurses (leadership mentor, new dean programs 2002—05, mem. program com. 2004—), state grassroots co-liaison for Mo. 2004—), Sigma Theta Tau (Internat. Beta Lambda Chpt.). Dfl. Lutheran. Avocations: walking, hiking, bicycling, photography, reading. Office: Avila Univ 11901 Wornall Rd Kansas City MO 64145 Home Phone: 913-764-4815; Office Phone: 816-501-3672. Office Fax: 913-501-2413. E-mail: susan.fetsch@avila.edu.

FETTER, ALEXANDER LEES, theoretical physicist, educator; b. Phila., May 16, 1937; s. Ferdinand and Elizabeth Lean Fields (Head) F.; m. Jean Holmes, Aug. 4, 1962 (div. Dec. 1994); children: Anne Lindsay, Andrew James; m. Lynn Bunim, Sept. 10, 2004. AB, Williams Coll., 1958; BA, Balliol Coll., Oxford U., 1960; PhD, Harvard U., 1963. Miller rsch. fellow U. Calif., Berkeley, 1963-65; mem. faculty dept. physics Stanford U., 1965—, prof., 1974—, chmn. dept. physics, 1985-90, assoc. chmn. dept. physics, 1998-99, asso. dean undergrad. studies, 1976-79, assoc. dean humanities and sci., 1990-93, dir. Hansen Exptl. Physics Lab., 1996-97, dir. lab. for adv. materials, 1999—2002; vis. prof. Cambridge U., 1970-71; Nordita vis. prof. Tech. U., Helsinki, Finland, 1976. Author: (with J.D. Walecka) Quantum Theory of Many Particle Systems, 1971, Theoretical Mechanics of Particles and Continua, 1980, Nonlinear Mechanics, 2006. Alumni trustee Williams Coll., 1974-79. Rhodes scholar, 1958-60; NSF fellow, 1960-63; Sloan Found. fellow, 1968-72; Recipient W.J. Gores award for excellence in teaching Stanford U., 1974 Fellow Am. Physics Soc. (chmn. div. condensed matter physics 1991), AAAS; mem. Sigma Xi. Home: 904 Mears Ct Palo Alto CA 94305-1029 Office: Stanford U Physics Dept Stanford CA 94305-4045 E-mail: fetter@stanford.edu.

FETTER, TREVOR, healthcare industry executive; b. San Diego, Jan. 16, 1960; married; 2 children. BS in Econs., Stanford U., 1982; MBA, Harvard U., 1986. With investment banking divsn. Merrill Lynch Capital Mkts.; sr. v.p. MGM/UA Comm. Co., 1988; exec. v.p., CFO Metro-Goldwyn-Mayer, Inc.; exec. v.p. Tenet Healthcare Corp., Dallas, 1995—96, exec. v.p., CFO, 1996—2000; chmn., CEO Broad Ln., Inc., San Francisco, 2000—02; pres. Tenet Healthcare Corp., Dallas, 2002—03, pres., acting CEO, 2003, pres., CEO, 2003—. Bd. trustees Healthcare Leadership Coun. Chmn. bd. Santa Catalina Island Conservancy; trustee Santa Barbara Zool. Garden. Office: Tenet Healthcare Corp 13737 Noel Rd Dallas TX 75240*

FETTERLY, BARBARA LOUISE, artist; b. Painesville, Ohio, May 28, 1930; d. Ralph Frances and Claire Louise (Marquis) Fetterly; m. Henry Joseph Hargis Jr., June 4, 1955 (dec.); children: Ben William, William John, Glenn D. AA, Citrus Coll., 1985. Artist Art Gallery, La Puente, Calif., 1984-94; gallery owner Hargis Chim Gregg Art Gallery, Pomona, Calif., 1994—. Grantee Millenn Prodn., Pomona, Calif., 1994-97. Mem. Carlsbad Oceanside Art League (life), DA Gallery Non Profit, Pomona Valley Art (dir. 1988, life), Corona Art Assn. (life), Women in Arts Mus. (charter mem.), Covina Arts and Crafts, Parks and Recreation (life). Republican. Baptist. Avocations: amateur radio, tennis, swimming, sewing, pool. Studio: BHUA El Cerrito CA 92881 Office: Gallery SoHo 300 A South Thomas St Pomona CA 91766 Office Phone: 951-340-1060. E-mail: FINEART28@aol.com.

FETTERMAN, DAVID MARK, anthropologist, educator; b. Danielson, Conn., Jan. 24, 1954; s. Irving and Elsie (Blumenthal) F.; m. Summer Fetterman; 1 child, Sarah Rachel BA, BS, U. Conn., 1976; MA in Anthropology, Stanford U., 1977, MA in Edn., 1979, PhD in Anthropology, 1981. Cert. tchr. Calif., Conn. Tchr. Richard C. Lee High Sch., New Haven, 1975-76; dir. Office of Econ. Opportunity Anti-Poverty, Danielson, 1976; tchr. Beth Am and Beth David, Cupertino and Palo Alto, Calif., 1976-78; sr. assoc., project dir. RMC Rsch. Corp., Mountain View, Calif., 1978-82; prin. rsch. scientist Am. Insts. Rsch., Stanford, Calif., 1982-91; dir. MA policy analysis and evaluation Stanford U., 1993—2003, dir. evaluation tng. program, 1993—, dir. evaluation, career devel. and alumni rels., 2003—04, dir. evaluation Sch. Medicine Calif., 2005—; dir. rsch. and evaluation Calif. Inst. Integral Studies, San Francisco, 1993—97. Mem. adv. bd. Ednl. Leadership, U.S. Dept. Edn., Washington, 1987—89, mem. adv. bd. Nat. Rsch. Ctr. Gifted and Talented; trustee Nueva Learning Ctr., Hillsborough, Calif., 1990—2001; chair accreditation team Calif. Inst. Integral Studies, San Francisco, 1994—. Author: Empowerment Evaluation Principles in Practice, 2005, Excellence and Equality, 1988 (Mensa award 1990), Ethnography: Step by Step, 1989, (G. & L. Spindler award Am. Anthropol. Assn., 1990), 2d edit., 1998, Foundations of Empowerment Evaluation, 2002 (Paul Lazarsfield award for contbns. to evaluation theory, Am. Evaluation Assn. 2002); editor: Speaking the Language of Power, 1993, Empowerment Evaluation, 1995. Pres. Mini-Infant Day Care Ctr., Palo Alto, 1992-93. Fellow Am. Anthrop. Assn. (bd. dirs. 1993), Soc. Applied Anthropology (liaison 1989); mem. Am. Evaluation Assn. (pres. 1992-94, Myrdal award 1999), Coun. Anthropology and Edn. (life, pres. 1988-92, Ethnographic Evaluation award 1988), Collaborative, Participatory, and Empowerment Group (chair 1995—, Pres.'s prize 1984). Avocations: computers, internet. Office: Stanford U Sch Medicine Stanford CA 94305 Home: 566 Hopkins St Menlo Park CA 94025-3593 Office Phone: 650-269-5689. Personal E-mail: profdavidf@yahoo.com.

FETTERMAN, JAMES CHARLES, lawyer; b. Charleston, W.Va., Apr. 13, 1947; s. Kenneth Lee and Sara Jane (Shaffer) F.; children: Janet, Paula, Kenneth, David. BA, Miss. State U., 1969, MA, 1970; JD, U. Miss., Oxford, 1972; MBA, St. Louis U., 1985. Bar: Miss. 1972, Sarasota County, U.S. Dist. Ct. (no. dist.) Miss. 1972, U.S. Ct. Mil. Appeals 1972, U.S. Dist. Ct. (mid. dist.) Fla. 1986, U.S. Tax Ct. 1986, U.S. Ct. Appeals (11th cir.) 1986. Staff atty. First Miss. Corp., Jackson, 1976-77; cert. of need adminstr. Office of Gov. State of Miss., Jackson, 1977-78; adminstrator, prin. investigator Miss. Bd. Nursing, Jackson, 1978-79; asst. prof., head dept. fin. Jackson State U., 1979-82; asst. prof. dept. mgmt sci. St. Louis U., Mo., 1982-86; ptnr. Borza Fetterman, Sardelis, Chartered, Sarasota, 1986-89, James C. Fetterman, P.A., Sarasota, Fla., 1989-2000; pres., ptnr. Fetterman & Zitani, P.A., 2001—03; prin., owner James C. Fetterman Chartered, 2003—. Sr. res. adviser to gen. counsel and assoc. gen. counsel Def. Logistics Agy., 1993-94; assoc. prof. Argosy U. at Sarasota, 1987—; judge advocate I.M.A. USAF, 1987; spl. master for zoning and code enforcement Sarasota County, 1991-2000; vol. counsel Am. Radio Relay League, 1995—; legal advisor Family Forum, CompuServe, 1996—. Editor Midwest Law Review U. Kans., 1984-86, also textbooks. Asst. scoutmaster Boy Scouts Am., 1991—95, 1999—, scoutmaster, 1995—98, scoutmaster nat. jamboree troop, 1998, dist. com., 1998—, venture crew advisor, 2001—, aquatics instr., 2003—; mem. sch. adv. coun. McIntosh Mid. Sch., 1999—2000; mem. Sarasota chpt. Eagles Club, 1999—, chaplain, 2001—02, v.p., 2002—03; life guard instr./trainer ARC, 2006—; active Incarnation Ch. Folk Group, 1986—90, 2000—; bd. dirs., v.p., chaperone Sarasota Boy's Choir, 1992—93; bd. dirs. Fla. Inst. Traditional Chinese Medicine, 1998—2002, chmn. bd. dirs., 1998—2002. Capt. USAF, 1972—76, ETO, col. res. USAF, 1972—. Named one of Outstanding Young Men of Am., Jaycees, 1982; recipient award of merit Boy Scouts Am., 1998, Order of the Bronze Pelican, Nat. Cath. Com. on Scouting, 2001, Silver Beaver award Boy Scouts Am., 2003, Venturing Leadership award Boy Scouts Am., 2006. Mem. Am. Bus. Law Assn., Res. Officer Assn. (Sarasota chpt. pres. 1989-91, v.p. 1991-92), Fla. Bar (vice chmn. mil. law com. 1991-94, chmn. 1994-95), Ret. Officer's Assn. (bd. dirs. Sarasota chpt. 1991-93), Am. Legion, Nat. Eagle Scout Assn., Loyal Order Moose. Republican. Roman Catholic. Avocations: running, swimming, amateur radio, ballroom dancing. Office: 4521A Bee Ridge Rd Sarasota FL 34233-2517 Office Phone: 941-377-9595. Personal E-mail: jfetterman@compuserve.com. Business E-Mail: FettermanLawOfc@cs.com.

FETTEROLF, DONALD EDWARD, physician executive, consultant; b. Scranton, Pa., Apr. 26, 1953; s. Donald James and Louise Ann (Pedrick) F.; m. Vicki Lynne Cochran. BA in Chemistry and Biochemistry, U. Pa., 1975, MD, 1979; MBA, U. Pitts., 1991. Diplomate Am. Bd. Internal Medicine, Nat. Bd. Med. Examiners, Am. Bd. Quality Assurance and Utilization Rev. Physicians, Am. Bd. Med. Mgmt.; lic. physician Pa., Ga. Intern and resident in internal medicine Hosp. U. Health Ctr. of Pitts., Presbyn. U. Hosp., 1979-82, fellow in occupational/environ. medicine, 1982-83; pvt. practice Pitts., 1982-88; group practice Allegheny Intermed, Ltd., Pitts., 1988-94; pres., chmn. St. Clair Hosp. LCO, Inc., Pitts., 1987-93; chmn. med. dir. Alpha Health Network, Pitts., 1990-93; sr. med. officer Highmark, Inc., 1994—2005; corp. v.p. health intelligence Matria Healthcare, Inc., Marietta, Ga., 2005—. Mem. staff Canonsburg (Pa.) Gen. Hosp., 1982-93, West Allegheny Hosp., Oakdale, Pa., 1985-86, Allegheny Medcare. Contbr. articles to profl. jours. Fellow Am. Coll. Utilization Rev. Physicians, Am. Coll. Physicians; mem. AMA, Pa. Med. Soc., Am. Coll. Physician Execs., Allegheny County Med. Soc., Mensa. Avocations: chess, computers. Home: 12 Laurel Hill Rd Mc Donald PA 15057-3503 Office: 120 5th Ave Ste 710 Pittsburgh PA 15222-3000 Office Phone: 770-767-7074.

FETTERS, DORIS ANN, retired secondary education educator; b. Bklyn. d. John Joseph and Loretta Gertrude (Stratford) F. BA, Calif. State Coll., LA, 1952. Cert. gen. secondary tchr. Tchr. Temple City (Calif.) H.S., 1954-55, L.A. City Schs., 1955-56; vice consul 3d sec. of embassy Dept. of State, Washington, 1957-60; tchr. U. Rafael Landivar, Guatemala, 1960-63, L.A. Unified Schs., 1964-90. Mem. Am. Fedn. Tchrs., United Tchrs. L.A. Democrat. Roman Catholic. Avocations: gardening, arts and crafts, reading.

FETTERS, NORMAN CRAIG, II, retired banker; b. Pitts., Aug. 27, 1942; s. Karl Leroy and Hazel (Lower) F.; m. Linda Wood, Aug. 14, 1965; children— Eric Craig, Kevin Edward, Brian Allan AB, Westminster Coll., 1964; MBA, U. Pitts., 1965. Various positions to v.p. Security Pacific Nat. Bank, Los Angeles, 1965-66, 69-74, v.p., 1974-82; sr. v.p. Rainier Bank, Security Pacific Bank Washington, Seattle, 1982-92, SeaFirst Bank, Seattle, 1992-93; sr. v.p., dir. Security Pacific Savs. Bank, Seattle, 1993-94; v.p. Key Bank of Wash., Seattle, 1994-96, sr. v.p., 1996-99; v.p., credit officer Fed. Home Loan Bank Seattle, 1999—2003, v.p., credit analysis mgr., 2003—05, ret., 2005. Served to lt. US Army, 1966—69. Decorated Commendation medal US Army. Mem. Risk Mgmt. Assocs., Lions Club (pres. 1988-89, 05-06, Melvin Jones fellow). Presbyterian (elder). Avocations: cross country skiing, travel, hiking, photography. Home Phone: 206-236-1634. Personal E-mail: ncfetters@aol.com.

FETTIG, JEFF M., manufacturing executive; b. Tipton, Ind., 1957; BS in Fin., Ind. U., MBA. Mem. fin. ops. Whirlpool Corp., 1981, various mgmt. positions, 1981-89, dir. product devel., 1988—89, v.p. mktg. KitchenAid, 1989-90; v.p. mktg., Philips Whirlpool Appliance Group Whirlpool Europe B.V., 1990—92; v.p., group mktg. and sales North Am. Appliance Group/Whirlpool, 1992—94; pres. Whirlpool Europe & Asia, 1994—99; exec. v.p. Whirlpool Corp., 1994—99, pres., COO, 1999—2004, chmn., pres., CEO, 2004—05, chmn., CEO, 2005—. Bd. dirs. Dow Chem. Co., 2003—, Whirlpool Corp., 2003—. Office: Whirlpool Corp 2000 N M 63 Benton Harbor MI 49022-2692*

FEUERMAN, CAROLE A., sculptor, artist; b. Hartford, Conn., Sept. 21, 1945; d. Milton and Doris Sue Ackerman; div.; m. Ron Cohen; children: Lauren Leahy, Craig, Sari Gibson, Hannah, Sam. Student, Hofstra U., 1963, Temple U., 1964, Sch. Visual Arts, 1967. Pres. Feuerman Studios, Inc., NYC, 1967—. One-woman shows include Basel Art Fair, Switzerland, 1979, O.K. Harris Gallery, Scottsdale, Ariz., 1982, Ackland Art Mus., Chapel Hill, N.C., 1985, Queens Mus., Flushing, N.Y., 1987, Arnesen Gallery, Vail, Colo., 1990, Internat. Swimming Hall of Fame, Ft. Lauderdale, Fla., 1993, So Alleghenies Mus. Art, Loretto, Pa., 2000 (award, 2002), Lobby Gallery The Durst Orgn., N.Y.C., 2001, Queensborough C.C. Mus. and Art Gallery, CUNY, Bayside, N.Y., 2005, Frederick R. Weisman Mus. Art, Malibu, Calif., 2003, Pepperdine U., 2003, Pavilion Paradiso, Giardini Venice, Italy, 2007, Art-St-Urban, Lucerne, Switzerland, 2007, Scott Richard Gallery, San Francisco, 2007, Pavilion Paradise, Giardini della Biennate, Venice, 2007, others, exhibited in group shows at The State Hermitage, St. Petersburg, Russia, Isetan Mus. Art, Tokyo, ACA Gallery, Harkone Open-Air Mus., Parrish Art Mus., Whitney Mus. Am. Art, Nat. Sculpture Soc., Riverside Art Mus., West Chelsea Arts Festival, N.Y.C., 1998, Frederick R. Weisman Mus. Art, Pepperdine U., Malibu, Calif., 1998, Florence Biennale Contemporary Art, Italy, 2001 (Lorenzo di Medici award, 2001), 2005 (award), So. Alleghenies Mus. Art, 2002, Queensborough C.C. Mus. and Art Gallery, 2002, Nat. Biennale fur Bildende Kunst, 2002 (Honor prize), Austria Biennale, 2002 (Honor prize, 2002), Boca Raton (Fla.) Mus., Chelsea (Mass.) Art Mus., Bass Art Mus., Circulo de Bellas Artes, Madrid, 2004, Janos Gat Gallery, NYC, 2005, Queensborough CC, NY, 2005, Open 2007, Lido Venice, Italy, 2007, others, Represented in permanent collections Lowe Art Mus., Fla., Tampa Mus. Art, Miami Children's Mus., So Alleghenies Mus. Art, Brandeis U., Queensborough CC at CUNY, Bayside, Bass Mus., Miami, Fla., Sen. Hilary Rodham Clinton, Pres. Bill Clinton, Dr. Henry Kissinger, Bass Mus., Fla., Ft. Lauderdale (Fla.) Mus. Art, Boca Raton Mus. Art, Fla., Caldic Collection, Rotterdam, The Netherlands, Pres. Mikael S. Gorbachov, Moscow, Lowe Art Mus., U. Miami, Tampa Mus. Art, Apollon Art Rsch. Found., Pepperdine U., Malibu, Calif., Good Samaritan Med. Ctr., Palm Beach, Calif., Swedish Wine and Spirits Corp., Stockholm, Frederick R. Weisman Art Found., LA, Rouse and Assocs., Columbus, Md., Hamilton Metro. Mus. of Art, NY, Grounds for Sculpture, Hamilton, NJ, Scott Richards Contemporary Art, San Francisco, Ctro Argentina, Buenos Aires. Recipient Betty Parsons Sculpture award 1970, Charles D. Murphy Sculpture award 1981, Amelia Peabody award for sculpture 1982, 1st prize U.S. Nat. Fine Arts Competition 1984, Fujisanskei Sculpture Biennale award, 1995, Artist's Showcase award Manhattan Art Internat., 2002, Medici award Biennale of Contemporary Art, Florence, 2005, Industry Svc. award, Dress for Success, Jersey City, 2007. Mem.: Internat. Women's Forum (N.Y.), Solomon R. Guggenheim Mus., Met. Mus. Art, Mus. Modern Art, Internat. Sculpture Ctr., Nat. Assn.Women Artists, Am. Women's Econ. Devel. Corp., Pro Arts, Nat. Women Caucus for Art, Woman's Leadership Forum, Sch. Visual Arts Alumni Assn., UNESCO. Home: 200 Mercer St Apt 1F New York NY 10012-1510 Studio: Feuerman Studios Inc 200 Mercer St 1F New York NY 10012 Office Phone: 212-228-9889. Personal E-mail: carol.feuerman@gmail.com.

FEUERSTEIN, ALAN RICKY, lawyer; b. Buffalo, Oct. 24, 1950; s. Aaron Irving and Doris Jean (Davis) F.; m. June, 1973 (div. Jan. 1984); children: Marni Lauren, Jami Lynn. BS cum laude, SUNY, Buffalo, 1974; LLB, U. Toledo, 1977. Bar: N.Y. 1978, Territorial and Dist. Ct. V.I. 1989, U.S. Supreme Ct. 1992, Fed. Ct. P.R. 1993. Assoc. Law Offices of Salvatore Martoche, Buffalo, 1977-79; ptnr. Martoche & Feuerstein, Buffalo, 1979-81; lectr. Erie County Cen. Police Svcs. Acad., Buffalo, 1981-82; pvt. practice Buffalo, 1981-93; ptnr. Feuerstein & Santapia, Buffalo, 1993-94; prin. Law Offices of Alan R. Feuerstein, Buffalo, 1994-97; ptnr. Feuerstein & Smith, LLP, Buffalo, 1998—. Lectr. Daemen Coll. Consortium, Buffalo, 1980-81; cons. in field. Mem. Erie County Reps., Buffalo, 1979—. Mem. Niagara Club, St.Thomas Yacht Club, The Buffalo Launch Club, Confrérie de la Châne des Rôtisseurs (officer). Republican. Jewish. Office: 17 St Louis Pl Buffalo NY 14202-1502 also: Woods & Woods 1 Comptroller Plz San Juan PR 00917 also: PO Box 502008 St Thomas VI 00805-2008 Office Phone: 716-856-9704. Personal E-mail: fsllp@aol.com.

FEUERSTEIN, DONALD MARTIN, lawyer; b. Chgo., May 30, 1937; s. Morris Martin and Pauline Jean (Zagel) F.; m. Dorothy Rosalind Sokolsky, June 3, 1962 (dec. Mar. 1978); children: Eliza Carol, Tony David; m. Summer Donnamarie Berben, May 25, 1987; 1 child, Ashley Paul. BA magna cum laude, Yale U., 1959; JD magna cum laude, Harvard U., 1962. Bar: N.Y. 1962. Assoc. firm Cleary, Gottlieb, Steen & Hamilton, NYC, 1962-63; law clk. to U.S. dist. judge NYC, 1963-65; assoc. firm Saxe, Bacon & Bolan, NYC, 1965; asst. gen. counsel, chief counsel instl. investor study SEC, Washington, 1966-71; ptnr., counsel Salomon Bros., NYC, 1971-81, mng. dir., sec., 1981-91; exec. v.p., chief legal officer Salomon, Inc., 1991; spl. asst. U.S. Dept. Edn., Washington, 1993-94, sr. advisor, 1994-99; pres. New Am. Schs., Arlington, Va., 1999-2000, sr. advisor, 2000-2001, Imaging Acceptance Corp., 2001—02, Nat. Coun. Accreditation of Tchr. Edn., Washington, 2001—. Spl. cons. Intersch. Group, N.Y.C., 1991-93; mem. bus. policy coun. com. on excellence in edn. Nat. Alliance of Bus., 2000-2001. Editor Harvard Law Rev., 1960-62; mem. editl. adv. bd. Securities Regulation Law Jour., 1973-90; bd. editors Nat. Law Jour., 1978-90. Mem. vis. com. Northwestern U. Law Sch., 1975—78; bd. dirs. 1st All Children's Theatre, 1976—85, chmn., 1976—82; mem. long-range planning and capital campaign coms. Brearley Sch., NYC, 1981—83; mem. adv. bd. Solomon R. Guggenheim Mus., 1984—91, chmn. bus. com., 1988—91, mem. internat. coun., 1991—; bd. dirs. Arts and Bus. Coun., 1980—85, v.p., 1985—88; trustee, v.p., mem. exec. com. Dalton Sch., 1983—89, 1990—93; mem. dean's adv. coun. Harvard U. Law Sch., 1988—95, mem. steering com. and capital campaign, 1991—95; mem. com. on univ. resources Harvard U., 1988—; mem. vis. com. Harvard Grad. Sch. Edn., 1993—99, mem. tech. adv. coun., 1996—2001; chmn. tech. com. Georgetown Day Sch., 1997—2000, trustee, 1997—2003, mem. exec. com., 2001—02, chmn., trusteeship commn., 2001—02, chmn. fin. aid com., 2002—03, mem. investment subcom., 2003—; mem. Brookings Coun., 1998—2001. Mem. ABA, Phi Beta Kappa, Pi Sigma Alpha. Home: 6430 Bradley Blvd Bethesda MD 20817-3246 Home Phone: 301-365-0776; Office Phone: 202-466-7496. E-mail: dfeuer13@cs.com.

FEUERSTEIN, HOWARD M., lawyer; b. Memphis, Sept. 16, 1939; s. Leon and Lillian (Kapell) F.; m. Tamra Lynn Saperstein, May 19, 1968; children: Laurie, Leon. BA, Vanderbilt U., 1961, JD, 1963. Bar: Tenn. 1963, Oreg. 1965. Law clk. to justice US Ct. Appeals (5th cir.), Montgomery, Ala., 1963-64; teaching fellow Stanford U., 1964-65; assoc. Davies, Biggs et al (now Stoel Rives LLP), Portland, Oreg., 1965-71; ptnr. Stoel Rives LLP, Portland, 1971—. Mem. Oreg. Gov.'s Task Force on Land Devel. Law, 1974; bd. realtors Condominium Study Com., Oreg., 1975-76. Editor-in-chief Vanderbilt Law Rev., 1962-63. Trustee Congregation Beth Israel, Portland, 1977-83; bd. dirs. Jewish Family & Child Service, Portland, 1975-81, Young Musicians and Artists Inc., 1991-96. Recipient Founder's medal Vanderbilt Law Sch., 1963. Mem. ABA, Oreg. State Bar, Community Assn. Inst. (bd. dirs. Oreg. chpt. 1980-86), Am. Coll. Real Estate Lawyers. Office: Stoel Rives LLP 900 SW 5th Ave Ste 2600 Portland OR 97204-1268 Office Phone: 503-294-9215. Business E-Mail: hmfeuerstein@stoel.com.

FEUERSTEIN, SANDRA JEANNE, judge; b. NYC, Jan. 21, 1946; d. Annette Elstein; BS, U. Vt., 1966; JD, Benjamin Cardozo U., 1979. Bar: N.Y. 1980, U.S. Dist. Ct. (so. and ea. dists.) N.Y. 1983, U.S. Ct. Mil. Appeals, 1988, U.S. Tax Ct. 1988, U.S. Supreme Ct. 1988. Sr. law asst. NY State Supreme Ct., Mineola, 1980-86, matrimonial referee, 1985-86; judge Nassau County Dist. Ct., Hempstead, NY, 1987—93; mem. discovery oversight com. US Dist. Ct. (ea. dist.) NY, 1983—86, mem. com. civil litig., 1989—91, judge, 2003—; assoc. justice NY State Supreme Ct. (10th judicial dist.), 1994—99, NY State Supreme Ct. (appellate divsn., 2d dept. from 10th jud. dist.), Nassau and Suffolk Counties, 1999—2003. Law sec. to adminstrv. judge Leo J. McGinity, Mineola, 1985-87; lectr. Trial Def. Bar of Nassau County, 1984, Town and Village Justice Continuing Jud. Edn., 1987; mem. Nassau County Exec.'s Blue Ribbon Panel on Domestic Violence, 1989; mem. jud. ethics adv. panel NY State; mem., chair Family Task Force; bd. dirs. Benjamin Cardozo Sch. Law; adj. prof. Hofstra Law Sch; lectr. state and local bar assns. Co-author: Handling a Criminal Case in New York: Practice Guide, 1994-2003; assoc. editor Nassau Lawyer, 1984-87, editor, 1987-89; contbr. numerous articles to profl. jours. Counsel Merrick Sr. Citizens Ctr., 1980-87; life mem. Hadassah, Long Beach Meml. Hosp. Aux.; bd. dirs. L.I. Arts Coun.; life mem., bd. dirs. Am. Cancer Soc.; dir., Benjamin N. Cardozo Sch. Law, Yeshiva U. Recipient Mesivta Torah award, 1985 and other numerous honors and awards. Mem. Women's Bar Assn. of NY State (v.p. 1990, pres. Nassau County chpt. 1988-89, founder pro bono project, judiciary com., spl. matrimonial com. 1985-86, v.p. 1986-87, 87-88, 90, chmn. judiciary com. 1984,. coun. Jud. Assns. 2d cir.), Nassau County Bar Assn. (bd. dirs. 1988, Pro Bono Recognition award 1990, jud. sect., gender bias com. Nassau County, dir.), Franklin D. Roosevelt Inns of Ct. (master), Bus. and Profl. Women of Nassau County, L.I. Ctr. Bus. and Profl. Women, Yeshiva U. Alumni Assn. (founding bd. dirs.), Acad. Law (pub. edn. com.), Nat. Assn. Women Judges (pres. chpt. NY State), Nassau County Women's Bar Assn. (pres.), NY State Women's Bar Assn. (v.p.). Office: US Dist Ct Ea Dist NY 1014 Federal Plz Central Islip NY 11722

FEUERWERKER, ALBERT, historian, educator; b. Cleve., Nov. 6, 1927; s. Martin and Gizella (Feuerwerker) F.; m. Yi-tsi Mei, June 11, 1955; children: Alison, Paul. AB, Harvard U., 1950, PhD, 1957. Lectr. history U. Toronto, Ont., Can., 1955-58; rsch. fellow Harvard U., Cambridge, Mass., 1958-60; assoc. prof. history U. Mich., Ann Arbor, 1960-63, prof., 1963-96, chmn. dept., 1984-87; dir. U. Mich. Ctr. for Chinese Studies, Ann Arbor, 1961-67, 72-83; A.M. and H.P. Bentley prof. of history U. Mich., Ann Arbor, 1986-96, prof. emeritus, 1996—; dir. d'études École des Hautes Etudes en Scis. Sociales, Paris, 1981; vis. scholar Acad. Social Scis., Shanghai, China, 1981, 88, Sichuan U., Chengdu, China, 1988. Joint com. on contemporary China, Social Sci. Research Coun.-Am. Council Learned Socs., 1966-78, 80-83, chmn., 1970-75; mem. com. on scholarly comm. with the People's Republic of China, Nat. Acad. Scis.-Social Sci. Rsch. Coun.-Am. Council Learned Socs., 1971-78, 81-83, vice-chmn., 1975-78 Author: China's Early Industrialization, 1958, History in Communist China, 1968, The Chinese Economy 1870-1911, 1969, Rebellion in 19th Century China, 1975, The Foreign Establishment in China, 1976, Economic Trends in the Republic of China, 1977, Chinese Social and Economic History from the Song to 1900, 1982, Studies in the Economic History of Late Imperial China, 1996, The Chinese Economy, 1870-1949, 1996; co-editor: Cambridge History of China, vol. 13, 1986; mem. editl. bd. Am. Hist. Rev., 1970-75, The China Quar., 1967-91, Comparative Studies in Soc. and History, 1964-2001. Served with AUS, 1946-47. Fellow NEH, 1971-72, Social Sci. Research Coun.-Am. Council of Learned Socs., 1962-63, Guggenheim Found., 1987-88. Fellow AAAS; mem. Assn. for Asian Studies (v.p. 1990, pres. 1991), Nat. Com. on U.S.-China Rels. Home: 827 Asa Gray Dr Apt 356 Ann Arbor MI 48105 Office: U Mich Ctr for Chinese Studies 1080 S University Ave Ste 3668 Ann Arbor MI 48109-1106 E-mail: afeuer@umich.edu.

FEUERWERKER, ELIE, biologist, educator; b. Paris, Dec. 2, 1948; arrived in U.S., 1989, naturalized, 1999; s. David Feuerwerker and Antoinette Gluck; m. Anne Esther Ackermann, Dec. 28, 2004. BSc in Biology, U. Montreal, Que., Can., 1971, MSc in Biology, 1976, PhD in Biology, 1983. Postdoctoral fellow Harvard U., Cambridge, Mass., 1985—87; rsch. assoc. Boston U., 1987—88; rsch. fellow McGill U., Montreal Neurol. Inst., 1987—89; mem. I-V team The Mount Sinai Med. Ctr., NYC, 1990—94; tchr. biology Lycee Français de N.Y., 1994—2000; tchr. N.Y.C. Bd. Edn., 2000—. Presenter in field. Contbr. articles to profl. jours. and newspapers. Grantee, The Hannah Inst. for the History of Medicine, NSF, The Rockefeller U. Mem.: N.Y. Acad. Scis. Jewish. Avocation: photography. Home: 1617 Cherry St Highland Park NJ 08904-3716

FEUERZEIG, HENRY LOUIS, lawyer; b. Chgo., Dec. 12, 1938; s. Samuel Alexander Feuerzeig and Esther Fleeger; m. Penny Zweigenhaft, Apr. 8, 1967; children: Paul Lawrence, Darcy Elizabeth Coty. BS, U. Wis., 1962; JD, George Washington U., 1970. Bar: D.C., V.I., Fla., Md. Reporter various newspapers, Dubuque, Iowa, Chgo., Madison, Wis., Cin. and Washington, 1962-64, 65-67; assoc. Sachs, Greenebaum, Frohlich & Tayler, Washington, 1970—72; asst. atty. gen. V.I. Dept. Law, St. Thomas, 1972-73, chief civil and adminstrv. law divsn., 1973-74, 1st asst. atty. gen., 1974; ptnr. Feuerzeig & Zebedee, St. Thomas, 1974-76; judge Territorial Ct. V.I., St. Thomas, 1977-87; del., chmn. jud. powers and functions com. 4th V.I. Constl. Conv., 1981; ptnr. Dudley, Topper and Feuerzeig, St. Thomas, 1987—. Mem. supervisory bd. V.I. Law Enforcement Planning Commn., 1978—87, Juvenile Justice and Delinquency Prevention, 1988—; mem. V.I. Juvenile Code Revision Task Force, 1978—83, V.I. Criminal Code Revision Task Force, 1978—87, Underwriters, Lloyd's US V.I. Rep., 1989—99; atty. In Fact, 1999—. Mem. Montgomery County (Md.) Dem. State Ctrl. Com., 1970-72; mem. V.I. Indsl. Devel. Commn., 1976; bd. dirs. Environ. Studies Program, St. Thomas, 1977-80, United Way, 1986-92; bd. reps. Hebrew Congregation of St. Thomas, 1983-90, 96-2002, co-chair Bicentennial Campaign com., 1993-97; trustee Antilles Sch., St. Thomas, 1983-91; mem. adv. coun. Youth Multi-Svc. Ctr., 1989-94; dir. Cmty. Found. of V.I., 1990-2003, pres., 1993-94, emeritus dir., 2003-. Sigma Delta Chi scholar, 1962; Congressional fellow Am. Polit. Sci. Assn., 1964-65; named Person of Yr. Hebrew Congregation of St. Thomas, 2003, St. Thomas & St. John C. of C. Cmty. Svc. award, 2004. Fellow Am. Bar Found.; mem. ABA (lawyers conf. jud. performance and conduct com. 1984—94), D.C. Bar Assn., Fla. Bar Assn., VI Bar Assn. (pres. 1976), Am. Law Inst. (life, cons. group for principles of family dissolution, 1992-2000, cons. group for restatement of law governing lawyers, 1992-99), Am. Judicature Soc., Assn. Trial Lawyers Am., Internat. Soc. Barristers, Order of Coif, Rotary, Harmonic Lodge No. 356, Sigma Delta Chi, Phi Delta Phi. Jewish. Office: Dudley Topper and Feuerzeig LLP 1000 Frederiksberg Gade PO Box 756 Charlotte Amalie VI 00804-0756 Office Phone: 340-715-4443. E-mail: hfeuerzeig@dtflaw.com, hfeuer@attglobal.net.

FEUILLE, RICHARD HARLAN, lawyer, director; b. Mexico City, June 10, 1920; s. Frank and Margaret (Levy) F.; m. Louann Johnston Hoover, Oct. 20, 1948; children: Louann H., Richard H., Robert R., Joseph L. (dec.), James M., Patrick F. (dec.), Margaret J. BA, U. Va., 1947, LLB, 1948; JD, 1970. Bar: Tex. 1948. Assoc. Jones, Hardie, Grambling & Howell, El Paso, Tex., 1948-53; ptnr. Hardie, Grambling, Sims & Feuille, El Paso, 1953-57; sr. ptnr. Scott, Hulse, Marshall & Feuille, El Paso, 1957—. Bd. dirs. El Paso Nat. Bank (now known as JPMorgan Chase Bank), 1964—93. Active United Fund El Paso, 1963—, pres., 1968, 75—, bd. dirs., 1966-72, founder, v.p. trust fund, 1969—; pres. El Paso Cmty. Concert Assn., 1961-67; mem. adv. coun. U. Tex. at El Paso, 1968—, mem. exec. com., 1968-70; bd. dirs. Providence Meml. Hosp., 1986-92; bd. dirs. St. Clement's Episcopal Parish Sch., El Paso, pres., 1993-95; trustee YWCA, El Paso; bd. dirs. El Paso Cmty. Found., 1980—, pres., 1983-84, chmn. bd., 2004-05. Maj. USAAF, 1942-46, PTO, Iwo Jima. Decorated bronze star; recipient Disting. Svc. award City of El Paso and Rotary Club, 2002. Mem. ABA (estate and gift tax com.), El Paso County Bar Assn. (pres. 1972-73), Tex. Bar Assn., Greater El Paso Tennis Assn. (bd. dirs.), Rotary Club of El Paso, Order Coif, Phi Beta Kappa, Omicron Delta Kappa. Episcopalian (vestryman, sr. warden). Clubs: Coronado Country (El Paso), El Paso Tennis (El Paso) (pres. 1973). Home: 1021 Broadmoor Dr El Paso TX 79912-2003 Office: Scott Hulse Marshall Feuille et al 201 East Main Dr 1100 Chase Tower El Paso TX 79901 Home Phone: 915-584-4064; Office Phone: 915-533-2493. Business E-Mail: rfeu@scotthulse.com.

FEULNER, EDWIN J., JR., research foundation executive; b. Chgo., Aug. 12, 1941; s. Edwin John and Helen J. (Franzen) F.; m. Linda C. Leventhal, Mar. 8, 1969; children: Edwin John III, Emily V. BS, Regis Coll., Weston, Mass., 1963; MBA, U. Pa., Phila., 1964; PhD, U. Edinburgh, Scotland, 1981; LHD (hon.), Nichols Coll., Dudley, Mass., 1981, Thomas More Coll., Crestview Hills, Ky., 2005; degree (hon.), Universidad Francisco Marroquin, Guatemala City, 1982; D in Social Scis. (hon.), Hanyang U., Seoul, Korea, 1982; LLD (hon.), Bellevue Coll., Nebr., 1987, Pepperdine U., Malibu, Calif., 2000, St. Norbert Coll., De Pere, Wis., 2002, Gonzaga U., Spokane, Wash., 1992; DLitt (hon.), Grove City Coll., Pa., 1994; D in Pub. Svc. (hon.), Hillsdale Coll., Mich., 2004; LHD (hon.), Thomas More U., Bowling Green, Ohio, 2005. Richard Weaver fellow London Sch. Econs., 1965; fellow Ctr. for Strategic and Internat. Studies, 1965—66; pub. affairs fellow Hoover Instn., 1966—68; rsch. analyst Rep. Conf. U.S. Ho. of Reps., 1968-69; confidential asst. to sec. def. Melvin Laird, 1969-70; campaign mgr. Crane for Congress Com., 1972; adminstrv. asst. to U.S. Congressman Philip M. Crane, 1970-74; exec. dir. Rep. Study Com., Ho. of Reps., 1974-77; pres. Heritage Found., Washington, 1977—; chmn. Inst. European Def. and Strategic Studies, 1977-96; counselor to v.p. candidate Jack Kemp, 1996. US del. IMF/World Bank, 1974—76; mem. exec. com. Presdl. Transition Pres.'s Commn. White House Fellows, 1980—81, mem., 1981—83; pub. del. UN 2nd Spl. Session on Disarmament, 1982; chmn. USIA, 1982—91, U.S. adv. com. pub. diplomacy, 1982—94; mem. Carlucci Comm. Fgn. Assistance, 1983; disting. fellow mobilization concepts Devel. Ctr. Nat. Def. U., 1983—89; nat. adv. bd. Ctr. Edn. and Rsch. in Free Enterprise Tex. A&M U., 1985—96; White House cons. on domestic policy, 1987; mem. US Com. Improving Effectiveness of UN, 1989—93; mem. adv. com. Am. Polit. Channel, 1994—96; vice-chmn. Nat. Com. Econ. Growth and Tax Reform, 1995—96; mem. Congrl. Policy Adv. Bd., 1997—2001, Internat. Fin. Inst. Adv. Com., 1999—2000; disting. vis. prof. Hanyang U., Seoul, 2001—; mem. Gingrich/Mitchell Task Force on UN Reform, 2005; mem. nat. adv. bd. Ctr. Edn. and Rsch. in Free Enterprise, Tex. A&M U., 1995—96. Author: Congress and the New International Economic Order, 1976, Looking Back, 1981, Conservatives Stalk the House, 1983, The March of Freedom, 1998, Intellectual Pilgrims, 1999, Leadership for America, 2000, Getting America Right, 2006; pub. Policy Rev., 1977-01; contbr. articles to profl. jours., newspapers, chpts. to books. Sec. Korea-U.S. Exch. Coun., 2001—04; chmn. Citizens for Am. Edn. Found., 1985—89; mem. coun. advisors Bryce Harlow Found.; trustee Nat. Chamber Found., 1998—; mem. exec. coun. Am.'s Future Found., 1998—; trustee Lehrman Inst., 1981—90, Sarah Scaife Found., 1988—, St. James Sch., 1990—98, Sequoia Nat. Bank, 1987—99, Regis U., 1991—2001, 2005—, Internat. Rep. Inst., 1995—2001, Acton Inst., 1995—2002; vice-chmn. bd. Aequus Inst., 1989—, Intercollegiate Studies Inst., 1979—, chmn., 1989—93, 2003—06; vice-chmn. bd. dirs. Roe Found., 1983—; mem. exec. com. Coun. Nat. Policy, 1993—2001; trustee Am. Coun. Germany, NY, 1982—92, Found. Francisco Marroquin, Inst. Rsch. Econs. Taxation, 1980—87; vice chmn., trustee Manhattan Inst. Policy Studies, 1977—86; mem. bd. visitors George Mason U., 1996—2004; mem. Multimedia Supercorridor Internat. Adv. Coun., Malaysia, 2001—05. Decorated Order of Brilliant Star with Grand Cordon Republic of China, Order of Diplomatic Svc. Merit-Gwanghwa medal Republic of Korea; named Free Enterprise Man of Yr., Tex. A&M U., 1985, Man of Yr., Wharton Sch., 1993; recipient Washington award, Freedom Found., 1979, 1980, Am. Eagle award, Invest-in-Am. Nat. Coun., 1983, Disting. Alumni award, Regis U., 1985, Superior Pub. Svc. award, Dept. of Navy, 1987, Presdl. Citizens medal, 1989, Dir.'s Svc. award, USIA, 1992, Thomas Jefferson Servant Leadership award, Coun. Nat. Policy, 1996, Walter Judd Freedom award, Fund for Am. Studies, 2004, Truman-Reagan medal of Freedom, 2006. Mem. Am. Econs. Assn., Internat. Inst. Strategic Studies, U.S. Strategic Inst., Inst. d'Etudes Politques, Phila. Soc. (treas. 1964-79, pres. 1982-83), Mont Pelerin Soc. (treas. 1979-96, 2000-, pres. 1996-98, sr. v.p. 1998-2000), Internat. Com. of the G.K. Chesterton Soc. (chmn. 1989-92), Union League (NYC), Met. Club, Reform Club (London), Bohemian Club (San Francisco), Old. Dominion Boat Club (Alexandria, Va.), Knights of Malta, Knights of the Holy Sepulchre, Alpha Kappa Psi. Republican. Roman Catholic. Office: The Heritage Found 214 Massachusetts Ave NE Washington DC 20002-4958 Office Phone: 202-546-4400. Personal E-mail: ed@feulner.us.

FEUSS, JUDITH FARRAR, musician, educator; b. El Dorado, Kans., Jan. 17, 1940; d. Roy and Velma Frost Farrar; m. John F. Hall (div.); children: Stephanie Hall, Suzanne Hall; m. Roger H. Feuss, July 4, 1987. MusB, Wichita State U., 1962; MFA, LI U., 1976, Juilliard Sch., 1977. Cert. Tchr. Queens Coll., NY, 1997. Organist Manhasset Congl. Ch., NY, 1992—; music educator Northside Elem. Sch., Farmingdale, NY, 1998—. Mem.: NY State Sch. Music Assn., Music Educators' Nat. Conf., Am. Guild Organists. Home: 5 Muriel Rd Port Washington NY 11050 Personal E-mail: rfeuss@optonline.net.

FEUSS, LINDA ANNE UPSALL, lawyer; b. White Plains, NY, Dec. 9, 1956; d. Herbert Charles and Edna May (Hart) Upsall; m. Charles E. Feuss, Aug. 16, 1980; children: Charles Herbert, Anne Hart. BA in French Lit., Colgate U., 1978; JD, Emory U., 1981. Bar: Ga. 1981, SC 1981, Minn. 2000. Assoc. Rainey, Britton, Gibbes & Clarkson, Greenville, SC, 1981-83; counsel Siemens Energy & Automation, Atlanta, 1983-91, Siemens Corp., Atlanta, 1991-93, sr. counsel, 1993-94, assoc. gen. counsel, 1994-98; v.p., gen. counsel Pillsbury Co., Mpls., 1998-2000; v.p., gen. counsel to exec. v.p. legal and human resources PEMSTAR Inc., Rochester, Minn., 2001—03; v.p., gen. counsel, sec. C.H. Robinson Worldwide Inc., Eden Prairie, Minn., 2003—. Rep. law coun. II Mfr.'s Alliance, Washington, 1995-98; rep. law com. Nat. Elec. Mfr.'s Assn., Washington, 1995-98; bd. govs. St. Thomas U. Sch. Law, 2006—; mem. adv. bd. PACER, 2005—. Adv. bd. PACER, 2005—; bd. govs. St. Thomas U. Sch. Law, 2006—; bd. mem. YWCA, 2006—. Mem. ABA, Am. Corp. Coun. Assn. (dir. Ga. chpt. 1995-98, v.p. Ga. chpt. 1996, pres. 1997), State Bar Ga., SC Bar, Minn. Bar Assn., Colgate Club Atlanta (pres. 1986-88, bd. dirs. 1989-98). Office: CH Robinson Worldwide Inc 8100 Mitchell Rd Eden Prairie MN 55344-2248 Office Fax: 952-937-7840.

FEVURLY, KEITH ROBERT, educational administrator; b. Leavenworth, Kans., Oct. 30, 1951; s. James R. Fevurly and Anne (McDade) Barrett; m. Peggy L. Vosburg, Aug. 4, 1978; children: Rebecca Dawn, Grant Robert. BA in Polit. Sci., U. Kans., 1973; JD, Washburn U. of Topeka Sch. Law, 1976; postgrad., U. Mo. Sch. Law, 1984; MBA, Regis U., 1988; LLM, U. Denver, 1992. Bar: Kans. 1977, Colo. 1986; cert. fin. planner. Pvt. practice, Leavenworth, 1977; atty. estate and gift tax IRS, Wichita and Salina, Kans., Austin, Tex., 1977-83; atty., acad. assoc. Coll. for Fin. Planning, Denver, 1984-91, program dir., 1991-95, v.p. edn., 1995-98; COO, U. St. Augustine (Fla.) for Health Scis., 1998-2000; exec. dir. fin. planning edn. program Kaplan U., Denver, 2000—07; vis. instr. fin. Denver Met. State Coll., 2007—. Contbg. author tng. modules, articles on tax mgmt., estate planning. Mem. Colo. Bar Assn., Fin. Planning Assn., Toastmasters Internat., Rotary Internat., Delta Theta Phi. Republican. Presbyterian. Avocations: softball, racquetball. Home and Office: 3007 E Otero Pl Centennial CO 80122-3666 Business E-Mail: keithfevurly@yahoo.com.

FEWEL, JOHN GERRARD, government agency administrator, director; b. Chickasha, Okla., Aug. 20, 1944; s. Kenneth Jack and Cleo Brees Fewel; m. Vicki Ann Huber, May 27, 2000; children: Jeffrey Scott Pickens, Sean Allen. BA in Microbiology, U. Tex., Austin, 1966; MS in Mgmt., U. Tex., San Antonio, 1980. Rsch. asst. U. Ky. Med. Ctr., Lexington, 1966—69; rsch. assoc. NJ Coll. Medicine, Newark, 1969—75; dir. cardiothoracic rsch. lab VA Med. Ctr., San Antonio, 1975—82, adminstrv. officer trainee Memphis, 1982—83; adminstrv. officer rsch. VA Outpatient Clinic, Boston, 1983—84, VA Med. Ctr., Boston, 1984—84, Dallas, 1984—2003; exec. dir. Dallas VA Rsch. Corp., Dallas, 1990—2002; ret., 2003. Rsch. coord. U. Tex. Southwestern Med. Ctr., Dallas, 1984—90. Author: Reflections from the Shaman's Tear; contbr. articles to profl. jours. Pres., chmn. bd. dir. Miracle Wish Found., 2006; hon. chmn. Nat. Rep. Congressional Com. Bus. Adv. Coun., Tex., 2006—, House Rep. Trust, Rep. Bus. Summit, 2007. Named Businessman of Yr., Nat. Rep. Congressional Com., 2006—; recipient Congl. medal of distinction, Nat. Leadership award, Nat. Rep. Congressional Com., Republican of Yr. Mem.: Soc. of Rsch. Adminstrs. (pres. govt. divsn. 1997—98). Achievements include development of quantitative analytical technique measuring variety of metabolites in tissue biopsies; research in underlying biochemistry of hemorrhagic/endo-toxin shock and cardio pulmonary bypass. Avocations: sailing, creative writing, running. Home and Office: 1307 High Ridge Drive Duncanville TX 75137 E-mail: feweljohn@aol.com.

FEWELL, CHARLES KENNETH, JR., lawyer; b. Washington, Jan. 26, 1943; s. Charles Kenneth and Mary Amanda (Hunt) F.; m. Christine Baker Huff, Jan. 23, 1971; children: Anna Catherine, John Maenner. BA magna cum laude, Dartmouth Coll., 1964; JD, Harvard U., 1967. Bar: N.Y. 1968, U.S. Dist. Ct. (so. dist.) N.Y. 1970, U.S. Ct. Appeals (2d cir.) 1975. Law clk. U.S. Dist. Ct. (so. dist.) N.Y, NYC, 1967-68; assoc. White & Case, NYC, 1968-75; v.p., counsel Nat. Westminster Bank, NYC, 1975-80; sr. counsel, sr. v.p. Deutsche Bank AG, NYC, 1980-92; chief counsel, mng. dir. Deutsche Bank N.Am., 1992-97; ptnr. Eaton & Van Winkle LLP, NYC, 1998—. Bd. dirs. Deutsche Bank Trust Co., Deutsche Fin. Svcs. Can. Corp.; v.p., sec. Deutsche Bank Fin., Inc., N.Y.C., 1980-97; v.p. and dir. DB Alumni Inc., 2003—. Mem. mediation panel U.S. Dist. Ct. (so. dist.) N.Y., 2001—; mem. vestry Grace Episc. Ch., Hastings-on-Hudson, N.Y., 2000-02. Mem. ABA (banking com. 1980—, co-chair internat. banking and fin. com. 1995-98), Am. Fgn. Law Assn. (v.p. 2000-01, bd. dirs. 2005—), Inst. Internat. Bankers (legis. and regulatory com. 1988-97), German Am. Law Assn. (dir. 1982-2004), N.Y. State Bar Assn. (internat. banking and securities markets 1987—, internat. employment law 1992—, publ. com., editl. bd. 2001—), Assn. Bar City N.Y. (banking law sect. 1992-95, co-op/condo mediation panel, 2006-), Phi Beta Kappa. Office: Eaton & Van Winkle LLP Three Park Ave New York NY 10016-2078 Home Phone: 914-478-0951; Office Phone: 212-561-3627. Business E-Mail: cfewell@evw.com.

FEY, ALBERT EUGENE, lawyer; b. Dearborn, Mich, June 6, 1933; s. Irving B. and Erma (Exley) Fey; m. Norma A. Pugh (dec.); m. Judy L. Crumley (dec.); children: Nancy, Holly, Daniel, Aimee. BSME, U. Mich., Ann Arbor, 1955; JD, George Washington U., Washington, 1958. Bar: DC 1958, Mich. 1959, NY 1959. Atty. GE Co., Washington and NY, 1956—59; patent trial lawyer Fish & Neave, NYC, 1959—2004; of counsel Ropes & Gray, 2005—. Lectr. in field. Active United Way, Little League, Am. Youth Soccer Orgn. With US Army, 1958—59. Mem.: Am. Coll. Trial Lawyers (listed in Best Lawyers in Am. 2007). Presbyterian. Avocations: golf, tennis, skiing, reading. Home: 365 Central Dr Briarcliff Manor NY 10510 Office: Ropes & Gray 1211 6th Ave New York NY 10020 Office Phone: 212-596-9079.

FEY, JOHN THEODORE, retired insurance company executive; b. Hopewell, Va., Mar. 10, 1917; s. Raymond B. and Ruth (Fultz) F.; m. Jane K. Gerber, Apr. 5, 1947 (dec.); 1 child, John Theodore; m. Deborah F. Fitzgerald, Dec. 6, 1986. Student, Washington and Lee U., 1935-37, LL.D., 1978; LL.B., U. Md., 1940; MBA, Harvard U., 1942; J.S.D., Yale U., 1952; LL.D., Middlebury Coll., Alma Coll., 1961, U. Vt., 1967, Washington and Lee U., 1980, St. Augustine Coll., 1981. Bar: Md. 1940, D.C. 1953, Vt. 1959, N.Y. 1977. County atty., Md., 1947-49; faculty Law Sch., George Washington U., 1949-53, dean, 1953-56, professorial lectr., 1956; clk. Supreme Ct. U.S., 1956-58; pres. U. Vt., 1958-64, U. Wyo., 1964-66, Nat. Life Ins. Co., 1966-74, also dir., 1966-74; chmn. bd. Equitable Life Assurance Soc. U.S., NYC, 1974-82, Nat. Westminster Bank U.S.A., NYC, 1982-85, Fidelity Union Life Ins. Co., Dallas, 1982-85. Bd. dirs. Sara Lee Corp., Certain-Teed Co., Norton Corp.; chmn. bd. dirs. Saint-Gobain Corp.; mem. Md. Legislature, 1946-50 Trustee Getty Mus., Malibu, Calif., 1979-92. Served to col. USMCR, 1942-46. Mem. Am. Coll. Life Underwriters, Order of Coif. Home Phone: 520-795-6624; Office Phone: 520-795-6624. Personal E-mail: fitzfey@cox.net.

FEY, LAURA CLARK, lawyer; b. Tulsa, Okla., Sept. 25, 1967; d. Robert Warren and Wanda Lee Clark; m. David Montgomery Fey, Nov. 6, 1993; children: Emily Elizabeth, Andrew Montgomery. BS in Journalism with distinction, U. Kans., Lawrence, 1989, JD, 1992. Bar: Kans. 1992, Mo. 1996. Trial atty. US Dept. Justice, Houston, 1992—95; assoc. Polsinelli, White, Vardeman & Shalton, Kansas City, Mo., 1995—96, Shook, Hardy & Bacon, Kansas City, 1996—2000, ptnr., 2001—. Sunday sch. tchr. Village Presbyn. Ch., Prairie Village, Kans., 2006—07. Named Best of the Bar, Kans. City Bus. Jour., 2006, 2007; named one of 40 under Forty, Ingram's Kansas City's Bus. Mag., 2007. Mem.: ABA. Office: Shook Hardy & Bacon LLP 2555 Grand Blvd Kansas City MO 64108-2613 Office Phone: 816-474-6550. Office Fax: 816-421-5547. Business E-Mail: lfey@shb.com.

FEY, TINA, actress; b. Upper Darby, Penn., May 18, 1970; m. Jeff Richmond, June 3, 2001; 1 child, Alice. BA in drama, U. Va., 1992. Writer: TV series Saturday Night Live: 25th Anniversary, 1999, The Colin Quinn Show, 2002, NBC 75th Anniversary Special, 2002, writer, composer: films Mean Girls, 2004; actor: (films) Mean Girls, 2004, Man of the Year, 2006; writer Saturday Night Live, 1997—2006, head writer, 1999—2006; actor: (TV series) Saturday Night Live, 2000—06; actor, writer, co-prodr.: 30 Rock, 2006— (Gracie award for best female lead in comedy, 2007); actor guest appearances (TV series) Upright Citizens Brigade, 1999, The Real World/Road Rules Extreme Challenge, 2001, Film 72, 2004, 60 Minutes, 2004. Named Entertainer of Yr., Entertainment Weekly, 2001; named one of The World's Most Influential People, TIME mag., 2007. Mailing: 3 Arts c/o David Miner 9460 Wilshire Blvd 7th Fl Beverly Hills CA 90212*

FEY, WILLARD, global environmental researcher, educator; b. Cin., June 29, 1935; s. Russell Richard and Irene Emma Fey; m. Mary Elizabeth Foley, June 21, 1958 (div. July 18, 1974); children: Lorenne Elizabeth, Leanne Susan, Erik Richard. BSEE, MIT, Cambridge, 1957, BS in Mgmt., 1957, MSEE, 1961. Instr. Sloan Sch. Mgmt. MIT, Cambridge, Mass., 1961—64; lectr. indsl. engring. dept. Northeastern U., Boston, 1963—68; asst. prof. Sloan Sch. Mgmt. MIT, Cambridge, 1964—67, dir. undergrad. sys. program, 1964—67; tech. staff The MITRE Corp., Bedford, Mass., 1967—68; assoc. prof. Indsl. and Sys. Engring. Sch. Ga. Inst. Tech., Atlanta, 1969—99; CEO Ecocosm Dynamics Ltd., Tucker, Ga., 2000—; global news commentator Signs of the Times, Comcast Pub. Svc. Cable TV, DeKalb, 2005—. Cons. The MITRE Corp., Bedford, 1962—67, Reynolds, Smith & Hills, Jacksonville, Fla., 1969—71, Guyana Mining, Ltd., Georgetown, Guyana, 1980—83, Coca Cola Co. USA, Atlanta, 1981—83; prin. rsch. investigator U.S. Law Enforcement Assistance Adminstrn., Washington, 1972—74, USAF, Tyndall AFB, Panama City, Fla., 1979—80, U.S. Forest Svc., U. Ga. Office, Athens, Ga., 1981—88. Contbr. book Some Theories of Organization, 1972; co-author (Luis Gutierrez): (book) Ecosystem Succession, 1980; co-prodr. Ann Lam: (video presentation) Pie in the Sky: A System Dynamics Perspective of Sustainability, 1998; co-prodr. The Bridge to Humanity's Future, 2000; contbr. reports and articles to profl. publs. Voting dep. Episcopal Ch., Detroit, 1988; bd. dirs. Episcopal Diocese Atlanta, 1983—85; mem. standing com. Episcopal Diocese, 1986—88, jr. warden, 2007; sr. warden Holy Cross Episcopal Ch., Decatur, Ga., 1986—88. Named to Leadership Atlanta, 1977. Mem.: Soc. Christian Ethics, Am. Schs. Oriental Rsch., Internat. Soc. for Sys. Scis., Sys. Dynamics Soc. (charter mem.), Bibl. Archaeology Study Group of Greater Atlanta, Inc. Episcopalian. Achievements include research in system dynamics philosophy and practice; dynamics of higher education, dynamics of Atlanta criminal justice system, forest management dynamics; development of environmental research that identified Ecocosm Paradox. Avocations: Biblical research, classical music, opera, sustainable architectural design, gardening. Business E-Mail: fey@ecocosmdynamics.org.

FEYER, THOMAS, editor; BA in History magna cum laude, Princeton U., 1975; MS in Journalism, Columbia U., 1976. With AP, 1976—80; formerly asst. fgn. editor, now editor, letters to the editor NY Times, 1980—. Office: Letters to the Editor NY Times 229 W 43rd St New York NY 10036 Office Phone: 212-556-1873. Office Fax: 212-556-3622. Business E-Mail: tfeyer@nytimes.com.

FEYLER, CARRIE A., elementary school educator; d. Dwight W. and Gayle Feyler; life ptnr. Mary Jo Snyder, May 5, 2006. BA, Gordon Coll., Wenham, Mass., 1998; MEd, Lesley U., Cambridge, Mass., 2002. Cert. experienced educator N.H., 1998. Lang. arts tchg. asst. Hamilton Wenham Sch. Dist., Mass., 1998—99; 4th grade tchr. Rochester Sch. Dist., NH, 1999—. Vol. Big Brother, Big Sister, 1994—99, Missionaries of Charity, Calcutta, India, 2001. Mem.: Am. Fedn. Tchrs. Democrat. Baptist. Avocations: travel, photography. Home: 7 Butler Way Middleton NH 03887 Home Phone: 603-755-2559. Personal E-mail: keepcroppin@adelphia.net.

FIACCO, ANTHONY VINCENT, retired educator, researcher; b. Herkimer, N.Y., Apr. 4, 1928; s. Umberto and Valentina (Palladini) F.; m. Diana Hannuna, Nov. 15, 1958 (div.); 1 child, Patricia; m. Sarah Echols, June 13, 1970; children— Kristen, Alicia, Anthony. B.S., Union Coll., 1950; Ph.D., Northwestern U., 1967. Ops. research analyst Rsch. Analysis Corp., McLean, Va., 1960-70; prof. ops. rsch. George Washington U., 1970-95; ret. 1995, prin. investigator rsch, 1970—; organized, chaired ann. symposia on optimization sensitivity George Washington U., 1979-98. Author: (with G.P. McCormick) Nonlinear Programming, 1964 (ORSA Lanchester prize, 1968); Sensitivity Analysis in NLP, 1983. Editor: MP Study: Sensitivity, 1984, others; assoc. editor: Jour. Optimization Theory and Applications, 1973-2002. Contbr. articles to profl. jours. Served to lt. USN, 1952-55. Fulbright scholar, 1950. Roman Catholic. Home: 20496 Broad Run Dr Sterling VA 20165-2511

FIALKOFF, FRANCINE SUSAN, editor; b. NYC, Aug. 24, 1946; d. Louis and Dorothy Ethel (Beck) F.; m. Glenn Robert Lewis, Mar. 31, 1974; children: Lindsay, Caroline. BA, CCNY, 1967; MA, U. Mass., 1969. Asst. editor Collier's Encyclopedia, NYC, 1969-71; assoc. editor Columbia U. Press, NYC, 1971-74; assoc. editor, book rev. Libr. Jour., NYC, 1977-89, mng. editor, book rev., 1989-90, editor, book rev., 1990-92, exec. editor, 1992-97, editor, 1997—2006, editor-in-chief, 2006—; editl. dir., libr. group Sch. Libr. Jour., Reed Bus. Info. divsn. Reed Elsevier, Inc. Mem. exec. bd. Friends of Librs. U.S.A., Phila., 1995—2005; judge NY Times Libr. award, 2001—. Columnist "Inside Track", Libr. Jour., 1989— (Neal award Am. Bus. Press 1997). Mem. ALA (advocacy subcom. 1996—98). Office: Libr Jour 360 Park Ave S New York NY 10010 Office Phone: 212-463-6807. Business E-Mail: fialkoff@reedbusiness.com.

FIASCHI-TAESCH, NATHALIE MADELEINE, medical educator; d. Gilbert Louis and Simone Josephine Fiaschi; m. Christophe Claude Taesch; children: Alix Karin Taesch, Constance Annick Taesch. PhD, Strasbourg, France, 2000. Asst. prof. medicine U. Pitts., 2006—. Recipient Young Investigator award, ASBMR, 2002. Mem.: Am. Soc. Bone and Mineral Rsch., Am. Diabetes Assn., Am. Heart Assn. Office: Univ Pitts BST E1140 200 Lothrop St Pittsburgh PA 15213 Home Phone: 412-521-2196; Office Phone: 412-648-9661.

FIBIGER, JOHN ANDREW, life insurance company executive; b. Copenhagen, Apr. 27, 1932; came to U.S., 1934, naturalized, 1953; s. Borge Rottboll and Ruth Elizabeth (Wadmond) F.; m. Barbara Mae Stuart, June 22, 1956; children: Karen Ruth McCarthy, Katherine Louise. BA, U. Minn., 1953, MA, 1954; postgrad., U. Wis. With Lincoln Nat. Life Ins. Co., Ft. Wayne, Ind., 1956-57; with Bankers Life Ins. Co. Nebr., Lincoln, 1959-73, sr. v.p. group, 1972-73; with New Eng. Mut. Life Ins. Co., Boston, 1973-89, vice chmn., pres., chief operating officer, 1981-89; with Transam Life Cos., 1991-94; exec. v.p., CFO, then pres. Transamerica Occidental Life Ins. Co., LA, 1994-95, chmn., 1995-97. Past vice chmn. Actuarial Bd. for Counseling and Discipline; bd. dirs. Fidelity Life Assn., Genworth Pvt. Asset Mgmt., Contra Fund. Life trustee, past chmn. Mus. Sci., Boston, 1989-91; past overseer New Eng. Med. Ctr., Boston Symphony Orch.; bd. dirs. Menninger Found., past v.p.; mem. fin. com., strategic planning com. L.A. Chamber Orch.; past chmn. Menninger Fund; past bd. dirs. U. So. Calif. Sch. Gerontology; bd. dirs. Austin Symphony Orch.; past trustee Calif. Mus. Sci. and Industry; bd. visitors, chmn. Menninger Baylor Meth. Found.; past chmn. Assn. Calif Life Insurance Co.; past founding dir. Boston Classical Orch., mem. fin. acctg. standards bd. adv. comm., 1984-88. With chem. corps US Army, 1957—59. Fellow Soc. Actuaries (past bd. dirs.); mem. Nat. Acad. Social Ins. (founding mem.), Am. Acad. Actuaries (past pres.). Personal E-mail: fibij@aol.com.

FICHTEL, RUDOLPH ROBERT, retired association executive; b. NYC, Dec. 12, 1915; s. Paul Gotthard and Helen (Szapka) F.; m. Elsie E. Terebesy, Dec. 24, 1942; children: Nancy Lynn, Robert Paul, Richard John. BBA cum laude, Coll. City N.Y., 1938; cert., Am. Inst. Banking, 1941; diploma fin. pub. relations, Northwestern U., 1950; MBA, NYU, 1951; diploma banking, Rutgers U., 1954. Tchr. N.Y.C. Pub. Schs., 1938-39; adminstr. East River Savs. Bank, 1939-42; dir. pub. relations, editor, asst. sec. Savs. Banks Assn. N.Y. State, 1945-53; dir. pub. relations council, savs. and mortgage div. Am. Bankers Assn., NYC and Washington, 1953-64; nat. dir. Am. Inst. Banking, 1964-78; regional v.p. United Student Aid Funds, Inc., NYC, 1978-87; ret. Mem. lender relations com. Higher Edn. Loan Programs; mem. faculty Am. Inst. Banking, Stonier Grad. Sch. Banking; contbg. editor Am. Inst. Banking textbooks; speaker. Contbr. articles to profl. jours. Vol. tutor Literacy Program, N.Y.C.; income tax counsellor Am. Assn. Retired Persons. Served to capt. AUS, 1942-45, ETO. Recipient highest award citation Internat. Council Indsl. Editors, 1948, Dr. Marcus Nadler award for excellence in finance; N.Y. U., 1951 Mem. Beta Gamma Sigma. Home: 65-19 170th St Flushing NY 11365-1949 *Success in my life has been the result of hard work, continuing search for knowledge, constant effort to understand and relate to people, and total dedication to excellence in full partnership with a loving family.*

FICHTNER, MARGARIA, journalist; b. Lakeland, Fla., May 4, 1944; d. August Albert and Margaret Louise (Kelly) Fichtner. BA, Fla. So. Coll., 1966. Feature writer, fashion editor Miami Herald, 1968—92, book editor, 1992—2001, book critic, 2001—03, sr. feature writer, 2003—. Recipient First Pl. Criticism award, Am. Assn. Sunday and Feature Editors, 1996, Fla. Soc. Newspaper Editors, 1997, First Pl. Criticism Green Eyeshade award, Soc. Profl. Journalists, 2000, First Pl. Critical Writing Sunshine State award, 2003. Office: The Miami Herald Pub Co One Herald Plz Miami FL 33132-1693 Home Phone: 305-858-6189; Office Phone: 305-376-3630. Business E-Mail: mfichtner@miamiherald.com.

FICHTNER, WILLIAM, actor; b. East Meadow, NY, Nov. 27, 1956; m. Betsy Aidem (div. 1996); 1 child; m. Kymberly Kalil, July 25, 1998; 1 child. BS, SUNY, 1978. Actor: (films) Malcolm X, 1992, Ramona!, 1993, Quiz Show, 1994, Underneath, 1995, Virtuosity, 1995, Strange Days, 1995, Heat, 1995, Albino Alligator, 1996, Contact, 1997, Switchback, 1997, Wing Commander Prophecy, 1997, Armageddon, 1998, The Settlement, 1999, Go, 1999, Endsville, 2000, Drowning Mona, 2000, Passion of Mind, 2000, The Perfect Storm, 2000, Pearl Harbor, 2001, What's the Worst that Could Happen?, 2001, Black Hawk Down, 2001, Julie Walking Home, 2002, Crash, 2004 (recipient, Outstanding Performance by a Cast in a Major Motion Picture, SAG awards, 2006), Nine Lives, 2005, The Chumscrubber, 2005, Mr. & Mrs. Smith, 2005, The Moguls, 2005, The Longest Yard, 2005, Ultraviolet, 2006, First Snow, 2006, Blades of Glory, 2007; (TV series) As the World Turns, 1987—93, MDs, 2002—03, Invasion, 2005—06, Prison Break, 2006—07; (TV films) A Father for Charlie, 1995, Empire Falls, 2005, (guest appearances): (TV series) Baywatch, 1989, Grace Under Fire, 1994, 1995, The West Wing, 2004, (voice) American Dad!, 2005.*

FICK, GARY WARREN, agronomist, educator; b. O'Neill, Nebr., July 10, 1943; s. Walter Henry and Doris Marie (Parks) F.; m. Mae Ellen Ruddell, June 29, 1969; children— Joseph, David, Charles BS, U. Nebr., 1965; diploma Agr. Sci., Massey U., 1968; PhD, U. Calif., Davis, 1971. Asst. prof. Cornell U., Ithaca, NY, 1971-76, assoc. prof., 1976-84, prof., 1984—, acting chair dept. soil crop and atmospheric scis., 1993, 95, tchg. leader soil crop and atmospheric scis., 1994—2006, tchg. leader dept. crop and soil scis., 2002—. Vis. scientist Lincoln Coll., New Zealand, 1977—78. Author: Food, Farming, and Faith; assoc. editor: Agronomy Jour., 1978-81, Jour. Prodn. Agr., 1987-93; mem. editl. bd. Jour. Sustainable Agr., 1996—; contbr. articles to profl. jours. and monographs. Fellow Crop Sci. Soc. Am., Am. Soc. Agronomy (tchg. award N.E. br. 1991); mem. Am. Forage and Grassland Coun. (Merit cert. 1989), Sigma Xi, Gamma Sigma Delta (Cornell pres. 1992-93), SUNY Chancellor's tchg. award 1995. Office: Cornell U Dept Crop and Soil Scis Ithaca NY 14853 Office Phone: 607-255-1704. Business E-Mail: gwf2@cornell.edu.

FICKE, GREGORY C., utilities executive; m. Carol Ficke; children: Lisa, Lindsay. BS, Miami U.; degree in Engring., The Ohio State U.; MBA, U. Cin.; JD, No. Ky. U.; grad. Adv. Mgmt. Program, Harvard Bus. Sch. Registered profl. engr., Ohio; bar: Ohio. With Bechtel Power Corp., Ann Arbor, Mich.; from mem. staff to pres. The Cin. (Ohio) Gas & Electric Co. Cinergy Corp., Cin., 1978—2001, pres. The Cin. (Ohio) Gas & Electric Co., 2001—. Bd. trustees Clovernook Ctr. Blind, Ohio Found. Ind. Colls. Mem.: Greater Cin. (Ohio) C. of C. (bd. trustees), Ohio C. of C. (bd. trustees). Office: Cinergy Corp 139 E 4th St Cincinnati OH 45202

FICKENSCHER, GERALD H., chemicals company executive; b. Buenos Aires, 1943; Graduate, Cath. U. Argentina, Buenos Aires, 1967; Post-Graduate, Cath. U. Argentina, 1970. V.p., CFO Uniroyal Chem. Corp., Middlebury, Conn.; v.p.-Europe, corp. officer Crompton Corp., Middlebury, 1994—. Home: 3200 Park Ave Unit 6b1 Bridgeport CT 06604-1147 Office: 199 Benson Rd Middlebury CT 06749 E-mail: gerald_fickenscher@cromptoncorp.com.

FICKER, ROBERTA SUE See FARRELL, SUZANNE

FICKETT, EDWARD HALE, architect, educator, arbitrator; b. LA, 1923; s. George Edward and Marguerite (Hale) F.; m. Joyce Helen Steinberg, Apr. 8, 1982. BArch, U. So. Calif., grad. studies in engring and archaelogy; M in City Planning, MIT, M in Arch. Registered architect, 50 states. Pvt. practice architecture, LA, 1950—. Archtl. advisor to Pres. Dwight D. Eisenhower, 1957-60; cons. to Federal Govt. on Housing; wrote guidelines and specifications for HUD, VA, FHA; Calif. Housing Bd. under Gov. Edmund G. Pat Brown; honored with fellowship in AIA, 1969; archtl. commr. City of Beverly Hills, Calif., 1977-86, chmn. Archtl. Commn., 1979-82; guest lectr., vis. prof. UCLA, U. Calif., Berkeley, MIT, Stanford U., U. So. Calif., U. Fla., Calif. Poly. State U.-San Luis Obispo, Rensselaer Poly. Inst., N.Y., U. Chgo.; arbitrator Nat. Panel Arbitrators, 1961—, Am. Arbitration Assn., 1963—. Archtl. works include L.A. Harbor (Port of L.A.) Cargo and Passenger Terminals, San Pedro, Sands Hotel, Las Vegas, Nev., La Costa Resort and Condominiums, Carlsbad, Calif., Las Cruces Resort Hotel, La Paz, Mex., Hacienda Hotel, Cabo San Lucas, Mex., Ocotillo Lodge Hotel, Palm Springs, Calif., Mammoth Mountain Inn, Mammoth, Calif., Murietta Hot Springs Resort, Murietta, Calif., Stallion Springs Resort, Tehachapi, Calif., Bistro Gardens Restaurant, Beverly Hills, Calif., Spago Restaurant, Beverly Hills, Scandia Restaurant, West Hollywood, Calif., Nicks Fishmarket Restaurant, West Hollywood, Univ. High Sch., UCLA Faculty Ctr., L.A. Police Acad., L.A., master plans for Edwards AFB, Calif., Norton AFB, Calif., Murphy Canyon Heights Naval Base, Calif., Los Alametos Naval Base, Calif., San Pedro Naval base, Calif., L.A. City Hall Hist. and Seismic Renovation, Nethercutt Antique Car Mus., Dodger Stadium, others; comml. devels., master planned communities, office bldgs., restaurants, resorts, hotels, homes, condominiums, shopping ctrs., air force bases, naval bases, schs., renovation of hist. bldgs., historic & seismic rehab, designed over 60,000 homes. Mem. Gov. Pat Brown's Housing Bd. for Calif.; U.S. del. to Internat. Congress of Archs. Lt. comdr. Sea Bees, USN. Recipient Merit of Honor award by Pres. of U.S., L.A. Conservancy Preservation Arch. award, 1999, National Progressive Architecture Design awards, city beautification awards from L.A., Beverly Hills, Reno, Seattle, numerous Nat. Assn. Home Builders awards, Sunset Magazine and House and Home awards, Better Homes and Gardens House of Yr. awards, Nat. Assn. Home Builders awards, Los Angeles Conservancy Archtl. Design Award, 1999, Nat. Hist. Monuments Archtl. Design Award, 1999, Housing Hall of Fame, other awards. Fellow AIA (AIA First Honor Awards, numerous AIA merit of honor awards, pres. So. Calif. chpt. 1958-62, pres. Calif. chpt. 1962, chmn. Nat. Ethics Com., featured speaker nat. convs., lectr., formulated and participated in AIA Univ. Lecture series, fellow 1969, U.S. del. internat. congress archs.), Nat. Comm. for Bldg. Industry (chmn. 1962-72), Nat. Assn. Home Builders (speaker nat. convs.), Calif. Coun. Architects (sec. 1960), Am. Archtl. Found. Octagon Soc. (charter mem.), U. So. Calif. Archtl. Guild (charter mem.). Avocations: tennis, golf. Office: 7421 Beverly Blvd Los Angeles CA 90036-2703 Office Phone: 323-939-7476. Fax: 323-935-4144.

FICKLER, ARLENE, lawyer; b. Phila., Apr. 21, 1951; BA cum laude, U. Pa., 1971, JD cum laude, 1974. Bar: Pa. 1974, D.C. 1980, U.S. Supreme Ct. 1989. Ptnr. Hoyle Fickler Herschel & Mathes LLP, Phila. Staff atty. Commn. on Revision of Fed. Ct. Appellate System, 1974-75; exec. asst. Bicentennial Com. Jud. Conf. of U.S., 1975-76. Comment editor U. Pa. Law Rev., 1973-74; co-reporter American College of Trial Lawyers Mass Tort Litigation Manual; contbr. chpt. to book and articles to law jours. Pres. U. Pa. Law Sch. Alumni Bd. Mgrs., 1997-99; trustee Jewish Fedn. of Greater Phila., 1981-88, 89-93, 94-98, 99—, Phila. Bar Found., 1993-98, Jewish Cmty. Rels. Coun. Greater Phila., 1983-94, 98-2000; trustee Jewish Cmty. Ctrs. of Phila., 1997—, chair, 2003—06; trustee HIAS Immigration Svcs. Phila., 1998—, treas., 1999-2003; mem. United Jewish Appeal Nat. Young Women's Leadership Cabinet, 1982-87; v.p. Phila. chpt. Am. Jewish Congress, 1995-2001; co-chmn. Phila. Jewish Cmty. Ctr. Maccabi Games, 2001; dir. Jewish Cmty. Ctr Assn., 2006—. Recipient Mrs. Isidore Kohn Young Leadership award Jewish Fedn. Greater Phila., 1981, Next Generation Leadership award Jewish Cmty. Ctrs. Assn., 2000, award of merit U. Pa. Law Sch. Alumni, 2001. Mem. ABA, Am. Law Inst., Am. Bar Found., Pa. Bar Assn., D.C. Bar, Phila. Bar Assn. (chmn. fed. cts. com. 1992), Fed. Bar Coun. of Second Cir., Third Cir. Bar Assn., U. Pa. Am. Inn of Ct. Office: Hoyle Fickler Herschel & Mathes LLP One South Broad St 1500 Philadelphia PA 19103 Home Phone: 215-735-0560; Office Phone: 215-981-5850. Office Fax: 215-981-5959. Business E-Mail: afickler@hoylelawfirm.com.

FIDANCE, CHRISTINA MARIE, human services administrator; b. Wilmington, Del., Nov. 24, 1980; d. Anthony Fidance and Ann Marie Lis. BA in Sociology, U. Del., Newark, 2004. Statis. analyst State of Del., Statistical Analysis Ctr., Dover, 2000—04; adminstrv. profl. State of Del., Dept Health & Human Svcs., New Castle, 2005—. Campaign solicitor Green Party, Wilmington, Del., 2004—06; rally organizing A.N.S.W.E.R. Coalition, Washington, 2004—06. Recipient Silver medal, VICCA Knowledge Bowl, 1998. Green Party. Achievements include research in statewide study on juvenile recidivism. Avocations: Scrabble, reading, travel, chess. Home: 219 N Bancroft Pky Wilmington DE 19805 Home Phone: 302-437-5281; Office Phone: 302-255-9633. Personal E-mail: faraway3283@aol.com.

FIDDICK, PAUL WILLIAM, public official, broadcast executive; b. St. Joseph, Mo., Nov. 20, 1949; s. Lowell Duane and Betty Jean (Manring) F.; m. Julie Hanna Lorms, July 31, 1983; children: Lea Elizabeth, Hanna Manring. BJ, U. Mo., 1971. Account exec. Sta. KCMO-KFMU, Kansas City, Mo., 1971-72, Sta. WEZW, Milw., 1972-74, dir. sales mktg., 1974-76, v.p., gen. mgr., 1976-81; sr. v.p. Multimedia Broadcasting Co., Milw., 1981; pres. Multimedia Radio, Cin., 1982-86, Radio Group, Heritage Communications, Inc., Des Moines, 1986-87, Radio Group, Heritage Media Corp., Dallas, 1987-98; dir, vice chmn. RadioWave.com, Inc., Schaumburg, Ill., 1998-99, acting pres., 1999; asst. sec. USDA, Washington, 1999-2001, dir. USDA Grad. Sch., 2000—; dir. Nat. Assn. of Broadcasters, Washington, 1994-98; pres. Emmis Internat., Wash., 2002—; dir. pres. Democracy Radio Inc., Wash., 2002—06. Dir. Radio Advt. Bur., NYC, 1983—99, chmn., 1993—94; trustee Washington Chorus, 2000—05; mem. acad. staff U. Wis., Milw., 1978—81; mem. adv. bd. Advanced Microbial Solutions LLC, Pilot Point, Tex., 2002—; mem. adv. coun. Bus. for Diplomatic Action, San Francisco, 2004—; mem. adv. bd. Siena Holdings LLC, Bethesda, Md., 2005—. Elder Westminster Presbyn. Ch., Dallas, 1997-99, Western Presbyn. Ch., Washington, 2004—. Named one of 40 Most Powerful People in Radio, Radio Ink Mag., 1996, Fifth Estater, Broadcasting Mag., 1990, Up and Coming Radio Exec. of Yr., Radio Only mag., 1983, Pub.'s Profile, Radio and Records mag., 1998. Mem. Phi Eta Sigma, Kappa Tau Alpha.

FIDEL, RAYA, information science educator; b. Tel Aviv, Jan. 18, 1945; came to U.S., 1977; BSc, Tel Aviv U., 1970; MLS, Hebrew U., Jerusalem, 1976; PhD, U. Md., 1982. Tchr. Adult Edn. Ctr., Jerusalem, 1971-72; br. libr. Hebrew U., Jerusalem, 1972-77; asst. prof. libr. sci. U. Wash., Seattle, 1982-87, assoc. prof. libr. sci., 1987-2000, prof. Info. Sch., 2000—, head Ctr. Human-Info. Interaction The Info. Sch., 2003—. Vis. libr. Duke U.

Libr., Durham, N.C., 1992-93. Author: Database Design, 1987; editor Advances in Classification, 1991-94 (award 1992-94); contbr. articles to profl. publs. Recipient Research award Am. Society for Information Science, 1994 Mem. AAUP (chair U. Wash. chpt. 1990-92, pres. state conf. 1992-97), Assn. Computing Machinery, Am. Soc. Info. Sci. (dir.-at-large 2000-02). Home: 5801 Phinney Ave N Seattle WA 98103-5862

FIEBACH, H. ROBERT, lawyer; b. Paterson, NJ, June 7, 1939; s. Michael M. and Silvia Irene (Nadler) F.; m. Elizabeth D. Carlton, Mar. 17, 1984; children: Michael, Emma; children by previous marriage: Jonathan, Rachel. BS, U. Pa., 1961, LLB cum laude, 1964. Bar: Pa. 1965, U.S. Supreme Ct. 1971. Law clk. to Chief Judge Biggs U.S. Ct. Appeals for 3d Cir., 1964-65; assoc. Wolf, Block, Schorr and Solis-Cohen, Phila., 1965-71, ptnr., 1971-79, sr. ptnr., 1979-95; mem., shareholder Cozen O'Connor, Phila., 1995—. Permanent mem. U.S. Jud. Conf. for 3d cir., 1967—; mem. Pa. Supreme Ct. Adv. Com. on Appellate Rules, 1987-93, Commn. on Jud. Elections, 1997-98; arbitrator, mediator U.S. Dist. Ct. (ea. dist.) Pa., 1966—, Commerc Ct., Phila., Pa., 1999—; lectr. Nat. Legal Malpractice Seminar, 2003, 04, 06, 07; course planner, lectr. PBI Litigating the Legal Malpractice Case Seminar, 2004. Contbg. author: Business and Commercial Litigation in the Federal Courts, 2005; rsch. editor U. Pa. Law Rev., 1964-65; contbr. articles to legal jours. Past mem. Phila. adv. bd. Anti-Defamation League of B'nai Brith, Greater Phila. Regional Commn. on Law and Social Action, Am. Jewish Congress; bd. dirs. Greater Phila. chpt. ACLU, past chmn. criminal justice and police practices com.; past bd. dirs. Pa. chpt. ACLU; bd. dirs. Rodeph Shalom Synagogue, v.p.; mem. Pub. Interest Law Ctr. of Phila.; mem. Mayor's Task Force on Gaming, 2005. Fellow: Am. Coll. Trial Lawyers; mem.: ABA (past chmn. jud. performance and conduct com., jud. adminstrn. divsn. 1986—91, nat. conf. bar pres. 1991—95, pres. nat. caucus state bar assns. 1994—95, chmn. standing com. on lawyers profl. liability 1994—95, bd. govs. 1997—2000, ho. of dels. 2001—07, nat. conf. bar pres. 2001—, state del. 2001—07, litigation sect., 1988 and 2002 midyear meeting host com., state chair), Pa. Bar Found., Am. Bar Found., Soc. of Fellows (state co-chmn. 2003—07), Phila. Trial Lawyers Assn. (bd. dirs. 1989—90, past chmn. bus. litig. com.), Am. Judicature Soc. (state membership chmn. 1988), Defender Assn. Phila. (bd. dirs.), Pa. Bar Inst. (pres. bd. dirs. 1984—90, 2000—01), Phila. Bar Assn. (chmn. spl. com. on ins. 1983—84, bd. govs. 1983—87, past chmn. fed. cts. com., spkr. various panels, past vice-chmn. arbitration com., civil jud. procedures com., past mem. spl. com. to study appellate cts.), Pa. Bar Assn. (past vice-chmn. jud. selection com., chmn. jud. retention election com 1980—83, chmn. polit. action com. for merit retention of judges 1980—83, ho. of dels. 1983—, chmn. com. on profl. liability 1984—87, bd. govs. 1987—95, pres.-elect 1992—93, pres. 1993—94, Pa. Bar Trust 1996—2004, chair 1999—2004, Spl. Achievement award 1986), Order of Coif (past dir. U. Pa. chpt.). Office: Cozen & O'Conner 1900 Market St Fl 3 Philadelphia PA 19103-3572 Home: 200 W Washington Sq Apt 2804 Philadelphia PA 19106-3536 Home Phone: 215-925-8141; Office Phone: 215-665-4166. Business E-Mail: rfiebach@cozen.com.

FIEBERT, MARTIN STEPHEN, psychology professor; b. NYC, June 6, 1939; s. Max and Grace F.; m. Paula Barbara Schwartz, June 1, 1963 (div. 1999); children: Bryan, Deirdre; m. Margo Law Kasdan, Dec. 22, 1999. PhD, U. Rochester, 1965. Lic. psychologist, Calif. Prof. psychology Calif. State U., Long Beach, Calif., 1965—. Contbr. articles to profl. jours. Mem.: Calif. Faculty Assn. (vice pres.), Am. Psychol. Soc. Avocations: tennis, travel, sculpting, meditation. Office: Calif State U 1250 Bellflower Blvd Long Beach CA 90840 Fax: 562-985-8004. E-mail: mfiebert@csulb.edu.

FIEDEROWICZ, WALTER MICHAEL, lawyer; b. Hartford, Conn., Aug. 23, 1946; s. Michael and Sylvia Christine (Ramunno) F.; m. Gerry Prattson, June 1, 1968; children: Michael, Catherine. BA, Yale U., 1968; JD (DuPont fellow), U. Va., 1971. Bar: Conn. 1971, U.S. Supreme Ct. 1977. Mem. firm Cummings & Lockwood, Stamford, Conn., 1971-76, ptnr. firm, 1979-88, of counsel, 1989-91; pres. Covenant Mut. Ins. Co., Hartford, 1985-92; White House fellow U.S. Dept. Justice, Washington, 1976-77; spl. asst. to Atty. Gen., Dept. Justice, Washington, 1976-77; assoc. dep. Atty. Gen., 1977-79. Bd. dirs. Photronics, Inc., Hematech; chmn. CDT Corp., Meacock Capital, Omega Ins. Holdings, Ltd. Mem. editl. Va. Law Rev., 1969-71. Grad. coun. Loomis-Chaffee Sch. Bd.; trustee Conn. Trust for Hist. Preservation; bd. dirs. Litchfield Hist. Soc.; comr. Conn. Commn. Culture and Tourism. Mem. ABA, Conn. Bar Assn., Order of the Coif, Hartford Golf Club, Univ. Club. Roman Catholic. Home: 102 North St PO Box 939 Litchfield CT 06759-0939 Office Phone: 860-567-9828. Personal E-mail: fiederowicz@juno.com.

FIEDLER, FRED EDWARD, retired organizational psychology educator, consultant; b. Vienna, July 13, 1922; arrived in US, 1938; s. Victor and Hilda (Schallinger) F.; m. Judith Joseph, Apr. 14, 1946; children: Decky, Ellen Victoria, Carol Ann. AM, U. Chgo., 1947, PhD, 1949. Clin. psychol. trainee US VA, Chgo., 1947-50; rsch. assoc., instr. U. Chgo., 1949-51; asst. prof. psychology to prof. U. Ill., Urbana, 1951-69; prof. U. Wash., 1969-93, prof. emeritus psychology, 1993—. Vis. prof. U. Amsterdam, 1958-59; guest prof. U. Louvain, Belgium, 1963-64; vis. rsch. fellow Templeton Coll., Oxford, 1986; cons. State of Wash., 1981-84, King County, Wash., 1970-80; cons. various govt., mil., pvt. orgns., U.S., Europe, 1953—; apptd. to SLA Marshall chair U.S. Army Rsch. Inst., 1988-89. Author: Boards, Management and Company Success, 1959; A Theory of Leadership Effectiveness, 1967; Improving Leadership Effectiveness, 1976; Leadership and Effective Management, 1974; New Approaches to Effective Leadership—Cognitive Resources and Organizational Performance, 1987; contbr. numerous articles to profl. jours. Mem. Wash. Gov.'s Transition Team, 1980, Task Force on Pers. Selection of Apptd. Ofcls; co-chmn. Tech. Transfer, State of Wash., 1980-81; pub. mem. State Med. Disciplinary Bd., 1981-85. With Med. Dept. and Mil. Govt. br. U.S. Army, 1942-45. Recipient Outstanding Rsch. award Am. Pers. and Guidance Assn., 1953, Stogdill award for disting. contbns. to leadership, 1978, award Outstanding Sci. Contbns. to Mil. Psychology, 1979, Walter F. Ulmer Jr. Applied Rsch. award Ctr. Creative Leadership, 2005; named Disting. Bicentennial lectr. U. Ga., 1985; Claremont Grad. Sch. and Claremont-McKenna Coll. 1991 Leadership Conf. dedicated to him. Fellow APA (Rsch. award in cons. psychology 1971), Soc. for Indsl./Orgnl. Psychology (Disting. Sci. Contbns. award 1996), Am. Psychol. Soc. (James McKeen Caltell award 1999), Am. Acad. Mgmt. (Disting. Educator award), Internat. Assn. Applied Psychology (Disting. Contrbns. award 2002), Internat. Assn. Applied Psychology (past pres. orgnl. psychology divsn.), Soc. Orgnl. Behavior. Office: U Wash Dept Psychology 351525 Seattle WA 98195-0001 Business E-Mail: fiedler@u.washington.edu.

FIEDLER, HAL (HAROLD), painter, printmaker; b. Bronx, Jan. 12, 1919; s. Eva Braun and Nathan Fiedler; children: Judith Aaron, Joan Barbara Mele. PhD, Inst. for Advanced Study Human Sexuality, San Francisco, 1988. Cert. Rational-Emotive Therapy and Techniques Inst. for Rational-Emotive Therapy, NY, 1990, diplomate Hypnotherapy Am. Bd. Hypnotherapy, Calif., 1995, Sex Therapy Am. Bd. Sexologists, DC, 1995. Art dir., graphic design, NYC, 1946—62; artist, painter S.P. Solomons Art, NYC, 1963—69; graphic designer, calligrapher Hal Fiedler Assocs., NYC, 1970—82; writer, editor Am. Bd. Sexology, Washington, 1992—93; sexologist, sex educator Pvt. Practice, Bayside, NY, 1993—2002, psychotherapist, hypnotherapist, 1995—2002; painter, printmaker Pvt. Practice/eBay, 2005—. Calligraphy instr. Cooper Union Sch. Art, NYC, 1957—59; seminar lectr. Nat. Guild Hypnotists, Nashua, NH, 1993—95. Author (illustrator): (textbook) Be Smart About Sex: Facts for Young People; author: (editor-in-chief) An Outline of Sexology; one-man shows include paintings Munsey Park Gallery, Rego Park Gallery, advertising, comm., graphics, Hal Fiedler Graphics, serigraph, Shipfitters (Purchase, Met. Mus. Art, 1944). Founding Clinical Fellow, Am. Acad. Clin. Sexologists, Calif., 1995. Mem.: Mensa (assoc.), Intertel (assoc.). Achievements include design of Type Designs: Fiedler Gothic, Egyptian, Baroque; research in sexual attitudes and behaviors, high IQ population; survey on sex education publications for high school age. Avocations: ballroom dancing, gerontological research. Home and Office: 6923 Bell Blvd Oakland Gardens NY 11364 Home Phone: 718-428-6469; Office Phone: 718-428-6469. Personal E-mail: halfiedler@aol.com.

FIEDLER, JOSEPH ROBERT, mathematician, educator; b. Dayton, Ohio, Aug. 26, 1948; s. Otto E and Winifred Cochran Fiedler. AB in Math., Harvard U., Cambridge, Mass., 1970; MS in Math., The Ohio State U., 1972, PhD in Math., 1988. Program assoc. Dept. of Math., The Ohio State U., Columbus, 1980—85; asst. prof. Dept. of Math., Calif. State U., Bakersfield, 1989—93, assoc. prof., 1993—99, prof., 1999—. Vis. assoc. prof. math. Ohio State U., 1995; co-dir. math. preparation initiative Calif. State U. Co-author (textbook) Calculus Laboratories with Maple: A Tool, not an Oracle, Calculus: Mathematics and Modeling. Grantee Prin. Investigator, Math. Profl. Devel. Inst., U. of Calif., 1001—, 2002—. Mem.: Am. Math. Assn. of Two Yr. Colls. (referee, amatyc rev. 1988), Assn. for Women in Math., Calif. Math. Coun. of Cmty. Colls., Bakersfield Math. Coun. (interim pres. 2000—02, Tchr. of the Yr. 2002), Calif. Math. Coun., Nat. Coun. Tchrs. Math., Teachers Tchg. with Tech. (coll. short course instr.), Am. Math. Assn. of Two Yr. Colleges, Nat. Coun. of Teachers of Math. (mem. math. tchr. adv. panel 2001—02), Math. Assn. of Am. (chair subcom. on svc. courses 1995—98). Home: 6513 S Half Moon Dr Bakersfield CA 93309 Office: California State University Bakersfield 9001 Stockdale Hwy Bakersfield CA 93311-1099 Office Phone: 661-664-2058. Business E-Mail: jfiedler@csub.edu.

FIEDLER, MARC, lawyer, advocate; b. New Haven, May 4, 1955; s. Ernest and Evelyn (Zimmerman) F. BA, Harvard U., 1978, JD, 1984. Bar: Mass. 1985, U.S. Ct. Appeals (D.C. cir.) 1987, D.C. 1988, U.S. Dist. Ct. D.C. 1988, U.S. Ct. Appeals (4th cir.) 1988, U.S. Supreme Ct. 1988. Law clk. to assoc. judge D.C. Ct. Appeals, Washington, 1984-85; assoc. Koonz, McKenney & Johnson P.C., Washington, 1985-93; ptnr. Koonz, McKenney, Johnson, DePaolis & Lightfoot LLP, Washington, 1994—. Co-founder, chmn. Disability Rights Coun. of Greater Washington; pres. NE Independent Living Program, Lawrence, Mass., 1982-84; v.p. Disability Law Ctr., Boston, 1982-84. Founder, assoc. dir. Mass. Office Handicapped Affairs, Boston, 1979-81. Recipient Lawyer of Yr. award Trial Lawyers Assn., 1989, Trailblazer award DC Cts., 2002, Alfred McKenzie award Washington Lawyers Com. Civil Rights and Urban Affairs, 2002. Mem. ABA, ATLA (co-chmn. Amicus Com. 1996-98), D.C. Bar Assn. (trustee rsch. found. 1992-95, young lawyers sect., civil jury instrn. com. 1988-91), Trial Lawyers Assn. Metro Washington (chmn. Amicus Com. 1987-2001, pres. 2001-02). Office: Koonz McKenney Johnson DePaolis & Lightfoot LLP 2001 Pennsylvania Ave NW Ste 450 Washington DC 20006 Office Phone: 202-659-5500. Business E-Mail: mfiedler@koonz.com.

FIEDLER, TOM (THOMAS EDWARD FIEDLER), retired editor; b. 1946; m. Suzanne Bowlin Fiedler, 1968; 2 children. Degree in Engring., Merchant Marine Acad.; MA in Journalism, Boston U., 1971; competed Advanced Exec. Program for Media Mgmt., Northwestern U., 2004. Fellow profl. journalism Duke U., 1984—85; polit. editor, columnist, White Ho. corr., war corr. Miami Herald, editl. page editor, 1999—2001, v.p., exec. editor, 2001—07. Author: Florida Institute of Government's Almanac of Florida Politics. Recipient Bronze Medallion, Soc. Profl. Journalists, 1988, Pulitzer prize reporting polit. influence extremist group, 1991, Pulitzer prize coverage Hurricane Andrew disaster, 1993.*

FIEGEL, JENNIFER, biomedical researcher, educator; m. Brian Fiegel, July 11, 1998; 1 child, Elijah. BS, U. Mass., Amherst, 1998; PhD, Johns Hopkins U., Balt., 2004. Postdoctoral fellow Harvard U., Cambridge, Mass., 2004—06; asst. prof. U. Iowa, Iowa City, 2006—. Fellow, NSF, 1999—2002. Mem.: AIChE, Soc. Women Engrs., Controlled Release Soc., Am. Assn. Pharm. Scientists, Soc. Biol. Engring., Internat. Soc. Aerosols in Medicine, Tau Beta Pi. Achievements include patents pending in field. Office: Univ Iowa 115 S Grand Ave S215 PHAR Iowa City IA 52242 Office Phone: 319-335-8830. Office Fax: 319-335-9349. Business E-Mail: jennifer-fiegel@uiowa.edu.

FIEGER, GEOFFREY NELS, lawyer; b. Detroit, Dec. 23, 1950; s. Bernard Julian and June Beth (Oberer) F.; m. Kathleen Janice Podwoiski, June 25, 1983. BA, U. Mich., 1974, MA, 1976; JD, Detroit Coll. Law, 1979. Bar: Mich. 1979, U.S. Dist. Ct. (ea. dist.) Mich. 1979, Fla. 1980, U.S. Dist. Ct. (mid. dist.) Fla. 1980, Ariz. 1980. Ptnr. Fieger Fieger Kenney & Johnson, P.C., Southfield, Mich., 1979—. V.p. Orgn. United to Save Twp., West Bloomfield, Mich., 1987; dem. nominee for gov. of Mich., 1998. Mem. ABA, Detroit Bar Assn., Assn. Trial Lawyers Am. Unitarian Universalist. Avocations: running, swimming. Office: Fieger Fieger Kenney Johnson & Giroux 19390 W 10 Mile Rd Southfield MI 48075-2463*

FIEL, STANLEY BRUCE, internist, pulmonologist, educator, researcher; b. Aug. 9, 1948; children: Jami Marissa, Seth Jordan, Marla Anne. BS, U. Conn., 1969; MD, Med. Coll. of Pa., 1973. Diplomate Am. Bd. Internal Medicine, Pulmonary Bd. Internal Medicine; lic. physician, Pa. Intern Temple U. Hosp., Phila., 1973-74, resident, 1974-76; pulmonary disease fellow Hosp. of U. Pa., Phila., 1976-78; attending physician Temple U. Sch. Medicine, Phila., 1978-91, Am. Oncologic Hosp., Phila., 1982-92, St. Christopher's Hosp. for Children, Phila., 1998—2003, Med. Coll. Pa., Phila., 1991—; asst. prof. medicine, assoc. prof. Temple U. Sch. Medicine, Phila., 1978-89, prof. medicine, 1990—, Med. Coll. Pa., Phila., 1991—, Allegheny U. Health Scis., Phila., 1994—; regional chmn. dept. medicine Atlantic Health Sus., 2004—; prof., chair dept. medicine Morristown (NJ) Meml. Hosp., 2004—; prof. medicine Drexel U. Coll. Medicine, 2004—, U. Medicine and Dentistry N.J.-N.J. Med. Sch., 2005. Chief pulmonary disease and critical care medicine sect. Drexel U. Coll. Medicine, 1991—2003, v.p. medicine, chief medicine, 2001; attending physician, chief pulmonary unit Drexel U. Coll. Medicine, 1991—2003, dir. fellowship tng. program, 1991—, dir. Adult Cystic Fibrosis Program, 1991—, dir. Respiratory Care Svcs., 1991—, exec. com. of faculty, 1992—, utilization com., 1992—, chmn. search com. Cmty. and Preventive Medicine, 1992-93, sec. Exec. Faculty Com., 1993—. Mem. editl. bd. Clin. Respiratory Medicine, 1993—, Jour. of Asthma, 1993—; assoc. editor New Insights into Cystic Fibrosis, 1993—; contbr. articles to profl. jours. and chpts. to books. Recipient Lange Book award in Medicine, 1973, Rittenhouse Book award, 1973, Mosby Book award, 1973, Golden Apple Teaching award, 1985, 88; named Finalist for Lindbach Teaching award, 1990; grantee NIH, 1978-83, 89-91, Maternal and Child Health Care, 1984-88, Cystic Fibrosis Found., 1987-89, 93, Rorer Pharms., 1991-92,Am. Lung Assn., 1989-90, Glaxo Pharm. Co., 1991-93, G.H. Besselaar Assocs., 1991-93, ICI Pharm. Group, 1991-2000, Cortech Pharm. Group, 1993-2000, Genentech, Inc., 1993. Mem. Am. Thoracic Soc., Am. Coll. Chest Physicians, Assn. Am. Med. Colls., Am. Coll. Physicians, Soc. Clin. Decision Making, Am. Fedn. Clin. Rsch., ASTE, Phila. County Med. Soc., Pa. Med. Soc., Pa. Thoracic Soc. Home: 9 S Gables Dr Chester NJ 07930 Office: Morristown Meml Hosp 100 Madison Ave Morristown NJ 07962 Office Phone: 973-971-5136. Business E-Mail: stanley.fiel@atlantichealth.org.

FIELD, ALEXANDER JAMES, economics professor, dean; b. Boston, Apr. 17, 1949; s. Mark George and Anne (Murray) F.; m. Valerie Nan Wolk, Aug. 8, 1982; children: James Alexander, Emily Elena. AB, Harvard U., 1970; MS, London Sch. Econs., 1971; PhD, U. Calif., Berkeley, 1974. Asst. prof. econs. Stanford (Calif.) U., 1974-82; assoc. prof. Santa Clara (Calif.) U., 1982-88, acad. v.p., 1986-87, prof., chmn. dept. econs., 1988-93, assoc. dean Leavey Sch. Bus. and Adminstrn., 1993-96, dean, 1996-97, Michel and Mary Orradre prof. econs., 1992—. Mem. bd. trustees Santa Clara U., 1988-91. Author: Educational Reform and Manufacturing Development in Mid-Nineteenth Century Massachusetts, 1989, Altruistically Inclined: The Behavioral Sciences, Evolutionary Theory and the Origins of Reciprocity, 2001, The Most Technologically Progressive Decade of the Century, 2003; assoc. editor: Jour. Econ. Lit., 1981—2004; editor: Rsch. in Econ. History, 1993—; mem. editl. bd.: Explorations in Econ. History, 1983—89, Jour. Econ. History, 2001—04, Jour. Bioecons., 2005—, Cliometrica, 2006—, NSF Econs. Panel, 2006—07; contbr. articles to profl. jours. Recipient Nevins prize Columbia U., 1975; NSF rsch. grantee, 1989. Mem. Am. Econ. Assn., Econ. History Assn. (exec. dir. 2004—), Cliometrics Soc., Phi Beta Kappa, Beta Gamma Sigma. Home: 3762 Redwood Cir Palo Alto CA 94306-4255 Office: Santa Clara Univ Dept Econs Santa Clara CA 95053-0001 Home Phone: 650-494-9133; Office Phone: 408-554-4348.

FIELD, ANDREA BEAR, lawyer; b. New London, Conn., Nov. 30, 1949; d Geurson Donald and Lorraine (Solomon) Silverberg; m. Thornton Withers Field, May 17, 1984; children: Benjamin, Geoffrey. Student, Wellesley Coll., 1967-69; BA, Yale U., 1971; JD, U. Va., 1974. Bar: Va. 1974, D.C. 1978, U.S. Ct. Appeals (3d, 4th, 5th, 7th, 8th and D.C. cirs.). Assoc. Hunton & Williams LLP, Washington and Richmond, Va., DC, 1974-81, ptnr. Washington, 1991—, mng. ptnr., resources, regulatory & environ. law, and mem. exec. com. Mem. ABA (chair sect. natural resources, energy and environ. law 1989-90, coun. 1984-87, 90-91, chair com. air quality 1982-84, vice chair teleconf. com. 1990—, environ. controls bus. law sect. 1990-91, vice chair com. environ. law, real property, probate and trust law sect. 1990-91; chair standing com. on natural conf. groups 1993-94, nat. conf. lawyers and scientists 1990-93, sect. ad hoc com. nat. insts. 1989-90, coun. sect. sci. and tech. 1991-92), Va. Bar, DC Bar. Office: Hunton & Williams 1900 K St NW Washington DC 20006-1109 Office Phone: 202-955-1558. Office Fax: 202-778-2201. Business E-Mail: afield@hunton.com.

FIELD, ARTHUR NORMAN, lawyer; b. NYC, Sept. 28, 1935; s. Harry and Rose (Lemberg) F.; m. Doris Helen Rabbiner, Sept. 1, 1957; children: Michael, Karen. BBA, CCNY, 1955; LLB, Harvard U., 1958. Bar: (NY) 1959, (Fla.) 1975. Assoc. Shearman & Sterling, NYC, 1959-68, ptnr., 1968-2000; pres. GXG Mgmt., LLC, NYC, 2000—; mem. Field Cons. LLC. Chair Tribar Opinion Com., 1985—90. Co-author (with Jeffrey M. Smith): Legal Opinions in Business Transactions, 2003; co-editor (with M. Moskin): Transactional Lawyers Deskbook, 2001. Chmn., bd. dirs. Community Action Legal Svcs., 1972-77 (chair 78-79); bd. dirs. Brookdale Found., 1983—, Wave Hill Inc., NYC, 1968-80, Washington Square Legal Svcs., 1979-95, Historic House Trust NY, 2000-; trustee Ramapo Trust, 1983; bd. dirs. Preservation League NY, 2003—; mem. adv. bd. N.E. Bus. Law Ctr. Fellow Am. Bar Found., NY Bar Found., NY County Lawyers Assn. (pres. 1990-92); mem. ABA (ho. of dels. 1990-92, chair bus. sect. opinion com., 2002-04, working group legal opinions, 2007-, mem. bus. sect. coun. 2004—), NY State Bar Assn. (v.p. 1992-97), Assn. Bar City NY, Am. Law Inst., Assn. of Arbitrators, NYC, (dir. 1998-2002). E-mail: anfield@igxg.com.

FIELD, BARBARA KAY, elementary school educator; d. Douglas George and Iva Mae Lorentz; m. Steven James Field, June 23, 1973; children: Melissa Kay, Nathaniel Peter. BS, U. Wis., Eau Claire, 1973, MS in Tchg. Reading, 2000. Cert. reading specialist Wis., elem. tchr. Wis., reading tchr. Wis. 6th grade tchr. Osseo (Wis.)-Fairchild Sch. Dist., 1974—76, 4th grade reading tchr., unit cons., 1976—85, Title I reading tchr., 1986—88, 4th grade tchr., 1988—91; grades 7-8 reading tchr. Opelika (Ala.) City Schs., 1991—92, K-2 Title I reading tchr., 1992—96; Title I reading tchr., dist. reading resource Whitehall (Wis.) Sch. Dist., 1996—99; K-5 reading tchr. Eau Claire Area Sch. Dist., 1999—, academic coord. Longfellow 21st Century Cmty. Learning Ctr., 2003—. Mem.: NEA (assoc.), Eau Claire Assn. Educators (assoc.), Wis. Edn. Assn. (assoc.), Eau Claire Area Reading Coun. (assoc.; treas, pres.), Wis. State Reading Assocation (assoc.; chmn. conv. com. evaluation 2004—05, Pat Bricker award 1998), Internat. Reading Assn. (assoc.), Alpha Delta Kappa (assoc.). Office: Longfellow Elem Sch 512 Balcom St Eau Claire WI 54703 Home Phone: 715-839-7835.

FIELD, BARRY ELLIOT, internist, gastroenterologist; b. Hartford, Conn., Apr. 21, 1947; s. Arnold and Selma (Nechrich) F.; m. Julie Farr, Jan. 6, 1991; children: Rachel Elizabeth, Hannah Margaret, Miles Jay. BA (scholar), Harvard U., 1968; MD, Albert Einstein Coll. Medicine, 1972. Intern in pediat. Montefiore Hops., Bronx, NY, 1972-73; intern in medicine Met. Hosp., NYC, 1973-74, resident in medicine, 1974-76; fellow in gastroenterology Harbor Gen. Hosp., Torrance, Calif., 1976-78; pvt. practice in internal medicine and gastroenterology North Tarrytown, NY, 1978—. Dir. medicine Phelps Meml. Hosp., North Tarrytown. Mem. Am. Gastroenterol. Assn., Alpha Omega Alpha. Office: 777 N Broadway Ste 305 Tarrytown NY 10591-1040 Home Phone: 718-548-8826; Office Phone: 914-366-6120.

FIELD, CAROL HART, writer, news correspondent, journalist; b. San Francisco, Mar. 27, 1940; d. James D. and Ruth (Arnstein) Hart; m. John L. Field, July 23, 1961; children: Matthew, Alison. BA, Wellesley Coll., 1961. Contbg. editor, assoc. editor, asst. editor City Mag., San Francisco, 1974-76; contbg. editor New West/Calif. Mag., San Francisco, L.A., 1975-80, San Francisco Mag., 1980-82; fgn. corr. La Gola, Milan, 1990-94, Il Sole 24 Ore, Milan, 2001—03. Lectr. Smithsonian Inst., Washington, 1991, 95, Schlesinger Libr., Radcliffe Coll., 1995; TV appearances with Lorenza de Medici, 1992, Julia Child, 1995, Mario Batali, 2004; bd. dirs. U. Calif. Press. Author: The Hill Towns of Italy, 1983 (Commonwealth Club award 1984), new edit., 1997, The Italian Baker, 1985 (Internat. Assn. Culinary Profls. award 1986), Celebrating Italy, 1990 (Commonwealth Club award, Internat. Assn. Culinary Profls. award 1991), paperback, 1997, Italy in Small Bites, 1993 (James Beard award), new edit., 2004, Focaccia: Simple Breads from the Italian Oven, 1994, In Nonna's Kitchen: Traditional Recipes and Culture from Italian Grandmothers, 1997 (Gold Medal, World Media awards, Australia, main selection Good Food Club, Book of the Month Club), Mangoes and Quince, 2001, paperback, 2002; mem. editl. bd. Gastronomica; contbr. articles to profl. jours. Lit. jury Commonwealth Club Calif., San Francisco, 1987-88, 92; bd. dirs. Women's Forum West, San Francisco, 1990-92, Bancroft Libr. U. Calif., Berkeley, 1991-97, Headlands Inst., San Francisco, 1992-93; bd. dirs. Mechanics' Inst., San Francisco, 1987-92, pres., 1990-92, Arion Press/Lyra Corp., 1998—; bd. dirs. Food Runners, San Francisco, 2000-05. Decorated Cavaliere Italian Govt., 2004; recipient Internat. Journalism prize Maria Luigia Duchessa di Parma, Italy, 1987, Barbi Colombini prize Tuscany, 1991, Nat. Journalism prize Vanghetto d'Oro, 1997; named Alumna of Yr. Head Royce Sch, Oakland, Calif., 1991, Honoree of Yr. Bread Bakers Guild of Am., 1999, recipient Contessa Premium Foods Who's Who of Food and Beverage in Am., James Beard Found., 2005. Mem. Accademia Italia della Cucina, Authors Guild, Les Dames d'Escoffier, Internat. Assn. Culinary Profls., Pen Ctr. USA West, Internat. Women's Forum. Home and Office: 2561 Washington St San Francisco CA 94115-1818 Personal E-mail: pedona@aol.com.

FIELD, DOROTHY MASLIN, minister; b. Port Chester, NY, June 10, 1925; d. Walter Adrian and Dorothy Hepworth Maslin; m. David Meredith Field, Sept. 14, 1946 (div. Oct. 16, 1976); children: Nancy Jean, Michael Maslin, Susan Field Nelson, Jeffrey David. BA in History and Polit. Sci. with honors, Douglass Coll., New Brunswick, NJ, 1946; MS, U. Pa., Phila., 1961; MDiv, Drew U., Madison, NJ, 1982. Pastor Packard Meml. United Meth. Ch., Media, Pa., 1980—81, Kedron United Meth. Ch., Morton, Pa.,

1981—84; v.p. for resident svcs. Cornwall Manor, Pa., 1984—86; pastor Chestnut St. and Ranshaw United Meth. Chs., Shamokin, Pa., 1986—92; pastor (serving in retirement) Crozerville United Meth. Ch., Aston, Pa., 1992—. Dir. Shamokin area ministry Ea. Pa. Conf. of the United Meth. Ch., Valley Forge, Pa., 1988—92. Pres., v.p. LWV, Delaware County, Pa., 1996, pres. Swarthmore, Pa., 1994—96; sec. Kiwanis Club, Chester, Pa., 1999; treas. Women's Internat. League for Peace and Freedom, Swarthmore, 1995—2003. Named Swarthmore Citizen of the Yr., Lions Club Swarthmore, 1994; named to Douglass Soc. for Disting. Alumnae, 1980. Mem.: Lions Club Swarthmore, Order of St. Luke (life), Pi Lambda Theta, Phi Beta Kappa Assn. of the Del. Valley (life). Methodist. Avocations: reading, walking, travel. Home: 100 Rutgers Ave 8 PO Box 379 Swarthmore PA 19081-0379 Office Phone: 610-543-8015. Personal E-mail: dotf1@aol.com.

FIELD, FRANCIS EDWARD, electrical engineer, educator; b. Casper, Wyo., Nov. 20, 1923; s. Jesse Harold and Persis Belle (St. John) F.; m. Margaret Jane O'Bryan, Oct. 13, 1945; children: Gregory A., Christopher B., Sheridan Diane. BSEE, U.S. Naval Acad., 1945; MA in Internat. Affairs, George Washington U., 1965; AMP, Harvard U., 1970. Master cert. graphoanalyst; comml. pilot. Owner Field Lumber Co., Lander, Wyo., 1948—50; commd. ensign U.S. Navy, 1945, advanced through grades to capt., 1966, ret., 1975; rsch. engr. George Washington U., Washington, 1975—90, adj. faculty, 1977—90. Pres. EXTANT, cons. firm, McLean, Va., 1981—; program dir. NSF, Washington, 1982-90. Author: Chronicle of a Workshop, 1977. Trustee Fremont County Mus. Bd., 1998—2003. Mem. Internat. Graphoanalysis Soc. (award of merit 1984), Mayflower Soc., Masons, Sigma Xi, Am. VFW. Republican. Home: 280 S 3rd St Lander WY 82520-3109 Office Phone: 307-332-3973. Personal E-mail: vacquero@bresnan.net.

FIELD, HENRY AUGUSTUS, JR., lawyer; b. Wis. Dells, Wis., July 8, 1928; s. Henry A. and Georgia (Coakley) F.; m. Patricia Ann Young, Nov. 30, 1957 (dec. 1980); children: Mary Patricia (dec. 1992), Thomas Gerard, Susan Therese (Mrs. Thomas Hempel); m. Molly Kelly Martin, Apr. 13, 1985. Student, Western Mich. Coll., 1946-47; PhB, Marquette U., 1950; LLB cum laude, U. Wis., 1952. Bar: Wis. 1952, U.S. Dist. Ct. (we. and ea. dists.) Wis. 1952, U.S. Ct. Appeals (7th cir.) 1957, U.S. Supreme Ct. 1980. Asst. U.S. atty. Western Dist. of Wis., 1956-57; assoc. Roberts, Boardman, Suhr, Bjork & Curry, 1957-62; jr. ptnr. Roberts, Boardman, Suhr & Curry, 1962-70; ptnr. Boardman, Suhr, Curry & Field, Madison, Wis., 1970—, chmn. exec. com., 1985-95; mem. Wis. Jud. Council, 1974-79. Dir. Family Service Soc., 1969-75, treas., 1971-72, pres., 1973-74; trustee Dane County Bar Pro Bono Trust Found., 1995-99. Served with C.I.C., AUS, 1952-55. Fellow: Wis. Law Found. (bd. dirs. 2003—, treas. 2005—), Am. Bar. Found., Am. Coll. Trial Lawyers (state chmn. 1982—83); mem.: ABA (Wis. chmn. legis. com. 1975—76), Wis. Law Found., Wis. Bar Assn. (chmn. litigation sect. 1971—72), Milw. and Dane County Bar Assn. (pres. 1971—72), 7th Fed. Cir. Bar Assn., Madison Club, Order of Coif, Sigma Tau Delta, Phi Delta Phi. Republican. Roman Catholic. Home: 3310 Valley Creek Cir Middleton WI 53562-1988 Office: Boardman Suhr Curry & Field 1 S Pinckney St Madison WI 53703-2892 Office Phone: 608-257-9521. Business E-Mail: hfield@boardmanlawfirm.com.

FIELD, JAMES BERNARD, internist, educator; b. Fort Wayne, Ind., May 28, 1926; s. Abraham and Clara (Ridner) F.; m. Dorothy Spivey, Sept. 25, 1954; children: Carolyn, Nancy, Douglas, Susan. Student, Harvard Coll., 1944, student, 1946—47; MD cum laude, Harvard Med. Sch., 1951. Diplomate: Am. Bd. Internal Medicine. Intern internal medicine Mass. Gen. Hosp., Boston, 1951-52, asst. resident internal medicine, 1952-53, resident internal medicine, 1953-54; practice medicine specializing in endocrinology Pitts., 1962-78, Houston, 1978-89. Med. officer USPHS, Nat. Inst. Arthritis and Metabolic Diseases, Bethesda, Md., 1954, sr. asst. surgeon, 1954-58, sr. investigator, 1958-60, surgeon, 1958-60, sr. surgeon, 1960-61; asst. in medicine diabetic dept. Kings Coll. Hosp., London, 1957-58; med. officer Nat. Inst. Metabolic Disease, Bethesda, Md., 1961-62; head divsn. endocrinology and metabolism U. Pitts. Sch. Medicine, 1962-78, assoc. prof. medicine, 1962-66, prof. medicine, 1966-78, dir. clin. research unit, 1962-78; Rutherford prof. medicine Baylor Coll. Medicine, Houston, 1978-89, head div. endocrinology and metabolism, 1978-87; vis. prof. dept. exptl. medicine Univ. Coll. Med. Sch., London, 1985-86; dir. Diabetes and Endocrinology Rsch. Ctr., Baylor Coll. Medicine, 1980-89; med. adv. bd. Nat. Pituitary Agy., 1967-69; research collaborator Brookhaven Nat. Lab., 1972-85; mem. nat. diabetes adv. bd. HEW, 1977-85, chmn., 1982-85; mem. endocrinology study sect. USPHS, 1965-69, chmn., 1968-69, endocrinology and metabolism tng. grant com., 1970-74, gen. clin. rsch. ctr. rev. com., 1976-79; mem. panel clin. scis. com. study nat. needs biomed. and behavioral rsch. pers. Nat Rsch. Coun., 1976-80; mem. VA merit rev. com. on endocrinology and metabolism, 1982-85; lectr. medicine Harvard Med. Sch., 1992—; mem. honors com. Harvard Med. Sch., 1993-2001. Editor (assoc. editor): Metabolism, 1959—69; editor: (editor-in-chief), 1969—; editor: (contbg.) Clin.Thyroidology, 1988—2000; contbr. numerous research articles on endocrinology to profl. jours. Bd. dirs. Gen. Clin. Research Centers, 1977-79; mem. Physician Vols. in Medicine, Hilton Head Island, S.C., 2001—. Served with U.S. Army, 1944-45. Decorated Purple Heart, Bronze Star; recipient Van Meter prize award Am. Goiter Assn., 1961, Prize Boylston Soc., 1951. Mem. Assn. Am. Physicians, Endocrine Soc. (mem. coun. 1972-75, internat. liaison com. 1972-75, mem. pub. affairs com. 1972-75, mem. awards com. 1972-75, chmn. 1974-75, nominating com. 1982-84, chmn. 1984), Am. Diabetes Assn. (dir. 1968-74, vice chmn. com. on rsch. 1972-73, chmn. com. rsch. 1975-77, mem. established investigator rev. bd. 1975-77, Eli Lilly award 1958), Am. Fedn. Clin. Rsch., Am. Clin. and Climatol. Assn., Am. Physiology Soc., Am. Soc. Clin. Investigation, Mass. Med. Soc. (chmn. com. on ret, physicians 1993-2002, Prize 1951, Vol. of Yr. 2001), Quechee Lakes Club (Quechee, Vt.), Harvard Med. Alumni Assn., (treas. 1997-2000), Sea Pines Country Club (Hilton Head), Alpha Omega Alpha. Home: 50 Stoney Creek Rd Hilton Head Island SC 29928

FIELD, JOHN LOUIS, architect; b. Mpls., Jan. 18, 1930; s. Harold David and Gladys Ruth (Jacobs) F.; m. Carol Helen Hart, July 23, 1961; children: Matthew Hart, Alison Ellen. BA, Yale U., 1952, MArch, 1955. Individual practice architecture, San Francisco, 1959-68; v.p. firm Bull, Field, Volkmann, Stockwell, Architects, San Francisco, 1968-83; ptnr. Field/Gruzen, Architects, San Francisco, 1983-86, Field Paoli Architects, San Francisco, 1986—. Guest lectr. Stanford, 1970; chmn. archtl. council San Francisco Mus. Art, 1969-71; mem. San Francisco Bay Conservation and Devel. Commn., Design Rev. Bd., 1980-84; founding chmn. San Francisco Bay Architects Review, 1977-80 Co-author, producer, dir.: film Cities for People (Broadcast Media award 1975, Golden Gate award San Francisco Internat. Film Festival 1975, Ohio State award 1976); film The Urban Preserve (Calif. Council AIA Commendation of excellence 1982); co-design architect: design for New Alaska Capital City (winner design competition). Bd. dir. Berkley Repertory Theatre; bd. mem. Ctr. for Urban Edn. About Sustainable Agriculture. Recipient Archtl. Record award, 1961, 1972; AIA, Sunset mag. awards, 1962, 64, 69; No. Calif. AIA awards, 1967, 82; Calif. Council AIA award, 1982; certificate excellence Calif. Gov.'s Design awards, 1966; Homes for Better Living awards, 1962, 66, 69, 71, 77; Albert J. Evers award, 1974, Best Bldg. award Napa (Calif.) C. of C., 1987, Design award Internat. Council Shopping Ctrs., 1988, Stores of Excellence award Nat. Mall Monitor, 1989, 92, 93, Pacific Coast Builders Gold Nugget award, 1989, 91, Urban Design award Calif. Coun. AIA, 1991, 93; Density Myth and Competition winner Boston Soc. Architects, 2003. Fellow AIA (com. on design, mem. coun. Calif. arch., Lifetime Achievement award, 2005); mem. Nat. Coun. Archtl. Registration Bds., Urban Land Inst. (Design award 1995), Yale Club, Lambda Alpha. Office: Field Paoli Architects 150 California St 7th Fl San Francisco CA 94111-1315 Home Phone: 415-922-0373; Office Phone: 415-788-6606. Business E-Mail: jlf@fieldpaoli.com.

FIELD, JUDITH JUDY, librarian; b. Bucyrus, Ohio, Sept. 30, 1939; d. William Harrison and Eva Gertrude (Miller) Judy; m. Nathaniel Lamson Field III, Jan. 25, 1959. BBA, U. Mich., 1961, M.L.S., 1963, MBA, 1969. Library mgr. Western Electric Bell Telephone Labs., Indpls., 1962-65; asst. librarian Natural Sci. Library, Ann Arbor, Mich., 1965-66; assoc. librarian Sch. Bus. Adminstrn., Ann Arbor, 1966-69; library mgr. Inst. Internat. Commerce, Ann Arbor, 1969-71, research assoc., 1971-72; head gen. reference Flint Pub. Library, Mich., 1972-86; dir. Legis. Ref. Libr., St. Paul, 1987; mgmt. cons., 1988—; sr. lectr. libr. and info. sci. Wayne State U., 1989—. Pres. Mich. Interorgn. Council on Continuing Library Edn., Lansing, Mich., 1983-85; bd. dirs. Continuing Library Edn. Network and Exchange, Washington, 1979-81. Editor: International Finance Bibliography, 1971, Apprentice and Training Program, 1972, Beginning Positions and Training Program, 1973, Michigan Legal Literature, 1991; editl. bd. The One-Person Lib. Mem. LVA. Mem. ALA (com. accreditation 1993-97, task force adv. com. White House Conf. 1990-92), Friends of Detroit Pub. Libr., Spl. Librs. Assn. (dep. conf. chmn. 1983, chmn. libr. mgmt. divsn. 1983-84, pres. Mich. chpt. 1981-82, bd. dirs. 1975-77, 86-89, 96-99, pres. 1997-98, conf. chair 1994, John Cotton Dana award, 2006), Am. Soc. Info. Sci. (pres. Mich. chpt. 1991-93, honors fellow 1996), ARMA Internat. Edn. Found. (bd. trustees 1998-2002), Internat. Fedn. Libr. Assn. (edn. and tng. 1999-2003, svc. sci. 2003-05, knowledge mgmt. 2005—, sec. 2005-06, chair 2006-). Republican. Avocations: archaeology, backgammon. Home: 20500 Clement Rd Northville MI 48167-1334 Office: Wayne State U 106 Kresge Lib Detroit MI 48202 Office Phone: 313-577-8539. Business E-Mail: aa4101@wayne.edu.

FIELD, KAREN ANN (KAREN ANN SCHAFFNER), real estate broker; d. Abraham Terry and Ida (Smith) Rogovin; m. Barry S. Crown, 1954 (div. 1969); children: Laurie Jayne, Donna Lynn, Bruce Alan, Bradley David; m. Michael Lehmann Field, 1969 (div. 1977); m. Ronald E. Schaffner, Apr., 1998. Student, Vassar Coll., 1953-54, Harrington Inst. Interior Design, 1973-74, Roosevelt U., 1987—. Cert. residential specialist. Owner Karen Field Interiors, Chgo., 1970-86, Karen Field & Assocs. Realtors, Chgo., 1980-81; pres., ptnr. Field-Pels & Assocs. Realtors, Chgo., 1981-86; with top sales volume Sudler-Marling, Inc., Chgo., 1989; sales broker Koenig & Strey GMAC, Chgo., 1992—. Mem. Women's Coun. Camp Henry Horner, Chgo., 1960; bd. dirs., treas. Winnetka Pub. Sch. Nursery (Ill.), 1961-63; pres. Jr. Aux. U. Chgo. Cancer Rsch. Found., 1960-66, mem. exec. com. women's bd., 1965-66, co-chair Grand Auction; bd. dirs., sec. United Charities, Chgo., 1966-68, Victory Gardens Theatre, Chgo., 1979; co-founder, pres. Re-Entry Ctr., Wilmette, Ill., 1978-80; mem. br. Child Abuse Svcs., Chgo., 1981-89, Stop AIDS Real Estate Divsn., 1988, AIDS Walkathon Com., 1990; bd. dirs. The Chgo. Ctr. for Self-Taught Art, 1993-96. Recipient Servian award Jr. Aux. of U. Chgo. Cancer Rsch. Found., 1966, Margarite Wolf award Women's Bd., U. Chgo. Cancer Rsch. Found., 1967, Founder's award, 1997, WAIT Woman of Day. Mem. Chgo. Real Estate Bd., Chgo. Assn. Realtors, English Speaking Union (jr. bd. 1958-59), Art Inst. Chgo., Field Mus., Arts Club of Chgo., Union League Club, Founders Club, Confrerie de la Chaine des Rotisseurs (Dame de la Chaine), Fulton River Dist. Assn., Friends of the River, Koenig and Strey GMAC Pres.'s Club. Office: Koenig & Strey GMAC 900 N Michigan Ave Ste 1700 Chicago IL 60611-1514 Office Phone: 312-893-3556.

FIELD, MARSHALL, retail executive; b. Charlottesville, Va., May 13, 1941; s. Marshall IV and Joanne (Bass) F.; m. Joan Best Connelly, Sept. 5, 1964 (div. 1969); 1 child, Marshall; m. Jamee Beckwith Jacobs, Aug. 19, 1972; children: Jamee Christine, Stephanie Caroline, Abigail Beckwith. BA, Harvard Coll., 1963. With N.Y. Herald Tribune, 1964-65; pub. Chgo. Sun-Times, 1969-80, Chgo. Daily News, 1969-78; dir. Field Enterprises, Inc., Chgo., 1965-84, dir., mem. exec. com., 1965-84, chmn. bd., 1972-84, The Field Corp., 1984—, Cabot, Cabot & Forbes, 1984—, chmn. exec. com., 1985-89, sr. dir., chief exec. officer, 1989—; pub. World Book-Childcraft Internat. Inc., 1973-78, dir., 1965-80. Trustee Art Inst. Chgo., Rush-Presbyn.-St. Lukes Med. Ctr., Chgo. Cmty. Trust, Field Mus. Natural History, Chgo. Pub. Libr. Found.; life trustee Music & Dance Theater, Chgo.; chmn. bd. Terra Found. for the Arts; adv. bd. Brookfield Zoo; charitable adv. coun. Office of Atty. Gen. of State of Ill.; active Chgo. Orchestral Assn.; bd. visitors, chair Nicholas Sch. of the Environment, Duke U.; bd. dirs. Field Found. Ill., Lincoln Park Zool. Soc.; chmn. Nat. Coun. of the World Wildlife Fund; bd. dirs. Atlantic Salmon Fedn. Mem. Nature Conservancy, River Club, Chgo. Club, Harvard Club, Racquet Club, Onwentsia Club, Jupiter Island Club, Shore Acres Club, McArthur Golf Club. Office: 225 W Wacker Dr Ste 1500 Chicago IL 60606-1235

FIELD, MARTHA AMANDA, law educator; b. Boston, Aug. 20, 1943; d. Donald T. and Adelaide (Anderson) Field; children: Maria Adelaide, Gabriel Hartry, Lucas Anthony. BA in Chinese History, Radcliffe Coll., 1965; JD, U. Chgo., 1968. Bar: DC 1969. Law clk. to Justice Abe Fortas, US Supreme Ct., 1968-69; asst. prof. U. Pa. Law Sch., Phila., 1969—72, prof., 1973—78; prof. law Harvard Law Sch., Cambridge, Mass., 1979—, Langdell prof. law, 1998—. Vis. prof. law Harvard Law Sch., 1978—79. Author: Surrogate Motherhood, 1991; co-author: Equal Treatment for People with Mental Retardation, 2000, Legal Reform in Central America: Dispute Resolution and Property Systems, 2001. Office: Harvard Law Sch 1563 Massachusetts Ave Cambridge MA 02138 Office Phone: 617-495-2962. Office Fax: 617-496-4947. Business E-Mail: mfield@law.harvard.edu.

FIELD, ROBERT EDWARD, lawyer; b. Chgo., Aug. 21, 1945; s. Robert Edward and Florence Elizabeth (Aiken) F.; m. Jenny Lee Hill, Aug. 5, 1967; children: Jennifer Kay, Kimberly Anne, Amanda Brooke. BA, Ill. Wesleyan U., Bloomington, 1967; MA, Northwestern U., Evanston, Ill., 1969, JD, 1973. Bar: Ill. 1973, U.S. Dist. Ct. (no. dist.) Ill. 1974, U.S. Supreme Ct. 1979. Exec. dir. Winnetka Youth Orgn., Ill., 1969-73; assoc. Seyfarth, Shaw, Fairweather & Geraldson, Chgo., 1973-79, ptnr., 1979-93, Field & Golan, Chgo., 1993—2005; of counsel Quinlan & Carroll, Chgo., 2006—. Bd. dirs. Gt. Lakes Fin. Resources, Matteson, Ill., 1983—, vice chmn., 1988-91, chmn. 1991—; bd. dirs. Gt. Lakes Trust Co., 2001--, chmn., 2001--; bd. dirs. Chgo. chpt. Ill. Wesleyan U. Assocs., Great Lakes Ins. Svcs., Alsip, Ill., 2001--; chmn. bd. dirs. 1st Nat. Bank of Blue Island, 1989-2001, Great Lake Bank, 2001—, Bank of Homewood, 1988-2001; bd. dirs. Winchester Mfg. Co., Wood Dale, Ill., Ludell Mfg. Co., Milw., Comml. Resources Corp., Naperville, Ill., 1984-93; dir., sec. Ellis Corp., Itasca, Ill., 1980—; chmn. bd. dirs. Cmty. Bank of Homewood-Flossmoor, Ill., 1983-92, Bank of Matteson, Ill., 1992-99; bd. dirs. Grand Prairie Svcs., Inc., 1999-2005, sec., 2001-05; mem. State Banking Bd. Ill., 1993-97. Bd. dirs. Ctr. for New Beginnings, 1997-2005, Svcs. Exch., 1998-2003, Family Svc. Ctrs. Cook County, Matteson, 1979-99, treas., 1981-82, pres., 1986-88, chmn., 1988-93; pres. Lakes of Olympia Condominium Assn., 1987-89; trustee Village of Olympia Fields, Ill., 1981-89, pres., 1991-97; trustee Ill. Wesleyan U., 1990—, treas., 1994—; bd. dirs. Northwestern U. Sch. Law Alumni Assn., 1990-94. Mem. ABA, Ill. Bar Assn., Am. Bankers Assn., Ill. Bankers Assn., United Meth. Bar Assn. (v.p. Chgo. chpt. 1989), Chgo. Bar Assn., Bankers Club Chgo., Union League Club Chgo., Calumet Country Club. Office: Quinlan & Carroll 30 N LaSalle St Ste 2900 Chicago IL 60602 Home Phone: 815-462-9033; Office Phone: 312-917-8856. Business E-Mail: refield@qclaw.com.

FIELD, ROBERT WARREN, chemistry professor; b. Wilmington, Del., June 13, 1944; s. Edmund and Kay (Huebsch) F. AB in Chemistry, Amherst Coll., 1965, DSc (hon.), 1997; MA, Harvard U., 1971, PhD, 1972. Adj. asst. prof. chemistry U. Calif.-Santa Barbara, 1974; asst. prof. chemistry M.I.T., Cambridge, 1974-78, assoc. prof. phys. chemistry, 1978-82, prof., 1982—99, Haslam and Dewey prof. chemistry, 1998—. Mem. editorial bd. Jour. Molecular Spectroscopy, contbr. articles to profl. jours. Alfred P. Sloan fellow, 1975-77. Fellow AAAS, Am. Acad. Arts and Scis., Am. Phys. Soc. (H.P. Broida prize 1980, E.K. Plyler prize 1988), Optical Soc. Am. (E. Lippincott award 1990, W. Meggers award, 1996); mem. Am. Chem. Soc. (Nobel Laureate Signature award to Y. Chen, co-preceptor with J.L. Kinsey 1990). Office: MIT Rm 6-219 Dept Chemistry 77 Massachusetts Ave Cambridge MA 02139 Office Phone: 617-255-1975. E-mail: rwfield@mit.edu.*

FIELD, SALLY MARGARET, actress; b. Pasadena, Calif., Nov. 6, 1946; m. Steven Craig, Sept. 16, 1968 (div. 1975); children: Peter, Eli; m. Alan Greisman, Dec. 15, 1984 (div. 1993); 1 son, Samuel. Student, Actor's Studio, 1973-75. Starred in TV series Gidget, 1965, The Flying Nun, 1967-70, The Girl With Something Extra, 1973, The Court, 2002, Brothers & Sisters, 2006-; film appearances include The Way West, 1967, Stay Hungry, 1976, Heroes, 1977, Smokey and the Bandit, 1977, Hooper, 1978, The End, 1978, Norma Rae, 1979 (Cannes Film Festival Best Actress award 1979, Acad. award 1980), Beyond the Poseidon Adventure, 1979, Smokey and the Bandit II, 1980, Back Roads, 1981, Absence of Malice, 1981, Kiss Me Goodbye, 1982, Places in the Heart, 1984 (Acad. award for best actress 1984), Murphy's Romance (also exec. producer), 1985, Surrender, 1987, Punchline, 1987 (also prodr.), Steel Magnolias, 1989, Soapdish, 1991, Not Without My Daughter, 1991, Homeward Bound: The Incredible Journey, 1993 (voice), Mrs. Doubtfire, 1993, Forrest Gump, 1994, Homeward Bound II: Lost in San Francisco, 1996 (voice)(also prodr.), Eye for an Eye, 1996 (also prodr.), Where the Heart Is, 2000, Say It Isn't So, 2001, Legally Blonde 2: Red, White & Blonde, 2003; TV movies include Maybe I'll Come Home In the Spring, 1971, Marriage: Year One, 1971, Home for the Holidays, 1972, Bridger, 1976, Sybil, 1976 (Emmy award 1977), All the Way Home, 1981, Merry Christmas George Bailey, 1997 (also prodr.), A Cooler Climate, 1999 (also prodr.), David Copperfield, 2000, Two Weeks, 2007; TV mini series David Copperfield, 1986, A Women of Independent Means, 1995 (also exec. prodr.), From the Earth to the Moon, 1998 (also dir.); exec. prodr. The Christmas Tree, 1996 (also writer, dir.), The Lost Children of Berlin, 1997; prodr. Dying Young, 1991; dir. Beautiful, 2000; guest appearances include The Hollywood Squares, 1966, Rowan & Martin's Laugh-In, 1968, Carol Burnett & Co., 1979, Saturday Night Live, 1993, King of Hill (voice), 1997, Murphy Brown, 1998, ER, 2000-2006 (several episodes), and several others. Recipient Golden Plate award, Acad. Achievement, 2005.*

FIELD, STEVEN PHILIP, medical educator; b. Newark, Feb. 21, 1951; s. Irving and Florence (Engel) F. BA, Yale U., 1973; MD, NYU, 1977, cert. in Bioethics and Med. Humanities, 2003. Diplomate Am. Bd. Internal Medicine, Am. Bd. Gastroenterology; cert. psychodynamic psychotherapy NYU Psychoanalytic Inst., Bioethics, Montefiore, NYU. Intern in internal medicine Bellevue Hosp., NYC, 1977-78, resident in internal medicine, 1978-81; instr. in medicine Mt. Sinai Hosp., NYC, 1981-83, NYU Sch. of Medicine, NYC, 1983—, clin. asst. prof. medicine, 1991—. Contbr. articles to med. jours., chpts. to med. textbooks. Recipient John Addison Porter Prize Yale U., 1973. Mem.: ACP, Crohn's and Colitis Found. Am. (sci. adv. coun.), N.Y. State Med. Soc., N.Y. Acad. Gastroenterology (v.p. 1995—96), Am. Gastroent. Assn., Yale Club Ctrl. N.J. (alumni schs. com.), Alpha Omega Alpha. Office: 245 E 35th St New York NY 10016-4283 Office Phone: 212-686-9477. Business E-Mail: steven.field@med.nyu.edu.

FIELD, SUELLEN R., not-for-profit developer; d. John Edwin and Mary Sue Payle Reid; m. Richard Joseph Field, Apr. 16, 1966; children: Richard, Marshall. BA, Birmingham So. U., Ala., 1966. Cert. fundraising exec. Assn. Fundraising Profls., 1991. Devel. officer Selby Gardens, Sarasota, Fla., 1986—89; exec. dir. Boy's Club Found., Bradenton, Fla., 1989—94; dir. devel. Pelican Man's Bird Sanctuary, Sarasota, 1994—95, All Faiths Food Bank, Sarasota, 1995—97; sr. dir. devel. Ringling Mus., Sarasota, 1997—. Exec. bd. SW Fla. Planned Giving Coun., Sarasota. Pres. Rotary Found., Sarasota, 1986, Zonta, Inc., Sarasota, 1988; first female pres. Rotary Club Sarasota, 1989—90. Named Fundraiser of Yr., Fla. State U. Mem.: Jr. League Sarasota (treas. 1984). Office: Ringling Museum 5401 Bayshore Rd Sarasota FL 34243

FIELD, TED (FREDERICK), film company and recording industry executive; b. Chgo. s. Marshall Field IV and Katherine W. Fanning; 8 children. Student, U. Chgo., Pomona Coll. Former race car driver; chmn., CEO Radar Pictures, 2002—; chmn. Artistdirect, Inc.; chmn., CEO Artistdirect Recs.; founder Interscope Communications; co-founder Interscope Records; former co-owner Field Enterprises, Chgo.; owner Panavision, 1985-87. Co-prodr.: (films) Critical Condition, 1987, Outrageous Fortune, 1987, Three Men and a Baby, 1987, Revenge of the Nerds II, 1987, Cocktail, 1988, The Seventh Sign, 1988, An Innocent Man, 1989; co-exec. prodr. (films) Bill and Ted's Excellent Adventure, 1989, Renegades, 1989; prodr. Revenge of the Nerds, 1984, Turk 182, 1985, Three Men and a Little Lady, Class Action, Jumanji, 1995, Mr. Holland's Opus, 1996, Runaway Bride, 1999; exec. prodr. The First Power, 1990, Bird on a Wire, 1990, The Hand That Rocks the Cradle, 1992, What Dreams May Come, 1998, Very Bad Things, 1998, Pitch Black, 2000, Texas Chainsaw Massacre, 2003, The Last Samurai, 2003, Le Divorce, 2003, The Amityville Horror, 2005, Zathura, 2005, The Heartbreak Kid, 2007; co-exec. prodr.: (TV films) The Father Clements Story, Everybody's Baby: The Rescue of Jessica McClure, A Mother's Courage; exec. prodr.: (feature film) Waist Deep, 2006. Avocations: chess, martial arts. Office: Radar Pictures 10900 Wilshire Blvd Ste 1400 Los Angeles CA 90024-6532

FIELD, (WILLIAM) TODD, actor, film director, scriptwriter; b. Pomona, Calif., Feb. 24, 1964; m. Serena Rathbun, July 25, 1987; 3 children. MFA, Am. Film Inst. Actor, musician Ark Theatre Co., NY; directing fellow Am. Film Inst. Actor: (films) Radio Days, 1987, The Allnighter, 1987, Gross Anatomy, 1989, Fat Man and Little Boy, 1989, Back to Back, 1990, Full Fathom Five, 1990, The End of Innocence, 1990, Queens Logic, 1991, Ruby in Paradise, 1993, The Dog, 1993, Frank & Jesse, 1994, Sleep With Me, 1994, Walking and Talking, 1996, Twister, 1996, Farmer & Chase, 1997, Broken Vessels, 1998, Eyes Wide Shut, 1999, The Haunting, 1999, Net Worth, 2000, Stranger Than Fiction, 2000, New Port South, 2001, Beyond the City Limits, 2001; (TV films) Lookwell, 1991, Jonathan Stone: Threat of Innocence, 1994; (TV series) Once and Again, 1999—2001, Aqua Teen Hunger Force, 2002—03; dir.: (films) Nonnie & Alex, 1995; dir., prodr. & screenwriter (films) In the Bedroom, 2001, Little Children, 2006 (Sonny Bono Visionary award Palm Spring Internat. Film Soc, Palm Springs Internat. Film Festival, 2007), dir., & screenwriter Too Romantic, 1992, When I Was a Boy, 1993, Delivering, 1993.*

FIELDEN, C. FRANKLIN, III, early childhood education consultant; b. Gulfport, Miss., Aug. 4, 1946; s. C. Franklin and Georgia (Freeman) F.; children: Christopher Michaux (dec.), Robert Michaux, Jonathan Dutton. Student, Claremont Men's Coll., 1964-65; AB, Colo. Coll., 1970; MS, George Peabody Coll. Tchrs., 1976, EdS, 1979. Tutor Proyecto El Guacio, San Sebastian, P.R., 1967-68; asst. tchr. GET-SET Project, Colorado Springs, Colo., 1969-70, co-tchr., 1970-75, asst. dir., 1972-75; tutor Early Childhood Edn. Project, Nashville, 1975-76; pub. policy intern Donner-Belmont Child Care Ctr., Nashville, 1976—77; asst. to urban min. Nashville Presbytery, 1977; intern to prin. Steele Elem. Sch., Colorado Springs, 1977-78, tchr., 1978-86; resource person Office Gifted and Talented Edn. Colorado Springs Pub. Schs., 1986-87; tchr. Columbia Elem. Sch., Colorado Springs, 1987-92; tchr., pre-sch. team coord. Helen Hunt Elem. Sch., Colorado Springs, 1992-93; validator Nat. Acad. Early

Childhood Programs, 1992—2006, mentor, 1994—2006, commr., 1996-2000, 2001—06, regional assessor, 2007—; cons. Colo. Dept. Edn., Denver, 1993—96, sr. cons., 1996—2001, state coord. Even Start Family Literacy Program, 1997—2006, prin. cons., 2001—06. Lectr. Arapahoe C.C., Littleton, Colo., 1981-82; instr. Met. State Coll., Denver, 1981; cons. Jubail Human Resources Devel. Inst., Saudi Arabia, 1982; mem. governing bd. GET-SET Project, 1969-79, 91-93. Mem. ad hoc bd. trustees Tenn. United Meth. Agy. on Children and Youth, 1976-77; mem. So. Regional Edn. Bd. Task Force on Parent-Caregiver Relationships, 1976-77; day care com. Colo. Commn. Children and Their Families, 1981-82; active Nashville Children's Issues Task Force, 1976-77, Tenn. United Meth. Task Force on Children and Youth, 1976-77, Citizens' Goals Leadership Tng., 1986-87, Child Abuse Task Force, 4th Jud. Dist., 1986-87, FIRST IMPRESSIONS (Colo. Govs. Early Childhood Initiative) Task Force, 1987-88, El Paso County Placement Alternatives Commn., 1990-96, White Ho. Summit on Early Childhood Cognitive Devel., 2001; proposal rev. team Colo. Dept. Edn., 1992-2006; co-chair City/County Child Care Task Force, 1991-92; charter mem. City/County Early Childhood Care and Edn. Commn., 1993-96; bd. dirs. Colo. Office of Resource and Referral Agys., 1996-99; appeals panel Divsn. Child Care, Colo. Dept. Human Svcs., 2002-06; bd. dirs. Colo. Parents as Tchrs., 2004-06. Recipient Arts/Bus./Edn. award, 1983, Innovative Tchg. award, 1984; fellow NIMH, 1976-77. Mem.: ASCD, Pikes Peak Assn. Edn. Young Children, Nat. Assn. Early Childhood Specialists in State Depts. of Edn. (v.p. 1997—99, pres. 1999—2001, past. pres. 2001—03), Colo. Assn. Edn. Young Children (legis. com. 1979—84, governing bd., sec., exec. com. 1980—84, rsch. conf. chmn. 1982, tuition awards com. 1983—86, governing bd. 1985—86, chmn. tuition awards com. 1985—86, governing bd. 1989—95, pub. policy com. 1989—96, exec. com., treas. 1993, primary grades conf. chmn. 1994), Nat. Assn. Edn. Young Children (founding mem. primary-grades caucus 1992—2001, co-chair Western States Leadership Network 1993, Membership Action Group grantee 1993, panel profl. ethics in early childhood edn. 1993—97, nominating panel 2000—02, co-facilitator primary-grades interest forum 2001—05, cons. editors panel 2006—), Nat. Trust Hist. Preservation, Huguenot Soc. Gt. Britain and Ireland., Phi Delta Kappa. Presbyterian. Home and Office: PO Box 7766 Colorado Springs CO 80933-7766

FIELDER, CHARLES ROBERT, retired oil industry executive; b. Lubbock, Tex., Mar. 9, 1943; s. Clarence Daniel and Ola Marie (Sewell) F.; m. Mary Ruth Wills, May 31, 1964; 1 child, Sara Elizabeth. BBA, Tex. Tech. U., 1965, MS in Acctg., 1972. C.P.A., Tex. Staff acct. Peat, Marwick, Mitchell & Co., Dallas, 1965-66, Arthur Andersen & Co., Dallas, 1968-69; treasury acct. Halliburton Co., Dallas, 1969-71, treasury supr., 1971-72, asst. treas., 1972-78, treas., 1978-89, v.p., treas., 1990-96; ret., 1997. Mem. AICPA, Fin. Execs. Inst., Tex. Soc. CPAs, Phi Eta Sigma, Beta Alpha Psi, Beta Gamma Sigma, Phi Kappa Phi. Republican. Mem. Ch. of Christ. Office: PMB 189 6757 Arapaho Rd Ste 711 Dallas TX 75248-4073

FIELDER, PRINCE SEMIEN, professional baseball player; b. Ontario, Calif., May 9, 1984; s. Cecil Fielder; m. Chanel Fielder; 1 child, Jaden. Draft pick Milw. Brewers, 2002, first baseman, 2005—. Named to Nat. League All-Star Team, Maj. League Baseball, 2007. Mailing: Miller Park One Brewers Way Milwaukee WI 53214-3652 Office Phone: 414-902-4400.*

FIELDING, ALLEN FRED, oral and maxillofacial surgeon, educator; b. Paterson, NJ, Jan. 22, 1943; s. Fred W. and Emily Claire (Boehm) F. BS, Fairleigh Dickinson U., 1961, DMD, 1963; postgrad. in oral surgery, N.Y. U., 1965-66; MD, U. Health Sci. Antigua, 2001; MBA, U. Phoenix, 2003. Diplomate Am. Bd. Oral and Maxillofacial Surgery (adv. bd. 1983-86), Am. Bd. Forensic Medicine, Dental Nat. Anesthesia Bd. Intern in oral surgery Roosevelt Hosp., NYC, 1966-67; resident in oral surgery Phila. Gen. Hosp., 1967-69; practice dentistry specializing in oral-maxillo facial surgery Phila., 1969—; prof., chmn. dept. oral and maxillofacial surgery Temple U., Phila., 1983-88, staff prof., chief dept. oral and maxillofacial surgery univ. hosp., 1982-87, prof. emeritus, 2006—; prof. Temple U. Sch. Medicine. Cons. VA Hosp., Wilmington, Del.; staff St. Christopher's Hosp. for Children, Phila., Northeatern Hosp.; staff, chief divsn. oral and Maxillofacial surgery Epics. Hosp.; sect. chief oral and maxillofacial surgery Quakertown (Pa.) Hosp., Lawndale Hosp., Phila.; cons. Gt. Lakes Naval Hosp., Ill., Brandywine Hosp.; lectr. in field. Contbr. articles to profl. jours. Mem. Chapel of Four Chaplains, Valley Forge, Pa.; amb. People To People, 2004. Served to capt. USAF, 1963-65. Fellow Am. Dental Soc. Anesthesiology, Royal Soc. Health, Am. Soc. Oral and Maxillofacial Surgeons (Pa. del.), World Affairs Coun. (Phila. chpt.), Am. Coll. Dentistry (editor local chpt.), Internat. Coll. Dentists, Internat. Assn. Oral and Maxillofacial Surgeons, Am. Assn. Oral and Maxillofacial Surgeons, Am. Coll. Oral and Maxillofacial Surgeons, Internat. Assn. Oral Maxillofacial Surgery; mem. AAUP, ADEA, ADA, Pa. Dental Soc., Phila. County Dental Soc. (bd. govs.), Assn. Mil. Surgeons, Am. Assn. Dental Schs., Del. Valley Soc. Oral Surgeons (com. resident tng. 1973-85, exec. com., pres. 1985), Am. Assn. Hosp. Dentists (sec.-treas. Del. County chpt. 1972-74, v.p. 1974, pres. 1976), Great Lakes Soc. Oral Maxillofacial Surgeons, Mid-Atlantic Soc. Oral Maxillofacial Surgeons, Temple U. Oral Surgery Honor Soc. (advisor), Pa. Soc. Oral and Maxillofacial Surgeons (exec. com., govt. affairs com., pres. 1995-96), Coll. Physicians and Surgeons Phila., Dental Assts. Nat. Bd. (adv. bd.), Internat. Assn. Oral Implantologists, Del. Valley Acad. Osseointegration, Pierre Fauchard Soc. (elected mem.), Omicron Kappa Upsilon (pres. 1985, Temple chpt.). Home: 1203 Rodman St Philadelphia PA 19147-1129 also: County Line Med Ctr Lincoln Hwy Gap PA 17527 Office: Temple U Episc Hosp Campus 100 E Lehigh Ave Philadelphia PA 19125 Office Phone: 215-707-3613. Personal E-mail: impactor@rcn.com.

FIELDING, ERIC, set designer, educator; b. Provo, Utah, Feb. 20, 1950; s. Franklin David and Virginia Zabriskie Fielding; m. Cecelia Ann Harris, June 1, 1978; children: Jefferson, Lincoln. BA, Brigham Young U., Provo, 1974; MFA, Goodman Sch. Drama, 1976. Lic. scenic designer United Scenic Artists. Freelance set & lighting designer Left-Handed Design, Orem, Utah, 1976—; asst. prof., resident set designer dept. theatre Brigham Young U., Provo, 1976—83, prof., resident set designer, 1992—, dept. chair, artistic dir. dept. theater, 1993—97; assoc. prof. Goodman Sch. Drama DePaul U., Chgo., 1983—86. Adj. faculty dept. theatre U. Utah, Salt Lake City, 1989—92; vis. prof./guest designer U. Tex., Austin, 1990. Scenic, lighting designer: (over 250 theatre, opera, TV, film prodns.); exhibitions include World Stage Design, Toronto, 2005, Mozart in America: USA Exhibition at Prague Quadrennial, Czech Republic, 1991 (Gold medal, 1991); editor: Theatre Design & Technology, 1988—95, WSD Catalogue, 2005; exec. editor: New Theatre Words, 1995. Missionary LDS Ch., Sao Paulo, Brazil, 1969—71. Named Outstanding Young Men of Am., Outstanding Ams. Found., 1978; recipient Hon. Membership award, Can. Inst. Theatre Tech., 2005. Fellow: US Inst. Theatre Tech. (bd. dirs. 1983—87, v.p. comm. 1999—2002, USITT Founders award 1992); mem.: Internat. Orgn. Scenographers, Technicians and Archs. Theatre (commr. publs. and communication 1991—99), Nat. Theatre Conf. (trustee 2005—), Theta Alpha Phi. Mem. Lds Ch. Office: Brigham Young Univ Dept Theatre D-581 HFAC Provo UT 84602 Home Phone: 801-225-0093; Office Phone: 801-422-7471. Office Fax: 801-422-0654. Business E-Mail: eric_fielding@byu.edu.

FIELDING, FRED FISHER, federal official, lawyer; b. Phila., Mar. 21, 1939; s. Fred P. and Ruth Marie (Fisher) F.; m. J. Maria Dugger, Oct. 21, 1967; children: Adam Garrett, Alexandra Caroline. AB, Gettysburg Coll., 1961; LL.B, JD, U. Va., 1964; LittD (hon.), U. Detroit, 1986; LLD (hon.), Pepperdine U., 1986, Mich. State U., 1986. Bar: Pa. 1965, D.C. 1974. Assoc. Morgan, Lewis & Bockius LLP, Phila., 1964-65, 67-70, ptnr. Washington, 1974-81; asst. counsel to Pres. The White House, Washington, 1970-72, dep. gen. counsel, 1972-74, gen. counsel to Pres., 1981-86, 2007—; sr. ptnr., corp. services, govt. affairs, crisis mgmt./white collar litig. Wiley, Rein & Fielding LLP, Washington, 1986—2007; pres. Gilmore Broadcasting Corp., 1988-90. Mem. Jud. Conf. D.C. Cir. Ct., 1976—; internat. adv. bd. Credit Internat. Bank, 1990-96; bd. dirs. Gilmore Broadcasting Corp., Coun. for Excellence in Govt.; spl. counsel Adminstrv. Conf. U.S., 1982-86, pub. mem., 1987-94, chmn. spl. com. on ethics in govt., 1988-92, com. on regulation, 1992-94; presdl. appointment to panel arbitrators Internat. Ctr. for Settlement Investment Disputes, 1987-95, 2002—; CPR panel Disting. Neutrals, 2000—: standing com. Fed. Judiciary ABA, 1996-2002; bd. dirs., vchmn. Nat. Legal Ctr. for Pub. Interest, 2002—; clearance counsel Bush-Cheney transition team, 2000-2001; commr., The Nat. Commn. on Terrorist Attacks Upon the U.S.(The 9-11 Commn.), 2002-04. Mem. Commn. on White House Fellowships, 1981-86, Pres.'s Commn. for German-Am. Tricentennial, 1983-84; presdl. del. to observe Philippine presdl. elections, 1986, pres.'s personal rep. Australia/Am. Friendship Week, 1986; spl. counsel to Rep. vice presdl. campaign, 1988, sr. legal advisor Bush-Quayle campaign, 1992; conflict-of-interest counsel Office of Pres.-Elect, 1980; gen. counsel 50th presdl. inaugural, 1984-85; dep. dir. presdl. transition, 1988-89; mem. Pres.'s Commn. on Fed. Ethics Law Reform, 1989; U.S. designated arbitrator Arbitration Tribunal on U.S.-U.K. Air Treaty Dispute, 1989-94, Sec. of Transp. Task Force on Air Disaster Victims, 1996-98; bd. vis. Sch. Law Pepperdine U., 1989-92; bd. dirs. Coun. for Excellence in Govt., 1989-95, Pediat. AIDS Found., 1998-2002; bd. fellows Gettysburg Coll., 1992—, trustee; bd. dirs. USAir Shuttle, 1992-97, Ethics Resource Ctr., 1993; sec.-treas., bd. dirs. Arlington Va. Hosp. Found., 1994—; mem. commn. on selection fed. judges U. Va. Miller Ctr., 1994-97; bd. dirs. Washington Scholarship Fund, 1994-97, Ctr. Democracy, 1995-98, vice-chmn. 1996-97, chmn., 1997. Capt. AUS, 1965-67. John McKee Found. fellow; recipient Gettysburg Coll. Disting. Alumni award, 1982; named Lawyer of Yr. Bar Assn. DC, 2004. Fellow ABA (life, standing com. on fed. judiciary CEELI), FBA, DC Bar Assn. (bd. govs. 1996-98), Pa. Bar Assn., Am. Arbitration Assn. (nat. panel, bd. dirs.), Law Initiative, Lawyers Club of Washington, Beachview Country Club, Washington Golf and Country Club, Met. Club, Phi Gamma Delta (Disting. Fiji 1987), Pi Delta Epsilon, Omicron Delta Kappa, Pi Lambda Sigma, Phi Delta Phi. Republican. Lutheran. Office: The White House 1600 Pennsylvania Ave NW 2nd Fl Washington DC 20502

FIELDING, HELEN, writer; b. Yorkshire, Eng., Feb. 19, 1958; 2 children. BA English, St. Anne's Coll., U. Oxford, Eng., 1979. Prodr. BBC-TV, England, 1979—89; freelance writer, 1989—; former columnist The Daily Telegraph; columnist The Independent of London, 2005—. Columnist London Ind., 1995—. Author: (novels) Cause Celeb, 1995, Bridget Jones's Diary, 1996, Bridget Jones: The Edge of Reason, 1999, Bridget Jones's Guide to Life, 2001, Olivia Joules and the Overactive Imagination, 2004; exec. prodr., screenwriter: (films) Bridget Jones's Diary, 2001 (London Critics Circle Film award for best screenwriter, 2002, Evening Standard British Film award for best screenplay, 2002); Bridget Jones: The Edge of Reason, 2004. Avocations: hiking, swimming, reading, movies. Office: c/o Viking Publicity 375 Hudson St New York NY 10014

FIELDING, JONATHAN EVAN, city health department administrator, pediatrician; b. Oct. 4, 1942; BA, Williams Coll., 1964; MA, MD, Harvard Coll., 1969, MPH, 1971; MBA, U. Pa., 1977. Diplomate Am. Bd. Pediats., Am. Bd. Preventive Medicine. Josiah Macy fellow Harvard U., Cambridge, Mass., 1969; intern, resident Boston Children's Hosp., 1969-71; fellow Harvard U., Boston, 1971; resident in pediats. Georgetown U. Med. Ctr., Washington, 1971-72, prin. med. svcs. nat. officer Job Corps, 1971-73; commr. pub. health Commonwealth of Mass., 1975-79; prof. health svcs. & pediats. UCLA, 1979—; dir. pub. health L.A. County, 1997—. Spl. asst. to dir. Bur. Cmty. Health Svcs. Health Svcs. & Mental Health Adminstrn. HEW, 1971-73; co-dir. Ctr. Health Enhancement Edn. & Rsch., 1979-84; co-dir. Ctr. for Healthier Children, Families & Cmtys., 1995—; lectr. Harvard U., Boston, 1973-75, Boston U., 1975-79, Brandeis U., 1975-79, Northwestern U., 1975-79; vis. lectr. UCLA, 1977; rsch. assoc. Urban Rsch. Ctr. Hunter Coll. CUNY, 1978; vis. prof. Nordic Sch. Pub. Health, Sweden, 1980, 83, 93. Editor: Ann. Revs. Pub. Health, 1995—; asst. editor Mercy-Rosenau Pub. Health and Preventive Medicine 1992-98, 14th edit. Vice-chair Partnership for Prevention, 1997—2002, chmn., 2002—, U.S. Cmty. Preventive Svcs. Task Force, 2001—. Fellow Assn. Health Svcs.; mem. NAS Inst. Medicine, Am. Acad. Pediats., Am. Assn. Pub. Health Physicians, Am. Med. Peer Rev. Assn., Am. Pub. Health Assn., Assn. Health Svcs. Medicine, Am. Heart Assn., Am. Coll. Preventive Medicine (pres. 1997-99). Office: UCLA Sch Pub Health Ctr Health Sci 61 253A Los Angeles CA 90095-0001

FIELDING, PEGGY LOU MOSS, writer; b. Davenport, Okla., Oct. 28, 1928; d. John Richard and Hazel (Matlock) Moss; B.S., Central State U., 1949, M.A., U. Santo Tomás, 1971. Tchr. various U.S. govt. overseas schs., Japan, Cuba and Philippines, 1955-71; owner Partners in Pub., Tulsa, 1975—; instr. writing Tulsa C.C., 1976—. Mem. Okla. Writers Fedn., Tulsa Night Writers Club, Romance Writers Am. Democrat. Baptist. Office: PO Box 50347 Tulsa OK 74150-0347

FIELDING, ROY THOMAS, software scientist; b. South Laguna, Calif., 1965; Attended, Reed Coll., Portland, Oreg., 1986; BS, U. Calif., Irvine, 1988, MS, 1993, PhD, 2000. Vol. tutor, Internat. Rels. and Model UN Laguna HS, Calif., 1985; programmer, analyst TRANSMAX, Santa Ana, Calif., 1983—86, Megadyne Information Sys., Santa Ana, Calif., 1986—88; software engr. PRC Pub. Mgmt. Svc. (San Francisco, Calif. and Portland, Oreg.), 1988—89, ADC Kentrox, Portland, Oreg., 1989—91; tchg. asst., info. and computer sci. U. Calif., Irvine, 1991—92; vis. scholar MIT Lab. Computer Sci., World Wide Web Consortium (W3C), 1995; grad. student researcher Inst. for Software Rsch., Info. and Computer Sci., U. Calif., Irvine, 1992—99; chmn. Apache Software Found., 1999—2002, dir., 1999—2003; chief scientist eBuilt, Irvine, Calif., 1999—2002, Day Software, Irvine, Calif., 2002—. Founding mem. Apache Group; mem. W3C Technical Architecture Group; external advisor Inst. for Software Rsch. Contbr. articles to profl. jours. Named Outstanding Grad. Student, U. Calif. Irvine Alumni Assn., 2000; named one of TR100 (top 100 young innovators), MIT Tech. Review, 1999; recipient Software Sys. award, Assn. Computing Machinery, 1999, Appaloosa award for Vision, O'Reilly Open Source 2000. Achievements include being the primary architect of the Hypertext Transfer Protocol (HTTP/1.1); author of the Internet standards for HTTP and Uniform Resource Identifiers (URI); founder of the Apache HTTP Server Project; defined the REST architectural style for network software. Avocations: board games, bridge, basketball, softball, football, fishing. Office: Day Software 23 Corporate Plaza Dr Ste 215 Newport Beach CA 92660 Office Phone: 949-706-5300. Office Fax: 949-706-5305. Business E-Mail: roy.fielding@day.com. E-mail: fielding@gbiv.com, fielding@apache.org.

FIELDS, ANTHONY LINDSAY AUSTIN, health facility administrator, oncologist, educator; b. St. Michael, Barbados, Oct. 21, 1943; arrived in Can., 1968; s. Vernon Bruce and Marjorie F.; m. Patricia Jane Stewart, Aug. 5, 1967. MA, U. Cambridge, 1969; MD, U. Alta., 1974. Diplomate Am. Bd. Internal Medicine. Sr. specialist Cross Cancer Inst., Edmonton, Alta., Canada, 1980-85, dir. dept. medicine, 1985-88, dir., 1988-2000; v.p. med. affairs and cmty. oncology Alta. Cancer Bd., 2000—. Asst. prof. medicine U. Alta., Edmonton, 1980-84, assoc. prof., 1984-98, prof., 1998—, dir. divsn. med. oncology, 1985-89, dir. divsn. oncology, 1988-93; v.p. Nat. Cancer Inst. Can., 2000-02, pres., 2002-04. Fellow ACP, Royal Coll. Physicians and Surgeons Can. (specialist cert. med. oncology, internal medicine); mem. Can. Assn. Med. Oncologists (pres. 1994-96), Am. Soc. Clin. Oncology, Can. Soc. for Clin. Investigation, Can. Med. Assn. Avocation: photography. Office: # 1220 10405 Jasper Ave Edmonton AB Canada T5J 3N4

FIELDS, BERTRAM HARRIS, lawyer; b. LA, Mar. 31, 1929; s. H. Maxwell Fields and Mildred Arlyn (Ruben); m. Lydia Ellen Minevitch, Oct. 22, 1960 (dec. Sept. 1986); 1 child, James Eldar; m. Barbara Guggenheim, Feb. 21, 1991. BA, UCLA, 1949; JD magna cum laude, Harvard U., 1952. Bar: Calif. 1953. Assoc. firm Shearer, Fields, Rohner & Shearer, and predecessor firms, 1955—57, mem. firm, 1957—82; ptnr. Greenberg, Glusker, Fields, Claman & Machtinger, LA, 1982—. Mem. editl. bd.: Harvard Law Rev., 1953—55; author (as D. Kincaid): The Sunset Bomber, 1986; author: The Lawyer's Tale, 1992; author: (as B. Fields) Royal Blood Richard III and the Mystery of the Princes, 1998, Players-The Shakespeare Mystery, 2005. 1st lt. USAF, 1953—55, Korea. Mem.: ABA, Coun. Fgn. Rels., LA County Bar Assn. Achievements include being the subject of profiles Calif. Mag., Nov. 1987; Avenue Mag., Mar. 1989; Am. Film Mag., Dec. 1989; Vanity Fair Mag., Dec. 1993; Harvard Law Sch. Bull., spring 1998; London Sunday Telegraph, June 1999; Sunday New York Post, July 1999; W Mag., Apr. 2002; L.A. Times, Apr. 2003; London Sunday Times, Apr. 2003; NY Times, May 2005; New Yorker Mag., July 2006. Office: Greenberg Glusker Fields Claman & Machtinger Ste 2000 1900 Avenue Of The Stars Los Angeles CA 90067-4590 Business E-Mail: bfields@ggfirm.com.

FIELDS, C(LARA) VIRGINIA, former city manager; b. Birmingham, Ala., Aug. 4, 1946; d. Peter and Lucille (Chappel) Clark; (div.) BA, Knoxville Coll., 1967; MSW, Ind. U., 1969; grad., NYU. Adminstr. social services Children's Aid Soc., 1971; supr. NYC Work Release Program; chair Cmty. Bd. 10, 1981-83; dist. leader 70th AD, Part C; city councilwoman Dist. 9, NYC, 1990-97; borough pres. Manhattan, NY, 1997—2006. Bd. mem., mem. Homeland Security Working Group Nat. League of Cities. Mem. NY State Coun. Black Elected Dems., NYC Coun. Black and Hispanic Caucus, Harlem Urban Devel. Corp., NY Urban League, Manhattan, Black Leadership Commn. on AIDS; bd. dirs. Morningside Daycare and Headstart Program; bd. mem. Jazz at Lincoln Ctr., Am. Mus. of Natural History, Mus. of City of NY, el Museo del barrio, Mus. of Art and Design. Mem. Ea. Star, Alpha Kappa Alpha, LINKS.

FIELDS, DEBBI (DEBRA FIELDS ROSE), cookie franchise executive; b. Oakland, Calif. m. Randy Fields (div.); children: Jessica, Jenessa, Jennifer, Ashley, McKenzie; m. Michael Rose, Nov. 29, 1997. Profl. water-skier Marine World; founder Mrs. Fields Chocolate Chippery (now Mrs. Fields Inc.), Palo Alto, 1977, Mrs. Fields Inc., Park City, Utah, 1978—, pres., CEO, 1977—93. Bd. dirs. Outback Steakhouse, 1996—, WKNO, The Orpheum Theater. Author: (cookbook) 100 Recipes from the Kitchen of Debbi Fields, I Love Chocolate, 1994, Debbi Fields Great American Desserts, (autobiography) One Smart Cookie. Mem.: Soc. Entrepreneurs. Office: Mrs Fields Original Cookies 2855 Cottonwood Pkwy Ste 400 Salt Lake City UT 84121-7050

FIELDS, DOUGLAS PHILIP, SR., building supply wholesale company executive; s. M. Emanuel and Priscilla (Wagner) F.; m. Paulette Susan Titko, Dec. 15, 1970 (div. Feb. 1990); children: Douglas Philip, Priscilla Wagner, Jessica Elizabeth; m. Maureen Virginia Hanmer, June 12, 1993; 1 child, Jacob Wagner. BS summa cum laude, Fordham U., 1964; MBA with distinction, Harvard U., 1966. Investment analyst Lehman Bros., NYC, 1966-67; asst. to pres. Talley Industries Inc., Mesa, Ariz., 1967-69; CEO, pres. TDA Industries Inc., NYC, 1969—; founder Unimet Corp., NYC, 1970-73; pres., chmn. Westcalind Corp., RI, 1971-87; CEO Acqueren, Inc., 1995-98. Chmn. bd. TDA Industries, Inc., NYC, 1970—, Westco Corp., Boston, 1970—79, Cooper Flooring Internat., Inc., Miami, 1972—98; chmn. bd. dirs., CEO Eagle Supply, Inc., Tampa, Fla., 1973—2004; CEO JEH/Eagle Supply, Inc., Dallas, 1997—2004; CEO, chmn. MSI/Eagle Supply Inc., Dallas, 1998—2000, Eagle Supply Group, Inc. (NASDAQ:EEGL), NYC, 1996—2004; chmn. Northeastern Plastics, Inc., NY, 1986—98; cons. U.S. Office Edn., 1973—74, Fed. Energy Adminstrn., 1974—75. Outside dir. NYU Grad. Sch. Bus., Mgmt. Decision Lab., 1973-78; mem. N.Y. State adv. com. U.S. Civil Rights Commn., 1974-85; bd. dirs. YMHA-YWHA of So. Westchester, Mt. Vernon, N.Y., 1981-92, Associated YMHA-YWHA of N.Y.C., Inc., 1989-91; mem. Young Pres.'s Orgn., 1973-92; road commr. Deer Park Assn., Greenwich, Conn., 2001-04, pres., 2005—. Mem. Chief Execs. Orgn., Met. Pres. Orgn., World Pres. Orgn., Deer Park Assn. (rd. commr. 2001-04, pres. 2005-), Belle Haven Club, Midtown Tennis Club (pres. 1969—).

FIELDS, FELICIA P., actress; b. Chgo. Actress (plays) Jammin' With Pops, Showboat, Lincolnshire Theatre, Carousel, Damn Yankees, Big River, Dreamgirls, The Wiz, Hot Mikado, Ain't Misbehavin', Hello Dolly!, Sophisticated Ladies (Joseph Jefferson award best actress in a musical), The Rose Tattoo, Goodman Theater, The Amen Corner, A Christmas Carol, Ties That Bind, Ma Rainey's Black Bottom, (Broadway plays) The Color Purple, 2005 (Theatre World award, 2006, Clarence Derwent award, Actors' Equity Found., 2006). Mailing: c/o Broadway Theatre 1681 Broadway New York NY 10019-5827

FIELDS, HENRY MICHAEL, lawyer; b. NYC, Feb. 11, 1946; s. Jack and Sylvia (Eggert) F.; m. Barbara Ann Schinman, June 20, 1971; children: Alexandra Wynne, Matthew Wyatt. BA magna cum laude, Harvard U., 1968; JD, Yale U., 1972. Bar: N.Y. 1973, N.J. 1974, Calif. 1981. Law clk. to presiding judge U.S. Dist. Ct. N.J. and U.S. Ct. Appeals (3d cir.), Newark, 1972-73; assoc. Cleary, Gottlieb, Steen & Hamilton, NYC and Paris, 1973-80, Morrison & Foerster, LA, 1980—81, ptnr., 1981—, mem. exec. com. Lectr. banking law various orgns., chair, Inst. for Corp. Counsel, 2000-01. Mng. editor Yale U. Law Rev., 1971-72; contbr. articles to profl. jours. Tower fellow Harvard U., 1968. Phi Beta Kappa. Clubs: Harvard-Radcliffe So. Calif, University (Los Angeles). Avocations: tennis, photography. Office: Morrison & Foerster LLP 555 W 5th St Ste 3500 Los Angeles CA 90013-1024 Office Phone: 213-892-5275. Office Fax: 213-892-5454. Business E-Mail: hfields@mofo.com.

FIELDS, HOWARD LINCOLN, neurologist, physiologist, educator; b. Chgo., Dec. 12, 1939; s. Charles and Mae (Pinkert) Fields; m. Carol Margaret Felts, Dec. 31, 1966; children: Rima Margaret Johnson, Gabriel Charles. BS, U. Chgo., 1960; MD, Stanford U., 1965, PhD in Neuroscience, 1966. Research neurologist Walter Reed Research Inst., Washington, 1967-70; clin. fellow Harvard Med. Sch., Boston, 1970-72; asst. prof. U. Calif., San Francisco, 1973-78, assoc. prof., 1978-82, prof., 1982—; vice chmn. neurology, 1993—; dir. Wheeler Ctr. for Neurobiology of Addiction. Cons. NIH, Bethesda, 1979—84; vis. fellow Clare Hall Coll. Cambridge U., England, 1979; vis. prof. Royal Soc. Medicine, 1988. Editor: Recent Advances in Pain Research and Therapy, 1985, Core Curriculum for Professional Education in Pain, 1991, 2d edit., 1995; author: Pain, 1987, Pain Syndromes in Neurology, 1990, Pharmacotherapy of Pain, 1994; contbr. articles to profl. jours. Recipient Rsch. Career Devel. award, NIH, Merit award, Nat. Inst. Drug Abuse, Kerr award, Am. Pain Soc., 1997. Mem.: Inst. Medicine of NAS, Soc. Neuroscience, Am. Neurol. Assn. (councillor 1991, mem. program com. 1991, R.D. Adams award 2006), Am. Acad. Neurology (Cotzias lectr. award 2000), Am. Soc. Clin. Investigation, Internat. Assn. Study Pain (program chmn. 1981—84, sec. 1990—93, editor-in-chief IASP Press 1993—2003). Office: U Calif Dept Neurology 5858 Horton St Ste 200 Emeryville CA 94608 Business E-Mail: hlf@phy.ucsf.edu.

FIELDS, JAMES PERRY, dermatologist, dermatopathologist, allergist, pharmacologist, pharmacist; b. Sherman, Tex., July 30, 1932; s. John Galloway and Alma (Goff) F.; m. Linda Hensley, May 30, 1958; children: Timothy Austin, Amy Elizabeth. BS, U. Tex., 1953, MS, 1957; MD, U. Tex., Galveston, 1958. Diplomate Am. Bd. Dermatology, Am. Bd. Allergy and Immunology, spl. competence cert. in dermatopathology. Dir. dept. dermatology USPHS, SI, N.Y., 1964-78; assoc. prof. medicine and pathology Vanderbilt U. Sch. of Medicine, Nashville, 1978-88; pvt. practice, Nashville, 1988—; dir. dermatopathology Lab. of the Mid-South, Nashville, 1988—. From instr. to assoc. clin. prof. dermatology and pathology Columbia-Presbyn. Hosp. and Coll. of Physicians and Surgeons, N.Y.C., 1968-88; assoc. clin. prof. medicine Vanderbilt U. Sch. Medicine, Nashville, 1988—. Author (with others): Mycobacterial Diseases, 1991, 2d edit., 2000; contbr. articles to profl. jours. Bd. dirs. Am. Leprosy Missions Internat., Greenville, S.C., 1974—; vol. med. missionary, United Meth. Vols. in Mission, 1984—. Capt. USPHS, 1958-79. Recipient citation for meritorious svcs. President's Com. on Employment of Handicapped, 1970, Meritorious Svc. medal USPHS, 1978, Good Samaritan award Nashville Acad. Medicine, 2002. Fellow ACP (Volunteerism and Cmty. Svc. award in Medicine, Tenn. chpt. 2000), Am. Acad. Allergy and Immunology, Am. Acad. Dermatology, Am. Coll. Allergy and Immunology, Am. Soc. Dermatopathology, Am. Soc. for Dermatologic Surgery, N.Y. Acad. Medicine (sec. 1976-77, chmn. sect. on dermatology 1977-78). Home: 411 Lynwood Blvd Nashville TN 37205-3434 Office: 4301 Hillsboro Rd # 222 Nashville TN 37215-3314 Home Phone: 615-298-1625. Personal E-mail: jpfields@earthlink.net.

FIELDS, JANICE L., food service executive; b. 1955; m. Doug Wilkins; 2 children. From crew mem. to regional v.p. Pitts. McDonald's Corp., 1978—94; v.p Pitts. region McDonald's USA, 1994—2000; v.p. Great Lakes divsn. McDonald's Corp., 2000; sr. v.p. SE divsn. McDonald's USA, sr. v.p. ctrl. divsn., 2000—03, pres. ctrl. divsn., 2003—06, exec. v.p., COO, 2006—. Mem. bd. dirs. United Cerebral Palsy, Catalyst. Bd. dirs. Ronald McDonald House Charities, Urban League. Named one of 25 Women to Watch, Crain's Chgo. Bus., 2007; recipient Golden Arch Partners Award, McDonald's, WON award, Women's Operator Network, 1988, Women Operators Network Recognition Award, McDonald's, 2001, Women's Leadership award, Women's Network, 2002. Office: McDonald's Corp 2111 McDonald's Dr Oak Brook IL 60523

FIELDS, MARK, automotive executive; b. Bklyn., 1961; BA in Economics, Rutgers U., 1983; MBA, Harvard U., 1989. Joined Ford Motor Co., Dearborn, Mich., 1989, served in a variety of sales and mktg. positions, 1990—96; mng. dir. Ford of Argentina, 1997—98; sr. adviser Mazda Motor Corp., 1998, sr. mng. dir. of mktg., sales & customer svc., 1998, rep. dir., pres., 1999—2002; group v.p., Premier Automotive Group Ford Motor Co., 2002—04, exec. v.p., Ford Europe, 2004—05, exec. v.p., pres. Americas, 2005—. Recipient Global Leader of Tomorrow, World Economic Forum, 2000, Innovator of the Year, CNBC's Asian Business Leader, 2001. Office: Ford Motor Co 21175 Oakwood Blvd Dearborn MI 48124-4079*

FIELDS, MARVIN LEON, secondary school educator; b. Mahanttan, NY, May 27, 1965; s. Ella Nora Fields. BS in Comm., U. New Haven, 1991; MS in Edn., Hamilton U., 2000. Mail carrier U.S. Postal Svc., Ridgewood, NJ, 1992—93; stockbroker trainee Gruntal and Co., NYC, 1993—95; prodr. ind. TV U.S. Cable, Paterson, NJ, 1993—; tchr. PAterson Pub. Schs., 1998—. Pres. Dolphn Sports, Paterson, 2000—. Youth advvisor NAACP, Paterson, 1993—97; mem. Athletics in Action Men's Basketball Team, 1991; founder Kids Without Parents Found., Joella Field Scholarship Fund. Recipient Achievement award, Christ Temple Bapt. Ch., Paterson, 2001. Mem.: Fellowship of Christian Athletes Assn., Phi Delta Kappa, Kappa Alpha Psi. Home: 376 E 28th St Paterson NJ 07514 Home Phone: 973-247-7955; Office Phone: 973-321-0140. E-mail: mlfields0@lycos.com.

FIELDS, SARA A., travel company executive; With Boeing Aircraft, Renton, Wash.; flight attendant UAL Corp., Elk Grove Village, Ill., 1963, various positions including mgr. flight attendant training, mgr. indsl. rels., dir. inflight svc internat., dir. employee rels., 1963—94, sr. v.p. onboard svc., 1994—. Office: UAL Corp 1200 E Algonquin Rd Arlington Heights IL 60005-4712 also: PO Box 66100 Chicago IL 60666-0100 Fax: 847-700-4899.

FIELDS, SHEILA CRAIN, elementary school educator; b. Big Sandy, Tex., Jan. 8, 1953; d. James Daniel and Janet Crain; m. Jerry Dale Fields, July 13, 1973; children: Carrie Fields Lentz, Angie Clack. BS in Elem. Edn., Tex. A&M U., 1975. Tchr. Bryan (Tex.) Ind. Sch. Dist., 1975—. Commr. Bryan Hist. Landmark Commn., Tex., 2005—07; vol. March of Dimes, Bryan, 2005—07, Am. Cancer Soc., Bryan, 2005—07. Named Tchr. of Yr., Fannin Elem. Sch., 2005. Mem.: PTA (parliamentarian 2004—05), Assn. Tex. Profl. Educators (treas. 1999—2000, state sec. 2000—01, state v.p. 2001—02, state pres. 2002—03, William B. Travis award 2002, Harvey Mitchell Cmty. Heritage award 1998), Delta Kappa Gamma (treas. 2004—06). Methodist. Home: 3106 Red Robin Loop Bryan TX 77802 Office: Fannin Elem 1200 Baker St Bryan TX 77803 Office Phone: 979-209-3800.

FIELDS, STUART HOWARD, labor relations specialist; b. Chgo., Dec. 15, 1943; s. Albert B. and Cecelia (Kessler) Fields; m. Birgit Willeke, Dec. 5, 1971; children: Jessica N., Jascha D. BS, UCLA, 1965; MS, U. Calif., Northridge, 1968. Cert. tchr. and instr. Calif. Labor rels. specialist Hughes Tool Co., Culver City, Calif., 1970, Dept. of the Navy, Point Mugu, Calif., 1971-76; employee rels. specialist Agrl. Rsch. Svc., Hyattsville, Md., 1976-81, labor rels. specialist, 1981-84, Pub. Health Svc., Rockville, Md., 1985-86; employee rels. specialist Def. Nuclear Agy., Bethesda, Md., 1986-88, Consumer Product Safety Commn., Bethesda, 1988-89, U.S. Dept. Commerce, Washington, 1989-97; sr. paralegal Gagliardo & Zipin, Attys. at Law, Silver Spring, Md., 1997—; labor rels. specialist IRS, Washington, 1997—2004; human resources specialist Fed. Election Commn., Washington, 2004—07; supervisory human resources specialist, nat. capital region Gen. Svcs. Adminstrn., Washington, 2007—. Presdl. classroom instr.; cons. in field. Author: Requirements for Top Positions in Personnel Administration, 1968. Lt. US Army, 1968—70. Mem.: Soc. Fed. Labor Rels. Profls., Mensa, Jewish Cmty. Ctr. Democrat. Avocations: classical music, coin collecting/numismatics, tax law, basketball. Home: 9449 Reach Rd Potomac MD 20854-2853 Office: Gen Svcs Adminstrn Nat Capital Region 301 Seventh St SW Washington DC 20407 Office Phone: 202-708-5314. Personal E-mail: stuarthfields@aol.com.

FIELDS, SUZANNE BREGMAN, syndicated columnist; b. Washington, Mar. 7, 1936; d. Samuel Holiday and Sadie (Hurwitz) Bregman; m. Theodore Martin Fields, June 16, 1957; children: Alexandra, Miriamne, Tobias. BA, George Washington U., 1957, MA, 1964; PhD, Cath. U., 1971. Freelance writer, Washington, 1965-71; editor Innovations Mag., Washington, 1971-79; columnist Vogue mag., Washington, 1982; author Like Father, Like Daughter (Little Brown), 1983; columnist Washington Times, 1984—; syndicated columnist L.A. Times Syndicate, Washington, 1988-2001, Chgo. Tribune Media Svcs., 2001—05, Creators Syndicate, 2005—. TV commentator, regular panelist CNN & Co. Mem. Phi Beta Kappa. Jewish. Home: 1934 Biltmore St NW Washington DC 20009-1510 Office: The Washington Times 3600 New York Ave NE Washington DC 20002-1996

FIELDS, VELMA ARCHIE, medical/surgical nurse; d. Charles and Ella Ruth Archie; m. Herrell Lee Fields Sr., July 29, 1972; children: Sherri Debnam, Herrell Jr., LaShonda Hairston. BSN, Winston-Salem State U., 1968. Cert. N. C. State Bd. Nursing. Nurse, oper. rm. nurse N.C. Bapt. Hosp., Winston-Salem, 1969—90; nursing instr. Forsyth Tech. Coll., Winston-Salem, 1990—93; client coord. Sr. Svcs. Meals-on-Wheels, Winston-Salem, 1993—96; nurse Nursefinders, Winston-Salem, 1997—. Segment based on story of Velma Field's hat and her daddy (off-Broadway play) Crowns, 2002—03. Vol. cardiopulmonary instr. ARC, Winston-Salem, NC, 1980; vol. Nurse Database for Bioterrorism Response Team Forsyth County Dept. Pub. Health, 2003—; vol. nightingale Nat. Black Theatre Festival, 2005; deacon Emmanuel Bapt. Ch., Winston-Salem, NC. Recipient Race Progress Promotors Achievement award in healthcare, Effort Club, New Bethel Bapt. Ch., Winston-Salem, N.C., 2001, Cert. Appreciation, NC Dept. Health and Human Svcs. Baptist. Office Phone: 336-995-8372.

FIELDS, VICTOR LEE, music educator; b. Hagerstown, Md., Nov. 11, 1959; s. Niles Emory and Caryl Lobe Fields. BMus, Mansfield U., 1981; MMus, Peabody Conservatory, 1983, U. Cin., 1990. Dir. music St. Paul's Episc. Ch., Petersburg, Va., 1985—88, Trinity Episc. Ch., Williamsport, Pa., 1991—94, Trinity United Ch. of Christ, York, Pa., 1998—; prof. music Mt. St. Mary's U., Emmitsburg, Md., 2004—. Sec. Am. Guild of Organists, York, Pa., 1998—2005. Composer: Celebrate God's Love, 2002. Recipient Frank Hines award, Peabody Conservatory, 1983. Democrat. Episcopalian. Avocations: travel, photography, reading. Home Phone: 717-858-4982. Business E-Mail: fields@msmary.edu.

FIELDS, WILLIAM ALBERT, lawyer; b. Parkersburg, W.Va., Mar. 30, 1939; s. Jack Lyons and Grace (Kelley) F.; m. Prudence Brandt Adams, June 26, 1964. BS magna cum laude, Ohio State U., 1961; postgrad., Harvard Law Sch., 1961-64. Bar: Ohio bar 1964. Since practiced in, Marietta; city prosecutor, 1964-65; acting Judge Marietta Mcpl. Ct.; dir. elections Washington County, 1967-74; profl. bass-baritone soloist. Bd. dirs. Bank One, Marietta, N.A.; lectr. on estate planning and probate matters. Mem. editl. bd. Probate Law Jour. of Ohio. Chmn. Washington County Heart Assn., 1965-67; mem. dist. exec. com. Boy Scouts Am., 1967-74; Treas. County Republican Exec. Com., 1966—; trustee YMCA, Salvation Army; pres. bd. trustees Washington State Community Coll., Marietta; exec. com., trustee Coll. Adminstrv. Scis., Ohio State U.; trustee Appalachian Bible Coll., Bradley, W.Va., 1974-77, Marietta Meml. Hosp., also treas.; bd. dirs. Ohio Valley Port Authority. Recipient Wall St. Jour. award, 1961; named Outstanding Young Man of Marietta, 1968, Outstanding Citizen of Marietta, 1992; named to Ohio Valley Sports Hall of Fame, 2001. Fellow Am. Coll. Trust and Estate Counsel; mem. Ohio Bar Assn. (chmn., bd. govs., probate and trust law sect., mem. splty. bd. Ohio Supreme Ct., splty approval bd. trust, probate, and estate planning), Washington County Bar Assn., Marietta Area C. of C. (v.p., trustee), Am. Mensa, Nat. Soc. of Arts and Letters (bd. trustees), Sigma Chi, Beta Gamma Sigma. Clubs: Rotarian (pres. 1970-71), Marietta Country (trustee). Home: 129 Hillcrest Dr Marietta OH 45750-9321 Personal E-mail: wafpaf@charter.net. *Without the light of Christ, all is darkness and vain machination.*

FIELDS-GOLD, ANITA, retired dean; b. Amarillo, Tex., Oct. 29, 1940; d. Dera and Mamie Maureen (Craig) Bates; m. Maurice Gold; 1 child, William Kyle. Grad. nursing, Jefferson Davis Hosp., 1962; BSN, Tex. Christian U., 1966; MSN, Northwestern State U. La., 1974; PhD, Tex. Women's U., 1980. C.E. coord., asst. prof. Northwestern State U., Shreveport; prof., dean McNeese State U., Lake Charles, La.; ret., 2000. Gov.'s appointee, chmn. S.W. La. Hosp. Dist. Commn., 1989—91; vice chair Region 5 Healthcare Reform Consortium. Mem. allocations com. and loaned exec. United Way, 1991—92, Am. Heart Assn.; vol. Am. Cancer Soc., ARC; bd. pres. Artists Civic Theatre and Studio, 2004—; vice chmn. Region 5 Health Care Reform Consortium, 2005; exec. dir. Region 5 Health Care Authority, 2006—, Region 5 Health Care Redesign Collaborative, 2006—07. Recipient Ben Taub award, 1962, Ann Magnussen award, ARC, 1977, Frances Windham award, ACTA, 2005—06. Mem.: ANA (del.), Lake Charles Dist. Nurses Assn. (bd. dirs., Nurse of Yr. award 1972, 1980), La. Nurses Assn. (past pres. and 1st v.p., Spl. Recognition award 1993, Nightingale Hall of Fame award 2002), Phi Kappa Phi, Delta Kappa Gamma, Sigma Theta Tau (Image of Nursing award 1993). Home: 2339 21st St Lake Charles LA 70601-7946 Personal E-mail: amgold1@suddenlink.net.

FIELDS-HARRIS, DEBORAH CAROL, mathematician, educator; d. Floyd Earl Fields and Mary Katheryn McGinnis Fields; m. Stevenson Harris III, May 26, 1979 (div. May 5, 1981). Degree in mgmt. and econs., Houston Bapt. U., 1974; M of Ednl. Leadership & Adminstrn., Tex. So. U., Houston, 2003; postgrad., Northcentral U., Phoenix, 2006—. Prin. Tex., 2003. Acct. Union Tex. Petroleum, Houston, 1981—88; tchr. English, lang. arts Kirby Mid. Sch., 1991—98; math. skill specialist Drew Acad. Magnet, 2003—06; chair math dept. Clifton Mid. Sch., 2007—. Author of poems; editor: (newsletter) Visioneers' Voice. Participant PUSH - Rainbow Coalition, Houston, 2006—; vol. Dems. for Am., 1990—. Named Tchr. of Year, Drew Acad., 2002—03; recipient Internat. Poet Merit award, Internat. Soc. Poets, 2002—03, Outstanding Cmty. Svc. award, Acres Homes Citizens Coun., 2003. Mem.: NAACP, Tex. Coun. Tchrs. English (v.p. affiliates 2000—02), Tex. Coun. Tchrs. English Lang. Arts, Nat. Coun. Tchrs. English (chair standing com. multilcultural concerns 1998—99, chair program recognize excellence student lit. mag. 1998—2000, del. 1999—2002), Nat. Coun. Tchrs. Math. (corr.), Acres Homes Citizens C. of C. Democrat. Baptist. Avocations: writing Christian literature, travel. Office Phone: 713-613-2516.

FIELEKE, NORMAN SIEGFRIED, economist, educator; b. Kankakee, Ill., Aug. 22, 1932; s. Lessly and Catharine M. (Nicholson) F.; m. Carol A. Curtiss, June 16, 1962 (div. Dec. 1985); children: Andrew, Eric, Michael. BA summa cum laude, Amherst Coll., 1954; AM, Harvard U., 1955, PhD, 1969. Economist, budget examiner Office Mgmt. and Budget, Washington, 1959—64; industry economist Office U.S. Trade Rep., Exec. Office Pres., 1964—65; v.p., economist Fed. Res. Bank of Boston, 1967—97. Dir. econ. rsch. U.S. Internat. Trade Commn., Washington, 1980; cons. IMF, Washington, 1993; adj. prof. Boston U., 1975-76, Brandeis U., 1988-90, Duke U., Durham, NC, 1998-2000; lectr. Duke Inst. for Learning in Retirement, 2001-05. Author: The Welfare Effects of Controls over Capital Exports from the United States, 1971, The International Economy under Stress, 1988; contbr. articles to profl. jours. Lt. USAF, 1955-57. Littauer fellow, NSF fellow Harvard U., 1969. Home: 101 Dundalk Dr Chapel Hill NC 27517-6583

FIELO, MURIEL BRYANT, interior designer; b. Bklyn., Dec. 11, 1921; d. Harry and Minnie (Dick) Bryant; m. Julius Fielo, June 17; one child, Michael Kenneth. Student, Rutgers U., 1965—69. Cert. NY Sch. Interior Design, 1970. Gen. mgr. Fidelity Discount Corp., Irvington, NJ; advt. supr. Lincoln Loan Co., Essex County, NJ, 1941—49; interior designer Alex Fielo Interior Decorators, Newark, 1942—49, prin., 1949—69, owner, 1969—. Designer, cons., space engr. Mudge Interior Design Studios, East Orange, NJ, 1969-; mem. adv. panel Interior Design mag., 1977-. Clk. Essex County Bd. Freeholders, 1972-76; commr. East Orange Bus. Devel. Authority, 1977-86; mem. US adv. coun. SBA-Region II, 1980-811 active LWV, 1950-55; organizer, first pres. South Orange chpt. Women's Am. ORT, 1952-54, mem. nat. speakers bur., 1952-65, parliamentarian No. NJ coun., 1955-65; pres. Amity chpt. B'nai B'rith, Newark, 1946-48, v.p. No. NJ coun., 1948-49, various nat. and state positions, 1948-80; mem. nat. com. on sect. fund raising Nat. Coun. Jewish Women, 1979-81, nat. tour chmn., 1979-81; trustee cmty. svc. coun. Oranges and Maplewood, United Way Essex and West Hudson, 1981-83; bd. dir. East Orange Ctrl. Ave. Mall Assn., 1979-83, chmn. new voter registration drive East Orange 2d Ward, 1955, entire city, 1969; pres. East Orange Dem. Club, 1957-58, campaign coord. for Dem. mayoral candidate, 1969; calendar coord. Essex County Dem. Com., 1970-76; mem. NJ Bipartisan Coalition for Women's Appointments, 1981. Named Outstanding Entrepreneur of 1984, Gov. of NJ, Outstanding Orgn. Pres., Kean Coll. Profl. Women's Assn., 1985, Wonder Woman of 1986, Bus. Jour. NJ, One of Eight Women To Watch, Jersey Woman mag., 1987, Bus. Person of Yr., East Orange C. of C., 1988. Mem. Internat. Soc. Interior Designers (bd. dir. 1981-85), Nat. Home Fashions League (NJ membership chmn. NY chpt. 1981-82), Interior Design Soc., Internat. Interior Design Assn. (charter), NJ Assn. Women Bus. Owners (state bd. dir. 1979-82), Women Entrepreneurs NJ (pres. 1981-85, CEO 1987—), NJ Home Furnishings Assn. (bd. dir. 1981-84, 86—), Constrn. Specifications Inst., NJ Soc. AIA profl. affiliate), Guild Designer Woodworkers, Women Bus. Ownership Ednl. Coalition (NJ pres. 1985-87, CEO 1987—, mem. steering com. interior designers for licensing in NY 1985—), East Orange C. of C. (bd. dir. 1977—, v.p. 1981-85), Bus. and Profl. Women's Club Oranges (bd. dir. 1958-66). Jewish. Home and Office: Mudge Interior Design Studio 185 S Clinton St East Orange NJ 07018-3099 Office Phone: 973-673-6008. Office Fax: 973-672-7287. Business E-Mail: mbfielo@rcn.com.

FIELS, KEITH MICHAEL, executive director American Library Association; b. June 1949; BA, MLS, SUNY, Buffalo. Dir. Mass. Bd. Libr. Commissioners, Boston, 1992—2002; exec. dir. ALA, Chgo., 2002—. Cons. NY State Libr., NJ State Libr. Recipient Nat. Advocacy Honor Roll, Assn. Libr. Trustees and Advocates, 2000, Leadership Achievement award, Assn. Specialized and Coop. Libr. Agencies, Libr. Pub. Relations Council award. Mem.: Chief Officers of State Libr. Agencies (pres.). Office: American Library Assn 50 E Huron St Chicago IL 60611 Office Phone: 312-280-1392. Office Fax: 312-944-3897. E-mail: kfiels@ala.org.

FIENBERG, STEPHEN ELLIOTT, statistician; b. Toronto, Ont., Can., Nov. 27, 1942; came to U.S., 1964; BS, U. Toronto, 1964; A.M., Harvard U., 1965, PhD, 1968. Asst. prof. dept. stats. and theoretical biology U. Chgo., 1968-72; asso. prof. dept. applied stats. U. Minn., St. Paul, 1972-76, prof., 1976-80, chmn. dept., 1972-78; prof. dept. stats. and social sci. Carnegie Mellon U., Pitts., 1980-85; Maurice Falk prof. Carnegie-Mellon U., Pitts., 1985-91, head dept. stats., 1981-84, dean Coll. Humanities and Social Scis., 1987-91; vice pres. acad. affairs York U., Toronto, 1991-93; chmn. com. on nat. stats. NRC, 1981-87; Maurice Falk prof. dept. stats Carnegie Mellon U., Pitts., 1992-97, Maurice Falk univ. prof., 1997—, prof., stats. and machine learning dept., 1997—, prof. Cy. Lab., 2002—. Author: (with others) Discrete Multivariate Analysis: Theory and Practice, 1975, Analysis of Cross-classified Categorical Data, 1977, 2d edit., 1980, (with others) Beginning Statistics with Data Analysis, 1983, (with M. Anderson) Who Counts? The Politics of Census-Taking in Contemporary America, 1999, revised paperback edit., 2001; editor: (with A. Zellner) Studies in Bayesian Econometrics and Statistics, 1975, (with D.V. Hinkley) R.A. Fisher: An Appreciation, 1980, (with A.J. Reiss, Jr.) Indicators of Crime and Criminal Justice: Quantitative Studies, 1980, (with others) Sharing Research Data, 1985, (with W. Mason) Cohort Analysis in Social Research, 1985, (with A.C. Atkinson) A Celebration of Statistics, 1985, (with others) Statistics and the Law, 1986, The Evolving Role of Statistical Assessments as Evidence in the Courts, 1989, (with others) A Statistical Model: Frederick Mosteller's Contributions to Statistics, Science and Public Policy, 1990, (with M. M. Meyer) Assessing Evaluation Studies: The Case of Bilingual Education Strategies, 1992, (with others) Intelligence, Genes, and Success: Scientists Respond to The Bell Curve, 1997, (with others) The Polygraph and Lie Detection, 2003, (with D.C. Hoaglin) Selected Papers of Frederick Mosteller, 2006, (with others, Statistical Network Analysis: Models, Issues and New Directions, 2006; editor Jour. Am. Stats. Assn., 1977-79, Chance, 1987-92; stats. editor Internat. Ency. Soc. Behavioral Sci., 2001, Annals of Applied Statistics, 2006—. Recipient Pres. award Com. Pres. Statis. Socs., 1982. Fellow AAAS, Am. Statis. Assn. (v.p. 1986-88, Wilks medal 2000), Inst. Math. Stats. (pres. 1998-99), Internat. Soc. Bayesian Analysis (pres.1996-97), Am. Acad. Polit. and Social Scis., Royal Soc. Can., Royal Statis. Soc., Am. Acad. Arts & Scis.; mem. Nat. Acad. Sci. (elected), Biometric Soc., Internat. Statis. Inst., Psychometric Soc., Statis. Soc. Can. Office: Carnegie Mellon U Dept Stats Pittsburgh PA 15213 Office Phone: 412-268-2723.*

FIENE, BRIAN D., protective services official, retired military officer; b. Kans. City, Mo., Apr. 2, 1969; s. Gary Fiene and Alice Rose, Carla Fiene (Stepmother); m. Angie Rogers, June 7, 1997 (div. Apr. 15, 2002); children: Zoey, Payton; m. Amber Lodge, Apr. 9, 2005. Lic. peace officer State Mo., 1997. Sgt. Camden County Sheriff's Dept., Camdenton, Mo., 1997—. Cpl. USMC, 1991—96, Camp Lejeune, NC. Decorated Nat. Def. Svc. medal USMC, 4th Expert Rifleman award, Armed Forces Expeditionary medal, Sea Svc. Deployment Ribbon award, Humanitarian Svc. medal, Joint Meritorious Unit award, Combat Action Ribbon award, Marine Good Conduct medal, Armed Forces Svc. medal, Meritorious Unit Commendation award, UN medal; recipient Sea Svc. Deployment Ribbon award, 1996, Humanitarian Svc. medal, 1996. Mem.: VFW, Nat. Criminal Enforcement Assoc., Mo. Dep. Sheriff's Assoc. R-Conservative. Roman Catholic. Avocation: hunting.

FIENNES, JOSEPH, actor; b. Salisbury, Wiltshire, Ireland, May 27, 1970; Student, Guildhall Sch. Music and Drama. With Royal Shakespeare Co. Appeared in The Woman in Black, A Month in the Country, Son of Man, Les Enfants du Paradis, Troilus and Cressida, The Herbal Bed; films include Vacillations of Poppy Carew, 1995, Stealing Beauty, 1996, Shakespeare in Love, 1998 (Screen Actors Guild awards 1999, Chgo. Film Critics Assn. award 1999, Broadcast Film Critics Assn. award 1999, Nominee Brit. Acad. award 1999, Nominee Block Buster Entertainment award 1999), Elizabeth, 1998, Martha, Meet Frank, Daniel and Laurence, 1998, Rancid Aluminum, 1999, Forever Mine, 1999, Enemy at the Gates, 2000, Leo, 2002, Killing Me Softly, 2002, Luther, 2003, Sinbad (voice), 2003, The Merchant of Venice, 2004, Nan to Man, 2005, The Great Raid, 2005, The Darwin Awards, 2006, Running with Scissors, 2006. Office: Ken McReddie Ltd 91 Regent St W1R 7TB London England*

FIENNES, RALPH (RALPH NATHANIEL TWISLETON-WYKEHAM FIENNES), actor; b. Ipswitch, Suffolk, Eng., Dec. 22, 1962; s. Mark and Jini (Jennifer Lash) Fiennes; m. Alex Kingston, 1993 (div. Oct 28, 1997). Student, Chelsea Coll. Art and Design, Royal Acad. Dramatic Art. Actor (theatre prodns.) with Royal Shakespeare Co., Broadway debut in Hamlet, 1995 (Tony award Lead Actor in a Play), Ivanov, 1997, Richard II and Coriolanus, 2000, The Talking Cure, 2002, Brand, 2003, Julius Caesar, 2005, Faith Healer, 2006; film appearances include Schindler's List, 1993 (Academy award nomination for best supporting actor 1993, New York Film Critics Circle award best supporting actor 1993), Quiz Show, 1994, Strange Days, 1995, The English Patient, 1996 (Academy award nominee, Golden Globe award nominee), Oscar & Lucinda, 1997, The Avengers, 1998, Spider, 2002, The Good Thief, 2002, Red Dragon, 2002, Maid in Manhattan, 2002, The Chumscrubber, 2005, The Constant Gardener, 2005, (voice) Wallace & Gromit: The Curse of the Were-Rabbit, 2005, Harry Potter and the Goblet of Fire, 2005, The White Countess, 2005; exec. prodr.: Taste of Sunshine, 1999, End of the Affair, 1999; (voice) Prince of Egypt, 1998, actor, prodr. Onegin, 1999; actor (TV films) Prime Suspect, 1991, A Dangerous Man: Lawrence After Arabia, 1992, Wuthering Heights, 1992, The Baby of Macon

FIERHELLER, GEORGE ALFRED, communications executive; b. Toronto, Can., Apr. 26, 1933; s. Harold Parsons and Ruth Hathaway (Bauld) F.; m. Glenna E. Fletcher, Apr. 17, 1957; children: Vicki Elaine, Lori Ann BA, U. Toronto, 1955; LLD, Concordia U.; DSLitt, Trinity Coll., U. Toronto. With IBM, Toronto, 1955-58, account mgr., 1962-65, mktg. mgr., 1966-68; founder, pres. Sys. Dimensions Ltd., Ottawa, Ont., 1968-79; pres., CEO Rogers Cable TV Broadcasting Co. Ltd., Vancouver, B.C., Canada, 1979-85, Cantel Inc., Toronto, 1985-90; chmn., CEO Rogers Cantel Mobile, Inc., 1990-93; vice chair Rogers Comm., Inc., Toronto, 1993-96; pres. Four Halls Inc., Toronto, 1997—. Bd. dirs. Extendicare Inc., Can. Inst. Advanced Rsch.; pres. Bd. of Trade of Met. Toronto, 1996-97. Author: Finnie's Family, Let Me Say This About That, others; contbr. articles to profl. jours. Gen. chmn. United Appeal Campaign, Ottawa, 1972; chmn. campaign Carleton U., 1975-77, also chmn. bd. govs., 1977-79; mem. adv. com. Norman Paterson Sch. Internat. Affairs; bd. dirs., v.p. United Way Ottawa, 1975-79 (United Way of Can. highest award 1998), Opera Ottawa, 1970-71; trustee, mem. exec. com. Nat. Arts Ctr., 1973-79; trustee Royal Ottawa Hosp., 1978-79, Vancouver Gen. Hosp. Found., 1981-85, Can. Ctr. for Advanced Rsch, 2001—; mem. Vancouver Centennial Commn., 1983-84; bd. govs. Simon Fraser U., Vancouver, 1981-84; chmn. United Way Vancouver, 1981, B.C. Coun. of 80's, 1980-83, Vision 2000, 1990-91; chair United Way Met. Toronto, 1994-96, chmn. gen. campaign, 1991; trustee Sunnybrook Hosp. Found., 1993-99, chair Sunnybrook Health Scis. Ctr. campaign, 1999—, McMichael Can. Art Collection, 1993-99; chair Trinity Coll. Campaign, 1996-99. Decorated mem. Order of Can.; recipient Award of Merit, City of Toronto, 1991, Award of Excellence, Can. Wireless Ind. Assn., 1996, Queen's Golden Jubilee medal, 2002, Salute to City award Toronto, 2002; named to Can. Info. Tech. Hall of Fame, 1998, Outstanding Vol. of Yr., Assn. Fundraising Profls., 2001; named to Sigma Chi Hall of Fame, Order of Constantine, 2005. Mem. Can. Info. Processing Soc. (pres. 1970-71), World Pres. Orgn., Chief Execs. Orgn., Can. Assn. Data Processing Svc. Orgns., Assn. Cert. Computer Profls. (founding com.), Can. Ctr. for Philanthropy (bd. dirs. 1987-91), Bus. Coun. on Nat. Issues, Coun. for Bus. and the Arts in Can. (bd. dirs. 2003—), Cellular Telecom. Industry Assn. (bd. dirs. 1986-94), Smart Toronto (chmn. 1996), Greater Toronto Mktg. Alliance (chmn. 1997-03), Vancouver Club, Rideau Club, Granite Club, Univ. Club, Nat. Club (pres. 1998-99), Rosedale Golf Club, Toronto Adventurers Club (chmn. 2003-04). Home: 24 Pearwood Crescent Toronto ON Canada M3B 2C2 Office: Four Halls Inc 77 King St W Ste 4545 Toronto ON Canada M5K 1K2 Home Phone: 416-443-1982; Office Phone: 416-861-1351. Home Fax: 416-443-9360. Personal E-mail: fierhel@attglobal.net.

FIERI, GUY, chef; married; 2 children. B in Hospitality Mgmt., U. Nev. Las Vegas, 1990. Mgr. Stouffer restaurants; gen. mgr. Louise's Trattoria, dist. mgr.; co-founder, mgr. Johnny Garlic's, 1996—, Johnny Garlic's catering divsn., 2001—, Tex Wasabi's, 2003—, Russell Ramsay's Chop House, 2004—. Mem., pres. Restaurant Assn. of Redwood Empire; bd. dir. Ednl. Found. of Calif. Restaurant Assn. Host Guy's Big Bite, Food Network, 2006—. Achievements include winning The Next Food Network Star contest, 2006. Office: Johnny Garlic's 8988 Brooks Rd Windsor CA 95492 Office Phone: 707-836-8300. Office Fax: 707-836-8365.*

FIERKE, THOMAS GARNER, lawyer; b. Boone, Iowa, Nov. 12, 1948; s. Norman Garner and Mary Margaret (Mullen) F.; m. Susan Marie Butler, July 17, 1976 (div. Mar. 1983); m. Debra Lynn Clayton, Sept. 17, 1988; children: Veronica Helen, Caroline Margaret. BSMetE, Iowa State U., 1971; JD, U. Minn., 1974; LLM, Boston U., 1978; M in Strategic studies, U.S. Army War Coll., 1999. Bar: Ill. 1974, U.S. Dist. Ct. Mass. 1976, U.S. Dist. Ct. (no. dist.) Ill. 1976, U.S. Ct. Appeals (1st cir.) 1976, U.S. Tax Ct. 1978, U.S. Supreme Ct. 1978, Mass. 1980, N.Y. 1981, U.S. Ct. Appeals (fed. cir.) 1989. Commd. 2nd lt. U.S. Army, 1971, advanced through grades to col., 1980, ret., 2002; trial ct. prosecutor Ft. Devens, Mass., 1974-77; group judge adv. 10th Spl. Forces Group, 1975-78; chief adminstrv. law sect. Ft. Devens, 1977-78; chief legal counsel, contracting officer U.S. Def. Rep., Am. Embassy, Tehran, Iran, 1979; chief adminstrv. law Ft. Devens, 1979-80; judge adv. gen. corps, 1974-80; atty.-advisor Army Materiel Command, 1980-82; mgr. contracts policy and review Martin Marietta Michoud Aerospace, Martin Marietta Corp., New Orleans, 1982; gen. counsel Lockheed Martin Manned Space Sys., Lockheed Martin Corp., New Orleans, 1984—. Apptd. to La. Gov.'s Mil. Adv. Commn., 1991; bd. dirs. La. Orgn. for Jud. Excellence, 1988—2004; mem. La. state com. Employer Support of Guard and Res., 1988—92, dep. state ombudsman, 1992—94, state ombudsman, 1994—2001, state chmn., 2001—07; mem. Mil. Adv. Com. of Greater New Orleans, 1993—, vice chair internat. rels., 2002—. Recipient Most Valuable Employer Support for the Guard and Res. award, NASA Pub. Svc. medal, 1992, La. Cross Merit award State of La., 1994, 5 Outstanding Vol. Svc. medals Dept. Def., 1994, 96, 97, 99, 2001, Legion of Merit, 1998, 2001, USN Superior Pub. Svc. medal, 1999, USCG commendation, 2001, 04, Exceptional Svc. medal Dept. Defense, 2004. Mem. Am. Corp. Counsel Assn. (bd. dirs. New Orleans chpt. 1987—, v.p. 1989-90), Internat. Assn. Def. Counsel, New Orleans C. of C. (bd. dirs. 1999-, chair pub. policy com. 2005-07), Metro-Vision Econ. Devel. Orgn. (bd. dirs.), French-Am. C. of C. (bd. dirs.), Sr. Army Res. Comdrs. Assn. (exec. com. 1998-2005, steering com. 1998-2006, by-laws counsel 1997-2005). Republican. Episcopalian. Avocations: skiing, reading, running. Office: Lockheed Martin Michoud Space Sys PO Box 29304 New Orleans LA 70189-0304 Home Phone: 504-218-4880; Office Phone: 504-257-4112. Business E-Mail: thomas.g.fierke@Lmco.com.

FIERMAN, ELLA YENSEN, retired psychotherapist; b. Cleve., June 20, 1922; d. Cecil Hoy and Dorthea Carolina Yensen; m. Chandler Garner Screven (div.); m. Louis B. Fierman, Sept. 25, 1947; children: Daniel B., Lauren C. BS, Case Western Res. U., 1944; MA, State U. Iowa, 1947; postgrad., Yale U., 1969—71; PhD, Saybrook Inst., 1982. Clin. psychiat. intern. Cleve. State Receiving Hosp., 1947—48; kindergarten tchr. US Army Dependents Sch., Fukuoka, Japan, 1948—49; clin. psychologist Mental Hygiene Clinic, Hartford (Conn.) Hosp., 1950—51; office adminstr. pub. health rsch. Yale U., New Haven, 1952—53, rsch. asst. psychiatry dept., 1953—55; psychotherapist Psychotherapy Assocs., New Haven, 1968—2002, adminstr., 1969—72, exec. dir., 1972—2002; ret., 2002. Cons. in field; trainer encounter groups Jewish Cmty. Ctr., New Haven, 1970—72; chmn. bd. dirs. Human Resource Ctr. Conn., New Haven, 1973—75. Author: The Role of Cues in Stuttering, 1955; co-author: Bibliotherapy in Psychiatry, 1947, 2d edit., 1978, Human Anxiety, 1956, 2d edit. Leader Girl Scouts US, Woodbridge, Conn., 1964—67. Recipient citation, State of Conn., 2005; grantee, Western Res. U., 1940—44. Mem.: APA, New England Psychol. Assn., Conn. Psychol. Assn. Avocations: gardening, birds, alternative medicine.

FIERO-MAZA, LORRAINE DORIS, music educator; d. Joseph Martin and Doris Lorraine Rodrigues; m. David Alfonzo Maza, Feb. 14, 2006; 1 child, André Rodrigo Trosan. MS in Music Edn., Ctrl. Conn. State U., New Britain, 1996; postgrad., Hartt Sch. Music, West Hartford, Conn. Tchr. music Pub. Sch. Sys., Fairfield, Conn., 1986—. Mentor best tng. Fairfield Pub. Schs., 1997—. Mem. PETA, Southbury, Conn., 2006; agt. Keeping Kids Safe Network, 2004. Grantee, Conn. Assn. Adminstrs., 2000. Mem.: NEA. Liberal. Roman Catholic. Avocations: travel, writing, exercise, reading, music. Home Phone: 203-888-5712; Office Phone: 203-255-8316. Personal E-mail: boccabella@sbcglobal.net.

FIERRO, MARCELLA FARINELLI, forensic pathologist, educator; b. Buffalo, May 24, 1941; d. Marcello Francis and Lena Louise (Luppino) Farinelli; m. Robert J. Fierro, May 30, 1966. BA in Biology (cum laude), D'Youville Coll., NY, 1962; MD in Forensic Pathology, SUNY, Buffalo, 1966. Diplomate Am. Bd. Pathology. Intern, resident Ottawa Civic Hosp., Ontario, Canada; resident, pathology Cleve. Clinic Ednl. Found., Ohio, 1973—74, Va. Commonwealth Univ., 1973—74; chief resident, pathology with fellowship in forensic pathology, dept. legal medicine Med. Coll. Va./Va. Commonwealth Univ., Richmond, Va., 1973—74; deputy chief med. examiner, city med. examiner State of Va., Richmond, 1975-92; prof. pathology East Carolina Sch. Medicine, Greenville, NC, 1992—94; designated med. exam. and forensic pathologist Med. Exam Sys., NC, 1992-94; chief med. examiner State of Va., Richmond, 1994—. Recipient Lifetime Achievement award, Sch. Medicine and Biomedical Scis. Med. Alumni Assn., State Univ., Buffalo, 2001. Office: Office Chief Med Examiner 400 E Jackson St Richmond VA 23219

FIERRO, ROBERT, JR., librarian; s. Robert L. and Avelica Fierro; m. Jane Stephanie Garcia, Feb. 14, 1993; children: Hisser, Randal Maurice Harvell, Juanito, Socks, Anna Belle, John, Pepper. BBA, Angelo State U., San Angelo, Tex., 1990. Employment interviewer Tex. Employment Commn., Houston, 1995—96; client mgmt. specialist Harris County Pvt. Industry Coun., Houston, 1996—99; family preservation specialist II Tex. Dept. Protective and Regulatory Svcs., Houston, 1999—2002; libr. br. supr. Harris County Pub. Libr., Houston, 2002—. Dep. comdr. Civil Air Patrol, San Angelo, 1997; vol. M.D. Anderson Cancer Ctr., Houston, 2004; mem. policy coun., cmty. ptnr., fin. liason Early Childhood Ctr., Galena Park, Tex., 2004; instnl. head, chartered rep. Boy Scouts of Am., Galena Park; dist. scout exec. Concho Valley coun. Boy Scouts Am., San Angelo, 1999, Sam Houston Area coun. Boy Scouts Am., Houston, 1992—94; treas. East Side Mobile Resources Collaborative, Inc., Galena Park, 2004. Recipient Order of Condor, InterAm. Scout Found., 2004, Internat. Scouters award, 2005. Mem.: ALA (life), Tex. Libr. Assn., League Latin Am. Citizens, Internat. Fellowship Scouting Rotarians (life Cliff Doehterman award), Rotary Internat. Democrat. Roman Catholic. Avocations: swimming, travel, reading. Office: Harris County Pub Libr 1500 Keene St Galena Park TX 77547-2400 Home Phone: 281-540-7252; Office Phone: 713-450-0982. Office Fax: 713-451-1131. Business E-Mail: rfierro@hcpl.net.

FIESE, RICHARD KELLY, music educator; b. Beloit, Wis., May 12, 1957; s. Richard and H. Joan Fiese; m. Robin Elizabeth Fiese, July 19. BS, U. Wis., Madison; MusM, PhD, U. Miami, Coral Gables, Fla. Dir. bands, dept. chair Cypress Lake HS, Ft. Myers, Fla., 1980—84; dir. bands West Lab. Sch., Coral Gables, 1984—89; assoc. prof. U. Houston, 1989—95, U. Miami, Coral Gables, 1995—2000; prof. Houston Bapt. U., 2000—. Cons. music edn. Models Assessment Musical Performances Ctr. Arts Adminstrn., Tallahassee, 1996—98. Co-author (with N. DeCarbo): Error Detection for Conductors, 2001, 4th edit., 2006; co-author: (with J.D. Boyle and N. Zavac) A Handbook for Preparing Graduate Papers in Music, 2001, 2d edit., 2004; contbr. chapters to books, articles to profl. jours. Mem.: Tex. Music Educators Assn. (columnist Southwestern Musician), Music Educators Nat. Conf. Republican. Baptist. Office: Houston Bapt Univ 7502 Fondren Rd Houston TX 77074-3298 Office Phone: 281-649-3000 2255.

FIETSAM, ROBERT, JR., physician; b. Columbus, Ohio, Dec. 15, 1956; s. Robert and Mary E. (Maccombie) F.; m. Jill Courtney Brach, Nov. 6, 1993; children: Dominique, Desiree, Alexandra, Robert Mac, Elle, Paris. BSChem., U. Mich., 1978; MD, Wayne State U., 1986. Diplomate Am. Bd. Surgery, Am. Bd. Thoracic Surgery. Cardiac surgeon Southeastern Cardiovasc. Assn., Dothan, Ala., 1995-96; asst. prof. surgery Duke U., Durham, NC, 1996-98; dir. cardiac surgery Village Surg. Assocs., 1998—2003; pres. Sandhills Heart Surgery P.A., Fayetteville, NC, 2003—. Contbr. chpt. Cardiac Issues, 1992; contbr. aritcles to profl. jours. Recipient Charles C. Guthrie award Vascular Surg. Soc., 1990, Charles Johnston award Detroit Surg. Assn., 1991. Mem. AMA, ACS, Soc. Thoracic Surgeons, Cumberland County Med. Soc. Home Phone: 910-465-4142; Office Phone: 910-323-9922. E-mail: dellnewjet@aol.com.

FIETSAM, ROBERT CHARLES, accountant; b. Oct. 18, 1927; s. Celsus J. and Viola (Ehret) F.; m. Miriam Runkwitz, Apr. 12, 1952; children: Robert C., Guy P., Nancy A., Lisa R. BS, U. Ill., 1955. CPA, Mo., Ill. Claims adjuster Ely & Walker Dry Goods, St. Louis, 1947-48; acct. Price Waterhouse & Co., St. Louis, 1949-54; staff acct. J.W. Boyle & Co., East St. Louis, 1955-59; owner R.C. Fietsam, CPA's, Belleville, Ill., 1959-68, mng. ptnr., 1969—. Mem. Belle-Scott Com., 1979—; bd. dirs, pres. Belleville Ctr., Inc., 1980-81; mem. Ill. Pub. Accts. Registration Com., 1985-87. Bd. dirs. Meml. Hosp., 1982-85, Meml. Found., Inc., 1986-91, Bellville Hosp. Golf Classic, mem., 1983-91, chmn. 1986-91, Ill. Bd. Examiners, 1994-2002, vice chair, 1997-98, chair 1998-99, coun. v.p., pres. St. Paul United Ch. of Christ, 1969-73; mem. accountancy com. U. Ill., St. Louis. With USAF, 1951-53. Recipient honor for completing equivalent of 4 trips around the world on a bicycle, Schwinn Fitness, Nautilus Inspiration award, Active Aging Week award, Nautilus, 2004, Outstanding Cmty. Svc. Citizen cert. recognition, Turkey Hill Grange, 2003, Lifetime Svc. award, Greater Belleville C. of C., Inc., 2007. Mem. AICPAs (coun. 1981-84, 85-90), Ill. CPA Soc. (Lifetime Achievement award, pres. so. chpt. 1972-73, Mr. Southern Chpt. award 1976, Chgo. state bd. dirs. 1979-81, sr. v.p. 1987-88, pres. 1988-89, bd. dirs. 1989-90, ICPAC PAC 1979-92, chmn. PAC 1989-92, coun. 1981-84, 85-90, 92, Pub. Svc. award 1982-83), Nat. Assn. State Bds. Accountancy (del. 1994-2002), Ill. State Bd. Accountancy, Mo. Soc. CPA's, U. Ill. Greater Belleville Illini Club (past pres.), Belleville C. of C. (pres. 1973-74, Lifetime Svc. award, 2007), Belleville Jr. C. of C. (life, key Man award 1959-60, Outstanding Citizen award 1976), Greater Belleville C. of C. Inc. (Ambassadors 1973—), U. Ill. Alumni Assn. (life), Lambda Chi Alpha Alumnae Assn., St. Clair County Club (treas. 1969, 71), Optimists (life, Belleville Chpt. pres. 1979-80, Disting. Pres. award 1979-80, Optimist of Yr. Belleville, 1977, Ill. Dist. 1980), Elks. Home: 23 Persimmon Rdg Belleville IL 62223-3946 Office: 325 W Main St Belleville IL 62220-1571 Office Phone: 618-234-4530.

FIFE, EDWARD H., landscape architecture educator; b. Mass., Oct. 18, 1942; s. Edwin Kenneth and Yvonne Barbara F.; children: Sarah Rodman and Mike Malcolm. BS in Landscape Architecture, R.I. Sch. Design, Providence, 1965; M in Landscape Architecture, Harvard U., 1967. Registered landscape architect, Ont. Designer Sasaki, Strong Assoc., Toronto, Ont., Canada, 1964-66; asst. prof. landscape architecture Ohio State U., Columbus, 1967-69, U. of Toronto, 1969-73, assoc. prof., 1973—, asst. chmn., 1983-85, chmn. program in landscape architecture, 1985-89, 92-96; dir. Ctr. for Landscape Rsch. U. Toronto, 1987—89, 2001—03; prin. E. H. Fife Landscape Architecture, Toronto, 1979—. Mem. roster vis. educators Landscape Archtl. Accreditation Bd., 1986-96. Bd. dirs. Koffler Gallery, Toronto, 1986-95, Landscape Architecture Can. Found., 1987-88, 94—; mem. adv. com. Restoration of Monserrate Park, Portugal, 1988-90; mem. sci. and edn. com. Royal Bot. Garden, 1988-91, mem. property com., 1991-93; mem. acad. bd. governing coun. U. Toronto, 1988-89. Fellow Can. Soc. Landscape Architects; mem. Internat. Fedn. Landscape Architects, Can. Soc. Landscape Architects (roster vis. educators), Ont. Assn. Landscape Architects (pres. 1987-88, bd. dirs. 1983-89, 2000-02). Avocations: painting, organic farming, canoeing, hiking. Home: 269 Waverley Rd Toronto ON Canada M4L 3T5 Home Phone: 416-946-3077; Office Phone: 416-946-3077. Office Fax: 416-971-2094. Business E-Mail: fife-e@ald.utoronto.ca.

FIFE, JONATHAN DONALD, education educator; b. Washington, Nov. 9, 1941; s. G. Donald and Marie (Wall) F.; m. Janice McKenna, Aug. 10, 1968 (div.); children: Patrick McKenna, Timothy Kingston, Brendan Martin; m. Ann Ferren, 1996. BBA, U. Mass., 1965; MS, SUNY, Albany, 1970; postgrad, U. Cin., 1965-67; EdD, Pa. State U., 1975. Asst. dir. student activities State U. Coll., Buffalo, 1967-69; rsch. asst. Pa. State U. Ctr. for Study Higher Edn., State College, 1970-72; assoc. dir. ERIC Clearinghouse on Higher Edn., George Washington U., Washington, 1972-77, dir., 1977-98, prof. edn., 1977-98; vis. prof. Va. Poly. Inst. and State U., Blacksburg, 1998—2005; adj. prof. Am. U. Bulgaria, 2005—. Edn. pilot team evaluator Malcolm Baldridge Nat. Quality Award, 1994, sr. evaluator, 1995-96, bd. examiners, sr. examiner, 1996-97, alumni examiner, 1999-2000, examiner, VA Sen. Productivity & Quality Award, 2002-04. Mng. editor Rev. Higher Edn., 1980-86; cons. editor Change, 1981-2001. Bd. dirs. Nat. Ctr. for Higher Ednl. Mgmt. Systems, Boulder, 1980-82; cons. Rosenberg Commn., Md., 1975; pres., Wheaton Sq. East Condominium, Wheaton, Md., 1973-78; pres. High Meadows Owners' Master Assn., Radford, Va., 2000-05. Mem. Assn. Study Higher Edn. (exec. sec. treas. 1978-87), Am. Ednl. Rsch. Assn. (sec. treas. spl. interest group postsecondary edn. 1977-81), Higher Edn. Group Washington (sec. 1979-81, v.p., 1997-98, pres. 1998-99), Assn. Instl. Rsch., Phi Kappa Phi. Avocations: tennis, golf, boating. Home Phone: 540-633-6662.

FIFE, WILMER KRAFFT, retired chemistry professor; b. Wellsville, Ohio, Oct. 19, 1933; s. Wilmer George and Lourene Elizabeth (Krafft) F.; m. Betsy Louise Jones, Dec. 26, 1959; children: Kimberly, Julia, Steven. B.Sc. in Chemistry, Case Inst. Tech., 1955; PhD in Organic Chemistry, Ohio State U., 1960. Applications chemist Monsanto Chem. Co., Dayton, Ohio, summers 1955, 57; instr. Muskingum (Ohio) Coll., 1959-60, asst. prof., 1960-64, asso. prof., 1964-70, prof., 1970-71, chmn. dept. chemistry, 1966-71; prof. chemistry Ind. U.-Purdue U. at Indpls., 1971—, chmn. dept., 1971-80; ret. NIH postdoctoral fellow Harvard U., 1965-66; NIH postdoctoral fellow Columbia U., 1968-69; NSF fellow, 1955-56; Sinclair Oil Co. fellow, 1958-59; DuPont fellow, 1960; Danforth assoc., 1969—; others; vis. scholar in chemistry Louis Pasteur U., Strasbourg, France, 1994, U. San Francisco, 1999; named Outstanding Rschr. in Sci. Ind. U.-Purdue U., Indpls. Mem. Am. Chem. Soc., AAAS, Sigma Xi, Tau Beta Pi, Phi Lambda Upsilon. Home: 7102 Dean Rd Indianapolis IN 46240-3626 Office: IUPUI Chemistry 402 N Blackford St Indianapolis IN 46202-3217 E-mail: fife@chem.iupui.edu.

FIFER, SALLY JO, broadcast executive, editor; b. Albuquerque, May 22, 1958; d. Reginald Dekoven and Shirley Rae (Canaday) F. BA in Art History, U. Calif., 1981. Dir. mktg., sales Serious Bus. Co., Oakland, Calif., 1981-84; program devel. dir., editor video news San Francisco, 1984—92; exec. dir. Bay Area Video Coalition, San Francisco, 1992—2001; pres. & CEO Ind. TV Svc. (ITVS), San Francisco, 2001—. Bd. dirs. Video Refuses, San Francisco, Marin County Regional Occupational Program. Editor: Art Video, Video Networks, Videomaker; exec. prodr.: (documentaries) The Education of Shelby Knox, 2005, A Lion in the House, 2006, The World According to Sesame Street, 2006; (TV series) Independent Lens, 2002—. Recipient Best Documentary award for Independent Lens: Be Good, Smile Pretty, News & Documentary Emmy Awards, 2004, Alfred I. duPont-Columbia award for Independent Lens: Seoul Train, 2007. Office: ITVS Ste 410 651 Brannan St San Francisco CA 94107 Office Phone: 415-356-8383 ext. 233. Office Fax: 415-356-8391. E-mail: sally_fifer@itvs.org.*

FIFFIE PROCTOR, JOANN, media and technology specialist; b. New Orleans; d. Joseph Paul Sr. and Elouise Marie Fiffie. BA in Comm., U. Southwestern, Lafayette, La., 1980; EdM, Minot State U., 1992; M of Libr. and Info. Sci., U. So. Miss., 1997. Tchr. St. James Sch. Bd., Lutcher, La., 1992-93, tchr. computers, 1994-96; spl. edn. tchr. Calif. Sch. Dist., Sacramento, 1993-94; instr. Southwestern U., Lafayette, La., 1997-98; media/tech. specialist St. John Sch. Bd., Reserve, La., 1998—; rschr. Lyndon Baines Johnson Presdl. Libr., 1996—2000. Dir. sta. WJLO-TV Magnet Sch., LaPlace, La., 2000. Founder mag. Tender Times, 2000. Active Parent-Tchr., St. James, La., 1994-96; pres./CEO House Hands & Hugs, Vacherie, La.; mem. adv. bd. Big Brothers & Sisters, Lafayette. Houma-Terabone grantee, 1998; Metrovision Sch.-To-Career grantee, 2002. Mem. ALA, AAUW, NEA, Libr. Info. Tech. Assn., Nat. Assn. Female Execs., Mothers of 21st Century Leaders. Office: John L Ory Magnet Sch 182 W 5th St La Place LA 70068-4501

FIFLIS, TED JAMES, lawyer, educator; b. Chgo., Feb. 20, 1933; s. James P. and Christine (Karakitsos) F.; m. Vasilike Pantelakos, July 3, 1955; children: Christina Eason, Antonia Fowler, Andreanna Lawson. BS, Northwestern U., 1954; LLB, Harvard U., 1957. Bar: Ill. 1957, Colo. 1975, U.S. Supreme Ct. 1984. Pvt. practice law, Chgo., 1957-65; mem. faculty U. Colo. Law Sch., Boulder, 1965—, prof., 1968—. Vis. prof. NYU, 1968, U. Calif., Davis, 1973, U. Chgo., 1976, U. Va., 1979, Duke U., 1980, Georgetown U., 1982, U. Pa., 1983, Am. U., 1983, Harvard U., 1988; Lehmann disting. vis. prof. Washington U., St. Louis, 1991; cons. Rice U.; arbitrator AT&T divesture disputes, 1984-87. Author: (with Homer Kripke, Paul Foster) Accounting for Business Lawyers, 1970, 3rd edit., 1984, Accounting Issues for Lawyers, 1991; editor-in-chief Corp. Law Rev., 1977-88; contbr. articles to profl. jours. Mem. ABA, Am. Assn. Law Schs. (past chmn. bus. law sect.), Colo. Bar Assn. (mem. coun. sect. of corp., banking and bus. law 1974-75), Am. Law Inst. (life, chmn. com. on rsch. proposed fed. securities code), Colo. Assn. Corp. Counsel (pres. 1998-99). Greek Orthodox. Home: 1602 Columbine Ave Boulder CO 80302-7832 Office: Univ Of Colo Law Sch Boulder CO 80309-0401 Home Phone: 303-443-4753; Office Phone: 303-492-6049. E-mail: ted.fiflis@colorado.edu.

FIFTY CENT, (CURTIS JAMES JACKSON), rap artist; b. Queens, NY, July 6, 1976; Performer: (songs) How to Rob, 1999, Wanksta, 2002, In Da Club, 2003 (Top R&B/Hip-Hop Song, ASCAP, 2004, Top Rap Song, ASCAP, 2004, Pop Songwriter of Yr., ASCAP, 2004), (albums) Power of the Dollar, 2000, Guess Who's Back, 2001, 50 Cent is the Future, 2001, Get Rich or Die Tryin', 2003, Massacre, 2005 (Am. Music Awards Favorite Rap Album, 2005, Billboard Album of Yr., 2005, Billboard 200 Album of Yr., 2005), God's Plan, 2006, No Mercy No Fear, 2006, Before I Self Destruct, 2007, Curtis, 2007; performer: (with G-Unit) Beg for Mercy, 2003; author (with Kris Ex): (autobiography) From Pieces to Weight, 2005; actor: (films) Get Rich or Die Tryin', 2005. Recipient Artist of Yr., Hip-Hop Artist of Yr., Rap Artist of Yr., Hot 100 Artist of Yr., Billboard Music Awards, 2005, Best-Selling Pop Male Artist, World Music Awards, 2005. Office: c/o Cara Lewis William Morris Agy 1325 Ave of the Americas New York NY 10019 also: c/o Jim Wiatt William Morris Agy 1 William Morris Pl Beverly Hills CA 90212*

FIGA, PHILLIP S., judge; b. Chgo., July 27, 1951; BA, Northwestern U., 1973; JD, Cornell U., 1976. Assoc. Sherman & Howard, Denver, 1976-80; ptnr. Burns & Figa, P.C., Denver, 1980-90, pres., 1988-90; pres., shareholder Burns, Figa & Will, PC, Englewood, Colo., 1991—2003; judge US Dist. Ct. for Dist. of Colo., 2003—. Articles editor: Cornell Internat. Law Rev., 1975—76.

FIGARI, ERNEST EMIL, JR., lawyer, educator; b. Navasota, Tex., Feb. 18, 1939; s. Ernest Emil and Louise (Campbell) F.; children: Alexandra Caroline, Audrey Elizabeth. BS, Tex. A&M U., 1961; LLB, U. Tex., 1964; LLM, So. Meth. U., Dallas, 1970. Bar: Tex. 1964, US Ct. Appeals (5th cir.) 1965, US Dist. Ct. (no. dist.) Tex. 1964, US Supreme Ct. 1967. Law clk. to judge U.S. Dist. Ct. (no. dist.) Tex., Dallas, 1964-65; assoc. Coke & Coke, Dallas, 1965-70, ptnr., 1970-75, Johnson & Swanson, Dallas, 1975-86, Figari & Davenport, Dallas, 1986—. Adj. prof. law So. Meth. U., Dallas, 1974-79, 81-82, U. Tex., 1980. Contbr. articles to profl. jours. Fellow ABA Found., Tex. Bar Found., Dallas Bar Found.; mem. State Bar Tex. Roman Catholic. Office: Figari & Davenport Bank of Am Plz 901 Main St Ste 3400 Dallas TX 75202-3796 Office Phone: 214-939-2000.

FIGI, MATTHEW L., secondary school educator; b. Monroe, Wis., Oct. 13, 1948; s. Dewayne L. and Ida Marie Larson Figi. BS in Edn., U. Wis., Whitewater, 1974; MS in Edn., Purdue U., Hammond, Ind., 1979. Educator Highland HS, Ind., 1974—2004; ret., 2004. Instr. adult edn. Highland HS, 1980—2004; instr. NW Ind. Computer Consortium, Highland, 1980—84. Author: A Tribute to Norwegian Parents Ambjorn & Oline Urness, 1985, I Shook the Family Tree, 1994, Enterprise School 1859-1964 Clarno, Green County, WI, 1997, Pictorial History of Highland, Indiana, 1999, Pictorial History of Highland, Indiana Part II, 2001, Pictorial History of Monroe, Wisconsin, 2006. With US Army, 1969—71, Vietnam. Mem.: Highland Hist. Soc. (bd. dirs. 1998—2004), Wis. State Geneal. Soc. (life), Green County Hist. Soc. (life; bd. dirs. 2004—07), NW Ind. Geneal. Soc. (life; pres. 1990—95). Avocations: genealogy, history. Home: 216 10th Ave Monroe WI 53566-1110 Home Phone: 608-325-6503.

FIGLEY, MELVIN MORGAN, radiologist, physician, educator; b. Toledo, Dec. 5, 1920; s. Karl Dean and Margaret (Morgan) F.; m. Margaret Jane Harris, Mar. 16, 1946; children: Karl Porter, Joseph Dean, Mark Thompson. Student, Dartmouth, 1938-41; MD magna cum laude (John Harvard fellow), Harvard, 1944. Diplomate: Am. Bd. Radiology (trustee 1967-72). Intern, then resident internal medicine Western Res. U., 1944-46; resident radiology U. Mich., 1948-51, instr., asst. prof., asso. prof. radiology, 1950-58; practice specializing in radiology Seattle, 1958-86; prof. radiology, chmn. dept. U. Wash., 1958-78, prof. radiology and medicine, 1979-85, emeritus prof. radiology and medicine, 1986—. Mem. radiation study sect. NIH, 1963-67; mem. com. on radiology Nat. Acad. Scis.-NRC, 1964-69, chmn., 1968-69. Editor: Am. Jour. Roentgenology, 1976-85; contbr. articles profl. jours. Bd. dirs. James Picker Found., 1970-80. Served to capt. M.C. AUS, 1946-48. John and Mary R. Markle scholar, 1952-57; named to Med. Hall of Honor, U. Mich., 2006. Fellow Am. Coll. Radiology (Gold medal 1987), Royal Coll. Radiologists (hon., London), Royal Australian Coll. Radiologists (hon.); mem. Royal Soc. Medicine (hon.), Assn. Univ. Radiologists (pres. 1966, Gold medal 1983), Am. Roentgen Ray Soc. (exec. council 1970-88, pres. 1983-84, Gold medal 1986), N. Am. Soc. Cardiac Radiology (pres. 1974), Fleischer Soc. (pres. 1986-87), Radiol. Soc. N.Am. (Gold Medal 1986), AMA, Boylston Med. Soc., Wash. Heart Assn. (past trustee), Soc. Chmn. Acad. Radiology Depts. (exec. council 1969-71), Phi Beta Kappa, Sigma Xi, Alpha Omega Alpha, Sigma Alpha Epsilon. Home: PO Box 859 Grantham NH 03753-0859 Personal E-mail: foxrun7010@adelphia.net.

FIGLIN, ROBERT ALAN, hematologist, oncologist; b. Phila., June 22, 1949; s. Jack and Helen Figlin; 1 child, Jonathan B. BA in Chemistry, Temple U., Phila., 1970; postgrad. in inorganic chemistry, Temple U., 1972; MD, Med. Coll. Pa., 1976. Diplomate Am. Bd. Internal Medicine, Am. Bd. Med. Oncology, Nat. Bd. Med. Examiners; lic. physician, Calif. Med. intern, resident in medicine Cedars-Sinai Med. Ctr., LA, 1976-79, chief resident in medicine, 1979-80; fellow in hematology-oncology UCLA, 1980-82, dir., hematology-oncology fellowship program, divsn. hematology-oncology, dept. medicine, 1992—2003, co-dir., oncology program area divsn. hematology-oncology, dept. medicine, 1993—95; asst. prof. medicine, divsn. hematology-oncology, dept. medicine UCLA Sch. Medicine, 1982-88, assoc. prof., divsn. hematology-oncology, dept. medicine, 1988-94, med. dir., thoracic oncology program, dept. medicine and surgery, divsns. hematology-oncology and thoracic surgery, 1994—, med. dir., genitourinary oncology, dept. medicine and surgery, divsns. hematology-oncology and urology, 1995—, Henry Alvin and Carrie L. Meinhardt chair in urol. oncology, 2000—; prof. medicine, divsn. hematology-oncology, dept. medicine UCLA David Geffen Sch. Medicine, 1994—, prof. clin. urology, divsn. urologic oncology, dept. urology, 2000—; asst. dir., Bowyer Multidisciplinary Oncology Clinic Jonsson Comprehensive Cancer Ctr., UCLA, 1985—90, dir. Bowyer Oncology Ctr., dir. outpatient clin. rsch. unit, 1990-92, dir. clin. rsch. unit, 1993-98, dir. hematology/oncology fellowship program, 1995—2003, assoc. program dir., solid tumor oncology, 1996—97, program dir., solid tumor oncology, 1997—98, program dir., solid tumor develop. therapeutics, 1998—2001, co-dir., genitourinary oncology, 2004—, co-dir., lung cancer rsch. program, 2005; assoc. dir. clin. rsch., Comprehensive Cancer Ctr. City of Hope, Duarte, Calif., 2006—, chair, divsn. med. oncology & exptl. therapeutics rsch., 2006—, Arthur and Rosalie Kaplan prof. med. oncology, 2006—. Co-principal investigator, mem. exec. bd. Lung Cancer Study Group, UCLA, 1982—89; co-principal investigator, mem. genitourinary com., mem. kidney cancer subcommittee Eastern Cooperative Oncology Group, 1988—93; mem. exec. bd. UCLA Med./Surgical Oncology Ctr., 1989—95; FDA cons., 1990—92; prin. investigator UCLA S.W. Oncology Group, 1990—2000, mem. lung com., 1990—2003, bd. gov., 1990—2000, mem. genito-urinary com., 1990—2003; mem. med. adv. bd. Nat. Kidney Cancer Assn., 1993—; med. dir. U. Calif. Preferred Oncology Networks of Calif., 1994—95; sci. founder Agensys, 1996—; chmn. instl. rev. bd., mem. human rsch. policy bd. UCLA, 1998—; co-prin. investigator, clin. dir. NCI Specialized Program of Rsch. Excellence, Lung Cancer, 2000—, NCI Bladder Cancer Prevention, 2003—; co-dir. Lung Cancer Rsch. Program, 2003—; chmn. scientific adv. bd. Phase One Found., 2005. Editor: Interferons in cytokines, 1988—90, Kidney Cancer Jour., 1993—94, Current Clin. Trials, 1992—96; UCLA Cancer Trials Newsletter, 1990—96, Seminars on Oncology-Kidney Cancer, 1995, Cancer Therapeutics, 1997, Cancer Biotherapy and Radio Pharms., 1997; contbr. articles and revs.; editor: Renal & Adrenal Tumors, 2002, Kidney Cancer Jour., 2003—. Named one of Best Doctors in Am., 1994-, America's Top Doctors for Cancer 2006. Fellow ACP, Internat. Soc. for Biologic Therapy; mem. Am. Soc. Clin. Oncology, Am. Fedn. Clin. Rsch., Am. Assn. for Cancer Rsch., Soc. for Biologic Therapy (chmn. ann. scientific meeting 1997, pres. cancer panel 1997, S.W. Oncology Group, Assn. Subspecialty Profs., Am. Urological Assn., Internat. Assn. for Study of Lung Cancer. Office: UCLA Ste 2333 10945 Le Conte Ave Los Angeles CA 90024-2828 also: City of Hope 1500 E Duarte Rd Duarte CA 91010 Office Phone: 310-825-5788. E-mail: rfiglin@mednet.ucla.edu.*

FIGUEROA, FRANCISCO ARMANDO, aerospace transportation executive, accountant; b. Del Rio, Tex., Feb. 4, 1945; s. Armando Garz and Flavia (Aldrete) F.; m. Sharon Marie Sanislo, Dec. 14, 1968; children: Derek Armando, Adam Joseph. BSEE, Tex. Tech. U., 1967; MS in Astronautics, Air Force Inst. Tech., 1969; MS in Systems Mgmt., UCLA, 1973; postgrad., Indsl. Coll., Fort McNair, DC, 1983-84. CPA; CFP. Commd. officer USAF, 1967, advanced to lt. col., various positions, 1969-79; staff officer Pentagon, Arlington, Va., 1979-83; mgmt. dir. HQ SD, Denver, 1984-86, ops. dir., 1986-87; ret. USAF, 1987; former bus. mgr. Martin Marietta, Denver, 1987; owner F.A. Figueroa, CPA, Aurora, Colo., 1984—; now v.p., bus. mgmt. & facilities svc, CFO Sandia Nat. Labs., Albuquerque. V.p. Lompoc (Calif.) Chpt. Jaycees, 1970-72; mem. Community Svcs. Commn., Denver, 1992—. Named one of 50 Most Important Hispanics in Govt., Edn., Hispanic Engineer and Info. Tech. mag., 2005. Mem. AICPA, AIAA, Colo. Soc. CPAs, Air Force Assn., Tau Beta Pi, Eta Kappa Nu. Avocations: reading, writing, poetry, mountain climbing, running. Home: PO Box 11337 Albuquerque NM 87192-0337 Office: Sandia Nat Labs PO Box 5800 Albuquerque NM 87185

FIGUEROA, JOSÉ MANUEL See SEBASTIAN, JOAN

FIGUEROA, ORLANDO, federal agency executive; b. San Juan, Sept. 9, 1955; m. Josephine Cerra; children: Daniel, Alexis. BSME, U. P.R., 1978; postgrad., U. Md. Mgr. superfluid helium On Orbit Transfer shuttle experiment Goddard Space Flight Ctr., 1986—89, head cryogenics tech. sect., 1987—89, mgr. Small Explorers project, 1990—94, mgr. explorers program, 1994—97, dir. sys., tech. and advanced concepts directorate, 1997—2000; dep. chief engr. sys. engring. NASA, Washington, 2000—01, dir. Mars exploration program Office Space Sci., 2001—. Named one of 50 Most Important Hispanics in Govt., Edn., Hispanic Engineer and Info. Tech. mag., 2005. Office: NASA Hdqrs Mail Code S 300 E St SW Washington DC 20546

FIJOLEK, RICHARD M., lawyer; b. Oak Park, May 31, 1958; AB with honors, Stanford U., 1979; JD, Columbia U., 1982. Bar: Ill. 1982, Tex. 1986. Assoc. Katten, Muchin and Zavis, Chgo., 1982-86, Haynes and Boone LLP, Dallas, 1986-89, ptnr., Bus., 1990—. Author: Complying with FIRPTA, 1989. Named one of best lawyers in Dallas, D Magazine, 2003, Tex. Super Lawyers, Tex. Monthly, World's Leading Tax Adv., Euromoney Guide, Leading US Tax Lawyers. Fellow: Am. Coll. Tax Counsel; mem.: Tex. Bar Assn., Internat. Fiscal Assn., ABA (chmn. Internat. Real Estate Com.). Office: Haynes and Boone LLP 901 Main St Ste 3100 Dallas TX 75202-3789 Office Phone: 214-651-5570. Office Fax: 214-200-0442. Business E-Mail: rick.fijolek@haynesboone.com.

FIKE, EDWARD LAKE, newspaper editor; b. Delmar, Md., Mar. 31, 1920; s. Claudius Edwin and Rosa Lake (Pegram) F.; m. Rosa Amanda Drake, Apr. 1, 1952; children: Rosa, Evelyn, Amy, Melinda. *Remarkably, Edward and his three siblings are all represented in Who's Who in America. Brother Dr. Claude E. Fike (deceased) was a Professor of History and Dean of Arts and Sciences at Mississippi Southern University, Hattiesburg, Miss. Sister Evelyn's late husband Dr. William Laupus was the founding first Dean of the Medical School at Eastern Carolina University, Greenville, NC Sister Ruth's husband Robert Pittman was editor, Editorial Page at the St. Petersburg, Fla. Times.* BA, Duke U., Durham, NC, 1941; postgrad., U. Cin., 1941-42. Editor, co-pub. Nelsonville Tribune, Ohio, 1945-48; dir. bur. pub. info. Duke U., Durham, NC, 1948-52; mem. US del. North Atlantic Coun., Paris, 1952-53; assoc. editor Rocky Mount Evening Telegram, NC, 1953-57; editor, pub. Fike Newspapers, Lewistown and Glendive, Mont., 1957-62, also Wilmington and Tujunja, Calif., 1957-68; assoc. editor Richmond News Leader, Va., 1968-70; dir. news and editl. analysis Copley Newspapers, 1970-77; editor editorial pages San Diego Union, 1977-90. Lectr. journalism San Diego State U., San Diego Evening Coll. Parole commr. San Diego County, 1993-94, pres. adv. coun. San Diego State U., 1988-93; bd. dir. Hubbs Seaworld Rsch. Inst. and Midway Aircraft/Carrier Mus. Grossmont Hosp. Found., Armed Svc. YMCA. Lt. USNR, 1942-45. Recipient George Washington award Freedoms Found., 1969-71, 73, 78, Editl. Writing award NC Press Assn., 1954-55, Va. Press Assn., 1969, Calif. Newspaper Pubs. Assn., 1969, 80; Hoover Inst. Media fellow Stanford U., 1990-91. Mem.: Omicron Delta Kappa. Republican. Methodist. Home: 17369 Plaza Maria San Diego CA 92128-2251 Personal E-mail: edfike@earthlink.net.

FIKES, JAY COURTNEY, anthropology educator, art dealer; b. San Luis Obispo, Calif., June 14, 1951; s. J.C. and Virginia Lee (Roberts) F.; m. Lebriz N. Tosuner, Apr. 17, 1979; 1 child, Leyla Tupina. BA in Comparative Culture, U. Calif., Irvine, 1973; MEd in Bilingual Edn., U. San Diego, 1974; MA in Anthropology, U. Mich., Ann Arbor, 1977, PhD in Anthropology, 1985. Tutor Palomar Coll., Pala Indian Reservation, Calif., 1974; instr. anthropology Allan Hancock Coll., Santa Maria, 1975—76; land use planner Navajo Nation, Window rock, Ariz., 1983; instr. anthropology US Internat. U., Oceanside, Calif., 1985; instr. rsch. methods soc. sci. Marmara U., Istanbul, 1985—87; prof. anthropology Yeditepe U., 1998—. Owner Cuatro Esquinas Traders, Carlsbad, Calif., 1979—; adj. prof. anthropology Highlands U., Las Vegas, N.Mex., 1989; lobbyist Friends Com. on Nat. Legislation, 1990—91; pres. Inst. Inter-cultural Issues, 1993—98. Author: Huichol Indian Identity and Adaptation, 1985, Step Inside the Sacred Circle, 1989, Carlos Castaneda, Academic Opportunism and the Psychedelic Sixties, 1993, Reuben Snake, Your Humble Serpent, 1996, Huichol Indian Ceremonial Cycle, 1997, Huichol Mythology, 2004, The Man Who Ate Honey, 2003; contbr. articles to profl. jours. Coord. Fiestas Patrias, Carlsbad Bicentennial Com., 1975. Anthropology Tchg. fellow U. Mich., Ann Arbor, 1976-79, Postdoctoral fellow Smithsonian Instn., Washington, 1991-92, 95; acad. scholar dept. anthropology, U. Mich., 1981-82; doctoral dissertation grantee Rackham Grad. Sch. U. Mich., 1981. Mem. Internat. Platform Assn., Rotary (dir. internat. svc. 1982-83). Mem. Religious Soc. Friends. Office: PO Box 517 Carlsbad CA 92018 Personal E-mail: jayfikes2004@yahoo.com. Business E-Mail: cfikes@yeditepe.edu.tr.

FIKRIG, EROL, rheumatologist, medical educator; b. Dec. 15, 1959; BA in Chemistry cum laude, Cornell U., 1981, MD, 1985. Diplomate Am. Bd. Internal Medicine, Am. Bd. Infectious Diseases. Resident in internal medicine Vanderbilt U. Hosp., 1985—88; fellow in infectious diseases and immunobiology Yale U., 1988—92, assoc. rsch. scientist in immunobiology, 1992, asst. prof. medicine sect. of rheumatology, 1992—96, assoc. prof. medicine sect. of rheumatology, 1996—. Contbr. articles to profl. jours.; ad hoc reviewer NIH study sect.: Bacteriology and Mycology I, 1994; spkr. in field. Recipient Young Investigator award, Nat. Found. Infectious Disease, 1991, award in vaccine devel., Infectious Disease Soc. Am., 1992, Young Investigator award, Am. Heart Assn., 1993, Investigator award, Arthritis Found., 1993, Apollo Kinsley award, State of Conn., 1993, NIH First award, 1994, Goodyear award, State of Conn., 1994, Established Investigator award, Am. Heart Assn., 1996; fellow NIH Clin. Investigation, 1990, Daland, Am. Philos. Soc., 1990; scholar Pew, 1993. Mem.: Phi Beta Kappa. Office: Yale U Sch Medicine Dept Rheumatology 333 Cedar St New Haven CT 06510-3289

FILA, JOHN CHARLES, psychoanalyst; b. Boston; s. John F. and Marion L. Fila. AB, Harvard U., Cambridge, Mass., 1992; PhD, U. Berkeley, Mich., 1995. Diplomate Am. Coll. Profl. Mental Health Practitioners. Pvt. practice, Wellesley, Mass., 1997—2000, Santa Monica, Calif., 2000—. Nat. bd. dirs. Internat. Acad. Philosophy, N. Hollywood, Calif. Contbr. articles to profl. jours. Vol. mentor for disadvantaged, 1995—; ombudsman, officer The Prometheus Soc. Internat., The Lewis Terman Soc.; mem. Nat. Com. on Am. Fgn. Policy, NYC, Nat. Campaign for Tolerance, Montgomery, Ala. Mem.: AAAS, Internat. Neuro-Psychoanalysis Soc., Royal Overseas Soc., NY Acad. Scis., Menninger Soc., Harvard Club (Boston, So. Calif., Palm Beach). Republican. Episcopalian. Achievements include research in post traumatic stress disorder and its comorbid relationship to a syndrome of mental health issues. Avocations: eclectic reading, sports, travel, theater, films. Home: Apt 40 2928 4th St Santa Monica CA 90405 Office: Ste 1215 5155 Rosecrans Ave Hawthorne CA 90250 Office Phone: 310-491-3680. Personal E-mail: psychdr721@hotmail.com.

FILBY, IVAN LEONARD, management educator; b. King's Lynn, Eng., Apr. 20, 1962; s. Leonard William and Mary Elizabeth (Day) Filby; m. Kathie Susanne Taggart, July 26, 1991; children: Samuel, Katie. BS in Mgmt. and Adminstrv. Scis., Aston U., Birmingham, Eng., 1984, PhD, 1990; MA, Dublin U., Ireland, 1993, Sheffield U., 2002. Lectr. bus. studies Trinity Coll., Dublin, 1989-99, dir. internat. student affairs, 1999—2004, chair Irish Coun. Internat. Students, 2000—03; prof. mgmt., chair mgmt. dept., assoc. faculty moderator Greenville Coll., Ill., 2005—. Vis. prof. U. Anahuac, Mexico City, 1999—, U. del Mayab, Merida, Mexico, 2002—04; expert European Commn., Brussels, 1994—2004. Contbr. articles to profl. jours.; mem. internat. editl. bd. Internat. Jour. Strategic Change Mgmt., Anahuac Jour. Founder, pres. Greenville Found. Program, 2005; dir. Cornerstone Christian Ch., Dublin, 1993—2004. Office: Greenville Coll Greenville IL 62246 Home Phone: 618-664-2414; Office Phone: 618-664-6827. Business E-Mail: ivan.filby@greenville.edu.

FILCHOCK, ETHEL, education educator; BS in Edn., Kent State U. Tchr. Cleve. Pub. Schs.; with EFC Creations, Solon, Ohio. Author: Voices in Poetics: Vol. 1, 1985 (Merit award), Hall of Fame, Ethel Filchock, Vol. 1, 1991, (poetry) Softer Memories Across a Lifetime, 1989, A Glimpse of Love, 1991; composer: Praise God, The Lord is Coming; lyricist (numerous songs including most recently) (Harmonious Honor award, Award for Excellence, 2000), (songs) Beautiful Lady of Medugorje, 1993, This Holy Morning, 1998, Theatre of the Mind, 2003, Only The Faces Change, 2003, Amerecord, 2003, My Beautiful America, 2003, this Holy Child, 2003, What About Tomorrow, 2003, Rolling On For Freedom, 2003, Something About You, 2003, Santa's Ho-Ho-Ho, 2003, Hilltop, 2003, Holiday Blues Circle of Life, 2003 (named into Nat. Lib. Poetry, 03). Chmn. sch. United Way, 1985-86. Recipient Cert. of Achievement N.Y. Profl./Amateur Song Jubilee, 1986, Editor's Choice award Disting. Poets of Am., Outstanding Achievement in Poetry, Nat. Libr. Poetry, 1993, Outstanding Poets of 1994, Interregnum Nat. Libr. Poetry, Best Poets of 1995, Transformation, Nat. Libr. of Poetry, Editor's Choice award Outstanding Achievement in Poetry, 1996, 2000-02, Nat. Libr. Poetry, 1995-96, 2001, Outstanding Poets of 1998 for Magnanimous Beauty, Nat. Libr. Poetry, 1998, Editor's Choice award, 1998. Mem. NAFE, Am. Fedn. Tchrs. Clubs: Akron Manuscript. Roman Catholic. Avocations: painting, travel, dance, fishing.

FILDES, RICHARD JAMES, lawyer; b. NYC, Nov. 9, 1952; s. Edgar E. and Lucille (Sanna) F.; m. Deborah D. Davenport, June 21, 1979; children: Matthew, Melissa, Heather. BS in Psychology and Econs. magna cum laude, Duke U., 1974; JD cum laude, U. Fla., 1977. Bar: Fla. 1977. Ptnr. Lowndes, Drosdick, Doster, Kantor & Reed, Orlando, Fla., 1977—. Past pres., gen. counsel Fla. Citrus Sports; trustee, dir. at large Fla. Citrus Sports Found., Inc. Dir. Orlando/Orange County Convention and VisitorsBur., Inc. Mem. Lake Nona Club. Democrat. Roman Catholic. Avocations: golf, working out, fishing, reading, running. Office: Lowndes Drosdick Doster et al 215 N Eola Dr Orlando FL 32801-2095 Office Phone: 407-843-4600.

FILER, EMILY SYMINGTON HARKINS, retired foundation administrator, writer, non-profit consultant, associate chaplain; b. Balt., May 12, 1936; d. Frank Fife and Grace (Cover) Symington; m. George Archer Harkins, June 21, 1958 (div. 1982); children: Montgomery Fox, Emily Harrison (dec. Apr. 1978); m. Robert Hoagland Filer, June 24, 1989. Degree, Villa Julie Med. Sec. Sch., Balt., 1955; CPE, Sentara Norfolk Gen. Hosp., Va., 2002—03. Cert. vol. adminstr., 1985; CPE Levell, CPE cert., Sentara Norfolk Gen. Hosp., 2003. Registrar Johns Hopkins Hosp., Balt., 1955-57, sec. hearing and speech ctr., 1957-58; pres. Distaff Wives, San Francisco, Boston, 1958-63; v.p., bd. dirs. The Planning Council, Tidewater, Va., 1969-78; pres. Jr. League of Norfolk (Va.)-Virginia Beach, 1972-74; founder, coord. Lee's Friends, Norfolk, 1978-86, exec. dir., 1986-2001; ret., 2001; dir. devel. YWCA S Hampton Rds., 2004—06; assoc. chaplain Sentara Norfolk Gen. Hosp., 2006—. Chmn. Tidewater dist. Va. Council Soc. Welfare, 1985-87, Va. Council Social Welfare, 1988; bd. dirs. Va. Wesleyan Coll., Norfolk, 1979-2001, Olde Huntersville Devel., Norfolk, 1985-87; mem. Glennan Geriat. Clerkship Faculty Ea. Va. Med. Sch., 1996-2001; nat. cons., trainer, vis. instr. Norfolk State U., Old Dominion U., Regent U., Tidewater C.C., Va. Wesleyan Coll. Lic. pastoral caregiver, lay reader The Ch. of Good Shepherd, 1992—, instr. adult Sunday sch., 1998, group leader Alpha program, 1999-2000, co-leader lay pastoral care, 2000-2004, lay eucharistic min., lay eucharist visitor; chair, Pastoral Care Coun., 2003-2004; bd. dirs., sec., exec. com. Westminster Canterbury of Virginia Beach, 1993-2001; mem. Mayor's Commn. on Aging, Virginia Beach, 1996-2000, vice chair, 1997-2000, chair, 1999-2001, mem. mayor's Census 2000 com.; bd. trustees Va. Wesleyan Coll., 1979-2001; mem., past pres. Tidewater dist. Va. Coun. on Social Welfare; steering com. Hampton Rds. Leadership Prayer Luncheon, 1999-2007, co-chair prayer luncheon, 2001—; del. Episcopal Diocese of So. Va., 1999-2000, co-chair Diocese Gala, 2001; mem. profl. adv. group Clin. Pastoral Edn., 2001—, co-chair, 2001-2003, self study group 2004-2005; vol. assoc. chaplain Westminster Canterbury, 2003; sec., Tidewater Pastoral Counseling Svc. Bd., 2006-. Named Gt. Citizen of Hampton Roads, 1987, Va. Vol. Adminstr. of Yr., Internat. Assn. for Vol. Adminstrn. Va. affiliates, 1992; recipient Women in Transition award YWCA of South Hampton Roads, 1989, Spl. award Outstanding Profl. Women of Hampton Roads, 1989, Disting. Merit citation NCCJ, 1992, Outstanding Cmty. Svc. award Delta Sigma Theta Norfolk Alumae chpt., 1997, Pub. Citizen of Yr. award NASW, Va. chpt., 1999, Jefferson award, WAVY 10, Cmty. Svc., 2003, First Woman in Bus. Achievement award, Inside Bus., 2004, Vol. Hampton Rds. Cmty. Achievement award, Lee's Friends Found., 2004, Leading Edge Adopter award YWCA So. Hampton Roads and Emily Filer, 2005. Mem. Internat. Assn. for Vol. Adminstrs. (cert. liaison, region IV 1986, profl. devel. liaison assn. 1987-88, region IV 1987-88, 93-94, recertification chair 1990-92, exec. planning com. Internat. Conf. on Vol. Adminstrn. 1997, chair subcom. peer assessment 2000-02), Southeastern Va. Assn. for Vol. Adminstrs. (dep. sec. 1986-87, pres. 1987-89), Tidewater Cancer Network (assoc. 1986), Nat. Hospice Orgn. (profl.), Va. Assn. for Hospice Orgn. (assoc.), Jr. League of Norfolk-Va. Beach (hon., sustainer, past pres., 1st Outstanding Sustainer award 1981), Assn. for Jr. Leagues Internat. (Disting. Vol. Centennial Cookbook profile 1996), Assn. for Fund Raising Profl. (Hampton Roads bd. 2005-06), Hampton Rds. C. of C. (co-chmn. bus. dist. forum 2006), CVA peer assessment, 2001-07. Episcopalian. Avocations: reading, walking, gardening, cooking, painting. Personal E-mail: emilyfiler@yahoo.com.

FILERMAN, GARY LEWIS, medical educator; b. Mpls., Nov. 16, 1936; s. Joseph H. and Bonnie (Kobrin) F.; m. Jane Harding, Sept. 15, 1962; children: Amy Beth, Joseph Harding, Suzanne Louise. BA, U. Minn., 1959, M.Health Adminstrn. (Phillips Found. fellow 1959-60), 1961, MA (W.K. Kellogg fellow 1961-64), 1963, PhD (Milbank travel grantee 1964, Orgn. Am. States fellow 1964), 1970. Adminstrv. resident Johns Hopkins Hosp., 1961-62; acting dir. Minn. Hosp. Assn., 1965; pres. Assn. Univ. Programs in Health Adminstrn., Washington, 1965-93; exec. sec. Accrediting Commn. Edn. Health Services Adminstrn., 1968-80; assoc. dir. PEW Health Professions Commn., Washington, 1993-95; dir. David A. Winston Fellowship, 1986—2007, pres., 1998—2003. Mem. faculty George Washington U., chmn., prof. dept. health mgmt. and policy, 1998-2000, prof. health svc. adminstrn., chmn. health sys., Georgetown U., 2000—; guest scholar Brookings Instn., 1962; sr. health advisor Acae. Ednl. Devel., 1998-2000; cons. in field. Author: A Future of Consequence, 1989; editor Jour. Health Adminstrn. Edn., 1982-93; author articles in field.; mem. editl. bds. profl. jours. Mem. nat. health professions adv. coun. HHS, 1983-87, coun. agy for health care policy and rsch., 1990-92; bd. dirs. Am. Refugee Commn., 1982-2004, Fairfax Audubon, 1989-93, Am. Internat. Health Alliance, Companion Care Assn., 2005; chmn. Planned Parenthood Metro Washington, 1990-91, bd. dirs. 1989-92; bd. dirs. Ctr. for Transformational Leadership, 2000-02; internat. adv. bd. Vols. of Am., 2003—; trustee Citizens Advocacy Ctr., 2006—, McLean Cmty. Found., 2007. Recipient Silver medal Leuven (Belgium) U., 1972, Disting. Contbn. award Assn. U. Programs Health Adminstrn., 1979, Outstanding Achievement award Regents of U. Minn., 1982, Outstanding Achievement award Ohio State U., 1992, Humanitarian award, Am. Refugee Com., 2005; Salzburg Seminar fellow, 2000. Fellow APHA, Am. Acad. Med. Adminstrs. (hon.), hon. alumni, Univ. Chgo.,1992, diplomate Am. Coll. of Health Care Execs., 1990—; mem. Royal Soc. Health, Assn. Am. Med. Colls., Cosmos Club (Washington), Phi Beta Kappa. Home: 1322 Banquo Ct Mc Lean VA 22102-2707 Office Phone: 202-687-8150.

FILERMAN, MICHAEL HERMAN, television producer; b. Chgo., May 4, 1938; s. Arthur Joseph and Anne Leah (Greenfield) F. BS in Communications, U. Ill., 1960. Gen. program dir. Sta. WGN-TV, Chgo., 1962-67; gen. program dir., dir. daytime programs CBS TV Network, NYC, 1967-72; dir. series devel. Paramount TV, 1972-74; v.p. series devel. Lorimar Prodns., 1976-83; with 20th Century Fox, 1983-85, NBC Prodns., 1985-88. Exec. prodr.: Knots Landing, Falcon Crest, Flamingo Road,

Secrets of Midland Heights, King's Crossing, Sisters, John Grisham's The Client, Four Corners, (Movie of the Week) Christmas Eve, Peyton Place: The Next Generation, A Letter to Three Wives, Assault and Matrimony, The Child Saver, Take My Daughters, Please, Turn Back the Clock, Coins in the Fountain, The Story Lady, The Return of Eliot Ness, Roommates, Deadly Family Secrets, Once You Meet a Stranger, Knots Landing: Back to the Cul-de-Sac, When Andrew Came Home, Knots Landing Together Again; prodr.: (theatre) 24th Day, I Love You!, You're Perfect!, Now Change!, Lypsinska: The Boxed Set, Our Lady of 121st Street, Tea At Five, Frozen, Sin: A Cardinal Deposed.

FILES, DOUGLAS SCOTT, surgeon, military officer; b. Ithaca, NY, Mar. 15, 1966; s. Donald Howard and Barbara Distin Files. BA in Linguistics, Mich. State U., East Lansing, 1987; MD, Wayne State U., Detroit, 1994; MPH, U. Utah, Salt Lake City, 2003. Diplomate Am. Bd. Preventive Medicine, cert. aerospace medicine Am. Coll. Preventive Medicine. Rsch. asst. Mich. State U., 1984—87; English totur Luth. Social Svcs., Lansing, Mich., 1987—90; resident in internal medicine Duke U. Med. Ctr., Durham, NC, 1994—97; internal medicine physician Omni Healthcare, Palm Bay, Fla., 1997—99; brigade surgeon 101st Airborne Divsn., Ft. Campbell, Fla., 1999—2002; resident in aerospace medicine Sch. Aerospace Medicine, Brooks City Base, Tex., 2003—05; chief aerospace medicine 47th Med. Group, Laughlin AFB, Tex., 2005—; commd. USAF, 2002, advanced through grades to maj., 2002. Bd. govs. Hugh O'Brian Youth Leadership, Tex., 2005—. Decorated Meritorious Svc. medal, Army Commendation medal. Mem.: Aerospace Medicine Assn., Soc. USAF Flight Surgeons, League World War I Aviation Historians, Alpha Omega Alpha, Phi Kappa Phi, Phi Beta Kappa. Avocations: travel, running, reading. Home: 111 King's Way # F44 Del Rio TX 78840 Office: 47 MDG/SGP 490 Mitchell Ave Laughlin A F B TX 78843

FILI-KRUSHEL, PATRICIA, media company executive; b. Nov. 12, 1953; BA, St. John's U., Jamaica, NY, 1975; MBA, Fordham U., Bronx, NY, 1982. Various positions including prog. contr. ABC Sports ABC, 1975—79; dir. sports adminstrn. HBO, 1979—80, dir. sports and spls. prog. budgeting, 1980—81, dir. of prodn., 1981—83, v.p. bus. affairs, 1984—88; sr. v.p. programming & prodn. Lifetime TV, 1988—89; grp. v.p. Hearts/ABC-Viacom Entertainment Svcs., 1990—93; pres. of ABC Daytime Walt Disney Co., 1993—98, pres., ABC TV, 1998-2000; pres., CEO Web MD Health, 2000—01; exec. v.p., adminstrn. AOL Time Warner Inc. (now Time Warner Inc.), 2001—. Bd. dirs. Oxygen Media, Inc. Co-chair child care initiative Mayor Bloomberg's Commn. on Women's Issues; trustee Pub. Theatre; bd. dirs. Ctrl. Pk. Conservancy; bd. comm., trustee Fordham U. Named Woman of Yr., Police Athletic League; named one of 50 Most Powerful Women, Fortune mag., 1998; recipient Muse award, Women in Film, 1993, Vision award, 1996, Women of Achievement award, Women's Project and Prodns., 1999, Matrix award, NY Women in Comm., Inc., Crystal Apple award, City of NY. Mem.: Acad. TV Arts and Scis. (exec. com., bd. govs.), NY Women in Film (past pres.). Office: Time Warner Inc One Time Warner Ctr Rm 12-235 New York NY 10019-8016

FILIMONOV, MIKHAIL ANATOLYEVITCH, investment company executive; b. Odessa, Ukraine, Oct. 26, 1956; came to the U.S., 1971; s. Anatoly M. and Ludmila G. (Yankelevitch) Filimonov; m. Natalia Baranova; 1 child, Nicholas M.; 1 child from previous marriage, Alexandra K. AAS, N.Y. Tech. Coll., 1982; student, Baruch Coll., 1983. V.p. Arnhold & S. Bleichroder, NYC, 1983, Cresvale Internat., London and NYC, 1984; 1st v.p. Quadrex Securities, NYC, 1985-87; v.p. Baring Securities, NYC, 1987-90; first v.p. London Investment Trust Am., Inc., NYC, 1990-92; chmn., chief investment officer, CEO Alexandra Investment Mgmt. (formerly Hermes Capital Mgmt.), NYC, 1992—. Bd. dirs. Alexandra Global Investment Fund, Brit. Virgin Islands. Republican. Office: Alexandra Investment Mgmt 767 3d Ave 39th Fl New York NY 10017

FILIPACCHI, DANIEL, publishing executive; b. Paris, Jan. 12, 1928; s. Henri Filipacchi. French corr. Ebony Mag., Paris; photographer Paris Match mag.; jazz disc jockey, radio prodr. Europe 1, Paris, 1955-60; chmn., prin. owner Publs. Filipacchi, Paris, 1960—; founder, owner, editor various mags., France, 1963—; chmn., CEO Warner-Filipacchi Music, S.A., Paris, 1970-85; chmn. Hachette Filipacchi Mags., NYC, 1990—; co-artistic dir. Sidney Bechet Centennial, New Orleans, 1997; prodr. Musisoft/Masters of Jazz. Chmn., prin. owner Paris Match, other French consumer mags. Editor: Surrealism: Two Pvt. Eyes, The Nesuhi Ertegun & Daniel Filipacchi Collections, 1999. Trustee S.R. Guggenheim Mus. Named one of Top 200 Collectors, ARTnews Mag., 2004. Avocation: collector modern art, especially surrealism. Address: Hachette Filipacchi Mags 1633 Broadway 40th Floor New York NY 10019-6708 Office: Hachette Filipacchi 149-151 rue Anatole France 92300 Levallois-Perret France

FILIPP BESEDA, CAROLYN FRANCINE, music educator, insurance agent; b. Houston, Oct. 11, 1950; d. Emil Frank and Augustina Joyce (Klozik) Filipp; m. Henry E. Beseda, Dec. 24, 2005. B in Music, U. Houston, 1973; Med., Stephen F. Austin State U., 1977; postgrad. Houston Baptist U., 1979-80. Band dir. Ft. Bend Ind. Sch. Dist., Stafford, Tex., 1973-74, choral dir., 1974-76; choral dir., Missouri City, Tex., 1976-77; band, choral dir. Houston Ind. Sch. Dist., 1977-95, band dir., 1985-86, 1994-95; choral dir. Aldine Ind. Sch. Dist., 1995—; pianist Houston Brethren Ch., 1964-73, choral dir., 1968-70; pianist Cy-Fair Cmty. Ch. Unity Brethren, Westheiner Cmty. Ch.; clarinetist, saxophonist, vocalist Space-City Dutchmen Orch., 1965-75; clarinetist Kovanda Orch., 1987-95; pvt. tchr. clarinet, saxophone and piano, Houston; mem. Houston Symphony Chorale, 1984-86; ins. agt. Western Frat. Life Assn., Cedar Rapids, Iowa, 1977-86, RVOS, 1982-, SPJST, 1986-; treas. Houston Brethren Ch. Christian Sisters Soc., 1991-94; pres. Cy-Fair Cmty. Ch. Christian Sisters, 2004-; trustee Hus Sch., sec., 1991-94. Mem. Congress Houston Tchrs. (rec. sec. 1980-82, exec. v.p. 1982-84), Tex. Music Educators Assn., Tex. Bandmasters Assn., Am. Choral Dirs. Assn. (life), Alpha Delta Kappa, Silver Sister (corr. sec. 2004-06), Tau Beta Sigma, Gamma Sigma Sigma (chpt. sec.-treas. 1971-73, life), Moores Sch. Music Soc. (U. Houston). Clubs: Coll. Women's, Houston Liederkranz. Lodges: Western Fraternal Life Assn. (lodge 289 sec. 1977-81, Tex. liaison officer 1985-86), SPJST, Lodge #88 (1st v.p. 2004, 05, 2nd v.p. 2006), Sons of Hermann, Sokol Houston, Czech Cultural Ctr. Home and Office: 2515 Lazybrook Dr Houston TX 77008-1003 Personal E-mail: cffilipp@earthlink.net.

FILIPPELLI, JAMES ANTHONY, literature and language educator; b. NY, Aug. 30, 1953; s. Anthony Michael Filippelli and Maria Immaculata Fiorillo; m. Carolyn Trudy Crecelius, May 8, 1977; children: James, Amanda. BA, St. Leo Coll., Fla., 1975; MFA, Bklyn. Coll., NYC, 1978; diploma in Adminstrn. and Supervision, Fordham U., Tarrytown, NY, 2003. Instr. English St. Cecilia's Sch., NY, 1975—78, Family Svc. West White Plains, NY, 1978, Lakeland Ctrl. Schs., Shrub Oak, NY, 1979—, asst. prin. Mid. Sch., 2003—05. Adj. instr. Dominican Coll., 1979—; adv. bd. Collegiate Press, 2003—04. Home: 36 Boxwood Rd Yonkers NY 10710 Office: Dominican Coll 470 Western Hwy Orangeburg NY 10962-1210 Office Phone: 914-739-2823.

FILIPPENKO, ALEXEI VLADIMIR, astrophysicist, educator; b. Oakland, Calif., July 25, 1958; s. Vladimir Ivan and Alexandra (Karmansky) F.; m. Diana Louise Lee, Aug. 5, 1989; children: Zoe, Simon. BA in Physics, U. Calif., Santa Barbara, 1979; PhD in Astronomy, Calif. Inst. Tech., 1984. Asst. prof. astronomy U. Calif., Berkeley, 1986-88, assoc. prof. astronomy, 1988-92, prof. astronomy, 1992—. Lectr. in field. Co-author (with Jay M. Pasachoff): The Cosmos: Astronomy in the New Millennium, 2001; contbr. articles to profl. jours. Named Presdl. Young Investigator, NSF, 1989—94; recipient Robert M. Petrie prize, Can. Astron. Soc., 1997, Guggenheim fellow, 2001, US Professors of Yr. Award for Outstanding Doctoral and Rsch. Universities Prof., Carnegie Found. for Advancement of Tchg. and Coun. for Advancement and Support of Edn., 2006, Richtmyer Meml. Award, Am. Assn. Physics Tchrs., 2007; Miller fellow, U. Calif., Berkeley, 1984—86, rsch. fellow astronomy, Calif. Tech. Inst., 1984. Mem. Am. Astron. Soc. (Newton Lacy Pierce prize 1992), Astron. Soc. Pacific, Internat. Astron. Union. Achievements include discovery of new type of exploding str; found that many nearby galaxies show low-level nonstellar activity similar to that of quasars; discovery of several probable black holes in the milky way galaxy; contributed to the discovery that the expansion of the universe appears to be accelerating; development of a robotic telescope. Office: U Calif Dept Astronomy 439 Campbell Hall Berkeley CA 94720-3411 Office Phone: 510-642-1813. Fax: 510-642-3411. E-mail: alex@astro.berkeley.edu.*

FILIPPINE, EDWARD LOUIS, federal judge; b. 1930; AB, St. Louis U., 1951, JD, 1957. Bar: Mo. 1957. Pvt. practice law, St. Louis, 1957—77; spl. asst. atty. gen. State of Mo., 1963—64; dist. judge U.S. Dist. Ct. (ea. dist.) Mo., St. Louis, 1977—, chief judge, 1990—95; U.S. sr. dist. judge U.S. Dist. Ct. for Ea. Dist. Mo., 1995—. Served with USAF, 1951-53 Mem. ABA, Mo. Bar Assn., Bar Assn. Met. St. Louis, Lawyers Assn. of St. Louis. Office: US Dist Ct Thomas F Eagleton US Cthse 111 S 10th St Rm 10 137 Saint Louis MO 63102 Office Phone: 314-244-7640. E-mail: edward_filippine@moed.uscourts.gov.

FILISKO, FRANK EDWARD, physicist, researcher; b. Lorain, Ohio, Jan. 29, 1942; s. Joseph John and Mary Magdalene (Cherven) F.; m. Doris Faye Call, Aug. 8, 1970; children: Theresa Marie, Andrew William, Edward Anthony. BA, Colgate U., 1964; MS, Purdue U., 1966; PhD, Case We. Res. U., 1969. Post doctoral fellow Case We. Res. U., Cleve., 1968—70; prof. materials sci. engring. and macromolecular sci. U. Mich., Ann Arbor, 1970—, acting dir. macromolecular sci. and engring., 1987—96. Dir. Polymer Lab., U. Mich. Editor: Progress in Electrorheology, 1995; contbr. more than 150 articles to profl. jours. Mem. Am. Phys. Soc., Am. Chem. Soc., KC, Soc. Rheology Roman Catholic. Achievements include patents for electric field dependent fluids and electric dependent fluids-CIP. Office: U Mich Materials Sci & Engring Ann Arbor MI 48109 Office Phone: 734-763-2240. Business E-Mail: fef@umich.edu.

FILKINS, DEXTER PRICE, newspaper reporter; b. Cin., May 24, 1961; s. Cedric Eugene and Helen Jean (Samp) F. BA in Polit. Sci. with high honors, U. Fla., 1983; MPhil in Internat. Rels., U. Oxford, Eng., 1986. Legis. aide to U.S. Sen. Lawton Chiles, Washington, 1983-84; reporter The Miami Herald, 1986—95, LA Times, 1995—97, bur chief New Delhi, 1997—2000; reporter NY Times, 2000—. Co-recipient Overseas Press Club award for best mag. reporting from abroad, 2006; recipient George B. Polk award for Iraq war coverage, 2005. Mem. Phi Beta Kappa. Office: Newsroom NY Times 229 W 43rd St New York NY 10036

FILLER, RONALD HOWARD, lawyer; b. St. Louis, Apr. 11, 1948; s. Leon Isaac and Jeanette Frances (Sanofsky) F.; m. Paula; children: Stephen Paul, Lindsay Ann. BS, U. Ill., 1970; JD, George Washington U., 1973; LLM in Taxation, Georgetown U., 1976. Bar: D.C. 1973, Ill. 1976, N.Y. 1993. Atty. SEC, Washington, 1973—76; assoc. Abramson & Fox, Chgo., 1976—77; assoc. counsel Conti Cmty. Svc., Chgo., 1977—78, dir. mgmt. accounts, 1978—80; mng. ptnr. Filler Zaner & Assocs., Chgo., 1980—85; ptnr. Vedder, Price, Kaufman & Kammholz, Chgo., 1985—93, corp. practice leader, 1989—91, mem. exec. com., 1991—93; dir. futures adminstrn. Lehman Bros., Inc., 1993—. Dir. Commodities Law Inst., Ill. Inst. Tech./Chgo-Kent Law Sch., 1978-97, adj. prof. law, 1977-93, bd. overseers, 1982-2005; lectr. Commodities Ednl. Inst., 1977-89; adj. prof. law Bklyn. Law Sch., 1994-96; vice chmn. Broker Tec Clearing Corp., 2002-04; bd. dirs. Clearing Corp. Contbr. articles to jours. and futures mags. Named one of top 315 lawyers State of Ill., 1991. Mem. ABA (chmn. sub futures commn. mchts. 1986-1995), Nat. Futures Assn. (bd. dirs. 1984-87), Am. Arbitration Assn. (arbitrator), Mid Am. Commodity Exch. (bd. dirs. 1984-86), Chgo. Bar Assn. (chmn. commodities law com. 1981-82, vice chmn. fin. and legal svcs. com. 1988-89, co-vice chmn. large law firm com. 1991-92), Nat. Assn. Futures Traders Assn., Futures Industry Assn. (bd. dirs. 1990-92, exec. com. Chgo. divsn. 1986-88, exec. com. Law and Comp. divsn. 1985-90, 92—, sec. 1995-98, pres. 1998-2000), N.Y. State Bar Assn., Ill. State Bar Assn. Democrat. Jewish. Office: Lehman Brothers Inc 745 7th Ave 6th Fl New York NY 10019 Home: 100 Warren St #1915 Jersey City NJ 07302 Home Phone: 201-333-6655; Office Phone: 212-526-0236. Business E-Mail: rfiller@lehman.com.

FILLEY, CHRISTOPHER MARK, neurologist, researcher; b. Saranac Lake, NY, July 31, 1951; s. Giles Franklin and Mary Brown (Klinefelter) F. BA, Williams Coll., 1973; MD, Johns Hopkins U., 1979. Diplomate Am. Bd. Psychiatry and Neurology. Intern U. Conn., Farmington, 1979—80; resident in neurology U. Colo., Denver, 1980—83; behavioral neurology fellow Boston U., 1983—84; from instr. to asst. prof. neurology U. Colo. Sch. Medicine, Denver, 1984—91, assoc. prof. neurology, 1991—97, prof. neurology, 1997—; interim dir. Alzheimers disease and cognition ctr. U. Colo., 2006. Prin. investigator studies in Alzheimers Disease NIH, Bethesda, Md., 1991-94. Author: Neurobehavioral Anatomy, 1995, Neurobehavioral Anatomy, 2d edit., 2001, The Behavioral Neurology of White Matter, 2001; contbr. articles to profl. jours. Health com. Denver Found., 1995-98. Fellow Am. Acad. Neurology; mem. Am. Neurol. Assn., Internat. Neuropsychol. Soc., Soc. for Behavioral and Cognitive Neurology, Colo. Soc. Clin. Neurologists. Avocations: piano, hiking, reading, guitar, skiing. Home Phone: 303-355-2672; Office Phone: 303-315-6461. Business E-Mail: christopher.filley@uchsc.edu.

FILLEY, WARREN VERNON, allergist; b. Topeka, Kans., Oct. 27, 1950; MD, U. Kans. Sch. Medicine, 1976. Diplomate Am. Bd. Allergy and Immunology, Am. Bd. Internal Medicine. Intern U. Okla., 1976-77, resident in internal medicine, 1977-79; fellow allergy and immunology Mayo Clin., Rochester, Minn., 1979-81; with Presbyn. Hosp., Oklahoma City; clin. prof. medicine U. Okla. Mem. AMA, Am. Acad. Allergy, Asthma and Immunology, Am. Coll. Allergy, Asthma and Immunology, Okla. Med. Assn. Office: Okla Allergy and Asthma Clin 750 NE 13th St Oklahoma City OK 73104-5051 Home Phone: 405-340-3448; Office Phone: 405-235-0040. Business E-Mail: wfilley@oklahomaallergy.com.

FILLIAT, ELIZABETH HARTLEY, retired secondary school educator; b. Albany, Ga., Oct. 8, 1942; d. Shell Elbert and Mary (Deese) Hartley; m. Ronald Wardall, June 6, 1963 (div. Jan. 15, 1971); 1 child, Thomas Ronald Wardall (dec.); m. Roland Paul Filliat, July 7, 1979 (dec.); 1 child, Annette Elizabeth. BA, The City Coll., CUNY, 1970; MEd, Ga. State U., 1973. Cert. tchg. in reading specialist T-5 Ga. Dept. Edn., 2005, leadership in instrnl. supervision - reading L-5 Ga. Dept. Edn., 2005, svc. in data collector S-5 Ga. Dept. Edn., 2005. Jr. HS tchr. English Lowndes County Sch. Sys., Valdosta, Ga., 1970—71; HS tchr. English DeKalb County Sch. Sys., Decatur, Ga., 1971—73, reading specialist - elem. sch., 1973—78, instrnl. lead tchr., 1978—84, HS reading tchr. and reading dept. chair, 1984—2000; ongoing substitute tchr. Fulton County Sch. Sys., Atlanta, 2001—. Secondary reading adv. com. mem. Ga. Dept. Edn., Atlanta, 1987. Mem. northside adv. com. Atlanta Jour. Constn., 2004—05; mem. writer's group North Fulton Dem. Party, Atlanta, 2004—05. Nominee Honor Tchr. award, Atlanta Jour. Constn., 1998; recipient Tchr. of Quarter, Ga. Power Co., DeKalb County's So. Dist., 1986, Citizenship award, Kiwanis Club South DeKalb County, 1989, Cert. of Merit, W.D. Clowdis chpt. Nat. Beta Club, 1994, Wal-Mart Tchr. of Yr., Wal-Mart Found., 1998. Mem.: NEA (life), Ga. Assn. Reading, Orgn. Dekalb Educators (life), Ga. PTA (life), Ga. Assn. Educators (life), Kappa Delta, Alpha Psi Omega. Democrat. Episcopalian. Avocations: writing, reading, travel, theater. Home: 580 S Riversong Lane Alpharetta GA 30022-1800 Personal E-mail: efilliat@aol.com.

FILLINGER, MARK F., vascular surgeon, researcher; b. Columbus, Ohio, Oct. 7, 1957; s. Robert J. and Charlotte A. Fillinger; m. Mary C. Pawlinga, Jan. 1, 1989. BS in Mech. Engring., Ohio State U., 1979, MD, 1984. Diplomate in surgery and vascular surgery Am. Bd. Surgery; diplomate Nat. Bd. Med. Examiners; registered vascular technologist; lic. physician, N.Y., N.H. Resident in gen. surgery SUNY Health Sci. Ctr., Syracuse, 1984-91, rsch. fellow dept. surgery, 1987-89; fellow in vascular surgery Dartmouth-Hitchcock Med. Ctr., Hanover, NH, 1991—93, asst. prof. vascular surgery, 1993—99, assoc. prof., 1999—2005, prof., 2005—. Contbr. chpts. to books, articles to profl. jours.; mem. editl. bd. numerous profl. jours. Recipient Peter B. Samuels award Soc. Clin. Vascular Surgery, 1989, Ralph A. Deterling award New Eng. Soc. for Vascular Surgery, 1993. Fellow ACS, Soc. Vascular Surgery (disting. fellow), European Soc. Vascular Surgery, Internat. Soc. Endovascular Specialists; mem. AMA, Internat. Soc. for Applied Cardiovascular Biology, Soc. for Vascular Tech., N.H. Med. Soc., Pi Tau Sigma. Avocations: golf, skiing, tennis. Home: 17 Mulherrin Farm Rd Hanover NH 03755-4907 Office: Dartmouth-Hitchcock Med Ctr Sect Vascular Surgery One Medical Ctr Dr Lebanon NH 03756 Office Phone: 603-650-8677. Business E-Mail: mark.fillinger@hitchcock.org.

FILLIOS, LOUIS CHARLES, retired science educator; b. Boston, Mass., July 1, 1923; s. Charles Louis and Pagona (Kefalas) F.; m. Iphigenia Loomis, June 15, 1947; children: Despena Fillios Billings, Diana Fillios Downey, Hilary Fillios Grant. AB, Harvard, 1948, MS, 1953, ScD, 1956. Rsch. assoc., then assoc. Harvard U., 1956-60; asst. prof. physiol. chemistry MIT, 1961-64, assoc. prof., 1964-66; assoc. rsch. prof. biochemistry and pathology Boston U. Sch. Medicine, 1966-68; prof. nutritional sci. Boston U., 1968-94; prof. biochemistry Boston U. Sch. Medicine, 1970-94; dir. divsn. basic sci. Boston U. Sch. Medicine (Sch. Grad. Dentistry), 1970-75, chmn. dept. nutritional scis., 1973-94; prof. biochemistry emeritus Boston U., 1994—. Chmn. Mass. Task Force Nutrition and Aging, 1970-71; cons. Mass. Office of Elder Affairs, 1971-73; co-chmn. nutrition sect. White House Conf. Aging, 1971-72; cons. VA, Bedford, Mass., 1982-87; mem. pres.'s adv. coun. Hellenic Coll., 1968-73. Author numerous research articles fields biochemistry, pathology and nutrition; contbr. sci. and profl. jours. 1st lt. USAAF, 1943-45. Decorated D.F.C., Air Medal with 3 oak leaf clusters (7 battle stars); recipient Outstanding Educator of Am. award Boston U., 1972, Spl. Honor, 1995. Fellow AAAS, Am. Heart Assn. (established investigator 1961-66); mem. Am. Inst. Nutrition (chmn. fellow award com. 1978-81), Am. Soc. for Nutritional Scis., Sigma Xi (Harvard chpt.), Omicron Kappa Upsilon (hon.). Home: 19 Eliot Rd Lexington MA 02421-5630

FILLMORE, JOHN DILLON, artist; b. Canoga Park, Calif., Nov. 24, 1951; s. Herbert Peter and Patricia Louise (Dillon) F. BFA, Art Ctr. Coll. Design, Hollywood, Calif., 1973. Fine artist, designer Chris O'Connell Inc./Ancient Echoes/Martex, Santa Fe, N.Mex., 1989-95; freelance fine artist Santa Fe, Tarzana, 1974—. Recipient Hubbard Art award for excellence, 1991. Republican. Roman Catholic. Avocations: art history, collecting art and books.

FILLMORE, PETER ARTHUR, mathematician, educator; b. Moncton, NB, Can., Oct. 28, 1936; s. Henry Arthur and Jeanne Margaret (Archibald) F.; m. Anne Ellen Garvock, Aug. 6, 1960; children: Jennifer Anne, Julia Margaret, Peter Alexander. B.Sc., Dalhousie U., 1957; MA, U. Minn., 1960, PhD, 1962. Instr. U. Chgo., 1962-64; asst. prof. math. Ind. U., 1964-67, assoc. prof., 1967-71, prof., 1971-72; vis. assoc. prof. U. Toronto, Canada, 1970-71; prof. math. Dalhousie U. , Halifax, Canada, 1972-2001; Killam sr. fellow Dalhousie U., Halifax, 1972-73, Killam rsch. prof., 1973-78, chmn. dept. math., stats. and computer sci., 1987-91, prof. emeritus, 2001—. Sr. vis. fellow U. Edinburgh, 1977; mem. Math. Scis. Rsch. Inst., Berkeley, Calif., 1984-85, Fields Inst. Rsch. Math. Sci., 1994-95; vis. prof. U. Copenhagen, 1990. Author: Notes on Operator Theory, 1970, A User's Guide to Operator Algebras, 1996; contbr. articles to profl. jours. Bd. mem. Nova Voce Male Voice Soc.; vice-chair bd. Opera of Nova Scotia. Fellow Royal Soc. Can., Fields Inst. for Rsch. Math. Sci.; mem. Can. Math. Soc. (life, council 1973-75, 77-79, v.p. 1975-77, pres. 1994-96), Am. Math. Soc. (council 1982-84). Office: Dalhousie U Math Dept Halifax NS Canada B3H 3J5 Office Phone: 902-494-2572. Business E-mail: fillmore@mathstat.dal.ca.

FILLMORE, ROBERT M., lawyer; b. Wichita, Kans., 1953; BGS, Univ. Kans., 1975, JD, 1977. Bar: Kans. 1977, Tex. 1986, lic.: US Supreme Ct. 1980. Asst. atty. gen., litig. divsn. State of Kans., 1979—80, spl. asst. atty. gen., 1981—85; ptnr., co-head, regulated industries, govtl. rels. team; head, regulated utilities practice area Hunton & Williams LLP, Dallas, 1985—. Adj. faculty, law Univ. Kans, 1981—82. Mem.: ABA (chmn., spl. com. on restructuring elec. industry 2003—05), State Bar of Tex. (chmn., vice chmn., sec./treas., mem. coun. pub. utility law section 1997—2001), Ctr. Am. and Internat. Law (mem. exec. com, chmn., power energy trading and mktg. com. 2002—04). Office: Hunton & Williams Energy Plz 30th Fl 1601 Bryan St Dallas TX 75201-3402 Office Phone: 214-979-3092. Office Fax: 214-979-3914. Business E-Mail: bfillmore@hunton.com.

FILNER, BOB, congressman; b. Pitts., Sept. 4, 1942; m. Jane Merrill; children: Erin, Adam. BA in Chemistry, Cornell U., 1963; MA in History, U. Del., 1969; PhD in History, Cornell U., 1973. Prof. history San Diego State U., 1970-92; legis. asst. Senator Hubert Humphrey, 1974, Congressman Don Fraser, 1975; spl. asst. Congressman Jim Bates, 1984; city councilman 8th dist. City of San Diego, 1987-92, dep. mayor, 1992; mem. U.S. Congress from 51st Calif. dist. (formerly 50th), 1993—; mem. transp. and infrastructure com., vets. affairs com. Pres. San Diego Bd. Edn., 1982, mem.-elect 1979-83; chmn. San Diego Schs. of the Future Commn., 1986-87. Democrat. Office: US Ho Reps 2428 Rayburn Ho Office Bldg Washington DC 20515-0551 also: Chula Vista Dist Office Ste A 333 F St Chula Vista CA 91910 Address: Imperial Dist Office Ste D 1101 Airport Rd Imperial CA 92251 Office Phone: 619-422-5963, 760-355-8800. Office Fax: 619-422-7290, 760-355-8802.*

FILO, DAVID, Internet company executive; b. Moss Bluff, La. BS in Computer Engring., Tulane U.; MSEE, Stanford U., 1990, PhD studies in Elec. Engring. Co-creator online navigational guide Yahoo!, Calif., 1994—; co-founder, chief Yahoo! Inc., Calif., 1995—, dir., 1995—96. Co-author (with Jerry Yang, Karen Heyman): (books) Yahoo! Unplugged: Your Discovery Guide to the Webb, 1995; co-author: (with Richard Raucci, Elizabeth Crane, Jerry Yang) Yahooligans!: Way Cool Web Sites, 1996. Named one of 400 Richest Americans, Forbes mag., 2004, 2005, 2006. Named company YAHOO! (acronym for Yet Another Hierarchical Officious Oracle). Office: Yahoo! Inc 701 First Ave Sunnyvale CA 94089

FILOSA, GARY FAIRMONT RANDOLPH, II, columnist, film producer; b. Wilder, Vt., Feb. 22, 1931; s. Gary F.R. de Marco de Varra and Rosaline M. (Falzaran) F.; m. Catherine Moray Stewart (dec.); children: Marc Christian Bazire de Villadon III, Gary Fairmont Randolph de Varra III. Grad., Mt. Hermon Sch., 1950; PhB, U. Chgo., 1954; BA, U. Americas, Mex., 1967; MA, Calif. Western U., 1968; PhD, U.S. Internat. U., 1970. Sports reporter Claremont Daily Eagle, Rutland Herald, Vt. Informer, 1947-52; pub. The Chicagoan, 1950—54; account exec., editor house publs. Robertson, Buckley & Gotsch, Inc., Chgo., 1953-54; account exec. Fuller, Smith & Ross, Inc., NYC, 1955; prodr./host Weekend KCET

Channel 13, NYC, 1956—67; editor Apparel Arts mag. (now Gentlemen's Quar.), Esquire, Inc., NYC, 1955-56; chmn. bd., CEO, pres. Filosa Publs. Internat., NYC, 1957—65; pub. Teenage, Rustic Rhythm, Teen Life, Mystery Digest, Top Talent, Rock & Roll Roundup, Celebrities, Stardust, Personalities, Campus monthly mags.; pres., chmn. bd. Teenarama Records, Inc., NYC, 1956-62; chmn. bd., pres. Produciones Mexicanes Internationales (S.A.), Mexico City, 1958—70; assoc. pub. Laundromatic Age, NYC, 1958-59; ptnr. with Warner LeRoy purchase of Broadway plays for Hollywood films, NYC, 1958—64; pres. Montclair Sch., 1958-60, Pacific Registry, Inc., LA, 1959-61; exec. prodr. Desilu Studios, Inc., Hollywood, Calif., 1958—62; exec. asst. to Benjamin A. Javits, 1963—64; propr. Gino's of Hollywood, 1961-70; dean adminstrn. Postgrad. Ctr. for Mental Health, NYC, 1962-64; chmn. bd., CEO Filosa Films Internat., Beverly Hills, Calif., 1962—; pres. Amateur Athletes Internat., Iowa City, 1996-2000; chmn. bd., pres. Cinematografica Americana Internationale (S.A.), Mexico City, 1964-84; pres. Casa Filosa Corp., Palm Beach, Fla., 1982-87; dir. Cmty. Savs., North Palm Beach, Fla., 1982-87. V.p. acad. affairs World Acad., San Francisco, 1967-68; asst. to provost Calif. Western U., San Diego, 1968-69; assoc. prof. philosophy Art Coll., San Francisco, 1969-70; v.p. acad. affairs, dean of faculty Internat. Inst., Phoenix, 1968-73; chmn. bd. dirs., pres. Universite Universelle, 1970-73, 2000-03; bd. dirs., v.p. acad. affairs, dean Summer Sch., Internat. C.C., L.A., 1970-72; chmn. bd., pres. Social Directory Calif., 1967-75, Am. Assn. Social Registries, L.A., 1970-76; pres. Social Directory U.S., N.Y.C., 1974-76; pres. Herbert Hoover Forum, Iowa City, 1996-2000; chmn. bd. dirs. Internat. Soc. Social Registers, Paris, 1974-2007; surfing coach U. Calif. at Irvine, 1975-77; v.p. Xerox-Systemic, 1979-80; CEO Internat. Surfing League, Palm Beach, 1987-95, Santa Barbara, Calif., 1996—; pres. Amateur Athletes Internat., Iowa City; internat. syndicated columnist Conservations with Am., 1997-. Editor: Sci. Digest, 1961-62; composer: (lyrics) The Night Discovers Love, 1952, That Certain Something, 1953, Bolero of Love, 1956; author: (stage play) Let Me Call Ethel, 1955, The Bisexual, 1961, Technology Enters 21st Century, 1966, (mus.) Feather Light, 1966, No Public Funds for Nonpublic Schools, 1968, Creative Function of the College President, 1969, The Surfers Almanac, 1977, The Filosa Newsletter, 1986-92, The Sexual Continuum, 1990, Traveltalk, 1991, God's Own Prince, 1995, Holy Hawai'i, 1996, (biography) A Plague on Paradise, 1994, (TV series) Danny Thomas Show, 1963, Surfing USA, 1977, Payne of Florida, 1985, rev. new series, 2007, Honolulu, 1991, The Gym, 1992, Sales Pitch, 1992, 810 Ocean Avenue, 1992, One Feather, 1992, Conversations with America, 1989, All American Beach Party, 1989, Riding High, 2000, Dreamsport, 2000, Icons, 2000; contbr. numerous articles, editorials, to profl. jours., newspapers, and encys., including Life, Look, Sci. Digest, Ency. of Sports, World Book Ency., New York Times, Cedar Rapids Gazete, L.A. Times, others. Trustee Univ. of the Ams., Pueblo, Mex., 1986-2000; candidate for L.A. City Coun., 1 959; chmn. Educators for Re-election of Ivy Baker Pirest, 1970; mem. So. Calif. Com. for Olympic Games, 1977-84. With AUS, 1954-55. Recipient DAR Citizenship award, 1959, Silver Conquistador award Am. Assn. Social Registers, 1970, Ambassador's Cup U. Ams., 1967, resolution Calif. State Legis., 1977, Duke Kahanamoku Classic surfing trophy, 1977, gold pendant Japan Surfing Assn., 1978, Father of Olympic Surfing award Internat. Athletic Union, 1995, Father of Surfing trophy Amateur Athletes Internat., 1997, Father of Surfing trophy Internat. Surfing Fedn., 2000; inducted into Rock & Roll Mus. & Hall of Fame, Cleve., 1995. Mem. NAACP, NCAA (bd. dels. 1977-82), AAU (gov. 1978-82), Am. Acad. Motion Picture Arts and Scis., Internat. Surfing Com., U.S. Surfing Com. (founder 1960—), Internat. Surfing League (founder, chmn., CEO 1988—), Internat. Surfing Fedn. (pres. 1960—), Am. Assn. UN, Authors League, Authors Guild, Alumni Assn. U. Ams. (pres. 1967-70), Surf Club of the Palm Beaches (pres. 1983-94), Sierra Club, Surfing Hui of Hawaii, Internat. Soc. Bibliotheraptists (Paris, pres. 1997-2007), Lords Corybantes (Berlin) (life pres. 1966—), Commonwealth Club (San Francisco), Town Hall (L.A.), Calif. Club (L.A.), Palm Beach Surf Club, Sigma Omicron Lambda (founder, pres. 1965-92). Episcopalian. Office: PO Box 299 Beverly Hills CA 90213-0299 Personal E-mail: filosa@att.net. Business E-Mail: ffilm@att.net.

FILPI, ROBERT ALAN, lawyer; b. Chgo., Oct. 8, 1945; s. John Andrew and Eunice Lorraine (Taylor) F.; m. Janice Elizabeth Crusoe, June 24, 1967; children: Jennifer Anne, Christopher Alan, Emily Elizabeth. BA in History, magna cum laude, Harvard U., 1967; JD, Northwestern U., 1970. Bar: Ill. 1970, U.S. Dist. Ct. (no. dist.) Ill. 1971, U.S. Ct. Appeals (7th cir.) 1971, U.S. Supreme Ct. 1975. Asst. U.S. atty. No. Dist. Ill., Chgo., 1971-75; dep. chief U.S. atty. No. Dist. Ill., Civil Divsn., Chgo., 1975-76; ptnr. Stack & Filpi, Chgo., 1976—. Assoc. editor Jour. Criminal Law, Criminology and Police Sci., 1969-70. Coach, Spring Lake Sports League, Lincolnshire, Ill. 1984-91; mem. Village of Lincolnshire Plan Commn., 1984-94. Recipient Hyde prize Northwestern U. Sch. Law, 1967. Mem. ABA, Chgo. Bar Assn., Union League, Harvard Club. Office: 140 S Dearborn St Ste 411 Chicago IL 60603-5201 Office Phone: 312-782-0690. Business E-Mail: rfilpi@stackfilpi.com.

FILSON, RONALD COULTER, architect, educator, dean; b. Chardon, Ohio, Dec. 11, 1946; s. Clifford Coulter and Mae Alice (Foster) F.; m. Susan Virginia Saward, Dec. 14, 1973 (div. May 1996); children: Timothy Coulter, Lily Virginia; m. Lea Ann Sinclair, Oct. 9, 1999. Diploma, Am. Acad. in Rome, 1970; B.Arch., Yale U., 1970. Registered arch., Calif., La., Mass., Ohio, Miss., Nat. Coun. Archtl. Registration Bds. Architect Atelier d'Etudes, Ghardaia, Algeria, 1971-73; asst. prof., asst. dean Sch. of Architecture UCLA, 1974-80; dean sch. architecture Tulane U., New Orleans, 1980-92, prof. sch. architecture, 1980—; prin. Ronald Filson, FAIA, Architects, New Orleans. Prin. works include Piazza d'Italia, New Orleans, 1978 (award 1976), Eola Hotel, 1980, Lee House, 1984, Hyatt Hotel, Poydras Plaza, 1987-88, Nat. Pk. Svc. Edn. Ctr., Nat. D-Day Mus., Trump Casino, L.A. Artists Guild, Natchez Visitors Ctr. Pres. Friends of the Schnidler House, L.A., 1978-80; bd. dirs. New Orleans Arts Coun., 1980-93, pres., 1989-92, Contemporary Arts Ctr., New Orleans, 1980-84, New Orleans Planning Commn., 1985-87. Recipient design citations Progressive Architecture mag., 1969, 76, Rome prize Am. Acad. in Rome, 1969 Fellow AIA (Design awards 1980, 81, 85, 87, 89, 92, 94, 98, 99, 2000, 01, Richardson medal 1992); mem. AIA La. (pres. 1998), New Orleans AIA (pres. 1994), Yale Alumni Assn. La. (pres. 1992-94), So. Yacht Club, New Orleans Lawn Tennis Club (bd. govs. 1998-2002). Avocations: watercolors, sailing. Home: 5700 Vrooman Rd Painesville OH 44077-8842

FILSTON, HOWARD CHURCH, pediatric surgeon; b. NYC, Dec. 29, 1935; s. Howard Samuel and Marion (Church) F.; m. Nancy Lee Jameson, June 3, 1961 (dec. Nov. 2002); children: Scott Jameson (dec.), Timothy Howard, Megan Lee Johnson; m. Sandra Kay Stoutt, May 7, 2005. AB, Harvard U., 1958; MD, Case Western Res. U., 1962. Diplomate Am. Bd. Med. Examiners. Intern in gen. surgery Univ. Hosps., Cleve., 1962-63, asst. resident in gen. surgery, 1963-64, 66-68, chief resident, 1968-69; asst. chief resident pediatric surgery Children's Hosp. Phila., 1969-70; instr. pediatric surgery U. Pa. Sch. of Medicine, Phila., 1969-71, chief resident pediatric surgery, 1970-71; asst. prof. pediatric surgery Case Western Res. U. Hosp., Cleve., 1971-76; assoc. prof. pediatric surgery and pediatrics Duke U. Med. Ctr., Durham, NC, 1976-82, chief pediatric surgery, 1976-90, prof. pediatric surgery and pediats., 1982—90, prof. pediatric surgery and pediatrics, U. Tenn. Med. Ctr., Knoxville, 1990-2000, chief pediatric surgery, 1990-2000, vice chmn. dept. surgery, 1992-2000; emeritus prof.of pediat. surgery, 2000—. Specialist site visitor, pediatric surgery, Accreditation Coun. Grad. Med. Edn., 1982-90, 95—2000. Author: Surgical Problems in Children, 1982; author: (with others) The Surgical Neonate, 1978, rev. 1985; assoc. editor, Jour. Pediatric Surgery, 1985-2000; mem. editorial bd. Pediatrics, 1990-97; contbr. articles to profl. jours. Bd. dirs. Pediatric Family Ctr. of N.C. (Ronald McDonald House), Durham, 1980-90, Surgeon Gen.'s Workshop on Drunk Driving, chmn. Citizens Adv. Panel, 1988; mem. exec. bd. Met. Drug Commn., Knoxville, 1993-2000, v.p., 1997-2000, chair DUI task force, 1994-99. Served to capt. U.S. Army, 1964-66. Nat. scholar Harvard U., 1954-58. Fellow ACS (gov. 1992-98), Am. Acad. Pediatrics (surg., exec. com. 1984-91, chmn. 1989-90), Am. Pediatric Surg. Assn. (edn. com. 1984-90, sec., bd. govs. 1994-97), Am. Surg. Assn., So. Surg. Assn.; mem. Alpha Omega Alpha. Republican. Presbyterian (Stephen Minister). Avocations: water sports, sailing. Office: Univ of Tenn Med Ctr Dept Surgery Box U-11 1924 Alcoa Hwy Knoxville TN 37920-6900 Personal E-mail: hnfilstonmd@comcast.net.

FILSTRUP, (E.) CHRISTIAN, library director, dean; b. North Hollywood, Calif., May 9, 1942; s. Edward Christian and Elizabeth Jane (Merritt) F.; m. Jane Merrill, Aug. 10, 1968 (div. June 1985); children—Emma Nilufar, Burton Thomas; m. Laurie Ellen Smith, Aug. 17, 1985 BA, Haverford Coll., 1965; MA, Harvard U., 1967; MS, Columbia U., 1974. Chief oriental div. NY Pub. Libr., NYC, 1978-85; asst. chief overseas ops. Library of Congress, Washington, 1985-87, chief overseas ops., 1987; assoc. dir. collection mgmt., orgn. and preservation NC State Univ. Librs.; now dean, dir. librs. SUNY, Stony Brook. Author: Beadazzled, 1982, China, 1982; contbr. articles to profl. publs. Mem. Middle East Studies Assn., ALA, Assn. for Asian Studies, Assn. Rsch. Librs., Phi Beta Kappa, Beta Phi Mu. Avocations: jogging, swimming, tennis. Home: 15 Eastbourne Cres East Patchogue NY 11772-4832 Office: Stony Brook Univ Librs Frank Melville Jr Meml Libr Stony Brook NY 11794-3300 Office Phone: 631-632-7100. Office Fax: 631-632-7116. E-mail: christian.filstrup@stonybrook.edu.*

FINALE, FRANK L., retired elementary school educator, writer; b. Bklyn., Mar. 10, 1942; s. Ralph and Mary (Guidone) F.; m. Barbara Ann (Long), Oct. 20, 1973; children: Michael, Alan, Steven. BS in edn., Ohio State U., 1964; MA in human devel., Fairleigh Dickinson U., 1976. Tchr. Toms River Regional Sch., NJ, 1964—2002; retired, 2002; writer Jersey Shore Publs., 1996—. Presenter, Young Authors Conf., 1985—, voted tchr. of the yr., 2002-2003, East Dover Elementary and named to the State of New Jersey's 2002 Governor's Tchr. Program. Author: To the Shore Once More, 1999, To the Shore Once More Vol. II, 2001, A Gull's Story, 2002, A Gull's Story Part 2: Counting at the Shore, 2006, A Gull's Story Part 3: Colors of the Shore, 2007; editor-in-chief: Without Halos, 1985-95; editor New Renaissance, 1996—; co-editor: Under A Gull's Wing, 1996, The Poets of New Jersey: From Colonial to Contemporary, 2005; author numerous poems. Recipient: Exemplary Svc. award, Internat. Reading Assn. and Ocean County Reading Coun., 1993 Mem. NEA, Acad. Am. Poets, N.J. Edn. Assn., Ocean County Poets Collective (founding mem.). Avocations: reading, films, music, comedians. Office Phone: 732-892-1276. E-mail: ffinale@aol.com.

FINAN, IRIAL, beverage company executive; b. Castlerea, Ireland; married; 2 children. B. of Commerce, Nat. U. Ireland, Galway. Acct. positions Trust House Forte, 1978—80, Bord na Mona, 1980—81; acct. positions Coca-Cola Bottlers Coca-Cola Co., Dublin, 1981—84, fin. contr., fin. dir. Coca-Cola Bottlers Ireland, 1984—90, mng. dir. Coca-Cola Bottlers Ulster, 1991—93, mng. dir. Coca-Cola Bottlers Romania and Bulgaria, 1994; mng. dir. Molino Beverages, 1995—97; joint mng. dir. Hellenic Bottling Co., 1997—99; region dir. then CEO Coca-Cola HBC Coca-Cola Co., Athens, Greece, 2000—03, pres. bottling investment Atlanta, 2004—, bd. dir., 2004—. Office: Coca-Cola Co One Coca-Cola Plaza Atlanta GA 30313*

FINBERG, JAMES MICHAEL, lawyer; b. Balt., Sept. 6, 1958; s. Laurence and Harriet (Levinson) Finberg; m. Melanie Piech; children: Joseph, John. BA, Brown U., 1980; JD, U. Chgo., 1983. Bar: Calif. 1984, U.S. Dist. Ct. (no. dist.) Calif. 1984, U.S. Dist. Ct. (ea. dist.) Calif. 1987, U.S. Ct. Appeals (9th and fed. cirs.) 1987, U.S. Dist. Ct. Hawaii, 1988, U.S. Supreme Ct. 1994. Law clk. to assoc. justice Mich. Supreme Ct., 1983-84; assoc. Feldman, Waldman and Kline, San Francisco, 1984-87, Morrison and Foerster, 1987-90; ptnr. Lieff, Cabraser, Heimann & Bernstein, L.L.P., San Francisco, 1991—2006, Altshuler Berzon, San Francisco, 2007—. Lawyer rep. to 9th Jud. Conf., 1999-2001 (chair No. Calif. del. 2000-01); adv. com. local rules for securities cases U.S. Dist. Ct., Calif., 1996. Exec. editor U. Chgo. Law Rev., 1982-83. Named one of Best Lawyers in Am., 2005—07, Top 100 Superlawyers in San Francisco Bay Area, 2005—07, Top 100 Lawyers in Calif., 2006. Fellow: Am. Coll. Labor and Employment Lawyers; mem.: ACLU (bd. dirs. No. Calif. chpt. 1995), ABA (chmn. securities subcom. class and derivative action com. 1998—2006, plaintiff's program chair equal employment opportunity com. 1999—2001), Lawyers Com. for Civil Rights of San Francisco Bay Area (fin. chmn. 1992—95, bd. dirs. 1992—98, sec. 1996, co-chmn. 1997—98), Calif. Bar Assn. (mem. standing com. on legal svcs. to poor 1990—94, vice-chmn. 1993—94), Bar Assn. San Francisco (jud. evaluation com. 1994, bd. dirs. 1999—2000, sec. 2002, treas. 2003, pres.-elect. 2004, pres. 2005). Office: Altshuler Berzon 177 Post St Ste 300 San Francisco CA 94108 Office Phone: 415-421-7151. Business E-Mail: jfinberg@altshulerberzon.com.

FINBERG, LAURENCE, pediatrician, educator, dean; b. Chgo., May 20, 1923; s. Joseph and Anne (Malkow) F.; m. Harriet Levinson, June 17, 1945 (dec. Jan. 1994); children: Robert, Jeanne, James; m. Joann Quane, Mar. 17, 1995. BS, U. Chgo., 1944, MD, 1946. Diplomate: Am. Bd. Pediatrics (examiner 1969-94, bd. dirs. 1974-79, 82-88 , pres. 1978, chmn. 1987). Intern U. Chgo. Clinics, 1946-47; asst. resident pediatrics Balt. City Hosps., 1949-50, resident in pediat., 1950-51; practice medicine specializing in pediat. Balt., 1951-63, NYC, 1963-94; asst. chief pediatrician Balt. City Hosps., 1951-61, dir. pediatric out-patient dept., 1951-63, dir. premature nursery, 1951-59, assoc. chief pediatrics, 1961-63; pediatrician Harriet Lane Home, 1951-63; chmn. dept. pediatrics Montefiore Hosp. and Med. Center, Bronx, NY, 1963-80, SUNY Health Sci. Ctr., Bklyn., 1982-95, prof. pediatrics, 1982-95, prof. emeritus, 1995—, dean, 1988-91; prof. clin. pediat. U. Calif., San Francisco, 1995—, Stanford U. Sch. Med., 1997—. Instr. pediatrics Johns Hopkins U., 1951-56; asst. prof., 1956-63; prof. pediatrics Albert Einstein Coll. Medicine, Yeshiva U., Bronx, 1963-82, chmn., 1968-80; cons. in field; pediatric adv. com. NYC Dept. Health, 1970-94 Mem. editl. bd. Jour. Pediat., 1973-83, Am. Jour. Diseases of Children, 1984-94, named changed to Archives of Pediat. and Adolescent Medicine, 1994-2002, editor nutrition sect., 1995-2002; editor Saunders Manual of Pediat. Practice, 1997, 2002 Served with USPHS, 1947-49. Recipient Bela Schick medal, 1992, Nutrition award Am. Acad. Pediatrics, 1992. Mem. AAAS, AMA (Goldberger Clin. Nutrition award 1993), Am. Pediatric Soc., Soc. Pediatric Research, Am. Acad. Pediatrics (com. on environ. hazards 1968-83, chmn. 1979-83, com. nutrition 1983-89—, chmn. 1984-89), Am. Coll. Nutrition, Am. Soc. for Nutritional Scis., Nat. Cholesterol Edn. Program Coordinating Com. (panel on children and adolescents 1989-93), Ambulatory Pediatric Assn., Am. Soc. Clin. Nutrition, Am. Fedn. Clin. Research, Sociedad Peruana de Pediatria, Sociedad Dominica De Pediatria, Harvey Soc., N.Y. Acad. Medicine (past chmn. pediatric sec.), Phi Beta Kappa, Sigma Xi, Alpha Omega Alpha. Achievements include research in electrolyte physiology. Home: 152 Lombard St Apt 602 San Francisco CA 94111-1134 Home Phone: 415-398-6205; Office Phone: 415-398-6205. Personal E-mail: laurence.finberg@ucsf.edu.

FINCH, CAROL, librarian; b. Ohio; married; 2 children. B, Ohio U., Athens; MLS, U. Iowa. Libr. Phoenix Pub. Libr., 1988—, coord. children & teen svcs., 2001—. Recipient Rising Moon Outstanding Youth Svc. award, Ariz. Libr. Assn., 2002, NY Times Libr. award, 2006. Office: Burton Barr Libr 1221 N Ctrl Ave Phoenix AZ 85004 Office Phone: 602-262-4636.

FINCH, CHRISTOPHER ROBIN, writer; b. Guernsey, Channel Islands, Great Britain, Dec. 31, 1939; s. Roy Colin Finch and Beatrice Amy Vaudin; m. Linda Rosenkrantz, Feb. 2, 1973; 1 child, Chloe. Co-author: (books) Gone Hollywood; author: In the Market, The Making of the Lion King, In the Market, Jim Henson: The Works, Nineteenth Century Watercolors, Beer: a Connoiseur's Guide the the World's Best, Special Effects, Of Muppets and Men, Norman Rockwell: 332 Magazine Covers, Norman Rockwell's America, The Art of the Lion King, The Art of Walt Disney, In the Market, The Art of the Lion King, Jim Henson: The Works, Highways to Heaven, Jim Henson: the Works, Special Effects: The Art of Movie Magic, Of Muppets and Men, The Art of Walt Disney, (artist monograph) Patrick Caulfield, (biographies) Rainbow: The Stormy Life of Judy Garland, (art history books) American Watercolors, Pop Art: Object and Image, 20th Century Watercolors, American Watercolors, Norman Rockwell: 332 Magazine Covers, Twentieth Century Watercolors, Norman Rockwell's America, 19th Century Watercolors, Image as Language, Pop Art: Object and Image, Image as Language, (art monograph) Chuck Close: Work, Patrick Caulfield. Personal E-mail: chriscresse@earthlink.net.

FINCH, EDWARD RIDLEY, JR., lawyer, educator, retired diplomat, ambassador; b. Westhampton Beach, NY, Aug. 31, 1919; AB with Atwater honors, Princeton U., 1941; JD, NYU, 1947; LLD (hon.), Mo. Valley Coll., 1963; DSc (hon.), Cumberland Coll., 1985. Bar: N.Y. 1948, U.S. Supreme Ct. 1953, D.C. 1978, Fla. 1980, Pa. 1992. Ptnr. Finch & Schaefler, NYC, 1950-85; of counsel Le Boeuf, Lamb, Leiby & MacRae, NYC, 1986-88; commr. City of N.Y., 1955-58. V.p. gen. counsel, dir. St. Giles Found., 1964—, Am. Internat. Petroleum Corp., 1988-92; U.S. del. 4th UN Congress, Geneva, 1970, 5th UN Congress, Japan, 1975; U.S. spl. ambassador to Panama, 1972; legal advisor, mem. U.S. Del. UNISPACE II, 1982, UNISPACE III, Vienna, Austria, 1999; lectr. in field. Author: Holes in Your Pockets, 3rd edit., Astro Business-A Guide to Commerce and Law of Outer Space, Judicial Politics; contbr. articles to profl. jours. Pres., bd. dirs. St. Nicholas Soc. N.Y., 1948—; past pres. N.Y. Inst. Spl. Edn., 1950—; bd. govs. Nat. Space Soc., 1984—; mem. faculty adv. com. dept. politics Princeton U.; bd. dirs., treas. Jessie Ridley Found., N.Y.C., Finch Trusts; pres. Adams Meml. Fund Inc.; v.p. St. Giles Found.; trustee St. Andrew's Dune Ch., Southampton, Cathedral of St. John the Divine, 1989-92, Whittell Trust, Am. Found. Cancer Rsch.; life trustee Met. Mus. of Art, N.Y.C.; mem. Coun. Am. Ambs. Col. JAG, USAFR, 1941-72. Decorated U.S. Legion of Merit with oak leaf cluster; Order Brit. Empire; Knight Order St. John; comdr. French Legion of Honor, Disting. Eagle Scout, Coun. of Am. Ambs Fellow Am. Bar Found. (chmn. aerospace coun. sect. sci. and tech 1986-92); mem. ABA (ho. of dels. 1971-72, chmn. corp. lawyers sr. lawyer divsn., chmn. aerospace law divsn. internat. law sect.1973-79), AIAA (sr.), FBA, Inter-Am. Bar Assn. (Hallgartern telecommunications award 1991), N.Y. State Bar Assn. (internat. law and practice sec., chmn. arms control and nat. security com.), Pa. Bar Assn., Fla. Bar Assn., Assn., Bar City of N.Y., Internat. Bar Assn., Judge Advs. Assn. U.S. (past pres.), Am. Law Inst., Am. Judicature Soc. (sr.), Internat. Astronautical Acad. (full elected mem.), Internat. Inst. Space Law (Lifetim Disting. Svc. award 1997), Nat. Space Soc. (bd. dirs.), Am. Arbitration Assn. (panelist), Univ. Clubs of Wash. and N.Y., Union League Club, Union Club, Princeton Club (bd. govs. 1982—), L.I. Club, Bathing Corp. of Southampton, Westhampton Country Club, Hillsboro Club (sr.). Office: 862 Park Ave New York NY 10021-1831 Office Phone: 212-327-0493. Office Fax: 212-327-0593. Personal E-mail: erfinchjr@aol.com.

FINCH, EVELYN VORISE, financial planner; b. Marietta, Ohio, Jan. 20, 1930; d. Richard Raymon Juantzee and Oreatha Fay (Carnes) Metcalf; m. Herman Frederick Ahrens, May 13, 1948 (dec. Apr. 2006); children: Erick K.F. Ahrens, Hilda Kate Ahrens(dec.) , Nicole Schwartz; m. James Derwood Finch, June 29, 1973 (dec. Oct. 1993). BS in Music Edn., Concord U., Athens, W.Va., 1961; postgrad., U. Md., Coll. Park, 1962—63, Am. U., Washington, 1964, Northeastern U., Boston, 1990. Registered Health Underwriter, Boston. Music tchr. Prince George's County Pub. Schs., 1961—72; pvt. piano tchr. Washington, 1961—73; sales rep. china and crystal Quality Products Co., Washington, 1973—80; ins. agt. Mut. of Omaha Cos., Washington, 1980—92, Memphis, 1992—94; pvt. practice Alamo, Tenn., 1994—; tax specialist H&R Block Inc., Jackson, Tenn., 2002—06. Ind. assoc. Pre-Paid Legal Svcs., Inc., 2000—. Supporting mem. Nat. Mus. Women in Arts, Washington, 1990—, Women's Philharm., San Francisco, 1993—. Mem.: LWV (Memphis br.), AAUW (br. pres. 1994—96, Tenn. chmn. ednl. found. 1996—98, mem. Nat. Diversity Resource Team 1997—2000), Internat. Assn. Fin. Planners, Nat. Assn. Health Underwriters (registered health underwriter), Nat. Assn. Ret. Fed. Employees, Chesapeake Bay Yacht Clubs Assn. (commodore 1982), Prince George's Yacht Club (commodore 1978), Potomas River Yacht Clubs Assn. (legis. chair 1978-87), Nat. Boating Fedn. (pres. 1985—87), Kappa Delta Pi, Pi Mu. Home and Office: 208 Finch Rd Alamo TN 38001-5923 Office Phone: 731-656-2002. Personal E-mail: evelynfinch@msn.com.

FINCH, FLOYD RAYMOND, JR., lawyer; b. Independence, Mo., Nov. 26, 1953; s. Floyd Raymond and Marjorie Lee (Marriott) F.; m. Joann Kay Stanley, Aug. 17, 1974; children: Aubrey, Nicholas. AB magna cum laude, U. Mo., 1974; JD, Harvard U., 1977. Bar: Mo. 1977, Kans. 1995, US Dist. Ct. (we. dist.) Mo. 1977, US Ct. Appeals (8th cir.) 1979, US Supreme Ct. 1981, US Ct. Appeals (10th cir.) 1988, US Dist. Ct. Kans. 1995. Law Clerk Hon. John W. Oliver Chief Judge US Dist. Ct. (we. dist.) Mo., Kansas City, 1977-79; assoc. Blackwell Sanders Matheny Weary & Lombardi, Kansas City, 1979-84, pntr., 1984—, Blackwell Sanders Peper Martin LLP, Kansas City, Mo., 1984—. Lctr. U. Kans. Sch. Law, 2002. Mem. Jackson County Dem. Com., Kansas City, 1984-90, Mo. Dem. Com., Jefferson City, 1986-90; bd. dirs. Dem. Victory Coalition, Kansas City, 1985—, com. County Progress, Youth Soccer Coach. Recipient Best Lawyers in Am., Blackwell Sanders, 2007. Mem.: Mo. Orgn. of Def. Lawyers, Mo Bar Assn. Office: Blackwell Sanders Peper Martin LLP 4801 Main St Ste 1000 Kansas City MO 64112 Office Phone: 816-983-8128. Office Fax: 816-983-8080. Business E-Mail: ffinch@blackwellsanders.com.

FINCH, JANET BUSWELL, musician; b. Columbus, Ohio, Aug. 26, 1955; d. Delbert LeRoy and Marjorie Rose Buswell; m. Monte Gene Finch; children: Stephanie Elise, Randall James. Student, Am. Inst. Musical Studies, 1977; MusB, Ohio State U., 1978; postgrad., U. Cin., 2000—. Staff, profl. accompanist Murray State U., Ky., 1996—99; instr. U. Cin., 2002. Profl. accompanist Murray State U., Murray, Ky.; adjudicator Murray Woman's Club Sophomore Scholarship Auditions, Murray, 1987, Ohio Music Tchr.'s Assn., Cin., 2003, Murray Music Tchr.'s Assn., 2005; accompanist U. Cin., 2000—03; rehearsal accompanist Dayton Opera Assn., Ohio, 1983; part-time faculty U. Akron, 1982—83. Sec. exec. bd. Murray Civic Music Assn., 2004; mem. Murray State U. Parent Orgn.; com. First Bapt. Ch., Murray, 2004, Fellowship of Christian Women, 2004; grant rev. bd. U. Cin. Grad. Student Governance Assn.; adult learning com. Nat. Pedagogy Conf., Princeton, NJ, 2001—03; monitor MTNA, Murray, 1999—; membership bd. Stuart Poston Wellness Ctr., 2003—04. Recipient Grad. Student of Yr., U. Cin. Grad. Student Governance Assn., 2000—03; scholar, U. Cin., Coll. Conservatory Music, 1999—, Dept. Secondary Piano and Pedagogy, 2002. Mem.: Ky. Music Tchr.'s Assn., Sigma Alpha Ipsilon (hon. Hon. Patroness Mem. 1999). Republican. Baptist. Avocations: exercise, reading, bible study, writing, travel. Home Phone: 270-753-0815.

FINCH, LAWRENCE NELSON, II, computer scientist, consultant; b. Bklyn., June 26, 1943; s. Lawrence N. and Amelia Julia (Weiss) F.; m. Patricia Moldauer, June 20, 1976 (div. July 1980); m. Wanda Richards, Sept. 27, 1981; 1 child, Abigail Emily. BEE, NYU, 1966; MS in Computer Sci., Stevens Inst. Tech., Hoboken, NJ, 1978. Engr. Airborne Instruments Lab., Deer Park, NY, 1966-70, Republic Electronic Industries Corp.,

Farmingdale, NY, 1970-73; tech. staff Schering Pharm., Bloomfield, NJ, 1973-74; regional analyst mgr. computer div. Tex. Instruments, Clark, NJ, 1974-80; v.p., tech. dir. Prolifics, NYC, NJ, 1980—. Recipient NSF rsch. grant, 1965. Achievements include patent for fixed compound lens scanning microwave antenna with moveable feed. Office: Prolifics 22 Cortlandt St Fl 18 New York NY 10007 Personal E-mail: finches@bellatlantic.net, finches@gmail.com. Business E-Mail: lfinch@prolifics.com.

FINCH, MICHAEL PAUL, lawyer; b. Galveston, Tex., Jan. 4, 1946; s. Albert Lynn and Ila Belle (Robertson) Finch; m. Rebecca Jean Minnear, Dec. 27, 1969; children: Michael Paul, Rachelle Jean. BA cum laude, Rice U., 1969, MEE, 1969; JD magna cum laude, U. Houston, 1972. Bar: Tex. 1973. Petroleum engr. Exxon Corp., Houston, 1969-72; assoc. Vinson & Elkins LLP, Houston, 1972—79, ptnr., 1980—. Bd. dirs. Rice Engring. Alumni, 1994—98; dir. Houston Pops Orch., 1988—89. Master: Am. Contact Bridge League (life); mem.: Houston Bar Assn., Tex. Bar Assn. Republican. Methodist. Avocations: electronics, woodworking, skiing, piano. Home: 12531 Overcup Dr Houston TX 77024-4915 Office: Vinson & Elkins LLP 2300 First City Tower 1001 Fannin St Houston TX 77002-6706 Business E-Mail: mfinch@velaw.com.

FINCH, RAYMOND LAWRENCE, judge; b. Christiansted, St. Croix, VI, Oct. 4, 1940; s. Wilfred Christopher and Beryl Elaine (Bough) Finch; m. Anne Marie Mohammed, May 8, 1996; children: Alison, Mark, Jennifer. AB, Howard U., 1962, JD, 1965. Bar: V.I. 1971, Ct. Appeals (3d cir.) 1976. Law clk. Judge's Municipal Ct. V.I., 1965-66, Hodge, Sheen Finch & Ross, 1969—70; ptnr. Hodge, Sheen, Finch & Ross, Christiansted, 1970-75; judge Territorial Ct. V.I., Charlotte Amalie, 1975-86, Ct. Appeals, V.I., Charlotte Amalie, 1986-94, US Dist. Ct. V.I., 1994—, chief judge, 1999. Instr. grad. divsn. Coll. V.I., Am. Inst. Banking, 1976—. Bd. dirs. Boy Scouts Am., Boys Club Am. Served to capt. US Army, 1966—69. Decorated Commendation medal U.S. Army, Bronze Star. Mem.: ABA, Internat. Assn. Chiefs Police, Nat. Bar Assn., Am. Judges Assn. Democrat. Lutheran. Address: PO Box 24051 Christiansted VI 00824-0051 Home Phone: 340-773-1130; Office Phone: 340-773-5021. E-mail: rfinch@vitelcom.net.

FINCH, ROBERT JONATHAN, communications engineer, consultant; b. Chgo., Sept. 21, 1955; s. Herman Manuel and Frances (Gutlow) Finch; m. Gayle Deborah Falk, Mar. 28, 1991; children: Layla Michelle, Grant Dillon. BA in Broadcast Mgmt., U. So. Calif., 1977. Engr.-in-charge LFI Prodns., Inc., Lafayette, Ind., 1990—92; comm. engring. cons. LA, 1978—90, Lafayette, 1992—. Developer ABC Hollywood's 1st satellite video-tape ctr., Saudi Arabia's 1st color TV studio; contbr. articles to profl. jours. Mem.: Hollywood Magic Castle, Tippecanoe Amateur Radio Assn. (trustee), Pasadena Casting Club (instr.). Achievements include development of 1st digitally based pub. transponder in a 2-way radio service in continental U.S; 1st large volume, pub. access and radio accessed computer database in U.S. Avocations: fly fishing, close-up magic. Home: 10436 Calle Perdiz NW Albuquerque NM 87114-1311 Business E-Mail: bfinch@computersthatwork.com.

FINCH, WARREN L., JR., library director, archivist; Archivist Office of Presdl. Libraries, Nat. Archives, Washington, Ronald Reagan Presdl. Libr. Project, Calif.; dep. dir. George H. W. Bush Presdl. Libr., College Station, Tex., dir., 2004—. Office: Bush Presdl Libr 1000 George Bush Dr W College Station TX 77845 Office Phone: 979-691-4000.*

FINCHEM, TIM, sports association executive; BA, U. Richmond, 1969; JD, U. Va., 1973. Dep. advisor econ. affairs White House, Washington, 1978—79; nat. staff dir. Jimmy Carter-Walter Mondale Presdl. Campaign, 1980; pres. Beckel, Finchem, Toricelli and Assocs., Washington, 1980—84; co-founder Nat. Strategies and Mktg. Group, Washington, 1984—87; v.p. bus. affairs PGA Tour, Ponte Vedra Beach, Fla., 1987—94, commr., 1994—. Co-founder World Golf Found., First Tee program; developer World Golf Hall of Fame, World Golf Village. Office: PGA Tour 112 PGA Tour Blvd Ponte Vedra Beach FL 32082

FINCHER, CAMERON LANE, psychology professor; b. Douglas County, Ga., Nov. 4, 1926; s. Andrew Jackson and Ada (Swafford) F.; m. Mary Frances Cutts, June 15, 1957; children: Marcel Andriette, Matthew Donnellan, Ada Amanda, Melissa Lane. B.C.S., Ga. State U., 1950; MA, U. Minn., 1951; PhD, Ohio State U., 1956. Lic. psychologist, Ga. Dir. testing and counseling Ga. State U., Atlanta, 1956-65; assoc. dir. Inst. Higher Edn., U. Ga., Athens, 1965-69, dir. Inst., 1969-99, prof. higher edn. and psychology, 1965—, Regents prof. higher edn. and psychology, 1981—. Cons. various indsl. and comml. cos., also state governing bds. colls. and univs., La., S.C., Ala., Tenn.; mem. Gov.'s Com. on Postsecondary Edn., Ga., 1978-83; mem. rsch. panel So. Edn. Found., 1978-86. Author: A Preface to Psychology, 1972, Challenge of Reform in Higher Education, 1991, Historical Development of the University System of Georgia, 1991, 2d edit., 2003, Administrative Leadership in Academic Governance and Management, 2003; co-author: One Hundred Classic Books in Higher Education, 2001; contbg. columnist: Athens Banner-Herald, 1970-90; editor: Planning Imperatives for the 1990s, 1989, Assessing Institutional Effectiveness in Higher Education, 1989, Defining and Assessing Quality, 1994, IHE Perspectives, 1999—; contbg. editor: Greenwood Dictionary of Education, 2003; contbg. editor Rsch. in Higher Edn., 1978—; contbr. articles to profl. jours. Served with USNR, 1944-46. Recipient Disting. Achievement in Public Service medallion U. Ga., 1980, 2000, Ben W. Gibson award So. Regional Council, Coll. Bd., 1982; Ga. Ho. of Reps. and Senate Resolution recognizing contbns. to higher edn. and State of Ga., 1986, Abraham Baldwin award U. Ga. Alumni Assn., 1991. Mem. APA, Ga. Assn. Instnl. Rsch., Planning, Assessment and Quality (1st recipient Cameron Lane Fincher outstanding svc. award 1997), Assn. Study of Higher Edn. (Howard Bowen Disting. Career award 1991), So. Assn. Instl. Rsch. (James R. Montgomery award 1991), Am. Assn. Higher Edn., Assn. Instnl. Rsch. (Disting. Mem. 1983, Outstanding Svc. award 1980, AIR/Suslow award, 1995), So. Assn. Instnl. Rsch. (disting.), Alpha Kappa Psi, Phi Delta Kappa, Golden Key Office: U Ga Inst Higher Edn Meigs Hall Athens GA 30602 E-mail: cfincher@uga.edu.

FINCHER, DAVID, film director and producer; b. Denver, Aug. 28, 1962; m. Donya Fiorentino (div.); 1 child. With Industrial Light & Magic, 1981—83; co-founder Propaganda Films, 1987. Dir.: (films) Alien 3, 1992, Seven, 1995, The Game, 1997, The Fight Club, 1999, Panic Room, 2002, Zodiac, 2007; (music videos) Don Henley, Sting, The Wallflowers, Paula Abdul, Aerosmith, Madonna, Michael Jackson, George Michael, Rolling Stones (Grammy award for best music video "Love is Strong", 1995), Steve Winwood, The Motels, Iggy Pop, Billy Idol, A Perfect Circle; exec. prodr. (films) Ambush, 2001, Chosen, 2001, The Follow, 2001, Star, 2001, Powder Keg, 2001, The Ticker, 2002, Lords of Dogtown, 2005, Love and Other Disasters, 2006; dir. (TV commericals) for Nike, Coca-Cola, Budweiser, Heineken, Pepsi, Levi's, Converse, AT & T, and Chanel. Office: Creative Arts Agy care Joe Rosenberg 9830 Wilshire Blvd Beverly Hills CA 90212-1804*

FINCHER, EDGAR FRANKLIN, dermatologic surgeon; b. Dallas, Apr. 23, 1966; s. Edgar Franklin Fincher, III and Elaine Allen Reinika; m. Helen Horn Fincher, July 13, 1991; children: Eden Montgomery, Avery Michele, Harrison Nichols. BS in Biology, Rhodes Coll., 1988; PhD in Physiology, U. Tenn., Memphis, 1997, MD, 1997. Bd. cert. dermatology Am. Bd. Dermatology, 2004. Postdoctoral rsch. fellow Stanford (Calif.) U., 1998—2001, dermatology resident, 2001—04; fellow Mohs micrographic surgery, laser and cosmetic surgery Ronald L. Moy, MD, LA, 2004—05; dermatologic surgeon Moy-Fincher Med. Group, LA, 2005—; clin. instr. David Geffen Sch. Medicine, UCLA, 2004—. Editor: (reference text) Advanced Facelift, 2006, Blepharoplasty; contbr. chapters to books, articles to profl. jours. Grantee, NIH, 1999—2001. Fellow: Am. Acad. Cosmetic Surgery, Am. Coll. Mohs Micrographic Surgery and Cutaneous Oncology, Am. Acad. Dermatology; mem.: Am. Acad. Dermatologic Surgery. Office: Moy-Fincher Medical Group 100 UCLA Medical Plaza suite 590 Los Angeles CA 90024 Home Phone: 310-794-7422; Office Phone: 310-794-7422.

FINCHER, MARGARET ANN, librarian, educator; b. Harrodsburg, Ky., June 2, 1934; d. Henry Alexander and Minnie Bee (White) Cathey; m. Willie John Fincher, Jr., Apr. 1, 1955; children: John Richard, Joseph Michael, Judy Darlene, James Andrew. BS in Bus. Edn., Auburn U., 1955; MEd, U. New Orleans, 1978. Bookkeeper, Markle's Drug Store, Auburn, Ala., 1952-54; asst. to dir. Auburn U. Library, 1955; elem. tchr., Birmingham, Ala., 1958-64; bus. edn. tchr. Abramson HS, New Orleans, 1964-01; ret., 2001; owner, mgr. craft shop Fanci Krafts, New Orleans, 1977-78; asst. supr. Shaklee Corp., 1979-85; libr., media ctr. dept. chmn. Abramson Sr. High Sch. Orleans Parish Sch. Bd., 1984-99, libr. media cons. Faith Christian Acad., 2004—. Supr. adult Bible tng. dept. Word of Faith Temple, 1982-94, cons. library devel., 1982, tchr., 1975-80, deaconess, 1983—; bd. dirs. Lamb Day Care Center, 1979-81; sustaining mem. Meth. Hosp. Aux., 1967—; adv./sponsor Christian Life on Campus Club. Recipient Am. Legion citation of appreciation, 1981; Future Bus. Leaders Am., award of Appreciation, 1976. Mem. ALA, Donna Villa Improvement Assn., Metro. Ednl. Media Orgn., Ch. and Synagogue Library Assn., So. Bus. Edn. Assn., Nat. Bus. Edn. Assn., La. Assn. Bus. Edn., La. Library Assn., La. Vocat. Assn., United Tchrs. New Orleans, Policemen's Assn. New Orleans (hon.), Tamaron Homeowners Assn. (treas. 1992—), Abramson Libr. Media Club (sponsor 1986-01), Phi Delta Kappa. Republican. Mem. Christian Ch. Home: 211 Lake Sabine Ct Slidell LA 70461

FINCHER, RUTH MARIE EDLA, medical educator, dean; b. Hartford, Conn., Dec. 16, 1949; d. Wilber Roe and Hannah Camilla (Andersen) Griswold; m. Michael Edward Fincher, June 26, 1977. BA, Colby Coll., 1972; BMS, Dartmouth U., 1974; MD, Emory U., 1976. Diplomate Am. Bd. Internal Medicine. Intern then resident internal medicine Emory Hosps., Atlanta, 1976-79; practicing internist Pub. Health Svc., Ludowici, Ga., 1979-81; pvt. practice internal medicine Hinesville, Ga., 1981-82; staff physician Am. Lake VA Med. Ctr., Tacoma, Wash., 1982-84; asst. prof. medicine Med. Coll. Ga., Augusta, 1984-89, assoc. prof., 1989-94, prof. medicine, 1994—, vice dean acad. affairs, 1994—. Pres. Clerkship Dirs. in Internal Medicine, Washington, 1992—93; com. chair Nat. Bd. Med. Examiners, Phila., 1995—96, bd. dirs., 2005—; co-chair rsch. in med. edn. com. Assn. Am. Med. Colls., Washington, 1995—96, chair group on ednl. affairs, 1996—97. Co-editor: Clinical Medicine 2nd Edit., 1995; contbr. articles to profl. jours. Bd. dirs. Nat. Bd. Med. Examiners at Large, 2005—07, mem. exec. com., 2007—. Fellow: ACP (gov. Ga. chpt. 2003—07, bd. dirs. ACP Found., J. Willis Hurst Tchg. award 1994, Disting. Tchg. award 1996); mem.: Assn. Am. Med. Colls. (Ednl. Affiars Career scholarship So. Group 2006, Merrel Flair award 2006), Alpha Omega Alpha (bd. dirs. 2003—, Robert J. Glaser Disting. Tchg. award 1996, Daniel S. Tostesen award 2003, Inaugural inductee U. Sys. Ga. Hall of Fame 2004). Avocations: woodworking, gardening, running. Office: Med Coll Ga CB 1843 1457 Laney Walker Blvd Augusta GA 30912 Office Phone: 706-721-3529. Business E-Mail: rfincher@mail.mcg.edu.

FINCHUM, GEORGE ALLEN, II, geography educator; b. Johnson City, Tenn., May 4, 1958; s. George Allen and Bernice Self Finchum; m. Tanya Lynn Ducker, Aug. 23, 1980; 1 child, Curtis. BS, East Tenn. State U., 1979; MA, U. Cin., 1985; PhD, U. Tenn., 1992. Cert. in data processing Inst. for the Cert. Computer Profls. Jr. programmer Gt. Am. Ins. Co., Cin., 1981-83; programmer, analyst Appalachian Nat. Life Ins., Knoxville, 1983-84; sys. specialist U. Tenn., Knoxville, 1984-93, rsch. assoc., 1995-96; asst. prof. Okla. State U., Stillwater, 1996—. Avocations: sports, travel. Office: Okla State U Dept Of Geography Stillwater OK 74078-0001 Fax: (405) 744-5620. E-mail: finchum@okstate.edu.

FINCK, CHRISTINE M., pediatric surgeon, educator; d. Stan and Joyce Finck; m. John J. Laplante, Feb. 8, 2003; 1 child, Isabelle Rose Laplante. MD, SUNY, Syracuse, 1994. Diplomate ACS, pediat. surgery ACS. Resident SUNY Health Sci. Ctr., Syracuse, 2000; fellow Ark. Children's, Little Rock, 2002; asst. prof. pediat. and surgery St. Christopher's Hosp., Phila., 2002—. Contbr. chapters to books, articles to profl. jours.; editor: (Resident's Column) Nutrition: The Internat. Jour. Applied and Basic Nutritional Scis., 1997—2000; manuscript reviewer: Critical Care Medicine, 2004, Tissue Engring., 2005. Organizer Erie Ave. Walk for Health and Fitness. Recipient Brookhaven Vol. Youth award, Brookhaven Twp., 1986, Resident Tchg. award, Syracuse U., 2000; grantee, CUMG, 2001—02, St. Christopher's Found. for Children, 2002, 2003, 2004, Mary Dewitt Found., 2004, Synergy, 2004, NIH, 2005. Mem.: AMA, ACS (assoc. Resident Paper award Upstate chpt. 1997), Am. Med. Women's Assn., Am. Soc. Bariatric Surgery, Am. Soc. Gen. Surgeons, Assn. Acad. Surgery (instnl. rep.), Am. Heart Assn. (cert. instr. advanced trauma and life support). Achievements include development of Healthy Weight Awareness Center to combat childhood obesity. Office: St Christophers Hosp Dept Surgery Erie at Front St Philadelphia PA 19134

FINCK, KEVIN WILLIAM, lawyer; b. Whittier, Calif., Dec. 14, 1954; s. William Albert and Ester (Gutbub) F.; m. Kathleen A. Miller, Oct. 7, 1989. BA in History, U. Calif., Santa Barbara, 1977; JD, U. Calif., San Francisco, 1980. Bar: Calif. 1980. Ptnr. Ord and Norman, 1985—88; pvt. practice San Francisco, 1989—. Lectr. Internat. Bar Assn., Learning Annex. Author: California Corporation Start Up Package and Minute Book, 1982, 10th edit., 2005; contbr. articles to various profl. jours. Avocations: hiking, golf, travel. Office: Ste 1670 Two Embarcadero Ctr San Francisco CA 94111 Office Phone: 415-296-9100. Personal E-mail: kevin@kevinfinck.com.

FINCKE, EDWARD MICHAEL (MIKE), astronaut; b. Pitts., Mar. 14, 1967; s. Edward and Alma Fincke; m. Renita Saikia; 2 children. BSc in Aero. & Astronautics, MIT, 1989, BSc in Earth, Atmospheric & Planetary Sci., 1989; MSc in Aero. & Astronautics, Stanford U., 1990; Msc in Physical Sci. (Planetary Geology), U. Houston, 2001. Commd. 2d lt. USAF, 1989, advanced through grades to lt. col., various assignments, 1990—94, lt. col., mem. 39th flight test squadron, flight test engineer Eglin AFB, Fla., 1994—96; flight test liaison USAF, Gifu Test Ctr., Gifu Air Base, Japan, 1996; astronaut NASA, Houston, 1996—. Astronaut Internat. Space Sta. Expedition , 2001. Decorated three Commendation medals USAF, two Achievement medals, Meritorious Svc. Medal; recipient DSM, NASA, Spaceflight Medal, ISS Leadership award. Mem.: British Interplanetary Soc., Geological Soc. Am. Achievements include technical duties in the Astronaut Office Station Operations Branch serving as an International Space Station Spacecraft Communicator (ISS CAPCOM); a member and flight engineer of the Crew Test Support Team in Russia; and as the ISS crew procedures team lead and flight engineer; currently back-up comdr. ISS Expedition-13. Avocations: hiking, flying, travel, geology, astronomy, reading, learning new languages. Office: Astronaut Office CB NASA Lyndon B Johnson Space Center Houston TX 77058*

FINCKENAUER, JAMES O., criminal justice educator, researcher; b. East Hampton, NY, July 16, 1939; s. Ezra M. and Sarah J. Finckenauer; m. Margaret J. Hadel, Feb. 10, 1961; children: Hedy L. McDermott, Scott D. BA, Gettysburg Coll., Pa., 1961; MA, NYU, 1965, PhD, 1971. Prof., dept. chair Trenton State Coll., Ewing, NJ, 1971—74; assoc. prof. Rutgers U., Newark, 1974—80, prof., 1980—2001, disting. prof., 2001—. Dir. internat. ctr. Nat. Inst. Justice, Washington, 1998—2002. Author: Scared Straight! and the Panacea Phenomenon, 1982, Juvenile Delinquency and Corrections: The Gap Between Theory and Practice, 1984, Organized Crime in America, 1995, Russian Youth: Law, Deviance, and the Pursuit of Freedom, 1995, Russian Mafia in America: Immigration, Culture and Crime, 1998, Scared Straight - The Panacea Phenomenon Revisited, 1999; editor: The Prediction and Control of Organized Crime: The Experience of Post-Soviet Ukraine, 2004; author: (monographs) The Threat of Russian Organized Crime, 2001, Asian Transnational Organized Crime and its Impact on the United States: Developing a Transnational Crime Research Agenda, 2006, Mafia and Organized Crime, 2007, Asian Transnational Organized Crime, 2007. 1st lt. US Army, 1961—63. Recipient Scholar Incentive award, NY State, 1963, Founder's Day award, NYU, 1971, Open Forum Distinguished Public Service award, US State Dept., 2001, Pro Humanitate Lit. award, N.Am. Resource Ctr. for Child Welfare, 2003, Jack Mark Memorial award for contbns. to criminal justice edn. at the state, nat. and internat. levels, 2005; Devel. fellow, Internat. Rsch. and Exchs. Bd., 1985. Mem.: Internat. Assn. Study of Organized Crime (pres. 1997—99), Am. Soc. Criminology, Acad. Criminal Justice Scis. (life; pres. 2004—05), Mensa. Democrat. Episcopalian. Avocations: walking, bicycling, physical fitness, reading. Office Phone: 973-353-3301.

FINDAKLY, HANI K., investment company executive; BSc in Civil Engring. magna cum laude, Baghdad U., 1966; MSc in Computer Simulation, MIT, 1971, DSc in Decision Theory, 1972. Prof. & rschr. decision theory and systems analysis MIT, 1972—75; various positions including dir, investment dept. & chief investment officer World Bank, Washington, 1975—86; mng. dir., global risk mgmt. PaineWebber Inc., NYC, 1986—88; dir., internat. div. Drexel Burnham Lambert, NYC, 1988—90; pres. Potomac Babson, Inc., NYC, 1990—99; vice chmn., dir. Clinton Group, Inc., NYC, 1999—. Visiting prof. Catholic U., Rio de Janeiro, 1973; mem. Council on Foreign Relations; gov. Middle East Inst., Wash. Office: Clinton Group 9 W 57 St 26th Fl New York NY 10019 Business E-Mail: findakly@alum.mit.edu.

FINDER, JOSEPH ALAN, writer; b. Chgo., Ill., Oct. 6, 1958; s. Morris and Natalie Finder; m. Michele Souda, Aug. 27, 1989; 1 child, Emma Josephine Souda Finder. BA summa cum laude, Yale Coll., 1980; MA, Harvard U., 1984. Writer, novelist, Boston, 1982—; writing faculty Harvard Coll., John F. Kennedy Sch. Govt., Harvard U., Cambridge, Mass., 1988, Harvard Coll./Harvard Ext. Sch., Cambridge, 1984—90. Author: Red Carpet: The Connection Between the Kremlin and America's Most Powerful Businessmen, 1983, The Moscow Club, 1991, Extraordinary Powers, 1993, The Zero Hour, 1996, High Crimes, 1998, Paranoia, 2004, Company Man, 2005, Killer Instinct, 2006; contbr. book revs. and articles to newspapers and publs. Mem.: SAG, PEN New Eng. (bd. dirs.), Boston Athaenaeum, Harvard Club Boston, Yale Club Boston, Phi Beta Kappa. E-mail: joe@josephfinder.com.

FINDLAY, DONALD CAMERON, lawyer, former federal agency administrator, insurance company executive; b. Chgo., Sept. 7, 1959; s. Donald C. and Judith R. (Lilly) F.; m. Amy Scalera, July 9, 1988; children: Alexander B., James M. BA summa cum laude, Northwestern U., 1982; MA 1st class, Oxford U., Eng., 1984; JD magna cum laude, Harvard U., 1987. Bar: Ill. 1987, D.C. 1988. Law clk. to Judge Stephen Williams US Ct. Appeals D.C. cir., Washington, 1987-88; law clk. to Justice Antonin Scalia US Supreme Ct., Washington, 1988-89; counselor to sec. US Dept. Transp., Washington, 1989-91; dep. asst. to pres. and counselor to chief of staff The White House, Washington, 1991-92; assoc. Sidley Austin Brown & Wood, Chgo., 1992-95, ptnr., 1995—2001; dep. sec. US Dept. Labor, Washington, 2001—03; exec. v.p., gen. counsel Aon Corp., Chgo., 2003—. Adj. prof. Northwestern U., Evanston, Ill., 1994-96. Trustee Northwestern U.; dir. Chgo. Coun. Global Affairs, Chgo. Shakespeare Theater, Children's Home & Aid Soc., Council Ins. Agents & Brokers; chmn. bd. visitors Weinberg Coll. Arts & Sci., Northwestern U. Office: Aon Corp 200 E Randolph St Chicago IL 60601

FINDLAY, MICHAEL ALISTAIR, art dealer, poet; b. Innellan, Scotland, May 13, 1945; came to U.S., 1964; s. Robert John Findlay and Mary Beatrice (Duffy) Collins; m. Naomi Sims, Aug. 4, 1973 (div. Jan. 1990); children: Bob, Beatrice; m. Victoria Wolfe, July 24, 1999. BA, York U., Toronto, Ont., Can., 1963. V.p., dir. exhbns. Richard L. Feigen and Co., Ltd., NYC, L.A., Chgo., 1964-70; founder, owner, dir. J.H. Duffy and Sons, Ltd., NYC, 1970-77; dir. William Beadleston Gallery, NYC, 1977-84; sr. v.p., sr. dir. Christie, Manson and Woods, NYC, 1984-94, sr. dir., 1994-97, internat. dir., 1997—; dir. fin., 1997-2000; dir. Acquevella Galleries, NYC, 2000—. Lectr. Moore Coll. Art, Phila., 1970-80; fine arts advisor N.Y.C. Parks Dept., 1979-84; mem. art adv. panel GSA, N.Y.C., 1985; keynote spkr. Oxford U. Alumnae Assn., N.Y.C., Rotary Clubs Internat., Taipei, Taiwan, Credit Suisse, Singapore, Young Pres.'s Orgn., N.Y.C., 1993-96; sr. faculty Christie's Edn., 1994-2000; bd. dirs. Christie's Internat.; mem., bd. dirs. Christie's Fine Art, Inc.; mem. art adv. panel IRS, 2002—; mem. adac. com. Christie's Edn., 2004—. Contbr. poetry and articles on art criticism to Arts, Artnews, mags. Bd. dirs. Peacemaker Found., Inc., Santa Fe, 1975—, Lacoste Sch. Arts, Vaucluse, France, Christie's Internat. Fine Arts, 1998—; hon. sec., v.p. for grants Brit. Sch. and Univs. Found., Inc., N.Y.C., 1975-85, bd. dirs., 1985—; trustee Parrish Mus., Southampton, N.Y., 1993-95; mem. adv. coun. Shanghai Mus., China, 1996; mem. scholarship com. Jade Found., N.Y.C., 1999—. Mem. ACLU, Amnesty Internat. Roman Catholic. Office: Acquavella Galleries 18 E 79th St New York NY 10021-0106

FINDLEN, PAULA ELIZABETH, history educator; b. May 19, 1964; BA, Wellesley Coll., 1984; MA, U. Calif., Berkeley, 1985, PhD, 1989. Prof. history U. Calif., Davis, 1989-96, Stanford (Calif.) U., 1996—. Vis. prof. history of sci. Harvard U., Cambridge, Mass., 1994; invited scholar-in-residence Getty Ctr., 1995-96; dir. sci., tech. and soc. program Stanford U., 1999—. Author: Possessing Nature, 1994 (Howard Marraro prize 1995, Pfizer prize 1996); editor Configurations, 1997—; mem. editl. bd. ISIS, 1996—. Recipient fellowship Am. Coun. Learned Societies, 1993-94; Guggenheim fellow, 1998—. Mem. History of Sci. Soc. (Derek Price award 1995), Sixteenth Century Studies, Renaissance Soc. Am. (Nelson prize 1990). Office: Stanford Univ Dept History Stanford CA 94305

FINDLEY, CARTER VAUGHN, historian, educator; b. Atlanta, May 12, 1941; s. John Clarke and Elizabeth (Steed) F.; m. Lucia LaVerne Blackwelder, Aug. 31, 1968; children: Madeleine Vaughn, Benjamin Carter. BA, Yale U., 1963; PhD, Harvard U., 1969. Asst. prof. Ohio State U., Columbus, 1971—79, assoc. prof., 1979—87, prof. Middle East and world history, 1987—2005, disting. prof. humanities, 2005—, co-founder world history program. Vis. mem. Inst. for Advanced Study, Princeton U., 1981-82; enseignant invité Ecole des Hautes Etudes en Scis. Sociales, Paris, 1994. Author: Bureaucratic Reform in the Ottoman Empire: The Sublime Porte, 1789-1922 , 1980, Ottoman Civil Officialdom, 1989 (Book award Ohio Acad. of History 1990, Turkish Studies Assn. 1990), The Turks in World History, 2005 (Al Mubarak Book prize, Brit.-Kuwait Friendship Soc.); co-author: Twentieth-Century World, 1986, 6th edit., 2006; contbr. articles to profl. publications. Capt. USAR, 1969-71. Recipient Disting. Scholar award, Ohio State U., 2000; Joint Com. on Near and Middle East/Am. Coun. Learned Socs./SSRC fellow, 1976-77, 79, 85-86, Nat. Endowment Humanities fellow, 2003, Guggenheim Found. fellow, 2004; Fulbright grantee, 1983, 1994, Inst. Turkish Studies grantee, 1986. Fellow Middle East Inst., Middle East Studies Assn.; mem. ACLU, Am. Hist. Assn., Am. Oriental Soc., Ohio Acad. History, Turkish Studies Assn. (pres. 1990-92), World History Assn. (exec. coun. 1991-94, pres. 2000-2002),

Turkish Acad. Sciences (hon.). Home: 2515 Sherwin Rd Columbus OH 43221-3623 Office: Ohio State U Dept History 106 Dulles Hall 230 W 17th Ave Columbus OH 43210-1361 E-mail: findley.1@osu.edu.

FINDLEY, DON AARON, manufacturing executive; b. Gadsden, Ala., June 11, 1926; s. Royal Guy and Hattie Elizabeth (Walden) F.; m. Mary Elizabeth Abernathy, Oct. 22, 1947; children: Elizabeth Jane Findley Dever, David Walden. BS, Auburn U., 1950. Acct. Buckeye Cellulose Corp. Augusta, Ga., 1950-51; acct. Tenn. Eastman Co., Kingsport, 1951-59, gen. supr. standard cost and analysis dept., 1959-64, gen. mgmt. staff, 1964-67, asst. comptroller, 1971-73, comptroller, 1975-79, v.p. fin. and adminstrn., 1979-88; mng. dir. Ectona Fibres Ltd., Cumberland, Eng., 1967-71; asst. comptroller Eastman Chem. Products, Eastman Chem. Internat. Ltd., Kingsport, 1971-73, comptroller, 1975-79, v.p. fin. and adminstrn., 1979-88; asst. comptroller Eastman Chem. Internat. Co., Kingsport, 1971-73, comptroller, 1975-79, Holston Def. Corp.; asst. v.p. Ark. Eastman Co., Carolina Eastman Co., Tex. Eastman Co. Dir. 1st Am. Nat. Bank, Kingsport Bd. dirs. Holston Valley Hosp. and Med. Ctr., Kingsport, 1978-90, treas., 1978-83; dir. United Way of Kingsport, 1994-97. Recipient Achievment award Ala. Soc. C.P.A.s, 1950, Outstanding Acctg. Alumnus award Auburn U., 1981 Fellow Inst. Dirs. (U.K.); mem. Nat. Assn. Accts. (pres. East Tenn. chpt. 1963-64), Tenn. Mfrs. and Taxpayers Assn. (bd. dirs. 1978-86), Delta Sigma Pi, Phi Kappa Phi, Beta Alpha Psi, Greater Kingsport C. of C. (bd. dirs. 1975-77) Clubs: Ridgefields Country (Kingsport) (bd. dirs. 1984-86). Republican. Methodist. Avocations: photography, coin collecting/numismatics, gardening, golf. Home: 524 Lakewood Rd Kingsport TN 37660-3420

FINDLEY, JOHN ALLEN, JR., publishing executive; b. Fulton, Mo., Feb. 25, 1951; s. John Allen and Naomi Joan (Reker) F.; m. Oneida Lynn Blackwell, Dec. 4, 1993; children: John III, Hugh. AB, Westminster Coll., 1973. Sales rep. Kingdom Daily News, Fulton, 1973-74; advt. dir. Colo. Daily, Boulder, 1973-74; advt. sales rep. Dallas Times Herald, 1976-77, advt. sales mgr., 1977-80, dir. consumer mktg., 1981-83, dir. circulation, 1983, dir. retail advt., 1983-84; regional sales mgr. Times Mirror Nat. Mktg., 1984-86; v.p. mktg. So. Conn. Newspapers, Stamford, 1986-88, sr. v.p. mktg. and prodn., 1989-93; pres. Charleston (W.Va.) Newspapers, 1993-97; pub., CEO Long Beach (Calif.) Press-Telegram, 1998—2001; v.p. newspaper rels. Parade Mag., LA, 2002—03, sr. v.p., 2003—. Bd. govs. Calif. State U., Long Beach; bd. dirs. Long Beach Found., Long Beach Venture Forum, Nat. Conf. Cmty. and Justice. Mem. Newspaper Assn. Am., Internat. Newspaper Promotion Assn., Sigma Chi. Office: 6300 Wilshire Blvd Los Angeles CA 90048

FINDLEY, KATHRYN E.C., psychologist; b. Detroit, Feb. 23, 1944; d. Oliver Clare Garwood and Elsie Madeline Everson-Garwood; m. J. D. Findley, Apr. 7, 1989; children: Raymond, Regina, Jacinda, Jason; m. Ralph Edward Cadger (div.); children: Steven Cadger, Karen Cadger, Rhonda Dauryn Cadger Soltysiak, Lauren Cadger Rogers. Diploma, Harper Hosp. Sch. Nursing, 1965; BA in Health Edn., Ottawa U., 1990; MA in Psychology, Forest Inst. Profl. Psychology, 2001, PsyD, 2003. RN. Owner, operator Sweetwater Ranch & Retreat, Edwards, Mo., 1986—; owner, pres. Sweetwater Therapeutics, Inc., 1986—; nurse mgr. Royal Oaks Hosp., Windsor, 1988—95; mental health nurse adminstr. Soleas Home Care, 1995—2002; staff nurse Lakeland Regional Hosp., Springfield, 2001—02; intern/resident Pointe Terre Wellness Ctr., Bolivar, 2002—04. Bd. dirs. Alternative Health Sys., Inc., Clinton, Mo., sec., 1997—; presenter in field; adj. prof. Forrest Inst., Springfield, Mont., 2004—. Author: Whole in One, 1995. Foster parent, 1992—97; amb. Warsaw C. of C., Warsaw, Mo., 1996—2001; commr. Warsaw City Airport Commn., 1999—2002; bd. dirs. Redlands YMCA, 1982—85; costume designer The Great Y Chorus, 1981—85. Mem.: APA (exec. divsn. 55 2004—), Mo. Psychol. Assn. Avocations: farming, gardening, sewing. Home and Office: 33292 Knabby Creek Ln Edwards MO 65326 E-mail: drkathrynf@yahoo.com.

FINDLEY, MILLA JEAN, nutritionist; b. Dallas, Aug. 14, 1934; d. Houston Henry and Juanita Imogene (Lisenbe) Shaw; m. Jack Stacy, may 29, 1952; children: Jere, David. Diploma, Rutherford Bus. Sch., Dallas, 1959; student, Mountain View C.C., 1978, El Centro C.C., 1976, Cedar Valley C.C., 1985. Tchrs. Aid diploma Stratford Career Inst., D.C., 2002, Early Childhood Edn. diploma Stratford Career Inst., D.C., 2002. File clk. Texaco Oil Co., Dallas, 1952-53; sales assoc. Toys R Us and Sears, Dallas, 1970s; nutrition specialist Cedar Hill Ind. Sch. Dist., Tex., 1983-87, Duncanville Ind. Sch. Dist., Tex., 1996—. Active cradle roll Cedar Hill Ch. of Christ, 1996. Recipient nutrition award Tex. Sch. Food Svcs. Assocs., Lewisville Ind. Sch. Dist., 1987. Mem. NAFE, Assn. Tex. Profl. Educators. Avocations: foods, church, parks, books. Home: 510 Meadow Ridge Dr Cedar Hill TX 75104-1977

FINDLEY, PAUL, former congressman, author, educator; b. Jacksonville, Ill., June 23, 1921; s. Joseph S. and Florence Mary (Nichols) F.; m. Lucille Gemme; children: Craig Jon, Diane Lillian. AB, Ill. Coll., 1943, LLD, 1972; LHD (hon.), Lindenwood Coll., 1969, Lincoln U., 1988, MacMurray Coll., 1997; LLD, Sana'a U., Yemen, 1997. Mem. 87th-97th Congresses from 20th Ill. dist., mem. Fgn. Affairs com., mem. Agr. com.; chmn. factfinding mission to Paris, 1965; chmn. Rep. NATO Task Force, 1965-68; chmn. com. to investigate internat. problems caused by agrl. support policies Ditchley (Eng.) Conf., 1973; del. N. Atlantic Assembly, 1965-70, 72-79, Munich Conf. German Rels., 1969-71; Ditchley Conf. Atlantic Trade, 1967; European Parliament, 1974-76; mem. 7th Congl. Del. to People's Republic China, 1975; chmn. Ill. Trade Mission to, USSR, 1972, People's Republic of China, 1978. Internat. food and agrl. devel. bd. AID, 1983-94; vis. prof. MacMurray Coll., 1994-96. Author: Abraham Lincoln: The Crucible of Congress, The Federal Farm Fable, They Dare to Speak Out: People and Institutions Confront Israel's Lobby, Deliberate Deceptions: Facing the Facts About the U.S.-Israel Relationships, Silent No More: Confronting America's False Images of Islam; contbr. numerous articles on fgn. policy and agr. to periodicals. Trustee emeritus Ill. Coll.; lectr. leadership program UN Leadership Acad., Amman, Jordan, 1987-88, 05; chmn. Coun. for the Nat. Interest, 1989-2000. Lt. (j.g.) USNR, WWII. Named laureate Lincoln Acad., 1980; decorated Grand Cross Order of Merit Fed. Republic of Ger.; recipient Outstanding Svc. to Agr. citation So. Ill. U., Kefauver award for promoting Fedn. of Atlantic Nations; Hon. Am. Farmer degree FFA, Outstanding Achievement award FFA Alumni Assn., citation Nat. Assn. State Univs. and Land-Grant Colls., EAFORD Humanitarian award, 1986, Alex Odeh Human Rights award Am. Arab Anti-Discrimination Com., 1992, Disting. Svc. award Assn. for Internat. Agr. and Rural Development, 1995; Malcolm X award Muslim Assn., 2000. Mem. Assn. to Unite Democracies (bd. dirs.), Am. Legion, Phi Beta Kappa. Republican. Presbyterian. Home and Office: 1040 W College Ave Jacksonville IL 62650-2306 Office Phone: 217-243-8444.

FINE, ANNE, writer; b. Leicester, Eng., Dec. 7, 1947; d. Brian and Eileen Mary (Baker) Laker; m. Kit Fine, Aug. 3, 1968 (div. 1991); children: Ione, Cordelia. BA with honors, U. Warwick, Eng., 1968. Tchr. Cardinal Wiseman Secondary Sch., Coventry, U.K., 1968-69; info. officer Oxfam, Oxford, England, 1969-71; tchr. Saughton Prison, Edinburgh, Scotland, 1971-72. Author: (children's fiction) The Summer-House Loon, 1978, The Other Darker Ned, 1979, The Stone Menagerie, 1980, Round Behind the Ice House, 1981, The Granny Project, 1983, Scaredy-Cat, 1984, Anneli the Art Hater, 1986, Madame Doubtfire, 1987, Crummy Mummy an Me, 1987, A Pack of Liars, 1988, Goggle-Eyes, 1989, Bill's New Frock, 1989, The Book of the Banshee, 1991, Flour Babies, 1992, Step By Wicked Step, 1995, The Tulip Touch, 1996, Charm School, 1999, Bad Dreams, 2000, Up on Cloud Nine, 2002, Stories of Jamie and Angus, 2002, The True Story of Christmas, 2003, Frozen Billy, 2004, The Road of Bones, 2006, others; (adult fiction) The Killjoy, 1986, Taking the Devil's Advice, 1990, In Cold Domain, 1994, Telling Liddy, 1998, All Bones and Lies, 2001, Raking the Ashes, 2005. Decorated Order Brit. Empire; named Children's Author of Yr., Brit. Book Awards, 1990, 1993, U.K. nominee for Hans Christian Andersen Author award, 1998, Children's Laureate, 2001—03; recipient Children's Lit. award, The Guardian, 1990, Carnegie medal, Brit. Libr. Assn., 1990, 1993, Whitbread Children's Novel award, 1993, 1996, Horn Book award, Boston Globe, 2003; fellow, Royal Soc. Lit., 2003. Avocations: reading, walking. Office: David Higham Assocs 5-8 Lower John St Golden Sq London W1R 4HA England

FINE, ARTHUR I., philosopher, educator; b. Lowell, Mass., Nov. 11, 1937; s. David Fine and Rae (Silverberg) Mintz; m. Helen S. Feldberg, June 16, 1957 (div. May 1980); children: Dana S. Mintz, Sharon D. Mintz; m. Micky Forbes, July 11, 1980. Student, Harvard U., 1955-56; BS, U. Chgo., 1958; MS, Ill. Inst. Tech., 1960; PhD, U. Chgo., 1963. Asst. prof. math and philosophy Ill. Inst. Tech., Chgo., 1961—63; asst. prof. philosophy U. Ill., Urbana, 1963—65; assoc. prof. philosophy Cornell U., Ithaca, NY, 1967—71, prof. philosophy, 1971—72, U. Ill., Chgo., 1972—82, Northwestern U., Evanston, Ill., 1982—85, John Evans prof. philosophy, 1985—2001; prof. philosophy U. Wash., Seattle, 2001—, adj. prof. physics, 2003—, adj. prof. history, 2003—. Mem. nat. com. Internat. Union History and Philosophy Sci. NAS, 1973—77; mem. adv. panel History and Philosophy Sci. NSF, 1975—77, 1987—88, 1992—93. Author: The Shaky Game, 1986, 2d edit., 1996; co-editor: Philosophical Rev., 1969—71; editor (with others): PSA, 1986, PSA, vols. I and II, 1990; subject editor: Philosophy fo Science Routledge Encyclopedia of Philosophy, 1993—98; contbr. articles to profl. jours. Fellow, Ctr. Advanced Study Behavioral Scis. Stanford, 1985—86; NSF fellow, 1966—67, NSF grantee, 1968, 1973, 1978, 1980, 1989, sr. fellow, NEH, 1974—75, Gugenheim fellow, 1982—83, vis. fellow, Dibner Inst., MIT, 1996. Mem.: Am. Philos. Assn. (ctrl. divsn. pres. 1997—98), Philosophy Sci. Assn. (pres. 1986—88). Office: U Wash Philosophy Dept Box 353350 Seattle WA 98195-3350 Business E-Mail: afine@u.washington.edu.

FINE, A(RTHUR) KENNETH, lawyer; b. NYC, June 29, 1937; s. Aaron Harry and Rose (Levin) F.; m. Ellen Marie Jensen, July 11, 1964; children: Craig Jensen, Ricki-Barie, Desiree-Ellen. AB, Hunter Coll., 1959; JD, Columbia U., 1963; CLU, Coll. Ins., 1973; diploma, Command and Gen. Staff Coll., 1978. Bar: N.Y. 1974; registered rep. and limited prin. Nat. Assn. Securities Dealers, Inc. Joined U.S. Army N.G., 1955, advanced through grades to maj., 1973, ret., 1980. Cons. U.S. Life Ins. Co., N.Y.C., 1970-74, atty., 1975-78, asst. gen. counsel, 1978; asst. counsel USLIFE Corp., N.Y.C., 1978-79, assoc. counsel, 1979-93; v.p., sr. counsel Western Res. Life Assurance Co. Ohio, Clearwater, Fla. Mem. ABA, Soc. Fin. Svc. Profls., N.Y. State Bar Assn., N.G. Assn. U.S., Militia Assn. N.Y. (chmn. vet. officers com. 1981-90), Am. Legion (7th regt. post), Mil. Officers Assn. of Am. (St. Petersburg chpt.). Republican. Lutheran. Home: 5953 36th Ave N Saint Petersburg FL 33710-1835 Office: Western Res Life Assurance Co of Ohio PO Box 5068 Clearwater FL 33758-5068 Office Phone: 727-299-1743. Business E-Mail: kfine@aegonusa.com.

FINE, DAVID R., lawyer; b. Toledo, Mar. 10, 1965; s. Burril B. and Marilynn (Abramson) F.; m. Beth Campbell, Sept. 1, 1990; 1 child, Kenneth Campbell. BS, Cornell U., Ithaca, NY, 1987; MS in Journalism, Northwestern U., 1988; JD, U. Toledo, 1992. Bar: Pa. 1992, (US Ct. Appeals (3d cir.)) 1993, (US Ct. Appeals (6th cir.)) 2001, (US Ct. Appeals (9th cir.)) 2004, (US Ct. Appeals (7th cir.)) 2006, Pa. (US Dist. (mid. dist.)) 1993, (US Supreme Ct.) 1996. Anchor/reporter WUTR-TV, Utica, NY, 1988-89; law clk. U.S. Dist. Ct., Mid. Dist. Pa., Harrisburg, 1992-94; assoc. to ptnr. Kirkpatrick & Lockhart, Harrisburg, 1994—2004; ptnr. & pro bono coord. Kirkpatrick & Lockhart Nicholson Graham LLP, Harrisburg, 2005—07, Kirkpatrick & Lockhart Preston Gates Ellis, LLP, 2007—. Mem. lawyers adv. com. US Dist. Ct. (mid. dist.) Pa., 1999—2005, chmn. lawyers adv. com., 2003—05; mem. lawyers adv. com. US Ct. Appeals (3rd cir.), 2006—. Co-author: The Middle District Manual, 6th edit., 2006; contbr. articles to profl. jours.; editor-in-chief U. Toledo Law Rev., 1991-92. Bd. dir. Ctrl. Pa. Autism Edn. & Resource Ctr.; mem. Pa. Autism Task Force, 2003—; Gubernatorial appointee Pa. Spl. Edn. Adv. Panel, 2004—. Named a Pa. Super Lawyer, Phila. mag., Law & Politics mag., 2005, 2006, 2007; named one of 30 Pa. Lawyers on the Fast Track, Am. Lawyer Media, 2004. Fellow Fed. Bar Found.; mem. ABA, Fed. Bar Assn. (pres. mid. dist. Pa. chpt. 2001-02), Pa. Bar Assn. (mem. coun. civil litig. sect. and appellate adv. com. 2003—, treas. civil litig. sect. 2005-06, vice chair civil litig. sect., 2006-), Dauphin County Bar Assn., Order of the Coif. Office: Kirkpatrick & Lockhart Preston Gates Ellis LLP 17 North 2d St 18th Fl Harrisburg PA 17101 Office Phone: 717-231-5820. Office Fax: 717-231-4501. Business E-Mail: david.fine@klgates.com.

FINE, DREW S., lawyer; b. Newark, 1962; BS, Georgetown Univ., 1984; JD, Northwestern Univ., 1987. Bar: N.Y. 1988. Ptnr. Global Transp. Fin. Group & mem. recruiting com. Milbank Tweed Hadley & McCloy, NYC. Contbr. articles to profl. jours. Office: Milbank Tweed Hadley & McCloy 1 Chase Manhattan Plz New York NY 10005-1413 Office Phone: 212-530-5940. Office Fax: 212-530-5219. Business E-Mail: dfine@milbank.com.

FINE, FREDERICK L., computer company and health products executive; BA in Econ., U. Ga. Founder, pres., CEO InfoCure Corp. (name changed to VitalWorks, Inc. in 2001), Atlanta; chmn., sr. advisor VitalWorks, Inc., 2001; co-founder Rialto Capital Partners, LLC, Atlanta. Mem. adv. bd. Asset Mgmt. Advisors.

FINE, GLENN A., federal agency administrator; AB magna cum laude, Harvard Coll., 1979; BA, MA, Oxford U.; JD magna cum laude, Harvard U., 1985. Asst. states atty. U.S. States Attys. Office, Washington, Del., 1986—89; atty. Washington, Del.; spl. counsel Dept. Justice Office Inspector Gen., Alexandria, 1995—96, dir. spl. investifations and rev. unit, 1996—2000, inspector gen., 2000—. Rhodes scholar. Office: US Dept Justice 950 Pennsulvania Ave NW Washington DC 20530-0001*

FINE, HOWARD ALAN, management consultant; BS, NYU, 1961, MBA, 1964. Internat. sales mgr. Pfaff, A.G., Fed. Republic of West Germany, 1964-67; regional sales dir. Brit. Transport Hotels, London, Eng., 1967-70; dir. internat. mktg. Sonesta Internat. Hotels, NYC, 1970-71; dir. Pacific mktg. Forte Hotels, LA, 1971-74, dir. Atlantic area and Latin Am. mktg. NYC, 1974-75, v.p. sales and mktg., 1975-78, exec. v.p., 1978-81; pres. Norwegian Am. Cruise Line, NYC, 1981-83; pres., chief exec. officer Costa Cruise Line, Miami, Fla., 1983-87; chmn., chief exec. officer Tourism Devel. Internat., Miami, 1987—; internat. mgmt. cons., advisor to corp. bds. and heads of state worldwide. Bd. dirs. Bahamas Devel. Found., Nassau, Traveling Times, L.A.; spkr., presenter Young Pres.'s Orgn, World Pres.'s Orgn., 1987—. Contbr. articles to profl. jours. Mem. mayors adv. bd. City of Los Angeles, 1972-74; mem. senatorial commn. Rep. Senatorial Inner Circle, Washington, 1984—, Presdl. task force to Pres. Bush, 1989—; bd. dirs. Calif. Dept. Agr. Wine Bd., 1974-75, Ptnrs. for Liveable Places, Washington, 1978-83, NYU Ctr. for Study of Foodservice, 1978-83, Fla. Crime Prevention Commn., 1984—, Boys Town of Italy, 1986—. Served to capt. USAR, 1961-66. Named Hon. Order Ky. Cols., 1986; named Man of Yr. Am. Jaycees, 1983, Man of Yr. Internat. Hotel Industry, 1980; recipient Disting. Marker of Yr. Sales and Mktg. Mgmt. Mag., 1979, Christopher Columbus award Nat. Columbus Day Com., 1986, Spirit of Life Humanitarian award City of Hope, 1987; numerous hotel and travel industry awards and citations from fgn. govts., 1972-87. Fellow Inst. Cert. Travel Agts.; mem. Young Pres.'s Orgn. (chmn. 1978—), World Pres.'s Orgn., Hotelier of World Com. (bd. dirs.), Italian C. of C. (bd. dirs.), Brit. C. of C. (bd. dirs.), Norwegian C. of C. (bd. dirs.), South African C. of C. (bd. dirs.), Greater Ft. Lauderdale C. of C. (bd. govs. 1986—), NYU Alumni Fedn., Sigma Alpha Mu, NYU Club (N.Y.C.), 110 Tower Club (bd. dirs.), Harbor Beach Club (bd. dirs.). Avocations: boating, travel, gardening, photography, flying. Office: Tourism Devel Internat PO Box 22323 Fort Lauderdale FL 33335-2323

FINE, J(AMES) ALLEN, insurance company executive; b. May 2, 1934; s. Samuel Lee and Ocie (Loflin) F.; m. Marie Nan Morris, Sept. 1, 1957 (dec. Apr. 1989); children: James A(llen), William. Student, Pfeiffer Coll., 1957—58; BS, U. N.C., 1961, MBA, 1965. Sr. acct. Haskins & Sells, CPAs, Charlotte, NC, 1961—62, Watson, Penry & Morgan, Asheboro, NC, 1962—64; instr. U. N.C., Chapel Hill, 1964—65; asst. prof. Pfeiffer Coll., Misenheimer, NC, 1956—66; treas., v.p. adminstrn. Nat. Lab. for Higher Edn. (formerly Regional Edn. Lab. Carolinas and Va.), Durham, NC, 1966—72; organizer, CEO, treas., dir. Investors Title Ins. Co., Inc., Chapel Hill, 1972—, Cpres., dir., 1976—; developer Carolina Forest Subdivsn., Chapel Hill, 1970—78, Springhill Forest Subdivsn., Chapel Hill, 1977—80, Stonycreek Subdivsn., 1978—. Lectr. acctg. U. N.C., Chapel Hill, 1967—70. Area officer ann. alumni giving U. NC, Chapel Hill, 1968—69, 1971—73, 1975—; trustee NC Mus. Art, 2003—; mem. Chapel Hill Downtown Partnership, 2004—06. With USN, 1953—57. Recipient Haskins & Sells Found. award for excellence in accounting, 1961, N.C. Assn. CPAs award for most outstanding accounting student, U. N.C., 1961. Mem.: AICPA, NC Museum of Art (bd. trustees), CEDAR Bus. Mgrs. (chmn. nat. exec. com. 1971), U. N.C. Nat. Devel. Com., Nat. Assn. Ins. Commrs. (liaison com. 1987—88, 1994—), Am. Land Title Assn. (rsch. com. 1983—2003, membership com. 1984—85, recruitment, retention subcom. 1985, exec. com. underwriters sect. 1986, 2002—), Am. Acctg. Assn., N.C. Assn. CPAs, Phi Beta Kappa, Beta Gamma Sigma (treas. 1961). Home: 112 Carolina First Chapel Hill NC 27516-9033 Office: 121 N Columbia St Chapel Hill NC 27514-3502 Office Phone: 919-968-2200. Business E-Mail: jafine@invtitle.com.

FINE, JAMES STEPHEN, physician; b. St. Paul, June 14, 1946; s. Ralph Irving and Beverlee Lois (Rockler) F.; m. Meredith Ann Blehert, June 20, 1970; children: Zachary, Esther, Gabriel. BA in Math., U. Minn., 1968, MD, 1972, MS in Biometry, Health Info. Systems, 1977. Intern in medicine St. Paul-Ramsey Hosp., 1972-73; residency U. Minn., Mpls., 1973-77; assoc. prof., dir. info. and specimen processing div. U. Wash. Hosp., Seattle, 1977-94, chmn. lab. medicine, 1994—. CIO U. Wash. Medicine, Seattle, 2005—. Mem. Am. Assn. Clin. Chemistry, Acad. Clin. Lab. Physicians and Scientists (Gerald T. Evans award 2001), Computer Soc. IEEE, Assn. Pathology (chmn.), Am. Med. Informatics Assn., Wash. State Med. Assn., King County Med. Soc. Office: U Wash Med Ctr Box 357110 1959 NE Pacific Ave NW 120 Seattle WA 98195-7110 Home Phone: 206-323-8417; Office Phone: 206-598-6137. Business E-Mail: jsfine@u.washington.edu.

FINE, JO RENÉE, management consultant; b. June 19, 1943; d. Ruby Arthur and Tillie Fern (Goldman) F.; m. Edward Trieber, Apr. 12, 1981; 1 child, Jessica. BA, Smith Coll., 1965; MA, NYU, 1968, PhD, 1973. Probation officer N.Y.C. Office Probation, 1966; rsch. asst. NYU, NYC, 1966-68; assoc. rsch. scientist Inst. Devel. Studies, NYC, 1968-73, rsch. scientist, 1973-77; program analyst N.Y. State Dept. Mental Health, NYC, 1977-78; pvt. practice psychotherapy NYC, 1978-81; pres. CVM Prodns., Inc., NYC, 1978-92; dir. Ctr. for Diversity and Quality Mgmt. Cicatelli Assocs., NYC, 1992-96; exec. v.p., dir. tng. Harris Rothenberg Internat., NYC, 1996—. Adj. asst. prof. dept. ednl. psychology, NYU, 1973-76, adj. asst. prof. ednl. comm. and tech., 1988-95; cons. to bds. edn., N.Y.C., also greater met. area, 1973-92, tng. cons., 1990-96. Co-author: The Synagogues of New York's Lower East Side, 1978. Co-chair bd. dirs. Project People Found. Mem. APA, ASTD, Am. Jewish Com. (v.p. N.Y. chpt., nat. bd. govs.). Home: 55 W 16th St New York NY 10011-6305 Office: Harris Rothenberg Internat 99 Wall St Fl 8 New York NY 10005-4389 Office Phone: 212-422-8847.

FINE, KIT, philosophy educator; b. Farnborough, Mar. 26, 1946; s. Maurice and Joyce Cicely (Woolf) F.; children: Ione, Cordelia. BA, Oxford U., Eng., 1967; PhD, U. Warwick, Eng., 1969; D (hon.), U. Bucharest, 2006. Asst. lectr. U. Warwick, 1967-69; jr. rsch. fellow St. John's Coll., Oxford, 1969—71; lectr. U. Edinburgh, Scotland, 1971-73; vis. asst. prof. Stanford U., 1974; assoc. prof U. Calif., Irvine, 1975—77, prof., 1977—78; vis. prof. U. Ariz., 1977; prof. U. Mich., Ann Arbor, 1978-88; vis. prof. UCLA, 1983, 1987, Flint chair of philosophy, 1993—97, prof., 1988—97; prof. philosophy NYU, 1997—, affiliated appt. with dept. math., Courant Inst., 2002—, Silver prof. philosophy, 2003—. Vis. fellow Australian Nat. U., 1985, Automatic Reasoning project, Australian Nat. U., 1990, All Souls Coll., Oxford, 1995-96; vis. prof. U. Melbourne, 1985, Princeton U., 1999-2001; assoc. mem. cognitive sci. grp., UCLA, 1990-97; invited spkr. Author: Reasoning with Arbitrary Objects, 1985; co-author: (with A.N. Prior) Worlds, Times and Selves, 1977, The Limits of Abstraction, 2002, Modality and Tense: Philosophical Papers, 2005; editor Jour. Symbolic Logic, 1979-87, coord. for the editors, 1983-85, Notre Dame Jour. Formal Logic, 1984-87, Studies in Logic, 1990-94, Lecture Notes on Logic, 1994-97; mem. editl. bd. Synthese, 1977-, Jour. Applied Non-Classical Logics, 1990-, Imprint; chair oversight com., Jour. Philos. Logic, 1988-. Robin Holloway Scholar, 1964-67, Guggenheim fellow, 1978-79, Am. Coun. Learned Socs. fellow, 1981-82, Inst. for Advanced Studies in the Humantities fellow, 1981-82, U. Mich. Rackham Fellowship, 1981, Inst. Advanced Studies in Humanities, U. Edinburgh, 1981-82, hon. fellow, Centre for Cognitive Sci., 1983-. Fellow Am. Acad. Arts & Sciences; mem. British Acad. (corr.), Assn. Symbolic Logic (editor logic series 1991-94, mem. exec. com., 1983-87), Am. Philos. Assn., Am. Math. Assn. Avocations: music, gardening, cooking. Office: NYU Dept Philosophy 100 Washington Pl New York NY 10003 Office Phone: 212-998-3558. Office Fax: 212-995-4179. Business E-Mail: kf14@nyu.edu.

FINE, LAWRENCE B., lawyer; b. June 20, 1951; BA, BS in Econs., U. Pa., 1973; JD, U. Va., 1976. Bar: Pa. 1976. Ptnr. Morgan, Lewis & Bockius, Phila., 1976—2006; v.p. labor and employment law Wyeth, Collegeville, Pa., 2006—.

FINE, MARJORIE LYNN, lawyer; b. Bklyn., Aug. 14, 1950; m. John Kent Markley, May 6, 1979; children: Jessica Paige Markley, Laura Anne Markley. BA, Smith Coll., 1972; JD, U. Calif., 1977. Bar: Calif. 1977. Assoc. to ptnr. Donahue Gallagher Woods, Oakland, Calif., 1977-87; sr. counsel Bank of Am., San Francisco, 1987-89; assoc., gen. counsel Shaklee Corp., San Francisco, 1989-90; gen. counsel, v.p. Shaklee U.S., Inc., San Francisco, 1990-94, Shaklee U.S., Shaklee Technica, 1995-99, Yamanouchi Pharma Techs., Inc., 1999-2001; gen. counsel, sr. v.p. Shaklee Corp., 2001—05, gen. counsel, exec. v.p., sec., 2005—. Judge pro tem Oakland Piedmont Emeryville Mcpl. Ct., 1982-89; fee arbitrator Alameda Co. Bar Assn., 1980-87. Mem. ABA, Calif. Bar Assn., Calif. Employment Law Coun. (bd. dirs. 1993-03, 05—). Jewish. Office: Shaklee Corp 4747 Willow Rd Pleasanton CA 94588-2740

FINE, MILTON, hotel company executive, lawyer; b. Pitts., May 18, 1926; s. Samuel and Ida (Krimsky) F.; m. Sara Mariam Fogel, June 15, 1952 (div. 1971); children: Carolyn Francis Fine Friedman, Sibyl Ann Fine King, David Jeremy; m. Sheila Dianne Cook, Nov. 24, 1989. BA magna cum laude, U. Pitts., 1949, JD, 1950. Bar: Pa. 1951. Pvt. practice, 1951-55; ptnr. Fine, Perlow & Stone, Pitts., 1955-75; co-chmn. Interstate Hotels Corp., Pitts., 1960-88, chmn., CEO, 1988-96, chmn. bd. dirs., 1996-98; chmn. FCC Capital Corp., 1998—. Mem. adv. bd. Greenwich St. Capital Ptnrs., Inc., 1996-00; bd. dirs. Wyndham Internat., Inc., Dallas, 2005.

Lifetime trustee Carnegie Inst., Pitts., 1983—; chmn. bd. dirs. Carnegie Mus. Art, 1992-00: trustee U. Pitts., 1997-00; mem. bd. dirs. Warhol Mus., Pitts., 1989—. Recipient Bicentennial Medallion of Distinction, U. Pitts., 1987, Cultural award Pitts. Ctr. for the Arts, 1995. Mem. Pa. Bar Assn., Duquesne Club. Republican. Jewish. Avocations: golf, collecting contemporary art. Office: FFC Capital Corp Dominion Tower Ste 3110 625 Liberty Ave Pittsburgh PA 15222 Office Phone: 412-444-3512. *With all the unexpected turns in my life, the thing which has been most predictable has been change. What remains constant is the need to be flexible and resilient, the need to take advantage of change rather than being overwhelmed by it, and, most importantly, the need to remain a student throughout one's life.*

FINE, MORRIS EUGENE, materials engineer, educator; b. Jamestown, ND, Apr. 12, 1918; s. Louis and Sophie (Berrington) F.; m. Mildred Eleanor Glazer, Aug. 13, 1950; children: Susan Elaine, Amy Lynn. B.Metall. Engring. with distinction, U. Minn., 1940, MS, 1942, PhD, 1943. Instr. U. Minn., 1942-43; mem. tech. staff Bell Telephone Labs., Murray Hill, N.J., 1946-54; prof. emeritus Northwestern U., Evanston, Ill., 1954—, prof., chmn. dept. metallurgy Tech. Inst., 1955-57, chmn. dept. materials sci., 1958-60, prof. and chmn. materials research center, 1960-64, Walter P. Murphy prof. materials sci., 1963-89, tech. inst. prof., 1985-89, dir. Am. Iron and Steel Inst. steel resource ctr., 1986-93, assoc. dean grad. studies and research Tech. Inst., 1973-85, prof. emeritus, 1989, mem. grad. faculty, 1989—. Vis. prof. dept. materials sci. Stanford U., 1967-68; JSPS vis. scholar, Japan, 1979; chmn., vis. prof. materials sci. and engring. U. Tex., Austin, 1984-95; assoc. engr. Manhattan Project, U. Chgo. and Los Alamos, N.Mex., WWII; mem. materials adv. bd. NRC, 1963-68; mem. com. geol. and materials scis. NRC, 1979-82; chmn. adv. bd. program on modular methods for tchg. materials Pa. State U., 1973-77; chmn. vis. com. metallurgy and materials Sci. and Materials Rsch. Ctr., Lehigh U., 1965-75; mem. vis. com. Lawrence Berkeley Lab., 1978-81, chmn., 1981, mem. vis. com. Ames Dept. Energy Lab., 1976-80, Materials Rsch. Ctr., Pa. State U., 1988-91, Colo. Sch. Mines, 1991-96; chmn., organizer numerous confs. in field. Author numerous tech. and sci. articles on mech. properties of metals and ceramics, fatigue of metals, phase transformations, high temperature alloys, and other subjects.; author: Introduction to Phase Transformation in Condensed Systems. Recipient Gilbert Speich award Iron and Steel Soc., 1993; named Chicagoan of Year in Sci., 1961 Fellow AAAS, Am. Phys. Soc., Japan Soc. Metals (hon.), Am. Soc. Metals (chpt. chmn. 1963, Campbell lectr. 1979, chmn. seminar com. 1979, hon. mem. com. 1993-96, gold medal 1986), Am. Acad. Arts and Scis., Metall Soc. of AIME (chmn. inst. metals divsn. 1966-68, bd. dirs. 1968-71, bd. dirs. inst. 1972-75, mem. Bardeen gold medals com. 1992-96, chmn. 1995-96, Mathewson gold medal for rsch. 1981, James Douglas gold medal 1982, Educator award 1993, hon. mem.), Am. Ceramic Soc. (keynote lectr. electronic materials div. 1972); mem. NAE (astronautics space engring. bd. 1973-77, membership com. 1974-79, chmn. 1977-78, mem. membership adv. com. 1991-94), Scripta Met et Mat (Outstanding Paper award 1991), The Metals, Materials, Minerals Soc. (inst. metals lecture and R.F. Mehl gold medal 1996), Sigma Xi, Tau Beta Pi, Alpha Sigma Mu, Sigma Alpha Sigma. Home: 1101 Manor Dr Wilmette IL 60091-1026 Office: Dept Materials Sci and Engring Northwestern U Evanston IL 60208-3108 Business E-Mail: m-fine412@northwestern.edu.

FINE, PAMELA B., newspaper editor; Grad., U. Fla. Reporter Daytona Beach News, 1979; several editl. positions with Atlanta Journal-Constitution, 1982—94; mng. editor, v.p. Mpls. Star Tribune, 1994—2002; mng. editor The Indianapolis Star, 2003—. Nat. conf. chair Associated Press Mng. Editors Assn., 2000; juror for Pulitzer Prize. Office: The Indianapolis Star PO Box 145 Indianapolis IN 46206-0145 Office Phone: 317-444-6168. Business E-Mail: pam.fine@indystar.com.

FINE, RANA ARNOLD, chemical and physical oceanographer; d. Joseph and Etta (Kreisman) Arnold; m. Shalle Stephen Fine, June 20, 1965 (div. 1979); m. James Stewart Mattson, Jan. 5, 1983. BA, NYU, 1965; MA, U. Miami, 1973, PhD, 1975. Systems analyst Svc. Bur. Corp. subs. IBM, Miami, 1965-69; rsch. assoc. Rosenstiel Sch. U. Miami, 1976-77, rsch. asst. prof., 1977-80, rsch. assoc. prof., 1980-84, assoc. prof., 1984-90, prof. marine and atmospheric chemistry, 1990—, chair divsn. marine and atmospheric chemistry, 1990-94; assoc. program dir. NSF, Washington, 1981-83. Mem. div. polar programs adv. com. NSF, Washington, 1987-90, geophys. study com. NAS, Washington, 1989-92, ocean studies bd., 1992-98, adv. panel Tropical Ocean/Global Atmosphere Program, 1990-93, chair adv. panel major ocean programs, 1996-98; bd. trustees UCAR 2005—, Inter-Am. Inst. Global Ch. SSC, 2004— Contbr. articles to profl. jours. Vol. guide Vizcaya Mus., Miami, 1967-78, adv. panel mem. methane hydrade rev. 2003-04. Grantee NSF, 1977—, NOAA, 1986—, Office of Naval Rsch., 1983-88, NASA, 1990-97. Fellow: AAAS (chair-elect atm and hydrospheric sci. sect. 2001—04), Am. Meteorol. Soc. (coun. mem. 2001—04), Am. Geophys. Union (sec. oceanography sect. 1986—88, pres.-elect oceanography sect. 1994—96, pres. 1996—98); mem.: Oceanography Soc. Avocations: sailing, scuba diving, fishing, tennis, reading. Office: RSMAS/MAC/U Miami 4600 Rickenbacker Cswy Miami FL 33149-1031 Business E-Mail: rfine@rsmas.miami.edu.

FINE, RICHARD ISAAC, lawyer; b. Milw., Jan. 22, 1940; s. Jack and Frieda F.; m. Maryellen Olman, Nov. 25, 1982; 1 child, Victoria Elizabeth. BS, U. Wis., Madison, 1961; JD, U. Chgo., 1964; PhD in Internat. Law, U. London, 1967; diplôme supérieur in Comparative Law, Faculté Internat. pour l'Enseignment du Droit Comparé, Strasbourg, France, 1967. Bar: Ill. 1964, DC 1972, Calif. 1973, cert.: Internat. U. Comparative Sci. (comparative law) 1965, Hague Acad. Internat. Law, The Netherlands (pvt. internat. law) 1965, Hague Acad. Internat. Law, The Netherlands 1966. Trial atty. fgn. commerce sect. antitrust divsn. US Dept. Justice, 1968-72; chief antitrust divsn. LA City Atty.'s Office, also spl. counsel gov. efficiency com., 1973-74; prof. internat., comparative and EEC antitrust law U. Syracuse Law Sch. (overseas program), NY, 1970-72; individual practice Richard I. Fine and Assocs., LA, 1974—. Mem. antitrust adv. bd. Bur. Nat. Affairs, 1981—; bd. dirs. Am. Friends London Sch. Econ. and Polit. Sci., 1984—, chmn. So. Calif. chpt., 1984—2005, chmn. LA adv. com.; mem. internat. cir. LA World Affairs Coun., 1990—, founder internat. cir.; vis. com. U. Chgo. Law Sch., 1992—95. Contbr. articles to legal publs. Bd. dirs. Retinitis Pigmentosa Internat., 1985-90, Citizens Island Bridge Co., Ltd., 1992-; founder LA Music Ctr. Named Atty. of the Decades, Calif. Black Rep. Women's Coun. and Judea-Christian Alliance, 2006. Mem. ABA (chmn. subcom. internat. antitrust and trade regulation, internat. law sect. 1972-77, co-chmn. com. internat. econ. orgn. 1977-79), ATLA, Am. Soc. Internat. Law (co-chmn. com. corp. membership 1978-83, exec. coun. 1984-87, budget com. 1992-97, regional coord. for L.A. 1994—, 1995 ann. program com. 1994-95, corr. editor Internat. Legal Materials 1983—), Am. Fgn. Law Assn., Internat. Law Assn., Brit. Inst. Internat. and Comparative Law, State Bar Calif. (chmn. antitrust and trade regulation law sect. 1981-84, exec. com. 1981-87), L.A. County Bar Assn. (chmn. antitrust sect. 1977-78, exec. com. sect. internat. law 1993—, treas. 1997, chmn. 2003-04), Ill. Bar Assn., Phi Delta Phi. Office: Ste 200 468 N Camden Dr Beverly Hills CA 90210 Home Phone: 818-996-8512; Office Phone: 310-277-5833. Business E-Mail: rfinelaw@earthlink.net.

FINE, RICHARD NISAN, pediatrician, educator, dean; b. Phila., Oct. 3, 1937; s. Eve Fine; children: Joanne, Michael; m. Shawney Wagner, Aug. 28, 1972. BS, Muhlenberg Coll., 1958; MD, Temple U., 1962. Intern Boston City Hosp., 1962-63, jr. asst. resident, 1963-64; sr. chief resident Children's Hosp. L.A., 1964-66; instr. pediatrics U. So. Calif., LA, 1966-68, asst. prof. pediatrics, 1968-72, assoc. prof. pediatrics, 1972-76, prof. pediatrics, 1976-80, U. Calif., LA, 1980-89, vice chmn. clin. affairs, 1985-90; prof., chmn. dept. pediatrics SUNY, Stony Brook, 1991—, dean Sch. Medicine, 2005—. Recipient Nat. Med. award in Nephrology, Nat. Kidney Found. N.Y./N.J., 1992. Mem.: N.Am. Pediatric Transplant Coop. Study (v.p.-treas.), Internat. Pediatric Transplant Assn. (sec.-treas.), Am. Soc. Transplantation (pres.). Office: Stony Brook Sch Medicen Dean's Office Health Sciences Ctr Level 4 Stony Brook NY 11794-8430 Office Phone: 631-444-2080.

FINE, ROGER SETH, lawyer, educator, former pharmaceutical executive; b. Bklyn., Sept. 22, 1942; s. Jack F. and Mildred (Perlmutter) F.; m. Rebecca Gold, June 14, 1964; children: David, Adam. BA, Columbia Coll., 1963; LLB, NYU, 1966. Bar: NY 1966, U.S. Dist. Ct. (so. dist.) NY 1967, U.S. Ct. Appeals (2d cir.) 1967. Assoc. Cahill, Gordon & Reindel, NYC, 1966-74; gen. atty. Johnson & Johnson, New Brunswick, NJ, 1974-78, asst. gen. counsel, 1978-84, assoc. gen. counsel, 1984-91, v.p. adminstrn., mem. exec. com., 1991-95, v.p., gen. counsel, mem. exec. com., 1996—2004. Mem. ABA.*

FINEBERG, GERALD, real estate company executive; m. Sandra Fineberg. Founder The Fineberg Companies, Fine Hotels Corp., 1990—, chmn., 1990—; ptnr. Frontier Capital Mgmt. LLC. Friend of Rose Art Mus., Brandeis U., 1990—, mem. bd. overseers, 1997—, chmn. bd. overseers, 2000—. Named in his honor Gerald S. & Sandra Fineberg Gallery, Rose Art Mus. of Brandeis U., 2005; named one of Top 200 Collectors, ARTnews Mag., 2004. Avocations: squash, golf, collector modern & contemporary art. Address: 5 Byron St Boston MA 02108 Office: The Fineberg Companies 1 Washington St Ste 402 Wellesley MA 02481 Office Phone: 781-239-1480. Office Fax: 781-239-1439.

FINEBERG, HARVEY VERNON, medical institute administrator; b. Pitts., Sept. 15, 1945; s. Saul and Miriam (Pearl) F.; m. Mary Elizabeth Wilson, May 16, 1975. AB, Harvard U., 1967, MD, M.P.P., Harvard U., 1972, PhD, 1980. Intern Beth Israel Hosp., Boston, 1972—73; asst. prof. Sch. Pub. Health, Harvard U., Boston, 1973—78; physician East Boston Health Ctr., 1974—76, Harvard Street Health Ctr., 1976—84; assoc. prof. Harvard U., Boston, 1978—81, prof., 1981—2002, dean Sch. Pub. Health, 1984—97, provost Cambridge, Mass., 1997—2001; pres. Inst. of Medicine, Washington, 2002—. Jr. fellow Harvard U., 1974—75; Mellon fellow, 1976. Co-author: Clinical Decision Analysis, 1980, The Epidemic That Never Was, 1983, Adverse Effects of Pertussis and Rubella Vaccines, 1991, Society's Choices: Social and Ethical Decision Making in Biomedicine, 1995, Innovators in Physician Education: The Process and Pattern of Reform in North American Medical Schools, 1996. Trustee Newton Wellesley Hosp., Mass., 1981-86; study sect. chmn. Nat. Ctr. Health Services Research, Rockville, Md., 1982-85; active Pub. Health Council, Mass., 1976-79; bd. dirs. Am. Found. AIDS Rsch., 1986-97, William and Flora Hewlett Found., 2003—. Mem.: Soc. Med. Decision Making (pres. 1980—81), Inst. Medicine. Jewish. Office: Inst Medicine 500 5th St NW Washington DC 20001-2721

FINEBERG, ROBERT ALAN, lawyer; b. Portland, Maine, May 29, 1948; s. Samuel and Lillian (Smith) F.; m. Virginia June Brealey, Aug. 22, 1970; children: Cynthia Joy, Daniel Harwood. BA, U. Conn., 1970; JD, Temple U., 1975. Bar: Pa. 1976, N.J. 1976, U.S. Dist. Ct. (ea. dist.) Pa. 1976, U.S. Dist. Ct. N.J. 1976, U.S. Supreme Ct. 1981; cert. civil trial atty.; Rule 1:40 qualified mediator. Assoc. Charles Blasband, Norristown, Pa., 1975—76, Perskie & Callinan, Wildwood, NJ, 1976—79; pvt. practice Wildwood, 1979—81; ptnr. Fineberg & Rodgers, North Wildwood, NJ, 1981—89; pvt. practice Cape May Court House, NJ, 1989—. Solicitor Borough of Avalon, N.J., 1979-87, Borough of Wildwood Crest, N.J., 1985-89, Bd. of Edn. of City of Cape May, N.J., 1983-91, 2005—, City of Cape May, 1991-99, City of Cape May Hist. Preservation Commn., 1999—. Bd. dirs. Assn. for Retarded Citizens of Cape May County, Rio Grande, N.J., 1982-87, Cape May Jazz Festival; pres. Wildwood Crest Civic Assn., 1985-87; mem. Bd. Edn. Mid. Township, N.J., 1990-2005 Mem.: ABA, ATLA, NJ Assn. Profl. Mediators, N.J. Inst. Mcpl. Attys., Cape May County Bar Assn., N.J. State Bar Assn., Union League (Cape May County, N.J.), Lions, Pi Sigma Alpha, Delta Sigma Rho, Phi Kappa Phi, Phi Beta Kappa. Democrat. Jewish. Home: 24 Chestnut Ave Cape May Court House NJ 08210-2623 Office: 208 N Main St Cape May Court House NJ 08210-2122 Office Phone: 609-463-0055. E-mail: courtlaw@bellatlantic.net.

FINEGAN, COLE, lawyer; b. Tulsa, Oct. 1, 1956; s. Philip Cole and Margaret (Hudson) F.; m. Robin Fudge, Dec. 29, 1984; children: Jordan Nicole, Ryan Andrew. BA in English, U. Notre Dame, Ind., 1978; JD, Georgetown U., 1987. Legis. asst., adminstrv. asst. Ctrl. Dist.-1st Dist. Okla., Tulsa and Washington, 1978-87; assoc. Brownstein Hyatt Farber & Strickland, Denver, 1987-91, shareholder, 1993—2003; dir. Office Policy and Initiatives Gov. State of Colo., Denver, 1991-93; city atty. City and County, Denver, 2003—06; atty. Hogan & Hartson LLP, Denver, 2007—. Chief of staff to Mayor John W. Hichinloafer, 2005—. Staff mem. The Tax Lawyer, 1984-86. Bd. mem. Greater Denver Corp., 1993-96, State Bd. of Agr., 1997-98, I Have A Dream Found.; bd. trustees State Colls. Colo., 1993-97; bd. mem. Auvaria Higher Edn. Commn., 1993-95; co-chair Downtown Denver Area Plan. Mem.: Urban Land Inst. Democrat. Roman Catholic. Home: 1934 Forest Pkwy Denver CO 80220-1337 Office: Hogan & Hartson LLP One Tabor Ctr Ste 1500 1200 Seventeenth St Denver CO 80202 Office Phone: 720-865-8600. Fax: 303-899-7333; Office Fax: 720-865-8796. E-mail: city.attorney@ci.denver.co.us.

FINEGOLD, ALAN H., lawyer; b. Oct. 1, 1942; BA, Yale U., New Haven, Conn., 1964; LLB, Harvard U., Cambridge, Mass., 1967. Bar: Pa. 1968. Assoc. Kirkpatrick, Pomeroy, Lockhart & Johnson, Pitts., 1968—72; ptnr. Kirkpatrick & Lockhart, Pitts., 1972—94; mem. Law Offices Alan. H. Finegold, Pitts., 1997—. Office: 6 Ppg Pl Ste 1150 Pittsburgh PA 15222-5427

FINEGOLD, MAURICE NATHAN, architect; b. Providence, Sept. 6, 1932; s. Samuel R. and Ruth (Marks) F.; m. Muriel Ann Savitz, Apr. 30, 1964; Jordan, Daniel Warren, Jonathan Eric, Michael Andrew. AB, Harvard Coll., 1954; MArch, Harvard U., 1958, LHD (hon.), 2007. Lic. architect. Mass., and 15 other states. Prin. Maurice N. Finegold & Assocs., AIA, Architect, Boston, 1964-69; ptnr. Finegold & Bullis, Architects, Boston, 1969-74; prin. Notter Finegold & Alexander, Boston, 1974-92; pres. Finegold Alexander & Assocs., Inc., Boston, 1992—. Chair Mass. Bd. of Registration of Architects, Boston, 1989-91. Bd. dirs. Downtown North Assn., Boston, 1990—, pres. 1997-99; mem. New Eng. Holocaust Meml. Com., Boston, 1990—; chair presdl. search com. Boston Archtl. Ctr., 1990-91, 96-97, bd. dirs., 1994-2007, vice chair bd. dirs., 1995-99, chair, bd. dirs., 1999-2003. Sgt. U.S. Army, 1958-64. Fellow AIA (mem. com. justice, numerous local and nat. design awards, Frey award 2002), Soc. for Arts, Religion and Contemporary Culture; mem. ALA, Boston Soc. Architects (chmn. several coms. 1961-), Soc. Coll. and Univ. Planning, Nat. Trust for Hist. Preservation, League Hist. Am. Theaters, Interfaith Forum Religion, Art and Arch., Harvard Club Boston, Harvard Club NYC. Democrat. Jewish. Avocations: sailing, travel. Office: Finegold Alexander & Assocs Inc 77 N Washington St Boston MA 02114-1908 Office Phone: 617-227-9272. Business E-Mail: mnf@faainc.com.

FINEGOLD, SYDNEY MARTIN, microbiology educator; b. NYC, Aug. 12, 1921; s. Samuel Joseph and Jennie (Stein) F.; m. Mary Louise Saunders, Feb. 8, 1947 (dec. June 1994); children: Joseph, Patricia, Michael; m. Gloria Weiss, Feb. 18, 1996. AB, UCLA, 1943; MD, U. Tex., 1949. Diplomate: Am. Bd. Med. Microbiology (mem. bd. 1979-85), Am. Bd. Internal Medicine. Intern USPHS, Galveston, Tex., 1949-50; fellow in medicine U. Minn. Med. Sch., 1950-52, research fellow, 1951-52; resident medicine Wadsworth Hosp., VA Ctr., Los Angeles, 1953-54; instr. medicine U. Calif. Med. Ctr., Los Angeles, 1955-57, asst. clin. prof., 1957-59, asst. prof., 1959-62, assoc. prof., 1962-68, prof., 1968—2000, emeritus, 2000—, prof. microbiology and immunology, 1983—2000, emeritus, 2000—; chief chest and infectious disease sect. Wadsworth Hosp., 1957-61, chief infectious disease sect., 1961-86, assoc. chief staff for research and devel., 1986-92; staff physician infectious disease sect. VA Med. Ctr., LA, 1992—. Mem. pulmonary disease rsch. program com. VA, 1961-62, infectious disease rsch. program com., 1961-65, merit rev. bd. (infectious diseases), 1972-74, med. rsch. program specialist, 1974-76, adv. com. on infectious disease, 1974-87; mem. NRC-Nat. Acad. Sci. Drug Efficacy Study Group, 1966-69; mem. subcom. on gram-negative anaerobic bacilli Internat. Com. on Nomenclature Bacteria, 1966—, chmn., 1972-78; mem. adv. panel U.S. Pharmacopoeia, 1970-75; chmn. working group on anaerobic susceptibility test methods Nat. Com. Clin. Lab. Standards, 1987-97, advisor, 1998-2002. Mem. editl. bd. Calif. Medicine, 1966-73, Applied Microbiology, 1973-74, Western Jour. Medicine, 1974-77, Am. Rev. Respiratory Disease, 1974-76, Jour. Clin. Microbiology, 1975-85, Infection, 1976—, Jour. Infectious Disease, 1979-82, 84-85, Antimicrobial Agts. Chemotherapy, 1980-89, Diagnostic Microbiology and Infectious Diseases, 1982-90; editor Revs. of Infectious Diseases, 1990-91, Clin. Infectious Diseases, 1992-2000; sect. editor: infectious diseases vols. Clin. Medicine, 1978-82, Microbiol. Ecology in Health and Disease, 1987-90; assoc. editor, consulting editor Anaerobe, 1994—. editor-in-chief, 1998—. Vice chmn. UCLA Acad. Senate, 1986-87, chair, 1987-88. Served with USMCR, with USNR, 1943-46, to 1st. lt. AUS, 1952-53. Co-recipient V.A. William S. Middleton award for biomed. rsch., 1984; recipient Profl. Achievement award UCLA, 1987, Mayo Soley award Western Soc. Clin. Investigation, 1988, Disting. Alumnus award U. Tex. Med. Br., 1988, UCLA Med. Alumni Assn. Med. Scis. award, 1990, Hoechst Roussel award Am. Soc. Microbiology, 1992, medal Helsinki U., Finland, 1996, Lifetime Achievement award Infectious Disease Assn. Calif., 1995, Wm. H. Oldendorf Lifetime Achievement awrd VA Med. Ctr., 1996, Lifetime Achievement award Internat. Soc. Anaerobic Bacteriology, 1998, Becton Dickinson award in Clin. Microbiology, 1999; organism named Fingeoldia magna, 1999; new species named Alistipes finegoldii, 2003. Master ACP; fellow APHA, AAAS, Am. Acad. Microbiology, Infectious Diseases Soc. Am. (councilor 1976-79, pres.-elect 1980-81, pres. 1981-82, exec. com. 1980-83, Bristol award 1987, Soc. citation 1999); mem. Assn. Am. Physicians, Am. Soc. Microbiology (chmn. subcom. on taxonomy of Bacteroidaceae 1971-74, 1st annual Alex Sonnenwirth award 1986), Am. Thoracic Soc., Western Soc. Clin. Rsch., Western Assn. Physicians, Wadsworth Med. Alumni Assn. (past pres.), Anaerobe Soc. of the Ams. (interim pres. 1992-94, pres. 1994-96), Soc. Intestinal Microbiology Ecology and Disease (interim pres. 1982-83, pres. 1983-87), Va. Soc. Physician in Infectious Diseases (pres. 1986-88), Am. Fedn. Clin. Rsch., Sigma Xi, Alpha Omega Alpha. Democrat. Jewish. Office: Infectious Disease Sect VA Med Ctr Wilshire & Sawtelle Blvds Los Angeles CA 90073 Home: 13082 Mindanao Way #17 Marina Del Rey CA 90292 Office Phone: 310-268-3678. Personal E-mail: sidfinegol@aol.com.

FINELSEN, LIBBI JUNE, lawyer; b. Encino, Calif., Apr. 14, 1968; BA in Polit. Sci. summa cum laude, U. Nev., 1990; JD magna cum laude, Lewis and Clark Coll., 1993. Bar: D.C. 1996, NY 2006, U.S. Ct. Appeals (9th, 11th and D.C. cirs.) 1996, U.S. Ct. Appeals (4th cir.) 1999, U.S. Ct. Appeals (fedl. cir.) 2001, Ct. Fed. Claims 2001. Jud. law clk. Gen. Svcs. Bd. Contract Appeals, Washington, 1993-94; assoc. McAleese & Assocs. P.C., McLean, Va., 1994-96; atty. USDA, Washington, 1996-99; trial atty. US Dept. Air Force, Wright Patterson AFB, Ohio, 2000—01, atty./adv. LA AFB, Calif., 2001—06; asst. county atty. Orange County, Goshen, NY, 2006—07; conflicts advisor Sonnenschein Nath & Rosenthal, NYC, 2007—. V.p. edn. Hadassah Young Profls. Group, Washington, 1998-99; mem. hospitality com. Kesher Israel Synagogue, Washington, 1998-99. Mem. ABA, Phi Alpha Delta, Phi Kappa Phi. Avocations: cooking, handicrafts, travel, art exhibitions.

FINEMAN, HOWARD DAVID, columnist, news correspondent; b. Pitts., Nov. 17, 1948; s. Charles Morton and Jean (Lederman) F.; m. Amy Lee Nathan, Apr. 21, 1984; children: Meredith Claire, Nicholas Lowell. AB, Colgate U., 1971; MS, Columbia U., 1973; JD, U. Louisville, 1980. Reporter The Courier-Jour., Louisville, 1973-79; corr. Newsweek, Washington, 1980-84, chief polit. corr., 1984—, dep. bur. chief, 1994—, sr. editor, 1996—, columnist, 2007—. Panelist "Washington Week in Review" PBS, Arlington, Va., 1982-95, "Capital Gang Sunday", CNN, Washington, 1995-98; contbr. MSNBC, CNBC, Fox News Network, 1996-98; news analyst NBC, 1998—. Recipient Front Page award NY Newspaper Guild, 1983, Silver Gavel award ABA, 1990, Nat. mag. award 1983, 92, 98, 2001, 03, 04, award Deadline Club, 2003, Alumni award Columbia U.; Pulitzer Traveling fellow Columbia U., 1976, Watson fellow Thomas J. Watson Found., 1971. Mem.: Phi Beta Kappa. Office: Newsweek Ste 1220 1750 Pennsylvania Ave NW Washington DC 20006-4578

FINEMAN, S. DAVID, lawyer; b. Phila., Oct. 23, 1945; BA, Am. U., 1967; JD with honors, George Washington U., 1970. Bar: Pa. 1971, U.S. Dist. Ct. (ea. dist.) Pa., U.S. Ct. Appeals (3d cir.) Pa. 1980. Trial atty. Defender Assn., Phila., 1971-72; law clk. Superior Ct. Commonwealth, Pa., 1972-73; mng. ptnr. Fineman Krekstein & Harris, P.A., Phila., 1981—, 1987—. Instr. bus. law Temple U., 1974-83; mem. Phila. Planning Commn., 1989-91, Industry Policy Adv. Com. to Advise Sec. of Commerce on Internat. Trade Issues, 1994-98. Bd. govs. US Postal Svc., 1995—2005, chmn., 2003—05, chmn. compensation com., 1997—2000, vice chmn., 2001—03, chmn. strategic planning com., 2001—03. Mem. ABA, Phila. Bar Assn., Pa. Bar Assn., Def. Rsch. Inst. Home: 335 Woodley Rd Merion Station PA 19066-1430 Office: 30 S 17th St 18th Fl Philadelphia PA 19103-5443 Office Phone: 215-893-8701. Business E-Mail: sdfineman@finemanlawfirm.com.

FINEMAN, STEVEN E., lawyer; b. LA, Feb. 13, 1963; BA, U. of California, San Diego, 1985; JD, University of California, Hastings College of the Law, 1988. Bar: California 1989, D.C., New York, U.S. Dist. Ct. 1995, U.S. Ct. of Appeals, Ninth Circuit 1995, U.S. Ct. of Appeals, Fifth Circuit 1996, No., Ea., Ctrl. Districts of California. Managing ptnr. Lieff Cabraser Heimann & Bernstein, LLP. Mem.: Lawyers Comm. for Human Rights, Supreme Ct. Historical Soc., Assoc. of Trial Lawyers of Am., Assoc. of the Bar for the City of N.Y., Trial Lawyers for Public Justice, D.C. Bar Assoc., Calif. Bar Assoc., N.Y. Bar Assoc., Am. Bar Assoc. Office: Lieff Cabraser Heimann & Bernstein LLP 780 Third Avenue 48th Floor New York NY 10017

FINERTY, MARTIN JOSEPH, JR., editor, military officer; b. Wilmington, Del., July 22, 1936; s. Martin Joseph and Jane Morris (McClenaghan) F.; m. Joan Eddleman, Dec. 3, 1960; children: Nancy Jane, Laura Tourison. BSE, U.S. Naval Acad., 1959; MS in Phys. Oceanography, U. Miami, Coral Gables, Fla., 1966; MS in Indsl. Mgmt., Indsl. Coll. of the Armed Forces, 1979. Commd. ensign USN, 1959, advanced though grades to capt., 1985; head, polar programs Office of Oceanographer of Navy, Alexandria, Va., 1975-76; spl. asst. submarines Office of Asst. Sec. of Navy, Washington, 1976-77; spl. asst. ocean environ. Office of Chief of Naval Ops., Washington, 1977-78; commdg. officer Naval Polar Oceanography Ctr., Washington, 1982-85; program officer NAS, Washington, 1985-87; asst. dir. rsch. ASME, Washington, 1987-88; exec. dir., COO Marine Tech. Soc., Washington, 1988-99; sr. cons. editor Compass Publs., Arlington, Va., 1999—. Expert in ocean and hydro survey ops., polar programs and assn. mgmt. Author/editor tech. publs. Fellow Marine Tech.

Soc.; mem. Assn. U.S. Naval Acad. Class of 1959 (sec. 1971-74), The Army Navy Club, Masons. Avocations: reading, gardening. Home: 1841 Northbridge Ln Annapolis MD 21401-6576 Personal E-mail: mjfna59@comcast.net.

FINESTONE, SHEILA, senator, retired legislator; b. Montreal, Que., Can., Jan. 28, 1927; d. Monroe and Minnie Abbey; m. Alan Finestone, June 9, 1947; children: David, Peter, Maxwell, Stephen. BS in Edn., McGill U. M.P. to Ho. of Commons for Mount Royal, 1984, 1988, 1993—99; critic for commn. and culture, 1985—93; Sec. of State Multiculturalism and the Status of Women, 1993—96; appt. Senate of Can., Ottawa, Ont., Canada, 1999—. Advisor to Parliament on eliminating anti-personal land mines; mem. transp. and comm., statutes and regulations; vice chair human rights; mem. spl. com. custody and access in divorce, constitution amendments edn.; past pres. La Fed. des Femmes du Quebec; mem. Quebec Referendum Organizer Les Yvettes, 1980; vice chair Amendment Equality Rights Can. Constn., 1985; min. of state Status of Women; leader Can. Delegation to Beijing World Conf. on Women's Rights, 1995; mem. exec. com. Can. Assn. Former Parliamentarians, Can. Land Mines Found., Adopt a Minefield Can. Pres. (hon.) Young Men and Young Women's Hebrew Assn.; ret. sec. Parliamentarian Assoc.; guide Canadian Mus. of Civilization; exec. World Exec. of Inter Parliamentary Union; mem. Nat. Coun. Jewish Women; hon. gov. Jewish Gen. Hosp.; mem. exec. com. Orgn. Jewish Parliament; bd. mem. Nat. Collection Fund, Mus. Civilization, 2005—. Named Person of the Yr., McGill U., 2001; recipient Jackie Robinson Leadership award, 1996, Samuel Bronfinan Leadership award, 1995, O.R.T. Sophie Benett award, 1996. Mem. Orgn. Rehab. and Tng. Liberal.

FINGAR, THOMAS, federal official; AB, Cornell U., 1968; MA, Stanford U., 1969, PhD, 1977. Co-dir. U.S.-China Edn. Clearinghouse NAS; adv. Congl. Office Tech. Assessment; various positions including sr. rsch. assoc., dir. U.S.-China Rels. Program Stanford U., 1975—86; chief China divsn. U.S. Dept. State, 1986—89, dir. office of analysis E. Asia and Pacific Washington, 1989—94, dep. asst. sec. for analysis, 1994—2000, prin. dep. asst. sec., 2001—03; acting asst. sec. for intelligence & rsch. US Dept. State, Washington, 2000—01, 2003—04, asst. sec. for intelligence & rsch., 2004—05; dep. dir. for analysis Office Nat. Intelligence, Washington, 2005—; chmn. Nat. Intelligence Coun., 2005—. Editor: (book) Higher Education in the People's Republic of China: Report of the Stanford University Delegation, 1980, China's Quest for Independence: Policy Evolution in the Nineteen Seventies, 1980; author: Modernizing China's Electronics Industry: Prospects for U.S. Business, 1985; co-author: Education in the People's Republic of China and U.S.: China Educational Exchanges, 1989, American Studies of Contemporary China, 1993; contbr. articles to profl. jours. German linguist, intellegence analyst US Army, 1969—72. Office: Office Nat Intelligence NEOB 725 17th St Washington DC 20500

FINGARETTE, HERBERT, philosopher, educator; b. Bklyn., Jan. 20, 1921; m. Leslie J. Swabacker, Jan. 23, 1945; 1 dau., Ann Hasse. BA, UCLA, 1947, PhD, 1949; LHD, St. Bonaventure U., 1993. Mem. faculty U. Calif.-Santa Barbara, 1948—, Phi Beta Kappa Romanell prof. philosophy, 1983—; William James lectr. religion Harvard U., 1971; W.T. Jones lectr. philosophy Pomona Coll., 1974; Evans-Wentz lectr. Oriental religions Stanford U., 1977; Gramlich lectr. human nature Dartmouth Coll., 1978; cons. NEH; Raphael Demos lectr. Vanderbilt U., 1985. Disting. tchr. U. Calif.-Santa Barbara, 1985, faculty rsch. lectr., 1977. Author: The Self in Transformation, 1963, On Responsibility, 1967, Self Deception, 1969, Confucius: The Secular as Sacred, 1972, The Meaning of Criminal Insanity, 1972, Mental Disabilities and Criminals Responsibility, 1979, Heavy Drinking: The Myth of Alcoholism as a Disease, 1988, Rules, Rituals, and Responsibility: Essays Dedicated to Herbert Fingarette, 1991, Death: Philosophical Soundings, 1996, Mapping Responsibility, 2004. Washington and Lee U. Lewis law scholar, 1980; fellow NEH, NIMH, Walter Meyer Law Rsch. Inst., Battelle Rsch. Ctr., Addiction Rsch. Ctr., Inst. Psychiatry, London; fellow Ctr. for Advanced Studies in Behavioral Sci., Stanford, 1985-86. Mem. Am. Philos. Assn. (pres. Pacific divsn. 1977-78). Home: 1507 APS Santa Barbara CA 93103 Office: U Calif Dept Philosophy Santa Barbara CA 93106

FINGER, HAROLD BEN, nuclear energy industry executive, consultant, government agency administrator; b. NY, Feb. 18, 1924; s. Beny and Anna (Perlmutter) F.; m. Arlene Karsch, June 11, 1949; children: Barbara Lynn Korengold, Elyse Sue Camozzo, Sandra Ruth Ciccarelli. BME, CCNY, 1944; MS in Aero Engring., Case Inst. Tech., 1950. With NASA and predecessor NACA, 1944-69; mgr. AEC-NASA Space Nuc. Propulsion Office, 1960-67; dir. nuc. sys. NASA, 1958-64, dir. space power and nuclear sys., 1964-67; dir. space nuc. sys. divsn. AEC, 1965-67; assoc. adminstr. for orgn. and mgmt. NASA, 1967-69; asst. sec. for rsch. and tech. HUD, 1969-72; mgr. electric utility engring. oper. GE, Schenectady, N.Y., 1972-74, gen. mgr. Ctr. for Energy Sys. Washington, 1972-80; staff exec. Power Sys. Strategic Planning and Devel., Fairfield, Conn., 1980-83; pres., CEO U.S. Com. for Energy Awareness, Washington, 1983-87, U.S. Coun. for Energy Awareness, Washington, 1987-91; energy, space, nuc. energy, housing, urban affairs, govt. mgmt. cons., 1991—. Recipient Manley Meml. award Soc. Automotive Engrs., 1958. Fellow: AIAA (James H. Wyld Propulsion award 1968), Nat. Acad. Pub. Adminstrn.; mem.: AAAS, AIA (hon.), Nat. Space Soc., Am. Astronautical Soc., NASA Alumni League (pres.), Nat. Housing Conf. (life trustee), Am. Nuc. Soc., Am. Soc. Pub. Adminstrn., Cosmos Club.

FINGER, JASON ROY, food service executive, internet entrepreneur; b. 1974; m. Stephanie Finger. BA, U. Md., 1994; JD, MBA, NYU, 1999. Assoc. O'Sullivan Graev, NYC, 1999; co-founder & CEO SeamlessWeb Profl. Solutions, Inc. (acquired by Aramark Co., 2006), NYC, 1999. Finalist Entrepreneur of Yr. award, Ernst & Young, 2005; named one of 40 Under 40, Crain's NY Bus., 2007.*

FINGER, STEPHEN N., aircraft manufacturing executive; B aerospace engring., Univ. Va.; M mgmt., MIT. Mgmt. positions United Technologies Corp., Hartford, Conn., 1970—, sr. v.p. op. mil. engines, Pratt & Whitney bus. unit, pres. mil. engines, Pratt & Whitney bus. unit, pres. Sikorsky bus. unit, 2003—06, pres. Pratt & Whitney bus. unit, 2006—. Recipient Laurels award, Aviation Week mag., 1991; Sloan Fellow. Mem.: Am. Inst. Aeronautics & Astronautics, Air Force Assn. Achievements include patents in field. Office: United Technologies United Technologies Bldg Hartford CT 06101*

FINGERHUT, ERIC D., academic administrator, former state legislator and congressman, lawyer; b. University Hts., Ohio, May 6, 1959; BS summa cum laude, Northwestern U., 1981; JD, Stanford U., 1984. Staff atty. older persons law office Legal Aid Soc., Cleve., 1984-85; assoc. dir. Cleveland Works, Cleve., 1987-89; atty. Hahn Loeser & Parks, Cleve.; campaign mgr., transition dir., spl. asst. to Mayor Mike White, 1989; mem. Ohio Senate from 25th Dist., Columbus, 1991-93, 103rd Congress from 19th Ohio dist., Washington, D.C., 1993-94, Ohio Senate from 25th dist., Columbus, 1999—2006; dir. econ.-devel. edn. and entrepreneurship Baldwin-Wallace Coll., Berea, Ohio, 2006—07; chancellor Ohio Bd. of Regents, Columbus, 2007—. Mem. Energy, Nat. Resources and Environ. com., Fin. com., Health and Human Svcs. com., Child Support Guidelines Adv. com., Ohio Adv. Coun. for Aging com., Task Force on Campaign Fin. reform com., Welfare Oversight Commission com., House Banking, Fin. and Urban Affairs com., Sci., Space and Tech. com., Fgn. Affairs Com. Author: Making Ohio Great Again. Bd. trustees Cleve. Zelma George Shelter; pres. Common Cause/Ohio, 1986-88; leader FITE; tchr. Sunday Sch. Synagogue Beth-Am. Recipient Future of Cleve. Jewry award, Stanford Law Review award; named to Cleve. Heights High Sch. Hall of Fame. Mem. Ohio Bar Assn., Cleve. Bar Assn. Democrat. Jewish. Home: 22675 Fairmont Blvd Cleveland OH 44118 Office: Ohio Bd Regents 30 E Broad St, 36th Fl Columbus OH 43215*

FINGERSON, LEROY MALVIN, engineering executive, mechanical engineer; b. Rochester, Minn., July 1, 1932; s. Malvin Ferdinand and Corolla Racelia (Sundet) F.; m. Ruth Anne Johnson, Nov. 26, 1960; children: Mark, Karin, Laura. BSME, U. Minn., 1954, MSME, 1955, PhDME, 1961. Chmn. bd. TSI, Inc., St. Paul, 1961-98, CEO, 1961-97, ret., 1998, chmn. emeritus. Contbr. articles to profl. jours. Mem. Nat. Acad. Engring. Lutheran.

FINGLETON, THOMAS D., retail executive; b. Kokomo, Ind. m. Kathleen L. Wentland; children: Rebecca, Elizabeth, Stephanie. Degree in bus., Ind. U. Acct. Arthur Andersen & Co., 1977; from dir. corp. acctg. to sr. v.p fin. May Dept. Stores Co., St. Louis, 1978—84, exec. v.p., CFO, 2000—; from sr. v.p. fin., CFO to chmn. Hecht's, Washington, 1985—2000. Office: May Dept Stores Co 611 Olive St Saint Louis MO 63101

FINK, CHARLES AUGUSTIN, behavioral systems scientist; b. McAllen, Tex., Jan. 1, 1929; s. Charles Adolph and Mary Nellie (Bonneau) F.; m. Ann Heslen, June 1, 1955 (dec. June 1981); children: Patricia A., Marianne E., Richard G., Gerard A. AA, Pan-Am. U., 1948; BS, Marquette U., 1950; postgrad., George Washington Med. Ctr., Walter Reed Army Med. Ctr., 1969-70, No. Va. C.C., 1973, George Mason U., 1974; MA, Cath. U. Am., 1979. Journalist UP and Ft. Worth Star-Telegram, 1950-52; commd. 2d lt. U.S. Army, 1952, advanced through grades to lt. col., 1966, various positions telecommunications, 1952-56, instr., 1956-58, exec. project mgmt., 1958-62, def. analysis and rsch., 1962-65, fgn. mil. rels., 1965-67, def. telecommunications exec., 1967-69, chief planning, budget and program control office Def. Satellite Communications Program, Def. Communications Agy., 1969-72, ret., 1972; pvt. practice cons. managerial behavior Falls Church, Va., 1972-77; pres. Behavioral Systems Sci. Orgn. (and predecessor firms), Falls Church, 1978—. Leader family group dynamics, 1958-67; home hemodialysis technician, 1969-81; pub (jour.) Circle, 1985—; computer program cons. Hubble Space Telescope Servicing Mission, NASA, 1993. Developer hierarchial theory of human behavior, 1967—, uses in behavioral, social and biol. sci. and their applications, 1972—, behavioral causal modeling research methodology, 1974—, computer-aided behavior systems coaching for persons and orgns., 1982—, telecoaching, 1989; microbiol. chromatographic profiling, 1989—; public domain Portable Personal Health Record, 1994, Computer Aid for Understanding Personal Behavior, 2005; adv. for copyrighting computer graphics displays and multi-media communications in scis. Adv. bd. Holy Redeemer Roman Cath. Ch., Bangkok, Thailand, St. Philip's Ch., Falls Church, Va., 1971-73. Decorated Army Commendation medals, Joint Services Commendation medal; named to Fink Hall of Fame, 1982; recipient Behavior Modeling award Internat. Congress Applied Systems Rsch. and Cybernetics, 1980, Mission Pin award NASA, 1993. Mem. AAAS, SAR, Nat. Genealogical Soc., Internat. Soc. Systems Scis., Am. Soc. Cybernetics, Internat. Assn. Cybernetics, Internat. Network Social Network Analysis, Assn. U.S. Army, Ret. Officers Assn., Finks Internat. (v.p. 1981—), KC. Home: 3305 Brandy Ct Falls Church VA 22042-3705 Office: PO Box 2051 Falls Church VA 22042-0051

FINK, CONRAD CHARLES, journalist, educator, communications executive, consultant; b. Marquette, Mich., Sept. 16, 1932; s. Donald Ellsworth and Mary Ruth (Fox) F.; m. Sue Carol Henry, Sept. 4, 1954; children: Karen Sue, Conrad Stephan. BS, U. Wis., 1954. Reporter Bloomington (Ill.) Daily Pantagraph; 1956-57; various positions to night city editor AP, Chgo., 1957-60, writer fgn. desk NYC, 1961, fgn. corr. Tokyo Bur., 1961-64, bur. chief South Asia New Delhi, 1964—67; dir. AP-Dow Jones Econ. Report, London, 1967-70; asst. to pres. AP, NYC, 1970, v.p., 1971-77, sec., 1974-77; 1st v.p., dir. Wide World Photos, Inc.; v.p. Press Assn., Inc.; v.p., dir. AP (Can.), Ltd.; sec., dir. N.Y.C. News Assn., Inc., 1974-77; exec. v.p. adminstrn., dir. Park Broadcasting, Inc., Ithaca, NY, 1977-81, Park Newspapers, Inc., 1977-81; disting. lectr. U. Ga. Sch. Journalism, Athens, 1982, prof. newspaper mgmt., 1983—; dir. James M. Cox Jr. Inst. for Newspaper Mgmt. Studies, Athens, 1990—, William S. Morris prof. newspaper strategy and mgmt., 1995—, Josiah Meigs disting. tchg. prof., 2004—. Sr. fellow emeritus U. Ga., Univ. Tchr. Acad., 2000—. Author: Strategic Newspaper Management, 1988, Media Ethics, 1988, Inside the Media, 1990, Introduction to Professional Newswriting, 1992, Introduction to Magazine Writing, 1993, Writing Opinion for Impact, 1999, Bottom Line Writing, 2000, Sports Writing: The Lively Game, 2001, Writing to Inform and Engage, 2003. Served to 1st lt. USMCR, 1954-56. Named Nat. Journalism Tchr. of year, Freedom Forum, 2002; recipient Disting. Svc. award, U. Wis., 1969, Regents Tchg. Excellence award, 2004. Home: 116 S Stratford Dr Athens GA 30605-3024 Office: U Ga Sch Journalism Athens GA 30602 Office Phone: 706-542-5031. Business E-Mail: CFink@uga.edu.

FINK, DANIEL JULIEN, management consultant; b. Jersey City, Dec. 13, 1926; s. Joseph and Dorothy (Weisberger) F.; m. Tobie E. Weiss, June 24, 1951; children: Kenneth Wayne, Betsy Ilene, Karen Patrice. BS, MIT, Cambridge, Mass., 1948, MS, 1949. Registered profl. engr., Mass. Aeromechanics engr. Cornell Aero. Lab., 1948; chief aircraft dynamics Bell Aircraft Corp., Buffalo, 1949—52; v.p. Allied Rsch. Assocs., Inc., Concord, Mass., 1952—63; asst. dir. def. rsch. and engring. Dept. Def., 1963—65, dep. dir. def. rsch. and engring., 1965—67; with GE, 1967—82, v.p., gen. mgr. space divsn., 1969—77, v.p., group exec. aerospace group Phila., 1977—79, sr. v.p. corp. planning and devel. Fairfield, Conn., 1979—82; pres. D.J. Fink Assocs., Inc., 1982—. Bd. dirs. Titan Corp., Orbital Scis. Corp.; def. sci. bd. Dept. Def., 1968—72, sr. cons., 1979—98; nat. indsl. adv. coun. Opportunities Industrialization Ctrs., 1977—79; sci. adv. panel Dept. Army, 1971—74; adv. coun. NASA, 1978—79, chmn. adv. coun., 1982—88; corp. vis. dept. aero. and astronautics MIT, 1972—82, Sloan Sch., 1982—85; chmn. dept. adv. bd. dept. mech. engring. Rensselaer Poly. Inst., 1981—84; mem. Vice Pres.'s Space Policy Adv. Bd., 1992. Patentee vibration isolation, weapon systems mgmt., aerospace mgmt. and corp. planning. Recipient Disting. Pub. Svc. award Dept. Def., 1967, NASA Disting. Svc. medal, 1986, NASA medal for Outstanding Leadership, 1988; Collier trophy, 1974 Hon. fellow AIAA (pres. 1974-75, von Karman lectr. 1980); fellow AAAS; mem. NAE (chmn. space applications bd. 1976-81, chmn. telecomms. and computer applications bd. 1984-87, chmn. com. on U.S.-Japan linkages in transport aircraft 1993, chmn. com. on space facilities 1994), Cosmos Club. Business E-Mail: dfink@nas.edu.

FINK, DAVID LEONARD, surgeon; b. St. Louis, June 6, 1936; s. Sidney Fink and Estelle Esses Goldstein; m. Frances Carole Bower, June 13, 1965; children: Dana Lynne, Denise Lysette. BA, Columbia Coll., 1957; MD, Cornell U., NYC, 1961. Diplomate Am. Bd. Surgery. Resident in surgery St. Luke's Hosp. Med. Ctr., NYC, 1961-64, U. Wis. Med. Ctr., Madison, 1964-66; pvt. practice, Paterson, N.J., 1970—; chief exec. officer Gen. Surgeons North Jersey, P.A., Paterson, 1970—. Chief surgery Barnert Meml. Hosp., Paterson, 1982-86, 2003—, pres. med. staff, 1988; assoc. clin. prof. surgery Seton Hall Postgrad. Sch. Medicine; asst. clin. prof. surgery U. Medicine and Dentistry of N.J. Maj. U.S. Army, 1966-70. Decorated Army Commendation medal; recipient Am. Top Surgeons. Fellow ACS, Soc. of Surgeons of N.J.; mem. Vascular Soc. N.J., Ea. Vascular Soc., Southeastern Surg. Soc., Cornell U. Med. Alumni Assn. (bd. dirs. 1986-89), Stuyvesant Yacht Club. Avocation: sailing. Office: Gen Surgeons North Jersey 707 Broadway Paterson NJ 07514-1425 Home Phone: 973-239-7431; Office Phone: 973-742-3371.

FINK, EDWARD MURRAY, lawyer, educator; b. NYC, Mar. 11, 1934; s. Nathaniel and Elsa Charlotte (Lenrow) F.; divorced; children: Jeffrey Neil, Andrea Sue; m. Rita Toby Cohen, Aug. 11, 1985. BS in Chemistry, CCNY, 1955; JD, Georgetown U., 1959. Bar: DC 1960, US Dist. Ct. DC 1960, US Ct. Appeals (DC cir.) 1960, NY 1962, NJ 1970, US Dist. Ct. NJ 1970, US Patent and Trademark Office 1960. Patent examiner U.S. Patent Office, Washington, 1955-60; atty. Bell Labs., Murray Hill, NJ, 1960-83, Bell Comm. Rsch. Inc., Livingston, NJ, 1984-91, Edward M. Fink, P.A., Edison, NJ, 1991—; v.p., gen. counsel Eastern RR Investment Corp., Watchung, NJ, 2000—, chmn. bd. dirs., 2001—, Somerset Terminal R.R. Corp., 2001—02. Adj. prof. torts, bus. law and civil litigation Middlesex County Coll., Edison, NJ, 1980-2000; adj. prof. partnerships and corps, contract law Montclair State U., Upper Montclair, NJ, 1984-2000. Mem. ABA, Am. Intellectual Property Assn., NJ Patent Law Assn., NJ State Bar Assn., DC Bar Assn., NY State Bar Assn. Democrat. Jewish. Home and Office: 23 Delaware Crossing Somerset NJ 08873 Home Phone: 732-564-6749; Office Phone: 732-563-0440. Personal E-mail: patemf@aol.com.

FINK, JEROLD ALBERT, lawyer; b. Dayton, Ohio, July 16, 1941; s. Albert Otto and Marjorie Carolyn (Scheidt) F.; m. Mary Jo McHone, Dec. 31, 1961 (div. July 1978); children: Marjorie, Kathryn, Erick; m. 2d, Deborah Lynn Bailey, Dec. 25, 1980 (div. Oct. 1986); 1 child, Justin. AB, Duke U., 1963, LLB, 1966. Bar: Ohio 1966. Assoc. Taft, Stettinius & Hollister, Cin., 1966-73, ptnr., 1973—. Bd. dirs. The Wm. Powell Co., Cin., 1974—, Great Trails Broadcasting Co., Cin., 1974-79. Co-author: (with Judy Cohn) Power Defensive Carding, 1988, (with Joe Lutz) The American Forcing Minor Bidding System, 1995, (with Joe Lutz) Defensive Carding in the 21st Century, 2001. Pres. Cin. Musical Festival Assn., 1978-79; trustee Cin. Playhouse, 1976-95, New Life Youth Svcs., Cin., 1971—. Republican. Presbyterian. Office: 1800 Firstar Tower 425 Walnut St Cincinnati OH 45202-3923 E-mail: fink@taftlaw.com.

FINK, JORDAN NORMAN, allergist, educator; b. Milw., Oct. 13, 1934; s. Jack and Ruth Fink; m. Phyllis Mechanic, Aug. 26, 1956; children: Leslie, Rosanne, Robert. BS, U. Wis.-Madison, 1956, MD, 1959. Diplomate Am. Bd. Internal Medicine, Am. Bd. Allergy and Immunology. Inst. Med. Coll. Wis., Milw., 1965-68, asst. prof. medicine, 1968-70, assoc. prof. medicine, 1970-73, prof., chief allergy and immunology, 1973—98, prof. medicine and pediats, 1994—. Chmn. adv. com. on pulmonary allergy FDA, Rockwell, Md., 1980-81, cons., 1983— Contbr. articles to profl. jours., chpt. to book Chmn. Camp Interlaken Com., Milw., 1978-81 bd. dirs. Jewish Community Ctr., Milw., 1977-81 Grantee NIH, 1982, VA, 1984 Fellow ACP, Am. Acad. Allergy (pres. 1984-85); mem. Assn. Am. Physicians, Am. Soc. Clin. Investigation, Am. Assn. Immunologists, Alpha Omega Alpha, Phi Delta Epsilon Avocations: swimming, travel. Home: 2829 W Golf Cir Mequon WI 53092-2446 Office: Med Coll Wis 9000 W Wisconsin Ave Milwaukee WI 53226-3518

FINK, JOSEPH ALLEN, lawyer; s. Allen Medford and Margaret Ruth (Draper) F.; m. Marcia L. Horton; children: Alexander Mentzer, Justin McGranahan. Student, Wayne State U., 1960-61; BA, Oberlin Coll., 1964; JD, Duke U., 1967. Bar: Mich. 1968, U.S. Dist Ct. (ea. dist.) Mich. 1968, U.S. Dist. Ct. (we. dist.) Mich. 1974, U.S. Ct. Appeals (6th cir.) 1987, U.S. Supreme Ct. 1998. Assoc. Dickinson, Wright, McKean & Cudlip, Detroit, 1967—72, Lansing, Mich., 1972—75; ptnr. Dickinson Wright PLLC, Lansing, 1976—. Instr. U.S. Internat. U. Grad. Sch. Bus., San Diego, 1971; adj. prof. trial advocacy Thomas M. Cooley Law Sch., Lansing, 1984-85; mem. com. on local rules U.S. Dist. Cts., 1985; chmn. trial experience subcom. U.S. Dist. Ct. (we. dist.) Mich., 1981. Contbg. author: Construction Litigation, 1979, Legal Considerations in Managing Problem Employees, 1988, Michigan Civil Procedure During Trial, 2d edit., 1989, Regulatory & Legislative Quarterly, CPRCU Soc.; co-author Honestly This May Not be The Best Policy, 2006; contbr. articles to profl. jours. Bd. dirs. Lansing 2000 Inc., 1985-92, Profl. Direct Inc., Universal Holding Corp.; bd. trustees Olivet (Mich.) Coll., 1985-94; mem. bd. advisors Mich. State U. Press, 1993-96. Lt. JACF USNR, 1968—72. Named one of Best Lawyers in Am., Commercial Litigation, Civil Litigation Defense Super Lawyers. Fellow: Mich. State Bar Found.; mem.: State Bar of Mich. (chmn. local disciplinary com. 1983—, com. for US Cts. 1984), Assn. Life Ins. Counsel, Internat. Assn. Ins. Receivers. Episcopalian. Avocations: writing, reading, golf. Office: Dickinson Wright PLLC 215 S Washington Sq Ste 200 Lansing MI 48933-1816 Home Phone: 517-339-4013; Office Phone: 517-487-4711. Business E-Mail: jfink@dickinsonwright.com.

FINK, JOSEPH RICHARD, academic administrator; b. Newark, Mar. 20, 1943; s. Joseph Richard and Jean (Chorazy) F.; m. Donna Gibson, 1965 (div. 1986); children: Michael, Taryn; m. Christine Gaudenzi, Oct. 4, 1992 (div. 2003); children: Madison, Joseph; m. Denise Riley, Nov. 17, 2006. AB, Rider U., 1963; PhD in Am. History, Rutgers U., 1971; DLitt (hon.), Rider U., 1982, Coll. of Misericordia, 1992, Golden Gate U., 1994. Asst. then assoc. prof history Immaculata (Pa.) Coll., 1964-72, adminstrv. asst. to pres., 1969-72; dean of Arts & Scis. City Colls. Chgo., 1972-74; pres. Raritan Valley Coll., Somerville, NJ, 1974-79, Coll. Misericordia, Dallas, 1979-88, Dominican U of Calif, San Rafael, 1988—. Pres. Regional Planning Coun. Higher Edn., Region 3/Northeastern Pa., 1986-88. Mem. exec. com. Philharm. Soc. Northeastern Pa., 1986-89; bd. dirs. Marin Symphony, 1989-2004, San Francisco Ballet, 1994-97, Ind. Coll. No. Calif., 1992—, Marin Forum, 1991—, Guide Dogs for the Blind, 1994-97, Alonzo Kings Lines Ballet, 2006—; bd. dirs. Am. Land Conservancy, 1995—, exec. com.; mem. campaign cabinet United Way San Francisco, 1990; bd. dirs. North Bay Coun., 1993—, chmn., 1996, exec. com. Mem. Nat. Assn. Ind. Colls. and Univs. (secretariat 1986), Nat. Assn. Intercollegiate Athletics (pres.'s adv. coun. 1986), Am. Coun. on Higher Edn. (commn. leadership devel. higher edn. 1978-82, commn. on internat. edn. 1993-96, acad. adminstrn. fellow 1974-75), Assn. Mercy Colls. (pres. 1985-87, exec. com. 1981-87), Coun. for Ind. Colls. (bd. dirs. 1989-92), Am. Hist. Assn., World Affairs Coun. No. Calif. (bd. dirs. 1990-96), Commonwealth Club Calif. (quar. chmn. 1989, chmn. Marin County chpt. 1989—, bd. dirs. 1992—, exec. com. 1997—, pres., 2003). Office: Dominican U Calif 50 Acacia Ave San Rafael CA 94901-2230 Business E-Mail: jrf@dominican.edu.

FINK, LAURENCE D., diversified financial services company executive; BA in Polit. Sci., U. Calif., LA, Calif., 1974, MBA in Real Estate, 1976. Mng. dir., mem. mgmt. com., head mortgage & real estate products group, co-head taxable fixed income div. First Boston Corp., 1976—88; chmn. & CEO BlackRock Inc., 1988—; chmn. Nomura BlackRock Asset Mgmt. Mem. bd. executives NYSE, 2003—; bd. dirs. PNC Asset Mgmt. Group Inc. Trustee, mem. exec. com., chmn. fin. affairs com. NYU; co-chmn. bd. trustees, mem. exec. com. Mount Sinai NYU Health; co-chmn. bd. trustees NYU Hosp. Ctr. Office: BlackRock Inc 40 East 52nd St New York NY 10022*

FINK, LESTER HAROLD, retired engineering company executive, educator; b. Phila., May 3, 1925; s. Harold D. and Edna B. (Hopkins) F.; m. R. Naomi Veit, Dec. 10, 1955; children: Lois Hope, Carol Anne. BSEE, U. Pa., 1950, MSEE, 1961. Supr. engr. rsch. divsn. Phila. Electric Co., 1950-74; asst. dir. Electric Energy Systems divsn. Dept. Interior, Washington, 1974-75, ERDA, Washington, 1975-77, Dept. Energy, 1977-79; pres. Systems Engring. for Power, Inc., Vienna, Va., 1979-83; chmn. Carlsen & Fink Assocs., Inc., 1983-89; exec. v.p. ECC, Inc., 1989-96, ret.; pvt. cons. Adj. prof. Drexel U., 1961-74, U. Pa., 1973, U. Md., 1979-80; Attwood assoc. Conf. Internationale de Grande Reseaux Electrique. Patentee underground power transmission and automatic generation control; contbg. author: Large Scale Systems, 1982, Power System Analysis and Planning, 1983; contbr. chpt.: Electronics Engring. Handbook, 1982, 97; editor, contbg. author: Power Systems Restructuring, 1988, Unlocking the Benefits of Restructuring, 1999. With U.S. Army, 1943-46. Recipient Meritorious Svc. award Dept. Energy, 1979 Fellow IEEE (life), Instrument Soc. Am., Sigma Tau, Eta Kappa Nu, Tau Beta Pi. Presbyterian. Home: 250 Pantops Mountain Rd # WCBR-4 Charlottesville VA 22911-8694 Personal E-mail: lfink@ieee.org.

FINK, MATTHEW E., health facility executive, educator; b. Phila., Jan. 15, 1951; BA cum laude, U. Pa., 1972; MD cum laude, U. Pitts., 1972-76. Diplomate Am. Bd. Critical Care Medicine, Am. Bd. Psychiatry and Neurology, Am. Bd. Internal Medicine, Nat. Bd. Med. Examiners. Intern then asst. resident in medicine Boston City Hosp., 1976-78, chief resident in internal medicine, 1978; asst. resident then chief resident in neurology Columbia-Presbyn. Med. Ctr., NYC, 1978-82, chief neurology clin., 1982-84, dir. neurology ICU, 1983-93, co-investigator Coma Clin. Rsch. Ctr., 1986-90, dir. neurology and neurosurgery ICU, 1991-93; clin. fellow Coll. Physicians and Surgeons Columbia U., NYC, 1978-82, assoc. in clin. neurology Coll. Physicians and Surgeons, 1982-83, from. asst. prof. to assoc. prof. in clin. neurology Coll. Physicians and Surgeons, 1983-90, dir. divsn. critical care neurology, 1988-93, assoc. prof. clin. neurology depts. neurology and neurosurgery, 1990; asst. attending neurologist Presbyn. Hosp., NYC, 1982-90; chmn. dept. neurology and comprehensive stroke ctr. Beth Israel Med. Ctr., NYC, 1993-97, co-dir. Inst. Neurology and Neurosurgery, 1996—, pres., CEO, 1997—2002; prof. neurology and medicine Albert Einstein Coll. Medicine, 1994—. Tchg. assoc. dept. medicine Sch. Medicine Boston U., 1979-80; emergency svcs. physician Health Ins. Plan N.Y., 1980-83; co-investigator Am. Critical Care, Inc., 1985, Nat. Inst. Neurol. and Communicative Disorders and Stroke, 1987-89, Nat. Inst. Neurol. Diseases and Stroke, 1991-95; sr. investigator Nat. Stroke Assn.; vis. prof. rounds Sch. Medicine Robert Wood Johnson U., New Brunswick, N.J., 1990, St. Vincent's Hosp. and Med. Ctr., N.Y.C., 1990, New Rochelle (N.Y.) Hosp., 1991, U. Med. and Dentistry NJ, Newark, 1992, Mt. Sinai Hosp., 1993, numerous others; vis. prof., grand rounds Yale-New Haven Med. Ctr., Sch. Medicine Yale U., 1990, Health Scis. Ctr. U. Oreg., Portland, 1991, Jersey Shore Med. Ctr., Neptune, 1993, others; course dir. neuro-critical care Child Neurology Soc., 1993, World Congress Neurology, Can., 1993, others; examiner Am. Bd. Psychiatry and Neurology, Inc., 1998; dir. Yarmen Stroke Ctr., 2003-; cons., lectr. and presenter in field. Ad hoc reviewer Archives Neurology, 1988—, Neurology, 1988—, Neurosurgery, 1988—, New England Jour. Medicine, 1988—; mem. editl. bd. Neurology Chronicles, 1991—; contbr. articles to profl. jours., chpts. to books. Nat. Inst. Neurol. Diseases and Stroke grantee, 1991-95; Nat. Stroke Assn. rsch. fellow, 1993-95. Mem. Am. Acad. Neurology (sec. sect. critical care and emergency medicine 1989, vice chmn. sect. critical care and emergency neurology 1991, chmn. sect. critical care and emergency medicine 1993), N.Y. County Med. Soc., World Fedn. Neurology (founding mem. rsch. group intensive mgmt. neurology 1989), Alpha Omega Alpha, Sigma Xi. Office: Beth Israel Medical Center 281 1st Ave New York NY 10003-2925

FINK, MATTHEW POLLACK, retired trade association administrator, lawyer; b. NYC, Jan. 8, 1941; s. Harry L. and Helen (Pollack) F.; m. Ellanor Thompson Stengel, June 22, 1945; children: Emily Pollack, Owen Thompson, Nina Pepper BA summa cum laude, Brown U., 1962; LLB cum laude, Harvard U., 1965. Asst. gen. counsel Investment Co. Inst., Washington, 1971-77, gen. coun., 1977-82, sr. v.p., 1982-91, pres., 1991—2004. Mem. adv. coun. SEC Hist. Soc.; bd. dirs. Oppenheimer Mut. Funds; trustee Com. for Econ. Devel. With U.S. Army, 1967-68. E-mail: mainsail@earthlink.net.

FINK, MITCHELL PHILLIP, surgeon, researcher; b. San Francisco, Calif., Dec. 27, 1948; s. Walter and Betty (Donnenfield) F.; m. Janis Wheeler, Feb. 2, 1973; children: Emily, Matthew. BS, U. Calif., Davis, 1970; MS, U. Calif., Irvine, 1971; MD, Washington U., St. Louis, 1976; MA, Harvard U., 1996. Diplomate Am. Bd. Surgery; cert., in Surgical Critical Care, Am. Bd. Surgery. Asst. prof. surgery Naval Rsch. Inst., Bethesda, Md., 1983—84; assoc. prof. surgery U. Mass. Med. Sch., Worcester, 1984—91, prof. surgery and anesthesia, 1990—91; dir. divsn. surgical critical care Mass. Gen. Hosp., Boston, 1992—93; chief divsn. surgical critical care Beth Israel Hosp., 1993—95; surgeon-in-chief Beth Israel Deaconess Med. Ctr., 1995—99; co-founder Critical Therapeutics Inc., Lexington, Mass. Mem. defense sci. rsch. coun. Defense Advanced Rsch. Project Agency; mem. surgery, anesthesiology and trauma study sect. NIH. Mem. numerous editl. bds. in field; Assoc. Editor Jour. Pharmacolofy and Experimental Therapeutics; Scientific Editor Critical Care Medicine; Editor, co-editor 16 books in field; contbr. over 200 articles to peer-reviewed pubs., over 100 chpts. to books. Lt. comdr. USNR, 1970-84. Decorated Joint Svc. Commendation medal; named Laerdal Meml. Lectr., Soc. Critical Care Medicine, 1994; recipient Kraft scholarship award, U. Calif. Berkley, 1966, Robert Carter Med. Sch. Prize, Wash. U. Med. Sch., 1974, 1977, Richard S. Brookings Med. Sch. Prize, 1975, Med. Alumni Scholarship award, 1976, Merck Manual award, 1977, Millennium Lectr. award, Soc. Critical Care Medicine, 2000, Presdl. Citation, 2002, Presdl. Citation Lecture award, Am. Coll. Chest Physicians, 2001. Mem.: Alpha Omega Alpha (Book Prize 1977). Office Phone: 412-647-6965.

FINK, NORMAN STILES, lawyer, educational administrator, fundraising consultant; b. Easton, Pa., Aug. 13, 1926; s. Herman and Yetta (Hyman) F.; m. Helen Mullen, Sept. 1, 1956; children: Hayden Michael, Patricia Carol. AB, Dartmouth Coll., 1947; JD, Harvard U., 1950. Bar: N.Y. 1951, U.S. Dist. Ct. (ea. and so. dists.) N.Y. 1954, U.S. Supreme Ct. 1964. Mem. legal staff Remington Rand, Inc., NYC, Washington, 1949-54; ptnr. Lans & Fink, NYC, 1954-68; counsel devel. program U. Pa., Phila., 1969-80; v.p. devel. and univ. rels. Brandeis U., Waltham, Mass., 1980-81; dep. v.p. devel., alumni rels., assoc. gen. counsel devel. Columbia U., NYC, 1981-89; sr. counsel John Grenzebach & Assocs., Inc., Chgo., 1989-91. Cons. v.p. Engle Consulting Group, Inc., Chgo. Editor: Deferred Giving Handbook, 1977; author: (with Howard C. Metzler) The Costs and Benefits of Deferred Giving, 1982. V.p. Am. Australian Studies Found.; bd. visitors Brevard Coll., NC, 1995—99, life trustee NC, 1999; bd. visitors Warren Wilson Coll., 1997—, Killough Trustee, NYC; trustee, treas., sec. Transylvania Cmty. Hosp. Found., 2003—. With US Army, 1945—46. Recipient Alice Beeman award Coun. Advancement and Support of Edn., 1984, Silver medal, 1988, Summit award Am. Fundraising Profls., 2006.; Lilly Endowment grantee, 1979-80. Master Mason; mem. ABA (mem. com. on exempt orgns. sect. taxation and com. estate planning and drafting, charitable givint), Coun. Advancement and support of Edn. (various coms.), Am. Arbitration Assn. (panelist), Assn. of Bar of City of N.Y.C. (com. on tax-exempt orgns. 1987-90), Dartmouth Lawyers Assn., Harvard Law Sch. Assn., Nat. Assn. Fundraising Profls. (Contbn. to Knowledge award 1985), Harvard Club Western N.C., Elks. Democrat. Jewish.

FINK, RAYMOND, medical educator; b. NYC, Apr. 21, 1927; s. William and Yetta (Rales) F.; m. Ruth Ursula Gebhard, May 28, 1961 (div. 1982); children: William D., David S.; m. Louise Berenson, Jan. 27, 1983. BBA, CCNY, 1947; MA, U. Denver, 1949; PhD, Cornell U., 1956. Statistician Opinion Rsch. Ctr. U. Denver, 1949; survey statistician U.S. Bur. Census, Suitland, Md., 1949-50, 56; rsch. assoc. human resources rsch. George Washington U., Washington, 1952-53; rsch. assoc. Bur. Social Sci. Rsch., Washington, 1957-60; assoc. dir. drinking practices study Calif. State Dept. Pub. Health, Berkeley, 1960-62; v.p. rsch. and stats. Health Ins. Plan Greater NY, NYC, 1962-78; prof. community and preventive medicine NY Med. Coll., Valhalla, 1978-2000, dir. health policy mgmt., 1982-90, dir. health svcs. rsch., 1990-2000; dir. rsch. Mid-Hudson Family Health Inst., New Paltz, NY, 1999—. Chmn. social sci. adv. com. Planned Parenthood Fedn. Am., NYC, 1966-71; chair task force on HMOs Nat. Inst. Mental Health, Rockville, Md., 1971-72. Contbr. articles to profl. jours. Trustee Health Svcs. Improvement Fund, NYC, 1986-2000; active United Hosp. Fund NY. Sgt. US Army, 1950-52. Grantee Nat. Inst. Mental Health, 1968-72, Nat. Cancer Inst., 1972-78, Social Sci. Rsch. Coun., 1982-83, Robert Wood Johnson Found., 1990-94. Mem. APHA, Am. Assn. Public Opinion Rsch. (co-editor 1968-69), Med. and Health Rsch. Assn. (chair 1975-2002), Assn. for Health Svcs. Rsch., Herman Biggs Soc. (pres. 1994-98, 2006—). Jewish. Home Phone: 212-222-0076. Personal E-mail: raymond.fink1@verizon.net.

FINK, RICHARD DAVID, chemist, educator; b. NYC, July 14, 1936; s. Merwin Jesse and Claudia (Lowenthal) F.; m. Alice Christine Hovenden, Sept. 8, 1961; children: Rebecca Elisabeth, Johanna Hovenden. AB, Harvard U., 1958; PhD, MIT, 1962; MA (hon.), Amherst Coll., 1971; LHD (hon.), Doshisha U., Kyoto, 1988. NSF fellow in chemistry Yale U., 1962-63; NIH fellow, 1963-64; asst. prof. chemistry Amherst (Mass.) Coll., 1964-67, assoc. prof., 1967-71, prof., 1971—, Mellon prof., 1977-80, chmn. dept., 1970-73, 79-82, dean of faculty, 1983-88. Vis. prof. U. London, 1972-73, 76-77, 96-97, 99-2000; vis. scholar U.S. Army War Coll., 1992, MIT, 1988-90, 93-95; cons. Edn. Assocs., Inc. Contbr. articles to profl. jours. NSF fellow U. London, 1968-69, Sloan Found. fellow, 1970-74; Dreyfus Found. tchr.-scholar prize, 1971; NSF Profl. Devel. award, 1979 Mem. Am. Phys. Soc., Am. Chem. Soc., AAAS, Sigma Xi. Home: 30 Orchard St Amherst MA 01002-2516 Office: Amherst Coll Amherst MA 01002

FINK, ROBERT MICHAEL, pharmacist; b. Greeneville, Tenn., June 11, 1960; s. Ralph Rye and Thelma Gertrude Fink. BS in Pharmacy, Mercer U., Atlanta, 1980—83, PharmD, 1983—84; MBA, E.Tenn. State U., Johnson City, Tenn., 1986—90. Cert. nutrition support pharmacist Bd. Pharm. Specialties, 1994, pharmacotherapy specialist Bd. Pharm. Specialties, 1995. Clin. pharmacy coord. Johnson City Med. Ctr., Tenn., 1984—97; assoc. dir. clin. pharmacy svcs. med. ctr. Baylor U., Dallas, 1997—98; dir. pharmacy svcs. Meth. Med. Ctr., Dallas, 1998—2001, Cmty. Health Sys., Franklin, Tenn., 2001—. Fellow: Am. Soc. Health Sys. Pharmacists; mem.: Tenn. Soc. Health Sys. Pharmacists (secretary-treasurer 1996—97, Tenn. Hosp. Pharmacist of Yr. award 1989), Am. Coll. Clin. Pharmacy, Am. Soc. Parenteral & Enteral Nutrition. R-Consevative. Meth. Avocations: golf, travel. Office: Cmty Health Sys 4000 Meridian Blvd Franklin TN 37068 Home Phone: 615-465-7404.

FINK, ROBERT RUSSELL, music educator and theorist, retired dean; b. Belding, Mich., Jan. 31, 1933; s. Russell Foster and Frances (Thornton) F.; m. Ruth Joan Bauerle, June 19, 1955; children: Denise Lyn, Daniel Robert. B.Mus., Mich. State U., 1955, M.Mus., 1956, PhD, 1965. Instr. music SUNY, Fredonia, 1956-57; instr. Western Mich. U., Kalamazoo, 1957-62, asst. prof., 1962-66, assoc. prof., 1966-71, prof., 1971-78, chmn. dept. music, 1972-78; dean Coll. Music U. Colo., Boulder, 1978-93; retired, 1994. Prin. horn Kalamazoo Symphony Orch., 1957-67; accreditation examiner Nat. Assn. Schs. Music, Reston, Va., 1973-92, grad. commr., 1981-89, chmn. grad. commn., 1987-89, assoc. chmn. accreditation commn., 1990-91, chmn., 1992. Author: Directory of Michigan Composers, 1972, The Language of 20th Century Music, 1975; composer: Modal Suite, 1959, Four Modes for Winds, 1967, Songs for High School Chorus, 1967; contbr. articles to profl. jours. Bd. dirs. Kalamazoo Symphony Orch., 1974-78, Boulder Bach Festival, 1983-90. Mem. Coll. Music Soc., Soc. Music Theory, Mich. Orch. Assn. (pres.), Phi Mu Alpha Sinfonia (province gov.), Pi Kappa Lambda. Home: 643 Furman Way Boulder CO 80305-5614 Business E-Mail: robert.fink@colorado.edu.

FINK, ROBERT STEVEN, lawyer, writer, educator; b. Bklyn., Dec. 7, 1943; s. Samuel Miles and Helen Leah (Bogen) F.; m. Abby Deutsch, Mar. 20, 1980; children: Juliet Leah, Robin Rachel. Diploma, U. Vienna, 1962; BA, Bklyn. Coll., 1965; JD, NYU, 1968, LLM, 1973. Bar: NY 1969, US Dist. Ct. (so. and ea. dists.) NY 1970, US Tax Ct. 1970, US Ct. Appeals (2d cir.) 1970, US Supreme Ct. 1972, US Dist. Ct. (we. dist.) NY 1975, US Ct. Claims 1984, US Dist. Ct. (no. dist.) NY 1985, US Ct. Appeals (fed. cir.) 1990, US Ct. Internat. Trade 1998. Assoc. Kostelanetz & Ritholz, NYC, 1968-75, ptnr., 1975-87, Kostelanetez, Ritholz, Tigue and Fink, NYC, 1987-94, Kostelanetz & Fink LLP, NYC, 1994—. Lectr. in field; expert witness IRS; adv. com. tax divsn. Dept. Justice; chmn. IRS/Bar Liaison Com. NE Region, 1996-99; adj. prof. law NYU. Author: Tax Controversies: Audits, Investigations, Trials, 2 vols., 1980, 26th rev. edit., 2007; co-author: How to Defend Yourself Against the IRS, 1987, 2nd rev. edit., 1988; dept. editor Jour. Taxation, contbr. numerous articles to profl. jours. Named one of Best Lawyers in Am., 1995—2007, Top Lawyers NY, SuperLawyers, 2006—. Fellow Am. Coll. Tax Counsel; mem. ABA (chmn. com. civil and criminal tax penalties 1983-85, chmn. task force for revision of tax penalties 1982, Jules Ritholz Meml. Merit Lifetime Achievement award 2003), NY State Bar Assn. (chmn. com. criminal and civil tax penalties 1982-85, 88-90, chmn. compliance and unreported income 1985-87, chmn. commodities and fin. futures 1987-88, chmn. com. compliance and penalties 1991-93, chmn. com. compliance practice and procedure 1993-2003, mem. ho. of dels. 1995-97), Fed. Bar Coun., NY County Lawyers Assn. (chmn. com. taxation 1988-92, 96-97, bd. dirs. 1989-95), NYC Bar Assn., Am. Arbitration Assn. (arbitrator). Office: Kostelanetz & Fink LLP 7 World Trace Ctr New York NY 10007-0034 Home Phone: 212-722-2256; Office Phone: 212-808-8100. Business E-Mail: rfink@kflaw.com.

FINK, SCOTT ALAN, lawyer; b. Aurora, Ill., Sept. 18, 1953; s. Harold Lawrence and Lois (Franch) F.; m. Kathy Ellen Klein, May 14, 1978; children: Lindsay Klein, Anna Klein. AB, Stanford U., 1974; JD, U. Mich., 1978. Bar: Calif. 1978, U.S. Dist. Ct. (no. dist.) Calif. 1978, U.S. Ct. Appeals 9th cir.) 1981, U.S. Supreme Ct. 1985. Assoc. Heller, Ehrman, White & McAuliffe, San Francisco, 1978-84, ptnr., 1985-87, Gibson, Dunn & Crutcher, San Francisco, 1987—. Office: Gibson Dunn Crutcher 1 Montgomery St Fl 31 San Francisco CA 94104-4505 Office Phone: 415-393-8200. Business E-Mail: sfink@gibsondunn.com.

FINK, THOMAS MICHAEL, lawyer; b. Huntington, Ind., Oct. 6, 1947; s. Francis Anthony and Helen Elizabeth (Hartman) F.; m. Sheila Ann Jeffers, Aug. 11, 1973; children: Mark, Matthew, Megan. BBA, U. Notre Dame, 1970; JD, Northwestern U., 1973. Bar: Ind. 1973, U.S. Dist. Ct. (no. dist.) Ind. 1973. Assoc. Barrett & McNagny, Ft. Wayne, Ind., 1973-78, ptnr., 1979—. Speaker Ind. Continuing Legal Edn., Estate Planning Coun., Ft. Wayne, 1987—. Pres. Bishop Luers H.S. Bd. Edn., Ft. Wayne, 1992-93; bd. dirs. Ft. Wayne Cmty. Found. Bus. Edn. Fund, 1990—; bd. dirs., treas. Planned Giving Coun. N.E. Ind., 1995—; dir. Lake George Conservancy, Inc., 2004—; dir. ARC of N.E. Ind., 2006—. Named Ind. Super Lawyer, 2005, 2006, 2007. Mem. Am. Coll. Trust and Estate Counsel, Ft. Wayne Country Club, Notre Dame Club of Ft. Wayne, Beta Gamma Sigma. Roman Catholic. Avocations: coaching basketball, golf, tennis, travel. Office: Barrett & McNagny 215 E Berry St Fort Wayne IN 46802-2705 Home: 10917 Birkdale Ct Fort Wayne IN 46814-9312 Office Phone: 260-423-9551. Business E-Mail: tmf@barrettlaw.com.

FINK, WILLIAM JAMES, retired surgeon; b. Washington, June 24, 1917; s. Gale J. and Elizabeth (Thomas) F.; m. Frances Kay Kerlin, Mar. 1945 (dec. Aug. 1985); children: Robert, Barbara, Barry; m. Arline Peeler, Jan. 1992. AB, DePauw U., 1939; MD, George Washington U., 1944. Diplomate Am. Bd. Surgery. Intern George Washington Hosp., Washington, 1944-45, resident in anesthesiology, 1948; resident in surgery Sibley Meml. Hosp., Washington, 1945-46, VA Hosp., Coral Gables, Fla., 1948-51, chief surg. svc. Fayetteville, Ark., 1951-79; advanced clin. assoc. prof. surgery to clin. prof. surgery U. Ark., 1967-80; ret., 1979. Pres. Universal Tongs, Inc., Fayetteville, 1979-90. Contbr. numerous articles to med. jours. Capt., M.C., AUS, 1946-48. Fellow ACS, S.W. Surg. Congress, Western Surg. Assn.; mem. Sigma Nu, Phi Chi. Republican. Methodist. Home: 1412 E Elmwood Dr Fayetteville AR 72703-3002 Personal E-mail: billypop@cox.net.

FINK, WILLIAM ORMAN, retired federal agency administrator, management consultant; b. Washington, Mar. 21, 1948; s. Orman S. and June B. Fink; m. Barry Elizabeth Brown, Aug. 7, 1970; children: Sara M., Jennifer L. BA in Polit. sci., U. Denver, 1970. Various nat. pk. ranger jobs Nat. Pk. Svc., 1971—80, site mgr. Friendship Hill Nat. Hist. Site Point Marion, Pa., 1980—85, supt., Ft. Necessity Nat. Battlefield and Friendship Hill Nat. Hist. Site Farmington, Pa., 1985—90, supt. Isle Royale Nat. Pk. Houghton, Mich., 1990—92, supt. Keweenaw Nat. Hist. Pk. Calumet, Mich., 1992—96, asst. regional dir. strategic planning and performance mgmt. Midwest region Houghton, Mich., 1996—2004. Mgmt. cons. Bill Fink Comm., Houghton, Mich., 2001—. Contbr. articles to profl. pubs. Leadership vol. Am. Nat. Red Cross, Washington, 1994—2005. Recipient Disting. Grad. award, Fed. Law Enforcement Tng. Ctr., 1973, Gov.'s award for tourism, State of Mich., 1994, Gold award, Upper Peninsula Travel and Recreation Assn., 2001. Mem.: Profl. Photographers of Am., Keweenaw Econ. Develop. Alliance, George Wright Soc., Assn. Nat. Pk. Rangers, Inst. Mgmt. Cons., Keweenaw C. of C. (life). Unitarian Universalist. Avocations: skiing, photography, canoeing. Home: 22083 Royalewood Rd Houghton MI 49931 Office: Bill Fink Comm LLC 616 Shelden Ave Rm 201 Houghton MI 49931 Office Phone: 906-370-9597. Personal E-mail: billfink@chartermi.net.

FINK, YOEL, science educator, researcher; BSc in Chem. Engring., Israel Inst. Tech.(Technion), 1994, BA in Physics, 1995; PhD in Materials Science, Mass. Inst. Tech., 2000. Rsch. asst. Israel Inst. Tech. (Technion), 1991—95, part-time instr. physics advancement project, 1993—95, lab instr. chemistry and physics track project, 1993—95; postdoctoral assoc. dept. physics MIT, Cambridge, asst. prof., 2000—04, Thomas B. King assoc. prof. materials sci., dept. materials sci. and engring., 2004—. Co-founder, pres. OmniGuide Comm., 2000—; prin. invesitgator Rsch. Lab Electronics. Contbr. articles to profl. jours. Recipient NAS award for Initiatives in Rsch., 2004. Achievements include research in optical materials synthesis, optical characterization, simulation and theory; design of novel optical structures and devices; development of processing method for photonic band gap fibers. Office: MIT Rm 13-5013 77 Massachusetts Ave Cambridge MA 02139 Office Phone: 617-258-6113. Fax: 617-452-3432. Business E-Mail: yoel@mit.edu.

FINKE, LEONDA FROEHLICH, sculptor, educator; b. NYC; d. Herman and Evelyn (Praeger) Froehlich; m. Arnold I. Finke; children: David, Erica, Rachel. Student, Art Students League, NYC, 1945. Instr. large bronze figure sculpture and samll art medals, Roslyn, NY, 1969-95; academician NAD, 1994—. One-woman shows include Oxford Gallery, Rochester, NY, Stonybrook U., 2005, Cedar Crest Coll., Allentown, Pa., 2006, others; exhibited in group shows at L.I. Mus., Stonybrook, NY, 2003, others; represented in permanent collections at Smithsonian Nat. Portrait Gallery (portrait of Georgia O'Keefe), Brit. Mus., Century Assn., Chrysler Mus., Butler Inst. Am. Art, CUNY, Bates Coll. Mus. Art, (outdoor sculpture) Brookgreens Gardens, S.C., Grounds for Sculpture, N.J., Stonybrook U., 2005; commd. works include 3 life-size bronzes for park in Altlanta, Max Som medal for Albert Einstein Med. Coll., 1991, Brit. Art Med. Soc. commn. of Virginia Woolf medal, 1989, Royal Philharm. Orch. commn. for medal, 1995, Aiken award poetry, Sewanee Rev., Tenn.; exhibited medals FIDEM, Helsinki, 1990, Brit. Mus., London, 1992; slide talk FIDEM, London, 1992, Germany, 2000; sculptor, writer (with photographs by David Finn) Leonda Finke, 2006; guest lectr., exhibitor Brit. Art Medal Soc., Loughborough U., Eng. Recipient medal of Honor Nat. Assn. Women Artists, 1972, Alex Ettl award NAD, 1990, J. Sanford Saltus award Am. Numismatic Soc., 1997. Fellow Nat. Sculpture Soc. (sec. 1987—, Gold medal 1989, Bas Relief award 1991, Maurice Hexter award 1992, Agop Agapoff award 1993, Silver medal and John Cavanaugh prize 1994, Sculpture House Annual award in recognition of a strong body of work throughout lifetime, 2005, Sculpture House Annual award, 2005), Sculptors Guild, (sculptors guild exhbn. in Kyoto, Japan 1993), Medallic Sculpture Assn., Audubon Artists (pres. 1984-85, medal of honor 1979, Kenan Master Scuptor in Residence, 2004, 75th Anniversary Brookgreen Gardens Designer medal, 2007). Jewish. Home: 10 The Locusts Roslyn NY 11576-1724 Office Phone: 516-484-5415.

FINKE, ROBERT FORGE, lawyer; b. Chgo., Mar. 11, 1941; s. Robert Frank and Helen Theodora (Forge) Finke. AB, U. Mich., 1963; JD, Harvard U., 1966. Bar: Ill. 1966, US Dist. Ct. (no. dist.) Ill. 1966, US Ct. Appeals (7th cir.) 1966, US Supreme Ct. 1970, US Ct. Appeals (9th cir.) 1980, US Ct. Appeals (4th and 6th cirs.) 1982, (8th cir.) 1998. Law clk., 1966—67; assoc. Mayer, Brown Rowe & Maw LLP, Chgo., 1967—71, ptnr., 1972—. Bd. dirs. Lyric Opera Guild, Chgo. Bot. Garden, Windy City Harvest; trustee Rush U. Med. Ctr. Mem. ABA (sects. litigation, bus., antitrust, legal edn. and admissions to the bar, vice chmn. 1974-75), Lawyers Club Chgo., Univ. Club, Econ. Club. Office: Mayer Brown LLP 71 S Wacker Dr Chicago IL 60606-4637 Home Phone: 847-256-3771; Office Phone: 312-701-7110. Business E-Mail: rfinke@mayerbrown.com.

FINKEL, ALAN GLEN, neurologist, educator; b. NYC, Aug. 6, 1953; s. Lawrence Finkel and Rhoda Gelbwaks; m. Carolyn J. Miller, May 19, 1979; children: Lee J. Miller-Finkel, Samuel R. Miller-Finkel, Oliver L. Miller-Finkel. MD, SUNY, Buffalo, 1985. Cert. in neurology 1991, in pain medicine 2003, headache medicine 2006. Prof. dept. neurology U. NC, Chapel Hill, 1989—; dir. headache ctr. U. NC, Sch. Medicine, Chapel Hill, 1993—. Mem. United Coun. Neurologic Subspecilaties, 2005—07. Fellow: Am. Headache Soc. (John R. Graham Sr. Clinicians' Forum award), Am. Acad. Neurology (Disting. Tchg. award 2006). Office: University of North Carolina 3114 Bioinformatics Building Chapel Hill NC 27599-7025 Home Phone: 919-929-8201; Office Phone: 919-966-2527. Office Fax: 919-843-8245.

FINKEL, DAVID, journalist; b. 1956; married; 2 children. Grad., U. Fla., 1977. Staff writer Tallahassee Dem., Fla., St. Petersburg (Fla.) Times, Washington Post, 1990—. Recipient Disting. Writing award, Am. Soc. Newspaper Editors, 1986, Mo. Lifestyles award, 1995, Sigma Delta Chi award, 1999, Robert F. Kennedy Journalism award, 2001, Pulitzer Prize for explanatory reporting, 2006. Office: Washington Post 1150 15th St NW Washington DC 20071

FINKEL, EUGENE JAY, lawyer; b. Phila., June 21, 1931; BA, Swarthmore Coll., Pa., 1952; MA, George Washington U., 1961, JD, 1965. Bar: U.S. Dist. Ct. D.C. 1966, U.S. Ct. Appeals (D.C. cir.) 1972, U.S. Supreme Ct. 1980. Various positions U.S. Dept. Treasury, Washington, 1952-74; dep. dir. Office Internat. Fin. Policy Coordination and Ops., Washington, 1963-67; dir. Office Latin Am., Washington, 1967-70, Multilateral Instns. Program Office, 1970-74, Developing Nations Fin., 1974-75; asst. exec. sec. World Bank-IMF Devel. Com., 1975-77; alt. U.S. exec. dir. Inter-Am. Devel. Bank, Washington, 1977-81; ptnr. Porter Wright Morris & Arthur, Washington, 1981—2006, counselor, 2006—. Lt. comdr. USNR ret. Office: Porter Wright et al 1919 Pennsylvania Ave NW Washington DC 20006-3434 Office Phone: 202-778-3033. Business E-Mail: jfinkel@porterwright.com.

FINKEL, EVAN, lawyer; b. Bklyn., Oct. 7, 1956; BS, Harpur Coll., SUNY, Binghampton, 1978; JD, Univ. Calif., Hastings, 1981. Bar: Calif. 1981, U.S. Patent & Trademark Office, U.S. Dist. Ct., (Calif. & Mich.), U.S. Ct. Appeals (9th, Fed. cir.), U.S. Supreme Ct. 1988, U.S. Dist. Ct. (Eastern Dist. Mich.). Ptnr., chmn. LA Intellectual Property group Pillsbury Winthrop Shaw Pittman, LA. Named a So. Calif. Super Lawyer, LA Mag., 2004. Mem.: USPTO, Intellectual Property Assn., Phi Beta Kappa, Order of the Coif, Thurston Soc. Office: Pillsbury Winthrop Shaw Pittman Suite 2800 725 S Figueroa St Los Angeles CA 90017 Office Phone: 213-488-7307. Office Fax: 213-629-1033. Business E-Mail: evan.finkel@pillsburylaw.com.

FINKEL, GERALD MICHAEL, lawyer; b. NYC, July 29, 1941; s. Abraham B. and Elizabeth B. (Michaels) F.; m. Beverly Lynne Jaffee, Aug. 26, 1962; children: Bruce Daniel, Judith Michelle. BA, NYU, 1962; JD, U. S.C., 1970. Bar: S.C. 1970, U.S. Dist. Ct. S.C. 1970, U.S. Ct. Appeals (4th cir.) 1973, U.S. Supreme Ct. 1973, D.C. 1973. Founding mem., of counsel Finkel Law Firm, LLC and predecessor firms, Columbia, SC, 1970—. Adj. prof. trial advocacy and ins. law U. SC, 1976-2006; lectr. Profl. Insts.; instr. SC Dept. Pub. Safety/Criminal Justice Acad.; disting. vis. prof. ins. law Charleston Sch. Law, 2005-06, prof. law, 2006-; spl. judge Richland County Family Ct., 1974-78, Ct. Gen. Sessions 5th Jud. Cir., 1976. Author: (with Ralph C. McCullough II) A Guide to South Carolina Torts, 1st edit., 1981, 2d edit., 1986, 3d edit., 1990, 4th edit., 1995, (with Elizabeth Rhodes) South Carolina Legal and Business Forms, Vols. 1 and 3, 1997. Hearing officer S.C. Dept. Health and Environ. Control, 1979-82; mem. S.C. Appellate Def. Commn., 1982-83, Gov.'s Sentencing Guidelines Commn., 1982-83. Served to capt. U.S. Army, 1962-67. Recipient Outstanding Alumni cert. Phi Alpha Delta, 1972 Mem. ABA (mem. faculty fed. trial practice), SC Bar Assn. (bd. govs. 1985-88, profl. responsibility com. and ethics adv. com., lectr.), Richland County Bar Assn. (lectr.), Assn. Trial Lawyers Am., Am. Law Inst. (consultative group for restatement of law 3d unfair competition, consultative group restatement law 3d torts, mem. faculty fed. trial practice), SC Trial Lawyers Assn. (exec. bd. 1978-81, pres. 1982-83, lectr.), Phi Alpha Delta (dist. justice 1976-78). Democrat. Jewish. Office: Finkel Law Firm LLC 1201 Main St Ste 1800 Columbia SC 29201-3294 Office Phone: 803-765-2935. Business E-Mail: jfinkel@finkellaw.com.

FINKEL, MARION JUDITH, internist, pharmaceutical administrator; b. NYC, Nov. 2, 1929; d. Israel and Bella (Stillman) Finkel; m. Simon V. Manson, Sept. 12, 1954. Student, L.I. U., 1945-48; MD (Howard Sloan Meml. scholar), Chgo. Med. Sch., 1952. Intern Jersey City Med. Ctr., 1952-53; resident in internal medicine Bellevue Hosp., NYC, 1954-56; med. editor Merck and Co., 1957-61; pvt. practice specializing in internal medicine, NYC, 1956-57, NJ, 1961-63; with FDA, 1963-85, dir. divsn. metabolic and endocrine drugs, 1966-70, dep. dir. bur. drugs, 1970-71, 72-74, dir. office new drug evaluation, 1971-72, 74-82, dir. office orphan products devel., 1982-85; exec. dir. R&D Berlex Labs., Inc., 1985-88; v.p. drug registration and regulatory affairs Sandoz Pharms., Inc., 1988-94, v.p. corp. regulatory compliance, 1994-95, cons. regulatory affairs, clin. R&D, 1995—. Contbr. chpts. to books, numerous articles to profl. jours. Recipient award of merit FDA, 1972, Superior Svc. award USPHS, 1976, 84, Fed. Woman's award Fed. Govt., 1976, Meritorious Exec. award, 1980; named Disting. Alumnus, Chgo. Med. Sch., 1977, L.I. U., 1980. Office: 21 Squirrel Run Morristown NJ 07960-6411

FINKEL, SANFORD NORMAN, lawyer; b. Troy, NY, Oct. 19, 1946; s. Max and Mildred (Fares) F.; m. Amy Lynn Gordon, Oct. 13, 1974 (div. July 1984); children: Marcy Jennifer, Melanie Gordon. BA, SUNY, Buffalo, 1968; JD, Union U., 1974. Bar: N.Y 1975, U.S. Dist. Ct. (no. dist.) N.Y. 1975. Tchr. sci. Enlarged City Sch. Dist. of Troy, N.Y., 1968-71; pvt. practice Troy, 1975—; counsel to dem. study group N.Y. State Assembly, Albany, 1977-78; instr. paralegal studies Jr. Coll. Albany divsn. Russell Sage Coll., 1977-81; dep. corp. counsel City of Troy, 1990-94. Mem. Rensselaer County Bar Assn. Avocations: reading, coin collecting/numismatics, stamp collecting/philately, travel. Home: 19 Capitol Pl Rensselaer NY 12144-9658 Office: 68 2nd St Troy NY 12180-3932 Home Phone: 518-434-6964; Office Phone: 518-272-2300. Personal E-mail: sanfordnfinkel@aol.com.

FINKELMAN COX, PENNEY, film producer; b. Ardmore, Pa., July 5, 1951; d. Jayne Miriam (Isaacs) Finkelman; m. James Douglas Cox, Feb. 9, 1986. BA, Barnard Coll., 1973. Exec. DreamWorks; exec. v.p. Sony Pictures Animation, 2002—. Asst. dir. (TV films) Skokie, 1981, co-prodr. (films) Terms of Endearment, 1983, Broadcast News, 1987; prodr.: (films) Honey, I Shrunk the Kids, 1989, Welcome Home, Roxy Carmichael, 1990, 'Til There Was You, 1997, The Prince of Egypt, 1998; exec. prodr. V.I. Warshawski, 1991, I'll Do Anything, 1994, Joseph: King of Dreams, 2000, Shrek, 2001; exec. prodr.: (films) Snakes on a Plane, 2006. Named one of 100 Most Powerful Women in Entertainment, Hollywood Reporter, 2006. Office: Sony Pictures Animation 10202 West Washington Blvd Culver City CA 90232*

FINKELSON, ALLEN, lawyer; b. NYC, June 23, 1946; BA magna cum laude, St. Lawrence Univ., 1968; JD, Columbia Univ., 1971. Bar: NY 1972. Assoc. Cravath Swaine & Moore LLP, NYC, 1971—77, ptnr., 1977—83, 1985—; mng. dir., mergers, acquisitions Lehman Bros., NYC, 1983—85. Editor: Columbia Law Rev. Mem.: Assn. of Bar of City of NY, Phi Beta Kappa. Office: Cravath Swaine & Moore LLP Worldwide Plz 825 Eighth Ave New York NY 10019-7475 Office Phone: 212-474-1262. Office Fax: 121-474-3700. Business E-Mail: afinkelson@cravath.com.

FINKELSTEIN, ALLEN LEWIS, lawyer; b. NYC, Mar. 19, 1943; s. David and Ella (Miller) F.; m. Judith Elaine Stutman, June 20, 1964 (div. Mar. 1980); children: Jill, Jennifer; m. Shelley Gail Barone, June 15, 1980; 1 child, Amanda. BS, NYU, 1964; JD, Bklyn. Law Sch., 1967; MBA, LI U., 1969. Bar: NY 1968, US Dist. Ct. (ea. and so. dists.) NY 1973, US Ct. Appeals (2d cir.) 1973, US Supreme Ct. 1976, US Tax Ct. 1979. Ptnr. Finkelstein, Bruckman, Wohl, Most & Rothman, NYC, 1974-97; sr. ptnr. Pressman Finkelstein, NYC, 1997-99; ptnr. Ganfer & Shore LLP, NYC, 1999—. Asst. prof. LI U., NYC, 1969-73, adj. assoc. prof., 1973-74. Chmn. bd. dirs. Amyotrophic Lateral Sclerosis Assn., 2004—07. Mem. ABA (bus. law and family law sect.), NY State Bar Assn., Assn. of Bar of City of NY, Queens County Bar Assn., Masons. Jewish. Home: 425 E 63rd St New York NY 10021-7804 Office: Ganfer & Shore LLP 360 Lexington Ave New York NY 10017-6502 Home Phone: 212-750-9154; Office Phone: 212-922-9250. Business E-Mail: afinkelstein@ganshore.com.

FINKELSTEIN, BERNARD, lawyer; b. NYC, Jan. 21, 1930; s. Irving and Sadie (Katz) F.; m. Adele S. (Levine), June 29, 1952; children: Sharon Ann, Marcia Lyn. BA, NYU, 1951; LLB, Yale U., 1954. Bar: N.Y. 1954, D.C. 1970. Assoc. Paul, Weiss, Rifkind, Wharton, and Garrison, LLP, NYC, 1956—64, ptnr., 1965—95, of counsel, 1996—. Trustee, mem. Altman Found., NYC, 1985—. Named one of Best Lawyers in N.Y. Mag., 1995. Fellow Am. Coll. of Trust and Estate Counsel (estate and gift tax com. 1987-); mem. ABA (com. on pre-death planning, probate and trust div. of sect. on real property, probate and trust law 1985-88), NY State Bar Assn. (chmn. gift and tax com. of tax sect. 1978-80), Assn. of Bar of City of NY (trusts, estate and surrogate's ct. com. 1986-89), NY Bar Found., Yale Law Sch. Assn. (exec. com. 1983-86), Phi Beta Kappa, Phi Alpha Delta, Order of Coif. Home: 1 Tory Ln Scarsdale NY 10583-2314 Office: Paul Weiss Rifkind Wharton and Garrison LLP 1285 Ave of the Americas New York NY 10019-6064

FINKELSTEIN, DANIEL, ophthalmologist; b. Phila., Apr. 13, 1940; s. Arthur and Leah Finkelstein; m. Catherine Marino, June 22, 2004; children: Carla, James. BA, Harvard Coll., 1962; MD, U. Pa., Phila., 1967; MA in Theology, St. Marys Seminary and U., 2007. Prof. Johns Hopkins U., Balt., 1990—. Mem. Order Of Malta, Balt. Home Phone: 410-955-3429.

FINKELSTEIN, DAVID RITZ, physicist, educator, consultant; b. NYC, July 19, 1929; s. Isidore and Esther (Rubinstein) F.; m. Helene Cooper, 1948 (div.); children: Daniel, Beth, Eve; m. Shlomit Ritz, 1981; 1 child, Aria. BS, CCNY, 1949; PhD, MIT, 1953. Asst., then assoc. prof. physics Stevens Inst. Tech., 1954-60; assoc. prof. Yeshiva U., then prof., chmn., dean, 1960-79; prof. physics Ga. Inst. Tech., 1979—2003, prof. emeritus, 2004—. Vis. prof. Tougaloo Coll., 1965, Hebrew U. Jerusalem, 1974 Author: Quantum Relativity, 1996; editor Internat. Jour. Theoretical Physics; mem. editl. bd. Jour. Math. Physics, 1991-93. Co-chmn. Miss. Project Parents Com., 1965. Ford Found. fellow, 1958; NSF grantee, 1954-96. Fellow Lindisfarne Assn.; mem. AAAS, Am. Phys. Soc., Internat. Quantum Structures Assn. (sec. 1990-93). Jewish. Achievements include research in black holes, high energy physics, space-time quanta, topological physics, gravity, quantum logic and set theory, Clifford algebra. Office: Ga Inst Tech Physics Dept Atlanta GA 30332-0430 E-mail: david.finkelstein@physics.gatech.edu.

FINKELSTEIN, DAVID S., lawyer; b. NYC, July 14, 1972; BA cum laude, Harvard Univ., 1994; JD magna cum laude, Fordham Univ., 1998; LLM, NYU, 2000. Bar: NY 1999. Assoc. Cravath Swaine & Moore LLP, NYC, 1998—2005, ptnr., trusts, estates, 2005—. Mem.: ABA, NY State Bar Assn. Office: Cravath Swaine & Moore LLP Worldwide Plz 825 Eighth Ave New York NY 10019-7475 Office Phone: 212-474-1304. Office Fax: 212-474-3700. Business E-Mail: dfinkelstein@cravath.com.

FINKELSTEIN, IRA ALLEN, lawyer; b. NYC, Oct. 7, 1946; s. Louis and Lillian (Reiser) F.; m. Madelyn Kay Hoffman, May 30, 1982; 1 child, Sarah Rebekah. BA, CCNY, 1967; JD, Harvard U., 1973. Bar: N.Y. 1974, U.S. Dist. Ct. (ea. and so. dists.) N.Y. 1974, U.S. Ct. Appeals (2d cir.) 1974, U.S. Supreme Ct. 1978. Assoc. firm Cahill, Gordon & Reindel, NYC, 1972-81, Tenzer, Greenblatt, Fallon & Kaplan, NYC, 1981-83, ptnr., 1983-99, Blank Rome Tenzer Greenblatt LLP, NYC, 2000—02, Harnik Wilker & Finkelstein, LLP, NYC, 2002—. Mem. Harvard Law Rev., 1970-72. Mem. N.Y. State Bar Assn., Assn. Bar City N.Y. Office: Harnik Wilker & Finkelstein LLP Olympic Tower 645 Fifth Ave 7th Fl New York NY 10022 Office Phone: 212-599-7575. Business E-Mail: finkelstein@harnik.com.

FINKELSTEIN, JAMES A., media executive; b. NYC; s. Jerry and Shirley Finkelstein; m. Pamela Gross, Feb. 1, 1998; children: Alexander, Gregory, Zachary, Jennifer, Eliza. BA, NYU, NYC, 1970; LLD honoris causa (hon.), Hofstra U., 1984. Pres. and CEO Nat. Law Pub. Co., NYC, 1979—98; pres. JAF Comm., Inc., NYC, 1998—2001; pres. and CEO News Comm., Inc. (publishers of Marquis Who's Who directories; The Hill; and Dan's Publications), NYC, 2001—; exec. chmn. Thompson Pub. Group, Washington, 2004—; chmn. Global Media Ptnrs. Credit Suisse First Boston, NYC, 2004—05; partner Avista Capital Partners, LP, 2005—; dir. WideOpen West, LLC. Media consultant DB Capital Ptnrs., NYC, 2001—03, Veronis Suhler Stevenson, NYC, 2002; bd. dirs. Advanstar Comm. Past bd. mem.-bd. overseers Faculty Arts and Sci., NYU; past bd. mem. Legal Aid Soc., NYC. Mem.: Yale Club, Harvard Club (assoc.). Avocations: tennis, chess. Office: 501 Madison Ave 23rd Fl New York NY 10022

FINKELSTEIN, JAMES ARTHUR, management consultant; b. NYC, Dec. 6, 1952; s. Harold Nathan and Lilyan (Crystal) F.; m. Lynn Marie Gould, Mar. 24, 1984; children: Matthew, Brett. BA, Trinity Coll., Hartford, Conn., 1974; MBA, U. Pa., 1976. Cons. Towers, Perrin, Forster & Crosby, Boston, 1976-78; mgr. compensation Pepsi-Cola Co., Purchase, NY, 1978-80; mgr. employee info. systems Am. Can. Co., Greenwich, Conn., 1980; mgr. bus. analysis Emery Airfreight, Wilton, Conn., 1980-81; v.p. Meidinger, Inc., Balt., 1981-83; prin. The Wyatt Co., San Diego, 1983-88; pres., chief exec. officer W. F. Corroon, San Francisco, 1988-95; founder, CEO FutureSense, Inc., 1995—97, chmn., CEO, 2001—; founder TallyUp Software, 1996—98; dir. En Wisen, Inc., 1996-98; ptnr. Andersen LLP, San Francisco, 1997-2001. Mem. regional adv. bd. Mchts. and Mfrs. Assn., San Diego, 1986-88; instr. U. Calif., San Diego, 1984-88. Mem. camp com. State YMCA of Mass. and R.I., Framingham, 1982-86; pres. Torrey Pines Child Care Consortium, La Jolla, Calif., 1987-88; founder, pres., CEO, Marin Football Club, Inc., 2003—; vice chmn. La Jolla YMCA, 1986-88; chmn. fin. com. YMCA, San Francisco, 1992-95, vice chmn., 1993-95, chmn., 1995-97, bd. dirs., 1988-2004; bd. dirs. San Domenico Sch., 1994-2000; trustee World Affairs Coun., 1998-2004; bd. dirs. Becket Chimney Corners YMCA, 1999—2003; treas. Ctrl. Marin Competitive Soccer Club, 2000-05. Avocations: soccer coaching and refereeing, music, theater, sports, camping. Home: 17 Bracken Ct San Rafael CA 94901-1587 Office: FutureSense Inc 369 B 3d St # 181 San Rafael CA 94901-3581 Personal E-mail: futuresense@yahoo.com.

FINKELSTEIN, JAMES DAVID, physician, educator; b. NYC, Oct. 16, 1933; s. Harry and Sylvia Z. (Bernstein) F.; m. Barbara Joan Eisenberg, Dec. 12, 1959; children: Donna Ilene, Laura Helene. AB, Harvard U., 1954; MD, Columbia U., 1958. Diplomate Am. Bd. Internal Medicine. Intern, resident in medicine Presbyn. Hosp., NYC, 1971-73; chief med. svc. VA Med. Ctr., Washington, 1979-99, chief gastroenterology, 1970-79, assoc. chief staff for rsch., 1975-79, med. investigator, 1970-75, clin. investigator, 1965-68, chief biochemistry rsch. lab., 1965—2005, sr. clinician, 1999—. Cons. Children's Hosp., Washington, 1968-85; prof. medicine George Washington U., 1969—; clin. prof. medicine Georgetown U., 1981-2001; prof. medicine Howard U., Washington, 1983-2001; mem. Nutrition Study sect. NIH, 1972-78; hon. pres. 2d Internat. Conf. on Homocysteine Metabolism, Nijmegen, Netherlands, 1998. Contbr. articles on biochemistry and nutrition of methionine to profl. jours. Served as surgeon USPHS, 1963-65. Recipient F.P. Gay Rsch. award Columbia U., NYC, 1956, Arthur S. Fleming award Jr. C. of C., Washington, 1971, Disting. Rschr. medal George Washington U., 1999; NIH grantee, 1966-95. Mem. Am. Soc. for Clin. Investigation, Am. Gastroent. Assn., Assn. of Am. Physicians, Am. Inst. Nutrition, Am. Soc. Clin. Nutrition (Robert H. Herman award 2001), Am. Fedn. Clin. Rsch., Harvard Club. Office: VA Med Ctr 50 Irving St NW Washington DC 20422-0001 Office Phone: 202-745-8373. E-mail: james.finkelstein@med.va.gov.

FINKELSTEIN, JESSE ADAM, lawyer; b. Rochester, NY, Mar. 25, 1955; s. Nisson A. and Rona G. (Glassman) F.; m. Elizabeth Bowman, Aug. 20, 1978; children: Sarah Moir, Danielle Bowman. BA cum laude, U. Rochester, 1977; JD cum laude, Boston Coll., 1980. Bar: Del. 1980. assoc. Richards, Layton & Finger, Wilmington, Del., 1980-86, ptnr., 1986—, pres., 2003-06, chmn. corp. dept., 2003-06. Del. Supreme Ct. Rules Com., 1990-96. Author: Corporation Law Review, 1982, Revue Internationale de Droit Comparé, 1982, The Business Lawyer, 1983, 90, 97, Review of Securities and Commodities Regulation, 1985-87, The Delaware Law of Corporations and Business Organizations, 1986, Meetings of Stockholders, 1987; contbr. the Securities Regulation Law Jour., 1986-87; bd. editors BNA Corp. Practice Series, Corp. Governance Law Reporter. Fellow Am. Coll. Trial Laywers; mem. ABA, Del. State Bar Assn. (chmn. supreme ct. rules com. 1990-96, mem. coun. corp. sect.). Office: Richards Layton & Finger 920 North King St Wilmington DE 19801 Office Phone: 302-651-7754. Business E-Mail: finkelstein@rlf.com.

FINKELSTEIN, JOSEPH SIMON, lawyer; b. Vineland, NJ, Feb. 28, 1952; s. Absalom and Goldie (Cukier) Finkelstein; m. Sara M. Green, May 30, 1976; children: Adam, Julia, Seth. BA, Rutgers U., 1973; JD, U. Pa., 1976. Bar: Pa. 1976, N.J. 1976, U.S. Supreme Ct. 1982. Assoc. Wolf, Block, Schorr and Solis-Cohen, Phila., 1976-85, ptnr., 1985—2007, Blank, Rowe LLP, Phila., 2007—. Pres. Perelman Jewish Day Sch., 1996—99, chmn. bd. trustees, 2005—; mem. Wexner Heritage Found., 1991—95; mem. exec. com., bd. dirs., chair funds distbn. United Way Southeastern Pa., 1997—99; exec. bd. young leadership coun. bd. Fedn. Jewish Agys., Phila., 1986—88; mem. nat. young leadership cabinet United Jewish Appeal, 1987—91; bd. dirs. Temple Beth Hillel Beth El; v.p., treas. Beth Am Israel; trustee Jewish Fedn. Greater Phila., 1996—2000; bd. dirs. State of Israel Bonds, Phila., SCRUB Found. Recipient New Life/New Leadership award, State of Israel, 1989, Hearts of Gold award, United Way Southeastern Pa., 1999; fellow, Am. Coll. Real Estate, 2007. Mem.: ABA, Am. Coll. Real Estate Lawyers, Pa. Land Title Assn., Phila. Bar Assn., N.J. Bar Assn., Pa. Bar Assn., Internat. Coun. Shopping Ctrs. Home: 716 Oxford Rd Bala Cynwyd PA 19004-2112 Office: Blank Rowe LLP 130 N 18th St Philadelphia PA 19103-6998 Office Phone: 215-569-5382. Business E-Mail: jfinkelstein@blankrowe.com.

FINKELSTEIN, MARK, mathematician, educator; b. NYC, Aug. 28, 1939; s. Isador and Bertha Finkelstein; m. Edith Gelles, June 1960; children: Adam, Noah; m. Beverly Bain, Jan. 2, 1991. BA, Cornell U., Ithaca, NY, 1959; PhD, Stanford U., Calif., 1966. Mathematician Nat. Security Agy., Ft. Meade, Md., 1960—62; prof. math. U. Calif., Irvine, 1966—. Contbr. articles to profl. jours. Recipient Outstanding Tchg. award, U. Calif. Sch. Phys. Sci., 1979, U. Calif., 1999, U. Calif. Alumni Assn., 1994, Disting. Tchg. award, Math. Assn. Am., 2003. Mem.: Am. Math. Soc. Office: U Calif Irvine Dept Math Irvine CA 92697-3875 Personal E-mail: mark.finkelstein@uci.edu.

FINKELSTEIN, PAUL D., personal care industry executive; BS, Wharton Sch. Univ. Pa.; MBA, Harvard Univ., 1966. Mgmt. positions Glemby Internat., 1966—81; chmn. beauty div. Seligman & Latz, 1981—84; CEO Turner Hall Corp., 1984—87; sr. v.p. Revlon Inc., 1987; exec. v.p. Regis Corp., Edina, Minn., 1987, pres., COO, 1988—96, pres., CEO, 1996—2004, chmn., pres., CEO, 2004—. Bd. dir. Eagle Supply Group Inc.; mem. adv. bd. NYSE. Mem.: Chief Executives Org., World Presidents Org. Office: Regis Corp 7201 Metro Blvd Minneapolis MN 55439*

FINKELSTEIN, PHIL, retail executive; BS economics, Wharton School, U. Penn; MBA, Harvard Business School. With Glemby Internat., 1966—81; chmn., Beauty Div. Seligman & Latz (S&L), 0191—1984; CEO Turner Hall Corp., 1984—87; sr. v.p. Revlon, 1987; exec. v.p. Regis Corp., 1987—88, pres., COO, 1988—96, pres., 1996—2004, CEO, 1996—, chmn., 2004—. Mem. World Pres. Org., Chief Executives Org. Office: c/o Regis Corp 7201 Metro Blvd Edina MN 55439

FINKELSTEIN, RICHARD ALAN, retired microbiology educator, consultant; b. NYC, Mar. 5, 1930; s. Frank and Sylvia (Lemkin) F.; m. Helen Rosenberg, Nov. 30, 1952; children: Sheri, Mark, Laurie; m. Mary Boesman, June 20, 1976; 1 dau., Sarina Nicole. BS, U. Okla., 1950; MA, U. Tex., Austin, 1952, PhD, 1955. Tchg. fellow, rsch. scientist U. Tex., Austin, 1950-55; fellow, instr. U. Tex. Southwestern Med. Sch., Dallas, 1955-58; chief bioassay sect. Walter Reed Army Inst. Research, Washington, 1958-64; dep. chief, chief dept. bacteriology and mycology U.S. Army Med. Component, SEATO Med. Research Lab., Bangkok, 1964-67; assoc. prof. dept. microbiology U. Tex. Southwestern Med. Sch., Dallas, 1967-73, prof., 1973-79; prof., chmn. dept. microbiology Sch. Medicine U. Mo., Columbia, 1979-93, Curators' prof., 1990-2000, Millsap Disting. Prof., 1985-2000, prof. emeritus, 2000—. Mem. Nat. Com. for Coordination Cholera Rsch., Ministry for Pub. Health, Bangkok, 1965-67; cons. WHO, 1970—, commdg. gen. U.S. Army Med. R&D Command, 1975-79, Schwarz-Mann Labs., 1974-79, ICN Biomeds., 1979—, Wyeth-Ayerst, 1992—, Amgen, 1992, Molecular Pharms., 1993—; Microbiolog. and Infectious Diseases Rsch. Com. Nat. Inst. Allergy and Infectious Diseases, NIH, 1994-98; vis. assoc. prof. U. Med. Scis., Bangkok, 1965-67; vis. prof. U. Chgo., Med. Sch., 1977; vis. scientist Japanese Sci. Coun., 1976, Ciba-Geigy lectr. Waksman Inst., Rutgers U., 1975; vis. lectr. Nat. Sci. Coun., Taipei, Taiwan, 1995, others. Contbr. articles on cholera, enterotoxins, gonorrhea, and role of iron in host-parasite interactions to profl. jours. Major med. svc. corps US Army, 1966. Recipient Robert Koch prize Bonn, Fed. Republic Germany, 1976; Chancellor's award for outstanding faculty rsch. in biol. scis. U. Mo.-Columbia, 1985, Sigma Xi Rsch. award U. Mo.-Columbia, 1986. Fellow Am Acad. Microbiology (bd. govs. 1990-93), Am. Soc. for Microbiology (pres. Tex. br. 1974-75, hon. Tex. br. divsn. councilor, chmn. program com. 1979-82, sec.-treas. Mo. br. 1985-87, v.p. 1987-89, pres. 1989-91, councillor, 1991-92, coun. policy com. 1992-95, Disting. Svc. award 1998), Am. Assn. Immunologists, Infectious Diseases Soc. of Am., Soc. Gen. Microbiology, Pathol. Soc. Gt. Britain and Ireland, Sigma Xi. Achievements include first purification of cholera enterotoxin; first purification of heat-labile enterotoxin from Escherichia coli; patent for living attenuated candidate cholera vaccine. Home: 3861 S Forest Acres Dr Columbia MO 65203-8608 Office: U Mo Sch Medicine Dept Molecular Microbiol Columbia MO 65212-0001 Home Phone: 573-446-2883; Office Phone: 573-882-4117. Business E-Mail: finkelsteinr@health.missouri.edu.

FINKELSTEIN, RICK, film company executive; Ptnr. Finley, Kumble, Wagner, Heine, Undreberg, Manley, Myerson & Casey, LA, Mitchell, Silverberg and Krupp, LA and London, 1978—86; exec. v.p. De Laurentiis Entertainment Group, 1986; pres. Nelson Films, 1987—94; exec. v.p. PolyGram Filmed Entertainment, 1994—99; sr. v.p. corp. devel. Universal Pictures, 1999, pres., 1999—2006, COO, 2000—06, vice chmn., 2006—; exec. v.p. Universal Studios, 2006—. Bd. dirs. Motion Picture Assn. Am. Office: Universal Studios Inc 100 Universal City Plz Universal City CA 91608-1002

FINKELSTEIN, STUART M., lawyer; b. NY, 1960; BBA with distinction, U. Mich., 1982, JD cum laude, 1985. Bar: N.Y. 1986. Assoc. Skadden, Arps, Slate, Meagher & Flom LLP, NYC, 1985-93, ptnr., 1993—. Office: Skadden Arps Slate Meagher & Flom LLP 4 Times Sq New York NY 10036-6595 Office Phone: 212-735-2841. Business E-Mail: sfinkels@skadden.com.

FINKLE, JEFFREY ALAN, professional association executive; b. Newark, Ohio, Apr. 22, 1954; s. Richard James and Margery (Orr) F.; m. Diane Elizabeth Letchford, Aug. 20, 1983 (div. July 1989). BSc cum laude, Ohio U., 1976; postgrad., Ohio State U., 1978-80. Legis. dir. Ohio Rep. Party, Columbus, 1976-78; legis. liason Ohio Dept. Mental Health, Columbus, 1978-80; mktg. dir. Systems 80, Bethesda, Md., 1980-81; exec. asst. HUD, Washington, 1981-83, dep. asst. sec., 1983-86; pres., CEO Coun. for Urban Econ. Devel., Washington, 1986—2001; pres. CEO Internat. Econ. Devel. Coun., 2001. Mem. adv. coun., Ohio U. Inst. for Local Govt. Adminstrn. and Rural Devel., 1986—. Bd. dirs., pres. Bollinger Found., 1989—, Arlington County Va. Econ. Devel. Corp., 1999—, D.C. Mktg. Ctr., 1998-2000. Mem. Housing Rehab. Assn. (bd. dirs. 1986-90), Nat. Assn. Ind. Living Ctrs. (nat. adv. bd. 1987-89), Sr. Living Choices (bd. dirs. 1991-98), Ohio U. Alumni Assn. (past pres. Washington chpt., past bd. dirs. nat. assn.). Republican. Roman Catholic. Avocations: golf, genealogy. Office: Internat Econ Devel Coun 734 15th St NW Ste 900 Washington DC 20005 E-mail: jfinkle@msn.com.

FINKLEA, TULA ELLICE See CHARISSE, CYD

FINKS, ROBERT MELVIN, paleontologist, educator; b. Portland, Maine, May 12, 1927; s. Abraham Joseph and Sarah (Bendette) F. BS magna cum laude, Queens Coll., 1947; MA, Columbia U., 1954, PhD, 1959. Lectr. Bklyn. Coll., 1955-58, instr., 1959-61; lectr. Queens Coll., CUNY, 1961-62, asst. prof., 1962-65, acting chmn., 1963-64, assoc. prof. geology, 1966-70, prof., 1971—2002, prof. emeritus, 2002—; geologist U.S. Geol. Survey, 1952-54, 63—; rsch. assoc. Am. Mus. Natural History, 1961—77, Smithsonian Instn., 1968—; rsch. assoc. in paleontology N.Y. State Mus.; rsch. prof. dept. geology Union Coll., Schenectady, NY. Doctoral faculty CUNY, 1983—; cons. in field. Author: Late Paleozoic Sponge Faunas of the Texas Region, 1960; co-author: Treatise on Invertebrate Paleontology, Part E, Porifera, vol. 2, 2003, vol. 3, 2004; editor: Guidebook to Field Excursions, 1968; contbr. articles profl. jours. Queens Coll. Scholar, 1947. Fellow AAAS, Geol. Soc. Am., Explorers Club; mem. AAUP, Paleontol. Soc. (vice chmn. Northeastern sect. 1977-78, chmn. 1978-79), Paleontol. Assn. Britain, Soc. Econ. Paleontologists and Mineralogists Soc. for Sedimentary Geology, Internat. Palaeontol. Assn., Geol. Soc. Vt. (charter mem.), Planetary Soc. (charter), Phi Beta Kappa (v.p. Sigma chpt. NY 1993-95, pres. 1995-99), Golden Key (hon.), Sigma Xi (exec. sec. Queens Coll. chpt. 1982-85; treas. Union Coll. chpt. 2006—). Office: Geology Dept Union Coll Schenectady NY 12308 Office Phone: 518-388-6770. Business E-Mail: finksr@union.edu. *Be humble in studying nature.*

FINLAY, JAMES CAMPBELL, retired museum director; b. Russell, Man., Can., June 12, 1931; s. William Hugh and Grace Muriel F.; m. Audrey Joy Barton, June 18, 1955; children: Barton Brett, Warren Hugh, Rhonda Marie. BSc, Brandon U., 1952; MSc in Zoology, U. Alta., Can., 1968. Geophysicist Frontier Geophys. Ltd., Alta., 1952-53; geologist, then dist. geologist Shell Can., Ltd., 1954-64; chief park naturalist and biologist Elk Island (Can.) Nat. Pk., 1965-67; dir. hist. devel. and archives, dir. hist. and sci. svc., dir. Nature Ctr., dir. interpretation and recreation City of Edmonton, Alta., 1967-92; ret., 1992; founder Fedn. Alta. Naturalists, 1969. Author: A Nature Guide to Alberta, Bird Finding Guide to Canada; (with Joy Finlay) Ocean to Alpine-A British Columbia Nature Guide, A Guide to Alberta Parks. Recipient Order of the Bighorn, Govt. of Atla., 1987, Heritage award Environment Can., 1990, Loran Goulden award Fedn. Alta. Naturalists, 1991, Can. 125th Anniversary award, 1993, Greenways Achievement award, BC Province Capital Commn., 2001, Douglas Pimlott award Nature Can., 1991; named to Edmonton Hist. Hall of Fame, 1976. Mem. Can. Mus. Assn. (pres. 1976-78), Alta. Mus. Assn. (founding mem., past pres.), Am. Mus. Assn. (past coun.), Am. Ornithol. Union. Home: 270 Trevlac Pl RR 3 Victoria BC Canada V9E 2C4 Personal E-mail: joyandcamfinlay@shaw.ca. *I will walk but once on this earth. In this short time I hope to help my fellow man come to a greater awareness, appreciation and understanding of the world environment of which we are very much a part. I am trying to ensure that our descendants have a fit planet on which to live.*

FINLAY, ROBERT DEREK, food products executive; b. U.K., May 16, 1932; s. William Templeton and Phyllis F.; m. Una Ann Grant, June 30, 1956; children: Fiona, Rory, James. BA with honors in Law and Econs, Cambridge U., Eng., 1955, MA, 1959. With Mobil Oil Co. Ltd., U.K., 1955-61; assoc. McKinsey & Co., Inc., 1961-67, prin., 1967-71, dir., 1971-79; mng. dir. H.J. Heinz Co. Ltd., U.K., 1979-81; sr. v.p. corp. devel. world hdqs. H.J. Heinz Co., Pitts., 1981-93, chief fin. officer world hdqrs., 1989-92, sr. v.p. corp. devel., area v.p., 1992-93. Chmn. Dawson Internat., 1995-98; mem. Inst. Mktg., 1976-2004. Mem. London com. Scottish Coun. Devel. and Industry, 1979-03; trustee Mercy Hosp., Pitts., 1983-93; bd. dirs. Pitts. Symphony Soc., 1989-92, U.S.-China Bus. Coun., 1984-92, Pitts. Pub. Theater, 1988-92; gov. Kingston Grammar Sch., 1997-2002. Capt. Gordon Highlanders, 1950-61. Fellow Inst. Dirs., Royal Soc. Arts; mem. Highland Brigade Club, Leander Club, Annabel's, Caledonian Club, Three Rivers Rowing Assn. (gov.).

FINLAY, TERENCE EDWARD, retired archbishop; s. Terence John and Sarah (McBryan) F.; m. Alice-Jean Cracknell, 1962; 2 daus. BA, U. We. Ont., London; BTh, Huron Coll., London, Ont.; MA, U. Cambridge, Eng.; DD (jure dignitatis), Huron Coll., 1987. Ordained deacon Anglican Ch., 1961, priest, 1962. Dean of residence Renison Coll., Waterloo, Canada; incumbent All Saints, Waterloo, 1964-66, St. Aidan's, London, Canada, 1966-68; rector St. John the Evangelist, London, 1968-78; archdeacon of Brant, 1978-82; incumbent Grace Ch., Brantford, Canada, 1978-82, St. Clement's, Eglinton, Toronto, Canada, 1982-86; suffragan bishop Diocese of Toronto, 1986, coadjutor bishop, 1987, bishop Toronto, 1989—2004; archbishop Met. of Ecclesiastical Province of Ont. Anglican. Avocations: music, skiing, travel. Home: 62 Wellesley St W Ste 1602 Toronto ON M5S 2X3 Canada

FINLAYSON, BRUCE ALAN, retired chemical engineering professor; b. Waterloo, Iowa, July 18, 1939; s. Rodney Alan and Donna Elizabeth (Gilbert) F.; m. Patricia Lynn Hills, June 9, 1961; children: Mark, Catherine, Christine. BA, Rice U., 1961, MS, 1963; PhD, U. Minn., 1965. Asst. prof. to prof. U. Wash., Seattle, 1967—2005, prof. dept. chem. engrng. and applied math., 1977-82, Rehnberg prof., 1989—2005, chmn. dept. chem. engrng., 1989-98; prof. emeritus, 2005—. Vis. prof. Univ. Coll., Swansea, Wales, U.K., 1975-76, Denmark Tekniske Hojskole, Lyngby, 1976, Universidad Nacional del Sur, Bahia Blanca, Argentina, 1980; Gulf vis. prof. Carnegie Mellon U., 1986; trustee Computer Aids to Chem. Engrng. Edn., Austin, Tex., 1980-92; mem. bd. on chem. sci. and tech. NRC, 1990-92. Mem. editl. bd. Internat. Jour. Numerical Methods in Fluids, Swansea, 1980—, Numerical Heat Transfer, 1981-2002, Numerical Methods for Partial Differential Equations, 1984—, Chem. Engrng. Edn., 1991—2007; author: The Method of Weighted Residuals and Variational Principles, 1972, Nonlinear Analysis in Chemical Engineering, 1980, Numerical Methods for Problems with Moving Fronts, 1992, Introduction to Chemical Engineering Computing, 2006. Lt. USNR, 1965-67. Recipient Undergrad. Computational Engring. and Sci. award, U.S. Dept. Energy, 1996. Fellow AIChE (CAST divsn. programming 1981-85, William H. Walker award 1983, bd. dirs. CAST divsn. 1984-86, vice chmn. 1987-88, chmn. 1989, bd. dirs. 1992-94, editorial bd. 1985-91, v.p. 1999, pres. 2000, past pres. 2001); mem. Am. Chem. Soc. (bd. dirs. Petroleum Rsch. Fund 1998-2004), Am. Soc. Engrng. Edn. (dir. Summer Sch. for Chem. Engrng. Faculty 1997, Martin award Ch.E. divsn. 1994, Dow Lectureship award, 2005), Soc. Indsl. and Applied Math., Soc. Rheology, Nat. Acad. Engring., N.Am. Alliance of Chem. Engrs. (pres. 2001). Home: 6315 22nd Ave NE Seattle WA 98115-6919 Office: U Wash Dept Chem Engring PO Box 351750 Seattle WA 98195-1750 Home Phone: 206-524-3375; Office Phone: 206-685-1634. Personal E-mail: bafinlayson@mindspring.com. Business E-Mail: finlayson@cheme.washington.edu.

FINLAYSON, JOHN SYLVESTER, retired biochemist; b. Phila., Sept. 19, 1933; s. Alexander Smeillie and Anna Eva (Sylvester) F.; m. Rasma Irêne Bramane; children: Mark Lars, Siglinda Erika Finlayson Beyeler. BA summa cum laude, Marietta Coll., 1953; MS, U. Wis., 1955, PhD, 1957. Rsch. fellow Inst. Radiophysics, Stockholm, 1957-58; biochemist NIH, Bethesda, Md., 1958-72; rsch. chemist FDA, Bethesda, 1972-75, chief Lab. Plasma Derivatives, 1975-86, chief Lab. Hepatitis, 1986-89, chief Lab. Hemostasis & Thrombosis, 1988-89, acting dir. divsn. hematology, 1990-92, assoc. dir. sci. office blood rsch. and review, 1993—2003, ret., 2003, guest worker, 2004—. Vis. prof., scientist Protein Rsch. Inst., Osaka, Japan, 1976; lectr. in biochemistry Found. Advanced Edn. in Sci., Bethesda, 1961-76, 86-96. Author: Basic Biochemical Calculations, 1969; co-editor: Immunoglobulins, 1980; contbr. articles to profl. jours. With USPHS, 1958-61. Mem. Internat. Soc. Thrombosis and Haemostasis (charter, emeritus), Soc. Exptl. Biology and Medicine (life), Sr. Biomed. Rsch. Svc.

FINLAYSON-PITTS, BARBARA JEAN, chemistry professor; b. Ottawa, Ont., Can., Apr. 4, 1948; d. James Colin and Jean Burwell (Moore) Finlayson; m. James N. Pitts Jr., May 27, 1976. BSc (Hons.) in Chemistry, Trent U., Ont., Can., 1970; MS in Chemistry, U. Calif., Riverside, 1971, PhD in Chemistry, 1973. Rsch. asst., then postdoctoral rsch. chemist U. Calif., Riverside, 1970-74; asst. prof. chemistry Calif. State U., Fullerton, 1974-77, assoc. prof., 1977-81, prof. chemistry, 1981-94, U. Calif., Irvine, 1994—. Mem. grants rev. panel EPA, 1980-86; mem. rsch. screening com. Calif. Air Resources Bd.; mem. editl. bd. Revista Internacional de Contaminacion Ambientel; mem. com. on tropospheric ozone NAS, 1989-91, com. atmospheric chemistry, 1989-92; mem. awards program adv. com. Rsch. Corp., 1993-95. Author: Atmospheric Chemistry: Fundamentals and Experimental Techniques, 1986, Chemistry of the Upper and Lower Atmosphere, 2000; mem. editl. bd. Rsch. on Chem. Intermediates, 1995—, Atmospheric Environ., 1996—, Internat. Jour. Chem. Kinet., 1996-2000, Jour. Environ. Sci. Health, 1996-97, Jour. Phys. Chemistry, 1998—; contbr. numerous articles to refereed jours. Fellow AAAS, NAS, Am. Acad. Arts and Sciences; mem. Am. Chem. Soc. (award for creative advances in environ. sci. 2004), Am. Geophys. Union, Am. Women in Sci., Iota Sigma Pi. Episcopalian. Avocation: fly fishing. Office: U Calif 328 Rowland Hall Mail Code 2025 Irvine CA 92697-0001

FINLEY, CLAUDIA D., secondary school educator, consultant; M of Sci. in Edn., No. Ill. U., DeKalb, 1976. Cert. reading specialist Ill., 1981. Reading specialist Glenbard HS, Glen Ellyn, Ill., 1976—88, social studies instr., 1988—. Sponsor Young Democrats of Glenbard West, Glen Ellyn, 2000—05; lector St. James the Apostle Cath. Ch., Glen Ellyn, 1992—2004. Mem.: Nat. Coun. for the Social Studies, Internat. Reading Assn. Independent. Roman Catholic. Achievements include development of American law course; college reading skills course. Avocations: history, reading, exercise, music, singing. Office: Glenbard West High Sch 670 Crescent Blvd Glen Ellyn IL 60137 Home Phone: 630-682-3992; Office Phone: 630-942-7417. Office Fax: 630-469-8615. Business E-Mail: claudia_finley@glenbard.org.

FINLEY, EMMA ROSEMARY, science educator; b. Gulfport, Miss., Sept. 23, 1935; d. Frank Ransom and Rosemary Blackmarr; m. Chester William Finley, Aug. 8, 1954; children: Margaret Finley Hase, Chester Lawrence, Robert Stacy. Ednl. Specialist, U. of So. Miss., 1995—2001; BS, U. of NC, 1968—70; MS, U. of So. Miss., 1971—75. Master Teacher Nat. Bd. for Profl. Tchg. Standards, 2001. Sci. educator Long Beach Sch. Dist., Miss., 1970—73, Harrison County Sch. Dist., Gulfport, Miss., 1973—. Sci. fair sponsor Harrison County Sch. Dist., Gulfport, Miss., 1973—; art fair sponsor North Woolmarket Sch. Parent Tchr. Student Assn., Biloxi, Miss., 1998—2002; candidates' mentor Nat. Bd. for Profl. Tchg. Standards, Long Beach, Miss., 2002—. Illustrator (resource guides) Oceanography and Coastal Processes, 1998, Global Awareness, Global Environmental Education, 1996. Vol. Friends of Libr., Gulfport, Miss., 2000—06; endowed Finley scholarship Miss. Gulf Coast CC Found., Perkinston, Miss., 2003—07. Named Tchr. of Yr., d'Iberville Mid. Sch., 1990, Woolmarket Sch., 1993, Ageless Hero for Love of Learning, Blue Cross/ Blue Shield of Miss., 2003; recipient Outstanding Instrn. in Marine Sci. award, Miss.-Ala. Sea Grant Consortium, 1991, 1994; Nature Trail grantee, BellSouth, Butterfly Garden grantee, 2001—03. Mem.: AAUW, NEA, Miss. Assn. Educators, Nat. Marine Educators' Assn., Nat. Sci. Teachers' Assn., Miss. Sci. Teachers' Assn. (v.p. and pres. 1988—90, Miss. Outstanding Elem. Sci. Educator 1980, Exemplary Mid. Sch. Sci. Tchr. 2002), Federated Women's Club, Gulf Coast Civic Club, Miss. Federated Women's Club, Gulfport Federated Women's Club, Phi Delta Kappa. Episcopalian. Avocations: nature artist, gardening, reading, conservationist. Office: West Wortham Middle Sch 20199 West Wortham Rd Saucier MS 39574 Office Phone: 228-831-1276. Office Fax: 228-539-5962. Business E-Mail: rfinley@harrison.k12.ms.us.

FINLEY, GEORGE ALVIN, III, wholesale executive, oil industry executive; b. Aurora, Ill., Apr. 25, 1938; s. George Alvin, II, and Sally Ann (Lord) F.; m. Sue Sellors, June 20, 1962 (dec. 1995); m. Phyllis Ann Finley; children: Valerie, George Alvin IV (dec. 2005). BBA, So. Meth. U., 1962; postgrad. Coll. Grad. Program, Ford Motor Co., 1963. Rep. for Europe Finco Internat., 1959-61; trainee Ford Motor Co., Dearborn, Mich., 1962-63; v.p. mktg. Internat. Motor Cars, Oakland, Calif., 1963-64, Sequoia Lincoln lease mgr., 1965; regional mgr. Behlen Mfg. Co., Dallas, 1965-67; pres. C C Distbrs., Corpus Christi, Tex., 1967—. Guest instr. Sch. Bus., So. Meth. U., pres., 1986-91, Nueces River Authority, 1975-2001; bd. dirs. Contract Svcs. Assn. Am. Sec. Bd. Washington, MD Anderson Hosp. U. Tex., Christus-Spohn Health Sys., exec. com., mem. McDonald Obs., U. Tex., exec. com.; mem. Del Mar Coll. Found. Mem. pres.'s coun. Tex. A&M U., Corpus Christi; pres. Nueces County Rural Rail Transp. Dist., 2005—; bd. dirs. Coastal Bend Alcohol and Drug Rehab. Ctr., 1973—97, 2005—. Mem. Tex. Wholesale Hardware Assn. (pres. 1991-92), Nat. Assn. Wholesalers, Am. Supply Assn., Wholesale Distbrs. Assn. (bd. dirs. 1994—), Impact Industries Inc. (chmn. bd. Sandwich, Ill. 1986-93), N.Am. Bldg. Material Distbn. Assn., Rotary Internat., State Bar of Tex. (grievance com. 1995-2001), Phi Delta Theta. Democrat. Episcopalian. Achievements include assisted in design, engineering, production, and marketing of the Apollo automobile. Home: 3360 Ocean Dr Corpus Christi TX 78411-1457 Office: PO Box 9153 210 Mcbride Ln Corpus Christi TX 78408-2338 Office Phone: 361-289-0200.

FINLEY, GLENNA, writer; b. Puyallup, Wash., June 12, 1925; d. John Ford and Gladys De Ferris (Winters) F.; m. Donald MacLeod Witte, May 19, 1951; 1 child, Duncan MacLeod. BA cum laude, Stanford U., Calif., 1945. Prodr. internat. divsn. NBC, 1945-49; film libr. March of Time, 1949; with news bur. Life Mag., 1950; publicity and radio writer Seattle, 1950-51; freelance writer, 1951-57; contract writer New Am. Libr. Inc., NYC, 1970—. Author numerous books including Master of Love, 1978, Beware My Heart, 1978, The Marriage Merger, 1978, Wildfire of Love, 1979, Timed for Love, 1979, Love's Temptation, 1979, Stateroom for Two, 1980, Affairs of Love, 1980, A Business Affair, 1983, Wanted for Love, 1983, A Weekend for Love, 1984, Love's Waiting Game, 1985, A Touch of Love, 1985, Diamonds for My Love, 1986, Secret of Love, 1987, The Marrying Kind, 1988, Island Rendezvous, 1990, Stowaway for Love, 1992, The Temporary Bride, 1993. Named Matrix Table Woman of Achievement, 1976. Mem.: Women's Univ. Club (Seattle). Republican. Anglican. Home: 7868-F Rea Rd Charlotte NC 28277 *I have always made a point of writing pleasant books that "turn out right"- believing that after readers have opened their wallets to purchase a book all suffering should cease.*

FINLEY, HARRY, artist, museum director; b. Long Branch, NJ, July 18, 1942; s. George and Marjorie Finley. BA, Johns Hopkins U., 1964; postgrad., U. Fla., 1966, U. Fla., 1969—71. Graphic designer Dept. Army, Washington and Germany, 1971—2004; mus. founder, dir. Mus. Menstruation, New Carrollton, Md., 1994—; artist, 1971—. Portraits. With US Army, 1964—66, with US Army, 1971—74. Decorated Commendation medal for Civilian Svc. Dept. Army; recipient Keith L. Ware award, 1974, Thomas Jefferson award, Dept. Def., 1974. Mem.: ACLU, Am. Assn. History Medicine, Soc. Menstrual Cycle Rsch. Independent. Avocations: astronomy, cultural history, classical music, languages. E-mail: hfinley@mum.org.

FINLEY, JAMES I., federal agency administrator; BS in Engring.; MS, Calif. State U. Chmn. bus. devel. coun. Gen. Dynamics Corp., pres. info. sys., corp. officer; pres., CEO SMARTSKIN, Inc.; pres., founder Finley Group, LLC; prin. dep. under sec., under sec. acquisition logistics and tech. US Dept. Def., Washington, 2006—. Office: US Dept Def 3015 Defense Pentagon Rm 3E1006 Washington DC 20301-3015 Office Phone: 703-697-7021.

FINLEY, JOHN CYRUS, III, lawyer, judge; b. Texarkana, Ark., Jan. 10, 1949; s. John Cyrus and LaVerne (Kenneweg) F., m. Andrea Weld Murry, 2004; BA magna cum laude, Ouachita Bapt. U., 1971; JD, U. Ark., 1974. Bar: Ark. 1974, US Dist. Ct. (we. dist.) Ark. 1974, US Supreme Ct. 1980. Ptnr. firm Finley and Finley, Attys.-at-Law, Ashdown, Ark., 1974—; judge Ashdown and Little River County Dist. Ct., 1983—; pres. Ark. Dist. Judges Coun., 2007, pres., 2007-. Mem. bd. dirs. Texarkana Area Cmty. Found., 2004-. Mem. ABA, Ark. Bar Assn. (mem. bd. govs. 2006-07), SW Ark. Bar Assn. (past pres.), Am. Judges Assn., Little River County Hist. Soc. (v.p. 1983, pres. 2002-), SAR (pres. chpt. 2003-). Baptist. Home: Highway 32 Ashdown AR 71822 Office Phone: 870-898-3147.

FINLEY, JOHN G., lawyer; b. White Plains, NY, Oct. 19, 1956; BA in History, U. Penn., 1978, BS in Econ., 1978; JD cum laude, Harvard U., 1981. Ptnr. Simpson Thacher & Bartlett LLP, NYC, 1988—, chmn. corp. governance practice group. Named a Dealmaker of the Yr., Am. Lawyer mag., 2006. Mem.: NY State Bar Assn., Internat. Bar Assn. (chmn. Internat. Annual Mergers & Acquisitons Conf.), Phi Betta Kappa. Office: Simpson Thacher & Bartlett LLP 425 Lexington Ave New York NY 10017

FINLEY, KATHERINE MANDUSIC, professional society administrator; b. Mansfield, Ohio, Nov. 8, 1954; d. Sam and Ann Julia (Konves) Mandusic; m. Edwin D. McDonell, Aug. 18, 1979 (div. Dec. 1994); m. Jeffrey A. Finley, June 12, 1999. BA, Ohio Wesleyan U.; MA in History and Mus. Studies, Case Western Res.; MBA, Ind. U. Rschr. Conner Prairie Mus., Fishers, Ind., 1978-82; exec. dir., rsch. historian Ind. Med. History Mus./Ind. Hist. Soc., Indpls., 1982-91; asst. dir. comm. and mktg. Ind. U. Ctr. Philanthropy, 1991-93; exec. dir. Roller Skating Assn. Internat., Indpls., 1993-2000, Assn. Rsch. Nonprofit Orgns. and Voluntary Action, 2000—05; mem. faculty philanthropic studies Ind. U.-Purdue U., Indpls., 2001—; rsch. dir. William E. Smith Inst. for Assn. Rsch., 2004—05; dir. Am. Coll. Sports Medicine Found., Indpls., 2005—06; exec. dir. Tenant-in-Common Assn. and Found., 2006—. Author: (book) The Journals of William A. Lindsay, 1989; contbg. editor: The Encyclopedia of Indianapolis, 1994; contbr. articles to profl. jours. Pres. Altrusa Internat. Indpls., 1995—97, treas., 1998—99, chmn. svc. com., 1999—2000; pres. Altrusa Found. Indpls., 2001—03; bd. dirs. Nat. Mus. Roller Skating, Lincoln, 1994—2000. Mem.: Assn. Fund Raising Profls. (bd. dirs. Ind. chpt. 2003—), Ind. Soc. Assn. Execs. (chair edn. com. 1997—98, chair conv. com. 1999—2000, bd. dirs. 1999—2001, chair found. 2000), Nat. Soc. Fund Raising Execs. (cert.), Am. Soc. Assn. Execs. (mem. ethics com. 2004—, Assn. Exec. of Yr. 2002, cert. meeting planner 2003), MINI Cooper Car Club Ind. (club advisor 2003—04), Toastmasters (v.p. edn. 1998—99, v.p. pub. rels. 2000, v.p. edn. 2000—02, gov. area 18 2001—02, v.p. edn. 2006—07), Rotary Internat. of Indpls., Phi Beta Kappa, Sigma Iota Epsilon, Beta Gamma Sigma. Avocations: reading, walking, gourmet cooking. Office: 10401 N Meridian St Ste 300 Indianapolis IN 46290 Business E-Mail: kfinley@ticassoc.org.

FINLEY, LEWIS MERREN, financial consultant; b. Reubens, Idaho, Nov. 29, 1929; s. John Emory and Charlotte (Priest) Finley; m. Virginia Ruth Spousta, Feb. 23, 1957; children: Ellen Annette Finley Guldenzopf, Charlotte Louise Finley Kinney. Student pub. schs., Spokane. With Household Fin. Co., Portland, Oreg. and Seattle, 1953-56, Doug Gerow Fin., Portland, 1956-61; pres. Family Fin. Planners Inc., Portland, 1961—. Assoc. broker Peoples Choice Realty, Inc., Milwaukie, Oreg., 1977-82, Lewis M. Finley, Real Estate Broker, Inc., 1982—; standing trustee Chpt. 13, Fed. Bankruptcy Ct., Dist. of Oreg., 1979. Author: The Complete Guide to Getting Yourself Out of Debt, 1975. With U.S. Army, 1951-53. Mem. Oreg. Assn. Credit Counselors (past pres.), N.W. Assn. Credit Counselors (past treas.), Am. Assn. Credit Counselors (v.p. 1982-85), Authors Guild, Nat. Assn. Realtors, Masons (past master), Scottish Rite (32d degree), Shriners (hosp. guide). Republican. Methodist. Home: 3015 SE Riviere Dr Portland OR 97267-5548 Office: PO Box 12287 Portland OR 97212-0287 Personal E-mail: yelnif@msn.com.

FINLEY, MICHAEL, professional basketball player; b. Mar. 6, 1973; Grad., Wis. State U., 1995. Guard, selected 1st round NBA draft Phoenix Suns, 1995-97; guard-forward Dallas Mavericks, 1997—2005, San Antonio Spurs, 2005—. Office: San Antonio Spurs One SBC Ctr San Antonio TX 78219

FINLEY, MICHAEL VALTON, foundation executive; b. Medford, Oreg., Apr. 8, 1947; s. Valton Austin and Anne Elsie (Huebner) F.; m. Lillie Eiteneir, June 14, 1969; children: Devon, Laura. BS in Biology, So. Oreg. State Coll., 1969. With Nat. Park Service, 1970-2001; park ranger Big Bend (Tex.) Nat. Park, 1970, Pinnacles Nat. Monument, Paicines, Calif., 1972-73, Yosemite (Calif.) Nat. Park, 1974-76; exchange ranger Calif. State Park System-Big Bas State Park, 1973-74; law enforcement specialist Grand Teton Nat. Park, Moose, Wyo., 1976-78; staff park ranger, Washington, 1978-80; legis. affairs specialist Washington, 1980-81; supt. Assateague Island Nat. Seashore Berlin, Md., 1981-83; assoc. regional dir. Anchorage, 1983-86; supt. Everglades Nat. Pk., Homestead, Fla., 1986-89, Yosemite Nat. Pk., Mammoth Hot Springs, 1989-94; pres. Turner Found., Atlanta, 2001—. Served to sgt. U.S. Army, 1968-70. Mem. Assn. Nat. Park Rangers (pres. 1980-82). Lodges: Rotary. Lutheran. Avocations: fishing, scuba, photography, hiking, skiing. Office: Turner Found Inc 133 Luckie St NW 2nd Fl Atlanta GA 30303

FINLEY, MORDECAI, rabbi; m. Meirav Finley; children: Lev, Kayitz, Shulamitz, Avigayil. PhD in Religion and Social Ethics, U. So. Calif. Cert. Rabbinic Ordination Hebrew Union Coll.-Jewish Inst. of Religion. Co-founder, co-CEO, Rabbi Ohr HaTorah Temple, LA, 1994—. Provost, prof. Liturgy and Jewish Ethics Acad. Jewish Religion, Calif., former pres.; faculty mem. Wexner Heritage Found.; mem. dept. Continuing Edn. U. Judaism; also taught Hebrew Union Coll.-Jewish Inst. Religion, Loyola Law Sch., Shalom Hartman Inst., Jerusalem. Actor: Fathers and Sons, 2005. Named one of The Top 50 Rabbis in America, Newsweek Mag., 2007. Office: Ohr HaTorah Ste 100 12410 Burbank Boulevard Valley Village CA 91607 Office Phone: 818-769-8223, 310-278-9049. Fax: 818-278-9049. Business E-Mail: rabbifinley@ohrhatorah.org.*

FINLEY, ROBERT VAN EATON, minister; b. Charlottesville, Va., May 2, 1922; s. William Walter and Melissa (Hoover) Finley; m. Ethel Drummond, Dec. 23, 1949; children: Deborah Ann, Ruth Ellen. BA, U. Va., 1944; postgrad., U. Chgo. Div. Sch., 1946-47; LittD, Houghton Coll., 1952. Ordained to ministry Bapt. Ch., 1957. Evangelist Youth for Christ Internat., Chgo., 1945-46, Inter-Varsity Christian Fellowship, Chgo., 1945-46, overseas, 1948-51; pastor Evang. Free Ch., Richmond, Calif., 1951-52; minister to fgn. students 10th Presbyn. Ch., Phila., 1952-55; founder, gen. dir. Christian Aid Mission, Charlottesville, 1953-70, CEO, 1970—2005, chmn. bd. dirs., 1970—; founder, gen. dir. Overseas Students Mission, Ft. Erie, Ont., Canada, 1954-68, pres., 1969-85; pastor Temple Bapt. Ch., Washington, 1965-66. Pres. Bharat Evang. Fellowship, Washington, 1973—87; founder, pres. Christian Aid Mission Can., 1985—88, chmn. bd. dirs., 1989—2003; pres. Internat. Congress Indigenous Missions, Harrisburg, Pa., 1988—2005. Author: The Future of Foreign Missions, 2002,

Reformation in Foreign Missions, 2005; editor: Conquest for Christ mag., 1954—74, Christian Mission mag., 1974—2005. Founder, pres. International Students, Inc., Colorado Springs, 1952—67, chmn., 1968—70. Mem.: Assn. Christians Ministering Internats. (bd. dirs. 1995—99), Omicron Delta Kappa. Office: Christian Aid Mission PO Box 9037 Charlottesville VA 22906-9037 *To indulge myself, beyond actual need, with the benefits of material wealth leaves me the poorer. But when my surplus resources are used to uplift those who lack opportunity, I am enriched.*

FINLEY, SARA CREWS, medical geneticist, educator; b. Lineville, Ala., Feb. 26, 1930; m. Wayne H. Finley; children: Randall Wayne, Sara Jane. BS in Biology, U. Ala., 1951, MD, 1955. Diplomate Am. Bd. Med. Genetics; cert. clin. geneticist; cert. clin. cytogeneticist. Intern Lloyd Noland Hosp., Fairfield, Ala., 1955-56; NIH fellow in pediatrics U. Ala. Med. Sch., Birmingham, 1956-60; NIH trainee in med. genetics Inst. Med. Genetics, U. Uppsala, Sweden, 1961-62; mem. faculty U. Ala. Med. Sch., 1960-96, co-dir. lab. med. genetics, 1966-96, prof. pediatrics, 1975-96, occupant Wayne H. and Sara Crews Finley chair med. genetics, 1986-96, prof. emerita, 1996—; Disting. Faculty lectr. Med. Ctr., U. Ala. at Birmingham, 1983; mem. staff U. Ala. Hosp., Children's Hosp. Ala. Mem. ad hoc com. genetic counseling Children's Bur., HEW, 1966; mem. ad hoc rev. panel for genetic disease and sickle cell testing and counseling programs, 1980; mem. genetic diseases program objective rev. panel Bur. Maternal and Child Health and Resources Div., HHS, 1989, mem. adv. group on lab. quality assurance, 1989. Birmingham Author papers on clin. cytogenetics, human congenital malformations, human growth and devel. Mem. White House Conf. Health, 1965; mem. rsch. manpower rev. com. Nat. Cancer Inst., 1977-81; mem. Sickle Cell Disease Adv. Com., NIH, 1983-87; chairperson physician's campaign bd. dirs. United Way, 1993-95. Recipient Disting. Alumna award U. Ala. Sch. Medicine Alumni Assn., 1989, Med. award Ala. Assn. for Retarded Children, 1969, Turlington award Planned Parenthood of Ala., 1982, Nat. Outstanding Alumnae award Zeta Tau Alpha, 1992, Disting. Alumna award U. Ala. Nat. Alumni Assn., 1994, Brother Bryan Prayer Point award Birmingham Women's Com. of 100, 2001, Gardner award Ala. Acad. Sci., 2002, Local Legend award Am. Med. Women's Assn. Nat. Libr. Medicine, 2004, Lifetime Achievement award Birmingham Bus. Jour., 2003, So. Women of Dist. award So. Women's Ctr., 2005; co-recipient Will Holmes award Children's Aid Soc. Birmingham, 1999; named Top Ten Women in Birmingham, 1989, Top 31 Most Outstanding Alumnae U. Ala., Tuscaloosa, 1993, Ala. Healthcare Hall of Fame, 2001; Finley-Compass Bank Genetics Conf. Ctr. with portrait opened, 2001. Fellow AMA (founding), Am. Coll. Med. Genetics; mem. Am. Soc. Human Genetics, Med. Assn. Ala. (Samuel Buford Word award 2003, Fifty Year Club 2005), Ala. Assn. Retarded Children (Ann. Med. awad 1969), Ala. Acad. Sci., Jefferson County Med. Soc. (pres. 1990), Jefferson County Pediatric Soc., So. Med. Assn., NY Acad. Sci., Caduceus Club, Rotary Club of Birmingham, Phi Beta Kappa, Sigma Xi, Alpha Omega Alpha, Alpha Epsilon Delta, Omicron Delta Kappa, Phi Kappa Phi, Zeta Tau Alpha. Office: U Ala Kaul Bldg 210E Birmingham AL 35294 E-mail: scfinley@webtv.net.

FINLEY, SARAH MAUDE MERRITT, retired social worker; b. Atlanta, Nov. 19, 1946; d. Genius and Willie Maude (Wright) Merritt; m. Craig Wayne Finley, Aug. 10, 1968; children: Craig Wayne Jr., Jarret Lee. BA, Spelman Coll., 1968; postgrad., Atlanta U., 1968-69. Cert. GPS/MAPP leader 2001. Job placement advisor Marsh Draughton Bus. Coll., Atlanta, 1971-72; child attendant Fulton County Juvenile Ct., Atlanta, 1972; social worker Fulton County Dept. Family and Children Svcs., Atlanta, 1972-2000, casework supr., 1976-98, Title VI customer svc. coord. Ctrl. City/North Area office, 1990-98, ret., 1998; counselor/asst. to the project dir. Right Way Home Project N.W. Area Office, 1998-99; social svcs. case mgr. Placement Resource Devel. N.W. Area Office, 2000; social worker Dept. Family and Children Svcs. Clayton County, Jonesboro, Ga., 2000—05, ret., 2005. Supr. Count on Me video Ga. Dept. Human Resources, 1987; mem. Spelman's Team of Alumni Recruiters, Spelman Coll. Vol. coord. family support program Family Support Group of Atlanta Detachment of 2d Army Maneuver Tng. Command.; vol. family support coun. 87th Maneuver Area Command (now 4th Brigade, 87th Divsn.), 1991-93; del. Ft. McPherson (Ga.) Army Family Symposium, 1992, 3d ann. worldwide USAR Family Support Conf., St. Louis, 1992 Mem.: Fulton County Ret. Employees Assn., Nat. Alumnae Assn. Spelman Coll., Womens Aux. Ga. VFW. Baptist. Avocations: poetry, reading, volunteer work, stress management, writing. Personal E-mail: maudngen@aol.com.

FINLEY, SKIP, communications executive; b. Ann Arbor, Mich., July 23, 1948; s. Ewell W. and Mildred Virginia F.; m. Karen Michele Woolard, May 6, 1971; children: Kharma I., R. Kristin. Student, Northeastern U., 1966-71. Owner Skifin Gallery, Boston, 1970-71; floor dir. Sta. WHDH-TV, Boston, 1971; floor mgr., asst. dir., prodr. Sta. WSBK-TV, Boston, 1971-72; account exec. Sta. WRKO-AM, Boston, 1972-73; account mgr. Humphrey, Browning, MacDougall Advt., Boston, 1973-74; sales mgr. Sta. WAMO-AM-FM Sheridan Broadcasting Corp., 1974-75, gen. mgr. Sta. WAMO-AM-FM, 1975-76, v.p. radio div. Pitts., 1976-77; dir. of sales Sheridan Broadcasting Network, NY, 1977-79, exec. v.p., gen. mgr., 1979-81, pres., 1981-82; gen. ptnr. Sta.-KEZO AM-FM, Omaha, 1983-88, Sta. KDAB-FM, Salt Lake City and Ogden, 1985-90; pres., gen. mgr. Sta. WKYS-FM, Washington, 1988-95; pres., CEO Albimar Comm., Washington, 1982-95, Answers, Solutions, 1999—2003; CEO, COO Am. Urban Radio Networks, Pitts., 1995-98; vice. chmn. Inner City Broadcasting Corp. Broadcast Holdings, Inc., NYC, 2003—. Contbr. numerous articles on media-related subjects to various publs. Testimony to House subcom. on Comm., 1977, FCC, 1977, Congl. Black Caucus, 1990; mem. bd. overseers, trustee Vineyard Open Land Found. Recipient Excellence in Media award Nat. Assn. Media Women, NY, 1981, Communicator of Yr. award Washington Area Media Orgn., 1982, New Horizons award DC Gen. Hosp., Washington, 1990, Advocacy in Edn. award DC Pub. Schs., Washington, 1990, Radio Wayne award best overall broadcaster Radio Ink mag., Dallas, 1994; named Top 25 African Ams. in radio Radio Ink mag., 1999-05. Mem. Nat. Assn. Black Owned Broadcasters (bd. dirs. 1982-95), Radio Advt. Bur. (bd. dirs. 1990—, chair 1997-98), Nat. Assn. Broadcasters (bd. dirs. 1981-82, 90-94, vice chair radio bd. 1993-94), Nat. Thespian Soc., The Advt. Coun., Inc. (bd. dirs. 1998-99), Martha's Vineyard Rod and Gun Club, Lowes Island Golf Club (founding adv. bd. govs. Sterling, Va. 1992-97), Libr. Am. Broadcasting Found. (bd. dirs. 2003-07), John Bayliss Found. (bd. dirs. 2004-07), Broadcaster's Found. (bd. dirs. 2005-). Avocations: deep sea fishing, model trains, shooting, automobiles, yoga. Office: ICBC Broadcast Holdings Inc 3 Pk Ave 40th Fl New York NY 10016-4244 Office Phone: 212-592-0406.

FINLEY, WAYNE HOUSE, medical educator; b. Goodwater, Ala., Apr. 7, 1927; s. Byron Bruce and Lucille (House) F.; m. Sara Will Crews, July 6, 1952; children: Randall Wayne, Sara Jane. BS, Jacksonville State U., 1948; MA, U. Ala., 1950, MS, 1955, PhD, 1958, MD, 1960; postgrad., U. Uppsala, Sweden, 1961-62. Cert. clin. cytogenetics Am. Bd. Med. Genetics, 1983. Sci. tchr. High Sch., Tuscaloosa, Ala., 1949-51; intern U. Ala. Hosps. and Clinics, 1960-61; from asst. prof. to assoc. prof. pediat. U. Ala. Sch. Medicine, 1962-70, prof., 1970-96, asst. prof. biochemistry, 1965-75, prof., 1975-96, asst. prof. physiology and biophysics, 1968-75, assoc. prof., 1975-96, chmn. med. student rsch. day, 1965-75, dir. Lab. Med. Genetics, 1966-96, prof. epidemiology, pub. health and epidmiology, 1975-96, prof. emeritus, 1996—, adj. prof. biology, 1980-96, chmn. faculty coun. Sch. Medicine, 1977-78, 84-87. Dir. med. genetics grad. program U. Ala. at Birmingham, 1983-96, dir. Am. Bd. Med. Genetics approved tng. program, 1978-96, dir. med. genetics residency program, 1995-98; chmn. Carey Phillips Travel Fellowship, 1972—; mem. com. on genetic counseling Children's Bur., Dept. HEW, 1966-67; nat. adv. rsch. resources coun. NIH and HEW, 1977-80; sr. scientist Comprehensive Cancer Ctr., Cystic Fibrosis Rsch. Ctr., Ctr. for Health Risk Assessment and Disease Prevention, 1982-96; bd. dirs. Southeastern Regional Genetics Group, 1982-2000, editor newsletter, 1997-2000; chmn. steering com. Reynolds Hist. Libr. Assocs., 1981-2007, Com. on Future Needs in Med. Genetics, Genetics Svc. Br., USPHS, 1987, Carmichael Fund for Grad. Students, 1989—; faculty rep. U. Ala. Sys. Bd. Trustees, 1995-96; senator U. Ala. at Birmingham Faculty Senate, 1995-96; mem. adv. and nominating com. Ala. Healthcare Hall of Fame, 1998—. Author University of Alabama Medical Alumni Association, 1859-2003; contbr. articles on human malformations and clin. cytogenetics to tech. jours. Deacon Dawson Meml. Bapt. Ch., 1960-. With Infantry US Army, 1945—46, Germany, officer Chemical Corps US Army, 1951—53, with USAR, 1946—74. Recipient Med. award Ala. Assn. Retarded Children, 1969, Outstanding Educators of Am., 1971, Turlington award, 1982, Disting. Faculty Lectr. award U. Ala. Med. Ctr., 1983, Wayne H. and Sara C. Finley chair in med. genetics U. Ala., Birmingham, 1986, Alumnus of Yr. award Jacksonville State U., 1989, Portrait Reynolds Libr., 1991, Will Gaines Holmes award Childrens Aid Soc., 1999, Brother Bryan Humanitarian award, 2001, Gardner award Ala. Acad. Sci., Samuel Buford Word award Med. Assn. State of Ala., 2003, Lifetime Achievement award Birmingham Bus. Jour., 2003, Disting. Svc. award U. Ala. Med. Alumni, 2005; named to Ala. Healthcare Hall of Fame, 2001; Finley-Compass Bank Genetics Conf. Ctr. established at U. Ala. Birmingham, 2001. Fellow Am. Coll. Med. Genetics (founder, edn. com. 1993-97, program dir. 1996), Royal Soc. Medicine; mem. AMA (Physicians Recognition award 1971, 75, 81, 84, 87, 90, 93, 96), AAAS, N.Y. Acad. Scis., Soc. Exptl. Biology and Medicine, Am. Inst. Chemists, Am. Fedn. Clin. Rsch., Am. Soc. Human Genetics, So. Med. Assn., So. Soc. Pediat. Rsch., Med. Assn. Ala. (counsellor 1990—), Jefferson County Med. Soc. (maternal and child health com. 1975-79, chmn. 1976-77, pres. 1983), Jefferson County Pediat. Soc., Ala. Acad. Sci. (trustee 1991—), Caduceus Club (pres. 1984-86), NIH Alumni Assn., U. Ala. Sch. Medicine Alumni Assn. (pres. 1974-75, Disting. Alumni award 1978, Disting. Svc. award 2005), Greater Birmingham Area C. of C. (bd. dirs. 1983-86), Newcomen Soc., Kiwanis (pres. Shades Valley 1973-74), Rotary Club Birmingham, SAR, Sigma Xi (pres. U. Ala. Birmingham chpt. 1972-73), Kappa Delta Pi, Phi Delta Kappa, Alpha Omega Alpha, Phi Beta Pi, Omicron Delta Kappa. Baptist. Avocations: reading, golf, genealogy, medical history. Home: 3412 Brookwood Rd Birmingham AL 35223-2023 Office: U Ala Birmingham Dept Genetics Kaul 210 1530 Third Ave S Birmingham AL 35294-0017 Office Phone: 205-934-4983. Personal E-mail: wfinley1942@charter.net.

FINN, A. MICHAEL, corporate communications specialist; b. Trenton, NJ, Oct. 4, 1929; s. Charles and Blanche (Englander) Finn; m. Antoinette Mary DiLeo, Feb. 2, 1957; children: Tracey Maureen, Alison Mary Finn Davis, Christopher Charles. Student, U. Pa., 1947-49; BA in Journalism, U. Md., 1952. Reporter Balt. Sun, 1947-54; sports editor Prentice Hall, Inc., NYC, 1955-57; dir. advt. and pub. rels. Cypress Gardnes, Winter Haven, Fla., 1957-58; account supr. Hill & Knowlton, Inc., NYC, 1958-64; v.p. PR Assocs., NYC, 1964-70; pres. Michael Finn Assocs., NYC, 1970-77; v.p. pub. affairs STP Corp., Ft. Lauderdale, Fla., 1977-78; dir. pub. rels. Esmark Inc., Chgo., 1978-79; sr. v.p., nat. dir. pub. rels. divsn. Cunningham & Walsh, Inc., NYC, 1979-87; chmn., CEO E.B. Wilson Pub. Rels., 1987-88; CEO FCS Comms. Inc., NYC, 1988—90; cons. mgmt. comm., 1990—; interviewer Southeastern Inst. Rsch., 2004—. Guest lectr. numerous colls. and univs.; interviewer Southeastern Inst. Rsch., 2004—. Editor, author: books on sports, recreation, self help, 1955—57; contbr. articles to publs. Mem. various coms. Bronxville PTA, 1970—76, pres., 1976—77; mem. Bronxville Adult Edn., 1980—81; bd. dirs. Cath. Comm. Found., 1987—2000; vol. Colonial Williamsburg Found., 1995—; mem. Williamsburg Land Conservancy, 1997—. With Intelligence US Army, 1952—55. Mem.: Pub. Rels. Soc. Am. (accredited), Ford's Colony Country Club. Home: 100 Eagle Williamsburg VA 23188-7428 Personal E-mail: toniandmike@cox.net.

FINN, ALBERT FRANK, JR., physician; b. Huntington, NY, Sept. 30, 1956; s. Albert F. and Margaret F. (May) F.; m. Anna M. Cannella, July 19, 1982; children: Anastasia, Alexandria, Abigail. BS cum laude, St. John's U., 1980; MD cum laude, SUNY, Syracuse, 1984. Diplomate Am. Bd. Internal Medicine, Am. Bd. Pathology, Am. Bd. Allergy and Immunology. Intern gen. medicine SUNY, Stony Brook, 1984-85, resident clin. pathology, 1985-88, resident internal medicine, 1988-89, allergy and clin. immunology fellow, 1989-91, clin. assoc. instr., 1985-91, cons. divsn. lab. medicine Med. Ctr., 1988-91, clin. asst. prof. medicine, 1991-92, head sect. on allergy, 1991-92; clin. assoc. prof. medicine, microbiology and immunology Med. U. S.C., Charleston, 1992—. Adj. asst. prof. St. John's U., N.Y.C., 1991-92 Contbr. articles to profl. jours. Mem. com. on advanced cardiac life support Am. Heart Assn., Nassau County, NY, 1988—92; mem. Am. Lung Assn., SC, 1992—94, pres. Coastal br. Nassau County, SC. Mem. ACP (bd. rev. course allergy and immunology sect. 1992), Am. Acad. Allergy and Immunology (task force 1994), Am. Soc. Clin. Pathology (course dir. lyme borreliosis 1989-92), S.C. Soc. Allergy & Immunology (pres. 1998-2000), Dorchester County Med. Soc. (pres. 1997-98), Rho Chi (pres.), Alpha Omega Alpha. Avocations: fishing, antiques, boating, skiing. Office: Allergy and Asthma Ctrs 9165 University Blvd Charleston SC 29406-9120

FINN, BRIAN D., financial services executive; b. 1960; BS in econ., Wharton Sch., U. Pa., 1982. Previous mng. dir. and co-head- mergers and acquisitions Credit Suisse First Boston, 1982—97; prin. Clayton, Dubilier & Rice, 1997—2002; co-pres. instl. securities Credit Suisse First Boston, NYC, 2002—04, pres., 2004—, also mem. Office Chmn., 2002—, also mem. exec. bd. and oper. com., 2002—; mem. exec. bd. Credit Suisse Group, 2003—. Mem. undergraduate exec. bd. Wharton Sch., U. Pa., chmn. undergraduate bd., 2005—; bd. dirs. City Kids Found. Office: Credit Suisse First Boston 11 Madison Ave New York NY 10010-3629

FINN, CHARLOTTE KAYE, interior designer; b. NYC, May 11; d. Edward and Florence (Karp) Kaye; m. Allen Charles Finn (dec. Oct. 2000); children: Andrew, Richard, Gregg. BA cum laude, Hunter Coll. Cert. Braille transcriber, Libr. of Congress. Apprentice designer J.H. Harvey, 1958-64; pvt. practice interior design White Plains, NY, 1965. Design cons. R.H. Macy's, 1977-78; product designer H.J. Stotter, George Kovacs, Grindley-of-Stoke, Sigma Marketing, Smith & Weigler. Work featured in publs. including House Beautiful, Interior Design, Residential Interiors, N.Y. Times, Palm Beach Life, Palm Beach Daily News, Home Furnishings Daily, The Designer, Home Environment, Sensuous Interiors, Prentice Hall; author Planning, Designing and Decorating a Room-Step by Step A How to Manual for Anyone, 2005. Recipient S.H. Hexter award, Burlington House award. Mem.: NOW, LVW, Phi Beta Kappa.

FINN, EDWIN ANTHONY, JR., publishing executive; BA in English and Polit. Sci., Tufts U., 1976; MA in Internat. Banking and Fin., Columbia U., 1983. Asst. mng. editor Blackstone Valley Tribune, 1970; mng. editor Southbridge (Mass.) Daily News, 1970; nat. copyreader The Wall St. Jour., NYC, 1980—81, editor fgn. desk, 1981—84, banking and fin. reporter Dallas bur., 1984—85; sr. editor internat. bus. and fin. Forbes Mag., 1986—89, asst. mng. editor, 1989—90; editor Am. Banker, 1990—92; mng. editor Barron's, The Dow Jones Bus. and Fin. Weekly, NYC, 1993—95, editor, 1995—, pres., 1998—, pub., 2000—01; chmn. SmartMoney, NYC, 2002—, editor-in-chief, 2002—06, editl. dir., 2006—. Office: Barron's 200 Liberty St New York NY 10281-1003 Business E-Mail: ed.finn@barrons.com.

FINN, JANE E., education educator; b. Mich. EdD, We. Mich. U., Kalamazoo, 2005. Lic. counselor Mich., 2005. Prof. Hope Coll., Holland, Mich., 2004—. Home Phone: 616-395-7739; Office Phone: 616-395-7740.

FINN, PETER, public relations executive; b. NYC, Mar. 31, 1954; s. David and Laura (Zeisler) F.; m. Sarah Duncan; children: Noah J., Emily M. BA, Brown U., 1976; MA, Columbia U., 1977. Researcher Research & Forecasts Inc., NYC, 1977-79, dir. ops., 1979-81, chmn., 1981-84; chmn. fin. com. Ruder-Finn, Inc. (formerly Ruder, Finn & Rotman, Inc.), NYC, 1984—, CFO, 1985-94, exec. v.p., 1986-87, chmn. exec. com., 1988—2001, CEO, 2001—. Chmn. Catskill Mt. Found., Inc., 1998—; bd. dirs. Hunter Found., Inc., 1998—. Office: Ruder-Finn Inc 301 E 57th St New York NY 10022-2900

FINN, PETER MICHAEL, broadcast executive; b. Milton, Mass., Feb. 19, 1936; s. Matthew Charles and Mary Germaine (Ireland) F.; m. Judith Mary Barry, Sept. 7, 1957 (div. Aug. 1996); children: Pamela Ann, Mary Kathryn, Matthew Ireland; m. Debra Jo McGraw, Oct. 18, 1997. AB, Holy Cross Coll., 1956; MBA, George Washington U., 1962; A.M.P., Harvard U., 1980. Account exec. J. Walter Thompson Co., NYC, 1962-64, account supr., 1966-67; account exec. Foote Cone & Belding, NYC, 1964-66, v.p., account supr., 1967-68, Doyle Dane Bernbach, NYC, 1968-70; sr. v.p., dir. F.W. Free, NYC, 1970-74; pres. Henderson Advt., Greenville, SC, 1974-80, Bozell & Jacobs, Dallas, 1980-85, also dir.; sr. ptnr., div. pres. Whittle Communications, Knoxville, Tenn., 1985-92; pres., CEO Peter Matthew Prodns., NYC, 1992—. Mem. Greater Greenville Planning Council, 1976-79, Dallas Citizens Council. Served to lt. USNR, 1957-62. Mem. Am. Assn. Advt. Agys. (bd. govs.), Am. Advt. Fedn., Am. Mktg. Assn. Office: Peter Matthew Prodns 523 W 45th St New York NY 10036

FINN, ROBERT, writer, educator; b. Boston, July 13, 1930; s. Edward Anthony and E. Caroline (Seifert) F.; m. Mary Pacana, Oct. 12, 1957; children: Laurence, Elaine. BA, Boston U., 1952. Staff reporter, music-drama critic New Bedford (Mass.) Standard-Times, 1956-59, Akron (Ohio) Beacon Jour., 1959-64; music critic Cleve. Plain Dealer, 1964-92. Mem. guest faculty Rockefeller Found. project for tng. music critics, 1965, 66 Author: Exploring Classical Music, 2000, A Musical Journey, Con Amore, 2003; contbr. to Opera News mag., Am. Record Guide. Served with AUS, 1953-56. Co-recipient ASCAP-Deems Taylor award for, 1972, 74, 78, 80 Mem. Music Critics Assn. (life, exec. bd. 1975-83, v.p. 1983-85, pres. 1985-89). Roman Catholic. Home: 1211 Blanchester Rd Cleveland OH 44124-1325 E-mail: robertfinn@aol.com.

FINN, ROBERT W., bishop; b. St. Louis, Mo., Apr. 2, 1953; s. Theodore and Betty (Schneider) Finn. Grad., St. Louis Preparatory Sem. North, 1971; BA in Philosophy, Cardinal Glennon Coll., 1975; M in Theology, Angelicum U., Rome, 1979; MEd, St. Louis U., 1989. Ordained priest, St. Louis, 1979; assoc. pastor Diocese of St. Louis; mem. faculty St. Francis Borgia Regional H.S., Washington, 1983—89; adminstr. St. Dominic H.S., O'Fallon, Mo., 1989—96; named dir. continuing formation of priests Archdiocese of St. Louis, Mo., 1996, editor St. Louis Review Mo., 1999—2004; ordained bishop, 2004; coadjutor bishop of Kansas City-St. Joseph, 2004—05; bishop of Kansas City-St. Joseph, Mo., 2005—. Roman Catholic. Office: Diocese of Kansas City-St Joseph PO Box 419037 300 E 36th St Kansas City MO 64141-6037

FINN, STEPHEN MARTIN, media producer, venture capitalist; b. Indpls., June 21, 1949; s. Martin Joseph and Theresa Diane (Mervar) F.; children: Shawn Marie, Stephanie Michelle, Rhyan Linthicum, Raimie Catherine (dec.). Pres. Equinox Systems, Grand Rapids, Mich., 1975-77, Solstice, Lake Helen, 1978—. Photographer Equitable Gallery, N.Y.C., 1978; contbr. articles profl. mags. City commr., Lake Helen, Fla., 2000—03. Recipient Kinsa award Kodak Internat., N.Y.C., 1978. Mem. Am. Film Inst., Profl. Photographers Am., Aircraft Owners and Pilots Assn., Mensa, Fla. Motion Picture Theater Assn. Home and Office: PO Box 129 Lake Helen FL 32744-0129 Personal E-mail: info@solsticeusa.com.

FINN, TERRENCE M., lawyer; b. Mpls., Feb. 13, 1948; BA, Yale U., 1970; JD, U. Pa., 1973. Bar: R.I. 1973, U.S. Dist. Ct. R.I. 1973, U.S. Ct. Appeals (1st. cir.) 1982, Mass. 1984. Mng. ptnr. Edwards & Angell, LLP; co-mng. ptnr. Edwards Angell Palmer & Dodge, LLP, 2005—. Mem. R.I. Bar Assn., Mass. Bar Assn., Fla. Bar., Boston Bar Assn. Office: Edwards Angell Palmer & Dodge 101 Federal St Fl 23 Boston MA 02110-1800

FINN, TIMOTHY JOHN, lawyer; b. Mpls., Nov. 23, 1950; s. Michael Charles and Muriel Ann (Findell) F.; m. Jacquelyn Greiner. AB, Harvard U., 1973, JD, 1976. Bar: DC, Ohio. Law clk. to chief judge Frank J. Battisti U.S. Dist. Ct. (no. dist.) Ohio, 1976-77; assoc. Jones, Day, Reavis & Pogue, Washington, 1977-81, mem., 1985—; dep. asst. atty. gen. U.S. Dept. Justice, Washington, 1981-83, assoc. dep. atty. gen., 1983-84; ptnr. Jones Day, Wash. Office: Jones Day 51 Louisiana Ave NW Washington DC 20001 Office Phone: 202-879-3789. Office Fax: 202-626-1700. Business E-Mail: tjfinn@jonesday.com.

FINNBERG, ELAINE AGNES, psychologist, editor; b. Bklyn., Mar. 2, 1948; d. Benjamin and Agnes Montgomery (Evans) Finnberg; m. Rodney Lee Herndon, Mar. 1, 1981; 1 child, Andrew Marshal Herndon. BA in Psychology, L.I. U., 1969; MA in Psychology, New Sch. for Social Rsch., 1973; PhD in Psychology, Calif. Sch. Profl. Psychology, 1981. Diplomate Am. Bd. Forensic Examiners, Am. Bd. Forensic Medicine, Am. Bd. Med. Psychotherapists and Psychodiagnosticians, Am. Bd. Disability Analysts (profl. adv. coun.), Am. Bd. Psychol. Specialties, Prescribing Psychologists Register (fellow), lic. psychologist Calif. Rsch. asst. med. sociology Cornell U. Med. Coll., NYC, 1969-70; med. abstractor USV Pharm. Corp., Tuckahoe, NY, 1970-71, Coun. Tobacco Rsch., NYC, 1971-77; editor, writer Found. Thanatology Columbia U., NYC, 1971-76, 1973-74; dir. grief psychology and bereavement counseling San Francisco Coll. Mortuary Scis., 1977-81; rsch. assoc. dept. epidemiology and internat. health U. Calif., San Francisco, 1979-81, asst. clin. prof. dept. family and cmty. medicine, 1985-93, assoc. clin. prof., dept. family and cmty. medicine, 1993—; active med. staff Natividad Med. Ctr., Salinas, Calif., 1984—2002, 2004—, chief psychologist, 1984—96. Asst. chief psychiatry svc. Natividad Med. Ctr., 1985—96, acting chief psychiatry, 1988—89, vice-chair medicine dept., 1991—93, sec.-treas. med. staff, 1992—94; cons. med. staff Salinas Valley Meml. Hosp., 1991—2003, Mee Meml. Hosp., 1996—97; dir. tng. Monterey Psychiat. Health Facility, 1996—97, chief clin. staff, 1996—97; expert cons. Calif. Bd. Psychology; cons. psychologist Calif. Forensic Med. Group, 1984—, Calif. Dept. Mental Health Sexually Violent Predator Program, 1996—. Editor: Jour. Thanatology, 1972—76, Cahtexis, 1976—81, Calif. Psychologist, 1988—95. Mem. Gov.'s adv. bd. Agnews Devel. Ctr., San Jose, Calif., 1988—96, chair, 1989—91, 1994—95. Mem.: APA, Internat. Soc. Police Surgeons, Internat. Rorschach Soc., Soc. Personality Assessment, Assn. Treatment Sexual Abuses, Am. Med. Writers Assn., Assn. Advancement Behavior Therapy, Western Psychol. Assn., Forensic Mental Health Assn. Calif., Mid-Coast Psychol. Assn. (sec. 1985, treas. 1986, pres. 1987, Disting. Svc. to Psychology award 1993), Soc. Behavioral Medicine, Calif. Psychol. Assn. (Disting. Svc. award 1989), Nat. Register Health Svc. Providers Psychology.

FINNEGAN, CYRIL VINCENT, retired dean, zoology educator; b. Dover, NH, July 17, 1922; emigrated to Can., 1958; s. Cyril Vincent and Hilda A. (McClintock) F.; children: Maureen A., Patrick S., Cathaleen C., Kevin S., Eileen D., Gormlaith R., Michaeleen S., Mairead B., Conal E. BS, Bates Coll., Lewiston, Maine, 1946; MS, U. Notre Dame, 1948, PhD,

1951. From instr. to asst. prof. St. Louis U., 1952-56; asst. prof. U. Notre Dame, South Bend, Ind., 1956-58; from asst. prof. to prof. zoology U. B.C., Vancouver, 1958-88, emeritus, 1988—, assoc. dean sci., 1972-79, dean sci., 1979-85, dean emeritus, 1988—, assoc. acad. v.p., 1986-88. Contbr. articles to profl. jours. Served to sgt F.A. and C.E. AUS, 1942-45, NATOUSA, CBI. Postdoctoral research fellow NIH, 1952-53; Killum sr. fellow, 1968-69 Mem. Soc. Devel. Biology, Can. Soc. Cell Biology, Tissue Culture Assn., Internat. Soc. Develop. Biology, Sigma Xi Roman Catholic. Office: U BC Dept Zoology Faculty of Science Vancouver BC Canada V6T 1Z4

FINNEGAN, JOHN D., insurance company executive; b. Jersey City, Jan. 31, 1949; m. Kathleen Finnegan; 2 children. BA in Polit. Sci., Princeton U., NJ, 1971; JD, Fordham U., NY, 1975; MBA, Rutgers U., NJ, 1976. Mem. tax. dept. GMAC, 1976—86, dir. strategic planning, 1985, exec. v.p., CFO, 1992—95, pres., 1997—99, chmn., pres., 1999—2002; CFO GMAC Mortgage Corp., 1986; asst. treas. worldwide benefits compensation GM, 1987—89, asst. treas. internat. financing ops., 1989—92, v.p., treas., 1995—97, exec. v.p., 1999—2002; pres., CEO, dir. Chubb Corp., 2002—, chmn., 2003—. Bd. dirs. Merrill Lynch & Co.; mem. Bus. Coun., Bus. Roundtable, Fin. Svcs. Roundtable. Office: Chubb Corp 15 Mountain View Rd Warren NJ 07059 Office Phone: 908-903-2000. Office Fax: 908-903-2027.*

FINNEGAN, MARCHAND MARIE (SHONNIE FINNEGAN), archivist, consultant; b. Washington, Oct. 9, 1931; d. Homer Alexander and Catherine McLeod Hall; m. Richard A. Finnegan (dec. 1986); children: Kate Becht, Sarah, Elizabeth H. BA magna cum laude, Trinity Coll., Washington, 1953; MA, Cath. U., 1955. Cert. in archives adminstrn. Instr. English Georgetown Visitation Jr. Coll., Washington, 1955, Newton (Mass.) Coll. of the Sacred Heart, 1955—57; univ. archivist SUNY, Buffalo, 1967—95, univ. archivist emerita, 1995—. Mem. grant rev. panels NEH, 1978—80; mem. NY State Hist. Records Adv. Bd., Albany, 1976—84, Nat. Archives Adv. Coun., Washington, 1980—84, NY Document Conservation Adv. Coun., Albany, 1983—86; mem. nat. coun. AAUP, 1979—82, pres. U. at Buffalo chpt., 1972—74. Contbr. articles to profl. jours. Mem. Erie County (NY) Records Commn. Recipient Chancellor's award for excellence in librarianship, SUNY, 1979. Fellow: Soc. Am. Archivists (v.p., pres. 1984—86, coun. 1978—82); mem.: Mid-Atlantic Regional Archives Conf., Buffalo and Erie County Hist. Soc. (bd. mgrs.). Roman Catholic. Home: 228 Darwin Dr Buffalo NY 14226 Office: Univ Archives U at Buffalo 420 Capen Hall Buffalo NY 14260 E-mail: mmfinn@buffalo.edu.

FINNEGAN, MICHAEL J., lawyer; b. LA, Dec. 14, 1962; BA cum laude, Loyola Marymount Univ., 1985; JD with honors, Loyola Law Sch., 1988. Bar: Calif. 1988. Ptnr., Litigation practice, mem. mng. bd. Pillsbury Winthrop Shaw Pittman, LA. Bd. dir. Public Counsel. Mem.: ABA, Am. Arbitration Assn., LA Bus. Trial Lawyers Assn., LA County Bar Assn. Office: Pillsbury Winthrop Shaw Pittman Suite 2800 725 S Figueroa St Los Angeles CA 90017 Office Phone: 213-488-7272. Office Fax: 213-629-1033. Business E-Mail: michael.finnegan@pillsburylaw.com.

FINNEGAN, NEAL FRANCIS, retired banker; b. Boston, Mar. 28, 1938; s. Neal Francis and Mary Theresa (McNeil) F.; children: Theresa, Lynn, Neal, Wayne. BS, Northeastern U., 1961; MBA, Babson Coll., 1969. With Shawmut Bank of Boston, 1961-80, sr. v.p. in charge of OIC comml. banking, 1977-80; pres., chief exec. officer Worcester Bancorp Inc., Mass., 1980-82; chmn., chief exec. officer Worcester County Nat. Bank, 1980-82; sr. exec. v.p. Shawmut Corp., Boston, 1982-83, vice-chmn., 1983-86, dir., 1982-86; exec. v.p. Shawmut Bank of Boston, N.A., 1983-86; pres., chief operating officer, dir. Bowery Savs. Bank, NYC, 1986-88; exec. v.p. Bankers Trust Co., NYC, 1988-93; chmn., CEO USTrust, Boston, 1993-99; ret., 2004. Former chmn. bd. trustees Cath. Charities; vice chmn. Mass. chpt. Multiple Sclerosis Soc.; chmn. bd. trustees Northeastern U., Boston, 1998; bd. dirs. Ireland C. of C. Office: Citizens Bank 28 State St Boston MA 02109 Office Phone: 617-725-5775.

FINNEGAN, PATRICK, dean, military officer, lawyer; b. Fukuoka, Japan; BS, U.S. Mil. Acad., West Point, 1971; MPA, Kennedy Sch. Govt., Harvard Univ.; JD, Univ. Va. Bar: Va., U.S. Supreme Ct. Commd. 2d lt. U.S. Army, advanced through grades to brig. gen.; dep. dir. & criminal law instr. JAG Sch., Charlottesville, Va.; staff judge advocate MacDill AFB, Fla.; legal adv. joint spl. ops. command, U.S. European command; staff judge advocate U.S. Mil. Acad., West Point, 1998—99, prof., head dept. law, 1999—2005, dean of academic bd., 2005—. Editor: Va. Law Rev.; contbr. articles to profl. legal jours. Mem.: Phi Kappa Phi, Order of the Coif. Office: USMA Office of the Dean Bldg 600 West Point NY 10996

FINNEGAN, SARA ANNE (SARA F. LYCETT), publisher; b. Balt., Aug. 1, 1939; d. Lawrence Winfield and Rosina Elva (Huber) F.; m. Isaac C. Lycett, Jr., Aug. 31, 1974. BA, Sweet Briar Coll., 1961; MLA, Johns Hopkins U., 1965; exec. program, U. Va. Grad. Sch. Bus., 1977. Tchr., chmn. history dept. Hannah More Acad., Reisterstown, Md., 1961-65; redactor Williams & Wilkins Co., Balt., 1965-66, asst. head redactory, 1966-71, editor book div., 1971-75, assoc. editor-in-chief, 1975-77, v.p., editor-in-chief, 1977-81, pres. book div., 1981-88, group pres., 1988-94; editor Kalends, 1973-78, 89-92; exec. sponsor jour. Histochemistry and Cytochemistry, 1973-77. Dir. Passano Found., 1979—91. Editor: Visions, Friends of Art of Sweet Briar Coll. Mag., 2001—03. Trustee St. Timothy's Sch., Stevenson, Md., 1974—83; mem. adv. bd. Balt. Ind. Schs. Scholarship Fund, 1977—81; mem. adv. coun. grad. study Coll. Notre Dame of Md., 1983; mem. bd. overseers Sweet Briar Coll., 1987—88, bd. dirs., 1988—2000, chmn.-elect, 1994, chmn., 1995—2000, dir. emerita, 2003—; docent The Walters Art Mus., 1994—; v.p. The Walters Art Mus. Docents, 2000—01, pres., 2001—02; bd. trustees The Walters Art Mus., 2001—02; bd. dirs. The Woman's Indsl. Exch., Balt., 1997—2000, v.p., 1998—2000; bd. dirs. Friends of Art of Sweet Briar Coll., 2000—06, The Hamilton St. Club, 2003—06, The Art Seminar Group, 2004—. Mem. Assn. Am. Pubs. (exec. coun. profl. and scholarly pub. divsn. 1984-85), Internat. Sci., Tech. and Med. Pubs. Assn. (group exec. 1986-93, chmn.-elect 1988, chmn. 1989-92). Republican. Lutheran.

FINNEGAN, SHEILA, lawyer; BS, Georgetown U., Edmund A. Walsh Sch. Fgn. Service, 1982; JD, U. Chgo., 1986. Law clerk to Hon. Milton I. Shadu US Dist. Ct. (no. dist.) Ill., 1986—87; atty. US Atty's Office No. Dist. of Ill., 1987—2000, dep. chief, Health Care Fraud Coord., Spl. Prosecutions, 1996—99, chief, criminal divsn., 1999—2000; ptnr. Mayer, Brown, Rowe & Maw LLP, Chgo., 2000—. Adj. prof. Trial Advocacy at Northwestern U. Law Sch. Author: (Law Guide) The First 72 Hours of a Govt. Investigation: A Guide to Identifying Issues and Avoiding Mistakes, 2007; Lectr. in field. Recipient Director's Award for Superior Performance, US Atty. Gen., 2000; fellow Am. Coll. of Trial Lawyers. Office: Mayer Brown Rowe & Maw LLP 71 S Wacker Dr Chicago IL 60606 Office Phone: 312-701-8943. Office Fax: 312-706-8418. E-mail: sfinnegan@mayerbrown.com.*

FINNELL, MICHAEL HARTMAN, mining executive; b. LA, Jan. 27, 1927; s. Jules Bertram and Maribel Hartman (Schumacher) F.; m. Grace Vogel, Sept. 11, 1954 (div. June 1964); children: Lesley Finnell Blanchard, Carter Hartman, Hunter Vogel. BA, U. Toronto, 1950; MBA, Harvard U., Cambridge, Mass., 1952; HHD (hon.), Capital U., Columbus, Ohio, 1980. Sec.-treas. Triad Oil Co. Ltd., 1952-62, v.p., dir., 1962-65; pres. Devon-Palmer Oils Ltd., 1966—70; v.p., dir. Can. Hydrocarbons, Ltd., 1970, pres., 1970—. Montreal River Internat. Silver Mines Ltd., 1972—. Trustee Capital U., Columbus, 1982—94; life trustee Columbus Mus. of Art. Mem. Calif. Club, Annandale Golf Club, Ranchmen's Club, Calgary Petroleum Club, Calgary Golf and Country Club, Nantucket Yacht Club, Calif. Club LA. Home: 724 Holladay Rd Pasadena CA 91106-4115 Office: 625 Fair Oaks Ave Ste 288 South Pasadena CA 91030-2668 Office Phone: 626-403-9588. Personal E-mail: finnellmh@yahoo.com.

FINNERAN, JOHN G., JR., lawyer, diversified financial services company executive; b. Feb. 1950; m. Catherine A. Cotter; 2 children. BA in History, Pa. State U., 1972; JD, Georgetown U. Bar: Va. 1981. Atty. Cleary, Gottlieb, Steen & Hamilton, Washington, 1981—91; assoc. gen. counsel resolutions FDIC, 1991—94, acting dep. gen. counsel, 1994; sr. v.p., gen. counsel, corp. sec. Capital One Fin. Corp., McLean, Va., 1994, exec. v.p., gen. counsel, corp. sec. Bd. dirs. Local Initiatives Support Corp., NYC, chmn. local adv. com. Richmond, Va. Recipient Outstanding Liberal Arts Alumni award, Pa. State U. Coll. Liberal Arts, 2003. Office: Capital One Fin Corp 1680 Capital One Dr Mc Lean VA 22102*

FINNERAN, JOHN PATRICK, JR., finance company executive, educator; b. NYC, Sept. 11, 1959; s. John Patrick and Mary Elenor (McCorry) F.; m. Dena Jo Golden, Mar. 19, 1983; children: John Patrick III, Meagan E., Brendan R., Ryan E., Katelyn J. BBA, Siena Coll., 1981; M Acctg., George Washington U., 1983. CPA, D.C., Va. Staff auditor Price Waterhouse, Washington, 1983-84; staff cons. KMG Peat Marwick (Main Hurdman), Washington, 1984-85; mgr. fin. analysis Finalco Group, Inc., McLean, Va., 1985-87; investment analyst Potomac Capital Investment Corp., Washington, 1987-89, mgr. fin. planning and investments, 1989-91, treas., 1991—, v.p., 1994—. Adj. lectr. acctg. and bus. No. Va. C.C., Annandale, 1984—. Named Team Leader of Yr., Dale Carnegie Ctr. Excellence, 1993. Mem. AICPA, D.C. Inst. CPAs, Va. Inst. CPAs, Nat. Assn. Corp. Treas., Fin. Execs. Inst., KC (3d degree). Republican. Roman Catholic. Avocations: golf, reading, children's sporting events, new york giants. Office: Potomac Capital Investment Corp 900 19th St NW Ste 600 Washington DC 20006-2105

FINNERAN, KATIE (KATHLEEN), actress; b. Chgo., Jan. 22, 1971; Attended, Carnegie Mellon U. Actor: (Broadway plays) On Borrowed Time, 1991—92, Two Shakespearean Actors, 1992, My Favorite Year, 1992—93, In the Summer House, 1993, The Heiress, 1995, Neil Simon's Proposals, 1997—98, The Iceman Cometh, 1999, Cabaret, 2000—01, Noises Off, 2001—02 (Tony award for Best Performance by a Featured Actor in a Play, 2002, Outer Critics Circle award, Drama Desk award nomination), (off-Broadway) Pig Farm, 2006; (films) Night of the Living Dead, 1990, You've Got Mail, 1998, Liberty Heights, 1999, Live at Five, 2005, Bewitched, 2005, Broken Bridges, 2006, Staten Island, 2007, Walk the Talk, 2007, Firehouse Dog, 2007; (TV films) Plainsong, 2004; (TV series) Bram and Alice, 2002, Wonderfalls, 2003, The Inside, 2005—, (guest appearance) Sex and the City, 1998, Frasier, 1999, All My Children, 1999, Oz, 2001.*

FINNERTY, BRYAN, sports association executive; b. 1967; Founder, CEO, Mng. Ptnr. High Velocity Sports Grp., 2005—; founder Sports Leadership Ctr. of Am.; co-founder Sports Facilities Adv. L.L.C., Dunedin, Fla. Former profl. soccer player Detroit Rockers. Named one of 40 Under 40, Crain's Detroit Bus., 2006. Office: High Velocity Sports Group 46245 Michigan Ave Canton MI 48188

FINNERTY, JOSEPH GREGORY, JR., lawyer; b. Balt., Jan. 25, 1937; s. Joseph Gregory and Sara Virginia (Porter) F.; m. Alice Ann Fannon, Sept. 14, 1958 (div. May 1989); children: Sara F. Kelly, Joseph G. III, Alice Ann Martin, Thomas P., Kathleen F. Curtis, Eileen F. McCoy; m. Deborah Barrett, Oct. 20, 1989; 1 child, Bridget P. BS in Physics, Loyola Coll., 1958; JD, U. Md., 1963. Bar: Md. 1963, D.C. 1981, N.Y. 1993. Law clk. Supreme Bench, Balt., 1960-63; assoc. Piper & Marbury, Balt., 1963-66; ptnr. Gallagher, Evelins & Finnerty, Balt., 1966-71; gen. counsel The Ryland Group, Columbia, Md., 1971-72; ptnr. Piper & Marbury, NYC, 1972—95; mng. ptnr. NY office Piper Rudnick LLP (now DLA Piper US LLP), NYC, 1995—2006; ptnr. DLA Piper US LLP, Balt., 2006—. 2nd lt. U.S. Army, 1958-59. Fellow Am. Coll. Trial Lawyers, Am. Bar Found.; mem. ABA, N.Y. State Bar Assn., Md. State Bar Assn. Avocation: farming. Office: DLA Piper US LLP 6225 Smith Ave Baltimore MD 21209 Home Phone: 410-366-3083; Office Phone: 4105804200. Office Fax: 410-580-3200. Business E-Mail: joseph.finnerty@dlapiper.com.

FINNERTY, JOSEPH GREGORY, III, lawyer; b. Balt., Apr. 25, 1960; s. Joseph Gregory, Jr. and Alice Ann (Fannon) Finnerty; m. Amy Caroline Shull, Nov. 12, 1988 (div. 1999); children: Katherine Pagett, Alice Olivia; life ptnr. Donna M. Paparella; 1 child, Samuel Joseph. AB in English Lit., Hamilton Coll., 1982; JD, U. Md., Balt., 1987. Bar: NY 1988, US Dist. Ct. (so., ea., no., we. dists.) NY, Ark., Colo., US Ct. Appeals (2d cir.), US Supreme Ct. Assoc. Rogers & Wells, NYC, 1988-94; prin. ptnr. McCarrick, Finnerty & Mayer, NYC, 1994-96; ptnr. Piper & Marbury, L.L.P., NYC, 1996-99, Piper Rudnick LLP, 1999—2004; ptnr. head NY litig. DLA Piper Rudnick Gray Cary, NYC, 2005—. Contbr. articles to profl. jours. Trustee Bklyn. Mus. Mem.: ABA (mem. task force corp. governance), NY Lawyers Pub. Interest (bd. dirs.), Assn. Bar City NY. Office: DLA Piper Rudnick Gray Cary 1251 Ave of Americas New York NY 10020-1104 Office Phone: 212-835-6260. Office Fax: 212-835-6001. Business E-Mail: joseph.finnertyIII@dlapiper.com.

FINNERTY, LOUISE HOPPE, food products executive; b. Alexandria, Va., Jan. 19, 1949; d. William G. and Ruth A. (Ehren) Hoppe; m. John D. Finnerty, May 21, 1988; 1 child, William Patrick Taylor. BA, Va. Commonwealth U., 1971; postgrad., Am. U., 1972—73. Staff asst. to Dr. Henry Kissinger NSC, Washington, 1971-73; adminstrv. asst. Nat. Petroleum Coun., Washington, 1973-75; profl. staff mem. Senate Armed Svc. Com., Washington, 1976-81; spl. asst. Office Legis. Affairs, U.S. Dept. State, Washington, 1981-84, dep. asst. sec. of state, 1984-88; mgr. govt. affairs PepsiCo, Inc., Purchase, NY, 1988-91; dir. govt. affairs PepsiCo Foods and Beverages Internat., Somers, NY, 1991-95; v.p. internat. govt. affairs PepsiCo., Inc., Purchase, 1995—2003, v.p. global health and wellness policy, 2004—. Mem. Spring Lake Bath and Tennis Club, Coveleigh Club. Republican. Lutheran. Avocations: reading, gardening, cooking. Home: 400 Park Ave Rye NY 10580-1213 also: 506 2nd Ave Spring Lake NJ 07762-1107 Office: PepsiCo Inc 700 Anderson Hill Rd Purchase NY 10577-1444 Business E-Mail: louise.finnerty@pepsi.com.

FINNERTY, WILLIAM J., oil industry executive; B, SUNY Maritime Coll., Throggs Neck, NY. Sr. v.p. trading and ops. Equiva Trading Co.; sr. v.p. Texaco Trading and Transp. Co.; v.p. Trading N.Am. Crude Chevron-Texaco, 2001—03; v.p. crude oil and logistics Tesoro Corp., San Antonio, 2003—04, sr. v.p. supply and distbn. Refining and Mktg., 2004—06, exec. v.p., COO, 2006—. Mem.: Nat. Petroleum Refining Assn. (bd. trustees, v.p. exec. com. 2005). Office: Tesoro Corp 300 Concord Plz San Antonio TX 78216-6999 Office Phone: 210-283-2000.

FINNEY, ALBERT, actor, director; b.Manchester, England, May 9, 1936; m. Jane Wenham, 1957 (div. 1961); 1 child; m. Anouk Aimee, Aug. 7, 1970 (div. 1978). Litt.D. (hon.), Sussex U., 1965, Salford U., 1979. Assoc. artistic dir. English Stage Co., 1972—; appearances include: The Party, New, London, 1958; Cassio in Othello, and Lysander, Stratford-on-Avon, 1959; The Lily White Boys, Royal Court, 1960; Billy Liar, Cambridge Theatre, 1960; Luther, in Luther, Royal Court Theatre and Phoenix Theatre, 1962-62, N.Y., 1963; Armstrong, in Armstrong's Last Goodnight, Miss Julie and Black Comedy, Chichester, 1965, Old Vic, 1966; A Day in the Death of Joe Egg, N.Y., 1968; Alpha Beta, Royal Court and Appollo, 1972; Krapp's Last Tape, Royal Court, 1973; Cromwell, Royal Court, 1973; Chez Nous, Globe, 1974; Uncle Vanya, and Present Laughter, Royal Exchange, Manchester, Eng., 1977, J.J. Farr, 1987; Nat. theatre appearances include: Love for Love, 1965, Much Ado About Nothing, 1965, A Flea in Her Ear, 1966, Hamlet, 1975, Tamburlaine, 1976, The Country Wife, 1977, The Cherry Orchard, Macbeth, Has "Washington" Legs?, 1978; stage dir. The Freedom of the City, Royal Court, 1973; Loot, Royal Court, 1975; dir. and appeared in The Biko Inquest, 1984, Serjeant Musgrave's Dance, 1984; films include: The Entertainer, 1960, Saturday Night and Sunday Morning, 1960, Tom Jones, 1963, The Victors, 1963, Night Must Fall, 1964, Two for the Road, 1967, Charlie Bubbles, 1967 (also dir.), The Picasso Summer, 1969, Scrooge, 1970, Gumshoe, 1971, Alpha Beta, 1973, Murder on the Orient Express, 1974, The Duellists, 1977, Wolfen, 1981, Loophole, 1981, Looker, 1981, Shoot the Moon, 1982, Annie, 1982, The Dresser, 1983, Under the Volcano, 1983, Orphans, 1987, Miller's Crossing, 1990, The Playboys, 1992, Rich in Love, 1992, The Browning Version, 1994, A Man of No Importance, 1994, The Run of the Country, 1995, Washington Square, 1997, Breakfast of Champions, 1999, Simpatico, 1999, Erin Brockovich, 2000, Traffic, 2000, Hemingway, the Hunter of Death, 2001, Delivering Milo, 2001, Big Fish, 2003, Ocean's Twelve, 2004, (voice) Corpse Bride, 2005, A Good Year, 2006, Amazing Grace, 2006, The Bourne Ultimatum, 2007; (TV films) Lights, Camera, Annie!, 1982, The Biko Inquest, 1984 (also dir.), Pope John Paul II, 1983, A Simple Man, 1987, The Green Man, 1990, The Wall: Live in Berlin, 1990, The Image, 1990, The Endless Game, 1990, A Rather English Marriage, 1998, The Gathering Storm, 2002, My Uncle Silas II, 2003; (TV series) Emergency Ward 10, 1957; (TV mini series) Cold Lazarus, 1996, Nostromo, 1997. *

FINNEY, GRAHAM STANLEY, management consultant; b. Greenwich, Conn., Sept. 6, 1930; s. William Stanley and Sarah Margaret (Boswell) F.; m. Katharine Pillsbury Becker, June 22, 1957; children: Sarah Boswell Finney Johnston, Martha Becker, Samuel Warner, Garrett Stevens. Student, Washington and Lee U., 1948-49; BA, Yale U., 1952; MPA, Harvard U., 1954. Planning dir. City of Portland, Maine, 1957-60; asst. exec. dir. Phila. City Planning Commn., 1961-65; exec. dir. Phila. Coun. for Cmty. Advancement, 1965-66; dep. supt. schs. Phila., 1966-69; commr. addiction svcs. agy. City of N.Y.; mng. ptnr. Greater Phila. Partnership, 1975-76; dir. Phila. Partnership, 1973-75; pres. Corp. for Pub./Pvt. Ventures, Phila., 1977-80; sr. ptnr. The Conservation Co., Phila., 1980-87, pres., 1988-95; mgmt. cons.; pres. 21st Century League, 1997-2000. Trustee Seybert Instn., Phila., 1978; dir. Mastery High Charter Sch., Phila., 2001—. Author: Administering Catastrophe, 1975; (with others) Philadelphia: 1776-2076, 1975. Vol. exec. Internat. Exec. Svc. Corps., 2001—; chair Nat. Ctr. on Adult Literacy; bd. dirs. Phila. Parks Alliance, 2003—, Awbury Arboretum. With U.S. Army, 1954-56. Recipient The Phila. award, 1998. Mem.: Yale Club (N.Y.C.). Democrat. Presbyterian. Avocations: gardening, tennis, hiking. Home: 615 W Hortter St Philadelphia PA 19119-3650 Personal E-mail: gkfinney@aol.com.

FINNEY, JERVIS SPENCER, lawyer, former prosecutor; b. Balt., Sept. 22, 1931; s. George Gross and Josephine (Stewart) F.; m. Patricia Voneiff, Nov. 16, 1974; children: Jervis Spencer Jr., John Emich. AB cum laude, Princeton U., 1953; LLM, Harvard U., 1958. Bar: Md. 1958, DC 1980, US Ct. Appeals (4th cir.), US Dist Ct. (dist. Md.). Ptnr., assoc. Ober, Kaler, Grimes & Shriver, Balt., 1958—75, ptnr., 1978—99, sr. counsel, 1999—2003, of counsel, 2007—; mem. Md. Senate, 1967—74, co-minority leader, 1971—74, legis. coun., 1971—74; US atty. dist. Md. US Dept. Justice, Balt., 1975-78; chief counsel, criminal justice adv., sr. policy adv. to Gov. State of Md., Annapolis, 2003—07. Mem. Taxation and Fiscal Reform Problem Study Commn., 1967—68; pres., chmn. Md. Criminal Justice Adminstrn., 1999—2003. Balt. county adminstr. Keep Md. Beautiful, 1960; chair, Balt. Crusade Am. Cancer Soc., 1966; mem. Balt. County Coun., 1962—66, mem., regional planning coun., 1963—66. Paratrooper, jumpmaster 11th Airborne Divsn. US Army, 1953—55. Recipient Md. Bar Found. award, 2003, Md. Leadership in Law award, Daily Record, 2003. Fellow Am. Bar Found., Am. Coll. Trial Lawyers (mem. legal ethics com. 1987—92, Md. State chair, 1993-94, chair, State Judiciary com., 1995-97), Md. Bar Found.; mem. Assn. Former US Attys, ABA, Md. Bar Assn. Avocation: squash. Office: Ober Kaler Grimes & Shriver 120 E Baltimore St Ste 800 Baltimore MD 21202-1643 Office Phone: 410-347-7363.

FINNEY, PAUL, acupuncturist, Chinese herbologist, entrepreneur; b. Humboldt, Kans., Apr. 19, 1944; s. Robert Arthur and Gertrude (Leitzbach) F. BS in Indsl. Engring., Stanford U., 1968; diploma in Acupuncture, Medicina Alternativa, Colombo, Sri Lanka, 1988; cert. Chinese herbalist, Herbal Traditions, Boston, 1993. Mgmt. asst. Signet Sci. Co., Burbank, Calif., 1971; pres. Atlantic Coastal Cmty., Cocoa Beach, Fla., 1972-81; lobbyist Am. Legion, Washington, 1982-83; legis. dir. Nat. Tax Limitation Com., Washington, 1983-84; pres. League for Ltd. Govt., Washington, 1985-86; intern Xi Yuan Hosp., Beijing, 1990; pvt. practice acupuncturist Humboldt, Kans., 1989—. Propr. Finney Enterprises, Humboldt, 1994—, India Tours Internat., Humboldt, 1996—, Bailey Hotel, Humboldt, 1997—2006, Finney Outdoor Advertising, Humboldt, 2004—. Mem. staff Reagan for Gov., San Francisco, 1966; founding pres. Humboldt Hist. Preservation Alliance, 1992-97, 99-2003; founder Sathya Sai Baba Ctr. of Humboldt, pres., 1998—. Lt. Signal Corp USAR, 1968, comm. officer 2/12 Arty. Bn., 23d Arty. group US Army, 1969—70, Vietnam. Decorated Bronze Star. Mem.: VFW (life), Acupuncture Assn. Kans. (polit. dir. 1998—), Lotus Life Car Club, Humboldt Rotary Club (Paul Harris Fellow). Libertarian. Office: Finney Acupuncture Clinic 714 Bridge St Humboldt KS 66748-1708

FINNEY, ROY PELHAM, JR., urologist, surgeon, inventor; b. Gaffney, SC, Dec. 7, 1924; s. Roy P. Finney Sr. and Mary Frances (Cannon) Woodard; m. Kay Harkness, Apr. 5, 1963; children: Wright C., James L., Joella R., Gray, Kevin. MD, Med. U. S.C., 1952. Diplomate: Am. Bd. Urology. Resident in urology Johns Hopkins U., Balt., 1952-57; prof. surg. urology U. South Fla., Tampa, 1972-84, dir. div. urology, 1972-84; ret. Designer and inventor implantable prostheses incontinence device inflatable penile prostheses treatment impotence, Double J ureteral stent, developer new surg. procedures treatment impotence; patentee in field. Fellow ACS; mem. Am. Urology Assn., Soc. Internationale D'Urologie, Internat. Continenece Soc., Urodynamic Soc. Republican. Home: 4382 Cortez Blvd Weeki Wachee FL 34607-1209

FINNIGAN, ROBERT EMMET, retired small business owner; b. Buffalo, May 27, 1927; s. Charles M. and Marie F. (Jacobs) F.; m. Bette E. van Horn, Apr. 1, 1950; children: Michael, Patrick, Robert E. Jr., Joan, Shawn, Thomas, Matthew. BS, U.S. Naval Acad., 1949; MS, U. Ill., 1954, PhD, 1957. Commd. lt. USAF, 1949, advanced through grades to capt., 1954; sr. scientist Livermore Lab., U. Calif., 1959, U. Calif. Lawrence Livermore Lab., 1957-62; sr. rsch. scientist Stanford Rsch. Inst., Menlo Park, Calif., 1962-63; dir. Electronic Assocs. Inc., Palo Alto, Calif., 1963-67; founder, vice chmn., sr. v.p., chief strategic officer Finnigan Corp., San Jose, Calif., 1967-92, vice chmn. emeritus, cons., 1992—. Mem. panel NAS, Washington, 1986—89; bd. dirs. Pacific Nanotechnology, Inc., Santa Clara, Calif.; bd. overseers Chem. Heritage Found., Phila., 2005. Author: Identification and Analysis of Organic Pollutants in Water, 1976, Advances in Identification and Analysis of Organic Pollutants in Water, 1981. Chmn., co-founder U.S. Nat. Working Group on Pollution, Internat. Orgn. for Legal Metrology, Washington, 1982-87; mem. pres.'s coun., U. Ill., Urbana, 2002—; mem. bd. overseers Chem. Heritage Found., Phila., 2005. Named Pioneer in Analytical Instrumentation-Mass Spectrometry, Soc. Analytical Chemists of Pitts. and Pitts. Conf. on Analytical Chemistry, 1994; named to Instrumentation Hall of Fame, Pitts. Conf. on Analytical Chemistry and Analytical Chem. Soc., 1999; recipient Alumni Honor award, Coll. of Engring., U. Ill., 1980, Disting. Alumnus award, U. Ill. Dept. Elec. Engring., 1975, Robert Finnigan professorship established, Keck Grad. Inst. Applied Life. Sci., Claremont, Calif., 2002. Mem. IEEE (sr.), Am. Soc. Mass Spectrometry (bd. dirs.), Am. Electronic Assn. (bd. dirs. 1982-84, 87, chmn., co-founder environ. and occupational health com.), U.S. Naval Acad. Alumni Assn. (pres.'s cir. 1996—), Sigma Xi. Avocations: wine, hiking, snowshoeing.

FINOCCHIARO, ALFONSO G., bank executive; b. Catania, Italy, Aug. 20, 1932; came to U.S., 1960; s. Giovanni and Giuseppina (Cavalieri) F.; m. Diana Louise Cavagnolo, Jan. 19, 1936; children: John Paul, Carol Anne. D in Polit. Sci., U. Catania, 1958; MBA in Internat. Fin., Pace U., NYC, 1967. V.p. Chem. Bank, NYC, 1966—77; pres., gen. mgr. Conn. Bank Internat., NYC, 1977—78; exec. v.p., regional dir. Banco Portugues do Atlantico, NYC, 1978—95; dir. BPA Futures Cayman, 1989—96, Internat. Strategy Svcs., 1990—96; vice-chmn. BPA Brazil, 1993—96; dir. BPA Overseas Ltd., 1993—96; advisor to bd. dirs. Banco Portugues do Atlantico, Lisbon, Portugal, 1996—97; chmn., CEO FINAB Internat. Corp. Svc. Ltd., 2000—; chmn. BPD Bank, NYC, 2005—. Bd. dirs. IMAG, N.Y.C., 1982-, BPD Internat. Bank, N.Y.C., 1997-2005, So. Fin. BAnk, Va., 1997-2004, Alfie Internat., Inc., 2005-; advisor to bd. dirs. Banco Internat. do Funchal, Lisbon, Portugal, 1997—. Mem. Friends of Queen Catherine, Inc., chmn. fin. com., trustee, 1988-2001. Decorated comdr. Order Infante D. Henrique (Portugal). Fellow: Internat. Mgmt. and Devel. Inst. (Leadership award); mem.: European-Am. C. of C. in the U.S. (bd. dirs. 1991—98, v.p.), Internat. Mgmt. and Devel. Inst., Global Leadership Inst. (bd. dirs. 1991—2001), Am. Portuguese Soc. (v.p., bd. dirs. 1979—), Portugal C. of C. (bd. dirs., pres. 1978—98). Republican. Roman Catholic. Avocations: piano, music, travel, foreign affairs. Personal E-mail: alfie333@yahoo.com.

FINS, JOSEPH JACK, internist, medical ethicist; b. NYC, Nov. 16, 1959; s. Herman and Ruth (Lovett) F.; m. Amy B. Ehrlich, July 2, 1989. BA with honors, Wesleyan U., Middletown, Conn., 1982; MD, Cornell U., Ithaca, NY, 1986. Diplomate Am. Bd. Internal Medicine. Intern in psychiatry NY Hosp. Payne Whitney Clinic, NYC, 1986—87; resident in medicine NY Hosp., NYC, 1987—89; instr. Cornell U. Med. Coll., NYC, 1990; fellow in medicine NY Hosp. Cornell Med. Ctr., NYC, 1990—92; vis. assoc. for medicine Hastings Ctr., Briarcliff Manor, NY, 1990—92; instr. Cornell U. Med. Coll., NYC, 1992—93; assoc. for medicine Hastings Ctr., Garrison, 1992—; asst. attending physician NY Hosp., 1992—98; asst. prof. medicine Cornell U. Med. Coll., NYC, 1993—98; assoc. attending physician NY Presbyn. Hosp., 1998—2003; assoc. prof. medicine and assoc. prof. medicine in psychiat. Weill Med. Coll. Cornell U., NYC, 1998—2003; assoc. prof. program clin. epidemiology/health sci. rsch. Weill Grad. Sch. Med. Scis. Cornell U., NYC; assoc. prof. of pub. health Weill Med. Coll. of Cornell U., NYC, 2001—03, chief divsn. med. ethics, 2001—, prof. medicine, 2003—, prof. public health, 2003—, prof. medicine in psychiatry, 2003—; attending physician NY Presbyn. Hosp., 2003—. Ethics com. dept. medicine NY Hosp., NYC, 1991-94; dir. med. ethics NY Presbyterian-Weill Cornell Hosp., chmn. com., 1994-2002; physician, ethicist in residence The Healthcare Chaplaincy, NY, 1994-2002; temp. advisor Regional Bioethics Ctr. of Pan Am. Health Orgn., 1995; faculty scholar Open Soc. Inst. Project on Death in Am., 1997-2000; bd. dirs. Fund for Modern Cts., 2004-07; adj. faculty Rockefeller U., 2003—; attending physician NY Presby. Hosp.; trustee Wesleyan U., 2004-07; dir.-at-large Am. Soc. Bioethics and Humanities. Author: A Palliative Ethic of Care: Clinical Wisdom at Life's End, 2006; mem. editl. bd. Jour. Am. Geriatrics Soc., 1991-92, BioMed Ctrl. Med.Ethics, The Oncologist; editor Bioethics, Cancer Investigation 1995-2000, Jour. Pain and Symptom Mgmt., 1997—; contbr. articles to profl. jours. Presdl. appt. commr. to White Ho. Commn. on Complementary and Alternative Medicine Policy, 2000—02; nat. adv. com. Woodrow Wilson Nat. Fellowship Found., 2003—06; quality care at the end of life commn. NY State Atty. Gen.'s Office, 1997—98; active NY State Task Force on Life and the Law, 2007—; bd. dirs. Partnership for Caring, 1999—2003. Recipient John P. McGovern ann. lectr., Am. Osler Soc., 2006, Robert Wood Johnson Health Policy Investigation award, 2007—; fellow, Woodrow Wilson Found., 1998—; scholar, Hastings Ctr., Briarcliff Manor, 1989. Fellow: ACP (chair 2003—06, councilor at large 2003—06, gov. 2007—, chmn. health and pub. policy com. NY chpt.), NY Acad. Medicine; mem.: Am. Geriat. Soc. (vice chair ethics com. 1994—96), Assn. Bar of City of NY (adj.). Office: Weill Med Coll Cornell U Divsn Med Ethics 435 East 70th St ste 4-J New York NY 10021 Office Phone: 212-746-4246.

FINTA, FRANCES MICKNA, secondary school educator; b. Stafford Springs, Conn., June 17, 1927; d. John Joseph Mickna and Mary Frances Breslin; m. Quinn Finta, Aug. 21, 1951; children: John Wright, Susan Frances Finta Phillips. BA in Math., Boston U., 1949; postgrad., U. Va., 1963—69, Prince George's C.C., Largo, Md., 1982, No. Va. C.C., Alexandria, 1982—84, postgrad., 1994, U. Va., Fairfax, 1988—89; MEd in Guidance and Counseling, George Mason U., 1975. Cert. tchr. Va. Food prodn. mgr., dining rm. mgr., waitress, field ops. rep., liaison to airlines Marriott Corp., Marriott In-Flight Svcs., Inc., Washington, 1950—62; tchr. math, Arlington (Va.) Pub. Schs., 1963—72, 1963—. Substitute tchr. Fairfax (Va.) Pub. Schs., 1972—73; 'substitute tchr. Arlington (Va.) County Pub. Schs., 1972—. Mem. Arlington County Scholarship Fund for Tchrs., Inc., 1995—, sec., 1996—2001, treas., 2002—; mem. Friends of Arlington Parks, 1995—, Maywood Cmty. Assn., 1966—; treas. Washington-Lee H.S. Band Booster Club, 1979—81, Evelyn Staples for County Bd., 1991; vol. coord. David Foster for Sch. Bd., 1994, 2003; mem. Arlingtonians for a Better County, 1999—2003, Arlington County Rep. Com., 1994—, chmn. hdqrs., 2000—, mem. fin. com., 1994—95, canvass chmn., 2000, 2000, 2002, 2004, 2006, chmn. nominations com., 2000—01, chmn. credentials com., 2006; mem. steering com. John Hager for Gov., 2000; del. to state conv. Rep. Party Va., 1996, 1998, 2000, Va. Fedn. Rep. Women, 1996—, co-chair credential com., 2007; mem. credential com. Va. 8th Dist. Rep. Conv., 1998; sec.'s adv. com. Commonwealth of Va., 1998—2002; mem. Organized Women Voters of Arlington, 1997—2004, mem. nominating com., 2000, treas., 2000—04. Recipient Hon. Guardian of Srs.' Rights award, 60 Plus Assn., 1999, Vol. Svc. award, Arlington County Rep. Com., 1995—99, Hilda Griffith Lifetime Achievement award, 1999, Leon Delyannis Cmty. Involvement award, 1997, award of Excellence, 2004, Cert. of Appreciation, Arlington County Civic Fedn., 1988, 1997, Jour. Newspapers trophy, 2001, Parent Vol. award, Washington-Lee H.S. Band Boosters Club, 1979, Appreciation award, 1981, Parent Vol. award, Woodmont Elem. Sch., 1975, Patrick Henry award, Commonwealth of Va., 2001, Disting. Meritorious Svc. award, Arlington County Civic Fedn., 2003, Vol. Svc. award, Arlington County Rep. Com., 2003, Cert. of Appreciation, Arlington County Voters in Partnership Program, 2001. Mem.: AAUW (del. to Arlington County Civic Fedn. 1994—, co-1st v.p. programs 2001—03, exec. com. 2001—, 1st v.p. programs 2002—03, policy chair 2003—05, co-policy chair 2005—), NEA, Arlington Ret. Tchrs. Assn. (v.p. programs 2004—06, 1st v.p. programs 2004—, exec. com. 2004—, pres. 2006—), Arlington Edn. Assn., Va. Edn. Assn., Va. Ret. Tchrs. Assn. (life), Arlington County Civic Fedn. (mem. numerous coms. 1985—, treas. 1998—2006, v.p. 2006—), Maywood Cmty. Assn. (del. Arlington Civic Fedn. 1982—, nominating com. 2006), Arlington County Taxpayers' Assn., Arlington Rep. Women's Club (auditor 1996, asst. treas. 1997, pres. 1998—99, newsletter editor 1998—99, exec. bd. 1998—, chmn. achievement awards 2000, chmn. bylaws com. 2000, chmn. Barbara Bush literacy com. 2000, dir. 2000—01, auditor 2002—03, chair fin. com. 2002—). Republican. Roman Catholic. Avocations: civic and political activities, reading. Home: 3317 23d St N Arlington VA 22201-4310

FINUCANE, ANNE M., communications executive, marketing executive; married; 4 children. BA with honors, U. N.H. Pub. info. officer Mayor of City of Boston; dir. creative svcs. Sta. WBZ-TV, Boston; head creative svcs. Hill, Holliday, Connors, Cosmopulos, Inc., Boston, dir. account mgmt., dir. corp. devel.; prin. Anne Finucane Mktg. and Telecomm., Boston; sr. v.p., dir. corp. mktg. and comm. Fleet Fin. Group, Boston, 1995—. Bd. dirs. Internat. Ctr. for Journalists. Bd. dirs. Urban Improv, Emerson Coll., New Eng. Coun., Mass. Women's Forum; co-chmn. tech. divsn. United Way of Mass. Bay Campaign, 1995, 96; mem. adv. coun. Children's Defense Fund, Washington, Conservation Law Found. Office: Fleet Fin Group Corp Mktg & Comm One Federal St Boston MA 02110 Fax: 617-346-4740.

FINUCANE, MELISSA LUCILLE, psychologist, researcher; d. Anthony and Veronica Finucane. BS with honors, U. Western Australia, Perth, 1991, M of Psychology, 1998, PhD, 1997. Lic. Psychologist Western Australia. Rsch. scientist Decision Sci. Rsch. Inst., Eugene, Oreg., 1997—2001; rsch. investigator Ctr. for Health Rsch., Hawaii, Kaiser Permanente Hawaii, Honolulu, 2001—. Recipient Australian Skeptics Eureka prize, 1999; grantee, NSF, 2000—07, Nat. Inst. on Aging, 2001—. Mem.: AAAS, APA, Assn. Psychol. Sci., Soc. Risk Analysis, Soc. Judgement and Decision Making. Achievements include research in affect heuristic, risk perception and decision-making competence. Office: Ctr Health Rsch Hawaii Kaiser Permanente Hawaii 501 Alakawa St Honolulu HI 96817 Home Phone: 808-783-8787; Office Phone: 808-432-4754. Office Fax: 808-432-4785. Business E-Mail: melissa.l.finucane@kp.org.

FINZER, CAROLYN LAUING, artist; b. Aurora, Ill., July 24, 1947; d. Royal Walter and Marcianna Julia (MIller) Lauing; m. Melvern Kent Finzer, July 26, 1969; children: Nicole Gabrielle, Deirdre Danielle. BS in Art Edn., Ill. State U., 1969; postgrad., Salzburg Coll., 1974. Cert. elem. and secondary tchr., Ill. Tchr. art Sch. Dist. # 90, Naperville, Ill., 1969—70; chmn. art dept. Sch. Dist. # 203, Naperville, 1970—75. Spkr., storyteller Native Am. enrichment programs.; tchr. weaving techniques, bead looming and quill embroidery, bookbinding workshops, 1990—; fashion model Marketplace Handwork of India Catalog. Illustrator Girl Scout field guide; featured in Birds and Blooms mag., 2000, (book) The Best of Birds and Blooms, 2005, Chicagoland Gardening mag., Mar./Apr. 2004; contbr. to several books. Vol./amb. Morton Arboretum, Lisle, Ill.; docent Naper Settlement, Naperville, Ill.; leader, trainer Girl Scouts U.S., badge lab facilitator DuPage Coun.; charter bd. dirs. Naperville Area Clean Cmty.; mem. edn. com. Conservation Found.; mem. Wild Ones; eucharistic min. Sts. Peter and Paul Ch. Recipient Disting. Svc. award Naperville Jaycees, 1985, 2005, Environ. Hero award Naperville Park Dist., 1991, Outstanding Alumnus award Ill. State U., 1992, Green Wood Environmentalist award Girl Scouts of DuPage County, Sts. Peter and Paul Disting. Grad. award Nat. Cath. Edn. Assn., 1999, Blazing Star award Willowbrook Wildlife Haven, 2004, Outstanding Contbns. to the Arts award Naperville Art League, 2006. Mem. Chgo. Art Inst. (historian, charter), Nature Conservancy, Ill. Storytellers Guild, Inc., DuPage Textile Artists Guild, Naperville Riverwalk Quilt Guild, United Air Lines Pilots Wives Friendship Club (historian 1989—), Naperville Cmty. Assocs. Avocations: natural gardening, fiber arts, cross county skiing, collecting Native American dolls, antiques, multi-cultural hats and gourd instruments. Home: 970 Sylvan Cir Naperville IL 60540-5532

FINZI, BENJAMIN, communications executive; s. Alberto Benedetto and Toni Finzi; m. Esther Uziel, Sept. 28, 1986; children: Lauren Emily, David Alexander. BA, Tel Aviv U., Israel, 1984; cert. sys. analyst, Inst. Mgmt. and Productivity, Tel Aviv, 1986; MBA with high distinction, INSEAD, Fontainebleau, France, 1988. V.p. sales and mktg. Almog Software Ltd., Tel Aviv, 1982—87; mgr. Boston Conss. Group, NYC, 1988—91; sr. mgr. APM Inc., NYC, 1991—94; ptnr. Monitor Group, NYC, 1995—99; coo Epik Comm. Inc., Orlando, Fla., 1999—2002; CEO Internet Satellite Platform Inc., Orlando, 2002—04; pres. WiNetworks Inc., NYC, 2004—. Founder, chmn. NAP Ams. LLC, Miami, Fla., 2000—03; chmn. bd. dirs. IT Fla., Tallahassee, 2001—04; founder, mng. ptnr. Secant Partners LLC, Summit, NJ, 2003—05; founder, pres. Ockham Consulting Group Inc, NYC, 2007—. 1st sgt. Israel Air Force, 1977—80. Scholar, Rothschild Found., 1987. Mem.: Internat. Exec. Resources Group. Home: 5800 Arlington Ave 17G Bronx NY 10471 Office: WiNetworks Inc 555 West 57th St Ste 326 New York NY 10019 Home Phone: 917-855-0162; Office Phone: 212-957-9302. Home Fax: 917-591-4191. Personal E-mail: bfinzi@gmail.com. Business E-Mail: benjaminf@winetworks.com.

FIOL MATTA, LIANA, judge; Grad., Trinity Coll.; M., Columbia U., 1988, JSD, 1996; JD, U. P.R. Prof. Inter-Am. U., 1978—88, Pontifical Catholic U.; judge PR Ct. of Appeals, 1992—2003; justice PR Supreme Ct., 2004—. Author numerous articles in professional journals. Mem.: P.R. Bar Assn. Office: PR Supreme Ct PO Box 9022392 San Juan PR 00902-2392*

FIORE, CAROLE DIANE, library consultant; b. Phila., May 5, 1946; d. Louis A. and Hortense (Menkes) Millendorf; m. Stanley Fiore, Jan. 2, 1980. BS in Edn., Temple U., 1969; MS in Library Sci., Drexel U., 1970; Cert. in Supr., Villanova U., 1977. Library page Free Libr. Phila., 1962—63; library asst. Sch. Dist. Phila., 1965—68, sch. librarian, 1969—82; dir. children's services Dunedin (Fla.) Pub. Library, 1982—85; head youth services cen. library Tampa-Hillsborough County (Fla.) Pub. Libr. Sys., Fla., 1985—90; pub. libr. cons. youth svcs. State Libr. Fla., Tallahassee, 1990—2005; LSTA coord. State Libr. and Archives Fla., 2005—06; ind. cons. and pres. Tng. and Libr. Consulting, 2006—; acquisitions editor Neal Schuman Pubs., 2006—. Leader vacation reading club Free Libr. of Phila., 1975-78; advisor ea. area br. div. sch. librs. Pa. Dept. Edn., 1976-82, cons. audio visual task force State Libr. of Fla., 1985-88; adj. instr. div. edn. U. Tampa, 1987-90; vis. instr. Sch. of Libr. and Info. Sci., Fla. State U., 1992-98; cons. children's svcs. manual com. Fla. Dept. State Div. Libr. and Info. Svcs., Tallahassee, 1987-88; mem. coun. advisors for inst. proposal, Fla. State U. Sch. Info. Studies, 1997-98; nat. libr. adv. com., Grolier Pub., 1996-2004; cons. in field. Author: Bridging the Gap: Books for Transitional Readers, 1987, Programming for Introducing Adults to Children's Literature, 1994, Programming for Young Children: Birth through Age Five, 1996, Running Summer Library Reading Programs: A How-To-Do-It Manual, 1998, Fiore's Summer Libr. Reading Program Handbook, 2005, other manuals; exec. prodr. (video) Born to Read—Florida Style, 1999; host, dir. (TV program) Under the Story Tree, 1983; contbr. articles to profl. jours. Pers. review bd. City of Dunedin, Fla., 1989-90; mem. adv. bd., Trejo Foster Found. Hispanic Libr. Edn., 1998-99, mem. planning com. One Goal Summer Confs., 2003-. Grantee Dominican U. Grad. Sch. Libr. and Info. Studies, 2007—; recipient Pub. Rels. award John Cotton Dana Libr., 1994, Davis productivity award, 1996, 2000, contbn. to literacy award Leon County Reading Assn., 2001. Mem. ALA (Booklist editl. adv. bd. 1997-2000, childrens book coun. jt. com. 2006—), Assn. Libr. Svcs. for Children (filmstrip evaluation com. 1987-90, chair filmstrip evaluation com. 1990-92, chair notable showcase 1990-91, Newbery award com. 1985-86, membership liaison com. 1984-2006, Caldecott award com. 1992, planning and budget com. 1996-97, priority group cons. 1997-99, rsch. and devel. com. 1998-00, dir. 1994-97, pres. 2001-02, Theodore Seuss Geisel award com. 2005-06, disting. svc. award com. 2007—), Nat. Assn. for Preservation and Perpetuation of Storytelling, Assn. Specialized and Cooperative Libr. Agys. (state libr. sect. 1991—, discussion group leader cons. for svc. to children and young people 1997-98, 2004-05), Young Adult Libr. Svcs. Assn. (chmn. vision task force 1999-2000), Fla. Libr. Assn. (audio visual caucus steering com. 1986-87, children and schs. caucus steering com. 1987-90, awards and citations com. 1993-95, chair 1994-95, charter by-laws and manual com. 1989-94, chair intellectual freedom com. 1996-97), Early Childhood Assn. Fla., Fla. Reading Assn., Fla. Suncoast Puppet Guild, Internat. Reading Assn., Leon County Reading Assn., Leon Assn. Edn. Young Children, Tallahassee Children's Lit. Cir., U.S. Bd. of Books for Young People, Young Adult Libr. Svcs. Assn. (serving the underserved II planning com. 1995), Beta Phi Mu (bd. dirs. Sigma chpt. 1978-81). Avocations: needlecraft, gardening. Office: Tng and Libr Consulting 4615 Fledgling Tallahassee FL 32311-1212 Personal E-mail: cfiore@earthlink.net. Business E-Mail: carole@fiore-tlc.biz.

FIORE, JOSEPH ALBERT, artist; b. Cleve., Feb. 3, 1925; s. Salvatore Emmanuel and Gemma Marie (Cominelli) F.; m. Mary Falconer Fitton, Oct. 10, 1952; children: Thomas, Susanna. Student, Black Mountain Coll., 1946—48, student, 1949, San Francisco Sch. Art Inst., 1948—49. Instr. painting, drawing Black Mountain (N.C.) Coll., 1949-56, chmn. art dept., 1951-56; free lance designer NYC, 1958-61; instr. painting Phila. Coll. Art, 1962-70, Md. Inst. Coll. Art, Balt., 1970-75; instr. landscape painting Nat. Acad. Design, NYC, 1979, Parson's Sch. Design Summer Program, Dordogne, France, 1980. Vis. artist-critic Artists for Environment Found., Walpack Center, N.J., 1972-83, Vt. Studio Sch., Johnson, Vt., 1987. One-man shows include Ten-Thirty Gallery, Cleve., 1944, 48, 50, Gallerie Parnass, Wuppertal, Germany, 1955, Round Top Ctr. for Arts, Damariscotta, Maine, 1997, 2002, Cathedral of St. John the Divine, N.Y.C., 1997, Black Mountain Coll. Mus. and Arts Ctr. at Zone One Contemporary, Asheville, N.C., 1995-96, Staempfli Gallery, N.Y.C., 1960, Robert Schoelkopf Gallery, N.Y.C., 1965, 69, Green Mountain Gallery, N.Y.C., 1973, John Bernard Myers Gallery, N.Y.C., 1974, Fischbach Gallery, N.Y.C., 1977, 81, Caldbeck Gallery, Rockland, Maine, 1988, Le Va-Tout Gallery, Waldboro, Maine, 1991, River Gallery, Damariscotta, Maine, 2002, Rider U. Art Gallery, Lawrenceville, N.J., 2004, Ctr. for Maine Contemporary Art, Rockport, 2004, Gallery One-Seventy, Damariscotta, Maine, 2006; exhibited in group shows Stable Gallery, N.Y.C., 1954, 55, Whitney Mus. Am. Art, 1959, U. Ill., Urbana, 1961, Am. Fedn. Art Travelling Exhbn., 1964, Corcoran Gallery Art, Washington, 1975, State Mus., Augusta, 1976, Cape Split Place, Addison, Maine, 1977, Am. Acad. Arts and Letters, N.Y.C., 1981, Landmark Gallery, N.Y.C., 1981, Jersey City Mus., 1982, Farnsworth Mus., Rockland, Maine, 1983, Artist's Choice Mus., 1983, Black Mountain Connection, Gilliam and Peden Gallery, Raleigh, 1987, Black Mountain Coll., Blum Art Inst., Bard Coll., N.Y.C., 1987, N.C. State Mus., Raleigh, 1987, Grey Art Ctr., NYU, 1987, Snyder Fine Arts, N.Y.C., 1992, Station Gallery, Katonah, N.Y., 1992, Anita Shapolsky Gallery, N.Y.C., 1997, Hofstra Mus., Hempstead, N.Y., 2001 Black Mountain Coll.: Experiment in Art Museo Nacional Centro De Arte Renia Sofia, Madrid, 2002-03, numerous others; represented in permanent collections Whitney Mus. Am. Art, N.Y.C., N.C. State Mus. Art, Raleigh, Corcoran Gallery, Art, Washington, Colby Art Mus., Waterville, Maine, Weatherspoon Gallery, Greensboro, N.C., NAD, N.Y., Chase Manhattan Collection, N.Y.C., Asheville Mus. of Art, N.C., Black Mountain Coll. Mus. and Art Ctr., Housatonic Mus. Art, Bridgeport, Conn., Farnsworth Mus., Rockland, Maine, 2004. Served with AUS, 1943-46. Recipient prize for painting San Francisco Mus. Ann., 1949, 1st prize Met. Young Artists 1st Ann. Nat. Arts Club, N.Y.C., 1958, Adolph and Clara Obrig Prize, NAD 178th Ann., 2003, Obrig prize Nat. Acad., 2005; Artists for Environment Found. residence grantee, 1976; Nettie Marie Jones fellow Ctr. Music, Drama and Art, Lake Placid, N.Y., 1983, purchase award Am. Acad. Arts and Letters, 1998. Mem. NAD (cert. of merit 168th Ann. Exhbn. 1993, Edwin Palmer Meml. prize 170th Ann. 1995, Cannon prize 175th Ann. 2000, Andrew Carnegie prize 176th Ann. 2001, Adolph and Clara Obrig prize 178th Ann. 2003), Artists Equity Assn. N.Y. Office Phone: 212-362-8897.

FIORENZA, FRANCIS P., religion educator; b. Bklyn., Feb. 27, 1941; married, 1967; 1 child. AB, St. Mary's U., 1961, STB, 1963; ThD, U. Münster, Fed. Republic of Germany, 1972. Asst. prof. theology U. Notre Dame, Ind., 1971-77, Villanova (Pa.) U., 1977-79; assoc. prof. theology Cath. U. Am., Washington, 1979-87; now Charles Chauncey Stillman prof. Roman Cath. theol. studies Harvard U., Cambridge, Mass. Vis. scholar Union Theol. Sem., N.Y.C., 1974-75; vis. prof. Yale U., 1995. Author: Critical Social Theory and Christology, 1975, Political Theology as Foundational Theology, 1977, Religion und Politik, Christliche Glaube, 1982; translator: Schleiermacher: Open Letters on the Glaubenslehre, 1981, Foundational Theology: Jesus and Church, 1984; editor: Systematic Theology, Roman Catholic Perspectives, 2 vols., 1991; co-editor: (with Don Browning) Habermas, Modernity and Public Theology, 1992, Handbook of Catholic Theology, 1995, (with James Livingston) Modern Christian Thought: Vol. 2 The Twentieth Century, 2000; contbr. articles to religious jours. Fellow Div., U. Chgo., 1978-79; rsch. fellow Am. Assn. Theol. Schs., 1982-83, 89, Henry Luce III fellowship, 2005-2006. Mem. Am. Acad. Religion, Cath. Theol. Soc. Am. (pres. 1985-86), Soc. Values Higher Edn., Coll. Theol. Soc., Hegel Soc. Roman Catholic. Office: Harvard U Div Sch 45 Francis Ave Cambridge MA 02138-1911 Office Phone: 617-495-4518.

FIORENZA, JOSEPH A., retired archbishop; b. Beaumont, Tex., Jan. 25, 1931; s. Anthony and Grace (Galiano) Fiorenza. Grad., St. Anthony HS, Beaumont, Tex., 1947. Ordained priest Sem. Chapel, St. Mary's Sem., La Porte, Tex., 1954; asst. pastor Queen of Peace Ch., Houston, 1954—57; prof. med. ethics Dominican Coll., Houston, 1957—59; adminstr. Sacred Heart Co-Cathedral, Houston, 1959—67; pastor St. Augustine Ch., Houston, 1967—69, St. Benedict Ch., Houston, 1969—72, Assumption Ch., Houston, 1972—73; named Prelate of Honor to his Holiness, 1973; vice chancellor Diocese of Galveston-Houston, Tex., 1972—73, chancellor Tex., 1973—79; consecrated bishop Sacred Heart Cathedral, San Angelo, Tex., 1979; bishop Diocese of San Angelo, 1979—85, Diocese of Galveston-Houston, 1985—2004; archbishop Archdiocese of Galveston-Houston, 2004—06, archbishop emeritus, 2006—. Bd. dirs. U. St. Thomas, Houston, Cath. Near East Welfare Assn., US. Mem.: US Conf. Cath. Bishops (adminstrv. com. 1995—, v.p. 1995—98, pres. 1998—2001). Roman Catholic. Office: Archdiocese of Galveston-Houston 1700 San Jacinto Houston TX 77001

FIORENZA, LISA A., music educator; b. Las Vegas, Apr. 11, 1964; d. Rudolf Salvatore Fiorenza and Linda Lee Kniess; 1 child, Jessica Ziebol. BA in Piano Performance, U. Nev. Las Vegas, 1986, BA in Music Theory, Composition, 1986, MusM in Composition, 1994. Cert. Tchr. Music Music Tchrs. Nat. Assn. Organist Ch. of Truth, Las Vegas, 1981—83; pianist Unity Ch. of Desert, Las Vegas, 1985—88; part-time music faculty Clark County CC Cheyenne Campus, North Las Vegas, 1986—87; rehearsal pianist Nev. Dance Theatre, Las Vegas, 1986—88; organist Holy Family Cath. Ch., Las Vegas, 1988—91; founder, promoter Jr. Piano Competition, Las Vegas, 1992—2002; pianist, organist, orch. leader, arranger Christ Servant Luth. Ch., Henderson, Nev., 1995—; webmaster serenepiano.com, Las Vegas, 1999—; pres. Las Vegas Music Tchrs. Assn., 1998—2000, founder, playathon, 1999—, webmaster, 2000—05, Christ Servant Luth. Ch., Henderson, Nev., 2003—04; blind ctr. Nev. music educator, coord. Blind Ctr. Nev., Las Vegas, 2003—; co-dir., founder Las Vegas Mandoliers, 2004—; accordionist Celtic Cove Band, Las Vegas, 2005—. Theory exam coord. Las Vegas Music Tchrs. Assn., 1991—94. Composer (pianist): (CD) Saturday Morning, Winter Journey, Western Sky; composer: (orchestrator) Lutheran Orchestrated Hymns, Concerto in A minor by Jean Williams, In Elfland; composer: With You At Christmastime; author: Lighthouse Piano Method for the Blind. Dir. Playathon Fundraiser for Lied Animal Shelter, Toys For Tots, Blind Ctr., Las Vegas, Nev., 1999—2005. Named Most Outstanding Music Student, U. Nev., Las Vegas, 1984; recipient Piano Concerto Competition, U. Nev. Las Vegas, 1987, Nev. State Piano Collegiate Divsn. award, Music Tchrs. Nat. Assn., 1986, Nat. Guild Honor Roll Tchr., Nat. Piano Auditions Guild, 2002, 2004, 2005. Mem.: ASCAP,

Nat. Fedn. Music Clubs, Am. Coll. Musicians, Am. Guild Organists, Las Vegas Music Tchrs. Assn. (pres. 1998—2000, Svc. award for vol. tchg. at the Blind Ctr. 2004, 2003), Musicians Local 369, Nev. Old Time Fiddlers Assn. Achievements include first to audio music learning method for the blind or visually impaired. Avocations: mandolin, celtic harp, irish button accordion, piano accordion, violin.

FIORI, PAMELA, publishing executive, writer; b. Newark, Feb. 26, 1944; d. Edward and Rita (Rascati) F.; m. Colton Givner. BA cum laude, Jersey City State Coll., 1966. Tchr. English Gov. Livingston HS, Berkeley Heights, NJ, 1966-67; assoc. editor Holiday Mag., NYC, 1968-71, Travel & Leisure Mag., NYC, 1971-74, sr. editor, 1974-75, editor-in-chief, 1975-80; editor-in-chief, exec. v.p. Am. Express Pub. Corp. (Travel & Leisure/Food & Wine), NYC, 1980-89, editorial dir., exec. v.p., 1989-93; editor-in-chief Town & Country, NYC, 1993—, Town & Country TRAVEL, NYC, 2003—. Columnist: Travel & Leisure, 1976—89, Town & Country, 1993—; contbr. articles to periodicals. Founding chmn. UNICEF Snowflake Project; bd. trustess US Fund for UNICEF. Recipient Chevalier de l'Ordre du Merite, 1985, Melva C. Pederson award for disting. travel journalism Am. Soc. Travel Afts., 1992, Outstanding Woman of the 90s award Found. for Neurosurg. Rsch., 1994, Bus. award Nat. Italian Am. Found., 1996, Fashion Oracle of Yr., Coun. Fashion Designers, 2004, Audrey Hepburn Humanitarian award UNICEF, 2005, Gem Award, Jewelry Info. Coun., 2006, Matrix Award, Women in Comms., Inc., 2007. Office: Town & Country 300 W 57th St New York NY 10019-3794 Office Phone: 212-903-5334.*

FIORI-BLANCHFIELD, JOAN, artist, historian; b. Tuxedo, NY, May 26, 1942; d. Anthony Justus Fiori and Janet Cynthia Pohl; m. William Charles Blanchfield; children: Lyn, Mark. BA, Coll. New Rochelle, 1964; MA in Studio Art, SUNY, Albany, 1972; MA in Art History with high honors, Syracuse U., 1999; postgrad., SUNY, Binghamton, 1993—94, Cornell U., 1995—97, CUNY, 2001—02, SUNY, Albany, 2004—07. Tutor in fine arts Empire State Coll., Saratoga Springs, N.Y., 1974-75; instr. in art Jewish Cmty. Ctr., Utica, N.Y.; adj. instr. Mohawk Valley C.C., Utica, 1976-83; instr. in art and fine art Herkimer (N.Y.) County C.C., 1979-80; dir. cultural exch. to Italy Utica Coll. of Syracuse U., Utica, 1988-89, lectr. in fine art, 1973, 82-93, dir. Edith Barrett Art Gallery, 1983-96; ind. scholar, artist, cons. Utica, 1996—. Contbr. articles to profl. publs.; executed sculpture at Museo d'Arte Moderna, Italy, Mostra Internazionale di Sculture all'Aperto, Italy, 1978, 79. Bd. dirs. Art Discovery Consortium, Herkimer, Madison, Oneida Counties, N.Y., 1985-87; dir. art-in-edn. program for Oneida, Herkimer and Madison Counties, N.Y. State Coun. on Arts, N.Y.C., 1985-96; art judge Munson Williams Proctor Inst. Art, Utica, 1992, Utica Pub. Libr., 1992-95; curator women's unity exhbn. Utica Coll. Women's History Mus., Seneca Falls, N.Y., 1984; mem. upstate N.Y. com. Nat. Mus. Women in Arts, Washington, 1989-90. Recipient 1st prize Albany Inst. Art, 1966, Hon. Mention award Albany Inst. Art, 1967, Best in Show award Cooperstown Art Mus., 1981, 1st prize in sculpture, 1979, 80; medal del Rettore, Università dell'Aquila, Italy, 1989; grantee Utica Coll. Syracuse U., 1988-91, N.Y. State Coun. Arts, 1983-89, N.Y. Coun. Humanities, 1984-85, others. Mem.: Assn. Historians Am. Art, Coll. Art Assn., Chamber Mus. Soc. Utica (sec. 2000—05, bd. dirs. 1992—), NOW, Medieval Acad. Am., Southeastern Medieval Assn. (sec., treas. 1989—96), Phi Alpha Theta. Avocations: piano, jogging. Home: 2610 Sunset Ave Utica NY 13502-6009 Office Phone: 315-733-6331. Personal E-mail: jfioriblanchfield@adelphia.net.

FIORILLA DI SANTA CROCE, JOHN LEOPOLDO, investment company executive, lawyer; b. Paterson, NJ, July 1, 1965; s. Giovanni and Maria Giuseppina (Mazzara) Fiorilla di Santa Croce; m. Annie Borello, Sept. 27, 2003; 1 child, Giovanni Maria. BS, Seton Hall U., NJ, 1987; JD, U. Pitts., 1990; LLM in Internat. Legal Studies, NYU, 1999. Bar: N.J. 1990, N.Y. 1991, D.C. 1991, U.S. Supreme Ct. 1995; master lic. USCG. Assoc. Sullivan & Cromwell, NYC, London, 1990-94, Brosio, Casati E Associati, Milan, 1992—93; prin. Elysium Group Inc., NYC, 1994—; of counsel Studio Legale Vassalli, Milan, 1994-2001, Studio Legale Caffi-Maroncelli & Associati, Bergamo and Milan, Italy, 1994—. Adviser to the nunciature, Permanent Observer Mission of the Holy See to the UN, 1997—, mem. Holy See Del. to the Gen. Assembly and other UN bodies, 1997—. Pres. standing com. Young Friends Save Venice, 1998-2007; bd. dirs. Internat. Cath. Orgns. Info. Ctr., 1999—; bd. dirs. Save Venice Inc., 2001—, sec., 2006—; hon. usher St. Patrick's Cathedral, 2003—; mem. adv. bd. Peggy Guggenheim Collection, 2004—; bd. dirs. Am. Found. Savoy Orders, 2006-. Decorated Knight Grand Order of Merit (Moto Proprio) Italy, knight Sovreign Mil. Order Malta, grand cross Equestrian Order Holy Sepulchre Jerusalem (Holy See), knight with star Sacred Mil. Constantinian Order St. George (Two Sicilies), officer Order Merit Savoy, silver cross of merit Red Cross of the Republic of San Marino, knight Order of Sts. Maurice and Lazarus (Savoy), Presdl. Unit citation USCG, grand cross Order of Prince Danilo I of Montenegro, grand officer Order St. Michael Wing (Braganca); recipient Presdl. Unit citation, UCG, Silver medal of merit, Italian Red Cross. Fellow: Fgn. Policy Assn.; mem.: Assn. Bar City NY, St. George's Soc. NY, Circolo Società dell'Unione Venice, Univ. Club NY, Met. Opera Club, Racquet Club Phila., Met. Club, Econ. Club Doubles NY, Down Town Assn., Circolo del Golf di Roma. Roman Catholic. Home: 555 Park Ave New York NY 10065-8166 Office: Elysium Group Inc 641 Lexington Ave 26th Fl New York NY 10022-4503 also: Corso Matteotti 10 20121 Milan Italy Office Phone: 212-661-6222. Personal E-mail: jlf@fiorilla.com.

FIORINA, CARLY (CARA CARLETON SNEED FIORINA), former computer company executive; b. Austin, Tex., Sept. 6, 1954; d. Joseph and Madelon Sneed; m. Frank J. Fiorina; 2 stepchildren BA in Medieval History and Philosophy, Stanford U., 1976; MBA, Robert H. Smith Sch. Bus. U. Md., College Park, Md., 1980; MSc in Mgmt., MIT, 1989; postgrad., UCLA. Account exec. Long Lines AT&T, 1980, sr. v.p. Global mfg. ops., pres., AT&T network systems, N. Am., 1994—95; exec. v.p. corp. ops. Lucent Technologies, Murray Hill, NJ, 1995—96, pres., consumer products bus., 1996—97, group pres. Global Svc. Provider bus., 1997—99; pres. Hewlett-Packard Co., Palo Alto, 1999—2000, CEO, 1999—2005, chmn., 2000—05. Bd. dirs., PowerUp, Hewlett-Packard, 1999-2005, Merck & Co. Inc., 1999-2001, Revolution Healthcare Group, 2005-, Cybertrust, 2005-, MIT, Taiwan Semiconductor Mfg. Co., 2006-; mem., US China Bd. Trade., 1999-, US Space Commn., 2004- Author: Tough Choices: A Memoir, 2006. Named one of Fortune Mag. Most Powerful Women in Am. Bus., Top 50 Women To Watch, Wall St. Jour., 2005; recipient Appeal of Conscience award, 2002, Concern Worldwide Seeds of Hope award, 2003, Leadership award, Private Sector Coun., 2004; grantee Hon. Fellow, London Bus. Sch., 2001. Business E-Mail: csfiorina@sbcglobal.net.

FIORITO, EDWARD GERALD, lawyer; b. Irvington, NJ, Oct. 20, 1936; s. Edward and Emma (DePascale) F.; m. Charlotte H. Longo (widowed 2-3-2004); children: Jeanne C., Kathryn M., Thomas E., Lynn M., Patricia A. BSEE, Rutgers U., 1958; JD, Georgetown U., 1963. Bar: U.S. Patent and Trademark Office 1960, Va. 1963, N.Y. 1964, Mich. 1970, Ohio 1975, Tex. 1984. Patent staff atty. IBM, Armonk, NY, 1958-69; v.p. patent and comml. relations Energy Conversion Devices, Troy, Mich., 1969-71; mng. patent prosecution Burroughs Corp., Detroit, 1971-75; gen. patent counsel B.F. Goodrich Corp., Akron, Ohio, 1975-83; dir. patents and licensing Dresser Industries, Inc., Dallas, 1983-93. Alt. mem. Dept. Commerce Adv. Commn. on Patent Law Reform, 1991-92; spl. master, arbitrator, neutral evaluator, expert providing opinion testimony in intellectual property litigation, 1986—; U.S. del. to World Intellectual Property Orgn. Diplomatic Conf., 1991. Bd. dirs. Akron's House Extending Aid on Drugs, 1976. Mem. ABA (chmn. sci. and tech. sect. 1984-85, chair intellectual property law sect. 2000-2001), IEEE, Tex. Bar Assn. (chmn. intellectual property law sect. 1990-91), Internat. Assn. for Protection Indsl. Property (exec. bd. 1989—), Assn. Corp. Patent Counsel (exec. com. 1982-84), Tau Beta Pi. Roman Catholic. Avocations: music, flying. E-mail: ipconsulting@msn.com. *Those of you who have received gifts in great abundance at the beginning of your journey here, should remember to use them before your journey ends in the service of your creator who gave them to you.*

FIORITO, FRANK ANTHONY, secondary educator; b. Newark, Oct. 21, 1927; s. Donald Anthony and Mary Ann (Carlomusto) F.; m. Mary Agliozzo, Aug. 21, 1965; 1 child, Frank A. Jr. BA, Columbia Coll., 1947, MA, 1950. Cert. tchr., N.J. Tchr. English Newark Bd. Edn., 1959—. Author: The Anatomy of a Strike, 1970., Del. Dem. Nat. Convention, N.Y.C., 1976. Cpl. U.S. Army, 1951-53. Mem. Am. Fedn. Tchrs. (exec. v.p. Newark tchrs.' union 1965-70), N.J. State Fedn. Tchrs. (pres. 1970-73, organizer of 8 N.J. state colls. and won bargaining rights for Am. Fedn. of Tchrs.), Maplewood Unico (pres. 1985-88). Roman Catholic. Home: 130 Oakland Rd Maplewood NJ 07040-2314 Personal E-mail: fafsr@comcast.net.

FIRCHOW, EVELYN SCHERABON, German language and literature educator, writer; b. Vienna; arrived in US, 1951, naturalized, 1964; d. Raimund and Hildegard (Nickl) Scherabon; m. Peter E. Firchow, 1969; children: Felicity (dec. 1988), Pamina. BA, U. Tex., 1956; MA, U. Man., 1957; PhD, Harvard U., 1963. Instr. coll. math. Balmoral Hall Sch., Winnipeg, Man., Canada, 1953—55; tchg. fellow in German Harvard U., Cambridge, Mass., 1957—58, 1961—62; lectr. German U. Md. in Munich, 1961; instr. German U. Wis., Madison, 1962—63, asst. prof., 1963—65; assoc. prof. German U. Minn., Mpls., 1965—69, prof. German and Germanic philology, 1969—, McKnight rsch. prof., 2004—07; vis. prof. U. Fla., Gainesville, 1973; Fulbright rsch. prof. Iceland, 1966—67, 1980, 1984; vis. rsch. prof. Nat. Cheng Kung U., Tainan, Taiwan, 1982—83; permanent vis. prof. Jilin U., Changchun, China, 1987—. Vis. prof. U. Graz, Austria, 1989, Austria, 91, Austria, 2002—03, U. Vienna, Austria, 1995, U. Bonn, 1996, Nat. U. Costa Rica, 2000. Editor and author: (under name E.S. Coleman) Taylor Starck-Festschrift, 1964, Stimmen aus dem Stundenglas, 1968, (under name E.S. Firchow) Studies by Einar Haugen, 1972, Studies for Einar Haugen, 1972, Was Deutsche lesen, 1973, Deutung und Bedeutung, 1973, Elucidarius in Old Norse Translation, 1989, The Old Norse Elucidarius: Original Text and English Translation, 1992, Notker der Deutsche von St. Gallen: De interpretatione, 1995, Categoriae, 2 Vols., 1996, De nuptiis Philologiae et Mercurii, 2 Vols., 1999, Notker der Deutsche von St. Gallen (950-1022): Ausführliche Bibliographie, 2000, De consolatione Philosophiae, 3 vols., 2003, Reluctant Modernists, Festschrift Peter Firchow, 2002, Gottfried von Strassburg: Tristan und Isolde, 2004, Wege und Irrwege der mittelalterlichen Textausgaben, 2007; translator: Einhard: Vita Caroli Magni, Das Leben Karls des Grossen, 1968, 84, 95, Einhard: Vita Caroli Magni, The Life of Charlemagne, 1972, 85, Icelandic Short Stories, 1974, 87, East German Short Stories, 1979, (with P.E. Firchow) Alois Brandstetter, The Abbey, 1998; dir., editor Computer Clearing-House Project for German and Medieval Scandinavian, to 2000; assoc. editor Germanic Notes and Revs., Am. Linguistics, Germanic Linguistics; contbr. articles and book revs. to profl. jours. Fulbright scholar Tex., 1951-52; fellow Alexander von Humboldt-Stiftung, Munich, 1960-61, Tuebingen, 1974, Marburg, 1981, Goettingen, 1985, Tokyo, 1991, Marburg and Berlin, 1993, Bonn, 2001, Fulbright Found., Iceland, 1967-68, 80, 94, Austrian Govt., 1977, NEH, 1980-81, Am. Inst. Indian Studies, 1988, BUSH fellow, 1989, Thor Thors fellow, 1994, Faculty summer fellow and Mc Knight summer fellow, 1995-96, 99, 2004, 07, Deutscher Akademischer Austausdienst (DAAD) rsch. fellow, 2000; named hon. mem. Multilingual Rsch. Ctr., Brussels, 1986. Mem. AAUP, MLA (chmn. divsn. German lit. to 1700 1979-80, 93-96, vice chmn. pedagogical seminar for Germanic philology 1979-86, 91-93, chair 1994), Medieval Acad. Am., Soc. German-Am. Studies (chair Linguistics I 1992), Internat. Comparative Lit. Assn., Soc. for Advancement Scandinavian Studies (chmn. Germanic philology 1979, text editing 1980, linguistics 1984, computers and Old Norse 1985), Assn. for Lang. and Linguistic Computing (founding mem.), Am. Comparative Lit. Assn., Midwest Modern Lang. Assn. (chmn. German I 1965-66, chmn. Scandinavian 1979), Am. Assn. Tchrs. German, Mediävisten Verband, Soc. for Germanic Philology, Österreichische Germanisten-Gesellschaft, Wolkenstein Gesellschaft, Assn. Lit. Scholars and Critics. Office: U Minn 205 Folwell Hall 9 Pleasant St SE Minneapolis MN 55455 Business E-Mail: firch001@umn.edu.

FIRCHOW, PETER EDGERLY, language professional, educator, writer; b. Needham, Mass., Dec. 16, 1937; s. Paul Karl August and Marta Loria (Montenegro) F.; m. Evelyn Maria Scherabon Coleman, Sept. 18, 1969; 1 dau., Pamina Maria Scherabon. BA, Harvard Coll., 1959; postgrad., U. Vienna, Austria, 1959—60; MA, Harvard U., 1961; PhD, U. Wis., 1965. Asst. prof. English U. Mich., 1965-67; asst. prof. English and comparative lit. U. Minn., Mpls., 1967-69, assoc. prof., 1969-73, prof., 1973—, chmn. Comparative Lit. Program, 1972-78. Disting. vis. prof. Nat. Cheng Kung U., Taiwan, 1982-83, Jilin U., Peoples Republic China, 1987, U. Munich, 1988, U. Graz, Austria, 1989, 2003; Fulbright prof. U. Bonn, Germany, 1995-96, Nat. U. Costa Rica, 2000. Author: Friedrich Schlegel's Lucinde and the Fragments, 1971, Aldous Huxley, Satirist and Novelist, 1972, The Writer's Place: Interviews on the Literary Situation in Contemporary Britain, 1974; (with E.S. Firchow) East German Short Stories: An Introductory Anthology, 1979; The End of Utopia: A Study of Huxley's Brave New World, 1984; The Death of the German Cousin: Variations on a Literary Stereotype, 1986; translator (with E.S. Firchow) The Abbey (Alois Brandstetter), 1998, Envisioning Africa: Racism and Imperialism in Conrad's "Heart of Darkness", 2000, W.H. Auden: Contexts for Poetry, 2002, Reluctant Modernists: Aldous Huxley and Some Contemporaries, 2002; contbr. articles on modern lit. subjects to profl. jours. Fellow Inst. Advanced Studies in Humanities, Edinburgh, 1977, Christopher Iskerwood fellow Huntington Libr., 2006. Mem. Midwest Modern Lang. Assn. (v.p. 1977, pres. 1978), Am. Comparative Lit. Assn., Assn. Lit. Scholars and Critics, Internat. Aldous Huxley Soc. Home: 135 Birnamwood Dr Burnsville MN 55337-6814 Office: U Minn Dept English 310D Lind Hall 207 Church St SE Minneapolis MN 55455-0134 Office Phone: 612-625-3363. E-mail: pef@tc.umn.edu.

FIRE, ANDREW Z., pathologist, educator, geneticist; b. Santa Clara, Calif., 1959; BA in Math., U. Calif., Berkeley, 1978; PhD in Biology, MIT, 1983; postdoctoral studies, Med. Rsch. Coun. Lab., Cambridge, UK, 1983—86. Microbiologist, dept. embryology Carnegie Instn., Washington, 1986—2003; adj. prof., biology Johns Hopkins U., Balt., 2000—; prof., depts. pathology and genetics Stanford U. Sch. Medicine, Calif., 2003—. Adj. prof. biology Johns Hopkins U., 1986—2003. Contbr. articles in profl. jours. Co-recipient Nobel Prize in Physiology or Medicine, Nobel Found., 2006; recipient Maryland Disting. Young Scientist award, 1997, medal, Genetics Soc. Am., 2002, Wiley Prize, Rockefeller U., 2003, Dr. H.P. Heinken prize in biochemistry and biophysics, Netherlands Acad. Arts and Sci., 2004, Gairdner award, Gairdner Found., 2005. Fellow: Am. Acad. Arts and Scis.; mem.: Inst. Medicine, NAS (award in Molecular Biology 2003). Achievements include discovery of process now known as RNAi (with Craig C. Mello). Office: Dept Pathology and Genetics Stanford Univ Sch Medicine 300 Pasteur Dr L235 Stanford CA 94305-5324 Office Phone: 650-723-2885. Office Fax: 650-725-6902, 650-724-9070. Business E-Mail: afire@stanford.edu.*

FIRE, EDWARD, retired labor union administrator; b. Lowellville, Ohio; 3 children. Student, Youngstown State U. Prodn. worker Packard Electric divsn. GM, Warren, Ohio, 1958; v.p. AFL-CIO, Ohio; chmn. Gen.Motors Conf. Bd. Internat. Union Elec., Salaried Machine and Furniture, Washington, mem. exec. bd., 1975—, sec.-treas., 1982-96, pres., 1996—2003, IUE-CWA, 2003—06; ret., 2006. Mem. Exec. Coun., 1996—. Served USN.

FIREBAUGH, FRANCILLE MALOCH, academic administrator; b. El Dorado, Ark., July 15, 1933; d. Delton Verdis and Dorothy Lucille (Measeles) Maloch; m. John David Firebaugh, Dec. 28, 1970. BS, U. Ark., 1955; MS, U. Tenn., 1956; PhD, Cornell U., 1962. Instr. U. Tex., Austin, 1956-58; asst. prof. home econs. Ohio State U., Columbus, 1962-65, assoc. prof., 1965-69, prof., 1969-88; dir. Sch. Home Econs., 1973-82; acting v.p. agrl. adminstrn.; exec. dean of agr., home econs., natural resources, 1982-83; assoc. provost Office Acad. Affairs, 1983-84; vice provost for internat. affairs, 1984-88; acting provost, v.p. acad. affairs, 1985-86; dean coll. human ecology Cornell U., Ithaca, NY, 1988-99, dir. spl. projects office of pres. and provost, 2000—01, vice provost for land grant affairs, spl. asst. to the pres., 2001—05, sr. cons. to provost, 2005—. Mem. joint com. on agrl. rsch. and devel. Bd. Internat. Food and Agr., 1982-87; fis. fellow Internat. Agr. Author: Home Management: Context and Concepts, 1975, Family Resource Management, 1981, 88. Bd. dirs. Columbus Coun. on World Affairs, 1987-88, Boyce Thompson Inst. for Plant Rsch., 1991-97; moderator First Baptist Ch., 1981-83; bd. dirs. Cayuga Med. Ctr., 1992-2001, Panamerican Agr. Sch., Zamorano, Honduras, 1994—, Kendal at Ithaca, 1995-2003; Families and Work Inst., N.Y.C., 1995—; trustee Ithaca (N.Y.) Coll., 2000—, Cmty. Found. of Tompkins County, 2000-02. Mem. Nat. Coun. Family Rels., AAAS, Am. Home Econs. Found. (bd. dirs. 1987-90), Am. Assn. of Family and Consumer Scis., Ohio State U. Faculty Club (pres. 1988), Assn. Women in Devel. (sec. 1988-89), Sigma Xi, Sigma Delta Epsilon, Kappa Omicron Nu, Phi Upsilon Omicron, Gamma Sigma Delta, Phi Kappa Phi, Epsilon Sigma Phi. Office: Cornell U Office of Provost 449 Day Hall Ithaca NY 14853-2801 Home Phone: 607-257-8179. Business E-Mail: fmf1@cornell.edu.

FIREBAUGH, MILLARD S., naval engineer; m. Barbara Firebaugh; 2 children. Grad., MIT, 1961, ScD in Ocean Engring., 1972. Commd. engring. duty officer USN, advanced through grades to rear admiral, with Naval Sea Sys. Command, 1979, mgr. program for design and constrn. Seawolf Class subs., chief engr. Naval Sys. Sea Command, ret., 1995; v.p. innovation, chief engr. Gen. Dynamics Electric Boat Corp., Groton, Conn. Editor: Naval Engineering and American Sea Power. Mem. NAE, Am. Soc. Naval Engrs. (Naval Engrs. Gold medal), Conn. Acad. Sci. & Engring., Cosmos Club. Office: Gen Dynamics Elec Boat Corp 75 Eastern Pt Rd Groton CT 06340-4989 Home Phone: 860-572-4405; Office Phone: 860-433-1950.

FIREMAN, PAUL BARRY, footwear and apparel company executive; b. Cambridge, Mass., Feb. 14, 1944; m. Phyllis Fireman; 3 children. Student, Boston U. Pres., chmn., CEO Reebok Internat. Ltd. (acquired by Adidas-Salomon 2006), Stoughton, Mass., 1979—2006; advisor to chmn., CEO Adidas-Salomon AG, 2006—. Founder The Reebok Found.; founder Paul & Phyllis Fireman Found.; co-founder One Family, Inc., 1998—. Named one of 400 Richest Ams., Forbes mag., 2006; recipient numerous industry awards, Pvt. Sector Achievement award, Nat. Alliance to End Homelessness, 2005, honored by Human Rights Law Grp. Office: Reebok Internat Ltd 1895 JW Foster Blvd Canton MA 02021

FIREMAN, PHILIP, pediatrician, allergist, immunologist; b. Pitts., 1932; MD, U. Chgo., 1957. Diplomate Am. Bd. Allergy and Immunology (chmn. 1992-93). Intern Phila. Gen. Hosp., 1957-58; resident in pediatrics Children's Hosp., Pitts., 1958-60; fellow in allergy and immunology NIH, Bethesda, Md., 1960-62; fellow allergist, immunologist Harvard Children's Hosp., Boston, 1962-64; prof. pediatrics, internal medicine U. Pitts. Med. Sch. Chmn. Am. Bd. Allergy & Immunology, 1990—91. Recipient Disting. Alumni award, U. Chgo. Mem.: Am. Acad. Allergy, Asthma and Immunology (pres. 1997—98). Office: Childrens Hosp 3705 5th Ave Pittsburgh PA 15213-2583 Office Phone: 412-692-5103. Business E-Mail: philip.fireman@chp.edu.

FIRESIDE, HARVEY FRANCIS, political scientist, educator; b. Vienna, Dec. 28, 1929; came to U.S., 1940, naturalized, 1945; s. Norbert and Frances F.; m. Bryna Joan Levenberg, Dec. 12, 1959; children: Leela Ruth, Douglas Leonard, Daniel Ephraim. BA magna cum laude, Harvard U., 1952, MA, 1955; PhD, New Sch. Social Research, 1968. Info. specialist AEC, 1957-58; editor Palmerton Publishing Co., NYC, 1959-60, Am. Cyanamid Co., NYC, 1960-61, Fgn. Policy Assn., NYC, 1961-62; freelance editor, 1962-64; asst. prof. polit. sci. N.Y. Inst. Tech., 1964-68; Charles A. Dana prof. politics Ithaca (N.Y.) Coll., 1968-96, prof. emeritus, 1998. Fulbright advisor Cornell U., 2003—04, vis. prof. Einaudi Ctr. Internat. Studies, 2003-04; cons. in field. Author: Icon and Swastika: The Russian Orthodox Church under Nazi and Soviet Control, 1971, Soviet Psychoprisons, 1979, Brown vs Board of Education, 1994, Young People from Bosnia Talk About War, 1996, Plessy vs. Ferguson, 1997, The Fifth Amendment, 1998, New York Times vs. Sullivan, 1999, Nuremberg Trials of Nazi War Criminals, 2000, The Mississippi Burning Civil Rights Murder Conspiracy Trial, 2002, Separate and Unequal: Homer Plessy and the Supreme Court Decision That Legalized Racism, 2004; also articles. Group leader Amnesty Internat., Ithaca, 1973-80; co-chmn. Socialist Studies Com., NY, 1977-83, Working Group Against Psychiat. Abuse, 1980-83; bd. dirs. Tompkins County chpt. ACLU, 1968-71, Ithaca Sanctuary Com., 1986-92, Tompkins County Mental Health Assn., 1986-89, 93-95, pres., 1995-96; bd. dirs. Com. on U.S.-Latin Am. Rels., 1990-92, Hillel Found., Ithaca Coll., 1991-93; coord. The Border Fund, 1989—, Bosnian Student Project, 1994-2000; Citizenship Project, 1997-99, Eleanor Roosevelt Loan Fund, 2000—, Ithaca City of Asylum, 2001-03. Recipient Tompkins County Human Rights award, 1992, 98, Carter G. Woodson award Nat. Coun. Social Studies, 2003; Harvard U. Russian Rsch. Ctr. fellow, summers 1975, 80; fellow Harvard U. Ukrainian Rsch. Inst., summer 1976; fellow Cornell U. Inst. for European Studies, 1995-98, 2004-05, Peace Studies Program, 1998-01, Cornell Law Sch., 2001-03; grantee N.Y. Dept. Edn., 1965; vis. scholar Russian Inst., Columbia U., 1966; Nat. Endowment Humanities fellow, summer, 1983, 94. Mem. Am. Polit. Sci. Assn. Democrat. Jewish. Home: 202 Eastwood Ave Ithaca NY 14850-6239 Personal E-mail: hfireside@juno.com.

FIRESTONE, CHARLES MORTON, lawyer, educator; b. St. Louis, Oct. 16, 1944; s. Victor and Betty (Solomon) F.; m. Pattie Winston Porter, Apr. 19, 1975; children: Laurel, Asa. BA, Amherst Coll., 1966; JD, Duke U., 1969. Bar: DC 1969, US Ct. Appeals (DC cir.) 1970, US Ct. Appeals (5th cir.) 1972, US Ct. Appeals (9th cir.) 1973, US Ct. Appeals (2d cir.) 1975, US Ct. Appeals (3d cir.) 1976, US Ct. Appeals (8th cir.) 1977, U.S. Supreme Ct. 1977, Calif. 1983. Litigation atty. FCC, Washington, 1969-73; dir. litigation Citizens Comm. Ctr., Washington, 1973-77; adj. prof. law, dir. comm. law program UCLA, 1977-86; counsel Mitchell, Silberberg & Knupp, LA, 1983-90; vis. lectr. UCLA Sch. Law, 1986-90; exec. dir. comm. and society program Aspen Inst., 1989—, exec. v.p. policy programs and internat. activities, 1997—2000. Vis. prof. Duke U., Terry Sanford Inst. Pub. Policy, 2003; faculty adviser Fed. Comm. Law Jour., LA, 1977-86; counsel statewide TV debates LVW Calif., 1978-90, counsel Calif. media Dukakis-Bentsen Com.; co-cmmn. adv. com. LWC Calif. Speak Out 1988 Election Project; pres. Bd. Telecom. Commrs., City of LA, 1984-86; mem. nat. adv. bd. Privacy and Am.Bus., 1993-2000; mem. Commn. on Radio and Tv Policy, 1996. Author: (with Ellen Mickiewicz) Television and Elections, 1992, (with Donald R. Browne and Mickiewicz)

Television/Radio News and Minorities, 1994, (with Robert Entman, Dee Reid and Mickiewicz) Television, Radio & Privatization, 1998, (with Craig L. Lamay and Mickiewicz) Television Autonomy & the State, 1999, (with Mickiewicz Browne LaMay) Democracy on the Air, 2000; editor: Television for the 21st Century: The Next Wave, 1993, (with Jorge Reina Schement) Toward An Information Bill of Rights and Responsibilities, 1995, (with Amy Korzick Garmer) Creating a Learning Society: Initiatives for Education and Technology, 1996, (with Anthony Corrado) Elections in Cyberspace: Toward A New Era in American Politics, 1996, (with Garmer) Digital Broadcasting and the Public Interest, 1998; mem. editl. bd. Aspenia, 2000-04; contbr. articles to profl. jours., chpts. to books. Bd. dirs. Corp. for Disabilities and Telecom., L.A., 1980-82; bd. dirs. KCRW Found., Santa Monica, Calif., 1982-90, vice chmn., 1987-90; trustee Ctr. for Law in Pub. Interest, 1988-89; mem. adv. com. campaign Mondale for Pres., LA, 1984; mem. adv. com. Ctr. for Govtl. Studies, 2003-05; Campaign Legal Ctr., 2004—; mem. adv. bd. Anwarul Quadir Found., 2006—. Recipient cert. of commendation Mayor of LA, 1986, resolution commendation award City Coun. LA, 1986; Luther Ely Smith scholar and Andrew Laurie scholar Amherst Coll., 1965-66; Glocom fellow Japanese Inst. Global Comms., 2001—. Mem. ABA (chmn. broadcast and spectrum use com., sect. sci. and tech. 1981-83, chmn. electronic campaigning com. 1984-86), Fed. Comm. Bar Assn., Soc. Satellite Profls. (sec. bd. dirs. So Calif. chpt. 1984-87), Coun. Fgn. Rels., Cosmos Club (chmn. membership com.). Jewish. Office: 1 Dupont Cir NW Ste 700 Washington DC 20036-1133 Home Phone: 301-654-5528; Office Phone: 202-736-5818. Business E-Mail: firestone@aspeninstitute.org.

FIRESTONE, DAVID E., editor; Congl. corr., Washington Bur. NY Times, enterprise editor. Office: NY Times 229 West 43rd St New York NY 10036 Office Phone: 212-556-1533. Office Fax: 212-556-3690. E-mail: fstone@nytimes.com.

FIRESTONE, JAMES A., printing company executive; b. Huntington, NJ, Oct. 8, 1954; B in Internat. Econs., Georgetown U.; M in Mgmt., Yale U., New Haven. Various fin. and gen. mgmt. positions including pres. Japan divsn., pres. Travelers Cheque divsn. Am. Express, 1978—93; head consumer divsn. Ameritech, 1993—95; head consumer products and svcs. IBM, 1995—98; sr. v.p. corp. strategy and mktg. group, pres. Xerox Channels Group Xerox Corp., Stamford, Conn., 1998—2001, pres. corp. ops. group, 2001—04, pres. Xerox N.Am., 2004—, exec. v.p., 2007—. Bd. dirs. Fuji Xerox Co. Ltd. Office: Xerox Corp 800 Long Ridge Rd Stamford CT 06904 Office Phone: 203-968-3000.*

FIRESTONE, LOUISE, lawyer; b. 1956; BA in Internat. Rels., Johns Hopkins U., 1979; JD, Fordham U., 1985. Bar: NY 1986. Assoc. Cole & Dietz, 1985—86; v.p. Citibank, NA, 1986—91; dir. Credit Suisse First Boston, 1991—98; atty. Art & Auction LLC; sr. v.p. legal affairs, gen. counsel LVMH Moët Hennessy Louis Vuitton Inc., 2003—. Office: LVMH Moët Hennessy Louis Vuitton Inc 19 E 57th St New York NY 10022 E-mail: louise.firestone@lvmhny.com.

FIRESTONE, NANCY B., federal judge; b. Manchester, NH, Oct. 17, 1951; d. Albert and Bernice (Brown) F. BA, Washington U., St. Louis, 1973; JD, U. Mo., 1977. Bar: Mo. 1977, US Ct. Appeals (2nd, 4th, 5th, 6th, 9th, 8th and 10th cirs.). Trial atty. US Dept. Justice, Washington, 1977-84, asst. chief, 1984-85, dep. chief environ. enforcement, 1985-89, dept. asst. atty. gen. environment & natural resources divsn., 1995—98; assoc. dep. adminstr. EPA, 1989-92, adminstrv. judge, 1992-95; judge US Ct. Fed. Claims, 1998—. Adj. prof. Georgetown U. Law Ctr., 1986—. Mem. ABA. Office: US Ct Fed Claims 717 Madison Pl Washington DC 20005 Office Phone: 202-357-6540.

FIREY, WALTER IRVING, JR., retired sociologist; b. Roundup, Mont., Aug. 13, 1916; s. Walter Irving and Marie (Oveson) F.; m. Mary Lou Powell, Aug. 23, 1952; children: Paul, John. BA, Univ. Wash., 1938, MA, 1940; PhD, Harvard U., 1945. Asst. prof. Mich. State U., East Lansing, 1945-46; from asst. prof. to prof. emeritus Univ. Tex., Austin, 1946-85, prof. emeritus, 1985—. Author: Land Use in Central Boston, 1947, 3d edit., 1975, Man, Mind & Land, 1960, 3d edit., 1999, Law & Economy in Planning, 1965; contbr. numerous articles to profl. jours. Ctr. for Advanced Study in Behavioral Scis. fellow Stanford, Calif., 1959-60. Mem. Am. Sociological Assn., Rural Sociological Assn. (award of merit 1983), Sociological Rsch. Assn. (pres. 1972), Phi Beta Kappa. Presbyterian. Avocation: reading. Home: 1307 Wilshire Blvd Austin TX 78722

FIRMAGE, EDWIN BROWN, lawyer, educator; b. Utah, Oct. 01; s. Edwin Raddon and Mary Myrtice (Brown) F.; children: Edwin James, Miriam, Sarah, Zina, Joseph, Jonathan, David. BS, Brigham Young U., 1960, MS, 1962; JD, U. Chgo., 1963, LLM, SJD, 1964. Bar: Utah, US Supreme Ct. Staff v.p. Hubert Humphrey White House, Washington, 1965-66; assoc, asst. prof. U. Utah Law Sch., Salt Lake City, 1966-70, prof. of law, 1970—. Vis. scholar UN, NYC, 1970-71; internat. affairs fellow Coun. Fgn. Rels., Geneva, Switzerland, 1970-71; fellow in law and humanities Harvard Law Sch., Cambridge, 1974-75; sr. fellow Keynes Coll. U. Kent, Canterbury, Eng., 1987; vis. prof. U. Tex. Sch. of Law, Austin, summer 1979, Clark Law Sch., Brigham Young U., Provo, summer 1983, 86, U. London, 1992; Reynold's lectr. U. Utah, 1987; Lane lectr. Creighton U. Law Sch., 1992; Kellogg lectr. Episcopal Div. Sch., Cambridge, Mass., 1993. Author: Zion in the Courts: A Legal History of the Church of Jesus Christ of Latter-Day Saints, 1988 (Alpha Sigma Nu book award 1989), To Chain the Dog of War: The War Power of Congress in History of Law, 1989, Religion and the Law: Biblical, Jewish & Islamic Perspectives, 1990; editor: The International Legal System: Cases and Materials, 1995. Found. pres. Utah Opera Co., 1976-80, Utahn's United Against Nuclear Arms Race, 1981-84. Recipient Gov.'s award in the Humanities, 1989, Rosenblatt prize U. Utah, 1991; named Samuel D. Thurman prof. of Law Utah Law Sch., 1990. Mem. ABA, Am. Soc. Internat. Law, Utah Bar Assn., Phi Alpha Delta, Phi Kappa Phi, Pi Sigma Alpha. Achievements include working actively with refugees and others in exile in Vietnam, Thailand, Hong Kong, India, China, Russia and Tibet. Office: U Utah Coll Law Bldg Salt Lake City UT 84112 Home Phone: 801-364-2023; Office Phone: 801-581-7819. Personal E-mail: ed.firmage@comcast.net.

FIRMIN, MICHAEL WAYNE, psychology professor; b. New Orleans, July 28, 1961; s. Lloyd John and Betty L. (Shepherd) F.; m. Karen Sue Tuttle, Aug. 4, 1984; children: Ruth, Sarah. BA, Calvary Bible Coll., 1983; MA, Calvary Theol. Sem., 1985; MS, Bob Jones U., 1987, PhD, 1988; MA, Marywood U., 1992; PhD, Syracuse U. Nat. cert. counselor; lic. psychologist, Ohio. Dir. counseling svcs. Bapt. Bible Coll. of Pa., Clarks Summit, 1988-98, assoc. prof., 1988-98, chmn. divsn. grad. studies, 1995-97; resident in psychology TCN: Behavioral Health Svcs., 2000—01; assoc. prof. psychology Cedarville (Ohio) U., 1998—2004, prof. psychology, 2004—, chmn. dept. psychology, 2000—. Cons. for psychol. svcs. Assn. Bapts. for World Evangelism, Harrisburg, Pa., 1991—94, 1999—2003; clin. assessment cons. Keystone City Residence, 1994—2000. Editor: Jour. Ethnographic & Qualitative Rsch., 2006—. Pastor Faith Fellowship Bapt. Ch., Danbury, Conn., 1991-94. Mem. Psi Chi. Republican. Home: 84 E Elm St Cedarville OH 45314-8513 Office: Cedarville Univ 251 N Main St Cedarville OH 45314-0601

FIRST, MICHAEL BRUCE, psychiatrist, educator; b. Phila., Nov. 25, 1956; s. E. David and Reda Bell (Dissin) First; m. Leslee Juanita Snyder, Nov. 12, 2006. BS in Engring., Princeton U., NJ, 1978; MS in Computer Sci., U. Pitts., 1981, MD, 1983. Diplomate Am. Bd. Psychiatry and Neurology. Intern in medicine Shadyside Hosp., Pitts., 1983—84; resident in psychiatry Columbia-Presbyn. Hosp., NYC, 1984—87, pvt. practice, 1987—; fellow in biometrics N.Y. State Psychiat. Inst., NYC, 1986—88, rsch. psychiatrist, 1988—; prof. clin. psychiatry Columbia U., NYC, 2005—. Author: The Structured Clinical Interview for DSM-IV (SCID), 1994, DSM-IV Guidebook, 1995, DSM-IV Handbook, 1995, (computer software) DTREE: The DSM-IV Expert, 1997, Am I OK? A Layman's Guide to the Psychiatrist's Bible, 1999; editor: DSM-IV Text and Criteria, 1990—. Mem.: AMA, Am. Psychiat. Assn. Office: NY State Psychiat Inst 1051 Riverside Dr New York NY 10032-1013 Home Phone: 718-768-6088; Office Phone: 212-543-5531. Business E-Mail: mbf2@columbia.edu.

FIRSTENBERG, JEAN PICKER, film institute executive; b. NYC, Mar. 13, 1936; d. Eugene and Sylvia (Moses) Picker; m. Paul Firstenberg, Aug. 9, 1956 (div. July 1980); children: Debra, Douglas BS summa cum laude, Boston U., 1958. Asst. producer Altman Prodns., Washington, 1965-66; media advisor J. Walter Thompson, NYC, 1969-72; asst. for spl. projects Princeton U., NJ, 1972-74, dir. publs. NJ, 1974-76; program officer John and Mary R. Markle Found., NYC, 1976—80; CEO Am. Film Inst., L.A., Washington, 1980—. Mem. Citizens' Stamp Advisory Com., US Postal Svc., 2002-; bd. dirs. Trans-Lux Corp.; former chmn. nat. adv. bd. Peabody Broadcasting Awards; bd. dirs. Trans-Lux Corp. Former trustee Boston U.; mem. adv. bd. Will Rogers Inst., N.Y.C.; chmn., bd. advisors Film Dept. N.C. Sch. of Arts. Recipient Alumni award for disting. service to profession Boston U., 1982; seminar and prodn. chairs at directing workshop for women named in her honor Am. Film Inst., 1986 Mem. Women in Film (Crystal award 1990), Trusteeship for Betterment of Women, Acad. Motion Picture Arts and Scis. Office: Am Film Inst 2021 N Western Ave Los Angeles CA 90027-1657 Office Phone: 323-856-7677.

FIRTH, EVERETT JOSEPH, timpanist; b. Winchester, Mass., June 2, 1930; s. Everett Emanuel and Rosemary (Scandura) F.; m. Olga Kwasniak, June 22, 1960; children— Kelly Victoria, Tracy Kimberly. Mus.B. with distinction, 1952. Faculty head New Eng. Conservatory, 1950—; mem. faculty Berkshire Music Center, 1956—. Pres., CEO Vic Firth Inc. (mfr. and distbr. worldwide drum sticks and mallets); CEO Vic Firth Mfg., Newport, Maine. Solo timpanist, Boston Symphony Orch., 1952—2002, Boston Pops Orch., 1952—2002, with, Boston Symphony Chamber Players; Recs. with, RCA Victor, Mercury, Columbia, Cambridge, Deutsche Grammophon. Mem. ASCAP, Phi Kappa Lambda, Phi Mu Alpha Sinfonia. Home: 3 Pinewood Rd Dover MA 02030-2521 Office: Vic Firth Inc 65 Sprague St Boston MA 02136 Office Phone: 617-364-6869. Business E-Mail: vic@vicfirth.com.

FIRTH, NICHOLAS, recording industry executive; b. London; With Chappell Group, 1964—85; pres. Chappell Internat., 1981—85; v.p. pub. divsn. PolyGram, 1981—85; shareholder & CEO Music Theatre Internat., 1985—87; pres. BMG Music Pub. Worldwide, NYC, 1987—2002, chmn. & CEO, 2002—. Bd. dirs. Third St. Music Sch. Settlement, NYC. Recipient Abe Olman Publishers award, Songwriters Hall of Fame, 2003. Mem.: ASCAP (bd. dirs. 1994—, exec. com, articles of assn. com., fgn. rels. com., law & licensing com., legis. com., long range planning & mktg. com), Internat. Music Pubs. Assn., Nat. Music Pubs. Assn. Office: BMG Music Publishing 245 5th Ave 8th Fl New York NY 10016 Office Phone: 212-287-1300. Office Fax: 212-930-4263.*

FISCH, NATHANIEL JOSEPH, physicist; b. Montreal, Quebec, Can., Dec. 29, 1950; s. Mandel and Helene (Greenfield) F.; m. Tobe Michelle Mann, Aug. 12, 1984; children: Jacob, Benjamin, Adam. BS, MIT, 1972, MS, 1975, PhD, 1978. Researcher Princeton (N.J.) Plasma Physics Lab., 1978-91, assoc. dir. for acad. affairs, 1993—; dir. program in plasma physics Princeton U., 1991—, prof. astrophys. scis., 1991—. Cons. Exxon Rsch. and Engring., Clinton, N.J., 1981-86; vis. scientist IBM, Yorktown Heights, N.Y., 1986. Recipient fellowship Guggenheim Found., 1985, 1992 APS award for Excellence in Plasma Physics, Am. Phys. Soc., 1992, Bronze medal for Outstanding Mentor, US Dept. Energy, 2002, E.O. Lawrence award, US Dept. Energy, 2004. Fellow Am. Phys. Soc. (vice chair divsn. plasma physics 1996, chair-elect 1997, chair 1998, James Clerk Maxwell prize, 2005). Achievements include patents in new ways to produce current in plasmas. Office: Princeton U Forrestal Campus PO Box 451 MS30 Princeton NJ 08543-0451 E-mail: fisch@princeton.edu.

FISCH, ROBERT OTTO, medical educator; b. Budapest, Hungary, June 12, 1925; came to U.S., 1957. s. Zoltan and Irene (Manheim) F.; 1 dau., Rebecca A. Med. diploma, U. Budapest, 1951; study art, Acad. Fine Arts, Budapest, 1943, Mpls. Coll. Arts and Design, 1970-76. Gen. practice medicine, Hungary, 1951-55; pub. health officer, 1955; pediatrician Hosp. for Premature Children, Budapest, 1956; intern Christ Hosp., Jersey City, 1957-58; intern pediatrics U. Minn. Hosps., 1958-59, researcher, 1959-60, research fellow, 1961; instr. U. Minn. Sch. Medicine, 1961-63, asst. prof., 1963-72, assoc. prof., 1972-79, prof., 1979—, dir. phenylketonuric clinic, 1961-97. Author: Respiratory Diseases; PKU, Child Development (Best Cover Minn. Med. 1975), Light from the Yellow Star: A Lesson of Love from the Holocaust, 1994, The Metamorphosis to Freedom, 2000, Dear Dr. Fisch: Children's Letters to a Holocaust Survivor, 2004; contbr. articles to profl. jours.; exhibited art works in various one-man and group shows. Mem. Soc. Pediatric Rsch., Am. Physician Art Assn. (Best of Show award 2002, numerous others). Home: 1201 Yale Pl 2301 Minneapolis MN 55403 Home Phone: 612-375-9760. Personal E-mail: fisch001@umn.edu.

FISCH, SANFORD MICHAEL, lawyer; b. Newark, July 27, 1955; s. Theodore W. and Iris Fisch. BA magna cum laude, Boston U., 1977; JD, U. San Diego, 1980; M of Law-Tax, Georgetown U., 1982. Tax specialist Coopers & Lybrand, San Diego, 1982-84; ptnr. Rosenberg and Fisch, San Diego, 1984-88, Armstrong, Fisch & Tutoli, PLC, San Diego, San Francisco and Santa Clara, Calif., 1988—. Tchr. Am. Coll., Bryn Mawr, Pa., 1983; co-founder Am. Acad. Estate Planning Attys., 1992. Co-founder San Diego Sr. Olympics, 1988; mem. law review U. San Diego, 1979-80. Recipient Program of Yr. award San Diego Jewish Community Ctr., 1988. Mem. Nat. Mortar Bd. Office: Am Acad Estate Planning Attys Ste 850 4365 Executive Dr San Diego CA 92121 Office Phone: 858-453-2128. Office Fax: 858-535-8241. Business E-Mail: sandyf@aaepa.com.

FISCH, WILLIAM BALES, law educator; b. Cleve., May 11, 1936; s. Max Harold and Ruth Alice (Bales) F.; m. Janice Heston McPherson, Sept. 2, 1961 (dec. 1987); m. Suzanne Fischer Good, June 19, 1993 (dec. 1998); children: Katherine Emily, Stephen McPherson. AB, Harvard Coll., 1957; LLB, U. Ill., 1960; M.Comparative Law (univ. fgn. law fellow), U. Chgo., 1962; JUD, U. Freiburg, Germany, 1972. Bar: Ill. 1961, Mo. 1982. Assoc. firm Kirkland & Ellis, Chgo., 1962-65; asst. prof. law U. N.D., 1965-68, assoc. prof., 1968-70, U. Mo., Columbia, 1970-74, prof., 1974—, Isador Loeb prof. law, 1977—2003, prof. emeritus, 2003—. Author: Die Vorteilsausgleichung im amerikanischen und deutschen Recht, 1974; co-author: Problems, Cases and Materials on Professional Responsibility, 1985, 3d edit., 2004; bd. editors: Am. Jour. Comparative Law; contbr. articles, revs. to law jours. Alexander von Humboldt-Stiftung Rsch. fellow, 1968-69, 89-90; Fulbright-Hays Rsch. scholar Hamburg, Germany, 1980-81, 89-90; Max Planck Soc. Rsch. fellow, Hamburg, 1992. Mem. ABA, AAUP, Am. Law Inst. Office: U Mo Law Sch Columbia MO 65211-4300

FISCHBACH, CHARLES PETER, rail transportation executive, consultant, lawyer, arbitrator, mediator; b. Apr. 3, 1939; s. Howard C. and Pauline Lillian (Wasserman) F.; m. Paula Rae Steinhorn, July 15, 1973. BS, U. Wis., 1960, JD, 1967; MA, Rutgers U., 1962. Bar: Wis. 1967, U.S. Supreme Ct. 1974. Pvt. practice, Madison, Wis., 1967-68; labor rels. rsch. analyst and cons. NYC, 1968-70; asst. to exec. officer labor rels. and pers. N.Y.C. Transit Authority, 1970; labor rels. rsch. analyst NYC, 1970-72; exec. dir. Classified Mcpl. Employees Assn. Balt. City, 1972-74; labor rels. cons./arbitrator Balt., 1974-77; dir. labor rels., chief labor rels. officer, spl. labor counsel Chgo., Rock Island and Pacific R.R. Co., 1977-81, dir. pers. and employee rels., spl. labor counsel Chgo., 1981-84; dir. adminstrn. and human resources Chgo. Pacific Corp., 1984-85. V.p. Rock Island Improvement Co., 1984—85; dir. Peoria and Bur. Valley R.R. Co., 1984—85; arbitrator, mediator, 1985—; lectr. Am. Mgmt. Assn., Am. Arbitration Assn. Collective Bargaining Inst. Contbg. editor: The Railway Labor Act, 1995; mem. editl. adv. panel Labor Rels. Bull. Aspen Pubs., Inc., 1999-2003; contbr. articles to profl. jours. Mem. Acad. Poli. Sci., Columbia U., 1972—75; advisor Balt. City Commn. on Aging, 1973—74; pub. sector labor rels. conf. bd. U. Md., 1973—77; advisor Balt. City Charter Revision Commn., 1974—75; landlord-tenant law study commn. State of Md., 1976—77; mem. Ill. Econ. Bd., 1988—90; coll. edn. adv. coun. Roosevelt U., 1990—93; gov.'s commn. on sci. and tech. State of Ill., 1990—98; Chgo. postal customer adv. coun. U.S. Postal Svc., 1994—95; Chgo. workforce bd. City of Chgo., 1999—2004, mayor's taskforce on employment of people with disabilities, 2002—05, chair employment barriers and model city work group, 2002—05; tax increment financing works adv. com. Mayor's Office of Workforce Devel., 2005—; bd. visitors dept. polit. sci. and LaFolette Sch. Pub. Affairs U. Wis., Madison, 2001—06, vice chair, 2002—05; chair Com. on Support for Tchg. and Rsch., 2002—05; referee Nat. R.R. Adjustment Bd., Ill. State Bd. Edn. Panel Hearing Officers; arbitration panel Herzog Transit Svcs./Transp. Workers Union; neutral mem. mediation and arbitration Warner-Lambert Arbitration Panel, Montgomery Ward Holding Corp. and Loewen Group Internat. Alternative Dispute Resolution Panels; neutral mem. ADR Sys., Am. Arbitration and Mediation Panel; commr. Chgo. Commn. on Human Rels., 2005—. Recipient Am. Jurisprudence prize in corp. law Joint Pubs. of Annotated Reports Sys., 1966, cert. for encouragement of vol. dispute settlement procedures Am. Arbitration Assn., 1981-84; Hon. fellow Harry S. Truman Libr. Inst., 1976. Fellow: Coll. Labor and Employment Lawyers; mem.: ACLU, ABA, United Airlines and Internat. Assn. Machinists and Aerospace Workers (sys. bd. adjustment), Am. Airlines and Airline Pilots Assn., So. Poverty Law Ctr., Labor and Employment Rels. Assn., Am. Arbitration Assn. (chmn. Chgo. regional office labor adv. com. 1998—2001), Nat. Hist. Soc., State Bar Assn. Wis., Am. Found. Automation and Employment, Ill. Pub. Employee Arbitration Mediation Panel, Nat. Mediation Bd. Register of Arbitrators, Fed. Mediation and Conciliation Svc. Roster of Arbitrators, Negro Leagues Baseball Mus., Nat. Civil Rights Mus., The Art Inst. Chgo., U.S. Holocaust Meml. Mus., Nat. Assn. R.R. Referees (regional v.p. 1996—2000), Rutgers Alumni Assn., Wis. Alumni Assn., Friends of the Nat. Baseball Hall of Fame and Mus., Soc. Am. Baseball Rsch., Statue of Liberty -Ellis Island Found. (charter). Avocations: coin collecting/numismatics, stamp collecting/philately, reading, baseball, art. Office: 1122 N Clark St Ste 2303 Chicago IL 60610-2866 also: Ste 305-PMB 110 3455 Peachtree Industrial Blvd Duluth GA 30096-6501 Office Phone: 312-664-3415. Personal E-mail: cpfischbach@gmail.com.

FISCHBACH, GERALD D., dean, neurobiology educator; b. New Rochelle, NY, Nov. 15, 1938; children: Elissa, Peter, Neal, Mark. AB, Colgate U., 1960; MD, Cornell U., 1965; MA (hon.), Harvard U., 1978. Intern U. Washington Hosp., Seattle, 1965-66; sr. surgeon, Pub. Health Svc., Lab. of Neurophysiology, Nat. Inst. Neurol. Diseases and Stroke NIH, Bethesda, Md., 1966-69; fellow Behavioral Biology Br. Nat. Inst. Child Health, 1969-73; assoc. prof. pharmacology Harvard Med. Sch., Boston, 1978-81, prof., 1978-81; Edison prof. neurobiology, chmn. dept. anatomy and neurobiology Washington U. Sch. Med., St. Louis, 1981-90; Nathan Marsh Pusey prof. neurobiology, chair dept. neurobiology Harvard Med. Sch., Mass. Gen. Hosp., Boston, 1990-98; dir. Neurol. Disorders and Stroke NIH, Bethesda, Md., 1998—2001; exec. v.p. for health and biomed. sciences, dean, faculty medicine Columbia U. Coll. of Physicians and Surgeons, NY, 2001—. Mem. exec. com. Program in Cell and Devel. Biology, Harvard Med. Sch., 1974-81; nonresident tutor Leverett House, Harvard Coll., 1974-77; clk. of corp. Marine Biol. Lab., Woods Hole, Mass, 1978-81, trustee, 1982—, exec. com., 1984-89; master Fuller Albright Acad. Soc., Harvard Med. Sch., 1979-81, faculty coun., 1980-81; chmn. Gordon Conf. on Molecular Pharmacology, 1983; dir. Ctr. for Cellular and Molecular Neurobiology, Washington U. Sch. of Med., 1983-90, dir. Jacob Javits Ctr. for Excellence in Neurosci., 1985-90, dir. Ctr. for Higher Brain Function, 1988-90, mem. Med. Ctr. Bd., 1989-90; dir. Neurosci. Ctr., Mass. Gen. Hosp., 1990—; mem. adv. bd. Nat. Spinal Cord Injury Assn., 1978—, Neurology B Study Sect., NIH, 1978-80, Alfred P. Sloan Found., 1984-89, Dept. Biology Adv. Coun., Princeton U., 1984-88, Fidia Rsch. Found., 1986—, McKnight Neurosci. Rsch. Awards Rev. Com., 1986—, Howard Hughes Med. Inst., 1988—, SUNY Health Sci. Ctr. at Bklyn, 1988—, Helen Hay Whitney Found., 1991, Children's Hosp., Boston, 1991; vis. prof. Dept. Pharmacology U. Calif. at San Francisco, 1978; lectr. Disting. Lecture Series in Pharmacology, U. Md. Sch. Medicine, 1978, 25th Ann. Bishop Lecture, Washington U. Sch. Medicine, 1980, Disting. Lecture Series, Dept. Zoology, U. Tex., 1981; invited speaker 5th Ann. Meeting European Neurosci. Assn., 1981; Alden Spencer lectr. Coll. Physicians and Surgeons, Columbia, U., 1981, Stephen W. Kuffler lectr. Harvard Med. Sch., 1990, numerous others; assoc. Neurosci. Rsch. Program, 1981—. Editor Jour. Cell Biolog, 1985-86; assoc. editor Devel. Biology, 1974-78, Jour. Neurophysiology, 1975-81, 1989—, Jour. Neurobiology, 1986—; corr. editor Proc. Royal Soc., Series B, London, 1989—; contbr. articles to profl. jours. Recipient Polk award Cornell U., 1965, Mathilde Solowey award Found. for Advanced Edn. in the Scis., NIH, 1975, W. Alden Spencer award Coll. Physicians and Surgeons, Columbia U., 1981; N.Y.State Regents scholar, 1956-60, N.Y. State med. scholar, Cornell U., 1962-65; Salk Inst. non-resident fellow, 1990. Mem. Soc. for Neurosci. (llth ann. lectr., pres.-elect 1982-83, pres. 1983-84), Soc. Gen. Physiologists, Am. Soc. Cell Biology, NAS (mem. governing coun. 2005-), Phi Beta Kappa. Office: Columbia U Coll Physicians and Surgeons 630 West 168th St P&S 2-401 New York NY 10032

FISCHBACH, PETER, pediatrician; b. NYC, Jan. 26, 1965; MA, Washington U., St. Louis, MD, 1993. Diplomate Am. Bd. Pediat., 2007. Assoc. prof. Emory U., Atlanta, 2006—. Fellow: Heart Rhythm Soc., Am. Coll. Cardiology; mem.: Pediatric and Congenital Electrophysiology Soc. (treas., exec. bd. mem.). Office: Sibley Heart Ctr Cardiology 2835 Brandywine Atlanta GA 30341 Office Phone: 404-256-2593.

FISCHBEIN, CHARLES ALAN, pediatrician; b. Newark, June 5, 1945; s. Martin and Naomi (Litzky) F.; m. Ellen Ruth Niemtzow, Aug. 10, 1969; children: Melissa Paige, Neil Todd. BA in Biology, Case Western Reserve U., 1966; MD, SUNY, Buffalo, 1970. Diplomate Am. Bd. Pediatrics. Resident in pediatrics Children's Hosp. Med. Ctr., Cin., 1970-72, fellow in pediatric cardiology Boston, 1972-74; pvt. practice pediatrics, 1974—; pres. Pediatric Assocs. of Conn., Waterbury, 1982—; asst. clin. prof. U. Conn. Med. Sch., Farmington, Conn., 1974—, Yale U. Sch. Medicine, New Haven, Conn., 1974—; acting co-chief dept. pediatrics St. Mary's Hosp., Waterbury, Conn., 1995-97. Fellow Am. Acad. Pediatrics; mem. AMA, Am. Coll. Sports Medicine. Avocation: mountain biking. Office: Pediatric Assocs Conn PC 160 Robbins St Waterbury CT 06708-2652 Office Phone: 203-755-2999.

FISCHEL, WILLIAM ALAN, economics professor; b. Bethlehem, Pa., Apr. 10, 1945; s. John Jacob and Lois T. (Yerger) F.; m. Janice M. Goldberg, Aug. 5, 1973; 1 child, Joshua. BA, Amherst Coll., 1967; PhD, Princeton U., 1973. Prof. Dartmouth Coll., Hanover, NH, 1973—, dept. chair, 2000—02, Patricia F. and William B. Hale prof. in arts and sci.,

2002—. Vis. assoc. prof. U. Calif., Davis, 1980-81; vis. prof. U. Calif., Santa Barbara, 1985-86, 2005-06, U. Wash., Seattle, 1998-99; adj. prof. Vt. Law Sch., South Royalton, 1985, 87-92. Author: Economics of Zoning Laws, 1985, Regulatory Takings, 1995, Homevoter Hypothesis, 2001; mem. editl. bd. Land Econs. Jour., 1984—, Ea. Econ. Jour., 1992-2005. Mem. Zoning Bd., Town of Hanover, N.H., 1987-97, chmn., 1993-97; dir. Lincoln Inst. Land Policy, 2006-. Olin fellow U. Calif., Berkeley, 1991-92. Mem. Phi Beta Kappa, Psi Upsilon. Home: 2 Read Rd Hanover NH 03755-1909 Office: Dartmouth Coll Dept Econs Hanover NH 03755 Business E-Mail: Bill.Fischel@Dartmouth.Edu, waf@dartmouth.edu.

FISCHELL, ROBERT ELLENTUCH, physicist; b. NYC, Feb. 10, 1929; s. Philip and Julia (Ellentuch) Fischell; m. Marian Standard (dec. May 2005); children: David R., Tim A., Scott J.S.; m. Susan Rudolph, Sept. 3, 2006. BSMechE cum laude, Duke U., 1951; MS in Physics, U. Md., 1953, ScD (hon.), 1996. Physicist U.S. Naval Ordnance Lab., Silver Spring, Md., 1951—56; prin. staff engr. Emerson Rsch. Labs., Silver Spring, 1956—60; various staff positions Applied Physics Lab., Johns Hopkins U., Laurel, Md., 1959—97, prin. profl. physicist, 1962—, chief engr. space dept., 1972—80, chief tech. transfer space dept., 1978—88; pres., chmn. bd. MedInnovations, Inc., Dayton, Md., 1988—90; chmn. bd. MedInTec, Inc., Dayton, Md., 1990—; pres. Fischell Biomed. LLC, 2000—; prof. practice of engring. U. Md., 2003—. Chmn. bd., v.p. R & D Cathco, Inc., 1991—; pres., chmn. bd. IsoStent, Inc., Dayton, Md., 1993—; chmn. emeritus NeuroPace, Inc., Dayton, 1997—; cons. Cordis, a J&J Co., 1998—; expert witness Brown and Bain, Palo Alto, Calif., 1992—93; rsch. assoc. in medicine Johns Hopkins U. Sch. Medicine, 1983—95, Yale U. Sch. Medicine, 1988—95; mem. exec. panel Chief of Naval Ops., Washington, 1983—87; expert witness Fish and Neave, NYC, 1986—92; field reviewer for orphan products FDA, 1984—90; mem. rsch. com. Md. affiliate Am. Heart Assn., 1985—87; mem. tech. com. on space guidance and control AIAA, 1972—75, chmn. nat. conf., 1973; mem. space com. Internat. Fedn. Automatic Control, 1970—75; mem., chmn. photovoltaic specialities com. IEEE, 1959—72; chmn., pres. Angel Med. Sys., Inc., 2001—, Neuralieve, Inc., 2002—; dir. U. Sys. Md. Author over 50 tech. publs.:, assoc. editor: AIAA Jour. Spacecraft and Rockets, 1972—75; holder 110 patents in field of biomed. engring., biomed. devices and spacecraft. Bd. visitors U. Md., 1997—; trustee U. Md. Found., 2000—. Named Disting. Citizen of Yr., "M" Club U. Md., 1984; named to Space Tech. Hall of Fame, U.S. Space Found., 1988; recipient Tech. Achievement award, ASME, 1962, Outstanding Young Engr. award, Washington Capitol area, 1963, awards for most significant inventions, Indsl. Rsch. mag., 1967, 1970, 1973, Inventor of Yr. award, Intellectual Property Owners Assn., 1984, Gold medal for contbn. to aerospace sci. and tech., N.Y. Acad. Sci., 1987, Exceptional Engring. award for MAGSAT satellite, NASA, 1980, Individual Achievement award for human tissue stimulator, 1982, Exceptional Engring. medal, 1984, Space Act prize, 1984, Disting. Engring. Alumnus award, Duke U., 1992, Tech. for Humanity award, Discover Mag., 1993, TED prize, Tech., Entertainment, Design Conf., 2004, Woodrow Wilson award for pub. svc., 2006. Mem.: NAE, N.Y. Acad. Scis., Internat. Soc. for Artificial Organs, Beta Omega Sigma, Pi Tau Sigma, Sigma Pi Sigma, Pi Mu Epsilon, Tau Beta Pi, Phi Beta Kappa. Avocations: tennis, sailing. Home and Office: MedInTec Inc 14600 Viburnum Dr Dayton MD 21036-1247 Home Phone: 301-854-0606; Office Phone: 301-854-0606. Personal E-mail: mfischell@aol.com.

FISCHELL, TIM ALEXANDER, cardiologist; b. Washington, Feb. 10, 1956; s. Robert Ellentuch and Marian (Standard) F.; m. Anne Elizabeth Arbetter, Sept. 23, 1984; children: Evan Daniel, Jonathan Morris, Emma Julia. AB, Cornell U., 1977, MD, 1981. Diplomate Am. Bd. Internal Medicine (subspeciality cardiovas. disease and interventional cardiology). Intern internal medicine Harvard/Mass. Gen. Hosp., Boston, 1981-82, resident, 1982-84; fellow cardiology Stanford U., Calif., 1984-87, asst. prof. medicine Calif., 1987-92; assoc. prof. medicine Vanderbilt U., Nashville, 1992-96; dir. cardiovascular rsch., Borgess Rsch. Inst. Mich. State U., Kalamazoo, 1996—, prof. medicine, 1996—; cardiologist Heart Ctr. for Excellence, Kalamazoo. Med. adv. bd. Scimed, Mpls., 1992—, Cardeon, Inc., Fremont, Calif., 1993—, Isostent, Inc., San Carlos, Calif., 1995-; lectr. in field. Patentee in field; contbr. articles to profl. jours., chpts. to books. Recipient Fischbach Residency Scholarship, 1986, Nat.Rsch. Svc. award grant NIH, 1986-87, clin. investigator award NIH, 1987-92, biomed. rsch. support grant NIH/Stanford U., 1988-90; Inventor of Yr. prize Thoraxcenter Course on Intracoronary Stenting, Rotterdam, The Netherlands, 1996. Fellow Am. Coll. Cardiology, Soc. Cardiac Angiography and Interventions, Andreas Gruntzig Soc., Am. Heart Assn. (coun. on circulation, advanced fellowship award Calif. affiliate 1987, grant in aid award 1988-90), Phi Beta Kappa, Phi Kappa Phi, Alpha Omega Alpha. Achievements include patents pending in field; patents in field; pioneered the world's first radioisotope stent; co-inventor of the BX Velocity Stent for the Johnson & Johnson Company inserted for blocked arteriesin 2000; co-inventor of the cardiosaver system. Avocations: basketball, tennis, skiing, golf. Home: 1701 Embury Rd Kalamazoo MI 49008 Office: Borgess Health Heart Center for Excellence 1722 Shaffer St Suite 1 Kalamazoo MI 49048 Office Phone: 269-226-8374, 269-226-8362, 269-381-3963. E-mail: taf1@net-link.net.

FISCHER, ALFRED GEORGE, geology educator; b. Rothenburg, Germany, Dec. 10, 1920; arrived in US, 1935; s. George Erwin and Thea (Freise) F.; m. Winnifred Varney, Aug. 26, 1939; children: Joseph Fred, George William, Lenore Ruth. Student, Northwestern Coll., Watertown, Wis., 1935-37; BA, U. Wis., 1939, MA, 1941; PhD, Columbia U., 1950. Instr. Va. Poly. Inst. and State U., Blacksburg, 1941-43; geologist Stanolind Oil & Gas Co., Kans. and Fla., 1943-46; instr. U. Rochester, NY, 1947-48; from instr. to asst. prof. U. Kans., Lawrence, 1948-51; sr. geologist Internat. Petroleum, Peru, 1951-56; prof. geology Princeton (N.J.) U., 1956-84, U. So. Calif., LA, 1984, now prof. emeritus. Co-Author: Invertebrate Fossils, 1952, The Permian Reef Complex, 1953, Electron Micrographs of Limestone, 1967; editor: Petroleum and Global Tectonics, 1975. Recipient Verrill medal Yale U. Fellow Geol. Soc. Am. (Penrose medal 1993), Geol. Soc. London (hon., Lyell medal 1992), Soc. Econ. Paleontologists (hon., Twenhofel medal); mem. AAAS, NAS, U.S. Nat. Acad. Sci., Am. Assn. Petroleum Geologists, Paleontol. Soc. (medal 1995), German Geol. Soc. (Leopold von Buch medal), Geol. Union (Gustav Steinmann medal 1992), Mainz Acad. Sci. Lit. (corr.), Lincei Acad. Rome (fgn.), U.S. Nat. Acad. Sci., Sigma Xi. Home: 1736 Perch St San Pedro CA 90732-4218 Office: U So Calif Dept Earth Scis Zumberge Hall of Sci 117 Univ Park Los Angeles CA 90089-0001

FISCHER, BRADLEY J., film company executive; b. Sept. 8, 1976; Grad. in Film Studies and Psych., Columbia U., NYC, 1998. Intern Brillstein-Grey, NYC; exec. asst. to Mike Medavoy Phoenix Pictures, 1998—99, dir. devel., 1999—2002, v.p. prodn., 2002—04, sr. v.p. prodn., 2004—. Co-exec. prodr.: (films) Basic, 2003; exec. prodr.: Pathfinder, 2007; prodr.: Resurrecting the Champ, 2007, Zodiac, 2007. Office: Phoenix Pictures Inc Frankovitch Bldg 10202 W Washington Blvd Culver City CA 90232 Office Phone: 310-244-6540. E-mail: bfischer@phoenixpictures.com.*

FISCHER, BRUCE G., gas industry executive; BS, Drexel U., 1976, MBA, 1983. Logistics and sys. mgr. Sunoco Inc., 1989—95; gen. mgr. Sunoco MidAmerica Mktg. and Refining, 1995—99, v.p., gen. mgr., 1999—2000; v.p. Sunoco Chems., 2000—02; sr. v.p. Sunoco Inc., Phila., 2002—. Office: Sunoco Inc Ten Penn Ctr 1801 Market St Philadelphia PA 19103-1699

FISCHER, CARL, photographer, graphic designer, actor; b. NYC, May 3, 1924; s. Joseph Albert and Irma (Schwerin) F.; m. Marilyn Wolf, Oct. 30, 1949; children: Kim Alison Lloyd-George, Douglas James, Kenneth Lee. BFA, Cooper Union Sch. Art, 1948; postgrad., Ctrl. St. Martins Coll. Art & Design, London, 1952. Designer Columbia Records, 1948, Look mag., 1949-51; asst. art dir. William H. Weintraub & Co., 1952-54; art dir. Sudler & Hennessey, 1954-56, Grey Advt., 1956-58; owner Carl Fischer Photography Inc., NYC, 1960—. Adj. prof. art Cooper Union; TV, film dir.; William A. Reedy Meml. lectr. Rochester Inst. Tech. Exhibited Mus. Modern Art, 1965, Whitney Mus. Am. Art, 1974, Pentagram Gallery, London, 2004, Galleria Carla Sozzani, Milan, 2004, Gallerie Colette, Paris, 2004, Nat. Portrait Gallery, London, 2005, Irvine Contemporary, Washington, DC, 2006, Staley & Wise Gallery, NY, 2006, Ludwig Mus., Cologne-Koblenz, Germany, 2007; represented in permanent collections, Met. Mus. Art, NYC, Corcoran Gallery Art, Washington, DC, Rose Art Mus., Amherst, Mass., Internat. Ctr. Photography, NYC, Internat. Mus. Photography at George Eastman House, Rochester, Spencer Mus. Art, Lawrence, Kans.; contbg. editl. photographer various mags. including London Observer, London Sunday Times, Time, Life, Fortune, Esquire, NY; author: Photographs: 1958 to 1988, Portraits: 1953 to 1984. With AUS, 1942-45, PTO. Fulbright grantee, 1951; recipient Profl. Achievement citation Cooper Union, 1966, St. Gaudens medal, 1969, Mark Twain Jour. award, 1971, Cleo award, 1980. Mem. Actors Equity Assn., SAG, Dirs. Guild, Art Dirs. Club (past pres., gold and silver medals), Century Assn. Office: 121 E 83d St New York NY 10028-0821 Office Phone: 212-794-0400. E-mail: FischerNY@mac.com.

FISCHER, CARL ROBERT, retired health facility administrator; b. Rahway, NJ, Nov. 15, 1939; s. Robert Carlton and Elsie Marie (Wolfarth) F.; m. Lynn Elaine Ekstrand, Mar. 12, 1966; children: Kristen, Leslie, Meredith, Kelly. BSN, Wagner Coll., 1964; MS, SUNY-Buffalo, 1966; MPH, Yale U., 1968. With Yale-New Haven Hosp., 1968-77, assoc. dir., 1975-77; exec. assoc. adminstr. U. Cin. Med. Ctr., 1977-80; exec. dir. clin. programs U. Ark. for Med. Scis., Little Rock, 1980-86; assoc. v.p. health scis., CEO Med. Coll. of Va. Hosps., Richmond, 1986-99; exec. v.p. corp. functions VCU Health Sys., 1999—2002; ret., 2003. Bd. dirs. Univ. Health Systems Consortium, exec. com. 1994-2000, chmn. bd. dirs. 1997-98, chmn. supply and svcs. divsn., 1988-89, 95-96; mem. exec. com. Nat. Assn. Pub. Hosps., 1999-2002. Pres. Ctrl. Va. Health Planning Agy., 1991-93, mem.-at-large, 1997-2002, exec. com., 2000-2002; bd. dirs. Richmond Luth. Home, 2000-01. Mem. Am. Assn. Med. Colls., Am. Hosp. Assn., Va. Hosp. Assn. (bd. dirs. 1986-91, 99-2000, chmn. coun. on adminstrn. and health planning 1988, coun. on assn. devel. 1987-88, physician liaison com. 1989-90, chmn. ctrl. Va. regional planning coun. 1997-99).

FISCHER, CRAIG LELAND, physician; b. Bklyn., Feb. 17, 1937; s. Emil Carl and Ruth Barbara (Minarcik) F.; m. Sandra Lucile Canfield, Feb. 17, 1962; children: Craig L. Jr., Emil Lewis, Lisa Anne. BS, Kans. State U., 1958; MD, U. Kans., 1962. Diplomate Nat. Bd. Med. Examiners, Am. Bd. Family Practice; cert. anat. and clin. pathology, nuclear medicine. Intern in anatomic pathology Kansas U. Med. Ctr., 1962—63, resident in anatomic pathology, 1963—64, rsch. fellow in pathology (pub. health svc.), nuc. medicine, 1962—64, rsch. fellow pathology, nuc. medicine, 1965—66; resident in clin. pathology, Meth. Hosp. Baylor U. Coll. Medicine, 1967—68; rsch. med. officer Manned Spacecraft Ctr., NASA, Houston, 1965—68, pathologist, chief clin. labs., 1968—71; chief med. ops. Johnson Space , NASA, Houston, 1980—82; assoc. dir. labs. to dir. labs. Eisenhower Med. Ctr., Rancho Mirage, Calif., 1971—78, dir. nuc. med., 1975—78, gen. practice medicine Palm Desert, 1978—80; pathologist, co-dir. Valley Clin. Labs., Palm Desert, 1982—99; gen. practice medicine Indio, Calif., 1982—99; dir. post grad. edn. J.F. Kennedy Hosp., 1982—92; dir. Fischer and Yao Cons. Pathologists, Indio, 1987—89; pres. Fischer Assocs., Cons. in Pathology, Indio, 1989—95; ptnr. Fischer and Starke Assocs., Indio, 1995—99; aviation med. examiner FAA, 1991—99; asst. dir. space medicine NASA Johnson Space Ctr., 1999—2001, assoc. dir. clin. lab., 1999—, chief, Space Medicine & health Care Sys. Office, 2001—03, asst. dir. internat. space medicine, 2003—07. Clin. prof. dept. preventive medicine and cmty. health U. Tex. Med. Br., Galveston, 2002-07; asst. clin. prof. U. Calif., Irvine, 1986-99; mem. sci. adv. bd. Dept. Air Force, Washington, 1986-90, NAE, NRC; mem. Air Force Studies Bd., Washington, 1987-93; mem. aerospace med. adv. com. Office Space Scis. and Applications, NASA Hdqrs., Washington, 1988-93, chmn. operational medicine discipline working group, Life Scis. Directorate, 1988-92, mem. Shuttle-Mir Joint Sci. Working Group, 1993-94, mem. Adv. Coun. Task Force on the Shuttle-Mir Rendezvous and Docking Missions, 1995; mem. Mir Sci. Program Rev. Panel, 1993-98; mem. Internat. Space Sta. Task Force (Stafford Commn.), 1998—; chmn. multinat. med. ops. panel Internat. Space , 2000-04, chmn. Space Medicine Ops. Team, 2000-04, co-chmn. crew safety working group, 2004-07; cons. lab. medicine project tektite U.S. Dept. Interior, 1969-70. Contbr. numerous articles to profl. jours. Capt. USAF, 1964-66; lt. col. USAFR, 1983-97. Recipient Group Achievement award NASA Manned Spacecraft Ctr., 1966, 69, 70, Group Achievement award Gemini support team NASA Manned Spacecraft Ctr., Apollo 7 Flight Ops. Team award NASA Manned Spacecraft Ctr., 1969, Sustained Superior Achievement award NASA Manned Spacecraft Ctr., 1969, Superior Achievement award, 1969, Skylab Group Achievement award NASA Johnson Space Ctr., 1974, Presdl. medal of Freedom Apollo 13 Mission Ops. Team, 1970, Group Achievement award NASA Space Shuttle Launch and Ops. Team NASA Manned Spacecraft Ctr., 1982, Meritorious Civilian Svc. award Dept. of Air Force, 1990, Spl. Profl. Achievement award, STS-107 Columbia Contingency Support Team, 2003, Russian Fedn. Space Agy. award for internat. coop. in space exploration, 2005, Exceptional Svc. medal NASA, 2006, Silver Snoopy award Shuttle Comdr. Robert Cabana, 2006, NASA Exceptional Achievement award, 2007. Fellow Am. Coll. Preventive Medicine, Am. Coll. Nuc. Physicians, Coll. Am. Pathologists, Am. Soc. Clin. Pathologists (CCE Commr.'s medal 1989), Aerospace Med. Assn., Riverside County Med. Assn. (councilor 1984-89, pres. 1990-91, alt. delegate 1991-96, councilor 1996-99, Outstanding Contbn. to Medicine award 1996), Palm Springs Acad. Medicine (pres. 1988-89). Republican. Avocations: sailing, tennis, flying. Home: 3134A NASA Rd 1 #113 Seabrook TX 77586 Home Phone: 832-326-8451. Personal E-mail: clfspacemed@aol.com.

FISCHER, DAVID CHARLES, lawyer; b. Columbia, SC, Oct. 10, 1952; s. Emeric and Bernice (Cooper) F.; m. Vicki Joyce Stoller, Nov. 9, 1985; children: Adam, Jeremy. BA, Vanderbilt U., 1975; JD, Coll. William & Mary, 1978. Bar: Mich. 1978, N.Y. 1980. Lawyer GM, Detroit, 1978-79, NYC, 1979-80; assoc. Finley Kumble Wagner Heine Underberg & Casey, NYC, 1980-82, Burns Summit Rovins & Feldesman, NYC, 1982-86; ptnr. Summit Rovins & Feldesman, NYC, 1986-90, Loeb & Loeb, LLP, NYC, 1990—; sec. Standard Microsystems Corp., 1998—2002. Achievements include patents in field. E-mail: dfischer@loeb.com.

FISCHER, DAVID HACKETT, historian, educator; b. Balt., Dec. 2, 1935; s. John Henry and Norma (Frederick) Fischer; m. Judith Hummel, Nov. 23, 1960; children: Susanna, Anne. AB, Princeton U., 1958; PhD, Johns Hopkins U., 1962; MA (hon.), Oxford U., 1985. Mem. faculty Brandeis U., Waltham, Mass., 1962—, prof. history, 1970—, Earl Warren prof., 1971—, chmn. Am. history program, Univ. prof., 2002—. Vis. lectr. Harvard U., 1964-65; vis. prof. U. Wash., Seattle, 1975, U. Otago, New Zealand, 1999, U. Waikato, 1995; Harmsworth prof. Oxford U., 1985-86; Fulbright lectr., New Zealand, 1994, China, 2007. Author: Revolution of American Conservatism, 1965, Historians Fallacies, 1970, Growing Old in America, 1977, Albion's Seed: Four British Folkways in America, 1989, Paul Revere's Ride, 1994, The Great Wave: Price Movements in Modern History, 1996, Bound Away: Virginia and the Westward Movement, 2000, Washington's Crossing, 2004 (Nat. Book Award finalist, 2004, Pulitzer Prize for history, 2005), Liberty and Freedom, 2005; contbr. (with James McPherson) Times Atlas of World History, 1978; editor: Concord: A Social History of a New England Town, 1983, Brookline: A Social History of a Boston Suburb, 1985; co-editor: New England Studies, 2007, Pivotal Moments in American History, 2007. Fellow Queens Coll., Oxford, 1985 Mem. Am. Hist. Assn., Hakluyt Soc., Orgn. Am. Historians, Soc. Am. Historians, Am. Antiquarian Soc., St. Botolph Club (Boston), Princeton Club (N.Y.), Century Assn., Soc. Cin. Independent. Lutheran. Office: Brandeis U MS 036 415 South St Waltham MA 02453-2728 Office Phone: 781-736-2270. E-mail: fischer@brandeis.edu.

FISCHER, DAVID J., retired mayor; b. Evanston, Ill., July 24, 1933; m. Margo Fischer (dec.); children: Susan, David, James, Allison. BA in Bus. Adminstrn., Duke U., 1955. Chartered mcpl. fin. advisor, mcpl. bond dealer, 1958-90; pres., owner Fischer Johnson, Inc., 1977-86; mayor City of St. Petersburg, Fla., 1991—2001. Pres. Fla. Mcpl. Bond Coun., 1982-83, mem., 1975-90. Vice mayor St. Petersburg City Coun., 1978-79, mem., 1975-79; pres. Lakewood H.S. Parent Coun., 1973-74; chmn. Environ. Devel. Commn., 1972-75, Bayfront Ctr. Found. and Adv. Coun., 1989, mem., 1989-91; chmn. United Way Allocations and Admissions Com., 1967, treas., 1968-70; co-chmn. Cmty. Alliance, 1970-71; chmn. bd. trustees Eckerd Coll., 1985-87, trustee, 1979—; pres. Neighborhood Housing Svcs., 2003-; CEO, pres. Community Found. of Tampa Bay, 2004-; Served to capt. USAF, 1956-58. Recipient Leadership award St. Petersburg Alumni Assn., 1979, Disting. Citizen award U. So. Fla., 1994. Dist. committeeman Nat. Assn. Securities Dealers, 1980-83; pres. C. of C., 1982 (Outstanding Contbns. to Community award 1986). Office Phone: 813-282-1975.

FISCHER, DAVID JON, lawyer; b. Danville, Ill., July 27, 1952; s. Oscar Ralph and Sarah Pauline (Pomerantz) F. BA, U. Miami, 1974, JD, 1977. Bar: Fla. 1977, Iowa 1978, (mid. dist.) Fla. 1993, U.S. Ct. Appeals (8th cir.) 1978, U.S. Ct. Appeals (D.C. cir.) 1979, U.S. Ct. Appeals (llth cir.) 1984, U.S. Tax Ct. 1987, Ga. 1989, U.S. Dist. Ct. (no. dist.) Ga. 1990, U.S. Supreme Ct. 1990, U.S. Dist. Ct. (mid. dist.) Fla., 1993. Atty. Iowa Dept. Social Svcs., Des Moines, 1978; assoc. Parrish & Del Gallo P.C., Des Moines, 1978-79, Donald M. Murtha & Assocs., Washington, 1979-80; assoc. editor Lawyers Coop. Pub. Co., Washington, 1980-82; pvt. practice law Washington, 1982-83, Des Moines, 1983-84, Atlanta, 1984-93, Tampa, Fla., 1993, Atlanta, 1995-2000, Columbia, SC, 2004—; asst. dist. legal counsel Fla. Dept. Health and Rehab. Svcs., Largo, 1993-95; case law editor LexisNexis Group, 2001—03. Part-time atty. Fla. Dept. of Children and Families, 1996-2000; prof. John Marshall Law Sch., Atlanta, 1986-88; instr. legal studies program dept. ins. and risk mgmt. Ga. State U., 1988-93, instr. aviation adminstrn. program Coll. Pub. and Urban Affairs, 1989-93; apptd. gen. counsel Techwerks, Inc., Mo., 1990-92; instr. Bridge the Gap seminar, Inst. CLE in Ga., 1993; presenter State of Fla. Dept. Health and Rehabilitative Svcs. Dist. Legal Counsel Workshop, 1994, 96, 97; spkr. Clearwater Bar Assn., 1993, 94, 95. Author: The Aeronaut's Law Handbook, 1986, (with others) Georgia Corporate Practice Forms for the Small Business Attorney, 1992; contbg. editor Balloon Life mag., 1986-96; editor: (suppl.) Georgia Corporate Forms, 1993—, Florida Criminal Sentencing, 1997-99; author, editor: Georgia Corporate Forms, 3d edit., 2005. Vol. liaison Atlanta Com. for the Olympic Games, 1991—92. Mem. ABA (sect. com. 1980-82), Fed. Bar Assn., Iowa Bar Assn., State Bar Ga., Atlanta Bar Assn., Fla. Bar Assn., D.C. Bar Assn., Polk County Bar Assn., Pros. Attys. Coun. Ga. (tech. editor Computer Crime Jour.), U. of Miami Alumni Assn., Balloon Fedn. Am. (chmn. com. 1986-91), Carolinas Balloon Assn., Ga. Balloon Assn. (chmn. com. 1985-90), Chesapeake Balloon Assn., Great Ea. Balloon Assn., Alpha Epsilon Pi (hon., faculty advisor). Jewish. Avocations: hot air balloon pilot, writing, competitive sports. Personal E-mail: theschnauzers@yahoo.com.

FISCHER, DOROTHY VIRGINIA, retired small business owner; b. New Era, Mich., June 3, 1920; d. Charles August Prill and Harriet Sophia Nelson; m. Henry Fischer (dec.); children: Glen Charles, Bruce Douglas, Diane Renee. Grad., Shelby HS, Mich. Sec.-treas. US Agrl. Adjustment Adminstrn., Shelby, Mich., 1937—48, office asst., 1964—67; co-owner, bus. mgr. Fischer Trees, Evergreen Nursery and Christmas Trees, Rothbury, 1941—82; treas. Grant Twp., Rothbury, Mich., 1972—76. Editor: National Asparagus Festival Cookbook, 1978. Master Sylvan Grange, Rothbury, 1945; sec. Rothbury Farm Bur., 1945, Oceana County 4-H Coun., Hart, Mich., 1964—68; pres., sec. Nat. Asparagus Festival Com., Hart, 1973—78, chmn., 1977; sec. Oceana County Internat. Coun., Hart, 1973—83; v.p. Oceana County Extension Clubs, 1950; pres. New Era PTA, 1966—67; friendship ambassador Russia and Poland, 1973. Mem.: Sunshine Strollers Sq. Dance Club, Oceana County Hist. and Genealogy Soc. (life), Melody Mates, Savanna Club Art League, Oceana County 4-H Clubs (hon.). Democrat. Lutheran. Avocations: genealogy, travel, reading, dance, painting. Home: 358 W Arthur Rd Rothbury MI 49452

FISCHER, DUNCAN KINNEAR, neurosurgeon; b. Chapel Hill, NC, Sept. 14, 1957; s. Newton Duchan and Janet (Jordan) F.; m. Anne Holmes Billington, Sept. 10, 1983; children: Luke Duncan, Kent Billington, Duncan Newton II. AB, Princeton U., 1979; MPhil, Yale U., 1982, MD, PhD, 1986. Cert. in neurosurgery. Intern in surgery Baylor Coll. Medicine Affiliated Hosps., Houston, 1986-87, resident in neurosurgery, 1987-92; rsch. assoc. Baylor Coll. Medicine, Houston, 1988-92; neurosurgeon San Angelo Cmty. Med. Ctr. and Neurosurg. Ctr., Tex., 1992—, vice-chief staff, 2007—. Contbr. numerous articles to profl. publs. Med. Scientist Tng. Program scholar NIH, ACS scholar. Fellow ACS; mem. Harvey Cushing Soc., Am. Assn. Neurol. Surgeons, Sigma Xi, Phi Beta Kappa. Republican. Episcopalian. Achievements include extensive experience in outpatient spinal microsurgery. Office: 3515 Executive Dr San Angelo TX 76904-6883 Office Phone: 325-947-2525.

FISCHER, EDMOND HENRI, biochemistry educator; b. Shanghai, Apr. 6, 1920; arrived in U.S., 53; s. Oscar and Renée (Tapernoux) Fischer. Lic. es Sciences Chimiques et Biologiques, U. Geneva, 1943, Diplome d'Ingenieur Chimiste, 1944, PhD, 1947; D (hon.), U. Montpellier, France, 1985, U. Basel, Switzerland, 1988, Med. Coll. of Ohio, 1993, Ind. U., 1993, U. Bochum, Germany, 1994. Pvt. docent biochemistry U. Geneva, 1950—53; research assoc. biology Calif. Inst. Tech., Pasadena, 1953; asst. prof. biochemistry U. Wash., Seattle, 1953—56, assoc. prof., 1956—61, prof., 1961—90, prof. emeritus, 1990—. Mem. exec. com. Pacific Slope Biochem. Conf., 1958—59, pres., 1975; mem. biochemistry study sect. NIH, 1959—64; symposium co-chmn. Battelle Seattle Rsch. Ctr., 1970, 73, 78; mem. sci. adv. bd. Biozentrum, U. Basel, Switzerland, 1982—86, Weizmann Inst. Sci., Rehovot, Israel, 1998—, bd. govs., 1997—; mem. sci. adv. bd. Principe Felipe Sci. Mus., Valencia, Spain, 1998—, Friedrich Miescher Inst., Ciba-Geigy, Basel, 1976—84, chmn., 1981—84; mem. bd. sci. govs. Scripps Rsch. Inst., La Jolla, Calif., 1987—; mem. scientific adv. bd. Basel Inst. for Immunology, 1996—2001; bd. sci. govs. Scripps Rsch. Inst., La Jolla, Calif. Contbr. numerous articles to sci. jours. Mem. sci. council on basic sci. Am. Heart Assn., 1977—80; sci. adv. com. Muscular Dystrophy Assn., 1980—88. Recipient Lederle Med. Faculty award, 1956—59, Guggenheim Found. award, 1963—64, Disting. Lectr. award, U. Wash., 1983, Laureate Passano Found. award, 1988, Steven C. Beering award, 1991, Nobel prize in physiology or medicine, 1992. Fellow: Am. Acad. Arts and Scis.; mem.: AAUP, NAS, AAS, Am. Chem. Soc. (editl. adv. bd. Biochemistry 1961—66, adv. bd. biochemistry divsn. 1962, assoc. editor 1966—91, exec. com. divsn. biology 1969—72, monograph adv. bd. 1971—73), fgn. assoc. (hon.), Korean Acad. Sci. and Tech. (hon.), Japanese Biochem. Soc. (hon.), Spanish Royal Acad. Scis. (assoc.; fgn.),

Venice Inst. Sci., Arts and Letters (assoc.; fgn.), Royal Acad. Medicine and Surgery (hon.; Cadiz, Spain), European Acad. Scis. (hon.), Am. Soc. Biol. Chemists (coun. 1989—93). Achievements include cellular regulation by phosphorylation/dephosphorylation cycle. Office: U Washington Med Sch PO Box 357350 Seattle WA 98195-7350 E-mail: efischer@u.washington.edu.

FISCHER, ELIZABETH (BETSY), television producer; b. New Orleans, Feb. 17, 1970; d. George Julius and Sally (Ford) Fischer; m. Gene Robert Raineri, Oct. 21, 1995; 1 child, Ella Elizabeth Raineri. BA cum laude, Am. U., 1992, MA, 1996. Polit. rschr. NBC News Meet the Press and Polit. Unit, Washington, 1992-94, assoc. prodr., 1995-96, prodr., 1997, sr. prodr., 1998—2002, exec. prodr., 2002—. Mem. Jr. League Washington. Recipient Emmy, Nat. Acad. TV Arts and Scis., 2005, Walter Cronkite/USC Annenberg award. Mem.: Am. Women Radio and TV, Radio and TV News Dirs. Assn., Coun. on Fgn. Rels., Women's Forum of Washington, Nat. Press Club, Delta Gamma. Presbyterian. Avocations: racquetball, genealogy, reading, tennis. Home: 6525 Orland St Falls Church VA 22043-1865 Office: NBC News Meet the Press 4001 Nebraska Ave NW Washington DC 20016-2733 Office Phone: 202-885-4752.

FISCHER, ERIC ROBERT, lawyer, educator; b. NYC, Aug. 22, 1945; s. Maurice and Pauline (Pilcer) F.; m. Anita Ellen Cohen, July 31, 1977; children: Joshua, Lauren BA, U. Pa., 1967; MBA, JD, Stanford U., 1971; LLM in Taxation, Boston U., 1982. Bar: NY 1975, Mass. 1977. Assoc. Fried, Frank, Harris, Shriver & Jacobson, NYC, 1971-76; v.p., asst. gen. counsel, asst. sec. First Nat. Bank of Boston, 1976-86; exec. v.p., gen. counsel, corp. sec. UST Corp., Boston, 1986-2000; sr. counsel Goodwin Procter LLP, Boston, 2000—02, ptnr., 2002—. Lectr. on law Boston U. Law Sch., 1984— Trustee Boston Lyric Opera, Inc., 1989-2001; bd. dirs. Boston Area Youth Soccer, 1989-90, Spirit of Mass. Boys Soccer Club, 1991-97. Mem. ABA (banking law com., former chmn. cmty. banking subcom., banking law com.), Bank Capital Markets Assn. (chmn. banking law subcom. 1984-90), UN Assn. Boston (treas. 1978-91), New Eng. Legal Found. (bd. dirs. 1990-92). Jewish. Home: 205 Waban Ave Waban MA 02468-2101 Office: Goodwin Procter Exchange Pl Boston MA 02109 Home Phone: 617-244-1298; Office Phone: 617-570-1522. Business E-Mail: efischer@goodwinprocter.com. *The pursuit of an objective which you believe is meaningful and constructive (whether you are right or wrong) gives definition to your life and allows you to accept your own limitations.*

FISCHER, FRED WALTER, physicist, engineer, educator; b. Zwickau, Germany, June 26, 1922; s. Fritz and Louiska (Richter) F.; m. Yongja Kim, Oct. 1, 1970. BS in Mech. Engring., Columbia U., 1949, MS, 1950; MS in Physics, U. Wash., 1957; D in Elec. Engring., Tech. U. Munich, 1966. Analyst Boeing Co., Seattle, Germany, 1950—84, cons., 1984—88; owner Fischer Cons., 1984—88. Instr. physics, math., and engring. North Seattle Community Coll., 1973-93; guest tchr. Perkins Sch. Author: Analysis for Physics and Engineering, 1982, Renaissance Mathematics, 1992. First v.p., trustee Wedgwood Cmty. Coun., 1994-2000; mem. Wedgwood Elem. Sch. Site Coun., Eckstein Middle Sch. Site Coun. With AUS, 1943-46. Boeing scholar Max Planck Inst. Plasma Physics, 1964-65. Mem. AAAS, N.Y. Acad. Sci., Mercedes Benz Club (Seattle sect. bd. dirs.), Sigma Xi (life). Office: North Seattle CC 9600 College Way N Seattle WA 98103-3514

FISCHER, HERBERT STEVEN, social studies educator; b. Flushing, NY, May 10, 1962; s. Alvin and Thelma Fischer; m. Karen Sussan, Oct. 12, 1996; 1 child, Rachel. BA, Lehigh U., Bethlehem, Pa., 1984; MA, NYU, NYC, 1991. Cert. social studies tchr. NY, NJ, lic. sightseeing guide NYC. Investigative reporter Elizabeth Daily Jour., NJ, 1988; mng. editor, photographer Housatonic Valley Pub. Co., New Milford, Conn., 1989—90; editor-in-chief, baseball columnist South Bergenite, Rutherford, NJ, 1990—91; social studies tchr. Evander Childs HS, Bronx, NY, 1991—2001, Teaneck (NJ) HS, 2001—04, Wadleigh HS, NYC, 2004—. Tchr. cons. Nat. Geog., Teaneck and NYC, 1995—. Mem. selection com. Nat. Youth Leadership Fellows, Washington, 1998—. Mem.: Nat. Coun. Social Studies. Avocations: weather, writing. Home: 7 Danbury Ct # 1608 Suffern NY 10901 Office: Wadleigh HS 215 W 114th St New York NY 10026 E-mail: hfischer2@nyc.gov.

FISCHER, IVAN, conductor; b. Budapest, Hungary, Jan. 20, 1951; s. Sandor and Evelyn (Boschan) F.; m. Anneke Boeke; 2 daus. Grad. Bela Bartok Conservatorium, Budapest, 1969; diploma Vienna Acad. Music, 1974. Mus. dir. No. Sinfonia, 1979-82; music dir., artistic dir. Kent Opera, England, 1982-2000; music dir. Lyon Nat. Opera, France, 2000-03; founder Budapest Festival Orch., 1983, Hungarian Mahler Soc.; debut appearance Los Angeles Philharm., 1983; prin. guest condr. Cin. Symphony, 1989-90, Nat. Symphony Orch., Washington, 2006-; past condr. Chgo. Symphony Orch., Cin. Symphony, Detroit Symphony, New Orleans Symphony Orch., Rochester Philharm., San Francisco Symphony, BBC Symphony, 1976; appearances with London Philharm., English Chamber Orch., Scottish Nat. Orch., Royal Liverpool Philharm. Recipient Premio Firenze, 1974, Rupert Found. Internat. Young Conductors award, BBC, 1976, Golden Medal, Republic of Hungary, Crystal award, World Econ. Forum, Kossuth prize, 2006. Office: Nat Symphony Orch PO Box 101510 Arlington VA 22210 also: c/o Edna Landau IMG Artists 152 W 57th St 5th Fl New York NY 10019*

FISCHER, JENNA (REGINA MARIE FISCHER), actress; b. Ft. Wayne, Ind., Mar. 7, 1974; d. Jim and Anne Fischer; m. James Gunn, Oct. 7, 2000. BA in Theatre, Truman State U., 1995. Receptionist, adminstrn. asst. Actress (films) Channel 493, 1998, Born Champion, 1998, The Specials, 2000, Picking Up Chicks with Harland Williams, 2001, Les Superficiales, 2002, Melvin Goes to Dinner, 2003, Doggie Tails, Vol 1: Lucky's First Sleep-Over, 2003, Employee of the Month, 2004, The Women, 2004, Lucky 13, 2005, Slither, 2006, Blades of Glory, 2007, (TV films) Rubbing Charlie, 2003, (TV series) The Office, 2005— (SAG award outstanding performance by an ensemble in a comedy series, 2007), (appeared on) Spin City, 2001, Off Centre, 2002, What I Like About You, 2002, Strong Medicine, 2003, Miss Match, 2003, Cold Case, 2004, Six Feet Under, 2005, writer, dir., actress (films) LolliLove, 2004 (SAG emerging actor award, St. Louis Film Festival, 2006, Tromadance Independent Soul award, Am. Film Market, 2006). Vol. Kitten Rescue. Named one of 100 Most Beautiful People, People Mag., 2006.*

FISCHER, JOEL, social work educator; b. Chgo., Apr. 22, 1939; s. Sam and Ruth (Feiges) F.; m. Renee H. Furuyama; children: Lisa, Nicole. BS, U. Ill., 1961, MSW, 1964; D in Social Welfare, U. Calif., Berkeley, 1970. Prof. sch. social work U. Hawaii, Honolulu, 1970—. Vis. prof. George Warren Brown Sch. Social Work, Washington U., St. Louis, 1977, U. Wis. Sch. Social Welfare, Milw., 1978-79, U. Natal, South Africa, 1982, U. Hong Kong, 1986; cons. various orgns. and univs. Author: (with Harvey L. Gochros) Planned Behavior Change: Behavior Modification in Social Work, 1973, Handbook of Behavior Therapy with Sexual Problems, vol. I, 1977, vol. II, 1977, Analyzing Research, 1975, Interpersonal Helping: Emerging Approaches for Social Work Practice, 1973, The Effectiveness of Social Casework, 1976; (with D. Sanders and O. Kurren) Fundamentals of Social Work Practice, 1982, Effective Casework Practice: An Eclectic Approach, 1978, (with H. Gochros) Treat Yourself to a Better Sex Life, 1980; (with H. Gochros and J. Gochros) Helping the Sexually Oppressed, 1985; (with Martin Bloom) Evaluating Practice: Guidelines for the Helping Professional, 1982; (with Kevin Corcoran) Measures for Clinical Practice and Research, 1987, 3d edit, vol. 2, 2006, Couples, Children and Families, Adults, vol. 2, 2000, East-West Connections: Social Work Practice Traditions and Change, 1992, Measures for Clinical Practice and Research, vol. 1, 2006, Couples, Children and Families, vol. 2, 2006; (with Daniel Sanders) Visions for the Future: Social Work and Pacific-Asian Perspectives, 1988; (with Martin Bloom and John Orme) Evaluating Practice, 2d edit., 1995, 5th edit., 2006, Instructor's Manual for Evaluating Practice, 1999, 3rd edit., 2006; mem. editl. bd. 12 profl. jours.; contbr. over 150 articles to profl. jours. Bd. dirs. U. Hawaii Profl. Assembly, Hawaii Peoples' Fund, Greenpeace; precinct pres. Dem. Party. With U.S. Army, 1958-61. Mem. NASW (Social Worker of Year for Social Justice 2005), ACLU, Hawaii Com. for Africa, Coun. Social Work Edn., Acad. Cert. Social Workers, Nat. Conf. Social Welfare, AAUP, Unity Organizing Com., Hawaii People's Legis. Coalition, People for the Ethical Treatment of Animals (bd. dirs.), Stop/The U. Utah Animal Rights Coalition, Bertha Reynold Soc., Amnesty Internat., Sierra Club. Democrat. Office: U Hawaii Sch Social Work Henke Hall Honolulu HI 96822-2217 Home Phone: 808-735-7582. Business E-Mail: jfischer@hawaii.edu.

FISCHER, JOSEPH L., pharmaceutical executive; BS in Acctg., Pa. State U., 1972. Former rschr. Fin. Acctg. Standards Bd.; various positions including group pres. of global personal care products, pres. J&J Canada, and corp. controller Johnson & Johnson, 1981—95; various mgmt. positions including sr. v.p. Dial Corp., 1995—2002; interim CEO ImClone Systems Inc., NYC, 2006. Bd. dirs. ImClone Systems Inc., 2003—06, mem. audit and compensation comt., 2003—06. Office: ImClone Systems Inc 180 Varick St New York NY 10014

FISCHER, JOYCE FAYE, engineering educator; b. Dayton, Ohio, May 24, 1945; d. Otis Crawford and Dorothy Margaret Brown; m. Robert Allen Fischer, Apr. 11, 1966; children: Robert Bryan, Jason Allen. BA, MA, Tex. State U.; PhD, U. Tex., Austin, 1995. Engring. tech. GE, Cin., 1966—68; asst. prof. Tex. State U., San Marcos, Tex., 1980—. Tchg., rsch., grant dir., cons. Tex. State U., San Marcos, 1990—; spkr. in field. Contbr. articles to profl. jours. Educator, rschr. Tex. State U, San Marcos, 1988—2005. Grantee, Tex. Edn. Agy., 2004, Math. for English Lang. Learners Initiative; Tchr. Quality grant, Coord. Bd. for Tchr. Edn. Mem.: Nat. Mus. Am. Indian (assoc. Cert. of Merit 2004), Kappa Delta Pi (assoc.), Nat. Honor Soc. (assoc.), Alpha Chi (assoc.), Phi Kappa Phi (life). Achievements include development of teacher curriculum and pedagogy workshops for preservice and inservice teachers. Home: 600 Dale Dr San Marcos TX 78666 Office: Tex State U 601 U Dr Math Bldg Rm 470 San Marcos TX 78666 Home Phone: 512-392-8027; Office Phone: 512-245-8023. Office Fax: 512-245-3425. E-mail: jf10@txstate.edu.

FISCHER, KURT WALTER, education educator; b. Balt., June 9, 1943; s. Kurt Wilhelm and Irmgaard Louise (Funke) Fischer; m. Sandra Pipp (div.); 1 child, Seth; m. Jane Haltiwanger, Dec. 7, 1986; children: Johanna, Lukas, Kara. BA in Psychology summa cum laude, Yale U., 1965; MA in Soc. Rels., Harvard U., 1968, PhD in Soc. Rels., 1971. Asst. prof. Univ. Denver, 1972-78, assoc. prof., 1978-85, prof., 1985-87; prof. edn. Harvard U., Cambridge, Mass., 1986—, Charles Bigelow prof., chair human devel., 1989—92, 1994—95, 1999—2000, dir. mind, brain and edn., 1999—. Vis. scholar Univ. Geneva, 1978—79; vis. prof. U. Pa., Phila., 1985—86; master lectr. U. Groningen, The Netherlands, 1996; vis. prof. Nanjing Normal U., China, 2000. Author: Cognitive Development, 1981, Levels and Transitions in Cognitive Development, 1983; co-author: Psychology Today: An Introduction, 2d and 3d edits., 1972, 75, Human Development from Conception to Adolescence, 1984, Development in Context, 1993, Human Behavior and the Developing Brain, 1994, Self Conscious Emotions, 1995, Development and Vulnerability in Close Relationships, 1996, Socioemotional Development across Cultures, 1998, The Educated Brain, 2007, Mind, Brain, and Education in Reading Disorders, 2007, Human Behavior, Learning, and the Developing Brain, 2007; founding editor jour. Mind, Brain, and Edn., 2007; contbr. articles to profl. jours. Fellow James McKeen Cattell Fund, 1985-86, Ctr. for Advanced Study, Palo Alto, Calif., 1992-93; grantee Carnegie Found., Nat. Inst. Child Health and Devel., 1994—2004, Sloan Found., Spencer Found., Rose Found., 1995—, Nat. Leadership Coll., 2003—, Ross Inst., 2007. Mem. Jean Piaget Soc. (pres. 1988-91), Internat. Mind Brain Edn. Soc. (founding pres. 2004-), Phi Beta Kappa, Sigma Xi. Home: 29 Vincent Ave Belmont MA 02478-4418 Office: Harvard U Grad Sch Edn Larsen 702 Cambridge MA 02138 Home Phone: 617-489-2212; Office Phone: 617-495-3446. E-mail: kurt_fischer@harvard.edu.

FISCHER, LAURENCE ELIOT, literature educator, consultant; b. Chgo., July 28, 1948; s. Joseph Green and Anne Fischer; m. Sarajane Dickey, Sept. 1, 1974; children: Jarrod Dickey, Zachary Abram. MS, San Francisco State U., Calif., 1974. Instr. English H.S. Fremont Unified Sch. Dist., Calif., 1974—89; co-dir. Bay Area Writing Project, Berkeley, Calif., 1989—91; prof. English Diablo Valley Coll., Pleasant Hill, Calif., 1991—. Named Tchr. of Yr., Contra Costa County Schs., 1996. Mem.: Nat. Coun. Tchrs. English. Office: Diablo Valley Coll 321 Golf Club Rd Pleasant Hill CA 94523 Office Phone: 925-685-1230. Business E-Mail: lfischer@dvc.edu.

FISCHER, LEROY HENRY, historian, educator; b. Hoffman, Ill., May 19, 1917; s. Andrew LeRoy and Effie (Risby) F.; m. Martha Gwendolyn Anderson, June 20, 1948; children: Barbara Ann, James LeRoy, John Andrew. BA, U. Ill., 1939, MA, 1940, PhD, 1943; postgrad., Columbia U., 1941. Grad. asst. history U. Ill., 1940-43; asst. prof. history Ithaca (N.Y.) Coll., 1946, Okla. State U. at Stillwater, 1946-49, assoc. prof. history, 1949-60, prof. history, 1960-73, Oppenheim Regents prof. history, 1973-78, Oppenheim prof. history, 1978-84, Oppenheim prof. emeritus, 1984—. Exec. sec. honors program, 1959-61; exec. coun. Emeriti Assn., 2000-02. Author: Lincoln's Gadfly, Adam Gurowski, 1964; (with Muriel H. Wright) Civil War Sites in Oklahoma, 1967, The Civil War Era in Indian Territory, 1974, The Western States in the Civil War, 1975, Territorial Governors of Oklahoma, 1975, The Western Territories in the Civil War, 1977, Civil War Battles in the West, 1981, Oklahoma's Governors 1907-1979, 3 vols., 1981-85, Oklahoma State University Historic Old Central, 1988; co-author: A History of Governance at Oklahoma State University, 1992; editor: The History of the Oklahoma State University Centennial Histories Project, 1993; contbr articles to profl. jours. Vice chmn. Honey Springs Battlefield Park Commn., 1968-92, Okla. Civil War Centennial Commn., 1958-65; chmn. Old Ctrl. com. Okla. State U., 1971-98; mem. Okla. State Hist. Preservation Rev. Commn., 1978—, vice chmn., 1978-81, chmn., 1981-83, 1997-2004; bd. dirs. Nat. Indian Hall of Fame, 1969-2002, YMCA, 1951-54, 83-85, 91—; bd. dirs. Assocs. Western History Collections, U. Okla., 1981-2002, pres., 1989-90; bd. dirs. Stillwater Mus. Assn., 1987-93, pres., 1990-91; mem. Okla. Chisholm Trail Centennial Commn., 1967-68; bd. dirs. Friends of Honey Springs Battlefield Park, 1991—, pres., 1994-97, sec. 1997-2000. With Signal Corps, AUS, 1943-45. Recipient Lit. award Loyal Legion U.S., 1963; named tchr. of Yr., Okla. State U.-Okla. Edn. Assn., 1969; inducted in Okla. Historians Hall of Fame, 1995, Centralia (Ill.) Hall of Fame, 1997, Okla. Higher Edn. Hall of Fame, 2002. Mem. Am. Hist. Assn., Southern Hist. Assn., Western History Assn., Am. Assn. State and Local History, AAUP, Okla. Heritage Assn. (Disting. Svc. award 1989), Okla. Hist. Soc. (bd. dirs. 1966—, treas. 1984-87), Ill. Hist. Soc., Orgn. Am. Historians, Omicron Delta Kappa, Pi Gamma Mu, Phi Alpha Theta, Alpha Kappa Lambda. Methodist (chmn. various coms. 1946—, adminstrv. bd. 1950-77, chmn. 1976-77, lay leader 1970-71). Home: 1010 W Cantwell Ave Stillwater OK 74075-4603

FISCHER, MARK ALAN, lawyer; b. Evanston, Ill., Sept. 28, 1950; s. Lee Earle and Zelda (Dlugo) F. BA magna cum laude, Emerson Coll., 1975; JD, Boston Coll., 1980. Bar: Mass. 1980, US Dist. Ct. Mass. 1980, US Ct. Appeals (1st cir.) Mass. 1985. Sole practice, Cambridge, Mass., 1980—83; mem. Cohen & Burg, Boston, 1983—86; ptnr. Wolf, Greenfield & Sacks, Boston, 1986—96, Palmer & Dodge, Boston, 1996—2002; prin. Fish & Richardson, Boston, 2002—, co-chmn. media and entertainment sect. and copyright sect. Lectr. copyright and trademark law Boston Coll. Law Sch., 1985—87; lectr. entertainment law New Eng. Sch. Law, Boston, 1983—93; assoc. prof. music law Berklee Coll. Music, 1989—90, 1994—95; lectr. intellectual property Northeastern Sch. Law, Boston, 1986; mem. adj. faculty advanced copyright law Suffolk U. Law Sch., 1999—. Contbr. articles to profl. jour.; columnist New Eng. Entertainment Digest, 1982-90; co-editor: Perle & Williams on Publishing Law, (3rd edit.). Named one of Boston's top lawyers, Boston Mag., 2002. Mem. ABA, Mass. Bar Assn., Boston Patent Law Assn. (chmn. copyright law com., 1985-96), Copyright Soc. USA (trustee 1997-2000), Copyright Soc. New Eng. (co-founder). Office: Fish & Richardson 225 Franklin St Boston MA 02110 Office Phone: 617-368-2121. Business E-Mail: fischer@fr.com.

FISCHER, MARK DAVID, lawyer; b. Manhasset, NY, May 2, 1961; s. Martin Joseph and Greta Priscilla Fischer; m. Marlene Kern, Aug. 16, 1987; children: Eric, Jonah, Isaac. BA, Brandeis U., 1983; JD, Boston U., 1987. Bar: Mass. 1987, N.Y. 1988, U.S. Dist. Ct. (so. and ea. dists.) N.Y. 1988. Assoc. Nixon. Hargrave, Devans & Doyle, NYC, 1987—89, Rosenman & Colin, NYC, 1989—96, ptnr., 1996—99; v.p., gen. counsel, sec. Phllips-Van Heusen Corp., NYC, 1999—. Equipment dir. Am. Youth Soccer Organ. Region 204, Armonk, 1998—, coach, 1998—. Mem.: ABA, NY State Bar Assn. (mem. bus. law and gen. counsel sects.), Assn. Corp. Counsel Am., Soc. Corp. Governance Profls. Office: Phillips-Van Heusen Corp 200 Madison Ave New York NY 10016-3903 E-mail: markfischer@pvh.com.

FISCHER, MAXIM, electronics engineer; b. Sibiu, Transylvan, Romania, June 14, 1946; s. Herman and Edita (Genad) F.; m. Aurelia Munteanu, Jan. 15, 1972; 1 child, Alina Christina. Diploma Engr., Poly. Inst., Bucharest, Romania, 1970. Prodn. engr. Electromagnetica, Bucharest, 1970-75; telecom. engr. Dept. Telecom., Beer Sheva, Israel, 1976-77; avionics engr. Tundra Tech. Industries, Edmonton, Alta., Can., 1978-82, chief engr., 1982-83; design engr. Northwestern Utilities, Edmonton, 1983-90, sr. engr. specialist, 1990-99; project leader Atco Pipelines, Edmonton, 1999—2004, group leader, 2004—. Dir. Can Trade Rsch., Inc., Edmonton, 1992—, Trunked Wireless Technologies, Edmonton. Contbr. articles to profl. jours. Mem. Instrument Soc. Am., Assn. Profl. Engrs., Geologists and Geophysicists of Alta., Romanian Radio Assn. (v.p. 1991-92, 95-96, sec. 1993-94, pres. 2001-2004). Jewish. Avocations: tennis, chess, golf. Personal E-mail: maximf@telusplanet.net. Business E-Mail: Max.Fischer@atcopipelines.com.

FISCHER, MICHAEL JOHN, computer science educator; b. Ann Arbor, Mich., Apr. 20, 1942; s. Carl Hahn and Kathleen (Kirkpatrick) F.; m. Alice Edna Waltz, June 1, 1963; children: Edward Michael, Robert Patrick, David Frederick. BS, U. Mich., 1963; MA (NSF fellow), Harvard U., 1965, PhD, 1968. Teaching fellow Harvard U., 1965-67; asst. prof. computer sci. Carnegie-Mellon U., 1968-69; asst. prof. math. MIT, 1969-73, assoc. prof. elec. engring., 1973-75; prof. computer sci. U. Wash., 1975-81, dir. Computer Sci. Lab., 1976-79; prof. computer sci. Yale U., New Haven, 1981—, dir. grad. studies in computer sci., 1992-99. Program chmn. IEEE Symposium on Founds. Computer Sci., 1976, 11th Assn. Computing Machinery Symposium on Theory Computing, 1979, Assn. Computing Machinery Symposium on Principles of Distributed Computing, 1982; sr. vis. fellow U. Warwick, Coventry, Eng., summer 1972; vis. assoc. prof. U. Toronto, spring, 1974; guest professor U. Frankfurt, Germany, summer 1974, ETH, Zurich, summer 1975; vis. scientist U. Saarbrücken, Germany, fall 1988; mem. adv. com. for math. and computer scis NSF, 1978-81; mem. com. on recommendations for U.S. Army Basic Sci. Rsch., 1978-81; cons. Xerox Palo Alto Research Ctr., 1982; co-organizer Oberwolfach Confs. on Math. Methods of VSLI and Distributed Computing, 1983, 87, 91; founding mem. subcom. on status women in computer sci. Computing Rsch. Assn., 1990-93; chmn. internat. sci. adv. bd. Max-Planck-Inst. for Informatik, Saarbrücken, 1993-2006; guest prof. Wuhan Univ. and mem. acad. com. State Key Lab. Software Engring., Wuhan, 2001-2004. Founding mem. TrueVoteCT.org, 2005—. Grantee NSF, 1974-92, 2000—; recipient Edsger W. Dijkstra prize in Distributed Computing, 2001. Fellow Assn. Computing Machinery (sec.-treas. spl. interest group on programming langs. 1971-73, local arrangements chmn. conf. 1973); mem. Am. Math. Soc., European Assn. Theoretical Computer Sci., Vote website, Yale Figure Skating Club (pres. 1989-91, 1997-2001), Phi Beta Kappa, Phi Kappa Phi. Office: Yale U Dept Computer Sci PO Box 208285 New Haven CT 06520-8285

FISCHER, MICHAEL LUDWIG, environmental executive; b. Dubuque, Iowa, May 29, 1940; s. Carl Michael and Therese Marie (Stadler) F.; m. Jane Pughe Rogers; children: Christina Marie, Steven Michael. BA in Polit. Sci., Santa Clara U., 1964; M in City and Regional Planning, U. Calif., Berkeley, 1967; grad. exec. program in environ. mgmt., Harvard U., 1980. Planner City of Mountain View, Calif., 1960-65; planner assoc. Bay Area Govts., 1966-67; planner County of San Mateo, Calif., 1967-69; assoc. dir. San Francisco Planning and Urban Rsch. Assn., nonprofit civc orgn., 1969-73; exec. dir. North Cen. region Calif. Coastal Zone Conservation Commn., San Rafael, 1973-76; chief dep. dir. Gov.'s Office Planning and Rsch., Sacramento, 1976-78; exec. dir. Calif. Coastal Commn., San Francisco, 1978-85; sr. assoc. Sedway Cooke Assocs., environ. cons., San Francisco, 1985-87; exec. dir. Sierra Club, San Francisco, 1987-93; resident fellow John F. Kennedy Sch. Govt., Inst. Politics, Harvard U., Cambridge, Mass., 1993; sr. cons. Natural Resources Def. Coun., San Francisco, 1993-95; exec. officer Calif. Coastal Conservancy, Oakland, 1994-97; program dir. environ. William & Flora Hewlett Found., Menlo Park, Calif., 1997—2002, sr. fellow, 2002—03; environ. and mgmt. cons., 2003—; sr. advisor Green Burial Coun., 2003—; prin. Conservation Burial Ptnrs., 2006—. Lectr. dept. city and regional planning U. Calif., Berkeley, 1984; mem., co-chair environ. com. adv. coun. Calvert Social Investment Fund, 1989—2005; mem. Harvard Commn. Global Change Info. Policy, 1993—95; mem. com. on impact of maritime facility devel. NAS/NRC, 1975—78; mem. nat. sea grant rev. panel NOAA, 1998—2001; mem. adv. bd. Sustainable Conservation, 2003—, Coastal States Stewardship Found., 2005—07; mem. steering com. Indigenous Cmtys. Mapping Initiative, 2000—05, Travel Just, 2003—07. Co-author Calif. state plan, An Urban Strategy for Calif., 1978, Building a New Municipal Railway, 1973, Oral History, Coastal Commn. Yrs., 1973-85, Oral History, Sierra Club Yrs., 1987-93; author intro. Ansel Adams: Yosemite, 1995; contbr. papers to profl. publs. Bd. dirs. High Country News Found., 2000—05, Resources for Cmty. Collaboration, 1999—2006, Am. Youth Hostels, Inc., 1985—87, Yosemite Restoration Trust, 1990—97, pres., 1995—97. Recipient Life Achievement award, Assn. Environ. Profls., 1986, Disting. Leadership award, Am. Soc. Pub. Adminstrn., 1987, Outstanding Nat. Leadership award, Coastal States Orgn., 1990, David Brower award for environ. leadership, Conservation Laborers Against Wrong, 1993, Exemplary Pub. Svc. award, San Francisco Bay Conservation and Devel. Commn., 1997, Spl. Recognition award, Calif. State Legis., 1998, Coastal Champion award, Nat. Resources Def. Coun. and Sierra Club, Calif., 2003, Coastal Hero award, Calif. Coastal Commn., 2005, Disting. Alumnus medal, U. Calif., Berkeley, Coll. Environ. Design, 2007. Fellow: Inst. Journalism and Nat. Resources (disting.); mem.: Calif. Planning and Conservation League (bd. dirs. 1970—76), Friends of the Earth (bd. dirs. 1988—94), The Oceanic Soc. (bd. dirs. 1983—88), Alliance Ethnic and Environ. Orgn. (founding bd. dirs. 1991—93), Sierra Club, Lambda Alpha. Achievements include making Renaissance keyboard instruments. E-mail: fischer@igc.org.

FISCHER, MICHELLE K., lawyer; BA in Econs. magna cum laude with distinction, Yale U., 1986; JD with honors, U. Chgo., 1989. Bar: Ohio 1989, D.C. 1991. With Jones Day, Cleve., 1989—, ptnr., 1999—. Mem.: ABA (antitrust law sect.), Ohio State Bar Assn. (bd. govs. antitrust law sect.). Office: Jones Day North Point 901 Lakeside Ave Cleveland OH 44114-1190

FISCHER, NORA BARRY, federal judge, lawyer; b. Pitts., June 13, 1951; d. Michael T. and Olga G. (Stipetich) Barry; m. Donald R. Fischer, Jan. 3, 1976; children: Erin, Lauren, Adam. BA magna cum laude, St. Mary's Coll., Notre Dame, Ind., 1973; JD, U. Notre Dame, 1976. Bar: Ill. 1976, Pa. 1977, U.S. Dist. Ct. (no. dist.) Ill. 1977, U.S. Dist. Ct. (we. dist.) Pa. 1977, U.S. Ct. Appeals (3rd cir.) 1981, U.S. Supreme Ct. 1982, W.Va. 1990, U.S. Dist. Ct. (so. dist.) W.Va. 1990, U.S. Dist. Ct. (no dist.) W.Va. 2002. Legal editor Callaghan's, Chgo., 1976-77; assoc. Meyer, Darragh, Buckler, Bebenek & Eck, Pitts., 1977-80, jr. ptnr., 1980-82, ptnr., 1983-92, mem. exec. com., 1987-89; ptnr. Pietragallo Bosick & Gordon, Pitts., 1992—2007, mem. practice mgmt. com., 1996—2007; judge US Dist. Ct. (we. dist.) Pa., 2007—. Pratice group leader Def. Litig. Group, 2002—. Mem. Pitts. Allegheny Co. Pvt. Industry Coun., 1982-84. Mem.: ABA, Acad. Trial Lawyers (past pres.), Allegheny County Bar Assn. Found., Exec. Womens Coun., Ins. Women Pitts., Allegheny County Bar Assn, (med.-legal com. 1984—89, interprofl. code com. 1985—86, judiciary com. 1985—88, health law sect. 1990—92, civil litig. coun. 1990—93, health law sect. vice chair 1992—93, health law sect. chair 1994, bd. govs., women in law com., edn. subcom., mem. fellows com.), Pa. Bar Assn. (civil litig. coun. 1985—87, ins. and surety law com. 1991), Am. Inns of Court (pres. 1999—2001). Democrat. Roman Catholic. Office: US Post Office & Courthouse Seventh Ave & Grant Ave Pittsburgh PA 15219

FISCHER, PAMELA SHADEL, public relations executive; b. Harrisburg, Pa., Feb. 28, 1959; d. Richard Lee and Pauline Louise (Nies) S.; m. Charles J. Fischer Jr., June 11, 1983; 1 child, Zachary Joseph. BA in English, Lebanon Valley Coll., Annville, Pa., 1981; AMP, U. Pa., 2005. Cert. child passenger safety technician AAA. Pub. rels. coord. Pa. Optometric Assn., Harrisburg, 1981-83; pub. rels. dir. Morris Ctr. YMCA, Cedar Knolls, NJ, 1983-85; pub. rels. coord. Delta Dental Plan of N.J., Parsippany, 1985-86; pub. rels. mgr. AAA N.J. Automobile Club, Florham Park, NJ, 1986-91, mgr. mem. svcs. and pub. affairs, 1991-94, asst. v.p. pub. rels. & safety, 1994-96, asst. v.p. pub. affairs and fin. svcs., 1996—2002, v.p. pub. affairs and fin. svcs., 2002—07; dir., gov. rep. NJ Divsn. Hwy. Traffic Safety, 2007—. Corp. capt. United Way of Morris County, Cedar Knolls, 1985—90, chmn. publs. com., 1989—90, chmn. mktg. com., 1991—95, v.p. mktg., 1996, mem. women's leadership initiative exec. com., 1999—2006, vice chmn., 2002—03, chmn., 2003—04; career counselor Lebanon Valley Coll., 1983—90, alumni amb., 2004—; mem. hwy. traffic safety policy adv. com. Gov.'s Office, 1998—2007; chair legis. com. Gateway Tourism Coun., 1997—2000; mem. Driver Edn. Commn. N.J., 1999—2005; bd. dirs. First Night of Morris County, 1999—2002, chmn., 2004; mem. NJ Motor Vehicle Commn., 2003—, vice chmn., 2004—05; mem. N.J. Child Passenger Safety Coalition, 2003—; mem. corp. leadership coun. Family Svc. Morris County, NJ, 2005—07; trustee Trans Options, 2005—07; co-chmn. Gov.-elect Jon Corzine's Transp. Transition Team, 2005—06; bd. dirs. Morris Ctr. YMCA, 1992—94, Hist. Morris County Visitors Ctr., 1999—2006, bd. pres., 2001—04; bd. mem. Exec. Women NJ. Rotary Found. scholar, 1981; recipient Gold award United Way of Morris County, 1988, Traffic Safety award Gov.'s rep., 2004, Salute to the Policy Maker award Exec. Women of NJ, 2006, Women in Leadership award Patriots Path coun. Boy Scouts Am., 2006. Mem. Pub. Rels. Soc. Am. (bd. dirs. 1995), N.J. Press Assn., N.J. Travel Industry Assn., N.J. Comm. Regional Plan Assn., Internat. Assn. Bus Communicators, Y's Club of Cedar Knoll (pres. 1986-91), Long Valley Ice Hockey Club (dir. media rels. 2003-2007), Govs. Hwy. Safety Assn., Nat. Assn. Women Traffic Safety Leaders, Exec. Women's Golf Assn. Republican. Roman Catholic. Avocations: reading, writing, photography, skiing, hockey. Office: NJ Divsn Hwy Traffic Safety PO Box 048 140 E Front St Trenton NJ 08625-0048 Office Phone: 609-633-9021. Business E-Mail: pfischer550@comcast.net.

FISCHER, RICHARD SAMUEL, lawyer; b. Buffalo, July 31, 1937; s. Richard D. and Isabel B. (Van Dorn) F.; m. Malinda Berry, June 3, 1960; children: Richard B., Van D. AB, Harvard U., 1959, JD, 1963. Bar: N.Y. 1963, Okla. 1996. Law clk N.Y. Ct. Appeals, Albany, 1963-65; assoc. Nixon, Hargrave, Devans & Doyle, Rochester, NY, 1965-71, ptnr., 1972-95, mem. policy com., 1991-95, head Rochester office, 1992-95; mem. faculty Okla. State U., Stillwater, 1997—2002. Past chair, trustee Highland Hosp.; past pres. Harley Sch.; past bd. dirs. Rochester Area Hosp. Corp., Primary Mental Health Project, United Way, Stillwater; past pres. Friends of Music and Allied Arts, 2000-01; mem. CHES exec. com. Okla. State U.; bd. dirs. Turning Point Ranch Found. Mem. ABA, N.Y. State Bar Assn. (past chmn. com. ins. programs and retirement plans), Monroe County Bar Assn., NYU Inst. Fed. Taxation (adv. com.), Okla. Bar Assn., Stillwater Country Club. Office: PO Box 1897 Stillwater OK 74076-1897

FISCHER, R.M., sculptor; b. NYC, Mar. 21, 1947; s. Bernard and Alva (Sherman) F.; m. Patti Paige, June 22, 1986; 1 child, Dena Paige. BA, L.I. U., 1971; MFA, San Francisco Art Inst., 1973. Numerous one-man shows, including Musee Ville Toulon, France, 1984, Whitney Mus. Am. Art, N.Y.C., 1984, Inst. Contemporary Art, Boston, 1985, Jay Gorney Modern Art, N.Y.C., 1989, Donald Young Gallery, Chgo., 1988, Sidney Janis Gallery, N.Y.C., 1991, Deitch Projects, N.Y.C., 1998, Sandra Gering Gallery, N.Y.C., 2002; exhibited in numerous group shows, including Mus. Modern Art, 1984, Whitney Mus. Am. Art, 1985, 88, 91, Aldrich Mus. Contemporary Art, 1988, Vienna (Austria) Seccession, 1990; represented in permanent collections Cin. Art Mus., Whitney Mus. Modern Art., Mus. Modern Art, Dallas Mus. Art, Carnegie Mus. Fine Arts, Pitts., Fundacao de Serrales Found., Oporto, Portugal; permanent pub. artworks include Kansas City Convention Ctr., Cleve. Gateway Plaza, Battery Park City, N.Y., Mass. State House, Boston, Seattle Tower, Sony Studios Fountain, Union Square, San Francisco. Studio: 126 13th St First Fl Brooklyn NY 11215

FISCHER, ROBERT BLANCHARD, academic administrator, researcher; b. Hartford, Conn., Oct. 24, 1920; s. Charles Albert and Matilda (Nylen) F.; m. Mary Ellen Mitchell, June 29, 1946; children: Lois, Marcia, Philip, Vivian, Valerie. BS, Wheaton Coll., 1942; PhD, U. Ill., 1946. Rsch. chemist U.S. Army Atomic Bomb Project, Chgo., 1944-46; instr. chemistry U. Ill., Urbana, 1946-48; prof. chemistry Indiana U., Bloomington, 1948-63; dean sch. of sci. Calif. State U.-Dominguez Hills, Carson, 1963-79, dean emeritus, 1979—; provost, sr. v.p. Biola U., La Mirada, Calif., 1979-88, disting. prof., 1988-89, provost, disting. prof. emeritus, 1989—. Research assoc. Calif. Inst. Tech., Pasadena, 1959-60; cons. in field. Contbr. articles to profl. jours. Fellow AAAS, Am. Sci. Affiliation (nat. pres. 1965-66); mem. Am. Chem. Soc. (sect. and region chmn.). Republican. Avocations: theology, amateur radio, sports. Home: 860 Morningside Dr C302 Fullerton CA 92835

FISCHER, RUSSELL LEONARD, public relations executive; b. East Orange, NJ, Feb. 4, 1958; s. Harold Martin and Annette Carol Fischer. BA, Boston U., 1980; JD, Antioch U., Washington, 1984. Importer, retailer, owner Fendi of Short Hills, NJ, 1982-92; pub. rels. dir., v.p. IME-Xaminations, Elizabeth, NJ, 1994—. Vol. World Trade Orgn., NYC, battered wives Unity Group, Short Hills, 1995-98; del. reform coun. Am. Jewish Congress, N.Y.C., 1991; adv. bd. Am. Assn. Reform Judaism, Washington, 1995-99; alumni advisor, pres. South Fla. chpt. Boston U. Alumni Assn., 2000-02; active Heritage Soc. Congregation Emanu-El, NYC. Recipient Meritorious and Outstanding Cmty. Svc. award Am. Nat. Red Cross, 1976. Mem.: NJ Importers Assn., Beach Club, Palm Beach, Club Colette, Ocean Point Beach Club, World Trade Ctr. Club, Williams Island Club, Crestmont Country Club. Avocation: sculpture.

FISCHER, THOMAS COVELL, law educator, consultant, writer; b. May 2, 1938; s. Vilas Uber and Elizabeth Mary (Holland) Fischer; m. Katherine Brenda Andrew, Sept. 29, 1972. AB, U. Cin., 1960; postgrad., U. Wash., 1960-62, Loyola U., Chgo., 1964-66; JD, Georgetown U., 1966. Asst. dir. U. Ill., Chgo., 1964-66; asst. dean Georgetown U. Law Ctr., 1966-72; cons. Antioch Sch. Law, 1972-73; asst. exec. dir. Am. Bar Found., Chgo., 1974-76; assoc. dean, prof. law U. Dayton, 1976-78; dean, prof. law New Eng. Sch. Law, Boston, 1978—81, prof., 1981—2003, prof. emeritus, 2003—; disting. acad. in residence Seattle U. Law Sch., 2003—. Vis. scholar, Cambridge, 1991, Exeter, 91, Edinburgh, 91, Konstanz U., 1993, Muenster U., 1993, U. Auckland, 1996; fellow Inst. Advanced Legal Studies, U. London, English Inns of Court, 1997; vis. fellow Wolfson Coll., Cambridge, England, 1997; sr. vis. fellow, LLM program U. Southampton Law Faculty, 2001, sr. vis. tutor, 02; cons. in field. Author: Due Process in the Student/Institutional Relationship, 1970; author: (with Duscha) The Campus Press: Freedom and Responsibility, 1973; author: (with Zenhle) Introduction to Law and Legal Reasoning, 1977, Legal Education, Law Practice and the Economy: A New England Study, 1990, The Europeanization of America: What Americans Need to Know About the European Union, 1996, The United States, the European Union, and the Globilization of World Trade: Allies or Adversaries?, 2000; author: (with Cox) Quick Review of Conflict of Laws, 4th edit., 2001. Project dir. Commn. Legal Edn. and Practice and Econ. New Eng. Recipient Elaine R. Maham award, U. Cin., 1960, Pub. Svc. award, Access to Justice Inst., 2006; Pi Kappa Alpha Meml. scholar, 1960—62. Fellow: Inns of Ct.; mem.: Phi Alpha Theta, Pi Delta Epsilon, Delta Theta Phi. Roman Catholic. Office: Seattle U Sch Law 901 12th Ave PO Box 222000 Seattle WA 98122 Office Phone: 206-398-4034. Business E-Mail: fischert@seattleu.edu. *Every one of us is a teacher in some way; we are also students. May we teach truthfully, and learn well.*

FISCHER, WILLIAM SAMUEL, composer, lecturer; b. Shelby, Miss., Mar. 5, 1935; s. Robert A. and Willye (Samuels) F.; m. Dolores Labrie, Feb. 14, 1934; children: Darius, Marc, Bryan, Paul. BS in Mus. Edn., Xavier U., 1956; postgrad., Vienne Acad. Music, 1965—66; studied in Music Theory and Composition, U. S.W. La., 1961; MA in Music Theory and Composition, Colo. Coll., 1962. Dir. band, choir Christianburg Inst., Cambria, Va., 1957-58, St. Landry Parish, Opelousas, La., 1958-62; faculty music Xavier U., 1962-66, High Sch. of Music and Art, NYC, 1969-76; dir. music Atlantic Rec. Co., NYC, 1967-71, record prodr., 1975—, Fantasy Rec. Co., Berkeley, Calif., 1976-79; freelance composer, arranger NYC, 1967—. Lectr. N.Y.C.; cons. bd. Edn., N.Y.C. Composer: (operas) Jesse, 1965-66, Simone, 1970, Touch Kiss, 1971, Dong Film opera, 1977, Choral Music for Mass Saint in honor of Katharine Drexel, 1988, Gospel Spirit, 1973, choirs concerto Grosso in D soloists and orch., 1969, Mass for a Saint, Vatican, Rome, 1988-2000, Cross Bronx Concerto violin concerto music saxophone, 1997, Experience in E orch. and jazz quintet, 1970; author: Music Theory, 2000, Mind to Music, 2001, Private Hours Trilogy and Meditation and Trance, LeBeau Mass, 1997, ballet music Alvin Ailey Dance Co., 1970—, Autumn Morn for Double String Orch., 2001. Mem. The LeBeau Mass com. for celebration 100 years of ch. established 1897 Immaculate Conception, St. Landry Parish, La. Served to corp. USMC, 1956-57. Recipient Deutsches Akademische Austaudienst award Fed. Republic of Germany, 1966; grantee Fulbright Found., 1965-66, Austrian govt., 1965, Pan Am. grantee, 1965, Tulane U., New Orleans. Mem. ASCAP., Internat. Platform Assn., Nat. Music Pubs. Roman Catholic. Avocation: astronomy. Personal E-mail: fishwd5565@aol.com.

FISCHER, ZOE ANN, real estate, property and marketing company executive; b. LA, Aug. 26, 1939; d. George and Marguerite (Carrasco) Routsos; m. Douglas Clare Fischer, Aug. 6, 1960 (div. 1970); children: Brent Sean Cecil, Tahlia Georgienne Marguerite Bianca; m. Paul Shillcock, Dec. 8, 2000. BFA in Design, UCLA, 1964. Pres. Zoe Antiques, Beverly Hills, Calif., 1973—; v.p. Harleigh Sandler Real Estate Corp., 1980-81; exec. v.p. Coast to Coast Real Estate & Land Devel. Corp., Century City, Calif., 1981-83; pres. New Market Devel., Inc., Beverly Hills, 1983—. Dir. mktg. Mirabella, L.A., 1983, Autumn Pointe, L.A., 1983-84, Desert Hills, Antelope Valley, Calif., 1984-85; cons. Lowe Corp., L.A., 1985. Artist landscape, plein air and still life oil on canvas; one-woman shows es posible Gallery at Boulders, Scottsdale, Ariz., 2007; designer interior and exterior archtl. enhancements and remodelling; designer album cover Clare Fischer Orch. (Grammy award nomination 1962); featured in West Coast Jazz: Artwork of Pacific Jazz Records. Soprano Roger Wagner Choir, UCLA, 1963-64; mem. bd. govs. artists coun. Palm Springs Art Mus., v.p. bd. govs. artist coun. Mem. UCLA Alumni Assn., So. Calif. Restaurant Writers, Laguna Plein Air Painters Assn., Coachella Valley Artist Alliance, Nat. Mus. women in Arts. Democrat. Roman Catholic. Avocations: designing jewelry, antiques. E-mail: zoeannfischer@aol.com.

FISCHHOFF, BARUCH, psychologist, educator; b. Detroit, Apr. 21, 1946; s. Henry and Shirley (Levine) F.; m. Andrea Marks, Dec. 22, 1968; children: Maya, Ilya, Noam. BS in Math., Wayne State U., 1967; MA in Psychology, Hebrew U., Jerusalem, 1972, PhD in Psychology, 1975. Rsch. assoc. Oreg. Rsch. Inst., Eugene, 1974-76, Decision Rsch., Eugene, 1976-85, Applied Psychology Unit Med. Rsch. Coun., Cambridge, England, 1981-82, Eugene Rsch. Inst., 1985-87; prof. Carnegie-Mellon U., Pitts., 1987—, Univ. prof., 1998—, Howard Heinz prof., 2002—. Vis. prof. U. Stockholm, 1982-83; mem. panels NRC; mem. sci. adv. bd. EPA; cons. in field. Author: Acceptable Risk, 1981, Mental Models, 2001; mem. editl. bd. Jour. Risk Uncertainty, Decision Analysis, Risk Analysis, also others; contbr. numerous articles to profl. jours. Mem. Eugene Commn. on Rights of Women, 1975-81; pres. Eugene Human Rights Coun., 1979-81; mem. sci. adv. bd. EPA, 2003—; mem. sci. tech. adv. com. Dept. Homeland Security, 2004—. Fellow APA (Disting. Sci. award 1981, psychology in Pub. Interest award 1991), Soc. for Risk Analysis (pres. 2004, Disting. Achievement award 1991), Soc. Judgment and Decision-Making (mem. coun. 1988-91, pres. 1990-91), Inst. Medicine, Phi Beta Kappa. Home: 1437 Denniston Ave Pittsburgh PA 15217-1332 Office: Carnegie Mellon U Dept Engring and Pub Policy Pittsburgh PA 15213-3890 Home Phone: 412-421-2298; Office Phone: 412-268-3246. Business E-Mail: baruch@cmu.edu.

FISCHL, ERIC, artist; b. NYC, 1948; BFA, Calif. Inst. Arts, 1972. Exhibitions include Dalhousie Art Gallery, Halifax, Canada, 1975, Studio, 1976, Galerie B., Montreal, Canada, 1976, 1978, Edward Thorp Gallery, New York, 1980, 1981—82, Emily Davis Art Gallery, Akron, OH, 1980, Sable-Castelli Gallery, Toronto, Canada, 1981—82, 1985, 1987, Sir George Williams Gallery, Montreal, Canada, 1983, Saidye Bronfman Centre, 1983, Larry Gagosian Gallery, Los Angeles, 1983, 1986, Mario Diacono Gallery, Rome, 1983, Boston, 1985, 1999, Multiples/Marian Goodman Inc., New York, 1983, Nigel Greenwood Gallery, London, 1983, Mendel Art Gallery, Saskatoon, Cananda, 1985, Stedelijk Van Abbe Museum, The Netherlands, 1985, Kunsthalle Basel, Basel, Switzerland, 1985, Institute of Contemporary Art, London, 1985, Art Gallery of Ontario, Toronto, Canada, 1985, Whitney Museum of Am. Art, New York, 1986, Mary Boone Gallery, 1984, 1986—88, 1990, 1992, 1994, 1996, 1999—2000, Daniel Weinberg Gallery, Los Angeles, 1986, Galerie Michael Werner, Koln, West Germany, 1988, Waddington Galleries, London, 1989, Akademie der Bildenden Kunste, Vienna, Austria, 1990, Musee Cantonal des Beaux-Arts de Lausanne, Lausanne, Switzerland, 1990, Aarhus Kunstmuseum, Aarhus, Denmark, 1991, Louisiana Museum of Modern Art, Humlebaek, Denmark, 1991, Michael Kohn Gallery, Santa Monica, CA, 1992, Center for the Fine Arts, Miami, FL, 1992, Galeria Soledad Lorenzo, Madrid, Spain, 1993, Galerie Daniel Templon, Paris, France, 1994, 1999, Daniel Weinberg Gallery, San Francisco, CA, 1994, Michael Nagy Fine Art, Potts Point, Australia, 1995, Baldwin Gallery, Aspen, CO, 1997, Gagosian Gallery, New York, 1998, London, 2000, Galleria Lawrence Rubin, Milan, Italy, 1998. Named National Academician, Nat. Acad. of Design, 1994. Mem.: Am. Acad. Arts and Letters. Office: c/o Baldwin Gallery 209 S Galena St Aspen CO 81611 also: c/o Mary Boone Gallery 745 Fifth Ave New York NY 10151 Office Phone: 970-920-9797, 212-752-2929. Office Fax: 970-920-1821, 212-752-3939.

FISCHLER, ABRAHAM SAUL, retired academic administrator, educator; b. Bklyn., Jan. 21, 1928; s. Morris and Esther P. Fischler; m. Shirley Balter, Apr. 9, 1949; children: Bruce Evan, Michael Alan, Lori Faye. BS in Soc. Sci., CUNY, 1951; MA in Sci. Edn., NYU, 1952; EdD, Columbia U., 1959; DSc (hon.), N.Y. Inst. Tech., 1981; LLD (hon.), Nova U., 1992; BSS (hon.), U. Maruzalis, 2006. Sci. tchr., supr. Ossining (N.Y.) Pub. Schs., 1952-58; instr. Columbia U., NYC, 1958-59; asst. prof. edn. Harvard U. Grad. Sch., Cambridge, Mass., 1959-62; assoc. prof. then prof. edn. U. Calif., Berkeley, 1962-66; dean grad. studies Nova U., Ft. Lauderdale, Fla., 1966-70, James Donn prof., 1966—, exec. v.p., 1969-70, pres., 1970-92; pres. emeritus, univ. prof., 1992—; mem. Broward County Sch. Bd., 1994-98, chair, 1996-97. Vis. prof. nat. and internat. univs., 1963-65; cons. numerous sch. dists., Calif., 1962-67; advisor ednl. pubs.; mem. bus.-edn. adv. com. Alameda-Contra Costa Counties, Calif.; mem. Calif. Elem. Sci. Adv. Com., Sacramento; mem. Overseas Tchrs. Examining Team, Berkeley; bd. dirs. Cardio-Metrics, Inc., Inst. Learning Techs., Inc., Hollywood Med. Ctr., Fla. Med. Ctr., 2000— Author: Modern Science, Grades 7,8,9, 1963; (with others) Science: A Modern Approach, 1966, Modern Science, 1967, Modern Elementary Science: Grades 1 through 8, 1971, Nova U.'s Three National Doctoral Degree Programs: An Analysis and Formative Evaluation, 1977; contbr. numerous articles to profl. jours., author monograph and rsch. reports. Pres. United Way Broward County (Fla.), 1984-85, bd. dirs., 1973-2000, chmn. budget com., 1976-81; chmn. Broward County Overall Econ. Devel. Com., 1980-88, Broward Edn. and Tng. Coun., 1989—; pres. S.E. Fla. Holocaust Meml. Ctr., 1985-87, Temple Beth El, Hollywood, 1988-90; adv. bd. Leadership Broward; mem. 17th Jud. Nominating Commn., Broward County, 1982-86, Ft. Lauderdale Mus. Art, Fla. Philharm., Broward County Crime Commn., Broward Workshop Edn. Task Force, Town of Davie, Fla. Econ. and Indsl. Devel. Bd.; bd. dirs. Hollywood (Fla.) Med. Ctr., 1982—, chmn. bd. dirs., 1985—; pres. Health Care Rsch. and Edn. Found., 1988-89, United Ways Fla., 1990-91; bd. govs. Fla. Bar, 1991-95, Fla. Bar Found., 1996-01; chmn. Hollywood City Master Plan; mem. Broward Ctr. Performing Arts Authority, 1998; co-chair Sun Sentinel Diversity Fund, 2000—; chair Broward Edn. Found., 2002, South Fla. Cmty. Blood Ctrs., 2002. With USN, 1945-47. Recipient Outstanding Mgmt. and Leadership award Sales and Mktg. Execs., Ft. Lauderdale, 1978, Leader of Yr. award Leadership Broward, 1991, Humanitarian of Yr. award E.A.S.E. Found., 1991, Disting. Educator award Assn. Ind. Schs. Fla., 1992, Tree of Life award Jewish Nat. Fund, 1993, Spirit of Broward award, 1994, Lifetime Achievement award Urban League, 1994; named Broward Educator of Yr., Women's Am. ORT, 1997, Disting. Pub. Svc. award ADL, 1998, Sun Sentinel Cmty. Leader of the Yr., 1999, Sun Sentinel Cmty. Svc. award, 2000, Fla. Bar medal of Hon., 2005; DuPont fellow UCLA, 1958, Sci. Manpower fellow Columbia U., 1958-59, Nova Southeastern U. Athletic Hall of Fame, 2007. Fellow AAAS, Phi Delta Kappa; mem. ASCD, NSTA, Assn. for Edn. Tchrs. Sci. (past pres.), Nat. Assn. Research in Sci. Teaching, Soc. Advancement Edn., Soc. Research Adminstrs., Am. Assn. Higher Edn., Nat. Council Univ. Research Adminstrs., Com. of 100, Hollywood, Hundred Club Broward County (pres. 1985-86), Tower Club, Woodmont Country Club, Kappa Delta Pi. Avocations: running, golf, travel. Office: Nova U Office Pres Emeritus 3301 College Ave Fort Lauderdale FL 33314-7796 Business E-Mail: fischler@nova.edu.

FISCHLER, SANDY LYNN, charitable and informational organization executive; b. Anchorage, Alaska, Dec. 28, 1962; d. Joseph Michael Fischler and Sharon Leigh (Blodgett) Smith. Student, U. Alaska, 1980-83, Circle in Square Theatre Sch., 1983. Spl. event coord. Universal Studios Fla., Orlando, 1993-95; prodn. mgr. Headdress Ball, Orlando, 1994; assoc. prodr. Nickelodeon "Guts", Orlando, 1994; event mgr. First Night Providence, 1995; prodr. bike stunt segment 1997 Holiday Bowl Halftime Show, San Diego, 1997; event prodr. ESPN X Games, San Diego, 1995-98; ptnr. Avalanche Events Group, 1998—; owner 4th Wall Events, 1998—; event mgr. NFL Experience, Super Bowl XXXIII, 1999; broadcast mgr. NFL Experience, Super Bowl XXXIV, XXXV, XXXVI, XXXVII; exec. dir., founder The Pilonidal Support Alliance, 2005—. Vol. Feral Cat Coalition, San Diego, 1998, Kisses for Kats Pet Rescue, 2000-01, Cat's Meow Cat Rescue, 2002-. Mem. Women in Sports and Events, Internat. Festival and Events Assn., Calfest, Nat. Sports Mktg. Network. Avocations: gardening, stained glass. Home: 5911 Cerritos Ave Long Beach CA 90805

FISCHMAN, MYRNA LEAH, accountant, educator; d. Isidore and Sally (Goldstein) Fischman. BS, Coll. City NY, 1960, MS, 1964; PhD, NYU, 1976. CPA N.Y. Asst. to contr. Sam Goody, Inc., NYC; tchr. accounting Ctr. Comml. H.S., NYC, 1960—63, vicat. adviser, 1963—66; instr. acctg. Borough of Manhattan C.C., NYC, 1963—66; self-employed acct. NYC, 1960—; chief acct. investigator rackets Office Queens Dist. Atty., 1969—70, cmty. fels. coord., 1970—71; adv. prof. L.I. U., 1970—79, prof. acctg. taxation and law, 1979—, coord. grad. capstone courses, 1982—86, dir. Sch. Profl. Accountancy Bklyn. Campus, 1984—, dir. Ctr. Acctg. and Tax Edn., 1986—, chmn. acctg. dept. Editor: Ea. Bus. Educators Jour., 1988. Rsch. cons. pre-tech. program N.Y.C. Bd. Edn., mem., 1992—; acct.-advisor Inst. for Advancement of Criminal Justice; acct.-cons. Coalition Devel. Corp., Interracial Coun. for Bus. Opportunities; treas. Breakfree Inc., Lower East Side Prep. Sch.; mem. ednl.task force Am. Jewish Com., 1972—; mem. Chancellor Com. Against Discrimination in Edn., 1976—97; chmn. supervisory com. Fed. Credit Union # 1532, NYC, 1983—; chmn. consumer coun. Astoria Med. Ctr., 1980—92; mem. subcom. on bus. edn. to the econ. devel. and mktg. com. Bklyn. C. of C., 1984—; mem. adv. bd. acctg. dept. burough of Manhattan C.C., 1997—; mem. Bus. Edn. Adv. Coun.; mem. steering com., youth div. N.Y. Dem. County Com., 1967—68; del. to Nat. Conv. Young Dems. Am., 1967, rep. assigned to women's activities com., 1967; mem. legis. adv. bd. N.Y. State Assemblyman Dennis Butler, 1979—97. Recipient award for meritorious svc., Cmty. Svc. Soc., 1969, Lifetime Achievement award, Soroptimist Internat. Bklyn., 1997. Mem.: NEA (bus. edn. assns.), AAUP, AICPA, Inst. Mgmt. Accts. (dir. N.Y. chpt. 1983—, dir. profl. devel. 1986—87, dir. pub. rels. 1987—88, dir. manuscripts 1991—92, dir. univ. rels. 1993—94), Tax Inst. L.I. U. (dir. Blyn. chpg. 1984—), N.Y. State Soc. CPAs (mem. com. on recruitment for CPA careers 1981—, auditing com. 1991—, gen. com. on edn. in colls. and univs. 1991—, pub. rels. com. 1992—, pres. Bklyn. chpt. 2001—02, bd. dirs. 2005—, Dr. Emanuel Saxe Outstanding CPA in Edn. award 1994—95), Fed. Credit Union (chmn. supervisory com. # 1532 n.Y.C. 1983—, bd. dirs. 1989—), Young Alumni Assn., Am. Assn. Jr. Colls., Doctorate Assn. N.Y. Educators (v.p. 1975—97), Assn. Govt. Accts. (dir. N.Y. chpg. 1983—, pres. elect n.Y. chpg. 1989—90, pres. N.Y. chpt. 1990—91), Fin. Execs. Inst., Grad. Students Orgn. NYU (treas. 1971—73), Internat. Soc. Bus. Edn., Nat. Eastern (co-chmn. ann. meeting 1967), Am. Acctg. Assn., Govt. Accts. (v.p. 1973—74, dir. rsch. and manuscripts 1985—, pres. elect N.Y. chpt. 1989—90, pres. 1990—91, bd. dirs. N.Y. chpt. 1994—), Emanu-El League Congregation Emanu-El, N.Y. (chmn. cmty. svcs. com. 1967—68), Jewish Guild for Blind, Jewish Braille Inst., Cmty. Welfare Com. Assn., Friends Met. Mus. Art, Friends Am. Ballet Theatre, Women's City Club (N.Y.), Delta Pi Epsilon (treas. 1976).

Democrat. Jewish. Achievements include development of new bus. machine course and curriculum Borough Manhattan Bus. C.C. Office: LI U Sch Bus Rm H700 1 University Plz Rm 700 Brooklyn NY 11201-5301 Office Phone: 718-488-1157. Business E-Mail: myrnafischman@liu.edu.

FISCHOFF, GARY CHARLES, lawyer; b. Manhasset, NY, Nov. 23, 1954; s. Harold and Ann (Yablon) F.; m. Linda Lee Sacca, Nov. 22, 1985 (div. Nov. 2002); 1 child, Lisa Frances. BA, U. Buffalo, 1976; JD, St. John's U., Jamaica, NY, 1983. Bar: N.J. 1983, U.S. Dist. Ct. N.J. 1983, N.Y. 1984, U.S. Dist. Ct. (so. and ea. dists.) N.Y. 1985, U.S. Dist. Ct. (no. and we. dist.) N.Y., U.S. Ct. Appeals (2d cir.) 1988. Asst. treas. IAP, Inc., Lyndhurst, N.J., 1980-82; assoc. Hannoch Weisman, Roseland, N.J., 1983-85; ptnr. Fischoff Gelberg & Director, Garden City, N.Y., 1985-96, Fischoff & Assocs., Garden City, 1996—, Steinberg, Fineo, Berger & Fischoff, Woodbury, NY, 2003—. Lectr. seminar Nat. Bus. Inst., Westbury, N.Y., 1990, 91, Practicing Law Inst., 1992, 93, N.Y. State Bar Assn., 1995. Rep. Greentree Homeowners Assn., Northport, N.Y., 1988-89; trustee Suffolk County Vanderbilt Mus., 1994-2002, corp. sec., 1995-97, treas. 1997-99, 1st v.p., 1999-2002. Mem. Am. Bankruptcy Bd. Cert. (cert. bus. bankruptcy and consumer bankruptcy), N.Y. State Bar Assn. (real property sect., seminar lectr. 1995, Practicing Law Inst., continuing legal edn. lectr. 1992, 93), Nassau County Bar Assn. (mem. bankruptcy com., jud. liaison 1988-89). Jewish. Avocation: bicycling. Office: Steinberg Fineo Berger & Fischoff 40 Crossways Park-Drive Woodbury NY 11797 Home Phone: 516-484-6710; Office Phone: 516-747-1136. Personal E-mail: gcf@title11.net.

FISCUS, PHILIP WAYNE, underwriter; b. Hastings, Nebr., Nov. 8, 1955; BA, Calif. State U., Northridge, 1978. CPCU. Underwriter St. Paul Fire and Marine Ins. Co., 1978-80, sr. underwriter, 1980-84, underwriter dir., 1984-92; v.p. Reliance Nat., NYC, 1992-94; sr. v.p. Minet, Inc., NYC, 1994-95; v.p. Chubb Group of Ins. Cos., Warren, NJ, 1995—2002, sr. v.p., 2002—. Mem. adv. bd. Biolaw and Bus. Publ. Contbr. articles to profl. jours. Mem. AAAS, Biotechnology Industry Assn., Risk and Ins. Mgmt. Soc. (assoc.). Office: Chubb & Son Inc 202 Hall's Mill Rd PO Box 1650 Whitehouse Station NJ 08889 Business E-Mail: pfiscus@chubb.com.

FISCUS, THOMAS J., former judge, career military officer; BSc in Computer Sci., USAF Acad., 1972; JD, Ohio State U., 1975; MSc in Nat. Security Strategy, Nat. War Coll., 1994. Bar: Iowa, U.S. Dist. Ct. (no. dist.), U.S. Court of Appeals (5th, 10th, 11th cir.), U.S. Ct. Appeals (fed. cir.), U.S. Ct. Appeals (armed forces), U.S. Supreme Ct., U.S. Ct. Fed. Claims. Advanced through ranks to maj. gen. USAF, 2000; asst. staff judge advocate, 1975—76; dep. staff judge advocate Zaragosa Air Base, Spain, 1976—78; chief appellate review divsn. Ramstein Air Base, Germany, 1978-80; litigation atty. office JAG USAF, Washington, 1980—83, asst. exec. JAG, 1983—85; staff judge advocate Mather AFB, Sacramento, 1985-88; chief preventive law and legal aid group USAF, 1988—91, exec. JAG, 1991—93, staff judge advocate Travis AFB, Calif., 1994-96, Hickam AFB, Hawaii, 1996-99, Langley AFB, Va., 1999—2000, dep. JAG, 2000—02, JAG, 2002—04. Decorated Legion of Merit with oak leaf cluster, Meritorious Svc. medal with two oak leaf clusters, Nat. Defense Svc. medal with bronze star, Vietnam Svc. medal with bronze star, Disting. Svc. medal, SW Asia Svc. medal. Mem. Judge Advocates Assn. (past pres.).

FISH, CHESTER BOARDMAN, JR., retired editor; b. Worcester, Mass., June 30, 1925; s. Chester Boardman and Mary Elizabeth Ada (Sheehan) F.; m. Claire Margaret Commo, Sept. 10, 1948; children: Craig Michael, Scott Kevin, Maribeth Ann, Andrea Dawn, Brian John. BA, Syracuse U., 1950, MA, 1952. Asst. editor Boys' Life mag., NYC, 1951-53; assoc. editor Sports Afield mag., NYC, 1953-55; copy chief Am. Home mag., NYC, 1955-57; assoc. editor Outdoor Life mag., NYC, 1957-63, article editor, 1963-67, mng. editor, 1967-73, editor in chief, 1973-76; sr. editor David McKay Co., Inc. book pubs., NYC, 1976-80, Charles Scribner's Sons (pubs.), NYC, 1980-81; pub. cons. The Competitive Edge, Greenlawn, N.Y., 1981-83; editorial dir. Stackpole Books, Harrisburg, Pa., 1983-85, exec. v.p., 1986-89, Stackpole Inc., Harrisburg, Pa., 1989-90; pub. Harness Horse mag., Harrisburg, 1989-91; pub. cons. and freelance writer Carlisle, Pa., 1990-94. Served with USNR, 1943-46, PTO. Mem. Carlindian Barbershop Chorus, Phi Beta Kappa. Republican. Roman Catholic. Home: 709 Sutton Dr Carlisle PA 17013-3546

FISH, HOWARD MATH, aerospace transportation executive; b. Melrose, Minn., Aug. 1, 1923; s. Nathaniel and Louise Margaret (Gaetz) Fish; m. Jamie Katherine Tom, May 15, 1948; 1 child, Howard Math Jr. Student, Air Command and Staff Coll., 1954; MBA, U. Chgo., 1957; postgrad., Armed Forces Staff Coll., 1960, Air War Coll., Montgomery, Ala., 1964; MAIA, George Washington U., 1964. Enlisted USAF, 1942, commd. 2d lt., 1944, capt., 1950, col., 1965, advance through grades to lt. gen., 1974, ret., 1979; deputy asst. sec. defense internat. security affairs Dept. Defense, Washington; asst. vice chief of staff USAF, Washington; chmn. US Mil. Delegation to UN; v.p. internat. LTV Aerospace and Defense Co., 1980—82, Loral Corp., 1992—96; sr. advisor Internat. Lockheed-Martin Missiles and Fire Control, Dallas, La., 1996—2005. Mem. Def. Policy Adv. Com. Trade, Washington, 1987—94; chmn. Am. League Exports and Security Assistance, Washington, 1986—94. Decorated Def. DSM, Air Force DSM, Legion of Merit, DFC, Air medal, Purple Heart, POW medal. Mem.: Washington Inst. Fgn. Affairs, Am. Def. Preparedness Assn. (chmn. internat. divsn. 1984—94), Air Force Assn., Army Navy Club, Beta Gamma Sigma. Roman Catholic. Avocations: tennis, fishing. Personal E-mail: genhmfish@aol.com.

FISH, JAMES HENRY, library director; b. Leominster, Mass., Feb. 21, 1947; s. Danny Mack and Doris Grace (Harvey) F. BA, U. Mass., 1968; MLS, Ind. U., 1971; MBA, Anna Maria Coll., Paxton, Mass., 1980. Dir. librs. Levi Heywood Meml. Libr., Gardner, Mass., 1971—72; dir. Leominster Pub. Libr., Gardner, 1972—77, Robbins Libr., Arlington, Mass., 1977—80, Springfield City Libr., Mass., 1982—90, Balt. County Pub. Libr., 1996—; state libr. Mass. State Libr., Boston, 1980—82; city libr. San Jose Pub. Libr., 1990—96. Author libr. reports and cons. projects cmty. analysis, planning and evaluation. Bd. dirs. United Fund Leominster, 1974-76, Vis. Nurses Assn., Leominster, 1974-76, Leominster chpt. ARC, 1975-77, Santa Clara Valley YMCA, 1991-94; chmn. Leominster Bicentennial Com., 1975-76. With US Army, 1969—71. Decorated Commendation medal; recipient Disting. Svc. award Arlington C. of C., 1979, Disting. Alumni award Ind. U. Sch. Libr. and Info. Sci., 2006, SirsiDynix-ALA-Allied Profl. Assn. award for Outstanding Achievement in Promoting Salaries and Status for Libr. Workers, 2006. Mem. ALA, Pub. Libr. Assn. (new stds. task force 1986-87, adv. com. chmn. pub. libr. data svc., mem. conf. prog. com. 1988-90, 90-91, mem. nominating com. 1993, mem. common concerns com. 1994, mem. ptnrs. prog. 1994, mem. exec. bd. 1998, mem. issues and concerns steering com. 1998), Calif. Libr. Assn. (mem. com. 1993-96, conf. planning com. 1994-95, chair local arrangements com. 1994-95), Urban Librs. Coun. (symposium planning com. chair 1998, steering com. 1994-97, video tng. project 1994-97, strategic dirs. com., bd. dirs. OCLC adv. com. pub. librs. 1998, vice chair, chair elect 2001), Beta Phi Mu. Office: Balt County Pub Libr 320 York Rd Towson MD 21204-5179 Office Phone: 410-887-6160. E-mail: bcpl@bcpl.info.

FISH, JANET ISOBEL, artist; b. Boston, May 18, 1938; d. Peter and Florence (Voorhees) F. BA, Smith Coll., Northampton, Mass., 1960; postgrad., Skowhegan Art Sch., 1961; BFA, MFA, Yale U., New Haven, Conn., 1963; DFA (hon.), Lyme Acad., 2000. Represented by D.C. Moore Gallery, NYC. One-woman shows D.C. Moore Gallery, NYC, Columbus Mus., Ga., Ogunquit Mus. Am. Art, Maine, Butler Inst. Am. Art, Youngstown, Ohio, 2006, also others; traveling exhbn. Yellowstone Art Ctr., Billings, Mont., 1995-97; represented in permanent collections Whitney Mus. Am. Art, NYC, Met. Mus. Art, NYC, Cleve. Mus. Art, Dallas Mus. Fine Arts, Am. Fedn. Arts, Am. Acad. Inst. Arts and Letters, Art Inst. Chgo., Kemper Mus., Kansas City, Albright-Knox Gallery, Buffalo, NY, Newark Mus., Mpls. Mus. of Art, Nat. Gallery of Victoria, Melbourne, Australia, Powers Inst., Sydney, Australia, Colby Coll., Waterville, Maine, Mus. of Fine Arts, Houston Art Ctr., RISD, Providence, Mus. Art, Providence, Va. Mus. Fine Arts, Richmond, Yale U., New Haven, Smith Coll. Mus. Art, Northampton, Mass., Albrecht Art Mus., St. Joseph, Mo., Milw. Art Mus., Hunter Mus. Art, Chattanooga, Butler Inst. Am. Art, Youngstown, Ohio, Am. Acad. Arts and Letters, John Szoke Gallery, NY, 1998-99, others. Bd. govs. Skowhegan Sch. Painting and Sculpture, Marie Walsh Sharpe Art Found. Recipient Harris award Chgo. Bienale award, 1974, Outstanding Woman Artist award Aspen Mus., 1992; MacDowell fellow, 1968, 70, 72; Yale scholar, Australian Coun. for Arts grantee, 1975. Mem. NAD (Henry Ward Ranger Purchase prize 2001, William A. Paton watercolor prize 2005, elected nat. academician 1994), Am. Acad. Arts and Letters (award 1994) Personal E-mail: jfcp1@earthlink.net.

FISH, LAWRENCE KINGSBAKER, bank executive; b. Chgo., Oct. 9, 1944; s. Alvin Kingsbaker and Beatrice (Brown) F.; m. Atsuko Toko, June 29, 1980; children: Leah Okajima, Edward Takezo, Emily Takako. BA, Drake U., 1966; MBA, Harvard U., 1968; D of Bus. Adminstrn. (hon.), Drake U., 2005; degree (hon.), Providence Coll., Bryant Coll., Johnson & Wales U., U. Mass. US aid officer US Agy. Internat. Capital Devel., 1970-72; internal officer Bank of Boston, Brazil, 1972, dir. internat. ops., 1972-74, asst. v.p., gen. mgr., 1974-75, v.p., dep. gen. mgr., 1975, v.p., 1975, v.p., gen. mgr. Tokyo, 1978-79, 1st v.p., 1979-80; 1st v.p., head Pacific Asia divsn., Bank of Boston, Hong Kong, 1980-81, sr. v.p., 1981-82, exec. v.p., 1982-83, exec. v.p., head of trust function Boston, 1983-84, exec. v.p, head New Eng. Group, 1984-88; pres., COO Columbia Savs. & Loan Assn., Beverly Hills, Calif., 1988-90; chmn., CEO Bank of New Eng., Boston, 1990-92; chmn., CEO and pres. Citizens Fin. Group, Inc., Providence, 1992—2007, chmn., 2007—; chmn. US ops. Royal Bank of Scotland Group PLC, 2007—. Bd. dirs. Fed. Reserve Bank of Boston, 2002, Textron Inc.; mem. bd. trustees Brookings Inst., Washington; bd. trustees MIT Corp., 2003—; mem. FDIC Commn. on Econ. Inclusion. Mem. exec. com. Children's Museum, Boston, 1984-85; pres. Boston/Kyoto Sister City Found., 1984-85; bd. dirs. Japan Soc. of Boston, 1984-85, Inst. Contemporary Art of Boston, Dimock Cmty. Found, Com. to Encourage Corp. Philanthropy; mem. exec. bd. USAID Pvt. Enterprise, Washington, 1984-88; overseer New Eng. Conservatory Music, Boston Symphony Orchestra. Grantee Frank Knox Fellowship; Woodrow Wilson Found. fellow, 1984. Fellow: Am. Acad. Arts & Scis.; mem.: Alfred P. Sloan Mgmt. Soc. (founding mem.), Longwood (Brookline, Mass.). Office: Citizens Financial Grp One Citizens Plaza Providence RI 02903-4089*

FISH, MARDY, professional tennis player; b. Edina, Minn., Dec. 9, 1981; s. Tom and Sally. Profl. tennis player ATP, 2000—. Named Comeback Player of Yr., 2006 ATP Awards; recipient Silver medal in tennis, Athens Summer Olympics, 2004. Achievements include winning 2 career singles titles, 3 career doubles titles, ATP. Avocations: hockey, baseball. Office: PO Box 4165 Vero Beach FL 32963*

FISH, MARY MARTHA, economics professor; b. Albert Lea, Minn., July 17, 1930; d. Charles H. and Olga (Stennes) Thomassen; m. Donald C. Fish, Oct. 1954 (dec.); children: Jill S., Lynn M., Jason M BBA, U. Minn., 1951; MBA Econs, Tex. Tech. Coll., 1957; PhD, U. Okla., 1963. Statis. asst. Iowa Bd. Control, 1951—53; pub. health analyst State of Calif., 1953—54; analytical statistician 46th Med. Gen. Lab., U.S. Army Forces, Tokyo, 1954—57; instr. econs. and bus. Odessa Coll., Tex., 1957—58; asst. prof., then assoc. prof. West Tex. State U., 1961—66; prof. econs. U. Ala., 1966—99, prof. emeritus, 1999—. Prof. econs. Landegg Internat. U., Wienacht, Switzerland, 2000-02; Fulbright lectr. U. Liberia, 1974-75, Gambian Govt., 1978-79; cons. in field Co-author: Convicts, Codes and Contraband, 1974; contbr. articles to profl. jours Founding mem. Nat. Campaign for Tolerance; mem. So. Poverty Tolerance Program, 1995. Grantee U. Ala., 1967-68, 87-89, Dept. Labor, 1978-79; Fulbright rsch. fellow, Taiwan, 1995; Phifer Faculty Scholar, 1998, fellow AAUW, 1960 Mem. Am. Econ. Assn., So. Econ. Assn Mem. Baha'i faith. Home: 1405 High Forest Dr N Tuscaloosa AL 35406-2153 Personal E-mail: mmf4473@bellsouth.net. Business E-Mail: mfish@cba.ua.edu.

FISH, STANLEY EUGENE, dean, language educator; b. Providence, Apr. 19, 1938; s. Max and Ida Dorothy (Weinberg) F.; m. Adrienne A. Aaron, Aug. 23, 1959 (div. 1980); 1 dau., Susan.; m. Jane Parry Tompkins, Aug. 7, 1982. BA, U. Pa., 1959; MA, Yale U., 1960, PhD, 1962. Instr. U. Calif., Berkeley, 1962-63, asst. prof., 1963-67, assoc. prof., 1967-69, prof., 1969-74; Kenan prof. English and Humanities Johns Hopkins U., Balt., 1978-85, chmn. dept., 1983-85; Arts and Sci. Disting. prof. English and prof. law Duke U., Durham, NC, 1985-98, chmn. dept., 1986-92; exec. dir. Duke U. Press, Durham, 1994-98; dean U. Ill. Coll. Liberal Arts and Scis., Chgo., 1999—2004; Davidson-Kahn Disting. Univ. Prof. humanities and Law Fla. Internat. U. Coll. Law, Miami, 2005—. Author: John Skelton's Poetry, 1965, Surprised by Sin: The Reader in Paradise Lost, 1967, 97 (Hanford Book award 1998), Seventeenth Century Prose: Modern Essays in Criticism, 1971, Self-Consuming Artifacts, 1972, The Living Temple: George Herbert and Catechizing, 1978, Is There a Text in This Class?, 1980, Doing What Comes Naturally, 1989, There's No Such Thing as Free Speech.And It's a Good Thing Too, 1994 (PEN/Spielvogel-Diamonstein award 1994), Professional Correctness: Literary Studies and Political Change, 1995, The Trouble with Principle, 1999, How Milton Works, 2001; mem. edit. bd. Milton Studies, Milton Quar. Recipient 2d place, Explicator prize, 1968; Am. Council Learned Socs. fellow, 1966; Guggenheim fellow, 1969 Mem. MLA, Am. Acad. Arts and Scis., Milton Soc. (hon. scholar 1991), Spenser Soc. Office: Fla Internat U Coll Law Univ Park Campus Green Library Ste 484 Miami FL 33199 Office Phone: 305-348-7820. Business E-Mail: fishs@fiu.edu.

FISH, TOM, special education and vocational school educator; b. Wyandotte, Mich., Mar. 18, 1936; s. Kenneth Lyle and Ann Julia Fish; m. Beverley Anderson, June 18, 1956 (div. Aug. 1976); children: Robert, Toni, Kenneth; m. Lynne Coates, Dec. 12, 1992. BA, Adrian Coll., Mich., 1962; MA, U. Pacific, Stockton, Calif., 1985; PhD in Spl. Edn. summa cum laude, Madison U., 2004. Cert. spl. edn. disabilities tchr. Calif. C.C., serv-safe instr. Nat. Restaurant Assn., 2004. Food svc. dir. Saga Adminstrv. Corp., Adrian, 1961-75, Cleve. Browns Pro Football Team, Hiram, Ohio, 1965-68, Del Monte Corp., San Francisco, 1975-80, Placer County Corrections, Auburn, Calif., 1980-83; intern Devel. Disabilities Svcs. Orgn., Sacramento, 1984-85; vocat./edn. tchr. Stockton Unified Sch. Dist., Calif., 1985—; tchr. nutrition and ind. living San Joaquin Delta Coll., 1993—. Founder Campus Cafe, A.A. Stagg High Sch., Stockton, 1987—, Deli Delivery, 1989, Greystone Cons. Group., 1992. Recipient Ednl. Enrichment award Stockton Enrichment Found., 1989, 90, Program Devel. award Jr. Aid Stockton, 1989, 90, Outstanding Person award San Joaquin County Juvenile Justice and Deliquency Prevention Commn., 1991. Mem. NEA, Coun. Exceptional Children (membership chair 1988-89, community svc. award 1989), Calif. Tchrs. Assn., Phi Delta Kappa (U. pacific chpt.). Democrat. Avocation: lecturing on spiritual development. Office: AA Stagg HS 1621 Brookside Rd H-8 Stockton CA 95207-7804 Office Phone: 916-849-2299.

FISHBACK, DENNIS, information technology executive; Mgmt. Va. Power; with Calif. Ind. Sys. Operator; sr. v.p. & chief info. officer Calpine Corp., San Jose, Calif., 2001—. Named one of the Premier 100 IT Leaders, Computerworld mag., 2004. Office: SVP & CIO Calpine Corp 50 W San Fernando St San Jose CA 95113

FISHBACK, IAN, military officer; b. Newberry, Mich., 1978; Grad., U.S. Military Acad., West Point. Capt. 1st Battalion 82nd Airborne Divsn. US Army, Afghanistan and Iraq. Named one of 100 Most Influential People in World, Time Mag., 2006. Brought prisoner abuses in Afghanistan and Iraq to light resulting in Sen. John McCain's successful sponsorship of antitorture legislation. Address: 82nd Airborne Divsn Cumberland County Fort Bragg NC 28307

FISHBEIN, PETER MELVIN, lawyer; b. NYC, June 20, 1934; s. Arthur L. and Lotta (Chary) F.; m. Bette Klinghoffer, June 16, 1957; children: Stephen, Bruce, Gregory. BA magna cum laude, Dartmouth Coll., 1955; JD, Harvard U., 1958. Bar: N.Y. 1959, U.S. Supreme Ct. 1973. Note editor Harvard Law Rev., Cambridge, Mass., 1956-58; law clk. to Justice William J. Brennan, Jr. U.S. Supreme Ct., Washington, 1958-59; dep. sec. gen. Internat. Peace Corps., Washington, 1962-64; ptnr. Kaye, Scholer LLP, NYC, 1967—2002, mng. ptnr., 1984-91; chief counsel N.Y. State Constl. Conv., Albany, 1967; mem. Presdl. Commn. to Nominate Candidates for Fed. Ct. of Appeals, NYC, 1980. Adj. prof. constl. law NYU Law Sch., 1970-84. Contbr. articles to profl. jours. Trustee Goddard Coll., 1967—75, Fedn. Jewish Philanthropies, NYC, 1975—81, Citizen's Budget Comm., 1995—99; mem. N.Y. State Gov.'s Bd. Pub. Disclosure, Albany, 1975—77; mgr. Justice Arthur J. Goldberg's Campaign for Gov., 1970; bd. dirs. Health Care Chaplaincy, 1993—99, Brennan Ctr. for Justice, 1995—, I Have A Dream Found., 2001—, White Plains Hosp., 2002—, Friends of the Supreme Ct. of Israel, 2003—, Purchase Coll., SUNY, 2005—. Recipient Disting. Cmty. Svc. award Brandeis U., Jurisprudence award Am. Ort. Fellow Am. Coll. Trial Lawyers, Am. Bar Found.; mem. ABA, Assn. of Bar of City of NY, NY State Commn. on Higher Edn., Harvard Club (NY), Beach Point Club (bd. govs. 1981-86), Phi Beta Kappa Home: 101 Woodlands Rd Harrison NY 10528-1423 Office: Kaye Scholer LLP 425 Park Ave New York NY 10022-3506 Business E-Mail: pfishbein@kayescholer.com.

FISHBEIN, THOMAS MARLON, general surgeon, transplant surgeon; b. Balt., Md., Jan. 28, 1963; MD, Georgetown Univ. Sch. Medicine, 1989. Cert. Surgery, 1996. Intern, surgery Boston Univ. Med. Ctr., 1990—91; resident Boston Univ. & Affiliated Hosp., 1991—95; transplant/hepatobiliary fellow Mt. Sinai Med. Ctr., NYC, 1995—97, asst. prof., 1997; fellow Univ. Pitts., Pa., 1997; assoc. prof., divsn. transplant surgery. dept. surgery Georgetown Univ. Hosp., dir., Intestinal & Pediatric Liver Transplantation. Achievements include being a nationally known surgeon in intestinal transplantation and has performed approximately 20% of all intestinal transplants performed in the US. Office: Georgetown U Hosp 3800 Reservoir Rd NW Main Hospital 2nd Floor Washington DC 20007 Office Phone: 202-444-3700.*

FISHBERG, GERARD, lawyer; b. Bronx, NY, May 23, 1946; s. Alfred and Sarah (Goldberg) F.; m. Eileen Taubman, Dec. 23, 1972; children: David, Dana. BA, Hofstra U., 1968; JD, St. John's U., Bklyn., 1971. Bar: N.Y. 1972, U.S. Dist. Ct. (ea. and so. dists.) N.Y. 1973, U.S. Ct. Appeals (2d cir.) 1975, U.S. Supreme Ct. 1976. Assoc. Cullen & Dykman LLP, Garden City, NY, 1972-79, ptnr., 1980—. Assoc. editor St. John's U. Law Rev., 1970-71. Legis. com. N.Y. Conf. of Mayors and Mcpl. Ofcls., Albany, 1976—; bd. dirs. Am. Heart Assn. L.I. region, 1995—, treas. 1997-98, vice chair, 1998-2000, chair, 2000-02; bd. dirs. Heritage Affiliate 1999-2005. Capt. USAR, 1968-77. St. Thomas Moore scholar, St. John's U. Sch. Law, 1969—71. Mem.: Nassau County Bar Assn. (chmn. mcpl. law com. 1981—83, 1985—87, chmn. labor law com. 1991-92 1991—92, bd. dirs. 1999—2002), N.Y. State Bar Assn. (mem. exec. com. 1978—, labor law sect. 1985, sec. 1985—87, mcpl. law 1985—, 1st vice chmn. 1989—91, chmn. 1991—93, mem. ho. of dels. 1993—), Rotacare (bd. dirs. 1992—, pres. 1993—99), Rotary (bd. dirs. 1988—94, treas. 1990—91, pres. 1992—93), Garden City C. of C. Jewish. Home: 1 Bucknell Dr Plainview NY 11803-1801 Office: Cullen & Dykman LLP 100 Quentin Roosevelt Blvd Garden City NY 11530-4850 Home Phone: 516-367-8583; Office Phone: 516-357-3703. Business E-Mail: gfishberg@cullenanddykman.com.

FISHBUNE, ROBERT, food products executive; CFO Specialty Foods Corp., Deerfield, Ill., US Food Service, Columbia, Md., 2004—. Office: US Foodservice 9755 Patuxent Woods Dr Columbia MD 21046 Office Phone: 410-312-7100. Office Fax: 410-312-7149.

FISHBURN, JANET FORSYTHE, dean; m. Peter Clingerman Fishburn, 1958; children: Susan, Katherine, Sally. BA magna cum laude, Monmouth Coll., 1958, LHD (hon.), 1984; PhD, Pa. State U., 1978. Ordained to ministry Presbyn. Ch., US, 1988. Dir. Christian edn. 1st United Presbyn. Ch., Cleveland Heights, Ohio, 1958-60; lectr. Pa. State U., 1977-78; asst. prof. Christian edn. Theol. Sch., Drew U., Madison, NJ, 1978-83, assoc. prof., 1983-90, asst. prof. Am. ch. history, 1982-83, assoc. prof., 1983-95, prof. tchg. ministry, 1990-95, prof. emeritus, 1995—, acting dean Theol. Sch., 1994-95. Parish assoc. Mt. Freedom Presbyn. Ch., 1991—94; manuscript reviewer Scholars Press, Fairleigh Dickinson Press, U. Pa. Press; lectr. in field, 1982—; panelist, spkr. profl. confs. and religious orgns.; cons. Books for Pastors Series Abingdon Press, 1987; mem. social justice com. Newton Presbytery, 1989—95, mem. coun., 1995—2001, 2004—, mem. com. on ministry, 2001—04, chmn. personnel com., 2005—. Author: (book) The Fatherhood of God and the Victorian Family: The Social Gospel in America, 1982, Confronting the Idolatry of Family: A New Vision for the Household of God, 1991, Parenting is for Everyone: Living Out Our Baptismal Covenant, 1996; editor: Drew Gateway, 1989—93; contbr. articles and revs. to profl. jours., clergy jours. and encys; editor: People of a Compassionate God: Creating Welcoming Congregations, 2003. Leader weekly bible study Madison Presbyn. Ch., 1985—89, mem. chancel choir, 1982—90, Morristown United Meth. Ch., 1992—96, co-leader spiritual growth group, 1990—; spkr. clergy confs.; tchr. adult edn. Mem.: Am. Soc. Ch. History, Presbyn. Profs. Social Witness Policy (panel coord. 1994, 2006), United Meth. Assn. Scholars Christian Edn. (chmn. rsch. com. 1995—97). Avocation: genealogy. Office Phone: 908-630-8787. Business E-Mail: jfishbur@drew.edu.

FISHBURNE, BENJAMIN POSTELL, III, lawyer; b. South Bend, Ind., Nov. 14, 1943; s. Benjamin Postell and Peggy (Gahan) F.; m. Edith E., Aug. 5, 1983. BA cum laude, U. Notre Dame, 1965; JD, U. Va., 1968. Bar: U.S. Ct. Mil. Appeals 1968, U.S. Army Ct. Mil. Rev. 1968, D.C. 1971. Capt. JAG Corps US Army, 1968-72; atty. Surrey & Morse, Washington, 1968, ptnr., 1975, mng. ptnr. Washington, 1981-84; ptnr. Jones, Day, Reavis & Pogue, 1986, ptnr.-in-charge Hong Kong office, 1986-91, ptnr., 1991-93, Winston & Strawn, Washington, 1993—. Gen. counsel Nat. Coun. U.S.-China Trade, 1981—87, assoc. coun., 1987—89, chmn. legal com., 1994—2001; mem. adv. com. China-U.S. Conciliation Ctr., 1993—; mem. Am. Arbitration Assn. spl. corp. com. East-West trade arbitration, 1973—79; mem. nat. coun. U.S.-China Trade Investment Del. to China; alt. mem. UN Assn.'s Nat. Policy panel study U.S.-China Rels., 1979; spkr. in field. Contbr. articles to profl. jours. Co-chmn. Am. C. of C. Hong Kong legal com., 1990, mem. bd. govs., 1991; mem. bd. advisors Johns Hopkins Nanjing Ctr., 1986-97. Mem.: Order of Coif. Home: 5535 Nevada Ave NW Washington DC 20015-1768 Office: Winston & Strawn LLP 1700 K St NW Washington DC 20006 Office Phone: 202-282-5792. Business E-Mail: bfishbur@winston.com.

FISHBURNE, JOHN INGRAM, JR., retired obstetrician/gynecologist, educator; b. Charleston, SC, Aug. 18, 1937; m. Jean Crawford, June 10, 1971; children: John Ingram III, Barron Crawford, Virginia Heyward. AB, Princeton U., NJ, 1959; MD, Med. Coll. SC, Charleston, 1963. Diplomate Am. Bd. Ob-Gyn. (sub. specialty maternal-fetal medicine), Am. Bd. Anes. Surg. intern Duke U. Hosp., Durham, NC, 1963-64; resident in ob-gyn. U. NC, Chapel Hill, 1966-70, resident in anesthesiology, 1970-72, instr. dept. ob-gyn., 1970-71, asst. prof., 1971-74, assoc. prof., 1974-75, asst. prof. dept. anesthesiology, 1972-75; assoc. prof. dept. ob-gyn. Bowman Gray Sch. Medicine, Wake Forest U., Winston-Salem, NC, 1975-78, prof., 1978-83, assoc. prof. anesthesiology, dept. anesthesiology, 1975-83; prof., chmn. dept. ob-gyn. U. Okla. Health Scis. Ctr., Oklahoma City, 1983-97, adj. prof. dept. anesthesiology, 1983-97, chmn. search com. for chair pathology dept., 1987-88, chmn. search com. for chair family medicine dept., 1993-94; residency program dir. dept. ob-gyn. Maricopa Med. Ctr., Phoenix, 1997—2001, chair dept. ob-byn., 1997—2000, vice chmn. dept. ob-gyn., 2000—04, assoc. program dir. dept. ob-gyn., 2001—04; prof. clin. ob-gyn. U. Ariz. Coll. Medicine, Tucson, 1997—2005; ret., 2005. Dir. maternal-fetal medicine dept. ob-gyn. Forsyth Meml. Hosp., Winston-Salem, 1977-83; vis. prof. U. W.I., Kingston, Jamaica, 1973-74, African-Health Tng. Instns. Project Nairobi, Kenya, 1975; cons. devel. mission US AID, Dacca, Bangladesh, 1980, Assn. Vol. Surg. Contraception World Fedn. Health Agys., Manila, 1984, Singapore, 1986, Zhordania Inst., Tbilisi, Republic of Georgia, 1992, 93, 97, Ivanovo, Russia, 1994, Almaty, Kazakhstan, 1994, St. Petersburg, Russia, 1995, Khojand, Tahjikistan, 1995, Odessa, Ukraine, 1995, Chechenov, Moldova, 1996, L'viv Ukraine; oral examiner Am. Bd. Ob-Gyn, 1980—2002; chmn. Gov.'s Task Force on Perinatal Care, 1984-86; mem. steering com. Robert Wood Johnson Healthy Futures of Okla., 1988-92; trustee Am. Assn. for Gynecologic Laparascopists, 1980-81; cons. Coun. on Resident Edn. in Ob-gyn., 1997—; presenter numerous sci. papers and lectures local, nat. and internat. profl. meetings. Author: (with others) The Prostaglandins, 1972, Endocrine-Metabolic Drugs, 1974, Gynecologic Laparoscopy: Principles and Techniques, 1974, Laparoscopy, 1977, Endoscopy in Gynecology, 1978, Clinics in Perinatology, 1982, Obstetric Anesthesia, 1982, Clinical and Diagnostic Procedures Obstetrics and Gyncecology, Part B, 1984, Advances in Clinical Obstetrics and Gynecology, Medical Economics Books, 1985, Clinical Obstetrics, 1987, Danforth's Obstetrics and Gynecology, 1994, 98, Bonica's Obstetric Analgesia and Anesthesia, 1995; contbr. update series Am. Colk Obstetricians and Gynecologists; editorial bd. Obstetrics and Gynceology, 1985-89; author self instructional programs in field; contbr. numerous articles to profl. jours. Capt. USAFR, 1964—66. Clin. fellow Am. Cancer Soc. U. NC, Chapel Hill, 1968-69, clin. fellow obstet. anesthesia Pub. Health Svc. U. Hosps. Case Western Res. U., Cleve., 1969; tng. rsch. grantee NIH Med. U. SC, Charleston, 1961-62. Fellow Am. Coll. Ob/Gyn (spl. interest rep. for obstet. anesthesia 1974-78, learning resources commn. 1981-82, mem. personal rev. of learning in ob-gyn. task force for obstetrics 1981-82, chair obs. IV, 1996-98, chair edn. commn. Accreditation Coun. for Grad. Med. Edn. (residency rev. com. ob/gyn 1991-93, chair 1994-96, dir.), Accreditation Coun. for Grad. Med. Edn. (exec. com. 2001-02, vice chair coun. of residency rev. com. chairs 1996, chair accreditation coun. for grad. med. edn. coun. res. rev. com. chairs, 1997-98, oral examiner 1980-2002), Am. Bd. Ob/Gyn, Am. Coll. Anesthesiologists (assoc. examiner 1974); mem. Am. Soc. Anesthesiologists, Soc. Maternal and Fetal Medicine (rep. liaison com. ob.-gyn. 1983-89, bd. dirs. 1981-84), South Atlantic Assn. Obstetricians and Gynecologists (assoc.), Internat. Soc. Advancement Humanistic Studies in Medicine (pres. 1997). Episcopalian. Avocations: golf, movies, reading, home repair. Home: 6 Cedar Marsh Retreat Savannah GA 31411-2922

FISHBURNE, LAURENCE, III, actor; b. Augusta, Ga., July 30, 1961; s. Laurence John Jr. and Hattie Bell Crawford F.; m. Hajna O. Moss, July 1, 1985 (div.); children: Langston Issa, Montana Isis; m. Gina Torres Sept. 20, 2002. Appearances include (theatre) Section D, 1975, Eden, 1976, Short Eyes, 1984, Loose Ends, 1988, Urban Blight, 1988, Two Trains Running, 1992 (Best Featured Actor Tony award 1992), Fences, 2006, (films) Cornbread, Earl and Me, 1975, Apocalypse Now, 1979, Fast Break, 1979, Willie and Phil, 1980, Death Wish II, 1982, Rumble Fish, 1983, The Cotton Club, 1984, The Color Purple, 1985, Band of the Hand, 1986, Quicksilver, 1986, Gardens of Stone, 1987, A Nightmare on Elm Street 3: Dream Warriors, 1987, School Daze, 1988, Red Heat, 1988, King of New York, 1990, Cadence, 1991, Class Action, 1991, Boyz N the Hood, 1991, Deep Cover, 1992, What's Love Got To Do With It, 1993 (Academy award nominee, Best Actor, 1993), Searching For Bobby Fischer, 1993, Higher Learning, 1995, Bad Company, 1995, Just Cause, 1995, Othello, 1995, Fled, 1996, Hoodlum, 1997, Event Horizon, 1997, The Matrix, 1999, Once in the Life, 2000 (also dir., writer, prodr.), Osmosis Jones, 2001, Biker Boyz, 2003, The Matrix Reloaded, 2003, Mystic River, 2003, The Matrix Revolutions, 2003, Assault on Precinct 13, 2005, Akeelah and the Bee, 2006, Mission Impossible III, 2006, Five Fingers, 2006, Bobby, 2006, (narrator) TMNT, 2007, (TV films) A Rumor of War, 1980, I Take These Men, 1983, The Father Clements Story, 1987, Decoration Day,1990, Miss Ever's Boys, 1997, Always Outnumbered, 1998; prodr. Miss Evers' Boys, 1997, Hoodlum, 1997, Always Outnumbered, 1998, dir., writer, prodr., actor: Once in the Life, 2000; TV guest appearances M*A*S*H, 1972, Hill Street Blues, 1981, Miami Vice, 1984, Spenser: For Hire, 1985, The Equalizer, 1985. Recipient Emmy award, 1993, 97, Image award, 1996, 98. Mailing: Landmark Artist & Mgmt 4116 W Magnolia Blvd, Ste 101 Burbank CA 91505*

FISHEL, ANDREW S., managing director; b. Apr. 7, 1948; married, 1969. BA, Am. U., 1969; EdD of Am. Politics and Edn., Columbia U., 1975; MEd, Am. U., 1970. Legis. planning coord. U.S. Dept. HEW, Washington; mgmt. dir. Office for Civil Rights U.S. Dept. Edn., Washington; dir. fin. and resource mgmt. EEOC, Washington, 1982-89; mng. dir. FCC, Washington, 1989—2006. Co-author: (with Jan Pottker) Sex Bias in the Schools: The Research Evidence, 1977, National Politics and Sex Discrimination in Schools, 1977. Recipient Quality Improvement Prototype award Office Mgmt. and Budget, 1987, Outstanding Mgr. award ASTD, 1992, Disting. Svc. medal FCC, 1992. Office: Fed Comm Commn 445 12th St SW Washington DC 20554

FISHEL, PETER LIVINGSTON, finance company executive; b. Chgo., Apr. 25, 1935; s. Philip W. and Dorothy B. (Livingston) F.; m. Donna Swift, Dec. 17, 1961; children: Pamela Leslie Fishel Saccocio, Patricia Jane Fishel, Françoise Suzanne Fishel. BS, U. Pa., 1959. CPA, Pa., Fla. Agt.-in-charge investigation and civil rights divsn. Commonwealth of Pa. Dept. Justice, 1961-62; contr. Internat. Playtex Corp., 1962-70, BVD Knitwear, 1970-71; corp. contr. BVD Co., Inc., NYC, 1971-73; v.p. fin. BVD Co., Inc. (BVD divsn.), NYC, 1973; chief fin. officer Colebrook Mills, divsn. Bobbie Brooks, Inc., Hialeah, Fla., 1973-77; owner Gen. Bus. Svcs., 1978-86, regional dir. S.E. Fla., 1982-86; pvt. practice acctg., 1987—; mem. adv. com. Oceanmark Fed. Savs. & Loan, 1983-88. Mem. Andover Civic Assn., 1973—2001; mem. citizens adv. com. Met. Dade Police, Miami, Fla., 1981—, treas., 1985—; mem. fin. com. Metro-Dade Pig Bowl, 1985; v.p. Andover Civic Assn., 1986—91; mem. NMB Pride, 1989—93, bd. dirs., 1991—93, Dade Alumni Club, U. Pa., 1991—; chmn. Bus. Devel. Com. of Aventura Mktg. Coun., 1995—; mem., treas. Coalition Improvement NW Dade, 1996—; bd. dirs. Rolling Hills Home Owners Assn., treas., 2003—; mem. Aventura Mktg. Coun., 1991—. With M.P. US Army, 1954—56. Mem. AICPA, Pa. Inst. CPAs, Fla. Inst. CPAs, Nat. Assn. Tax Practitioners, Mensa, North Dade C. of C. (bd. dirs. 1978-97, v.p., Businessman of Yr. 1990, Mem. of Month, 1987, 91). Home: 8119 S Savannah Cir Davie FL 33328-3033 Office: 2396 NE 172nd St Aventura FL 33160-2923 Home Phone: 305-720-7531; Office Phone: 305-944-0040. Personal E-mail: plfishel@aol.com.

FISHER, ALAN HALL, guidebook writer; b. Evanston, Ill., July 16, 1945; s. Howard Taylor and Marion Ethel (Hall) F.; m. Margaret Ellen Williams, July 3, 1974; children: Ellen Williams, Howard Williams. BA, Harvard U., 1967; JD, Boston U., 1977. Bar: Md. 1977. English tchr. Trinity-Pawling (NY) Sch., 1967-68, Acton (Mass.)-Boxborough H.S., 1968-70; rsch. asst. Grad. Sch. Design Harvard U., Cambridge, Mass., 1971-72; assoc. Venable, Baetjer and Howard, Balt., 1977-80; guidebook writer Balt., 1980—. Author: Country Walks Near Boston, 1976, 3rd edit., 2000, Country Walks Near Baltimore, 1981, 4th edit., 2001, Country Walks Near Philadelphia, 1983, Country Walks Near Washington, 1984, 2d edit., 1996, Country Walks Near Chicago, 1987, Day Trips in Delmarva, 1992, 2d edit., 1998, Country Walks and Bikeways in the Philadelphia Region, 1994, Country Walks in the Chicago Region, 2003. Home and Office: 1430 Park Ave Baltimore MD 21217-4230 Office Phone: 410-523-5257. Business E-Mail: ramblerbooks@aol.com.

FISHER, ALAN WASHBURN, historian, educator; b. Columbus, Ohio, Nov. 23, 1939; s. Sydney Nettleton and Elizabeth E. (Scipio) F.; m. Carol L. Garrett, Aug. 24, 1963; children: Elizabeth, Ann Christy, Garrett. BA, DePauw U., 1961; MA, Columbia U., 1964, PhD, 1967. Instr. history Mich. State U., East Lansing, 1966-67, asst. prof., 1967-70, assoc. prof., 1970-78, prof. Russian and Turkish history, 1978—2003, assoc. dean grad. studies and research, Coll. Arts and Letters, 1987-89, dir. Ctr. for Integrative Studies in Arts and Humanities, 1989-97, emeritus prof., 2003—. Author: Russian Annexation of the Crimea, 1772-1783, 1970, The Crimean Tatars, 1978, revised edit., 1987, Ottoman Studies Directory, I, 1979, II, 1981, III, 1983, Between Russians, Ottomans and Turks: Crimea and Crimean Tatars, 1998, A Precarious Balance: Conflict, Trade and Diplomacy on the Russian-Ottoman Frontier, 1999. Am. Rsch. Inst. in Turkey fellow, 1969, 73, 76; Am. Coun. Learned Socs. grantee, 1976-77 Fellow Royal Hist. Soc., Turkish Hist. Assn. (corr.), Am. Rsch. Inst. Turkey (mem. bd. dels. 1990-99, v.p. 1995-99), Mid. East Studies Assn., Turkish Studies Assn. (pres. 1982-84, editor bull. 1984-87), Inst. Turkish Studies (dir. 1995-97, chmn. 1997-99). Home: 830 Lantern Hill Dr East Lansing MI 48823 Office Phone: 517-355-7500. Business E-Mail: fishera@msu.edu.

FISHER, ALICE S., federal agency administrator, lawyer; b. Louisville, 1967; BA, Vanderbilt U., 1989; JD, Catholic U., 1992. Bar: DC 1993. Assoc. Sullivan & Cromwell LLP; dep. spl. counsel US Senate Spl. Com. to Investigate Whitewater Devel. & Related Matters, 1995—96; ptnr. Latham & Watkins, LLP, Washington, 1996—2001, 2003—05; dep. asst. atty. gen. criminal divsn. US Dept. Justice, Washington, 2001—03, asst. atty. gen. criminal divsn., 2005—. Named one of Top 40 Lawyers Under 40, Nat. Law Jour., 2005, The 50 Most Influential Women Lawyers in Am., 2007, Litigation's Rising Stars, The Am. Lawyer, 2007. Office: US Dept Justice Robert F Kennedy Bldg Tenth St & Constitution Ave NW Rm 2107 Washington DC 20530 Office Phone: 202-637-2148. Office Fax: 202-637-2201.*

FISHER, ANDREW, management consultant; b. Richmond, Va., Dec. 17, 1920; s. Marion Nimmo and Sarah Randolph (Talcott) F.; m. Cornelia Johnson, Oct. 10, 1942; children: Peter R., Carolyn, Andrew R. BA, Amherst Coll., 1943; MBA, Harvard U., 1947; D.Sc. (h.c.), Albany Med. Coll. Dir. indsl. relations Internat. Braid Co., Providence, 1947; with N.Y. Times, 1947-71, v.p., 1963-70, exec. v.p., 1971; mgm. cons., 1972-76; chmn., pres., pub. News Jour. Co., 1976-78. Mgmt. cons. Trustee emeritus Albany Med. Coll. Capt. AUS, 1943-46. Mem. Moorings Club. Home: 1780 Cedar Ln Vero Beach FL 32963-2621

FISHER, ANDREW, IV, newswriter, television producer; b. Richmond, Va., Jan. 15, 1944; s. Andrew III and Dorothy Dale (Crannis) Fisher; m. Sharon Mary Cozza, Aug. 16, 1969 (dec. Feb. 2006). BA, Columbia U., 1965. News anchor Sta. WIP Radio, Phila., 1965, investigative reporter, 1968-69; writer, editor WNEW News, NYC, 1969-74; overnight news anchor Sta. WNEW-AM, NYC, 1974-79; morning news anchor Sta. WNEW-FM, NYC, 1979-81; radio news corr. NBC News, NYC, 1981-89, prin. news writer Today Show, 1990-99; fin. journalist CNBC, Englewood Cliffs, NJ, 1999—. Guest lectr. NYU, 1978, 80, Rutgers U., New Brunswick, NJ, 1984, Ramapo Coll., Mahwah, NJ, 2002; adj. prof. journalism Columbia U., NYC, 1989—90; judge TV Emmy Award, 2002, 04; panelist Nat. Publicity Summit, NYC, 2005, 06. Reporter, prodr. Sunday News Closeup, 1969—79, corr. Source Report, 1981—88, host, prodr. Catch of the Day, 1985—88, Andy Fisher Reporting on Religion, 1986—89, network radio anchor Winter Olympics, Calgary, Can., 1988, Summer Olympics, Seoul, Republic of Korea, 1988; consulting editor: Joyful Noiseletter, 1988—, contbg. writer: Marketplace, Am. Publ. Radio, 1989, More Holy Humor, 1997, Dick Clark's American Bandstand: An Anniversary Celebration of Music and Dance, 1997, Holy Hilarity, 2000; writer (TV spl.) Christmas in Rockefeller Center, 1999, Attack on America, 2001, Wall St. Responds, 2001, The U.S. vs. Martha Stewart, 2004. Mem. Denville Hist. Soc.; founding patron Flying Boat Mus., Foynes, Ireland, 1990—; founding sponsor Nat. Mus. of US Army, 2007; clk. vestry St. Peter's Ch., Morristown, NJ, 1979; mem. various coms. Episcopal Diocese, Newark, 1982—87; lay reader Ch. of Saviour, Denville, NJ, 1982—87. With US Army, 1965—68, spl. agt. Army Intelligence US Army, 1966—68. Decorated Disting. Mil. Svc. medal; recipient Headliner Reporting award, Nat. Headliners Club, 1985, Media award, Am. Women in Radio & TV, 1985, NY State Bar Assn., 1985, Gold medal, Internat. Radio Festival, 1989. Mem.: AFTRA, Writers Guild Am., NY Acad. Scis., Actors Fund (life), Albany Acad. Alumni Assn., Boston St. Rlwy. Assn., Fellowship Merry Christians, Nat. Rlwy. Hist. Soc., NYC Transit Mus. (sustaining), Indian Lake Cmty. Club. Office: CNBC 1 CNBC Plaza 900 Sylvan Ave Englewood Cliffs NJ 07632 Office Phone: 201-735-3098. Business E-Mail: andrew.fisher@nbcuni.com.

FISHER, ANDREW TAYLOR, computer software developer; b. Oakland, Calif., Nov. 22, 1950; s. Walter Dummer Fisher and Marjorie Catherine Lynis Smith. BA in Computer Studies, Northwestern U., 1988. Programmer Health Info. Reporting Co., Chgo., 1988-90; programming cons. Blue Cross and Blue Shield Assn., Chgo., 1990-91; programmer ACCO USA, Wheeling, Ill., 1992; programmer, tech. writer Healthcare Transformations, Hobart, Ind., 1992-93; programming cons. Abbott Labs., Abbott Pk., Ill., 1993, tech. writing cons., 1995; programming cons. A.C. Nielson, Bannockburn, Ill., 1993-94; data mgmt. software devel. cons. Amoco, Chgo., 1995; programming contractor Northrop Grumman, Rolling Meadows, Ill., 1996; database programmer, tech. writer The Good Group, Inc., Evanston, Ill., 1997-2000; pvt. practice, 2000—; database, office mgr. Svc. Corps Ret. Execs., Chgo., 2003—06. Webmaster Nutrition for Optimal Health Assn. Chair environ. task force from Chgo. area Unitarian Universalists for Social Justice, 2004—. Recipient Steve Sutton Meml. award Chgo. Metro. Ski Coun., 1996; co-recipient Arthur B. Hanson Rescue medal Safety at Sea Com. Nat. Gov. Body Sport of Sailing, 2000, 2d Pl. trophy Art McGee Sailing Race, 2003, 1st Pl. trophy, 2004, Fleet Championship award for cruising Sheridan Shores Yacht Club, 2005. Mem. Nutrition for Optimal Health Assn. (wood apple award 1998), Union Concerned Scientists, Worldwatch Inst., Students for Ecol. and Environ. Devel. Northwestern U. (founder, 1st pres. 1986-88), Greenpeace, Snowseekers Club (rec. sec. 1995-96, webmaster 2004-06). Democrat. Avocations: choral singing and acting, long distance biking, skiing, sailing, web site designing. Home: 1580 Sherman Ave Unit 1108 Evanston IL 60201-4494 Personal E-mail: fisher.a@sbcglobal.net.

FISHER, ANN BAILEN, lawyer; b. NYC, Oct. 15, 1951; d. Eliot and Elise (Thompson) Bailen; m. John C. Fisher, Apr. 6, 1980. BA magna cum laude, Radcliffe Coll., 1973; JD, Harvard U., 1976. Bar: N.Y. 1977. Assoc. Sullivan & Cromwell, NYC, 1976-80, 82-84, ptnr., 1984—, assoc. Paris, 1980-82. Mem. ABA, N.Y. State Bar Assn. Clubs: Cosmopolitan, Harvard (N.Y.C.). Episcopalian. Office: Sullivan & Cromwell 125 Broad St Fl 32 New York NY 10004-2400

FISHER, ANN LEWIS, judge; b. Reading, Pa., Mar. 31, 1948; d. William E. and Florence (Makowiecki) Lewis; m. Donald E. Fisher, Dec. 27, 1965 (div. July 1986); children: Caroline E., Catherine E., John Michael (dec.); m. David H. DeBlasio, May 28, 1988; 1 child, Michael Joseph DeBlasio. BS in Liberal Studies, Oreg. State U., 1975; JD, Willamette U., 1983. Bar: Oreg. 1984, U.S. Dist. Ct. Oreg. 1984, U.S. Ct. Appeals (9th cir.) 1984, Wash. 1987, U.S. Dist. Ct. (we. dist.) Wash. 1987, U.S. Dist. Ct. (ea. dist.) Wash. 1996, U.S. Ct. Appeals (fed. cir.) 1996. Atty. Spears, Lubersky, Portland, Oreg., 1983-85, Greene & Markley, Portland, 1985-89; asst. gen. counsel Portland GE, 1988-93; atty. Schwabe, Williamson & Wyatt, Portland, 1993-96; founder Ann L. Fisher Legal and Consulting Svcs., Portland, 1997—. Judge Pro Tem, Multnomah County Cir. Ct., Portland, 1995-2006; spkr. on corp. ethics, 1993-95; spkr. on energy issues, 1997—. Contbg. author: (treatise) ABA Year in Review, 1994, 95, Fed. Energy Bar Yr. Rev., 1997, 2000. Named Mem. of Yr., Bldg. Owners and Mgrs. Assn., 2001. Mem.: ABA, Fed. Energy Bar Assn. (electric utility regulation com. 1996—99, ethics com. 1999—00), Multnomah Bar Assn. (mem. com. 1987—91, Multnomah Lawyer Pubs. com. 1994—96, chair Multnomah Lawyer Pubs. com. 1995—96, professionalism com. 1996—98, ct. liason com. 2001—04), Oreg. Bar Assn. (ins. and bar sponsored program com. 1985—87, sec. 1986—87, chair 1987—88, MCLE bd. 1991—94, disciplinary bd. region 5 1991—97, sec. 1993—94, chair 1995—96, ethics com. 1998—01, bd. govs. region 4, 2007—), Oreg. State Bar (bar-sponsored programs com. 1985—88, sec. bar-sponsored programs com. 1986—87, chair, bar-sponsored programs com. 1987—88, new lawyer's com. 1990—91, MCLE bd. 1991—94, sec. MCLE bd. 1992—93, chair MCLE bd. 1993—94, disciplinary bd. 1993—97, region 5 chair disciplinary bd. 1995—97; fin. instns. com. 1996—98, 03-04, 06, ethics com. 1999—02, exec. bd. mem., energy telecomm. and utility sect. 2000—, energy telecom. and utility sect. chair 2001, 07-, energy telecomm. and utility sect. past chair 2004, energy telecomm. sect. sec. 2004, energy telecomm. and utility sect. chair elect 2006-07, exec. com. mem., adminstrv. law sect. 2002—, adminstrv. law sect. sec. 2004, adminstrv. law sect. chair-elect 2005, adminstrv. law sect. chair 2006, administrative law sect. immediate past chair 2007), Wash. State Bar Assn., Fed. Bar Assn. (vice chair gas pipelines com. 1994—96, vice chair electric power com. sect. natural resources, energy and environ). Avocations: reading, writing, golf. Office Phone: 503-721-0181. Home Fax: 503-291-1556. Business E-Mail: energlaw@aol.com, afisher1@qwest.net.

FISHER, ARNOLD L., real estate company executive; Sr. ptnr. Fisher Bros., NYC. Chmn., CEO Fisher House Found., 1999—2003, vice chmn.; chmn. Intrepid Mus. Found., 2003—; hon. chmn. Interpid Fallen Heroes Fund; head Fisher Brothers Ann. Scholarship Fund; chmn. bd. Hall of Honor; bd. mem. NY chpt. USO. Served in US Army, 1953—54, Korea. Recipient Ellis Island Medal of Honor, 1995. Office: Fisher Bros 299 Park Ave New York NY 10171*

FISHER, ARON BAER, physiology educator; b. Phila., Apr. 20, 1936; m. Joan C. Fisher, 1957; children: Marc L., Steven A., Eric R., Mara E. BS in Chemistry summa cum laude, Dickinson Coll., 1956; MD, U. Pa., 1960. Diplomate Am. Bd. Internal Medicine; diplomate Nat. Bd. Med. Examiners. Intern and resident in medicine U. Hosps., Cleve., 1960-61, 64-65; resident in pulmonary medicine Hosp. U. Pa., 1965-66; fellow dept. physiology U. Pa., 1966-68, assoc. in medicine, assoc. in physiology, 1968-70, from asst. prof. to assoc. prof. medicine, 1970-80, prof. medicine, 1980—, from asst. prof. to assoc. prof. physiology, 1970-1980, prof. physiology, 1980—, prof. environmental medicine, 1986—; staff physician VA Hosp., Phila., 1968-73, clin. investigator, 1973-76, cons. in pulmonary medicine, 1976-82; mem. med. staff Hosp. U. Pa., 1976—, dir. hyperbaric medicine clin. practice, 1985—; dir. Inst. Environ. Medicine U. Pa., 1985—. Mem. Am. Heart Assn. student rsch. fellowship adv. com. U. Pa., 1983-97, mem. diabetes ctr. adv. com., 1985—, mem. teaching awards com., 1989-92, chmn. animal care com. 1982-84, 87-89, chmn. com. for animal facility planning, 1985-86, chmn. transgenic mouse facility com., 1989, chmn. instnl. animal care and use com., 1989-92, mem. bioengring. grad. group, 1988—, chmn. biochemistry grad. group rev. com., 1989-90, others, supr. grad. students; fellow dept. biophysics and phys. chemistry U. Pa., 1971-72; mem. study sect. Pa. Coal Worker's Respiratory Disease Program, 1976-78; mem. cardiovascular study sect. A NIH, 1979-81, mem. respiratory and applied physiology sect., 1981-83; mem. adv. panel U.S. Army Med. R&D Command, 1980-85; mem. VA Merit rev. com. for respiration, 1998—. Editor: (with others) Handbook of Physiology: The Respiratory System (Section 3), vol. 1, 1980-85; mem. editorial bd. Exptl. Lung Rsch. 1979-88, Am. Rev. Respiratory Diseases, 1981-87, Jour. Applied Physiology, 1984-87, Am. Jour. Physiology, 1988—; guest editor Symposium on Lung Surfactant Apoproteins, 1984; contbr. numerous articles and revs. to profl. jours., chpts. to books. With USPHS, 1958, 59-61; capt. MC USAR, 1961-65. Grantee NIH, 1986-91, 1988—; recipient Clin. Investigator award VA Res. Svc., 1973-76, Established Investigator award Am. Heart Assn., 1977-82, Christian R. and Mary F. Lindback Found. award for Disting. Teaching, 1984. Mem. AAAS, ACP, Am. Physiol. Soc. (chmn. respiration dinner 1991, councillor respiratory sect. 1991-95), Am. Thoracic Soc. (sec. assembly on structure, function and metabolism 1973-74, chmn. 1981, sec. sect. on pulmonary circulation 1979, councillor ea. sect. 1973-77, chmn. ann. meeting program com. 1976, pres. 1983), Am. Fedn. Clin. Rsch., Am. Soc. Clin. Investigation, Am. Heart Assn. (cardiopulmonary coun.), Am. Soc. Cell Biology, Undersea and Hyperbaric Med. Soc., Oxygen Soc., Aerospace Med. Assn., John Morgan Soc. U. Pa., Laennec Soc. Phila., Pa. Thoracic Soc. (chmn. rsch. com. 1985-87), Phi Beta Kappa, Alpha Omega Alpha. Achievements include co-determination that lung lamellar bodies maintain an acidic internal pH, that phospholipids co-isolated with rat surfactant protein-C account for the apparent protein-enhanced uptake of liposomes into lung granular pneumocytes, that secretogues for lung surfactant increase lung uptake of alveolar phospholipids, that adenosine cyclic monophosphate increases synthesis of surfactant-associated protein A by perfused rat lung; research on secretory granule calcium loss after isolation of rat alveolar type II cells, on alveolar uptake of lipid and protein components of surfactant, on oxygen-dependent peroxidation during lung ischemia, on choline transport by lung epithelium, and on role of acidic compartment in synthesis of disaturated phosphatidylcholine by rat granular pneumocytes; isolation and molecular cloning of a new calcium-independent phospholipase A2. Home: 239 E Gowen Ave Philadelphia PA 19119-1021 Office: U Pa Inst Environ Medicine One John Morgan Bldg 36th St and Hamilton Walk Philadelphia PA 19104-6068

FISHER, ARTHUR, magazine editor; b. NYC, Mar. 10, 1931; s. Abraham G. and Sadie (Gold) F.; m. Liliane E. Kowarsky, Aug. 18, 1951; 1 child, Anthony E. BA, NYU, 1951. Sr. rsch. aide NYU, 1954-56; mng. editor Dodge Books, 1957-62, Sci. World & Sr. Sci., 1962-68; sci. and tech. editor Popular Sci., NYC, 1969-94, exec. editor, 1994-96, sci. editor emeritus, 1996—. Author: The Healthy Heart, 1981; co-author: (with Ernest V. Heyn) Century of Wonders, 1972, Fire of Genius, 1976; contbr. articles to mags. Recipient citations for excellence in sci. writing Deadline Club, 1973, 74, Claude Bernard Sci. Journalism award Nat. Soc. Med. Rsch., 1978, Sci. Writing award Am. Heart Assn., 1981, Am. Inst. of Phys. Sci. Writing award, 1985, Sci. Writing award AAAS, 1986, Grady-Stack Sci. Writing award Am. Chem. Soc., 1988, Writing award Ednl. Writers Assn.,

1993, Journalism award Engring. Found., 1997. Mem. Nat. Assn. Sci. Writers, Coun. for Advancement of Sci. Writing (bd. dirs. 1989—). Home: 120 Cabrini Blvd New York NY 10033-3438

FISHER, BARBARA A., former broadcast executive; b. 1954; m. Michael Scott; children: Kyle, Zachary. BA, Oberlin Coll., Ohio. Publicist A&M Records; prodr. Dave Bell Assoc.; v.p. creative affairs New World Pictures, MCA TV Entertainment; dir. movies and miniseries Universal TV Entertainment, 1987—91, pres., 1991—99; exec. v.p. Lifetime Entertainment Svcs., 2002—04.

FISHER, BARRY ALAN, lawyer; b. LA, May 15, 1943; s. Harry Benjamin and Fay Doris (Sternfeld) F.; m. Susan E. Landman, June 16, 1968 (dec. 1995); children: J. Benjamin, Jonathan J., Robert A. A.B., UCLA, 1965, J.D., 1968. Bar: Alaska 1969, R.I. 1969 (spl.), Calif. 1971, U.S. Supreme Ct. 1972. law clk. to chief justice Alaska, 1968-69; Reginald Heber Smith fellow U. Pa., Law Sch., 1969-71; staff counsel Sierra Club Legal Def. Fund, San Francisco, 1972-74; mem. Fleishman, Brown, Weston & Rhode, Beverly Hills, Calif., 1974-77; ptnr. Fleishman, Fisher & Moest (now Fleishman & Fisher), L.A., 1977—; v.p. Human Rights Advs. Internat.; justice of peace, R.I., 1971. Signatory, Multinational Holocaust Claims Settlement Treaties with Germany and Austria. Recipient Cert. of Appreciation UN Internat. Criminal Tribunal for former Yugoslavia, 1995. Mem. ABA (co-chair 1st amendment com., co-chair nat. inst. on tort and religion, chair religious freedom subcom., vice chair 1st Ammendment com.), Calif. Acad. Appellate Lawyers, World Jurist Assn. Contbg. author Government Intervention in Religious Affairs, 1982; mem. adv. bd. Religious Freedom Reporter. Office: Fleishman & Fisher 1875 Century Park E Ste 2130 Los Angeles CA 90067-1736 Home Phone: 310-395-8905; Office Phone: 310-557-1077. Personal E-mail: BFisher557@aol.com.

FISHER, BARRY G., orthopedist, surgeon; b. 1951; m. Jodi Beth Spiegel, July 1, 1990 (dec.); children: Jordan, Samantha, Charlie. Grad., U. Cin.; MD, U. Chgo., 1976. Intern Nassau County Med. Ctr., 1976—77; resident LI Jewish Med. Ctr., 1977—78, Bellevue Hosp. Ctr., 1978—81, NYU Med. Ctr., 1978—81, fellowship, 1981—82; pvt. practice Great Neck, NY; staff mem. LI Jewish Med. Ctr. Team orthopedist NJ Devils, 1982—; head physician Team USA, World Cup of Hockey, 1996, USA Olympic Hockey Team, Nagano, Japan, 1998; clin. instr. Dept. Orthop. Surgery NYU Med. Ctr. Avocations: boating, golf, tennis. Office: 560 Northern Blvd # 106 Great Neck NY 11021-5100 Office Phone: 516-466-6160. Office Fax: 516-466-7814.*

FISHER, BART STEVEN, lawyer, educator, investment banker; b. St. Louis, Feb. 16, 1943; s. Irvin and Orene (Moskow) F.; m. Margaret Cottony, Mar. 1, 1969; 1 child, Ross Alan. AB, Washington U., 1963; MA, Johns Hopkins Sch. Advanced Internat. Studies, 1967, PhD, 1970; JD, Harvard U., 1972. Bar: D.C. 1972. Assoc. Patton, Boggs & Blow, Washington, 1972—78, ptnr., 1978—94, Arent Fox Kintner Plotkin & Kahn, Washington, 1994—95; mng. ptnr. Capital House, LLC, 1995—, JJ & B, LLC, 2005—, Law Office of Bart S. Fisher, 2004—; of counsel Porter Wright Morris & Arthur, 1996—2001, Bryan Cave, 2002—03, Dorsey & Whitney, 2003—04. Adj. prof. internat. rels. Georgetown U. Sch. Fgn. Svc., Washington, 1974-82, 97; profl. lectr. internat. rels. Johns Hopkins U. Sch. Advanced Internat. Studies, 1983-96, 2005—, George Mason U., 1991, 93, George Washington U., 2002-04; chmn. IFC Global Mgmt., Inc.; co-chmn. NetVision Internat., LLC. Author: The International Coffee Agreement, 1972, (with John H. Barton) International Trade and Investment: Regulating International Business, 1986; editor: Regulating the Multinational Enterprise, 1983, Barter in the World Economy, 1985. Pres. Aplastic Anemia Found. Am. Inc., Balt., 1983—92, pres. emeritus, 1993; bd. dirs. Marrow Found.; chmn. Give Life Found., 2004—; ex-officio bd. govs. Internat. Practice sect. Bar Va.; participating mem. Internat. Trade Working Group, Pres. Coun. on Year 2000 Conversion. Recipient Dean's Cert. Appreciation Georgetown U. Sch. Fgn. Svc., Washington, 1984. Mem. ABA, Internat. Bar Assn., Am. Soc. Internat. Law (rapporteur, panel trade policy and insts. 1974-77), Va. State Bar (bd. govs. internat. law sect.), Parkville Post Am. Legion, Great Falls Swim and Tennis Club Va. Jewish. Home: 9009 Potomac Forest Dr Great Falls VA 22066-4110 Office: 700 12th St NW Ste 700 Washington DC 20005 Office Phone: 202-659-2979. Personal E-mail: bart_fisher2002@yahoo.com.

FISHER, BERNARD, surgeon, educator; b. Pitts., Aug. 23, 1918; s. Reuben and Anna (Miller) F.; m. Shirley Kruman, June 5, 1947; children: Beth, Joseph, Louisa. BS, U. Pitts., 1940, MD, 1943; DSc (hon.), Mt. Sinai Sch. Medicine, CUNY, 1986; HHD (hon.), Carlow Coll., Pitts., 2003; DMS (hon.), Yale U., 2004. Diplomate Am. Bd. Surgery. Intern Mercy Hosp., Pitts., 1943—44, resident in surgery, 1944—48; fellow in surg. research, resident in gen. surgery Harrison Dept. Dept. Surg. Research U. Pa., Phila., 1950—52; fellow London Postgrad. Med. Sch. Hammersmith Hosp., 1955—56; tchg. fellow in pathology U. Pitts., 1944—45, 1945—47, assoc. prof., 1956—59, prof. surgery, 1959—86, Disting. Svc. prof., 1986—; Fulbright Commn. award appointee to Peru, 1965; med. surg. staff Presbyn.-Univ. Hosp., 1953—98. Past mem. cons. staff Children's Hosp., Pitts.; mem. cons. staff Magee-Women's Hosp., VA Hosp., Pitts.; chmn. Nat. Surg. Adjuvant Breast and Bowel Project, 1967—94, sci. dir., 1995—2005; chmn. Adjuvant Therapy Ctr., 1973—94, Breast Care and Diagnostic Ctr., 1980—93, Pitts. Cancer Inst., 1985—, Comprehensive Breast Care Ctr., 1992—98; mem. spl. del. to China, 1977; mem. President's Cancer Panel, 1979—82, Nat. Cancer Adv. Bd., 1986—92, Inst. Medicine of NAS. Mem. editl. bd.: Transplantation, 1966—71, Cancer, 1970—88, 1975, Year Book of Cancer, 1973—85, Internat. Jour. Radiation Oncology Biology Physics, 1975—78, Cancer Clin. Trials, 1977, Invasion and Metastasis, 1981—85, Cancer Metastasis Revs., 1981—85, Jour. Clin. Oncology, 1982—87, Internat. Jour. Breast and Mammary Pathology, 1982—84, Cancer Rsch., 1976, Seminars in Oncology, 1979, Breast Cancer Rsch. and Treatment, 1980, 1992—, Clin. and Exptl. Metastasis, 1980—94, Breast Diseases: Yr. Book Quar., 1989—95, Annals Surg. Oncology, 1993—94, Internat. Jour. Oncology, 1993—94, Advances in Oncology, 1992—96, Breast Disease: Internat. Jour., 1993—96, Cancer Jour., 1994—, Internat. Jour. Cancer, 1993—94, European Jour. Cancer, 1995—97; contbr. more than 585 articles to med. jours. Named Bernard Fisher prof. surgery established in his honor, U. Pitts., 2006, Bernard Fisher chair surgery established in his honor, 2006; recipient Man of Yr. award in medicine, Pitts. Jr. C. of C., 1966, Philip Hench Disting. Alumnus award, U. Pitts. Sch. Medicine, 1976, McGraw medal, Detroit Surg. Assn., 1978, Lucy Wortham James Clin. Rsch. award, 1981, Heath Meml. award, 1982, Joseph H. Morton Meml. award, 1983, Julia Hudson Freund Meml. award, 1983, Albert Lasker Med. rsch. award, 1985, Hammer Cancer prize, 1988, Am. Cancer Soc. Medal of Honor, 1986, Susan Komen Found. Sci. Distinction award, 1988, Milken Med. Found. Ctr. Rsch. award, 1989, Assn. Commn. Cancer Ctrs. award, 1990, Chancellors Dist. Rsch. award U. Pitts., 1992, Nat. Health Couns. Med. Rsch. award, 1992, Brinker Internat. Breast Cancer award, 1992, Durham N.C. City of Medicine award, 1992, Dr. Josef Steiner Cancer Rsch. prize, 1992, GM Cancer Rsch. Found. Kettering prize, 1993, Bristol-Myers Squib award, 1993, James Ewing Lectr. award SSO, 1993, Gottlieb Meml. award, 1993, Sheen award, 1993, Claude Jacquillet award, 1995, Lifetime Achievement award in Breast Cancer Rsch., Senologic Internat. Soc., 1996, Health Care Lifetime Achievement award, Pitts. Bus. Times, 1998, Potamkin Internat. award for breast cancer rsch., Pa. Breast Cancer Coalition, 1999, Celebrating Survival: A Century of Advancements in Early Breast Cancer award, 2000, Am. Surg. Assn. Medallion for Sci. Achievement, 2000, Flance-Karl award for contbns. to sci. of clin. surgery, 2001, St. Gallen Internat. Breast Cancer award, 2003, AstraZeneca Hist. Milestone Excellence Clin. Rsch. award, 2003, Jill Rose award, Breast Cancer Rsch. Fond., 2003, Internat. Spirit of Life Rsch. award, 2003, C. Chester Stock award, Meml. Sloan Kettering Cancer Ctr., 2004, Breast Cancer Awareness Month award, 2004; Markle scholar in med. sci., John and Mary Markle Found., 1953—58, Fisher Breast Cancer lectureship established in his honor, U. Pitts., 1989. Fellow: AAAS, Am. Med. Writers Assn. (hon.), Am. Coll. Radiology (hon.); mem.: ACS, AAUP, Am. Italian Fedn. Cancer Rsch., Internat. Assn. Breast Cancer Rsch., Assn. Italiana per la Divulgaxione Sci. della Cancerologia Clinica, Italian Surg. Rsch. Assn., Pitts. Surg. Soc. (pres. 1979), Pitts. Acad. Medicine, Allegheny County Med. Soc. (Man of Yr. award 1983), Pa. Med. Soc., Am. Socs. for Exptl. Biology, Soc. Univ. Surgeons, Soc. Surg. Oncology, N.Y. Acad. Scis., Am. Surg. Assn. (v.p. 1996), Cell Kinetic Soc., Assn. Am. Med. Colls., Am. Physiol. Soc., Am. Soc. Clin. Oncology (pres. 1992-93, bd. dirs., Karnofsky award 1980, Disting. Svc. award for sci. achievement 1999), Am. Assn. Cancer Rsch. (bd. dirs., 3d Jos. H. Burchenal Clin. Rsch. award 1998, Lifetime Achievement award 2006), Assn. Cancer Edn., Oncology Nursing Soc. (hon.), Peruvian Acad. Surgery (hon.), Am. Soc. Therapeutic Radiology and Oncology (hon.), Phi Beta Kappa, Alpha Omega Alpha. Office: U Pitts Dept Surgery 200 Lothrop St Ste 7098 Pittsburgh PA 15213

FISHER, CALVIN DAVID, food products executive; b. Nerstrand, Minn., June 10, 1926; s. Edward and Sadie (Wolf) F.; m. Patricia Vivian Capriotti, July 28, 1950; children: Cynthia, Nancy Joann, Michael. BS, U. Minn., 1950. Dairy specialist U.S. Dept. Agr., Mpls., 1950-54, chemist and dairy specialist Omaha, 1954-58; with Roberts Dairy Co., Omaha, 1958-80, sr. v.p., chief operating officer, 1967-70, pres., chief exec. officer, 1970-80, owner, chief exec. officer, 1975-80, Fisher Foods Ltd., Lincoln, Nebr., 1980—; pres., dir. Master Dairies, Indpls., 1968-80; bd. dirs. Internat. Assn. Ice Cream Mfrs. Milk Industry Found., 1973-80. Patentee spray-dried ice cream mix, pasteurized egg products. Bd. dirs., v.p. Omaha Safety Council, 1981; bd. dirs. Arthritis Found., 1972-81; mem. adv. council SBA; bd. dirs. Nebr. State Patrol Found., 1990—. With USN, 1944-47. Mem. Omaha C. of C. (pres.'s coun. 1976, 78), Internat. Food Scientists Assn., Inst. Food Tech., Nat. Ind. Dairies Assn., Rotary, Univ. Club (Lincoln), Firethorn Country Club. Republican. Methodist. Home: 18940 E Via Hermosa Rio Verde AZ 85263 Office: Fisher Foods Ltd 220 S 20th St Lincoln NE 68510-1007

FISHER, CARRIE FRANCES, actress, writer; b. Beverly Hills, CA, Oct. 21, 1956; d. Eddie Fisher and Debbie Reynolds; m. Paul Simon, 1983 (div. 1984); 1 child, Billie Catherine. Ed. high sch., Beverly Hills, Calif.; student, London Cen. Sch. Speech and Drama. Mem. chorus in Broadway musical Irene, 1972, also in Broadway prodn. Censored Scenes from King Kong; appeared in films The Groove Tube, 1972, Shampoo, 1975, Star Wars, 1977, Mr. Mike's Mondo Video, 1979, The Blues Brothers, 1980, The Empire Strikes Back, 1980, Under the Rainbow, 1981, Return of the Jedi, 1983, Garbo Talks, 1984, The Man with One Red Shoe, 1985, Hannah and Her Sisters, 1986, Hollywood Vice Squad, 1986, Amazon Women on the Moon, 1987, Appointment With Death, 1988, Time Guardian, 1989, When Harry Met Sally., 1989, The 'Burbs, 1989, Loverboy, 1989, Sweet Revenge, 1990, Sibling Rivalry, 1990, Drop Dead Fred, 1991, Soapdish, 1991, This Is My Life, 1992, Austin Powers: International Man Of Mystery, 1997, Scream 3, 2000, Lisa Picard is Famous, 2001, Jay and Silent Bob Strike Back, 2001, A Midsummer Night's Rave, 2002, Charlie's Angels: Full Throttle, 2003, Wonderland, 2003, Stateside, 2004, Undiscovered, 2005, Cougar Club, 2007; TV movies include Come Back, Little Sheba, (spl.) 1977, Ringo, 1978, Leave Yesterday Behind, 1978, Frankenstein, 1984, From Here to Maternity, 1986, Liberty, 1986, Sunday Drive, 1986, Present Tense, Past Perfect, 1995, These Old Broads, 2001 (also co-exec. prodr.), Romancing The Bride, 2005; TV series Leaving L.A., 1997; guest appearances Laverne & Shirley, 1982, Thumbelina, 1982, Frasier, 1995, Gun, 1997, Nero Wolfe Mystery, 2002, Good Morning, Miami, 2003, Jack & Bobby, 2004, Smallville, 2005, Family Guy (3 episodes-voice), 2005-2006; author: Postcards from the Edge, 1987, (also screenplay, 1990), Surrender the Pink, 1990, Delusions of Grandma, 1994, Hollywood Moms, 2001, The Best Awful There is, 2004; host, Conversations from the Edge; co-host, The Essentials, 2007-.*

FISHER, CHARLES HAROLD, chemistry educator, researcher; b. Hiawatha, W.Va., Nov. 20, 1906; s. Lawrence D. and Mary (Akers) F.; m. Elizabeth Dye, Nov. 4, 1933 (dec. 1967); m. Lois Carlin, July 1968 (dec. June 1990); m. Elizabeth Snyder Kiser, Nov. 29, 1991. BS in Chemistry, Roanoke Coll., 1928, ScD (hon.), 1963; MS in Chemistry, U. Ill., 1929, PhD, 1932; DSc (hon.), Tulane U., 1953. Tchg. asst. in chemistry U. Ill., Urbana, 1928—32; instr. Harvard U., 1932—35; leader rsch. group U.S. Bur. Mines, Pitts., 1935—40; head carbohydrate divsn. Ea. Regional Rsch. Ctr. USDA, 1940—50; dir. So. mktg. and nutrition rsch. divsn. So. Regional Rsch. Ctr., USDA, New Orleans, 1950—72. Adj. rsch. prof. Roanoke Coll., Salem, Va., 1972-2006. Co-author: Profiles of Eminent American Chemists, 1988; contbr. over 200 articles to profl. jour. Co-inventor 72 patents. Pres. New Orleans Sci. Fair, 1967-69; bd. dir. Salem Hist. Soc., 1982-85, Salem Ednl. Found., 1991-99; established Lawrence D. and Mary A. Fisher Scholarship Roanoke Coll., 1978, Lois Carlin Fisher Scholarship, 1991, Elizabeth Snyder Fisher Scholarship, 1992. Recipient So. Chemists award, 1956, Herty medal, 1959; named Polymer Science Pioneer, 1981, Roanoke Coll. medal, 1996; named to Hall of Fame, Salem Ednl. Found., 1996; named Charles H. Fisher Lectures in his honor Roanoke Coll., 1990, Laboratory of Organic Chem. in his honor Roanoke Coll., 2002. Mem. AAAS, Am. Inst. Chemists (hon., pres. 1962-63, chmn. bd. dir., Chem. Pioneer award 1966, Presdl. citation of merit 1986), Oil Chem. Soc., Am. Chem. Soc. (dir. region IV 1969-71), Chemurgic Coun. (dir.), Am. Assn. Textile Chemists and Colorists, Hidden Valley Country Club (Salem, Va.), Cosmos Club (Washington), Internat. House, Round Table Club (New Orleans); Chemists Club (NYC). Achievements include co-inventor of acrylic rubber. *I have worked hard as a physical scientist and research administrator because research is fun and offers the best way of benefiting humankind.*

FISHER, CHERYL SMITH, lawyer; b. Corning, NY, Sept. 4, 1951; d. Norman Albert and Betty (Manzella) Smith; 1 child, Daniel Terence. BA cum laude, SUNY, Oswego, 1973; JD cum laude, SUNY, Buffalo, 1976. Bar: N.Y. 1977, U.S. dist. Ct. (we. dist.) N.Y. 1977, U.S. Ct. Appeals (2d cir.) 1980, U.S. Supreme Ct. 1992. Assoc. Runfola, Birzon & Renda, Buffalo, 1976-77, Kavinoky Cook et al, Buffalo, 1977-79; asst. U.S. Atty. Western Dist. N.Y., Buffalo, 1979-84; assoc. Cohen Swados Wright Hanifin Bradford & Brett, Buffalo, 1984-86, Magavern & Magavern, Buffalo, 1986-87; ptnr. Magavern, Magavern & Grimm, 1988—. Spl. asst. U.S. atty. Dept. Justice, Buffalo, 1984, mem. com. character and fitness 8th Jud. Dist., Supreme Ct. N.Y. Pres. Cathedral Park Counseling Svc., Inc., Buffalo, 1979—83; mem. Civil Justice Reform Act, 1993—96, adv. panel, 1993—98; chmn. Lord of Life Adult and Child Svcs., 1999—2002; mem. vestry St. Paul's Cathedral, Buffalo, 1979—82, 1984—87, 2002—05; mem. bd. dirs. Child and Family Svc. Erie County, Buffalo, 1982—, chmn. bd. dirs., 1993—96; bd. dirs. Lord of Life Adult and Child Svcs., 1997—. Recipient Bishop Lauriston Scaife award, Episcopal Cmty. Svcs., 1999, John N. Walsh Jr. award, Child & Family Svcs. of Erie County, 2000. Mem. N.Y. State Bar Assn. (com. on profl. ethics, chair com. on conduct jud. elections), Erie County Bar Assn. (bd. dirs. 1996-99, v.p., pres.-elect 2006, pres. 2007—), N.Y. State Women's Bar Assn., Women Lawyers Assn., Alpha Psi Omega. Democrat. Episcopalian. Home: 306 Highland Ave Buffalo NY 14222-1751 Office: Law Offices 1100 Rand Building Bldg Buffalo NY 14203-1911 Home Phone: 716-881-7024; Office Phone: 716-856-3500. Business E-Mail: cfisher@magavern.com.

FISHER, CONNIE MARIE, physical therapist; b. Johnstown, Pa., Dec. 29, 1972; d. James Michael and Janet Fisher. BS with honors in Athletic Tng. and Sports Medicine, Calif. U. of Pa., California, Pa., 1995; MA in Phys. Therapy, St. Francis U., Loretto, Pa., 2002. Cert. in phys. therapy Am. Phys. Therapy Assn., 2003, athletic trainer Nat. Athletic Tng. Bd. Certification, Nebr., 2004. Student athletic trainer The U. Notre Dame, Ind., 1994; phys. therapist, athletic trainer Conemaugh Health Sys., Johnstown, Pa., 1996—2007, Resta Home Health, No. Cambria, Pa., 2007—. Athletic trainer Vantage Phys. Therapy, Johnstown, Pa., 2004—05; phys. therapist Phoenix Rehab., Cresson, Pa., 2006. Recipient Clin. Excellence award, St. Francis, Q.P.A. award, Calif. U. of Pa., WOW award, Conemaugh Health Sys.; Presdl. scholar, Calif. U. of Pa. Mem.: Nat. Athletic Tng. Assn. (licentiate), Am. Phys. Therapy Assn. (licentiate). Roman Cath. Achievements include selected as first female trainer for men's basketball team at California University of Pennsylvania. Avocations: walking, swimming, reading. Home: 1513 Jefferson Ave Portage PA 15946 Office: Resta Home Health 4219 Crawford Ave Northern Cambria PA 15714 Home Phone: 814-736-3382; Office Phone: 814-242-9881. Personal E-mail: conkey3@verizon.net.

FISHER, D. MICHAEL, judge; b. Pitts., Nov. 7, 1944; s. C. Francis and Dolores (Darby) Fisher; m. Carol Hudak, Aug. 25, 1973; children: Michelle Lynn Fisher Reyes, Brett Michael. AB, Georgetown U., 1966; JD, Georgetown Law Ctr., 1969. Bar: Pa. 1970. Asst. dist. atty. Allegheny County, Pitts., 1970—74; assoc. Brenlove & Fisher, 1970—75; rep. Pa. Ho. of Reps., Harrisburg, 1974—80; assoc. Fisher & McGinley, 1975—80; mem. Pa. Senate, Harrisburg, 1980—97; ptnr. Fisher & Flynn, 1981—83, Houston Harbaugh, Pitts., 1984—97; atty. gen. Commonwealth of Pa., Harrisburg, 1997—2003; judge US Ct. Appeals (3d cir.), Pitts., 2003—. Chmn. House Subcom. on Crime and Corrections, 1979—80, Senate Environ. Resources & Energy, 1981—90, Senate Majority Policy Com., 1988—90, Senate Rep. Caucus, 1992—; vice-chmn. Senate Jud. Com., 1981—90; Majority Whip, 1990—96. Contbr. articles to profl. jours. Active Environ. Quality Bd., 1980—90, Pa. Commn. on Crime and Delinquency, 1979—2003; mem. Pa. Security Task Force, 2001—03; chmn. Office of Nat. Drug Control Policy's Phila./Camden High Intensity Drug Trafficking Area, 2003—; mem. exec. working group for fed., state and local prosecutorial rels. US Dept. Justice, 2001—03; v.p. Nat. Assn. Attys. Gen. Exec. Bd., 2000—01; Rep. candidate for lt. gov. State of Pa., 1986; active Pa. Gov.'s Energy Coun., 1981—86, Pa. Energy Devel. Authority, 1984—86; del. Rep. Nat. Conv., 1988, 1992; Rep. nominee for gov. State of Pa., 2002; bd. dirs. Am. Legacy Found., 2003—04. Named Man of Yr., Upper St. Clair Rep. Club, 1980, Vector's Law & Govt., 1991; named one of Outstanding Young Men Am., 1977—79. Mem.: Fed. Bar Assn., Allegheny County Bar Assn., Pa. Bar Assn., Rotary, Am. Legion, Elks. Republican. Roman Catholic. Avocations: golf, hockey, football, baseball. Office: US Circuit Ct Appeals 3rd Cir 5360 US PO & Courthouse Pittsburgh PA 15219*

FISHER, DALE DUNBAR, animal scientist, dairy nutritionist; b. Lewisburg, Pa., Feb. 13, 1945; s. Glenn Murray and Elsie May (Bryson) F.; divorced; children: Elsie Maria, Maria Vanessa. BS Animal Sci., Pa. State U., 1967, MS Animal Industry, 1978, PhD Animal Industry, 1980. Vol. animal husbandry Peace Corps, Ciudad Quesada, Costa Rica, 1967—71; area animal husbandry-pasture specialist Costa Rican Ministry Agr., Ciudad Quesada, 1971—73; vis. scientist Internat. Ctr. for Tropical Agr., Cali, Colombia, 1973—75; animal nutritionist Co-op. Feed Dealers, Inc., Chenango Bridge, NY, 1981—. Contbr. articles to profl. jours. Eva B. and G. Weidman Groff Meml. scholar Pa. State U., 1979. Mem. Am. Soc. Animal Sci., Am. Dairy Sci. Assn., Am. Soc. Agronomy, Am. Acad. Vet. Nutrition, N.Y. Acad. Scis., Am. Coll. Nutrition, Sigma Xi, Phi Kappa Phi, Gamma Sigma Delta. Democrat. Avocations: jogging, reading. Home Phone: 607-724-3384; Office Phone: 607-651-9078 x 312. Business E-Mail: nutrition@co-opfeed.com.

FISHER, DALE JOHN, retired chemist, medical investigator; b. Omro, Wis., June 4, 1925; m. Ruth J. Laird, Apr. 27, 1957; 1 child, Shelley Dale. BS, U. Wis., Oshkosh, 1947; PhD (Univ. fellow), Ind. U., 1951. Staff mem. Inst. Paper Chemistry, Appleton, Wis., summer 1945; chemist City of Oshkosh, Wis., summers 1946-48; chemist ionic analyses group Oak Ridge Nat. Lab., 1951-52, group leader analytical instrumentation group, 1952-72, mem. dir.'s staff, 1972-73; physicist (nuclear medicine) VA Hosp., Gainesville, Fla., 1973-74, tech. dir. nuclear medicine, 1974-76; grad. studies faculty U. Fla., Gainesville, 1974-76; physicist FDA, 1976-91, physicist divsn. in vitro diagnostic device standards, 1976-83, physicist Office Sci. and Tech., divsn. life scis., health scis. br., 1983-91; ret., 1991. Recipient Disting. Alumni award U. Wis., Oshkosh, 1982. Mem. ASTM (sr.), Am. Chem. Soc. (emeritus; nat. award chem. instrumentation), U. Wis. Oshkosh Alumni Assn. (life), Sigma Xi (emeritus), Phi Lambda Upsilon. Achievements include design and new applications of instrument systems and methods for analysis, process monitoring and research; creation electronic and mechanical designs and administration of research. Patentee in field. Research with computer-based nuclear medicine imaging instrumentation for the improvement of patient care. Development of med. device standards and performance requirements. Establish sci. basis for med. diagnostic and clin. lab. instruments. Improve safety and effectiveness of medical devices through toxicology and statistics research. Home: 6319 Golden Hook Columbia MD 21044-3710

FISHER, DAVID RUSSEL, business educator; b. Detroit, Mar. 23, 1946; s. Russel J. and Olive J. (Bilyea) F.; m. Janet I. Coolman; children: Christopher D., Autumn D., Matthew D. BBA, Mich. State U., 1968; MBA, Fla. inst. Tech., 1984. Human resources dir. Omaha dist. U.S. Army Corps of Engrs., 1979-81; dir. recruitment and placement U.S. Army Missile Command Redstone Arsenal, Huntsville, Ala., 1981-85; human resources officer Def. Reutilization and Mktg. Svcs., Battle Creek, Mich., 1985-94, detailed v.p. reinvention, 1994, CFO, 1994-95, v.p. resources, 1995-96, exec. v.p. corp. planning, 1996-98, dir. Army and Marine Corps cataloging ctr., 1998-99, dir. customer products and svcs. def. logistics info. svc., 1999—2006; adj. prof. Miller Coll., Battle Creek, 2006—. Adj. prof. Fla. Inst. Tech., 1983-84; bd. dirs. Dept. of Def. Fed. Credit Union; sr. fellow JFK Sch. Govt., Harvard U., 2002. Bd. dirs., past v.p. human resources S.W. Mich. coun. Boy Scouts Am., Kalamazoo, Mich., 1991-2000; industry rep. dist. improvement com. Battle Creek Pub. Schs., 1994-2001; rep. Coun. Logistics Mgmt., Lansing, Mich., 1997-2000; deacon, elder, trustee United Presbyn. Ch. Decorated Bronze Star; named to Hall Fame, DLA, 2007; named to Hall Fame, Def. Logistics Agy., 2006. Mem. Vietnam Vets. Am., Mich. State Alumni Assn., Battle Creek C. of C. (rep. 1995-99), Harvard U. Alumni Avocations: exercise, golf, reading, sports. Office: Robert B Miller College 450 North Ave Battle Creek MI 49017 Office Phone: 269-965-2709. Personal E-mail: davejanfisher@aol.com.

FISHER, DEENA KAYE, social studies education administrator; b. Elk City, Okla., Dec. 20, 1950; d. Earl Dean and Rosa Lee (Stone) Music; m. Mike Fleck, May 29, 1970 (div. June 1988); children: DeeAnna Michelle, Carrie Denise, William Michael; m. Tom Fisher, Nov. 13, 1993; 1 stepchild, Eleni. BA in Edn.-Social Sci., Southwestern Okla. State U., 1979, MEd in Social Sci., 1983, MEd in Sch. Counseling, 1987; EdD, Okla. State U., 2004. Instr. in social sci. Cordell (Okla.) H.S., 1979-85, El Reno (Okla.) C.C., 1985-88, Upward Bound guidance and career counselor, instr., 1987-89; instr. Am. History Yukon (Okla.) H.S., 1986-87; instr. polit. sci. and Am. history Southwestern Okla. State U., 1987-89; chair dept. Am. history, instr. Am. govt. Woodward (Okla.) H.S., 1989-96; instr. social studies Northwestern Okla. State U., Alva, 1989—, assoc. prof., 2004; dean Northwestern Okla. State U., Woodward Campus, 2002—.

Author ednl. materials in field. Del. Dem. Nat. Conv., Okla. Dem. Party, Chgo., 1996; law day coord. Okla. Bar Assn., Woodward, 1990-96; regional coord. Citizen Bee, Tulsa World, 1994-97; panelist U.S. History Nat. Assessment of Ednl. Progress, St. Louis, 1994. Recipient Outstanding Am. History Tchr. award Okla. Soc. DAR, 1993, Tchr. of Yr. award Okla. Supreme Ct., 1992; Bill of Rights Edn. Collaborative grantee, 1991. Mem. Nat. Coun. for Social Studies (ho. dels., co-chmn. resolution com. 1996), Okla. Social Studies Suprs.' Assn. (membership bd. 1997), Okla. Coun. for Social Studies (del.-at-large 1996, pres. 1994-96), Woodward Edn. Assn. (pres. 1996), Woodward C. of C. (mem. edn. com. 1997), Delta Kappa Gamma (pres. Psi chpt. 1996-98), Phi Delta Kappa. Mem. Christian Ch. (Disciples Of Christ). Avocations: reading, chess. Home: 3308 Bent Creek Dr Woodward OK 73801-6931 Office: Northwestern Okla State U Woodward Campus PO Box 1046 Woodward OK 73802-1046 Office Phone: 580-256-0047.

FISHER, DELBERT ARTHUR, pediatric endocrinologist, educator, retired health facility administrator; b. Placerville, Calif., Aug. 12, 1928; s. Arthur Lloyd and Thelma (Johnson) Fisher; m. Beverly Carne Fisher, Jan. 28, 1951; children: David Arthur(dec.) , Thomas Martin, Mary Kathryn. BA, U. Calif., Berkeley, 1950; MD, U. Calif., San Francisco, 1953. Diplomate Am. Bd. Pediat., Sub Bd. Pediatric Endocrinology. Intern, resident in pediat. U. Calif. Med. Ctr., San Francisco, 1953—55; resident in pediat. U. Oreg. Hosp., Portland, 1957—58; Irwin Meml. fellow in pediatric endocrinology, 1958—60; from asst. prof. to assoc. prof. pediat. Med. Sch. U. Ark., Little Rock, 1960—67, prof. pediat., 1967—68, UCLA, 1968—73, prof. pediat. and medicine Med. Sch., 1973—91, prof. emeritus, 1991—; chief, pediat. endocrinology Harbor-UCLA Med. Ctr., 1968—75, rsch. prof. devel. and perinatal biology, 1975—85, chmn. pediat., 1985—89, sr. scientist Rsch. and Edn. Inst., 1991—, chmn. bd. Rsch. and Edn. Inst., 2001—02; dir. Walter Martin Rsch. Ctr., 1986—91; pres. Nichols Inst. Reference Labs, San Juan Capistrano, Calif., 1991—93; pres. acad. assocs., chief sci. officer Nichols Inst., San Juan Capistrano, Calif., 1993—94, Quest Diagnostics-Nichols Inst., San Juan Capistrano, Calif., 1994—97, sr. sci. officer, 1997—98, chief sci. officer, 1998—99; v.p. sci. and innovation Quest Diagnostics Inc., 1999—2005, sr. sci. officer, 2005—07, acad. assoc., 2007—. Cons. genetic disease sect. Calif. Dept. Health Svcs., 1978—98; mem. organizing com. Internat. Conf. Newborn Thyroid Screening, 1977—88; examiner Am. Bd. Pediat., 1971—80, mem. subcom. on pediat. endocrinology, 1976—79. Co-editor: Pediatric Thyroidology, 1985, 10 other books; editor-in-chief: Jour. Clin. Endocrinology and Metabolism, 1978—83, Pediat. Rsch., 1984—89; contbr. over 450 articles to profl. jours., over 100 chpts. to books. Capt. M.C. USAF, 1955—57. Named to Hall of Honor, NICHHD, NIH, 2003; recipient Career Devel. award, NIH, 1964—68. Master: Am. Coll. Endocrinology; mem.: Am. Assn. Clin. Chemistry (So. Calif. sect., Albert L. Nichols award 2004), Clin. Ligand Assay Soc. (Disting. Scientist award 2001), Western Soc. Pediat. Rsch. (pres. 1982—83), Lawson Wilkins Pediatric Endocrine Soc. (pres. 1982—83), Assn. Am. Physicians, Am. Soc. Clin. Investigation, Am. Thyroid Assn. (pres. 1988—89, Disting. Lectr. 1982), Endocrine Soc. (pres. 1983—84, Leadership award 1998), Am. Pediat. Soc. (pres. 1992—93, John Howland medal 2001), Soc. Pediat. Rsch. (v.p. 1973—74), Am. Acad. Pediat. (Borden award 1981), Nat. Acad. Clin. Biochemistry, Inst. Medicine of NAS, Alpha Omega Alpha, Phi Beta Kappa. Home: 24582 Santa Clara Ave Dana Point CA 92629-3031 E-mail: fisherdl@cox.net.

FISHER, DEREK, former professional basketball player; b. Aug. 9, 1974; Graduated, Univ. Arkansas-Little Rock. Basketball player LA Lakers, 1996—2004, Golden State Warriors, 2004—06, Utah Jazz, 2006—07. Named Sunbelt Conference Player Yr., 1996; named to All-Rookie Team, NBA Western Conf., 1997.

FISHER, DONALD G., retail executive; b. 1928; m. Doris Fisher. BS, U. Calif., 1950. With M. Fisher & Son, 1950-57; former ptnr. Fisher Property Investment Co.; co-founder Gap Stores, San Bruno, Calif., 1969; chmn. Gap Inc., San Bruno, Calif., 1969—2004, pres., 1969—83. Mem. adv. coun. Office of US Trade Rep., 1987—98. Dir Schwab Charles Corp.; trustee Presidio Trust, 1997—; bd. mem. Calif. State Bd. Ed. Named one of Top 200 Collectors, ARTnews Mag., 2004, Forbes Richest Americans, 2006. Avocation: art collector. Office: Gap Inc 2 Folsom St San Francisco CA 94105 Address: 3456 Washington St San Francisco CA 94118

FISHER, DONALD WAYNE, medical association administrator; b. Pitts., Mar. 2, 1946; s. David H.W. and Jean K. F.; children by previous marriage: Kimberly Elizabeth, Jeffrey Wayne. AA, Hinds Jr. Coll., 1966; BS in Biology and Chemistry, Millsaps Coll., 1968; MS in Anatomy, U. Miss., 1970, PhD in Anatomy, 1973; postgrad. in assn. mgmt., U. Md., 1977-79. Cert. assn. exec. Instr. dept. chemistry and biology Hinds Jr. Coll., Raymond, Miss., 1968-74; instr. dept. anatomy U. Miss. Sch. Medicine, Jackson, 1973-74, co-dir. and exec. officer physician asst. program, 1972-74; asst. professorial lectr. George Washington U. Sch. Medicine, 1974—; exec. dir. Assn. Physician Asst. Programs, Arlington, Va., 1974-80, Am. Acad. Physician Assts., Arlington, 1974-80; pres., CEO Am. Med. Group Assn., Alexandria, Va., 1980—; chmn. Am. Med. Group Corp., Inc., Anceta, 2001—; chmn. bd. Anceta; treas. polit. action com. Am. Med. Group, 1980—. Mem. Nat. Commn. on Allied Health Edn., 1977-80; mem. adv. com. for tng., devel. and utilization of physician extenders Systems Scis., Inc., 1975-80; pres. Am. Acad. Physician Assts. Ednl. and Rsch. Found., 1977-80; sec., treas. Am. Med. Group Found., 1980—; mem. Am. Express Health Care Faculty, 1985-88. Robert Wood Johnson Found. grantee, 1973-80 Mem. Am. Soc. Assn. Execs. (govt. rels. com. 1980—), Assn. Am. Med. Colls., AAAS, Am. Internat. Health Alliance (bd. dirs. 1992—, treas. 1995-2003, chair 2004--), Disease Mgmt. Assn. Am. (bd. dirs. 2o004—), Greater Washington Soc. Assn. Execs., Fairfax County Hosp. Assn., Arlington (Va.) C. of C, Am. Internat. Alliance (chair, 2004—). Home: 3814 Ivanhoe Ln Alexandria VA 22310-2170 Office: Am Med Group Assn 1422 Duke St Alexandria VA 22314-3430

FISHER, DORIS, retail executive; m. Donald G. Fisher; 1 child, Robert J. Co-founder Gap, Inc., 1969, merchandiser, 1969—2003, bd. dir., 1969—. Trustee Stanford U. Named one of most powerful women, Forbes mag., 2005. Office: Gap Inc Two Folsom St San Francisco CA 94105 Office Phone: 650-952-4400.

FISHER, ERIC O'NEILL, economist; b. NYC, Feb. 9, 1954; s. Leonard and Lora (Segall) Porter; m. Kathryn G. Marshall, June 15, 1991; children: Jane Marshall, Marshall Havard. AB in Philosophy, Princeton U., NJ, 1974; MA in Internat. Rels., Johns Hopkins U., Washington, 1979; PhD, U. Calif., Berkeley, 1984. Economist bd. govs. FRS, Washington, 1984—87; asst. prof. Cornell U., Ithaca, NY, 1987—93; asst. then assoc. prof. Ohio State U., Columbus, 1993—2006; prof., dir. econs. lab. Calif. Poly. State U., San Luis Obispo, 2006—. Vis. fellow Inst. Internat. Econ. Studies, Stockholm, 1987, Australian Nat. U., Canberra, 1994, Tinbergen Inst., Rotterdam, 1993; vis. prof. U. Sao Paulo, 1990, Va. Polytech. Inst., 2004, U. Calif., Santa Barbara, 2005-07, Chulalongkorn U., 2007; vis. asst. prof. U. Chgo., 1990-91; vis. fgn. scholar Inst. Social and Econ. Rsch., U. Osaka, Japan, 1998; Associazione Generale Italiana di Petrol prof. Johns Hopkins U., 2002-03; Jean Monnet fellow European U. Inst, 2002-03; rsch. assoc. Fed. Res. Bank, Cleve., 2003-2004; mem. editl. coun. Rev. Internat. Econs., 1994—; mem. editl. bd. Jour. Econ. Integration, 1994-2000; mem. COTA Legacy Coun., 2000-04; assoc. editor Jour. Internat. Econs., 2004—, Jour. Money, Credit and Banking, 2005—. Contbr. articles to profl. jours. Vol. Peace Corps, Morocco, 1975-77; mem. City of Ithaca Rep. Com., 1991-93; village coun. Riverlea, Ohio, 2000-02; mem. staff Amnesty Internat./USA, 1978. Recipient Outstanding Tchr. award, Sigma Chi Fraternity, Ohio State U. chpt., 1993—94, Srs. Recognition Outstanding Faculty, Ohio State U., 1995; fellow, Found. Def. Democracies, 2003; scholar, Fed. Res. Bank, San Francisco, 2007. Mem. Econometric Soc., Am. Econ. Assn., Internat. Econs. and Fin. Soc. (sec. 1998-2000). Republican. Episcopalian. Avocation: fly fishing. Office: Calif Poly Inst Orfalea Coll Bus 1 Grand Ave San Luis Obispo CA 93407 Home: 522 Stoneridge Dr San Luis Obispo CA 93401-5669 Office Phone: 805-756-2764. Office Fax: 805-756-1473. Personal E-mail: eric.on.fisher@gmail.com.

FISHER, EUGENE, marketing professional, community leader; b. Sept. 30, 1927; s. Morris and Sarah (Edelstein) Fisher; m. Joline Cobb, July 28, 1956 (dec.); children: Robin Downing, Amy Homer, Douglas; m. Penny Blanchard, Dec. 18, 1988. PhB, U. Chgo., 1945, MBA in Mktg., 1948. With Brunswick Corp., Lake Forest, Ill., 1955-95, dir. mktg. planning bowling divsn., 1955-72, dir. corp. mktg. rsch., 1972-87, corp. mktg. dir., 1987-95; pres. Fisher Mktg. Intelligence, Inc., 1982—; chmn. Conf. Bd. Mktg. Rsch. Coun., 1988-89, mem. exec. com., 1989-95. Guest lectr. in field. Mng. editor: Profile Mag., 1988—98; prodr.: Maritime Festival, 1988—91, Brunswick 150th Anniversary Exhbn., 1995. Cmty. leadership civic planning com. Ill. State Hist. Soc., 1994—2002; exec. dir. Diversey Harbor Lakeview Assn., 2000—; chmn., pres. Diversey Harbor Lakeview Preservation Assn., 2001—; bd. dirs. Park West Cmty. Assn., 2001—04, pres., 2003—04; bd. dirs. 2626 Lakeview Condominium Assn., 1995—2000, 2004—, pres., 1996—2000, 2004—; 50th reunion dinner chmn. U. Chgo. Alumni Assn., 1995; 55th reunion program chmn. U. Chgo. Class of 1945, 2000, vice chmn. emeritus classes, 2002—03; mem. cmty. rels. com. Children's Meml. Hosp., 2003—. Mem.: Nat. Bowling Coun. (mktg. com. 1975—83), Chgo. Maritime Soc. (bd. dirs. 1991—95), Am. Mktg. Assn., Phi Sigma Delta. Home and Office: Apt 4103 2626 N Lakeview Ave Chicago IL 60614-1832 Home Phone: 773-281-7072; Office Phone: 773-388-9190. E-mail: Fishermarketing@aol.com.

FISHER, FENIMORE, business development consultant; b. NYC, 1926; s. Benn and Sadie (Cohan) F.; m. Marcia Obler, Nov. 9, 1952; children: Bennett G., Alan L., Karen Soo. BS in Physics, Columbia U., 1951; MBA, U. Pa., 1952. Staff physicist USN Rsch. Lab., Phila., 1951-52; ops. mgr., chief engr. instrument divsn. Thomas A. Edison Industries, West Orange, NJ, 1952-60; pres. Analogue Controls Inc., Hicksville, NY, 1960-67; corp. v.p. IMC Magnetics Corp., Jericho, NY, 1967-77, pres., CEO, 1977-89, also bd. dirs. Chmn. bd. Hansen Mfg. Co. Inc., Princeton Ind., IMC Ariz. Divsn., Tempe, IMC Fla. Divsn., Miami Lakes, IMC Tenn. Divsn., Camden, IMC Tex. Divsn., Mexia, IMC Western Divsn., Cerritos, Calif., New Eng. Alloys Inc., Lawrence, Mass., Pacific Propeller Inc., Kent Washington, Universal Magnetics Corp., Cerritos, 1989—; exec. v.p. Synergy Gas Corp., 1989-93; bus. devel. cons., 1993-96; v.p. bus. and fin. Dowling Coll., Oakdale, N.Y., 1996-98; exec. dir. Action Long Island, 1999—2001. Contbr. numerous articles on bus. econs., tech. edn., relation with the Far East. Bd. dirs. L.I. Philharm., West Suffolk YM & YWHA, United Way L.I.; chmn. L.I. Forum for Tech., Suffolk Cmty. Planning Coun., Old Westbury Coll. Found.; trustee Dowling Coll. Served to 1st lt. U.S. Army, 1944-46, PTO. Mem.: Eastpoint Golf and Racquet Club (West Palm Beach, Fla.). Home: 6451 Woodthrush Ct Palm Beach FL 33418-1429 Office Phone: 561-801-0100. E-mail: ff1570@aol.com.

FISHER, FRANCES, actress; b. Milford-on-Sea, Eng., May 11, 1952; d. William I. and Olga (Moen) F.; 1 child, Francesca Ruth Fisher-Eastwood. Student, Lee Strasberg, Stella Adler, Marilyn Fried, Sandra Seacat, HB Studios. Appearances include (films) Can She Bake a Cherry Pie?, 1985, Tough Guys Don't Dance, 1986, Patty Hearst, 1987, Lost Angels, 1988, Pink Cadillac, 1989, Welcome Home Roxy Carmichael, 1989, L.A. Story, 1991, Unforgiven, 1992, Baby Fever, 1992, The Stars Fell on Henrietta, 1994, Molly and Gina, 1992, Female Perversions, 1993, Striptease, 1995, Wild America, 1996, Titanic, 1997, True Crime, 1998, The Big Tease, 1998, The Rising Place, 2002, Gone in 60 Seconds, 2000, (TV) Elysian Fields, 1987, Sudie & Simpson, 1988, Cold Sassy Tree, 1989, Promises to Keep, 1990, Lucy & Desi: Before the Laughter, 1991, Devlin, 1987, Crime and Punishment, 1989, Law and Order, 1990, Praying Mantis, 1992, Attack of the 50 Foot Woman, 1993, The Other Mother, 1994, Strange Luck, 1995, Becker, 2000, Audrey Hepburn, 1999, Titus, 2001, Jackie, 2000, Glory Days, 2001, (theater) Cat on a Hot Tin Roof, 1981, Hay Fever, 1981, The Chain, 1983, Desire Under the Elems, 1982, Still Life, 1983, Ruffian on the Stair, 1979, A Midsummer Night's Dream, 1981, Hunchback of Notre Dame, 1981, Orpheus Descending, 1986, The Hitchhikers, 1985, Crackwalker, 1987, Fool for Love, 1985, Three More Sleepless Nights, (Drama Logue award 1996), 1996, 1984, 1984, Jammed, 1997. Mem. Actors Studio. Office: Nevin Dolcefino Innovative Artists 1505 10th St Santa Monica CA 90401

FISHER, FREDRICK LEE, lawyer; b. Charleston, W.Va., Nov. 12, 1952; s. Ahaz and Lois Mildred (O'Dell) F.; m. Roberta Lee Lane, Sept. 16, 1972; children: Jamie Elizabeth, John Fredrick, Jennifer Katherine. BA in Econs. summa cum laude, Ohio State U., 1973; JD cum laude, Harvard U., 1976. Bar: Ohio 1976, U.S. Dist. Ct. (no. dist.) Ohio 1976, U.S. Claims Ct. 1978, U.S. Tax Ct. 1978. Assoc. Squire, Sanders & Dempsey, Cleve., 1976-80, Columbus, Ohio, 1981-85, ptnr., 1985-87, Schottenstein, Zox & Dunn, Columbus, 1987—; pvt. pratice Worthington, Ohio. Trustee Players Theatre Columbus, 1982-93, pres., 1987-88; sec., treas., trustee The Bill and Edith Walter Found., Columbus, 1982—; trustee Meadow Park Ch., Columbus, 1985-88, 95-97, ctrl. Ohio chpt. Arthritis Found., 1988-89, Directions for Youth, Columbus, 1992-94. Mem. ABA, Ohio Bar Assn., Columbus Bar Assn., Phi Beta Kappa, Capital Club (Columbus). Republican. Avocations: reading, swimming, skiing, biking. Office: 6711 Elmers Ct Worthington OH 43215 Office Phone: 614-746-9028. Fax: (614) 462-5135; Office Fax: 614-885-1088. E-mail: breck400@ameritech.net, ffisher@szd.com.

FISHER, (DONALD) GARTH, plastic surgeon; b. Sacto, MS, May 24, 1958; s. Donald Fisher; m. Brooke Burke, 2001 (div. 2005); children Neriah, Sierra Sky BA in Biology, U. Miss., Oxford, 1980; MD, U. Miss., Jackson, 1984. Diplomate Am. Bd. Plastic Surgery, Am. Bd. Surgery. Intern in gen. surgery U. Calif., Irvine, 1984-85, resident in gen. surgery, 1985-89, resident in plastic surgery, 1989-91; fellow in aesthetic plastic surgery Santa Ana, Calif., 1991; pvt. practice Beverly Hills, Calif., 1991—. Instr. dept. surgery U. Miss. Sch. Medicine, 1980, dept. anatomy, 1980; lectr. in field; consulted extensively for many TV , news and magazine interviews. Author: (5 part ednl. video series) The Naked Truth About Plastic Surgery, The Informed Patient; contbr. articles to sci. and profl. jours.; appeared in: (TV series) Extreme Makeover; guest appearances Good Morning America, Oprah, Today Show, CBS Evening News, NBC Evening News, CNN, Entertainment Tonight, Access Hollywood, EXTRA, E!, and the Discovery Channel, featured in Elle, Allure, GQ, People, Details, In Touch, LA Mag., Town & Country, TV Guide, Wall Street Journal, US Weekly, Parade, LA Times, and USA Today. Fellow ACS; mem. AMA, Calif. Med. Assn., Los Angeles County Med. Assn., L.A. Soc. Plastic Surgeons. Achievements include first plastic surgeon selected to appear on ABC's hit show "Extreme Makeover". Office: 120 S Spalding Dr Ste 222 Beverly Hills CA 90212-1840 Office Phone: 310-273-5995. Office Fax: 310-273-9079. Personal E-mail: garthmd@earthlink.net.

FISHER, GENE JORDAN, retired chemical company executive; b. Quitman, Miss., Mar. 26, 1931; s. Ira R. and Gertrude (Jordan) F.; m. Christine Ann Hodges, May 28, 1954; children— Denise, Darrell BS, U. Tex., 1952. From research chemist to sr. research chemist Celanese Chem. Co., Corpus Christi, Tex., 1952-59, group leader, 1959-67, research mgr., 1967-77, dir. research, 1977-83, tech. dir., 1983-85, ret., 1985; tech. and mgmt. cons., 1985—. Contbr. articles to profl. jours.; patentee in field. Baptist. Home: PO Box 1944 Rockwall TX 75087-2044 E-mail: genefisher@sbcglobal.net.

FISHER, GENE LAWRENCE, financial executive; b. Chillicothe, Ill., Nov. 15, 1929; s. Lawrence Hubert and Alyce Anne (Niggemeyer) F.; m. Sandra Kay Burns, Sept. 19, 1959; children— Kyle Butler, Kelley Anne. B.S., U. Ill., 1957. Staff acct. Inland Container Corp., Indpls., 1957-63, mgr. corp. acctg., 1964-65, asst. corp. controller, 1966-78, dir. fin. systems, 1979-93; ret., 1993. Chmn. fin. com.-exec. com, Winona Meml. Hosp., Indpls., 1979-81, chmn. bd. dirs., 1982-83. Served with U.S. Army, 1951-53. Mem. Beta Alpha Psi, Sigma Iota Epsilon. Republican. Avocations: fishing, swimming. Home: 5427 N Washington Blvd Indianapolis IN 46220-3027 E-mail: genofish@aol.com.

FISHER, GEORGE ROSS, III, physician, educator; b. Erie, Pa., May 8, 1925; s. George Ross and Margaret (Schwitay) F.; m. Mary Stuart Blakely (dec. April 24, 2006); children: George Ross IV, Miriam Schaefer, Margaret Fisher-Rosenthal, Stuart Blakely. BS, Yale U., 1945; MD, Columbia U., 1948. Diplomate Am. Bd. Internal Medicine. Intern Pa. Hosp., Phila., 1948-50, med. resident, 1953-54, dir. house staff, 1954-56; fellow in endocrinology Jefferson Hosp., Phila., 1950-51; surgeon endocrinology br. Nat. Cancer Inst., NIH, Bethesda, Md., 1951-53; from instr. to asst. prof. clin. medicine Jefferson U., Phila., 1955—; asst. prof. clin. medicine U. Pa., Phila., 1960—. Pres. Phila. Profl. Standards Rev. Orgn., 1981-84; med. dir. Heritage Health Systems, King of Prussia, Pa., 1986—; chmn. Ross and Perry, Inc. Book Pubs., Haddonfield, NJ; cons. in field. Author: The Hospital That Ate Chicago, 1980; contbr. articles on endocrinology and med. econs. to profl. jours. Served as sr. asst. surgeon USPHS, 1951-53. Fellow ACP, Phila. Coll. Physicians; mem. AMA (ho. of dels. 1978—), Pa. Med. Soc. (ho. of dels. 1969-89, chmn. coun. of med. econs. 1985-88, trustee 1989—), Phila. County Med. Soc. (bd. dirs. 1969-81), Pa. Soc. Internal Medicine (pres. 1980), Am. Soc. Internal Medicine (ho. of dels. 1974—), Union League (life), Right Angle Club Phila. (pres. 2007—). Republican. Mem. Soc. Of Friends. Avocations: computer science, Phila. history. Home: 203 Chews Landing Rd Haddonfield NJ 08033-3837 Office: 3 South Haddon Ave Haddonfield NJ 08033-1882 Office Phone: 856-427-6135. Business E-Mail: gfisher@rossperry.com.

FISHER, ISLA LANG, actress; b. Muscat, Oman, Feb. 3, 1976; arrived in Australia, 1980, arrived in England, 1997; Actor: (TV series) Bay Cove, 1993, Paradise Beach, 1993—94, Home and Away, 1994—97, 2005, Hearts and Bones, 2000; (TV miniseries) Oliver Twist, 1999, Pilot Season, 2004; (TV films) Attila, 2001, Random Acts of Intimacy, 2002; (films) Bum Magnet, 1997, Furnished Room, 1998, Out of Depth, 2000, Swimming Pool - Der Tod feiert mit, 2001, Scooby-Doo, 2002, Spyz, 2003, The Wannabes, 2003, Dallas 362, 2003, I Heart Huckabees, 2004, Wedding Crashers, 2005 (Breakout Performance, MTV Movie awards, 2006), London, 2005, The Pleasure of Your Company, 2006, The Lookout, 2007; author: (novels) Bewitched, Seduced by Fame.*

FISHER, JAMES LEE, lawyer; b. Akron, Ohio, Apr. 10, 1944; s. James Lee and Maxine (Sumner) Fisher; m. Nancy Lorenz, Dec. 20, 1980. BSCE, U. Akron, 1968, JD, 1971. Bar: Ohio 1971. Staff atty. Brunswick Mgmt. Co., Akron, 1972-77; prin. James L. Fisher Co., L.P.A., Akron, 1977-88, Buckingham, Doolittle & Burroughs, Akron, 1988—. City planner City of Akron, 1968—71, cmty. devel. atty., 1971—73; mem. Metro Regional Transit Authority Bd., 1992—; sec.-treas. Summit County Planning Commn., 1978—99. Mem.: ABA, Ohio Planning Conf., Am. Planning Assn., Home Builders Assn., Akron Bar Assn., Ohio Bar Assn., Copley Lions (pres. 1982). Republican. Mem. United Ch. Of Christ. Home: 1135 Forest Pool Rd Akron OH 44333-1509 Office: Buckingham Doolittle & Burroughs 3800 Embassy Pkwy Akron OH 44333

FISHER, JAMES WILLIAM, pharmacologist, medical educator; b. Tucapau (now Startex), SC, May 22, 1925; s. Ernest Amaziah and Mamie V. (Turner) F.; m. Carol Barbara Brodarick, June 5, 1947 (dec.); children: Candis Loreen Fisher Rush Smith, Patricia Eileen Fisher Valladares, Richard W., William E., John C., Elaine Marie Fisher Spurr; m. Maryann Hillyer Annis, Sept. 30, 2006. BS, U. S.C., 1947; PhD in Pharmacology (USPHS fellow), U. Louisville, 1958. Devel. chemist Armour Pharm. Rsch. Labs., Chgo., 1950-53, Ayerst Pharm. Labs., Rouses Point, NY, 1953—54; pharmacologist Lloyd Bros. Pharm. Co., Cin., 1954-56; instr. pharmacology U. Tenn., 1958-60, asst. prof., 1960-62, assoc. prof., 1962-66, prof., 1966-68; prof., chmn. dept. pharmacology Med. Sch., Tulane U., 1968-96; Regents prof. Tulane U., 1996—99, Regents prof. emeritus, chmn., 1999—. Vis. prof. U. Zambia, Lusaka, 1987, Keio U., Tokyo, 1987, U. Nairobi, 1993; external examiner U. W.I., Trinidad, 1992; vis. scientist Christie Hosp. and Holt Radium Inst., Manchester, Eng., 1963-64; dir. Tulane-Universidad Nacional del Nordeste, Corrientes, Argentina, Pan Am. Health Orgn. Physiol. Scis. Tng. Program, 1972-77; lectr. in field; mem. Nat. Heart, Lung and Blood Inst. (erythropoietin com. 1971-74), mem. NIH hematology tng. grants com., 1977; mem. Cooley's Anemia Nat. Rsch. Com., 1974; pres. So. Blood Club, 1975-77; mem. Wellcome Professorships Com., 1976, 93, 94, 95; mem. pharmacology com. Nat. Bd. Med. Examiners, 1988-92; mem. ad hoc group med. rsch. funding AAMC, 1990-93. Author: Readings on the History of Pharmacology, 1970, History of Pharmacology at Tulane, 2004; editor: Kidney Hormones, Vol. I, 1971, Vol. II, 1977, Vol. III, 1986, Renal Pharmacology, 1971, Handbook of Pharmacology: Blood and Blood Forming Organs, 1992, History of Pharmacology at Tulane, 1834-2004; co-editor: Erythropoiesis, 1975, Erythropoietin and Erythropoiesis, 1981; cons. editor: Erythropoietin, 1968; mem. editl. bd. Proc. Soc. Exptl. Biology and Medicine, 1971-86; contbr. articles to profl. jours. Served to lt. (j.g.) USNR, 1943-46, PTO. Recipient rsch. career devel. award USPHS, 1960-65, Purkinje medal Czechoslovakia Med. Soc., 1975, Golden Sovereign award, 1976, Aspet Exptl. Therapeutics award, 1992, U. Louisville Med. Sch. Alumni award, 1999; named Disting. faculty AOA Honor Med. Soc., 1993; Ann. Tulane Fisher Lectureship established in his honor, 1992. Mem. AAAS, AAUP, Am. Soc. Pharmacology and Exptl. Therapeutics (Sollman awards com. 1981, exptl. therapeutics award com. 1982, 94, alerting network 1986-90, edtl. affairs com. 1986-89, Krayer awards com. 1990, Exptl. Therapeutics award 1992, nominating com. 1997), Soc. Exptl. Biology and Medicine, Am. Soc. Nephrology, Am. Soc. Hematology (sci. affairs com. 1973-74, chmn. erythropoietin subcom. 1973), Assn. Med. Sch. Pharmacology (exec. com. 1979-82, nominating com. 1975, 86, 94, 96, 99, chmn. essential knowledge base in pharmacology com. 1984-95, pres. 1990-92), N.Y. Acad. Scis., Sigma Xi. Home: 67 Grand Canyon Dr New Orleans LA 70131 Business E-Mail: jfisher@tulane.edu. *Creativity and brilliance are very important in science but in order to test one's ideas these qualities must be adequately supplemented by the necessary amount of work at the bench.*

FISHER, JEFF, professional football coach; b. Culver City, Calif., Feb. 25, 1958; m. Juli; children: Brandon, Trenton, Tara. Student, U. Southern California. Professional football player Chicago Bears, 1981-85; defensive backs coach Philadelphia Eagles, 1986-88, defensive coordinator, 1989-90, Los Angeles Rams, 1991; defensive backs coach San Francisco 49ers, 1992-93; defensive coordinator Tenn. Titans, 1994; head coach Tenn. Oilers (now Titans), 1995—; exec. v.p. Tenn. Titans, 2000—. Avocations: fly fishing, golf, sushi, travel. Office: Tennessee Titans Baptist Sports Park 460 Great Circle Rd Nashville TN 37228-1404

FISHER, JEFFREY L., lawyer; b. 1970; BA in English, Duke U., 1992; JD, U. Mich. Law Sch., 1997. Bar: Wash. 2000. Law clk. to Justice John

Paul Stevens U.S. Supreme Ct., Washington; law clk. to Hon. Stephen Reinhardt US Ct. Appeals (9th cir.); assoc. Davis Wright Tremaine LLP, Seattle, 1999—2004, ptnr., 2005—; assoc. prof. Stanford Law Sch., Palo Alto, Calif., 2006—, co-dir. Supreme Ct. Litig. Clinic Palo Alto., Calif., 2006. Vis. lectr. U. Wash. Law Sch.; vice chair, amicus com., co-chair supreme ct. oral argument com. Nat. Assn. Criminal Def. Lawyers; spkr. in field. Contbr. articles to profl. jours. Named one of Top 40 Lawyers Under 40, Nat. Law Jour., 2005, Top 100 Influential Lawyers, 2006, Litigation's Rising Stars, The Am. Lawyer, 2007; recipient Professionalism award, Wash. Young Lawyers Divsn., Wash. State Bar, 2004, William O. Douglas Award, Wash. Assn. of Criminal Defense Lawyers. Mem.: Wash. State Bar Assn., ACLU of Washington (mem. legal com.). Office: Davis Wright Tremaine LLP 2600 Century Sq 1501 Fourth Ave Seattle WA 98101-1688 Office Phone: 206-622-3150. Business E-Mail: jefffisher@dwt.com.*

FISHER, JEFFREY L., psychologist; b. Michigan City, Ind., Nov. 21, 1945; s. George and Alice Marie Fisher; m. Wynn Jessica Hummel, Nov. 10, 2001; children: Matt Hummel, Nicholas Hummel; m. Patricia Ann Milcarek (dec.); children: Kimberly Milcarek, Benjamin Milcarek, Kathy Milcarek. AB, Ind. U., Bloomington, 1969; MA in Applied Behavioral Sci., Valparaiso U., Ind., 1989; D of Psychology, Ill. Sch. Profl. Psychology, Chgo., 1999. Psychologists asst. Rehab. Achievement Ctr., Hazel Crest, Ill., 1996—98; cons. psychologist Swanson Ctr., Michigan City, Ind., 1999; staff psychologist Westville Correctional Ctr., Nestville, 2000—01, Munster Cmty. Hosp., 2002—03, St. Catherines Hosp., East Chicago, Ill., 2003; clin. psychologist Assocs. Clin. Practice, Merrillville, Ind., 2002—04, St. Margaret Outpatient Behavioral Health, Hammond, 2004—. V.p., sec. Jesseff Corp., Michigan City, 2004—. Recipient Hospitality award, LaPorte City Visitors Bur., Michigan City, 2006. Mem.: APA, Ind. Psychol. Assn., Michigan City C. of C. Methodist. Avocation: chess. Home: 731 Washington St Michigan City IN 46360 Office: St Margaret Mercy Hosp 5500 Hohman Ave Hammond IN 46321

FISHER, JEROME, apparel executive; m. Anne C. Fisher; children: Marc, Jodi. Founder Nine West Group, chmn. emeritus. Jerome & Anne C. Fisher Charitable Found.; overseer Wharton Sch., U. Pa.; trustee U. Pa. Named one of Top 200 Collectors, ARTnews Mag., 2004; recipient Humanitarian Award, 1997, Humanitarian of Yr., Shoes on Sale, 2003. Mem.: Acad. of U. Pa., Coll. House Adv. Bd. Avocation: collector modern art. Office: Nine West Group 1129 Westchester Ave White Plains NY 10604

FISHER, JOEL MARSHALL, political scientist, educator, wine consultant; b. Chgo., June 24, 1935; s. Dan and Nell (Kolvin) F.; children: Sara Melinda, Matthew Nicholas. AB, U. So. Calif., 1955; LLB, MA, U. Calif.-Berkeley; PhD in Govt., Claremont Grad. U., 1968. Orgn. dir. Republican Citizens Com. of U.S., Washington, 1964-65; dir. arts and scis. state legis. divs. Rep. Nat. Com., Washington, 1968-69; asst. dep. counsel to pres. U.S. White House, 1969-70; dep. asst. sec. econ. and social affairs U.S. Dept. State, Washington, 1969-71; vis. prof. comparative and internat. law Loyola U. Sch. Law, LA, 1972-73; dir. World Bus. Inst., LA, 1974-75; prof. constl. law Southwestern U. Sch. Law, LA, 1974-76; dir. World Trade Inst. So. Calif., 1976-84; prof. internat. law, asst. dean Whitter Coll. Sch. Law, LA, 1977-80; prin. Ziskind, Greene and Assocs., 1980-83; v.p. Wells Internat., 1983-84; pres. LawSearch Inc., 1984-91; v.p. Clarke Cos., 1991-93; pres. Fisher Group, 1993—; adj. prof. Calif. Internat. U., LA, 1993-99. Spl. projects Hollywood Palace, 1998—2002, pub. affairs, 2002—; ofcl. visitor The European Cmtys., 1974, 76; wine instr. AILA/culinary arts, 1999—2006; mem. US dels. UN confs., 1969—71; chmn. Strategy for Peace Conf. Panel on US and UN, 1972—; coord. Series on the Contemporary Am. Presidency, 1972—73; cons. Robert Taft Inst., 1977—82, World Trade Inst., NY, 1977—80; chair Bid Renewal Steering Com., Hollywood Entertainment Dist.; pres. Hollywood United Neighborhood Coun., 2000—06; chair Bid Security Com., 2001—03, 2003—06; bd. dirs., treas. Hollywood Bus. Improvement Dist., 2001—, v.p., 2003—05, 2006; organizer, pres. Lawine Fest, Inc., 2005—. Co-author three books; contbr. articles to profl. jours. Steering com. Calif. Com. Reelection of Pres., 1972; nat chmn. Cmty. Leaders Ford, 1976; trustee Rep. Assocs., 1978—, exec. com., 1986—; mem. vestry, sr. warden St. Michael and All Angeles Ch., Studio City, Calif., 1983-86, 89-93, mem. diocesan coun. L.A., 1986-88, chmn. budget com. 1987; bd. dirs. Corp. of the Cathedral, 1988-91, com. on constn. and canons, 1993—; mem. bd. dirs. Hollywood-Wilshire YMCA, 2005-. Fellow Nobel Found., 1958; Falk fellow, 1961-62 Mem. Am. Polit. Sci. Assn. (state legis. fellow 1970-73). Home: 4358 Mammoth Ave Unit 26 Sherman Oaks CA 91423-3692 Office: 1735 Vine St Hollywood CA 90028-5248 Office Phone: 818-429-6770. Personal E-mail: jmfisher@aol.com.

FISHER, JOELY, actress; b. Burbank, Calif., Oct. 29, 1967; d. Eddie Fisher and Connie Stevens; m. Christopher Duddy, 1996; 2 children. Student, Univ. Paris, Emerson Coll. Actor: (films) I'll Do Anything, 1994, The Mask, 1994, Mixed Nuts, 1994, Family Plan, 1998, Inspector Gadget, 1999, Nostradamus, 2000, Slingshot, 2005; (TV films) Dedicated to the One I Love, 1991, Jitters, 1997, Seduction in a Small Town, 1997, Icebergs: The Secret Life of a Refrigerator, 1998, Perfect Prey, 1998, Thirst, 1998, Coming Unglued, 1999, Kidnapped in Paradise, 1999, (TV series) In the Loop, 1998, Ellen, 1994-98, Normal, Ohio, 2000-01, Baby Bob, 2002-03, Til Death, 2006, (Broadway plays) Grease; performed with Connie Stevens and Bob Hope overseas during Persian Gulf War; sang before Pres. and Mrs. Bush at Kennedy Ctr. Office: c/o Fox Entertainment Group Inc 1211 Avenue of the Americas Ste 302 New York NY 10036

FISHER, JOHN MORRIS, association official, business executive, educator; b. Fairhaven, Ohio, Apr. 20, 1922; s. Marion Hays and Bessie (Morris) F.; m. Thelma Ison, Feb. 2, 1947; children: Steven Roger, Linda Lucille. AB, Miami U., Oxford, Ohio, 1947; postgrad., Bklyn. Law Sch., 1950-51, Northwestern U., Evanston, Ill., 1954-55; LLD (hon.), Nasson Coll., 1972. With Belden Mfg. Co., Richmond, Ind., 1941; spl. agt. FBI, 1947—53; exec. staff asst. to v.p. personnel and employee rels. Sears Roebuck & Co., Chgo., 1953—57, chmn. corp. security com., 1957—61; chmn., CEO, oper. dir. Am. Security Coun., 1956—2002, pres., 1957—2002. Pres. Am. Rsch. Found., 1961-90; pres., CEO Am. Security Coun. Found., 1962-87, CEO, 1987-2002, chmn., 1992-2002; pres. Comm. Corp. Am., 1972-80, chmn., 1980—; pres. Am. Coalition Patriotic Socs., 1978-91; adminstrv. chmn. Coalition for Peace Through Strength, 1978-2002; dir. Ctr. for Internat. Security Studies, 1977-83; organizer, pres. Fidelifax, Inc., 1956-57; chmn. merc. divsn. Nat. Safety Coun., 1959-60, 1st vice chmn. trades and svcs. sect., 1961-62. Chmn. Chgo. Retail Safety Conf., 1959-60; spl. adviser Ill. Supt. Pub. Instrn., 1963-64; cons. to Gov. Fla.; cons. to chmn. com. cold war edn. Nat. Gov.'s Conf., 1962-65, Ill. CD Adv. Coun., 1965-68; pres. Am. Coun. World Freedom, 1971-72; mem. exec. com. Nat. Captive Nations Com., 1968-70; bd. visitors Freedoms Found., 1964-65; bd. dirs. Am. Fgn. Policy Inst., 1976-84, Security and Intelligence Fund, 1976-84, James Monroe Libr., 1977-85; pres. Culpeper Meml. Hosp. Found., 1984-86; exec. chmn. U.S. Congl. Adv. Bd., 1982-2002; chmn. Nat. Security Caucus Found., 1997-2002. 1st lt. USAAF, 1943-45. Decorated Air medal with clusters; recipient 10th Anniversary medal and scroll Assembly Captive European Nations, Order Lafayette Freedom award, 1973, Disting. Svc. award Chapel of 4 Chaplains, 1979, Pres. Eagle, Pres. Reagan, 1982, others. Mem. Am. Soc. Indsl. Security (dir. 1959-62), Phi Kappa Tau. Republican. Presbyterian. Office: Comms Corp Am 13195 Freedom Way Boston VA 22713 Home: 1210 S Blue Ridge Ave Culpeper VA 22701 Office Phone: 540-547-1700. Personal E-mail: johnmorrisfisher@comcast.net. Business E-Mail: john.fisher@cca.net.

FISHER, JOHN R., district supreme court justice; b. Knox County, Ohio; s. George and Helen Fisher. BA magna cum laude, Harvard Coll., 1968; JD cum laude, Harvard Law Sch., 1974. Law clk. to Hon. Joseph P. Kinneary US Dist. Ct. (so. dist) Ohio; atty. US Attorney's Office, 1976—83; asst. U.S. atty. (so. dist.) Ohio US Dept. Justice, 1983—86; of counsel Vorys, Sater, Seymour & Pease, Columbus, 1986—89; chief appellate divsn. US Atty's Office DC US Dept. Justice, 1989—2005; assoc. judge DC Ct. Appeals, 2005—. Served in US Army. Recipient John Marshall award, U.S. Atty. Gen. Mem.: Asst. U.S. Attorneys Assn. (Harold Sullivan award), DC Bar Assn. (legal ethics com.). Office: DC Ct Appeals Moultrie Courthouse 500 Indiana Ave NW Washington DC 20001 Office Phone: 202-879-2751.*

FISHER, JOHN W., insurance company executive; With Auto-Owners Ins., Lansing, Mich., 1978—, pres., 1993—. Pres., bd. dirs. Lake Country Corp.; dir. Mut. Reinsurance Bur. Mem.: Nat. Assn. Mut. Ins. Cos. (chmn. 2002—03). Office: Auto Owners Ins PO Box 30660 6101 Anacapri Blvd Lansing MI 48917

FISHER, JOHN WELTON, II, lawyer, educator, academic administrator; b. Fisher, W.Va., Dec. 11, 1942; s. John Welton and Orrie (Shobe) F.; m. Susan Carol Vass, June 6, 1964; children: John Welton III, Jennifer Lynn. BA, W.Va. U., 1964, JD, 1967. Bar: W.Va. 1967, U.S. Dist. Ct. (no. and so. dists.) W.Va. 1967, U.S. Ct. Appeals (4th cir.) 1969. Law clk. to chief judge U.S. Dist. Ct. (no. dist.) W.Va., 1967-68; assoc. Farmer & Farmer, Morgantown, W.Va., 1968-71; mem. faculty W.Va. U. Coll. Law, 1971—, prof. law, 1977—, acting dean, 1981-82, 92-93, 97-98, dean, 1998—, exec. officer univ., 1982-86; magistrate judge U.S. Dist. Ct. No. Dist. W.Va., 1977-98. Reporter Speedy Trial Planning Group, No. Dist. W.Va. Reporter: Local Rules of Practice, Northern District of West Virginia, 1980. Fellow Am.Bar Found., W.Va. Bar Found.; mem. W.Va. State Bar, W.Va. Bar Assn., Fourth Cir. Jud. Conf., Order of Coif. Office: PO Box 6130 Morgantown WV 26506-6130 Office Phone: 304-293-3199. Business E-Mail: John.Fisher@mail.wvu.edu.

FISHER, KATHLEEN V., lawyer; b. Aug. 9, 1948; AB, UCLA, 1971; JD, U. Calif., Davis, 1976. Bar: Calif. 1976. Extern to Hon. Raymond Sullivan Calif. Supreme Ct., 1975; assoc. Morrison & Foerster LLP, San Francisco, 1976—82, ptnr., 1982—2005, chair litigation dept., 1993—96; ptnr. Calvo & Clark LLP, San Francisco, 2005—. Recipient Leadership award, San Francisco AIDS Found., 2004. Mem. Order of Coif. Office: Calvo & Clark LLP One Lombard St San Francisco CA 94111 E-mail: kfisher@calvoclark.com.*

FISHER, KENNETH, real estate company executive; m. Tammy Fisher; 3 children. Student, Ithaca Coll. Ptnr. Fisher Bros., NYC, 1991—2003, sr. ptnr. mgmt., leasing and new ventures, 2003—. Mem. real estate bd. NY Bd. Govs.; mem. exec. com. City Investment Fund, LP; bd. dirs. Realogy Corp., 2006—. Vice chmn. Fisher House Found., 2001—03, chmn., CEO, 2003—; bd. trustees NY City Assn. for Help of Retarded Children; bd. dirs. Intrepid Mus. Found., NY's Finest Found. Recipient Sec.'s award, Dept. Vets. Affairs, 2004, Decoration for Disting. Civilian Svc., Sec. Army, 2005, Lives that Make a Difference award, Arts & Entertainment Network, 2005. Office: Fisher Bros 299 Park Ave New York NY 10171 Office Phone: 212-752-5000.*

FISHER, KENNETH LAWRENCE, investment management firm executive; b. San Francisco, Nov. 29, 1950; s. Philip Arthur and Dorothy (White) F.; m. Sherrilyn Ellis, Nov. 4, 1970; children: Clayton, Nathan, Jesse. AB in Econs., Humboldt State U., 1972. Rsch. assoc. Fisher & Co., San Francisco, 1972-73; sole proprietor K.L. Fisher & Co., San Francisco, 1973-76; ptnr. Fisher Investments, San Francisco, 1976-78; chief exec. Fisher Investments, Inc., Burlingame, Calif., 1978-85, Woodside, Calif., 1985—, now chmn., chief investment officer. Mem. adv. bd. Investment Co. Inst., Washington, 1989-92. Author: Super Stocks, 1984, The Wall Street Waltz, 1987, 100 Minds That Made the Market, 1992; outside columnist Forbes Mag., 1984—. Mem. bd. San Mateo County Hist. Assn., San Mateo, Calif., 1990-92. Named one of Forbes Richest Americans, 2006. Mem. The Kings Grove, Sons of Norway, Bohemian Club. Republican. Avocation: history of 19th century redwood lumbering. Office: Fisher Investments Inc 13100 Skyline Blvd Woodside CA 94062-4542

FISHER, LANE J., lawyer; b. Phila., Pa., Sept. 3, 1963; s. Howard Ronald Fisher and Ina Lee Meyers; m. Michele Fisher, Apr. 18, 1998; children: Ryan Brett, Cole Edward. BBA, George Washington U., 1985, MBA, 1986; JD, Am. U., Washington, 1989. Atty. Abraham Pressman & Bave, Phila., 1989—95; ptnr. Fisher Zucker, Phila., 1995—. Mem.: Internat. Franchisee Assn. (bd. dirs. 2005—06, 2007—, mem. exec. com. 2005—06). Jewish. Office: Fisher Zucker LLC 121 S Broad St Ste 1200 Philadelphia PA 19187

FISHER, LAURA LANI, physician, medical educator; b. East Orange, NJ, July 13, 1959; d. Hyman Wendell and Rosalie Jane (Joseph) F.; m. Adi Raviv; children: Micaela Sara, Jessica Alana, Gabriella Noa. BA in Biology and Biomed. Ethics, Brown U., 1981, MD, 1984. Intern in internal medicine N.Y. Hosp., 1984-85, resident in internal medicine, 1985-87, chief resident in medicine, 1989-90, dir. Lyme Disease Ctr., 1990—; from clin. to rsch. fellow in infectious diseases Mass. Gen. Hosp., Boston, 1987-89; dir. student health svc. Cornell Med. Coll., NYC, 1990-93, asst. prof. medicine, 1990—. Contbr. articles to profl. jours. Mem. nat. cabinet Israel Bonds-Young Leadership, U.S., 1992-94, mem. city bd. dirs., 1993-94; mem. Anti-Defamation League, N.Y.C., 1993-94. Recipient Rsch. Scientist award NIH, 1988-89. Fellow ACP; mem. AMA, N.Y. Med. Soc., Mass. Med. Soc., Brown Med. Soc., Infectious Disease Soc. Am. Republican. Jewish. Avocations: painting, sports, sculpture, reading, travel. Office: 1385 York Ave New York NY 10021-3904 Office Phone: 212-717-5920.

FISHER, LAWRENCE EDGAR, market research executive, anthropologist; b. Los Alamos, N.Mex., Jan. 13, 1946; s. Leon H. and Phyllis (Kahn) F.; m. Valerie Joseph, Mar. 25, 1979; children: Lael Sharon, Jonathan Daniel, Matthew Joseph. AB, U. Calif., Berkeley, 1968; MA, Northwestern U., 1969, PhD, 1973; postdoctoral fellow, U. Chgo., 1973—74; postgrad. in bus. adminstrn., U. Pa., 1982. Asst. prof. U. Ill., Chgo., 1974—83; dir. Ethnographic Field Sch. Northwestern U., Evanston, Ill., 1975—78, adj. assoc. prof., 1984—86; dir. client svc. MRCA Info. Svc., Northbrook, Ill., 1983—88; group mgr. Test Mktg. Group, Control Data Corp., Chgo., 1988—89; dir. client svc. Info. Resources, Inc., Chgo., 1989—90, v.p., 1991—94, sr. v.p., 1994—2000, NFO WorldGroup, Chgo., 2000—04, Rsch. Internat., Chgo., 2006, Global Online Strategy, Synovate, Inc., 2004—05, dir., 2004—05; faculty dept. integrated mktg. comm. Roosevelt U., Chgo., 2007—. Vis. scholar Stanford U., 1978; vis. asst. prof. U. Mich., Ann Arbor, 1979—80; mem. external adv. bd. A.C. NielsenCtr., Grad. Sch. Bus. U. Wis., Madison, 1991—, chmn. bd., 1998—99; founding bd. govs. Interactive Market Rsch. Orgn., 2000—. Author: Colonial Madness, 1985; also numerous articles; mem. editl. rev. bd., Jour. Online Rsch., 2001—. Program com. mem. Market Rsch. Assn. Annual Conf., 2005, 2006, 2007, chair online rsch. track, 2005—, 2006, 2007. Fellow Woodrow Wilson Found., 1972-73, NIH, 1973-74, NEH, 1975. Mem.: ESOMAR, Mktg. Rsch. Assn., Market Rsch. Assn., Am. Anthrop. Assn., Am. Mktg. Assn. (EXPLOR award com. 2001—, conf. com. Exec. Insights Forum 2003, program com. Mktg. Rsch. Summit 2004, 2006). Home: 324 S Euclid Ave Oak Park IL 60302-3508

FISHER, LAWRENCE N., lawyer, engineering and construction management company executive; BA, U. So. Calif., LA, 1965, JD, 1968. Bar: Calif. 1969. Assoc. ptnr. Hahn & Hahn, Pasadena, Calif., 1969-74; tax atty. Fluor Corp., Calif., 1974-76; sr. tax counsel Fluor Corp., Calif., 1976-78; v.p. corp. law, asst. sec. Fluor Corp., Calif., 1984—96, sr. v.p. law, corp. sec., chief legal officer Calif., 1996—; v.p. adminstrn. Fluor Arabia Ltd., 1978-79. Pres. Nat. Constructor's Assn. Tax Com., 1983—84. Fluor's bd. rep. Orange County Performing Arts Ctr. Office: Fluor Enterprises 3 Polaris Way Aliso Viejo CA 92698 Office Phone: 949-349-2000. Office Fax: 949-349-2585.*

FISHER, LEE I., lieutenant governor, former state attorney general; b. Ann Arbor, Mich., Aug. 7, 1951; m. Peggy Zone Fisher; children: Jason, Jessica. Grad., Oberlin Coll., 1973; JD, Case Western Res. U. Law clk. US Ct. Appeals (6th cir.); mem. firm. Hahn Loeser and Parks, Cleve.; mem. Ohio Gen. Assembly, 1981—82, Ohio State Senate, 1982—90; atty. gen. State of Ohio, Columbus, Ohio, 1991—95; pres., CEO Ctr. for Families and Children, 1999—2006; lt. gov. State of Ohio, 2007—. Chair Nat. Commn. Crime Ctrl. and Prevention; mem., World Bd. Governors United Svc. Organizations. Contbr. articles to profl. jours. Founder, co-chair Mental Health Advocacy Coalition; bd. mem. Cleve. Clinic Cancer Ctr., Nat. Ctr. for Missing and Exploited Children, Oberlin Coll. Recipient Visionary Innovation in Bus. award, Medical Mutual, 2001, Nonprofit Exec. of Yr. award, Smart Bus. mag., 2004. Mem. Greater Cleveland Bar Assn. (Merit Svc. award), Ohio Acad. Trial Lawyers (Legislator of Yr.), Case Western Res. U. Alumni Assn. (Disting. Recent Grad. award). Democrat. Office: Lieutenant Governor 77 High St 23rd Fl Columbus OH 43215 Office Phone: 614-466-3636. Office Fax: 614-644-0575.*

FISHER, LEONARD EVERETT, artist, educator, writer; b. NYC, June 24, 1924; s. Benjamim M. and Ray Mera (Shapiro) F.; m. Margery Meskin, Dec. 21, 1952; children: Julie Anne, Susan Abby, James Albert BFA, Yale U., 1949, MFA, 1950. Dean Whitney Art Sch., New Haven, Conn., 1951-53; mem. faculty Paier Art Sch., Hamden, Conn., 1966-78; acad. dean Paier Coll. of Art, Hamden, 1978-82, dean emeritus, 1982—, vis. prof., 1982-87, Fairfield U., Conn., 1983-85. Del. at large White House Conf. Libr. and Info. Svcs., Washington, 1979; lectr. in field, 1957-; mem. adv. bd. MFA program Western Conn. State U., Danbury. Author 90 childrens books; illustrator approximately 260 childrens books; author, illustrator: A Russian Farewell (Nat. Jewish Book award), 1981; designer 10 U.S. postage stamps including 1972 and 1977 U.S. Bicentennial Commemorative issues; paintings and illustrations represented in permanent collections Butler Art Inst., Youngstown, Ohio, Mt. Holyoke Coll., Mass., Union Coll., Schenectady, N.Y., Housatonic Mus., Bridgeport, Conn., New Britain Mus. Am. Art, Conn., U. Conn., Storrs, U. Minn., Mpls., U. Oreg., Eugene, U. So. Miss., Hattiesburg, Brown U., Providence, Libr. of Congress, Washington, N.Y. Pub. Libr., Mus. Am. Illustration, N.Y.C., Norwalk (Conn.) Transp. Ctr. Trustee Westport Pub. Library, Conn., 1982-89, v.p., 1985-86, pres. 1986-89; founding mem. Westport-Weston Arts Coun., 1969, pres., bd. dir., 1973-74, trustee, 1969-76; mem. Lowe com. New Britain Mus. Am. Art, Conn. With U.S. Army, 1942-46, NATOUSA, PTO, ETO. Recipient Premio Grafico Internat. Book Fair, Italy, 1968, Medallion, U. So. Miss., 1979, Christopher medal, 1980, Non-Fiction award Childrens Book Guild Washington and the Washington Post, 1989, Regina medal Cath. Libr. Assn., 1991, Kerlan award U. Minn., 1991, Arbuthnot Honor Lectr. citation ALA, 1995, New Eng. Booksellers award for children's lit., 2002, Westport Arts Heritage award, 2003, Pulitzer Art scholarship, 1950; Winchester fellow Yale U., 1949. Mem. Soc. Illustrators, Silvermine Guild (life, trustee 1970-74), Authors Guild N.Y., P.E.N., New Haven Paint and Clay Club (life). Home and Studio: 7 Twin Bridge Acre Rd Westport CT 06880-1028 Office Phone: 203-227-0133. Personal E-mail: l.e.fisher@sbcglobal.net.

FISHER, LESTER EMIL, retired zoo administrator; b. Chgo., Feb. 24, 1921; s. Louis and Elizabeth (Vodicka) F.; m. Wendy Fisher, Jan. 23, 1981; children: Jane Serrita, Katherine Clark. MDV, Iowa State U., 1943. Supr. animal care program Northwestern U. Med. Sch., 1946-47; attending veterinarian Lincoln Park Zoo, Chgo., 1947-62, zoo dir., 1962-92, dir. emeritus, 1992—; owner, dir. Berwyn (Ill.) Animal Hosp., 1947-68. Producer, moderator ednl. closed circuit TV for nat. vet. meetings, 1949-66; asso. prof. dept. biology DePaul U., 1968-98; adj. prof. zoology U. Ill., from 1972 Editor: Brit. Small Animal Jour. and Small Animal Clinician, 1958-72. Mem. citizens com. U. Ill.; chmn. zoo and wildlife div. Morris Animal Found. Served to maj., Vet. Corps AUS, 1943-46. Recipient Alumni Merit award Iowa State U., 1968, Stange award Iowa State U., 1988, Chgo. Superior Pub. Svc. award Chgo. Park Dist., 1973, 92, Laureate Ill. Lincoln Acad., 1993. Mem. Am. Animal Hosp. Assn. (regional dir., outstanding Service award 1969), Am. Vet. Med. Assn., Nat. Recreation and Park Assn., Internat. Union Dirs. Zool. Gardens (v.p. 1980-83, pres. 1983-86), Am. Assn. Zoo Veterinarians (pres. 1966-69), Am. Assn. Zool. Parks and Aquariums (pres. 1972-73, chmn. gorilla species survival plan 1982-92), Chgo. Geographic Soc. (v.p.), Adventures Club (pres. 1971-72), Execs. Club of Chgo. (bd. dirs. 1968-71), Arts Assoc., Chgo. Econs. Club (membership com.), Theta Xi. Home: PO Box 606 Alexandria Bay NY 13607-0606

FISHER, LINDA J., former federal agency administrator; b. Saginaw, Mich., June 26, 1952; BA, Miami U., Oxford, Ohio, 1974; MBA, George Washington U., 1978; JD, Ohio State U., 1982. Legis. asst. to Hon. Clarence J. Brown, Ohio, 1974-75, Hon. Ralph S. Regula, Ohio, 1976-80; special asst. to asst. adminstr. solid waste and emergency response EPA, 1983-84, chief staff to adminstr., 1985-87, asst. adminstr. policy and evaluation, 1988, asst. adminstr. pesticides and toxic substances Washington, 1989—93, dep. adminr., 2001—03; of counsel Latham & Watkins, 1993—95; v.p. govt. and pub. affairs Monsanto, 1995—2000.

FISHER, LLOYD EDISON, JR., lawyer; b. Medina, Ohio, Oct. 23, 1923; s. Lloyd Edison and Wanda (White) F.; m. Twylla Dawn Peterson, Sept. 11, 1949 (dec. Apr. 1996); children: Karen S., Kirk P. BS, Ohio State U., 1947, JD, 1949. Bar: Ohio 1950. Mem. gen. hearing bd. Ohio Dept. Taxation, 1950-53; trust officer Huntington Nat. Bank, Columbus, 1953-62; ptnr. Porter, Wright, Morris & Arthur and predecessor firm, Columbus, 1962—. Adj. prof. law Ohio State U., Columbus, 1967—69, Columbus, 1984—91. Bd. dirs Wesley Glen Retirement Ctr., 1974-80, 88-95, Home Reach Hospice, 1997—. Served with AUS, 1943-45. Fellow Am. Coll. Trust and Estate Counsel; mem. ABA, Ohio Bar Assn., Columbus Bar Assn., Order of Coif. Home: 6478 Strathaven Ct E Worthington OH 43085-2985 Office: 41 S High St Columbus OH 43215-6101 Office Phone: 614-227-2285. Business E-Mail: lfisher@porterwright.com.

FISHER, LUCY, film producer; b. NYC, Oct. 2, 1949; d. Arthur Bertram and Naomi (Kislak) F.; m. Douglas Z. Wick, Feb. 16, 1986; children: Sarah, Julia, Tessa. BA in English, cum laude, Harvard U., 1971. Reader United Artists; v.p. prodn. 20th Century Fox, LA, 1979-80; v.p. worldwide prodns. Zoetrope Studios, Burbank, Calif., 1980-81; v.p., sr. prodn. exec. Warner Bros. Pictures, Burbank, 1981-87, sr. v.p., 1987-89, exec. v.p. prodn., 1989-96; vice chmn. Columbia Tristar Motion Picture Co., Culver City, Calif., 1996-2000; prodr. Red Wagon Productions, Culver City, Calif., 2000—, pres. Prodr.: (films) Stuart Little 2, 2002, Peter Pan, 2003, Win a Date with Tad Hamilton!, 2004, Bewitched, 2005, Jarhead, 2005, Memoirs of a Geisha, 2005, Stuart Little 3: Call of the Wild, 2005; exec. prodr.: (TV series) Stuart Little, 2003. Recipient Crystal award, 1998, David O. Selznick Achievement award in Theatrical Motion Pictures, Producers Guild Am., 2007. Office: Red Wagon Entertainment Hepburn West 10202 Washington Blvd Culver City CA 90232-3119*

FISHER, MARK JAY, neurologist, neuroscientist, educator; b. Bklyn., Aug. 23, 1949; s. Ralph Aaron and Dorothy Ann (Weissman) F.; m. Janeth Godeau, Aug. 5, 1994. BA in Polit. Sci., UCLA, 1970; MA in Polit. Sci., U. S.D., 1972; MD, U. Cin., 1975; JD, Loyola U., 1997. Diplomate Am. Bd. Psychiatry and Neurology. Intern UCLA Sepulveda VA Hosp., 1975-76; resident UCLA Wadsworth VA Med. Ctr., 1976-79, chief resident, 1979-80; faculty mem., dir. stroke rsch. program U. So. Calif. Sch. of Medicine, LA, 1980-98, prof. neurology, 1995-98; dir. residency tng. program U. So. Calif. Sch. Medicine, LA, 1992-96; chmn. dept. neurology U. Calif. at Irvine, Orange, 1998—2006, prof. neurology and anatomy and neurobiology, 1998—, prof. polit. sci., 2003—; dir. U. Calif. at Irvine Stoke Ctr., 2002—. Editor: Medical Therapy of Acute Stroke, 1989. Recipient Tchr. Investigator award NIH, Bethesda, Md., 1984-89, Program Project grantee, 1994-99. Mem.: Internat. Soc. Polit. Psychology, Am. Polit. Sci. Assn., State Bar Calif., Internat. Soc. for Thrombosis and Haemostasis, Am. Polit. Sci. Assn., Am. Heart Assn. (stroke coun.), Am. Neurol. Assn., Am. Acad. Neurology. Office: U Calif Irvine Dept Neurology 101 The City Dr S Orange CA 92868-3201

FISHER, MARK LEIGHTON, software engineer; b. South Bend, Ind., Dec. 11, 1956; s. Leighton Ernest and Nancy Ann (Abbott) F.; m. Melinda Sue Chambers, July 30, 1988; children: Michelle Lorainne, Morgan Leighton. BSEE, Purdue U., 1979. Rsch. asst. Purdue U., West Lafayette, Ind., 1978-79; software engr. Northrop Def. Sys., Rolling Meadows, Ill., 1979-81, Micro Data Base Sys., Lafayette, Ind., 1981-84, Wintek, Lafayette, 1984-91; mem. tech. staff Thomson Consumer Electronics, Indpls., 1991—2003; pvt. practice cons. Indpls., 2003—05; sys. engr. Regenstrief Inst., Indpls., 2005—. Mem. Internet Engring. Task Force. Libertarian. Lutheran. Achievements include creation of of electronic reference document repository corporate technical memory using world-wide web and WAIS, co-creator of PCB autoreplacement tool using simulated annealing. Mailing: 612 E Greyhound Pass Carmel IN 46032 Personal E-mail: mark-fisher@mindspring.com.

FISHER, MICHAEL D., retail executive; Bachelors Degree, Univ. Fla. With Maas Brothers Dept. Stores, Robinson's Dept. Stores, The May Co.; exec. v.p. stores Stein Mart, Inc., 1993—2001, pres., COO, 2001—03, pres., CEO, 2003—. Office: Stein Mart Inc 1200 Riverplace Blvd Jacksonville FL 32207 Office Phone: 904-398-9945.

FISHER, MICHAEL ELLIS, physicist, educator, chemist; b. Trinidad, W.I., Sept. 3, 1931; m. Sorrel Castillejo; children: Caricia J., Daniel S., Martin J., Matthew P.A. BS with 1st class honors in Physics, King's Coll., London, 1951, PhD, 1957; DSc (hon.), Yale U., 1987, Tel Aviv U., 1992. Lectr. math. RAF, 1952-53; lectr. theoretical physics King's Coll., 1958-62, reader physics, 1962-64; prof. physics U. London, 1965-66; prof. chemistry and math. Cornell U., 1966-73, Horace White prof. chemistry, physics and math., 1973-89, chmn. dept. chemistry, 1975-78; Disting. U. prof. Inst. for Phys. Sci. and Tech. & dept. physics U. Md. Sys., 1987—, Regents prof. Inst. for Phys. Sci. & Tech. & dept. physics, 1993—. Guest investigator Rockefeller Inst., 1963-64; vis. prof. applied physics Stanford U., 1970-71; Buhl lectr. theoretical physics Carnegie-Mellon U., 1971; Richtmyer Meml. lectr. Am. Assn. Physics Tchrs., 1973; S. H. Klosk lectr. NYU, 1975; 17th F. London Meml. lectr. Duke U., 1975; Walker-Ames prof. U. Wash., Seattle, 1977; Loeb lectr. physics Harvard U., 1979; vis.prof. physics MIT, 1979; Welsh Found. lectr. in physics U. Toronto, Ont., Can., 1979; 21st Alpheas Smith lectr. Ohio State U., 1982; Fairchild scholar Calif. Inst. Tech., 1984; Cherwell-Simon lectr., vis. prof. Oxford U., 1985; Schlapp scholar Edinburgh U., 1987; Marker lectr. Pa. State U., 1988, Nat. Sci. Coun. lectr., Taiwan, 1989; Hamilton Meml. lectr. Princeton U., 1990, 65th J. W. Gibbs lectr. Am. Math. Soc., 1992; E. U. Condon lectr. U. Colo., 1992; M. S. Green Meml. lectr. Temple U., 1992; R&B Sackler Disting. lectr. in solid state physics Tel Aviv U., 1992; 1st Lars Onsager lectr., Norway, 1993; Phi Beta Kappa vis. scholar, 1994; Lennard-Jones lectr. Royal Soc. Chemistry, 1995; Joseph O. Hirschfelder Prize lectr. U. Wis., 1995; Gilbert Newton Lewis Meml. lectr. U. Calif., Berkeley, 1995; George Fisher Baker lectr. chemistry Cornell U., 1997; distng. lectr. in theoretical Physics, The Technion, 2004; bd. governor Weizmann Inst. Sci., 2005, co-chair, scietific and academic adv. com., 2005; Homi J. Bhabha lectr., Tata Inst. Fundamental Rsch., Bombay, 2007; CV Raman Meml. lectr., Indian Inst. Sci., Bangalore, 2007. Author (with D.M. MacKay): Analogue Computing at Ultra-High Speed, 1962; author: The Nature of Critical Points, 1964, The Theory of Equilibrium Critical Phenomena, 1967; assoc. editor Jour. Math. Physics, 1965—68, 1972—75, 1986—89, mem. adv. bd. Jour. Theoretical Biology, 1969—82, Chem. Physics, 1972—84, Discrete Math., 1971—78, Jour. Phys. A. Math. & Gen., 1972—75, 1996—, Jour. Statis. Physics, 1978—81, Physica A, 1995—, mem. editl. bd. Comms. Math. Phys., 1984—2000, Phys. Rev. A, 1987—93, Revs. Math. Phys., 1998—2000. Recipient Guthrie medal and prize Inst. Physics, London, 1980, Wolf prize in physics, Wolf Found., Israel, 1980, Michelson-Morely award Case Western Res. U., 1982, Boltzmann medal IUPAP, 1983, Guggenheim fellow, 1970-71, 78-79. Fellow: AAAS, Kings Coll. London, Am. Phys. Soc. (Langmuir prize 1970, Lars Onsager Meml. prize 1995), Phys. Soc. London, Am. Acad. Arts and Scis., Royal Soc. Edinburgh (hon.), Indian Acad. Scis. (hon.), N.Y. Acad. Scis. (hon. award in Physics and Math. Sciences 1978), Royal Soc. London (regional editor 1989—93, v.p. 1993—95, Royal medal 2005); mem.: NAS (fgn. assoc., J.M. Luck award 1983), Biophysical Soc., Royal Norwegian Soc. Scis. and Letters (fgn. assoc.), Brazilian Acad. Scis. (fgn. assoc.), Math. Assn. Am., Soc. Indsl. and Applied Math., Am. Philos. Soc., Am. Chem. Soc. (Hildebrand award 1995). Office: U Md Inst Phys Sci & Tech College Park MD 20742-2431 E-mail: xpectnil@ipst.umd.edu.

FISHER, MICHELE RENEE, lawyer; b. Champlin, Minn., May 29, 1974; BA in Criminal Justice and Spanish, St. Cloud U., 1997; JD, William Mitchell Coll. Law, 2000. Bar: Minn. 2000, US Dist. Ct. (dist. Colo.), US Dist. Ct. (dist. Minn.), Minn. Supreme Ct. Assoc., mem. nat. wage and hour litig. team Nichols, Kaster & Anderson, P.L.L.P., Mpls. Named a Rising Star, Minn. Super Lawyers mag., 2006. Mem.: Assn. Trial Lawyers of Am., Fed. Bar Assn., Minn. Women Lawyers, ABA, Minn. State Bar Assn., Hennepin County Bar Assn., Nat. Employment Lawyers Assn. Office: Nichols Kaster & Anderson PLLP 4600 IDS Ctr 80 S 8th St Minneapolis MN 55402 Office Phone: 612-256-3229. E-mail: fisher@nka.com.*

FISHER, MILES MARK, IV, education and religious studies educator, minister; b. Huntington, W.Va., Sept. 25, 1932; s. Miles Mark and Ada Virginia (Foster) F. BA, Va. Union U., 1954, M.Div., 1959; MA, N.C. Central U., 1968; D.Min., Howard U., 1978. Ordained to ministry Baptist Ch., 1961; tchr. pub. schs. Durham, N.C., 1959-67; assoc. min. White Rock Bapt. Ch., Durham, N.C., 1959-65; asst. prof. edn., counselor Norfolk (Va.) State U., 1967-69; cons. Model Cities Area of Recreation, Norfolk, 1968-69; exec.-sec., CEO Nat. Assn. Equal Opportunity in Higher Edn., Washington, 1969-78; spl. cons. Inst. for Services to Edn., Washington, 1969-70; vis. asst. prof. Sch. Divinity Howard U., 1978-80; staff dir., com. clk. Com. of Whole, Council of D.C., Washington, 1979-83; spl. asst. to v.p. acad. affairs U. D.C., Washington, 1983-84, dir. policy rev. and analysis Office of the Bd. of Trustees, 1985-88, exec. dir. Office of the Bd. of Trustees, 1989-90, interim pres., 1990-91, disting. U. prof., 1991—. Chaplain counselor Lincoln Hosp. Sch. Nursing, Durham, N.C., 1962-67; chaplain Fisher Funeral Parlor, Durham, 1963-67; mem. task force employment of minority populations Nat. Recreation and Park Assn., 1970-71; mem. task force on edn. and Vietnam Era vet. VA, 1971-72; mem. steering com. U.S. Office of Edn. Common Core Data for the 70's, 1971-78, Congl. Black Caucus Nat. Policy Conf. on Black Edn., 1972; mem. Nat. task force on Student Financial Aid Problems, 1974-75; bd. trustees Consortium of U. of the Washington Met. Area, 1990-91; bd. dirs. Washington Rsch. Libr. Consortium, 1990-91. Bd. dirs. Cooperative Coll. Registry, 1973-75; mem. adv. bd. Four-Year Servicemen's Opportunity Coll., 1974-77; mem. adv. com. to bd. dirs. Nat. Student Ednl. Fund, 1974-78; v.p. bd. dirs. Reading is Fundamental Program, 1977-79, Vis. Nurse Assn., 1974-80; bd. dirs. D.C. Citizens for Better Public Edn., 1977, pres., 1981-83; bd. dirs. Voice Informed Community Expression, pres., 1982-84; trustee Va. Union U., 1983-85, Shaw U. Div. Sch., 1982-88. Mem. ACA, Am. Assn. Higher Edn., Am. Acad. Polit. and Social Scis., Am. Acad. Religion, Assn. Multicultural Counseling and Devel., Assn. Spiritual Ethical and Religious Values in Counseling, Am. Soc. Ch. History, Internat. Alumni Assn. Va. Union U. (pres. 1983-85), Am. Tennis Assn. (life), Assn. for Study of Afro-Am. Life and History (life), Assn. for Study of Higher Edn., U.S. Tennis Assn. (life). Home: 4444 Connecticut Ave NW Apt 402 Washington DC 20008-2319 Office: PO Box 2340 Washington DC 20013-2340 Office Phone: 202-744-8141. Personal E-mail: milesmfisher@yahoo.com.

FISHER, MORTON POE, JR., lawyer; b. Balt., Aug. 17, 1936; s. Morton Poe Sr. and Adelaide (Block) F.; m. Ann P. Fisher, Aug. 12, 1962; children: Stephen N., Marjorie P. AB, Dartmouth Coll., Hanover, NH, 1958; LLB, Yale U., 1961. Bar: Md. 1961, D.C. 1961. Law clk. to presiding justice U.S. Dist. Ct. Md., Balt., 1961-62; assoc. Piper & Marbury, 1962-68; asst. gen. counsel Rouse Co., 1968-73; ptnr. Frank, Bernstein, Conaway & Goldman, Balt., 1973-92; mng. ptnr. Ballard Spahr Andrews & Ingersoll, Balt., 1992—. Faculty mem. U. Md. Law Sch., 1978-87. Mem. Balt. County Econ. Devel. Commn., 1988-90, Mayor's Adv. Commn., Balt. City, Risk Mgmt. Com. Balto City, 1999; bd. dirs. Balt. Downtown Partnership, 1998-2004, Johns Hopkins U. Real Estate Inst., 2004; dean U. of Shopping Ctrs., 1998-99; trustee U. Md. Balt. Found., 2003—. Mem. ABA (vice chmn. real property divsn 1990-92, chmn. sect. real property, probate and trust law 1993-94), Am. Coll. Real Estate Lawyers (pres. 1988-89), Am. Coll. Constrn. Lawyers, Am. Law Inst., Anglo-Am. Real Property Inst., Internat. Coun. Shopping Ctrs. (co-chmn. law conf. 1995-97). Office: Ballard Spahr Andrews & Ingersoll LLP Ste 1800 300 E Lombard St Baltimore MD 21202-6739 Office Phone: 410-528-5615. Business E-Mail: fisher@ballardspahr.com.

FISHER, NANCY DEBUTTS, library director; b. Pitts., Apr. 10, 1945; d. Jacob John DeButts and Marie Christine Grills; m. Bruce C. Fisher, May 29, 1971. BS, Cleve. State U., 1968; MSLS, Case Western Res. U., 1973. Reference libr. Cleveland Heights-University Heights Pub. Libr., 1968-79; mgr. Beachwood (Ohio) br. Cuyahoga County Pub. Libr., 1980-90; dir. Wickliffe (Ohio) Pub. Libr., 1990—. Mem. adv. coun. Wickliffe United Way, 1991—2001; key communicator Wickliffe City Schs., 1992; mem. comm. com. Lake County United Way, 2002—, mem. cabinet, 2003—04; mem. Wickliffe Cmty. Adv. Panel, 1995—; grad. Leadership Lake County, 2003; bd. dirs. Wickliffe Civic Ctr., Inc., 1999—, pres. bd. dirs., 2004—; mem. adv. com. Holden Aboretum Warren H. Corning Libr., 1999—2002; mem. alumni planning com. Case Western Res. U. Libr. Sci., 1997—; mem. Lake Hosp. Sys., women's health adv. bd., 1999—. Mem.: ALA, Cleve. Area Met. Libr. Sys. (bd. dirs. 1994—96, mem. pers. com. 2003—), Ohio Libr. Coun., Lake County C. of C. Bd., Wickliffe C. of C. (v.p. 1998—99, pres. 2001—03, Civic Leader of Yr. 1999), Rotary (pres. 1992—94, chair charity ball 2002—03). Home: 939 Stuart Dr South Euclid OH 44121-3425 Office: Wickliffe Pub Libr 1713 Lincoln Rd Wickliffe OH 44092-2499 Home Phone: 216-382-0774; Office Phone: 440-944-6010. Business E-Mail: nfisher@wickliffe.lib.oh.us.

FISHER, NANCY LOUISE, pediatrician, geneticist, retired nurse; b. Cleve., July 4, 1944; d. Nelson Leopold and Catherine (Harris) F.; m. Larry William Larson, May 30, 1976 (div. Oct. 2000); 1 child, Jonathan Raymond. Student, Notre Dame Coll., Cleve., 1962-64; BSN, Wayne State U., 1967; postgrad., Calif. State U., Hayward, 1971-72; MD, Baylor Coll. of Medicine, 1976; M in Pub. Health, U. Wash., 1982, certificate in ethics, 1993. Diplomate Am. Bd. Pediatrics, Am. Bd. Med. Genetics. RN coronary care unit and med. intensive care unit Highland Gen. Hosp., Oakland, Calif., 1970-72; RN coronary care unit Alameda (Calif.) Hosp., 1972-73; intern in pediatrics Baylor Coll. of Medicine, Houston, 1976-77, resident in pediatrics, 1977-78; attending physician, pediatric clinic Harborview Med. Ctr., Seattle, 1980-81; staff physician children and adolescent health care clinic Columbia Health Ctr., Seattle, 1981-87, founder, dir. of med. genetics clinic, 1984-89; maternal child health policy cons. King County div. Seattle King County Dept Pub. Health, 1983-85; dir. genetic svcs. Va. Mason Clinic, 1986-89; dir. med. genetic svcs. Swedish Hosp., 1989-94; pvt. practice Seattle, 1994-97; med. cons. supr. office of managed care Wash. State Dept. Social and Health Svcs., Olympia, 1996-97; med. dir. Medicaid Dept. of Social and Health Svcs., Wash., 1997-99; assoc. med. dir. Govt. Programs Regence Blue Shield, 1999; med. dir. Regence Blue Shield, 2000—02; chief med. officer Wash. State Health Care Authority, 2003—. Nurses aide psychiatry Sinai Hosp., Detroit, 1966—67; charge nurse Women's Hosp., Cleve., 1967; rsch. asst. to Dr. Shelly Liss, 76; with Baylor Housestaff Assn., Baylor Coll. Medicine, 1980—81; clin. asst. prof. grad. sch. nursing U. Wash., Seattle, 1981—85, clin. asst. prof. dept. pediat., 1982—92, clin. assoc. prof. dept. pediat., 1992—; com. appointments include Seattle CCS Cleft Palate Panel, 1984—97; bd. dirs., first v.p. King County Assn. Sickle Cell Disease, 1985—86, acting pres., 1986, pres., 1986—87; hosp. affiliation include Childrens Orthopedic Hosp. and Med. Ctr., Seattle, 1981—, Virginia Mason Hosp., Seattle, 1985—89, Harborview Hosp., Seattle, 1986—89; mem. Wash. State Steering Coun. Stroke and Heart Disease, 2006—, Wash. State Vaccine Adv. Com., 2006—. Contbr. articles to profl. jours. Active Seattle Urban League, 1982-96, 101 Black Women, 1986-94; bd. dirs. Seattle Sickle Cell Affected Family Assn., 1984-85, Am. Heart Assn., 2001—, March of Dimes 2002—; mem. People to People Citizen Ambassador Group; sec. Health and Human Svcs. Com. on Infant Mortality, 1993—2003; mem. Twins Com. Inst. of Medicine, 1995-2000; Evaluation, Rsch. and Planning Group Ethical Legal and Social Implications Nat. Human Gerome Rsch. Inst., 1997-2000. Served to lt. USN Nurse Corps, 1966-70; active State Steering Com. on Heart Disease and Stroke, 2005—, Washington State Govs. Coun. on Disparities, 2006—. Fellow Am. Coll. Medicine Genetics (founder); mem. AMA, APHA, Am. Heart Assn. (bd. dirs. King County 2001—, Pacific NW affiliate bd. 2006—, Physician of Yr.), Am. Acad. Physician Execs., Student Governing Body and Graduating Policy Com. Baylor Coll. Medicine (founding mem. 1973-76), Loans and Scholarship Com. Baylor Coll. Medicine (voting mem. 1973-76), Am. Med. Student Assn., Student Nat. Med. Assn., Admission Com. Baylor Coll. Medicine (voting mem. 1974-76), Am. Med. Women's Assn., Am. Acad. Pediatrics, Am. Soc. Human Genetics, Nat. Spkrs. Assn., Nat. Quality Found. (steering com.), Wash. State Assn. Black Providers of Health Care, Soc. Health and Human Values, Wash. State Soc. Pediatrics, Wash. State Med. Assn. (women in medicine com., intersplty. coun., fin. com.), Seattle C. of C. (mem. Leadership Tomorrow 1988—), Sigma Gamma Rho, Phi Delta Epsilon. Office: Wash State HCA 676 Woodland Sq Loop SE MS-42701 Olympia WA 98504-2701 Office Phone: 360-923-2709. Business E-Mail: nancy.fisher@hca.wa.gov.

FISHER, NEAL FLOYD, religious organization administrator; b. Washington, Ind., Apr. 4, 1936; s. Floyd Russell and Florence Alice (Williams) F.; m. Ila Alexander, Aug. 18, 1957; children: Edwin Kirk, Julia Bryn. AB, DePauw U., 1957, LHD (hon.), 1982; MDiv, Boston U., 1960, PhD, 1966; STD, MacMurray Coll., Jacksonville, Ill., 1991; DD, Coe Coll., 1994. Ordained to ministry United Meth. Ch., 1958; pastor 1st United Meth. Ch., Revere, Mass., 1960-63, North Andover, Mass., 1963-68; planning assoc. United Meth. Bd. Global Ministries, NYC, 1968-73, dir. planning, 1973-77; assoc. dean, asst. prof. theology and society Boston U. Sch. Theology, 1977-80; pres., prof. theology and society Garrett-Evang. Theol. Sem., Evanston, Ill., 1980-2001, pres. emeritus, sr. scholar, 2001—. Mendenhall lectr. DePauw U., Greencastle, Ind., 1982, Willson lectr., Nashville, 1983, Voigt lectr. McKendree Coll., 1984, McKendree Blair lectr. MacMurray Coll., 1986, Henry Martin Loud lectr. U. Mich., Ann Arbor, 1987; Wright lectr. Morningside Coll., 1991, Bransford lectr., 1999; chaplain, preacher, Chautauqua, NY, 1984, 88, Lakeside, Ohio, 1996; mem. theol. edn. commn. United Meth. Ch., 1992-2000, former mem. univ. senate; mem. bd. of ordained ministry No. Ill. Conf. United Meth. Ch.; chmn. com. on acad. affairs DePauw U. Bd. Trustees. Author: Parables of Jesus: Glimpses of the New Age, 1979, rev. edit., 1990, Context for Discovery, 1980, Parables of Jesus: Glimpses of God's Reign, 1990; contbg. editor: Truth and Tradition: A Conversation about the Future of United Methodist Theological Education, 1995. Trustee DePauw U., Greencastle, Ind., 1996-2000; mem. bd. visitors Boston U. Sch. Theology, 2002-05, bd. overseers, 2006—. Recipient Disting. Alumnus award Boston U. Sch. Theology, 1985, Disting. Alumni citation DePauw U., 1993; Jacob Sleeper fellow, 1960-61. Mem. Assn. United Meth. Scis., Assn. Chgo. Theol. Schs. (pres. 1985-87, 95-97). Mem. United Methodist Ch. Home: 2008 Elmore Pond Road Wolcott VT 05680 Business E-Mail: nfisher@garrett.edu.

FISHER, ORA T., lawyer; BS in Econ., Univ. Pa., 1984; JD cum laude, Univ. Mich., 1991. Bar: Calif. 1991. Internal cons. and public fin. banking officer JPMorgan, NYC; atty. Latham & Watkins LLP, San Francisco, 1991—97, atty., Silicon Valley office Menlo Park, 1997—2004, mng. ptnr. Silicon Valley office, 2004—, and co-chair, venture & tech. practice group. Mem.: ABA, San Francisco Bar Assn., State Bar of Calif. Office: Latham & Watkins LLP 140 Scott Dr Menlo Park CA 94025-1008

FISHER, PAUL CARY, writing supplies company executive; b. Lebanon, Kans., Oct. 10, 1913; s. Carey A. Fisher and Alice Bales-Fisher; children: Terry Hough, Cary Fisher, Pomm Hepner, Marteen Moore, Morgan Fisher, Scott Fisher. BS, Kans. State U., 1939. Gen. mgr. Butter-Nut Bakery, Cedar Rapids, Iowa, 1936-38, Aetna Ball Bearing Co., Chgo., 1942—45; pres. Fisher-Armour Mfg. Co., Chgo., 1945-50; owner Fisher Space Pen Co., Boulder City, Nev., 1950—. Dem. presdl. candidate, NH Primary, 1960. Named Small Bus. Person of Yr., State of Nev., U.S. Small Bus. Adminstrn., 1980, Exporter of Yr., Gov.'s Office State of Nev., 1995, 97, Inventor of Yr. Nev. Tech. Coun., 1998, Pres.'s Inventor award, Nev. Desert Rsch., 2001. Mem. Boulder city Rotary, Phi Kappa Phi. Achievements include invention of pressurized space pen for NASA. Avocations: handball, tennis, chess. Office: Fisher Pen Co 711 Yucca St Boulder City NV 89005-1905 Home Phone: 702-293-0076; Office Phone: 702-293-3100. E-mail: fisher@spacepen.com.

FISHER, PETER R., investment company executive, former federal agency administrator; b. 1956; 2 children. BA in History, Harvard U., 1980, JD, 1985. With Bank for Internat. Settlements, Basle, Switzerland, 1989—90; sr. v.p. fgn. exch. Fed. Res. Bank N.Y., NYC, 1993—94, exec. v.p., 1994—2001; under sec. domestic fin. US Dept. Treasury, Washington, 2001—03; mng. dir. BlackRock, Inc., NYC, 2004—. Bd. dirs. Securities Investor Protection Corp.; chair Advanced Counterfeit Deterrence Steering Com. Recipient Disting. Svc. award, Bond Market Assn., 2004. Office: BlackRock Inc 40 E 52nd St New York NY 10022

FISHER, PHILIP J., English language and literature educator; b. Pitts., Oct. 11, 1941; s. Leo and Anna (Walker) F.; 1 child, Mark. BA, U. Pitts., 1963; AM, Harvard U., 1966, PhD, 1970. Asst. prof. U. Va., Charlottesville, 1970-72, Brandeis U., Waltham, Mass., 1973-80, assoc. prof. English and Am. lit., 1980-87; Reid prof. English and Harvard U. Coll. prof., Cambridge, Mass., 2005—; prof. Brandeis U., Waltham, Mass., 1987—; chair dept. English Harvard U., Cambridge, Mass., 1990-93, prof., 2005—. Asst. prof. Andrew Mellon Harvard U., 1976-77; vis. prof. Free U. Berlin, 1981, Yale U., 1985-86, U. Konstanz, W.Ger., 1986, Harvard U., 1986-87; adv. bd. Inst. Advanced Study, Berlin, 1994—. Author: Making Up Society, 1981, Hard Facts: Setting and Form in the American Novel , 1984 (finalist Nat. Book Critics Circle prize for criticism), Making and Effacing Art: Modern American Art in a Culture of Museums, 1991, The New American Studies, 1991, Wonder, the Rainbow and the Aesthetics of Rare Experiences, 1998, Still The New World, American Literature in a Culture of Creative Destruction, 1999 (Truman Capote prize for literary criticism, 2000), The Vehement Passions, 2002. Recipient Howard Mumford Jones prize, Harvard U., 1971; fellow, Inst. Advanced Study, Berlin, 1987—88, Stanford Ctr. for Advanced Study in Behavioral Scis., 2003—04; Nat. Endowment Humanities fellow, 1972—73, Mellon fellow, 1976—77, Exxon fellow program in sci., tech. and soc., MIT, 1984—85, Guggenheim fellow, 1996—97, sr. fellow, Getty Mus., 1998—99. Office: Harvard U Dept English Barker Ctr Cambridge MA 02138 Business E-Mail: PJFisher@fas.harvard.edu.

FISHER, PIERRE JAMES, JR., physician; b. Chgo., Oct. 29, 1931; s. Pierre James and Evelyn F.; m. Carol Ann Walton, Mar. 16, 1951; children: James Walton, David Alan, Steven Edward, Teresa Ann. Student, Taylor U., 1949-51, Ball State U., 1951-52; MD, Ind. U., 1956. Diplomate Am. Bd. Surgery. Intern U.S. Naval Hosp., San Diego, 1956-57, resident in surgery, 1957-61; pvt. practice specializing in surgery Surgeons Inc., Marion, Ind., 1965—, pres., 1977—; mem. staff Marion Gen. Hosp., chief staff, 1970. Trustee Meth. Hosp., Indpls., 1972-94; bd. dirs. Charlotte County Cultural Ctr., 2005—. Served with USN, 1956-65. Recipient Physicians Recognition award AMA, 1974, 77, 80, 83, 89. Fellow ACS; mem. AMA, Grant County Med. Soc. (pres. 1980), Marion Area C. of C. (v.p. 1979-81), N.Am. Med. Golf Assn. (v.p. 1989-90, pres. 1991-93), Rotary (pres. Marion 1983-84, Dist. 656 Disting. Svc. award 1989), Kingsway Country Club (bd. dirs., pres. 1997-99), Royal Order of Ponce de Leon Conquistadors (treas. 2000-). Methodist. Home: 11250 SW Essex Dr Lake Suzy FL 34269 Office: Surgeons Inc 330 N Wabash Ave Ste 450 Marion IN 46952-2600 Personal E-mail: fpjfisher@aol.com.

FISHER, RAYMOND CORLEY, federal judge; b. Oakland, Calif., July 12, 1939; s. Raymond Henry and Mary Elizabeth (Corley) Fisher; m. Nancy Leigh Fairchilds, Jan. 22, 1961; children: Jeffrey, Amy. BA, U. Calif., Santa Barbara, 1961; LLB, Stanford U., 1966. Bar: Calif. 1967, U.S. Supreme Ct. 1967. Law clk. to Hon. J. Skelly Wright US Ct. Appeals (DC cir.), Washington, 1966—67; law clk. to Hon. William J. Brennan US Supreme Ct., Washington, 1967—68; ptnr. Tuttle & Taylor, L.A., LA, 1968—88, Heller, Ehrman, White & McAuliffe, LA, 1988—97; assoc. atty. gen. US Dept. of Justice, Washington, 1997—99; judge US Ct. Appeals (9th cir.), 1999—. Pres.: Stanford Law Rev., 1965—66. Dir. Constl. Rights Found., LA, 1978—, pres., 1983—87, LA City Bd. Civil Svc. Commn., 1987—88; dep. gen. counsel Christopher Commn., LA, 1991—92; pres. LA City Bd. Police Commrs., 1996—97; dir. Western Justice Ctr. Found., 2000—; spl. asst. to Gov. of Calif., 1975. With USAR, 1957—64. Fellow: Am. Bar Found., Am. Coll. Trial Lawyers; mem.: ABA, Am. Law Inst., L.A. County Bar Assn., Calif. State Bar, Fed. Bar Assn. (exec. com. 1990—96), Chancery Club, Order of Coif. Office: US Ct Appeals 125 S Grand Ave Rm 400 Pasadena CA 91105*

FISHER, REBECCA RHODA, lawyer; b. Milw., 1971; BA in Polit. Sci., U. Minn., Mpls., 1993; JD, William Mitchell Coll. Law, St. Paul, 1999. Bar: Minn. 1999, US Dist. Ct. (dist. Minn.) 2000, Wis. 2005. Law clk. criminal appeals Office of Minn. Atty. Gen., 1998—99; assoc. Ramsey & DeVore, 1999—2003; atty. Law Office of Rebecca Rhoda Fisher, P.L.L.C., Roseville, Minn. Contbr. articles to profl. publs. Named a Rising Star, Minn. Super Lawyers mag., 2006; named one of Up and Coming Attys., Minn. Lawyer, 2004. Mem.: Nat. Assn. Criminal Def. Lawyers, Minn. Assn. Criminal Def. Lawyers, Minn. Soc. Criminal Justice, ABA, Minn. Women Lawyers, Warren E. Burger Inn of Ct., Ramsey County Bar Assn.,

Minn. State Bar Assn. (chair criminal law sect. 2006—, vice chair criminal law sect. 2005—06, sec., treas. criminal law sect. 2003—05, chair new lawyers sect. 2005—06, vice chair new lawyers sect. 2004—05, sect. new lawyers sect. 2003—04). Office: Law Office of Rebecca Rhoda Fisher PLLC 2589 Hamline Ave North Ste B Roseville MN 55113 Office Phone: 651-251-3838. E-mail: rebecca@rrflaw.com.*

FISHER, RICHARD FORREST, research scientist, editor-in-chief; b. Champaign, Ill., May 15, 1941; S. Richard Forrest Fisher and Hannah Elizabeth Ponath; m. Karen Dangerfield, Sept. 4, 1959; children: William Forrest, Marilu, Kevin Royden. BS, U. Ill., 1963; MS, Cornell U., 1967, PhD, 1968. Rsch. scientist Can. Forestry Svc., Sault Sainte Marie, Ont., 1968-69; asst. prof. forestry U. Ill., Urbana, 1969-72; assoc. prof. U. Toronto, Ont., 1972-77; prof. U. Fla., Gainesville, 1977-82; prof., head dept. forest resources Utah State U., Logan, 1982-90; prof., head dept. forest sci. Tex. A&M U., 1990-96, prof., 1996-99; dir. rsch. Temple-Inland, Diboll, Tex., 1999—. Author: (with others) Ecology and Management of Forest Soil, 3d edit.; contbr. articles to profl. jours. Fellow Soc. Am. Foresters, Soil Sci. Soc. Am. (co-editor in chief Forest Ecology and Mgmt.); mem. Internat. Soc. Tropical Foresters, Ecol. Soc. Am., Nat. Assn. Profl. Forestry Schs. and Colls. (pres. 1994-96), Internat. Assn. Round Dance Tchrs. (gen. chmn. 1997-99). Democrat. Avocations: round dance cuer, tchr. Home: 1004 Augusta Dr Lufkin TX 75901-7412 Office: Temple-Inland Forest PO Drawer N Diboll TX 75941 Home Phone: 936-639-9582. Business E-Mail: dickfisher@templeinland.com.

FISHER, RICHARD PAUL, chemist; b. Alameda, Calif., Feb. 10, 1948; s. George Paul and Mary Augusta (Caldeira) F.; m. Melinda Ruth Maledy, June 2, 1973. BS, U. Calif., Berkeley, 1970; PhD, U. Calif., Davis, 1974. Rsch. chemist U.S. Borax Rsch. Corp., Anaheim and Boron, Calif., 1974-79, sr. rsch. chemist Boron, 1979-87, asst. mgr., 1987-91, mgr. chem. rsch. Anaheim, Valencia, Calif., 1991-93, rsch. fellow Valencia, Boron, 1993—. Contbr. articles to profl. jours. Kiwanis scholar, 1966-70; U. Calif. Berkeley Alumni scholar, 1966; NDEA fellow, 1971-73. Mem. Am. Chem. Soc. Home: 8850 Hickory Ave Hesperia CA 92345-3845 Office: Rio Tinto Minerals Pilot Plant Ctr 14486 Borax Rd Boron CA 93516-2017 Home Phone: 760-244-6516; Office Phone: 760-762-7167. Business E-Mail: richard.fisher@riotinto.com.

FISHER, RICHARD WELTON, bank executive; b. LA, Mar. 18, 1949; s. Leslie Welton and Magnhild (Fisher; m. Nancy Collins, Sept. 8, 1973; children: Andersen, Alison, James, Texana. BA cum laude, Harvard U., 1971; student, Oxford U., Eng., 1972-73; MBA, Stanford U., 1975. Asst. to Robert Roosa Brown Bros. Harriman & Co., NYC, 1975-77, sr. mgr., 1983-87; exec. asst. to sec. U.S. Dept. Treasury, Washington, 1977-79; mng. ptnr. Fisher Capital Mgmt., Dallas, 1987-98, Fisher Ewing Ptnrs. (Value Ptnrs., Ltd.), Dallas, 1989-98; dep. U.S. Trade Rep. Exec. Office of the Pres., Washington, 1998-2001; vice-chmn. Kissinger McLarty Assocs., Washington, 2002—05; pres., CEO Fed. Res. Bank Dallas, 2005—. Chmn. Stanford U. Sch. Bus. Trust, Palo Alto, Calif., 1982-84, Am. Assembly, N.Y., 2003—; adj. prof. L.B.J. Sch., U. Tex., 1996-98; Weatherhead fellow Harvard U., 2001. Bd. dirs., mem. exec. com. Dallas Mus. Art, 1985-89; bd. dirs. Goodwill Industries Dallas, 1989-98, treas., 1991-93, chmn., 1993-95; bd. dirs. Boys Club Dallas, 1984-84, Dallas Assembly, 1983-97, Russian Am. Enterprise Fund, 1993-98; active Dallas Com. Fgn. Rels., chmn., 1987-98; trustee Brookings Instn., 2001-05, Eisenhower Fellowships, 2001-2003, Pacific Coun., 2002—; mem. Trilateral Commn., 2002-; Dem. candidate U.S. Senate, 1994. Decorated gran oficial Order of Bernardo O'Higgins (Chile); U.S.-Japan leadership fellow Japan Soc., 1989; recipient Outstanding Achievement award Stanford U. Assocs., 1986; hon. fellow Hertford Coll., Oxford U., 2002; named Admiral of Tex. Navy, 1987. Fellow Am. Acad. Arts and Scis.; mem. Inst. Ams. (chmn. 1987-93), Inter-Am. Dialogue (exec. com. 1992), Am. Coun. on Germany (bd. dirs. 1985-94, 2004—), Philos. Soc. Tex., Harvard Club, Petroleum Club, Met. Club (Washington). Presbyterian. Office: Fed Res Bank Dallas 2200 N Pearl St Dallas TX 75201 Office Phone: 214-922-6000.*

FISHER, ROBERT, gastroenterologist, health facility administrator; b. Bklyn., July 28, 1939; married. BSE, Princeton U., 1960; MD, U. Pa., 1964. Intern Chgo. Wesley Meml. Hosp., 1964-65; resident in internal meedicine Temple U. Hosp., Phila., 1967-70; fellow in gastroenterology Hosp. U. Pa., 1970-72; from asst. prof. to assoc. prof. Temple U. Sch. Medicine, 1972-80, prof. medicine, 1980—; dir. Functional Gastrointestinal Disease Ctr. Temple U. Hosp., Phila., 1984—, chief gastroenterology sect., 1985—. Mem. Am. Coll. Gastroenterology, Am. Gastroent. Assn., Am. Soc. Gastrointestinal Endoscopy, Am. Fedn. Clin. Rsch., Rsch. Soc. Alcoholism. Office: Temple Univ 3400 N Broad St Philadelphia PA 19140-5104 Office Phone: 215-707-3433. Business E-Mail: robert.fisher@temple.edu.

FISHER, ROBERT ALAN, laser physicist; b. Berkeley, Calif., Apr. 19, 1943; s. Leon Harold and Phyllis (Kahn) F.; children: Andrew Leon, Derek Martin. AB, U. Calif., Berkeley, 1965, MA, 1967, PhD, 1971. Programmer Stanford (Calif.) linear accelerator Stanford U., 1965; staff mem. Granger Assocs., Palo Alto, Calif., 1966; lectr. U. Calif., Davis, 1972-74; physicist Lawrence Livermore Lab., Calif., 1971-74; laser physicist Los Alamos (N.Mex.) Nat. Lab., 1974-86. Cons. R.A. Fisher Assocs., Santa Fe, 1986—; instr. Engring. Tech., Inc., 1982—; mem. Air Force ABCD Panel, 1982; program com. mem. Internat. Quantum Electronics Conf., 1982, 86; program com. CLEO Conf., 2002—05, chair subcom. nonlinear optics, 2006—07; vice chmn. Gordon Conf. on Lasers and Non-linear Optics, 1981; chmn. Soc. Photo-Optical Instrumentation Engrs. Conf. on Optical Phase Conjugation/Beam Combining/Diagnostics, 1987—; mem. Air Force Red Team for Space-Based Laser, 1983—86, HEDS II SDI Red Team, 1986, U.S. Ballistic Missile Office Options Team, 1986; mem. secretariat SDI Red/Blue Sensor Teams, 1986, SDI GBL Red/Blue Team Interaction, 1987—88; mem. architecture panel SDI SDS Phase I, 1990, Air Force Laser 21 Working Group, 1990. Assoc. editor Optics Letters, 1984-86, Applied Optics, 1984-91, Topical Edit. Optics Letters, 2002-04; editor: Optical Phase Conjugation, 1973; contbr. articles to profl. jours. Vol. coach elem. sch. chess team Pojoaque Elem. Sch. (winner nat. elem. championship 1984), Santa Fe, 1984. Fellow Optical Soc. Am. (guest editor jour. spl. issue on optical phase conjugation, mem. Engring. Excellence award com. 2003, chmn. 2004), SPIE (bd. dirs. 2002-04, scholarship com. 2001-04, edn. com. 2004-); mem. IEEE (sr.), Optical Soc. Am. Found. Avocation: performing and teaching bluegrass and fiddle tune music. Home and Office: 2996 Plaza Blanca Santa Fe NM 87507-5340 Office Phone: 505-992-3930.

FISHER, ROBERT BRUCE, priest; b. Paragould, Ark., Feb. 6, 1937; s. Lawrence Bruce Fisher and Georgia M. (Paris) Kasper. BA, Divine Word Seminary, Techny, Ill., 1961, MA, 1965; STB, STL, Gregorian Univ., Rome, 1966; STD, Pont. Ateneo di Sant' Anselmo, Rome, 1969. Ordained priest Roman Cath. Ch., 1965. Adminstrv. attache Nunciature of Holy See, Accra, Ghana, 1982-83; pastor Good Shepherd Ch., Tema, Ghana, 1984-86; asst. pastor St. Matthias Ch., New Orleans, 1990-94; pastor St. Martin de Porres Ch., Prairie View, 1996-2000, St. Anthony's Ch., Lafayette, La., 2000—03, St. Bartholomew Ch., Little Rock, 2003—04; dir. William J. Kelley, SVD Retreat Ctr., Bay St. Louis, Miss., 2004—05; parochial vicar St. Philip the Apostle Ch., El Campo, Tex., 2006—. Asst. prof. Xavier U., New Orleans, 1988—95; dir. studies A. Tolton Ho. of Studies, New Orleans, 1991—96; dist. superior Divine Word Soc., New Orleans, 1990—96; promoter New African Cinema film series; instr. ethics and critical thinking Prairie View (Tex.) A&M U., 1998—2000, adj. prof., 1997—2000. Author: West African Religious Traditions: Focus on the Akan of Ghana, 1998; editor: (liturgical ordo) Ordo for the Philippines, 1972. Co-chmn. Cath. Returnee Crisis Com., Accra, 1982-83; active Cmty. Oriented Govt. Program, Lafayette, 2002-03 Mem. Am. Soc. Missiology, Coll. Theology Soc., Am. Acad. Religion, KC (chaplain Met. chpt. 1993-96, chaplain Bay St. Louis chpt. 2004-05), African Assn. for Study of Religions, Divine Word Soc. Democrat. Address: 304 West Church St El Campo TX 77437 Office Phone: 979-543-8770. Personal E-mail: africoco@aol.com.

FISHER, ROBERT CHARLES HARU, publishing executive, editor; b. Burlington, Iowa, Mar. 3, 1930; s. Ray Erwin and Blanche Columbia (Brolin) Fisher. BA cum laude, Harvard U., 1955; postgrad., Columbia U. Law Sch., 1955-56, Tokyo U., 1957-59. Analyst, adjutant gen's. office U.S. Army, Kansas City, Mo., 1949-50, Washington, 1950-51; adv. Prime Minister Takeo Miki of Japan, 1957-64; Far Eastern rep. Fodor Travel Guides, Tokyo, 1959-64, exec. editor NYC, 1964-66, 75-77, exec. v.p., 1975-77, pres., 1977-80, exec. editor London, 1966-74; Far Eastern rep. US Nat. Student Assn., Tokyo, 1956—59; v.p. David McKay Co., NYC, 1976-80; pres. Fisher Travel Guides, 1980-88; gen. editor Crown Insider's Travel Guides, 1988-89; editl. dir. Gault Millau Guides, 1989-90; cons. Simon & Schuster, NYC, 1990-92; editl. dir. Maco Comm., NYC, 1992-94; exec. editor Arthur Frommer, Inc., NYC, 1995—2000; exec. editor, columnist www.frommers.com, NYC, 2000—. Founder, dir. Kansas City Open Forum, 1949—50; bd. dirs. Internat. Assn. Med. Assistance to Travelers, 1972—, v.p., 1985—; chmn. Hotel and Restaurant Unsafe Food Labeling Action com., 1995—; pres. Fisher Publs. Inc., 1997—; founder Key West Travel Writers Workshop, 1991—; T. Author: Picasso, 1967, Klee, 1967, Guide to Japan, 1981, Insider's Guide to Japan, 1986; co-author: Off-Season Riviera, 1997, Off-Season London, 1999. Served with CIC US Army, 1952—54, Korea. Grantee for study in Japan, Balt. Scholarship Fund, 1956—59. Mem.: Soc. Am. Travel Writers Found. (pres. 1985—90), Brit. Guild Travel Writers (vice-chmn. 1970—71), N.Y. Travel Writers Assn. (pres. 1979—81), Soc. Am. Travel Writers (dir. 1978—80, v.p. 1981—83, pres. 1983—84), Internat. House of Japan, Am. Club of Japan, Harvard Club N.Y.C. Personal E-mail: BobHaru@aol.com.

FISHER, ROBERT DALE, stockbroker, retired naval officer; b. Memphis, July 30, 1924; s. Hollis Welton and Anna Sue (Parrish) Fisher; m. Joy Lee Chandler, Mar. 30, 1946. BS, Am. U., 1957. Commd. ensign USN, 1944, advanced through grades to comdr., 1963; tng. officer Polaris Missile program, 1955-58, comdr. destroyer, 1959-61, ret., 1963; stockbroker, 1963—; v.p. investments Smith Barney, Washington, 1979—. Mem.: Army-Navy Club, Jesters, Shriners, Masons, Kiwanis (pres. Falls Church 1969, pres. McLean 1979—80), Mil. Order Carabao. Republican. Methodist. Home: 6033 Chesterbrook Rd Mc Lean VA 22101-3213 Office: 1850 K St NW Ste 900 Washington DC 20006-2222 Office Phone: 202-862-2866. Business E-Mail: robert.d.fisher@smithbarney.com.

FISHER, ROBERT I., lawyer; b. Bklyn., July 10, 1939; s. Sidney B. and Jeanette (Talisman) F.; m. Debra Kram Fisher, June 30, 1974; children: Daniel I., Elizabeth R. BA, Columbia U., 1960; JD cum laude, Harvard U., 1963; LLM, N.Y.U., 1967. Bar: N.Y. 1964. Assoc. Dewey, Ballantine, Bushby, Palmer & Wood, NYC, 1964-67, Sullivan & Cromwell, NYC, 1967-72; ptnr. Greenbaum, Wolff & Ernst, NYC, 1972—82, Katten Muchin Roseman LLP, NYC, 1982—. Lectr. Practicing Law Inst. Fulbright fellow, Israel, 1963-64. Mem. ABA, N.Y. State Assn. Home: 150 Factory Pond Rd Locust Valley NY 11560-1416 Office: Katten Muchin Rosenman LLP 575 Madison Ave Fl 11 New York NY 10022-2585 Home Phone: 516-759-3289; Office Phone: 212-940-8827. E-mail: robert.fisher@kattenlaw.com.

FISHER, ROBERT J., retail executive; b. 1954; s. Donald G. and Doris (Feigenbaum) Fisher; married; 3 children. BA, BS, Princeton U., NJ, 1976; MBA, Stanford U., Calif., 1980. Store mgr. Gap, Inc., 1980-85, exec. v.p. mdse. Banana Republic, 1985-89, pres. Banana Republic, 1989-90, exec. v.p., 1992—99, COO, 1992—93, 1995—97, CFO, 1993-95, pres. Gap Brand, 1997—2004, non-exec. chmn., 2004—07, interim CEO, 2007—. Bd. dirs. The Gap, Inc., 1990—, Sun Microsystems, Inc., 1995—2006. Chair exec. com. Conservation Internat.; vice chair bd. Natural Resources Def. Coun.; bd. mem. San Francisco Mus. Modern Art. Named one of Forbes' Richest Ams., 2006. Office: Gap Inc 2 Folsom St San Francisco CA 94105 Office Phone: 650-952-4400.*

FISHER, ROBERT MORTON, foundation and academic administrator; b. St. Paul, Oct. 15, 1938; s. S.S. and Jean Fisher; m. Elinor C. Schectman, June 19, 1960; children: Laurie, Jonathan. AB magna cum laude, Harvard Coll., 1960; JD, Harvard U., 1963; PhD, London Sch. Econs, Polit. Sci., 1967; LLD, West Coast U., LA, 1981; DHL, Profl. Sch. Psychology, San Francisco, 1986; DPS, John F. Kennedy U., Orinda, Calif., 1988. Rsch. assoc. Mass. Mental Health Ctr., Cambridge, 1957-62; rsch. asst. Ctr. Study Juvenile Delinquency, Cambridge, 1961-63; spl. asst. to chief psychologist British Prison Dept. Home Office, London, 1963-67; prof. Sch. Criminology U. Calif., Berkeley, 1965-71; profl. race car driver, 1972-77; pres. John F. Kennedy U., Orinda, Calif., 1974-85; exec. dir. 92d St. YMHA, NYC, 1984-85; dir., CEO The San Francisco Found., 1987-97; pres. non-profit edn. and founds. Rusher, Loscavio & LoPresto Exec. Search, San Francisco, 2005—. Mayor, councilman Lafayette, Calif., 1968-76; mem. Minn. and Calif. Bar Specialty: charitable gift planning; CEO Fisher Cos., 1997—; exec. dir. Alonzo King's Line Ballet, 2002; prin. cons. Robert Fisher Assocs. Non-Profit Cons., 2003—. Scholar-in-residence Rockefeller Found., Bellagio, 1994; Polit. Sci. vis. fellow London Sch. Econs. and Polit. Sci., 1994; named Outstanding Fundraising Exec. Nat. Soc. Fund Raising Execs. Home: 85 Southwood Dr Orinda CA 94563-3026 Office: Rusher Loscavio and LoPresto Exec Search 100 Spear St # 935 San Francisco CA 94105 Home Phone: 925-254-1566; Office Phone: 415-765-6584. E-mail: rmfisher@earthlink.net.

FISHER, ROBERT PERRY, environmental scientist, researcher; b. Houston, May 30, 1945; s. George Robert and Brownie (Perry) F.; m. Cari Patrice Guritz, Sept. 6, 1969; children; William Robert, Jay Kenneth. BS in Chemistry cum laude, Centenary Coll., 1967; PhD in Analytical Chemistry, U. Fla., 1971. Postdoctoral rsch. assoc., asst. prof. U. Fla., Gainesville, 1971-72; rsch. chemist Nat. Coun. for Air and Stream Improvement, Gainesville, 1972-83, investigative programs mgr., 1983-88, regional mgr., 1988-92, program dir., 1992-95, v.p., 1995—. Chmn. methods com. APHA-Standard Methods, Washington, 1980—; co-chair, mem. tech. com. EPA Gulf of Mexico Program, 1999—. Contbr. articles to Analytical Chemistry, Jour. Tech. Assn. Pulp and Paper Industry, Pulp and Paper Canada and chpt. to ASTM Quality Assurance Monitoring. Leader Cub Scouts Boy Scouts Am., Gainesville, 1985-95. Recipient Teaching award DuPont, U. Fla., 1969. Fellow Am. Inst. Chemists (Outstanding Chemistry Student 1967), Mem. ASTM (methods com. 1980—), Am. Chem. Soc., Am. Indsl. Hygiene Assn. Achievements include methodology for controlling sulfur gas releases from kraft pulp mills; 2 patents for methods of generating chlorine dioxide gas. Office: Nat Coun Air/Stream Improve PO Box 13318 Research Triangle Park NC 27709 Office Phone: 919-941-6409. E-mail: rfisher@ncasi.org.

FISHER, ROGER DUMMER, negotiation expert, law educator; b. Winnetka, Ill., May 28, 1922; s. Walter Taylor and Katharine (Dummer) F.; m. Caroline Speer, Sept. 18, 1948; children: Elliott Speer, Peter Ryerson. AB, Harvard U., 1943, LLB magna cum laude, 1948; LHD, Conn. Coll., 1994; DHL, Bay Path Coll., 1999. Bar: Mass. 1948, D.C. 1950. Asst. to gen. counsel, then asst. to dep. U.S. spl. rep. ECA, Paris, 1948-49; with firm Covington & Burling, Washington, 1950-56; asst. to solicitor gen. U.S., 1956-58; lectr. law Harvard Law Sch., Cambridge, Mass., 1958-60, prof. law, 1960-76, Samuel Williston prof. law, 1976-92, dir. Harvard negotiation project, 1980—, prof. emeritus, 1992—. Vis. prof. internat. rels. dept. London Sch. Econ., 1965-66; cons. pub. affairs editor WGBH-TV, Cambridge, 1969; tech. adivsor Found. for Internat. Conciliation, Geneva, 1984-87; sr. advisor Mercy Corps'; lectr. in field. Originator, 1st exec. editor: (pub. TV series) The Advocates, 1969-70, moderator, 1970-71; co-originator, exec. editor: (pub. TV series) Arabs and Israelis, 1975; author: International Conflict for Beginners, 1969, Dear Israelis, Dear Arabs, 1972, International Mediation: A Working Guide, 1978, International Crises and the Role of Law: Points of Choice, 1978, Improving Compliance with International Law, 1981; co-author: Getting to Yes: Negotiating Agreement Without Giving In, 1981, 2d edit., 1991, Getting Together: Building Relationships as We Negotiate, 1988, Beyond Machiavelli: Tools for Coping with Conflict, 1994, Getting Ready to Negotiate: The Getting to Yes Workbook, 1995, Coping with International Conflict: A Systematic Approach to Influence in International Negotiation, 1997, Getting It Done: How to Lead When You're Not in Charge, 1998, (with Daniel Shapiro) Beyond Reason: Using Your Emotions as You Negotiate, 2005 (awarded as outstanding book on alternate dispute resolution Internat. Inst. for Conflict Prevention and Resolution, 2005); co-author, editor: International Conflict and Behavioral Science--The Craigville Papers, 1964; contbr. articles to profl. jours. Bd. dirs. Coun. for Livable World, 1962-2006; trustee Hudson Inst., 1962-95. 1st lt. USAF, 1942-46. Recipient Sziland Peace award 1981, Peace Advocate award Lawyers Alliance for Nuclear Arms Control, 1988, Spl. Contbn. award Ctr. Pub. Resources, 1993, Steve Brutschè award Assn. Atty. Mediators, 1994, D'Alemberte-Raven Outstanding Achievements and Contributions to Dispute Resolution award, 1995, Honorato Vasquez Nat. Order Insignia Great Cross Republic Ecuador, 1999, helping settle in 1998 the fifty-yr. boundary war between Ecuador and Peru, Lifetime Achievement award Am. Coll. Civil Trial Mediators, 1999, Pioneer award New Eng. Soc. Profls. Dispute Resolution, 1999, St. Thomas More award St. Mary's U. Law Sch., 1999; named Guggenheim fellow 1965-66. Fellow Am. Acad. Arts and Sci.; mem. ABA (sect. dispute resolution), Am. Soc. Internat. Law (exec. coun. 1961-64, 66-69, v.p. 1982-84), Mass. Bar Assn., Commn. to Study Orgn. of Peace, Coun. Fgn. Rels., Phi Beta Kappa. Clubs: Metropolitan (Washington); Harvard (NYC). Office: Harvard U Law Sch Harvard Negotiation Project Pound Hall # 525 Cambridge MA 02138 Address: Mercy Corps 9 Waterhouse St Cambridge MA 02138-3607 Home: Cadbury Commons 66 Sherman St Cambridge MA 02140 Office Phone: 617-495-7786.

FISHER, SEYMOUR, psychologist, educator; b. NYC, Nov. 4, 1925; s. George and Fannie (Hesselson) F.; m. Carmen Eldridge, June 20, 1959; children: Mark, Andrew. BA, NYU, 1948; PhD, U. N.C., 1952; postgrad., Washington Sch. Psychiatry, 1954-55. Diplomate Am. Bd. Examiners in Psychol. Hypnosis. Clin. psychologist trainee VA Hosp., Roanoke, 1950, psychology trainee, 1952; intern Psychol. Clinic, U. N.C., Chapel Hill, 1950-51; supervising clin. psychologist Walter Reed Army Inst. Rsch., Washington, 1952-58; rsch. psychologist Psychopharmacology Svc. Ctr., NIMH, Bethesda, Md., 1958-60; chief spl. studies unit Psychopharmacology Rsch Br., NIMH, Bethesda, 1960-63; prof. psychiatry (psychology), dir. rsch. tng., dir. psychopharmacology lab., divsn. psychiatry Boston U. Sch. Medicine, 1963-78; prof. dept. psychiatry and behavioral scis., U. Tex. Med. Br., Galveston, 1978—, prof. emeritus, 2000—, assoc. chmn. for rsch., 1978-80, rsch. advisor to chmn. dept., 1980-91, dir. Ctr. for Medication Monitoring, 1987-2000. Vis. prof. Harvard U., Boston U., May to Nov., 1988; cons. NIMH, Chevy Chase, Md., 1964-66, mem. clin. psychopharmacology rsch. rev. com., 1973-77, mem. treatment devel. and assessment rsch. rev. com., 1979-83; cons. Office Naval Rsch., Washington, 1964-66, Mass. Dept. Mental Health, 1969-78, FDA, 1973-77; pres. Boston Mental Health Found., Inc., 1970-72; mem. Commn. on Cmty. Care of Mentally Ill, chmn. tech. com. Hogg Found., 1987-90, planning com. for 50th anniversary rsch. conf., 1988-89 Mem. editl. bd. Psychopharmacology Svc. Ctr. Bull., 1959-63; assoc. editor Psychol. Record, 1960-66; sr. editor vol. on clin. and biobehavioral aspects of cocaine, Oxford U. Press, 1987; mem. adv. bd. Internat. Jour. Methods Psychiatry, 1998-2000; contbr. numerous articles to profl. jours., chpts. in books. Recipient Disting. Alumnus award U. N.C., 1981, Donald E. Francke award for best paper Drug Info. Jour., 1987. Fellow APA (mem. exec. coun. divsn. psychopharmacology 1979-82), Am. Coll. Neuropsychopharmacology (life, pres. 1984, asst. sec.-treas. 1974-77, chmn. hon. awards com. 1985-87, mem. other coms. 1973-87, emeritus), Soc. Clin. and Exptl. Hypnosis, Internat. Coll. Psychosomatic Medicine, Collegium Internat. Neuro-Psychopharmacologicum (emeritus); mem. Am. Psychopathol. Assn. (exec. coun. 1970-72), Psi Chi, Sigma Xi, Beta Lambda Sigma. Office Phone: 409-763-6610. Business E-Mail: sfisher@utmb.edu. *The difference between intelligence and wisdom: intelligence is knowing that half of what you hear or read is garbage; wisdom is knowing which half.*

FISHER, STEPHEN CAREY, musicologist, editor; b. Norfolk, Va., May 18, 1948; s. Bryce B. and Ruth B. Fisher. BA, U. Va., Charlottesville, 1969; PhD, U. Pa., Phila., 1985. Lectr. U. Pa., Phila., 1984—93; adj. asst. prof. Widener U., Chester, Pa., 1985—87; bibliographic specialist U. Pa. Libr., Phila., 1987—2004; staff editor Packard Humanities Inst., Cambridge, Mass., 2004—. Editor: (music) Joseph Haydn Werke, Reihe I, Band 9: Sinfonien um 1777-1779, The Symphony 1720-1840, Series B, Volume X: Witt, Reicha, Eberl; contbr. to music encyclopedias. Fulbright-Hays grant, Fulbright Commn., 1976—77. Mem.: Music Libr. Assn., Mozart Soc. Am., Internat. Musicological Soc., Haydn Soc. N.Am., Am. Musicological Soc. (sec., treas. mid-atlantic chpt. 1985—87), Soc. Eighteenth Century Music (dir. 2006—). Methodist. Avocations: entomology, hiking, writing. Home: 266 Harvard St Apt 2 Cambridge MA 02139 Office: Packard Humanities Inst 11A Mt Auburn St Cambridge MA 02138 E-mail: docsfisher@aol.com.

FISHER, STEVEN, real estate company executive; 3 children. Asst. field supt. Park Ave. Plz.; ptnr. Fisher Bros., NYC; chmn., CEO Plz. Constrn. Co., NYC; chmn. Terra Mark Devel. Co. Bd. govs. Police Athletic League; v.p. bd. trustees Police Mus.; bd. trustees Intrepid Mus. Named one of 40 Under 40, Crain's NY Bus., 1999; recipient Ellis Island Medal of Honor, Outstanding Leadership award, Greater NY Constrn. Users Coun., Queens Bot. Garden Rose Ball award, 2006. Office: Fisher Bros 299 Park Ave New York NY 10171 Office Phone: 212-752-5000.*

FISHER, STEVEN KAY, neurobiology educator; b. Rochester, Ind., July 18, 1942; s. Stewart King and Hazel Madeline (Howell) F.; m. Dinah Dawn Marschall, May 2, 1971; children: Jenni Dawn, Brian Andrew, Steven William. BS, Purdue U., 1964, MS, 1966; postgrad., Johns Hopkins U., 1967—69; PhD, Purdue U., 1969. Postdoctoral fellow Johns Hopkins U., Balt., 1969-71; prof. U. Calif., Santa Barbara, 1971—, dir. Inst. Environ. Stress, 1985-88, dir. Neurosci. Rsch. Inst., 1989-2001. Cons. Ultrastructure Tech., Goleta, Calif., 1984—, Regeneron Pharms., Inc., 1993, 94, Amgen, Inc., 1994, 95; mem. NIH Visual Scis. A2 Study Sect. Contbr. numerous articles to profl. jours. Recipient Devel. award, NIH, 1980—84, M.E.R.I.T. award, 1989—99, Ludwig von Sallmann prize for vision rsch., 2002; grantee, NIH, 1971—, NSF, 2003. Mem. Assn. Rsch. in Vision and Ophthalmology (mem. program com. 1979-80, K-12 edn. com. 1997-2001); Internat. Soc. for Eye Rsch., Soc. Neurosci. Avocations: music, gardening, guitar, literature, weightlifting. Home: 6890 Sabado Tarde Rd Goleta CA 93117-4305 Office: U Calif Neurosci Rsch Inst Santa Barbara CA 93106-5060 E-mail: fisher@lifesci.ucsb.edu.

FISHER, STEWART WAYNE, lawyer; b. Phila., Mar. 5, 1950; s. Frederick and Evalyn (Wilson) F.; m. Melinda Ruley, Oct. 1, 1994; children: Henry J., Isabel Rose; children from previous marriage: Kira H., Amos N., Emily E. BA magna cum laude, Duke U., 1972; MA, Yale U., 1974; JD with honors, U. N.C., 1982. Bar: N.C. 1982, U.S. Dist. Ct. (ea.

and ctrl. dists.) N.C. 1982, U.S. Dist. Ct. (we. dist.) N.C. 1997, U.S. Ct. Appeals (4th cir.) 1993, U.S. Supreme Ct. 1997, bd. cert. Civil Trial Advocate: Nat. Bd. Trial Advocacy 1998. Atty. Haywood, Denny & Miller, Durham, N.C., 1982-85; ptnr. Glenn, Mills & Fisher, PA, Durham, 1985—. Faculty Nat. Inst. for Trial Advocacy, Durham, 1988—. Coop. atty. ACLU, Raleigh, 1992—. Mem. ABA, ATLA, Nat. Employment Lawyers, N.C. Acad. Trial Lawyers, N.C. Bar Assn., Phi Beta Kappa. Democrat. Avocations: fishing, gardening. Office: Glenn Mills & Fisher PA PO Box 3865 Durham NC 27702-3865

FISHER, TERESA MARIE, psychologist, forensic specialist; b. Canyon Country, Calif., Feb. 23, 1975; d. Robert Alstrand and Susan Jeanne Fisher. BA, U. Calif., Irvine, 1996; MA, Calif. Sch. Profl. Psychology, 1998, PhD in Psychology, 2000. Lic. psychologist Calif., 2002. Intern psychology Alliance Healthcare Corp., Sun Valley, Calif., 1998—99, Dorothy Kirby Detention Ctr., LA, 1999—2000; postdoctoral fellow Northeast Valley Health Corp., San Fernando, Calif., 2000—01; postdoctoral resident Job Corps Ctr., Long Beach, Calif., 2000—01; staff psychologist Calif. Instn. Men, Chino, Calif., 2001—. Adj. prof. Argosy U., Costa Mesa, Calif., 2004; evaluator San Bernardino (Calif.) County Ct., 2002—; coord. Developmental Disabilities Program Calif. Instn. Men, 2004—06. Author: Psychological Violence: A Handbook for Assisting Stalking Victims, 1999. Mem.: APA, Am. Psychology-Law Assn., Am. Assn. Correctional and Forensic Psychology, Calif. Correctional Psychology Assn., Mensa, Psi Chi. Avocations: fencing, golf, theater, basketball, art museums. Home: 17887 Lone Ranger Trail Chino Hills CA 91709 Office: PMB 121 4200 Chino Hills Pkwy Ste 820 Chino Hills CA 91709

FISHER, THOMAS GEORGE, lawyer, retired media company executive; b. Debrecen, Hungary, Oct. 2, 1931; came to U.S., 1951; s. Eugene J. and Viola Elizabeth (Rittersporn) F.; m. Rita Knisley, Feb. 14, 1960; children: Thomas G. Jr., Katherine F. Vaaler. BS, Am. U., 1957, JD, 1959; postgrad., Harvard U., 1956. Bar: D.C. 1959, Iowa 1977. Atty. FCC, Washington, 1959-61, 65-66; pvt. law practice, 1961-65, 66-69; asst. counsel Meredith Corp., NYC, 1969-72, assoc. gen. counsel Des Moines, 1972-76, gen. counsel, 1976-80, v.p. gen. counsel, 1980-94, corp. sec., 1988-94, ret., 1994. Comml law liaison ABA Ctr. and East European Law Initiative, Krakow, Poland, 1994—95; atty. Iowa Legal Aid, 1996—. Contbr. articles to profl. jours. Bd. dirs. Des Moines Met. Opera Co., Indianola, 1980-94, pres., 1990-91; bd. dirs. Civic Music Assn., Des Moines, 1982-92, pres., 1987-88; chmn. legis. com. Greater Des Moines C. of C., 1976-77; bd. dirs. Legal Aid Soc. Polk County, 1986-93, pres., 1993. With U.S. Army, 1952-54. Mem. ABA, Iowa State Bar Assn. (chmn. corp. counsel subcom. 1979-82), Polk County Bar Assn., Embassy Club. Office: Iowa Legal Aid Ste 230 1111 9th St Des Moines IA 50314-2527 Office Phone: 515-243-1198 ext. 1687.

FISHER, THOMAS GEORGE, JR., lawyer; b. Washington, June 1, 1961; s. Thomas George and Rita (Knisley) F.; m. Susan Jane Koenig, June 23, 1990. BA, Iowa State U., 1983; JD with high distinction, U. Iowa, 1986. Bar: Iowa 1986, U.S. Dist. Ct. (so. dist.), Iowa 1987, U.S. Ct. Appeals (8th cir.) 1987, U.S. Dist. Ct. (no. dist.) Iowa 1993. Jud. clk. Iowa Supreme Ct., Davenport, 1986-87; assoc. Duncan, Jones, Riley & Finley, P.C., Des Moines, 1987-91; asst. atty. gen. State of Iowa, Justice Dept., Des Moines, 1991-95; counsel Am. Mut. Life Ins. Co., Des Moines, 1995-96; ptnr. Hogan & Fisher, PLC, Des Moines, 1997—2003, Whitfield & Eddy, P.L.C., Des Moines, 2003—04; atty. in pvt. practice, 2004—. Mem. Des Moines Leadership Inst., 1998—99; candidate Iowa Ho. of Reps. Dists. 73, 1994; precinct chair Polk County Dem. Party, Des Moines, 1988—90, 1994—96, 1998—2000, 2002—; bd. dirs., chair Metro Arts Alliance of Greater Des Moines; bd. dirs. Des Moines Emergency Food Pantry, Iowa Forest Heritage Found. Mem. Blackstone Inn of Ct. Democrat. Roman Catholic. Office: 100 Walnut St Ste 324 Des Moines IA 50309 Office Phone: 515-288-1901. E-mail: tfisher@dwx.com.

FISHER, TIMOTHY ROY, protective services official; b. Ft. Ord, Calif., Sept. 29, 1967; s. Charles Glen Fisher and Juanita Deletha Fishser; m. Heather Joanna Campbell, Apr. 13, 1991; children: Brandon Eugene, Alicia Leann. Cert. in mobile electronics, Installers Inst., Daytona, Fla., 1993; cert., Ctrl. Tng. Acad. Dept. Energy. Cert. comml. art Tex. State Tech. Inst., Amarillo, 1989. Sgt. corrections officer Tex Dept. Criminal Justice, Pampa, Tex., 1994—2001; security pro force BWX Tech. Pantex, Amarillo, 2001—. Staff cartoonist: Drum Corp. World, 1988—89. With USN, 1990—93. Decorated Co. Honorman award USN, Achievement award; recipient 1st pl., Pampa Area Art League, 1989. Mem.: Harley Owners Group, Pantex Guard Union. Republican. Assembly Of God. Avocations: art, motorcycling. Office: BWXT Pantex Hwy 60 and FM 2373 Amarillo TX 79109 Personal E-mail: trfisher67@yahoo.com.

FISHER, VERNON, artist, educator; b. Ft. Worth, Tex., 1943; BA, Hardin-Simmons U., 1967; MFA, U. Ill., 1969. Assoc. prof. art Austin Coll., Sherman, Tex., 1969-78; prof. art North Tex. State U., Denton, 1978—. One-man shows Asher-Faure Gallery, L.A., 1986, 91, Barbara Gladstone Gallery, N.Y.C., 1987, Hiram Butler Gallery, Houston, 1987, 90, Lannan Mus., Lake Worth, Fla., 1987, Fred Hoffman Gallery, Buffalo, 1989, Karsten Schubert Ltd., London, 1989, Mus. Fine Arts, Houston, 1990, Rena Bransten Gallery, San Francisco, 1992, Charles Cowles Gallery, 1996, 1998, 2001, 2002, Devin Borden Hiram Butler Gallery, Houston, Tex., 1999, Dunn and Brown Contemporary, Dallas, 2000, 2003, Mark Moore Gallery, Santa Monica, Calif., 2002, 2004; exhibited in group shows Bronx (N.Y.) Mus. Arts, 1984, Hirshhorn Mus. and Sculpture Garden, Washington, 1984, New Orleans Mus. Art, 1986, Bklyn. Mus., 1986, Walker Art Ctr., Mpls., 1987, Los Angeles County Mus. Art, 1987, Inst. Contemporary Arts, London, 1987, A Singualar Vision: Prints from Landfall Press, MoMA, NY, 1997, Story: Language as Image, Sheldon Meml. Art Gallery and Sculpture Garden, U. Nebr., 1998, Altered States, Charles Cowles Gallery, NY, 1999, Flip, Dunn and Brown Contemporary, 2003, There, there: painting and photography, Zolla/Lieberman Gallery, Chgo., 2004, Misleading Trails, China Art Archives and Warehouse, Beijing, China, 2004-2006; represented in permanent collections Hirshhorn Mus. and Sculpture Garden, Guggenheim Mus., N.Y.C., Mus. Modern Art, N.Y.C., Albright-Knox Gallery, Art Inst. Chgo., Balt. Mus. Art, Corcoran Gallery Art, Washington, DC, Denver Art Mus., Colo., High Mus. Art, Atlanta, Ga., LA County Mus. Art, Milw. Art Mus., Mus. Contemporary Art, Chgo., New Orleans Mus. Art, San Diego Mus. Art, Calif., San Francisco Mus. Modern Art, Calif.; Author: Navigating by the Stars, 1989, editor, 1992. Grantee SECCA, 1981, 88, Louis Comfort Tiffany Found., 1980-81, 84; Individual Artist's Fellowship, NEA, 1974, 1980, 1981, John Simon Guggenheim Fellowship, 1995; Award in Visual Arts, Southeastern Ctr. Contemporary Art, 1988, Disting. Tchg. Art award, Coll. Art Assn., 1992. Mailing: c/i Charles Cowles Gallery 537 West 24th St New York NY 10011

FISHER, WILLIAM LAWRENCE, geologist, educator, dean; b. Marion, Ill., Sept. 16, 1932; s. Henry Adam and Madge Lenora (Moore) F.; m. Marilee Booth, Dec. 18, 1954; children: Leah, Karl, Peter. BS, So. Ill. U., 1954, DSc, 1986; MS, U. Kans., 1958, PhD, 1961; DEng, Colo. Sch. Mines, 2002. Cert. Profl. Geologist Am. Inst. Profl. Geologists, Petroleum Geologist Am. Assn. Petroleum Geologists, Profl. Earth Scientist Soc. Ind. Profl. Earth Scientists. Rsch. scientist Tex. Bur. Econ. Geology, Austin, 1960-68, assoc. dir., 1968-70, dir., 1970-75, 77-94, John A. and Katherine G. Jackson Sch. Geoscis., 2001—05, dean, 2005—06; asst. sec. for energy and minerals Dept. Interior, Washington, 1976—77; prof. dept. geol. scis. U. Tex., Austin, 1969—, dep. asst. sec. energy, 1975—76, Morgan J. Davis prof. petroleum geology, 1984-86, Leonidas T. Barrow chair in mineral resources, 1986—, participating faculty LBJ sch. pub. affairs, 1977—81, chmn. dept. geol. scis., 1984-90, dir. Geology Found., 1984—2006. Vis. prof. dept. geology So. Ill. U., 1967; bd. dirs. Pogo Producing Co.; geology assoc. bd. U. Kans., 1972-74, 83—; adv. coun. Gas Rsch. Inst., Tex. Energy and Natural Resource; mem. Tex. Sci. Adv. Coun., Gov.'s Energy Coun., White House Sci. Coun., Nat. Petroleum Coun., Pres.' Coun. of Advisors on Sci. and Tech. Panel on Energy R & D and Sec. Energy Adv. Bd.; mem. Tex. 2000 Commn.; bd dirs. Diamond Shamrock, 1987-98. Trustee, chmn. Southwest Rsch. Inst. With AUS, 1954—56. Shell fellow, 1961; recipient Hedberg medal Inst. for the Study of Earth and Man, 1995, Robert Earll McConnell award Am. Inst. Mining, Metall. and Petroleum Engrs., 2004. Fellow AAAS, Soc. Econ. Geology, Geol. Soc. Am. (councillor); mem. NRC (commn. on geoscis., environ. and resource, chmn. bd. mineral and energy resources, US nat. com. on geology, chmn. bd. on earth scis. and resources, bd. on energy and environ. sys.), Nat. Acad. Engring., Nat. Assoc., Nat. Acads. (nat. assoc. 2003), Am. Inst. Profl. Geologists (pres. Tex. sect. 1979, pres. 1993, Galey Pub. Svc. award, 1985, Parker medal, 1996), Assn. Am. State Geologists (hon. pres. 1981-82), Am. Assn. Petroleum Geologists (hon., pres. 1985-86, trustee, chmn. Found., Sidney Powers Meml. medal award 1994, Heritage award 2006), Am. Geol. Inst. (pres. 1991, trustee, chmn. Found., Campbell medal, 1991, Heroy award, 1997, Milling Legendary Geoscientist medal 2007), Austin Geol. Soc. (hon., pres. 1973-74), Gulf Coast Assn. Geol. Scis. (hon. 1986, pres. 1994, Boyd medal 2002), Tex. Ind. Prodrs. and Royalty Owners (Hats Off award, 2002), Tex. Acad. Medicine, Engring. and Sci., Acad. Medicine, Engring. Sci. Tex. (founding mem.), Soc. Sedimentary Geology (Twenhofel medal 2001), Soc. Petroleum Engrs., Soc. Ind. Profl. Earth Scientists, Brazilian Assn. Petroleum Geologists Republican. Achievements include first to introduce the concept of depositional systems linking modern depositional environments to ancient counterparts in 1967; introduce the concept of additional mobile oil recovery and its significance to oil and gas reserves growth. Home: 8705 Ridgehill Dr Austin TX 78759-7342 Office: Univ Tex Dept Geological Scis Austin TX 78712 Office Phone: 512-471-5600. Business E-Mail: wfisher@mail.utexas.edu.

FISHER, WILLIAM RALPH, retired geologist; b. Chattanga, Tenn., May 17, 1935; s. Ralph Alexander and Oneta Blanche (White) Fisher; m. Beverly Jean Anderson (div.); children: Terry Lee, Tracy Lee. Associates (hon.), ARE, Va., 1968; Doctorate (hon.), Am. Fellow Seminary, Monterey, 1972; degree in engring. and geology, South Western Coll., Chula Vista. Various rsch. Nat. Hist. Mus., San Diego, 1973—94, Bibby Fisher Lab., Imperial Beach, Calif., 1985—94, Machlin-Fisher Lab., Greeley, Kans., 1995—2001. Assoc. Pacific Geology Soc., San Francisco, 1976, NY Acad. Sci., NYC, 2005—06. With special ops group USN, 1952—73, Korea, Vietnam. Grantee, Josephine Scripps, 1974—87, Joan Croc, 1974—87, Helen Coperty, 1974—87. Independent. Avocations: sculpting, music, art. Home and Office: 33999 NE 2400 Rd Greeley KS 66033

FISHER, WILLIAM THOMAS, business administration educator; b. Central Falls, RI, Mar. 15, 1918; s. William L. and Sarah (Foley) F.; m. Mary Rowena Donnelly, Dec. 26, 1949; 1 son, William Thomas. BS with high honors, Am. Internat. Coll., 1949; MEd in Econs. and Edn., Boston U., 1951; PhD, U. Conn., 1956; postgrad., Clark U., 1954, Columbia U., 1957, St. Thomas Sem., Bloomfield, Conn., 1970-73. Prodn. planner local industry, Putnam, Conn., 1938-42; prin. Templeton (Mass.) Sch., 1949-50, Tourtellotte High Sch., Thompson, Conn., 1950-57; instr. Becker Jr. Coll., Worcester, Mass., 1955-57; assoc. prof. State U. N.Y. at, Albany, 1957; asst. dean Sch. Ins., U. Conn., 1957-76; asst. dean adminstrn. U. Conn. Sch. Bus. Adminstrn., 1976-77; adminstrv. dir. (Hartford MBA program), 1957-64; vis. prof. Ohio U., summer 1962; dir. (IBM Advanced Ins. Industry Sch.), 1960-70; ednl. cons. IBM Corp., 1960-80; adminstr., asst. dir. Ctr. for Ins. Edn. and Rsch., Hartford, 1976-81; assoc. prof. mgmt. and adminstrv. scis. dept. Sch. Bus. Adminstrn., U. Conn., Storrs, 1976-81, assoc. prof. mgmt. and orgn. dept., 1981-89, prof. emeritus, 1989—, adj. prof., 1989-90, 92; ordained permanent deacon Roman Cath. Ch. for Archdiocese of Hartford, 1973; assigned St. Joseph Cathedral, Hartford, part-time 1973-83; rsch. fellow Divinity Sch. Yale U., New Haven, 1989-91, Theol. Opportunities Program Harvard U., Cambridge, Mass., 1994-95. Vis. scholar Divinity Sch., Duke U., Durham, N.C., 1995, 96, 98, 99, Divinity Sch., Vanderbilt U., Nashville, 1996-97, Emory U., Candler Sch. Theology, Atlanta, 1997; real estate broker, 1973-93; mem. Conn. State Ins. Com. and Conn. State Ins. Purchasing Bd., 1963-73, 75-91, chmn. bd., 1971-73; past pres., dir. Conn. Assn. Mcpl. Devel. Commns., 1963-91; mem. Conn. adv. coun. SBA, 1964-70, chmn., 1967; chmn. various comms. Greater Hartford Coun. Econ. Edn., 1958-81; mem. Thompson Bd. Fin., 1963-75; chmn. Thompson Indsl. and Devel. Com., 1964-70, 71-80, 81-91. Editor: Selective Readings in Human Resources Management, 1985, 87, 89; contbr. articles to profl. jours. Pres. Thompson Indsl. Found., 1965-66; mem. Gov.'s Conf. on Human Rights and Opportunities, 1967, Gov.s Conf. on Innovation, 1989; Organizer Conn. small bus. divsn. Businessmen for V.P. Humphrey, 1968; alumni dir. Am. Internat. Coll., 1961-63, 89-93, trustee, 1963-71, mem. corp., 1972—; chmn. adv. bd. govs. Conn. Libr. Svc. Ctr., Willimantic, 1964-68; bd. dir., sec. Edn. and Rsch. Found. IMA-PIA for States N.Y., N.J. and Conn., Glenmont, N.Y., 1973-83; past trustee, past pres. Thompson Libr.; corporator Day Kimball Hosp., Putnam, Conn.; mem. region 3 adv. and planning coun. Conn. Dept. Mental Retardation, 1987-92; trustee Annhurst Coll., Woodstock, Conn., 1977-84; active Conn. Small Bus. Devel. Ctr., summer 1982, 83, 84, 85; bd. dir. Norwich-Quinebaug unit Am. Cancer Soc. Served with AUS, 1942-45, 39.5 months continuous overseas svc. Recipient Yr. award Hartford Assn. Ins. Women, 1969; Presdl. Appreciation cert. Conn. Assn. Mcpl. Devel. Commns., 1968, Alumni Achievement award Am. Internat. Coll., 1999. Mem. NEA (life), AAUP, KC (hon. life), Am. Risk and Ins. Assn. (fellowship 1960, 62), Risk and Ins. Mgmt. Soc., Am. Soc. Personnel Adminstrn., Am. Acad. Mgmt., Am. Acad. Religion, Northeastern Indsl. Developers Assn., Conn. Hist. Soc., Nat. Trust Historic Preservatio, Am. Legion, Phi Delta Kappa, Delta Pi Epsilon.: Loomis Village Apt A310 10 Bayon Rd South Hadley MA 01075

FISHER, WINFIELD STITT, III, medical educator; b. Highland Park, Ill., Oct. 1, 1952; MD, St. Louis U., 1978. Lic. Am. Bd. Neurol. Surgery, 1987. Prof. U. Ala., Birmingham, 1991—. Capt. USN, 1978—90, Bethesda, Md. Office: 1040 Fot 510 20th Street S Birmingham AL 35294

FISHER, WINSTON CRAWFORD, real estate company executive; s. Richard L. and Sandra Fisher; m. Jessica Helen Eckle, July 28, 2001. Grad., Syracuse U. Ptnr. fin., acquisitions and new devel. Fisher Bros., NYC. Mem. real estate and constrn. coun. Lincoln Ctr. Exec. vice chmn. Fisher House Found.; bd. visitors Syracuse Coll. Arts and Scis. Office: Fisher Bros 299 Park Ave New York NY 10171 Office Phone: 212-752-5000.*

FISHKIN, ANNE SONYA, retired special education educator; b. Bklyn., Nov. 25, 1938; d. Harry Aaron and Judith Esther Pollack; m. F. William Kroesser, Oct. 26, 1996; children: Ruth Ellen, Amy Lynne Caplan. AB, Shimer Coll., 1958; MA in Psychology, U. Colo., 1970; PhD in Applied Behavioral Studies in Edn., Okla. State U., 1989. Cert. sch. psychologist Okla. Dept. Edn. Enrichment tchr. Guthrie (Okla.) Pub. Schs., 1975—76, Millwood Pub. Schs., Oklahoma City, 1976—78; enrichment tchr./sch. psychologist Edmond (Okla.) Pub. Schs., 1978—90; asst. prof. Marshall U. Grad. Coll., South Charleston, W.Va., 1990—94, assoc. prof. spl. edn. of gifted edn., 1994—97, rsch. specialist, 1997—2000; ret. Parent edn. coord. for family judge cir. W.Va. Supreme Ct. Appeals, Charleston, 1998—2002, parent edn. evaluator, 1998—2002; dir. Eastman Acad. Summer Sch., 2006—. Editor: Investigating Creativity in Youth: Research and Methods, 1999; contbr. chapters to books, articles to profl. jours. Chair social action com. Congregation B'nai Israel, Charleston, W.Va., 2003—; mem. Commn. on Social Action, Union Reform Judaism, 2006—; v.p. Okla. Odyssey of the Mind, 1982—89; vice-chair W.Va. Odyssey of the Mind, 1992—98, W.Va. Creative Adventures Network (Destination Imagination), 1999—. Recipient Hon. Mention for outstanding rsch. article, Rsch. and Evaluation Divsn. of the Nat. Assn. for Gifted Children, 1994; grantee, W.Va. Grad. Coll. and GMI Engring. and Mgmt. Inst., 1991, Summer Tng. Inst., Educating Gifted Students with Learning Disabilities, Albuquerque, 1995, Parent Edn. Project Evaluator, W.Va. Supreme Ct. of Appeals, 1998, 1999, 2000, 2002, The Greater Kanawha Valley Found., 2006, 2007; grant, Mission W.Va., 2005. Mem.: Okla. Assn. for Gifted/Creative/Talented (v.p. 1989—90), W.Va. Assn. for Gifted and Talented (pres., newsletter editor 1995—96), Creativity Divsn. Nat. Assn. for Gifted Children (Guest (Issue) Editor of Creativity Divsn. Newsletter 1990, 1993, 2001), Nat. Assn. for Gifted Children (chair creativity divsn. 1990—91), Am. Mensa (gifted children's adv. com. 1987—90), Ctrl. Okla. Mensa (scholarship chair, proctor, gifted children's coord. 1982—89), Vandalia Mensa (scholarship chair, proctor coord. 1991—). Home: 813 Whispering Way South Charleston WV 25303 Personal E-mail: anne_fishkin@hotmail.com.

FISHKIND, WILLIAM J., ophthalmologist; b. Bklyn., Oct. 16, 1946; m. Wendy Weston, Aug. 24, 1968; children: Jennifer, Brett Michael. BA, Adelphi U., Garden City, NY, 1968; MD, Tufts U., Boston, 1972. Diplomate Am. Bd. Ophthalmology, 1982, Am. Bd. Internal Medicine, 1977. Intern Mt. Auburn Hosp., Cambridge, Mass., 1972—73; resident internal medicine Harvard Primary Care Internal Medicine, Cambridge, 1975—77; resident ophthalmology La. State U., New Orleans, 1977—80; mem. staff emergency rm. Touro Hosp., New Orleans, 1979—80; ophthalmologist Westside Eye Physicians, Tucson, 1980—81; co-dir. Fishkind and Bakewell Eye Care, Tucson, 1981—. Clin. instr. sch. medicine U. Ariz., Tucson, 1998—; clin. prof. ophthalmology U. Utah, Utah, 1996—. Editor: Complications in Phacoemulsification: Avoidance, Recognition, and Management; prodr.: (films) Pop Goes the Microbubbles: Exploring the Microcosm of the Phaco Tip, Revelation, Velocity Subsonic; contbr. chapters to books. Fellow: ACS, Fellow Am. Acad. Opthalmology; mem.: Am. Coll. Eye Surgeons, European Soc. Cataract and Refractive Surgeons (Overall Best Videos award 1997), Outpatient Ophthal. Surgery Soc. (pres. 1987—), Am. Soc. Cataract and Refractive Surgery (mem. program com. 1984—2006, mem. govt. rels. com. 1998—, prodr. Magnificent Phaco, First Pl. Film Festival Quality Tchg. Category award 2001, 2002), Ariz. Ophthal. Soc. Achievements include research in corneal endothelium in diabetes mellitus. Office: Fishkind and Bakewell Eye Care 5599 N Oracle Rd Tucson AZ 85704 Home Phone: 520-299-5779; Office Phone: 520-293-6740. Office Fax: 520-293-6771.

FISHMAN, ALAN H., mortgage company and former bank executive; b. Mar. 16, 1946; married. BA, Brown U., 1968; MA in Econs, Columbia U., 1968. V.p. Chem. Bank, 1974-76, sr. v.p., 1976-79, sr. v.p. fin., 1979-81, exec. v.p. fin., 1983—88; exec. v.p., CFO Chem. N.Y. Corp., 1981-83, sr. exec. v.p.; with Neuberger & Berman, 1988—89; mng. ptnr. Adler & Shaykin, 1990—92, Columbia Financial Partners, L.P., 1992—2001; pres., CEO ContiFinancial Corp., 1999—2001, Independence Community Bank, Bklyn., 2001—06; pres., COO Sovereign Bank, Wyomissing, Pa., 2006; chmn. Meridian Capital Group LLC, NYC, 2007—. Bd. dirs. KeySpan Corp., 1998—; chmn. bd. trustees Bklyn. Acad. Music. Office: Meridian Capital Group LLC 1 Battery Pk Plz New York NY 10004*

FISHMAN, ALFRED PAUL, physician; b. NYC, Sept. 24, 1918; s. Isaac Fishman and Anne (Tinter) Fishman; m. Linda Fishman, Oct. 7, 1984; children: Mark, Jay, Hannah Rae. AB, U. Mich., 1938, MS, 1939; MD, U. Louisville, 1943; MA (hon.), U. Pa., 1971. Diplomate Am. Bd. Internal Medicine, Nat. Bd. Med. Examiners. Intern Jewish Hosp., Bklyn., 1943—44; Dazian Found. fellow pathology Mount Sinai Hosp., NYC, 1946—47, asst. resident, resident medicine, 1947—48; Dazian Found. fellow cardiovascular physiology Michael Reese Hosp., Chgo., 1948—49; Am. Heart Assn. rsch. fellow Bellevue Hosp., NYC, 1949—50, established investigator Am. Heart Assn. cardiopulmonary lab., 1951—55; Am. Heart Assn. rsch. fellow in physiology Harvard U., Boston, 1950—51; instr. physiology NYU, NYC, 1951—53; assoc. in medicine Columbia Coll. Physicians and Surgeons, NYC, 1953—55, asst. prof., 1955—58, assoc. prof., 1958—66; prof. medicine U. Chgo., 1966—69; dir. Inst. and Divsn. Cardiovasc. Disease Michael Reese Hosp., Chgo., 1966—69; prof. medicine U. Pa., Phila., 1969—72, William Maul Measey prof. medicine, 1972—, assoc. dean Sch. Medicine, 1969—99, dir. cardiovasc.-pulmonary divsn., 1969—90, chmn. dept. rehab. medicine, 1990—97, steering com. dept. chmn. Med. Ctr., 1992, mem. coun. grad. med. edn., 1992—93, assoc. dean program devel., 1998—99, sr. assoc. dean program devel., 1999—. Dir. Robinette Found., Clin. Cardiovascular Rsch. Ctr., U. Pa. Med. Ctr., 1969—82; mem. steering com. dept. chmn. U. Pa. Med. Ctr., 1992, coun. on grad. med. edn., 1992—93; dir. Specialized Center of Rsch. (Lung), 1973—81; attending physician Hosp. U. Pa., 1969—, Presbyn. Hosp. Phila., 2000—; sr. attending physician Phila. Gen. Hosp., 1970—78; physician Mass. Gen. Hosp., 1979; cons. to chancellor U. Mo., Kansas City, 1973—78; vis. prof. Harvard U., 1970, Oxford (Eng.) U., 1972, Washington U., St. Louis, 1973, Johns Hopkins U., 1974, Ben Gurion U., 1975, Emory U., Atlanta, 1976, U. Porto Alegra, Brazilia, Brazil, 1976, U. Zurich, Switzerland, 1978, Duke U., 1986, U. N.C., 1986; vis. scientist for NIH to Peking, China, 1980, to USSR, 1985; cons. Exec. Office Pres., 1961—69, U. Athens, Greece, 1980; mem. WHO Expert Panel, Geneva, 1973—76, Nat. Adv. Heart and Lung Council, NIH, 1968—71, 1979—83, Steering Com. of Dept. Chmn U. Pa. Med. Ctr., 1992, Coun. on Grad. Med. Edn. U. Pa. Med. Ctr., 1992—93; coun. mem. Coll. Physicians of Phila., 1993—2006, bd. govs., 2006; chmn. Gov.'s Com. for Rsch. on Respiratory Diseases in Coal Miners, 1974—90, Internat. Conf. on Lung, Titisee, Germany, 1976, Florence, Italy, 84, Prague, Czech Republic, 86, Prague, 89, NIH Conf. Proliferative & Obliterative Vascular Disease; chair steering com. Nat. Emphysema Treatment Trial, 1996—; U.S. chief del. Internat. Union of Physiol. Scis., Helsinki, Finland, 1989; cons. N.Y. State Bd. Health, 1987—91, Cleve. Found., 1984—; vis. com. Case Western Res. Sch. Medicine, Cleve., 1989—, Rsch Inst., Lankenau Hosp., Phila., 1990; chmn. Scientific Edn. Partnership U. Mo-U. Kans.-Merrill Dow, 1989—2001. Editor (with D.W. Richards): Circulation of The Blood-Men and Ideas, 1964; editor: (with H.H. Hecht) The Pulmonary Circulation and Interstitial Space, 1969; editor: Handbooks of Respiratory Physiology, Am. Physiol. Soc., 1967—72, 1979—87, Physiology in Medicine, New Eng. Jour. Medicine, 1969—79, Jour. Applied Physiology, 1981—89, 1989—99; editor: (with D.W. Richards) Circulation of the Blood Men and Ideas, 1982; editor: Merck Manual, 1972—80, Ann. Rev. Physiology, 1977—81, Heart Failure, 1979; editor: (with E. M. Renkin) Pulmonary Edema, 1979; editor: Pulmonary Diseases and Disorders, 1979, 2d edit., 1988, Classics in Biology and Medicine, 1989—97, The Pulmonary Circulation: Normal and Abnormal, 1990;: 3d edit., 1998, Pulmonary Rehabilitation, 1994, Fishman's Pulmonary Diseases and Disorders, 3rd edit., 1998—, Fishman's Manual of Pulmonary Diseases and Disorders, 2002; contbr. articles to profl. jours.; reviewer Health Care Financing Adminstrn., 1995—97, Washington Adv. Group, 2000—. Bd. dirs. Polachek Found., Phila. Zool. Soc.; mem. Kansas City Life Scis. Inst., 2000—01. Recipient Disting. Alumni award, U. Louisville, 1984, Disting. award in nephrology, A.N. Richards, 1998. Fellow: ACP, Royal Coll. Physicians, Am. Coll. Chest Physicians (hon.); mem.: AAAS, NAS (com. on sci., edn. and pub. policy 1987—90, policy bd. complementary/alternative medicine 2003), Am. Thoracic Soc. (Trudeau medal 2001), Heart Assn. Southeastern Pa. (bd. dirs.), Coll. of Physicians of Phila. (coun. 1993—, governance com. 2006, pres. 1996—97), N.Y. County Med. Soc., Nat. Space Biomed. Rsch. Inst. (bd. dirs. 1999—), Health Care Financing Adminstrn. (mem. lung transplant ctr. rev. com. 1996—, NIH-HCFA nat. emphysema treatment trial 1996—, chair steering com.), Am. Coll. Cardiology (A.N. Richards Disting. Achievement award 1997), Fedn. Am. Socs. for Exptl. Biology (exec. bd. 1983—85), Internat. Union Physiol. Scis. (U.S. Nat. Com. 1982—89, chmn. 1986—89), N.Y. Heart Assn. (pres. 1965—67), Am. Heart Assn. (chmn. coun. on cardiopulmonary disease 1972—74, rsch. coun. 1974—79, sci. pub. com. 1986—88, bd. dirs. 1988—92, chmn. 1988—94, sci. adv. com. 1992—98, founder, Disting. Achievement award 1980, Merit award 1989, Gold Heart award 1992, Sr. Rsch. award 2003), Assn. Am. Physicians, Royal Soc. Medicine (London), Am. Acad. Arts and Scis., Am. Soc. Clin. Investigation, Am. Physiol. Soc. (chmn. publs. bd. 1974—81, pres. 1983, chmn. centennial celebration com. 1985—87, editor handbook 1986, Ray G. Daggs award 2004, Trudeau medal 2005), Inst. Medicine of NAS (chmn. health scis. bd. 1990—95, com. on social and ethical impact of advances in biomedicine 1992—94, com. on use of CAM by the pub. 2004—), Interurban Clin. Club, Alpha Omega Alpha. Home: 2401 Pennsylvania Ave Apt 20a7 Philadelphia PA 19130-3004 Office: 316 Blockley Hall 423 Guardian Dr Philadelphia PA 19104-6102

FISHMAN, BARRY STUART, lawyer; b. Chgo., June 14, 1943; s. Jacob M. and Anita (Epstein) Fishman; m. Meredith Porte, Mar. 27, 1976; 1 child, Janna. BA, U. Wis., 1965; JD, DePaul U., 1968. Bar: Ill. 1968, Fla. 1969, Calif. 1969. Ptnr. firm Fishman & Fishman, Chgo., 1968-72; counsel real estate fin. dept. Baird & Warner, Inc., Chgo., 1972-75; counsel Biscayne Fed. Savs. and Loan Assn., Miami, Fla., 1976-79; mem. firm, Ea. regional counsel Logs Nationwide Representation of Lenders; mem. firm Pallott, Poppell, Goodman & Slotnick, Miami, 1977-80; sr. ptnr. Shapiro & Fishman, Aventura, Tampa, Deerfield Beach, Fla., 1984—. Dir. investment divsn. Cushman and Wakefield Fla., 1978—. Dir. Neighborhood Housing Svcs., Dade County, Fla., 1977—; mem. big gifts com. Greater Miami Jewish Fedn., 1977—. Mem.: Comml. Law League, Fla. Mortgage Bankers Assn., Mortgage Bankers Assn., Real Estate Securities and Syndication Inst., Nat. Assn. Realtors, Dade County Bar Assn., Chgo. Bar Assn., Ill. Bar Assn., Ill. Bar Assn., Calif. Bar Assn., Fla. Bar Assn., Turnberry Country Club, Turnberry Isle Yacht and Racquet Club. Jewish. Home: 912 Captiva Dr Hollywood FL 33019-5045 Office: 2424 N Federal Hwy Ste 360 Boca Raton FL 33431 E-mail: barryf.mia@logs.com.

FISHMAN, BERNARD, mechanical engineer; b. Bklyn., June 26, 1920; s. Max and Mollie (Greenberg) F.; m. Sara Fishman, July 3, 1947; 1 dau., Carol Beth. Student, Bklyn. Coll., 1937-39; B.M.E., CCNY, 1942; M.M.E., Bklyn. Poly. Inst., 1951. Instr. CCNY Sch. Tech., 1942-44; design and mfg. engr. Star Auto Radio, 1944-45; rocket propulsion engr. M.W. Kellogg Co., 1946-53; chief hydro-mech. engr. Simmonds Precision Products, 1953-65; engring. specialist Reaction Motors div. Thiokol Corp., 1965-67; dir. research, dir. ops. exec. office ASME, NYC, 1967-89; freelance consulting engr., 1989—. Contbr. articles to profl. jours.; patentee in field. Mem. Bd. Edn., Ft. Lee, N.J., 1968-72. Served with USAF, 1945-46. Fellow ASME; mem. Nat. Soc. Profl. Engrs., Tau Beta Pi, Pi Tau Sigma. Personal E-mail: fishmanb@asme.org.

FISHMAN, BERNARD PHILIP, museum director; b. NYC, July 25, 1950; m. Elizabeth Andersen, Jan. 8, 1983; 1 child, Philip. BA summa cum laude, Columbia U., 1972; MA, U. Pa., 1982. Rsch. fellow Mus. Applied Sci. Ctr. for Archaeology, U. Pa., Phila., 1976-79; Egyptologist Epigraphic Survey Oriental Inst., U. Chgo., Luxor, Egypt, 1979-82; dir. Fenster Mus. Art, Tulsa, 1982-85, Jewish Mus. Md., Balt., 1985-98, Lehigh County Hist. Soc., Allentown, Pa., 1998—2002, R.I. Hist. Soc., Providence, 2002—. Tchr., lectr. in field. Author, co-author, editor numerous books, exhibit catalogues, jours., articles; art critic World newspaper, Tulsa. Participant Getty Mus. Leadership Inst. Fellow R.I. Found.; mem. Phi Beta Kappa. Home: 499 Seven Mile Rd Hope RI 02831 Office: The RI Hist Soc 110 Benevolent St Providence RI 02906 Office Phone: 401-331-8575 ext. 36. Business E-Mail: bfishman@rihs.org. *Without the study of history there can be no civilization; without the cultivation of the arts there can be no immortality.*

FISHMAN, EDWARD MARC, lawyer; b. Cambridge, Mass., Apr. 28, 1946; s. Eli Manuel and Marian (Goldberg) F.; m. Barbara Ellen Stern, June 29, 1969 (div. Sept. 1982); children: Andrea Stern, Bradley Craig; m. Tracy Ann Lind, July 13, 1985; children: Alison Leigh, Kendall Paige. AB, Bowdoin Coll., 1968; JD, Columbia U., 1972. Bar: Tex. 1972. Assoc. Akin, Gump, Strauss, Hauer & Feld, Dallas, 1972-73, Luce, Hennessy, Smith & Castle, Dallas, 1973-76; corp. counsel Centex Corp., Dallas, 1976-78; from assoc. to ptnr. Brice & Barron, Dallas, 1978-82; v.p. Baker, Smith & Mills, Dallas, 1982-86; pres. Fishman, Jones, Walsh & Gray, Dallas, 1986-99; v.p. Clements, Allen, Fishman, Woods & Walsh, P.C., Dallas, 1999-2000; with Glast, Phillips & Murray, P.C., Dallas, 2000—. Bd. dirs. Space Found. Roundtable, Dallas, 1985-87, Hope Cottage, Dallas, 1990-96; officer local pub. TV sta., Dallas, 1976—. Mem. ABA, Tex. Bar Assn., Dallas Bar Assn. Avocations: reading, bicycling, swimming, running, skiing. Home: 4723 Stonehollow Way Dallas TX 75287-7525 Office: Glast Phillips & Murray PC Ste 2200 13355 Noel Rd Dallas TX 75240-6657 E-mail: efishman@gpm-law.com.

FISHMAN, ELLEN BETH, lawyer; b. Bklyn., 1953; d. Stanley Irving and Elizabeth Flynn Fishman. BA summa cum laude, Tufts U., 1974, MA, 1974; JD, U. Pa., 1978. Bar: N.Y. 1979. Asst. corp. counsel NYC Law Dept., 1978—86, asst. chief. appeals divsn., 1986—2000, sr. coun. appeals divsn., 2000—03; ptnr., appellate coun. Martin Clearwater & Bell LLP, NYC, 2003—. Pres. Epiphany Parish Coun., NYC, 1988—89. Mem.: Def. Rsch. Inst., Am. Health Lawyers Assn., N.Y. Cir. Translators, N.Y. County Lawyers Assn., N.Y. State Bar Assn. (chair com. on appellate cts. 1992—94), Phi Beta Kappa. Democrat. Roman Catholic. Office: Martin Clearwater & Bell LLP 220 E 42nd St New York NY 10017 Home Phone: 212-679-1950; Office Phone: 212-697-3122.

FISHMAN, FRED NORMAN, lawyer; b. NYC, Aug. 21, 1925; s. Arthur Elihu and Frederica (Greenspan) F.; m. Claire S. Powsner, Sept. 19, 1948 (dec. Dec. 17, 2006); children: Robert J., Nancy K. S.B. summa cum laude, Harvard U., 1946, LL.B. magna cum laude, 1948; postgrad., Yale U., 1945-46. Bar: N.Y. State 1950, U.S. Supreme Ct. 1954. Law clk. to Chief Judge Calvert Magruder, U.S. Ct. Appeals, 1st Circuit, Boston, 1948-49; to Asso. Justice Felix Frankfurter, Supreme Ct. U.S., 1949-50; assoc. firm Dewey Ballantine LLP (and predecessors), NYC, 1950-57; with Freeport Minerals Co., NYC, 1957-61, asst. sec., 1958-59, asst. v.p., 1959-61; partner firm Kaye Scholer LLP, NYC, 1962-92, mem. exec. com., 1970-87, chmn. exec. com., 1981-83, spl. counsel, 1993-95. Editor, officer: Harvard Law Rev. Chmn. Harvard Law Sch. Fund, 1977—79; mem. bd. overseers' com. to visit Harvard Law Sch., 1975—81, 1988—94, mem. dean's adv. bd., 2001—; chmn. com. Harvard Law Sch. Class of 1948 Twenty-Fifth Anniversary Gift, Forty-Fifth Anniversary Gift; mem. bd. overseers' com. to visit Grad. Sch. Edn., Harvard U., 1971—77, bd. overseers' Com. on Univ. Resources, 1991—, permanent class com. Harvard Coll. Class of 1946; mem. bd. overseers' com. to visit Med. Sch. and Sch. of Dental Medicine Harvard U., 1997—2003; trustee Pub. Edn. Assn., NYC, 1956—73, chmn. bd., 1970—71; dir. Harvard Alumni Assn., 1981—83; trustee Hosp. for Joint Diseases and Med. Ctr., 1971—73, Lawyers' Com. for Civil Rights under Law, 1979—2004, bd. dirs., 1983—2004, co-chmn., 1983—85, hon. lifetime trustee, 2005—; mem. steering com. Campaign for Harvard Law Sch., 1991—95; mem. leadership coun. Harvard Sch. Pub. Health, 2003—. Recipient Alumni award, Harvard Alumni Assn., 2004. Fellow: Am. Bar Found.; mem.: ABA, Harvard Law Sch. Assn. (coun. 1978—82, exec. com. 1980—82, 1st v.p. 1984—86, pres. 1986—88, exec. com. 1988—90), Legal Aid Soc. (bd. dirs. 1991—94), Am. Law Inst. (adviser corp. governance project 1980—92), Assn. Bar City N.Y. (chmn. com. fed. legis. 1963—66, exec. com. 1966—70, chmn. com. corp. law 1980—82, treas. 1993—94), N.Y.C. Harvard Law Sch. Assn. (trustee 1966—69, pres. 1988—89, v.p. 1974—75), Harvard Club N.Y.C., Phi Beta Kappa. Home: 650 Park Ave Apt 3D New York NY 10065-6115 Office: Kaye Scholer LLP 425 Park Ave New York NY 10022-3598 Office Phone: 212-836-8348.

FISHMAN, IRA, lawyer; b. Chgo., Nov. 6, 1957; BA magna cum laude, Yale Univ., 1979; JD cum laude, Harvard Univ., 1982. Bar: DC 1982. Assoc. to ptnr. Patton Boggs LLP, Washington, 1983—93; v.p. Congl. & External Affairs Import-Export Bank, Washington, 1993—95; dep. asst. Legis. Affairs to Pres. of U.S., Washington, 1995—96; spl. counsel & dir. Task Force on Edn. FCC, Washington, 1996; founder & past bd. chmn. NetDay, Irvine, Calif.; ptnr., Public Policy, Edn. practices Patton Boggs LLP, Washington, 2001—, COO, 2004—. Trustee KIPP Key Acad. Office: Patton Boggs LLP 2550 M St NW Washington DC 20037-1350 Office Phone: 202-457-6330. Office Fax: 202-457-6315. Business E-Mail: ifishman@pattonboggs.com.

FISHMAN, JAY STEVEN, diversified financial services company executive; b. NYC, Nov. 4, 1952; s. Edward and Shirley (Cantor) F.; m. Randy Lee Chapman, Sept. 25, 1976; children: Jordan Elliot, Scott Martin. BS in Econs. magna cum laude, U. Pa., 1974, MS in Acctg., 1974. CPA, N.Y. Audit supr. Coopers & Lybrand, NYC, 1974-79; dir. mergers and acquisitions Am. Can Co., Greenwich, Conn., 1979-83; sr. v.p. Goergen & Sterling, Greenwich, 1983-86; sr. v.p. mcht. banking Shearson Lehman Bros., NYC, 1986-89; exec. v.p., CFO Comml. Credit Co., NYC, 1989-91; sr. v.p., treas. Primerica Corp., NYC, 1991-94; sr. v.p. Travelers Group, NYC, 1994; vice chmn., CFO ins. group Travelers Inc., Hartford, Conn., 1994, pres., CEO, 1998—2004, chmn., 2000—04; pres., CEO St. Paul Travelers Cos., Inc., St. Paul, 2004—05; chmn., pres., CEO St. Paul Travelers Cos., Inc. (now The Travelers Cos., Inc.), St. Paul, 2005—. Mem. Wharton Club. Avocations: golf, running, skiing. Office: The Travelers Companies Inc 385 Washington St Saint Paul MN 55102*

FISHMAN, JERALD G., semiconductor executive; BSEE, CCNY; MSEE, Northeastern U.; MBA, Boston U.; JD, Suffolk Law Sch. Mgr. in product mktg., ops., strategic planning Analog Devices, Norwood, Mass., 1971-79, gen. mgr. semicondr. divsn., 1979-80, v.p., 1980-82, group v.p., 1982-88, exec. v.p., 1988-91, pres., COO, 1991-96, pres., CEO, 1996—. Bd. dirs. Xilinx, Lahey Clinic, Cognex Corp. Office: Analog Devices 1 Technology Way Norwood MA 02062*

FISHMAN, JOSHUA AARON, sociolinguist, educator; b. Phila., July 18, 1926; s. Aaron S. and Sonia (Horwitz) F.; m. Gella Jeanne Schweid, Dec. 23, 1951; children: M. Manuel, David Elliot, Avrom Avi. BS, MS (Mayor Phila. competitive scholar 1944-48), U. Pa., 1948; PhD, Columbia U., 1953; Ped.D. (hon.), Yeshiva U., 1968; LittD (hon.), Free U. Brussels, 1986. Tchr. elem. and secondary Yiddish secular schs., 1945-50; ednl. psychologist, sr. research asso. dept. research and experimentation Jewish Edn. Com. N.Y., 1951-54; from lectr. to vis. prof. psychology CCNY, 1955-58; research assoc. to dir. research Coll. Entrance Exam. Bd., 1955-58; assoc. prof. human relations and psychology U. Pa., 1958-60; prof. psychology and sociology, dean Grad. Sch. Edn. Yeshiva U., 1960-66, disting. univ. research prof. social scis. Ferkauf Grad. Sch. Psychology, 1966-88, emeritus, 1988—, univ. v.p. acad. affairs, 1973-76; vis. rschr., vis. prof. Stanford (Calif.) U., 1990—. Cummings lectr. McGill U., 1979; Linguistics Soc. Am. prof. Linguistics Inst., 1980; disting. vis. prof. Monash U., Melbourne, Australia, summers 1985, 2000; mem. com. on sociolinguistics Social Sci. Rsch. Coun.; adviser, cons. Am. Jewish Congress, Nat. Scholarship Svc. and Fund for Negro Students, Coll. Entrance Exam. Bd., Am. Assn. Jewish Edn., Ministry of Fin., Republic of Ireland; cons. Ctr. for Applied Linguistics, Internat. Rsch. Ctr. on Bilingualism, Secretariat Linguistic Policy Basque Govt., 1986—, Maori Lang. Commn., 1995—; vis. prof. linguistics L.I. U., 2000, NYU, 1998—, Grad. Ctr. CUNY, 1999—; bd. dirs. Consortium for Study of Lang. Problems, 2001—; expert witness Ministry of Edn. Edmonton Province Can., 1995. Author: Studies on Polish Jewry, 1974, Sociology of Bilingual Education, 1976, The Spread of English, 1977, Advances in the Study of Societal Multilingualism, 1978, Never Say Die: A Thousand Years of Yiddish in Jewish Life and Letters, 1981, Bilingual Education for Hispanic Students in the U.S., 1982, The Rise and Fall of the Ethnic Revival, 1985, Readings in the Sociology of Jewish Languages, 1985, Ethnicity in Action, 1985, The Fergusonian Impact (2 vols.), 1986, Ideology, Society and Language, 1987, Language and Ethnicity in Minority Sociolinguistic Perspective, 1988, Yiddish: Turning to Life, 1991, Reversing Language Shift, 1991, The Earliest Stage of Language Planning, 1993, Post-Imperial English, 1996, In Praise of the Beloved Language, 1997, The Multilinges Apple: Languages in New York City, 1997, Handbook of Language and Ethnic Identity, 1999, Can Threatened Languages Be Saved?, 2000, Llenga i identitat, 2001, Test Construction for Students of the Behavioral and Social Sciences, 2003, Do Not Leave Your Language Alone, 2006, Developing Minority Language Resources, 2006, Along the Paths to Power, 2006, The Sociology of Language and Religion, 2006, Language Loyalty: Continuity and Change, 2006, Language Loyalty, Lange Planning and Language Revitalization, 2006, also numerous profl. publs. including Afn shvel, 1980—, Forverts, 1996—; assoc. editor: Jour. Ednl. Sociology, 1963-65, Yivo Ann., 1970-77, Yidishe Sprakh, 1970—; editor: Yivo Bleter, 1974-77; editor Jour. Social Issues, 1964-69; editor: (series) Contributions to the Sociology of Lang., 1971—, Internat. Jour. Sociology of Lang., 1973—, (series), Contributions to the Sociology of Jewish Languages, 1985-88. Pres.'s scholar E.C. Morris fellow Columbia Tchrs. Coll., 1952-53, postdoctoral rsch. tng. fellow Social Sci. Rsch. Coun., 1954-55, fellow Ctr. Advanced Study Behavioral Scis., 1963-64, Princeton Inst. Advanced Study fellow, 1975-76, fellow Netherlands Inst. Advanced Study, 1982-83, Israel Inst. Advanced Studies, 1983, Nat. Fgn. Lang. Ctr., 1995-96; NSF European Conf. grantee, 1960, Office of Edn. grantee, 1960-63, 66-68, 72-74, 79-80, Social Sci. Rsch. Coun. European Conf. grantee, 1961, NIMH grantee, Latin Am., 1963, 66, NSF grantee, Europe, 1966, 79-83, Ford Found. grantee, 1969-72, 75-76, Meml. Found. Jewish Culture grantee, 1970-71, 78-79, 82-83, Nat. Inst. Edn. grantee, 1978-79, 79-81; sr. specialist Inst. Advanced Projects, East-West Ctr., 1968-69; sr. assoc. Multicultural-Bilingual divsn. Nat. Inst. Edn., 1976-77. Fellow APA, Am. Sociol. Assn., Am. Anthrop. Assn.; mem. AAAS, Am. Ednl. Rsch. Assn., Linguistic Soc. Am., Yivo Inst. Jewish Rsch., Nat. Assn. Bilingual Edn. (Man of Yr. 1992), TESOL, Terralingua. Personal E-mail: joshuaafishman@aol.com. *I have had the incredible good fortune to be exposed simultaneously to modern Western as well as both classical and modern Jewish thought, to secular and religious values, beliefs and ideals, and theoretical and applied emphases, to the comforts of a language of wider communication (English) and a language of ethnic intimacy (Yiddish), to the infinite world of science, the eternal land of my ancestors and the new world of democracy, opportunity and pluralism to which my parents came as immigrants. I have tried to combine all of these forces within myself and to contribute to them. I consider both the tensions and the creativity resulting from these varied stimuli to be a unique heritage: an American-Jewish heritage to be treasured, cultivated, improved and handed on.*

FISHMAN, LEWIS WARREN, lawyer, educator; b. Bklyn., Dec. 19, 1951; BA in Polit. Sci., Syracuse U., 1972; MPA, Maxwell-Syracuse U., 1973; JD, U. Miami, 1976. Bar: Fla. 1976, U.S. Dist. Ct. (so. dist.) Fla. 1977, U.S. Dist. Ct. D.C. 1978, U.S. Ct. Appeals (5th and 11th cirs.) 1981. Assoc. Simons & Fishman P.A. (and predecessor firm), Miami, 1976-80, ptnr., 1980-81; assoc. Wood, Lucksinger & Epstein, Miami, 1981—82; pres. Lewis W. Fishman, P.A., Miami, 1982—. Adj. prof. law Fla. Internat. U., 1981, 83, 84, 91; mem. bd. legal specialization and edn. Fla. Bar, 1999—. Mem. Fla. Acad. Healthcare Attys. (bd. dirs., sec. 1986-88, pres. 1990-92), Nat. Health Lawyers Assn. (lectr. 1983, 88-89), Fla. Hosp. Assn. (lectr. 1983, 88-89), Fla. Hosp. Assn. (lectr.), Fla. Med. Record Assn. (lectr. 1982, 83, 84), Am. Acad. Hosp. Attys. (lectr. 1989, 90, 91), Nat. Health Lawyers Assn., Cath. Health Assn., Fla. Bar Assn. (mem. exec. coun. health law sect. 1988-97, 2006-, chmn. health law sect. 1988-97, chmn. health law sect. 1995-96, cert. health law atty., mem. health law cert. com. 1994-99, vice chmn. 1995-96, chmn. 1996-98, bd. legal specialization and edn. 1999-2005, profl. ethics com. 2005—). Jewish. Home: 14140 SW 104th Ave Miami FL 33176-7064 Office Phone: 305-670-2100. Personal E-mail: lwfpa@aol.com.

FISHMAN, MARK CHARLES, biomedical researcher; married; 2 children. B., Yale U.; MD, Harvard Med. Sch. Prof. medicine Harvard Med. Sch.; chief of cardiology, dir. Cardiovasc. Rsch. Ctr., Mass. Gen. Hosp., Boston; pres., CEO Novartis Inst. BioMed. Rsch., Cambridge, Mass., 2002—. Exec. com. Novartis Inst. BioMed. Rsch., Cambridge, Mass., 2002—; editorial bds. NIH, NAS, Wellcome Trust. Author: (textbooks) Medicine. Fellow: Am. Acad. Arts & Sciences; mem.: Inst. Medicine. Office: Novartis Institute for BioMedical Research 250 Mass Ave Cambridge MA 02139 Office Phone: 617-871-8000.

FISHMAN, MARK I., lawyer; b. NYC, Sept. 25, 1945; AB magna cum laude, Harvard U., 1967, JD, 1970. Bar: Mass. 1970, U.S. Dist. Ct. Mass. 1971, N.Y. 1972, U.S. Dist. Ct. (so. and ea. dists.) N.Y. 1972, U.S. Ct. Appeals (2d cir.) 1972, U.S. Supreme Ct. 1974, U.S. Ct. Appeals (D.C. cir.) 1976, U.S. Dist. Ct. Conn. 1979, Conn. 1980, U.S. Tax Ct. 1981. Law clk. Supreme Jud. Ct. Mass., 1970-71; atty. Sullivan & Cromwell, NY, 1978; mem. Pullman & Comley, Bridgeport, Conn.; ptnr. Pepe & Hazard LLP; prin. Neubert, Pepe & Monteith PC, New Heaven, Conn., 2006—. Mem. adv. com. on article 6 of uniform comml. code Conn. Law Revision Commn. Chmn. profl. divsn. United Way Eastern Fairfield County, 1989; mem. (bd dir.) Jewish Cmty. Found., 2004. Mem. Comml. Law League Am., Conn. Bar Assn. (mem. exec. com. comml. law and bankruptcy sect. 1986—), NY State Bar Assn. (mem. spl. ethics subcom. paralegal assts. 1975-76), Bridgeport Bar Assn., mem. Adv. Com. State Law Revision Commn. Repeal Article 6 Uniform Comml. Code 1990, Assn. Bar NYC, chmn. (com. comml. law) Greater Bridgeport Bar Assn. 1997 — 1998, co-chmn. (bankruptcy com.) Regional Bar Assn. 2002 - 2003. Office: Neubert Pepe & Monteith PC 195 Church St 13th Fl New Haven CT 06510-2009 Office Phone: 203-821-2000. Office Fax: 203-821-2009. Business E-Mail: mfishman@npmlaw.com.

FISHMAN, MARVIN ALLEN, pediatric neurologist, educator; b. Chgo., Feb. 16, 1937; s. Joseph and Mary (Schneider) F.; m. Gloria Brenda Greenberg, Dec. 20, 1959; children: Bradley Steven, Patricia Ann. BS, U. Ill., 1959, MD, 1961. Diplomate Am. Bd. Pediatrics, Am. Psychiatry and Neurology. Intern, then resident in pediat. Michael Reese Hosp. and Med. Center, Chgo., 1961—64; resident in neurology Mass. Gen. Hosp., Boston, 1966—67; fellow in pediat. neurology St. Louis Children's Hosp., 1967—70, dir. Birth Defects Ctr., 1971—79; prof. pediat., neurology and preventive medicine Washington U. Med. Sch., St. Louis, 1970—79, dir. Irene Walter Johnson Inst. Rehab., 1974—79; prof. pediat. and neurology Baylor Coll. Medicine, Houston, 1979—2007, dir. pediat. neurology tng. program, 1979—2004, vice chmn. dept. pediat., 1992—2007; chief neurology svc. Tex. Children's Hosp., Houston, 1979—2004, chief Blue Bird Clinic for Child Neurology, 2003—05. Mem. residency rev. com. for neurology Accreditation Coun. for Grad. Med. Edn., 1991-96, chmn., 1995-96; bd. dirs. Am. Bd. Psychiatry and Neurology, 1991-97, exec. com., 1995-97, v.p., 1996, pres., 1997, cons., 1999-05; cons. Am. Bd. Pediat., 1999-05. Contbr. articles in field, chpts. in books; mem. editl. bd. Jour. Pediat., 1980-87; Jour. Child Neurology, Pediat. Neurology, Annals of Neurology; editor textbook. With USAR, 1964-66. Grantee HEW, Grant Found., Ga. Warm Springs Found., Nat. Found.-March of Dimes. Mem. Am. Soc. Neurochemistry (councilor 1977-79), Child Neurology Soc. (exec. com., councillor 1980-82, sec.-treas. 1984-86, pres.-elect 1986-87, pres. 1987-89, past pres. 1989-90, John B. Hower award 1999), Houston Neurol. Soc. (pres.-elect 1989-90, pres. 1990-91), Am. Acad. Pediat., Am. Acad. Neurology, Am. Neurol. Assn., Am. Pediat. Soc., Soc. Pediat. Rsch., Soc. Neuroscis. Home: 1523-B Potomac Dr Houston TX 77057-1925 Personal E-mail: mfishman@bcm.tmc.edu.

FISHMAN, MITCHELL STEVEN, lawyer; b. NYC, July 27, 1948; s. Abraham and Sylvia (Sher) F.; m. Alison Rivard, Sept. 7, 1980 (div.) children: Danielle, Matthew, Jeremy; m. Mary Ellen Spiegel, Sept. 21, 2003. BA cum laude, Harvard U., 1970; JD cum laude, Harvard Law Sch., 1973; LLM in Taxation, NYU Law Sch., 2005. Bar: N.Y. 1974, D.C. 1984, Conn. 2006. Assoc. Breed, Abbott & Morgan, NYC, 1973-74, Paul, Weiss, Rifkind, Wharton & Garrison, NYC, 1975-81; ptnr., 1981-99. Exec. dir. Temp. State Commn. on Banking, Ins. and Fin. Svcs., N.Y., 1983-84; cons. Sirius Satellite Radio, Inc., N.Y.C., 2000-01. Mem. ABA, N.Y. State Bar Assn., Assn. of Bar of City of N.Y. (com. on corp. law 1976-79, mem. com. on securities regulation 1998-01), Conn. Bar Assn. Democrat. Home and Office: 18 Osborn Ln PO Box 1879 Litchfield CT 06759 Office Phone: 860-567-2461. Business E-Mail: fishmanlegal@aol.com.

FISHMAN, RICHARD GLENN, lawyer, accountant; b. Orange, NJ, June 2, 1952; s. Irving and Eleanor (Tanenbaum) F.; m. Jean Goldhammer, Aug. 11, 1974; children: Neil Samuel, Peter Lawrence, Ellen Melissa BA in Econs. highest honors and highest distinction, Rutgers U., 1974; JD, Yale U., 1977; LLM in Taxation, NYU, 1980. Bar: NY 1978, NJ 1978, US Dist. Ct. NJ 1978, US Ct. Claims 1978, US Tax Ct. 1978, US Dist. Ct. (so. dist.) NY 1979, US Ct. Appeals (3d cir.) 1994. Assoc. Stroock & Stroock & Lavan, NYC, 1977—80, Roberts & Holland, NYC, 1980—85; tax mgr. Spicer & Oppenheim (formerly Oppenheim, Appel, Dixon & Co.), NYC, 1985—87, ptnr., 1987—88; from sr. tax. counsel to assoc. gen. tax counsel AlliedSignal Inc., Morristown, NJ, 1988—97, assoc. gen. tax counsel, 1997—99; dir. tax planning for bus. units, assoc. gen. tax counsel Honeywell Internat., Inc., Morristown, 1999—2001, dir. internat. & bus. tax planning, 2001—06, assoc. gen. tax counsel, 2001—06; tax dir., chief tax counsel Albermarle Corp., Baton Rouge, 2006—. Contbr. articles to profl. jours Mem. ABA, AICPA, NY State Bar Assn., NJ State Bar Assn Home: 6 Tilden Ct Livingston NJ 07039-2419 Office: Albemarle Corp 451 Florida St Baton Rouge LA 70801 Business E-Mail: richard.fishman@albemarle.com.

FISHMAN, ROBERT A., lawyer; b. Malden, Mass., Apr. 23, 1948; BA magna cum laude, Harvard U., 1970, JD cum laude, 1973. Bar: Mass. 1973. Mem. Nutter, McClennen & Fish, Boston, ptnr. Instr. law sch. Boston Coll., 1980-83; chaired NAIOP's Pub. Affairs Com., co chaired Growth Mgmt. Task Force. Contbg. author: Massachusetts Conveyancers Handbook, 3d edit., 1984, contbr. articles to profl. journs. Recipient NAIOP Pub. Affairs award, Am.'s Leading Bus. Lawyers, Chambers USA, Mass. Super Lawyer, Law & Politics and Boston mag., Internat. Who's Who of Real Estate Lawyers, Best Lawyers in Am., 18 Nutter partners, 2007. Mem. ABA, Mass. Bar Assn., Boston Bar Assn., Phi Beta Kappa, Nat. Assn. Indsl. and Office Properties (Mass. chapter). Office: Nutter McClennen & Fish 155 Seaport Blvd World Trade Center W Boston MA 02210 Office Phone: 617-439-2204. Office Fax: 617-310-9204. Business E-Mail: rfishman@nutter.com.

FISHMAN, ROBERT ALLEN, retired neurologist, educator, department chair; b. NYC, May 30, 1924; s. Samuel Benjamin and Miriam (Brinkin) F.; m. Margery Ann Satz, Jan. 29, 1956 (dec. May 29, 1980); children: Mary Beth, Alice Ellen, Elizabeth Ann.; m. Mary Craig Wilson, Jan. 7, 1983. AB, Columbia U., 1944; MD, U. Pa., 1947. Mem. faculty Columbia Coll. Physicians and Surgeons, 1954-66, asso. prof. neurology, 1962-66;

asst. attending neurologist N.Y. State Psychiat. Inst., 1955-66, Neurol. Inst. Presbyn. Hosp., NYC, 1955-61, asso., 1961-66; co-dir. Neurol. Clin. Research Center, Neurol. Inst., Columbia-Presbyn. Med. Ctr., 1961-66; prof. neurology U. Calif. Med. Ctr., San Francisco, 1966-94, chmn. dept. neurology, 1966-92, prof. emeritus, 1994—; ret., 2005. Cons. neurologist San Francisco Gen. Hosp., San Francisco VA Hosp., Letterman Gen. Hosp.; dir. Am. Bd. Psychiatry and Neurology, 1981-88, v.p., 1986, pres., 1987 Author: Cerebrospinal Fluid in Diseases of the Nervous System, 1992; chief editor Annals of Neurology, 1993-97; contbr. articles to profl. jours. Nat. Multiple Sclerosis Soc. fellow, 1956-57; John and Mary R. Markle scholar in med. sci., 1960-65; recipient Disting. Alumnus award U. Pa. 1996. Mem. Am. Neurol. Assn. (pres. 1983-84), Am. Fedn. for Clin. Research, Assn. for Research in Nervous and Mental Diseases, Am. Acad. Neurology (v.p. 1971-73, pres. 1975-77), Am. Assn. Physicians, Am. Soc. for Neurochemistry, Soc. for Neurosci., N.Y. Neurol. Soc., Am. Assn. Univ. Profs. Neurology (pres. 1972-73), AAAS, Am. Epilepsy Soc., N.Y. Acad. Scis., AMA (sec. sect. on nervous and mental diseases 1964-67, v.p. 1967-68, pres. 1968-69), Alpha Omega Alpha (hon. faculty mem.), NAS Insts. Medicine. Home: 205 Paradise Dr Belvedere Tiburon CA 94920-2534 Personal E-mail: raf530@comcast.net.

FISHMAN, STEVEN S., retail executive; BA, Columbia Coll. Sr. v.p., gen. mdse. mgr. Caldor Inc., 1988—93; chmn., pres., CEO Pamida Inc., 1993—99; founder, pres. SSF Resources, Omaha, 1999—; chmn., CEO Frank's Nursery & Crafts Inc., 2001—02; pres., CEO, chief restructuring officer Rhodes Inc., 2004—05; chmn., pres., CEO Big Lots Inc., Columbus, Ohio, 2005—. Bd. dir. Internat. Mass Retail Assn. Office: Big Lots Inc 300 Phillipi Rd Columbus OH 43228-5311*

FISHMAN, STEVEN T., psychologist; b. St. Louis, Sept. 19, 1941; s. Paul Leon and Frances Fishman; m. Cheryl Dee Sheinberg, Nov. 23, 1972; 1 child, Stephanie Carie. BA, Washington U., 1963; MA, PhD, U. Mo., 1970. Cert. behavioral psychology Am. Bd. Profl. Psychology, 1987, clin. psychology Am. Bd. Profl. Psychology, 1985. Intern VA, Palo Alto, Calif., 1967—68, Stanford U., Palo Alto, 1967—68; postdoctoral fellow SUNY, Stony Brook, 1970—71; founder and dir. Inst. For Behavior Therapy, NYC, 1971—. Vis. clin. faculty Columbia U., NYC, 1971—72; vis. assoc. prof. Grad. Sch. Applied Profl. Psychology, Rutgers U., New Brunswick, NJ, 1975—85; adj. grad. faculty Yeshiva U., NYC, 1983—, Hofstra U., Hempstead, NY, 1989—2000. Author: (audiotape series) Agoraphobia:multiform Behavioral Treatment; contbr. chapters to books, articles to profl. jours. Mem. Mental Health Commn., Rockland County, NY, 1983—89. Fellow clin. psychology, USPHS, 1968—69. Mem.: APA (com. mem.), Assn. for the Advancement of Behavior Therapy (chairperson numerous coms. 1971—2005, Outstanding Svc. award 2002), Behavior Soc. N.Y. (pres. 1975—80), Am. Acad. Behavioral Psychology (pres. 1998—2001), Am. Bd. Behavioral Psychology (dir., sec./treas. 1985—2001). Office: Institute For Behavior Therpay Ste 206 104 East 40th St New York NY 10016 Home Phone: 845-371-8355; Office Phone: 212-692-9288. Office Fax: 212-692-9305. Personal E-mail: sfishman@ifbt.com.

FISHWICK, JOHN PALMER, retired lawyer, railroad executive; b. Roanoke, Va., Sept. 29, 1916; s. William and Nellie (Cross) F.; m. Blair Wiley, Jan. 4, 1941 (dec. June 1987); children: Ellen Blair (Mrs. Guyman Martin III), Anne Palmer (Mrs. Wesley Posvar), John Palmer Jr.; m. Doreen Allton, Nov. 17, 1989. AB, Roanoke Coll., 1937, DHL (hon.), 1971; LL.B., Harvard U., 1940; DL (hon.), Washington & Lee Univ., 2000. Bar: Va. 1939. Assoc. Cravath, Swaine & Moore, NYC, 1940-42; asst. to gen. solicitor N. & W. Ry., Roanoke, Va., 1945-47, asst. gen. solicitor, 1947-51, asst. gen. counsel, 1951-54, gen. solicitor, 1954-56, gen. counsel, 1956-58, v.p., gen. counsel, 1958-59, v.p. law, 1959-63, sr. v.p., 1963-70, pres., chief exec. officer, 1970-80, chmn., chief exec. officer, 1980-81, also dir.; ptnr. Windels, Marx, Davies & Ives, NYC, 1981-84; of counsel Fishwick, Jones and Glenn, Roanoke, Va., 1984-95; ret. Chmn., chief exec. officer Erie Lackawanna Ry. Co., 1968-70; pres., chief exec. officer Del. and Hudson Ry. Co., 1968-70; pres., dir. Dereco, Inc., 1968-81; chmn. investment com., bd. dirs. Norfolk So. Corp., 1981-89. Trustee Roanoke Coll., 1964-72; trustee Va. Theol. Sem.; former chancellor Diocese S.W. Va.; former bd. dirs. Va. Found. Humanities; former trustee Va. Mus. Fine Arts, Richmond. Served as lt. comdr. USNR, 1942—45. Mem. Met. Club (Washington). Episcopalian. Office: 110 Franklin Rd SE Roanoke VA 24042-0002 Personal E-mail: fish87@cox.net.

FISK, CATHERINE LAURA, lawyer, educator; m. Erwin Chemerinsky. AB summa cum laude, Princeton Univ., 1983; JD, Univ. Calif., Berkeley, 1986; LLM, Univ. Wis., Madison, 1995. Bar: Calif. 1986, D.C. 1988. Staff atty. U.S. Ct. Appeals 9th cir., San Francisco, 1986—87, law clerk, 1987—88; assoc. Rogovin Huge & Schiller, Washington, 1988—90; atty. Appellate Staff, Civil Div., U.S. Dept. of Just., Washington, 1990—91; lectr. Univ. Wis. Law Sch., Madison, 1991; assoc. prof. Loyola Marymount Univ., 1992—96, prof., 1996—2003; vis. prof. Univ. Calif., Los Angeles, 1997—2002, Duke Univ., 2002; prof. Univ. Calif., Los Angeles, 2003—04, Duke Univ., 2004—. Contbr. articles prof. law jour. Vice-chair spec. comm. Investigative Oversight, City of Los Angeles, 1998; bd. dir. ACLU So. Calif., 1996—2004, exec. comm., 1998—2000, 2003—04, v.p., 2000—04; mem. nat. comm. commercial speech ACLU, 2003—; chair Willard Hurst Prize comm., Law & Society Assn., 2003—04. Recipient Pro Bono Svc. award, ACLU So. Calif., 2004, Distinguished Law Prof., 2003, Excellence in Education award, Indsl. Relations Rsch. Assn., 2000. Mem.: Am. Soc. Legal Hist. (mem. comm. membership 1997—99), Labor Law Group. Office: Duke Univ Sch Law Sci Dr & Towerview Rd Durham NC 27708-0360

FISK, CHARLES JOHN, meteorologist, researcher, consultant; s. Everett Vincent Fisk and Florence Linnea Carlson. BSBA, U. Minn., 1968; MS in Meteorology, U. Wis., 1984; MBA, Mankato State U., 1973. Meteorologist/climatologist Naval Base Ventura County, Point Mugu, Calif., 1986—; fin. analyst IBM Corp., Rochester, 1974—79. Cons. long-range forecasting of so. Calif. temperatures and precipitation, 1996—2000. Author: The First Fifty Years of Continuous Recorded Weather History In Minnesota (1820-1869) - A Narrative Chronology; contbr. articles to profl. jours.; author procs. Pvt. US Army, 1968—69. Mem.: Am. Statis. Assn., Am. Meteorol. Soc. Avocations: reading, travel, web publishing. Home: 590 Gilbert St Newbury Park CA 91320 Personal E-mail: cjfisk@worldnet.att.net.

FISK, DORIS ROSALIE SCANLAN, volunteer; b. Mpls., Aug. 20, 1915; d. Arthur William and Lea Marie (Beauchaine) Scanlan; m. Ellsworth William Fisk, Aug. 31, 1942; children: Gregory, Janine, Marilyn, Kathleen. Student, Mpls. Bus. Coll., 1935, U. Minn., 1940, San Antonio Jr. Coll., 1964. Hosp. vol. ARC, 1940-71; vol. Audie Murphy Vets. Hosp., 1972—; med. transcriber Radiology Assocs., San Antonio, 1962-64; nurse office mgr. for surgeon San Antonio, 1964-77; vol. Sr. Svc. Orgn., San Antonio, 1970—; vol., fund raiser Vis. Nurse Assn. S.W. San Antonio, 1992-97; vol. Quantum Brookhollow Med. Ctr., 1999—. Sec. vol. Demo-Ne Demos, San Antonio, 1960-64; pres. YWCA Wives, San Antonio, 1964-65, Espada Mission Aux., San Antonio, 1965-66; chair March of Dimes, San Antonio, ARC, 1940-1971, chmn. of vols.; vol. usher and seamstress Harlequin Theatre, from 1971; treas. altar soc. St. Mary's Cath.Ch., 1984-92; pres. flu shot prog. VNA, vol. Brookhollow Libr., 1995-96; chmn. Brooke Gen. Hosp. Vols. Recipient Golden Globe award Vol. Vis. Nurse of the Yr., San Antonio, 1993, Gold Key ring J.C. Penney; Letter of Congratulation, Pres. Clinton. Mem. AAUW, La Societé Francaise Canadian, Ret. Sr. Vols. (bd. mem. 1970—), Officers Wives Club (tour guide 1996-97, tel. chairperson 1999-2000, 2000-2001), Smithsonian Instn., Williamsburg, Met. Mus., Beta Sigma Phi (life), Kappa Kappa Gamma. Democrat. Roman Catholic. Avocations: travel, reading, sewing. Home: 109 Timaaron Ct Weatherford TX 76085-3025

FISK, EDWARD RAY, retired civil and structural engineer, author, educator; b. Oshkosh, Wis., July 19, 1924; s. Ray Edward and Grace O. (Meyer) Barnes; married, Oct. 28, 1950; children: Jacqueline Mary, Edward Ray II, William John, Robert Paul. BCE, Marquette U., Milw., 1949; student, Fresno State Coll., Calif., 1954, UCLA, 1957-58. Registered profl. engr., Ariz., Calif., Colo., Fla., Idaho, Ky., La., Mont., Nev., Oreg., Utah, Wash., Wyo.; lic. land surveyor, oreg., Idaho; lic. gen. engring. contractor, Calif.; cert. arbitrator Calif. Constrn. Contract Arbitration Com. Engr. Calif. Div. Hwys., 1952-55, Bechtel Corp., Vernon, Calif., 1955-59; project mgr. Toups Engring. Co., Santa Ana, Calif., 1959-61; dept. head Perliter & Soring, Los Angeles, 1961-64; Western rep. Wire Reinforcement Inst., Washington, 1964-65; cons. engr. Anaheim, Calif., 1965; assoc. engr. Met. Water Dist. So. Calif., 1966-68; chief specification engr. Koebig & Koebig, Inc., Los Angeles, 1968-71; mgr. constrn. svcs. VTN Consol., Inc., Irvine, Calif., 1971-78; pres. E.R. Fisk Constrn., Orange, Calif., 1978-81; corp. dir. constrn. mgmt. James M. Montgomery Cons. Engrs., Inc., Pasadena, Calif., 1981-83; v.p. Lawrance, Fisk & McFarland, Inc., Santa Barbara and Orange, 1983—; pres. E.R. Fisk & Assocs., Orange, 1983—, Gleason, Peacock & Fisk, Inc., 1987-92. V.p. constrn. svcs. Wilsey & Hamm, Foster City, Calif., 1993-94; adj. prof. engring., constrn. Calif. State U., Long Beach, 1987-90, Orange Coast Coll., Costa Mesa, Calif., 1957-78; instr. U. Calif., Berkeley, Inst. Transportation Studies, 1978—, engring. prof. programs U. Wash., 1994—2003, internationally for ASCE Continuing Edn. Author: Machine Methods of Survey Computing, 1958, Construction Project Administration, 1978, 8th edit., 2006, Construction Engineers Complete Handbook of Forms, 1981, 2d edit., 92, Resident Engineers Field Manual, 1992; co-author: Contractor's Project Guide, 1988, Contracts and Specifications for Public Works Projects, 1992, Introduction to Engineering Construction Inspection, 2004. With USN, 1942-43, res. USAFR, 1951-52. Fellow ASCE (life, past chmn. exec. com. constrn. divn., past chmn. nat. com. inspection 1978—), Nat. Acad. Forensic Engrs.; mem. Calif. Soc. Profl. Engrs. (past pres. Orange County), Structural Engrs. Assn. Calif. (engrs. joint contracts documents com. 1993-95), US Com. Large Dams, Order Founders and Patriots Am. (past gov. Calif.), Soc. Colonial Wars (dep. gov. gen. Calif. chpt.), S.R. (past dir.), Engring. Edn. Found. (trustee), Tau Beta Pi. Office Phone: 714-321-7200. Personal E-mail: efisk@ca.rr.com.

FISK, HAYWARD DAN, lawyer, computer services company executive; b. Las Vegas, Nev., Mar. 5, 1943; BS, U. Kans., Lawrence, 1965, JD, 1968; LLM, U. Mo., Columbia, 1971. Bar: Kans. 1968, Pa. 1972, DC 1986, US Dist. Ct. (dist. Kans.) 1968, US Ct. Appeals (5th cir.) 1970, US Supreme Ct. 1971. V.p., gen. counsel, sec. United Tel. Sys. Ea. Group, Carlisle, Pa., 1971—82; v.p., Washington counsel Sprint Corp., Washington, 1982—88, v.p., assoc. gen. counsel Kansas City, 1988—89; v.p., gen. counsel, sec. Computer Scis. Corp., El Segundo, Calif., 1989—. Bd. dirs. Atlantic Legal Found., 1971—, chmn., 1997—; legal adv. bd. Nat. Legal Ctr. for Pub. Interest, 1991—; editl. bd. The Computer and Internet Lawyer, 1989—; Common Carrier and Emergency Preparedness Adv. Com. FCC, 1985—; Govt. and Regulatory Affairs Com. US C. of C., 1985—. Mem.: Calif. Bar Assn., Am. Soc. Corp. Secs. (bd. dirs.), Am. Corp. Counsel Assn. (bd. dirs., pres. So. Calif. Chpt. 1999, Excellence in Corp. Practice Award 2000), DC Bar, Pa. Bar Assn., Kans. Bar Assn., ABA. Office: Computer Scis Corp 2100 E Grand Ave El Segundo CA 90245-5024

FISK, IRWIN WESLEY, financial investigator; b. Byers, Kans., Nov. 20, 1938; s. Walter Roleigh Fisk and Mae Pearle Irwin; m. Susie Bea Walters, Sept. 9, 1973; children: Mark Christopher, Paul Steven. Student, LA City Coll., 1958—60, Calif. State U., LA, 1960—64, Pasadena C.C., 1987—88. Lic. pvt. investigator, Calif. Asst. exec. dir. Stores Protective Assn., LA, 1962-66; sr. spl. investigator Calif. Dept. Corps., LA, 1966-83, chief investigator, 1983-94; pres. Bus. and Fin. Investigations, Inc., La Crescenta, 1994—. Mem. Multi-State Law Enforcement Task Force of Fraudulent Telemarketing, LA, 1987—94, Nat. Coun. Policy Advisors, 1994—; mem. nat. coun. of policy advisors Inst. for Law and Econ. Policy, 1994—; mem. criminal justice adv. bd. Bethany Coll., 2002—. Contbr. articles to profl. publs. (Cramer journalism award 2004). Bd. dirs., v.p. Anatoly Karpov Internat. Sch. Chess. Recipient Cramer Journalism award, 2004. Mem. U.S. Chess Fedn. (life), Am. Radio Relay League (DXCC award 1993, Cramer Journalism award 2004), Authors Guild, So. Calif. Fraud Investigators Assn., Masons, Nat. Coun. Policy Adv. for Inst. Law and Econ. Policy, 1994-2004, Criminal Justice Adv. Bd. Bethany Coll., 2002-, Internat. Chess Inst. Midwest (bd. dirs., 2006—). Republican. Avocations: chess, amateur radio. Home: 701 Emerald Dr Lindsborg KS 67456-2004 Home Phone: 785-227-4121. Personal E-mail: iwfisk@yahoo.com.

FISK, JEAN BAUDER, music educator, director; d. Arthur Bauder and Ruth Warrington-Bauder; m. Elmer R. Fisk, Oct. 2, 1970; children: Marilyn Jean Fisk-Romero, Barry Jay. MusB in Performance with Edn., Ea. N.Mex U., Portales, 1961—63; post-grad. in choral conducting, Royal Coll. Music, London, 1986—86; attended, Stanford U., Palo Alto, Calif., 1988—89. Cert. tchr. Calif., 1969. Music tchr. Clovis Sch. Dist., N.Mex., 1963—64, Dumas Sch. Dist., Tex., 1964—65, Fallon Sch. Dist., Nev., 1966—68; music, classroom & gifted tchr. Richmond Unified Sch. Dist., Calif., 1969—96; music dir., organist Pinole United Meth. Ch., Calif., 1969—. Gifted seminar tchr. Richmond Unified Sch. Dist., 1996—2000. Composer: (choral, organ & handbell compositions) various; watercolors, various; composer: (handbells & choir) The Last Seven Words. Mem. Edn. Adv. Com., Contra Costa County, Calif., 1995—96; scholarship com. chairperson Fellowship United Meth. Music & Worship Arts, national, 1995—98, we. jurisdiction rep., 2001—05, co-convenor Calif., Nev. chpt. Calif., 1992—2000; founder Organ Scholars' Program for young organ scholars, 1991—. Recipient PTA Founders' Day award of yr., Parent Tchr. Assn., 1982, Richmond Unified Sch. Dist. Tchr. of Yr. award, Richmond Unified Sch. Dist., 1984, Youth Svc. award recipient, Pinole Rotary, 1997. Mem.: Am. Guild Organists (bd. mem.-at-large 2006), Pinole Artisans (bd. mem. 2005—06), Exchangettes Svc. Club (pres. 1975—77), Alpha Delta Kappa. Home Phone: 510-724-2563.

FISK, MARTIN H., lawyer; b. St. Paul, Apr. 11, 1947; BA, U. Minn., 1969; JD, Harvard U., 1976. Bar: Minn. 1976. Mem. Briggs and Morgan P.A., St. Paul, shareholder. Recipient Best Lawyers in Am., 2006. Mem. ABA, Phi Beta Kappa. Office: Briggs and Morgan PA 332 Minnesota St W 2200 1st Nat Bank Bldg Saint Paul MN 55101-3210 Office Phone: 651-808-6522. Office Fax: 651-808-6450. Business E-Mail: mfisk@briggs.com.

FISK, SCOTT, graphics designer, educator; b. Monmouth, Ill., Aug. 27, 1974; s. Fisk Gary and Fisk Rhonda; m. Fisk Timarie, Dec. 28, 2003. MFA, Memphis Coll. Art, 2001. Art dir. Elitevideo, Hot Springs, Ark., 1997—2003; asst. prof. graphic design Samford U., Birmingham, Ala., 2001—. Photojournalist Army Reserves, Birmingham, 2001—06. Ednl. chair Birmingham Am. Inst. Graphic Arts, 2002—06. Decorated Bronze Star US Army. Mem.: Am. Inst. Graphic Arts (assoc.; bd. mem. 2002—06). Home Phone: 205-533-6063; Office Phone: 205-726-2193.

FISKE, EDWARD B., editor, educator, journalist, consultant; b. Phila., June 4, 1937; s. Edward R., Jr. and Jean B.; m. Dale Alden Woodruff, July 12, 1963 (div. May 1997); children: Julia F. Hogan, Suzanna F. Wilson; m. Helen F. Ladd, June 29, 1997. BA, Wesleyan U., Middletown, Conn., 1959; MA, Princeton Theol. Sem., 1963, Columbia U., 1965; LL.D. (hon.), Occidental Coll., 1991; and others. Religion reporter and editor N.Y. Times, 1964-74, edn. editor, 1974-91. Cons. Pew Forum on Edn. Reform, 1991-92, Bus. Roundtable Edn. Initiative, 1991-92, Dana Found., 1992-99, UNICEF Edn. Mission to Bangladesh, 1993, Internat. Rescue Com. in Cambodia, 1993-94, Acad. Ednl. Devel., 1993—, World Bank, 1995—, UNESCO, 1996—, USAID, 2003-; edn. analyst Asian Devel. Bank, 1994; vis. scholar Victoria U. Wellington, New Zealand, 1998, U. Cape Town, South Africa, 2002. Author: Fiske Guide to Colleges, (annual) Smart Schools, Smart Kids, 1990, (with Bruce Hammond) Fiske Guide to Getting into The Right College, 1997, 3d edit., 2005, (with Hammond) When Schools Compete, 2000, (with Helen Ladd) Fiske What to Do When for College, 2004, (with Hammond) Fiske Nailing the New SAT, 2005, (with Ladd) Elusive Equity: Education Reform in Post-Apartheid South Africa, 2004; contbr. articles to nat. periodicals. Trustee Found. for Excellent Schs., 2000—, chair NC Ctr. Internat. Understanding, 2001—, Central Park Sch. Children, Durham, 2002—. Wolynsky-Joukowsky fellow Brown U., 1990, Montgomery fellow Dartmouth Coll., 1991. Mem.: Phi Beta Kappa. Home: 1723 Tisdale St Durham NC 27705-5631 Personal E-mail: efiske@aol.com.

FISKE, JANET MURRAY, volunteer, elementary school educator, researcher; b. Cedar Rapids, Iowa, Nov. 23, 1912; d. Frederick Gray and Janette (Stevenson) Murray; m. John Codman Fiske, Sept. 14, 1940 (dec.); children: Lindsay Fiske Hoemag, Jonathan, Anne Fiske Long, Fred. BA, Coe Coll., 1934; diploma, Athens, Greece, 1937; MA, Columbia U., 1941. Cert. tchr. Iowa. Vol. tchr. US Fgn. Svc., East Pakistan, 1957—59, Heidelberg, Germany, 1960—63, Kinshasa, Congo, 1965—68, Reykjavik, Iceland, 1968—70; substitute tchr. Washington; ret. Co-author 2 books. Vol. Moscow Preservation Comm., 1988—2006, Palouse Path Commn., 1989—; precinct worker Dem. Party, Moscow, Idaho, 1970—. Recipient Human Rights award, city of Moscow. Mem.: LWV (editor newsletter), Delta Delta Delta. Avocations: birdwatching, walking, writing. Home: 910 E B St Moscow ID 83843

FISKE, NEIL S., retail executive; b. Colo. Degree in Polit. Economy, Williams Coll.; MBA, Harvard U. Polit. speechwriter; bus. cons. Boston Consulting Group, 1989—99, mng. ptnr., 2000—02; CEO Bath & Body Works, Reynoldsburg, Ohio, 2003—07; pres., CEO Eddie Bauer Holdings, Inc., Redmond, Wash., 2007—, bd. dir., 2007—. Co-author (with Michael Silverstein): Trading Up: The New American Luxury, 2003. Past legis. adv. Congressman and Senator Timothy E. Wirth. Office: Eddie Bauer Holdings Inc 15010 NE 36th St Redmond WA 98052*

FISKE, ROBERT BISHOP, JR., lawyer, former prosecutor; b. NYC, Dec. 28, 1930; s. Robert Bishop and Lenore (Seymour) F.; m. Janet Tinsley, Aug. 21, 1954; children: Linda Goucher, Robert Bishop, Susan Williams. BA, Yale U., 1952; JD, U. Mich., 1955, LLD (hon.), 1997, Vt. Law Sch., 2005. Bar: Mich. 1955, NY 1956, US Ct. Appeals (2nd cir.) 1957, US Supreme Ct. 1961. Assoc. Davis, Polk, Wardwell, Sunderland & Kiendl, NYC, 1955-57; asst. US atty. (so. dist.) NY US Dept. Justice, NYC, 1957-61; assoc. Davis Polk & Wardwell, NYC, 1961-64, ptnr., 1964—; US atty. (so. dist.) NY US Dept. Justice, NYC, 1976-80; ind. counsel for Whitewater Investigation Little Rock, 1994. Chmn. NY State Jud. Commn. on Drugs and the Cts., 1999—2000; mem. Commn. for the Rev. of FBI Security Programs, 2001—02. Fellow Am. Coll. Trial Lawyers (pres. 1991-92), Am. Acad. Appellate Lawyers; mem. ABA (chmn. standing com. on fed. judiciary 1984-87), Assn. of Bar of City of NY, Fed. Bar Coun. (pres. 1982-84), NY State Bar Assn., Noroton Yacht Club, Wee Burn Country Club. Republican. Congregationalist. Office: Davis Polk & Wardwell 450 Lexington Ave New York NY 10017-3911 Office Phone: 212-450-4090.

FISS, OWEN M., law educator; b. 1938; BA, Dartmouth Coll., 1959; BPhil, Oxford U., 1961; LLB, Harvard U., 1964. Bar: N.Y. 1965. Law clk. to Judge Thurgood Marshall US Ct. Appeals 2d Cir., 1964—65; law clk. to Justice Brennan US Supreme Ct., 1965; spl. asst. atty. gen. civil rights divsn. US Dept. Justice, Washington, 1966—67; acting dir. Office of Planning Coordination, 1968; prof. U. Chgo. Law Sch., 1968—74, Yale Law Sch., New Haven, 1974—84, Alexander M. Bickel prof. pub. law, 1984—92, Sterling prof., 1992—. Vis. prof. Stanford U., 1973; mem. Harvard Law Rev. Author: Injunctions, 1972, The Civil Rights Injunction, 1978; author: (with R.M. Cover) The Structure of Procedure, 1979; author: (with D. Rendleman) Injunctions, 2d edit., 1984; author: (with Cover and J. Resnik) Procedure, 1988, The Fed. Procedural Sys., 1988, The Fed. Procedural Sys. 3d edit., 1991, Holmes Devise Hist. of the Supreme Ct.: Troubled Beginnings of the Modern State, 1888-1910, 1993, Liberalism Divided, 1996, The Irony of Free Speech, 1996, The Law As It Could Be, 2003, A Community of Equals, 1999, A Way Out, 2003; author: (with J. Resnik) Adjudication and Its Alternatives, 2003; mem. edtl. bd.: Philosophy and Pub. Affairs and Found. Press, Yale Jour. Criticism, Yale Jour. Law and Humanities, Law, Econs. and Orgns. Mem.: Am. Acad. Arts and Scis. Office: Yale Law Sch PO Box 208215 New Haven CT 06520 Office Phone: 203-432-4963. E-mail: owen.fiss@yale.edu.

FISTER, BARBARA RUTH, librarian, educator, writer; b. Madison, Wis., 1954; d. Bruce Hutchinson and Rosemary Nist Westley; m. William T. Fister, 1975; children: Timothy, Rosemary. BA, U. Ky., Lexington, 1976; MLIS, U. Tex., Austin, 1981. Prof., acad. libr. Gustavus Adolphus Coll., St. Peter, Minn., 1987—. Author: (book) Third World Women Writers: A Dictionary and Guide to Materials in English, 1995, (novels) On Edge, 2002; contbr. articles to profl. jours. Office: Gustavus Adolphus Coll 800 W College Ave Saint Peter MN 56082 Office Phone: 507-933-7553. Business E-Mail: fister@gustavus.edu.

FISTER, MICHAEL J., computer company executive; b. Savannah, Ga. m. Teresa Fister; children: Allison, Sarah. BSEE, U. Cin., 1977, MSEE, 1978. Various exec. and engring. mgmt. positions Wyse Tech., Machine Vision Internat., Cin. Milacron; ops. mgr. 8-bit focus group Intel Corp., Chandler, Ariz., 1987—88, engring. mgr. application-specific integrated circuit group, 1988—90, mgr. microcomputer engring. group, 1990—91, gen. mgr. end user components divsn., 1991—95, gen. mgr. microprocessor divsn., 1995—99, v.p., 1996—2000, gen. mgr. enterprise server group, 1999—2000, gen. mgr. enterprise platform group, 2000—04, corp. v.p., 2000—02, sr. v.p., 2002—04; pres., CEO Cadence Design Systems, Inc., San Jose, Calif., 2004—, also bd. dirs. Bd. dirs. Autodesk Corp., San Rafael, Calif. Office: Cadence Design Systems Inc 2655 Seely Ave San Jose CA 95134

FISZEL, GEOFFREY LYNN, investment banker, investment advisor; b. NYC, Aug. 9, 1942; s. John Henry and Rebecca (Wexman) F.; m. Barbara Ann Foohey, Jan. 30, 1970; children: Sharon Lynn, Morgan Bernard, Austin Tyler, Alexander William. BS in Mgmt. and Ops. Rsch., NYU, 1974; MS in Acctg. and Tax (Seminar award), U. Hartford, 1976; grad. scholar program econs. of fin., Trinity Coll., 1980. Registered securities rep., gen. securities prin., investment adviser. Cost acct. O'Malley Cos., Phoenix, 1974; regional acct., asst. regional contr. Sanitas Svc. Corp., Hartford, Conn., 1974-75; asst. to corp. contr. Bristol Brass Corp., Conn., 1975-76; asst. contr. Security Ins. Co. of Hartford, 1976-80; contr. Chase Enterprises, 1980-81, v.p., contr., 1981, sr. v.p., contr., 1985, sr. v.p. corp. and real estate devel., banking, ins., telecom., and mergers and acquisitions, 1988-89; CEO, pres., chmn. Equity Investors Holding Co., Glastonbury, Conn., 1989—; v.p. investments Advest, Inc., Hartford, 1993-94, Tucker Anthony, Inc., Hartford, 1994-2000, first v.p. investments, 2000—01; v.p., fin. advisor Morgan Stanley, Hartford, 2001—. Tax and fin. cons. U. Conn.; lectr., cons. in field. Author: How to Start Your Own Private Investment Partnership, 1997; pub., author investment adv. newsletter Continuing Walks On The Wild Side. Mem. Juvenile Diabetes Found. Served with

USMC, 1959-63. Mem. Real Estate Bd. N.Y., Fin. Execs. Inst. (mem. corp. fin. and taxation coms.), The Nature Conservancy. Home: 245 Farmcliff Dr PO Box 578 Glastonbury CT 06033-0578 Office: Morgan Stanley One City Pl Hartford CT 06103 Office Phone: 860-275-6592. Personal E-mail: geoffrey_fiszel@msn.com.

FISZER-SZAFARZ, BERTA (BERTA SAFARS), research scientist; b. Feb. 1, 1928; m. David Safars; children: Martine, Michel. MS, U. Buenos Aires, 1955, PhD, 1956. Lab. chief Cancer Inst. Villejuif, France, 1961—67; vis. scientist Nat. Cancer Inst., Bethesda, Md., 1967—68; lab. chief Institut Curie, Orsay, France, 1969—93. Vis. scientist Ins. Applied Biochemistry, Mitake, Gifu, Japan, 1986; gen. sec. dep. French-Israel Assn. Sci. Rsch. and Tech., 1994. Contbr. articles to profl. jours. Mem.: French Soc. Cell Biology, European Cell Biology Orgn., Am. Assn. Cancer Rsch. (emeritus mem.), European Assn. Cancer Rsch., Internat. Soc. Hyaluronan Scis. (life). Personal E-mail: bfiszer-szafarz@wanadoo.fr.

FITCH, COY DEAN, internist, educator; b. Marthaville, La., Oct. 5, 1934; s. Raymond E. and Joey (Youngblood) F.; m. Rachel Farr, Mar. 31, 1956; children: Julia Anne, Jaquelyn Kay. BS, U. Ark., 1956, MS, MD, U. Ark., 1958. Diplomate Am. Bd. Internal Medicine and Endocrinology. Intern U. Ark. Sch. Medicine, 1958—59, resident, 1959—62, instr. biochemistry, 1959—62, asst. prof. medicine and biochemistry, 1962—66, dir. honors med. student rsch. program, 1965—67, asso. prof., 1966—67; practice medicine, specializing in internal medicine Little Rock, 1962—67; asso. prof. internal medicine and biochemistry St. Louis U. Sch. Medicine, 1967—73, prof. internal medicine, 1973—, prof. biochemistry, 1976—, head sect. metabolism, 1969—76, dir. div. endocrinology and metabolism, 1977—85; practice medicine, specializing in internal medicine St. Louis, 1969—; chief med. service St. Louis U. Hosps., 1976—77, vice-chmn. dept. internal medicine, 1983—85, acting chmn. dept. internal medicine, 1985—88, chmn. dept., 1988—2000; chief med. svc. St. Louis VA Med. Ctr., 2005—. Dir. Diabetic Clinic, U. Ark. Med. Ctr., 1962-67, head sect. metabolism and endocrinology, 1966-67; mem. nutrition study sect. div. research grants NIH, 1967-71 Assoc. editor: Nutrition Revs., 1964; contbr. articles to profl. jours. Served from capt. to lt. col., M.C. AUS, 1967-69. Recipient Lederle Med. Faculty award, 1966-67; Russell M. Wilder-Nat. Vitamin Found. fellow, 1959-62. Master ACP (gov. Mo. chpt. 1995-99); mem. Am. Inst. Nutrition, Am. Soc. Biol. Chemists, Ctrl. Soc. Clin. Rsch., Phi Beta Kappa. Office: VAMC 111JC 915 N Grand Blvd Saint Louis MO 63106-1621 Office Phone: 314-289-7030. Business E-Mail: coy.fitch@va.gov.

FITCH, FRANK WESLEY, pathologist, immunologist, dean, educator; b. Bushnell, Ill., May 30, 1929; s. Harold Wayne and Mary Gladys (Frank) F.; m. Shirley Dobbins, Dec. 23, 1951; children— Mary Margaret, Mark Howard. MD, U. Chgo., 1953, S.M., 1957, PhD, 1960; MD (hon.), U. Lausanne, Switzerland, 1990. Postdoctoral research fellow USPHS, 1954-55, 57-58; faculty U. Chgo., 1957—, prof. pathology, 1967—, Albert D. Lasker prof. med. sci., 1976—, emeritus prof., 1996, assoc. dean med. and grad. edn. div. biol. scis., 1976-85, dean acad. affairs, 1985-86, dir. Ben May Inst., 1986-95. Vis. prof. Swiss Inst. Exptl. Cancer Research, Lausanne, Switzerland, 1974-75. Editor-in-chief The Jour. of Immunology, 1997-2002; contbr. chpts. to books, articles to profl. jours. Recipient Borden Undergrad. Research award, 1953, Lederle Med. Faculty award, 1958-61; Markle Found. scholar, 1961-66; Commonwealth Fund fellow U. Lausanne (Switzerland) Institut de Biochimie, 1965-66; Guggenheim fellow, 1974-75 Mem. Fedn. Am. Socs. for Exptl. Biology (pres. 1993-94), Am. Assn. Immunologists (pres. 1992-93), Am. Soc. for Investigative Pathology, Am. Assn. for Cancer Rsch., Chgo. Path. Soc., Transplantation Soc., Sigma Xi, Alpha Omega Alpha. Business E-Mail: ffitch@uchicago.edu.

FITCH, JANET, writer; b. LA; Grad., Reed Coll. Mng. editor Am. Film mag.; editor The Mancos Times Tribune; book reviewer Speak mag., San Francisco. Author: (novels) Kicks, 1996, White Oleander, 1999, Paint It Black, 2006, short stories. Office: c/o Heather Rizzo Little Brown and Co 1271 Avenue of the Americas New York NY 10020

FITCH, NANCY ELIZABETH, historian, educator; b. White Plains, NY, June 17, 1947; d. Robert Franklin and Nancy Elizabeth (Harvey) F. BA in Polit. Sci./English Lit., Oakland U., Rochester, Mich., 1969; MA in History, U. Mich., 1971, PhD in History, 1981. Danforth tchg. intern dept. history U. Mich., Ann Arbor, 1970; asst. prof. history and lit. Sangamon State U., Springfield, Ill., 1972-74; sr. social sci. rsch. analyst The Congl. Rsch. Svc. of Libr. of Congress, Washington, 1975-78; asst. to the chmn./historian U.S. EEO Commn., Washington, 1982-89; asst. prof. history Lynchburg Coll. of Va., 1989-91; asst. prof. African Am. studies Temple U., Phila., 1991-92; Jesse Ball Dupont vis. scholar Randolph-Macon Woman's Coll., Lynchburg, Va., 1992-93; assoc. prof. history U. N.C. at Asheville, 1993-95; assoc. prof. history and English Coll. New Rochelle, NY, 1995—, chair dept. NY, 1999—2003. Chmn.'s rep. White House Inst. on Hist. Black Colls. and Univs., U.S. Dept. Edn., 1985-89, EEO com.; pub. rels. vol. S. Africa Exhibit Project, Washington, 1986-88; mem. adv. com. DuPont Vis. Scholars Project, Va. Found. Ind. Colls., 1990-91; adj. prof. in history Shaw U., Asheville, 1994; lectr. Jesse Ball DuPont Found. Coll. Confs. on Diversity, The Aspen Inst., Queenstown, Md., 1995, 96; participating historian, spkr. Schomburg Ctr. for Rsch. in Black Culture, N.Y.C., 1994, Booker T. Washington Jr. Anniversary Commemoration. Editor, compiler: (anthology) How Sweet the Sound: The Spirit of African American History, 1999; editl. assoc.: Jour. South Asian Lit., 1969-79; co-editor: Diversity: A Jour. of Multicultural Issues, 1995-98; mem. editl. adv. bd. Kente Cloth: African Am. Voices in Tex.; contbr. book reviews to Jours.; author: (series) Essays on Liberty, 1988; contbr. articles to profl. jours. Organizer, producer Ann. Dr. Martin Luther King Jr. Celebration prog., Washington, 1986-88; guest lectr. on history of Am. music Blue Ridge Music Festival, Lynchburg, 1991; participant Radio America African-Am. contbrs. to art and lit., 1990; vol./cons. The Holiday Project, Washington, 1986-88; mem. Widening Horizons Prog. of D.C. Pub. Schs., 1986-88; trustee Sister to Sister Internat, 2004. Recipient Achievement award Mt. Vernon Day Care Ctr., 1983, Spl. Commendation, U.S. EEO Commn., 1985-89, Ft. Drum Sgt. Maj.'s medal for svc. 10th Mountain div. Light Inf., Ft. Drum, N.Y., 1992; fellow Ford Found., 1971-72, Nat. Def. Fgn. Lang., 1970, U. Mich., 1970-71, 78-79, John Hay Whitney Found., 1969-70; Faculty summer seminar fellowship Nat. Endowment for the Humanities, U. Kans., Lawrence, 1996; Alden B. Dow creativity fellow Northwood U., 1998; Millennium writer Westchester Libr. Sys. Inc., 2000. Fellow Soc. Values in Higher Edn.; mem. Assn. for Study African Am. Life and History, Orgn. Am. Hists., Phi Alpha Theta (faculty advisor 1990-91). Republican. Episcopalian/Buddhist. Avocation: photography. Office: Coll New Rochelle 29 Castle Pl New Rochelle NY 10805-2338 Home: 304 W Post Rd White Plains NY 10606 Office Phone: 914-654-5390. Business E-Mail: nfitch@cnr.edu.

FITCH, RACHEL FARR, health policy analyst; b. July 27, 1933; d. Allen Edward and Rosie Leola (Jones) Farr; m. Coy Dean Fitch, Mar. 31, 1956; children: Julia Anne, Jaquelyn Kay. Student, Little Rock U., 1965-67; BS, St. Louis U., 1974, MS, 1976, PhD, 1983. RN, Mo. Psychiat. staff nurse VA Ft. Root Hosp., North Little Rock, Ark., 1954-57; surg.-med. staff nurse St. Vincent Infirmary, Little Rock, Ark., 1957-65; acute care nurse Georgetown U. Hosp., Washington, 1968-69; pub. health nurse to adminstr. South office Vis. Nurse Assn. Greater St. Louis, 1970-73; cons. in edn. St. Louis City Health Dept., 1977-80; rsch. specialist Sen. John C. Danforth, St. Louis, 1980; owner RFF Assocs., 1983-86. Project dir. study of infant mortality in city of St. Louis, 1978. Mem. community health edn. com. Am. Heart Assn., 1977-87; bd. dirs. LWV of Mo., 1984-2001, 2003—, dir. health issues, 1987-99, 1st v.p. 1999-2001, 2003-07; chmn. Mo. Consumer Health Care WATCH, 1996-2002; mem. adv. com. Mo. Medicaid Consumer, 1996-97; mem. Mo. Welfare Coord. Com., 1997-99; mem. health-care mgmt. and policy adv. com. Maryville U., 2002-04; mem. Mo. Found. for Health Advocates steering com., 2003-04; sec. St. Louis U. Hosp. Aux. Editor: (newspaper) LWV of Mo., 1984—87. Mem. APHA, Acad. Polit. Sci., Grand Jury Assn. St. Louis (bd. dirs.), Woman's Club St. Louis U. Sch. Medicine (past pres., bd. dirs. 2004—), St. Louis Vol. Assn., Jr. League St. Louis, Sigma Theta Tau. Address: 23 Lenox Pl Saint Louis MO 63108-1901 Office Phone: 314-961-6869. Personal E-mail: rachel.farr.fitch@sbcglobal.net.

FITCH, ROBERT MCLELLAN, research and development company executive, consultant; b. Shanghai, Apr. 30, 1928; came to U.S., 1937; s. George A. and Geraldine (Townsend) F.; m. Reta Peck, Aug. 21, 1955; children: David H.A., Douglas G., Christopher M. AB, Dartmouth Coll., 1949; PhD, U. Mich., 1954. Prof. U. Conn., Storrs, 1962-83; v.p. corp. rsch. SC Johnson, Racine, Wis., 1983-85, sr. v.p. R & D, 1985-89; pvt. practice cons., 1990—. Author: Polymer Colloids, A Comprehensive Introduction, 1997; editor: Polymer Colloids, 1971, Polymer Colloids II, 1980; contbr. over 100 articles to profl. jours.; patentee in field. Mem. adv. bd. Nat. Sci. Resources Ctr., Smithsonian Inst. and Nat. Acad. Science, 1992-96, chmn., 1994-96; mem. adv. team Nat. Inst. for Sci. Edn., 1995-2000; chmn. Taos Talking Pictures, 1998-2000; bd. dirs. Taos Chamber Music group, 2001—. Recipient Disting. Svc. award Am. Chem. Soc., 1987; named to S.E. Wis. Educators Hall of Fame, 1992. Fellow AAAS. Avocations: skiing, scuba diving, photography.

FITCH, VAL LOGSDON, physics professor; b. Merriman, Nebr., Mar. 10, 1923; s. Fred B. and Frances Marion (Logsdon) Fitch; m. Elise Cunningham Fitch, June 11, 1949 (dec. 1972); children: John Craig(dec.) , Alan Peter; m. Daisy Harper Sharp, Aug. 14, 1976. B in Engring., McGill U., 1948; PhD, Columbia U., 1954; degree (hon.), McGill U., Toronto, Can., Columbia U., NYU, U. Northeast, Biddeford, Maine, Princeton U., NJ. Instr. Columbia, 1953; instr. physics Princeton, 1954—56, asst. prof., 1956—59, assoc. prof., 1959—60, prof., 1960—94, Class 1909 prof. physics, 1968—76, Cyrus Fogg Bracket prof. physics, 1977—84, James S. McDonnell Distinguished Univ. prof. physics, 1984—94, prof. emeritus, 1994—. Mem. Pres.'s Sci. Adv. Com., 1970—73. Trustee Assoc. Univ., Inc., 1961—67. With USAR, 1943—46. Recipient Rsch. Corp. award, 1967, E.O. Lawrence award, 1968, John Price Wetherill medal, Franklin Inst., 1976, Nobel prize in Physics, 1980, Grad. Alumnus award, Am. Assn. State Colls. and Univs., 1984, Disting. Alumnus award, Columbia U., 1985, Nat. medal of Sci., 1993; fellow Sloan, 1960. Fellow: Am. Assn. for Advancement of Sci., Am. Phys. Soc. (pres. 1987—88); mem.: NAS, Am. Philos. Soc., Am. Acad. Arts and Scis. Office: Princeton U Dept Physics 391 Jadwin Hall Princeton NJ 08544-0001

FITCHEN, ALLEN NELSON, publisher; b. Syracuse, Aug. 8, 1936; s. John Frederick and Mary (Nelson) F. III; m. Jane Cady, June 13, 1959 (div. Feb. 1986); children— Anne Wheeler, Christopher Hardy, William Mills; m. Shirley Bergen, May 23, 1991. BA in English cum laude, Amherst Coll., 1958; MA in English, Cornell, 1960. Coll. traveler Macmillan Co., NYC, 1960-62, editor, 1962-67; humanities editor U. Chgo. Press, 1968-82, sr. editor, 1971-82; dir. U. Wis. Press, 1982-98, ret., 1998. Mem.: Psi Upsilon. Home: 603 Eugenia Ave Madison WI 53705-3404 E-mail: afitchen@wiscmail.wisc.edu.

FITCHEN, DOUGLAS BEACH, physicist, researcher; b. NYC, June 8, 1936; s. Paul R. and Eleanor B. Fitchen; m. Janet Mathews (dec. 1995); children: John, Katherine, Sylvia; m. Nancy Mathews, 1996 (dec. 2000); m. Karen Brazell, 2002. AB, Harvard U., 1957; PhD, U. Ill., 1962. Asst. prof. physics Cornell U., Ithaca, NY, 1962-65, assoc. prof., 1965-71, prof., 1971—, chmn. dept. physics, 1977-82, 86-91, 94-99. Vis. prof. Oxford U., 1968, U. Paris, Orsay, 1975 Alfred P. Sloan fellow, 1964-68 Achievements include research in optical studies of solids, Raman spectroscopy. Office: Cornell U Clark Hall Ithaca NY 14853

FITCHETT, TAYLOR, law librarian; b. 1947; BA, Kans. State U., 1970; MLS, U. Ala., 1979. Acting dir. Law Libr. U. Ala., 1981—83; assoc. libr. Law Libr. Tulane U., 1983—86; dir. Law Libr. U. Cin., 1986—98; assoc. libr. Law Libr. U. Va., 1998—2000, dir. Law Libr. and lectr. gen. faculty, 2000—. Mem.: Va. Assn. Law Libr. (chmn., publications com.), Am. Libr. Assn., Am. Assn. Law Libr. Office: Office of Law Libr Dir U Va 580 Massie Rd Charlottesville VA 22903-1789 Office Phone: 434-924-7725. Business E-Mail: tf2u@virginia.edu.*

FITE, TOM W., retired mathematics educator, farmer; b. Bethel, Ohio, June 19, 1937; s. Charles Lloyd Fite and Esther Iota Ogden; m. Mary Ann Lyons, July 27, 1963 (dec.); children: Lisa Teegarden, Michael. BS in Edn., Wilmington Coll., Ohio, 1959; MS in Math., U. Okla., Norman, 1969. Math. tchr. Western Brown H.S., Mount Orab, Ohio, 1960—64, West Clermont H.S., Glen Este, Ohio, 1965—90; math. instr. So. State C.C., Sardinia, Ohio, 1967—77, 1998—2003, No. Ky. U., Alexandria, 1982—83, Maysville C.C., Ky., 1992—97; ret. Leader 4H, 1957—60, Boy Scouts Am., 1958—62. Republican. Mem. Ch. Of Christ. Avocations: hunting, fishing, gardening, reading. Home: 4355 Sunshine Rd Georgetown OH 45121

FITIAL, BENIGNO REPEKI, governor; b. No. Mariana Islands, Nov. 27, 1945; m. Josie P. Fitial; 6 children. BA, U. Guam, 1976. Budget officer Commonwealth No. Mariana Islands Legislature, 1978—80, rep. Dist. 3, 1980—2006, spkr., 1982—84, 2000—02, 2004—06, minority leader, 1980—82, 1984—86, chmn. Commn. on Fed. Laws, 1985—88, vice spkr., 1986—88; gov. Commonwealth No. Mariana Islands, 2006—. News dir. KJQR Radio Station; chmn. Bank of Saipan, 1990—94; cons. Tan Holdings Corp.; pres. Century Ins. Co., 1988—96, Century Travel Corp., Consolidated Transp. Svcs. Inc., Pacific Oriental Inc., Home Improvement. Chmn. Trusteeship Termination Task Force, Civil Svc. Commn., Saipan Mcpl. Scholarship Bd.; founder Covenant Party; delegatge 1st No. Marianas Constl. Convention, chmn. Tax, Pub. Dept, Edn. and Local Govt. Com.; mem. Tax Task Force, Rep. Presdl. Task Force; chmn. No. Marianas Rep. Party, Zoning Bd., Bush for Pres. Com. for Commonwealth No. Mariana Islands. Recipient Disting. Alumni Award, U. Guam, 1982. Mem.: Oxford Club. Catholic. Office: Office of Gov Caller Box 10007 Saipan MP 96950 Office Fax: 670-233-5112. E-mail: fitial@vzpacifica.net.

FITOUSSI, JEAN-PAUL SAMUEL, economics professor; b. Aug. 19, 1942; s. Joseph and Mathilde (Cohen) F.; m. Annie Krief, July 11, 1964; children: Lisa, David. Student, U. Paris, 1961-63; licencie in Econs., U. Strasbourg, 1966, D d'Etat in Econs., 1971, Agrege in Econs., 1973. From asst. to hon. dean Louis Pasteur U., Strasbourg, France, 1968-77, hon. dean, 1977—; prof. European U. Inst., 1979-83, Inst. d'Etudes Politiques de Paris, 1983—. Cons. EEC, 1978-82, 84—; dir. Bur. Theoretical and Applied Econs., U. Strasbourg, 1974-82, rsch. dept. Observatoire Francais des Conjonctures Econs., 1982-89, pres. 1990—; adv. com. Econ. and Social Scis. Rsch. Coun., U.K., 1986; mem. French Nat. Com. Sci. Rsch., 1987-90; bd. dirs. GAN Ins. Co; mem. exec. com. Aspen Inst. Italia, 2001—; mem. rsch. coun. European U. Inst., Florence, Italy, 2003—; mem. com. nat. polit. evaluation ville, 2002; d'initiative et de proposition par la recherche, 2004—; mem. sci. bd. Austrian Inst. Econ. Rsch., 2004—; hon. prof. U. Trento. Author: Inflation, Equilibre et Chômage, 1973, Le Fondement microéconomique de la theorie Keynésienne, 1974; co-author: (with Edmond Malinvaud) Unemployment in Western Countries, 1980, (with Pierre-Alain Muet) Macrodynamique et Déséquilibres, 1987, (with Edmund S. Phelps) The Slump in Europe, 1988, La crisi economica in Europa, 1989, A l' Est, En Europe, 1990, Le débat interdit, 1995, (with P. Rosanvallon) Le Nouvel Age des Inégalitès, 1996, (with Oliver Blanchard) Croissance et Chômage, 1998 (dir. Jean-Paul Fitoussi) Rapport sur l'État de l'Union Européenne, 1999-00, 02-04, L'enseignement supérieur de l'économie en question, 2001, La Règle et le choix, 2002, (with J. Creel) How to Reform the ECB, 2002, Il dittatore benevolo, 2003, EDF, le marché et l'Europe, 2003, Rapport sur l'état de l'union européenne 2003, 04, 07, L'idéologie du monde, 2004, (with Eloi et Laurent e Joël Naurice) Ségrégation urbaine et intégration sociale, 2004, Nacioeconomic Theory and Economic Policy Essay in honor of J.P. Fitoussi, 2004, La démocratie et le marché, 2004, La politique de l'impuissance, 2005, L'état de L'union européenne, 2005, Report on the State of the European Union, 2006. Mem. Econ. Commn. of the Nation, 1996—, Coun. Econ. Analysis of the Prime Min., 1997—; pres. sci. coun. Inst. d'Etudes Politiques de Paris, 1997—; expert Commn. of the European Parliament, 2000—; mem. adv. bd. inst. rsch. UN Social Develop., 2001-; adminstrv. coun. mem. Ecole Normale Supérieure, 2004-; adv. bd. mem. Ctr. Capitalism Soc., Columbia U., 2004. Decorated chevalier Order of Nat. Merit, chevalier Legion of Honor (France), grand officier de l'Infant Henri (Portugal); recipient prize Acad. Scis. Morales et Politiques, 1974. Mem. Internat. Assn. Applied Econometrics, Internat. Econ. Assn. (gen. sec. 1984, European chpt., French chpt. prize 1972, Am. chpt.). Office: Observatoire Francais des Conjonctures Economiques 69 quai d'Orsay 75007 Paris France Office Phone: 0144185401. Business E-Mail: presidence@ofce.sciences-po.fr.

FITTON, HARVEY NELSON, JR., former government official; b. Washington; s. Harvey Nelson and Ada Hortense (Marshall) F.; m. Bernice Jeanette Sutton, Jan. 8, 1946 (dec. Sept. 1998); m. Judith Ann Krauss, Dec. 11, 2006 Student, Nat. Acad. Theater, 1940; degree in Am. Studies, George Washington U., 1949, MA in Am. Lit. and Cultural History, 1956; postgrad., Am. U., 1963. Editor, rsch. asst. Nat. Acad. Scis., Nat. Rsch. Coun., Washington, 1949-56; med. writer and editor NIH, Bethesda, Md., 1956-58; info. specialist farmer cooperative svc. USDA, Washington, 1958-61, publs. editor office of info., 1961-63, chief editorial br. office of info., 1963-66, head pub. divsn. office govtl. and pub. affairs, 1966-84, dep. dir. of info., office govt. and pub. affairs, 1984. Instr. USDA Grad. Sch., Washington, 1962-92, chmn. editl. adv. com., 1976-85, mem. comm. skills adv. com., 1986-97. Editor, rsch. asst. Atlas of Tumor Pathology, 1949-56; editor NIH Record, 1956-58; contbr. articles to profl. jours. Pres. Clermont Woods Community Assn., Fairfax County, Va., 1968, No. Va. Family Svc., Falls Church, 1972-73; elder local Presbyn. Ch. With USN, 1942-45. Recipient Horace Hart award Edn. Coun. of Graphic Arts Industry, 1980; inductee Internat. Poetry Hall of Fame, 1996. Fellow Soc. for Tech. Comm. (pres. Washington chpt. 1972-73, asst. to pres. for recognition programs 1976-77); mem. Acad. Am. Poets, Internat. Soc. Poets, Haiku Soc. Am., Agrl. Communicators in Edn. (pres. Washington chpt. 1968, Spl. Achievement award 1986), Nat. Assn. Govt. Communicators (pres. Washington chpt. 1979, nat. pres. 1980, mem. editl. bd. Govt. Comm., 1994—, Communicator of Yr. 1984), St. Andrews Soc., Nat. Assn. Scholars, Assn. Lit. Scholars and Critics, Toastmasters (pres. Alexandria chpt. 1959-60), SAR. Avocations: gardening, singing, book collecting, poetry, tap dancing. Home and Office: 6030 Ashby Heights Cir Alexandria VA 22315-3804 Personal E-mail: hnfitton@cox.net.

FITTON, TOM (THOMAS J. FITTON), legal foundation administrator; Student, George Washington U. Editor and publisher Opinion Inc.; pres. Judicial Watch Inc., 2003—; political analyst America's Voice (TV Network). Office: Judicial Watch Inc PO Box 44444 Washington DC 20026 Home Phone: 202-237-2870.*

FITTS, ALSTON, III, writer; b. Tuscaloosa, Ala., Nov. 19, 1939; s. Alston and Anna Catherine Fitts; m. Anne Malone Fitts, Dec. 23, 1972; children: Lida Malone, Mary Alston Kerllenevich, Ruth Withnell. BA, U. Ala., 1961; MA, Harvard U., 1964; PhD, U. Chgo., 1974. Acting dir. men's housing U. Ala., Tuscaloosa, 1962—63; instr. English U. Ky., Lexington, 1963—65, Northwestern U., Evanston, Ill., 1967—69; asst. prof. English U. Ala., Tuscaloosa, 1970—73; dir. info. Edmundite Missions, Selma, Ala., 1977—2005. Author: Selma, Queen City of the Black Belt, 1989, (brochure) Selma's Historic Churches, 2005; assoc. editor: Edmundite Missions Newsletter, 1977—2005. Mem., former co-chair One Selma, 1990—; sec., former pres. Old Depot Mus., Selma, 1986—; lector Queen of Peace Parish. Mem.: Rotary Club Selma. Roman Catholic. Home: 2101 Church St Selma AL 36701 Personal E-mail: alstonfitts@yahoo.com.

FITTS, CATHERINE AUSTIN, investment advisor; b. Phila., Dec. 24, 1950; d. William Thomas Jr. and Barbara Kinsey (Willits) Fitts. AA, Bennett Coll., 1970; student, Chinese U., Hong Kong, 1971; BA, U. Pa., 1974, MBA, 1978; postgrad., MIT, 1995. With Dillon, Read & Co., Inc., NYC, 1978-89, sr. v.p., 1984-86, mng. dir., 1986-89, also bd. dirs.; asst. sec. housing, urban devel., fed. housing commr. HUD, Washington, 1989-90; pres., chmn. Hamilton Securities Group, Inc., Washington, 1990-97, Solari, Inc., Tenn., 1998—, Solari Investment Adv. Svcs. LLC, 2006—. Adv. bd. Fedn. Nat. Mortgage Assn. Fannie Mae, 1992—93; emerging markets adv. com. SEC, 1990—93; mem. Gold Anti-Trust Action Com. Columnist: Mapping the Real Deal, Scoop Media. Bd. dir. Student Loan Mktg. Assn. Sallie Mae, 1991—94; mem. grad. adv. bd. Wharton Sch., U. Pa., Phila., 1986—95. Office Phone: 731-609-2412. Business E-Mail: catherine@solari.com.

FITTS, DONALD DENNIS, chemist, educator; b. Concord, NH, Sept. 3, 1932; s. Russell P. and Elisabeth (Reille) F.; m. Beverly Hoffman, July 11, 1964; children: Robert K., William R. AB, Harvard U., 1954; PhD, Yale U., 1957. NSF postdoctoral fellow U. Amsterdam, Netherlands, 1957-58; research fellow Yale U., 1958-59; mem. faculty U. Pa., 1959—, assoc. prof. chemistry, 1964-69, prof. chemistry, 1969—, asst. chmn. dept., 1965-72, assoc. dean grad. studies faculty arts and scis., 1978-82, 83-94, acting dean arts and scis., 1982-83. Cons. Am. Cyanamid Co., 1959-63 Author: Nonequilibrium Thermodynamics, 1962, Vector Analysis in Chemistry, 1974, Principles of Quantum Mechanics, 1999; also articles. Mem. Am. Phys. Soc. Achievements include research on theory of optical activity, statis.-mech. theory of transport processes, nonequilibrium thermodynamics, molecular quantum mechanics, theory of liquids, intermolecular forces, surface phenomena. Home: 634 Revere Rd Merion Station PA 19066-1008 Office: Dept Chemistry U Pa Philadelphia PA 19104-6323 E-mail: dfitts@sas.upenn.edu.

FITTS, MICHAEL ANDREW, dean, law educator; b. Phila., Mar. 1, 1953; s. William Thomas Jr. and Barbara Kinsey (Willits) F.; m. Renee Judith Sobel, Jan. 2, 1982; children: Alexis, Whitney. AB, Harvard Coll., 1975; JD, Yale U., 1979; MA (hon.), U. Pa., 1991. Law clk. Hon. A. Leon Higginbotham, Jr., U.S. Ct. Appeals (3d cir.), Phila., 1979-81; atty. office legal counsel Dept. of Justice, Washington, 1981-85; asst. prof. law U. Pa., Phila., 1985-90, assoc. prof., 1990-92, prof., 1992—, assoc. dean acad. affairs, 1996-98, Robert G. Fuller Jr. prof. law, 1996-2000, Bernard G. Segal prof. law, 2000—, dean Sch. of Law, 2000—. Vis. prof. dept. polit. sci. Swarthmore Coll., 1999; adv. com. Weseda Law Sch.; bd. dir. World Affairs Coun.; adv. bd. Reinvestment Fund. Editor Yale Law Jour., 1978-79; contbr. articles to profl. jours. and chpts. to books. Harvard U. scholar, 1971. Mem.: Pa. Bar Assn., Am. Polit. Sci. Assn. (law and polit. process working group), Com. of Seventy, Phi Beta Kappa. Mem. Soc. Of Friends. Office: U Pa Law Sch 3400 Chestnut St Philadelphia PA 19104-6204 Office Phone: 215-898-7061. Office Fax: 215-573-2025. Business E-Mail: deanfitts@law.upenn.edu.

FITTS, NELSON ORUS, lawyer; b. Nashville, Feb. 26, 1975; s. Jerre Nelson and John Orus Fitts; m. Elizabeth Alice Crouch; 1 child, Evelyn Kay. AB, Princeton U., NJ, 1996; JD, Columbia U. Sch. Law, NYC, 1999. Bar: Tenn. 1999, NY 2001, US Dist. Ct. (we. dist.) Ky. 2000. Law clk. to Hon. John G. Heyburn II US Dist. Ct., we. dist., Louisville, 1999—2000; assoc. Wachtell, Lipton, Rosen & Katz, NYC, 2000—. Antitrust & trade regulation com. Assn. Bar of City of NY, NYC, 2004—07. Bd. Kentuckians of NY, NYC, 2004—06. Regional Scholarship, Coca-Cola Scholars Found., 1993. Independent. Presbyterian. Office: Wachtell Lipton Rosen & Katz 51 W 52nd St New York NY 10019 Office Phone: 212-403-1361. Office Fax: 212-403-2361. Business E-Mail: nofitts@wlrk.com.

FITZALAN-HOWARD, BENNETT-THOMAS HENRY ROBERT, news analyst, consultant, political scientist, theologian; b. Geneva, Oct. 10, 1955; came to U.S., 1959; s. S. and A. (Argyle-Campbel) FitzA.-H. BA, BS, BA, Union Coll., Schenectady, NY, 1973; MDiv, New Brunswick Theol. Sem., 1978; MS, Rutgers U., 1980; MA, Russell Sage Coll., 1987; postgrad., NYU, 1989, Yale U., 1989. Cert. fin. analyst, broker, contractor in Nigeria, 1993-98; cert. min. Bride in the Light New Testament Ministry. Adminstrv. analyst Todd Logistics, Inc., NJ, Saudi Arabia, 1980—81; owner, cons. Fitz Co., Internat., Albany, 1981—; contractor Nigeria, 1988—98. Mem. N.Y. Merc. Exch.; insr. Gaton Sch., Yale U., 1987-89, NYU, 1987-89. Author: Expropriation Predictability and Politics, 1979, The Politics of the U.S. Budget, 1987, The Courts in a Democratic System, 1987, White House-Wall Street: The October 87 Crash and the Post Regan Persidency, 1987, The Politics of Deficits, 1988, Enemyless: Can We Survive?, 1989, Responsibility and Accountability: The Forgotten Cornerstones of Democracy, 1990, The Eagle and the UN: Is the US Mature Enough to be the Sole Super-Power?, 1998: contbg. author: Toward a Global Government, 1972, Conservetism: New World Order?, 1990, Tory vs. Labour: Tory: The New English Order, 1992, Hyperinflation, 1992, Eschatology Now, 1992, Eschatology and Current Events, 1992, Bride in the Light: New Testament Church, The Opened Seals of Revelation, How Bush Ambushed America, 2002. Active local ARC, RP Found. With U.S. Army, 1974-77. Mem. AIGA, AAAS, APA, SAR, VFW, Acad. Polit. Sci. (life), Am. Philatelic Soc. (life). Am. Vietnam Vets. Assn., Audubon Soc., Am. Numismatic Assn. (life), Fin. Analysts Fedn. (at large), Fin. Execs. Inst. (at large), Nat. Assn. Securities Dealers (at large), N.Y. Mercantile Exchange, Am. Enterprise Inst., Brookings Inst., Am. Legion, MENSA, Am. Soc. Internat. Law, Am. Bach Found., Am. Soc. Info. Sci., Blind Vets. Assn. (life), Am. Conservative Union, Nat. Press Club, Equestrian Club, Gideons, Mus. Modern Art, Barons of Magna Carta. Avocations: oriental antiques and silver, stamp collecting/philately, photography, reading, cello. Home: 334 Clinton Ave 1-A Albany NY 12206-1301 Personal E-mail: norfolk90@aol.com.

FITZ-CARTER, ALEANE, retired elementary school educator, composer; b. Council Bluffs, Iowa, July 24, 1929; d. Andrew Wilburt and Beatrice Mildred (Maddox) Fitz; m. James Benny Carter, Dec. 10, 1958 (wid. Aug. 1964); children: Angel Beatrix, Angel Sherrie. BSEd, U. Nebr., 1956. Elem. sch. tchr. Omaha Pub. Schs., 1956—69; instr. Black history and music U. Nebr., Omaha, 1970—74; nat. faculty mem. Gospel Music Workshop Am. Inc., 1986—2005; tchr. music Ascension Luth. Sch., LA, 1990—94; min. music Messiah Luth. Ch., LA, 1996—2003; ch. musician Tamarind Seventh Day Adventist Ch., Compton, Calif., 1997—2003; performing artist Nebr. Arts Coun., Omaha, 1980—, Iowa Arts Coun., Des Moines, 1998—; tchr. adult edn. L.A. Unified Schs., 1998—; ednl. cons. Torrance Unified Schs., Calif., 1997—99; ret., 2005. Min. music Olivet Luth. Ch., Hawthorne, 2003-05; program prodr. KETV TV, Omaha, 1970-73; talk show host, Radio Sta. KOWH, Omaha, 1973-74; comm. cons. Mayor's Human Rels. Bd., Omaha, 1970-73; midwest bd. rep. Nat. Black Media Coalition, Washington, 1973-76, others; tchr. Black Awareness Opportunities Industrialization Ctr., 1969-74; instr. history of jazz, Oasis, L.A., 1997-2001; arranger, librettist, lyricist, elocutionist, storyteller, lectr. in field Recs. include I Love Jesus, 1965, A Mighty Fortress, 1986; performer: (one-woman show) Rosa Parks, 1979—, Omaha Junior Theater, 1980—85; actress: I Elvis; Hard Copy, 1992; Ice Cube video Dead Homie MTV, 1990; (films) A Man Apart, 2003; music dir. (stage) One Last Look, Marla Gibbs Theater, 1990; contbr. articles to profl. jours.; composer: One Child, 1993, (sacred hymns) Psalm 91, 1993—97, Children's TV workshop, Strawberry Square II: Take Time, NETV, 1983; performer: South African Chs. of KwaZulu Natal and African Enterprises, 1995. Presentation Visiting With Huell Howser, KCET; rschr. soul food history and cooking; amb. storytelling programs Dwight D. Eisenhower's People to People, to South Africa, 2004. Nominee Best Supporting actress, Great White Hope Ctr. Stage, Omaha, Nebr., 1982; recipient Comty. Christian Leadership award, Salem Baptist Ch., Omaha, Nebr., 1987, Woman in Fine Arts award, Alyce Wilson Womens Ctr., Omaha, 1987, 5 yr. ACT-SO award, NAACP, Omaha, 1986, Outstanding Songwriter award, 1987—88, Psalm 91 Song of Yr. award, Thurston Frazier Chorale, 1987, Nebr. Chpt. Gospel Music Workshop of America Inc. award, 1987—88, Fine Arts award, Bethesda Seventh Day Adventist Ch., 1988, Comty. Guest Day, Bethesda Seventh Day Ch., Omaha, Nebr., 1988, Outstanding Svc. award, L.A. Union Seventh Day Acad., 1992, Creativity in music award, Thurston Frazier Chorale, Gospel Music Workshop Am., 1993, Svc. comty. award, Salem Baptist Mission, Norfolk, Nebr., 1995; grantee, L.A. Dept. of Cultural Affairs. Mem.: ASCAP, SAG, Nat. Storytelling Network, Rec. Acad., Profl. Musicians Union - Local 47, Nebr. Congress of Parents and Tchrs. (hon. life), Gold Star Wives Am., L.A. Pianist Club, VFW Ladies Aux., Sigma Gamma Rho (Gamma Beta Sigma chpt.). Adventist. Avocations: walking, swimming, cooking. Mailing: PO Box 90087 Los Angeles CA 90009 Home: 200 E Hyde Pk Blvd 1 Inglewood CA 90302 Home Phone: 310-330-8350. Personal E-mail: psalm91@mymailstation.com.

FITZ-ENZ, DAVID G., retired military officer, television producer; b. Aurora, Ill., Oct. 18, 1940; s. John Arthur and Kathryn M. Fitz-Enz; m. Carol J. Fitz-Enz, Aug. 12, 1961; children: David Scott, Timothy Robert, Jonathan Gregory. BA, Marquette U., 1963; postgrad., Command and Gen. Staff Coll., Ft. Leavenworth, Kans., 1974-75, U.S. Army War Coll., Carlisle, Pa., 1985-86. Comd. 2d lt. U.S. Army, 1963, advanced through grades to col.; ret., 1993; v.p. Cannonade Filmworks, Plattsburgh, N.Y., 1994—. Lectr. Brit. Nat. Army Mus., London, Eng., 2000—, U.S. Army War Coll., Nat. Archives, 2005. Author: Why a Soldier?, 2000, The Final Invasion, 2001, Nineteenth Century U.S. Army History, 2001 (Disting. Writing award Am. Hist. Found.), Old Ironsides, Eagle of the Sea, 2004; script writer: (films) The Final Invasion, 1999. Trustee Francis Scott Key Found., Frederick, Md., 1979-83, Battle of Plattsburgh Assn., 1999—. Decorated Bronze Star Valor with 4 oak leaf clusters, Soldiers medal, Legion Merit with 3 oak leaf clusters, knights templar Sovereign Mil. Order of Temple of Jerusalem. Mem. Am. Mil. Retirees (nat. pres. 1994-98), Mil. Order St. Louis, Naval and Mil. Club (Eng.). Office Phone: 518-891-6792. E-mail: coldfitzenz@earthlink.net.

FITZGEARLD, GAYL, musician, educator; b. Albany, Calif., Mar. 30, 1941; d. Glen Oldham and Nadine Edith Center; m. Fredric Edward Fitzgearld, May 27, 1961; children: Fredric Edward, Mark Galen. MusB, N.Mex State U., Las Cruces, 1982, MusM, 1984. Tchr. pvt. voice studio, Las Cruces, 1983—; coord. accompanists Music Dept. N.Mex State U., Las Cruces, 1983—85, voice instr. Music Dept., 1983—86, instr. Music Dept., 2001—; adminstr. Calvary Bapt. Ch. Fine Arts Acad., Las Cruces, 1988—91, First Bapt. Fine Arts Acad., Las Cruces, 1997—2000. Music dir. First Bapt. Ch., Clearlake Highlands, Calif., 1971—80, choir coord., Las Cruces, 1980—82, organist, 2005—; music dir. Mendo-Lake Bapt. Assn., Clearlake Highlands, 1975—78, Mesilla Pk. Cmty. Ch., Mesilla Park, Calif., 1990—96; workshop leader Calif. So. Bapt. Conv., Fresno, 1975—78; organist Calvary Bapt. Ch., Las Cruces, 1982—90. Singer: (plays) Music Man, 1984, Quilters, 1988, (Operas) The Old Maid and the Thief, 1984, Ahmal and the Night Visitors, 1986. Staff mem. Youth Music Camp, Inlow Camp, N.Mex., 1982—. Recipient Achievement award in Fine Arts, Bank of Am., 1958, Norseman award, Diablo Valley Coll., 1960, Youth Concert Competition award, Las Cruces Symphony, 1983, Concerto Competition award, 1984. Mem.: Nat. Assn. Teachers of Singing. Baptist. Home and Office: 2283 Uranus Ave Las Cruces NM 88012 Home Phone: 505-382-1885.

FITZGERALD, DENNIS D., federal agency administrator; b. New Haven, Conn., Feb. 28, 1943; m. Deborah Fitzgerald; 2 children. BS, Fairfield U., 1964; four Master's degrees, John Hopkins U. Cert. Profl. Engr., NY, Va.; lic. Master Electrician Va. Field engr. Sperry Gyroscope, 1964—66, Vitro Labs., 1966—74; various positions with directorate of sci. and tech., office of devel. and engring. and nat. reconnaissance office CIA, 1974—, assoc. dir. Nat. Photographic Interpretation Ctr.; dep. dir. Nat. Reconnaissance Office, 2001—, acting. dir., 2005. Avocation: running. Office: Nat Reconnaissance Office Office of Inspector Gen 14675 Lee Rd Chantilly VA 20151-1715

FITZGERALD, EDMUND BACON, electronics executive; b. Milw., Feb. 5, 1926; s. Edmund and Elizabeth (Bacon) F.; m. Elisabeth McKee Christensen, Sept. 6, 1947; children: Karen, Kathleen, Edmund Greer, Rogers Christensen. BSEE, U. Mich., 1946. With Cutler-Hammer, Inc., Milw., 1946-78, v.p. in charge engring., 1959-61, adminstrv. v.p., 1961-63, pres., CEO, 1964-69, chmn., chief exec. officer, 1969-78; vice chmn. Eaton Corp., Cleve., 1978-79; mng. dir. Hampshire Assocs., Milw., 1979-80; pres., dir. No. Telecom, Inc., Nashville, 1980-82; pres. No. Telecom Ltd., 1982-84, chmn. bd. dirs. Mississauga, 1985-90; mng. dir. Woodmont Assocs., Nashville, 1990—. Adj. prof. mgmt. Vanderbilt U., Nashville, 1990—; former chmn., bd. dirs. Milw. Brewers Baseball Club, Inc.; former chmn. Com. for Econ. Devel.; mem. President's Nat. Security Telecom. Adv. Com. Capt. USMCR, 1943-46, 51-52. Named Man of Yr., Milw. Jr. C. of C., 1956 Mem. Nat. Elec. Mfrs. Assn. (pres. 1968). Office: Woodmont Assocs 3434 Woodmont Blvd Nashville TN 37215-1422

FITZGERALD, EDWIN ROGER, physicist, researcher; b. Oshkosh, Wis., July 14, 1923; s. James C. and Edwina (Brown) F.; m. Carolyn H. Johnson, Aug. 30, 1946; children: Lucia Edwina, Margaret Mary, William Maurice, Alice Ann, Roger Edwin, Douglas Brendan, Thomas Michael, Jane Carolyn. BS in Elec. Engring, U. Wis., 1944, MS in Physics, 1950, PhD in Physics, 1951. Registered profl. engr., Md. Physicist Phys. Research Lab., B.F. Goodrich Co., 1944-46; Project asso. chemistry U. Wis., 1951-52; faculty Pa. State U., 1953-61, prof. physics, 1959-61; prof. dept. mechanics Johns Hopkins U., 1961—99, dr. of u., 1999—; ret., 1999. Vis. prof. chemistry U. Wis., Madison, 1981. Author: Particle Waves and Deformation in Crystalline Solids, 1966; contbr. articles to profl. jours., sects. in books; patentee in field. Fellow: Am. Phys. Soc. (exec. com., chmn. high polymer physics 1958—59); mem.: Am. Chem. Soc. (poly. materials divsn.), Materials Rsch. Soc., Acoustical Soc. Am., Tau Beta Pi, Eta Kappa Nu, Sigma Xi, Phi Beta Kappa. Achievements include research in mechanical and dielectric properties solids including dynamic mechanical properties of violin wood in relation to tone qualities of violins and viscoelastic properties of marine mammal tissues, dynamic mechanical measurements during freezing and thawing of ice. Home: 2445 Traceys Store Rd Parkton MD 21120-9642

FITZGERALD, EUGENE FRANCIS, management consultant; b. Jersey City, Mar. 15, 1925; s. Arthur Gregory and Anna (O'Rourke) F.; m. Ellen M. O'Connor, Sept. 1, 1951; children— Timothy, Mary Ellen, Eugene Francis, Maura, John, Ann, Katherine. BS in Bus. Adminstrn, Georgetown U., 1949. Spl. agt. FBI, 1951-52; mgr. Prudential Ins. Co. Am., Newark, 1953-65; agy. v.p. K.C., New Haven, 1965-67; v.p. Minn. Mut. Life Ins. Co., St. Paul, 1967-70; pres., dir. North Star Equities Co., St. Paul, 1969-70; exec. v.p. Southland Life Ins. Co., Dallas, 1970-72, also dir.; exec. v.p. Equitable Life Ins. Co., Washington, 1972-73, also trustee; v.p. Liberty Life Ins. Co., Greenville, S.C., 1974-81; pres. Mountain View Orchard, Inc., 1981-85; mgmt. cons. Phillips Resource Group, Greenville, S.C., 1986—. Dir. Nathan Hale Life Ins. Co.; cons. Phillips Resource Group; bd. dirs. Nat. Peach Council, 1984-85 Chmn. bd. United Ministries, Greenville Free Med. Clinic; chmn. Greenville County Human Rels. Commn., 1991—; bd. dirs. Catholic Charities, Diocese of Charleston. Served with USMCR, 1943-45. Decorated Bronze Star. Mem. Nat. Assn. Life Underwriters, Sales and Mktg. Execs. Internat., Newcomen Soc. Clubs: Green Valley Country. Roman Catholic. Home: 305 Aberdare Ln Greenville SC 29615-2406 Office: Phillips Resource Group PO Box 5664 Greenville SC 29606-5664 E-mail: dadfitz@aol.com.

FITZGERALD, FAITH THAYER, internist; b. Boston, Sept. 24, 1943; d. Edward Timothy Fitzgerald and Irene Synnerberg. BA, U. Calif., Santa Barbara, 1965, MD, 1969. Lic. Am. Bd. Internal Medicine, 1973. Intern U. Calif., San Francisco, 1969—70, resident, 1970—72, asst. prof. medicine, 1973—78; chief resident San Francisco Gen. Hosp., San Franciso, 1972—73; asst. prof. medicine U. Mich., Ann Arbor, 1978—80; assoc. prof. to prof. medicine U. Calif., Davis, 1980—. Asst. chief medicine San Francisco Gen. Hosp., 1973—78; dir. internal medicine Parent and ICU Svc., Ann Arbor, 1978—80; dean students U. Calif. Davis Sch. Medicine, 1980—82; assoc. dean bioethics and humanities U. Calif Davis Health Sys. Contbr. articles to profl. jours.; co-author: (textbook) Chemical Diagnosis. Master: Am. Coll. Physicians (regent 2005—). Office: Univ Calif Davis Divisn Gen Medicine 4150 V St Ste 2400 Sacramento CA 95817

FITZGERALD, HAROLD KENNETH, social work educator, consultant; b. Lakewood, Ohio, Apr. 28, 1921; s. Edward James and Julia Florence (Klell) F.; m. Caroline Lee Graham, May 31, 1951; children: Mark, Matthew, Mary, Maura, Kristin. AB, John Carroll U., 1942; MSSW, Cath. U. of Am., 1948, PhD, 1953. Social worker ARC, Cin., 1950-53; exec. dir. Cath. Social Svcs., Atlanta, 1953-56; dir. social services Muscular Dystrophy Assn. of Am., NYC, 1957-58; regional cons., survey dirs. Am. Found. for the Blind, NYC, 1958-66; assoc. dir. Commn. on Standards and Accreditation for the Blind, NYC, 1963-66; prof. social work Syracuse (N.Y.) U., 1966-88, prof. emeritus, 1988—. Dir. internat. projects Coun. on Social Work Edn., N.Y.C., 1956-67; bd. dirs. Lighthouse, Syracuse, 1967-90, Ctrl. N.Y. Assn. for Hearing Impaired, Syracuse, 1976-90, Support, 1990-96, Aurora, 1991—; cons. Nat. Conf. Cath. Charities, Washington, 1966-80, UN, Teheran, Iran, 1975-76. Contbr. articles to profl. jours. Mem. Commn. on Peace and Social Justice, Diocese of Syracuse, 1989-91. Lt. USN, 1943-46. Mem. NASW, AAUP, N.Y. State Assn. Human Svcs. (bd. dirs. 1980-93), Internat. Assn. Schs. Social Work, Inter Univ. Consortium Internat. Social Devel. Roman Catholic. Avocation: swimming. Home and Office: 301 Greenwood Rd Syracuse NY 13214-2327 Personal E-mail: hkenfitz1@msn.com.

FITZGERALD, HELEN TERESA, social worker, writer; b. Jackson, Minn., Nov. 12, 1938; d. John Raymond and Mayme Mary (Benes) Cihak; m. Richard Carl Olson; stepchildren: Mark Albert Olson, Thomas Parker Olson, Jeffrey Paul Olson, Melissa Karen Franger; m. Jerald Charles Fitzgerald (dec. Apr. 1, 1974); children: Patti Ann Rauld, Sarah Jane Turosak, Charles Edwin, Mary Elizabeth. Diploma, Jackson HS, Jackson, MN, 1956. Cert. in thanatology Assn. for Death Edn. and Counseling, 2006. Creative therapist Fairfax Hosp., 1972—82; coord. grief program Mt. Vernon Ctr. for Cmty. Mental Health, Alexandria, Va., 1977—2000; dir. tng. Am. Hospice Found., Washington, 1996—2007. Mem. adv. bd. Haven of No. Va., Annandale, Va. Author: The Grieving Child, 1992, 2003, The Mourning Handbook, 1994, The Grieving Teen, 2000, (tng. manuals) Grief At School, 1998, Grief At Work, 1999. Recipient Outstanding Performance award, Cmty. Svcs. Bd. Fairfax County, 1998, Cmty. Svc. award, Social Work Assn. Fairfax County, 1999. Mem.: Assn. for Death Edn. and Counseling (bd. dirs. 1993—96, Clin. Practices award 1999). Avocation: painting. Home: 3601 Devilwood Ct Fairfax VA 22030 Office Phone: 703-273-3454. Personal E-mail: helen38@cox.net.

FITZGERALD, JAMES FRANCIS, broadcast executive; b. Janesville, Wis., Mar. 27, 1926; s. Michael Henry and Chloris Helen (Beiter) F.; m. Marilyn Field Cullen, Aug. 1, 1950; children: Michael Dennis, Brian Nicholas, Marcia O'Loughlin, James Francis, Carolyn Jane, Ellen Putnam. BS, Notre Dame U., 1947; LLD, U. Wis., Whitewater, 1999; LHD, Baldwin-Wallace U., 2001. With Std. Oil Co. (Ind.), Milw., 1947-48; pres. F.-W. Oil Co., Janesville, 1950—, Total TV, Inc. (cable TV Systems), Wis., 1965-86. Bd. dirs. Milw. Ins. Co., Bank One, Janesville N.A.; chmn. bd. Golden State Warriors, Oakland, Calif., 1986-95, Total TV Calif., 1987-96. Bd. govs., chmn. TV com. NBA; chmn. bd., pres. S.P.A.C.E. Inc. subs. Milw. Bucks NBA team, 1976-85; chmn. Greater Milw. Open PGA Tournament, 1985, Notre Dame Bus. Adv. Coun., 1989—. Lt. (j.g.) USNR, 1944-46, 51-53. Named to Wis. Sports Hall of Fame, 1999, Wis. Bus. Hall of Fame, 2001. Mem. Chief Execs. Forum, World Bus. Coun., Wis. Petroleum Assn. (pres. 1961-62), The Quarry at LaQuinta, Janesville Country Club, Vintage Club (pres. 1989-91), San Francisco Golf Club, El Dorado Country Club. Roman Catholic. Home and Office: PO Box 348 Janesville WI 53547-0348

FITZGERALD, JAMES J., III, state supreme court justice; BA, U. Pa., Phila., 1962; JD, Villanova U., Pa. With Office of Dist. Atty., Phila.; chief counsel Pa. Liquor Control Bd.; pvt. practice atty.; head govt. affairs divsn. Greater Phila. C. of C.; judge Phila. Ct. Common Pleas; adminstrv. judge trial divsn. Supreme Ct. Pa., assoc. justice, 2007—. Office: Supreme Ct Pa 1 Oxford Ct Ste 3130 Pittsburgh PA 15219-1407*

FITZGERALD, JANET ANNE, philosophy educator, academic administrator; b. Woodside, NY, Sept. 4, 1935; d. Robert W. and Lillian H. (Shannon) F. BA magna cum laude, St. John's U., 1965, MA, 1967, PhD, 1971, LLD (hon.), 1982. Joined Sisters of St. Dominic of Amityville, Roman Catholic Ch., 1953; NSF postdoctoral fellow Cath. U. Am., summer 1971; prof. philosophy Molloy Coll., Rockville Centre, NY, 1969—, pres., 1972-96, pres. emerita, 1996—. Trustee L.I. Regional Adv. Coun. on Higher Edn., 1972-96, chmn., 1981-84; trustee Commn. on Ind. Colls. and Univs., 1981-84, 89-92, Cath. Charities, Diocese of Rockville Centre, 1979-82; trustee Fellowship of Cath. Scholars, 1977—, v.p., 1977-80; invited expert peritus Vatican Internat. Conf. on Cath. Higher Edn., Rome, 1989; prof. S. John Neumann, Archdiocese of N.Y.; invited auditor St. Thomas Aquinas Pontifical U., Rome, 1999. Author: Alfred North Whitehead's Early Philosophy of Space and Time, 1979. Mem. bd. advisors Sem. of Immaculate Conception, 1975-80; mem. adv. bd. pretheology program Dunwoodie Sem., Archdiocese of N.Y.; mem. pub. policy com. N.Y. State Cath. Conf., 1992-94; mem. N.Y. State Edn. Dept.-Blue Ribbon Panel on Cath. Schs., 1992-93; 1st woman grand marshal St. Patrick's Day Parade, Glen Cove, 1992. Recipient Disting. Leadership award L.I. Bus. News, 1988, plaque of recognition L.I. Women's Coun. for Equal Edn. Tng. and Employment, 1989, Pathfinder award Town of Hempstead, 1990, Disting. Long Islander in Edn. award Epilepsy Found. L.I., 1991, Educator of Yr. award Assn. Tchrs. N.Y., 1980, Spl. award for arts in edn. L.I. Arts Coun., 1994; honored by L.I. Cath. League for Religious and Civil Rights, 1989; named L.I.'s 100 Influentials, L.I. Bus. News, 1992, 93, 94, 95, 96. Mem. Soc. Cath. Social Scis. (bd. advisors). Office: Molloy College PO Box 5002 Rockville Centre NY 11571-5002 Office Phone: 516-678-5000. Business E-Mail: jfitzgerald@molloy.edu.

FITZGERALD, JOAN V., artist; b. Batavia, NY, Jan. 24, 1930; d. Russell Edward Voyer and Marian Ruth Voyer Montague; children: Remy C. Orffeo, Jerome P. Orffeo, Andres Orffeo. BS in Art Edn., Buffalo State Coll., 1963, MS in Art Edn., 1968. Tchr. art Hamburg Ctrl. Schs., NY, 1964—85; asst. prof. Erie C.C., Buffalo, 1985—92, acting asst. acad. dean, 1989—90, instr. fine arts, 1992—98. Author: The Magic Lunch Box, 2003, Not Another Christmas!, 2004, The Iris House, 2006, Dark Towers, 2007, (poetry) Glamor, 2006, The Sweet Life, 2007; Exhibited in group shows at Period Gallery, 2000—05 (Spl. Recognition award), exhibitions include Broome St. Gallery, NYC, Somarts Gallery, San Francisco, Indigo Gallery, Norfolk, Va., Gallery 219, Decatur, Ill., Afif Gallery, Phila., Main St. Gallery, Groton, NY, Viridian Gallery, NYC, Schoharie Nat. Small Works, Cobleskill, NY, 2004 (Dirs. Choice award), Boise State Women's Ctr., NJ Ctr. for the Visual Arts, First Frontier Collage Soc., Austin, The Stage Gallery, Merrick, NY, Art West Gallery, Jackson, Wyo., Brand Exhbn. Ctr., Glendale, Calif., Nat. Collage Soc., Hudson, Ohio, Cork Gallery, Lincoln Ctr. for Performing Arts, NY Cuyahoga Art Ctr., Cuyahoga Falls, Ohio, Butler Inst. Am. Art, Salem, Ohio, Nat. Arts Club, NYC, Masur Art Ctr., Monroe, La., exhibitions include Katherine Lorillard Wolfe Exhbn. (Winnie Borne Sherman Meml. award painting), Meml. Art Gallery, Rochester, NY, Ceres Gallery, NY, New Century Gallery, NYC, North East Collage and Assemblage Soc., Burlington, Vt., Springfield Mus. Art, Chautauqua Inst. Art, NY, Cooperstown Nat. Exhbn., DelMar Nat. Drawings and Sculpture Exhibit, Corpus Christi, Tex., Spar Nat., Shreveport, La., Assn. for Cult. Alternatives, NYC, Wind River Nat., Utah, Boise Art Ctr., Las Vegas Mus. Art, Impact Gallery Nat., Buffalo, Carnegie Art Ctr., North Tonawanda, NY, Tubac Ctr. Arts, Ariz., Impact Gallery, Buffalo (hon. mention), Upstream People Gallery. Co-chair Environ. Conservation Commn., Hamburg, 1990—92; mem. People for Parks, 2001—05. Recipient Dir.'s Choice award, Main St. Gallery Small Works Exhbn., Eight Spl. Recognition awards, Period Gallery Internat. Internet Exhbns., award, Buffalo Soc. Artists, Pres.'s award, Erie C.C., Buffalo, others. Mem.: Nat. Collage Soc. (signature mem.), Western NY Artists Group (bd. dir. 2000—06, chmn. 2002), Buffalo Soc. Artists (pres. 1980). Personal E-mail: jcjvfitz@adelphia.net.

FITZGERALD, JOHN CHARLES, JR., investment banker; b. Sacramento, May 23, 1941; s. John Charles and Geraldine Edith (McNabb) F.; m. Mildred Ann Kilpatrick, June 26, 1965; children: Geraldine Kathrine, Erec John. BS, Calif. State U., Sacramento, 1964; MBA, Cornell U., 1965. Dir. corp. planning Bekins Co., LA, 1966-73; mgr. corp. planning Ridder Publs., Inc., LA, 1973-75; CFO City of Inglewood, Calif., 1975-77; treas./contr. Inglewood Redevel. Agy., 1975-77; v.p. mcpl. fin. White, Weld & Co., Inc., LA, 1977-78; v.p. pub. fin. paine Webber Jackson & Curtis, LA, 1978-79; v.p. and mgr. for Western region, mcpl. fin. dept. Merrill Lynch Capital Markets, LA, 1979-82, mng. dir. Western region, mcpl. fin. dept., 1982-86; mng. dir. Seidler-Fitzgerald Pub. Fin., LA, 1986—2002; sr. v.p. The Seidler Cos., Inc., LA, 1986—2002; mng. dir. John C. Fitzgerald & Assocs. (Divsn. Wulff, Hansen & Co.), 2002—. Instr. fin./adminstrn. El Camino Coll., Torrance, Calif., 1977-80. Chmn. bd. dirs., exec. com., treas., chmn. fundraising com. L.a. chpt. Am. Heart Assn., 1977—; bd. dirs. Daniel Freeman Hosps. Inc., Corondelet Health Care corp.; trustee Mt. St. Mary's Coll., L.A., 1992-2001, regent, 2004—; bd. dirs. Tau Kappa Epsilon Ednl. Found., Indpls., 1995-2003; bd. dirs. Calif. Soc. for Biomed. Rsch., 1998; alumni coun. mem. Johnson Grad. Sch. Mgmt. Cornell U., real estate coun.; bd. dirs. Civergebcy Ethanol Inc., 2007—. Mem. Fin. Execs. Inst., Mcpl. fin. Officers, League Calif. Cities, So. Calif. Corp. Planners Assn. (past pres.), L.A. Bond, Lido Isle Yacht Club, Jonathan Club, The Calif. Club, Lake Arrowhead Country Club, Rotary, Navy League, Beta Gamma Sigma. Address: PO Box 765 27447 Bayshore Dr Lake Arrowhead CA 92352 Office Phone: 213-955-5977.

FITZGERALD, JOHN EDWARD, III, lawyer; b. Cambridge, Mass., Jan. 12, 1945; s. John Edward Jr. and Kathleen (Sullivan) FitzGerald. BCE, U.S. Mil. Acad., West Point, NY, 1969; JD, M in Pub. Policy Analysis, U. Pa., Phila., 1975. Bar: Pa 1975, NY 1978, Calif 1983, US Supreme Ct 1991. Commd. 2d lt. US Army, 1969, advanced through grades to capt., 1971, resigned, 1972; assoc. Saul Ewing Remick & Saul, Phila., 1975-77, Shearman & Sterling, NYC, 1977-78; atty., dir. govt. rels. and pub. affairs Pepsico, Inc., Purchase, NY, 1978-82; sr. v.p., dept. head Security Pacific Corp., LA, 1982-83; ptnr. Schlesinger, FitzGerald & Johnson, Palm Springs, Calif., 1983-87; mng. ptnr. FitzGerald & Mulé, Indian Wells, Calif., 1987—. Chmn., pres. United Way Desert, 1998—2007; trustee Palm Springs Art Mus., 1998—2007; past pres. exec. bd. Coachella Valley coun. Boy Scouts Am, 2000; bd. dirs., past chmn., dir. for life Palm Springs Boys and Girls Club, 1990—; treas. Desert Youth Found., 2000; bd. dirs., vice chair Desert Regional Med. Ctr., 2004—06. Named Palm Springs Disting. Citizen of Yr., 1999; recipient Friend of Youth award, Boys and Girls Clubs, 1998, Disting. Eagle award, Boy Scouts Am., 1999, Jefferson Bronze Medallion award, 2004. Mem.: Am. Arbitration Assn. (arbitrator), Desert Bar Assn. (pres. 2003—04), Calif. Bar Assn., Desert Bus. Roundtable. Personal E-mail: jackfitzgerald3@aol.com.

FITZGERALD, JOHN T., JR., lawyer; b. Worcester, Mass., 1947; AB magna cum laude, Harvard Coll., 1969; JD magna cum laude, U. Pa., 1972. Bar: NY 1973, Fla. 1986, US Tax Ct., Mass. 2005. Ptnr., pvt. clients group leader Nixon Peabody LLP, Rochester, NY, also Boston. Bd. govs. Hillside Family of Agencies; trustee U. Rochester Med. Ctr. Mem.: Mass Bar Assn., Fla. Bar Assn., Estate Planning Coun. of Rochester, Monroe County Bar Assn., NY State Bar Assn. Office: Nixon Peabody LLP 1100 Clinton Square Rochester NY 14604 Address: Nixon Peabody LLP 100 Summer St Boston MA 02110 Office Phone: 585-263-1357, 617-345-1081. Office Fax: 866-947-0918. E-mail: jfitzgerald@nixonpeabody.com.

FITZGERALD, JOHN THOMAS, JR., religious studies educator; b. Birmingham, Ala., Oct. 2, 1948; s. John Thomas and Annie Myrtle (Walters) Fitzgerald; m. Karol Bonneaux, May 23, 1970; children: Kirstin Leigh, Kimberly Anne. BA, Abilene Christian U., 1970, MA, 1972; MDiv, Yale U., 1975, PhD, 1984. Instr. Yale Coll., New Haven, 1979, Yale Div. Sch., New Haven, 1980—81; from instr. to asst. prof. U. Miami, Coral Gables, Fla., 1981—88, assoc. prof., 1988—, dir. honors program, master Hecht Residential Coll., 1987—91. Vis. assoc. prof. Brown U., Providence, 1992, Yale Div. Sch., New Haven, 1998—99, New Haven, 2004; vis. rsch. scholar North-West U., Potchefstroom, South Africa, 2006. Author: Tabula of Cebes, 1983, Cracks in an Earthen Vessel, 1988; editor: Christian Origins sect. Religious Studies Rev., 1994—2002, Friendship, Flattery and Frankness of Speech, 1996, Greco-Roman Perspecitves on Friendship, 1997, Early Christianity and Classical Culture, 2003, Philodemus and the New Testament World, 2004, The Writings of St. Paul, 2007; contbr. articles to profl. jours. Judge for Silver Knight awards Miami (Fla.) Herald, 1988, 1990. Named Two Bros. fellow, Yale Div. Sch., 1974—75; recipient Max Orvitz Summer Rsch. award, U. Miami, 1985, 1987, 1994, 1995, 1998, 2002; fellow, Rotary, Tuebingen, Germany, 1975—76. Mem.: Soc. Bibl. Lit. (chmn. com. 1989—96, editor Texts and Translations Series: Greco-Roman Religion 1993—2000, editor Writings from the Greco-Roman World Series 2001—06, chmn. com. 2003—04, coun. 2003—, sec. 2003—, rsch. grantee 1997—99), Golden Key Nat. Honor Soc., Iron Arrow Hon. Soc., Omicron Delta Kappa, Phi Kappa Phi (chpt. pres. 1988—89). Home: 15215 SW 78 Ct Palmetto Bay FL 33157-2349 Office: U Miami PO Box 248264 Coral Gables FL 33124-4651 Home Phone: 305-235-4298; Office Phone: 305-284-3698. Business E-Mail: john.fitzgerald@miami.edu.

FITZGERALD, JOSEPH PATRICK, artist; b. DC, May 26, 1950; s. John Joseph and Mary Irene Fitzgerald; m. Jean Ellen Hill, Sept. 27, 1975. BA, U. Md., 1972. Illustrator, designer US Consumer Product Safety Comm., Bethesda, Md., 1973—80; chief graphics Nat. Libr. Medicine, Bethesda, 1980—2005; ret., 2005. Painting, Looking for Little Egging, Ocean in View US Nickel, 2005. Recipient Dir.'s award, Nat. Libr. Medicine, 1998. Mem.: Am. Numis. Assn., Assn. Oldest Inhabitants. Avocation: travel. Home and Office: 828 Sligo Ave Silver Spring MD 20910-4701 Personal E-mail: nickelman2005@yahoo.com.

FITZGERALD, JUDITH KLASWICK, federal judge; b. Spangler, Pa., May 10, 1948; d. Julius Francis and Regina Marie (Pregno) Klaswick; m. June 5, 1971 (div. Dec. 1982); 1 child; m. Barry Robert Fitzgerald, Sept. 20, 1986; 1 child. BSBA, U. Pitts., 1970, JD, 1973. Legal rschr. Assocs. Fin., Pitts., 1972-73; law clk. to pres. judge Beaver County (Pa.) Ct. Common Pleas, 1973-74; law clk. to judge Pa. Superior Ct., Pitts., 1974-75; asst. U.S. atty. U.S. Dist. Ct. (we. dist.) Pa., Pitts. and Erie, 1976-87, U.S. bankruptcy judge Pitts., Erie and Johnstown, 1987—, U.S. Dist. Ct. (ea. dist.) Pa., U.S. Dist. Ct. U.S. V.I., U.S. Dist. Ct. Del. Adj. prof. law U. Pitts., 2003-2004, 2005-2006. Co-author: Bankruptcy and Divorce, Support and Property Division, 1991; editor: Pennsylvania Law of Juvenile Delinquency and Deprivation, 1976; contbr. articles to profl. jours. Mem. Pitts. Camerata, 1978-80, Allegheny County Polit.-Legal Edn. Project, 1980, Mendelssohn Choir Pitts., 1982—07; mem. coun. Program to Aid Citizen Enterprise, 1985-87. Recipient Spl. Achievement awards Dept. Justice, Spl. Recognition award Pittsburgh mag., Operation Exodus Outstanding Performance award Dept. Commerce, 1986. Mem. Am. Coll. Bankruptcy, Internat. Women's Insolvency and Restructuring Conf., Allegheny County Bar Assn., Women's Bar Assn. of Western Pa., Nat. Conf. Bankruptcy Judges, Am. Bankruptcy Inst., Nat. Conf. Bankruptcy Clks., Comml. Law League of Am., Fed. Criminal Investigators Assn. (Spl. Svc. award 1988), Zonta. Republican. Lutheran. Avocations: singing, reading, travel. Office: US Bankruptcy Ct 600 Grant St Ste 5490 Pittsburgh PA 15219-2805

FITZGERALD, KATHERINE, molecular biologist, educator; m. Daniel Caffrey. BSc, Univ. Coll., Cork, Ireland, 1995; PhD, Trinity Coll., Dublin, Ireland, 1999. Postdoctoral fellow dept. biochemistry Trinity Coll., Dublin, 1999—2001; postdoctoral rschr. divsn. infectious disease U. Mass. Med. Sch., Worcester, 2001—03, asst. prof. medicine, 2004—. Contbr. articles to profl. jours. Recipient Wellcome Trust Rsch. award, 2001. Office: Immunology and Virology Prog U Mass Med Sch 55 Lake Ave Worcester MA 01655 Office Phone: 508-856-6518. Office Fax: 508-856-5463. E-mail: Katherine.Fitzgerald@umassmed.edu.*

FITZGERALD, KELLY PATRICK, lawyer; BA in Physics with distinction, U. Iowa, 1997, JD magna cum laude, 2000. Bar: Minn. Legal clk., patent agt. Intermec Technologies Corp.; atty. Fish & Richardson, Shumaker & Sieffert, P.A., St. Paul, 2001—. Named a Rising Star, Minn. Super Lawyers mag., 2006. Mem.: Am. Intellectual Property Law Assn., Minn. Intellectual Property Law Assn., Minn. Bar Assn. Office: Shumaker & Sieffert PA 8425 Seasons Pky Ste 105 Saint Paul MN 55125 Office Phone: 651-286-8343. E-mail: fitzgerald@ssiplaw.com.*

FITZGERALD, KEVIN C., lawyer; b. Redlands, Calif., 1962; BA, George Washington Univ., 1985, MA, 1988, JD, 1991. Bar: Mass. 1991, DC 1994, Supreme Ct. 2001. Assoc. Reid & Priest, 1991—95; of counsel Troutman Sanders LLP, 1995—97, ptnr., energy, project develop., fin., 1997—, mng. ptnr., Washington office, 1999—. Adv. coun. Cath. Charities, Archdiocese, Washington. Mem.: ABA, Mass. Bar Assn., Energy Bar Assn., DC Bar Assn. Office: Troutman Sanders LLP Ste 1000 401 Ninth St NW Washington DC 20004-2134 Office Phone: 202-274-2955. Office Fax: 202-654-5600. Business E-Mail: kevin.fitzgerald@troutmansanders.com.

FITZGERALD, KEVIN GERARD, oil industry executive; b. New Orleans, Oct. 31, 1955; s. Patrick Harold Fitzgerald and Rosary Claire (Carallero) Eble; m. Janice Faye Mender, Dec. 20, 1975; children: Kevin Gerard Jr., Shelly Lynn. B magna cum laude in Acctg., U. New Orleans, 1977. CPA, La. Ptnr. Vizzoni & Cooley, CPAs, Kenner, La., 1975-82; asst. treas. Ocean Drilling and Exploration Co., New Orleans, 1982; dir. investor rels. Murphy Oil Corp., 1996—2001, treas., 2001—06, sr. v.p., CFO, 2007—. Mem. AICPA, La. Soc. CPAs (New Orleans chpt.). Clubs: Corp. 25 Investment (Metairie, La.) (treas. 1986), Metaurice Carnival. Roman Catholic. Avocations: fishing, softball. Office: Murphy Oil Corp PO Box 7000 El Dorado AR 71731-7000 Office Phone: 870-862-6411.*

FITZGERALD, KEVIN MICHAEL, lawyer, mediator; b. Kansas City, Kans., May 10, 1956; s. Thomas Francis and Theresa Ann (Grosdidier) FitzG.; m. Susan Patricia Parker, June 21, 1980; children: Kathryn Ann, Shannon Elizabeth, Erin Parker. BBA, U. Tex., Arlington, 1981; JD, U. Ark., 1985. Bar: Mo. 1985, U.S. Dist. Ct. Mo. 1985, U.S. Ct. Appeals (8th cir.) 1985. Assoc. Taylor, Stafford, Woody, Cowherd and Clithero, Springfield, Mo., 1985-90; ptnr. Taylor, Stafford, Woody, Clithero and FitzGerald, Springfield, 1990-2000, Taylor, Stafford, Clithero, FitzGerald & Harris, Springfield, 2001—. Mediator, neutral U.S. Dist. Ct. (we. dist.) Mo. Atty. Roman Cath. Diocese of Springfield-Cape Girardeau. Mem.: Mo. Orgn. Def. Attys., Nat. Diocesan Attys. Assn., Legal Aid S.W. Mo. (bd. dirs. 1993—96), Springfield Met. Bar Assn. (sec. 1997, chmn. alternative dispute com. 2000), Mo. Bar Assn. Office: Taylor Stafford et al 3315 E Ridgeview St Ste 1000 Springfield MO 65804-4083 Office Phone: 417-887-2020. Business E-Mail: kfitzgerald@taylorstafford.com.

FITZGERALD, KYRIAKI ANTONIA, theologian, psychologist; b. Boston, Jan. 17, 1956; d. Michael E. and Tula (Archontula) M. (Tsopeis) Karidoyanes; m. Rev. Dr. Thomas E. FitzGerald. BA, Hellenic Coll., 1977; certificate advanced studies, U. Thessalonika, Greece, 1979; MDiv, Holy Cross Greek Orthodox Sch. Theology, 1980; PhD, Boston U., 1985. Lic. psychologist/health svc. provider Commonwealth of Mass., fellow Am. Assn. Pastoral Counselors. Dir. edn., assoc. dir. tng. Worcester Pastoral Counseling Ctr., 1986—91; vis. prof. pastoral theology St. Vladimir's Sem., 1994; psychologist/psychotherapist Paloma Ctr. for Christian Psychology, Switzerland, 1995—99; cons. and instr. World Coun. Chs., Geneva, 1996—99; psychologist, pastoral psychotherapist, ind. scholar, 1999—. Commr. faith and order commn. World Coun. Chs., 1984—99; adj. asst. theol. faculty Holy Cross Greek Orthodox Sch. Theology, 1984—90; pastoral counselor Holy Cross Greek Orthodox Sch., 1984—90; adj. assoc. prof. theology Holy Cross Greek Orthodox Sch. Theology, 2007—; adj. clin. faculty Andover-Newton Theol. Sch., 1987—90; bd. dirs. Interfaith Sexual Trauma Inst., 1991—96; founder, project coord. St. Catherine's Vision, Inc.; del. internat. dialogue Ecumenical Patriarchate Constantinople, Jerusalem, 2007; presenter in field. Author: Women Deacons in the Orthodox Church, 1999, Persons in Communion: A Theology of Authentic Relationships, 2006; editor: Orthodox Women Speak: Discerning the Signs of the Times, 1999, Encountering Women of Faith, 2005; co-author: Living the Beatitudes: Perspectives in Orthodox Spirituality, 2006. Fellow: Am. Assn. Pastoral Counselors; mem.: Orthodox Theol. Soc., Mass. Psychol. Assn., APA.

FITZGERALD, MARY EILEEN, museum program director; b. Dayton, Ohio, Dec. 21, 1944; d. William McAvoy and Irene Ann (Dougherty) F. BA in Studio Art, U. Dayton, 1966; MA in Art History, Ohio State U., 1970; PhD in Humanities, Syracuse U., 1986. Lectr. Colgate U., Hamilton, NY, 1984-85; asst. prof. Ithaca (N.Y.) Coll., 1987-89, Syracuse (N.Y.) U., 1989-90, Roanoke Coll., Salem, Va., 1990-96; curator of edn. Maier Mus. of Art, Lynchburg, Va., 1996—2002; head of adult edn. and programs Art Mus. Western Va., Roanoke, 2002—. Vis. prof. Ohio U., Athens, 1986-87; adj. asst. prof. Sweet Briar (Va.) Coll., 2001—. Mem. editl. bd. Artemis, 1994-95. Grantee St. James Ch. (Italy), 1983, NEH, 1994; Mednick fellow Va. Found. Ind. Coll., 1991, Florence fellow Syracuse U., 1977-79. Mem. Artemis (pres. bd. dirs. 1994-98). Avocations: photography, hiking, yoga. Home: 2571 Brambleton Ave SW Roanoke VA 24015-4303 Office: Art Mus Western Va Roanoke VA 24011-1436 E-mail: mfitzgerald@artmuseumroanoke.org.

FITZGERALD, MICHAEL LEE, state official; b. Marshalltown, Iowa, Nov. 29, 1951; s. James Martin and Clara Francis (Dankbar) F.; m. Janet Roewe; children: Ryan, Chris, Erin, Bridie. BBA, U. Iowa, 1974. Campaign mgr. Fitzgerald for Treas., Colo., Iowa, 1974; market analyst Massey Ferguson Co., Des Moines, 1975-83; treas. State of Iowa, Des Moines, 1983—. Mem.: Am. Soc. Pub. Adminstr., Govt. Fin. Officers Assn., Nat. Assn. Unclaimed Property Adminstr. (past pres.), Nat. Assn. State Auditors, Comptrollers, and Treasurers (past pres.), Midwest Treasurer's Assn. (past pres.), Nat. Assn. State Treasurers (past pres.). Democrat. Roman Catholic. Office: Office of State Treas Capitol Bldg Rm 114 Des Moines IA 50319-0001 Office Phone: 515-281-5368. Office Fax: 515-281-7562. Business E-Mail: treasurer@iowa.gov.*

FITZGERALD, PATRICK J., JR., prosecutor; b. Bklyn., Dec. 22, 1960; s. Patrick and Tillie Fitzgerald. BA in Econ. and Math., Amherst Coll., 1982; JD, Harvard U., 1985. Litigation assoc. Christy & Viener, 1984—87; asst. US atty. (So. Dist.) NY US Dept. Justice, 1988—2001, chief narcotics unit, 1994, co-chief organized crime-terrorism unit, 1995—2001, nat. security coord., 1996—99, US atty. (no. dist.) Ill., 2001—. Prosecutor in case against Sheikh Omar Abdel Rahman for 1993 World Trade Ctr. bombings US Dept. Justice, 1994, mem. atty. gen's advisory com., 2001—05, spl. prosecutor investigating government leak in the identification of Valerie Plame as a CIA operative, 2003—; mem. Pres. Corp. Fraud Task Force. Named Lawyer of the Yr., Nat. Law Jour., 2005; recipient Atty. Gen.'s award for Exceptional Service, 1996, Stimson Medal, NY Bar Assoc., 1997, Atty. Gen.'s award for Dist. Svc., 2002. Mem.: Phi Beta Kappa Soc. Office: US Dist Ct No Dist Ill Dirksen Federal Bldg 219 S Dearborn St 5th Fl Chicago IL 60604*

FITZGERALD, PETER GOSSELIN, former senator, lawyer; b. Elgin, Ill., Oct. 20, 1960; s. Gerald Francis and Marjorie (Gosselin) F.; m. C. Nina Kerstiens, July 25, 1987; 1 child, Jake Buchanan. AB, Dartmouth Coll., 1982; cert. of attendance, Aristotelian U., Salonica, Greece, 1983; JD, U. Mich., 1986. Bar: Ill. 1986, U.S. Dist. Ct. (no. dist.) Ill. 1986. Assoc. Isham, Lincoln & Beale, Chgo., 1986-88; ptnr. Riordan, Larson, Bruckert & Moore, Chgo., 1988-92; mem. Ill. Senate, Springfield, Ill., 1993—98, chmn. state govt. ops. com., 1997—98; senator from Ill. US Senate, Washington, 1999—2005, chmn. sub com. consumer affairs and product safety com. on commerce, sci., transp., chmn. subcom. fin. mgmt., budget and internat. security com. on govt. affairs, 2003—05; chmn. Chain Bridge Bancorp, Inc., McLean, Va., 2006—. Counsel Harris Bankmont, Inc., 1992—96; dir. Nat. Coun. Econ. Edn., 2005—; trustee Nat. Constitution Ctr., 2005—; adv. dir. Transurban Devel., Inc., 2006—. Rotary Found. internat. grad. scholar, 1982-83. Mem. Econ. Club Chgo., Union League Club. Republican. Roman Catholic. E-mail: dgumino@fitzgeraldpeter.com.

FITZGERALD, REBECCA ANNE, curator, historian; b. Tucson, Mar. 25, 1956; d. Jack Bates Johnson and Hope Anne Charity Springer; m. Robert Francis Fitzgerald, Jan. 3, 1977; children: Zachary Randal Townsend, Reba Louise. BA in History, Okla. Bapt. U., Shawnee, 1997; MA in History and Mus. Studies, U. Ctrl. Okla., Edmond, 1999. Dir., curator Pottawatomie County Hist. Soc., Shawnee, 1989—90; student asst. Okla. Bapt. U. Archives, Shawnee, 1994—97; registrar, collections mgr. Mabee-Gerrer Mus. Art, Shawnee, 1997—2000; exec. dir. Erlander Home Mus., Rockford, Ill., 2000—03; curator collections Muskegon County Mus., Mich., 2003—. Peer reviewer Am. Assn. Museums, Washington, 2001—. Author: (weekly column) Shawnee News Star, 1989—90, singer. Asst. leader, leader Girl Scouts, Shawnee, asst. leader Williams Bay, Wis.; leader Missionettes, Whitehall, Mich., 2004; alumni Okla. Scholar Leadership Enrichment Program, 1996; bd. mem. Midwest Registrars Com., archivist, 2004—05. Scholar, Okla. Bapt. U., 1997, U. Ctrl. Okla., 1998, 1999. Mem.: Phi Alpha Theta. Office: Muskegon County Mus 430 W Clay Ave Muskegon MI 49446

FITZGERALD, ROBERT MAURICE, financial and retired bank executive; b. Chgo., Jan. 8, 1942; s. James Patrick and Catherine (McNulty) Fitzgerald; children: Stephen, Peter, Susan, Martin. BS, Loyola U., Chgo., 1971; postgrad., U. Wis., 1974-76, Northwestern U., 1980. Sr. v.p. Fed. Reserve Bank, Chgo., 1979-85; pres. Chgo. Clearing House Assn., Chgo., 1985—. Cons. Currency Bd., Abu Dhabi, United Arab Emirates, 1979; past bd. dirs. Nat. Automated Clearing House Assn., Washington; advisor U.S. Coun. on Internat. Banking, NYC. Pres. Coun. on Alcoholism, Ann Arbor, Mich., 1978, Diocesan Bd. Edn., Joliet, Ill., 1981—84; former dir. Frances Xavier Warde Sch.; vice chair. Chgo. Crime Commn.; trustee Union League Boys and Girls Clubs; sec. Civic and Arts Found.; former mem. adv. bd. St. Mary of Nazereth Hosp.; past pres., bd. dirs., vice chmn. exec. com. LaLalle St. Coun.; former chair, bd. trustees Old St. Patrick's Ch., Chgo.; bd. dirs. Concern Worldwide (U.S.), Inc. Mem.: City Club Chgo., Bankers Club Chgo. (sec., treas., exec. com.), Union League Club Chgo. (past pres.), Econ. Club Chgo., Execs. Club of Chgo. (bd. dirs., treas.). Democrat. Roman Catholic. Office: Chgo Clearing House Assn 230 S La Salle St Ste 700 Chicago IL 60604-1410 E-mail: fitz@chgo.org.

FITZ-GERALD, ROGER MILLER, lawyer; b. NYC, July 13, 1935; s. Gerald Hartpence and Rovenia Francis (Miller) F.-G.; m. Martha Ann Odell, 1967 (div. 1985); children: Kathleen Odell, Maureen Roxanne, Arthur Thomas; m. Janice Evens, 1993. BS with honors, U. Ill., 1957, JD with honors, 1961. Bar: Ill. 1961, U.S. Dist. Ct. (no. dist.) 1961, U.S. Patent and Trademark Office, 1965, U.S. Ct. Customs and Patent Appeals, 1978, U.S. Ct. Appeals (fed. cir.) 1982, U.S. Dist. Ct. (so. dist.) Ill. 1992, U.S. Dist. Ct. (cen. dist.) Ill. 1994. Assoc. Kirkland, Ellis, Hodson, Chaffetz & Masters, Chgo., 1961-64; assoc. specializing in fgn. patent law Fitch, Even, Tabin & Luedeka, Chgo., 1964-72; patent atty. Bell & Howell Co., Chgo., 1972-74, sr. patent atty., 1974-75, group patent atty., 1975-76, group patent counsel, 1976-82, sr. patent counsel, 1982-85, sr. tech. law counsel, 1985-86, chief tech. law counsel, 1986-90; pvt. practice Urbana, Wilmette, Belleville, Ill., 1990—, St. Louis, 1990—. Author: (with Ferdinand J. Zeni) Precinct Captain's Guide, 1968; contbg. author: Materials on Legislation (Read, MacDonald, Fordham and Pierce), 1973 Constl. revision chmn. Ill. Young Republican Orgn., 1968-70. Served with AUS, 1957 Mem. ABA, Ill. Bar Assn., Chgo. Bar Assn., Champaign County Ill. Bar Assn., Intellectual Property Law Assn. Chgo., Am. Intellectual Property Law Assn., Assn. Corp. Patent Counsel, Computer Law Assn., Order of Coif, Phi Beta Kappa, Phi Eta Sigma, Phi Delta Phi, Delta Upsilon (province gov. 1969-75). Office: 1104 S Orchard St Urbana IL 61801-4852 Personal E-mail: rogerthebrave@juno.com.

FITZGERALD, SHANE MICHAEL, engineer; b. Landstuhl, Germany, Oct. 20, 1958; s. William Joseph and Anne T. Fitzgerald; m. Jessica D. Dimaggio, Feb. 14, 1985. BSEE, Calif. State U., Long Beach, 2000. Dir. engring. ElectroCom Comm., Santa Fe Springs, Calif., 1991—99; chief scientist IPMobileNet, Irvine, 1999—2007; group mgr. RF Design Broadcast Microwave Svcs., Poway, Calif., 2007—. Mem.: IEEE. R-Conservative. Roman Catholic. Achievements include patents in field. Avocations: swimming, target shooting, weight training. Home: 31930 Calle El Potrero Pauma Valley CA 92061 Home Phone: 760-742-4292. Personal E-mail: fitzgerald@ieee.org.

FITZGERALD, THOMAS ROBERT, state supreme court justice; b. Chgo., July 10, 1941; s. Thomas Henry and Kathryn (Touhy) Fitzgerald; m. Gayle Ann Aubry; 5 children. Attended, Loyola U., Chicago, 1959—63; JD, John Marshall Law Sch., Chicago, 1968. Bar: Ill. 1968. Trial asst. State Atty. Office Cook County, 1968—72, asst. state atty., 1968—76, felony trial supr., 1973—76; judge criminal div. Circuit Ct. Cook County, 1976—2000; justice Ill. Supreme Ct., 2000—. Adj. prof. law Kent Coll. Law, 1977—2000. Served in USN. Recipient Outstanding Jud. Performance award Chgo. Crime Commn., Herman Kogan Media award for excellence in broadcast jour., John Powers Crowley award Lawyers' Assistance Program, 2000, John Marshall Law School Freedom award, 2001, Joel Flaum award Chgo. Inn of Ct., 2003; named Celtic Man of Yr. Celtic Legal Soc., Catholic Lawyer of Yr. Catholic Lawyers Guild Chgo., 2005; fellow Ill. Bar Found. Office: Ill Supreme Ct 160 N LaSalle St Rm N-2013 Chicago IL 60601*

FITZGERALD, TIMOTHY J., corporate financial executive; Audit mgr. Arthur Andersen LLP; corp. contr. Middleby Corp., Elgin, Ill., 1998—2003, v.p., 2000—, CFO, 2003—. Named one of Top 40 Under 40, Crain's Chgo. Bus., 2006. Office: Middleby Corp 1400 Toastmaster Dr Elgin IL 60120*

FITZGERALD, TIMOTHY K., writer, political organizer, non-profit administrator; b. San Jose, Calif., Jan. 3, 1946; BA in Econs., San Jose State Coll., 1971; BA in History, San Jose State U., 1980, MA in Social Sci., 1985, MA in History, 1997. Treas. Associated Students San Jose State Coll., 1969-70; camp bus. mgr. Boy Scouts Am., Sonora, Calif., 1973; co. budget analyst Allstate Equity Investments, 1980; adminstrv. asst. Summer Employment of Youth program CETA, San Jose, 1981; pres. Corp. for Shared Responsibility, San Jose, 1983-84; rschr. San Jose, 1992-96; owner/operator Raccoon Pubs., San Jose, 1991-92; freelance writer San Jose, 1986—; rschr., 1992-96. Sec. Discovery, Inc, 1991-93; adminstrv. trustee Inst. for Social Orgnl. Rsch., 1992-94, 98-2001, exec. dir., 2001-; instr. Cerro Coso CC, Mammoth Lakes, Calif., 1998-2000, Columbia CC, Sonora, Calif., 2004; staff writer David Cobb Campaign for U.S. pres., 2004. Author: Trail to Black Mountain, 1978, Impressions from Idle Rock, 1981, Essays in Capitalism, 1986, Inner City, 1993, Twilight in the Afternoon, 1997, Challenge To America, 1998, (trilogy) The Quest: The Cut of the Diamonds, 2001—03, Statecraft and War, 2004; corr.: Mono County Rev. Herald, 1997—98; talk show host KSJS Radio, San Jose, 1995—97. Mgr., candidate State Assembly, San Jose, 1994, San Jose City Coun., 1982, Mono County Bd. Edn., 1998; del. nat. conv. Green Party US, 2000, 04, presdl. screening com. for '08; co-coord. State Green Party Platform, Calif., 1993, State Green Party campaigns and candidates, Calif., 1995-97; elected mem. Green Party County Coun., Santa Clara County, Calif., 1992-94, Mono County, 2000-03; staff writer David Cobb Campaign for U.S. Pres., 2004; elector Electorial Coll., 2004, vol. Cmty. Companions, Inc., San Jose, 1990-91; commr. City of San Jose Disability Adv., 1993-97, vice-chair, 1997; task force on poverty Santa Clara County, 1995-97; active Mono County Mental Health Adv. Bd., 1998-2002, chair, 1999-2000. Advanced cadet U.S. Army ROTC, 1966-67 Mem. Acad. Poets, Nat. Writers Union, Amnesty Interant., Fellowship of Reconciliation, Ams. for Dem. Action, Commonwealth Club, Sierra Club, Tau Delta Phi. Lutheran. Avocations: hiking, wilderness photography, chess, bridge. Home: 419 E Santa Clara St # B San Jose CA 95113 Personal E-mail: timkf@hotmail.com.

FITZGERALD, WARREN FRANKLIN, lawyer; b. Methuen, Mass., Feb. 4, 1955; s. Donald Franklin and Ruth Elizabeth (Mann) F.; children: Sara Elizabeth, Dillon Charles. BA magna cum laude with distinction, Boston U., 1976, JD, 1979. Bar: Mass. 1979, U.S. Dist. Ct. Mass. 1980, U.S. Ct. Appeals (1st cir.) 1985, U.S. Supreme Ct. 2005. Assoc. Hutchins & Wheeler, Boston, 1979-84, Parker, Coulter, Daley & White, 1984-85,

Meehan, Boyle & Cohen, P.C., 1985—2002; ptnr. Meehan, Boyle, Black & Fitzgerald, P.C. Mem. ABA, ATLA, Mass. Acad. Trial Attys. (pres. 1999-2000), Mass. Bar Assn. (pres. 2005), Boston Bar Assn., Fed. Bar Assn., Phi Beta Kappa. Avocations: skiing, boating, scuba diving, reading. Office: Fitzgerald Law Firm LLC One Constitution Ctr Ste 100 Boston MA 02129 Office Phone: 617-241-4288. Business E-Mail: wf@fitzgerald.com.

FITZGERALD, WILLIAM ALLINGHAM, savings and loan association executive, director; b. Omaha, Nov. 18, 1937; s. William Frances and Mary (Allingham) F.; m. Barbara Ann Miskell, Aug. 20, 1960; children—Mary Colleen, Katherine Kara, William Tate. BSBA in Fin., Creighton U., 1959; grad. Savs. and Loan League exec. tng. program, U. Ga., 1962, U. Ind., 1969. With Comml. Fed. Savs. & Loan Assn., Omaha, 1959—, v.p., asst. sec., 1963-68, exec. v.p., 1968-73, pres., 1974-82, CEO, 1983—, chmn., CEO, 1994—. Trustee Ind. Coll. Found.; vice chmn. bd. dirs. Creighton U.; bd. dirs. Coll. of St. Mary, United Way of Midlands; trustee Archbishop's com. for ednl. devel. Roman Catholic Ch. Served to lt. Fin. Corps, U.S. Army. Chmn. Am. Cmty. Bankers, 1998—. Clubs: Omaha Country, Kiewit Plaza. Lodges: Knights of Ak-Sar-Ben (gov.).

FITZGIBBON, DANIEL HARVEY, lawyer; b. Columbus, Ind., July 7, 1942; s. Joseph Bales and Margaret Lenore (Harvey) FitzGibbon; m. Joan Helen Meltzer, Aug. 12, 1973; children: Katherine Lenore, Thomas Bernard. BS in Engring., U.S. Mil. Acad., 1964; JD cum laude, Harvard U., 1972. Bar: Ind. 1972, U.S. Dist. Ct. (so. dist.) Ind. 1972, U.S. Tax Ct. 1977. Commd. 2d lt. U.S. Army, 1964, advanced through grades to capt., 1967, served with inf. in West Berlin and Vietnam, resigned, 1969; assoc. Barnes & Thornburg, Indpls., 1972-79, ptnr., 1979-99, of counsel, 2000—. Spkr. various insts.; comml. law liaison ABA-CEELI, Moscow, 1998—99. Author: To Bear any Burden, A Hoosier Green Beret's Letters from Vietnam, 2005. Mem. sch. bd. Met. Sch. Dist. Lawrence Twp., 1988—96, pres., 1990—91, 1994—95; bd. advs. Eiteljorg Mus. Am. Indian and Western Art, 1993—2003. Fellow: Am. Bar Found., Am. Coll. Tax Counsel; mem.: ABA (internat. law sect.), Indpls. Bar Assn. (chmn. tax sect. 1982—83, coun. 1982—86), Ind. State Bar Assn. (tax sect.), Am. Law Inst., Lit. Club, Woodstock Club, Lawyers Club. Home: 6460 Lawrence Dr Indianapolis IN 46226-1035 Office: Barnes & Thornburg 1313 Merchants Bank Bldg Indianapolis IN 46204-3506 Office Phone: 317-231-7247. Business E-Mail: dfitzgib@btlaw.com.

FITZHUGH, KATHRYN CORROTHERS, law librarian; b. Little Rock, Feb. 4, 1950; d. Charles Edward and Billie Jean (Burns) Corrothers; m. Benjamin Dewey Fitzhugh, Nov. 28, 1970; 1 child, Erica Janine. BA, U. Ark., 1971; MSLS, U. Ill., 1976; JD, U. Ark., Little Rock, 1983. Bar: Ark. 1983, US Dist. Ct. (ea. dist.) Ark. 1983. Sci./tech. libr. Grad. Inst. Tech., Little Rock, 1977-79; br. libr. U.S. Cts. Br. Libr., Little Rock, 1980-83, 89-92; law clk. Hon. George Howard Jr., Little Rock, 1983-84; ptnr. Fitzhugh & Fitzhugh, Little Rock, 1985-87; ref./circulation libr. U. Ark.-Little Rock/Pulaski County Law Libr., 1987-89, pub. svcs. libr., 1992-97, ref./spl. collections libr. and prof. of law librarianship, 1997—. Contbg. author: Handbook of Law for Arkansas Women, 1987; contbr. chpt. to book; editor in field. Mem. North Little Rock NAACP, 1990—5; mem. Ouachita coun. Girl Scouts U.S., 1986-88, troop leader, 1997-98; mem. Shorter Coll. Adult Edn. Bd., 1986-87, Carver Magnet Elem. Sch. PTA, 1989-96. Co-recipient Pub. Svc. award U. Ark.-Little Rock Bowen Sch. Law, 2003; The Herbert Lehman Edn. Fund scholar, 1967-71. Mem. ABA, Am. Assn. Law Librs., Ark. Bar Assn., Ark. Assn. Women Lawyers (corr. sec. 1989-90), Soc. of Am. Archivists, Soc. Southwest Archivists, Southwestern Assn. Law Librs. (pres. 2002-03) Ark. Hist. Assn., Delta Sigma Theta, Afro-Am. Genealogical & Historical Soc., 2003-. Methodist. Office: U Ark at Little Rock William H Bowen Sch of Law Pulaski County Law Libr 1203 McMath Ave Little Rock AR 72202-5142

FITZMAURICE, LAURENCE DORSET, social services administrator; b. Worcester, Mass., Aug. 7, 1938; s. John Vincent and Alice (Earle) F.; m. Ann McQuaid, Apr. 15, 1961; children: Laura, Peter, Meghan. BS in Mgmt., Babson Coll., 1959; postgrad. in law, Boston Coll., 1961. NASD Series 6. Prodn. control Sylvania, Needham, Mass., 1959-61; divsn. controller EG&G, Inc., Bedford, Mass., 1961-69; asst. corp. controller Tyco Labs., Waltham, Mass., 1970; corp. controller Analog Devices, Norwood, Mass., 1971-73; v.p. fin. Balco, Inc., Newton, Mass., 1974-75; comptroller Commonwealth of Mass., Boston, 1976-78, commr. of revenue, 1978; sr. cons. Am. Mgmt. Systems, Arlington, Va., 1979; prin. cons. Boston, 1980-81; v.p. State St. Bank & Trust Co., Boston, 1982—2002, ret., 2002; prin. Dorset Mgmt. Group, Wellesley, Mass., 2002—; CEO New Eng. Shelter Homeless Vets., Boston, 2005—. Adj. prof. Northeastern U. Grad. Sch. Polit. Sci., Boston, 1977-78; mem. faculty New Eng. Coll. Fin., 1998—; mem. Bd. Bank Incorp., Boston, 1978; cons. Exec. Svc. Corps. of New Eng., 2003—. Contbr. articles to profl. jours. Commr. Mass. State Lottery, Braintree, 1976-78; sec. Mass. Housing Fin. Agy., Boston, 1978; pres. Human Rels. Svc., Wellesley, Mass., 1988-89, trustee, 1986-2000; bd. dirs. Social Policy Rsch. Group, Boston, 1981-92, Boston Mcpl. Rsch. Bur., 1985-2001, exec. com. 1999-2001; mem. allocations com. United Way of Mass. Bay, 1998, 2001-02, multi-yr. audit task force, 1999, 2000; bd. overseers USS Constitution Mus., 1999-2001, trustee, 2001—; mem. hearings com. Mass. Bd. Bar Overseers, 2002—; bd. mem. Nat. Coalition for Homeless Veterans, 2007-. Cpl. USMCR, 1957—62. Recipient Better Govt. award, Pioneer Inst., Boston. Mem.: Union Club of Boston. Democrat. Roman Catholic. Avocation: golf. Office Phone: 617-371-1772. E-mail: Dorsets4@comcast.net.

FITZMYER, JOSEPH AUGUSTINE, theology studies educator, priest; b. Phila., Nov. 4, 1920; s. Joseph Augustine and Anna Catherine (Alexy) F. AB, Loyola U., Chgo., 1943, AM, 1945; Licentiate in Sacred Theology, Facultés St. Albert de Louvain, Belgium, 1952; PhD, Johns Hopkins U., 1956; Licentiate in Sacred Scripture, Pontifical Bibl. Inst., 1957. Joined S.J., 1938, ordained priest Roman Cath. Ch., 1951. Asst. prof. N.T. and Bibl. langs. Woodstock (Md.) Coll., 1958-59, assoc. prof., 1959-64, prof., 1964-69; prof. Aramaic and Hebrew dept. Nr. Ea. langs.-civilizations U. Chgo., 1969-71; prof. N.T. and Bibl. langs. dept. theology Fordham U., Bronx, NY, 1971-74, Weston Jesuit Sch. Theology, Cambridge, Mass., 1974-76; prof. dept. Bibl. studies Cath. U. Am., Washington, 1976—2004, prof. emeritus, 2004—. Tchr. Gonzaga H.S., Washington, 1945-48; Spkr.'s lectr. Bibl. studies Oxford (Eng.) U., 1974-75. Author: Essays on the Semitic Background of the New Testament, 1971, The Genesis Apocryphon of Qumran Cave I, 1966, 3d edit., 2004; editor (with R.E. Brown and R.E. Murphy) The New Jerome Biblical Commentary, 1990; The Gospel According to Luke (Anchor Bible), vol. 28, 1981, vol. 28A, 1985, Romans (Anchor Bible), vol. 33, 1993, The Acts of the Apostles, vol. 31, 1998, The Letter to Philemon, vol. 34C, 2000. Mem. Cath. Bibl. Assn. (pres. 1970, editor Quar. 1980-84), Soc. Bibl. Lit. (pres. 1978-79, editor Jour. 1971-76), Studiorum Novi Testamenti Societas (pres. 1992-93). Home: Georgetown U Jesuit Cmty PO Box 571200 Washington DC 20057-1200 E-mail: fitzmyja@georgetown.edu.

FITZPATRICK, BRIAN, Canadian legislator; b. Assiniboia, Can., Nov. 18, 1945; m. Zinaida Fitzpatrick; 2 children. BA in History, Bemidji State U., Minn.; LLB, U. Saskatchewan, Can. Cert. tchr. Can. Mem. 37th, 38th, and 39th parliament House of Commons, Ottawa, Canada, mem. standing com. on pub. accounts. Trustee Nipawin Bd. Edn.; mem. Reform's Nat. Task Force on Criminal Justice, Dem. Populism and Provincial Party Involvement. Office: House of Commons Justice Bldg Ste 402 Ottawa ON K1A 0A6 Canada Address: 201 118 12th St E Prince Albert SK S6V 1B6 Canada

FITZPATRICK, DANIEL M., trust company executive, lawyer; b. Plattsburgh, NY, Mar. 5, 1958; s. James A. and Joan M. FitzPatrick; m. Helen Ix, Aug. 24, 1985; children: Whitney G., Caroline I., John R. AB cum laude, Dartmouth Coll., Hanover, New Hampshire, 1980; JD, Vanderbilt U. Sch. Law, Nashville, Tennessee, 1983. Bar: NY 1984. Atty. Davis Polk & Wardwell, NYC, 1983—92; mng. dir. J.P. Morgan & Co., Inc., 1992—2000, Goldman, Sachs & Co., 2000—05, Citigroup, Inc., 2005—; global CEO, Citigroup Trust, 2005—. Trustee The Health Care Chaplaincy, NYC, 2005—; bd. mem. Greenwich Emergency Med. Svc., Inc., Greenwich, Conn., 2004—; bd. councillors Am. Assn. of Sovereign Mil. Order of Malta, NYC, 2006—. Editor-in-chief Vanderbilt Journal of Transnational Law. Mem.: Assn. of the Bar of the City of NY, NY State Bar Assn., ABA, Trust & Investment Divsn., NY Bankers Assn. (exec. com. mem. 2002—04), Trust Mgmt. Assn. (exec. com. mem. 2002—05), The Anglers Club, NYC, The Preston Mountain Club, Kent, Conn., The Belle Haven Club, Greenwich, Conn., The Univ. Club, NYC. Roman Catholic. Office: Citigroup Trust 485 Lexington Ave 10th Fl New York NY 10017 Home Phone: 203-869-5634; Office Phone: 212-559-9862. E-mail: dan.fitzpatrick@citigroup.com.

FITZPATRICK, HAROLD FRANCIS, lawyer; b. Jersey City, Oct. 16, 1947; s. Harold G. and Anne Marie F.; m. Joanne M. Merry, Sept. 22, 1973; children: Elizabeth, Kevin, Matthew, Christopher. AB, Boston Coll., 1969; MBA, NYU, 1971; JD, Harvard U., Cambridge, Mass., 1974. Bar: N.J. 1974, U.S. Dist. Ct. N.J. 1974, U.S. Ct. Internat. Trade 1986, U.S. Supreme Ct. 1994. Securities analyst Chase Manhattan Bank, NYC, 1970-71, Brown Bros., Harriman & Co., NYC, 1971; staff asst. U.S. Senate, Washington, 1972; law clk. to assoc. justice NJ Supreme Ct., Trenton, 1974-75; assoc. Cleary, Gottlieb, Steen & Hamilton, NYC, 1975-78; mng. ptnr. Fitzpatrick & Merritt, Bayonne, NJ, 1978—. Gen. counsel Housing Authority City of Bayonne, 1976—, Color Pigments Mfrs. Assn., Alexandria, Va., 1978—, N.J. Assn. Housing and Redevel. Authorities, Brick, N.J., 1979—, Housing Authority Town of Secaucus, N.J., 1980-88, Rahway (N.J.) Geriatrics Ctr. Inc., 1981-92, Housing Authority City of Englewood, N.J., 1985-91, Housing Authority City of Rahway, 1986-2000, Edgewater Mcpl. Utilities Authority, 1986-93, Housing Authority City of Woodbridge, N.J., 1988-94, Housing Authority City of Asbury Pk., N.J., 1991-94, Bd. Edn. City of Rahway, 1994-97, N.J. Pub. Housing Authority Joint Ins. Fund, 1995-2001. Recipient Silver medal, Soc. Dyers and Colourists, Bradford, Eng., 2006. Mem.: ABA, Hudson County Bar Assn. (trustee, officer 1984—92, pres. 1993), N.J. Bar Assn., Beta Gamma Sigma. Office: Fitzpatrick & Merritt 90 W 40th St Bayonne NJ 07002-6127 Office Phone: 201-339-4000.

FITZPATRICK, JAMES A., JR., lawyer; b. Plattsburgh, NY, July 1, 1949; BA cum laude, Dartmouth Coll., 1971; JD, Albany Law Sch., Union Univ., 1974. Bar: N.Y. Ptnr. Dewey Ballantine LLP, NYC, 1989—, global chmn. corp. dept., 1989—. Trustee Winston Churchill Found. U.S.; dir. Ultimate Software Group. Mem.: ABA. Office: Dewey Ballantine LLP 1301 Ave of the Americas New York NY 10019-6092 Office Phone: 212-259-6220. Office Fax: 212-259-6333. Business E-Mail: jfitzpatrick@dbllp.com.

FITZPATRICK, JAMES DAVID, lawyer; b. Syracuse, NY, Oct. 21, 1938; s. William Francis and Margaret Mary (Shortt) F. BS, Holy Cross Coll., Worcester, Mass., 1960; JD, Syracuse U., 1963. Bar: N.Y. 1963, U.S. Dist. Ct. (no. dist.) N.Y. 1965. Assoc. Bond, Schoeneck & King, Syracuse, 1963—76, mem., 1976—88, ptnr., 1988—. Pres. Hiscock Legal Aid Soc., Syracuse, 1975-76; faculty Nat. Bus. Inst., Eau Claire, Wis., 1990—; del. Russian Conf. on Banking-The Kremlin, Moscow, 1992, 93; spkr. Internat. Conf. on Terrorism, Madrid, 2002. Mem. Presdl. Roundtable, Washington, 1991-92; founding mem. pres.'s task force Nat. Coalition Against Pornography, Common Cause; chmn. adv. bd. Rep. Nat. Coms., 1994; mem. The Studio Mus. in Harlem, Am. Mus. Nat. History; founding mem. Am. Air Mus.; nat. adv. coun. USN Meml. Found. Recipient Afghanistan Freedom Fighter award Afghan Mercy Fund, 1989, Rep. Senatorial Medal of Freedom, Honored Friend of El Salvador award, 1991, Wisdom award of Honor, Wisdom Soc. for Advancement of Knowledge, Learning and Rsch. in Edn., named to Wisdom Hall of Fame, 1999. Mem. ABA, NAACP, N.Y. State Bar Assn., Onondaga County Bar Assn. (chmn. real estate com. 1990-96), Internat. Bar Assn., Am. Land Title Assn., UN Assn. of U.S.A., Habitat for Humanity Internat., Amnesty Internat. U.S.A., Nat. Audubon Soc., Ctr. for Nat. Independence in Politics, Smithsonian Nat. Assocs., Nat. Trust for Hist. Preservation, Navy League U.S., World Future Soc., Ams. Guild, Internat. Platform Assn. (spkr. Internat. Youth Ctr., New Delhi), Inst. Global Ethics, World Jurist Assn. Republican. Roman Catholic. Avocations: housing education, reading, walking. Home: 201 Croyden Rd Syracuse NY 13224-1917 Office: Bond Schoeneck & King 1 Lincoln Ctr Fl 18 Syracuse NY 13202-1324 Office Phone: 315-218-8184. Business E-Mail: fitzpatrick@bsk.com.

FITZPATRICK, JAMES FRANKLIN, lawyer; b. Bluffton, Ind., Jan. 18, 1933; s. Raymond North and Evelyn (Baughman) F.; m. Sandra McNear, July 22, 1961; children: Michael, David, Benjamin. AB, Ind. U., 1955, JD, 1959; postgrad., Cambridge U., 1956. Law clk. to chief judge U.S. Ct. Appeals, Chgo., 1959-61; assoc. Arnold & Porter, Washington, 1961-67, ptnr., 1967—. Adj. prof. law Georgetown U., Washington, 1971-75, 2003—; acad. vis. London Sch. Econs., 1978-79, Trinity Coll., Dublin, Ireland, 1987-88; chmn. Global Rights, 1999—; vis. prof. law U. N.Mex., 1999, 2005-06. Author: Law and Roadside Hazards, 1975. Bd. dirs. ACLU, 1983-85, pres. Nat. Capital chpt., Washington, 1982-83; pres. Washington Project for the Arts, 1984-90; dir. Ctr. for Auto Safety, 1984—, Phillips Collection, 1990-2005, Shakespeare Theatre, 1991-2007, Site Santa Fe, 1997—, Ctr. for Arts and Culture, 1998—2006, Brit. Am. Arts Assn., 1999—; nat. chmn. Young Citizens for Johnson, 1964. Mem. ABA, Order of Coif, Phi Beta Kappa. Democrat. Presbyterian. Office: Arnold & Porter 555 12th St NW Washington DC 20004-1206 Office Phone: 202-942-5878.

FITZPATRICK, JAMES WARD, JR., retired engineering educator; b. Birmingham, Ala., June 17, 1921; s. James Ward and Ellen Barbara (Vogtle) Fitzpatrick; m. Ruth Bertha Horn, June 19, 1948; 1 child, James Ralph (dec.). BS in Indsl. Engring., Auburn U., Ala., 1942, BSME, 1947; student, MIT, 1949—50, Auburn U., Ala., 1951—53. Registered profl. engr., Ala. Indsl. engr. O'Neal Steel, Birmingham, 1947-48; plant engr. Stockham Valves & Fittings, Birmingham, 1948-49; instr. mech. engring. Auburn U., 1950-53; structural engr. Decatur (Ala.) Iron & Steel Co., 1953-56, chief engr. jail and prison equipment, 1956-64; engring. and project mgr. Monsanto Co., St. Louis, 1964-72, engring. supt., 1972-82; v.p. personnel and ops. Continental Commodities, Inc., Charlotte, N.C., 1982-83; instr. York Tech. Coll., Rock Hill, SC, 1986—98, dept. mgr., indsl. and engring. tech. and constrn. trades, continuing edn. divsn., 1999—2001, cons. continuing edn. divsn., 2002—07; ret. Cons. in field. Author: (software) Workplan, 1984. Capt. US Army, 1942—46, ETO. Decorated Bronze Star. Mem.: Charlotte Philatelic Soc. (pres. 1985—89). Republican. Presbyterian. Avocations: fantasy baseball, stamp collecting/philately. Home: 5006 Gamton Ct Charlotte NC 28226-7920 Personal E-mail: ogoytc@bellsouth.net.

FITZPATRICK, JANE, entrepreneur; b. Cuttingsville, Vt., Nov. 18, 1923; m. John H. Fitzpatrick, Sept. 7, 1944; children: Nancy Jane, JoAnn Fitzpatrick Brown. HHD (hon.), N. Adams State Coll., Mass., 1978; LHD (hon.), U. Mass., 1987, Am. Internat. Coll., Springfield, Mass., 1994. Co-founder, chmn. bd. Country Curtains, Stockbridge, Mass., 1956—. Life trustee Boston Symphony Orch., trustee, 1982—96; trustee emerita The Norman Rockwell Mus., Stockbridge, Mass. Chmn. Berkshire Theatre Festival, Stockbridge, Mass, (bd. pres. 1977-98). Office: PO Box 954 Stockbridge MA 01262-0955

FITZPATRICK, JOHN CHARLES, humanities educator, curator; b. Streator, Ill., July 17, 1947; s. Eileen Veronica Leber and John Bernard Fitzpatrick. BA, Principia Coll., Elsah, Ill., 1965—69; EdS, U. Iowa, Iowa City, 1969—79; postgrad., UCLA, 1986. Cert. tchr. State of Iowa, 1980. Grad. asst., asst. varsity swim coach U. Iowa, Iowa City, 1969—73; lectr., health and phys. edn. Cornell Coll., Mount Vernon, Iowa, 1973—78; art history chmn. Kirkwood CC, Cedar Rapids, Iowa, 1977—78; tchr. and coach Iowa City Cmty. Sch. Dist., 1978—80; curriculum program facilitator Cedar Rapids Cmty. Sch. Dist., Iowa, 1981—82. We. regional dir. for supervision and adminstrn. Nat. Art Edn. Assn., Washington, 2003—05; pres. Humanities Iowa, Iowa City, 2004—; art tchr. Polk Elem. Sch., Cedar Rapids, 2002—03; adj. art edn. methods Coe Coll., 2001—03. Contbr. anthology, educational programming (NEH Swartz Award, 2002). Mem. Iowa Old Capitol restoration com., 1976; judge Cmty. Betterment Programs, Iowa Devel. Commn., 1976-77; bd. mem. Friends of the Jeffrey Ballet, N.Y.C., 1985-89; bd. mem. Dance Focus of Iowa, 1986-90, pres. 1988-90; mem. arts com. Iowa City C. of C., 1986-91; mem. Iowa Arts Festival Com., 1988-90; chmn. Grant Wood Centennial Celebration State Com., 1991; mem. Cedar Rapids Literary Club, Cedar Rapids Country Club, 1992-96; spkr. Nat. Endowment for the Arts in ednl. programs with Kitty Carlisle Hart, Lincoln Ctr., U.S. Senate subcom., 1993; presenter, Lt. Gov.'s Conf. on Diversity, 1995; mem. Am. Theatre Organ Soc., 1966-, Nat. Edn. Com., 1994-96; mem. arts advisory bd., Grant Wood Edn. Agy., 1991-; mem. design com., Regional Arts Facility-Ctr. Space, 1991-98; mem. City of Cedar Rapids Visual Arts Com., 1994-2001, v.p., 1998, chmn., 1999, 2000; mem. Art in State Bldgs. Com., U. Iowa Hosps. & Clinics, 1996-2003; events chair U. Iowa Mus. Art, 1997; bd. mem. Cedar Rapids Opera Theater, 1998-2004; mem. River Way Design Team, City of Cedar Rapids, 1998-2001; mem. exhbns. com., the History Ctr., 1999-; cons. Humanities Iowa, Born Again project, 2001-02, treas. and chair programming and grants com., 2002-03, v.p., 2003-04, pres., 2004-05; mem. fundraising com. Friends of the Paramount Theatre, 2001-04; bd. dirs. Cedar Rapids Oak Hill Cemtery, 2001-; Performance Pavilion chair, band commn. City of Cedar Rapids, 2001- Named Arts Adminstr. of the Yr., Iowa Art Edn. Assn., 2001; recipient Arts Edn. Award, Rockefeller Bros. Fund, 1982, John Fitzpatrick Day, City of Cedar Rapids, 2001. Mem.: Nat. Art Edn. Assn. (we. region dir., adminstrn. and supervision 2003, nat. dir.-elect 2005—, Nat. Educator of the Yr. 2002). Avocations: travel, reading, swimming, jogging. Home: 721 North Linn Iowa City IA 52245-1937 Office: Cedar Rapids Cmty Schs 346 Second Ave SW Cedar Rapids IA 52404-2099 Home Phone: 319-337-3223; Office Phone: 319-558-1132. Office Fax: 319-558-2900. Personal E-mail: historicphillips@aol.com. Business E-Mail: jfitzpatrick@cr.k12.ia.us.

FITZPATRICK, JOHN WEAVER, ornithologist, researcher; b. St. Paul, Minn., Sept. 17, 1951; s. Joseph Taylor and Persis Weaver Fitzpatrick; m. Molly Wyer Mary Ellen (Molly) Wyer, Dec. 10, 1954; children: Sarah Warner, Dylan James. AB, Harvard U., 1974; PhD, Princeton U., 1978—78. Curator of birds, chmn. zoology Field Mus. Natural History, Chgo., 1978—89; exec. dir. Archbold Biol. Sta., Lake Placid, Fla., 1988—95, Cornell Lab. Ornithology, Ithaca, NY, 1995—. Mem. endangered species recovery teams U.S. Fish and Wildlife Svc., Washington, 1993—; bd. govs. The Nature Conservancy, Arlington, Va., 1995—2005; bd. dirs. Nat. Audubon Soc., NYC, 1996—2001; pres. Am. Ornithologists' Union, Washington, 2000—02. Author: (scientific book) The Florida Scrub-Jay: Demography of a Cooperative-breeding Bird (William Brewster Award, Am. Ornithologists' Union, 1985), Neotropical Birds: Ecology and Conservation; contbr. scientific book. Mem. The Nature Conservancy, Arlington, Va., 1995—2005, Finger Lakes Land Trust, Ithaca, NY, 2002. Recipient Hairy Painton award, Cooper Ornithol. Soc., 1981, Cruickshank award, Fla. Audubon Soc., 1995, Oak Leaf award, The Nature Conservancy, 1995; grantee, NSF, 1982—. Achievements include patents for Internet-based archiving of georeferenced data; discovery of seven previously undescribed bird species; rediscovery of Ivory-billed Woodpecker; first to popularized Internet-based citizen science for research and education. Avocations: bird-watching, watercolor painting, skiing, hiking, golf. Home: 1636 Ellis Hollow Rd Ithaca NY 14850 Office: Cornell Laboratory Ornithology 159 Sapsucker Woods Rd Ithaca NY 14850 Home Phone: 607-273-1284; Office Phone: 607-254-2410. Business E-Mail: jwf7@cornell.edu.

FITZPATRICK, JOSEPH MARK, lawyer; b. Jersey City, May 27, 1925; s. Joseph Francis Stephen and Meave (Wilson) F.; m. Elizabeth Anne Keane, June 18, 1949; children: Elizabeth A., Susan E., Christopher M., Stephen R. ME, Stevens Inst. Tech., 1945; JD, Georgetown U., 1951. Bar: Va. 1950, U.S. Patent Office 1950, N.Y. 1954. Trial atty. anti-trust divsn. Dept. Justice, 1951-53; mem. firm Ward, McElhannon, Brooks & Fitzpatrick, NYC, 1954-70, Fitzpatrick, Cella, Harper & Scinto, NYC, 1970—. With USNR, 1943-46. Fellow Am. Coll. Trial Lawyers; mem. ABA, Va. Bar Assn., N.Y. Bar Assn., Assn. of Bar of City of N.Y., Am. Intellectual Property Law Assn., N.Y. Intellectual Property Law Assn., Manasquan River Yacht Club. Home: 17 Oak Ln Scarsdale NY 10583-1628 Office: Fitzpatrick Cella Harper Scinto 30 Rockefeller Plz Fl 38 New York NY 10112-3800 Office Phone: 212-218-2100. Business E-Mail: jfitzpatrick@fchs.com.

FITZPATRICK, KAREY ROSE, music educator, director; b. Jefferson City, Mo., July 12, 1979; d. Larry William and Peggy Anne Wieberg; married, June 9, 2007; 1 child, Kaylin Berendzen. BS in Music Edn., S.W. Mo. State U., Springfield, 2002. Dir. choir Webster Groves Sch. Dist., St. Louis, 2003—04, Francis Howell Sch. Dist., St. Charles, Mo., 2004—. Singer: St. Louis (Mo.) Chamber Choir, 2003—. Mem.: Mo. Choral Dirs. Assn. (R&S chair multi cultural music 2006), Music Educators Nat. Conf., Am. Choral Dirs. Assn. Avocations: swimming, reading, movies. Office: Francis Howell High Sch 7001 Hwy 94 South Saint Charles MO 63304

FITZPATRICK, LOIS ANN, library administrator; b. Yonkers, NY, Mar. 27, 1952; d. Thomas Joseph and Dorothy Ann (Nealy) Sullivan; m. William George Fitzpatrick, Jr., Dec. 1, 1973; children: Jennifer Ann, Amy Ann. BS in Sociology, Mercy Coll., 1974; MLS, Pratt Inst., 1975. Clk. Yonkers Pub. Libr., 1970-73, libr. trainee, 1973-75, libr. I, 1975-76; reference libr. Carroll Coll. Libr., Helena, Mont., 1976-79, acting dir., 1979, dir., 1980—; asst. prof. Carroll Coll., Helena, 1979-89, assoc. prof., 1989-99, prof., 2000—. Bd. dirs. Mont. Shares 2000-; chmn. arrangements Mont. Gov.'s Pre White House Conf. on Libraries, Helena, 1977-78; mem. steering com. Reference Point coop. program for librs., 1991; mem. adv. com. Helena Coll. of Tech. Libr., 1994—; adv. coun. Mont. Libr. Svcs., 1996-2000; mem. Networking Task Force, 1998-2003, Laws Revision Task Force, 1998-2001, Not Ready for Prime Time Freedom Fighters, 2004-; pres. elect Helena Area Health Sci. Libraries Cons., 1979-84, pres., 1984-88; bd. dirs. Mont. FAXNET; chair govt. affairs Mont. Libr. Assn., 1997-2005, 2006-. Co-chmn. interst group OCLC; chmn. local arrangements Mont. Gov.'s Pre White House Conf.;; mem. Soroptimist Internat. of Helena, 1977—, Mont. Race for the Cure, 1998-2004; bd. dirs. ACLU-MT, 1998—2007, pres., 2005-2007; mem. adv. com. Am. Cancer Soc. Lewis and Clark County; bd. dir. Montana Shares, 2004-. Mem. Mont. Libr. Assn. (task force for White House conf. 1991, chair govt. affairs com. 1997-2003, 2005-, EdLINK-MT 1997-99, 2000-01, spl. recognition award 1999), Soroptimist Internat. of Helena (2d v.p. 1984-85, pres. 1986-87, Women Helping Women award 1988), Am. Cancer Soc. (mem. lapel program, 2005—, mem. Cancer Advocacy Network program, 2005—, legislative ambassador, 2007-); Mont. Cancer Control Coalition (mem. adv. bd. 2005-, steering com., 2006-, chair legislative work group, 2006-). Home: 1308 Shirley Rd Helena MT 59602-6635 Office: Carroll Coll Jack & Sallie Corette Libr 1601 N Benton Ave Helena MT 59625-0001 Home Phone: 406-431-6122; Office Phone: 406-447-4341. Business E-Mail: lfitzpat@carroll.edu.

FITZPATRICK, M. LOUISE, dean, nursing educator; b. South River, NJ, May 24, 1942; d. John Francis and Bettina (Galassi) F. Diploma in nursing, Johns Hopkins U., 1963; BSN, Cath. U. Am., 1966; MA, Columbia U., 1968, MEd, 1969, EdD, 1972; cert., Harvard U., 1985. Former assoc. prof., dept. nursing edn. Tchrs. Coll., Columbia U., NYC; Connelly Endowed dean, prof. nursing Villanova U. Coll. Nursing, Pa., 1978—. Cons. Mid. States Assn., Phila.; cons. to numerous univs., also univs. in Morocco, Egypt, Jordan, West Bank, Sultanate of Oman; cons., reviewer USPHS; bd. dirs. Nurses Ednl. Funds, Inc., N.Y.C. Author: The National Organization for Public Nursing, Development of a Practice Field, 1975; editor: Present Realities/Future Imperatives, 1977, Historical Studies in Nursing, 1978, Nursing in Society: A Historical Perspective, 1983; also 21 articles in profl. jours. Recipient Disting. Alumni award Columbia U. Tchrs. Coll., 1966, Cath. Univ. McManus medal, 1992; WHO fellow, Scandinavia and U.K., 1974; Am. Acad. Nursing fellow, 1978. Mem. Am. Nurses Assn. (past chmn. cabinet on nursing edn.), Am. Assn. Colls. Nursing, Nat. League for Nursing (bd. of govs.). Democrat. Roman Catholic. Avocations: music, theater, cooking, international travel. Home: 80 Woodstone Ln Villanova PA 19085-1425 Office: Villanova U Coll Nursing 800 Lancaster Ave Villanova PA 19085-1690 Office Phone: 610-519-4909. E-mail: louise.fitzpatrick@villanova.edu.

FITZPATRICK, MICHAEL G., former congressman, lawyer; b. Phila., June 28, 1963; m. Kathleen Fitzpatrick; 6 children. BA with honors, St. Thomas U., Miami, Fla., 1985; JD, Pa. State U. Dickinson Sch. Law, 1988. Bar: Pa., NJ. Spl. counsel Saul Ewing LLP, Phila.; mem. Bucks County Bd. Commrs., Pa., 1995—2004, US Congress from 8th Pa. dist., 2005—07, mem. fin. svcs. com., mem. small bus. com. Bd. dirs. Temple Lower Bucks County Hosp.; bd. advs. Conwell Egan Cath. HS. Mem.: ABA, Pa. State Bar Assn., Bucks County Bar Assn., Brehon Law Soc., Ancient Order of Hibernians, Levittown Bristol Kiwanis, KC. Republican. Roman Catholic. Mailing: PO Box 308 Langhorne PA 19047 Office Phone: 215-750-0110. E-mail: mfitzpatrick@begleycarlin.com.

FITZPATRICK, NANCY HECHT, editor; b. Dec. 29, 1942; d. Ira Youngwood and Bettie Jane (Van Cleave) Hecht; m. Alan Rush Fitzpatrick, Dec. 15, 1973 (dec.); m. Thomas H. Gervais, May 17, 2003. Student, Upsala Coll., 1960-62, New Sch. Social Rsch., 1962-64, Johns Hopkins U., summer 1987, Bennington Coll., summer 1988; MFA in writing, Union Inst., 2005. Asst. copy editor Am. Home mag., NYC, 1964-68; v.p. Creative Comms. Assocs., Newark, 1968-70; sr. editor Family Circle mag., NYC, 1970-77; corp. sec., v.p. mktg. Alternative Telecom. Corp., NYC, 1977-92; exec. editor Meeting News mag., NYC, 1993-95; assoc. news editor, book and art reviewer The Vineyard Gazette, 1997—2001; archivist and publs. editor Wampanoag Tribe of Gay Head/Aquinnah, 2002—04; editor Spice Arts and Entertainment Guide, 2005—06. Editor various publs. Mem.: LWV, NOW, Lower Adirondack Regional Arts Coun. (adv. bd.), Eastern Bedford Environ. Assn. (treas.), Empire women in Telecom. (pres.), N.Y. Women in Comms.

FITZPATRICK, RAYMOND JOHN, retired urologist; b. NYC, Feb. 27, 1919; s. John Aloysiouse Fitzpatrick and Susan Veronica Dowie; children: Kevin Scot, Jean Ellen, Raymond John Jr. BS, Fordham U., NYC; MD, Columbia U., NYC. Diplomate Am. Bd. Urology. Surg. intern Bellevue Hosp., NYC, 1943; gen. intern Orange Meml. Hosp., Orlando, Fla., 1946; gen. practice Bishop, Va., 1946—48; preceptorship Orr Urol. Group, Orlando, 1948—53; urology practice Alaghua Gen. Hosp., Gainesville, Fla., 1953—85. Editor: Mus. Natural History, Fla. U., 1986—90, author 3 books poetry; contbr. articles to profl. jours. Capt. US Army, 1943—47. Fellow: ACS. Republican. Roman Catholic.

FITZPATRICK, ROBERT JOHN, museum director; b. Toronto, Ont., Can., May 18, 1940; came to U.S., 1952, naturalized, 1962; s. John and Maxine (Dunn) F.; m. Sylvie M. Blondet, Jan. 1966; children: Joel Denis, Michael Sean, Claire Valerie. BA magna cum laude, Spring Hill Coll., 1963, MA magna cum laude, 1964; student (Woodrow Wilson fellow), Johns Hopkins U., 1964-65. Asst. prof. French U. Maine, 1965-68; mem. staff McCarthy Nat. Campaign Hdqrs., 1968; staff asst., campaign aide to Sen. Joseph D. Tydings, Washington, 1970; chmn. dept. modern langs. Gilman Sch., Balt., 1968-72; dean of students Johns Hopkins U., 1972-75; pres. Calif. Inst. of Arts, Valencia, 1975-87, Euro Disneyland, Burbank, Calif., 1987—93; CEO RFC, Paris, 1993—95; dean Sch. of the Arts Columbia U., NYC, 1995—2001; Pritzker dir., CEO Museum of Contemporary Art, Chicago, 2001—. Mem. Balt. City Council, 1971-75; v.p. Mayor's Com. on Cultural Affairs, Los Angeles, 1976-79, Calif. Confedn. of Arts, 1977-79; dir. Olympic Arts Festival, Los Angeles, 1984, Los Angeles Festival, 1985-87; mem. Md. Democratic State Central Com., 1970-74; mem. adv. com. Next Wave Festival, Bklyn. Coll.; trustee Craft and Folk Art Mus., Los Angeles, 1976-82; bd. dirs. Los Angeles Chamber Orch., 1977-81; trustee Dunn Sch., Los Olivos, Calif., 1980-84, Bennington Coll., Vt. Democrat. Office: Museum of Contemporary Art 220 E Chicago Ave Chicago IL 60611

FITZPATRICK, SUSAN, biochemist, neurologist, foundation administrator; married. Grad., St. John's U.; PhD in Biochemistry and Neurology, Cornell U. Postdoctoral tng. Yale U., New Haven; dir. edn. Miami Project To Cure Paralysis, Miami, Fla., assoc. exec. dir.; adminstr. grants program Brain Trauma Found., Miami; program dir. James S. McConnell Found., St. Louis. Office: James S McDonnell Found Ste 1850 1304 S Brentwood Blvd Saint Louis MO 63117

FITZPATRICK, TERRY, public radio reporter, producer; Student, Univ. Wis. Anchor, reporter and assignment editor NPR stations, Amarillo, Dallas; reporter Dallas Morning News, Texas Monthly mag.; prodr. MacNeil/Lehrer NewsHour; former sr. editor and Pacific Northwest bureau chief NPR. Co-recipient AAAS Sci. Journalism award for radio reporting, 2006; recipient NY Times Critic's Pick award, 1995. Mailing: c/o Living on Earth 20 Holland St Ste 408 Somerville MA 02144-2749 Home: Seattle WA

FITZPATRICK, THOMAS MARK, lawyer; b. Anaconda, Mont., June 12, 1951; s. Marcus Leo and Natalie Stephanie (Trbovich) F. BA, U. Mont., 1973; JD, U. Chgo., 1976. Bar: Ill. 1976, Wash. 1978. Asst. to pres.-elect ABA, Chgo., 1976-77, asst. to pres., 1977-78; assoc. Karr, Tuttle, Campbell, Seattle, 1978-85, ptnr., 1985-89, Stafford, Frey, Cooper, Seattle, 1989-99; asst. chief civil divsn. Snohomish County Prosecuting Atty.'s Office, Everett, Wash., 1999—2005; exec. dir. Snohomish County County Exec. Office, Everett, 2005—06; ptnr. Talmadge Law Group PLLC, Tukwila, Wash., 2006—. Editor: ABA: A Century of Service, 1979. Fellow Am. Bar Found.; mem. ABA (chmn. lawyer and media conf. 1985-88, profl. discipline com. 1988-94, LRIS com. 1994-97, ethics com. 2001-04, chmn. nat. conf. groups 1982-85, ho. of dels. 1990—, state del. 1993-98, bd. govs. 1998-2001), Wash. Bar Assn. (pres. young lawyer divsn. 1986-87), Snohomish County Bar Assn., Seattle-King County Bar Assn., U. Chgo. Law Sch. Alumni Assn. (bd. dirs., Seattle regional pres. 1980-86). Roman Catholic. Home: 7345 13th Ave NW Seattle WA 98117-5306 Office: Talmadge Law Group PLLC 18010 Southcenter Pkwy Tukwila WA 98188 Office Phone: 206-574-6661. Business E-Mail: tom@talmadgelg.com.

FITZPATRICK, WHITFIELD WESTFELDT, lawyer; b. New Orleans, Jan. 31, 1942; s. William Harry and Frances (Westfeldt) F.; m. Jean Phipps, July 6, 1984. BA, Washington & Lee U., 1964; JD, Tulane U., 1967; LLM, Grenoble U., France, 1969, Doctorate, 1972. Bar: La. 1967, Va. 1972, NY 1974, US Dist. Ct. (ea. dist.) La. 1974, DC 1975, US Dist. Ct. (we. dist.) La. 1975, US Ct. Appeals (5th cir.) 1975. Law clk. Supreme Ct. Commonwealth of Va., Norfolk, 1969-70; assoc. Coudert Bros., NYC, 1972-74; sr. assoc. Phelps, Dunbar, Marks, Claverie & Sims, New Orleans, 1974-76; counsel Mobil Oil Corp., New Orleans, 1976-79, Mobil North Sea Ltd., London, 1979-82; gen. counsel Mobil, The Hague, Netherlands, 1982—87; sr. counsel, asst. sec. Mobil Exploration and Producing U.S., Inc., Midland, Tex., 1987-89; asst. sec. Mobil Producing Tex. and N.Mex., Inc., Midland, 1987-89; with direction juridique Elf Aquitaine, Europe and U.S. coord., 1989-94; spl. advisor to dir. of comml. and lic. adminstrn. divsn. ELF Petroleum Norge, 1994-97; exec. v.p. and gen. counsel Fountain Oil Inc., 1997—99; of counsel The Silecky Firm, 1999—; ptnr., gen. counsel Scandinavian Bus. Ptnrs., 2005—. Contbr. articles to profl. pubs. Dir. Am. Coordinating Coun. of Norway, 1990—92. Named Mem. Soc. of the Friends of the Legion of Honor, Ordres de Chevalerie; Grenoble U. Law Sch. scholar, 1967-69; fellow Govt. of France, 1970-72. Mem. ABA, Maritime Law Assn., Internat. Bar Assn., La. Bar Assn., Va. Bar Assn., NY Bar Assn., DC Bar Assn., Boston Club of New Orleans, Racquet and Tennis Club of NY, Royal Auto Club of London, Soc. Colonial Wars, Societé des Amis du Musée National de la Légion d'Honneur. Avocations: golf, skiing, reading, tennis. Home: Camilla Collets vei No 8 0258 Oslo Norway also: 2206 Neely Ave Midland TX 79705 Home Phone: 432-684-9055; Office Phone: 432-684-9055, 011-47-22-56-1837. Personal E-mail: whitfitzpatrick@yahoo.com.

FITZPATRICK, WILL, lawyer; b. Montgomery, Ala. m. Phyllida Burlingame; children: Oona, Arlo. BA, Harvard Coll., 1989; JD, Columbia U., 1994. With Ala. Capital Representation Resource Ctr.; law clk. for Chief U.S. Dist. Judge Myron H. Thompson; assoc. Fenwick & West, Mountain View, Calif.; in-house counsel Loudcloud Inc., @Home.Corp. (now Excite@Home); pvt. practice San Francisco; corp. counsel Omidyar Network, 2005—. Office: Omidayar Network Svcs LLC 1991 Broadway St Ste 200 Redwood City CA 94063-1958 Office Phone: 650-482-2500.

FITZROY, NANCY DELOYE, engineering executive, mechanical engineer; b. Pittsfield, Mass., Oct. 5, 1927; d. Jules Emile and Mabel Winifred (Burr) deLoye; m. Roland Victor Fitzroy, Jr., Mar. 24, 1951. BChemE, Rensselaer Poly. Inst., Troy, 1949; DEng (hon.), Rensselaer Poly. Inst., 1990; DSc (hon.), N.J. Inst. Tech., 1987. Registered profl. engr., N.Y. Heat transfer engr. corp. R & D GE, Schenectady, NY, 1950-71, mgr. heat transfer consulting, 1971-74, strategy planner, 1974-76, mgr. program devel. gas turbine divsn., 1976-82, mgr. energy and environ. program, 1982-87. Dir. West Hill Devel. Corp., Rotterdam, NY, 1955—65; mem. adv. com. rsch. NSF, Washington, 1972—75; mem. transp. rsch. bd. coordinating com. rsch. and tech. NRC, 1996—99; cons. in field; bd. dirs. ASME Found., 1989—95, 1997—, trustee, 1998—. Author, editor: book Heat Transfer and Fluid Flow, Data Books, 1955—75. Charter mem. Rensselaer Poly. Inst. Coun., 1972—. Named to Rensselaer Poly. Inst. Hall of Fame, 1999; recipient Demers medal, Rensselaer Poly. Inst., 1975, Achievement award, Fedn. Profl. Women, 1984, Disting. Alumna medal, Rensselaer Poly. Inst., 1996. Fellow: ASME (1st woman nat. pres. 1986—87, trustee Gear Rsch. Inst. 1987—89), Soc. Women Engrs. (Outstanding Achievement award 1972), Instn. Mech. Engrs. London (hon.); mem.: Assn. Engrings. Socs. (gov. 1987—89), Nat. Acad. Engring., Coral Ridge Yacht Club (Ft. Lauderdale, Fla.), Mohawk Golf Club, Whirly-Girls Club, Ninety-Nines Club. Republican. Episcopalian. Achievements include patents in field.

FITZSIMMONS, B. JOSEPH, JR., lawyer; b. Weymouth, Mass., Oct. 18, 1940; s. B. Joseph Sr. and Rita M. (Mitchell) F. AB in History cum laude, Boston Coll., 1963; JD, New Eng. Sch. Law, 1967. Bar: Mass. 1967, U.S. Dist. Ct. Mass. 1969, U.S. Ct. Appeals (1st cir.) 1969, U.S. Supreme Ct. 1979; cert. U.S. Profl. Tennis Registry instr.; PGA golf profl. Pvt. practice, Weymouth, 1967-77, 93—; spl. asst. atty. gen., asst. dist. atty. Commonwealth of Mass., Boston and Dedham, 1970—72; equity clk. Norfolk County/Commonwealth of Mass., Dedham, 1972-80; trial judge Mass. Trial Ct., Boston, 1980-93. Author: Representing the Plaintiff, 1980; contbr. articles to profl. jours. Pers. officer Town of Weymouth, 1970-73, selectman, 1973-77, chmn., 1976, chair Nike site acquisition task force. Mem. Mass. Bar Found., Mass. Bar Assn., Bar Assn. Norfolk County, Quincy Bar Assn. (bd. govs. 1967—, Alfred P. Malaney award for leadership in legal field 1991). Roman Catholic. Avocations: tennis, golf, reading. Office: Fitzsimmons & Fitzsimmons 63 Homestead Ave Weymouth MA 02188

FITZSIMMONS, BECKY BARLOW, lawyer; b. Princeton, NJ, Apr. 2, 1968; BA, Western Md. Coll., 1990; JD, U. Md. at Baltimore, 2000. Bar: Ohio 2000. Assoc. Dinsmore & Shohl LLP, Cin. Named one of Ohio's Rising Stars, Super Lawyers, 2006. Mem.: Ohio State Bar Assn., Cin. Bar Assn., ABA. Office: Dinsmore & Shohl LLP 255 E Fifth St Ste1900 Cincinnati OH 45202-4700 Office Phone: 513-977-8200. Office Fax: 513-977-8141.

FITZSIMMONS, BETH DUSTON (CAROLYN BETH FITZSIMMONS), library and information scientist; BS in Chemistry, Simmons Coll.; MLS, SUNY Albany; PhD in Pub. Policy, George Mason U., Va. Founder, pres. Info. Strategists LLC, 1987—; chmn. Depository Libr. Coun. to US Pub. Printer, 1993—94; info. specialist Aerodyne Rsch., Inc.; with Commerce, Energy, NASA, Def. Info. Managers Grp., 1993—96, US Patent and Trademark Office, 1996—99. Presdl. appointee to adv. bd. White House Conf. on Libraries and Info. Services, 1991, chair tech. com.; bd. mem. Nat. Mus. and Libr. Services; mem. nat. libr. leadership com. U. Mich. Dir. YMCA, Ann Arbor, Mich., Rotary Club, Ann Arbor, Mich. Recipient Disting. Svc. award, Pub. Printer's. Mem.: US Nat. Commn. on Libraries and Info. Sci. (chairwoman 2004—), AAAS, Spl. Libraries Assn., Am. Chem. Soc. Office: US Nat Commn on Libraries and Info Sci Ste 350 North Tower 1800 M St NW Washington DC 20036 Office Phone: 202-606-9200. Office Fax: 202-606-9203. Business E-Mail: bfitzsimmons@nclis.gov.*

FITZSIMMONS, ELLEN MARIE, lawyer; b. May 1960; BS, Va. Poly. Inst. & State Sch.; JD, Georgetown U. Assoc. Hunton & Williams, Richmond, Va.; sr. counsel CSX Corp., Jacksonville, Fla., 1991—95, asst. gen. counsel, 1995-97, gen. counsel corporate, 1997—2001, sr. v.p. law, gen. counsel, 2001—03, sr. v.p. law, corp. sec., gen. counsel, 2003, sr. v.p. law & pub. affairs, sec., gen. counsel, 2003—. Office: CSX Corp 15th Fl 500 Water St Jacksonville FL 32202*

FITZSIMMONS, JAY (JOSEPH J. FITZSIMMONS), food service executive; BS in Acctg., U. Notre Dame; MBA, U. Chgo., 1974. CPA. Sr. v.p., dir. CFO Nat. Pizza Co., 1985—93; sr. v.p., CFO S&A Restaurant Corp., 1993; sr. v.p. and securities analyst Rauscher Pierce Refsnes, Inc., 1993—94; v.p. fin. Wal-Mart Stores, Inc., 1994—95, sr. v.p. fin., 1995—98, sr. v.p. fin. and treas., 1998—2007; exec. v.p., CFO Wendy's Internat. Inc., 2007—. Bd. dirs. Mexican Restaurants Inc., 1996—. Advisory bd. Bus. Consortium Fund an affiliate Nat. Minority Diversity Coun., U. Chgo. Grad. Sch. Bus. Mem.: Fin. Executives Inst. Office: Wendy's Internat Inc 288 W Dublin Granville Rd Dublin OH 43017-0256*

FITZSIMMONS, WILLIAM R., dean; AB, Harvard U., 1967, EdM, 1969, EdD, 1971. Mem. admissions office Harvard Coll., 1972—, dir. Harvard Coll. Fund, dean admissions and fin. aid; mem. faculty arts and scis. Harvard U.; dir. Harvard Summer Inst. Trustee Coll. Entrance Examination Bd.; bd. dirs. Summerbridge Cambridge. Office: Harvard U Faculty Arts and Scis 86 Brattle St Cambridge MA 02138 Office Phone: 617-495-1557. Office Fax: 617-495-8321.*

FITZSIMONS, DENNIS JOSEPH, broadcast and publishing executive; b. NYC, June 26, 1950; s. Genevieve Theresa (English) F.; m. Ann Christie, Sept. 27, 1980; children: Matthew, Christine. BA, Fordham U., 1972. Account exec. Blair TV, NYC, 1975-77; sales mgr. TeleRep, Inc., Chgo., 1977-78, NYC, 1979-81, dir. spl. projects, 1978-79; dir. advt. sales Viacom Internat., NYC, 1981; dir. sales and mktg. Sta. WVIT-TV, Hartford, Conn., 1981-82; dir. sales Sta. WGN-TV, Chgo., 1982-84, v.p., gen. mgr., 1987—92, Sta. WGNO-TV, New Orleans, 1984-85; v.p. ops. Tribune Broadcasting Co., Chgo., 1985-87; pres. Tribune Television, 1992—94, Tribune Broadcasting Co., 1994—2003; exec. v.p. Tribune Co., 2000—01, bd. dirs., 2000—, COO, 2001—03, pres., 2001—, CEO, 2003—, chmn., 2004—. Vice chmn. United Negro Coll. Fund of Chgo. With U.S. Army, 1970-76. Mem. Ill. Assn. Broadcasters (bd. dirs.), INTV (bd. dirs.). Roman Catholic. Office: Tribune Co 435 N Michigan Ave Chicago IL 60611*

FIUMARA, ETTORE, neurosurgeon; b. Alcamo, Sicily, Italy, May 20, 1954; s. Gabriele Fiumara and Maria Calamia; m. Maria Impellizzeri, Dec. 30, 1978; children: Roberta, Gabriele. Med. diploma, Palermo U., 1978; postgrad., Cath. U. Rome, 1983. Asst. to top neurosurgeon Hosp. Niguarda, Milan, 1979-90; vice-head neurosurgeon Casa Sollievo della Sofferenza Hosp. S. Giovanni, Rotondo, Italy, 1990-98, Villa Sofia Hosp., Palermo, Italy, 1998—. Univ. tchr. spl. svc. sch. neurosurgery, Catania, Italy, 1998—2002, Catania, 2007—. Contbr. articles to profl. jours. Fellow: Italian Neurosurgical Soc. Achievements include research in intracranial vascular maliformations. Office: Villa Sofia Hosp Dept Neuro piazzetta Salerno 1 Sicily Palermo Italy Personal E-mail: ettorefiumara@virgilio.it.

FIUMEFREDDO, CHARLES A., brokerage house executive; b. Bayonne, NJ, May 12, 1933; s. Charles F. and Alice (Guiliana) F.; m. Joan Kuczynski, June 18, 1955; children— Joanne Fiumefreddo Lewicki, Charles M. BS, St. Peter's Coll., Jersey City, 1955; postgrad., NYU Sch. Bus. Adminstrn., 1955-57. Asst. v.p. First Jersey Nat. Bank, Jersey City, 1953-65; asst. v.p. investment mgmt. Anchor Corp., Elizabeth, NJ, 1965-69; from v.p. to pres., CEO Standard & Poor's/InterCapital, NYC, 1969—77; pres. Morgan Stanley Investment Advisors Inc., NYC, 1977—84, treas., 1977—82, chmn., 1982—98, CEO, 1977—98; pres. Morgan Stanley Investment Cos., NYC, 1982—99, dir., trustee, 1991—, chmn., 1992—; exec. v.p., bd. dirs. Dean Witter Reynolds Inc., until 1998. Chmn. Morgan Stanley Trust FSB, Jersey City, 1989-98; bd. dirs., mem. exec. com. Investment Co. Inst., Washington, 1983-98; mem. investment co. com. SIA, N.Y.C., 1984-86. Bd. dirs. Bayonne Hosp., N.J., 1983-89. Mem.: K.C. (Bayonne, N.J.). Avocations: stamp collecting/philately, fishing.

FIVEL, STEVEN EDWARD, lawyer, communications executive; b. Aug. 26, 1960; Atty. Melvin Simon & Assoc., Inc., 1988—93, Simon DeBartolo Group, Inc., 1988—97, Simon Property Group, Inc., 1993—97; exec. v.p., gen. counsel, sec. Brightpoint, Inc., Plainfield, Ind., 1997—. Lectr. in field. Office: Brightpoint, Inc 2601 Metropolis Parkway, Ste 210 Plainfield IN 46168 Office Phone: 317-707-2355. Office Fax: 317-707-2514.*

FIX, IRENE M., pianist; b. Phila., Mar. 26, 1935; d. Werner Frederick Mueller and Marie Anna Westermann; m. David W. Fix (div.); children: Paul David, Sybil. Studied with Jose Echaniz; MusB cum laude, U. Rochester, NY, 1956. Performers cert. Eastman Sch. Music, U. Rochester, 1956. Mem. staff piano dept. Eastman Sch. Music Prep. Sch., Rochester, 1956—57; piano instr. St. Anne's Sch., Charlottesville, Va., 1958—60, Neighborhood Music Sch., New Haven, 1960—62, Music Arts Sch., Highland Park, Ill., 1962—68, Collegium Musicale, Montepulciano, Italy, 1974—79, Nazareth Schs., Rochester, 1991—2003; pvt. piano instr. Chgo., 1968—71, Rochester, 1991—2003, Westchester, Pa., 2004—. Pianist, collaborator Accedemia Chigiana, Siena, Italy, 1976—80. Musician (soloist): Reading Symphony Orch., Eastman-Rochester Symphony; musician: (solo recitals) Nat. Gallery, U. Va., others. Avocations: cooking, gardening, tennis, cats. Home: 671 Fairview Rd PO Box 224 Glenmoore PA 19343

FIX, JOHN NEILSON, banker; b. Evanston, Ill., Apr. 10, 1937; s. John Leonard and Margaret (Neilson) F.; m. Linda Harris, Dec. 21, 1961; children: John, Christopher, David, Wendy. BS, U. Ill., 1959; grad., Rutgers U., 1971. Asst. cashier, v.p. No. Trust Co., Chgo., 1962-77; v.p., divsn. head Continental Ill. Nat. Bank & Trust Co., Chgo., 1977-80; sr. v.p., group head Continental Bank N.A., Chgo., 1980-83, sr. v.p., dept. head, 1983-94; sr. v.p, dir. corp. devel. global payment svcs. Bank of Am. N.T.S.A., Chgo., 1994-95, ret., 1995; mng. dir. Fixco, Inc., 1996—; prin. Treasury Strategies, Inc., Chgo., 1997—, dir., 2001—. Bd. dirs. Kenilworth Dist. 38 Sch. Bd., Ill., 1969-75; trustee, pres. Kenilworth Park Bd., 1981-89; mem. exec. com. Chgo. Area Boy Scouts, 1981-89; pres., treas. Kenilworth Baseball Assn., 1976-85; trustee Kenilworth Union Ch., 1988-93; bd. dirs. Western Golf Assn., 1989—, audit com., 1992—. Lt. U.S. Army, 1959-61. Recipient George Huff award U. Ill., Champaign, 1955; Good Scout award Chgo. Area Boy Scouts Am., 1982 Mem. Bankers Club of Chgo., Ill. State C. of C. (bd. dirs., treas. 1980-82), Exec. Club of Chgo., Econ. Club of Chgo., U. Ill. Alumni Assn. (mem. bd. trustees 1987, exec. com. 1990-93, chmn. investment com. 1992-93), Nat. Corp. Cash Mgmt. Assn. (mem. publs. com. 1987-91, strategic planning com.), Indian Hill Club (bd. govs. 1984-87, 98-02, sec. 1999-2001, pres. 2001-03), Old Elm Club (Highland Park, Ill.), Western Golf Assn. (exec. com., par club chmn. 2000—, vice chmn., 2006-07). Clubs: Chicago; Minneapolis; Indian Hill (bd. govs. 1984-87). Avocations: golf, skiing, paddle tennis. Office Phone: 847-251-5578. E-mail: fixco@earthlink.net.

FIXMAN, MARSHALL, chemist, educator; b. St. Louis, Sept. 21, 1930; s. Benjamin and Dorothy (Finkel) F.; m. Marian Ruth Beatman, July 5, 1959 (dec. Sept. 1969); children: Laura Beth, Susan Ilene, Andrew Richard; m. Branka Ladanyi, Dec. 7, 1974. AB, Washington U., 1950; PhD, MIT, 1954. Jewett postdoctoral fellow chemistry Yale U., 1953-54; instr. chemistry Harvard U., 1956-59; sr. fellow Mellon Inst., Pitts., 1959-61; prof. chemistry, dir. Inst. Theoretical Sci., U. Oreg., 1961-64, prof. chemistry, research asso. inst., 1964-65; prof. chemistry Yale U., New Haven, 1965-79; prof. chemistry and physics Colo. State U., Ft. Collins, 1979-2000, prof. emeritus, 2000—. Mem. editorial bd. Jour. Chem. Physics, 1962-64, Jour. Phys. Chemistry, 1970-74, Macromolecules, 1970-74, Accounts Chem. Rsch. 1982-85, Jour. Polymer Sci. B, 1991-93; assoc. editor Jour. Chem. Physics, 1994—2006. Wwith U.S. Army, 1954-56. Fellow Alfred P. Sloan Found., 1961-63; recipient Governor's award Oreg. Mus. Sci. and Industry, 1964 Mem. NAS, Am. Acad. Arts and Scis., Am. Chem. Soc. (award pure chemistry 1964, award polymer chemistry 1991), Am. Phys. Soc. (high polymer physics award 1980), Fedn. Am. Scientists. Office: Colo State U Dept Chemistry Fort Collins CO 80523-0001 Business E-Mail: mf@fibm.mfbl.colostate.edu.

FJORDBOTTEN, ALF LEE, language educator; b. Camrose, Alta., Can., Apr. 26, 1952; arrived in U.S., 1960, naturalized, 1987; s. Alf Lee and Helene Josephine (Hansen) Fjordbotten; m. Beverly Elaine Lee, Oct. 22, 1983. BA in Religion, St. Olaf Coll., 1974; MDiv, Luther Theol. Sem., 1978; MA in English and Comparative Lit., Fairleigh Dickinson U., 1989; PhD in English Lang. and Lit., Fordham U., 1999. Ordained to ministry Evang. Luth. Ch. Am., 1978. Vicar, chaplain Grace Luth. Ch., Good Shepherd Home, Allentown, Pa., 1976-77; pastor St. Mark's Luth. Ch., Ridge, NY, 1978-83, Holy Spirit Luth. Ch., Leonia, NJ, 1983—2002, Grace Luth. Ch., North Arlington, NJ, 2002—, First Luth. Ch., Kearny, NJ, 2002—; sr. editor Bishop Books, NYC, 2000—02; freelance editor, 2002—. Tchg. fellow Fordham U., 1989—92, adj. instr., 2003—, Fairleigh Dickinson U., 1994—, St. Peter's Coll., 2004—, Felician Coll., 2004—.

Recipient Charles J. Donahue prize, Fordham U., 1990; Presdl. scholar, 1989—92. Home: 580 Gail Ct Teaneck NJ 07666-4128 Personal E-mail: aleefjord@aol.com. E-mail: drfjord@optonline.net.

FLACHMANN, MICHAEL CHARLES, English language educator; b. St. Louis, Nov. 3, 1942; s. Charles Randall and Charlotte W. (Widen) F.; m. Josephine Kumbera Marschel, June 30, 1969; children: Christopher Michael, Laura Marschel. BA, U. of the South, 1964; MA, U. Va., 1965; PhD, U. Chgo., 1972. Asst. prof. English So. Ill. U., Edwardsville, 1965-68; from asst. prof. to prof. English Calif. State U., Bakersfield, 1972—, chair honors consortium, 1995—. Dir. univ. honors programs Calif. State U., 1985—; dir. Camp Shakespeare Utah Shakespearean Festival, 1986—, company-dramaturg, 1985—; vis. prof. Calif. Inst. Arts, Valencia, 1988; mem. Western Region Adv. Coun. Shakespeare Globe Ctr., 1983—; mem. Internat. Com. for the Bibliography of Shakespeare Quarterly, 1985—. Author: Shakespeare's Lovers, 1983, Teaching Excellence, 1998, Shakespeare: From Page to Stage, 2005, Shakespeare's Women, 1986, The Prose Reader, 1986, 8th edit., 2007, Beware the Cat, 1988; editor: Image of Idleness, 1990; contbr. articles to profl. jours. Named CSU System-Wide Outstanding Prof., 1993, Carnegie Found. U.S. Prof. of Yr., 1995; recipient Wang Tchg. Excellence award Calif. State U., 2001. Mem. MLA, Shakespeare Assn. Am., Early English Text Soc., Renaissance Soc. Am., Assn. for Theatre in Higher Edn., Shakespeare Theatre Assn. Am. Avocations: Judo (Fifth Degree Black Belt), tennis. Home: 1236 Fairway Dr Bakersfield CA 93309-2422 Office: Calif State Univ Dept English 9001 Stockdale Hwy Bakersfield CA 93311-1022 Office Phone: 661-654-2121. Business E-Mail: mflachmann@csub.edu.

FLACK, ROBERTA, singer; b. Black Mountain, NC, Feb. 10, 1939; d. Laron and Irene F.; m. Stephen Novosel, 1966 (div. 1972). BA in Music Edn., Howard U., 1958. Tchr. music and English lit. pub. schs., Farmville, N.C., Washington, 1959-67; rec. artist Atlantic Records, 1968—. Star ABC TV spl. The First Time Ever, 1973; composer: (with Jesse Jackson and Joel Dorn) Go Up, Moses; albums include: First Take, 1969, Chapter Two, 1970, Quiet Fire, 1971, Killing Me Softly, 1973, Feel Like Makin' Love, 1975, Blue Lights In The Basement, 1977, Roberta Flack, 1978, The Best of Roberta Flack, 1981, I'm The One, 1982, Born To Love, 1983, Hits and History, 1984, Roberta Flack, 1985, Oasis, 1989, Set the Night to Music, 1991, Roberta, 1994; writer TV theme song Valerie. Recipient Gold Record for The First Time Ever I Saw Your Face, 1972; Grammy awards for best record, best song (The First Time Ever I Saw Your Face), 1972, best record, best female vocalist (Killing Me Softly With His Song), 1973, best pop vocal duo (Where Is The Love), 1972, Star on the Hollywood Walk of Fame, 2000; winner Downbeat's reader poll as best female vocalist, 1971-73; City of Washington celebrated Roberta Flack Human Kindness Day, 1972. Mem. Sigma Delta Chi. Office: care Atlantic Records 75 Rockefeller Plz New York NY 10019-6908

FLACKE, JOAN WAREHAM, physician, anesthesiologist, educator; b. Evanston, Ill., Dec. 16, 1931; d. Loyal Delbert and Alice (Cummings) Wareham; m. Werner E. Flacke, Aug. 7, 1957; children: Christopher, Gary, Timothy. BA, Scripps Coll., Claremont, Calif., 1953; MD, Harvard U., Cambridge, Mass., 1959. Rsch. fellow Med. Sch., Harvard U., Boston, 1964-67, rsch. assoc., 1967-69, instr., 1969-70; asst. prof. med. sci. U. Ark., 1972-75, assoc. prof. med. sci., 1975-76; adj. assoc. prof. UCLA, 1977-82, adj. prof., 1982-89, prof.-in-residence, 1989-95, prof. emeritus, 1995—. Cons. to FDA, 1989-93; assoc. examiner Am. Bd. Anesthesiology, L.A., 1974-76; program chmn. Anesthesia Ednl. Found., La.A., 1986-91; dir. cardiovascular anesthesiology UCLA Hosp., 1990-91. Contbr. numerous articles to profl. jours. Mem. Am. Soc. Anesthesiologists, Assn. Univ. Anesthesiologists, Internat. Anesthesia Rsch. Soc., Soc. Cardiovascular Anesthesiologists, Calif. Soc. Anesthesiologists, Mass. Med. Soc. Roman Catholic. Avocations: reading, skiing, needlecrafts, horseback riding. Home and Office: PO Box 308 Wolcott CO 81655-0308 E-mail: flacke@colorado.net.

FLADUNG, RICHARD DENIS, lawyer; b. Kansas City, Mo., Aug. 1, 1953; s. Jerome Francis and Rosemary (Voeste) Fladung; m. Leslie Lynn Cox, June 1, 1985; children: Daniel Edwin, Erica Anne, Derek Richard. BSCE, U. Kans., 1976, postgrad., 1977; JD, Washburn U., 1980. Bar: Kans. 1980, U.S. Dist. Ct. Kans. 1980, Ind. 1981, U.S. Dist. Ct. (so. dist.) Ind. 1981, U.S. Patent and Trademark Office 1982, Mo. 1983, U.S. Dist. Ct. (we. dist.) Mo. 1983, Tex. 1984, U.S. Dist. Ct. (so. dist.) Tex. 1984, U.S. Ct. Appeals (fed. cir.) 1984, U.S. Ct. Appeals (5th cir.) 1987, U.S. Supreme Ct. 1987, U.S. Dist. Ct. (we. dist.) Tex. 1988, U.S. Dist. Ct. (ea. and no. dists.) Tex. 2000. Engr. Black and Veatch Cons. Engrs., Kansas City, 1975—80; corp. counsel CTB Inc., Milford, Ind., 1980—82; patent atty. Chase & Yakimo and predecessor firm, Kansas City, 1982—83, Bush, Moseley, Riddle and Jackson and predecessor firm, Houston, 1983—87, Pravel, Hewitt & Kimball, Houston, 1987—98, Akin, Gump, Strauss, Hauer & Feld LLP, Houston, 1999—2006, Strasburger & Price, LLP, 2006—. Contbr. articles to profl. ednl. programs. Com. chmn. Troop 1089 Boy Scouts Am., Houston, 2000—03; legal aide to spkr. Kans. Ho. of Reps., Topeka, 1980. Named one of Outstanding Young Men of Am., 1985. Fellow: Houston Young Lawyers Found. (founding mem.), Houston Bar Found., Tex. Bar Found.; mem.: ASCE, ABA (vice chmn. patent, trademark sect. young lawyer divsn. 1988—89), Houston Intellectual Property Law Assn., Kansas City Bar Assn., Houston Young Lawyers Assn. (pres. 1987—88, exec. mem. bd. dirs. 1987—88, Outstanding Com. Chmn. award 1984—86), Ind. Bar Assn., Mo. Bar Assn., Tex. Young Lawyers Assn. (bd. dirs. 1988), Am. Intellectual Property Law Assn., Houston Bar Assn. (ex officio bd. dirs. 1987—88, vice chmn. profl. responsibility com. 1991—), Pi Alpha Kappa (treas. 1974—75). Roman Catholic. Avocations: tennis, jogging, bicycling, golf. Office: Strasburger & Price LLP Ste 2200 1401 McKinney Houston TX 77010 Office Phone: 713-951-5626. Business E-Mail: richard.fladung@strasburger.com.

FLADUNG, THOM, editor-in-chief; b. Canton, Ohio; m. Jeanette Meyer-Fladung; 2 children. Grad., Univ. Dayton, 1982. Various ed. positions Detroit Free Press, Mich., 1994—2000; mng. ed. Akron Beacon Journal, Ohio, 2000—02, Detroit Free Press, 2002—05; editor & v.p. St. Paul Pioneer Press, 2005—. Mem.: Am. Soc. Newspaper Editors. Office: Pioneer Press 345 Cedar St Saint Paul MN 55101 Office Phone: 651-228-5487. E-mail: tfladung@pioneerpress.com.*

FLAGAN, RICHARD CHARLES, chemical engineering educator; b. Spokane, Wash., June 12, 1947; s. Robert and Frances F.; m. Aulikki Pekkala, Aug. 4, 1979; children: Mikko, Suvi, Taru. BSE in Mech. Engring., U. Mich., 1969; MS, MIT, 1971, PhD, 1973; TechD (hon.), Lund Tech U., Sweden, 2004. Research assoc. MIT, Cambridge, 1973-75; asst. prof. environ. engring. sci. Calif. Inst. Tech., Pasadena, 1975—81, assoc. prof., 1981—84, assoc. prof., environ. engring. and mech. engring., 1984—85, prof., 1986—90, prof. chem. engring., 1990—2000, Irma and Ross McCollum prof. chem. engring., 2000—, prof. environ. sci. and engring., 2003—04, William H. Corcoran prof. chem. engring., 2004—, acting exec. officer, chem. engring., 1996, exec. officer, chem. engring., 1997, 2004—. Vis. prof. Helsinki U. Tech., 1987. Assoc. editor Aerosol Sci. and Tech.; editor-in-chief Aerosol Sci. and Tech., 2003—. Recipient NASA Cert. of Recognition for Creative Develop., 1984, 1989; Japan Soc. for the Promotion of Sci. Fellow, 1992. Mem. AIChE (Thomas Baron award in fluid particle sys. 1997), Am. Assn. Aerosol Rsch. (pres. 1996-97, David Sinclair award 1993, Nicholas Fuchs award 2006), Am. Chem. Soc. (Divsn. Environ. Chemistry Outstanding Paper award 1987, ACS award for creative advances in environ. chemistry 2007), Gesellschaft fur Aerosolforschung (Marion Smoluchowski award for Aerosol Rsch., 1990). Office: Calif Inst of Tech Dept Chem Engring 213 Spalding Mail Code 210-41 Pasadena CA 91125 Business E-Mail: flagan@cheme.caltech.edu, flagan@caltech.edu.

FLAGEL, MARK ALAN, lawyer; b. LA, Sept. 18, 1958; s. Bertram Flagel and Wendy Moloshco; m. Sandra Elizabeth Williams, Apr. 20, 1991; children: Christina, Matthew William, Cameron David. BA magna cum laude, U. Calif., LA, 1980; JD, U. Calif., Berkeley, Calif., 1983. Bar: Calif. 1983, U.S. Dist. Ct. (ctrl. dist.) Calif. 1984, U.S. Ct. Appeals (fed. cir.) 1991, U.S. Ct. Appeals (9th cir.) 1986, U.S. Supreme Ct. 1995. Litig. assoc. Munger, Tolles & Olson, LA, 1983—84, Reboul, MacMurray, Hewitt, Maynard & Kristol, LA, 1984—87, Irell & Manella, LA, 1987—90, litig. ptnr., 1991—96, Latham & Watkins LLP, LA, 1996—. Adj. prof. Loyola Law Sch., LA, 2003—05; spkr. in field. Vol. lawyer Kayne-ERAS Ctr., Culver City, Calif., 1994—. Mem.: ABA, Order of Coif. Home: 450 South Camden Drive Beverly Hills CA 90212 Office: Latham & Watkins LLP 633 West Fifth Street Suite 4000 Los Angeles CA 90071-2007 Office Phone: 213-891-7581. Office Fax: 213-891-8763. Business E-Mail: mark.flagel@lw.com.

FLAGG, C.A. (CHUCK FLAGG), oil industry executive; B in Chem. Engring., Villanova U., Pa. Mgmt. positions Texaco Inc.; gen. mgr. Bay/Valley Refining Complex Equilon Enterprises, LLC; gen. mgr. supply optimization Shell Oil Products US; sr. v.p. planning and optimization Tesoro Corp., San Antonio, 2005, sr. v.p. supply and optimization, sr. v.p. strategy. Office: Tesoro Corp 300 Concord Plz San Antonio TX 78216-6999 Office Phone: 210-283-2000.

FLAGG, RONALD SIMON, lawyer; b. Milw., Dec. 3, 1953; s. Arnold and Marian (Levy) F.; m. Patricia Sharin, June 20, 1982; children: Laura Sharon, Emily Rachel, Naomi Erica. AB, U. Chgo., 1975; JD, Harvard U., 1978. Bar: Wis. 1978, US Dist. Ct. (ea. dist.) Wis. 1978, US Ct. Appeals (7th cir.) 1979, DC 1980, US Dist. Ct. DC 1980, US Ct. Appeals (DC cir.) 1980, US Ct. Appeals (3d cir.) 1984, US Supreme Ct. 1986, US Ct. Appeals (5th cir.) 1987, US Ct. Appeals (8th cir.) 1989. Law clk. to presiding judge U.S. Dist. Ct. (ea. dist.) Wis., Milw., 1978-80; atty., adv. office of intelligence policy and rev. U.S. Dept. Justice, Washington, 1980-82; assoc. Sidley & Austin, Washington, 1982-85, ptnr., 1986—2001, ptnr. comml. and adminstrv. litig., 1986—, and chair pro bono and public interest law com. Bd. dirs. Nat. Vets. Legal Svcs. Program, chair; bd. dir. Legal Counsel for the Elderly, Wash. Lawyers Com. on Civil Rights and Urban Affairs Mem. ABA, DC Bar Assn. (bd. gov.), Phi Beta Kappa. Office: Sidley Austin LLP 1501 K St NW Washington DC 20005-1401 Office Phone: 202-736-8171. Office Fax: 202-736-8711. Business E-Mail: rflagg@sidley.com.

FLAGG DAVIS, VIVIAN ANNETTE, librarian, researcher, public information officer; b. Milledgeville, Ga., July 18, 1960; d. Rufus and Sandra Ann (Seals) F.; m. Joe H. Davis Jr., Jan. 16, 1993. BA, Ga. State U., 1982, MPA, 1988. Purchasing and sales clk. Reed Drugs, Atlanta, 1980-81; libr. assoc. Atlanta Jour. & Constn., 1981-84, libr. asst., 1984-89, assoc. libr., rsch. supr., 1989-91, systems libr., 1991—. Tutor Lit. Action, Atlanta, 1981-83, Alonzo Herndon Elem. Sch., 1999-2001; bd. dirs. Odyssey Family Counseling Ctr., Hapeville, Ga., 1983-85; adv. coun. Vol. Atlanta, 1984-87, pres., 1983-85; vol. spl. projects Changed Living Recovery, 1994—; svc. coun. Youth Devel. Allocations and Evaluation Com., Atlanta, 1987—, planning and allocations com. United Way, Atlanta, 1987—, co-chair Task Force for Homeless and Hungry, 1992-1996; chmn. social action com. social svcs. and human resources dir. Greater Piney Grove Bapt. Ch.; mem. Atlanta Ballet Assocs.; bd. dirs. Higher Plain Ministries, 1994—, chair adminstrn. com., 2003; co-chair edn. com. AJC in Action; founder reading program Will You Read To Me?, 2003. Recipient Outstanding Leader award Vol. Ga., 1984, Vol. of Yr. Golden Link, 2004. Mem. ASPA, Nat. Young Profls. Forum, NAACP, Am. Soc. Info. Sci., Spl. Librs. Assn. Democrat. Avocations: piano, sewing, tennis, gardening, travel. Home: 3735 Landgraf Cv Decatur GA 30034-4775 Office: Atlanta Jour Constn 72 Marietta St NW Atlanta GA 30303-2804

FLAHERTY, CLEMENTINA SANTI, corporate communications specialist, writer; b. Memphis; d. Clement Alexander and Dale (Pendergrast) Santi; m. William Edward Flaherty, Feb. 22, 1985. BA, U. Memphis; doctorate (hon.), St. John's U., Balt. Commentator host interview program Sta. WMC-TV, Memphis; newscaster, commentator Sta. WHER, Memphis; cmty. rels. specialist Western Electric Co., NYC; v.p. pub. rels. divsn. Grey Advt., NYC; dep. dir. corp. rels. Colgate-Palmolive Co., NYC, dir. corp. rels., corp. v.p., v.p. in charge of communications; v.p. pub. affairs GTE Corp., Stamford, Conn.; pres., chief exec. officer Image Mktg. Internat., NYC. Author: The Savvy Woman's Success Bible, 1997 (one of Top Motivational Books of Yr., Books for a Better Life 1997), Talk Your Way to the Top, 1999, What Jackie Taught Us: Lessons from the Remarkable Life of Jacqueline Kennedy Onassis, 2004. Former chmn. Bus. Coun. of UN Decade for Women; bd. dirs. Nat. Jr. Achievement, Palm Beach Zoo, Statue Liberty/Ellis Island Found.; mem. The White House Pub. Affairs Advisors; nat. bd. dirs. Animal Med. Ctr. Recipient Jr. Achievement Meml. award; named One of N.Y.C.'s Outstanding Women of Achievement, NCCJ, One of 100 Top Corp. Women, Bus. Week, One of 73 Women Ready to Run Corp. Am., Working Woman, Woman of Distinction, Birmingham So. Coll., One of 100 Amazing Ams. Mem. DAR, Com. of 200, Internat. Women's Forum. Home and Office: Image Mktg Internat 1040 Fifth Ave New York NY 10028-0137 Office Phone: 212-535-0025. Personal E-mail: imi1040@aol.com. *Persistence alone is omnipotent.*

FLAHERTY, CYNTHIA MEAD, music educator; b. Silver Creek, NY, Jan. 29, 1957; d. Lewis Stephen and Carol D. Mead; children: Travis Martin, Meghan Grace. MusB magna cum laude, SUNY, Fredonia, 1979, MusM summa cum laude, 1982. Elem. music tchr. Dunkirk City Schs., NY, 1979—99, workshop leader BOCES, 1981—, mid. sch. music tchr., 1999—, creator music instrn. music program, writer, arranger; workshop leader SUNY (Fredonia Sch. Music), 1981—, music tchr., 1999—. Dir. Marauder Steel Drum Band, Dunkirk, 1999—, Dunkirk Mid. Sch. Musicals, 2001—. Composer: (songs) Beware Invaders, 2001. Vol. various local charities, Dunkirk, Fredonia, 1999—; vol. United Way, 2005—06, Humane Soc., 2004. Scholar, Fulbright Meml. Fund, Japan, 2001. Mem.: NY State Union Tchrs. and United U. Profs., Dunkirk Tchrs. Assn., Chautau County Music Tchrs. Assn., Am. Fedn. Tchrs. Avocations: kayaking, swimming, cross country skiing, bicycling, travel. Office: Dunkirk Mid Sch 525 Eagle St Dunkirk NY 14048 Office Fax: 716-366-9357. Business E-Mail: cynthia.flaherty@fredonia.edu.

FLAHERTY, FRANCIS XAVIER, state supreme court justice; b. Providence, Jan. 8, 1947; son of Eugene and Gertrude (Strong) F.; married Donna Marie Anderson, 1969; children: Nicole, Michael, Brendan. BA, Providence Coll., 1968; JD, Suffolk U. Sch. of Law, 1975. Dir. Warwick Drug Abuse Program, RI, 1971—73, Federal Program, 1973—75; labor relations adminstr. City of Warwick, 1975—78, asst. city solicitor, city prosecutor, 1975—87, councilman ward 6, 1978—84, mayor, 1985—90; litigation partner Edwards & Angell; mnging partner Wynn & Wynn, Flaherty, Orton, and Flaherty, 1995—2003; justice RI Supreme Ct., 2003—. chmn. Warwick Community Action Program; bd. dirs. Warwick Boys and Girls Club; mem. R.I. Nat. League Cities. Served to 1st lieutenant US Army, 1968—70. Decorated 3 Bronze Stars, 3 Air medals, Vietnam Campaign medal, Vietnamese Cross for Gallantry, Combat Infantryman's award, Vietnamese Civic Action award, Vietnamese Service medal. Member VFW, Am. Legion, ABA, R.I. Bar Assn., Kent County Bar Assn., Kent County Bd. Realtors. Office: Frank Licht Judicial Complex 250 Benefit St Providence RI 02903*

FLAHERTY, JOHN JOSEPH, quality assurance company executive; b. Chgo., July 24, 1932; s. Patrick J. and Mary B. Flaherty; m. Norrine Grow, Nov. 20, 1954 (dec. Sept. 1995); children: John, Bridgette, George, Eileen, Daniel, Mary, Michael, Amy; m. Rosemarie Clausen, Dec. 27, 2001. BEE U. Ill., 1959. Design engr. Admiral Corp., Chgo., 1959—60; project engr. Magnaflux Corp., Chgo., 1960—79, v.p., mgr. rsch. and engring., 1979—84, v.p., mgr. mktg. and sales, 1984—86, v.p., gen. mgr. electronic products, 1986—88; pres. Flare Tech., Chgo., 1988—. With AUS, 1951—53. Fellow: Am. Soc. Non-Destructive Testing; mem.: IEEE, Am. Soc. Metals. Roman Catholic. Achievements include patents and publications on nondestructive testing, including medical ultrasonic; laser scanning. Office: 401 Meadow Lark Rd Bloomingdale IL 60108 Home: 401 Meadowlark Rd Bloomingdale IL 60108-1331 Office Phone: 630-980-4537. Personal E-mail: johnflare@aol.com.

FLAHERTY, JOHN PAUL, JR., chief justice emeritus; b. Pitts., Nov. 19, 1931; s. John Paul and Mary G. (McLaughlin) F.; m. Linet Flaherty; 7 children, 2 stepchildren. BA, Duquesne U., 1953; JD, U. Pitts., 1958; LLD (hon.), Widener U., 1993. Bar: Pa. 1958. Pvt. practice, Pitts., 1958-73; mem. faculty Carnegie-Mellon U., 1958-73; judge Ct. Common Pleas Allegheny County, 1973-79, pres. judge civil divsn., 1978-79; justice Supreme Ct. Pa., 1979-96, chief justice, 1996—2001, chief justice emeritus. USIA speaker in Far East, 1985-86. Mem. Pa. Hist. Soc.; chair Pa. County Records Com., Pa. Judicial Independence Commn. Recipient Medallion of Distinction U. Pitts., 1987, Judicial award Pa. Bar Assn., 1993, Pres. award Pa. Bar Assn., 1999; Chief Justice John P. Flaherty award, Pa. Bar Assn. Conf. of Bar Leaders, 2001; named Man of Yr. in law and govt., Greater Pitts. Jaycees, 1978, named to Century Club of Disting. Alumni, Duquesne U., 1994. Mem. Pa. Acad. Sci. (chmn. hon. exec. bd. 1978-89, Disting. Alumnus award 1977), Am. Law Inst., Pa. Soc., Pa. Bar Assn. (award 2001), Pa. Judicial Ind. Commn. (chair), Mil. History Soc. Ireland, Friendly Sons St. Patrick, Am. Legion. Office: Pa Supreme Ct Rm 810 City County Bldg Pittsburgh PA 15219 *The law is the energy of the living world, and although developed and defined by the judiciary in our Anglo-American society, it is applied and is derived by and from the people. It exists only to protect one person from being hurt, physically or economically, by another. Serious problems face our age. In the final analysis, the judiciary must accomodate the various solutions which will be forthcoming. I hope that my brothers have the foresight and the stamina to accommodate what might be quite novel innovations in the law, which is the living energy, to make this world a place in which it's worth living, since that is the function of the law. Every case involves people. There is no such thing as a small case.*

FLAHERTY, KATHLEEN RUTH, telecommunications industry executive; b. Boston, May 19, 1951; d. John P. and Annette (Baker) Flaherty; m. Kenneth D. Davis, Dec. 30, 1973. BA, Northwestern U., 1973, MS, 1975, PhD in Indsl. Engring., 1979. Policy analyst US Dept. Commerce, Gaithersburg, Md., 1976-79; sr. mgr. sales programs Gen. Electric Info. Services Co., Rockville, Md., 1979-80; sr. mgr. network planning MCI, Washington, 1981-82, dir. network engring., 1982-84, v.p. fin. ops., 1984-86; v.p. communications network services MCI N.E., Rye Brook, NY, 1986—90; v.p. product mktg. MCI, 1990, named sr. v.p., 1993; sr. v.p. worldwide sales & mktg. Concert Services (joint venture of MCI & Brit. Telecom), 1993—95; sr. v.p., marketing dir. nat. bus. communications Brit. Telecom, 1995—97; sr. v.p. global product architecture MCI, 1997—98; pres., COO WinStar Europe SA, 1998—99, WinStar Internat., 1999—2001; chief mktg. officer AT&T bus. services AT&T Corp., 2004—. Dir. CMS Energy Corp., 1995—2004; mem. Industry Adv. Coun. McCormick Sch. Engring., Northwestern U. Coordinator Cmty. Garden Program, Washington, 1983; treas. Woodbine Condominium Assn., Washington, 1979-81. Named one of Outstanding Young Women of Am., Jaycees, 1982; Walter P. Murphy Fellow, 1973. Mem. Sigma Xi. Avocations: reading, camping, gardening, swimming. Office: AT&T Bus Services One AT&T Way Bedminster NJ 07921

FLAHERTY, LOIS TALBOT, editor, psychiatrist, educator; b. Nashville, Apr. 28, 1942; BA, Wellesley Coll., 1963; MD, Duke U., 1968. Diplomate Nat. Bd. Med. Examiners. Intern D.C. Gen. Hosp., 1968-69; resident in psychiatry Georgetown U. Hosp., 1969-71; resident in child psychiatry Johns Hopkins Hosp., 1971-73; pvt. practice Cross Keys, Md., 1973-81; dir. tng. divsn. child and adolescent psychiatry U. Md., 1981-89, assoc. prof. med. sch. divsn. child and adolescent psychiatry, 1982-93, dir. divsn. child and adolescent psychiatry, 1984-92, adj. assoc. prof., 1994—; clin. assoc. prof. psychiatry U. Pa., 1997-2000; pvt. practice Blue Bell, Pa., 1994-99; editor Adolescent Psychiatry, 2000—. Instr. depts. psychiatry and pediatrics Johns Hopkins U. Sch. Medicine, 1973-92; attending staff psychiatrist family, child and adolescent divsn. Sinai Hosp. Balt., 1974-77; staff child psychiatrist Walter P. Carter Ctr., 1977-78, dir. child and adolescent svcs., 1978-92, acting dir. inpatient adolescent unit, 1979-80; clin. asst. prof. U. Md., 1977-81; lectr. psychiatry Harvard U., 2002—; cons. Northwest Drug Alert Sinai Hosp. Balt., 1971-72, St. Vincent's Child Care Ctr., 1973-78, Children's Guild, Inc., 1975-82, SSA, Balt., 1985, many others. Contbr. chpts. to books, articles and book revs. to profl. jours. NIMH grantee, 1983-86. Fellow: Am. Soc. for Adolescent Psychiatry, Am. Psychiat. Assn. (disting.); mem.: Group for Advancement of Psychiatry, Am. Coll. Psychiatrists, Am. Acad. Child Psychiatry. Office: 4 Charlesgate East #605 Boston MA 02215-2369 Personal E-mail: lflaher770@aol.com.

FLAHERTY, SISTER MARY JEAN, dean; Dean, prof. Sch. Nursing, Cath. U. Am., Washington. Office: Cath U Am Sch Of Nursing Washington DC 20064-0001

FLAHERTY, PAMELA POTTER, bank executive; b. Jefferson City, Mo., July 1, 1944; d. Reese H. and Mary Jane (Stagg) Potter; m. Peter A. Flaherty, Nov. 28, 1970; children: Jonathan Peter, David Alexander. BA, Smith Coll., 1966; MA in Internat. Rels., Johns Hopkins U., 1968. Various positions internat. banking Citicorp, NYC, 1968-76, various position consumer banking, 1976-85, head of human resources, 1985-89, head of consumer banking in N.E., 1989—95, sr. v.p., dir. community rels., 1995—98; sr. v.p., global community rels. Citigroup Inc. (formerly Citicorp), NYC, 1998—2007; pres., CEO Citigroup Found., NYC, 2007—. Bd. dirs. Rockefeller Fin. Svcs., Inc., N.Y.C.; mem. adv. coun. Bass plc U.S., 1990—; bd. dirs., mem. exec. com. Am. Women's Econ. Devel. Corp., N.Y.C., 1987—. Bd. trustees Johns Hopkins U., 1997—, chmn.-elect, 2007—; bd. trustees Johns Hopkins Medicine, 2000—, Colonial Williamsburg Found. Named one of Women Who Make a Difference by Smith Coll. Club of N.Y., 1991. Mem. Com. of 200. Office: Citigroup Found 850 Third Ave 13th Fl New York NY 10022*

FLAHERTY, PETER, legal association administrator; m. Rose Flaherty; children: Ashleigh, Winston. Pres. Nat. Legal and Policy Ctr., Falls Church, Va., 1991—. Co-author: (book) The First Lady: A Comprehensive View of Hillary Rodham Clinton, 1996; contbr. articles to profl. jours. Chmn. Citizens for Reagan, 1984—88. Office: Nat Legal and Policy Ctr 107 Park Washington Ct Falls Church VA 22046

FLAHERTY, STEPHEN, composer, orchestrator; b. Pitts., Sept. 18, 1960; Ed., Cin. Coll. Conservatory, 1982. Composer (with Lynn Ahrens): Lucky Stiff, 1988, Once on this Island, 1990, 1995, My Favorite Year,

1993, Ragtime, 1996 (Tony award best orginal score, 1998, Drama Desk award outstanding music), 2003, Anastasia, 1997, Bartok the Magnificent, 1999, With Voices Raised, 1999, Seussical, 2000, A Man of No Importance, 2002, We Tell the Story, 2002, Dessa Rose, 2005, Chita Rivera: The Dancer's Life, 2005, The Glorious Ones, 2007; composer: Love Repeating: A Musical of Gertrude Stein, 2005. Recipient Tony award for original musical score "Ragtime", also Drama Desk award, Outer Critics Cir. award. Mem.: ASCAP, Drama Dept., Dramatists Guild. Mailing: c/o Peter Franklin William Morris Agy 1325 Avenue of the Americas New York NY 10019*

FLAHERTY, TIMOTHY THOMAS, radiologist; b. Fond du Lac, Wis., 1933; m. Joan Flaherty; 4 children. MD, Marquette U., 1959. Diplomate Am. Bd. Radiology. Intern St. Marys Hosp., Milw., 1959—60; resident in radiology, chief resident U. Wis., Madison, 1963—66; fellowship U. Wis. Hosps., Madison, 1964—65; pvt. practice, 1965—. Bd. dirs., sec. Nat. Patient Safety Found.; founding dir. Physicians Ins. Co.-Wis., exec. com. and underwriting com., chair investment com., chmn. bd. dirs.; mem. Govs. task force on health reform, Wis.; founding dir. SMS Svcs., Inc.; bd. dirs. Bank One of Appleton, N.A.; chair Profl. Svcs. Network, Inc.; trustee Novus Health Group Inc., Appleton, Wis., 1988-94; mem. med. exec. com., bd. trustees dept. radiology Theda Clark Regional Med. Ctr., Neenah, Wis., chmn. dept. radiology, 1980-95; clin. prof. dept. radiology U. Wis. Ctr. for Health Scis., Madison, Med. Coll. of Wis., Milw. Maj. gen. USAF, ret. Fellow Am. Coll. Radiology (councilor); mem. AMA (exec. com. 1995—, chair fin. com., chair com. on membership 1996-97, chair com. on orgn. and operation, mem. compensation com., commr. to joint commn. on accreditation of healthcare orgns. 1994, dir. Commn. on Office Lab. Assessment, 1996—, bd. trustees 1994—, chair bd. trustees, 2001-02, sec.-treas. exec. com.), AMPAC (bd. dirs.), State Med. Soc. of Wis. (vice chair bd. dirs., commn. chair), Wis. Radiol. Soc. (past pres.), Radiol. Soc. of N.Am. (counselor 1991-97), Soc. of Med. Cons. of the Armed Forces, Aerospace Med. Assn., Assn. of Mil. Surgeons, Soc. of Air Force Flight Surgeons. Office: AMA 515 N State St Chicago IL 60610-4325 Address: Radiology Assoc Fox Valley 547 E Wisconsin Neenah WI 54956-2966

FLAHERTY, WILLIAM E., chemicals executive, metal products executive; m. Tina Santi. Formerly with GM Overseas Corp., Reynolds Metals Co.; with Gulf & Western, 1974-81, past COO zinc and chems. divsn.; past chmn. bd., CEO Horsehead Industries, NYC. Home Phone: 561-833-1151; Office Phone: 561-832-7060. Personal E-mail: wef561@bellsouth.net.

FLAITZ, CATHERINE M., dean, dental educator; BA in Psychology, Creighton U., 1974, DDS, 1978; MS in Pediat. Dentistry, U. Iowa, 1981. Bd. cert. oral and maxillofacial pathology. With Creighton U., U. Iowa, U. Colo.; pvt. practice pediat. dentistry Denver; prof., chair diagnostic sci. Dental Branch, U. Tex., Houston, dir. oral and maxillofacial pathology residency program, 2001—02, interim dean, 2002—04, dean, 2004—. Prof. pediat. dentistry Dental Branch, U. Tex., 1992; mem. editl. bd. Pediat. Dentistry, Jour. Dentistry Children, Am. Jour. Dentistry; cons. commn. dental accreditation advanced specialty edn. programs ADA; bd. mem. Friends of the Nat. Inst. of Dental and Craniofacial Rsch., 2005—. Mem. editl. bd.: Archives of Pathology and Laboratory Medicine. Named Tex. Dentist of Yr., Tex. Acad. Gen. Dentistry, 2005; recipient George W. Teuscher Silver Pen award, Jour. Dentistry Children, 2001, William N. Finnegan III Professorship in Dental Scis., U. Tex. Health Sci. Ctr.-Houston, 2005, Pres.'s Scholar award for excellence in tchg., 2004. Fellow: Am. Acad. Pediat. Dentistry (mem. grants and fellowship com., mem. pres. circle); mem.: ADA, Internat. Coll. Dentists, Omicron Kappa Upsilon, Tex. Dental Assn., Internat. Assn. Dental Rsch., Am. Assn. Dental Rsch., Am. Acad. Oral Medicine (mem. clinical investigation and abstract com.), Greater Houston Dental Soc., Am. Acad. Oral and Maxillofacial Pathology (exec. coun.), Am. Dental Edn. Assn., Am. Coll. Dentists. Office: Univ Tex Health Sci Ctr Dental Branch 6516 MD Anderson Blvd Rm 147 Houston TX 77225-0068 Office Phone: 713-500-4021. Office Fax: 713-500-4089. Business E-Mail: catherine.m.flaitz@uth.tmc.edu.

FLAKE, FLOYD HAROLD, former congressman; b. LA, Jan. 30, 1945; m. M. Elaine McCollins; children: Aliya, Nailah, Robert, Harold BA in Psychology, Wilberforce U., 1967; D in Ministry, United Theol. Sem., Dayton, Ohio, 1995; postgrad., Northeastern U. Social worker, 1968-69; sales rep. Reynolds Tobacco Co., 1969; mktg. analyst Xerox Corp., 1969-70; assoc. dean students, dir. student activities Lincoln U., Pa., 1970-73; dean students, univ. chaplain, dir.Martin Luther King Jr. Afro-Am. Ctr. Boston U., 1973-76; mem. 101st-105th Congresses from 6th N.Y. dist., Washington, 1987-97, mem. banking and fin. svcs. com., mem. domestic & internat. monetary policy subcom., mem. small bus. com.; pastor Allen A.M.E. Cathedral, Jamaica, NY, 1976—; pres. Edison Charter Schs. Pres., Edison Charter Sch. 2000; sr. fellow Manhattan Inst., 1998—; pres., Wilberforce U., 2002-present, bd. dir. Fannie Mae Found. Columnist N.Y. Post, 1999; author: The Way of the Bootstrapper: Nine Action Steps For Achieving Your Dreams, co-author, Practical Virtues, African American Church Management Handbook Pastor Allen A.M.E. Ch., Jamaica, N.Y., past chmn. affiliate corps. including Allen Sr. Citizen Complex, Allen Christian Sch. and Multi-Purpose Ctr., Allen Home Care Agy., Allen Housing Corp., So. Jamaica Multi-Svc. Ctr. Alfred Sloan fellow Northeastern U., Danforth fellow Payne Theol. Sem.; Gilbert H. Jones scholar Wilberforce U. 1986, Ebony Mag. Black Achievement award in Religion. Office: Greater Allen AME Cathedral NY 11031 Merrick Blvd Jamaica NY 11433-3440 Office Phone: 718-206-4600.

FLAKE, GARY WILLIAM, computer software company executive; BS, Clemson U., SC, 1989; PhD in Computer Sci., U. Md., College Park, 1993. Rsch. asst., dept. computer sci. Clemson U., 1988, rsch. asst., dept. mgmt., 1989; rsch. asst. Los Alamos Nat. Lab., 1989, 1990; tchg. asst. U. Md., Univ. Coll., 1992; rsch. asst. UMIACS, U. Md., College Park, 1990—93; scientist, rsch. project mgr., adaptive info. & signal processing dept. Siemens Corp. Rsch., 1995—96, mem. tech. staff, adaptive info. & signal processing dept., 1994—98; vis. summer scientist Siemens Med. Solutions, 1998; vis. summer scientist, Ctr. for Biol. and Computational Learning MIT, 1998; sci. columnist Fatbrain.com (now owned by barnesandnoble.com), 1999—2000; scientist, computer sci. divsn. NEC Rsch. Inst., 1998—2000, rsch. scientist, computer sci. divsn., 2000—02; chief sci. officer Overture Svcs., 2002—03; head, founder, principal scientist Yahoo! Rsch. Labs, 2003—05; tech. fellow, disting. engr. Microsoft, MSN Divsn., 2005—; dir., Live Labs (rsch. partnership between MSN and Microsoft Rsch.) Microsoft Corp., 2006—. Lectr. in field; served on numerous academic conferences and workshop orgn. committees; mem. SACS accreditation self-study com., dept. computer sci. Clemson U., 1989; mem. dept. coun. com., dept. computer sci. U. Md., 1991, mem. coll. coun. com., dept. computer sci., 92; dean's adv. panel Sch. Informatics, Indiana U., 2004. Author: The Computational Beauty of Nature; editl. bd. Transactions on Internet Technologies, Assn. for Computing Machinery; contbr. articles to profl. jours., to books, book chapters, conf. proceedings, tech. reports, user manuals & teaching guides; editl. adv. bd. mem. NeuroVe$t Journal, 1995, past or current reviewer or referee for Kluwer Academic Publishers, IEEE Transactions on Neural Networks, Neural Computation, Neural Networks, Computational Learning Theory and Natural Language Systems, Journal of Artificial Intelligence Research, Neural Information Processing Systems, and NeuroVe$t Journal. Named to Alumni Hall of Fame, Dept. Computer Sci. (First Inductee), U. Md. Mem.: Upsilon Pi Epsilon, Phi Kappa Phi. Achievements include patents in field. Office: Microsoft Corp One Microsoft Way Redmond WA 98052 Office Fax: 425-707-4955, 425-936-7329. Business E-Mail: gary.flake@usa.net. E-mail: flake@microsoft.com.

FLAKE, JEFF, congressman; b. Snowflake, Ariz., Dec. 31, 1962; m. Cheryl, 15 yrs.; 5 children. BA in Internat. Rels., Brigham Young U., 1986, MA in Polit. Sci., 1987. Worked in pub. rels., Wash., DC, 1987; exec. dir. Found. Democracy, Nambia, Goldwater Instit., Ariz., 1992; mem. U.S. Congress from 1st Ariz. dist., 2001—. Mem. House Judiciary com.; serving on House Internat. Rels. com. Republican. Mem. Lds Ch. Office: US Ho Reps 424 Cannon Ho Office Bldg Washington DC 20515-0306 Office Phone: 202-225-2635. Office Fax: 202-226-4386. E-mail: jeff.flake@mail.house.gov.*

FLAKES, SUSAN, playwright, theater director; b. San Diego, July 9, 1943; d. Herbert Franklin and Dorothy Jean (Loafman) Barrows; m. Donald Lewis Flakes, Dec. 31, 1964; 1 child, Daniel Keith. BA, U. N.Mex., Albuquerque, 1965; MA, San Diego State U., 1969; PhD, U. Minn., Mpls., 1973. Asst., then assoc. prof. Tisch Sch. Arts N.Y. U., NYC, 1973-76, dept. chair Tisch Sch. Arts, 1973-76; founder, artistic dir. Blue Tower Theatre, Stockholm, 1977-80, Strindberg's Intima Teater, Stockholm, 1981-83, Source Prodns., NYC, 1984-90. Instr. U.S. Internat. Univ., San Diego, 1972-73; founder, artistic dir. 1st Strindberg Festival, Stockholm, 1977; mem. Women's Project and Prodns., N.Y.C., 1984-90; v.p. Ibsen Soc. Am., N.Y.C., 1986-99; coord. writers unit W. Coast Ensemble Theatre, Hollywood, Calif., 1991-93. Author: (plays) The Woman Will Play Strindberg's Christina, Laura, Silent Star, And Immortality, Marilyn's Rose, Portrait of Psyche, Daddy's Eyes, Trespasser, To Take Arms, Cafe L.A., Café Heaven, (with Shirl Hendryx) 4F; (libretto with Galt MacDermot) Take It Higher, Maid of Lorraine; (with Gabe Green) Any Saints Out There?, It Girls, Trespasser; (screenplays) To Take Arms, Stand the Storm, Hometown, Inc., Café L.A., Café Heaven, Francois Poet/Thief, Lifetime Achievement, Immortality, The Sacred Garden; (with Stephane Haskell) Immortalité: Daddy's Eyes, The Sacred Garden, The Acting Teacher, The Acting Lesson, Eighteen Candles, The Last Gasp of Madelaine Barone; dir. Hughie, 1989, Mother Love, 1994; contbr. articles to profl. jours., chpts. to books; creator Exptl. Theatre Wing, U.G. Drama Tisch Sch. Arts, NYU, 1975-76; contbr. (play) And Immortality to Baltic Seasons Mag., Russia, 2003; author 2 screenplays (1st Pl. award, 2d Pl award, Screenwriting Competition winner Film Industry Network, 2005). Ensign USN, 1965-67. Recipient winner 10-minute play festival, Fire Rose Productions, 2004, Fullerton Coll. Playwriting Festival, Resident Theater Co., 2004, Alliance of L.A. Playwrights New Works Lab 2004 at the Co. of Angels, LA, Lamia Ink Internat. competition, 1991; fellow Am. Film Inst., 1990; grantee Nat. Endowment for Arts, 1972, Travel grantee Am. Scandinavian Found., Norwegian and Swedish Govts., 1985-86, 89, 94, 2001. Mem. Dramatists Guild, Actor's Studio (playwright/dirs. unit), Am. Film Inst. (finalist directing workshop for women 2003), Alliance L.A. Playwrights, Phi Beta Kappa. Address: 7552 Amazon Dr #1 Huntington Beach CA 92647 Personal E-mail: sflakes@socal.rr.com.

FLAM, JACK DONALD, art historian, educator; b. Paterson, NJ, Apr. 2, 1940; s. Max and Rose Leila (Silverberg) F.; m. Bonnie Suzanne Burnham, Oct. 7, 1972 (div.); 1 child, Laura Rose. BA, Rutgers U., 1961; MA, Columbia U., 1963; PhD, NYU, 1969. Instr. Rutgers U., Newark, 1962-66; asst. prof. U. Fla., Gainesville, 1966-69, assoc. prof., 1969-72, Bklyn. Coll., 1975-80, prof. grad. ctr., 1980-90, disting. prof., 1991—. Author: Matisse on Art, 1973, Bread and Butter, 1977, Robert Motherwell, 1983, Matisse, the Man and His Art, 1986, Motherwell, 1991, Richard Diebenkorn: Ocean Park, 1992, Matisse: The Dance, 1993, Western Artists/African Art, 1994, Robert Smithson: The Collected Writings, 1996, Judith Rothschild: An Artist's Search, 1998, Frankenthaler, 1999, The Modern Drawing, 1999, Matisse in the Cone Collection, 2001, Matisse and Picasso: The Story of Their Rivalry and Friendship, 2003, Primitivism and Twentieth-Century Art: A Documentary History, 2003, Manet: Un Bar Aux Folies Bergere Ou L'abysse Du Miroir, 2005, Matisse in Transition: Around Laurette, 2006; art critic Wall St. Jour., 1984-92. Guggenheim Found. fellow, 1979, NEH, 1986. Mem. Internat. Art Critics Assn., Internat. PEN, Coll. Art Assn. Am. Office: Bklyn Coll Art Dept Bedford Ave # H Brooklyn NY 11210-2889

FLAMM, JUSTIN D., lawyer; b. Dayton, Ohio, June 10, 1974; BA, Miami U., 1996; JD, Washington and Lee U., 1999. Bar: Ohio 1999. Assoc. Taft, Stettinius & Hollister LLP, Cin. Bd. trustee Friends of William Howard Taft Birthplace. Named one of Ohio's Rising Stars, Super Lawyers, 2005, 2006. Office: Taft Stettinius & Hollister LLP 425 Walnut St Ste 1800 Cincinnati OH 45202 Office Phone: 513-381-2838. Office Fax: 513-381-0205.

FLAMM, LEONARD N(ATHAN), lawyer; b. Newark, May 23, 1943; s. Sydney Lewis and Lillian (Schreiber) F. Cert., London Sch. Econs., 1964; BA, Dartmouth Coll., Hanover, NH, 1965; JD, Harvard U., Cambridge, Mass., 1968. Bar: NJ 1968, NY 1970, US Ct. Appeals (2d cir.) 1970, Fla. 1976, US Dist. Ct. (so. and ea. dists.) NY 1976, US Ct. Appeals (7th cir.) 1986, US Ct. Appeals (3d cir.) 1987, US Supreme Ct. 1989. Assoc. Marshall, Bratter, Greene, Allison & Tucker, NYC, 1968-70, Donovan, Leisure, Newton & Irvine, NYC, 1970-72, Glass, Greenberg & Irwin, NYC, 1972-75; ptnr. Hockert & Flamm, NYC, 1975-90; pvt. practice NYC, 1990—. Contbg. author Employee Rights Litigation: Pleadings and Practice, 1991. Named one of Best Lawyers in US, Town & Country Mag., 1985. Mem. Assn. Bar City NY (legal referral panel 1975—), Nat. Employment Lawyers Assn. (v.p. NY chpt., nat. co-chmn. Age Discrimination in Employment Act com.) Office: 880 3rd Ave Ste 1300 New York NY 10022-4730 Office Phone: 212-752-3380. Personal E-mail: drelano@aol.com.

FLAMM, MELVIN DANIEL, JR., cardiologist; b. LA, Jan. 29, 1934; s. Melvin Daniel and Mary (Peterek) F.; m. Carla Baker, June 24, 1955; children: Scott Daniel, Bradley John, Jason Andrew, Amanda Paige. BA, UCLA, 1956; MD, Stanford U., 1960. Diplomate Am. Bd. Internal Medicine, Am. Bd. Cardiovascular Disease. Rotating intern Walter Reed Gen. Hosp., Washington, 1960-61; med. resident Stanford U., 1964-66, fellow in cardiology, 1966-68; cardiologist in pvt. practice No. Calif. Cardiology Assocs., Sacramento; clin. prof. medicine U. Calif., Davis; med. dir. Cardiac Catheterization Labs. Sutter Meml. Hosp., Sacramento, 1976-92. Chmn. instl. rev. com. Sutter Comty. Hosps., 1987-93; examiner Subspecialty Bd. of Cardiovasc. Diseases of Am. Bd. Internal Medicine, 1971-75; vis. prof. cardiology Nat. Def. Med. Sch. and Vets. Gen. Hosp., Taiwan U. Sch. Medicine, 1978, Queen Mary Hosp. of Hong Kong, U. Sch. Medicine and Hong Kong Cardiologic Soc., 1978. Contbr. numerous articles to profl. jours. Trustee Sutter Hosps. Found., 1987-89. Col. M.C., USAF, 1959-74, active res., 1974-84. Fellow ACP, Am. Coll. Cardiology, Coun. on Clin. Cardiology of Am. Heart Assn. (chmn. and mem. rsch. com. and rsch. allocation com. Golden Empire chpt.); mem. AMA, Am. Fedn. Clin. Rsch., Sacramento-El Dorado Med. Assn., Calif. Med. Assn. Avocations: gardening, travel, music. Office: No Calif Cardiology Assocs 5301 F St Ste 117 Sacramento CA 95819-3220 also: Mercy Gen Hosp 4001 J St Sacramento CA 95819*

FLANAGAN, BARBARA, journalist; b. Des Moines; d. John Merrill and Marie (Barnes) F.; m. Earl S. Sanford, 1966. Student, Drake U., 1942-43. With promotion dept. Mpls. Times, 1945-47; reporter Mpls. Tribune, 1947-58; women's editor, spl. writer Mpls. Star and Tribune, 1958-65; columnist Mpls. Star, 1965—. Author: Ovation, Minneapolis. Active Junior League Mpls., Womans Club Mpls. Mem. Mpls. Soc. Fine Arts (life), Mpls. Inst. Arts (founding mem. Minn. Arts Forum), Mpls. Club, Minikahda Club, Kappa Alpha Theta, Sigma Delta Chi. Episcopalian. Office: Mpls Star Tribune 5th And Portland Sts Minneapolis MN 55488-0001

FLANAGAN, CHRISTIE STEPHEN, lawyer; b. Port Arthur, Tex., June 28, 1938; s. Christie John and Rita Catherine (Hancock) F.; m. Gretchen Dowling Neuhoff; children: Mary Eileen, Margaret, Christopher, Michael. BBA, U. Notre Dame, 1960; LLB, U. Tex., Austin, 1962. Bar: Tex. 1962. Assoc. Hutchenson & Grundy, Houston, 1962-68; ptnr. Jenkens & Gilchrist, Dallas, 1968-88, mgr. ptnr., 1982-87, mem., 1988—94, of counsel, 2002—06; exec. v.p., gen. counsel Calif. Fed. Bank, 1994—2002; counsel Hunton & Williams, Dallas, 2007—. Active Dallas Citizens Coun., 1982-92; trustee Hockaday Sch., 1980-86, St. Marks Sch. Tex., 1986-92, Sierra Internat. Found., 1984-88. Mem. ABA, Tex. Bar Assn., Dallas Bar Assn., Salesmanship Club, Serra Club Dallas, Fishers Island Club, Brook Hollow Gold Club, Coon Creek Club, Dallas Country Club, Jupiter Island Club. Office: Hunton & Williams 1445 Ross Ave Ste 3700 Dallas TX 75202-2785 Office Phone: 214-468-3323.

FLANAGAN, CLYDE HARVEY, JR., psychiatrist, psychoanalyst, educator; b. Louellen, Ky., Aug. 21, 1939; s. Clyde H. Sr. and Ruby M. Flanagan; m. Gloria Kay Glymph, June 1, 1961 (div. Feb. 1974); children: Clyde H. III, Christopher Shane; m. Carol Anne Ross, Apr. 13, 1974; children: Patrick Ross, Colleen Helen. BS, Maryville Coll., 1962; MD, U. Tenn. Med. Unit, Memphis, 1966. Cert. Am. Bd. Psychiatry and Neurology in Adult, Child, Adolescent Psychiatry; diplomate Nat. Bd. Med. Examiners. Commd. 2d lt. U.S. Army, 1965, advanced through grades to col. MC, 1980; rotating med. intern U.S. Army Tripler Gen. Hosp., Honolulu, 1966-67; gen. psychiatry resident U.S. Army Walter Reed Gen. Hosp, Washington, 1967-69; child psychiatry resident Walter Reed Hosp., Washington, 1969-71; asst. chief child guidance svc. Walter Reed Army Med. Ctr., Washington, 1971-80; chief Cmty. Mental Health Activity, Ft. Belvoir, Va., 1980-86; asst. head tri-svc. alcohol rehab. dept. Nat. Navy Hosp., Bethesda, Md., 1986-88; dir. gen. psychiat. residency program W.S. Hall Psychiat. Inst., Columbia, SC, 1988-92; prof. psychiatry dept. of psychiatry/behavioral sci. Sch. Medicine U. S.C., Columbia, 1988—, dir. divsn. psychoanalysis dept. psychiat./behavioral sci., 1992—. Candidate in psychoanalysis Washington Psychoanalytic Inst., 1978-88; tng. and supervising analyst, asst. dir. PSA Inst. Carolinas, Chapel Hill, 1991—. Contbr. chapters to books. Recipient Tchr. Yr. award Resident's Gen. Psychiat. Rsch. Program William S. Hall Psychiat. Inst., 1995, Spl. Alumni citation Maryville Coll., 2000. Fellow: Am. Acad. Child and Adolescent Psychiatry (Franklin Robinson award 1975), Am. Coll. Psychiatrists (com. pub. edn. 1998—99, Laughlin fellow selection com. 2000—03, membership devel. com. 2003—05), Am. Psychiat. Assn. (disting. life fellow); mem.: Am. Assn. Child Psychoanalysis, Internat. Psychoanalytic Assn., Am. Group Psychotherapy Assn. (founder, cert. group psychotherapist), SC Psychiat. Soc. (chair membership com. 1991—), NC Psychoanalytic Soc. (councilor 1990—98), Am. Psychoanalytic Assn. (councilor 1989—2004, cert. in adult, adolescent, and child psychoanalysis 1991). Avocations: fishing, boating. Office: U SC Sch Medicine Dept Neuropsychiatry 3555 Harden St Ext Ste 104A Columbia SC 29203-6894 Office Phone: 803-434-4250. Business E-Mail: cflanagan@gw.mp.sc.edu.

FLANAGAN, FIONNULA MANON, actress, writer, theater director; b. Dublin; came to U.S., 1968; d. Terence Niall and Rosanna (McGuirk) F.; m. Garrett O'Connor, Nov. 26, 1972; 2 stepchildren. C.I.H.E., U. Fribourg, Switzerland, 1962; student, Abbey Theatre Sch., Dublin, 1964-66. Pres. The Rejoycing Co., 1978—. Stage appearances include: Ulysses in Nighttown, N.Y.C., 1974, Lovers, 1968, Ghosts, 1989, Happy Days, 1991, Unfinished Stories, 1992, Countess Cathleen, 1992, Summerhouse, 1994; author, actress one-woman shows: James Joyce's Women, 1977 (L.A. Drama Critics award, San Francisco Theatre Critics award, Drama-Logue award); films include: Ulysses, 1967, In the Region of Ice, 1980, Mr. Patman, 1980, James Joyce's Women, 1984, Reflections, 1984, Chain Reaction, 1985, Death Dreams, 1992, Mad at the Moon, 1992, Money for Nothing, 1993, Some Mother's Son, 1996, Waking Ned Devine, 1998, With or Without You, 1999, The Others, 2000, Divine Secrets of the Ya-Ya Sisterhood, 2002, Tears of the Sun, 2003, One of the Oldest Con Games, 2004, Blessed, 2004, Man About Dog, 2004, Transamerica, 2005, Four Brothers, 2005; TV appearances include: The Picture of Dorian Gray, 1973, The Legend of Lizzie Borden, 1975, Rich Man Poor Man, 1976 (Emmy award for most outstanding support role 1976), How the West Was Won, 1977-79 (Emmy nominee 1978), A Winner Never Quits, 1986, White Mile, 1994, Kings in Grass Castles, 1998, To Have and To Hold, 1998, For Love or Country: The Arturo Sandoval Story, 2000, Murder She Wrote: The Celtic Riddle, 2003, Revelations, 2005; dir. Freedom of the City, Theatre West L.A., 1988 (Dramalogue award), Faith Healer, 1989, Away Alone, Court Theatre, L.A., 1991, Abbey Theatre, Dublin, 1992, A Secret Affair, 1999, Havana Nocturne, 2000; TV guest appearances include: Chicago Hope, 1999, Enterprise, 2002, Law & Order: Special Victims Unit, 2003, Nip/Tuck, 2004. Mem. AFTRA, SAG, Actors' Equity, Irish Actors Equity. Office: Don Buchwald & Assocs 6500 Wilshire Blvd Ste 2200 Los Angeles CA 90048-4942

FLANAGAN, JAMES HENRY, JR., lawyer, finance educator; b. San Francisco, Sept. 11, 1934; s. James Henry Sr. and Mary Patricia (Gleason) F.; m. Charlotte Anne Nevins, June 11, 1960; children: Nancy, Christopher, Christina, Alexis, Victoria, Grace. AB in Polit. Sci., Stanford U., 1956, JD, 1961. Bar: Calif. 1962, U.S. Dist. Ct. (no. dist.) Calif. 1962, U.S. Ct. Appeals (9th cir.) 1962, U.S. Dist. Co. (so. dist.) Calif. 1964, U.S. Dist. Ct. (ea. dist.) Calif. 1967, Oreg. 1984. Assoc. Creede, Dawson & McElrath, Fresno, Calif., 1962-64; ptnr. Pettitt, Blumberg & Sherr and successor firms, Fresno, 1964-75; pvt. practice Clovis, Calif., 1975—92, North Fork, Calif., 1992-98; counsel Standing Chpt. 13 Trustee, 2003—06; staff Greater Fresno Area C. of C., 2006—. Instr. Humprey's Coll. Law, Fresno, 1964-69; instr. bus. Calif. State U., Fresno, 1986—; instr. MBA program Coll. of Notre Dame, Belmont, 1990-91; instr. Nat. U., 1991—, Emerson Inst., 1998—; judge pro tem Fresno County Superior Ct., 1974-77; gen. counsel Kings River Water Assn., 1976-79; founder, CEO Bus. and Non-profit Devel. Ctr; staff greeter Fresno Area C. of C., 2006-. Author: California Water District Laws, 1962; columnist. Choir mem. Our Lady of Sierra, 1998—; exec. com. parish coun. St. Helen's Ch., 1982-85, chmn. exec. com., 1985; pres. parish coun. St. John's Cathedral, 1974-82; pres. bd. dirs. 3d Floor Ctrl. Calif.; bd. dirs. Fresno Facts Found., 1969-70, Fresno Dance Repertory Assn., St. Anthony's Retreat Ctr., Three Rivers, Calif.; sec. Coarsegold Resource Conservation Dist.; co-founder Clovis Big Dry Creek Hist. Soc.; past chmn. Sierra Vista Nat. Scenic Byway Assn.; past judge adv. Mountain Detachment, Marine Corps League. Recipient President award Fresno Jaycees, 1964. Mem. Calif. Bar Assn., Fresno County Bar Assn., Calif. Trial Lawyers Assn. (chpt. pres. 1975, 83, state bd. govs. 1990-94), Fresno Trial Lawyers Assn., Am. Arbitration Assn., Stanford Alumni Assn. (life, svc. award), Fresno Region Stanford Club (pres. 1979-80), Celtic Cultural Soc. Ctrl. Calif. (pres. 1977-78), Fresno County and City C. of C. (chmn. natural resources com. 1977-78), Clovis C. of C., North Fork C. of C. (pres. 1993-96, sec. 1998-00, exec. dir. 2000—), Serra Club (pres. Fresno chpt. 1980-81, v.p. 1986-87), Rotary, Elks, KC (past grand knight, 4th degree honor guard knight, assembly navigator), Western Assn. Chamber Exec. Republican. Roman Catholic. Avocations: writing, music, gardening, golf, fishing. Office: PO Box 1555 North Fork CA 93643-1555 Office Phone: 559-760-9045. Personal E-mail: jayflanagan@sbcglobal.net.

FLANAGAN, JAMES LOTON, electrical engineer, educator, researcher; BSEE, Miss. State U., 1948; SMEE, MIT, 1950, ScDEE, 1955; PhD (hon.), U. Madrid, 1992, U. Paris, 1996. Elec. engring. faculty Miss. State U., 1950-52; tech. staff Bell Labs., Murray Hill, N.J., 1957-61, head dept. speech and auditory rsch., 1961-67, head dept. acoustics rsch., 1967-85, dir. info. prins. rsch. lab., 1985-90; dir. ctr. for advanced info. processing Rutgers U., Piscataway , NJ, 1990—, v.p. for rsch. Piscataway, NJ, 1993—.

Evaluation panel Nat. Bur. Standards/NRC, 1972—77; adv. panel on White House tapes U.S. Dist. Ct. for D.C., 1973—74; sci. adv. bd. Callier Center, U. Tex., Dallas, 1974—76; sci. adv. panel on voice comm. Nat. Security Agy., 1975—77. Author: Speech Analysis, Synthesis and Perception, 1972; contbr. articles to profl. jours. Recipient Disting. Svc. award in sci., Am. Speech and Hearing Assn., 1977, L.M. Ericsson Internat. prize in telecomms., 1985, Nat. Medal Sci., Nat. Medal Sci. Com., Pres. Clinton, 1996, N.J. R&D Coun. Sci. and Tech. medal, 2000; fellow, Marconi Internat., 1992. Fellow: IEEE (selection com. 1979—81, Edison medal 1986, Honor medal 2005), Am. Acad. Arts and Scis., Acoustical Soc. Am. (assoc. editor Speech Comm. 1959—62, exec. coun. 1970—73, v.p. 1976—77, pres. 1978—79, Gold medal 1986); mem.: NAS (chmn. engring. sect. 1996—99), NAE, Acoustics, Speech and Signal Processing Soc. (v.p. 1967—68, pres. 1969—70, Achievement award 1970, Soc. award 1976), Eta Kappa Nu. Achievements include patents in field.

FLANAGAN, JOSEPH PATRICK, advertising executive; b. Chgo., Jan. 6, 1938; s. Charles Larkin and Helen Mary (Sullivan) F.; children: Charlotte Ahern, Joseph P. Jr., Michael S., Larkin S., Brian A.; m. Carol Perkins, Nov. 6, 1999. BA, Mich. State U., 1959; MBA, U. Chgo., 1961. Dist. mgr. sales Time mag., Pitts. and Chgo., 1961-69; gen. mgr. Ctr. Advanced Research in Design, Chgo., 1969-75; v.p., dir. client services BBDO, Chgo., 1975-77; sr. v.p. IMPACT subs. Foote, Cone & Belding Comm. Co., Chgo., 1977-85, pres., 1985-99; corp. dir. sales promotion Foote, Cone & Belding Comm. Co., Chgo., 1987-99; pres. Flanagan Mktg., 1999—. Pres. Coun. of Sales Promotion Agys., 1986-89, also bd. dirs. Mem. governing bd. Chgo. Symphony Orch., 1974; v.p. Lyric Opera Guild, Chgo., 1974; trustee Loyola Acad.; bd. dirs. Count Theater; dir. arts and letters bd. Nat. Adv. Coun., Mich. State U.; bd. dirs. Total Focus Leo Burnett, Root-Lowell Mfg; client relationship exec. Diamond Cluster Internat., 1999—. Named Sales Promotion Profl. of Yr., Coun. Sales Promotion Agys., 1989; recipient Disting. Alumni award Mich. State U., 1991. Mem. Am. Assn. Advt. Agencies (chmn. sales promotion com.), Assn. of Promotion Mktg. Agys. Worldwide (Hall of Fame award 1998), Creek Club (Locust Valley, N.Y.), Centre Island, Seawanahaka Yacht Club (Oyster Bay, N.Y.). Roman Catholic. Avocations: classical music, opera. Home and Office: Flanagan Mktg 369 South Lake Dr Palm Beach FL 33480 Home (Summer): 334 Yacht Club Rd Oyster Bay NY 11771 Office Phone: 561-833-1607. E-mail: jpflanagansr@aol.com.

FLANAGAN, JOSEPH PATRICK, JR., retired lawyer; b. Wilkes-Barre, Pa., Sept. 18, 1924; s. Joseph P. and Grace B. Flanagan; m. Mary Elizabeth Mayock, Aug. 5, 1950; children: Maureen Elizabeth, Joseph P. III. BS, U.S. Naval Acad., 1947; JD, U. Pa., 1952. Bar: Pa. 1953, U.S. Dist. Ct. (ea. dist.) Pa. 1953, U.S. Ct. Appeals (3d cir.) 1953, U.S. Supreme Ct. 1997. Assoc. Saul, Ewing, Remick & Saul, Phila., 1952-56; ptnr. Ballard, Spahr, Andrews & Ingersoll, Phila., 1956-94, chmn. pub. fin. dept., 1961-90; ret., 1994. Editor: Practicing Law Inst., Health Facilities Financing, 1976; co-author: In Search of Capital-A Trustee's Guide to Hospital Financing; reviewing editor: Disclosure Roles of Counsel in State and Local Government Securities Offerings, editor-in-chief: U. Pa. Law Rev., 1951—52; contbr. articles to profl. jours. Bd. dirs. Phila. Com. 70, 1952—56; former trustee Wyo. Sem., Kingston, Pa.; mem. adv. coun. federalism Nat. Govs. Assn., 1988; former mem. bd. visitors U. Pa. Law Sch.; bd. dirs. John Bartram Assn., 1993—2003, v.p., 2000—03. Served to lt. (j.g.) USN, 1946—49. Fellow: Am. Bar Found.; mem.: ABA (past chmn. urban, state and local govt. sect.), Pa. Bar Inst. (chmn. curriculum and course planning com. 1976—88, pres. 1983), Pa. Bar Assn., Phila. Bar Assn. (past chmn. bus. law sect., bd. govs., past founding chmn. tax exempt fin. com., past chmn. profl. edn. com., mem. client's security fund com., mem. fee disputes com.), Nat. Assn. Securities Dealers (arbitrator 1998—), Army Navy Country Club Va., Chesapeake Bay Yacht Club, Phila. Cricket Club, Racquet Club, Phila. Club. Republican. Roman Catholic. Office: Ballard Spahr Andrews & Ingersoll 1735 Market St Fl 49 Philadelphia PA 19103-7501 Home: 4903 Quarry Row Lafayette Hill PA 19444 Office Phone: 215-864-8517. Business E-Mail: flanagan@ballardspahr.com.

FLANAGAN, JUDY, director, special events consultant; b. Lubbock, Tex., Apr. 28, 1950; d. James Joseph II and Jean (Breckenridge) F. BS in Edn., Memphis State U., Tenn., 1972; postgrad., Disney U., Orlando, Fla., 1975—81, Valencia C.C., 1977—79, Rollins Coll., Winter Park, Fla., 1979; MS in Comm., U. Tenn., Knoxville, 2004. Area/parade supr. entertainment divsn. Walt Disney World, Orlando, Fla., 1972—81; parade dir. Gatlinburg C. of C., Tenn., 1981-85; entertainment prodn. mgr. The 1982 World's Fair, Knoxville, 1982; cons. Judy Flanagan Prodns./Spl. Events, Gatlinburg, 1982—, Miss U.S.A. Pageant, Knoxville, 1983; prodn. coord. Nashville Network, 1983; dir. sales River Terr. Resort, Gatlinburg, 1985-86; account exec. Park Vista Hotel, Gatlinburg, 1986-88; project coord. Universal Studios, Fla., 1988-90; dir. spl. events U. Tenn., Knoxville, 1990—2006; creative cons. for spl. events, parades, 2006—. Dir. Neyland Stadium Expansion Dedication, 1996—, U. Tenn. Bicentennial Events, 1994, 21st Century Campaign Major Events, Main St. Dir. City Savannah, 2006-; prodn. mgr. 1984 World's Fair Parades and Spl. Events, New Orleans, (rock video) Neil Sedaka, (daytime soap opera) Days of Our Lives; spkr. in field. Extraordinary eucharistic minister, lectr. Cath. Ch. Recipient Gatlinburg Homecoming award, 1986, World Lifetime Achievement award, 1993. Mem.: ASPCA, Nat. Women's History Mus. (charter mem.), Nat. Wildlife Found., Ocean Conservancy, African Wildlife Found., Natural Resources Defence Council, Tenn. Festivals and Events Assn. (bd. dirs.), Internat. Festivals and Events Assn. (cert. festival and events exec., found. bd.), Internat. Spl. Events Soc., The Ocean Conservancy, Return Wild Horses to Freedom, World Wildlife Fund, Defenders of Wildlife, Humane Soc. U.S., Doris Day Animal League, Sierra Club, U. Tenn. Soc. Pres. Club. Roman Catholic. Home and Office: 835 Breckenridge L Savannah TN 38372 Personal E-mail: judy-flanagan@charter.net.

FLANAGAN, LAWRENCE, finance company executive; married. BS, Univ. New Haven. Mktg. positions in beauty care div. Procter & Gamble, 1986—94; asst. v.p. mktg., cosmetic & fragrance div. L'Oreal, 1994—96; v.p. U.S. advt. MasterCard Worldwide, Purchase, NY, 1996—99, sr. v.p., No. Am. mktg., 1999—2000, exec. v.p., chief mktg. officer, 2000—. Office: MasterCard Worldwide 2000 Purchase St Purchase NY 10577*

FLANAGAN, MICHAEL P., school system administrator; m. Anna Flanagan; children: Mike, Brian, Christa. Bachelor's degree, Notre Dame U.; Master's degree, Ea. Mich. U. Supt. Farmington/Farmington Hills Sch. Dist., Mich., 1989—94, Wayne Regional Ednl. Svcs. Agency, Mich., 1994—2001; exec. dir. Mich. Assn. of School Adminstrs. (MASA), 2001—05; edn. adv. to Gov. Jennifer M. Granholm, 2003; state supt. pub. instrn. Mich. Dept. Edn., 2005—. Chair Edn. Alliance of Mich.; served on former Mich. Gov. John Engler's Reading Plan for Mich. Coun.; edn. commr. Detroit 300 Commn. Past mem. Mich. Commn. on Asia in Schs.; bd. mem. Ready to Succeed Partnership, North Ctrl. Assn. State Com., Detroit Regional C. of C. Bus. and Edn. Training Alliance, Mich. Leadership Inst., Botsford Hosp., Mich. Virtual U., Midwest Regional Edn. Lab. Recipient Notre Dame Scholar award, Mich. Sch. Bus. Officials Disting. Svc. award, Mich. Assn. for Bilingual Edn. award, Educator of Yr. award, Mich. Assn. State and Fed. Program Specialists, Mich. Spl. Olympics Outstanding Sch. Dist. award, PTA-PTO Lifetime Achievement Award, Crystal Apple Award, Mich. State U., Eagle award for Disting. Svc. and Leadership, Mich. C. of C., 2006. Mem.: Mich. Sch. Bus. Officials, Mich. Liquid Asset Fund, Nat. County Supts. Assn. (past pres.). Office: Mich Dept Edn 608 W Allegan St PO Box 30008 Lansing MI 48909 Office Phone: 517-373-3324.*

FLANAGAN, NANCY A., nursing educator, researcher; b. Erie, Pa., June 27, 1951; d. William E. and Rosemary Rosenbaum; m. Timothy J. Flanagan, Aug. 4, 1973; children: Erin E. Coglianese, Kevin C. BS, Gannon U., Erie, Pa., 1973; MS, Russell Sage Coll., Troy, NY, 1980; PhD, Tex. Woman's U., Houston, Tex., 1997. RN NY, 2007. Nurse med. surg. unit St. Peter's Hosp., Albany, NY, 1973—74, nurse intensive care unit, 1975—76; clin. instr. dept. nursing Marshall U., Huntington, W.Va., 1975; scrub nurse oper. rm. Cabell-Huntington Hosp., Huntington, W.Va., 1975; charge nurse pvt. duty, hosp. staffing Tri-Cities and Helpmates Nursing Svcs., Latham, NY, 1977—86; staff nurse Albany Allergy Assocs., NY, 1986—87; asst. instr. sch. nursing Ellis Hosp., Schenectady, NY, 1987—91; staff nurse open heart step down unit Conroe Med. Ctr., Tex., 1992; coord. nursing skills lab. North Harris C.C., Houston, 1993—96; asst. prof. Tex. Woman's U., Houston, 1997—98, SUNY, Brockport, 1998—2000, Buffalo, 2000—06; pvt. practice cons. Framingham, Mass., 2006—. Presenter in field. Contbr. articles to profl. jours. Vol. Rochester Area Interfaith Hospitality Network, NY, 2004—06. Named Outstanding McNair Faculty Mentor, SUNY, Buffalo, 2006; recipient Gen. Excellence in Nursing award, Villa Maria Coll., 1973, New Investigator award, Rehab. Nursing Found. Assn. Rehab. Nurses, 1996, Accomplishment award, SUNY Inst. Rsch. and Gender, Buffalo, 2005, Dr. Nuala McGann Drescher Affirmative Action award, United U. Professions and SUNY, Buffalo, 2005; fellow, Sch. Nursing, U. Pa., 2003; scholar, Bur. of Health Manpower Edn., 1976—79. Mem.: ANA (assoc.), Nat. Commn. Correctional Health Care (assoc.), Coun. Advancement Nursing Sci. (assoc.), Sigma Theta Tau (hon.; pres. Gamma Kappa chpt. 2002—04). Achievements include research in transitional health care planning for ex-offenders. Avocations: camping, reading, travel, needlecrafts, snowshoeing. Office Phone: 508-626-4960. Business E-Mail: nflanagan@frc.mass.edu.

FLANAGAN, NORMAN PATRICK, lawyer; b. Pitts., Feb. 3, 1953; s. Norman Patrick and Janice (Smith) F.; m. Caroline E.E. Reverdin, Aug. 2, 1975; children: Erin Elizabeth, Sean Patrick. BS in Edn., Duquesne U., 1975; JD, Calif. Western U., 1978. Bar: Pa., Nev., U.S. Dist. Ct. Nev., U.S. Ct. Appeals (9th cir.), U.S. Supreme Ct. Dep. pub. defender Washoe County Pub. Defender's Office, Reno, 1979-81; asst. pub. defender Pub. Defender's Office, Reno, 1982—90; atty. Hale, Lane, Peek, Dennison & Howord, 1990—. Mem. Nev. State Bar Assn. (continuing legal edn. sect., pres-elect, 2002-03), Legal Def. Fund (capital litigation sect.). Republican. Roman Catholic. Avocations: tennis, cross country skiing. E-mail: pflanagan@halelane.com.

FLANAGAN, ROBERT JOSEPH, economics professor; b. New Haven, Dec. 16, 1941; s. Russell Joseph and Anne (Macauley) F.; m. Susan Rae Mendelsohn, Aug. 23, 1986. BA, Yale U., 1963; MA, U. Calif., 1966, PhD, 1970. Economist U.S. Dept. Labor, Washington, 1963-64; asst. prof. labor econs. Grad. Sch. Bus. U. Chgo., 1969-75; assoc. prof. labor econs. Grad. Sch. Bus. Stanford (Calif.) U., 1975-86; sr. staff economist Coun. of Econ. Advisors, Washington, 1978-79; sr. fellow The Brookings Instn., Washington, 1983-84; prof. labor econs. Grad. Sch. Bus., Stanford (Calif.) U., 1987-92, Matsushita prof. internat. labor econs. and econ. policy, 1993—, assoc. dean, 1996-99. Cons. OECD, Paris, 1988, U.S. Civil Rights Commn., Washington, 1982-83, NOAA, Washington, 1981; vis. scholar IMF, 1994, Australian Nat. U., 1990, 2000. Author: Labor Relations and Litigation Explosion, 1987, Globalization and Labor Conditions, 2006; (with others) Unionism, Economic Stabilization and Income Policy, 1982, Economics of the Employment Relationship, 1989, numerous others; contbr. articles to profl. jours. Mem. Am. Econs. Assn., Indls. Rels. Rsch. Assn., Soc. Labor Economists. Office: Stanford U Grad Sch Bus Palo Alto CA 94305

FLANAGAN, SEAN PATRICK, publishing executive; b. Oct. 16, 1963; m. Donna; children: Riley, Owen. BA, Villanova U., 1985. Territory mgr. Playboy, Nat. Geographic Traveler, Am. Bar Assn. Journal, N.Y. mgr.; advertising dir. Men's Health Mag., NYC, 1993-96, assoc. publisher, 1996-97, publisher, 1997—2000; eastern ad. dir. Yahoo! Internet Life, 2000—01; assoc. pub. Nat. Geographic Mag., NYC, 2001—03, U.S. pub., 2003—. Mem. AAAA, ACNY, BPAA, CTFA, MPA, NACDS, TFA, Fragrance Found., Beacon Hill Country Club. Avocations: family, irish music, golf, landscape horticulture. Office: Nat Geographic 711 Fifth Ave New York NY 10022*

FLANAGAN, THOMAS JAMES, medical products executive; Grad., US Naval Acad., Annapolis, Md., MIT, Cambridge, US Naval War Coll., Newport, RI, Harvard U. John F. Kennedy Sch. Govt., Cambridge. Officer USN; various exec. positions including chief info. officer and sr. v.p. global svc. delivery MCI, 1995—2004; v.p. info. systems Amgen, Inc., Thousand Oaks, Calif., 2004—05, head global enterprise resource planning program, 2005—06, sr. v.p., chief info. officer. Office: Amgen Inc One Amgen Center dr Thousand Oaks CA 91320-1799 Office Phone: 805-447-1000. Office Fax: 805-447-1010.*

FLANAGAN, TIMOTHY JAMES, academic administrator, criminal justice educator; b. Pitts., May 16, 1951; s. Norman Patrick and Dorothy Helen (Hoffmann) F.; m. Nancy Ann Rosenbaum, Aug. 4, 1973; children: Erin E., Kevin C. BA, Gannon U., 1973; MA, SUNY, Albany, 1974, PhD, 1980. Asst. prof., then assoc. prof. Sch. Criminal Justice, SUNY Rockefeller Coll. Pub. Affairs and Policy, 1982—91; prof. criminal justice, dean Coll. Criminal Justice Sam Houston State U., Huntsville, Tex., 1991—98; provost SUNY, Brockport, 1998; pres. Framingham State Coll., Mass., 2006—. Presenter numerous papers to profl. meetings, also panel convenor, chmn., discussant; exec. dir. Michael J. Hindelang Criminal Justice Rsch. Ctr., Inc., Albany, 1981-83. Co-editor: Sourcebook of Criminal Justice Statistics - 1978-92; editor: Jour. Criminal Justice Edn., 1989-93; contbr. articles to profl. jours., chpts. to books. Recipient Disting. Alumnus award SUNY Rockefeller Coll. Pub. Affairs and Policy, 1992. Fellow: Acad. Criminal Justice Scis.; mem.: Harvard U. Inst. for Ednl. Mgmt., Am. Coun. on Edn. (coun. fellows, leadership devel. fellow 1988—89), Am. Soc. Criminology, Pi Gamma Mu, Blue Key, Golden Key. Roman Catholic. Avocations: photography, bicycling, computers, sports, reading. Office: Framingham State Coll 100 State St Framingham MA 01701 Office Phone: 508-626-4575. Business E-Mail: president@frc.mass.edu.

FLANAGAN, VAN KENT, journalist; b. San Antonio, Sept. 20, 1945; s. Marquiss Monroe and Nina Louise (Fowler) F.; m. Janet Dorothy Robinson, Dec. 16, 1972. BA, Angelo State U., 1968. Reporter, editor San Angelo Standard-Times, Tex., 1966-68; copy editor Fort Lauderdale News, Fla., 1973-74; from news editor to editor Sun. Express-News, San Antonio, 1974-79; from newsman to bur. chief AP, Phila., 1979-80, Columbia, SC, 1980-82, Bismarck, ND, 1982-83, Nashville, 1983—2004; editor, adj. instr. Vanderbilt U., Freedom Forum Diversity Inst., Nashville, 2005—06. Disting. journalist-in-residence, asst. prof. Mid. Tenn. State U., 2005—. Served with U.S. Army, 1968-72, Vietnam. Decorated Bronze star. Mem.: Investigative Reporters and Editors, Inc., Journalism Edn. Assn., Tenn. Intercoll. Press Assn., Tenn. Coalition for Open Govt. (founding mem., sec. 2004—), Soc. Profl. Journalists (pres. Mid. Tenn. chpt. 1986—87, 2000—03). Presbyterian. Avocations: walking, hiking, reading. Home: 613 Riverview Dr Franklin TN 37064-5514 Office: Ezell Hall Rm 117-B MTSU Murfreesboro TN 37132 Office Phone: 615-898-2495. Personal E-mail: vankent45@comcast.net.

FLANAGAN KELLY, ANNE MARIE, academic administrator; b. North Kingstown, RI, Apr. 13, 1954; d. John James Flanagan and Margaret Mary Ortstein; children: Timothy Kelly, Brigid Kelly. Cert. advanced studies, SUNY, BA; MEd, Pa. State U. Cert. sch. dist. adminstr., sch. adminstrv. supr., nursery, kindergarten and grades 1-6, spl. edn. K-12. Grade 4 tchr. Narrowsburgh Ctrl. Sch. Dist., Narrowsburgh, NY, 1976; spl. edn. tchr. Tompkins-Seneca-Tioga BOCES, Ithaca, NY, 1977—80; learning disabilities specialist Ithaca City Sch. Dist., Ithaca, NY, 1980—81; head tchr. Adolescent Day Sch./Cmty. Treatment Ctr., Worcester, Mass., 1981—83; resource/cons./remedial tchr. Onteora Ctrl. Sch. Dist., Boiceville, NY, 1986—93; supr. spl. edn. Ulster BOCES, New Paltz, NY, 1993—. Adv. bd. 21st Century Grant- Ulster BOCES and Ellenville CSD, New Paltz, NY, 2001—; mem. NY State Coun. of Admstrs. Spl. Edn., NY; student success mgr. SUNY-Ulster, Stone Ridge; lectr., presenter in field. Contbr. articles to profl. jours. Religious edn. tchr. St. Joseph's Ch., Kingston, NY, 1989—2000, eucharistic min., 1996—2003; merit badge counselor Boy Scouts of Am. Troop 20, Hurley, NY, 1999—2003; mem. Kingston H.S. Alumni Choir, 2002—, St. Joseph's Music Ministry, Kingston. Fellow Spl. Edn., US Office Edn., 1976-1977; grantee VATEA, NY State Edn. Dept., 1995—97. Mem.: Regional Bd. N.Y. State Parent Tchr. Assn. (scholarship chairperson 1993—95, Hudson Valley chpt.), N.Y. State United Tchrs., SUNY Cortland Alumni Assn., SUNY New Paltz Alumni Assn., Penn State U. Alumni Assn., Coun. for Exceptional Children, Assn. Supervision and Curriculum Devel. Roman Catholic. Avocations: reading, singing, church activities, athletic events. Home: 28 Village Ct Kingston NY 12401 Office: Ulster BOCES 175 Route 32 N New Paltz NY 12561 Personal E-mail: kellya@sunyulster.edu. Business E-Mail: akelly@mhric.org.

FLANAGAN-SOULEN, MARY SUSAN, secondary school educator, adult education educator; b. Aug. 14, 1952; d. Hugh William and Rose A. (Holland) Flanagan; m. William R. Soulen; children: Margaret R. Soulen, David A. Soulen. BA, U. Notre Dame, Ind., 1974; MA, Ohio State U., Columbus, 1978. Tchr. Columbus Pub. Schs., 1974—2007; lectr. Ohio State U., Lima, Ohio, 2002—04, 2005, Newark, 2005—. Mem.: Phi Delta Kappa, Iota Lambda Sigma (Tchr. of Yr. 2000). Avocation: quilting. Home: 6790 Oakfair Ave Columbus OH 43235 Office: Columbus City Schs 1919 Northcliff Dr Columbus OH 43219

FLANDERS, DONALD HARGIS, manufacturing executive; b. Memphis, Apr. 26, 1924; s. Henry Jackson and Mae (Hargis) Flanders; m. Phala Kathryn Davis, Dec. 15, 1946; children: Donald Hargis, Dudley Kennedy, Kathryn Cotten. Student, Tex. Christian U., 1943; BBA, Baylor U., 1947. Dir. cost acctg., purchasing agt. McCoy-Couch Furniture Mfg. Co., Benton, Ark., 1947-50, Garrison Furniture Co., Ft. Smith, Ark., 1950-54; pres., founder Flanders Mfg. Co., Ft. Smith, 1954-70, Flanders Industries, Inc., Ft. Smith, 1970—. Chmn. bd., CEO Lloyd/Flanders Industries, Inc., Menominee, Mich., bd. dirs. 1st Nat. Bank, Ft. Smith. Chmn. exec. com. Ft. Smith Freight Bur., 1960-61; chmn. furniture bd. govs. Dallas Mkt. Ctr., 1968; exec. com. Ark. Coun. on Econ. Edn., 1964-67; mem. Ark. Small Bus. Adv. Coun., 1966-68; chmn. Ft. Smith United Fund drive, 1962; dist. chmn. Boy Scouts Am., Ft. Smith, 1960-62, pres. Westark Area coun. 1963-65, regional exec. com., 1964-72, vice chmn. region 5, 1967-69, chmn. region 5, 1969-72, nat. exec. bd., 1969-77; Com. of 100, 1965—; exec. dir. Ark. Indsl. Devel. Commn., 1981-83; trustee, vice chmn. Sparks Regional Med. Ctr., Hendrix Coll., U. Ark.-Ft. Smith Found., North Ark. Conf. 1986-95; bd. dirs. Meth. Ch. Served from apprentice seaman to lt. (s.g.) USNR, 1943-46. Recipient Silver Antelope, Silver Beaver, Silver Buffalo, Disting. Eagle Scout awards Boy Scouts Am., Free Enterprise award, 1964; named Industrialist of Yr. Ft. Smith Realtors Bd., 1965. Mem. SW Furniture Mfg. Assn. (pres. 1963), Ft. Smith C. of C. (dir. 1961-63, 73-75), Ark. Wood Products Assn. (dir. 1965-68), Summer Casual Furniture Mfrs. Assn. (pres. 1992-94, chmn. 1994-96), Masons (33 degree), Shriners, KT, Delta Sigma Pi. Methodist. Office: PO Box 1788 1901 Wheeler Ave Fort Smith AR 72902-1788 Personal E-mail: dhf@ipa.net.

FLANDERS, ELEANOR CARLSON, community volunteer; b. Spearville, Kans., Mar. 27, 1916; d. Carl Edward and Laura Rebecca (Pine) Carlson; m. Laurence Burdette Flanders, Jr., June 6, 1941; children: Laurel F. Umile, John C., Lynette F. Moyer, Paul L. BA, cert. journalism, U. Colo., 1938; family inst. cert., Vassar Coll., 1958. Examiner of credits U. Colo., Boulder, 1938-41; stock market analyst trust dept. First Nat. Bank, Longmont, Colo., 1970-85; landlady Historic Library Hall Apt. House. V.p. St. Vrain Valley Sch. Bd., 1978—84. Contbr. articles to profl. jours. Mem. PEO Sisterhood, 1948—; nat. treas. Am. Mothers NY, 1988—90; club leader 4-H Boulder County, 1947—63; pres., charter mem. Boulder County Mental Health Clinic, 1947—60; N. Colo. area rep. Am. Field Svc., Longmont, 1965—70; coord. tutoring program Boulder County Juvenile Ct., 1965—81; trustee, farm mgr. Carl and laura Carlson trust, Oberlin, Kans., 1971—85; trustee, dir. Colo. 4-H Youth Fund, Ft. Collins, 1973—86; trustee, investment counsel Am. Mothers Endowment Fund, NYC, 1979—90; founder, pres. St. Vrain Edn. Found. Endowment Fund, Longmont, 1985—2004; trustee, bd. dirs. Longmont Cable Trust, 1986—89; dir. St. Vrain Valley Sch. Bd., 1978—86; active Boulder County Ext. Svc. Com., 1985—90; precinct worker, del. Reps., Longmont, Boulder, 1941—; trustee, investment com. 1st Congl. Ch., Longmont, 1960—2001. Mem.: AAUW (charter), St. Vrain Hist. Soc. (dir., pres. 1970—), Sunshine Club, U. Colo. Alumni Assn. (dir., sec. 1950—58), Delta Kappa Gamma (hon.). Avocations: gardening, travel, duplicate bridge, reading, writing. Home: Covenant Village 9153 Yarrow St #1418 Broomfield CO 80021

FLANDERS, KAREN, consumer products company executive; married; 3 children. Mgr. internat. advocacy campaigns World Wildlife Fund, 1996—2001; dir. corp. responsibility Coca-Cola Co., NYC, 2001—. Bd. dir. Women's Network for Sustainable Future. Named one of America 's Top Women in Bus.-Game Changers, Pink mag. & Forté Found., 2007. Fluent in French, Dutch. Address: Coca-Cola Co One Coca-Cola Plz Atlanta GA 30313 Office: Corporate Responsibility Coca-Cola Co 711 5th Ave New York NY 10022 Office Phone: 404-676-2121, 212-759-4270.*

FLANDERS, RAYMOND ALAN, dentist, governmental health agency administrator, author; b. Bangor, Maine, Jan. 4, 1929; s. Carroll Benjamin and Mary (Watson) F.; m. Anne-Liss Teisen; children: Molly Olivia and Michael Benjamin (twins), Katherine Todd Mohan, James C. Todd. Student, Colgate U., 1948-50; BS, U. Miami, Fla., 1955; DDS, U. Md., 1959; MPH, U. Mich., 1979. Mem. faculty W.Va. U., Morgantown, 1964-65; program dir. Project Hope, Brazil, 1976-78; mem. faculty Coll. Dentistry U. Alagoas, Maceio, Brazil, 1976-78; regional dental dir. Va. State Health Dept., Richmond, 1970-76, 79-85; mem. faculty Med. Coll. Va., Richmond, 1980-85; state dental dir. Ill. Dept. Health, Springfield, 1985-96; mem. faculty Coll. Dental Medicine So. Ill. U., Alton, 1985-96; mem. faculty Coll. Dentistry Sch. Pub. Health U. Ill., Chgo., 1990-96; dental cons. Aetna U.S. Healthcare, 1998—. Cons. Project Esperanca, Amazon River, Brazil, 1981, Project HOPE/U.S.A.I.D., Grenada, West Indies, 1984, Project HOPE, Honduras, 1986, Am. Dental Assn., Brazil and Guyana, 1992. Author: Murder on the Sea Wolf and Other Stories, 2006; contbr. more than 35 articles to profl. jours. Served to capt. U.S. Army, 1946-47, 50-51, 60-63. Recipient Sec's Excellence in Health Promotion Award, 1990, Ranking 5th, Age Group 60-65, Western Tennis Assn., 1989, Gold Medal, Singles and Doubles Tennis, Ranked 4th Nat., Age Group 65-70, Sr. Olympics, 1994, Gold Medal, Singles Tennis, Age Group 70-75, 1999; fellow USPHS fellow, 1978—79. Mem. ADA (Preventive Dentistry award 1983, Cmty. Preventive Dentistry award 1990, 95), Va. Dental Assn., Assn. State Territorial Dental Dirs. (exceptional achievement award 1998), Am. Assn. Pub. Health Dentists, Ill. Pub. Health Assn., Va. Dental Assn. Home: 5 Whittakers Mill Williamsburg VA 23185 E-mail: rafalt@aol.com.

FLANDERS, ROBERT G., JR., lawyer, educator, association administrator; b. Freeport, NY, July 9, 1949; m. Ann I. Walls, May 29, 1971; children: Danielle, Heather, Zachary. AB magna cum laude, Brown U., 1971; JD, Harvard Law Sch., 1974. Bar: N.Y. 1975, Mass. 1976, R.I. 1976,

U.S. Ct. of Appeals (1st and 2d. cir.), U.S. Dist. Ct. (so. dist., ea. dist.) N.Y., R.I., Mass. Assoc. Paul, Weiss, Rifkind, Wharton & Garrison, NYC, 1974-75; ptnr., chmn. litig. dept. Edwards & Angell, Providence, 1975-87; founding ptnr. Flanders & Medeiros Inc., 1987-96; assoc. justice R.I. Supreme Ct., 1996—2004; ptnr. Ainckley, Allan & Snyder, 2004—; disting. visiting prof. Roger Williams U. Sch. of Law, 2004—. Mem. Am. Law Inst., 2000—; bd. dirs. Rsch. Engring. and Mfg., Inc., Nestor, Inc. Contbr. articles to profl. publ. Bd. dirs. Brown Sports Found., 2000, Greater Providence YMCA, 1995—, Providence Performing Arts Ctr., 1997—, Vets. Meml. Auditorium, 1999—, Women and Infants Hosp., 1996—. Mem. ABA, Phi Beta Kappa. Avocations: tennis, clarinet, jazz, poetry, cigars.

FLANIGAN, JAMES J(OSEPH), journalist; b. NYC, June 6, 1936; s. James and Jane (Whyte) F.; m. Patricia Quatrine, Nov. 28, 1997; children: Michael, Siobhan Jane. BA, Manhattan Coll., 1961. Fin. writer N.Y. Herald Tribune, 1957-66; bur. chief, asst. mng. editor Forbes Mag., 1966-86; bus. columnist, sr. econs. editor L.A. Times, 1986—. Office: LA Times 202 W 1st St Los Angeles CA 90012 Office Phone: 213-237-7167. E-mail: jim.flanigan@latimes.com.

FLANIGAN, ROBERT CHARLES, urologist, educator; b. Lima, Ohio, May 2, 1946; children: Nancy, Charles. BA in Chemistry, Coll. of Wooster, 1968; MD, Case Western Res. U., 1972. Resident in surgery and urology Case Western Res. U., 1972-78; vol. asst. prof. urology U. Nebr., 1978-80; asst. prof. surgery U. Ky. Med. Ctr., Lexington, 1980-84, assoc. prof. surgery, 1984-86; prof. urology, chmn. dept. Loyola U. Med. Ctr., Maywood, Ill., 1986—. Chief urology Hines VA Hosp., 1986—; trustee Am. Bd. Urology. Officer M.C., USAF, 1978-80. Recipient Cardinal's Medallion, Archdiocese of Chgo., 1995. Fellow ACS; mem. Am. Bd. Urol. (pres. 2005-), Am. Urol. Assn., Am. Assn. Genito-Urinary Surgeons, Soc. Pelvic Surgeons, Am. Soc. Transplant Surgeons, Chgo. Urol. Soc. (past pres.), Soc. Univ. Urologists (sec.-treas.), Soc. Urologic Oncology (sec.), Loyola U. Physicians Found. (v.p. 1995—). Office: Loyola U Med Ctr 2160 S 1st Ave Maywood IL 60153-3304 E-mail: rflanig@luc.edu.

FLANIGEN, EDITH MARIE, materials scientist, consultant; BA in Chemistry magna cum laude, D'Youville Coll., 1950; MS in Inorganic Physical Chemistry, Syracuse U., 1953; DSc (hon.), D'Youville Coll., 1983. Rsch. chemist Union-Carbide Corp., 1952—56, researcher, molecular sieve group, 1956—73, corp. rsch. fellow, 1973—82, sr. corp. rsch. fellow, 1982—88; sr. rsch. fellow materials sci. UOP Tarrytown Tech. Ctr., NY, 1988—91, UOP fellow, 1991—94, ret. NY, 1994; cons. White Plains, NY, 1994—. Amb. World for Zeolites, lectr. Named to Nat. Inventors Hall of Fame, 2004; recipient Disting. Svc. award, Am. Chem. Soc. (Western NY Sect.), 1980, Chemical Pioneer award, Am. Inst. Chemists, 1991, Perkin medal (first women to win this award), Soc. Chem. Ind. (Am. Sect.), 1992, Francis P. Garvan-John M. Olin medal, Am. Chem. Soc., 1993, Internat. Zeolite Assn. award, 1994, Outstanding Women Scientist, NY Acad. Sciences, 1996, Achievement award, Indsl. Rsch. Inst., 2004, Lemelson-MIT Lifetime Achievement award, 2004. Mem.: NAE. Achievements include patents in field. Home: 502 Woodland Hills Rd White Plains NY 10603-3136

FLANNERY, ELLEN JOANNE, lawyer; d. William Rowan and Mary Jane (Hamilla) Flannery. AB cum laude, Mount Holyoke Coll., 1973; JD cum laude, Boston U., 1978. Bar: Mass. 1978, DC 1979, US Ct. Appeals (DC cir.) 1979, US Dist. Ct. DC 1980, US Ct. Appeals (4th cir.) 1981, US Supreme Ct. 1983. Spl. asst. to commr. of health Mass. Dept. Pub. Health, Boston, 1973—75; law clk. US Ct. Appeals DC cir., Washington, 1978—79; assoc. Covington & Burling LLP, Washington, 1979—86, ptnr., 1986—, co-chmn. Food & Drug Regulatory Practice Group. Lectr. ins. U. Va. Sch. Law, 1984—90, Boston U. Sch. Law, 1993, bd. visitors, 1995—; lectr. ins. U. Md. Sch. Law, 1994; mem. Nat. Conf. Lawyers and Scientists, AAAS-ABA, 1989—92; chair Fellows Adv. Rsch. Commn., 2002—06. Contbr. articles to profl. jour. Fellow: Am. Bar Found. (chair fellows adv. rsch. com. 2002—06, sec. fellows 2005—06, chair elect fellows 2006—); mem.: ABA (chmn. life scis. divsn. 1982—84, chmn. com. med. practice 1987—88, chmn. life scis. divsn. 1988—91, vice chair food and drug law com. 1991—97, chmn. sect. sci. and tech. 1992—93, del. sci. and tech. sect. to house of dels. 1993—, chmn. coordinating group on bioethics and the law 1998—2000, vice chair House Tech. Com. 2002—04, chmn. conf. sect. and divsn. dels. 2003—), Cosmos Club. Office: Covington & Burling LLP 1201 Pennsylvania Ave NW Washington DC 20004-2401 Office Phone: 202-662-5484. Office Fax: 202-662-6291. Business E-Mail: eflannery@cov.com.

FLANNERY, JOHN PHILIP, lawyer; b. NYC, May 15, 1946; s. John Philip and Agnes Geraldine (Applegate) F.; 1 child by a previous marriage: Diana Elizabeth; m. Holly Lynne Smith, Mar. 1, 2003; 1 stepchild, Alexandra Elizabeth. BS in Physics, Fordham Coll., 1967; BS in Engring., Columbia U., 1969, JD, 1972; student, Art Students League, 1972-73; MS in Info. Sci., George Washington U., 2002. Bar: N.Y. 1973, U.S. Dist. Ct. (so. dist.) N.Y. 1973, U.S. Ct. Appeals (2d cir.) 1973, Va. 1983, U.S. Ct. Appeals (4th cir.) 1985, U.S. Ct. Appeals (D.C. cir.) 1985, U.S. Dist. Ct. (ea. dist.) Va. 1985, U.S. Supreme Ct. 1985. Mem. staff Ford Found. Project to Restructure Columbia U., NYC, 1968; news rep. nat. press rels. IBM, 1970; law clk. Adminstrv. Conf. U.S., 1971, U.S. Ct. Appeals (2d cir.), 1972-74; asst. U.S. atty. Narcotics and Ofcl. Corruption units, So. Dist. N.Y., NYC, 1974-79; sr. assoc. Poletti Freidin Prashker Feldman & Gartner, NYC, 1979-82; spl. counsel U.S. Senate Judiciary Com., 1982, U.S. Senate Labor Com., 1982-83; Dem. candidate U.S. Congress from Va. 10th Dist., 1983-84; pvt. practice in civil and criminal litigation, 1984—. Spl. counsel Sen. Howard Metzenbaum, 1985-87; asst. dist. atty., Bronx, N.Y., 1986-87; counsel, bd. dir. Washington Internat. Horse Show Assn., 1989-91; legal expert "Crime in D.C.", Fox TV, 1993, "Crime Bill" Wis. Pub. Radio, 1994, "People vs. O.J. Simpson" ABC Network Radio, 1994-95, "Va.'s No Parole" Larry King Live CNN, 1994, "Imprisonment" CBS Morning Show, 1994, Habeas Reform Court TV, 1996, Terrorism, 1996, O'Reilly Factor, Fox News, "Torture", 2004, Fox News "Supreme Court," 2004-05; spl. counsel U.S. House Judiciary Com., 1996-97; project dir., spl. counsel U.S. Edn. and Work Force Com., 1997-98; spl. counsel (impeachment proceedings) U.S. Rep. Zoe Lofgren, 1998-99, Washington staff chief, spl. counsel, 1999-2001; vis. exec. George Washington U. Sch. Bus. and Pub. Mgmt., 2002-04; of counsel, Campbell, Miller, Zimmerman, P.C., 2002—; officer, dir. Campbell Miller Zimmerman, PC, 2005—; lectr. in field. Author: Commercial Information Brokers, 1973, Habeas Corpus Bores Hole in Prisoners' Civil Rights Action, 1975, Pro Se Litigation, 1975, Prison Corruption: A Mockery of Justice, 1980, Conspiracy: A Primer, 1988, Is Innocence Relevant to Execution? If Not, Isn't that Murder?, 1994, Equal Justice For All, 1995, Virginia Governor Allen's No-Parole Plan: A Billion Dollar Wasteland of Prisons, 1995, Pain in America and How our Government Maked it Worse, 2006; tech. columnist, Loudoun Times Mirror, May 2002-04; contbg. columnist Loudoun Times Mirror, 2004—; on-air commentator O'Reilly Factor, Fox News, Chris Matthews' Hardball, MSNBC, 2004—. Mem. legis. commn. Citizen's Union, 1971—72; mem. Arlington Transp. Commn., 1983—85; chmn. bus. coun. Va. Gov.'s War on Drugs Task Force, 1983—84; pres. Franklin Soc., 1979—80; committeeman Dem. Party N.Y. County, 1979—80, Dem. Party Arlington County, 1983—84; coord. N.Y. State Lawyers Com. for Sen. Edward M. Kennedy, 1979—80; dir. Citizens for Sen. M. Kennedy, 1980; del. Dem. Nat. Conf., 1988, Va. Assembly Univ. W.Va., 1990; committeeman Loudoun County Dem. Com., 1995—, sec., 1995—, chmn., 1995—97, mem., 2006—, v.p., 2001; del. 10th Congress and Dist. Com., 1997—; mem. Ctrl. State (Va.) Com., 1997—; del. Dem. Nat. Conv., 2000, 2004; Va. coord. Kerry for Pres., 2003—04. Recipient U.S. Justice Dept. award for Outstanding Contbns. in Field of Drug Law Enforcement, 1977, U.S. Atty. Gen.'s Spl. Commendation for Outstanding Svc., 1979, FLEOA award, Fed. Law Enforcement Officer's Assn., 1984, NACDL's Marshall Stern award Outstanding Legis. Achievement, 1997. Mem. ABA, Assn. Bar City N.Y., N.Y. County Lawyers Assn., Arlington County Bar Assn., Loudon County Bar Assn., Nat. Assn. Criminal Def. Lawyers (chair briefbank com. 1990-91, legis. co-chair 1991-96, dir. 1993-97, President's commendation 1991, 92, 95), Acad. Polit. Sci., Va. Coll. Criminal Def. Attys. (bd. dir. 1993-96), Restoration and Preservation Soc. (bd. dir. 2004-05), Leesburg Rotary (bd. dir. 2004-05). Democrat. Home: Ithaca Manor 38469 Triticum Ln Lovettsville VA 20180 Office Phone: 703-771-8344. Personal E-mail: jonflan@aol.com.

FLANNERY, JOSEPH PATRICK, manufacturing executive, director; b. Lowell, Mass., Mar. 20, 1932; s. Joseph Patrick and Mary Agnes Egan F.; m. Margaret Barrows, June 1957; children: Mary Ann, Diane, Joseph, James, David, Elizabeth. BS in Chemistry, Lowell Tech. Inst., 1953; MBA, Harvard U., 1955; PhD, U. Lowell, Mass., 1981. Pres. Uniroyal Chem. Co., Naugatuck, Conn., 1975-77; exec. v.p. Uniroyal, Inc., Middlebury, Conn., 1977, pres., 1977—, chief exec. officer, 1980—, chmn. bd., 1982—; chmn., pres., chief exec. officer Uniroyal Holding, Inc., Naugatuck, Conn., 1986—. Bd. dirs. The Scotts Co., ArvinMeritor. Mem.: Country Club of Fla., Oyster Harbors (Mass.), Vesper Country Club (Lowell), Country Club of Waterbury (Conn.), Knights of Malta. Roman Catholic. Office: Uniroyal Holding Inc 70 Great Hill Rd Naugatuck CT 06770-2224

FLANNERY, KATE, actress; b. Phila., Pa., June 10, 1964; BFA, Univ. Arts, Phila. Mem. Second City's Nat. Touring Co., Chgo. Annoyance Theater; former off-Broadway actress. Music dir. LA Drama Club for Kids; radio personality Air America. Actor: (off-Broadway) Valley of the Dolls, Phacts of Life, Hildy, Hildy, Three Feet Under, Evidence Room; (TV series) Bernie Mac Show, Boomtown, 2003, Curb Your Enthusiasm, 2002, Cross Balls, 2004, Jimmy Kimmel Live, 2005, The Office, 2005— (winner Outstanding Performance by an Ensemble in a Comedy Series, SAG awards, 2007). Office: NBC 30 Rockefeller Plz New York NY 10112*

FLANNERY, MICHAEL SIDNEY, environmental scientist; b. Logan, W. Va., Sept. 11, 1952; s. Wilbur Elmer and Mildred Davis Flannery; m. Terrie Mackin Lee, Nov. 24, 1984; children: Lauren Lee, Brian Mackin. MS, U. Fla., 1984, BS in forestry, 1975. Biologist U. Fla., Gainesville, Fla., 1975—81; biologist, botanist Northwest Fla. Water Mgmt. Dist., Havana, Fla., 1984—85; sr. environ. scientist Soutwest Fla. Water Mgmt. Dist., Brooksville, Fla., 1985—2005. Office: SW Fla Water Mgmt Dist 2379 Broad St Brooksville FL 34604-6899

FLANNERY, SUSAN MARIE, library administrator; b. Newark, Feb. 18, 1953; d. John Patrick Flannery and Assunta (Lardieri) Ege; m. Stephen A. Coren, Oct. 6, 1984. BA in History of Art, U. Pa., 1974; MLS, Simmons Coll., 1975. Dir. of libr. Newton Country Day, 1975-77, Am. Sch. in Switzerland, Montagnola, 1977-78; young adult libr. Somerville (Mass.) Pub. Libr., 1979-81; reference libr. Cary Meml. Libr., Lexington, Mass., 1981-83; asst. dir. Lucius Beebe Libr., Wakefield, Mass., 1983-87; dir. Reading (Mass.) Pub. Libr., 1987-91; assoc. dir. Cambridge (Mass.) Pub. Libr., 1991-1993, dir., 1993—. Steering com. Mass. delegation to White Ho. Conf. on Librs., 1990; corporator East Cambridge Savs. Bank. Reviewer Sch. Libr. Jour.; contbr. articles to profl. jours. Incorporator Cambridge (Mass.) Family YMCA , 1991—93; bd. dirs. Guidance Ctr., Inc., Cambridge, 1994—2000, sec., 2001—. Recipient Friend to Writers award, PEN New Eng., 2004, Leading Role award, Cambridge Cmty. TV, 2005. Mem. ALA (Mass. councilor 1993-97, John Cotton Dana award 1989, Outstanding Libr. Adv. 20th Century 2000), ACLU Mass. (adv. bd. 1994-96, bd. dirs. 1996—2004), Mass. Libr. Assn. (pres. 1985-87, v.p. 1983-85), Rotary (bd. dirs. Cambridge 1993-99, v.p. 1995-96, pres. 1997-98, pres. Reading club). Office: Cambridge Pub Libr 359 Broadway Cambridge MA 02139 Home Phone: 617-661-0882; Office Phone: 617-349-4032. E-mail: sflannery@cambridgema.gov.

FLANZIG, DANIEL, lawyer; b. Huntington, NY, Aug. 7, 1968; s. Marcia Flanzig. BA, Rutgers U., New Brunswick, NJ, 1990; JD, CUNY, Queens, 1991. Assoc. Joachim, Flanzig, Mineola, NY, 1995—2002; ptnr. Flanzig and Flanzig, LLP, Mineola, 2002—. Home and Office: Flanzig and Flanzig LLP 323 Willis Ave Mineola NY 11501 Home Phone: 516-741-8222; Office Phone: 516-741-8222. Home Fax: 516-741-8889.

FLASTER, DONALD J., retired pharmaceutical executive; s. Murray J. and Theresa Flaster; m. Susan J. Alexander, Dec. 16, 1988. AB in Biol. Scis., Johns Hopkins U., Balt., 1953; MD, U. Naples, Italy, 1959. Intern Meyer Meml./Erie County Hosp., Buffalo; resident Millard Fillmore Hosp., Buffalo, Emergency Hosp., Buffalo; pvt. practice physician Valley Cottage, NY, 1961—67; assoc. med. dir. Pfizer Labs., NYC, 1967—69; dir. clin. rsch. USV Pharm., NYC, 1969—72; assoc. dir. clin. rsch. Sandoz Inc., East Hanover, NJ, 1972—74; pres., CEO SRS Inc., Morristown, NJ, 1974—90; ret., 1990. Cons. SRS Inc., Morristown, 1974—90. Author: Malpractice: A Guide to the Legal Rights of Patients and Doctors, 1983—84. Recipient Outstanding Contbn. award, NY State Acad. Family Physicians, 25 Yrs. Comprehensive Svc. award. Fellow: Am. Acad. Family Physicians (life); mem.: NJ Med. Soc. (emeritus). Avocation: music.

FLATEN, ARNE R., art educator; b. Northfield, Minn., Nov. 11, 1966; s. Robert Arnold and Carroll Jean Flaten; m. Rebecca Rhodes Rhodes, July 25, 1992; children: Erika Laine, Natasha Marie, Lara Nicole. BA, St. Olaf Coll., Northfield, Minn., 1989; MA, Ind. U., Bloomington, 1996, D, 2001. Asst. prof. Coastal Carolina U., Conway, SC, 2003—. Co-founder, co-dir. Ashes2Art, Conway, SC, 2003—; vis. asst. prof. Va. Tech U., Blacksburg, 2002—03. Author: (book) The Middeldorf Collection: Medals and Plaquettes 15th to 20th Centuries, (catalogue) Selected Medals and Plaquettes from the Middeldorf Collection, (catalogue entries) Renaissance Medals in the Chazen Collection; Encyclopedia of Sculpture; Encyclopedia of the Renaissance; contbr. articles to profl. jours.; Lead singer, songwriter and keyboardist: rock band Virtue Trap, 2003—. Recipient Outstanding Tchg. award, Pan-Hellenic Soc., Va. Tech, 2003; fellow, Fulbright Commn., 1998—99, Samuel H. Kress Found., 1999—2000, Ctr. Advanced Study Visual Arts, Nat. Gallery Art, Washington, 2000—01, Samuel H. Kress Found., 2001—02, Sweet Briar Coll., Va., 2001—03; grantee, Getty Rsch. Inst., 2005, NEH, 2006, 2007. Mem.: Assn. Art Historians, Italian Art Soc., Coll. Art Assn., Renaissance Soc. Am. (fellow 2001—02), Phi Beta Kappa. Home: 101 East Coker Ln Conway SC 29526 Office: Coastal Carolina U Edwards Coll Conway SC 29528 Home Phone: 843-347-3989; Office Phone: 843-234-3463. Business E-Mail: arflaten@coastal.edu.

FLATER, MORRIS EUGENE, lawyer; b. Augusta, Ga., Sept. 1, 1943; s. Morris E. Flater and Sue (Ransom) Bell; m. Susanne R. Flater (div. 1987); children: Lara, Morris E. III. BS, Tulane U., 1966; JD magna cum laude, Washington and Lee U., 1973; LLM, Georgetown U., 1997. Bar: Va. 1973, Mass. 1991. Of counsel Hunton and Williams, Norfolk, Va., 1973-84; pres. Channel Labs., Ltd., Norfolk, 1984-85, Hub Express Airlines, Boston, 1986-91; exec. dir., gen. counsel Am. Helicopter Soc., Alexandria, Va., 1991—. Pub. Vertiflite mag. Capt. USMC, 1966-70. Recipient Helicopter Assn. Internat. Excellence in Comm. award. Fellow Royal Aeronautical Soc., Order of Coif, AIAA (assoc.), Omicron Delta Kappa. Office: Am Helicopter Soc 217 N Washington St Alexandria VA 22314-2520 E-mail: rflater@vtol.org.

FLATO, WILLIAM ROEDER, JR., software development company executive; b. Corpus Christi, Tex., Apr. 20, 1945; s. William Roeder and Juanita Flato; m. Beatrice Pesl, Aug. 22, 1974; children: Amanda Leigh, William Roeder III. BBA, U. Houston, 1967. CPA, Tex. Acct. Hughes Tool Co., Houston, 1966-67, Milchem, Inc., Houston, 1967-72, accounting mgr., asst. contr., corp. contr., 1972-78; v.p. fin., sec., treas. Baker Performance Chems. Inc. (formerly Magna Corp.), Houston, 1978-82, exec. v.p. fin. and planning, sec.-treas., 1982-93; CFO, v.p. fin. CoToCo Techs., Inc., Houston, 1993-97; founder, CFO, v.p. fin. Connective Techs., Inc., Houston, 1996—2001, CEO, 2001—, pres., 2001—. Active Country Village Civic Assn.; state chmn. Young Ams. for Freedom, 1964; precinct chmn. Harris County Rep. Exec. Com., 1966-67; chmn. Acctg. Adv. Com., Houston CC Sys., 1996-. With U.S. Army, 1968-69. Decorated Army Commendation medal. Mem. Tex. Soc. CPA, Houston Chpt. TSCPA, Mensa, Tex. Rifle Assn. (life), NRA. Conservative. Presbyterian. Home: 11931 Drexel Hill Dr Houston TX 77077-3009 Office: 7676 Hillmont St Ste 120 Houston TX 77040-6468 Office Phone: 713-690-6789 ext. 129. Personal E-mail: bflato@houston.rr.com. Business E-Mail: bflato@connectivetech.com.

FLATT, ADRIAN EDE, surgeon; b. Frinton, Eng., Aug. 26, 1921; came to U.S., 1956, naturalized, 1960; s. Leslie Neeve and Barbara F.; m. Judith Johnson. BA, Cambridge U., 1942, MA, 1945, MBBchir., 1946, MD, 1953, M. chir., 1972. Diplomate: Am. Bd. Orthopedic Surgery. Rotating intern, then resident in gen., plastic and orthopaedic surgery London (Eng.) Hosp., 1946-54, 55-56; mem. faculty U. Iowa Med. Sch., 1956-79; prof. orthopaedic surgery and anatomy, dir. div. hand surgery, chmn. dept. surgery Norwalk (Conn.) Hosp., 1979-82; clin. prof. Yale U. Med. Sch., 1979-82; chief dept. orthopaedics Baylor U. Med. Ctr., Dallas, 1982-92, coord. rsch. Tom Landry Sports Medicine Ctr., 1992-94, dir. edn. dept. orthopaedics, 1995—. Hunterian prof. Royal Coll. Surgeons, 1962; McIlrath guest prof. Royal Prince Alfred Hosp., Sydney, Australia, 1972; Sir R. Watson-Jones lectr. Brit. Orthopaedic Assn., 1986; cons. in hand surgery to surg. gen. U.S. Air Force, 1962— Editor in chief Jour. Hand Surgery, 1981-91; author textbooks, papers in field; patentee artificial wrist and finger joints. Served as officer RAF, 1948-50. Recipient Kappa Delta award Am. Acad. Orthopaedic Surgeons, 1972 Mem. Am. Soc. Surgery Hand, Brit. Hand Soc., Brit. Assn. Plastic Surgery (hon.), Group Etude de la Main, Am. Orthopaedic Assn., Am. Acad. Orthopaedic Surgeons, Am. Soc. Plastic and Reconstructive Surgery. Office: Baylor U Med Ctr George Truett James Orthopedic Inst 3500 Gaston Ave Dallas TX 75246-2096 Office Phone: 214-820-1989. Business E-Mail: adrianf@baylorhealth.edu.

FLATTÉ, STANLEY MARTIN, physicist, researcher; b. LA, Dec. 2, 1940; s. Samuel and Henrietta (Edelstein) Flatté; m. Renelde Marie Demeure, June 26, 1966; children: Michael, Anne. BS, Calif. Inst. Tech., 1962; student, NYU, 1960-61; PhD, U. Calif.-Berkeley, 1966. Rsch. particle physicist Lawrence Berkeley Lab., Calif., 1966-71; asst. prof. physics U. Calif., Santa Cruz, 1971-73, assoc. prof., 1973-78, prof., 1978—2004, prof. emeritus, 2004—; dir. Ctr. Studies Nonlinear Dynamics La Jolla Inst., 1982-86, dept. chmn., 1986-89. Cons. phys. oceanography and underwater sound U.S. Govt.; vis. rschr. Cern, Geneva, 1975, Scripps Inst. Oceanography, 1980, Cambridge (Eng.) U., 1981. Author (with others): Sound Transmission Through a Fluctuating Ocean, 1979; contbr. articles to profl. jours. Woodrow Wilson fellow, 1962, NSF fellow, 1962—66, Guggenheim Found. fellow, 1975. Fellow: AAAS, Optical Soc. Am., Acoustical Soc. Am., Am. Phys. Soc.; mem.: Am. Geophys. Union, Sigma Xi (pres. Santa Cruz chpt. 1999—2000). Achievements include discovery of cusp phenomenon in particle physics; development of methods for using sound and light waves to probe statistical atmosphere, ocean and earth processes; analysis method for a particle decaying by two channels, one near threshold. Office: Univ Calif Physics Dept Santa Cruz CA 95064 Home Phone: 831-426-7021. Business E-Mail: sflatte@ucsc.edu.

FLATTERY, THOMAS LONG, lawyer, administrator; b. Detroit, Nov. 14, 1922; s. Thomas J. and Rosemary (Long) F.; m. Gloria M. Hughes, June 10, 1947 (dec.); children: Constance Marie, Carol Dianne Lee, Michael Patrick, Thomas Hughes, Dennis Jerome, Betsy Ann Sprecher m. Barbara J. Balfour, Oct. 4, 1986; children: Laura B. Lundquist, Linda B. Flint, William D. Balfour III. BS, U.S. Mil. Acad., 1947; JD, UCLA, 1955; LLM, U. So. Calif., 1965. Bar: Calif. 1955, U.S. Patent and Trademark Office 1957, U.S. Customs Ct. 1968, U.S. Supreme Ct. 1974, Conn. 1983, N.Y. 1984. With Motor Products Corp., Detroit, 1950, Equitable Life Assurance Soc., Detroit, 1951, Bohn Aluminum & Brass Co., Hamtramck, Mich., 1952; mem. legal staff, asst. contract adminstr. Radioplane Co. (divsn. Northrop Corp.), Van Nuys, Calif., 1955—57; gen. counsel, asst. sec. McCulloch Corp., LA, 1957—64; sec., corp. counsel Technicolor, Inc., Hollywood, Calif., 1964—70; v.p., sec. and gen. counsel Amcord, Inc., Newport Beach, Calif., 1970—72; v.p., sec., gen. counsel Schick Inc., LA, 1972—75; counsel, asst. sec. C.F. Braun & Co., Alhambra, Calif., 1975—76; sr. v.p., sec., gen. counsel Automation Industries, Inc. (now PCC Tech. Industries Inc. a unit of Penn Ctrl. Corp.), Greenwich, Conn., 1976—86; v.p., gen. counsel G&H Tech., Inc. (a unit of Penn Ctrl. Corp.), Santa Monica, Calif., 1986—93; temp. judge Superior Ct. Calif. L.A. Jud. Dist. and Santa Monica Unified Cts., 1987—; settlement officer L.A. Superior Ct., 1991—; pvt. practice Palisades, Calif., 1993—. Panelist Am. Arbitration Assn., 1991—; jud. arbitrator and mediator Alternative Dispute Resolution Programs LA Superior Ct., 1993—, Calif. Ct. Appeals 2d Appellate Dist., 1999—; alternative dispute resolution com. LA Superior Ct., 2001—. Contbr. articles to profl. jours. Served to 1st lt. AUS, 1942-50. Master L.A. West Am. Inns Court, mem. ABA, Nat. Assn. Securities Dealers (bd. arbitrators 1996, bd. mediators 1997), State Bar Calif. (co-chmn. corp. law dept. com. 1978-79, lectr. continuing legal edn. program, mandatory fee arbitrator 2001—), L.A. County Bar Assn. (chmn. corp. law dept. com. 1966-67, dispute resolution svcs. atty.-client fee dispute arbitrator and mediator 1993—), Century City Bar Assn. (chmn. corp. law dept. com. 1979-80), Conn. Bar Assn., Santa Monica Bar Assn. (trustee 1999-2003, chmn. alt. dispute resolution sect. 2000-2007, atty.-client fee dispute arbitrator and mediator, chmn. alt. dispute resolution sect. 2000-), N.Y. State Bar Assn., Am. Soc. Corp. Secs. (L.A. regional group pres. 1973-74), L.A. Intellectual Property Law Assn., Irish-Am. Bar Assn. Calif., Am. Ednl. League (trustee 1988—, sec. 1998-2007), Am. Legion (life), West Point Alumni Assn., Army Athletic Assn., Friendly Sons St. Patrick, Jonathan Club (dir. 1996-99, 2d v.p. 1997-98, Trumbull award 2005), Phi Alpha Delta Law Fraternity. Roman Catholic. Home and Office: 439 Via De La Paz Pacific Palisades CA 90272-4633 Personal E-mail: flatterytl@verizon.net.

FLAUCHER-FALCK, VELMA RUTH, retired special education educator; b. Hazleton, Iowa, Feb. 10, 1935; d. Amos Burdette and Florence Ella (Short) Flaucher; m. Kenneth Elgin Bienfang, Nov. 26, 1958 (div. Oct. 1975); children: Kende Sue Wynn, Victor Nolan Bienfang, Rodney Dean Bienfang; m. James Leo Falck, July 30, 1994. BA, U. No. Iowa, 1973, MA, 1977. Tchr. kindergarten Orange Ctr. Elem. Sch., Waterloo, Iowa, 1954—59; tchr. Van Eaton Elem. Sch., Waterloo, 1962; tchr. Headstart Exceptional Persons, Waterloo, 1967—68; tchr. kindergarten Hudson Sch. Dist., Hudson, Iowa, 1969—71; dir. activities Friendship Village, Waterloo, 1973—74; tchr. resource AEA7 Spl. Edn., Cedar Falls, Iowa, 1975—94; ret., 1994. Author: Whatever Became of LuAnn?, 2002, Where Did Sally Go?, 2004, Have You Seen Hannah?, 2004, Christina's House, 2004; contbr. poems to Internat. Libr. Poetry. Mem.: Iowa Ret. Sch. Pers., Tues. Tourists Book Club of Oelwein. Avocations: writing, reading, music, painting. Home: 1111 1st St NE Oelwein IA 50662

FLAUM, JOEL MARTIN, federal judge; b. Hudson, NY, Nov. 26, 1936; s. Louis and Sally (Berger) Flaum; m. Delilah Brummet, June 4, 1989. BA, Union Coll., Schenectady, 1958; JD, Northwestern U., 1963, LLM, 1964; LLD, John Marshall Law Sch., 2002. Bar: Ill. 1963. Asst. state's atty. Cook County, Ill., 1965—69, 1st asst. atty. gen. Ill. Ill., 1969—72; 1st asst. U.S. atty. (no. dist.) US Dept. Justice, Chgo., 1972—75; judge US Dist. Ct. (no. dist.) Ill., Chgo., 1975—83, US Ct. Appeals (7th cir.), 1983—, chief judge, 2000—06. Mem. Ill. Law Enforcement Commn., 1970—72; cons. US Dept. Justice, Law Enforcement Assistance Adminstrn., 1970—71; lectr. DePaul U. Coll. Law, 1987—88; adj. prof. Northwestern U. Sch. Law, 1993—2000. Mem.: Northwestern U. Law Rev., 1962—63; contbr. articles to legal jours. Mem. vis. com. U. Chgo. Law Sch., 1983—86; law bd. Northwestern U. Sch. Law, 1983—; mem. adv. com. USCG Acad., 1990—93. Lt. comdr. JACG USNR, 1981—92. Fellow Ford Found., 1963—64. Fellow: Chgo. Bar Found. (licentiate), Am. Bar Found. (licentiate); mem.: FBA, ABA, Am. Judicature Soc., Navy-Marine Corps Ret. Judges Advs. Assn., Maritime Law Assn., Chgo. Bar Assn., Chgo. Inn of Ct., 7th Cir. Bar Assn., Ill. Bar Assn., Naval Res. Assn., Lawyers Club Chgo. Jewish. Office: US Ct Appeals 7th Ct 219 S Dearborn St Chicago IL 60604-1702 Office Phone: 312-435-5626.*

FLAUM, KEITH AVERY, lawyer; b. Bklyn., Aug. 14, 1963; married. BA, UCLA, 1986; JD, U. Calif., Davis, 1989. Bar: Calif. 1989, Colo. 1993. Assoc. Cooley Godward LLP, Palo Alto, Calif., 1995—97, ptnr. Bus. Dept., 1997—. Author: Antitrust Provisions: A Dealmaker's Guide; contbr. articles to law jours.; spkr. in field. Named a Dealmaker of the Yr., Am. Lawyer Mag., 2006; named Top 20 Calif. Lawyers Under the Age of 40, Calif. Law Bus., 1999; named one of Calif. Lawyer/Attys. of Yr. (CLAY), Calif. Lawyer mag., 2005. Mem.: ABA (Com. on Negotiated Acquisitions), Colo. Bar Assn., State Bar Calif. Office: Cooley Godward LLP Five Palo Alto Sq 3000 El Camino Real Palo Alto CA 94306-2155 Office Phone: 650-843-5141. Office Fax: 650-849-7400. E-mail: flaumka@cooley.com.

FLAUM, MARSHALL ALLEN, television producer, writer, director; b. Bklyn. s. Mayer and Ethel (Lamkay) F.; m. Gita Faye Miller; children: Erica, Seth Baruch. BA, U. Iowa, 1948; DFA (hon.), So. Ill. U., Edwardsville, 1974. Story editor, writer, assoc. producer TV series for 20th Century, 1957-62; producer, writer, dir. TV spls. for Wolper Prodns., 1962-65; founder Flaum-Grinberg Prodns., 1966; v.p. Metromedia Producers Corp., 1968-76; pres. Marshall Flaum Prodns., Inc., 1976—. Prodr., writer, dir.: TV spls. Day of Infamy, 1963, Hollywood: The Great Stars, 1963, The Yanks Are Coming, 1964, Battle of Britain, 1964, Berlin: Kaiser to Kruschev, 1964, Let My People Go, 1965 (Ohio State award, George Foster Peabody award), Miss Goodall and the Wild Chimpanzees, 1966 (Edinburgh Festival award), Bogart, 1967 (Melbourne Festival award) Hollywood: The Selznick Years, 1969 (Silver Lion award Venice film Festival), The Time of Man, 1969 (Silver Hugo award Chgo. Internat. Festival), Yabba Dabba Doo! The Happy World of Hanna-Barbera, 1977, Bing Crosby: His Life and Legend, 1978 (Christopher award), Playboy's 25th Anniversary Celebration, 1979, A Bing Crosby Christmas.Like the Ones We Used to Know, 1979, Bob Hope's Texaco Star Theatre, Life's Most Embarrassing Moments, 1984, Portrait of Dorothy Stratten, 1985, A Yabba Dabba Doo Celebration, 50 Yrs. of Hanna Barbera, 1989, Arts and Entertainment's Ancient Mysteries, 1996, Celebrate the Century, 1998-99, The Desilu Story, 1999-2000; prodr., writer TV spls. Killy Le Champion, 1969; exec. prodr., co-writer: (TV series) Undersea World of Jacques Cousteau, 1970-76, Jane Goodall and The World of Animal Behavior, 1972-76, The Wild Dogs of Africa, 1973 (Emmy award best documentary, Chgo. Internat. Festival Gold Hugo award), Baboons of Gombe, 1974, Hyena, 1975, Lions of Serengeti, 1976; prodr. Am. Film Inst. Salute to Bette Davis, 1977; prodr., co-writer (with others): TV spls. Ripley's Believe It or Not, 1982, Bob Hope's Who Makes the World Laugh, 1983. Recipient Emmy award as best documentary for A Sound of Dolphins, 1972, The Unsinkable Sea Otter, 1972, George Foster Peabody award for TV spls. for Miss Goodall and The Wild Chimpanzees, 1966, Monte Carlo Internat. TV Festival Golden Nymph award for TV spl. The Yanks are Coming, 1964, Silver medal Atlanta Film Festival for Wild Dogs of Africa, 1973, Octopus, Octopus, 1972, Chgo. Internat. Film Festival Silver Hugo award for Tragedy of the Red Salmon, 1971, Oscar nomination sfor best documentary feature for The Yanks Are Coming, 1964, Let My People Go, 1966, Golden Globe nomination for The Fogotten Mermaids, 1972, Writers Guild of Am. nomination for The Time of Man, 1969, 16 Emmy award nominations. Mem. Writers Guild Am., Dirs. Guild Am., Acad. Motion Picture Arts and Scis., Acad. TV Arts and Scis. Address: 301 S Rodeo Dr Beverly Hills CA 90212-4206

FLAUM, RUSSELL M., engineering executive; BA in Psychology, Vanderbilt U., Nashville; MBA, Lake Forest Grad. Sch. Mgmt., Ill. Sales rep. Signode Corp. (acquired by Ill. Tool Works), 1975, dir. mktg., 1984-86, v.p. mktg., 1986-90, pres. US bus. Glenview, 1990-92; exec. v.p. Ill. Tool Works (ITW), Glenview, 1993—. Bd. dirs. Quanex Corp. Bd. dirs. Evanston Hosp. Corp., Ill., 1993—, Lake Forest Grad. Sch. Mgmt. Mem. Am. Mktg. Assn., Am. Mgmt. Assn. (mem. conf. bd.). Office: Ill Tool Works 3600 W Lake Ave Glenview IL 60026-1215 Office Phone: 847-724-7500. Office Fax: 847-657-4572.*

FLAUM, SANDER ALLEN, advertising and marketing executive; b. Apr. 5, 1937; s. Joseph and Rose (Deutsch) F.; children: Pamela, Jonathon; m. Mechele Plotkin, Apr. 25, 1990. BA, Ohio State U., 1958; MBA, Fairleigh Dickinson U., 1970. Mktg. dir. Lederle Labs. divsn. Am. Cyanamid Co., Wayne, NJ, 1964-84; exec. v.p. Klemtner Advt., NYC, 1984-88; chmn., CEO Robert A. Becker, Inc., NYC, 1988-98, 1998—. Vice chmn. Euro RSCG, Healthcare; chmn. Fordham Grad. Sch. Bus., NYU Stern Sch. Bus. Author: The Shortest Road to Success, Focusing Is for Tough Guys, The Leader's Edge, There's a Little Consumer in Every M.D., Great Is Better than Good, Hocus Focus, Darwin 2000; Survival of Fastest, Focus on the Future Direction: Outward. Trustee Hollins Coll. Comms. Rsch. Inst.; bd. mem. Atrix Labs., Neopharm Corp. With US Army, 1959—61. Mem. Am. Mktg. Assn. Avocations: running, golf. Office: Robertr A Becker Euro Rscg 75 9th Ave Frnt 2 New York NY 10011-7029

FLAUTZ, NANCY A., librarian; b. Akron, Ohio, Dec. 20, 1931; d. Roland and Ruth A. (Whitman) Page; m. John T. Flautz, June 26, 1951; children: Judy, Susan. BA, Cedar Crest Coll., 1967. Acquisitions libr. Cedar Crest and Muhlenberg Coll. Librs., Allentown, Pa., 1969-92. Mem. AAUW (booksale com. 1994-95, Gateway to Equity dir. 2006—, cmty. awards com., named outstanding woman 194). Home: 1413 Exeter Rd Allentown PA 18103-6314

FLAWS, JAMES B., technology executive; B in Engring., Tufts U.; Masters degree, Dartmouth Coll. Fin. analyst internat. divsn. Corning (N.Y.) Inc., 1973-83, dir. fin. and adminstrn. for consumer products divsn., 1983-89, v.p. planning and bus. devel., 1989-92, v.p., CFO Corning Consumer Products Co., 1992-97, asst. treas., 1993—97, v.p., contr., fin., treas., 1997, sr v.p., treas., CFO, 1997—99, exec. v.p., CFO, 1999—2002, vice chmn., CFO, 2002—. Bd. dirs. Dow Corning Corp., Corning Mus. Glass. Bd. mem. United Way, bd. chmn., treas. Office: Corning Inc 1 Riverfront Plz Corning NY 14831-0002

FLAX, HERMAN JACOB, physiatrist; b. Richmond, Va., Mar. 31, 1917; s. Bernard Nathan Flax and Jennie Hannah Jaffe; m. Josefina S. Guarch (dec.); children: Hjalmar L., Judith J. Flax Guarch, Jennifer J. Flax Guarch; m. Melanie Hermina Grishman, Sept. 1, 1986. BS, U. Richmond, 1936; MD, Med. Coll. Va., 1940; M.Med.Sci., U. Pa., 1952; prof. degree (hon.), Universidad Catolica, Santiago, 1985. Diplomate Am. Bd. Phys. Medicine and Rehab. Dir. pub. charities Municipia de Manati, PR, 1941—44; asst. dir. rehab. State Ins. Fund, San Juan, 1945—50; dir. dept. phys. medicine and rehab. Dept. Vets. Adminstrn. Hosp., San Juan, 1951—90; from assoc. prof. to prof. phys. medicine and rehab. U. PR, Rio Piedras, 1952—90; staff physiatrist Dept. Vets. Affairs Med. Ctr., Washington, 1990—94, cons. phys. med. and rehab. dept., 1994—; clin. prof. phys. medicine and rehab. Med. Coll. Va., Richmond, 1999—2005. Author: Life to Years, 1995, (book of poetry) September Songs, 1984, Songs of My Sixties, 1987, Four Score and Five, 2002. Recipient Outstanding Alumnus award, Med. Coll. Va., 2002. Fellow: ACP, Am. Acad. Phys. Medicine and Rehab. (Disting. Clinician award 1991), Am. Congress of Rehab. Medicine (pres. 1971, Gold Key award 1981, Edward W. Lowan award 2000); mem.: Crippled Children and Adult Soc. P.R., Internat. Soc. Phys. and Rehab. Medicine (hon.), Internat. Rehab. Med. Assn. (pres. 1982—86, Lifetime Achievement award 1994). Jewish. Avocations: travel, reading, hiking. Home: 11401 Commonwealth Dr Apt 1 North Bethesda MD 20852 Personal E-mail: mgrish7715@aol.com.

FLAX, HERSCHEL, surgeon; b. Capetown, South Africa, Feb. 9, 1941; came to U.S., 1974; s. Alexander Elliah and Mary Freda (Pasvolsky) F.; m. Elana Yehudith Matzkin; children: Joshua, Daniel, Rachel, Alexander. MB ChB, U. Capetown, 1964; ChM, U. Capetown Med. Sch., 1974; MA, NYU, 1978. Diplomate Am. Bd. Surgery. Intern Groote Schuur Hosp., Cape Town, South Africa, 1965-66; surg. registrar U. Cambridge, London, Birmingham, Eng. and Cape Town, 1966-72; chief resident Albert Einstein Coll. of Medicine, Bronx, NY, 1974-75, attending surgeon, asst. clin. prof., 1975—, attending surgeon, 1975—, assoc. clin. prof. surgery, 1989-97, prof. clin. surgery, 1997—; attending surgeon, specializing in diseases of the breast Mt. Sinai Hosp., NYC, 1999—. Contbr. articles to profl. jours. Recipient Frank Forman prize, Moffat Meml. prize, Sir Abe Bailey Travel Bursar, Paul Martini European prize, Bronte-Stewart Rsch. prize. Fellow ACS, Royal Coll. Surgeons (Eng.); mem. Med. Soc. State N.Y., N.Y. Surg. Soc., N.Y. Met. Breast Cancer Soc. Avocations: piano, photography, politics, travel, skiing. Office: 9 E 63rd St New York NY 10021 Home Phone: 516-487-3185; Office Phone: 212-755-3833. E-mail: hflax@hotmail.com.

FLAX, MARTIN HOWARD, pathologist, retired educator; b. NYC, Jan. 19, 1928; s. Abraham and Sadie (Finkel) F.; m. Ann E. Brockway, June 26, 1955; children: Adam, Jonathan, Elizabeth. AB, Cornell U., 1946; AM, Columbia U., 1948, PhD, 1951; MD, U. Chgo., 1955; MS in Health Mgmt., MIT, 1979. Intern Mt. Sinai Hosp., NYC, 1955-56; fellow pathology U. Chgo., 1956-57; chief biophysics br. Armed Forces Inst. Pathology, Washington, 1957-59; clin. fellow Mass. Gen. Hosp., Boston, 1959-61, asst. pathologist, 1961-66; fellow pathology Harvard U. Med. Sch., 1959-61, instr. pathology, 1961-63, assoc. pathology, 1961-66, asst. prof., 1966-69; prof., chmn. pathology dept. Tufts U. Sch. Medicine, 1970-97; chmn. pathology dept. Tufts U. Sch. Vet. Medicine, 1985-96; pathologist-in-chief New Eng. Med. Ctr. Hosp., Boston, 1970-97; emeritus prof. pathology Tufts U., 1998—. Cons. pathology B study sect. NIH, 1970-74. Vol. Peabody Mus. Anthropology and Ethnology, Cambridge, Mass., 1998—2005, George Eastman House, Rochester, NY, 2001—05. Capt. M.C. USAF, 1957—59. Recipient Rsch. Career Devel. award NIH, 1966-69; Nat. Cancer Inst. fellow, 1959-61, Med. Found. fellow, 1963-65, Sloan fellow MIT, 1979. Mem.: Sigma Xi, Phi Beta Kappa. Home: 32 Gate House Rd Chestnut Hill MA 02467-1335 Personal E-mail: martinflax@earthlink.net.

FLAXMAN, FRED, broadcast producer, host; b. NYC, May 9, 1940; s. Philip and Helen F.; m. Annick Story, Sept. 10, 1963; children: Michel, Tana Flaxman Jencks. BA, Cert. in Journalism, U. Mich., 1962; Cert. in French Studies, Sorbonne U. Paris, 1962; MA, Stanford U., 1964. Founding mgr. WETA-FM (90.9), Washington, 1970-74; program dir. WETA-TV Channel 26, Washington, 1974-77; v.p. programming, 1977-78; pres. Pub. Broadcasting Internat., Paris, 1978-79; asst. gen. mgr., dir. programming and prodn. KUAT-TV Channel 6, Tucson, 1980-83; v.p. nat. programming WTTW, Chgo., 1984-89; v.p., gen. mgr. So. Oreg. Pub. TV, Medford, Oreg., 1990-91; pres., exec. prodr. Teleflax Prodns., Medford, 1991-98; v.p. devel. WXEL-TV-FM, W. Palm Beach, Fla., 2000—06. Prodr., writer, host nationally syndicated pub radio program Compact Discoveries. Author: Sixty Slices of Life.On Wry; editor: The Timeless Tales of Reginald Bretnor, 1997; contbr. articles to newspapers and mags. Recipient Emmy award NATAS, 1989, First pl. Nat. Soc. Newspaper Columnists, 1989, Put It in Writing award Placerville Creative Writing Conf., 1990. Avocations: classical music, writing, travel, reading. Home and Office: 36 Pickens Ln Weaverville NC 28787 Personal E-mail: fred@fredflaxman.com.

FLAXMAN, JON E., computer company executive; B in Fin., U. Ill. Urbana-Champaign; MBA, Washington U., St. Louis. Cost acct. Hewlett-Packard Co., Palo Alto, Calif., 1981, v.p., CFO Bus. Customer Orgn., 1999—2001, v.p., contr., 2001—02, sr. v.p., contr., 2002—07, exec. v.p., chief adminstrv. officer, 2007—, mem. exec. council leadership team, 2007. Office: Hewlett Packard Co 3000 Hanover St Palo Alto CA 94304-1185*

FLAY, BOBBY, chef, restaurateur; b. NYC, Oct. 9, 1964; s. Bill and Dorothy F.; m. Debra Ponzek, 1991 (div. 1993); m. Kate Connelly (div.); 1 child, Sophie; m. Stephanie March, 2005. Diploma, French Culinary Inst., 1984. Exec. chef Miracle Grill, NYC, 1984—91; chef, ptnr. Mesa Grill, NYC, 1991—; ptnr. Bolo, NYC, 1993—, Mesa Grill Las Vegas, Caesar's Palace, 2004—, Bar Americain, NYV. Celebrity judge Wickedly Perfect TV series, 2005; co-star Iron Chef Am., Food Network; chef's coun. Chefs for Humanity. Author: (cookbook) Bold American Food, 1994 (IACP award for design, 1995), From My Kitchen to Your Table, 1998, Boy Meets Grill, 1999, Bobby Flay Cooks American, 2001, Boy Gets Grill, 2004, Bobby Flay's Grilling for Life: 75 Healthier Ideas for Big Flavor from the Fire, 2005; host (TV series) Grillin' & Chillin', The Main Ingredient, Hot Off the Grill, Food Nation, BBQ with Bobby Flay, Throwdown, 2007—. Named Rising Star Chef of Yr., James Beard Found., 1993; recipient Outstanding Graduate award, French Culinary Inst., 1993. Office: Mesa Grill 60 W 23rd St Apt 630 New York NY 10010-5288*

FLECHTNER, HARRY MARSHAL, law educator; b. Fostoria, Ohio, Apr. 8, 1951; s. August Marshall and Dorothy Mary (Reardon) F.; m. Joan Patricia Kammer, Aug. 5, 1978; children: Emily Lora, Andrew Robert. AB, Harvard U., 1973, AM, 1975, JD, 1981. Bar: D.C. 1981. Assoc. Wilmer Cutler and Pickering, Washington, 1981-84; asst. prof. law U. Pitts., 1984-88, assoc. prof. law, 1988-94, prof. law, 1994—. Faculty adviser Journal Law and Commerce Sch. Law U. Pitts., 1986—; nat. corr. for U.S., UN Commn. on Internat. Trade Law. Contbr. articles to profl. jours. Mem. ABA, Assn. Am. Law Schs., Am. Bankruptcy Inst. Office: U Pitts Sch of Law Pittsburgh PA 15260 Business E-Mail: flechtner@law.pitt.edu.

FLECK, BELA, country musician; Albums Deviation, 1985, Bela Fleck and The Flecktones, 1989, Drive, Places, Flight of the Cosmic Hippo, 1991, UFO Tofu, 1992, Three Flew Over the Cuckoo's Nest, 1993, Tabula Rosa, 1994, Tales from the Acoustic Planet, 1995, Live Art, 1996, Left of Cool, 1998, Outbound, 2000 (Grammy award for Best Contemporary Instrumental Jazz Performance), Perpetual Motion, 2001, Live at the Quick, 2002, Little Worlds, 2003, Little World, 2004, Ten From Little Worlds, 2003, Music for Two, 2004, The Hidden Land, 2006 (Grammy award for Best Contemporary Jazz Album, 2007), songs The Sinister Minister, 1996 (Grammy award for Best Pop Instrumental Performance), Almost 12, 1998 (Grammy award for Best Instrumental Composition), Leaving Cottondale, 2000 (Grammy award for Best Country Instrumental Performance), Doctor Gradus as Parnassum, 2001 (Grammy award for Best Instrumental Arrangement). Office Phone: 310-278-5657. E-mail: artistsinc@aol.com.

FLECK, RAYMOND ANTHONY, JR., retired academic administrator; b. Bklyn., Mar. 9, 1927; s. Raymond Anthony and Dorothy (Canavan) F.; m. Dorothy Marie Rossow, Aug. 22, 1970; children: Andrew Jerome, Casey Thomas. Student, Manhattan Coll., 1946-48; BS, U. Notre Dame, 1951, PhD, 1954; student Ins. Coll. and Univ. Adminstrs., Harvard U., 1959. Brother of Holy Cross, 1949-70. Prof. chemistry St. Edward's U., 1954-69, pres., 1957-69; assoc. research chemist dept. environ. toxicology U. Calif. at Davis, 1969-72; pres. Marygrove Coll., Detroit, 1972-79; acting dir. Food Protection and Toxicology Ctr., U. Calif., Davis, 1979-83; dir. research Calif. State Poly. U., Pomona, 1983-95. Cons. EPA, La. Bd. Regents, U. Wis., Eau Claire, NSF; dir. Monterey Basin Pilot Monitoring Project, 1971-72; pres. Our Lady of the Assumption Conf., St. Vincent de Paul Soc., Claremont, Calif., 1999-05. Vice pres., bd. dirs. Harmony Village Home Corp. N.W., Detroit, 1977-79. Served with USN, 1945-46. NSF fellow, 1952, 1969; recipient U. Notre Dame Centennial of Sci. medal, 1965; bldg. at St. Edward's U. named Fleck Hall. Home: 4273 Guava St La Verne CA 91750-3010 E-mail: raymonda2@aol.com.

FLEDER, GARY, film director, producer; b. Norfolk, Va., Dec. 19, 1965; Attended, Boston U. Dir.: (films) Things to Do in Denver When You're Dead, 1995 (winner critics award and spl. jury prize Cognac Festival du Film Policier), Kiss the Girls, 1997, Don't Say a Word, 2001; (TV series) Tales from the Crypt, 1989, Homicide: Life on the Street, 1993, L.A. Doctors, 1998, Falcone, 2000, The Shield, 2002, The Evidence, 2006; dir.: (TV films) The Companion, 1994, From Earth to the Moon, 1998; dir., prodr. Air Time, 1992, Impostor, 2002, Runaway Jury, 2003; actor, dir.: Just the Facts, 2004, Love Hollywood Style, 2004; dir., exec. prodr.: (TV series) October Road, 2007. Office: care David Wirtschafter William Morris Agy 151 El Camino Dr Beverly Hills CA 90212-3300*

FLEDER, ROBERT CHARLES, lawyer; b. New London, Conn., Aug. 31, 1948; s. Samuel and Pearl (Perelman) F.; m. Laura Louise Waltuch, Dec. 19, 1971; children: Daniel, Anna, Michael. BA, Columbia U., 1969, MA, 1971, LLB, 1973. Bar: N.J. 1974, N.Y. 1977, D.C. 1991. Law clk. to presiding justice N.J. Supreme Ct., Trenton, 1973-74; assoc. Stryker, Tams & Dill, Newark, 1974-75, Kramer, Levin, Nessen, et al, NYC, 1976-80, ptnr., 1981-86, Paul, Weiss, Rifkind, Wharton & Garrison., NYC, 1986—. Contbr. articles to profl. jours. Mem. ABA, N.Y. State Bar Assn. Office: Paul Weiss Rifkind Wharton & Garrison 1285 Ave Of The Americas New York NY 10019-6028

FLEEGER, DAVID CLARK, colon and rectal surgeon; b. Neubrucke, Germany, July 11, 1959; s. James Elliott and Madge Ellen (Iseminger) F.; m. Jamie Greenstreet, Aug. 16, 1984; 1 child, Lauren Ann. BS, Baylor U., 1981; MD, Tex. A&M U., 1985. Diplomate Am. Bd. Surgery, Am. Bd. Colon and Rectal Surgeons. Resident in gen. surgery Mayo Clinic, Rochester, Minn., 1985-90; fellow in colon and rectal surgery La. State U., Shreveport, 1990-91; ptnr. Austin Colon and Rectal Clinic, Tex., 1991—; chief surgery Columbia St. Davids. S. Hosp., 1996-97; chair Cancer Ctr. St. David's Med. Ctr., 1997—, co-chair Pain Mgmt. Ctr., 2000—05, chair dept. surgery, 2004—05; exec. bd. Travis County Med. Soc., 2004—. Pres. Travis County Med. Soc., 2007—; sec., treas., med. exec. St. David's Med. Ctr., 2006—. Fellow ACS, Am. Soc. Colon and Rectal Surgeons (socio-econs. com. 2000-02), Tex. Soc. Colon and Rectal Surgeons (pres-elect 1994, pres. 1994-95); mem. AMA (alt. mem. ho. of dels.), Am. Soc. Gastrointestinal Endoscopy Surgeons, Soc. Am. Gastrointestinal Endoscopy, Tex. Med. Assn. (chmn. young physician sect., mem. governing coun. 1992-99, chmn. com. on physician distbn. 1999-02, chair coun. practice mgmt. svcs. 2006-). Avocations: fishing, hunting, photography, kayaking. Office: 4208 Medical Pkwy Austin TX 78756-3310 Office Phone: 512-452-9551.

FLEER, KEITH GEORGE, lawyer, film company executive; b. Feb. 28, 1943; s. Samuel Robert and Sophia M. (Scherer) Fleer. BA in Govt., Am. U., 1964, JD, 1967. Bar: N.Y. 1968, D.C. 1968, Calif. 1976. Asst. dir. athletics Fordham U., 1967—68; assoc. Gettinger, Gettinger & Manheimer, NYC, 1968—72, Kaye, Scholer, Fierman, Hays & Handler, NYC, 1972—75; sr. counsel Avco-Embassy Pictures, Hollywood, Calif., 1976; assoc. Schiff, Hirsch & Schreiber, Beverly Hills, Calif., 1977; sr. v.p. bus. and legal affairs Melvin Simon Prodns., Inc., Beverly Hills, 1978—81; exec. v.p. Simon, Reeves, Landsburg Prodns., Beverly Hills, 1982—84; v.p. bus. affairs Warner Bros., Beverly Hills, 1984—88; ptnr. Denton Hall Burgin and Warrens, Beverly Hills, 1987—88, Sinclair Tenenbaum & Emanuel & Fleer, Beverly Hills, 1989—98, Loeb & Loeb, Century City, Calif., 1998—. Guest lectr. U. West LA Law Sch., 1979—80; legis. counsel N.Y. State Assemblyman, 1969—70; adj. prof. Law Ctr. U. So. Calif., 1995. Bus. editor: Am. U. Law Rev., 1966—67. Bd. trustees Am. U., 1992—97. Recipient Bruce Hughes award, Am. U., 1964, Alumni award, Am. U. Law Sch., 1967, Stafford H. Cassell award, 1979. Mem.: ABA, Acad. Motion Picture Arts and Scis., LA Copyright Soc. (trustee 1983—90, pres. 1988—89), Beverly Hills (Calif.) Bar Assn. Office: 10100 Santa Monica Blvd Los Angeles CA 90010

FLEETWOOD, CLIFFORD GENE ("THE FATHER OF PHILOSOPHICAL ART"), lawyer, publishing and recording industry executive, author; b. Tulsa, Mar. 25, 1961; s. Henry R. and Bernice (Rose) Fleetwood. PhD in Philosophy, So. Calif. Coll., Chula Vista, 1996; JSD in Internat. Law, Northwestern Internat. U., Gibraltar, Eng., 2007, JD, 2007. Chmn., CEO Clifford G. Fleetwood Co., Nashville, 1992—; bur. chief and pub. Rio Grande Pub. S.W. Inc., Santa Fe, pres., 2001—; assoc. prof. Am. Soc. Law, Medicine, Ethics, 2005; exec. pub. Nat. News Network, 2007; JSD rschr., 2004—07. Controlling shareholder Emerson C. Winchester and Co., 1995, Sir Lloyd of London Films Co., 1999—, Rio Grande Publishing Southwest, 2000—, Coupe DeVille Broadcasting Co., 2001—, Fleetwood Master Art Works Co., 2005—, Bluegrass & Cadillacs Record and Pub. Corp., 2007—, Chama Land & Cattle Co., 2007—, Nat. News Network, 2007—; mem. physician's adv. bd. Nat. Rep. Congl. Com., Washington, 2003—, mem. bus. adv. coun., 2003—. Author: The Presidential Collection President George W. Bush, Jr. and Family (placed in Smithsonian Mus., 2004), The Vatican Prayers and Passages Pope John Paul II, 2003 (letter of acceptance from Pope John Paul II, 2003), Royal Family Collection Queen Elizabeth and The Royal Family, 2007—, The Tri-Angular Equation, 2005; composer: 207 catalogued top 40 country music hit songs; record prodr.: The Ballad of Jacob Wright, 1990, Hank Sr. Died With the Blues, 1990, Highways, Bluegrass & Cadillacs, 1990, From Texas to Dixie, 1990, The Indian and the Cowboy, 1990, Big Timber Cowboy, 1992, Dancin' Across Texas, 1993, Southern Style, 1993, Calling All Hearts, 1994, The Blues Cadillac, 2000, Watermelon Mountain, 2001, Your Quarter Bar and Grille, 2003, 58 Freight Shaker, 2005. Mem. Am. Legion, Smithsonian Mus. and Inst. With US Army and USCG, 1981—87. Named Businessman of Yr., Nat. Rep. Congl. Com., 2003, Rep. of Yr., 2003; named to Colo. Country Music Hall of Fame, 1999; recipient Congl. Order of Merit (2), U.S. Congress and Pres. George W. Bush, Jr.; law fellowship, Coll. Law Eng. and Whales, 2007. Mem.: BMI, ASCAP, ABA (assoc.), Fgn. Policy Rsch. Inst., Am. Lawyer Assn., Nat. Republican Congl. Com., Fgn. Policy Assn., Tex. Bar Assn., Nat. Med. Assn., Broward County Bar Assn., UPI, Pub. Rels. News Wire, AP Mng. Editors, Am. Soc. Law Medicine, and Ethics, Rep. Nat. Lawyers Assn., Nat. Lawyer's Assn., Internat. Law Assn., Internat. Bar Assn., Bookings Inst., Assn. Acad. Country Music. Republican. Roman Catholic. Avocations: walking, chess, writing, shipwatching, music. Office: 2629 N State Rd 7 Ste 13 Fort Lauderdale FL 33313 Office Phone: 954-703-1325. Office Fax: 954-618-0832. Business E-Mail: drcliffordgfleetwoodphd@lawyer.com.

FLEETWOOD, MARY ANNIS, education association executive; b. Winfield, Ala., July 31, 1931; d. George A. and Martha Ann (Perry) Sullivan; m. Lewis N. Fleetwood, Aug. 19, 1950; children: Juanita, Dexter Lewis, Melanie Louise. Student, HCC Community Coll., 1973-80. Gen. office staff Able Rose Mercentile Co., Birmingham, Ala., 1949-51; with auditing dept. Bank for Savs. & Trusts, Birmingham, Ala., 1951; account receivables clk. I.W. Phillips, Tampa, Fla., 1972-77; account clk. Sch. Bd. Hill County, Tampa, Fla., 1980, office mgr., 1981-90. V.p. PTA, 1961-62; pres. Woman's Missionary Union, Birmingham, 1963-64. Mem. DAR, Nat. Inst. Govt. Purchasing (cert. profl. buyer). Baptist. Avocations: photography, genealogy, travel.

FLEGLE, JIM L., lawyer; b. Paducah, Ky., Dec. 3, 1951; s. J.L. and Alice M. (Goodman) F.; m. Ophelia Flegle Camina; children: Lauren Tyler, Brittanie Len, James Brendan, Alexandra Carlisle, James Armand. BA, U. Ky., 1974; JD, U. Va., 1977. Bar: Tex. 1977, US Dist. Ct. (so. dist.) Tex. 1977, US Dist. Ct. (no. dist.) Tex. 1984, US Dist. Ct. (we. dist.) Tex. 1988, US Dist. Ct. (ea. dist.) Tex. 1989, US Dist. Ct. Colo. 2002, US Ct. Appeals (5th and 11th cirs.) 1981, US Ct. Appeals (9th cir.) 1991, US Ct. Appeals (7th cir.) 2004, US Ct. Appeals (fed. cir.) 1994, US Supreme Ct. 1994. Assoc. Bracewell & Patterson, Houston, 1977-83, ptnr., 1983-89, Dallas, 1989—2002, head Dallas office, 1992-98, adv. com., 1996-98; ptnr. Loewinsohn Flegle, LLP, Dallas, 2002—07, Loewinsohn Flegle Deary, LLP, 2007—. Mem. Coll. of the State Bar of Tex., 2003-05, criminal justice act vol. atty. panel US Dist. Ct. (no. dist.) Tex.; mem. dean's counsel, U. Va. Law Sch., 1997-; fellow U. Ky., 2006-. Vol. Houston Pro Bono Program; active Tex. Lawyers and Accts. for Arts, Houston, 1982-85, St. Paul's Chamber Music Soc.; mem. corp. campaign com. Dallas Mus. Art, 1994-95, Dallas Hist. Soc., 1991-92. Named Tex. Super Lawyer, Tex. Monthly Mag., 2004, 2005, 2006, 2007; named one of Best Lawyers in Am., Woodward/White, Inc., 2007. Mem. ABA, Tex. Bar Assn. (grievance com. 1996-99, advt. rev. com. 2003-06), Houston Bar Assn., Dallas Bar Assn., Houston Bar Found. (life fellow), Tex. Bar Found., Dallas Bar Found., Am. Bd. Trial Advocates (mem. exec. com., chair membership com. 2004-06, rep. nat. bd. 2006—, treas. 2007), Higginbotham Inn of Ct. (barrister), Raven Soc., Phi Beta Kappa, Omicron Delta Kappa, Sigma Nu. Methodist. Office: 12377 Merit Dr No 900 Dallas TX 75251 Office Phone: 214-572-1701. Office Fax: 214-572-1717. Business E-Mail: jimf@texasverdict.com.

FLEISCHAKER, GORDON HENRY, JR., pediatrician; b. Louisville, July 1, 1928; s. Gordon H. and Agnes Rose (Shatzen) F.; m. Barbara Lorraine Draeger, Aug. 15, 1954 (dec. 1998); children: Rachel, Judith, James. BA in Zoology, U. Louisville, 1949, MD, 1953. Diplomate Am. Bd. Pediatrics, 1960. Intern Univ. Hosp., Madison, Wis., 1953-54; resident in pediat. The Children's Hosps., Denver, 1956-58; fellow in pediatric rheumatology State U. Iowa, Iowa City, 1958-60; practice medicine specializing in pediat. Denver, 1960—. Assoc. clin. prof. pediat. U. Colo. Sch. Medicine, Denver, 1960—; mem. active med. staff The Children's Hosp., Denver. Served to capt. MC, USAF, 1953-56. Fellow Am. Acad. Pediat.; mem. AMA, AAAS, Colo. Med. Soc., Clear Creek Valley Med. Soc. (pres. 2002-03). Office: G H Fleischaker MD 4485 Wadsworth Blvd Wheat Ridge CO 80033-3318 Office Phone: 303-421-0194. Personal E-mail: PeeDaTrx@aol.com.

FLEISCHAKER, MARC L., lawyer; b. Cin., Feb. 22, 1945; s. Leopold and Betty Jane (Spritz) F.; m. Phyllis S. Schmidt, June 16, 1969; children: Deborah, Julia. BS in Econs., Wharton Sch. U. Pa., 1967; JD, George Washington U., 1971. Bar: D.C. 1971, U.S. Dist. Ct. D.C. 1971, U.S. Supreme Ct. 1974, U.S. Ct. Mil. Appeals, U.S. Ct. Appeals D.C., U.S. Ct. Appeals (3d cir.) 1986, U.S. Ct. Appeals (4th, 5th and 11th cirs.). From assoc. to chmn. Arent Fox PLLC, Washington, 1971—, head environ. practice, 1978—2000, interim mng. ptnr., 1993, mng. ptnr., 2002, exec. com., 1983—, vice chmn., 1986—96, chmn., 1997—, non-profit initiative chair, 2004—. Exec. com. lawyers com. civil rights and urban affairs, Washington, 1989—, co-chmn., 1990-91, 99—, chair fin. com. 1992-93; bd. dirs. Coun. for Ct. Excellence, 2002—; mentor U. Md. Sch. Pub. Affairs, 2002—. Contbr. articles to profl. jours. Mem. Fed. City Coun., 2000—; bd. dirs. The Appleseed Found., 2004, co-chair, 2005—. With USNG, 1969-75. Recipient Triangle award, Motor and Equipment Mfrs. Assn., 1976, Whitney North Seymour award, Nat. Lawyers' Com. for Civil Rights Under Law, 2003, Kintner award, Nat. Assn. Coll. Stores, 2006, Wiley A. Branton award, Washington Lawyers Com. Civil Rights and Urban Affairs, 2006. Mem.: ABA, Am. Soc. Assn. Execs. (chmn. tech. com. legal sect. 1995—96, bd. dirs. tchg., learning and tech. group), Fed. Bar Assn., Econ. Club Washington. Avocations: politics, competitive running, golf, tennis. Home: 6308 Broad Branch Rd Bethesda MD 20815-3342 Office: Arent Fox 1050 Connecticut Ave NW Washington DC 20036-5339 E-mail: fleischaker.marc@arentfox.com.

FLEISCHER, ALAN BERNARD, JR., dermatologist, educator; b. St. Louis, June 6, 1961; s. Alan Bernard and Eileen Barbara (Meyer) F.; m. Anne Bridget Fitzsimmons, Aug. 12, 1989; children: Gerrit James, Sarah Elizabeth, Rebecca Anne. AB, U. Mo., 1982, MD, 1987. Diplomate Am. Bd. Dermatology, Nat. Bd. Med. Examiners. Internal medicine intern U. N.C., Chapel Hill, 1988, resident in dermatology, 1988-91; asst. prof. dermatology Bowman Gray Sch. Medicine, Winston-Salem, NC, 1991-96, assoc. prof. dermatology, 1996—2003; prof., chair dermatology Wake Forest U. Sch. Medicine, Winston-Salem, 2003—. Writer or co-editor 6 books; contbr. numerous articles to profl. jours. Med. Found. Teaching scholar, 1993. Mem. Am. Acad. Dermatology, European Acad. Dermatology, Phi Beta Kappa, Sigma Xi, Alpha Omega Alpha. Office: Wake Forest U Sch Medicine Dept Dermatology Medical Center Blvd Winston Salem NC 27157-0001

FLEISCHER, ARI (LAWRENCE ARI FLEISCHER), former White House press secretary; b. Pound Ridge, NY, Oct. 13, 1960; m. Becki Davis; 2 children. Grad., Middlebury Coll., 1982. Press sec. for Jon Fossil; press sec. for Congressman Norman Lent; field dir. Nat. Rep. Congl. Com., 1985—88; press sec. for Congressmna Joseph DioGuardi, 1988; press sec. for Sen. Pete Domenici, 1989—94; dep. comm. dir. for George H.W. Bush re-election campaign, 1992; spokesman House Ways & Means Com. US Congress, 1994—99; press sec. The White House, Washington, 2001—03; pres. Ari Fleischer Comm., Inc., 2003—. Bd. dirs. Rep. Jewish Coalition. Author: Taking Heat: The President, the Press, and My Years in the White House, 2005. Mem.: Kappa Delta Rho.*

FLEISCHER, ARTHUR, JR., lawyer; b. Hartford, Conn., Jan. 27, 1933; s. Arthur and Clare Lillian (Katzenstein) F.; m. Susan Abby Levin, July 6, 1958; children: Elizabeth, Katherine. BA, Yale U., 1953, LLB, 1958. Bar: NY 1959. Assoc. Strasser, Spiegelberg, Fried & Frank, NYC, 1958-61; legal asst. SEC, Washington, 1961-62, exec. asst. to chmn., 1962-64; assoc. Fried, Frank, Harris, Shriver & Jacobson, NYC, 1964-67, ptnr., 1967—, chmn., 1989-97, sr. ptnr., 1997—. Vis. lectr. law Columbia U., NYC, 1972-73; adviser to adv. com. Fed. Securities Code Project, Am. Law Inst., 1970-78; adviser to com. to consider new issue proposals Nat. Assn. Securities Dealers, 1973-75, mem. com. corp. financing, 1976-80; bd. dirs. Haleakala Inc. (The Kitchen), NY, 1987-2002; chmn. Ann. Inst. on Securities Regulation, Practising Law Inst., 1969-81; mem. indsl. issuers adv. com. SEC, 1972-73; mem. adv. com. corp. disclosure, 1976-77; bd. govs. Am. Stock Exch., 1977-83; legal adv. com, bd. dirs. NY Stock Exch., 1987-91 Co-author: Tender Offers, 1978, 6th edit., 2002, Board Games, 1988; co-editor: Annual Institute on Securities Regulation, 1970-81; contbr. articles to profl. jours. Mem. adv. coun. Ctr. for study of fin. instns. U. Pa.; former trustee Whitney Mus.; trustee Ind. Curators Internat., 1990-2002. Recipient Disting. Cmty. Svc. award Brandeis U., 1983, Judge Learned Hand Human Rels. award Am. Jewish Com., 1983, Harold P. Seligson award Practicing Law Inst., 1988, Judge Joseph W. Proskauer award UJA Fedn., 1994. Mem. ABA (mem. com. on fed. regulation of securities regulation 1969—), Assn. Bar City NY (mem. spl. com. on lawyers role in securities transactions 1973-77, chmn. com. securities regulation 1972-74), Century Country Club (NYC). Office: Fried Frank Harris 1 New York Plz Fl 27 New York NY 10004-1980 Office Phone: 212-859-8120. Business E-Mail: fleisar@friedfrank.com.

FLEISCHER, ARTHUR C., medical educator, radiologist; b. Miami, Fla., May 15, 1952; s. Eugene and Lucille Fleischer; m. Leona Fleischer, May 25, 1975; children: Braden, Jared, Amy. BS in Biology, Emory U., 1973; MD, Med. Coll. Ga., 1976. Diplomate Am. Bd. Radiology. Prof. radiology Vanderbilt U. Med. Ctr., Nashville, 1987—, prof. ob-gyn., 1988—. Author: Principles and Practice of Ultrasonography in Ob/Gyn, 2004, 20 books on diagnostic sonography. Recipient Disting. Alumnus award, Med. Coll. Ga., 2007. Fellow: Am. Inst. Ultrasound in Medicine (bd. govs. 1989—91, William Fry award 1999), Am. Coll. Radiology, Soc. Radiologists in Ultrasound (Larry Mack award 1999, Frank H. Boehm award for continuing med. edn. 2005, C.A.N.D.L.E. award for med. student tchg. 2005). Office: Vanderbilt Univ Med Ctr 1161 21st Ave S Nashville TN 37232

FLEISCHER, EVERLY BORAH, academic administrator, department chairman; b. Salt Lake City, June 5, 1936; s. Arthur and Clare (Katzenstein) F.; m. Harriet Eve Perlysky, June 14, 1959; children: Deborah, Adam Joseph. BS, Yale U., 1958, MS, 1959, PhD, 1961. Asst. prof., then assoc. prof. chemistry U. Chgo., 1961-69; prof. U. Calif., Irvine, 1970-80, dean phys. sci., 1975-80, exec. vice chancellor, prof. chemistry Riverside, 1988-94; prof. chemistry, dean Coll. Arts and Scis. U. Colo., Boulder, 1980-88; program exec. Am. Acad. Arts and Scis., Western Ctr., 1996; project dir. NSF Math. Sci. Partnership Focus! grant, 2003—05; interim chair Dept. Environ., Health, Sci. and Policy, 2006—. Author articles on metalloporphyrins, bioinorganic chemistry. NSF fellow, 1959-61; Alfred P. Sloan fellow, 1962-66; recipient Univ. Svc. award U. Calif., Irvine, 1980. Fellow AAAS; mem. Am. Chem. Soc., Sigma Xi, Alpha Chi Sigma. Office: Univ California Dept Chemistry Irvine CA 92697-0001 Home: 62 Shade Tree Ln Irvine CA 92603 Business E-Mail: ebfleisc@chem.ps.uci.edu.

FLEISCHER, GERALD ALBERT, industrial engineer, educator; b. St. Louis, Jan. 7, 1933; s. Louis Saul and Rita Bashkow F.; m. Ann Ivancic, Dec. 17, 1960 (div. 1992); children: Laural Andrea, Adam Steven; m. Carolyn M. Boyum, Apr. 13, 1993. BS, St. Louis U., 1954; MS, U. Calif., Berkeley, 1959; PhD, Stanford U., Calif., 1962. Ops. analyst Consolidated Freightways, Menlo Park, Calif., 1959-60; instr. Stanford U., Calif., 1961-63; asst. prof. U. Mich., Ann Arbor, 1963-64; assoc. prof. engring. U. So. Calif., Los Angeles, 1964-71, prof. engring., 1971-97, univ. marshal, 1981-87, pres. faculty senate, 1986-87, prof. emeritus, 1998—. Author: Capital Allocation Theory, 1969, Risk and Uncertainty, 1975, Contingency Table Analysis, 1981, Engineering Economy, 1984, Introduction to Engineering Economy, 1994; contbr. to Handbook of Industrial Engineering, 2001, Industrial Engineering Handbook, 2001, Manufacturing Engineering Handbook, 2004. Served to lt. (j.g.) USN, 1954-57 Ford Found. fellow, 1960-62, Fulbright sr. lectr. Ecuador, 1974; fellow Inst. Advancement of Engring., 1976 Fellow Inst. Indsl. Engrs. (region v.p. 1984-86); mem. Am. Soc. Engring. Edn., Inst. Mgmt. Scis. Home: 4449 Chateau Dr Loveland CO 80538-1591 Business E-Mail: fleische@usc.edu.

FLEISCHER, HUGH WILLIAM, lawyer; b. Riverside, Calif., Aug. 14, 1938; s. Frederick John and Helen Marie (Bendorf) F.; m. Lanie Lacey, May 31, 1960; children: Robin, Erin, Ian. BA, Washington U., St. Louis, 1961; JD, U. Denver, 1964. Bar: Colo. 1964, U.S. Supreme Ct. 1970, Alaska, 1971, Mo. 1972. Atty. U.S. Dept. Justice, Washington, 1964-70, Alaska Legal Svcs. Corp., Anchorage, 1971-72; atty., adviser St. Louis Legal Aid Soc., 1972; ptnr. Hedland, Fleischer, Friedman, Brennan & Cooke, Anchorage, 1972-96. Co-dir., McGovern for Pres. campaign, Anchorage, 1972; pres. Bartlett Dem. Club, Anchorage, 1987; bd. dirs. Alaska Pub. Interest Group, 1974—, Out North Theater, 1988-94; pres. Anchorage Friends of Libr., 1989-92; bd. dirs. Alaskans Against the Death Penalty, 1993—, pres., 2003—. Avocations: reading, mountain climbing. Home: 1401 W 11th Ave Anchorage AK 99501-4248 Office: 310 K St Ste 200 Anchorage AK 99501-2064 Office Phone: 907-264-6635.

FLEISCHER, MARIAN, surgeon; MD, U. Milan, Italy, 1972. Diplomate Am. Bd. Colo-rectal Surgery. Clin. instr. surgery SUNY, Bklyn., 1986—. Fellow: ACS. Office: 9707 4th Ave Brooklyn NY 11209-8129 Office Phone: 718-836-3603.

FLEISCHER, NORMAN SAMUEL, endocrinology administrator, medical educator; b. Springfield, Tenn., Jan. 24, 1936; s. Paul and Eva (Cohen) F.; m. Eva Lessy, Apr. 7, 1966; children: Deborah, Arlene. AB, Vanderbilt U., 1958, MD, 1961. Med. resident Albert Einstein Coll. of Medicine, Bronx, 1961-64; fellow in endocrinology Vanderbilt U., Nashville, 1964-66; dir. endocrinology Albert Einstein Coll. of Medicine, Bronx, 1976—, prof., 1978—; fellow in endocrinology Sch. of Medicine Vanderbilt U., Nashville, 1964-66; asst. prof. Coll. of Medicine Baylor U., Houston, 1966-71, assoc. prof. Sch. of Medicine, 1971-73; assoc. prof. Albert Einstein Coll. of Medicine, Bronx, 1973-77. Author chpts. in books; contbr. numerous articles to profl. jours. NIH grantee, 1966—. Fellow ACP; mem. Am. Fedn. Clin. Rsch., Am. Soc. Clin. Investigation, Am. Assn. Physicians, Am. Diabetes Assn., Endocrine Soc. Office: Yeshiva U Albert Einstein Coll Medicine 1300 Morris Park Ave Bronx NY 10461-1926

FLEISCHER, ROBERT LOUIS, geology professor; b. Columbus, Ohio, July 8, 1930; s. Leo H. and Rosalie (Kahn) F.; m. Barbara L. Simons, June 10, 1954; children: Cathy Ann, Elizabeth Lee. AB, Harvard U., 1952, AM, 1953, PhD, 1956. Asst. prof. metallurgy MIT, 1956—60; physicist GE Rsch. Lab., Schenectady, 1960—92; rsch. prof. earth and environ. scis. Rensselaer Poly. Inst., Troy, NY, 1992—97; rsch. prof. geology Union Coll., Schenectady, 1997—. Sr. rsch. fellow physics Calif. Inst. Tech., 1965-66; adj. prof. physics and astronomy Rensselaer Poly. Inst., 1967-68; adj. prof. geol. sci. SUNY, Albany, 1982-87; cons. U.S. Geol. Survey, 1967-70, GE R&D Ctr., 1992-93; vis. scientist Nat. Ctr. for Atmospheric Rsch., NOAA, 1973-74; adj. prof. applied physics and mech. engring. Yale U., 1984; vis. scientist Materials Rsch. Soc., 1995. Author: Nuclear Tracks in Solids, 1975, Tracks to Innovation, 1998; co-editor: Intermetallic Compounds: Principles and Practice, vols. 1 and 2, 1995, vol. 3, Progress, 2002, Crystal Structures of Intermetallic Compounds, Basic Mechanical Properties of Intermetallic Compounds, Magnetic, Electrical and Optical Properties, and Applications of Intermetallic Compounds, 2000, others; assoc. editor: 1st-4th Lunar Sci. Conf. Procs., 1970-73. Pres. Zoller Sch. PTA, 1968-69; mem. com. on candidates Schenectady Citizens Conv. for Sch. Bd., 1969-72, 82-83, chmn., 1969-70, 71-72, vice chmn. conv., 1977-78, chmn., 1978-79; mem. com. on priorities Schenectady Sch. Bd., 1974-75; bd. dirs. Schenectady Citizens' League, Freedom Forum, Inc; mem. Mayor's Com. on Transp. and Infrastructure, 2000. Recipient awards Indsl. Rsch., 1964, 65, 72, Spl. award Am. Nuc. Soc., 1964, Ernest O. Lawrence award AEC, 1971, Gen. Elec. Silver medallion Inventor's award, 1971, Gold Medallion Inventor's award, 1991, Golden Plate award Am. Acad. Achievement, 1972, Coolidge award Gen. Electric Rsch. and Devel. Ctr., 1972; NASA Exceptional Sci. Achievement award, 1973, spl. recognition, 1979; Disting. Career award Hudson-Mohawk chpt. AIME, 1991. Fellow: NAE, AAAS, Am. Soc. Metals, Health Physics Soc., Am. Geophys. Union, Am. Acad. Arts and Scis., Am. Phys. Soc.; mem.: Materials Rsch. Soc., Internat. Nuc. Track Soc. (hon.), Sigma Xi. Achievements include research in charged particle tracks in solids and their use in several fields, including cosmic ray and meteorite sci., geochronology, nuclear physics, radiobiology, environmental radon, personal radon dosimetry, Hiroshima neutron dosimetry, mineral exploration; defects in solids and their effects on mech. properties and superconducting properties, high temperature materials. Office: Union Coll Dept Geology Schenectady NY 12308 Office Phone: 518-388-6985. Business E-Mail: fleischr@union.edu.

FLEISCHER, ROLAND EDWARD, art history professor; b. Balt., Feb. 12, 1928; s. Edward Charles and Freda Anna (Denker) Fleischer; children: Edward Brandt, Frederick Roland. BA, Western Md. Coll., 1952; MA, Johns Hopkins U., 1954, PhD, 1964; DFA, Western Md. Coll., 1993. Instr. art history Johns Hopkins U., Balt., 1955—56; assoc. prof. U. Miami, Coral Gables, Fla., 1956—66; prof. art history George Washington U., 1966—74, Pa. State U., State College, 1974—96, prof. emeritus, 1996—. Cons. in field. Author (editor): The Age of Rembrandt, 1988; author: Ludolf de Jongh, 1989. Recipient Fulbright award, U.S. Govt., 1954—55; fellow, Pa. State U., 1989; scholar, 1990. Mem.: Found. Cornelis Hofstede de Groot, Am. Assn. Netherlandic Studies, Coll. Art Assn., Moose. Democrat. Lutheran. Avocations: theater, acting, singing, fishing, travel. Home: 30355 Falcon Ln Big Pine Key FL 33043 E-mail: rrolandf@aol.com.

FLEISCHER, WALTER HERSCH, lawyer; b. Washington, Feb. 2, 1940; s. Michael and Helen Anna (Isenberg) F.; m. Candace S. Kovacic, 1990; 1 child, Ilona Saari. BA, Yale U., 1961; LLB, Harvard U., 1964. Bar: DC 1965, US Supreme Ct. 1968, US Ct. Appeals (DC, 4th and 9th cirs.) 1965, US Ct. Appeals (6th and 7th cirs.) 1966, US Ct. Appeals (10th cir.) 1967, US Ct. Appeals (3d cir.) 1969, US Ct. Appeals (8th cir.) 1970, US Ct. Appeals (1st cir.) 1972, US Ct. Appeals (2d cir.) 1978, US Ct. Appeals (fed. cir.) 1982. Atty.civil div. U.S. Dept. Justice, Washington, 1964-71, asst. chief appellate sect., 1971-73; assoc. Cole & Groner, P.C., Washington, 1973-76, v.p., 1976-90; pvt. practice Washington, 1990—2002, Va., 2002—. Mediator Superior Ct. DC, 1987-00, US Ct. Appeals (DC cir.), 1992—; arbitrator Superior Ct. DC, 1990-00. Mem.: ABA. Home: 7318 Hooking Rd Mc Lean VA 22101-2718 Office: 1320 Old Chain Bridge Rd Ste 435 Mc Lean VA 22101 Office Phone: 703-821-0613. Personal E-mail: wfleish1060@aol.com.

FLEISCHMAN, AARON I., lawyer; b. Chgo., Jan. 8, 1939; BA with honors, Trinity Coll., Conn., 1960; LB, Harvard Law Sch., 1963. Bar: DC 1965. Sr. ptnr. Fleischman & Walsh LLP, 1976—, mng. ptnr.; dir. Citizen's Comm. Co. Dir. Citizen's Comm. Co., So. Union Co., 1990—2002. Named one of Top 200 Collectors, ARTnews Mag., 2004, 2005, 2006. Mem.: Fed. Comm. Bar Assn., DC Bar, Miami Art Mus. (trustee), Nat. Gallery Art, DC (trustee coun.), Whitney Mus. Am. Art (bd. mem.), Pi Gamma Mu, Phi Beta Kappa. Avocation: collector modern & contemporary art. Office: Fleischman & Walsh LLP Ste 600 1919 Pennsylvania Ave NW Washington DC 20006 Office Phone: 202-939-7940. Business E-Mail: afleischman@fw-law.com.

FLEISCHMAN, ALBERT SIDNEY (SID FLEISCHMAN), writer; b. Bklyn., Mar. 16, 1920; s. Reuben and Sadie (Solomon) F.; m. Beth Elaine Taylor, Jan. 25, 1942; children— Jane, Paul, Anne. BA, San Diego State Coll., 1949. Newspaper reporter San Diego Daily Jour., 1949-50; freelance screenwriter. Lectr. fiction writing UCLA. Author: (children's books) Mr. Mysterious & Company, 1962, By the Great Horn Spoon!, 1963, The Ghost in the Noonday Sun, 1965, Chancy and the Grand Rascal, 1966, McBroom and the Great Race, 1970, Longbeard the Wizard, 1970, Jingo Django, 1971, Kate's Secret Riddle Book, 1977, Me and the Man on the Moon-Eyed Horse, 1977, Jim Bridger's Alarm Clock and Other Tall Tales, 1978, Humbug Mountain, 1978, McBroom and the Beanstalk, 1978, The Hey Hey Man, 1979, McBroom and the Great Race, 1980, The Bloodhound Gang in the Case of the Cackling Ghost, 1981, The Bloodhound Gang in the Case of the Flying Clock, 1981, The Bloodhound Gang in the Case of the Princess Tomorrow, 1981, The Bloodhound Gang in the Case of the Secret Message, 1981, The Bloodhound Gang in the Case of the 264-Pound Burglar, 1982, McBroom's Zoo, 1982, McBroom's Ear, 1982, McBroom and the Big Wind, 1982, The Bloodhound Gang's Secret Code Book, 1983, McBroom's Almanac, 1984, The Whipping Boy, 1986 (John Newbery medal 1987), The Scarebird, 1988, The Midnight Horse, 1990, Jim Ugly, 1992, Here Comes McBroom, 1992, McBroom's Wonderful One-Acre Farm, 1992, The 13th Floor, 1995, The Abracadabra Kid, A Writer's Life, 1996, Mr. Mysterious & Company, 1997, Chancy and the Grand Rascal, 1997, The Ghost on Saturday Night, 1997, Bandit's Moon, 1998, McBroom's Ghost, 1998, McBroom Tells the Truth, 1998, McBroom the Rainmaker, 1999, McBroom Tells a Lie, 1999, A Carnival of Animals, 2000, Bo and Mzzz Mad, 2001, Disappearing Act, 2003, The Giant Rat of Sumatra, 2005, Escape! The Story of the Great Houdini, 2006, The White Elephant, 2006; (screenplays) Blood Alley, 1955, Goodbye, My Lady, 1956, Lafayette Escadrille, 1958, The Deadly Companions, 1973, Scalawag, 1973, Prince Brat and the Whipping Boy, 1995. Served with USNR, 1941-45. Recipient Spur award Western Writers Am., Commonwealth Club award, Lewis Carrol Shelf award, Mark Twain award, Calif. Young Reader award, John and Patricia Beatty award. Mem. Writers Guild Am., Authors Guild, Soc. Children's Book Writers and Illustrators. Democrat. Jewish. Office: care Greenwillow Books 1350 Avenue Of The Americas New York NY 10019-4702

FLEISCHMAN, BARBARA GREENBERG, public relations consultant; b. Detroit, Mar. 20, 1924; d. Samuel J. and Theresa (Keil) Greenberg; m. Lawrence A. Fleischman, Dec. 18, 1948; children: Rebecca, Arthur, Martha. BA, U. Mich., 1944. Tchr. Detroit Pub. Schs., 1944-45; psychoanalyst's sec., 1947-49; sec. Greenberg Ins. Agy., 1947-49; customer/pub. rels. cons. Kennedy Galleries, NYC, 1976—2005. Bd. dirs. Detroit Artists Market, 1958-66, Planned Parenthood, N.Y.C., 1990-96, Am. Craft Coun., 1980-83, Friends of Channel 13, 1968-80, pres., N.Y.C., 1975-79, chmn. auction, 1975, trustee, 1975-84; mem. women's com. Detroit Inst. Arts, 1957-66; pres. Friends of N.Y. Pub. Libr., 1979-84, trustee, 1980—, v.p., bd., 1987-2002; trustee The Acting Co., 1986-89, pres., 1988-89; mem. gov. bd. Off the Record Luncheons, Fgn. Policy Assn., 1978-85; assoc. prodr. Channel 13 Auction, 1978-80; trustee Mus. TV and Radio, 1988-92, Archives of Am. Art, 1997—, caryatids chmn., 1998-2003; vis. com. Am. Wing, Met. Mus., 1998—; commr. Art Commn. of the City of N.Y., 1995-98; hon. patron Brit. Mus., 1996—, Caryatids com., pres., 1995—2003, chmn.; v.p. Archives of Am. Art, pres.; pres. Archives of Am. Art, 1998—; mem. devel. trust Brit. Mus., 1999-2003; v.p. Assocs. of Art Commn., 1999—; chmn., vis. com. Met. Mus. Am. Painting and Sculpture, 2002—; adv. com. NY Skin Cell Found.; trustee J. Paul Getty Trust, 2002-06. Mem. Cosmopolitan Club. Office: 870 United Nations Plz New York NY 10017 E-mail: bgf324@aol.com.

FLEISCHMAN, BRIAN WILLIAM, mathematics educator; b. Lincoln, Nebr., Apr. 14, 1975; s. William Glenn and Barbara Jane Fleischman; m. Leah Ann Feeney, Jan. 20, 1979; children: Haley Helen, Braden William, Brody Andrew. BA, Midland Luth. Coll., Fremont, Nebr., 1998. Cert. tchr. Nebr. Dept. Edn., 1998. Tchr. math. grades 7-12 Cedar Bluffs Pub. Sch., Nebr., 1998—; constrn. layman (part time) Pebley Constrn., Fremont, Nebr., 1994—. Math dept. chairperson Cedar Bluffs Pub. Sch., 1998—, girls golf coach, 1998—, boys basketball coach, 1998—2005, jr. class sponsor/prom advisor, 2000—06, boys golf coach, 2001—. Mem.: Nebr. Edn. Assn., Assn. Supervision and Curriculum Devel., Nebr. Coun. Sch. Adminstr., Nat. Coun. Tchrs. of Math. (assoc.), Nebr. Coaches Assn.

(assoc.). Democrat. Methodist. Avocations: golf, woodworking, basketball, swimming. Home: 1780 Victoria Lane Fremont NE 68025 Office: Cedar Bluffs Public Sch 110 East Main St Cedar Bluffs NE 68015 Home Phone: 402-721-9201; Office Phone: 402-628-2080. Office Fax: 402-628-2108. Business E-Mail: bfleisch@esu2.org.

FLEISCHMAN, EDWARD HIRSH, lawyer, consultant; b. Cambridge, Mass., June 25, 1932; s. Louis Isaac and Jean (Grossman) F.; m. Joan Barbara Walden, Dec. 27, 1953 (dec. 1993), m. Judy Vernon, Sept. 27, 1998. BA, Harvard U.; LLB, Columbia U., 1959. Bar: N.Y. 1959, U.S. Supreme Ct. 1980. Assoc. Beekman & Bogue, NYC, 1959-67, ptnr., 1968-86; commr. SEC, Washington, 1986-92; ptnr. Rosenman & Colin, 1992-94; sr. counsel Linklaters, NYC, 1994—. Bd. dirs. Soundview Tech. Group, Inc. (previously Wit Capital Corp.), 1998—2003; bd. govs. Security Traders Assn., 1997—2000; chmn. exec. com. Corps., Secs. and AntiTrust Practice Group. Federalist Soc., 2004—. Served with U.S. Army, 1952-55. Mem.: ABA (chmn. bus. law subcom. rule 144 1970—72, subcom. broker-dealer matters 1973—78, subcom. model simplified indenture 1980—83, adminstrv. law com. on securities, commodities and exchs. 1981—84, bus. law com. on devels. in bus. financing 1987—91, com. on counsel responsibility 1995—99, internat. law com. on internat. securities transactions 1999—2002), Internat. Law Assn. (chmn. com. on internat. securities regulation 1998—), Internat. Bar Assn., Soc. Corp. Governance Profls., Am. Coll. Investment Counsel (pres. 1990—91), Am. Law Inst. Republican. Jewish. Office: Linklaters LLP 1345 6th Ave New York NY 10105-0302 Home: 897 Franklin Lake Rd Franklin Lakes NJ 07417-2115 Home Phone: 201-847-2004; Office Phone: 212-903-9011. Business E-Mail: edward.fleischman@linklaters.com, edward@fleischman.org.

FLEISCHMAN, FRANCINE D., secondary school educator; b. Bklyn., Jan. 28, 1951; d. Alvin and Lillian Rachel Moskowitz; m. Herman Israel Fleischman, Feb. 3, 1973; children: Meredith, Brandon, Gary. BS, West Conn. State U., 1973; MS, CUNY, 1975. Tchr. Bd. Edn., Bklyn., 1973—. Assoc. prof. Nassau C.C., Garden City, NY, 1994—; v.p. United Mutual Industries, Inc., Merrick, NY, 1987—. Home: 2970 Hewlett Ave Merrick NY 11566

FLEISCHMAN, HERMAN ISRAEL, lawyer; b. Bklyn., Aug. 30, 1950; s. Boris and Bella (Weisbrot) F.; m. Francine Moskowitz, Feb. 3, 1973; children: Meredith, Brandon, Gary. BA, Bklyn. Coll., 1972; JD, Bklyn. Sch. Law, 1976; MPA, NYU, 1974. Bar: NY 1977, US Dist. Ct. (ea., so., we. and no. dists.) NY 1977, US Ct. Appeals (DC cir.) 1979, US Tax Ct. 1982, US Supreme Ct. 1980. Asst. counsel Amalgamated Ins. Fund, NYC, 1976; spl. asst. atty. gen. State of N.Y., NYC, 1977-79; asst. counsel N.Y. State Dept. Mental Hygiene, Staten Island, N.Y., 1979; assoc. Ackerman, Salwen & Glass, NYC, 1979-80; sole practice NYC, 1980—. Mem. Thomas Jefferson Dem. Club, Bklyn., 1983-85; chmn. B'nai Brith Youth Orgn., 1980-82; bd. dirs. Big Apple Region, vice chmn., 1970-80, treas. bd. dir., 1976; bd. dirs. Nassau and Suffolk Counties, NY, 1990-2001; mem. bd. gov. B'nai Brith Dist. 1, 1979-80; alumni reunion coord., Bklyn BBYO, 2006. Recipient Citation, Town of Hempstead, 1986, Dist. Key award, B'nai B'rith Youth Org., 1979, Man of Yr. award, B'nai B'rith Youth Org., 1980; named Coach of Yr., North Merrick-North Bellmore Basketball League, 1998. Mem. ABA, NY State Bar Assn., Bklyn. Bar Assn., United Mut. Industries, Inc. (pres. 1983—). Office Phone: 516-867-3100. E-mail: HFleischma@aol.com.

FLEISCHMAN, JOSEPH JACOB, lawyer; b. Jersey City, Mar. 10, 1946; s. Benjamin Emanuel and Esther (Robfogel) F.; m. Gloria Damast, May 31, 1975; children: Michael, Richard. BA with highest honors, Rutgers U., 1968; JD, Columbia U., 1972. Bar: N.J. 1972, U.S. Dist. Ct. N.J. 1972, U.S. Ct. Appeals (3d cir.) 1983, U.S. Ct. Appeals (9th cir.) 1986, U.S. Ct. Appeals (2d cir.) 1994, U.S. Supreme Ct. 1983. Assoc. Hannoch Weisman, Roseland, NJ, 1972-77, ptnr., 1977-99, Norris, McLaughlin & Marcus, P.A., Somerville, NJ, 1999—. Contbr. articles to legal publs. Mem. ABA, N.J. Bar Assn., Essex County Bar Assn., Phi Beta Kappa. Avocations: reading, golf. Home: 209 Lyncrest Rd Englewood Cliffs NJ 07632-2020 Office: Norris McLaughlin & Marcus PO Box 1018 Somerville NJ 08876-1018 Office Phone: 908-252-4265. Personal E-mail: jjfleisch@aol.com. Business E-Mail: jjfleischman@nmmlaw.com.

FLEISCHMAN, KEITH M., lawyer; BA, U. Vt., 1980; JD, Calif. Western Sch. Law, 1984. Bar: NY, US Dist. Ct. (so. dist.) NY, US Dist. Ct. (ea. dist.) NY, US Dist. Ct. (ea. dist.) Wis., US Dist. Ct. Colo., US Ct. Appeals (1st cir.), US Ct. Appeals (2nd cir.), US Ct. Appeals (11th cir.), US Supreme Ct. Prosecutor Investigations and Major Offense Bureau, Bronx Dist. Atty.'s Office; trial lawyer, fraud sect. US Dept. Justice; asst. US Atty. US Atty.'s Office; litigator, trial lawyer numerous plantiff firms; trial lawyer, ptnr. Milberg Weiss LLP, NYC; ptnr. Grant and Eisnhofer, NYC. Trial practice instr. Atty. Gen. Advocacy Inst., US Dept. Justice; mem. Dallas and New Eng. Bank Fraud Task Force, Conn. Bank Fraud Working Group; co-chmn. Practicing Law Inst.'s Annual Conf. on Class Actions; lectr. in field. Named Super Lawyer, Super Lawyer Mag., 2006—07; named one of 500 Leading Plantiff Lawyers in Am., LawDragon; recipient awards, FBI Dir. and Atty. Gen., US Dept. Justice. Avocations: skiing, climbing. Office: Grant & Eisenhofer 485 Lexington Ave 29th Fl New York NY 10017 Office Phone: 646-722-8512. Business E-Mail: kfleischman@gelaw.com.

FLEISCHMAN, PAUL, children's author; BA, Univ. of N.Mex., 1977. Author: The Birthday Tree, 1979, The Half-a-Moon Inn, 1980 (Silver medal Commonwealth of Calif. 1980, Golden Kite honor book Soc. Children's Book Writers 1980), Graven Images: Three Stories, 1982 (Newbery honor book 1983), The Animal Hedge, 1983, Finzel the Farsighted, 1983, Path of the Pale Horse, 1983 (Golden Kite honor book Soc. Children's Book Writers 1983, Parents' Choice award Parents' Choice Found. 1983), Phoebe Danger, Detective, in the Case of the Two-Minute Cough, 1983, Coming-and-Going Men: Four Tales, 1985, I Am Phoenix: Poems for Two Voices, 1985, Rear-View Mirrors, 1986, Rondo in C, 1988, Joyful Noise: Poems for Two Voices, 1988 (John Newbery medal 1989), Saturnalia, 1990, Shadow Play, 1990, Time Train, 1991, The Borning Room, 1991, Townsend's Warbler, 1992, Copier Creations, 1993, Bull Run, 1993 (Scott O'Dell award), Dateline: Troy, 1996, A Fate Totally Worse than Death, 1997, Seedfolks, 1997, Whirligig, 1998, Weslandia, 1999 (Pen West Lit. award, Calif. Young Readers medal), Mind's Eye, 1999, Cannibal in the Mirror, 2000, Big Talk: Poems for Four Voices, 2000, Lost!: A Story in String, 2000, Seek, 2001, Sidewalk Circus, 2003, 04, Animal Hedge, 2003, Breakout, 2003 (Nat. Book award finalist), Zap, 2005. Office: PO Box 646 Aromas CA 95004

FLEISCHMAN, PAUL ROBERT, psychiatrist, writer; b. Newark, Aug. 4, 1945; s. Martin L. and Etta G. Fleischman; m. Susan K., June 15, 1974; 1 child, Forrest. BA, U. Chgo., 1967; MD, Albert Einstein Coll. Medicine, 1971. Diplomate Am. Bd. Psychiatry and Neurology. Seminar leader in psychiatry and religion Yale U., New Haven, 1981-87; pvt. practice psychiatry Amherst, Mass., 1975—. Keynote spkr. Highland Hosp., Asheville, NC, 1992, Albany Med. Coll., Coll. St. Rose, Albany Jewish Family Svcs., 1993, Values in Psychotherapy conf. Nashville Inst. Psychotherapy, 1995, Brussels Conf. Trauma, 2006; 31st Williamson lectr. in religion and medicine U. Kans., 1995; cons. in psychiatry, Amherst, 1975—; lectr., spkr. U. Mass., Amherst, Hampshire Coll., Smith Coll., Amherst Coll., 1989—98, Med. Group Rounds Albany Med. Coll., 1990, Beth Israel, Boston, 1994; cons. in field. Author: Therapeutic Action of Vipassana Meditation, 1986, The Experience of Impermanence, 1990, The Healing Spirit, 1990, Spiritual Aspects of Psychiatric Practice, 1993, Cultivating Inner Peace, 1997, 2d edit., 2004, Karma & Chaos, Collected and New Essays, 1999, Snowstorm in a Cabin in the Woods, 2001, Tapas, 2001, The Buddha Taught Nonviolence, Not Pacifism, 2002, Cultivating Inner Peace, rev. edit., 2004, You Can Never Speak Up Too Often, 2004; contbr. articles to profl. jours. Recipient Oskar Pfister award for important contbns. to spiritual and humanistic side of psychiatry Am. Psychiat. Assn., 1993. Mem. Phi Beta Kappa, Alpha Omega Alpha. Office: 1394 S East St Amherst MA 01002-3030

FLEISCHMANN, DENNIS C., lawyer; BA, Fordham U., 1971, JD, 1975. Mng. ptnr., mem. exec. com. Bryan Cave LLP, NYC. Office: Bryan Cave LLP 1290 Ave of the Americas New York NY 10104 Office Phone: 212-541-2000. E-mail: dcfleischmann@bryancave.com.

FLEISCHMANN, ERNEST MARTIN, performing arts executive, consultant; b. Frankfurt, Germany, Dec. 7, 1924; came to U.S., 1969; s. Gustav and Antonia (Koch) F.; children: Stephanie, Martin, Jessica. B of Commerce, U. Cape Town, South Africa, 1950, MusB, 1954; postgrad., South African Coll. Music, 1954-56; MusD (hon.), Cleve. Inst. Music, 1987. Gen mgr. London Symphony Orch., 1959-67; dir. Europe CBS Masterworks, 1967-69; exec. v.p., mng. dir. LA Philharm. Assn. and Hollywood Bowl, 1969-98; artistic cons. LA Philharm. Assn., 1998—; pres. Fleischmann Arts, Internat. Arts Mgmt. Cons. Svc., 1998—. Mem. French Govt. Commn. Reform of Paris Opera, 1967-68; steering com. U.S. nat. commn. UNESCO Conf. Future of Arts, 1975; artistic dir. Ojai Festival, 1998-03; bd. counselors U. So. Calif. Thornton Sch. Music; bd. dirs. Monday Evening Concerts, Am. Youth Symphony; hon. lifetime dir. LA Philharm. Assn. Debut as condr. Johannesburg (Republic of South Africa) Symphony Orch., 1942; asst. condr. South African Nat. Opera, 1948-51, Cape Town U. Opera, 1950-54; condr. South African Coll. Music Choir, 1950-52, Labia Grand Opera Co., Cape Town, 1953-55; music organizer Van Riebeeck Festival Cape Town, 1952; dir. music and drama Johannesburg Festival, 1956; contbr. to music publs. Decorated officier Ordre des Arts et Lettres (France), comdrs. cross Order of Merit (Germany), knight 1st class Order of the White Rose (Finland); recipient award of Merit, L.A. Jr. C. of C., John Steinway award, Friends of Music award, Disting. Arts Leadership award U. So. Calif., 1989, L.A. Honors award, L.A. Arts Coun., 1989, Live Music award Am. Fedn. Musicians Local 47, 1991, Disting. Authors/Artists award U. Judaism, 1994, Treasures of L.A. award, Ctrl. City Assn. L.A., 1996, Los Amigos de Los Angeles award, L.A. Conv. and Vis. Bur., 1996; honored Mayor and City Coun. as First Living Cultural Treasure of L.A., 1998, Gold Baton award Am. Symphony Orch. League, 1999. Mem. Assn. Calif. Symphony Orchs., L.A. Philharm. Assn. (bd. dirs. 1984—), Salzburg Seminar/Alberto Vilar Conf. on Orch. Mgmt. (co-chmn. 2002). Office: Fleischmann Arts 2225 Maravilla Dr Los Angeles CA 90068 Office Phone: 323-851-5822. Business E-Mail: efleischmann@laphil.org. *Progress in the arts involves taking risks. Safety and blandness go hand in hand and should be banished from the artistic experience: better to stick your neck out and fail than to err on the side of correctness and caution.*

FLEISHER, ERIC WILFRID, retired foreign service officer; b. Washington, Jan. 31, 1926; s. Wilfrid and Greta Agda (Sundberg) F.; m. Elizabeth Fredrikson, Dec. 22, 1948 (div. 1974); children: Emily Susanne, Eric Torsten; m. Thale Gunneng, Aug. 5, 1974 (dec. Feb. 2000); 1 child, Arne Ericsson. Cert., U. Stockholm, 1948; BA, George Washington U., 1950; PhD, U. Lund, Sweden, 1953. Orientation officer U.S. Displaced Persons Commn., French Zone, Germany, 1950-51; program and ops. officer Refugee Relief Dept. State, Washington, 1954-55, intelligence rsch. analyst, 1955-58; polit. officer Am. Embassy, Copenhagen, 1959-63; consul Faroe Islands, 1959-63; polit. counselor Helsinki, Finland, 1964—69; dep. country dir., then dir. Nordic countries Washington, 1969—73; press attache Am. Embassy, Stockholm, 1974—76; spl. asst. human rights and refugee affairs Washington, 1977-80; fgn. affairs cons., sr. cons., 1980—. Author: Viking Times to Modern, 1953; translator, editor: Scandinavia in Great Power Politics, 1905-1908, 1958; contbr. articles to various publs. 1st lt. U.S. Army, 1944-47, Tokyo. Mem. Am. Fgn. Svc. Assn., Diplomatic and Consular Officers Ret., Am. Scandinavian Found. Avocations: hiking, hunting, photography. Home: 8300 Thoreau Dr Bethesda MD 20817-3164 Office: Rm 7000 SA2 Dept State Washington DC 20522-6001 Office Phone: 202-663-3837. Personal E-mail: flycatcher26@comcast.net.

FLEISHER, FREDERIC ELLIOTT, communications executive; b. Tokyo, Jan. 31, 1933; s. Wilfrid and Greta (Sundberg) F.; divorced; children: Linn M., Rebecca M. BA, U. Stockholm, 1951, MA, 1954, PhD, 1967. Lectr. Scandinavian lit. U. Stockholm, 1967-71; producer, dir. TV programs Sta. TRU-TV, Stockholm, 1968-77; lectr. Am. lit. U. Stockholm, 1970-71; producer, dir. TV programs Sveriges Utbildningsradio (Swedish Ednl. Broadcasting Co.), Stockholm, 1978-90, head internat. rels., 1990-98; cons., 1998—. Author: Seven Swedish Poets, 1963, 5th rev. edit., 1972, The New Sweden: The Challenge of a Disciplined Democracy, 1967, Eight Swedish Poets, 1969, Voices from Black America, 1975, Americans and the United States, 1987; contbr. articles to profl. jours.; co-host internat. prodn. sessions, Munich, 1993-94, Berlin, 1995, 97, Fla., 1995, Bern, 1996, Chgo., 1996, Pa. State U., 1997, Phoenix, 1997; mem. editl. bd. Ednl. Media Internat., 1993—. Jury mem. MediaNet Awards, 1994, Rotterdam Market, 1998, Rotterdam Erasmus, 1998; jury pres. Basle Ednl. Awards, 1997. Recipient Poetry Translations award Sweden, 1964; various grants. Mem. Internat. Coun. Ednl. Media (exec. com. 1991-98), European Broadcasting Union (program com. for edn. 1995-98). Office: Swedish Film AB Vretenvaegen 12 SE-17154 Solna Sweden Personal E-mail: fredf@swipnet.se, f.fleisher@comhem.se.

FLEISHER, MICHAEL D., music company executive; b. 1965; B Econs., U. Pa. Cons. Bain and Co., 1987-90; head conf. and bus. events Gartner Group, Inc., Stamford, Conn., 1993-95, sr. v.p. emerging bus., 1995-96, exec. v.p., pres., 1996-99, CFO, exec. v.p., 1999; pres., CEO, bd. dirs. Gartner Inc. (formerly Gartner Group Inc.), Stamford, Conn., 1999—2001, chmn., 2001—05; exec. v.p & CFO Warner Music Group, NYC, 2005—. Bd. dirs. TruSecure and Tech. Edn. Network. Office: Warner Music Group 75 Rockefeller Plaza New York NY 10019 Fax: (203) 316-1100. E-mail: genilly:help@gartner.com.*

FLEISHER, SEYMOUR, manufacturing executive; b. Highland Park, NJ, Jan. 21, 1923; s. Benjamin Fleisher and Mary (Grossman) Kivitz; m. Estelle Uram, Aug. 12, 1944; 1 son, Bruce Michael. BS in Mech. Engring., Newark Coll. Engring., 1951. Rsch. engr. Eclipse Pioneer div. Bendix Corp., Teterboro, N.J., 1951-53; asst. gen. mgr. Wayne Engring. Corp., Hackensack, N.J., 1953-56; pres. Pilot Metal Fabricators, Inc., Wayne, 1956-89, chmn. bd., 1989-95, Pilot Technologies (now Chatham Technologies), 1995—2004; ret., 2004. Patentee motorized bicycle with removeable fuel tank. Bd. dirs. YM and YWHa of Wayne, 1985-91, Kenneth L. Jordan Heart Fund, 1985—, Jewish Fedn. North Jersey, 1991—, Wayne Area C. of C., 1991—, United Way, 1990-93; trustee Found. for Handicapped, Wayne, 1986—, St. Joseph's Hosp. and Med. Ctr., Patterson, 1988—, Found. of St. Joseph's Hosp. and Med. Ctr., 1991—, exec. com., 1992—; mem. campaign cabinet United Way Passaic Valley, 1989-91; mem. adv. com. Sch. Indsl. Mgmt., N.J. Inst. Tech., 1990, chmn. athletic adv. bd., 1992-94; exec. bd. Passaic Valley Coun. Boy Scouts Am., 1992—; chmn. Wayne Township Indsl. Commn., 1994; bd. dirs. Am. Friends Tel Aviv U., 1993-2000; trustee Wash. Inst., 1990-2000. Capt. U.S. Army, 1942-46, PTO. Decorated Air medal; recipient Edward F. Weston medal for disting. svc. N.J. Inst. Tech., 1985, Benefactors award United Way of Passaic Valley, 1990, Wayne Twp. Corp. Citizen award, 1990; inducted into Athletic Hall of Fame, N.J. Inst. Tech., 1992, Newark Athletic Hall of Fame, 2006. Mem. ASME, Precison Metalforming Assn., Soc. Mfg. Engrs., Aircraft Owners and Pilots Assn., Rotary (bd. dirs., past pres.), Masons, Shriners, Preakness Hills Country Club, Frenchman's Creek Yacht, Beach and Country Club, Pi Tau Sigma, Omicron Delta Kappa, Tau Beta Pi. Republican. Jewish. Avocations: flying, fly fishing, golf, jogging, exercise. Home: 3121 Monet Dr E Palm Beach Gardens FL 33410

FLEISHER, THOMAS ARTHUR, physician; b. Rochester, Minn. s. Gerard and Gisela Fleisher; m. Mary Fleisher; children: Jeffrey, Jeremy, Matthew. BS, U. Minn., 1969, MD, 1971. Diplomate Am. Bd. Pediats., Am. Bd. Allergy and Immunology. Staff physician bone marrow transplant svc. Naval Med. Rsch. Inst., Bethesda, Md., 1975—77; commd. lt.comdr. USNR, 1975—77; commd. USPHS, 1977—80, advanced through grades to capt., 1983—2001; ret., 2001; clin. assoc. metabolism br. Nat. Cancer Inst., NIH, Bethesda, 1977—80; asst. chief allergy clin. immunology svc. Walter Reed Army Med. Ctr., Washington, 1980—83; chief immunology svc. Warren G. Magnuson Clin. Ctr., NIH, Bethesda, 1983—, chief dept. lab. medicine, 1998—. Tng. program dir. clin. lab. immunology NIH, Bethesda, 1992—; bd. dirs. Am. Bd. Allergy and Immunology, Phila., 1991—2001, chair, 1996. Editor Clin. Immunology, 1985—89, 1993—, Immunology, 1983—86, Clin. Diag. Lab. Immunology, 1993—, Cytometry, 1996—, contbr. numerous articles to sci. jours., —. House capt. Christmas in April, Montgomery County, Md., 1991—2000; deacon, elder St. Mark Presbyn. Ch., Rockville, Md., 1983—88; bd. dirs. Bethesda Soccer Club, 1987—95. Fellow: Am. Acad. Allergy, Asthma and Immunology (bd. dirs. 2003—); mem.: Clin. Immunology Soc. (pres. 2004—), Clin. Cytometry Soc., Soc. for Pediat. Rsch., Am. Assn. Immunologists. Avocations: travel, skiing, woodworking. Office: NIH 10/2C306 9000 Rockville Pike Bethesda MD 20892-1508 E-mail: tfleisher@nih.gov.

FLEISHHACKER, DAVID, school administrator; b. San Francisco, May 30, 1937; s. Mortimer and Janet (Choynski) F.; m. Victoria Escamilla, Aug. 1965; children: William, Eleanor, Jeffrey. AB, Princeton U., 1959; MA, U. Calif., 1965. Tchr. Lick-Wilmerding High Sch., San Francisco, 1959-61, Peace Corps, Afghanistan, 1962-64, Marin Country Day Sch., Corte Madera, Calif., 1965, Town Sch., San Francisco, 1965-70; headmaster Katherine Delmar Burke Sch., San Francisco, 1970-95; ret.; interim head Hillbrook Sch., Los Gatos, 1997-98, South Peninsula Hebrew Day Sch., 1998-99. Pvt. ednl. cons. Author: (book) Lessons from Afghanistan, 2002; contbr. articles to profl. jours. Trustee Internat. Ho., Berkeley, Calif., 1987—95; pres. Fleishhacker Found., San Francisco, 1990—, Music in Sch. Today, 2002—; bd. dirs. St. Joseph's Hosp./Queen of Angels, LA, 1976—, San Francisco Youth Orch., 1981—, San Francisco Boys Chorus, 1997—2003, Booker T. Washington Cmty. Ctr., 1995—2004, Educating Girls Globally, 2002—, Berkeley Repertory Theater, 2007—. Mem. Nat. Assn. Prins. Schs. Girls. (bd. dirs. 1979-82), Elem. Sch. Heads Assn., Calif. Assn. Ind. Schs. (treas. 1978-81). Home: #8 1958 Vallejo St San Francisco CA 94123 Personal E-mail: trampc@aol.com.

FLEISHMAN, PHILIP ROBERT, internist; b. Hartford, Conn., Apr. 17, 1935; s. Morris and Anna Lillian (Farber) Fleishman; m. Anita Rose Coopersmith, Oct. 18, 1964; children: David, Beth, Rachael. BS, Trinity Coll., Hartford, 1957; MD, SUNY, Bklyn., 1961. Diplomate Am. Bd. Internal Medicine. Med. intern Bklyn. Jewish Hosp., 1961—62, med. resident, 1962—65; practice specializing in internal medicine East Islip, NYC, 1967—; attending physician, dir. medicine Southside Hosp., Bay Shore, NY, 1993—; attending physician Good Samaritan Hosp., W. Islip, NY; v.p. med. bd. Southside Hosp., 1986-89; pres., 1989—; clin. asst. prof. SUNY Med. Sch., Stony Brook, 1967—; asst. dir. medicine, 1988—; dir. med. sch., 1993—; founder, co-dir. diabetic clinic Southside Hosp.; also bd. dirs., 1999—. Bd. dir. Southlake Hosp. Contbr. articles to profl. jours. Co-author, chmn. constn. and bylaws Pro-Arts Group Islips, 1979; asst. basketball coach Police Athletic League, 1979; v.p., trustee Bay Shore Jewish Ctr., 1979—, pres., 1988—90. Capt. M.C. US Army, 1965—67. Fellow: ACP; mem.: AMA, Suffolk County Med. Soc., N.Y. State Soc. Internal Medicine (past chpt. pres.), N.Y. State Med. Soc., Am. Diabetes Assn. Office Phone: 631-968-7373.

FLEISZIG, SUZANNE MARIANE JANETE, optometry educator; b. Melbourne, Australia, Sept. 5, 1960; came to U.S., 1990; d. Kornel Fleiszig and Judith Mary (Falus) Fleiszig-Farkas. BSc in Optometry, U. Melbourne, 1983, MSc in Optometry, 1985, PhD, 1990. Lic. optometrist, Victoria, Australia. Postdoc. fellow Harvard U. Med. Sch., Boston, 1990-93, instr., 1993-94; prof. optometry U. Calif., Berkeley, 1994—, assoc. dean rsch., 2003—06. Cons. to contact lens industry, 1993—. Mem. editl. bd. Eye and Contact Lens. The Ocular Surface Jour.; contbr. articles to Investigtive Ophthalmology and Vision Sci., Jour. Clin. Microbiology, Infection and Immunity. Postdoctoral fellow Nat. Soc. To Prevent Blindness, 1991, C.J. Martin fellow Nat. Health and Med. Rsch. Coun. Australia, 1992; rsch. grantee NIH, 1995-; recipient Borish award, 1997, Glenn A. Fry award, 2005. Mem. Am. Soc. Microbiology, Assn. Rsch. in Vision and Ophthalmology, Internat. Soc. Contact Lens Rsch. (pres. 2005), Tear Film and Ocular Surface Soc. (governing bd. 2005-). Achievements include discovery that contact lens wear enhances bacterial binding to human corneal cells, discovered that Pseudomonas aeruginosa invades epithelial cells. Office: U Calif 688 Minor Hall Optometry Berkeley CA 94720-0001 Office Phone: 510-643-0990.

FLEKSHER, CASSANDRA C., psychology and research rehabilitation professional; b. NJ, 1975; d. Daphne T. Berger; m. Mark Fleksher, 2002; 1 child, Dillon. BA in Psychology and Criminal Justice Studies, Alfred U., 1997; MA in Forensic Psychology, John Jay Coll. Criminal Justice, 2000. Neuropsychology RA II neuropsychology and neurosci. lab. Kessler Med. Rehab. Rsch. & Edn. Corp., West Orange, NJ, 2001—03, rsch. coord. II rehab. engring. analysis lab., 2003—04, neuropsychology rsch. coord. II virtual reality lab, 2004—. Author (researcher): (journal abstract) Archives of Clinical Neuropsychology, Archives of Physical Medicine & Rehab.; author: (research assistant) Jour. Internat. Neuropsychological Soc.; research coordinator (cognitive research): Examining the Demands of Driving in Multiple Sclerosis; research assistant II Assessment & Rehabilitation of Cognitive Symptoms of Multiple Sclerosis. Mem.: APA, Nat. Acad. Neuropsychology. Home Phone: 973-209-1951. Personal E-mail: cfleksher@gmail.com.

FLEMING, DOUGLAS RILEY, journalist, publishing executive, consultant; b. Fairmont, W.Va., Jan. 25, 1922; s. Douglas Riley and Sarilda Artemes (Short) F.; m. Irene Stachowicz, Oct. 28, 1944 (dec. 1979); m. Nancy Evelyn Kincaid, May 30, 1992. BS, Georgetown U., 1953. Commd. ensign U.S. Navy, 1944, advanced through grades to comdr.; naval aviator; chief protocol NATO, Naples, Italy, 1962-67; ret. U.S. Navy, 1967; with Francis I. DuPont & Co., Investment Banking, Rome, 1968-70; exec. editor, gen. mgr. Daily American, Rome, 1970-75; pres. Stampa Generale, S.R.L., Pubs., Naples, 1975—80; mng. dir. Italo-Am. Assn., Naples; dir. Am. Studies Ctr., Naples, 1975-80; pres. Gen. Press Svcs., Washington, 1979—. Dir. Va. Winery Coop., Inc., Culpeper, 1985-93; propr., operator Campicello Vineyards, Madison, Va., 1982-92. Active Nat. Trust Hist. Preservation, Smithsonian Assocs., Assn. Naval Aviation. Mem. Associazione della Stampa Estera in Italia, The Cogswell Soc., The Murray Clan Soc., St. Andrew's Soc. of Washington D.C., Georgetown U. Alumni ASsn. (pres. Italy 1972-80), Am. C. of C. in Italy, Military Officers Assn., Navy League of U.S., Nat. Press Club, Vinifera Wine Growers Assn., Jeffersonian Wine Grape Growers Soc., Va. Vineyards Assn., Naval and Mil. Club, Steering Wheel Club, Royal Aero Club (London), Circolo Canottieri (Naples), N.Y. Athletic Club, Dist. Yacht (Washington). Address: 400 Madison St Apt 1408 Alexandria VA 22314-1724

FLEMING, FRANCINE FAYE, legal nurse consultant; b. Houston, Apr. 17, 1947; d. Francis Elmer Turner and Evelyn Frances Fieseler; m. Garrel

Vern Fleming, Dec. 23, 1995. Diploma, Brackenridge Hosp. Sch. Nursing, 1968; BS, Tex. State Coll., 1989. RN. Staff nurse Brachenridge Hosp., Austin, Tex., 1968—70, Galveston County Meml. Hosp., Texas City, 1970—72, Seton Med. Ctr., 1979—84; staff nurse, head nurse St. David's Hosp., Austin, 1972—78; office nurse Med. Pk. Orthop. Group, 1982—83; rsch. nurse Biomed. Rsch. Group, 1983—84; paralegal Brown McCarroll LLP, 1984—. Chair Concepts Care Adv. Com., Austin, 1989—90, vice chair, 1991—93, 1995. Mem. Vol. Assistance Program, Austin, 1984, ARC, 1965—; bd. dirs. Windermer Homeowners Assn., Pflugerville, Tex., 1986. Mem.: Am. Assn. Legal Nurse Cons. (pres. 1990—92, 1997, co-founder), State Bar Tex. (paralegal divsn.), Capital Area Paralegal Assn., Alpha Chi. Mem. Ch. Of Christ. Avocations: genealogy, gardening, music, singing, birdwatching. Office: Brown McCarroll LLP 111 Congress Ave #1400 Austin TX 78701 E-mail: ffleming@mailbmc.com.

FLEMING, GAVIN JOHN, lawyer; b. Knowsley, Eng., July 13, 1978; s. John and Margaret Katherine Fleming; m. Melissa Ponder; 1 child, Noah John. BA in Gen. Studies, U. Mich., Ann Arbor, 2000, JD cum laude, 2003. Bar: Ill. 2003, Mich. 2005. Assoc. atty. Jones Day, Chgo., 2003—04, Bush Seyferth Kethledge & Paige, Troy, Mich., 2004—05, Beals Hubbard, PLC, Farmington Hills, Mich., 2005—. Recipient award for Excellence in Oral Advocacy, Internati. Acad. Trial Lawyers; Angel Scholar, U. Mich., 2000. Mem.: Ill. Bar Assn., Mich. State Bar (assoc.), Phi Beta Kappa, Am. Inn Cts. (assoc.). Home Phone: 248-596-9614; Office Phone: 248-932-1101. Office Fax: 248-932-4186. Business E-Mail: gfleming@bealshubbard.com.

FLEMING, GEORGE ROBERT, psychologist; 1 child, Maisha Amira. BA, Hillsdale Coll., 1969; MA in Clin. Psychology, Mich. State U., 1972, PhD in Clin. Psychology, 1975. Lic. psychologist Mich., Am. Bd. Profl. Disability Cons., Psychol. Am. Coll. Forensic Examiners, Emergency Crisis Response, Am. Acad. Experts in Traumatic Stress, cert. Profl. Qualification in Psychology, Assn. State and Provincial Bd. Staff mem. Allied Health-Detroit Med. Ctr.; staff dept. psychiatry and behavioral neuroscis. Harper Hosp. and Detroit Receiving Hosp., 1990—; ind. psychiatric examiner mental divsn. Wayne County Probate Ct., 1991—; psychologist risk mgmt. divsn. Detroit Police Dept., 1997—; psychologist dept. behavioral medicine St. John Detroit Riverview Hosp., 1998—; prof. med. staff Detroit Riverview Hosp. St. John Health Sys., 1998—; clin. dir. Wayne County Juvenile Assessment Ctr., Mich., 2000—03. Cons. Sacred Heart Rehab. Ctr., Inc., Detroit, 1981-84, Detroit Pub. Schs., 1981, 1986, Southgate Regional Ctr. for Devel. Disabilities, Mich. Dept. Mental Health, 1989-90, 1995; cons., facilitator Morehouse Rsch. Inst., Morehouse Coll., Atlanta, 1990-92; advisor African Am. Males at Risk, Rockefeller Found., NYC, 1989-90; workshop panelist Congl. Black Caucus Found., Washington, 1988; asst. prof. dept. cmty. medicine Wayne State U., 1991-. Bd. trustees Optometric Inst. and Clinic of Detroit, 1995—, pres., 1998—2001. Named one of Outstanding Young Men in Am., U.S. Jaycees, 1982; recipient Spirit of Detroit award, 1986; fellow Nat. Inst. Mental Health, Mich. State U., 1974—75. Fellow Am. Orthopsychiatric Assn.; mem. Am. Psychol. Assn., Assn. Black Psychologists (past pres. Mich. chpt., 1981-82), Nat. Register Health Svc. Providers in Psychology, Am. Bd. Profl. Disability Cons. , Am. Coll. Forensic Examiners (diplomate 1997—), Nat. Black Child Devel. Inst., Am. Acad. of Experts in Traumatic Stress (diplomate 1999-), Internat. Soc. for Traumatic Stress Studies, Soc. Cmty. Rsch. and Action. Office: 243 W Congress Ave Ste 350 Detroit MI 48226 Office Phone: 313-567-2234. Personal E-mail: gpsychdet@sbcglobal.net.

FLEMING, GRAHAM RICHARD, chemistry educator; b. Barrow-in-Furness, Lancashire, Eng., Dec. 3, 1949; came to U.S., 1979; s. Maurice Norman and Ena (Winter) F.; m. Jean McKenzie, Sept. 16, 1977; 1 child, Matthew. BS with honors, U. Bristol, Eng., 1971; PhD in Phys. Chemistry, U. London, 1974. Rsch. fellow Calif. Inst. Tech., Pasadena, 1974-75; univ. rsch. fellow U. Melbourne, Australia, 1975, Australian Rsch. Grants Commn. rsch. asst., 1976; Leverhulme fellow Royal Instn., London, 1977-79; asst. prof. U. Chgo., 1979-83, assoc. prof., 1983-85, prof., 1985-87, A.H. Compton Disting. Svc. prof., 1987-97, chmn. dept. chemistry, 1988-90; prof. U. Calif., Berkeley, 1997—, Melvin Calvin disting. prof., 2002—; dir. phys. bioscis. divsn. Lawrence Berkeley Nat. Lab., 1997—, assoc. lab. dir. for phys. sci., 2002—. Co-chmn. Ultrafast Phenomena V Meeting, Snowmass, Colo., 1986; co-dir. Inst. Bioengrng., Biotech., Quantitative Biomedicine, U. Calif., Berkeley, San Francisco, Santa Cruz. Author: Chemical Applications of Ultrafast Spectroscopy, 1986; mem. editl. bd. Chem. Physics Letters, Jour. of Phys. Chemistry, Chem. Physics; contbr. 235 rsch. articles to profl. publs. Recipient Coblentz award, Coblentz Soc., 1985, Earle K. Plyler award, Am. Phys. Soc., 2002; fellow Alfred P. Sloan Found. fellow, 1981, J.S. Guggenheim fellow, 1987; scholar Dreyfus tchr.-scholar, 1982. Fellow Am. Acad. Arts and Scis., Royal Soc. London; mem. Optical Soc. Am., Inter-Am. Photochem. Soc. (award 1996), Royal Soc. Chemistry (Marlow medal 1981, Tilden medal 1991, Centenary medal 1996), Am. Chem. Soc. (Nobel Laureate Signature award for grad. edn. in chemistry 1995, Peter Debye award in phys. chemistry 1998, Harrison Howe award 1999), NAS. Avocation: mountain climbing. Office: Univ of Calif-Berkeley Dept Chemistry B77 Hildebrand Hall Berkeley CA 94720-0001 Office Phone: 510-643-7609. Office Fax: 510-643-7012.*

FLEMING, GREGORY JAMES, investment company executive; b. Feb. 27, 1963; m. Melissa Danne Shaw, Apr. 28, 1990. BA summa cum laude in Econs., Colgate U., 1985; JD, Yale U., 1988. Prin. Booz-Allen & Hamilton; co-head global fin. instns. grp. Merrill Lynch & Co., Inc., NYC, 1992—2003, mng. dir., 1998—2003, head US fin. inst. group, 1999—2003, COO global investment banking, 2003, exec. v.p., pres. global markets and investment banking, 2003—07, co-pres., 2007—. Office: Merrill Lynch & Co Inc 4 World Fin Ctr 250 Vesey St New York NY 10080*

FLEMING, HORACE WELDON, JR., academic administrator; b. Elberton, Ga., Jan. 14, 1944; s. Horace Weldon Sr and Alma G (Dove) Fleming; m. Orene Stephens Greene, Feb. 8, 1970; children: Susan Renee, Patrick Weldon. BA, U. Ga., 1965, MA, 1966; PhD, Vanderbilt U., 1973. Mem. faculty Clemson (S.C.) U., 1971-87; chief economist U.S. Senate Judiciary Com., 1981; staff dir. Office of Pres. Pro Tem U.S. Senate, 1981-82; founding dir. Strom Thurmond Inst. Govt. and Pub. Affairs, Clemson, 1982-90; exec. v.p. U. of the Pacific, Stockton, Calif., 1990-92; exec. v.p., provost Mercer U., Macon, Ga., 1992-96; pres. U. So. Miss., Hattiesburg, 1997—2001. Consult to fed, state and local govt agys on fin, orgn and mgt, energy and water policy; frequent media columnist and speaker; bd dirs Miss Technology Inc, Inst Technology Develop. Charter trustee Dropout Prevention Fund, 1986—90, Palmetto Project, 1987—90; vpres Hill Found, 1982—96; mem SC Reorganization Commn., 1987—90, Stockton-San Joaquin Conv and Visitors Bur, Calif., 1990—92; mem Vision 2000 task force Stockton Bus Coun, 1990—92; bd visitors Air Univ, 1998—; mem Pres's Nat Vol Adv coun, 1986—89, Assembly Future SC, 1988, Gov's Transition Task Force Govt Reform, 1986—87. Capt US Army, 1969—71, Vietnam. Recipient Order Palmetto, SC, 1990, Award of Merit, SC Water Resources Comn, 1990, Palmetto Pride Award, Palmetto Project, 1990; fellow Faculty, Leadership Hilton Head Island, 1989. Mem.: Tiger Brotherhood, Blue Key, Scabbard and Blade, Phi Kappa Phi, Omicron Delta Kappa, Sigma Phi Epsilon, Pi Sigma Alpha, Phi Mu Alpha. Office Phone: 478-301-2110.

FLEMING, JANE WILLIAMS, retired elementary school educator, writer; b. Bethlehem, Pa., May 26, 1926; d. James Robert and Marion Pauline (Melloy) Groman; m. George Elliott Williams, July 2, 1955 (div. July 1965); children: Rhett Dorman, Santee Stuart, Timothy Cooper; m. Jerome Thomas Fleming, Sept. 25, 1980 (dec. 2002). BS, UCLA, 1951; MA, Calif. State U., Long Beach, 1969. Tchr. San Diego Unified Sch Dist., 1951-55, Costa Mesa (Calif.) Sch. Dist., 1955-56, Long Beach (Calif.) Sch. Dist., 1956-58, 62-87, 90-92; ret. Author: Why Janey Can't Teach, 2001. Mem. Phi Kappa Phi, Ret. Tchrs. Assn., UCLA Alumni Assn., Planetary Soc. (charter), Red Hat Soc., Mus. of Tolerance. Avocations: theater, travel. Address: PO Box 13053 Long Beach CA 90803-8053 Personal E-mail: jwilli5687@aol.com.

FLEMING, JAYNE ELIZABETH, lawyer; children: Anthony, Isabel. BA in Polit. Sci., U. Calif., Berkeley, 1994; JD, U. Calif. Boalt Hall Sch. Law. Bar: Calif. 2000. Assoc. Crosby Heafey Roach & May LLP (merged with Reed Smith LLP), 2000—03, Reed Smith LLP, Oakland, Calif., 2003—. Named Calif. Lawyer Atty. of Yr., Calif. Lawyer mag., 2005; named one of The 50 Most Influential Women Lawyers in Am., Nat. Law Jour., 2007; recipient Sean Halpin award, Reed Smith LLP, 2005, Father Moriarity award, Lawyers Com. for Civil Rights, 2005. Mem.: ABA, Lawyers' Com. Civil Rights San Francisco Bay Area, First Dist. Appellate Project, Ctr. Gender & Refugee Studies, San Francisco Bar Assn.: Internat. Human Rights Section. Office: Reed Smith LLP 1999 Harrison St Ste 2400 Oakland CA 94612 E-mail: jfleming@reedsmith.com.*

FLEMING, JENNIE M, retired education educator; b. Elba, Ala., Aug. 8, 1948; d. Amie Junior Fleming and Lessie Mae Broxton-Burrows-Fleming; children: Jenna Helena Fleming-Matthews, Bashiri Phillips, Nia Dafina Diggs-Evans. Graduate, Herbert H. Lehman Coll., Bronx; Battaliton Mgmt., BMTS, Ft. Taylor Harding, Montgomery, Ala., 1985; Pastorial Counseling, Speak the Word Sch. of Ministry-Dothan, Dothan, Ala., 2002—04; Adminstrv. Specialist, Civilian Acquired Skills Program, Ft. McClellan, Ala., 1975; Logistics Exec. Devel. Course, The Army Logisitcs Manangement Coll., Ft. Lee, Va., 1999—99; BS in Early Childhood Edn., Troy State U., Dothan, Ala., 1980; MS- ECE Specialist, Troy State U., Ala., 1993; Adj. Gen. Corps- Basic Officer Course, Ft. Benjamin Harrison, Lawrence, Ind., 1978—79; Advanced Officer Course, Adj. Gen. Corps, Lawrence, Ind., 1981—82; Clergy Leadership Tng., Fla. Bapt. Sem., Graceville, Fla, 1997—99; Family Support Tng., 81st RSC (Reserve Service Components), Birmingham, Ala. Congregational Elder Northview Christian Ch., 1999; Early Childhood Specialist Troy State U., 1995. Early childhood educator Geneva County Schools Sys. - Samson Elem., Samson, Ala., 1975—2001; ceo/ founder Angelic Cultural Ctr., Inc., Dothan, Ala., 1974—; sec./ cmty. liaison Seven Loaves Cmty. Arts Coalition, East Village, New York, NY, 1972—74; spl. staff officer USAR Control Group (REINF), St. Louis, 1987; founder, CEO Beacon Produztions Unlimited, Dothan, Ala., 2003. Coord. Student Mock Election, Samson, Ala., 1998—99. Participant Family Action Plan Symposium, Fort Rucker, Ala., 1987, Centennial Commn., Enterprise, Ala., 1992; coord. and cultural cons. African-American History Celebration, Fort Rucker, Ala., 1992; founder Angelic Cultural Ctr., Inc, Dothan, Ala., 1974; coord. and ednl. cons. Northview Christian Ch.- Learning With Dignity Program, Dothan, Ala., 2003. Served Army Nat. Guard, Ala. Scholar TSU tuition, Kappa Delta Pi, 1979, Tech. Scholarship, Ala. State Dept. of Edn., 1993. Mem.: S.E. Ala. Regional Arts Alliance, SE Ala. Arts Alliance (assoc.; CEO Angelic Cultural Ctr., Inc. 1974), Kappa Delta Pi, Gamma Delta Pi. Democrat. Achievements include being the first African-Native American to graduate from Alabama Military Academy. Avocations: gospel singing, writing, performing arts, interior decorating, landscaping. Home: 102 Montrose Ctt Apt 6 Dothan AL 36305 Office Phone: 334-434-9290. Personal E-mail: jfleming07@comcast.net.

FLEMING, JOHN E., retail executive; b. Rochester, Minn. With Target Corp., 1981—2000, sr. v.p. merchandising, fashion; chief merchant Walmart.com, Brisbane, Calif., 2000—01, COO, 2001—02, pres., CEO, 2002—; exec. v.p., chief mktg. officer Wal-Mart Stores USA, Bentonville, Ark., 2005—07, exec. v.p., chief merchandising officer, 2007—. Office: Wal-Mart Stores 702 SW 8th St Bentonville AR 72716*

FLEMING, JOHN JACOB, music educator, director; b. Joliet, Ill., Oct. 19, 1977; s. J. Edward and Deborah Lee Fleming; m. Gina Marie Pehlke, June 18, 2005. B in Music Edn., Murray State U., Ky., 2003. Band dir. Indian Trail Mid. Sch., Plainfield, Ill., 2003—. Instr. percussion Plainfield Sch. Dist., Ill., 2003—, solo and ensemble judge, 2003—. Leader Boy Scouts Am., Plainfield, Ill., 1995—. Named an Eagle Scout. Mem.: Music Educators Nat. Conf., Percussive Arts Soc. Avocations: rock climbing, bicycling.

FLEMING, JOSEPH Z., lawyer; b. Miami, Fla., Jan. 30, 1941; s. Richard Marion and Lenore C. Fleming; m. Betty Corcoran, Feb. 12, 1947; 1 child, Katherine Anne. BA in English, U. Fla., 1958; postgrad., U. Chgo., 1959, Hague Acad. Internat. Law, 1966; JD, U. Va., 1965; LLM in Labor Law, NYU, 1966. Bar: Fla. 1965, D.C. 1981. Assoc. Paul & Thomson, Miami, 1966-72, ptnr., 1972-74, Fleming & Neuman, 1974-81, Fleming & Huck, Miami, 1981-86; pvt. practice Miami, 1986-87; with Fleming & Klink, 1987-88; pvt. practice, 1988—96; with Ford & Harrison, 1996—2001, Greenberg Traurig PA, 2001—. Lectr. in field. Author: Airline and Railroad Labor Law, 1981-; editor, contbg. author Environmental Regulation and Litigation in Florida, 1980, 82, 84-85, 87-88, 90-91, 93-95, 97, 99-2000, 03-06, Environmental Pollution and Individual Rights, 1978, Reporter's Handbook, 1979—, Historic Preservation Law, 1984-87, 89, 99, 2001, 04-05, 07, Entertainment, Arts, & Sports Law, 1989-91, 97-99, 2001, 03, 05, 07. Trustee Met. Dade County Ctr. for Fine Arts, 1982-86; mem. Biscayne Bay Environ. Task Force Subcom., 1982-83, well field protection adv. com. Dade County Task Force, 1984-87; mem. Noguchi-Bayfront Park Trust, Miami, 1983-89; pres., bd. dirs. Fla. Rural Legal Svcs., 1967-78, Pres.'s Water Policy Implementation Workshops, Dept. of Interior Water Task Force, 1979; bd. dirs. Miami chpt. Am. Jewish Com. Recipient Conservation award Fla. Audubon Soc., 1981, 89, Tropical Audubon Soc., 1979, award Dade County Mental Health Assn., 1974, award Miami Design Preservation League, 1982-83, award Progressive Architecture, 1982, Am. Jewish Com. award. Mem. Am. Law Inst., ABA (continuing profl. edn. com. 1985—), Fla. Bar Assn. (past chmn. environ. and land use law sect., labor law and employment discrimination law sect., entertainment, arts and sports law sect., cert. labor and employment law). Home: 34 LaGorce Cir Miami Beach FL 33141-4520 Office: 1221 Brickell Ave Miami FL 33131 Office Phone: 305-579-0517. E-mail: flemingj@gtlaw.com.

FLEMING, JULIAN DENVER, JR., lawyer; b. Rome, Ga., Jan. 12, 1934; s. Julian D. and Margaret Madison (Mangham) F.; m. Sidney Howell, June 28, 1960; 1 dau., Julie Adrianne. Student, U. Pa., 1951-53; BChemE, Ga. Inst. Tech., 1955, PhD, 1959; JD, Emory U., 1967. Bar: Ga. 1966, D.C. 1967; registered profl. engr., Ga., Calif. Rsch. engr., prof. chem. engring. Ga. Inst. Tech., 1955-67; ptnr. Sutherland, Asbill & Brennan, Atlanta, 1967—. Contbr. articles to profl. jours.; patentee in field. Bd. dirs. Mental Health Assn. Ga., 1970-80; bd. dirs. Mental Health Assn. Met. Atlanta, 1970-80, pres., 1974-75; mem. coun. legal advisors Rep. Nat. Com., 1981-85. Fellow: Am. Bar Found., Am. Coll. Trial Lawyers, Am. Inst. Chemists; mem.: AIChE, AAAS, ABA (coun. sect. sci. and tech. 1980—, vice chmn. 1982—84, chmn. 1985—86, ho. dels. 1990, bd. govs. 1994—95, ho. dels. 1994—96, chmn. spl. citation issues com. 1995—96, coord. commn. legal tech. 1995—97, standing com. tech. and info. sys. 1997—2001), Bleckley Inn of Ct. (master of bench), Nat. Conf. Lawyers and Scientists (chmn. ABA del. 1988—90, standing com. nat. conf. groups 1990, ABA liaison 1990—93, chmn. 1992—93). Achievements include patent for data apparatus. Home: 1248 Oxford Rd NE Atlanta GA 30306-2610 Office: Sutherland Asbill & Brennan 999 Peachtree St NE Ste 2300 Atlanta GA 30309-3996

FLEMING, MAC ARTHUR, retired labor union administrator; b. Walnut Grove, Miss., Sept. 22, 1945; s. Austin J. and Dorothy (Downey) F.; m. Phyllis Jean Tatro, May 18, 1984; children: Vaughn L. Voth, Vaughn L. Voth II AA, Jones County Jr. Coll., Laurel, Miss., 1967; student, So. Colo. State Coll., Pueblo, 1967-68; student in trade union program, Harvard U., 1979. System organizer Atchison, Topeka & Santa Fe System Fedn., Pueblo, 1972, asst. gen. chmn. San Bernardino, Calif., 1972-73, asst. chmn., sec.-treas. Newton, Kans., 1974-75, vice chmn., 1975-80, gen. chmn., 1980-86; grand lodge sec.-treas. Brotherhood Maintenance Ways Employees, Detroit, 1986-90; pres. Brotherhood Maintenance of Way Employees, Detroit, 1990—2004; v.p. AFL-CIO, 1995—2004, ret., 2004. Democrat. Avocations: tennis, golf. Home: 39921 Urbana Dr Sterling Heights MI 48313-5678

FLEMING, MACKLIN, retired judge; b. Chgo., Sept. 6, 1911; s. Ingram Macklin Stainback and Hazel (Caldwell) Fleming; m. Polly Naething, May 17, 1941; children: Penelope, Frances, Ingram. BA, Yale U., New Haven, Conn., 1934, LLB, 1937; LLD, Pepperdine U., Malibu, Calif., 1968. Bar: NY 1938, Calif. 1946. Assoc. Sullivan & Cromwell, NYC, 1937-39; atty. Bituminous Coal divsn. US Govt., Washington, 1939-41; pvt. practice San Francisco, 1946-49; asst. US atty. US Atty.'s Office, San Francisco, 1949-53; assoc. Mitchell, Silberberg & Knupp, LA, 1954-59; judge Superior Ct., LA, 1959-64; justice Calif. Ct. Appeal, LA, 1964-81; of counsel Troy and Gould, LA, 1981-91; assigned judge Superior Ct., LA, 1992-98, ret., 1998. Author: The Price of Perfect Justice, 1974, Of Crimes and Rights, 1978, Lawyers, Money, & Success, 1997, Perfect Justice, 2001. Chmn. Far Eastern Art Coun. LA County Mus., LA, 1967—69; dir. Ctr. Theater Group, 1970—78. Capt. US Army, 1941—46. Fellow Am. Bar Found.; mem. ABA, Inst. Jud. Adminstrn. Episcopalian. Avocations: tennis, gardening. Home: 331 N Carmelina Ave Los Angeles CA 90049-2701

FLEMING, MARJORIE FOSTER, freelance writer, artist; b. Phila., Sept. 12, 1920; d. Major Bronson and Helen Margaret (Vertner) Foster; m. John Joseph Hundermark, Sept. 24, 1949 (div. Sept. 1955); children: John Foster Hundermark, David Laurence Hundermark; m. Paul Stewart Fleming, May 6, 1961. BA, Ursinus Coll., 1942; studied painting with Morris Blackburn, Pa. Acad. Fine Arts and Cheltenham Ctr. for Arts; studied Robert Goldman, Cheltenham Twp. Ctr. Arts; studied painting with Paul Wieghardt, Chgo. Art Inst. and Cheltenham Twp. Ctr. for Arts. Cert. tchr. Cost acct. Philco Corp., Phila., 1942-43; asst. bank auditor Liberty Title and Trust, Phila., 1943-44; asst. dept. spl. events Phila. Evening Bulletin, 1945-47; asst. stage TV and radio show prodr. Phila., 1947-49. Appeared on Wit's End (live pilot TV show), 1948, guest Poetry Today, Sta. WRTN radio, N.Y.C., 1997. Author: Whispers of Escaped Thoughts, 2003; Whispers of Escaped Thoughts, 2003; contbr. poetry to local newspapers. Vol. occupl. therapist ARC; spl. duty hostess for Purple Heart and Stage Door Canteen, WWII. Mem. Internat. Poetry Mus., Internat. Libr. Poetry, Internat. Soc. Poets (inducted into Hall of Fame Mus.), Poetry Guild, Am. Diabetes Assn., Cheltenham Ctr. Arts, Kappa Chi Delta, Omega Chi. Republican. Methodist. Avocations: sculpture, photography, creative needlework, pianist, collecting sheet music, art, creative writing. Home: 82 Holly Dr Crystal Lake IL 60014-5022

FLEMING, MARTIN, economist, strategist; b. Lowell, Mass., Mar. 19, 1953; s. M. Brendan and Bernice (Kenney) F.; m. Patricia Marie Magnan; children: Brian Martin, Katherine Mary. BS, Lowell Tech. Inst., Mass., 1974; MA, Tufts U., 1976; PhD, Tufts U., 1980. Tech. dir. MIT, Cambridge, 1974-75; project dir. Tufts U., Medford, Mass., 1978-81; v.p. strategy Reed Elsevier Inc., Newton, Mass., 1982-95; prin. cons. Abt Assocs. Inc., Cambridge, Mass., 1995-99; v.p. strategy global bus. ptnrs. IBM Corp., White Plains, NY, 1999—2003, v.p. strategy, global sales and distbn., 2003—06, v.p. corp. strategy Armonk, NY, 2006—. Mem. Am. Econ. Assn., Nat. Assn. Bus. Economists (bd. dirs. 1990), Boston Assn. Bus. Economists (pres., various offices 1984-86), N.Y. Assn. of Bus. Economists Roman Catholic. Home: 38 Oval Ave Greenwich CT 06878-2128

FLEMING, MICHAEL F., medical educator; MPH. U. of NC at Chapel Hill. Resident, family practice, Milwaukee, 1977; sole practitioner, 1977—81; prof. U. NC, Chapel Hill, 1981—86; prof. family medicine U. Wis. Med. Sch., 1986—; dir. NIH rsch. fellowship; dir. pain consult svc. U. Wis. Hosp., dir. inpatient addiction medicine consult svc. Mem.: Inst. Medicine. Office: Dept Family Medicine 777 S Mills St Madison WI 53715-1896 Office Phone: 608-263-9953. E-mail: mike.fleming@fammed.wisc.edu.

FLEMING, MICHAEL O., physician; b. Monroe, La., June 16, 1950; m. Sally Fleming; 4 children. MD, La. Med. Ctr., 1975. Intern Confederate Meml. Med. Ctr., Shreveport, 1975—76; resident LSU Med. Ctr., Shreveport, 1976—78; asst. clinical prof. Dept. Family Medicine, LSU Health Sci. Ctr. Mng. sr. ptnr. The Family Doctors. Mem.: Northwest La. Soc. Family Physicians, Shreveport Med. Soc., La. Acad. Family Physicians, La. State Med. Soc., Am. Acad. Family Physicians (pres. 2003—). Office: Am Acad Family Physicians PO Box 11210 Shawnee Mission KS 66207-1210

FLEMING, MICHAEL PAUL, lawyer; b. Orlando, Fla., June 25, 1963; s. Joseph Patrick and Therese (Eccles); m. Natalie Jackson, Oct. 15, 1988; children: Shannon Isabel, Nicholas Patrick, Patrick Edward, Michael Paul, Eamon John, Celeste Natalie. BA, U. St. Thomas, 1984; JD, U. Houston, 1987. Bar: Tex. 1987; U.S. Dist. Ct. (so. dist.) Tex. 1988; U.S. Ct. Appeals (5th cir.) 1988, U.S. Supreme Ct. 1991; cert. personal injury; bd. cert. residential real estate law. Ptnr. Fleming & Fleming, Houston, 1987-91; asst. county atty. Harris County, Houston, 1991-96, elected Harris county atty., 1996, re-elected, 2000; ptnr. Bracewell & Patterson, Houston, 2001—02; pvt. practice, 2002—; vice chair Harris County Housing Authority, 2003—05. Bd. dirs. U. St. Thomas, 2002—. Named Irish Person of Yr., 2000. Mem.: State Bar of Tex., Houston Bar Assn., KHS, Equestrian Order of Holy Sepulchre of Jerusalem, Irish Soc., 100 Club of Houston, Ancient Order of Hibernians, KC. Roman Catholic. Avocations: genealogy, Castlemahon history. Home: 643 W Forest Dr Houston TX 77079-6915 Office: 19221 I-45 South Conroe TX 77385 Office Phone: 281-296-9544. Personal E-mail: mick1996@swbell.net. Business E-Mail: mfleming@flemingattorneys.com.

FLEMING, PATRICIA STUBBS (PATSY FLEMING), artist; b. Phila., Mar. 17, 1936; d. Fredrick Douglass Stubbs and Marion Turner Stubbs Thomas; m. Harold S. Fleming, June 1958 (div. Feb. 1971); children: Douglass, Craig, Gordon. BA, Vassar Coll., 1957; postgrad., NYU, 1958-60, U. Pa., 1957-58, Pa. Acad. Fine Arts, 1957-58. Legis. asst. to reps. U.S. Ho. of Reps., Washington, 1971-77; asst. to sec. HEW, Washington, 1977-78, dir. intergovtl. and legis. affairs Office Civil Rights, 1979-80; asst. to sec. U.S. Dept. Edn., Washington, 1979-80, dep. asst. sec. legis., 1980-81; sr. pub. policy assoc. James H. Lowry & Assocs., Washington, 1981-83; chief staff Rep. Ted Weiss U.S. Ho. of Reps., Washington, 1983-86, profl. staff mem. subcom. human resources & intergovtl. rels, 1986-93; spl. asst. to sec. HHS, Washington, 1993-94; dir. Office Nat. AIDS Policy The White House, Washington, 1994-97, cons. on govt. rels. and AIDS policy and programs, 1997—2000; freelance artist Bethesda, Md., 2006—. Washington rep. Joint Co-sponsored UN Programme on HIV/AIDS, 1997-99; mem. bd. Prevention Works: Needle Exch. Program in the Nation's Capitol. One-person shows include NYU, Foundry Gallery, Washington, Anne C. Fisher Gallery, Washington; exhbns. include NYC, Washington and St. Petersberg, Russia, New Delhi, Cairo and numerous others. Democrat. Avocations: travel, music, reading.

Home and Studio: 6009 Massachusetts Ave Bethesda MD 20816-2041 Office Phone: 301-320-5420. E-mail: pfleming@erols.com.

FLEMING, PEGGY GALE, professional ice skater; b. San Jose, Calif., July 27, 1948; d. Albert Eugene and Doris Elizabeth (Deal) F.; m. Greg Jenkins, June 13, 1970; children: Andy, Todd. Student, Colo. Coll., 1966. Skating commentator for ABC Wide World of Sports; appears in commls. for Concord Watch Performer with Ice Capades, from 1968, Ice Follies; performer 7 TV spls.; guest appearance, Fantasy Island; Ambassador of goodwill, UNICEF; actor: (films) Blades of Glory, 2007. Nat. chmn. Easter Seals; trustee Womens Sports Found. Recipient Sports award ABC-TV, 1967; named Woman of Year Reader's Digest, 1969, Female Athlete of Year A.P., 1968; named to Colo. Hall of Fame, 1969 Mem. U.S. Figure Skating Assn. Clubs: Broadmoor Figure Skating (Colorado Springs, Colo.). Juvenile ice skating champion S.W. Pacific and Pacific Coast, 1960, novice champion, 1961, sr. champion, 1963, jr. champion S.W. Pacific, 1962; 2d place nat. novice champion, 1962, 3d nat. jr. champion, 1963; U.S. ladies champion, 1964-68; 2d place N.Am. competition, 1965; 3d place world championship competition, 1965; world champion, 1966, 67, 68; N.Am. ladies champion, 1967; 1st place gold medal for women's figure skating Olympic Games, 1968. Address: care William Morris Agy 151 S El Camino Dr Beverly Hills CA 90212-2704

FLEMING, PETER EMMET, JR., lawyer; b. Atlantic Highlands, NJ, Aug. 18, 1929; s. Peter Emmet and Anna (Sullivan) F.; m. Jane Breed, June 2, 1956 (dec.); children— Peter Emmet III, James M., William B., David W., Jane H. AB, Princeton U., 1951; LL.B., Yale U., 1958. Bar: N.Y. 1959, U.S. Dist. Ct. (so. and ea. dists.) N.Y. 1960, U.S. Ct. Appeals (2d cir.) 1963, U.S. Ct. Appeals (4th cir.) 1979, U.S. Supreme Ct. 1985. Assoc. Davis, Polk & Wardwell, NYC, 1958-61; asst. U.S. atty. U.S. dist. Ct. (so. dist.) N.Y., NYC, 1961-70; mem. Curtis, Mallet-Prevost Colt & Mosle, NYC, 1970—. Home: 122 Old Church Rd Greenwich CT 06830-4821 Office: Curtis Mallet-Prevost Colt & Mosle 101 Park Ave Fl 34 New York NY 10178-0061 Office Phone: 212-696-6008. Business E-Mail: pfleming@cm-p.com.

FLEMING, RENÉE L., opera singer; b. Indiana, Pa., Feb. 14, 1959; d. Edwin Davis Fleming and Patricia (Seymour) Alexander; m. Richard Lee Ross, Sept. 23, 1989 (div. 2000). BM in Music Edn., Potsdam State U., 1981; MM, Eastman Sch. Music, 1983; student, Juilliard Am. Opera Ctr., NYC, 1983—84, Juilliard Am. Opera Ctr., 1985—87; PhD (hon.), Juilliard, 2003. Exclusive rec. artist Decca Records, London, 1995—. Debut engagements include Spoleto Festival, Charleston and Italy, 1986-90, Houston Grand Opera & N.Y.C. Opera, 1988, 89, San Francisco Opera, 1991, Met. Opera, Paris Opera at the Bastille, 1991, Covent Garden, London, 1989, Teatro Colon Buenos Aires, 1991, Vienna State Opera, 1993, La Scala, 1993, Lyric Opera of Chgo., 1993, Paris Opera at Palais Garnier, 1996; author: The Inner Voice (also German, Japanese, French and U.K. publs.), 2004. Bd. trustees Carnegie Hall Corp., 2004—; mem. adv. bd. White Nights Found. Am., 2005—, Louise T. Blouin Found., 2005—. Decorated Chevalier de la Légion d'Honneur, 2005; winner Met. Opera Nat. Auditions, 1988; recipient George London prize, 1988, Richard Tucker award, 1990, Solti prize l'Acad. du Disque Lyrique, 1996, Prix Maria Callas, Academie due Disque Lyrique, 1997, Prize l'Acad. du Disque Lyrique, 1998, Lotos Medal of Merit, 2005; Fulbright scholar, Frankfurt, Germany, 1984-85, Classical Brits award for outstanding contbn. to music, 2004; named Vocalist of Yr. Mus. Am., 1997, Female Artist of the Yr., Classic Brits Awards, 2003, Prix Maria Callas, Acad. du Disque Lyrique, 2004; nominated 9 Grammy awards, 1997-2006; recipient 2 Grammy awards, 1999, 2003; 3 gramophone awards, 1999, Record of yr., Opera award, Recital award, Gift of Music award Orch. of St. Luke's, 2000; named one of top 10 classical singers of the 90s, AP, 2000; La Diva Renée dessert named in her honor by chef Daniel Boulud, 1999; Commandeur de l'Ordre des Arts et des Lettres, France, 2002; Renee Fleming iris introduced, 2004, Prix Toscanini, 2006, Echo award, 2006, Prix Marial Callas Orphee d'Or, 2007. Mem.: Royal Acad. Music (hon.). Office: care ML Falcone Pub Rels 155 W 68th St Apt 1114 New York NY 10023-5817

FLEMING, REX JAMES, meteorologist; b. Omaha, Apr. 25, 1940; s. Robert Leonard and Doris Mae (Burrows) F.; m. Kathleen Joyce Ferry, Sept. 3, 1969; children: Thane, Manon, Mark, Noel. BS, Creighton U., 1963; MS, U. Mich., 1968, PhD, 1970. Commd. 1t. U.S. Air Force, 1963, advanced through grades to capt., 1972; research scientist Offutt AFB, Nebr., 1963-67; sci. liaison to Nat. Weather Service for Air Weather Service, Suitland, Md., 1970-72; resigned, 1972; mgr. applications mktg. advanced sci. computer Tex. Instruments, Inc., Austin, 1972-75; dir. U.S. Project Office for Global Weather Expt., NOAA, Rockville, Md., 1975-80, Spl. Research Projects Office, 1980-82, Office of Climate and Atmospheric Research, 1983-84, Internat. Tropical Ocean and Global Atmosphere Project Office and Nat. Storm Program Office, 1984-86; pres. Tycho Tech. Inc., Boulder, Colo., 1986-87, Creative Concepts, Boulder, Colo., 1987-91; sr. mgr., coord. FAA rsch. Nat. Ctr. for Atmospheric Rsch., 1991-92, vis. scientist, 1987-88; NOAA, Boulder, 1993-2001; program mgr. U. Corp. for Atmospheric Rsch., 2001—04; pres. Global Aerospace, LLC, Boulder, Colo., 2005—. Contbr. articles to profl. jours. Recipient Gold Medal award Dept. Commerce, 1980 Fellow AAAS; mem. Am. Meteorol. Soc. (chmn. probability and statistics com. 1976-77), The Planetary Soc., Am. Geophys. Union (sec. atmospheric scis. sect. 1984-86). Republican. Patents for aerial sampler system, temparature sensor system for mobile patrforms; patents pending for an aerial sampler system, atmospheric turbulence analysis system and method, atmospheric turbulence analysis system, airplane system for an atmospheric turbulence analysis system. Home: 7225 Spring Dr Boulder CO 80303-5115 Office: NCAR PO Box 3000 Boulder CO 80307-3000 *One need only be inspired by its spring-morning freshness, stimulated by its magnificent variety of color and form, and humbled by the power of its ever-present energy, to be driven to unveil the secrets of our life-sustaining atmosphere.*

FLEMING, RHONDA, actress, singer; b. LA; d. Harold Cheverton and Effie (Graham) Louis; m. Darol W. Carlson; 1 child, Kent Lane. Student, pub. and pvt. schs., LA, Beverly Hills. Appeared in 40 motion pictures, including Spellbound, 1945, Spiral Staircase, 1945, Out of the Past, 1947, A Connecticut Yankee in King Arthur's Court, 1949, The Great Lover, 1949, The Eagle and the Hawk, 1950, Cry Danger, 1951, Last Outpost, 1951, Hong Kong, 1952, Tropic Zone, 1953, Tennessee's Partner, 1955, Gunfight at OK Corral, 1956, Slightly Scarlett, 1956, Home Before Dark, 1958, Pony Express, 1953, The Nude Bomb, 1980; Broadway debut in The Women, 1973; appeared in musical and plays, including The Boyfriend, 1975, Marriage Go Round, 1960, Bell, Book and Candle, 1962, Kismet at Music Center, 1976; sang Gershwin concert in; 10-week tour, 1963; starred in Las Vegas, Nev., 1959, one-woman concert at Hollywood Bowl, 1964, numerous guest appearances on TV series and talk shows including MacMillan and Wife, Love Boat; TV movies include The Last Hours Before Morning, 1975; NBC's Legends of the Screen, 1980, Metromedia Spl. Road to Hollywood, 1983, Wildest West Show of the Stars, 1986. Founder Rhonda Fleming Clinic for Women's Comprehensive Care and Rhonda Fleming Resource Ctr. for Women With Cancer at UCLA, PATH (People Assisting the Homeless) Rhonda Fleming Family Ctr.; benefactor Music Ctr.; supporter Childhelp USA, Achievement Rewards Coll. Scientists; life assoc. Pepperdine U.; founding mem. French Found. for Alzheimer Rsch.; adv. bd. Olive Crest Treatment Ctrs. for Abused Children; supporter Freedoms Found. at Valley Forge, City of Hope, Excellence in Media, SPCA, Humane Soc. USA; patron of the arts Music Ctr. Blue Ribbon; bd. dirs. World Opportunities Internat., St. John's Med. Ctr.; mem. nat. adv. cabinet Guideposts. Recipient award NCCJ, Gold Angel award Excellence in Media, Woman of the World award Childhelp, USA, Eve award Mannequins of the Assistance League, 1986, Our Lady of Perpetual Inspiration award; named Woman of Year City of Hope, Oper. Children, 1991, honoree of the Music Ctr. Club 100, 1992, UCLA Alumni Assn. Disting. Contbns. award to UCLA Cmty., 2000; Rhonda Fleming Rsch. fellowship for women's cancer established at City of Hope, 2000.

FLEMING, RICHARD H., finance executive; b. Milw., July 22, 1947; s. David M. and Mildred (Codere) F.; m. Diana Loane, Mar. 21, 1970; children: Douglas Codere, Petria Anne. BA, U. Pacific, 1969; MBA, Dartmouth, 1971. Fin. analyst Graco, Inc., Mpls., 1971-72, mgr. banking and fgn. exchange, 1972-73; fin. analyst Masonite Corp., Chgo., 1973-74, mgr. capital investment, 1974-77, asst. treas., 1977-82, treas., 1982-84, v.p. fin., chief fin. officer, 1985-89; dir. corp. fin. and asst. treas. USG Corp., Chgo., 1989-90, v.p., treas., 1991-94, v.p., CFO, 1994-95, sr. v.p., CFO, 1995-99, exec. v.p., CFO, 1999—. Trustee USG Found., 1989—; bd. dirs. Columbus McKinnon Corp. Bd. dirs. Family Care Services Met. Chgo., 1977—, pres. 1983-86; bd. dirs. Child Welfare League Am., Washington, 1987—, pres. 1999-2000. Alumni fellow U. Pacific Sch. Bus. Adminstrn. and Pub. Policy, 1990. Office: USG Corp PO Box 6721 125 S Franklin St Chicago IL 60680-6721 Home: Apt 2802 195 N Harbor Dr Chicago IL 60601-7532*

FLEMING, RONALD A., lawyer; b. May 24, 1967; BA summa cum laude, Columbia Univ., 1991, JD, 1991. Bar: NY 1992. Ptnr., co-chmn. Emerging Growth & Tech. practice Pillsbury Winthrop Shaw Pittman, NYC. Harlan Fiske Stone scholar. Mem.: Phi Beta Kappa. Office: Pillsbury Winthrop Shaw Pittman 1540 Broadway New York NY 10036 Office Phone: 212-858-1143. Office Fax: 212-858-1500. Business E-Mail: ron.fleming@pillsburylaw.com.*

FLEMING, SUZANNE MARIE, academic administrator, freelance/self-employed writer; b. Detroit, Feb. 4, 1927; d. Albert T. and Rose E. (Smiley) F. BS, Marygrove Coll., 1957; MS, U. Mich., 1960, PhD, 1963. Joined Congregation of Sisters Servants of Immaculate Heart of Mary, Roman Catholic Commn., 1945. Chmn. natural sci. div. Marygrove Coll., Detroit, 1970-75, v.p., dean, 1975-78, acad. v.p., 1978-80; asst. v.p. acad. affairs Eastern Mich. U., Ypsilanti, 1980-82, acting assoc. v.p. acad. affairs, 1982-83; provost, acad. v.p. Western Ill. U., Macomb, 1983-86; vice chancellor U. Wis., Eau Claire, 1986-89; freelance writer, 1989—. Vis. scholar U. Mich., 1989-2001; pres. Mich. Coll. Chemistry Tchrs. Assn., 1975; councilor Mich. Inst. Chemists, 1973-77; bd. dirs. Nat. Ctr. for Rsch. to Improve Postsecondary Teaching and Learning, 1988-90. Contbr. articles to profl. publs. NIH rsch. grantee, 1966—69. Home and Office: 2888 Cascade Dr Ann Arbor MI 48104-6659

FLEMING, THOMAS A., retired administrative assistant; b. Reading, Pa., 1933; m. Diane Rosinski, 1975; 1 child, Malcolm;children from previous marriage: Thomas, Sharon. BA in Religious Edn., William Tyndale Coll., 1964; MA in Spl. Edn., Ea. Mich. Univ. Spl. asst. to the provost Ea. Mich. U., Ypsilanti, Mich. Baptist min. With US Army N.G., 1950—55. Named Tchr. of Yr. Mich., 1991, Nat. Tchr. of Yr., 1992.

FLEMING, THOMAS JAMES, writer; b. Jersey City, July 5, 1927; s. Thomas James and Katherine (Dolan) F.; m. Alice Mulcahey, Jan. 19, 1951; children: Alice, Thomas, David, Richard. AB, Fordham U., 1950; postgrad., Sch. Social Work, 1950-51. Reporter Yonkers (N.Y.) Herald Statesman, 1951; asst. to Fulton Oursler, 1951-52, lit. executor estate, 1953; asso. editor Cosmopolitan mag., 1954-58, exec. editor, 1959-61; writer, 1961—. Author: (book) Now We Are Enemies, 1960, All Good Men, 1961, The God of Love, 1963, Beat the Last Drum, 1963, One Small Candle, 1964, King of the Hill, 1966, A Cry of Whiteness, 1967, West Point, The Men and Times of the U.S. Military Academy, 1969, The Man from Monticello, 1969, Romans Countrymen Lovers, 1969, The Sandbox Tree, 1970, The Man Who Dared the Lightning, 1971, The Forgotten Victory, 1973, The Good Shepherd, 1974, 1776: Year of Illusions, 1975, Liberty Tavern, 1976, Rulers of the City, 1977, New Jersey, 1977, Promises to Keep, 1978, A Passionate Girl, 1979, rev. edit., 2004, (book) The Officers' Wives, 1981, Dreams of Glory, 1983, rev. edit., 2001, (book) The Spoils of War, 1985, Time and Tide, 1987, Downright Fighting: The Story of Cowpens, 1988, Over There, 1992, Loyalties: A Novel of World War II, 1994, Remember The Morning, 1997, Liberty! The American Revolution, 1997, The Wages of Fame, 1998, Lights Along the Way, 1998, Hours of Gladness, 1999, Duel: Alexander Hamilton, Aaron Burr and the Future of America, 1999, The New Dealers' War: FDR and the War Within World War II, 2001, When This Cruel War is Over, 2001, Conquerors of the Sky, 2003, The Illusion of Victory, America World War I, 2003, The Louisiana Purchase, 2003, Mysteries of My Father: An Irish-American Memoir, 2005, Washington's Secret War: The Hidden History of Valley Forge, 2005 (Frances Tavern Best Book on Am. Revolution award, 2006), The Secret Trial of Robert E. Lee, 2006, Everybody's Revolution, 2006, The Perils of Peace: America's Struggle to Survive After Yorktown, 2007; editor: Affectionately Yours, George Washington, 1967, Benjamin Franklin, A Biography in His Own Words, 1972, The Living Land of Lincoln, 1980, The Secrets of Inchon, 2002; contbr. book Reader's Companion to American History, 1991, book Young Reader's Companion to American History, 1991, book Past Imperfect: History According to the Movies, 1995, book Forgotten Heroes, 1997, book What If, 1999, book To The Best of My Ability: The American Presidents, 2000, book What If, 2001; contbr. (book I Wish I Was There, 2006); contbr. also various TV scripts, articles, short stories; cons. (movie) The American Revolution The History Channel, 1994, prin. commentator Long Journey Home - The Irish in America, 1998, (TV films) C-Span In Depth, 2004. Chmn. N.Y. Am. Revolution Round Table, 1970-81, Sr. scholar, Nat. Ctr. for the Am. Revolution of Valley Forge. Recipient achievement award in comm.arts Fordham U., 1961, Encaenia award, 1965, Mass Media award NCCJ, 1963, Christopher award, 1970, Colonial Dames Am. ann. book award, 1970, 72, award of merit Am. Assn. for State and Local History, 1974, fiction award Nat. Cath. Press Assn., 1974, Best Book award Am. Revolution Round Table, 1975, 97, 99, award of recognition N.J. Hist. Commn., 1992, Burack award for lifetime achievement Boston U., 2001, Best Mag. Article award Army Hist. Found., 2002, Abraham Lincoln Lit. award Union League Club, 2003. Fellow N.J. Hist. Soc., Soc. Am. Historians (pres. 2007—); mem. Am. PEN (pres. 1971-73), The Century Assn. Office Phone: 212-988-9160. Personal E-mail: tflem37048@aol.com.

FLEMING, TOM, chef; Grad., Kendall Coll., 1990. Chef Everest, Chgo., Brasserie Jo, Lobster Ranch, Lombardi Mare, Pappas Brothers' Steak House; stage Paul Bocuse, France, L'Auberge de l'Ille, France; exec. chef Old Hickory Steakhouse, Tex., Riviera, Dallas; chef de cuisine Mediterranneo, Dallas; host chef Central 214, Dallas. Named one of Dallas' Rising Stars, StarChefs.com, 2007. Office: Central 214 5680 N Ctrl Expressway Dallas TX 75206 Office Phone: 214-443-9339. Office Fax: 214-443-9372.*

FLEMING, TOMMY WAYNE, lawyer; b. Canyon, Tex., Nov. 13, 1941; s. Benjamin Dalby and Willie Mildred (Vineyard) F.; m. Sally Ann Moore, Nov. 30, 1968; children: Benjamin Dalby II, Hunter Leah. Student, West Tex. State U., 1960-61; BBA, U. Tex., 1964, JD, 1966. Bar: Tex. 1969, U.S. Dist. Ct. (so. dist.) Tex. 1971, U.S. Supreme Ct. 1978, U.S. Ct. Appeals (5th cir.) 1983. Asst. dist. atty. Office Dist. Atty., Amarillo, Tex., 1969-70; asst. criminal dist. atty. Cameron County Criminal Dist. Atty.'s Office, Brownsville, Tex., 1970-72; ptnr. Wiech, Lewis & Fleming, Brownsville, 1972-74, Wiech, Fleming, Hamilton & Uribe, Brownsville, 1974-82, Wiech & Black, Brownsville, 1982-89, Atlas & Hall, Brownsville, 1989-94, Fleming, Hewitt & Olvera, Brownsville, 1994-98, Fleming & Olvera, Brownsville, 1998-2001, Fleming & Hernandez, Brownsville, 2001—. Mem. Supreme Ct. Grievance Oversight Com., 1983-2000. Chmn. Brownsville Cmty. Health Clinic, 1978-79. 1st lt. U.S. Army, 1966-69. Fellow Tex. Bar Found. (life, bd. dirs. 1984-87); mem. Tex. Assn. Bank Counsel, State Bar Tex. (bd. dirs. 1981-84), Cameron County bar Assn. (bd. dirs. 1972-79, pres. 1979-80), Brownsville Hist. Assn. (bd. dirs. 1977-80). Home: 915 Santa Ana Ave Rancho Viejo TX 78575-9749 Office: Fleming & Hernandez 1650 Paredes Line Rd Ste 102 Brownsville TX 78521-1602 Office Phone: 956-982-4404.

FLEMING, WAYNE, professional hockey coach; b. Snowlake, Man., Can. m. Carolyn Fleming; children: Angie, Allie, Jarett, Jordan. Asst. coach U. Man. Bisons, 1979—80, head coach, 1980—87, 1988—90; asst. coach/gen. mgr. Can. Nat. Team, 1990—92; head coach Leksand IF, Swedish Elite League, 1992—94; asst. coach NY Islanders, 1997—99, Phoenix Coyotes, 1999—2001, Phila. Flyers, 2002—06, Calgary Flames, 2006—. V.p. hockey, head coach Nat. Men's Team, Can. Hockey Assn.; mem. coaching staff Team Can., Olympic Games, Albertville, France, 1992, assoc. coach, Salt Lake City, 2002, Torino, Italy, 06, Team Can., World Cup of Hockey, 2004. Named Coach of the Yr. CIAU, 1983-84, GPAC Coach of the Yr., 1981-82, 83-84. Office: Calgary Flames PO Box 1540 Stn M Calgary AB Canada

FLEMING, WENDELL HELMS, mathematician, educator; b. Guthrie, Okla., Mar. 7, 1928; s. James Lucian and Helen (Helms) F.; m. Florence Tatum, Apr. 4, 1948; children: Randall, Daniel, William. BS, Purdue U., 1948, MS, 1949, D honoris causa, 1991; PhD, U. Wis., 1951. Mathematician RAND Corp., 1951-55, cons., 1960-65; asst. prof. Purdue U., 1955-58; mem. faculty Brown U., 1958—, prof. math., 1963—, prof. applied math., 1969-95, chmn. dept., 1965-68, 82-85, 1991-94; prof. emeritus, 1995—. Author: Functions of Several Variables, 1965, (with R.W. Rishel) Deterministic and Stochastic Optimal Control, 1975, (with H.M. Soner) Controlled Markov Processes and Viscosity Solutions, 1992; editor SIAM Rev. NSF fellow, 1968-69; Guggenheim fellow, 1976-77 Mem. Am. Math. Soc. (chmn. com. on employment and ednl. policy 1975-77, Steele prize 1987), Soc. Indsl. and Applied Math. (Reid prize 1994), Am. Acad. Arts and Sci. Home: 9 Dolly Dr Bristol RI 02809-1578 Office: Brown U Div Applied Math Providence RI 02912-0001 E-mail: whf@dam.brown.edu.

FLEMING, WILLIAM CARY, retired physician, consultant; b. Lee Hall, Va., Jan. 16, 1918; s. Thomas Hayes and Martha (Kirby) F.; m. Mabel Clare Green, Mar. 19, 1944; children: Martha Frances, Sharon Anne, Joan Marie. BS in Chemistry, U. Va., 1942, MD, 1945. Diplomate: Am. Bd. Phys. Medicine and Rehab. Intern Del. Hosp., Wilmington, 1945-46; gen. practice Glasgow, Va., 1948-49; mem. staff student health U. Kans., 1949-51; indsl. physician E.I. duPont de Nemours & Co., Inc., Waynesboro, Va., 1951-53; resident phys. medicine and rehab. VA Hosp.-Med. Coll. Va., Richmond, 1953-56; phys. medicine and rehab. physician VA hosps., Richmond, 1956-58, Pitts., 1959, Coral Gables, Fla., 1959-64, VA Hosp., Birmingham, Ala., 1970-78, cons. 1978-88, ret., 1988; prof. phys. medicine and rehab. U. Ala. Med. Sch., 1964-88, chmn. dept., 1964-70; physiatrist in chief Univ. Hosp. Birmingham, 1964-70. Med. dir. Spain Rehab. Ctr., Birmingham, 1964-69, physiatrist, 1969-88, ret.; dir. U. Ala. Rehab. Research and Tng. Ctr., 1966-69,; med. staff, chmn. med. bd. Lakeshore Rehab. Hosp., 1973—88; cons. staff Children's and St. Vincent's Hosps., 1965—88; cons. rehab. pavillion, courtesy staff Druid City Hosp., Tuscaloosa, Ala., 1984—88; courtesy staff Med. Ctr. East, Birmingham, 1989—90, med. dir. rehab. St. Francis Hosp., Topeka, 1989-91; dir. chronic illness project, Dade County, Fla., 1962-63; mem. med. adv. bd. Birmingham Vis. Nurse Assn., 1965-86, Central Ala. chpt. Nat. Multiple Sclerosis Soc., 1966—93, chmn., 1976, 85-87; bd. dirs. N. Central Ala. Occupational Rehab. Ctr., 1966-70, 73-79, chmn. bd., 1978-79; surveyor Commn. on Accreditation Rehab. Facilities, 1984—93; mem. State Profl. Adv. Council for Home Health Service, 1986-88. Bd. dirs. Birmingham Civic Ballet, 1971-77. Served to capt. M.C. AUS, 1946-48. Mem. AMA, So. Med. Assn. (chmn. sect. 1966-67), Ala. Med. Assn., Am. Acad. Phys. Medicine and Rehab., So. Soc. Phys. Medicine (founding mem., chmn. 1970-72), Ala. Soc. Phys. Medicine and Rehab. (founding mem., v.p., pres.), Assn. Acad. Physiatrists, Raven Soc. (v.p. 1942-43), Assn. Med. Rehab. Dirs. and Coordinators (cert. bd. 1964—87), Alpha Chi Sigma, Nu Sigma Nu. Clubs: Poinsettia Men's (founding mem. 1970, pres. 1971-72), Shoal Creek, The Club (Birmingham, Ala.). Lodges: Rotary (Paul Harris fellow). Spl. research rehab. aspects stroke, emphysema, kidney disease, heart disease, spinal cord injury, electromyography. Home: 3528 Belle Meade Way Birmingham AL 35223-1522

FLEMING, WILLIAM SLOAN, energy and computer company executive; b. Long Beach, Calif., Aug. 13, 1937; s. William Sloan and Helen Jean (Disler) Fleming; m. Jacquline M. Carrio, Mar. 9, 1960; children: Katherine A., Kimberly A. BSME, Calif. Maritime Acad., 1958; MBA, Syracuse U., 1970. Commd. ensign USN, 1958, advanced through grades to lt., 1967, attack pilot, 1958—67, disabled in the line of duty, ret., 1967; mech. engr. Carrier Corp., Syracuse, NY, 1967—70; regional sales mgr. Rheem Mfg., Atlanta, 1970—71; market devel. supr. Owens Corning Fiberglas, Toledo, 1971—73; pres. W. S. Fleming & Assocs., Inc., Syracuse, 1975—86, Fleming Group, Syracuse, 1986—87, CEO, chmn. bd., 1987—94; bus. devel. mgr., energy systems group Sci. Applications Internat. Corp. SAIC/Fleming Group, Syracuse, 1994—96; bus. devel. mgr. Sci. Applications Internat. Corp./Energy Sys. Group, 1996—97; exec. v.p. Jacwill Svcs. Inc., Cazenovia, NY, St. Petersburg, Fla., 1997—2007, owner, 2007—. Pres. Enterlog Sys., Inc., Syracuse, 1985—94; chmn. bd. Assn. Intelligent Sys. Tech., Inc., Syracuse, 1986—90. Author: Singer Energy & Economic Building Simulation Computer Program; contbr. articles to profl. jours. Recipient Energy awards, Ctrl. N.Y., 1981. Fellow: ASHRAE (life; chmn. tech. com. 9.6, sys. energy utilization 1981—83, chmn. ad hoc com. 90, energy stds. 1983—84, chmn. tech. com. 6.7, solar energy utilization 1984—86, chmn. nat. program com. 1985—86, mem. edn. coun. 1989—90, rsch. and tech. com. 1991—95, chmn. spl. publs. com. 1998—99, rsch. adminstrn. com. 2000—01, mem. handbook com. 2001—05, chmn. handbook fund subcom. 2004—05, chmn. handbook com. 2005—06, honors and awards com. 2007—, mem. nom. com. 2007—, Disting. Svc. award 2006); mem.: DAV, Assn. Energy Engrs. (charter, 1 of 34 in Hall of Fame), Mil. Officers Assn., Am. Legion. Roman Catholic. Avocations: skiing, boating. Office: Jacwill Svcs PO Box 8249 Saint Petersburg FL 33738-8249 Personal E-mail: flemg@aol.com.

FLEMING, WILLIAM WRIGHT, JR., pharmacology educator, department chairman; b. Washington, Jan. 30, 1932; s. William Wright and Esme (Reeder) F.; m. Dolores D. Atchison, Sept. 1, 1952; children: Lisa Marie, Jennifer Amelia, David William. AB cum laude, Harvard U., 1954; PhD (Procter fellow), Princeton U., 1957. Mem. faculty W.Va. U. Med. Ctr., Morgantown, 1960—, prof. pharmacology, 1966—, chmn. dept., 1966-86, Mylan Chmn. of Pharmacology and Toxicology, 1986-99, prof. emeritus, 1999—. Vis. prof. U. Melbourne, Australia, 1969, St. George's Hosp. Med. Sch. U. London, 1978, Flinders U., Adelaide, Australia, 1985, 87, U. Adelaide, 1987; adj. prof. pharmacology U. Pitts. Sch. Medicine, 2005-; cons. Mead Johnson Rsch. Ctr., Evansville, Ind., 1970-77, Spriggs & Hollingsworth Law Firm, Washington, 2004-06; mem. pharmacology-toxicology rsch. program. Nat. Inst. Gen. Med. Scis., NIH, 1973-77, chmn., 1975-77; mem. drug abuse rsch. rev. com. Nat. Inst. Drug Abuse, 1985-89; mem. pharmacology study sect., div. rsch. grants NIH, 1990-94. Mem. editl. bd. Jour. Pharmacology and Exptl. Therapeutics, 1966-85, Life Scis., 1978-90; contbr. articles to profl. jours. USPHS postdoctoral fellow Harvard U., 1957-60; Fogarty sr. internat. fellow, 1978; recipient P.L. MacLachlan award W.Va. U. Med. Sch., 1964, 67, 78, 89, 92, 97, 99; named Outstanding Tchr., W.Va. U. Found., 1978. Mem. AAAS, Am. Soc. Pharmacology and Exptl. Therapeutics (councilor 1975-78, pres. 1981-82, chmn. bd publs. trustees 1984-90, Otto Krayer award 1986, Croker Meml. lectr. 1988, Torald Sollman award 1999), Assn. Med. Sch. Pharmacology (councilor 1977-79, treas. 1977-78, pres. 1986-88), Fedn. Am. Socs. for Exptl. Biology (dir. 1980-83), Internat. Union Pharmacology (del. 1980-83, 91-94, mem. internat. adv. com. for Congress of Pharmacology 1987, exec. com. 1994-98, 2002—06, pres. 1998-2002). Home: HC 3 Box 22 A Tionesta PA 16353 Office: WVa U Health Scis Ctr Dept Physiology & Pharmacology Morgantown WV 26506 Personal E-mail: wfle216184@aol.com.

FLEMING-BROWN, JULIE A., attorney, legal consultant; b. Atlanta, Dec. 22, 1968; d. Julian Denver and Sidney Howell Fleming; m. William M. Brown, Aug. 26, 2004. BA, Vanderbilt U., Nashville, 1990; JD, Emory U., Atlanta, 1993; BS, Ga. State U., Atlanta, 1998. Bar: Ga. 1993, DC 2005, Fla. 2005, registered: US Patent and Trademark Office (patent atty.) 1998. Law clk. US Dist. Ct. (no. dist.) Ga., Atlanta, 1993—95; assoc. Law Offices B.J. Powell, Atlanta, 1998—99, Jones Day, Atlanta, 1999—2005, Allen, Dyer, Doppelt, Milbrath & Gilchrist, Orlando, Fla., 2005; founder Fleming Brown Coaching, Orlando, 2005—; of counsel Keegan Fed. & Assoc., Atlanta, 2006—. Fellow: Am. Bar Found.; mem.: ABA (chair biotech. com. sect. sci. and tech. law 1997—2002, coun. 1999—2004, spl. com. on bioethics and the law 2000—06, chair life scis. and phys. scis. divsn. 2001—04, mem. edtl. bd. The SciTech Lawyer 2004—06, editor-in-chief 2007—). Office: 3610 Cherry Hill Dr Orlando FL 32822 Home Phone: 404-374-7500; Office Phone: 800-758-6214. Fax: 404-348-4202. Business E-Mail: jfb@juliieflemingbrown.com.

FLEMINGS, MERTON CORSON, engineering educator, materials scientist; b. Syracuse, NY, Sept. 20, 1929; s. Merton C. and Marion (Dexter) F.; m. Elizabeth Goodridge, Sept. 7, 1956 (div. 1976); children: Anne, Peter; m. R. Elizabeth ten Grotenhuis, Feb. 20, 1977; children: Cecily, Elspeth. SB, MIT, Boston, 1951, SM, 1952, ScD, 1954; PhD (hon.), Swiss Fed. Inst. Tech., Lausanne, 2004. Mem. faculty MIT, Cambridge, 1956—70, ABEX prof. Metallurgy, 1970—75, Ford prof. engring., 1975—81, dir. materials processing ctr., 1979—82, Toyota prof. materials processing, 1981—94, Toyota prof. emeritus, dept. materials sci. and engring., 1994—, dept. head materials sci. and engring., 1982—95; dir. MIT-Singapore Alliance, 1999—2001, Lemelson-MIT Program, Cambridge, Mass., 2001—. Vis. prof. U. Tokyo, 1989, Ecole des Mines de Paris, 1996; bd. dir. Hitchiner Corp., Metal Casting Tech., Inc., Silk Road Project, Inc. Author: Foundry Engineering, 1959; Solidification Processing, 1974. Contbr. numerous articles on metallurgy to profl. jours. Mem. Mass. Gov.'s Coun. Econ. Growth and Tech., 1994-2000. Recipient Simpson Gold medal Am. Foundrymen's Soc., 1961, Henri Sainte-Claire Deville medal Soc. Francaise de Metallurgie, 1977, John Chipman award, Am. Inst. of Mining, Metallurgical, and Petroleum Engineers, (AIME) 1980, James Douglas Gold medal, AIME, 1985, Merton C. Fleming award, Worcester Polytechnic Inst., 1991, Herbert J. Holloman award Acta Metallurgica, 1997, David Turnbull lectureship Materials Rsch. Soc., 1997, Benjamin Franklin medal in Materials Engring., 2007. Fellow Minerals, Metals & Materials Soc. (Leadership award 1990, Bruce Chalmers award 1993, Educator award 1999), ASM Internat. (bd. trustees 1994-97, Henry Marion Howe medal 1973, 90, Albert Sauveur Achievement award, 1978, Edward DeMille Campbell Meml. lectr. 1990, Albert Einstein White Disting. Tchr. award, 2006); mem. Am. Inst. Metall. Engrs. (hon.; Mathewson Gold medal 1969), Am. Acad. Arts and Scis., Japan Foundrymen's Soc. (hon.), Iron and Steel Inst. Japan (hon., Yukawa Meml. lectr. 1985, Tawara award 2000), Italian Metall. Assn. (Luigi Losana Gold medal 1986), Japan Inst. Metals (hon., Gold medal 2005), Nat. Acad. Engring., Fed. Materials Socs. (Nat. Materials Advancement award 1999), Korean Acad. Sci. and Tech. Achievements include patents in field. Home: 975 Memorial Dr Apt 605 Cambridge MA 02138-5803 Office: Dept Materials Sci and Engring MIT 4-415 Cambridge MA 02139 Office Phone: 617-253-3233. Business E-Mail: flemings@mit.edu.*

FLEMMING, DAVID PAUL, biologist; b. Kittanning, Pa., Oct. 23, 1953; s. Paul Ross and Jeanne Marie (Seaton) F.; m. Diane Frances MacKenzie, Sept. 17, 1983; children: Daniel Robert, Peter David. BS in Biology, Grove City Coll., 1975; MS in Biology, Bowling Green State U., 1977. Child care worker George Jr. Rep., Grove City, Pa., 1978-79; park naturalist State of Pa.-McConnell's Mill State Park, Portersville, 1979; biologist sect. 7 U.S. Fish & Wildlife Svc., Washington, 1979-80, Atlanta, 1980-83, recovery coord. Denver, 1983-87, biologist endangered species Vero Beach, Fla., 1987-88, chief divsn. endangered species Atlanta, 1988-96, chief ecol. svcs., 1997-98, ecol. svcs. supr., 1998—. Contbg. author: Conservation and Resource Management, 1993. Asst. coach T-ball and soccer YMCA, Lawrenceville, Ga., 1991—92, premier soccer coach Snellville, Ga., 1995—2001; USS Ofcl., 1996—2003. Business E-Mail: dave_flemming@fws.gov.

FLESCHER, SHARON, art historian, educator; d. Harry and Esther Flescher. BA in English Lit., Barnard Coll., NYC; MA in English Lit., NYU; MA in Art History, Columbia U., NYC, PhD in Art History, 1977. Program officer Nat. Endowment for Humanities, DC, 1983—86; dir. grants & programs The Equitable Found., NYC, 1987—91; dir. Heineman Galleries, NYC, 1993—94; dir. instl. rels. Ctrl. Park Conservatory, NYC, 1996—98; exec. dir., editor-in-chief Internat. Found. for Art Rsch., NYC, 1998—. Adj. assoc. prof. NYU, NYC, 1993—; cons. development & marketing, NY, 1991—96. Author: (book) Zacharie Artruc: Critic, Artist & Japoniste, 1977; contbr. articles to numerous journs. & mags. Bd. mem. Am. Globe Theatre, NY, 1991—96. Mem.: Art Table, Am. Assn. Museums, Coll. Art Assn., Am. Cancer Soc. (bd. mem. 1989—96). Avocations: piano, travel. Office: Internat Found Art Rsch 500 Fifth Ave Ste 935 New York NY 10110

FLESHMAN, JAMES W., medical association administrator; b. New Orleans, Aug. 2, 1954; BA summa cum laude, Wash. U., 1975; MD, Wash. U., St. Louis, 1980. Surgery residency Jewish Hosp., St. Louis, 1980—86; fellowship colon & rectal surgery U. Toronto, 1986—87; now prof. surgery Wash. U. Sch. of Medicine, St. Louis; chief colon & rectal surgery. Mem.: Am. Bd. Surgery, Am. Bd. Colon & Rectal Surgery (sec.). Office: Wash U Sch of Medicine Box 8109 660 S Euclid Campus Saint Louis MO 63110 Home Phone: 314-878-9030; Office Phone: 314-454-7204.

FLESSNER, PAUL, information technology executive; b. Roberts, IL, Jan. 1959; m. Sue Flessner; children: Andy, Jonathan. BS in Computer Sci. & Bus. Adminstrn., Ill. State U., 1981. With Microsoft, 1994—, sr. v.p. .NET enterprise servers divsn. Redmond, Wash., sr. v.p., server platform div. Mem. bus. leadership team Microsoft, leader devel. & coord. combined enterprise bus. strategy plan. Office: One Microsoft Way Redmond WA 98052-6399

FLETCHER, ANTHONY LEE, lawyer; b. Washington, Dec. 12, 1935; s. Robert J. and Lyndell (Pickett) F.; m. Juliana Schump, Sept. 3, 1960 (div. 1977); children: Leigh Anne Grinstead, Kristin Marie Giffin, Julie Bowen Cimino; m. Zelda L. Fletcher, Mar. 30, 1986. BA, Princeton U., 1957; JD, Harvard U., 1962. Bar: NY 1963, U.S. Ct. Appeals (2d cir.) 1966, U.S. Ct. Appeals (7th cir.) 1966, U.S. Supreme Ct. 1966, U.S. Ct. Appeals (3d cir.) 1969, U.S. Ct. Appeals (fed. cir.) 1972, U.S. Ct. Appeals (5th cir.) 1973, U.S. Ct. Appeals (1st cir.) 1981, U.S. Ct. Appeals (9th cir.) 1983. Assoc. Simpson Thacher & Bartlett, NYC, 1962-71, Conboy, Hewitt, O-Brien & Boardman, NYC, 1971-74, ptnr., 1974-86, Hunton & Williams, NYC, 1986-97; prin. Fish & Richardson P.C., NYC, 1997—2002, sr. counsel, 2003—. Editor-in-chief Trademark Reporter, 1982-84; contbr. articles to profl. jours. With infantry US Army, 1957—59. Mem. Internat. Trademark Assn. (bd. dirs. 1983-85, Pres.'s award 2003). Episcopalian. Office: Fish & Richardson PC 153 E 53d St New York NY 10022 Business E-Mail: fletcher@fr.com.

FLETCHER, BETTY BINNS, federal judge; b. Tacoma, Mar. 29, 1923; BA, Stanford U., 1943; LLB, U. Wash., 1956. Bar: Wash. 1956. Mem. firm Preston, Thorgrimson, Ellis, Holman & Fletcher, Seattle, 1956—79; judge US Ct. Appeals (9th cir.), Seattle, 1979—98, sr. judge, 1998—. Mem.: ABA (Margaret Brent award 1992), Fed. Judges Assn. (past pres.), Am. Law Inst., Wash. State Bar Assn., Phi Beta Kappa, Order of Coif. Office: US Ct Appeals 9th Cir 1200 6th Ave 21st Fl Seattle WA 98101*

FLETCHER, BILL, JR., political organization executive, activist; Attended, Harvard U. Organizer Dist. 65-united Auto Workers; org. sec., admin. dir. Nat. Postal Mail Handlers Union; vice-pres. internat. trade unit devel. prog. George Meany Ctr./ Nat. Labor Coll. AFL-CIO; edn. dir., asst. to pres. AFL-CIO; pres. TransAfrica Forum, 2002—06. Adj. faculty U. Mass.-Boston. Co-chair United for Peace and Justice; founder Black Radical Congress. Named one of 100 Most Influential Black Americans, Ebony mag., 2006. Office: BRC Nat Office PO Box 24795 Saint Louis MO 63115 also: United for Peace and Justice PO Box 607 New York NY 10108 Office Phone: 202-223-1960. Office Fax: 202-223-1966.

FLETCHER, DENISE KOEN, strategic and financial consultant; b. Istanbul, Turkey, Aug. 31, 1948; came to U.S., 1967, naturalized, 1976; d. Moris and Kety (Barkey) Koen; m. Robert B. Fletcher, Nov. 11, 1969; children— David, Kate. AB (Coll. scholar), Wellesley Coll., 1969; M in City Planning, Harvard U., 1972. Analyst Ea. div. Getty Oil Co., NYC, 1972-73, sr. analyst, 1973-74, cash mgmt. and bldg. supr., 1974-76, Getty Oil Co. (Eastern), 1976; asst. treas. N.Y. Times Co., NYC, 1976-80, treas., 1980-88; pres. Fletcher Assocs. Inc., Larchmont, NY, 1988-96; CEO Comm. Venture Group, Ltd., NYC, 1989-90; v.p., CFO Bowne & Co., 1996-98, sr. v.p., CFO, 1998—2000; exec. v.p., CFO Mastercard, 2000—03; sr. v.p., CFO Davita, Inc., 2004—05; CFO, exec. v.p. fin. Vulcan Inc., 2005—. Bd. dirs. Unisys Corp. Bd. dirs. Overseas Edn. Found. Internat., 1989-90, Boy Scouts Am., Exploring, 1991-93; bd. dirs., trustee and v.p. bd. dirs., exec. com. YWCA, N.Y., 1987-2002, Girl Scouts USA, 2000-02; mem. budget com. City of Larchmont, N.Y., 1981-83, chmn. zoning bd. appeals, 1987—, mem. selection com., 1985-87; mem. alumni exec. coun. Harvard U. Sch. Govt., 1982-87. Mellon scholar, 1970 Mem. Academy of Women Achievers, The Business Leadership Coun., Fin. Execs. Internat., Fin. Women's Assn., Women's Forum, Treasurers Club N.Y., Harvard Club (N.Y.C.), Phi Beta Kappa.

FLETCHER, DONALD RODGERS, writer, religious studies educator; b. Ventnor, NJ; s. Archibald Grey and Jessie (Rodgers) Fletcher; m. Martha Clayton Bradway, May 19, 1942; children: Donna Poole, Sylvia, Thomas, Marilyn Keith, Alan, Lawrence Fletcher-Hill. BA in English, Princeton U., 1939; MDiv, Princeton Theol. Seminary, 1943; PhD in English, Princeton U., 1951. Ordained Presby. Elizabeth, 1943. Fgn. missionary Presbyn. Ch., Chile, 1944—56, field rep. Caribbean, 1956—60; tchr. bibl. studies U. Tex., Austin, 1960—65; chair, divsn. of humanities Stillman Coll., Tuscaloosa, Ala., 1965—67; sec. of continuing edn. Presbyn. Bd. of Christian Edn., Phila., 1967—73; tchr. English Cherry Hill H.S. West, Cherry Hill, 1973—86; sr. pastor Rossmoor Cmty. Ch., Monroe, NJ, 1993—99; ret., 1999. Interim pastor St. Paul's Presbyn. Ch., Laurel Springs, NJ, 1978—79; organizing pastor Bethel Presbyn. Ch., 1981—83; supply pastor First Presbyn. Ch., Janvier, NJ, 1987—93. Author: Gates of Brass, 1942, (book) I, Lukas Wrote the Book, 2003, View from the Playroom Floor, 2005. Elected mem. Sch. Bd., Cherry Hill, NJ, 1970—73; mem., officer Kiwanis Club Rossmoor, Monroe, NJ, 1998—; dir. Mutual 15, Rossmoor, Monroe, 2003—06. Recipient Disting. Alumnus, Princeton U., 1979. Mem.: U.S. Croquet Assn. Democrat. Presbyterian. Avocations: writing, poetry, watercolor, sailing. Office Phone: 609-860-0981. Personal E-mail: donmarflet@verizon.net.

FLETCHER, DONNA ANGELLA, secondary school educator; b. Spanish Town, St. Catherine, Jamaica, Jan. 17, 1973; d. Melvin Fletcher and Beverly Vinnetta Thaxter, Cebert Glenn (Stepfather). BA, SUNY, Stony Brook, 1995; MA, EdM, Columbia U., NYC, 1997. Cert. 7-12 English tchr. NY, 1999, 7-12 social studies tchr. NY, 2003. Classroom tchr. NYC Bd. Edn., 1997—2004, 2007; mentor tchr. NYC Dept. of Edn., 2004—. Home instrn. tchr. NYC Bd. of Edn., NYC, 2000—04; youth coord., sec. Bright Horizon Women's Group, 2007. Mem. Rainbow PUSH Coalition, NYC, 2005—06; master guide, tchr. Adventist Youth/Pathfinder, Bronx, NY, 2001—03; mem. Faithful Youth Challengers, Roosevelt, NY, 2003—06. Mem.: Nat. Coun. Social Studies, Nat. Coun. Tchrs. English, Schomburg Ctr., Kappa Delta Pi. Democrat. Seventh Day Adventist. Avocations: writing, reading, travel, opera, theater. Home: 276 Tudor St Waterbury CT 06704 Office: NYC Dept Edn Brooklyn NY 11201 Personal E-mail: dnnfletcher@aol.com.

FLETCHER, DOROTHY JEAN, hospital administrator, educator; b. Cleve., May 14, 1932; d. Melvin Albert Heidloff and Dorothy Florence Geiger; m. Archibald Eaton Fletcher, Jr., Oct. 9, 1932; children: David Jeffrey, Sally, Thomas Eaton. Degree in Nursing, St. Luke's Hosp., Cleve., 1953; BS in Health Studies, Barat Coll., Lake Forest, Ill., 1981; MA in Human Resource Devel., Webster U., St. Louis, 1986. RN Ill., cert. addictions counselor, Ill., addictions nurse, Ill.; ordained Presbyn. Ch., 1999. From staff nurse to discharge planning RN Ctrl. DuPage Hosp., Winfield, Ill., 1972—75, discharge planning RN, 1975—76; dir. nursing Nursing Home, Waukegan, Ill., 1981—82; from staff nurse to case mgr. behavioral svcs. Highland Pk. Hosp., Ill., 1982—94, case mgr. behavioral svcs., 1992—94. Mem. long range planning com. Sch. Dist. 65, Lake Bluff, 2003—. Vol. Lake County Forest Preserves, Ill., 1994—97; elder Presbyn. Ch., Lake Forest, 1999, chmn. program, 1995—2003; bd. dirs. Lake Bluff Libr., Ill., 1985—90. Recipient Outstanding Alumni award, Barat Coll., 2003, Mother Burke award, 2003. Mem.: LWV (chmn. voting com. 2004—05), Shields Township Dems. (observer sch. dist. voting 2002—), Lake Forest Lake Bluff Arts (assoc.), Botanic Gardens (docent 1995—). Democrat. Presbyn. Avocations: history, genealogy, reading, baseball, gardening. Home: 323 Park Ln Lake Bluff IL 60044

FLETCHER, DOUGLAS CHARLES, lawyer; b. Rockford, Ill., Mar. 5, 1943; s. Fred Leland and Dorothy Edwards Fletcher; children: Adrian, Lauren, Robin. BA in Econs. and Engring., U. Nev., Reno, 1969, MBA in Fin. cum laude, 1972; JD, U. of Pacific, 1975; postgrad., Colo. State U., 1976. Bar: Nev. 1975, U.S. Ct. Appeals (9th cir.) 1976. Exec. v.p. PanWorld Engring., 1967-68; design engr. Nev. Bell, 1968-70; economist Sierra Pacific Power Co., 1970-72, gen. counsel, 1975-78; operating trustee William Lear Motors Co., 1978-79; ptnr. Leslie Gray & Assocs., 1979-81; oper. trustee Horseshoe Club Casinos, 1981-82, Mapes Hotel and Money Tree Casinos, 1982-85; owner, ptnr. Douglas C. Fletcher, Ltd., 1985—; operating receiver Echo Summit Tahoe Ski Resort, 1989-92. Advisor U. Nev. Grad. Bus. Sch., Reno, 1976-85; mem. U.S. Trustee Panel, 1978-95; judge pro tem Reno Mcpl. Ct., 1980-82. Author: Bond Reverse Yield Gaps of Public Utilities, 1972. Mem. ctrl. planning com. Republican Party of Washoe County, 1978-82; bd. dirs. Washoe County Youth Found., Reno, 1983-92, Eagles Nest Assn., Reno, 1998; founder, bd. dirs. Sierra League, Reno, 1989-99; bd. dirs., pres. ski team advisors U. Nev., Reno, 1982—. Mem. No. Nev. Bankruptcy Bar Assn. (founding mem.), Washoe County Bar Assn., State Bar Nev. (environ. law com. 1975—), Reno Tennis Club (pres., bd. dirs.), U.S. Ski Coaches Assn. (cert.), Reno Ski and Recreation Club (bd. dirs., pres. 1982—), Prospectors Club (bd. dirs.), Prof. Ski Instr. of Am. (cert.), Sigma Nu, Phi Kappa Phi, Beta Gamma Sigma. Office: 20 Sharps Cir Reno NV 89509-8009 Personal E-mail: fletchlaw1@aol.com.

FLETCHER, ERNIE (ERNEST LEE FLETCHER), governor, former congressman; b. Mt. Sterling, Ky., Nov. 12, 1952; m. Glenna Foster; children: Rachael, Benjamin. BS, U. Ky., 1974, MD with distinction, 1984. Physician, Lexington, Ky., 1984—96; CEO St. Joseph Med. Found., Lexington, 1997—99; mem. from 78th dist. Ky. Ho. Reps., 1994—96; mem. U.S. Congress from 6th Dist. Ky., 1999—2003; gov. State of Ky., Frankfort, 2003—. Mem. Ho. Budget Com., Agr. Com., Com. on Edn. and the Workforce (vice chmn. subcom. on Employer-Employee Rels.); elected freshman liaison to the Ho. Leadership; chmn. bd. So. States Energy; bd. dirs. Achieve, Inc. Served on numerous coms. including the Ky. Commn. on Poverty and the Task Force on Higher Edn.; chosen by gov. to play an important leadership role in reforming Ky.'s ailing health care sys.; lay min. Porter Meml. Baptist Ch.; vol. in cmty. With USAF, 1974—79. Republican. Baptist. Office: Office of Gov 700 Capital Ave Ste 100 Frankfort KY 40601 Office Phone: 502-564-2611. Office Fax: 502-564-2517.

FLETCHER, HARRY GEORGE, III, library director; b. Bklyn., Mar. 25, 1941; s. Harry G. and Helen T. (Dawson) F.; m. Toni A. Owen, 1966 (div. 1987); children: Alexandra, Thomas; m. 2d, Florence Sussman, 1987. AB, Fordham Coll., 1962, MA, 1970. Asst. editor, editor, dir. Fordham U. Press, 1966-91; Astor curator of printed books and bindings Pierpont Morgan Libr., NYC, 1991-98; Brooke Russell Astor dir. spl. collections NY Pub. Libr., NYC, 1998—, acting dir. Humanities and Social Scis. Libr., 2003—04. Adj. assoc. prof. NYU, 1996—, Pratt Inst., 2006. Author: Gutenberg and the Genesis of Printing, 1994, New Aldine Studies, 1988, In Praise of Aldus Manutius, 1995, Izaak Walton's The Complete Angler 1653-2003, 2003, (with Bertrand Dorny) Ma bibliothèque, c'est moi, 2006; co-author: Art Deco Bookbindings: the work of Pierre Legrain and Rose Adler, 2004; editor: The Heritage of New York, 1970, A Miscellany for Bibliophiles, 1979, The Wormsley Library, 1999, 2nd ed., 2007; co-editor: Paradosis, 1976; contbr. articles to profl. jours., chpts. to books. Served with AUS, 1963-66. DAAD fellow, 1962-63. Mem. Baker Street Irregulars. Clubs: Grolier. Office: NY Pub Libr Fifth Ave and 42d St New York NY 10018-2788 E-mail: hgfletcher@nypl.org.

FLETCHER, HOMER LEE, librarian; b. Salem, Ind., May 11, 1928; s. Floyd M. and Hazel (Barnett) F.; m. Jacquelyn Ann Blanton, Feb. 7, 1950; children— Deborah Lynn, Randall Brian, David Lee. BA, Ind. U., 1953; MS in L.S, U. Ill., 1954. Librarian Milw. Pub. Library, 1954-56; head librarian Ashland (Ohio) Pub. Library, 1956-59; city librarian Arcadia (Cal.) Pub. Library, 1959-65, Vallejo (Calif.) Pub. Library, 1965-70, San Jose, Calif., 1970-90; ret., 1990. Contbr. articles to profl. jours. Pres. S. Solano chpt. Calif. Assn. Neurol. Handicapped Children, 1968-69; mem. Presbyn. Ch. Sunnyvale, 1997. Served with USAF, 1946-49. Mem. ALA (intellectual freedom com. 1967-72), Calif. Library Assn. (pres. pub. libraries sect. 1967), Phi Beta Kappa. Democrat. Presbyterian. Home: 7921 Belknap Dr Cupertino CA 95014-4973 *Standing up for what I believe regardless of the consequences. Accepting all human beings as important regardless of their circumstances. Emphasizing honest and forthright behavior in personal and professional life. Retaining a sense of humility and thankfulness.*

FLETCHER, JUDITH ELLEN, music educator; b. Lafayette, Ind., Aug. 5, 1950; d. Edward Abraham and Roslyn Silber Fletcher; m. John F. Rathé, Nov. 25, 1977; children: Zarya D.F. Rathé, Anuta X.F. Rathé. BA in Biology, Swarthmore Coll., Pa., 1972; studied with Patinka Kopec, Syoko Aki, Peter Oundjian, Szymon Goldberg, Harris Goldsmith, Mannes Coll. Music and Sch. Strings. Cert. creative ability devel. Editor Biol. Abstracts, Phila., 1972—73; resident tchr. Whitby Sch., Greenwich, Conn., 1973—74; freelance violinist, 1974—; music tchr. Horace Mann Sch., Bronx, NY, 1974—83; violin tchr. Hoff-Barthelson Music Sch., Scarsdale, NY, 1982—83; music tchr. Riverdale Country Sch., Bronx, NY, 1981—. Founder Musicians United to Save the Environment, Bronx, NY, 2000—. Summer fellowships, NSF, 1970—72. Mem.: Chamber Music Am., Suzuki Assn. of the Ams., Am. String Tchrs. Assn. Jewish. Avocation: environmental activism and memberships. Office: Riverdale Country Sch 5250 Fieldston Rd Bronx NY 10471 Office Phone: 718-519-2719. Business E-Mail: jfletcher@riverdale.edu.

FLETCHER, LEROY STEVENSON, mechanical engineer, educator; b. San Antonio, Oct. 10, 1936; s. Robert Holton and Jennie Lee F.; m. Nancy Louise McHenry, Aug. 14, 1966; children: Laura Malee, Daniel Alden. BS, Tex. A&M U., 1958; MS, Stanford U., 1963, Engr., 1964; PhD, Ariz. State U., 1968. Registered profl. engr., Ariz., N.J., Va., Tex., Australia; chartered engr., U.K. Rsch. scientist NASA-Ames Rsch. Ctr., Moffett Field, Calif., 1958-62, dir. aeronautics/aerospace, 1999—2005; instr. Ariz. State U., Tempe, 1964-68; prof. aero., engring. Rutgers U., New Brunswick, 1968-75, assoc. dean, 1974-75; prof., chmn. dept. mech. and aero. engring. U. Va., Charlottesville, 1975-80; dir. Ctr. Energy Analysis, 1979-80; assoc. dean Tex. A&M U., College Station, 1980-88, assoc. dir. Tex. Engring. Expt. Sta., 1985-88, Dietz prof. mech. engring., 1988—2006, Regents prof., 1998—2006, rsch. chair Tex. Engring. Expt. Sta., 2006—. Vis. prof. Tokyo Inst. Tech., 1993; hon. prof. Ruhr U., Bochum, Germany, 1988—; disting. vis. prof. Am. U., Cairo, 1998, Am. U. Sharjah, United Arab Emirates, 2000—; cons. to various industries, govt. labs. and univs.; mem. exec. com. Internat. Ctr. Heat and Mass Transfer, Ankara, Turkey, 1994—, chmn., 1999—2003, fellow, 1998; disting. vis. scholar Hong Kong Poly. U., 2002. Author: Introduction to Engineering Including FORTRAN Programming, 1977, Introduction to Engineering Design with Graphics and Design Projects, 1979; editor: Aerodynamic Heating and Thermal Protection, 1978, Heat Transfer and Thermal Control Systems, 1978. Served to capt. USAF, 1958-61. Recipient Disting. Alumni award Ariz. State U., 1985, Exceptional Achievement medal NASA-Ames, 2002, Outstanding Leadership medal NASA, 2005. Fellow: AIAA (dir. 1981—84, v.p. edn. 1992—95, dir. 1992—98, pres. 1996—97, Lee Atwood award 1982, Enery Sys. award 1984, Thermophysics award 1992, Disting. Svc. award 2002, hon. fellow 2004), AAAS (chair sect. M-engring. 1988—89, Internat. Sci. Coop. award 2003), ASME (bd. govs. 1983—87, pres. 1985—86, Charles Russ Richards award 1982, Heat Transfer Meml. award 1996, hon., medal 2002), Internat. Acad. Astronautics, Pan Am. Acad. Engring., Internat. Astron. Fedn. (Frank J. Malina award 1997), Royal Aero. Soc. U.K., Inst. Engrs. Australia, Accreditation Bd. Engring. and Tech. (dir. 1979—89, 1991—94, 2003—, pres.-elect 2006—, Linton Grinter award 2002), Am. Astron. Soc. (bd. dirs. 1993—96), Inst. Mech. Engrs. U.K. (James Watt Internat. Gold medal 2005), Am. Soc. Engring. Edn. (dir. 1974—77, v.p. 1978—89, George Westinghouse award 1982, Ralph Coats Roe award 1983, Donald E. Marlowe award 1986, Leighton W. Collins award 1993, Benjamin Garver Lamme award 2001); mem.: Union Panam. Assns. Engrs. (Vector de Oro award 2000), Phi Kappa Phi, Sigma Gamma Tau, Pi Tau Sigma, Tau Beta Pi, Sigma Xi. Office: Tex A&M Univ Dept Mech Engring College Station TX 77843-3123

FLETCHER, MARGARET ANN, religious studies educator; b. Fairmont, W.Va., Sept. 21, 1948; BA in Edn., Fairmont State Coll., W.Va., 1970; MDiv, Regent U., Va. Beach, 1989. Adminstrv. asst. Regent U. Sch. Divinity, 1988—89; instr. Tidewater C.C., Va. Beach, 1998—. Recipient Cmty. award, Sch. Div. Regent U., 1989. Avocations: reading, exercise. Home: 738 Ridge Cir Chesapeake VA 23320 Office: Tidewater Cmty Coll 1700 Coll Crescent Virginia Beach VA 23453 Office Phone: 757-822-7100.

FLETCHER, MARJORIE AMOS, librarian; b. Easton, Pa., July 10, 1923; d. Alexander Robert and Margaret Ashton (Arnold) Amos; m. Charles Mann Fletcher, May 14, 1949; children: Robert Amos, Elizabeth Ashton, Anne Kennard. AB, Bryn Mawr Coll., 1946. Asst. to dir. rsch., then rsch. asst. to pres. Penn Mut. Life Ins. Co., 1946—49; officer A.R. Amos Co., Phila., 1949—66; part-time tchr., 1965—68; libr. Am. Coll., Bryn Mawr, Pa., 1968—77, archivist, 1977—2007, dir. oral history collection, 1975—, lectr. on archives, 1975—, asst. prof. edn., 1973—87, dir. archives and oral history, 1977—2007, curator art collection, 1981—; pres. pub. rels. MAF Enterprises, 1987—. Contbr. articles to profl. jours. Bd. dirs. Emergency Aid Pa. Found. Recipient awards, Phila. Flower Show, 1965—. Mem.: Hist. Soc. Pa., Hist. Soc. Pa., Oral History Assn., Soc. Am. Archivists (chairperson oral history sect. 1981—87, award of merit 1987), Spl. Librs. Assn. (pres. Phila. 1977—78), Emergency Aid Pa. Found., Bridlewild Trails Club (Gladwyne), Bridlewild Pony Club (sponsor), Davis Creek Yacht Club, Phila. Skating Club, US Pony Club, Nat. Soc. Colonial Dames in Commonwealth of Pa., DAR. Republican. Episcopalian. Home: 1135 Norsam Rd Gladwyne PA 19035-1419 Home Phone: 610-525-5720; Office Phone: 610-525-5720.

FLETCHER, MARY LEE, retired marketing professional; b. Farnborough, Eng. d. Dugald Angus and Mary Lee (Thurman) Fletcher. BA Pembroke Coll., Brown U., 1951. Ops. officer CIA, Washington, 1951—53; exec. trainee Gimbels, NYC, 1953—54; head rschr. Ed Byron TV Prods., NYC, 1954; copywriter Benton and Bowles Inc., NYC, 1955—63; creative dir. Alberto-Culver Co., Melrose Park, Ill., 1964—66; v.p. advt. and publicity Christian Dior Perfumes, NYC, 1967—71; v.p. Christian Dior-N.Y., 1972—78, exec. v.p., dir., 1978—85. Home: 15 Shelter Lane Locust Valley NY 11560

FLETCHER, NORMAN S., retired state supreme court justice; b. July 10, 1934; s. Frank Pickett and Hattie Sears Fletcher; m. Dorothy Johnson, 1957; children: Mary Kiker, Elizabeth Coan. BA, U. Ga., 1956, LLB, 1958; LLM, U. Va., 1995. Assoc. Matthews, Maddox, Walton and Smith, Rome, Ga., 1958-63; pvt. practice LaFayette, Ga., 1963—89; city atty. City of LaFayette, 1965-89; county atty. County of Walker, 1973-88; spl. asst. atty. gen. State of Ga., Atlanta, 1979-89; justice Ga. Supreme Ct., Atlanta, 1995—2001, chief justice, 2001—05; ret., 2005. Mem. State Disciplinary Bd., 1984-87, chair investigative panel, 1986-87. Bd. visitors U. Ga. Sch. Law, 1992-95, chmn., 1994-95. Master Joseph Henry Lumpkin Inn of Ct.; fellow Am. Bar Found., Ga. Bar Found.; mem.ABA, State Bar Ga. (chair local govt. sect. 1977-78), Atlanta Bar Assn., U. Ga. Law Sch. Alumni Assn. (pres. 1977), Lawyers Club Atlanta, Rotary. Home Phone: 706-290-1745; Office Phone: 706-291-8853. Business E-Mail: nsfletcher@brinson-askew.com.

FLETCHER, RAYMOND RUSSWALD, JR., lawyer; b. Schenectady, NY, June 7, 1929; s. Raymond Russwald and Elsie Dorothea (Hovemeyer) F.; m. Elsa Ellen Tillema, Dec. 20, 1949 (div. 1973); children— Raymond Russwald III, Nicholas H., Pamela L., William E., Catherine A. B.Ch.E., Rensselaer Poly. Inst., 1949; LL.B., Harvard U., 1956. Bar: N.Y. 1956. Vice-pres., gen. counsel Trans World Airlines, Inc., NYC, 1969-78; ptnr. Chadbourne, Parke, Whiteside & Wolff, NYC, 1978-84; counsel Gilbride, Tusa, Last & Spellane, NYC, 1984—2004. Vice chmn. legal com. Internat. Air Transport Assn., Geneva, Switzerland, 1976-77 Served as lt. (j.g.) USN, 1949-53; Korea Decorated Air medal Mem. Harvard Club. Democrat. Presbyterian. Home and Office: 453 Albany Hill Rd Rensselaerville NY 12147-2705 Office Phone: 518-797-3863.

FLETCHER, ROBERT, retired lawyer; b. Birmingham, Ala., May 4, 1920; s. Robert Hall and Beatrice (Skelding) Jones; m. Florence K. Szuba, Sept. 12, 1942; children— Andrew R., William Alan. BFA, Ohio U., Athens, 1943; LLB, JD, Case Western Res U., Cleve., 1948. Bar: Ohio 1948. Asst. gen. counsel Cleve. Transit System, 1951-56; with firm Jamison, Ulrich, Johnson & Burt, Cleve., 1956-59, Meyers, Stevens & Rea, Cleve., 1959-61; pvt. practice Cleve., 1961-82; horologist Parma, Ohio, 1982—. Lectr. Am. Heart Assn. Served with AUS, World War II, Korea. Recipient Speakers Bur. award Am. Heart Assn., 1973-76 Mem.: Rosicrucian Order, Masonic Order. Republican. Presbyterian. Home: 5801 Hollywood Dr Cleveland OH 44129-5220

FLETCHER, ROBERT ALEXANDER, artist, writer; b. North Haledon, NJ, Aug. 3, 1931; s. Adam Fletcher and Kittie Roon; m. Elizabeth Ann Breeman, Sept. 26, 1956; children: Brenda, Douglas, Jane, Robert B. A, Newark Sch. Fine and Indsl. Art, 1952. Asst. art dir. Conti Advt., Ridgewood, NJ, 1955—60; gen. ptnr. Fletcher, Daniels Advt., Midland Park, NJ, 1961—68, Fletcher, Walker, Gessell Advt., Midland Park, 1969—85; artist, illustrator, author Warwick, NY, 1986—. Author, illustrator: Remembrance: A Tribute to America's Veterans, 2002 (Best Essay, Creative Non Fiction, Ind. Pub. Assn., 2003), The Little Red Jeep: 12 Months on the Farm, 2006, Jeeps at War, 2007; exhibitions include Cannon Bldg. Rotunda, US Ho. of Reps., Washington, 2000, Rayburn Bldg Rotunda, US Senate, 2002. Mem. archtl. rev. bd. Town of Warwick, 1986—96. Cpl. US Army, 1953—55. Mem.: VFW (life), Am. Legion (sgt.-at-arms 2004—, Orange County Legionnaire of Yr. 2001). Avocations: farming, kayaking. Home: 33 Iron Mountain Rd Warwick NY 10990 Personal E-mail: bob.fletcher@gmail.com.

FLETCHER, RONALD DARLING, microbiologist educator; b. Foxboro, Mass., Jan. 18, 1933; s. Howard Wendel and Ada Louise (Darling) F.; m. Barbara Gundersen, Jan. 30, 1954; children: Deborah, Mark Ronald, Christopher Gary. BS, U. Conn., 1954, MS, 1959, PhD, 1963. Mule skinner U.S. Forest Svc., St. Maries, Idaho, 1952; instr. U. Conn., Storrs, 1959-63; rschr. Am. Cyanamid Co., Pearl River, N.Y., 1964-67; dir. microbiology McKeesport Hosp., Pa., 1971-79; prof., assoc. chair dept. microbiology U. Pitts., 1967—86, prof. microbiology dept. clin. lab. scis., 1989—; assoc. dir. Armed Forces Med. Intelligence Ctr. Dept. Def., Frederick, Md., 1984—85, sr. analyst Armed Forces Med. Intelligence Ctr., 1986—89; v.p. Affordable Tech., Inc., Pitts., 1990—91; exec. v.p. ATI Bioremediation, Inc., Pitts., 1991—92. Biotech. steering com. U.S. Dept. Def., 1987-89; cons. U.S. Army, Frederick, 1978-82, Mellon Inst., Pitts., 1981, Cons.'s Brokerage, Mountain View, Calif., 1981, Battelle Meml. Inst., Columbus, Ohio, 1989-90. Contbr. articles to prof. jours. Judge Internat. Sci. and Engring. Fair, Mpls., 1980, Milw., 1981, Dallas, 1982, Nat. Jr. Sci. and Humanities Symposium, West Point, N.Y., 1983, 85; dept. state lectr. med. schs. in Ankara and Istanbul, Turkey, 1982. Col. USA & USAR, 1954-85. USPHS fellow U. Zurich, Switzerland, 1963-64; grantee U.S. Army, Am. Cancer Soc., NIH; Postdoctoral fellow U. Saskatchewan, Can., 1965, Harvard Med. Sch., 1966, cert. of achievement in microbiology Surgeon Gen. U.S. Army, 1973. Fellow AAAS, Am. Acad. Microbiology (registered microbiologist, specialist microbiologist); mem. Internat. Assn. Dental Research (pres. Pitts. 1979-80), ADA, Assn. Mil. Surgeons, Am. Assn. Microbiologists, N.Y. Acad. Scis., Am. Soc. for Cell Biology, Nat. Mil. Intelligence Assn., Internat. Assn. Chiefs of Police, Am. Legion Personal E-mail: fletchuconn@yahoo.com.

FLETCHER, STEPHEN L., art appraiser; Ptnr., exec. v.p., chief auctioneer & appraiser Skinner, Inc., Boston, 1975—, and dir., Am. Furniture and Decorative Arts. Appraiser Antiques Roadshow, WGBH-PBS. Contbr. writer Art & Antiquities in Estates, lectr. in field. Mem.: Provincetown Art Assn., Mus. (bd. trustees), Mus. Fine Arts, Boston. Office: Skinner Inc 63 Park Plz Boston MA 02116 Office Phone: 617-350-5400. Office Fax: 617-350-5429. Business E-Mail: tvappraisers@skinnerinc.com.

FLETCHER, SUZANNE WRIGHT, epidemiologist, medical educator, editor; b. Jacksonville, Fla., Nov. 14, 1940; d. Robert Dean and Helen (Selmer) Wright; m. Robert H. Fletcher; children: John Wright, Grant Selmer. BA, Swarthmore Coll., 1962; MD, Harvard Med. Sch., 1966; MSc, Johns Hopkins U., 1973. Diplomate Nat. Bd. Med. Examiners, Am. Bd. Internal Medicine. Intern Stanford (Calif.) U. Med. Ctr., 1966—67, resident, 1967—68; physician 22nd med. detachment U.S. Army, New Ulm, Germany, 1969—70; asst. prof. epidemiology and health Mc Gill U., Montreal, Canada, 1974—77, assoc. prof., 1977—78, asst. prof. medicine, 1973—78; dir. med. clinic dept. medicine NC Meml. Hosp., 1978—82; assoc. prof. medicine U. NC, 1978—83, co-chief divsn. gen. medicine and clin. epidemiology dept. medicine, 1978—86, rsch. assoc. health svcs. rsch. ctr., 1978—90, vice chmn. clin. svcs., 1981—90, prof. medicine, clin. prof. epidemiology, 1983—90, program dir. faculty devel. gen. medicine and gen. pediatrics, 1985—90, co-dir. internat. clin. epidemiology network program Rockefeller Found., 1986—90; prof. ambulatory care and prevention Harvard Med. Sch., 1994—; editor Annals of Internal Medicine, Phila., 1990—93. Adj. prof. medicine U. Pa., Phila., 1990—93, Jefferson Med. Coll., 1991—93, U. NC, 1994—; physician internal medicine; chmn. NIH Tech. Assessment Conf., 1992, Nat. Cancer Inst. Internat. Workshop, 1993; faculty World Bank Seminar on Preventive Strategies in Med. Edn., Hangzhou, China, 1986; active Ad Hoc NCI Com. on Breast Cancer Detection Rsch., 1986; chair Macy Conf. on Continuing Edn. of Health Profls., 2007. Author: Clinical Epidemiology—The Essentials, 1982, 4t edit., 2005; contbr. chapters to books, articles to profl. jours. Named rsch. grantee, Conseil de la Recherche en Sante du Quebec, 1975—77; recipient Can. Nat. Health Rsch. Scholar award, Can. Govt., 1975—78; grantee, Health and Welfare Can., 1976—78, Robert Wood Johnson Teaching Hosp. Gen. Medicine Group Practice Program, 1980—84, Nat. Ctr. Health Scis. Rsch. and Health Tech., 1985—89, Rockefeller Found. Clin. Epidemiology Resource and Tng. Ctr., 1986—90, NIH, 1987—90, 1997—. Master: ACP (med. knowledge self assessment program 1984—85, clin. practice subcom. 1987, pub. policy subcom. 1988—89); fellow: Coll. Physicians Phila., Am. Coll. Epidemiology (bd. dirs. 1990—93, chmn. pub. com. 1992—94); mem.: APHA, Am. Bd. Internal Medicine (bd. govs. 1981—87), NCI Bd. Sci. Advisors, World Assn. Med. Editors (v.p. 1997—2001), Internat. Clin. Epidemiology Network (bd. dirs.), Inst. Medicine (coun. 1993—96, exec. com. 1993—96), Soc. Gen. Internal Medicine (counsellor 1978—81, pres.-elect 1982—83, pres. 1983—84, co-editor Jour. Gen. Internal Medicine 1984—89, mem. publs. com. 1990—, chmn. Glaser award com. 1991). Unitarian Universalist. Office: 208 Boulder Bluff Chapel Hill NC 27516 Business E-Mail: Suzanne_Fletcher@hms.harvard.edu.

FLETCHER, VERNON JEROME, dental association administrator, director; b. Augsburg, Germany, Mar. 11, 1974; s. James Edward and Dana Fletcher; m. Patty Marie DeGregori, Apr. 24, 1975. BS, US Air Force Acad., 1996; MBA, Webster U., 2000. Cert. Microsoft Profl. Calif., 2000. Network security officer US Air Force, Maguire AFB, NJ, 1996—98, acquisitions officer El Segundo, Calif., 1998—2001; sales engr. TAAR-COM, Mountain View, Calif., 2001—03; bus. devel. mgr. Tyco Internat., San Francisco, 2003—04; nat. dir. bus. devel. Onsite Dental, San Mateo, Calif., 2004—; enterprise account mgr. Hewlett-Packard, San Francisco. Capt. USAF, 1996—2001, NJ, Calif. Roman Catholic. Avocations: triathlons, travel. Home Phone: 650-375-8049.

FLETCHER, WILLIAM A., federal judge, educator; b. June 6, 1945; BA, Harvard U., 1968, Oxford U., 1970; JD, Yale U., 1975. Law clk. to presiding justice US Dist. Ct. Calif., San Francisco, 1975—76; law clk. to Justice William J. Brennan US Supreme Ct., Washington, 1976—77; acting prof. law U. Calif., Berkeley, 1977—84, prof. law, 1984—98; judge US Ct. Appeals (9th cir.), San Francisco, 1998—. With Office of Emergency Preparedness, Exec. Office of the Pres., 1970—72; prof. Salzburg Seminar on Am. Legal Institutions; mem. Am. Law Inst. Lieutenant USN, 1970—72. Mem.: Calif. Bar Assn. Office: 95 7th St San Francisco CA 94103*

FLETCHER, WINONA LEE, theater educator; b. Nov. 25, 1926; m. Joseph Grant; 1 child, Betty. BA, Johnson C. Smith U., 1947; MA, U. Iowa, 1951; PhD, Ind. U., 1968. Prof. speech and theatre Ky. State U., Frankfort, 1951-78; prof. theatre and afro-Am. studies Ind. U., Bloomington, 1978-94, prof. emeritus, 1994; assoc. dean COAS, 1981-84. Costumer, dir. summer theatre, U. Mo., Lincoln, 1952-60, 69. Sr. editor: Community Memories: A Glimpse of African American Life in Frankfort, Ky., 2003. Recipient Lifetime Achievement award, 1993; Am. Theatre fellow, 1979. Mem. Am. Theatre for Higher Edn., Black Theatre Network, Ky. Hist. Soc., Nat. Assn. Dramatic and Speech Arts, Nat. Theatre Conf., Alpha Kappa Alpha. Home: 317 Cold Harbor Dr Frankfort KY 40601-3011

FLETTNER, MARIANNE, opera administrator; b. Frankfurt, Germany, Aug. 9, 1933; d. Bernhard J. and Kaethe E. (Halbritter) F. Bus. diploma, Hessel Bus. Coll., 1953. Sec. various cos., 1953-61, Pontiac Motor Div., Burlingame, Calif., 1961-63, Met. Opera, NY, 1963-74, asst. co. mgr. NY, 1974-79; artistic adminstr. San Diego Opera, 1979—. Avocations: travel, hiking, swimming, cooking. Home: 4015 Crown Point Dr San Diego CA 92109-6270 Office: San Diego Opera 1200 Third Ave 18th Fl San Diego CA 92101-4112 Office Phone: 619-232-7636, 619-533-7004. Business E-Mail: marianne.flettner@sdopera.com.

FLEURY, MARC, application developer; b. Paris, Nov. 22, 1968; m. Nathalie Fleury; 3 children. BS, Ecole Polytechnique, 1991; M in Theoretical Physics, Ecole Normale, 1992; PhD, Ecole Polytechnique, 1996. With Sun Microsystems, France, programmer Silicon Valley, Calif., 1997—99; founder, chmn., CEO JB Boss, Inc., 1997—. Vis. scientist Mass. Inst. Tech. Office: JBoss Inc 3340 Peachtree Rd Ste 1200 Atlanta GA 30326 Office Phone: 404-467-8555. Office Fax: 404-948-1496.

FLEURY, PAUL AIMÉ, dean, physicist; b. Balt., July 20, 1939; m. Carol Anne Moss, Aug. 22, 1964; children: Ellen, Laura, Jennifer. BS in Physics, John Carroll U., 1960; PhD in Physics, MIT, 1965. Mem. tech. staff AT&T Bell Labs., Murray Hill, NJ, 1965-70, head condensed state physics rsch., 1970-79, dir. materials rsch., 1979-84, dir. phys. rsch., 1984-92; v.p. rsch. Sandia Nat. Lab., Albuquerque, 1992-93; dir. materials & process rsch. AT&T Bell Labs., Murray Hill, NJ, 1993-96; dean engring. U. N.Mex., Albuquerque, 1996-2000, Yale U., New Haven, 2000—. Editor: Coherence and Energy Transfer in Glasses, 1983; contbr. over 120 articles to Phys. Rev., Sci., others. Fellow AAAS, NAE, NAS, Am. Acad. Arts and Scis., Am. Phys. Soc. (Michaelson Morley prize 1985, Frank Isakson prize for optical effects in solids 1992). Achievements include 5 patents for optical devices, lasers, optical fibers; research in laser spectroscopy. E-mail: paul.fleury@yale.edu.

FLEXNER, KURT FISHER, economist, educator; b. Vienna, Sept. 26, 1915; arrived in U.S., 1928; s. Otto Gerard and Wilhelmine (Fisher) Flexner; m. Josephine Moncure, Dec. 20, 1942; children: Thomas Moncure, Peter Wallace. BS in Econs., Johns Hopkins U., 1946; PhD in Econs., Columbia U., 1954. From asst. prof. to prof. econs. NYU Grad. Sch. Arts and Scis., U. Coll. and Sch. Commerce, 1946-59; chief economist, dep. mgr. The Am. Bankers Assn., 1959-66; adj. prof. banking and fin. NYU, 1965-66, prof., chmn. dept. econs., 1966-78; prof. econs. U. Memphis, 1978-87, prof. emeritus, 1987—. Cons. U.S. Savs. and Loan League, 1955—59, N.Y. State Savs. and Loan League, 1955—59; P. K. Seidman vis. distin. prof. Christian Bros. U., Memphis, 1990—94; lectr. intergenerational seminars Bard Coll., Annandale on the Hudson, NY, 1987—, Ctr. for Life Studies, Marist Coll., Poughkeepsie, NY, 1995—; chief fin. instns. advisor U.S. Agy. for Internat. Devel., Seoul, Republic of Korea, 1966—68; spkr. in field; adv. com. to Chancellor Franz Vranitzky Prime Minister of Austria, 1991—93; guest lectr. USA and Can. Acad. Sci., Moscow, 1991—95; advisor to coun. Pres. Mikhail Gorbachev, 1990—91, Pres. Boris Yeltsin, 1991—94. Author: The European Payments Union 1950 to 1954, 1957, The Savings and Loan Associations in the State of New York, 1958, Mortgage Lending by Commercial Banks, 1964, The Enlightened Society: The Economy with a Human Face, 1989, The 21st Century-The Best or the Last, 2005; columnist Memphis Daily News, 1986—90, Comml. Appeal, 1980—87; contbr. articles to profl. jours. Trustee M. L. Seidman Town Hall Meml. Lecture Series, 1968—87; mem. Gov. Alexander's Action Team, 1980—85. With US Army, 1944—45. Mem.: Econ. Club Memphis (exec. dir. 1973—85, pres. 1985—92). Home and Office: The Fountains at Millbrook 17 Crestview Rd Millbrook NY 12545

FLICK, CARL, electrical engineer, consultant; b. Vienna, June 22, 1926; came to U.S., 1939; s. Henry Chaim Ber and Sofie (Dornhelm) F.; m. Frances Ethel Berman, July 4, 1954; children: Lawrence David, Susan Naomi, Jack Bennet. BEE, Poly. U. of N.Y., 1951; MEE, Poly. U., 1953. Registered profl. engr., Fla., Pa. Various engring. positions, adv. engr. Westinghouse Electric Corp., East Pittsburgh, Pa., 1952-84, adv. engr., Orlando, Fla., 1984-89; cons. Techno-Lexic, Orlando, 1989—. Co-author: Handbook of Electric Machines, 1987; contbr. articles to profl. jours.; patentee in field. With U.S. Army, 1945-47, PTO. Fellow IEEE (life; various coms., Centennial medal 1984, Outstanding Engr. award Orlando sect. 1989, Fla. coun. 1989, Region 3 1990, Nikola Tesla award 1994), Power Engring. Soc. (com. Disting. Svc. award, Millenium medal 2000); mem. B'nai B'rith. Democrat. Jewish. Avocations: writing, photography, painting.

FLICK, FERDINAND HERMAN, surgeon, preventive medicine physician; b. Bklyn., Feb. 19, 1925; s. Paul Albert and Elizabeth Kath (Herz) F.; m. Marie T. Flick, Apr. 7, 1945; children: Paul, Ferdinand, Annette Flick Riddle. BS, MS, Fordham U.; MD, Yale U., 1951. Diplomate Am. Bd. Preventive Medicine. Intern SUNY Downstate, 1951-52; resident in ob-gyn Coll. Physicians & Surgeons Columbia U., NYC, 1952; asst. prof. Columbia U. Coll. Physicians & Surgeons, NYC, 1959-62; surgeon 77th Divsn. USAR, NYC, 1962-76; chief plant physician Fort Motor Co., Mahwah, N.J., 1976-80, Edison, N.J., 1980—. Asst. prof. U. Calif., Berkeley, 1946-47; trauma lectr. Middlesex C.C., 1984-85. Contbr. articles to profl. jours. including Nature and Am. Jour. Ob-gyn. Mem. smoking intervention team Am. Cancer Soc., New Brunswick, N.J., 1993-95. Col. USAR, 1946-76. Decorated Meritorious Svc. medal. Mem. Am. Coll. Occupl. and Environ. Medicine, Am. Coll. Preventive Medicine, Am. Soc. Abdominal Surgeons, Sigma Xi (Yale chpt.). Avocations: hunting, skiing. Home: 233 Evans Ave Piscataway NJ 08854-2937

FLICK, JOHN EDMOND, retired lawyer; b. Franklin, Pa., Mar. 14, 1922; s. Edmond Leroy and Mary M. (Weaver) F.; m. Lois Anna Lange, Apr. 20, 1946; children: Gregory Allan, Scott Edmond, Lynn Ellen, Ann Elizabeth. Student, Northwestern U., 1941—44, U. Pa., 1945; JD, Northwestern U., 1948. Bar: Ill. 1948, Calif. 1971, U.S. Dist. Ct. (ctrl. dist.) Calif. 1971, U.S. Ct. Appeals (9th cir.) 1971, U.S. Supreme Ct. 1974. Commd. 1st lt. Judge Adv. Gen. Corps U.S. Army, 1950, advanced through grades to lt. col. Res., 1968; ret., 1972; faculty U.S. Mil. Acad., 1954-57, Judge Adv. Gen. Sch., U. Va., 1960-61; counsel Litton Industries, 1963-67; sr. v.p., sec., gen. counsel, dir. Bangor Punta Corp., 1967-69; sr. v.p., gen. counsel Times Mirror Co., Los Angeles, 1970-87, cons., 1987-88, ret., 2004. Past chmn. Los Angeles adv. bd. Salvation Army; past mem. nat. adv. bd. Salvation Army. Recipient Am. Bar Assn. Acad. award, 1961 Mem. State Bars Calif. and Ill., Wigmore Club (life benefactor, Northwestern U. Law Sch.).

FLICK, THOMAS MICHAEL, mathematician, educator, educational association administrator; b. Covington, Ky., July 14, 1954; s. Thomas Lawrence and Crystel (Moore) F.; m. Jeanine M. Moran, Nov. 23, 1991. BS, No. Ky. U., 1976, MA, 1981; MEd, Xavier U., 1977; PhD, Southea. U., 1979; EdD, U. Sarasota, 1989. Cert. secondary tchr., Ohio, Ky. Assoc. vice prin., dean, chmn. math., prin. summer sch. Purcell Marian H.S., Cin., 1977—89; asst. prof. Xavier U., Cin., 1989—95, assoc. prof., 1995—2004, prof., 2004—; dir. Xavier Ctr. for Cath. Edn., 2004—; chair dept. secondary and special edn. Xavier U., 2006—. Lectr. astronomy Wilmington Coll., Ohio, 1977-78, engring. and nat. sci., U. Cin., 1979—; dir. Ctr. Excellence Edn. Xavier U., 2004—. Author: Guidelines for Astronomy Courses, 1976, 1978; author: (with J. Ventre & J. Boothe) Astronomy Teaching Handbook, 1992; author: Introduction to the Universe, 1991, 1993, 2002, Eclipses: Presentations for Educators, 1999; author: (with J. Ventre, J. Boothe and L. Rutherford) Handbook for Astronomy Educators, 2004; contbr. articles to profl. jours. Guest lectr. Cin. Nature Ctr., Milford, 1976—; chmn. edn. Astron. League, Washington; tchr. Super Saturday Program for Gifted and Talented., Cin., 1983; commn. mem. Archdiocese Cin., 1986; Commd. Ky. Col. Gov. Ernie Fletcher, 2006. Recipient Ohio NSF Presdl. Award for Excellence in Math. Edn., 1986, Greater Cin. Found./GE grantee, 1987. Mem. Ohio Coun. Tchrs. Math. (contest coord. 1983—, Outstanding Math. Tchr. award 1982), Nat. Astron. League (v.p. 1980-82, chmn. edn. 1975—), Nat. Coun. Tchrs. Math., Math. Assn. Am., Ohio Acad. Sci. (Jerry Acker Outstanding Math. Tchr. award 1986-87), Sigma Xi (Outstanding Math. Tchr. award 1985), Pi Mu Epsilon; Midwestern Astronomers Club Roman Catholic. Avocations: golf, piano, bicycling, model railroading. Office: Xavier U Ctr for Excellence in Edn 3800 Victory Pkwy Dept Edn Cincinnati OH 45207-7321 Office Phone: 513-745-3477. Business E-Mail: flick@xavier.edu.

FLICKINGER, CHARLES JOHN, anatomist, educator; b. Bethlehem, Pa., July 13, 1938; s. Wilbur James and Verna (Diehl) F.; m. Agnes Elizabeth Dickel, Feb. 23, 1963; children: Laura Jill, David Paul. AB, Dartmouth Coll., 1960; MD, Harvard U., 1964. Rsch. fellow dept. anatomy U. Colo., Denver, 1964-65, Harvard Med. Sch., Boston, 1965-66; rsch. assoc. Inst. Devel. Biology, U. Colo., Boulder, 1966-67, asst. prof., 1967-70; assoc. prof. dept. anatomy Sch. Medicine, U. Va., Charlottesville, 1971-75, Harvey E. Jordan prof. anatomy, 1982—2002, chmn. dept. cell biology, 1982—2002, prof., 1975—2006; ret.; prof. emeritus Sch. Medicine, U. Va., 2007—. Mem. reproductive biology study sect. NIH, 1979-83; mem. anatomy test com. Nat. Bd. Med. Examiners, 1981-84. Author: (with Brown, Kutchai, Ogilvie) Medical Cell Biology, 1979; contbr. articles to profl. jours.; assoc. editor: Jour. Andrology, 1989-92; adv. editor: Internat. Rev. Cytology, 1974-98; mem. editl. bd. Biology of Reprodn., 1986-89, 2002-04, Jour. Andrology, 1986-89, Anatomical Record, 1972-98. NIH rsch. career devel. award grantee, 1968-70. Mem. Am. Soc. Cell Biology, Am. Assn. Anatomists, Soc. Study Reproduction, Am. Soc. Andrology, Phi Beta Kappa, Alpha Omega Alpha. Home: 2009 Meadowbrook Rd Charlottesville VA 22903-1247 Office: University of Virginia Dept Cell Biology PO Box 800732 Charlottesville VA 22908-0732 Office Phone: 434-924-2731. Business E-Mail: cjf@virginia.edu.

FLICKINGER, DON JACOB, lawyer; b. Massillon, Ohio, Dec. 31, 1933; s. John Jacob and Elizabeth Ann (Slinger) F.; m. Sonja Loy Jersild (dec. Aug. 1987); 1 child, Packy J. Flickinger. Student, Kent State U., Ohio, 1951-54, U. Ariz., 1958; BA, Ariz. State U., 1963, MA, 1964. Bar: U.S. Patent and Trademark Office, 1973. Apprentice tool and die maker Spun Steel Corp., Canton, Ohio, 1951-54; staff Ariz. State U., Tempe, 1963-65; law clerk, paralegal Drummond, Cahill & Phillips, Phoenix, 1966-73; reg. patent agent Drummond, Nelson & Ptak, Phoenix, 1973-77, self employed, Phoenix, 1977-94; counsel Parsons & Goltry, Phoenix, 1995—2001. Lectr., instr. Patent Seminars & Courses, Phoenix, 1977—; staff Rio Salado C.C., Phoenix, 1982-84; intellectual property counselor SCORE Phoenix Chpt.

105, 2001. Patentee Collapsible Dust Pan, Hort. Growing Unit. Comdg. officer Poolee Enrichment Program, Family Marine Force, Poolee Assistance Co., Phoenix; sponsor Thunderbird Little League, Phoenix, 1985, 86, 87; big brother Valley Big Brothers, Phoenix, 1968-70; participant, staff Valley Big Bros./Big Sisters Fish-a-Ree, 1984-87; judge Crown Royal Kinetic Contraption Compeition, 1990. With USMC, 1954-57. Am. Soc. Tool. scholar, Tucson, 1960; recipient Disting. Svc. cert. Valley Big Brothers, Phoenix,1970, Honor award Westside Area Career Project, Glendale, 1981. Mem.: NRA (endowment), Svc. Corps of Ret. Execs. (intellectual property counselor Phoenix chpt. 105 2001—), Defenders of Wildlife, Legal Def. Fund, Heritage Alliance, Nat. Wildlife Fedn. (leaders club), Wilderness Soc., Mensa, Kappa Delta Pi. Republican. Buddhist. Avocations: philosophy, reading, woodworking, arts and crafts. Office: Phoenix Score Chpt 105 2828 N Central Ave Ste 800 Phoenix AZ 85004 Office Phone: 602-745-7250. E-mail: padsha@aol.com.

FLICKINGER, DONALD E., mathematics educator; b. Scranton, Pa., Mar. 21, 1947; s. Jesse Emory and Ann Florence Flickinger; m. Carolyn Carmella Rome, Aug. 15, 1981. BS, U. Scranton, 1969, MS, 1972. Tchr. 7th grade math. Wyo. Area Sch. Dist., Exeter, Pa., 1969—82, tchr. 8th grade math., 1982—, prin. mid. sch., 1990. Head vol. program Wyo. Area Sch. Dist., 1994—97. V.p. W.A. Credit Union, Wyoming, 1985—89. Mem.: NEA, Pa. Coun. Math. Tchrs., Pa. State Edn. Assn. Roman Catholic. Avocations: golf, reading, sports. Home: 106 Chase St West Pittston PA 18643 Office: Wyo Area Sch Dist 10 Meml St Exeter PA 18643

FLICKINGER, HARRY HARNER, management consultant; b. Hanover, Pa., July 27, 1936; s. Harry Roosevelt and Goldie Anna (Harner) F.; m. Hsin Yang, May 30, 1961; children: Audrey Mae, Deborah Lynn. BS in Psychology, U. Md., 1958. Investigator U.S. Civil Service Commn., Washington, 1962-64; personnel specialist U.S. Naval Ordinance Lab., Silver Spring., Md., 1964-66; from asst. dir. to dir. personnel U.S. OMB, Washington, 1966-73; asst. dir. personnel AEC and Dept. Energy, Washington, 1973-78; dir. personnel U.S. Dept. Justice, Washington, 1978-79, dep. asst. atty. gen. adminstrn., 1979-85, assoc. asst. atty. gen., 1985-87, asst. atty. gen., 1987-92; exec. dir. Am. Consortium for Internat. Pub. Adminstrn., Washington, 1993; pres. Flickinger Enterprises, Gaithersburg, Md., 1994—2003. Recipient Presdl. Disting. Exec. Rank award, 1988.

FLICKINGER, JOE ARDEN, telecommunications educator, department chairman; b. Cadillac, Mich., Feb. 4, 1949; s. Arden Henry and Stella Frances (Hurst) F.; m. Judith Marie Gardner, Sept. 18, 1971; children: Jan Elsa, Jill Kimberly. BA, Kalamazoo Coll., Mich., 1971; MA, U. So. Calif., 1975; AS, Clatsop Community Coll., 1985; PhD, U. Oreg., 1993. Asst. chief engr. Sta. KUSC-FM, LA, 1972-74; sta. engr. Sta. KAST-AM-FM, Astoria, Oreg., 1974-75; studio operator, instr. Clatsop CC, Astoria, 1975-88; grad. tchg. fellow in telecom. U. Oreg., Eugene, 1988-90; sr. mktg. cons. RKM Corp., Vancouver, Wash., 1990-93; vis. asst. prof. com. Lewis and Clark Coll., Portland, Oreg., 1991-92; assoc. prof. media studies Radford U., Va., 1992—, dir. grad. program, corp. and profl. comm., 1996-98, chair media studies dept., 1998—. Session organizer on high definition TV, Northcon, 1989, IEEE and ERA Tech. Conf., 1989. Dir. TV muscular dystrophy telethon Astoria Jaycees, 1980, 81; canvasser Friends of Coll., Astoria, 1982; pres. bd. dirs. Sta. KMUN-FM Tillicum Found., Astoria, 1983-84. Mem. IEEE, IEEE Computer Soc., IEEE Comm. Soc., Am. Radio Relay League (life), Pacific Telecomm. Coun., Northcom Inner Circle, N.Y. Acad. Scis., Nat. Model R.R. Assn., Sunset Empire Amateur Radio Club (sec. 1978-81), Lions Club (region chair dist. 24-E 1999-2002). Democrat. Presbyterian. Avocations: amateur radio, golf, fishing, astronomy, cooking. Office Phone: 540-831-6039. Business E-Mail: jflickin@radford.edu.

FLIEGELMAN OLLI, AMY, lawyer, computer company executive; BS, SUNY, Oswego; JD, Western New England Sch. Law. Assoc. gen. counsel Software Group IBM, Europe, Middle East and Africa, assoc. gen. counsel Global Svcs., assoc. gen. counsel Southwest Europe, v.p., gen. counsel Americas, co-global coord. sales and distribution; exec. v.p., co-gen. counsel CA, Inc., Islandia, NY, 2006—. Office: CA, Inc One CA Plaza Islandia NY 11749

FLIER, JEFFREY S., dean, endocrinologist; b. NYC, 1948; BS in Biology, CCNY, 1968; MD, Mt. Sinai Sch. Medicine, 1972; MD (hon.), U. Athens, 1997. Diplomate Am. Bd. Internal Medicine. Intern Mt. Sinai Hosp., NYC, 1972—73, resident in internal medicine, 1973—74; fellow in endocrinology NIH, Bethesda, Md., 1974—77; asst. prof. medicine Harvard Med. Sch., Boston, 1978—82, assoc. prof. medicine, 1982—93, prof. medicine, 1993—, George C. Reisman prof. medicine, 1999—, dean, 2007—; chief diabetes unit Beth Israel Hosp., Boston, 1978—90, chief divsn. endocrinology, 1990—2000; vice chair for rsch. dept. medicine Beth Israel Deaconess Med. Ctr., Boston, 1998—2002, chair rsch. strategy com., 1999, Harvard faculty dean academic programs, 2000, chief acad. officer, 2002. Vis. scientist Whitehead Inst., MIT, Cambridge, Mass., 1985—86; lectr. in field; Smith Kline Beecham vis. prof. U. Cambridge, 1998. Contbr. articles to profl. jours. Recipient Eli Lilly award for outstanding sci. achievement, Am. Diabetes Assn., 1991, Transatlantic medal, Brit. Endocrine Soc., 2004. Fellow: Am. Acad. Arts and Scis., AAAS; mem.: Assn. of Am. Physicians, Inst. Medicine (life; pres. 2001), Inter Urban Clin. Club. Avocations: golf, skiing. Office: Flier Lab Research North 390 99 Brookline Ave Boston MA 02215 also: Harvard Med Sch Gordon Hall 25 Shattuck St Boston MA 02115 Office Phone: 617-667-8575. Office Fax: 617-667-2927. E-mail: jflier@bidmc.harvard.edu.*

FLIER, MICHAEL STEPHEN, Slavic languages educator; b. LA, Apr. 20, 1941; s. Albert and Bonnie Flier; m. Glenn Patton Wright, Sept. 19, 2004. BA, U. Calif., Berkeley, 1962, MA, 1964, PhD, 1968. Acting vis. asst. prof. Slavic langs. and lits. U. Calif., Berkeley, 1968; asst. prof. Slavic langs. and lits. UCLA, 1968-73, assoc. prof., 1973-79, prof., 1979-91, chmn. dept., 1978-84, 87-89. Vis. prof. Slavic langs. Columbia U., fall 1988, Harvard U., fall 1989; Oleksandr Potebnja prof. Ukrainian Philology Harvard U., 1991—, chmn. dept. Linguistics, 1994-99, chmn. dept. Slavic langs. and lits., 1999—2005, acting chmn. dept. linguistics, 2002; acting dir. Harvard Ukrainian Rsch. Inst., 2001, dir., 2004-. Author: Aspects of Nominal Determination in Old Church Slavic, 1974, Say It In Russian, 1982; editor: Slavic Forum: Essays in Slavic Linguistics and Literature, 1974, Am. Cont. to the Intl. Congress of Slavists, 1983, Ukrainian Philology and Linguistics, 1994; co-editor: Medieval Russian Culture, 1984, Issues in Russian Morphosyntax, 1985, The Scope of Slavic Aspect, 1985, Language, Literature, Linguistics, 1987, Medieval Russian Culture, vol. 2, 1994, For SK: In Celebration of the Life and Career of Simon Karlinsky, 1994, The Language and Verse of Russia: In Honor of Dean S. Worth on His Sixty-fifth Birthday, 1995, Francis J. Whitfield, Old Church Slavic Reader, 2004, Henrik Birnbaum, in Memoriam, 2006; mem. editl. bd. Slavic and East European Jour., 1989—, Movoznavstvo, 1991—, Harvard Ukrainian Studies, 1991—, Russkii iazyk v nauchnom osveshchenii, 2000—. Vice chmn. Am. Com. Slavists, 1989-94, chmn., 1994—. Internat. Rsch. and Exchs. Bd. travel grantee Russia, Czechoslovakia, 1966-67, 71, 78, 93, 96; U. Calif. Pres.'s fellow, 1990, John Simon Guggenheim Meml. Found. fellow, 1990-91. Mem. Linguistics Soc. Am., Am. Assn. Tchrs. Slavic and East European Langs., Am. Assn. Advancement Slavic Studies, Western Slavic Assn., Coll. Art Assn., Am. Assn. for Ukrainian Studies (sec.-treas. 1989-93, bd. dirs.). Home: 76 Fresh Pond Ln Cambridge MA 02138-4641 Office: Harvard U Dept Slavic Langs and Lits Barker Ctr, 12 Quincy St Cambridge MA 02138 Office Phone: 617-495-4065. Business E-Mail: flier@fas.harvard.edu.

FLIFLET, ARNE WOOLSEY, research scientist; b. Aiken, SC, Dec. 22, 1947; s. Arne Thorleif and Effie Woolsey Fliflet; m. Deborah Ann Levin, Apr. 13, 1978; children: Naomi Elena, Ruth Elise, Max Levin, Shirley Catharine. BSc, Duke U., Durham, NC, 1970; PhD, U. Va., Charlottesville, 1975. Rsch. fellow Calif. Inst. Tech., Pasadena, 1975—79; project scientist B-K Dynamics, Inc., Rockville, Md., 1979—82; rsch. physicist Naval Rsch. Lab., Washington, 1982—. Contbr. articles to profl. jours. Fellow: Am. Phys. Soc.; mem.: IEEE. Jewish. Achievements include research in gyrotrons and gyrotron applications; patents for gyrotrons and microwave processing of materials. Avocations: sailing, farming. Home: 3400 Russell Rd Alexandria VA 22305 Home Phone: 703-683-5659. Personal E-mail: arne.fliflet@verizon.net.

FLIGGE, JÖRG, librarian, library director; b. Königsberg, Germany, Dec. 1, 1940; s. Armin and Ursula (Schroeter) F.; m. Gabriele Edner, July 6, 1968; children: Christina, Claudia. PhD, U. Bonn, Germany, 1972. Cert. sci. libr. Jr. libr. U. Libr., Bonn, 1972-74, libr. adminstr. Duisburg, Germany, 1974-77, head libr. adminstr., 1978-79, dep. dir., 1979, libr. dir., 1980; dep. dir. City Libr., Duisburg, 1983-90; dir., ltd. libr. dir. Bibliothek der Hansestadt Lübeck, Germany, 1990—. Head commn. AV-media in librs. German Libr. Inst., Berlin, 1980-90; mem. German-Russian Libr. Commn. Restitution, Berlin, and St. Petersburg, Russia, 1993—. Author: Herzog Albrecht von Preussen und der Osiandrismus, 1972; author: (editor) Bibliotheca Baltica, 1994, Stadt und Bibliohek, 1997, Die Wissenschaffliche Stadtbibliothek, 2001; contbr. articles to profl. jours. Active Assn. zur Beförderung gemeinnütziger Tätigkeit, Lübeck, 1991—. Mem. Verein Deutscher Bibliothekare, Verein der Bibliothekare an Öffentlichen Bibliotheken, Rotary. Lutheran. Avocations: music, studying cultural history. Home: Hermann-Lönsweg 24 23562 Lübeck Germany Office: Bibliothek der Hansestadt Lübeck Hundestr 5-17 23552 Lübeck Germany Office Phone: 49 (0) 451 122 4111.

FLINCHBAUGH, DAVID EDWARD, physicist; b. Poughkeepsie, NY, Oct. 11, 1934; s. Louis David and Lolita Mildred (Hook) F.; m. Heidi Maria Rose, June 15, 1957; children: William David, Laura Jean, Karen Marie, Karl Louis. BS in Physics and Math., Union Coll., 1957; MS in Physics, U. Conn., 1960, PhD in Modern Physics, 1964; cert. computer database mgmt., Harvard U., 1979. Registered profl. engr., Fla., Pa.; cert. tchr., Fla. Rsch. physicist IBM Corp., Poughkeepsie, 1956-57; rsch. assoc. Argonne Nat. Labs., Lemont, Ill., 1958; rsch. scientist United Techs. Rsch. Labs., East Hartford, Conn., 1959-60, 63-65; mgr. R&D Andersen Labs., Bloomfield, Conn., 1965-68; dir. R&D Orlando (Fla.) Rsch. Corp., 1968-69; v.p. R&D Control Laser Corp., Orlando, 1968-71; staff cons. Martin Marietta Aerospace Corp., Orlando, 1971-73, 86-87, Internat. Laser Corp., Orlando, 1975; sr. staff cons. Sperry Microwave Electronics Corp., Clearwater, Fla., 1977-78; program mgr., P.I. Planning Rsch. Corp., Kennedy Space Center, 1978-80; cons. team leader Westinghouse Electric Corp., Pitts., 1980-81; systems engring. mgr. McDonnell Douglas Astronautics Co., Titusville, Fla., 1982-86; v.p., dir. mfg., CEO UroSolutions, Orlando, Fla., 2000—05; sr. v.p. Global Med. Rsch. LLC, Orlando, 2005—. Chief cons., CEO Aerobeam Corp., Orlando, 1971—2002, Dr. David Flinchbaugh & Assoc., P.A., Orlando. Patentee refractive acousto-optic modulators, robotic manipulator system, urinary drainage control valve, others. Vol. instr. ARC, Orlando, 1968-90; lead counselor Boy and Girl Scouts Am., Orlando, 1968—; mem. Nat. Dem. Policy Com., 1984-86. Named Engr. of Yr. Fla. Engring. Soc., Tallahassee, 1984, Fla. Inventor of Yr. Palm Beach Soc. Am. Inventors, 1986—, Nat. Inventor of Yr. Inventor's Soc. South Fla., Ft. Lauderdale, 1988; recipient Environ. Award, Orange Co., Fla., 1998, DaVinci Award, 2002, Albert M. Sargent Progress Award, Soc. Mfg. Engrs., 2003. Fellow IEEE (Engr. of Yr. Orlando sect. 1982, 83, Entrepreneur of Yr. 1998), AIAA (assoc.), Optical Soc. Am., Soc. Mfg. Engrs./Robotics Internat., Laser Inst. Am. (bd. dirs. 1975-79); mem. NSPE, Fla. Coun. Engring. Socs. (exec. com., pres. 1985-86), Inventors Coun. Cen. Fla. (exec. com., pres. 1984—). Presbyterian. Achievements include invention of the UroCycler®; ROSA Westinghouse nuclear service robot. Avocations: music, photography, aviation, swimming, boating. Home: 4855 Big Oaks Ln Orlando FL 32806-7826 Office: Dr David Flinchbaugh & Assoc PA 5509A Commerce Dr Orlando FL 32839 Office Phone: 407-760-7200. Personal E-mail: drflinchbaugh@aol.com.

FLINCHBAUGH, JAMIE, training services executive; b. 1972; Mfg. plant supr. Harley-Davidson Motors Inc.; lean mfg. dir. Daimler Chrysler AG, DTE Energy Co.; co-founder, ptnr. Lean Learning Ctr., Novi, Mich., 2001—. Author: The Hitchhiker's Guide to Lean. Named one of 40 Under 40, Crain's Detroit Bus., 2006. Office: Lean Learning Center 40028 Grand River Ste 300 Novi MI 48375 Office Phone: 248-478-1480. Office Fax: 248-478-1589.

FLINN, CHARLES GALLAGHER, lawyer, priest; b. Ft. Lauderdale, Fla., Feb. 22, 1938; s. Robert Galloway and Gertrude (Gallagher) F. AB, Princeton U., 1959; LLB, U. Va., 1962; BD, U. London, 1980; ThM, Westminster Theol. Sem., 1994; MA, Cath. U., 2001. Bar: Fla. 1962, Va. 1962, U.S. Supreme Ct. 1966, D.C. 1970; ordained to ministry Episcopal Ch. as deacon, 1991, as priest, 1992. Assoc. Charles B. Fulton, Esq., West Palm Beach, Fla., 1962-63; asst. counsel Office Gen. Counsel U.S. Dept. Navy, Washington, 1963-71; asst. commonwealth's atty. County of Arlington, Va., 1971-72, asst. county atty. Va., 1972-75, dep. county atty. Va., 1975-81, county atty. Va., 1981-93; atty. Arlington Sch. Bd., 1981-93; curate Grace Episcopal Ch., Brunswick, Md., 1991-93; vicar Trinity Episcopal Ch., Monmouth, Ill., 1994-96; vice-chancellor Episcopal Diocese, Quincy, Ill., 1996—. Vis. lectr. in bibl. lang. Reformed Theological Seminary, Orlando, Fla., 1997-2000; adj. faculty Protestant Episcopal Theol. Sem., Alexandria, Va., 1999-2000; pres. Nathanael Inst., 2001—. Mem. Va. Local Govt. Attys. Assn. (bd. dirs. 1988-92), Va. Coun. Sch. Bd. Attys. (dir.-at-large 1988-93). Office: PO Box 100921 Arlington VA 22210 Business E-Mail: cgflinn@alumni.princeton.edu.

FLINN, MARK VAN DOREN, education educator; s. Richard and Edwina Flinn; m. Carol Ward, May 19, 1990; children: Rick, Warren, Jack. PhD, Northwestern U., Evanston, Ill., 1983. Postdoctorate U. Mich., 1987. Prof. U. Mo., Columbia, 1987—. Author: (sci. article) Hormones and the human family. Recipient Disting. Scientist award, Bowen Ctr. for Study of the Family. Office: Univ Mo Dept Anthropology 107 Swallow Hall Columbia MO 65211 Office Phone: 573-882-9404.

FLINN, MICHAEL DE VLAMING, investment company executive; b. Durham, NC, June 15, 1941; s. Lawrence and Marion (de Vlaming) Flinn; m. Elizabeth Jamison Folk, Aug. 3, 1962 (div. Mar. 1985); children: William III, Michael de Vlaming, T. Rex, Randall E.; m. Ann G. Hanes, Feb. 14, 1993. BA magna cum laude, Yale U., 1962; JD, Harvard U., 1965. Bar: Conn. 1968. Ltd. ptnr. Ingalls & Snyder, 1970-96; mem. Conn. Ho. of Reps., Hartford, 1983-86; v.p. Spears, Benzak, Salmon & Farrell, Inc. (name now Victory, NYC, 1996—2005, mng. dir., 1997, Tocqueville Asset Mgmt. LP, NYC, 2005—. Mng. dir. Victory SBSF Capital Mgmt. Active Town Meeting, Greenwich, Conn., 1970—82; pres., bd. dirs. Greenwich Boys Club Assn., 1977—92, Round Hill Assn., 1972—81, Boys and Girls Club Greenwich, 1993—94; trustee Green-Wood Cemetery, 1983—; bd. dirs. Coldwater Conservation Fund, 2002—; mem. Conn. Rep. Fin. Com., 1972, Greenwich Rep. Town Com., 1980—85, mem. exec. com., 1982—84. Capt. US Army, 1966—68. Mem.: ABA, Greenwich Bar Assn., Conn. Bar Assn., Yale Alumni Assn. Greenwich (gov. 1982—85), Hotchkiss Alumni Assn. (gov. 1979—83), Burning Tree Club, Links. Home: PO Box 1309 Greenwich CT 06836-1309 Office: Tocqueville Asset Mgmt 40 West 57th St 19th Fl New York NY 10019 Office Phone: 212-698-0803. Business E-Mail: mflinn@tocqueville.com.

FLINN, MICHAEL JAMES, lawyer; b. Pitts., June 9, 1949; s. George E. and Iris R. (Schartl) F.; m. Eileen McGrady, Aug. 7, 1971; children: Erin, Kevin. BA, U. Notre Dame, 1971; JD, U. Pitts., 1974. Bar: Pa. 1974, U.S. Dist. Ct. (we. dist.) Pa. 1974. Assoc. Moorhead & Knox, Pitts., 1974-81; ptnr. Buchanan Ingersoll & Rooney, P.C., Pitts., 1981—. Pres. Nat. Aviary, 1992-97, 07—; mem. adv. bd. The Salvation Army, Southwestern Pa., 1993—; mem. Bd. Nat. Aviary, 1998—. Home: 728 Harden Dr Pittsburgh PA 15229-1107 Office: Buchanan Ingersoll PC 301 Grant St Ste 21 Pittsburgh PA 15219-1408 Home Phone: 412-366-5012; Office Phone: 412-562-1027. E-mail: flinnmj@bipc.com.

FLINN, PAUL ANTHONY, materials scientist; b. NYC, Mar. 25, 1926; s. Richard A. and Anna M. (Weber) F.; m. Mary Ellen Hoffman, Aug. 20, 1949; children: Juliana, Margaret, Donald, Anthony, Patrick. AB, Columbia Coll., 1948, MA, 1949; ScD, MIT, 1952. Asst. prof. Wayne U., Detroit, 1953-54; research staff Westinghouse Research Lab., Pitts., 1954-63; prof. Carnegie-Mellon U., Pitts., 1964-78; sr. staff scientist Intel Corp., Santa Clara, Calif., 1978-95; cons. prof. dept. material sci. and engring. Stanford (Calif.) U., 1985—. Vis. prof. U. Nancy, France, 1967-68, U. Fed. do Rio Grand du Sol, Porto Allegro, Brazil, 1975, Argonne (Ill.) Nat. Lab., 1977-78, Stanford (Calif.) U., 1984-85. Contbr. sci. articles to profl. jours. Served with USN, 1944-46, PTO. Fellow Am. Phys. Soc.; mem. Metall. Soc., Materials Rsch. Soc., Phi Beta Kappa, Tau Beta Pi. Home Phone: 808-878-3799. Personal E-mail: pflinn@stanford.edu.

FLINT, DOUGLAS J., investment company executive; b. July 8, 1955; s. David and Dorothy (Jardine) Flint. Articled clerk KPMG (formerly Peat Marwick Mitchell & Co.), 1977—80, chartered acct., 1980—88, ptnr., 1988-95; group fin. dir. HSBC Holdings plc, London, 1995—. Bd. dirs. HSBC Holdings plc, HSBC Bank Malaysia Berhad. Office: HSBC Holdings plc 8 Canada Square London E14 5HQ England

FLINT, GEORGE SQUIRE, lawyer; b. Ft. Wayne, Ind., Oct. 28, 1930; s. A. Verne and Alberta (Minor) F.; m. Emily Gregg McLees, Nov. 23, 1968; 1 son, Alexander C.; children by previous marriage: Julia M., Melissa A., Anthony E. AB, U. Mich., 1952, JD, 1955. Bar: N.Y. 1956. Assoc., then sr. assoc. Fulton, Walter & Duncombe, NYC, 1955-65; ptnr. Fulton, Duncombe and Rowe, 1983-89; with Tenneco Chems., Inc., 1965-82, v.p., sec., gen. counsel, 1969-82; counsel Jackson & Nash, NYC, 1989—2002. Arbitrator Small Claims Part. Civil Ct., N.Y.C. With USN, 1955-57. Mem. N.Y. State Bar Assn., Assn. Bar City N.Y., Order of Coif. Clubs: Indian Harbor Yacht, Wadawanuck, Stonington. Home: 1185 Park Ave New York NY 10128-1308

FLINT, JOHN E., retired historian; b. Montreal, May 17, 1930; s. Alfred Edgar and Sarah (Pickup) F.; m. Nezhat Sepanj, Sept. 19, 1975; children: Helen Sarah, Richard John. BA, U. Cambridge, 1952, MA, 1954; PhD, U. London, 1957. Asst. lectr., lectr., reader colonial history King's Coll., U. London, 1954-67; vis. prof., Fulbright fellow U. Calif., Santa Barbara, 1960-61; vis. prof., head history dept. U. Nigeria, Nsukka, 1963-64; prof. history Dalhousie U., 1967—, dir. African Studies Centre, 1967-92; prof. emeritus, 1993—. Mem. acad. panel Can. Council, 1967-68, Social Scis. and Humanities Research Council Can. Author: Sir George Goldie and the Making of Nigeria, 1960, Nigeria and Ghana, 1966, Cecil Rhodes, 1974; co-author: Oxford History of the British Empire, Vol. V, 1999; editor: Cambridge History of Africa, Vol. V, 1790-1870, 1977. Fellow Royal Hist. Soc., Royal Soc. Can.; mem. Canadian Assn. African Studies, Canadian Hist. Assn., Nigerian Hist. Assn., African Studies Assn. U.K. Personal E-mail: johnflint@rogers.com.

FLINT, ROBERT WALLACE, neuroscientist, educator; b. Washington, Mar. 3, 1970; s. Robert Wallace and Cynthia Kay Flint; m. Susan Marie Castor; children: Evan Richard, Noah Robert. BS, Allegheny Coll., Meadville, Pa., 1992; MA, Kent State U., Ohio, 1994, PhD, 1997. Asst. prof. psychology Minn. State U., Mankato, Minn., 1997—99; assoc. prof. psychology Coll. St. Rose, Albany, NY, 1999—. Contbr. articles to profl. jours. Recipient Guy Emerson Buckingham Psychology award, Allegheny Coll., 1992, Tchg. award, Kent State U., 1996; grantee, NIH, NIMH, 1991, 1992. Mem.: NE Undergrad. Rsch. Orgn. Neuroscience (mem. steering com. 2002—07), Faculty Undergraduate Neuroscience Edn., Ea. Psychol. Assn., Soc. Neuroscience (assoc.), Psi Chi, Delta Tau Delta. Office: The Coll Saint Rose 432 Western Ave Albany NY 12203-1490 Home Phone: 518-373-9119; Office Phone: 518-458-5379. Business E-Mail: flintr@strose.edu.

FLINT, WILLIS WOLFSCHMIDT (WILLI WOLFSCHMIDT), artist, sculptor; b. Kenton, Ohio, Dec. 27, 1936; s. Wilbur Henry and Ilo Edna (Obenour) Flint. Student, Art Career Sch., NYC, 1957—60, Ins. Allende, San Miguel Allende, Mex., 1961. Artist trainee Kossack Advt., Tucson, 1961; gen. boardman Mithoff Advt., El Paso, 1962-63; tech. illustrator Volt Tech. Corp., NYC, 1967; gen. illustrator Salesvertising Advt., Denver, 1968; gen. boardman/cons. Burr-Brown Rsch. Corp., Tucson, 1969-71; musician, actor Paul Barons Harmonica Rascals, Bklyn., 1965-85; musician Wild Ones, Tucson, 1982-83; muralist San Diego, Tucson, NYC, 1976-80; artist Tucson, 1985—; originator Fantasy-Expressionism, 1984; musician, comedian Desert Rats, Tucson, 1999-2000, Willi Wolfschmidt, N.W. Sr. Ctr., Tucson, 2003—; founder Ragged Edge, 2003, Sch. Ragged Edge, 2003. Pvt. tchr. art, Tucson, 1981—85; cons. muralist Yaqui Indian-Pascua Ctr., Tucson, 1989; freelance muralist and graphic artist Wolfschmidt & Washburn, 1994—96. Co-author: (poems) Best-Loved Contemporary Poems, 1979, Famous Poems of Today, 1995, A Delicate Balance, 1996, Poetic Voices of America, 1996, Best Poems of the '90s, 1996, Best Poems of the 20th Century, 1996, Best Famous Poems of '96, 1997, Best Poems of '97, 1997, Soaring with the Wind, 1998, Ten Years Excellence, 1998; one-man shows include sculptor Old Pascua Village, Tucson, 1996, exhibited in group shows at United Way Fund Dr. Exhibit, United Servicemen's Orgn. Exhibit, Mobile, Ala., Student Union Exhibit, U. Ariz., Tucson, La Galeria Instituto, San Miguel de Allende, Margarita de Mena Gallery, N.Y.C., Represented in permanent collections So. Ariz. Hist. Soc., Tombstone, Hardin County Hist. Mus., Inc., Kenton, Ohio, Williams County Hist. Soc., Montpelier, Ohio, Cherokee Nat. Mus., Tahlequah, Okla., Bisbee Mining and Historical Mus., Bisbee, Ariz., Bryan HS, Bryan Ohio, So. Ariz. Trans. Mus., Tucson, Ariz.; author: A Treatise on Fantasy—Expressionism from the School of the Ragged-Edge, 2003. Vol. harmonica soloist, comic Willi Wolfschmidt Sr. Citizen Ctr., Tucson, 2004—. With USN, 1954—57, with USN, 1979—81. Recipient award of merit, Latham Found., 1958, letter of commendation, U. Ariz. Family Practice, Tucson, 1978, U.S. Dept. Navy, San Diego, 1979; scholar, Latham Found., 1958. Mem.: Internat. Soc. Poets, Maverick Artists, Tucson Harmonica Club. Avocations: antique vehicles, travel, motorcycling. Home: 707 W Calle Progreso Tucson AZ 85705-6446

FLIPPEN, EDWARD L., lawyer; b. Richmond, Va., Dec. 2, 1939; s. Hannie Thomas Flippen; m. Pearcy light, Feb. 14, 1970; children: Elizabeth Hunter, Margaret Harlan. BS, Va. Commonwealth U., 1965; MBA, Coll. of William and Mary, 1967, JD, 1974. Bar: Va. 1974, NC 1981. Gen. atty. Va. State Corp. Commn., Richmond, 1975-78, assoc. gen. counsel, 1978-80, dep. gen. counsel, 1980; asst. gen. counsel Duke Power Co., Charlotte, NC, 1980-81, assoc., 1981-83; ptnr. Mays & Valentine, LLP, Richmond, 1983-99, McGuireWoods, LLP, Richmond, 1999—. Lectr. U. Va. Sch. Law, 1978—82, 2004—, Duke U. Sch. Law, 2006—; adj. prof. Coll. William and Mary, 1996—2000, Washington and Lee U., 1997—99, U. Richmond, 2000; vis. fellow U. London, 1998—99; vis. prof. George Mason Sch. Law, 2001—02, disting. sr. fellow, 2004—, Va. Commonwealth U Sch. Govt. Pub. Policy Affairs and Sch. Edn. Author: Practical Networking: How to Give and Get Help with Jobs, 2001. Bd. visitors Va.

Commonwealth U., Richmond, 1994-2002, rector, 2000-02; adv. bd. Va. Ctr. on Aging, Richmond, 1994-98; trustee River Rd. United Meth. Ch., Richmond, 1995-98;; chmn. Gov.'s Blue Ribbon Commn. Higher Edn., 1998-00, Atty. Gen.'s Task Force on Access to Higher Edn., 2003; bd. VCU Health Sys., 2000-02. With US Army, 1958-61. Mem. Va. State Bar (chmn. adminstrv. law sect., 1986-87), Soc. for Advanced Legal Studies (assoc. fellow). Republican. Avocations: writing, teaching, assisting others in job placements. Office: McGuireWoods LLP One James Ctr 901 E Cary St Richmond VA 23219-4057 Office Phone: 804-775-4380. Business E-Mail: eflippen@mcguirewoods.com.

FLIPPO, KIRK, research scientist; PhD, U. Mich., Ann Arbor, 1997—2003. Grad. rsch. asst. Ctr. Ultrafast Optical Sci., Ann Arbor, 1998—2003; postdoctoral rsch. assoc. Los Alamos Nat. Lab., N.Mex., 2003—. Mem.: Am. Phys. Soc. Achievements include one of first researchers to discover superthermal ions from short-pulse laser plasma interaction; member of the research team that first discovered mono-energetic ions from short-pulse laser plasma interactions; co-inventor of a system and apparatus to create isotopes using short-pulse lasers. Office: Los Alamos Nat Lab Po 1663 Ms E526 Los Alamos NM 87507

FLIPSE, JOHN EDWARD, naval architect, mechanical engineer; b. Montville, NJ, Feb. 4, 1921; SB, MIT, 1942; MME, NYU, 1948. Registered profl. engr., NY, Va., Tex. Sr. engr., ship stabilization dept. head, marine div. Sperry Gyroscope Co., Great Neck, NY, 1955-57; rsch. engr., dir. rsch., mgr. systems dept., asst. to pres. Newport News (Va.) Shipbuilding and Dry Dock Co., 1957-68; chmn., pres., chief exec. officer Deepsea Ventures, Inc., Gloucester, Va., 1968-77; pres., chief exec. officer Tex. A&M Rsch. Found., College Station, 1983-84; dep. dir. Tex. Engring. Experiment Sta., 1985-88; disting. prof. civil and ocean engring. Tex. A&M U., 1982-92, assoc. dean engring. College Station, 1984-88, assoc. dep. chancellor for engring., 1984-89, Wofford Cain prof. engring., 1988-91, dir. Offshore Tech. Rsch. Ctr., 1988-91, dir. emeritus, 1991—2000. Chmn. Nat. Adv. Com. on Oceans and Atmosphere, 1985-86; mem. marine bd. Nat. Rsch. Coun., 1979-84, chmn., 1982-84; mem. marine facilities panel U.S./Japan Coop. Program in Natural Resources, 1980-96; mem. marine petroleum and minerals adv. com. Dept. Commerce, 1974-75; expert mem. U.S. delegation to Law of the Sea Conf., UN, 1975-76; cons., lectr. in field. Contbr. articles to profl. jours. Mem. dean's adv. coun. Sch. Engring. & Applied Sci., U. Va., 1995-98. Fellow Marine Tech. Soc. (pres. 1985-87), Soc. Naval Architects and Marine Engrs. (past chmn. tech. and rsch. steering com.); mem. Nat. Acad. Engring. (membership policy com. 1987-90, membership com. 1987-90, peer rev. com. 1985-86), Va. Inst. Marine Sci. (vice chmn. bd. dirs. 1968-76). Achievements include patents in field.

FLITCRAFT, RICHARD KIRBY, II, former chemical company executive; b. Woodstown, NJ, Sept. 5, 1920; s. H. Milton and Edna (Crispin) F.; m. Bertha LeSturgeon Hitchner, Nov. 14, 1942; children: Alyce, Anne, Elizabeth, Richard. BS, Rutgers U., 1942; MS, Washington U., 1948. With Monsanto Co., St. Louis, 1942—, dir. inorganic rsch., 1960-65, dir. mgmt. info. and systems dept., 1965-67, asst. to pres., 1967-68, group mgr. electronics enterprises, 1968-69, gen. mgr. electronic products div., 1969-71; v.p. Monsanto Rsch. Corp., 1971-75; dir. Mound Lab., 1971-75, v.p. ops., 1975-76; pres. Monsanto Resh. Corp., Dayton, 1976-82, ret., 1982. Past chmn., bd. dirs. United Way, Dayton; bd. dirs. City-Wide Devel. Corp.; former trustee and chmn. bd. Miami Valley Hosp.; past bd. dirs. Pvt. Industry Coun., Srs., Inc.; chmn. bd. Headstart program Miami Valley Child Devel., Inc. Mem. AAAS, AICE, Am. Chem. Soc., Am. Inst. Chemists, Am. Mgmt. Assn., N.Y. Acad. Scis., Ohio Acad. Scis. (past exec. com.), Dayton C. of C. (past bd. dirs., chmn. small bus. adv. bd., mil. affairs com.), Engrs. Club of Dayton (past bd. dirs.), Engrs. Club Dayton Found. (bd. trustees, chmn.), Moraine Country Club, Dayton Racquet Club. Presbyterian. Personal E-mail: rkf2@aol.com.

FLITSIYAN, ELENA S., physicist, physics educator; d. Samuel Y. and Maria M. Flitsiyan; m. Garry I. Gofen, May 5, 1966; 1 child, Yana G Shatkhin. PhD, Moscow State U., 1975; second doctoral degree, Joint Inst. Nuc. Rsch., Dubna, Moscow region, Russia, 1995. Prof. Tashkent State U., Uzbekistan, 1995—98; vis. prof. Marburg U., Germany, 1994—96; adj. professor U. Ctrl. Fla., Orlando, 1998—2003, vis. prof., 2003—. Head dept. Inst. of Nuc. Physics, Tashkent, Uzbekistan, 1996—98. Contbr. articles to profl. jours. Recipient World Yr. of Physics award, UCF, 2005. Mem.: Am. Phys. soc., European Rare-Earth Actinide Soc., Internat. Nuc. Track Soc. Office: Univ of Ctrl Fla (UCF) 4000 Ctrl Florida Blvd Orlando FL 32816-2385 Home Phone: 407-388-1602; Office Phone: 407-823-1156. Personal E-mail: flitsiyan@aol.com. E-mail: esf@physics.ucf.edu.

FLITTIE, CLIFFORD GILLILAND, retired petroleum company executive; b. Brookings, SD, Mar. 10, 1924; s. Theodore Ignatius and Grace Eliza (Gilliland) F.; m. Dawn Marie Lee, May 22, 1954. Student, Okla. State U., 1944, Colo. Sch. Mines, 1946; BS (Nat. scholar Am. Inst. Mining and Metall. Engrs.), S.D. Sch. Mines and Tech., 1948. Geologist Arabian Am. Oil Co., Dhahran, Saudi Arabia, 1948-57; v.p. exploration Conorada Petroleum Corp., NYC, 1958-63, dir., 1963-65; v.p., mgr. Amerada Petroleum Corp. of U.K., London, 1964-65, Amerada Petroleum Corp. of Australia, Brisbane, 1966-69; exploration supr. Amerada Hess Corp., NYC, 1970-73; v.p. Shaheen Natural Resources Co., Inc., NYC, 1974-75, Macmillan Oil Co., NYC, 1975-82, Natomas Co., San Francisco, 1982-86. Dir. Amerada Exploration Ltd., 1964-65 Served with USNR, 1944-46. Mem. Am. Assn. Petroleum Geologists, Soc. Exploration Geophysicists, Theta Tau, Sigma Tau. Episcopalian. Home: 46 San Jacinto Way San Francisco CA 94127-2033

FLOCK, HOWARD, psychology professor; b. Phila., Nov. 24, 1924; s. Salomon and Della (Buschel) F. BA, Yale U., 1944; MA, Harvard U., 1958; PhD, Cornell U., 1962. Asst. prof. CUNY, 1961-64; assoc. prof. Dartmouth Coll., 1964-65, York U., Toronto, Ont., Can., 1965-70, prof. psychology, 1970—. Contbr. articles to profl. publs., chpts. to books, also to films. Lt. (j.g.) USN, 1943-45, ETO. Grantee NSF, NSERC, NRC Can., 1964-82. Fellow APA; mem. Psychonomic Soc., Ea. Psychol. Assn., Harvard Club. Avocations: skiing, travel, films, photography. Home: 20 W 64th St Apt 10E New York NY 10023-7180 Office: York U Dept Psychology North York ON Canada M3J 1P3 Office Phone: 212-595-2895. Personal E-mail: hrflock@aol.com.

FLOCKHART, BARBARA TOWNSLEY, publishing executive; b. Paterson, NJ, Apr. 11, 1940; d. John J. and Rachel Chapman Townsley; children: Ian T., Rhoderick T., Craig T. Student, Columbia U., NYC, 1964; grad. in graphic design, New Eng. Sch. of Art and Design, Boston, 1978; student, Northeastern U., Boston, 1984—87. Propr. Barbara Flockhart Design, Winchester, Mass., 1980—83; dir. of prodn. Silver Burdett & Ginn, Needham, Mass., 1983—90; v.p., dir. of ops. Prentice Hall Sch., Needham, 1990—97; v.p. consulting ops. Mgmt. Process Integrators, Scottsdale, Ariz., 1998—99; mng. editor, dir. of ops. Home Portfolio, Inc., Newton, Mass., 1999—2000; v.p., exec. dir. GTS Pub. Svcs. divsn. TechBooks, Boston, 2000—03; CEO Pub. Solutions Group, Inc., Boston, 2003—06; ret. Spkr. BookTech 1999, NYC, 1999, Rsch. & Engring. Coun. Seminar on Prepress, Orlando, Fla., 1992—98, Seybold Seminars, Boston, 1993, Graphic Arts Tech. Foundation's Ann. Meeting, The Cloisters, SC, 1991, Electronics in Prepress/Lasers in Graphics, Orlando, 1990. Author: (book) Guidelines for Electronic Publishing. Vol. Peace Corps, Tunisia, 1964—66. Named to InnerCity Entrepreneurs of Boston, Boston U., 2005—; recipient Invited Del. to Joint U.S./China Edn. Conf. in Beijing, People to People Amb. Program, 2005. Mem.: NSTA, Nat. Coun. of Social Studies, Internat. Reading Assn., BookBuilders of Boston (com. mem.), Greater Lynn Photographic Assn. (libr. 2002—06, multiple photography ribbons 1998—2006). Avocations: photography, travel. Home: #837 3 Seal Harbor Rd Winthrop MA 02152

FLOCKHART, CALISTA, actress; b. Freeport, Ill., Nov. 11, 1964; d. Ronald and Kay Flockhart; 1 adopted child, Liam BFA, Rutgers U., 1988. Actress Ally McBeal Twentieth Century Fox, LA. Appeared in Broadway plays, including The Glass Menagerie, The Three Sisters; actress (films) Quiz Show, 1994, Getting In, 1994, Naked in New York, 1994, Pictures of Baby Jane Doe, 1996, The Birdcage, 1996, Milk and Money, 1997, Drunks, 1997, Telling Lies in America, 1997, A Midsummer Night's Dream, 1999, Like a Hole in the Head, 1999, Jane Doe, 1999, Things You Can Tell Just By Looking at Her, 2000 The Last Shot, 2004, Fragiles, 2005; (TV movies) Darrow, 1991, Lifestories: Families in Crisis-The Secret Life of Mary Margaret: Portrait of a Bulimic, 1992, Bash: Latter Day Plays, 2001; (TV series) Guiding Light, 1989, Ally McBeal, 1997-2002, Brothers and Sisters, 2006-; (TV appearances) The Practice, 1998, (voice only) Happily Ever After: Fairy Tales for Every Child (Rip Van Winkle episode), 1999. Recipient Golden Globe award for Best Actress award, 1998 Office: Internat Ceative Mgmt Inc 8942 Wilshire Blvd Beverly Hills CA 90211

FLOECKHER, LOUISE BYRNE WELDON, volunteer; b. NYC, July 28, 1928; d. Arthur Cornelius Byrne and Mary Elizabeth Colton; m. Peter Wren Floeckher (dec.). Student, Finch Jr. Coll., NY, 1946. Vol. N.Y. Presbyn. Hosp., 1962—75, prof. dir., vol. svcs., 1975—85. Mem.: Soc. of the Four Arts, Nat. Croquet Ctr., Colony Club. Avocations: croquet, travel. Home: 225 Everglades Ave 7 Palm Beach FL 33480

FLOERSCH, RICHARD, human resources specialist; BS, MBA, State U. NY. Cons. human resources Meredith Assocs., Conn.; with human resources mgmt. Internat. Playtex, Conn.; joined General Foods, 1984; v.p. compensation Kraft Foods N.Am.; v.p. corp. compensation Philip Morris; v.p. human resources Kraft Foods Internat., Rye Brook, NY, 1998—2003; exec. v.p. worldwide human resources McDonalds, Oak Brook, Ill., 2003—. Bd. dirs. AIESEC Yale. Office: McDonalds One Kroc Dr Oak Brook IL 60523

FLOM, EDWARD LEONARD, retired metal products executive; b. Tampa, Fla., Dec. 10, 1929; s. Samuel Louis and Julia (Mittle) F.; m. Beverly Boyett, Mar. 31, 1956; children— Edward Louis, Mark Robert, Julia Ruth. B.C.E., Cornell U., 1952. With Fla. Steel Corp., Tampa, 1954-93, v.p. sales, 1957-64, pres., dir., 1964-93, ret., 1993. Bd. dirs., mem. exec. com. Com. of 100, Tampa, United Fund Tampa; mem. adv. com. St. Joseph's Hosp., Tampa; bd. dirs. Family Svc. Assn. Tampa, Jewish Welfare Fedn. Tampa; bd. dirs. temple. With C.E., U.S. Army, 1952-54. Mem. Am. Iron and Steel Inst. (bd. dirs.), Fla. Engring. Soc., Young Pres. Orgn., Univ. Club, Palma Ceia Golf and Country Club, Tampa Yacht Club, Gasparilla Krewe, Rotary (bd. dirs. Tampa). Home: 4936 Saint Croix Dr Tampa FL 33629-4831

FLOM, GERALD TROSSEN, lawyer; b. Neenah, Wis., Feb. 6, 1930; s. Russell Craig and Lois Eva (Trossen) F.; m. Martha Herrington Benton, Aug. 21, 1954 (div. June 25, 1980); children— Katherine Simmons, Sarah Elizabeth Kiecker, Russell Craig. BA magna cum laude, Lawrence U., Appleton, Wis., 1952; JD, Yale U., New Haven, Conn., 1957. Bar: Minn. 1957, U.S. Dist. Ct. Minn. 1957. Assoc. Faegre & Benson LLP, Mpls., 1957-64, ptnr., 1964-95; ret., 1995. Adj. asst. prof. Law Sch., U. Minn., Mpls., 1966. Mem. editl. bd. Yale Law Jour. Trustee Mpls. Soc. Fine Arts, 1970-76, Lawrence U., 1974-81, Plymouth Congl. Ch., 1978-81, William Mitchell Coll. Law, St. Paul, 1983-89; bd. dirs. Met. Med. Ctr. Research Found., Mpls., 1975-85. Served with U.S. Army, 1952-54. Mem. ABA, Minn. State Bar Assn., Hennepin County Bar Assn., Assn. Bar City of N.Y., Mace, Mpls. Club, Interlachen Country Club (Edina, Minn.), Phi Beta Kappa, Phi Delta Theta, Phi Alpha Delta. Congregationalist. Home: 3434 Zenith Ave S Minneapolis MN 55416-4663 Office: Faegre & Benson LLP 2200 Wells Fargo Ctr 90 S 7th St Minneapolis MN 55402-3901

FLOM, JASON, music company executive; With A&R music Atlantic Records Group; pres. Lava Records Warner Music Group, 1995—2004, chmn., CEO Atlantic Group, 2004—05; chmn., CEO Virgin Records EMI Music, NYC, 2005—. Bd. dirs. Innocence Project, Legal Action Centre, Families Against Mandatory Minimums. Office: Virgin Records Am Inc 150 5th Ave New York NY 10010 Office Phone: 212-786-8200. Office Fax: 212-786-8343.

FLOM, JOSEPH HAROLD, lawyer; b. Balt., Dec. 20, 1923; s. Isadore and Fannie (Fishman) Flom; m. Claire Cohen, Nov. 14, 1958; children: Peter Leslie, Jason Robert. Student, CCNY, 1948; LLB cum laude, Harvard U., 1948; LHD (hon.), Queens Coll., 1984; LLD (hon.), Fordham U., 1990. Bar: NY 1949. Joined Skadden Arps Slate, NYC, 1948—; now ptnr. Skadden Arps Slate Meagher & Flom LLP, NYC. Spl. counsel subcom. on admisntrn. of internal revenue laws House Ways and Means Com., 1951—52; mem. SEC Com. on Tender Offers, 1996—2006; bd. dirs. Wm. Wrigley Jr. Co., 1977—94, Urban Am., LLC, 1998—. Editor Harvard Law Rev., 1947—48; co-editor: Disclosure Requirements of Public Corporations and Insiders, 1967, Texas Gulf Sulphur-Insider Disclosure Problems, 1968, Lawyer's Conflicts-The Evolving Case Law, 1991. Trustee Fedn. Jewish Philanthropies NY, 1977—89, Mt. Sinai-NYU Med. Ctr. Health Sys., 1978—99, Barnard Coll., 1983—93, NY Hist. Soc., 1989—94, Skadden Fellowship Found., Constl. Edn. Found., 1989—93; mem. NYC Commn. on Status of Women, 1975—76, NYC Holocoaust Meml. Commn., 1982—87, Mayor's Coun. Econ. Advisors, NYC, 1990—93, Mayor's Mgmt. Adv. Task Force, 1991—93; bd. dirs. United Way NYC, 1991—97, Am.-Israel Friendship League, 1996—2000; co-chair task force on capital fin. and constrn. NYC Bd. Edn., 1987—89; co-chair NYC Commn. on Bicentennial of US Constn., 1986—89, NYC Operation Welcome Home Commn., 1991; chair emeritus Woodrow Wilson Internat. Ctr. for Scholars, 1994—98; chair adv. com. Export-Import Bank of US, 1995; adv. coun. Bologna Ctr. of the Paul H. Nitze Sch. Advanced Internat. Studies Johns Hopkins U., 2000—03; mayor's rep. Met. Mus. Art, 1990—93; mem. Woodrow Wilson Coun., Archdiocesan Task Force on Crime Prevention and Youth, 1982—87. Recipient Whitney North Seymour Jr. Award, Fed. Bar Coun., 1989, DSM, Dept Def., 1992, Lifetime Achievement award, The Am. Lawyer, 2004, CCNY Presdl. medal for Disting. Achievement and Pub. Svc. Fellow: Am. Acad. Arts & Sciences; mem.: Coun. on Fgn. Rels., Assn. Bar City NY. Office: Skadden Arps Slate 4 Times Sq Fl 41 New York NY 10036-6522 Office Phone: 212-735-3100. Business E-Mail: jflom@skadden.com.

FLOMENBOM, OPHIR, biophysicist, researcher; b. Tel Aviv, Nov. 1, 1974; s. Masha and Amnon Flomenbom. BsC in Chemistry, Tel Aviv U., 2000, BsC in Life Sci., 2000, PhD in Chemistry, 2005. Rschr. neurobiochemistry Tel Aviv U., 1999—2000; rschr. NIH, Bethesda, Md., 2004, MIT, Cambridge, Mass., 2005—. Tchr. asst. Tel Aviv U., 2000—05. Capt., 1993—97, Israel. Scholar, Trotzki Scholar Orgn., 2004. Liberal. Jewish. Avocations: basketball, chess. Home: 12 Greenough Ln #205 Boston MA 02113 Home Phone: 617-650-6742; Office Phone: 617-253-1538. Business E-Mail: flomenbo@mit.edu.

FLOOD, ANGELA, interior designer, artist; b. NYC, Jan. 22, 1945; d. Americo Montes and Candace M. Hansen; m. Oscar William Rocafort, June 2, 1963 (div.); 1 child, Angélique Rocafort-Ward; m. Steven Arthur Flood, June 12, 1988. Student, NYU, 1965—66, Pace U., 1973—76; AAS, Suffolk C.C., 1992. Artist, curator F.O.R.E., Bedford, NY, 1976—86; owner, designer A&S Interiors, Westhampton Beach, NY, 1992—; owner design and art exhbns. Exhibitions include Easthampton (NY) Town Hall, 2001, 2006, Westhampton Beach Libr., 2002, 2006, Southampton RML Gallery, 2003, Easthampton Guild Hall Mus., 2004—07, Easthampton Artist Alliance Hall, 2005—07, L.I. Maritime Mus., 2006, Brookhaven Town Hall, NY, 2006—07. Counselor ARC, White Plains, NY, 1974—77. Republican. Avocations: horseback riding, kayaking, canoeing, sailing, skiing. Office: A&S Interiors PO Box 413 Westhampton Beach NY 11978 Personal E-mail: lilly11967@yahoo.com.

FLOOD, H. GAY (HULDA GAY FLOOD), editor, consultant; b. Plainfield, NJ, Aug. 14, 1935; d. William Edward and Lucy (Dycker) Flood. BA, Smith Coll., 1957. With picture dept. Sports Illustrated, Time Inc., NYC, 1957-58, with letters dept., 1958-59, reporter, 1959-60, writer-reporter, 1960-71, assoc. editor, 1971-85, sr. editor, 1985-90. Mem. Greater Consistory First Reformed Ch., Nyack, NY; assoc. mem. The Ch. of the Pilgrimage, Plymouth, Mass. Mem.: Plymouth Garden Club, Smith Coll. Students Aid Soc., Alumnae Assn. Smith Coll., Boston Smith Coll. Club, Garden Club Nyack (chair cmty. flower show 2001). Office: 7 Sampson Commons Plymouth MA 02360

FLOOD, HENRY, non-profit organization executive; b. Charleston, SC, Nov. 26, 1949; s. Joseph Harrison Jr. and Patricia (Johnson) F.; m. Nilde Martinez, Oct. 21, 1990. Student, Charleston So. U., 1968-70, Coll. of Charleston, 1970-74; MA in Legal Studies, Antioch U., 1985. Admitted to St. Regis Mohawk Bar. Dir. rsch. Ednl. Svcs. Inst., Arlington, Va., 1985; cons. Constn. Bicentennial Commn., Washington, 1986-88; dir. R & D, Falmouth Inst., 1988-92; program specialist Adminstrn. for Native Ams., Washington, 1992-93; devel. specialist, spl. counsel St. Regis Mohawk Tribe, Hogansburg, NY, 1993-97; pres. Self-Determination Inst., Aventura, Fla., 1993—. V.p. DKW Internat., Miami, Fla., 1996—; prin. drafter Mohawk constn. and laws, 1993-97. Author: Writing and Revising Constitutions in Indian Country, 1998; contbg. editor Value Engring. Digest, 1981-88. Pres. Com. To Incorporate Folly Beach, S.C., 1973. Recipient cmty. leadership award City of Folly Beach, 1973. cert. of merit Del. Assn. for Pub. Adminstrn., 1978. Mem. St. Regis Mohawk Bar Assn., Toastmasters (area 3 gov., dist. 47). Episcopalian. Avocations: reading, writing, music, public speaking. Office: 20533 Biscayne Blvd Ste 224 Aventura FL 33180-1529

FLOOD, JOAN MOORE, paralegal; b. Hampton, Va., Oct. 10, 1941; d. Harold W. and Estalena (Fancher) M.; 1 child by former marriage, Angelique. B.Mus., North Tex. State U., 1963; postgrad., So. Meth. U., 1967-68, Tex. Women's U., 1978-79, U. Dallas, 1985-86. Clk. Criminal Dist. Ct. Number 2, Dallas County, Tex., 1972-75; reins. libr. Scor Reins. Co., Dallas, 1975-80; corp. ins. paralegal Assocs. Inc. Group, 1980-83; corp. securities paralegal Akin, Gump, Strauss, Hauer & Feld, 1983-89; asst. sec. Knoll Internat. Holdings Inc., Saddle Brook, N.J., 1989-90, 21 Internat. Holdings, Inc., NYC, 1990-92; dir. compliance Am. Svc. Life Ins. Co., Ft. Worth, 1992-93; v.p., sec. Express Comm., Inc., Dallas, 1993-94; fin. transactions paralegal Thompson & Knight, Dallas, 1994-96; corp. transactions paralegal Jones, Day, Reavis & Pogue, Dallas, 1996-97, Weil, Gotshal & Manges, LLP, 1998—99; corp. paralegal PennCorp. Fin. Group, Inc., Dallas, 1999-2001; debt trade mgr. Patton Boggs LLP, 2001—03, sr. paralegal bus. transactions, 2003; corp. paralegal Carrington, Coleman, Sloman & Blumenthal, LLP, Dallas, 2003—05; freelance paralegal, 2005—. Mem. ABA, Tex. Bar Assn. Home and Office: PO Box 190165 Dallas TX 75219-0165 Home Phone: 214-599-0906; Office Phone: 214-236-7591. Personal E-mail: jmfdallas@msn.com.

FLOOD, RALPH F., educational association administrator; s. Allen and Edna Flood; m. Constance Finnerty, Feb. 10, 1973; children: Charles, Elizabeth, Joseph, Matthew. BS, SUNY, New Paltz, 1971, MS, 1975, cert. in Advanced Study, 1985. Cert. tchr. NY State, 1971, sch. dist. administr. NY State, 1985, sch. administr. supr. NY State, 1985. Tchr. Wallkill Ctrl. Sch. Dist., NY, 1971—86, 1989—2004; asst. dir. Mid-Hudson Tchr. Ctr., New Paltz, NY, 1986—89, exec. dir., 2004—. Adv. bd. Devereux NY, Red Hook, NY, 1992—2002; site coord. Spl. Olympics, Kingston, NY, 1974—78; mem. tech. com. Statewide Tchr. Ctr., Albany, NY, 1986—89; mem. planning com. NY State Tchr. Ctrs., Albany, 2000—03, mem. higher edn. com., 2004—, mem. pub. rels. com., 2006—; tchr. summer program Hebrew Acad. Spl. Children, Parksville, NY, 1982—86, asst. prin., 1991—2006; adj. prof. SUNY, New Paltz, 1990—, mem. adv. com. dept. spl. edn., 1990; cons. in field. Editor: Perceptions: Jour. of NYS Educators of the Emotionally Disturbed, 1989—92; co-editor: Parent Connection: Devereux NY, 1998—2001; contbr. articles to profl. jours. Mem. edn. com. Hudson Valley Philharm., Poughkeepsie, NY, 1988—89; mem. edn. adv. com. Ulster County Head Start, Kingston, NY, 1988—89. Mem.: ASCD, Wallkill Tchrs.' Assn. (pres. 2000—06), Coun. Exceptional Children, Nat. Staff Devel. Coun., NY State United Tchrs. (life), Am. Fedn. Tchrs. (life), Phi Delta Kappa. Dfl. Avocations: cooking, reading. Office: Mid-Hudson Tchr Ctr OM 212 State U of NY 800 Hawk Dr New Paltz NY 12561 Home Phone: 845-389-1600; Office Phone: 845-257-2885.

FLOOD, RICHARD SIDNEY, curator; b. Nov. 10, 1943; BA, St. Joseph's Coll., Phila., 1965; MA Annenberg Sch. Commn., U. Pa., 1967. Tchr. film, video & English Phila. pub. schools; dir. Cmty. Sch. Phila.; co-founder, editor Art Exchange mag., Phila., 1976—79; mng. editor to books editor ArtForum Mag., 1980—83; dir. Barbara Gladstone Gallery, NYC, 1983—94; chief curator Walker Art Ctr., Mpls., 1994—2005, New Mus. Contemporary Art, NYC, 2005—. Adv. grad. sculpture dept. RI Inst. Art & Design, Providence, 1981—83, Nat. Coll. Art & Design, Dublin, 2005—06; adv. dept. photography Yale U., New Haven, 2007—. Office: New Mus Contemporary Art 210 11th Ave New York NY 10001 Office Phone: 212-219-1222. Office Fax: 212-431-5328.

FLOOR, RICHARD EARL, lawyer; b. Lynn, Mass., Aug. 3, 1940; s. Albert C. and Blanche (Goldthwait) F.; m. Elizabeth Wilson, Apr. 19, 1969; children: Amy, Lucy, Rebecca. AB, Fairfield U., 1962; JD, Harvard Law Sch., 1965. Bar: Mass. 1965, N.Y. 2001. Law clk. to Hon. C.P. O'Sullivan U.S. Ct. Appeals (6th cir.), 1965-66; assoc. Goodwin, Procter & Hoar, Boston, 1966-74; ptnr. Goodwin Procter LLP (formerly Goodwin, Procter & Hoar), Boston, 1974—; mem. mgmt. com. & exec. com. Goodwin, Procter & Hoar, Boston, 1987-93; mem. mgmt. com., co-chair corp. dept. Goodwin Procter LLP, Boston. Lectr. Harvard Bus. Sch., Cambridge, 1988-92; bd. dirs. Affiliated Mgrs. Group, Inc., New Am. High Income Fund, NYSE; mem. supervisory bd. Basell S.A. Contbr. articles to profl. jours. Co-chmn. reverse investment com. internat. trade adv. bd. Commonwealth Mass., 1994; organizer Inst. Mgmt. Edn. Thailand; trustee Regis Coll., Wellesley, Mass., 1990-97, 99-; chmn. Harvard Ctr. Eating Disorders, 2000-01. Mem. ABA, Boston Bar Assn. Office: Goodwin Procter LLP Exchange Pl 53 State St Boston MA 02109-2881 Home Phone: 617-484-9118; Office Phone: 617-570-1260. E-mail: rfloor@goodwinprocter.com.

FLOR, CLAUS PETER, conductor; b. Leipzig, Saxonia, Germany, Mar. 16, 1953; adopted s. Richard and Sigrid (Langer) F.; m. Sabine Winni Niedziella, Mar. 15, 1984; 1 child, Claus Peter Jr. Grad., Music Sch., Weimar, Germany, 1971; Diploma, High Sch. Music, Weimar/Leipzig, 1971-77; grad. in conduction, High Sch. Music, Leipzig, 1975-78. Chief condr. Philarm. Orch., Suhl, Germany, 1981-84; chief condr., gen. music dir. Berliner Sinfonie Orchester, 1984-92; artistic adv. Tonhalle Orchestra, 1991—96; prin. guest condr. Dallas Symphony Orch. Prin. guest condr. Philharmonia Orchestra, 1991-96, Dallas Symphony Orch., 1998—, Sinfonica di Milano Giuseppe Verdi, 2003- Guest condr. numerous symphonic orchs. including Munich and Berlin Philarm. Orchs., various famous London, Paris, Vienna orchs., L.A. Philarm., N.Y. Philarm., and many others, also various opera houses in Munich, Berlin, Hamburg. Avocations:

collecting red wines, history and genealogy of the european nobility, horses, sailing. also: Intermusica Artists Mgmt 16 Duncan Terr London N18BZ England Office Phone: 1712785455. E-mail: swflor@AOL.com.*

FLORA, JAIRUS DALE, JR., statistician; b. Northfield, Minn., Mar. 27, 1944; s. Jairus Dale and Betty Ruth (Garvin) F.; m. Sharyl Ann Hughes, Aug. 18, 1967; 1 child, Edward Hughes BS magna cum laude, Midland Luth. Coll., 1965; postgrad., Tech. U. Karlsruhe, Fed. Republic Germany, 1965-66; MS, Fla. State U., 1968, PhD, 1971. Asst. prof. biostats Sch. Pub. Health U. Mich., Ann Arbor, 1971-73, asst. prof., asst. rsch. scientist Hwy. Safety Rsch. Inst., 1973-76, assoc. rsch. scientist Hwy. Safety Rsch. Inst., 1976-81, assoc. prof. biostats. Sch. Pub. Health, 1976-81, prof. biostats. Sch. Pub. Health, rsch. scientist Transp. Rsch. Inst., 1981-84; prin. statistician Midwest Rsch. Inst, Kansas City, Mo., 1984-90; sr. advisor for stats. Midwest Rsch. Inst., Kansas City, Mo., 1991-99, pres. coun. prin. scientists, 1986; clin. prof. biostats. Sch. Medicine U. Mo., Kansas City, 1984—; prin. statistician Ken Wilcox Assocs., Inc., Grain Valley, Mo., 1999, statis. cons., 1999—. Cons. statistician Nat. Burn Info. Exchange, 1971-76 Editl. collaborator Annals of Thoracic Surgery, Mathematical Bioscis., Biometrics, Accident Analysis and Prevention, 1979-90; contbr. articles to profl. jours.; patentee in field. Mem. adminstrn. bd. Valley View U. Meth. Ch., 1989-92; vol. leader Boy Scouts Am. Recipient CPS Enterprise award, 1985, Dir.'s award, 1987; German Acad. Exch. Svc. fellow, 1965-66; NASA trainee, 1966-69; NIH trainee, 1969-71; Nat Hwy. Traffic Safety Adminstrn. rsch. grantee, 1974-81. Mem. Am. Statis. Assn., Biometric Soc., Inst. Math. Stats., Masons (area dep. Grand Master 2003-05, Knight comdr. ct. hon.), Scottish Rite, Masonic Societas Rosiercruciana in Civitatibus Foederatus, Blue Key, Sigma Xi (pres. Kansas City chpt. 1990-91, v.p. 1994-96). Republican. Home: 9921 Foster St Shawnee Mission KS 66212-2452 Personal E-mail: jdflora2002@yahoo.com.

FLORA, JOSEPH M(ARTIN), language educator; b. Toledo, Feb. 9, 1934; s. Raymond D. F. and Frances (Ricica) Neumann; m. Glenda Christine Lape, Jan. 30, 1959; children: Ronald James, Stephen Ray, Peter Joseph, David Benjamin. BA, U. Mich., 1956, MA, 1957, PhD, 1962. Instr. U. Mich., Ann Arbor, 1961-62, U. N.C., Chapel Hill, 1962-64, asst. prof., 1964-66, assoc. prof., 1966-77, prof. English, 1977—, Atlanta prof. so. culture, 2001—, acting chmn. dept. English, 1980-81, chmn., 1981-91, asst. dean grad. sch., 1967-72, assoc. dean grad. sch., 1977-78. Author: Vardis Fisher, 1965, William Ernest Henley, 1970, Frederick Manfred, 1974, Hemingway's Nick Adams, 1982 (Mayflower Cup award 1982), Ernest Hemingway: A Study of the Short Fiction, 1989, Vardis Fisher: Centennial Essays, 2000; editor: The English Short Story, 1880-1945, 1985; co-editor: Southern Writers, 1979, Fifty Southern Writers Before 1990, 1987, Fifty Southern Writers After 1900, 1987, Contemporary Fiction Writers of the South, 1993, Contemporary Poets, Dramatists, Essayists, Novelists of the South, 1994, The Companion to Southern Literature, 2001, Southern Writers: The New Biographical Dictionary, 2006; editorial bds. Mem. MLA, South Atlantic MLA (v.p. 1997-98, pres. 1998-99), Western Lit. Assn. (bd. dirs. 1978-81, 83-86, v.p. 1990, pres. 1992), Soc. for Study So. Lit., Thomas Wolfe Soc. (v.p. 1993-95, pres. 1995-97), Phi Beta Kappa, Phi Eta Sigma. Home: 505 Caswell Rd Chapel Hill NC 27514-2705 Office: UNC Dept Of English Chapel Hill NC 27599-0001 Business E-Mail: jflora@email.unc.edu.

FLORA, KATHLEEN M., retired state representative; b. Dearborn, Mich., Nov. 10, 1952; m. James A. Flora; two children. BA, Mich. State U., 1975, MA, 1977. State rep. N.H. Ho. of Reps., 1996—2002. Mem. Bedford Rep. Com., 1996— Vol. adv. bd. VNA Hospice, 1996-97. Mem. ASTD. Office: NH State Legis State House Concord NH 03301 Office Phone: 941-907-6063. E-mail: kflora@tampabay.rr.com.

FLORENCE, JOYCE FRITZ, mathematics professor; b. Lexington, Ky., July 17, 1956; d. Joe and Elaine Humphrey Fritz; children: Donald Joe, Jillian Florence Anderson. Associates, Maysville C.C., 1997; Bachelors, U. Ky., 2000; Masters, Georgetown Coll., 2003, Ea. Ky. U., 2005. Travel agt. Wilco Travel Agy., Lexington, 1974—75; bookkeeper Fritz Distbg. Co. Inc., Cynthiana, Ky., 1977—90; travel agt. Going Places Travel, Georgetown, Ky., 1986—91, The Travel Shoppe, Winchester, Ky., 1991—2001; preschool tchr. United Preschool, Cynthiana, 1996—97; algebra, prealgebra tchr. Harrison County HS, Cynthiana, 2000—03; algebra, problem solving tchr. Harrison County Mid. Sch., Cynthiana, 2003—. Life mem. Girl Scouts, NYC, 1962—2006, troop leader Cynthiana, 1975—2006, day camp dir., 1975—2000; sec. Trials and Trowels Garden Club, Cynthiana, 1985—87; harrison county svc. unit chmn. Girl Scouts, 1987—90, 1996—99; Sunday sch. tchr. First United Meth. Ch., Cynthiana, 1986—90. Recipient Silver Cup award, Trials and Trowels Garden Club, 1985, Honor Pin, Wilderness Rd. Girl Scout Coun., 1990, Thanks Badge, 1999; Cmty. scholarship, Maysville C.C., 1998, Mason County Alumni scholarship, Mason County Alumni Assn., 1998. Mem.: Nat. Tchrs. Math. (assoc.), Ky. Edn. Assn. (assoc.), Ky. Tchrs. Math. (assoc.), Girl Scouts (life). Home: 207 Wilson Ave Cynthiana KY 41031 Office: Harrison County Mid Sch 269 Edn Dr Cynthiana KY 41031 Home Phone: 859-234-5710; Office Phone: 859-234-7123.

FLORENCE, TYLER, chef; b. SC, Mar. 3, 1971; 1 child, Miles. Grad. with honors, Coll. Culinary Arts, Johnson & Wales U., SC, 1991. Chef Aureole, NYC, Mad 61, NYC, River Cafe, NYC; exec. chef Cibo, NYC, 1995, Cafeteria, NYC, 1998—2000. Chef Grilling Fresh menu, Applebee's Restaurants. Host (TV series) Food 911, 1999, Planet Food, All American Festivals, My Country, My Kitchen, Tyler's Ultimate, 2006—, guest appearances Rosie, The Today Show, The View, E!, Access Hollywood, Food Network; author: Tyler Florence's Real Kitchen, Eat This Book: Cooking with Global Fresh Flavors, Tyler's Ultimate. Achievements include receiving recognition from Food & Wine Mag., GQ, The Wall Street Journal, USA Weekend, People Mag., The NY Times, NY Mag., and Crain's NY Business. Office: Food Network Studios 604 W 52nd St New York NY 10019*

FLORES, ANTONIO R., educational association administrator; BBA, Universidad de Guadalajara, Mex.; BA in Elem. Edn., Centro Normal Regional, Mex.; MA in Counseling and Pers., Western Mich. U.; PhD in Higher Edn., U. Mich., Ann Arbor; EdD (hon.), Madonna U., Mich., 1995; LHD (hon.), Woodbury U., Calif., 2002. Dir. progs. and svcs. Mich. Higher Edn. Assistance Authority, Mich. Higher Edn. Student Loan Authority; pres., CEO Hispanic Assn. Colls. and Univs., Washington, 1996—. Chmn. Adelante! Leadership and Scholarship Fund, Hispanic Assn. Corp. Responsibility; bd. dir. Am. Coun. Edn., Mexico Am. Cultural Ctr., Nat. Hispanic Leadership Agenda, Nat. Commn. on Workforce of Am. Hosp. Assn. Named to Wall of Honor as disting. alumnus, Western Mich. U., 1986; recipient Disting. Alumni award, 2003, Lifetime Achievement award, Hispanic Bus. mag., 2003, Alumni of Yr. award, Western Regional U., 2003, Presdl. Medal award, Ana G. Méndez U. Sys., PR, 2004. Mem.: Ind. Sector, Am. Assn. Higher Edn., Am. Ednl. Rsch. Assn., Washington Higher Edn. Secretariat. Office: Hispanic Assn Colls and Univs One Dupont Cir NW Ste 605 Washington DC 20036 Office Phone: 202-833-8361. Office Fax: 202-261-5082.*

FLORES, BELINDA BUSTOS, bilingual educator, administrator; b. San Antonio, June 17, 1955; d. Arturo Silvano and Frances S. Bustos; m. Mario Enrique Flores, June 5, 1976; 1 child, Janelle Beth. BA, U. Tex., San Antonio, 1980, MA, 1987; PhD, U. Tex., 1999. Cert. bilingual edn. , early childhood, elem. tchr. Tex., 1980, profl. sch. counselor Tex., 1987, lic. profl. counselor Tex., 1989. Bilingual kindergarten tchr. Harlandale Ind. Sch. Dist., San Antonio, 1980—84; bilingual prekindergarten tchr. Northside Ind. Sch. Dist., San Antonio, 1984—87, elem. sch. counselor, 1987—92; asst. prof. U. Tex., San Antonio, 1999—2004, assoc. prof., dept. chair, 2004—. Contbr. articles to profl. jours., chapters to books. , US Dept. Edn. grantee, 2003—. Mem.: Assn. of Tchr. Educators, Assn. for Childhood Edn. Internat., Nat. Assn. for Bilingual Edn., Am. Edn. Rsch. Assn. Home: 9623 Misty Trails San Antonio TX 78254-5522 Office: Univ Tex 6900 N Loop 1604 W San Antonio TX 78249 Home Phone: 210-647-0872; Office Phone: 210-458-5969. Business E-Mail: belinda.flores@utsa.edu.

FLORES, GREG, retail executive; married; 2 children. BS in Psychology and Stats., U. Tex., 1977; student in Indsl. Psychology, North Tex. State U. Human resources position H.E. Butt Grocery Co.; mgr. human resources Tex. region Pepsi Bottling Group PepsiCo; dir., officer human resources Thriftway Food & Drug, Inc., Cin.; sr. v.p. human resources Daymon Worldwide; sr. v.p. human resources, comm. and rsch. Reed Bus. Info., 2000—06; exec. v.p., chief human resources officer TJX Cos., Inc., 2006—. Office: TJX Cos Inc 770 Cochituate Rd Framingham MA 01701 Office Phone: 508-390-1000. Office Fax: 508-390-2091.*

FLORES, KATHRYN LOUISE, mathematics educator; b. Midland, Mich., Sept. 28, 1963; d. George Homer and Mary Ruth Flores. BS in Chem. Engring., Tex. A&M U., Kingsville, 1985; MS in Chem. Engring., Tex. A&M U., College Station, 1989; PhD in Applied Math., U. Tex., Dallas, 2002. Asst. prof. math. McMurry U., Abilene, Tex., 2002—. With US Army, 1992—97, PTO. Mem.: Am. Math. Soc., Math. Assn. America, Tau Beta Pi. Avocation: running. Office: McMurry U McMurry Sta Box 668 Abilene TX 79697

FLORES, YOLANDA, speech pathology/audiology services professional, consultant; d. Samuel and Consuelo Flores; m. Manuel Moreno Jr., Nov. 17, 1985; children: Sasha Monik Moreno, Danielle Erika Moreno. BA in Speech, Hearing and Lang. Disability, U. Tex., El Paso, 1983, MS in Speech and Lang. Pathology, 1985. Cert. speech and lang. pathologist N.Mex., Tex., clin. competence in speech lang. pathology Am. Speech and Hearing Assn., 1990. Speech lang. pathologist Ysleta Ind. Sch. Dist., 1983—, Providence Meml. Hosp., 1995—98. Instr. ESL El Paso C.C., Tex.; off-campus grad. supr. U. Tex. El Paso, 1992—2004, Tex. Women's U., 2002—03; class sponsor Ysleta Ind. Sch. Dist., Tex., 2002—; technology and inclusion trainer Speak Up, Tex., Tex., 2005—. Mem.: N.Mex. Speech and Hearing Assn., El Paso Speech and Hearing Assn. (sec., pres. elect, pres.), Tex. Speech Lang. and Hearing Assn., Am. Speech and Hearing Assn. (continuing edn. award 1999, 2002, 2005). Roman Catholic. Avocations: travel, gardening, exercise, dance, sports. Home: 1363 Pony Trail Pl El Paso TX 79936

FLORESCU, JOHN MAURICE, broadcast executive; b. Boston, Apr. 14, 1954; s. Radu Radu and Nicole (Michel) F.; m. Gina Diane Christensen, July 31, 1993; 1 child, Peter Vlad. Degree, Campion Hall, Oxford U., England, 1974; BA, Boston Coll., Chestnut Hill, 1976. Correspondent Associated Press, Paris, 1977-79; staff Sen. Edward Kennedy Presdl. Campaign, Washington, 1979-80; exec. prodr. Great Confrontations at Oxford Union/PBS-BBC, 1982-85; v.p. Am. Program Bur., Boston, 1981-85; dir. comms. Dem. Nat. Com., Washington, 1985-86; exec. prodr. PBS Talking with D. Frost, LA, 1991—98; CEO David Paradine TV, Inc., LA, 1987—; exec. prodr. A&E George Bush: A President's Story, 1998, Decisive Battles (History Channel), 2000. Commentator U.S. Politics TFI-French Television, N.Y.C., 1984; mem. bd. dirs. Centrade Saatchi & Saatchi, Bucharest, Romania, 1991-, CEO Bates Centrade USA, Saatchi & Saatchi, 1998—. Contbr. editl. pages The Washington Post, The Boston Globe, The Christian Sci. Monitor. Election observer Nat. Dem. Inst., Romania, 1990, Kenya, 1992. Mem. Oxford-Cambridge Soc. Calif. and Romania, Boston Coll. Alumni Soc. Democrat. Roman Catholic. Avocations: tennis, skiing. E-mail: jmflor@aol.com.

FLORESCUE, LEONARD GEORGE, lawyer; b. Rochester, NY, Nov. 29, 1946; s. Harold M. and Sarah (Miller) F.; m. Susan Thypin, Aug. 13, 1972 (dec. 1975); m. Marilyn Cronenberg, Apr. 10, 1976; 1 child, Heather. BA, U. Rochester, 1967; JD, NYU, 1972. Bar: N.Y. 1973, U.S. Dist. Ct. (so. and ea. dists.) N.Y. 1974, U.S. Ct. Appeals (2d cir.) 1974. Assoc. Fried Frank Harris Shriver & Jacobson, NYC, 1972-83; ptnr. Ruskin Schlissel Moscou Evans & Faltischek, Mineola, N.Y., 1983-91; counsel Tenzer Greenblatt LLP (now Blank Rome LLP), NYC, 1991-96; ptnr. Blank Rome LLP, NYC, 1997—. Adj. prof. Fordham Law Sch., Benjamin Cardozo Sch. Law, N.Y.C.; lectr. in field. Co-author: Tax Aspects of Divorce and Separation, 1989; contbr. columns to N.Y. Law Jour., 1983—. Mem. Interstate Commn. on High Conflict Divorce. Mem. NY State Bar Assn., Assn. Family and Concilation Courts (founding mem., past-pres., bd. mem. NY chpt.) Avocations: miltary history, golf, reading, sports. Office: Blank Rome LLP 405 Lexington Ave New York NY 10174-0208 Office Phone: 212-885-5396. Business E-Mail: lflorescue@blankrome.com.*

FLORET, EVELYN, sculptor; b. Paris; arrived in USA, 1941; d. Joseph and Rose Floret. BA, Washington U., St. Louis, 1961. Three yr. cert. Nat. Acad. Sch. Fine Arts. Contbg. photographer People Mag., NYC, 1976—94; sculptor NYC, 1995—. Exhibitions include United Nations, 1986, Internat. Ctr. Photography, 1988, Hubert Gallery, 1995, Nat. Sculpture Soc. Ann. Exhbn., 1998, Cork Gallery, 1999, Nat. Arts Club, 1999, Nat. Sculpture Soc. Ann. Exhbn., 2001, Pen and Brush 54th Ann. Sculpture and Medallic Exhbn., 2000 (Elliot Liskin Meml. award, 2000), Pen and Brush 58th Ann. Sculpture and Medallic Exhbn., 2004 (Elliot Liskin Meml. award, 2004), Nat. Sculpture Soc. In Remembrance: Sept. 11th Exhbn., 2002, Audubon Artists 61st Ann. Exhbn., 2003, Allied Artists of Am. 91st Ann. Exhbn., 2004, Audubon Artists 64th Ann. Exhbn., 2006. Mem.: Soc. N.Am. Goldsmiths, Am. Soc. Media Photographers, Pen and Brush, Inc., Audubon Artists Inc. Home: 8 East 83rd St New York NY 10028 Home Phone: 212-472-3179.

FLOREY, KLAUS GEORG, chemist, pharmaceutical consultant; b. Dresden, Germany, July 4, 1919; came to U.S., 1947, naturalized, 1952; s. Friedrich Georg and Margarethe Käthe (Pick) F.; m. Anne Major, Nov. 22, 1956; children: Peter, Andrea. Student, U. Munich, U. Heidelberg, Germany; PhD, U. Pa., 1954. Research asst. Bayer, Leverkusen, Germany, 1944-45; research asso. Merck & Co., Rahway, N.J., 1949-50; research chemist Squibb Inst. Med. Research, New Brunswick, N.J., 1954-59, dir. analytical research and devel., 1959-84, cons., 1984-90. Mem. com. revisions U.S. Pharmacopeia, 1970-95, hon. mem., 2000; mem. WHO Expert Adv. Panel Internat. Pharmacopeia, 1976-93; docent The Princeton U. Art Mus., 1991--. Editor: Analytical Profiles of Drug Substances, 22 vols., 1971—; contbr. articles to profl. jours.; patentee in field. Recipient Justin L. Powers award, 1987. Fellow AAAS, Acad. Pharm. Scis. (chmn. pharm. analysis and control sect. 1967-68, pres. 1980-81); mem. Am. Chem. Soc., Soc. Nuclear Medicine, Am. Assn. Pharm. Scientists (Disting. Svc. award 1990), Coun. Sci. Soc. Pres. (chmn. 1983) Home: 151 Loomis Ct Princeton NJ 08540-3438

FLOREZ, MARY A., artist; married; 5 children. Student, Boca Raton Art Mus., U. Cin., Thompson Art Studio. Exhibitions include Southeastern Ind. Art Guild, Aurora, Breast Cancer Awareness Brick Auction, Cin., 2002, Sharon Ctr. Hilltop Artists, 2003, 2004, Women in Visual Arts, Boca Raton, Fla., 2003, 2005, Fed. Credit Union Cin., 2003, Fitton Ctr. Creative Arts, Hamilton, Ohio, Cin. Acad. Medicine, Farbach Warner Nature Preserve, Cin., Town Club Cin, Ansonia High Sch., Conn., Evengale Recreation Ctr., Cin., 2004, Hamilton County Pub. Libr., 2004. Mem. Good Samaritan Hosp. Guild, Cin., St. Francis-St. George Hosp. Guild, Providence Hosp. Guild; fundraising chair Acad. Sacred Heart, St. Mary's Hosp. Mem.: Cin. Acad. Medicine Women's Aux., Hilltop Artists, Women Visual Arts, Cin. Town Club, Woman's Art Club, Cin. Woman's Club. Avocation: golf. Home: 797 Windings Ln Cincinnati OH 45220 E-mail: mflorez1@cinci.rr.com.

FLOREZ, VIOLA E., academic administrator, dean; b. Bloomfield, N.Mex., July 30, 1947; d. Jose M. and Florence (Hancock) Florez; m. Girard A. Tighe, June 27, 1980; children: Kathryn Marie, Joseph A. BA, Ft. Lewis Coll., Durango, Colo., 1970; MA, U. Colo., 1976; EdD, Tex. A & I U., 1980. Cert. tchr., Tex. Tchr. Sch. Dist. #11, Colorado Springs, Colo., 1971-76, Ft. Defiance Sch. Dist., Window Rock, Ariz., 1976-78; cons. Region VI Edn. Svc. Ctr., Huntsville, Tex., 1980; asst. prof. U. Nebr., Lincoln, 1980-81, Tex. A&M U., College Station, 1982-87, assoc. prof., 1987-92, coord. grad. programs, 1990—, asst. head dept. edn., 1990; dean Coll. Edn. U. N.Mex., Albuquerque, 1997—, interim provost, exec. v.p. academic affairs, 2007—. Dir. Bilingual Edn. Ctr., Tex. A&M Coll., 1983—; ednl. cons. Region VI ECS, Huntsville, Tex., 1980-92. Book reviewer: Literacy and Bilingualism, 1990; contbr. articles to profl. jours. Named Outstanding Woman of the Yr. Tex. A&I U., 1979, Disting. Teaching award Tex. A&M U., 1987, Lone Star Showcas e& Salute award Community Svc. Program, 1992. Mem. Nat. Coun. tchrs. English, Nat. Assn. for Bilingual Edn., Internat. reading Assn., Teaching English to Speakers of Other Langs., Am. Ednl. Rsch. Assn., Hispanic Profl. Network. Democrat. Roman Catholic. Avocations: music, reading, travel. Office: U NMex Academic Affairs & Office of Provost Scholes Hall 221 Albuquerque NM 87131 Office Phone: 505-277-7267. E-mail: vflorez@unm.edu.

FLORI, ANNA MARIE DIBLASI, nurse anesthetist, educational administrator; b. Amsterdam, N.Y., Oct. 29, 1940; d. Tony and Maria (Macario) DiBlasi; children: Tammy, Tina, Toni; m. Gilberto Flori, May 24, 1986. Grad., Albany Med. Ctr. Sch. Nursing, 1962, Fairfax Hosp. Sch. Nurse Anesthetists, Va., 1972; BS in Anesthesia, George Washington U., 1979; M. in Bus. and Pub. Adminstrn., Southeastern U., Washington, 1982; PhD, Columbia Pacific U., 1983. Cert. registered nurse anesthetist. Staff nurse West Seattle Gen. Hosp., 1962-64; office nurse Filmore Buckner, M.D., Seattle, 1964-66; staff nurse anesthetist Fairfax Hosp., 1972-73; staff nurse anesthetist Potomac Hosp., Woodbridge, Va., 1973, chief nurse anesthetist, 1973—; dir. Potomac Hosp. Sch. for Nurse Anesthetists and Sch. for Nurse Anesthesia; faculty mem. Columbia Pacific U., 1973-90; chief nurse anesthetist No. Va. Anesthesia Assn., 1988—; guest lectr. No. Va. Community Coll., Inservice Potomac Hosp., George Washington U.; coord. Free Clinic Prince William County, Woodbridge, Va. Contbr. books on anesthesia. Mem. Am. Assn. Nurse Anesthetists, Va. Nurse Anesthesia Assn., Nat. Italian Am. Found. Home: 12954 Pintail Rd Woodbridge VA 22192-3831 Office Phone: 703-490-5496.

FLORIAN-LACY, DOROTHY, psychologist, educator; b. Dearborn, Mich., Oct. 27, 1958; d. Raymond Joseph and Dorothy Mae Florian; m. Bill George Lacy, July 25, 1981; children: Jason M., Miles, Anderson. BS in Psychology and Edn., Ea. Mich. U., Ypsilanti, 1978, MA in Guidance and Counseling, 1979; EdD in Counselor Edn., Tex. Southeastern U., 1998. Lic. profl. counselor, Tex. Realtor Century 21, Ann Arbor, Mich., 1978—79; tchr. Adult Exception Ctr., Compton, Calif., 1979—81; owner, dir. Village Learning & Play Ctr., Houston, 1982—94; dept. chair spl. edn. Milby Sr. H.S., Houston, 1994—2000; therapist Houston Achievement Place, 1998—. Author: Fundamentals of Mathematics I, Fundamentals of Mathematics II, Consumer Math; co-author: Reference Manual for Special Education Department Chairpersons. Vol. Child Abuse Prevention, Houston, 1989-91, vol. coach YMCA, Houston, 1987-90. Recipient Adaptor grant Impact II, 1997, Study Group grant Impact II, 1998. Mem. ACA, Children's Mus Avocation: golf coach. Office: Houston Achievement Place 236 W 17th St Houston TX 77008-4002 Office Phone: 713-868-2909 x272. Personal E-mail: dflorian@houstonisd.org. Business E-Mail: dlacy@h-a-p.org.

FLORIDA, RICHARD LOUIS, finance educator, writer; b. Newark, Nov. 26, 1957; s. Louis and Eleanor Florida. BA, Rutgers U., 1979; MPh in Urban Planning, Columbia U., 1984, PhD in Urban Planning, 1986. Instr. Dept. City and Regional Planning, Ohio State U., 1984—85, asst. prof., dir. undergraduate program, 1985—87; asst. prof. mgmt. and pub. policy H. John Heinz III Sch. Pub. Policy and Mgmt., Carnegie Mellon U., Pitts., 1987—90, assoc. prof., 1990—94, dir. Ctr. Econ. Devel., 1993—98, prof., 1994, Heinz prof. regional econ. devel., 1996—2004, dir. Software Industry Ctr., 2001—05; Hirst prof. pub. policy George Mason U., 2004—07; non-resident sr. fellow Brookings Inst., 2004—07; dir. Inst. Jurisdictional Advantage and Prosperity, prof. bus. and creativity Rotman Sch. Mgmt., U. Toronto, 2007—. Rsch. assoc. Ctr. Urban Policy Rsch., Rutgers U., 1980—83; lectr. Dept. Environ. Design and Planning, SUNY, Buffalo, 1983; adj. scholar Am. Enterprise Inst., 1993; vis. prof. John F. Kennedy Sch. Govt., Harvard U., 1995—96; vis. scholar Internat. Motor Vehicle Program, MIT, 1996; non-resident sr. fellow Brookings Inst., 2004—07; sr. scientist Gallup Orgn., 2005—07; adv. White House Office of Sci. and Tech. Policy, US Dept. Commerce. Author: Beyond Mass Production, 1993, The Breakthrough Illusion, 1990, Rise of the Creative Class, 2002 (Washington Monthly Polit. Book award), Flight of the Creative Class, 2005, (editor) Industrializing Knowledge: University-Industry Linkages in Japan and the United States, 1999; contbr. articles to profl. jours., newspapers including The N.Y. Times, The Wall St. Jour., Washington Post; commentator on PBS documentaries about US economy, global competitiveness, future of jobs. Active Coun. Gt. Lakes Govs.; bd. dirs. TeamPa., Pa.'s 21st Century Environ. Commn. Named one of Best and Brightest, Esquire mag., 2005; recipient Inaugural Parnes Creativity Award, Creative Problem-Solving Inst., 2005. Office: Richard Florida Creativity Group 4500 Connecticut Ave NW Apt 512 Washington DC 20008-4336 also: Joseph L Rotman Sch of Mgmt U Toronto 105 St George St Toronto ON Canada Office Phone: 412-782-5211, 703-993-2280. Business E-Mail: florida@gmu.edu.*

FLORINE, JANE L., musicology educator; b. Waseca, Minn., July 22, 1953; d. Martin Clifford Florine and Alice Dorothy Ostergren. BA summa cum laude, U. Minn., 1975; MA, Lesley Coll., 1992; PhD, Fla. State U., 1996. Flutist Nat. Symphony Orch., Buenos Aires, 1975-83; bilingual asst. to the pres. Braun Argentina, Buenos Aires, 1983-86; fgn. student advisor Boston U., 1991-92; assoc. prof. ethnomusicology/musicology Chgo. State U., 1997—. Cons. Chgo. Symphony Orch., 1999-2001. Author: Cuarteto Music and Dancing from Argentina: In Search of the Tunga-Tunga in Cordoba, 2001; contbr. articles to profl. jours. Fulbright fellow, 1994, Dissertation fellow Fla. State U., 1995, Fulbright-Hays fellow, 2004, NEH fellow, 2005. Mem.: L.Am. Studies Assn., Coll. Music Soc., Argentine Musicology Assn., Soc. for Ethnomusicology (pres. Midwest chpt. 1999—2000), Internat. Assn. for Study Popular Music, Nat. Flute Soc. (life). Home: 5000 S Cornell Ave Apt 4C Chicago IL 60615 Office: Chgo State Univ Music Dept/HWH 331 9501 S King Dr Chicago IL 60628-1598 Office Phone: 773-995-2119. Business E-Mail: jflorine@csu.edu.

FLORIO, STEVEN T., magazine executive; b. NYC, Apr. 19, 1949; s. F. Steve and Sophia (Masciale) F.; m. Marianne McNeill, June 1, 1974; children: Steven John, Kelly Anne. AA, NYU, 1970, BS, 1972. Rschr. Esquire mag., NYC, 1972-73, New Eng. mgr., 1974-76, advt. dir., 1976-79, v.p., 1979-80; pub. Gentlemen's Quar., NYC, 1980-85; pres., CEO New Yorker mag., NYC, 1985-94, pub., 1985-88; pres. Condé Nast Publs., Inc., NYC, 1994—2004, CEO, 1996—2004; vice chmn., Advanced Mag. Group Conde Nast Publs., Inc., NYC, 2004—. Guest spkr. lecture series Harvard U., Rice U., NYU, Yale U. Chmn. Namesake Com. USS N.Y.C. USN. Mem.: Mag. Pubs. Assn. (chmn. conf. 1989), Men's Fashion Assn. Office: Conde Nast Publ 4 Times Sq New York NY 10036-6561

FLORIO, THOMAS A., publishing executive; B, NYU. Formerly advt. dir. Conde Nast Traveler, NYC, pub., 1990-94; pres. The New Yorker, NYC, 1994-99; v.p., pub. Gentleman's Quarterly, NYC, 1999—2002; v.p. Vogue, NYC, 2002—, pub., 2002—. Named one of NY's 40 under Forty Rising Stars, Crain's NY Business, 1994. Office: Vogue Conde Nast 4 Times Sq New York NY 10036-6522*

FLORSHEIM, RICHARD STEVEN, lawyer; b. Milw., Apr. 2, 1949; s. Ernst Frederick and Ingeborg Miriam Florsheim; m. Neena B. Florsheim; children: Ali Brynn, David Ira, Rebecca Lynn. BS, MIT, 1971; JD magna cum laude, Marquette U., 1974. Bar: Wis. 1974, Fla. 1983. Assoc. Foley & Lardner, Milw., 1974-81, ptnr., 1981—, leader intellectual property litigation group, 1987-97, chair intellectual property dept., 1997—2006, chair industry teams dept., 2006—, chair regulated industries dept., 2006—07, mem. mgmt. commn., 2006—. Co-author: Biotechnology Patent Practice, 1994, Inside the Minds: Leading Intellectual Property Lawyers, 2001. Pres. North Shore Libr., Milw., 1985-87, Jewish Found. Econ. Opportunity, Milw., 1992-96, 05-; bd. dirs. Milw. Jewish Fedn., 1987-93, 96-02, NCCJ Wis. region, 1990-2000, Ohr Hatorah Jewish Heritage Ctr., 2002-2007, pres., 2002-2007, Children's Rsch. Inst., 2005— Mem. ABA, Am. Intellectual Property Law Assn. (subcom. chmn. 1992-97), Fed. Cir. Bar Assn., Wis. Bar Assn., Milw. Bar Assn., Marquette Law Alumni Assn. (pres. 1985-86). Office: Foley & Lardner LLP 777 E Wisconsin Ave Ste 3800 Milwaukee WI 53202-5367 Office Phone: 414-297-5515. Business E-Mail: rflorsheim@foley.com.

FLORY, CURT ALAN, research physicist; BS in Physics with distinction, Stanford U., 1975; MS in Physics, U. Wash., 1977; PhD in Physics, U. Calif., Berkeley, 1981. R&D fellow, rsch. physicist Agilent Technologies, Palo Alto, Calif., 1984—; postdoc. SLAC, 1981-84. Recipient Indsl. Physics prize Am. Inst. Physics, 1993-94. Fellow Am. Phys. Soc. Office: Agilent Technolgies 3500 Deer Creek Rd # 26M Palo Alto CA 94304-1317 E-mail: curt_flory@agilent.com.

FLORY, MARGARET MARTHA, retired religious organization administrator; b. Wauseon, Ohio, May 13, 1914; d. Arthur Henry and Laura Grace (Gorsuch) F. BA, Ohio U., 1936, MA, 1938; postgrad., Union Theol. Seminary, 1940-43; LLD, Maryville Coll., 1988. Tchg. fellow Ohio U., Athens, 1936-38, dir. Westminster Found., 1940-44; tchr. Bainbridge (Ohio) H.S., 1938-39; drama and speech faculty Ala. State Coll., Montevallo, 1939-40; Eastern area sec. Presbyn. Ch. Nat. Hdqrs., NYC, 1944-51, staff student world rels., 1951-68, staff new dimension in mission, 1969-73; staff ecumenical sharing program dir. Presbyn. Ch. U.S.A., 1973-80; short-term tchr. missions and ecumenical rels. San Francisco Theol. Sem., 1979-80; min. in residence Pacific Sch. Religion, Berkeley, Calif., 1981; mem. Stony Point (N.Y.) ctr. program staff Presbyn. Ch. U.S.A., 1981-87; ret., 1987. Author: Moments in Time, 1995, From Past to Future: Experiments in Global Bridging, 1997, Dear House, 2001; contbr. articles to profl. jours. Active Pres. Kennedy's Women's Com. on Civil Rights, 1963; trustee Maryville (Tenn.) Coll., 1963-78; pres. bd. trustees World Student Christian Fedn., N.Y.C., 1968-90; coun. ch. rels. Warren Wilson Coll., N.C., 1993—. Named Outstanding Alumnae Ohio U.; recipient Human Rights award Korean Christian Scholars, 1985, Woman of Faith award Presbyn. Women, 1987, Cert. of Appreciation Silliman U., 1981; conf. hall named in her honor John Knox Internat. Studies Ctr., Geneva, 1993. Mem. AAUW (exec. bd.), Assn. for Women's Edn. in Asia (pres. 1973-85), Ch. Relationships with Eastern Europe, Ch. Women United, Phi Beta Kappa. Avocations: reading, theater, walking, gardening, floral decoration. Home and Office: 276 College Walk Ln Brevard NC 28712-3161 E-mail: margaretflorycw@yahoo.com.

FLORY, MARJORIE ANNE, writer, editor; d. Harry Russell and Florence Gilman Flory. BA, Smith Coll., Northampton, Mass., 1951; postgraduate, Columbia U., NYC, 1952—53. Libr. asst. French Embassy Cultural Svcs., NYC, 1951—52; rschr. Reader's Digest, NYC, 1953—60, assoc. editor Pleasantville, NY, 1960—80, sr. editor Pleasantville and NYC, 1980—85; freelance writer and editor NYC, 1985—. Editor Fourth Write Press, Shelbourne, Vt., 1993—; vice chair Freedom Press Assocs., NH, 1998—. Copy editor Made in Italy, 1988; co-author: Reel Life/Real Life, 1994; editor: More Cooking with Pecans, 2003. Vol. tutor Vol. Svcs. for Children, NYC, 1980—85; interpreter NY Rd. Runners Club, NYC, 1998—2006. Mem.: Smith Coll. Club NYC (bd. mem. 2003—05), Phi Beta Kappa. Avocations: travel, tennis, language study, choral singing. Home: 610 West End Ave Apt 7E New York NY 10024

FLORY, PETER CYRIL WYCHE, federal agency administrator; b. Oct. 1955; m. Kathleen M. Flory; 6 children. BA, McGill U., 1979; JD, Georgetown U. Spl. asst. to under sec. for policy US Dept. Def., Washington, 1989—92; assoc. coord. counter-terrorism US Dept. State, Washington, 1992—93; atty. Hughes, Hubbard & Reed LLP, Washington, 1993—97; chief investigative counsel & spl. counsel, select. com. on intelligence U.S. Senate, Washington, 1997—2001; prin. dep. asst. sec. for internat. security affairs US Dept. Def., Washington, 2001—05, asst. sec. for internat. security policy, 2005—.*

FLOTTE, TERENCE ROBIN, pediatrician, pulmonologist; b. New Orleans, Dec. 4, 1961; s. Arthur Victor and Marie Therese (Indest) F.; children: David Edward, Lindsay Hanna, Jesse Cole. BS summa cum laude, U. New Orleans, 1982; MD, La. State U., 1986. Diplomate Am. Bd. Pediatrics, subspecialty in pulmonary pediatrics. Pediatric resident Johns Hopkins Hosp., Balt., 1986-89; pediatric pulmonary fellow Johns Hopkins U., Balt., 1989-92, instr., 1992-93, asst. prof., 1993-96; postdoctoral rsch. fellow NIH, Bethesda, Md., 1989-92; asst. prof. pediats. and molecular genetics 1998U. Fla., Gainesville, 1996—98; co-dir. Powell Gene Therapy Ctr. U. Fla., Gainesville, 1996—2000; dir. Powell Gene Therapy Ctr., 2000—02, UF Genetics Inst., 2000—02; prof., chmn. pediat., 2002—. Contbr. articles to profl. jours. Recipient Leroy Mathews Physician Scientist award Cystic Fibrosis Found., 1991, Chancellor's award La. State U. Sch. Medicine, 1986, E. Mead Johnson award, 2005; NIH CF Gene Therapy Ctr. Rsch. grantee, 1993; Nemours Eminent scholar. Mem. AMA, Am. Thoracic Soc., Alpha Omega Alpha. Roman Catholic. Achievements include research on first NIH recombinant DNA advisory committee - approved gene therapy protocol using an adeno-associated virus vector in humans; inventor 2 patents of AAV-Vectors for cystic fibrosis gene therapy and production process for these vectors. Office: Univ Fla Pediat Gene Therapy Ctr PO Box 100296 Gainesville FL 32610-0296 Office Phone: 352-392-3337.

FLOUM, JOSHUA R., finance company executive, lawyer; BA, Univ. Calif., Berkeley; JD, Harvard Univ. Ptnr. Legal Strategies Group, San Francisco, Heller Ehrman White & McAuliffe, San Francisco; ptnr., chmn. Calif. litigation practice Holme Roberts & Owen, San Francisco; exec. v.p., gen. counsel, sec. Visa USA, San Francisco, 2004—. Mem. Lawyers Com. for Civil Rights; legal adv. Earth Island Inst. Mailing: Visa USA PO Box 194607 San Francisco CA 94119-4607*

FLOURNOY, JOHN CHARLES, SR., retired civilian military employee, officer; b. Florala, Ala., Nov. 30, 1936; s. Q. P. and Alice Ruby (Cope) Flournoy; m. Charlene Reneé Lett, June 7, 1957; children: Jamie Lynn, John Charles Jr., Jeffrey Allan. BS, Auburn U., 1959. Commd. 2d lt. USAF, 1959, advanced through grades to col., dep. chief of staff for ops. 23rd Air Force Hurlburt Field, Fla., 1983—88; site mgr., tng. mgr. Raytheon Sys., Kirkland AFB, N.Mex., 1988-98, tng. analyst, Air Force Rsch. Lab. Albuquerque, 1998—99; training cons. Air Force Rsch Lab, Mesa, 2003—06; cons., 2006—. Decorated Legion Merit; recipient German Gratitude medal, Fed. Republic of Germany, 1962. Mem.: Pedro Rescue Helicopter Assn. (member at large), Air Rescue Assn. (pres.), Air Commando Assn., USAF Helicopter Pilot Assn., Tanker/Airlift Assn., Jolly Green Assn. (1st v.p. 1983—84, pres. 1985—86), Order of Daedalians (former flight capt.). Republican. Avocations: fishing, walking, coin collecting/numismatics, NASCAR. Home: 6817 Medinah Ln NE Albuquerque NM 87111-6419 Personal E-mail: jflournoy2@comcast.net.

FLOURNOY, JOHN CRAIG, journalism educator; b. Shreveport, La., June 26, 1951; s. Camp Rogers and Carolyn (Clay) F.; m. Nina Planchard, May 21, 1977; children: Kathryn Helene, Louise, Emma. BA in History with honors, U. New Orleans, 1975; MA in History, So. Meth. U., 1986; PhD in Mass. Comm., La. State U., 2003. Freelance writer, landscaper The Courier, New Orleans, 1975; polit. reporter Houma (La.) Daily Courier, La., 1976; polit. reporter, columnist Shreveport Jour., 1977—78; investigative reporter Dallas Morning News, 1978—2000; prof. journalism So. Meth. U., 2002—. Recipient First pl. Investigative Reporting Dallas Press Club, 1981-83, 85, 93, Pub. Svc. award Assn. Press Managing Editors Assn., NYC, 1986, Silver Gavel award ABA, NYC, 1986, Pulitzer prize, NYC, 1986, Outstanding Investigative Reporting award Investigative Reporters and Editors, 1989, Worth Bingham prize for investigative reporting, 1993, Edward Meeman award for environ. reporting, 1993. Avocation: gardening. Home Phone: 214-696-2041; Office Phone: 214-768-3395. Business E-Mail: cflourmo@smu.edu.

FLOURNOY, NANCY, statistician, educator; b. Long Beach, Calif., May 4, 1947; d. Carr Irvine Flournoy and Elizabeth Flournoy; m. Leonard B. Hearne, Aug. 28, 1978. BS, UCLA, 1969, MS, 1971; PhD, U. Wash., 1982. Dir. clin. stats. Fred Hutchinson Cancer Rsch. Ctr., Seattle, 1974-86; dir. stats. and probability NSF, Washington, 1986—88; prof. stats. American U., Washington, 1988—2002; chmn., prof. stats. U. Mo., Columbia, Mo., 2002—. Mem. of corp. Nat. Inst. Statis. Scis., Research Triangle Park, N.C., 1990-97, coun. Inst. Math. Stats., 2004—. Editor Multiple Stats. Integration, 1991, Adaptive Designs, 1995, New Developments and Applications in Experimental Designs, 1998, Adaptive Designs in Clinical Trials, 2005. USPHS fellow, 1969-71. Fellow AAAS, Inst. Math. Stats., Am. Statis. Assn. (chair coun. sects. 1994), World Acad. Art and Sci., Washington Acad. Sci.; mem. Caucus for Women in Stats., Internat. Stats. Inst., Internat. Biometric Soc., Nat. Inst. Stats. Scis. (Disting. Svc. award, 2006). Democrat. Achievements include development of new statistical procedures for clinical trials and response-driven experimental designs; research on bone marrow transplantation, on graft versus leukemia, on infectious diseases in immuno-compromised hosts, on information management. Office: U Mo Dept Stats 146 Middlebush Columbia MO 65211-4100 Office Phone: 573-882-6376.

FLOURNOY, WILLIAM LOUIS, JR., landscape architect; b. Raleigh, NC, May 6, 1945; s. William Louis and Flossie (Combs) F. Student, Gardner-Webb Jr. Coll., 1964-66; BS in Recreation and Parks Adminstrn., N.C. State U., 1969, M of Landscape Architecture, 1972. Cons. to City of Raleigh N.C. State U. Sch. Design, 1971—72; community planner Wake County Planning Dept., Raleigh, NC, 1972-80; environ. analysis program mgr. Office Legis. and Intergovtl. N.C. Dept. Environ. and Natural Resources, Raleigh, 1980—2002, sr. conservation specialist Office Conservation and Cmty. Affairs, 2002—05, dir. conservation incentive program, Office Conservation and Cmty. Affairs, 2005—. Mem. alumni adv. bd. dept. landscape architecture N.C. State U., 1999—, chair, 2003—05. Contbr. articles to profl. jours. Bicycle com. NC Dept. Transp., 1974—83, chair, 1974—76, 1978—79; mem. nat. recreational trails adv. com. U.S. Dept. Transp., 1992—94; steering com. Wake County Cmty. Assessment, 1992—94; organizing com. NC Greenways Conf., 1986—95, conf. chair, 1992; active Triangle Open Space Network, 1997—99; bd. dirs. Southeastern U.S. Masters Track and Field, Inc., Raleigh, 1976—82, Triangle Land Conservancy, Rsch. Triangle Pk., NC, pres., 1991—94; bd. dirs. Triangle Greenways Coun., pres., 1989—91; bd. dirs. People for Parks, Wake County, NC, pres., 2002—04. Fellow Am. Soc. Landscape Architects (treas. N.C. chpt. 1982-86, v.p. 1978-79, awards 1978, 86, 90, 95), N.C. Trails Assn. (bd. dirs. 1977-82, acting pres. 1977), Landscape Architecture Founds., Landscape Architecture Urban Parks Honor Roll, others. Democrat. Methodist. Avocations: trail construction/maintenance, jogging, canoeing, hiking, bicycling. Home: 520 Polk St Raleigh NC 27604-1960 Office: NC ENR Office Conservation and Cmty Affairs 512 N Salisbury St Raleigh NC 27604-1170 Personal E-mail: bill.flournoy@ncmail.net.

FLOWE, BENJAMIN HUGH, JR., lawyer; b. Durham, NC, Feb. 8, 1956; s. Benjamin H. and Dorothy Amelia (Bell) F.; children: Samantha Kathleen, Andrew Benjamin; m. Margaret Mahoney; stepchildren: Jane Mahoney, Daniel Mahoney. AB in Sociology and Psychology cum laude, Duke U., Durham, NC, 1978; JD with high honors, U. NC, Chapel Hill, 1981. Bar: U.S. Ct. Appeals (D.C. cir.) 1981, U.S. Supreme Ct. 1990. Assoc. Arent, Fox et al, Washington, 1981-84, Bowman, Conner & Touhey P.C., Washington, 1984-87, Verner, Liipfert, Bernhard, McPherson & Hand, Washington, 1987-89, ptnr., 1990-96; pvt. practice, Washington, 1996-97; ptnr. Berliner, Corcoran & Rowe, L.L.P., Washington, 1997—. Contbr. congl. testimony on export controls Ctr. for Stratetic and Internat. Studies. Author: Export Compliance Guide, 1995; contbr. articles to profl. jours. Mem.: ABA (chair export controls and econ. sanctions com. 1995—2006), Dept. Commerce (vice chair regulations and procedures adv. com), Am. Electronics Assn. (co-chair export controls com. 2004), Order of the Coif. Democrat. Presbyterian. Avocations: skiing, writing, golf, tennis. Office: Berliner Corcoran & Rowe LLP 1101 17th St NW Ste 1100 Washington DC 20036-4798 Home: 13720 Canal Vista Ct Potomac MD 20854-1024 Office Phone: 202-293-5555. Business E-Mail: bflowe@bcr-dc.com.

FLOWE, CAROL CONNOR, lawyer; b. Owensboro, Ky., Jan. 3, 1950; d. Marvin C. Connor and Ethel Marie (Thorn) Smith; children: Samantha Kathleen, Andrew Benjamin. BME magna cum laude, Murray State U., 1972; JD summa cum laude, Ind. U., 1976. Bar: Ohio 1977, DC 1981, US Dist. Ct. (so. dist.) Ohio 1977, US Dist. DC 1981, US Dist. Ct. Md. 1983, US Ct. Appeals (1st, 2d, 3d, 4th, 5th, 6th, 7th, and DC cirs.), US Supreme Ct. 1987. Assoc. Baker & Hostetler, Columbus, Ohio, 1976—80, Arent Fox Kintner Plotkin & Kahn, Washington, 1980—87; dep. gen. counsel Pension Benefit Guaranty Corp., Washington, 1987—89, gen. counsel, 1989—95; ptnr. Arent Fox, LLP, Washington, 1995—. Mem.: ABA, DC Bar Assn., Order of Coif, Phi Alpha Delta, Alpha Chi. Avocations: computers, reading. Home: 8608 Aqueduct Rd Potomac MD 20854-6249 Office: Arent Fox PLLC 1050 Connecticut Ave NW Ste 500 Washington DC 20036-5339 Home Phone: 301-251-2656; Office Phone: 202-857-6054. Business E-Mail: flowe.carol@arentfox.com.

FLOWERS, BETTY SUE, library director, educator; b. Waco, Tex., Feb. 2, 1947; d. Paul Davis and Betty Lou (Lewis) Marable; m. John G. Flowers III; 1 child, John Michael. BA with high honors, U. Tex., 1969, MA, 1970; PhD, U. London, 1973. With U. Tex., Austin, 1968—, dir. plan II honors program, 1987-91, assoc. dean Graduate Studies, 1979-82, 88-90, Kelleher prof. English, dir. creative writing English Dept.; dir. Lyndon Baines Johnson Libr. and Mus., Austin, Tex., 2002—. Cons. Exxon, IBM, Shell Internat., London. Author: Browning and The Modern Tradition, 1976, Four Shields of Power, 1987, Extending the Shade, 1990; editor: A World of Ideas, 1988, Joseph Campbell and the Power of Myth: Bill Moyers and Joseph Campbell in Conversation, 1988, (with Lynda E. Boose) Daughters and Fathers, 1988, Moyers: Healing and the Mind, 1992; contbr. chpts. to books, articles to profl. jours. Adv. bd. Salado Inst. for Humanities, 1980-84, bd. dirs., 1988; mem. exec. com. Tex. Com. for Humanities, 1987-90; bd. trustees Tex. Humanities Alliance, 1986-87. Recipient Amoco Teaching Excellence award 1979, Leadership Tex., 1985; Andrew W. Mellon fellow, 1976; grantee faculty U. Rsch. Inst., 1983. Mem. MLA, Tex. Assn. Coll. Tchrs., Tex. Assn. Creative Writing Tchrs., AAUP, Nat. Poetry Therapy Assn. (bd. dirs. 1987—), NEH, Rotary, Phi Beta Kappa, Omicron Delta Kappa. Office: Lyndon Johnson Libr and Mus 2313 Red River St78705 Austin TX 78705-5702 Office Phone: 512-721-0200.*

FLOWERS, BRANDON RICHARD, singer; b. Las Vegas, Nev., June 21, 1981; m. Munblowski Tara Flowers, Aug. 2, 2005; 1 child. Lead singer & keyboardist The Killers, 2002—. Singer: (albums) Hot Fuss, 2004, Sam's Town, 2006 (Best Internat. Album, BRIT Awards, 2007), (songs) Somebody Told Me, 2004, Mr. Brightside, 2004, Bones, 2006 (Best Video, NME Awards, 2007), Spider-Man 3 soundtrack, 2007. Co-recipient Best New Artist award (with The Killers), MTV Video Music Awards, 2005, World's Best-selling New Group award, World Music Awards, 2005, Best Rock award (with The Killers), MTV Europe Music Awards, 2006; recipient Best Dressed award, Sexiest Man award, New Musical Express (NME) Mag., 2005, Best Internat. Group, BRIT Awards, 2007. Office: c/o Lauren Schneider Island Records 825 8th Ave New York NY 10019*

FLOWERS, DAVID J., corporate financial executive; Grad., Carleton Coll. V.p. Liberty Media Corp., Englewood, Colo., 1995—97, v.p., treas., 1997—2000, sr. v.p., treas., 2000—06, sr. v.p., treas., CFO, 2006—. Office: Liberty Media 9197 S Peoria St Englewood CO 80112*

FLOWERS, GARRY W., engineering and construction management company executive; BS, Furman U., Greenville, SC. With Fluor Corp., 1978—, dir. security, 1987—91, sr. dir. corp. security, 1991—94, v.p., 1994—2004, sr. v.p. indsl. rels., security and health, safety & the environment, 2004—. Mem. Exec. Coun. of US Dept. State, Overseas Security Adv. Coun. Mem.: Internat. Security Mgmt. Assn., Chief Spl. Agts. Assn., Inc. Office: Fluor Corp 6700 Las Colinas Blvd Irving TX 75039 Office Phone: 469-398-7000. Office Fax: 469-398-7255.*

FLOWERS, J. CHRISTOPHER, investment banker; b. Oct. 27, 1957; s. Woodford L. and Ann A. Flowers; m. Mary H. White. AB, Harvard U., 1979. Gen. ptnr. Goldman Sachs & Co., NYC, 1988—96, mng. dir. Fin. Institutions Group, 1996—98; vice chmn. Enstar Group, 1998—2003; founder, chmn. J.C. Flowers & Co., LLC, 2002—. Bd. dirs. Enstar Group, 1996—, Shinsei Bank, 2000—. Trustee Rockefeller U. Named one of Forbes' Richest Americans, 2006. Office: 717 Fifth Ave 26th Fl New York NY 10022

FLOWERS, KRISTE K., financial analyst; b. Jackson, Miss., Dec. 16; d. Henry W. and Limmie M. Flowers. BS in Acctg., Hampton U., Va., 1988—92; MS in Pub. Acctg., Jackson State U., Miss., 1992—95. Revenue collections supr. City Jackson, 1994—96, dirs. office analyst spl. projects, 1996—. Mem. spl. projects policies & procedures City Jackson, 1996—, mem. performance budgeting reveiw com., mayor's clean team/quality of life, 1998—2004. Alumni Leukemia Soc., Jackson; coord. Adopt-a-School Program, Jackson. Recipient Jackson's Best award for performance of duties above & beyond ordinary job responsibilities, Mayor, Successful Implementation Performance Based Budgeting Process award, Cert. Achievement award for excellence in fin. reporting, Govt. Fin. Officers Assn., Untangling the Web of ADA, FMLA, and Workers' Comp Regulations award, Am. Mgmt. Assn. Mem.: Assn. Study Higher Edn., Am. Ednl. Rsch. Assn., Govt. Fin. Officers Assn., Assn. Govt. Accts., Delta Sigma Theta. Bapt. Avocations: reading, writing. Home: 104 Lofty Pine Ln Clinton MS 39056 Office: City Jackson 200 S President St Jackson MS 39205 Home Phone: 601-259-6015. Office Fax: 601-960-1049. Personal E-mail: kriste02@bellsouth.net. Business E-Mail: kflowers@city.jackson.ms.us.

FLOWERS, LANGDON STRONG, food company executive; b. Thomasville, Ga., Feb. 12, 1922; s. William Howard and Flewellyn Evans (Strong) Flowers; m. Margaret Clisby Powell, June 3, 1944 (dec. Nov. 22, 1003); children: Margaret Flowers Rich, Langdon Strong, Elizabeth Powell, Dorothy Howard Flowers Swinson, John Howard. BS, MIT, Boston, 1944, MS, 1947; H.H.D., Presbyn. Coll., Clinton, SC, 1984. Engr., Douglas Aircraft, Los Angeles, 1947; supr. Flowers Baking Co., Thomasville, 1947-50, sales mgr., 1950-58, v.p. sales, 1958-65; pres., chief operating officer Flowers Industries, Inc., Thomasville, 1965-76, vice chmn. bd., chief exec. officer, 1976-80, chmn. bd., 1980-85, ret., 1985. Past pres. Thomasville YMCA, 1958-62; past trustee Presbyn Coll., Clinton, S.C., Archbold Meml. Hosp., Thomasville. Served as lt. (j.g.) USNR, 1943-46. Named Man of Year, Thomas County C. of C., 1974 Mem. Am. Bakers Assn. (exec. com. 1974-75, chmn. 1975-76), So. Bakers Assn. (chmn. bd. 1969-70), NAM (dir., exec. com.), Thomasville C. of C. (pres. 1953-54), Sigma Alpha Epsilon. Presbyterian (chmn. bd. deacons 1952-56, elder 1956—, rep. Gen. Assembly 1966). Club: Rotarian. Home: 207 Fairways Dr Thomasville GA 31792-7626 Office: PO Box 997 Thomasville GA 31799-0997

FLOWERS, MURHL LYNN, retired pharmacist; b. Charleston, W.Va., Feb. 25, 1940; s. Lowell Edward and Mable Irene Flowers; m. Regina Semel Flowers, Dec. 30, 1982; children: Kelly, Christopher. BS in Pharmacy, W.Va. U., Morgantown, 1965. Registered Pharmacist Md. Bd. Pharmacy. Pharmacist, asst. mgr. Peoples Drug, Oxon Hill, Md., 1965—68; asst. dir. pharmacy Morris Cafritz Meml. Hosp., Washington, 1968—72; pharmacist, owner Cmty. Med. Ctr. Pharmacy, La Plata, Md., 1972—76, Ye Olde Apothecary, Upper Marlboro, Md., 1974—80; pharmacist, mgr. Temple Hills Pharmacy, Md., 1980—82; dir. pharmacy Safeway Inc., Eastern Divsn., Landover, Md., 1982—2002; ret., 2002. Moderator Pharmcon, Pharm. Continuing Edn., Conway, SC, 2003—. Pres. Upper Marlboro C. of C., Md., 1978. Mem.: Md. Pharmacists Assn. (pres. 2000, Siedman Achievement award 2003). Republican. Baptist. Avocations: golf, gardening. Home: 668 W Bay Front Rd Lothian MD 20711

FLOWERS, V. ANNE, retired academic administrator; b. Dothan, Ala., Aug. 29, 1928; d. Kyrie Neal and Annie Laurie (Stewart) Flowers. BA, Fla. State U., 1949; MEd, Auburn U., 1958; EdD, Duke U., 1963. Teaching asst. Duke U., Durham, NC, 1963; elem. and secondary sch. tchr., adminstr. Dothan, Dalton, Ga., 1949-61; from assoc. prof. to prof. edn., head dept. Columbia (S.C.) Coll., 1963-68, from assoc. dean to dean, 1969-72; prof. edn. Va. Commonwealth U., 1968-69; tchg. asst. Duke U., 1963, assoc. dean, asst. provost, acting dean, vice provost Trinity Coll. Arts and Scis., 1972-74, prof. edn., chmn. dept., asst. provost ednl. program devel., 1974-80; dean Sch. Edn. Ga. So. Coll., Statesboro, 1980-85; asst. vice chancellor acad. affairs Univ. Sys. Ga., Atlanta, 1985-88, vice chancellor, 1988-90, ret., 1990, vice chancellor emerita, 1990—. Mem. coun. aging and human devel. Duke U., 1974—80; cons. in field. Co-author: Law and Pupil Control, 1964, Readings in Survival in Today's Society, 2 vols., 1978; mem. editl. bd. Ednl. Gerontology, 1979, Jour. Tchr. Edn., 1980—82; contbr. articles to profl. jours. Bd. dirs., mem. exec. com. Learning Inst. N.C., 1976—80; vice chmn. continuing commn. study black colls. related to United Meth. Ch., 1973—76; pres. univ. senate Bd. Higher Edn. and Ministry United Meth. Ch., 1977—80; adv. trustee Queens Coll., Charlotte, NC, 1976—78; mem. bd. visitors Charleston So. U., 1992—93. Delta Kappa Gamma scholar, Duke U., 1963, State of Fla. scholar, Fla. State U., 1949. Mem.: NEA, Nat. Orgn. Legal Problems Edn., Am. Assn. Colls. Tchr. Edn. (bd. dirs., mem. exec. com. 1979—84, pres. 1983—84), Kappa Delta Pi. Home and Office: 41 Williamsburg Pl Dothan AL 36305

FLOWERS, WILLIAM HAROLD, JR., lawyer; b. Chgo., Mar. 22, 1946; s. William Harold Sr. and Ruth Lolita (Cave) Flowers; m. Pamela Ann Mays, Sept. 13, 1980. BA, U. Colo., 1967, JD, 1971. Bar: Colo. 1973, U.S. Ct. Appeals (10th cir.) 1973, U.S. Dist. Ct. Colo. 1973, U.S. Supreme Ct. 1985, U.S. Ct. Appeals (4th cir.) 1994. Atty. Pikes Peak Legal Svcs., Colorado Springs, Colo., 1973; ptnr. Tate, Tate & Flowers, Denver, 1973-76; dep. dist. atty. Office Adams County Dist. Atty., Brighton, Colo., 1977-78; ptnr. Taussig & Flowers, Boulder, 1978-81; pvt. practice Boulder, 1981-89; ptnr. Holland & Hart, LLP, Denver, 1989-97, Hurth Yeager, Sisk & Blakemore LLP, Boulder, 1997—. Mem. Boulder County Cmty. Corrections Bd., 1985—90. Mem. Boulder Bd. Zoning Adjustment, 1973-78, chmn., 1977-78; mem. Boulder Growth Task Force, 1980-82; mem. exec. bd. Longs Peak coun. Boy Scouts Am., 1983-98; bd. dirs. Sta. KGNU, Boulder County Broadcasting, 1981-84, Coloradans Against the Death Penalty, 2001-04; trustee Nat. Coll. Advocacy, 2002-06. Mem.: ATLA (chair Coun. of Pres. 2001—02, exec. com. 2001—03, chair state dels. 2002—03, bd. govs. 2002—04), Am. Bd. Trial Advs., Colo. Bar Assn. (bd. govs. 2000, v.p. 2002—03), U. Colo. Found. (bd. dirs. 1995—2002), U. Colo. Boulder Alumni Assn. (bd. dirs. 1987—96, pres. 1994—95), Sam Cary Bar Assn. (pres. 1987), Boulder County Bar Assn. (civil litig. com. 1978—, criminal law com. 1979—, bd. dirs. 2003—, pres. 2007—), Colo. Trial Lawyers Assn. (bd. dirs. 1989—, exec. com. 1996—2006, pres. 1999—2000), Colo. Criminal Def. Bar (bd. dirs. 1982—83), Nat. Bar Assn. (regional dir. 1983—86, bd. govs. 1983—96, v.p. 1990—91). Democrat. Methodist. Office: Hurth Yeager Sisk & Blakemore LLP PO Box 17850 4860 Riverbend Rd Boulder CO 80308 Office Phone: 303-443-7900.

FLOWERS-SCHOEN, MARYLU UTLEY, art educator; d. Lynwood Hugh and Mary Jane Utley Flowers. BA, Meredith Coll., Raleigh, NC, 1974. Cert. art tchr. K-12 Dept. Pub. Instrn., N.C., 1974, Dept. Edn., NSW, Australia, 1975, art specialist Dept. Edn., Victoria, Australia, 1977, visual arts tchr. K-12 Dept. Pub. Instrn. N.C., 1985. Visual arts specialist Miller HS, New South Wales, Australia, 1974—76; contract creating art programs Dept. Edn., Carringbah, Taree, Coffs Harbour and Corowa, New South Wales, Australia, 1976—80; visual arts specialist St. Anne's and Gippsland Grammar Sch., Sale, Victoria, Australia, 1980—81, Dept. Edn., Ballimore and Dubbo, New South Wales, 1981—85; graphic artist Fine Designs, Durham, NC, 1985—90; visual arts specialist Durham City and Public Schs., 1987—; contract educator Ackland Art Mus., Chapel Hill, NC, 1990—; mixed media tchr. Durham Arts Coun., 1992—. Lead tchr., fellow Thomas Day Edn. Project, Durham, 1994—2004; A+ fellow Kenan Inst. for the Arts/ A+ Schs., Greensboro, NC, 1993—; presenter NCAEA Confs., 1993, 94, 98, 2005, PDS Conf., Louisville, 1995, Columbia, SC, 2000, Integrated Arts Conf., Tucson, 2003, Tucson, 05, N.C. Environ. Edn. Conf., 2005. Author (editor): (published history) Ballimore Public School, Centenary 1884-1984; mural, Our Ballimore; contbr. articles to profl. jours. Mem. Five Oaks Assn., Durham, 1994—99; cultural arts liaison PTA, Durham, 1996—. Recipient Miss NC Outstanding Arts Educators award, NC Dept. Pub. Instrn. and N.C. PTA, 1992, award for Excellence in Internat. Edn., Goldman Sachs Found., 2003; grantee Cultural Edn. Through the Arts, Bright Ideas/ Gen. Electric, 1988, Race Rels. through Arts, Z. Smith Reynolds Found., 1989, One World, Many Faces, Durham Pub. Edn. Network Tchr. Initiative Grants, 1995, Thomas Day Edn. Project, Nat. Endowment for the Humanities and N.C. Arts Coun., 1997, Mary Mac Mullen Fund for Art Edn., Nat. Art Edn. Found., 1999, History in a Green Box, Durham Pub. Edn. Network Tchr. Initiative Grants, 2003, New Hope Creek Project, 2005. Mem.: NEA, NC Art Edn. Assn. (treas., sec., mem. at large, and long range planning 1993—, N.C. Art Educator of Yr. 1996), Forest View Elem. PTA (membership chair 2003—06), Durham Assn. Educators (site rep. 1987—), Nat. Art Edn. Assn. (NC Art Educator of Yr. 1998), Phi Delta Kappa (Outstanding Educator of Yr. 2003). Achievements include students' artworks published in three Shakti for Children's books and Unicef 2000 Calendar. Avocations: cooking and catering, Japanese style gardening.

FLOYD, ALTON DAVID, cell biologist, consultant; b. Henderson, Ky., July 17, 1941; s. Frank and Queen Tina (Melton) F.; m. Barbara Wilson, Aug. 18, 1962; children: Fara Alison, Heather Lynn. BS, U. Ky., 1963; PhD, U. Louisville, 1968. From lectr. to asst. prof. U. Mich., Ann Arbor, 1967-72; from asst. to assoc. prof. Sch. of Medicine Ind. U., Bloomington, 1972-83, assoc. prof. Sch. of Medicine Indpls., 1983-84; sect. head cell biology Miles Sci., Inc., Naperville, Ill., 1984-85; sr. staff scientist Miles, Inc., Elkhart, Ind., 1985-89; pvt. practice cons. Edwardsburg, Mich., 1989—; assoc. dir. Ctr. Light Microscope Imaging and Biotech. Carnegie Mellon U., Pitts., 1991. Bd. dirs. Endotech Corp., Indpls.; mem. subcom. immunohistochem. stains NCCLS, 1995-96; industry rep. adv. panel hematology and pathology devices FDA, 1996-99; trustee Biol. Stain Commn., 1997—. Mem. Am. Assn. Anatomists, Tissue Culture Assn., Soc. Analytical Cytology, Histochem. Soc., Soc. Quantitative Morphology, Soc. Histotech. Avocations: sailing, reading, wood and metal shopwork, computing. Home and Office: 23126 S Shore Dr Edwardsburg MI 49112-8502 Office Phone: 269-699-7182. Personal E-mail: al.floyd@juno.com.

FLOYD, BARRY, information systems educator, consultant; b. Mich. BS in Math., Mich. State U., East Lansing, 1973, MS, 1975; MBA, U. Mich., Ann Arbor, 1983, PhD, 1985. Asst. prof. NYU, NYC; mgr. academic computer svcs. U. Petroleum and Minerals, Dhahran, Saudi Arabia, 1975—80; prof. info. systems Calif. Poly. State U., San Luis Obispo, 1990—, dir. grad. programs, 2002—03. Owner Barry D. Floyd and Assocs., San Luis Obispo, 1992—. Office: California Polytechnic State University 1 Grand Ave San Luis Obispo CA 93407 Home Phone: 805-544-2876; Office Phone: 805-756-6551. Business E-Mail: bfloyd@calpoly.edu.

FLOYD, DAISY HURST, dean, law educator; BA, MA in Polit. Sci., Emory U., 1977; JD cum laude, U. Ga., 1980. Bar: Ga., TEx. Dir. Legal Rsch. and Writing Prog. U. Ga. Sch. Law; atty. Alston, Miller & Gaines, Atlanta; prof. law Tex. Tech U. Sch. Law, assoc. dean academic affairs; dean Walter F. George Sch. Law, Mercer U., 2004—. Faculty mem. Nat. Inst. Trial Advocacy (NITA), Nat. Jud. Coll., Tex. Jud. Acad., Tex. Ctr. for Judiciary. Mem. bd. dirs. Lubbock Legal Aid Soc. Named Phi Alpha Delta Prof. of Yr., 2001, Carnegie Scholar, 2001; recipient New Prof. Excellence in Tchg. Award, 1995. Fellow: Am. Bar. Found.; mem.: Tex. Bar Found. Office: Mercer U Sch Law 1021 Georgia Ave Macon GA 31207-0001 Office Phone: 478-301-2602. E-mail: floyd_dh@mercer.edu.

FLOYD, ELSON SYLVESTER, academic administrator; b. Henderson, NC, Mar. 1, 1956; s. Elson and Dorothy (Garrett) F.; m. Pearl Burris, Sept. 14, 1979; children: Jessica, Elease. BA, U. N.C., 1978, MEd, 1982, PhD, 1984. Asst. dean U. NC, Chapel Hill, 1978-81, asst. to the dean, 1981-83, assoc. dean, 1983-88, asst. v.p., 1988-90, chief adminstrv. and operating officer, sr. official, 1995—98; v.p. student svcs., adminstrn., exec. v.p. Eastern Wash. U., Cheney, 1990—93, COO; pres. Western Mich. U., Kalamazoo, 1998—2002, U. Mo. Sys., Columbia, 2003—07, Wash. State U., Pullman, 2007—. Bd. visitors Darlington Sch., Rome, Ga., 1987—. Mem. Africans Am. Forum, Spokane, Wash., 1990—; mem. exec. com. Triangle Bus. Assn., Raleigh, N.C., 1989; v.p. Durham (Ala.) Mentor Devel. Assn., 1990—. Mem. Nat. Assn. Student Pers. Admintrs. (state bd. dirs. 1989-90), Am. Coun. of Educators, Coll. Pers. Assn., Am. Educators Rsch. Assn. (exec. bd. dirs. Washington chpt. 1988-90), Alpha Phi Alpha (v.p. 1988). Democrat. Methodist. Avocations: tennis, swimming, skiing, handball, racquetball. Office: Office of Pres Wash State U PO Box 641048 Pullman WA 99164-1048 Office Phone: 509-335-6666. E-mail: PresidentsOffice@wsu.edu.*

FLOYD, GARY LEON, plant cell biologist; b. Moline, Ill., Dec. 23, 1940; s. Leland L. and Zenta (Henderson) F.; m. Myrna A. Floyd, Aug. 18, 1963. BA, U. No. Iowa, 1962; MS, U. Okla., 1966; PhD, Miami U., Oxford, Ohio, 1971. Sci. tchr. Grinnell (Iowa) Jr. High Sch., 1962-65; instr. Miami U., 1966-68; asst. prof. Rutgers U., New Brunswick, NJ, 1971-75; asst. prof. plant biology Ohio State U., Columbus, 1975-78, assoc. prof., 1978-83, prof., 1983-96, assoc. dean biol. scis., 1986-88, dean, 1989-96, prof. and dean emeritus, 1996—. Dir. TEM facility plant biology dept. Ohio State U., Columbus, 1978-86. Contbr. articles to profl. jours. NSF scholar, 1965-66; recipient Alumni Teaching award Ohio State U., 1980, Disting. Rsch. award, 1982, Darbaker prize Bot. Soc. Am., 1993, award of excellence Phycological Soc. Am., 2003; Phycological Soc. Am. nat. lectr., 1983-85. Avocation: golf. Home: 936 Kendale Rd S Columbus OH 43220-4148 Business E-Mail: floyd.1@osu.edu.

FLOYD, HAZEL MCCONNELL, special education educator; b. Cumming, Ga., June 4, 1953; d. E.W. and Reatha Mae (Sosebee) McConnell; m. Nolan Trent Floyd, June 8, 1975; children: Jared Gordon, Nalanna Hope. BS in Elem. Edn., Ga. Southwestern Coll., 1974; MEd in Elem. Edn., North Ga. Coll., 1977; Specialist in Edn., U. Ga., 1991. Tchr. 2nd grade Midway Elem. Sch., Alpharetta, Ga., 1974-81; tchr. visually impaired Chestatee Elem. Sch./Forsyth County Schs., Gainesville, Ga., 1981—2002; ret.; tchr. visually impaired Dawson County Sch., Dawsonville, Ga., 2005—. Part-time Ga. Pines, 2005—. Composer songs: He Will Hear Me When I Pray, 1989, I Want to Work Till Jesus Comes Again, 1991. Panel mem. State Adv. Bd. for Spl. Edn., Atlanta, 1988-91, Local Edn. agy. for Vision tchrs., Macon, 1988-90; treas. Chestatee Elem. Sch. PTO, 1989-91; choir leader Children's Choir, Salem Bapt. Ch., Gainesville, 1986—. Named Tchr. of the Yr. Midway Elem. Sch., 1981. Mem. Ga. Assn. Educators (legis. chmn. 1987-92), Coun. for Exceptional Children, Assn. for edn. and Rehab. of Visually Impaired. Baptist. Avocations: singing, playing organ. Home: 6285 Keith Bridge Rd Gainesville GA 30506-3907 E-mail: canuchazel@juno.com.

FLOYD, ISRAEL J., lawyer, chemicals executive; BA, Lincoln U., Nebr., 1969; MBA in fin., Temple U., 1973; JD, Villanova U., 1973. From atty. to corp. sec., gen. counsel Hercules Inc., Wilimington, Del., 1973—2001, gen. counsel, corp. sec., 2001—. Office: Hercules Inc 1313 N Market St Wilmington DE 19894 Office Phone: 302-594-5000. E-mail: ifloyd@herc.com.*

FLOYD, JACK WILLIAM, lawyer; b. Columbia, SC, May 14, 1934; s. Edward Immanuel and Edith Fletcher (Herlong) F.; m. Ruth Parker Matthews, Jan. 10, 1957; children: Connie, Cindy, Jay. BS, U. N.C., 1958, JD with honors, 1961. Bar: N.C. 1961, U.S. Supreme Ct. 1971. Assoc. Smith, Moore, Smith, Schell & Hunter, Greensboro, NC, 1961-67, ptnr., 1967-87, Floyd, Greeson, Allen & Jacobs, Greensboro, 1988-90, Floyd, Allen & Jacobs, Greensboro, 1991-97, Floyd & Jacobs, Greensboro, 1998—. Lectr. acctg. U. N.C., 1960-61; lectr. bus. law Guilford Coll., 1962-64; spkr. on jury trials ABA, Am. Patent Law Assn.; arbitrator U.S. Dist. Ct. Annexed Arbitration Program. Bd. editors N.C. Law Rev., 1960—61. Mem. parents' bd. dirs. Meredith Coll., Raleigh, NC, 1977—79, chmn., 1980—81. With USN, 1951—55. Mem. ABA, N.C. Bar Assn. (panelist on family law), Am. Law Inst., N.C. Assn. Trial Lawyers, Elks Club, Order of Coif. Democrat. Baptist. Home: 1404 Valleymeade Rd Greensboro NC 27410-3938 Office: Floyd & Jacobs 401C N Eugene St Greensboro NC 27401-2644 Office Phone: 336-273-1797. Personal E-mail: jwf1404@aol.com. E-mail: jackfloyd@bellsouth.com.

FLOYD, JAMES M., JR., adult education educator; s. James M. and Carolyn S. Floyd; m. Linda J. Mosier, Feb. 12, 1999. AS in Liberal Arts, U. State N.Y., Albany, 1989; BFA in Visual Comm. summa cum laude, Am. Intercontinental U., Hoffman Estates, Ill., 2004, MEd in Instrnl. Tech., 2005. Cert. in brain rsch. edn. U. Wash. Ext., Seattle, 2005, in neuroanatomical dissection: human brain and spinal cord Marquette U., Milw., 2005; in distance edn. Ind. U., Bloomington, 2005, tng. cons. Ball State U., master naturalist Ind. Dept. Natural Resources. Mem. adj. faculty Ivy Tech State Coll., Indpls., 2001—. EMS educator, program mgr. St. Vincent Indpls. Hosp., 2001—; reviewer in field. Contbr. articles to profl. jours. Recipient Ky. Col. Commn., Commonwealth Ky., Office of Gov., Appreciation cert., Ind. Law Enforcement Acad., Indpls. Police Dept., Wayne Township Fire Dept., Dept. Safety Tng. award, Washington Township Fire Dept., 2004, Ednl. Achievement award, Washington Township Fire Dept. Contbn. Fund, 2005. Mem.: Wilderness Med. Soc., Nat. Assn. for Interpretation, Ind. Acad. Sci., Am. Arachnological Assn., Am. Ednl. Rsch. Assn. (mem. brain, neuroscience and edn., mem. sys. thinking in edn.). Office: St Vincents Hosp EMS Edn Dept 2001 W 86th St Indianapolis IN 46240 Home Phone: 317-356-7786; Office Phone: 317-338-3059.

FLOYD, JOHN ALEX, JR., editor; b. Selma, Ala., Feb. 21, 1948; s. John Alex Sr. and Louise (Johnson) F.; m. Pamela Lorene Billups, Aug. 14, 1982; children: Ryan Thomas, James Alex. BS, Auburn U., Ala., 1970; MS, Clemson U., SC, 1972, PhD, 1975. Instr. Jefferson State Jr. Coll., Birmingham, Ala., 1975-77; sr. horticulturist So. Living Mag., Birmingham, 1977-84; editorial dir. Classics-So. Accents, Birmingham, 1985-87, Creative Ideas and Cooking Light, Birmingham, 1987-88; dir. mktg. svcs., editor So. Progress Corp, Birmingham, 1988-91; v.p., editor So. Living, Birmingham, 1991—. Author: (with others) Southern Living Trees & Shrubs, 1980, Southern Living Garden Guide, 1982, Southern Living Vegetable & Herbs, 1984. Mem. adv. com. Landscape Architecture Adv. Coun., Auburn U., 1988-93; bd. dirs. U. N.C. Bot. Gardens, Chapel Hill, 1988-90; program com. Brookgreen Gardens; bd. dirs. Ea. Health Found., Trussville Tree Commn.; bd. dirs., co-chair steering com. Trussville Schs. Ency. of Ala. Grantee NSF, 1977. Mem. Am. Soc. Hort. Sci., Garden Writers Am., Birmingham Bot. Soc. (pres. 1981, trustee 1984—), Am. Hort. Soc. (bd. dirs. 1991-94), Gamma Sigma Delta, Pi Alpha Xi. Methodist. Office: So Progress Corp 2100 Lakeshore Dr Birmingham AL 35209-6721 Office Phone: 205-445-6365. E-mail: john_floyd@timeinc.com.*

FLOYD, JOHN DAVID, theology studies educator, minister; b. Lockesburg, Ark., Sept. 28, 1934; s. William Chaney Floyd and Alice Thadine (Park) Trammell; m. Helen Nutt, June 3, 1955; children: Elizabeth Ann Stivers, John Paul. BA, Ouachita Bapt. U., 1952-56; BD, Southwestern Bapt. Theol. Sem., 1962, M in Div., 1969; PhD, Mid-Am. Bapt. Theol. Sem., 1976; post doctoral studies, Fuller Theol. Sem., 1980-81. Ordained to ministry Bapt. Ch., 1952. Pastor various So. Bapt. Chs., 1952-65; missionary Fgn. Mission Bd. So. Bapt. Conv., Philippines, 1965-75; v.p. adminstrn., prof. missions Mid-Am. Bapt. Theol. Sem., Memphis, 1975-84; dir. missionary enlistment Fgn. Mission Bd. So. Bapt. Conv., Richmond, Va., 1984-85; v.p., dir. ministry program Mid-Am. Bapt. Theol. Sem., Memphis, 1985-93; dir. fgn. mission bd. for Europe The So. Bapt. Conv., 1993-2000, trustee internat. mission bd., 2001—; v.p., chmn. missions dept. Mid-Am. Bapt. Theol. Sem., 2000—. Head Missions Dept. Mid-Am. Bapt. Theol. Sem., Memphis, 1977-84, cons. ch. growth, 1979-84, dir. sch. world missions, 1982-84; trustee Internat. Mission Bd. So. Bapt. Conv., 2002—, chmn. trustees, 2006—. Editor: Inductive Bible Study Series, 1970, 1971 Church Growth Survey in the Philippines, 1972, Modern Cults, 1979; editor numerous articles Mid-Am. Bapt. Theol. Jour., 1976-86; editor Jour. Evangelism and Missions. Campaigner Rep. Party in Va., Richmond, 1984-85. Served as 1st lt. inf. US Army, 1957-59. Recipient Eye of the Eagle award 101st Airborne Div. Ft. Campbell, 1984, Key to the City award Booneville City Govt., 1982. Mem. Am. Assn. Missiologists, Assn. Mission Profs., Internat. Missiological Soc., Nat. Planned Giving Assn., Am. Mgmt. Assn. Home: 2533 Brotherwood Cv Collierville TN 38017-8972 Office: Mid-Am Bapt Theol Sem 2095 Appling Rd Cordova TN 38016 Office Phone: 901-751-8453. Business E-Mail: jdfloyd@mabts.edu.

FLOYD, JOHN TAYLOR, electronics executive; b. Quincy, Mass., Jan. 17, 1942; s. John Taylor and Virginia Marie (Watts) Floyd; m. Denise Angela Dufault, Oct. 4, 1969; children: Jennifer, Aimee. BA, Northeastern U., 1965; MBA in Fin., Boston Coll., 1972. Product group controller Tex. Instruments, Attleboro, Mass., 1972-75; asst. to v.p. fin. Waters Assocs., Milford, Mass., 1975-76; group fin. mgr. Digital Equipment Corp., Maynard, Mass., 1976-82; v.p. mfg. Computer Devices, Burlington, Mass., 1982-83; dir. fin. and adminstrn. Wang Labs., Lowell, Mass., 1984-85; v.p. ops. Charleswater Products, Newton, Mass., 1985-90; v.p. Devon Group, Waltham, Mass., 1991—, also bd. dirs. Served to capt. US Army, 1965—70, Vietnam. Mem.: Fin. Execs. Inst., Am. Legion. Independent. Office: Devon Group 800 South St Waltham MA 02453-1478

FLOYD, MICHAEL O'S., lawyer; b. Woodbury, NJ, 1939; s. Frederick W. and Anne O. Floyd; m. Mary Louise Santor, May 30, 1970; children: Michael F., Edward W., Stephen A. AB, St. Joseph's Coll., 1961; student, Hague Acad. Internat. Law, 1963; LLB cum laude, Univ. Pa., 1964. Bar: NJ 1965, Pa. 1967. Of counsel Drinker Biddle & Reath LLP, Phila., co-chair products liability practice group. Co-founder Phila. Chamber Ensemble; former v.p., dir. Navy League of US, Phila. Chapter. Capt. USAR, 1973. Mem.: ABA, NJ Bar Assn., Pa. Bar Assn., Phila. Bar Assn., US Naval Inst., Union League Phila., Def. Rsch. Inst., Order Coif. Office: Drinker Biddle & Reath LLP One Logan Sq 18th & Cherry Sts Philadelphia PA 19103-6996 Office Phone: 215-988-2941. Office Fax: 215-988-2757. Business E-Mail: michael.floyd@dbr.com.

FLOYD, OTIS HENRY, retired military officer, adult education educator; b. York, SC, June 4, 1951; s. John Mason Barnette and Mozelle Phillips Lindsay; m. Shirley Jane Sims, Aug. 21, 1997; 1 child, Nashara Yvette Hopkins. AAS, C.C. of Air Force, Maxwell, AFB, Ala., 1988; BS, Gardner-Webb U., Boiling Springs, NC, 2000; MS, N.C. Agrl. and Tech. State U., Greensboro, 2001; post grad., U. N.C., Charlotte, 2001—. Aircraft maintenance technician US Air Force, Washington, 1969—90; cmty. devel. instr. Ctrl. Piedmont C.C., Charlotte, NC, 2001—. V.p. Gaston Cmty. Action Inc., Gastonia, NC, 2004—. Decorated Vietnam Gallantry Cross US Air Force, Vietnam Svc. medal, 4 commendation medals; named to Nat. Deans List, Gardner-Webb U., 2000. Mem.: Am. Assn. Adult and Continuing Edn. (assoc.), Am. Mil. Soc., Kappa Delta Pi. Home Phone: 704-862-0069. E-mail: otis_floyd@cpcc.edu.

FLOYD, RAYMOND LORAN, professional golfer; b. Ft. Bragg, NC, Sept. 4, 1942; s. Loren B. and Edith (Brown) F.; m. Maria; children: Raymond Loran, Robert Loran, Christina Loran. Student, U. N.C., 1960. Profl. golfer PGA, 1961-92; profl. golfer Sr. PGA, 1992—; mem. Ryder Cup team, 1969, 75, 77, 81, 83, 85, 89, 91, 93; capt. Ryder Cup Team, 1989. Winner 2000 Ford Sr. Players Championship, Doral Ryder Open, 1992, GTE North Classic, 1992, Northville Long Island Classic Senior PGA, 1993, Sr. Tour Championship, 1994, Ford Sr. Players Championship, 2000; named Rookie of Year Golf Mag., 1963, 77, Player of Yr., 1976. Winner PGA tournament, 1969, 82 St. Petersburg Open, 1963, St. Paul Open, 1965, Jacksonville Open, 1969, Am. Golf Classic, 1969, Kemper Open, 1975, Masters, 1976, World Open, 1976, Byron Nelson Golf Classic, 1977, Pleasant Valley Golf Classic, 1977, Brazilian Open, 1978, Greater Greensboro Open, 1979, Canadian PGA, 1981, Vardon Trophy, 1983, Ryder Cup, 1969, 75, 77, 81, 83, 85, Doral Ea. Open, 1980, 81, Tournament Players Championship, 1981, Westchester Classic, 1981, Meml. Tournament, 1982, Memphis Classic, 1982, PGA Championship, 1982, $1Million Sun City Challenge, 1982, Houston Open, 1985, Chrysler Team Championship, 1985, U.S. Open, 1986, Walt Disney/Oldsmobile Classic, 1986, Skins Game, 1988, RMCC Invitational, 1990, Doral-Ryder Open, 1992, GTE North Classic, 1992, Ralph's Sr. Classic, 1992, Sr. Tour Championship, 1992, Thailand Srs., 1992, Northville L.I. Classic, 1993, The Tradition, 1994, Sr. Skins Game, 1994, 95, 96, 97, 98, 06, Las Vegas Srs. Classis, 1994, Sr. Tour Championship, 1994, PGA Srs. Championship, 1995, Burnet Sr. Classic, 1995, Ford Sr. Players Championship, 1996; capt. Ryder Cup, 1989; inducted in PGA/World Golf Hall of Fame, 1989, winner father-son tourn. w/son Raymond Jr., 1995, 96, 97, w/son Robert, 2000, 01, winner Par 3 Shootout, 2000. Office: 505 S Flagler Dr West Palm Beach FL 33401

FLOYD, SUZANNE ELVIRA IZZO, music educator; b. Norristown, Pa., Sept. 27, 1950; d. Nicholas and Virginia Marsh Izzo; children: Jennie Rebecca, Andrea Roberta. MusB, U. Miami, Coral Gables, Fla., 1978; MusM, U. Miami, 1983. Music specialist Miami-Dade County Pub. Schs., Miami, Fla., 1978—; music tchr. L'Ouverture Elem. Sch., Miami. Supt.'s leadership cir. Miami-Dade County Pub. Schools/United Way, Miami, Fla., 2002—; dir. music First United Meth. Ch., Homestead, Fla., 1992—2001; adj. prof. Barry U., Miami Shores, Fla., 1997—; mem. U. Miami Pres. Cir., 2002—. Chair bd. trustees Greater Miami Youth Symphony. With WAC, 1970—72, Ft. McClellan, Alabama. Named Tchr. of Yr., Miami Dade County Pub. Schs./Perrine Elem. Sch., 1989; recipient Outstanding Svc. award, U. Miami, Frost Sch. Music, 1988, 1990, 1992. Mem.: U. Miami Frost Sch. Music Alumni Assn. (pres. 1989—92), U. Miami Alumni Assn. (bd. dirs. 1992—95), Miami Dade County Music Educators Assn., Miami Dade County Music Tchrs.' Assn. (pres. 1990—2007), Sigma Alpha Iota (life; nat. dir. music edn. 1997—2000, nat. v.p., alumnae chapters 2000—06, Ring of Excellence 2005, Rose of Dedication 2003, Diamond Sword of Honor 1997, Rose of Honor 1991). Independent. Presbyterian. Avocations: gourmet cooking, counted cross stitch, travel, reading. Home: 10340 SW 120th St Miami FL 33176 Office Phone: 305-758-2600. E-mail: suefloyd@dadeschools.net.

FLOYD, TED, ornithologist, writer; b. Pitts., Apr. 12, 1968; s. Edwin Douglas and Mary (Beaty) F.; m. Kei Sochi, Aug. 5, 1995. BA cum laude, Princeton U., NJ, 1990; PhD, Pa. State U., 1995. Sr. lectr. Pa. State U., University Park, 1995; rsch. assoc. SUNY, Stonybrook, 1996-97; career counselor U. Pa., Phila., 1997-99; coord. projects Great Basin Bird Obs., Reno, Nev., 1999—. Vis. asst. prof. Williams Coll., Williamstown, Mass., 1995-96; state coord. N.Am. Migration Count, Phila., 1998; with Pa. Ornithol. Tech. Com., Phila., 1998-99, Pa. Ornithol. Records Com., Phila., 1998-99, Nev. Bird Records Com., Reno, 1999—. Sr. author: Atlas of the Breeding Birds of Nevada, 2007; contbr. over 125 articles to jours. and mags. Interpretive naturalist Tinicum Nat. Wildlife Refuge, Phila., 1998-99; chair edn. Nev. Ptnrs. in Flight, 1999-2000; bd. dirs. Western Field Ornithologists, 2001-07; deacon Presbyn. Ch., Reno, 2001. Fellow NSF, 1991, grantee, 1993; grantee Orgn. Tropical Studies, 1992. Mem. AAAS, Am. Birding Assn. (editor Birding 2002-07), Delaware Valley Ornithol. Club. (chmn. awards com. 1997). Democrat. Avocations: birding, writing, baseball, classical music, Go. Office: Am Birding Assn PO Box 7974 Boulder CO 80306 Home: 2009 S Fork Dr Lafayette CO 80026 Business E-Mail: tedfloyd@aba.org.

FLOYD, TIM, men's college basketball coach, former professional basketball coach; b. Hattiesburg, Miss. m. Beverly Floyd; 1 child, Shannon. BS, La. Tech. Univ., 1977. Coach Univ. El Paso, 1977-86, Idaho Univ., 1986-88, Iowa State Univ., 1994-98; head coach Chgo. Bulls, 1999—2001, New Orleans Hornets, 2003—04, U. So. Calif., 2005—. Named Coach of Yr. Office: c/o USC Athletic Dept 3501 Watt Way HER 203 A Los Angeles CA 90089

FLOYD, WALTER LEO, lawyer; b. St. Louis, May 29, 1933; s. Walter L. Sr. and Estelle E. (Kiess) F.; children: Michael W., Mary Ann, Mark L.; m. Patricia A. Knapko, Sept. 3, 1994. BS, St. Louis U., 1955, LLD, 1959. Bar: Mo. 1959, Ill. 1959, U.S. Dist. (ea. dist.) Mo. 1959. Owner The Floyd Law Firm P.C., St. Louis, 1959—. Contbr. articles to profl. jours. Fellow: Orgn. Nat. Bd. Trial Advocacy; mem. Mo. Assn. Trial Attys. (sec. 1961, v.p. 1962, 85), Am. Trial Lawyers Assn. (lectr.), Mo. Bar Assn., Ill. Assn., Phi Delta Phi. Democrat. Unitarian Universalist. Address: Floyd Law Firm 8151 Clayton Rd Ste 202 Saint Louis MO 63117-1111 Office Phone: 314-863-4114. Business E-Mail: walter@thefloydlawfirm.com.

FLOYD, WILLIAM R., former health facility administrator; b. Oct. 16, 1944; BA, U. Pa., 1967, MBA, 1969. With Gillette; various positions to v.p. mktg. Bennigan's chain Pillsbury, 1975; exec. v.p., gen. mgr. Safeguard Business Systems, Inc.; Northeast brand mgr. PepsiCo, COO, Ky. Fried Chicken, 1994, COO, Taco Bell, 1995—96; CEO Choice Hotels Internat., 1997—98; pres., COO Beverly Enterprises Inc., 2000—01, pres., CEO, 2001—06, chmn., 2001—06. Bd. dirs. Beverly Enterprises Inc., 2000—06. Bd. trustees Valley Forge Military Academy.

FLÜGELMAN, MÁXIMO ENRIQUE, financier, composer; b. Buenos Aires, Nov. 2, 1945; s. Cirilo and Matilde (Rhein) F. Lic. es Sci. Econ., U. Geneva; diploma in econ. policy, Cath. U., Buenos Aires; MBA, Harvard U., Cambridge, Mass.; BM, Manhattan Sch. Music; M in Composition, Juilliard Sch., NYC. Credit officer Citibank, Buenos Aires and NYC, 1970; sr. investment officer World Bank Group Internat. Fin. Corp., Washington, 1972-77; internat. mgr., chief external funding, negotiator Nat. Devel. Bank, Buenos Aires, 1981-84; v.p. banker 1st Chgo. Internat. Capital Markets Group, Chgo. and NYC, 1985-89; v.p., exec. com. Inter-Am. Investment Corp., Washington, 1989—94; prin. Corfina Global Advisors, LLC, 1995—. Mem. ofcl. Argentine del. to IMF/World Bank meetings, Inter Am. Devel. Bank gen. assemblies; lectr. Buenos Aires Nat. U., Cath. U., Washington. Author: Argentina and the Debt Crisis; composer: Symphonic Variants for orch., Concertino for woodwinds and orch., Sea Sonnets for soprano and orch., Sonatina for chamber orch., Rhapsody for Cello and Orch., Concerto for Piano and String orch., Concerto for Cello and Orchestra, Dialogues for Orchestra, chamber works performed at Aspen Festival, Latin Am. Chamber Music Festival, Quinteto Rego, orchestral works performed Indpls. Symphony, Seattle Symphony, Puerto Rico Symphony, Interam. Festival Orch., Kennedy Ctr., Carnegie Hall, Northwestern U. Orch., Nat. Argentine Symphony, Buenos Aires Philharm. at Teatro Colon, Conn. Chamber Orch., Fla. Philharm., Am. Composers Orch., Orchestre de la Cité; contbr. articles. Bd. dirs. Am. Composers Orch. Recipient 14th ann. contemporary orchestral composition award Ind. State U./Indpls. Symphony; 1st prize LRA Argentine State Radio Chamber Orch. composition contest, Outstanding Young Musician of Yr. award Argentine Jr. C. of C.; Amigos de la Musica composition contest; finalist Nissim Orchestral Composition Competition, Plymouth Music Series award; fellow Bunge and Born Found. Mem. ASCAP, Am. Composers Orchestra (dir.), Argentine Coun. on Fgn. Rels., Teatro Colón Found. (trustee, founding), A. Ginastera Found. (dir.), Soc. Argentina de Autores y Compositores, Soc. Rural Argentina, Cosmos Club (Washington), Doubles, Harvard Club (N.Y.C.), Club Nautico San Isidro (Buenos Aires). Home: 2817 Dumbarton St NW Washington DC 20007-3366

FLUHARTY, DAVID ARTHUR, automotive executive, statistician, consultant; b. Steubenville, Ohio, Feb. 28, 1951; s. Ralph Osborn and Grace Elaine (Martin) Fluharty; m. Mary Margaret Reiter, Nov. 25, 1978; 1 child, Margaret Rose Elaine Fluharty-Reiter (dec.). BA, Wheeling Jesuit U., W.Va., 1973; MBA, U. Chgo., 1975, MA in Internat. Rels., 1978; cert. in applied stats., Oakland U., Rochester, Mich., 1992; PhD, Wayne State U., Detroit, 2007. Loan guarantee analyst Maritime Adminstrn. U.S. Dept. Commerce, Washington, 1976—77; fin. analyst Ford Motor Co., Dearborn, Mich., 1977—85, statistician, 1985—88; program mgr., warranty/reliability mgr. Alcoa Fujikura Ltd., Allen Park, Mich., 1988—99, sr. statistician, 1999—2001; mgr. reliability and warranty adminstrn. statistician Continental Teves, Auburn Hills, Mich., 2001—03; statistician Remy Inc., Anderson, Ind., 2004—. Contbr. Statistical Case Studies: A Collaboration Between Academe and Industry. Math. steering com. Macomb Intermediate Sch. Dist., Clinton Township, Mich., 1998—2003. Mem.: Am. Statis. Assn. (officer Detroit chpt. 1990—2002, com. on tchr. enhancement 2000—03, chmn. sect. on quality and productivity 1988—89, chpt. svc. recognition award 1999). Roman Catholic. Avocations: reading, history, philosophy, movies.

FLUHR, HOWARD, consulting firm executive; b. Bklyn., Feb. 20, 1943; s. Morton and Evelyn (Cohen) F.; m. Margaret Appel, Sept. 7, 1963; children: Lisa Metaxas, Allison Kaufman. BS in Math. and Philosophy cum laude, NYU, 1964. Various actuarial positions Guardian Life Ins. Co., 1964-66, Eastern Life Ins. Co., 1966-69; various actuarial and mgmt. positions The Segal Co., NYC, 1969-73, v.p., 1973-76, sr. v.p., 1976-87, exec. v.p., 1987-93, pres., CEO, 1994—2005, chmn., 2006—. Contbr. articles to profl. jours.; speaker in field. Fellow Soc. Actuaries, Conf. Cons. Actuaries (bd. dirs. 1990-96, v.p. 1991-96), Can. Inst. Actuaries; mem. Internat. Actuarial Assn., Am. Acad. Actuaries (bd. dirs. 1989-95, v.p. 1993-95), Employee Benefit Rsch. Inst. (trustee 1994—, chmn. 2000-2002). Office: The Segal Co 1 Park Ave New York NY 10016-5895 E-mail: hfluhr@segalco.com.

FLUHR, JEFF, Internet company executive; BS summa cum laude in Fin., Elec. Engring., Univ. Penn., Phila. Formerly with The Blackstone Group, NYC; profl., private equity investing group Thomas Weisel Ptnrs.; co-founder, CEO, strategic dir. StubHub.com, 2000—.*

FLUKE, LYLA SCHRAM (MRS. JOHN M. (LYLA) FLUKE SR.), publisher; b. Maddock, ND; d. Olaf John and Anne Marie (Rodberg) Schram; m. John M. Fluke, June 5, 1937 (dec. 2002); children: Virginia Fluke Gabelein, John M. Jr., David Lynd. BS in Zoology and Physiology, U. Wash., Seattle, 1934, diploma tchg., 1935. H.S. tchr., 1935-37; tutor Seattle schs., 1980-84; pub. Portage Quar. mag. Hist. Soc. Seattle and King County, 1980-84. Hon. chmn. nanotech. rsch. U. Wash., 2000, hon. chmn. campaign, 2006—. Contbr. articles to profl. jours. Co-founder N.W. chpt. Myasthenia Gravis Found., 1953, Wash. Tech. Ctr., 1996, pres., 1960-66; obtained N.W. artifacts for Navy destroyer Tender Puget Sound., 1966; mem. Seattle Mayor's Com. for Seattle Beautiful, 1962; sponsor Seattle World's Fair, 1962; charter and founding mem. Seattle Youth Symphony Aux., 1974; benefactor U. Wash., 1982-01, sponsor first chair mfg., U Wash., 1982, nat. chmn. ann. giving campaign, 1983-84; benefactor Cascade Symphony, Salvation Army, Sterling Cir. Stanford U., MIT, 1984, Seattle Symphony, 1982-2002, Wash. State Hist. Soc., Pacific Arts Coun., Pacific Sci. Ctr., 2003-04, Twenty-Twelve Club, 1962-2002; mem. condr.'s club Seattle Symphony, 1978-; mem. U. Wash. Campaign Exec. Com., 2003-04, hon. mem. Campaign Com. NSF Grant to Nat. Nanotechnology Infrastructure Network, 1984; hon. exec. com. on nanotech. U. Wash. Coll. Engring., 2003-; benefactor Seattle Symphony, 2004, U. Wash., 2004; mem. Seattle Beautification Com., 1965-68. Recipient Crystal plaque Coll. Engring. U. Wash., 2002, Framed document Pres. US; fellow Seattle Pacific U., 1972; named Father of Electronics in Wash. State, Gov. John Spellman, 1983; honored by Repub. Nat. Com. Eisenhower Commn., 2006. Mem. IEEE Aux. (chpt. charter mem., pres. 1970-73), Wash. Trust Hist. Preservation, Nat. Trust for Hist. Preservation, N.W. Ornamental Hort. Soc. (benefactor, life, hon.), Nat. Assn. Parliamentarians (charter mem., pres. N.W. unit 1961-64), Wash. Parliamentarians Assn. (charter), Seattle C. of C. (women's divsn. 1965-66), Seattle Symphony Women's Assn. (life, charter, sec. 1982-84, pres. 1985-87), Hist. Soc. Seattle and King County (exec. com. 1975-78, pres. women's mus. league 1975-79, pres. Moritz Thomsen Guild of Hist. Soc., 1978-80, 84-87), Highlands Orthopedic Guild (life), Wash. State Hist. Soc., Antiquarian Soc. (v.p. 1986-88, pres. 1988-90, hon. mem. John Fluke Mfg. Co. 20 Year Club 1987—), Rainier Club, Seattle Golf Club, U. Wash. Pres.'s Club, Twenty-Twelve Club, Pacific Sci. Ctr, Seattle. Republican. Lutheran. Achievements include sponsorship of the Fluke Chair in Coll. of Engring. U Wash. Home: 1206 NW Culbertson Dr Seattle WA 98177-3942 Office Phone: 425-453-4590.

FLUMENBAUM, MARTIN, lawyer; b. Bronx, NY, July 22, 1950; AB summa cum laude, Columbia Coll, 1971; JD cum laude, Harvard Law Sch., 1974. Bar: NY 1975, DC 1985, US Dist. Ct. (so. and ea. dists. NY) 1975, US Ct. Appeals (2nd cir.) 1975, US Ct. Appeals (5th cir.), US Supreme Ct. 1986, US Dist. Ct. (dist. DC). Clk. to Hon. Whitman Knapp US Dist. Ct. (so. dist. NY), asst. US atty., 1979—82; with Paul, Weiss, Rifkind, Wharton & Garrison, LLP, NYC, 1975—, ptnr., 1983—, co-chair litig. dept., 1999—2005. Exec. com. mem. NY Lawyers for Pub. Interest. Monthly columnist Second Cir. Rev., NY Law Jour. Named one of Top 10 Trial Lawyers in Am., Nat. Law Jour., 2005, Nat.'s Top Litigators, 2005. Mem.: DC Bar, Assn. Bar City NY, ABA, Fed. Bar Coun. Office: Paul Weiss Rifkind Wharton & Garrison 1285 Avenue Of The Americas New York NY 10019-6064 Office Phone: 212-373-3191. Office Fax: 212-373-2226. Business E-Mail: mflumenbaum@paulweiss.com.*

FLUTH, JOHN ADAM, medical educator; b. Beeville, Tex., May 19, 1954; s. John and Elouise (Perdue) F.; m. Martye René Glenn, June 22, 1991; children: Craig, Kent, Chad. PhD, Tex. A&M U., 1986; computer technician, Apple Computer, Inc., Culpertino, Calif., 1994. Cert. ednl. adminstr., Tex. Surrogate parent Coastal Bend Youth City, Driscol, Tex., 1977-78, dir. halfway house Corpus Christi, Tex., 1978; tchr. spl. edn. Robstown, Tex., 1978-81; grad. asst. Tex. A&M U., College Station, Tex., 1981-86; coord. assistive tech. Region 5 Edn. Svc. Ctr., Beumont, Tex., 1986-97; dir. Tex. Acad. Leadership in the Humanities, Beaumont, 1997-98. Peer reviewer US Dept. Edn., Washington, 1995—; grant reviewer Entergy, Inc., Beaumont, Tex., 1995-98. Pres. Ptnrs. Resource Network, Tex., 1994-96, Cerebral Palsy Rehab. Ctr., 1994-96; mem. exec. bd. Boy Scouts Am., Beaumont, Tex., 1996-98; sr. chaplain Tex. Dept. Pub. Safety Critical Incident Response Team; ordained elder United Meth. Ch. Olympic Torch Bearer Atlanta Com. for The Olympic Games, 1996; named Cmty. Hero, United Way, Beaumont, Tex., 1996; recipient Perkins-Prothro fellowship, Perkins Sch. of Theology, Dallas, 1998. Mem. Order of Eastern Star (worthy patron), Masons (worshipful master). E-mail: john@fluth.com.

FLUTIE, DOUG (DOUGLAS RICHARD FLUTIE), retired professional football player; b. Manchester, Md., Oct. 23, 1962; m. Laurie Flutie; 1 child, Doug Jr. BS in Comm. and Comp. Sci., Boston Coll., 1984. Quarterback NJ Generals, 1985, LA Rams, 1985, Chgo. Bears, 1986—87, New England Patriots, 1987—89, 2005—06, BC Lions, 1990—91, Calgary Stampeders, 1992—95, Toronto Argonauts, 1996—97, Buffalo Bills, 1998—2001, San Diego Chargers, 2001—04; coll. football analyst ABC and ESPN, 2006—. Founder, pres. Doug Flutie Jr. Found. for Autism, Inc., 1998—. Named Most Outstanding Player, Can. Football League, 1991—94, 1996—97, MVP, Grey Cup CFL championship game, 1992, 1996, Coll. Football Player of Yr., The Sporting News, 1984, quarterback coll. All-Am. first team, 1984, Comeback Player Yr., NFL, 1998—99; named to Coll. Football Hall of Fame, 2007, Pro-Bowl Team, NFL, 1998—99; recipient Heisman Meml. trophy, 1984, GMC Profl. Grade Play award (Drop Kick), ESPY award, 2006. Office: Doug Flutie Jr Foundation for Autism PO Box 767 Framingham MA 01701

FLYE, CAROLYN MARIE, minister; d. L.A. and Marjorie Janette Flye. Ordained min. Lighthouse Fellowship of Chs., Fla., 1995; cert. Mandt tng. Anthony Wayne Svcs., 2005, CPR and first aid for infants, children and adults YWCA, 2004. Follow-up min. Calvary Chapel, Fort Wayne, Ind., 1991—93, pastoral and ch. com. chairperson, 1992—, deaconness, 1992—94, singles and womens conf. event planner, spkr., 1993—, evangelism ministry head, instr., 1993—95; sr. elder, assoc. min. Lighthouse Deliverance Cathedral, Fort Wayne, Ind., 1995—, worship leader, 1998—2000, dir. faith based initiative program, 1999—2000; edn., employment adv. YWCA Domestic Violence Svcs., Fort Wayne, Ind., 2001—04, supr. shelter program, 2005; trainer Anthony Wayne Svcs., Fort Wayne, Ind., 2004—. Spkr. Youth Svcs., Fort Wayne, 1993—95, Wood Youth Svcs., Fort Wayne, 1993—95, Greater Mt. Ararat Bapt. Ch., Fort Wayne, 1999—2003, Kingdom Door Worship Ctr., Fort Wayne, 1999, Lion of Judah, Huntington, Ind., 2000, Taylor U., Chapel Svc., Fort Wayne, 2004; adv. YWCA Domestic Violence Svcs., Fort Wayne, 2001—04, supr., 2001—04; min. to youth Calvary Chapel, Wood Youth Ctr., Youth Svcs., Fort Wayne. Treas. Lighthouse Deliverance Cathedral, Fort Wayne, 1995—2005. Grantee, Taylor U., 2002—05; scholar, Grabill Bank, Ft. Wayne, 2002—05; Levi and Pearl Moser scholar, Ft. Wayne, 2005—. Avocations: travel, mentoring, singing, reading. Home Phone: 260-447-6580. Personal E-mail: carolflye7@yahoo.com.

FLYE, M. WAYNE, surgeon, immunologist, educator, writer; b. Tarboro, NC, June 23, 1942; s. Charlie A. and Martha E. (Bullock) F.; m. Phyllis Webb, June 7, 1964; children: Christopher Warren, Brandon Reid. BS, U. N.C., 1964, MD, 1967; MA in Immunology, Duke U., 1972, PhD in Immunology, 1980; MA (hon.), Yale U., 1985. Diplomate Am. Bd. Surgery, Am. Bd. Thoracic Surgery, Am. Bd. Vascular Surgery. Intern. surg. Case-We. Res. U., Cleve., 1967-68, res. gen. and cardio-thoracic surgery, 1968-75; instr., teaching scholar, vascular and transplantation surgery Duke U. Med. Ctr., Durham, NC, 1975-76; sr. investigator , chief thoracic surg. svc. NIH, Bethesda, Md., 1977-79; chief vascular surgery U. Tex. Med. Br., Galveston, 1979-82, assoc. prof. surgery and microbiology, 1980-82; dir. div. organ transplantation and immunology, prof. transplantation, dir. sect. gen. surgery Yale U. Sch. Medicine, New Haven, 1983-85; prof. surgery, molecular microbiology and immunology Washington U. Med. Sch., St. Louis, 1985—, prof. radiology, 2000—, mem. admissions com., 2000—. Trustee New Eng. Organ Bank, Boston, 1984-85; com. mem. United Network Orgn. Sharing, Richmond, Va., 1986-89; mem. anesthesiology and trauma study sect. NIH Surgery, 1991-95; merit rev. com. for surgery VA, 1994-96, chmn., 1996—; merit rev. com. Am. Heart Assn. study sect., 2001–; chief of surgery St. Louis Regional Hosp.; 1996; chief thoracic surgery St. Louis VA Hosp., 1996—. Editor: Principles of Organ Transplantation, 1989, The Thymus: Regulator of Cellular Immunity, 1993, Atlas of Organ Transplantation, 1994; mem. editl. bd. Clin. Transplantation, 1986—, Prospectives in Gen. Surgery, 1988-94, Transplantation, 1989-2000, Xanthus Intelligence Unit Reports, 1990—, Shock: Molecular, Cellular and Systemic Pathobiology of Injury, 1993-99, Transplantation Sci., 1993—, Jour. Surg. Rsch., 1995-2000, Surgery, 1997—, Graft, Jour. Organ and Cellular Transplantation, 1998—, New Surgery, 2000—; assoc. editor Jour. Immunology, 1996-99, Hepatology, 2003—. Lt. col. U.S. Army, 1976-78. Recipient James W. McLaughlin medal U. Tex.-Galveston, 1982. Fellow ACP, So. Thoracic Surg. Assn. (Best Sci. Paper award 1980); mem. Am. Assn. Immunologists, Internat. Cardiovascular Soc., N.Y. Acad. Sci., Soc. Thoracic Surgeons, Am. Soc. Transplant Physicians, Am. Soc. Transplant Surgeons (program com. 1984-86, Ethics Com. 1994-95), Brit. Soc. Immunology, Transplantation Soc., Mid-Am. Transplant Assn. (bd. dirs. 1986-89), Am. Fedn. Clin. Rsch., Royal Soc. Medicine, AAAS, Surg. Infection Soc. (edn. and fellowship com. 1998-2002), Reticuloendothelial Soc., Soc. Univ. Surgeons, Soc. Clin. Vascular Surgery, Brit. Transplantation Soc., So. Assn. Vascular Surgery, Am. Coll. Chest Physicians, Soc. Surg. Oncology, Am. Assn. Thoracic Surgery, Surg. Biology Club I, Am. Assn. Study Liver Diseases, Am. Surg. Assn., So. Surg. Assn., Cen. Surg. Assn., Soc. Internat. de Chirurgie, Midwestern Vascular Surg. Soc., Soc. Vascular Surg., World Ann. Hepato-Pancreato-Bilary Surg., Soc. Surgery of Alimentary Tract, Shock Soc., Gen. Thoracic Surgery Club, Soc. Thoracic Surg., St. Louis Surg. Soc. (v.p. 2002-03, treas. 2003—), Sigma Xi, Alpha Omega Alpha., Chi Psi, Young Republicans N.C. Episcopalian. Avocations: sports, genealogy, medical history. Home: 585 Coeur De Royale Dr Apt 402 Saint Louis MO 63141-6915 Home Phone: 314-991-4535; Office Phone: 314-362-7145. Business E-Mail: flyew@wustl.edu.

FLYER, MICHAEL R., lawyer; b. Bklyn., Nov. 13, 1937; AB, U. Mich., 1959; JD, U. Mich. Law Sch., 1962. Bar: DC 1963. Atty. IRS, 1962—69, section chief, corp. reorganization branch, 1968—69; co-founder, ptnr. Tucker Flyer, 1969—99; (Tucker Flyer PC merged with Venable LLP, 1999); ptnr., tax & business law Venable LLP, Washington, 1999—. Adjunct prof. George Washington U. Law Sch., 1972—2001; former mem., steering com. DC Div. of Taxation; lecturer U. Mich. Law Sch. Inst. of Continuing Legal Ed., Great Plains Federal Tax Inst., Tenn. Tax Inst., Federal Bar Assn. Inst. on Federal Taxation, NYU Tax Inst. Bd. dirs. Jewish Social Service Agency, Jewish Federation of Washington. Mem.: ABA (mem. corp. tax com., taxation section), DC Bar Assn. Office: Venable LLP 575 7th St NW Washington DC 20004 Office Phone: 202-344-8520. Office Fax: 202-344-8300. Business E-Mail: mrflyer@venable.com.

FLYNN, HARRY JOSEPH, archbishop; b. Schenectady, NY, May 2, 1933; BA in English, MA in English, Siena Coll., Loudonville, NY; student, Mt. St. Mary's Coll., Emmitsburg, Md. Ordained priest Roman Cath. Ch., 1960. Assoc. pastor, pastor, teacher, retreat master, and spiritual leader Diocese of Albany; dean, vice rector then rector Mount St. Mary's Seminary, 1965—79; coadjutor bishop Diocese of Lafayette, La., 1986—89, bishop La., 1989—94; coadjutor archbishop Archdiocese of St. Paul and Minneapolis, Minn., 1994—95, archbishop Minn., 1995—. Chmn., bd. of trustees St. Paul Seminary, U. St. Thomas; pres. of bd. St. John Vianney Seminary; mem. Com. for Black Catholics US Catholic Conference of Bishops. Address: Archdiocese of St Paul and Minneapolis 226 Summit Ave Saint Paul MN 55102-2121

FLYNN, JOHN J., museum curator; b. Wilkes-Barre, Pa., Aug. 10, 1955; s. John J. and Phyllis B. Flynn; m. Alison L. Flynn; children: Rachel, Peter. BS cum laude, Yale U., 1977; MA, Columbia U., 1979, MPhil, 1980, PhD, 1983. Lectr. dept. geology and geophysics Yale U., New Haven, 1982; asst. prof. geol. scis. Rutgers U., New Brunswick, NJ, 1982-88; assoc. curator dept. geology Field Mus. Natural History, Chgo., 1988-92, curator dept. geology, 1992—2004, chmn. dept. geology, 1993-2000, MacArthur curator dept. geology, 1995—2004; Frick curator Am. Mus. Natural History, NYC, 2004—, chmn. divsn. paleontology, 2005—, dean Richard Gilder grad. sch., 2007—. Co-chair Earth History and Global Change com. Systematics Agenda 2000, 1991-96; lectr. Com. on Evolutionary Biology, U. Chgo., 1990-2005, assoc. chair, 1995-2004; adj. prof. dept. biol. scis. U. Ill., Chgo., 1994-2004, CUNY, 2005—; adj. prof. dept. earth and environ. scis. Columbia U., 2005—. Co-editor: Vertebrate Paleontology in the Neotropics: The Miocene Fauna of La Venta, Colombia, 1997, Mesozoic/Cenozoic Vertebrate Paleontology: Classic Localities, Contemporary Approaches, 1989; assoc. editor Jour. Vertebrate Paleontology, 1988-91, Systematic Paleontology, 2001—; contbr. articles to profl. jours. Grantee in field; recipient William R. Belknap prize, 1977, Best Mus. Curator award Chgo. Mag., 1995, Premio Roberto Araya award Sociedad Geologica de Chile, 2002; John S. Guggenheim fellow, 2001-02. Mem. Soc. Vertebrate Paleontology (chair affiliated soc. liaison 1986-93, mem. devel. com. 1987-89, 2002—, chair collections computerization com. 1990-93, sec. 1993-96, v.p. 1996-98, pres. 1998-2000, past pres. 2000-02, Alfred Sherwood Romer prize 1982), Geol. Soc. Am., The Paleontological Soc., Soc. Systematic Biologists. Achievements include discovery of the oldest South American rodent, oldest well-preserved South American monkey skull and exceptional Triassic vertebrates from Madagascar; research on geologic time scales. Office: Am Mus Natural History Divsn Paleontology Central Park W at 79th St New York NY 10024

FLYNN, KIRTLAND, JR., accountant; b. Orange, NJ, Aug. 27, 1922; s. Kirtland and Jane Elizabeth (Miller) F.; m. Lucy Jane Andrews, June 11, 1948 (dec. Oct. 2002); children: Patricia Carson Flynn Moore, Gail Miller, James Kirtland; m. Anne Blankenship Jones, Apr. 26, 2003. BA, Colgate U., 1943. Enrolled Agt. Acctg. staff Celanese Corp., Newark, Houston, Charlotte, 1947-65; sec.-treas. Little Constrn. Co., Inc., Charlotte, 1965-66; mem. contr.'s staff J.P. Stevens & Co., Inc., Charlotte, 1966-81, mgr. info. svcs. divsn. Charlotte and Greer, S.C., 1981-85; pvt. practice acctg., 1985-92; mem. staff Larry R. Swartz, CPA, 1993—. Chmn. Tryon Fire Protection Dist. Bd. Commrs., 1986—; bd. dirs., treas. Charlotte Exch. Student Program, 1979—83, Polk County Sheltered Workshop, 1987—91, exec. v.p., 1991—93, pres., 1994—96; bd. dirs. Tryon Fine Arts Ctr., 1987—89, Tryon Little Theater, 2004—07. 1st lt. USMCR, 1943—46. Decorated DFC, Air medals. Mem. Inst. Mgmt. Accts. (chpt. pres. 1966-67, nat. dir. 1971-73, pres. Carolinas Coun. 1973-74, nat. v.p. 1978-79), Stuart Cameron McLeod Soc. (bd. govs. 1979-81, treas. 1981-82, sec. 1982-83, v.p. 1983-85, pres. 1985-86), Tryon C. of C. (bd. dirs. 1985-93, treas. 1985-90, v.p. 1990-92), Tryon Riding and Hunting Club (bd. dirs. 2000-03), Masons, Shriners, KT. Home: 390 Sourwood Ridge Rd PO Box 1138 Tryon NC 28782-1138 Office: 20 Jervey Rd Ste 103 Tryon NC 28782-3709

FLYNN, MARIE COSGROVE, retired portfolio manager, corporate financial executive; b. Honolulu, Jan. 1, 1945; d. John Aloysius and Emeline Frances Cosgrove; m. John Thomas Flynn, Jr., June 3, 1968; children: Jamie Marie, Jacqueline Elizabeth. BA, Trinity Coll., 1966. CPA; CFP. Analyst U.S. Govt., Washington, 1967-70; coord. nat. reading coun. F.X. Doherty Assocs., NYC, 1970-71; security analyst Corinthian Capital Co., NYC, 1971-73; portfolio mgr. Clark Mgmt. Co., Inc., NYC, 1973-78; 1at v.p., sr. portfolio mgr. Lexington Mgmt. Corp., Saddle Brook, NJ, 1978-96; pres. Corinthian Capital Mgmt. Co., Inc., Morristown, NJ, 1996-99; 1st v.p., mng. dir., sr. portfolio mgr. Glenmede Trust Co., 1999—2007; ret. Bd. dirs., v.p. First Call for Help, 1996—2000; bd. trustees NJ Pension and Annuity Fund, 1996—, vice chair bd. trustees, 2006—; elected mem. Somerset County Rep. Com., 1994—98; treas. Bernardsville Rep. Com., 1996—98, Bernardsville Planning Bd., 1996—98; mem. Bernardsville Borough Coun., 1998—2004; mayor Bernardsville, 2002, 2004; commr. Bernardsville Police Commn., 2000—04; pres. Women's Polit. Caucus NJ, 2001—03; bd. dirs. Soc. Women's Health Rsch., 2004—07. Recipient Tribute to Women award, Patriots' Path Coun., 2002, Somerset Commn. on Women, 2004. Mem.: NY Soc. Security Analysts, Inst. Chartered Fin. Analysts, Fin. Analysts Fedn. Home: 50 Pickle Brook Rd Bernardsville NJ 07924-1909

FLYNN, PATRICIA M., director, special education and gifted and talented educator; b. East Cleveland, Ohio, Sept. 11, 1952; d. Harry L. and Eleanore (Mahon) Flynn. BS in Edn. magna cum laude, St. John Coll., Cleve., 1974, MS in Edn., 1975; cert., Notre Dame Coll., 1992, Ursuline Coll., 2001. Cert. elem. edn., prin., edn. handicapped Ohio Detp. Edn. Reading specialist East Cleveland City Schs., 1974—98, reading coord., 1998—2000, curriculum specialist, 2000—01; dir. pupil svcs. Fairview Park (Ohio) Schs., 2001—. Local coord. Reading Is Fundamental Project, East Cleveland, 1996—2000; coord. East Cleveland Elem. Acad., East Cleveland, 1999. Scholar, St. John Coll., 1974. Mem.: Nat. Assn. Fed. Edn. Program Adminstrs., Internat. Reading Assn., Ohio Assn. Adminstrs. State and Fed. Edn. Programs, Ohio Assn. Pupil Svcs. Adminstrs., Irish Am. Club, City Club Cleve., Kappa Gamma Pi. Roman Catholic. Office: Fairview Park City Schs 20770 Lorain Rd Fairview Park OH 44126 E-mail: pflynn@leeca.org.

FLYNN, PAUL BARTHOLOMEW, foundation executive; b. Quincy, Mass., Sept. 17, 1935; s. Bartholomew Joseph and Katherine Marie (Coleman) F.; m. Aline Therese Nicholson, Feb. 11, 1961; children: Bonnie Marie, Laureen P., Elizabeth A., Bernadette J. AB, Stonehill Coll., 1957; LL.D. (hon.), Allentown Coll., 1985. Sportswriter The Patriot Ledger, Quincy, 1955-63, cmty. rels. dir., 1963-65; dir. pub. rels. Mass. Tchrs. Assn., Boston, 1965-66; asst. dir. pub. svc. Rochester (N.Y.) Democrat and Chronicle and The Times-Union, 1966-71, dir. pub. svc. and rsch., 1971-72; dir. advt. Huntington (W.Va.) Herald-Dispatch and Advertiser, 1972-74, Binghamton (N.Y.) Press and Sun-Bulletin, 1974-76; dir. mktg. services Gannett Co., Rochester, N.Y., 1976-77; gen. mgr. Jour.-News, Nyack, N.Y., 1977; pres., pub. Fort Myers (Fla.) News-Press, 1977-84; S.E. regional v.p. Gannett Co., 1981-83; exec. v.p. USA Today, Washington, 1983-84, pres., 1984; pres., pub. Pensacola News-Jour., Fla., 1984-87; v.p. Gannett South Newspaper Group, 1985-87; exec. v.p. Foster's Daily Democrat, Dover, N.H., 1989-93; dir. mktg. and pub. rels. Strawbery Banke Mus., Portsmouth, N.H., 1993-95; mktg. cons. Jour.-Transcript Newspapers, N.H., Maine, 1995-96; v.p. Susan Bennett Mktg. & Media, Fort Myers, Fla., 1996-97; exec. dir. Southwest Fla. Community Found., Ft. Myers, Fla., 1997—2004, pres., CEO, 2004—. V.p. Gannett Newspaper Advt. Sales, N.Y.C., 1976-77 Author: You Can Make News, 1996; co-editor: Promoting the Total Newspaper, 1977. Pres. Lend-A-Hand Fund S.W. Fla., S.W. Fla. coun. Boy Scouts Am., 1981, adv. bd., 1997—, commr. Daniel Webster coun., 1989-96, v.p., 1995-96; bd. dirs. Lee County United Way, 1979-84, campaign chmn., 1981; bd. dirs. Edison C.C. Endowment Fund, 1978-83, Sr. Friendship Ctrs., Inc., 1981-83, United Way Pensacola, Sacred Heart Hosp. Found., Pensacola Jr. Coll. Found.; mem. adv. bd. Stonehill Coll., 1984, trustee, 1987-92. With U.S. Army, 1957-58. Recipient Disting. Service award B'nai B'rith of Cape Coral, Fla., 1979; Gold medal for good citizenship SAR, 1980; disting. alumni award Stonehill Coll., 1984; Patriotism citation Freedom's Found., 1986, Legacy award ARC, 2003. Mem. Internat. Newspaper Promotion Assn. (bd. dirs. 1977-78), Fla. Fedn. Cmty. Founds. (treas. 2003-07), Greater Dover C. of C. (bd. dirs. 1989-93), Stonehill Coll. Alumni Assn., Rotary Ft. Myers. (bd. dirs. 2000-02, 05-06). Roman Catholic.

FLYNN, TERRANCE PATRICK, prosecutor, lawyer; b. Warsaw, NY, Aug. 18, 1963; s. Jeremiah Wilham and Elizabeth Joan (Cloonan) F. BBA, U. Notre Dame, 1985; JD, SUNY, Buffalo, 1988. Bar: NY 1989, US Dist. Ct. (we. dist.) 1989. Assoc. Saperston & Day, P.C., Buffalo, 1987-91, Karinoky & Cook LLP, Buffalo, 1991-92; ptnr. Gibson, McAskill & Crosby LLP, Buffalo, 1992—2006; US atty. (we. dist.) NY US Dept. Justice, Buffalo, 2006—. Pres. U. Buffalo Law Sch. Alumni Assn., 2004—05. Vol. Ronald McDonald House, Buffalo, 1988—; bd. dirs. Notre Dame Alumni, Buffalo, 1988-92. Republican. Roman Catholic. Avocations: golf, running, swimming, travel. Office: US Attys Office 138 Delaware Ave Buffalo NY 14202*

FLYNN, TIMOTHY P., finance company executive; m. Susan Flynn; children: Laura, Tyler. BA in Acctg., U. St. Thomas. With KPMG LLP, NYC, 1988—, various positions including vice chair audit and risk advisory svcs., vice chair human resources, chmn., CEO, 2005—. Mem. dean's advisory coun. Coll. Commerce and Fin. Villanova U.; mem. fin. com. Most Blessed Sacrament parish, Franklin Lakes, NJ; bd. dirs. YMCA, NY. Office: KPMG LLP 345 Park Ave New York NY 10154-0102 Office Phone: 212-909-5029. Office Fax: 212-758-9819.*

FLYNN, WILLIAM JOSEPH, insurance company executive; b. NYC, Sept. 6, 1926; s. William and Anne (Connors) F.; m. Margaret M. Collins, Mar. 21, 1952; children: William, Maureen, James, Robert. MA in Econs., Fordham U., 1951. V.p. group ops. Equitable, NYC, 1953-71; pres. Mut. Am. Life Ins., NYC, 1971-72, pres., CEO, 1972-82, chmn. bd., CEO, 1982—. Bd. dirs. Richmond Hill Savs. Bank, Floral Park, N.Y. Pres. bd. dirs. N.Y. Foundling Hosp., N.Y.; bd. dirs. U.S. Cath. Hist. Soc., S.I., N.Y., United Student Aid Funds, Indpls., Coll. Constrn. Loan Ins. Assn., Washington, Elie Wiesel Found. for Humanity, N.Y.C., Williamsburg Charter Found., Washington, United Student Aid Fund, N.Y.C., United Way Internat., Alexandria, Va; past chmn. adv. com. U.S. Holocaust Meml. Council, Bd. Life Ins. Council N.Y., St. Vincent's Svcs. Served with USAF, 1951-53, Korea. Recipient Disting. Community Service award Brandeis U. 1980, Ubi Cantas Deus Ibi award Cath. Charities 1983, Nat. Profl. Leadership award United Way Am. 1984, Brotherhood award NCCJ, 1984, Disting. Service award United Way Bergen County, 1985. Mem. Am. Council Life Ins. Clubs: University (N.Y.C.); Garden City (N.Y.) Country. Avocations: golf, reading. Home: 69 2nd St Garden City NY 11530-4322 Office: Mutual of Am Life 680 5th Ave New York NY 10019-5429

FLYNN-CONNORS, ELIZABETH KATHRYN, reporter, editor; b. Chgo., Aug. 17, 1939; d. Timothy Carver Flynn and Elizabeth Eleanor (Tait) Scanlon; m. Gerald Martin Connors, Dec. 30, 1978; children: Andrew, Kathryn, Elizabeth. Student, Monmouth Coll., Ill., 1957-59; BA in Journalism, U. Wis., 1961, postgrad., 1965-66. Cityside reporter Mpls. Tribune, 1961-62, Chgo. Daily News, 1962-66, UN/N.Y. corr., 1966-75, Washington corr., 1968; writer, press officer UN, NYC, 1975-82; sr. writer UN Chronicle, NYC, 1982-85, editor-in-chief, 1985-96; chief editor Yearbook of UN, NYC, 1996-99; chief UN pubs., NYC, 1999—. Troop leader Girl Scouts U.S., Tarrytown, N.Y., 1993-95. Russell Sage fellow U. Wis., 1965-66; recipient Investigative Reporting award Sigma Delta Chi, 1962, 1st Pl. Spot News award AP, 1970. Mem. UN Corrs. Assn. (alumni), White House Corrs. Assn., Congrl. Reporter Assn., Sleepy Hollow Sr. Citizens Club (sec.), White Plains Garden Club, Phi Beta Kappa, Kappa Delta. Avocations: reading, watching old movies. Home: 238 Hunter Ave Sleepy Hollow NY 10591-1317 E-mail: betty1153@aol.com.

FLYNN PETERSON, KATHLEEN A., lawyer; b. St. Paul, July 7, 1954; d. Richard Edward and Margaret (Flaig) Flynn; m. Steven R. Peterson; children: Christopher, Colin. BA in Nursing, Coll. St. Catherine, 1976; JD cum laude, William Mitchell Coll. Law, 1981. Bar: Minn. 1981, US Ct. Appeals (8th cir.) 1981, N.D. 1987. Assoc. Robins, Zelle, Larson & Kaplan, St. Paul, 1981-88, Robins, Kaplan, Miller & Ciresi, Mpls., 1988—. Lectr. health law issues various med. orgns., 1979—; adj. prof. med. malpractice William Mitchell Sch. Law, St. Paul, 1984-94. Named one of The 50 Most Influential Women Lawyers in Am., Nat. Law Jour., 2007. Mem. ABA, Am. Bd. Trial Advocates (Minn. chpt. pres.),Am. Assn. Nurse Attys. (past pres. Minn. chpt.), Minn. Bar Assn., Minn. Trial Lawyers Assn. (bd. governors 1987-, pres. 1995-96), Minn. Women Lawyers, Hennepin County Bar Assn., Gt. Plains Orgn., Perinatal Health Care (bd. dirs., pres. 1994), Am. Assn. for Justice (pres.-elect, mem. exec. com.), fellow Am. Coll. Trial Lawyers, Internat. Acad. Trial Lawyers, Internat. Soc. Barristers Am. Bar Found. Democrat. Office: Robins Kaplan Miller & Ciresi 800 Lasalle Ave Ste 2800 Minneapolis MN 55402-2015*

FLYNT, LARRY CLAXTON, JR., publisher; b. Magoffin County, Ky., Nov. 1, 1942; s. Larry Claxton and Edith (Arnett) F.; m. Kathy Barr, Dec. 1968 (div. 1969); m. Althea Leasure, Aug. 21, 1976 (dec. June 27, 1987); m. Elizabeth Berrios, June 20, 1998; children: Tonya, Lisa, Teresa, Larry Claxton, III. Student public schs., Saylersville, Ky. Factory worker Gen. Motors, Dayton, Ohio, 1958, 64-65; owner, operator Hustler Club, Dayton, Columbus, Toledo, Akron and Cleve., 1970-74; owner, pub. Hustler and Chic mags., Los Angeles, 1974—; owner, operator Larry Flynt Publications, Los Angeles, 1976—. Actor: (films) The People vs. Larry Flynt, 1996; author: An Unseemly Man: My Life as a Pornographer, Pundit, and Social Outcast, 1996, Sex, Lies and Politics: The Naked Truth, 2004. Served with U.S. Army, 1958-59; Served with USN, 1960-64. *I intend to devote my entire life to the cause of civil liberties and civil rights for all mankind in an effort to bring about peace on earth. I absolutely refuse to compromise my unorthodox strategy concerning my principles, ideas, goals, and conduct that have brought me this far.*

FOARD, DOUGLAS W., historian; b. Balt., Oct. 23, 1939; s. George Winfield and Anna (Herrmann) F.; m. Janet Hess, Aug. 26, 1961; children: Wendy Lynn, Scott Douglas. BA, Randolph-Macon Coll., 1961; MA, U. Va., 1965; PhD, Washington U., 1972; LHD (hon.), Randolph-Macon Coll., 1992, Hampden Sydney Coll., 2001. Asst. to dir. pub. rels. Ferrum (Va.) Coll., asst. prof. history, 1965-70, chair social sci., 1970-79, prof. history, 1972-85, assoc. dean, 1979-81; program officer NEH, Washington, 1985-89; exec. sec. Phi Beta Kappa, Washington, 1989-2001. Adj. prof. history George Mason U., Fairfax, Va. Author: The Revolt of the Aesthetes, 1989; contbr. articles to profl. jours.; guest editor Mag. of History, 1991. Bd. dir. Nat. Humanities Alliance, 1994-2001, mem. exec. com., 1997-2000; bd. dir. Nat. History Day, Washington, 1987-2001; bd. dir. Va. Found. Humanities and Pub. Policy, 1990-96, chmn., 1995-96; trustee Randolph-Macon Coll., 2001—. Grantee Ford Found. 1969-70; James Still fellow U. Ky. 1983, Nat. Defense Act fellow Washington U., 1967-70, Philip DuPont fellow U. Va., 1961-62, Ford Found. fellow Asian Studies, 1967, Nat. Meth. scholar Randolph-Macon Coll., 1960-61; NEH summer seminar Vanderbilt U., 1976. Mem. Soc. Spanish & Portuguese Hist. Studies (newsletter editor 1982-85) Va. Soc. History Tchrs. (pres. 1981-83), Phi Beta Kappa. Address: 38998 Bolington Rd Lovettsville VA 20180

FOBERT, PAMELA HART, music educator; b. San Francisco, Feb. 15, 1949; d. Thomas Albert and Gloria Hagler Hart; m. Norman Douglas Fobert, Apr. 13, 1974; children: Thomas, Benjamin, Aaron, Jared. MusB, Brigham Young U., Provo, 1972. Tchr. choral and gen. music Granite Pk. Jr. HS, Salt Lake City, 1972—75; music specialist San Lorenzo Unified Sch. Dist., La., 1991—, co-chair music dept., 2006—. Mentor Beginning Tchr. Support and Asst. Calif. Tchrs. Assn., San Lorenzo, 2002—. Stake music chair Ch. of Jesus Christ LDS, San Leandro, Calif., 1986—90, ward music chair, 2000—06. Recipient Hon. Svc. award, PTA, San Lorenzo, 1986, Continuing Svc awrd, 1997. Mem.: CTA, MENC, San Lorenzo Edn. Assn. (mem. exec. bd. 2004—). Avocations: reading, walking, singing.

FOCH, NINA, actress, creative consultant, film director, educator; b. Leyden, The Netherlands, Apr. 20, 1924; arrived in US, 1927; d. Dirk and Consuelo (Flowerton) Foch; m. James Lipton, June 6, 1954; m. Dennis de Brito, Nov. 27, 1959; 1 child, Dirk de Brito; m. Michael Dewell, Oct. 31, 1967 (div.). Grad., Lincoln Sch., 1939; studies with Stella Adler. Adj. prof. drama U. So. Calif., Grad. Sch. Cinema & TV, LA, 1966—68, 1978—80, adj. prof. film, 1987—; creative cons. to dirs., writers, prodrs. of all media. Founder, actress LA Theatre Group, 1960—65; artist-in-residence U. NC, 1966, Ohio State U., 1967, Calif. Inst. Tech., 1969—70; mem. sr. faculty Am. Film Inst., 1974—77; founder, tchr. Nina Foch Studio, Hollywood, Calif., 1973—. Actor: (films) Nine Girls, 1944, Return of the Vampire, 1944, Shadows in the Night, 1944, Cry of the Werewolf, 1944, Escape in the Fog, 1945, A Song to Remember, 1945, My Name is Julia Ross, 1945, I Love a Mystery, 1945, Johnny O'Clock, 1947, The Guilt of Janet ames, 1947, The Dark Past, 1948, The Undercover Man, 1949, Johnny Allegro, 1949, An American in Paris, 1951, Scaramouche, 1952, Young Man with Ideas, 1952, Sombrero, 1953, Fast Company, 1953, Executive Suite, 1954 (Oscar award nominee), Four guns to the Border, 1954, You're Never Too Young, 1955, Illegal, 1955, The Ten Commandments, 1956, Three Brave Men, 1957, Cash McCall, 1959, Spartacus, 1960, Such Good Friends, 1971, Salty, 1973, Mahogany, 1976, Jennifer, 1978, Rich and Famous, 1981, Skin Deep, 1988, Silver, 1993, Morning Glory, 1993, 'Til There Was You, 1996, Hush, 1998, Shadow of Doubt, 1998, How to Deal, 2003; (Broadway plays) John Loves Mary, 1947, Twelfth Night, 1949, A Phoenix Too Frequent, 1950, King Lear, 1950, Second String, 1960; (plays) Am. Shakespeare Festival in Taming of the Shrew, Measure for Measure, 1956, San Francisco Ballet and Opera in the Seven Deadly Sins, 1966, Seattle Repertory Theatre, TV, 1947—; (TV series) Playhouse 90, Studio One, Pulitzer Playhouse, Playwrights 56, Producers Showcase, Lou Grant (Emmy nominee, 1980), Mike Hammer, Shadow Chasers, 1985, War and Remembrance, 1988, LA Law, 1990, Hunter, 1990, Dear John, 1990, 1991, Tales of the City, 1993, Dharma and Greg, 1999, Just Shoot Me, 2000, Bull, 2000—01, State of Grace, 2003, When We Were Grown-ups, 2004, NCIs, 2005, 2006, The Closer, 2007, numerous other series, network spls. and TV films; panelist, guest (TV series) The Dinah Shore Show, Merv Griffin Show, The Today Show, Dick Cavett, The Tonight Show, moderator Let's Take Sides, 1957—59; dir.: (films) The Diary of Anne Frank, 1959; (plays) Tonight at 8:30, 1966—67, Family Blessings, 1997; assoc. prodr.: Ford's Theatre, 1968. Bd. dirs. Nat. Repertory Theatre, 1967—75; hon. chmn. LA chpt. Am. Cancer Soc., LA, 1970. Recipient Film Daily award, 1949, 1953. Mem.: AAUP, Hollywood Acad. TV Arts and Scis. (bd. govs. 1976—77), Acad. Motion Picture Arts and Scis. (co-chair exec. com. fgn. film award, mem. membership com., chair fgn. lang. award com. 1998—99). Avocation: work. Office: PO Box 1884 Beverly Hills CA 90213-1884 Office Phone: 310-553-5805.

FOCHT, JOHN ARNOLD, JR., engineer; b. Rockwall, Tex., Aug. 31, 1923; s. John Arnold and Fay (Goss) F.; m. Edith Rials, Aug. 8, 1950; children: John Arnold III, Judith Lynn Schweitzer. BSCE, U. Tex., 1944; MSCE, Harvard U., 1946. Soils engr. U.S. Waterways Expt. Sta., Vicksburg, Miss., 1947-50, 52-53; sr. soils engr. McClelland Engrs., Inc., Houston, 1953-55, v.p. engring., 1955-72, exec. v.p., 1972-87; v.p. TERA, Inc., 1965-85; chmn. bd. Fugro-McClelland Inc., 1987-90; cons., 1991-99, Focht Consultants, Inc., 1999—2004. Contbr. articles to tech. jours. Chmn. ofcl. bd. Grace Methodist Ch., 1960-62; bd. dirs. N.W. YMCA, 1957-59; chmn. vis. com. dept. civil engring. U. Tex., Austin, 1974. Served to capt. AUS, 1944-46, 50-52. Recipient Disting. Engring. Grad. award, U. Tex., Austin, 1964, Tech. Pioneer for Found. Design, Offshore Energy Ctr., 2001. Fellow: ASCE (pres. Tex. sect. 1970—71, nat. dir. 1980—83, nat. pres. 1989—90, Thomas A. Middlebrooks award 1957, Karl Terzaghi lectr. 1993, William H. Wisely Am. Civil Engr. award 1999, GeoInst. Hero 2002, Tex. Sect. Lifetime Svc. award 2002); mem.: NSPE, Instn. Engrs. Ireland, Inst. Profl. Practice (dir. 1996—99), Houston Engring. and Sci. Soc. (treas., dir. 1973—76), Tex. Coun. Engring. Labs. (dir. 1972—75), Cons. Engrs. Coun. Tex. (dir. 1965—67), Am. Cons. Engrs. Coun., Tex. Soc. Profl. Engrs. (Engr. of Yr. award 1987), Nat. Acad. Engring., Tau Beta Pi, Chi Epsilon (Nat. Honor Mem. 2000). Methodist. Home: 12226 Perthshire Rd Houston TX 77024-4244

FOCHT, THEODORE HAROLD, lawyer, educator; Teaching assoc. Columbia U. Sch. Law, N.Y.C., 1959-60; atty. Office of Gen. Counsel SEC, Washington, 1960-61, legal asst. to Commr., Washington, 1961-63; mem. faculty U. Conn. Sch. Law, Hartford, 1963-71 (leave of absence, 1969-71); spl. counsel on securities legislation Interstate and Fgn. Commerce Com., U.S. Ho. of Reps., Washington, 1969-71; gen. counsel Securities Investor Protection Corp., Washington, 1971-94, pres., 1984-94; adj. prof. law American U. Sch. Law, Washington, 1979-84; mem. Fla. State Comptroller's Task Force on Regulatory DeCoupling, 1995. Home: 8436 Pinafore Dr New Port Richey FL 34653-6739

FOCKLER, HERBERT HILL, foundation executive; b. Summersville, W.Va., Feb. 18, 1922; s. William Okey and Annie Lee (Fitzwater) Fockler; m. Mary Hildegarde Ziegler, May 15, 1950; 1 child, Herbert. BA, W.Va. U., 1947, MA, 1948; cert., Oxford U., Eng., 1948, Harvard U., Cambridge, Mass., 1949; MS in Libr. Sci., Cath. U. Am., Washington, DC, 1952. Adminstr. libr. Princeton U., NJ, 1952-54, Library of Congress, Washington, 1956-58; advisor White House Confs., Washington, 1959-60; exec. NIH, Bethesda, Md., 1961-69; chmn. Sci. and Tech. Coms., Washington, 1969-70; exec. dir. Sci. Founds., Washington, 1971-72; trustee, chmn. Am. Arts Internat. Found., Washington, pres., 1984—, also bd. dirs.; trustee Nat. Mus. of Health and Medicine Found., 1989—. Adv. Nat. Coun. for Sci. and Environment, 2000—; chmn., trustee World Tech. Found., Washington, 1988-89; bd. dirs. Nat. Info. Tech. Ctr.; advisor NSF, 1975, White House Conf. on Bus., 1975, 78, Montgomery Coll., Rockville, Md., 1978, World Bank, 1986, Winston Churchill Found., 1988, IMF, 1991, others; adv. coun. Coolfont Found., Berkeley Springs, W.Va., 1980-87; mem. Presdl. Rsch. Group; assoc. Woodrow Wilson Internat. Ctr., 1988—; mem. Bd. on Sci. Edn.; advisor Global Internet, 2000-01; bd. dirs. Calif. Ctr. for Strategic Studies, 2001—. Editor: Contemporary South, 1968, also conf. records and newsletters; contbr. articles to profl. jours. Adv. Stanford U., 1967-69, Georgetown U., 1975-85; trustee Threshold Environ. Found., Washington, 1969-75, Nat. Mus. Health and Medicine Found., 1989-90, adv. coun., 1991—; mem. pres.'s coun. Shenandoah Coll., Winchester, Va., 1982-87; mem. Found. Advancement Edn. in Scis., 1980—, Joint Bd. Edn. in Sci. and Engring., 1991—; bd. dirs. Nat. Mus. of Lang., 1999—, Global Children's Health Fund, 1999—, Nat. Fgn. Lang. Ctr., 2000—; chmn. Sustainable Value Found., 2003—. Staff sgt. US Army, 1941-45. Mem. AAAS, Acad. Polit. Sci., Am. Polit. Sci. Assn., Washington Acad. Scis. (bd. dirs.), UN Assn., Smithsonian Assocs., Am. Assn. Mus., Air and Space Mus., Nat. Trust Hist. Preservation, Libr. Congress Assocs., Colonial Williamsburg Found., SAR, Fgn. Policy Inst., World Affairs Coun., Policy Studies Orgn., Found. for Advancement Edn. in Sci., Internet Soc., Smithsonian Assocs., Am. Film Inst., Harvard Club, Princeton Club, W.Va. Club, W.Va. Acad. Sci., Nat. Press Club. Home and Office: 10710 Lorain Ave Silver Spring MD 20901-1512

FODA, RABIZ NASIR, industrial and electrical engineer; b. Bombay, May 14, 1949; arrived in Can., 1994; s. Nasir Huseinibhai Foda and Amena (Yahya) Khairullah; m. Nermin Zoyeb Kantawala, Dec. 5, 1977; children: Maria, Zulqarnain, Farzeen. B Tech. with honors, Indian Inst. Tech., Bombay, 1973; grad. diploma in mgmt. studies, U. Bombay, 1981. Sr. asst. engr. Tata Electric Cos., Bombay, 1973-85; elec. engr. Sceco-Western Region, Jeddah, Saudi Arabia, 1985-92, corp. tech. mgmt. group for transmission dept., 1986-90, chief of sub-stations, 1990-92, acting dir. transmission, 1989-92; sr. engr. Indsl. Power Projects, Jeddah, 1993-94, Elecsar Engring. Ltd., Can., 1995-99, Atomic Energy Can. Ltd., Mississauga, Ont., 1999—2003; sr. project engr. Marshall Macklin Monaghan, 2003—. Cons. energy conservation Econ. Cons., Bombay; guest lectr. exec. MBA class St. Bonaventure U., NY, 2004—; lt. gov.'s appointed mem. health professions review bd. Gov. Ont., Can. Sr. mgr. global, assoc. editor: PiTech Pan IIT Tech. Review, 2005—; contbr. articles to profl. jours. Mem. Cir. of Champions Triec, Toronto, Canada, 2005—. Recipient Disting. Alumni Svc. award, Indian Inst. Tech., Bombay, 2005. Mem.: IEEE (sr.), CIGRE Can., IEEE Engring. Mgmt. Soc. (Toronto), Inst. Elec. Engrs. U.K., Profl. Engrs. Ont. (experience requirements com.), Soc. Power Engrs. India, Project Mgmt. Inst., N.Y. Acad. Scis., Indian Inst. Tech. Alumni Assn. Can. (exec. bd. 1996—, treas. 2000—01, gen. sec. 2001—03, v.p. 2003—, pres. 2004—), Econ. Forum of Indian Expatriates (exec. com. 1987—88), India Forum, Embassy of India, Jeddah (mng. com. 1990—94). Avocations: painting, reading, music, tennis, swimming. Home: 1511 Hollywell Ave Mississauga ON Canada L5N 4P6 Personal E-mail: foda@computer.org. Business E-mail: fodar@mmm.ca.

FODERA, LEONARD V., lawyer; b. Bklyn., Sept. 9, 1956; s. Vito Leonard and Nancy Rose (Calderola) F.; m. Kathleen M. Scanlon, Sept. 4, 1981; children: Leonard, Nancy. BA, LaSalle Coll., Phila., 1978; JD, Temple U., Phila., 1989. Bar: Pa. 1989, U.S. Dist. Ct. (ea. dist.) Pa. 1989. Gen. counsel Plymouth Risk Mgmt., Plymouth Meeting, Pa., 1990-92; assoc. Sheller Ludwig & Badey, Phila., 1992-95; ptnr. Monheit, Monheit, Silverman & Fodera, PC, Phila., 1995—. Legal counsel Roosevelt Adv. Counsel, 1989—; mem. Cinnaminson Curriculum Com., N.J., 1992-93, Cinnaminson planning bd., 1998—; advisor Com. of 70, Phila., 1986—. Mem. ABA, Assn. Trial Lawyers Am., Phila. Bar Assn., Million Dollar Advocates Forum, Phila. Trial Lawyers Assn. Roman Catholic. E-mail: LFodera@civilrights.com.

FODERARO, ANTHONY HAROLDE, nuclear engineering educator; b. Scranton, Pa., Apr. 3, 1926; s. Edward and Myrtha (Bachman) F.; m. Rita Lacey, May 4, 1953; children— Anthony, John, Diana. BS in Physics, U. Scranton, 1950; PhD in Physics, U. Pitts., 1955. Supervisory scientist Westinghouse Atomic Power Div., Pitts., 1954-56; sr. nuclear physicist Gen. Motors Research, Warren, Mich., 1956-60; assoc. prof. nuclear engring. Pa. State U., University Park, 1960-63, prof., 1963-88; prof. emeritus, 1989—. Cons. on radiation protection govt. and industry. Author: The Elements of Neutron Interaction Theory, 1971, The Photon Shielding Manual, 1976; co-author: The Reactor Shielding Design Manual, 1956, The Engineering Compendium on Radiation Shielding, 1968; contbr. articles to pubs. in field. Served with US Army, 1943—46. Home: 301 S Gill St State College PA 16801-3963 E-mail: tony@foderaro.com.

FODERARO, LISA, reporter; m. Don Pollard; children: Amelia Jane, Sawyer James. Grad., Brown U., 1985. Reporter White Plains Bur. NY Times. Office: NY Times White Plains Bur 235 Main St White Plains NY 10601 Office Phone: 914-949-0538. Office Fax: 914-949-2613. E-mail: foderaro@nytimes.com.

FODERO, JOSEPH PETER, plastic surgeon; b. Jan. 28, 1967; BS in Biology, Georgetown U. Coll. Arts and Scis.; MD, Yale U. Sch. Medicine, New Haven, Conn., 1993. Lic. NJ, cert. Am. Bd. Plastic Surgeons. Resident, plastic surgery U. Mich.; hosp. appointments St. Barnabas Med. Ctr., Livingston, NJ, Morristown Hosp., NJ, Overlook Hosp., Summit, NJ; private practice Livingston, NJ, 1993—. Named one of Top Rated Doctor in NJ; recipient Dingman Clin. Rsch. award, U. Mich. Mem.: Phi Beta Kappa. Office: 239 W Northfield Rd Livingston NJ 07039 Office Phone: 973-992-3818. Office Fax: 973-992-2466.*

FODIMAN, AARON ROSEN, publishing executive; b. Stamford, Conn., Oct. 10, 1937; s. Yale J. and Thelma F. BS, Tulane U., 1958; LLB, NYU, 1960, MBA, 1961; grad., L'Academie de CuisineCanardier, Washington, 1977. Bar: N.Y. 1960, D.C. 1961, Va. 1965. With FTC, Washington, 1961-65; practiced in Arlington, Va., 1965-78; pres. Fast Food Operators, Inc., NYC, 1978-84, Hampton Healthcare, 1984-91, Kapok Tree Restaurants, Tampa Bay Publs., 1986—. Author: Life is not an Illusion, it Just Looks That Way, 1998; pub., editor: Tampa Bay Mag.; TV host local sports show, Dine Line, Tampa Bay Mag. Bd. dirs. Tampa Players Inc., Washington Ballet, Manhattan Punch Line Theatre, Kent Jewish Cmty. Ctr., Mahaffey Theater Found., Outdoor Art Found., Clearwater Arts Found., pres., chmn., 2003; bd. advisors Fla. Orch.; pres. Dunedin Art Ctr., Bay Ballet Theatre; chmn. Pinellas County Arts Coun., Golda Meir Ctr., Bay Ballet Theatre, A Taste of Pinellas; cmty. advisor Clearwater Dunedin Jr. League; mem. adv. bd. Am. Film Inst.; chmn. Ford Presdl. Campaign, 1976; advisor Fed. Res. Bank Atlanta; participant Leadership Pinellas; participant, founder Leadership Tampa Bay, Nat. Conf. Christians and Jews; Pinellas County amb. to Ringling Mus. Art. Recipient Hyam Soloman Freedom award, 1974, Miniature Palette award Miniature Art Soc. of Fla., 1987, Order of Salvador medal Dali Mus., 1989, Lifetime Achievement award Internat. Restaurant and Hospitality Rating Bur., 2000, Friends of Arts Pinellas County award, Svc. to Mankind award Sertoma Club, Arts Patron award Tampa Bay Bus. Com. for the Arts, 2003; knighted as Baron Order of St. John of Jerusalem, 1999; inducted into Ct. of Honor, Krewe of Venus, 2006. Mem. Pinellas County Restaurant Assn. (pres.), Tampa Bay Restaurant Assn. (pres.), Fla. Restaurant Assn. (bd. dirs.),

Tampa Bay Food and Wine Soc. (founder and pres.), Chaine des Rotisseurs (chpt. officer), Internat. Legal Frat., Phi Delta Phi, Barrister Inn Club (Washington, pres.), B'nai Brith (pres. Washington). Office Phone: 727-791-4800.

FODOR, PETER BELA, plastic surgeon, educator; b. Cluj, Romania, May 14, 1942; MD, U. Wis. Med. Sch., 1966. Cert. Am. Bd. Surgery, Am. Bd. Plastic Surgery, lic. Colo., Conn., Mich., NY, Calif., Wis. Intern, gen. surgery Parkland Meml. Hosp., Dallas, 1966—67; resident, plastic surgery Columbia-Presbyn. Med. Ctr., 1967—68; resident St. Luke's Hosp., NYC, 1974—76; faculty, plastic surgery St. Luke's-Roosevelt Hosp.; faculty, reconstructive plastic surgery and gen. surgery Columbia U. Coll. Physicians and Surgeons; assoc. clin. prof. plastic surgery UCLA Med. Ctr., LA; plastic surgeon Century Aesthetics, LA. Hosp. appointment Santa Monica/UCLA Med. Ctr.; staff mem., plastic surgery Century City Doctors Hosp., LA, Olympia Hosp., LA, St. John's Hosp., Santa Monica, Calif.; mem. adv. bd., exec. editl. cons., round table moderator Consumer Guide to Plastic Surgery. Contbr. scientific papers articles to peer-reviewed jours., chapters to books. Bd. mem. and patron Coun. of Children's Burn Found., Helen Keller Manhattan League for the Blind, Music Ctr. LA, Sonance-House Ear Inst., LA Wild Beat Soc., Music Ctr.-Fraternity of Friends, Peterson Auto Mus. Checker 200, Thalians-President's Club, Bel Air Navy League and Calif. Hwy. Patrol Found. Capt. USAF. Fellow: Internat. Coll. Surgeons Plastic Surgery, ACS; mem.: Semmelweiss Scientific Soc. (past pres.), Royal Soc. Medicine, Northeastern Soc. Plastic Surgeons (founding mem.), NY Acad. Medicine, NY County Med. Soc., NY Regional Soc. Plastic and Reconstructive Surgeons, LA Soc. Plastic Surgeons, Lipoplasty Soc. N.Am. (immediate past pres., past treas.), Internat. Soc. Aesthetic Plastic Surgery, Conn. Soc. Plastic and Reconstructive Surgeons (founding mem.), Conn. State Med. Soc., Calif. Soc. Plastic Surgeons (past sec.), Bay Surgical Soc., Am. Soc. Plastic Surgeons, Am. Soc. for Aesthetic Plastic Surgery (current pres.-elect, past v.p., past treas., past clin. investigator), Am. Assn. Plastic Surgeons. Office: Century Aesthetics 2080 Century Park E Ste 710 Los Angeles CA 90067 Office Phone: 866-203-9818. Office Fax: 310-203-9798.*

FOEGE, WILLIAM HERBERT, public health administrator, educator; b. Decorah, Iowa, Mar. 12, 1936; s. William August and Anne Erika (Ermisch) F.; m. Paula S. Ristad, Dec. 23, 1958; children: David, Michael, Robert. BA, Pacific Luth. U., 1957; MD, U. Wash., 1961; MPH, Harvard U., 1965. Intern USPHS Hosp., SI, NY, 1961-62; epidemic intelligence svc. officer Communicable Disease Ctr., Atlanta, 1962-64; med. officer Immanuel Med. Ctr., Yahe, Nigeria, 1965-66; epidemiologist smallpox eradication/measles control program Nigeria, 1969-70; dir. smallpox eradication program Ctr. Disease Control, Atlanta, 1970-73, dir., 1977-83; med. epidemiologist smallpox program Southeast Asia Regional Office WHO, New Delhi, 1973-75; exec. dir. Carter Ctr., Atlanta, 1987-92; Presdl. Disting. prof. internat. health Rollins Sch. Pub. Health Emory U., Atlanta, 1997—2001, emeritus Presdl. Disting. prof. internat. health, 2001—; exec. dir. Task Force for Child Survival and Devel., 1984—99; sr. medical advisor Bill and Melinda Gates Found., 1999—2001, sr. fellow. Cons. WHO, Bangkok, Thailand, 1967, Kinshasha, Zaire, 1968; dep. field coord. Internat. Red Cross Joint Relief Action, Nigeria. Trustee Rockefeller Found. Recipient Public Welfare medal, Nat. Acad. Sci., 2005. Office: Emory U Rollins Sch Pub Health 1518 Clifton Rd NE Atlanta GA 30322-4201

FOER, FRANKLIN, editor; b. 1975; Editorial asst., staff writer Slate, 1996—98; staff writer, assoc. editor US News & World Report, 1998—2000; sr. editor New Republic, Washington, 2000—06, editor, 2006—. Contbr. editor NY mag., NY Times, Washington Post, Lingua Franca, Spin. Author: How Soccer Explains the World: An Unlikely Theory of Globalization, 2004. Office: The New Republic Ste 700 1331 H St NW Washington DC 20005 Office Phone: 202-508-4444. Office Fax: 202-628-9383.

FOER, JONATHAN SAFRAN, writer; b. Washington, Feb. 21, 1977; m. Nicole Krauss; 1 child, Sasha. BA, Princeton U. Held various positions before publ. such as morgue asst., receptionist, math tutor, ghostwriter, and asst. archivist; sr. editor New Republic. Author: (short story) A Primer for the Punctuation of Heart Disease, 2003, other short stories published in Paris Review, Conjunctions, NY Times, & The New Yorker, (novels) Everything Is Illuminated, 2002 (basis of film by same name, 2005, Nat. Jewish Book award, Guardian First Book award, William Saroyan Internat. prize for writing, 2003), Extremely Loud and Incredibly Close, 2005, (opera libretto) Seven Attempted Escapes From Silence, 2005; editor: Convergence of Birds: Original Fiction and Poetry Inspired by Joseph Cornell, 2001. Named one of People of Yr., Rolling Stone Mag., Best and Brightest, Esquire Mag.; recipient Zoetrope: All Story Fiction prize, 2000. Mailing: care Houghton Mifflin Trade Divsn Adult Editl 8th Fl 222 Berkeley St Boston MA 02116-3764

FOERST, JOHN GEORGE, JR., retired fundraising executive; b. Queens, NY, June 8, 1927; s. John George and Mary Elizabeth (McGinn) F.; m. Marion Theresa Cassidy, June 27, 1953; children: Gerard M., Kathryn J. BA, St. Johns U., Queens, 1950, LHD (hon.), 2005. Regional rep. Nat. Found. for Infantile Paralysis, NYC, 1950-52; campaign dir., v.p. Cmty. Counselling Svc., NYC, 1952-59, v.p., asst. to pres., 1965-69, pres., 1969-87, chmn., 1987-96, chmn. emeritus, 1997-2001; pres. John G. Foerst, Inc., NYC, 1959-65. Spl. advisor to chmn. and bd. dirs. Changing Our World, Inc., 2001—. Contbg. author: complete Guide to Corporate Fund Raising, 1982. Trustee Pope John Paul II Libr. and Cultural Ctr., Washington, 1998—, Telecare, Uniondale, NY; chmn. Am. Assn. Fund Raising Counsel, 1982; mem. Cardinal's Com. of Laity Roman Cath. Archdiocese NY, 1984—; bd. dirs. St. Francis Hosp., Roslyn, NY, 1972—2002, The Ctr. for Devel. Disabilities, Woodbury, NY, 1974—87, Nat. Ctr. for Disability Svcs. Inc., Albertson, NY, 1988—99, Cath. Health Sys. of L.I., 1998—99, Help for the Poor Found., 1998—99, Mid-Atlantic Hosp. Trust, Bermuda. Mem. Union League, Knights of Malta. Republican. Home: 77 Dover Rd Manhasset NY 11030-3717

FOERSTER, BERND, architecture educator; b. Danzig, Dec. 5, 1923; came to U.S., 1947, naturalized, 1954; s. Joseph and Martha (Brumm) F.; m. Enell Dowling, May 13, 1950; children: Kent, Mark (dec.). Student, Columbia U., 1948-49; BS in Architecture, U. Cin., 1954; MArch, Rensselaer Poly. Inst., 1957. Various positions Govt. The Netherlands, 1945-47; with various engrs. and architects offices, 1950-59; cons. Ch. bldgs., design cons., 1954—; instr. architecture U. Cin., 1954, Rensselaer Poly. Inst., Troy, N.Y., 1954-56, asst. prof., 1956-62, assoc. prof., 1962-65, prof., 1965-71, dean, 1969—71; prof. Kans. State U., Manhattan, 1971—99, dean, 1971-84; adjunct prof. Grad. Program in Hist. Preservation Goucher Coll., 1995—. Cons. archtl. and cmty. surveys N.Y. State Coun. Arts, 1962-71; chmn. Gov.'s Adv. Com. Hist. Preservation N.Y. State, 1968-71; cons. Albany Hist. Sites Commn., 1967-71, Independence (Mo.) Heritage Commn., 1975-77; leader U.S. del. Preservation Planning to China, 1982, USSR and Ea. Europe, 1989; leader faculty team Coll. Architecture and Design, Kans. State U. to Poland, The Czech and Slovak Republics, and Hungary, 1990; cons. selection of archs. and design cons. for Fed. projects U.S. GSA, 1994-96. Author: Man and Masonry, 1960, Pattern and Texture, 1961, Architecture Worth Saving in Rensselaer County, N.Y., 1965; (with others) Independence, Missouri, 1978, 2d printing, 1989; (films) Man and Masonry, 1961 (Am. Film Festival selection), What Do You Tear Down Next?, 1964, Earth and Fire, 1964, Assault on the Wynantskill, 1967; editorial adv. bd. Preservation Forum, 1987-93. Bd. dirs. Albany Inst. History and Art, 1967-71, Mohawk-Hudson Council on Edn. TV, 1968-71, v.p., 1970-71; co-chmn. Conf. on Rensselaer County, 1966; pres. Rensselaer County Council for Arts, 1963-64, 66-67; trustee Olana Historic Site, 1969-71; pres. bd. trustees Riley County Hist. Mus., 1977; chmn. Manhattan Downtown Redevel. Adv. Bd., 1979-85, City Fountain Restoration Com., 1983-86; mem. coun. Drayton Hall, Charleston, S.C., 1985-93; mem. Hist. Dist. Rev. Bd. Manhattan, 1997-99; mem. Manhattan Hist. Resources Bd., 1999-2005, vice chmn., 1999-2001; mem. planning bd. Riley County, Kans., 1997-99; chair Road and Bridge Adv. Com. Riley County, 1997-98; chair steering com. Downtown Tomorrow, Manhattan, 1998-2000. Named Disting. prof. Assn. Collegiate Schs. Architecture, 1988; recipient Kans. Gov.'s award for historic preservation, 1995, James Marston Fitch Lifetime Achievement award Nat. Coun. for Preservation Edn., 2000, Disting. Svc. award Kansas State U., 2004, Lifetime Achievement award Kansas Preservation Alliance, 2004. Fellow AIA (com. hist. resources 1977-92, vice chmn. 1986, chmn. 1987, state preservation coordinator 1979-92); mem. AIA Kans. (sec. 1975, exec. com. 1975-80, pres. 1979), Nat. Trust Hist. Preservation (bd. advs. 1979-81, trustee 1981-90, trustee emeritus 1990—), AAUP (chpt. pres. Rensselaer Poly. Inst. 1963-64, Kans. State U. 1987-88, v.p. Kans. conf. 1988-90, pres. 1990-92), The Land Inst. (bd. dirs. 1976-87), Manhattan Arts Coun. (bd. dirs. 1973-78, pres. 1976-77), LWV of Manhattan-Riley County (2d v.p. 1988-91, pres.-elect 91-92, pres. 92-93), Kans. Preservation Alliance (bd. dirs. 1979-85, hon. trustee 1999—), Nat. Council Preservation Edn. (bd. dirs. 1980-93, vice-chmn. 1981-85), Nature Conservancy, Audubon Soc., Scarab, Tau Sigma Delta, Phi Kappa Phi. Lodges: Rotary (Paul Harris fellow). Home: 920 Ratone St Manhattan KS 66502-5136 *Some places are so important, so fragile, or so beautiful that we must leave them alone.*

FOERSTER, DAVID WILLIAM, plastic surgeon; s. Hervey A. and Hazel Ann (Lower) Foerster; m. Montine Louise Price (div.); m. Barbara Jane Dans; children: Stephen, Stanton, Lesia, Leslee, Lara. BA, Yale U., 1954; MD, Okla. U., 1958. Diplomate Am. Bd. Plastic Surgery. Plastic and cosmetic surgeon, Oklahoma City, 1965—. Author: Memoirs of a Yale Man, Class of '54, 2005. Bd. dirs. Jim Thorpe Orgn., Oklahoma City, 1972—. Maj. USAR, 1960—65. Mem.: Internat. Soc. Clin. Plastic Surgeons (pres. 1975—77), Am. Soc. Aesthetic Plastic Surgeons, Am. Soc. Plastic Surgery. Republican. Achievements include pioneering surgical procedures in gender dysphoria patients. Avocation: Senior Olympics shot put and discus. Home: 1602 Coventry Park Nichols Hills OK 73120 Office: 6304 Waterford Blvd Oklahoma City OK 73118 Office Phone: 405-848-3459. Office Fax: 405-848-5401.

FOGARTY, CHARLES JOSEPH, former lieutenant governor; b. Providence, Sept. 15, 1955; s. Charles Joseph and Martha Jane (Hague) F. BA, Providence Coll., 1977; MPA, U. RI, 1980. Policy assoc. Office Gov., Providence, 1978-84; spl. asst. to commr. RI Dept. Edn., Providence, 1985; town councilman Glocester, RI, 1985-91; sr. policy analyst Office Gen. Treas., Providence, 1985-88; dir. policy Office Lt. Gov., Providence, 1989-91; senator RI State Senate, Providence, 1991-99, majority whip, 1993-95, pres. pro tem, 1995-99; lt. gov. State of RI, 1999—2007. Chmn. Glocester Dem. Town Com., 1979-85, RI Longterm Care Coord. Coun., 1996—; del. Dem. Nat. Conv., NYC, 1980, 96, 2000; bd. dirs. NW Cmty. and Nursing Health Svc., 1994-2001, RI chpt. ARC, 1994— Mem. Lions (pres. Glocester chpt. 1991—). Democrat. Roman Catholic. Home: 230 Paris Irons Rd Harmony RI 02829*

FOGARTY, CHARLES MICHAEL, pulmonologist, researcher; b. Sioux City, Iowa, Sept. 18, 1944; s. Charles F. and Wilma M. Fogarty; m. Jane C. McNerney, June 24, 1968; children: Charles D., Thomas F., John W. BS, Providence Coll., 1961; MD, U. Rochester, NYC, 1970. Diplomate Am. Bd. Internal Medicine, 1978. Intern internal medicine Strong Meml. Hosp., Rochester, NY, 1970—71, resident internal medicine, 1973—75; resident pulmonary diseases Hosp. U. Pa., Phila., 1975—78; ptnr. Lung & Chest Med. Assoc., 1978—; med. dir. Spartanburg Med. Rsch., 1994—, Spartanburg Bone Density Ctr., 1997—. Chmn. dept. internal medicine Spartanburg Regional Med. Ctr., 1994—2000; med. dir. respiratory therapy Spartanburg Tech. Coll., 1990—. Capt. US Army, 1971—73. Mem.: European Respiratory Soc., Am. Soc. Bone and Mineral Rsch., Am. Thoracic Soc., Internat. Soc. Clin. Dentsitometry, Acad. Pharm. Physicians and Investigators, Am. Coll. Physicians. Catholic. Avocation: travel. Home: 450 Mudd Creek Rd Inman SC 29349 also: 485 Simuel Rd Spartanburg SC 29303-4755 Office Phone: 864-583-1556. E-mail: cmf@medresearch.com.

FOGARTY, EDWARD MICHAEL, lawyer; b. Woonsocket, RI, Feb. 25, 1948; s. Raymond Henry and Mary (Hogan) F.; m. Gail Higgins, Jan. 8, 1977. BA, Providence Coll., 1969; JD, Georgetown U., 1972. Bar: R.I. 1972, D.C. 1973, U.S. Supreme Ct. 1977. Law clk. U.S. Dist. Ct. R.I., Providence, 1972-73; assoc. Wilkinson, Cragun & Barker, Washington, 1973-79, ptnr., 1979-82, Baenen, Timme, De Reitzes & Middleton, Washington, 1982-83; counsel Spriggs & Hollingsworth, Washington, 1983-98. Legal counsel to speaker R.I. Ho. of Reps., Providence, 1987-93; legal counsel to majority leader R.I. Senate, Providence, 1993-2003, 04—, legal counsel to senate pres., 2003-04; arbitrator R.I. Superior Ct., 1989—. Trustee Festival Ballet Providence, 1988—, pres., 1994—96. Mem.: ABA, Am. Arbitration Assn. (nat. panel of arbitrators 1985—96), D.C. Bar, R.I. Bar Assn. (ho. dels. 1992—94), Univ. Club Providence, Univ. Club Washington. Democrat. Roman Catholic. Home: 488 Lloyd Ave Providence RI 02906-4550 Office Phone: 401-222-3310. Business E-Mail: efogarty@rilin.state.ri.us.

FOGARTY, ROBERT STEPHEN, historian, educator, editor; b. Bklyn., Aug. 30, 1938; s. Michael Joseph and Marguerita (Carmody) F. BS, Fordham U., 1960; PhD, U. Denver, 1968. Instr. Mich. State U., 1963-67; asst. prof. Antioch Coll., Yellow Springs, Ohio, 1968-73, chmn. humanities area, 1973-74, 78-79, assoc. prof., 1974-80, prof. history, 1980—, John Dewey prof. emeritus; prof. Advanced Internat. Studies, Ctr. for Chinese-Am. Johns Hopkins U., 1986-87; editor Antioch Rev., 1977—; dir. Associated Colls. Midwest/Gt. Lakes Coll. Assn., Program in Humanities, Newberry Library, 1978-79; cons. Nat. Endowment for Arts, 1975-81, U. Waterloo, Ont., Canada, 1981. Vis. fellow NYU Inst. for Humanities, 1992—93; Darwin lectr. human biology Galton Inst., London, 1994; lectr. U. Leece, 2006, U. Calabria, 2006, U. So. Miss., 2006. Author: Dictionary of American Communal and Utopian History, 1980, The Righteous Remnant-The House of David, 1981, All Things New: Communes and Utopian Movements, 1860-1914, 1990, Special Love/Special Sex, 1994, Desire and Duty at Oneida: Tirzah Miller's Intimate Memoir, 2000; editor Antioch Rev., 1977—; contbr.: American Encyclopedia of American Culture, 2001; contbr. essays to The Nation, TLS, Mo. Rev.; contbr. articles to profl. jours. Recipient Martha K. Cooper award for editl. achievement, 1981, Nora Magid Award for Editing PEN Am. Ctr., 2003; grantee Am. Philos. Soc., 1976, Am. Coun. Learned Socs.; fellow NEH, 1980, All Souls Coll., Oxford U., 1988, Lloyd Lewis fellow Newberry Libr., 1995, Galton Inst. fellow, 1995; Fulbright Disting. Lectr. to Korea, 2000, Gilder Lehrman fellow 2001, Mary Baker Eddy libr. fellow, 2004. Mem.: PEN/Am. Ctr., Orgn. Am. Historians, Nat. Hist. Communal Sites Assn. (exec. com. 1975—2002), Am. Studies Assn. (bibliography com. 1981—). Office: Antioch Rev Inc PO Box 148 Yellow Springs OH 45387-0148 Office Phone: 927-769-1365. E-mail: rfogarty@antioch.edu.

FOGARTY, THOMAS JAMES, surgery educator; b. Cin., Feb. 25, 1934; s. William Henry and Anna Isabella (Ruthemeyer) F.; m. Rosalee Mae Brennan, Aug. 28, 1965; children: Thomas James Jr., Heather Brennan, Patrick Erin, Jonathan David. BS in Biology, Xavier U., 1956; MD, U. Cin., 1960; D (hon.), Xavier U., 1987. Intern U. Oreg. Med. Sch., Portland, 1960-61, resident, 1962-65, instr. surgery, 1967-68; chief resident, instr. surgery divsn. cardiovascular surgery Stanford (Calif.) U. Med. Ctr., 1969-70, asst. prof. surgery, 1970-71, asst. clin. prof. surgery, 1971-73; cardiovascular surgeon pvt. practice, Stanford, 1973-78; pres. med. staff Stanford U. Med. Ctr., 1977-79; cardiovascular surgeon pvt. practice, Redwood City, Calif., 1978-93; dir. cardiovascular surgery Sequoia Hosp., Redwood City, Calif., 1980-93; clin. prof. surgery Stanford U. Med. Ctr., 1993—. Bd. dirs. Acorn Cardiovascular Inc., Satellite Dialysis Ctrs., Inc.; co-founder, bd. dirs. AneuRx, Inc., Biopsys Med., Inc., Cardiac Pathways, Inc., Emergency Med. Sys., Windy Hill Tech., Inc., Gen. Surg. Innovations, Inc., LocalMed, Inc., Vital Insite, Inc., Raytel Med. Corp., Cardiovascular Imaging Sys., Inc., Devices for Vascular Intervention, Inc., Hancock Labs., Imagyn Med., Inc., Physiometrix, Inc., Ventritex, Inc., Xenotech; mem. scientific adv. bd. Autogenics, BioLink Corp., Cardio Thoracic Sys., Inc., bd. dirs.; pres., founder Fogarty Engring., Inc.; co-founder, sr. ptnr. Three Arch Ptnrs., Baccitus Vascular, Novare Surg., Vascular Archs. Safety; founder, proprietor Thomas Fogarty Winery, 1981-. Portrait included in Bay Area Hon. Mus., 1998; contbr. articles to profl. jours.; patentee in field. Fellow U. Cin. Coll. Medicine, Good Samaritan Hosp., 1961-62, Nat. Heart Inst. Surgery br., Bethesda, Md., 1965-67, rsch. fellow divsn. cardiovascular surgery Stanford Med. Ctr., 1968-69; recipient AstroLobe award Roger Bacon High Sch., 1974, Disting. Alumnus award U. Cin. Med. Sch., 1989, Lifetime Achievement award Phoenix Hall of Fame, 1997, No. Calif. 1998 Entrepreneur of Yr. award Ernst & Young, 1998, Lemelson-MIT $500, 000 Prize invention and innovation, 2000, Assn. Advancement Med. Instrumentation's Found.'s Ann. Laufman-Greatbatch prize, 2000, Sci. Leadership award Nat. Breast Cancer Coalition, 2000, Internat. Soc. award Excellence in Endovascular Innovation Internat. Soc. Endovascular Specialists, 2001, Jacobson Innovation award Am. coll. Surgeons, 2001; named Inventor of Yr., San Francisco Patent and Trademark Assn., 1980; inducted into the Nat. Inventors Hall of Fame, 2001. Mem. AMA, ACS, Am. Assn. Thoracic Surgery, Am. Bd. Thoracic Surgery, Am. Coll. Physican Inventors, Am. Heart Assn. (grantee), Am. Inst. Med. and Biol. Engring., Assn. for Advancement Med. Instrumentation, Med. Device Mfrs. Assn., Am. Med. Polit. Action Com., Am. Surg. Assn., Internat. Soc. Specialists Surgery, Western Thoracic Surg. Soc., Calif. Med. Soc., Pacific Coast Surg. Assn., San Francisco Surg. Soc., San Mateo County Med. Assn., Santa Clara County Med. Assn. (Achievement award in medicine), Internat. Soc. Cardiovascular Surg. (N.Am. chpt.), Soc. Clin. Vascular Surgery, Soc. Vascular Tech., Soc. Thoracic Surgeons, Soc. Vascular Surgery (past pres. 1995), Copco Lake Sportsmen Assn., Santa Cruz Mountain Winegrowers Assn., South Skyline Assn., Sports Car Club Am., Rapley Trail Improvement Assn., Soc. Med. Friends of Wine. Republican. Achievements include invention of balloon embolectomy catheter. Avocations: hunting, fishing, pond gardening, woodworking, genealogy. Office: 3274 Alpine Rd Portola Valley CA 94028 also: Thomas Fogarty Winery 3270 Alpine Rd Portola Valley CA 94028

FOGED, LESLIE OWEN, mathematician, educator; b. Cheyenne, Wyo., Sept. 26, 1953; s. Leif Clifford and Darlene Ann (Lutz) F.; m. Robyn Rachel Gilliom, May 30, 1981 (div. 1984); 1 child, Leif Erik. BA in Math., Midland Luth. Coll., 1974; PhD in Math., Washington U., St. Louis, 1979. Asst., assoc. prof. U. Tex., El Paso, Tex., 1979—, chmn. dept. math., 1987-88. Dir. U. Tex. H.S. Math. Contest, 1990—. Contbr. articles to profl. jours. Recipient Master Tchr. award Midland Luth. Coll., 1991. Achievements include discovery of an internal characterization of topological spaces which are closed images of metric spaces; constrn. of a consistent example of a quotient space of a separable metric space which is not stratifiable; construction of open-compact image of metric space with no point-countable closed quasibase. Office: U Tex at El Paso Dept Math El Paso TX 79968-0001

(KAHN) FOGEL, DANIEL MARK, academic administrator, literature educator, writer; b. Columbus, Ohio, Jan. 21, 1948; s. Ephim and Charlotte Edith (Finkelstein) F.; m. Rachel Kahn, June 24, 1973; children: Nicholas Alden Kahn-Fogel, Rosemary Luttrell. BA in English magna cum laude, Cornell U., 1969, MFA in Creative Writing, 1974, PhD in English, 1976. Tchr. English East Lyme (Conn.) High Sch., 1969-71; asst. prof. English La. State U., Baton Rouge, 1976-80, assoc. prof. English, 1980-84, prof. English, 1984—2002, assoc. dean grad. sch., 1990-92, assoc. vice chancellor acad. affairs, dean grad. sch., 1992-97, exec. vice-chancellor and provost, 1997—2002, prof. emeritus, 2002—; pres. U. Vt., Burlington, 2002—. Tchr. poetry writing workshops, Baton Rouge, 1980-87; instr. creative writing and lit. Instituto Allende, San Miguel de Allende, Guanajuato, Mex., 1972; mem. adv. com. Publs. MLA, 1986-90. Author: Henry James and the Structure of the Romantic Imagination, 1981 (Pulitzer prize nomination), Daisy Miller: A Dark Comedy of Manners, 1990, Covert Relations: James Joyce, Virginia Woolf, and Henry James, 1990, A Companion to Henry James Studies, 1993; author: (with others) The Aspern Papers Souvenir Book, 1988, The World Book Encyclopedia, 1991; author (poetry): A Trick of Resilience, 1975; author foreword: The Henry James Encyclopedia, 1989; editor/co-editor, author introduction: American Letters and the Historical Consciousness, 1987, New Essays on the Portrait of a Lady, 1987; editor: The Princess Casamassima, The Tragic Muse, The Reverberator, 1989; editor, founder Henry James Rev., 1979-95; mem. editorial staff Epoch, 1974-76; poetry editor Epoch, 1974, Nat. Forum 1981-86; editorial cons. Nat. Forum, 1980-84; consulting editor UMI Rsch. Press, 1983-89; author articles in field; contbr. poems to anthologies and periodicals. NEH summer stipend, 1977, 87; grantee La. Endowment for Humanities, 1990, Manship rsch. grantee, 1991-92. Mem. MLA, Henry James Soc. (exec. dir. 1979-2000). Jewish. Office: U Vt Pres Office Room 350B Waterman Bldg 85 S Prospect St Burlington VT 05405-0160 Home: 235 Thayer Bay Rd Colchester VT 05446-6618 Home Phone: 802-864-5138; Office Phone: 802-656-7878. Business E-Mail: daniel.fogel@uvm.edu.*

FOGEL, ESTHER MARIAN (ESTHER MARIAN ROSEIG), veterinary researcher; b. Bklyn., July 23, 1917; d. Chone and Rebecca (Kaplan) Fogel; m. Seymour Roseig, Jan. 21, 1967. Cert., Med. Assts. Sch., NYC, 1967; student, Orange County CC, Middletown, NY, 1967—68. Cert. clin. lab. technician, N.Y. Gen. lab. technician Arden Hill Hosp., Goshen, NY, 1967-68; tech. rsch. asst. Lamont-Doherty Geol. Obs., 1968-70. Achievements include research on the organism saccharomyces cerevisiae in its inactive dry state as brewers yeast or bakers yeast, and its ability to repel the parasites, fleas and ticks from domestic pets through a biochemical process of metabolism in conjunction with meat protein: the end product as CO(NH2)2 in solution in sweat; a coincidental process of coat pigment losses in both dogs and cats fed the initial Yeast was resolved by adjusting the B, A, D Vitamins and Calcium.

FOGEL, IRVING MARTIN, consulting engineer; b. Gloucester, Mass., Apr. 15, 1929; s. Jacob and Ethel (David) F.; children: Ethan, Ronit. BS, Ind. Inst. Tech., 1954, D of Engring. (hon.), 1982. Registered profl. engr., 20 states, Israel. Civil engr. Ill. Hwy. Dept., Peoria, 1954-55; field engr. Peter Kiewit Sons Co., East Gary, Ind., 1955, field engr., progress engr., cost engr. Ogdensburg, NY, 1955-56; supt. grading and paving Merritt, Chapman & Scott, Binghamton, NY, 1956; cost engr. Drake-Merritt, Goose Bay, Labrador, 1956-57; constrn. mgmt. engr. Mil. Estimating Corp., Madrid, Spain, also P.I., 1957-58; project mgr. Ministry of Def., State of Israel, 1958-59, Frederic R. Harris (Holland) N.V., The Hague, also Tehran, Iran, 1959-61, Solel Boneh & Assocs., Addis Ababa, Ethiopia, 1961-63; asst. to tech. dir. Frederic R. Harris, Madrid, 1963-64; chief engr. McKee-Berger-Mansueto, Inc., NYC, 1964-65, v.p. constrn. mgmt., 1965-69; pres. Fogel & Assocs., Inc., NYC, 1969—. Lectr. in field. Author guides, and handbooks on constrn. mgmt.; author: AMA Handbook of Project Mgmt. 2d edit., 2006; contbr. chpts. to books; contbr. articles to profl. jours. Fellow ASCE (life); mem. NSPE (life), NY State Soc. Profl. Engrs. (bd. dir. N.Y.C. chpt.) Home: 404 E 79th St #28D New York NY 10021-1404 Office: 61 Broadway Ste 1605 New York NY 10006-2714 E-mail: fogeleng@pangulf.com.

FOGEL, PAUL DAVID, lawyer; b. Santa Monica, Calif., Sept. 19, 1949; s. Phillip and Betty (Distler) Fogel; m. Yvette Chalom, Feb. 11, 1981; 1 child, Daniele. AB, U. Calif.-Berkeley, 1971; postgrad., U. Paris II, 1972-73; JD, UCLA, 1976. Bar: Calif. 1976, US Dist. Ct. (ctrl. dist.) Calif. 1977, US Dist. Ct. (no. dist.) Calif. 1987, US Supreme Ct. 1990, US Ct. Appeals (9th cir.) 1981, US Ct. Appeals (DC cir.) 2004, US Ct. Appeals (7th cir.) 2006. Grad. fellow Ctr. for Law in Pub. Interest, LA, 1976-77; dep. state pub. def. State Pub. Defender, LA, 1977-79; Fulbright fellow U. Paris II Law Sch., 1979-80; dep. state pub. def. State Pub. Def., San Francisco, 1980-82; sr. supervising atty. Calif. Supreme Ct., San Francisco, 1982-87; assoc. Hinton & Alfert, Walnut Creek, Calif., 1987-88, Crosby, Heafey, Roach & May, San Francisco, 1988-89, ptnr., 1990—2002, Reed Smith LLP, San Francisco, 2003—. Lectr. Am. law U.S. State Dept., Washington, 1980, 87, 99, 2006; lectr. U. Calif. Berkeley Boalt Hall Sch. Law, 1995, practitioner-advisor, 1991-94, 96—. Fellow Am. Acad. Appellate Lawyers, Calif. Acad. Appellate Lawyers (sec., treas. 2003-04, 2d v.p. 2004-05, 1st v.p. 2005-06, pres. 2006-07); mem. Calif. State Bar Assn. (chmn. appellate cts. com. 1990-91), Bar Assn. San Francisco (chair appellate practice sect. 1999-2000), 9th cir. rules com. 1999-2005, appellate rules task force 1998-2004, Calif. jud. coun., appellate adv. com. 2004-, Amnesty Internat. Office: Reed Smith LLP 2 Embarcadero Ctr Ste 2000 San Francisco CA 94111-4191 Home Phone: 510-540-8402; Office Phone: 415-543-8700, 415-659-5929. Business E-Mail: pfogel@reedsmith.com.

FOGEL, RICHARD, lawyer, educator; m. Sheila Feldman; children: Bruce, Lori Ellen. BA, York Coll., CUNY, 1971; JD, N.Y. Law Sch., 1974. Bar: N.J. 1976, U.S. Dist. Ct. N.J. 1976, N.Y. 1981, U.S. Dist. Ct. (so. dist.) N.Y. 2000, U.S. Tax. Ct. 1977. Tax law specialist IRS, Newark, 1975-77; sr. pension cons., atty. N.Y. Life, NYC, 1977-81; pvt. practice Franklin, N.J., 1981-85, Wayne, N.J., 1985-88, McAfee, N.J., 1988—. Lectr. Inst. for Continuing Legal Edn., Newark, 1977—; mem. adj. faculty Upsala Coll., East Orange, N.J., 1978-88; presenter 34th ann. meeting. Internat. Soc. for Systems Scis., Portland State U., 1990. Recipient Certs. of Appreciation, IRS, Newark, 1977, Inst. Continuing Legal Edn., Newark, 1981-82, 84, Cert. in Recognition of Accomplishments, Coop. Extension Cook Coll., Rutgers U., 1982, Disting. Grad. award York Coll., 1984, Founder's Day Dist. Alumni award, 1992. Mem.: Columbian Lawyers Assn. (1st jud. dept. State of N.Y.). Home: 28 Elizabeth Dr Sussex NJ 07461 Office: Vernon Colonial Pla PO Box 737 Rt 94 Mc Afee NJ 07428 Home Phone: 973-875-7232; Office Phone: 973-827-3933. Business E-Mail: rfogel@nac.net.

FOGEL, ROBERT WILLIAM, economist, educator, historian; b. NYC, July 1, 1926; s. Harry Gregory and Elizabeth (Mitnik) Fogel; m. Enid Cassandra Morgan, Apr. 2, 1949; children: Michael Paul, Steven Dennis. AB, Cornell U., 1948; AM, Columbia U., 1960; PhD, Johns Hopkins U., 1963; MA (hon.), U. Cambridge, Eng., 1975, Harvard U., 1976; DSc (hon.), U. Rochester, 1987, U. de Palermo, Argentina, 1994, Brigham Young U., 1995, SUNY, Binghamton, NY, 1999. Instr. Johns Hopkins U., 1958—59; asst. prof. U. Rochester, 1960—64; Ford Found. vis. rsch. prof. U. Chgo., 1963—64, asso. prof., 1964—65, prof. econs., 1965—69, prof. econs. and history, 1970—75; prof. econs. U. Rochester, 1968—71, prof. econs. and history, 1972—75; Taussig rsch. prof. Harvard U., Cambridge, Mass., 1973—74, Harold Hitchings Burbank prof. polit. economy, prof. history, 1975—81; Charles R. Walgreen Disting. Svc. prof. Am. institutions U. Chgo., 1981. Pitt prof. Am. history and insts. U. Cambridge, 1975—76; chmn. com. math. and statis. methods in history Math. Social Sci. Bd., 1965—72; rsch. assoc. Nat. Bur. Econ. Rsch., 1978—, co-dir. Cohort Studies program, 1998—, dir. DAE program, 1978—91; dir. Ctr. for Population Econ., Chgo. Author: The Union Pacific Railroad: A Case in Premature Enterprise, 1960, Railroads and American Economic Growth: Essays in Econometric History, 1964, Ten Lectures on the New Economic History, 1977, Without Consent of Contract: The Rise and Fall of American Slavery, Vol. 1, 1989, The Fourth Great Awakening and the Future of Egalitarianism, 2000, The Slavery Debates, 1952-1990: A Retrospective, 2003, The Escape from Hunger and Premature Death 1700-2100: Europe, America, and the Third World, 2004; author: (with others) The Reinterpretation of American Economic History, 1971, Dimensions of Quantitative Research in History, 1972, Without Consent of Contract: The Rise and Fall of American Slavery, Vols. 2-4, 1992; author: (with S.L. Engerman) Time on the Cross: The Economics of American Negro Slavery, 1974; author: (with G.R. Elton) Which Road to the Past? Two Views of History, 1983. Co-recipient The Bancroft prize, 1975, Gustavus Myers prize, 1990, Nobel prize, Nobel Found., 1993; recipient Arthur H. Cole prize, 1968, Schumpter prize, 1971, Disting. Alumnus award, Johns Hopkins U., 2000; fellow, Gilman, 1957—60, Social Sci. Rsch. Coun., 1960, Ford Found. Faculty Rsch., 1970; grantee Faculty Rsch., 1966, NSF, 1967, 1970, 1972, 1975—76, 1978, 1992—96, Fulbright, 1968, NIH, 1991—. Fellow: AAAS, Royal Hist. Soc., Econometric Soc., Brit. Acad. (corr.); mem.: NAS, Am. Philos. Soc., Internat. Union for Sci. Study of Population, Population Assn. Am., Am. Acad. Arts and Scis., Agrl. History Soc., Social Sci. History Assn. (pres. 1980—81), Assn. Am. Historians, Am. Hist. Assn., Econ. History Soc., Econ. History Assn. (trustee 1972—81, pres. 1977—78), Royal Econ. Soc., Am. Econ. Soc. (pres. 1998), European Acad. Arts, Scis. and Humanities, Phi Beta Kappa. Office: U Chgo Grad Sch Bus Ctr for Population Econ 5807 S Woodlawn Ave Chicago IL 60637-1511 Office Phone: 773-702-7709.*

FOGELMAN, ANN FLORENCE, nutrition consultant, educator, researcher; b. Reading, Pa., Oct. 12, 1924; d. George Franklin Fogelman and Ruth Amelia Swartley Fogelman. BS, U. Del., 1950; MPH, U. Calif., Berkeley, 1957. Registered dietitian Am. Dietetic Assn., lic. dietitian Tex. Cook Art Camp, Cragsmoor, NY, 1948; asst. dir. YWCA Camp Otonka, Dagsboro, Del., 1949; asst. dietitian Meml. Hosp., Wilmington, Del., 1950—51; dietetic intern Frances Stern Food Clinic, Boston, 1952; clinic and tchg. dietitian Vanderbilt U. Hosp., Nashville, 1953—56; nutritionist Charlotte (N.C.)-Mecklenburg Health Dept., 1957—60; nutrition cons. Md. State Dept. Health, Balt., 1960—63; nutritionist dept. ob-gyn. U. Tex. Med. Br., Galveston, 1963—91; ret. Dietary dir. Tex. Nutrition Survey, 1968—69; liaison Tex. Home Econs. Assn. Tex. Dietetic Assn. Exec. Bd., 1968—69; pres., various other offices and coms. Tex. State Nutrition Coun., 1976—78; Tex. del. Am. Home Econs. Assn. Nat. Conv., 1971, 73; rec. sec. Houston Area Home Econs. Assn., 1967—68; pres. South Tex. Dietetic Assn., 1969—70. Contbr. chapters to books, articles to profl. jours. Vol. Clear Lake Regional Med. Ctr., Webster, Tex., 1992—96, Meml. Hermann S.E. Hosp., Houston, 1994—, Vitas Healthcare, Friendswood, Tex., 1994—, Sr. Learning Ctr., Webster, 1997—; active Clear Lake Presbyn. Ch., 1992—, deacon, 1996, Stephen min., 2000. With WAVES, 1944—46. Named one of 10 Most Outstanding Students, Sch. Home Econs. U. Del., 1962. Mem.: Waves Nat. (life), Bay Area Writers League, U. Tex. Med. Br. Retirees, Sr. Friends (Clear Lake chpt.), The Women's Meml. (charter), Beta Sigma Phi (pres. Charlotte chpt. 1959—60, pres. Pasadena chpt. 1974—75, Dickinson chpt. Girl of Yr. 1966—67, Girl of Yr. 1974—75). Avocations: travel, dance, reading. E-mail: annbird@hotmail.com.

FOGELNEST, ROBERT, lawyer; b. Phila., Aug. 29, 1946; s. Phillip Harold and Charlotte (Wolkov) F.; m. M.J. Wolf, Jan. 21, 1972 (div. 1980); 1 child, B. Jacob; m. Susan W. Van Dusen, Mar. 27, 1991. BA, Temple U., 1973; JD, Rutgers U., 1976. Bar: Pa. 1976, N.Y. 1987, U.S. Dist. Ct. (ea. dist.) Pa. 1976, U.S. Dist. Ct. (ea. and so. dists.) N.Y. 1987, U.S. Dist. Ct. (we. dist.) Pa. 1988, U.S. Tax Ct. 1984, U.S. Ct. Appeals (3d cir.) 1985. Asst. dist. atty. Phila., 1976-79; ptnr. Ellis, Fogelnest & Newman, P.C., Phila., 1979-85; pvt. practice, N.Y.C., 1985—; mem. bd. regents Nat. Criminal Def. Coll.; faculty mem. Gerry Spence's Trial Lawyers Coll. Editorial adviser Inside Drug Law, 1984-89. Fellow Am. Bd. Criminal Lawyers (gov.), Pa. Assn. Crimininal Def. Lawyers, N.Y. Assn. Criminal Def. Lawyers (dir.); mem. Nat. Assn. Criminal Def. Lawyers (pres. 1995-96). E-mail: fogelnest@aol.com.*

FOGER, FRANCES MURCHISON, minister; b. Alexandria, La., Dec. 31, 1941; d. Duncan Cameron and Marietta Mills Murchison; m. Carl Allen Foger, Dec. 18, 1982; m. Wallace Montgomery Driskell (dec.); 1 child, Stephen Driskell. Student, Rhodes Coll., Memphis, 1959—61; BA, La. Tech. U., Ruston, 1963; MS, Tex. Woman's U., Denton, 1984; MDiv, So. Meth. U., 2000. Adminstrv. mgr. The U. of Tex. Health Sci. Ctr. at Houston, 1970—84; adminstrv. asst. Baylor Coll. Medicine, 1989—93; min. United Meth. Ch., 1995—. Preschool bd. mem. First United Meth. Ch., LaPorte, Tex., 2000—02; ptnrs. in mission United Meth. Ch., Houston, 2001; spkr. Rotary Club Internat., Houston, 2001. Police chaplain LaPorte Police Dept., 2002; clinical mem. Assn. Clinical Pastoral Edn., 1995—96; mem. Coll. of Chaplains, 1995—96. Fellow: Am. Coll. Healthcare Execs.; mem.: Ministerial Alliance (sec. 2002—05). Democrat. Methodist. Avocations: piano, swimming, walking, crafts, organ. Home: 9825 Radio Rd Houston TX 77075

FOGERTY, JOHN CAMERON, musician, composer; b. Berkeley, Calif., May 28, 1945; Singer, guitarist Creedence Clearwater Revival, 1968-72; solo performer, 1973—; albums include (with Creedence Clearwater Revival) Creedence Clearwater Revival, 1968, Bayou Country, 1969, Willy & the Poor Boys, 1969, Green River, 1969, Cosmo's Factory, 1970, Pendulum, 1970, Creedence Gold, 1972, Mardi Gras, 1972, More Creedence Gold, 1973, Live in Europe, 1973, Chronicle, Vol. 1, 1976, Vol. 2, 1986, Down on the Corner, 1976, Hot Stuff, 1977, Greatest Hits, 1979, Concert, 1980, Creedence Country, 1981, Rollin' on the River, 1988, Travelin' Band, 1990; (solo) Blue Ridge Rangers, 1973, John Fogerty, 1975, Hoodoo, 1976, Centerfield, 1985, Knockin' on Your Door, 1986, Eye of the Zombie, 1986, Blue Moon Swamp, 1997, Deja Vu All Over Again, 2004. Inducted to Rock and Roll Hall of Fame, 1993; recipient: Golden Plate award, Acad. Achievement, 2005. Office: Warner Bros 3300 Warner Blvd Burbank CA 91505-4694*

FOGG, BLAINE VILES, lawyer; b. Boston, Mar. 29, 1940; s. Sanford L. and Dorothy (Viles) F.; m. Diane Abitbol, June 22, 1964; children: William, Matthew, Katherine. AB cum laude, Williams Coll., 1962; JD cum laude, Harvard U., 1965. Bar: NY 1966. Assoc. Skadden, Arps, Slate, Meagher & Flom LLP, NYC, 1966-71, ptnr., of counsel, 1971—, sr. advisor, Continental Europe, chair, fin. oversight and audit com. Spkr. in the field. Co-author: a major treatise on the Hart-Scott-Rodino Antitrust Improvements Act; author: numerous articles. Trustee Mount Sinai Med. Ctr., Inc. Named "senior statesman", Chambers USA, America's Leading Lawyers for Business, 2004—05. Office: Skadden Arps Slate Meagher & Flom LLP Four Times Sq New York NY 10036 Address: Skadden Arps Slate Meagher & Flom LLP 68 rue du Faubourg Saint-Honoré 75008 Paris France Office Phone: 212-735-3900, 011.33.1.55.27.11.00. Office Fax: 011.33.1.55.27.11.99, 917-777-3900. Business E-Mail: bfogg@skadden.com.

FOGG, RICHARD LLOYD, food products executive; b. Boston, Jan. 22, 1937; s. Lloyd Clark and Mildred Ann (Cass) F.; m. Carolyn Ann Kane, Feb. 12, 1966; children— Amanda C., Jennifer S., Timothy L. AB, Bowdoin Coll., Brunswick, Maine, 1959; MBA, Cornell U., 1961. With brand mgmt. dept. Procter & Gamble Co., Cin., 1961-66; dir. mktg. mgmt. Hunt-Wesson Foods, Fullerton, Calif., 1967-76; sr. v.p. Amfac Food Group, Portland, Oreg., 1977; pres. subs. Fisher Cheese Co., Wapakoneta, Ohio, 1978-83; group v.p., COO Land O'Lakes Dairy Foods, Mpls., 1983-93; pres., CEO Orval Kent Food Co., Wheeling, Ill., 1994-96; pvt. investor, 1997—. Mem. Am. Mktg. Assn. Office Fax: 707-939-7859. Personal E-mail: sonomafogg@aol.com.

FOGG, WILLIAM V., lawyer; b. NYC, Feb. 21, 1966; BA magna cum laude, Brown Univ., 1988; JD, Columbia Univ., 1991. Bar: NY 1992. Assoc. Cravath Swaine & Moore LLP, NYC, 1991—99, ptnr., corp., 1999—. Mng. editor Columbia Jour. of Law and Social Problems. Named a Stone Scholar. Mem.: ABA, Assn. of Bar of City of NY, NY Bar Assn., NY Lawyers for the Pub. Interest. Office: Cravath Swaine & Moore LLP Worldwide Plz 825 Eighth Ave New York NY 10019-7475 Office Phone: 212-474-1131. Office Fax: 212-474-3700. Business E-Mail: wfogg@cravath.com.

FOGGE, LEN, advertising executive; b. NYC; children: Adam, Gina, Vanessa. BA in Philosophy, St. Peter's Coll., 1973. Traffic asst. Charles Schlaifer & Co., NYC, 1973, acct. coord., 1974; acct. coord., acct. exec. Grey Entertainment, NYC, 1974-75, account supr., 1977, v.p. account supr., 1979-84, v.p. mgmt. supr., 1984-86, sr. v.p., gen. mgr., 1986-92, pres., 1992-95, Franklin Spier, Inc., NYC, 1995-96; exec. v.p. creative, mktg., rsch. and digital media Showtime Networks, Inc., 1996—. Office: Showtime Networks Inc 1633 Broadway New York NY 10019-6708 Home: 113 W 87th St New York NY 10024-2903

FOGIEL, MAX, publishing executive; b. Magdeburg, Germany, Aug. 29, 1929; came to U.S., 1940; s. Abram and Sara (Pergericht) F. BME, Cooper Union U., NYC, 1952; MME, Poly. Inst., Bklyn., 1954; PhD in Elec. Engring., Tech. U., Munich, Germany, 1965. Bar: U.S. Patent Office, 1958; registered profl. engr., N.Y., N.J. Sr. engr. Ford Instrument, Long Island City, NY, 1952-56, Control Instrument, Bklyn., 1956-59; rsch. engr. Loral Electronics, Bronx, NY, 1959-61; project engr. RCA, NYC, 1961-64; pres., CEO, Rsch. & Edn. Assn., Piscataway, NJ, 1964—2004, dir. engring. seminars, 1964-66. Instr. in elec. engring. N.J. Inst. Tech., 1965-66. Author: Microelectronics, 1968, 1973, Life Insurance, 1972, Beauty Care, 1993, AIDS and HIV, 1995, Handbook of Electrical Engineering, 1996, Handbook of Chemical Engineering, 1998, Handbook of Mechanical Engineering, 1998; editor: 41 Problem Solvers, 1973—, Energy Technology, vol. I and II, 1975, Pollution Control, vol. I and II, 1978, Calculus Textbook, 2002, series bus. and math. 57 books, 1999; pub. H.S. and coll. study guides and handbooks in sci. and tech.; editor: Basic Electronics, 2003, (test preparation books for) No Child Left Behind series, 2003. Achievements include patents in field. Avocation: painting. Home: 44 Maple Ct Highland Park NJ 08904-1922 Office Phone: 732-214-8892.

FOGLE, SHERYL KAY, voice educator, music educator; b. Ft. Hood, Tex., Mar. 27, 1947; d. J.B. and Ophelia Kathryn Denn; m. John Samuel Fogle, July 28, 1984; children: John Peter Fish, Calvenn Starre. MusB in Sacred Music and Voice summa cum laude, East Tex. Bapt. U., Marshall, 1996; MusM in Voice Pedagogy and Lit., Southwestern Bapt. Theol. Sem., 1999, D of Musical Arts in Voice Pedagogy and Lit., 2005. Voice adj. faculty East Tex. Bapt. U., Marshall, 2000—02, Tarrant County South Campus, Ft. Worth, 2003—05; pvt. voice adj. faculty, tchg. asst. Southwestern Bapt. Theol. Sem., Ft. Worth, 2004—05; pvt. voice and piano instr. Salt Lake City, 2006, Marshall, Tex., 2007—. Active Cumberland Presbyn. Ch., Marshall, 2007—. Recipient Music Dept. Outstanding Student award, East Tex. Bapt. U., 1996, Southwestern Seminary Presdl. award, 1996. Mem.: Nat. Assn. Tchrs. Singing, Sigma Alpha Iota (life). Home and Studio: 2512 Grangeway Marshall TX 75672-4483

FOGLEMAN, GUY CARROLL, physicist, mathematician, educator; b. Lake Charles, La., Dec. 29, 1955; s. Louis Carroll and Peggy Joyce (Trahan) F.; m. Jenny S. Kishiyama, Mar. 14, 1993; children: Elyssa Mayumi, Myles Masaru. BS in Physics, La. State U., 1977; MS in Physics, Ind. U., 1979, MA in Math., 1981, PhD in Physics, 1982. Rsch. assoc. Tri Univ. Meson Facility U. B.C., Vancouver, Canada, 1982—84; assoc. prof. San Francisco State U., 1984—87, adj. prof., 1987—; project scientist RCA Govt. Svcs., Moffett Field, Calif., 1987—88; prin. investigator Search for Extraterrestrial Intelligence Inst., Mountain View, Calif., 1988—89; mgr. advanced programs life scis. divsn. NASA Hdqrs., Washington, 1990—93; acting chief environ. sys. and tech. br. Life and Biomed Scis. and Applications divsn. NASA Hdqrs., Washington, 1993—95; program exec. human exploration and devel. of space advanced human support techs. program Life Scis. divsn. NASA, Washington, 1996—2000; acting dir. bioastronautics rsch. divsn. NASA Hdqrs., Washington, 2000—03, dir. bioastronautics rsch. divsn., 2003—06; exec. dir. Fedn. Am. Societies Exptl. Biology, Bethesda, Md., 2006—. Vis. physicist Stanford (Calif.) Linear Accelerator Ctr., 1984-86. Contbr. articles to sci. jours. Travel grantee NSF and NATO, 1980; rsch. grantee NASA, 1988, 89. Mem. AIAA (sr.), AAAS, Am. Phys. Soc., Prometheus Soc. (ombudsman 1998-99), Mega Soc., Sigma Xi (assoc.), Sigma Pi Sigma, Internat. Acad. Astronautics (corr. mem.). Achievements include research in physics of particles in microgravity, theoretical elementary particle physics, technologies for the collection of cosmic dust particles, the origins of life and the philosophy of mind. Business E-Mail: gfogleman@faseb.org.

FOGLEMAN, JULIAN BARTON, lawyer; b. Memphis, Apr. 17, 1920; s. John Franklin and Marie Julia (McAdams) F.; m. Melba Margaret Henderson, Aug. 11, 1950; children: Margaret Elisabeth Heath, Julian Barton, John Nelson, Jennifer Leigh Vaughan, Frances Lorie Irwin. BS, U. Ark., 1941, LL.B., 1943, JD, 1969. Bar: Ark. 1943. Practiced in Marion, 1946-54, West Memphis, 1954—; pvt. practice, 1946-52; assoc. Hale & Fogleman, 1952-66, ptnr., 1967-73, Hale, Fogleman & Rogers, 1974—2001, Fogleman & Rogers, 2002—. City atty., Marion, 1951-81, dep. pros. atty., 1957-64 Chmn. fin. dir. Crittenden dist. Chickasaw coun. Boy Scouts Am., 1969, mem. exec. bd. coun., 1970-71, 75-80; bd. dirs. Crittenden County Charities, 1994-97, v.p., 1995; bd. dirs. Ark. Good Rds. Transp. Coun., 1976-96; mem. Ark. Cmty. Based Rehab. Commn., 1978-86, Crittenden County Bd. Edn., 1987-92. With inf. AUS, 1943-45, ETO. Fellow Am. Bar Found., Ark. Bar. Found. (bd. dirs. 1989-92); mem. ABA, Ark. Bar Assn. (ho. of dels. 1972-75, 81-84, exec. council 1972-75, 81-84, outstanding lawyer citizen award 1995-96), N.E. Ark. Bar Assn. (past pres.), Crittenden County Bar Assn. (past pres.), Phi Alpha Delta, Sigma Chi. Methodist. Home: 84 Turner Ave Marion AR 72364-1932 Office: PO Box 1666 123 W Broadway West Memphis AR 72301 Office Phone: 870-735-1900.

FOGLEMAN, RONALD ROBERT, retired air force officer, consultant; b. Juniata County, Pa., Jan. 27, 1942; s. Harry R. and Sara (Landis) F.; m. M. Jane Lauver, June 22, 1963; children: Harry R., William E. BS, USAF Acad., 1963; MA, Duke U., 1971. Commd. 2d lt. USAF, 1963, advanced through grades to gen., 1992, fighter, mobility and command pilot; chief Tactical Forces Divsn., The Pentagon, Washington, 1979-81; vice comdr. 388th Tactical Fighter Wing, Hill AFB, Utah, 1981-82; dir. fighter ops. Hdqrs. Tactical Air Command, Langley AFB, Va., 1982-83; comdr. 56th Tactical Tng. Wing, MacDill AFB, Fla., 1983-84, 836th Air Divsn., Davis-Monthan AFB, Ariz., 1984-86; dep. dir. Programs and Procedure, Hdqrs. USAF, Washington, 1986-88, dir., 1988-90; comdr. 7th Air Force, 1990-92; comdr. in chief U.S. Transp. Command, 1992-94; comdr. Air Mobility Command, 1992-94; chief of staff USAF, Washington, 1994-97, ret. gen., 1997; chmn., CEO Durango Aerospace Inc. Bd. dirs. Mesa Airgroup, N.Am. Airlines, Mitre Corp., World Airways, Rolls-Royce N.Am.; mem. Def. Policy Bd., 2001-. Chmn. Falcon Found., Airlift/Tanker Assn.; bd. dirs. Ft. Lewis Coll. Found., Mitre Corp.; mem. NASA Shuttle Return to Flight Task Group; chmn. Vision 2050: An Integrated Transp. Sys., Nat. Rsch. Council. Mem. Air Force Assn., USAF Acad. Assn. Grads., Daedalians (flight capt. 1983-84, 89-90), Coun. Fgn. Rels. Republican. Methodist. Avocation: rugby. Home: 406 Snow Cap Ln Durango CO 81303-3636

FOGLER, DAN, actor; b. Bklyn., Oct. 20, 1977; Grad., Boston U. Performer: (off-broadway plays) The Detective Sketches, The Voyage of the Carcass, Bridges and Harmonies, Joe Fearless, 2000, The 25th Annual Putnam County Spelling Bee, 2005 (Lucille Lortel award for Outstanding Featured Actor, 2005), (off-off broadway) Bobby Gould in Hell, 2004, C-R-E-P-E-S-C-U-L-E, 2004, (Broadway plays) Joe Fearless, 2000, The 25th Annual Putnam County Spelling Bee, 2005— (Drama League award nomination for Disting. Performance, 2005, Outer Critics Circle award for Outstanding Featured Actor in a Musical, 2005, Theatre World award, 2005, Tony award for Best Performance by a Featured Actor in a Musical, 2005), (off-Broadway) The Voyage of the Carcass, 2006; stand-up comic appeared in comedy clubs such as Caroline's Comedy Club, Gotham Comedy Club, Stand Up NY and NYCC; performer: (Nat. Tour) Scooby Doo/Stage Fright; actor: (films) Brooklyn Thrill Killers, 1999, Home Field Advantage, 2000, Bust a Move, 2000, Hyper, 2002, Slippery Slope, 2005, School for Scoundrels, 2006, Balls of Fury, 2007. Address: c/o Circle in the Square Theatre 1633 Broadway New York NY 10036*

FOGLESONG, JAMES STATON (JIM), retired music company executive; b. Lundale, W. Va., July 1922; m. Toni Foglesong; 4 children. Grad., Eastman Sch. of Music, Rochester, NY. Joined Columbia Records, NYC, 1951; artists and repertoire head Epic Records, NYC; exec. prodr. RCA Records, NYC, 1963—70; pres. ABC/Dot Records, Nashville, 1970—79, MCA Nashville, Nashville, 1979—84, Capitol Records, Nashville, 1984—89; now cons., independent prodr, Nashville; adj. prof. music, Blair Sch. of Music Vanderbilt Univ., Nashville, 1991—; dir., music bus. program. Trevecca Nazarene Univ. Former chmn. of bd. Country Music Found., 1976, 87, trustee emeritus. Named to Country Music Hall of Fame non-performer category, 2004. Achievements include being credited with furthering careers of Garth Brooks, Reba McEntire, George Strait, Oak Ridge Boys, Tanya Tucker, others.

FOGLESONG, ROBERT H., academic administrator, career military officer; b. W. Va. m. Mary Thrasher Foglesong; children: David, Mark. BS in Chem. Engring., W. Va. U., 1968, MSc in Chem,. Engring., 1969, PhD in Chem. Engring., 1971; student, Nat. War Coll., Ft. Lesley McNair, Washington, 1989; participant, Seminar XXI MIT, on Fgn. and Internat. Rels., 1996. Commd. 2d lt. USAF, 1972, advanced through grades to gen., 2001; instr. pilot 557th Flying Tng. Squadron USAF Acad., Peterson Field, Colo., 1973-76; aide de campe to comdr. Air Forces Korea, 314th Air Divsn., Osau Air Base, S. Korea, 1976-77; instr. pilot, comdr. ops. officer, spl. asst to NORAD region comdr. USAF, Malmstrom AFB, Mont., 1977-80; pilot, squadron scheduler, 9th tactical fighter squadron chief quality 49th figher wing, comdr repair squadron USAF, Holloman AFB, N. Mex., 1980-82; spl. asst. tactical issues, exec. officer dep. chief of rsch, devel. and acquisition Headqtrs USAF, Washington, 1983-85; spl. asst. to comdr., chief combat analysis divsn. Hdqs. Tactical Air Command, Langley AFB, Va., 1985-87; chief of staff of the air force, chair, prof. joint and combined warfare Nat. War Coll. Ft. Lesley McNair, Washington, 1988-90; pilot F-16, chief of maintenance, 347th Air Tactical Wing USAF, Moody AFB, Ga., 1990-91, comdr. 14 flying tng. wing Columbus AFB, Miss., 1993, comdr. 51st fighter wing Osau Air Base, Republic of Korea, 1994-95; dep. dir. politico-mil. affairs Joint Staff, Washington, 1995-97, asst. to chmn., 1997—99; comdr. 12th Air Force and U.S. Southern Command Air Forces USAF, Davis-Monthan AFB, Ariz., 1999—2000, dep. chief of staff Air and Space Ops. Washington, 2000—01, vice chief of staff, 2001—03, comdr. Allied Air Component Command, air component comdr. U.S. European Command Ramstein AFB, Germany, 2003—06; dir. Multinational Joint Air Power Competence Ctr., Kalkar, Germany, 2006. Pres. USAF Europe U.; pres., exec. dir. Appalachian Leadership and Edn. Found.; pres. Miss. State U., 2006—. Contbr. articles to mil. and profl. jours. Decorated Defense Superior Svc. medal, Legion of Merit with oak leaf cluster, Meritorious Svc. medal with 3 oak leaf clusters, Aerial Achievement medal with 2 oak leaf clusters, Air Force Commendation medal with 2 oak leaf clusters, Air Force Achievement medal, Korean Nat. Security medal (Samil), Korean Nat. Security medal (Cheon-Su). Office: Miss State U PO Box 6018, 610 Allen Hall Mississippi State MS 39762 Office Phone: 662-325-3221. E-mail: president@msstate.edu.*

FOHL, TIMOTHY, investment company executive; b. Pitts., Apr. 21, 1934; s. Edward Zinn and Dorothy (Umbenhauer) F.; m. Nancy Lee Hattox, Apr. 15, 1961; children: Nicholas, Jeffrey, Peter. AB, Dartmouth Coll., 1956; MS, MIT, 1959, PhD, 1963; postgrad. exec. devel. program, Whittemore Sch. Bus. and Econs., 1977. Rsch. scientist Itek Corp., Lexington, Mass., 1962-63, Mt. Auburn Rsch. Assos., Newton, Mass., 1963-68, prin. scientist, dir., 1968-72; with GTE Products Corp., Danvers, Mass., 1972—88, mgr. new product devel. lighting group, 1977-82, mgr. engring. devel., 1982-85, dir. engring. devel., 1985-88; scientist GTE Labs., Inc., Waltham, Mass., 1988-92; pres. Tech. Integration Group, Carlisle, Mass., 1992—; v.p. Light Time in Space, Inc., 1992—; dir. chief sci. officer Qualume Corp., 2002—. Contbr. articles to profl. jours.; patentee in field. Pres., trustee Carlisle Conservation Found., 1972-79; v.p. Carlisle Trails Assn., 1975—; fin. chmn. Town Republican Com., 1980; mem. land stewards com. Carlisle Conservation Commn., 2006. Recipient Leslie H. Warner Tech. Achievement award, 1990. Mem. Mass. Bus. Roundtable. Home: 681 South St Carlisle MA 01741-1517 Office Phone: 978-371-0194. E-mail: tfohl@tigco.com.

FOHRER, ALAN J., utilities company executive; BS, MS, U. So. Calif.; MBA, Calif. State U., Los Angeles. V.p., treas., CFO Southern Calif. Edison (SCE), 1991—93; sr. v.p., treas., CFO Edison Internat., SCE, Rosemead, Calif., 1993; chmn., pres., CEO Edison Mission Energy, Irvine, Calif., 2000—02; CEO Southern Calif. Edison (SCE), 2002—. Office: So Calif Edison 2244 Walnut Grove Ave Rosemead CA 91770

FOK, AGNES KWAN, retired cell biologist, educator; b. Hong Kong, China, Dec. 11, 1940; came to US, 1962; d. Sun and Yau (Ng) Kwan; m. Fok, June 8, 1965; children: Licie Chiu-Jane, Edna Chiu-Joan. BA in Chemistry, U. Great Falls, 1965; MS in Plant Nutrition and Biochemistry, Utah State U., 1966; PhD in Biochemistry, U. Tex., 1971. Asst. rsch. prof. pathology U. Hawaii, Honolulu, 1973-74, Ford Found. postdoctoral fellow, anatomy dept., 1975, asst. rsch. prof., 1975-82, assoc. rsch. prof., 1982—88, rsch. prof. Pacific Biomed. Rsch. Ctr., 1988-96, grad. faculty, dept. microbiology, 1977—2003, dir., 1994-96, dir., prof. biology program, 1996—2003, prof. emeritus, 2003—. Contbr. articles to profl. jours. Mem. Am. Soc. for Cell Biology, Soc. for Protozoologists, Sigma Xi (treas. Hawaii chpt. 1979-2002). Avocations: reading, gardening, hiking, sewing. Office: U Hawaii Biology Program Honolulu HI 96822 Business E-Mail: fok@hawaii.edu.

FOK, THOMAS DSO YUN, civil engineer; b. Canton, China, July 1, 1921; came to U.S., 1947, naturalized, 1956; s D. H. and C. (Tse) F.; m. Maria M.L. Liang, Sept. 18, 1949. B.Eng., Nat. Tung-Chi U., Szechuan, China, 1945; MS, U. Ill., 1948; MBA Dr. Nadler Money Marketeer scholar, NYU, 1950; PhD, Carnegie-Mellon U., 1956. Registered profl. engr., N.Y., Pa., Ohio, Ill., Ky., W.Va., Ind., Md., Fla. Structural designer Lummus Co., NYC, 1951-53; design engr. Richardson, Gordon & Assocs., cons. engrs., Pitts., 1956-58; assoc. prof. engring. Youngstown U., Ohio, 1958-67, dir. computing ctr. Ohio, 1963-67; ptnr. Cernica, Fok & Assocs., cons. engrs., Youngstown, Ohio, 1958-64; prin. Thomas Fok & Assocs., cons. engrs., Youngstown, Ohio, 1964-65; ptnr. Mosure-Fok & Syrakis Co., Ltd., cons. Engrs., Youngstown, Ohio, 1965-76; cons. engr. to Mahoning County Engr. Ohio, 1960-65; pres. Computing Systems & Tech., Youngstown, Ohio, 1967-72; chmn. Thomas Fok and Assocs., Ltd., cons. engrs., Youngstown, Ohio, 1977—. Contbr. articles to profl. jours. Trustee Pub. Libr. of Youngstown and Mahoning County, 1973—; trustee Youngstown State U., 1975-84, chmn., 1981-83; mem. Ohio State Bd. Registration for Profl. Engrs. and Surveyors, 1992-96. Recipient Walter E. and Caroline H. Watson Found. Disting. Prof.'s award Youngstown U., 1966, Outstanding Person award Mahoning Valley Tech. Socs. Council, 1987. Fellow ASCE; mem. Am. Concrete Inst., Internat. Assn. for Bridge and Structural Engring., Am. Soc. Engring. Edn., Nat. Soc. Profl. Engrs., AAAS, Soc. Am. Mil. Engrs., Ohio Acad. Sci., N.Y. Acad. Sci., Sigma Xi, Beta Gamma Sigma, Sigma Tau, Delta Pi Sigma Lodges: Rotary. Achievements include development of a design method by computer for a solid-ribbed tied, through arch Ft. Duquesne Bridge; development of Analysis of Continuous Truss by Digital Computer. Home: 325 S Canfield Niles Rd Youngstown OH 44515-4020 Office: 3896 Mahoning Ave Youngstown OH 44515-3022

FOLAND, JEFFREY T., air transportation sales executive; BS in Mech. Engring., Purdue U.; MBA, U. Mich. With Allison Gas Turbine Divsn. GM; with Detroit Diesel Corp.; prin. cons. ZS Assocs.; v.p. N.Am. sales United Airlines, Chgo., 2005, sr. v.p. worldwide sales, 2005—. Guest lectr. Northwestern U. Kellogg Grad. Sch. Mgmt., U. Chgo. Grad. Sch. Bus.; mem. exec. com. of bd. dirs. Chgo. Convention and Tourism Bur., 2006—. Named one of Top 40 Under 40, Crain's Chgo. Bus., 2006. Office: United Air Lines Corp World Hdqs PO Box 66100 Chicago IL 60666*

FOLAND, KENNETH A., geological sciences educator; b. Frederick, Md., May 25, 1945; s. Austin Franklin and P. Lillian (Wachter) F.; m. Ellen Lee Spero, June 18, 1968. BS, Bucknell U., 1967; MSc, Brown U., 1969, PhD, 1972. Postdoctoral fellow U. Pa., Phila., 1972-73, from asst. prof. to assoc. prof., 1973-80; assoc. prof. Ohio State U., Columbus, 1980-87, prof. geological scis., 1987—. Cons. divsn. nuclear chemistry Lawrence Livermore Nat. Lab., 1982-86, adv. com. nuclear waste U.S. Nuclear Regulatory Commn., 1990-99; mem. indoor radon panel Am. Lung Assn. Ohio, mem. steering and rev. com. Columbus and Franklin County Radon Study, Columbus Health Dept. Assoc. editor Isotope Geosci., 1982-99, Jour. Geophys. Rsch., Solid Earth, 1992-98; adv. editor Jour. Geol. Soc.; reviewer rsch. papers, rsch. proposals; author, co-author numerous rsch. papers, abstracts, revs. Recipient numerous grants NSF, NIH, DAAD and NATO. Fellow Geol. Soc. Am.; mem. Am. Geophys. Union, Geochem. Soc., Sigma Xi. Home: 4090 Fenwick Rd Columbus OH 43220-4870 Office: Ohio State U 125 South Oval Mall 379 Mendenhall Lab Columbus OH 43210 E-mail: foland.1@osu.edu.

FOLBERG, HAROLD JAY, lawyer, educator, dean; b. East St. Louis, Ill., July 7, 1941; s. Louis and Matilda (Ross) F.; m. Diana L. Taylor, May 1, 1983; children: Lisa, Rachel, Ross. BA, San Francisco State U., 1963; JD, U. Calif., Berkeley, 1968. Bar: Oreg. 1968. Assoc. Rives & Schwab, Portland, Oreg., 1968-69; dir. Legal Aid Service, Portland, 1970-72; exec. dir. Assn. Family and Conciliation Cts., Portland, 1974-80; prof. law Lewis and Clark Law Sch., Portland, 1972-89; clin. asst. prof. child psychiatry U. Oreg. Med. Sch., 1976-89; judge pro-tem Oreg. Trial Cts., 1974-89; dean, prof. U. San Francisco Sch. Law, 1989-99, prof. law, 1999—. Chair jud. coun. Calif. Task Force on Alternative Dispute Resolution and the Jud. Sys., 1998-99, Calif. Blue Ribbon Panel Experts on Arbitration Ethics, 2001-2002, chair jud. coun.; Rockefeller Found. scholar in residence Bellagio, Italy, 1996; vis. prof. U. Wash. Sch. Law, 1985-86; mem. vis. faculty Nat. Jud. Coll., 1975-88; mem. Nat. Commn. on Accreditation for Marriage and Family Therapists, 1984-90; cons. Calif. Jud. Coun., U.S. Dist. Ct. (no. dist.) Calif., JAMS. Author: Joint Custody and Shared Parenting, 1984, 2d edit., 1991; (with Taylor) Mediation-A Comprehensive Guide to Resolving Conflicts without Litigation, 1984; (with Milne) Divorce Mediation, 1988; (with others) Divorce and Family Mediation: Models, Techniques and Applications, 2004, Resolving Disputes: Theory, Practice and Law, 2005, (with Golann) Lawyer Negotiation, 2006; mem. editl. bd. Family Counts Rev., Jour. of Divorce, Conflict Resolution Quar.; contbr. articles to profl. jours. Bd. dirs. Internat. Bioethics Inst., 1989-95, Oreg. Dispute Resolution Adv. Coun., 1988-89. Recipient Bernard E. Witkin award, Jud. Coun. Calif., 2002. Mem. ABA (chmn. mediation and arbitration com. family law sect. 1980-82, chmn. ethics com. dispute resolution sect. 2002-04), Oreg. State Bar Assn. (chmn. family and juvenile law sect. 1979-80), Am. Bd. Trial Advs., Multnomah Bar Assn. (chmn. bd. dirs. legal aid svc. 1973-76), Assn. Family and Conciliation Cts. (pres. 1983-84), Assn. Marriage and Family Therapists (disting. mem.), Am. Assn. Law Schs. (chmn. alternative dispute resolution sect. 1988), Acad. Family Mediators (bd. dirs., pres. 1988), CPR Inst. (panel disting. mediators), World Assn. Law Profs. (sec.-gen. 1995-2000). Office: U San Francisco Sch Law 2130 Fulton St San Francisco CA 94117-1080 Office Phone: 415-422-6279. Business E-Mail: folbergj@usfca.edu.

FOLCH-SERRANO, KAREN D., psychologist, consultant; b. Mayagüez, PR, Feb. 20, 1969; d. José Folch and Digna J. Serrano. BA in Psychology, U. P.R., Mayaguez, 1991; MS in Clin. Psychology, Carlos Albizu U., San Juan, 1994, PhD in Clin. Psychology, 1998. Cert. forensic psychologist Carlos Albizu U., P.R., 1999, in gerontology U. P.R., San Juan, 2006. Asst. to dir. clin. tng. program Carlos Albizu U., San Juan, 1997—98; dir. Centro Clinico Roig Lucy Lopez Roig and Assocs., San Juan, 1999; clin. psychologist Ramsay Youth Svcs. of P.R., San Juan, 1999—2000, Inst. Psychol. Treatment, San Juan, 2000—02, Clin. Support Group, Inc., San Juan, 2002—; pvt. practice San Juan, 2002—. Support Therapy Ctr., Inc., Caguas, PR, 2004—05. Cons. in field; lectr. in field; presenter in field. Named Outstanding Student Counselor of Yr., U. PR, 1990, Outstanding Student Gerontology Program, Med. Scis. Campus U. PR, 2006. Mem.: APA. Roman Catholic. Avocations: reading, travel, collecting barbies. Office: Calle Manuel Pavia # 611 Ste 213 San Juan PR 00910-2239 also: Clin Support Group Inc 65th Infantry Plaza Iturregui Ste 217-A San Juan PR 00924 Office Phone: 787-722-3944. Personal E-mail: kdfolch@yahoo.com.

FOLDEN, NORMAN C. (SKIP FOLDEN), information systems executive, consultant; b. San Francisco, July 28, 1933; BS in Math./English/Engring., U.S. Mil. Acad., 1956. With IBM, various locations, 1966-83; U.S. program mgr. I/S Tech. IBM-US, 1983—86; arch. program process Architecture ETVX, 1984; owner Folden Mgmt. (Palladin Advocacy), 1986-91, Folden Mgmt., Las Vegas, 1991—. Author: Drug Criminalization: Organized Crime Cash Cow, 1996, Delegation of Legislative Authority, 1997, Payback to Lippo Group or Grand Coincidence at Grand Staircase, 1997, Kosovo Negotiations Provisions-Five by Five Plan, 1999, ICTY Charges and Submission, 1999, Matrix of Deception: The Iraq War and the Betrayal of American Values, 2005; contbr. poetry to anthologies. Mem. Assn. Grads. U.S. Mil. Acad., Little Big Horn Assocs., Calif. Scholarship Fedn., Team Marcus. Avocations: antiques, history. Home and Office: 4329 Silvercrest Ct North Las Vegas NV 89032-0116 Personal E-mail: sfolden@cox.net.

FOLDI, ANDREW HARRY, retired vocalist; b. Budapest, Hungary, July 20, 1926; arrived in U.S., 1939, naturalized, 1947; s. Alexis and Ann Foldi; children from previous marriage: David John, Nancy Susanne; m. Marta Justus. PhB, U. Chgo., 1945, MA, 1948; pvt. student singing and piano. Pvt. tchr. voice, 1949-61; cantor, mus. dir. Temple Isaiah Israel, Chgo., 1949-61, English-Speaking Jewish Community of Geneva, 1963-71; vis. prof. voice and music Cleve. Inst. Music, 1978-81; chmn. opera dept. Cleve. Inst. Mus., 1981-91; dir. Chgo. Lyric Opera Ctr. for Am. Artists, 1991-95; ret., 1995; mem. faculty U. Chgo., 1947-49, dept. adult edn., 1951-61; instr., dir. opera workshop DePaul U., 1949-57. Vis. instr. voice Augustana Coll., 1950-51; mem. faculty apprentice tng. program Santa Fe Opera, 1959, 64, 76, 77, also stage dir.; stage dir. Pa. Opera Festival, 1982, 83, Utah Opera, 1986, 88, 91, Wolf Trap Festival, 1987, Toledo Opera, 1987, 89, Atlanta Opera, 1989, Chgo. Opera Theater, 1990, Chgo. Lyric Opera Ctr., 1992. Author: recorded text An Introduction to Music, 1959; also criticism, program notes; contbr. articles to profl. publs.; Leading bass, Met. Opera, N.Y.C., La Scala, Milan, Vienna Staatsoper, Teatro San Carlo, Naples, Vienna Festival, Grand Théâtre, Geneva, Théâtre Royale de la Monnaie, Brussels, Teatro Regio, Torino, Am. Nat. Opera, Cin. Opera, Stadttheater, Zurich, Teatro Comunale, Genoa, Nederlandsche Opera, Amsterdam, San Francisco Opera Co., Lyric Opera Chgo., Santa Fe Opera, Sociedad Pro Arte Mus., Havana, Cuba; guest soloist, Vienna Festival, Bavarian State Radio, Munich, Concertgebouw Orch., Amsterdam, Orch. de la Suisse Romande, Geneva, Nat. Orch. Monte Carlo, Pitts. Symphony Orch., Clarion Concerts, N.Y., Gulbenkian Found., Lisbon, Concerti sinfonici, Genoa, Atlanta Symphony Orch., Aldeburgh, Lucerne, Lausanne, Ravinia, Glyndebourne, Florence Maggio Musicale festivals, Chgo. Symphony Orch., N.Y. Philharmonic Orch., Boston Symphony, Cleve. Orchestra, San Francisco Symphony, Little Orch. Soc., N.Y., Rochester, Kansas City (Mo.) philharmonic orchs., Radio Sottens, Geneva, Radio Beromunster, Zurich, Grant Park Concerts, Chgo., Indpls. Symphony Orch., Internat. Soc. Contemporary Music, also numerous recitals, radio and TV appearances, recordings for Columbia, Vanguard, Concert Hall, La Voix d'Eglise.

FOLDS, FRANK ELLIOTT, music educator; b. Atlanta, Ga., July 13, 1957; s. Charlie Clifford Folds and Martha Frances McKee; m. Cheri Lynn Jones, Mar. 31, 1964; children: Frank Elliott, Ansley Elizabeth, Emily Katherine, Abigail Katelyn. MusB, U. of Ga., 1975—79, MusM, 1980—82, Edn. Specialist in Music Edn., 1999—2002. T-6 Ga. Profl. Standards Commn., 2002. Band dir. Baldwin County Pub. Schools, Milledgeville, Ga., 1980—80, Jeff Davis Bd. of Edn., Hazlehurst, Ga., 1983—86, Camden County Pub. Schools, Woodbine, Ga., 1986—88, Clayton County Pub. Schools, Jonesboro, Ga., 1988—89, Camden County Bd. of Edn., Woodbine, Ga., 1989—95, Gwinnett County Pub. Schools, Lawrenceville, Ga., 1995—. Mem. bd. dirs. U. of Ga. Alumni Band, 1986—2001; treas. Tara Winds Scholarship Found., Jonesboro, Ga., 2003—; chmn. of band masters hall of fame Phi Beta Mu Hon. Band Masters Frat., Atlanta, 2002—. Contbr. book; featured performer: Michael Colegrass Festival, Ga. State U. Orch. dir. W. R. Cannon United Meth. Ch., Snellville, Ga., 2001—; lead tchr. Gwinnett County Pub. Schools, Lawrenceville, Ga., 2002—04. Recipient Tchr. of the Yr., Camden County Bd. of Edn., 1992—93, Selected as featured performing group, Ga. Music Educators Assn., 1997. Mem.: Music Edn. Leadership Inst. at Ga. State U., U. of Ga. Ednl. Enhancement Fund, PA of Ga. Educators (assoc.), Ga. Music Educators Assn. (assoc.; state band divsn. chmn. 1997—99), Ga. Music Educators Assn. (assoc.; v.p. 1991—93), Phi Beta Mu Hon. Band Masters Frat. (assoc.; mem. at large of exec. com. 2001—03). Christian, Protestant, United Meth. Home: 565 Georgian Hills Dr Lawrenceville GA 30045 Office: Alton C Crews Middle Sch 1000 Old Snellville Highway Lawrenceville GA 30044 Office Phone: 770-982-6940. Office Fax: 770-982-6942. Home Fax: 770-982-6942. Personal E-mail: folder57@aol.com. E-mail: frank_folds@gwinnett.k12.ga.us.

FOLDVARY, FRED EMANUEL, economist, educator; b. Haifa, Israel, May 11, 1946; came to U.S., 1952; s. Otto and Tina (Klein) F.; m. Janet Waara. BA in Econs./Computer Sci., U. Calif., Berkeley, 1970; MA in Econs., George Mason U., 1990, PhD in Econs., 1992. Editor Topical Time mag., 1981-87; prof. U. Latvia, Riga, 1993, Latvian U. Agr., Jelgava, 1992-93; prof. econs. Mary Washington Coll., Fredericksburg, Va., 1994, Va. Poly. Inst. and State U., Blacksburg, 1994-95, Calif. State U., Hayward, 1995—98; lectr. econ. Santa Clara U., 1998—. Dir. Embarcadero Fed. Credit Union, San Francisco, 1979-81. Author: Soul of Liberty, 1980, Public Goods and Private Communities, 1994, Dictionary of Free MarketEconomics, 1998. Chmn. Libertarian party, Alameda County, Calif., 1981-82. Bradley fellow Ctr. for Study of Pub. Choice, George Mason U., 1989-91. Mem. Am. Econ. Assn., Congress Polit. Economists, Common Ground Va. Office: Dept Economics Santa Clara Univ 500 El Camino Real Santa Clara CA 95053 Office Phone: 408-554-6968. Office Fax: 408-554-2331. Business E-Mail: ffoldvary@scu.edu.

FOLDY, SETH LEONARD, physician, educator; b. Cleve., Sept. 3, 1955; s. Leslie Lawrence and Roma (Bisgyer) F; m. Joan Marie Bedinghaus, June 7, 1986; children: Benjamin, Eva. BA in Human Biology with distinction, Stanford U., 1977; MD, Case Western Res. U., 1982; M in Pub. Health, Medical Coll. Wis., Milw., 2005. Dilomate Am. Bd. Family Practice, Am. Bd. Preventive Medicine, Nat. Bd. Med. Examiners. Intern in family practice Cleve. Met. Gen. Hosp., 1982-83, resident in family practice, 1983-85, chief resident in family practice, 1984-85; family physician Great Brook Valley Health Ctr., Worcester, Mass., 1985-87; med. dir. MetroHealth Family Practice, Cleve., 1987-94, dir. cmty. health svcs., 1994-96; med. dir. City of Milw. Health Dept., 1996-98, health commr., 1998—2004; prin. health.e.volution Consulting, 2004—; prin. investigator Wis. Health Info. Exch., 2004—05; med. dir. Healthcare for the Homeless, Milw., 2005—. Asst. prof. family medicine Case Western Res. U., Cleve., 1987-96; assoc. clin. prof. family and cmty. medicine Health Policy Inst. Preventive Medicine, Med. Coll. Wis., Milw., 1996—, clin. prof. health adminstrn. and informatics, U. Wis., 2001-; pub. health systems cons., Ctr. Internat. Health, 2005—, sr. pub. health cons., e Health Initiative, 2005—; spl. term fac. appointee Argonne Nat. Lab., Ill., 2004— Co-author: Health Information Exchange: From Start-Up to Sustainability, 2007; asst. editor: Urban Family Practice: A Resource Monograph, 1994; editor (newsletter) Urban Health News, 1990-96; assoc. editor Advances in Disease Surveillance, 2006—. Trustee Friends Sch. in Cleve., 1972-74; nat. com. War Resisters League, NYC, 1970-74; mem. Nat. Health Policy Leadership Coun., Washington, 1991-92, Ohio legis. adv. com. on environ. lead abatement, Columbus, 1994-95, Wis. Turning Point Transformation Team, 1998—, Wis. pub. health system terrorism and pub. health emergencies legis. coun. com., 2002; mem. info. coun. US CDC, 2000-04, steering com. Rand Inst. Summits on Info. Tech. Infrastructure for Bioterrorism, Operation Combined Assistance, US Navy Project Hope Tsunami Task Force, 2005; founder Milw. Pub. Health Found. and Health Champion Award, 2002; bd. dirs. eHealth Initiative & eHealth Inititative Found., 2002—, Greater Milw. Bus. Group on Health, 2002-, Southeast Wis. Bioterrorism Prepardness Group, Inc., 2003-, Benedict Ctr., 2007-, Planning Coun. Health and Human Svcs., 2007-. Recipient award for Excellence in Info. Tech., Nat. Assn. County and City Health Officers, 1999, Pres.'s Vol. Svc. award, 2005, 2007. Fellow Am. Acad. Family Physicians; mem. AMA, APHA (gov. coun. 1992-94, 96-98, Roemer award, 2002), Nat. Assn. City and County Health Officers (various coms.), Pub. Health Leadership Soc., Wis. Med. Soc., Milw. Acad. Medicine (bd. dirs. 2003-), Milw. County Med. Soc. (chair pub. health com. 1996—, Cmty. Svc. award 1997), Phi Beta Kappa. Achievements include participated in detecting and elimination of monkeypox virus outbreak from Western Hemisphere. Avocations: fishing, hiking, birding. Office: health evolution 3061 N Marietta Ave Milwaukee WI 53211 Home Phone: 414-906-0036. Personal E-mail: sfoldy@sbcglobal.net.

FOLEY, APRIL H., ambassador; b. Avon Lake, Ohio, Aug. 9, 1947; Grad., Smith Coll.; MBA, Harvard U. With Pfizer Pharm. Co.; dir. strategy Reader's Digest Assn.; various positions in fin. mgmt., strategic planning, and mergers and acquisitions PepsiCo, Inc.; first v.p., vice chmn. Export-Import Bank U.S., 2003—05; U.S. amb. to Hungary, 2006—. Chmn. Alexis de Tocqueville Soc. Westchester and Putnam counties. Office: 5270 Budapest Pl Washington DC 20521*

FOLEY, BRIAN JOSEPH, philosophy educator; s. Michael Edward and Susan Jane Foley; m. Mary Ellen Foley, May 9, 1998. B in Humanities, Pa. State U., Harrisburg, 1999; MA in Philosophy, West Chester U., Pa., 2000. Adj. prof. philosophy Northampton Area C.C., Bethlehem, Pa., 2001—02, Alvernia Coll., Reading and Pottsville, Pa., 2001—, Lebanon Valley Coll., Annville, Pa., 2002—, Cedar Crest Coll., Allentown, Pa., 2003—, Reading Area C.C., 2005—06, Temple U., Phila. and Ambler, 2004—, West Chester U., 2006—. Cofounder, contbr. Socrates' Cafe, Orwigsburg, Pa., 2004—. Mem. environ. group Schuylkill Keep It Pretty, Pottsville, 1999. Recipient Paul Hagan Acad. award, Pa. State U., 1998—99, Beyard Kunkle Acad. award, 1998—99, Pa. State Undergrad. Studies award, 1998, West Chester U. Philosophy Dept. grad. assistanship, West Chester U., 1999—2000, Superior Acad. Achievement award, Pa. State U., 1998—99, Acad. award, Pa. State U. Honors Program, 1998, Fischer award, Pa. State U., 1999. Mem.: Am. Philos. Assn., West Chester U. Grad. Student Assn. (assoc.), West Chester U. Philosophy Club (assoc.), Religious and Philosophic Forum (assoc.; pres. 1997—99), Pi Sigma Tau. Avocations: music composition/performance, landscaping, hiking. Office: Lebanon Valley Coll 101 N College Ave Annville PA 17003-1400 Home Phone: 570-366-1049; Office Phone: 610-436-2994. Business E-Mail: foley@lvc.edu.

FOLEY, BRIAN SCOTT, physiatrist, medical educator; b. Glens Falls, NY, Jan. 15, 1967; s. David Frank and Sharon Ann Foley; m. Linda M. McDole, Oct. 10, 1998; 1 child, Zoe Brianna. AS in Liberal Arts, Adirondack CC, Glens Falls, NY, 1984—87; BA, Binghamton U., NYC, 1987—89; MD, Upstate Med. Ctr., Syracuse, NY, 1990—94; MBA, Kelley Sch. Bus., Ind. U., 2003—06. Diplomate Am. Bd. Phys. Medicine and Rehab., cert. Am. Bd. Pain Medicine, Am. Bd. Electrodiagnostic Medicine. Phys. medicine & rehab. residency Ohio State U. Sch. Medicine, Columbus, 1995—98, internal medicine internship, 1995—98; physiatrist Tri-State Orthop. Surgeons, Evansville, Ind., 1998—2003; asst. prof. Ind. U. Sch. Medicine, Indpls., 2003—. Med. dir., occupl. health Wishard Hosp., Indpls., 2003—06; med. dir. Comty. Spine Ctr., Indpls., 2007—. Contbr. chapters to books, articles to profl. jours. and pubs.; author: (computer program) Roader. Dir. U. Physiatric Assoc., Indpls., 2003—06. Recipient Tchg. Excellence award, Ind. U. Sch. Medicine, 2004. Fellow: North Am. Spine Soc. (practice mgmt. com. mem. 2005—06); mem.: Am. Acad. Electrodiagnostic Medicine, Am. Acad. Pain Medicine, Internat. Spine Intervention Soc., Toastmaster's Internat. Achievements include research in electromyography; occupational musculoskeletal injuries & outcomes. Office: Cmty Spine Ctr 7120 Clearvista Dr Ste 1500 Indianapolis IN 46256 Office Phone: 317-621-9292.

FOLEY, CHERYL M., electric power industry executive; V.p., gen. counsel PSI Energy, Inc., Ind., 1989-91; v.p., gen. counsel, corp. sec. PSI Energy, Inc. and PSI Resources Inc., Ind., 1991-94; v.p., sec., gen. counsel Cinergy Corp., Cin., 1994-99, v.p., sec., 1999—; pres. Cinergy Global Resources subs. Cinergy Corp., Cin. Office: Cinergy Corp 221 E 4th St # 30 Cincinnati OH 45202-4124

FOLEY, CHRISTOPHER P., lawyer; b. 1953; BS, USN Acad., 1975; JD, Georgetown U., 1983. Bar: DC 1983, US Ct. Appeals (Fed. Cir.) 1983, Va. 2003, registered: US Patent & Trademark Office. Ptnr., Trademark & Copyright Practice Group Finnegan, Henderson, Farabow, Garrett & Dunner LLP, firm mng. ptnr., chmn. mgmt. com., mng. ptnr. Reston Office Va. Mem.: Am. Intellectual Property Law Assn., ABA, Bar Assn. DC, DC Bar. Office: Finnegan Henderson Farabow Garrett & Dunner LLP Two Freedom Sq 11955 Freedom Dr Reston VA 20190-5675 Office Phone: 571-203-2700. Office Fax: 202-408-4400. Business E-Mail: christopher.foley@finnegan.com.

FOLEY, CORNELIA MACINTYRE, retired artist; b. Honolulu, Jan. 31, 1909; d. Malcolm and Florence (Hall) M.; m. Paul Foley Jr., June 4, 1936 (dec. July 1990); children: Jean Drake, John Malcolm, Mark Lincoln. Student, U. Hawaii, 1926-27, Slade Art Sch., London, 1929-31; BA in Fine Arts, U. Wash., Seattle, 1932. One-woman shows at Honolulu Art Acad., Long Beach (Calif.) Pub. Libr., Army-Navy Club, Long Beach, Newport (R.I.) Art Assn., Hofstra U. Libr., Mallette Gallery, Garden City, N.Y., also 6 banks in L.I.; 3 woman show at Manhasset Pub. Libr.; exhibited in numerous group shows, including Hofstra U., L.I. Fedn. Women Artists, Rockefeller Center, N.Y., Seattle Art Mus., Corcoran Gallery of Art, Washington, Nat. Art Gallery of NSW, Australia, Honolulu Acad. Arts, Mfrs. Hanover Trust, N.Y.C., Glen Cove Boy's Club, Lever House, N.Y.C., Equitable Life Assurance, N.Y.C., Nassau F.A. Mus., Manhasset Libr., Great Neck Libr., Post Coll., Great Neck House, others; represented in permenent collections at Libr. of Congress, Washington, Honolulu Printmakers Assn., Castle Collection, Honolulu, Harold Mertz Collection, L.I., Whitney Mus. of Am. Art, N.Y.C., Honolulu Acad. of Arts, Mitchell Wolfson Collection, Miami, Fla., also many pvt. collections; works reproduced in Islands, Discover Am. travel book, Island Home. Recipient Purchase prizes and Best in Show award Honolulu Printmakers, 1st and 2d prize Jr. League Regional Shows, 1st prize Nat. Jr. League Frontespiece Contest, Grand prize and Hon. Mention award Honolulu Artists, 4th prize L.I. Fedn. Women Artists, numerous 1st, 2d, 3d, and hon. mention awards Manhasset Art Assn., 1st prize Nassau County Cerebral Palsy, Molly M. Canaday Meml. prize Nat. Assn. Women Artists, Grumbacher Gold medal Nat. Assn. Women Artists, award of excellence Ind. Art Soc., Hon. Mention award Suburban Art League. Mem. Manhasset Art Assn. (past pres.), Nat. Assn. Women Artists. Avocations: needlecraft, creative writing. Home: 141 Chapel Rd Manhasset NY 11030-3635

FOLEY, DANIEL RONALD, personnel director, lawyer; b. Chgo., Dec. 13, 1941; s. Daniel Edward and Louise Jean (Connolly) Foley; m. Mae Geraldine Muscarello, Jan. 30, 1965; children: Louise Ann, Sarah Elizabeth. AB in Psychology, Marquette U., 1965; JD, Depaul U., 1971. Bar: Ill. 1971, U.S. Dist. Ct. (no. dist.) Ill. 1971, U.S. Supreme Ct. 1975. Pers. recruiter Civil Svc. Commn. City of Chgo., 1965-66; pers. adminstr. Alberto Culver Co., Melrose Park, Ill., 1966-67; pers. dir. Litton Industries, Des Plaines, Ill., 1967-68; equal opportunity coord., mgr. labor rels. Canteen Corp., Chgo., 1968-71; mgr. labor rels. Internat. Telephone and Telegraph World Hdqs., NYC, 1971-79, dir. employee rels., 1979-81, 1981-85; dir. employee rels., environ. health and safety, group v.p. human resources IBP, Dakota City, Nebr., 1985-88; v.p. adminstrn., gen. counsel Domino's Pizza Inc., Ann Arbor, Mich., 1988-93; pres. Exec. Bus. Ptnrs., Inc., 1993-94; v.p. human resources MascoTech, Inc., 1994-96, Masco Corp., Taylor, Mich., 1996—. Spkr. labor law and bus. seminars Wharton Sch., U. Pa., St. Mary's Coll., LEGATUS; faculty mem. Mich. U. Named Mich. Human Resource Exec. of Yr., 2006. Mem.: Knights of Holy Sepulchre, Knights of Malta. Roman Catholic. Avocation: photography. Home: 3399 Robinwood Dr Ann Arbor MI 48103-1748 Office Phone: 313-792-6691. Personal E-mail: dcndan@aol.com. E-mail: daniel_foley@mascohq.com.

FOLEY, EUGENE ARTHUR, accountant, consultant; b. San Jose, Calif., May 6, 1953; s. Eugene Frank and Shirley Ann (Merrill) Foley; m. Elaine Sayre, July 9, 1995; children: Eugene Welles, Patrick Michael, Brian Ross. BSBA, U. Hartford, 1976; MS in Taxation, Golden Gate U., 1979; MDiv, Princeton Theol. Sem., 1994; M in Acctg., Rutgers U., 2000. CPA Calif., N.J., cert. mgmt. acct., info. sys. auditor, internal auditor, govt. fin. mgr.; computer profl., networking specialist, info. tech. profl. Acct. J. K. Lasser et al, San Jose, 1976-79; internal auditor Carter Hawley Hale, LA, 1979-81; lectr., asst. prof. Calif. State U., Sacramento, 1979-84; owner, cons. E. A. Foley Accountancy, Sacramento, 1981-84; corp. audit mgr. Emhart Corp., Farmington, Conn., 1984-86; controller Powers Mfg. div. Emhart Corp., Elmira, NY, 1986-88; owner, cons. Foley Cos., Elmira, 1988-92; asst. prof. Rider U., Lawrenceville, NJ, 1992-94; pastor Court House Presbyn. Ch., 1996-2000; mgr., CFO Lower Twp., Lower, NJ, 1994—97; tchr. Cape May County Tech. Sch., 1999-2000; mcpl. auditor, contr. State of NJ, Camden, NJ, 2000—02; dir. fin. Parking Authority of City of Camden, 2003—04; adminstr., CFO Tuckerton Borough, NJ, 2004; pvt. practice Camden, 2000—06, New Brunswick, 2006—. Bus. mgr. Calif. Polit. Rev., 1987—; asst. Christian edn. Cold Spring Presbyn. Ch., 1993—96; pastor Court House Presbyn. Ch., 1996—2000; lectr. Rutgers U., 2001—. Sec.-treas., exec. dir. Elmira YMCA, 1986—87; treas. Supreme Ct. Project, Calif., 1985—86; v.p. fin. Sullivan Trail Coun. Boy Scouts Am., 1987, treas., 1988, dist. commr. George Washington Coun., 1992—94, dist. commr. So. N.J. Coun., 1994—96, dist. exec., 1996—99, mem. N.E. region religious com., 2001—, mem. N.E. region Sea Scout com., 2003—; treas. Calif. Pub. Policy Found., 1987—; commr. Learning Life/Venturing, 1999—2003; mem. Scoutreach com., Camden, 2000—05, co-chair, 2003; ruling elder West Collingswood Presbyn. Ch., 2002—04. Recipient Whitney M. Young Jr. Svc. award, Boy Scouts Am., 1989; Baden-Powell fellow, World Scout Found., 2002. Fellow: N.J. Soc. CPAs, AICPA Acad. Exempt Orgns.; mem.: AICPA, Nat. Assn. Comm. Sys. Engrs., Assn. Govt. Accts., Am. Numismatic Assn. (life), Info. Sys. Audit and Control Assn., Inst. Cert. Mgmt. Accts., Inst. Internal Auditors (cert.), Nat. Assn. Presbyn. Scouters (regional dir. 1995—), Am. First Day Cover Soc., Mensa, Am. Topical Assn. (life), Scottish Rite, Masons. Avocations: coin collecting/numismatics, genealogy. Mailing: PO Box 416 New Brunswick NJ 08903 Business E-Mail: eafoley@eden.rutgers.edu.

FOLEY, GARY J., chemical engineer, researcher, computer scientist, federal agency administrator; b. Staten Is.n, NY, Mar. 20, 1943; m. Barbara Ickes, 1986; children: William, Karen, Kevin, Ryan, Courtney. BChE, Manhattan Coll., 1964; MS, U. Wis., 1965, PhD in Chem. Engring., 1968. Engr. Am. Oil Co., 1968-73, EPA, 1973—76, 1979—86; dir. Nat. Exposure Rsch. Lab, 1987—93, 1995—2005, acting asst. adminstr. R&D, 1993—2005; dir. Nat. Ctr. for Env. Rsch., 2005—. Mem. AiChE. Achievements include rsch. in air pollution, acid rain, emissions, transport and fate, human and ecosystem exposure and earth observing systems, total quality mgmt. in rsch. orgns. Office Phone: 202-343-9800. Business E-Mail: foley.gary@epa.gov.

FOLEY, GERARD F., history educator; b. Boston, June 5, 1970; s. John Anthony Foley and Anna Mary Diener; m. Kathleen St. Peter, July 15, 2000; children: Carter Brian, Meredith Kathleen. BA in Econ., Westfield State Coll., Mass., 1992, BA in Polit. Sci., 1992; MA in History, Bridgewater State Coll., Mass., 2005. Tchr. Qualters Mid. Sch., Mansfield, Mass., 1999—. Curriculum assoc. Mansfield Pub. Sch., 2002—05, mock trail advisor, 2002—05. Named Rookie of Yr., Bristol County Educators Orgn., 2001. Home: 814 Main St Dighton MA 02715-1113

FOLEY, JACK (JOHN WAYNE HAROLD FOLEY), poet, writer, editor-in-chief; b. Neptune, NJ, Aug. 9, 1940; s. John Harold and Juana (Terio) F.; m. Adelle Joan Abramowitz, Dec. 21, 1961; 1 child, Sean Ezra. BA, Cornell U., 1963; MA, U. Calif., Berkeley, 1965. Exec. prodr.-in-charge poetry program Sta. KPFA-FM, Berkeley, 1988—; editor-in-chief Poetry USA, Oakland, Calif., 1990-95. Resident artist The Djerassi Program, 1994. Author: (poetry and prose) Letters/Lights-Words for Adelle, 1987, (poetry) Gershwin, 1991, Exiles, 1996, (prose) O Her Blackness Sparkles! The Life and Times of the Batman Art Gallery, San Francisco, 1960-1965, 1995, O Powerful Western Star, 2000, Foley's Books: California Rebels, Beats and Radicals, 2000, (poetry) Greatest Hits 1974-2003, 2004; editor, contbr. The Fallen Western Star Wars, 2001, (with Ivan Arquelles) New Poetry From California: Dead, Requiem, 1998, Advice to the Lovelorn, 1998, (translations from the French) Some Songs by Georges Brassens, 2001; contbr. (film jour.) Bright Lights; contbg. editor Poetry Flash, 1992—, performances of poetry with wife Adelle, 1985—, columnist Foley's books, The Alsop Rev., 1998—. Woodrow Wilson fellow U. Calif., 1963-65; Poetry grant Oakland Arts Coun., 1992-95. Mem. MLA, Poets and Writers, Nat. Poetry Assn. (sec. San Francisco 1989-95), PEN Oakland (program dir. 1990-97). Avocations: playing guitar, tap dancing, writing songs. Home and Office: 2569 Maxwell Ave Oakland CA 94601-5521 E-mail: JASFOLEY@aol.com.

FOLEY, JAMES, film director; b. NYC, Dec. 28, 1953; Attended, U. So. Calif. Film Sch. Dir. (films) Reckless, 1984, At Close Range, 1986, Who's That Girl, 1987, Glengarry Glen Ross, 1992, Two Bits, 1995, No Fear, 1996, The Chamber, 1996, The Corruptor, 1999, Confidence, 2003, Perfect Stranger, 2007; screenwriter, dir.: (films) After Dark, My Sweet, 1990. Office: Creative Artists Agy 9830 Wilshire Blvd Beverly Hills CA 90212-1825*

FOLEY, JANE DEBORAH, foundation executive; b. Chgo., May 30, 1952; d. Colin Gray Stevenson and Bette Jane (Cullenbine) Coleman; m. George Edward Foley, Jan. 29, 1972; children: Sy Curtis, Shelly. BA, Purdue U., 1973, MS, 1977, PhD, 1992. Cert. elem. adminstr., Ind., cert. elem. adminstrn. and supervision. Tchr. phys. edn. and health Lafayette (Ind.) Jefferson H.S., 1973-74; tchr. music and phys. edn. Valparaiso (Ind.) Cmty. Schs., 1974-79, tchr. elem. phys. edn., 1979-90; prin. South Ctrl. Elem. sch., Union Mills, Ind., 1990-93, Flint Lake Elem. Sch., Valparaiso, 1993-98; v.p. Milken Family Found., Santa Monica, Calif., 1998—2003, sr. v.p., 2003—. Mem. panel experts The Master Tchr., 1996—98, NEH; coord. Milken Nat. Educator Awards, Milken Scholars, Children of Willesden Ln, Milken Festival For Youth; spkr., presenter in field. Author: Technology Integration: A School Administrator's Guide, 1998, Success in Restructuring: A Road Map for Administrators, 1998, The Administrator's Technology Training Booklet, 1998; contbr. articles to profl. jours. and books. Mem. Valparaiso Sch. Sys. PTA, mem. exec. bd., 1993-98; co-chair Hold Onto Your Music Found.; bd. dirs. Wings Inc.; pres. adv. bd., sr. advisor Lowell Milken Ctr.; sr. advisor Am. the Last Best Hope. Recipient Hoosier Sch. award, 1992, Ind. 2000 Designation award 1994, Outstanding Dissertation award Internat. Soc. Ednl. Planning, 1993, Milken Educator award, Milken Family Found., 1994, Ind. Bell Ringer award Ind. Dept. Edn., 1994, Ind. 4 Star Sch. award, 1995, 96, 97, 98, Internat. Tech. Edn. Assn. award, 1995, Cmty. Improvement award Valparaiso C. of C., 1994, NCREL Pathways to Improvement Pilot Site, 1995, Ind. Sch. Improvement award, Ind. Dept. Edn., 1998, others; Ind. 2000 Planning grantee, 1993, Milken Educator Tech. Project leader, 1997, other grants. Mem.: ASCD (assoc.), Valparaiso Tchrs. Assn. (treas. 1989—90), Phi Kappa Phi. Avocations: running, reading, writing, computers. Office: Milken Family Found 1250 4th St Santa Monica CA 90401-1350 Office Phone: 310-570-4782. Business E-Mail: jfoley@mff.org.

FOLEY, JEREMY N., athletic director; b. Washington, DC, Dec. 1, 1952; m. Molly McCaughy. BA, Hobart Coll., 1974; MEd in Sports Adminstrn., Ohio U., 1976. Ticket mgr. U. Fla., Gainesville, 1977—79, dir. ticket game ops., 1979—80, asst. athletic dir., 1980—81, assoc. athletic dir. bus. affairs, 1981—86, interim athletic dir., 1986—87, sr. assoc. athletic dir., 1987—92, athletic dir., 1992—. Named Nat. Athletic Dir. of Yr., Street & Smith's SportsBusiness Jour., 2006; recipient Disting. Alumni award, Ohio Grad. Sch., 1995, John L. Toner Award, Nat. Football Found. and Coll. Football Hall of Fame, 2007. Mem.: NCAA. Office: U Fla Office of Dir Athletics PO Box 14485 Gainesville FL 32604-2485 Office Phone: 352-375-4683. E-mail: jeremy@gators.uaa.ufl.edu.*

FOLEY, FATHER JOHN P., school system administrator, reverend; BA in Latin, Xavier U.; MA in Sociology, Loyola U., Chgo.; EdD (hon.), Georgetown U. Entered Soc. of Jesus, 1954; pres. Jesuit K-12 schs., Peru, 1961—95; co-founder Cristo Rey Jesuit HS, Chgo., 1995, pres., 1996—2005, Cristo Rey Network, Chgo., 2005—. Recipient Seton Award, Nat. Cath. Edn. Assn. (NCEA), 2007. Office: Cristo Rey Network Pres 2244 S Wolcott #1N Chicago IL 60608 Office Phone: 773-890-6879. Office Fax: 773-890-6808. E-mail: jfoley@cristoreynetwork.org.*

FOLEY, JOHN PATRICK, archbishop; b. Darby, Pa., Nov. 11, 1935; s. John Edward and Regina Beatrice (Vogt) Foley. BA summa cum laude, St. Josephs Coll., Phila., 1957; BA, St. Charles Borromeo Sem., Phila., 1958; PhL, U. St. Thomas Aquinas, Rome, 1964, PhD cum laude, 1965; MS magna cum laude, Columbia U., 1966; LHD (hon.), St. Joseph's U., Phila., 1985, Allentown Coll., Pa., 1990, Cath. U. Am., 1996, John Cabot U., 1998, St. John's U., 2001, U. Portland, 2007; DST (hon.), Assumption Coll., Worcester, Mass., 1997; D Journalism (hon.), Regis U., 1997. Ordained priest Roman Cath. Ch., 1962, archbishop 1984. Asst. pastor Sacred Heart Ch., Havertown, Pa., 1962—63; Rome corr. Cath. Standard & Times, Phila., 1963—65; asst. pastor St. John the Evangelist Ch., Phila., 1966; faculty Cardinal Dougherty H.S., Phila., 1966—67; assoc. prof. philosophy St. Charles Borromeo Sem., Phila., 1967—84; titular archbishop Neapolis in Proconsulari, 1984—. Vice-chmn. Pa. State Ethics Commn., 1979—84; apptd. pres. Pontifical Commn. for Social Comm., Vatican City, 1984; pres. Vatican TV Ctr., 1984—89; bd. govs. Internat. Eucharistic Congress, 1974—76; mem. Pontifical Coun. for Culture, 1993—, Commn. for L.Am., 1984—89; comm. com. U.S. Cath. Conf., 1979—82; news sec. gen. meetings Nat. Conf. Cath. Bishops, 1969—84. Author: Natural Law, Natural Right and the Warren Court, 1965; mem. editl. bd. Cath. Standard & Times, 1963, 1967—70; editor: Cath. Standard & Times, 1970—84. Regional bd. dirs. NCCJ, 1969—82. Decorated knight comdr. with grand cross Order the Holy Sepulchre, Order the No. Star (Sweden), comdr. with grand cross Order St. Martin (Argentina), Order Bernardo O'Higgins (Chile); named hon. prelate, Pope Paul VI, 1976, Hon. chaplain with Grand Cross, Sovereign Mil. Order of Malta; recipient Sourin award, Cath. Philopatrian Lit. Inst., Phila., 1990, Pres.'s medal, Holy Family Coll., Phila., 1996, Shield of Loyola award, St. Joseph's U., Phila., 1997, Cath. Leadership award, Cath. Leadership Inst., Phila., 2001, Ignatian award, St. Joseph's Prep. Sch., Phila., 2003, Orden de Libertador de San Martin, Argentina, 2003, Pres.'s award, Cath. Acad. Comm. Arts Profls., 2005. Mem.: Cath. Press Assn. (St. Francis de Sales award 1984), Am. Cath. Philos. Assn., Am. Cath. Hist. Soc. (Barry award 1997). Roman Catholic. Home: Villa Stritch Via della Nocetta 63 00164 Rome Italy Office: Pontifical Coun Social Comm 00120 Vatican City Italy Office Phone: 011-39-06-698-83197. Fax: 011-39-06-6988-5373. Business E-Mail: pccs@vatican.va, pres@pccs.va. *The most important reality in life is the existence of God, His love for every person exemplified in our redemption by His Son, Jesus Christ, and our eternal destiny to live with Him forever in heaven.*

FOLEY, JOSEPH LAWRENCE, sales executive; b. Albuquerque, June 14, 1953; s. Joseph Bernard and Joan Marie (Johnston) F.; m. Michelle Troglia, Jan., 1992; children: Joseph Louis, Kyle Benjamin. BS in Polit. Sci. & Mktg., Niagara U., 1975. Asst. retail buyer Lord & Taylor, NYC, 1975, E.J. Korvette Co., NYC, 1976-78, retail buyer, 1978-80, retail mdse. mgr., 1980; import sales coord. Block Industries, NYC, 1980-81; v.p. sales Sutton Shirt Co., NYC, 1981-83; exec. v.p. V.I.P. Imports, NYC, 1984-97; prin. Long-Term Care Cons. of Ill., Inc., 1998—. Mem.: Million Dollar Roundtable, Chi Are Racing Assn. Republican. Roman Catholic. Avocations: marathon running, baseball, tennis, skiing, golf. Home and Office: 225 Sunset Ridge Rd Willowbrook IL 60527-8406

FOLEY, JOSEPH PATRICK, public relations executive; b. June 5, 1949; married; two children. BA, Elon U., 1971; MA, Am. U., 1980. State health and social worker Fla. Health Dept., 1971-74; legis. floor asst. U.S. Ho. Reps., Washington, 1974-80; dir. legis. affairs, program analyst, congrl. liaison officer Fed. Emergency Mgmt. Agy. & Selective Svc. System, 1980-86; pres., sr. assoc. Foley Govt. and Pub. Affairs Inc., Potomac, Md., 1986—. Adj. prof. Sch. of Govt., Am. U. Office: Foley Govt and Pub Affairs Inc PO Box 61303 Potomac MD 20859 Office Phone: 301-294-0937. Business E-Mail: info@foleycoinc.com.

FOLEY, L(EWIS) MICHAEL, real estate company officer; s. Raymond B. and Mabel F.; m. Pamela Wagner, June 16, 1962; children: Michael D., Kimberly B., Robin E. BS in Sci. Engring., U. Mich., 1960; MBA in Fin. and Mktg., Harvard U., 1964. Pres. Econ. Devel. Corp., Detroit, 1969-71; v.p. Chrysler Realty Corp., Troy, Mich., 1972-77; exec. v.p. Bell and Howell Video Group, Chgo., 1977-79; v.p. fin., chief fin. officer Bell and Howell Corp., Chgo., 1979-80; sr. v.p. Homart Devel. Co., Chgo., 1981-84, exec. v.p., 1984-93; sr. exec. v.p. Coldwell Banker Real Estate Group Inc., Chgo., 1986-93; chmn., CEO Sears Savs. Bank, Chgo., 1989-93; sr. v.p., CFO Coldwell Banker Corp., 1995-96. Chmn. Borrowers Choice Corp., 1992-93; ret. non exec. chmn. bd. BRE Properties, Inc. Author: Management of Racial Integration in Business, 1965. Former vestry, jr. warden St. James by the Sea Episcopal Ch. Mem. Internat. Coun. Shopping Ctrs. (former v.p., trustee), Sigma Alpha Epsilon. Episcopalian. Office: 5824 Camino de la Costa La Jolla CA 92037-6551 Home Phone: 858-459-7095.

FOLEY, LOUISE, medical educator, retired military officer; d. Archibald and Janet Cameron; m. John Foley, May 20, 1972. EdM, U. Ctrl. Okla., Edmond, 1981. Registered respiratory therapist AZ Bd. Respiratory Examiners, 1995. Officer USAF, 1971—92; respiratory care practitioner NW Med. Ctr., Tucson, 1995—2002; respiratory therapy instr. Pima Med. Inst., 2003—. Decorated Meritorous Svc. medal USAF. Mem.: Am. Assn. Respiratory Care, Air Force Assn. (life), Ret. Officers Assn. (life), Kappa Delta Pi, Lambda Beta (life). Office: Pima Medical Inst 3350 E Grant Tucson AZ 85716 Home Phone: 520-749-5242; Office Phone: 520-326-1600. E-mail: louise@wvcnet.com.

FOLEY, MARILYN LORNA, artist; b. Arlington, NJ, Aug. 30, 1929; d. Archibald and Mary Ellen (Hall) Lyon; m. William Edward Foley, June 19, 1954; children: Katherine Ann Hastings, William Edward III. BA, Wellesley Coll., Mass., 1950; postgrad., Rutgers U., 1950-52; postgrad studies, Art Students' League, NYC, 1953. Art instr. Wellesley (Mass.) Coll., 1953—54; chair artists com. Art Show: Bedford, 1985—92. One-woman shows include St. Mary's Gallery, NYC, 1989, Northridge Art Gallery, Ridgefield, Conn., 1990, 1992, Kim Iocovozzi Gallery, Savannah, Ga., 1997, 1999, 2000, 2002, Looking Glass Gallery, Hawley, Pa., 2006, 2007, exhibited in group shows at St. Peter's Gallery, Savannah, Ga., 1997—2007, Salmagundi Club, NYC, 1986, Nat. Arts Club, 1988, Knickerbocker Artists 40th Ann., 1990, Newington-Cropsey Gallery, Hastings on Hudson, N.Y., 1997 (1st prize watercolor), Broome St. Gallery, NYC, 1997 (2d prize watercolor), Copley Soc. Mem. Show, 1982 (Juror's Choice prize), Art Show, Bedford, NY, 1983—97 (Emille Baker award, 1993), Landings Art Assn. Ann. Exhibitions (Best of Show 1996-2000, People's Choice award, 2005, 2006), Mo. Nat. Winston Churchill Meml., 2003, 2004, 28th Ann. So. Watercolor Exhbn., 2005, Gallery One, Nashville, 2005—07, Telfair Mus. Art Fair, 2006, 2007—, Washington Nat. Cathedral, 2007—; author: The Artists Mag., 1998, Watercolor Basics, 2003. Named Wellesley scholar, 1950. Mem. Hudson Valley Art Assn., Landings Art Assn., Catharine Lorillard Wolfe Art Club, Natl. Watercolor Soc. (signature mem.), Hilton Head Art League. Republican. Episcopalian. Avocations: travel, designer of church needlework. Studio: Foley Watercolors 2 Scotch Bonnet Ct Savannah GA 31411-2859 Home Phone: 912-598-8314; Office Phone: 912-598-8314. E-mail: mlfoley@bellsouth.net.

FOLEY, MARK ADAM, former congressman; b. Newton, Mass., Sept. 8, 1954; s. Edward and Fran F. Foley. Student, Palm Beach C.C., 1973—75. Owner, mgr. The Lettuce Patch Restaurant, 1975-81; real estate broker, pres. Foley-Smith & Assocs., Inc., 1975-94; commr. City of Lake Worth, 1977-79, 1982-84, vice mayor, 1983—84; mem. Fla. Ho. Reps. from Dist. 85, 1991—93, Fla. State Senate from Dist. 35, 1993—95, U.S. Congress from 16th Fla. dist., 1995—2006; mem. ways and means com.; dep. majority whip. Named Outstanding Young Floridian, Jaycees, 1987; recipient Up and Comers award, South Fla. Bus. Jour., 1990, Disting. Layman award, Fla. Med. Assn., 1993, Legis. of Yr., Fla. Farm Bur., 1993, Nat. Merit award, Cities in Schools, 1993, Nat. Health Leadership award, Nat. Org. for Rare Disorders, 2002, Legis. of Yr., Biotechnology Industry Org., 2003, Most Promising Newcomer, The Voters Coalition, 1991. Republican. Roman Catholic.*

FOLEY, MARTIN JAMES, lawyer; b. Nebr., Nov. 7, 1946; s. James Gleason and Mary Elizabeth (O'Brien) Foley; children: James Gleason Foley II, Daniel Patrick, Michelle Sivyer. Cert. Completition, Cambridge U., 1967; BA in Philosophy, U. So. Calif., L.A., 1968, JD, 1974, MBA, 1975. Bar: Calif. 1975, U.S. Dist. Ct. (cen. dist.) Calif. 1980, U.S. Dist. Ct. (ea., so. and no. dists.) Calif. 1980, U.S. Ct. Appeals (9th cir.) 1980, U.S. Ct. Fed. Claims 1991, U.S. Supreme Ct. 1990. Acct. Ford Motor Co., San Jose, Calif., 1968, cost analyst, 1970-71; assoc. Adams, Duque & Hazeltine, 1975-80; sr. ptnr. Bryan, Cave, McPheeters & McRoberts, LA, 1980-89, Sonnenschein Nath & Rosenthal, LA, 1990—, gen. counsel, 2001—05. Mem. bd. govs. Gen. Alumni Assn. U. So. Calif., 1982—84; ct. appt. settlement officer Calif. State, 1992—94, U.S. Dist. Ct. (cen. dist.), 1998—2001; lectr. groups and profl. confs. Contbr. articles to profl. jours. Lt. j.g. USNR, 1968—70. Mem.: ABA (numerous coms.), L.A. County Bar Assn., Calif. Bar Assn. (conf. of dels. 1979—93), Annandale Golf Club Pasadena, Calif., Jonathan Club LA. Republican. Roman Catholic. Office: Sonnenschein Nath Rosenthal 601 S Figueroa St Ste 2500 Los Angeles CA 90017-5704 Office Phone: 213-892-5004. Business E-Mail: mfoley@sonnenschein.com.

FOLEY, MAURICE B., federal judge; b. Ill., 1960; BA, Swarthmore Coll., 1982; JD, U. Calif., Berkeley, 1985; LLM in Taxation, Georgetown U., 1988. With Office of Chief Counsel IRS, Washington, 1985-88; tax counsel, majority staff Com. on Fin., US Senate, Washington, 1988-93; dep. tax legis. counsel US Dept. Treasury, Washington, 1993-95; judge US Tax Ct., Washington, 1995—. Mem. State Bar Calif. Office: US Tax Ct 400 2nd St NW Washington DC 20217-0001 Office Phone: 202-521-0681. E-mail: jfoley@ustaxcourt.gov.

FOLEY, NEAL T., cardiovascular surgeon; b. Aug. 11, 1952; BA, Northwestern U., Evanston, Ill., 1973; MD, U. Ill., Chgo., 1976. Diplomate Am. Bd. Thoracic Surgery, Am. Bd. Thoracic Surgery, 2005, Am. Bd. Surgery. Chief cardiac surgery Houston VA Med. Ctr., 1984—85; pvt. practice Austin, Tex., 1985—. Named Tex. Super Dr., 2006. Mem.: ACS, Tex. Med. Assn., Michael E. DeBakey Cardiovascular Soc., Travis County Med. Soc., Soc. Thoracic Surgeons. Office: 5656 Bee Cave Ro H 201 Austin TX 78746

FOLEY, REGINA M., lawyer; b. 1967; BA, Cath. U. Am., 1989; JD, Widener U., 1992; grad., Nat. Inst. Trial Advocacy. Bar: Pa., NJ, US Dist. Ct., NJ 1992. Mem. Raynes McCarty, Phila. Elected mem. Alumnae Bd., Mt. St. Joseph Acad. Mem.: ABA, Desmond J. McTighe Chap., Am. Inn of Cts., Montgomery County Bar Assn., Phila. Trial Lawyers Assn., Pa. Bar Assn., Pa. Trial Lawyers Assn. (bd. govs.), Phila. Bar Assn. Office: Raynes McCarty 1845 Walnut St, 20th Fl Philadelphia PA 19103 Office Phone: 212-568-6190. Office Fax: 212-998-0618. E-mail: rmfoley@raynesmccarty.com.*

FOLEY, RIDGWAY KNIGHT, JR., lawyer, writer; b. Portland, Oreg., Oct. 7, 1937; s. Ridgway Knight and Eunice Alberta (Ammer) F. BS magna cum laude, with honors, Lewis & Clark Coll., 1959; JD, U. Oreg., 1963. Bar: Oreg. 1963. Assoc. Mautz, Souther, Spaulding, Kinsey & Williamson, Portland, 1964-71; gen. ptnr. Schwabe, Williamson & Wyatt (and predecessor firms), Portland, 1972-84, sr. ptnr., 1985-92; ptnr., shareholder Foley & Duncan, P.C., Portland, 1993-96; of counsel Greene & Markley PC, Portland, 1997—, med. office mgr., 1999—2004. Com. mem. Multnomah Lawyer Com., 1964-68, 90-93, chair, 1992-93. Contbr. more than 100 articles, essays to profl. jours. Trustee Found. Econ. Edn., Inc., Irvington-on-Hudson, N.Y., 1974-91, 93-96; founding dir. Paulist Fathers Cath. Ctr., Portland, 1978-85. Mem. ABA, Oreg. State Bar, Multnomah County Bar (dir. 1993-97), Univ. Club (Portland), Mt. Hood Philos. Soc. (founding trustee, officer 1972-85), Lang Syne Soc., Order of Coif. Episcopalian. Avocations: writing, lecturing, genealogy, publishing, golden retrievers. Office: Greene & Markley PC 1515 SW 5th Ave Ste 600 Portland OR 97201-5449 Office Phone: 503-295-2668. Business E-Mail: ridgway.foley@greenemarkley.com.

FOLEY, TERESA A., psychologist; BA in Psychology, Antioch U., LA, 1995; MA in Clin. Psychology, Calif. Sch. Profl. Psychology, LA, 1998, PsychD in Clin. Psychology, 2000. Intern Cornerstone Day Care, Marina Del Rey, Calif., 1993, Windows Between Worlds, Marina Del Rey, 1994—96, Sojourn Battered Women's Shelter, Marina Del Rey, 1994—96; assessment intern Booth Meml., Lincoln Heights, 1997; intern therapist Pacific Ctr., LA, 1997, AIDS Svc. Ctr., Pasadena, Calif., 1998—99, Glendale Family Svc., Calif., 1998—99, LA Police. Dept., LA, 1999—2000, fellow behavioral scis. sect., 2000—01; self employed, 2000—05; rschr., liaison so. Ariz. area CFIDs Assn. Am. So., 2006—. Home: 2990 S Placinta Sam Javier Green Valley AZ 85614

FOLEY, THOMAS COLEMAN, ambassador, investor; b. Evanston, Ill., Jan. 9, 1952; s. Gifford Pinchot and Catherine (Coleman) F. AB, Harvard U., 1975, MBA, 1979. Chmn. bd. The Bibb Co., Macon, Ga., 1985-1996, T.B. Woods Sons Co., Chambersburg, Pa., 1987—2006; chmn. bd., CEO The NTC Group Inc., Greenwich, Conn., 1985—2003; chmn. bd. Stevens Aviation Inc., Greenville, S.C., 1989—; dir. pvt.-sector devel. Coalition Provisional Authority, Baghdad, Iraq, 2003—04; US amb. to Ireland US Dept. State, Dublin, 2006—. Recipient Disting. Pub. Svc. award, US Dept. Def., 2004. Mem. Am. Textile Mfrs. Inst. (bd. dirs. 1987-88). Office: US Embassy 42 Elgin Rd Dublin Ireland

FOLEY, THOMAS JOHN, lawyer; b. Detroit, July 3, 1954; s. Thomas John and Mary Catherine (Gluekert) F.; m. Virginia Lee, Aug. 20, 1977; 1 child, Kaitlin Shea. BA, Mich. State U., 1976, JD, 1979. Bar: Mich. 1980, Ohio 1992, U.S. Dist. Ct. (ea. and we. dists.) Mich. 1980, U.S.Ct. Appeals (6th cir.) 1980. Assoc. Kitch, Drutchas, Wagner, Denardis & Valitutti, Detroit, 1980—84, assoc. prin., 1984—87, prin., shareholder, 1987—2003; founder Foley, Baron & Metzger, PLLC, Farmington Hills, Mich., 2003—. Contbr. articles to profl. jours. Mem.: Food and Drug Law Inst., Def. Rsch. Inst., Internat. Assn. Def. Counsel. Avocations: swimming, private pilot. Office: Foley Baron and Metzger PLLC Ste 350 38777 W Twelve Mile Rd Farmington Hills MI 48331 Office Phone: 248-488-1535. Business E-Mail: tfoley@fbmlaw.com.

FOLEY, TOM (THOMAS STEPHEN FOLEY), former ambassador, former congressman; b. Spokane, Wash., Mar. 6, 1929; s. Ralph E. and Helen Marie (Higgins) F.; m. Heather Strachan, Dec. 1968. BA, U. Wash., 1951, LL.B., 1957. Bar: Wash. Ptnr. Higgins & Foley, 1957-58; dep. pros. atty. Spokane County, Spokane, 1958-60; asst. atty. gen. State of Wash., Olympia, 1960-61; spl. counsel interior and insular affairs com. U.S. Senate, Washington, 1961-64; mem. US Congresses from 5th Wash. dist., Washington, 1965—95, House majority whip, 1981-86, House majority leader, 1987-89, speaker, 1989-94; ptnr. Akin, Gump, Strauss, Hauer & Feld LLP, Washington, 1995-97, 2001—; U.S. amb. to Japan US Dept. State, Tokyo, 1997—2001. Instr. law Gonzaga U., 1958-60; mem. bd. advisors Ctr. Strategic and Internat. Studies; mem. adv. council Am. Ditchley Found., mem. Def. Policy Bd., Homeland Security Advisory Coun., 2006-; chmn., Pres. Fgn. Intelligence Advisory Bd., 1995-97, N. Am. Trilateral Commn. Author: Honor in the House. Bd. overseers Whitman Coll.; bd. advisors Yale U. council; bd. dirs. Council on Fgn. Relations. Mem. Phi Delta Phi. Democrat. Office: Akin Gump Strauss Hauer & Feld LLP Robert S Strauss Bldg 1333 New Hampshire Ave NW Washington DC 20036 E-mail: tfoley@akingump.com.

FOLEY, WILLIAM PATRICK, II, insurance company executive; b. Austin, Tex., Dec. 29, 1944; s. Robert P. Foley; m. Carol J. Johnson, Nov. 15 1969; children: Lindsay, Robert P. II, Countney Diane, William P. III. BS, U.S. Mil. Acad., 1967; MBA, Seattle U., 1970; JD, U. Wash., 1974. Assoc. Streich, Lang, Weeks, Cardon & French P.A., Phoenix, 1974-76; ptnr., pres., dir. Foley, Clark & Nye P.A., Phoenix, 1976-84; pres., CEO Land Resources Corp., Scottsdale, Ariz., 1983-84; chmn., pres., CEO Fidelity Nat. Fin. Inc., Jacksonville, Fla., 1981—2007, chmn., 2007—, Checkers Drive-In Restaurants, Inc., Clearwater, Fla. Chmn. bd., dir., pres., chief exec. officer Fidelity Nat. Fin., Inc., Fidelity Nat. Title Ins. Co. of Calif., Fidelity Nat. Title Ins. Co. of Tenn., Fidelity Nat. Title Ins. Co. of Tex., So. Title Holding Co., Pacific Western Aviation, Inc., Western Am. Exch. Corp., Western Pacific Property & Casualty Agy., Inc., Fidelity Appraisal Group, Inc., Folco Devel. Corp., Western Pacific Acquisitions, Inc., Bristol Investment Corp.; chmn. bd., dir. Western Fin. Trust Co., Rocky Mountain Aviation, Inc.; chmn. bd. dir., chief exec. officer Fidelity Nat. Title Agy., Inc. Fidelity Nat. Title Agy. of Maricopa County, Inc., Fidelity Nat. Title Agy. of Pinal County, Inc., Fidelity Nat. Title Co. of El Paso, Fidelity Nat. Title Co. of Oreg., Ramada Inn Old Town Mgmt., Inc.; numerous other chairmanships and directorships in fin. industry; founder & mng. ptnr. Foley Estates Vineyard & Winery of Calif.; founder & mng. ptnr. LinCourt Vineyards of Calif.; chmn. bd. CKE Restaurants Inc. Mem. Jacksonville C. of C., Fla.; del. Rep. Nat. Conv., 1996; adv. bd. mem. U. Wash. Sch. Law; trustee Found. Bd. U. Calif. Santa Barbara. Capt. USAF. Recipient Semper Fidelis award, Marine Corps Scholarship Found., 1997. Avocations: golf, chess, winemaking. Office: Fidelity Nat Fin Inc 601 Riverside Ave Jacksonville FL 32204-2950*

FOLIO, JAMES M., publishing executive; BS in Acctg., SUNY, 1981. CPA. Various positions including sr. audit mgr. Grant Thornton, 1984—94; v.p. fin. and ops., exec. v.p., CFO, treas. Gen. Media Internat., Inc., 1994—98; sr. v.p. fin., comptroller Martha Stewart Living Omnimedia, Inc., 1998—2001, CFO, chief adminstrv. officer, 2001—06; sr. v.p., CFO The NY Times Co., NYC, 2007—. Mem.: AICPA. Office: The NY Times Co 229 W 43rd St New York NY 10036*

FOLK, DAVID WILBUR, occupational health and safety administrator; b. Bellevue, Ohio, Aug. 31, 1955; s. Donald Wilbur and Mary M. Folk; children: Eric David, Jason Allen. BS in Pub. Health and Safety, Trinity U., 1998; MS in Occupl. Safety and Health, Madison U., Gulfport, Miss., 2004, PhD, 2007. Command safety and health mgr. USN, 1979—2007, occpl. safety and health profl., 2007—. Contbr. articles to profl. jours. Recipient medal of heroism, VFW, 1966, Impact award, Sec. Labor, 1997, Exceptional Achievement award, Asst. Sec. Labor, 1998. Achievements include research in philosophy of trends in accident prevention. Office: US Dept Navy NAVFAC Box 30 Bldg 902 Naval Air Station Jacksonville FL 32212 E-mail: folkzvidw@aol.com.

FOLK, FRANK ANTON, surgeon, educator; b. Chgo., Dec. 15, 1925; s. Frank A. and Anna (Pilisauer) F.; m. Lorna C. Hill, June 18, 1949; children: Laura, Lawrence, Patricia, Elizabeth, Thomas, James, Mary, Tracy Ann, William. BS, Northwestern U., 1945; postgrad., U. Wis., 1945-46; MD, U. Ill., 1949. Diplomate Am. Bd. Surgery, Nat. Bd. Med. Examiners; lic. Ill., Wis. Rotating intern Cook County Hosp., Chgo., 1949-51; resident in gen. surgery Cook County/Columbus Hosp., Chgo., 1951, Cook County Hosp., Chgo., 1954-57, surgeon, 1958-69, dir. of surgery, 1969-72; mem. faculty Stritch Sch. Medicine Loyola U., Maywood, Ill., 1958—, prof. surgery Stritch Sch. Medicine, 1972-96; prof. emeritus, 1997—; rsch. fellow Hektoen Inst., Chgo., 1959-64; asst. chief surgery VA Hosp., Hines, Ill., 1972-95, chief surg. svc., 1995-96. Mem. editl. bd.: The Am. Surgeon, 1984-92; contbr. articles to med. jours. including Am. Jour. Physiology, Jour. Occupl. Medicine, Annals of Surgery, Archives of Surgery, Jour. Trauma, Surg. Clinics of N.Am. Unit pres., exec. bd. Am. Cancer Soc., Chgo., 1972-89; mem. pres.'s adv. com. Benedictine U., Lisle, Ill., 1965-90. Lt. USN, 1951-53, Korea. Decorated Bronze Star, 1953. Fellow ACS (gov., chmn. gen. surgery Chgo. com. on trauma 1975-83, pres. met. chpt. 1977-78, mem. SESAP com. II and III, instr. ACS advanced trauma life support course 1980-87); mem. Am. Surg. Assn., Am. Assn. for Surgery of Trauma, Assn. Mil. Surgeons of U.S., Assn. for Acad. Surgery, Soc. for Surgery of Alimentary Tract, Assn. VA Surgeons, Internat. Soc. Digestive Surgry, Ctrl. Surg. Assn., Midwest Surg. Assn. (pres. 1974-75), Western Surg. Assn., Ill. Surg. Soc. (pres. 1971-72), Chgo. Surg. Soc. (pres. 1989-90), Inst. Medicine of Chgo. Roman Catholic. Avocations: medical history, civil war history, central american civilizations. Home: 446 S Columbia St Naperville IL 60540-5418 Personal E-mail: fafolk@aol.com.

FOLK, ROBERT LOUIS, geologist, educator; b. Cleve., Sept. 30, 1925; s. George Billmyer and Marjorie Marshall (Kinkead) F.; m. Marjorie Thomas, Sept. 7, 1946; children: Robert T., Jennifer Louise, Charles Marshall. BS, Pa. State Coll., 1946, MS, 1950, PhD, 1952. Research geologist Gulf Oil Co., Houston, 1951-52; mem. faculty U. Tex., Austin, 1952—, prof. geol. scis., 1960—, Dave Carlton prof. geol. scis., 1977-88. Vis. lectr. Australian Nat. U., Canberra, 1965, Tong-Ji U., Shanghai, China, 1980; vis. researcher Universita degli Studi, Milan, Italy, 1973 Author: Petrology of Sedimentary Rocks, 1980; contbr. articles to sci. publs. Neil Miner award Nat. Assn. Geology Tchrs., 1989, H.C. Sorby medal Internat. Assn. Sedimentologists, 1990. Fellow Geol. Soc. Am. (Penrose medal 2000); mem. Soc. Econ. Paleontologists and Mineralogists (hon., Twenhofel medal 1979). Methodist. Achievements include first discovery of mineralized nannobacteria on earth; the same-appearing organisms were discovered by NASA in Martian meteorite. Home: 1107 Bluebonnet Ln Austin TX 78704-2005 Office: U of Tex Dept Geol Scis Austin TX 78801 Office Phone: 512-471-5294. *My unique characteristic is that I run my life randomly. At home each day, I put all the things I have/want to do in a list. Then I roll dice to see which thing to do and do that immediately whether it be a painful or pleasurable choice. Since I adopted this method I get immeasurably more work done and much greater pleasure out of daily life. Try it.*

FOLK, THOMAS ROBERT, lawyer; b. Milford, NJ, Jan. 9, 1950; s. Conrad Frank and Isabella Ramsey (Sickels) F.; m. JoAnn Elizabeth Lo Pinto, June 21, 1975; children: Elizabeth Frances, Karina Marie. BS, U.S. Mil. Acad., 1972; JD, U. Va., 1978. Bar: Va. 1978, U.S. Ct. Mil. Appeals 1978, U.S. Ct. Appeals (4th cir.) 1978, U.S. Supreme Ct. 1983, U.S. Ct. Claims 1985, U.S. Ct. Appeals (9th and fed. cirs.) 1985, D.C. 1986., U.S. Dist. Ct. D.C. 1987, U.S. Dist. Ct. Md. 1987. Commd. 2d lt. U.S. Army, 1972, advanced to maj., 1983, resigned, 1986, asst. to gen. counsel Washington, 1980-82, atty. litigation, 1983-86; assoc. Hazel & Thomas, P.C., Fairfax, Va., 1986-88, owner, 1989-99; ptnr. Reed Smith LLP, Fairfax, 1999—. Contbr. articles to profl. jours. Mem. Com. Armed Svcs. and Vets. Affairs, 1985-88. Col. USAR, 1995, ret. Mem.: Fairfax Bar Assn. (bd. govs. 1993—97), Va. State Bar (bd. govs. constrn. and pub. contracts 1993—99), West Point Soc. D.C (bd. govs. 1993—99). Home: 4902 Asquith Ct Fairfax VA 22032-2102 Home Phone: 703-503-9475; Office Phone: 703-641-4294. Personal E-mail: tfolk1@cox.net. Business E-Mail: tfolk@reedsmith.com.

FOLKMAN, DAVID H., retail, wholesale and consumer products consultant; b. Jackson, Mich., Nov. 6, 1934; s. Jerome D. and Bessie (Schomer) F.; m. Susan Kleppner, June 22, 1958; children: Louis, Sarah, Karen, Jeffrey. AB, Harvard U., 1957, MBA, 1960. Mdse. mgr. Foley's, Houston, 1957-69; v.p. dir. stores Famous-Barr, St. Louis, 1969-74; sr. v.p., gen. mdse. mgr. Macy's Calif., San Francisco, 1974-82; pres., chief exec. officer Emporium Capwell, San Francisco, 1982-87; gen. ptnr. U.S. Venture Ptnrs., Menlo Park, Calif., 1987-90; venture ptnr., 1991-93; pres., chief exec. officer Laurel Burch, Inc., San Francisco, 1990-91; retail investor, cons., 1991-93; CEO Esprit de Corp, San Francisco, 1993-95; mng. dir. Regent Pacific Mgmt. Corp., San Francisco, 1995—. Instr. U. Houston, 1968—69, Washington U., St. Louis, 1970—73; bd. dirs. Regent Pacific Mgmt. Corp.; MBA students mentor Ctr. Entrepreneurial Studies, Stanford Grad. Sch. Bus., 2005—; cons. Harvard Bus. Sch., Cmty. Ptnrs. Projects, 2006—. Mem. Harvard Club (N.Y.C.). Office: Regent Pacific Mgmt Corp 433 California St Ste 210 San Francisco CA 94104 Office Phone: 415-391-8500. Business E-Mail: dfolkman@regent-pacific.com.

FOLKMAN, MOSES JUDAH, surgeon, educator; b. Cleve., Feb. 24, 1933; s. Jerome D. and Bessie Folkman. BA, Ohio State U., 1953; MD, Harvard U., 1957; MD (hon.), Uppsala U., Sweden, 1998, Göteborg U., 2000; MD, U. Torino, Italy, 2006; DSc (hon.), Mt. Sinai Sch. Medicine, 1996, Northwestern U., 1998, Muhlenberg Coll., 1999, Albany Med. Coll., 1999, Thomas Jefferson U., 2001, U. Conn., 2002, Oberlin Coll., 2002, NE Ohio U., 2002, U. Mass., Dartmouth, 2003, Northeastern U., 2004, McGill U., 2004, Ohio State U., 2005, Brandeis U., Waltham, Mass.; LHD (hon.), U. Mass., Lowell, 1999; DHL (hon.), Salem State Coll., Mass., 2004; LD (hon.), Jewish Theol. Sem., NY. From intern to asst. resident in surgery Mass. Gen. Hosp., Boston, 1957—60, sr. asst. resident in surgery, 1962—64, chief resident, 1964—65; chief resident in pediat. surgery Phila. Children's Hosp., 1969; instr. surgery Harvard U. Med. Sch., 1965—66, assoc. in surgery, 1967, prof. surgery, 1967—, Julia Dyckman Andrus prof. pediat. surgery, 1968—, prof. anatomy and cellular biology, 1989—. Asst. surgeon Boston City Hosp., 1965—66; assoc. dir. Sears Surg. Lab., 1966—67; sr. surgeon Children's Hosp. Med. Ctr., Boston, 1968—, surgeon-in-chief, 1968—81; dir. Surg. Rsch. Labs., 1968—. Author 389 original peer-reviewed papers and 106 book chpts. and monographs. With M.C. USN, 1960—62. Recipient Career Devel. award, NIH, 1966, Lila Gruber award, Am. Acad. Dermatology, 1974, Ledlie prize, Harvard U., 1987, Gairdner Found. Internat. award, Toronto, Can., 1991, Christopher Columbus Commemorative Sci. medal, U.S. Congress/NIH, Wolf award, Wolf Found., Jerusalem, 1992, Lucian award, Royal Coll. Surgeons Can., 1993, Steiner award, Josef Steiner Found., Switzerland, 1994, Bristol-Myers Cancer Rsch. award, 1995, Ernst Schering award, Germany, 1996, Gen. Motors Cancer Rsch. award, 1997, Ernst Jung Found. award, Germany, 1997, Med. prize, Keio (Japan) U., 1998, Chiron award in medicine, Italy, 1999, award in life sci., Benjamin Franklin Inst., Phila., 2001, Prince of Asturias award, Spain, 2004, Henry Bigelow medal, Boston Surg. Soc., 2005, Grand Prix Scientifique, Inst. France, 2005, Scientific Achievement award, 2005, award, Helen Keller Found., 2006, Nature Biotechnology Lifetime Achievement award, 2006, Warren Alpert prize, Harvard Med. Sch., 2006. Fellow: ACS (Sheen award 1989, Jacobson Innovation award 2006), German Surg. Soc. (hon.), Royal Coll. Surgeons (Ireland) (hon.); mem.: NAS (mem. Inst. Medicine), Assn. Am. Physicians, Mass. Med. Soc., Am. Pediat. Surg. Assn. (pres. 2005—06), Assn. Acad. Surgery, Am. Surg. Assn., Am. Acad. Arts and Scis., Am. Philos. Soc. Achievements include development of the first atrio-ventricular implantable pacemaker; discovery of the field of angiogenesis research; first to report the use of silicone rubber implantable polymers for the sustained release of drugs; first to propose the mechanism of angiogenesis in neoplastic disease. Office: Children's Hosp Karp Rsch Bldg Fl 12 One Blackfan Cir Boston MA 02115-5724

FOLKMAN, SUSAN, research psychologist; b. NYC, Mar. 19, 1938; d. Otto and Beatrice (Taub) Kleppner; m. David H. Folkman, June 22, 1958; children: Louis, Sarah, Karen, Jeffrey. BA, Brandeis U., 1959; MEd, U. Mo., 1974; PhD, U. Calif., Berkeley, 1979. Asst. rsch. psychologist U. Calif., Berkeley, 1979-84, assoc. rsch. psychologist, 1984-88, prof. medicine San Francisco, 1989—, Osher Found. disting. prof. integrative medicine, 2001—, dir. Osher Ctr. Integrative Medicine, 2001—. Co-author: Stress, Appraisal and Coping, 1984; contbr. articles to profl. jours. Pres. Peninsula Temple Beth El, San Mateo, Calif., 1985-87, Bur. Jewish Edn., 1993-95; bd. dirs. Jewish Cmty. Fedn., San Francisco, 1988-96. Rsch. grantee NIH, NIMH, Nat. Ctr. Complementary Alternative Medicine, 2001—. Fellow APA; mem. Soc. Behavioral Medicine, Psychosomatic Soc., Acad. Behavioral Medicine Rsch. Jewish. Office: U Calif PO Box 1726 San Francisco CA 94143-1726 Office Phone: 415-353-7719.

FOLLETT, KENNETH MARTIN, author; b. Cardiff, Wales, June 5, 1949; s. Martin D. and Lavinia C. (Evans) F.; m. Mary Emma Ruth Elson, Jan. 5, 1968 (div. 1985); children: Emanuele, Marie-Claire; m. Barbara Broer, Nov. 8, 1985. BA, U. Coll., London, 1970. Reporter, music columnist South Wales Echo, 1970-73; reporter Evening News, London, 1973-74; editorial dir. Everest Books Ltd., London, 1974—76, dep. mng. dir., 1976-77. Pres. The Dyslexia Inst.; chair Nat. Year of Reading, 1998-99; trustee Nat. Literary Trust; patron Stevenage Home-Start, 2000—; pres. Stevenage Cmty. Trust, 2005—. Author: The Shakeout, 1975, The Bear Raid, 1976, Secret of Kellerman's Studio, 1976, Eye of the Needle, 1978, Triple, 1979, The Key to Rebecca, 1980, The Man from St. Petersburg, 1982, On Wings of Eagles, 1983, Lie Down with Lions, 1985, The Pillars of Earth, 1989, Night over Water, 1991, A Dangerous Fortune, 1993, Pillars of the Almighty, 1994, A Place Called Freedom, 1995, The Third Twin, 1996, The Hammer of Eden, 1998, Code to Zero, 2000, Jackdaws, 2001, Hornet Flight, 2002, Whiteout, 2004, World Without End, 2007; (as Martin Martinsen) The Power Twins and the Worm Puzzle, 1976; (as Symon Myles) The Big Needle, 1974, The Big Black, 1974, The Big Hit, 1975; (as Bernard L. Ross) Amok: King of Legend, 1976, Capricorn One, 1978; (as Zachary Stone) The Modigliani Scandal, 1976, Paper Money, 1977; screenwriter: Fringe Banking, 1978, A Football Star, 1979, Lie Down with Lions, 1987. Bd. govs. Roebuck Primary Sch. and Nursery, 1998—, chair govs., 2001—05; mem. coun. Nat. Literacy Trust, 1996—; pres. The Dyslexia Inst., 1998—; chair Nat. Yr. of Reading, 1998—99; chair adv. com. Reading Is Fundamental U.K., 2003—; mem. Yr Academi Gymreig; bd. dirs. Nat. Acad. Writing, 2003—. Recipient Edgar award Mystery Writers Am., 1979, Corine award, Germany, 2003; fellow Univ. Coll., London, 1994. Fellow Royal Soc. Arts. Office: PO Box 4 Stevenage SG3 6UT England

FOLLETT, ROBERT JOHN RICHARD, publisher; b. Oak Park, Ill., July 4, 1928; s. Dwight W. and Mildred (Johnson) F.; m. Nancy L. Crouthamel, Dec. 30, 1950; children: Brian L., Kathryn R., Jean A., Lisa W. AB, Brown U., 1950; postgrad., Columbia U., 1950-51. Editor Follett Pub. Co., Chgo., 1951-55, sales mgr., 1955-58, gen. mgr. ednl. divsn., developer first multi-racial textbook program, first textbooks for disadvantaged, first beginning-to-read books, 1958-68, pres., 1968-78; chmn., dir. Follett Corp., 1979-94. Pres. Alpine Guild, Inc., 1977—; dir. Assn. Am. Pubs., 1972—79; chmn. Sch. Pubs., 1971—73; dir. Ednl. Sys. Corp.; mem. Ill. Gov.'s Commn. on Schs, 1972; pres. Alpine Rsch. Inst., Adv. Coun. on Edn. Stats., 1975—77; chmn. Book Distbn. Task Force of Book Industry, 1978—81; adv. coun. Krannert Sch. of Mgmt., 1988—93; pres. Soda Creek Open Space Assn. Inc., 1994—; dir. Continental Divide Land Trust, 1996—2002; chmn. Rocky Mountain Resource Ctr., Inc., 1997—2002; lectr. Denver U. Pub. Inst., 1997—; mem. adv. bd. Ctr. for Living Democracy, 1997—2000; mem. Consortium on Renewing Edn., 1997—2000; chmn. Open Space for Summit, 1999; pres. Snake River Comty. Assoc., 2001—, Continental Divide Land Trust, 2001—03; dir. Keystone Ctr., 2006—. Author: Your Wonderful Body, 1961, What to Take Backpacking and Why, 1977, How to Keep Score in Business, 1978, The Financial Side of Book Publishing, 1982, rev. edit., 1988, Financial Feasibility in Book Publishing, 1988, rev. edit., 1996, Wolf Trapped: The Death of a Young Artist in Hitler's Europe, 2006. Bd. dirs. Village Mgr. Assn., 1964-84, Cmty. Found. Oak Park and River Forest, 1959-86, Fund for Justice, 1974-77, For Character, 1983-93, Ctr. Book Rsch., 1985-88; trustee Inst. Ednl. Data Sys., 1965-; trustee, pres. Rotary Found., 2000-06; elected mem. Rep. State Com. from 7th dist. Ill., 1982-90, vice chmn., 1986-90; chmn. Ill. Reps. Strategic Planning Com., 1986-87; Presdl. Elector, 1988; pres. Keystone Citizens League, 1997-2004; mem. Keystone Mountain Responsibility Team, 1998-2000; mem. adv. coun. Colo. Mountain Coll., 2003-; hon. co-chair Colo. Mountain Coll. Campaign, 1998-99; mem. Wildlife/Wetlands Citizens Adv. Group, 2001-02; mem. adv. com. Keystone Sci. Sch., 2003—; mem. sustaining bd. Nat. Repertory Orch., 2006—. Served in AUS, 1951-53. Named one of Torchbearers, Olympics, 2004; recipient Citizen of Yr. award, Summit County, 1999, Philanthropist of Yr. award, 2003. Mem.: Soc. Midland Authors, Ill. C. of C. (chmn. edn. com. 1977—79), Am. Book Coun. (v.p. 1987—88), Rocky Mountain Book Pubs. Assn., Mid.-Am. Pubs. Assn. (mng. dir. 1987—88, dir. 1988—93), Chgo. Pubs. Assn. (pres. 1976—94), Rotary Club Summit County, River Forest Tennis Club, Sierra Club. Office: Alpine Guild Inc PO Box 4848 Dillon CO 80435-4848 Home: 0160 Kinnikinnik Rd Keystone CO Home Phone: 970-262-1038. Business E-Mail: bob@alpineguild.com.

FOLLETT, RONALD FRANCIS, soil scientist; b. Laramie, Wyo., June 26, 1939; s. Roy Lawrence and Frances (Hunter) F.; m. Dorothy Mae Spangle, Jan. 1, 1967; children: William, Jennifer, Michael. BS, Colo. State U., 1961, MS, 1963; PhD, Purdue U., 1966. Rsch. soil scientist Agrl. Rsch. Svc., USDA, Mandan, ND, 1968-75, nat. rsch. program leader Beltsville (Md.) and Ft. Collins (Colo.), 1976-86, rsch. leader soil-plant-nutrient rsch. unit Ft. Collins, 1986—; postdoctoral rsch. U.S. Plant-Soil-Nutrition Lab., Ithaca, NY, 1975-76. Co-author: The Potential of U.S. Cropland to Sequester Carbon and Mitigate the Greenhouse Effect, 1998; editor: Soil Erosion & Crop Productivity, 1985, Soil Fertility and Organic Matter as Critical Components of Production Systems, 1987, Nitrogen Management and Ground Water Protection, 1989, Managing Nitrogen for Ground Water Quality and Farm Profitability, 1991, Soil Processes & The Carbon Cycle, 1997, Soil Properties & Their Management for Carbon Sequestration, 1997, The Potential of U.S. Grazing Lands to Sequester Carbon and Mitigate the Greenhouse Effect, 2000, Nitrogen in the Environment, Sources, Problems and Management, 2001, Agricultural Practices and Policies for Carbon Sequestration in Soil, 2002; guest editor spl. issue Jour. Containment Hydrol.; contbr. over 150 articles to profl. jours. Officer 1st Presbyn. Ch., Mandan, then Ft. Collins; adult leader local Boy Scouts Am., Beltsville, then Ft. Collins. Capt. arty., U.S. Army, 1966-68; maj. Res. Named Scientist of Yr., Agr. Rsch. Svc./USDA, 2005; recipient Disting. Svc. award, USDA, 1984, 1992, Superior Svc. award, 2000, Appreciation cert., Soil Conservation Svc./USDA, 1992, Merit cert., Agr. Rsch. Svc./USDA, 1990, 1996, 1999—2003, 2005, 2006, U.S. Presdl. Rank Meritorious Svc. award, 2004, Innovator award, No-Tell, 2007. Fellow Soil Sci. Soc. Am. (divsn. chmn. bd. dirs. 1985-88), Am. Soc. Agronomy, Soil and Water Conservation Soc. Am. (pres. Colo. chpt. 1993, 2006, dir. 2007, Colo. chpt. Presdl. citation 2002). Avocations: working with youth, skiing, fishing, gardening, woodworking. Office: USDA Agrl Rsch Svc Soil-Plant-Nutrient Rsch Unit 2150 Centre Ave Bldg D Ste 100 Fort Collins CO 80526-8119 Office Phone: 970-492-7220. Business E-Mail: ronald.follett@ars.usda.gov.

FOLLIARD, THOMAS J., automotive executive; s. Thomas J. and Audrey Lee Folliard. BS, Fla. Inst. Tech., 1989. Sr. buyer CarMax Inc., Richmond, Va., 1993, dir. purchasing, 1994—96, v.p. merchandising, 1996—2000, sr. v.p. store operations, 2000—01, exec. v.p. store operations, 2001—06, pres., CEO, 2006—. Bd. dirs. Nat. Assn. Basketball Coaches. Office: CarMax Inc 12800 Tuckahoe Creek Pkwy Richmond VA 23238*

FOLLICK, EDWIN DUANE, law educator, dean, chiropractor; b. Glendale, Calif., Feb. 4, 1935; s. Edwin Fulfford and Esther Agnes (Catherwood) Follick; m. Marilyn K. Sherk, Mar. 24, 1986. BA in Social Sci., Calif. State U., LA, 1956, MA in Edn., 1961; MA in Social Sci., Pepperdine U., 1957, MPA, 1977; PhD in Social Sci., Sem. Free Prot. Episc. Ch., London, 1958, DTh, 1958; MS in LS, U. So. Calif., 1963, MEd in Instrnl. Materials, 1964, AdvMEd in Edn. Adminstrn., 1969; postgrad., Calif. Coll. Law, 1965; LLB, Blackstone Law Sch., 1966, JD, 1967; DC, Cleve. Chiropractic Coll., LA, 1972; PhD in Eccles. Law, Academia Theatina, Pescara, 1978; MA in Orgnl. Mgmt., Antioch U., LA, 1990. Tchr., libr. adminstr. L.A. City Schs., 1957-68; law libr. Glendale U. Coll. Law, 1968-69; coll. libr. Cleve. Chiropractic Coll., LA, 1969-74, dir. edn. and admissions, 1974-84, prof. jurisprudence, 1975—2003, dean student affairs, 1976-92, coll. chaplain, 1985—2003, dean of edn., 1989—2003, rector, 2003—04, rector emeritus, 2004—; assoc. prof. Newport U., 1982; extern prof. St. Andrews Theol. Coll., London, 1961; dir. West Valley Chiropractic Health Ctr., 1972-2000, West Valley Chiropractic Consulting, 2001—04; cons. instnl. chaplain, 2004—; libr. dir. South Baylo U., 2004—, u. chaplain, 2004—; libr. dir. Calif. U. Mgmt. and Sci., 2004—. Adj. prof. law Calif. U. Mgmt. and Sci., 2004—, univ. chaplain, 2004—. Contbr. articles to profl. jours. Chaplain's asst. US Army, 1958—60. Decorated cavaliere Internat. Order Legion of Honor of Immaculata (Italy); Knight of Malta, Sovereign Order of St. John of Jerusalem; Knight Grand Prelate, comdr. with star, Order of Signum Fidei; comdr. chevalier Byzantine Imperial Order of Constantine the Gt.; comdr. ritter Order St. Gereon; chevalier Mil. and Hospitaller Order of St. Lazarus of Jerusalem (Malta), Chaplain to the Order of St. Stanislas; numerous others. Mem. ALA, NEA, Am. Assn. Sch. Librarians, LA Sch. Libr. Assn., Calif. Sch. Libr. Assn., Assn. Coll. and Rsch. Librarians, Am. Assn. Law Librarians, Am. Chiropractic Assn., Internat. Chiropractors Assn., Nat. Geog. Soc., Internat. Platform Assn., Phi Delta Kappa, Sigma Chi Psi, Delta Tau Alpha. Democrat. Episcopalian. Home: 6435 Jumilla Ave Woodland Hills CA 91367-2833 Office: 590 N Vermont Ave Los Angeles CA 90004-2115 also: 7022 Owensmouth Ave Canoga Park CA 91303-2005 Address: 1126 N Brookhurst St Anaheim CA 92801 Office Phone: 323-906-2114, 714-533-6077. Business E-Mail: edwin.follick@cleveland.edu, edfollick@southbaylo.edu.

FOLLIT, EVELYN V., former retail executive; b. Sept. 10, 1946; BA in Math., MBA in Fin. and Info. Sys.; degree in Exec. Planning and Tech., Cornell U., MIT. With Dunn & Bradstreet, 1984—96; v.p. ops. & engring. AC Nielson, 1996—97; sr. v.p., chief info. officer RadioShack Corp., 1997—2005, chief orgnl. enabling svcs., 2003—05. Bd. dirs. Catalina Mktg. Corp., 2000—, chmn. audit com., mem. fin. com.; chmn. CIO Coun. Nat. Retail Fedn., 2000—; mem. adv. bd. Ctr. Values Based Leadership, 2002—; bd. dirs. Winn-Dixie Stores Inc., 2006—. Bd. visitors Tex. Christian U., Fort Worth. Named one of Top 10 CIOs in Retailing, Retail Tech. Mag., 1999, Top 10 CIOs Across Am., Info. Week, 1999, 100 Premier IT Leaders in Country, Computerworld, 2001, 25 Most Influential People in Retail, Retail Info Sys. News, 2001, Pioneering Women in Tech., Am. Friends Jerusalem Coll. Tech., 2002; recipient Leadership and Innovation award, Exec. Tech. Mag./Compaq Computer, 2002.*

FOLSOM, JIM (JAMES ELISHA FOLSOM JR.), lieutenant governor, former governor; b. Montgomery, Ala., May 14, 1949; s. James E. Folsom Sr. and Jamelle Dorothy Moore; m. Marsha Guthrie, 1977; children: Meghan, James BA, Jacksonville State U., 1974. With Ala. Dept. Indsl. Rels., 1974-76; pub. rels. rep. Reynolds Metal Co., 1976-79; mem. Nat. Dem. Arrangement Com., 1979-80; pub. svc. commr. State of Ala., Montgomery, 1980, lt. gov., 1986—93, 2007—, gov., 1993-95; pres. Chama Conss., Inc.; v.p. pub. fin. Raymond James & Associates, 1995—2007. State chmn. Leukemia Soc., 1992; Served in Ala. Nat. Guard, 1968-70. Recipient Outstanding Communications award Toastmasters Ala., 1980, Outstanding Progress Communications award Black Mayors Assn. Ala., 1980, Outstanding Young Men of Am., U.S. Jaycees, 1981. Mem. Pub. Rels. Soc. Ala., Nat. Assn. Regulatory Commrs., Masons, Kiwanis. Democrat. Episcopalian. Office: Office Lt Gov 11 S Union St Ste 725 Montgomery AL 36130*

FOLSOM, LOWELL EDWIN, language educator; b. Pitts., Sept. 30, 1947; s. Lowell Edwin and Helen Magdalene (Roeper) Folsom; m. Patricia Ann Jackson, Aug. 30, 1969; 1 child, Benjamin Bradford. BA, Ohio Wesleyan U., 1969; MA, U. Rochester, 1972, PhD, 1976. Chmn. English dept. Lancaster (Ohio) H.S., 1969-70, 71-72; instr. Eastman Sch. Music, Rochester, NY, 1974-75; vis. asst. prof. SUNY, Geneseo, 1975-76; asst. prof. U. Iowa, Iowa City, 1976-82, assoc. prof., 1982-87, prof., 1987—, chair English dept., 1991-95, F. Wendell Miller disting. prof., 1991—2002, Carver prof., 2002—. Cons. Am. Coll. Testing Co., Iowa City, 1980—, Nat. Assessment Ednl. Progress, Denver, 1980—84; dir. Walt Whitman Centennial Conf., Iowa City, 1992, Walt Whitman Conf., Beijing, 2000, Leaves of Grass: The 150th Anniversary Conf., Lincoln, Nebr., 2005; Fulbright sr. prof. U. Dortmund, Germany, 1996. Author: Walt Whitman's Native Representations, 1994 (Choice Best Acad. Book, 1995), Re-Scripting Walt Whitman, 2005, Whitman Making Books/Books Making Whitman, 2005; editor: Walt Whitman: The Centennial Essays, 1994, Walt Whitman: The Measure of His Song, 1981 (Choice Best Acad. Book, 1982), rev. edit., 1998 (Ind. Publisher Book award, 1999), Walt Whitman and the World, 1995, (CD-ROM) Walt Whitman, 1997 (Choice Best Acad. Book, 1998), Walt Whitman Quar. Rev., 1983—, Whitman East and West, 2002; co-dir.: Walt Whitman Hypertext Archive, 1997—; editl. bd. Walt Whitman Encyclopedia, 1994—98, PMLA, 1999—2002, Profession, 2002—05. Named Disting. Scholar, U. Rochester, 1995; recipient Rsch. award, NEH, 1991—94, Collaborative Rsch. award, 2000—04, Faculty Excellence award, Iowa Bd. Regents, 1996, U. Iowa Collegiate Tchg. award, 2003, Preservation award, 2004, Pres. and Provost award Tchg. Excellence, 2005; fellow, Guggenheim, 2007—. Mem.: MLA, Whitman Scholars Assn. (dir. 1992—), Am. Studies Assn., Am. Lit. Assn. Home: 739 Clark St Iowa City IA 52240-5640 Office: Univ Iowa Dept English 308 EPB Iowa City IA 52242 Business E-Mail: ed-folsom@uiowa.edu.

FOLSOM, TYLER CLEVELAND, computer engineer, educator; b. Seattle, Nov. 10, 1948; s. Tyler Cleveland Folsom and Phylis Emily Greer; m. Frances Paula Solomon, July 12, 1981. BS in Math., Villanova U., Pa., 1970; MA in Math., U. Md., College Park, 1972; MSEE, U. Wash., Seattle, 1980, PhD in Elec. Engring., 1994. Cert. profl. engr., Wash. Scientific programmer Sperry UNIVAC, DC, 1973—76; software engr. Macotech Corp., Seattle, 1980—84; sr. software engr. Quest Integrated, Inc., Kent, Wash., 1984—90, project mgr., 1994—2000; rschr. U. Wash., Seattle, 1990—94; prof. Digipen Inst. Tech., Redmond, Wash., 2000—. Vis. prof. NW U., Xian, China, 2004; robotics advisor Level 5 CIS, LLC, Sequim, Wash., 2004—05, U. British Columbia, Vancouver, Canada, 2006—. Author: (software) IEEE Trans Pami, 1998. Organizer High Tech. Profl. Peace, Seattle, 1983; spkr. Computer Profl. Social Responsiblity, Seattle, 1987—98. Recipient Small Bus. Innovation Rsch. award, US Army, 1985, 1997, Nat. Sci. Found., 1989, USAF, 1995, 1998—2000. Mem.: IEEE (sr.), Toastmasters Internat. (local v.p. 2002—, ATMS award 2006). Democrat. Mem. Soc. Of Friends. Avocations: bicycling, travel, backpacking.

FOLTA, CARL D., communications executive; b. Holyoke, Mass., 1957; Attended, Boston U., 1980. Account supr. Ruder Finn; joined Paramount Comm., Inc., 1984, sr. dir., corp. comm., 1992—94; v.p. corp. relations Viacom, Inc., NYC, 1994, sr. v.p., corp. relations, 1994—2005, exec. v.p., 2005—. Office: Viacom Inc 1515 Brdwy New York NY 10036

FOLTER, ROLAND, historian, rare book dealer, writer; b. Fulda, Germany, May 27, 1943; s. Heinz and Annemie (Bennewitz) F.; m. Siegrun Heinecke, Aug. 28, 1967 (dec. 1988); m. Mary Ann Kraus, Apr. 29, 1989; 1 child, Elizabeth. MA, Brown U., 1967, PhD, 1969. Rare books cataloger Yale U., New Haven, 1966-68; prof. U. Ill., Urbana, 1969-77; dir. H.P. Kraus Rare Books, NYC, 1977—2003; ret., 2003. Jury Internat. League Antiquarian Booksellers Prize for Bibliography. Author: Deutsche Dichterbibliotheken, 1975, The Gutenberg Bible in the antiquarian book trade, 1999; co-author: Bibliography: Its History, 1984; contbr. to ency. and articles to profl. jours. Violinist Frankfurt Youth Symphony Orchestra, Germany, 1960—65. Fellow Brown U., 1968, Faculty fellow U. Ill., 1970-75. Fellow Pierpont Morgan Libr.; mem. Bibliog. Soc. Am. (coun. 1982-90), Bibliog. Soc. London, N.Y. Philharm. Soc., Assn. Internat. de Bibliophilie, Maximilian Gesellschaft, Gesellschaft der Bibliophilen, Antiquarian Booksellers Assn. Am., Old Book Table (pres. 1995-97), Yale Libr. Assocs. Avocations: violin, chamber music, book collecting, mountain climbing. Office: H P Kraus Rare Books PO Box 949 Larchmont NY 10538 Business E-Mail: rolandfolter@hpkraus.com.

FOLTZ, RODGER LOWELL, chemistry professor; b. Milw., Feb. 10, 1934; s. Ross Milton and Ida Louise (Campbell) F.; m. Ruth Lynch Bilbe, June 9, 1956; children: Richard C., Camilla M. BS, MIT, 1956; PhD, U. Wis., 1961. Research chemist Battelle Meml. Inst., Columbus, Ohio, 1961-76, sr. research leader, 1976-79; adj. prof. pharmacy Ohio State U., 1972-76, adj. assoc. prof. pharmacology, 1976-79; assoc. dir. Center for Human Toxicology, U. Utah, Salt Lake City, 1979—; rsch. assoc. prof. dept. pharmacology and toxicology U. Utah, Salt Lake City, 1980-85, rsch. prof. pharmacology/toxicology dept., 1985—; pres. CHT, Inc., 1985-87; exec. v.p., lab. dir. N.W. Toxicology Inc., 1987-94; lab dir. Northwest Bioanalytical, 1994—99; tech. dir. Tandem Labs., 2000—. Contbr. articles to profl. jours.; editl. adv. bd. Biomed. Mass Spectrometry, 1979-87, 90-95. Pres. N.W. Area Human Relations Council, Columbus, 1968-70; deacon First Congregational Ch., 1971-75; trustee Denison U. Research Found., 1977-79. Mem. Am. Chem. Soc. (chmn.-elect Columbus chpt. 1978, award Columbus chpt. 1977), Am. Soc. Mass Spectrometry (chmn. nominating com. 1980, 82, bd. dirs. 1988-90), Calif. Assn. Toxicologists (bd. dirs. 1990-91, v.p. 1994, pres. 1995-96), Am. Acad. Forensic Scis. (Alexander O. Gettler award 2000), Am. Assn. Pharm. Scientists. Home: 2080 Belaire Dr Salt Lake City UT 84109-1409 also: Tandem Labs 1121 E 3900 S Salt Lake City UT 84124-1215 Office Phone: 801-587-8810. Personal E-mail: rodgerf@aol.com.

FOLZ, CAROL ANN, benefits compensation analyst; b. Cedar Rapids, Iowa, Dec. 28, 1951; d. D. Glenn Frederick and Ruth Frances (McIntosh) Rullman; m. Donald Harold McElderry, Oct. 3, 1970 (div. 1981); m. David Charles Folz, Mar. 19, 1983 (dec.). AA, ASLS, St. Louis C.C., 1973; BSBA, U. Mo., St. Louis, 1980; MBA, Am. Intercontinental U., Ga., 2006. Libr. asst. Bloomfield Pub. Libr., Iowa, 1968—70, Ferguson Pub. Libr., Mo., 1972—77; payroll clk. U. Mo., St. Louis, 1977—79, sr. sec., 1979—80, acct., 1980—82, sr. acct., 1982, sr. fiscal analyst, 1982—89; payroll analyst Blue Cross and Blue Shield Mo., St. Louis, 1990—91, sr. payroll acct., 1991; acct. Harris-Stowe State Coll., St. Louis, 1996—98, Accountemps, St. Louis, 1998; benefits specialist May Dept. Stores Co., St. Louis, 1998—2005; coord. Macy Corp. Svcs., Inc., St. Louis, 2005—. Methodist. Avocations: genealogy, music, reading, sports, needlecrafts. Office: 611 Olive St Saint Louis MO 63101 Office Phone: 314-342-6529. Personal E-mail: carol.folz@macy.com.

FOMON, SAMUEL JOSEPH, pediatrician, educator; b. Chgo., Mar. 9, 1923; s. Samuel and Isabel (Sherman) F.; m. Betty Lorraine Freeman, Aug. 20, 1948 (div. Apr. 1978); children: Elizabeth Ann Fomon Seiberling, Kathleen Lenore Fomon Anderson, David Bruce, Christopher, Mary Susan Fomon; m. Louise G. Thomson, June 27, 1986. AB cum laude, Harvard U., 1945; MD, U. Pa., 1947; D (hons.), U. Catolica de Cordoba, Argentina, 1974; prof. (hon.), U. Guadalajara. Diplomate Am. Bd. Pediatrics, Am. Bd. Nutrition. Intern Queen's Gen. Hosp., Jamaica, NY, 1947-48; resident Children's Hosp., Phila., 1948-50; research fellow Cin. Children's Hosp. Research Found., 1950-52; asst. prof. pediatrics U. Iowa, Iowa City, 1954-58, assoc. prof., 1958-61, prof., 1961-93, prof. emeritus, 1993—; hon. prof. U. Guadalajara, Mexico, 2005. Adj. prof. pediat. Baylor Med. Coll., Houston, 2002-05; rev. com. child health and human devel. program project NIH, 1966-69, nutrition study sect., 1978-81; select com. Generally Recognized as Safe Substances Life Sci. Rsch. Office, 1974-80; expert to working group on infant formula US FAO of UN and WHO, 2003; hon. prof. U. Guadalajara, 2005. Author: Infant Nutrition, 1st edit., 1967, 2d edit., 1974, Nutrition of Normal Infants, 1993. Recipient Career Devel. award NIH, 1962-67, Rosen von Rosenstein award Swedish Pediatric Soc., 1975, F. Cuenca Villoro Found. award, Zaragosa, Spain, 1981, Commr.'s spl. citation FDA, 1984, Nutricia Found. award, Rotterdam, The Netherlands, 1991, Bristol-Myers Squibb/Mead Johnson award, 1992, Harry Schwachman award N.Am. Soc. Pediatric Gastroenterology and Nutrition, 1992, A.O. Atwater 2000 Lectureship, Spl. award L.Am. Nutrition Soc., 2000, 03. Fellow AAAS; mem. Am. Inst. Nutrition (pres. 1989-90, fellow 1989, Conrad A. Elvehjem award 1990), Am. Acad. Pediatrics (chmn. com. nutrition 1960-63, Borden award 1956, Nutrition award 2004), Am. Soc. Clin. Nutrition (pres. 1981-82, McCollum award 1979), Fedn. Am. Socs. Exptl. Biology, Midwest Soc. Pediat. Rsch. (pres. 1963-64, Founder's award 1986), Am. Dietetic Assn. (hon.), El Colegio de Pediat. de Jalisco (hon.). Personal E-mail: samfomon@aol.com.

FONDA, BRIDGET, actress; b. LA, Jan. 27, 1964; SAG; d. Peter and Susan Fonda.; m. Danny Elfman, 2003; 1 child, Oliver Henry Milton. Films: Aria, 1987, You Can't Hurry Love, 1988, Shag, 1988, Scandal, 1989, Strapless, 1989, Frankenstein Unbound, 1990, The Godfather, Part III, 1990, Doc Hollywood, 1991, Out of the Rain, (also known as Remains), 1991, Single White Female, 1992, Singles, 1992, Bodies Rest and Motion, 1993, Point of No Return, 1993, Little Buddha, 1994, It Could Happen To You, 1994, Camilla, 1994, The Road to Wellville, 1994, Rough Magic, 1995, Balto (voice), 1995, Grace of My Heart, 1996, City Hall, 1996, South of Heaven, West of Hell, 2000, Delivering Milo, 2001, The Whole Shebang, 2001, Kiss the Dragon, 2001; TV appearances: (series) 21 Jump Street, 1989, Jacob Have I Loved, WonderWorks episode, 1989, (made for cable movie) Leather Jackets, 1991, Jackie Brown, 1997, A Simple Plan, 1998, Finding Graceland, 1998, The Break Up, 1998, South of Heaven West of Hell, 1999, South From Hell's Kitchen, 1999, Monkey Bone, 1999, Lake Placid, 1999; (TV movies) In the Gloaming, 1997, After Amy, 2001, The Snow Queen, 2002; (TV series) The Chris Isaak Show, 2001.

FONDA, JANE, actress; b. NYC, Dec. 21, 1937; d. Henry and Frances (Seymour) F.; m. Roger Vadim Aug. 14, 1965, (div. Jan. 16, 1973); 1 child, Vanessa; m. Tom Hayden, Jan. 20, 1973 (div. 1990); children, Troy Garity, Mary Luana Williams; m. Ted Turner, Dec. 21, 1991 (div. May 22, 2001). Student, Vassar Coll. Appeared on Broadway stage in There Was a Little Girl, 1960, The Fun Couple, 1962; appeared in Actor's Studio prodn. Strange Interlude, 1963; appeared in films Tall Story, 1960, A Walk on the Wild Side, 1962, The Chapman Resort, 1962, Period of Adjustment, 1962, Sunday in New York, 1963, In the Cool of the Day, 1963, The Love Cage, 1963, La Ronde, 1964, Cat Ballou, 1965, The Chase, 1966, Any Wednesday, 1966, The Game Is Over, 1967, Hurry Sundown, 1967, Barefoot in the Park, 1967, Barbarella, 1968, Spirits of the Dead, 1969, They Shoot Horses, Don't They?, 1969 (NY Film Critics Circle award for Best Actress), Klute, 1970 (NY Film Critics Circle award for Best Actress, Nat. Soc. Film Critics award, Golden Globe award for Best Actress, Acad. award for Best Actress), All's Well, 1972, Steelyard Blues, 1973, A Doll's House, 1973, The Blue Bird, 1976, Fun with Dick and Jane, 1977, Julia, 1977 (Golden Globe award for Best Actress), California Suite, 1978, Comes a Horseman, 1978, Electric Horseman, 1979, Nine to Five, 1980, On Golden Pond, 1981, Rollover, 1981, Agnes of God, 1985, The Morning After, 1986, Retour, 1987, Leonard Part 6, 1987, Old Gringo, 1988, Stanley and Iris, 1990, Monster-in-Law, 2005, Georgia Rule, 2007; actor, prodr., Coming Home, 1978 (LA Film Critic Assn. award for Best Actress, Golden Globe for Best Actress, Acad. award for Best Actress), The China Syndrome, 1979; (TV movies) A String of Beads, 1961, Lily: Sold Out, 1981, The Dollmaker(Emmy award for Best Actress), 1984; (TV miniseries) A Century of Women, 1994; author: Jane Fonda's Workout Book, 1981, Women Coming of Age, 1984, Jane Fonda's New Workout & Weight-Loss Program, 1986, Jane Fonda's New Pregnancy Workout & Total Birth Program, 1989, (autobiography) My Life So Far, 2005 (New York Times bestseller list); video: Jane Fonda Workout Video, 1982, 12 additional videos. Recipient Golden Globe award for Most Promising Newcomer, 1962, Golden Apple prize for Female Star of Year Hollywood Women's Press Club, 1977, People's Choice award for Favorite Motion Picture Actress, 1980-83, Career Achievement award Nat. Bd. Review, 2005. Office: Creative Artists Agy care Kim Hodgert 9830 Wilshire Blvd Beverly Hills CA 90212-1804*

FONDA, PETER, actor, director, producer; b. NYC, Feb. 23, 1939; s. Henry and Frances (Seymour) F.; m. Susan Brewer, Oct. 8, 1961 (div. Apr. 1972); 2 children; m. Portia Rebecca Crockett, Nov. 11, 1975. Student, U. Omaha. Film appearances include Tammy and The Doctor, 1963, The Victors, 1963, Lilith, 1964, The Young Lovers, 1964, The Trip, 1967, The Wild Angels, 1966, The Last Movie, 1971, Two People, 1973, Dirty Mary, Crazy Harry, 1974, Race With The Devil, 1975, 92 in the Shade, 1975, Killer Force, 1975, Fighting Mad, 1976, Futureworld, 1976, Outlaw Blues, 1977, High Ballin', 1978, Wanda Nevada, 1979, Open Season, Smokey and the Bandit II, 1980, Split Image, 1982, Certain Fury, 1985, Dead Fall, 1993, Nadja, 1994, Love and a .45, 1994, Painted Hero, 1996, Grace of My Heart (voice), 1996, Escape From L.A., 1996, Idaho Transfer, Spasm, 1983, Fatal Mission, 1990, The Tempest, 1998, The Passion of Ayn Rand, 1999, The Limey, 1999, Keeping Time, 1999, South of Heaven, West of Hell, 2000, Thomas and the Magic Railroad, 2000, Second Skin, 2001, Wooly Boys, 2001, The Laramie Project, 2002, The Heart Is Deceitful Above All Things, 2004, El Cobrador: In God We Trust, 2006, Ghost Rider, 2007, Wild Hogs, 2007; dir., actor in The Hired Hand, 1971, Two People, 1973; writer, co-producer, actor movie Easy Rider, 1969; TV movie appearances include The Hostage Tower, 1980, A Reason To Live, Don't Look Back, 1996, Ulee's Gold, 1997(won Golden Globe Award, Best Actor), Me and Will, 1998, South of Heaven West of Hell, 1999, The Passion of Ayn Rand, 1999, The Limey, 1999, Keeping Time, 1999, The Maldonado Miracle, 2003, Back When We Were Grown Ups, 2004; author Don't Tell Dad, 1998.*

FONDA, RONALD ALAN, epistemologist; b. Asheville, NC, Dec. 14, 1940; s. Alan and Louise (Moore) F.; m. Mary Louise Mayfield, Jan. 29, 1964; children: Dirk, Rolf, Brandt. Student, Davidson Coll., 1958-60. Presenter confs. Staff writer: American Populist Review; author: Age & Origin of the Human Species, numerous essays and poems, the novella Magnus, Rafe's Saga. Mem. Natural Philosophy Assn. Achievements include first: to hypothesize that the time metric is quantized, and to demonstrate that view consistent with established formulae and observations; thereby to elucidate a physically plausible explanation of gravity; to explicate time related indeterminancy, the significance of Planck's constant, and aspects of photon and electron behavior; to suggest differentiated spacial formation to explain cosmic structure and expansion characteristics. Home: 1271 Stewart Rd Andrews NC 28901-8033

FONDAHL, JOHN WALKER, civil engineering educator; b. Washington, Nov. 4, 1924; s. John Edmund and Mary (DeCourcy) F.; m. Doris Jane Plishker, Mar. 2, 1946; children: Lauren Valerie, Gail Andrea, Meredith Victoria, Dorian Beth. BS, Thayer Sch. Engring., Dartmouth, 1947, MSCE, 1948. Instr., then asst. prof. U. Hawaii, 1948-51; constrn. engr. Winston Bros. Co., Mpls., 1951-52; project engr. Nimbus Dam and Powerplant project, Sacramento, 1952-55; mem. faculty Stanford U., 1955—, prof. civil engring., 1966-90, Charles H. Leavell prof. civil engring., 1977-90, prof. emeritus, 1990—. Author reports in field. Served with USMCR, 1943-46. Recipient Golden Beaver award Heavy Constrn. Industry, 1976. Fellow ASCE (Constrn. Mgmt. award 1977, Peurifoy Constrn. Rsch. award 1990), Project Mgmt. Inst. (hon. life, Fellow award 1981, Jim O'Brien Lifetime Achievement award 2007); mem. Nat. Acad. Engring., Nat. Acad. Constrn., Phi Beta Kappa. Achievements include patent in field. Home and Office: 12810 Viscaino Rd Los Altos Hills CA 94022-2520 E-mail: fondahlj@aol.com.

FONDAW, RONALD EDWARD, artist, educator; b. Paducah, Ky., Apr. 25, 1954; s. Lex Alan and Rose Mary (Holley) Kilgore; m. Lynn S. Shepard, Oct. 7, 1987; children: Andrea Rose, Wyler S. BFA, Memphis Coll. Art, 1976; MFA, U. Ill., 1978. Instr. Ohio U., Athens, 1978; assoc. prof. art U. Miami, Coral Gables, Fla., 1978-95, prof., 1997—; prof. art Washington U., St. Louis, 1995—. Lectr., presenter workshops Ohio State U., Chgo. Art Inst., Tokyo U. Fine Art, Chautauqua Sch. Art. Exhbns. nat. and internat.; several public art commissions. Ford Found. fellow, 1977, Fla. Arts Coun. fellow, 1981, Guggenheim fellow, 1985, Pollack/Krasner fellow, 1997-98; grantee NEA, 1988; Kransberg award St. Louis Art Mus., 1998. Office: Wash U 721 Kingsland Ave Saint Louis MO 63130-3107 Home: 2004 Stemler Rd Columbia IL 62236-2926 E-mail: refondaw@art.wustl.edu.

FONDER, MARK LESLIE, music educator; b. Green Bay, Wis., June 24, 1955; s. Leslie Charles Fonder and Jeanne Leona Heinz; m. Wendy Kay Sayler, Aug. 11, 1984; 1 child, Bryan Mark. MusB, Lawrence Conservatory, Appleton, Wis., 1977; MS in Music, U. Ill., Champaign/Urbana, 1978, EdD, 1983. Dir. bands Park Falls HS, Wis., 1978—81; asst. prof. U. Wis., Green Bay, 1983—88, U. Tex., San Antonio, 1988—89; prof. Ithaca Coll., NY, 1989—. Guest condr. numerous honor bands, 1990—; presenter in field. Editor: Grandmaster Series, 2003, Jour. Hist. Rsch. in Music Edn., 2003—, (mus. composition (by Albert Roussel) A Glorious Day, 2006; chmn. editl. bd.: Music Educators Jour., 1998—2002; contbr. more than 25 articles to profl. jours. Recipient citation of excellence, Wis. chpt. Nat. Band Assn., 1986. Mem.: Pi Kappa Lambda, Phi Delta Kappa, Phi Kappa Phi. Avocation: running. Office: Ithaca Coll 953 Danby Rd Ithaca NY 14850

FONDILLER, SHIRLEY HOPE ALPERIN, nursing educator, journalist, historian; b. Holyoke, Mass. d. Samuel and Rose (Sobiloff) Alperin; m. Harvey V. Fondiller, Dec. 27, 1957 (div. June 1984); 1 child, David Stewart. BS, Columbia U., 1962, MA, 1963, MEd, 1971, EdD, 1980. Editor Am. Nurse, Kansas City, Mo., 1975-78; assoc. prof., asst. to dean for spl. projects Rush-Presbyn.-St. Luke's Med. Ctr., 1979-86; exec. dir. Mid-Atlantic Regional Nursing Assn., NYC, 1986-89; adj. assoc. prof. Columbia U., 1986—99; founder, prin. Pub. for Health Dimensions, phd,

1990—. Author of books; contbr. articles to profl. jours. Fellow Am. Acad. Nursing; mem. Kappa Delta Pi, Sigma Theta Tau. Office Phone: 212-663-4557. E-mail: sfondiller@worldnet.att.net.

FONER, ERIC, historian, educator; b. NYC, Feb. 7, 1943; s. Jack D. and Liza F.; m. Lynn Garafola, May 1, 1980. BA, Columbia U., NYC, 1963, PhD, 1969; BA, Oxford U., Eng., 1965. Prof. history City Coll., CUNY, NYC, 1973-82, Columbia U., NYC, 1982—; Pitt prof. Am. history and instns. Cambridge U., England, 1980-81. Harmsworth prof. Am. history Oxford U., Eng., 1993-94. Author: Free Soil, Free Labor, Free Men, 1970, Tom Paine and Revolutionary America, 1976, Politics and Ideology in the Age of the Civil War, 1980, Nothing But Freedom, 1983, Reconstruction: America's Unfinished Revolution, 1988, Readers' Encyclopedia of American History, 1991, Freedom's Lawnmakers, 1993, The Story of American Freedom, 1998, Who Owns History?, 2002, Give Me Liberty!: An American History, 2004, Voices of Freedom, 2004, Forever Free, 2005; editor: The New American History, 1990, The Reader's Companion to American History, 1991. Recipient Bancroft prize Columbia U., 1989, LA Times Book award, 1989, Parkman prize Soc. Am. Historians, 1989, Owsley prize So. Hist. Assn., 1989, Lit. Lion prize NY Pub. Libr., 1994; named Scholar of Yr., NY Coun. for the Humanities, 1995; fellow ACLS, 1972-73, NEH, 1983-84, Guggenheim fellow, 1974-76. Mem. Am. Hist. Assn. (pres. 2000), Orgn. Am. Historians (Avery O. Craven prize 1989, pres. 1993-94), Soc. Am. Historians (pres. 2006-07), Am. Antiquarian Soc., Am. Acad. Arts and Scis., Brit. Acad. Home: 606 W 116th St New York NY 10027-7011 Office Phone: 212-854-5253. Business E-Mail: ef17@columbia.edu.

FONG, BERNARD W.D., physician, educator; b. Honolulu, May 18, 1926; s. Leonard K. and Francis C. Fong; m. Roberta Wat, Aug. 14, 1950; children: Phyllis K., Jeffrey S., Camille K., Allison K. BS, Bucknell U., 1948; MD, Jefferson Med. Coll., 1952. Diplomate Am. Bd. Internal Medicine. Intern Germantown Hosp., Phila., 1952-53, chief med. resident, 1953-55; teaching fellow cardiology Jefferson Med. Coll. Hosp., Phila., 1955-56; attending physician Queen's Med. Ctr., Honolulu, 1956—2002, St. Francis Hosp., Honolulu, 1956-89; clin. prof. medicine U. Hawaii, Honolulu, 1982—2004; med. dir. medicare part B Aetna Ins. Co., Hawaii, Guam, 1988-97, Transamerica Occidental Life Ins. Co., Hawaii and Guam, 1997-2000, Noridian Adminstrv. Svcs., Hawaii and Guam, 2000—04; ret., 2004. Adv. coun. Nat. Heart, Lung and Blood Inst., NIH, Bethesda, Md., 1976-80, chmn. 3d forum on cardiovascular risk factors, 1985; adv. com. cardiovascular risk factors in minorities NIH, 1976-89; pres. Triple C, 1996-2001. Pres. Hawaii Heart Assn., Honolulu, 1962-63; bd. dirs. Am. Heart. Assn., N.Y.C., 1963-66; pres. Chung Shan Assn., Honolulu, 1969-70, United Chinese Soc. Hawaii, Honolulu, 1973-74; 1st v.p. Wong Leong Doo Benevolent Soc., Honolulu, 1973-2003; 1st v.p. Ocean View Cemetery, Honolulu, 1973-2003; bd. dirs. Palolo Home, 2004—. With USNR, 1944-46, PTO. Fellow ACP (bd. govs. 1972-76, inaugural laureate internal medicine Hawaii chpt. 1986), Am. Coll. Cardiology (bd. govs. 1992-96, chair 1995-96, trustee 1997-2002), Am. Coll. Chest Physicians, Am. Heart Assn; mem. Am. Soc. Internal Medicine (pres. Hawaii chpt. 1980-82). Republican. Roman Catholic. Home: 97 Dowsett Ave Honolulu HI 96817-1107 Personal E-mail: bernard4568@aol.com.

FONG, DONALD P., psychiatrist; b. Waukegan, Ill., Oct. 1, 1962; s. Don Leon and Lily Fong. BA, Baylor U., Waco, Tex., 1984; MD, Tex. Tech. Sch. Medicine, Lubbock, Tex., 1991. Resident Georgetown U. Med. Sch., Washington; fellow Johns Hopkins Hosp.; med. dir. Comprehensive Mental Health Svcs., Pennington, NJ, 1997—. Cons. NJ Cts., Trenton, NJ, 1997—. Supporter Make A Wish Found., Drs. Without Borders. With USN. Mem.: AMA, Am. Psychiat. Assn. Avocations: golf, tennis, skiing. Office: Comprehensive Mental Health Svcs 100 Stranbe Ctr Blvd Ste H-1 Pennington NJ 08534

FONG, IVAN KENNETH, health products executive, lawyer; b. NYC, Aug. 3, 1961; s. Jeffrey T. and Elizabeth N. (Chang) Fong; m. Sharon K. Ty, Nov. 30, 1985; children: Kelley Christine Ty, Caitlin Elizabeth Ty, Caroline Olivia Ty. SB in Chem. Engring., MIT, 1983, SM in Chem. Engring., 1984; JD with distinction, Stanford U., 1987; BCL, Oxford U., Eng., 1988. Bar: Calif. 1987, DC 1989. Law clk. to Judge Abner J. Mikva US Ct. Appeals (DC cir.), Washington, 1988-89; law clk. to Justice Sandra Day O'Connor US Supreme Ct., Washington, 1989-90; assoc. Covington & Burling, Washington, 1990-95, ptnr., 1995-97; dep. assoc. atty. gen. US Dept. Justice, Washington, 1997—2000; sr. v.p. Vendor Fin. Svcs. bus. GE, 2000—05; exec. v.p., chief legal officer, sec. Cardinal Health, Inc., Dublin, Ohio, 2005—. Adj. prof. law Georgetown U. Law Ctr., 1997-2000 Contbr. articles to profl. jours. Trustee Stanford U., 1995-2000, bd. visitors, 1993-96; treas. Edward Bennett Williams Am. Inn of Ct., 1997, barrister, 1997, assoc. and assoc.-at-large, 1993-97. Recipient Cmty. Svc. award Asian Am. Bar Assn., 1987; Fulbright scholar, 1987. Mem. ABA, AIChE, Asian Pacific ABA (pres. 1993-94), Nat. Asian Pacific Am. Bar Assn. (bd. govs. 1995-97), Phi Beta Kappa, Sigma Xi. Office: Cardinal Health Inc 7000 Cardinal Pl Dublin OH 43017*

FONG, KEVIN MURRAY, lawyer; b. 1955; AB magna cum laude, Harvard U., 1976, JD cum laude, 1979. Bar: Calif. 1979. Law clk. Judge Constance Baker Motley, U.S. Dist. Ct. (so. dist.) N.Y., NYC, 1979-80; ptnr. Pillsbury, Madison & Sutro LLP, San Francisco, 1980—2001, Pillsbury Winthrop LLP, 2001—05; ptnr. litigation practice, co-leader appellate practice, chmn. diversity com. Pillsbury Winthrop Shaw Pittman LLP, 2005—. Editor-in-chief Law Rev. Harvard civil rights-civil liberties, 1979. Mem. ABA (mem. com. racial and ethnic diversity), Calif. Acad. Appellate Lawyers (sec., treas.), Asian Am. Bar Assn. (pres. 1989), Asian Pacific Bar Calif. (pres. 1990), Bar Assn. San Francisco (bd. dirs. 1991-92), Legal Aid Soc. San Francisco (treas. 1995-97, mem. exec. com.). Democrat. Office: Pillsbury Winthrop Shaw Pittman LLP 50 Fremont St San Francisco CA 94105 Office Phone: 415-983-1270. Office Fax: 415-983-1200. Business E-Mail: kevin.fong@pillsburylaw.com.

FONG, MARYANNE T.P., telecommunications industry executive, researcher; Fellow: Inst. Direct Mktg., Inst. Dirs., Inst. Health Promotion and Edn., Inst. Sales and Mktg., Royal Soc. Health, Inst. Mfg., Inst. Travel and Tourism; mem.: Ohio Arts and Crafts Guild, United Nations Girls Edn. Initiative, United Nations World Heritage Ctr., European Assn. Sports Mgmt., Adult Learning Australia, Brit. Occupl. and Hygiene Soc., Am. Soc. Internat. Law, Environ. Assessment Assn. (cert. environ. inspector, cert. environ cons.), Australian Inst. Mgmt., Irish Inst. Tng. and Devel., Instn. Occupl. Safety and Health, Acad. Execs. and Adminstrs., Inst. Mgmt. Specialists, Inst. Profl. Bus. and Tech. Mgmt., Inst. Adminstrv. Mgmt., Inst. Pub. Sector Mgmt., Inst. Comml. Mgmt., Assn. Project Mgmt., Hotel Catering Internat. Mgmt. Assn. (assoc.), Inst. Profl. Fin. Mgrs. (assoc.), Chartered Inst. Pub. Rels. (assoc.), Inst. Welfare Officers (assoc.), Inst. Leisure and Amenity Mgmt. (assoc.), Australian Inst. Tng. and Devel. (assoc.), Inst. Cost and Exec. Accts. (assoc.), City and Guilds Inst., Chartered Inst. Logistics and Transport, Inst. Leadership and Mgmt., Chartered Mgmt. Inst., Richmond Hill C. of C., Guild Grads. U. Wales, Stanford U. Alumni Assn. Avocations: reading, music, bicycling, gardening, painting. Office: Ste 1221 Fl 12 32 Clarissa Dr Richmond Hill ON L4C 9R7 Canada Office Fax: 905-508-7496. Business E-Mail: mfongc575@rogers.com.

FONG, PETER C. K., lawyer, judge; b. Honolulu, Oct. 28, 1955; s. Arthur S.K. and Victoria K.Y. (Chun) F. BBA with honors, U. Hawaii, 1977; JD, Boston Coll., 1980. Bar: Hawaii 1980, U.S. Dist. Ct. Hawaii 1980, U.S. Ct. Appeals (9th cir.) 1980, U.S. Supreme Ct. 1983. Law clk. to presiding justice Supreme Ct. Hawaii, Honolulu, 1980-81; dep. pros. atty. Pros. Atty.'s Office, Honolulu, 1981-84; with Davis, Reid & Richards, Honolulu, 1984-89; chief legal counsel, chief clk. Senate jud. com. Hawaii State Legislature, 1989—; judge per diem Dist./Family Ct., Hawaii, 1989—; ptnr. Hong, Kwock & Fong, Honolulu, 1990-91, Fong & Fong, Honolulu, 1989—; pres., CEO, dir. Chun Kim Chow, Ltd., Honolulu, 1998—. Gen. legal counsel Hawaii Jr. C. of C., 1983-84; pres., bd. dirs. Legal Aid Soc. Hawaii, 1984-90; pres., 1986-87; arbitrator Hawaiian Cir. Ct., 1986—, Am. Arbitration Assn., 1989—; mediator Arbitration Forums, Inc., 1989—. Editorial staff Boston Coll. Internat. and Comp. Law Rev., 1978-80. Mem. City and County Honolulu Neighborhood Bd., 1981-83; campaign treas. for Hawaii state senator, 1981-89; mem. aux. admissions com. Boston Coll. Law Sch., 1982—, major gifts com. and sustaining membership fundraising drive com. YMCA, 1988; del. Gov.'s Congress on Hawaii's internat. role, 1988; del. Hawaii Jud. Forsight Congress, 1991; mem. hearings com. Hawaii State Atty.'s Disciplinary Bd., 1991—. Recipient Pres.'s award Hawaii Jr. C. of C., 1984; named one of ten Outstanding Persons of Hawaii, 1990, 92. Mem. ABA, ATLA, Hawaii State Bar Assn. (co-chmn. and vice-chmn., jud. salary com., mem. legis. com., coord. legis. resource bank, mem. task force on disciplinary counsel), Hawaii Developer's Coun., Am. Judicature Soc., Hawaii Supreme Ct. Hist. Soc., Hawaii Trial Judges Assn., Nat. Coun. Juvenile and Family Ct. Judges, Rsch. Bd. of Advisors, Nat. Assn. Dist. Attys., U.S. Supreme Ct. Hist. Soc., Mortar Bd., Tu Chiang Shen (past pres.), Waialae Country Club. Home: 5255 Makalena St Honolulu HI 96821-1808 Office: Fong & Fong Pacific Guardian Ctr Makai Tower 733 Bishop St Ste 1550 Honolulu HI 96813-4003 Office Phone: 808-528-2889. Office Fax: 808-521-1550.

FONG, PHYLLIS KAMOI, federal agency administrator, lawyer; b. Phila., Pa., Oct. 16, 1953; d. Bernard W.D. and Roberta (Wat) F.; m. Paul E. Tellier, Nov. 25, 1978. BA in Asian Studies, Pomona Coll., 1975; JD, Vanderbilt U., 1978. Bar: Tenn. 1978, DC 1982. Atty. U.S. Commn. on Civil Rights, Washington, 1978-81; asst. gen. counsel Legal Svcs. Corp., Washington, 1981-83; assoc. counsel to the insp. gen. U.S. Small Bus. Admin., Washington, 1983-88, asst. insp. gen. for mgmt. and policy, 1988-94, asst. insp. gen. for mgmt. and legal counsel, 1994-99, insp. gen., 1999—2002, USDA, Washington, 2002—. Mem. ABA, Tenn. Bar Assn., D.C. Bar Assn. Office: USDA Rm 117 W Jamie Whitten Bldg 1400 Independence Ave SW Washington DC 20250

FONGWA, MARIE NGETIKO, nurse midwife; arrived in US, 1978; d. Tita and Lydia Beyongha Fongwa. BS in Health Sci., San Jose State U., Calif., 1979—83, MPH, 1983—85; MS in Nursing, U. Calif., San Francisco, 1993—94, PhD in Nursing, 1994—98. RN State Bd. Calif., 1981. RN Bd. Registered Nursing & Midwifery, Bamenda, Cameroon, 1973—, midwife, 1976—78. Recipient Resource Ctrs. Minority Aging Rsch. award, NIH/NIA, 2002, Faculty Career Devel. award, U. Calif. Academic Senate, 2005; Academic Senate grant, UCLA Academic Faculty, 2002. Presbyn. Achievements include development of a patient satisfaction instrument that is sensitive to health care concerns of African Americans and Whites. Office: UCLA Sch Nursing 700 Tiverton Ave 3-238 Factor Bldg Los Angeles CA 90095 Home Phone: 310-677-0143. Office Fax: 310-267-0413. Business E-Mail: mfongwa@sonnet.ucla.edu.

FONKALSRUD, ERIC WALTER, pediatric surgeon, educator; b. Balt., Aug. 31, 1932; s. George and Ella (Fricke) F.; m. Margaret Ann Zimmermann, June 6, 1959; children: Eric Walter Jr., Margaret Lynn, David Loren, Robert Warren. BA, U. Wash., 1953; MD, Johns Hopkins U., 1957. Diplomate Am. Bd. Surgery, Am. Bd. Pediatric Surgery, Am. Bd. Thoracic Surgery. Intern Johns Hopkins Hosp., Balt., 1957-58, asst. resident, 1958-59, U. Calif. Med. Ctr., Los Angeles, 1959-62, chief resident surgery, 1962-63, asst. prof. surgery, chief pediatric surgery, 1965-68, assoc. prof., 1968-71, prof. LA, 1971—2001, emeritus prof., 2001—, vice chmn. dept. surgery, 1981-89; resident pediatric surgery Columbus (Ohio) Childrens Hosp. and Ohio State U., 1963-65; practice medicine specializing in pediatric surgery LA, 1965—. Mem. surg. study sect. NIH; James IV surg. traveller to, Gt. Britain, 1971 Mem. editl. bd. Jour. Surg. Rsch., Archives Surgery, Am. Jour. Surgery, Annals Surgery, Surgery, Current Problems in Surgery, Jour. Pediat. Surgery, World Jour. Surgery, Japanese Jour. Surgery, Turkish Jour. Pediat. Surgery, Med. Video Jour. Surgery; contbr. over 650 articles to profl. jours., chpts. to books; co-author: The Undescended Testis, 1981, Infections and Immunologic Disorders in Pediatric Surgery, 1993, Essentials of Pediatric Surgery, 1995, Gastroesophageal Reflux in Childhood; Current Problems in Surgery, 1996, Pediatric Surgery, 1998, 2d edit., 2006, Principles of Pediatric Surgery, 2003. Recipient Golden Apple award UCLA Sch. Medicine, 1968; John and Mary R. Markle scholar, 1963-68; named Nat. Champion Rowing Crew, U. Wash., 1950, 53, Tree Farmer of Yr. Western Wash., 1998; Johns Hopkins U. Soc. of Scholars, 2003; Profl. Achievement Award, UCLA Sch. of Medicine, 2003. Fellow ACS (surg. forum com., bd. govs. 1978-84, pres. So. Calif. chpt. 1995-96, Mead Johnson award 1963), Am. Acad. Pediat. (exec. bd., chmn. surg. sect. 1986-87, Salzberg award 2000, William E. Ladd medal 2006), German Assn. for Surgery (hon.), Polish Assn. Pediat. Surgery (hon.), Japanese Pediat. Surgery Assn. (hon.), John Hopkins Soc. Scholars (hon.); mem. AMA, Am. Thoracic Surg. Assn., Am. Acad. Sci., Am. Assn. Acad. Surgery (pres. 1972), Soc. Univ. Surgeons (pres. 1976, sec. 1972-76), Calif. Med. Assn., Crohns and Colitis Found. of So. Calif. (Man of Yr. 1999), Internat. Surg. Group (treas. 1993-2003), Lilliputian Surg. Soc. (chmn. 1989), L.A. County Med. Assn., Am. Surg. Assn., Pan Pacific Surg. Assn., Pacific Coast Surg. Assn. (recorder 1979-85, pres. 1989), Am. Pediat. Surg. Assn. (bd. govs. 1975-78, pres. 1989), Pacific Assn. Pediat. Surgeons (pres. 1983-84, Coe medal 1998), S.W. Pediatric Soc., L.A. Pediat. Soc., Soc. for Clin. Surgery, Transplantation Soc., Pediat. Surgery Biology Club, Bay Surg. Soc., L.A. Surg. Soc. (sec. 1988-90, pres. 1991), Town Hall (L.A.), Pithotomy Club (pres. 1956-57), Sigma Xi, Alpha Omega Alpha. Methodist. Home: 428 24th St Santa Monica CA 90402-3102 Office: U Calif Med Ctr Dept Surgery Los Angeles CA 90095 Office Phone: 310-825-6712. Business E-Mail: efonkalsrud@mednet.ucla.edu.

FONKEN, GERHARD JOSEPH, retired chemistry professor, academic administrator; b. Krefeld, Germany, Aug. 3, 1928; came to U.S., 1930, naturalized, 1935; s. Henry A. and Wilhelmina Katerina (von Eyser) F.; m. Carolyn Lee Stay, Dec. 20, 1952; children: David, Katherine, Steven, Karen, Eric. BS, U. Calif., Berkeley, 1954, PhD, 1957. Chemist Procter & Gamble Co., 1957-58; chemist Stanford (Calif.) Research Inst., 1958-59; instr. U. Tex., Austin, 1959-61, from asst. to assoc. prof., 1961-72, prof. chemistry, 1972-94, asso. provost, 1972-75, acting v.p. acad. affairs, 1975-76, exec. asst. to pres., 1976-79, v.p. research, 1979-80, v.p. acad. affairs and research, 1980-85, exec. v.p., provost, 1985-94; retired, 1994. Contbr. articles to chemistry jours. Served with U.S. Army, 1946-49, 50-51, Korea. Decorated Order of the Crown, Kingdom of Belgium; grantee NIH, 1961-64, Robert A. Welch Found., 1962-79. Mem. Am. Chem. Soc. Home: 6612 Lost Horizon Dr Austin TX 78759-6116 Personal E-mail: fonken@mail.utexas.edu.

FONS, ERIC WALLACE, physics professor; b. Dallas, May 3, 1964; s. Theodore Raymond and Leah Carol (Steinberg) Fons; 1 child, Zoe Rachel. BA in Physics & Astrophysics, U. Calif., Berkeley, 1989; MS in Physics, U. Fla., Gainesville, 1994, postgrad., 1995—99. Satellite ops. assoc. engr. Lockheed Tech. Ops. Co., Sunnyvale, Calif., 1989—92; prof. physics Okla. Sch. Sci. and Math., Oklahoma City, 2000—02; asst. prof. physics Anne Arundel C.C., Arnold, Md., 2002—. Adj. instr. physics and math. Santa Fe C.C., Gainesville, 1996—97. Composer, musician, singer:. Fellow, U. Fla., 1992—94; Grad. Grinter fellow, 1993—95. Mem.: ASCAP, Am. Assn. Physics Tchrs. Jewish. Achievements include research in optical studies of Pr and Tb doping in YBa(2)Cu(3)O(7-ffi) single crystals. Avocations: songwriting/composing, guitar, hiking, environmental activism. Home Phone: 410-263-5813; Office Phone: 410-777-2154. Personal E-mail: efons@msn.com. E-mail: ewfons@aacc.edu.

FONS, MARGARET E., elementary school educator; d. James Louis and Nancy Ann Fons. BS in Recreation Adminstrn., U. Wis., LaCrosse, 1982; M of Ednl. Leadership, No. Ariz. U., 1992. Cert. tchr. Ariz. State U., 1986, English as 2d lang. tchr. Ariz. State U., 1992. Tchr. elem. sch. Maricopa Unified Sch. Dist., Ariz., 1986—92; tchr. 4th grade Mesa Unified Sch. Dist., 1992—. Contbr. articles to profl. jours. V.p., pres. elect, pres. Ariz. Ski Coun., Phoenix, 2003—05; pres. Scottsdale Sea & Ski Club, 1994—99; bd. mem. Far West Ski Assn. Named Woman of Yr., Far West Ski Assn., 1994; recipient, 2004; grantee, Salt River Project, 1996, Mesa Found., 1996. Mem.: ASCD (assoc.). Roman Catholic. Avocations: skiing, travel, golf, dance, gardening. Office: Mesa Unified Sch Dist 591 W Mesquite Chandler AZ 85225 Home Phone: 480-940-3634; Office Phone: 480-472-3600. Business E-Mail: mefons@mpsaz.org.

FONSECA, ALEJANDRA, language educator; arrived in US, 1972; d. Guillermo and Emilce Fonseca. BS in Biology, U. Costa Rica, 96; MS, Middlebury Coll., Vt., 2006. Cert. 7-12 Spanish and biology tchr. NY. English tchr. Centro Orgn. Integrada, San José, Costa Rica, 1996; GED sci. tchr. Escuela Juan XXI, San José, 1998—2000; sci. tchr. Liceo Escazu, San José, 1998—2000; Spanish tchr. Bibb County Edn. Dept., Macon, Ga., 2000—02, Valley Stream Ctrl. HS Dist., NY, 2002—. Vol. guide Assn. Vols. Svc. in Nat. Parks, San José, Costa Rica, 1993—95. Mem.: Am. Coun. Tchg. Fgn. Langs. (Superior Spanish Oral Proficiency award 2000). Roman Catholic. Avocations: reading, biographies, history. Home: 149 Meyer Ave Valley Stream NY 11580 Office: Wyandanch Meml HS 32nd St Wyandanch NY 11798

FONSECA, JOSEPH MOJICA, JR., political science professor; b. Seattle, Wash., Sept. 27, 1951; s. Joseph Mojica Fonseca Sr. and Maria Flores (Torres) Fonseca; m. Eva Rivas, Jan. 14, 1989; children: Monica, Frank Daniel, Jason, Nicole Jolene, Joseph Anthony, Jacob Matthew. AA, San Antonio Coll., Tex., 1979; BA in Polit. Sci. and Psychology, St. Mary's U., 1998, MA, 2002. Adminstrv. aide Senator Glenn H. Kothmann, San Antonio, 1982-89; tax and mortgage analyst Bexar County Tax Office, San Antonio, 1989-95; fed., state and county process server Daniel Rivans Jr. owner, San Antonio, 1995-97; fin. analyst CitiGroup Investment Svcs., San Antonio, 1998—2002; prof. Northwind Vista Coll., San Antonio, 2003—. Pres., SIMCONG leg St. Mary's U., San Antonio, 1996—97, chair coll. dems., 1995—97, 1st pres. Mem. Bexar County Dems., San Antonio, 1995—; rape crisis vol. Rape Crisis Ctr., Seattle, 1973—74; spousal abuse vol. Spousal Abuse Ctr., Phoenix, 1973—74. Decorated 3 Purple Hearts, Silver Star for valor, Congl. Medal of Honor presented by Pres. Richard M. Nixon. Mem.: K.C. (chancellor 1977—79), Acad. of Polit. Sci., Am. Legion, Rho Ki. Roman Catholic. Avocations: quarter horse racing, reading, football. Office: Northwest Vista Coll 3535 N Ellison Dr San Antonio TX 78251 E-mail: jaqijugi777@yahoo.com.

FONTAINE, JOHN C., foundation administrator, lawyer, former newspaper company executive; BA, U. Mich., 1953; LLB, Harvard U., 1956. Bar: NY 1957. Pres. Knight-Ridder, Inc., Miami, Fla.; ptnr. Hughes Hubbard & Reed LLP, NYC, 1997—. Bd. mem. Samuel H. Kress Found., 1975—, chmn., 1994—; mem. bd. trustees Nat. Gallery Art, Washington, DC, 1984—2000, 2002—; bd. mem. Jacob's Pillow Dance Festival, Nat. Exec. Svc. Corp. Office: Samuel H Kress Found 174 E 80th St New York NY 10021

FONTAINE, KATHLEEN STUREY, policy analyst; b. Balt., Mar. 22, 1962; d. Peter Sturey and Geraldine Marie Teodori; m. Mark Roselius Fontaine, Dec. 21, 1997; children: Elissa Anne Pedelty, Andrew Dylan Pedelty, Scott Gerald Pedelty, Michelle Rossi, Matthew. BS in Physics with Astrophysics Option, N.Mex Inst. Mining and Tech., 1984; MA in Sci. Tech. and Pub. Policy, George Washington U., 2002. Master trainer AchieveGlobal, 1999, MBTI (Myers Briggs Type Indicator) qualified Ctr. for Applications of Psychol. Type, 1998. Human resources devel. specialist NASA GSFC (Goddard Space Flight Ctr.) Office Human Resources, Greenbelt, Md., 1998—2002; policy analyst NASA GSFC Global Change Data Ctr., Greenbelt, 2002—. Contbr. articles to profl. jours. Bd. dirs. Anne Arundel County Sch. Bd. Nominating Conv. Com., Annapolis, Md., 2001—; vol., leader Girl Scout Coun. of the Nation's Capitol, Bowie, Md., 1993—97; adult vol. Girl Scout Coun. Ctrl. Md., Annapolis, 1997—2005. Mem.: AGU, AIAA, Women in Aerospace. Democrat. Avocations: music, travel, cooking, sailing. Office: NASA Goddard Space Flight Ctr Code 610.2 Greenbelt MD 20771 Personal E-mail: ksfontaine@juno.com. Business E-Mail: kathy.fontaine@nasa.gov.

FONTAINE, R. RICHARD, computer game company executive; Exec. positions B. Dalton Booksellers, Software Etc., Michaels Stores Inc., Ingram Distribution; CEO GameStop Corp., Grapevine, Tex., 1996—2000, chmn., CEO, 2000—. Office: GameStop Corp 625 Westport Pkwy Grapevine TX 76051*

FONTAINE NEWSOME, LYNN, lawyer; b. East Orange, NJ, Dec. 22, 1955; BA, Seton Hall U., 1977, JD, 1981. Bar: NJ 1981, US Dist. Ct. (Dist. NJ) 1981. Law sec. to Hon. George P. Helfrich Superior Ct. Morris County, 1981—82; ptnr. Donahue Hagan Klein & Newsome PC, Morristown, NJ. Mem. Dist. X Ethics Com., 1990—93; lectr. NJ Inst. Continuing Legal Edn., Nat. Bus. Inst. Master: Family Law Inns of Ct.; mem.: Morris County Bar Found. (past pres.), Assn. Trial Lawyers Am., Essex County Bar Assn., Morris County Bar Assn. (bd. trustees 1990—, pres. 1999, past chair Morris county family law com.), NJ State Bar Assn. (pres.-elect 2006—07, supreme ct. family practice com., treas., past chair exec. com. family sect.), ABA. Office: Donahue Hagan Klein Newsome & O'Donnell PC 360 Mt Kimble Ave Morristown NJ 07960 Office Phone: 973-467-5556. Office Fax: 973-467-0636.

FONTANA, ADAM VINCENT, music educator, musician; b. Bronx, NY, Sept. 15, 1980; s. John Arthur Fontana and Patricia Ann Cooper-Fontana; m. Lisa Marie Pizzo, Aug. 19, 2006. MusB in Music Edn., SUNY, Potsdam, 2002; MA in Music Edn., Columbia U., NYC, 2007. Cert. K-12 music NY, 2002. Chorus and gen. music tchr. South Orangetown Ctrl. Sch. Dist., Blauvelt, NY, 2002—03; band tchr. Taft Elem. Sch., Washingtonville, NY, 2003—, Little Britain Elem. Sch., Washingtonville, 2003—. Advisor Odyssey of Mind, Washingtonville, 2005—06; mentor NYSUT, NY, 2006—; clarinetist OCMEA Wind Ensemble, Orange County; freelance clarinetist, NY. Ch. musician Sacred Heart Ch., Monroe, NY, 1990—2000. Mem.: Internat. Clarinet Assn., Conductor's Guild, NY State Sch. Music Assn., MENC, Phi Mu Alpha Sinfonia. Roman Catholic. Home: 102 Cartwheel Ct #24 Washingtonville NY 10992 Office: Washingtonville Ctrl Sch Dist 20 Toleman Rd Washingtonville NY 10992 Home Phone: 845-629-5681; Office Phone: 845-497-2200.

FONTANA, GARY LYNN, lawyer; b. Roscoe, NY, Apr. 9, 1946; s. Robert W. and Lois E. (Baxter) F.; m. Barbara J. Lubker, Aug. 31, 1968 (div. Nov. 1987); children: Brent, Ryan. AB with honors, Cornell U., 1968; JD, Yale U., 1971. Bar: Calif. 1972, U.S. Ct. Appeals (9th cir.) 1972, D.C. 1981, U.S. Ct. Appeals (5th cir.) 1981, U.S. Supreme Ct. 1981. Assoc. Heller, Ehrman, White & McAuliffe, San Francisco, 1971-77; mem. staff Office of Energy Policy White House, Washington, 1977-78, dep. dir. legis. affairs Office of Mgmt. & Budget, 1978-81; ptnr. Van Ness, Feldman, Sutcliffe & Curtis, Washington, 1981-86, Thelen, Marrin, Johnson & Bridges, San Francisco, 1986—, Thelen Reid Brown Raysman & Steiner LLP. Cons.

Am. Ins. Assn., Wash. 1989-90; mem. ins. law adv. com. Practising Law Inst. 1993, spkr. in feilds. Recipient Super Lawyer, San Francisco mag., 2004, Cornell Nat. Scholar. Mem. ABA, World Affairs Coun., C. of C. (adv. pub. affairs com. San Francisco chpt.) 1986, Nat. Health Lawyers Assn., Calif. Dept. Ins. (rate regulation task force), Bar Assn. San Francisco Com. Ins. Law, Men's Glee Club. Democrat. Avocation: basketball. Office: Thelen Reid Brown Raysman & Steiner LLP 101 2nd St Ste 1800 San Francisco CA 94105 Office Phone: 415-371-1200, 415-369-7337. Office Fax: 415-371-1211. Business E-Mail: glfontana@thelen.com.

FONTANA, JOHN ARTHUR, employee benefits specialist; b. NYC, Feb. 24, 1955; s. Joseph and Gloria (Rosiello) F.; m. Patricia Ann Cooper, Nov. 10, 1979; children: Adam Vincent, Brian Patrick, Jennifer Ann. BA in Econs., Fordham U., 1977, MBA in Acctg., 1984. Pension analyst George Buck Cons. Actuaries, NYC, 1977-79; retirement plan analyst Sperry Corp., NYC, 1979-80; ops. specialist Bankers Trust Co., NYC, 1980-83; mgr. employee benefits Fidata Corp., NYC, 1983-85; mgr. benefit plan devel. N.Y. Power Authority, White Plains, 1985-90; dir. employee benefits Random House, Inc., NYC, 1990-98; dir. benefits and Human Resources Info. Sys. Polygram Holding, Inc., NYC, 1998-99; sr. cons. Price-Waterhouse Coopers, NYC, 1999—; pres. The Fontana Group, LLC, Montvale, NJ, 1999—; adj. prof. Manhattanville Coll., 2006—. Bd. dirs. Monroe (N.Y.) Dem. Com., 1985-87; capt. United Way, N.Y.C., 1992—; musician Ch. of the Sacred Heart, Monroe, 1989—, fin. com.; team mgr. M-W Little League, 1987-90; mem. Orange County C. of C., Orange County Partnership. Mem. U.S. C. of C. (benefits com. 1987-89), Am. Mgmt. Assn., Soc. Human Resource Mgmt., Mid-Hudson Valley Soc. for Human Resources Mgmt. (pres.-elect, pres. chpt. contact advocate). Republican. Roman Catholic. Avocations: music, golf, collecting baseball memorabilia. Home and Office: The Fontana Group LLC 61 Peter Bush Dr Monroe NY 10950 Office Phone: 845-729-5818. E-mail: john.fontana@employeestrategy.com.

FONTANA, MARIO H., nuclear engineer; b. West Springfield, Mass., Mar. 30, 1933; s. Remo and Sabina F.; m. Sue Janeway, Apr. 12, 1958; children: Richard, Edward. BS, U. Mass., 1955; MS, MIT, 1957; PhD, Purdue U., 1968. Registered engr., Tenn. Mem. rsch. staff Oak Ridge (Tenn.) Nat. Lab., 1957-63, 65-81, asst. dir. nuc. safety rsch., 1968-72, head advanced concepts devel. engrng. tech. divsn., 1972-81, asst. to dir. engrng. tech. divsn., 1990-92; group leader Advanced Concepts, 1993-94; instr. Purdue U., Oak Ridge, Tenn., 1964-65; dir. industry degraded core program Tech for Energy, Inc., Knoxville, Tenn., 1981-84; v.p. engrng. Energex Oak Ridge, 1984-85; dir. nuclear safety tech. IT Corp. and Tenera, L.P., Knoxville, 1985-90; sr. scientist Avco Rsch. and Advanced Devel., Wilmington, Mass., 1963-64. Cons. AEC, Washington, 1972-73, Nuc. Regulatory Commn., Washington, 1979-81, 91—, U.S. Dept. Energy, Washington, 1986-89; rsch. prof. U. Tenn., 1995—; mem. Adv. Com. on Reactor Safeguards, 1995-99. Author more than 100 reports and articles. Fellow Am. Nuclear Soc. (chmn. nuclear reactor safety divsn. 1972-73, 94-95); mem. ASME, Rotary Internat., Sigma Xi, Tau Beta Pi. Achievements include patents for method of arc synthesis of uranium carbide from UF6 and Graphite, others.

FONTANA, MARK ALLAN, lawyer; b. Sewickley, Pa., June 6, 1957; s. Louis Paul and Marie (Bruni) F.; m. Susan Marie Maravich, May 15, 1982; children: Matthew, Amanda. BA magna cum laude, Indiana U. Pa., 1979; JD magna cum laude, U. Pitts., 1982. Bar: Pa. 1982, US Dist. Ct. (we. dist.) Pa. 1982, US Ct. Appeals (3d cir.) 1984. Ptnr. labor group Reed, Smith, Shaw & McClay LLP, Pitts., 1982—2004; ptnr. employment svcs. group Wolf, Block, Schorr & Solis Cohen LLP, Pitts., 2004—. Mem. ABA, Legal Aid Soc. Allegheny County, Order of Coif. Democrat. Roman Catholic. Avocations: golf, racquetball. Home: 1 Drayton Ct Mechanicsburg PA 17055-8023 Office: Wolf Block Schorr & Solis Cohen LLP 213 Market St 9th Fl Harrisburg PA 17101 Office Phone: 717-237-7183. Business E-Mail: mfontana@wolfblock.com.

FONTANA, ROBERT EDWARD, electrical engineer, educator, retired military officer; b. Bklyn., Nov. 26, 1915; s. Valentino and Secondina (Lesca) F.; m. Victoria E. Mauriello, Dec. 2, 1945; children: Robert Edward, Thomas Paul, Mary Joan. B Elec. Engring, NYU, 1939; MS, U. Ill., 1947, PhD, 1949. Commd. 2d lt. USAAF, 1942; advanced through grades to col. USAF, 1959, ret., 1969; research scientist Sandia Corp., 1949-54; spl. asst. nuclear devel. Hdqrs. USAF, 1954-58; head nuclear applications (Air R&D Command), 1958-61; dir. (Aerospace Rsch. Labs.), Wright-Patterson AFB, Ohio, 1961-66; chmn. dept. elec. engring. Air Force Inst. Tech., Wright-Patterson AFB, 1966-84, prof. emeritus, 1984—. Pres. Honors Seminars Met. Dayton, 1966-86. Decorated Legion of Merit with oak leaf cluster, Exceptional Civilian service award Dept. Air Force, 1985 Fellow IEEE (life; chmn. Dayton sect. 1971, editor edn. group newsletter 1970-81, meritorious service award 1983); mem. Am. Soc. Engring. Edn. (editor elec. engring. div. newsletter 1970-81, chmn. energy conversion com. 1978-80), Sigma Xi, Tau Beta Pi, Eta Kappa Nu. Home: 6534 Brook Lake Dr Dallas TX 75248-3915

FONTANA, SANDRA ELLEN FRANKEL, special education educator; b. NYC, July 12, 1951; d. Robert Lowell and Mildred (Tropan) Sharoff; m. Jay Tommy Frankel, May 25, 1973 (div. 1993); children: Austin, Lauren; m. David Fontana, July 27, 2002; stepchildren: Troy, Tara. BS in Med. Tech., Rochester Inst. Tech., NY, 1973; MA in Linguistics, Galludet U., 1984. Cert. comprehensive permanent S.I.G.N. Nat. Assn. Deaf SIGN Instr. Guidance Network, 1985. Coord. bus. affairs/sign lang. program dept. bus. affairs Gallaudet U., 1980-83; head tchr. dept. sign communication faculty retreat N000, winter 1981; instr. dept. interpreter/translator instruction Gallaudet U., 1981-84, instr. in sign lang. dept. sign communication, spring 1982, ASL instr. dept. sign communication, 1982-84, coord. NDC sign lang. program dept. sign communication, 1984-88, instr. dept. sign communication, 1984-88, head instr./trainer, ASL instr. dept. sign communication, 1988-89, ASL instr. Coll. Continuing Edn. extension/summer programs, 1988; assoc. prof. interpreting preparation program CC Balt. County, 1990—2002; assoc. prof. interpreting preparation program/world langs. Riverside (Calif.) CC, 2002—. Evaluator Sign Instr. Guidance Network, Indpls., 1989-90; mem. Sign Instr. Guidance Network; bd. dir. State Md. Office Govr. Assistive Tech. Guaranteed Loan Program, 1999-2002. Mem. Am. Sign Lang. Tchr. Assn. (profl. cert. 1986—, nationwide evaluator 1990—, mem. L.A. chpt. 2002-), Nat. Assn. of the Deaf, Metro. Wash. Assn. of the Deaf, Md. Assn. of the Deaf. Home: 1540 Highridge Rd Riverside CA 92506 Office: Riverside CC 4800 Magnolia Ave Riverside CA 92506 Personal E-mail: sandrell@aol.com.

FONTANA, THOMAS MICHAEL, television producer, scriptwriter; b. Buffalo, Sept. 12, 1951; s. Charles Louis and Marie Angelica (Internicola) Fontana. BA in Theater, State U. Coll., Buffalo, 1973; LittD (hon.), SUNY, 1997. Playwright in residence The Writers Theatre, NYC, 1975-93; prodr., writer St. Elsewhere, NBC-TV, 1982-88; writer The Fourth Wiseman, MOW/ABC-TV, 1985; exec. prodr., writer Tattinger's NBC-TV, 1988-89, Nick and Hillary, 1989, Home Fires NBC-TV, 1991, Homicide: Life on the Street NBC-TV, 1993-99, Oz HBO-TV, 1997—2003, The Jury FBC-TV, 2004, Strip Search MOW/HBO, 2004, Homicide: Life Everlasting, MOW, NBC-TV, 2000, The Beat, UPN, 2000, Judas, MOW/ABC, 2003, The Bedford Diaries, WB, 2006. Exec. prodr.: (TV films) The Press Secretary, PBS, 2001, Shot in the Heart, MOW, HBO, 2001, American Tragedy, CBS, 2000; exec. prodr.: (TV films) In Good Conscience, 2006; contbr. articles to NY Times, TV Guide, Esquire, Written By, TV special, A Tribute to Heroes. Named Amnesty Internat. Filmmaker of Yr., 2005; named to Buffalo Theatre Hall of Fame, 2003; recipient Peabody Award, 1983, 1993, 1996, 1998, Humanitas Prize, 1984, Emmy Award for St Elsewhere, 1985, 1987, Emmy Award for Homicide-Life in the Street, 1993, Christopher Award, Nat Asn Cath Broadcasters, 1986, Autism Award, Nat Asn Autistic Children, 1986, Maggie Award, Planned Parenthood Asn, 1986, Distinguished Alumnus Award, State Univ Col, Buffalo, 1987, Founder's Award, VQT, 1995, Best Drama Series Award, 1996, Best Drama Series and Program of Yr award, TV Critics Assn., 1996—98, Nancy Susan Reynolds Award, 1996, Marylander of the Yr Award, Baltimore Sun, 1996, Best Drama Series Oz, Cable Ace Award, 1997, Prix Poula Meillevre Series Oz, 1997, Literacy in Media award for Oz, 1999, Caths in the Media Award, 1999, Lifetime Achievement Award, Casting Soc Am, 2000, Evelyn Burkey Lifetime Achievement award, WGA East, 2000, Fortune Soc. Award for Oz, 2000, award, Media Action Network for Asian-Ams., 2002, Outstanding TV Writer's award, Austin Film Festival, 2003, Excellence award, Can. Film Ctr., 2002—03, Spl. Edgar award, Mystery Writers Am., 2005, Lifetime Achievement award, Caucus of TV Writers, Prodrs. and Dirs., 2005, Real Deal award, Scenarios USA, 2005. Mem.: Prodrs. Guild Am., Auths League Am, Writers Guild Am. East (Ann Award 1987, 1993, 1994), Dramatists Guild, Friars Club, Players Club, West Side Rowing Club (Buffalo). Democrat. Roman Catholic. Office: Fatima Prodns 185 Broome St New York NY 10002 Office Phone: 212-206-3585. E-mail: tomfontana@aol.com.

FONTANAROSA, PHIL BERNARD, medical journal executive editor, emergency physician, educator; b. Youngstown, Ohio, 1954; m. Kristine Fontanarosa, Aug. 1977; children: Jennifer, Joel, Beth, Julie. Youngstown State U., 1975; MD, Med. Coll. Ohio, 1978; postgrad., Kent St. U., 1992-93. Diplomate Am. Bd. Emergency Medicine. Intern Akron (Ohio) City Hosp., 1978-79, resident in emergency medicine, 1979-81; assoc. prof., rsch. dir. emergency medicine Northeastern Ohio Universities Coll. Medicine, 1983-93; adj. prof. medicine Northwestern Med. Sch., Chgo. Editor, Emergency Medicine Reports; dep. editor, dir. editl. affairs Jour. AMA, now exec. editor; editor-in-chief text: Physicians' Evaluation and Educational Review in Emergency Medicine, 1996, Alternative Medicine: An Objective Assessment, 2000. Mem. Am. Coll. Emergency Physicians. Office: AMA 515 N State St Chicago IL 60610-4325

FONTANE, EMILY, physician, educator; BS, CUNY Lehman Coll., 1989; MD, U. Pa., 1996. Clin. asst. prof. East Carolina U., NC, 2001—. Contbr. articles to profl. jours. Recipient Jonas E. Salk award, City U. NY, 1992, Faculty Tchg. award, East Carolina U., NC, 2003. Fellow: Am. Assn. Pediat., Am. Coll. Emergency Physicians; mem.: AMA, North Carolina Med. Soc., Soc. Academic Emergency Medicine.

FONTANES, A. ALEXANDER, insurance company executive; Sr. v.p., chief investment officer Liberty Mut. Ins. Co., exec. v.p., chief investment officer. Office: Liberty Mut Ins Co 175 Berkeley St Boston MA 02116 Office Phone: 617-357-9500. Office Fax: 617-574-5637.*

FONTÉ, RICHARD W., educational consultant, former academic administrator; BS in Internat. Affairs, Georgetown U., 1967; M in Am. Dem. Theory, Ind. U., 1969; PhD in C.C. and Higher Edn. Fin., U. Mich., 1988. Asst. for workforce edn. to Gov. Edgar, Ill.; asst. to Gov. Edgar, workforce cons., 1970-77; v.p., interim pres. Triton Coll., Ill.; pres. South Suburban Coll., Ill., 1988, Austin CC, Tex., 1997—2003; nat. dir. We the People, NEH, Washington, 2004—06; pres. Coll. of Lake, Grayslake, Ill., 2006—07, spl. asst. nat. edn., 2007—. Co-author: (books) Shaping the Community College Image, Strategic Marketing for Presidents; contbr. articles to profl. jours. Bd. dirs. numerous comty. orgns. including Ill. Philharm. Orch., Austin 2010, Tex. Edn. Agy. Task Force on Adult Edn. Accountability, State Theatre Bd., Capital Area Workforce Devel. Bd., Austin, Capital Area Tng. Found. Mem. Greater Austin C. of C. (bd. dirs.). Office: Coll of Lake 19351 W Washington St Grayslake IL 60030-1198 Office Phone: 847-543-2201. E-mail: rfonte@clcillinois.edu.

FONTENOT, ANDREA DEAN, communications executive; b. Drumright, Okla., Mar. 14, 1944; d. Howard G. and Ruby Jewell (Harvison) Harris; m. Lloyd John Culver, Aug. 12, 1962 (widowed Feb. 1966); m. Ronald Ray Fontenot. BS in Speech and Broadcasting, McNeese State U., Lake Charles, 1978, MFA in Creative Writing, 1985; ABD in English, Tex. Tech. U., Lubbock, 1997, PhD in English, 1998. Cert. Distance Educator. Jr. acct. exec. Harris & Weinstein Ad Agy., Atlanta, 1973-75; grad. tchg. asst. McNeese State U., Lake Charles, La., 1981-85, adjunct prof., 1985-89, Davis Monthan Air Force Base, Pima CC Tucson, 1989-90; grad. teaching asst. Tex. Tech. U., Lubbock, Tex., 1990-96; rsch. asst. Distance Edn. Coll. Engring., Lubbock, Tex., 1996, sr. dir. engring. outreach and literacy, 2003—27; mng. dir. CLEAR project Southwestern Bell Comms. Found., Lubbock, Tex., 1997—2006; dir. Tex. Tech U. T-Stem Ctr., 2006—. Mem. Tchg. Learning and Tech. Ctr., Lubbock, Tex., 1996-98; tchg. on internet ind. cons. Lubbock, Tex., 1993—; rsch. asst. Internet Cons. SCATE, Lubbock, Tex., 1996-97; sr. dir. engring. outreach and lit., 2003. Author: (short story) Minotaur, 1985, Hayden's Ferry Review, 1986; contbr. articles to profl. jours. Mem. Rural Assistance Initiative Task Force, 1998—2001, Collaborative Cmty. Network Task Force, 1998—, Ctr. for Partnerships in Sci. and Tech., Svc. Learning Adv. Coun., High Plains Rural Broadband Network; mem. scholarship com. Lubbock Area Found., 2007—; mem. Ptnrs. in Edn., 2005—. Recipient Paul Whitfield Horn scholarship, 1995, Outstanding Grad. Tchr., 1993, 95, McNeese Award in Fiction, 1984, 85, Outstanding Classroom Practices award Conf. Coll. Composition and Comm., 1998. Mem.: Soc. Women in Engring., Tex. Partnerships in Aerosci. Edn., NASA-Revolutionary Aerospace Concepts-Acad. Linkage, Am. Soc. Engring. Educators, Grad. English Soc., Soc. for Tech. Comm., South Ctrl. MLA, Nat. Coun. Tchrs. English, Alliance Minority Engrs., Tex. Learning Orgn., Assoc. Writing Program. Home: 5020 Kenosha Ave Apt A Lubbock TX 79413-3948 Office: Ctr for Engring Outreach COE Tex Tech Univ Lubbock TX 79409 Office Phone: 806-742-3451. Business E-Mail: dean.fontenot@ttu.edu.

FONTES, EDWARD MICHAEL, graphics designer; b. Paso, Tex., Apr. 30, 1934; s. Eduardo Michael Fontex and Josfina Ramirez Fontez; m. Sue J. Flatland, Sept. 1, 1992; 1 child, Robert M. 1 stepchild, Michael D. Williams; m. Bonnie Faherty (div.); stepchildren: Nancy T. Montoya, Lisa Y. Eikseth, Patrick M. Montoy. Cert., LA Trade Tech. Coll., LA Harbor Coll., El Camino Coll., Torrance, Calif., Mil. Leadership Sch., Carmel, Calif. With Howard/Winneshiek Cmty. Sch., Cresco, Iowa. Dir. Harbor Area Civic Improvement, LA; dir. city beautification City of San Pedro, Calif.; dir. law enforcement adv. coun. LA; dir. Youth Motivation Task Force, LA; mem. Harbor Area Ethnic Polit. Coalition; mayor City of Cresco, Iowa, 2002—03; ctrl. com. mem. Calif. Dem., LA County Dem.; past chmn. 32d Congl. Dist. Dem. Coun. Col. USAR, 1953—73. Mem.: VFW, United Filipino-Am. Svc. Orgn. (past pres.), Mexicn-Am. Assn., Am. Legion (2d vice comdr. #135 1973), Toastmasters (divsn. gov. 1974). Republican. Roman Catholic. Avocations: art, ballroom dancing, photography, history. Home: 604 6th Ave E Cresco IA 52136 Office: Howard/Winneshiek Cmty Sch 1000 Schroder Dr Cresco IA 52136

FONTES, MANUEL LOPES, medical educator, researcher; arrived in US, 1975; s. Charles L. Fontes and Alda S. Soares; m. Joanna T. Tavares, Nov. 27, 1982; 1 child, Monique T. BS in Biology, Tufts U., Medford, Mass., 1983; MD, U. Mass., Worcester, 1988. Diplomate Am. Bd. Anesthesiology, 1993. Resident Cornell U., NYC, 1988—92; commd. US Army, 1989, advanced through grades to lt. col., 2003; post doctoral fellow U. Calif., San Francisco, 1992—94; asst. prof. Yale U., New Haven, 1994—99; assoc. prof. anesthesiology and critical care Weill Med. Coll., Cornell U., NYC, 1999—. Co-dir. cardiothoracic icu Yale U. Sch. Medicine, New Haven, 1994—99; dir. cardiac rsch. Weill Med. Coll. Cornell U., NYC. Contbr. articles to profl. jours. Active Healing the Children, 1995—2007; fund raiser, educator, advisor Almozov Found. N.Am., New Haven, 2006—07. Decorated Army Commendation medal US Army. Fellow: Soc. Critical Care Medicine (adv. group 1999, President's Citation award 2000); mem.: Am. Soc. Anesthesiologists (spkr., presenter 1993—2007), NRCC Physician Adv. Bd. (corr. Ronald R. Gold Medal award 2005, 2006, 2007), Soc. Cardiovasc. Anesthesiologists (mem. program com. 2000—06). Achievements include first to report on pulse pressure as a better predictor of stroke, renal failure, and death in coronary bypass surgery tha systolic or distolic blood pressure; research in atrial fibrillation after cardiac surgery requiring cardiopulmonary bypass is associated with monocyte activation; multicenter risk index for atrial fibrillation after cardiac surgery. Avocations: music, sports, reading, cooking, travel. Home Phone: 212-746-0395; Office Phone: 212-746-0395. Business E-Mail: maf2029@med.cornell.edu.

FONTES, PATRICIA J., psychologist; b. Providence, Dec. 10, 1936; d. Manuel William and Sadie Elizabeth (Conceicao) Sousa F. BS in Edn., Boston U., 1957; MEd, Boston Coll., 1965, PhD, 1968. Tchr. Warwick (R.I.) pub. schs., 1957-59; religious sister/superior Sisters of Our Lady of Providence, 1959-65; asst. prof. U. R.I., Kingston, 1968-69; asst./assoc. prof. Salve Regina Coll., Newport, RI, 1969-72; cons. psychologist Girl Scouts of R.I., Inc., Providence, 1972-73; research fellow Ednl. Research Ctr., St. Patrick's Coll., Dublin, 1973-88; cons. psychologist Girl Scouts R.I., Providence, 1989-92; prof. CEFOPE/IEC U. Minho, Braga, Portugal, 1992—2003; ret. Lectr. in field. Author: Equality in Primary Teaching 1985, As Crianças como Agentes de Mudança Ambiental, 1998, Os Alunos com Necessidades Educativas Especiais, 1998; contbr. articles to profl. jours., chpts. to books. Sec. Hopkinton, RI Conservation Commn.; mem. Women's Crew, South County Habitat for Humanity, RI; activist Progressive Democrats, South County Justice and Peace Action Group. Boston U. scholar, 1953-57; Boston Coll. fellow, 1965-68; Inst. for Portuguese Lang. and Culture grantee, 1982. Mem. APA, Internat. Coun. Psychologists (sec.-gen. 1991-94), The Nature Conservancy, Internat. Wildlife Found., Nat. Wildlife Found., Girl Scouts, Pax Christi, Sierra Club. Roman Catholic. Avocations: biking, mountain walking, travel, gardening, reading, cooking. Personal E-mail: patfontes@netscape.com.

FONTES, PAULO A., surgeon, educator; b. Sao Paulo, Ala., Jan. 20, 1962; came to U.S., 1991; s. Paulo B. and Mildred (Chaves) F.; m. Monica M. Mollerstrand, Sept. 9, 1991; children: Rafaella M., Karl Liam M. MD, Sao Paulo State U., 1985. Bd. cert. gen. surgery Brazilian Coll. Surgeons; cert. transplant surgeon, Am. Soc. Transplant Surgery. Intern Sao Paulo State U. Sch. Medicine, Botucatu, Brazil, 1984-85; resident Prof. Edmundo Vasconcelos Hosp., Sao Paulo, 1986-88, mem. med. staff, 1990-91, supr. gen. surgery residents, 1990-91; rsch. fellow Sao Paulo Fed. U., 1990-91, U. Pitts. Med. Ctr., 1991-93, vis. asst. prof. surgery, 1993-96, clin. fellow, 1996-98, attending surgeon, asst. prof., 1998—, med. dir. Organ Referral Ctr., 2004—. Dir. S. & Am. divsn. U. Pitts. Med. Ctr. Overseas Inc., 1998—, assoc. prof. surgery, dir. liver transplant transplantation med. dir. Organ Referral Ctr. Contbr. articles to profl. jours. Recipient Bradesco Found. prize, 1988, 89, hon. award, Brazilian Nat. Congress; scholar Sao Paulo State Govt., 1980-85. Fellow: ACS; mem.: ACS, AMA, Internat. Liver Transplantation Soc., Transplantation Soc., Am. Soc. Transplant Surgeons, Am. Assn. Advancement of Sci., Cell Transplant Soc. (founding mem. 1991), Internat. Coll. Surgeons, Brazilian Coll. Abdominal Surgeons, Brazilian Soc. for Advancement of Sci., Brazilian Coll. Surgeons. Avocations: sailing, biking, working out, surfing. Home: 1244 Beechwood Blvd Pittsburgh PA 15206-4548 Office: U Pitts Med Ctr 725N MUH 3459 5th ave Pittsburgh PA 15213-3403 Office Phone: 412-692-4184. Office Fax: 412-692-4180.

FONVIELLE, CHARLES DAVID, lawyer; b. Melbourne, Fla., Dec. 28, 1944; s. Charles David Fonvielle Jr. and Margaret Jordan Palmer; m. Deborah Konas, July 25, 1970; children: C. Caulley, D. Jordan. BA, U. Fla., 1968; JD, Fla. State U., 1972. Bar: Fla. 1972, U.S. Dist. Ct. (no., mid. and so. dists.) Fla. Asst. pub. defender Fla. Pub. Defender Assn., Tallahassee, 1972-74; pvt. practice Tallahassee, 1974-77; ptnr. Thompson, Wadsworth, Messer, Turner & Rhodes, Tallahassee, 1977-80, Green & Fonvielle, Tallahassee, 1980-84, Green, Fonvielle & Hinkle, Tallahassee, 1984-85, Fonvielle & Hinkle, Tallahassee, 1986—94, Fonvielle Hinkle & Lewis, Tallahassee, 1995—2002, Fonvielle Lewis Foote & Messer, Tallahassee, 2002—. Bd. dirs. Fla. State U. Coll. Law, endowed prof. litigation. Mem. ATLA (sustaining), Tallahassee Bar Assn. (bd. dirs. 1978-79), Acad. Fla. Trial Lawyers (Eagle sponsor 1990—), Nat. Bd. Trial Advocacy (cert.), Fla. Bar Assn. (bd. legal specialization and edn. 1991—). Avocations: physical fitness, flying, spearfishing, sports cars. Office: Fonvielle Lewis Foote & Messer 3375 Capital Cir NE Ste A Tallahassee FL 32308-3778 Home Phone: 850-893-3626; Office Phone: 850-422-7773. E-mail: david@flfmlaw.com.

FOO, SUSANNA, chef; b. Inner Mongolia, China; arrived in US, 1967; m. E-Hsin Foo. Co-owner, chef Susanna Foo Chinese Cuisine, Philadelphia, 1987. Commencement spkr. Culinary Inst. Am., 1996. Author: Susanna Foo Chinese Cuisine, 1995, 1997, 2002, Susanna Foo Fresh Inspiration: New Approaches to Chinese Cuisine, 2005; featured chef (articles) Susanna Foo Cooking at Home, Gourmet Mag., 1998, Susanna Foo Chinese Cuisine, NY Times Mag., 1998. Named one of Finest Chef's Worldwide, Am. Acad. Hospitality Sciences, 2004; recipient Best New Chef, Food and Wine Mag., 1989, Woman of the Yr. in Food Service, Del. Valley Restaurant Assoc., 1990, Best Chinese Cook in the Country, Eating Well Mag., 1992, Internat. Cook Book award, James Beard Found., 1996, Best Chef, Mid Atlantic Region, 1997, Chef of the Yr., Internat. Food and Wine Soc., Phila. Chpt., 1996—97, 1999, 2002, Confrerie de la Chaine de Rotisseur, 1992, 1994, 1998—99, 2002. Office: Susanna Foo Chinese Cuisine 1512 Walnut St Philadelphia PA 19102 Office Phone: 215-545-2666. Office Fax: 215-546-9160. E-mail: susannafoo@susannafoo.com.*

FOOSANER, ROBERT STEPHEN, telecommunications industry executive, lawyer; b. Newark, Feb. 1, 1943; s. George and Gertrude (Rood) F.; m. Carol Baber; children: Eve, Matthew, Nellie Ann. BA, Rutgers U., 1965; JD, Washington Coll. Law, 1968. Bar: U.S. Dist. Ct. D.C. 1968, U.S. Ct. Appeals D.C. 1969. Atty. Broadcast Bur., FCC, Washington, 1968-73, atty. Office Gen. Counsel, 1973-77, supervisory atty., 1977-79, chief policy task force Office of Sci. and Tech., 1979-80, chief policy and mgmt. staff, 1980-81, dep. chief Pvt. Radio Bur., 1981-83; chief Pvt. Radio Bur., 1983-86; ptnr. Jones, Day, Reavis & Pogue, Alexandria, VA., 1986-92; sr. v.p. govt. affairs Nextel Communications, Inc., Washington, 1992—2005; sr. v.p., govt. affairs, chief regulatory officer Sprint Nextel, Reston, Va., 2005—. U.S. del. MF Broadcasting Conf., Buenos Aires, Argentina, 1980, Mobile WARC Conf., Geneva, Switzerland, 1983 Trustee Leukemia Soc. Am., Washington, 1976-82. Fellow Radio Club Am., 1985. Mem. D.C. Bar Assn., Bar Assn. D.C. Office: Sprint Nextel 2001 Edmund Halley Dr Reston VA 20191 Office Phone: 703-433-4000.*

FOOSE, CHIP, automotive designer, television personality; b. Santa Barbara, Calif., Oct. 6, 1963; s. Sam Foose; m. Lynne Foose; children: Brock, Katie. Grad., Art Ctr. Coll. Design, 1990. Staff designer, fabricator Asha Corp., 1986—89, dir., 1989; automotive designer Stehrenberger Design; chief designer, fabricator Baker Sportronics; automotive designer Project Design; with Hot Rods by Boyd, 1990—98, mng. dir., pres.; founder Foose Design, Huntington Beach, Calif., 1998—. Host (TV series) Overhaulin, 2004—. Vice chmn. Progeria Rsch. Found. Calif. Chpt. Recipient Good Guys Trendsetter award, 1998, America's Most Beautiful Roadster award, 1995, 1996, 1999, 2000, 2001, 2003, 2006, Detroit Autorama Ridler award, 2002, 2003, 2005, 7 Good Guy Streetcar of Yr. awards; inductee, Hot Rod Hall of Fame, 1997, Darryl Starbird Rod

&Custom Car Mus. Hall of Fame, 2002, Grand Nat. Roadster Show Hall of Fame, 2003, San Francisco Rod and Custom Motorcycle Hall of Fame, 2004. Office: Foose Design Inc 17811 Sampson Ln Huntington Beach CA 92647*

FOOTE, AVON EDWARD, web developer/producer, communications educator; b. Sept. 24, 1937; s. Avon Ruble and Lila Frances (Broughton) F.; m. Dorothy Veronica Gargis, Mar. 15, 1960; children: Anthony E., Kevin A., Michele. *Richard Foote, kinsman of half-brother Samuel and Samuel's son Topham of Windsor in Berkshire, settled in the 1680's in Virginia. The migration was documented in Chotankers: A Family History (Thornwood Publishers, 1982) and at Chotank.com. Family moves included: Cornwall; London; Chotank; Caswell County, North Carolina; Chester County, South Carolina; Lancaster County, South Carolina; Giles County, Tennessee; Tishomingo County, Mississippi, where Avon Ruble Foote and Lila Frances Broughton Foote resided on January 1, 2004. Chotankers reminds descendants, "To all those who came before; they make this book possible. To all those who follow; the possibility is all theirs."* Cert., NYU, 1961; BS, Florence State U., 1963; MS, U. So. Miss., 1968; PhD, Ohio State U., 1970. Announcer Sta. WJOI, Florence, Ala., 1958-60; prodn. mgr. Sta. WOWL-TV, Florence, 1960-64; advt. coord. Plough Inc., Memphis, 1964-66; faculty adviser Sta. WMSU, U. So. Miss., Hattiesburg, 1966-67; prodr.-dir. telecomm. Ohio State U., Columbus, 1967-69; assoc. prof. broadcasting U. Miss., Oxford, 1971-72; project dir. (part-time) Ohio Valley TV Sys., Columbus, 1972-74, Ohio State, 1972—74; faculty, coord. grad. studies Sch. Journalism/Mass Comm. U. Ga., Athens, 1974-80; prof. broadcasting U. North Ala., Florence, 1980—. Prof., London, 1990-91; awards judge Ohio State Awards, 1968-73; chmn. faculty screening com. Peabody Radio-TV Awards, 1976-79; jury chair NY Festivals Internat. TV awards, 2002-04; founder Worldwide Web pages including Worldserver, 1995, Web cons. chotank.com, flytheshoals.com, fasthealth.com; developer Gulf War Video Collection, 1992-2001, Libr. Am. Broadcasting, U. Md., College Park, 2002—; faculty Ohio State U., 1972-74; cons. in field. Editor: The Challenges of Educational Communications, 1970, CBS and Congress: The Selling of the Pentagon Papers, 1972, Nat. Assn. Ednl. Broadcasters Broadcasting Rev., 1969-73; author: (with Koenig and others) Broadcasting and Bargaining, 1970, Chotankers, 1982, online author: Burke's Peerage and Gentry, 2003; prodr. ednl. TV programs; editor ref. shelf materials Nat. Pub. Broadcasting Archives, U. Md., College Park, 2002; contbr. and author: www.burkes-peerage.net; contbr. articles to profl. jours. Bd. dirs. Florence YMCA, 1982-86. Recipient Cmty. Svc. award Florence Civitan Club, 1990, 1st pl. award Corp. Video Profl. Competition Nat. Broadcasting Soc., 1991, regional 1st pl. award, Nat. 3d pl. award Coll. Emmy award Hollywood Acad. TV Arts and Scsi., 1984, Honorable Mention Comedy awards Nat. Broadcasting Soc., 1987; Industry Faculty Seminar fellow Internat. Radio-TV Soc., 1987, NDEA fellow, 1967, NATAS Meml. fellow, 1970. Mem.: BBC Networking Club, Radio TV News Dirs. Assn. Republican. Anglican. Home: 222 Shirley Dr Florence AL 35633-1434 Office: Comm Bldg PO Box 5158 Florence AL 35632-0001 Office Phone: 256-765-4489. Personal E-mail: chotank@aol.com.

FOOTE, CHANDRA JEANET, education and elementary school educator, writer; b. Rochester, NY, Jan. 20, 1970; d. Theron A. and Patricia M. Foote; m. Christopher A. Robins, July 3, 1999; children Aidan M. Robins, Carson A. Robins. BS, Syracuse U., 1992, MA, 1994, PhD, 1996. Cert. in elem. edn., N.Y. Tchg. assoc. Syracuse U., NY, 1994-96; chair, prof. edn., dept. chair Niagara U., NY, 1996—. Project dir. Niagara Falls (N.Y.) Bd. Edn., 1998-99. Co-author: (book) Constructionist Teaching Practices; contbr. chpt. to books, articles to profl.jours. Leadership rep. The Higher Edn. Task Force for Quality Inclusion, N.Y. State, 1998—; cmty. rep. LaSalle Mid. Sch. Quality Coun., 2001—. Recipient Golden Apple award Niagara Falls City Sch. Dist., 1998-99, Dean's award Coll. Edn. at Niagara U., 1998; Goals 2000 grantee N.Y. State Dept. Edn., 1998-99; Office of Vocat. and Ednl. Svcs. for Individuals with Disabilities grantee, 2000, 02,03. Mem. Am. Ednl. Rsch. Assn., Assn. Tchr. Educators. Avocations: reading, travel. Office: Niagara U Dept Edn B 11 O'Shea Hall Niagara University NY 14109-2042 Office Fax: 716-286-8561. Business E-Mail: cjf@niagara.edu.

FOOTE, DOROTHY GARGIS, nursing educator; b. Sheffield, Ala., Jan. 27, 1942; d. Tracy E. and Mary Helen (Cox) Gargis; m. Avon Edward Foote, Mar. 15, 1960; children: Anthony E., Kevin A., Michele. Student, U. So. Miss., 1966-67; AS in Nursing, NW Coll., 1985; BS in Nursing, U. N. Ala., Florence, 1987; MS in Nursing, U. Ala., Huntsville, 1989; postgrad., U. North Ala., England and Scotland, 1990-91; PhD in Higher Edn. Adminstrn., Miss. State U., 2003. RN Ala., cert. family nurse practitioner, gerontol. nurse practitioner. Real estate assoc. McWaters Realty & Appraisal Co., Athens, Ga., 1977-79; acctg. clk. U. Ga., Athens, 1979-81; nursing supr., nurse practitioner Mitchell Hollingworth Annex Eliza Coffee Meml. Hosp., Florence, 1985-92; v.p. Thornwood Books, Florence, 1982-93; instr. N.W. CC, Phil Campbell, Ala., 1992-93; asst. prof. U. Ala., Huntsville, 1993—; nurse practitioner N. Ala. Clinics, 2002—. Rsch. dir. Leadership Long Term Care, 1995—; co-donor Gulf War video collection U. Md., College Park, 2002; prin. investigator LTC Nursing Adminstr. Ednl. Needs, 2004; faculty chair health fair U. Ala. Coll. Nursing Faculty Coun., Huntsville, 2001—, chair health fair, 2003—06; prof. studies abroad U. Ala., London, 2006—. Editor: (newsletter) Dames Digest, 1970. Pres. Band Boosters, Athens, 1976. Mem.: ANA, Am. Assn. Colls. Nursing (Elnec Grad. award 2007), Advanced Practice Council (chair 1999—2001), Ala. State Nurses Assn. (pres. dist. 1 1989—92, bd. dirs. 1989—92, chair gerontol. coun. 1992—93), Phi Theta Kappa, Beta Sigma Phi, Sigma Theta Tau (Beta Phi chpt. pres 2002—04). Home: 222 Shirley Dr Florence AL 35633-1434 Office Phone: 256-824-2439. Business E-Mail: footed@uah.edu.

FOOTE, EDWARD THADDEUS, II, academic administrator, lawyer; b. Milw., Dec. 15, 1937; s. William Hamilton and Julia Stevenson (Hardin) F.; m. Roberta Waugh Fulbright, Apr. 18, 1964; children: Julia, William, Thaddeus. BA, Yale U., 1959; LLB, Georgetown U., 1966; LLD (hon.), Washington U., St. Louis, 1981, Barry U., 1991; degree (hon.), Tokai U., Tokyo, 1984; LLD (hon.), Barry U., 1991. Bar: Mo. 1966. Reporter Washington Star, 1963-64, Washington Daily News, 1964-65; exec. asst. to chmn. Pa. Ave. Commn., Washington, 1965-66; assoc. Bryan, Cave, McPheeters & McRoberts, St. Louis, 1966-70; vice chancellor, gen. counsel, sec. to bd. trustees Washington U., St. Louis, 1970-73, dean Sch. Law, 1973-80, spl. adv. to chancellor and bd. trustees, 1980-81; pres. U. Miami, Coral Gables, Fla., 1981—2001, chancellor, 2001—. Mem. exec. com., bd. dirs. Am. Coun. Edn., 1986-88; chmn. citizens com. for sch. desegregation, St. Louis, 1980; chmn. desegregation monitoring and adv. com., St. Louis, 1980-81. Author: An Educational Plan for Voluntary Cooperation Desegregation of School in the St. Louis Met. area, 1981 Mem. Coun. on Fgn. Rels.; founding pres. bd. New City Sch., St. Louis, 1967-73; mem. gov.'s task force on reorganization State of Mo., 1973-74, steering com., chmn. governance com. Mo. Gov.'s Conf. on Edn., UN Assn. Greater St. Louis chpt., 1977-79, adv. com. Naval War Coll., 1979-82, Fla. Coun. of 100, Southern Fla. Metro-Miami Action Plan, exec. com. Miami Citizens Against Crime; founding chmn. Miami Coalition for a Drug Free Community, 1988—. Recipient Order of Sun (Peru). Democrat. Office: U Miami PO Box 248006 Miami FL 33124-8006

FOOTE, EVELYN PATRICIA, retired military officer; b. Durham, NC, May 19, 1930; d. Henry Alexander and Evelyn Sevena (Womack) Foote. BA summa cum laude, Wake Forest U., 1953, LLD (hon.), 1989; student, U.S. Army Command & Gen. Staff Coll., Leavenworth, Kans., 1971-72, U.S. Army War Coll., Carlisle, Pa., 1976-77; MS in Govt. and Pub. Affairs, Shippensburg State U., 1977; student, U. Va. Sch. Bus. Adminstrn., 1980. Commd. 1st lt. U.S. Army, 1960, advanced through grades to brig. gen., 1986, platoon officer WAC Ft. McClellan, Ala., 1960-61, selection officer 6th recruiting dist. Portland, Oreg., 1961-64; comdr. WAC Co. U.S. Army Engr. Brigade, Ft. Belvoir, Va., 1964-66; student Adj. Gen. Officer Advanced Course, Ft. Benjamin Harrison, Ind., 1966; exec. officer, chief adminstrv. div. pub. affairs office U.S. Army, Vietnam, 1967; exec. officer, office personnel ops. WAC, Washington, 1968-71, plans and programs officer OFC, dir., 1972-74; personnel mgmt. officer U.S. Army Forces Command, Ft. McPherson, Ga., 1974-76; comdr. 2d basic tng. bn. U.S. Army Tng. Brigade and Military Police Sch., Ft. McClellan, Ala., 1977-79; faculty mem. U.S. Army War Coll., 1979-82; student Fgn. Service Inst., Dept. of State, Washington, 1982-83; comdr. 42d Mil. Police Group, Mannheim, Fed. Republic of Germany, 1983-85; spl. asst. to comdg. gen. 32d Army Air Def. Command Hdqrs., Darmstadt, Fed. Republic of Germany, 1985-86; dep., insp. gen. for inspections Hdqrs. Dept. of the Army, Washington, 1986-88; dep. comdg. gen. Mil. Dist. Washington, comdr. Ft. Belvoir, Va., 1988-89; ret. U.S. Army, 1989, recalled to active duty Sr. Rev. Panel, 1996-97, ret., 1997. Lectr. various U.S. Army and civilian groups. Contbr. articles to mil. jours. and books. Mem. Am Battle Monuments Commn., 1994—2001; bd. visitors Wake Forest U., 1991—2003, chmn. bd. visitors, 2001—03; trustee Fund for Peace, 2002—; bd. dirs. U.S. Army Women's Mus. Found., 1995—2005. Decorated DSM, Legion of Merit with oak leaf clusters, German Cross of Svc. 1st class; named Spokesperson of the Yr., Dept. Army, 1997—98; named to Disting. Fellows Hall of Fame, U.S. Army War Coll., 1996, Regimental Hall of Fame, U.S. Army MP Corps, 1998; recipient Disting. Pub. Svc. award, Wake Forest U., 1987, DSM, Am. Battle Monuments Commn., 2001. Mem.: Vets. United For Truth (bd. dirs.). Democrat. Lutheran. Avocations: music, reading, hiking.

FOOTE, GWENDOLYN SUE, middle school educator, artist; b. Oklahoma City, Apr. 9, 1953; d. John Thurman and Dorothy Clow Foote; 1 child, Shawn Robert Scarbrough. BS in Biomed. Sci., Tex. A&M U., 1975; MA in Interdisciplinary Studies, U. Tex., 1985; BS in Elem. Edn. and Spl. Edn., Oglala Lakota Coll., Pine Ridge Indian Reservation, SD, 2004. Registered med. technologist; cert. tchr. Spl. edn. tchr., Miami Beach, Fla., 2006; owner Foote Fine Art Studio, 1983—97; supr. med. tech. St. Joseph's Hosp., Denver, 1988—90, St. Mary's Hosp., Tucson, 1990—91; tchr. Little Wound Sch., Pine Ridge Indian Reservation, SD, 2001—05; instr. dept. edn. Oglala Lakota Coll., 2003—05; tchr. 8th grade sci. Nautilus Middle Sch., Miami Beach, Fla., 2006—; instr. Johns Hopkins U. Ctr. Talented Youth, 2006—07. Instr. Johns Hopkins U., Balt., 2006—07, Ctr. for Talented Youth; ednl. del. to Egypt People to People Internat., amb., 2007; spkr. in field. Exhibitions include, Dallas, Denver, Las Vegas, L.A., 1985—95, Australia, France, Ireland, Universal Studios, UNESCO, 1994 (Royal Rainer Family award, 1995), Human Civil Rights, Namibia, Africa; mem. rev. bd.: Science Scope Mag., 2006—. Rehabilitator Fed. Fish and Wildlife, Tex., 1983—87. Recipient award, Pediat. AIDS Soc., 1992, Recognition award, Oglala Lakota Tribe, 2004, 2005;, Toshiba NASA ednl. grantee, 2005. Mem.: Am. Med. Tech. Soc., Tex. A&M U. Former Students, Internat. Sr. Citizens Assn. (v.p. 1994—97), Nat. Sci. Tchrs. Assn. Avocations: travel, hiking, writing, music, art. Office: Nautilus Middle Sch 4301 N Michigan Ave Miami Beach FL 33140 Office Phone: 305-532-3481. Personal E-mail: gwendolyn00@excite.com.

FOOTE, HORTON, playwright, scriptwriter; b. Wharton, Tex., Mar. 14, 1916; s. Albert Horton and Hallie (Brooks) Foote; m. Lillian Vallish, June 4, 1945; children: Barbara Hallie, Albert Horton, Walter Vallish, Daisy Brooks. Student, Pasadena Playhouse Sch. Theatre, Calif., 1933-35, Tamara Daykarhanova Sch. Theatre, NYC, 1937-39. Actor, NYC, 1939-42; mgr. prodn. co. Productions Inc., Washington, 1942-45; vis. disting. dramatist Baylor U., 2002—. Tchr. playwriting. Author: (plays) The Chase, 1956, (screenplays) Storm Fear, 1956, To Kill a Mockingbird, 1962 (Academy award best screenplay, 1962, Writers Guild Am. award, 1962), Baby, The Rain Must Fall, 1965, Hurry Sundown, 1966, Tomorrow, 1971, Tender Mercies, 1983 (Academy award best screenplay, 1983), 1918, 1984, On Valentine's Day, 1985, The Trip to Bountiful, 1985 (Academy Award nomination best screenplay, 1985), Spring Moon, 1987, Convicts, 1991, Of Mice and Men, 1992, (plays) Texas Town, Out of My House, 1942, Only The Heart, 1944, Celebration, 1948, The Chase, 1952, The Trip to Bountiful, The Midnight Caller, 1953, A Young Lady of Property, 1954, The Traveling Lady, The Roads to Home, 1955, Harrison, Texas: Eight Television Plays, 1959, Tomorrow, 1960, Three Plays, Roots in a Parched Ground, 1962, Getting Frankie Married.and Afterward, 2002—, (musical adaption) Gone with the Wind, 1971, The Road to the Graveyard, 1985, Blind Date, 1986, Selected One Act Plays of Horton Foote, Habitation of Dragons, 1988, Dividing the Estate, 1989, Talking Pictures, 1990, Horton Foote: Four New Plays, 1994, The Young Man From Atlanta, 1994 (Pulitzer Prize for drama, 1995), Night Seasons, Laura Dennis, Talking Pictures, 1994, The Carpetbagger's Children, also (play series) The Orphans' Home Cycle, 2001, The Last of the Thorntons, 2002, (TV films) Only The Heart, 1947, Ludie Brooks, 1951, The Travelers, 1952, The Old Beginning, The Trip to Bountiful, Midnight Caller, John Turner Davis, Young Lady of Property, The Oil Well, Rocking Chair, Expectant Relations, Death of the Old Man, Tears of My Sister, 1953, The Shadow of Wilie Greer, The Dancers, 1954, The Roads to Home, 1955, Flight, 1956, Drugstore: Sunday Noon, 1956, Member of the Family, Traveling Lady, 1957, Old Man, 1959, Tomorrow, 1960, 1971, The Shape of the River, 1960, The Night of the Storm, 1961, Gambling Heart, 1964, The Displaced Person, 1977, Barn Burning, 1980, Keeping On, 1983, The Habitation of Dragons, 1992, Mr. and Mrs. Loving, 1996; dir.: When They Speak of Rita, 2000. Recipient Evelyn Burkey award Writer's Guild, 1989, Nat. medal of Arts, 2000.

FOOTE, NATHAN MAXTED, retired physical science educator; b. Woodlawn, Pa., Oct. 8, 1913; s. Myron Tinkham and Ada May (Maxted) F.; m. Laura Belle Gruey, Sept. 5, 1936 (dec. June 2001); children: Jonathan W., L. Nadine, Frances C., Willard G. AB, DePauw U., 1935; MS, Purdue U., 1939. Jr. chemist U.S. FDA, Phila., 1939-40; Rsch. engr. RCA, Camden, NJ, 1940-49; rsch. scientist Colgate Palmolive, Jersey City, 1950-52; rheologist B.F. Goodrich Chem. Co., Avon Lake, Ohio, 1953-58; acting head, Dept. Physics Baldwin Wallace Coll., Berea, Ohio, 1958-60; vis. asst. prof. Physics Pa. State U., University Park, 1960-61, asst. prof. Physics, Behrend Coll. Erie, 1964-78, ret., 1979; assoc. prof. Phys. Sci. SUNY, Geneseo, 1961-64. Author: Industrial and Engineering Chemistry, 1944, rev. edit., 1947. Del. Ohio Coun. Am. Bapt. Men, 1955-58. Mem.: AAAS, Am. Chem. Soc. (50 Yr. award 1993), Sigma Xi. Avocation: stratospheric chemical change. Home: Elyria United Methodist Village 807 W Ave Apt 5309 Elyria OH 44035-9204

FOOTE, PAUL SHELDON, business educator, administrator, consultant; b. Lansing, Mich., May 22, 1946; s. Harlon Sheldon and Frances Norene (Rotter) Foote; m. Badri Seddigheh Hosseinian, Oct. 25, 1968; children: David, Sheila. BBA, U. Mich., 1967; MBA, Harvard U., 1971, postgrad, 1971—72, New Eng. Sch. Law, 1971—72; PhD, Mich. State U., 1983. Advanced prof. cert. NYU, 1975. Br. mgr., divisional mgr. Citibank, NYC, 1972—74, Bombay, 1972—74, Beirut, 1972—74; mgr. planning and devel. Singer Co. Africa/Middle East, 1974—75; lectr. acctg. Mich. State U., East Lansing, 1977; instr. U. Mich., Flint, 1978—79; asst. prof. U. Windsor, Ont., Canada, 1979—81, Oakland U., Rochester, Mich., 1982—83, NYU, 1983—87; assoc. prof. Saginaw Valley State U., University Center, Mich., 1981—82, Pepperdine U., Malibu, Calif., 1987—89; prof. Sultan Qaboos U., Muscat, Oman, 1994—96; assoc. dean Chapman U., 2004—05; prof. dept. acctg. Coll. Bus. and Econs., Calif. State U., Fullerton, 1989—. Lectr. Chapman U., 1998, U. Calif., Irvine, 2004; vis. prof. U. Wash., Seattle, 1999—2000; cons., spkr. in field. Mem. editl. bd. Jour. Bus. Forecasting, 1983—; author: Corporate Profitability: Determinants and Forecasts, 1983; contbr. articles to jour. Lt. AUS, 1968—69, Vietnam. Loomis-Sayles fellow, Harvard U., Doctoral Consortium fellow, Haskins and Sells, 1977. Mem.: Inst. Bus. Forecasting, Am. Acctg. Assn. Achievements include research in biometrics, information security, and automatic identification using SAP R/3 and bioLock (realtime North America). Office: Calif State U Dept Acctg PO Box 6848 800 N State Coll Fullerton CA 92834-6848 Office Phone: 714-278-2682. Personal E-mail: pfoote@mba1971.hbs.edu. Business E-Mail: pfoote@fullerton.edu.

FOOTE, ROBERT HUTCHINSON, medical educator; b. Gilead, Conn., Aug. 20, 1922; s. Robert E. and Annie (Hutchinson) F.; m. Ruth E. Parcells, Jan. 12, 1946 (dec. Jan. 1992); children: Robert W., Dale H.; m. Barbara J. Johnson, Sept. 25, 1993. BS, U. Conn., 1943; MS, Cornell U., 1947, PhD Animal Physiology/Biochem. Genetics, 1950. Grad. asst. Cornell U., Ithaca, NY, 1946-50, asst. prof. animal physiology, 1950-56, assoc. prof., 1956-63, prof., 1963-93, Jacob Gould Schurman chair, 1980-93; emeritus, 1993—. Mem. study sect. NIH, 1974-78; cons. Shell Oil, 1985-89, EPA, 1988-96; program mgr. USDA competitive grants, 1986-87. Author: Animal Reproduction, 1954, AI to Cloning, 1998; mem. editl. bds. 5 jours., 1958-96, Cloning, 1999-2002, Reproductive Physiology, 1992-99, Cryobiology, 1991-94; contbr. some 500 articles to profl. jours., chpts. to books. Chmn. trustees Congregation Ch., Ithaca, 1955-60. Served to capt. inf. US Army 1943-46, ETO. Recipient Sci. medal NY Farmers, 1969, Nat. Physiology and Endocrinology award Am. Soc. Animal Sci., 1970, SUNY Chancellor award, 1980, Superior Svc. award USDA, 1988, Alumni Merit award U. Conn., 1996, Casida Physiology Reprodn. award, 1991, JSPS award, 1996, CALS Alumni Outstanding Faculty award, 2003, Outstanding Alumnus award U. Conn., 2005; named hon. prof. Beijing Agrl. U., 1995. Fellow: AAAS; mem.: Internat. Embryo Transfer Soc. (Pioneer Biotech. award 2002), Am. Soc. Theriogenology (editl. bd. 1976—89, Robert H. Foote Symposium in his honor 1992), Am. Soc. Andrology (editl. bd. 1982—88, Outstanding Andrologist 1984, Upjohn physiology award 1985), Nat. Assn. Animal Breeders (Physiology award 1970), Soc. Study Reprodn. (bd. dirs. 1976—78, pres. 1985, Hartman Lifetime Rsch. award 2000, Pioneer award 2007), Am. Dairy Sci. Assn. (spkr.), Gamma Sigma Delta, Phi Kappa Phi, Sigma Xi. Republican. Home: 474 Savage Farm Dr Ithaca NY 14850-6508 Office: Cornell U Dept Animal Sci 204 Morrison Hall Ithaca NY 14853-4801 Business E-Mail: rhf4@cornell.edu.

FOOTE, WARREN EDGAR, neuroscientist, psychologist, educator; b. Boston, Nov. 5, 1935; s. Warren Edgar and Edith Irene Foote; m. Cynthia Sue Hall, July 21, 1973; children: Pamela Fowler, Sarah Canby, Julia Landry, Christopher Warren. BA, Hamilton Coll., 1958; MA, Boston U., 1960; PhD, Tufts U., Medford, Mass., 1965. Rsch. assoc. Harvard U. Med. Sch., 1966—67, vis. asst. prof. psychology, 1970—73, asst. prof., 1974—83, assoc. prof., 1983—. USPHS postdoctoral fellow Yale U., 1967—69; rsch. scientist Norwich State Hosp., Conn., 1969—70; sr. Fulbright scholar Max-Planck Inst., Munich, 1973—74; assoc. pscyologist Mass. Gen. Hosp., Boston, 1974—, psychologist, 1984—95, sr. psychologist, 1995—; cons. Gen. Foods Corp., 1970—74, Neurotech Corp., 1987—88; advisor Wayland Pub. Sch. Found., 1982—. Contbr. articles and revs. to profl. jours. With M.C. US Army, 1959—60. Recipient McCurdy prize, Mass. Soc. Rsch. in Psychiatry, 1962; fellow Sr. Fulbright fellow, 1973—74; grantee Nat. Inst. Neurol. Disease and Stroke grantee, 1974—77, NIMH grantee, 1970—73, Nat. Eye Inst. grantee, 1979—, Nat. Inst. Communicative Disorders and Stroke grantee, 1983—. Mem.: AAAS, APA, Soc. Neurosci., N.Y. Acad. Sci., Harvard Club (Boston), Sigma Xi. Home: 5 Hilltop Park Wilbraham MA 01095-1753 Office: Mass Gen Hosp PO Box 70 Boston MA 02114 Office Phone: 617-726-3832. Business E-Mail: wfoote@partners.org.

FOOTE, WAYNE C., military officer; s. Warren C. and Will Eva Foote; m. Ruth Y. Foote, July 1, 1989; children: Audrey K., Eva A. MS, Air Force Inst. Tech., Wright-Patterson AFB, Ohio, 1986. Commd. 2d lt. USAF, 1981, advanced through grades to col., 2004, dir. internat. affairs Air Force Security Assistance Ctr. Wright-Patterson AFB, 2002—05, B-2 sys. support mgr. Tinker Air Logistics Ctr. Tinker AFB, Okla., 2005—. Named USAF Logistics Plans Sr. Mgr. of Yr., USAF, 1999. Republican. Avocations: swimming, running, Bible study, homeschooling. Office: 556 ACSS/CC 7180 Reserve Rd Bldg 1083 Tinker AFB OK 73145-8760

FOOTE, WILLIAM CHAPIN, manufacturing executive; b. Milw., Mar. 15, 1951; s. Peter Chapin and Mary Jane (Manierre) F.; m. Kari H. Foote, July 27, 1969; children: Tracy, Leslie Suzanne. BA, Williams Coll., 1973; MBA, Harvard U., 1977. Asst. treas. Chase Manhattan Bank, NYC, 1973-75; sr. engagement mgr. McKinsey & Co., Inc., Chgo., 1977-83; v.p. USG Corp., Chgo., 1984-94, pres., COO, 1994-99; pres. CEO L&W, USG Interiors Inc., 1994, chmn., pres., CEO, 1996-2000; chmn. bd., pres., CEO USG Corp., Chgo., 1999—2005, chmn., CEO, 2005—. Mem.: Economics Chgo.*

FOOTMAN, GORDON ELLIOTT, educational administrator; b. LA, Oct. 10, 1927; s. Arthur Leland and Meta Fay (Neal) F.; m. Virginia Rose Footman, Aug. 7, 1954; children: Virginia, Patricia, John. BA, Occidental Coll., 1951, MA, 1954; EdD, U. So. Calif., 1972. Tchr., Arcadia, Calif., 1952, Glendale, Calif., 1956; psychologist Burbank (Calif.) Schs., 1956-64, supr., 1964-70, dir. pupil pers. svcs., 1970-72; dir. divsn. ednl. support svcs. L.A. County Office Edn., Downey, Calif., 1972-91; cons. ednl. adminstrn., counseling and psychol. svcs., 1991—. Pres. Calif. Assn. Adult Devel. and Aging, 1994-95; lectr. ednl. psychology U. So. Calif., 1972-75, asst. prof. ednl. psychology, 1976-85. Pres. Coun. for Exceptional Children, 1969-70; pres. Burbank Coordinating Coun., 1969-70; mem. Burbank Family Svc. Bd., 1972-72. Served with AUS, 1945-47. Mem. ACA (senator 1983-86, gov. coun. 1989-93, exec. com. 1990-93, parliamentarian 1991-92, western region br. assembly publs. editor 1985-87, chair 1988-89, chair bylaws com. 1995-97), Am. Ednl. Rsch. Assn., Am. Assn. Humanistic Edn. and Devel. (bd. dirs., treas. 1996—), Calif. Assn. for Counseling & Devel. (pres. 1981-82, exec. coun. 1996—. bylaws chair 2000--), Calif. Assn. for Counseling and Devel. Found., Nat. Assn. Pupil Pers. Adminstrs., Calif. Assn. Pupil Pers. Adminstrs. (monograph editor 1977-80), Calif. Assn. Counselor Educators and Suprs. (trustee), Calif. Soc. Ednl. Program Auditors and Evaluators (sec. 1975-76, v.p. 1976-77, pres.), Calif. Assn. Measurement and Evaluation in Counseling and Devel. (sec. 1976, pres. 1979-80, 96-97, pres. 1997-98, cons. ednl. and pupil svcs. adminstrn. 1991—), Calif. Inst. Tech. Assocs., Assn. Humanistic Edn. and Devel. (bd. dirs. 1996-99, treas. 1996—, pres. 2000-2001, conv. coord. 1999--), Huntington Libr. Soc. Fellows, Phi Delta Kappa, Phi Beta Kappa, Phi Alpha Theta, Psi Chi. Republican. Presbyterian. Home and Office: 1259 Sherwood Rd San Marino CA 91108-1816

FORAN, JESSICA LEA, veterinary technician, educator; b. Spring Lake, NJ, Apr. 7, 1979; d. Joseph Foran and Monica Galasetti-DAgostino. AS in Sci., Midlands Tech. Coll., Columbia, SC, 2001; BS in Forensic Studies, U. Balt., 2006; MS in Forensic Studies, Villa Julie Coll., Stevenson, Md., 2007. Emergency vet. technician Emergency Animal Hosp., Ellicott City, Md., 2002—; internship Crime Scene Unit, Balt., 2005—06. Student rotations MSP forensic divsn. Balt. County Forensic Dept., Owings Mills, 2006—; tchrs. asst. gen. chemistry lab. Villa Julie Coll., Stevenson, Md., 2006—; tchrs. asst. serology U. Balt., 2006. Mem.: Am. Acad. Forensic Sci. (assoc.), Internat. Assn. Bloodstain Pattern Analysts (assoc.), Internat. Assn. Identification (assoc.), Alpha Chi (assoc.). Personal E-mail: jessica.foran@gmail.com.

FORBATH, WILLIAM E., law educator; b. 1952; AB, Harvard U., 1974; BA, Cambridge U., 1976; JD, Yale U., 1983, PhD, 1992. Law clk. to Hon.

Louis H. Pollak, Phila., 1981-82; instr. Am. studies Yale U., 1983-84; acting prof. UCLA, 1984-89, prof. law, 1989—; prof. U. Tex. Sch. Law, Austin, Tex. Editl. bds. of law & hist. ABA Found.; vis. prof. Columbia Law Sch., 2001—02. Author: Law and the Shaping of the Am. Labor Movement, 1991, Social and Economic Rights in the Am. Grain, 2007; co-author: The Nixon Years, 1976. Bd. dirs. Am. Soc. Legal Hist., Tex. Low Income Housing Svcs., Other Pub. Interest Orgns. Golieb fellow in legal history NYU, 1982-83. Office: U Tex Sch Law 727 E Dean Keeton St Austin TX 78705 Office Phone: 512-232-1326. Office Fax: 512-471-6988. Business E-Mail: wforbath@mail.law.utexas.edu.

FORBES, ALFRED DEAN, religious studies researcher; b. Pomona, Calif., Mar. 2, 1941; s. Paul Edward and Lela Irene Forbes; m. Ellen Moss, May 8, 1971. BA in Physics, Harvard Coll., 1962; MDiv, Pacific Sch. Religion, 1969. With U.S. Peace Corps, Nigeria, 1962—64; prin. med. dept. scientist Hewlett-Packard Labs., Palo Alto, Calif., 1971—98; vis. scholar U. Calif., San Diego, 1999—2002. Vis. scholar Stanford (Calif.) U., 1986-89, U. Calif., Berkeley, 2003—05; adj. prof. Jewish studies Pa. State U., 1998-2003; lectr. Assn. Internat. Bible et Informatique, 2000; charter mem. Bibl. Colloquium West, 2002—; adv. bd. Turgama, Leiden U. Author: (with F.I. Andersen) Spelling in the Hebrew Bible, 1986, The Vocabulary of the Old Testament, 1989; (with F.I. Andersen and D.N. Freedman) Studies in Hebrew and Aramaic Orthography, 1992; co-creator: Andersen-Forbes text and phrase marker analysis of the Hebrew Bible, 2006; co-editor: Foundations for Syriac Lexicography, 2005, others; algorithms editor Jour. Clin. Monitoring and Computing, 1985-2001; contbr. articles to profl. jours. Trustee, v.p. Whitney Edn. Found., Los Altos, Calif., 1981—88. Mem. Soc. Bibl. Lit., IEEE (sr. mem.), Internat. Brotherhood of Magicians (Order of Merlin). Avocations: travel, magic. Home: 820 Loma Verde Ave Palo Alto CA 94303-4112 Personal E-mail: adforbes@ix.netcom.com.

FORBES, BRIAN L., lawyer; BA, Univ. Calif., Berkeley, 1970; JD, Univ. Calif., Hastings, 1974. Bar: Calif. 1974, Tex., US Dist. Ct. (so. dist. Calif.) 1974, US Dist. Ct. (no. dist. Calif.) 1989, US Ct. Appeals (9th cir.) 1990, US Tax Ct. 1989, US Supreme Ct. 1980. Gen. counsel Gray Cary & Freidenrich, 1999—2004; profl. responsibility ptnr. DLA Piper Rudnick Gray Cary, San Diego, 2005—. Mem.: Thurston Soc., Order of the Coif. Office: DLA Piper Rudnick Gray Cary Suite 1100 4365 Executive Dr San Diego CA 92121 Office Phone: 858-638-6842. Office Fax: 858-677-1401. Business E-Mail: brian.forbes@dlapiper.com.

FORBES, CHRISTOPHER (KIP FORBES), publisher; b. Morristown, NJ, Dec. 5, 1950; s. Malcolm Stevenson and Roberta Remsen (Laidlaw) F.; m. Baroness Astrid Cornelia Mathilde Von Heyl Zu Herrnsheim, Sept. 7, 1974; 1 child, Charlotte Adelaide Mathilde. BA in Art History magna cum laude, Princeton U., NJ, 1972; LHD (hon.), NH Coll., Manchester, 1986. Curator Forbes Mag. Collection, NYC, 1970-80; ad salesman Forbes Mag., NYC, 1972-76, assoc. pub., v.p., 1978-89, sec., 1981-92, vice-chmn., corp. sec., 1989—, also dir. Pub. Nineteenth Century, Phila., 1976-78. Author books and catalogues, including: Victorians in Togas, Paintings by Sir Lawrence Alma-tadem from the Collection of Allen Funt, 1973; the Royal Academy (1836-1901) Revisited, 1975; (with Margaret Kelly) War a la Mode: Meisonier Detaille, de Neuville, and Berne-Bellecour, 1975; (with Hermione Waterfield) Faberge: Imperial Eggs and Other Fantasies, 1978; (with Dr. Armand Hammer) Faberge Eggs, 1980, (with Susan Casteras) Victorian Childhood, 1986; editor: Masterpieces from the House of Faberge, 1984, (with Robyn Trommeur Brenner) Faberge, 2000. Active Cultural and Hist. Commn. Somerset County, N.J., 1984-96; bd. dirs. Newark Mus., Prince of Wales Found.; vice-chmn., bd. advisers Princeton U. Art Mus., N.J., Bklyn. Mus. Art, Victorian Soc.; nat. trustee Balt. Mus. Art; chmn. bd. trustees Am. Friends of the Louvre; formed Nat. Jewelry Inst. Decorated assoc. knight Venerable Order St. John Jerusalem. Mem. Grolier Club, Nat. Arts Club, Salmagundi Club, Century Club. Republican. Episcopalian. Office: Forbes Inc 60 5th Ave New York NY 10011-8882 Business E-Mail: cforbes@forbes.com.

FORBES, DANIEL MERRILL, minister; b. Savannah, Ga., June 20, 1954; s. Marion and Mary Edna (Godbee) F.; m. Wanda Iris Rosa, Sept. 25, 1977; children: Daniel Felix, Amanda Iris. BA in Theology, So. Coll., Tenn., 1977; MA in Counselor Edn., U. South Fla., 1988, EdS, 1992; EdD in Counseling Psychology, Argosy U., 2004. Ordained to ministry 7th Day Adventist Ch., 1982; cert. cognitive behavior therapist, lic. mental health counselor, cert. Nat. Cert. Counselor, family life educator, family mediator Fla. Supreme Ct. Min. Fla. Conf. of Seventh-day Adventists, Orlando, 1977—. Cons. in field. Democrat. Seventh-day Adventist. Avocations: music, reading, nature, walking. Office: Univ Seventh Day Adventist Ch 9191 University Blvd Orlando FL 32817-1704 Office Phone: 407-657-4696. Business E-Mail: dmforbes1@earthlink.net. *Life, both temporal and eternal, is a gift of God to mankind. It is in our physical life that we are to prepare to partake of the eternal life. I think that the wise man, Solomon, said it best in Eccl. 12:13 when he wrote of the purpose of man's life and said, "Let us hear the conclusion of the whole matter: Fear God keep His commandments, for this is the whole duty of man".*

FORBES, DAVID CRAIG, musician; b. Seattle, Feb. 12, 1938; s. Douglas James and Ruby A. (Niles) F.; m. Sylvia Sterling, Aug. 29, 1965 (div. Apr. 1973); 1 child, Angela Rose. Grad., USN Sch. Music, 1957; student, Western Wash. U., 1960-64. Prin. horn La Jolla (Calif.) Civic Orch., 1958-60, Seattle Worlds Fair Band, 1962, Seattle Opera Co., 1964—, Pacific Northwest Ballet, Seattle, 1964—; asst. prin. horn Seattle Symphony Orch., 1964—2003, ret., 2003; prin. horn Pacific Northwest Wagner Fest., Seattle, 1975—. Instr. horn Western Wash. State U., 1969-81, Cornish Inst., Seattle, 1964-78. Served with USN, 1956-60. Mem. NARAS, Internat. Horn Soc. Avocations: piano, golf, fishing. Home: 9050 15th Ave NW # 2 Seattle WA 98117-3429 E-mail: DavidForbes@webtv.net.

FORBES, DORSEY CONNORS, commentator, journalist; b. Chgo. d. William J. and Sarah (MacLain) C.; m. John E. Forbes; 1 dau., Stephanie. BA cum laude, U. Ill. Fl. reporter WGN-TV Rep. Nat. Conv., Chgo., Dem. Nat. Conv., LA, 1960. Conducted: Personality Profiles, WGN-TV, Chgo., 1948-49, Dorsey Connors Show, WMAQ-TV, Chgo., 1949-58, 61-63, Armchair Travels, WMAQ-TV, 1952-55, Homeshow, NBC,1954-57, NBC Today Show, Dorsey Connors program, WGN, 1958-61, Tempo Nine, WGN-TV, 1961, Society in Chgo, WMAQ-TV, 1964; writer: column Hi! I'm Dorsey Connors, Chgo. Sun Times, 1965—; Author: Gadgets Galore, 1953, Save Time, Save Money, Save Yourself, 1972, Helpful Hints for Hurried Homemakers, 1988. Founder Ill. Epilepsy League; mem. woman's bd. Children's Home and Aid Soc., mem. women's bd. USO. Named one of Am.'s Outstanding Irish Am. Women, World of Hibernia mag., 1995. Mem. AFTRA, NATAS (Silver Cir. award 1995), SAG, Mus. Broadcast Comm. (founding mem.), Soc. Midland Authors, Chgo. Hist. Soc. (guild com., costume com.), Chi Omega. Roman Catholic. Office: Chicago Sun Times 350 N Orleans St Ste 1270 Chicago IL 60654-2148

FORBES, GEORGE NEAL, minister; b. Richmond, Ky., Sept. 9, 1946; s. Howard Neal and Virginia McKinney Forbes; m. Phyllis Ann Ewen, Dec. 31, 1998; 1 child, Bryan Neal. BA in Psychology, U. Ga., Athens, 1967; MA in Counseling, U. Cin., 1968; BS, Cin. Bible Sem., 1968; D in Ministry, Christian Bible Coll. and Sem., Independence, Mo., 2006. Lic. counselor Ark., Ky. Owner, counselor Omega Svc., Ltd., Rogual, Ark., 1971—88, Lexington, Ky., 1988—2002; minister Rose Hill Christian Ch., Va., 2002—05, First Christian Ch., Aberdeen, Miss., 2005—. Presenter in field. Capt. USMC, 1969—70, Vietnam. Office: First Christian Ch College Pl at Hickory St Aberdeen MS 39730

FORBES, GORDON MAXWELL, sportswriter, commentator; b. Bellport, NY, Feb. 6, 1930; s. Harlow Campbell and Grace Bain (DeVall) F.; m. June Lolita Cassidy, July 16, 1960 (dec. Jan. 1994); children— James Douglas, Christopher Bryan BA in English, Duke U., 1955. Sports writer Fla. Times Union, Jacksonville, 1957-62; pro-football writer Phila. Inquirer, 1962-82; pro-football editor USA Today, McLean, Va., 1982—2002; sports commentator Home Box Office Cable TV, 1988, Sta. WIP Radio, Phila., 1992-95. Corr. Sports Illustrated, N.Y.C., 1963-89; selector Pro Football Hall of Fame, Canton, Ohio, 1975-87. Author: How to Win at the Trotters, 1966, Tales from the Eagles Sidelines, 2002; contbr. numerous articles to jours. and mags. Served to cpl. U.S. Army, 1952-54 Recipient Dick McCann award for outstanding pro football coverage, 1988; named to Suffolk County (N.Y.) Sports Hall of Fame, 2001. Mem. Duke U. Alumni Assn., Pro Football Writers of Am. Republican. Episcopalian. Avocations: jogging, tennis, weightlifting, thoroughbred horses (with Write Stuff Stable). Home and Office: USA Today 5 Summerlawn Dr Lakewood NJ 08701-7542 Office Phone: 732-477-4740. Personal E-mail: gmforbes30@aol.com.

FORBES, JAMES RANDY, congressman; b. Chesapeake, Va., Feb. 17, 1952; m. Shirley Forbes, 1978; 4 children. BA, Randolph-Macon Coll., Ashland, Va., 1974; LLB, U. Va. Sch. Law, Charlottesville, 1977. Lawyer pvt. practice; mem. Va. State Ho. Dels., 1989—97, Va. State Senate, 1997—2001, US Congress from 4th Va. dist., 2001—, mem. armed svcs. com., mem. judiciary com., mem. sci. com. Chmn. Rep. Party Va., 1996—2001. Republican. Baptist. Office: US Ho Reps 307 Cannon Ho Office Bldg Washington DC 20515 Office Phone: 202-225-6365.*

FORBES, JIM (JAMES D. FORBES), investment banker; BBA, Loyola Coll. With debt capital markets group Credit Suisse First Boston; joined Merrill Lynch & Co. Inc., NYC, 1995—, now mng. dir., global healthcare group. Recipient Rainmaker prize in healthcare banking, Dealmaker mag., 2006. Office: Merrill Lynch Healthcare Banking 4 World Fin Ctr 250 Vesey St New York NY 10080 Office Phone: 212-449-1000.*

FORBES, JOHN DOUGLAS, architectural and economic historian; b. San Francisco, Apr. 9, 1910; s. John Franklin and Portia (Ackerman) F.; m. Margaret Funkhouser, Feb. 4, 1937 (dec.); children: Pamela, Peter; m. Mary Elizabeth Lewis, July 26, 1980 and Dec. 24, 1999; 1 child, Michael. AB, U. Calif.-Berkeley, 1931; MA, Stanford U., 1932; A.M., Harvard U., 1936, PhD, 1937. Accountant J.F. Forbes & Co. (C.P.A.'s), San Francisco, 1937-38, 42-43; asst. to dir. fine arts, curator paintings San Francisco World's Fair, 1938-40; chmn. dept. fine arts U. Kansas City, Mo., 1940-42; faculty history Bennington Coll., 1943-46; assoc. editor Am. Enterprise Assn., 1944-46; assoc. prof. history and fine arts Wabash Coll., 1946-50, prof., 1950-54; prof. bus. history Darden Sch. U. Va., 1954-80; prof. emeritus U. Va., 1980—, lectr. art history sch. continuing edn., 1982—2003; adv. bd. Historic Am. Bldgs. Survey, 1974-78. Author: Israel Thorndike, 1953, Victorian Architect, 1953, Murder in Full View, 1868, Death Warmed Over, 1971, Stettinus, Sr., Portrait of a Morgan Partner, 1974, J.P. Morgan, jr. (1867-1943), 1981, Death Among the Artists, 1993, I'd Be Tempted to Dip into Capital First, 2004; editor Jour. Soc. Archtl. Historians, 1953—58, adv. editor industry Ency. Britannica, 1956—58. 2d lt. AUS, 1942. Decorated officier Ordre des Palmes Académiques (France); cavaliere Ordine al Merito (Italy); named Hon. Alumnus Class of 1950, Assn. of Wabash Men, 1993. Fellow Soc. Archtl. Historians (pres. 1962-64, life); mem. Am. Hist. Assn. (life), Coll. Art Assn. (life), Mystery Writers Am., Colonial Soc. Mass. (life), AIA (hon.), Wilderness Soc. (life), Sierra Club (life), Nature Conservancy (life), Mechanics Inst. (life), Victorian Soc. (life), Calif. Hist. Soc., Soc. Calif. Pioneers (life), Friends of Sea Otter (life), Tamalpais Conservation Club (life), Am. Kitefliers Assn. (life), Am. Soc. Dowsers (life), Save-the Redwoods League (life), Phi Beta Kappa. Clubs: Colonnade (Charlottesville) (life), Pacific-Union (San Francisco); Farmington Country (Charlottesville, life); Cambridge (Mass.) Boat. Home: PO Box 3607 Charlottesville VA 22903-0607 also: 1250 Jones St San Francisco CA 94109-4261

FORBES, JOHN EDWARD, retired financial consultant; b. Chgo., Sept. 18, 1925; s. Harry Charles and Jeanette Anne (Field) F.; m. Dorsey Connors, Aug. 10, 1961. Student, Rensselaer Poly. Inst., 1943-44, Franklin and Marshall Coll., Lancaster, Pa., 1943; BA, Monmouth Coll., 1949; postgrad., Northwestern U., 1949-50. Account exec. and commodity mgr. Merrill Lynch, Pierce, Fenner and Smith, Inc., Chgo., 1949-61; pres. San Jose Cigarette Co., Calif., 1958-68; account exec. Hornblower & Weeks, Hemphill, Noyes, Inc., Chgo., 1961-71, assoc. resident mgr., 1971-75, v.p., resident mgr., 1975-78; corp. v.p. Loeb, Rhoades, Hornblower & Co., Chgo., 1981—, Shearson Lehman Bros., Chgo., 1961—; sr. v.p. fin. cons. Smith Barney, Chgo., 1995—2005; ret., 2005. Pres. 227 E. Delaware Corp, Chgo., 1980-86; bd. dirs. Trend Industries, Chgo. With USN, 1943-46, PTO. Mem.: Saddle and Cycle Club (bd. dirs. 1983—86), Tavern Club (pres. 1981—82), Hundred Club of Cook County, Soc. St. Andrew. Home: 227 E Delaware Pl Chicago IL 60611-7758

FORBES, KENNETH ALBERT FAUCHER, retired urological surgeon; b. Waterford, NY, Apr. 28, 1922; s. Joseph Frederick (dec.) and Adelle Frances (Robitaille) Faucher; adopted s. James Peter Forbes; m. Jeanne Ann Bonacci, June 18, 1947 (dec.); 1 child: Michael; m. Eileen Ruth Gibbons, Aug. 4, 1956; children: Diane, Kenneth E., Thomas, Maureen, Daniel. BS cum laude, U. Notre Dame, Ind., 1944; MD, St. Louis U., 1947. Diplomate Am. Bd. Urology. Intern St. Louis U. Hosp., 1947-48; resident in urol. surgery Barnes Hosp., VA Hosp., Washington U., St. Louis. U. schs. medicine, St. Louis, 1948-52; asst. chief urology Letterman Army Hosp., San Francisco, 1952-54; fellow West Roxbury (Harvard) VA Hosp., Boston, 1955; asst. chief urology VA Hosp., East Orange, N.J., 1955-58; practice medicine specializing in urology Green Bay, Wis., 1958-78, Long Beach, Calif., 1978-85; ret., 1999. Cons. staff Fairview State Hosp. U. Calif. Med. Ctr., Irvine, VA Hosp., Long Beach; commr. State Med. Soc. Wisc., 1975—77, chmn. legal def. com., 1976—77; pres. Wis. Urological Soc., 1977—78; asst. clin. prof. surgery U. Calif., Irvine, 1978—85; cons. in field. Contbr. articles to profl. jours. Served with USNR, 1944-46, ensign 1947-51; capt. US Army, 1952-54. Named Outstanding Faculty Mem. by students, 1981. Fellow ACS, Royal Soc. Medicine (emeritus), Internat. Coll. Surgeons; mem. AMA, AAAS, Calif. Med. Assn., Am. Urol. Assn. (exec. com. North Ctrl. sect. 1972-75, Western sect. 1980—), NY Acad. Scis., Surg. Alumni Assn. U. Calif.-Irvine, Justin J. Cordonnier Soc. Washington U., Urologists Corr. Club, Notre Dame Club (Man of Yr. award 1965), Union League Club of Chgo., Miles City Club (Mont.), Phi Beta Pi. Republican. Roman Catholic. Home: 3222 Port Pacific Ln Elk Grove CA 95758-3606 Personal E-mail: kfef@comcast.net.

FORBES, KRISTIN J., economics professor, former federal official; BA summa cum laude in Econ., Williams Coll., 1992; PhD in Econ., MIT, 1998. Fin. analyst, investment banking divsn., Fin. Institutions Group Morgan Stanley, NYC, 1992—93; project asst., policy rsch. dept. The World Bank, Washington, 1993—94; rsch. fellow Nat. Coun. of Applied Econ. Rsch, New Delhi, 1996; dep. asst. sec. quantitative policy analysis U.S. Dept. Treasury, Washington, 2001—02, dep. asst. sec of quantitative policu analysis, Latin Am. & Caribbean nations, 2002; asst. prof. mgmt. in Applied Econ. Group MIT Sloan Sch. Mgmt., Cambridge, Mass., 1998—2002, Mitsubishi devel. chair internat. mgmt., 2001—, assoc. prof. mgmt. applied econ. group, 2002—04, assoc. prof. mgmt., 2004—; mem. Coun. Econ. Advisers The White House, Washington, 2003—05; faculty rsch. fellow Nat. Bur. Econ. Rsch. Faculty rsch. fellow Nat. Bur. Econ. Rsch., 2000—05; vis. scholar Indian Coun. Rsch. on Internat. Econ. Rels. and Internat. Monetary Fund (ICRIER), 2000; vis. fellow U.S. Fed. Reserve Bd., 2001; vis. scholar IMF, 2002, Fed. Reserve Bank of Mpls., 2002; co-chair IMF rsch. program Project on Global Linkage, 2001—03; assoc. editl. bd. Emerging Markets Review, 2002—03; mem. editl. bd. Jour. Econ. Integration, 2002—03; mem. Coun. Fgn. Relations, 2004—; rsch. assoc. Nat. Bur. Econ. Rsch., 2005—. Contbr. articles to profl. jours. Named a Young Global Leader, World Econ. Forum, 2005; named 1 of 100 Global Leaders for Tomorrow, 2003; recipient David Wells prize in Econ., Williams Coll., 1992, Solow prize for Excellence in Rsch. & Teaching, 1998, Milken award Disting. Econ. Rsch., 2000, Teacher of the Year award, MIT Sloan Sch. Mgmt, 2001. Office: MIT Sloan Sch Mgmt 50 Memorial Dr Rm E52-455 Cambridge MA 02142 E-mail: kjforbes@mit.edu.

FORBES, MARY ALLISON, psychology educator; b. Culpeper, Va., Jan. 29, 1978; d. Richard and Barbara Forbes. BS in Family and Child Devel., Va. Tech. U., 2000, BS in Psychology, 2000, MA in Counselor Edn., 2002. Rschr. dept. human devel. Va. Tech. U., Blacksburg, Va., 2000—01, rschr. dept. psychology, 2000—02; substitute tchr. Poe Mid. Sch., Annandale, Va., 2002—03; mem. faculty Gibbs Coll., Vienna, Va., 2002—. Nominee Tchr. of Yr. award, Gibbs Coll., 2004, Tchr. of Quarter award, 2004. Republican. Avocations: exercise, reading, scrapbooks. E-mail: maforbes02@hotmail.com.

FORBES, MICHAEL PATRICK, former congressman; b. Riverhead, NY, July 16, 1952; m. Barbara; children: Abigail, Theodore, Samuel, Maximilian. BA, SUNY Albany, 1983; LLD (hon.), LI U., 1999. Coord. various local, state and fed. polit. campaigns, 1979—89; exec. asst. to US Senator Alfonse D'Amato, 1981-84; chief of staff to US Rep. Connie Mack, 1985-87; owner pub. rels. small bus., 1985-89; regional administr. US SBA, 1989-92; legis. dir., regional mgr. US C. of C., 1993-94; mem. 104th-106th Congress from LI 1st NY dist., 1995-2001; pres., CEO, PR/Strategies Internat., 2001—. Democrat. Personal E-mail: congforbes@aol.com.

FORBES, MORTON GERALD, lawyer; b. Atlanta, July 12, 1938; s. Arthur Mark and Mary Dean (Power) F.; m. Eunice Lee Haynsworth, Jan. 25, 1963; children: John, Ashley, Sarah. AB, Wofford Coll., Spartanburg, SC, 1962; JD, U. Ga., Athens, 1965. Bar: Ga. 1965, US Dist. Ct. (mid. dist.) Ga. 1965, US Dist. Ct. (so. dist.) Ga. 1968, US Dist. Ct. (no. dist.) Ga. 1993, US Ct. Appeals (5th cir.) 1974, US Ct. Appeals (4th cir.) 1972, US Ct. Appeals (11th cir.) 1981. Assoc. Pierce, Ranitz, Lee, Berry & Mahoney, 1967-70; ptnr. Pierce, Ranitz, Berry, Mahoney & Forbes, 1970-76, Pierce, Ranitz, Mahoney, Forbes & Coolidge, 1976-81; ptnr., sec. Ranitz, Mahoney, Forbes & Coolidge, P.C., 1981-91, Forbes & Bowman, Savannah, Ga., 1991—2007, Forbes, Foster & Pool, 2007—. Gen. counsel Ga. Fed. Young Rep. Clubs, 1971-72; guest lectr. dept. dental hygiene Armstrong State Coll., 1970-72. Mem. Savannah Port Authority (now Savannah Econ. Devel. Authority), 1973-2003, chmn., 1979-81; mem. Chatham County Devel. Authority, 1973-80; nat. com. Nat. Fedn. Young Reps., 1973; econ. adv. coun. Coastal Area Planning and Devel. Authority, 1980—; bd. dirs. Savannah Symphony Soc., 1971-75; Ga. del. to Japan/Southeast Trade Mission, Kyoto, Japan, 1983, S.E. Asia USA/Japan Assn. meeting, Birmingham, Ala., 1984. With USN, 1965-67. Recipient Outstanding Service award, Savannah Port Authority, 1981. Mem. ABA, Internat. Assn. Def. Counsel, Fedn. Def. and Corp. Counsel (state rep.), State Bar Ga., Ala. Def. Lawyer Assn. (hon.), Am. Judicature Soc., Nat. Assn. Bond Counsel, Ga. Def. Lawyers Assn. (v.p. 1987—, mem. exec. com. 1988, bd. dirs., exec. v.p. 1990-91, pres. 1991-92), Savannah Bar Assn. (exec. com. 1989-94, pres. 1992-93), Libel Def. Resource Ctr., Def. Rsch. Inst. (state chmn. 1992-99, bd. dirs. 1999-2002), Savannah Econ. Devel. Action Coun. (founding), Savannah Area Wofford Coll. Alumni Club (past pres.), Soc. of the Cincinnati (Va.), St. Andrews Soc. (bd. stewards), Soc. Colonial Wars (sec.), Sons of Revolution (sec. 1988-92), Chatham Club, Savannah Yacht Club, The Landings Club. Republican. Presbyterian. Office: Forbes Foster & Pool PO Box 13929 Savannah GA 31416-0929 Office Phone: 912-352-1190. Business E-Mail: salty@ffp-law.com.

FORBES, PETER, architect; b. Berkeley, Calif., May 22, 1942; s. John Douglas and Margaret (Funkhouser) F.; m. Patricia Ann Marsh, Aug. 27, 1966 (div. 1982); children: Alexander John, Anne deMarken; m. Erica Longfellow deBerry, July 21, 1990 (div. 2007); 1 child, Allegra Longfellow. BArch, U. Mich., 1966; MArch, Yale U., 1967; Dr. Engring. Tech. (hon.), Wentworth Inst. Tech., 1991. Registered arch., Mass., Va., Calif., Maine, NY, Mich., Conn., DC; cert. Nat. Council Archtl. Registration Bds. Project designer Skidmore, Owings & Merrill, Chgo., 1965-66; assoc. ptnr. PARD Team, Inc., Boston, 1967-71; pres. Forbes Hailey Jeas Erneman, Inc., Boston, 1972-80, Peter Forbes and Assoc., Inc., Boston, 1980-2000, Peter Forbes, FAIA Arch., Seal Harbor, Maine, 2000—. Mem. Commonwealth of Mass. Designer Selection Bd., 1986-89; mem. Spl. Commn. Concerning State and County Bldgs., 1978-81; bd. dirs. continuing edn. Boston Archtl. Ctr.; vis. critic U. Mich., 1980-82, Cath. U. Am., Rome, 1982; vis. lectr. Cath. U., Washington, 1997, U. Turin, Italy, 2007; lectr., vis. critic Va. Poly. Inst. and State U., 1989-92, 96, Columbia U., 1984; vis. critic N.C. State U., 1997; Thomas S. Monaghan Disting. vis. prof. U. Mich., 1987; vis. prof. Harvard U., 1989, 91, 94, G. Truman Ward vis. lectr. Va. Poly. Inst. and State U., 1996; vis. lectr. Lawrence Tech. U., 1996, Evergreen State Coll., 1996, U. B.C., 1996; guest lectr. Boston Mus. Fine Arts, 1997, Guido A. Binda vis. lectr. U. Mich., 1997, vis. prof. Wentworth Inst. of Tech., Gargonza, Italy, 2003; vis. lectr. U. Turin, Italy, 2007. Author: Ten Houses: Peter Forbes and Associates, 1995; exhbns. include Cath. U. Am., 1982, 97, U. Mich., 1982, 87, 97, Va. Poly. Inst. and State U., 1983, Boston Athenaeum, 1986, Harvard U., 1986, Lawrence Tech. U., 1996, Am. Inst. Architects/Continental Europe, Milan, Italy, 2007; contbr. articles to profl. jours. Recipient Record House award, 1983, 86, 87, 89, New Eng. Design awrd, 1986, 87, 89, 91, 94, 96, 97, 98, Archtl. Excellence award Am. Inst. Steel Constrn., 1987, Tucker award Bldg. Stone Inst., 1987, 90, Best and Brightest award, 1995, Honor award Am. Wood Inst., 1989, Nat. Housing Design award, 1990, Silver award Indsl. Designers Soc. Am., 1993, 94, Am. Arch. award Chgo. Athenaeum Mus. Arch. and Design, 1999. Fellow AIA (nat. jud. coun. 1987—, Nat. honor award 1986, 92, New Eng. regional coun./design award 1986, 87, 89, 91, 94, 96, 97, 98, Washington D.C. merit award 1994; Excellence in Arch. award Maine chpt. 1995), Boston Soc. Archs. (bd. dirs., commr. pub. affairs, chmn. ethics com., v.p., pres. 1988-89, Excellence in Arch. award 1988-89, 91-94, 98, Honor award 1995, 97, 98, Excellence in Housing design award 1996, 98); mem. Soc. Archtl. Historians (life), Century Club, Newport Reading Rm., Racquet and Tennis Club, Nat. Tennis Club, Yale Club, Boston Athenaeum. Home: Greenings Is Southwest Harbor ME 04679 also: Viale Giovanni Milton 65 50129 Florence Italy Office: 12 Main St Seal Harbor ME 04675 Home Phone: 39-055-4627458; Office Phone: 207-276-0970. E-mail: pfamaine@adelphia.net, pfafirenze@dada.it.

FORBES, PETER EDWIN, sculptor; b. Detroit, Mich. s. Edwin Fisher and Grace Campbell Forbes; m. Leona Collins Forbes, July 1, 1961; 1 child, Wyndham. BS in design, U. Mich., 1961, MA in design, 1963. Art instr. Mich. State U., 1964, U. Ill., 1964—69, SUNY, 1974—86, Syracuse U., 1991—99; vis. artist Rochester Inst. of Tech., 1999—2000; art instr. Syracuse U., 2000—03; Pollock-Krasner grantee in sculpture, 2006—. Freelance indsl. designer Syracuse area, 1980; resident artist Sculpture Space Inc., Utica, 2002. Sculpture, Norfolk Internat. Airport, 1995, Shaffer Art Bldg., Syracuse U., 1994, Downtown Syracuse area, 1992, exhibitions include 4th Biennale Internazionale dell'ArteContemporanea, Florence, Italy, 2003, Meml. Art Gallery, Rochester, NY, 2007, multimedia presentation, Vienna, Austria, 2000, juried shows, Schweinfurth Meml. Art Ctr., NY, 2001, Meml. Art Gallery, Rochester, NY, 1999, Nexus Gallery, NYC, 1998, Paint Creek Ctr. for the Arts, Rochester, 1998, Zaner Gallery, 1985, Chelsea, N.Y., 2005 (winner Amsterdam Whitney Internat. Fine Arts Chelsea Global Showcase competition, 2005), Everson Mus. Art, Syracuse,

NY, 2006, Coll. Art Gallery, Utica, NY, 2006. Vol. art cons. and builder of displays Erie Canal Mus., Syracuse, 2003—04; mem. Outer Comstock Neighbor Assn., Syracuse, 1994—2005. Recipient Spl. Opportunity Stipend, NY Found for the Arts, 2002; grantee Pollock-Krasner Grant, 2006—07. Avocations: walking, jogging. Home: 336 Vincent St Syracuse NY 13210 Personal E-mail: forbes010@aol.com.

FORBES, SALLY, researcher, editor, curator; d. William Shackleford Koontz and Mary Louise Kibler; m. Kenneth Frith Forbes, Oct. 15, 1944 (dec.); children: Philip Andrews, Melanie Kibler. BA in English and Speech, Ctrl. Meth. U., 1941. Libr., rschr., curator Standard Oil Co. NJ, NYC, 1945—57; freelance art rschr., curator NYC, 1957—. Exec. dir. The Beaux Arts Alliance, NYC, 1995—. Co-founder, prodr.: The Penny Bridge Players, 1976—97. Recipient Disting. Alumni award, Ctrl. Meth. U., 1980. Democrat. Episcopalian. Office: The Beaux Arts Alliance 119 East 74th St New York NY 10021

FORBES, SARAH ELIZABETH, gynecologist, real estate company officer; b. Currituck, NC, May 4, 1928; d. Dexter and Mary (Brock) Forbes. BA, U. Rochester, 1949; MD, Med. Coll. of Va., 1954. Diplomate Am. Bd. Ob-Gyn. Intern Norfolk (Va.) Gen. Hosp., 1954-55; resident ob-gyn Johnston-Willis Hosp., 1955-56, Norfolk Gen. Hosp., 1956-57, chief resident, 1957-58; pvt. practice gynecologist Newport News, Va., 1958—; pres., real estate investor Mary B. Forbes Land Corp., Newport News, 1972—; pres. Sebrof Corp., Newport News, 1978—, Haras, Inc., Newport News, 1984—, S.S. U.S., Inc., Newport News, 1984—. Bd. dirs. Family Planning Coun.; mem. teaching staff ob-gyn dept. Riverside Hosp. Pres. Peninisula Soc. for Prevention Cruelty to Animals, 1966—; mem. adv. bd. Peninisula chpt. Parents without Ptnrs.; bd. dirs. Newport News chpt. Am. Cancer Soc., pres., 2d v.p., 1971-72, 1st v.p., 1972-73, pres., 1973-74, chmn. rsch., 1961-69; candidate for Newport News City Coun., 1986; bd. dirs. Va. Peninsula Boys and Girls Club, 1991-99, 1st v.p., pres. Va. Peninsula Boys and Girls Club, 2000—. Recipient AMA Physicians Recognition award for Continuing Edn., 1973-76, Twin award Va. Peninsula YWCA, 1987, Medallion award Peninsula Boys and Girls Club, 1993; named Woman of Yr. for Peninsula Area, 1975. Mem. Va. Peninsula Acad. Medicine (pres. 1973-74, v.p. 1972-73, sec., treas. 1971-72); fellow AMA, Va. Med. Soc., Newport News Med. Soc. Am. Coll. Ob-Gyn, Tidewater Ob-Gyn Soc. Office: 12420 Warwick Blvd Newport News VA 23606-3001

FORBES, STEVE (MALCOLM STEVENSON FORBES JR.), publishing executive; b. Morristown, NJ, July 18, 1947; s. Malcolm Stevenson and Roberta Remsen (Laidlaw) Forbes; m. Sabina Beekman, June 19, 1971; children: Sabina, Roberta, Catherine, Moira, Elizabeth. BA in history, Princeton U., 1970; LHD (hon.), Lycoming Coll., Jacksonville U., Kean Coll., Seton Hill U.; LLD (hon.), Lock Haven U., Westminster Coll., Sacred Heart U., Centenary Coll., Iona Coll., Pepperdine U., Lehigh U., New Hampshire U., Siena Coll.; LittD (hon.), Spring Arbor U.; LLD (hon.), Caldwell Coll.; ScD (hon.), N.Y. Inst. Tech., Lynn U., U. Francisco Marroquin; D.P.S. (hon.), U. Rio Grande; PhD (hon.), Hillsdale Coll., UEES Universidad Espiritu Santo, Ecuador; DBA (hon.), Lincoln Coll., New Bulgarian Univ.; AA (hon.), Raritan Valley CC. With Forbes Inc., NYC, 1970—, pres., COO, 1980-90, dep. editor-in-chief, 1982-90, editor-in-chief, pres., CEO, 1990—. Author: The Moral Basis of A Free Society, 1999; co-author (filmscript): Some Call It Greed, 1977, A New Birth of Freedom, 1999; editor: Fact and Comment, 1974. Pres. Somerset County Park Commn., 1981—91; mem. Bd. for Internat. Broadcasting, 1983—93, chmn., 1985—93; trustee Brooks Sch., North Andover, Mass., 1978—97; pres., bd. trustees Freedom House, 1993—, Heritage Found., 2001—, Found. for the Def. Democracies, 2001—; bd. visitors Pepperdine U., 2002—; bd. trustees Princeton U., 1992—2002, pres., 1987—96; Ronald Reagan Presdl. Found., 1990; Rep. presdl. primary campaign candidate, 1995—96, 1999—2000; internat. adv. bd. Brit. Am. Bus. Coun., 2001; pres. bd. trustees Brooks Sch., 1987—96; bd. overseers Meml. Sloan-Kettering Cancer Ctr., 1989—; chmn. bd. dirs. Empower Am., 1993—96, Ams. Soc., 1992—; bd. dirs Nat. Endowment for Democracy, 1994—98; bd. dirs. Nat. Taxpayers Union, 1997, Jackie Robinson Found., 1996—; mem. Coun. for Nat. Policy, 1998; bd. dirs. Abraham Lincoln Presdl. Libr., 2001—. Republican. Office: Forbes Inc 60 Fifth Ave New York NY 10011-8882 Office Phone: 212-620-2200. Office Fax: 212-620-2245. E-mail: sforbes@forbes.com.*

FORBES, THEODORE MCCOY, JR., arbitrator, mediator, retired lawyer; b. Atlanta, Oct. 28, 1929; s. Theodore M. and Mary Beatrice (Christie) F.; m. Margaret Paty, Dec. 12, 1953; children: Theodore McCoy, Margaret Paty. BS in Chemistry, Ga. Inst. Tech., 1950; LLB, U. Va., 1953. Bar: Ga., 1952, D.C. 1973, U.S. Ct. Appeals (5th cir.) 1976, U.S. Ct. Appeals (11th cir.) 1981. Instr. Culver (Ind.) Summer Naval Sch., 1950; from assoc. to ptnr. Smith, Gambrell & Russell, and predecessor firms, Atlanta, 1953—58, ptnr., 1958-91; solo practice, 1992-95. Bd. dirs. Travelers Aid Soc., Atlanta, 1974-90, pres., 1975-76, 86-89; bd. dirs., corp. sec. Shepherd Spinal Ctr., Atlanta, 1975-95; bd. dirs. Ga. Fund for Edn., 1986-89. Lt. (j.g.) USNR, 1950-62. Fellow Ga. Bar Found.; mem. Atlanta Bar Assn., State Bar Ga. (emeritus), Ga. C. of C. (bd. dirs. 1986-95), Capital City Club (life). Avocations: golf, american history, fishing. Home: 2520 Peachtree Rd NW Apt 202 Atlanta GA 30305-3617

FORBES, TIMOTHY CARTER, publishing executive; b. Morristown, NJ, Oct. 5, 1953; s. Malcolm Stevenson and Roberta (Laidlaw) F.; m. Anne Shepard Harrison, Mar. 4, 1983. AB with honors, Brown U., 1976, LHD (hon.), 1996. Prodr. Seven Seas Cinema, NYC, 1977-81; prodr., screenwriter NYC, 1981-85; pres. Am. Heritage Mag., NYC, 1986—2000; v.p. Forbes Inc., NYC, 1986—, COO, 1996; chmn. bd. dirs. Forbes.com, NYC. Dir., producer: (films) Some Call It Greed, 1977, Lost to the Revolution, 1979, Golden Age of Toy Boats, 1981, Happily Ever After?, 1992. Mem. bd. fellows Brown U., 2000—; bd. dirs. Margaret Thatcher Found., 1993—, Hist. House Trust N.Y.C., 1990—. Mem. Am. Antiquarian Soc. Office: Forbes Inc 60 5th Ave New York NY 10011-8882

FORBES-RICHARDSON, HELEN HILDA, state agency administrator; b. Detroit, July 26, 1950; d. Henry and Trunetta (Adams) Forbes; m. Leon Richardson (div.); 1 child, Leon Ronald Jr. BA in Edn. and Human Svcs., U. Detroit, 1972; MPA, Harvard U., 1989. Cert. tchr. Mich. Substitute tchr. Detroit Bd. Edn., 1972-75; assistance payment worker State Dept. Social Svcs., Detroit, 1975-79, supr. assistance payment, 1979-85, section mgr., 1985—; adminstrv. asst. to chief dep. dir. Wayne County Dept. Social Svcs., Detroit, 1989-90. Mem. case rev. com. Mich. Dept. Social Svcs. Gen. Assistance, 1985, 87, labor rels. subcom., quality initiative task force tng. com., 1985; co-chairperson quality initiative error reduction com. and conf. planning com.; mem. tng. com. quality initiative task force Mich. Dept. Social Svcs., 1984, client svc. subcom., 1989—, coord. employee recognition program, 1989-90, chmn. procedure com., Grand River Warren local office, 1990—, coord. state employee recognition program, Wayne County, 1980-90; chair security plan com. client info. system County of Wayne, 1989, mem. UAW Secondary Contract Negotiations Team, 1988; mem. conf. planning com. Mich. County Social Svcs. Assn., 1988; chairperson Grand River/Warren Procedures Com., 1990, employee recognition awards program level 1 Grand River/Warren Dept. Social Svcs., 1990; pres. Forbes-Richardson Ltd., 1990—, mgmt. cons., 1990; owner, editor Adams-Forbes Pub. Co., Detroit. Pub.: (poetry) I Am, 1997. Coordinator Social Svc. United Found. Dr., Lafayette local office 1985, Social Svc. Black United Fund Dr. 1987, speaker Nat. Polit. Congress Black Women, 1986; student project coord. Wayne County Community Coll., Wayne County Dept. Social Svcs., 1989; coord. scholarship project Mary Holmes Coll. Spirit of Detroit Leadership award, 1985. Mem. Am. Pub. Welfare Assn. (planning com. 1986), Am. Legion Aux. Avocations: reading, sewing, billiards.

FORBESS, JOSEPH MATTHEW, thoracic surgeon, educator; b. Mobile, Ala., June 9, 1964; s. Thomas Edward and Wanda (Watkins) Forbess; m. Lisa Karen Weiss, Oct. 30, 1953; children: Madeline Belle, Caroline Joy. AB, Harvard U., Cambridge, Mass., 1986; MD, Harvard U., Boston, 1990. Diplomate Am. Bd. Surgery. Asst. cardiovasc. surgery Children's Hosp., Boston, 1999, assoc. cardiovasc. surgery, 2000; cardiothoracic surgeon Emory Hosps., Atlanta, 2002, Children's Healthcare Atlanta, 2002—04, vice chair cardiothoracic surgery, 2004; dir. cardiothoracic surgery Children's Med. Ctr., Dallas, 2004—; Pogue disting. chmn. divsn. pediatric cardiothoracic surgery U. Tex. Southwestern Med. Ctr., Dallas, 2004—. Consulting affiliate Meth. Hosp. Dallas Med. Ctr., 2006. Ad hoc reviewer: Jour. Thoracic and Cardiovasc. Surgery, 2000, Annals Thoracic Surgery, 2001, Jour. Pediat., 2004. Recipient Meritorious Svc. award, Am. Soc. Entrocorporeal Technicians, 2006. Mem.: Soc. Thoracic Surgeons (co-chair workforce annual meeting 2004), Congenital Heart Surgeon's Soc., 21st Century Cardiothoracic Surg. Soc. Avocations: fishing, tennis, reading. Office: Childrens Med Ctr Dallas 1935 Motor St Ste E03-320Z Dallas TX 75235

FORCE, PIERRE MARIE, French language and literature educator; b. Toulon, France, Apr. 4, 1958; came to U.S., 1984; s. Louis Joseph and Marie (Hapette) F.; m. Christel Hollevoet, 1997; children: Charlotte, Eliot. BA, Sorbonne, Paris, 1979, MA, 1980, PhD, 1987; MBA, NYU, 1990. Fgn. svc. officer French Embassy, Mexico City, 1981-83; lectr. Yale U., New Haven, 1984-86, Johns Hopkins U., Balt., 1986-87; project mgr. Banque Pallas France, Paris, 1990-91; asst. prof. French Columbia U., NYC, 1987-90, assoc. prof., 1992—95, prof., 1995—2000, Nell Singer prof. of contemporary civilization, 2000—05, chmn. dept. French, 1997—, prof. French and history, 2005—. Adv. bd. Maison Francaise. Author: Le Probléme Herméneutique Chez Pascal, 1989, Moliére ou Le Prix des Choses, 1994, Self-Interest Before Adam Smith, 2003; mem. editl. bd. Romanic Rev. Decorated chevalier Ordre nat. du Merite; Ecole Normale Superieure fellow, Paris, 1978-81 Mem. Soc. des Amis de Port-Royal, Assn. Internat. des études Francaises (governing bd.) Democrat. Roman Catholic. Home: 21 Claremont Ave # 91 New York NY 10027 Office: Columbia Univ Dept French 517 Philosophy Hall New York NY 10027 Home Phone: 212-864-5691; Office Phone: 212-854-2500. E-mail: pf3@columbia.edu.

FORCE, ROBERT, law educator; b. Phila., Aug. 11, 1934; s. Charles and Dora (Woloshin) F.; m. Ruth Morris, Aug. 18, 1962; children: Joshua Simon, Seth Daniel. BS, Temple U., 1955, LL.B., 1958; postgrad., U. Adelaide, 1958-59; LL.M., NYU, 1960. Bar: Pa. 1961. Law clk. to presiding justice Pa. Ct. Common Pleas., Phila., 1960-61, U.S. Dist. Ct., Phila., 1961-62; instr. Temple U., Phila., 1960-61; assoc. Kleinbard, Bell & Brecker, Phila., 1963-64; asst. prof. Ind. U. Law Sch., Indpls., 1964-67, assoc. prof., 1968; prof. Tulane U., New Orleans, 1969—, Thomas Pickles prof. law, 1979-89, Niels F. Johnsen prof. maritime law, 1989—, acting dean, 1977-78. Dir. emeritus Tulane Maritime Law Ctr. Co-author: Hall's Criminal Law, 1993, Admiralty and Maritime Law: Cases, Notes and Text, vols. 1 and 2, 1997, Marine Pollution: Conventions, Statutes, Cases and Text, 1998, (with M. Norris) The Law of Seamen, 5th edit., 2003, (with M. Norris) The Law of Maritime Personal Injuries, 2004, Admiralty and Maritime Law, 2005. Fulbright fellow, 1958-59 Mem. ABA, Beta Gamma Sigma, Omicron Delta Kappa Home: 1038 Eleonore St New Orleans LA 70115-4311 Office: 6329 Freret St Ste 255 New Orleans LA 70118-6231 Office Phone: 504-865-5947. Business E-Mail: rforce@law.tulane.edu.

FORCE, RONALD WAYNE, retired librarian; b. Sioux City, Iowa, Sept. 7, 1941; s. Robert N. and Madeline (Heine) F.; m. Jo Ellen Hitch, May 31, 1964; children: Emily, Alicia. BS, Iowa State U., 1963; MA, U. Minn., 1968; MS, Ohio State U., 1975. Asst. to head dept. librs. Ohio State U., Columbus, 1968-70, head engring. librs., 1970-72, head edn./psychology libr., 1972-79; asst. dir. pub. svcs. Wash. State U. Librs., Pullman, 1979-82; asst. sci. libr. U. Idaho Libr., Moscow, 1982-84, pub. svcs. libr., 1984-85, humanities libr., 1985-88, assoc. dean libr. svcs., 1988-91, dean libr. svcs., 1991—2006; ret., 2006. Mem. adv. coun. Libr. Svcs. and Constrn. Act. Author: Guide to Literature on Biomedical Engineering, 1972; contbr. articles to profl. jours. Mem. Sacajawea Coun. Campfire Bd., 1980-85, mem. Pullman Dist. Campfire Com., fin. com., 1980-82, chair, 1983-84, treas., 1985, Sacajawea County Self-Study Com., 1986; mem. adv. bd. N.W. Net Info. Resources, 1994-95, 2000—; mem. Idaho Network Adv. Com., 1993-95; mem. LSCA Adv. Coun., 1989-95; mem. Libraries Linking Idaho Bd., 2000—. Mem. ALA, Idaho Libr. Assn. (2d v.p. 1997-98, 1st v.p. 1998-99, pres. 1999-2000). Home: 545 N Blaine St Moscow ID 83843-3626

FORCHESKIE, CARL S., former apparel company executive; b. Shamokin, Pa., Feb. 3, 1927; s. John A. and Helen F.; m. Barbara Ann Pierz; children from previous marriage: Carl, Gail, Caroline Karen. BA, Pa. State U., 1951. Mgr. Coopers & Lybrand, 1951-62; cons. U.S. Dept. Treasury, 1962-63; chief fin. officer Loral Corp., 1963-69; exec. v.p. Salant Corp., NYC, 1969-81, pres., chief exec. officer, 1981-85; ret., 1985. Bd. mem. Pike County Indsl. Devel. Corp., Pike County Indsl. Devel. Authority. Served with AUS, 1945-46. Mem. AICPA, N.Y. State Soc. CPAs, Fin. Execs. Inst., Paupack Hills Golf and Country Club. Roman Catholic. Home: 101 Beechwood Ln Greentown PA 18426-9052

FORD, ALMA REGINA, retired union official, educator; b. Owings, W.Va., Oct. 4, 1939; d. Charles Feathers and Pearl (Costello) Ford. AB, Fairmont State Coll., 1960; MA, W.Va. U., 1964, Ball State U., 1984; postgrad., Sorbonne. Cert. counselor. Tchr., Ohio, 1961—78, W.Va., 1961—78, Turkey, 1961—78, England, 1961—78, France, 1961—78, Italy, 1961—78, Germany, 1961—78; v.p., dep. rep. Dept. Def. Dependents Schs.-Europe; negotiator Overseas Fedn. Tchrs., 1978—80; tchr. Zweibrucken, Germany, 1980—, counselor, 1997; ret., 1999. Recipient Sustained Superior/Performance award, Dept. Army, 1972—76, Exceptional Performance award, 1984; NDEA fellow, 1968. Mem.: LWV, AARP, AAUW, Marion County Ret. Tchrs. Assn., W.Va. Sheriff's Assn., Overseas Fedn. Tchrs., Am. Fedn. Tchrs., Speech Assn. Am., Nat. Assn. Ret. People, Nat. Coun. Tchrs. English, Nat. Assn. Ret. Fed. Employees, Zweibrucken Alumnus Assn., Fairmont State Coll. Alumnus Assn., Ret. Eagles Club, W.Va. Travelers Club, Moose, Elks, Eagles Ladies Aux., Am. Legion Ladies Aux., VFW Ladies Aux., Alpha Psi Omega, Phi Delta Kappa. Home: RR 2 Box 365 Shinnston WV 26431-9616 Home Phone: 304-534-4091; Office Phone: 304-534-4091.

FORD, ANDREA MICHELLE, mathematics educator; b. Vincennes, Ind., Apr. 10, 1967; d. James Robert and Kathy Ann Hoalt; children: Alexis, Austin. B, Ind. State U., 1989; postgrad., Ind. Wesleyan U. Jr. high math. tchr. North Daviess Jr./Sr. High, Elnora, Ind., 1989—96; h.s. math. tchr. North Knox High, Bicknell, Ind., 1996—. Avocations: sports, cross stitch. Home: 8002 E Bobe Rd Bruceville IN 47516 Office: North Knox HS 10890 N Hwy 159 Bicknell IN 47512 Office Phone: 812-735-2990. E-mail: aford@hp.nknox.k12.in.us.

FORD, ANDREW THOMAS, former academic administrator; b. Cambridge, Mass., May 22, 1944; s. Francis Lawler and Eleanor (Vahey) F.; m. Anne M. Monahan, July 2, 1966; 1 dau., Lauren Elizabeth. BA, Seton Hall U., 1966; MA, U. WIs., 1968; PhD, U. Wis., 1971. Asst. prof. history Stockton State Coll., Pomona, NJ, 1971-72, asst. to v.p. for acad. affairs, 1972-74; acting dir. Nat. Materials Devel. Ctr. for French and Portuquese, Bedford, NH, 1976-77; acad. programs coordinator N.H. Coll. and Univ. Council, Manchester, 1975-78; v.p. acad. affairs R.I. Sch. Design, Providence, 1978-81; dean Allegheny Coll., Meadville, Pa., 1981-93, provost, 1983-93; pres. Wabash Coll., Crawfordsville, Ind., 1993—2006. Mem. adv. bd. Marine Bank, 1987-93; founding mem. Commonwealth Partnership. Author: (with R. Chait) Beyond Traditional Tenure, 1982; mem. editl. bd. Liberal Edn., 2000—. Bd. dirs. Vis. Nurse Assn., Providence, 1979-81, Allegheny Summer Music Festival, Meadville, 1981-89, Meadville Med. Ctr., 1985-87; bd. incorporators Spencer Hosp., 1981-85; mem. Nat. Com. on U.S.-China Rels., 1986—; trustee Higher Learning Commn. North Ctrl. Assn. Schs. and Colls., 2002—; dir. Crawfordsville Main St. Program, 2001—. Democrat. Home: 1112 Golf Ln Wheaton IL 60187 Office Phone: 765-361-6221. E-mail: forda@wabash.edu.

FORD, ANN K., lawyer; b. Cleve., July 12, 1954; BA, Georgetown Univ., 1976; JD, Duke Univ., 1980. Bar: DC 1981, NY 1987. Ptnr., nat. chair Trademark, Copyright and Media Practice Group DLA Piper US LLP. Contbr. articles to profl. jours. Mem.: ABA, Internat. Trademark Assn. Office: DLA Piper US LLP 1200 19th St NW Washington DC 20036-2412 Office Phone: 202-861-3920. Office Fax: 202-689-7540. Business E-Mail: ann.ford@dlapiper.com.

FORD, BARBARA JEAN, librarian, educator; b. Dixon, Ill., Dec. 5, 1946; BA magna cum laude with honors, Ill. Wesleyan U., 1968; MA in Internat. Rels., Tufts U., 1969; MS in Libr. Sci., U. Ill., 1973. Dir. Soybean Insect Rsch. Info. Ctr. Ill. Natural History Survey, Urbana, 1973-75; from asst. to assoc. prof. U. Ill., Chgo., 1975-84, asst. documents libr., 1975-79, documents libr., dept. head, 1979-84, acting audiovisual libr., 1983-84; asst. dir. pub. svcs. Trinity U., San Antonio, 1984-86, assoc. prof., assoc. dir., 1986-91, acting dir. librs., 1989, 91; prof., dir. univ. libr. svcs. Va. Commonwealth U., Richmond, 1991-98; asst. commr. Chgo. Pub. Libr., 1998—2002; dir., disting. prof. Mortenson Ctr. Internat. Libr. Programs, U. Ill., Urbana, 2003—. Women's re-entry adv. bd. U. Ill., Chgo., 1980-82, student affairs com., 1978-80, student admissions, records, coll. rels. com., 1981-84, univ. senate, 1976-78, 82-84, chancellor's libr. coun. svcs. com. 1984, campus lectrs. com. 1982-83; admissions interviewer for prospective students Trinity U., 1987-91, reader for internat. affairs theses, 1985-91, libr. self-study com., 1985-86, internat. affairs com., 1986-91, inter-Am. studies com., 1986-91, faculty senate, 1987-90; libr. working group U.S./Mex. Commn. Cultural Coop., 1990; presenter in field Contbr. articles to profl. jours. Bd. dirs. Friends of San Antonio Pub. Libr., 1989-91; adv. com. chair Office for Libr. Pers. Resources, 1994-95; steering com. Virtual Libr. Va., 1994-98, chair user svcs. com., 1995-96. Celia M. Howard fellow Tufts U., 1969; sr. fellow UCLA Grad. Sch. Libr. and Info. Sci., 1993. Mem. ALA (conf. program com. 1985-91, libr. edn. assembly 1983-84, membership com. 1978-79, status of women in librarianship com. 1983-85, exec bd., 1996-99, Lippincott Award Jury 1979-80, Shirley Olofson Meml. award 1977), ALA Coun. (at-large councilor 1985-89, chpt. councilor Ill. Libr. Assn. 1980-84, com. on coms. 1987-88, spl. coun. orientation com. 1982-83, ALA exec. bd., 1996-99, pres.- elect 1996-97, pres. 1997-98), Assn. Coll. and Rsch. Librs. (bd. dirs. 1989-92, pres.-elect 1989-90, pres. 1990-91, publs. com. 1990-91, conf. program planning 1990-91), Nat. Assn. State Univs. and Land Grant Colls. (commn. info. tech. 1992-94), Internat. Fedn. Libr. Assns. and Instns. (sec. ofcl. pubs. sect., gen. info. com. 1985 conf., moderator Latin Am. seminar on ofcl. pubs. 1991, univ. and other rsch. librs. sect. standing com. 1999-2007, governing bd. 2005-07), Spl. Librs. Assn. (program com. 1976-77, 80-82, publicity com. 1977-79, chair 1978-79, chair spl. projects com. 1981-82, sec./treas. divsn. social sci. internat. affairs sect. 1984-86), Assn. Libr. Info. Sci. Edn. (chair local arrangements conf. planning com. 1988, 92), Ill. Libr. Assn. (chair election com. 1976-77, exec. bd. 1978-79, 80-84, bd. govt. documents round table 1976-79, chair 1978-79, long range planning com. 1980-84), Tex. Libr. Assn. (pubs. com. 1985-87, legis. com. 1986-87, judge best of exhibits award 1987, task force Amigos Fellowship 1990, del. conf. on librs. and info. svcs., 1991), Va. Libr. Assn. (ad hoc. com. distance learning 1992), Va. State Libr. and Archives (Va. libr. and info. svcs. task force 1991-93, steering com. Arbuthnot lecture 1992-93, coop. continuing edn. adv. com. 1992-94), VIVA (steering com. 1994-98), Chgo. Libr. Club (2d v.p. 1983-84), Richmond Acad. Libr. Consortium (v.p. 1991-92, pres. 1992-93), Beta Phi Mu, Phi Kappa Phi, Phi Alpha Theta, Kappa Delta Pi. Office Phone: 217-244-1898. Business E-Mail: bjford@uiuc.edu.

FORD, BETTY ANN (ELIZABETH ANN FORD), former First Lady of the United States, health facility executive; b. Chicago, Apr. 8, 1918; d. William Stephenson and Hortence (Neahr) Bloomer; m. William G. Warren, 1942 (div. 1947); m. Gerald R. Ford (38th Pres. U.S.), Oct. 15, 1948; children: Michael Gerald, John Gardner, Steven Meigs, Susan Elizabeth. Studied, Bennington Sch. of Dance, 1936-37; studied with Martha Graham, Graham Sch. of Dance, NYC, 1937; LL.D. (hon.), U. Mich., 1976. Dancer Martha Graham Concert Group, NYC, 1939-41; fashion dir. Herpolsheimer's Dept. Store, Grand Rapids, Mich., 1943-48; dance instr. Grand Rapids, 1932-48; First Lady of the United States, 1974—77. Co-founder Susan G. Komen Foundation, 1982; chmn., co-founder The Betty Ford Ctr., Rancho Mirage, Calif., 1982—. Author: (autobiography) The Times of My Life, 1978, Betty: A Glad Awakening, 1987. Bd. dirs. Nat. Arthritis Found. (hon.); trustee Martha Graham Dance Ctr., Eisenhower Med. Ctr., Rancho Mirage; hon. chmn. Palm Springs Desert Mus.; nat. trustee Nat. Symphony Orch.; bd. dirs. The Lambs, Libertyville, Ill.; co-founder (with Leonard Firestone) Betty Ford Ctr., Rancho Mirage, Calif., 1982. Named to Mich. Women's Hall of Fame, 1987; recipient Presidential Medal of Freedom, 1991, Living Legacy award, Women's Internat. Ctr., 1998, Congressional Gold Medal, 1999, C. Everett Koop Health award, Am. Hosp. Assn., 1999, Woodrow Wilson Pub. Svc. award, 2003. Republican. Episcopalian. Office: Gerald R Ford Library 1000 Beal Ave Ann Arbor MI 48109*

FORD, BILL (WILLIAM CLAY FORD JR.), automotive company executive; b. Detroit, May 3, 1957; s. William Clay Ford Sr. and Martha Parke (Firestone); m. Lisa Vanderzee; 4 children. BA, Princeton U., 1979; MBA in Mgmt., MIT, 1984. Prodn. planning analyst, advisor vehicle devel. design ctr., mfg. engr. auto assembly divsn., mgr. Ford Motor Co., Ala., 1979-82, mem. nat. bargaining team Ford/UAW labor talks, mktg. strategy analyst No. Am. Auto Opns., advt. specialist, 1982-83, internat. fin. specialist, mem. fin. staff, 1984-85, planning mgr. car prodn. devel., 1985-86, dir. com. vehicle mktg. Europe divsn., 1986-87, chmn., mng. dir. Switzerland divsn., 1987-89, mgr. heavy truck engr. and mfg. Ford Truck Opns., 1989-90, dir. bus. strategy Ford Auto Group, 1990-91, exec. dir. bus. strategy Ford Auto Group, 1991-92, gen. mgr. climate control divsn., 1992-94, v.p. com. Trucking Vehicle Ctr. Ford Auto Ops., 1994-95, chmn. fin. com., 1995—2001, chmn., 1998—, CEO, 2001—06. Vice chmn. Detroit Lions; mem. fin. com., properties com. NFL; bd. dir. eBay, Inc., 2005-. Chmn. bd. trustees Henry Ford Mus., Greenfield Village; trustee Henry Ford Health Sys., Detroit Renaissance; mem. World Econ. Forum's Global Leaders for Tomorrow. Alfred P. Sloan fellow MIT, 1983-84. Office: Ford Motor Co 1 American Rd Dearborn MI 48126-2798*

FORD, BRENDAN A., health facility administrator; B in Acctg., Miami U., Oxford, Ohio; JD, Ohio State U., Columbus. With Baker-Hostetler LLP; dir. legal affairs Cardinal Health, Inc., 1991—93, v.p. corp. devel., 1993—96, sr. v.p. corp. devel., 1996—99, exec. v.p. corp. devel., 1999—, interim gen. counsel, 2005. Office: Cardinal Health Inc 7000 Cardinal Pl Dublin OH 43017*

FORD, BURCH TRACY, headmaster; BA, Boston U.; MSW, Simmons Coll.; EdM, Harvard U. Teacher and sch. counselor Groton Sch., 1978—88; teacher & dean of students Milton Acad., 1988—93; head of sch. Miss Porter's Sch., Conn., 1993—. Former pres. Nat. Coalition of Girls Schools; former chair Commn. on Independent Schools, New England Assn. of Schools and Colleges; bd. mem. Nat. Assn. of Principals of Schools for Girls. Bd. mem. Chewonki Found., Nutmeg Big Brothers Big Sisters Found. Office: Miss Porter's Sch 60 Main St Farmington CT 06032 Office Phone: 860-409-3632. Business E-Mail: burch_ford@missporters.org.*

FORD, CARL W., JR., consulting firm executive, former federal agency administrator; b. Hot Springs, Ark., 1943; married. BA in Asian Studies, Fla. State U., 1968, MA in East Asian Studies. China analyst CIA, 1974—78, congl. fgn. affairs fellow, 1978; legis. asst. for arms control and fgn. policy Office of Senator John Glenn; staff mem. Senate Com. on Fgn. Rels., 1979—81; fgn. policy and def. issues dir. Office of Senator John Glenn, 1981—84; fgn. policy and def. advisor John Glenn Presl. Campaign, 1984; nat. intelligence officer for East Asia CIA, 1985—91; prin. dep. asst. sec. of def. for internat. security affairs U.S. Dept. Def., 1989, acting asst. sec., 1991, dep. asst. sec. for Near East and South Asian affairs, 1991—93; ret. CIA, 1993; asst. sec. for intelligence & rsch. U.S. Dept. State, Washington, 2001—03; exec. v.p. Cassidy & Associates, Washington, 2003—. With US Army, 1963—66, Vietnam, with US Army, 1969—74. Office: Cassidy & Associates 700 13th St NW Ste 400 Washington DC 20005

FORD, CECILIA SPARKS, federal agency administrator; Grad., U. Va. Atty. Bus. and Adminstrv. Law Divsn. Health and Human Svcs. Office Gen. Counsel; bd. mem. U.S. Dept. Health and Human Svcs., Washington, 1980—99, chair departmental appeals bd., 1999—, also bd. dirs. Office: Dept Health & Human Svcs Departmental Appeals Bd MS 6127 DAB Chair & Appellate Division 330 Independence Ave Cohen Bldg Rm G-644 Washington DC 20201 Office Phone: 202-565-0200. Office Fax: 202-565-0238. Business E-Mail: cecilia.ford@hhs.gov.

FORD, CHARLES A., ambassador; b. May 31, 1950; s. Marvin and Wanda F.; m. Lillian Malave, Dec. 8, 1973; children: Monica Ann, Michael BA in Econmics, William and Mary Coll., 1972; MA in Latin Am. Studies, George Washington U., 1975. Policy analyst Inter-Am. Devel. Bank, 1974-78; internat. economist Motor Vehicle Mfg. Assn., 1978-82; from comml. attache to sr. adv. U.S. Dept. Commerce, Buenos Aires, 1982—2003; sr. advisor to dep. asst. sec. internat. ops. U.S. and Fgn. Comml. Svc. U.S. Dept Commerce, 2003—05; US amb. to Honduras US Dept. State, Tegucigalpa, 2005—. Author: Past Trends and Developments in Mexican Automotive Policy and Potential Implications for U.S./Mexican Trade Relations, 1981. Wolcott fellow Wolcott Found./George Washington U., 1974-75; Recipient Silver medal, US Dept. Commerce, Gold medal for Disting. Achievement in Fed. Svc., Bronze medal for Outstanding Achievement Mem. Am. Fgn. Svc. Assn., Inter Am. Coun., Sigma Chi. Methodist. Avocations: travel, reading, jogging. Office: Am Embassy 3480 Tegucigalpa Washington DC 20521 Home: Unit 3030 Box 1 Apo AA 34022

FORD, CHARLES NATHANIEL, otolaryngologist, educator; b. NYC, June 25, 1940; s. Charles Nathaniel and Marie (Casa) F.; children: C. David, Brian C.; m. Sharon L. James, Feb. 3, 1990; stepchildren: Scott James, Julie James. BA, SUNY, Binghamton, 1961; MD, U. Louisville, 1965. Intern and resident Henry Ford Hosp., Detroit, 1965-70, staff, 1970-71; with Gundersen Clinic, LaCrosse, Wis., 1973-81; chief otolaryngology Middleton VA Hosp., Madison, Wis., 1982-94; prof. otolaryngol. divsn. dept. surgery U. Wis., Madison, 1981-93, chmn. otolaryngol. divsn. dept. surgery, 1993—. Mem.-at-large med. bd. U. Wis. Ctr. for Health Scis., 1989-91, sec., 1992-93, v.p., 1994-95, pres. med. staff, chair med. bd. 1996-98; DeWeese lectr. U. Oreg., 1994; Manion Meml. lectr. Ind. U., 1995; Hough lectr. U. Okla., 1996; Sartian lectr. U. Tex., 1998; keynote lectr. Brit. Voice Assn., 2000, Voice Symposium Australia, 2002, G. Paul Moore lectr. Voice Found., Phila., 2003. Author, editor: Phonosurgery: Assessment and Surgical Management of Voice Disorders, 1991; mem. editl. bd.: Jour. Voice, Otolaryngol. Head and Neck Surgery, Laryngoscope, Microsurgery; author editor numerous sci. papers, chpts. and abstracts. Maj. USAF, 1971-73. Avalon Found. scholar, 1962-63; named to Best Drs. in Am., Woodward/White, Inc., 1991—. Fellow ACS, Am. Laryngol., Rhinol. and Otolog. Soc., Am. BronchoEsophagological Assn. (past pres.), Am. Laryngol. Assn., Am. Soc. for Head and Neck Surgery, Am. Acad. Otolaryngology, Head and Neck Surgery (honor award 1992); mem. AMA, Soc. Univ. Otolaryngologists-Head and Neck Surgeons (past pres.), Internat. Assn. Phonosurgeons, Am. Speech-Lang.-Hearing Assn. Democrat. Unitarian Universalist. Avocations: tennis, golf, theater, art, music. Office: U Wis Ctr Health Sci 600 Highland Ave Madison WI 53792-0001 Office Phone: 608-263-0192.

FORD, CHARLES WILLARD, medical educator; b. Bloomsburg, Pa., Oct. 28, 1938; s. John Willard and Pauline Teresa Ford; m. Barbara Marie Hanawalt, June 6, 1959; children: Lane(dec.) , Lori, Lanae, Lanette. BA, Taylor U., Upland, Ind., 1960; BS, Pa. State U., 1961, MEd, 1962; PhD, SUNY, Buffalo, 1970; postgrad., U. Mich., 1976—77. HS tchr., 1961-64; mem. faculty Erie CC, 1965-70; fgn. svc. officer Peace Corps, Ghana, 1970-72; various positions Sch. Health Related Professions, SUNY, Buffalo, 1972-75, 77-79, assoc. dean Sch. Health Related Professions, 1978—79; with Grand Rapids Med. Edn. Ctr., Mich., 1975-77; dean U. Health Scis./Chgo. Med. Sch., 1979—80; dean undergrad. colls. U. New Eng., Biddeford, Maine, 1982-84, pres., 1984-91, prof. health sci., 1983—. Active in accreditation and curriculum program develop in 40 states and 6 countries; vis. prof. Israel, Tel Aviv, Jerusalem, Haifa, spring, 1999—. Author (with M. K. Morgan): (book) Teaching in the Health Professions, Clinical Education for the Allied Health Professions; contbr. articles to profl jours. Pres. Maine Higher Edn. Coun., 1987—88, Maine Ind. Coll. Assn., 1988—89; bd. govs. Am. Assn. Coll. Osteo. Medicine, 1984—91. Recipient Study Exch., Rotary, Germany and Turkey, 1995. Mem.: NEA (life), Assn. Schs. Allied Health Profls. (life), Am. Assn. Higher Edn. (life). Office: U New Eng Biddeford ME 04005 Office Phone: 207-283-0171.

FORD, CHERYL, professional basketball player; b. Homer, La., June 6, 1981; d. Karl Malone and Bonita Ford. Grad. in Health and Phys. Edn., La. Tech U., Ruston, 2003. Forward WNBA Detroit Shock, 2003—; forward (off-season) Nat. Women's Basketball League Dallas Fury, 2003—04. Mem. USA Women's Nat. Team, 2004—. Named WNBA Rookie of Yr., 2003, All-Star Game MVP, 2007; named to Ea. Conf. All-Star Team, WNBA, 2003, 2005—07, Select All-Star Team, 2004. Achievements include winning the 2003 and 2006 WNBA Championships as a member of the Shock. Avocations: painting, drawing. Mailing: Detroit Shock Palace Sports & Entertainment 5 Championship Dr Auburn Hills MI 48326*

FORD, CHRISTOPHER ASHLEY, federal official, lawyer; s. Ashley Lloyd and Barbara Hill Ford; m. Jennifer Lynn Davis-Ford, June 27, 1992; 1 child, Stella-Grace Annabelle. AB summa cum laude, Harvard Coll., 1989; DPhil, Oxford U., 1992; JD, Yale Law Sch., 1995. Bar: 4th Cir. Ct. Appeals 1996, Va. 1996, DC 1998, Ct. Veterans Appeals 1997. Assoc. Shea and Gardner, Washington, 1995—97; asst. counsel Pres. Intelligence Oversight Bd., Washington, 1996; counsel spl. investigation Senate Govtl. Affairs Com., Washington, 1997, chief investigative counsel, 1999; nat. security advisor for Senator Susan Collins, Washington, 1998; chief coun./staff dir. Permanent Subcommittee Investigations, Washington, 2000; minority counsel/gen. counsel Senate Select Com. Intelligence, Washington, 2001—03; prin. dep. asst. sec. US State Dept., Washington, 2003—06, spl. rep. nuc. nonproliferation, 2006—. Office Phone: 202-320-5164.

FORD, CLARENCE QUENTIN, mechanical engineer, educator; b. Glenwood, N.Mex., Aug. 6, 1923; s. Clarence Noel and Elsie May (Jones) F.; m. Ruth Madge McKinney, June 11, 1950; children— Glenn Mac, Dabney Ann. BS, U.S. Mcht. Marine Acad., 1944; BS in Mech. Engring., N.Mex. State U., 1949; MS in Mech. Engring., U. Mo., 1950; PhD, Mich. State U., 1959. Registered profl. engr. Inst. U. Mo., 1949-50; instr. Wash. State U., 1950-53, asst. prof., 1953-56; instr. Mich. State U., 1956-59; prof. N.Mex. State U., Las Cruces, 1959-88, head dept. mech. engring., 1960-70, assoc. dean engring., 1974-80, 81-88, dean engring., 1980-81, prof. and assoc. dean emeritus, 1988—; prin. Ford & Assocs., 1964—. Mem. N.Mex. Bd. Registration Profl. Engrs. and Land Surveyors, 1978-88, chmn., 1980-81, 86-87, mem. emeritus, 1989—; mem. N.Mex. State Hwy. Commn., 1989-95, sec., 1991-95. Editor: Space Technology and Earth Problems, Vol. 23 Sci. and Tech. Series, 1969 Served to lt. USNR, 1942-46 Fellow AAAS; mem. ASME, Am. Soc. Engring. Edn., Nat. Coun. Examiners for Engring. and Surveying (v.p. 1986-88, Disting. Svc. award 1989, Disting. Svc. award with spl. commendation 1990), N.Mex. Soc. Profl. Engrs. (Outstanding Engr. 1964), Masons, York Rite, Kiwanis, Sigma Xi, Phi Kappa Phi, Pi Tau Sigma, Tau Beta Pi, Pi Mu Epsilon. Presbyterian. Home: 1985 Crescent Dr Las Cruces NM 88005-3300 Office Phone: 505-524-6753. E-mail: Chapache@aol.com.

FORD, DANIEL (DANIEL FRANCIS FORD), writer; b. Nov. 2, 1931; s. Patrick Joseph and Anne Theresa Ford; m. Sarah Lansing Paine; 1 child, Katharine Serena. BA, U. NH, 1954; postgrad., U. Manchester, Eng., 1954-55, King's Coll. London, 2006—. Reporter Overseas Weekly, Frankfurt, Germany, 1958; asst. editor N.H. Profiles mag., Portsmouth, 1959-60; publs. editor U. N.H., 1961-68; freelance writer Durham, N.H., 1969—. Corr. The Nation, South Vietnam, 1964; contbg. editor Air & Space/Smithsonian Mag., 1994—; pub. Warbird's Forum, 1997—. Author: Now Comes Theodora, 1965, Incident at Muc Wa (transl. in Dutch, filmed as Go Tell the Spartans), 1967, The High Country Illuminator, 1971, The Country Northward, 1976, Flying Tigers: Claire Chennault and the American Volunteer Group, 1991, rev. edit., 2007, Glen Edwards: The Diary of a Bomber Pilot, 1998, Remains, 2000, The Only War We've Got: Early Days in South Vietnam, 2001, Michael's War, 2003; editor: The Lady and the Tigers, 2002; contbr. Wall St. Jour., 2001—. With U.S. Army, 1956-57. Recipient award of excellence Aviation-Space Writers, 1992; Fulbright fellow U. Manchester, 1954-55, Verville fellow Nat. Air & Space Mus., 1989-90; Stern Found. Mag. Writers grantee, 1964; resident scholar U. N.H., 1996—. Mem. Met. Opera Guild, Phi Beta Kappa, Phi Kappa Phi. Office: 433 Bay Rd Durham NH 03824-3439

FORD, DEXTER, retired insurance company executive; b. Utica, NY, Nov. 18, 1917; s. David E. and Anna Mae (Dexter) F.; m. Jean Brand McGowan, Nov. 1, 1944; children: David K., Dexter T., Nancy E. BS, St. Lawrence U., 1939. With Aetna Life & Casualty Co., Hartford, Conn., 1946—80, v.p. mktg., 1968-76, v.p. personal ins. dept., 1976-80. Chmn. bd. mgmt. YMCA, 1978-80. Served to lt. (s.g.) USNR, 1941-45. Recipient St. Lawrence U. Alumni citation, 1978 Mem. St. Lawrence U. Alumni Assn. (pres. 1974-75) Republican. Congregationalist (chmn. bd. trustees 1970). Home: Apt 213 156 Lawrence St Saratoga Springs NY 12866-1351

FORD, DONALD HERBERT, psychologist, educator; b. Sioux City, Iowa, Aug. 15, 1926; s. Herbert Owen and Esther (Sanow) F.; m. Carol Clark, May 30, 1948; children— Russell, Martin, Douglas, Cameron. BS, Kans. State U., 1948; MS, 1951; PhD, Pa. State U., 1955. Counselor Kans. State U., 1948-52; asst. prof. psychology Pa. State U., University Park, 1955-64, assoc. prof., 1964-67, assoc. prof. human devel., 1967-72, prof. human. devel., 1972—, prof. biobehavioral health, 1992—. Asst. dir. div. counseling, 1956-59, dir., 1959-67; dean Coll. Human Devel., 1967-77, head dept. Communications Disorders, 1988-89, head biobehavioral health, 1992. Author: Systems of Psychotherapy; A Comparative Study, 1963, Humans as Self-Constructing Living Systems, 1987, 2d edit., 1992, Developmental Systems Theory, 1992, Contemporary Models of Psychotherapy, 1998. Served with USAAF, 1944-45. Mem. AAAS, Am. Psychol. Assn., Am. Psychol. Soc., Ea. Psychol. Assn. Home: 130 Slab Cabin Rd State College PA 16801-6971 Office: Penn State U Coll Health & Human Devel University Park PA 16802 E-mail: dhf6@psu.edu. *My basic values are rooted in the "teaching by example" of my parents, serving the objectives of being of service to others as well as to self, utilizing a strong, caring family unit as the best cornerstone of psychological, social, and economic health. My basic professional goal is to help harness the fruits of technological advances, resulting from the intensive application of the principle of specialization, to the evolution of humanistic societies designed to serve people as open, living systems. This requires a new scientific model of Man as a coherent unit, enabling us to synthesize the fruits of analytical science and to put "Humpty Dumpty" back together again as a person with purposes and values as well as productive potential.*

FORD, EILEEN OTTE (MRS. GERARD W. FORD), modeling agency executive; b. NYC, Mar. 25, 1922; d. Nathaniel and Loretta Marie (Laine) Otte; m. Gerard William Ford, Nov. 20, 1944; children: Margaret (Mrs. Robert Craft), Gerard William, M. Katie (Mrs. Andre Balazs), A. Lacey (Mrs. John Williams). BS, Barnard Coll., 1943. Stylist Elliot Clarke Studio, NYC, 1943-44, William Becker Studio, 1945; copywriter Arnold Constable, NYC, 1945-46; reporter Tobe Coburn, 1946; co-founder Ford Model Agy., NYC, 1946—, now chmn. bd. Author: Eileen Ford's Model Beauty, Secrets of the Model's World, A More Beautiful You in 21 Days, Beauty Now and Forever, 1977. Bd. dirs. London Philharmonic, 1948—. Recipient Harpers Bazaar award for promotion internat. understanding, Woman of Yr. in Advt. award, 1983 Office: Ford Models Inc 111 5th Ave New York NY 10003*

FORD, FORD BARNEY, retired federal official; b. Norton, Va., Nov. 19, 1922; s. William Zachary and Annis Louvinia (Ford) Godbey; m. Norma Isabel Lentz, Jan. 16, 1945; children: Robert Barney, Jack T. (dec.). Student, Va. Mil. Inst., Lexington, 1942-43; BS, U. Calif., Berkeley, 1948; LLD (hon.), Huston Tillotson Coll., 1985. Registered indsl. and safety engr. Acting postmaster, Bishop, Calif., 1951-54; adminstrv. analyst Calif. Joint Legis. Budget Com., Sacramento, 1955-59; exec. dir. Calif. Senate Fact-Finding Com. on Natural Resources, Sacramento, 1959-67; dep. sec. Calif. Resources Agt., Sacramento, 1967-73; chmn. and mem. Calif. Occupl. Safety and Health Appeals Bd., Sacramento, 1973-78; v.p. Calif. Inst. Indsl. and Govtl. Rels., Sacramento, 1978-81; asst. sec. labor for mine safety and health US Dept. Labor, Arlington, Va., 1981-83, undersec. Washington, 1983-85, acting sec., 1984-85; chmn. Mine Safety and Health Rev. Commn., 1985-92; ret., 1992. Rsch. publs. on fire prevention, geothermal devel. East Wilmington oil field. With U.S. Army, 1943-46, ETO. Decorated Combat Infantryman badge. Mem. DAV, SAR, VFW (comdr. Bishop, Calif. 1948-50), Elks, Masons, Shriners. Methodist. Personal E-mail: fordbarneyford@cs.com.

FORD, GEORGE BURT, retired lawyer; b. South Bend, Ind., Oct. 1, 1923; s. George W. and Florence (Burt) Ford; m. Charlotte Ann Kupferer, June 12, 1948; children: John, Victoria, George, Charlotte. BS in Engring. Law, Purdue U., 1946; LLB, Ind. U., 1949. Bar: Ind. 1949, US Dist. Ct. (no. dist.) Ind. 1949. Assoc. Jones, Obenchain & Butler, South Bend, 1949-52; ptnr. Jones, Obenchain, Ford, Pankow & Lewis, South Bend, 1953-93, of counsel, 1994—2003; ret., 2003. Co-author: (book) Forms for Indiana Corporations, 1967, 2d edit., 1977. With US Army, 1943—45, ETO. Fellow: Am. Coll. Trust and Estate Counsel; mem.: ABA, St. Joseph County Bar Assn. (pres. 1976—77), Ind. Bar Assn., Phi Delta Phi, Phi Gamma Delta.

FORD, GERALD J. (JERRY), finance company executive; b. Tex., Aug. 1944; BA in Econs., So. Meth. U., 1966, JD, 1969. Bar: Tex. Chmn., CEO First Gibraltar Bank, Tex., 1988-93; chmn. bd. dirs. First Madison Bank; pres., owner Madison Fin., Inc.; founder First United Bank Group, Inc.; chmn., CEO First Nationwide Mortgage Corp., 1994—2002, Calif. Fed. Bank (formerly First Nationwide Bank), 1994—2002, Calif. Fed. Preferred Capital Corp., 1996—2002, Golden State Bancorp (acquired by Citigroup), 1998—2002, CEO, 1996—2002; chmn. First Acceptance Corp. (formerly Liberte Investors, Inc.), 1996—. Bd. dir. Freeport-McMoRan Cooper & Cold, 2000—, AmeriCredit Corp., Fort Worth, Tex., 2003—, McMoRan Exploration Co.; bd. trustees So. Meth. Univ., Dallas, 1992—, chmn. bd. trustees, 2002. Named Among 40 Most Generous, Fortune Mag., 1998; recipient, Disting. Alumni award, SMU, 1995, Mustang award, SMU, 1997. Office: Chairman First Acceptance Corp 3813 Green Hills Village Dr Nashville TN 37215

FORD, GREGORY RAY, investment banker; m. Gale C. Cobb, Oct. 31, 1990. BBA, Baylor U., Waco, Tex., 1980, MBA, 1981. V.p. Tex. Commerce Bank, Houston, 1981—96; pres. GRFAI, Houston, 1996—2003; mng. prin. The Legacy Equity Group, LLC, Houston, 2003—. Avocations: wingshooting, golf, fly fishing. Home Phone: 281-330-7617. Personal E-mail: eagleford@aol.com.

FORD, HAROLD EUGENE, retired congressman; b. Memphis, Tenn., May 20, 1945; s. Newton J. and Vera (Davis) F.; m. Dorothy Bowles, Feb. 10, 1969; children: Harold, Newton Jake, Sir Isaac. BS, Tenn. State U., 1967; AA, John Gupton Coll., 1969; MBA, Howard U. Mem. Tenn. Ho. of Reps., 1970-74; mem. US Congress from 9th Tenn. dist., 1975—96, edn. and workforce com., govt. reform and oversight com.; consult., founder The Harold Ford Group, Memphis, 2001—. Ways and means com., subcom. on oversight, mem. subcom. human resources, Dem. whip representing Tenn., La., Miss. during 99th Congress. Bd. dirs. Met. Memphis YMCA affiliated with Alpha Phi Alpha frat.; nat. adv. bd. St. Jude Children's Research Hosp. Named Outstanding Young Man of Year Memphis Jaycees, 1976, Outstanding Young Man of Year Tenn. Jaycees, 1977, Child Advocate of Yr. Child Welfare League Am., 1987. Democrat. Office: The Harold Ford Group 6060 Poplar Ave #150 Memphis TN 38119-0917

FORD, HAROLD EUGENE, JR., law educator, former congressman; b. Memphis, May 11, 1970; s. Harold E. and Dorothy (Bowles) Ford. BA in Am. Hist., U. Pa., 1992; JD, U. Mich. Law Sch., 1996. Spl. asst. Clinton & Gore Transition Team, 1992, Econ. Devel. Adminstrn., US Dept. Commerce, 1993; mem. US Congress from 9th Tenn. dist., 1997—2007, budget com., com. on fin. services, com. on edn. & the workforce, Cong. E 911 Caucus, 2003—04; chmn. Dem. Leadership Coun., Washington, 2007—; vice chmn, sr. policy adv. Merrill Lynch & Co., Inc., NYC, 2007—. Vis. prof. pub. policy Vanderbilt U., 2007—; polit. contbr. FOX News Channel, 2007—. Named one of 100 Most Influential Black Americans, Ebony mag., 2006; recipient Trumpet Awards Young STAR award, 2001, Homeownership Hero award, Homeownership Alliance, 2003. Democrat. Baptist. Office: Dem Leadership Coun 600 Pennsylvania Ave SE Ste 400 Washington DC 20003 also: Merrill Lynch & Co Inc Four World Financial Ctr New York NY 10080*

FORD, HARRISON, actor; b. Chgo., July 13, 1942; m. Mary Marquardt, June 18, 1964 (div. 1979); children: Willard, Benjamin; m. Melissa Mathison, Mar. 14, 1983 (div. Jan. 6, 2004); children: Malcolm, Georgia. Attended, Ripon Coll. Appeared in motion pictures including: Dead Heat on a Merry-Go-Round, 1966, Luv, 1967, The Long Ride Home, 1967, Getting Straight, 1970, Zabriske Point, 1970, American Graffiti, 1973, The Conversation, 1974, Star Wars, 1977, Heroes, 1977, Force 10 From Navarone, 1978, Hanover Street, 1979,More American Graffiti, 1979, The Frisco Kid, 1979, Apocalypse Now, 1979, The Empire Strikes Back, 1980, Raiders of the Lost Ark, 1981, Blade Runner, 1982, Return of the Jedi, 1983, Indiana Jones and the Temple of Doom, 1984, Witness, 1985, Mosquito Coast, 1986, Frantic, 1988, Working Girl, 1988, Indiana Jones and the Last Crusade, 1989, Presumed Innocent, 1990, Regarding Henry, 1991, Patriot Games, 1992, The Fugitive, 1993, Clear and Present Danger, 1994, Sabrina, 1995, A Hundred and One Nights, 1995, Devil's Own, 1996, Air Force One, 1997, Six Days Seven Nights, 1998, Random Hearts, 1999, What Lies Beneath, 2000, K-19: The Widowmaker, 2002, Hollywood Homicide, 2003, Firewall, 2006; appeared in TV movies The Intruders, 1970, Judgement: The Court-Martial of Lt. William Calley, 1975, James A. Michener's Dynasty, 1976, The Possessed, 1977; numerous TV appearances including Ironside, The Mod Squad, The F.B.I., My Friend Tony, Gunsmoke, Kung-Fu, The Virginian, Young Indiana Jones Chronicles.

FORD, JACK, lawyer, news correspondent; m. Dorothy Ford; children: Ashley, Colin. BA in History, Yale U.; JD, Fordham U. Asst. prosecutor Prosecutor's Office, Monmouth County, NJ; pvt. practice; legal commentator Sta. WCBS-TV, NYC, 1983; chief legal corr. NBC News, 1994; anchor weekend edits. Today, 1995; anchor, corr. Courtroom TV, 1991—94, guest anchor, 2004, co-host, Trial Heat, co-anchor, Banfield & Ford: Courtside. Adj. prof. law Fordham U. Sch. Law. Moderator (TV series) That Delicate Balance II: The Bill of Rights, 1992. Vol. Susan Komen Breast Cancer Found., Alzheimer's Assn., NJ Spl. Olympics, Jimmy V. Found. Recipient Emmy, 1989, Emmy nomination, 1991, Silver Anniversary award NCAA, 1997; named Nat. Father of Yr., 1998. Mailing: c/o Courtroom TV 600 Third Ave New York NY 10016

FORD, JEREMIAH, III, architect; b. Phila., Apr. 22, 1932; s. Jeremiah II and Mary Sterling (Hewitt) F.; m. Judith Oakes Seidler, June 17, 1954 (div. 1973); children: Amanda Hewitt, Katherine Brewster; m. Elizabeth Dana Stewardson, Mar. 1, 1975; children: Elizabeth Connolly, Caroline Thornewill, Dana H. Stewardson. AB, Princeton U., 1954, MFA, 1959. Registered architect, N.J., Mass., Pa., Fla., Del. Designer Harrison and Abramovitz Architects, NYC, 1960-61, Port of N.Y. Authority World Trade Ctr., NYC, 1961-62; archtl. apprentice Kenneth Kassler Architect, Princeton, 1962-64; ptnr. Walker Sander Ford and Kerr Architects, Princeton, 1965-74, Short and Ford Architects, Princeton, 1974-93, Ford Farewell Mills and Gatsch Architects, Princeton, 1993—2004, Ford 3 Architects, Princeton, 2004—. Prin. works include Marriott Hotel and Conf. Ctr., Trenton, N.J. State House, Trenton, Summit (N.J.) City Hall, 1973, Morristown (N.J.) Libr., 1985, Princeton Cmty. Housing, 1982, Cranbury (N.J.) Sr. Housing, 1990, Summit Unitarian Ch., 2000, Christ Ch., Summit, N.J., 2002, Blawenburg Reformed Ch., 2005, D&R Greenway HQs, 2006, pvt. residences. Capt. USMC, 1954-57, Korea, Japan. Episcopalian. Avocations: painting, gardening. Home: 820 Pretty Brook Rd Princeton NJ 08540-7532 Office: Ford 3 Architects 32 Nassau St Princeton NJ 08542 Home Phone: 609-921-2412; Office Phone: 609-924-0043. Personal E-mail: jerryfiii@aol.com. Business E-Mail: jerryf@Ford3.com.

FORD, JOE THOMAS, telephone company executive, former state senator; b. Conway, Ark., June 24, 1937; s. Arch W. and Ruby (Watson) F.; m. Jo Ellen Wilbourn, Aug. 9, 1959; children: Alison, Scott. BS, U. Ark., 1959. With Allied Telephone Co., Little Rock, 1959-83, v.p.-treas., 1963-77, pres., 1977-83, Alltel Corp., 1983-87, pres., chief exec. officer, 1987-91, chmn., pres., chief exec. officer, 1991-93, chmn., CEO, 1993—2002, chmn. Little Rock, 2002—. Mem. Ark. Senate, 1967-82; dir.

Comml. Nat. Bank, 1970-85, Little Rock, Security Bank, Conway, Dial Corp., Textron Inc., EnPro Industries Inc. Recipient Disting. Alumni cert. U. Ark., 1987. Baptist. Office: Alltel Corp PO Box 2177 1 Allied Dr Little Rock AR 72203 Home: 2500 N Jackson St Little Rock AR 72207-3718*

FORD, JOHN CHARLES, artist; b. Choudrant, La., Sept. 29, 1929; s. John Leon Ford and Jessie Faye Dugdale; m. Margaret Ann Preston, Sept. 1959 (div. Apr. 1964); 1 child, John Charles Jr. BFA, La. Poly. Inst., 1950; BDiv, Austin Pres. Theol. Sem., 1953; MFA, U. Oreg., 1960. One-man shows at Leicester Galleries, London, 1967, Otto Seligman Gallery, Seattle, 1962, 72, Francine Seders Gallery, Seattle, 1972, Avanti Gallery, N.Y., 1972, L.I. Painters Awards Exhbn., 1974, Country Art Gallery, Locust Valley, 1974, La. State U., Baton Rouge, 1974, Neuberger Mus., Purchase, N.Y., 1977, Sid Deutsch Art Gallery, N.Y., 1977, RR Gallery, N.Y., 1980, Jack Gallery, N.Y., 1982, Phillip Dash Gallery, N.Y., 1986, Ruston (La.) Art Assn., 1991, Shreveport (La.) Arts Coun., Centenary Gallery, Shreveport, 2001; two-man shows at Labette C.C., Parsons, Kans., 1998; represented in permanent collections at Solomon R. Guggenheim Mus., NYU, N.Y., Hirshhorn Mus. and Sculpture Garden, Washington, Corcoran Gallery of Art, Washington, Neuberger Mus., Purchase, N.Y., Herbert F. Johnson Mus., Ithaca, N.Y., Seattle Art Mus., Addison (Mass.) Gallery Am. Art, Nuffield Found., London, Birmingham (Ala.) Mus. Art, U. Oreg., Ark. Arts Ctr., Little Rock, Ea. Oreg. Coll., La Grande. Avocations: writing, gardening. Home: 1592 Highway 145 Choudrant LA 71227-3600

FORD, JOHN STEPHEN, treasurer; b. Clinton, Mass., Apr. 27, 1957; s. James Joseph and Rita (Hart) F.; m. Mary Andrejczyk, Apr. 15, 1978; children: Michelle, Amanda, William. BS, Lowell U., 1979. CPA, Mass.; notary pub., Mass. Staff acct. Main, Hurdman, Cranston, CPA's, Worcester, Mass., 1979; sr. acct. William S. Reagan & Co. CPA's, Fitchburg, Mass., 1979-82; treas. Peterborough Oil Co., Inc., Leominster, Mass., 1982—2006, bd. dirs., 2006—. Bd. dirs. Peterborough Oil Co. Inc.; cons. in field. Former treas. Lancaster Soccer; former mem. Lancaster Recreation Com.; former coach Pop Warner football; former treas. Lancaster Baseball Assn.; bd. dirs. Worker's Credit Union, Fitchburg, Mass., chmn. bd., Worker's Fin. Svcs., Inc. Fellow Mass. Soc. CPAs; mem. AICPA, Am. Turners, Elks. Roman Catholic. Avocations: sports, local politics, home improvements. Office: Peterborough Oil Co PO Box 787 665 N Main St Leominster MA 01453-1894

FORD, JUDITH ANN TUDOR, retired natural gas distribution company executive; b. Martinsville, Ind., May 11, 1935; d. Glenn Leyburn and Dorotha Mae (Parks) Tudor; m. Walter L. Ford, July 25, 1954 (dec. 1962); children: John Corbin, Christi Sue. Student, Wichita State U., 1953-55; student, U. Nev.-Las Vegas. Legal sec. S.W. Gas Corp., Las Vegas, 1963-69, asst. corp. sec., 1969-72, corp. sec., 1972-82, v.p., 1977-82, sr. v.p., 1982-88, also bd. dirs., dir. 7 subs. Bd. dirs. NBA Svcs., Nev., residence for handicapped, 1989-97, treas., 1990-91, chmn., 1994-97; trustee Nev. Sch. Arts, Las Vegas, 1979-90, chmn. bd. dirs., 1985-86; trustee Disciples Sem. Found., Claremont Sch. Theology and Pacific Sch. Religion, San Francisco, 1985-91, 92-98, 99-2005, vice chmn., 1993-94, chmn., 1994-98; mem. Ariz. Acad., Ariz. Town Halls, 1986-92. Mem. Am. Soc. Corp. Secs., Greater Las Vegas C. of C. (bd. dirs. 1979-85), Pacific Coast Gas Assn. (bd. dirs. 1984-88), Ariz. Bus. Women Owners (exec. com. 1985-88). Democrat. Mem. Christian Ch. (Disciples Of Christ).

FORD, KATHERINE MICHELLE, special education educator; b. Gloversville, NY, Oct. 16, 1965; d. Michael Joseph Conte and Belle Mae Bruse; m. John Allen Ford, Aug. 16, 1997; 1 child, Garrett Michael. BS, U. Tenn., 1997, MEd, 2002; EdS in Ednl. Leadership, Lincoln Meml. U., 2004. Lic. spl. edn. tchr. Ga. Instr. Lexington Ctr., Gloversville, NY, 1987—95; mgr. group home Orange Group Ctr., Chattanooga, 1996—98; from tchr. spl. edn. Mid. Sch. to lead tchr. spl. edn. Elem. Sch. Whitfield County Pub. Schs., Dalton, Ga., 1997—2001, lead tchr. spl. edn. Elem. Sch., 2001—. Trainer new tchrs. Whitfield County Pub. Schs., 2003—; mem. leadership team New Hope Elem. Sch., Dalton, 2001—, Whitfield County Spl. Edn. Dept., Dalton, 2001—. Leader pioneer team Varnell (Ga.) United Meth. Ch., 2004—. Mem.: PTA (pres. 2004—05), Profl. Assn. Ga. Educators. Republican. Meth. Avocations: travel, camping, swimming, hiking. Office: New Hope Elem 1175 New Hope Rd Dalton GA 30720

FORD, KENNETH M., computer scientist, educator; b. Hampton, Va. BS in mgmt., NH Coll., 1982; MS in computer sci., U. West Fla., 1984; PhD in computer sci., Tulane U., 1987. Founder, dir. Inst. Human and Machine Cognition U. West Fla., Pensacola, 1990—. Bd. dirs. Nat. Sci. Bd., 2002—, itFloriada.com; assoc. dir. to dir. Ctr. Excellence and Info. Tech. Ames Rsch. Ctr., NASA, 1997—99; mem. bd. supervisors Fla. Space Authority; editor-in-chief AAAI/MIT Press; past pres. Fla. Artificial Intelligence Rsch. Soc. Author: over 100 sci. papers, Android Epistemology, 1995, Expertise in Context: Human and Machine, 1997, Knowledge Acquisition as Modeling, 1993; co-author (with Patrick J. Hayes): Advances in Human & Machine Cognition, 1999, On Computational Wings: Rethinking the Goals of Artificial Intelligence, 2003. Fellow: Am. Assn. Artificial Intelligence. Office: Inst for Human and Machine Cognition 40 S Alcaniz St Pensacola FL 32502 Office Phone: 850-202-4462. Office Fax: 850-202-4440.

FORD, KENNETH WILLIAM, physicist; b. West Palm Beach, Fla., May 1, 1926; s. Paul Hammond and Edith (Timblin) F.; m. Karin Stehnike, Aug. 27, 1953 (div. 1961); m. Joanne Baumunk, June 9, 1962; children: Paul T., Sarah E., Caroline A., Adam B., Jason L., Ian L.; 1 stepdau., Nina Tannenwald. Student, John Carroll U., 1945, U. Mich., 1945—46; AB, Harvard Coll., 1948; PhD, Princeton U., 1953. Rsch. asst. Los Alamos Sci. Lab., 1950-51; rsch. assoc. Princeton U., 1951-52; from rsch. assoc. to assoc. prof. Ind. U., 1953-58, asst. prof. physics, 1954-57; from assoc. prof. to prof. Brandeis U., 1958-64; prof. U. Calif., Irvine, 1964-70, chmn. dept. physics, 1964-68; prof. physics U. Mass., Boston, 1970-75; pres. N.Mex. Inst. Mining and Tech., Socorro, 1975-82; exec. v.p. U. Md., Adelphi, 1982-83; pres. Molecular Biophysics Tech. Inc., 1983-85; edn. officer Am. Phys. Soc., 1986-87; exec. dir. Am. Inst. Physics, 1987-93; tchr. Germantown Acad., 1995-98; sci. program dir. David and Lucile Packard Found., 1998-99; tchr. Germantown Friends Sch., 2000-2001. Mem. Commn. Coll. Physics, 1968—71; cons. in field. Author: The World of Elementary Particles, 1963, Basic Physics, 1968, Classical and Modern Physics, 3 vols., 1972-74; (with John Wheeler) Geons, Black Holes, and Quantum Foam: A Life in Physics, 1998, The Quantum World: Quantum Physics for Everyone, 2004, In Love with Flying, 2007; mem. editl. bd. Phys. Rev., 1960-62, The Physics Tchr., 2000-06; contbr. articles to profl. jours. With USN, 1944—46. Fulbright fellow Max Planck Inst., Germany, 1955-56, NSF sr. postdoctoral fellow Imperial Coll. London, 1961-62, MIT, 1962. Fellow AAAS (coun. del. physics electorate 1983-86), Am. Phys. Soc. (chmn. forum on physics and soc. 1981, councilor 1984-87, sec.-treas. forum on history of physics 2001-05); mem. Am. Assn. Physics Tchrs. (pres. 1972, Disting. Svc. citation 1976, Oersted medal 2006), Fedn. Am. Scientists.

FORD, LORETTA C., retired dean, educator, consultant, nurse; b. NYC, Dec. 28, 1920; d. Joseph F. and Nellie A. (Williams) Pfingstel; m. William J. Ford, May 2, 1947; 1 child, Valerie. BSN, U. Colo., Boulder, 1949, MS, 1951, EdD, 1961; DSc (hon.), Ohio State Med. Coll., Columbus, 1997, Simmons Coll., Boston, 1997, U. Colo., Boulder, 1997; LLD (hon.), U. Md., College Park, 1990; DSc (hon.), U. Rochester, NY, 2000, Ind. State U., Terre Haute, 2007; LHD (hon.), Binghamton U., NY, 2001. RN N.J. Staff nurse New Brunswick Vis. Nurse Svc., 1941—42; supr., dir. Boulder County (Colo.) Health Dept., 1947—58; from asst. prof. to prof. U. Colo. Sch. Nursing, 1960—72; dean Sch. Nursing, DON, prof. U. Rochester, NY, 1972—86, acting dean Grad. Sch. Edn. and Human Devel. NY, 1988—89; vis. prof. U. Fla., 1968, U. Wash., Seattle, 1974, St. Lukes Coll. Nursing, Tokyo, 1987. Mem. educators adv. panel GAO; dir. Security Trust Co., Rochester, Rochester Telephone Co.; internat. cons. in field. Contbr. chapters to books, articles to profl. jours. Mem. adv. com. Commonwealth Fund Exec. Nurse Fellowship PRogram; bd. dirs. Threshold Alt. Youth Svcs., Easter Seal Soc., ARC, Monroe Cmty. Hosp. With Nurse Corps USAF, 1942—46. Named Colo. Nurse of Yr, Colo. Nurses Assn., Alumni of Century, U. Colo. Sch. Nursing Alumni Assn., 1998; recipient N.Y. State Gov.'s award for women in sci., medicine and nursing, Modern Healthcare Hall of Fame award, Modern Health Care Jour., 1994, Lillian D. Wald Spirit of Nursing award, N.Y. Vis. Nurse Svc., 1994, Lifetime Achievement award, Nat. Conf. Nurse Practitioners, 1999, Trailblazer award, Am. Coll. Nurse Practitioners, 2003, Elizabeth Blackwell award, Hobart and William Smith Colls., 2003, Amazing Exemplar award, Friends of Nat. Inst. Nursing, 2005, Second Century Excellence in Health Care award, Columbia U., 2006. Fellow: Nat. League Nursing (Linda Richards award), Am. Acad. Nursing (Living Legend award 1999); mem.: NAS Inst. Medicine (Gustav O. Leinhard award 1990), ANA, APHA (Ruth B. Freeman award), Am. Coll. Nurse Practitioners (Crystal Trailblazers award 2003), Am. Coll. Health Assn. (Boynton award), Sigma Theta Tau, Alpha Omega Alpha (hon.). Personal E-mail: lorettaford@cfl.rr.com.

FORD, LUCILLE GARBER, economist, educator; b. Ashland, Ohio, Dec. 31, 1921; d. Ora Myers and Edna Lucille (Armstrong) Garber; m. Laurence Wesley Ford, Sept. 1, 1946; children: Karen Elizabeth, JoAnn Christine. AA, Stephens Coll., 1942; BS in Commerce, Northwestern U., 1944, MBA, 1945; PhD in Econs., Case Western Res. U., 1967; PhD (hon.), Tarkio Coll., 1991, Ashland U., 1995. Cert. fin. planner. Instr. Allegheny Coll., Meadville, Pa., 1945-46, U. Ala., Tuscaloosa, 1946-47; personnel dir., asst. sec. A.L. Garber Co., Ashland, Ohio, 1947-67; prof. econs. Ashland U., 1967-95, chmn. dept. econs., 1970-75; dir. Gill Ctr. for Econ. Edn. Ashland Coll., 1975-86, v.p., dean Sch. Bus., Adminstrn. and Econs., 1980-86, v.p. acad. affairs, 1986-90, provost, 1990-92; exec. asst. to pres., 1993-95; pres. Ashland Comm. Found., 1995—. Bd. dirs. Peco II, Inc., Western Res. Econ. Devel. Coun., Ohio Coun. Econ. Edn.; lectr. in field; mem. govs. adv. com. on econ. devel. Author: University Economics-Guide for Education Majors, 1979, Economics: Learning and Instruction, 1981, 91; contbr. articles to profl. jours. Mem. Ohio Gov.'s Commn. on Ednl. Choice, 1992; candidate for lt. gov. of Ohio, 1978; trustee Stephens Coll., 1977-80, Ashland U., 1995—, North Cen. State Coll., 1998-2005; elder Presbyn. Ch.; bd. dirs. Presbyn. Found., 1982-88; chair, trustee Synod-Presbyn. Ch., 1994-2000; active ARC. Named to Ohio Women's Hall of Fame, 2001; recipient Outstanding Alumnus award, Stephens Coll., 1977, Outstanding Profl. award, Ashland U., 1971, 1975, Roman F. Warmke award, 1981, Women of Achievement award, 1998, Outstanding Fundraiser award, Assn. Fund Raising Profls., 2001, Spirit of Chamber award, Ashland Area C. of C., 2001, Disting. Ashland H.S. award, Ashland City Sch. Acad. Found., 2002, Gleanch Clayton award, Ashland U., 2003. Mem. Am. Econs. Assn., Nat. Indsl. Rsch. Soc., Am. Arbitration Assn. (profl. arbitrator), Assn. Pvt. Enterprise Edn. (pres. 1983-84), North Ctrl. Assn. Colls. and Schs. (commr.), Omicron Delta Epsilon, Alpha Delta Kappa. Republican. Office: Ashland Co Comm Found 300 College Ave Ashland OH 44805-3803 Home Phone: 419-289-0668; Office Phone: 419-281-4733. Business E-Mail: accf@hmltd.net.

FORD, MARK PATRICK, publishing executive; b. Euclid, Ohio, Nov. 17, 1956; s. Clyde Robert Ford and Shirley Ann (Kloss) Fuhry; m. Margaret Mary Noonan, Mar. 15, 1987; children: Molly Bridget, Shannon Mary. BS, Kent State U., Oh., 1979. Media planner J. Walter Thompson, Chicago, Ill., 1979-82; midwest advt. mgr. Hearst Corp., Chicago, 1982-85; internat./midwest advt. mgr. Time Mag., Chicago, 1985-89; midwest sales mgr. Entertainment Weekly, Chicago, 1989—91; midwest ad sales mgr., Entertainment Weekly, People and Life mags., 1991—93; corp. accts. dir. Time Inc., 1993—97; pres. Media Networks Inc. (subs. Time, Inc.), Stamford, Conn., 1997—2001; CEO, Time4Media Time Inc., 2001—06, pres., pub., Sports Illus. Group NYC, 2005—. Mem. Chicago Advertising Club, Agate Club, Evanston Golf Club. Avocations: skiing, golf. Office: Sports Illustrated Time Inc 1271 Ave of Americas New York NY 10020 Office Phone: 212-522-1212.*

FORD, MARY ANN, secondary school educator; b. Delhi, La. d. George William Evans and Sarah Elizabeth Deggans (Evans); m. Randall Frank Ford, Oct. 2, 1982; children: Vicki Lynn Russell, Todd Glenn Longino. BA in English, McNeese State U., Lake Charles, La., 1985; MEd in Adminstrn. and Supervision, U. La. Monroe, 2000. English Edn. Receptionist Delhi Clinic, Delhi, La., Coenen, Berry & Bruyninckx, Rayville, La.; lang. arts tchr. Calcasieu Parish Sch. Bd., Lake Charles, La., spl. edn. tchr., Ouachita Parish Sch. Bd., Monroe, La., 2003—. Mem.: NEA, La. Assn. Educators, Ouachita Assn. Educators. Home: 110 Lacrosse Cir West Monroe LA 71291 Personal E-mail: mfordw@bellsouth.net. Business E-Mail: maryford@opsb.net.

FORD, MARY (POLLY) WYLIE, retired physical education educator; b. Rock Hill, SC, Oct. 20, 1927; d. William Calvin and Orene Poe Wylie; m. Jack Buening Ford, June 25, 1960 (dec. Aug. 25, 1992). BS cum laude, Winthrop U., 1948; MEd, U. Va., 1953; PhD, U. Iowa, Iowa City, 1957. Instr. Anderson (S.C.) Coll., 1948—50, Stratford Coll., Danville, Va., 1950—55; grad. asst. U. Iowa, Iowa City, 1955—57; asst. prof. Ea. Ill. U., Charleston, 1957—60; prof. dept. chair Winthrop U., Rock Hill, 1960—92; ret., 1992. Mem. phys. edn. textbook selection panel State Dept. Edn., Columbia, SC, 1995—95. Bd. dirs. Rock Hill YMCA, 1975—78; mem. adv. coun. home care Catawba Health Dist., Lancaster, SC, 1998—; adv. bd. Fewell Pk. Recreation Ctr., Rock Hill, 1998—2002; trustee Presbyn. Home S.C., Columbia, 2005—, Winthop U., Rock Hill, 2002—06; bd. dirs. Shepherd's Ctr. Rock Hill, 1993—95, pres., 1995; profl. adv. com. Home Health, Inc., Rock Hill, 1995—. Named to First Class of Disting. Phys. Edn. Alumni, Winthrop U., 2000. Mem.: AAHPERD (bd. govs., pres. So. dist. 1986—90, Honor award So. Dist. 1975, Profl. Svc. award So. Dist. 1991), S.C. Assn. for Health, Phys. Edn., Recreation and Dance (pres. 1970—71, President's Honor award 1970, Pres. Svc. award 1993), So. Assn. Phys. Edn. Coll. Women (pres. 1984—86), Perihelion Club (pres. 1994—96), Phi Kappa Phi. Democrat. Presbyterian. Avocations: bridge, tennis, travel. Home: 335 Shurley St Rock Hill SC 29732 Personal E-mail: pford@cetlink.net.

FORD, MICHAEL RAYE, lawyer; b. Blackwell, Okla., Sept. 1, 1945; s. Oscar Raye and Lucille Belton (Ray) Ford; m. Rebecca Deal, Nov. 5, 1993; children: Trevor Hawkins, Devin Connor;children from previous marriage: Seth Michael, Jared Raye. Student, Northwestern U., Evanston, Ill., 1963-64; BA, U. Okla., Norman, 1967, JD, 1970; postgrad. (scholar), U. Wis., 1967, Georgetown U., Washington, DC, 1971-72; LLM, George Wash. U., Washington, DC, 1974. Bar: Okla. 1970, US Dist. Ct. (no. dist.) Okla. 1974, US Supreme Ct. 1974, US Ct. Appeals (10th cir.) 1975, US Dist. Ct. (we. dist.) Okla. 1978, US Ct. Appeals (5th cir.) 1989. Mem. legal dept. Cities Svc. Oil Co., Tulsa, 1970; assoc. Gable, Gotwals, Rubin, Fox, Johnson & Baker, Tulsa, 1974-77; ptnr. Baker, Baker, Wilson, Selph & Ford, Oklahoma City, 1977-79, McKnight, Gasaway, Beck, Seals & Ford, Enid, Okla., 1979-84; pvt. practice, Enid, 1984; ptnr. Ford & Brown, Enid, 1984-86; ptnr., pres., exec. com. mem. Fellers, Snider, Blankenship, Bailey & Tippens, P.C., Oklahoma City, 1987—. Lectr. legal edn. seminars. Articles and book rev. editor: U. Okla. Law Rev., 1969—70; contbr. articles to law jours. Trustee Ctrl. Christian Ch., Enid, 1982—84, deacon, 1981—85, 1985—, bd. dirs., 1981, vice chmn., 1984—; deacon Westminster Presbyn. Ch., Oklahoma City, 2006—. Capt. JAGC US Army, 1971—74. Master: Luther Bohanon Am. Inn of Ct.; fellow: Okla. Bar Found., Am. Bar Found.; mem.: ABA (mem. com. sect. taxation 1978, chmn. closely held bus. com. taxation sect. 2003—05, vice chair profl. svcs. com. 2005—), Enid Estate Planning Coun. (v.p. 1982—83, pres. 1983—84), Am. Law Inst., Okla. Bar Assn. (program chmn. CLE seminar 1982, v.p. taxation sect. 1982—83, chmn. 1983—84), Greater Enid C. of C. (bd. dirs. 1983—85), Kiwanis (1st v.p. 1979—80, com. chmn. Enid 1980—81, bd. dirs. 1982—83, 2d v.p. 1982—83, pres. 1984—85, lt. gov. 1986—87), Order of Coif, Pi Kappa Alpha, Phi Delta Phi. Democrat. Office: Chase Tower 100 N Broadway Ave Ste 1700 Oklahoma City OK 73102 Home Phone: 405-359-7233; Office Phone: 405-232-0621. Business E-Mail: mford@fellerssnider.com.

FORD, NELSON M., civilian military employee; B in History, Duke U.; M in Edn., U. Del.; attended, U. Pa. COO Georgetown U. Med. Ctr., 1990—97; ptnr. Coopers & Lybrand; pres., CEO Clinipad, 1997—2000; dir. sr. products Humana, 2004—05; dep. asst. sec. for health budgets & fin. policy. Dept. Army, US Dept. Def., 2001—04, prin. dep. for. fin. mgmt. & comptr., 2005—06, asst. sec. for. fin. mgmt. & comptr., 2006—. Bd. dirs. AcademyHealth. Office: US Army 109 Army Pentagon Washington DC 20310*

FORD, PATRICK KILDEA, Celtic studies educator; b. Lansing, Mich., July 31, 1935; s. Oliver Patrick and Ina Mildred (Spence) F.; m. Carol Mae Larsen, June 20, 1959 (div. 1978); children: Anne Kristina, Paul Kildea, James Oliver; m. Chadine Pearl Bailie, Nov. 17, 1979. BA, Mich. State U., 1959; MA, Harvard U., 1966, PhD, 1969. Asst. prof. English Stanford U., 1968-70; asst. prof. Indo-European studies UCLA, 1970-71, asst. prof. English, 1971-74, assoc. prof., 1974-79, prof. English and Celtic studies, 1979-91, dir. Folklore and Mythology Ctr., 1979-84, chmn. Indo-European studies program, 1972-73, 74-75, 79-82, dir. writing programs, 1989-91; Wallace E. and Grace Connolly prof. Celtic Stanford U., 1986; Margaret Brooks Robinson prof. Celtic Harvard U., Cambridge, Mass., 1991—2005, Robinson rsch. prof. Celtic, 2006—. Hon. prof. Welsh, U. Wales, Bangor; founder, pres. Ford & Bailie Pubs./Book Distbrs. Author: The Poetry of Llywarch Hen, 1974, The Mabinogi and Other Medieval Welsh Tales, 1977, Ystoria Taliesin, 1992, The Celtic Poets: Songs and Tales from Early Ireland and Wales, 1999, Math uab Mathonwy, 1999, Manawydan uab Llyr, 2000; editor, contbr.: Celtic Folklore and Christianity: Essays in Memory of William W. Heist, 1983; co-author: Sources and Analogues of Old English Poetry: Celtic and Germanic, 1984, The Irish Literary Tradition, 1992. With AUS, 1956-57. NEH fellow, 1972, UCLA fellow, 1973, Fulbright fellow, 1973-74; grantee Skaggs Found., 1981-83, Am. Council Learned Socs., 1985, NEH, 1986, 94, 96, 99, 2002; hon. fellow Ctr. for Advanced Welsh and Celtic Studies/U. Wales. Mem. Internat. Arthurian Soc. (pres. N.Am. br. 1981-83), Medieval Acad. Am., Celtic Studies Assn. N.Am. (v.p. 1984-86, pres. 1987-89), Modern Humanities Rsch. Assn. (pres. 2005). Office: Harvard U Dept Celtic Lang and Lit Barker Ctr 12 Quincy St Cambridge MA 02138-2030 Home Phone: 617-489-6683. Business E-Mail: pford@fas.harvard.edu.

FORD, PAUL B., lawyer; b. Augusta, Ga., Dec. 1, 1943; s. Paul Brendan Ford and Augustine Marie Roy; m. Nancy Young; children: Brendan, Ian, Hunter, Jade. BA magna cum laude, Boston Coll., 1965; JD, Duke U., 1968. Of counsel Simpson Thacher & Bartlett LLP, NYC, 1976—. Contbr. articles to profl. jours. Active Nat. Com. on U.S. China Rels., NYC, 1999—; chmn. U.S. Fgn. Policy Assn., NYC, 1993—2000; dir. New Haven Symphony Orch., New Haven, 1992—. Mem.: ABA, Coun. Fgn. Rels., Japan Soc., Korea Soc., Inter Pacific Bar Assn., Internat. Bar Assn., Union Internat. des Avocats, Assn. Bar City of NY. Avocations: sailing, skiing. Office: Simpson Thacher & Bartlett LLP 425 Lexington Ave New York NY 10017 Business E-Mail: pford@stblaw.com.

FORD, PETER C., chemistry professor; b. Salinas, Calif., July 10, 1941; s. Clifford and Thelma (Martin) F.; children: Vincent, Jonathan; m. Mary E. Howe-Grant. BS with honors, Calif. Inst. Tech., 1962; MS, Yale U., 1963, PhD, 1966. Postdoctoral fellow Stanford U., 1966-67; asst. prof. chemistry U. Calif., Santa Barbara, 1967-72, assoc. prof. chemistry, 1972-77, prof. chemistry, 1977—. Grad. advisor dept. chemistry U. Calif., 1980-81, co-grad. advisor, 1985-92, 99—, chmn., 1994-96; vis. fellow Australian Nat. U., 1974; guest prof. H.C. Oersted Inst., Denmark, 1981; lectr. U. Berne, Switzerland, 1989, MITI-ASTI, Japan, 1990; guest investigator radiation biology br. Nat. Cancer Inst., 1994. Contbr. to profl. jours. Fellow NIH, 1963-66, NSF, 1966-67, Sterling fellow Yale U., 1963, sr. fellow Fulbright Found., 1974; Dreyfus Found. Tchr. scholar, 1971-76; recipient Alexander von Humboldt-Stiftung U.S. Sr. Scientist Rsch. award, 1992, Richard C. Tolman medal Am. Chem. Soc., 1993. Fellow: AAAS; mem.: Inter-Am. Photochem. Soc. (v.p. 2002—04, pres. 2004—). Achievements include research in the photochemical, photocatalytic and photophysical mechanisms of transition metal complexes and with homogeneous catalysis mechanisms as probed by modern kinetics techniques; the bioinorganic chemistry of metal nitrosyl complexes. Office: Univ of California Dept of Chemistry 552 University Rd Santa Barbara CA 93106-0001

FORD, PETER HILARY, music educator; s. John Randolph and Gladys (Hiller) Ford; children: Erik T., Hyllaerye Y. MusB, Yale U., New Haven, 1954; MusM, Converse Coll., Spartanburg, SC, 1956; MusD of Arts, Stanford U., Calif., 1964. Cert. hypnotherapist Gil Boyne Sch. Hypnotism. Pvt. practice hypnotherapist, Sumter, SC, 1981—; pvt. practice music tchr. Author numerous poems. Organist various chs. Recipient Kellogg F. prize, Yale U., 1954, Sch. prize, Stanford U., 1964. Mem.: Pi Kappa Lambda. Avocations: poetry, yoga. Home: 206 Crosswell Dr Sumter SC 29150

FORD, RALPH A., lawyer, moving and relocation company executive; b. 1946; BA in Polit. Sci., Morgan State U., 1968; JD, Boston U. Sch. Law, 1971. Bar: Md. 1972, US Dist. Ct. Dist. Md. 1972. Assoc. Venable, Baetjer & Howard, 1971—73; atty. Dupont Co., 1973—77; group counsel Bell and Howell Co., 1977—81; mem. legal dept. GE, 1981—99; gen. counsel GE Indsl. Control Systems, 1992—99; sr. v.p., gen. counsel, sec. Sirva, Inc., Westmont, Ill., 1999—2006; ptnr. GenNx360 Capital Partners, 2006—. Mem.: Am. Corp. Counsel Assn. Office: GenNx360 Floor 17 300 Park Ave New York NY 10022*

FORD, RALPH LEE, academic administrator; s. William Wilson and Verda Handley Ford; m. Cheryl M. Warrick, June 14, 1973; children: Marian Allyson, Lee Warrick, Anna Elizabeth. Doctorate, U. Ala., Tuscaloosa, 1985. Dean enrollment mgmt. Odessa (Tex.) Coll., 1997—2005; v.p. student svcs. Union County Coll., Cranford, NJ, 2005—. Pres. Jr. and C.C. Student Pers. Assn. of Tex., Odessa, Tex., 2002—03. V.p. Lion's Club, Odessa, Tex., 2005. Recipient Strategic Enrollment Mgmt. Faculty, Am. Assn. Collegiate Registrars and Admissions Officers, 2002, Outstanding Young Men of Am., U.S. Jaycees, 1981, 1983, 1984; grantee ESL/Bilingual Tchr. Preparation, U.S. Dept. of Edn., 2002. Achievements include development of Established Livingston International Friendship Assn; Established Monroe Internat. Friendship Assn. Home Phone: 432-559-4027. Business E-Mail: ford@ucc.edu.

FORD, RICHARD, writer; b. Jackson, Miss., Feb. 16, 1944; s. Parker Carrol and Edna (Akin) F.; m. Kristina Hensley, 1968. BA in English, Mich. State U., 1966; MFA, U. Calif., 1970. Bd. dir. PEN/Faulkner awards. Author: (novels) A Piece of My Heart, 1976, The Ultimate Good Luck, 1981, The Sportswriter, 1986 (PEN/Faulkner citation for fiction 1986), Wildlife, 1990, Independence Day, 1995, Women with Men: Three Stories, 1997, The Lay of the Land, 2006; author: (short stories) Rock Springs, 1987, A Multitude of Sins, 2002; author: (play) American Tropical, 1983, (screenplay) Bright Angel, 1991; editor: (with Shannon Ravenel) The Best

American Short Stories, 1990, The Granta Book of the American Short Story, (with Michael Kreyling), Eudora Welty: Complete Novels, 1998, Eudora Welty: Stories, Essays, and Memoir (Eudora Welty), 1998, The Granta Book of the American Long Story, 1999; contbr. articles to popular publs. Recipient Pulitzer prize for fiction, 1996, PEN/Faulkner prize for fiction, 1996, PEN/Malamud award for excellence in the short story, 2003; Guggenheim fellow, 1977-98, Endowment for the Arts, 1979-80, 85-86. Mem. U. Mich. Soc. Fellows, Am. Acad. Arts and Letters. Home: PO Box 510 East Boothbay ME 04544-0510*

FORD, RICHARD EDMOND, lawyer; b. Ronceverte, W.Va., May 3, 1927; s. Grady Williams and Hazel Loraine (Fry) F.; m. Sally Frances Alexander, June 14, 1952; children: Richard Edmond Jr., Sally Anne, Melinda J. Student, U. N.C., 1950; BS in Bus. Adminstrn., W.Va. U., 1951, LL.B., 1954. Bar: W.Va. 1954. Assoc. Holt & Haynes, Lewisburg, W.Va., 1954-55; ptnr. Haynes & Ford, Lewisburg, 1955-74, Haynes, Ford & Rowe, Lewisburg, 1975-96, The Ford Law Firm, Lewisburg, 1997—. Dir. First Nat. Bank Ronceverte. Bd. dirs. W.Va. U. Found., Daywood Found., v.p., 1986—; bd. dirs. Faculty Merit Found. W.Va., W.Va. Legal Svcs. Plan, 1973—79; trustee Greenbrier Coll. for Women, 1960—73; mem. exec. bd. Buckskin Coun. Boy Scouts Am.; mem. adv. bd. Greenbrier C.C. Ctr.; mem. vis. com. Coll. Law W.Va. U., 1972—74; mem. W.Va. Legislature, 1961—64. Served as ensign U.S. Maritime Svc., 1945—47. Recipient Outstanding Alumnus award W.Va. U. Law Sch., 1980, W.Va. U., 88. Mem. ABA (ho. of dels. 1977-80), W.Va. Bar Assn. (v.p. 1965-66, 75-76, pres. 1987-88), Greenbrier County Bar Assn. (pres. 1964-66, 81-82), W.Va. Law Sch. Assn. (pres. 1966-67), Nat. Conf. Commrs. Uniform State Laws, Am. Coll. Real Estate Lawyers, W.Va. U. Alumni Assn. (pres. 1971), W.Va. State Bar (pres. 1978-79), Phi Beta Kappa, Sigma Chi, Phi Delta Phi, Order Vandalia, Masons, KT, Shriners, Lewisburg Elks club; fellow Am. Bar Found., Am. Judicature Soc. Democrat. Methodist. Office: The Ford Law Firm 203 W Randolph St Lewisburg WV 24901-1023 Office Phone: 304-645-1858.

FORD, RICHARD EDWIN, volunteer; b. Wabash, Ind., Feb. 27, 1939; s. Wilbur Edwin and Florence Gertrude (Joup) Ford. BS, Ind. U., Bloomington, 1961; LHD (hon.), Manchester Coll., North Manchester, Ind., 2005. Sales rep. Ford Meter Box Co., Wabash, Ind., 1961—69; liaison officer US EPA, Washington, 1971—75; vol. various charitable orgns., Washington, 1976—, Wabash, 1976—. Bd. dirs. Ind. U. Found., Bloomington, Culver Ednl. Found. Chmn. Charley Creek Found., Wabash, 2002—; active Dr. James Ford Hist. Home, Wabash, 2005; bd. dirs. Indpls. Mus. Art, Wabash County Hist. Mus., 2006. Mem.: Mark's Club (London), Lyford Cay Club (Nassau), Univ. Club Winter Pk. (Fla.), Capitol Hill Club, Arts Club (Washington), Wabash Country Club, Propylaeum Club (Ind.), Woodstock Club, Univ. Club, Skyline Club, Press Club, Columbia Club (Indpls.), Elks. Republican. Methodist. Avocation: travel. Home and Office: 540 N Wabash St PO Box 454 Wabash IN 46992 Personal E-mail: reford@richardeford.com.

FORD, ROBERT DAVID, lawyer; b. New Orleans, Oct. 30, 1956; s. Thomas Paul and Inez Mary (Rodriguez) F.; m. Jean Ann Burg, May 5, 1979; children: Robert David Jr., Charlene Elizabeth, Timothy Michael. BA, U. New Orleans, 1978; JD, Loyola U., 1983. Bar: La. 1983, U.S. Dist. Ct. (ea. dist.) La. 1983, U.S. Dist. Ct. (mid. dist.) La. 1997, U.S. Ct. Appeals (5th cir.) 1985. Claims rep. State Farm Mut. Auto Ins. Co., Metairie, La., 1978-80; assoc. Hammett, Leake & Hammett, New Orleans, 1983-86; ptnr. Thomas, Hayes & Beahm, New Orleans, 1986—95; mem. Chehardy, Sherman, Ellis, Breslin & Murray, Metairie, La., 1995-96; ptnr. Hailey, McNamara, Hall, Larmann & Papale, Metairie, 1996—2003, Mang, Batiza, Gaudin, Godofsky & Penzato, Metairie, 2003—04, Batiza, Godofsky, Penzato, Schroeder & Ford, Metairie, 2004—. Mem. ABA (coms. on health law, profl. liability and products liability litigation 1992, subcoms. on hosp. and clinic med. devices and med. malpractice liability 1992), La. Bar Assn., La. Assn. Def. Counsel, Am. Soc. Law and Medicine, La. Soc. Hosp. Attys. of La. Hosp. Assn., Def. Rsch. Inst., Phi Kappa Theta, Pi Alpha Delta. Republican. Roman Catholic. Avocations: golf, softball. Home: 8 Caney Ct Kenner LA 70065-3944 Office: Batiza Godofsky Penzato Schroeder & Ford 1 Galleria Blvd Ste 700 Metairie LA 70001-7543 E-mail: rford@hmhlp.com, rford@lemmico.com.

FORD, ROBERT MACDONALD, III, architect, educator; b. Seattle, Apr. 4, 1934; s. Robert MacDonald Jr. and Nancy Elizabeth (McFate) F.; m. Ruth Evelyn Keene, 1957 (div. 1980); children: Karen, Judith, Robert IV; m. Martha Evelyn Cooper, Mar. 11, 1983 (div. 2000); m. Deborah Mahoney Nettles, Feb. 28, 2003 (div. 2006); m. Mary Lynn Moore, July 24, 2007. BArch, U. Wash., Seattle, 1962; MArch, U. Ill., 1963. Registered architect, Miss. Asst. prof. architecture U. Ill., Urbana, 1963-66, Wash. State U., Pullman, 1966-69, assoc. prof. architecture, 1969-74, prof. architecture, 1974-75, Miss. State U., Starkville, 1975-96, prof. emeritus architecture, 1996—. Vis. prof. Oreg. Sch. Design, Portland, fall 1982, U. P.R., San Juan, spring 1990; pres. Ford & Assocs., Architects, Miss., 1975-92; pres. Architecture/South, Miss., Tenn., 1992-97, Ford Properties, 1997—, Ford/Architecture/Planning, 2006—; Miss. commr. Clan Donald, 2002—. Councilman City of Pullman, 1969-74. With U.S. Army, 1953-56. Recipient award of excellence, McGraw-Hill, 2006. Fellow AIA (bd. dirs. Miss. 1987, 90, 98, 2000--, sec.-treas. 1988, v.p. 1989, pres.-elect 1991, pres. 1992, state design awards 1981, 82, 83, 88, 99, regional design awards 1981, 84, 85, 91, 92, 2006), Archtl. Found., Tau Sigma Delta. Democrat. Avocations: sailing, genealogy, travel. Home and Office: 308 Mangrove Palm St Starkville MS 39759 Office Phone: 662-323-0649. Personal E-mail: robmford3@hotmail.com.

FORD, ROLLIN, retail executive; BS in Bus. Adminstrn. and Sys. Analysis, Taylor U. With Wal-Mart Stores, Inc., 1983—, with distbn. and logistics ops., v.p. splty. distbn./transp., 1996—98, v.p. distbn. ops., 1998—2000, sr. v.p. logistics, 2000—03, exec. v.p. logistics, 2003—06, exec. v.p., CIO, 2006—. Bd. dirs. Thurgood Marshall Scholarship Found. Office: Wal-Mart Stores Inc 702 SW Eighth St Bentonville AR 72716

FORD, SCOTT T., telecommunications industry executive; married; 3 children. B in Fin., U. Ark., Fayetteville, 1984. With Merrill Lynch Capital Markets, NY, Stephens Group Inc., Little Rock, 1986—96; exec. v.p. Alltel Corp., Little Rock, 1996, pres., 1997—, COO, 1998, CEO, 2002—, bd. dir., 1996—. Chmn. Cellular Telecommunications and Internet Assn. Mem. Little Rock Branch of the Fed. Reserve Bank of St. Louis. Office: Alltel Corp One Allied Dr Little Rock AR 72202*

FORD, SHIRLEY GRIFFIN, science educator, pharmacist; b. Peoria, Ill., Dec. 21, 1946; d. Jesse Andrew Griffin and Dorothy Mae Lampert; m. William Herschel Ford, Dec. 19, 1970; children: Bret Andrew, Bryce Merritt, Heather Louise. BS, U. Ill., Urbana, 1968, MA in Tchg., 1970; PharmD, U. Pacific, Stockton, Calif., 1978. Registered pharmacist Calif., 1979. Tchr. East Lynn H.S., Ill., 1972—73, Wren H.S., Anderson, SC, 1973—74, Tri County Tech. Coll., Pendleton, SC, 1974—75, Stockton Unified Sch., Calif., 1976—87, Lodi Unified Sch., Stockton, 1987—, tchr. dept. sci., choir Bear Creek H.S., 2006—; pharmacist Dameron Hosp., Stockton, Calif., 1987—2006, Kaiser Permanente, Stockton, Calif., 2006—. Coach Sci. Olympiad team Lodi Unified Schs., 1987—; pharmacy intern Dameron Hosp., 1990—2006. Com. mem. Golden State Exams Com., Sacramento, 1985—2002, Supt's. Adv., Stockton, 2005—06; health acad. coord. Bear Creek H.S., Stockton, 1995—2002. State Tchr.'s scholar, State of Ill., 1964. Mem.: Minn. Bd. Pharmacy (licentiate), State of Calif. Pharmacists Assn. (licentiate; local officer 1987—91), NSTA (assoc.). Independent. Presbyterian. Avocations: singing, theater, scuba diving, travel. Office: Bear Creek High Sch 10555 N Thornton Rd Stockton CA 95204 Home Phone: 209-462-2800; Office Phone: 209-953-8060. E-mail: sford@lodiusd.k12.ca.us.

FORD, STEVEN J., lawyer, manufacturing executive; b. Queens, NY, Sept. 20, 1959; s. Joseph and Helen Ford; m. Patricia A. Lynn, Mar. 28, 1987. BS, Villanova U., 1981; JD, St. John's U., 1985; LLM in Taxation, NYU, 1988. Bar: NY 1986. With Coopers & Lybrand, Cowan, Liebowitz & Latman, Bond, Schoeneck & King, Syracuse, NY; v.p. Carlisle Cos., Inc., Charlotte, NC, 1995—, sec., 1995—, gen. counsel, 1995—. Mem.: ABA, NY State Bar. Office: Carlisle Cos Inc 250 S Clinton St Ste 201 Syracuse NY 13202*

FORD, THOMAS W., JR., lawyer; b. Austin, Tex., 1955; BA in Acctg., U. Tex., Austin, 1978; JD, U. Houston, 1981. Bar: Tex. 1981. Ptnr., tax dept. Andrews Kurth LLP, Houston. Mem.: Coalition of Publicly Traded Partnerships, ABA, State Bar Tex., Houston Bar Assn., Phi Delta Phi, Beta Alpha Psi, Gamma Delta Sigma, Order of Barons. Office: Andrews Kurth LLP 600 Travis St Ste 4200 Houston TX 77002-3090 Office Phone: 713-220-4498. Office Fax: 713-238-4285. Business E-Mail: tford@andrewskurth.com.

FORD, TOM, apparel designer and executive; b. Austin, Tex., 1962; Postgrad., NYU, Parsons Sch. Design, NY, Paris. Sr. designer Cathy Hardwick, 1986—88; design dir. Perry Ellis Women's Am. Divsn., 1988—90; chief women's ready-to-wear designer Gucci, 1990—92, design dir., 1992—94, creative dir., 1994—2004, creative dir. Yves Saint Laurent Rive Gauche, YSL Beauté line, 2000—04; CEO, pres. Tom Ford Co., 2005—. Collaborator fragrance and beauty products line Tom Ford for Estee Lauder, 2005—. Named Internat. Designer of Yr., Coun. Fashion Designers Am., 1996, Womenswear Designer of Yr., 2001, Accessory Designer of Yr., 2002, Internat. Designer of Yr., Fashion Editor's Club of Japan, 1996, Best Designer of Yr., 2001, Internat. Man of Yr., British GQ, 2000, Best Fashion Designer, Time Mag., 2001, Designer of Yr., GQ Am., 2001, Future's Best New Designer, VH1/Vogue Fashion Awards, 1995, Menswear Designer of Yr., 1996, Womenswear Designer of Yr., 1996, 1999; recipient Style Icon award, Elle Style Awards, 1999, Commitment to Life award, AIDS Project, L.A., 1999, Designer of Yr. Yves Saint Laurent Rive Gauche, VH1/Vogue Fashion Awards, 2002, Superstar award, Fashion Group Internat. Night Stars, 2000. Office: Creative Artists Agency 9830 Wilshire Blvd Beverly Hills CA 90212*

FORD, VICTORIA, retired public relations executive, writer, oral historian; b. Carroll, Iowa, Nov. 1, 1946; d. Victor Sargent and Gertrude Francis (Headlee) F.; m. John K. Frans, July 4, 1965 (div. Aug. 1975); m. David W. Keller, May 2, 1981 (div. Nov. 1985); m. Jerry W. Lambert, Mar. 30, 1991 (div. Aug. 2002). AA, Iowa Lakes C.C., 1972; BA summa cum laude, Buena Vista Coll., 1974; MA in Journalism, U. Nev., Reno, 1988. Parole officer juvenile Iowa Dept. Social Services, Sioux City, 1974—78; staff reporter Feather Pub. Co., Quincy, Calif., 1978—80; tng. counselor CETA, Quincy, 1980; officer libr. pub. info. U. Nev., Reno, 1982—84; exec. pub. rels. Brodeur/Martin Pub. Rels., Reno, 1984—87; dir. pub. rels. Internat. Winter Spl. Olympics, Lake Tahoe (Calif.) and Reno, 1987—89; owner Ford Factor Pub. Rels. cons. firm, Reno, 1989—2002. Staff writer Publs. and Pub. Info. Office Truckee Meadows C.C., 2001—05; comm. specialist U. Nev. Coop. Ext., Reno, 2005—. Author: Making Their Mark: Reno-Sparks YWCA History, 1997; author: (with R.T. King and Ken Adams) War Stories, 1997; author: Jean Ford: A Nevada Woman Leads the Way (oral history), 1998, Silver Peak Oral History Project, 2001, Charlotte Hunter Arley, 2001, Never a Ghost Town: Silver Peak, Nevada, 2002, Cliff Young, Chief Justice, Nevada Supreme Court, 2002, Arthur Bernard, Nevada Mine Inspector and PrisonWarden, 2003, Victor Kral (oral history), 2004, Through the Glass Ceilings, Sue Wagner, A Life in Nevada Politics, 2005, The Civilian Conservation Corps in Nevada: From Boys to Men, 2006; contbr. articles to profl. jours. Mem. adv. bd. Reno Philharm., 1985-87, Reno-Sparks Conv. and Visitors Authority, 1985-93; bd. dirs. Truckee Meadows Habitat for Humanity, 1992-93, half-time exec. dir., 1994; mem. Gov.'s Com. on Fire Prevention, 1991-92; mem. U. Nev. Reno Oral History Program, 1994; bd. dirs. Nev. Women's Archives, 1996; state sec. and roll of honor Nev. Women's History Project, 1998, 2001, com. Nev. Writers Hall of Fame, 1993-96; bd. dirs. Friends of the U. Nev. at Reno Libr., 1995-98. Mem.: NOW, Women Writing the West, Assn. Personal Historians, S.W. Oral History Assn. (bd. dirs. 2000—02, State Hist. Rec. adv. bd. 2002—), Pub. Rels. Soc. Am. (charter v.p. Sierra Nev. chpt. 1986—87, pres. 1987—88), Sigma Delta Chi. Democrat. Home and Office: PO Box 33993 Reno NV 89533-3993 Office Phone: 775-784-7070.

FORD, WILLIAM CLAY, automotive and professional sports team executive; b. Detroit, Mar. 14, 1925; s. Edsel Bryant and Eleanor (Clay) F.; m. Martha Firestone, June 21, 1947; children: Martha, Sheila, William Clay, Elizabeth. BS, Yale U., 1949. Sales and advt. staff Ford Motor Co., 1949; indsl. relations, labor negotiations with UAW, 1949; quality control mgr. gas turbine engines Lincoln-Mercury Div., Dearborn, Mich., 1951, mgr. spl. product ops., 1952, v.p., 1953, gen. mgr. Continental Div., 1954, group v.p. Lincoln and Continental Divs, 1955, v.p. product design, 1956-80; dir., 1948—; vice chmn. bd., 1980-89; mem. fin. com. Ford Motor Co., 1987—, dir. emeritus; owner, chmn. Detroit (Mich.) Lions, Inc., 1964—. Mem. adv. coun. Tex. Heart Inst.; chmn. emeritus Edison Inst.; hon. life trustee Eisenhower Med. Ctr. Mem. Soc. Automotive Engrs. (asso.), Automobile Old Timers, Econ. Club Detroit, Masons, K.T., Phelps Assn., Psi Upsilon. Office: Ford Motor Co Design Ctr PO Box 6012 Dearborn MI 48121-6012 also: The Detroit Lions Inc 222 Republic Dr Allen Park MI 48101

FORD, WILLIAM E., investment company executive; BA, Amherst Coll., 1983; MBA, Stanford U., 1987. Investment banker Morgan Stanley & Co; with Gen. Atlantic LLC (formally Gen. Atlantic Ptnrs.), 1991—, mng. dir., chmn. Investment Com., 2001—, pres., 2005—. Bd. dirs. Archipelago Holdings, Inc., 2004—06, NY Stock Exch., 2004—06, NYSE Group, Inc., 2006—. Trustee Amherst Coll., 2001—, chair Investment Com.; mem. bd. trustees Common Ground Cmty., New Mus. Contemporary Art, Echoing Green Found., Spence Sch. Office: Gen Atlantic LLC Three Pickwick Plaza Greenwich CT 06830 also: NYSE Group Inc c/o Corp Sec 11 Wall St New York NY 10005 Office Phone: 203-629-8600. Office Fax: 203-622-8818.

FORD, WILLIAM F., banker; b. Huntington, NY, Aug. 14, 1936; s. William Freithaler; m. Diane McDonald, June 11, 1960; children: Eric W., Kristin E. BA in Econs. summa cum laude, U. Tex., 1961; MA, U. Mich., 1962, PhD, 1966; DSc (hon.), Fla. Inst. Tech., 1981; grad. sr. exec. program, Stanford U., 1983. Part-time teaching asst. U. Mich., 1962-63, instr., 1965-66; economist Rand Corp., 1966, cons., 1967-68, 70-71; asst. prof. econs. U. Va., 1967-69; assoc. prof. Tex. Tech. U., Lubbock, 1969-70; prof. econs., dean Transylvania Coll., Lexington, Ky., 1970-71; exec. dir., chief economist rsch. and planning group Am. Bankers Assn., 1971-75; sr. v.p., chief economist Wells Fargo Bank, San Francisco, 1975-80; pres., chief exec. officer Fed. Res. Bank Atlanta, 1980-83; pres., chief operating officer First Nationwide Savs., 1983-85; pres., chief exec. officer Broadview Savs. Bank, Cleve., 1986-89; dean coll. bus. U. Denver, 1990-91; prof. and chair fin. Mid. Tenn. State U., Murfreesboro, 1992—. Mem. faculty Stonier Grad. Sch. Banking, 1976—80; mem. fed. open market com. Fed. Res. Sys., 1982—83; sr. econ. advisor TeleCheck Svcs. Inc., 1992—2001; spkr. in field. Author: Mexico's Foreign Trade and Economic Development, 1968; also over 100 articles, revs., TV script. Bd. vis. Berry Coll., 1984—89. With USN, 1954—57. Woodrow Wilson fellow, 1961; NDEA fellow, 1961-63; Ford Found. fgn. area fellow, Mex., 1964-65; Rotary fellow, Chile, 1970; co-winner Fred M. Taylor Prize U. Mich. Mem. Stanford Grad. Sch. Bus. Adminstrn. Alumni Assn. (bd. dirs. 1985-86), Am. Econ. Assn., Nat. Assn. for Bus. Econs. (bd. dirs. 2002-05), U.S. C. of C. (bd. dirs. 1989-91, chmn. econ. policy com. 1990-93), Phi Beta Kappa. Methodist. Office: Mid Tenn State U Coll Bus PO Box 27 Murfreesboro TN 37133-0027 Business E-Mail: wfford@mtsu.edu.

FORD, WILLIAM FRANCIS, retired bank holding company executive; b. Albany, NY, Mar. 11, 1925; s. Patrick J. and Ellen M. F.; m. Marcia J. Whalen, Jan. 7, 1956; children: William Francis, Michael P., Timothy K., Daniel J., Cathleen A. BA in Acctg. with honors, St. Michaels Coll., 1950. V.p. Equitable Credit Corp., Albany, 1950-60, Am. Fin. Systems Inc., Silver Spring, Md., 1960-65, Gen. Electric Credit Corp., Stamford, Conn., 1965-74; chmn., chief exec. officer Security Pacific Fin. Corp., San Diego, 1974-81; exec. v.p., adminstr. specialized fin. services group Security Pacific Corp., Los Angeles, 1981-84, vice chmn., 1984-91. Bd. dirs., vice chmn. Ford Fin. Svcs., 1991—. Served with USN, 1943-46. Mem. Am. Fin. Svcs. Assn. (chmn., dir. emeritus exec. com.) Clubs: Stone Ridge Country. Home: 741 Cypress Hills Dr Encinitas CA 92024-2376

FORDEMWALT, JAMES NEWTON, microelectronics engineering educator, consultant; b. Parsons, Kans., Oct. 18, 1932; s. Fred and Zenia (Chambers) F.; m. Suzan Lynn Hopkins, Aug. 26, 1958 (div. June 1961); m. Elizabeth Anna Hoare, Dec. 29, 1963; children: John William, James Frederick. BS, U. Ariz., 1955, MS, 1956; PhD, U. Iowa, 1960. Sr. engr. GE Co., Evandale, Ohio, 1959-60, U.S. Semcor, Inc., Phoenix, 1960-61; sect. mgr. Motorola Semiconductor Products Div., Phoenix, 1961-66; dept. mgr. Philco-Ford Microelectronics Div., Santa Clara, Calif., 1966-68; assoc. dir. R & D Am. Microsystems Inc., Santa Clara, 1968-71; assoc. rsch. prof. U. Utah, Salt Lake City, 1972-76; dir. microelectronics lab. U. Ariz., Tucson, 1976-87; assoc. prof., lab. mgr. Ariz. State U., Tempe, 1987—2001, prof. emeritus, 2001—, assoc. chair microelectronics, 1992—2001, asst. chair dept. electronic and computer tech., 1993—2001. Cons. Integrated Cirs. Engring., Scottsdale, Ariz., 1976—, Western Design Ctr., Mesa, Ariz., 1980—; mem. semiconductor com. United Techs. Corp., Hartford, Conn., 1978-87. Author: Silicon Wafer Processing Technology, 1979; editor: Integrated Circuits, 1965; contbr.: MOS Integrated Circuits, 1972. Mem. IEEE, Internat. Soc. for Hybrid Microelectronics (chpt. pres. 1982-83), Electrochem. Soc. Avocations: pilot, photographer. Home: 613 W Summit Pl Chandler AZ 85225-7798 E-mail: jfordemwalt@cox.net.

FORDEN, DIANE CLAIRE, magazine editor; b. NYC, Apr. 6, 1951; d. Joseph Anthony and Helen (Nash) F. BA in English Edn. summa cum laude, Montclair State U., NJ, 1973. Fashion editor Seventeen Mag., NYC, 1975-81; fashion and beauty dir. YM Mag., NYC, 1981-85; fashion dir. Avon Fashions, NYC, 1985-87, Prima Mag., NYC, 1987-88; from fashion and beauty editor to editor in chief and v.p. Bridal Guide Mag., NYC, 1989—. Author: How to Have an Elegant Wedding-Without Going Broke, 2002, How to Find the Perfect Wedding Dress, 2003, New Etiquette for Today's Bride, 2004. Mem. Am. Soc. Mag. Editors, Fashion Group Internat., N.Y. Women in Comms. Avocations: piano, biking, skiing, photography. Home: 10 River Rd Apt F Nutley NJ 07110-3459 Office: Bridal Guide Mag 3 E 54th St New York NY 10022-3108 E-mail: dforden@ebridalguide.com.

FORDHAM, CHRISTOPHER COLUMBUS, III, dean, academic administrator, medical educator; b. Greensboro, NC, Nov. 28, 1926; s. Christopher Columbus and Frances Long (Clendenin) Fordham; m. Barbara Byrd, Aug. 16, 1947; children: Pamela Fordham Richey, Susan Fordham Crowell, Betsy Fordham Templeton. Student, U. NC, 1943—45, student, 1946—47, cert. in medicine, 1949; MD, Harvard U., 1951. Diplomate Am. Bd. Internal Medicine. Intern Georgetown U. Hosp., 1951—52; asst. resident Boston City Hosp., 1952—53; sr. asst. resident NC Meml. Hosp., Chapel Hill, 1953—54; fellow in medicine U. NC Sch. Medicine, 1954—55, instr. medicine, 1958—60, asst. prof., 1960—64, assoc. prof., asst. dean Sch. Medicine, 1964—68, prof., assoc. dean, 1968—69, prof. medicine, 1971—, vice chancellor for health affairs, 1977—80, chancellor, 1980—88, chancellor emeritus and prof. medicine, 1988—93, prof. medicine emeritus, 1993—, chancellor emeritus, dean emeritus, prof. medicine emeritus, 1993—; practice medicine, specializing in internal medicine Greensboro, 1957—58; prof. medicine, v.p. for medicine, dean Sch. Medicine, Med. Coll. Ga., Augusta, 1969—71; dean Sch. Medicine U. NC, 1971—79; acting asst. sec. for health Dept. HEW, Washington, 1977. Chair Gov.'s Com. on NC Awards, 1993—2000; chmn. NC Awards Com., 1993—2000; bd. dirs. Royal Soc. Med. Found., NYC, 1990—95. Officer USAF, 1955—57. Master: ACP; fellow: AAAS; mem.: AMA (Spl. award 1990), AAUP, Elisha Mitchell Sci. Soc., Inst. Medicine of NAS (coun. 1985—90), NY Acad. Scis., Am. Assn. Med. Coll. So. Regional Deans (chmn. 1972—73, 1975—75, chmn. nat. coun. deans 1977), Am. Assn. Med. Colls. (exec. coun. 1975—78, rep. liaison com. med. edn. 1977—79), Soc. Health and Human Values, Am. Fedn. Clin. Rsch., Am. Soc. Nephrology, So. Soc. Clin. Investigation, NC Med. Soc., Nat. Assn. State Univs. and Land Grant Colls. (chair coun. univ. governance 1990—91), Order Golden Fleece, Alpha Omega Alpha, Sigma Xi. Office: Office Med Alumni Affairs G OSO Bonduvant Hall Campus Box 9530 Chapel Hill NC 27599-9530 Office Phone: 919-966-8622.

FORD III, DON D., lawyer; b. Houston, Sept. 15, 1971; s. Don D. and Ann S. Ford. BBA, Baylor U., Waco, Tex., 1994; JD, Baylor U. Sch. Law, Waco, 1997. Bar: Tex. 1997. Tax atty. KPMG, Houston, 1997—98; atty. Van Pelt & Frank, Houston, 1998—99; mng. ptnr./atty. Ford & Mathiason LLP, Houston, 1999—. Mem. Guardianship Certification Bd., Austin, 2006—; editl. bd. mem. Houston Lawyer Mag., 2000—; bd. dirs. Houston Lawyer Referral Svc., 2001—, Crystal Shores East Assn., Nev., 2004—; mem. adv. bd. The Joshua Found., Houston, 2005—. Author: articles in field of law. Fellow: Houston Bar Found.; mem.: Houston Bar Assn. (probate, trusts & estate sect.), Attys. in Tax & Probate, Disability & Elder Law Attys. Assn. Office: Ford & Mathiason LLP 5151 San Felipe Ste 1950 Houston TX 77056 Office Phone: 713-260-3926. Office Fax: 713-260-3903. Business E-Mail: dford@ford-math.com.

FORDIS, JEAN BURKE, lawyer; b. Ashiya AFB, Japan, Feb. 25, 1956; BA in Biology with distinction, Calif. State U., 1978; JD cum laude, Am. U., 1985. Bar: Md. 1985, US Ct. Appeals (Fed. Cir.) 1986, DC 1988, US Supreme Ct. 1993, Calif. 2005, registered: US Patent & Trademark Office. Law clk. to Hon. Philip Nichols Jr., Sr. Cir. Judge US Ct. Appeals (Fed. Cir.), 1985—86; biologist Nat. Inst. Health, Uniformed Services U. for Health Sci.; ptnr. Finnegan, Henderson, Farabow, Garret & Dunner LLP, Palo Alto, Calif., mng. ptnr. Pa. office. Mem. Am. U. Law Rev., 1983—85. Mem.: Md. Patent Law Assn. (sec. 1990—92, v.p. 1993—94, pres. 1995—97), Licensing Exec. Soc., Am. Intellectual Property Law Assn. (chmn. awards com. 1988—90), Phi Kappa Phi. Office: Finnegan Henderson Farabow Garrett & Dunner LLP 3300 Hillview Ave Palo Alto CA 94304-1203 Office Phone: 650-849-6600. Office Fax: 650-849-6666. Business E-Mail: jean.fordis@finnegan.com.

FORD-REED, LILLIE MAE, geriatrics services professional; b. Near Blackville, SC, Oct. 9, 1939; d. William Henry and Joanne Coleman Reed; m. Phinnize Ford; children: Monica D. Ford, Marie C. Ford, William H. Ford, Maude L. Ford, Phinnize E. Ford, Lee A. Ford, Merlinda Ford, Christopher E. Ford. A in Paralegal, Orangeburg Calhoun Tech. Coll., 2000. Pres. usher bd. Thankful Bapt. Missionary, Bamberg, SC; program chairperson Bapt. Usher Bd. Union, Bamberg; therapeutic asst. Northhampton Assocs., Orangeburg, SC, S.C. Mentor Network, Columbia; insp. quality control Allied Signal Aerospace Electronics, Orangeburg; vol.

solicitor's office, victim witness sect. Helpline, Aiken, SC; vol. VITA Tax Svc.; pvt. caregiver Aiken. Named to Wall of Tolerance So. Poverty Law Ctr., Mont.; recipient Honor award for Internship, Senator Strom Thurmon, 1984, Spl. Recognition award, Continental Challenge II Team, 2003, cert. of Appreciation, Girl Scouts U.S. Mem.: NAACP, Christian Burial Aid Assn. (pres. lodge #46), Smith-Hazel Phraise Modeling Team, Smith-Hazel Phraise Dance Group, Smith-Hazel Sr. Citizens Art and Crafts Club. Avocations: quilting, crafts, reading, sewing, dance.

FORDTRAN, JOHN SATTERFIELD, physician; b. San Antonio, Nov. 15, 1931; s. William M. and Josephine (Bell) F.; m. Jewel Evans, July 25, 1953; children: William, Bess, Josephine, Amy. Student, U. Tex., 1949-52; MD, Tulane U., 1956; DSc (hon.), Med. Coll. Wis., 1988; MD (hon.), Karl Franzens U., Graz, Austria, 1995. Internal medicine intern Parkland Meml. Hosp., Dallas, 1956-57, asst. resident internal medicine, 1957-58; research fellow gastroenterology Mass. Meml. Hosp., Boston, 1960-62; instr. internal medicine U. Tex. Southwestern Med. Sch., Dallas, 1962-63, asst. prof. internal medicine, 1963-67, assoc. prof. internal medicine, 1967-69, prof., 1969-79, chief sect. gastroenterology, 1963-79; chief dept. internal medicine Baylor U. Med. Center, Dallas, 1979-96; pres. Baylor Rsch. Inst., Baylor U. Med. Ctr., Dallas, 1991-2000. Mem. attending staff Parkland Meml. Hosp., Dallas, 1963-79; cons. gastroenterology Dallas VA Hosp., 1963-79. Contbr. articles to profl. jours.; editorial bd. Jour. Clin. Investigation, 1968-73; editor Gastroenterology, 1977-81; co-editor: Gastrointestinal Disease, 5th edit., 1993. Served with USPHS, 1958-60. Recipient King Faisal prize in medicine Saudi Arabia, 1984 Fellow Royal Coll. Physicians Eng.; mem. ACP, Am. Soc. Clin. Investigation (past pres.), Am. Gastroent. Assn. (Disting. Achievement award 1971, Kirsner prize 1990, Disting. Educator award 1991, Friedenwald medal 1993), Am. Gastroenterology Assn. (Lifetime Achievement in Digestive Sci. award, 1999). Office: Baylor U Med Ctr 3500 Gaston Ave Dallas TX 75246-2096 Home: 3408 Hanover St Dallas TX 75225-7643 Office Phone: 214-820-2672. E-mail: johnfo@baylorhealth.edu.

FORDYCE, JAMES GEORGE, physician; b. Detroit, Jan. 9, 1945; s. James Alexander and Stella Marie (Pakron) F.; m. Kathleen Marie Ray, June 17, 1967; children: James A., Jonathan A., Jared A. BS, Mich. State U., 1966, DVM, 1968; MD, Wayne State U., 1974. Diplomate Am. Bd. Pediats., Am. Bd. Allergy and Immunology. Intern, resident Children's Hosp. Mich., Detroit, 1973-76; fellow allergy and clin. immunology Henry Ford Hosp., Detroit, 1976-78; physician Dearborn (Mich.) Allergy and Asthma Clinic, PC, 1978—. Cons. Metro Med. Group, Detroit, 1979-95. Author: Asthma in Clinical Pulmonary Medicine, 1992. Bd. trustees Oakwood Healthcare, Inc., 1996-2000. Fellow Am. Acad. Pediats., Am. Acad. Allergy, Asthma and Immunology, Am. Coll. Allergy, Asthma and Immunology; mem. Mich. Allergy and Asthma Soc. (pres. 1991-92). Avocations: fishing, flying, sailing. Office: Dearborn Allergy & Asthma Clinic PC 20200 Outer Dr Dearborn MI 48124-2634 Office Phone: 313-565-3565. Personal E-mail: jgfordyce@comcast.net.

FORDYCE, JAMES STUART, non-profit organization executive; b. London, Dec. 10, 1931; arrived in US, 1947, naturalized, 1994; s. James Wilfred and Doris Vera (McRae) F.; m. Beverly Ann Arnold, June 12, 1954; children: Cameron James, Jean Margaret. AB, Dartmouth Coll., 1953; PhD in Phys. Chemistry, MIT, 1959. Rsch. scientist Parma (Ohio) rsch. lab. Union Carbide Corp., 1959-66; rsch. scientist Lewis rsch. ctr. NASA, Cleve., 1966-68, head electrochemical fundamentals, 1968-73, mgr. environ. monitoring office, 1973-76, chief electrochemistry br., 1976-80, dep. chief space power tech. divsn., 1980-81, chief, 1981-84, dep. dir. aerospace tech., 1984-85, dir., 1985-91, dep. ctr. dir., 1991-94; v.p., chief scientist Ohio Aerospace Inst., Cleve., 1995-2000, sr. cons., 2000—. Spl. lectr. Internat. Space U.; disting. space tech. lectr. Columbia U., 1988; bd. trustees Edison Polymer Innovation Corp., Akron, Ohio, 1991—. Author: (with others) Solar Power Satellites, 1993; contbr. articles to profl. jours. Mem. spl. com. Mus. Natural History, Cleve., 1991-96, 2000-02; active Leadership Cleve., 1992-93; internat. mem. program adv. bd. Ctr. for Rsch. in Earth and Space Tech., Toronto, 2001-04; mem. Eng. adv. bd. Ohio U., Athens, 2002-06. Fellow AIAA (assoc.); mem. AAAS, Am. Chem. Soc., Fedn. Am. Scientists, Electrochem. Soc. (lectr. 106th mtg. 1985), Sigma Xi, Phi Beta Kappa. Democrat. Unitarian Universalist. Avocations: sailing, hiking, travel, music. Home: 21295 Cromwell Ave Fairview Park OH 44126-2714 Personal E-mail: stfordyce@cox.net.

FORE, HENRIETTA HOLSMAN, federal agency administrator; m. Richard L. Fore. AB, Wellesley Coll., 1970; MS, U. No. Colo., 1975. Pres. Stockton Wire Products, Burbank, Calif., 1977-89; chmn., pres. Pozacorp, Inc., 1981—89; asst. adminstr. for pvt. enterprise US Agy. for Internat. Devel., Washington, 1990-91, asst. adminstr. for Asia, 1991-93; dir. US Mint US Dept Treasury, Washington, 2001—05; under sec. for mgmt. US Dept. State, Washington, 2005—, dir. US Fgn. Assistance, 2007—; acting adminstr. US Agy. Internat. Devel., Washington, 2007—. Chmn. US Asia Environ. Partnership, 1991—93. Mem. Com. of 200. Mem. Young Pres. Orgn. Office: US Dept State 2201 C St NW Rm 7207 Washington DC 20520

FORELLE, CHARLES, reporter; BA in math, Yale Univ., 2001. Intern NY Observer, Miami Herald; intern to staff reporter Wall St. Journal, Boston, 2002—. Editor (mng.): Yale Daily News, 2000—01. Co-recipient Breaking or Hard News award, Edn. Writers Assn., 2003, Polk award for bus. reporting, 2006. Mailing: Wall St Journal 200 Liberty St New York NY 10281 Business E-Mail: charles.forelle@wsj.com.*

FOREMAN, ALFRED G., theologian, philosopher; b. Sulfur, La., Mar. 19, 1960; s. Grover Foreman and Stella Kibodeaux. BA, U. La., Lafayette, 1987; MA, Liberty U., 1991. Founder S. La. Weather Sta., Crowley, 1986—; pastor Ch. of God, Crowley, 1986—2002; with Imam Al-Ruh-Al-Amin Masjid, Crowley, 2003—. Lectr. Islamic Ctr., Lafayette, La., 1983-84, La. Philos. Inst. Humanities, Crowley, 1993-2004. Author: The Ecclesiastic Order: The Apology, 2002, The Christian and Islamic Thesis in History, 2002, Sadr Al-Din Shirazi and Hajji Sabziwari, Trans-substantial Motion and History: Toward a Definition of Unified Field of Knowledge from the Microcosm to the Macrocosm, 2006; dir. South La. Weather Jour., 1986—. Mem. Internat. Palm Soc., Ctr. for Islam and Sci. Home: 130 Palms Rd Crowley LA 70526-1907 Personal E-mail: faithandreason2004@yahoo.com.

FOREMAN, BARBARA BLATT, healthcare facility administrator; b. Phila., Pa., Apr. 8, 1951; d. Raymond and Charlotte (Schiller) Blatt; m. Stewart Barry Foreman, May 15, 1981; children: Vicki Spitalnick Densen, Benjamin Blatt Spitalnick. BS, Pa. State U., 1971, MS, 1975. Secondary English instr. Abington (Pa.) Sch. Dist., 1972—81, faculty advisor, 1972—81; practice adminstr. Dr. S.B.F. Assoc., Inc., Pa., 1981—94; practice integrator multipractice program devel. U. Pa. Health Sys., Phila., 1994—97; healthcare cons. Health Power Assocs., Phila., 1998—2002; program dir. Cogent Healthcare, Boca Raton (Fla.) Cmty. Hosp., 2005—. Mem. exec. bd. Am. Heart Assn., Boca Raton, 2003—04. Mem.: Soc. Hospitalist Medicine, Rotary Club (mem. exec. bd. Boca Raton club 2003—04). Avocations: swimming, gardening, cooking. Office: Cogent Healthcare Boca Raton Cmty Hosp 800 Meadows Rd Boca Raton FL 33486 Office Phone: 561-955-3677. Business E-Mail: foreman.barbara@cogenthealthcare.com.

FOREMAN, CAROL LEE TUCKER, consumer advocate; b. Little Rock, May 3, 1938; d. James Guy and Willie Maude (White) Tucker; m. Jay Howell Foreman, June 13, 1964; children: Guy Tucker, Rachel Marian. AA, William Woods Coll., 1958; AB, Washington U., 1960; postgrad., Am. U.; LLD (hon.), William Woods Coll., 1976. Rsch. asst. Com. Govt. Ops. U.S. Sen., 1961; assoc. Fed. Counsel Assocs., 1961-63; instr. Am. govt. William Woods Coll., Fulton, Mo., 1963-64; exec. asst. to Rep. James Roosevelt, 1964; dir. rsch. & publs. Dem. Nat. Com., 1965-66; Congl. liaison aide HUD, 1967-69; chief info. liaison Ctr. Family Planning Program Devel. Planned Parenthood-World Population, 1969-71; dir. policy coordination Commn. on Population and Am. Future, 1971-72; exec. dir. Citizens Com. on Population and Am. Future, 1972-73, Paul Douglas Consumer Rsch. Ctr., 1973-77, Consumer Fedn. Am., 1973-77; asst. sec. food and consumer svcs. Dept. Agriculture, Washington, 1977-81; dir. U.S. Commodity Credit Corp., 1977-81, U.S. Consumer Coop. Bank, 1977-81; pres. Foreman & Co., 1981-86, Foreman Heidepriem & Mager, 1986—99; disting. fellow, dir. The Food Policy Inst. Consumer Fedn. Am., 1999—. Mem. Pres.'s Commn. on White House Fellows, 1996—2001, Nat. Adv. Com. Meat and Poultry Inspection, 1997—2002, EU/US Consultative Forum Biotech., 2000, US Agriculture Policy Adv. Com. for Trade, 2002-; adv. com. Joint Inst. Food Safety and Applied Nutrition, 2000-05; mem. adv. com. on agrl. biotech. USDA, 2000—. Editor: Regulating for the Future, 1991. Exec. dir. Ctr. Women Policy Studies, 1983-84, mem. Interdeptl. Task Force on Women, 1973-74; bd. dirs. Consumer's Union, 1982-83, chmn., 1993—; bd. dirs. Food Rsch. & Action Ctr., 1983, Christianity and Crisis, 1990-92; vice chmn. Ctr. Nat. Policy, 1982-84, bd. dirs., 1981-99; trustee Washington U., St. Louis, 1987-95; bd. dirs. Bread for the World, 2000—. Recipient disting. alumni award Washington U., 1979, 2000. Mem. Women's Equity Action League (past pres. local chpt.), Nat. Policy Assn. (dir. 1985-97), Phi Beta Phi. Presbyterian. Home: 5600 Wisconsin Ave Ste 502 Chevy Chase MD 20815 Office: Consumer Federation Of America 1620 I St NW Ste 200 Washington DC 20006-4030 Office Phone: 202-797-8551. Personal E-mail: tuckfore@aol.com.

FOREMAN, EDWARD RAWSON, retired lawyer; b. Atlanta, May 15, 1939; s. Robert Langdon and Mary (Shedden) F.; m. Margaret Reeves, Oct. 19, 1968; children: Margaret Langdon, Mary Rawson. BA, Washington & Lee U., 1962; JD, Emory U., 1965. Bar: Ga. 1965. Assoc. Jones, Bird & Howell, Atlanta, 1965-70, ptnr., 1970-82, Alston & Bird, Atlanta, 1982-99; ret., 1999. Chmn. McAliley Endowment Trust, 1978—; lectr. Inst. for Continuing Legal Edn. in Ga., 1989; panelist, moderator Bus. Atlanta's Office Leasing and Tenant Opportunities in 1990s. Mem. editl. bd. Comml. Leasing Law and Strategy, 1996-98. Bd. dirs. Ansley Park Beautification Found., Atlanta, 1984-99, Midtown Alliance, Atlanta, 1988-96, sec., chmn. fundraising com., 1989-91, v.p., 1991, pres., 1992; trustee Paidela Sch. Endowment Fund, Atlanta, 1980-99, Woodruff Arts Ctr., Atlanta, 1985-90; chmn. Emory U. Law Fund, Atlanta, 1981; chmn. legal divsn. United Way Met. Atlanta, 1984; chmn. strategic planning com. High Mus. Art, 1986-95, chmn., bd. dirs. 1998—99, chmn. nominating com., 1993-95; vestryman, sr. warden St. Luke's Episc. Ch., 1975, 94, 2001, com. mem., 1975-90; pres. Atlanta Legal Aid Soc., 1975-76; comm. chair and pres. Atlanta Preservation Ctr., 1986-91; trustee Miss Hall's Sch., Pittsfield, Mass., 1990-2001. Recipient Cmty. Svc. award Martin Luther King Jr. Ctr. Nonviolent Social Change, 1980, Outstanding Svc. award Atlanta Preservation Ctr., Inc., 1983. Mem. ABA (mem. comml. leasing com. 1987-95), State Bar Ga. (chmn., panelist, moderator comml. leasing seminars 1979-86), Atlanta Bar Assn. (chmn., panelist, moderator leasing seminars 1979-86, chmn. hdqrs. search com. 1988-96), Lawyers Club Atlanta (chmn. long-range planning com. 1989-90), Atlanta Bar Found. (bd. dirs.), Old War Horse Lawyers Club, Nine O'Clocks Club (mem. centennial com. 1983), Piedmont Driving Club, Highlands Country Club N.C. Democrat. Episcopalian. Personal E-mail: pforeman@mindspring.com.

FOREMAN, GEORGE EDWARD, retired boxer, minister, boxing commentator; b. Marshall, Tex., Jan. 10, 1949; s. J. D. and Nancy Foreman; m. Mary Foreman, children: Michi, Freeda, Natalie, George Jr., George III, George IV, George V, George VI. Profl. boxer, 1969—77, 1987—97; minister, 1977—; founder, minister Ch. Lord Jesus Christ, Houston, 1984—; promoter The George Foreman Lean Mean Grilling Machine, 1995—, The George Foreman Signature Collection, 2004—; expert commentator HBO's World Championship Boxing; founder George Foreman Enterprises Inc., 2005. Co-author: (with Joel Engel) By George: the Autobiography of George Foreman, 1995, George Foreman's Knock-Out-The-Fat: Barbecue and Grilling Cookbook, 1996,(with Barbara Witt) George Foreman's Big Book of Grilling, Barbecue, and Rotisserie: More than 70 Recipes for Family and Friends, 2000, (with Linda Kulman) George Foreman's Guide to Life: How to Get up Off the Canvas When Life Knocks You Down, 2003, (with Kathryn Kellinger) George Foreman's Indoor Grilling Made Easy: More Than 100 Simple, Healthy Ways to Feed Family and Friends, 2004, (with Ken Abraham) God in My Corner: A Spiritual Memoir, 2007; actor (films) Lets Do It Again, 1975; (TV series) George, 1993; (TV appearances) The Six Million Dollar Man, 1975, Sanford and Son, 1976, Good Sports, 1990, Home Improvement, 1991, The Larry Sanders Show, 1992, (voice only) King of the Hill, American Inventor, 2007; numerous TV commercials and endorsements. Founder George Foreman Cmty. Ctr., Houston. Named Boxer of the Year, World Boxing Assn., 1974, Male Athlete of Yr., AP, 1994; named to The US Olympic Hall of Fame, 1990, The World Boxing Hall of Fame, 2002, Internat. Boxing Hall of Fame, 2003. Achievements include winning a gold medal for boxing in the 1968 Olympic Games, Mexico City; Nat. AAU Heavyweight Champion, 1968, World Heavyweight Boxing Champion, 1973-74, 1994-95; becoming the oldest Heavyweight Champion in boxing history, Nov. 5, 1994 (45 yrs. old).*

FOREMAN, JAMES LOUIS, retired judge; b. Metropolis, Ill., May 12, 1927; s. James C. and Anna Elizabeth (Henne) F.; m. Mabel Inez Dunn, June 16, 1948; children: Beth Foreman Banks, Rhonda Foreman Wittig, Nanette Foreman Love. BS in Commerce and Law, U. Ill., 1950, JD, 1952. Bar: Ill. Ind. practice law, Metropolis, Ill.; ptnr. Chase and Foreman, Metropolis, until 1972; state's atty. State of Ill., Massac County, asst. atty. gen.; chief judge U.S. Dist. Ct. (so. dist.) Ill., Benton, 1979-92, sr. status, 1992—2007; ret., 2007. Pres. Bd. of Edn., Metropolis. With USN, 1945-46. Mem. Ill. State Bar Assn., Metropolis C. of C. (past pres.). Republican. Home: 660 Whitney Dr Paducah KY 42001

FOREMAN, JOHN PATRICK, electrical engineer; b. Lake Charles, La., Aug. 16, 1954; s. John Calvin Foreman and Daisy Mae (Finley) Foreman Milsted; m. Nadine Rachelle Dudek, Nov. 10, 2001. BSEE, McNeese State U., Lake Charles, La., 1976. Registered profl. engr., Tex., Calif., La., Oreg., Mass., Wash., Nev. Elec. engr. Fluor Engrs. & Contractors, Houston, 1977-83, Jacobs Engring. Group, 1983, Burgess & Niple, Ltd., 1984-86; project mgr. Turpin & Rattan Engring., San Diego, 1986-92, TH Rogers & Assocs., Oakland, 1993, Alfa Tech. Cons. Engrs., San Jose, 1994-99; assoc. TKG Cons. Engrs., San Diego, 2000—03, Bechard Long & Assocs., Inc., 2003—05, Aillett, Fenner, Jolly & McClelland, Shreveport, La., 2005—06, John J. Guth, 2006—07. Mem.: NSPE, IEEE, Tex. Soc. Profl. Engrs. Democrat. Roman Catholic. Avocations: darts, skiing, volleyball, softball, martial arts. Home: 4907 General Ashley Dr Bossier City LA 71112 Office: John J Guth & Assocs 208 Milam St Shreveport LA 71101-3226

FOREMAN, JOHN WILLIAM, pediatrician, educator; b. Washington, June 23, 1947; s. William Roy and Elizabeth Roberts (McLean) F.; m. Linda Poffenberger, May 27 1973; children: Matthew John, Jennifer Lynne. BS, Duke U., 1969; MD, U. Md., 1973. Diplomate Nat. Bd. Med. Examiners, Pa., Va., N.C., Am. Bd. Pediatrics, subbd. pediatric nephrology. Intern, resident Montreal (Que., Can.) Children's Hosp., 1973-75; asst. chief resident pediatrics Children's Hosp. Phila., 1975-76, fellow pediatric nephrology, 1976-79, staff physician, 1979-86; instr. pediatrics U. Pa. Sch. Medicine, Phila., 1976-79, clin. asst. prof., asst. prof., 1979-85, assoc. prof., 1985-86; assoc. prof. pediatrics Med. Coll. Va., Va. Commonwealth U., Richmond, 1986-90, prof., 1990-93; prof., chief divsn. pediatric nephrology Duke U. Med. Ctr., Durham, NC, 1993—. Cons. WHO, 1984; chmn. med. adv. bd. Nat. Kidney Found. Va., 1989-92, mem. exec. com. pediatric urology and nephrology coun.; mem. pediatric delegation to Chinese Med. Assn. of People's Republic of China. Contbr. articles to profl. jours., chpts. to books. Bd. dirs. Transplant Found., Richmond, 1991. Daland fellow Am. Philos. Soc., Phila., 1980-81; grantee Am. Heart Assn., 1984-88, NIH, 1988-91. Fellow Am. Acad. Pediat.; mem. Soc. Pediatric Rsch., Am. Pediatric Soc., So. Soc. Pediatric Rsch. (councillor 1989-91), Internat. Pediatric Nephrology Soc. (councillor 1993-98), Am. Soc. Pediatric Nephrology (coun. mem. 2002-06), Am. Soc. Nephrology, chair exec. com. sect. on Nephrology Am. Acad. Pediatrics. Avocation: reading. Home: 9 Streamley Ct Durham NC 27705-5396 Office: Duke U Med Ctr PO Box 3959 Durham NC 27710-0001 Office Phone: 919-684-4246. Business E-Mail: forem001@mc.duke.edu.

FOREMAN, MICHAEL J., astronaut; b. Columbus, Ohio, Mar. 29, 1957; s. James W. and Nancy C. Foreman; m. Lorrie Lee Dancer; 3 children. BSc in Aerospace Engring., U.S. Naval Acad., 1979; MSc in Aeronautical Engring., U.S. Naval Postgraduate Sch., 1986. Commd. lt. USN, 1975, advanced through grades to capt., naval aviator Brunswick, Maine, 1981—89, various assignments, 1990—93, chief engr. Crystal City, Va., 1993—98; astronaut NASA, Houston, 1998—. Technical duties Astronaut Office Space Station; liaison, Space Shuttle Branch Johnson Space Ctr. and Kennedy Space Ctr.; dep. Space Shuttle Branch; mission specialist STS-120 mission to Internat. Space Station, 2006. Decorated Meritorious Svc. medal USN, Navy Commendation medal; recipient Adml. William Adger Moffett Aeronautics award, U.S. Naval Postgraduate Sch., Navy Achievement medal. Mem.: Assn. Naval Aviation, U.S. Naval Acad. Alumni Assn. Avocations: golf, running, skiing, home repair/improvement, time with family. Office: Astronaut Office CB NASA Johnson Space Center Houston TX 77058

FOREMAN, RICHARD, theater director, playwright; b. NYC, June 10, 1937; s. Albert and Claire (Levine) F. BA, Brown U., 1959, ArtsD (hon.), 1993; MFA, Yale U., 1962. Artistic dir. Ontological-Hysteric Theater, NYC, 1968—. Dir.-in-residence N.Y. Shakespeare Festival, N.Y.C., 1975-76; artistic dir. Theatre O.H., Paris, 1973-85. Dir. Broadway and off-Broadway plays including 3-Penny Opera, 1976; author, dir. Dr. Selavy's Magic Theater, 1972, Rhoda in Potatoland, 1976 (Obie award Village Voice 1976), Film Is Evil: Radio is Good, 1987 (Obie award Village Voice, 1987), Pearls for Pigs, 1997 (Obie award Village Voice, 1997), Benita Canova, 1998 (Obie award Village Voice, 1998); over 40 others; author: Unbalancing Acts, 1992 and others. Mem. panel theatre div. Nat. Endowment for Arts, Washington, 1976-79. Guggenheim fellow, 1972, Rockefeller fellow, 1974, Creative Artist's Pub. Svc. fellow, 1974, Creative Artist's Pub. Svc. fellow N.Y. State Arts Coun., 1971, MacArthur fellow, 1995-2000; recipient Lifetime Achievement award NEA, 1990, Am. Acad. Arts and Letters prize in lit., 1992, PEN/Laura Pels Master Am. Dramatist award, 2001; officer Order Arts and Letters, France, 2003. Mem. Dramatist's Guild, Soc. Stage Dirs., PEN. Jewish. Avocations: philosophy, psychoanalysis. Home and Office: 152 Wooster St New York NY 10012-5330 E-mail: mmeedwarda@earthlink.net.

FOREMAN, SPENCER (SPIKE FOREMAN), pulmonologist, retired hospital administrator; b. Phila., Nov. 10, 1935; s. Samuel and Freda F.; m. Sandra Lee Finkelstein, June 10, 1961; children: Corinne, Todd, Cheryl, Andrea. BS, Ursinus Coll., 1957; MD, U. Pa., 1961. Diplomate in internal medicine and pulmonary disease Am. Bd. Internal Medicine. Intern Henry Ford Hosp., Detroit, 1961-62; med. officer USPHS, San Pedro, Calif., 1962-63; resident in internal medicine USPHS Hosp., New Orleans, 1963-65; fellow in pulmonary diseases Tulane U., 1965-67; asst. chief dept. internal medicine USPHS Hosp., Balt., 1967-68, chief dept. internal medicine, 1968-73, hosp. dir., 1971-73; CEO Sinai Hosp., Balt., 1973-86; pres. Montefiore Med. Ctr., Bronx, NY, 1986—2007. Prof. medicine, prof. social medicine and epidemiology Albert Einstein Coll. Medicine, Bronx; mem. Accreditation Coun. on Med. Edn., 1981-87, ProPAC (Prospective Payment Assessment Commn.) 1996. Contbr. articles to med. jours. Commr. Md. Health Resources Commn., 1982-86, Liaison Com. for Med. Edn., 1989-91; bd. dirs. Am. Jewish Joint Distbn. Com., Inc., Ursinus Coll., Collegeville, Pa.; chmn. Biomed. Rsch. Alliance N.Y., 1998-2000, chmn., 2000-; vice chmn. Ursinus Coll., 2002-04, chmn., 2004-. Capt. USPHS, 1962-73. Fellow ACP, N.Y. Acad. Medicine; mem. Inst. Medicine Nat. Acad. Scis., Assn. Am. Med. Colls. (rep. assembly, chmn. 1986, adminstrv. bd. Coun. Tchg. Hosps., chmn.-elect assembly 1991-92, chmn. 1992-93), Am. Hosp. Assn. (bd. dirs. 1995-98), Health Forum (bd. dirs. 1998-99), Greater N.Y. Hosp. Assn. (bd. dirs., vice chmn., chmn.), League Vol. Hosps. (bd. dirs., sec.-treas., chmn.), N.Y. Bot Garden (bd. mgrs. 2007—), Soc. Med. Adminstrs. (pres. 2000-02).

FOREMAN, THOMAS ALEXANDER, dentist; b. Tionesta, Pa., Oct. 24, 1930; s. James Aura and May Lanson Foreman; m. Dorothy Jean Wolf, June 12, 1953; children: Bonnie Jean, Julie Marie, Mary Aleta, Lloyd George. Student, Grove City Coll., 1948—50; BS, Allegheny Coll., 1952; DDS cum laude, U. Pitts., 1957, DMD, 1970. Gen. practice dentistry, Clarion, Pa., 1961—. Active Clarion Hosp. Assn., 1965—; exec. bd. Colonel Drake coun. Boy Scouts Am., 1969-72, mem.-at-large French Creek coun., 1972-73, vice-chmn. Indian Trails dist., 1971-73; governing coun. Alpha Christian Acad. Sch., 1977-81. Capt. with Dental Corps USAF, 1957—61. Fellow, Pierre Fauchard Acad. Fellow Acad. Dentistry Internat., Am. Coll. Dentists, Internat. Coll. Dentists, Royal Soc. Health; mem. ADA, Pa. Dental Assn. (dir. 8th dist. 1964-87, 91—, pres. 1974-76, 2006—, trustee 1987-91), Acad. Gen. Dentistry (master), AMA (affiliate), Clarion County Dental Soc. (pres. 1983-87), SAR (pres. Capt. Samuel Brady chpt. 1970-71, 77-80), Soc. Mayflower Descs., Pilgrim Edward Doty Soc., Fedn. Dentaire Internat., Pa. Soc., We. Pa. Conservancy, Cook Forest Ctr. for Arts, Clarion County Hist. Soc., Masons, Shriners, Phi Beta Phi, Omicron Kappa Upsilon, Delta Sigma Delta, Theta Chi. Presbyn. (pres. bd. trustees 1966-67, supt. Sunday sch. 1966-67, chmn. endowment trust fund dirs. 1980-84, 2006-, elder 2001—). Home: 147 S 7th Ave Clarion PA 16214-2006 Office: 832 E Main St Clarion PA 16214-1168

FOREMAN, TODD MATTHEW, professional sports team owner, communications executive; s. Spencer Foreman; m. Tracy Ellen Schafer; children: Samuel, Joshua, Katelyn. BBA, Emory U.; MBA, George Washington U. CPA. Pub. acct.; sales and leasing rep. Julien J. Studley Inc., Bethesda, Md.; ptnr. United Comm. Grp., Rockville, Md., 1992—; prin. Atlanta Spirit, LLC (parent co. of NBA Atlanta Hawks and NHL Atlanta Thrashers). Office: United Comm Grp Ste 1100 11300 Rockville Pike Rockville MD 20852-3030*

FORER, ARTHUR H., biology professor, researcher, editor; b. Trenton, NJ, Dec. 17, 1935; arrived in Can., 1972; s. Bernard and Rose Ethel Forer; m. Alexandra Engberg Westengaard, Dec. 18, 1964; children— Michael, David. B.Sc., MIT, Cambridge, 1957; postgrad., U. Rochester, 1957-59, U. Wash.-Friday Harbor, summer 1959; PhD in Molecular Biology, Dartmouth Med. Sch., 1964. Postdoctoral fellow Am. Cancer Soc. Carlsberg Labs., Copenhagen, 1964-66; research asst. Cambridge U., England, 1966-67, Helen Hay Whitney Found. fellow, 1967-69, Duke U., Durham, NC, 1969-70; lektor Odense U., Denmark, 1970-72; assoc. prof. biology York U., Toronto, Canada, 1972—75, prof. biology, 1975—2001, prof. emeritus, sr. scholar, 2001—. Mem. grant selection panel Natural Scis. and Engring. Rsch. Coun., 1976-78. Editor: Mitosis/Cytokinesis, 1981; mem. editorial bd. Jour. Cell Sci., 1972-84, Can. Jour. Biochemistry and Cell

Biology, 1982-93, Cell Biology Internat. Reports, 1984—; contbr. articles to profl. jours. Active Amnesty Internat., Ottawa, Ont., 1980—, Cmty. Theatre Orchs., Toronto, A Pack-O-Lips Now Saxophone Quartet, Toronto. Fellow Royal Soc. Can., Acad. Scis.; mem. Am. Soc. Cell Biology, Stankel Ben Soc. (charter mem. 1960—), Tarragon Theatre, Shaw Festival (supporting). Avocations: music, gardening, bicycling, hiking. Home: 17 Michigan Dr Willowdale ON Canada M2M 3H9 Office: York U Biology Dept 4700 Keele St Downsview ON Canada M3J 1P3 Business E-Mail: aforer@yorku.ca.

FORESE, JAMES JOHN, business machine company executive; b. Coatesville, Pa., Dec. 31, 1935; s. Samuel and Edith (Mastrangelo) Forese; m. Florine Skutnik, June 27, 1959; children: Laura Lee, James Anthony, Diane Edith, John Thomas. BSEE, Rensselaer Polytech. Inst.; MBA, MIT. With IBM, Armonk, NY, 1959—95; exec. v.p., COO Alco Std., 1996; exec. v.p., pres. internat. ops. IKON Office Solutions, Inc., 1997—98, pres., CEO, 1998—2000, chmn., 2000—03. Bd. dirs. NUI Corp., Am. Mgmt. Sys., IBM Latin Am., IBM Credit Corp., Lexmark Internat. Trustee Rensselear Polytech. Inst.; mem. CBA Found. adv. coun. Coll. Bus. Adminstrn.; mem. engring. found. adv. coun. Coll. Engring. U. Tex.-Austin.

FORESE, LAURA LEE, hospital administrator, orthopedist; b. Suffern, NY, Aug. 17, 1961; m. Robert J. Downey; 3 children. BSE in civil engring. and ops. rsch. (summa cum laude), Princeton U., 1983; MD, Columbia U. Coll. Physicians and Surgeons, 1987; M in Health Svc. Mgmt., Columbia Sch. Pub. Health (now called Mailman Sch. Pub. Health), 1995. Intern, orthop. surgery NY Presbyterian Hosp., NYC, NJ, 1987—88, asst. attending orthop. physician, 1994, v.p. med. affairs, 2003—05; asst. attending physician Helen Hayes Hosp., West Haverstraw, NY, 1993—97, chief surgical and anesthesia services, 1994—97; resident, orthop. surgery Columbia U., 1988—93, vice chair, dept. orthopaedic surgery, 1998—2002; sr. v.p., chief med. officer NY Presbyterian Hosp./Weill Cornell Med. Ctr., NYC, 2005—, COO, 2006—. Faculty mem. specializing in pediatric orthopaedic surgery, assoc. clin. prof. Columbia U., 1993—; teaches physician-patient comm. to orthopaedic surgeons in the US; lectr. in field. Mem.: Am. Coll. Physician Executives, NY Acad. Medicine, Am. Acad. Orthopaedic Surgeons (editor-in-chief, Orthopedic Medical Legal Advisor, comm. skills mentor), Assn. Am. Med. Coll., Health Mgmt. Acad., Alpha Omega Alpha, Phi Beta Kappa. Office: NY Presbyterian Hosp/Weill Cornell Med Ctr M-106 525 E 68th St New York NY 10021

FORESMAN, GEORGE W., federal agency administrator; b. Lexington, Va. BS, Va. Military Inst. With Va. Dept. Emergency Mgmt., 1985—2002, dep. state coord., 1994—2002; dep. asst. to Gov for commonwealth preparedness State of Va., Richmond, 2002—05; under sec. for preparedness US Dept. Homeland Security, Washington, 2005—. Mem., vice chmn. Congl. Advisory Panel to Assess Domestic Response Capabilities for Terrorism Involving Weapons of Mass Destruction, 1999—2003. Mem.: Va. Emergency Mgmt. Assn., Nat. Emergency Mgmt. Assn. Office: US Dept Homeland Security 3801 Nebraska Ave NW Washington DC 20528

FORESTER, JOHN GORDON, JR., lawyer; b. Wilkesboro, NC, Jan. 14, 1933; s. John Gordon and Mary Hope (Hendren) F.; m. Georgina Ramirez, June 26, 1957; children: John Gordon III, Robert Raoul, Georgina Yasué, Richard Alexander. BS; in Indsl. Rels., U. NC, 1955; LLB, George Washington U., 1962. Bar: DC 1962, Md. 1993. Internat. economist Dept. Commerce, 1958-62; confidential asst. to dep. asst. sec. commerce, 1962-63; law clk. US Dist. Judge L.P. Walsh, 1963-64; pvt. practice Washington, 1964-80; ptnr. Pohoryles & Greenstein, P.C., Washington, 1980-89, Greenstein Delorme & Luchs, P.C., Washington, 1989-95; pvt. practice, 1995—. Mem. Jud. Conf. DC Cir., 1981, 82, 92, adv. com. Civil Justice Reform Act, US Dist. Ct., 1991-93; pres. Lawyers Mut. Ins. Co. DC, 1990-92. Author: A Different Cadence, 1997, Death by Due Process, 2006; contbr. articles to profl. jours. Pres. Friendly Citizens Assn., 1963, Gonzaga Fathers Club, 1974-76; chmn. bd. dirs. Henson Valley Montessori Sch.; bd. dirs. Sursum Corda Neighborhood Ctr., 1975-77. Lt. comdr. USNR, 1955-58. Mem. ABA (mem. ho. dels. 2000-2002), DC Bar Assn. (pres. 2001-02), Md. Bar Assn., Coun. Ct. Excellence (chmn. ct. improvement com.), George Washington U. Law Alumni Assn. (pres. DC chpt. 1988-89), Counsellors (pres. 1984-85), Barrister Inn (pres. 1976-77), Order Golden Fleece, Kappa Alpha Order, Phi Delta Phi. Roman Catholic. Office: 1914 Sunderland Pl NW Washington DC 20036 Office Phone: 202-293-3353. Personal E-mail: jgfcadence1@verizon.net.

FORET, MICKEY PHILLIP, retired air transportation executive; b. McComb, Miss., Oct. 23, 1945; s. Fadias Phillip and Christine (Brown) F.; m. Mary Ann Tramonte, Aug. 12, 1966; 1 child, Keri. BS in Fin., MBA in Fin., La. State U., 1971. Dir. credit/interim dir. internal audit Tex. (Houston) Internat. Airlines, 1975-77, dir. cash mgmt., 1977-78, asst. treas., 1978-81, v.p. fin. svcs., 1981-82; v.p., treas. Continental Airlines, LA, 1982-84, v.p., chief fin. officer, 1984-86, also bd. dirs.; sr. v.p. fin. and internat. Eastern Airlines, Miami, Fla., 1987-88, v.p., chief fin. officer, 1986—, also bd. dirs.; sr. v.p. Tex. (Houston) Air Corp., 1988—; exec. v.p. fin. and planning Continental Airlines, Houston, 1988-89, pres., 1989-90; exec. v.p., CFO Northwest Airlines, 1992-96; pres. Atlas Air, Inc., 1996-1997; spec. projects offcr. Northwest Airlines, 1998, CFO, exec. v.p., 1998—2002. Chmn. bd. dirs., chief exec. officer Chelsea Catering Co., Houston; bd. dir. URS Corp. 2003- Pres. Clear Wood Improvement Assn., Houston, 1975-78; coach Friendswood (Tex.) Girls Softball Team, 1981. Served with USAF, 1966-69, Vietnam. Mem. Phi Kappa Phi, Beta Gamma Sigma. Republican. Baptist. Avocations: boating, water-skiing, bicycling. Mailing: URS Corp Bd Directors 600 Montgomery St San Francisco CA 94111-2728

FORGANG, DAVID M., curator; b. NYC, Mar. 26, 1947; s. Joseph Hyman and Clarice (Ishbia) F.; m. Joyce Enid Blumenthal, June 15, 1968 (div. May 1979); children: Adam, Bradley. B in Anthropology, U. Ariz., 1968, M in Anthropology, 1971. Mus. curator So. Ariz. Group Nat. Pk. Svc., Phoenix, 1971-77, regional curator we. region San Francisco, 1977-82, curator Yosemite (Calif.) Mus., 1982—. Pres. Yosemite Renaissance Art Competition, 1983-94; dir. Yosemite Artist in Residence Program, 1985—. Mariposa County advisor El Portal (Calif.) Town Planning Adv. Bd., 1984-94. Recipient Unit Award citation US Dept. Interior, 1974. Democrat. Jewish. Avocations: fishing, canoeing, hunting, gardening. Office: Nat Pk Svc PO Box 577 Yosemite National Park CA 95389-0577

FORGER, ROBERT DURKIN, retired professional association administrator; b. Norwalk, Conn., May 24, 1928; s. Alois John and Elsie Marie (Durkin) F.; m. Eleanor Marie Goddard, May 14, 1951; children: Gary Robert, Jeffrey Alois. BS, Norwich U., Northfield, Vt., 1949; grad., U.S. Army Command and Gen. Staff Coll., 1970. Research and devel. engr., mgr. tech. publicity Dorr-Oliver Inc., Stamford, Conn., 1949-59; conf. mgr., pub., exec. dir. Soc. Plastics Engrs., Brookfield, Conn., 1959-93; ret., 1993. Chmn. Westport (Conn.) Pub. Housing Authority, 1959-64; treas. Plastics Edn. Found., 1971-75; bd. dirs. Norwich U. Alumni Assn., 1981-86, pres., 1984-86; trustee Norwich U., 1987-92, Nat. Plastics Mus., 1983-93; mem. plastics engring. curriculum adv. com. U. Mass., Lowell, 1974-93. Lt. col. USAR. Named Conn. Assn. Exec. of Yr., 1983, elected to Plastics Hall of Fame, 1996; named Disting. Alumnus, Norwich U., 1999. Mem. Soc. Plastics Engrs. (disting. mem. 1984, pres.'s cup, 1992), Am. Soc. Assn. Execs. (life), Coun. Engring. and Sci. Soc. Execs. (bd. dirs. 1983-85, sec. 1985-86, v.p. 1986-87, pres. 1987-88), Plastics Pioneers Assn. Home: 79 Suzie Dr Newtown CT 06470-1260

FORGET, BERNARD G., hematologist, educator; BA, Univ. Montreal, 1959; MD, McGill Univ., Montreal, 1963. Chief, hematology sect. Yale Univ. Sch. Medicine, New Haven; and prof., medicine, genetics Yale Univ., New Haven. Fellow: Am. Acad. Arts & Scis. Office: Hematology-Internal Medicine Yale Univ Sch Medicine PO Box 208021 New Haven CT 06520-8021 Office Phone: 203-785-4144, 203-785-4154. Business E-Mail: bernard.forget@yale.edu.*

FORGET, MARK ALAN, educational consultant, educator; s. Timothy Paul and Marie Caroline Forget; m. Kim Elaine Weitz Forget, July 25, 2002; m. Karen Wilson Forget (div.); children: Jon Andre, Ian Andrew, Nathan Willis, Andrew Jeffrey. BA in Polit. Sci., U. Rochester, 1973, MA in Edn., 1974; PhD in Urban Scis., Edn., Old Dominion U., 1999. Tchr., coach McQuaid HS, Rochester, NY, 1974—77, Hampton Roads Acad., Newport News, Va., 1977—78, Green Run HS, 1985—94; investment advisor Paine-Webber, Virginia Beach, 1978—84; tchr. Va. Beach Friends Sch., 1984—85; tchr., dir. Ocean Lakes HS, 1994—99; dir. reading staff devel. So. Regional Edn. Bd., Atlanta, 1999—2001; pres., dir. staff devel. Max Teaching, Inc., Findlay, Ohio, 2001—. Author: MAX Teaching with Reading and Writing, 2004; co-author: Reading for Success, 1996. Dir. youth coaching William & Mary Soccer Camp, Williamsburg, Va., 1986—94. Chief warrant officer US Army, 1968—70. Decorated 2 Purple Hearts U.S. Army, Disting. Flying Cross, Bronze Star. Mem.: Findlay Country Club. Avocation: golf. Office Phone: 404-441-7008.

FORGEY, BENJAMIN FRANKLIN, architecture and art critic; b. Ashland, Ky., July 31, 1938; s. Chauncey Eaton F. and Joyce Evangeline (Shafer) Heinzen; m. Julie A. Savage, Sept. 1963 (div. 1967); 1 son, Benjamin Eric; m. 2d Gabriella A. von Joeden, Aug. 14, 1967; children: Elisa Gabriella, Martina Jane. BA, Princeton U., 1960. Reporter, editor, art critic Washington Star, 1964-81; architecture critic Washington Post, 1981—. Juror, profl. awards Am. Soc. Landscape Architects, 2003. Contbr. articles to Landscape Architecture mag. Served with USAR, 1961-67. Fulbright fellow, Japan, 1985-86. Mem.: Am. Inst. Architects (hon.). Home: 2856 28th St NW Washington DC 20008-4110 Office: Washington Post 1150 15th St NW Washington DC 20071-0002

FORGIONE, DANA ANTHONY, accounting educator; BBA, U. Mass., Amherst, 1975; MBA, 1977, MS in Acctg., 1980, PhD, 1987; cert. in Christian Leadership with high honors, Heritage Bapt. Inst., Springfield, Mass., 1979, cert. in Ch. Ministries, 1983. CPA Md., Tex., Fla., CMA, cert. fraud examiner. Asst. prof. C.W. Post Ctr. Sch. Profl. Accountancy LI U., Greenvale, NY, 1981-83; asst. prof. Sch. Bus. We. New Eng. Coll., Springfield, Mass., 1983-87; asst. prof. Coll. Bus. Adminstrn., Grad. Sch. Bus. Tex. A&M U., College Station, 1987-93; assoc. prof. Merrick Sch. Bus. U. Balt., 1993-2000, prof., 2000-2001, dir. profl. MBA program Merrick Sch. Bus., 1993-2000, advisor MBA specialization in healthcare mgmt., 1993-2001; affiliate assoc. prof. Sch. Pharmacy U. Md., Balt., 1996-2000, affiliate prof., 2000-2001; dir., prof. Sch. Acctg. Fla. Internat. U., Miami, 2001—05, prof., dir. Ctr. for Acctg., Auditing and Tax Studies, Sch. Acctg., 2006; Janey S. Briscoe endowed chair in bus. health, dept. acctg. U. Tex. Coll. Bus., San Antonio, 2006—. Prin. Global Anti-Fraud Cons., Inc., Balt., 1998—2001; cons. U.S. Dept. Vets Affairs, 1997; cons in field. Author: Costly Reflections in a Midas Mirror, 1994, Costly Reflections in a Midas Mirror, 2d edit., 1999; co-author: Pet Polygon Mfg. Company Management Accounting Case, 1992, Pet Polygon Mfg. Company Management Accounting Case, 3d edit., Laser Logos, Inc., 1994, Laser Logos, Inc., 2d edit., 1997; editor: Rsch. in Healthcare Fin. Mgmt., 1994—2000, 2000—, chmn. editl. rev. bd. The White Paper, 1996—99, columnist Jour. Health Care Finance, reviewer Internat. Jour. Pub. Adminstrn., Govt. Accts. Jour., Govtl. and Non Profit Acctg., 1992—, mem. editl. bd. Today's CPA, 1992—93, Jour. Econs. and Fin., 1992—95, Pub. Budgeting, Acctg. and Fin. Mgmt., 1994—, Jour. Health Care Fin., 1996, Rsch. in Govt. and Nonprofit Acctg., 1996—, rev. Issues in Acctg. Edn., 1997—, mem. editl. bd., 1998—, Fin. Accountability and Mgmt., 1994—, assoc. editor N.Am., 1998—; contbr. articles to profl. jours.; rev.: Internat. Jour. Pub. Adminstrn., 2001—. Litig. support, expert testimony, cons. Tex. Atty. Gen., 1992—93. Symposium fellow Office for Govt. Acctg. Rsch. and Edn. U. Ill. Chgo., 1984; recipient Chancellor's Citation for Undergrad. Instrs., U. Mass., 1973, Hon. Mention Manuscript award Mass. Soc. CPAs, 1976, Outstanding Fac. Mem. award, Beta Alpha Psi (acctg. Hon. Fraternity), 1992, Incentive Grant for Tchg., Ctr. for Tchg. Excellence, Tex. A&M U., 1992, Curriculum Funds Development Awd., Merrick Sch. Bus., 1994, Manuscript award Nat. Assn. Accts., Black and Decker Rsch. Awd., Merrick Sch. Bus., U. Balt., 1995, 99, Top 10 List, Merrick Sch. of Bus., 1995, Diploma of Honor, U. San Marcos, Peru, 2004; named hon. prof. Ricardo Palma U., Peru, 2004—. Mem.: Inst. Pub. Sector Acctg. Rsch. U. Edinburgh (internat. assoc.), Assn. Cert. Fraud Examiners (bd. regents 1999—2000, regent emeritus 2001—), Internat. Soc. Rsch. in Healthcare Fin. Mgmt. (dir. 1994—, founder), Internat. Assn. Mgmt. (Internat. Regional Publ. award 1996, sr. editor jour. 1996—98, chmn. healthcare mgmt. divsn. 1997—98, Divsn. award 1998), Am. Acctg. Assn. (mem. exec. com. Mid-Atlantic region 1994—2001, pres. Mid-Atlantic region 1996—97, sec., treas. govt. and nonprofit sect. 2003—04, pres. govt. and nonprofit sect. 2005—06, mem. nat. coun. 1996—97, 2005—06). Baptist. Avocations: computers, biblical chronology, woodworking. Office: U Texas at San Antonio One UTSA Circle San Antonio TX 78249-0632 Business E-Mail: dana.forgione@utsa.edu.

FORIEST, JOANN M., education educator; b. New Orleans, Oct. 20, 1950; d. August L. and Mable Lloyd Monier; m. Joseph Lenard Foriest, Sept. 27, 1980; children: Jamil Joseph, Janeen Jene. BS, Chgo. State U., 1971; MEd, No. Ill. U., DeKalb, 1973, EdS, 1997, EdD, 2002. Tchg. asst. No. Ill. U., 1971—73; reading specialist Elgin Sch. Dist., Ill., 1973—79; instr. English Chgo. State U., 1979—86; instr. reading Chgo. Urban Skills Inst., 1979—86; lectr. reading, English U. Ill., Chgo., 1986—97; prof. reading, English Prairie State Coll., Chicago Heights, Ill., 1997—. Peer evaluator Higher Learning Commn., Chgo., 2004—; commr. Ednl. Comm. Olympia Fields, Ill., 2007. Fellow, No. Ill. U., 2002. Mem.: Assn. Black Women Higher Edn. (v.p. 2002—03).

FORKAN, EVELEEN, counselor, educator, researcher; b. Cloonmore, Mayo, Ireland, Jan. 8, 1927; arrived in U.S., 1970; d. Michael J. Forkan and Winnie Kate Sherlock. Studied Anthropology, Spirituality, Marist Inst., Eng., 1944—45; studied Philosophy, Psychology, Marist Inst., Paris, 1945—48; BA, Ottawa U., Canada, 1954, MEd, 1963; M in Counseling, St. Paul's U., Ottawa, 1980. Tchr. Primary Devel. Pub. Schs., New Brunswick, Canada, 1948—51, tchr. H.S., 1951—64; adminstr. Children's Home, Edmondton, Canada, 1964—70; tchr. St. Albert's Cath. Sch., Dearborn Heights, Mich., 1970—72, Wheeling Cath. Schs., W.Va., 1972—80; personal growth workshops PRH Internat., Detroit, 1982—, healing counselor personal growth, 1982—. Recipient Pepper award, 2004. Mem.: Marist Sisters. Avocations: reading, philosophy, anthropology, spirituality, psychology. Home: 16057 Hauss Eastpointe MI 48021 Office: St James Parish 241 Pearson Ferndale MI 48220 Office Phone: 248-542-8836 x 15.

FORKAN, PATRICIA ANN, foundation executive; b. NYC, June 13, 1944; d. Robert James and Elaine May F. BA in Polit. Sci., Pa. State U., State College, 1966; postgrad., Am. U., Washington, DC, 1968-69. Manpower analyst Dept. Labor, Washington, 1967-69; nat. coord. Fund for Animals, NYC, 1970-76; v.p. program and comms. Humane Soc. of US, Washington, 1976-86, sr. v.p., 1987-91, exec. v.p., 1992—. Weekly web-active commentator Soap Box, 1999—2004; bd. dirs. Solar Elec. Light Fund, 1990-2000; mem. US del. Internat. Whaling Commn., 1978, 93, 94 Re-negotiation of Conv. for Regulation of Whaling, 1978, US del. North Pacific Fur Seal Commn., 1985; mem. US Pub. Adv. Com. to Law of the Sea, 1978-83; bd. dirs. Coun. for Ocean Law; advisor, contbr. weekly TV show Living with Animals, 1985-91; advisor Animal Polit. Action Com.; sr. v.p. Humane Soc. Internat., 1991-2004; pres. Humane Soc. Internat., 2004—, Global Alliance Humane and Sustainable Devel., 2004—; coun. woman Friendship Heights Village, Md., 1993-2001; pres. Nat. Assn. Humane and Environ. Edn., 1994—; pres. Worldwide Network (Women in Devel. and Environ.), 1998-2004; presdl. appointed mem. trade and environment policy adv. com. US Trade Rep., 2000—; bd. mem. Humane Farm Animal Care. Contbr. articles to environ. and animal welfare publs.; co-host weekly radio show, 1986-87. Office: Humane Soc of US 2100 L St NW Washington DC 20036

FORKER, ALAN DUANE, medical educator; b. Kingman, Kans., Apr. 21, 1938; BA in Chemistry, U. Kans., 1960; MD, U. Kans., Kansas City, 1964. Diplomate Am. Bd. Internal Medicine, Am. Bd. Cardiovasc. Disease. Intern U. Minn. Hosps., Mpls., 1964-65; resident in medicine Mayo Clinic, Rochester, Minn., 1965-69, resident in cardiology, 1967-69; prof. medicine, chief cardiac medicine U. Mo., Kansas City, 1990-2000, prof. medicine, 1990—; mem. staff Truman Med. Ctr., Kansas City, 1990-2000. Program dir., cardiovascular fellow Univ. Mo.-Kans. City Sch. Medicine, Mid Am. Heart Ins., 1990—. Named a Kans. City Super Doctor, Kans. City mag., 2007. Fellow ACP, Am. Coll. Cardiology (pres. Mo. chpt. 2007). Office: Mid Am Heart Inst Fl 5 St Luke's Hosp 4401 Wornall Rd Kansas City MO 64111-3220 Office Phone: 816-932-5797. Fax: 816-932-5613. E-mail: aforker@saint-lukes.org.*

FORLINES, FRANKLIN LEROY, minister, educator; b. Winterville, NC, Nov. 14, 1926; s. John Leroy and Leta Nanny (Manning) F.; m. Carolyn Le Fay Gilbert, Aug. 4, 1956; children: Jonathan Gilbert, James Franklin. BA, Freewill Bapt. Bible Coll., Nashville, 1952; MA, Winona Lake Sch. of Theology, Ind., 1959; BD, No. Bapt. Theol. Sem., Chgo., 1962; ThM, Chgo. Grad. Sch. of Theology, 1970. Ordained to ministry Free Will Bapt. Ch., 1951. Pastor 1st Free Will Bapt. Ch., Newport News, Va., 1952-53; mem. faculty Free Will Bapt. Bible Coll., 1953-59, 1962—, chmn. Bible dept., 1965—93, dean of men, 1953-59, 65-71, dean of students, 1971-74, prof. emeritus, 1999—. Guest lectr. Bapt. sems. and insts., Kiev and Odessa, Ukraine, 1996, Moscow, 1996, 2001, 04, 05, Kazakhstan, 2003; preacher Free Will Bapt. Internat. Missions, Russia, 1996-; chmn. theol. commn. Nat. Assn. Free Will Baptists, 1962—; condr. pastors' conf., India, 1999; spkr. in field. Author: Biblical Ethics, 1973, Biblical Systematics, 1975 (transl. into Russian and Spanish), Romans, The Randall House Bible Commentary, 1987, Quest for Truth, 2001; columnist Contact mag., 1970-80. Mem. Evang. Theol. Soc., Bible Sci. Assn. Nashville (v.p. 1988-96). Home: 3801 Rolland Rd Nashville TN 37205-2537 Office: Free Will Bapt Bible Coll 3606 W End Ave Nashville TN 37205-2403

FORMAN, CHARLES WILLIAM, religious studies educator; b. Gwalior, India, Dec. 2, 1916; s. Henry and Sallie (Taylor) F.; m. Helen Janice Mitchell, Mar. 12, 1944; children: David, Sarah, Harriet. BA, MA, Ohio State U., 1938; PhD, U. Wis., 1941; BD, Union Theol. Sem., NYC, 1944, STM, 1947. Ordained to ministry Presbyn. Ch., 1944. Prof. North India United Theol. Coll., Saharanpur, 1945-50; sec. program emphasis Nat. Coun. Chs., 1951-53; mem. faculty Divsn. Sch., Yale U., New Haven, 1953—; D. Willis James prof. missions Div. Sch., Yale U., New Haven, 1961-87, D. Willis James prof. missions emeritus, 1987—. Chmn. theol. edn. fund World Coun. chs., 1965-70, mem., 1970-77; mem. commn. ecumenical mission United Presbyn. Ch., 1962-71, chmn., 1965-71; chmn. Found. for Theol. Edn. in SE Asia, 1970-89, mem. 1966-69, 90—. Author: A Faith for the Nations, 1958, The Nation and the Kingdom, 1964, Christianity in the Non-Western World, 1967, The Island Churches of the South Pacific, 1982, The Voice of Many Waters, 1986. Mem. bd. edn., Bethany, Conn., 1957-66; bd. dirs. Community Action Agy., New Haven, 1978-81, Overseas Ministries Study Center, New Haven, 1979-2000. Home: 200 Leeder Hill Dr Hamden CT 06517-2726 Home Phone: 203-230-1214.

FORMAN, DONALD T., biochemist, educator; b. NYC, Feb. 27, 1932; s. Jack and Fannie (Jaffee) F.; m. Florence Sporn, Aug. 22, 1953; children: Joan Diane, Steven Lawrence, Debra Helene. BS, Bklyn. Coll., 1953; MS, Wayne State U., 1957, PhD, 1959. Clin. biochemist Mercy Hosp. Med. Center, Chgo., 1959—63; dir. clin. biochemistry, asso. prof. biochemistry and pathology Evanston Hosp./Northwestern U. Med. Sch., Chgo., 1963—78; rsch. prof. U. Stockholm and Royal Postgrad. Med. Sch., London, 1975; prof. pathology and biochemistry U. NC, Chapel Hill, 1978—2002, dir. clin. chemistry, 1978—2002, prof. emeritus pathology and biochemistry, 2002. Cons. clin. chemist, industry and govt., 1965—. Editor: Clinical Chemistry, 1976. Served with AUS, 1953-55. Recipient Chgo. Clin. Chemists award, 1974, Sunderman award as clin. scientist for 1986, Spl. Recognition award for clin. chemistry Am. Chem. Soc., 2000; Mich. Heart Assn. fellow, 1957-59 Mem. AAAS, AAUP, Assn. Clin. Scientists (pres. 1973-74), Am. Assn. Clin. Chemistry (dir., award for outstanding contbn. to animal clin. chemistry 1995), Sigma Xi, Phi Lambda Upsilon. Achievements include research on enzymology, inborn errors of metabolism, tumor-associated markers, atherosclerosis, human alcohol metabolism, clinical biochemistry and critical care chemistry. Home: 2559 Owens Ct Chapel Hill NC 27514-1737 Office: U NC Med Sch Dept Pathology Chapel Hill NC 27514 Office Phone: 919-967-9958. E-mail: dforman@nc.rr.com.

FORMAN, EDGAR ROSS, mechanical engineer; b. Camden, NJ, Oct. 5, 1923; s. Edgar Charles and Annie (Baragwanath) F.; m. Alma Kuppinger, Sept. 26, 1953; children: Bruce, Dianne. BSME, Drexel U., 1950, MBA, 1953. Registered profl. engr., Pa. Project engr. Penn Instrument div. Burgess Manning Co., Phila., 1950—55; application engr. Moore Products Co., Phila., 1955—59; chief instrument engr. Catalytic Co., Phila., 1959—67, mgr. mgmt. sys. dept., 1967—71; supervising instrument engr. United Engrs. & Constructors, Inc., Phila., 1971—78; mgr. instrument and controls dept. Day & Zimmermann, Inc., Phila., 1978—89; dir. Automation Tech., 1989—93; cons., 1993—2002. Guest lectr. U.S. Naval Acad., Sun Oil Co., U. Del. Contbr. articles to profl. jours. Past mem. Boy Scouts Am.; mem. pres. coun. Spring Garden Coll., 1979-83, chmn. indsl. adv. com., 1984-89; past pres. Erdenheim Civic Assn. Served with AUS, 1943-46. Fellow: Instrument Soc. Am. (Phila. sect. pres. 1960, v.p. dist 2 1982—84, chmn. food and pharm. divsn. 1986—87, nat. v.p. 1989—93, nat. honrs and awards com. 1993—96, China visitation team 1996, Engrs. Week liaison 1997—2001, founder Outstanding Tech. Achievement award 1998—2002, cert. instr. 1998—2002, rev. Power Industries Divsn. 2002—07, past chmn. edn. commn., Eckman award 1982, Man of Yr. 1987, Golden Achievement award 1989, Outstanding Svc. award 1990, Dist. 2 Svc. award 1999, Old Shoe award 2001); mem.: NSPE (pres. Valley Forge chpt. 1982—83, Engrs. Week coun. 1990—99, county Mathcounts coord. 1994—95, Man of Yr. award Del. Valley Engrs. 1990), ASME (life; past chmn. dynamic sys. and controls divsn., old guard com.), NFE Resident's Assn. (pres. 2007), 94th Inf. Divsn. Assn. (pres. Del. Valley chpt. 2003—05), Ea. Star, Commandry, Shriners, York Rite, Masons, Scottish Rite, Pi Tau Sigma (pres.), Pi Nu Epsilon, Alpha Phi Omega (nat. pres.). Episcopalian.

FORMAN, J(OSEPH) CHARLES, chemical engineer, consultant, writer; b. Chgo., Dec. 22, 1931; s. Joseph O. and Marie (Smith) F.; m. Ursula Diane Weston, July 22, 1953; children: Stephen Charles, Diane Brigitte, Mary Erika. S.B., M.I.T., 1953; MS, Northwestern U., 1957, PhD, 1960. Registered profl. engr., Ill. Trainee chem. engring. Dow Chem. Co., Midland, Mich., 1953-54; from sr. chem. engr. to dir. mfg. ops. agrl. vet. div. Abbott Labs., North Chicago, Ill., 1956-77; assoc. exec. dir. Am. Inst.

Chem. Engrs., NYC, 1977-78; exec. dir., sec., pub. Am. Inst. Chem. Engrs. Jour., Internat. Chem. Engring., Biotech Progress, Plant/Ops. Progress, Energy Progress, Environ. Progress, 1978-87; pres. and prin. Forman Assocs. Cons. and Tech. Svcs., 1987—. Cons. in field, accreditation insp. chem. engring. curricula; mem. ednl. council MIT, 1961-74, 78-95; mem. chem. engring. consultor coun. Manhattan Coll., N.Y.C., 1985—. Mem. Lake Bluff (Ill.) Bd. Edn., 1967-73, pres., 1971-73; pres. Lake County (Ill.) Sch. Bd. Assn., 1969-71; mem. Lake Bluff Plan Commn., 1973-77, chmn., 1976-77; mem. Darien (Conn.) Pers. Adv. Commn., 1986-92, Darien Park and Recreation Commn., 1999-2005; dist. chmn. Boy Scouts Am., 1994-97. With USAF, 1954—56. Fellow AIChE, AAAS; mem. Am. Chem. Soc., Am. Soc. Assn. Execs., Coun. Engring. and Sci. Soc. Execs. (dir. 1980-83, sec. 1983-84, v.p. 1984-85, pres. 1985-86), Nat. Eagle Scout Assn., Darien Sr. Men's Assn. (bd. dirs. 2005—), Sigma Xi, Tau Beta Pi, Phi Lambda Upsilon, Alpha Tau Omega. Achievements include patents in field. Home and Office: 77 Stanton Rd Darien CT 06820-5128 Office Phone: 203-655-4189. Business E-Mail: jcforman@alum.mit.edu.

FORMAN, LEE LAVINTHAL, museum administrator; b. Trenton, NJ, Feb. 22, 1950; d. Albert and Gladys Meyers Lavinthal; m. Howard Jay Forman, Feb. 28, 1976; children: Grant, Lauren. BA, Am. U., 1971. Prodn. artist Jones Composition Co., Bladensburg, Md., 1972—73, Design House, Alexandria, Va., 1973—75; graphic designer John F. Holman Co., Washington, 1975—77, Colortone Press, Washington, 1977, Wickham & Assocs., Washington, 1978—81; freelance designer Washington, 1977—78; art dir., designer Lee Forman Design, Alexandria, 1981—90; founder, trustee Mus. Bags Found., McLean, Va., 1999—. US Olympic shooting team logo, hot air balloon for Bicentennial of Treaty of Paris, ofcl. bag Cherry Blossom Festival, Washington. Amb. Women's Ctr., Vienna, Va., 1994—2000; mem. McLean Citizens Assn., 1990—; v.p., pres. Jr. Women's Club, McLean, 1990—91; founder, pres. New Dominion Women's Club, McLean, 1991—93; mem. Oversight Com. on Drinking and Driving, Fairfax County, Va., 1998—2003; vol. helpline Nat. Alliance of Mentally Ill, Arlington, Va., 2001—03; mem. Greenway Heights Citizens Assn., 2000—; founder, dir. Women for L.F. Payne for Lt. Gov. Va., 1997; mem. Women's Leadership Forum, Dem. Nat. Com., Washington, 1997—99, Temple Rodef Shalom Sisterhood, 1988—; bd. dirs. Temple Rodef Shalom, Falls Church, Va., 1998—2000. Recipient Design Excellence award, Art Dirs. Club Met. Washington, 1981, 1982. Mem.: Am. Assn. Museums, Va. Assn. Museums, Friends of Blair House, Capitol Spkrs. Club. Avocations: collecting bags, interior decorating, graphic design. Office: Mus of Bags 8300 Greensboro Dr Ste 800 Mc Lean VA 22102

FORMAN, LEONARD P., former publishing executive; b. NYC, June 7, 1945; s. William and Jean (Feldman) F.; m. Barbara Rubin, June 2, 1968; children: Daniel, Matthew. BA in Econs., CUNY, 1967; PhD, NYU, 1975. Asst. prof. econs. Fordham U., NYC, 1971-72; rsch. econs. Fed. Res. Bank, NYC, 1973—74; dir. planning N.Y. Times Corp., NYC, 1974-86; sr. v.p. ops. Telemundo, Inc., NYC, 1986—89; pres., CEO Newspaper Advt. Bur., 1989—92; COO Newspaper Assn. Am., 1992—94; pres., CEO Nynex/Newsday electronic svc. joint venture, 1994—95; media cons., 1995—96; sr. vp. corp. devel. N.Y. Times Corp., NYC, 1996-98; pres., CEO N.Y. Times Mag. Group, 1998—2001; sr. v.p. The N.Y. Times Co., 2001, sr. v.p., CFO, 2002—04, exec. v.p., CFO, 2004—07. Adj. asst. prof. Queens Coll. CUNY, 1972-75; assoc. prof. Pace U., 1975-77; lectr. Fordham U., 1977-80; adj. prof. Fordham U. Grad. Sch., 1972-73, Yale U., 1981, prin. researcher CEAR, N.Y.C., 1982—; chmn. telecommunications com. Am. Newspaper Pubs. Assn.; cons. Social Systems Inc., Chapel Hill, N.C., 1977-82. Editor Managerial and Decision Econs. jour., 1981-84; contbg. editor Managerial Planning jour.; contbr. articles to profl. jours. Named teaching fellow U. Mass., 1969-70; recipient research assistantship N.Y.U., 1972-73. Mem. Am. Econ. Assn., Managerial Econ. Assn., Econometric Soc., Nat. Assn. Bus. Economists, N.Am. Soc. Corp. Planning, Planning Execs. Inst., Ops. Research Soc., Inst. Mgmt. Sci., Omicron Delta Epsilon. Avocations: race car driving, reading, tennis.

FORMAN, MICHAEL H., lawyer; b. Newark, July 17, 1946; BA, Rutgers U., 1968, JD, 1972; LLM in Taxation, NYU, 1976. Bar: NJ 1972, US Dist. Ct. (dist. NJ) 1972, US Tax Ct. 1975, US Claims Ct. 1975. Assoc. Cole, Schotz, Meisel, Forman & Leonard, Hackensack, NJ, 1975-76, ptnr., 1976—, mng. ptnr., 1990—. Adj. prof. Am. Coll. Tax Planning, 1979-81; pres. Estate Planning Coun. Bergen County, 1992-93. Chmn. atty.'s divsn. State of Israel Bonds, 1993-98; mem. of Gov. State of NJ Tax Adv. Grp., 1999-2002; trustee Montclair State U. Found., 2003. Named one of Top 100 Attys., Worth mag., 2005—06; named to Best Lawyers in NJ, 1997. Mem. ABA (taxation, corp. and probate sects.), NJ State Bar Assn. (taxation and probate sects.), Tax Soc. NYU, Passaic County Bar Assn. (taxation and probate sects.), Bergen County Bar Assn. (taxation and probate sects.). Office: Cole Schotz Meisel Forman & Leonard Court Plz North 25 Main St Hackensack NJ 07601-7015 Office Phone: 201-525-6333. Office Fax: 201-678-6333. E-mail: mforman@coleschotz.com.*

FORMAN, MICHELE, secondary school educator; b. Biloxi, Miss., Apr. 7, 1946; m. Dick Forman; children: Elissa, Laura, Tim. BA in hist., Brandeis U., 1967; MA in tchg., U. Vt. Cert. Profl. Tchg. Standards Nat. Bd. Tchr., social studies Middlebury (Vt.) Union HS, 1986—. Alcohol drug edn curriculum spec. Vt. Dept. Edn. Mem. Vt. State Dept. Edn., Task Force HS Reform; vol. Peace Corp., Nepal, 1960. Named Nat. Tchr. of Yr., 2001, Vt. State Tchr. of Yr., 2001; recipient Mary K. Bonsteel Tachau Pre-Collegiate Tchg. award, 1999. Mem.: Academic Coun. The Coll. Bd., Hist. Soc. Studies Academic Adv. Com., Nat. Bd Profl. Tchg. Standards. Office: Middlebury Union HS Hist Social Studies Dept 73 Charles Ave Middlebury VT 05753*

FORMAN, ROBERT EDGAR, retired sociology professor; b. Mpls., July 17, 1924; s. Phillip Erwin and Lotta Louise (Holmgren) Forman; m. Ruth Anne Linsley (dec.); children: Lucy Jeanne, Mark Richard, Dan Robert. BA cum laude, U. Minn., Mpls., 1948, MA in Sociology, 1949, PhD in Sociology, 1959. Instr. sociology U. Minn., Duluth, 1949—50, St. Olaf Coll., Northfield, Minn., 1951—53; counselor Dean of Students Office U. Minn., Mpls., 1954—59; asst. prof. sociology Rockford Coll., Ill., 1959—61; from asst. prof. to prof. and dept. chair Wis. State U., Oshkosh, 1961—69; prof. sociology U. Toledo, 1969—86, prof. emeritus, 1986—. Author: Black Ghettos, White Ghettos, 1971, How to Control Your Allergies, 1979; co-author: The University & It's Foreign Alumni, 1964; contbr. chapters to books, articles to profl. jours. Cpl. US Army, 1944—46. Avocations: music, home workshop. Home: 611 E 6th Ave Colville WA 99114

FORMAN, SYDNEY, finance company executive; b. Boston, Mar. 13, 1925; B of Bus. Mgmt. in Mech. Engring., Northeastern U.; postgrad., Boston Coll., Boston U., MIT; M in Sales and Mktg., Northwestern U.; PhD in Bus. Adminstrn., Franklin U., Phila.; D of Clin. Hypnotherapy, Strassford U., London. Draftsman Riveted Lathe & Grinder, Watertown, Mass., prodn. tool designer, mem. design team; sales Cheverlot, Am. Photocopy Equipment Co., regional mgr. Boston; New Eng. regional mgr. Consolidated Internat., Boston; founder Forman Internat., Inc., Forman Leasing, Inc., Fla., Force Funding Internat., Fla. With US Army, 1941—44.

FORMENTO, DANIEL, radio company executive, writer; b. Pitts., Aug. 11, 1954; s. Stephen P. and Betty Jean (McCorkle) F.; m. Alison Ashley, Oct. 7, 1995; children: Alexander Daniel, Natalie Annette. Grad. high sch., Mt. Lebanon, Pa. Program mgr. The Source/NBC Radio Network, NYC, 1979-82; prin. Dan Formento Prodns., NYC, 1982-84; pres. Radio Today Entertainment, NYC, 1984—, West Hill Studios, NJ, 1993—. V.p., creative dir. ABC Radio Network, 1998. Author: Rock Chronicle, 1982; producer radio programs including Flashback, 1984 , Rock Stars, 1985—, Walter Cronkite's 20th Century, 1988, Pop Quiz, 1992—; radio comml. Grog Shop, 1976 (Aftra award 1976); announcer radio feature Today in Rock History, 1979—; TV comml. Short Cuts, 1989—; producer radio feature One Minute With, 1976 (Golden Quill award 1976), Pop Quiz, 1992—(Internat. Radio Festival of N.Y. grand award 1992). Democrat. Avocations: swimming, tennis, audio enthusiast. Office: ABC Radio Network 444 Madison Ave New York NY 10022-6903 Office Phone: 212-735-1700.

FORNADEL, MARTHA SUE, elementary school educator; b. Madison, Ohio, Mar. 3, 1952; d. Robert E. and Esther M. Moll; m. David J. Fornadel, Sept. 8, 1974; children: Lenora, Todd. BS in Edn., Ohio State U., Columbus, 1974; MA in Edn., Curriculum and Instrn., U. Phoenix, Ariz., 2005. Cert. tchr. Tex. 6th grade tchr. Archdiocese of San Antonio, 1984—86, Judson-Converse Ind. Sch. Dist., Tex., 1986—88; 5th grade reading/lang. arts tchr. Belton Ind. Sch. Dist., Tex., 1988—93; 6th grade reading/lang. arts tchr. Allen Ind. Sch. Dist., Tex., 1993—. Nominee Tchr. of Yr., Allen Ind. Sch. Dist., 1998, 2003. Mem.: Internat. Reading Assn., Delta Kappa Gamma (sec. 2004—06). Republican. Lutheran. Avocations: gardening, camping, hiking, sewing, reading. Office: Kerr Elem 1325 Glendover Dr Allen TX 75013 Office Phone: 214-495-6765. E-mail: marti_fornadel@allenisd.org.

FORNAGE, BRUNO DENIS, radiologist, educator; b. Reims, France, July 2, 1949; came to U.S., 1987; s. Louis and Genevieve (Mercier) F.; m. Brigitte Wittmer, Oct. 18, 1991; 1 child, Louis Bruno. MD, Med. Sch. Reims, 1974. Diplomate French Bd. Radiology, French Bd. Oncology. Resident in oncology Inst. Jean-Godinot Regional Cancer Ctr., Reims, 1974-76, resident in radiology, 1976-79, asst. dept. biophysics and nuc. medicine, 1976-82, dir. dept. radiology, 1982-87; assoc. prof. radiology U. Reims, 1986-87; assoc. prof. radiology, chief sect. ultrasound U. Tex. M.D. Anderson Cancer Ctr., Houston, 1987-2000, prof. radiology, 1990—, prof. surg. oncology, 1999—. Author 5 textbooks; editor 2 textbooks; mem. editl. bd. various jours.; editor-in-chief Jour. of Clin. Ultrasound, 1997—; reviewer jours.; contbr. chpts. to books, articles to profl. jours.; patentee in field. Fellow Am. Inst. Ultrasound in Medicine, Soc. Radiologists in Ultrasound, Soc. Breast Imaging; mem. Am. Roentgen Ray Soc., Radiol. Soc. N.Am., Am. Coll. Radiology, Am. Soc. Breast Disease, Internat. Skeletal Soc., numerous others. Office: U Tex MD Anderson Canc Ctr 1515 Holcombe Blvd Houston TX 77030-4009 Personal E-mail: fornage@swbell.net. Business E-Mail: bfornage@di.mdacc.tmc.edu.

FORNARA, CHARLES WILLIAM, historian, classicist, educator; b. NYC, Nov. 19, 1935; s. Charles and Dorothy Mae (Stind) F.; 1 son, Charles William III. BA, Columbia U., 1956; MA, U. Chgo., 1958; PhD, UCLA, 1961. Instr. Ohio State U., Columbus, 1961-63; from asst. prof. to prof. classics and history Brown U., Providence, 1963—, David Benedict prof. classics, 1989—. Vis. prof. U. Tex., Austin, 1976; prof. Greek history Inst. Ancient History, Ann Arbor, Mich., summer 1977; vis. fellow Humanities Rsch. Ctr. Australian Nat. U., Canberra, spring 1983; lectr. Australian univs., 1983, English univs., 1987, U. Amsterdam, 1995. Author: Herodotus, An Interpretative Essay, 1971, The Athenian Board of Generals, 1971, Archaic Times to the End of the Peloponnesian War, 1977, 2d edit., 1983, The Nature of History in Ancient Greece and Rome, 1983, (with Loren Samons II) From Cleisthenes to Pericles, 1991 (commentary) Continuation of Felix Jacoby, Die Fragmente der griechischen Historiker III c, 1994; contbr. articles and revs. in field to profl. jours. John Simon Guggenheim fellow, 1988-89. Mem. Am. Philol. Assn., Soc. for Promotion Hellenic Studies. Clubs: Providence Art. Home: 527 Mooresfield Rd Saunderstown RI 02874-1208 Office: Brown Univ Dept Classics Providence RI 02912-0001 Office Phone: 401-863-2123.

FORNARI, VICTOR M., psychiatrist; b. NYC, June 20; s. Ermanno and Alice (Notrica) F.; m. Alice Johnson, Mar. 27, 1977; children: Eric, Amy, Marci. BS in Biology, Cornell U., 1974; MS in Human Nutrition, Columbia U., 1975; MD, SUNY-Downstate Med. Ctr., Bklyn., 1979. Diplomate Am. Bd. Psychiatry and Neurology, Am. Bd. Child and Adolescent Psychiatry and Neurology. Intern LI Coll. Hosp., Bklyn., 1979-80; resident in psychiatry Hosp. U. Pa., Phila., 1980-82; fellow in child and adolescent psychiatry LI Jewish Med. Ctr., New Hyde Park, 1982-84; staff child psychiatrist Schneider's Children's Hosp./LI Jewish Med. Ctr., 1984-85; physician-in-charge Child Psychiatry Inpatient Unit/LI Jewish Med. Ctr., 1985-86; physician-in-charge, child psychiatry cons. liaison svc., eating disorders program North Shore-Cornell U. Hosp., Manhasset, NY, 1986-91, dir. tng./clin. svcs. div. child and adolescent psychiatry, 1991—98; assoc. chmn. edn. and tng. North Shore U. Hosp./NYU Sch. Medicine, 1998—2006; acting dir. divsn. child and adolescent psychiatry Zucker Hillside Hosp. North Shore-LI Jewish Health Sys., 2006—. Assoc. prof. psychiatry and pediatrics Cornell U. Med. Coll., NYC, 1991—; assoc. prof. NYU Sch. Medicine, 1993—; clin. dir. dept. psychiatry North Shore U. Hosp., 2007-. Fellow Am. Psychiat. Assn. (disting.), Am. Acad. Child and Adolescent Psychiatry; mem. Greater LI Psychiat. Soc. (pres.), Am. Assn. Dirs. of Psychiat. Resident Tng., Soc. Profs. of Child and Adolescent Psychiatry. Office Phone: 516-562-3206. Business E-Mail: vfornari@nshs.edu.

FORNERIS, JEANNE M., lawyer; b. Duluth, Minn., May 23, 1953; d. John Domenic and Elva Lorraine (McDonald) F.; m. Michael Scott Margulies, Feb. 6, 1982. AB, Macalester Coll., 1975; JD, U. Minn., 1978. Bar: Minn. 1978. Assoc. Halverson, Waters, Bye, Downs & Maki, Ltd., Duluth, 1978-81, Briggs & Morgan, P.A., Mpls., St. Paul, 1981-83; ptnr. Hart & Bruner, P.A., Mpls., 1983-86; assoc. gen. counsel M.A. Mortenson Co., Mpls., 1986-90, v.p., gen. counsel, 1990-96; with Gen. Counsel, Ltd., Mpls., 1997-98; v.p., sr. counsel Medtronic, Inc., Mpls., 1999—. Instr. women's studies dept. U. Minn., Mpls., 1977-79. Author profl. edn. seminars; contbr. articles to profl. jours. Bd. dirs. Good Will Indusries Vocat. Enterprises, Inc., 1979-81; chmn. bd. trustees Duluth Bar Libr., 1981; mem. United Way Family and Individual Svcs. Task Force, Duluth, 1981. Nat. Merit Assn. scholar, 1971. Fellow Am. Coll. Constrn. Lawyers (bd. dirs.); mem. AMA, Am. Arbitration Assn. (mem. large complex case panel), Minn. State Bar Assn., Minn. Women Lawyers (bd. dirs.), U.S. Dist. Ct. Hist. Soc. (pres.). Democrat. Roman Catholic. Office: Medtronic Inc 7000 Central Ave NE Minneapolis MN 55432-3576

FORNESS, STEVEN ROBERT, educational psychologist; b. Denver, May 13, 1939; s. Robert E. and Rejeana C. (Houck) F. BA in English, U. No. Colo., 1963, MA in Ednl. Psychology, 1964; EdD in Spl. Edn., UCLA, 1968. Tchr. Santa Maria (Calif.) H.S., 1964—66; counselor Sch. Edn. UCLA, 1966—68; spl. educator Neuropsychiat. Inst., 1968—2003, chief ednl. psychology child outpatient dept., 1970—2003, mem. mental retardation rsch. ctr., 1970—2003, prof. dept. psychiatry, 1972—2003, prin. inpatient sch., 1976—2003, dir. mental retardation and devel. disabilities tng. program, 1985—92, disting. prof. emeritus, 2003—. Grant rev. panelist U.S. Dept. Edn., 1974-2000; cons. Nat. Assn. Exceptional Children, Venezuela, 1974-2000; commn. ednl. psychology Calif. State Bd. Behavioral Scis. Examiners, 1977-99. Author: (with Frank Hewett) Education of Exceptional Learners, 3d edit., 1984, (with K. Kavale) Science of Learning Disabilities, 1985, (with Kavale and Bender) Handbook of Learning Disabilities, vols. I, II and III, 1987, 88; (with K. Kavale) Nature of Learning Disabilities, 1995, Efficacy of Special Education, 1999, (with E. Sinclair) Learning Disabilites and Related Disorders, 2002; cons. editor various jours. Sr. scholar Shaklee Inst. on Spl. Edn., 1996-2001. Recipient Disting. Alumni award U. No. Colo., 2006; Fulbright scholar Ministry of Edn., Portugal, 1976. Fellow Internat. Acad. Rsch. in Learning Disabilties, Am. Assn. Mental Retardation; mem. Tchr. Educators of Children with Behavior Disorders (pres. 1985-86), Coun. Children with Behavior Disorders (pres. 1987-88, Leadership award 1995, Forness Regional Scholarship 2003), Am. Assn. Univ. Affiliated Programs in Developmental Disabilities (interdisciplinary coun. 1972-89), Internat. Coun. for Exceptional Children (del. Assembly 1988-91, Wallin award 1992, Excellence in Tchr. Edn. award 1995, honors com. 1999-2002), Acad. on Mental Retardation (exec. com. 1989-91), Nat. Mental Health and Spl. Edn. Coalition (co-chair of Definition Task Force 1987-2000), Am. Psychiat. Assn. (DSM IV subcom. on learning disorders 1988-94), Profl. Group for Attention and Related Disorders (com. profl. advisors 1990-91), Midwest Symposium on Behavioral Disorders (Leadership award 1993), Am. Acad. Child and Adolescent Psychiatry (co-chmn. practice parameters on learning disabilities 1996-98, Sidney Berman award on learning disorders 2000), Knights of Malta (Order of St. John 1994). Home: 11901 W Sunset Blvd Los Angeles CA 90049-4240 Office: UCLA Dept Psychiatry 760 Westwood Plz Los Angeles CA 90095-8353 Office Phone: 310-825-0159.

FORNEY, G(EORGE) DAVID, JR., retired electronics executive; b. NYC, Mar. 6, 1940; s. George David Forney and Priscilla (Brush) Forney McDonnell; m. Harriett A. Bascom, June 9, 1962 (div. 1989); children: Mark Hamilton, Priscilla Jean, William McDonnell; m. Elizabeth D. Coxe, Aug. 26, 2006. BS in Engring., Princeton U., 1961; MSc, MIT, 1963, ScD, 1965; PhD (hon.), Ecole Poly. Fed. Lausanne, Switzerland, 2007. Mem. tech. staff Codex Corp., Watertown, Mass., 1965-70, v.p. rsch. Newton, Mass., 1970-75, v.p. R&D, 1975-78, v.p. rsch. Mansfield, Mass., 1978-82, v.p. tech. and bus. devel., 1986-89; v.p., dir. tech. and planning Motorola Info. Sys. Group, Mansfield, 1982-86; v.p. tech. staff Motorola, Inc., Mansfield, 1980-99. Vis. scientist Stanford U., Stanford, 1971—72, vis. prof., 1990, 2007, adv. coun., 1990—94; adv. coun. dept. elec. engring. Princeton U., NJ, 1977—99, Columbia U., NYC, 1986—93, Harvard U., Cambridge, Mass., 1995—2003, EPFL, Lausanne, Switzerland, 1999—2006; adj. prof. MIT, Cambridge, 1980—82, Cambridge, 1996—. Author: Concatenated Codes, 1966; contbr. articles to profl. jours. Overseer Shady Hill Sch., Cambridge, 1980—86; bd. dirs. Am. Field Svc., NYC, 1971—74, Aware, Inc., 1999—; trustee Lehrman Inst., NYC, 1973—80, Mt. Auburn Hosp., Cambridge, 1986—2004. Named to Mass. Telecom. Hall of Fame, 2001; recipient Christopher Columbus award in Internat. Comm., 1996; Marconi Internat. fellow, 1997. Fellow: IEEE (editor jour. 1970—73, Info. Theory Group award 1970, Browder J. Thompson prize paper award 1972, Centennial medal 1984, Donald G. Fink prize paper award 1990, Edison medal 1992, Shannon award 1995, Info. Theory Golden Jubilee award 1998), AAAS, Am. Acad. Arts and Scis.; mem.: NAS, NAE, IEEE Info. Theory Soc. (pres. 1992), Popov Soc. (Russia) (hon.). Achievements include patents in field. Home and Office: 1010 Memorial Dr Apt 3G Cambridge MA 02138-4853 Home Phone: 617-868-4855; Office Phone: 617-868-4855. Business E-Mail: forneyd@comcast.net.

FORNEY, JAN LYNETTE, geophysicist; b. Mpls., Sept. 5, 1954; d. Robert Ellsworth and Joanne Carol (Jones) Forney; 1 child, Sarah Winspeare Merriam George. BA in Geology, Smith Coll., Northampton, Mass., 1977; MS in Geology, U. Mass., Amherst, 1980; postgrad., Rice U., 1992. Cert. profl. geoscientist Tex. Tech. Gulf Coast exploration geophysicist Amoco, 1980—86, new ventures geoscientist internat. and deepwater Gulf of Mex., 1986—97; new ventures geoscientist, West Africa Texaco, 1997—99; reservoir simulation geoscientist Core Labs., 2001—04; new ventures geophysicist, deepwater Gulf of Mex. Amerada Hess, 2004—06, Samson, Houston, 2006—. Vol. Girl Scouts, Pvt. Sector Initiatives. Recipient Exploration Strategy award, Amoco, 1991, Angola Team award, 1994. Mem.: Houston Geol. Soc., Soc. Exploration Geophysics, Am. Assn. Petroleum Geologists. Progressive. Avocations: travel, music. Home: 607 Kipling St Houston TX 77006

FORNEY, LARRY J., chemical engineer, educator; b. Waterloo, Iowa, Nov. 1, 1944; s. Loren John and Ramona Leary F.; m. Paula Hickey, Aug. 3, 1974; 1 child, Megan Catlin. BS, Case Inst. Tech., Cleve., 1966; MS, MIT, Boston, 1968, ME, 1969; PhD, Harvard U., Cambridge, Mass., 1974. Rsch. engr. Norton Rsch. Corp., Cambridge, Mass., 1968, Walden Rsch. div. Abcor, Inc., Cambridge, Mass., 1972-74; asst. prof. dept. civil engring. U. Ill., Urbana, 1974-79; assoc. prof. chem. engring. Ga. Inst. Tech., Atlanta, 1979—. Cons. Comml. Union Ins. Co., 1977, Lockheed Ga. Co., 1982-83, Sverdrup Tech. Inc., 1983-87, Dupont, 1989-91, Leeds & Northrup, 1991, Dow Corning Corp., 1994-96, Chem. Products Corp., 2004; phys. scientist USAF Rocket Propulsion Lab., Edward AFB, Calif., 1983. Contbr. articles to profl. jours. Active Clean Air Coun., Ga. Lung Assn., 1980-82. NIH fellow, 1968, SCEEE fellow, 1982, NASA fellow, 1988; grantee NSF, 1975-77, EPA, 1976-78, U.S. Dept. Energy, 1977-81, USAF, 1983-84, 1989-95 Ga. FoodPAC, 2002-06. Mem. Am. Inst. Chem. Engrs. (coordinator of sessions 1983, 88, 2000 ann. meetings), Harvard Soc. Engrs. and Scientists, North Am. Mixing Forum, Harvard Club, MIT Club. Achievements include patents for Taylor-Couette Flow: UV disinfection of fluids. Office: Ga Inst Tech Sch Chem Engring Atlanta GA 30332-0001 Office Phone: 404-894-2825. Personal E-mail: flll44@aol.com. Business E-Mail: larry.forney@chbe.gatech.edu.

FORNI, PATRICIA ROSE, nursing educator; b. St. Louis, Feb. 14, 1932; d. Harold and Glenda M. (Keay) Brown. BSN, Washington U., St. Louis, 1955, MS (USPHS trainee), 1957; PhD (USPHS fellow), St. Louis U., 1965; postgrad. (USPHS scholar), U. Minn., summers 1968, 70. Staff nurse McMillan EENT Hosp., St. Louis, summer 1955, Renard Psychiat. Hosp., St. Louis, part-time 1955-57; rsch. asst. Washington U. Sch. Nursing, St. Louis, 1957-59, rsch. assoc., 1959-61, asst. prof., 1964-66, assoc. dean in charge grad. edn., assoc. prof. gen. nursing sci., 1966-68; assoc. prof. pub. health nursing Wayne State U., Detroit, 1968-69; asst. dir. for manpower and edn. Ill. Regional Med. Program, Chgo., 1969-71; project dir. Midwest Continuing Profl. Edn. for Nurses, St. Louis U., 1971-75; dean, prof. nursing So. Ill. U., Edwardsville, 1975-88; dean Coll. Nursing U. Okla., Oklahoma City, 1988—2004, prof. Coll. Nursing, 1988—. Grant proposal reviewer Divsn. Nursing, USPHS, 1972-79, 88, 91, NSF, 1978, U.S. Dept. Edn., 1980; mem. Ill. Implementation Commn. on Nursing, 1975-77, Okla. State Health Plan Adv. Com., 1994—. Mem. peer rev. panel Nursing Outlook, 1987-91; mem. editl. bd. Health Care for Women Internat., 1984—, Jour. Profl. Nursing, 1988-90. Chairwoman articulation of nursing programs task force Okla. State Regents for Higher Edn., 1990-91; bd. dirs. Greater St. Louis Health Sys. Agy., 1976-81, Adult Edn. Coun. Greater St. Louis, 1973-76, Edwardsville unit Am. Cancer Soc., 1981-88. Fellow WHO, Sweden, Finland, 1985. Mem. Nat. League for Nursing (accreditation site visitor 1979—, nominating com. Coun. Baccalaureate and Higher Degree Programs 1979-82, pub. policy and legis. com. 1981-85, bd. dirs. 1991-93, treas. 1991-93, fin. com. 1991-95), Nat. League for Health Care (trustee 1991-93), Nat. League for Nursing Accrediting Commn. (peer review panel, baccalaureate and higher degree programs 1997-2000, 06, commr. 2000-06, chmn. 2001-06), Am. Nurses Assn. (chmn. continuing edn. publs. com. 1975-76), Mo. Nurses Assn. (chmn. edn. com. 1973-77), Greater St. Louis Soc. Health Manpower Edn. and Tng. (chmn. legis. com. 1974-75), Midwest Alliance in Nursing (1st governing bd. 1979-80, 93-96, chmn. nominations com. 1980-81, fin. com. 1993-94, chair fin. com. 1994-96, treas. 1994-96, pres. 1998-2000), Am. Assn. Colls. Nursing (hon., program com. 1978-82, mem.-at-large, bd. dirs. 1990-92, chair rsch. com. 1990-92), Ill. Coun. Deans/Dirs. Baccalaureate and Higher Degree Programs in Nursing (chmn. 1979-81), Am. Acad. Nursing (treas., chair fin. com., gov. coun. 1989-93, editor Newsletter 1982-87), Ill. Nurses Assn. (commn. on adminstrn. 1983-87, commn. on edn. 1987-89), Okla. Nurses Found. (pres. bd. trustees 1990-93), Sigma Theta Tau Internat. (charter mem. Epsilon Eta chpt. 1980). Office: U Okla Coll Nursing PO Box 26901 Oklahoma City OK 73190-0001

FORREST, DANIEL ERNEST, composer, music educator; b. Elmira, NY, Jan. 7, 1978; s. Daniel Ernest, Sr. and Bonita Jean Forrest; m. Adelyn Elaine Johnson, May 8, 2001; children: Leah Adelyn, Daniel Ernest III. BMus in Piano Performance, Bob Jones U., 1999, MMus in Piano Performance, 2001; DMusA in Composition, U. Kans., Lawrence, 2007. Prof. music Bob Jones U., Greenville, SC, 2001—. Composer: (choral work, a cappella) Words From Paradise (ACDA Raymond Brock Meml. Composition Contest, 2005, ASCAP Morton Guild Young Composer award, 2006), (choral anthem) The King of Love My Shepherd Is (John Ness Beck Found. award, 2005). Recipient Std. awards, ASCAP, 2003—06. Fellow: Melodious Accord; mem.: Am. Choral Dir. Assn. Home: 202 Pine Spring Ct Greenville SC 29609

FORREST, DAVID VICKERS, psychiatrist, educator; b. NYC, July 8, 1938; s. Melbourne Arthur and Cleo Florence (Garello) Forrest; m. Lynne Putnam Stetson; children: Daniel Stetson, Susannah Forrest Karajannis. AB summa cum laude, Princeton U., 1960; MD, Columbia U., 1964, cert. in psychoanalysis, 1974. Cert. in psychiatry Am. Bd. Psychiatry and Neurology. Intern in medicine St. Luke's Hosp., NYC, 1964-65; resident in psychiatry N.Y. State Psychiat. Inst., Columbia Presbyn. Med. Ctr., NYC, 1965-68; chief psychiatric clinic 935th Med. Det. (KO) 93d Evacuation Hosp., Long Binh, Vietnam, 1968-69; chief psychiatric consultation Letterman Army Med. Ctr., San Francisco, 1969-70; pvt. practice psychiatry NYC, 1970—; mem. psychiatry faculty Columbia U., NYC, 1970—; dir. edn. ednl. rsch. dept. N.Y. State Psychiat. Inst., 1970-77; assoc. prof. clin. psychiatry Columbia U., Coll. Physicians and Surgeons, NYC, 1984—, faculty psychoanalytic ctr., 1974—, consultation-liaison psychiatrist neurology (movement disorders), 1977—, clin. prof. of psychiatry NYC, 2000—. Lectr. psychiatry U. Saigon Med. Sch., Vietnam, 1968-69; lectr. abnormal psychology Far East div. U. Md., Long Binh, Vietnam, 1969. Author: Selected American Expressions, 1974, 76, 82; co-author: Treating Schizophrenic Patients, 1983, (video cassette series) Electronic Textbook of Psychiatry, 1972-77; co-author, pub: The Ballet Company Game, 1973; founding editor, pub. Spring: The Jour. of the E. E. Cummings Soc., N.Y.C., 1980—; editor: Neural Net News, N.Y. State Psychiat. Inst., 1989-91; technical cons. Star Trek TV series, 1997—; contbr. articles to profl. jours., textbooks. Psychiat. cons. N.Y.C. Ballet Co., 1973; first aid instr. Boy Scouts Am., 1983—. Capt. USAF, 1968-70, Vietnam. Decorated Bronze Star; Gen. Motors nat. scholar. Fellow Am. Psychiat. Assn., Am. Coll. Psychiatrists, Am. Acad. Psychoanalysis (program chair), Am. Coll. Psychoanalysts (program chair 1987-89, bd. regents 1989-92, v.p. 1993, pres.-elect 1994, pres. 1995), Explorers Club; mem. Am. Acad. Neurology (assoc.), NY Clin. Soc. (v.p. 1995, pres. 1996), Med. Strollers (v.p. 2007). Episcopalian. Avocations: invention, discovery, magic. Office: 133 E 73rd St Ste 211 New York NY 10021-3556 also: 155 W 68th St Apt 1219 New York NY 10023-5818 Office Phone: 212-988-4800.

FORREST, HERBERT EMERSON, lawyer; b. NYC, Sept. 20, 1923; s. Jacob K. and Rose (Fried) F.; m. Marilyn Lefsky, Jan. 12, 1952; children: Glenn Clifford, Andrew Matthew. Student, CCNY, 1941, Ohio U., 1943-44; BA with distinction, George Washington U., 1948, JD with highest honors, 1952. Bar: Va. 1952, DC 1952, US Supreme Ct. 1956, Md. 1959, US Ct. Appeals (DC cir.) 1953, US Ct. Appeals (1st cir.) 1992, US Ct. Appeals (2d cir.) 1971, US Ct. Appeals (3d cir.) 1957, US Ct. Appeals (4th cir.) 1956, US Ct. Appels (5th cir.) 1981, US Ct. Appeals (7th cir.) 1996, US Ct. Appeals (8th cir.) 1991, US Ct. Appeals (9th cir.) 1994, US Ct. Appeals (11th cir.) 1981. Plate printer Bur. Engraving and Printing, Washington, 1942-43, 1946-52; law clk. to chief judge Bolitha J. Laws US Dist. Ct., Washington, 1952-55; pvt. practice Washington, 1952-87; with Welch & Morgan, 1955-65, Steptoe & Johnson, 1965-85, of counsel, 1986-87; trial atty. fed. programs br. civil divsn. US Dept. Justice, Washington, 1987—; chmn. adv. bd. DC Criminal Justice Act, 1971-74; sec. com. admissions and grievances US Ct. Appeals, DC, 1973-79; title-1 audit hearing bd. US Office Edn. HEW, 1976-79; edn. appeals bd. US Dept. Edn., 1979-82. Mem. Lawyer's Support Com. for Visitors Service Ctr., 1975-87 Contbr. articles to profl. jours.; mem. editl. bd. Duke Law Jour, 1969-75. Pres. Whittier Woods PTA, 1970—71. With F.A., Signal Corps US Army, 1943—46, We. PTO, Manana, Palau. Recipient Walsh award in Irish history, 1952, Goddard award in commerce, 1952. Fellow Am. Bar Found. (life), ABA (council 1972-75, 1981-84, budget officer 1985-88, vice chmn. task force on sect. devel. 1987-89, chmn. com. on agy. rule making 1968-72, 1976-81, chmn. membership com. 1984-85, editor ann. reports 1973-88, adminstrv. law sect., fellow adminstrv. law and regulatory practice, mem. comm. com. public utilities law sect., vice chmn. industry regulation com. 1985-86, chmn. comm. subcom. 1983-85, antitrust law sect., internat. law sect., sec. judicial adminstrn., sect. sci. and tech., comm. forum); mem. George Washington Law Assn., Am. Judicature Soc., Va. State Bar Assn., Fed. Bar Assn. (chmn. jud. rev. com. 1981-85, vice chmn. adminstrv. law sect. 1985-87), Fed. Comm. Bar Assn. (del. to ABA Ho. Dels. 1979-81, exec. com. 1967-71, 76-84, v.p. 1981-82, pres. 1982-83, chmn. telecomm. com. 1983-87), DC Bar Assn. (past sec., exec. com.), NAM, Nat. Conf. Bar Pres., Washington Council Lawyers, Legal Aid and Pub. Defender Assn., Am. Arbitration Assn. (comml. panel 1976-87), DC Unified Bar (bd. govs. 1976-79, chmn. com. on employment discrimination complaint service 1973-79, chmn. task force on services to public 1974-78, chmn. com. on appointment counsel in criminal cases 1978-88, co-chmn. com. on participation govt. employees in pro bono activities 1977-79), Broadcast Pioneers, Order of Coif, B'nai Brith, Phi Beta Kappa, Pi Gamma Mu., Artus, Phi Eta Sigma, Phi Delta Phi. Democrat. Home: 8706 Bellwood Rd Bethesda MD 20817-3033 Office: US Dept Justice 20 Massachusetts Ave NW Rm 7112 Washington DC 20530 Office Phone: 202-514-2809. Business E-Mail: herbert.forrest@usdoj.gov.

FORREST, JULIET, dancer, educator, choreographer; b. Chgo., Apr. 4, 1954; d. Norman Forrest and Rochelle Shor. MFA, NYU, NYC, 1977. Cert. Laban/Bartenieff movement analyst U. Utah, 2006. Dir. Forrest Collection Dance Co., Balt., 1986—91; assoc. prof. dance Goucher Coll., Towson, Md., 1982—2006. Master tchr. modern technique Howard County Ballet Sch., Ellicott City, Md., 1993—2006. (group choreography) Red Zone II, (movement theater) Near Miss-A Calamity in Nine Acts. Chair AIDS walk performing arts com. Health Edn. Resource Orgn., Balt., 1990—91. Md. State Arts grantee, 1987—2001. Avocations: writing, dance, hiking. Office: Dance Dept of Goucher Coll 1021 Dulaney Valley Rd Towson MD 21204-2794 Office Phone: 410-337-6393. Office Fax: 410-337-6433. Business E-Mail: jforrest@goucher.edu.

FORREST, KATHERINE B., lawyer; b. NYC, Feb. 13, 1964; BA with honors, Wesleyan Univ., 1986; MA, NYU, 1987, JD, 1990. Bar: NY 1991. Summer assoc. Cravath Swaine & Moore LLP, NYC, 1989, assoc., 1990—97, ptnr., litig., 1998—. Lectr. in field of antitrust, intellectual property law, gen. comml. litig.; bd. mem. Lawyers' Com. for Civil Rights, Fund for Modern Cts. Contbr. chapters to books, articles to profl. jours. Named one of Am. Lawyer's Fab 50, 2007, recognized in Global Competition Rev. 40 under 40, 2004. Mem.: Am. Acad. Trial Lawyers, Am. Acad. Trial Counsel, NY State Bar Assn., Assn. of Bar of City of NY. Office: Cravath Swaine & Moore LLP Worldwide Plz 825 Eighth Ave New York NY 10019-7475 Office Phone: 212-474-1155. Office Fax: 212-474-3700. Business E-Mail: kforrest@cravath.com.

FORREST, KENNETH B., lawyer; b. Bklyn., Jan. 16, 1952; BA magna cum laude, Bklyn. Coll., 1973; JD magna cum laude, SUNY, Buffalo, 1976. Bar: N.Y. 1977, US Dist. Ct. (so. & ea. N.Y.), US Ct. Appeals (2d, 9th & 11th cir.), US Supreme Ct. Ptnr. Wachtell, Lipton, Rosen & Katz, NYC, 1982—, assigning ptnr. litigation dept. Editor (sr.): Buffalo Law Rev. Mem. Dean's Adv. Council SUNY Buffalo Law Sch. Mem.: ABA, Fed. Bar Council, N.Y. State Bar Assn., Assn. Bar City of N.Y. (mem. com. Fed. legislation & com. profl. responsibility). Office: Wachtell Lipton Rosen & Katz 51 W 52nd St New York NY 10019-6150 Office Phone: 212-403-1211. Office Fax: 212-403-2211. Business E-Mail: kbforrest@wlrk.com.

FORREST, PATRICIA ANNE, publishing executive, editor; b. Kingstree, SC, July 16, 1935; d. John Symonds Hale and Clara Mae Smith; m. Richard Stockton Forrest, June 26, 1999; m. Dwight Ellsworth Whitton (div.); children: Laura Katherine, Robert Kennedy. BA, Agnes Scott Coll., 1955; MA, CUNY, 1969. Pub. New Plays Inc., Charlottesville, Va., 1962—, editor, 1962—. Lectr. in field. Author: Capture Them With Magic, 1982, Bringing the World Alive, 1996, (plays) The Little Mermaid, 1996, Puppet Heroes Around the World, 2006. Bd. dirs. Internat. Assn. of Theatre for Children and Youth, 1981—87. Recipient Oustanding Svc. award, East Ctrl. Theatre Coop., 1996, Sace Spencer Lifetime Achievement award, 1997, award, Children's Theatre Found., 2004, Woodrow Wilson Centennial Celebration Commn. Plays winner, Hall Mirr. Fellow: Coll. Fellows Am. Theatre; mem.: Am. Alliance Theatre and Edn. (chmn. exhibits 1991). Democrat. Avocations: camping, water aerobics, snorkeling, cats. Office: New Plays Inc PO Box 5074 Charlottesville VA 22905 Personal E-mail: patwhitton@aol.com.

FORREST, SIDNEY, clarinetist, music educator; b. NYC, Aug. 21, 1918; s. Paul and Esther Forrest; m. Faith Levine, Nov. 16, 1941; 1 child, Paula Forrest. Student, Juilliard Sch. Music, 1935—37; BA, U. Miami, Fla., 1939; MA, Columbia U., 1941; studied with Simeon Bellison, Otto Conrad, Alexander Williams. Prof. Peabody Conservatory of Music, Johns Hopkins U., Balt., 1946-85, prof. emeritus, 1985, dir. placement and career counseling, 1969-85. Clarinet soloist U.S. Marine Band and Symphony Orch., Washington, 1941-45; prin. clarinet Nat. Symphony, 1946-50; adj. prof. faculty Cath. U., 1954-2003; faculty Interlochen Ctr. for the Arts, Mich., 1959-2004, Am. U., Washington, 1961-81, George Washington U., Washington, 1970-74, Levine Sch. Music, Washington, 1980—, Amalfi Coast Festival, Italy, 2006; adjudicator Nat. Fulbright Commn., 1980-84, Que. Can. Nat. Conservatoire, 1969-84. Editor and arranger clarinet solos including Entrance March of the Boyars: Halvorsen, Theme and Variations: Baermann Divertimento: Baermann, Nocturne No. 20: Chopin, Pastorale: Baermann, Twelve Fantasies for Solo Clarinet: Telemann, Variations on a Theme of Corelli: By Tartini, Four Hebraic Pictures (arranged by S. Bellison), Twelve Fantasies for Solo Saxophone: Telemann, Twelve Fantasies for Solo Oboe: Telemann, others; major full clarinet recitals include Carnegie Recital Hall, Bklyn. Mus., Nat. Art Gallery, Phillips Collection, Libr. Congress, others; solo clarinet recordings and recitals with Galimir Quartet, Erno Balogh, Bernard Greenhouse, Carlton Cooley, Leonid Hambro, others; recs. include (clarinet quintet) Mozart K.581, (with viola and piano) Mozart Trio K.498, (with cello and piano) Brahms Trio op. 114, (clarinet and piano) Hindemith Sonata, (with piano) Grand Duo Concertant op. 48, Variations op. 33: Von Weber, Alban Berg Vier Stuecke (with piano); contbr. articles to profl. jours.; former students in major Am. and overseas opera and symphony orchs.; co-designer (with J. Hall) of Sidney Forrest Signature Clarinet Mouthpiece. Mem. Internat. Clarinet Assn., Music Tchrs. Nat. Assn. Avocations: photography, gardening, stamp collecting/philately, travel. Home: 9611 Kingston Rd Kensington MD 20895-3521 Personal E-mail: sidneyforrest@aol.com.

FORRESTER, ALFRED WHITFIELD, psychiatrist, educator; b. Springfield, Mass., May 15, 1953; s. Wallace Lomax and Alma Mae (Brooks) F. BA magna cum laude, Yale U., 1975; MD, Johns Hopkins U., 1979. Diplomate Nat. Bd. Med. Examiners, Am. Bd. Psychiatry and Neurology. Med. resident dept. medicine Mt. Auburn Hosp., Cambridge, Mass., 1979-82; psychiatry resident dept. psychiatry and behavioral scis. Johns Hopkins Med. Insts., Balt., 1982-85, research fellow, 1985-86, instr., 1986-93; clin. asst. prof. dept. psychiatry U. Md., Balt., 1987—; pvt. psychiat. practice, 1988—. Staff psychiatrist Cann Health Resources, Fallston, Md., 1987-88, The Sheppard and Enoch Pratt Hosp., 1988-97; dir. psychiat. svcs. Chase-Brexton Health Svcs., Balt., 1988-90, staff psychiatrist, 1985-2000; med. dir. Behavioral Sci. Assocs., Lutherville, Md., 1993-97, Nicotine Addiction Treatment Ctrs., Lutherville, 1997-2002; med. cons. Bon Secours Hosp., Balt., 1983-90; psychiat. cons. Shock-Trauma Ctr. U. Md. Hosp., 1987-90. Contbr. articles to profl. jours. Active Groton (Mass.) Sch. Bd. Govs., 1983-85, AIDS com., Med. and Chirurgical Faculty State of Md., 1988-91. Nat. Achievement scholar, 1971—75. Fellow APA; mem. AMA, ACP, Med. and Chirurgical Faculty State Md., Md. Psychiat. Soc., Md. Psychiat. Liaison Assn., Yale Alumni Assn. (fundraiser 1975-2003), Greater Balt. Bus. Profl. Assn., Mory's Assn. (New Haven), Yale Club (Md.), Johns Hopkins Club. Democrat. Episcopalian. Avocations: classical music, theater. Home: 115 Saint Dunstans Rd Baltimore MD 21212-3311 Office: 9515 Deereco Rd Ste 1001 Timonium MD 21093 Office Phone: 410-453-0901. Business E-Mail: a.w.forrester@att.net.

FORRESTER, JAMES STUART, cardiologist, medical educator; b. Phila., July 13, 1937; s. James S. and Mildred W. (Smith) F.; m. Deborah MacAdam, 1963 (div. 1974); children: Jeffrey Lance, Brent Worth; m. Barbara Ann Bick, May 27, 1975; 1 child, Justin Bick. BA, Swarthmore Coll., 1959; MD, U. Pa., 1963. Diplomate Am. Bd. Internal Medicine; bd. cert. cardiovascular disease. Intern U. Pa. Hosp.; resident Harbor Gen. Hosp.; fellow Peter Bent Brigham Hosp.; prof. medicine, David Geffen Sch. Medicine UCLA, 1986—; dir. divsn. cardiology Cedars-Sinai Med. Ctr., LA, 1989-95, dir. cardiovascular rsch. inst., 1993—, George Burns and Gracie Allen prof. cardiology, 1989—. Recipient Goldman award for laser rsch. SPIE, 1990, Kellerman award for prevention cardiology rsch. Internat. Soc. Heart Failure, 1996; named Best Doctors in Am., 1994, 95, 96, 97, 98, Best Heart Doctors in Am., Good Housekeeping, 1996. Mem. Am. Coll. Cardiology (bd. trustees 1993-98), Am. Heart Assn. (bd. dirs. 1993—, Disting. Sci. Achievement award 1990). Office: Cedars Sinai Med Ctr 8700 Beverly Blvd Los Angeles CA 90048-1865 also: David Geffen Sch Medicine SINAI-5347 UCLA Los Angeles CA 90095*

FORRESTER, JAY WRIGHT, management consultant, educator; b. Anselmo, Nebr., July 14, 1918; s. Marmaduke M. and Ethel Pearl (Wright) F.; m. Susan Swett, July 27, 1946; children: Judith, Nathan Blair, Ned Cromwell. B.Sc., U. Nebr., 1939, D.Eng. (hon.), 1954; M.Sc., MIT, 1945; D.Sc. (hon.), Boston U., 1969, Union Coll., 1973; D.Eng. (hon.), Newark Coll. Engring., 1971, U. Notre Dame, 1974; D.Polit. Sci. (hon.), U. Mannheim, 1979; LHD (hon.), SUNY, 1988; PhD (hon.), U. Bergen, Norway, 1990; Doctorate (hon.), U. de Sevilla, Spain, 1998. Instr., X-ray equipment rschr. MIT, Cambridge, 1939-40, co-founder Servomechanisms Lab., 1940, devel. electric and hydraulic servomechanisms for gun mounts and radar, 1940-44, asso. dir. servomechanisms lab., also supr. Whirlwind I digital computer devel., 1944-51, founder Digital Computer Lab., dir., 1951-56, div. head Lincoln Lab. for Air Def., 1951-56, prof. mgmt. Sloan Sch. Mgmt., 1956-72, Germeshausen prof., 1972-89, Germeshausen prof. emeritus, sr. lectr., 1989—. Former owner Forrester Cattle Ranch, Dunning, Nebr.; head System Dynamics Group, Sloan Sch., 1960-89. Lectures and tech. papers on digital computers and indsl. mgmt.; also dynamics indsl. and econ. behavior.; author: Industrial Dynamics, 1961, Principles of Systems, 1968, Urban Dynamics, 1969, World Dynamics, 1971, Collected Papers, 1975; patentee servomechanisms, digital info. storage, indsl. control. Recipient Inventor of Yr. award George Washington U., 1968, Valdemar Poulsen Gold medal Danish Acad. Tech. Scis., 1969, Outstanding Accomplishment award Systems, Man and Cybernetics Soc. of IEEE, 1972, Computer Pioneer award IEEE Computer Soc., 1982, Benjamin Franklin fellow Royal Soc. Arts, London, 1972, New Eng. award Engring. Socs. New Eng., 1973, Potts medal Franklin Inst., 1974; Harry Goode Meml. award Am. Fedn. Info. Processing Socs., 1977, Common Wealth award of Disting. Service, 1979, James R. Killain Jr. Faculty Achievement award MIT, 1987, Agricultura 2000 award, Italy, 1987, Info. Storage award IEEE Magnetics Soc., 1988, Lord Found. Leadership award, 1988, U.S. Nat. Medal of Tech., 1989, Pioneer award IEEE Aerospace & Electronic Systems Soc., 1990, Fellow award, Computer History Mus., 1995; named to Nat. Inventors Hall of Fame, 1979, Hall Fame, Internat. Fedn. Operational Rsch. Socs., 2006; Jay W. Forrester chair named in his honor, MIT. Fellow IEEE (medal of Honor 1972, Pioneer award 1990), Am. Acad. Arts and Scis., Acad. Mgmt.; mem. Nat. Acad. Engring., Inst. Mgmt. Scis., Soc. Mfg. Engrs. (hon.), Am. Phys. Soc., Assn. Computing Machinery, Eta Kappa Nu, Sigma Xi, Sigma Tau.

FORRESTER, PATRICK G., astronaut; b. El Paso, Tex., Mar. 31, 1957; s. Redmond V. and Patsy L. Forrester; m. Diana Lynn Morris; 2 children. BSc in Applied Sci. & Engring., US Mil. Acad., West Point, NY, 1979; MSc in Mech. & Aerospace Engring., U. Va., 1989. Commd. 2d lt. U.S. Army, 1979, advanced through grades to col., various assignments, 1980—89; flight test engr., R&D coord. Army Aviation Engring. Flight Activity, Edwards AFB, Calif., 1989—92; graduate USN Test Pilot Sch., 1992; engring. test pilot U.S. Army Aviation Tech. Test Ctr., Ft. Rucker, Ala., 1992—93; ret. U.S. Army, 2005; aerospace engr. NASA, Houston, 1993—, mission specialist, astronaut, 1996—. Astronaut STS-105 Mission, Discovery mission to Internat. Space Sta., 2001; crew mem., spacewalker STS-117 Mission Atlantis, 2007. Decorated Def. Superior Svc. medal, Legion of Merit, Meritorious Svc. medal with 2nd oak leaf cluster, Army Commendation medal, Army Achievement medal, Nat. Defense Svc. medal, Expert Infantryman Badge; recipient Lyndon B. Johnson Space Ctr. Cert. Commendation, 1995, NASA Space Flight medal, 2001, Order St. Michael, 2001. Mem.: Am. Helicopter Soc., Army Aviation Assn. Am., Soc. Exptl. Test Pilots (Jack Northrop award 1996), West Point Soc. Greater Houston, U.S. Mil. Acad. Assn. Graduates, Order of St. Michael. Avocations: baseball, running. Office: Astronaut Office CB Johnson Space Center Houston TX 77058*

FORRINGER, LETITIA MARIE, music educator; b. Kittanning, Pa. d. Kenneth Robert and Deborah Lee Forringer. BS in Music Edn., Pa. State U., 2004; MEd in Curriculum and Instrn., Gannon U. Cert. music tchr. Music tchr. Hopewell Area Sch. Dist., Allquippa, Pa., 2004—. Musician (horn substitute): Butter (Pa.) County Symphony. Sponsor Drama Club, Aliquippa, Baldwin Whitehall Sch. Dist. Mem.: NEA, Nat. Educators Nat. Conf., Pa. State Edn. Assn., Pa. Music Educators Assn., Pi Lambda Theta. Home: 297 Pleasant Dr #A-1 Aliquippa PA 15001

FORRY, JOHN INGRAM, lawyer; b. Washington, Feb. 9, 1945; s. John Emerson and Marion Carlotta (MacArthur) Forry; m. Carol Ann Micken, Jan. 12, 1980; children: Alicia Ann, Camilla Lorraine. BA, Amherst Coll., 1966; JD, Harvard U., 1969. Bar: Calif. 1970, U.S. Supreme Ct. 1975, U.S. Tax Ct. 1977, DC 1998, N.Y. 1998. Founding ptnr. Forry Golbert Singer & Gelles, LA, 1973—80; sr. ptnr. Morgan, Lewis & Bockius, LA, 1980—97, McDermott, Will & Emery, NYC, 1997—98, Ernst & Young LLP, NYC, 1999—2003, Withers Bergman LLP, NYC, 2004—05, Dunnington Bartholow & Miller LLP, NYC, 2007—; prof. internat. fin. and taxation, 2005—. Co-author, editor: A Practical Guide to Foreign Investment in the United States, 1979, 3d edit., 1989, Joint Ventures in the United States, 1988, Differences in Tax Treatment of Foreign Investors, 1984, others; contbr. articles to profl. jours. Mem. adv. group to U.S. Commr. IRS, Washington, 1985—86; co-founder Fund in Philosophy and Sci., Amherst (Mass.) Coll., 1984—. Mem.: Internat. Fiscal Assn., Internat. Bar Assn. Republican. Roman Catholic. Avocations: auto racing, mountain climbing, scuba diving, philosophy. Office Phone: 646-345-0586. Personal E-mail: forryjo@aol.com.

FORRY, ROBERT H., lawyer; b. Indpls., 1947; BA magna cum laude, Emory Univ., Atlanta, 1969; JD, Univ. Va., 1972. Bar: Ga. 1972. Assoc. Troutman Sanders LLP, Atlanta, 1972—76, ptnr., energy, govtl. law, 1977—, and sect. chief, pub. law. Named a Super Lawyer, Atlanta Mag., 2004—; named one of America's Leading Lawyers for Bus., Chambers USA, 2004—. Mem.: ABA, Fed. Energy Bar Assn., State Bar Ga. (past chmn., adminstrv. law sect.), Atlanta Bar Assn. Office: Troutman Sanders LLP 600 Peachtree St NE Ste 5200 Atlanta GA 30308-2216 Office Phone: 404-885-3142. Office Fax: 404-962-6559. Business E-Mail: robert.forry@troutmansanders.com.

FORRY, STEVEN, not-for-profit fundraiser; b. Bellflower, Calif., Aug. 30, 1952; s. Earl Forry and Darlys Gallagher; 1 child, Sarah Cathrine. BA French magna cum laude, U. Calif., Santa Barbara, 1978, BA English cum laude, 1978; MA English, Columbia U., 1984, PhD English, 1988. Dir. stewardship Columbia U., NYC, 1987—89; sr. devel. officer Sharp Hosps. Found., San Diego, 1990—96; assoc. dir. devel. U. Calif., San Diego, 1996—99; dir. corp. rels. Orange County HS Arts, Santa Ana, Calif., 2000—01; dir. devel. Children's Hosp. of Orange County, 2001—. Author: (Critical Study) Hideous Progenies: Dramatizations of Frankenstein in the 19th Century, 1990, (screenplays) Squiggets, 2002. Recipient award for Best Essay on Theatre, Am. Theatre Assn., 1987, award for outstanding pub. speaking, Toastmasters Internat.; fellow, Columbia U., 1978—81, fellowship, 1982—83, English Dept. Tchg. fellowship, 1984—87; scholar Whiting scholar, 1984—86. Mem.: Assn. Fundraising Profls., Nat. Soc. Fund Raising Profl. (chair Fund Raising Day San Diego chpt. 1993, chair fund raising day San Diego chpt. 1995, Orange Co. Chpt. 2001—02), Orange County Triathlon Club. Avocations: jogging N.Y.C. and LA marathons, men's over thirty baseball, sailing, tennis.

FORSBERG, MYRA, editor; b. 1951; Features editor Ft. Myers News-Press, Fla., Atlanta Constitution; arts & entertainment editor San Jose Mercury News, Calif.; Weekend sect. dep. editor NY Times, 1983—92, editor Weekend sect., 1992—. Office: NY Times Culture Desk 229 W 43rd St New York NY 10036 Office Phone: 212-556-7413. Office Fax: 212-556-1516.

FORSBERG, PETER, professional hockey player; b. Ornskoldsvik, Sweden, July 20, 1973; Center MoDo, Swedish Elite League, 1990-94, Sweden, 2004—05, Quebec Nordiques, Colo. Avalanche, 1994—2005, Phila. Flyers, 2005—07, Nashville Predators, 2007. Mem. Swedish Olympic Hockey Team, Lillehammer, Norway, 1994, Nagano, Japan, 98, Torino, Italy, 2006, Team Sweden, World Cup of Hockey, 1996, 2004. Named NHL First Team All-Star, 1998, 1999, 2003; named to NHL All-Rookie Team, 1995, NHL All-Star game, 1996, 1998, 1999, 2001, 2003; recipient Calder Trophy, 1995, Art Ross Trophy, 2003, Hart Memorial Trophy, 2003. Achievements include being a member of gold medal Swedish Hockey Team, Lillehammer Olympics, Norway, 1994, Torino Olympics, Italy, 2006; being a member of Stanley Cup Champion Colorado Avalanche, 1996, 2001.

FORSBERG, SUZANNE, humanities educator; b. Salt Lake City, May 16, 1940; d. J. Ernest and Maureen (Kendall) Forsberg; m. Raymond A. Joseph, Dec. 13, 1974; 1 child, André E.F. Joseph. MusB, U. Utah, 1962; MA, Harvard U, 1966; PhD, NYU, 1990. Instr. Brigham Young U, Provo, Utah, 1969—71; vis. instr. St. Francis Coll., Bklyn., 1975—76, adj. prof., 1976—91, prof., 1991—; instr. Newark Sch. of Arts, 1997—. Con. NYC Bd. of Ed., New York, NY, 1990; spkr. NY Coun. for the Humanities, New York, NY, 2003—. Author: (articles) music ency. and jour., 2000—01. Participant in Franciscan leadership pilgrimage to Assisi St. Francis Pilgrimages, Assisi, Italy, 1999. Grantee fellowship, Woodrow Wilson/Harvard U, 1962—63, German Academic Exch./ Munich, Germany, 1971—72. Mem.: Am. Musicological Soc., Soc. for Eighteenth

Century Music, Am. Bach Soc., Phi Beta Kappa. Achievements include discovery of the symphonic output of the Bavarian composer Joseph Anton Camerloher. Avocations: travel, art history. Home: 865 W End Ave Apt 8C New York NY 10025-8405 Office: St Francis College 180 Remsen St Brooklyn NY 11201 Office Phone: 718-489-5387. Business E-Mail: sforsberg@stfranciscollege.edu.

FORSEE, GARY D., telecommunications industry executive; b. Kansas City, Apr. 10, 1950; m. Sherry Forsee; children: Melanie, Kara. B in Engring., U. Mo. at Rolla, 1972. With Southwestern Bell Tele., 1972—80, AT&T, 1980—89; v.p., gen. mgr. govt. sys. divsn. Sprint Corp., 1989—91, pres.govt. sys., bus. svcs. group, 1991—93, sr. v.p. staff ops., long distance divsn., 1993—95, interim CEO, Sprint PCS, 1995, pres., COO long distance divsn., 1995—98, CEO, 2003—05; chmn. bd. dir. Sprint Corp. (now Sprint Nextel Corp.), 2003—05; CEO, pres. Global One, Brussels, 1998—99; pres. Bell South Internat., 1999—2003; vice chmn. Bell South Corp., Atlanta, 1999—2003; pres., CEO Sprint Nextel Corp., Reston, Va., 2005—06, chmn., pres., CEO, 2007—. Bd. dirs. Goodyear Tire & Rubber Co., Sprint Corp., 2003—; appointed to Nat. Security Telecommunications Adv. Com., 2004. Vol. leader March of Dimes Birth Defects Found., 1988, bd. trustee, 1995, vice chair, 2000, former chmn. nat. bd. trustees, 2001; chmn. March of Dimes WalkAmerica; adv. coun. sch. engring. U. Mo.-Rolla, bd. trustee; mem. Bus. Roundtable, mem., CEO Com. to Encourage Corp. Philanthrophy; mem. Bus. Coun., Kansas City Civic Coun.; mem. nat. exec. bd. Boy Scouts of Am. Named one of 19 Best Managers, BusinessWeek, 2004. Office: Sprint Nextel Corp 20001 Edmund Halley Dr Reston VA 20191*

FORSHEE, GLADYS MARIE, insurance agent, writer; b. Loveland, Colo., July 1, 1942; d. Henry William Hansen and Bird Marie Smith; m. Larry Bill Forshee, Aug. 27, 1960 (widowed Dec. 1992). Score grad., Small Bus. Adminstrn., 2003. Cert. ins. agt. Customer svc. rep., acct. mgr. various ins. agys., Denver, 1970—2000; property and casualty divsn. agy. mgr., 2004; owner Superior Janitorial Svc., Colo., 1975—2000, A Appletree Pub., Superior, 1991—2007. Tribal Assistance Program US Environ. Protection Agy., 2006—07; sr. tax work off Boulder County Pub. Health Immunizations Program, 2006—07. Author, pub.: (history book) Where Memories Linger, 1994, (cookbook) A Superior Centennial, Culinary Fest Cookbook, 1996; contbr. articles to profl. jours. Asst. organizer Superior Hist. Soc., 1998; town clk., recorder Town of Superior, 1970—73; cmty. svc. dir. Colo. State Grange, Aurora, 1992—99, Boulder county dep., 1999—2001; rsch. asst. Nat. Archives, Lakewood, Colo.; asst. organizer Superior Vol. Fire Dept., Colo., 1972—81; mem., vol. Adams County Hist. Soc., Henderson, Colo., 1991—2006; mem., vol. citizens adv. com. Boulder County Recycling and Composting Authority, 2000—05; mem. com. Boulder County Hist. Preservation, 2002—05; mem. Boulder County Resource Conservation Adv. Bd., 2002—04, chair, 2003—04; mem. Adams County Centennial Roundtable, 2002; mem. scholarship Colo. Preservation Conf., 2004, 2006; citizen shareholder Colo. Dept. Transp. Environ. Impact statements for US36 corridor and northwest parkway corridor projects, 2004—06; mem. Town of Superior Parks, Recreation, Open Space and Trails Adv. Com., 2006—07; citizen adv. Town of Superior, Colo., 2003—07; event coord. Christian Clown Posse, 2003. Mem.: Nat. Womens History Mus. (50 Yr. Mem.), Green Valley Grange. Achievements include development of National Children's Day, 2006; organized placement of sign on Boulder County, Colo. open space property regarding the Denver and interurban railroad electric trolley line from Denver to Boulder, 2005 circa 1908-1926; organized placement of plaque honoring coal miners killed in industrial mine in Superior, Colorado from 1860 to 1946. Avocations: gardening, crocheting, reading, playing the stock market, photography. Home: 404 S 3d Ave Superior CO 80027

FORSHEY, MICHAEL S., lawyer; b. Akron, Ohio, May 30, 1956; BA, Univ. So. Fla., 1977; JD magna cum laude, Univ. Houston, 1981. Bar: Tex. 1981, US Dist. Ct. (no., so., ea. & we. dist.) Tex., US Ct. Appeals (5th cir.). Ptnr., Litigation & Dispute Resolution, Bus. Law practices Patton Boggs LLP, Dallas, co-chair wide pro bono com. Contbr. articles to profl. jours. Mem.: Tex. Bar Assn., Dallas Bar Assn. (mem. Bus. Litigation & Sports & Entertainment Law sect., mem. pro bono activities com.), Order of the Barons. Office: Patton Boggs LLP Suite 3000 2001 Ross Ave Dallas TX 75201-8001 Office Phone: 214-758-3540. Office Fax: 214-758-1550. Business E-Mail: mforshey@pattonboggs.com.

FORSMAN, ALPHEUS EDWIN, retired lawyer; b. Montgomery, Ala., May 12, 1941; m. Greta Friedman, July 5, 1964; children: Ellen E., Jennifer Ann. BA with distinction, George Washington U., 1963, JD, 1967. Bar: Va. 1968, D.C. 1969, U.S. Supreme Ct. 1973, Mo. 1979. Trademark examiner U.S. Patent Office, Washington, 1967-69; atty. Marriott Corp., Washington, 1969-72; assoc. Roylance, Abrams, Berdo and Kaul, Washington, 1972-75, ptnr., 1975-78; trademark atty. Ralston Purina Co., St. Louis, 1978-81, trademark counsel, 1981-91, v.p., sr. trademark counsel, 1991-96; asst. v.p. Eveready Battery Co., Inc., St. Louis, 1986-98; asst. sec. Ralston Purina Co., St. Louis, 1999—2001, v.p., sr. counsel, 1996—2002; v.p. Eveready Battery Co., 1998-2000; v.p., sr. counsel Nestle Purina PetCare Co., 2001—02. Asst. sec. Continental Baking Co., 1990-95; adj. prof. trademark practice Washington U., 2000. Mem.: Bar Assn. Met. St. Louis. Home: 417 Glan Tai Dr Manchester MO 63011-4067 Personal E-mail: alforsman@sbcglobal.net.

FORSON, HEATHER LEAH, physician assistant; BS in Physician Assisting, U. Ala., Birmingham, 2001; BS in Biology, Queens U. Charlotte, NC, 1997. Cert. physician asst. Nat. Commn. Cert. Physician Assts., 2001. Physician asst. divsn. neurosurgery U. Ala., Birmingham, 2002—. Preceptor physician asst. program U. Ala., 2002—; spinning instr. Pro-fitness, Birmingham, 2006—. Mem.: Am. Assn. Neurol. Surgeons (assoc.). Christian. Avocations: travel, bicycling, painting, home decorating. Office Phone: 205-934-8971.

FORST, EDMUND CHARLES, JR., communications educator, administrator, consultant; b. Chgo., June 25, 1961; s. Edmund Sr. and Patricia Ann (Dopek) Forst; m. Kelly Lee Globke; children: Morgan Mae, Shannon Rose, Maximillian, Charles. BA, Ea. Ill. U., 1983, MA, 1984; EdD, W. Va. U., 1994. Leader, mem. staff Neighborhood Boys Club, Chgo., summer 1975-84; instr. in communication DePaul U., Chgo., 1988-93; instr. Waubonsee C.C., Sugar Grove, Ill., 1993-94, assoc. dean comms. and humanities, 1994-98; dean arts and scis. Triton Coll., River Grove, Ill., 1998—2006; dean instrn. Morton Coll., Cicero, Ill., 2006—. Cons. comm. for Leon Spinks, 1990; pres.-elect Ill. Coun. CC Adminstrs., 2003—04, pres., 2004—05. Contbr. articles to profl. jours. Eucharist minister Our Lady of Mercy, Chgo., 1989-90; bd. dirs. Neighborhood Boys Club, Chgo., 1988-92,; bd. dirs. St. Leonard Sch., Berwyn, Ill., 2000-01, mem. parish coun., 2002-2005, mem. fin. com., chair fundraising com., 2003—. Mem. Aurora-Naperville Rotary, Forest Park C. of C. Republican. Roman Catholic. Avocations: sports, reading, collecting comic books, model railroads. Home: 6509 Sinclair Ave Berwyn IL 60402-3737

FORST, EDWARD C., investment company executive; m. Susan Kelly Ryan, Dec. 4, 1993. BA cum laude, Harvard U.; MBA, U. Pa. Mng. dir. loan sales and trading Bankers Trust Securities Bankers Trust Co., 1993—94; with Goldman Sachs Group Inc., 1994—, mng. dir., 1996, COO leveraged fin., head of global loan syndications, 1998, chmn. capital com. fixed income, currency, and commodities and chief of staff, 2000, co-head Global Credit Markets, fixed income, currency and commodities divsn., 2002—03, chief staff equities divsn., 2003—04, chief staff fixed income, currency, and commodities divsn., 2000—02, 2003—04, exec. v.p., chief adminstrv. officer NYC, 2004—07, London, 2007—. Treas. Market Bond Assn., 2003—04, vice chmn., 2004—. Corp. mem. Woods Hole Oceanographic Instn., 2002—; co-chmn. Harvard U. Com. Student Excellence and Opportunity. Mem.: Securities Industry and Financial Markets Assn. (co-chair). Office: Goldman Sachs Internat Peterborough Ct 133 Fleet St London EC4A 2BB England*

FORSTADT, JOSEPH LAWRENCE, lawyer; b. Bklyn., Feb. 21, 1940; BA, CCNY, 1961; LLB, NYU, 1964. Bar: N.Y. 1965, U.S. Supreme Ct. 1968. Spl. legal counsel to bd. justices Supreme Ct. N.Y. County, 1965-67; dep. commr. N.Y.C. Dept. Licenses, 1967-68, acting commr., 1968-69, N.Y.C. Dept. Consumer Affairs, 1969; asst. adminstr. Econ. Devel. Adminstrn., 1969; assoc. Stroock & Stroock & Lavan, NYC, 1969-75, ptnr., 1976—. Lectr. trial practice N.Y. County Lawyers Assn., Practising Law Inst., 1993-94, Title Ins. Litig.; mem. N.Y.C. Rent Guidelines Bd., 1984-97; arbitrator U.S. Dist. Ct. (ea. dist.) N.Y.; spl. counsel Appellate Div. First Dept., Disciplinary Com.; mem. Housing Ct. Adv. Bd., 2001-02. Contbr. articles to profl. jours. Dist. campaign mgr. John V. Lindsay for Mayor of N.Y.C., 1965; campaign mgr. Congressman Theodore Kupferman, 1966; chmn. N.Y.C. Young People for Nixon, 1968, pres. N.Y. State Assn. Young Rep. Clubs, 1970-72; pres. N.Y. Young Rep. Club, 1969-71; vice-chmn. N.Y. Com. to Re-elect Pres. Nixon, 1972. Judge Jacob Markowitz scholar NYU Law Sch., N.Y.C., 1964; recipient Brotherhood award NCCJ, 1987. Mem. ATLA, Fed. Bar Coun., Am. Judicature Soc., NYU Sch. Law Alumni Assn. (trustee 2006—), Phi Alpha Delta. Office: Stroock & Stroock & Lavan 180 Maiden Ln Suite 32108 New York NY 10038-4937 Home Phone: 212-877-1996; Office Phone: 212-806-5662. Business E-Mail: jforstadt@stroock.com.

FORSTER, ARNOLD, lawyer, author; b. NYC, June 25, 1912; s. Hyman Lawrence and Dorothy (Turits) Fastenberg; m. May Kasner, Sept. 29, 1940 (dec.); children: Stuart William (dec.), Janie Forster Berman. LLB, St. John's U., 1935. Bar: N.Y. 1935, U.S. Supreme Ct. 1949. Gen. practice law, 1935-40; dir. law dept. Anti-Defamation League of B'nai Brith, 1940-46; asso. dir. Anti-Defamation League of B'nai B'rith, 1946-78, gen. counsel, 1946—; of counsel Shea & Gould, NYC, 1979-94, Baer Marks and Upham, NYC, 1994—. Police justice N.Y. State, 1954-57 Author: Anti-Semitism in the United States, 1947, A Measure of Freedom, 1950, The Troublemakers, 1952, Cross-Currents, 1956, Some of My Best Friends, 1962, Danger on the Right, 1964, (with B.R. Epstein) Report on the Ku Klux Klan, 1965, Report on the John Birch Society, 1966, Radical Right: Report on the John Birch Society and Its Allies, 1967, Report From Israel, 1969, The New Anti-Semitism, 1974, Square One, 1988, Stubs-A Letter to His Children, 1994; author (TV/radio) Dateline Israel, 1967-83 Mem. bd. edn., New Rochelle, N.Y., 1962-66. Recipient Emmy award for film Avenue of the Just, 1980, Emmy award for film Zubin and the I.P.O., 1983 Home: 79 Wykagyl Ter New Rochelle NY 10804-3207 Office: Baer Marks and Upham 805 Third Ave New York NY 10022-7513 *In one's vintage years, it becomes unarguably clear that the only true satisfaction is in understanding that one's achievements, however small or large, made others happy and this earth a better place for living.*

FORSTER, CARL-PETER, automotive executive; b. London, May 9, 1954; B in Econs., Bonn U.; post grad in Aviation, Space Tech., Munich Tech. U. Cons. McKinsey & Co., Munich, 1982; dept. head, planning, logisitics BMW, 1986, sys. project mgr., 1988, dept. head test pilot car mfg., 1990, overseer, 1993—96; mng. dir. BMW South Africa, 1996—99; overseer vehicle devel. projects BMW AG Mgmt. Bd., 1999—2000; v.p. GM Europe, 2001—04, pres., 2004—; v.p. GM, 2004—05; chmn., mng. dir. Adam Opel AG Supervisory Bd., 2004—; chmn. Saab Automobile AB, 2005—; group v.p. GM, 2005—. Office: GM PO Box 300 Detroit MI 48265-3000 also: GM Europe Stelzenstrasse 4 CH-8152 Zurich Switzerland

FORSTER, GEOFFREY PETER, engineering executive; b. Sydney, NSW, Australia, 1953; s. Anthony Ashley Forster and Mary Edna Flynn; m. Lorraine Maria Pfahl; children: Alexander Ashley, Mercedes Sophia. BEE, U. NSW, 1976; degree in Bus. Adminstrn., Sydney U., 1999; PhD, So. Cross U., NSW, 2006. Product devel. mgr. ROLM Corp., Santa Clara, Calif., 1984—88; dir. bus. devel. IBM, Sydney, 1988—99, MediaDNA, La Jolla, Calif., 1999—2001; dir. and v.p. Fairbanks Polo Club, Del Mar, Calif.; exec. v.p., sales & mktg. Fujitsu Software Divsn., Washington DC, DC, 2001—03; co. dir. and CFO Assured Geoengineering Corp., San Diego, 2004—. Fellow: Inst. Co. Dirs. Office: Assured Technology Corporation PO Box 7265 San Diego CA 92067 Home Phone: 858-472-0247; Office Phone: 760-472-0247.

FORSTER, JONATHAN M., lawyer; b. NY, Feb. 25, 1964; BS in Fin., U. Md., 1986; JD, George Mason U., 1989. Bar: Va. 1989, Md. 1990, DC 1991. Law clk. IRS, 1988, SEC, 1989; co-mng. shareholder, nat. chair wealth mgmt. grp. Greenberg Traurig, LLP, McLean, Va. Com. mem. DC Soc. Fin. Svc. Profls.; bd. mem. Suburban Md. Life Underwriters Assn., No. Va. Life Underwriters Assn., DC Life Underwriters Assn.; mem. Md. Office Econ. Devel. Bus. Mentor Com. Contbr. articles to profl. publs. Mem. U. Md. Athletics Campaign Cabinet; chmn. Nat. Capital Bus. Ethics award; mem. legis. and info. tech. coms. Md. High Tech. Coun.; bd. dirs. U. Md. Terrapin Club; bd. mem. Hebrew Home Greater Washington. Named one of Washington's Top Lawyers in Field of Tax Planning, Washingtonian Mag., 1994, Top Washington Lawyers in Field of Tax, Washington Bus. Jour., 2006, Top 100 Attys., Worth mag., 2006; recipient Md. Leadership award for Establishing Pub./Pvt. Bus. Partnerships, Montgomery County. Mem.: Md. State Bar Assn. Office: Greenberg Traurig LLP 1750 Tysons Blvd 12th Fl Mc Lean VA 22102 Office Phone: 703-903-7504. Office Fax: 703-714-8314.*

FORSTER, MERLIN HENRY, foreign languages educator, writer, researcher; b. Delta, Utah, Feb. 24, 1928; s. Henry and Ila Almeda (Rawlinson) F.; m. Vilda Mae Naegle, Apr. 25, 1952; children: Celia Marlene, David Merlin, Angela, Daniel Conrad, Elena Marie. BA, Brigham Young U., 1956; MA, U. Ill., 1957, PhD, 1960. Instr. in Spanish U. Tex., Austin, 1960-61, asst. prof., 1961-62; asst. prof. Spanish and Portuguese U. Ill., Urbana, 1962-65, assoc. prof., 1965-69, prof., 1969-78, dir. Latin Am. studies, 1972-78; prof., chmn. dept. Spanish and Portuguese, U. Tex., Austin, 1978-87; disting. prof. Latin Am. lit. Brigham Young U., Provo, Utah, 1987-98, chmn. dept. Spanish and Portuguese, 1989-93, prof. emeritus, 1998—. Dir. summer seminars NEH, 1978, 89, 90, 93, 96, 98. Author: Los Contemporáneos, 1964, Fire and Ice, 1976, Historia de la poesía hispanoamericana, 1981, The Committed Word: Studies in Spanish American Poetry, 2002, Many Stages: Studies in Latin American Drama, 2004, Arbol de imágenes: Nueva historia de la poesía hispanoamericana, 2007; editor: Index to Mexican Journals, 1966, Tradition and Renewal, 1975, De la Crónica a la Nueva Narrativa, 1986, Vanguardism in Latin American Literature: An Annotated Bibliographical Guide, 1990, La vanguardia literaria en México y la América Central, 2001. Rsch. grantee Social Sci. Rsch. Coun., Mexico City, 1965, Fulbright-Hays, Buenos Aires, 1971, NEH, Austin, 1986-87, Am. Coun. Learned Socs. and German Acad. Exch. Svc., 1993-94; fellow Ctr. for Advanced Study, Urbana, 1976-77. Mem. MLA, Latin Am. Studies Assn., Am. Assn. Tchrs. Spanish and Portuguese, Internat. Inst. Iberoam. Lit. (pres. 1981-83, 94-96). Mem. Lds Ch. Avocations: classical music, quartet singing, gardening, woodworking. Personal E-mail: merlinforster@yahoo.com.

FORSTER, PETER C., construction executive; m. Betsy Forster; 2 children. Grad. in Bus. Adminstrn. and Civil Engring., Tex. A&M U., College Station, 1963; student in Civil Engring., Northeastern U., Boston. Civil engring. officer USAF; positions up to pres., COO Blount Internat., Ltd., Montgomery, Ala., 1968—87; pres., COO Blount Bros. Corp., 1978—87, George Hyman Constrn., 1987—96, CEO, 1989—96; chmn., CEO Clark Constrn. Group, LLC, Bethesda, Md., 1996—. Bd. mem. Weston Jesuit Sch. Theology; coun. pres. Nat. Capital Area Boy Scouts; mem. bd. advisors Georgetown Ctr. Liturgy, Washington, 2006—07; bd. dirs. City Ctr. Consortium. Mem.: ASCE, Constrn. Industry Round Table (chmn., vice-chmn. 2000), Knights of Malta. Office: Clark Constrn Group LLC 7500 Old Georgetown Rd Bethesda MD 20814 Office Phone: 301-272-8100. Office Fax: 301-272-1928.*

FORSTER, ROBERT, actor, educator; b. Rochester, NY, July 13, 1941; s. Robert Wallace and Grace (Montanarella) F.; m. June Carol Provenzano May 14, 1966 (div. 1975); children: Robert, Elizabeth, Kathrine, Maeghen; m. Zivia Foster, 1978 (div. 1980). BA in History and Psychology, U. Rochester, 1964; student, Heidelberg Coll., Tiffin, Ohio, 1959-60, Alfred U., NY, 1960-62. Actor, 1966—; motivational speaker Interacting, LA; instr. actor workshops. Appeared in Broadway plays Mrs. Dally Has a Lover, 1965, Streetcar Named Desire; Off-Broadway plays include Glass Menagerie, Twelve Angry Men, The Sea Horse, others; films include Reflections in a Golden Eye, 1966, Medium Cool, 1968, The Don is Dead, Stunts, Avalanche, Jackie Brown, 1997 (Acad. award nominee), American Perfekt, Psycho, 1998, Outside Ozona, 1998, Family Tree, 1999, All the Rage, 1999, Kiss Toledo Goodbye, 1999, It's a Shame About Ray, 2000, Supernova, 2000, The Magic of Marciano, 2000, Lakeboat, 2000, Me, Myself & Irene, 2000, Diamond Men, 2000 (also exec. prodr.), Strange Hearts, 2001, Dr. Mulholland, 2001, Human Nature, 2001, Finder's Fee, 2001, Lone Hero, 2002, Like Mike, 2002, Confidence, 2003, Where's Angelo?, 2003, Charlie's Angels: Full Throttle, 2003, Grand Theft Parsons, 2003, Firewall, 2006, others; TV series include Banyon, 1971-72, Nakia, 1974, Once a Hero, 1987, (voice) Spawn, 1997; TV films include The Death Squad, 1974, The City, 1977, Standing Tall, 1978, The Darker Side of Terror, 1979, Goliath Awaits, 1981, Adventures of William Tell, 1986, In the Shadow of a Killer, 1992, Rear Window, 1998, Like Mother Like Son: The Strange Story of Sante and Kenny Kimes, 2001, Due East, 2002, Murder in Greenwich, 2002, Undefeated, 2003, Bounty Hunters, 2005, The Hunt for the BTK Killer, 2005, others, TV movie Rear Window, 1998; prodr., dir. Hollywood Harry, 1985.

FORSTER, WILLIAM HULL, management consultant; b. Shelby, Miss., June 24, 1939; s. William Oskar Hermann and Amy B. (Hull) F.; m. Francine O'Neill, June 1999; children: William Hull Jr., Robert Brown. BS in Chemistry, U. Ala., 1960; PhD in Nuclear Chemistry, U. Calif., 1965; grad., Air Force War Coll., Navy Test Pilot Sch. Entered U.S. Army, 1965, advanced through grades to lt. gen.; comdr. Battery C, 6/56th Arty., Vietnam, 1965-66, TUSLOG Det. 74, Turkey, 1967, 173d Assault Helicopter Co., Vietnam, 1971-72, 10th Combat Aviation Bn., Ft. Lewis, Wash., 1976-78; detailed NASA Manned Spaceflight Ctr., Houston, 1973—75; chief aviation systems div. hdqrs. U.S. Army, Washington, 1981-82; project mgr. Army Helicopter Improvement Program, 1982-85; dep. comdg. gen. Army Aviation Systems Command, 1985-86; program mgr. Apache Advanced Attack Helicopter, 1986-87; program exec. officer Combat Aviation, 1987-88; dir. requirements hdqrs. U.S. Army, Washington, 1988-91; comdr. Army Operational Test and Evaluation Command, Alexandria, Va., 1991-92; dep. asst. sec. rsch., devel., and acquisition U.S. Army, Washington, 1992-95; ret., 1995; v.p. land combat sys. Northrop G. Corp., 1996—2004; ret., 2004. Chmn. Nat. Acad. Sci. bd. Army Sci. and Tech., 1996—2001. Decorated D.F.C., D.S.M. with oak leaf cluster, Bronze Star with oak leaf cluster, Legion of Merit with oak leaf cluster; recipient Air medal (15 awards), US Dept. Def., Carlucci award, 1983. Fellow: Am. Helicopter Soc. Internat. (pres. 2004—05, chmn. bd. dirs. 2005—06); mem.: Nat. Aeronautic Assn., Army Aviation Assn., Russian Acad. Natural Sci., Am. Phys. Soc. Presbyterian. Avocations: boating, automobile repair. Office: PO Box 12 Gibson Island MD 21056

FORSTMANN, THEODORE J., investment firm executive; b. Greenwich, Conn., 1940; adopted children: Everest, Siya. Grad., Yale U., 1961, Columbia Law Sch.; JD (hon.), Siena Coll., Pepperdine U.; PhD in edn. leadership (hon.), Seton Hall U. Co-founder, sr. ptnr. Forstmann Little & Co., NYC, 1978—2006. Bd. dirs. Citadel Broadcasting Corp., 2001—, McLeodUSA, 1996—, chmn. exec. com., 2001—. Co-founder Huggy Bear Invitational Tennis Tournament, 1984—, Benedict-Forstmann Silver Lining Ranch, Colo., Boggy Creek Gang Camp, Fla.; co-founder (with John Walton), mem. nat. bd. advisors Children's Scholarship Fund, 1998—; mem. bd. Nelson Mandela's Children's Fund; bd. trustees Freedom House; overseer Internat. Rescue Com. Named one of Forbes 400 Richest Americans, 1998—2005; recipient Disting. Humanitarian Award, Internat. Rescue Com., 1994, Patron of the Arts award, Nat. Acad. Popular Music, 1995. Avocation: Brooklyn Dodgers.

FORSTOT, STEPHAN LANCE, ophthalmologist; b. NYC, Aug. 19, 1943; s. Shepard and Edith Forstot; m. Lynne Rochelle Bitton, June 15, 1945; children: Michele, Jordan. AB, Princeton U., 1965; MD, Johns Hopkins U., 1969. Diplomate Am. Bd. Ophthalmology. Ophthalmologist Corneal Cons. of Colo., Denver, 1982—, U. Colo. Sch. of Medicine, Denver, 1976-82, clin. prof., 1982—. Contbr. articles to profl. jours. Recipient Honor award Am. Acad. Ophthalmology, Sr. Honor award Am. Acad. Ophthalmology. Mem. Contact Lens Assn. Ophthalmology (bd. dirs. 1985-87, 2004- , pres.-elect 2006, pres. 2007-), Internat. Soc. Refractive Surgery (bd. dirs. 1995-96). Avocation: tennis. Office: Corneal Cons Colo 8381 Southpark Ln Littleton CO 80120-4508 Office Phone: 303-730-0404. Personal E-mail: SL4STOT@aol.com.

FORSTROM, LEE ARTHUR, physician; b. Alpha, Minn., Oct. 4, 1936; s. Elmer Leroy and Ione Grace (Simpson) F.; m. Nancy Mulcahy, June 17, 1964; children: Michael, Jennifer, Kerstin, Eric. BA, U. Minn., 1957; MD, Yale U., 1962; PhD, Cambridge U., Eng., 1977. Diplomate Am. Bd. Internal Medicine, Am. Bd. Nuclear Medicine. Asst. prof. Simm Fraser U., Burnaby, B.C., Canada, 1965—66; resident U. Minn., Mpls., 1968-72, fellow in nuclear medicine, 1972-73; grad. rsch. asst. Cambridge (Eng.) U., 1974-75; asst. prof., physician U. Minn., Mpls., 1976-84; nuclear medicine cons., assoc. prof. Mayo Clin., Rochester, Minn., 1984—. Contbr. articles to profl. jours. including Jour. Nuclear Medicine, Radiology, among others. Pres. Am.-Swedish Inst. Ch., Mpls., 1978-80; bd. dirs. Luth. Ch. Good Shepherd, Mpls., 1980-82. Fellow Am. Scandinavian Found., 1959-60, NIH, 1975, HSF, 1963-65; grantee Am. Cancer Soc., 1958. Mem. AMA, Am. Coll. Nuclear Physicians, Soc. Nuclear Medicine, Brit. Soc. Philosophy Sci., European Assn. Nuclear Medicine, Am. Soc. Nuclear Cardiology. Lutheran. Avocations: music, photography, travel. Office: Mayo Clin 200 1st St NW Rochester MN 55901 Business E-Mail: lforstrom@mayo.edu.

FORSYTH, BEN RALPH, retired academic administrator, medical educator; b. NYC, Mar. 8, 1934; s. Martin and Eva Forsyth; m. Elizabeth Held, Aug. 19, 1962; children: Jennifer, Beverly, Jonathan. Attended, Cornell U., 1950-53; MD, NYU, 1957. Diplomate Am. Bd. Internal Medicine. Intern, then resident Yale Hosp., New Haven, 1957-60; postdoctoral fellow Harvard U. Med. Shc., Boston, 1960-61; rsch. assoc. NIH, Bethesda, Md., 1963-66; assoc. prof. med. microbiology and prof. medicine U. Vt., Burlington, 1966—90, prof. emeritus medicine, 1990; sr. exec. asst. to pres. Ariz. State U., Tempe, 1990—2002, pres., 2002—, prof. health adminstrn. and policy, 1992—2002, prof. emeritus health adminstrn. and policy, 2002—. Sr. cons. Univ. Health Ctr., Burlington, 1986-90; sr. adv. Ctr. Future Ariz., Phoenix, Ariz., 2003—. Contbr. articles to profl. jours. V.p., chmn. United Way Planning Com., Burlington, 1974—75, mem. ops. com., 1975—76, bd. dirs., officer, 1977—89; mem. New Eng. Bd. Higher Edn. Com., Burlington, 1985—89; chmn. U. Vt. China Project Adv. Bd., Burlington, 1989—90; trustee U. Vt., Burlington, 1996—2002. Lt. comdr.

USN, 1962—63. Sinsheimer Found. faculty fellow, 1966-71. Fellow ACP, Infectious Diseases Soc. Am.; mem. Phi Beta Kappa, Alpha Omega Alpha. Avocations: hiking, gardening, travel. Personal E-mail: forsyth@asu.edu.

FORSYTH, DONALD WILLIAM, geophysics educator; b. Berkeley, Calif., Jan. 8, 1948; s. J. Ford and Margret R. (Campbell) F. BA, Grinnell Coll., 1969; PhD, MIT, Cambridge, 1974. Rsch. asst. MIT, 1969—73; rsch. scientist Lamont-Doherty Geol. Obs., Columbia U., Palisades, NY, 1973, rsch. assoc., 1974—76; asst. prof. Brown U., Providence, 1977-81, assoc. prof., 1981—87, prof., 1988—95, James L. Manning prof., 1995—. Summer fellow Woods Hole Oceanog. Instn., 1969-1970; chair Global Seismic Network Com., 1990—, dept. geol. scis., Brown U., 1993-1999. Assoc. editor Jour. Geophys. Rsch., 1976-78; contbr. articles to profl. jours. Deacon Cen. Congl. Ch., Providence. Sloan fellow, 1977-1979, Guggenheim fellow, 1988-1989; recipient George Woollard award, Geol. Soc. Am., 2000, Arthur L. Day medal, 2005. Fellow Am. Geophys. Union (Macelwane award 1982); mem. Seismol. Soc. Am., R.I. Audubon Soc., Sigma Xi, Phi Beta Kappa, NAS. Avocations: birds, squash. Office: Brown U Dept Geol Scis 324 Brooks St Box 1846 Providence RI 02912-9079

FORSYTH, GARYFALLIA LILLIAN, nurse educator; b. Taunton, Mass., Sept. 22, 1920; d. Peter Halekas and Sophia Zakopoulos; m. Charles Clifford Forsyth, June 15, 1945 (dec.); 1 child, Charles Jr. BA in English, Fort Hayes State U., 1950; MS in Nursing, U.Colo., 1967; PhD in Nursing, Tex. Women's U., 1977. U.S. Army nursing U.S. Hosp. Ship Okasa, 1943—46; op.rm. supr. Veteran's Hosp., Wichita, Kans., 1953—63; nursing faculty Wichita State U., 1963—70; v.p. nursing affairs Rush Presbyn., 1978—84; assoc. prof. nursing St. Luke's Med. Ctr., 1978—84. Contbr. articles to profl. jours. Mem. Am. Red Cross, 1942—80. Republican. Presbyn. Home: 1829 W Via Del Recodo Green Valley AZ 85614

FORSYTH, GEORGE LIONEL, psychotherapist, author; b. Bridgetown, NS, Can., July 14, 1934; came to US, 1969, naturalized, 1978, dual citizen Can./U.S. s. Frederick Chesley and Mildred Estella (MacNeill) F.; m. Carolyn Gail Rood, Aug. 20, 1955 (div. June 1982); children: George Eric, Gail Lori Forsyth Smith; m. Helen-Ray Norton, Oct. 2, 1983 (dec. April 2000); step-children: Pamela Darie Norton White, Helen Jeanne Norton Berry; m. Carolyn Gail Forsyth, Aug. 20, 2000. BS, Thomas A. Edison Coll., Palm Beach, Fla., 1969, MS in Psychology, 1970, PhD in Psychotherapy, 1972, DD, 1975; BD, Universal Brotherhood, Atlanta, 1993. Lic. psychotherapist, hypnotherapy, psychology, biofeedback, instr.-tchr., coll. prof.; ordained priest Order of St. John of Jerusalem, 1975; ordained min. Universal Brotherhood Movement, Inc., 1994. With Maritime Telegraph & Telephone Co. Ltd., 1952-56, 58-68; with spl. projects dept. Bell Can., 1956-58; master electrician Glen Dorman Electric; part owner Evangeline Enterprises, 1959-68; liaison officer RCAF/USAF Bell Telephone Co. Can., Montreal, Que., Can., 1956-58; with United Tel. Co., Freeport, The Bahamas, 1968, Sunair Comm., Ft. Lauderdale, Fla., 1969, Overbrook Music, Ft. Lauderdale, Fla., 1969, So. Bell Telephone Co., Ft. Lauderdale, 1970-84; owner Marvo Talent Agys.; pvt. practice hypnotherapy Ft. Lauderdale, Fla., 1972-76; tchr. hypnosis Broward County Schs., 1972-84; mem. Lauderdale Psychiat. Group, Ft. Lauderdale, 1975-85. Rsch. assoc. World Rsch. Ctr. for Hypnosis Studies, Inc., Miami, Fla., 1975-76; adminstrv. v.p. Internat. Coll. Hypnosis Studies, Inc., Miami Beach, 1975-78; prof. Broward C.C., Ft. Lauderdale, 1972-80, Miami-Dade C.C., North Miami Campus, 1972-80; adult edn. instr., coll. prof. Broward County Cmty. Schs., 1972-85; owner Video Memories; charter mem., co-founder, treas., preacher, isntr., psychic healer Inner Light Metaphys. Ctr., Ft. Lauderdale, 1977-80; instr., prof. Nova-Davie Cmty. Sch., Piper Cmty. Sch., Pembroke Pines Cmty. Sch., Broward C.C., Miami Dade C.C., Applied Hypnosis Inst.; cons. Ocean Med. Hypnotherapy and Biofeedback Ctr. Inc., 1974-84. Author: How to Enjoy Eating the North Atlantic Lobster, 1994, All About Lobsters and Dulse, 1995; stage mgr., actor, singer, hypnotist, magician's asst., lighting and sound engr. various stage shows over the years; inventor in field including spl. hypnosis induction light, 1975. TV antenna insepctor Town of Wolfville, N.S., 1954-56; dir. civil defence Town of Kentville, N.S., 1960-65; choir mem., soloist, mem. bd. stewards United Ch. of Can., Berwick, N.S., 1950—; chmn. N.S. Folk Arts Coun., 1967. Served Royal Can. Army, 1946—53, served Royal Can. Army Res., 1950—53, liaison officer USAF, 1956—60. Recipient various awards and plaques for pub. orgns. for hypnosis, N.S. and Ft. Lauderdale, Fla., 1969-80's. Mem. Hypnosis Soc. N.S. (hon. life), Clan Forsyth Soc. (life), Telephone Pioneers Am. (life), Fla. State Assn. Spiritualist Ministers Inc., Internat. Brotherhood Elec. Workers (hon. life), Comm. Workers Am. (hon. life), Comm. Workers Am. Retiree's Club, Can. Inst. Hypnotism, Nat. Guild Hypnotherapists, Nat. Guild Hypnotists (N.H.), N.S. Hypnotists Soc. (hon.), Can. Inst. Hypnotism (Montreal), Soc. for the Preservation and Encouragement of Barbershop Quartet Singing in Am., Masons (32 degree), Lions Club. Avocations: amateur radio, photography, videography, model building, radio. Home (Summer): 9180 Long Point Rd Harbourville NS Canada BOPLEO Home Phone: 902-538-0521. Personal E-mail: cngforsyth@aura.com.

FORSYTH, ILENE HAERING, art historian; b. Detroit, Aug. 21, 1928; d. Austin Frederick and Eleanor Marie (Middleton) H.; m. George H. Forsyth, Jr., June 4, 1960. AB, U. Mich., 1950; AM (univ. fellow), Columbia U., 1955, PhD (Fulbright, AAUW, Fels Found. fellow), 1960. Lectr. Barnard Coll., 1955-58; instr. Columbia U., 1959-61; mem. faculty U. Mich., Ann Arbor, 1961—, prof. history of art, 1974-97, prof. emerita, 1998—, Arthur F. Thurnau prof., 1984—; vis. prof. Harvard U., 1980; Mellon vis. prof. U. Pitts., 1981; vis. prof. U. Calif., Berkeley, 1996. Mem. Nat. Com. History Art, 1975-97; bd. dirs. Internat. Ctr. Medieval Art, 1970-95, 2005-, v.p., 1981-85; mem. supervisory com. Woodrow Wilson Found., 1985-88; Rome prize juror Am. Acad. in Rome, 1986-88; bd. advisors Ctr. Advanced Study in the Visual Arts, Nat. Gallery Art, 1985-88; mem. vis. com. medieval dept. Met. Mus. Art, N.Y.C., 1990-95; Samuel H. Kress prof. Ctr. Advanced Study in the Visual Arts, Nat. Gallery Art, 1998-99, bd. advisors, 1999-2000, U. Mich. Mus. of Art, 2005- Author: The Throne of Wisdom, 1972 (Charles Rufus Morey Book award 1974), The Uses of Art: Medieval Metaphor in The Michigan Law Quadrangle, 1993 (Annie award for non-fiction 1994); co-editor: Current Studies on Cluny, 1988; contbr. articles to profl. jours. Rackham research grantee and fellow, 1965-66, 75-76; grantee Am. Council Learned Socs., 1972-73; mem. Inst. Advanced Study Princeton, 1977 Mem. Coll. Art Assn. (dir. 1980-84), Archaeol. Inst. Am., Medieval Acad. Am. (fellow, 2006-, bd. advs. 1985-86, editorial bd. 1986-90), Medieval Club N.Y., Soc. francaise d'archéologie, Soc. Archtl. Historians, Acad. Arts, Scis. et Belles Lettres Dijon (France), Centre de recherches et d'études préromanes et romanes. Home: 5 Geddes Hts Ann Arbor MI 48104-1724 Office: U Mich Dept Art History Ann Arbor MI 48109

FORSYTH, NICOLE YOUNG, animal scientist; d. John Lloyd and Evelyn Kay Forsyth. BA in English and Edn., U. Colo., Boulder, 1993; MA in Comm., U. Maine, Orono, 1998; MS in Animal Biology, U. Calif., Davis, 2007. Tchr. English C.O. Finest Alternative HS, Englewood, Colo., 1993—94; tchr. lang. arts Bangor Mid. Sch., Maine, 1994—95; pub. rels. specialist MDI Hosp., Bar Harbor, Maine, 1998—2000; devel. dir. Am. Wildlands, Bozeman, Mont., 2001—02; fund devel. assoc. Placer SPCA, Roseville, Calif., 2003—04; CEO, pres. United Animal Nations, Sacramento, 2006—. Bd. dirs. Sacramento Area Animal Coalition. Chair fundraising com. Wildlife Care Assn., Sacramento, 2004; mem. mktg. com. MDI Cmty. Health Plan, Bar Harbor, Maine, 2000; mem. Nat. Com. Planned Giving. Recipient Excellence award, Maine Hosp. Comm. Assn., Chester Writing award, 1998. Mem.: AAAS, Phi Sigma. Avocations: hiking, skiing, gardening. Office: United Animal Nation 1722 J St Ste 11 Sacramento CA 95818

FORSYTH, RAYMOND ARTHUR, civil engineer, consultant; b. Reno, Mar. 13, 1928; s. Harold Raymond and Fay Exona (Highfill) F.; m. Mary Ellen Wagner, July 9, 1950; children: Lynne, Gail, Alison, Ellen; m. Adeline Skog, Nov. 15, 1996. BS, Calif. State U., San Jose, 1952; MCE, Auburn U., 1958. Jr. engr., asst. engr. Calif. Divsn. Hwys., San Francisco, 1952-54; assoc. engr., sr. supervising, prin. engr. Calif. Dept. Transp., Sacramento, 1961-83, chief geotech. br., 1972-79, chief soil mechanics and pavement br., 1979-83; chief Transp. Lab., Sacramento, 1983-89. Cons., lectr. in field; geotech. engr. cons., 1989—. Contbr. articles to profl. jours. Served with USAF, 1954-56. Fellow ASCE (pres. Sacramento sect., chmn. Calif. coun. 1980-81); mem. Transp. Rsch. Bd. (chmn. embankments and earth slopes com. 1976-82, chmn. soil mechanics sect. 1982-88, chmn. group 2 coun. 1988-91), ASTM. Home: 5017 Pasadena Ave Sacramento CA 95841-4149 Personal E-mail: slvrfox800@aol.com.

FORSYTH, RICHARD J., chemist; b. Darby, Pa., Feb. 6, 1953; s. James J. and Sara M. Forsyth; m. Betsy Fetterolf, Feb. 13, 1976; children: Richard J., Stephen J., Leslie Anne, James J. BS in Chemistry, St. Joseph's U., Phila., 1975, MS in Chemistry, 1977, MBA in Adminstrn., 1987. Chemist Gen. Electric, King of Prussia, Pa., 1975—76; lit. reviewer Inst. Sci. Info., Phila., 1976—77; from quality control chemist to sr. mgr. Merck & Co., Inc., West Point, Pa., 1977—2005, assoc. dir., 2005—; chemistry instr. Montgomery County CC, Pottstown, Pa., 2004—. Adj. prof. Temple U., Phila., 2007—. Contbr. articles to profl. jours. Youth coach Cath. Youth Orgn., Collegeville, Pa., 1994—2003. Mem.: Am. Assn. Pharm. Scientists. Home Phone: 610-948-2970; Office Phone: 215-652-7462.

FORSYTH, ROSALYN MOYE, middle school educator; b. Pavo, Ga., Sept. 14, 1942; d. David Cody and Mary (Chapman) Moye; m. Jamos Floyd Forsyth, Aug. 7, 1965. AB, Wesleyan Coll., Macon, Ga., 1964. Cert. paraprofl. Tchr. edn. Dougherty County Bd. of Edn., Albany, Ga., 1965-70, substitute tchr., 1972-88, paraprofl., 1988—. Editor: Membership Roll and Register of Ancestors, 1986. Mem. at large exec. com. South Ga. conf. United Meth. Women, 1972-74, dist. pres. Thomasville dist., 1977-78, rec. sec., 1979-83, sec. publicity and pub. rels., 1983-87, mem. com. on nominations Southeastern jurisdiction 1988-92). Mem. DAR (regent Chenaw chpt. 2005-), Profl. Assn. Ga. Educators, Bus. and Profl. Woman's Club (pres. 1973-75, dist. dir. Ga. Fedn., state chmn. Young Careerist 1977-79, state chmn. nat. found. 1979-81), DAR (regent Thronateeska chpt. 1986-88, state chmn. Am. Heritage 1986-88, dist. dir. Ga. soc. 1988-90, state officer, historian 1990-92, state chmn. textbook study nat. soc. 1992-94, state officer, registrar 1994-96, state officer, libr. 1996-98). Methodist. Avocations: reading, jogging, georgia bulldog activities, basketball, football. Home: 1706 Pineknoll Ln Albany GA 31707-3770 Office: Alice Coachman Elem 1425 Oakridge Dr Albany GA 31707

FORSYTH, STEPHEN A., venture capitalist, department chairman; Prin. financier Accsys Chemicals PLC, Medicsight PLC; chmn., founder The Internat. Capital Co., 1998; chmn. Medicsight, Inc., 2004. Founding trustee Found. Early Detection of Disease, Libr. of Life Trust; chmn. Libr. of Life. Address: Medicsight Inc 46 Berkeley Sq London W1Y 7FF England

FORSYTHE, PATRICIA HAYS, development professional; b. Curtis, Ark. d. John Chambers and Flora Jane (Eby) Hays; m. Kurt G. Pahl, Dec. 15, 1962 (div. Dec. 1980); children: Thomas Walter, Susan Clara; m. Robert E. Forsythe, June 20, 1981; 1 child, Nathaniel Ryan. BA, Calif. State U., Los Angeles, 1974; MSLS, U. So. Calif., 1976. Asst. to dir. devel. office The Assocs., Calif. Inst. Tech., Pasadena, 1978-81; exec. dir. Iowa City Pub. Library Found., 1982-89; dir. devel. Hoover Presdl. Libr. Assn., West Branch, Iowa, 1989-94, exec. dir., 1994—. Contbr. articles to profl. jours. Recipient Outstanding Fund Raising Exec. award Ea. Iowa, 1990, honorary Paul Harris fellow, 1994, West Br. C. of C. Person of Yr., 2005, Main St. Iowa Vol. Yr., West Br., 2006. Mem. ALA, LWV (editor 1985-87), Assn. Fund Raising Execs. (bd. dirs. 1987-89, chmn. Ea. Iowa Philanthropy Day 1990-91, bd. dirs. Ea. Iowa chpt. 1986-91), Assn. Am. Execs., Blacksmith Assn. N.Am., Iowa City C. of C., West Branch C. of C. (bd. dirs.), Temple Ter. C. of C., Iowa Life Shares Assn. (bd. dirs., pres. 1995-96), Libr. Adminstrn. and Mgmt. Assn., Hancher Guild (audience devel. 1981-85, pres. 1985-86), Univ. Athletic Club, Rotary (program chair 1992-98, permanent fund chair 1999—, sec., 2006—). Congregationalist. Avocations: travel, writing, cooking, drama, tai chi chu'an. Office: Hoover Presdl Libr Assn PO Box 696 West Branch IA 52358-0696

FORSYTHE, RANDALL NEWMAN, paralegal, educator; b. Hammond, Ind., Mar. 24, 1959; s. Perry Newman and Elwanda (Cox) F.; children: Kenneth Newman, Keith Randall. AA in Law Enforcement, Calumet Coll., Whiting, Ind., 1979, BA in Criminal Justice magna cum laude, 1982, BS in Mgmt. magna cum laude, 1982; Lawyer's Asst. Cert., Roosevelt U., Chgo., 1986. Labor leader/painter Inland Steel Co., East Chicago, Ind., 1978-86; ins. and securities rep. Primerica, Portage, Ind., 1984-91; paralegal Katz, Brenman & Angel, Merrillville, Ind., 1987-91, Richard P. Komyatte & Assocs., P.C., Highland, Ind., 1991—; coord. paralegal divsn. Sawyer Coll., Merrillville, 1989-92, paralegal instr., 1989—95. Ct. apptd. spl. advocate Juvenile divsn. Lake County Superior Ct., Gary, Ind., 1987—97. Manuscript/book reviewer West Pub. Co., St. Paul, 1991—. Parliamentarian Orchard Dr. Bapt. Ch., Hammond, Ind., 1981-91. Mem. Assn. Trial Lawyers Am., Nat. Assn. Legal Assts., Ind. Legal Assts. (Ind. Legal Asst. of Yr. 1990, liaison to nat. orgn. 1989-92, 97). Avocations: coaching children's little league baseball, basketball, football teams, adult softball, hunting, fishing, camping. Office: Richard P Komyatte & Assocs PC 9650 Gordon Dr Highland IN 46322-2909

FORSYTHE, ROBERT ELLIOTT, economics professor; b. Pitts., Oct. 25, 1949; s. Robert Elliott and Dolores Jean (Davis) F.; m. Lynn Maureen Zollweg, June 17, 1970 (div. July 1978); m. Patricia Ann Hays, June 20, 1981; 1 child, Nathaniel Ryan. BS, Pa. State U., Phila., 1970; MS, Carnegie-Mellon U., Pitts., 1972, MS, 1974, PhD, 1975. Ops. rsch. analyst PPG Industries Inc., Pitts., 1970-72; instr. Carnegie-Mellon U., Pitts., 1974-75; asst. prof. Calif. Inst. Tech., Pasadena, 1975-81; assoc. prof. U. Iowa, Iowa City, 1981-86, prof. econ., 1986-90, chmn. dept. econ., 1990-94, sr. assoc. dean Coll. Bus., 1994—, Cedar Rapids Area Bus. Chair, 1992-2000, Leonard A. Hadley Chair in Leadership, 2000—06; dean Coll. Bus. Adminstrn. U. South Fla., Tampa, 2006—. Founder Iowa Polit. Stock Market; pres. Iowa Market Systems, Inc., 1993-2000. Author: Forecasting Presidential Elections: Polls, Markets, Models; assoc. editor Jour. Econ. Behavior and Orgn., 1996-97, Jour. Exptl. Econs., 1997-2004. Recipient State of Iowa Regents award for faculty excellence, 2002; Univ. faculty scholar U. Iowa, 1985-88. Mem. Econometric Soc., Am. Econ. Assn., Econ. Sci. Assn. (sect. head 1989-92, pres.-elect 1992-93, pres. 1993-95). Congregationalist. Home: 1806 E Court St Iowa City IA 52245-4643 Office: Univ South Fla Coll Bus Adminstrn 4202 Fowler Ave BSN 3403 Tampa FL 33620-550 Business E-Mail: rforsyth@coba.usf.edu.

FORSYTHE, THOMAS M., communications executive; b. Crookston, Minn., Feb. 6, 1958; s. Ernil L. and Malvina J. (Stahlback) F. BS magna cum laude, Moorhead State U., 1980. Coord. comm. Nat. Alliance Bus. of N.D., Fargo, 1981; dir. comm. divsn. N.D. Econ. Devel. Com., Bismarck, 1981—82; press sec. Gov. Allen Olson, Bismarck, 1982—85; account exec. Flint Comm., Inc., Mpls., 1985; pres. Flint, Forsythe & Assocs., Mpls., 1985—91; dir. state govt. rels. General Mills, Inc., Mpls., 1991—, dir. corp. comm., v.p. corp. comm., 1994—. Campaign mgr. Lee A. Christoferson for U.S. Congress, Fargo, 1980; field dir. Mark Andrews for U.S. Senate, Fargo, 1980. With USMC, 1977. Mem. Internat. Assn. Bus. Communicators, Pub. Rels. Soc. Am. Republican. Lutheran. Office: General Mills One General Mills Blvd Minneapolis MN 55426

FORSYTHE, VELMA BROWN, accountant, consultant, literature educator; b. California, Pa., Apr. 27, 1928; d. Ernest and Anne Leyland Brown; m. Forrest Evans Forsythe, Aug. 6, 1950 (dec. Oct. 1982); children: Leslie Ann, Lynn Allyson. BS in Bus. Edn., Indiana U., Pa., 1950; student various univs. and colls., Pa. and Wis., 1952-96. High sch. tchr. bus. edn., Pa. and Ohio, 1954-58; v.p., tax preparer Kincaid Tax Svc., Akron, Ohio, 1968-74; pub. acct. Pitts. and Akron, 1974-82; controller Holiday Inn, Dubois, Pa., 1982-86; asst. controller Radisson Hotel, Lexington, Ky., 1986-87; asst. to pres. Petrolec Inc.-Jadel Inc., Clearfield, Pa., 1987-88; acct., cons. Forsythe Bus. Svcs., Dubois, 1982—; tchr. ELI Ulaanbartar, Mongolia, 1999—. Vol. Internat. Exec. Svc. Corps., Egypt, Ghana, Slovak Republic, Stanford, Conn., 1992—; lay missionary fin. and edn. United Meth. Ch. Uganda, Mozambique, 1991—; missionary amb. to Indonesia, 1998; vol. exec. Citizens Democracy Corps, Republic of Georgia, spring, 2000, Russia, summer and fall, 2000; active Velma Scholarships, 97 children and adults, Uganda, 1992—. Mem. AAUW (program chair 1997-99, Woman of Yr. award 1998), Kappa Delta Pi, Delta Sigma Epsilon. Republican. Methodist. Avocations: travel, reading, hiking, canoeing. Home and Office: 717 Treasure Lk Du Bois PA 15801-9019 Personal E-mail: vel4sythe@yahoo.com.

FORSYTHE, WILLIAM, actor; b. Bklyn., June 7, 1955; Actor: (films) Cloak & Dagger, 1984, Once Upon A Time In America, 1984, The Lightship, 1985, Raising Arizona, 1987, Extreme Prejudice, 1987, Weeds Deg, 1987, Patty Hearst, 1988, Dead-Bang, 1989, Torrents of Spring, 1989, Blind Faith, 1990, Dick Tracy, 1990, Career Opportunites, 1991, Out For Justice, 1991, Stone Cold, 1991, The Waterdance, 1992, The Gun in Betty Lou's Handbag, 1992, Things To Do In Denver When You're Dead, 1995, Palookaville, 1995, The Substitute, 1996, Beyond Desire, 1996, For Which He Stands, 1996, The Rock, 1996, Firestorm, 1998, The Pass, 1998, Ambushed, 1998, Soundman, 1998, Hell's Kitchen, 1998, Paradise Lost, 1999, 18 Shades of Dust, 1999, Deuce Bigalow: Male Gigolo, 1999, Big City Blues, 1999, Four Days, 1999, Blue Streak, 1999, The Last Marshal, 1999, Civility, 2000, Row Your Boat, 2000, Luck of the Draw, 2000, Outlaw, 2001, Camouflage, 2001, Blue Hill Avenue, 2001, Coastlines, 2002, Run for the Money, 2002, City by the Sea, 2002, The Technical Writer, 2003, The Librarians, 2003, The Last Letter, 2004, The L.A. Riot Spectacular, 2005, The Devil's Rejects, 2005, Freedomland, 2006, (TV series) The Untouchables, 1993-94, UC: Undercover, 2001-02, (TV films) Stories from the Edge, 1996, Gotti, 1996, First Time Felon, 1997, Dollar for the Dead, 1998, John Doe, 2002, Larva, 2004. Office: United Talent Agy 9560 Wilshire Blvd Fl 5 Beverly Hills CA 90212-2400

FORT, ARTHUR TOMLINSON, III, obstetrician, educator; b. Lumpkin, Ga., Sept. 24, 1931; s. Thomas Morton and Gladys (Davis) F.; m. Jane Wilmer McClelland, June 15, 1957; children: Abby Lucinda, Arthur Tomlinson IV, Juliana Melody, Ernest Arlington, II. BBA, U. Ga., 1952; MD, U. Tenn., 1962. Diplomate: Am. Bd. Ob-Gyn, Am. Bd. Family Practice. Intern, then resident in ob-gyn U. Tenn.-City of Memphis Hosp., 1962-66; asst. prof. U. Tenn. Med. Sch., 1966-70; prof. ob-gyn, head dept. Sch. Medicine La. State U., Shreveport, 1970-73; prof. maternal-child health and family planning, head program family health Sch. Pub. Health Tulane U., 1973-74; practice medicine specializing in rural family medicine Vacharie, La., 1974-79; prof. ob-gyn and family medicine, head dept. family medicine and comprehensive care Sch. Medicine La. State U., Shreveport, 1980—. Author articles in field. Adv. bd. mem. State of La. Dept. Health and Human Resources, 1986-88. With USAF, 1952-57. Recipient Golden Apple Teaching award Student AMA, 1969, Golden Apple Teaching award Western Interstate Commn. on Higher Edn., 1973 Fellow Am. Coll. Ob-Gyn, Am. Acad. Family Practice; mem. AMA. Office: PO Box 33932 Shreveport LA 71130-3932

FORT, JEFFREY C., lawyer; b. Burlington, Iowa, Oct. 10, 1950; s. Lyman R. and Lucille (Gibb) F.; m. Diane Locandro; children: Christopher Glen, Elizabeth Anne. BA, Monmouth, 1972; JD, Northwestern U., 1975. Bar: Ill. 1975, U.S. Dist. Ct. (no. dist.) Ill. 1976, U.S. Ct. Appeals (7th cir.) 1977, U.S. Ct. Appeals (D.C. cir.) 1985, U.S. Supreme Ct. 1980. Law clk. to John M. Karns, Jr. Appellate Ct., Belleville, Ill., 1975-76; assoc. Martin Craig Chester, et al, Chgo., 1976-83, ptnr., 1983-88, Gardner Carton & Douglas, Chgo., 1988-90, Sonnenschein Nath & Rosenthal, Chgo., 1990—. Adj. prof. Northwestern U. Sch. Law, Chgo., 1990-92; bd. dir. Delta Inst., 2000—; chair Environmentalist Trading Congress, NYC, 2006, Chgo., 2007; presenter in field. Author: Establishing an Effective Environmental Law Compliance Program, 1993-2007, Avoiding Liability for Hazardous Waste: RCRA CERCLA and Related Corporate Law Issues, 2002, 3d edit., 2007; mem. editl. bd. Environmental Law for the Transactional Lawyer, 1991, rev. edit., 1994, 2001, Illinois Environmental Law, 1993, 3d edit., 2007; contbr. articles to profl. jours. Chair Lake Mich. States sect. Air and Waste Mgmt. Assn., Chgo., 1988-89, Am. Leading Bus. Lawyers, Ill. Environ., 2002-, Leading Lawyers in Ill. Environ. Law, 2002-; pres. Trevian Girls Softball Assn., 2004—; elder 1st Presbyn. Ch. Wilmette, Ill., 1990-93, 2001—04. Mem. ABA (vice chair spl. com. on environ. disclosures), Chgo. Bar Assn. (chair environ. law com. 1987-88), Met. Club. Office: Sonnenschein Nath & Rosen LLP 7800 Sears Tower Chicago IL 60606 Office Phone: 312-876-2380. Business E-Mail: jfort@sonnenschein.com.

FORT, RANDALL MARTIN, federal agency administrator; b. Richmond, Ind., July 4, 1956; Student, U. Cin., 1974-76; BA in Pub. Affairs with distinction, George Washington U., 1978. Various positions with Rep. Willis D. Gradison Jr. US Congress, Cin. and Washington, 1976-80; rsch. asst. Office of Hon. Roo Watanabe M.P., Tokyo, 1980-81; asst. dir., dep. exec. dir. Pres's. Fgn. Intelligence Adv. Bd., Washington, 1982-87; spl. asst. to sec. nat. security, dir. Office Intelligence Support US Dept. Treasury, Washington, 1987-89; dep. asst. sec. for functional analysis and rsch. US Dept. State, Washington, 1989-93; dir. spl. projects TRW, Inc., Washington, 1993-96; chief of staff to pres., COO then co-head global security Goldman, Sachs & Co., NYC, 1996—2006; asst. sec. for intelligence & rsch. US Dept. State, Washington, 2006—. Luce scholar Henry Luce Found., 1980. Mem. Phi Beta Kappa. Republican. Methodist. Office: US Dept State Bur Intelligence & Rsch Harry S Truman Bldg 2201 C st NW Rm 6531 Washington DC 20520

FORT, ROBERT BRADLEY, minister; b. Portsmouth, Va., Dec. 27, 1948; s. Richard Gould and Hazel Naomi (McBride) F.; m. Esther Faith Hardin, June 10, 1967; children: Yvonne René, Nathan Michael. Ordained to ministry United Evang. Ch., 1973. Evangelist United Evang. Chs., Monrovia, Calif., 1966, nat. youth dir., 1968-70, asst. to the pres., 1970-73, Calif. dist. supt., 1973-75; evangelist Assemblies of God, Springfield, Mo., 1976-78; sr. pastor Lynden (Wash.) Assembly of God, 1978-81, County Christian Ctr., Bellingham, Wash., 1981-87, First Assembly of God, Salinas, Calif., 1988—. Exec. dir. Life Mgmt. Sems., Salinas, 1989—; pres. Ft. Ministries, Salinas, 1967—; exec. v.p., chmn. bd., CEO United Evang. Chs., Hollister, Calif., 1996—; faculty NY Coll. Advanced Studies, 2002-05; plenary spkr. World Congress Evang. Chs., Nairobi, Kenya, Africa, 1993. Composer Love was the Color, 1980 (Grand prize Music City Songfest, Nashville, 1981); singer, musician 15 recordings. Chmn. resolutions com. NorCal/Nev. Dist. of the Assemblies of God, 1997-2000; mem. bd. adminstrn. Pentecostal/Charismatic Chs. N.Am., 2001—. Fellow: N.Am. Acad. Arts and Scis.; mem.: Am. Assn. Christian Counselors (charter mem.). Republican. Business E-Mail: rbfort@uecol.org.

FORT, TOMLINSON, chemist, chemical engineering educator; b. Sumter, SC, Apr. 16, 1932; s. Tomlinson and Madeline A. Kean (Scott) F.; m. Martha Kirby, Oct. 13, 1956; children: Tomlinson, III, Frances Clare; m. Nancy H. Blackwelder, Dec. 19, 1998. BS in Chemistry, U. Ga., 1952; MS,

U. Tenn., 1957, PhD in Phys. Chemistry, 1957; A.E. and F.A.Q. Stephens postdoctoral fellow, U. Sydney, Australia, 1957-58; cert., Inst. Edn1. Mgmt., Harvard U., 1978. Instr. surface chemistry U. Sydney, 1957—58; rsch. chemist, then sr. rsch. chemist and project leader duPont Co., 1958—65; mem. faculty Case Western Res. U., 1965—73, prof. chem. engring., dir. surfaces research lab., 1971—73; prof. chem. engring. and chemistry, head dept. chem. engring. Carnegie-Mellon U., 1973—80, adj. prof., 1980—83; prof. chemistry and chem. engring., provost U. Mo., Rolla, 1980—82; v.p. acad. affairs Calif. Poly. State U., San Luis Obispo, 1982—83, provost, 1983—86, prof. chemistry and materials sci., 1986—89; Centennial prof. chem. engring., prof. materials sci. Vanderbilt U., Nashville, 1989—2002, Centennial prof. chem. engring. emeritus, 2002—, chair dept. chem. engring., 1989—96. Summer vis. prof. Nat. U. Mex., 1973, U. Copenhagen, 1978, 80; pres. Frances Fort Brown Realty Co., Chattanooga, 1970-94. Author papers on surface and colloid sci. Mem. AAAS, Am. Chem. Soc., Am. Inst. Chem. Engrs., Internat. Assn. of Colloid and Interface Scientists, KP, Sigma Xi, Phi Beta Delta, Gamma Sigma Epsilon, Alpha Chi Sigma, Sigma Chi. Home: 1015 Carlisle Ln Franklin TN 37064-4802 Office: Vanderbilt U Dept Chem Engring PO Box 1604 Station B Nashville TN 37235 Business E-Mail: tomlinson.fort@vanderbilt.edu.

FORTADO, MICHAEL GEORGE, lawyer; b. Wichita Falls, Tex., Oct. 29, 1943; s. Antonio and Flossie Juanita (Bowers) F.; m. Avis Ann Smith, Mar. 12, 1964; children: Michael Scott, Angela Avis, Shannon Michelle. BBA, Midwestern U., Wichita Falls, 1965; LLB, U. Tex., Austin, 1968. Bar: Tex. 1968. Assoc. atty. firm McClure & Sharpe, Houston, 1968-69; atty. Enserch Corp. (and predecessor), Dallas, 1969-71, corp. sec., asst. gen. counsel, 1971-88, v.p., corp. sec., asst. gen. counsel, 1988-96; sr. v.p., gen. counsel, corp. sec. Enserch Exploration, Inc., Dallas, 1996-97; v.p., gen. counsel, corp. sec. Trinity Indus., Inc., Dallas, 1997—. Mem. ABA, Am. Soc. Corp. Secs. (bd. dirs. 1980-83), State Bar Tex., Dallas Bar Assn., DAC Country Club, Kappa Alpha Order, Delta Sigma Pi, Phi Alpha Delta. Office: Trinity Industries Inc 2525 N Stemmons Fwy Ste 1000 Dallas TX 75207-2400 E-mail: mike.fortado@trin.net.

FORTE, WESLEY ELBERT, former insurance company executive, lawyer; b. Worcester, Mass., Dec. 1, 1933; s. Elbert W. and Ethel M. (Lyons) F.; m. Margaret Ellen Layman, July 29, 1961; children: Laura Jean, Scott Montgomery. BBA, Clark U., 1956; JD, N.Y. U., 1959, LL.M., 1965. Bar: Pa. 1960, Ohio 1972, U.S. Supreme Ct 1972, Tex. 1974, D.C. 1975, N.Y. 1980. Atty. Dechert, Price & Rhoads, Phila., 1959-62; atty. corporate law dept. Standard Brands, Inc., NYC, 1962-66; atty., foods div. counsel Borden, Inc., NYC, 1966-71, sr. counsel domestic ops., 1971-72; sr. v.p. legal affairs Campbell-Taggart, Inc., Dallas, 1972-73, exec. v.p., gen. counsel, dir., 1973-79; sr. v.p. law USLIFE Corp., NYC, 1979-85, exec. v.p., gen. counsel, 1985-97. Contbr. articles to profl. jours. Home: 35 Green Meadow Ln East Falmouth MA 02536-6954 Personal E-mail: margief@aol.com.

FORTENBAUGH, SAMUEL BYROD, III, lawyer; b. Phila., Nov. 6, 1933; s. Samuel Byrod Jr. and Katherine Francisca (Wall) F.; children: Samuel Byrod IV, Cristina Fortenbaugh Alemany, Katherine Fortenbaugh Silliman, Francesca Cowden, Harrison Selden; m. Sharon A. Swartz, Nov. 17, 2001. BA, Williams Coll., 1955; LLB, Harvard U., 1960. Bar: NY 1961, US Dist. Ct. (so. dist.) NY 1961. Assoc. Kelley Drye & Warren, NYC, 1960—69, ptnr., 1970—79, Morgan, Lewis & Bockius, 1980—2001, chmn., 1990—91, 1999, sr. counsel, 2001—02; pvt. practice, 2002—. Bd. dirs. Baldwin Tech. Co., Inc., Shelton, Conn., Security Capital Corp., Greenwich, Conn.; bd. dirs., sec. Furgueson Capital Mgmt. Inc., N.Y.C.; chmn. bd. dirs., sec. Wall Industries, Inc., Kannapolis, N.C.; chmn. bd. dirs. Knight Textile Corp, Saluda, S.C.; trustee Patroni Scholastici, New Brunswick, N.J., 1978—, sec. 1985—; lectr. profl. seminars. Contbr. articles to profl. jours. Mem. Assn. of Bar of City of N.Y. (mem. Young Lawyers com. 1962-65, corp. law com. 1976-79, com. on securities regulation 1982-85, chmn. com. on issue distbn. of securities 1984-85), Univ. Club (N.Y.C.), N.Y. Yacht Club, Indian Harbor Yacht Club (Greenwich, Conn.) (bd. dirs. 2000—, rear commodore 2003-05, vice commodore 2006-), Phi Beta Kappa Office Phone: 212-596-3379. Business E-Mail: sam@sfortenbaugh.com.

FORTENBERRY, JEFFREY LANE, congressman; b. Baton Rouge, Dec. 27, 1960; m. Celeste Gregory; 5 children. BA Econs., La. State U., 1982; M in Pub. Policy, Georgetown U., Washington, 1986; MA in Theology, Franciscan U., Steubenville, Ohio, 1996. Mem. econ. analysis team US Senate Subcommittee for Intergovernmental Rels., 1986; rsch. assoc. economist Gulf South Rsch. Inst., New Iberia, La., 1987—89; asst. dir. Downtown Devel. Dist., Baton Rouge, 1989—92; pub. rels.-fund. activities dir. Sandhills Pub., Lincoln, Nebr., 1995—98, sales rep., 1998—2005; at-large mem. City Coun., Lincoln, Nebr., 1997—2001; mem. US Congress from 1st Nebr. dist., 2005—. Mem. agr. com. US Congress, mem. fgn. affairs com., mem. small bus. com. Republican. Roman Catholic. Office: US House Reps 1517 Longworth House Office Bldg Washington DC 20515-2701 Office Phone: 202-225-4806. E-mail: jeff.fortenberry@mail.house.gov.*

FORTES, BRENDA JOYCE, language educator; d. Laurence Antonio Fortes and Emma Hill; m. Philip Elmore Jenks (div.); children: Lauren Brenda Jenks, Angela Christine Jenks, Elita Joyce Fortes Jenks. BA, Ea. U., St. Davids, Pa., 1972, MEd, 1998. Cert. elem., English tchr. Pa. Tchr. H.S. English Boyertown Area Sch. Dist., Pa., 1993—; English adj. faculty Montgomery County C.C., Pottstown, Pa., 1998—. Pres.'s adv. bd. on diversity Montgomery County C.C., Blue Bell, Pa., 1997—. Publicity chairperson NAACP, Pottstown, Pa., 1993—; com. adv. panel Occidental Chem., Pottstown, Pa., 1995—98; mem. No Place for Hate com. Police Dept., Pottstown, Pa., 2003—. Mem.: Boyertown Area Edn. Assn., Pa. State Edn. Assn., Am. Fedn. Tchrs., NEA, Kappa Delta Pi. Baptist. Achievements include writing reading remediation program for Boyertown Area Sch. Dist. Avocations: reading, bread baking, sewing, piano lessons, community service. Home: 1133 Grandview Cir Pottstown PA 19465 Office: Boyertown Area Sch Dist 911 Montgomery Ave Boyertown PA 19512 Office Phone: 610-369-7435. Personal E-mail: bfortes@aol.com. E-mail: brendafortes@yahoo.com.

FORTH, KEVIN BERNARD, beverage distributing industry consultant; b. Adams, Mass., Dec. 4, 1949; s. Michael Charles and Catherine Cecilia (McAndrews) F.; m. Alice Farnum (dec. 1994); children: Melissa, Brian; m. Deborah Newport. AB, Holy Cross Coll., 1971; MBA with distinction, NYU, 1973, Benjamin Levy fellow. Divsn. rep. Anheuser-Busch, Inc., Boston, 1973-74, dist. sales mgr. LA, 1974-76, asst. to v.p. mktg. staff St. Louis, 1976-77; v.p. Straub Distbg. Co., Ltd., Orange, Calif., 1977-81, pres., 1981-93, chmn., CEO, 1986-93. Commr. Orange County Sheriff's Adv. Coun., 1988—; mem. adv. bd. Rancho Santiago C.C. Coll. Dist., 1978-80; exec. com., bd. dirs. Nat. Coun. on Alcoholism, 1980-83; mem. pres. coun. Holy Cross Coll., 1987-91; bd. dirs., pres. Calif. State Fullerton Titan Athletic Found., 1983-85, 89-90; mem. Calif. Beer Wholesalers Assn., dir., 1978-89, v.p., 1984, chmn., 1985; bd. dirs. Orange County Sports Hall of Fame, 1980-89, Children's Hosp. of Orange County Padrinos Found., 1983-85, Freedom Bowl, 1984-93 (founders award, 1993), v.p., 1984-85, pres., 1986, chmn., 1986-87, Orangewood Children's Found., 1988-93, St. Joseph's Hosp. Found., Anaheim Vis. and Conv. Bur., 1989-93, Wilcox Health Found., 2003-05; mem. Calif. Rep. State Ctrl. Com., 1988-93, Orange County Probation Dept. Cmty. Involvement Bd., 1992-93. Recipient Vol. of Yr. award, Calif. State U., Fullerton, Calif., 1990. Mem. Nat. Beer Wholesalers Assn. (bd. dirs. 1986-93, asst. sec. 1989-90, sec. 1989-91, vice-chmn. 1992, chmn. 1993; Lifetime Achievement Svc. award 2001), Holy Cross Alumni Assn., Sports Car Club Am. (Ariz. state champion 1982). Roman Catholic. Home and Office: 1326 Mandi Ct Prescott AZ 86301 Personal E-mail: kforth1204@aol.com.

FORTHUN, LARRY F., social sciences educator, consultant; s. Lloyd and Beverly Forthun; m. Tracy A. Carroll, June 15, 1991; children: Laykin, Tristan. BS in Psychology, Utah State U., 1992, MS in Marriage & Family Therapy, 1995; PhD, Tex. Tech U., Lubbock, 1999. Cert. family life educator Nat. Coun. Family Rels., 2000. Assoc. prof. Pa. State U., DuBois, 1998—. Rsch. cons., Pa., 2003—07. Editl. bd. mem. Jour. Youth and Adolescence; contbr. articles to jour. Pres. Mid-Atlantic Coun. Family Rels., 2005—06; mem. Pa. State U./Pa. Liquor Control Bd. Partnership for Prevention, DuBois, 1998—2007, Drug Free Cmtys. Coalition, 2006—, Pa. State U. Youth & Family Consortium. Recipient Commonwealth Coll. award for Innovation, Penn State U., 2002, Commonwealth Coll. award for Disting. Faculty Svc. and/or Outreach, 2005. Mem.: APA, Soc. Rsch. Identity Formation, Nat. Coun. Family Rels., Soc. Rsch. Adolescence, Phi Kappa Phi. Office: Pa State Univ College Pl Du Bois PA 15801 Office Phone: 814-375-4852. Business E-Mail: lff3@psu.edu.

FORTI, LENORE STEIMLE, business consultant; b. Houghton, Mich., Sept. 9, 1924; d. Russell Nicholas and Agnes (McCloskey) Steimle; m. Frank Forti, May 29, 1950 (dec.). BBA summa cum laude, Northwood U., 1973, Dr.Laws, 1969. Asst. corp. sec., purchasing agt. Fed. Life & Casualty Co., Detroit, 1942-53; supr. sectl. J.L. Hudson Co., Detroit, 1953-57, adminstrv. asst. to exec. v.p., 1957-86; instr. Wayne State U. and U. Mich. Adult Edn., Detroit, 1958-71; creator, dir. Seminars for Profl. People, 1971—. Co-author: The Professional Secretary; contbr. articles to profl. jours. Asst. br. dir. planning City of Detroit for Civil Def.; chmn. bd. trustees PSI Rsch. and Ednl. Found.; trustee PSI Retirement Home Complex, Albuquerque; elected dir. Property Owners and Residents Assn., Sun City West Mcpl. Govt., 1994—97; past pres. Women's Bd. Northwood U., Midland, Mich.; past pres. parish coun. Our Lady of Lourdes Ch., Sun City West, Ariz., 1988, pres. ladies guild, 1990, 1995; 1st v.p. Vol. Bur. of Sun Cities, 1989; pres. Sun City West Found., 2002—03; bd. dirs. Sun City West Cmty. Fund, 1998—99. Elected One of Detroit's Top Ten Working Women, 1969; elected to Exec. and Profl. Hall of Fame. Mem. Internat. Assn. Adminstrv. Profls. (internat. pres. 1967-69), Future Secs. Assn. (nat. coord.), Lioness Club (pres. 1991-92), Sun City West Singles Club (pres. 1988). Republican. Roman Catholic. Avocations: bridge, Mah Jongg, dance. Home and Office: 12613 W Seneca Dr Sun City West AZ 85375-4635

FORTI, WILLIAM BELL, manufacturing executive; b. Washington, Dec. 6, 1941; s. Francis and Margaret Lee (Bell) F.; m. Martha Louise Goding; children: Scott, Jennifer, Meredith, Kimberly, Mark, Andrea. BS, U. Richmond, 1963, MComm., 1964. Fin. analyst SEC, Washington, 1964—66; economist Joint tax, House judiciary, Senate commerce coms. US Congress, Washington, 1966—71; mgmt. positions in bus. planning and devel. Bendix Corp., Southfield, Mich., 1971—75, Internat. Paper Co., NYC, 1975—78, Gen. Dynamics, St. Louis, 1978—92; founder, chmn. William Mark Corp., Claremont, Calif., 1992—. Patentee flying recreational products. Bd. visitors Sch. of Edn. Claremont Grad. U.; mem. World Affairs Coun., LA, 2007; participant current strategy forum Naval War Coll., RI, 2006, nat. security forum Air War Coll., Maxwell AFB, Ala., 1997; trustee Naval War Coll. Found., 2001—; co-chmn. LA County Aerospace Task Force, LA, 1992; chmn. internat. trade legislation working group Def. Planning Adv. Com. on Trade, 1986. Recipient Recognition of Dedicated Svc. County of LA, 1992, Recognition of Contribution Naval War Coll. Found., 1997, Joint Civilian Orientation Conf., 1999. Mem.: Def. Orientation Conf. Assn. (bd. dirs. 2007—), Naval War Coll. Found. (trustee 2001—07), Claremont U. Club. Republican. Avocations: travel, reading, hiking. Office: William Mark Corp 112 Harvard Ave Claremont CA 91711-4716

FORTIER, ALBERT MARK, JR., lawyer; b. Cambridge, Mass., July 22, 1936; s. Albert M. and Marie R. (Tagney) F.; m. Bente Mortensen, Nov. 10, 1964; children: John, Mark. AB, U. Chgo., 1955; LLB, Harvard U., 1958. Bar: Mass. 1958. Assoc. Richard S. Bowers, Boston, 1958-65; ptnr. Bowers, Fortier & Lakin, Boston, 1966-76, Rackemann, Sawyer & Brewster, Boston, 1976—. Contbr. articles to profl. jours. Mem. ABA, Am. Bar Found., Boston Bar Assn. (probate sect. former chair), Am. Coll. Trust and Estate Counsel (past state chair), Union Club (Boston, past bd. govs.). Home: 90 Craftsland Rd Chestnut Hill MA 02467-2632 Office: Rackemann Sawyer & Brewster One Financial Ctr Boston MA 02111 Home Phone: 617-277-2572; Office Phone: 617-542-2300. E-mail: afortier@rackemann.com.

FORTIER, L. YVES, barrister; b. Quebec City, Que., Can., Sept. 11, 1935; s. Francois and Louise (Turgeon) F.; m. C. Carol Eaton, Sept. 26, 1959; children: Michel, Suzanne, Margot. BA summa cum laude, U. Montreal, 1955; BCL, McGill U., 1958; BLitt, Oxford U., 1960, LLD (hon.), 1989, LLD (hon.), 1992, LLD (hon.), 1993, LLD (hon.), 1999, LLD (hon.), 2004, LLD (hon.), 2005. Created Queen's counsel, 1976. Sr. ptnr., chmn. Ogilvy, Renault Advs., Barristers and Solicitors, Montreal, 1960—; Can. amb. to UN NYC, 1988-92. Counsel Can. in Can.-USA, Gulf Maine Case in World Ct., 1984, Royal Commns., Commn. Inquiry War Criminals, Commn. Inquiry Lang. Air Tarffic Control, Commn. Inquiry R.C.M.P.; mem. Permanent Ct. Arbitration The Hague, 1984-1991; pres. London Ct. Internat. Arbitration, 1998-2001; chief negotiator Can.-France fishing dispute, 1987-89, Can.-U.S. Pacific Salmon Treaty dispute, 1993-98; Can.'s chief del. to 43d, 44th, 45th, 46th, sessions UN Gen. Assembly, Can. rep. UN Security Coun., 1989-90; v.p. UN 45th Gen. Assembly; gov. Hudson's Bay Co.; bd. dirs. Nova Chems. Corp.; chmn. bd. dirs. Alcan Inc. Bd. dirs. Can. Inst. Advanced Legal Studies, Internat. Peace Acad., UN Internat. Sch., Montreal Gen. Hosp. C.D. Howe Inst., Clin. Rsch. Inst., Can. Found. for AIDS Rsch.; trustee Internat. Acctg. Stds. Com., Can., 2000-06. Decorated Companion Order Can.; Rhodes scholar, 1960. Mem. ABA (hon.), Can. Bar Assn. (pres. 1982-83, founding dir. Law for Future Fund), Internat. Commn. Jurists (Can. sect.), Internat. Law Assn. (Can. br.), Am. Coll. Trial Lawyers (regent 1991-95), Internat. Assn. Permanent Reps. to UN (exec. bd.), Mount Royal Club (pres. 2002-03), Univ. Club, Montreal Indoor Tennis Club, Hermitage Country Club (pres. 1983-84), The Brook Club (N.Y.), The Toronto Club. Roman Catholic. Avocations: tennis, squash, skiing, golf. Home: 19 Rosemount Ave Westmount PQ H3Y 3G6 Canada Office Phone: 514-847-4740. Business E-Mail: yfortier@ogilvyrenault.com.

FORTIN, RAYMOND D., lawyer, bank executive; b. 1952; BA, U. Fla., Gainesville, 1974, JD, 1977. Bar: Ga. 1977. Pvt. practice atty., 1977-81; staff counsel The Citizens & So. Corp., 1981-89; mng. atty. SunTrust Banks, Inc., Atlanta, 1989-91, sr. v.p., gen. counsel, 1991—2004, corp. exec. v.p., gen. counsel, 2004—. Office: SunTrust Banks Inc PO Box 4418 Atlanta GA 30302-4418 Office Phone: 404-588-7165. Office Fax: 404-827-6173.*

FORTMANN, STEPHEN PAUL, medical educator, researcher, epidemiologist; b. Burbank, Calif., Oct. 13, 1948; s. Daniel John and Mary (Van Halteren) F.; married; children: Nicolas, Michele. AB, Stanford U., 1970; MD, U. Calif., San Francisco, 1974. Diplomate Am. Bd. Internal Medicine, Am. Coll. Epidemiology. Clin. instr. Stanford (Calif.) U. Sch. Medicine, 1979-83, asst. prof., 1983-90, assoc. prof., 1990-99, prof., 1999—. Advisor World Health Orgn., Geneva, 1980-86. Contbr. articles to profl. jours; co-author: The Blood Pressure Book, 2001. Fellow ACP, Am. Heart Assn. (coun. on epidemiology and prevention), Am. Coll.Epidemiology, Soc. Behavioral Medicine; mem. Inst. Medicine. Avocations: photography, running.

FORTNER, HUESTON GILMORE, lawyer, writer, composer; b. Tacoma, Nov. 1, 1959; s. Hueston Turner Jr. and Deborah Hewes (Berry) F. BS, Tulane U., 1981; JD, U. Miss., 1985. Bar: Miss. 1986, La. 1987, U.S. Dist. Ct. (no. and so. dists.) Miss. 1986, U.S. Dist. Ct. (ea., mid. and we. dists.) La. 1987, U.S. Ct. Appeals (5th cir.) 1986, bar: Calif. 1989, U.S. Dist. Ct. (cen. dist.) Calif. 1989, U.S. Dist. Ct. (so. dist.) Calif. 1999. Clk. Farrer and Co., London, Miss., 1985; assoc. Cliff Finch & Assocs., Batesville, Miss., 1986; pvt. practice New Orleans, 1987-88; atty. Parker, Milliken, Clark, O'Hara & Samuelian, LA, 1989-90; pvt. prctice LA, 1990—. Vis. lectr. Anhui U., Hefei, People's Rep. of China, Bejing Inst. of Petrochem. Tech., 1994; participanted in Leicester vs. Leicester Rugby Union, House of Lords, Eng., 1985; assisted Queen's Counsel in Yussuf Islam (Cat Stevens) vs. Bank of Westminster P.L.C. royalties litigation 1985, Newton vs. NBC, 1988; judge pro tem LA County Superior Ct., 1991—; pres., CEO Orange Records, 1997—. Contbg. photographer Flix mag., 1993—; contbr. editor Rental, 1987-89. Recipient Space Devel. Strategies award NASA/U. Houston Advanced Rsch. Ctr., 1995; grantee NSF, 1976. Mem. Miss. Bar Assn., La. Bar Assn., State Bar Calif., Broadcast Music Internat., Phi Alpha Delta. Presbyterian. Avocations: music, film, scuba diving.

FORTNER, JOSEPH GERALD, surgeon, educator; b. Bedford, Ind., May 30, 1921; s. Everett Rex and Lula Alice (Robbins) F.; m. Roberta Olson, Nov. 4, 1948; children: Kathleen Alice Fortner, Joseph Jr. BS, U. Ill., 1944, MD, 1945; MSc in Immunology, Birmingham U., Eng., 1965. Diplomate: Am. Bd. Surgery. Intern St. Luke's Hosp., Chgo., 1945-46; resident in pathology Tulane U., New Orleans, 1948-49; surg. resident Bellevue Hosp., NYC, 1949-51, Meml. Hosp., NYC, 1951—54, clin. asst. surgeon, asst. to clin. dir., 1955-59, asst. attending surgeon, 1958-66, assoc. attending surgeon, 1966-69, attending surgeon, 1969-94, chief transplantation svc. and gastric and mixed tumor svc., 1970-78, chief surg. research service, 1978-91, assoc. chmn. for lab. affairs dept. surgery, 1978-84, chief div. surg. research, 1968-77; chief Gen. Motors Surg. Rsch. Lab., 1977-92; instr. surgery Sloan-Kettering Inst., NYC, 1954-58, asst. prof. clin. surgery, 1958-64; clin. asst. prof. surgery Cornell U. Med. Coll., NYC, 1964-70, assoc. prof. surgery, 1970-72, prof., from 1972. Contbr. articles to profl. jours.; editor Accomplishments in Cancer Research. Pres. Gen. Motors Cancer Rsch. Found., 1978-96, pres. emeritus, 1996—, trustee mem. awards assembly. With U.S. Army, 1946-48. Recipient Alfred P. Sloan award Sloan-Kettering Inst. Cancer Research, 1963 Fellow ACS, Royal Coll. Surgeons Edinburgh (hon.); mem. AAAS, Am. Assn. Cancer Research, Am. Gastroent. Assn., Am. Radium Soc., Am. Soc. Clin. Oncology, European Soc. Exptl. Surgery, Harvey Soc., Soc. Surg. Oncology, N.Y. County, N.Y. State med. socs., Am. Surg. Assn., N.Y. Surg. Soc., Soc. Univ. Surgeons, Hellenic Surg. Soc. (hon.), Chgo. Surg. Soc., Korean Surg. Soc., Am. Soc. Transplant Surgeons, Transplantation Soc., N.Y. Cancer Soc., Econ. Club of N.Y., Explorer Club N.Y., Met. Club N.Y., Madison Beach Club, Sigma Xi, Alpha Omega Alpha. Republican. Home: New York, NY. Died Feb. 18, 2007.

FORTNER, ROSANNE WHITE, environmental scientist, educator; b. Logan, W.Va., Nov. 13, 1945; d. William Edward and Annabel (Blevins) White; m. Richard Donald Fortner, Aug. 20, 1966; children: Christopher Neil, Craig Michael. BA, W.Va. U., 1967; MA, Oreg. State U., 1973; EdD, Va. Poly. Inst. and State U., 1978. Curriculum developer NSTA, Washington; curriculum cons. U.S. Nat. Park Svc., Washington; edn. coord. Ohio Sea Grant Coll. Program, Columbus; prof. emeritus natural resources Ohio State U., Columbus. Dir. COSEE Great Lakes, assoc. dir. F.T. Stone Lab., Put-in-Bay, Ohio; dir. Earth Sys. Edn. Program, Columbus, Ohio. Author: (with Mayer) The Great Lake Erie; author, editor 12 vols. curriculum activities for Earth Sys. Edn.; editor: Proceedings of 2d Internat. Conf. on Geosci. Edn.; exec. editor Science Activities; contbr. numerous articles on edn. and communication to profl. jours. Recipient Rsch. award N. Am. Assn. for Environ. Edn., 1992, Disting. Alumni award Va. Poly. Inst. and State U., 1989; Ohio Sea grantee, 1981—, grantee Nat. Estuarine Sanctuary, George Gund Found., Ohio Bd. Regents, Spencer Found., Great Lakes Protection Fund, NSF, USEPA; named 1st Edn. Liaison Nat. Oceanic and Atmospheric Adminstrn.; Fulbright Sr. scholar, Cyprus, 1999. Fellow AAAS Edn. Secretary; mem. Nat. Marine Educators Assn. (pres.), Coalition Earth Sci. Edn. (bd. dirs.), N.Am. Assn. Environ. Edn. (bd. dirs.), Ohio Acad. Sci. (v.p.). Business E-Mail: fortner.2@osu.edu.

FORTON, GREGORY A., secondary school educator; b. Hortonville, Wis., June 12, 1964; s. Robert John LaVern Forton and Helen Mae Lindholm; m. Kay I. Forton, May 23, 1993; children: Gwen, Brad, Nadine, Erin. BA, St. Norbert Coll., DePere, Wis., 1987. Tchr. Battle Creen H.S., Mich., 1987—89, Hortonville H.S., Hortonsville, Wis., 1989—. Videography sound engr. Thompson Hill Studios, Black Creek, Wis. Mem.: Music Educators Nat. Conf., Internat. Assn. Jazz Educators. Lutheran. Avocations: pottery, photography. Office: Hortonsville High Sch 211 Towne Dr Hortonville WI 54944

FORTUNA, JULIAN ANTHONY, lawyer, accountant; b. NYC, Feb. 19, 1956; s. Fred and Violet (Ruffini) F.; m. Theresa R. Colangelo, Sept. 3, 1983; 1 child, Anthony. BA, CUNY, 1977; JD, Rutgers U., Camden, NJ, 1980; LLM, Emory U., 1984. Bar: NY 1981; CPA, Ga., Ill. Tax atty. IRS, Atlanta, 1980-84; sr. tax mgr. Deloitte & Touche, 1984—95; v.p., gen. tax counsel InterContinental Hotels Grp., 1995—2007; ptnr. Duane Morris LLP, Atlanta, 2007—. Co-author: Depreciation Methods, 1988; contbr. articles to profl. publs. Sect. leader, United Way, Atlanta, 1989. Recipient Am. Jurisprudence award. Mem. ABA (tax sect.), AICPA, Midtown Bus. Assn., Atlanta Bar Assn., NY Bar Assn., Ga. Bar Assn., Internat. Fiscal Assn., Orgn. for Internat. Investment, Northside Athletic Club, Peachtree Athletic Club. Roman Catholic. Avocations: photography, golf, tennis, mountain biking, hiking. Office: Duane Morris LLP Atlantic Ctr Plz 1180 W Peachtree St NW Ste 700 Atlanta GA 30309-3448 Office Phone: 404-253-6969. Office Fax: 404-253-6901. Business E-Mail: jafortuna@duanemorris.com.*

FORTUNE, JOHN B., medical educator; b. Indpls., Mar. 19, 1950; s. William Brooks and Joan Helen Fortune; m. Janellen Neely Fortune; children: Brooks, Neely. BA, Duke U., 1972, MD, 1975; DSc (hon.), Ind. Wesleyan U., 1999. Cert. MD. Asst. prof. surgery U. Calif., San Diego, 1982—84; assoc. prof. surgery Albany (NY) Med. Coll., 1984—94; prof. surgery U. Ariz., Tucson, 1994—2001, So. Ill. U., Springfield, 2002—04, chief gen. surgery, 2002—04, dir. residency, 2003—04; prof. surgery, chief sect. trauma and critical care SUNY Upstate Med. U., Syracuse, 2004—. Contbr. articles various profl. jours. Dir. So. Ariz. Trauma Network, Tucson, 1994—2001. Fellow: ACS; mem.: Soc. Univ. Surgeons. Achievements include invention of Retrograde Intubation Kit. Avocation: creative writing. Office: SUNY Upstate Dept Surgery 750 E Adams St Syracuse NY 13210 Home Phone: 315-446-4579; Office Phone: 315-464-4776. Business E-Mail: fortunej@upstate.edu.

FORTUNE, LARRY M., real estate broker; b. Fresno, Calif., Feb. 3, 1948; s. Donlad A. and Matheda B. Fortune; m. Jane B. Fortune, Apr. 26, 1980; children: Katherine, Patrick. BA, Stanford U., 1970; MBA, Trinity Coll. and U., 2002. Cert. Real Estate Broker Mgr. Realtors Nat. Mktg. Inst., Nat. Assn. Realtors, 1985, Residential Specialist Realtors Nat. Mktg. Inst., Nat. Assn. Realtors, 1986, Residential Broker Nat. Assn. Realtors, Arbitrator and Mediator Calif. Assn. Realtors, 1985, lic. in Real Estate Sales

Calif., 1975, Broker 1978. Loan officer, asst. v.p. consumer and auto loan ctr. Bank. Calif., San Francisco, Sacramento, 1972—74; broker, owner Fortune Property Mgmt., Fresno, Calif., 1982—94, Fortune Assocs., Fresno, 1974—. Ct. receiver Fresno County Superior Ct.; trustee US Bankruptcy Ct., Ea. Dist. Calif.; real estate expert witness civil, criminal cts.; mediator in field; mem. BBB, 1982—, bd. dirs., 1995—98, chmn. membership devel. com., 1996—98; mem. Fresno Bus. Coun., 1999—, mem. pub. safety com., 2000—01; investor Econ. Devel. Corp. Serving Fresno County, 2002—, bd. dirs., 2004—, co-chmn. bus. pk. task force, 2004—; joint powers authority bd. dirs. Ctr. Advanced Rsch. and Tech., 2005—. Cub scout pack leader Boy Scouts Am., 1994—97, leadership mem., 1994—, asst. scout master, 1997—2002; mem. Fresno Athletic Hall of Fame, 1974—, bd. dirs., 1976—94, sec., 1980—90; mem. Fresno Multiple Listing Svc., 1975—99, bd. dirs., 1984—87, vice chmn., 1984, chmn., 1985; mem. Fig Garden Police Protection Dist., 1986—, bd. dirs., 2001—02, chmn., 2002—; mem. ctrl. area planning task force City of Fresno, 1986—87, chmn. redevelopment agy. project area com., 1998—, mem. mayor's task force Fresno empowerment zone, 2001; bd. dirs. Cmty. Housing Leadership Bd., 1987—90; pub. alt. local agy. formation commn. County of Fresno, 1990—96, pub. mem. local agy. formal commn., 1996—, chmn. local agy. formation commn., 2002—04, chmn. pub. safety citizens adv. com., 0203—2004, pub. mem. Indian gaming local cmty. benefit commn., 2004—; mem. cmty. rels. adv. com. Ctrl. Calif. Blood Ctr., 1991—96, bd. dirs., 2002—, mem. fin. com., 2002—, mem. exec. com., 2002—, sec., 2004—; mem. Tree Fresno, 1995—, treas., 2003—04, mem. projects com., 2003—, bd. dirs., 2003—05; mem. strategic planning com. facilities Fresno Unified Sch. Dist., 1999—2000; bd. dirs. Fresno Police Activities League, 2000—, mem. exec. com., 2001—, treas., 2001—; bd. dirs. Fresno County Workforce Investment Bd., 2001—, mem. info. tech. com., 2001—, chmn. info. tech. com., 2003—, mem. youth coun., 2002—, mem. exec. com., 2003—, vice chmn., 2004—, chmn., 2004—; mem. leadership coun. Regional Jobs Initiative, 2004—, chmn. infrastructure com., 2004—. Recipient Realtor of Yr., Fresno Assn. Realtors, 1987, Hon. Dir. Life, Calif. Assn. Realtors, 1991, Best Ednl. Program award, 1988. Mem.: Leadership Fresno Alumni Assn., Fresno City and County C. of C. (membership com. mem. 1976—80, Fresno beautiful com. mem. 2000—02, bd. dirs. FresPAC 2002—03), Stanford Alumni Assn. (life), Fresno Region Stanford Club (founding dir. 1979, bd. dirs. 1979—86, pres. 1984—85). Avocation: gardening. Office: Fortune Associates Ste 200 680 W Shaw Ave Fresno CA 93704-2450

FORTUNE, LOWELL, judge; b. Colorado Springs, Colo., Dec. 12, 1941; s. Benjamin Acres and Wilma E. (Henry) Fortune; m. Beverly Jane Sanborn, June 30, 1963; children: Sabrina Fortune Allen, Christina Fortune Howery. BA, U. Denver, 1963, JD, 1966. Bar: U.S. Dist. Ct. Colo. 1966, U.S. Ct. Appeals (10th cir.) 1966, U.S. Supreme Ct. 1976. Assoc. White & Steele, Denver, 1966—71, ptnr., 1971—75; pres. Lowell Fortune, P.C., 1975—79, Fortune & Lawritson, P.C., 1979—95, Fortune Law Firm, P.C., 1995—99, 2002—; spl. counsel Montgomery, Kolodny, Amatuzio, Dusbabek and Parker, L.L.P., 1999—2001; U.S. adminstrv. law judge, 2005—. Mem.: Am. Bd. Trial Advs. Office: 605 N Arrowhead Ave Ste 200 San Bernardino CA 92401 E-mail: lowfort@mac.com.

FORTUÑO, LUIS, congressman; b. San Juan, Oct. 31, 1960; m. Luce Fortuno. BS, Georgetown Univ.; JD, Univ. Va. Pvt. practice; exec. dir. Puerto Rico Tourism Co., 1993—97; sec. econ. devel. & commerce Commonwealth of PR, San Juan, 1994—97; resident commr. U.S. Ho. Reps., 109th & 110th Congresses, PR at-large, 2005—; mem. ed. and workforce com. U.S. Ho. Reps., 109th Congress, PR at-large, mem. transp. and infrastructure com., mem. resources com. Co-chair Congrl. Friends Spain Caucus; chmn. Congrl. Hispanic Conf. Republican. Roman Catholic. Office: US Ho of Reps 126 Cannon Ho Office Bldg Washington DC 20515-5401 also: Dist Office 250 Calle Fortaleza San Juan PR 00901 Office Phone: 202-225-2615.

FORTUNO, VICTOR M., lawyer; b. NYC, Jan. 24, 1952; s. Victor M. Fortuno and Ceda Aguayo; m. Vicki Ann Clark; children: Adam, Victor III, Scott, Erica, Bryce. AB in Econs., Columbia U., 1974, JD, 1977. Bar: Pa. 1977, US Dist. Ct. (ea. dist.) Pa. 1977, US Ct. Appeals (3rd cir.) 1977, US Supreme Ct. 1980, US Ct. Appeals (DC cir.) 1987, DC 1988, US Dist. Ct. DC 1988, US Ct. Appeals (4th cir.) 1988, US Dist. Ct. Ariz. 1991. Staff atty. Cmty. Legal Svcs., Inc., Phila., 1977—78; asst. dist. atty. Phila. Dist. Atty., 1978—83; staff atty. Legal Svcs. Corp., Washington, 1983—85, acting dir. compliance divsn., 1985—86, asst. gen. counsel, 1986, sr. litig. counsel, 1986—88, acting gen. counsel, 1987, 1991, dep. gen. counsel, 1988—91, gen. counsel, 1991—, corp. sec., 1995—, v.p. legal affairs, 1999—. Bd. dirs. Columbia Coll. Alumni Assn., 1981-83, Phila. Health Plan, 1980-83, Middleford HOA, 2001—, Friends of Legal Svcs. Corp., 2001-04, Ayuda, Inc., 2005—. Pulitzer Found. scholar, 1970-74, Assn. of Bar of City of NY C. Bainbridge Smith scholar, 1974-77. Mem. ABA, DC Bar Assn., Assn. Corp. Counsel, Fed. Small Agy. Coun. Methodist. Office: Legal Svcs Corp 3rd Fl 3333 K St NW Washington DC 20007-3522 Office Phone: 202-295-1620. Office Fax: 202-337-6831. Business E-Mail: vfortuno@lsc.gov.

FOSCARINIS, MARIA, lawyer; b. NYC, Aug. 8, 1956; d. Nicolas and Rosa F.; m. Nathan Alan Stoltzfus. BA, Barnard Coll., 1977; MA, Columbia U., 1978, JD, 1981. Bar: NY 1982, US Dist. Ct. (so. and ea. dists.) NY 1983, DC 1986, US Dist. Ct. DC, US Ct. Appeals (DC cir.). Law clk. to judge U.S. Ct. Appeals (2d cir.), NYC, 1981-82; assoc. Sullivan & Cromwell, NYC, 1982-85; counsel Nat. Coalition for Homeless, Washington, 1985-89; founder and dir. Nat. Law Ctr. on Homelessness and Poverty, Washington, 1989—. Adj. prof. Cornell U., 2003. Notes editor Columbia U. Law Rev., 1980-81; contbr. articles to scholarly pubs., chpts. to books. Bd. dir. US Human Rights Network; mem. nat. adv. bd. Fannie Mae Corp. Harlan Fiske Stone scholar, 1978-79; John Dewey fellow, 1977-78; Recipient John W. Macy award, Nat. Alliance to End Homelessness, 1995, Public Interest Achievement award, Public Interest Law Found., Columbia Law Sch., 2006. Fellow Cephalonian Soc. Am. (hon.); mem. ABA (commr. homelessness and poverty, 1989-95, 2004—). Office: Nat Law Ctr Homelessness and Poverty 1411 K St NW Ste 1400 Washington DC 20005-3404 Home: 1752 Swann St NW Washington DC 20009-5535 Office Phone: 202-638-2535. Business E-Mail: mfoscarinis@nlchp.org.

FOSDICK (BEEBE), CORA PRIFOLD, management consultant; b. San Francisco, Nov. 3, 1937; d. George and Beatrice (Ehni) Prifold; m. Ronald Beebe, Jan., 1959 (div.); m. Donald James Fosdick, Oct. 12, 1997. Student, Hollins Coll., Va., 1955-57, Am. U., DC, 1957-58; BA, U. Mich., Ann Arbor, 1959, MA, 1961; LHD (hon.), Southeastern U., DC, 1993. Adminstrv. asst. Am. Polit. Sci. Assn., 1962-64; rsch. assoc. Inst. Comparative Studies of Polit. Systems, Washington, 1963-65; program planning and evaluation specialist U.S. Office Edn., Washington, 1965-68, planning coord., 1968-73, dir. planning and budget div., 1973-80; prin. dep. asst. sec. for elem. and sec. edn. Dept. Edn., Washington, 1980-81; asst. sec. adminstrn. U.S. Treasury Dept., Washington, 1981-84; dir. office of policy, budget and program mgmt. OSWER, EPA, Washington, 1984-86; dir. office of planning, budget and evaluation Dept. Commerce, Washington, 1986-87; commerce & justice br. chief Office of Mgmt. and Budget, 1987-94, advisor to assoc. dir. gen. govt. and fin., 1994; exec. dir. adminstrn., chief fin. officer Office of Thrift Supervision, Washington, 1994-99; v.p. Jefferson Consulting Group, Washington, 1999—2002; sr. assoc. Kelly, Amdersen & Assocs., Inc., Alexandria, Va., 2002—. Active Coun. for Excellence in Govt.; bd. dirs. Treasury Hist. Assn., 2005—. Recipient HEW Superior Svc. award, Presdl. Rank award, 1989; Inst. World Affairs fellow, 1956, Am. Edn. Abroad former fellow, 1960. Fellow: Nat. Acad. Pub. Adminstrn. (vice chair 2002—03); mem.: Nat. Press Club, Exec. Women in Govt. Program and Budget Analysis. Home: 1415 N Pegram St Alexandria VA 22304-1933 Office Phone: 703-518-8828. Personal E-mail: corabeebe@aol.com.

FOSDICK, JACQUE JANELLE, literature and language educator, theater educator; d. William Edward and Lucille Marie Grooms; children: Julene, Jayme Goscha, Jeana Geringer, Joy. BA in Religion and Philosophy, Phillips U., Enid, Okla., 1969; BA in Secondary English, Adams State U., Alamosa, Colo., 1990. Tchr. English as 2d lang. Sahabamrung Acad., Nakhon Pathom, Thailand, 1969—71; tchr. Head Start Program, La Junta, Colo., 1972; supr. supplemental svcs. Otero Jr. Coll., 1982—89; tchr. English, drama Crowley County H.S., 1990—. Scholar, Masons, Fowler, Colo., 1965. Mem.: Tri-M Music Soc. (life), Fowler Woman's Club, Kappa Delta Pi, Delta Kappa Gamma. Avocations: singing, writing. Office: Crowley County High Sch PO Box 338 Ordway CO 81063-0338 Office Phone: 719-267-3582.

FOSHEE, DOUGLAS L., gas industry executive; BBA, S.W. Tex. State U., 1982; MBA, Rice U., 1992; grad., So. Meth. U. Active comml. banking; various positions in fin. and new bus. ventures ARCO Internat. Oil and Gas Co.; COO, CEO Torch Energy Advisors, Inc., 1993—97; chmn., CEO, pres. Nuevo Energy Co.; CFO Halliburton, 2001, exec. v.p., COO, 2003; pres., CEO, dir. El Paso Corp., Houston, 2003—. Pres., bd. mem. Small Steps Nurturing Ctr.; bd. mem. Goodwill Industries, Houston, Tex. Bus. Hall of Fame Found.; mem. coun. of overseers Jones Grad. Sch. Adminstrn., Rice U. Mem.: Houston Prodrs. Forum, Ind. Petroleum Assn. Am. Office: El Paso Corp PO Box 2511 1001 Louisiana St Houston TX 77252-2511*

FOSKETT, CYNTHIA, nurse, analyst; b. Kansas City, Mo., Dec. 1, 1956; d. Clifford and Marlene Hedstrom; m. Francis Allan Foskett, Oct. 8, 1993; children: Sarah Hinton, Charles Hinton, Kimberly. BSN, St. Lukes Coll., Kansas City, Mo., 1994. Cert. informatics nurse, ANCC, 2007. Clincal analyst St. Lukes Home Care and Hospice, Kansas City, Mo., 2000—01; clin. analyst II St. Lukes Info. Svcs., Kansas City, Mo., 2001—06; clin. informatics analyst Liberty Hosp., Mo., 2006—. Sec. Kansas City Clin. Infomatics, 2006—; parish nurse Partners in Health Svcs., Liberty, 2001—. Mem.: ANA, Health Ministry Assn., St. Lukes Coll. Alumni Assn., Capital Area Roundtable on Informatics in Nursing, Am. Med. Informatics Assn. Home: 3013 NE 73rd St Gladstone MO 64119 Office: Liberty Hosp 2525 Glenn Hendren Dr Liberty MO 64069 Home Phone: 816-436-9441; Office Phone: 816-415-3123.

FOSLER, GAIL D., economist, government official; b. LA, Dec. 7, 1947; d. Richard E. and Helen Elizabeth (O'Gorman) Deschner; m. R. Scott Fosler; 1 son, Michael. AB in Econs. U. So. Calif., 1969; MBA in Fin., NYU, 1972. Rsch. analyst Chgo. Dept. Human Resources, 1970-72; research assoc. I.C.F., Inc., 1972-74; asst. v.p., economist Manufacturers Hanover, 1974-78; chief economist Senate Budget Com., Washington, 1981-89, dir. and chief economist, 1986-89; exec. v.p., chief economist The Conf. Bd., Inc., NYC, 1989-. Bd dirs. Unisys Corp., Baxter Internat., Caterpillar Inc., DBS Holdings, Singapore. Office: The Conference Bd Inc 845 3rd Ave Fl 2 New York NY 10022-6600

FOSS, CLIVE FRANK WILSON, history professor; b. London, Aug. 30, 1939; came to U.S., 1945, naturalized, 1980; s. Victor Albert and Jeanne Francoise (Beurton) W. AB magna cum laude, Harvard U., 1961, MA, 1965, PhD, 1973. Instr. U. Mass., Boston, 1967-69, lectr., 1969-73, asst. prof., 1973-76, assoc. prof., 1976-80, prof. history, 1980—2002. Faculty Boston Coll., 1968-69; vis. prof. U. Lyon, France, 1977-79, U. South Africa, 1981, U. Calif., 1985, Harvard U., 1990-91, Georgetown U., 2001—; mem. Sardis Expdn., 1969-75, 79-83; dir. Medieval Castles Survey of Anatolia, 1982-85; assoc. Ephesus Excavations, 1973-74. Author: Byzantine and Turkish Sardis, 1976, Rome and Byzantium, 1977, Ephesus After Antiquity, 1979, Medieval Castles Survey I: Kutahya, 1985, II, Nicomedia, 1996, Byzantine Fortifications, 1986, History and Archaeology of Byzantine Asia Minor, 1990, Roman Historical Coins, 1991, Nicea, 1996, Cities, Fortresses and Villages of Byzantine Asia Minor, 1996, Juan and Eva Peron, 1999, Fidel Castro, 2000, The Tyrants, 2006; contbr. articles to profl. jours. Norton fellow Am. Sch. Classical Studies, Athens, 1961-62; Am. Coun. Learned Socs. grantee, 1974, 80; Indo-U.S. fellow (CIES), 1983; CNRS rsch. assoc., Paris, 1983; NEH fellow, 1975-76; Guggenheim fellow, 1983-84; vis. fellow Dumbarton Oaks, 1973-74, 99-2000, All Souls Coll., Oxford U., 1983-84, Trinity Coll., Oxford U., 1997, 2005; fellow Inst. Advanced Studies, Hebrew U., Jerusalem, 1993. Fellow Soc. Antiquaries, Royal Numismatic Soc.; mem. Am. Philol. Assn., Am. Numismatic Soc., Brit. Inst. Archaeology of Ankara, Numismatic Soc. India, Harvard Club (N.Y.C.), Tavern Club (Boston), Cosmos Club (Washington), Phi Beta Kappa. Republican. Episcopalian. Office: Georgetown Univ Dept History Washington DC 20057 Home: 3536 T St Washington DC 20007-1818 Office Phone: 202-687-3264. E-mail: cff@georgetown.edu.

FOSS, EMMA THOREN, retired social worker; b. Hamill, SD, Sept. 23, 1921; d. Elmer Vincent Thoren and Christine Nielsen; m. George Thomas Foss (dec.); children: Douglas, Georgia, Ronald. BA (magna cum laude), Pacific Lutheran U., Tacoma, Washington, 1945; MSW, U. Wash., 1947. Social worker Assoc. Lutheran Welfare, Seattle, Lutheran Welfare, Tacoma; brought people from refugee camp Luth. Refugee Svc., Tacoma; social worker Mpls. Schs.; ret., 1985; social worker Luth. Social Svcs., Mpls. Vol. S.W. Dakota Area Resources; mem. Amnesty Internat., Mpls. Mem.: VFW, Eastern Star. Democrat. Lutheran. Avocations: reading, knitting. Home: 14813 Wildwood Rd Burnsville MN 55306-4859 E-mail: emma.foss@frontiernet.net.

FOSS, ERIC J., consumer products company executive; b. Mar. 13, 1968; BS, Ball State Univ. Sales, mktg. & mgmt. positions Pepsi Cola Co., 1982—90, v.p. retail strategy No. Am., 1990—94, gen. mgr. No. Am. Great West bus. unit, 1994—96, gen. mgr. Ctrl. Europe, 1996—99; sr. v.p. US sales & field mktg. Pepsi Bottling Group, Inc., Somers, NY, 1999—2000, exec. v.p., gen. mgr. No. Am., 2000—01, pres. No. Am., 2001—05, COO, 2005—06, pres., CEO, 2006—. Bd. dirs. Pepsi Bottling Group, Inc., 2006—, United Dominion Realty Trust; mem. industry affairs council Grocery Manufacturers Am. Office: Pepsi Bottling Group 1 Pepsi Way Somers NY 10589*

FOSS, JOHN FRANK, mechanical engineering educator; b. Washington, Pa., Mar. 24, 1938; s. Maurice Felker and C. Catharine (Reynard) F.; m. Jacqueline Kay Voss, July 24, 1960; children: Judith Kathleen, Janette Diane. Student, Wilmington Coll., 1956—58; BS, Purdue U., 1961, MS, 0162, PhD, 1965. Mem. faculty Mich. State U., East Lansing, 1964—, assoc. prof. mech. engring., 1968-75, prof., 1975—; owner, pres. Digital Flow Techs., Inc., Mich., 1994—. Dir. fluid dynamics & hydraulics program NSF, 1998-2000; cons. McDonnel Douglas Helicopter Co., Ford Motor Co., Bd. Water and Light, Lansing, Tranter Corp., United Techs. Rsch. Ctr., East Hartford, Conn. Author: (with M.C. Potter) Fluid Mechanics, 1975; N.Am. editor Measurement Sci. and Tech., 1995-; assoc. editor AIAA Jour., 1982-85, ASME Jour. Fluids Engring., 1988-91. Mem. Oaks Recreation Program staff, 1976-78; moderator Edgewood United Ch., 1975-77. Sloan fellow John Hopkins U., Balt., 1970-71; Alexander von Humboldt fellow U. Karlsruhe, Fed. Republic Germany, 1978-79, U. Erlangen, Fed. Republic Germany, 1985-86, rsch. fellow U. Melbourne, Australia, 1995. Fellow ASME; mem. AIAA, AAAS, AAUP, Am. Soc. Engring. Edn., Am. Phys. Soc. (mem. exec. com. divsn. fluid dynamics 2003-2006), Soc. Scholars Johns Hopkins U., Sigma Xi, Tau Beta Pi, Pi Tau Sigma. Mem. United Ch. of Christ. Avocation: handball. Home: 2353 Sapphire Lane East Lansing MI 48823 Office: Mich State U Dept Mech Engring East Lansing MI 48824 Home Phone: 517-324-9991; Office Phone: 517-355-3337. Business E-Mail: foss@egr.msu.edu.

FOSS, LUKAS, composer, conductor, pianist; b. Berlin, Aug. 15, 1922; came to US from Paris, 1937, naturalized, 1942; s. Martin and Hilde (Schindler) F.; m. Cornelia Brendel, Sept. 1951; 2 children. Student, Paris Lycée Pasteur, 1932-37; grad., Curtis Inst. Music, 1940; independent study, Yale U., 1940-41; studied with Paul Hindemith, studied with Julius Herford, studied with Serge Koussevitzky, studied with Fritz Reiner, studied with Isabelle Vengerova; doctorate (hon.), Yale U., 1991. Pianist Boston Symphony Orch., Boston, 1944—50; prof. composition U. Calif., Los Angeles, 1953—62; music dir. Buffalo Philharmonic, 1963—71, Brooklyn Philharmonic, 1971—90; musical adviser Jerusalem Symphony, 1972—75; music dir. Milwaukee Symphony, 1982—86, condr. laureate, 1986—. Founder & condr. Improvisation Chamber Ensemble, 1957—62; composer-in-residence Harvard, Manhattan Sch. of Music, Carnegie Mellon U., Yale U.; guest conductor Boston Symphony, Chicago Symphony, Cleveland Orch., Los Angeles Philharmonic, NY Philharmonic, Phila. Symphony Orch., San Francisco Symphony, Berlin Philharmonic, Leningrad Symphony, London Symphony Orch., Santa Cecilia Orch., Tokyo Philharmonic. Former condr., music dir., Buffalo Philharmonic; music dir., condr., Bklyn. Philharmonic, 1971-90, condr. laureate, 1990—; music dir., condr. Milw. Symphony Orch., 1981-86, condr. laureate, 1986—; orchestral compositions performed by many major orch.; best known works include (opera) Griffelkin, Baroque Variations (orch.), Echoi (4 instruments), Time Cycle (songs with orch.), Renaissance concerto (flute and orch.); orch., chamber music, ballets, works commd. by, League of Composers, Nat. Endowment for Arts, NY Arts Coun., NBC opera on TV, Am. Choral Condrs. Assn., Ind. U., 1979 Olympics, Boston Symphony, Chgo. Symphony; (recipient NY Critic Circle citation for Prairie 1944, Soc. for Pub. Am. Music award for String Quartet in G 1948, Rome prize 1950, Horblit award for Piano concerto #2 1951, Naumburg Rec. award for Song of Songs 1957, Creative Music grant Inst. Arts and Letters 1957, NY Music Critics Circle award for Time-Cycle orch. songs 1961, for Echoi 1963, Ditson award for condr. who has done the most for Am. music 1973, NYC award for spl. contbn. to arts 1976, ASCAP award for adventurous programming 1979, CRI rec. award for Thirteen Ways of Looking at a Blackbird 1979). Guggenheim fellow, 1945; Creative arts award Brandeis U., 1983; Laurel leaf award Am. Composers Alliance, 1983; elected to Am. Acad. & Inst. of Arts & Letters, 1983; inductee Am. Classical Music Hall of Fame, 2002. Mem. Am. Acad. of Arts and Letters (Gold medal 2000).

FOSS, MICHELLE MICHOT, think-tank executive, economist; BS, Univ. La., Lafayette, 1976; MS, Colo. Sch. Mines, 1985; PhD with honors, Univ. Houston, 1995; postgraduate, Tex. A&M Univ., Rice Univ. Coord. Energy & Minerals Field Inst., Colo. Sch. Mines, 1982—85; sr. assoc. & dir. rsch. Rice Ctr., 1985—88; dir. rsch. Simmons & Co. Internat., 1988—89; exec. dir. Inst. Energy Law & Enterprise, U. Houston, 1991. Ptnr. Harvest Gas Mgmt. LLC, Tex. Mem. bd. editors Internat. Jour. Regulation & Governance. Mem. vis. com. div. Economics & Business, Colo. Sch. Mines. Mem.: Women's Energy Network, Houston Geol. Soc., Assn. Internat. Petroleum Negotiators, Council on Fgn. Rels., U.S. Assn. Energy Economics (pres. 2001), Internat. Assn. Energy Economics (pres. 2003). Office: Institute for Energy Law & Enterprise University of Houston 100 Law Ctr Houston TX 77204-6060

FOSS, RICHARD JOHN, bishop; b. Wauwatosa, Wis., Dec. 27, 1944; s. Harlan Funston and Beatrice Naomi (Lindaas) F.; m. Nancy Elizabeth Martin, June 21, 1969; children: Susan, Naomi Foss Welsh, Elizabeth, Peter, Andrew. BA, St. Olaf Coll., 1966; MDiv, Luther Theol. Seminary, 1971; ThM, Luther N.W. Theol. Seminary, 1984. Ordained to ministry Luth. Ch., 1971. Pastor St. Andrews Ch. and Ch. of Christ the Redeemer, Mpls., 1971-77; assoc. pastor First Luth., Fargo, NC, 1977-79; sr. pastor Prince of Peace Luth., Seattle, 1979-86, Trinity Luth., Moorhead, Minn., 1986-92; bishop Ea. N.D. Synod, Fargo, 1992—. Soloist F-M Opera Co., Fargo, 1979; coach St. James Girls' Basketball Team, Settle, 1982-84; vol. Wash. State Patrol Crisis Chaplaincy, Seattle, 1983-86; bd. dirs. Discovery, Inc., Mpls., 1972-77, Highline Boys' and Girls' Club, Burien, Wash., 1980-81, Luth. Compass Ctr., Seattle, 1983-86, v.p., 1985-86; mem. Master Chorale, 1987-99; bd. regents Concordia Coll., 1992—; bd. dirs. Daily Bread, 1991-2000, Luth. Social Svcs. of N.D., 1992—, Oak Grove Luth. H.S., 1990—, Luth. Resources Network, 1994-97, Healthy Congregations Adv. Bd., 1997-2005, chair 2004-05, N.D. Conf. Chs., 1993—; mem. adv. bd. Thrivent Fin. for Luths., 2000—, Ctr. for Ethical Leadership, 2001-05; mem. United Way Cmty. Bd., 2001-02; bd. regents Luther Sem., 2002—. Lutheran. Avocations: golf, reading, travel, vocal performance. Home: 1510 2nd St S Moorhead MN 56560-4014 Office: Ea ND Synod 1703 32nd Ave S Fargo ND 58103-5936 Home Phone: 218-233-9678; Office Phone: 701-232-3381. E-mail: rick.foss@ecunet.org.

FOSSELLA, VITO JOHN, JR., congressman; b. SI, NY, Mar. 9, 1965; s. Vito John and Elizabeth Lucey Fossella; m. Mary Patricia Rowan, 1990; 3 children. BS, U. Pa. Wharton Sch., Phila., 1987; JD, Fordham U. Sch. Law, NYC, 1993. Atty.; real estate mgmt. cons. Deloitte & Touche; mem. Cmty. Bd. 3, Staten Island, 1989-90, City Coun., NYC, 1994-97, US Congress from 13th NY dist., 1997—, mem. energy & commerce com., chmn. Rep. Task Force on Capital Market Competitiveness, 2007. Mem. fin. svcs. com. US Congress, mem. energy and commerce com. Recipient Taxpayer Hero award, Coun. Citizens Against Govt. Waste, 1999. Mem.: Phi Sigma Epsilon. Republican. Roman Catholic. Office: 4434 Amboy Rd Fl 2 Staten Island NY 10312-3858 Office Phone: 718-356-8400, 202-225-3371. Office Fax: 718-356-1928.*

FOSSETT, STEVEN (J. STEVEN FOSSETT), retired investor, adventurer; b. Calif., Apr. 22, 1944; m. Peggy Fossett. Investor Lakota Trading, Inc., Marathon Securities, Inc. Bd. trustee Washington U. Named Rolex Yachtsman of Yr., US Sailing Assn., 2001; named an Disting. Eagle Scout, Boy Scouts of Am., 1998, Silver Buffalo, 1999; named one of Ballon and Airship Hall of Fame, FAI-CIA, 1997; named to Hall of Fame, Aviation Week and Space Technology, Laureate for Ops., 2003; recipient Victor award (Special), Victor Sports Awards, 1995, 1997, 2003, Prix De La Vauix, Fédération Aéronautique Internationale, 1995, 1997, 1998, 2002, Diplôme de Montgolfier, 1996, Gold Air Medal, 2002, Distinction in Exploration, Nat. Geographic Soc., 1998, Harmon Trophy, Nat. Aeronautic Assn., 1998, 2002, Prix de l'Aventure Sportive, Académie des Sports, France, 2002, Medaille de l'Aéronautique, Republique Francaise, 2003, Gold Medal, Royal Aero Club, UK, 2002, Grand Medaille de l'Aéro Club de France, 2003. Fellow: Royal Geographical Soc., Explorers Club (Explorers medal 2002); mem.: Academie Nationale de l'Air et de l'Elspace, Circumnavigators Club (hon. Magellan award 2003), Yacht Club de France (hon.), Nat. Yacht Club of Ireland (hon.), Aero Club de France (hon.), Adventurers Club (hon.). Holds current official World Records in five sports: Six Solo Round The World Attempts in Ballooning (First to fly solo across the Pacific Ocean, flying from Seoul, South Korea, to Mendham, Saskatchewan, 1995, first to cross the African continent in a ballon, 1997, first to cross the European Continent in a Ballon, 1998, first to cross the South Atlantic and the Indian Oceans, 1998, first Solo Ballon Flight Round the World-Speed Record (nonstop) in the Bud Light Spirit of Freedom, June-July, 2002, 24 Hour Record (Speed), June-July, 2002); Two major Ballon Flights (with multi-persons); Thirteen Outright World Records in Sailing; Three Singlehanded Records in Sailing(Round the World, 58 days, 9 hours, 32 minutes, 45 seconds, 15.52 knots, 2004, TransAtlantic (NY to England) 4 dyas, 17 hours, 28 minutes, 6 seconds, 25.78 knots, 2001); Eight Race Records in Sailing (World's Fastest Yacht

Race Record-Newport to Ensenada, 6 hours, 46 minutes, 40 seconds, 18.45 knots, 1998); One Solo Transatlantic Race in Sailing; Eleven Glider Records (with co-pilot Terry Delore); One Airship Speed Record (Absolute Airship Speed Record, Zeppelin NT, 2004); Three U.S. Transcontinental Records in Airplanes; Two Round the World Records in Medium Airplane-H Class; 6 other Airplane records; Two Cross Country Skiing records; piloted the Virgin Atlantic GlobalFlyer, first to fly solo, non-stop around the world without refueling, 2005, plans to fly around the world and cross the Atlantic Ocean a second time, landing outside of London, 2005; other sports adventures include: English Channel Swim (France to England), 1985, Leadville 100, 1991, Iditarod Dogsled Race, 1992, Ironman Triathalon (Hawaii), 1996, 24 Hours of Le Mans Sports Car Race, 1993 & 1996; donated the gondola of his ballon to the Smithsonian National Air and Space Museum in Washington, DC; In 3 1/2 days, approximately 76 hours in the Virgin Atlantic Global Flyer broke the airplane flight distance and ballon record for the longest non-stop flight (26,389 miles), once around the world and then across the Atlantic again, with a landing at Bournemouth Internatiional Airport in Southern England on February 11, 2006; flew in GlobalFlyer farther than anyone departing and landing at the same spot, traveling more than 25,000 miles in three days, March, 2006. Mailing: Marathon Racing Inc/ Steve Fossett Challanges Attn Brian Spaeth 401 South La Salle Ste 200 Chicago IL 60605

FOSSUM, JERRY GEORGE, electrical engineering educator; b. Phoenix, July 18, 1943; s. George Clayton and Lillian Edith (McNeilis) F.; m. Mary Ellen; children: Kerry Ray, Kelly Lynn. AA, Phoenix Coll., 1963; BSEE, U. Ariz., 1966, MS, 1969, PhD, 1971. Mem. tech. staff Sandia Labs., Albuquerque, 1971-78; assoc. prof. elec. engring. U. Fla., Gainesville, 1978-80, prof., 1980—2006, disting. prof., 2006—. Cons. Burr-Brown Rsch. Corp., Tucson, 1970-71, Jet Propulsion Lab., Pasadena, Calif., 1979, Harris Corp., Melbourne, Fla., 1984, Tex. Instruments, Inc., Dallas, 1988-89, 94-96, Ibis Tech. Corp., Danvers, Mass., 1995, Meta-Software, Campbell, Calif., 1995-96, Dynamics Rsch. Corp., San Diego, 1996-02; mem. adv. com. Semiconductor Rsch. Corp., 1991-95; mem. exec. com. IEEE SOI Conf., 1994-97. Contbr. articles to profl. jours.; assoc. editor: Solid-State Electronics, 1979— , IEEE Trans. Computer-Aided Design, 1988-91; patentee in field. Recipient Outstanding Rsch. award, Am. Soc. Engring. Edn., 1979. Fellow: IEEE (Best Paper award SOI Conf. 1992, J.J. Ebers award Electron Devices Soc. 2004). Office: U Fla Dept Elec and Computer Engr Gainesville FL 32611-6130 Home Phone: 352-377-5887; Office Phone: 352-392-4921. Business E-Mail: fossum@tec.ufl.edu.

FOSSUM, MICHAEL E., astronaut; b. Sioux Falls, SD, Dec. 19, 1957; s. Merlyn E. and Patricia A. Fossum; m. Melanie J. London; 4 children. BSME, Tex. A&M U., 1980; MS in Sys. Engring., Air Force Inst. Tech., 1981; disting. grad., USAF Test Pilot Sch., 1985; MS in Phys. (Space) Sci., U. Houston, Clear Lake, Tex., 1997. Commd. USAF, 1980, flight test engr. F-16 test squadron Edwards AFB, Calif., 1985—89, flight test mgr. detachment 3 Air Force Flight Test Ctr., 1989—92; resigned, 1992; sys. engr. NASA, 1993, rep. Flight Crew Ops. Directorate on Internat. Space Sta. redesign, 1993—96, tech. asst. space shuttle, 1996—97, flight test engr. X-38, 1997—98; astronaut, mission specialist candidate NASA, Johnson Space Ctr., Houston, 1998—. Astronaut office lead Space Station flight software development; capsule communicator (CAPCOM) in Mission Control; lead CAPCOM Space Station Expedition-6; crew mem. STS-121 (Discovery), a return-to-flight test mission and assembly flight to the Internat. Space Station, 2006. Col. USAF Reserves. Decorated Meritorious Svc. medal with one oak leaf cluster USAF. Avocations: jogging, fishing, backpacking. Office: Astronaut Office/CB NASA Johnson Space Ctr Houston TX 77058

FOSSUM, ROBERT MERLE, mathematician, educator; b. Northfield, Minn., May 1, 1938; s. Inge Martin and Tina Otelia (Gaudland) F.; m. Cynthia Carol Foss, Jan. 30, 1960 (div. 1979); children: Karen Jean, Kristin Ann; m. Barbara Joel Mason, Aug. 4, 1979 (div. 1993); children: Jonathan Robert, Erik Anton; m. Robin Karyl Goodman, Aug. 10, 1997. BA, St. Olaf Coll., 1959; MA, U. Mich., 1961, PhD, 1965. Instr. U. Ill., Urbana, 1964-66, asst. prof., 1966-68, assoc. prof., 1968-72, prof., 1972—, elect. and computer engring. Urbana, 2003—; prof. Beckman Inst., 2000. Lectr. Aarhus U., Denmark, 1971-73, Copenhagen U., Denmark, 1976-77; vis. prof. U. Paris VI, 1978-79, Oslo U., 1968-69. Contbr. articles to profl. jours. Recipient Disting. Alumni award Northfield H.S.; Fulbright fellow U. Oslo, 1967-68. Fellow: AAAS, Det Kongelig Norske Videnskabers Selskab (elected nat. sci. sect.); mem.: IEEE, Soc. Advancement Scandinavian Studies, European Math. Soc., Inst. Algebraic Meditation (sec.), Am. Math. Soc. (assoc. sec. cen. sect. 1983—87, sec. 1989—99), Soc. for Indsl. and Applied Math., Assn. Computing Machinery, Nordmanns Forbundet, Heimskringla (Urbana), Sigma Pi Sigma, Sigma Xi, Phi Beta Kappa. Democrat. Lutheran. Office Phone: 217-244-3572. E-mail: rmfossum@uiuc.edu.

FOSTER, BARRY ALAN, cultural organization researcher, educator; b. Tacoma, Wash., Dec. 11, 1956; s. Glen H. Foster and Selma Landers; m. Sue Rose Foster, July 20, 1954; children: Nathan M., Zachary A., Kristen B. BA in Theology, Southeastern Coll., Lakeland, Fla., 1994; MBA in Managerial Leadership, City U., Renton, Wash., 1996; MA in Orgnl. Devel., The Fielding Inst., Santa Barbara, Calif., 1998, PhD in Human and Orgnl. Sys., 2000. Orgnl. culture change leader The Boeing Co., Seattle, 1999—. Author: (organizational change model) Essential Foundations of the Engaged Organization. Dir. Lemonaid Fund, Chgo., 1999—2002. Mem.: Am. Sociol. Assn. (assoc.; cert.). Achievements include research in barriers to servant leadership and large scale organizational culture change. Avocations: mountain biking, racquetball, flag football. Office: The Boeing Co PO Box 3707 MS 5F-98 Seattle WA 98124 Office Phone: 253-951-8161. Home Fax: 646-607-3329. Personal E-mail: barryfoster777@bellsouth.net. E-mail: barry.a.foster@boeing.com.

FOSTER, BETTY LOUISE, educator; b. Lincoln, Nebr., Nov. 12, 1943; d. Burt Willis and Elizabeth Julia Hunt; m. Gary A. Foster; children: Ann Louise, Geofrey Algot; foster children: Matt Urbauer, Don Simmons, Ronda Real. BS in Elem. Edn., U. Nebr., 1965, postgrad. in Elem. Edn. Reading; postgrad. in Elem. Edn. and Reading, Kearney State Coll.; MA in Edn., Doane Coll., Crete, Nebr., 1994. Endorsement in teaching reading. Tchr. reading departmentalized grades 5-6 South Sioux City (Nebr.) Schs., 1967-69, supplemental reading tchr. Title I, 1970-71; supplemental reading tchr. Title I Grand Island Schs., Nebr., 1971-76; tchr. Jefferson Sch., Grand Island, 1976-2001; tech. tchr. Christ the King Sch., Omaha, 2001-05; tech. tchr., sys. adminstr. St. Thomas More Sch., Omaha, 2005-; adj. prof. Hamilton Coll., Council Bluffs, Iowa, 2005—. Contbr. articles to profl. jours. Organizer, tchr. Head Start in South Sioux City Cmty. Ctr. and Chs., 1968-69; active Girl Scouts U.S.A., 1970— , mentor for girls interested in art; v.p. Neighborhood Taskforce, Inc., 1980-82; pres. S. Locust/Barr Neighborhood Assn., 1980-81; mem. Mayor's Taskforce for Tornado Recovery, 1980-81; v.p. YWCA Grand Island, 1983; organizer Grand Island Women's Network, 1984; local rep., host family Grand Island Internat. Visitors Program, 1977-94, North Atlantic Cultural Exch. League, 1987-92; coach elem. level Olympics of the Mind, 1986-88, Oddyessy of the Mind, 1987-88; bd. dirs., dir. Aurora Art Workshops, Nebr., 1989-91; mem. amb. People to People Citizen Program, Japan, 1992, Grand Island Prarie Visions Team; chmn. Artel Show, Antiquariam Gallery, 1994-95. Mem. DAR (Major I Saddler La Belle Vue Cho 2004—), Nat., Nebr., Grand Island Edn. Assns. (chairwoman instrn. and career enhancement com. 1990-91), Internat. (sec. Central Coun. 1974—2000), Nebr., State reading assns., PTA of Children with Learning Disabilities (Jefferson Sch. chairwoman student assistance team 1989-92), AAUW (pres. Grand Island br. 1979-80, state v.p. 1981-82, state topic chmn. 1980-81), Nebr. Ednl. Tech. Assn., Coalition of Women, LWV, Nat. Women's Caucus for Art (bd. dirs. 1995-2004), Nebr. Women's Cacus for Art (Nebr. state treas. 1995—), Artel Artist Networking Cmty, Assn. of Nebr. Art Clubs (chmn. state conv. 1987, sec. 1987-2000), Grand Island Art Club (pres. 1985-86), Grand Island Sketch Club, Meadows Cmty. Assn. (sec./treas. 2004—), Daus. Union Vets (Betsy Ross tent #1, treas. 2007-), DAV (Maj. I. Sadler-LaBette Vue chpt.),Alpha Delta Kappa, Sigma Kappa. Developed self correcting games. Certified in elementary edn., kindergarten-8th grade, Nebr., Iowa; specialist in diagnosis and remediation of reading problems with learning disabilities problems, gifted children; trained to teach Jr. Great Books program, Productive Thinking Skills, Cooperative Learning, Quest-Skills for Growing K-5,trained discipline with a purpose. I'm Special 3-4; cert. foster home, Nebr. Office: St Thomas Moore Sch 3515 S 48th Ave Omaha NE 68106 Home: 13920 Lisa Cir Omaha NE 68138 Personal E-mail: bateach3@aol.com.

FOSTER, B.J. See SHOEMAKER, BOBBY

FOSTER, BOB See FOSTER, ROBERT

FOSTER, CARTER, curator; b. Atlanta; B in Art History, U. Ga.; M in Art History, Brown U., 1991. Intern Nat. Gallery Art, Washington; curatorial intern Phila. Mus. Art; print specialist, divsn. arts, prints, and photographs NY Pub. Libr.; staff mem. drawing dept. Cleveland Mus. Art, 1996—2004, chief drawing dept., 2002—04; curator, co-chair dept. prints and drawings LA County Mus. Art, 2004—05; curator of drawings Whitney Mus. Am. Art, NYC, 2005—. Office: Whitney Mus Am Art 945 Madison Ave New York NY 10021 Office Phone: 212-570-3651. Business E-Mail: carter_foster@whitney.org.

FOSTER, C(HARLES) ALLEN, lawyer; b. Aug. 26, 1941; s. Charles Shearer and Bessie Lea (Long) F.; m. Susan Coomes; children: Charles Shearer Sanders II, Susan Elizabeth Coomes, Charles Henry Edward. BA summa cum laude, Princeton U., 1963; BA in Jurisprudence 1st class honors, Oxford U., Eng., 1965, MA in Jurisprudence, 1971; JD magna cum laude, Harvard U., 1967. Bar: N.C. 1967, D.C. 1994, U.S. Dist. Ct. (mid. dist.) N.C. 1968, U.S. Dist. Ct. (we. dist.) N.C. 1968, U.S. Dist. Ct. (ea. dist.) N.C. 1968, U.S. Tax Ct. 1970, U.S. Ct. Appeals (4th cir.), U.S. Ct. Appeals (5th cir.) 1970, U.S. Ct. Appeals (11th cir.) 1991, U.S. Ct. Appeals (9th cir.) 2003, U.S. Ct. Appeals (10th cir.) 1993, U.S. Ct. Appeals (fed. cir.) 1995, U.S. Supreme Ct. 1971, U.S. Dist. Ct. D.C. 1985, U.S. Dist. Ct. (no. dist.) Tex. 1990, U.S. Dist. Ct. (so. dist.) Tex. 1991, U.S. Ct. Fed. Claims 1994. Assoc. McLendon, Brim, Brooks, Pierce & Daniels, Greensboro, NC, 1967-72, ptnr., 1972-73; sec., dir., gen. counsel Spanco Industries, Inc., Greensboro and Sanford, NC, 1973-75, Conestee, SC, 1973-75; ptnr. Turner, Enochs, Foster, Sparrow & Burnley, Greensboro, 1975-81, Foster, Conner & Robson, 1983-88, Patton, Boggs LLP, 1988-99, Greenberg Traurig, Washington, 1999—. Sr. lectr. law Duke U., 1981-88; arbitrator Am. Arbitration Assn., mem. Nat. Acad. Arbitrators; pub. mem. N.C. Tax Rev. Bd., 1972-76; mem. N.C. Judicial Selection Study Commn., 1987-88; U.S. rep. Internat. Energy Agy. Dispute Resolution Ctr., Paris, 1984—; permanent panel arbitrator Martin Marietta and Atomic Trades and Labor Coun.; others. Author: Construction and Design Law, 1984—, Construction and Design Law Digest, 1981—, Law and Practice of Commercial Arbitration in North Carolina, 1984; contbr. articles to profl. jours. Co-founder, sec., bd. dirs. Greensboro Day Sch.; exec. com. Princeton U. Alumni Assn.; exec. com. Harvard Law Sch. Assn. N.C., 1970; Rep. candidate for atty.-gen. N.C., 1984; spl. counsel Rep. Nat. Com., 1989—; spl. litigation counsel N.C. Rep. Cen. Com., 1987—. Named one of top 20 trial lawyers in D.C., 2003. Mem. ABA (litigation sect., labor and employment discrimination law sect., forum com. on constrn. industry), Am. Law Inst., Am. Arbitration Assn. (bd. dirs. 1980-83, nat. panels labor, constrn., internat. comml. arbitrators 1975—, chmn. N.C. regional adv. coun. 1979-83), Am. Coll. Constrn. Arbitrators (pres. 1983-84), Princeton U. Alumni Assn. (exec. com. 1978-79, pres. mid. N.C. chpt. 1968-80), Phi Beta Kappa, Cap and Gown Club. Home: 4827 Foxball Crescents NW Washington DC 20007 Office Phone: 202-331-3102. Business E-Mail: fostera@gtlaw.com.

FOSTER, CHARLES CRAWFORD, lawyer, educator; b. Galveston, Tex., Aug. 1, 1941; s. Louie Brown and Helen (Hall) F.; m. Marta Brito, Sept. 7, 1967 (div. Apr. 1986); children: John, Ruth; m. Lily Chen, Jan. 7, 1989; children: Zachary, Anthony. AA, Del Mar Jr. Coll., 1961; BA, U. Tex., 1963, JD, 1967. Bar: Tex. 1967, N.Y. 1969. Assoc. Reid & Priest, NYC, 1967-69, Butler & Binion, Houston, 1969-73; ptnr. Tindall & Foster, Houston, 1973—. Hon. consul gen. Kingdom of Thailand, 1996—; adj. prof. immigration law U. Houston, 1985-89; bd. dirs. Greater Houston Partnership, 1997-2006, chmn. econ. devel. adv. bd., chmn., 2000 World Trade Adv. Bd., 1997; chmn. Asia Soc.-Tex., bd. trustees, 1990—; bd. dirs. Houston World Affairs Coun., 1990; mem. Inst. Internat. Edn., Houston Ballet Found., Houston Holocaust Mus.; mem. Mayoral Adv. Bd. for Internat. Affairs and Devel./Asia, 1999—; pres. Houston Forum, 2002-04; co-chmn. George Bush Monument Project, 2003-04; pres. The Houston Club, 2000. Contbr. articles to profl. jours. Chmn. immigration reform Gov.'s Task Force of Tex., 1984—87; mem. Bush-Cheney Transition Adv. Com., 2000—01. Admiral Texan Navy, 2003. Decorated knight comdr. 2d class Order of the Crown (Thailand), comdr. 2d class Exalted Order of White Elephant (Thailand); Rotary Internat. fellow U. Concepción, Chile, 1964; recipient Houston Internat. Svc. award Houston Jaycees, 1996, Disting. Friend of China award U.S. China Friendship Found., 2000; honoree Am. Immigration Law Found., 1998' commd. adm. Tex. Navy, Gov. Rick Perry, 2003, Svc. to Humanity award, Rotary Found., 2006; Wall of Honor Alumni award Del Mar Coll., 2006. Mem. ABA (chmn. immigration com. internat. law and practice sect. 1982-90, chmn. coordinating com. on immigration and law 1987-89, fgn. rels. com. 2000—), Am. Immigration Lawyers Assn. (pres. 1981-82, Outstanding Svc. award 1985), Tex. Bar Assn. (chmn. com. law on immigration and nationality 1984-86), Tex. Bd. Legal Specialization (chmn. immigration adv. commn. 1979—), Houston Bar Assn., Asia Soc. (trustee 1992—, chmn. Houston Ctr. 1992—). Methodist. Avocations: mountain climbing, photography, travel. Home: 17 Courtlandt Pl Houston TX 77006-4013 Office: Tindall & Foster 600 Travis St Ste 2800 Houston TX 77002-3094 Business E-Mail: cfoster@tindallfoster.com.

FOSTER, CHARLES H., title insurance company executive; BA, Princeton Univ.; MBA, Univ. Va. With Lawyers Title, 1979-80, sr. v.p.-CFO, 1980-88, pres., 1988-90, CEO, 1990-91, LandAm. Fin. Group, Inc., 1991—2004, chmn., 1991—. Mem. nat. adv. coun. Fannie Mae, 1999-2000; bd. dirs. Universal Corp., SunTrust Bank. Past chmn. Greater Richmond C. of C. Mem. Am. Land Title Assn. (pres.) Office: LandAm Fin Group Inc 101 Gateway Ctr Pky Richmond VA 23235

FOSTER, CHARLES HENRY WHEELWRIGHT, former foundation officer, consultant, author; b. Boston, Mar. 18, 1927; s. Reginald Candler and Frances Helen (Hoar) F.; m. Barbara Ann Duchaine, Sept 19, 1953; children: Frances H., Jonathan R., Susan C. BA, Harvard U., 1951; BSF, U. Mich., 1953, MS, 1956; PhD, Johns Hopkins U., 1969; DPA (hon.), Suffolk U., 1971; MA (hon.), Yale U., 1977. Exec. sec. Wildlife Conservation Inc., Boston, 1953-55; cons. Mass. Water Resources Commn., Boston, 1956-59; commr. Mass. Dept. Natural Resources, Boston, 1959-66; pres. Nature Conservancy, Washington, 1966-67; sr. staff mem. Conservation Found., Washington, 1967-68; chmn. bd. N.E. Natural Resources Ctr., Boston, 1969-70; sec. Mass. Exec. Office Environ. Affairs, Boston, 1971-75; sr. staff mem. A. D. Little, Inc., Cambridge, Mass., 1975-76; prof. environ. policy U. Mass., Amherst, 1975-76; dean Sch. Forestry and Environ. Studies Yale U., 1976-81; vis. scholar Stanford U., 1981-82; rsch. assoc. U. Calif., Santa Cruz, 1982; scholar in residence U. Va., 1983; pres. W. Alton Jones Found., Charlottesville, Va., 1983. Adj. prof. environ. studies Tufts U., 1984-85; vis. rsch. prof. Clark U., 1985-86; adj. rsch. fellow Harvard U., 1986—; vis. prof. environ. studies Brown U., 1987; cons., lectr. in field. Trustee of numerous natural resources and ednl. orgns. With U.S. Army, 1945-47. Bullard fellow Harvard U., 1969-70 Fellow AAAS; mem. Soc. Am. Foresters, Am. Water Resources Assn., Harvard Club (Boston). Office Phone: 617-495-1351. E-mail: charles_foster@harvard.edu.

FOSTER, CRAIG ALLEN, plastic surgeon; b. Mpls., Aug. 31, 1948; MD, U. Minn., 1974. Diplomate Am. Bd. Plastic Surgery, Am. Bd. Otolaryngology. Intern U. Minn., Mpls.; resident in gen. surgery U. Minn. Hosps., resident in otolaryngology; resident in plastic surgery NYU, NYC; pvt. practice plastic surgery NYC; plastic surgeon Manhattan EE Hosp., NYC. Office: 850 Park Ave New York NY 10021-1845 Office Phone: 212-744-5746. E-mail: plasticrn1@aol.com.

FOSTER, DALE WARREN, political scientist, educator, real estate agent, accountant, management consultant; b. Bryan, Tex., Mar. 7, 1950; s. William Henry and Maysie Blanche (Hembree) F. BBA, Tex. A&M U., 1972, MA, 1979, Cert. in Profl. Teaching, 1987; BS, U. Houston, 1981, MEd, 1983; AAS, Houston C.C. Sys., 1982. Cert. in property mgmt. Dept. mgr. J.C. Penney Co., Bryan, 1973-74; shopper advt. mgr. Harte-Hanks Newspapers/Daily Eagle, Bryan, 1975-76; bus. mgr., contr. S.M. Hardee Enterprises, College Station, Tex., 1976-78; ops. mgr. Western Food Svcs., Inc., Pasadena, Tex., 1978-80; internal auditor Hermann Hosp., Houston, 1980-82; high sch. tchr. Cypress-Fairbanks Independent Sch. Dist., Houston, 1983-84; alternative sch. tchr. Alief Independent Sch. Dist., Houston, 1984-88; gov. prof. Houston C.C. System, 1980—, chmn. govt. dept. co-op program, 1992—; lead instr. Houston C.C. Sys., 1993—; supr. student tchr. U. Houston, 1989-90. Adj. instr. North Harris County Coll., Houston, 1983-96; fin. cons. Pro-Trac Econ. Planning Adv. Bd., Denver, 1985-86; Presdl. Scholars lectr. Minority Students Honors Program, Houston, 1986-89; coord. legis. practicum Harris County Congl. Internship Program, 1988—; exch. tchr., The Netherlands, 1992. Co-editor textbook supplement, curriculum guide, departmental political reader; author classroom instructional project. Mem. adv. com. Hermann Affiliated Fed. Credit Union, Houston, 1980-82; mem. fin. coun. Harris County Dem. Com., 1991-93; mem. dean's coun. U. Houston, 1992-96; trustee, treas. Wilmington-Barnard Found., 1992—. Named Tchr. of Yr., Cy.-Fair H.S., 1984, Alief Individualized Study Ctr., 1987, Master Tchr. Nat. Leadership Inst, U. Tex., Austin, 1991, host tchr. Washington Week Intern Program, 1995; recipient Adj. Teaching and Comty. Svc. award North Harris County Coll. Dist., 1990, Teaching Excellence medal Nat. Inst. Staff and Orgn. Devel., 1991, 98; Fulbright scholar, 1992, 98; Robert A. Taft fellow L.B.J. Sch. Pub. Affairs, 1995, Fulbright-Hays fellowship U.S. Dept. Edn., 1998. Fellow Am. Bd. Master Educators; mem. Tex. Jr. Coll. Tchrs. Assn., Tex. Coun. Social Studies, Inst. Mgmt. Accts., , Am. Fin. Assn., Fulbright Assn., Houston C.C. Sys. Faculty Assn. (treas. 1997-2000, v.p. 2000-01, pres.-elect 2001-02, pres. 2002-03, Outstanding Tchr. award 1991, Tchr. of Yr. 1997), Phi Theta Kappa, Alpha Phi Omega, Kappa Delta Pi. Democrat. Baptist. Avocations: travel, reading, bowling, water sports, outdoor activities. Office: Houston C C NW 1010 W Sam Houston Pkwy N Houston TX 77043 E-mail: corps1972@yahoo.com.

FOSTER, DANIEL WILLETT, medical educator; b. Marlin, Tex., Mar. 4, 1930; married, 1955; 3 children. BA, Tex. Western Coll., 1951; MD, U. Tex., 1955. Intern internal medicine Parkland Meml. Hosp., 1955-56, asst. resident, 1956-58, chief resident, 1958-59; fellow biochemistry U. Tex. Southwestern Med. Sch., 1959-60; investigator Nat. Inst. Arthritis and Metabolic Disease, 1960-62; from asst. prof. to assoc. prof. U. Tex. Southwestern Med. Sch., 1962-69, prof. Dallas, 1969-86, Jan and Henri Bromberg prof., 1986-89, chmn. dept. internal medicine, 1988—2003, Donald W. Seldin Disting. chair, 1989—2003, John Denis McGarry Disting. chair, 2003—. Mem. metabolism study sect. NIH, 1968-70, chmn. sect., 1970-72, mem. NIDDK adv. coun., 1987-90, bd. sci. counselors Clin. Ctr., 1991-95, 98—; chief internal medicine Parkland Meml. Hosp. and Univ. Med. Ctr., Tex.; mem. Nat. Diabetes Adv. Bd., 1981-84; chair sci. adv. bd. Hartford Found.; cons. VA Hosp., Dallas, Presbyn. Hosp., Baylor U. Med. Ctr.; mem. sci. adv. bd. Merck, Inc., 1991-94; mem. sci. adv. coun. Abbott Labs., 1998—; mem. Pres.'s Coun. on Bioethics, 2002—. Assoc. editor: Jour. Clin. Investigation, 1972-77; editor: Diabetes, 1978-83. Master ACP; fellow AAAS, Am. Acad. of Arts and Scis.; mem. Assn. Profs. of Medicine (pres. 1997-98), Inst. Medicine-NAS, Am. Soc. Clin. Investigation, Am. Diabetes Assn. (Banting medal 1984, Joslin medal 1984, Upjohn award 1988), Am. Fedn. Clin. Rsch., Am. Soc. Biol. Chemists, Assn. Am. Physicians. Office: U Tex Health Sci Ctr Dept Internal Medicine Dallas TX 75235-9030

FOSTER, DAVID LEE, lawyer; b. Des Moines, Dec. 13, 1933; s. Carl Dewitt and Dorothy Jo (Bell) F.; m. Marilyn Lee Bokemeier, Aug. 12, 1957 (div. June 1978); children: Gwendolyn Foster Reed, Cynthia Foster Curry, David Lee Jr. (dec.); m. Kathleen Carol Walsh, Mar. 24, 1979; 1 child, John Wickersham. Student, Simpson Coll., 1951-52; BA, U. Iowa, 1954, JD, 1957. Bar: Iowa 1957, N.Y. 1958, Ohio 1964, U.S. Supreme Ct. 1975. Assoc. Cravath, Swaine & Moore, NYC, 1957-63; from assoc. to ptnr. Jones, Day, Cockley & Reavis, Cleve., 1963-72; ptnr., counsel Willkie Farr & Gallagher, NYC, 1972—2004; counsel Trachtenberg Rodes & Friedberg, NYC, 2007—. Lectr. So. Meth. U., 1979-84, U. Pitts., 1984, Practicing Law Inst., N.Y.C., 1984-85; mem. adv. bd. Civil RICO Report LRP Publs., 1988-2007; bd. govs. N.Y. Ins. Exch., 1987-96; bd. dirs. Dowling Corp. Contbr. chpts. to book, articles to legal jours. Mem., bd. trustees Cardigan Mountain Sch., 1995-2004, v.p., 2002-2003. Served with USNR, 1952-60. Fellow Am. Coll. Trial Lawyers, Internat. Acad. Trial Lawyers (bd. dirs. 1987-92); mem. Am. Counsel Assn. (pres. 1994-95, bd. dirs. 1992-98), River Club, Order of Coif, Phi Beta Kappa. Home Phone: 845-677-8189; Office Phone: 845-677-8189. Personal E-mail: qkwick@msn.com.

FOSTER, DAVID SCOTT, lawyer; b. White Plains, NY, July 13, 1938; s. William James and Ruth Elizabeth (Seltzer) F.; m. Eleanore Stalker, Dec. 21, 1959; children: David Scott, Robert McEachron. BA in Physics, Amherst Coll., 1960; LLB, Harvard U., 1963. Bar: NY 1963, DC 1977, Calif. 1978. Jud. law clk. US Dist. Ct. (so. dist.) N.Y., 1963-64; assoc. Debevoise & Plimpton, NYC, 1964-72; from atty.-advisor to internat. tax counsel US Treasury Dept., Washington, 1972-77; ptnr. Brobeck, Phleger & Harrison, San Francisco, 1978-90, Coudert Bros., San Francisco, 1990-91, Thelen Reid Brown Raysman & Steiner LLP, San Francisco, 1991—. Mem. ABA, San Francisco Bar Assn., Western Pension and Benefits Conf., St. Francis Yacht Club (San Francisco), Phi Beta Kappa, Sigma Xi. Presbyterian. Office: Thelen Reid Brown Raysman & Steiner LLP Ste 1800 101 2nd St San Francisco CA 94105-3606 Office Phone: 415-369-7020. Business E-Mail: dsfoster@thelen.com.

FOSTER, DUDLEY EDWARDS, JR., musician, educator; b. Orange, NJ, Oct. 5, 1935; s. Dudley Edwards and Margaret (DePoy) Foster. Student, Occidental Coll., 1953—56; AB, UCLA, 1957, MA, 1958; postgrad., U. So. Calif., 1961—73. Lectr. music. Immaculate Heart Coll., LA, 1960—63; dir. music Holy Faith Episcopal Ch., Inglewood, Calif., 1964—67; lectr. music Calif. State U., LA, 1968—71; assoc. prof. music LA Mission Coll., 1975—83, prof., 1983—, chmn. dept. music, 1977—. Mem. dist. acad. senate LA CC's, 1991—92; dir. music 1st Luth. Ch., LA, 1968—72. Organist, pianist, harpsichordist: numerous recital; composer: O Sacrum Convivium for Trumpet and Organ, 1973, Passacaglia for Brass Instruments, 1969, Introduction, Atroso & Fuque for Cello and Piano,

1974. Recipient Associated STudents Faculty award, 1988; fellow Trinity Coll. Music, London, 1960. Mem.: Mediaeval Acad. Am., LA Coll. Tchrs. Assn., Town Hall Calif., Acad. Senate, Nat. Assn. of Scholars, Am. Musicol. Soc., Am. Guild Organists. Republican. Anglican. Office: LA Mission Coll Dept Music 13356 Eldridge Ave Sylmar CA 91342-3200 Personal E-mail: fostermusic@eartlink.net. Business E-Mail: defoster@lamc.org.

FOSTER, EARL JAMES, orthopedist; b. Brocklyn, Iowa, Jan. 4, 1948; s. Lawrence Franklyn and Lila Irene Foster; m. Carol Marie Blanchord, May 29, 1951; children: Taryn, Kyle. BS in Gen. Sci., U. Iowa, 1970, MD, 1974. Intern U. Ind., Indpls., 1975; orthopedic resident U. Syracuse, NY, 1979; hand surgery fellow New Orleans, 1979—80; physician Scott Orthopedic Ctr., Huntington, W.Va., 1980—, pres., 1996—; chmn. of bd. Three Gable Surgery Ctr. Chief orthopedics Cabell Hosp. and St. Mary Hosp., Huntington, 1988—90; pres. med. staff Cabell Huntington Hosp., 1994—96. Fellow: ACS, Am. Acad. Orthopedic Surgery; mem.: Am. Soc. Surgery Hand. Avocations: fitness, golf, reading. Home: 85 Camelot Dr Huntington WV 25701 Office: Scott Orthopedic Ctr 2828 1st Ave Huntington WV 25702 Office Phone: 304-525-6905. Personal E-mail: earljfoster@gmail.com.

FOSTER, EDWARD JOHN, engineer physicist; b. NYC, Aug. 10, 1938; s. John Paul and Mildred Julia (Hassiak) F.; m. Sandra Thornton Christie (div. 1989); children: Sandra Foster Swindler, Mary Elizabeth Foster. BS in Physics cum laude, Fordham U., 1959; MS in Physics, Syracuse U., NY, 1965; MBA, Iona U., 1973. Mgr. magnetics dept. Shephard Industries, Inc., Nutley, NJ, 1960-61; founder, CEO S.E.D. Memories, Inc., Rutherford, NJ, 1961-63; br. mgr. rsch. CBS Labs., Stamford, Conn., 1963-73; v.p. tech. ByWord Corp., Armonk, NY, 1973-76; pres. Diversified Sci. Labs., Brevard, NC, 1976—. Cons. Electronics Industries Assn., Washington; dep. tech. advisor to U.S Nat. Com. Internat. Electrotech. Com. TC100, Geneva, Switzerland, 1982—. Author: Effects and Degrees of Error of Modulation-Demodulation, 1965; contbg. editor: Acquisition Reduction and Analysis of Acoustical Data, 1974; contbr. articles to profl. jours. Woodrow Wilson fellow, 1959, fellowship NSF, 1959-60. Fellow: Audio Engring. Soc. (v.p. ea. U.S./Can.); mem.: IEEE (sr.), Delta Mu Delta, Sigma Xi. Achievements include patents for Automatic Recording Level Control, Directional Microphone Arrays. Home and Office: 79 Isuhdavga Ct Brevard NC 28712-9221 Personal E-mail: divscilab@gmail.com.

FOSTER, EDWARD PAUL (TED FOSTER), process industries executive; b. Pawtucket, RI, Aug. 23, 1945; s. Edward Francis and Vivian Adrienne (Davagne) F.; m. Barbara Philomena Cook, Dec. 17, 1965 (div. Apr. 1978); children: Edward Robert, Gwendolyn Lucy; m. Johanna Helena Klaassen, June, 1985 (div. 1988). BSChemE with distinction, U. R.I., 1967; MSChemE, Worcester Poly. Inst., 1970; MBA, Lehigh U., 1981. Mfg. melting engr. Corning Glass Works, Central Falls, R.I., 1966-67; group leader rsch. and devel. The Babcock & Wilcox Co., Alliance, Ohio, 1968-71, mgr. tampella process Barberton, Ohio, 1972-74; from comml. devel. engr. to dir. bus. devel. in gases, metallurgy, coal, energy, chems. and polymers, and environ. areas Air Products and Chem., Inc., Allentown, Pa., 1974—. Cons. U.S. Army Natick (Mass.) Lab., 1966-67. Contbr. articles to profl. jours. Chmn. fin. Unitarian Ch., Bethleham, Pa., 1985, chmn. social, 1983-84. NDEA fellow HEW, 1967-69; ROTC scholar U.S. Army, 1965, Nat. Merit scholar, 1963. Mem. AIChE, Comml. Devel. Assn. (vice chmn. fall meeting 1996, nat. program chmn. 1997-99, bd. dirs.), Am. Chem. Soc., Comml. Devel. and Mktg. Assn. (bd. dirs. 2000—03), Gasification Tech. Coun. (bd. dirs., 2004-.), Phi Kappa Phi, Tau Beta Pi, Theta Chi. Achievements include patents in field. Avocations: tennis, downhill skiing, sailing. Home: 6023 Fairway Ln Allentown PA 18106-9610 Office: Air Products and Chems 7201 Hamilton Blvd Allentown PA 18195-1526 Office Phone: 610-481-5307.

FOSTER, ERIC HAROLD, JR., retail executive; b. Nov. 8, 1943; s. Eric H. Sr. and Dorothy (Schwarz) F.; married; children: Dawn, Eric III, Kimberly, Meredith. BS in Mgmt., Rutger's U., 1969; student grad. sch. acctg. and taxation, Farleigh Dickinson U., 1973-74. Computer and peripheral equipment operator N.J. Bell Tel. Co., 1965-66; mem. prodn. planning and scheduling 3M Co., St. Paul, 1966-68, data analyst, 1968-69; supr. customer and geog. info. ctr. McGraw-Hill Book Co., Hightstown, N.J., 1969-71, staff asst. to gen. mgr. distbn. ctr., 1971-75, 78, mgr. retail accounts receivable credit and collection dept., 1975-78, 79, responsible McGraw-Hill club and retail customer svc. depts., 1979, mgr., 1979-80, mgr. spl. svcs. and returns, 1980-82, gen. mgr. profl. pub. svcs., 1982-88. Councilman Borough of Freehold, pres., chmn. water and sewer dept., mem. planning bd., fin. and econ. devel. com.; bd. dirs. Freehold Presbyn. Nursery Sch.; chmn. bd. The Rugby Sch.; vice chmn. Freehold Borough Zoning Bd.; mem. vestry, bus. and pers. com., maintenance and repair com. St. Peter Episc. Ch., chmn. fin. com.; advisor Youth Group; charter mem., 1st pres., mem. founding group East Freehold Fire Co.; coord. troop 151 Boy Scouts Am. Recipient Bronze Palm award Eagle Scouts Am., 1960. Mem. Direct Mktg. Assn., Direct Mktg. and Credit Assn. (bd. dirs.), Internat. Consumer Credit Assn. (bd. dirs. region II N.Y./N.J. chpts.), N.J. Assn. Schs. and Agys. for the Handicapped, Internat. Credit Assn. (cert. consumer credit exec.). Episcopalian. Home: 380 Schanck Rd Freehold NJ 07728

FOSTER, EVALINE L., education educator, researcher; b. Natchez, Miss., Aug. 7, 1953; d. John and Augustine W. Lewis; m. James L. Foster, Apr. 16, 1972; children: Tanya Shontae Demby, Cedrick James, Laura Alisha Simmons, Jamie Ryan. Degree in elem. edn. and gen. studies, Alcorn State U., 1996, MEd, 2000; PhD, Nova Southeastern U., 2005. Cert. elem. tchr., guidance counselor La. Guidance counselor intern Natchez (Miss.) Adams Sch. Dist., 2000—01, guidance counselor, social worker, 2000—02, behavior enrichment instr., 2002—03, rschr., 2003—04, prin. investigator, rschr., 2003—04; adj. prof. Alcorn State U., Natchez, 2005—. Mem. disciplinary rev. com. mem. Natchez Adams Sch. Dist., 2000—02. Sec., Bible class tchr. Ch. of Christ, Natchez, 1973—2006. Named Bible Class Tchr. of Yr., Ch. of Christ, Natchez, 1986; recipient Trillium Staff Spl. Recognition award, Copiah-Lincoln C.C., Natchez, 1993, Spl. Recognition Student Support Svcs., 1994. Mem.: ASCD (assoc.). Achievements include research in implementation of a social skills curriculum to reduce behavior problems of African American boys in elementary classroom settings. Home: 376 Concordia Pk Vidalia LA 71373 Office: Alcorn State U 15 Campus Dr Natchez MS 39120 Office Phone: 601-392-9503. Office Fax: 1-318-336-5480; Home Fax: 318-336-5480. Personal E-mail: evalinefoster@yahoo.com.

FOSTER, HOPE S., lawyer; b. 1948; BA, Wellesley Coll., 1970; JD with honors, George Washington U., 1973. Bar: DC 1973. Mem. Mintz Levin Cohn Ferris Glovsky & Popeo PC, Washington, co-mgr., Health Care Sect. Contbr. articles to profl. jour.; spkr. in field. Mem.: Am. Health Lawyers Assn., ABA (white collar crime com., health care com., antitrust com., health care fraud & abuse subcom.), DC Bar. Office: Mintz Levin Cohn Ferris Glovsky & Popeo PC 701 Pennsylvania Ave NW Washington DC 20004 Office Phone: 202-661-8758. Office Fax: 202-434-7400. Business E-Mail: hsfoster@mintz.com.

FOSTER, IAN TREMERE, computer scientist; b. Wellington, New Zealand, Jan. 1, 1959; arrived in US, 1989; s. Peter Kinnear and Eileen June (Gapes) F.; m. Angela Claire Smyth; children: Alexander Peter, Imogen Teresa. BSc with honors, U. Canterbury, Christchurch, New Zealand, 1979, DSc honoris causa, 2006; PhD, Imperial Coll., London, 1988. Rsch. assoc., dept. computing Imperial Coll., London, 1985-88; asst. computer scientist Argonne Nat. Lab., Ill., 1989-93, scientist, 1993-96; assoc. prof. U. Chgo., 1996-2000; sr. scientist Argonne Nat. Lab., 1997-2000, assoc. div. dir., sr. scientist, head, Distributed Systems Lab Math. & Computer Sci. Argonne, Ill.; Arthur Holly Compton prof. computer sci. U. Chgo., 2000—. Software architect I-Way Experiment U. Chgo., 1995; co-founder Global Grid Forum; program chair High Performance Distributed Computing Conf., 1997, gen. chair, 2000, 01; program chair Frontiers of Massively Parallel Computation Conf., 1998; application evangelist chair Information Arch. Com. Conf., 2000; mem. SCxy Steering Com.; co-program chair HPC Asia, 2001; information arch. chair SC'2001, 2001; mem. World Tech. Network, 2003. Author: Strand: New Concepts in Parallel Programming, 1990, Systems Programming in Parallel Logic Languages, 1990, Designing and Building Parallel Programs, 1995, The Grid: Blueprint for a New Computing Infrastructure, 1999, 2nd edit., 2004; contbr. to 300 tech. papers and reports. Named Innovator of Yr., InfoWorld, 2003, R&D Mag., 2003; named one of Top 50 Agenda Setter, Silicon.com, 2003, Ten Technologies that Will Change the World, MIT Tech. Review, 2003; recipient Tech. Innovation award, Brit. Computer Soc., 1989, Next Generation award, Global Info. Infrastructure, 1997, Gordon Bell award, 2001, Lovelace Medal, 2002, Most Promising New Technology award, R&D Mag., 2002, Fed. Lab. Consortium Tech. Transfer award, 2002, Ill. Innovation award, 2003. Fellow: British Computer Soc., AAAS; mem.: Assn. for Computing Machinery. Achievements include co-design of Strand parallel programming language; contributions in algorithms and technologies for parallel computing; leadership in design of middleware for wide area computing; co-design of Globus network computing system. Address: U Chgo 1100 E 58th St Ryerson Hall Rm 155 Chicago IL 60637 Office Phone: 630-252-4619, 773-702-3487. Office Fax: 630-252-9556, 773-702-8487. Business E-Mail: foster@mcs.anl.gov, foster@cs.uchicago.edu.

FOSTER, JACKIE GREEN, voice educator; d. Jack and Geneva Green; children: Jamie, Keegan. BA, U. of SC., 1981; M in Elem. Edn., Francis Marion U., 1988. Math tchr. Moore Mid. Sch., Florence, SC, 1988—94, Sneed Mid. Sch., 1994—2003, chorus tchr., 2003—. Mem.: SC Music Educator's Assn., Music Educators Nat. Conf., SC Edn. Assn., Am. Choral Dirs. Assn. Baptist. Office: Sneed Mid Sch 1102 South Ebenezer Road Florence SC 29501 Home Phone: 843-662-0393; Office Phone: 843-673-1199. Personal E-mail: jfoster@fsd1.org.

FOSTER, JAMES CALDWELL, dean, historian; b. Madison, Wis., Apr. 10, 1943; s. Mark A. and Ruth C. (Caldwell) Foster; m. Diane L. Mohn, Sept. 3, 1966 (dec. Sept. 2001); children: Jeffrey, Justin, Joshua; m. Mary Louise Pusch, June 25, 2004. BS, U. Wis., 1967; PhD, Cornell U., 1972. Assoc. dir. Wis. Humanities Commn., NEH, Madison, 1977-78; asst. prof. U. Alaska, College, 1971-74; dir. labor studies Ariz. State U., Tempe, 1974-81, Sch. for Workers, U. Wis., Madison, 1981-84; assoc. dean of campus Ohio State U., Newark, 1984-87; dean Coll. Arts, Scis. and Lit. U. Mich., Dearborn, 1987-92; dir. acad. affairs Pa. State U.-Fayette, Uniontown, 1993-95; v.p. acad. affairs Walsh U., Canton, Ohio, 1995-99, Mt. Senario Coll., Wis., 1999—2000, Mount Marty Coll., Yankton, SD, 2001—. Presenter North Ctrl. Assn. Coll. and Schs./ Higher Learning Comn., 2003, 05, 07, cons. evaluator, 2005—. Author: The Union Politic, 1975, American Labor in the Southwest, 1982; newspaper columnist, Kenosha (Wis.) Labor, 1981— (1st, 2d and 3d best story awards for column Lest We Forget, AFL-CIO 1984); commentator Wis. Pub. Radio, Madison, 1981-84. Exxon Edn. grantee, Tempe, 1976, Rockefeller Found. grantee, Tempe, 1977, German Marshall Fund grantee, Madison, 1981. Mem. Indsl. Rels. Rsch. Assn., Am. Arbitration Assn. Home: PO Box 509 Yankton SD 57078 Office: Mt Marty Coll 1105 W 8th St Yankton SD 57078 Home Phone: 605-665-2238; Office Phone: 605-668-1584. Personal E-mail: jcfosterml@earthlink.net. Business E-Mail: jfoster@mtmc.edu.

FOSTER, JAMES FRANKLIN, professional sports management executive; b. Iowa; s. M. (Egerer) F.; m. Susan Jane Salsi, July 19, 1976. BGS, U. Iowa, 1972; postgrad., U. Pa., 1982. Retail advt. specialist Maytag Co., Newton, Iowa, 1972-78; founder, gen. mgr. Iowa Nite Hawks AAA Pro Football Club, 1974-78; founder, dir. Am. Pro Football Tour of Europe, 1977, 79; promotion mgr. NFL Properties, Inc., NYC, 1979-82; asst. gen. mgr. Ariz. Wranglers Pro Football Club, 1982-83; exec. v.p. Chgo. Blitz Pro Football Club, 1983-84; v.p. mktg. Chgo. Sting Indoor Soccer Promotions-Burke Promo Mktg. Inc., 1984—85; founder Arena Football, Chgo., 1985—92, commr., 1985-92, spl. cons., 1992-94; founder, mng. owner, bd. dirs. Iowa Barnstormers Arena Football, Des Moines, 1994—; founder, mng. owner Quad City Steamwheelers Arena Football, Davenport, Iowa, 1999—2006; spl. projects cons. af2, 2006—. Co-founder, bd. dirs. Arena Football 2 League. Mem. Davenport (Iowa) One Chamber; active YMCA. Recipient Golden Helmet Excellence award NFL Properties, Inc., 1981-82; named Minor Pro Football Exec. of Yr., Pro Football Weekly, 1976, No. States League Gen. Mgr. of Yr., AAA Football, 1976, Exec. of Yr., Arena Football League, 1995-96; named to Minor Pro Football Hall of Fame, 1982, one of Inaugural Class, Arena Football Hall of Fame, 1998. Mem. Iowa State Hist. Soc., Antique and Classic Boat Soc., Boat Owners Assn. U.S., U. Iowa Alumni Assn. (pres.'s club), Aircraft Owners and Pilots Assn., Nat. Iowa Varsity Lettermans Club, Iowa Assn. R.R. Passengers, Sons and Daughters Pioneer Riverman, U. Iowa Champions Ath. Club. Methodist. Achievements include patents for arena football game system. Home and Office: 901 Mississippi Ave Davenport IA 52803-3936

FOSTER, JAMES HENRY, advertising and public relations executive; b. Kansas City, Mo., May 14, 1933; s. Wendell F. and Lillian M. (East) F. BA, Drake U., 1955, postgrad., 1957. Reporter, editor Des Moines Register, 1951-61; pub. rels. and advt. exec. J. Walter Thompson Co., NYC, 1961-73, 79-99, v.p., 1970-73; sr. v.p., gen. mgr. Brouillard Comm. divsn., NYC, 1979-81, exec. v.p., gen. mgr., 1981-84, pres., CEO, 1984-94; chmn., CEO Brouillard Comm., 1994-97, chmn., 1997-99, chmn. emeritus, 1999—2003; v.p. pub. affairs Western Union Corp., Upper Saddle River, 1973-79; pres. Reputation Mgmt. Strategies, Durango, Colo., 1999—; bd. dirs. Music in the Mountains, Inc., Durango, 1999—, pres., 2000—03. Bd. dirs. Fort Lewis Coll. Found., 1999—, sec., 2005-06, v.p., 2006. Mem. Union League Club (N.Y.C.), Petroleum Club, Glacier Club. Presbyterian. Office: Reputation Mgmt Strategies 1472 E Third Ave Durango CO 81301-5244

FOSTER, JAMES J(OHN), lawyer; b. Pitts., Oct. 27, 1945; BSEE, MIT, 1967; JD, Harvard U., 1970. Bar: NY 1971, US Dist. Ct. (so. and ea. dists.) NY 1972, US Ct. Appeals (2d cir.) 1972, US Ct. Appeals (8th cir.) 1984, US Dist. Ct. (no. dist.) NY 1985, US Dist. Ct. (no. dist.) Calif. 1988, Mass. 1989, US Dist. Ct. Mass. 1989, US Ct. Appeals (fed. cir.) 1989, US Ct. Appeals (4th cir.) 1991, US Dist. Ct. (no. dist.) Ill. 1992, US Dist. Ct. (no. dist.) Miss. 1992, US Dist. Ct. (we. dist.) Wis. 1993, US Dist. Ct. (ea. dist.) Tex. 1993, US Ct. Appeals (1st cir.), 1994, US Dist. Ct., Mont. 1995, US Patent and Trademark Office. Of counsel Davis, Hoxie, Faithfull & Hapgood, NYC, 1983-87; ptnr. Wolf, Greenfield & Sacks, P.C., Boston, 1987, shareholder. Contbr. articles to profl. jour. Named one of Mass. Super Lawyers, Boston mag., The Best Lawyers in Am., 2007. Mem.: ABA (fed. practice, procedure com., intellectual property law sect.), Fed. Cir. Bar Assn., Boston Patent Law Assn. (litig. com.). Office: Wolf Greenfield & Sacks PC 600 Atlantic Ave Boston MA 02210-2211 Office Phone: 617-646-8225, 617-646-8000. Office Fax: 617-646-8646. Business E-Mail: jfoster@wolfgreenfield.com.

FOSTER, JAMES REUBEN, travel company executive; b. Chgo., May 28, 1930; s. Reuben Aaron and Marion (Philipson) F.; m. Claire Lynn Block, Aug. 16, 1953; children: Kim Petracca, Craig James, Kyle Foster Weinstein. BA, Trinity Coll., 1952; JD, Yale U., 1955. Bar: Ill. 1955, U.S. Ct. Claims 1955, U.S. Ct. Mil. Appeals 1956, U.S. Ct. Customs and Patent Appeals, 1956. Trial atty. U.S. Dept. of Justice, Washington, 1955—57; v.p. L.B. Foster Co., Pitts., 1957—82; pres. Fosco Fabricators, Chgo., 1961—64; v.p., sec. Foster Industries, Inc., Pitts., Pa., 1977—97; gen. ptnr. Real Estate Partnerships, 1975—93; v.p., sec. Fostin Securities, Inc., 1978—; pres., 1994—98; chmn. bd., chief exec. officer Travel Profls. Inc., 1984—; v.p. Foster Holdings Co., Pitts., 1998—2000; also bd. dirs. Fostin Mgmt. Co., Chgo. Sec. United Comms. Sys. Inc., Chgo., 1993—; bd. dirs. Foster Industries, Inc., Pitts., Fostin Capital Co., Pitts., L.B. Foster Co., Pitts., Travel Profls., Inc., Chgo., Pelouze Scale, Evanston, Ill., 1990-94, United Comm. Sys., Inc., Chgo., Fostin Securities, Inc., Fostin Mgmt. Inc.; chmn., pres. Foster Charitable Trust. Pres. Temple Jeremiah, Northfield, Ill., 1980-83; chmn. com. Chgo. Assn. Commerce and Industry, 1971-73; trustee, chmn. com. Lakeland Health Svcs./Highland Park Hosp., 1978-84, life trustee, 1985—; vice chmn., committeeman Lake County Reps. Ctrl. Com., Ill., 1964-74; bd. dirs., sec., treas. Groveland Health Svcs., Highland Park, 1982-90, sec., 1987-90; v.p. Am. Jewish Com., 1990-96, nat. coun., 1996—, exec. bd. Chgo. chpt. 1981—; mem., chmn., exec. bd. Am. Assocs. Ben Gurion U. of the Negev, 1991-95,2002; treas. collectors forum Mus. of Contemporary Art, Chgo., 1994-97. Mem. ABA, Am. Inst. Mgmt. (pres. coun.), Std. Club (bd. dirs. 1985-92), Northmoor Country Club. Republican. Jewish. Avocations: art collector, travel, golf, photography. Office: Travel Profls Inc 500 W Madison Ave Ste 411 Chicago IL 60611-4544 Office Phone: 312-681-2500 x23. Business E-Mail: jfoster@travpros.net.

FOSTER, JIM (JAMES S. FOSTER), women's college basketball coach; Grad., Temple U., 1980. Head coach St. Joseph's U., Pa., 1978—91, Vanderbilt U., 1991—2002, Ohio State U., 2002—. Head coach Jr. Nat. Team, 1991, USA Jr. World Championship Team, 1993, World U. Games, Marsala, Italy, 1997, USA Basketball World Championship For Young Women Team, 2003; interim athletics dir. Vanderbilt U., 1995—96; mem. NCAA Women's Basketball Rules Com., 2003—. Named Coach of Yr., NCAA, 1985, US Basketball Writers Assn., 1993, Devel. Coach of Yr., USA Basketball, 2003, Ohio Women's Coll. Basketball Coach of Yr., Columbus Dispatch, 2003, Ohio Collegiate Coach of Yr., 2005. Mem.: Women's Basketball Coaches Assn. (pres. 1992). Office: Ohio State U Womens Basketball 1080 Jerome Schottenstein Ctr 555 Borror Dr Columbus OH 43210 Office Phone: 614-292-5222. E-mail: foster.384@osu.edu.*

FOSTER, JOE C., JR., lawyer; b. Lansing, Mich., Feb. 5, 1925; s. Joe C. and Grace E. (McComb) F.; m. Janet C. Shanks, July 6, 1946; children: Cathy Foster Young, Susan Foster Ambrose, Thomas, John, Amy Foster Trenz. Student, Wabash Coll., Ind., 1943—44; JD, U. Mich., 1949. Bar: Mich. 1949, Fla. 1986. Assoc. Fraser, Trebilcock, Davis & Foster, and predecessors, Lansing, 1949-53, ptnr. and shareholder, 1954-2000; shareholder, sr. counsel Foster Zack Little Pasteur & Manning, P.C., Okemos, Mich., 2001—. Co-author: Independent Probate Administration, 1980, 3d edit., 1995, Informal Estat Procs. in Mich., 2000, supplements, 2002, 03. Trustee, sec. Renaud Found., Lansing, 1960-87; bd. dirs., sec. Abrams Found., Lansing, 1960—; bd. dirs., officer ACTEC Found., L.A., 1983-87, 98-2004; trustee Jr. League Endowment Found., Lansing, 1984-90; trustee, chmn. Sparrow Hosp., Lansing, 1970-84; trustee, pres. Okemos Bd. Edn., 1962-66; bd. dirs., pres. county unit Am. Cancer Soc., 1950-60; bd. dirs., pres. Cmty. Nursing Bur., Lansing, 1956-57. Lt. USNR, 1943-46, PTO. Fellow Am. Coll. Trust and Estate Counsel (pres. 1985-86), Am. Coll. Tax Counsel, Am. Bar Found., Mich. Bar Found.; mem. ABA, Fla. Bar Assn., Mich. Bar Assn. (chmn. probate and estate planning sect. 1977-78), Internat. Acad. Estate and Trust Law (exec. coun. 1990-94), Rotary (bd. dirs. Lansing 1968-70), Phi Beta Kappa, Phi Gamma Delta. Avocations: sailing, running, tennis. Office: Foster Zack Little Pasteur & Manning PC PO Box 27337 Lansing MI 48909-7337 Business E-Mail: joe.foster@fosterzack.com. *Honesty and kindness are two of our best precepts. They also are good business.*

FOSTER, JOHN HORACE, consulting environmental engineer; b. Quincy, Mass., June 2, 1927; s. Horace Herbert and Alice Gertrude (Hatch) F.; m. Claire Alice Sabean, Aug. 31, 1952; children— Janet, Mark, David. BS, Tufts U., 1952; MS, Harvard U., 1953. Engr. Malcolm Pirnie Engrs., White Plains, NY, 1953-63; partner Malcolm Pirnie, Inc., 1963-70, pres., 1970-88, chmn. bd. dirs., 1988-95; chmn. emeritus, 1997—. Contbr. articles to profl. jours. Served with USN, 1945-47. Recipient Distinguished Service award Dept. Civil Engring. Tufts U., 1977 Mem. ASCE, Water Environment Fedn., Am. Water Works Assn., Am. Cons. Engrs. Coun. (v.p. 1989-91, pres. 1992-93), N.Y. Assn. Cons. Engrs. (v.p. 1987-92, Engr. of Yr. 1995). Clubs: Cedar Point Yacht (commodore 1975-76). Home: 53 Farrell Rd Weston CT 06883-2306 Office: Malcolm Pirnie Inc PO Box 751 104 Corporate Park Dr White Plains NY 10604-3335

FOSTER, JOHN STUART, JR., physicist, former defense industry executive; b. New Haven, Sept. 18, 1922; s. John Stuart and Flora (Curtis) F.; m. Frances Schnell, Dec. 28, 1978; children: Susan, Bruce, Scott, John. BS, McGill U., 1948; PhD in Physics, U. Calif., Berkeley, 1952; DSc (hon.), U. Mon., 1979. Dir. Lawrence Livermore (Calif.) Lab., 1952-65; dir. def. rsch. and engring. Dept. Def., Washington, 1965-73; v.p. TRW Energy Systems Group, Redondo Beach, Calif., 1973-79; v.p. sci. and tech. TRW Inc., Cleve., 1979-88, also bd. dirs. Chmn. Def. Sci. Bd., 1989-93; chmn. GKN Aerospace Transparency Sys.; ptnr. Tech. Strategies & Alliances. Decorated knight comdr.'s cross, badge and star Order of Merit (Germany); comdr. Legion of Honor (France); recipient Ernst Orlando Lawrence Meml. award AEC, 1960, Disting. Pub. Svc. medal Dept. Def., 1969, 73, 93, Crowell medal, 1972, Enrico Fermi Award, U.S. Dept. of Energy, 1992, Eugene Fubini award, U.S. Dept. Def., 1998. Mem. NAE (Founders award 1989), AIAA, Am. Def. Preparedness Assn., Nat. Security Indsl. Assn. Office: Northrop Grumman 1 Space Park Bldg E1-5010 Redondo Beach CA 90278-1071

FOSTER, JOHN WITHERSPOON, lawyer; b. Columbia, SC, Nov. 6, 1948; s. Charles Cantzon and Isabel (Witherspoon) F.; m. Vesta Anne Haselden, Nov. 5, 1977; children: Vesta Murray, Isabel Witherspoon. BA, Davidson Coll., 1970; BA, MA 1st honours, Oxford U., Eng., 1972; JD cum laude, Harvard U., 1976. Bar: NY 1978, SC 1977, 4th cir. Jud. Conf., 1983. Analyst econ. Govt. Research Group, Washington, 1972-73; assoc. Sullivan & Cromwell, NYC, 1976-79; from assoc. to ptnr. Boyd, Knowlton, Tate & Finlay, Columbia, 1979-83; ptnr. McNair Law Firm, P.A., Columbia, 1983—, Kilpatrick Stockton LLP, Atlanta. Bd. dirs., mem. exec. com. Foster-Dixiana Corp., Columbia, 1979—; chmn. S.C. Tax Bd. Rev., Columbia, 1981-88; pres. Palmetto Seed Capital Corp. 1st lt. U.S. Army, 1972-73. Mem. ABA, Nat. Assn. Bond Lawyers. Office: Kilpatrick Stockton LLP 1100 Peachtree St Ste 2800 Atlanta GA 30309 Office Phone: 404-815-6322. Office Fax: 404-815-6555. Business E-Mail: jfoster@kilpatrickstockton.com.

FOSTER, JUDI, interior designer, artist; d. Harold Gordon and Edith Mae (Stevens) Miller; m. Peter H. Foster, Aug. 8, 1959 (dec. Nov. 20, 2004); children: Juliet Elise, Christel Elise. BSc cum laude, U. Conn., 1959; student in Art, U. N.Mex., 1960. Buyer Federated Dept. Stores, Albuquerque, 1960—65; tchr. home econs. So. Union Gas Co. Schs., Albuquerque, 1965—70; with inventory control Comml. Warehouse, Albuquerque, 1970—75; sales Amana/Quasar, Albuquerque, 1975—80; prin. owner Pinon Tree Gallery, Albuquerque, 1975—80; interior decorator pvt. practice, Albuquerque, 1980—; exec. asst. Dyncorp., Albuquerque, 1980—90; owner Nob Hill Art Gallery, N.Mex. The Art of Layering, 2004, Making Connections, 2004, New Mexico Women in Business Directory, 25th Anniversary Edition, 2006. Mem.: Nat. Soc. Layerists Multimedia (mem. planning com. for nat. convention), Nat. Watercolor Soc., Am. Watercolor Soc., MasterWorks of N.Mex. (steering com. 2002—), Soc. Layerists Multimedia, N.Mex. Watercolor Soc. (mem. exhbn. com., MasterWorks rep.), Taos Nat. Watercolor Soc. (hon.; exhibitor). Avocations: jazzercise, travel, painting, historic restoration. Home and Office: 28 Juniper Hill Ct NE Albuquerque NM 87122 Office Phone: 505-249-7167. Personal E-mail: judistudio@aol.com.

FOSTER, JUDITH CHRISTINE, lawyer, writer; b. Columbus, Ohio, Nov. 25, 1952; d. Paul Marvel and Jean Harper (Uhland) F.; m. Sabah Amin Wali, Dec. 28, 1973; children: Samed Michel, Russeen Paul. BS in Natural Sci. and BA in Linguistics, Pa. State U., University Park, 1973; JD, Coll. William and Mary, Williamsburg, Va., 1979. Bar: Va. 1979, U.S. Ct. Appeals (4th cir.) 1979, U.S. Ct. Appeals (9th cir.) 1996, U.S. Supreme Ct. 1984. Pvt. practice, Fairfax, Va., 1980-90, Encino, Calif., 1992—2002, Glendale, Calif., 2002—. Mem. Am. Immigration Lawyers Assn. (legis. com. 1985, D.C. chpt. 1980-90, L.A. chpt. 1992—). Business E-Mail: jfoster_attorney_at_law@yahoo.com.

FOSTER, KEN, writer, educator; b. Williamsport, Pa., Sept. 2, 1964; s. William Hepler and Gladys Marbeth Foster. BA, Lock Haven U., 1987; MEd, Northeastern U., 1989; MFA, Columbia U., 1996. Lit. curator The Drawing Ctr., NYC; curator KGB Bar Lit. Readings, NYC, 1994—98; instr. The New Sch. U., NYC; vis. instr. Fla. State U., Tallahassee, 2002—04; vis. asst. prof. Tulane U., New Orleans, 2006—. Author: The Kind I'm Likely to Get (NY Times Notable Book, 1999), The Dog Who Found Me, 2006; editor: (anthology) Dog Culture: Writers on the Character of Canines, (literary anthology) The KGB Bar Reader; contbr. book revs. to NY Times, San Francisco Chronicle, others. Fellow, Yaddo, 1996, NY Found. Arts, 2000. Mem.: Nat. Book Critics Cir., Authors Guild. D-Liberal. Personal E-mail: kenrfoster@gmail.com.

FOSTER, KENNARD P., magistrate judge; b. 1944; Student, Purdue U., 1962-64; BS, Ball State U., 1966; JD, Ind. U., 1970. Bar: Ind. Spl. agt. FBI, 1970-71; atty. Jones, Foster & Loveall, 1971-76; asst. U.S. Atty., 1976-86; magistrate judge U.S. Dist. Ct. (so. dist.) Ind., Indpls., 1985—2002, recalled magistrate judge, 2002—. Mem. Fed. Bar Assn., Johnson County Bar Assn., Fed. Magistrate Judges Assn. Office: Birch Bayh Fed Bldg and US Courthouse Ste 255 Indianapolis IN 46204-1903 Office Phone: 317-229-3620.

FOSTER, KENT B., information technology executive; b. 1944; BS in Elec. Engring., NC State U.; MS in Mgmt., U. SC. Bd. dirs. GTE Corp., Irving, Calif., 1992—99, vice chmn. bd., 1993—99, pres., 1995—99; chmn., pres., CEO Ingram Micro Inc., Santa Ana, Calif., 2000—05, non-exec. chmn., 2005—. Bd. dir. Campbell Soup Co., J.C. Penney Co., NY Life Ins. Co. Bd. mem. Dallas Opera, Dallas Symphony. Capt. USAF, 1966—70. Named Forbes' America's Most Powerful People. Office: Ingram Micro Inc 1600 E St Andrew Pl Santa Ana CA 92705-4931 Office Phone: 714-566-1000. Office Fax: 714-566-7900.*

FOSTER, LAWRENCE G., orthopedist, surgeon; BA, Cornell U., 1984; MD, Columbia U., 1988. Cert. Am. Bd. Orthopaedic Surgery, 1996. Intern NYU Med. Ctr., NYC, 1988—89; resident Hosp. for Joint Diseases, NYC, 1989—96; fellowship hand and upper extremity surgery Allegheny Gen. Hosp., Pitts., 1993—94; orthop. surgeon Somers Orthop. Surgery & Sports Medicine Group, PC, Carmel, NY. Clin. asst. prof. Dept. Orthop. Surgery, NYU Med. Ctr.; lectr. in field. Author: Dr. Divot's Guide to Golf Injuries, 2004; numerous TV and radio appearances. Fellow: Am. Acad. Orthop. Surgeons; mem.: AMA. Office: Somers Orthopedic Surgery & Sports Medicine Group 664 Stoneleigh Ave Carmel NY 10512 Office Phone: 845-278-8400.*

FOSTER, LESTER ANDERSON, JR., metal products executive; b. Apr. 4, 1929; s. Lester Anderson and Annie Lee (Swink) F.; m. Patricia White, July 9, 1955; children: Leslie Ann, Caroline Suzann, Lester Anderson, Samuel Timothy. Student, Elon Coll., 1947-50; BS, N.C. State U., 1952. With Bethlehem Steel Corp., Sparrows Point, Md., 1952-94, engr., 1956-57, med. foreman, 1957-59, asst. gen. foreman, 1959-61, asst. master mechanic, 1961-67, master mechanic, 1967-92; pres. L&M Cons. Steel Plant Facilities, Inc., 1992—. Pres. PTA, Sparrows Point, 1963—65; mem. exec. bd. nominating com. Balt. County Sch. Bd., 1964—65; dist. field svc. chmn. Boy Scouts Am., Balt., 1972—78, bicentennial show program chmn., 1976, dist. commr., 1979—83, dist. chmn., 1983—; pres. 7th Dist. Rep. Club, 1969—72; mem. Md. Rep. State Ctrl. Com., 1980—90. With US Army, 1952—54, col. Md. Def. Force, 1995—. Recipient Silver Beaver award Boy Scouts Am., 1975, award of Merit, 1984. Mem. SAR (pres. Md. Soc. 1993, v.p. gen. Mid-Atlantic, Silver Good Citizenship medal, Meritorious medal, Patriot meda, Minuteman medal 1999), Am. Inst. Iron and Steel Engrs., Soc. Mfg. Engrs., Am. Mgmt. Assn., Soc. Advancement Mgmt., Nat. Football Found. and Hall of Fame, Sparrows Point Country Club, Sparrows Point Engrs. Clubs, Masons, Shriners, K.T. (Grand Comdr.). Lutheran. Home: 3006 Dunmore Rd Baltimore MD 21222-5131 Home Phone: 410-282-0758; Office Phone: 410-282-0758. Personal E-mail: lespatfoster@erols.com.

FOSTER, LINDA TIMBERLAKE, state legislator; b. Portland, Maine, Feb. 8, 1943; m. Bernard Scott; 3 children. BS, U. Maine, 1965. Mem. from Hillsborough Dist. 4 N.H. State Ho. of Reps., 1992—, dep. spkr. Bd. dirs. Family Strength; com. on fin. and rules Dem. Party. Mem. N.H. Assn. Residential Care Homes (adv. bd.), So. N.H. Svcs. (exec. bd.), Phi Kappa Phi. Office: NH Ho of Reps Dep Spkr State Capitol Concord NH 03301

FOSTER, MARK D., information technology executive; Ind. cons., comm. industry svcs. Lockheed Martin, 1994—99; sr. v.p., chief tech. officer Neustar Inc., Sterling, Va., 1999—. Named one of Top 25 Chief Tech. Officers, InfoWorld mag., 2006, Top 100 Voices of IP Comm., Internet Telephony mag., 2006. Office: Neustar Inc 46000 Center Oak Plz Sterling VA 20166 Office Phone: 571-434-5400. Business E-Mail: mark.foster@neustar.biz.*

FOSTER, MARK EDWARD, lawyer, consultant, international lobbyist; b. Detroit, May 12, 1948; s. Herbert Edward and Joyce Mary (Campbell) F.; m. Miyoko Katabami, Apr. 20, 1974; children: Lorissa Chieko. BA, Alma Coll., 1970; MA, U. Calif., Berkeley, 1972; JD, U. Calif., Hastings, 1981; postgrad., Stanford Ctr., Tokyo, 1983. Japanese lang. cert., 1982; bar: Calif. 1981, Oreg. 1989. Law clk. U.S. Dist. Ct., San Francisco, 1980-81; atty. Hetland & Hansen, Berkeley, 1981-82, Braun Moriya Hoashi, Tokyo, 1982-84; spl. counsel U.S. Embassy, Tokyo, 1984-85; Japan counsel U.S. Electronic Industries Assn., 1985-86; mng. ptnr. Law Offices Mark E. Foster, Portland, Tokyo, 1988—2002; v.p., gen. counsel Natus Med. Inc., San Carlos, Calif., 2002—. Lectr., cons. on internat. law and tech. stds., tech. transfer, product compliance, energing. Internat. Stds. Orgn., Geneva, Ministry of Internat. Trade and Industry of Japan, U.S. Dept. Commerce, U. So. Calif., World Trade Inst.; mem. tech. stds. com. for Optoelectronics, Japanese Ministry of Posts and Telecom., 1984-86, tech. stds. com. for Intelligent Office Systems, Japanese Patent Office, Japanese Ministry of Internat. Trade and Industry, 1984-86. Author articles, books in internat. law and tech. Trustee U. Calif. Hastings Law Sch. 1066 Found. Grantee Rockefeller Found. Presbyn. Ch., Geneva and Tokyo, 1972-74; sr. fellow Conf. of World Regions. Mem. ABA, Am. Soc. Quality Control, Internat. Bar Assn., Calif. Bar Assn., Oreg. Bar Assn., Am. C. of C. in Japan, World Affairs Coun. Presbyterian. Office: Natus Med 1501 Industrial Rd San Carlos CA 94070 E-mail: mfoster@markfoster.com.

FOSTER, MARK STEPHEN, lawyer; b. Edgerton, Mo., Feb. 6, 1948; s. George Elliott and Annabel Lee (Bradshaw) F.; m. Camille Pepper, June 27, 1970; children: Natalie Ashley, Stephanie Ann. BS, U. Mo., 1970; JD, Duke U., 1973. Bar: Mo. 1973, U.S. Ct. Mil. Appeals 1974, Hawaii 1975, U.S. Dist. Ct. Hawaii 1975, U.S. Dist. Ct. (we. dist.) Mo. 1977, U.S. Ct. Appeals (8th cir.) 1986, U.S. Supreme Ct. 1994. Assoc. Stinson, Mag & Fizzell, Kansas City, 1977-80, ptnr., 1980—2002, mng. ptnr., 1987-90, chmn. bd. dirs., 1998—2002; ptnr. Stinson Morrison Hecker LLP, Kansas City, 2002—, mng. ptnr., 2002—. Arbitration panelist Nat. Assn. Securities Dealers, N.Y.C., 1985—, Pvt. Adjudication Found., Durham, N.C., 1988-2000. Active Citizens Assn., Kansas City, 1982-92; pres. Spelman Med. Found., Smithville, Mo., 1984-88; bd. dirs. Alzheimers Assn. Metro. Kansas City, 1997—2004, 1st v.p., 1998, pres., 1999; mem. bd. visitors Park U., 2005—; bd. mem. Legal Aid Western Mo., 2007-, Kans. City Area Devel. Coun., 2007-. Lt. comdr. USNR, ret. Named Mo. Super Lawyer, 2005, 2006; named to Best Lawyers in Am., 2006. Mem. ABA, CCSA Kansas City (bd. dir. 2001—05), Hawaii Bar Assn., Mo. Bar Assn., Kansas City Met. Bar Assn., Am. Arbitration Assn. (panelist 1990—, large complex case adv. com. 1993—), Lawyers Edn. Assistance Program (bd. dirs. 2000—, sec. 2004-06), Carriage Club (bd. dir. 2000-04, 2d v.p. 2001, 1st v.p. 2002, pres. 2003), United Wat Alexis de Tocqueville Soc., U. Mo. Davenport Soc., Masons. Home: 1035 W 65th St Kansas City MO 64113-1813 Office: Stinson Morrison Hecker LLP PO Box 419251 1201 Walnut St Ste 2800 Kansas City MO 64106-2117 Office Phone: 816-842-8600. Business E-Mail: mfoster@stinson.com.

FOSTER, MARTHA TYAHLA, pre-school administrator; b. Coaldale, Pa., Apr. 22, 1955; d. Stephen and Frances (Solomon) Tyahla; m. David Marion Foster, Jan. 3, 1981. BA with distinction, U. Va., 1977, MEd, EdS, U. Va., 1981. Legis. asst. US Ho. of Reps., Washington, 1977-79; asst. dean summer session U. Va., Charlottesville, 1981; program cons. campus activities U. Houston, 1981; coord. student affairs Capitol Inst. Tech., Kensington, Md., 1982-83, asst. dean students Laurel, Md., 1983-84, assoc. dean students, 1984-86, dean students, 1986-87; dir. Resurrection Luth. Presch., 1997—. Bd. dirs. Curry Sch. Edn. Found. U. Va., 1987-90. Mem. Arlington County Commn. on Status of Women, 1985—88; coun. mem.-at-large Arlington United Way, 1995—98; pres. PTA Arlington Traditional Sch., 1997—98, treas., 1994—95; troop leader Girl Scouts, 1999—; chair advancement Boy Scouts Am., 2001—; bd. dirs., exec. com. Arlington Arts Coun., 2005—; chmn. Christian edn. Christ Meth. Ch., 1994—97. Named Woman of Yr., Bus. and Profl. Women's Club, Vienna, Va., 1986. Mem. Order Eastern Star (worthy matron 1988-89, trustee 1993-96). Methodist.

FOSTER, MARY CHRISTINE, film producer, writer; b. LA, Mar. 19, 1943; d. Ernest Albert and Mary Ada (Quilici) Foster; m. Paul Hunter, July 24, 1982. BA, Immaculate Heart Coll., LA, 1967; M in TV News Documentary, UCLA, 1968. Dir. R & D Metromedia Producers Corp., LA, 1968-71; dir. devel. and prodn. svcs. Wolper Prodns., LA, 1971-76; mgr. film programs NBC-TV, Burbank, Calif., 1976-77; v.p. movies and mini series Columbia Pictures TV, Burbank, 1977-81, v.p. series programs, 1981; v.p. program devel. Group W. Prodns., LA, 1981-87; agt. The Agency, LA, 1988-90, Shapiro-Lichtman Agy., LA, 1990-99; ind. prodr., 1999—. Lectr. in field. Creator (TV series) Sullivan, 1985, Auntie Mom, 1986; author: Immaculate Heart High School: Memories of 100 Years 1906-2006, 2005. Trustee Immaculate Heart H.S., LA, 1980—; exec. com. Humanitas awards Human Family Inst., 1985—; cmty. devel. com. Immaculate Heart Cmty., 2001—; exec. com. LA Roman Cath. Archdiocesan Comm. Commn., 1986—90; bd. dirs., treas. Catholics in Media, 1992—2004; vol. com., writer tour script, vis. book, newsletter and website Cathedral of Our Lady of Angels, 2002—; chmn. pastorial coun. St. Francis of Assisi, 2003—05, chmn. stewardship com. and renovation com. Democrat. Personal E-mail: fosterc@aol.com. *Fidelity to God's will yields life's greatest satisfaction. Love of family and community gives life fulfillment.*

FOSTER, MICHAEL KIRK, anthropologist, linguist; b. Athens, Greece, June 2, 1938; s. Andrew Brisbin and Barbara (Kirk) F.; m. Doris Elizabeth Wilkinson, Sept. 7, 1974 (dec. Nov. 23, 2005); 1 child, Andrew Erskine. BA, Lawrence Coll., 1961; MAT, Harvard U., 1962; PhD, U. Pa., 1974. Instr. Ursinus Coll., Collegeville, Pa., 1964-66; ethnologist, curator Can. Mus. Civilization, Ottawa, Ont., Can., 1970-89; sessional lectr. Carleton U., Ottawa, 1975, 93; curator emeritus Can. Mus. Civilization, Ottawa, 1989—. Editor, co-editor 6 books; contbr. numerous articles on Iroquoian langs. and cultures to scholarly jours. and books. Grantee NSF, 1970-71, NEH, 1982-85, Am. Philos. Soc., 1990, 92, 97. Fellow Am. Anthrop. Assn.; mem. Can. Ethnology Soc., Soc. for Study of Indigenous Langs. of the Ams., Soc. for Linguistic Anthropology, Current Anthropology (assoc.). Home: 746 Pattrell Rd Norwich VT 05055-9479

FOSTER, MICHAEL T., architect; b. Portsmouth, Va., Apr. 19, 1962; s. Donald Patrick and Barbara Anne (Groce) F.; m. Vicki Scheer, Sept. 9, 1989; children: Alexandra, Jessica. BArch, Va. Poly. Inst. and State U., 1985. Registered arch. Nat. Coun. Archtl. Registration Bds.; lic. in Va., DC, Md. Intern, draftsman Design 3, Inc., Virginia Beach, Va., 1982; intern Williams & Tazewell, Norfolk, Va., 1983; architect HOK, Washington, 1983-84; owner, sr. asst. Cooper-Levky Archs., Washington, 1985-94; owner, prin. MTFA Architecture, Inc., Arlington, Va., 1989—. Mem. adv. bd. George Mason Bank, Va., 1996. Mem. Site Plan Rev., Arlington, 1996. Fellow AIA (Merit award 1992); mem. Interfaith Forum of Religious Art and Architecture (Honor award 1994), Toastmasters (pres. 1995). Avocations: sailing, tennis, golf, photography. Office: MTFA Architecture Inc 2311 Wilson Blvd Arlington VA 22201-3307 Office Phone: 703-524-6616. Office Fax: 703-524-6618.*

FOSTER, MILO GEORGE, manufacturing executive; b. San Diego, Aug. 2, 1957; s. Milo Hughes and Kathryn G. (Sevastos) F.; m. Barbara A. Vandenberg, Mar. 25, 1988; children: Kathleen Elaine, Anthony Hughes. BS, U. Mo., Rolla, 1979; MBA, Harvard U., 1983. Prodn. team mgr. Procter & Gamble, Cape Girardeau, Mo., 1979—81; various mfg. roles Kimberly-Clark Corp., 1983—86, feminine care plant mgr. Neenah, 1987-89, dir. ops., feminine care, 1989-91, dir. feminine care expansion project, 1992-93; dir. World Support Group-Tissue, Neenah, 1993-94, v.p. ops. and engring. family care Kimberly-Clark Europe, 1994—99, gen. mgr. family care Australia, 2000—05; v.p. Family Care, South Asia, 2006—. Avocations: skiing, cooking, singing, triathlons. Office: Kimberly-Clark 52 Alfred St Milsons Point NSW Australia Office Phone: 61-2-9963-8980. Business E-Mail: mfoster@kcc.com.

FOSTER, NANCY HASTON, columnist, writer; b. Austin, Tex., June 07; d. Arch B. and Verlea Haston; m. Joe D. Foster Jr. (div.). BJ, U. Tex., BA in Sociology. Writer, pub. rels. dept. Trinity U., San Antonio, Tex.; social worker pub. welfare dept. State of La., Lafayette; instr. sociology U. Tex., Austin; columnist San Antonio Light, 1982-83, San Antonio Express-News, 1989-90; freelance writer, 1977—. Author: San Antonio, A Texas Monthly Guidebook, 1983, rev. edit., 1989, 94, 98, San Antonio, Lone Star Guide, 1999, 2000, The Alamo and Other Texas Missions to Remember, 1984, Texas Missions, A Texas Monthly Guidebook, 1995, Texas Missions, Lone Star Guide, 1999; contbg. editor, writer: Texas, Fodor's Travel Guides, 1985, rev. edit., 1991, Fodor's American Cities, 1986, rev. edit., 1988, Texas, A Texas Monthly Guidebook, 1993, 98; contbr. articles to popular mags. Mem. Women in Comm., Phi Beta Kappa. Avocations: conversation, photography, collectibles. Home and Office: 201 Prinz Dr San Antonio TX 78213-1921

FOSTER, PATRICK R., historian, writer; b. Burlington, Vt., July 25, 1953; s. Wilfred C. and Liane Foster; m. Diane M. Powichrowski, Apr. 26, 1980; 1 child, Caitlin L. Columnist Hemmings Classic Car, Old Cars Weekly; feature writer Collectible Automobile, Hemmings Classic Car, Automobile Quarterly, Old Cars Weekly. Author: (history books) The Story of Jeep (Thomas McKean Cup for best hist. book, AACA, 1999), American Motors The Last Independent (Book of Distinction award, AACA, 1993), The Metropolitan Story (Bronze medal, Automotive Media Coun., 1997); contbr. articles to profl. jours., literature and photographs. Recipient Outstanding Book award, Antique Automobile Club Am., 1994, Bronze medal, Internat. Automobile Media Coun., 1996, Best Periodical Article of Yr. award, Soc. Automotive Historians, 1997, Thomas McKean Mem. Cup award, Antique Automobile Club Am., 1998, James J. Bradley Distinguished Svc. award, Soc. Automotive Historians, 2003. Mem.: Soc. Automotive Historians (dir., founder 1996—99, Best Periodical Article of Yr. award 1997). Avocations: antique automobiles, photography, literature, films, reading. Home: 108 Clark Hill Rd Milford CT 06460 Office: Olde Milford Press PO Box 5342 Milford CT 06460 Home Phone: 203-878-6672; Office Phone: 203-877-6717. Office Fax: 203-877-6717; Home Fax: 203-877-6717. Personal E-mail: oldemilfordpress@msn.com.

FOSTER, PAUL, playwright; b. Penn's Grove, NJ, Oct. 15, 1931; s. Elderidge M. and Mary (Manning) F. BA, Rutgers U., 1954; LLB, St. John's U., 1958. Pres. La Mama Theater Club, NYC, 1962—; tchr. drama dept. NYU and U. Calif.-San Diego, 1983. Author: The Birthday Party Stories, 1962, Hurrah for the Bridge, 1963, The Recluse, 1964, Balls, 1964, Madonna In the Orchard, 1965, The Hessian Corporal, 1966, Tom Paine, 1967, Heimskringla, 1969, Satyricon, 1970, Elizabeth I, 1971, Silver Queen Saloon, 1972, Marcus Brutus, 1973-74, Murderers' Row, 1976, A Kiss is Just a Kiss, 1983, (stage trilogy) The Dark and Mr. Stone, 1985-87, (TV) The Tragedy of the Commons, 1979, The Vampyre and Dr. Frankenstein, 1980, Silver Saloon, 1992, (film) Andrew Mellon and the National Gallery of Art, 1980, Cop and the Anthem, 1982, Smile, 1983, Cinderella Story, 1984, (stage play based on Dickens) A Tale of Two Cities, 1988, Kisses, Bites and Scratches, 1990, Elizabeth Eins, 1992, Make Believe Musical Book and Lyrics, 1993, Murder in the Hollyhocks, 1995; translator: (Horvath) Back & Forth, Faith, Hope, Charity, 1983, Fritz Lang's M for stage, 1997, Masquerade, 1999-2000; contbr. e-zine opera revs. to Arts4All.com, 2000; The Lives of Artists, 14 minimovies for Discovery-.com, 2004, 05, song lyrics for musical Kisses, Bites and Scratches, 2004-05; donated collection of theatrical lit. to Rutgers U. Libr. Served to lt. (j.g.) USNR, 1955-57. Recipient Play award Irish Univs., 1967, 71, N.Y. Drama Critics award, 1968, Tony award nomination, 1973; Rockefeller Found. fellow, 1967-68; Creative Artists Pub. Service grantee, 1972; Nat. Endowment Creative Writing fellow, 1973; Guggenheim fellow, 1974. Mem. Eugene O'Neill Meml. Theater Found., New Dramatists, Dramatists Guild, Player's Club, Societe des Auteurs. Home: 115 Saint Marks Pl Staten Island NY 10301-1600 E-mail: pfoster@virtualforum.com.

FOSTER, PAUL L., oil industry executive; BBA, Baylor Univ., 1979. CPA Ariz., 1986. Acctg. supr. So. Union Refining Co.; oil & gas cons. KPMG Peat Marwick; contr. Pride Refining Co.; gen. mgr. mktg. El Paso Refinery; v.p., gen. mgr. Border Refining Co., 1993—97; pres., CEO WRC Refining Co., 1997—2000, Western Refining Co., El Paso, Tex., 2000—. Bd. dir. Bank of the West. Chmn. El Paso Regional Econ. Develop. Corp., El Paso Am. Red Cross; mem. Tex. Higher Edn. Coord. Bd.; bd. mem. Am. Heart Assn. El Paso, Tex. Econ. Develop. Corp., El Paso Cmty. Found., Sun Bowl Assn.; chmn. Young Presidents Org.; cmty. govt. affairs com. El Paso Bus. Leadership Council; mem. exec. com. El Paso C. of C.; mem. bus. adv. council Univ. Tex., El Paso. Mem.: We. States Petroleum Assn., We. Petroleum Marketers Assn., Nat. Petroleum Refiners' Assn., Am. Inst. CPAs, Ariz. Soc. CPAs, Rep. Senatorial Inner Circle (life), El Paso Downtown Rotary Club. Office: Western Refining Co 6500 Trowbridge Dr El Paso TX 79905*

FOSTER, RICHARD S., urologist, educator; BA, Miami U., Oxford, Ohio, 1976; MD, Ind. U., Indpls., 1980. Prof. urology Ind. U., 1986—. Home: 535 Barnhill Dr Indianapolis IN 46202

FOSTER, ROBERT CARMICHAEL, banker; b. Toledo, Ohio, Apr. 1, 1941; s. Robert Albert and Kate (Thompson) F.; m. Phyllis Lorainne Schmidt, Nov. 25, 1974; children: Brian Clinton, Suzanne Pamela, Robert Carmichael Jr. AB, Colo. Coll., 1963; MBA, U. Chgo., 1965; AMP, Harvard U., 1982. Analyst, programmer McDonnell-Douglas Corp., St.Louis, 1965—67; systems cons. Bristol-Myers Co., NYC, 1967—70; comptroller Toledo Trust Co., 1970—73, sr. v.p., 1973—77, exec. v.p., 1977—87, also bd. dirs.; v.p. Trustcorp, Inc., 1975—86, exec. v.p., 1986—87; pres., dir. SeaGate Aviation Corp., Toledo, 1983—2000; pres., chief exec. officer West Mich. Nat. Bank & Trust, Frankfort, Mich., 1987—2006, bd. dirs., 1987—. Bd. dirs. Traverse Bay Econ. Devel. Corp., 1988—, exec. com. 1998—2005, treas. 2000-01, vice chmn. 2001—. Bd. dirs. Riverside Hosp., Toledo, 1978-85, Northcoast Health Sys., Inc., 1983-88, Lucas County Children Svcs., Toledo, 1981-85, Munson Healthcare Inc., 1990—, Traverse City, Mich.; trustee YMCA, Toledo, 1974-87; assoc. trustee Boys Club of Toledo, 1984-86, trustee, 1986-87; chmn. Lucas County U.s. Savs. Bond Program, Toledo, 1972-87; mem. planning commn. Crystal Lake Twp., 1988-97; sec.-treas. Paul Oliver Meml. Hosp., 1989-90, bd. dirs., pres., 1990-98; pres. Frankfort Indsl. Pk. Devel. Corp., 1989—; mem. Traverse Bay Cmty. Found., 1995-2000; chmn. Frankfort City-County Airport Authority, 1995—2006. Mem. Am. Inst. Banking, Bank Adminstrn. Inst., Toledo Area Govtl. Rsch. Assn. (pres., bd. dirs. 1974-79), Toledo C. of C. (aviation com.), Ottawa Skeet Club (treas.), Crystal Downs Country Club (treas. 1993-99), Rotary. Presbyterian. Avocations: flying, water and snow, hunting, tennis. Home: 70 Thomas Rd Frankfort MI 49635-9538

FOSTER, ROBERT FRANCIS, communications executive; b. Chgo., June 4, 1926; s. William John and Anna Alice (O'Farrell) F.; m. Mary D. Palella, May 4, 1963; children: Sean Terence, Nancy Marie, Patrick Daniel. Student, Cath. schs., Chgo. and Evanston, Ill. News and sports writer Sta. WGN, Chgo., 1943-55; with Chgo. Pub. Rels. Counselors, 1955-60, WGN Continental Broadcasting Co., Chgo., 1960-82, news bur. chief Springfield, Ill., 1961-63, Washington news bureau chief Washington, 1964-82; press sec. to Ill. Congressman Philip M. Crane, 1982-96; reporter and analyst at 10 nat. polit. convs. WGN-TV and WGN-Radio. Chgo. Stadium announcer Chgo. Blackhawks, 1955-64. Goalie 78th Divsn. ice hockey team, 1946. With AUS, 1944-46. Decorated Combat Inf. badge, Bronze Star. Recipient award best pub. service news Am. Coll. Radio Arts, Crafts and Scis., 1961. Mem. Radio-TV Corr. Assn. Washington (pres. 1976), Broadcast Pioneers, Radio TV News Dirs. Assn., Am. Legion, Chgo. Press Vets. Assn. Roman Catholic. Home: 5718 Marble Arch Way Alexandria VA 22315-4037

FOSTER, ROBERT G. (BOB FOSTER), mayor; b. Brooklyn, Jan. 1, 1947; BS in Pub. adminstrn., San Jose State University. Formerly with Calif. State Senate, Calif. Energy Commn.; with So. Calif. Edison, 1984—2006, v.p. pub. affairs, 1993—96, sr. v.p. pub. affairs, 1996—2001, sr. v.p. external affairs, 2001—02, Edison Internat., 2001—02; pres. So. Calif. Edison, 2002—06; mayor City of Long Beach, Calif., 2006—. Dep. dir. Calif. State Energy Resources Conservation Commn.; bd. dirs. Calif. Inst., Calif. Found. on the Environment and Economy, Long Beach Aquarium of the Pacific; trustee Calif. State Univ. Sys.; bd. dirs. Pub. Corp. for the Arts' CEO Leadership Bd.; mem. spkrs. com. on initiative reform Govs. Work Force Investment Bd.; mem. L.A. World Airports Bus. Coun. Trustee Calif. State U.; mem. Long Beach Public Library Found.; bd. mem. Long Beach Aquarium; adv. bd. mem. Long Beach Memorial Miller Children's Hosp. Office: 333 W Ocean Blvd Long Beach CA 90802*

FOSTER, ROGER SHERMAN, JR., surgeon, educator, health facility administrator; b. Washington, Jan. 8, 1936; s. Roger Sherman and Genevieve Wakeman (Bartlett) F.; m. Joan Crile, June 25, 1960 (dec. Feb. 2000); children: Roger Sherman III, Charles Bartlett, Elizabeth Crile, Halle

Crile Foster Moore; m. Baiba J. Grube, July 3, 2004. AB, Haverford Coll., 1957; MD, Case Western Res. U., 1961. Diplomate Am. Bd. Surgey, Nat. Bd. Med. Examiners; lic. Vt. Intern then resident in surgery Univ. Hosps., Cleve., 1961-66; research fellow Roswell Park Meml. Inst., Buffalo, 1966-68; asst. prof. surgery U. Vt., Burlington, 1970-73, assoc. prof. surgery, 1973-80, prof. surgery, 1980-92, dir. comprehensive cancer ctr., 1984-92; attending surgeon Med. Ctr. Hosp. of Vt., 1970-92; Wadley Glenn prof. surgery Emory U., Atlanta, 1992-99; chief surgical svcs. Crawford Long Hosp. of Emory U., 1992-99. Mem. cancer clin. investigation rev. com. NIH, 1987-92, chmn., 1991-92, chmn. various coms.; cons. Am. Internat. Health Alliance for Tblisi, Georgia Hosp., 1992-96. Assoc. editor: Clinical Surgery, 1987; co-editor: Essentials of Clinical Surgery, 1991; editor-in-chief: Breast Surgery: Index and Reviews, 1993-95; assoc. editor: Surgery: Problem-Solving Approach, 2d edit., 1995; co-editor: Q & A Review for Surgery, 1995; manuscript reviewer: Jour. AMA, Jour. Trauma, others; contbr. more than 100 articles to profl. jours. Trustee Univ. Health Ctr., Burlington, 1986-89, Vt. Ethics Network, 2001—06. Served to maj. U.S. Army, 1968-69. Grantee NIH, 1971-92; summer rsch. fellow Josiah Macy Jr, Found., 1958-59. Fellow ACS (bd. regents 1991-2000, bd. govs. 1981-87, adv. coun. for gen. surgery 1989-92, 95-2000, sec./treas. Vt. chpt. 1979-80, v.p. 1980-81, pres. 1981-82), Am. Surg. Assn.; mem. AMA, AAAS, New Eng. Surg. Soc. (treas. 1986-89, exec. com. 1981-92, 2001-03, pres. 2001-02), Soc. Univ. Surgeons, So. Surg. Assn., Southeastern Surg. Congress, Soc. Surg. Oncology, Ea. Surg. Soc. (pres. 1994), Am. Endocrine Surg. Soc. (coun. 1992-95), Am. Soc. Clin. Oncology (pub. rels. 1989-91 and pub. issues coms. 1989-94), Transplantation Soc., New Eng. Cancer Soc. (treas. 1983-87, v.p. 1988-89, pres. 1989-90), Assn. Acad. Surgery, Newfoundland Club Am. (bd. dirs. 1976-78, 1st v.p. 1979), Nat. Surg. Adjuvant Breast Project, 1971-92 (exec. com. 1978-81). Avocations: white water canoeing, breeding newfoundland dogs, wilderness travel, chamber music. Home: 395 Stevenson Rd New Haven CT 06515 E-mail: halirock@aol.com.

FOSTER, RON, agricultural products supplier and executive; BS in Agr. Bus., Calif. Poly-San Luis Obispo Coll., 1981. Gen. mgr. McHenry Ave plant Foster Farms, Modesto, Calif., 1981—96, gen. mgr. Kans. Ave plant Fresno, Calif., 1981—96, pres. Livingston, Calif., 1996—, CEO, 1996—. Chmn. campaign com. Calif. Dairy Tech. Ctr.; mem. dean's adv. coun. U. Calif., Davis, Calif. Office: Foster Farms PO Box 457 Livingston CA 95334

FOSTER, ROSEANNE H., business educator; d. Thora E. Hollums; m. Clifton L. Foster, Nov. 6, 1970; children: Ferrell Lee, Rita Faye. BS in Bus. Edn., U. Ctrl. Fla., 1989. Cert. tchr. Nat. Bd. of Profl. Tchrs., 2003. With Wood & Merritt, CPAs, Oak Hill, W.Va., 1975—83; bookkeeper, office mgr. Gen. Mills, Orlando, Fla., 1983—86; tchr. Osceola County Sch. Dist., Kissimmee, Fla., 1989—. Lead peer tchr. Denn John Mid. Sch., Kissimmee, Fla., 1991—, treas. sch. adv. counsel, 1991—2003; sec. profl. devel. coun. Osceola County Dist. Schs., Kissimmee, Fla., 2003—04. Recipient Best Practices Gold award, Valencia CC, 2001, Cert. of Excellence in Tchg. award, Osceola County Career and Tech. Edn., 2002, 2007, Tchr. of the Yr. award, Denn John Mid. Sch./Osceola County Schs., 2004. Mem.: ASCD, Fla. Bus. Edn. Assn., Delta Kappa Gamma. Avocations: reading, cooking, motorcycle riding. Office Phone: 407-935-3560. Business E-Mail: fosterr@osceola.k12.fl.us.

FOSTER, SERRIN MARIE, non-profit organization executive; b. Washington, Sept. 17; d. William A. and Donna R. (Hayden) F. BA in Pub. Rels., Old Dominion U., 1977. Freelance pub. rels. specialist, Springfield, Va., 1978-82; program mgr., regional rep. St. Jude Children's Rsch. Hosp., Arlington, Va., 1982-89; dir. devel. Nat. Alliance for Mentally Ill., Washington, 1989-94; exec. dir. Feminists for Life of Am., Washington, 1994-99, pres., 1999—. Mem. adv. bd. Ivy League Coalition for Life, Harvard U., 1997—, Am. Collegians for Life, Washington, 1998—. Author: (books) Pro-Women Answers to Pro-Choice Questions, 2003, Great Speeches in History, 2004—; contbr. Women's Rights, Boston Globe, Cost of Choice; editor-in-chief, contbr. The Am. Feminist mag., 1994—. Susan B. Anthony List, Alexandria, 1997—. Mem. Alpha Phi Women's Found. Avocations: gardening, travel, painting. Office: Feminists for Life of Am PO Box 206 Alexandria VA 22314

FOSTER, SUTTON, actress; b. Statesboro, Ga., Mar. 18, 1975; Postgrad., Carnegie Mellon U., Hunter Coll., NYC. Actor: (Broadway musical) Grease, Annie; (Broadway plays) Scarlet Pimpernel, Les Misérables, Thoroughly Modern Millie (winner Tony award for Best Performance by a Leading Actress in a Musical, 2002), Little Women, 2004—05, The Drowsy Chaperone, 2005 (LA Ovation award lead actress in a musical, 2006). Mailing: c/o Ahmanson Theatre 135 N Grand Ave Los Angeles CA 90012

FOSTER, TIMOTHY EDWARD, educational association administrator; b. Schenectady, NY, Dec. 12, 1951; s. William Edward and Mary Emmet Foster; m. Ellen Patrice Nash, May 22, 1982; children: James Timothy, William Robert. BA in Econs., Union Coll., Schenectady, NY, 1973. V.p., treas. Gen. Electric Venture Cap. Co., Fairfield, Conn., 1981—83; v.p. Foster Mgmt. Inc., NYC, 1983—86; from sr. v.p. ops. to CFO NovaCare Inc., King of Prussia, Pa., 1986—98, CEO, 1998—2000, Liberty Higher Edn. LLC, York, Pa., 2005—; chmn., CEO YTI Career Inst., 2005—, Ross U., Edison, NJ, 2000—04, Concorde Career Colls., 2006—. Adv. health policy and mgmt. exec. coun. Sch. Pub. Health Harvard U., Boston, 1998—. Chmn. cap. campaign Rosemont (Pa.) Sch. The Holy Child, 2003—. Avocations: fly fishing, horseback riding, cross country skiing, outdoors. Office: YTI Career Inst 1405 Williams Rd York PA 17402 Office Phone: 717-757-8132.

FOSTER, VICKI ANNE, secondary school educator; b. Sapulpa, Okla., Apr. 21, 1952; d. James Robert and Mary Louise Long; m. E. Bernard Foster, July 14, 1976; children: Seth Alden, Chelsea Marie Burgardt. BA, U. Wyo., Laramie, 1974, MS in Tchg., 1978, PhD, 2005. Tchr., grades 1-9 multiple sch. districts, Wyo., 1974—98; instrnl. assessment specialist Natrona County Sch. Dist., Casper, 1998—2001, mentoring program facilitator, 2001—03, coord. secondary curriculum, 2003—. Adj. faculty U. Wyo., Casper Ctr., 1999—2001. Dist. commr. US Pony Club branches, Casper, 1993—2000. Recipient Presdl. award Excellence Elem. Sci. Tchg., NSF, 1991. Mem.: ASCD, Nat. Staff Devel. Coun., Nat. Sci. Tchrs. Assn., Nat. Coun. Tchrs. Math., Phi Delta Kappa. Avocation: equestrian sports. Office: Natrona County School District 970 N Glenn Rd Casper WY 82601 Home Phone: 307-473-2083; Office Phone: 307-577-0200. Business E-Mail: vicki_foster@ncsd.k12.wy.us.

FOSTER, VIRGINIA, retired botany educator; b. Joseph, Oreg., Feb. 4, 1914; d. Perry Alexander and Genevieve (Shain) F. BS, U. Wash., 1949, MS, 1950; PhD, Ohio State U., 1954. Prof. Judson Coll., Marion, Ala., 1956-58; prof. Miss. State Coll. for Women, Columbus, 1958-59, LaVerne (Calif.) Coll., 1959-60, Calif. Western U., San Diego, 1960-61, Pensacola (Fla.) Jr. Coll., 1962-84. Author: (lab. manual) The Botany Laboratory, 1976, rev. edit., 1985, 3d edit., 1991. Avocations: gardening, travel, photography. Home: 1335 3rd Ave Ste 315 Longview WA 98632-6003

FOSTER, WALTER HERBERT, JR., real estate company executive; b. Belmont, Mass., Nov. 2, 1919; s. Walter Herbert and Gertrude (Sullivan) F.; m. Hazel Campbell, Aug. 7, 1942 (div. July 1979); children: Katherine D., Walter H. III, Stephen C., Banton T.; m. Nedra Ann Thompson, July 3, 1981; 1 child, Timothy John. Student, Harvard U., 1937-38; BS, U. Maine, 1947; grad. in real estate, Tri-State Inst., 1968-70. Cert. gen. appraiser, Maine. Owner, mgr. Foster Bros., Lyndeborough, N.H., 1947-56; ter. sales mgr. Beacon Milling Co., Oakland, Maine, 1956-64; v.p. Sherwood & Foster, Inc., Old Town, Maine, 1964-67; sales rep. Bangor (Maine) Real Estate, 1967-73; chief appraiser James W. Sewall Co., Old Town, 1970-73; mgr. J.F. Singleton Co., Bangor, 1973-80; pres. Coldwell Banker Am. Heritage, Bangor, 1980—. Dean Tri-State Inst., 1981; mem. Maine Real Estate Commn., 1987-93, chmn. 1991. Active Rep. Nat. Com., Washington, 1980; assessment bd. appeals Old Town, Maine, Holden Assessment Bd. of Appeals; bd. dirs. Penobscot Theatre, 1987-92, treas., 1989, mem. Maine State Bd. Property Rev., 1998—. Capt. USAF, 1941-46, USAFR ret., 1966. Mem. Nat. Assn. Realtors (bd. dirs. 1980-81), Maine Assn. Realtors (life, bd. dirs. 1976-80, pres. 1980, Realtor of Yr. 1984), Bangor Bd. Realtors (bd. dirs. 1973-74, pres. 1976, Realtor of Yr. 1976, 84), Maine Real Estate Commn. (chmn. 1991-92), Maine State Bd. Property Tax Review, Commn. to Study Real Estate Appraiser Cert. and Licensing, Nat. Assn. Rev. Appraisers, Am. Assn. Cert. Appraisers, Res. Officers Assn., Appraisal Inst. (assoc.), Nat. Assn. Ind. Fee Appraisers (sr.), Harvard Club of Ea. Maine (treas.), Rotary (bd. dirs. local club, Paul Harris fellow 2005), Am. Legion., Ret. Offices Assn., Mil. Officers Assn. Am. Episcopalian. Avocations: woodworking, gardening. Home: 68 Dole Hill Rd Holden ME 04429-9802 Office: Coldwell Banker Am Heritage 510 Broadway Bangor ME 04401-3468 Office Phone: 207-942-6773. Business E-Mail: cbah@midmaine.com.

FOSTER, (PAUL) WESLEY, JR., real estate broker; b. McDonough, Ga., Nov. 25, 1933; s. Paul Wesley Sr. and Sara Frances (Chappell) F.; m. Betty Lane Flanders, Sept. 7, 1962; children: Rodney, Paul Wesley III, Amanda. BA, Va. Mil. Inst., 1956; postgrad., Am. U., Washington, 1963-64. Salesman Residential Products Divsn. Kaiser Aluminum, Chgo., 1956-57; commd. 2d lt. U.S. Army, 1957, resigned, 1959; mktg. dir. Kaiser Aluminum, Oakland, Calif., 1959-63; sales mgr. New Homes Minchew Corp., Annandale, Va., 1963-66; v.p., sales mgr. Nelson Realty, Annandale, 1966-68; pres. Long & Foster Real Estate, Inc., Fairfax, Va., 1968, chmn. and CEO. Bd. dirs. Lane Construction Corp., Inc., Meriden, Conn., Carl Freeman Constrn. Corp., Potomac, Md., Greater Washington Bd. Trade, Washington, George C. Marshall Found., Relo, The Leading Real Estate Companies of World. Bd. dirs. Washington/Balt. Regional Assn., Balt., 1984—. Named Entrepreneur of Yr. for Real Estate in Great Washington, DC area, Ernst & Young, 1991; named one of Real Estate's 25 Most Influential Thought Leaders, Realtor Mag., 2006. Mem.: Washington Golf and Country (Arlington, Va.); City of Washington. Republican. Episcopalian. Avocations: tennis, jogging. Office: Long & Foster Cos Inc 11351 Random Hills Rd Ste 100 Fairfax VA 22030-7409 Office Fax: 703-591-6978.*

FOSTER, WILLIAM EDWIN (BILL FOSTER), nonprofessional basketball coach; b. Ridley Park, Pa., Aug. 19, 1929; s. Howard M. and Viola Jane (Beaston) F.; m. Shirley Ann Junkin, June 17, 1957; children: Vicki R., Debra Jo, Julia Ann, Mary K. BS, Elizabethtown Coll., 1954; MEd, Temple U., 1957. Coach, tchr. Chichester (Pa.) High Sch., 1954-57, Abington (Pa.) High Sch., 1957-60; coach, instr. Bloomsburg (Pa.) State Coll., 1960-63; head basketball coach Rutgers U., New Brunswick, NJ, 1963-71, U. Utah, Salt Lake City, 1971-74; head basketball coach, asst. athletic dir. Duke U., Durham, NC, 1974-80, U. S.C., Columbia, 1980-86; head basketball coach, interim athletic dir. Northwestern U., Evanston, Ill., 1986-93, athletic dir., 1993; assoc. commr. S.W. Conf., Dallas, 1993-96; cons. Com. of Big 12 Conf. for basketball, 1996-99; spl. asst. to the commr. Western Athletic Conf., 1999—2005. Chmn. of the bd. Naismith Meml. Basketball Hall of Fame, 1997-98, bd. trustees; pres. Nat. Sports Video Seminars. Served with USAF, 1951-52. Named Nat. Coach of Yr., Sporting News Playboy Mag., 1978, S.C. Coach of Yr., 1981, Nat. Invitation Tournament's Man of Yr., Met. Coaches Assn., 2003; named to Sports Hall Fame Elizabethtown Coll., Pa., Rutgers. U., Hall Fame Delaware County (Pa.), Hall Fame Interboro H.S, 2004, Glen-Nor H.S., 2004. Mem. Nat. Assn. Basketball Coaches (past pres., co-coach of yr. 1978), Met. Intercollegiate Basketball Assn. (elected 2003, Man-of-Yr. Nat. Invitation Tournament). Office: PO Box 635 Galveston TX 77553 Home: The Club of the Isle 3433 Cove View Blvd 1408 Galveston TX 77554 Office Phone: 409-996-4545. Personal E-mail: bfosterbb@aol.com.

FOSTER, WILLIAM R., zoological park administrator; DVM. Dir., CEO Louiville (Ky.) Zool. Garden, Louisville, 1997—. Office: Louisville Zool Garden PO Box 37250 Louisville KY 40233-7250

FOSTER, WOODBRIDGE A., medical entomologist, educator; BS in Entomology & Parasitology, Univ. Calif., Berkeley, 1963, PhD in Entomology & Parasitology, 1967. Asst. prof. Haile Sellassie I Univ., Addis Ababa, Ethiopia, 1967—70; rsch. fellow Univ. Bristol, 1970—71; rsch. assoc. Univ. Ga., 1971—73; asst. prof. Ohio State Univ., 1973—76, assoc. prof., 1976—. Invited spkr. in field. Contbr. articles to profl. jours.; chair editl. bd. Journal of Vector Ecology, American Entomologist. Macdonald Scholarship, Univ. Calif., Berkeley, 1961, NSF Undergraduate Grant, 1962, NIH Predoctoral Fellow, 1965—67, Ministry of Overseas Develop. (UK) Rsch. Fellowship, 1970—71. Mem.: Ohio Mosquito Control Assn. (bd. dir., sec., newsletter editor). Achievements include leading a team of collaborators to develop a proposal to study the nutritional ecology of the most important vector of maleria, Anopheles gambiae, in Kenya & Tanzania, now approved for funding by NIH; creating a matrix of mating-behavior characters from video analysis, being used to construct hypotheses for the phylogeny of sabethine mosquitos & the origin & evolution of courtship; revealing the importance of energy status to decision-making & vectorial capacity of Ochlerotatus triseriatus and anopheles gamgiae, two important vectors of pathogens. Office: Dept Entomology Ohio State Univ 486 ARONOFF LB 318 W 12TH Ave Columbus OH 43210 Office Phone: 614-292-2204. Office Fax: 614-292-2180. Business E-Mail: foster.13@osu.edu.

FOSTER-CHEEK, KAYE I., health products executive; With Yellow Pages, Pfizer, Inc.; v.p. human resources North Am. Consumer Products Cos. Johnson & Johnson, New Brunswick, NJ, 2003—04, v.p. human resources Consumer and Personal Care Grp., mem. human resources leadership team, mem. consumer and personal care grp. operating com., 2004—05, v.p. human resources, mem. exec. com., 2005—. Office: Johnson & Johnson 1 Johnson & Johnson Plz New Brunswick NJ 08933

FOSTER-WELLS, KAREN MARGARET, artist; b. Pasadena, Calif., Oct. 26, 1942; d. Ray Russell Foster and Margaret Victoria Ray; m. David Roycroft Rory Wells, Sept. 17, 1988; children; John McCarthy, Sabisha Friedberg. AA, Orange Coast Coll., Costa Mesa, Calif., 1962; student, U. Calif., Irvine, 1967-68, Laguna Beach Sch. Art/Design, Calif., 1965-67. Illustrator, 1963—. One-woman shows include Santa Barbara (Calif.) of Natural History, 1979, Morro Bay (Calif.) Mus. of Natural History, 1988, Great Western Bank, San Luis Obispo, Calif., 1989, Cayucos (Calif.) Art Assn., 1993, Chelsea Bookshop, Paso Robles, Calif., 1993, Paso Robles Art Assn. Gallery, 1993, Wild Horse Found., Santa Barbara, Summerwood Winery, 2002; group exhbns. include Waterside Gallery, Morro Bay, Calif., 1997, 98, Johnson Gallery and Framing Studio, San Luis Obispo, 1999, 2000, Coll. of Creative Studies, Santa Barbara, 2000, Santa Barbara Mus. Natural History, 2000, Carnegie Western Art Gallery, Paso robles, 2000-2001, San Luis Obispo Art Ctr., 2001, Cayucos Art Assn., 2001, Biennale Internazionale Dell'arte Contemporanea, Florence, Italy, 2003, Mid-State Fair (Artist Achievement award 2003), Quick Draw Cowboy Festival, Santa Clarita, 2003, 2004, Cattlemen's Western Art Show, Paso Robles, 2004, (with pianist Hilary Anderson) Painting Concert, 2004; artist (cover) The Path of Return, 2001, Monterey Mus. Art, 2002. Recipient Bronze medal Art of Calif. Discovery awards, 1993, 1st Pl. Calif. Mid-State Fair Art Show, 1994, 98, 1st Pl. and Coord. award Calif. Mid-State Fair Art Show, 2000, Best of Show Paso Robles Art Assn., 2000, Color of Autumn award Paso Robles Art Assn., 2004. Mem. The Oak Group, Calif. Art Club, San Luis Outdoor Painters Enterprise (co-founder), Am. Soc. Portrait Artists, Women Artists of the West. Avocations: horses, natural history. Office: Karen Foster Artist dot com PO Box 1114 Templeton CA 93465 Home Phone: 805-239-9260; Office Phone: 805-239-8413. E-mail: horseart@tcsn.net.

FOTI, CHARLES C., JR., state attorney general; b. New Orleans, Nov. 30, 1937; s. Charles C. and Eleanore (Palmisano) Foti. Degree, U. New Orleans; JD, Loyola U., New Orleans, 1965. Bar: La., US Dist. Ct. (ea. dist.) La., US Ct. Appeals, US Supreme Ct. Litig. atty. FHA, New Orleans; trial atty. Dist. Attys. Office, New Orleans, Legal Aide Bur., New Orleans; atty. New Orleans Police Dept.; head criminal divsn. City Attys. Office, New Orleans; criminal sheriff Orleans Parish, New Orleans, 1973—2004; atty. gen. State of La., 2004—. Judge ad hoc Mcpl. Ct. City New Orleans; chmn. La. Commn. on Peace Officers Standards and Tng.; chmn. Total Cmty. Action; mem. adv. bd. Nat. Am. Bank, Internat. Trade Mart Br.; lectr. criminal justice Our Lady State U., La. State U.; mem. Gov.'s Prison Overcrowding Task Force; mem. adv. bd. Housing Authority New Orleans; mem. La. Commn. on Law Enforcement and Adminstrn. Criminal Justice; mem. exec. com. Mayor's Criminal Justice Coord. Coun., City New Orleans; bd. mem. Mayor's Interagency Coun. Govt. chmn. United Way campaign; mem. Emergency Preparedness Adv. Com.; mem. adv. bd. 4-H Club; campaign dir. March of Dimes; mem. exec. bd. Times Picayune Doll and Toy Fund; mem. steering com. Barthelemy Campaign Fin. Com.; mem. adv. com. Health Promotion Continuing Edn. Grant; bd. trustees La. Children's Mus.; mem. cmty. rels. bd. New Orleans Job Corps Ctr.; co-chmn. Tulane's Athletic Devel. Com.; mem. adv. bd. Children's Crisis Mgmt. Prog. Served in US Army, 1955—58. Mem. ABA (nat. com. on prisons, pardons and paroles), Nat. Sheriff's Assn. (law and legis. com., detention and corrections com.), La. Sheriff's Assn. (mem. exec. bd., chmn. state supplemental pay com.), Am. Correctional Assn., Am. Correctional Food Svc. Assn., Am. Correctional Health Svcs. Assn., Am. Fedn. Police, Am. Pub. Works Assn., Am. Soc. Indsl. Security, Am. Soc. Pers. Adminstrn., Am. Trial Lawyers Assn., Correctional Edn. Assn., Internat. Assn. Chiefs Police, La. State Bar Assn. Democrat. Roman Catholic. Office: Office of Atty Gen PO Box 94095 Baton Rouge LA 70804-4095 Office Phone: 504-827-8501, 225-326-6000.*

FOTI, MARGARET, medical association administrator, editor, consultant; b. Phila., Dec. 15, 1944; d. Samuel A. and Margaret M. (DiBiase) F. BA, Temple U., 1975, MA in Comm., 1985, PhD in Comm., 1995; MD (hon.), U. Rome, 2003. Tech. editor U. Pa., Phila., 1962—64, asst. to bus. adminstr., 1964—65; sr. editl. asst. Cancer Rsch. Jour., Phila., 1965—69, mng. editor, 1969—; CEO Am. Assn. Cancer Rsch., Phila., 1982—; sec.-treas., CEO Am. Assn. Cancer Rsch. Found. for Prevention and Cure of Cancer. Adminstrn., pub. edn., devel., editl. and pub. cons., lectr. in field. Contbr. articles to profl. jours. Pres. Nat. Coalition Cancer Rsch., 1994-96, bd. dirs. 2004. Recipient Cert. Appreciation, Am. Assn. Cancer Rsch., 1975, 1985, 1990, 1999, Award for Leadership and Extraordinary Achievements in Cancer Rsch., 2007, Women of Distinction award, 1999, Cino del Duca award, 2000, Ville de Paris award, 2000, award, City of Trento, Italy, 2002, Solemn Encomium recognition, U. Palermo, Italy, 2003, Cmty. Caring award, William S. Graham Found. for Melanoma Rsch., Am. Soc. Clin. Oncology Spl. Recognition award, Disting. Svc. award, Assn. Am. Cancer Insts. Mem.: NCCR (bd. dirs.), AAAS, Coun. Engrs. and Sci. Soc. Execs., Coun. Biology Editors (pres. 1980—81), Soc. Scholarly Publs. (pres. 1996—97), Internat. Fedn. Sci. Editors, European Assn. Sci. Editors, Am. Assn. Cancer Rsch., Am. Soc. Assn. Execs., Japanese Cancer Assn. (hon.), European Assn. Cancer Rsch. (hon.; disting.). Democrat. Roman Catholic. Office: Am Assn Cancer Rsch 615 Chestnut St 17th Fl Philadelphia PA 19106-4404 Office Phone: 215-440-9300. Office Fax: 215-440-9313. E-mail: foti@aacr.org.*

FOTOPOULOS, JAMES, artist; b. Norridge, Ill., 1976; Guest lectr."Film One" production class U. Tex., Austin, 2001, 2003; guest lectr. NY City U., 2003; founder Fantasma Inc., 1998. Dir.: (films) ZERO, 1997, Migrating Forms, 1999 (Best Feature Award, NY Underground Film Festival, 2000, Made in Chgo. Award, Chgo. Underground Film Festival, 2000), Back Against the Wall, 2000, Consumed, 2001 (Chgo. Underground Film Fund Grant, Chgo. Underground Film Festival, 2001), Christabel, 2001, The Lighthouse, 2004 (No Budget Award, Cinematexas Internat. Short Film & Video Festival, 2004), Spine Face, 2005; exhibitions include with Cory Arcangel Fotopoulos/Arcangel Part 5, NY Underground Film Festival, 2004, exhibitions include Whitney Biennial, Whitney Mus. Am. Art, 2004, and others. Office: Fantasma Inc 1400 West Devon 440 Chicago IL 60660 Business E-Mail: info@jamesfotopoulos.com.

FOTOPOULOS, SOPHIA STATHOPOULOS, medical research scientist, administrator; b. Kansas City, Mo., Nov. 6, 1936; d. Marinos G. and Stavroula (Fotopoulos) Stathopoulos; m. Chris K. Fotopoulos, Aug. 27, 1963 (div.) BA, U. Kans., 1958, MA, 1964, PhD, 1970. Diplomate Behavioral Scis. Regulatory Bd. State of Kans., Council for Nat. Register of Health Svc. Providers. Rsch. asst. U. Kans. Med. Ctr., Kansas City, 1958-61; rsch. assoc. Inst. Cmty. Studies, Kansas City, Mo., 1965-66; lectr. U. Kans., Lawrence, 1969-70; dir. Psychophysiology-pharmacology Lab. Greater Kansas City (Mo.) Mental Health Found., 1970-73; staff assoc. neuropsychophysiology, 1973, Midwest Rsch. Inst., Kansas City, Mo., 1974-75, sr. scientist, head Psychophysiology Lab., 1975-77, assoc. dir. chem. scis. div., 1977-79, dir. life scis. div., 1979-84; dir. rsch. Am. U., Washington, 1984-87; exec. v.p., CEO Immucomp, Inc., 1987-92; pres., CEO Bioactive Tech., 1992—. rsch. prof. dept. medicine Kansas U. Med. Ctr., 1987-97; spl. rev. com. Nat. Cancer Inst., 1978-98; mem. adv. com. Am. Cancer Soc., 1982-96; lectr. U. Mo.-Kansas City Sch. Medicine, 1970-84. NIH research fellow, 1962-64, HHS research fellow, 1965-69; recipient Creative Scientist award Am. Inst. Research, 1971. Mem. AAAS, Claude Bernard Soc., Internat. Soc. for Antiviral Rsch., N.Y. Acad. Scis., Biofeedback Soc. Am., Mo. Biofeedback Soc. (pres. 1979-80), Sigma Xi. Greek Orthodox. Clubs: Zonta Internat. (pres. KCII 1983-85), Philoptochos Soc. Contbr. articles to profl. jours. and books.

FOTSCH, GEORGE BERNARD, III, chemical addiction counselor; b. Abbeville, La., May 9, 1945; s. George Bernard Fotsch Jr. and Norma Jeanne Fotsch; m. Evelyn Colleen Hunziker, Oct. 17, 1971 (div. Dec. 1988); children: Sandra, George, Seth, Evelyn, Troy; m. Jamie Linn Harper, June 21; 1 child, Candice Nicole. Student, U. Md., 1962—64, U. S.W. La., 1967—68, Am. Petroleum Inst., Long Beach, Calif., 1974—75. Lic. chem. dependency counselor TCADA, 1998. Mgr. Hollywood Diamond Exch., Long Beach, Calif., 1969; regional mgr. LeeRoy Barrys Jewelers, Riverside, Calif., 1970; ops. mgr. Armstrong Petroleum, Newport Beach, Calif., 1971—72; gen. mgr. Burmah Phillips Petroleum, Huntington Beach, Calif., 1973—83; counselor-in-tng. VA Chem. Dependency Treatment, Canandeiqua, NY, 1983—86; chem. dependency counselor Tex. Alcoholism Found., Houston, 1987—92; clin. dir. Cenikor Found., Inc., Deer Park, Tex., 1993—2004; exec. dir. Multi Addiction Counseling, 2004—. Author: Thee True Book, 2002. Avocations: astronomy, cosmology, physics. Office: George B Fotsch PO Box 1012 La Porte TX 77572 Home: 5150 Red Bluff Rd Apt 505 Pasadena TX 77503-4441 Office Phone: 713-384-5217.

FOUAD, MOHAMED RAOUF, science educator; b. Alexandria, Egypt, June 4, 1969; s. Raouf F. Abdel Kader and Amal A. Mostafa; m. Dina A. Abd El-Moneim, Aug. 27, 1999; 1 child, Ahmed R. BS in Auto. Control Computer Sci., Alexandria U., 1992, MS in Math., 1999; MS in Computer

Sci., Purdue U., West Lafayette, Ind., 2003, MS in Indsl. Adminstrn., 2005. Software engr. MobiCom (IBM agt.), Alexandria, 1995—97; tchg. asst. Alexandria U., 1993—2000, Purdue U., West Lafayette, Ind., 2002. Soldier Egyptian Air Def., 1993—94. Recipient Excellence awards, Egyptian Govt., 1987—92, CETA Excellence in Tchg. award, Purdue U., 2005; fellow, Egyptian Govt., 2001—05; summer rsch. grantee, Purdue U. Rsch. Found., 2004. Master: Egyptian Student Assn. (pres. 2004—05); mem.: Upsilon Pi Epsilon (hon.). Avocations: soccer, tennis, squash. Home: 400 North River Rd Apt 811 West Lafayette IN 47906 Office: Purdue U 305 N University St West Lafayette IN 47907 Home Phone: 765-743-9938. Personal E-mail: mohraouf@hotmail.com.

FOUDREE, BRUCE WILLIAM, lawyer; b. Des Moines, Mar. 27, 1947; s. Shie and Dorothy F.;m. Suzanne J. F. Reade, May 31, 1986; children: Andrew A., Grant R., Zarina. BA, Drake U., 1969; student, U. Geneva, Switzerland, 1968, U. Vienna, Austria, 1968; JD, Drake U., 1972; LLM, U. Pa., 1975. Bar: Iowa 1972, U.S. Ct. Appeals (8th cir.) 1976, U.S. Supreme Ct. 1977, Ill. 1986. Asst. atty. gen. Iowa Dept. Justice, Des Moines, 1976-80; ins. commnr. Iowa Ins. Dept., Des Moines, 1980-86; of counsel Mitchell, Williams, Selig and Tucker, Little Rock, 1986-88; shareholder Keck, Mahin & Cate, Chgo., 1988-96; of counsel Lord, Bissell & Brook, Chgo., 1996—. Commr., chmn. Iowa Ins. Dept., 1980-86; commr. Iowa Health Data Commn., 1983-86, chmn. 1985. Assoc. editor Drake Law Rev., 1971-72; dir. Jour. Ins. Regulation, 1982-89. Mem. ABA (TIPS scope and correlation com. 1991-94, chmn. fin. svcs. com. 1990-91, professionalism com. 1994-96), Nat. Assn. Ins. Commrs. (chmn. 1984, pres. 1985), Ins. Regulatory Examiners Soc. Found. (bd. dirs. 1991—, chmn. 1999-2000), Iowa State Bar Assn., Life and Health Compliance Assn., Union League Club of Chgo. (chmn. ins. group 1989-92), The Chgo. Lighthouse (bd. dirs. 1995—, sec. 1998, chmn. 2002-05), Chaine des Rotisseurs Chgo. (vice charge de missions-caviste 2006). Office: Lord Bissell & Brook 111 S Wacker Dr Chicago IL 60606 Office Phone: 312-443-1830. Business E-Mail: bfoudree@lordbissell.com.

FOUDREE, CHARLES M., financial consultant; BS in Acctg., Truman State U., 1966. CPA Kans., Mo. Mem. audit staff Peat, Marwick, Mitchell, and Co., Kansas City, Kans., 1966-72; CFO, bd. dirs. Harmon Industries, Inc., Blue Springs, Mo., 1972-99. Bd. dir. OTR Express, Inc., Olathe, Kans., 1995—2001, Carondelet Health, Kansas City, Mo., Sceptor Industries, Mo., SLS Internat., Springfield. Past chmn. bd. assocs. St. Mary's Hosp., Blue Springs; bd. dir. treas. Harry S. Truman Libr. Inst., 1997-2006; treas., trustee St. Paul Sch. Theology, Kansas City, Mo.; chmn. St. Mary's Hosp. Found., 2003-2005, Truman State U. Found., 2003-05; bd. dirs. Truman Heartland Cmty. Found., Independence, Mo. Mem.: AICPA, Independence C. of C. (past dir., treas.), Fin. Exec. Inst. (bd. dirs., past pres. Kansas City chpt., nat. bd. dirs. 1995—98), Mo. Soc. CPAs, Rotary Club of Independence (bd. dirs.), Sigma Tau Gamma, Blue Key. Home: 4124 N E Pembroke Ln Lees Summit MO 64064-1622 Office Phone: 816-591-5109. E-mail: cfoudree@aol.com.

FOUDY, JULIE MAURINE, retired professional soccer player, Olympic athlete; b. San Diego, Jan. 23, 1971; m. Ian Sawyers, July 1995. BSW in Biology, Stanford U., 1993. Mem. U.S. Women's Nat. Soccer Team, 1987—2004, capt., 1992—2004; profl. soccer player San Diego Spirit, 2001—03. Color commentator Men's World Cup, ESPN, 1998. Mem. Tyresco Football Club, Sweden, 1994; pres. Women's Sports Found. Named World Cup Champion, 1991, 1999; named to U.S. Nat. Soccer Hall of Fame, 2007; recipient Gold medal, Centennial Olympic Games, 1996, Athens Olympic Games, 2004, FIFA Fair Play award, 1997, Silver medal, Sydney Olympic Games, 2000, Bronze medal, World Cup, 2003. Achievements include being a member of the Bronze medal winning team World Championships, Sweden, 1995; CONCACAF, Montreal, 1994; being voted number 1 most powerful in sports, Sports Business Journal, 2004. Office: c/o US Soccer Fedn 1801 S Prairie Ave # 1811 Chicago IL 60616-1319

FOUILLADE, JEAN-PAUL ERIC, management consultant; b. Neuilly-Sur-Seine, France, Aug. 7, 1950; arrived in U.S., 1989; s. Paul Henri and Andrèe Françoise Fouillade; m. Fabienne Patricia Ide, June 17, 1972 (div. June 1994); children: Jean-Sèbastien, Aurèlie, Lorraine; m. Katherine Ruth Hensel, Sept. 24, 1994 (div. Dec. 2001). MBA, Hautes Etudes Commerciales, HEC, Jouy-en-Josas, France, 1972. Asst. treas. Lesieur Group, Paris, 1972—74, UTA French Airlines, Paris, 1975-76, treas., 1977-80; dir. control Usinor Sacilor Group, Paris, 1981-89; sr. v.p. fin. and adminstrn. Francosteel Corp., NYC, 1990-96; pres. Whitridge Enterprises, Jersey City, 1997—2001. Prof. Inst. Formation Continue, Paris, 1978—79. Dir. Summit Child Care Ctr., NJ, 1996-99; trustee Com. French Speaking Soc., 2000-03, French Am. Conservatory of Music, 2001—. Union Pour La Democratie Francaise. Roman Catholic. Avocations: horseback riding, skiing, flying. Home and Office: 179 Hawk Creek Dr Spartanburg SC 29301 Personal E-mail: fouillade@bellsouth.net.

FOUKE, JANIE M., academic administrator, educator; BS, St. Andrews Presbyn. Coll., 1973; MS, U. NC, Chapel Hill, 1980, PhD in Biomed. Math. and Engring., 1981. Prof. Dept. Biomedical Engring. Case Western Reserve U., Cleve., 1981—99; div. dir. Div. of Bioengineering and Environ. Sys., NSF, Washington, DC; dean Coll. Engring. Mich. State U., 1999—2005; provost, sr. v.p. academic affairs U. Fla., Gainesville, 2005—. Adv. bd. mem. Engring. Directorate, NSF, Nat. Inst. of Bioimaging and Bioengineering, NIH. Author: Engineering Tomorrow, 2000 (Dexter Prize, Soc. for History of Tech.); contbr. articles to profl. jours. Fellow: AAAS, IEEE, Biomed. Engring. Soc., Am. Inst. Med. and Biol. Engring. Office: U Fla 235 Tigert Hall PO Box 113175 Gainesville FL 32611 Office Phone: 352-392-2404. Office Fax: 352-392-8735. E-mail: jfouke@aa.ufl.edu.

FOULADVAND, HENGAMEH, artist; b. Tehran, Iran; naturalized U.S. citizen, 1974; d. Mansour and Mahin F.; m. Masoud B. Mansouri, Feb. 20, 1981; 1 child, Tia. BA, San Jose State U., 1976; M, Calif. State U., 1979. Exec. dir. Ctr. Iranian Modern Arts, 1998—. Art cons. T.H.E. Graphics & Design, 1990-96; graphic & prodn. cons. Metro Lables, 1994-96. Exhibited in solo and group shows including Columbia U., N.Y.C., 1989, L.I. U., 1989, 91, Strathmore Arts Ctr., Md., 1991, Port Washington Pub. Libr., 1991, Huntington Arts Coun., Hecksher Mus., 1993, 95, McArthur Airport Terminal Bldg., L.I., 1996-97, Columbia U., Hamilton Bldg., N.Y.C., 1997, Lindberg Gallery, N.Y.C., 1999, GORA Gallery, Montreal, 1999, La Maison Francaise, Columbia, 2000; represented in permanent collections Ency. Iranica Found., N.Y., Line & Tone Typographics, N.Y., numerous pvt. collections; mem. editl. bd.: Tavoos Art Quarterly, 1999--. Mem. N.Y. State Coun. Arts, N.Y. Found. Arts, Huntington Art League and Coun. Long Island. Home: 34 Lisa Dr Dix Hills NY 11746 E-mail: hengamehf@earthlink.net.

FOULKE, EDWIN GERHART, JR., federal agency administrator, lawyer; b. Perkasie, Pa., Oct. 30, 1952; s. Edwin G. and Mary Claire (Keller) F. BA, N.C. State U., 1974; JD, Loyola U., New Orleans, 1978; LLM, Georgetown U., 1993. Bar: S.C. 1979, U.S. Dist. Ct. S.C. 1979, U.S. Ct. Appeals (4th cir.) 1979, Ga. 1986, U.S. Ct. Appeals (11th cir.) 1986, D.C. 1989, U.S. Ct. Appeals (D.C. cir.) 1989, U.S. Supreme Ct. 1990, N.C. 1997. Assoc. Thompson, Mann & Hutson, Greenville, SC, 1978-83, Rainey, Britton, Gibbes & Clarkson, Greenville, 1983-85; ptnr. Constangy, Brooks & Smith, Columbia, SC, 1985-90; chmn. OSHA Rev. Commn., Washington, 1990-95; ptnr. Jackson Lewis LLP, Greenville, SC, 1995—2006; asst. sec., OSHA US Dept. Labor, Washington, 2006—. Instr. St. Mary's Dominican Coll., New Orleans, 1977-78. Field rep. Reagan/Bush Campaign, Columbia, 1980, S.C. state coord., 1984; sec., treas. Employment Labor Law Sect., Columbia, 1981-82. Mem. ABA, S.C. Bar Assn., Ga. Bar Assn., Greenville County Bar Assn. (chmn. pub. rels. com. 1984-85), SAR, Rotary. Roman Catholic. Avocations: swimming, tennis, skiing, golf. Office: US Dept Labor 200 Constitution Ave NW Rm S2315 Washington DC 20210 Office Phone: 202-693-2000.

FOULKE, LAURA TAYLOR, not-for-profit fundraiser; b. Phila., Sept. 20, 1969; d. Walter Longfellow and Wendy Taylor Foulke. BA, Bowdoin Coll., Brunswick, Maine, 1991; MEd, Harvard U., Cambridge, Mass., 1995. Dean student support svcs. Neighborhood Ho. Charter Sch., Dorchester, Mass., 2001—04; dir. devel. Aim High, San Francisco, 2004—. Bd. mem. Killing My Lobster, San Francisco, 2006—07. Recipient Neighborhood Builders award, Bank Am., 2007. Mem.: Assn. Fundraising Profls. Democrat-Npl. Home: 415 Kirkham St San Francisco CA 94122 Office: Aim High PO Box 410715 San Francisco CA 94141 Office Fax: 415-551-2626. Business E-Mail: lfoulke@aimhigh.org.

FOULKES, LLYN, artist, educator; b. Yakima, Wash., Nov. 17, 1934; m. Katie Foulkes; children: Laurey, Jenny, Breck. Student, Ctrl. Wash. Coll., 1952-53, U. Wash., 1954, Chouinard Art Inst., 1957-59. Prof. painting and drawing, artist-in-residence UCLA, 1965—71; resident painter painting workshop Art Ctr. Sch., LA, 1971—77; vis. prof. art U. Calif., Irvine, 1981—82, Santa Barbara, 1983—84; prof. Otis Art Inst., LA, 1986—87. Exhibited group shows LA County Mus. Art, 1960, 61, 63, 67, 73, 83, Pomona Coll., Calif., 1961, San Francisco Mus. Art, 1961, 63, 68, 76, Pasadena Art Mus., Calif., 1964, 68, 70, 73, São Paulo, Brazil, 1964, 66, Allan Frumpkin Gallery, Chgo., 1964, NY Worlds Fair, 1965, U. Mich., 1965, U. Ill., 1965, Mus. 20th Century, Vienna, 1965, Guggenheim Mus., 1966, 78, Mus. Modern Art, NYC, 1966, 76, Whitney Mus., NYC, 1967, 69, 70, 71, 74, 77, Robert Frazier Gallery, London, 1966, São Paulo Biennale, 1968, Paris Biennale, 1967, Mus. Modern Art, Paris, 1967, Seattle Art Mus., 1968, Portland Art Mus., Oreg., 1968, San Francisco Mus., 1968, 76, Brandeis U., 1968, traveling exhbn. Found. Maeght, France, 1968, Art Coun. London, 1968, U. Nev., 1969, Va. Mus., Richmond, 1970, Inst. Contemporary Art, Phila., 1972, Art Inst. Chgo., 1972, 74, 75, 77, LA County Art Inst., 1971, LA Mcpl. Art Gallery, 1973, 76, LA Inst. Contemporary Art, 1975, 76, 79, Visual Arts Mus., NYC, 1975, Aldridge Mus. Contemporary Art, Ridgefield, Conn., 1975, Corcoran Gallery, Washington, 1975, Gallery Darathea Speyer, Paris, 1975, 78, 86, U. Tex., 1977, Nat. Collection Fine Arts, Washington, 1977, Mus. Contemporary Arts, Chgo., 1976, 78, retrospective, 1978, Whitney Mus., NYC, 1980, Mus. Modern Art, Paris, 1980, Santa Barbara Mus. Art, 1981, San Francisco Mus. Modern Art, 1982, U. Wash., Seattle, 1982, 86, U. Calif. Santa Barbara, 1983, 86, Arco Ctr. Visual Arts, LA, 1984, U. So. Calif., LA, 1985, Willard Gallery, NY, 1985, Calif. State U., LA, 1985, Asher Faure Gallery, LA, 1986, Kent Fine Art, NY, 1986, 87, U. Calif. Irvine, 1987, U. Calif. Berkeley, 1987, Va. Mus. Fine Arts, Richmond, 1987, "Real Allusions" Whitney Mus., 1990, "Helter Skelter" Mus. Contemporary Art, LA 1992, Altered States: Selections from the Permanent Collection, Mus. Contemporary Art, LA, 1993, Human Environment and Future, Sonte Mus. Contemporary Art, Korea, 1994, Bestiaire, Galerie Darthea Speyer, Paris, 1995, Be Specific, Rosamund Felsen Gallery, Santa Monica, 1996, Seattle Collects Paintings, Seattle Art Mus., 1997, Goldrush to Pop: Calif. Art in Context, Orange County Mus.Art, Newport Beach, 1998, Size Matters, Patricia Faure Gallery, Santa Monica, 1999, Pop Culture, Norton Simon Mus., Pasadena, Calif., 2001, LA Post Cool, San Jose Mus. Art, Calif., 2002, Paperwork, Patricia Correia Gallery, 2003, POP from San Francisco Collections, San Francisco Mus. Modern Art, 2004, 181st Ann. Invitational Exhbn., Nat. Acad., NYC, 2006; one-man shows: Nelson Gallery, 1963, 64, Oakland Art Mus., Calif., Ferus Gallery, 1961, Pasadena Art Mus., 1962, Rolf Nelson Gallery, LA, 1966, David Stuart Gallery, LA, 1969, 73, 74, Galerie Darathea Speyer, 1970, 75, Willard Gallery, NYC, 1975, Gruenebaum Gallery, Ltd., NYC, 1977, Asher Faure Gallery, LA, 1983, LA Inst. Contemporary Art, 1984, Zola-Lieberman Gallery, Chgo., 1984, Gallery Paule Anglim, San Francisco, 1985, 88, Henry Art Gallery U. Wash., Seattle, 1986, Santa Barbara Contemporary Arts Forum, 1986, Forum, Zurich, Switzerland, 1987, Kent Fine Art, NY, 1987, The Sixties, Kent Fine Art, NYC, 1988, Herter Art Gallery, U. Mass., Amherst, 1989, The First Picture, Kent Gallery, NYC, 1990, I Space, Chgo., 1993, Patricia Faure Gallery, Santa Monica, Calif., 1994, Palm Springs Desert Mus., Calif., 1995, The Legend of Mick Rat, Patricia Faure Gallery, Santa Monica, 1996, Gallery Paula Anglim, San Francisco, 1997, Post-POP, Kent Gallery, NYC, 2004; retrospective exhbn. Newport Harbor Art Mus., Newport Beach, Calif., 1974; represented in permanent collections, Mus. 20th Century, Vienna, La Jolla Mus. Art, Calif., LA County Mus. Art, Oakland Art Mus., Pasadena Art Mus. (now Norton Simon Mus.), Whitney Mus., Mus. Modern Art, NYC, and Paris, Stanford, Palo Alto, Chgo. Art Inst., Beaubourg Mus., Paris, Mus. Boymans, Rotterdam, Guggenheim Mus., NYC, Newport Harbor Art Mus., Newport Beach, Calif., San Francisco Mus. Modern Art, Seattle Art Mus., Laguna Beach Mus. Art, Calif. Served with AUS, 1954-56. New Talent purchase grantee LA County Mus. Art, 1964; medal of France (1st award for painting), 5th Paris Bienniale, Mus. Modern Art, Paris, 1967; Guggenheim fellow, 1977-78 Office: c/o Kent Gallery 541 W 25th St New York NY 10001

FOUNTAIN, EDWIN BYRD, minister, librarian, poet; b. Manassas, Ga., Mar. 11, 1930; s. David Theodore and Laura Bertha (Phillips) F. BFA, U. Ga., 1951; BRE, ThB, Lexington Bapt. Coll., 1980, MRE, 1981, DD (hon.), 1990; MLS, U. Ky., 1984; PhD in Edn., Am. Bible Coll. and Seminary, 1998. Ordained to ministry Bapt. Ch., 1982. Pastor Riverview Bapt. Ch., Lexington, Ky., 1982-87; libr. asst. Lexington Bapt. Coll., 1980-81, tchr., libr., 1989—90; divisional chmn. libr. svcs. Tenn. Temple U., Chattanooga, 1990-91; librarian Statesboro (Ga.) Regional Libr., 1991-93. Author: The Sovereignty and Rightousness of God, 1997, Election and Redemption, 2000, (bibliography) Reformation in Italy and Southern France, 16th, 17th, 18th and 19th Centuries, 2000; compiler indexes for religious books: (by B.H. Carroll) An Interpretation of the English Bible, (by T.P. Simmons) A Systematick Study of Bible Doctrine, (with Jim Jeffries) A Student's Writers Guide, Fountains and Related Families, 2001, Hymn There Was a Night in Israel, 2002, (young adult novel) Whispers From the Past, 2004, (with Pastor Willard Ramsey) The Signature of God, 2007; contbr. articles to profl. publs., poetry to anthologies. U. Ky. fellow, 1990. Mem. ALA, SAG, SAR (local sec.), S.R., SCV, Christians Librs. Assn., Actors Equity Assn., Bulloch County Hist. Soc., Darlington County Hist. Commn., Lexington Bapt. Coll. Alumni Assn. (pres. 1982-87, 89-90), Armstrong State Coll. Alumni Assn., Beta Phi Mu. Home: 311 Jerriel St Vidalia GA 30474 Personal E-mail: edwin@cybersouth.com.

FOUNTAIN, KAREN SCHUELER, retired physician; b. Aberdeen, SD, Oct. 14, 1947; BA, No. State Coll., Aberdeen, SD, 1968; MD, U. Md., Balt., 1972. Diplomate Nat. Bd. Med. Examiners, Am. Bd. Radiology in Therapeutic Radiology. Intern Md. Gen. Hosp., Balt., 1972-73, resident in radiation oncology, 1973-74; fellow in radiation oncology Mayo Clinic, Rochester, Minn., 1974-76, cons. in oncology, 1976-81; clin. asst. prof. Columbia U., NYC, 1981-83, residency program dir. dept. radiation oncology, 1981—93, clin. assoc. prof., 1983—2001, ret., 2004. Mem. med. bd. Presbyn. Hosp., N.Y.C., 1983-86, Med. Res. Corps., 2004-; faculty coun. mem. Columbia U., 1982-89; del. N.Y. State Radiological Soc., N.Y.C., 1987-2004. Fellow Am. Coll. Radiology (councilor 1999-04), Am. Radium Soc. (exec. com. 2004-06), N.Y. Acad. Medicine; mem. Am. Soc. Therapeutic Radiology and Oncology, Radiol. Soc. N.Am., Am. Soc. Clin. Oncology, Am. Assn. for Women Radiologists (bd. dirs. 1995-96), So. Med. Assn., N.Y. Roentgen Soc. (sect. chmn. 1989-90), N.Y. State Radiol. Soc. (bd. dirs. 1996-02), N.Y. Acad. Scis.

FOUNTAIN, LINDA KATHLEEN, health science association executive; b. Fowler, Kans., Apr. 30, 1954; d. Ralph Edward and Ruth Evelyn (Cornelson) Young; m. Andre Fountain. BS in Nursing, Cen. State U., Edmond, Okla., 1976. RN, Okla. Staff nurse med./surg. and coronary care unit Presbyn. Hosp., Oklahoma City, 1976-79; mgr. nursing Hillcrest Osteo. Hosp., Oklahoma City, 1979-80; staff nurse, mgr. Oklahoma U. Teaching Hosp., Oklahoma City, 1981-82; pres. New Life Programs, Oklahoma City, 1981-88, Nursing Entrepreneurs, Ltd., Oklahoma City, 1988—; mgr. Internat. Health Supply, Oklahoma City, 1988—. Coord. lactation cons. program State of Okla., 1981-98, new life car seat rental program at various hosps., 1983-92, also speaker Success Co., Oklahoma City, 1984—; owner Rainbows Overhead Graphic Media, Oklahoma City, 1984-91; speaker in field. Founder Praxis Coll., Oklahoma City, 1988. Named Mentor of Yr., Okla. Metroplex Childbirth Network, Oklahoma City, 1984; honored for vol. work with families and rescue after Oklahoma City bombing, U.S. Dept. Justice, 1995. Mem. Am. Nurses Assn., Internat. Lactation Cons. Assn., Internat. Platform Assn., Bodyworkers and Wellness Therapies Assn. Avocations: gemology, travel. Office Phone: 405-879-0224. Business E-Mail: Lfountain@praxiscollege.com.

FOUNTAIN, ROBERT ROY, JR., retired engineering company executive, farmer, military officer; b. Norfolk, Va., Jan. 25, 1932; s. Robert Roy and Hilda (Burton) F.; m. Elizabeth Whitmarsh Bean, June 4, 1955; children: Robert, Dorothy, Sally, Edwin. Student, U. Rochester, 1950-51; BS Engring. with distinction, U.S. Naval Acad., 1955. Commd. ensign U.S. Navy, 1955, advanced through grades to rear adm., 1980; nuclear engr. serving in destroyers, cruisers, and nuclear submarines; comdg. officer U.S.S. Sea Devil, 1970-74; comdr. Submarine Devel. Squadron 12, New London, Conn., 1976-78; comdr. U.S. Naval Forces Marianas, comdr. U.S. Naval Base Guam comdr. in chief Pacific rep. Guam and Trust Ter. Pacific Islands, 1979-81; dep. chief Naval Sea Sys. Command, ASW and Undersea Warfare Sys., Navy Dept., Washington, 1981-85; ret., 1985; dir. Offshore Sys. Marine Sys. divsn. Honeywell, Seattle, 1986-88; v.p. Honeywell Advanced Marine Sys. Operation, Mpls., 1988, San Diego, 1989, Arlington, Va., 1990-91; dir. tech. plans & resources Alliant Techsystems Inc., Arlington, Va., 1991-92. Presdl. elector, 1996; chmn. Westmoreland County Rep. Com.; active Va. Nat. Def. Indsl. Authority, 2005—. Decorated Legion of Merit (3), Def. Superior Service medal, Meritorious Service medal (2), Navy Commendation medal. Mem.: SAR, Assn. Preservation Va. Antiquities, Va. Small Grains Assn., No. Neck Hist. Soc., Naval Acad. Alumni Assn., Mil. Officers Assn., Naval Submarine League. Home: Stillwater 4750 Zacata Rd Montross VA 22520-3510

FOUNTAIN, RONALD GLENN, management consultant, corporate financial executive, entrepreneur, educator; b. Mason City, Wash., Feb. 12, 1939; s. Aldine Shirah and Ella Maude (Fordham) F.; m. Ethel Joan Hightower, Aug. 22, 1968; children: John Hightower, Dana Leigh. AS, Ga. Southwestern Coll., 1959; BS, Valdosta State U., 1965; MBA, Case Western Res. U., 1983, ExecDrMgmt, 1999. V.p. nat. accounts Ctrl. Bancshares, Birmingham, Ala., 1973-74; cash control mgr. White Consol., Cleve., 1974-76, asst. treas., 1976-79, treas., dir. investor rels., 1979-82, v.p., treas., 1982-83, v.p. fin., treas., 1983-86; pres. Dix & Eaton, 1986-88; v.p. fin., CFO M.A. Hanna Co., Cleve., 1988-93; mng. prin. The Commonwealth Group, Cleve., 1993-04; sr. exec. v.p. Roulston & Co., Cleve., 1994-96; adv. dir. InfoSource, Harris Co., 1995-98; ptnr. The Parkland Group, 1996—2003; pres., CEO United Truck Fin. & Mktg., 1998—2001; prof. mgmt. Walsh U., North Canton, Ohio, 2003—; mng. ptnr. Capital Acceleration Ptnrs. LLC, 2003—. Adj. faculty Weatherhead Sch. Mgmt., 1996-, exec. dir. profl. fellow program, 2000-02; bd. dirs. Dise & Co.; pres. Delta Sys. Inc., 2004-06, bd. dirs., 2001-07; pres. Ironrock Capital. Trustee Notre Dame Coll., Cleve., 1984-90, Laurel Sch., 1986-90, Pub. Radio Sta. WCPN, 1990-93, MetroHealth Sys., 1996—; chmn. N.E. Hospice Study Com., 1989-93; bd. dirs. Jr. Achievement Cleve., 1982, Nat. Adoption Exch., Phila., 1983, Cleve. Edn. Fund, 1983-87 Mem.: Planning Forum (pres. 1992—94), Nat. Investor Rels. Inst. (pres. 1978—79), Assn. Corp. Growth, Fin. Execs. Inst. (membership chmn. 1983—84), Alumni Assn. Weatherhead Sch. Mgmt. (pres. 1985—88), Country Club, Union Club. Home: 2908 Paxton Rd Cleveland OH 44120-1824 Personal E-mail: rgf2908@msn.com.

FOURNELLE, RAYMOND ALBERT, engineering educator; b. St. Louis, Dec. 9, 1941; s. August Carl and Adella Emma (Fleer) F. BS in Metall. Engring., U. Mo., 1964, MS in Metall. Engring., 1968, PhD in Metall. Engring., 1971; Profl. Degree of Metall. Engring. (hon.), U. Mo., Rolla. Registered profl. engr., Wis. Rsch. engr. Shell Oil Co., Wood River, Ill., 1964-66; rsch. assoc. Northwestern U., Evanston, Ill., 1971-72; asst. prof. Marquette U., Milw., 1972-78, assoc. prof., 1978-86, prof., 1986—; interim chairperson Dept. of Mech. and Indsl. Engring., 1998—2001. Contbr. articles to profl. jours. 1st lt. U.S. Army, 1964-66, Fed. Republic Germany. Rsch. grantee NSF, 1975, 79, 86; Fulbright fellow U. Stuttgart (Germany), 1983-84, 90-91, Alexander von Humboldt fellow, 1985-88, Mac-Planck-Forschungspreis, 1994, ASM Internat. fellow, 1996. Mem. ASME, AAUP, ASM Internat. (bd. rev. 1981—), Minerals, Metals and Materials Soc. (com. mem.), Am. Soc. Engring. Edn. Republican. Achievements include development of theories and models for various solid state reactions in metals and alloys, including discontinuous precipitation, coarsening, and dissolution, diffusion induced grain boundary and liquid film migration. Home: 1029 N Jackson St Apt 509A Milwaukee WI 53202 Office: Marquette U Dept Mech Engring PO Box 1881 Milwaukee WI 53201-1881 Office Phone: 414-288-3541. Business E-Mail: raymond.fournelle@mu.edu.

FOURNET, PATRICIA SIBLEY, retired secondary school educator; b. Beaumont, Tex., Aug. 21, 1936; d. George W. and Irma Turnbull Sibley; m. Kenneth Leon Fournet, June 26, 1990; 1 child, George Ray Jones. Med, U. Southwestern La., Lafayette, 1975. HS tchr. St. Martin Parish Sch. Bd., St. Martinville, La., 1963—93. Cons. local bar assn. St. Martin Ville, La., 1972—74; singer Return to Bethlehem, 2005. Author: Experiments and Exercises, 1974; actor: Twelve Plays of Christmas, Opera House, 2006; stage mgr.: Miracle of 34th Street, 2006; Cinderella, 2007; singer: (albums) Return to Bethlehem, 2005; stage mgr.: Our Town, 2006. Mem. Found. for the Blind, 1995—2005; missions dir. Evangeline Assn. Vacation Bible Sch., Lafayette, La., 2006—07; treas. Little Theater, St. Martinville, La., 2002—07; bd. dirs. Evangeline Players, 2002—07. Recipient Outstanding Vol. award, 2004. Mem.: La. Ret. Tchrs. Assn., So. Med. Aux. Soc. Baptist. Avocations: travel, organ, bridge, walking. Home: 206 Allan St PO Box 224 Saint Martinville LA 70582 Home Fax: 337-394-4118. Personal E-mail: pati4@bellsouth.net.

FOURNIE, RAYMOND RICHARD, lawyer; b. Belleville, Ill., Jan. 3, 1951; s. Raymond Victor and Gladys M. (Muskopf) F.; m. Mary Lindeman, Sept. 2, 1978; children: Sarah Dozier, John David, Anne Gerard, David Raymond. BS, U. Ill., 1973; JD, St. Louis U., 1979. Bar: Mo. 1979, Ill. 1980. Assoc. Moser, Marsalek, et al., St. Louis, 1979-80, Brown, James & Rabbitt, P.C., St. Louis, 1981-82, Shepherd, Sandberg & Phoenix, P.C., St. Louis, 1982-86; shareholder Shepherd, Sandberg & Phoenix, St. Louis, 1986-88; ptnr. Armstrong Teasdale LLP, St. Louis, 1988—. U. Ill. fellow, 1974. Mem. Mo. Bar Assn., Ill. Bar Assn., St. Louis Bar Assn. (sec. trial sect.), Lawyers Assn. (v.p. 1987-88, pres. 1990-91), Actors Equity Assn. Roman Catholic. Avocations: singing, baseball, golf, acting. Home: 4 Ridgetop St Saint Louis MO 63117-1021 Office: Armstrong Teasdale LLP One Metropolitan Sq Ste 2600 Saint Louis MO 63102-2740

FOURNIER, DUDLEY JOHN, surgeon; b. Capreol, Ont., Can., June 23, 1923; s. Dudley Thomas and Margaret Mary (Conway) Fournier; m. Barbara Jane Arnold, Dec. 2, 1950; children: Dudley John Jr., Michele

Fournier McLellan. BSc, Northwestern U., Evanston, Ill., 1945, MB, 1947, MD, 1948. Served with USN, Chgo., 1943—45; intern Queen of Angels Hosp., LA, 1947—48; med. officer USN, 1949—51; resident in surgery St. Mary's Hosp., San Francisco, 1953—55; fellow in cancer rsch. U. Calif. Med. Sch., San Francisco, 1955—56, mem. surg. faculty, 1956—63; pvt. practice surgeon San Francisco, 1956—. Surgeon emergency hosps. San Francisco Health Dept., 1956—78; team physician San Francisco Warriors (now Golden State Warriors), 1962—66. With USN, 1943—45, lt. comdr. USN, 1949—51. Recipient Man and Youth award, San Francisco Boys and Girls Club, 1990. Mem.: Olympic Club (San Francisco), Bohemian Club (San Francisco), The Guardsmen (San Francisco) (life). Republican. Roman Catholic. Avocations: golf, skiing. Office Phone: 415-986-4247. Personal E-mail: dfournier948@md.northwestern.edu.

FOURNIER, MAUREEN MARY, physical education educator; b. Chgo., Feb. 27, 1952; d. George Joseph and Lauretta Marie (Tangney) Lewis; m. Thomas Joseph Fournier, Sept. 21, 1979; children: Jennifer Lynn, Michele Marie. BS in Edn., No. Ill. U., 1973; MS in Edn., Chgo. State U., 1983. Recreation leader Alsip Park Dist., Ill., 1973-75; tchr. phys. edn. Sch. Dist. 126, Alsip, 1974—. Mem. Alsip Coun. Local 943 IFT, 1973—, pres., 1985—87, 1992—97, 2005—. Mgr. Oak Lawn (Ill.) Girls Softball, 1990—91, 1994—98, sec., 1998, Richard Area Swim Club, 1997—98; mem. internal rev. com. Sch. Dist. 126, Alsip, 1999—2006; NCA com. mem., sec. Richards HS Parent Boosters Club, 2000—. Mem.: AAHPERD, Ill. Assn. Health, Phys. Edn., Recreation and Dance (evaluator Blue Ribbon com.). Avocations: bowling, swimming, reading. Office: Sch Dist 126 Lane Sch 4600 W 123rd St Alsip IL 60803-2522 E-mail: mofournier@sd12.k12.il.us.

FOURNIER, R. E. KEITH, biologist; b. Attleboro, Mass., July 26, 1949; BS, Providence Coll., RI, 1971; PhD, Princeton U., NJ, 1974. Asst. prof. U. So. Calif., LA, 1978—84, assoc. prof., 1984—86, prof., 1986—87; full mem. Fred Hutchinson Cancer Rsch. Ctr., Seattle, 1987—2007; ret., 2007. Adj. prof. W. Alton Jones Cell Sci. Ctr., Lake Placid, NY, 1978—82. Author: over 100 articles in sci. publs. Office Phone: 206-667-5217. Office Fax: 206-667-6522. Business E-Mail: kfournie@fhcrc.org.

FOURT, BERNARD-FRANCOIS P., retired engineer; b. Vermelles, France, Oct. 12, 1927; s. Antoine-Jean Fourt and Denise Angele Hanot-Fourt; m. Henriette Mortamet, Sept. 22, 1956; children: Benoit (dec.), Gilles, Catherine, Frederique (dec.), Jerome, Beatrice, Martin, Xavier, Marie-Laure. Degree in Elec. Engring., Ecole Supr. Electricity, Malakoff, 1952; MBA, Harvard Bus. Sch., Boston, 1955; Ancien Auditeur, IHEDN, Paris, 1969. Profl. engr. Sales engr. Le Carbone Lorraine, Paris, 1952-53; prodn. mgr. Compagnie Electromecanique and subs., Villeurbane, France, 1955-59, svc. mgr. Paris, 1959-62; plant mgr. Darex, DeWalko, W.R. Grace, Epernon, France, 1962-64; internal cons. Alcatel Alsthom (formerly CGE), France, 1964-67; pres. Le Joint Français, Bezons, France, 1967-76; pvt. cons. Le Vesinet, France, 1976-88; expert at the ct. of appeal Versailles, 1978—. Lt. French Army, 1947-48, hon. maj. Roman Catholic. Avocations: golf, bridge. Home: 11 Rue des Reservoirs Le Vesinet 78110 France Personal E-mail: fourt@free.fr.

FOUSE, JACQUALYN A., consumer products company executive; b. Duncanville, Tex. BA in Econs., MA in Econs., Univ. Tex., Arlington. Fin. analyst Alcon, Ft. Worth, 1986—93, sr. v.p., CFO, 2002—07; asst. controller, pharm., cosmetics group Nestle (Alcon corp. parent), Switzerland, 1993—2001; CFO Swissair Group, 2001—02, Bunge, White Plains, NY, 2007—. Bd. dir. ORBIS Internat. Named a Great Woman of Tex., Ft. Worth Bus. Press, Global Leader for Tomorrow, World Econ. Forum; recipient Fin. Exec. Yr. award, Inst. Mgmt. Accts. and Robert Half Internat., 2005, Disting. Alumni award, Univ. Tex. Arlington. Office: CFO Bunge Ltd 50 Main St White Plains NY 10606 Office Phone: 914-684-2800.

FOUST, LAWRENCE L., lawyer; b. Houston, Apr. 22, 1953; s. William L. and Barbara J. Foust; m. Christine E. Wagener, Sept. 1, 1948. BA, Duke U., Durham, NC, 1975; JD, U. of Va., 1978, LLM, 1980; MBA, U. of St. Thomas, Houston, 1996. Bar: Va. 1978, Tex. 1980, Calif. 2006, bd. cert. health law: Tex. Bd. Legal Specialization; Master of Vessels USCG, 2004. Fellow U. of Va. Schs. of Medicine and Law, Charlottesville, 1978—80; atty. Wood, Lucksinger & Epstein, Houston, 1980—83; assoc. gen. counsel Sisters of Charity, Houston, 1983—95; shareholder Jenkens & Gilchrist, Houston, 1996—2006; sr. counsel Kaiser Found. Health Plan, 2006—. Audit com. U. Tex. Physicians, Houston, 2004—06. Bd. dirs. Houston Taping for the Blind Radio, 2002—06, exec. v.p., 2002—06; bd. dirs. Southampton Civic Assn., Houston, 2005—06. Named Tex. Super Lawyer Health Law, Tex. Monthly Mag., 2003—05, Outstanding Physician Practice Atty., Beard Group, 2004, Outstanding Hosp. Atty., 2005. Mem.: Calif. State Bar, Va. State Bar, Tex. State Bar, Houston Bar Assn., Am. Health Lawyers Assn. Lutheran. Avocations: sailing, travel. Home: 2240 Robinhood Houston TX 77005 Office: Kaiser Found Health Plan One Kaiser Plz Ste 1900 Oakland CA 94612 Home Phone: 713-669-8930; Office Phone: 510-271-6674. Personal E-mail: lawrencefoust@houston.rr.com. Business E-Mail: lawrence.l.foust@kp.org.

FOUST, ROBERT SCHMERTZ, retired legislative staff member, educator; b. New Holland, Pa., Jan. 20, 1941; s. Wilson Arbogast and Elizabeth (Schmertz) F. BA in Polit. Sci., Upsala Coll., 1964; MA in Internat. Rels., Lehigh U., Bethlehem, Pa., 1971. Asst. dir. admissions Upsala Coll., East Orange, NJ, 1965-69; legis. asst. Office of Senator Claiborne Pell, Washington, 1970-89; cons. Indochinese Cmty. Ctr., Washington, 1990-91; sr. policy adv. Office of Senator Kent Conrad, Washington, 1991—2005; ret.; mem. faculty George Washington U., Washington. Named Outstanding Young Men of Am., Jaycees, 1973; recipient commendations USCG, U.S. Dept. Vets. Affairs, Disabled Am. Vets., Career Resources Network Assn., Nat. Assn. Federally Impacted Schs., Nat. Head Start Assn. Mem.: Asia Soc., The Army and Navy Club. Personal E-mail: jurongsq@aol.com.

FOUTS, JAMES FREMONT, mining company executive; b. Port Arthur, Tex., June 3, 1918; s. Horace Arthur and Willie E. (Edwards) F.; m. Elizabeth Hanna Browne, June 19, 1948; children: Elizabeth, Donovan, Alan, James. BChemE, Tex. A&M U., 1940. Div. supt. Baroid divsn. N.L. Industries, U.S. Rocky Mountain area and Can., 1948-60; pres. Riley-Utah Co., Salt Lake City, 1960-67, Fremont Corp., Monroe, La., 1967—, Auric Metals Corp., Salt Lake City, 1972-2000. Bd. dirs. La Fonda Hotel, Santa Fe, High Plains Natural Gas Co., Canadian, Tex. Hon. asst. sec. of State of La. Served to lt. col. arty U.S. Army, 1942-46. Mem. Wyo. Geol. Assn. (v.p. 1958), Rocky Mountain Oil & Gas Assn. (bd. dirs. 1959), Res. Officers Assn. Wyo. (pres. 1948), Am. Assn. Petroleum Geologists, Internat. Geol. Assn., Mont. Geol. Assn., Ind. Petroleum Producers Assn. Clubs: Univ. Lodges: Elks. Republican. Episcopalian. Home: 4002 Bon Aire Dr Monroe LA 71203-3015 Office: Fremont Corp PO Box 7070 Monroe LA 71211-7070

FOWKE, BENJAMIN G.S., III, energy executive; BS in Fin. and Acctg. magna cum laude, Towson U. CPA 1982. Auditor KPMG; supr. internal audits Dart Group; mgr. fin. reporting DWG Corp.; various fin. positions FP&L Group; v.p. retail bus. unit New Century Energies; v.p., CFO Energy Markets; v.p., treas. Xcel Energy Inc., 2002—03, v.p., CFO, treas., 2003—. Bd. mem. Milestone Growth Fund.*

FOWLE, BRUCE S., architect; m. Marcia Fowle; 3 children. BArch, Syracuse U., 1960. Assoc. Edward Larrabee Barnes, FAIA, 1970—77; co-founder, sr. principal FXFOWLE Archs., P.C. (formerly Fox & Fowle Architects, P.C.), 1978—. Co-founder Architects, Designers, and Planners for Social Responsibility, NYC, 1982; chmn. Syracuse U. School of Architecture Adv. Comm. Named Nat. Academician, Nat. Acad. of Design, 1994; named to Am. Institute of Architects College of Fellows, 1985; recipient George Arents Pioneer Medal, Syracuse U., 2001. Fellow: Institute for Urban Design; mem.: Am. Institute of Architects Design Comm. Office: FXFOWLE Architects PC 22 W 19th St New York NY 10011

FOWLER, ALAN BICKSLER, retired physicist; b. Denver, Oct. 15, 1928; s. Alan Bruce and Minnie Edna (Bicksler) F.; m. Kathleen Teresa Devlin, Sept. 4, 1950; children: Stephen B., Susan Fowler-Finn, Andrew A., Sarah A. BS, Rensselaer Poly. Inst., 1951, MS, 1952; PhD, Harvard U., 1958. Rsch. staff mem. Raytheon Mfg. Co., Rsch. Div., Waltham, Mass., 1953-56, IBM Rsch. Div., Yorktown Heights, NY, 1958-83; IBM fellow Yorktown Heights, NY, 1983-93; IBM fellow emeritus, 1993—2005. With U.S. Army, 1946-48, 1st lt. Signal Corps, 1952-53. Recipient John Price Wetherill medal Franklin Inst., 1981, Alexander von Humboldt Preistraeger, 1982, David Sarnoff medal IEEE, 1987, Buckley prize Am. Phys. Soc., 1988. Mem.: NAE, NAS, IEEE, Royal Soc. of London (fgn.), Am. Acad. Arts and Scis., Am. Phys. Soc. Personal E-mail: alnfwl@aol.com.

FOWLER, BARBARA J., middle school educator; b. Emporia, Kans. d. Calvin and Leona Zirnstein; m. Stanley A. Fowler; children: Kelsey, Matthew. BSE, Emporia State U., Kans., 1979. Cert. Nat. Bd. Profl. Tchg., 2000. Tchr. Lowther Mid. Sch., Emporia, 1982—88, Emporia Mid. Sch., 1988—. Mentor tchr. Emporia State U., 1991—; team leader Emporia Mid. Sch., 2002—; keen presenter Kans. State Dept. Edn., Topeka, 2003—. Project leader Kans. 4-H, Lyon County, 1996—; mem. rev. team Kans. State/Nat. Coun. Accreditation of Tchr. Edn.; sec. Kans. State Dem. Party, 2003—; Bible sch. tchr. Ch. of Christ, Emporia. Recipient Horace Mann Tchg. award, 2003, Kans. Master Tchr. award, State of Kans., 2002, Kans. Tchr. of Yr. award, Kans. Dept. Edn., 2003, Disting. Alumni award, Emporia State U., 2003; grantee Gov.'s Tchg. Excellence scholarship, U.S. Peace Inst., Summer Inst., 2004. Mem.: ASCD, NEA (sec. 2004, del., Tchg. Excellence award 2003), Nat. Coun. Social Studies. Democrat. Avocations: reading, politics. Home: 14 S Barbie Emporia KS 66801 Office: Emporia Mid Sch 2300 Graphic Arts Rd Emporia KS 66801 Business E-Mail: bfowler@usd253.org.

FOWLER, BETH, actress; b. Jersey City, Nov. 1, 1940; Actor: (Broadway plays) Gantry, 1970, A Little Night Music, 1974, 1600 Pennsylvania Avenue, 1976, Peter Pan, 1979—81, Baby, 1984, Take Me Along, 1985, Teddy & Alice, 1987—88, Sweeney Todd, 1989—90 (Tony nominee best actress musical, 1990), Beauty and the Beast, 1994 (LA Ovation award), Bells Are Ringing, 2001, The Boy From Oz, 2003 (Tony nominee best featured actress musical, 2004), Escape, 2005, Inherit the Wind, 2007.*

FOWLER, BRUCE ANDREW, toxicologist, researcher, public health service official; b. Seattle, Dec. 28, 1945; s. Andrew and Dolores Yvonne F.; children from previous marriage: Glenn Andrew, Randall Bruce. BS in Fisheries, U. Wash., 1968; PhD in Pathology, U. Oreg., 1972. From staff fellow to head metal toxicology Nat. Inst. Environ. Health Scis., Research Triangle Park, NC, 1972—86, head metal toxicology, 1986—87; dir. toxicology program U. Md., 1987—2001; sr. rsch. advisor Agy. for Toxic Substances and Disease Registry, Atlanta, 2002—03, asst. dir. for sci., divsn. toxicology, 2003—; scientist environ. health Sr. Biomed. Rsch. Svc. USPHS, 2003—; Pres.'s rotating prof. U. Alaska, 2006—. Prof. pathology U. Md. Med. Sch., 1987—2001, prof. epidemiology and toxicology, 2001—03, dir. lab. of cellular and molecular toxicology dept. of epidemiology and preventive medicine, 2001—03; dir. office collaborative studies on adaptive responses estuarine species U. Md., 1988—2001; Meyer Bodansky lectr. Dept. Pathology, U. Tex. Med. Br., Galveston; adj. assoc. prof. U. NC, NC; temporary adv. WHO; work group mem. Internat. Agy. Rsch. Against Cancer; mem., chmn. Sci. Com. on Toxicology of Metals; mem. Md. Gov.'s Coun. on Toxic Substances, 1988—93, chmn., 1990—93, Dahlem Workshop on Mechanisms of Cell Injury: Implications for Human Health, Berlin, 1985; mem. toxicology info. program com. on toxicology; chmn. com. on measuring lead in critical populations; mem. com. on women in sci. and engring., com. on biologic markers in urologic toxicology NAS/NRC, 1989—93, com. on evaluation on viability of augmenting potable water supplies with reclaimed water, 1996—97, subcom. on arsenic in drinking water, 1997—99; co-chmn. NY Acad. Scis. Conf. on Mechanisms of Chem.-Induced Porphyrinopathies, Rye, NY; Swedish Med. Rsch. Coun. vis. prof. Karolinska Inst., 1994—95; Colgate-Palmolive vis. prof. U. Wash., 1998—99; mem. Fulbright scholarship rev. com., Scandinavia, 1999—2001, chair, Scandinavia, 2000—01; mem. nat. metals assessment panel sci. adv. bd. U.S. EPA, 2002—03, mem. nat. metals risk assessment framework review panel sci. advisory bd., 2004—05, mem. all ages lead model review panel sci. adv. bd., 2005—, mem. clean air sci. adv. lead review panel sci. adv. bd., 2006—; mem. expert panel Ctr. Evaluation of Risks to Human Reproduction Nat. Toxicology Program, 2003—. Editor: Biological and Environmental Effects of Arsenic, 1983, Mechamisms of Cell Injury: Implications for Human Health; co-editor: Mechanisms of Chemical Induced Porphyrinopathies, Handbook on the Toxicology of Metals, 3d edit.; mem. editl. bd. Chemico-Biol. Interacctions, 1980—85, Environ. Health Perspectives, 1981—97, Toxicology and Applied Pharmacology, 1985—96, Internat. Archives of Environ. Health, 1986—, Renal Failure, 1988—, Internat. Jour. Occupl. and Environ. Health, 1994—96, Jour. Biochem. and Molecular Toxicology, 2000—, Open Toxicology Revs., 2006—, Chemistry Ctrl. Jour., 2007—; contbr. articles to profl. jours., chapters to books. Rsch. fellow Japanese Soc. Promotion of Sci., 1990; Fulbright scholar Karolinska Inst., 1994; finalist Charles C. Shepard award CDC, 2007. Fellow Acad. Toxicol. Scis. (bd. dirs. 2006-); mem. AAAS (recruitment and screening panel ct. apptd. sci. experts project 2000—), Am. Inst. Biol. Scis., Am. Soc. Pharmacology and Exptl. Therapeutics, Soc. Toxicology (councilor mechanisms of toxicity sect., pres. metals splty. sect. 1996, councilor nat. capitol area regional chpt. 1994-95, v.p. in-vitro splty. sect. 2001-02, pres. in-vitro splty. sect. 2003-04, councilor 2005-07), Am. Coll. Toxicology (councilor 1995-98), Soc. Occupl. and Environ. Health (councilor 1988, v.p. 1993), Fulbright Assn., NY Acad. Sci., Internat. Commn. Occupl. Health (chmn. sci. com. toxicology of metals 1996-2002), Profl. Assn. Diving Instrs., Sigma Xi. Office: ATSDR MSF-32 1600 Clifton Rd NE Atlanta GA 30333 Office Phone: 770-488-7250. Personal E-mail: drtox@earthlink.net. E-mail: bxf9@cdc.gov.

FOWLER, CHARLES ALBERT, electronics engineer; b. Centralia, Ill., Dec. 17, 1920; s. Clarence J. and Bess (Maxwell) F.; m. Kathryn Elizabeth Grimes, Oct. 23, 1943; children: Patricia Ann Paul, Mary Catherine Leathem. BS in Engring. Physics, U. Ill., 1942. Mem. staff radiation lab. MIT, 1942-45; head radar systems dept. Airborne Instruments Lab., Deer Park, N.Y., 1946-66; dep. dir. (tactical warfare) def. research and engring. Dept. Def., 1966-70; v.p., mgr. equipment devel. labs. Raytheon Co., Sudbury, Mass., 1970-76; sr. v.p., gen. mgr. Bedford (Mass.) ops. Mitre Corp., 1976-85; pres C.A. Fowler Assocs., 1986—. Mem. sci. adv. com. Def. Intelligence Agy., 1971—2000, chmn. sci. adv. com., 1976—82; mem. Air Force Sci. Adv. Bd., 1971—77, Def. Sci. Bd., 1972—98, chmn., 1984—88, vice chmn., 1988—90. Contbr. articles in field. Mem. East Norwich Sch. Bd., 1955-61, East Norwich Library Bd., 1956-62. Fellow IEEE, AAAS, AIAA; mem. Nat. Acad. Engring. Office: 100 Newbury Ct Ste 309 Concord MA 01742 E-mail: bertfowler@verizon.net.

FOWLER, CHARLES ALLISON EUGENE, retired architect, civil engineer; b. Halifax, NS, Can., Jan. 24, 1921; s. Charles Allison and Mildred (Crosby) Fowler; m. Dorothy Christine Graham, Aug. 30, 1947 (dec. Sept. 1998); children: Graham Allison, Beverly Anne; m. Ruby Joyce Crooks, Aug. 21, 2002. BSc, Dalhousie U., 1942; B in Engring., McGill U., 1944; BArch., U. Man., 1948; DEng (hon.), Tech. U. of Nova Scotia, 1975. With C.A. Fowler, Bauld & Mitchell, Ltd. (and predecessor firms), Halifax, 1946-80, sr. ptnr., 1950-70, pres., 1970-80, chmn., 1980-81; pres. C.A. Fowler & Co., 1950-70, 81-95; ret., 1995. Prin. works include Miners Mus., Glace Bay, N.S., Dalhousie U. Fine Arts Ctr., 1970, univ. ctr. Acadia U., Acad. Ctr. at Mt. St. Vincent U., Halifax Law Cts., Canadian Martyrs Ch., Can. Permanent Bldg. Hfx., Halifax Metro Ctr., Stadacona Hosp., Victoria Gen. Hosp., Centre 200, Sydney, N.S. Past chmn. bd. dirs. N.S. Coll. Art and Design. With Can. Army, 1943-46. Fellow AIA (hon.), Royal Archtl. Inst. Can. (pres. 1965), Can. Soc. for Civil Engring.; mem. Engring. Inst. Can. (life). Mem. United Ch. Home: 2 Hall's Rd Halifax NS Canada B3P 1P3

FOWLER, DANIEL MCKAY, lawyer; b. Chgo., Mar. 25, 1950; m. Julia M. Duffy, Apr. 20, 1990; children: Douglas M., Peter M. BA, Monmouth Coll., 1972; JD, U. Denver, 1975. Bar: Colo. 1975, Wyo. 1994, U.S. Dist. Ct. Colo. 1975, U.S. Ct. Appeals (10th cir.) 1975. Pres. Fowler, Schimberg & Flanagan, P.C., Denver. Mem. ABA, Colo. Bar Assn., Denver Bar Assn., Def. Rsch. Inst., Fedn. Def. and Corp. Counsel, Colo. Def. Lawyers Assn., Denver Athletic Club, Lakewood Country Club. Avocations: motorcycle touring, skiing, boating, travel. Office: Fowler Schimberg & Flanagan PC 1640 Grant St Ste 150 Denver CO 80203-1640 E-mail: d_fowler@fsf-law.com.

FOWLER, DAVID LUCAS, corporate lawyer; b. Heidelberg, Germany, Sept. 26, 1952; s. James Daniel and Nannie Romay (Lucas) F.; m. Cynthia Lou Smith, Aug. 19, 1989. BS, US Mil. Acad., 1974; JD, Georgetown U., 1981. Bar: NJ 1982, Calif. 1990, US Ct. Fed. Claims 1990, US Dist. Ct. (cen. dist.) Calif. 1990. 2d lt. US Army, 1974, advanced through grades to maj., infantry platoon leader Berlin, 1975-76, asst. protocol officer, 1976-77, aide-de-campe US comdr., 1977—78; minority augmentation recruit officer US Mil. Acad., 1978; chief adminstrv. law sect. US Army Tng. Ctr., Ft. Dix, NJ, 1981—84; command judge adv. US Army Field Sta., Sinop, Turkey, 1984—85; govt. contracts trial atty. US Army Legal Svcs. Agy., Falls Church, Va., 1986-89; resigned US Army, 1989; corp. staff counsel Hughes Aircraft Co., LA, 1989-94, sr. sgt. counsel Electro-Optical Sys. El Segundo, Calif., 1994-95, asst. gen. counsel Arlington, Va., 1996-97; v.p., dep. gen. counsel Raytheon Sys. Co., Arlington, 1998-99; v.p. legal Raytheon Washington Ops., 1999—; v.p., gen. counsel, sec. Raytheon Internat. Inc., Arlington, 2000—05; sr. v.p., gen. counsel Raytheon Tech. Svcs. Co., Reston, 2005—. Mem. AIA (chair legal com.). Avocations: reading, weightlifting, golf. Office: Raytheon Tech Svcs Co 12160 Sunrise Valley Dr Reston VA 20191

FOWLER, DAVID WAYNE, architectural engineering educator; b. Sabinal, Tex., Apr. 25, 1937; s. Otis Lindley and Sadie Gertrude (Cox) F.; m. Maxine Yvonne Thomson, Mar. 31, 1961; children: Teresa, Leah. BS in Archtl. Engring., U. Tex., 1960; MS, U. Tex., Austin, 1962; PhD in Civil Engring., U. Colo., 1965. Design engr. W.C. Cotten (Cons. Engr.), Austin, Tex., 1961-62; asst. prof. archtl. engring. U. Tex., Austin, 1964-69, assoc. prof., 1969-75, prof., 1975—, Taylor prof., 1981—, dir. Internat. Ctr. Aggregates Rsch., 1992—, Joe J. King chair, 1998—, chair intercoll. athletics coun. for men. Vis. prof. Nihon U., Japan, 1981, Chulalongkorn U., Thailand, 2001; bd. dirs. Univ. Fed. Credit Union, 1976-84; pres. Internat. Congress on Polymers in Concrete, 1981-87, bd. dirs. Univ. Coop, 2000—. Editor procs. 2d Internat. Congress on Polymers in Concrete, 1978, 2001; contbr. articles to profl. jours. Recipient Teaching award Gen. Dynamics, 1975, Teaching award Amoco Found., 1978, Disting. Engring. Alumnus award U. Colo., 1993, Owen Nutt award ICPIC, 1995, Joe J. King Profl. Achievement award, 2000, Claude Hocott Rsch. award, 2002; named to Acad/ Disting. Tchrs., 2000; cited by Engring.-News Record, 1975, Concrete Repair, 1995; Ford Found. faculty devel. grantee, 1962-64, Disting. Grad. Dept. Civil Archl. and Environ. Engring. U. Tex., 2005. Fellow ASCE (pres. Austin br. 1976-77), Am. Concrete Inst. (Delmar L. Bloem award 1985, bd. dirs. 1993-96, Robert Philleo award 2003), Archtl. Engring. Inst.; mem. NAE, Concrete Rsch. Coun. (chmn. 1996-2002), Concrete Rsch. Found. (chmn. 2000-2001), Am. Soc. Engring. Edn. (chmn. archtl. engring. divsn. 1971-72), Tex. Soc. Profl. Engrs. (bd. dirs. Travis chpt. 1968), Russian Acad. Engring. (hon.), Tau Beta Pi, Chi Epsilon. Mem. Ch. of Christ. Home: 612 Brookhaven Trl Austin TX 78746-5455 Office: Univ Tex ECJ 5208 Archtl Engring Group Austin TX 78712 Office Phone: 512-232-2575. Personal E-mail: dwfowlerpe@austin.rr.com. Business E-Mail: dwf@mail.utexas.edu.

FOWLER, DENNIS L., surgeon, director; BS with honors, Phillips U., Enid, Okla., 1970; MD, U. Kans. Sch. Medicine, Kans. City, 1973. Cert. Am. Bd. Surgery. Internship St. Luke's Hosp., Kans. City, Mo., 1974—75, surgery residency, 1975—79; surg. endoscopy fellowship Mass. Gen. Hosp., Boston, 1979—80; active staff Olathe Med. Ctr., Kans., 1985—97; dir. Allegheny Ctr. Laparoscopic and Minimally Invasive Surgery, Allegheny Gen. Hosp., Pitts., 1997—2000; dir. Minimal Access Surgery Ctr. NY Presbyn. Hosp./Columbia U. Med. Ctr., 2000—04, v.p., med. dir. perioperative svcs., 2004—. Asst. clin. prof. surgery U. Mo. Kans. City Sch. Medicine, 1987—93; courtesy staff Miami County Med. Ctr., Paola, Kans., 1988—97; assoc. prof. surgery MCP-Hahnemkann Sch. Medicine, Phila., 1997—2000; Leon C. Hirsch prof. clin. surgery Cornell U. Weill Med. Coll., 2000—04, chief divsn. gen. surgery, 2002—04; US surg. prof. clin. surgery Columbia U. Coll. Physicians & Surgeons, 2003—; cabinet mem. dept. surgery Columbia U. Coll. Physicians and Surgeons; clin. adv. bd. Ultracision, Inc.; presenter in field. Contbr. articles to profl. jours., chapters to books. Mem.: AMA, ACS (gov.-at-large NY 2002—05), Soc. Surgery of Alimentary Tract, Soc. Laparoendoscopic Surgeons, Soc. Am. Gastrointestinal Endoscopic Surgeons, Am. Soc. Gastrointestinal Endoscopy (Resident/Fellow Essay award 1980). Office: NY Presbyn Hosp/Columbia U Med Ctr PH Rm 126 622 W 168th St New York NY 10032 Office Phone: 212-305-0577. Office Fax: 212-543-8790.*

FOWLER, DON WALL, lawyer; b. Apr. 19, 1944; s. Slayden Grimes and Dorothy Lavenia (Wall) Fowler; m. Ruthann Arneson, Sept. 16, 1968 (div.); 1 child; m. Deborah Dewar, Sept. 15, 1984 (dec. Feb. 1986); m. Marcia Petlin, Oct. 1, 1988 (div.). BA, Emory U., 1966; JD, U. Chgo., 1969. Bar: Ill. 1969, U.S. Dist. Ct. (no. dist.) Ill. 1969, U.S. Ct. Appeals (7th cir.) 1980. Assoc. Lord Bissell & Brook, Chgo., 1969—77, ptnr., 1977—2005, of counsel, 2005—. Mem.: ABA, Ill. Bar Assn. Unitarian Universalist. Office: Lord Bissell & Brook 111 S Wacker Dr Chicago IL 60606-4302 Office Phone: 312-443-0237. Business E-Mail: dfowler@lordbissell.com.

FOWLER, FLORA DAUN, retired lawyer; b. Washington, Aug. 11, 1923; d. Herman Hartwell and Flora Elizabeth (Adams) Sanford; m. Kenneth Leo Fowler, Aug. 22, 1941; children: Kenneth Jr., Micheal, Kathleen, Daun, Jonathan, Colin, Kevin, James, Shawn, Maureen, Wendelyn, Liam, Tobias, Melanie. Student, Wilson Tchrs. Coll., 1940-41; AA, U. Md., 1973; JD, U. Balt., 1976. Bar: Fla. 1977, US Dist. Ct. (mid. dist.) Fla. 1979, US Ct. Appeals (5th and 11th cirs.) 1981. Staff atty. Cen. Fla. Legal Services Inc., Daytona Beach, 1978-80, mng. atty., 1980-81; pvt. practice, Daytona Beach, 1981-93; ret., 2001. Past editor: Seabrook Acres Citizens' League Newsletter, columnist: Bowie Express & Cmty. Times; contbr. poems to New Voices Am. Poetry. Past v.p. Prince Georges County Civic Fedn., Md.; past unit chmn. LWV Prince Georges County; past pres., v.p., publicity chmn. Lanham-Bowie Dem. Club, Seabrook; v.p. Seabrook Acres Citizens

League, Md., 1970. Recipient Evening Star Trophy award, Prince Georges County Civic Fedn., 1969. Mem.: Fla. S. Ct. Hist. Soc. Democrat. Roman Catholic. Avocations: swimming, creative writing, cursillo. Personal E-mail: daunfowler@msn.com.

FOWLER, FLOYD JACKSON, JR., researcher; b. Akron, Ohio, July 4, 1939; s. Floyd Jackson Fowler and Marion Vaughn Holoman; m. Julia Ann Chambliss, Nov. 19, 1977; m. Diane Davant West, Sept. 3, 1960 (div. June 1974); children: Alex J., Randolph W., Elizabeth D. BA, Wesleyan U., 1960; MA, U. Mich., 1962, PhD, 1966. Asst. dir. Cmty. Rsch. Project Combined Jewish Philanthropies, Boston, 1965—68; asst. dir. Survey Rsch. Program Joint Ctr. for Urban Studies MIT and Harvard U., Cambridge, Mass., 1968—71; sr. rsch. fellow Ctr. for Survey Rsch. U. Mass., Boston, 1971—. Pres. Found. for Informed Med. Decision Making, Boston, 2002—; rschr. Dartmouth Med. Sch., Hanover, NH, 1984—. Author: Improving Survey Questions, 1995, Survey Research Methods, 2002; co-author: Standardized Survey Interviewing, 1990, Survey Methodology, 2004; mem. editl. bd.: Pub. Opinion Quarterly, 2003—06. Mem.: Am. Statis. Assn., Am. Assn. Pub. Opinion Rsch. Avocation: writing. Office: Center for Survey Research U Mass Boston 100 Morrissey Blvd Boston MA 02125

FOWLER, FRED J., energy executive; b. Braman, Okla., 1946; m. Jan Fowler; 3 children. B in Fin., Okla. State U., 1968. With Conoco, Inc., 1968—74; v.p. natural gas liquids supply Enterprise Products Co, 1974—76; sr. v.p. Gulf States Oil & Refining, 1976—78; pres. Wynn-Fowler Trading Co., 1978—85; from gen. mgr. to v.p., gen. mgr. Panhandle Trading Co., 1985—87; v.p. mktg., transp. and exch. Panhandle Ea. Pipe Line Co., 1987—88, Trunkline Gas Co., 1987—88, Panhandle Ea., Trunkline and Tex. Ea. Transmission Corp., 1989; pres. Trunkline, 1991; corp. v.p. mktg. PanEnergy, 1992—93, group v.p., 1996; pres. Tex. Ea., 1994—96; group pres. energy transmission Duke Energy, Charlotte, NC, 1997—2002, pres., COO, 2002—06, group exec., pres. Duke Energy Gas, 2006; pres., CEO Spectra Energy, Houston, 2007—. Mem.: Interstate Natural Gas Assn. Am. (chmn. bd.). Office: Spectra Energy 5400 Westheimer Ct Houston TX 77056-5310*

FOWLER, FRED JOSEPH, human services manager; s. Burnell F. and Myrle Unsworth Fowler; life ptnr. Linda A. Falorio. BA in Philosophy, U. Pitts., 1968—74, EdD, 1990—97; MEd, Duquesne U., Pitts., 1977—79. Houseparent supr. Montanari Clin. Sch. & Residential Treatment Ctr., Miami, Fla., 1971—72; asst. tchr. Quimby Regional Sch., Worcester, Mass., 1973—74; child care worker Variety Children's Hosp., Miami, 1974—75; milieu counselor Highland Pk. Gen. Hosp., Miami, 1975—76; laborer United Mine Workers Am., 1976—78; intake clinician No. Cmtys. Mental Health/Mental Retardation Program, Pitts., 1978—79, intake supr., 1979—82, project dir., 1982—84; instr. CC Allegheny County, Pitts., 1984—88; dir. assessment No./SW Mental Health/Mental Retardation Program, Pitts., 1984—88; child and adolescent mental health program specialist, cassp coord. Allegheny County Dept. Human Svcs., Office Behavioral Health, Pitts., 1988—98, supr. children/adolescent svcs., 1998—2001, sr. planning coord., 2001—02, mgr. behavioral health spl. projects, 2002—. Mem., right to edn. task force Pitts. Pub. Schs., 1988—98, mem. safe schools/healthy students steering com., 1999—2004, mem. steering com. Gang Free Schs. & Cmtys., 2003—; mem. adv. bd. Ctr. Sch. Mental Health Analysis & Action, Balt., 2001—. Contbr. chapters to books. Bd. dirs. Am. Coll. Mental Health Adminstrn., Pitts., 2003—04. Recipient Svc. award, Shuman Detention Ctr., 1989, 1991, Achievement award, Children's Coun. We. Pa., 1990, Cmty. Citation of Merit award, County of Allegheny, Bd. County Commnrs., 1991. Mem.: Pa. Assn. Student Assistance Profls., Amen Corner. Avocations: W.African hand-drumming, guitar. Office: Allegheny County Dept Human Svcs 304 Wood St Pittsburgh PA 15222 Business E-Mail: ffowler@dhs.county.allegheny.pa.us.

FOWLER, FREDERICK VICTOR, JR., import company executive; b. Newton, Mass., May 27, 1933; s. Frederick Victor and Priscilla (Coffin) F.; m. Nancy White, Apr. 18, 1959; children: Cynthia, Frederick III. BSBA, Boston U., 1955. Salesman Fred V. Fowler Co., Newton, 1958-69; v.p. UNA Corp., Boston, 1969-72; pres., CEO Fred V. Fowler Co., Inc., Newton, 1972—. Col. USAF, 1955-78. Mem. Soc. Mgr. Engrs., Am. Measuring Tools Mfrs. Assn. (pres.), Nat. Machine Tool Builders Assn., Nat. Bus. Aircraft Assn., Aircraft Owners and Pilots Assn., Air Force Assn., Res. Officers Assn., Rep. 500 Club, Boston U. Alumni Club (v.p. 1975-78). Episcopalian. Avocations: flying, golf, skiing, travel. Office: Fred V Fowler Co Inc 66 Rowe St Auburndale MA 02466-1530 Business E-Mail: fredjr@fvfowler.com.

FOWLER, JAMES D., JR., leadership executive; b. Washington, Apr. 24, 1944; s. James D. and Romay (Lucas) F.; m. Linda Marie Raiford, May 25, 1968; children— Scott, Kimberly Student, Howard U., Washington, 1962-63; BS, U.S. Mil. Acad., West Point, NY, 1967; MBA, Rochester Inst. Tech., 1975. With Xerox Corp., Rochester, N.Y., 1971-75; sr. cons. D.P. Parker & Assocs., Inc., Wellesley, Mass., 1975-76; mgr. staffing ITT World Hdqrs., NYC, 1976-78; v.p. dir. of adminstrn. ITT Aetna, Denver, 1978; sr. v.p., dir. adminstrn. ITT Consumer Fin. Corp., Mpls., 1978-84, sr. v.p., dir. adminstrn. and mktg., 1984-87, exec. v.p., dir. adminstrn. and mktg., 1987-90, exec. v.p., dir. product mgmt., mktg. and adminstrn., 1990-92; exec. v.p., dir. of adminstrn., 1992-93; dir. govt. rels. ITT Washington Office, 1993-96; pres. Fowler & Assocs., 1996-97; exec. dir. Exec. Leadership Coun., 1997-99, pres., 1999-2000, ITT Industries, Inc., 2000—. Trustee U.S. Mil. Acad., West Point, N.Y., 1977-86, 87—; bd. dirs., chmn. ITT Ednl. Svcs., Inc.; bd. dirs. Duke Ellington Sch. Arts, 1993-2000, Suburban Hosp., Bethesda, Md., 1997-2000, Folger Shakespeare Libr., Washington; charter mem., bd. dirs. Exec. Leadership Coun., 1992-97. Capt. U.S. Army, 1967-71, Vietnam. Decorated Bronze Star with oak leaf cluster. Mem. Sigma Pi Phi. E-mail: james.fowler@itt.com.

FOWLER, JEFFREY L., academic administrator, career military officer; b. 1956; m. Katie Fowler; children: Lynne, Connor, Brittany. BS with distinction, US Navel Acad., 1978; MBA, Chaminade U., 1985; MPA, Harvard U., 1990; grad., Nat. Security Studies Program, Syracuse U., 2002. Commn. USN, 1978, advanced through grades to vice admiral, 2007; officer USS Bremerton, USS Alaska; exec. officer Unit Montpelier, USS Hyman G. Rickover; comdr. USS Charlotte, Submarine Squadron 3; staff mem. of Comdr. in Chief, US Atlantic Fleet; head submarine programs sect. Programming Div., Staff of Chief of Navel Ops.; dep. exec. asst. to Dep. Chief Navel Ops.; vice chmn. Joint Chiefs of Staff; prospective commdg. officer instr. Pacific Submarine Force; exec. asst. to comdr. US Strategic Command; dir. Navel Forces Europe/6th Fleet Plans and Ops.; dep. comdr. 6th Fleet; comdr. Submarines, Allied Navel Forces South, Submarine Grope 8, Task Force 69 and Task Force 164, Naples, Italy, 2006—07; supt. US Naval Acad., Annapolis, Md., 2007—. Submarine tactics instr. Navel Submarine Training Ctr., Pacific; jr. mem. Nuclear Propulsion Examining Bd. Decorated Defense Superior Svc. Medal, Legion of Merit, Meritorious Svc. Medal, Joint Svc. Commendation Medal, Navy Commendation Medal, Navy Achievement Medal. Mem.: Coun. Fgn. Rels. (life; mil. fellow 2002—03). Office: US Naval Academy Office of Supt 121 Blake Rd Annapolis MD 21402*

FOWLER, JOANNA S., chemist; b. Aug. 9, 1942; BA, U. South Fla., 1964; PhD in Chem., U. Colo., 1967. Sr. rsch. assoc. U. East Anglia, Norwich, England, 1968; rsch. assoc., med. dept. Brookhaven Nat. Lab., 1969—71, assoc. chemist, med. dept., scientist, 1974—76, chemist, chem. dept., 1976—88, sr. chemist, 1988, dir., Ctr. Translational Neuroimaging. Adj. prof. chem. dept. and biomedical engring. dept. Stony Brook U. Named Disting. Basic Scientist of Yr., Acad. Molecular Imaging, 2005; recipient Ernest Orlando Lawrence award, Dept. Energy, 1999, Alfred P. Wolf award, Soc. Nuclear Imaging in Drug Devel., 2000, Glen T. Seaborg award, nuclear and radiochemistry, Am. Chemical Soc., 2002. Mem. Soc. Nuclear Medicine, Am. Chem. Soc. (co-recipient Gustavus John Esselen Award for Chemistry in the Pub. Interest, northeastern sect., 1988, Francis P. Garvin & John M. Olin Medal, 1998), Nat. Acad. Sciences (mem. 2003). Office: Brookhaven Nat Lab Chem Dept Bldg 555A Upton NY 11973 Office Phone: 516-344-4365. E-mail: fowler@bnl.gov.

FOWLER, JOHN, information technology executive; Various engring. mgmt. positions Java Software, Solaris, Unix Desktop and Graphics Sun Microsystems, Inc., dir. engring. Software Devel. Tools, chief tech. officer Software, exec. v.p. x64 Systems Group, exec. v.p. systems. Office: Sun Microsystems Inc 4150 Network Cir Santa Clara CA 95054 Office Phone: 650-960-1300.*

FOWLER, JOHN M., finance executive; b. Youngstown, Ohio, Apr. 12, 1949; s. William E. Jr and Jean L. (Moore) Fowler; m. Brooke McMurray, Oct. 1999; children: Evan, Ned, Grey McMurray. BS, Yale U., 1971; JD, U. Pa., 1974. Bar: Pa 1974, US Dist Ct (ea dist) Pa 1974. Assoc. White and Williams, Phila., 1974-77; v.p., chief fin. officer Reading Co., Phila., 1977-81; gen. counsel U.S. Dept. Transp., Washington, 1981-83; exec. v.p., pres. Warner Amex Cable Comm., Inc., Blue Bell, Pa., 1983-86; pres., CEO Gulf Ins. Co., Dallas, 1986-94, chmn., 1991-94; exec. v.p., chief adminstrv. officer Primerica Co. (now Citigroup Inc.), NYC, 1986-94; exec. v.p., CFO MoneyGram Payment Systems, Inc., 1996-98. Office: 149 E 73rd St New York NY 10021 Office Phone: 908-508-0092. Office Fax: 908-508-0093.

FOWLER, MARTIN, software engineer, consultant; b. Walsall, Eng., Dec. 18, 1963; arrived in US, 1994, naturalized; s. Denys William and Ivy Fowler; m. Cindy BSc, Univ. Coll., London, 1986. Asst. cons. Coopers & Lybrand, London, 1986-89; cons. Associative Design Tech., London, 1989-91; freelance cons. software engr. London, 1991—; chief scientist ThoughtWorks, Chgo., 1999—. Cons. James Odell Assocs., Ann Arbor, Mich., 1991; spkr. in field. Author: Analysis Patterns: Reusable Object Models, 1997, UML Distilled: Applying The Standard Object Modeling Language, 1997 (Software Development Productivity award, 1998), Refractoring: Improving the Design of Existing Code, 1999, Patterns of Enterprise Application Architecture, 2002; co-author (with Kent Beck) Planning Extreme Programming, 1999; columnist Distributed Computing mag.; adv. bd. Software Development mag., IEEE Software(also editor, design column); contbr. articles to profl. jours. Chair Blackheath and Greenwich Amnesty, London, 1991-93. Mem. IEEE, Assn. Computing Machinery. Avocations: hiking, food, music, cross country skiing. Home: 15 Damon Ave Melrose MA 02176-2013 Office: ThoughtWorks 200 E Randolph 25th Fl Chicago IL 60601-6501 Business E-Mail: fowler@acm.org.

FOWLER, PAUL RAYMOND, physician, lawyer; b. Washington, Apr. 30, 1958; s. Charles Raymond and Dora E. (Burger) Fowler; m. Mary Jane Weber, Oct. 4, 1986; children: Christina D., Laura M., Joshua P. BS, U. Md., 1980, postgrad., 1980—81; DO, U. Des Moines, 1985; JD with honors, Drake U., 1994. Bar: U.S. Supreme Ct., Fla. 1995, Ill. 1996, D.C. 1996, Ky. 1998; diplomate Am. Bd. Forensic Examiners, Am. Osteo. Bd. Family Practice, Am. Osteo. Bd. Preventive Medicine, cert. Am. Bd. Disability Analysts, diplomate Am. Bd. Family Practice. Intern Des Moines Gen. Hosp., 1985—86; resident Ea. Va. Grad. Sch. Medicine, Norfolk, 1986—88; pvt. practice medicine Norfolk, 1988—90; staff Iowa Meth. Med. Ctr., Des Moines, 1990—95, Mercy Med. Ctr., Des Moines, 1992—94; med. dir. Occupl. Health Svcs., Des Moines, 1990—95; pvt. practice law Washington, 1994—; chief physician Ford Motor Co., Hapeville, Ga., 1995—97; med. dir. Quorum Health Sys., Spartanburg, SC, 1997—2000; legal medicine officer to surgeon gen. U.S. Army, Washington, 2000—; Health Policy scholar Ctrs. Medicare and Medicaid Svs., Balt., 2003—04. Mem. mock trial team Med. Malpractice Rev. Bd., Commonwealth of Va., 1988—90, Drake U. Law Sch., 1992; assoc. clin. prof. U. Des Moines, 1990—; judge Nat. Mock Trial Coll. Comp., 1992; pvt. practice law, 1994—; clin. prof. Pikevill Coll. Osteo. Medicine, 1997—. Reviewer: Am. Forensic Examiner, 1997—, Fed. Practitioner, Family Practice Mgmt.; contbr. articles to profl. jours. Active Silver Spring Vol. Fire Dept., 1978—81; mem. bioethics com. Iowa Meth. Med. Ctr., Des Moines, 1992—95; mem. Montgomery County Commn. Health, 2005—; apptd. Md. State Task Force on Electronic Med. Records, 2006—. Recipient Good Citizen award, Clifton Park Citizens Assn.; Health Policy Scholars fellow, Ctrs. for Medicare and Medicaid, 2003—. Fellow: Am. Osteo. Coll. Preventive and Occupl. Medicine (gen. counsel, trustee, treas., v.p., pres., treas.), Am. Coll. Legal Medicine, Am. Acad. Family Physicians; mem.: D.C. Osteomed. Assn., Am. Osteo. Assn. (tech. task force, ho. dels., coun. specialty societies), Md. Acad. Family Physicians (bylaws com., chmn. resolutions com.), Am. Bd. Med. Specialties, D.C. Bar Assn., Ill. Bar Assn., Ky. Bar Assn., Fla. Bar Assn., Phi Sigma (pres. 1984—85). Avocations: tennis, running, stamp collecting/philately. Home: 18313 Leedstown Way Olney MD 20832 Office: Walter Reed Army Med Ctr Bldg 1 Rm A-316 Washington DC 20307-5001 Office Phone: 202-782-8233. Personal E-mail: prfowler@pol.net.

FOWLER, RAYMOND DALTON, psychologist, educator; b. Jasper, Ala., Dec. 22, 1930; s. Raymond Dalton and Willie (Sanders) F.; m. Nancy Allebach, Aug. 13, 1955 (dec.); children: Karen Sydney, Derek Tyson, Michael Allan; m. Sandra Mumford, May 5, 1984. Student, Vanderbilt U., 1948-50; BA, U. Ala., 1952, MA, 1953; PhD, Pa. State U., 1957. Diplomate in clin. psychology Am. Bd. Profl. Psychology; lic. psychologist, Ala. Rsch. asst. Psychoacoustics Lab., Pa. State U., University Park, 1953-54; fellow USPHS, 1954-56; asst. prof. psychology, asst. dir. Psychol. Clinic, U. Ala., Tuscaloosa, 1956-59, assoc. prof., dir. Psychol. Clinic Birmingham, 1959-65, prof., chmn. dept., 1965-83, prof. (on leave), 1983-86, prof. emeritus, 1986—; sr. cons. Psych. Sys. and Nat. Computer Sys., Balt. and Washington, 1983-86; prof. psychology, head dept. U. Tenn., Knoxville, 1986-89; exec. v.p., CEO APA, Washington, 1989—2002. Participant White House Conf. on Health, 1965, Nat. Conf. on Criminal Justice Stds. and Goals, 1973; mem. nat. adv. com. on alcoholism HEW, 1970-72, chmn. com. on rsch., 1970; mem. task panel on manpower and pers. President's Commn. on Mental Health, 1977-78; mem. Ala. Gov.'s Adv. Com. on Alcoholism and Drug Abuse, 1973-82; vice chmn. program com. N.Am. Congress on Alcohol and Drug Addiction, 1974; mem. sci. adv. com. Nat. Coun. on Alcoholism, 1974-78; mem. rsch. tng. rev. com. Nat. Inst. Alcohol Abuse and Alcoholism, 1975-78; dir. Ala. Prison Classification Project, 1976-77; chmn. So. Sch. Alcohol Studies, 1960-62; cons. Ala. Commn. on Alcoholism, 1958-70, VA, 1959-65, Estate of Howard R. Hughes, 1976-84; prin. cons. Roche Psychiat. Svc. Inst., Nutley, N.J., 1966-77, Med. Computer Svc., Basel, Switzerland, 1968-76, Med. Computer Svc., Hans Huber Verlag, Berne, Switzerland, 1976-89; cons. to adminstr. Law Enforcement Assistance Adminstrn., U.S. Dept. Justice, Washington, 1971-73; program cons. div. alcoholism Ala. Dept. Mental Health, 1973-75; sr. cons. Nat. Computer Sys., Mpls., 1983-89 Contbg. author: Assessment for Decision, 1987, Handbook of Psychological Assessment, 1990; editor Am. Psychologist, 1989-2002; contbr. articles and revs. to profl. jours. Vice pres. Ala. Coun. on Human Rels., 1965-68, Rehab. Rsch. Found., 1965-80; alumni fellow Pa. State U., 1988—; bd. dirs. Rosalynn Carter Inst. for Human Devel., 1988-98. Named Disting. Practitioner, Nat. Acad. Practice, 1986; recipient significant Minn. Multiphasic Personality Inventory contbn. award U. Minn., 1988; grantee Ala. Commn. on Alcoholism, 1962-63, 64-68, NIMH, 1963-64, Roche Psychiat. Svc. Inst., 1967-76, Ala. Dept. Mental Health, 1969-70, U.S. Dept. Justice, 1971-82, Ala. Bd. Corrections, 1972-73, Ala. Law Enforcement Planning Agy., 1972-74, Nat. Inst. Alcohol Abuse and Alcoholism, 1973-83. Fellow APA (pres. div. 13, 1978-79, coun. reps. 1965-68, 70-73, 75-78, bd. dirs. 1979—, treas. 1983-87, pres.-elect 1987-88, pres. 1988-89, presdl. citation 1990), Soc. for Personalaity Assessment; mem. AAUP (pres. U. Ala. chpt. 1969-70), Southeastern Psychol. Assn. (pres. 1971-72, dir. continuing edn. 1973-89, dist. speaker 1982, 87), Ala. Psychol. Assn. (pres. 1962, award for outstanding contbns. 1979), Alcohol and Drug Problems Assn. N.Am. (program chmn. 1974-76, bd. dirs. 1975-77), Internat. Assn. Applied Psychology (pres.-elect 2006—), Sigma Xi (life), Psi Chi (nat. v.p. 1980-84, disting. speaker 1977, 88), Omicron Delta Kappa, Phi Kappa Phi. Democrat. Avocations: running, gardening, cooking. Home: 8276 Caminito Maritimo La Jolla CA 92037

FOWLER, ROBERT MARTIN, oil industry executive, consultant; b. Tribbey, Okla., Dec. 9, 1919; s. Robert Martin Fowler and Lois Ann Atwood; m. Virginia Anderson, Aug. 23, 1943; 1 child, Jane Clare Fowlen Root. Student, Munnay State U., Tishimingo, Okla., 1938—40, Okla. U., Norman, 1940—41. Oil field supt. Bunk Royalty Co., Sherman, Tex., 1954—61, Borge, Tex., 1961—69, Rerryton, Tex., 1969—78, v.p. prodn. Wichita Falls, Tex., 1978—90, cons., 1990—2007. Capt. US Army, 1941—53. Decorated Silver Star US Army, Bronze State; recipient Belgium Bulge, Tex. Senate, 2005. Mem.: N. Tex. Oil, Panhandle Producers. Home: 3 Fawnwood Ct Wichita Falls TX 76310

FOWLER, THOMAS KENNETH, physicist; b. Thomaston, Ga., Mar. 27, 1931; s. Albert Grady and Susie (Glynn) F.; m. Carol Ellen Winter, Aug. 18, 1956; children: Kenneth, John, Ellen. BS in Engring, Vanderbilt U., 1953, MS in Physics, 1955; PhD in Physics, U. Wis., 1957. Staff physicist Oak Ridge Nat. Lab., 1957-65, group leader plasma theory, 1961-65; staff physicist Gen. Atomic Co., San Diego, 1965-67, head plasma physics divsn., 1967; group leader plasma theory Lawrence Livermore Lab., Livermore, Calif., 1967-69, div. leader, 1969-70, assoc. dir. magnetic fusion, 1970-87; prof., chmn. dept. nuclear engring. U. Calif., Berkeley, 1988-94, prof. emeritus, 1995—. Calif. Coun. Sci. Tech. fellow, 1997—. Fellow Am. Phys. Soc. (chmn. plasma physics div. 1970); mem. Nat. Acad. Scis., Sigma Xi, Sigma Nu. Home: 221 Grover Ln Walnut Creek CA 94596-6310 Office: U Calif Dept Nuclear Engring Berkeley CA 94720-1730 Business E-Mail: fowler@nuc.berkeley.edu.

FOWLER, VIVIAN DELORES, insurance company executive; b. Knoxville, Tenn., Sept. 26, 1946; d. Rance James Pierce and Margaret Willadene (Crowe) Compton; m. James Hubert Fowler, May 12, 1979. Student, U. Tenn., Knoxville. CPCU. Clk. The Travelers Ins. Co., Knoxville, 1967-84, adminstv. staff, 1984, comml. mktg. asst., 1984-86, comml. account analyst Nashville, 1986-89, sr. account analyst, 1989-90, account mgr., 1990-93, regional asst. mgr. small bus. unit coml. lines Atlanta, 1993—2005; regional underwriting mgr. select accounts mktg. Travelers/Aetna Ins. Co. (name changed to St. Paul Travelers), Atlanta, 1996; comml. sr. profl. Fireman's Fund Ins. Co., Alpharetta, Ga., 2006—. Lay witness speaker, United Meth. Ch., Knoxville 1979-82; charter mem. St. Thomas Hosp. Found. Soc., 1990; mem. Arthritis Found., 1991. Mem. NAFE, Soc. CPCU, Soc. Cert. Ins. Counselors (cert. 1987), Nat. Assn. of Ins. Women (cert. Profl. Ins. Woman 1975), Internat. Platform Assn., Ins. Professionals of Atlanta, 1998. Republican. United Methodist. Home: 604 Ashley Forest Dr Alpharetta GA 30022-6133 Office: Firemans Fund Ins Co Royal Ctr Three 111475 Great Oaks Way Alpharetta GA 30022 Home Phone: 770-998-5039; Office Phone: 770-497-5367. Personal E-mail: vdfowler@earthlink.net.

FOWLER, W. RANDALL, energy executive; CPA inactive. Dir. investor rels. Enterprise Products Ptnrs., Houston, 1999; treas., v.p. Enterprise Products GP and EPCO, 2000—05, sr. v.p., treas., 2005; CFO EPCO, 2005; sr. v.p., CFO Enterprise GP Holdings LP, Houston, 2005—; sr. v.p., treas., dir. Duncan Energy Ptnrs., 2006—. Office: Enterprise GP Holdings LP PO Box 4323 Houston TX 77210-4323 Office Phone: 713-381-6500.*

FOWLER, WAYNE LEWIS, SR., internist; b. Topeka, Kans., Jan. 5, 1923; s. Morrill George and Grace Anna (Carlson) F.; m. Violet June Ransom, Sept. 4, 1948; children: Wayne Jr., Deborah. BS, Washburn U., 1945; MD, U. Ind., 1947. Diplomate Am. Bd. Internal Medicine. Intern Kansas City (Mo.) Gen. Hosp., 1947-48, resident internal medicine, 1948-51; internist Galvin-Haughey Clinic, Concordia, Kans., 1953-95, NCK Med. Clinic, Concordia, Kans., 1995—. Past pres. med. staff St. Joseph Hosp., Concordia, Kans. Capt. US Air Force, 1951-53, Fellow Am. Coll. Physicians (Laureate award Kans. chpt. 1994), Am. Coll. Chest Physicians; mem. AMA, Cl. County Med. Soc., Kans. Med. Soc., Am. Soc. Internal Medicine, Elks, Moose, Masons, Shriners. Republican. Episcopalian. Avocation: amateur radio. Office: NCK Med Inc 1010 3rd Ave Concordia KS 66901-4003 Home: 7300 W 107th St Apt 712 Overland Park KS 66212-6607 Personal E-mail: wfowler23@kcrr.com.

FOWLER, WESLEY CASWELL, JR., obstetrician, gynecologist; b. Dunn, NC, Feb. 18, 1940; MD, U. N.C., 1966. Diplomate Am. Bd. Ob.-Gyn. Intern N.C. Meml. Hosp., Chapel Hill, 1967; resident N.C. Meml. Hosp, Chapel Hill, 1967-71; obstetrician-gynecologist U. N.C. Hosps., Chapel Hill, 1972—; prof., vice chmn. dept. ob.-gyn. U. N.C. Sch. of Medicine, Chapel Hill, 1972—. Mem. ACS, ACOG, Soc. Gynecologists and Obstetricians. Office: Univ NC Dept Ob-gyn CB #7570 - Macnider Chapel Hill NC 27599-0001 Office Phone: 919-966-1196.

FOWLKES, NANCY LANETTA PINKARD, social worker; d. Amos Malone and Nettie (Barnett) Pinkard; m. Vester Guy Fowlkes, June 4, 1955 (dec. 1965); 1 child, Wendy Denise. BA, Bennett Coll., 1946; MA, Syracuse U., 1952; MSW, Smith Coll., 1963; MPA, Pace U., 1982. Dir. publicity Bennett Coll., Greensboro, NC, 1946-47, 49-50; asst. editor Va. Edn. Bull. ofcl. organ Va. State Tchrs. Assn., Richmond, 1950-52; asst. office mgr. Cmty. Svc. Soc., NYC, 1952-55; social caseworker, asst. supr. Dept. Social Svcs. Westchester County, White Plains, NY, 1959-67, supr. adoption svcs., 1967-77, supr. adoption and foster care, 1977-89. Mem. adv. bd. White Plains Adult Edn. Sch. First v.p. Eastview Jr. HS, 1970-71; area chmn. White Plains Cmty. Chest, 1964; sec. Mt. Vernon Concert Group, 1952-54; fund raising co-chmn. Urban League Guild of Westchester, 1967; pres. White Plains Interfaith Coun., 1972-74; pres. northeastern jurisdiction United Meth. Ch., 1988-92; chmn. adminstrv. bd. Meth. Ch., 1970-72, 82-83, vice chmn., 1978-80, vice chmn. trustees, 1973-77, treas., 1978-83; lay spkr., v.p. Met. dist. United Meth. Women, 1977-79, exec. bd. NY conf.; NY conf. rep. Upper Atlantic Regional Sch., 1981-83, mem. nominating com., 1982-83, trustee NY conf., 1982-88, pres. NY conf., 1983-87; bd. dirs. Global Ministries United Meth. Ch., 1988-96, women's divsn., 1988-96, v.p., chair sect. finance women's divsn., 1992-96, supt., 1997—, chair program divsn. NY conf., 1989-93; v.p. superintendency commn. Met. North Dist., 1997—; chair Episcopal residence NY Conf. Episcopacy Com., 1997-2002; mem. NY Conf. Bd. Ordained Ministry, 2000—, Bishop's Ptnrs. in Mission Leadership Coun., 2005—, mem. nominating com. N.Y. conf., 2006—, mem. bd. laity N.Y. conf., 2006—; chmn. Dist. Coun. on Ministry, 2002-05, lay leader 2005—; bd. dirs. Family Svc. Westchester, Bethel Meth. Home, Ossining, NY, White Plains YWCA, 1985-93, Scarritt Bennett Ctr., Nashville, 1990-2000, Gum Moon Women's Residence, San Francisco, 1992-96, White Plains-Greenburg NAACP, 1993-98. Mem. NASW, Acad. Cert. Social Workers, Jack and Jill of Am. Inc. (chpt. pres. 1954-56, regional sec.-treas. 1967-71), Nat. Bus. and Profl. Women's Club (chpt. sec. 1954-56), Internat. Platform Assn., Theta Sigma Phi (sec.-treas.), Zeta Nu Omega, Alpha Kappa Alpha (pres. 1960-64, treas. 1975-78), Regency Bridge Club (pres. 1963-65). Home: 107 Valley Rd White Plains NY 10604-2316 E-mail: npfvalley@aol.com.

FOX, ALAN, philosophy educator; b. Oct. 1, 1955; BA in Psychology, Johns Hopkins U., 1977; MA in Religious Studies, Temple U., 1983, PhD in Religious Studies, 1988. Adj. prof., dept. Eastern Religions Reconstructionist Rabbinical Coll., Wyncotte, Pa., 1988, 1992, 1996, 1996; asst. prof., Intellectual Heritage Program Temple U., Phila., 1988—90; asst. prof., dept. Philosophy U. Delaware, 1990—96, assoc. prof., dept. Philosophy, 1996—. Contbr. articles to numerous profl. jours. Recipient Nat. Merit Scholar, Johns Hopkins U., RCA Corp., 1973—77, Arts and Sci. Outstanding Tchr. award, U. Delaware, 1999, US Prof. Yr. State of Del., Carnegie Found. Advancement of Tchg., 2006; grantee Russell Conwell Fell., Temple U., Fulbright-Hays Scholar, 1987. Office: Dept Philosophy U Delaware Newark DE 19716

FOX, ANDREW, entertainment productions executive; Ptnr. Tumble Interactive, 1997—99; founder 3-G Wireless Communications, 2000; formerly CEO Way Communications; CEO Track Entertainments, NYC, 2005—. Co-founder ClubPlanet.com night-life interactive website. Office: Track Entertainment 21st Fl 485 Madison Ave New York NY 10022*

FOX, ARTHUR CHARLES, cardiologist, educator; b. Newark, Sept. 16, 1926; s. Jacob and Mae (Bonda) F. Student, Harvard U., Cambridge, Mass., 1943-44; MD, NYU, 1948. Cert. Am. Bd. Internal Medicine, 1956, in internal medicine Am. Bd. Internal Medicine, 1974, in cardiovascular disease Am. Bd. Internal Medicine, 1975. Intern, asst. resident, chief resident medicine Bellevue Hosp., NYC, 1948—52; from asst. to full prof. medicine NYU Sch. Medicine, NYC, 1954—, chief cardiology sect., 1968—2001. Cons. Manhattan VA Hosp.; attending physician, NYU Hosp., Bellevue Hosp. Contbr. articles to profl. jours. 1st lt. to capt. USAF, 1952—54, prof. asst., 1953—54, Divsn. Med. Scis., Nat. Rsch. Coun. NIH fellow, 1954-56; grantee, 1956-80 Master ACP (gov. region 1981-86, Laureate award NY Chpt.); fellow Am. Coll. Cardiology, Am. Heart Assn.; mem. AAAS, Am. Fedn. Clin. Rsch., NY Heart Assn. (pres. 1987-89), NY Cardiologic Soc. (pres. 1992-93), Alpha Omega Alpha, Sigma Xi. Home: 330 E 33rd St Apt 20-L New York NY 10016-9466 Office: 550 1st Ave New York NY 10016-6402 Office Phone: 212-263-7229. Business E-Mail: arthur.fox@med.nyu.edu.

FOX, ARTHUR JOSEPH, JR., editor; b. Bklyn., Sept. 19, 1923; s. Arthur Joseph and Mary Loretta (Foley) F.; m. Ann Marie McElroy, Sept. 7, 1946; children: Jane Ann, John Arthur; m. Lorraine Cecelia Hodge, Sept. 10, 1993. BS in Civil Engring, Manhattan Coll., 1947, DSc (hon.), 1982. Structural designer Sanderson & Porter, NYC, 1947-48; asst. editor Engring. News-Record, McGraw-Hill Publs., NYC, 1948-54, asso. editor, 1954-58, sr. editor, 1956-57, sr. staff editor, 1957-60, mng. editor, 1960-64, editor-in-chief, 1964-88; mng. dir. Constrn. Industry Presidents Forum, Potomac, Md., 1989-97; exec. dir. Constrn. Industry Round Table, 1998. Mem. N.Y.C. Environ. Control Bd., 1974-77. Served with AUS, 1943-45. Decorated Bronze Star; recipient award of merit Am. Cons. Engrs. Council, 1975, medal of profl. excellence, 1985; recipient Met. Civil Engr. of Year award, 1975, We Dig America award Nat. Utility Contractors Assn., 1987, Golden Beaver svc. award, 1988; recipient Silver Shovel award Am. Subcontractors Assn., 1975, hon. mem. 1987, Carroll H. Dunn award Constrn. Industry Inst., 2000; elected to Nat. Acad. of Constructon, 2001; named hon. mem. AIA, 1986. Fellow ASCE (pres. 1975-76); mem. Am. Acad. Environ. Engrs. (past trustee), Engrs. Coun. for Profl. Devel. (dir. 1969-75), Nat. Constrn. Industry Coun. (exec. com. 1976-77, Saul Horowitz Career Achievement award 1987), N.Y. Bldg. Congress (bd. govs. 1969-73, 78-86), Engrs. Joint Coun. (dir. 1976-77, v.p. 1978-80), The Moles, Manhattan Coll. Alumni Soc. (past pres.), Chi Epsilon, Tau Beta Pi. Clubs: Congrl. Country. Home and Office: 10108 Garden Way Potomac MD 20854-3966 Personal E-mail: artfox1944@comcast.net.

FOX, ARTURO ANGEL, Spanish language educator; b. Hoguín, Cuba, Aug. 2, 1935; came to U.S., 1962, naturalized, 1972; s. Arturo Roberto and Dulce Maria (Macle) F.; m. Rosa del Carmen Portilla, Jan 17, 1959 (dec. June 1998); children: Franz, Alexandra; m. Carol E. Fox, Dec. 8, 2003. B Letters and Scis., Friends Sch., Holguin, Cuba, 1952; LLD, U. Havana, 1960; MA in Spanish, U. Minn., 1968, PhD, 1971. Bar: Cuba 1960. Pvt. practice law, Holguin, 1960—62; instr. Spanish Luther Coll., Decorah, Iowa, 1963—66; asst. prof. Spanish Dickinson Coll., Carlisle, Pa., 1966—72, assoc. prof., 1972—79, prof., 1979—98, chmn. dept. modern langs., 1972—74, chmn. depts. Spanish and Italian, 1978—79, chmn. dept. Spanish, 1981—84, 1990—93. Coord. Latin Am. Studies program, 1968-77; dir. Colombia Semester program Ctrl. Pa. Consortium, 1977-78, Dickinson in Spain, Malaga, 1985-86, 88-90, 93-95; apptd. William W. Edel prof. humanities; honorary chair, 1992. Author: three Spanish textbooks, (novel) Anecdotario del Comandante, 1976; (lit. criticism) El Edipo en Unamuno, 2001; contbr. articles in field to profl. publs. Ford grantee, 1969-70; Lilly and Mellon faculty devel. grantee, 1978, 79; recipient Christain R. and F. Lindback Found. Disting. Teaching award, 1981 Mem. Am. Assn. Tchrs. Spanish and Portuguese Office: Dickinson Coll Dept Spanish Carlisle PA 17013 Home: 28 Coventry Drive Carlisle PA 17015 Personal E-mail: foxar@aol.com.

FOX, BETTE-LEE, journal editor; b. Bklyn., Mar. 16, 1950; d. Samuel and Rose (Kaufman) F. BA, CUNY, 1971. Editl. asst. Libr. Jour., NYC, 1972-74, asst. editor, 1974-76, assoc. editor, 1976-85, sr. editor, 1985-87, mng. editor, 1987—. Avocations: theater, sports, sunday times crossword puzzles, reading, walking. Office: Libr Jour 360 Park Ave S New York NY 10010 Office Phone: 212-463-6802. Business E-Mail: bl.fox@reedbusiness.com.

FOX, CHARLES DUNSMORE, IV, lawyer; b. Roanoke, Va., Jan. 12, 1953; s. Charles Dunsmore III and Preston (Wescoat) F.; m. Elizabeth McCabe, Dec. 16, 1989; children: Charles Dunsmore V, Edward Lee McCabe. AB, Princeton U., 1975; MA, Yale U., 1977; JD, U. Va., 1980. Bar: Va. 1980, Ill. 1980. Assoc. Schiff, Hardin & Waite, Chgo., 1980-86, ptnr., 1987—2005, McGuire Woods LLP, Charlottesville, Va., 2005—. Ptnr. chmn. Econs. of Practice of Trusts and Estates Mag., Atlanta, 1995-98; adj. prof. Northwestern U. Sch. Law, 1998-2005; lectr. U. Va. Law Sch., 2005-. Author: Estate Planning with Life Insurance, 1998, Estate Planning Strategies After Estate Tax Reform, 2001, Estate Planning Manual, 2002, Trust and Fiduciary Law Guide, 2004, Tax Law Guide, 2004; mem. editl. bd. Trusts and Estates Mag., 1997-2001, Trust and Investment Mag., 2001—, chair, 2003—. Active U. Va. Law Sch. Found., Charlottesville, 1992-95, vice-chair nat. appeals, 1997-98, chair nat. appeals, 1998-2000; trustee Va. Law Sch. Found., 1998—, LaGrange Meml. Found., 1994-96, Episcopal HS, Alexandria, Va., 1995-2001, chair capital campaign, 1998-2001; gen. counsel Cmty. Meml. Found., LaGrange, Ill., 1995—; co-chair planned giving task force Episcopal Diocese of Chgo., 2001-05; bd. dirs. St. Annes-Bolfield Found., 2005—, Arc of Piedmont, 2005—. Fellow Am. Coll. Trust and Estate Counsel (co-chair legal edn. com. 2002-05, asst. editor jour. 2004-05, editor 2005-06, regent 2006—, vice chair editl. bd. 2005—); mem. ABA. Democrat. Episcopalian. Avocation: golf. Home: 506 Wellington Pl Charlottesville VA 22903 Office: McGuire Woods LLP Ste 300 Box 1288 310 Fourth St NE Charlottesville VA 22902-1288 Office Phone: 434-977-2500. Personal E-mail: skipfoxiv@earthlink.net. Business E-Mail: cfox@mcquirewoods.com.

FOX, CYNTHIA F., journalist, writer; b. Boston, June 17, 1961; d. Francis and Cynthia Fox. BA, Brown U., Providence, RI, 1983; MFA, Columbia U., NYC, 1990. Newspaper reporter The Patriot Ledger, 1985—87; mag. editor Vox, 1989—91; mag. writer, reporter LIFE, NYC, 1994—98; freelance writer, 1998—. Contbr. articles to profl. jours.; author: Cell of Cells, 2007. Writing Fellow residency, Ragdale Found. Artist Colony, 1993, Va. Ctr. Creative Arts, 1993, MacDowell Artist Colony, 1993, 2003, Sci. Writing fellowship, Woods Hole Oceanog. Inst., 2001, fellowship, Jerome Found., 2003, Fgn. Press Ctr. Japan, 2004. Office: 118 Montague St Brooklyn NY 11201 Home Phone: 718-624-1269.

FOX, DANIEL EMERY, orthopedic surgeon; b. Bronx, NY, Mar. 19, 1957; s. Maurice and Rina Fox; m. Michelle Frank, Apr. 24, 1995; 1 child, Brandon; 1 child from previous marriage, Brian. BA in Biol. Scis., Rutgers U., 1979; MD, U. Medicine and Dentistry N.J., 1983. Intern in surgery St. Joseph's Hosp. and Med. Ctr., Paterson, N.J., 1983-84; resident in orthopedics Lebanon Hosp. Ctr., Bronx, 1984-88; fellow U. Fla., Gainesville, 1988-89; staff emergency rm. dept. orthopedic surgery Booth Meml. Hosp., Queens, N.Y., 1987-88; assoc. attending orthopedic surgeon Cmty. Med. Ctr., Toms River, N.J., 1989—, chmn., dept. orthop., 2005—06. Mem. courtesy staff orthopedic surgery Rsch. Med. Ctr., Kansas City, Mo., 1990, Kimball Med. Ctr., Lakewood, N.J., 1990-92; mem. edn. com. Cmty. Med. Ctr., 1993—; mem. insight physician cons. panel Ciba Grigy Corp., 1994—; head team physician, NY/NJ Gov's Bowl Classic, official team dr. Nat. H.S. All-Star Football Classic, 2000, NJ E-treme arena football team, 2005. Fellow ACS, AMA, Am. Acad. Orthopaedic Surgeons, Ocean County Med. Soc. (nom. com. 1995), Lake Placid Sports Medicine Soc., Acad. of Medicine of N.J., U. Fla. Coll. of Medicine Alumni Assn., Med. Soc. N.J., N.J. Med. Sch. Alumni Assn.; mem. Ocean County C. of C., Disabled Am. Vets. Comdrs. Club. Office: Orthopedics 111 W Water St PO Box 5016 Toms River NJ 08754-5016 Business E-Mail: info@foxorthopedics.com.*

FOX, DANIEL MICHAEL, foundation executive, writer; b. NYC, Aug. 20, 1938; s. Alexander E. and Rose (Leitner) F.; m. Carol Anne Kemps, Sept. 8, 1963 (div. 1985); children: Aaron, Miriam, Joshua, Benjamin; m. Louise O. Vasvari, Dec. 26, 1988 (div. 2003). AB, Harvard U., Cambridge, Mass., 1959, AM, 1961, PhD, 1964. Instr. Harvard U., Cambridge, Mass., 1964—65, asst. prof., 1967—72; dir. field ops. Applachian Vols., Berea, Ky., 1965—66; assoc. dir. Commonwealth of Mass. Svc. Corps, 1965—67; prof., v.p. SUNY, Stony Brook, 1972—89. Assoc. dir. Nat. Ctr. for Health Svcs. Rsch., Rockville, Md., 1975-78; pres. Milbank Meml. Fund, NYC, 1990-2007, pres. emeritus, 2007-; cons. in field. Author: Engines of Culture, 1963, rev. edit., 1995, The Discovery of Abundance, 1967, electronic edit., 2002, Economists and Health Care, 1979, Health Policies, Health Politics, 1986, Photographing Medicine, 1988, AIDS: The Burdens of History, 1989, AIDS: The Making of a Chronic Disease, 1992, Power and Illness: The Failure and Future of American Health Policy, 1993, 2d edit., 1995. Bd. dir. Village Care NY Inc., vice chmn., 1996—; treas. Employee Benefit Rsch. Inst., 2003—04; bd. dir. ECRI, The Health Tech. Ctr., Health Quality Coun. Sask., Suicide Prevention Internat. Shaw traveling fellow Harvard U., 1959-60, Sheldon traveling fellow, 1962; also numerous grants. Mem.: APHA, NY Acad. Medicine, Am. Assn. for the History of Medicine, Nat. Acad. Social Ins., Am. Hist. Assn. (Beveridge prize 1965), Coun. on Fgn. Rels., Inst. Medicine of NAS, Century Assn., Harvard Club of NY. Jewish. Business E-Mail: dmfox@milbank.org.

FOX, DAVID, lawyer; b. NYC, 1958; LLB, Hebrew U., Jerusalem, 1982. Bar: Israel 1983, N.Y. 1984. Ptnr., mem. policy com. Skadden, Arp, Slate, Meagher & Flom LLP, NYC. Founder, mem. exec. com. Kaminker Project; bd. mem. Am. Friends Israel Democracy Inst. Named one of "45 Under 45: The Rising Starts of the Private Bar", The Am. Lawyer mag. Office: Skadden Arps Slate Meagher & Flom LLP 4 Times Sq Fl 24 New York NY 10036-6595 E-mail: dfox@skadden.com.

FOX, DAVID ALAN, rheumatologist, immunologist; b. Montreal, July 5, 1953; s. Lester L. and Zelda L. (Rothbart) F.; m. Paula L. Bockenstedt, July 10, 1977; children: Sharon Elizabeth, Michelle Caroline, Jonathan William. BS, MIT, 1974; MD, Harvard U., 1978. Diplomate Am. Bd. Internal Medicine, Am. Bd. Rheumatology. Intern, then resident Brigham and Women's Hosp., Boston, 1978-81; fellow in rheumatology and immunology Harvard U. Med. Sch., Boston, 1981-85; asst. prof. U. Mich., Ann Arbor, 1985-90, assoc. prof., 1990-95, prof., 1995—, acting chief divsn. rheumatology, 1990-91, chief divsn., 1991—. Dir. U. Mich. Multipurpose Arthritis Ctr., Ann Arbor, 1990—2001, U. Mich. Rheumatic Disease Core Ctr., 2001—; trustee Arthritis Found., 1992—. Assoc. editor Jour. Clin. Investigation, 1997-2002; contbr. chpts. to books, articles to profl. jours. Mem.: Assn. Am. Physicians, Am. Soc. Clin. Investigation, Am. Assn. Immunologists, Am. Coll. Rheumatology (pres.-elect 2006—07). Achievements include discovery of T lymphocyte surface molecules and development of various monoclonal antibodies. Office: U MichMed Ctr Rackham Arthritis Rsch Unit 3918 Taubman Ctr Ann Arbor MI 48109

FOX, DEBRA L., educational association administrator, business owner; m. Jules Rosen; children: Adam, Josh, Daniel, Rebecca. Reporter, anchor WTAE-TV, 1976—86; founder, owner, pres., CEO Fox Learning Systems Inc. (formerly Fox FarSight Prodn.), 1997—. Named One of Pa. Best 50 Women in Bus., 2004. Office: Fox Learning Systems Inc Manor Oak II 1910 Cochran Rd Ste 920 Pittsburgh PA 15220 Office Phone: 412-531-1889. Business E-Mail: debra@foxlearningsystems.com.

FOX, DIANE PORRETTA, nursing educator; d. Marvin and Mary Lou Porretta; m. Robert Curtis Fox, Nov. 7, 1975; children: Jesse Thomas Morgan, Patrick Robert. AS with honors, Washtenaw C.C., 1978; BA magna cum laude, Siena Heights Coll., 1989; BSN magna cum laude, U. Mich., 1997; MS in Nursing, Ea. Mich. U., 2003. Cert. tchg. healthcare sys., Ea. Mich. U., 2001; asthma educator Nat. Asthma Educator Certification Bd., 2003. Staff nurse, contingent ecmo nurse U. Mich. Hosp., Ann Arbor, 1990—; part-time faculty Monroe County C.C., 1990—2004; reg. respiratory therapist U. Mich., 1995—2000; staff nurse U. Mich.-Mich. Congenital Heart Ctr., 1997—99; asst. prof. nursing Sch. Nursing, Ea. Mich. U., Ypsilanti, 2004—. Dir. cardiopulmonary svcs. Saline Cmty. Hosp., Mich., 1988—95; adj. faculty Washtenaw C.C., Ann Arbor, 2000—04; presenter in field; ednl. leadership doctorate cohort Ea. Mich. U., 2005. Vol. Big Bros./Big Sisters, Adrian, Mich., 1997—2002. Named Outstanding Grad. Nursing Student, Ea. Mich. U., 2003; Joan Rodman Schrandt Nursing scholar, Saline Cmty. Hosp., 1995—97, Angell scholar, U. Mich., 1997. Mem.: AACN, Nat. Bd. Respiratory Care, Am. Assn. Respiratory Care, Transcultural Nursing Soc., Am. Assn. Adult and Continuing Edn., Stratford Shakespeare Soc., Golden Key Nat. Honor Soc., Sigma Theta Tau (assoc.; v.p. 2002—04, rsch. award 2003). Avocation: master gardener. Office: Ea Mich U 306 Marshall Ypsilanti MI 48197 Home Phone: 517-423-7243; Office Phone: 734-487-2154. Business E-Mail: dfox2@emich.edu.

FOX, DONALD THOMAS, lawyer; b. Council Bluffs, Iowa, June 12, 1929; s. Donald and Genevieve (Tinley) F.; m. Ana Clemencia Tercero-Graham; children: Mark, Matthew, Genevieve, Melissa. AB magna cum laude, Harvard U., 1951; LLB, N.Y. U., 1956; Brevet de Traduction et de Terminologie Juridiques, U. Paris, 1957, Diplome de Droit Comparé, 1961. Bar: N.Y. 1957, U.S. Ct. Claims 1960, U.S. Dist. Ct. (so. and ea. dists.) N.Y. 1960, U.S. Ct. Appeals (2nd cir.) 1960, D.C. 1968, U.S. Tax Ct. 1973. Instr. Inst. Comparative Law, NYU, 1957-59; assoc. Davis, Polk, Wardwell, Sunderland & Kiendl, NYC, 1958-67; ptnr. Fox Horan & Camerini, LLP and predecessor firms, NYC, 1968—. Bd. dirs. Michelin Licensing Svcs. Inc., Horphag Rsch., Save Venice Inc.; mem. adv. com. on history and theory Harvard U. Grad. Sch. Design, 1990—95. Author: Conciliation of International Economic Disputes, 1964, Human Rights in Guatemala, 1979, Report on Contra Activity in Nicaragua, 1985, Violence in Colombia, 1989, Hungarian Constitutional Reform and the Rule of Law, 1993, Elections in Ethiopia, 1995, Elections in Nicaragua, 1996, 2000, Elections in Mexico, 1997, Lessons of the Colombian Constitutional Reform of 1991 (U.S. Inst. of Peace), 2002; editor: The Cambodian Incursion: Legal Issues, 1971; mem. panel advisors Jour. Internat. Law and Politics, 1968-99; contbr. articles to legal jours. Trustee Law Ctr. Found., N.Y.U., 1975-86, chmn. campaign fund, 1980; mem. Am. Soc., 1975—, pres.'s coun., 2005—; Coun. on Fgn. Rels., 1973—; Pres.'s assocs. Harvard U., 2000—; mem. Havard Coll. Fund Gift Com. 1st lt. USAF, 1951-53. Named to Com. of Honor, Giulio Romano Exhbn., Mantova, Italy, 1989; Albert Gallatin fellow, 1978; Nat. scholar Harvard U., Root-Tilden scholar NYU, Fulbright scholar U. Paris. Fellow: Am. Bar Found. (life); mem.: The Century Assn. (chmn. wine com.), Humanitarian Found. for Nicaragua (exec. com. bd. dirs. 1991—96), NYU Alumni Fedn. (pres. 1983—85), NYU Law Alumni Assn. (pres. 1971—73), Assn. of Bar of City of N.Y. (chmn. com. lawyers role in search for peace 1969—71, chmn. com. profl. responsibility 1971—74, chmn. com. audit 1978—80, treas. 1982—84, chmn. fin. com. 1982—84), Am. Arbitration Assn. (panel arbitrators 1970—), Am. Assn. Internat. Commn. Jurists (exec. com., bd. dirs. 1970—, chmn. 1991—), Am. Law Inst. (sustaining life), Harvard Club of N.Y.C. Office: Fox Horan & Camerini LLP 825 3rd Ave New York NY 10022-7519 Office Phone: 212-480-4800. Fax: 212-269-2383. Business E-Mail: dtfox@foxlex.com.

FOX, DONNA M., dean, biology professor; d. Hatsuko Tanaka and John Forte; m. Alan I. Fox, June 12, 1976; children: Allison J., Kimberley A. PhD, George Mason U., Fairfax, Va. Patent examiner US Patent and Trademark Office, Crystal City, Va., 1992—93; asst. dean George Mason U., 2000—, biology instr. Recipient Excellence in Tchg. award, George Mason U., 1998, U. Citizenship award, 2004. Mem.: Acad. Affairs Adminstrs. (assoc.; bd. mem. 2004—), Alpha Lambda Delta (hon. named Advisor of Yr. 2004), Alpha Epsilon Delta (hon.), Golden Key Internat. Honour Soc. (hon.). Office: George Mason Univ 4400 University Dr Fairfax VA 22030-4444

FOX, EDWARD ALAN, retired finance company executive; b. NYC, July 17, 1936; s. Herman and Ruth Fox; children from previous marriage: Brian, Laura, Jacqueline. AB, Cornell U., 1958; MBA, NYU, 1975. Pres., CEO Student Loan Mktg. Assn., Washington, 1973-90; dean Amos Tuck Sch. Dartmouth Coll., Hanover, NH, 1990-94; chmn. SLM Corp. (Sallie Mae), Reston, Va., 1997—2005. Bd. dirs. Delphi Fin. Group, Inc., Capmark Fin. Corp. Chmn. bd. dirs. Am. Ballet Theater.

FOX, ELEANOR MAE COHEN, lawyer, educator, writer; b. Trenton, NJ, Jan. 18, 1936; d. Herman and Elizabeth (Stein) Cohen; children: Douglas Anthony, Margot Alison, Randall Matthew. BA, Vassar Coll., 1956; LLB, NYU, 1961. Bar: N.Y. 1961, U.S. Dist. Ct. N.Y. 1964, U.S. Supreme Ct. 1965. Ptnr. Simpson Thacher & Bartlett, 1970—76, of counsel, 1976—; prof. Law Sch. NYU, NYC, 1976—, Walter J. Derenberg prof. trade regulation, 1999—. Mem. Pres. Carter's Nat. Commn. Rev. Antitrust Laws and Procedures, 1978-79; mem. adv. bd. Bur. Nat. Affairs Antitrust and Trade Regulation Reporter, 1977—; trustee NYU Law Ctr. Found., 1974-92; exec. com. Lawyers' Com. Civil Rights Under Law, 1988—, bd. dirs.; mem. Coun. Fgn. Rels., 1993—; mem. Pres. Clinton's internat. competition policy adv. com. to advise the U.S. Atty. Gen., 1997-2000; lectr. on antitrust law, European Union law, world competition, trade, and econ. devel. Author (with Byron E. Fox): Corporate Acquisitions and Mergers, 1968, 1970, 1973, 1981, 2005; author: (novel) W.L., Esquire, 1977; author: (with Lawrence A. Sullivan and Rudolph Peritz) Cases and Materials, U.S. Antitrust in Global Context, 2000; author: (with G. Bermann, R. Goebel, W. Davey) European Union Law, Cases and Materials, The Competition Law of the European Union--Cases and Materials, 2002; author: (with J. Fingleton, D. Neven, P. Seabright) Competition Policy and the Transformation of Central Europe, 1996; mem. editl. bd. NY Law Jour., 1976—99, Antitrust Bull., 1986—, Rev. Indsl. Orgn., 1990—2001, EEC Merger Control Reporter, 1992—, Gaceta Juridica de la CE y de la Competencia, 1992—2001, World Competition: Law and Economics Rev., 1999—, Inst. for Consumer Antitrust Studies, 2002—. Fellow Am. Bar Found., N.Y. Bar Found.; mem. ABA (chmn. merger com. antitrust sect. 1974-77, chmn. publs. com. 1977-78, chmn. Sherman Act com. 1978-79, coun. antitrust sect. 1979-83, 90-94, vice chmn. antitrust sect. 1992-94, chair NAFTA Task Force, 1993-99), N.Y. State Bar Assn. (chmn. antitrust sect. 1978-79, exec. com. antitrust sect. 1979-83), Fed. Bar Coun. (trustee 1974-76, v.p. 1976-78), Assn. of Bar of City of N.Y. (v.p. 1989-90, exec. com. 1977-81, chmn. trade regulation com. 1973-76, lawyer advt. com. 1976-77, chmn. com. on U.S. in global economy, 1991-94), Am. Law Inst., Assn. Am. Law Schs. (chmn. sect. antitrust and econ. regulation 1981-83), NYU Law Alumni Assn. (bd. dirs. 1974-79, 87-91), Am. Fgn. Law Assn. (v.p. 1979-82, 98-2001). Business E-Mail: eleanor.fox@nyu.edu.

FOX, FRANCIS HANEY, lawyer; b. Attleboro, Mass., May 28, 1933; s. Francis Joseph and Mary Frances (Brady) F.; m. Cynthia Ann Blundell, Dec. 27, 1959; children: Cynthia, Martin, Matthew, Kalarn. BS in Econs., Coll. Holy Cross, 1955; LLB, Harvard U., 1963. Bar: Mass. 1963, U.S. Ct. Appeals (1st cir.) 1963, U.S. Supreme Ct. 1977. Assoc. Bingham, Dana & Gould, Boston, 1963-70; ptnr. Bingham McCutchen LLP and predecessor firms, Boston, 1970—. Mem. adv. com. on civil rules Jud. Conf. of U.S., 1992-98. Overseer U.S.S. Constn. Mus. Capt. USNR, 1955—78. Fellow Am. Coll. Trial Lawyers; mem. Am. Law Inst. Home: 77 Cottage St Sharon MA 02067-2132 Office: Bingham McCutchen LLP 150 Federal St Boston MA 02110-1726 Office Phone: 617-951-8352. Business E-Mail: francis.fox@bingham.com.

FOX, G. RICHARD, lawyer; b. Galveston, Tex., Feb. 17, 1942; s. George J. and Margaret (Kolar) F.; m. Carol L. Halbert, July 22, 1967; children: Stacey, Jessica, Alison. BS, St. Louis U., 1964, JD, 1967. Bar: Mo. 1969, US Dist. Ct. (ea. dist.) Mo. 1971, US Ct. Appeals (8th cir.) 1971. Assoc. Rooney, Webbe, Davidson & Schlueter, St. Louis, 1971-76; ptnr. Kell & Fox, St. Louis, 1976-80; pvt. practice St. Louis, 1981-87; ptnr. Lane, Lahey & Fox, St. Louis, 1987—91, Fox, Heller, Gallagher & Finley LLP, St. Louis, 1991—. Pros. atty. City of Ballwin, Mo., 1975—, City of Clarkson Valley, Mo., 1990—; mcpl. judge City of Eureka, Mo., 2001-. Bd. dirs. Camp Wyman, Inc., Eureka, Mo., 1975—, pres. bd. dirs., 1983-86; bd. dirs. Wyman Ctr., St. Louis, 1975-, Camp Wyman Found., 1986—, St. Louis County Spl. Sch. Dist., Spl. Edn. Enrichment Found., 1990-97. Mem. Mo. Bar Assn., Bar Assn. Metro St. Louis, Assn. Trial Lawyers Am., Mo. Assn. Trial Attys., Mo. Athletic Club. Avocations: golf, swimming. Office: Fox Heller Gallagher & Finley LLP 1034 S Brentwood Blvd Saint Louis MO 63117-1223 Office Phone: 314-725-1780. E-mail: grf@stlouislawyer.net.

FOX, GALEN W., state representative; b. Hilo, Feb. 24, 1943; children: Derek, MeiMei. BA, U. Redlands, 1965; MPA, Princeton U., 1967, PhD, 1978. Fgn. svc. officer U.S. Dept. of State, 1966—82; rsch. fellow East-West Ctr., Honolulu, 1982—84; exec. asst. Mayor of Honolulu, 1985—91; chief bus. devel. and mkrg. divsn. Hawaii Dept. of Econ. Devel., 1991—96; mem. Hawaii State Ho. of Reps., 1996—, Rep. whip, 1998—2000, Rep. leader, 2000—05. Chair Sec. of State's Open Forum, 1978—79; sec. Am. Fgn. Svc. Assn., 1979—81; chair, vice chair Neighborhood Bd. #3, 1989—96. Mem., treas. Oahu Pvt. Industry Coun., 1985—91; pres. Hawaii Cmty. Svcs. Coun., 1995—96; sec., treas. exec. com. East-West Ctr. Internat. Alumni, 1995—2000; mem. allocations com. Aloha United Way, 1996—; exec. bd. Ch. of the Crossroads, 2001—04. Mem.: Waikki Residents Assn., Waikki Improvement Assn. Republican. United Ch. Of Christ. Home Phone: 808-946-5223; Office Phone: 808-586-8520. E-mail: repfox@capitol.hawaii.gov.

FOX, HAMILTON PHILLIPS, III, (PHIL FOX), lawyer; b. Salisbury, Md., Sept. 18, 1945; s. Hamilton Phillips and Evelyn Louise (Jefferson) F.; m. Mary Shannon Lafans, Aug. 31, 1968 (dissolved); children: Gretchen

Robinson, Hamilton Duke, Caleb Savage; m. Barbara Daniels Robinson, Dec. 13, 1986. BA with honors, U. Va., 1967; LLB, Yale U., 1970. Bar: Maine 1971, D.C. 1972, U.S. Dist. Ct. Md., U.S. Ct. Appeals (1st, 9th and D.C. cirs.), U.S. Supreme Ct. Law clk. to judge U.S. Ct. Appeals (1st cir.), Portland, Maine, 1970-71; law clk. to Hon. Stanley Reed and Lewis F. Powell Jr. U.S. Supreme Ct., Washington, 1971-72; asst. U.S. atty. U.S. Atty.'s Office, Washington, 1972-73, 74-77; asst. spl. prosecuter Watergate Prosecution Force, Washington, 1973-74; dep. chief organized crime sect. U.S. Dept. Justice, Washington, 1977-80; sole practice Washington, 1980-84; ptnr. Dewey, Ballantine, Bushby, Palmer & Wood, Washington, 1984-90; now ptnr. Sutherland, Asbill & Brennan, Washington. Lectr. law U. Va., Charlottesville, 1980-82; assoc. dep. counsel com. on standards of official conduct U.S. Ho. of Reps., 1983-84. Home: 729 Massachusetts Ave NE Washington DC 20002-6007 Office: Sutherland Asbill Brennan 1275 Pennsylvania Ave NW Ste 1 Washington DC 20004-2415

FOX, HAROLD EDWARD, obstetrician, researcher, gynecologist, educator; b. East Orange, NJ, Feb. 19, 1945; s. Willis Edward and Elizabeth (Strathearn) F.; m. Rhea Keller, June 18, 1966; children: Harold Hamilton, Andrhea Alicia. BA, U. Rochester, 1967, MS, MD with honors, 1972. Diplomate Am. Bd. Ob-Gyn., Am. Bd. Maternal-Fetal Medicine. Intern, resident Strong Meml. Hosp., Rochester, NY, 1972-75; dir. Regional Perinatal Program, Rochester, NY, 1975-79; dir. obstetrics and maternal fetal medicine U. Rochester, 1977-79; dir. maternal fetal medicine Columbia U., NYC, 1979-95, dir. obstetrics, 1985-88, vice-chmn. ob-gyn., 1988-91, chmn. protem dept. ob-gyn., 1991-95; Oscar I. and Mildred S. Dodek prof., chmn. ob-gyn. George Washington U., Washington, 1995-96, exec. dir. Ctr. Excellence for Women's Health, 1995-96; ob-gyn. in-chief Johns Hopkins Medicine, Balt., 1996—, Dr. Dorothy Edwards prof. ob-gyn., 1996—, chair women's health ctr. oversight com., 1997—, chmn., dir. ob-gyn. Trustee Johns Hopkins Med. Svc. Corp., Johns Hopkins Home Care Group, 1996—, Kennedy Kreige Inst., 1996—2003; bd. dirs. JH Cmty. Physicians, JH Health Care; vice chair med. bd. Johns Hopkins Hosp., 1999-2002, chair med. bd., 2002-05, bd. dirs., 2002-05; mem. adv. bd. Johns Hopkins Medicine, bd. govs., chmn. govt. affairs com.; mem. Gov.'s Commn. on Infant Mortality, State of Md., 2000—; chmn. women and infant transmission study NIH, 1988-93; mem. pediat. com. AIDS clin. trials group, 1988-91; organizing mem. women's com.; mem. obstet. adv. com. N.Y.C. Dept. Health; bd. midwifery N.Y. State Edn. Dept., 1994-95; chmn. N.Y. Acad. Medicine Ob-gyn. sect., 1993-94; mem. Gov.'s Commn. on Infant Mortality, State Md., 1999—; co-chair innovations in patient care; chair med. adv. bd. United Prewmiere Med. Group, Johns Hopkins Internat., 2003—; mem. med. adv. bd. Bridgtech Asia, 2004—, Barnev Inc., Israel, 2000—. Editor Pediatric AIDS, 1991-95, Practical Revs. in Ob-Gyn., 2001—; contbr. articles to profl. jours. Grantee NIH, 1988-95, USPHS, 1991-95, March of Dimes. Fellow Soc. Gynecologic Investigation, Am. Coll. Ob-Gyn.; mem. Internat. AIDS Soc., Am. Gynecol. and Obstet. Soc., Am. Inst. Ultrasound in Medicine, Perinatal Rsch. Soc., Washington Acad. Medicine, Washington Gynecol. Soc., N.Y. Obstet. Soc., Med.Soc. State of Md. (chair maternal mortality com. 2003—), Alpha Omega Alpha, Phi Beta Delta. Avocations: boating, art, exercise. Home: PO Box 142 Gibson Island MD 21056-0142 Office: Johns Hopkins Medicine Dept Gyn-Ob 600 N Wolfe St Rm 264 Baltimore MD 21287-0005 Office Phone: 410-614-0178. Business E-Mail: hfox@jhmi.edu.

FOX, INGRID, curator; b. Shoemaker, Calif., June 14, 1945; d. Mel V. and Margaret (Hubert) Allex; m. Frederick B. Fox Jr., Sept. 1, 1973; children: Vanessa Verena, Frederick Bain. AD in Design, Parsons Sch. Design, NYC, 1968; BFA, The New Sch., NYC, 1977. Graphic designer Pfizer, Inc., NYC, 1988-1992, curator, 1992—2004, Gallery at Nicholas F. Rizzo Fine Arts, Chatham, NJ, 2005—; ind. curator/art advisor, 2004—. Designer Montgomery Winecoff & Assocs., NYC, 1969—75., 1976—87. Mem. adv. bd. Pro Arts, Jersey City, 2007—. Mem.: Art Table, Nat. Art Exhbns. by the Mentally Ill (bd. mem.). Episcopalian. Avocations: crafts, designing. Home and Office: 22 Pomander Walk Ridgewood NJ 07450-3711

FOX, JAMES CARROLL, federal judge; b. Atchison, Kans., Nov. 6, 1928; s. Jared Copeland and Ethel (Carroll) F.; m. Katharine deRosset Rhett, Dec. 30, 1950; children: James Carroll, Jr., Jane Fox Brown, Ruth Fox Jordan. BSBA, U. N.C., 1950, JD with honors, 1957. Bar: N.C. 1957. Law clk. U.S. Dist. Ct. (ea. dist.) N.C., Wilmington, 1957-58; assoc. Carter & Murchison, Wilmington, NC, 1958-59; ptnr. Murchison, Fox & Newton, Wilmington, NC, 1960-82; sr. fed. judge U.S. Dist. Ct. (ea. dist.) N.C., Wilmington, 1982—. Lectr. in field. Contbr. articles to profl. jours. Vestryman, St. James Episcopal Ch., 1973-75, 79-82. Office: US Dist Ct Alton Lennon Fed Bldg PO Box 2143 Wilmington NC 28402-2143

FOX, JAMES GAHAN, veterinarian, educator, researcher; b. Reno, Mar. 8, 1943; married; 2 children DVM, Colo. State U., 1968; MS, Stanford U., 1972. Resident veterinarian Biol. Lab. Animal Div. U.S. Army Vet. Corps, Ft. Detrick, 1968-70; asst. prof., staff veterinarian Med. Ctr. U. Colo., 1973-74; inst. veterinarian, dir. animal care facility MIT, Cambridge, 1974-75, inst. veterinarian, assoc. prof., dir. div. comparative medicine, 1975-82, dir., prof. comparative medicine, 1983—. Adj. prof. U. Pa. Sch. of Vet. Med., 1989; faculty affiliate dept. clinics and surgery Colo. State U., 1973-74; adj. assoc. prof. dept. comparative medicine Tufts U. Sch. Vet. Medicine, 1981-82, adj. prof., 1983—; prin. investigator NIH Diagnostic Investigative Lab. grant, 1975—, NIH/Nat. Cancer Inst. Campylobacter and Helicobacter Infections in Animals and Man, 1983—, NIH postdoctoral tng. grant in lab. animal medicine, 1989—; chmn. com. lab. animal usage NAS, 1986—; mem. NIH/DRR/ARB Study Sect., 1981-85, chmn., 1985; cons. in field, 1976-78; mem. editl. bd. Lab Animal Science, 1983-86, Am. Jour. Vet. Rsch., 1990-92, Helicobacter, 1995—, Jour. Clin. Microbiology, 1995—. NIH fellow in lab. animal medicine and med. microbiology Stanford U., 1970-72; grantee Animal Rsch. Ctr., Nat. Cancer Inst., 1977-80, 83—, Nat. Cancer Inst./NIH, 1988—. Fellow Soc. Infectious Diseases Am.; mem. AVMA (Charles River award 1990), Am. Assn. Accreditation Lab. Animal Care (chmn. animal medicine 1983-85), Am. Coll. Toxicology, Am. Assn. Lab. Animal Sci., Am. Coll. Lab. Animal Medicine (pres. 1990), Mass. Soc. Med. Rsch. (exec. com. 1984—, pres. 1990-93), Am. Lab. Animal Diseases (exec. com. 1984—, pres. 1990-92). Home: 349 Littleton Rd Harvard MA 01451-1236 Office: MIT Dept Biol Engring 16-825C 77 Mass Ave Cambridge MA 02139-4307 Office Phone: 617-253-1757. Office Fax: 617-252-1877. E-mail: jgfox@mit.edu.

FOX, JOAN PHYLLIS, environmental engineer, engineering executive; b. Rockledge, Fla., July 16, 1945; d. John A. and Nonie L. (Knutson) Fox. BS in Physics with high honors, U. Fla., 1971; PhD in Civil/Environ. Engring., U. Calif., Bekeley, 1980. Registered profl. engr., Ariz., Fla., Calif., Ga., Wash., Wis., diplomate, Am. Acad. Environ. Engrs., cert. air pollution control, registered environ. assessor class I/II, Calif., qualified environ. profl., Inst. Profl. Environ. Practice. Engr. Bechtel, Inc., San Francisco, 1964—66, 1971—76; dir. program, prin. investigator Lawrence Berkeley Lab., 1977-81; prin. engr., pres. Environ. Mgmt., Berkeley, Calif., 1981—2006; cons. engr. Fla., 2006—. Guest lectr. dept. conservation and resource studies U. Calif., Berkeley, 1980—84; expert witness in field. Contbr. articles to profl. pubs. Grantee, Dept. Energy, 1976—81, EPA, 1976—81. Mem.: NAS (past mem. com. surface mining and reclamation), Air and Waste Mgmt. Assn., Am. Chem. Soc., Phi Beta Kappa, Sigma Pi Sigma. Achievements include design and development of methods to analyze air pollutants. Office Phone: 321-626-6885. Personal E-mail: phyllisfox@gmail.com.

FOX, JOHN, professional football coach; b. Virginia Beach, Va., Feb. 8, 1955; m. Robin Fox; children: Matthew, Mark, Cody, Halle. Student, Southwestern Coll., 1974—75; PhB, San Diego State; degree in sec. edn. tchg., 1977. Grad. asst. San Diego State, 1978; asst. coach U.S. Internat. U., 1979; sec. coach Boise State, 1980, Long Beach State, 1981, Utah, 1982, Kans., 1983, Iowa State , 1984, L.A. Express (USFL), 1985; defensive coord., sec. coach U. Pitts., 1986—88; sec. coach Pitts. Steelers, 1989—91; sec. coach San Diego Chargers, 1992—93; defensive coord. Oakland Raiders, 1994—95; cons. St. Louis Rams, 1996; defensive coord. N.Y. Giants, 1997—2001; head coach Carolina Panthers , 2002—. Named Asst. Coach of Yr., Pro Football Weekly. Office: Carolina Panthers 800 S Mint St Charlotte NC 28202

FOX, JOHN, film company executive; b. May 13, 1974; B in English, UCLA. Intern Baumgarten/Prophet Entertainment; prodn. asst. Timecop ABC; asst. to prodn. head Casey La Scala Gaylord Films; dir. devel. DreamWorks, 2002—04, v.p. devel., 2004—. Achievements include overseeing development and production for Anchorman: The Legend of Ron Burgundy, 2004, and the upcoming releases Norbit and Transformers. Office: DreamWorks 1000 Flower St Glendale CA 91201*

FOX, JOHN BAYLEY, JR., university dean; b. Cambridge, Mass., Nov. 6, 1936; s. John Bayley and Eunice (Jameson) F.; m. Julia Garrett, July 22, 1967; children: Sarah Cleveland Kreckel, Thomas Bayley. AB, Harvard U., 1959; BA, Oxford U., Eng., 1961, MA, 1962. Assoc. div. internat. fellowships Commonwealth Fund of N.Y., NYC, 1963-67; dir. Office Career Services Harvard U., Cambridge, 1967-71, spl. asst., asst. dean of faculty, 1971-76, dean Harvard Coll., 1976-85, adminstrv. dean Grad. Sch. Arts and Scis., 1985-94, sec. Faculty Arts and Scis., sec. faculty coun., 1992—2005, sr. advisor to dean Faculty of Arts and Scis., 2005—. Unitarian. Home: 125 Prince St West Newton MA 02465-2603 Office: Harvard Univ Faculty Arts and Scis University Hall 401 Cambridge MA 02138-5722 Home Phone: 617-527-0295; Office Phone: 617-495-1522. Business E-Mail: John_Fox@harvard.edu.

FOX, KARL AUGUST, retired economist, educator, eco-behavioral scientist; b. Salt Lake City, July 14, 1917; s. Feramorz Young and Anna Teresa (Wilcken) Fox; m. Sylvia Olive Cate, July 29, 1940; children: Karl Richard, Karen Frances Anne. BA, U. Utah, 1937, MA, 1938; PhD, U. Calif., 1954. Economist USDA, 1942-54; head divsn. statis. and hist. rsch. Bur. Agrl. Econs., 1951-54; economist Coun. Econ. Advisers, Washington, 1954-55; head dept. econs. and sociology Iowa State U., Ames, 1955-66, head dept. econs., 1966-72, disting. prof. scis. and humanities, 1968-87, prof. emeritus, 1987—. Vis. prof. Harvard, 1960-61, U. Calif., Santa Barbara, 1971-72, 78, vis. scholar, Berkeley, 1972-73; William Evans vis. prof. U. Otago, N.Z., 1981; Bd. dirs. Social Sci. Rsch. Coun., 1963-67, mem. com. econ. stability, 1963-66, chmn. com. areas for social and econ. statistics, 1964-67; mem. Com. Reg. Accounts, 1963-68 Author: Econometric Analysis for Public Policy, 1958, (with M. Ezekiel) Methods of Correlation and Regression Analysis, 1959, (with others) The Theory of Quantitative Economic Policy, 1966, rev. edit., 1973, Intermediate Economic Statistics, 1968, rev. edit., (with T.K. Kaul), 1980, (with J. K. Sengupta) Economic Analysis and Operations Research, 1969, (with W.C. Merrill) Introduction to Economic Statistics, 1970, Social Indicators and Social Theory, 1974, Social System Accounts, 1985, The Eco-Behavioral Approach To Surveys and Social Accounts for Rural Communities, 1990, repub., 1994, Demand Analysis, Econometrics and Policy Models, 1992, Urban-Regional Economics, Social System Accounts and Eco-Behavioral Science, 1994; author-editor: Economic Analysis for Educational Planning, 1972; co-editor: Readings in the Economics of Agriculture, 1969, Economic Models, Estimation and Risk Programming (essays in honor of Gerhard Tintner), 1969, Systems Economics, 1987; contbr. articles to profl. jours. Recipient superior service medal USDA, 1948, award for outstanding pub. research Am. Agrl. Econs. Assn., 1952, 54, 57, for outstanding doctoral dissertation, 1953 Fellow Econometric Soc., Am. Statis. Assn. (Census Research fellow 1980-81), Am. Agrl. Econs. Assn. (v.p. 1955-56, award for publ. of enduring quality 1977), AAAS; mem. Am. Econs. Assn. (rsch. and publs. com. 1963-67), Regional Sci. Assn., Ops. Rsch. Soc. Am., Am. Edni. Rsch. Assn., Phi Beta Kappa, Phi Kappa Phi. Home: 1801 20th St Apt J-31 Ames IA 50010-5166 Office: Iowa State U Econs Dept Ames IA 50011-0001

FOX, KEITH, publishing executive; B in History, Brown U., Providence; MBA, Columbia U., NYC. With Booz Allen Hamilton, Unilever; v.p. new media Reader's Digest Assn.; sr. v.p. mktg. and bus. devel. BusinessWeek McGraw-Hill Cos., 2000, pres. McGraw-Hill Profl., pres. BusinessWeek, 2007—. Office: BusinessWeek McGraw Hill Bldg 43rd Fl 1221 Ave of the Americas New York NY 10020-1093 Office Phone: 212-512-2511.*

FOX, LAWRENCE J., lawyer; b. Phila., July 17, 1943; s. William and Elainne B. Fox; m. Vicki Hessan (div.); children: Emily, Anthony. BA, U. Pa., 1965, LLB, 1968. Bar: Pa. 1968, NY 1970, US Dist. Ct. So. Dist. NY 1970, US Dist. Ct. Ea. Dist. Pa. 1972, US Ct. Appeals 3rd Cir. 1972, US Ct. Appeals 5th Cir. 1975, US Ct. Appeals 2nd Cir. 1978, US Supreme Ct. 1994. Law clk. to Justice Samuel J. Roberts Pa. Supreme Ct.; legal services lawyer Cmty. Action Legal Services, NYC; assoc. Drinker Biddle & Reath, Phila., 1972-76, ptnr., 1976—, former mng. ptnr. Lectr. in law U. Pa.; law firm rep. CPR Inst. for Dispute Resolution (formerly Ctr. for Pub. Resources), mem. disting. panel neutrals, mem. bd. editors Alternatives newsletter, mem. Commn. on Ethics and Standards of Dispute Resolution. Author: Legal Tender: A Lawyer's Guide to Professionalism Dilemmas, 1995; co-author (with Susan R. Martyn): Traversing the Ethical Minefield: Problems, Law, and Profl. Responsibility, 2004. Mem. bd. overseers U. Pa. Sch. Law, 1992—, nat. chmn. ann. giving, 1987-89; assoc. trustee U. Pa., 1992—; trustee Friends Select Sch., 1982-93, Beth Zion-Beth Israel Synagogue, 1988—; mem. bd. advisors United Way; active USCG Aux. Recipient Wachovia Fidelity Award, Phila. Bar Assn., 2004. Mem. ABA (former chair sect. litig.; mem. Standing Com. on Ethics and Profl. Responsibility 1990-97, chair 1996-97) , Pa. Bar Assn., Am. Law Inst., Am. Coll. Trial Lawyers. Democrat. Avocations: sailing, writing.

FOX, MARGALIT (EVE), journalist, editor, writer; b. Glen Cove, NY, Apr. 25, 1961; d. David and Laura (Garfield) Fox; m. George Richard Robinson, Sept. 13, 1986. BA, SUNY, Stony Brook, 1982, MA, 1983; MS, Columbia U. Sch. Journalism, 1991. Fgn. lang. editor Dover Publs., NYC, 1984-85; freelance arts journalist NYC, 1985-94; staff editor Book Rev. NY Times, NYC, 1994—2004, obituary writer, 2004—. Contbr. articles on lang. and culture to NY Times. Regents fellow, U. Calif., San Diego, 1983—84. Office: NY Times 229 W 43rd St New York NY 10036-3959 Business E-mail: fox@nytimes.com.

FOX, MARK, men's college basketball coach; m. Cindy Fox; children: Parker, Olivia. Student, Garden City CC, Kans., 1987—89; BS magna cum laude in Phys. Ed., Ea. N.Mex. U., Portales, 1991; MS in Athletic Adminstrn. and Sports Psych., U. Kans., 1996. Grad. asst. to asst. coach U. Wash., 1991—93; asst. coach Kans. State U., 1994—2000; assoc. head coach U. Nev., Reno, 2000—04, head coach, 2004—. Named Don Haskins Western Athletic Conf. Coach of Yr., 2005, 2006. Office: U Nev Mens Basketball Legacy Hall MS 264 1664 N Virginia St Reno NV 89557-0110 Office Phone: 775-682-6949. Office Fax: 775-327-5022.*

FOX, MARY ANN WILLIAMS, librarian; b. Savannah, Ga., Jan. 16, 1939; d. Alton F. and Arthur (Colquitt) Williams; m. William Francis Fox, Dec. 26, 1960 (div. 1984); children: Katherine Frances, William Francis Jr. BA, U. Ga., 1960; MLS, Rutgers U., 1984. Libr. Metuchen (N.J.) Pub. Libr., 1983-85, Mable Smith Douglas Libr. Rutgers U., New Brunswick, NJ, 1984, Firestone Libr. Princeton (N.J.) U., 1985, The Hun Sch. of Princeton, 1985—. Bd. dirs. Ctrl. Jersey Regional Libr. Coop., 1997-2005, Region 5 Libr. Coop., N.J., 1985-92. Trustee East Brunswick (N.J.) Pub. Libr., 1979-92; bd. dirs. Ctrl. Jersey YWCA, New Brunswick, 1985-88, Ctrl. Atlantic Conf. United Ch. of Christ, 1985-88. Mem. ALA, N.J. Libr. Assn., N.J. Ind. Sch. Assn. (chair libr. sect. 1988—), Edn. Media Assn. N.J. (bd. dirs. 1987-92), Librs. of Middlesex (pres.). Democrat. Mem. United Ch. of Christ. Home: 10 Redcoat Dr East Brunswick NJ 08816-2759 Office: Hun Sch Princeton 176 Edgerstone Rd Princeton NJ 08540 Home Phone: 732-257-4228. E-mail: mafox@hunschool.org.

FOX, MATTHEW, actor; b. Crowheart, Wy, July 14, 1966; m. Margherita Ronchi; children: Kyle, Byron. Grad., Columbia U., 1989. Actor: (TV series) Freshman Dorm, 1992, Party of Five, 1994—2000, Haunted, 2002, Lost, 2004— (Outstanding Performance by an Ensemble in a Drama Series, Screen Actors Guild award, 2006); (films) My Boyfriend's Back, 1993, A Token for Your Thoughts, 2003, We Are Marshall, 2006; (TV films) If I Die Before I Wake, 1993, Behind the Mask, 1999; appeared: (TV miniseries) I Love the 80's, 2002. Office: c/o ABC 77 W 66th St New York NY 10023*

FOX, MATTHEW IGNATIUS, publishing executive; b. NYC, Apr. 10, 1934; s. Matthew I. and Lucille V. (Reilly) F.; children: Cathleen, Matthew, Patricia. AB, Rutgers U., 1956. Field rep. Prentice-Hall, Inc., NYC, 1958-60, editor engring., 1960-67, exec. editor, asst. v.p., 1967-71, exec. editor, 1981-83, editor-in-chief, 1983-85, pub., 1985—; pres. Reston Pub. Co., Va., 1971-81. Cons. in pub., 1987—; bd. dirs. Fairmont Press, Atlanta. Dep. mayor, mayor, Rivervale (NJ), 1964-67, commr., Bergen County, NJ, 1966-70; del. Fairfax County (Va.) Dem. Com., 1976-81; leader City of Cape May Dem. Party. Mem. Rutgers U. Alumni Assn., Cape May Cottagers and Beach Club, Corinthian Yacht Club, Villas Fishing Club. Democrat. Roman Catholic. Home: 1103 Illinois Ave Cape May NJ 08204-2608

FOX, MAURICE SANFORD, retired molecular biologist, educator; b. NYC, Oct. 11, 1924; s. Albert and Ray F.; m. Sally Cherniavsky, Apr. 1, 1955; children: Jonathan, Gregory, Michael. BS in Meteorology, U. Chgo., 1944, MS in Chemistry, 1951, PhD, 1951; Docteur honoris causa, Université Paul Sabatier, Toulouse, France, 1994. Instr. U. Chgo., 1951-53; asst. Rockefeller Inst., 1953-55, asst. prof., 1955-58, assoc. prof., 1958-62, MIT, Cambridge, 1962-66, prof., 1966-79, Lester Wolfe prof. molecular biology, 1979-96, head dept. biology, 1985-89; ret., 1997. Mem. Radiation Effects Rsch. Found., Hiroshima, 1997—2000. Mem. Internat. Bioethics Com. UN Ednl., Sci. and Cultural Orgn., 1997-2003. Served with USAAF, 1943-46. USPHS fellow, 1952-53; Nuffield Rsch. fellow, 1957; Fogarty scholar, 1991. Fellow: AAAS; mem.: NAS, Am. Acad. Arts and Scis., Inst. Medicine. Office: MIT Dept Biology 77 Massachusetts Ave Cambridge MA 02139-4307 Office Phone: 617-253-4728. Business E-Mail: msfox@mit.edu.

FOX, MERRITT B., lawyer, educator; b. 1946; BA, Yale U., 1968, JD, 1971, PhD, 1980. Bar: N.Y. 1975. Acting instr. econs. Yale U., 1973; assoc. Cleary, Gottlieb, Steen & Hamilton, NYC, 1974-80; assoc. prof. Ind. U., Bloomington, 1980-86, prof., Ira C. Batman faculty fellow, 1986-88; prof. law U. Mich., Ann Arbor, 1988—2000, Alene & Allan F. Smith prof. law, 2000—03; vis. prof. Columbia Univ. Sch. Law, 2001, Michael E. Patterson Prof., 2003—; co-dir. Ctr. Law & Econ. Studies, Columbia Univ., 2003—. Vis. lectr. econs. Yale U., 1976; vis. assoc. prof. Fordham U., 1976-80; vis. prof. Mich. U., spring 1988. Author: (with Lasswell) The Signature of Power, 1979, Finance and Industrial Performance in a Dynamic Economy, 1987. Mem. Am. Soc. Internat. Law, Am. Law Inst., Am. Econs. Assn., Assn. Am Law Sch. (chmn. Business Assn. sect. 1997-98), Am. Law & Econ. Assn. Office: Columbia University Law School Room 837 435 W 116th St New York NY 10027 Business E-Mail: mfox1@law.columbia.edu.

FOX, MICHAEL DAVID, retired art educator; b. Dec. 29, 1937; s. Donald F. and Ethel (Allen) Sullivan; m. Carol Ann Hampstson, Nov. 5, 1967; 1 child, Kathryn Gabrielle. BS, SUNY, Buffalo, 1962, MS, 1969; cert. in sculpture, Bklyn. Mus. Sch., 1964. Tchr. art City Schs., Rochester, NY, 1962-63, 64-65; prof. art Morehead State U., Ky., 1965-67, SUNY, Oswego, 1967—2000; ret., 2000. Vis. artist univs. and art ctrs. in U.S., univs. and art ctrs. in Can.; dir. Popular Image Gallery, Oswego, 1967—2006; spkr. in field; lectr. in field; judge local, state, regional and nat. exhibitions. One-man shows include in U.S. and Can., work featured on CBS-TV, 1976, 1978, 1980, also featured in N.Y. Times, Look, Evergreen Rev., Nat. Lampoon, Scanlon's Monthly, Cavalier, Sch. Arts, others, Represented in permanent collections, U.S., Can., Japan, Africa, Asia, Europe, S.Am.; reviewer textbooks; featured in texbook, Sculpture: Techniques, Form and Content, 1988, Beginning Sculpture, 2004, The Sculpture Reference, 2004. Recipient numerous awards for drawing, painting and sculpture, 1962—, Outstanding Tchg. award, Morehead State U., 1967, Chancellor's award for excellence in tchg., SUNY, 1981. Mem.: United Univ. Profs. (v.p., del). Home: 38 W End Ave Oswego NY 13126-1758 Office Phone: 315-591-3392. E-mail: cfox@oswego.edu.

FOX, MICHAEL J. (MICHAEL ANDREW FOX), actor; b. Edmonton, Alberta, Can., June 9, 1961; s. Bill and Phyllis Fox; m. Tracy Pollan, July 16, 1988; children: Sam Michael, Aquinnah Kathleen, Schuyler Frances, Esme Annabelle. GED, 1995. Head Lottery Hill Entertainment, The Michael J. Fox Found. for Parkinson's Rsch., 2000-. TV series include Leo and Me (CBC), 1976, Palmerstown USA, 1980, Family Ties, 1982-89 (Emmy award, 1986, 87, 88, Golden Globe best actor 1989), Spin City (also exec. prodr.), 1996-2000 (Emmy award best actor in comedy 2000, Golden Globe best actor 1998, 99, 2000); TV films include Letters From Frank, 1979, Poison Ivy, 1985, High School USA, 1985, I Am Your Child, 1997, Tales From the Crypt: The Trap (guest dir.), Don't Drink the Water, 1994, The Magic 7 (voice), 2005; exec. prodr. TV series Anna Says, 1999, Otherwise Engaged, 2002; TV guest appearances include Lou Grant, 1979, Family, 1980, Trapper John, M.D., 1981, The Love Boat, 1983, Night Court, 1984, Tales from the Crypt, 1991, Scrubs, 2004, Boston Legal, 2006; film appearances include Midnight Madness, 1980, Class of '84, 1981, Back to the Future, 1985, Teen Wolf, 1985, Light of Day, 1986, The Secret of My Success, 1987, Bright Lights, Big City, 1988, Casualties of War, 1989, Back to the Future, Part II, 1989, Back to the Future, Part III, 1990, The Hard Way, 1991, Doc Hollywood, 1991, (voice over) Homeward Bound: The Incredible Journey, 1993, Life with Mikey, 1993, For Love or Money, 1993, Where the Rivers Flow North, 1993, Greedy, 1994, Cold Blooded, 1995, Blue in the Face, 1995, The American President, 1995, Mars Attacks!, 1996, Homeward Bound II: Lost in San Francisco, 1996, The Frighteners, 1996, Stuart Little (voice), 1999, Atlantis: The Lost Empire (voice), 2001, Interstate 60, 2002, Stuart Little 2 (voice), 2002, Stuart Little 3: Call of the Wild, 2006; Author: Lucky Man: A Memoir, 2001, Always Looking Up, 2008. Named one of The World's Most Influential People, TIME Mag., 2007; recipient Golden Plate award, Acad. Achievement, 2005. Office: Creative Artists Agy care Kevin Huvane 9830 Wilshire Blvd Beverly Hills CA 90212-1804 also: Michael J Fox Foundation for Parkinson's Research PO Box 4777 New York NY 10163*

FOX, MICHAEL VASS, theology studies educator; b. Detroit, Dec. 9, 1940; s. Leonard W. and Mildred (Vass) F.; m. Jane Schulzinger, Sept. 4, 1961; children: Joshua, Ariel BA, U. Mich., 1962, MA, 1963; PhD, Hebrew U., Jerusalem, 1972. Ordained rabbi, 1968. Lectr. Haifa U., Israel, 1971-74, Hebrew U., Jerusalem, 1975-77; prof. Hebrew U. Wis., Madison, 1977—, chmn. dept., 1982-88, 92-99, Weinstein-Bascom prof. in Jewish studies, 1990—, Halls-Bascom prof.; 1999—; Moss exch. prof. Hebrew U., 2006. Author: The Song of Songs and the Ancient Egyptian Love Songs, 1985, Shirey Dodim Mimitzrayim Ha'atiqa, 1985, Qohelet and his Contradictions, 1988, The Redaction of the Books of Esther, 1991, Character and Ideology in the Book of Esther, 1991, 2001, A Time to Tear Down and a Time to Build Up: A Rereading of Ecclesiastes, 1999; editor: Anchor Bible: Proverbs, vol. I, 2000, Ecclesiastes--JPS Commentary, 2004; contbr. articles to profl. jours. Named Vilas assoc., U. Wis., 1988—90; recipient Wahrburg prize, Hebrew U., 1971—72, Kellett Mid-Career award, U. Wis., 1999; fellow, Brit. Friends of Hebrew U., Liverpool, 1974—75, NEH, 1992; Leverhulme fellow, U. Liverpool, Eng., 1974—75, Am. Coun. Learned Socs. fellow, 2001, Am. Acad. for Jewish Rsch. fellow. Mem. Soc. for Bibl. Lit. (editor SBL Dissertation Series 1994-99, editl. bd. Jour. Bibl. Lit. 1991-95; pres. midwest region 1998-2000), Nat. Assn. Profs. Hebrew (editor Hebrew Studies 1985-93, v.p. 2000-03, pres. 2003—). Home: 2815 Chamberlain Ave Madison WI 53705-3607 Office: U Wis Dept Hebrew 1220 Linden Dr Rm 1338 Madison WI 53706-1525 Office Phone: 608-238-5644.

FOX, MICHAEL WILSON, veterinarian, animal scientist; b. Bolton, Eng., Aug. 13, 1937; came to U.S., 1962; s. Geoffrey and Elizabeth (Wilson) F.; m. Deanna L. Krantz, May 1989; children by previous marriage: Michael Wilson, Camilla, Mara. B. in Vet. Medicine, Royal Vet. Coll., London, 1962; PhD, U. London, 1967, D.Sc., 1975. Postdoctoral fellow Jackson Lab., Bar Harbor, Maine, 1962-64; med. research assoc. State Research Hosp., Galesburg, Ill., 1964-67; assoc. prof. psychology Washington U., St. Louis, 1967-76; v.p. Humane Soc. U.S., Washington, 1986-98, sr. scholar bioethics, 1998—2002; chief cons./vet. India Project for Animals & Nature, 1996—. Columnist (syndicated) Ask Your Animal Doctor; author: Canine Behavior, 1965, Canine Pediatrics, 1966, Integrative Development of Brain and Behavior in the Dog, 1971, Behavior of Wolves, Dogs and Related Canids, 1971, Understanding Your Dog, 1972, Understanding your Cat, 1974, Concepts in Ethology: Animal and Human Behavior, 1974, Between Animal and Man: The Key to the Kingdom, 1976, The Dog, Domestication and Behavior, 1977, (juveniles) Wild Dogs Three, 1977, What Is Your Cat Saying?, 1978, The Wolf, 1973 (Christopher award), Vixie, The Story of a Fox, 1973, Sundance Coyote, 1974, Ramu and Chennai, 1975 (Sci. Tchrs. award); co-author: (juveniles) What is Your Dog Saying?, 1977, Dr. Fox's Fables, 1980, The Touchlings, 1981, Animals Have Rights Too, 1991, (adult) Understanding Your Pet, 1978, The Soul of the Wolf, 1980, One Earth One Mind, 1980, Returning to Eden: Animal Rights and Human Responsibility, 1980, How to be Your Pet's Best Friend, 1981, The Healing Touch, 1982, Love is a Happy Cat, 1982, Farm Animal Husbandry, Behavior and Veterinary Practice, 1983, The Whistling Hunters: Field Studies of the Asiatic Wild Dog (Cuon alpinus), 1984, The Animal Doctor's Answer Book, 1984, Laboratory Animal Care, Welfare and Experimental Variables, 1986, Agricide-The Hidden Crisis That Affects Us All, 1986, The New Animal Doctor's Answer Book, 1989, The New Eden, 1989, Superdog, 1990, Inhumane Society, The American Way of Animal Exploitation, 1990, You Can Save The Animals; 50 Things to Do Right Now, 1991, Supercat, 1991, Superpigs and Wondercorn: How the Brave New World of Biotechnology Will Affect Us All, 1992, The Boundless Circle: Caring for Creatures and Creation, 1996, Eating With Conscience: The Bioethics of Food, 1997, Beyond Evolution: The Genetically Altered Future of Plants, Animals, The Earth-.and Humans, 1999, Bringing Life to Ethics: Global Bioethics for a Humane Society, 2001, The Healing Touch for Dogs, 2004, The Healing Touch for Cats, 2004, Killer Foods, 2004, Dog Body Dog Mind, 2007, Cat Body Cat Mind, 2007; editor: Abnormal Behavior in Animals, 1968, Readings in Ethology and Comparative Psychology, 1973, The Wild Canids, 1975, On the Fifth Day: Animal Rights and Human Ethics, 1978, Internat. Jour. for study of Animal Problems, Advances in Animal Welfare Sci. Mem.: AVMA, Brit. Vet. Assn. *My life was shaped in childhood by close contact with animals and nature. Empathy and concern for the well-being of non-human beings led to a veterinary degree and curiousity about their behavior and inner awareness to several years research. Most influential teacher: the wolf. My philosophy: reverence for all life; humankind as steward living in co-creative communion with nature and all.*

FOX, MIKE, college baseball coach; m. Cheryl Fox; children: Matthew, Morgan. BA in Phys. Edn., U. NC, Chapel Hill, 1978, MA in Tchg., 1979. Grad. asst. U. NC, Chapel Hill, 1979, head coach, 1998—, Millbrook HS, Raleigh, NC, 1980—81, NC Wesleyan Coll., Rocky Mount, 1982—98, athletic dir., 1985—98. Named Divsn. III Nat. Coach of Yr., Am. Baseball Coaches Assn., 1989, Atlantic Region Coach of Yr., 2006. Achievements include winning the 1989 NCAA Division III National Championship as head coach. Office: Athletics Dept U NC PO Box 2126 Chapel Hill NC 27515*

FOX, MITCHELL B., publishing executive; married; 3 children. Degree, SUNY. Sr. v.p. sales and promotion Bergdorf Goodman; pub. Vanity Fair mag., NYC, 1994—97, v.p., 1997—99; sr. v.p., corp. sales Conde Nast, NYC, 1999—2000, exec. v.p. sales and mktg., 2000—01; pres. The Golf Digest Cos., NYC, 2001—05, CEO, 2001—05; pres. Golf Digest Divsn., Conde Nast Publications, NYC, 2005—. Office: Golf Digest Four Times Square New York NY 10036*

FOX, MURIEL, retired public relations executive; b. Newark, Feb. 3, 1928; d. M. Morris and Anne L. (Rubenstein) F.; m. Shepard G. Aronson, July 1, 1955 (dec. Nov. 10, 2003); children: Eric R., Lisa S. Student, Rollins Coll., 1944-46; BA summa cum laude, Barnard Coll., 1948. Art critic, bridal editor Miami (Fla.) News, 1946; reporter U.P.I., 1946-48; polit. speechwriter, publicist, 1949-50; from TV-radio writer to exec. v.p. Carl Byoir & Assos., NYC, 1950-85; pres. subs. MediaCom Comm. Tng., 1975-85, By/Media Inc., 1981-85; sr. cons. Hill & Knowlton, Inc., 1986-90. Dir. Harleysville Ins. Co., Rorer Group Inc.; Co-chmn. Vice Presdl. Task Force on Women, 1968; mem. steering com. Women's Forum, 1974-79, pres., 1976-78; mem. Women's Econ. Adv. Com., N.Y.C., 1974-78; mem. nat. adv. com. Nat. Women's Polit. Caucus; nat. adv. bd. Women Today, Ethnic Woman Sr. editor: Feminists Who Changed America 1963-1975, 2006. Bd. dirs. N.Y. Diabetes Assn., 1956-66, Holy Land Conservation Fund, United Way of Tri-State, Internat. Rescue Com., 1977-84; v.p. Rockland Ctr. for the Arts, 1985-2004, pres., 2004—; pres. Hickory Hill Coop., Inc., 1995-99; chair bd. dirs. Vet. Feminists of Am., 1997—. Named one of 100 Top Corp. Women Bus. Week mag., 1976; recipient Matrix award Women in Communications, 1977, Bus. Leader of Year award ADA, 1979; Disting. Alumna award Barnard Coll., 1985, Eleanor Roosevelt Leadership award, 1985 Mem.: NOW (v.p. 1967—70, chmn. bd. 1971—73, chair nat. adv. com. 1973—74, bd. dirs. legal def. and edn. fund 1974—, v.p. fund 1977—78, pres. 1978—81, chair bd. 1981—92, hon. chair bd. 1993—, founder, Muriel Fox Comm. Leadership award 1991, Our Hero award 1995, Caroline Lexow Babcock award 1997), Am. Arbitration Assn. (bd. dirs. 1983—87), Am. Women in Radio and TV (bd. dirs. 1950—51, chair nat. publicity com. 1955—57, chair nat. pub. rels. com. 1957—59, Achievement award 1983), Vet. Feminists of Am. (chair bd. dirs. 2000—). Home and Office: 66 Hickory Hill Rd Tappan NY 10983-1804 Office Phone: 845-359-6075. Personal E-mail: mfox66@optonline.net. *As a business executive, a founder and leader of the modern women's movement, and a fulfilled wife and mother, I hope I have helped to prove that women can enjoy success at many levels-professionally, politically and personally-without being forced to sacrifice one aspect of life for another. I also hope I've helped make such multifaceted success more attainable for other women in the present and future.*

FOX, PATRICK JOHN, sociology educator; b. Ramey AFB, PR, Sept. 25, 1953; s. Leon James and Frances Valeria Fox; m. Sabrina Watson, July 30, 1978. BS in Social Sci., MA in Edn., Calif. Poly. State U., 1976; MSW in Social Welfare, U. Calif., Berkeley, 1978; MA in Sociology, U. Calif., San Diego, 1977; CPhil in Sociology, U. Calif., San Francisco, 1984, PhD in Sociology, 1988. Pub. adminstrn. analyst Inst. Health & Aging U. Calif. Sch. Nursing, San Francisco, 1985-87, sr. pub. adminstn. analyst Inst. Health & Aging, 1987-89, prin. pub. adminstn. analyst Inst. Health & Aging, 1989-90, from asst. prof. to assoc. prof. sociology in residence, 1990—, assoc. dir. for rsch./strat. planning Inst. Health & Aging, 1996-99, assoc. dir. Ctr. Healthy & Active Aging/Inst. Health & Aging, 1999—, prof. sociology in residence dept. social/behavioral scis., 1999—, co-dir. Inst. Health & Aging, 1999—. Guest prof. Inst. Population Studies, East China Normal U., Shanghai, 1997-2000; mem. Ctr. Health and Cmty., U. Calif., San Francisco, 1996—; mini residency in geriatrics U. Calif. San Diego Med. Ctr., 1987; reviewer books and jours. for Scott, Foresman & Co., 1989—; Helen Nahm rsch. lectr. U. Calif., San Francisco; reviewer various panels and confs.; presenter in field. Reviewer: Social Science and Medicine, 1989—, The Gerontologist, 1989—, PharmacoEconomics, 1989—, Am. Jour. Preventive Medicine, 1989—, Am. Jour. Pub. Health, 1989—, Am. Jour. Managed Care, 1989—, Health Care for Women Internat., 1989—, Brain Research, 2002, Health Policy, 2002, Drugs and Aging, 2000-04, Geriatric Nursing, 2006, Jour. AMA, 2007, Can. Jour. on Aging, 2006. Named 25th Helen Nahm Rsch. lectr. Sch. Nursing U. Calif., San Francisco, 2005,; Regents fellow U. Calif.-San Diego, 1981-82, Pew doctoral fellow, U. Calif., San Francisco, 1985-87; Laura Hawkins scholar U. Calif., San Diego, 1981-82; Chancellor's Patent Fund grantee U. Calif., San Francisco, 1986. Fellow Gerontol. Soc. Am.; mem. APHA, AAAS, Am. Soc. Aging, Am. Sociol. Assn., Assn. Health Svcs. Rsch., Pi Gamma Mu. Avocations: music, swimming, films. Office: U Calif Ste 340 3333 California St San Francisco CA 94118 Business E-Mail: pat.fox@ucsf.edu.

FOX, PAUL T., lawyer; b. NYC, Jan. 17, 1953; m. Andrea Fox; children: Emily, Bennett, Eli. BA, Northwestern U., 1975, JD cum laude, 1978. Bar: Ill. 1978, Wis. 1989, US Dist. Ct. (no. dist. trial bar) Ill. , US Dist. Ct. (ctrl. dist.) Ill., US Dist. Ct. (so. dist.) Ill., US Dist. Ct. (ea. dist.) Wis., US Dist. Ct. (we. dist.) Wis. 2006, US Dist. Ct. Mass., US Dist. Ct. (ea. dist.) Mich., US Dist. Ct.(we. dist.) Mich., US Dist. Ct. (we. dist.) Mont., US Ct. Appeals (1st cir.) , US Ct. Appeals (6th cir.), US Ct. Appeals (7th cir.), US Ct. Appeals (9th cir.), US Ct. Appeals (fed. cir.), US Supreme Ct. Appeals (7th cir.) 1979, U.S. Ct. Appeals (fed. cir.) 1987, U.S. Ct. Appeals (1st cir.) 2005, U.S. Ct. Appeals (9th cir.) 2006, U.S. Supreme Ct. 1986,. Co-mng. shareholder Greenberg Traurig LLP, Chgo. Faculty mem. Nat. Inst. for Trial Advocacy; adj. prof. Northwestern U. Sch. Law. Active Leukemia and Lymphoma Soc., Ravinia Music Festival; former chair Glencoe, Ill. Nominating Caucus, Jewish United Fund; former bd. mem. New Trier HS Endowment Fund, US Holocaust Meml. Mus., Chgo. Com. on Diversity in Large Law Firms; dir. Albany Bank & Trust Co., N. Am. Named, Ill. Super Lawyer, 2005—07; named to, Leading Lawyers Network, 2005—07; recipient Martindale Hubbel AV rating. Fellow Am. Bar Found.; mem. ABA (mem. bus. and litigation sect.), State Bar Wis., Chgo. Bar Assn. (com. on large law firms), Chgo. Bar Found., Commn. Mng. Ptnrs., Order of Coif, Green Acres Country Club. Avocations: tennis, golf, history, travel. Office: Greenberg Traurig 77 W Wacker Drive Ste 2500 Chicago IL 60601 Office Phone: 312-456-8420. Business E-Mail: foxp@gtlaw.com.

FOX, PAULA, writer; b. NYC, Apr. 22, 1923; d. Paul Hervey and Elsie (de Sola) F.; m. Richard Sigerson (div. 1954); children: Adam, Linda, Gabriel; m. Martin Greenberg, June 9, 1962. Student, Columbia U. Condr. writing Seminars U. Pa. Author: 22 children's books and 6 novels, including How Many Miles to Babylon, 1966, Portrait of Ivan, 1968, Blowfish Live in the Sea, 1970; (novels) Poor George, 1967, Desperate Characters, 1970, The Western Coast, 1972, The Slave Dancer, 1974 (John Newbery medal), The Widow's Children, 1976, The Little Swineherd and Other Tales, 1978, A Place Apart, 1983 (Am. Book award), A Servant's Tale, 1984, One-Eyed Cat, 1985 (Newbery honor book 1985), Maurice's Room, 1985, The Moonlight Man, 1986, The Stone-Faced Boy, 1987, The Village by the Sea, 1988, Lily and the Lost Boy, 1989, The God of Nightmares, 1990, Monkey Island, 1991, Amzat and His Brothers, 1993, Western Wind, 1993, The Eagle Kite, 1995, Radiance Descending, 1997, Borrowed Finery: A Memoir, 2000 (PEN/Martha Albrand award), (memoir) The Coldest Winter, 2005. Recipient Arts and Letters award Nat. Inst. Arts and Letters, 1972, Hans Christian Andersen medal, 1978, fiction citation Brandeis U., 1984, Empire State award for children's lit., 1994; Guggenheim fellow, 1972. Mem. Authors League, Am. Acad. Arts and Letters (recipient medal and cash award). Office: care Robert Lescher 47 E 19th St New York NY 10003-1323

FOX, RENÉE CLAIRE, sociology educator; b. NYC, Feb. 15, 1928; d. Paul Fred and Henrietta (Gold) F. AB summa cum laude, Smith Coll., 1949, LHD, 1975; PhD, Harvard U., 1954; MA (hon.), U. Pa., 1971, U. Oxford, 1996; ScD (hon.), Med. Coll. Pa., 1974, St. Joseph's Coll., Phila., 1978; D (hon.), Katholieke U., Leuven, 1978; LHD (hon.), La Salle U., Phila., 1988; DSc (hon.), Hahnemann U., 1991, U. Nottingham, Eng., 2002. Rsch. asst. Bur. Applied Social Rsch., Columbia U., 1953-55, rsch. assoc., 1955-58; lectr. dept. sociology Barnard Coll., 1955-58, asst. prof., 1958-64, assoc. prof., 1964-66; lectr. sociology Harvard U., 1967-69; rsch. fellow Ctr. Internat. Affairs, 1967-68, rsch. assoc. program tech. and soc., 1968-71; prof. sociology, psychiatry and medicine U. Pa., Phila., 1969-98, Annenberg prof. social scis., 1978-98, chmn. dept. sociology, 1972-78, Annenberg prof. social scis. emerita, 1998—, sr. fellow Ctr. for Bioethics, 1999—2002, sr. fellow emeritus Ctr. for Bioethics, 2005—, affiliated faculty Solomon Asch Ctr. for the Study of Ethnopolit. Conflict, 2001—07. Rsch. assoc. Refugee Studies Centre, Queen Elizabeth House, U. Oxford, 1998-2006; sci. advisor Centre de Recherches Sociologiques, Kinshasa, Zaïre, 1963-67; vis. prof. sociology U. Officielle du Congo, Lubumbashi, 1965; vis. prof. Sir George Williams U., Montreal, summer 1968; Phi Beta Kappa vis. scholar, 1973-75; dir. humanities seminar med. practitioners NEH, 1975-76; maitre de cours U. Liège, Belgium, 1976-77; vis. prof. Katholieke U., Leuven, Belgium, 1976-77; Wm. Allen Neilson prof. Smith Coll., Mass., 1980; dir. d'Etudes Associé, Ecole des Hautes Etudes en Sciences Sociales, Paris, summer 1989; George Eastman vis. prof. Oxford U., 1996-97; vis. scholar Tokyo Med. and Dental U., 2001; mem. bd. clin. scholars program Robert Wood Johnson Found., 1974-80; mem. Pres.'s Commn. on Study of Ethical Problems in Medicine, Biomed. and Behavioral Rsch., 1979-81; dir. human qualities of medicine program James Picker Found., 1980-83; Fae Golden Kass lectr. Harvard U. Sch. Medicine and Radcliffe Coll., 1983, Kate Hurd Mead lectr. Med. Coll. Pa./Coll. Physicians Phila., 1990, Lori Ann Roscetti Meml. lectr. Rush-Presbyn.-St. Luke's Med. Ctr., Chgo., 1990; vis. scholar Women's Ctr., U. Mo., Kansas City, 1990, vis. scholar Case Western Res. Sch. of Med., 1992; opening address 13th Internat. Conf. on Social Scis. and Medicine, Hungary, 1994, vis. prof. U. Calif., San Francisco Sch. of Medicine, 1994; lectr. founds. of medicine Faculty of Medicine McGill U., Montreal, 1995; Supernumerary fellow Balliol Coll. Oxford U., 1996-97; WHR Rivers disting. lectr. dept. social medicine Harvard Med. Sch., 1998; assembly series lectr. Washington U., St. Louis, 1998; William J. Rashkind Meml. lectr. Am. Heart Assn., 1998, Salinger-Forlang lectr. U. Tex. Health Scis. Ctr. at San Antonio, 1999, Frances H. Schlitz lectr. U. Kans., Wichita, 2002; Stambaugh lectr. U. Louisville Sch. Medicine, 2004. Author: Experiment Perilous, 1959; author: (with Willy De Craemer) The Emerging Physician, 1968; author: (with Judith P. Swazey) The Courage to Fail, 1974, rev. edit., 1978, 2002; author: Essays in Medical Sociology, 1979, 2d edit., 1988, L'Incertitude Medicale, 1988, The Sociology of Medicine: A Participant Observer's View, 1989; author: (with Judith P. Swazey) Spare Parts: Organ Replacement in American Society, 1992; author: In the Belgian Château: The Spirit and Culture of European Society in an Age of Change, 1994, French lang. edit., 1997, Organ Transplantation: Meanings and Realities (edited with Stuart Youngner and Laurence O'Connell), 1996; author: (in Japanese) Looking Intimately at Bioethics: Fifty Years as a Medical Sociologist, 2003; editor (with Victor N. Lidz and Harold J. Bershady): After Parsons: A Theory of Social Action for the Twenty-First Century, 2005; assoc. editor Am. Sociol. Rev., 1963—1196, Social Sci. and Medicine, Jour. Health and Social Behavior, 1985—87, Perspectives in Biology and Medicine, 1996—, mem. editl. com. Ann. Rev. Sociology, 1975—79, mem. editl. adv. bd. Tech. in Soc., Sci., 1982—83, mem. editl. bd. Bibliography of Bioethics, 1979—, Culture, Medicine and Psychiatry, 1980—86, Jour. of AMA, 1981—94, Am. Scholar, 1994—99, Current Revs. in Publs., 1994—, Am. Jour. Bioethics, 1999—, vice chair adv. bd. Am. Jour. Ethics and Medicine, A Festschrift published in her honor Society and Medicine: Essays in Honor of Renée Fox, 2003; contbr. articles to profl. jours. Bd. dir. Medicine in Pub. Interest, 1979-94; mem. tech. bd. Milbank Meml. Fund, 1979-85; mem. overseers com. to visit univ. health svcs. Harvard Coll., 1979-86; trustee Russell Sage Found., 1981-87; vice chmn. bd. dir. Acadia Inst., 1990-97; mem. adv. com. Sch. Nursing LaSalle U., 1998—; mem. advancement com. King Baudouin Found. US Inc., 1998—, mem., sec. bd. dir. Acadia Inst., 2002—; mem. info. sci. adv. coun. Innovia Found., Netherlands, 2002—; mem. external bd. Ctr. Bioethics, Columbia U., 2002—; mem. Internat. and Sci. Adv. Coun., 2002—. Recipient E. Harris Harbison Gifted Tchg. award Danforth Found., 1970, Radcliffe Grad. Soc. medal, 1977, Lindback Found. award for tchg. U. Pa., 1989, Centennial medal Grad. Sch. Arts and Scis. Harvard U., 1993, Chevalier de l'Ordre de Leopold II (Belgium), 1995, M. Powell Lawton Quality of Life award Phila. Corp. Aging, 2006, Lifetime Achievement award Am. Soc. for Bioethics and Humanities, 2007; Wilson Ctr., Smithsonian Instn. fellow, 1987-88, Guggenheim fellow, 1962, Andrew W. Mellon Emeritus fellowship, 2004-05; Fulbright Short-Term Sr. scholar to Australia, 1994; 1st W.H.R. Rivers Disting. lectr. Harvard Med. Sch., 1998. Fellow African Studies Assn., AAAS (dir. 1977-80, chmn. sect. K 1986-87), Am. Sociol. Assn. (coun. 1970-73, 79-81, v.p. 1980-81), Am. Acad. Arts and Scis. (co-chair Class III section I membership com., 1994-96), Inst. Medicine of NAS (coun. 1979-82), Inst. Soc., Ethics and Life Scis. (founder, gov.); mem. AAUP, AAUW, Assn. Am. Med. Colls., Social Sci. Rsch. Coun. (v.p., dir.), Ea. Sociol. Soc. (pres. 1976-77, Merit award 1993), NY Acad. Scis., Soc. Sci. Study Religion, Inst. Intercultural Studies, 1969-93, (asst. sec. 1969-78, sec. 1978-81, 89-92, v.p. 1987-89), Am. Bd. Med. Specialists, Coll. of Physicians of Phila. (coun. 1993-98), Phi Beta Kappa (senate 1982-87, Ralph Waldo Emerson book award com. 1998-2001), Alpha Omega Alpha (hon.). Home and Office: The Wellington 135 S 19th St 1104 Philadelphia PA 19103-4912 Business E-Mail: rcfox@ssc.upenn.edu.

FOX, RICHARD GABRIEL, anthropologist, educator; b. NYC, Mar. 3, 1939; s. Joseph Fox and Elizabeth(Cetron) Swig; m. Judith Lynn Huff, Dec. 18, 1974; 1 child, Sarah. BA, Columbia U., 1960; MA, U. Mich., 1961, PhD, 1965. Asst. prof. Brandeis U., Waltham, Mass., 1965-68; assoc. prof. Duke U., Durham, N.C., 1968-74, prof. anthropology, 1974-93; prof. Washington U., St. Louis, 1993-99. Pres. Wenner-Gren Found. for Anthropological Rsch., 2000—; vis. scholar Sch. Am. Rsch., Santa Fe, 1987-88; mem. Inst. Advanced Study, Princeton, N.J., 1972-73. Author: Kin, Clan, Raja and Rule, 1972, Urban Anthropology, 1977, Lions of the Punjab, 1985, Gandhian Utopia, 1989. John Simon Guggenheim Found. fellow, N.Y.C., 1987-88; grantee NSF, NEH, NIH. Fellow Am. Anthropol. Assn. Office: Wenner-Gren Found 470 Park Ave South New York NY 10001-7708 E-mail: rfox@wennergren.org.

FOX, RICHARD L., lawyer; BBA, Temple U., 1981, JD, 1986; LLM in Taxation, NYU, 1990. CPA Pa., 1983; bar: NY 1987, Pa. 1988. Ptnr. tax practice area Dilworth Paxson, LLP, Phila. Adj. lectr. Temple U. Sch. Bus., 1983—86. Contbr. articles to profl. jours. Named one of Top 100 Attys., Worth mag., 2005—06. Mem.: Pa. Inst. CPA, AICPA, ABA, Phila. Bar Assn. Office: Dilworth Paxson LLP 3200 Mellon Bank Ctr 1735 Market St Philadelphia PA 19103-7595 Office Phone: 215-575-7163. Office Fax: 215-575-7200. E-mail: rfox@dilworthlaw.com.*

FOX, ROBERT FREDERICK, JR., architect; b. White Plains, NY, Dec. 3, 1941; s. Robert F. Fox and Dorothy (Kennedy) Fox Hickling; m. Judith Rosuck, Feb. 29, 1964 (div.); 1 child, Lisa; m. Gloria Fox. BArch, Cornell U., Ithaca, NY, 1965; MArch, Harvard U., 1973. Registered arch., NY, NJ, Calif., Conn. Designer J. Victor Bagnardi, Ithaca, 1965—67; draftsman Emery Roth & Sons, NYC, 1967—69, assoc., 1973—77; project arch. Brown, Daltas and Assocs., Rome, 1969—72; prin. Fox & Fowle Archs., P.C., NYC, 1978; ptnr. Cook+Fox Archs., 2003—. Cons. Mayor's Blue Ribbon Panel, NYC, 1985; chmn. Nat. Inst. Archtl. Edn.; vis. lectr. Harvard U. Grad. Sch. Design, Cambridge, Mass., Cornell U. Coll. Archtl. Arts and Planning; mem. adv. bd. Harvard Ctr. Health and the Global Environment; co-chair sustainable design com. Real Estate Bd. NY; mem. adv. team Interface Sustainability. Mem. adv. coun. Cornell U. Coll. Art, Architecture and Planning; mem. adv. bd. Syracuse U. NY Indoor Environ. Quality Ctr., Indoor Environment Ctr., Green Ground Zero; mem. planning bd. City of Scarsdale; trustee Scarsdale Citizens for Sr. Housing, Warren Affordable Housing Corp.; active Warren Vol. Fire Co.; town arch. Warren, Conn.; lead sustainable design cons. NYC Transit Authority; founding chmn. US Green Bldg. Coun. NY chpt.; bd. mem. De La Salle Acad., 2003—. Named one of 100 Tastemakers, Forbes mag., 2007; recipient NY State Hist. Preservation Cert. of Achievement, NY State Office of Pks. and Recreation, 1982, Cert. of Merit, Mcpl. Art Soc., NYC, 1982, Ofcl. Citation for Leadership in Clean Energy, State of Conn., Urban Visionary award, Cooper Union for Advancement of Sci. and Art, 2002, Leadership award, US Green Bldg. Counsel, 2006, Big Green Apple award for Environ. Leadership, NY City Coun., 2006. Mem.: AIA (Nat. Honor award), NY Soc. Archs. Office: Cook+Fox Archs 641 Ave of the Americas New York NY 10011 Office Phone: 212-477-0287. Office Fax: 212-477-4521.*

FOX, ROBERT WILLIAM, mechanical engineering educator; b. Montreal, Que., Can., July 1, 1934; s. Kenneth and Jessie (Glass) F.; m. Beryl Williams, Dec. 15, 1962; children— David, Lisa. BS in Mech. Engring, Rensselaer Poly. Inst., 1955; MS, U. Colo., 1957; PhD, Stanford U., 1961. Instr. mech. engring. U. Colo., Boulder, 1955-57; research asst. Stanford (Calif.) U., 1957-60; mem. faculty Purdue U., Lafayette, Ind., 1960-99, assoc. prof., 1963-66, prof., 1966-99, asst. head mech. engring., 1971-72, asst. dean engring. for instrn., 1972-76; acting head Purdue U. (Sch. Mech. Engring.), 1975-76, asso. head, 1976-98, chmn. univ. senate, 1971-72, prof. emeritus, 1999. Cons. Owens-Corning Fiberglass Co., Edn. Services Inc., Nelson Mfg. Co., Peoria, Ill., B. Offen Co., Chgo., Agard Co., Johns-Marsville Co., Richmond, Ind., Babcox & Wilcox, Alliance, Ohio. Named Standard Oil Outstanding Tchr. Purdue U., 1967; recipient Harry L. Solberg Outstanding Tchr. award, 1978, 83, Donald E. Marlowe awd., Am. Soc. for Engineering Education, 1992. Fellow ASME, Am. Soc. for Engrng. Edn.; mem. Sigma Xi, Pi Tau Sigma, Tau beta Pi, Delta Tau Delta. Home: 3627 Chancellor Way Lafayette IN 47906-8809 Office: Purdue U Sch Mech Engring Lafayette IN 47907

FOX, RONALD FORREST, physicist, educator; s. Sidney Walter and Raia (Joffe) F.; children: Daniel, Lara. BA, Reed Coll., 1964; PhD, Rockefeller U., 1969. Postdoctoral fellow Miller Inst., U. Calif., Berkeley, 1969-71; asst. prof. Ga. Inst. Tech., Atlanta, 1971-74, assoc. prof., 1974-79, prof., 1979—, Regents prof. physics, 1991—, asst. dir. Sch. Physics, 1982-84, assoc. dir. Sch. Physics, 1986-89, 97-99, acting chair, 1999-2000, chair, 2001—05. A.A. Knowlton lectr. Reed Coll., 1999. Author: Biological Energy Transduction, 1982, Energy and the Evolution of Life, 1988; contbr. over 100 articles to sci. jour., over 20 chpt. to books. Recipient W. Roane Beard Outstanding Tchr. award Ga. Inst. Tech., 1992, Sigma Xi

Sustained Rsch. award Ga. Inst. Tech., 1997; fellow Alfred P. Sloan Found., 1974-78, Guggenheim fellow, 1985; grantee NSF, 1973-2003. Fellow Am. Phys. Soc.; mem. NY Acad. Sci. Avocations: racquetball, jazz piano. Office: Ga Inst Tech Dept Physics Atlanta GA 30332-0430 Office Phone: 404-894-5260. Business E-Mail: ron.fox@physics.gatech.edu.

FOX, SANDRA GAIL, insurance marketing executive; b. NYC, Aug. 12, 1960; d. Joseph A. and Rhoda (Levine) Fried; m. David A. Fox, Sept. 21, 1986; children: Alexander, Peter. BA, Ind. U., 1982. Lic. Series 26 and 7, NASD. Examiner nat. compliance Dean Witter, NYC, 1983—84, from sales supr. active assets acct. to mktg. assoc., 1984—86; pvt. practice Hackensack, NJ, 1986—87; dir. alt. distbn. mktg. Mut. of N.Y., Teaneck, NJ, 1987—89, dir. spl. markets and annuities, 1989—94, asst. v.p. annuities mktg., 1994—97; dir. product development Prudential, Newark, 1997—2004, v.p. annuity product devel. and mgmt., 1998—2004; leader variable product mktg. Genworth Fin., Richmond, 2005—. Mem. work life force com. Mut. N.Y., Teaneck, 1991-97. Vol. presch. activities YW-YMHA, Wayne, N.J., 1993-94; trustee Shomrei Torah Sisterhood, 2004-2005, chmn. fundraising programs, 2004; vol. Wayne PTA (fundraisers), 1996—; fundraiser United Jewish Fedn., Bergen and Passaic, N.J., 1992-96, Kidney Found., 1994; mem. annuity exam. rev. panel LOMA, 1998-2003, annuity programs steering com., 1999, 2002, expert reviewer for Annuity Principles and Products book, 2003-2004. Griswald acad. scholar Ind. U., 1980, 81. Mem. Nat. Assn. Variable Annuities (edn. com. 1996—, publ. chmn. 1996), Shomrei Torah Sisterhood (bd. trustee, chair fundraising programs 2004), Phi Beta Kappa. Avocations: tennis, running, theater. Office: Genworth Fin Bldg 4 6610 W Broad St Richmond VA 23230 Office Phone: 804-922-5121. Business E-Mail: sandra.fox@genworth.com.

FOX, STACY L., lawyer; b. Ann Arbor, Mich., 1953; m. Michael Van Hemet; children: Kyle, Callan. BS with high distinction, U. Mich., 1974, JD, 1983. Assoc. Mintz, Levin, Cohn, Ferris, Glovskky & Popeo, P.C., Boston, 1983—88; gen. counsel Unisys Fin. Corp., 1988—89; group counsel automotive systems group and plastics tech. group Johnson Controls, Inc., 1989—93, group v.p., gen counsel automotive systems group, 1993—2000; sr. v.p. corp. transactions and legal affairs Visteon Corp., Dearborn, Mich., 2000—05; chief adminstrv. officer, gen. counsel Collins & Aikman, Southfield, Mich., 2005—. Named one of 100 Leading Women in Automotive Industry, Automotive News, 2000. Office: Collins & Aikman 26533 Evergreen Rd Southfield MI 48076*

FOX, STEPHEN E., lawyer; BA magna cum laude, U. Notre Dame, 1983; JD, U. Va. Law Sch., 1987. Bar: Tex. 1987. Prin. Fish & Richardson, P.C., Dallas. Contbr. articles to profl. jours. Named a Tex. Super Lawyer, Tex. Monthly, 2003—06; named one of Best Lawyers in Dallas, D Mag., 2001, 2005. Mem.: Soc. Human Resources Mgmt. Profls., ABA (mem. non-competition and trade secret litig. subcommittee 1996—). Office: Fish & Richardson PC 5000 Bank One Ctr 1717 Main St Dallas TX 75201 Office Phone: 214-292-4060. Office Fax: 214-747-2091. E-mail: sfox@fr.com.*

FOX, STEPHEN LEE, language educator; b. Denver, Nov. 14, 1955; s. Lionel and Barbara Virginia Fox; m. Jeanine Marie Sellmer; children: Rachel Frances, Sarah Renee, Hannah Lee. BA, U. Ga., Athens, 1973—76; MA, Duke U., Durham, NC, 1976—77; MDiv, So. Bapt. Theol. Sem., Louisville, Ky., 1979—84; PhD, U. Wis., Madison, 1987—92. Asst. lectr. Hong Kong Bapt. Coll., 1980—82; instr. Jefferson CC, Louisville, 1983—87; assoc. prof. IUPUI, Indpls., 1992—. Dir. ITW Writing Project, Indpls., 1997—. Editor: (academic book) Teaching Academic Literacy. Mem. Marion County Green Party, Indpls., 2004—. Mem.: Nat. Coun. Tchrs. English. Green Party. Office: Indiana Univ 425 University Blvd Indianapolis IN 46202 Home Phone: 317-357-8582. Business E-Mail: sfox@iupui.edu.

FOX, STEVE, editor-in-chief; B in English, Yale U. Mng. editor Omni mag.; with Popular Mechanics, IEEE; editor-in-chief The Web Mag., 1996—98; various editl. positions PC World mag., 1991—96, editor, 1998—99; editor in chief pcworld.com, 1999; editl. dir. CNET, 1999—2003; editor-in-chief InfoWorld Media Group, 2003—. Spkr. in field. Office: Inforworld Media Group 501 Second St San Francisco CA 94107 Office Fax: 415-978-3120. Business E-Mail: stevefox@inforworld.com.

FOX, STUART IRA, physiologist; b. Bklyn., June 21, 1945; s. Sam and Bess Fox; m. Ellen Diane Berley; 1 child, Laura Elizabeth. BA, UCLA, 1967; MA, Calif. State U., LA, 1967; postgrad., U. Calif., Santa Barbara, 1969; PhD, U. So. Calif., 1978. Rsch. assoc. Children's Hosp., LA, 1972; prof. physiology LA City Coll., 1972-85, Calif. State U., Northridge, 1979-84, Pierce Coll., 1986—. Cons. McGraw-Hill, 1976—. Author: Computer-Assisted Instruction in Human Physiology, 1979, Laboratory Guide to Human Physiology, 10th edit., 2003, 12th edit., 2007, Textbook of Human Physiology, 1986, 10th edit., 2007, Human Anatomy and Physiology, 1986, Perspectives on Human Biology, 1991, Laboratory Manual for Anatomy and Physiology, 1986;: 5th edit., 1999;; co-author: Biology, 5th edit., 1999, Synopsis of Anatomy and Physiology, 1997. Mem.: AAAS, Am. Anatomy and Physiology Soc., Am. Physiol. Soc., Sigma Xi. Home: 5556 Forest Cove Ln Agoura Hills CA 91301-4047 Office: Pierce Coll 6201 Winnetka Ave Woodland Hills CA 91371-0001 Office Phone: 818-710-2832. Business E-Mail: Foxsi@piercecollege.edu.

FOX, SYLVAN, journalist, educator; b. Bklyn., June 2, 1928; s. Louis and Sophie (Shapiro) F.; m. Gloria R. Endleman, Sept. 8, 1948; 1 child, Erica. BA, Bklyn. Coll., 1951; MA, U. Calif., Berkeley, 1952. Reporter Little Falls (N.Y.) Evening Times, 1954, Schenectady (N.Y.) Union Star, 1954-55, Buffalo Evening News, 1955-59; successively rewriteman, asst. city editor, city editor N.Y. World Telegram and Sun, 1959-66; dep. police commr. for press relations City of N.Y., 1966-67; successively rewriteman, reporter, dep. met. editor, Saigon bur. chief N.Y. Times, NYC, 1967-73; Nassau editor Newsday, LI, NY, 1973-77, nat. editor, then asst. mng. editor nat. and fgn. news, 1977-79, editor editorial pages, 1979-88; travel columnist, 1994-95. Tchr. journalism NYU, 1965, L.I.U., 1967, Baylor U., Waco, 1985, 88; asst. prof. journalism NYU, 1989-90. Author: The Unanswered Questions About President Kennedy's Assassination, rev. edit., 1975. Recipient Pulitzer prize local reporting, 1963. Mem. Soc. of Silurians. Home: 401 E 65th St New York NY 10021-6943 E-mail: sylglo@aol.com.

FOX, THOMAS C., lawyer; b. McKees Rocks, Pa., June 1, 1941; BA in polit. sci., Muskingum Coll., New Concord, Ohio, 1963; LLB, George Washington U., 1966. Bar: Va. 1966, DC 1967. With Reed Smith LLP, 1970—, now ptnr. healthcare group & mem. exec. com.; spl. counsel Com. on Standards of Official Conduct Ho. of Reps., 1976, 1979. Trustee Muskingum Coll. Capt. US Army, 1967—69. Mem.: Am. Health Lawyers Assn. Office: Reed Smith LLP 1301 K St NW Ste 1100 - East Tower Washington DC 20005 Office Phone: 202-414-9222. Office Fax: 202-414-9299. Business E-Mail: tfox@reedsmith.com.

FOX, THOMAS GEORGE, academic administrator; b. NYC, Sept. 15, 1942; s. Thomas Peter and Alice Cecilia (Ehler) F.; m. Mary Patricia Palmer, Aug. 29, 1980; children: Christopher Adam, Thomas Andrew, Stephen Baron. BA, Coll. NJ, Trenton, 1964; MEd, U. Vt., Burlington, 1966; PhD, U. Mich., Ann Arbor, 1972. Asst. to dean U. Mass., Amherst, 1966; dir. counseling and student svcs. U. Mich., Ann Arbor, 1966-68, sr. adminstrv. asst. Med. Ctr., 1968-69, adminstrv. assoc., 1969-71; asst. dean Robert Wood Johnson Med. Sch., Piscataway, NJ, 1972-77, assoc. dean, 1977-83; sr. v.p. Robert Wood Johnson U. Hosp., New Brunswick, NJ, 1983-86; exec. v.p. U. Health System of N.J., New Brunswick, 1986-90; prof., v.p. devel. and univ. rels. Oreg. Health Scis. U., Portland, 1990-94; CEO Univ. Found., 1990-94; pres., CEO, Liberty Sci. Ctr., Jersey City, 1994-96; CEO, Operation Smile, Norfolk, Va., 1996-2000; sr. v.p. advancement and sponsored programs Wheeling Jesuit U., W.Va., 2000—03; sr. v.p. advancement Fla. Inst. Tech., 2003—. Asst. prof. U. Medicine and Dentistry NJ, 1973-79, assoc. prof., 1979-83, clin. assoc. prof., 1983-90. Contbr. articles to profl. jours. Trustee Francis E. Parker Meml. Home, 1981-90, 96—. Fellow: Acad. Medicine NJ; mem.: Coun. for Advancement and Support of Edn. (instl. lead), Am. Coll. Healthcare Execs. (diplomate). Home: 895 Chatsworth Dr Melbourne FL 32940-2174 Office: Fla Inst Tech 150 W University Blvd Melbourne FL 32901-6975 Business E-Mail: tfox@fit.edu.

FOX, THOMAS J., communications executive; b. 1968; B, Va. Tech, Blacksburg, Va. Bus. account mgr. Verizon Wireless Comm. Inc., telesales mgr., major account sales mgr., dir. bus. sales, Southern Calif. region, dir. bus. sales, Desert Mountain region, dir. retail sales, Southwest region, pres., Ill./Wis. region Schaumburg, Ill. Mem. Chicagoland Chamber of Commerce. Office: Verizon Wireless 1515 Woodfield Road Ste 1400 Schaumburg IL 60173 Office Phone: 847-706-2655. Office Fax: 847-706-2477.*

FOX, VIVICA, actress; b. Indpls., July 30, 1964; Actor: (films) Independence Day, 1996, Set It Off, 1996, Booty Call, 1997, Batman & Robin, 1997, Soul Food, 1997, Why Do Fools Fall in Love, 1998, Idle Hands, 1999, Teaching Mrs. Tingle, 1999, Kingdom Come, 2001, Two Can Play That Game, 2001, Little Secrets, 2001, Juwanna Mann, 2002, Boat Trip, 2002, Kill Bill: Vol. 1, 2003, Ride or Die, 2003, Motives, 2004, Ella Enchanted, 2004, Kill Bill: Vol. 2, 2004, Blast!, 2004, The Salon, 2005, Getting Played, 2005, Citizens Duane, 2006, The Hard Corps, 2006, Kickin It Old Skool, 2007, (video) Natural Born Komics, 2007; (TV films) Salomon, 1997, A Saintly Switch, 1999, Hendrix, 2000; (TV series) Getting Personal, 1998, City of Angels, 2000, 1-800-Missing, 2004—(Outstanding Actress in a Drama Series, NAACP Image Awards, 2006), (voice) Ozzy & Drix, 2002; (TV films) Kim Possible: A Sitch in Time, 2003; performer: Dancing with the Stars, 2006; guest appearances Alias, 2004, Loonatics Unleashed, 2005, All of Us, 2006, Icons, 2006. Office: William Morris Agy 151 S El Camino Dr Beverly Hills CA 90212-2775*

FOX, WAYNE C., stock exchange and corporate financial executive; BA, U. Waterloo, 1971; MBA, McMaster U., 1973; grad. in Advanced Mgmt., U Pa., 1992. With Can. Imperial Bank Commerce, head of world markets global capital markets activities, vice chmn. and chief risk officer, 1999—2005; chmn. Toronto Stock Exch., 2001—. Bd. govs. McMaster U.; gov. emeritus Appleby Coll.; bd. dirs. and chmn. CanadaHelps.org Inc.; founder Wayne C. Fox Graduate Scholarship in Arts. Office: Toronto Stock Exch PO Box 450 3rd fl 130 King St W Toronto ON Canada M5X-1J2

FOX, WILLIAM F., dean, law educator; BS, George Washington U., 1970; JD, Catholic U. Am. Sch. Law, 1972; LLM, Harvard Law Sch., 1974. Law clerk N.Mex Ct. Appeals, 1972—73; atty. vom Baur, Coburn, Simmons & Turtle, 1973—74; instr. Boston U. Law Sch., 1973—74; asst. prof. Indpls. Sch. Law, Indiana U., 1974—75; prof. Columbia Sch. Law, Cath. U. Am., 1975—, assoc. dean, 1975—78, dean, 2003—. Vis. prof. London Sch. Econs. and Polit. Sci., 1983—84; sr. assoc. mem. St. Anthony's Coll., Oxford U., 1983—84; vis. lectr. U. Dundee, Ctr. Petroleum & Mineral Law; mem. permanent faculty ALI-ABA prog. Author: Understanding Administrative Law, International Commercial Agreements, The Law of Veterans Benefits: Judicial Interpretation. Fulbright Scholar, Parahyangan Cath. U. Law Sch., Indonesia, 1993, Veterans Law Scholar, Paralyzed Veterans Am., 1994. Office: Columbus Sch Law Catholic U Am 3600 John McCormack Rd NE Washington DC 20064 E-mail: foxw@law.edu.

FOX, WILLIAM J., bank executive, former federal official; b. Nebraska; m.; two children. BA in History, JD, Creighton U., Omaha. Atty., sr. counsel, then deputy chief counsel Bureau of Alcohol, Tobacco & Firearms, 1988—2000; acting dep. asst. gen. counsel for enforcement US Dept. Treasury, 2000—01, principal asst. and sr. advisor to gen. counsel, 2001—03, acting dep. gen. counsel, 2002, assoc. dep. gen. counsel, 2002—03, dir. Financial Crimes Enforcement Network, 2003—06; sr. compliance exec. for fin. crimes Bank of Am. Corp., Charlotte, NC, 2006—. Recipient Meritorious Rank award, US Dept. of Treas. Office: Bank of Am Corp 100 N Tryon St Bank of Am Corp Ctr Charlotte NC 28255

FOX-CLARKSON, ANNE C., fundraising company executive; 1 child. BS in Edn., Bucknell U., 1967; MS in Reading, Syracuse U., 1973, PhD in Tchr. Edn., 1975. Cert. elem. tchr., adminstr., Idaho. Postdoctoral work in edn. adminstrn. U. Idaho; elem. sch. tchr.; prin., supt. pub. schs., 1978-84; assoc. prof. ednl. adminstrn. Gonzaga U., 1987-94; supt. pub. instrn. State of Idaho, 1995-98; v.p. ednl. markets Shop2gether.com, 2000; pres. Grant Writers, Inc., Boise, 2004—, Mem. State Bd. Edn., State Land Bd., State Libr. Bd., State Endowment Fund, State Investment Bd.; pres., co-founder Children's Village, Homes for Abused Children; grant writer, mgmt. cons.; spkr. in field. Former pres. Idaho State Elem. Prin. Assn., Wash. State Univ. Profl. Adminstr. Assn. Personal E-mail: raand29@hotmail.com.

FOXE, MARYE ANNE, academic administrator; b. Canton, Ohio, Dec. 9, 1947; m. James K. Whitesell, 1990; stepchildren: Christopher Whitesell, Robert Whitesell; children: Robert Fox, Michael Fox, Matthew Fox. BS, Notre Dame Coll. of Ohio, 1969; MS, Cleve. State U., 1970; PhD, Dartmouth Coll., 1974; postgrad., U. Md., 1974-76; DSc (hon.), Notre Dame Coll., 1994, Cleve. State U., 1998; JD (hon.), Sandhills Cmty. Coll., 2000; degree (hon.), Universite Pierre et Marie Curie, 2001; LHD (hon.), Texas A&M, 2002; degree (hon.), Universidad Nacional de Educacion a Distancia, Madrid, 2003. Prof. chemistry U. Tex., Austin, 1976-91, Rowland Pettit Centennial prof., 1986-92, M. June and J. Virgil Waggoner regents chair chemistry, 1992-98, v.p. rsch., 1994-98; chancellor N.C. State U., Raleigh, 1998—2004, U. Calif. San Diego, 2004—. Mem. Nat. Sci. Bd., 1991-96, vice-chair, 1994-96; bd. dirs. Kenan Inst. Engring., Tech., and Sci., 1998—, Microelectric Ctr., NC, 1998—, mem. sci. adv. bd. Robert A. Welch Found., 1998—, David and Lucile Packard Found., 1998—; mem. Coun. on Competitiveness, 1999—; bd. trustees Nat. Inst. Statistical Sciences, 2000—; bd. dirs. Nat. Inst. Environment, 2001—, Boston Sci. Inc., 2001—, mem. President's Adv. Coun. of Advisors on Sci. and Tech., 2001—; bd. dirs. NC Bd. Sci. and Tech., 2002—, PPD Inc., 2002—, Red Hat Inc., 2002, Nat. Assn. State Universities and Land Grant Coll., 2003— Assoc. editor Jour. Am. Chem. Soc., 1986-94; mem. adv. bd. Jour. Organic Chemistry, Chem. Engring. News, Chem. Rev. Bd. trustees U. Notre Dame, 2002—; bd. dirs. N.C. Citizens for Bus. and Industry, 2003—. Recipient Agnes Faye Morgan Rsch. award Iota Sigma Pi, 1984, Arthur C. Cope scholar award Am. Chem. Soc., 1988; Garvan medal Am. Chem. Soc., 1988, Havinga medal Leiden U., 1991, Monie A. Ferst award, 1996; named to Hall of Excellence, Ohio Found. Ind. Colls., 1987, The Best of the New Generation, Esquire Mag., 1984; Alfred P. Sloan Rsch. fellow, 1980-82, Camille and Henry Dreyfus tchr. scholar, 1981-85. Fellow AAAS, Assn. Women in Sci.; mem. NAS (co-chair, Govt.-Univ.-Industry Rsch. Roundtable, 1999-), Am. Acad. Arts and Sci., Am. Philos. Soc., Sigma Xi (pres. 2001-02). Office: U Calif San Diego Chancellors Office 9500 Gilman Sr La Jolla CA 92093-0005*

FOXEN, RICHARD WILLIAM, manufacturing executive; b. NYC, Nov. 12, 1927; s. William alyisus and Mae Dorothea (Scully) F.; m. Hilda Duran-Ballen, Feb. 11, 1956; children: Richard, Theresa, Thomas, Patricia, Anthony. BME, Bklyn. Poly. Inst., 1950. V.p. corp. staffs Westinghouse Air Brake Co., Pitts., 1961-69; pres. European indsl. group Am. Std., Brussels, 1969-73; v.p. Europe bus. divsn. GE, Brussels, 1973-78; sr. v.p. Rockwell Internat., 1978-88. Adj. prof. bus. adminstrn. Carnegie Mellon U., U. Pitts.; chmn. Mercy Health Sys., Inc., Pitts.; bd. dirs. Cordis Corp. Bd. trustees N.Y. Poly. U.; bd. dirs. Mannesmann U.S. Adv. Conflict Resolution Ctr. Internat.; chmn. Mendelssohn Choir Pitts., Pressley-Ridge Schs., We. Pa. Family Ctr., Pitts. With U.S. Army, 1946-48. Mem. Pitts. Athletic Assn., Duquesne, Pitts. Athletic, Seabrook Is., Tau Beta Pi, Pi Tau Sigma. Roman Catholic. Home: 1292 Puritan Ave Birmingham MI 48009-4815

FOXHOVEN, JERRY RAY, lawyer; b. Yankton, SD, July 24, 1952; s. Elmer William and Ida Elizabeth (Lubbers) F.; m. Julie Ann Greco, Apr. 6, 1985; children: Anthony Michael, Peter Joseph. BS summa cum laude, Morningside Coll., Sioux City, Iowa, 1974; JD, Drake U., Des Moines, 1977. Bar: Iowa 1977, US Dist. Ct. (so. and no. dists.) Iowa 1977, US Ct. Appeals (8th cir.) 1977, US Supreme Ct. 1981, Nebr. 1985, US Dist. Ct. Nebr. 1985, Wis. 1986. Assoc. Critelli & Pille, Des Moines, 1977-79, ptnr., 1979-82, Foxhoven & McCann, Des Moines, 1982-88, Peddicord, Wharton, Thune, Foxhoven & Spencer, P.C., 1988-91; pvt. practice, 1991-2000; adminstr. Child Advocacy Bd., Des Moines, 2000—06; sr. fellow Ctr. Adoption Rsch. U. Mass., 2002—04; dir. Middleton ctr. children's rights law sch. Drake U., 2006—. Instr. criminaljustice dept. Des Moines Area C.C., Ankeny, Iowa, 1978-81, Am. Inst. Banking, 1982-85. Mem. steering con. Culver for US Senate, Des Moines, 1980; chmn. Iowa State Foster Care Rev. Bd., 1986-99; bd. dirs., nat. pres. Nat. Assn. Foster Care Reviewers, 1988-01; mem. parish coun. Sacred Heart Roman Cath. Ch., West Des Moines, 1982. Recipient Angel in Adoption award, Congl. Adoption Coalition, 2004. Lodge: Masons (master 1990). Democrat. Home: 1608 NW 101st St Clive IA 50325-6716 Office: Drake Legal Clinic 2400 University Ave Des Moines IA 50311 Office Phone: 515-271-2073. Personal E-mail: jfoxhoven@aol.com. Business E-Mail: jerry.foxhoven@drake.edu.

FOXMAN, ABE (ABRAHAM HENRY FOXMAN), advocacy organization administrator; b. Warsaw, 1940; came to U.S., 1950; s. Helen and Joseph F.; m. Golda BA in Polit. Sci., CCNY, 1962; postgrad., Jewish Theol. Sem., 1958-60, New Sch. Social Rsch., 1963-64; JD, NYU, 1965; LLD (hon.), Fla. Internat. U., 1992. Asst. dir. law dept. Anti-Defamation League of B'nai B'rith, NYC, 1965-68, dir. Mid. Ea. affairs, 1968-73, nat. leadership dir., 1973-79, assoc. nat. dir., 1979-87, nat. dir., 1987—. Author: Never Again: The Threat of the New Anti-Semitism, 2003. Mem. Pres.'s U.S. Holocaust Meml. Coun., N.Y.C. Holocaust Meml. Commn. (adv. coun.), Am. Gathering, Jewish Holocaust Survivors.

FOXMAN, BRUCE MAYER, chemist, educator; b. Youngstown, Ohio, Mar. 12, 1942; s. Jerome Jay and Phyllis E. (Altshuler) Foxman; m. Carole J. Wittkopf, Sept. 14, 1968; children: Gregory Michael, Andrew Craig. BS with distinction, Iowa State U., 1964; PhD in Inorganic Chemistry, MIT, 1968. Rsch. fellow Australian Nat. U., Canberra, 1968-72; asst. prof. Brandeis U., Waltham, Mass., 1972-78, assoc. prof., 1978-85, prof., 1985—. Vis. prof. Thomas J. Watson Rsch. Ctr., IBM, Yorktown Heights, NY, 1975, Max-Planck-Inst. fuer Polymerforschung, Mainz, Germany, 1995—96; hon. prof. U. Birmingham, England, 2001; invited prof. U. Louis Pasteur, Strasbourg, France, 2002; cons. Polaroid Corp. Mem.: Coll. Bd. Advanced Placement Exam. Com. (chair chemistry 1993—96), Royal Soc. Chemistry, Materials Rsch. Soc., Am. Crystallographic Assn., Am. Chem. Soc., Sigma Xi, Phi Lambda Upsilon, Phi Kappa Phi. Home: 74 N Hill Ave Needham MA 02492-1223 Office: Brandeis Univ Dept Chemistry Waltham MA 02454-9110 Office Phone: 781-736-2532. Business E-Mail: foxman1@brandeis.edu.

FOXWORTH, JOHNNIE HUNTER, retired state agency administrator; b. Anderson, SC, Feb. 13, 1921; d. John Ira and Bessie (Hatton) Hunter; m. Marvin Ardell, Sept. 21, 1941. Attended colls., univs., Atlanta, Bridgeport, Conn. Cashier examiner, office supr. Motor Vehicle Dept., State Conn., Bridgeport, 1957—72; br. office mgr. various locations in state, 1972—77; br. office dist. supr. Wethersfield, Conn., 1977—81; asst. dir., 1981—85; cons., tng. instr., 1985—88; ret. Writer: manual in field. Mem. Commrs. Affirmative Action Com., 1987; bd. trustees Waterbury Cmty. Found., Conn. Cmty. Found., In Search of Excellence Fund. Named to Donors Hall of Fame, Spelman Coll. Ga.; recipient Profl. Achievement award, Bridgeport chpt. Nata. Bus. and Profl. Women, 1972, (2) Disting. Managerial Svc. award, State of Conn., Wethersfield, 1982, Woman of Yr. award, Nat. Coun. Negro Woman, Bridgeport, 1972. Mem.: The Links, Inc. (Waterbury) (pres. 1980—85), Les Treize (Bridgeport) (pres. 1966—68). Home: 496A Heritage Village Southbury CT 06488-1525

FOXWORTHY, JEFF, comedian, writer, actor; b. Atlanta, Ga., Sept. 6, 1958; m. Pamela Gregg Grethe, 1985; children: Jordan, Juliane. Grad., Ga. Inst. Tech., 1979. Computer engr. IBM, 1979-84; performing and rec. artist, comedian, writer, 1984—. Actor: (films) (voice) Racing Stripes, 2005, Fox and The Hound II, 2006; (TV series) The Jeff Foxworthy Show, 1995-97 (People's Choice Award, Favorite Male Newcomer); (TV films) Banner Times, 1993, Blue Collar Comedy Tour Rides Again, 2004, Blue Collar Comedy Tour-One For The Road in Washington, DC, 2006; actor, exec. prodr. (TV series) Blue Collar TV, 2004-; writer (TV films) Jeff Foxworthy: Totally Committed, 1998; author: You Might Be a Redneck If., 1989, Hick Is Chic: A Guide to Etiquette for the Grossly Unsophisticated, 1990, Red Ain't Dead: 150 More Ways To Tell If You're a Redneck, 1991, Check your Neck: More of You Might Be a Redneck If., 1992, You're Not a Kid Anymore, 1993, (with Vic Henley) Games Rednecks Play, 1994, Redneck Classic: The Best of Jeff Foxworthy, 1995, Jeff Foxworthy's Redneck Dictionary, 2005; albums include You Might Be a Redneck If., 1994 (platinum cert.), Games Rednecks Play, 1995 (platinum cert.), Have Your Loved Ones Spayed or Neutered, 2004; host (game show) Are You Smarter Than a 5th Grader?, 2007-. Hon. chmn. Duke Children's Classic Golf Tournament. Named Comedian of Yr. (Three times), TNN.*

FOXX, JAMIE (ERIC BISHOP), actor, comedian; b. Terrell, Tex., Dec. 13, 1967; s. Shaheed Abdulah and Louise Annette D.(div.); raised by great grandparents Mark and Ester Talley. Student, U.S. Internat. U., San Diego, 1986—88; studied classical piano, Juliard Sch. Fine Arts. Stand-up comedian. Actor, dir., prodr., writer (TV series) The Jamie Foxx Show, 1996 (NAACP Image award for Outstanding Lead Actor in a Comedy Series, 1997), comedian, exec. prodr., writer (TV Spl.) Jamie Foxx: I Might Need Security, 2002; actor: (films) Toys, 1992, The Truth About Cats and Dogs, 1996, The Great White Hype, 1996, Booty Call, 1997, The Players Club, 1998, Held Up, 1999, Any Given Sunday, 1999, Bait, 2000, Date from Hell, 2001, Ali, 2001 (NAACP Image award for Outstanding Supporting Actor in a Motion Picture, 2002), Shade, 2003, Breakin' All the Rules, 2004, Collateral, 2004, Ray, 2004 (Named Best Actor Nat. Bd. Rev. Motion Pictures, 2004, Best Actor, Washington, DC Film Critics award, 2004, Best Actor, Boston Film Critics award, 2004, Golden Globe award for best actor musical or comedy, 2005, Screen Actors Guild Award, outstanding performance by male actor in leading role, 2005, Academy award for best actor in a leading role, 2005), Stealth, 2005, Jarhead, 2005, Miami Vice, 2006, Dreamgirls, 2006; (TV films) Redemption: The Stan Tookie Williams Story, 2004; (TV series) In Living Color, 1991—94, (voice) C-Bear and Jamal, 1996; host MTV Video Music Awards, 2001, ESPY Awards, 2003; singer: (albums) Peep This, 1994, Unpredictable, 2005 (Best Album, Soul Train awards, 2007), (songs) (with Kanye West) Gold Digger, 2005 (Best Duet & Video of Yr., BET awards, 2006). Named one of Time Mag. 100 Most Influential People, 2005, The 10 Most Fascinating People of 2005, Barbara Walters Special; recipient Outstanding Male Artist, NAACP Image awards, 2006, Favorite Male Artist, Soul/Rhythm & Blues, Am. Music awards, 2006. Office: The Gersh Agy 232 N Canon Dr Beverly Hills CA 90210*

FOXX, VIRGINIA ANN, congresswoman, small business owner; b. NYC, June 29, 1943; m. Thomas A. Foxx; 1 child, 2 grandchildren. AB in English, U. NC, Chapel Hill, 1968, MACT, 1972; EdD Curriculum and Tchg./Higher Edn., U. NC, Greensboro, 1985. Sec., rsch. asst. U. NC, Chapel Hill; prof. Caldwell CC, Hudson, NC; prof. sociology Appalachian State U., Boone, NC, asst. dean gen. coll.; dept. sec. mgmt. NC Dept. Adminstrn.; pres., cons. Mayland CC, Spruce Pine, NC, 1987—94; owner, operator Grandfather Nursery, Banner Elk, NC; mem. NC State Senate, 1995—2004, US Congress from 5th NC dist., 2005—. Mem. agr. com. US Congress, mem. govt. reform com., mem. edn. and the workforce com. Mem. Watauga County Bd. Edn., 1976-88. Recipient Outstanding Pub. Official award, NC Christmas Tree Assn., Award for Outstanding Citizenship, Exceptional Pub. Svc., Watauga County League Women Voters, 1988, NC Disting. Women's award, 1990, Order of the Long Leaf Pine, NC Gov. Jim Martin, 1992, Disting. Fundraising award, YMCA, 1993, NC Carpathian award, 1994, Guardian of Small Bus. award, Nat. Fedn. Ind. Bus., 2000, Alan Keith-Lucas Friend of Children award, NC Child Care Assn., 2002, Contbns. to Sociology award, NC Sociol. Assn., 2002. Mem. Nat. Assn. Women Legislators, Am. Legis. Exch. Conf., NCCBI, NC Ctr. Pub. Policy Rsch., NC Women's Forum. Republican. Office: 6000 Meadowbrook Mall Ste 3 Clemmons NC 27012 Office Phone: 202-225-2071, 336-778-0211. Office Fax: 336-778-2290.*

FOY, BETSY D., health facility administrator, educator; b. Milw., Apr. 5, 1953; d. Homer Charles Foy and Dorothy Louise Rohlfing; m. Mark T. Cockson, Sept. 2, 1978; children: Emily L. Cockson, Luke T. Cockson, Dylan J. Cockson. BA, St. Louis U., 1975; M in Health sci., Wash. U., St. Louis, 1996. Cert. Health Edn. Specialist Nat. Commn. for Health Edn. Credentialing, 1997; Qualified Profl. Mo. Dept. of Mental Health/Divsn. of Alcohol and Drug Abuse, 2001. Supr. social svc. worker Mo. Dept. of Social Svcs., St. Louis, 1975—90; child care specialist Mo. Dept. of Health, St. Louis, 1990—97; asst. dir. Wash. U. Student Health & Counseling Ctr., St. Louis, 1997—. Founder, chair St. Louis Higher Edn. Health & Wellness Collaborative. Author: (several articles) Jour. of Am. Coll. Health, (article) Health Promotion Practice Jour., Health Edn. and Behavior Jour.; cons. editor Jour. Am. Coll. Health, 2002—04. Parents adv. bd. Voluntary Interdistrict Coordinating Coun., St. Louis, 1995—99; fundraising Wash. U. Arts & Scis. Alumni Assn., St. Louis, 1998—2003; leader Girl Scouts of Am., St. Louis, 1992—94. Alcohol Prevention Grant, NCAA, 2002—05. Mem.: Soc. for Pub. Health Edn., Am. Coll. Health Assn. (alcohol & drug task force 1999—2005), Alpha Sigma Nu, Nat. Honor Soc. Achievements include development of WU Walks-Campus Walking Club. Avocations: walking, letter writing. Home: 7418 Hoover Saint Louis MO 63117 Office: Washington U Campus Box 1201 One Brookings Dr Saint Louis MO 63130 Office Phone: 314-935-7386. Personal E-mail: betsy_foy@wustl.edu.

FOY, BETTY LOU JONES, educational administrator; b. Balt., July 31, 1935; d. Henry Hiram and Agnes Bertha (Caster) Jones; m. Lorenzo Earl Foy, July 31, 1960; 1 child, Kimberli Agnes. BA, Morgan State Coll., Balt., 1961, postgrad., Coppin State Coll., Johns Hopkins U.; HLD (hon.), Eastern Theol. Sem., Lynchburg, Va., 2002. Cert APC. Dir. edn. Opportunities Industrialization Ctr. Balt., Inc., Westinghouse Learning, Inc., Balt.; secondary tchr. Dept. Edn., Balt., Talmudical Acad., Balt.; dean acad. svcs. Park Heights Street Acad., Balt. Dir. Sylvan Learning Sys., Inc., Balt.; adj. prof. Coppin State U., Balt. Deacon Sharon Bapt. Ch. Mem.: ASCD, Nat. Assn. Bus. and Profl. Women's Clubs, Gamma Theta Upsilon.

FOY, CHARLES DALEY, retired soil scientist; b. Buena Vista, Ky., Aug. 19, 1923; s. Charles Clinton and Zylphia Gertrude (Binkley) F.; m. Doris Blanche Hornbaker, June 4, 1950; 1 child, David Alden. BS in Agriculture, U. Tenn., Knoxville, 1949; MS in Soil Sci., Purdue U., Lafayette, Ind., 1953, PhD in Soil Fertility, 1955. Tchr. Vets. Inst. on Farm Tng. Program, Connersville, Ind., 1949-51; rsch. fellow Purdue U., West Lafayette, Ind., 1951-55, asst. prof. agronomy, 1955-57; rsch. soil scientist, dept. agronomy USDA U. Ark., Fayetteville, 1957-61; rsch. soil scientist, climate stress lab. USDA Agrl. Rsch. Sta., Beltsville, Md., 1961-95; collaborator, 1995—. Cons. and lectr. in US and abroad. Contbr. articles to profl. jours. With U.S. Army, 1943-46, PTO. Recipient Environ. Quality award Am. Soc. Hort. Sci., 1974, Cert. of Recognition for outstanding contbn. Orgn. Com. of IV Internat. Symposium on Plant-Soil Interactions at Low pH and Nat. Maize and Sorghum Rsch. Ctr., Belo Horizonte, Brazil, 1996; Purdue U. grad. rsch. fellow, 1953-55. Fellow Am. Soc. Agronomy, Soil Sci. Soc. Am., Crop Sci. Soc. Am. Personal E-mail: cdfoy@verizon.net.

FOY, HERBERT MILES, III, lawyer, educator; b. Statesville, NC, Mar. 22, 1945; s. Herbert Miles Jr. and Perci Aileen (Lazenby) F.; m. Eleanor Jane Meschan, June 27, 1970; children: Anna Meschan, Sarah Aileen. AB, U. NC, 1967; MA, Harvard U., 1968; JD, U. Va., 1972. Bar: NC 1973, U.S. Dist. Ct. (mid. and we. dists.) NC, 1973, U.S. Ct. Appeals (4th cir.) 1975, U.S. Supreme Ct. 2002. Jud. clk. U.S. Ct. Appeals (5th cir.), Atlanta, 1972-73; assoc. Smith, Moore, Smith, Schell & Hunter, Greensboro, NC, 1973-77, 81-83, ptnr., 1983-84; sr. atty. advisor office legal counsel U.S. Dept. Justice, Washington, 1977-81; assoc. prof. Sch. Law Wake Forest U., Winston-Salem, NC, 1984-87, prof., 1987—, assoc. dean acad. affairs, 1990-95, 2000—. Contbr. articles to legal jours. Morehead scholar, 1963; Woodrow Wilson fellow, 1968. Mem. ABA, NC Bar Assn., NC State Bar Assn., Fosythe County Bar Assn., Order of Coif, Phi Beta Kappa. Democrat. Mem. Soc. Of Friends. Avocations: banjo playing, gardening, athletics, poetry. Office: Wake Forest U Sch Law PO Box 7206U Winston Salem NC 27109-7206 Office Phone: 336-758-5434.

FOY, THOMAS PAUL, lawyer, retired state legislator, bank executive; b. Silver City, N.Mex., Oct. 19, 1914; s. Thomas J. and Mary V. Foy; m. Joan Carney, Nov. 17, 1948 (dec. June 1994); children: Celia, Thomas Paul Jr. (dec.), Muffet (Mary Ann), J. Carney, James B. BS in Commerce, Notre Dame U., 1938, JD, 1939; DHL (hon.), Western N.Mex U., 2004. Bar: N.Mex. 1946. Dist. atty. N.Mex. 6th Jud. Dist., Silver City, 1949-57; atty. Village of Bayard, N.Mex., 1954-68, Village of Ctrl., N.Mex., 1960-70; v.p., counsel, bd. dirs. Sunwest Bank, Silver City, 1946-84, chmn. bd. dirs., 1969-84, chmn. emeritus, 1971—98; state rep. Dist. 39 State of N.Mex., Grant-Hidalgo, 1984—97; chmn. jud. com. N.Mex. State Legis., Santa Fe, 1984-98; pres. Foy & Vesely and Foy, Foy & Castillo, Silver City, 1946-99, Foy Law Firm PC, 1999—. 1st lt. U.S. Army, 1941-46; prisoner of war, PTO, 1942-45. Decorated Bronze Star, Purple Heart, Asiatic-Pacific Ribbon with 3 oak leaf clusters; recipient Citizen of Yr. award Silver City-Grant County C. of C., 1965, Dedication to Advancement award Trial Lawyers Assn., 1993, N.Mex. Disting. Svc. medal, 1994. Mem. ABA, N.Mex. Bar Assn. (bar commr. 1967-85, v.p. N.Mex. bar commn. 1978-79, Disting. Svc. of Laws award 1987), Am. Judicature Soc., Bataan Vets. Orgn. (state comdr. 1965-66, 98-99, 2004—), KC (Grand Knight 1936-37), VFW (state comdr. 1959-60), Lions (dist. gov. 1956-57), Elks. Democrat. Roman Catholic. Avocations: football, baseball, travel, conventions. Office: Box 266 Bayard NM 88023-2660 Home: PO Box 266 Bayard NM 88023-0266 Office Phone: 505-537-3355.

FOYE, RANDY, professional basketball player; b. Newark, Sept. 9, 1983; s. Regina and Antonio Foye. Student, Villanova U., Pa., 2002—06. Draft pick Boston Celtics, 2006; guard Minn. Timberwolves, 2006—. Named First Team All-Am., Nat. Assn. Basketball Coaches, 2006, Nat. Collegiate Basketball Writers Assn., 2006, Sporting News, 2006, Big East Player of Yr., 2006, Big 5 Outstanding Player of Yr., 2006; named to Big East First Team All-Conf., 2006, Bayer Advantage Sr. CLASS First Team, 2006, NBA All-Rookie First Team, 2007. Office: Minn Timberwolves 600 First Ave N Minneapolis MN 55403*

FOYE, THOMAS HAROLD, lawyer; b. Rapid City, SD, Nov. 23, 1930; s. Harold Herbert and Jean Winifred (McCormick) F.; m. Laurene Fowler, Aug. 7, 1972; children: David Snyder, Stewart Snyder BS in Commerce, Creighton U., Omaha, Nebr., 1952; LLB, Georgetown U., Washington, DC, 1955. Bar: SD 1955, DC 1955, US Supreme Ct. 1968. Trial atty. tax div. US Dept. Justice, Washington, 1955-58; assoc. Bangs, McCullen, Butler, Foye & Simmons, predecessor firms, Rapid City, 1958-60, ptnr., 1960—. Lectr. in field Fellow Am. Coll. Trust and Estate Counsel, Am. Bar Found.; mem. ABA, State Bar SD (pres. 1982-83), Pennington County Bar Assn. (pres. 1962), Am. Coll. Real Estate Lawyers, Internat. Acad. Estate and Trust Law., Am. Coll. Tax Counsel. Clubs: Arrowhead Country (Rapid City). Democrat. Roman Catholic. Avocations: skiing, water-skiing, hiking. Office: Bangs McCullen Butler Foye & Simmons PO Box 2670 Rapid City SD 57709-2670 Home Phone: 605-343-8053; Office Phone: 605-343-1080. Business E-Mail: tfoye@bangsmccullen.com.

FOYOUZI-YOUSSEFI, REYHANEH, pharmacologist; b. Tehran, Iran, Dec. 6, 1964; arrived in Switzerland, 1983. d. Amin and Seyedeh (Salimi-Eshkevari); m. Hamid R. Mostafavi, 2001; 1 child, Mahan Ali. Diploma of Asst. Pharmacist, Sch. Pharmacy, Geneva, Switzerland, 1988, Diploma of Pharmacy, 1991; PhD in Pharmacy, U. Geneva, Geneva, Switzerland, 1999. Pharmacist, Geneva, 1991—; sr. scientist Estee Lauder Cos., Inc., 2000—04. Contbr. articles to profl. jours.

FOYSTON, FREDERICK L. (RICK FOYSTON), literature and language educator, coach; b. Seattle, Oct. 28, 1945; s. Sidney C. and Marylin R. Foyston; m. Cherie L. Eacret; children: Trevor, Jacob, Heidi L. Nykaza, Heather L. Bryant, Haley A. Pozzi, Jershon C. BA in Edn., Western Wash. U., 1972; MEd, Lesley Coll., 1993; MA in Ednl. Adminstrn., Seattle Pacific U., 1995; student, Breyer State U., 2004—06. Cert. prin. Wash. Shipping/receiving staff Tradewell Stores Inc., Kent, Wash., 1972—84; new constrn. sales mgr. Windermere Real Estate, Belleview, Wash., 1984—86; English lang. arts instr. Kent Sch. Dist., 1987—; field supr. Evergreen State Coll., 2004—05, subcontractor program devel., 2004—05. Football, track coach Sequoia Mid. Sch., 1987—2006, curriculum devel./implementation staff, 1991—, athletic dir., 1997—2004. Mem., tchr. LDS Ch., Kent, 1977—. Sgt. USAF, 1965—69. Mem.: Assn. Supervision and Curriculum Devel., Wash. Secondary Sch. Athletic Adminstrs. Assn. (assoc.). Achievements include development of Reality Edn.-Keys for Success curriculum; speed writing curriculum. Avocations: coaching, reading, outdoor activities, travel, remodeling older homes.

FRACKMAN, NOEL, art critic; b. NYC, May 27, 1930; d. Walter David and Celeste (Barman) Stern; m. Richard Benoit Frackman, July 2, 1950 (dec. Jan. 2, 2002); 1 child, Noel Dru Pyne. Student, Mt. Holyoke Coll., 1948—50; BA, Sarah Lawrence Coll., 1952, MA, 1953; postgrad., Columbia U., 1964—67; MA Inst. Fine Arts, NYU, 1976, PhD Inst. Fine Arts, 1987. Art critic Scarsdale (N.Y.) Inquirer, 1962—67, Patent Trader, Mt. Kiscoo, NY, 1962—71; assoc. Arts Mag., NYC, 1968—92. Lectr. Aldrich Mus. Contemporary Art, Ridgefield, Conn., 1967—75, Gallery Passport Ltd., NYC, 1968—96; curator edn. Storm King Art Ctr., Mountainville, NY, 1973—75; instr. continuing edn. divsn. SUNY, 1988—2002; contractual lectr. Met. Mus. Art, NYC, 1994—95; adj. assoc. prof. humanities SUNY, 1997—. Contbr. articles and revs. to various mags., including Arts Mag., Harper's Bazaar, Feminist Art Jour., Art Voices. Bd. dirs. Friends of the Neuberger Mus. Art, 1994—; bd. trustees Purchase Coll. Found., 2006—. Scholar Sarah Williston scholar, 1948—50. Mem.: Coll. Art Assn., Art Table Inc., Internat. Assn. Art Critics.

FRACKMAN, RUSSELL JAY, lawyer; b. NYC, July 3, 1946; s. Sam and Doris (Wasserberg) F.; m. Myrna D. Morganstern, Aug. 3, 1980; children: Steven Howard, Abigail Zoe. BA in History, Northwestern U., 1967; JD cum laude, Columbia U., 1970. Bar: Calif. 1971, U.S. Dist. Ct. (ctrl., ea. and no. dists.) Calif., U.S. Ct. Appeals (2d and 9th cirs.), U.S. Supreme Ct. Assoc. Mitchell, Silberberg & Knupp LLP, LA, 1970-76, ptnr., 1976—, chmn. litigation dept., 1994-96. Lectr. on intellectual property and entertainment law various instns. including Practising Law Inst., L.A. Copyright Soc., Beverly Hills Bar Assn., U. So. Calif. Sch. Law, Am. Film Mktg. Assn., Calif. Copyright Conf. Bd. editors Columbia Law Rev., 1969-70; contbr. articles and revs. to legal jours. Co-chmn. internat. leadership devel. forum CARE, 1990; bd. trustees CARE Found., 1991—, Twitty, Milsap, Sterban Found., 1988-92. Named Entertainment Lawyer of the Year, Beverly Hills Bar Assn.; named one of Top 100 Most Influential Lawyers in Calif., Calif. Law Bus., Los Angeles' Top 50 Litigators, Los Angeles Bus. Jour., Best Lawyers in Am., Entertainment Law, The Best Lawyers in Am., Los Angeles Mag., 2005, 2006, 100 Most Influential Lawyers, Nat. Law Jour., 2006. Mem. ABA (chmn. copyright subcom. litigation sect. 1990-93, lectr. various confs.), Am. Film Mktg. Assn. (mem. arbitration tribunal). Democrat. Jewish. Office: Mitchell Silberberg & Knupp LLP 11377 W Olympic Blvd Los Angeles CA 90064-1625 Home Phone: 310-471-2787; Office Phone: 310-312-3119.*

FRADE, PETER DANIEL, chemist, educator, administrator; b. Highland Park, Mich., Sept. 3, 1946; s. Peter Nunes and Dorathea Grace (Gehrke) F.; m. Karen L. Kovich, Mar. 14, 1992. BS in Chemistry, Wayne State U., 1968, MS, 1971, PhD, 1978. Chemist Henry Ford Hosp., Detroit, 1968-75, analytical chemist, toxicologist dept. pathology, divsn. pharmacology and toxicology, 1975-86, sr. clin. lab. scientist dept. pathology divsn. clin. chemistry and pharmacology, 1987-96; assoc. prof. Eugene Applebaum Coll. Pharmacy and Health Sci. Wayne State U., Detroit, 1996—, interim chair dept. mortuary sci., 2000—03, chair dept. mortuary sci., 2003—04, chair dept. fundamental and applied scis., 2004—06. Rsch. assoc. in chemistry Wayne State U., Detroit, 1978—79; vis. scholar U. Mich., Ann Arbor, 1980—90; vis. scientist dept. hypertension rsch. Henry Ford Hosp., Detroit, 1986—88; adj. prof. Eugene Applebaum Coll. of Pharmacy and Health Scis. Wayne State U., 1991—96, dir. anat. pathologist assts. program, dir. mortuary sci. program. Contbr. sci. articles to profl. jours.; peer reviewer for profl. jours., 1988—; mem. editl. bd. Annals of Pharmacotherapy, 2003-. Mem. Rep. Presdl. Task Force, 1984-88; organist St. John's Episcopal Ch., Royal Oak, Mich., 1995-97. Recipient David F. Boltz Meml. award, Wayne State U., 1977, Teaching Excellence award. Fellow Am. Inst. Chemists, Nat. Acad. Clin. Biochemistry, Assn. Clin. Scientists; mem. Am. Coll. Forensic Examiners, Am. Chem. Soc., Am. Soc. Forensic Odontology, Am. Assn. Clin. Chemistry, Am. Guild Organists, Assn. Analytical Chemists, Mich. Inst. Chemists (treas. 1994—), NY Acad. Scis., Am. Coll. Toxicology, Royal Soc. Chemistry (London), Sigma Xi, Phi Lambda Upsilon, Alpha Chi Sigma. Episcopalian. Home: 20200 Orleans St Detroit MI 48203-1356 Office: Wayne State U 5439 Woodward Ave Detroit MI 48202-4009 Home Phone: 313-892-4514; Office Phone: 313-577-7874. Business E-Mail: ab8123@wayne.edu.

FRADIN, ROGER BRENT, manufacturing executive; b. NYC, Aug. 5, 1953; s. Irving and Margery (Wolf) Fradin; m. Susan Schemen; children: Russell, Michelle, William. BS, U. Pa., Phila., 1975, MBA, 1976, JD, 1978. Sr. rsch. assoc. indsl. rsch. unit U. Pa., 1974—76; v.p. Ademco divsn. Pittway Corp., Syosset, NY, 1976, pres. Ademco divsn., 1985—2000; pres., CEO Honeywell Security and Fire Solutions, 2000; pres. Automation and Control Products Honeywell Automation and Control Solutions, pres., CEO, 2004—. Bd. dirs. MSC Indsl. Direct, 1998—. Author: Unionizing the Armed Forces, 1977, Objective Selection of Supervisors, 1979. Office: Honeywell Internat Inc 101 Columbia Rd Morristown NJ 07962 Office Phone: 973-455-2000. Office Fax: 973-455-4807.*

FRADIN, RUSSELL P., human resources company executive, former computer company executive; b. Aug. 6, 1955; MBA, Harvard U., 1978. Sr. ptnr. McKinsey & Co.; sr. v.p. Automatic Data Processing, Inc., group pres. ADP Employee Svc. Group Roseland, NJ, 1998—2003; pres., CEO The BISYS Group, Inc., Lincolnshire, Ill., 2004—06; chmn., CEO Hewitt Associates, Inc., Lincolnshire, Ill., 2006—. Office: Hewitt Associates Inc 100 Half Day rd Lincolnshire IL 60069*

FRADKIN, DAVID MILTON, physicist, researcher; b. Los Angeles, Apr. 20, 1931; s. Aaron and Annie (Gordon) F.; m. Dorothea Edna Fairweather, Nov. 25, 1959; children: Lee, Mark, Steven. BS, U. Calif., Berkeley, 1954; PhD, Iowa State U., 1963. Exploitation engr. Shell Oil Co., Los Angeles, 1954-56; research assoc. Iowa State U. and Ames Lab., Ames, Iowa, 1963-64; NATO postdoctoral fellow U. Rome, 1964-65; asst. prof. physics Wayne State U., Detroit, 1965-69, assoc. prof., 1969-75, prof., 1975-94, chmn. dept. physics, 1981-91; prof. emeritus, 1994—. Del. Argonne (Ill.) Univs. Assn., 1981-83; vis. fellow U. Durham, Eng., 1991-92. Contbr. articles to profl. jours. Vice chmn. adv. bd. Detroit pub. schs., 1972-73; trustee Detroit Sci. Ctr., 1986-94. Recipient award Probus Club, 1973; sr. postdoctoral fellow U. Edinburgh, Scotland, 1977-78. Mem. Am. Phys. Soc., Sigma Xi. Avocations: tennis, fishing, golf, sailing, gardening.

FRADLEY, FREDERICK MACDONELL, retired architect; b. Bronxville, July 31, 1924; s. Justis Frederick and Helen Josephine (Macdonell) F.; m. Dorothy Davis Richard, Aug. 7, 1948; children: Stephen Davis, Wendy Fradley Monroe. BS, Brown U., 1948; M.F.A. (Lowell M. Palmer fellow), Princeton, 1954. Office engr. Turner Constrn. Co., Phila., 1948-51; project arch. Vincent G. Kling, Phila., 1954-61; ptnr. Bower & Fradley Archs., Phila., 1961-78. Important works with Bower in Phila. area include 1500 Walnut St. Office Bldg., Internat. House Student Ctr., Wharton Grad. Ctr. (Vance Hall), Gallery at Market East, 1234 Market St. Office Bldg., Yarway Corp. Hdqs., SKF Industries Hdqrs., in Balt. the W.R. Grace Bldg. Served with USAAF, 1942-46, PTO. Mem. Phi Delta Theta. Home (Summer): 20 McFarland Shore Rd New Harbor ME 04554-4827 Home (Winter): 5000 Estate Enighed PMB 332 St John VI 00830

FRAENKEL, GEORGE KESSLER, chemistry professor; b. Deal, NJ, July 27, 1921; s. Osmond Kessler and Helene (Esberg) F.; m. Johanna-Maria Herzog, June 30, 1951 (div. Aug. 1965); m. Elizabeth R. Rosen, Nov. 11, 1967 (div. Jan. 1990); m. Eva S. Cantwell, Feb. 3, 1990. BA, Harvard U., 1942; PhD, Cornell U., 1949. Research group leader National Def. Research Com., 1943-46; instr. chemistry Columbia U., NYC, 1949-53, asst. prof., 1953-57, assoc. prof., 1957-61, prof., 1961-91, Eugene Higgins prof. Grad. Sch. Arts and Scis., 1986-91, prof. emeritus, 1992—, chmn. dept. chemistry, 1966-68, dean grad. sch. arts and scis., 1968-83, dean emeritus, 1983—, v.p. spl. projects, 1983-86. Mem. postdoctoral fellowship com. Nat. Acad. Sci.-NSF, 1964-65; chmn. Gordon Research Conf. Magnetic Resonance, 1967; mem. Arts Coll. adv. council Cornell U., 1964-74; mem., bd. dirs. Atran Found., N.Y.C., 1968—2005, com. on budget and fin., 1986—2005; treas. Atran Found., 1988—2005. Assoc. editor: Jour. Chem. Physics, 1962-64; Mem. adv. editorial bd.: Chemical Physics Letters, 1966-71; editorial bd.: Jour. Magnetic Resonance, 1969-70. Trustee Columbia U. Press, 1968-71, Walden Sch., N.Y.C., 1964-66. Recipient Army-Navy certificate of appreciation, 1948; Harold C. Urey award Phi Lambda Upsilon, 1972; decorated officer Ordre des Palmes Académiques. Fellow AAAS, Am. Phys. Soc., Am. Chem. Soc., Internat. Electron Spin Resonance Soc.; mem. Assn. Grad. Schs. (exec. com. 1976-80, v.p. 1977-78, pres. 1978-79, chmn. com. policies on grad. edn. 1969-71), Phi Beta Kappa, Sigma Xi, Phi Kappa Phi. Achievements include research in field of electron spin resonance with particular emphasis on the electron spin resonance of organic free radicals. Home: 520 W 114th St Apt 82 New York NY 10025-7852 E-mail: gkf520@cs.com.

FRAGEN, ANDREW J., surgeon; MD, St. Louis U., 1991. Lic. physician, surgeon Calif., 1997. Pvt. practice cosmetic and gen. surgeon, Palm Springs, Calif., 1997—. Chmn. dept. surgery Desert Regional Med. Ctr., Palm Springs, Calif. Office Phone: 760-327-1885. Business E-Mail: office@fragensurgery.com.

FRAGER, ALBERT S., retired food products executive; b. Boston, Dec. 29, 1922; s. Oscar and Anna (Polterak) F.; m. Marion Nathan, June 15, 1950; children: Owen R., Bonnie L. Frager Franks, Laurie J. Burton, Sherri Frager Goodstein. Student, Amos Tuck Sch. Bus., Dartmouth Coll., 1943; BS in Bus. Adminstrn, Northeastern U., 1944. Internal revenue agt. IRS, 1945-56; v.p., controller Stop & Shop, Inc., Boston, 1956-67, treas., 1967-86, fin. v.p., 1969-79, sr. v.p., 1979-86. Past trustee South Palm Beach County Jewish Fedn.; bd. dirs. Donna Klein Jewish Acad.; mem. corp., past bd. overseers Northeastern U.; past pres. Jewish temple. With USNR, 1943-44. Mem. AICPA, Mass. Soc. CPAs. Home: 4740 S Ocean Blvd Apt 911 Highland Beach FL 33487-5354

FRAGILE, PATRICK CHRISTOPHER, physics professor, astrophysicist, researcher; b. Columbus AFB, Miss., Oct. 12, 1970; s. Pat C. and Mary Lou Fragile; m. Jessica Lynn Embry, Aug. 18, 2001; 1 child, Julia Lauren. BS, Duke U., Durham, NC, 1993; MS, PhD, U. Notre Dame, Ind., 2001. Postdoctoral rsch. staff mem. DNT-AX divsn. Lawrence Livermore Nat. Lab., 2001—04; postdoctoral rschr. dept. physics U. Calif., Santa Barbara, 2004—05; asst. prof. dept. physics and astronomy Coll. Charleston, SC, 2005—. Contbr. articles to profl. jours. Regional sci. fair judge Intel Internat. Sci. and Engring. Fair, South Bend, Ind., 2000—01, Walnut Creek, Calif., 2002—04, Mount Pleasant, SC, 2006—. Capt. USAF, 1993—97. Decorated Commendation medal USAF; grantee, TeraGrid Medium Resource Allocation, 2005—06, SC Space Grant Consortium, 2006, Coll. Charleston Faculty R&D Com., 2006; Arthur J. Schmitt Grad. fellow, U. Notre Dame, 1997—2001. Mem.: Am. Phys. Soc., Am. Astron. Soc. Roman Catholic. Avocations: golf, hiking, travel, snowboarding, bicycling. Office: College Charleston Dept Physics 58 Coming St Charleston SC 29424 Home Phone: 843-278-2549; Office Phone: 843-953-3181. Office Fax: 843-953-4824. Business E-Mail: fragilep@cofc.edu.

FRAGNER, MATTHEW CHARLES, lawyer; b. NYC, Jan. 12, 1954; s. Berwyn N. and Marcia R. (Salkind) F.; m. Mariann Donahue, June 19, 1983; children: Rachel Jade, Jaron Roark, Bailyn Natalie, Talia Colby. BA, Yale U., 1975; JD, U. Calif., Berkeley, 1978. Bar: Calif. 1978, U.S. Tax Ct. 1979, U.S. Ct. Appeals (9th crct.) 1979. Atty. Thomas Shafran & Wasser, LA, 1978-83; ptnr. Shafran & Fragner, LA, 1984-87, Lane & Edson, LA, 1987-88, Mayer Brown & Platt, LA, 1989-92, Sonnenschein Nath & Rosenthal, LA, 1992-2000; pres. Somnolence, Inc., LA, 1989—96; gen. cousel, dir. investments Citadel Capital Mgmt. Corp., 2000—02; founder, chmn. Tools to Talent Non Profit Corp., 2001—; ptnr. Liner Yankelevitz Sunshine & Regenstreif, Santa Monica, Calif., 2002—03; prin. Fragner & Pace Law Corp., Los Angeles, 2003—05; ptnr. Fragner Seifert Pace & Winograd, LLP, LA, 2005—; gen. counsel CIM Group, LA, 2006—. Lectr. U. So. Calif., 1994—99. Active Berkeley (Calif.) Law Found., 1978-83. Mem. Los Angeles County Bar Assn. (chair comml. devel. and leasing subsect.). Office: Fragner Seifert Pace & Winograd LLP 300 S Grand Ave 14th Fl Los Angeles CA 90071 Office Phone: 213-687-2320. Business E-Mail: mfragner@fspwlaw.com.

FRAGOMENI, JAMES MARK, mechanical engineer, educator; b. Columbus, Ohio, Sept. 24, 1962; s. John and Kathleen Fragomeni. BS in Metall. Engring., U. Pitts., 1985; MS in Engring., Purdue U., West Lafayette, Indiana, 1988, PhD, 1994. Cert. quality technician ASQ, 2005. Sumer rsch. intern Allegheny Ludlum Steel Corp. Rsch. Ctr., Brackenridge, Pa., 1984; mgmt. assoc. engr. US Steel Corp., Gary, Ind., 1985—86; asst. rschr. Dept. Defense Analysis Ctr., U. Purdue, West Lafayette, Ind., 1995; asst. prof. U. Ala., Tuscaloosa, 1995—97, Ohio U., Athens, 1997—2000; summer faculty fellow Wright Patterson AFB Materials and Mfg. Directorate, AFOSR, Dayton, 1998; asst. prof. U. Detroit Mercy, 2000—. Grad. rsch. asst. Purdue U., Engring. Rsch. Ctr., West Lafayette, Ind., 1986—94; summer faculty fellow NASA Marshall Space Flight Ctr., Huntsville, Ala., 1996, Huntsville, 97. Contbr. articles to profl. jours., scientific papers to sci. confs. Cmty. svc., Portage, Ind., 1985—87; vol. Comcast Television Studio, Southfield, Mich., 2005—. U. Pitts. Merit scholar, 1981-1985, Carpenter Tech. Corp. scholar, Order of Engr. 1989. Fellow: Am. Biographical Inst. (life; lifetime deputy gov. 2005—, ambassador gen. cultural convention 2006—, ambassador of grand eminence 2005, Man of Yr. 2005, 2006, Outstanding Profl. award 2006, Internat. Peace Prize 2006, 500 Greatest Geniuses of the 21st Century 2006, dir. of experts and expertise 2006); mem.: Mich. Edn. Assn., Materials Soc. (corr.; mem. of Titanium com. 2000—04), Soc. Advancement Materials and Process Engring. (assoc.; faculty advisor student chpt. Ohio U. 1998—2000), Sigma Xi, Pi Tau Sigma (faculty advisor student chpt. U. Detroit Mercy 2002—04), Tau Beta Pi (inter-honorary coun. rep. student chpt. U. Pitts. 1983—85). Conservative. Roman Catholic. Achievements include research in aluminum-lithium alloys for aerospace applications. Avocations: photography, scuba diving, canoeing, skiing, archery, golf. Home: 25105 Biarritz Circle C Oak Park MI 48237-4021 Office: Engring and Sci Cons Svc PO Box 1446 Royal Oak MI 48068-1446 Home Phone: 412-371-1517; Office Phone: 248-245-4843. Personal E-mail: jamesfrag@yahoo.com. Business E-Mail: jamesmark88@yahoo.com.

FRAHM, SHEILA, association executive, academic administrator, former government official; b. Colby, Kans., Mar. 22, 1945; m. Kenneth Frahm; children: Amy, Pam, Chrissie. BS, Ft. Hays State U., 1967. Mem. bd. edn. State of Kans., 1985-88; mem. Kans. Senate, Topeka, 1988-94, senate majority leader, 1993-94; lt. gov. State of Kans., 1995-96; mem. from Kans., U.S. Senate, Washington, 1996; exec. dir. Kans. Assn. C.C. Trustees, Topeka, 1996—. Mem. AAUW (Outstanding Br. Mem. 1985), Thomas County Day Care Assn., Shakespeare Fedn. Women's Clubs, Farm Bur., Kans. Corn Growers, Kans. Livestock Assn., Rotary (Paul Harris fellow 1988). Republican. Home: 410 N Grant Colby KS 67701-2036 Office: 700 SW Jackson St Ste 1000 Topeka KS 66603-3757 Personal E-mail: sfrahm@st-tel.net.

FRAIDIN, STEPHEN, lawyer; b. Boston, July 29, 1939; s. Morris and Freda (Rozeff) F.; m. Lori Kramer, Oct. 27, 2001; children from previous marriage: Matthew, Sam, Sarah AB, Tufts U., 1961; JD, Yale U., 1964. Bar: NY 1965. Assoc. Fried, Frank, Harris, Shriver & Jacobson, NYC, 1964—71, ptnr., 1971—2003, Kirkland & Ellis LLP, NYC, 2003—. Vis. lectr., Yale U. Law Sch., 1988—; exec. com. Yale Law Sch. Assn., 1990-94; bd. overseers Tufts U. Arts and Scis., 1992-99; bd. dirs. Lawyers Divsn. of UJA-Fedn. NY, chmn. 1995-97; bd. dirs. Coll. Summit. Contbr. numerous articles to profl. jours. Past chmn. N.Y. Lawyers Divsn. United Jewish Appeal Fedn. Recipient Judge Joseph M. Proskauer award, 2002. Mem.: ABA (reporter com. on fed. regualtion securities, sect. corp., banking and 1974—76, subcom. 1974—), Assn. of Bar of City of NY (sec. securities regulation com. 1971—74, chmn. subcom. tender offers 1987—90, securities regulation com. 2004—). Office: Kirkland & Ellis LLP Citigroup Ctr 153 E 53rd St New York NY 10022

FRAIZER, MICHAEL D., insurance company executive; BA in Political sci., Carleton Coll. Mgr. G.E. Fin. Mgmt., 1980—89; pres., mng. dir. G.E. Japan, 1989—91; v.p. portfolio acquisitons and ventures G.E. Captial Comml. Real Estate Fin. and Svcs., 1991—93, pres., 1993—96; pres., CEO G.E. Fin. & G.E. Insurance, 1996—2004; sr. v.p. G.E. Co., 2000—04; chmn., pres., CEO Genworth Fin., Richmond, Va., 2004—. Trustee Va. Found. for Independent Colleges; bd. mem. Andre Agassi Charitable Found., Va. Commonwealth Univ. Sch. Bus. Found. Office: Genworth Financial 6620 W Broad St Richmond VA 23230*

FRAKER, FORD M., ambassador; b. Princeton, 1948; m. Linda M.H. Fraker; 3 children. BA, Harvard Coll., 1971. Various positions including v.p., regional manager Chemical Bank, Bahrain, 1972—79; division head, banking, credit and client develop. Saudi Internat. Bank, London, 1979—91; founder Fraker and Co., London, 1991—93; mng. dir. MeesPierson Investment Fin. Ltd., London, 1993—97; founding ptnr., chmn. Trinity Group Ltd., London, 1997—2007; mng. dir., sr. v.p. fund formation Flagship Ventures, 2007—; US amb. to Kingdom of Saudi Arabia US Dept. State, Riyadh, 2007—. Consultant Internat. Real Estate Corp., Boston. Office: Flagship Ventures One Memorial Dr Cambridge MA 02142 also: Am Embassy PO Box 94309 Riyadh 11693 Saudi Arabia also: DOS Amb 6300 Riyadh Pl Washington DC 20521-6300*

FRAKER, PAMELA J., science educator; BA, Purdue U., 1966; PhD, U. Ill., 1971. Postdoctoral assoc. U. Ill. Med. Ctr., 1971—73; prof. dept. biochemistry and molecular biology Mich. State U. Contbr. articles to profl. jours. Mem.: NAS. Office: Mich State U 419 Biochemistry Bldg East Lansing MI 48824-1319 Office Phone: 517-353-3513. Office Fax: 517-353-9334. Business E-Mail: fraker@msu.edu.*

FRAKES, RODNEY VANCE, plant geneticist, educator; b. Ontario, Oreg., July 20, 1930; s. Wylie and Pearl (Richardson) F.; m. Ruby L. Morey, Nov. 27, 1952; children: Laura Ann, Cody Joe. BS, Oreg. State U., 1956, MS, 1957; PhD, Purdue U., 1960. Instr. dept. agronomy Purdue U., West Lafayette, Ind., 1959-60; asst. prof. dept. crop sci. Oreg. State U., Corvallis, 1960-64, assoc. prof., 1964-69, prof., 1969—, assoc. dean research, 1981-88, emeritus dean of rsch., prof. emeritus crop sci., 1989—. Author numerous papers and abstracts; contbr. to books in field Served with USCG, 1950-53 Named Man of Yr., Pacific Seedsmen's Assn., 1972; recipient Elizabeth P. Ritchie Disting. Prof. award Oreg. State U., 1980. Fellow Am. Soc. Agronomy, Crop Sci. Soc. Am.; mem. AAAS, Soc. Research Adminstrs., Nat. Council Univ. Research Adminstrs., Western Soc. Crop Sci. (pres. 1978), Model A Ford Club of Am., Model T Ford Club of Am., Rotary. Avocations: antiques, history, amateur radio. Home: 2615 NW Linnan Cir Corvallis OR 97330-1221 Office: Oreg State U Rsch Office Corvallis OR 97331

FRAKNOI, ANDREW, astronomer, educator; b. Budapest, Hungary, Aug. 24, 1948; came to US, 1959; naturalized; s. Emery I. and Katherine H. (Schmidt) F.; m. Lola Goldstein, Aug. 16, 1992; 1 child, Alexander. BA in Astronomy, Harvard U., 1970; MA in Astrophysics, U. Calif., Berkeley, 1972. Instr. astronomy and physics Cañada Coll., Redwood City, Calif., 1972-78; exec. dir. Astron. Soc. Pacific, San Francisco, 1978-92; chmn. dept. astronomy Foothill Coll., Los Altos, Calif., 1992—. Prof. San Francisco State U., 1980-92; fellow Com. for Sci. Investigation of Claims of Paranormal, 1984—; bd. dirs. Search for Extra Terrestrial Intelligence Inst., Mountain View, Calif.; host radio prog. Exploring the Universe Sta. KGO-FM, San Francisco, 1983-84. Author: Resource Book for the Teaching of Astronomy, 1978; (with others) Effective Astronomy Teaching and Student Reasoning Ability, 1978, Universe in the Classroom, 1985; (with T. Robertson) Instructor's Guide to the Universe, 1991, (with others) Exploration of the Universe, 1995; (with others) Voyages Through the Universe, 1997, Voyages to the Planets, 2000, Voyages to the Stars and Galaxies, 2004, Disney's Wonderful World of Space, 2007; editor: The Planets, 1985, Interdisciplinary Approaches to Astronomy, 1985, The Universe, 1987, The Universe at Your Fingertips Resource Notebook, 1995, Cosmos in the Classroom, 2000; editor Mercury Mag., 1978-92, The Universe in the Classroom Newsletter, 1985-92, Astronomy Education Review, 2002—; assoc. editor: The Planetarian, 1986-88. Bd. dirs. Bay Area Skeptics, San Francisco, 1982-91. Recipient award of merit Astron. Assn. No. Calif., 1980, award Astron. League, 1993, Klumpke-Roberts award, 1994, Annenberg Found. prize in astronomy edn., 1994, Carl Sagan prize for sci. popularization, 2002; Asteroid 4859 named Asteroid Fraknoi, 1992. Fellow Calif. Acad. Scis.; mem. AAAS (astronomy sect. com. 1988-92), Am. Astron. Soc. (astronomy edn. adv. bd. 1988-2004), Astron. Soc. Pacific (Richard H. Emmons award for Excellence in Coll. Astronomy Tchg. 2007), Am. Assn. Physics Tchrs., Nat. Assn. Sci. Writers. Avocations: music, astronomy, science, literature. Office: Foothill Coll Dept Astronomy 12345 El Monte Rd Los Altos CA 94022-4504 Office Phone: 650-949-7288. E-mail: fraknoiandrew@fhda.edu.

FRALEIGH, CHRISTOPHER J., food products executive; B, Lehigh U., Bethlehem, Pa.; MBA, Columbia U., NYC. With PepsiCo, 1989—2001, v.p. colas; exec. dir. advt. and corp. mktg. GM, 2001, gen. mgr. GMC-Buick-Pontiac divsn.; CEO Food & Beverage, exec. v.p. Sara Lee Corp., 2005—. Bd. dirs. Sabre Holdings. Office: Sara Lee Corp 3500 Lacey Rd Downers Grove IL 60515 Office Phone: 630-598-6000.*

FRALEY, ANDREA LYN, physiatrist; b. Oklahoma City, Aug. 19, 1974; d. Gary Bob and Linda P. Fraley; life ptnr. Julie D. Watson. BS, So. Nazarene U., Bethany, Okla., 1997; MD, U. Okla., Oklahoma City, 2002. Bd. cert. in phys. medicine and rehab. Am. Bd. Phys. Medicine and Rehab. Resident Rehab. Inst. Chgo., 2002—06, attending physician, 2006—. Named Walter E. Heller Chief Resident, Rehab. Inst. Chgo., 2005—06. Mem.: Internat. Spine Interventional Soc., N.Am. Spine Soc., Am. Assn. Neuromuscular and Electrodiagnostic Medicine (assoc.). Office: 345 E Superior St Chicago IL 60611 Home Phone: 312-765-0039; Office Phone: 312-238-1164.

FRALEY, LINDA WILLIAMS DARNELL, music educator; b. Lamesa, Tex., Mar. 11, 1953; d. Floyd Holley and Helen Alice Williams; m. James Raymond Fraley, Mar. 12, 1982; children: Emily Anne, Sarah Elizabeth. MusB magna cum laude, U. Tex., Austin, 1971—75. Cert. tchr. all level music Tex. Edn. Agy., 1975, Orff level three Memphis State U., 1981. Tchr. music Austin Ind. Sch. Dist., Tex., 1975—82, 1994—95, 1996—99, Leander Ind. Sch. Dist., 1999—; tchr. kindergarten Grace Covenant Christian Sch., 1991—94. Pvt. piano instr., Austin, Tex., 1982—91; coach univ. interscholastic league music memory teams Austin Ind. Sch. Dist., 1996—99, dir. Highland Pk. Scottie Singers, 1996—99; dir. Bagdad Bobcat Choir Leander Ind. Sch. Dist., 2000—07. Fundraising Leander Band Boosters, Leander, Tex., 2000—06; charter mem. Blanton Mus. Art U. Tex., Austin, 2006—. Mem.: Percussive Arts Soc., Tex. Music Educators Assn., Tex. Exes U. Tex. (life), Leander Band Boosters, Alpha Lambda Delta, Phi Delta Kappa. Presbyterian. Avocations: West African drumming, travel, scrapbooks, reading, gardening. Office: Leander Ind Sch Dist 204 W South St Leander TX 78641 Home Phone: 512-388-5005; Office Phone: 512-434-5000. E-mail: linda.fraley@leanderisd.org.

FRALEY, ROBERT T., biotechnologist; b. Danville, Ill. m. Laura Fraley; children: Steven, Devin, Katherine. BS in Biology, U. Ill., 1974, PhD in Microbiology/Biochemistry, 1978; postgrad., Northwestern U., 1991. Postdoctoral fellow U. Calif., San Francisco, 1979—80; co-pres. agrl. sector Monsanto Co., St. Louis, 1980—2000, exec. v.p., chief tech. officer, 2000—. Past mem. adv. com. Agriculture Biotechnology Rsch.; past mem. health molecular cytology study sect. NIH; tech. advisor to US Dept. Agriculture, NSF, Office of Technology Assessment, CAST, Agency for Internat. Develop., NAS and Internat. Svc. for the Acquisition of Agri-Biotech Applications. Contbr. articles to profl. jours.; mem. editl. bds. of several scientific jours. Named Man of the Year, Progressive Farming mag., 1995; recipient Nat. Award for Agrl. Excellence in Sci., Nat. Agri-Mktg. Assn., 1995, Kenneth A. Spencer award for Outstanding Achievement in Agrl. and Food Chemistry, 1995, Nat. Medal Tech., 1998. Fellow: AAAS. Achievements include development of part of the team that developed the world's first practical system to introduce foreign genes into crop plants and development of insect-and-herbicide-resistant plants. Avocations: skiing, gardening, tennis. Office: Monsanto Co 800 N Lindbergh Blvd Saint Louis MO 63167-0001

FRALIX GOLD, CAROLYN M., medical/surgical nurse, educator, consultant; b. Pulaski, Tenn., Oct. 12, 1951; d. Gardner and Louetta (Miller) Fralix; children: Sean Adams, Amber Holcomb-Keene; m. Ronald David Gold, Jan. 1, 2000. ADN, San Antonio Coll., 1982; BSN, U. Tex. Health Sci. Ctr., San Antonio, 1988; MSN, U. Tex., San Antonio, 1995. RN; cert. EMT, BLS, CPR instr. Tchr., rsch. assoc. U. Tex. Health Sci. Ctr., San Antonio; staff devel. coord. St. Rose and Villa Rosa Hosp., San Antonio; neonatal ICU Santa Rosa Hosp., San Antonio, 1982; cons. for ednl. resources, med. surg. staff nurse Santa Rosa Health Care Corp., San Antonio, 1984-88; med.-surg. pool nurse Meth. Hosp., San Antonio, 1994-95; vocat. nursing instr. St. Philip's Coll., San Antonio, 1991-95; nursing instr. U. Tex. Health Sci. Ctr., San Antonio, 1995-98, rsch. nurse coord., 1999, asst. prof., 2006—; assoc. prof. Dept. Nursing San Antonio Coll., 1998-99; intake coord. SNU Methodist Hosp., 1999—2001. Adj. faculty dept. nursing U. Tex. Health Sci. Ctr., San Antonio, 2002, S.W. Tex. Meth. Women's Ctr., 2002-05; founder, owner Hearts Alive Inc., 2003—; cons. in field. Founder, first aid ministry Oak Hills Ch., San Antonio, 2004—, dir., first aid ministry, 2004—. Recipient various scholarships. Mem. ANA, Holistic Nurses Assn., Am. Urol. Assn. Allied, Tex. Nurses Assn., U. Tex. Nursing Alumni Assn. (past treas.), Tex. Jr. Coll. Tchrs. Assn., Rotary, Sigma Theta Tau.

FRAME, ROGER EVERETT, school psychologist; b. Lansing, Mich. s. James Sutherland and Emily (Boyce) F.; m. Marsha Wiggins, Dec. 18, 1982 (div. 2006); children: Brian, Cameron. BS, Denison U., 1971; MA, Western Mich. U., 1973; PhD, Mich. State U., 1979. Children's therapist North Ctrl. Mich. Mental Health Svcs. Bd., Cadillac, 1973-76; rsch. assoc., lectr. Mich. State U., East Lansing, 1978-79; cons. Mich. Dept. Edn., Lansing, 1979; vis. asst. prof., project dir. So. Ill. U., Carbondale, 1979-81; sch. psychologist Collier County Pub. Sch., Naples, Fla., 1981-83, Denver Pub. Schs., 1993—94, Douglas County Pub. Schs., 1994—2002; clin. measurement cons. Psychol. Corp./Harcourt Assessment, 2002—07; pvt. practice mental health counselor Gainseville, Fla., 1983—93; pres. Frameworks 4 Learning, 2007—. Therapist, family mediator, trainer, workshop leader, 1984—1993; pres., mental health counselor, assessment, counseling, tng. svcs., Gainesville, Fla., 1983-88, 89-93, Port St. Lucie, Fla., 1988-89; grant writing cons., 1993-95. Contbr. articles to profl. jours. Mem. adv. bd. dist. III Dept. Health & Rehab. Svcs. Interim Planning Group, 1991—; pres. Rocky Mountain Condo, LLC 2000-03. Mem. APA, Fla. Soc. Psychotherapists (rec. sec. 1991-92), Fla. Assn. Profl. Family Mediators. Methodist. Avocations: skiing, bicycling, sailing, scuba diving. Home and Office: 8830 E Mineral Pl Centennial CO 80112-2733 Personal E-mail: reframe3@comcast.net.

FRAME, SUSAN S., special education educator; b. Napoleon, Ohio, June 6, 1952; d. George Raymond and Virginia Sappington (Clabaugh) Schey; m. Thomas F. Baslaugh (div.); children: Thomas Adam Boslaugh, Benjamin Schey Boslaugh, Elizabeth V. Skinner; m. Dennis C. Frame, Jan. 2, 1999. BS in Edn. in Vocal Music, S.W. Mo. State U., Springfield, 1996, MS in Edn. in Spl. Edn., 2003. Lic. practical nurse, Mo.; cert. tchr. visual impairments Mo., tchr. learning disabilities Mo., tchr. vocal music Mo. Tax checker H&R Block, Springfield, 1981; nurse Vis. Nurses Assn., Springfield, 1990—92; tchr. visually impaired Marshfield (Mo.) Pub. Schs. Owner Fair Grove Plumbing. Co-author: (book) 50 Years of Flight with My Guardian Angel, 1990, composer songs. Choir mem. St. James Ch. Ozark Anglican Coun., 1979—; adviser Boy Scouts, Fair Grove, 1985—93, 4-H Club, Fair Grove, 1985—93. Mem.: DAR, Mo. State Tchrs. Assn., Assn. for Edn. and Rehab. of the Blind and Visually Impaired. Republican. Avocations: quilting, music. Office: Marshfield Pub Schs 650 N Locust Marshfield MO 65706

FRAME, TED RONALD, lawyer; b. Milw., June 27, 1929; s. Morris and Jean (Lee) F.; m. Lois Elaine Pilgrim, Aug. 15, 1954; children: Kent, Lori, Nancy, Owen. Student, UCLA, 1946-49; AB, Stanford U., 1950, LLB, 1952. Bar: Calif. 1953. Gen. agri-bus. practice, Coalinga, Calif., 1953—; sr. ptnr. Frame & Matsumoto and predecessor , Coalinga, 1965—. Dir. West Hills Coll. Found. Mem. ABA, Calif. Bar Assn., Fresno County Bar Assn., Kings County Bar Assn., LA County Bar Assn., Am. Agrl. Law Assn., Coalinga C. of C. (past pres.), Masons, Shriners, Elks. Avocations: bicycling, hiking. Home: 1222 Nevada St Coalinga CA 93210-1239 Office: 201 Washington St Coalinga CA 93210-0895 Office Phone: 559-935-1552. Business E-Mail: ted@frame_matsumoto.com.

FRAMME, LAWRENCE HENRY, III, political organization administrator, lawyer; b. Louisville, Oct. 8, 1949; s. Lawrence Henry and Margaret Gertrude (Hayes) F.; m. Frances Claire Schwacke, Dec. 27, 1969; children: Jessica Marie, Lawrence Henry IV, Benjamin Hayes. BA, Centre Coll., 1971; JD cum laude, Washington and Lee U., 1974. Bar: Va. 1974, U.S. Dist. Ct. Va., 1974, U.S. Ct. Appeals (4th cir.) 1974. Assoc. McGuire, Woods & Battle, Richmond, Va., 1974-81, Lacy & Baliles, Richmond, 1981-82; mem. firm, dir. Mezzullo, McCandlish & Framme, Richmond, 1982-90; sec. econ. devel. (gov's. cabinet) Commonwealth of Va., 1990-92; chmn. Virginians for Progress Found., 1992; v.p. LeClair, Ryan, Joynes, Epps & Framme, Richmond, 1992-95; prin. Framme Law Firm, 1995—; co-chmn. gov's. adv. coun. Workforce 2000, 1990-91. Chmn. Dem. Party Va., 1986-90, 2001-03. Va. State Bd. Cmty. Colls., mem. 1987-90, chmn. 1989-90; bd. visitors Va. Commonwealth U., 1992-96; bd. dirs. Downtown YMCA, 1986-95, chmn. 1992-94; bd. dirs., sec. Va. Biotech. Rsch. Park Authority, 1991-92, 93-95, 2002-04, Va. Biotech. Rsch. Park Corp., 1994-2002, Leadership Metro Richmond, 1991-94; bd. dirs., legal advisor Richmond Urban League, 1985-86, Metro Richmond YMCA, 1995-2000; policy bd. mem. Va. Tech Bioinformatics Ctrs., 2001-; Recipient Legal award Housing Opportunities Made Equal, Richmond, 1983; named Alumni of Yr., Leadership Metro Richmond, 1990. Mem. ABA, VSB, Va. Bar Assn., Richmond Bar Assn., Omicron Delta Kappa. Roman Catholic. Office: Framme Law Firm PC 2812 Emerywood Pky Ste 220 Richmond VA 23294-3539 Home: 2420 Hanover Ave Richmond VA 23220 Business E-Mail: lframme@frammelaw.com.

FRAMPTON, PAUL HOWARD, physics researcher, educator; b. Kidderminster, Eng., Oct. 31, 1943; came to U.S., 1968; naturalized citizen, 1989; s. Harold Albert and Grace Elizabeth (Howard) Frampton; m. Anne-Marie Frampton, 1993. BA, U. Oxford, 1965, MA, DPhil, U. Oxford, 1968, DSc, 1984. Rsch. assoc. U. Chgo., 1968—70; fellow CERN, Geneva, 1970—72; vis. prof. Bielefeld U., Germany, 1972, 1999, Syracuse U., 1972—75; vis. assoc. prof. UCLA, 1975—77; vis. scholar Harvard U., Cambridge, Mass., 1978—81; from asst. prof. physics to prof. U. N.C., Chapel Hill, 1981—96; disting. prof. physics Louis D. Rubin Jr., 1996—. Vis. prof. U. Tex., fall 1983, Boston U., 1986-87, U. d'Aix-Marseille, 1993, CERN, 1996, 98, 2000, 2003, Perimeter Inst., 2005; chmn. steering com. Workshops on Grand Unification, 1980-89; chmn. organizing com. 1st workshop U. N.H., 1980, 3d workshop, U. N.C., 1982, 10th and last workshop U. N.C., 1989; symposium chair 8th Internat. Symposium on Particles, Strings and Cosmology, U. N.C., 2001 Author: Dual Resonance Models, 1974, 2d edit., 1986, Gauge Field Theories, 1986, 2d edit., 2000, Frampton Festschrift: The Launching of La Belle Epoque of High Energy Physics and Cosmology, 2004; editor books in field; contbr. 350 articles to profl. jours., also chpts. to books. Gov.'s project dir. for supercollider in N.C., 1987. Fellow AAAS, Am. Phys. Soc., Brit. Inst. Physics. Achievements include research in high-energy theoretical physics including particle phenomenology, string theory and theoretical cosmology. Home: 101 Cedar Ridge Way Durham NC 27705 Office: U NC Dept Physics And Astronomy Chapel Hill NC 27599-3255 Office Phone: 919-962-7207. Business E-Mail: frampton@physics.unc.edu.

FRAN, GRANDMA **See BROWN, FRANCES**

FRANCAVILLA, DONNA T., journalist; b. Camden, NJ, Dec. 4, 1960; d. Lelio and Aurora (DeVuono) Ciccotelli; m. Thomas Louis Francavilla, May 29, 1957; children: Michael, Lisa, Jessica, Gregory. BS, Emerson Coll., Boston, 1985. Talk show prodr. WWDB-FM Talkradio, Phila., 1980-81; desk asst., prodn. asst. KYW Newsradio 1060 AM, Phila., 1981-82; talk show prodr. WRKO-AM, Boston, 1982-85; news anchor radio network Internat. Media News, Washington, 1986-88; program dir., news dir. Westinghouse WPGC AM & FM, Washington, 1988-90; traffic reporter Metro Traffic Control, Phila., 1990-92; news anchor, all news radio WINZ-AM, Miami, 1993-94; news reporter NBC, WVTM-TV, Birmingham, Ala., 1996—99; radio corr. CBS Radio News, 1999—; freelance reporter/anchor Radio Ala., Alabaster; contbr. Westwood One's Am. in the Morning Program, 1999—; freelancer reporter, 2002—; freelance reporter Agy. France Presse, Washington, 2000—, CBS News Path, 2003—, Am. Urban Radio Networks, 2003—, Voice of Am.; radio and TV news dir. RTNDA, 2006—. Owner Frankly Speaking Comm., LLC; participant RIAS German Journalist Exch. Program, 1999, 2006; freelance writer Birmingham Mag., 1999; news reporter APTV Ala. Pub. TV, Montgomery, 1999. Freelance wire svc. reporter Agy. French Press, 2000—. V.p. Greystone Ladies Club, Birmingham, 1995; bd. dirs., sec. The Cottages at Camp Creek Home Owners Assn., 2006—. Mem. Jefferson County Med. Alliance; public rels. dir., Jefferson County Med. Alliance. Roman Catholic. Avocations: exercising, dance, skiing, cooking, writing. Home: 5079 Greystone Way Birmingham AL 35242-6456 Office Phone: 205-991-4461. Personal E-mail: newsmom@hotmail.com.

FRANCE, BELINDA TAKACH, lawyer, business owner; b. Jacksonville, Fla., June 10, 1964; d. Bruce Albert and Bertha Loretta (Hawkins) Takach. BS, U. Tampa, Fla., 1985; JD, Stetson U., 1987; LLM in Taxation, U. Fla., 1989. Bar: Fla. 1989, U.S. Dist. Ct. (mid. dist.) Fla. 1989, U.S. Ct. Claims 1989, U.S. Tax Ct. 1989, U.S. Ct. Appeals (11th cir.) 1989, U.S. Ct. Appeals (Fed. cir.) 1990. Tax preparer H&R Block, Tampa, 1983-84; acct. Robert Osborne & Assocs., Tampa, 1984-85; assoc. Thomas C. Little, P.A., Clearwater, Fla., 1987-88; co-counsel Bruce R. Young, P.A., Clearwater, 1988; prin. pvt. practice, Tallahassee, 1988—. Prof. Ft. Lauderdale Coll., Tallahassee, 1989; adj. instr. Tallahassee C.C., 1991—; expert witness in taxation and pension matters. Named Best Atty., Tallahassee Mag., 2000; named to Legal Elite, Fla. Trend, 2004, 2005. Mem. ABA (com. domestic rels. tax problems, com. attys. in small law firms), Fla. Bar Assn., Tallahassee Bar Assn., Tallahassee Women Lawyers Assn., Tallahassee C. of C. Office: 1625 Summit Lake Dr Ste 240 Tallahassee FL 32317 Office Phone: 850-224-1040. Business E-Mail: btf@francelawfirm.com.

FRANCE, BRIAN Z., sports association executive; b. Daytona Beach, FL, Aug. 2, 1962; s. Bill France, Jr.; m. Megan France; 3 children. Mem. mktg. dept. and touring divs. NASCAR, Daytona Beach, Fla., 1994—, CEO, 2003—. Founder, former chmn. Diversity Coun., NASCAR; head Brandsense. Named Sports Industrialist of Yr., Sports Bus. Daily, 1999, SMEI

Mktg. Statesman of Yr., Sales and Mktg. Execs. Internat. (SMEI), 1999; named one of 100 Most Influential People, Time Mag., 2006. Office: c/o NASCAR 1801 W International Speedway Blvd Daytona Beach FL 32114*

FRANCE, DOROTHY DANIEL, minister; b. Danieltown, Va., Nov. 23, 1926; d. Arthur R. and Susan G. (Waller) Daniel; m. Carl G. France, Aug. 6, 1946 (dec. Nov. 1997); 1 child, Dorothy Gail France Frankle. BA, Bethany Coll., 1950; post grad., William and Mary Coll., 1964, Va. Commonwealth U., 1966. Dir. Army Dir. Svc., Camp Pickett, Va., 1944-46; tchr. Nottoway County Pub. Sch., Crewe, Va., 1950-55, Henrico Pub. Sch., Richmond, Va., 1961-63, Petersburg Pub. Sch., Va., 1964-68; dir. Cmty. Devel., New River Cmty Action, Radford, Va., 1969-73; min. Petunia Christian Ch., Wytheville, Va., 1969-72, Galilee Christian Ch., Wytheville, 1973-75; assoc. dir. CROP/Ch. World Svc., Va., NC, 1975-76; dir. CROP/Ch. World Svc. for Va., Richmond, 1977-80; dir. resource devel. Va. Inst. of Pastoral Care, Richmond, 1980-81; min. Prospect Christian Ch., Dinwiddie, Va., 1982-87; dir. Refugee Resettlement CWS/EMM, Va. Coun. of Ch., Richmond, 1981-91. Cons. on Am. corp. involvement in South Africa Christian Ch., Indpls., 1971. Author: Special Days of the Church Year, 1969, Newness of Life, 1970, Partners in Prayer, 1986, Welcome to the United States An Orientation Guide for Refuges, 1988, Blessed Assurance, 1999, (with Jason and David Frankle) You Might Be a Football Fan If.Simplified Game Notes for Would Be Fans, 2000; (with Jason and David Frankle) You Might Be a Basketball Fan If. Simplified Game Notes for Would Be Fans, 2003, Listening With the Heart Brings Healng and Hope, 2004, Bless Us, O God Services and Prayers for Special Days, 2007; author: (with others) Go Quickly and Tell, 1973; author, editor: At Christ's Table, 1997; mem. editl. com. Toward Better Grouping in Reading, 1968. Recipient Valiant Woman award Ch. Women United. Mem. AAUW, Va. Coalition on Nutrition, Delta Kappa Gamma (chair personal growth and devel. com. 1968). Avocations: writing, travel. Home and Office: DDF Enterprises 3534 Elmhurst Cir Uniontown OH 44685 Personal E-mail: ddfenprise@aol.com.

FRANCE, JAMES C., professional sports executive; b. Daytona Beach, Fla. married; 3 children. Bus. degree, Fla. So. Coll., Lakeland, 1968. Various positions including parker Internat. Speedway Corp., Daytona Beach, Fla., 1959, ticket stubber, ticket seller, mgr. ticket gate opers., sec., asst. treas., v.p., COO, exec. v.p., pres., 1987—2003, bd. dirs., CEO, 2003—, chmn., 2007—. Starter U.S. Motorcycle Grand Prix; active Legends Car racing; competitor Allison Legacy Car Series; bd. dirs. SunTrust Bank, East Ctrl. Fla. With US Army, 1969—70, Vietnam. Named nat. tour champion, BF Goodrich Legends Cars, 1992; named one of Forbes' Richest Americans, 2006. Mem.: Am. Motorcyclist Assn., NASCAR (exec. v.p., sec., bd. dirs. 2000). Achievements include Legends Cars national tour champion, 1992. Office: Internat Speedway Corp 1801 W International Speedway Blvd Daytona Beach FL 32114

FRANCE, JENNIFER JEAN, lawyer, educator; b. Sault Sainte Marie, Mich., Dec. 26, 1976; d. Glenys Joy Miller. BSc in Polit. Sci., Pre-Law, Lake Superior State U., 1998; JD, Thomas M. Cooley Law Sch., 2001. Bar: Mich. 2003, Chippewa County Bar Assn. 2003, Sault Tribe Chippewa Indians 2003, Bay Mills Tribal Ct. 2004. Law clerk Mahjoory, Mahjoory & Berry PC, Lansing, 1999—2001, Law Office WM. Dyke Justin, PC, 2001—02, Law Office of Mark Dobias PC, 2001—02; law clerk, atty. Chippewa County Pub. Defender, 2002—04; pvt. practice, 2003—. Adj. prof. Lake Superior State U., 2002—. Office Phone: 906-632-4157. Personal E-mail: jjflaw@sbcglobal.net.

FRANCE, JOSEPH DAVID, financial analyst; b. Smithville, Mo., July 24, 1953; s. Raymond Hughes and Bonnie Lee (Cavin) F.; m. Priscilla L. Gilbert; children: Lucille Terrell, Margaret Anne. BS in Pharmacy, U. Kans., Lawrence, 1977, MBA, 1980. Chartered fin. analyst. Staff pharmacist U. Kans. Med. Ctr., Kansas City, 1977-80; securities analyst First Nat. Bank Chgo., 1980-82, Smith Barney, Harris Upham & Co., Inc., NYC, 1982-86, mng. dir., 1986-93; 1st v.p. Merrill Lynch, NYC, 1993-95; sr. v.p. Dillon, Read & Co., 1995-96; dir. CS First Boston, NYC, 1996—2003; mng. dir. Banc Am. Securities, 2003—. Mem. Am. Fin. Assn., Boston Security Analyst Soc., Am. Econ. Assn., Am. Math. Soc., NY Soc. Securities Analysts, Assn. for Investment Mgmt. and Rsch. Republican. Roman Catholic. Avocations: reading, writing. Office: Banc America 100 Federal St 12th Fl Boston MA 02110

FRANCE, KIM, editor-in-chief; Staff writer Sassy mag., Elle mag., 7 Days; sr. editor NY mag., dep. editor; editor-at-large Spin mag.; editor-in-chief Lucky mag. Contbr. Vibe, Rolling Stone mag., Allure mag., NY Times Book Review, Mademoiselle, Harper's Bazaar, NY Times Mag., The Village Voice. Named one of NY's Most Poweful Women, 2004, 40 Under 40, Crain's Bus., 2004. Office: 4 Times Sq 6th Fl New York NY 10036*

FRANCE, NEWELL EDWIN, retired health facility administrator; b. Massillon, Ohio, Sept. 30, 1927; s. Lawrence Joel and Marcella Ruth (Nelson) F.; m. Eve Elisabeth Voluter, 1953; children: Philip J., Corinne E., Anne-Claire I., Stephen C., Louise A. BS, Northwestern U., 1953, MS in Hosp. Adminstrn, 1955. Adminstrv. resident Herrick Meml. Hosp., Berkeley, Calif., 1954-55; evening supt. Chgo. Wesley Meml. Hosp., 1955-56; asst. adminstr. St. Lukes Episcopal and Tex. Children's hosps., Houston, 1956-58, assoc. adminstr., 1958-64, adminstr., 1964-73, exec. dir., 1973-83; pres. emeritus Tampa Gen. Hosp., Fla., 1983-91, 91—; pres. Patrick Philbin & Assocs., Austin, 1993—; cons. Hok Architecture, 1995—. Assoc. adminstr. Tex. Heart Inst., Houston, 1958-64, adminstr., 1964-73, exec. dir., 1973-83; cons. adv. council HEW and NIH; staff cons. AID, 1969—; cons. program projects rev. com. Nat. Inst. Neurol. and Communicative Disorders and Stroke; mem. com. pediatrics NRC-Nat. Acad. Scis., 1975—; chmn. Greater Houston Hosp. Coun., Children's Hosps. Execs. Council, 1972-73; dir. Child Care Center, Tex. Med. Ctr., 1967—; adj. assoc. prof. Sch. Architecture, Rice U.; prof. health scis. Tex. Women's U. Bd. dirs. Met. Houston chpt. Nat. Found. March of Dimes, First City Bank Med. Center; trustee Pin Oaks Charity Horse Show Assn., Houston Bot. Soc.; mem. exec. bd. South Main Center Assn., Inc.; active Houston/Baku Sister City Assn. Served with USNR, 1946-48, 51-52. Fellow Am. Coll. Hosp. Adminstrs.; mem. Am. Hosp. Assn., Tex. Hosp. Assn. (chmn. coun. hosp. auxs. 1969-73, trustee 1972—, adviser, chmn. coun. on profl. svc. 1976—), Houston Area Hosp. Assn. (pres. 1968-69), Nat. Assn. Childrens Hosps. and Related Instns. (pres. 1969-70, conf. chmn. 1969, trustee 1971—, chmn. coun. past pres.'s 1973-74), Am. Assn. Hosp. Planning, Statutory Teaching Hosps. Coun. (Fla.) (chmn. 1988-91). Clubs: Rotary Internat; Doctors (Houston). Methodist. Home: 6609 Coolglen Dr Dallas TX 75248-2902

FRANCE, OLIN KENNETH, JR., psychologist; b. Miami Beach, Fla., Feb. 22, 1949; s. Olin Kenneth and Eva (Center) F.; m. Mary Duncan, Aug. 16, 1969; 1 child, Micah Duncan. BA, Wake Forest U., 1971; MS, Fla. State U., 1973, PhD, 1975. Lic. psychologist, Pa.; registrant Nat. Register of Health Svc. Providers in Psychology. Asst. prof. Francis Marion Coll., Florence, SC, 1975-78; prof. Shippensburg (Pa.) U., 1978—; ind. practice psychology SC, 1975—78, Pa., 1979—. Coord. Pa. Summer Acad. Advancement Coll. Tchg., 1999-2005, Ann. Conf. Advancement Coll. Tchg. and Learning, Pa. State Sys. Higher Edn., 2001-03; tng. coord. Warm Line, Carlisle, Pa, 2004—. Author: Crisis Intervention, 1982, 5th edit., 2007, Body Conditioning, 1985, The Hospital Patient, 1987, Basic Psychological Skills, 1993, Helping Skills for Human Service Workers, 1995, 2d edit., 2006. Recipient Salute to Teaching, Shippensburg U. and the Pa. State Sys. of Higher Edn., 1990, Excellence Tchg. award Pa. Soc. Tchg. Scholars, 1999; named Vol. of Yr. New Hope Online, 2001. Mem. APA, Pa. Psychol. Assn., Am. Assn. Suicidology. Office: Shippensburg U Psychology Dept 1871 Old Main Dr Shippensburg PA 17257-2299

FRANCES, MARIE CECILIA, theater producer, television producer; b. Bklyn., Jan. 18, 1937; d. Rocco Joseph Lucadamo and Yolanda Frances Romano; children: Arthur Robert, Elissa Marie, Marie Peggy. AA, George Washington U., 1962; BS, Md. U., 1966; MS, Northfield U., 2003. Pres., owner Marie Frances Prodns., Inc., Las Vegas, 1971—; nat. dir. Anti Drug Program, Exec. Office of Pres., Washington, 1972—75; field prodr. ABC's Ripley's Believe it or Not, 1980—85; exec. prodr. Mt. Kilimanjaro Marathon, Tanzania, 1991—, Miss Egypt Universe, Cairo, 1987—97, The Paramids Marathon, 1987—97. Pub. info. officer USAID, Cairo, 1981—85. Exec. prodr.: (video presentations projects) USAID, 1983—86 (Best Video Prodn. Food for Peace, 1983); exec. prodr.: (films) Acupuncture the Eastern Cure, 1971; prodr.: (radio show) The Marie Frances Hour, 1998, Miss Latin Star, 2005. Founder, pres. The Frances Found., Las Vegas, 2005—. Recipient Outstanding Achievement, Office of Pres., Washington, 1967. Mem.: Rotary. Roman Catholic. Avocations: music, piano, art. Home: 8120 Bay Harbor Dr Las Vegas NV 89128 Office: Marie Frances Prodns Inc 8370 W Cheyenne Ave Ste 109-365 Las Vegas NV 89129 Office Phone: 702-952-9940.

FRANCES, RICHARD JOSEPH, psychiatrist; b. NYC, Mar. 3, 1946; s. Joseph and Julia (Levy) F.; 1 child, Jenny. BA, Columbia U., 1967; MD, NYU, 1971. Diplomate Am. Bd. Psychiatry and Neurology (added qualifications in addiction psychiatry, 1992). Resident and chief resident in psychiatry Albert Einstein Sch. Medicine, Bronx, N.Y., 1971-74, instr. in psychiatry, 1976; asst prof. New York Hosp., Cornell, White Plains, 1976-83; assoc. prof. psychiatry N.Y. Hosp., White Plains, 1983-86; prof. clin. psychiatry N.J. Med. Sch., Newark, 1986—; pvt. practice NYC, 1976—; CEO, pres., med. dir. Silver Hill Hosp., New Canaan, Conn., 1997—. Vice chmn. residency tng., 1986-93, AIDS grant review com. Nat. Inst. Drug Abuse; vice chair Coun. on Addiction Psychiatry; dir. psychiatry Hackensack Med. Ctr., 1993-97; mem. faculty NYU, 1997—. Author: Concise Guide to Addiction Treatment, 1989; editor: Self Assessment in Psychiatry, 1986, Clinical Textbook of Addictive Disorders, 1991, 2d edit., 1998. Lt. comdr. USN, 1974-76. Fellow Am. Coll. Psychiatrists (Commr. 1998), Am. Psychiat. Assn. (chmn. com. on alcoholism 1990); mem. Am. Acad. Psychiatrists on Alcoholism and Addictions (founding pres. 1985), Am. Assn. Gen. Hosp. Psychiatrists, Coun. on Addiction Psychiatry, Am. Bd. Psychiatry and Neurology Addiction (psychiatry exam. com.) Home: 208 Valley Rd New Canaan CT 06840-3812 Office: 510 E 86th St Apt 1D New York NY 10028-7547 also: 200 E End Ave Apt 9B New York NY 10128-7891

FRANCESCA, MIKE, radio personality; b. NY, 1961; Grad., St. John's U. Analyst CBS Sports; with MSG; co-host Mike and the Mad Dog WFAN-AM 660, NYC, 1989—. Host (radio shows) The NFL Now with Mike Francesca, appearances in (TV series) ESPN's Sports Century, 2000—03, (TV films) Undefeated, 2003, (films) Jim Brown All American, 2002. Co-recipient Marconi Radio award for Major Market Personality of Yr., Nat. Assn. Broadcasters, 2000; named one of New York's Influentials, New York Mag., 2006. Office: WFAN-AM 34-12 36th St Astoria NY 11106 Office Phone: 718-706-7690.

FRANCESCHETTI, DONALD RALPH, physicist, educator; b. Oceanside, NY, Nov. 21, 1947; s. Nicholas and Lucile Frances (Powell) F.; m. Alice Frizzell, Oct. 2, 1982. BS, Bklyn. Coll., 1969; MA, Princeton U., 1971, PhD, 1974. Rsch. assoc. U. Ill., 1973—75, U. N.C., Chapel Hill, 1975—77, rsch. asst. prof., 1977—79; asst. prof. U. Memphis, 1979—83, assoc. prof., chmn. dept. physics, 1983—86, prof. physics, chmn. dept. physics, 1986—91, interim assoc. v.p. for rsch., 1990—93, interim vice provost for rsch., 1993—96, disting. svc. prof. physics and chemistry, 1996—. Vis. lectr. State U., Utrecht, Netherlands, 1982; Dunavant prof., 2003—, Faundree univ. prof., 2005-; dir. Learning Communities, 2005—. Consulting editor (reference works) Biog. Ency. Mathematicians; contbr. articles to profl. jours. Woodrow Wilson Grad. fellow, 1969-70, NSF Grad. fellow, 1969-72, Postdoctoral Energy-related fellow, 1975-76 Mem.: Am. Phys. Soc., Cognitive Sci. Soc., History of Sci. Soc., Am. Chem. Soc., Sigma Xi, Phi Beta Kappa. Achievements include patent in field. Office: University of Memphis Dept Of Physics Memphis TN 38152-0001 Office Phone: 901-678-5257. Business E-Mail: dfrncsch@memphis.edu.

FRANCESCHI, ERNEST JOSEPH, JR., lawyer; b. LA, Feb. 1, 1957; s. s. Ernest Joseph and Doris Cecilia (Beluche) Franceschi. BS, U. So. Calif., 1978; JD, Southwestern U., LA, 1980. Bar: Calif. 1984, U.S. Dist. Ct. (cen. dist.) Calif. 1984, U.S. Dist. Ct. (ea. dist.) Calif. 1986, U.S. Dist. Ct. (no. and so. dists.) Calif. 1987, U.S. Ct. Appeals (9th cir.) 1984, U.S. Supreme Ct. 1989. Pvt. practice law, LA, 1984—; judge pro tem L.A. Superior Ct., 1999—. Mem. Assn. Trial Lawyers Am., Calif. Trial Lawyers Assn., L.A. Trial Lawyers Assn., Trial Lawyers for Pub. Justice, Fed. Bar Assn. Office: 445 S Figueroa St Ste 2600 Los Angeles CA 90071-1630 Office Phone: 213-612-7723. Office Fax: 213-612-7724.

FRANCESCONI, LOUISE L., defense equipment manufacturing company executive; b. Calif., Mar. 1953; BA, Scripps Coll., 1975; MBA, UCLA, 1978. With Hughes Missile Systems Co., 1976—98, CFO, 1993, pres., 1996—98; sr. v.p. Raytheon Systems Co., 1998—99; v.p. Raytheon Co., 1999—; dep. gen. mgr. Raytheon Missile Systems, Tucson, 1998—99, gen. mgr., 1999—2002, pres., 2002—. Bd. dirs. Stryker Corp., 2006—; bd. trustees Tucson Med. Ctr. Healthcare, Tucson Airport Authority. Mem. Ariz. Gov.'s Coun. on Innovation and Tech., 2003—; nat. bd. advisors Eller Coll. Bus. and Pub. Adminstrn., U. Ariz.; bd. trustees Tucson Med. Ctr. Healthcare, Tucson Airport Authority. Named Tech. Exec. of the Yr., Eller Coll. & U. Ariz. Coll. Engring. & MInes, 2002; recipient Lifetime Achievement award, Women in Aerospace, 2005. Office: Raytheon Missile Systems 1151 E Hermans Rd Tucson AZ 85706*

FRANCH, RICHARD THOMAS, lawyer; b. Melrose Park, Ill., Sept. 23, 1942; s. Robert and Julia (Martino) Franch; m. Patricia Staufenberg, Apr. 18, 1971 (dec. Apr. 1994); children: Richard T. Jr., Katherine J.; m. Susan L. Rice, Sept. 1, 1995. BA cum laude, U. Notre Dame, 1964; JD, U. Chgo., 1967. Bar: Ill. 1967, U.S. Dist. Ct. (no. dist.) Ill. 1967, U.S. Ct. Appeals (7th cir.) 1971, U.S. Supreme Ct. 1980, U.S. Ct. Appeals (3d and 8th cirs.) 1981, U.S. Ct. Appeals (2d cir.) 1984, U.S. Dist. Ct. (no. dist.) Wis. 1989, U.S. Ct. Appeals (6th cir.) 1991, U.S. Tax Ct. 1994, U.S. Ct. Appeals (9th cir.) 1997, U.S. Ct. Appeals (4th cir.) 2003. Assoc. Jenner & Block, Chgo., 1967-68, 70-74, ptnr., 1975—. Former mem. Ill. Supreme Ct. Rules Com. Served to capt. US Army, 1968—70. Decorated Bronze Star, Army Commendation medal. Fellow: Am. Coll. Trial Lawyers; mem.: Am. Law Inst. Office: Jenner & Block Ste 4600 330 N Wabash Ave Chicago IL 60611 Home Phone: 847-446-0792; Office Phone: 312-923-2965. Personal E-mail: dickfranch@aol.com. Business E-Mail: rfranch@jenner.com.

FRANCHIONE, DENNIS, university football coach; b. Girard, Kans., Mar. 28, 1951; s. Peter and Theda; divorced; 1 child, Brad; m. Kim Franchione; children: Ashley, Libby. BA, Pittsburg State U., Kans., 1973. Asst. coach Kans. State U., 1978—80; head coach Southwestern Kans. Coll., 1981—82; offensive coord. U. Tenn., 1983—84; head coach Pittsburg State U., 1985—99, Southwestern Tex. St., 1990—91, U. New Mexico, 1992—97, Tex. Christian U., 1998—2000, Univ. Ala., 2001—02, Texas A&M U., 2002—. Recipient Nat. Coll. Football Coach Yr., AP, 1986—87. Achievements include coaching Western Athletic Conference Champions in 1996, 2000. Office: Athletic Dept Tex A & M U PO Box 30017 College Station TX 77842-3017*

FRANCIOSA, JOSEPH ANTHONY, healthcare consultant; b. Easton, Pa., Apr. 24, 1936; s. Joseph and Letitia Beatrice (Cascioli) F.; m. Antonietta Battistoni, Feb. 8, 1964 (div. 1972); m. Barbara Ann Neilan, Aug. 3, 1973 (div. 1989); 1 child, Christopher David; m. Robin J. McGarry, Oct. 4, 1998. BA, U. Pa., 1958; MD, U. Rome, 1963. Diplomate Am. Bd. Internal Medicine; lic. in Pa., Md., Ark. Intern USPHS Hosp., SI, N.Y., 1964-65; resident Washington Hosp. Ctr., 1967-69; cardiology fellow VA Hosp.-Georgetown U., Washington, 1969-71; chief ICU Va. Hosp., Washington, 1971-73; asst. prof. medicine Georgetown U. Med. Sch., 1971-73, assoc. dir. cardiovascular tng. program, 1974-75; dir. CCU Va. Hosp., Mpls., 1974-76; asst. prof. medicine U. Minn., Mpls., 1977-79; chief cardiology VA Hosp., Phila., 1979-82; assoc. prof. U. Pa., Phila., 1979-82. Adj. prof. 1987-98; adj. prof. medicine Mt. Sinai Med. Sch., N.Y.C., 1989—, Cornell U. Coll. Med., N.Y.C., 1999—; dir. cardiology div. U. Ark., Little Rock, 1982-86; prof., 1982-86; dir. cardio-renal drugs ICI Americas Inc., Wilmington, Del., 1986-88; v.p. R&D Zambon Corp., East Rutherford, N.J., 1988-90; exec. dir. med. affairs Ciba-Geigy Pharm., Summit, N.J., 1990-91; exec. dir. med. svcs. Ciba-Geigy, 1992-95; health care/pharm. cons., N.Y.C., 1995—. Contbr. numerous articles to med. jours. Mem. med. rsch. com. Am. Heart Assn., Mpls., 1976-79, Phila., 1981-82. Lt. comdr. US Pub. Health Svc., 1965—67. VA grantee, 1974-84, U. Ark. grantee, 1982-83, NIH grantee 1985-86. Fellow ACP, Am. Coll. Cardiology, Am. Coll. Chest Physicians (chmn. hypertension com. 1981-83, gov. Ark. 1984-86), Am. Heart Assn. (circulation coun. 1978—, coun. high blood pressure rsch. 1982—, clin. cardiology coun. 1984, bd. dirs. N.J. affiliate 1994-98); mem. Am. Soc. Clin. Pharmacology and Therapeutics (vice chmn. cardiopulmonary com. 1981-89), Assn. Univ. Cardiologists, Am. Acad. of Pharm. Physicians (charter mem. v.p. pubis. com. 2002-2004), Heart Failure Soc. Am. Avocations: computers, physical fitness. Office: 350 E 79th St Apt 9C New York NY 10075 Office Phone: 212-879-2366. E-mail: josephafranciosa@aol.com.

FRANCIS, BARBARA JOAN, nurse, paralegal; b. Toledo, Ohio, Oct. 28, 1957; d. Robert Arthur and Patricia Louise (Hansen) Francis; children: Jessica Lynn, Zachary Alfred, Katherine Elizabeth. RN, Toledo Hosp. Sch. of Nursing, Toledo, Ohio, 1978; Nurse Paralegal, U. Toledo, Toledo, Ohio, 2001; BSN, Lourdes Coll., Sylvania, Ohio, 2002. RN Ohio, 1978, registered In Patient Ob., NCC, 1991, lic. Elec. Fetal Monitoring, NCC, 1998, cert. Advanced Life Support in Ob. Instr., The Am. Acad. of Family Physicians, 1998, Neonatal Resucitation Instr., Am. Acad. of Pediat./ Am. Heart Assn., 1989, Basic Life Support Instr., Am. Heart Assn., 1998. Staff nurse Toledo Hosp., Toledo, 1978—82, Flower Hosp., Sylvania, Ohio, 1982—97, Toledo Hosp., Toledo, 1986—97, 2004—; asst. nurse mgr. St. Vincent Hosp., Toledo, 1997—98, staff nurse, 1998—2004. Day care educator Day Cares, Toledo, 1997—2002. Mem.: NACC, ACNM, Assn. Women's Health Obstetric and Neonatal Nurses (cert. prins. and practices fetal monitoring instr. 2005), Bus. and Profl. Women (assoc.), Sigma Theta Tau/Zeta Theta Chpt. (Clin. Practice Award 2002). Home: 3314 Stanhope Dr Toledo OH 43606 Office: Toledo Hosp 2142 N Cove Toledo OH 43607 Home Phone: 419-536-1464; Office Phone: 419-291-4325.

FRANCIS, CHARLES K., medical educator; b. Newark, May 24, 1939; BA, Dartmouth Coll., 1961; MD, Jefferson Med. Coll., 1965. Med. intern Phila. Gen. Hosp., 1965—66; med. resident Boston City Hosp., Tufts U., 1969—70; clin. fellow cardiology Tufts Circulation Lab., 1970—71; clin. and rsch. fellow cardiology Mass. Gen. Hosp., 1971—72, sr. med. resident, 1972-73; chief cardiac catheterization lab. divsn. cardiology Martin Luther King Jr. Gen. Hosp., LA, 1973—74, chief cardiology divsn., 1974—77; dir. cardiology divsn. Mt. Sinai Hosp., Hartford, Conn., 1977—80; assoc. dir. hypertension svc., assoc. prof. medicine, dir. cardiac catheterization lab. Yale Med. Sch., Hartford, Conn., 1980-87; dir. dept. medicine Harlem Hosp. Ctr., NYC, 1987—98; prof. clin. medicine Columbia U. Coll. Physicians and Surgeons, 1987—98; pres. Charles R. Drew U. Med. and Sci., 1998—. Clin. instr. medicine Sch. Medicine Tufts U., 1970—71; tchg. fellow Harvard Med. Sch., 1971—72, clin. fellow, 1972—73; asst. prof. medicine Charles R. Drew Postgrad. Med. Sch. & Sch. Medicine U. Calif., 1973—75; asst. prof. medicine, dir. Burgdorf Hypertension Clin., Med. Sch. U. Conn., 1977—80; mem. cardiac adv. com. Nat. Heart, Lung & Blood Inst., NIH, 1977—79; asst. prof. medicine Sch. Medicine Yale U., 1980—81, assoc. prof., 1981—87; pres. Am. Coll. of Physicians, 2004—05. Fellow: ACP, Am. Coll. Cardiology; mem.: Assn. Black Cardiologists (chmn. bd. 1994—), Am. Heart Assn., Am. Fedn. Clin. Rsch., Inst. Medicine-NAS. Address: Charles Drew U Med & Sci 1621 E 120th St Los Angeles CA 90059-3025

FRANCIS, EDWARD D., architect; b. Cleve., Aug. 15, 1934; s. Michael and Anna (Buchinsky) F.; m. Betty-Lee Seydler, Aug. 25, 1956 (div. 1982); children— Tameron, Theron; m. Lynne Marie Merrill, Sept. 6, 1984. B.Arch, Miami U., 1957. Draftsman, designer David Maxfield, Oxford, Ohio, 1953-59; draftsman Austin Co., Cleve., summers 1954, 56; designer Meathe, Kessler & Assoc., Grosse Pointe, Mich., 1959-68; prin. William Kessler & Assoc., Detroit, 1968—, pres., 1985-95, Kessler Assoc. Inc., 1995-99; CEO Kessler/Francis/Cardoza Architects, 1999—2004; prin. Gunn Levine Archs., Detroit, 2004—. Archtl. adv. com. Ferris State U., Big Rapids, Mich. Chmn. Franklin Village Hist. Commn., Mich., 1971-79; pres. Friends of Capitol, Lansing, 1984-85, State Hist. Preservation Rev. Bd., 1984-94. Fellow AIA (Gold medal Detroit and Mich. chpts.); mem. Frank Lloyd Wright Found., Frank Lloyd Wright Preservation Trust, Nat. Trust for Hist. Preservation, Mich. Hist. Preservation Network (Lifetime Achievement award 2001), Gabriel Richard Hist. Soc. (bd. dirs.). Office: Gunn Levine Archs 726 Lothrop Detroit MI 48202 Home Phone: 313-393-0103; Office Phone: 313-873-3868. Business E-Mail: edwardf@gunnlevine.com.

FRANCIS, GEORGIA, music educator; Music/band instr. Charlotte Amalie (VI) H.S., 1981—. Named St. Thomas-St. John Tchr. of Yr., 2005, VI Tchr. of Yr., 2006. Office: Charlotte Amalie High Sch PO Charlotte Amalie Charlotte Amalie VI 00802*

FRANCIS, GREGORY R., lieutenant governor; m. Cheryl Francis; 4 children. Student, U. VI, 1984. VI dir. Office Vets. Affairs, 1999—2001; adminstr. St. Croix, 2001—06; lt. gov. Ter. of VI, 2007—; commr. VI Divsn. Banking & Ins., 2007—. Chair dist. St. Croix VI Dem. Party; mem. VI del. Nat. Dem. Conv., Boston, 2004. Mem. Yesterday, Today, Tomorrow Emancipation Com., Crusaders Fraternity, Inc., Red Brick Reading Club, Ballet Folkorico Hispanos Unidos; founder Friends Helping Friends Fitness Club; vol. Boy Scouts and Girl Scouts of Am. Command prog. support specialist US Army, supervisory mil. personal specialist US Army, recruiting and retention mgr. US Army, chief warrant officer 4 US Army, 1999. Decorated Army Meritorious Svc. medal, Army Commendation medal, Army Achievement medal, Army Good Conduct medal, Army Res. Components Achievement medal, Nat. Def. Svc. medal, Humanitarian Svc. medal, Armed Forces Res. medal, Silver Hourglass, Army Svc. Ribbon, Oversees Svc. Ribbon. Mem.: Vets. Svc. Orgn., Myron G. Danielson Am. Legion Post 85 (first vice comdr.), King Soloman Grand Lodge (dep. dist. grand master), Caribbean Lodge (pearl). Office: Office Lt Gov 1131 King Street Ste 101 Christiansted VI 00820 Office Phone: 340-773-6449. Office Fax: 340-773-0330. E-mail: Gregory.francis@lgo-vi.gov.*

FRANCIS, JAMES DELBERT, oil industry executive; b. Orange, NJ, Jan. 8, 1947; s. Delbert Matthew and Margaret Janet F.; m. Shirley Ann Waters; children: Elizabeth M., John A., David S., Virginia a., Grace A., J. Thornley. BS in Commerce, U. Va., 1970; JD, U. Fla., 1973. Bar: Fla. 1973. Ptnr. Smith and Hulsey, Jacksonville, Fla., 1973-82; exec. v.p. Charter Oil Co., Fla., 1982-83, pres. Fla., 1983-86; chmn., CEO Ray Distbg. Co., 1987—; ptnr. First Coast Energy, LLP, 1997—. Bd. dirs. Petro Distbg., Inc.

Bd. dirs., chmn. Children's Home Soc., Jacksonville, 1976-2003; elder St. Johns Presbyn. Ch., 1985—; pres. CHS Found., Inc., 2000-03; trustee Riverside Presbyn. Day Sch., 2001-02; bd. trustee The Bolles Sch., 2005-; bd. dirs. Seamark Ranch, Christian Healing Ministries, 2004-. Mem. ABA, Fla. Bar, Jacksonville Bar Assn., Fla. Yacht Club, River Club (Jacksonville), Timuquana Country Club. Republican. Home: 4284 Mcgirts Blvd Jacksonville FL 32210-4368 Address: First Coast Energy LLP 7014 A C Skinner Pkwy Ste 290 Jacksonville FL 32256-6940

FRANCIS, JAMES STEPHEN, JR., psychology professor, psychologist; b. Norwalk, Conn., Sept. 29, 1945; s. James Stephen and Elaine Fiske Francis; m. Sandra Maria Eisworth, Oct. 18, 1951; children: James Stephen III, Grover Magee. BA, U. Miami, 1969, MS, 1972, PhD, 1975. Instr. lab U. Miami, Coral Gables, 1970—75; rsch. assoc. Miami Heart Inst., Miami Beach, 1974—76, VA Hosp., Columbia, SC, 1976—77; asst. prof. U. Houston, 1977—80; prof. San Jacinto Coll., 1989—. Adj. asst. prof. Alvin Coll., Tex., 1980—89. Contbr. articles to profl. jours. Mem.: APA, Psi Beta (faculty advisor 1998—2005), Phi Delta Theta (pres. 1967—68). Democrat. Roman Catholic. Achievements include development of Internet Psychology Courses. Avocations: tennis, jogging, travel, teaching, reseach. Home: 2319 Colleen Dr Pearland TX 77581 Office: San Jacinto Coll 13735 Beamer Rd Houston TX 77089 Home Phone: 281-485-6993; Office Phone: 281-484-1900. Office Fax: 281-929-4693; Home Fax: 281-485-6993. Personal E-mail: jfphd@sbcglobal.net. Business E-Mail: james.francis@sjcd.edu.

FRANCIS, JEROME LESLIE, lawyer; b. Seattle, May 25, 1941; s. Leslie J. and Phyllis G. (Pike) F.; m. Jen H. Hough, Nov. 2, 1968; children: David S., Catherine E. BA in Bus. Adminstrn., U. WAsh., 1963; JD, San Francisco Law Sch., 1968. Bar: Mass. 1970. Sole practice, Sudbury, Mass., 1970-74; atty. legal dept. Texaco Inc., Boston, 1974-76, Cherry Hill, N.J., 1976-84, Denver, 1984-89; sr. atty. Star Enterprise (Texaco-SRI), Houston, 1989-98; atty. legal dept. Equiva Svcs. (Texaco-Shell-SRI), Houston, 1998—2002; ret. Mem. ABA, Mass. Bar Assn. Republican. Episcopalian. E-mail: jfrancis4@houston.rr.com.

FRANCIS, JULIE, beverage company executive; d. Butch and Tonie. BBA, Alfred U., 1993. Dir. mktg. Rabun, Hatch & Assoc., Atlanta, 1993—95; key account category mgr. Coca-Cola Enterprises, Atlanta, 1995—96, key account mgr., 1996—97, market devel. mgr. NY divsn. NY, 1998—99, dir. sales NY divsn. NY, 1998—99, sales ctr. mgr. NY divsn. NY, 1999—2001, area v.p. Eastern Great Lakes divsn. Rochester, NY, 2001—02, area v.p. Lakeshore divsn., 2002—04, v.p., gen. mgr. Midwest Bus. Unit, 2005—. Named one of 40 Under 40, Crain's Chgo. Bus., 2005. Office: Coca-Cola Enterprises 2500 Windy Ridge Parkway Atlanta GA 30339

FRANCIS, KAREN, painter, television producer, writer; b. Memphis, Apr. 27, 1950; BA in Comm. Arts, Rhodes Coll., 1971; MA, U. Mo., 1973. Cert. tchr., Tenn. Secondary sch. tchr. Memphis City Schs., 1971-72; speech tchr. U. Ga., Athens, 1973-75; dir. computer systems installations Planning Rsch. Corp., McLean, Va., 1976-78; dir. account mgmt. TDX Systems, Cable & Wireless, Vienna, Va., 1978-80; cons. telecommunications MCI, Washington, 1985-87; producer Fairfax Cable Access, Merrifield, Va., 1991-96. Owner Art Promotions, 1989—. Exhibited paintings in numerous group and one-woman shows and in cyberspace including Mus. Contemporary Art, Washington, 1996, Arts Coun. Fairfax County, Va., 1999, many others; paintings numerous pvt. collections; author screenplay Sisters, 2003. Founder Non-Violence Award Program, 1998; bd mem., vol. several non profit cmty. orgns. Avocations: bridge, poetry, piano. Office Phone: 901-289-4939, 901-752-5029. E-mail: kfrancis427@bellsouth.net.

FRANCIS, LYNNE ANN, elementary school and music educator; b. Parkersburg, W.Va., May 18, 1961; d. Gale Meyer and Mabel Eileen Hains; m. Randal Craig Francis, June 17, 1989; 1 child, Brent. MusB, SUNY, Fredonia, 1982, MusM, 1984. Cert. Pathwise mentor, music tchr. Ohio, N.Y., W.Va., lic. supr. Ohio, supr., prin. and supt. W.Va. Summer employee E.I. DuPont, Washington, W.Va., 1980—82; music specialist elem. sch. Marietta City Schs., Ohio, 1984—2007; tchr. adaptive music for spl. learners. Owner Edendale Jewelry Designs; freelance harpist, Marietta, Ohio, 1982—2000; lectr. in field. Mem.: NEA, W.Va. Music Edn. Assn., Music Educators Nat. Conf., Ohio Edn. Assn., Sigma Alpha Iota. Avocations: crocheting, music, counted cross stitch, photography, computers, jewelry design. Home: 165 Edendale Ln Parkersburg WV 26101 Office Phone: 740-374-6500. Personal E-mail: wvharpo@core.com.

FRANCIS, MARION DAVID, consulting chemist; b. Campbell River, BC, Can., May 9, 1923; arrived in U.S., 1949; s. George Henry and Marian (Flanagan) F.; m. Emily Liane Williams, Aug. 27, 1949 (dec. 1995); children: William Randall, Patricia Ann; m. Jacqueline S. Lohman, June 14, 1997. BA, U. B.C., Vancouver, 1946, MA, 1949; PhD, U. Iowa, 1953. Instr. U. B.C., Vancouver, Canada, 1946—49; chemist Can. Fishing Co., Vancouver, Canada, 1946; rsch. asst. U. Iowa, Iowa City, 1949—51; rsch. chemist Procter & Gamble Co., Cin., 1952—76, sr. scientist, 1976—85, Norwich Eaton Pharms., Inc., Norwich, NY, 1985-89; rsch. fellow Victor Mills Soc., Cin., 1990-93; cons. Cin., 1993—. Chmn. Gordon Rsch. Conf., N.H., 1968, 79, session chmn., 1985; panel mem. Internat. Conf. on Crystal Deposition and Dissolution in Tissues, Evion, France, 1985; session chmn. workshop, Sienna, Italy, 1992; co-chmn. Bisphosphonate Therapies for Osteoporosis: Today and Tomorrow Symposium, Davos, Switzerland, 1996, 2006, chmn. Internat. Conf. on Phosphorus Chemistry, Cin., 1998, others; session chmn. Internat. Congress on Arts and Comms., Lisbon, Portugal, 1999, Washington, 2000, Cambridge, Eng., 2001, Vancouver, B.C., 2002, Dublin, 2004, Honolulu, 2005; spkr. and lectr. in field. Contbr. articles to sci. jours.; patentee in field. Dist. chmn. Cin. United Appeal, 1956-60. Recipient Profl. Accomplishment award Tech. and Sci. Socs. Cin., 1979, Tech. Innovation award Victor Mills Soc., 1990, Perkin medal Soc. of Chem. Industry, 1996, Disting. Alumnus Achievement award U. Iowa Carver Coll. Medicine, 2003; U.S. Pub. Health predoctoral fellow, 1951-52. Fellow AAAS, Am. Inst. Chemists; mem. Am. Soc. Bone and Mineral Rsch., Am. Chem. Soc. (program chmn. ctrl. regional meeting 1983, invited symposium spkr. nat. meeting 1987, 92, invited awards symposium spkr. 1994, Cin. Chemist of Yr. award 1977, Nat. Indsl. Chemist award 1994, Morley medal 1996, Heros of Chemistry award 2000), Am. Coll. Rheumatologists, Dance Club (pres. 1972-73), Wyo. (Ohio) Sunday Supper Club (pres. 1998-99, 2003-04). Republican. Roman Catholic. Home and Office: 23 Diplomat Dr Cincinnati OH 45215-2074 Office Phone: 513-772-3940. Office Fax: 513-772-3039. Personal E-mail: mfrancis3@cinci.rr.com.

FRANCIS, MARY FRANCES VAN DYKE, small business owner, real estate company executive, retired editor; b. Sedalia, Mo., Nov. 17, 1925; d. Frank B. and Mary Irene (Sims) Van Dyke; m. Harold E. Francis, Apr. 23, 1944 (div. 1980); children: David Eugene, Lois Irene Valero, Roland Wayne, Eric Brian. Student, Ctrl. Mo. State Coll. Tchr. grade sch. Pettis County, Mo., 1943-44; timekeeper Montgomery Ward & Co., Kansas City, Mo., 1944-45; instr. new operators Southwestern Bell Telephone Co., Independence, Mo., 1945-47; real estate salesman Russell Realtors, Independence, 1958-66; owner Mary Francis, Realtor, Independence, 1967—. Exec. sec., editor Ea. Jackson County Bd. Realtors, 1962-68; exec. asst., pub. rels. dir., editor Kansas City Realtor, 1968-71; mktg. asst. South Ctrl. region Chgo. Title Ins. Co., Kansas City, 1971-75; pres. Maranco, Inc., 1975-; v.p. Raintree Lake Realty, 1980-83. Contbr. articles to profl. jours. Den leader Boy Scouts Am. Recipient Outstanding Svc. award Ea. Jackson County Bd. Realtors, 1964, Salesmanship award, 1965, CPW Real Estate Exch. award, Expo, 1983. Mem. Nat. Assn. Real Estate Bds. (charter pres. Greater Kansas City chpt., gov., pres. Mo. Women's Coun.), Mo. Real Estate Assn. (Spkrs. Bur.), Soroptimist (past pres.), Metro Kansas City Assn. Realtors (life), Mo. Assn. Realtors (life). Address: PO Box 1158 Independence MO 64051-0658

FRANCIS, MICHAEL R., retail executive; Grad., U. Mich. Sr. v.p. mktg. Marshall Fields, 1995—96, sr. v.p. mktg. and visual mdse., 1996—2001; sr. v.p. mktg. Registrant, 2001—03; exec. v.p. mktg. Target Corp., Mpls., 2003—. Named one of 25 Masters of Innovation, BusinessWeek, 2006. Office: Target Corp 1000 Nicollet Mall Minneapolis MN 55403

FRANCIS, NORMAN C., academic administrator; b. Lafayette, La., Mar. 20, 1931; s. Joseph Abel and Mabel F.; m. Blanche MacDonald, June 6, 1955; children: Michael, Timothy, David, Kathleen, Patrick, Christine. BA, Xavier U. of La., 1952; JD, Loyola U., New Orleans, 1955; EdD (hon.), Villanova U., 1969; LLD (hon.), Holy Cross Coll., 1969, Seton Hall U., 1969, St. Michael's Coll., 1972, Marquette U., 1977. Dean of men Xavier U. of La., New Orleans, 1957-63, dir. student pers. svcs., 1963-64, asst. to pres. for student affairs, 1964-65, asst. to pres. for devel., 1965-67, exec. v.p., from 1968, pres., 1968—. Trustee Coll. Entrance Exam. Bd., 1972-76, chmn., 1976-78. Commr. New Orleans Civil Svc. Commn., 1969-76; former pres. Urban league New Orleans; former chmn. New Orleans Aviation Bd.; mem. Pontifical Peace & Justice Commn., 1977. Recipient Presdl. Medal of Freedom, 2006.*

FRANCIS, PHILIP HAMILTON, management consultant; b. San Diego, Apr. 13, 1938; s. William Samuel and Ruth Kathryn (Allison) F.; m. Regina Elizabeth Kirk, June 10, 1961 (div. May 1971); m. Diana Maria Villarreal, July 15, 1972; children: Philip Scott, Edward Philip, Mary Allison, Kenneth Joseph. BSME, Calif. Poly. State U., 1959; MSME, U. Iowa, 1960, PhD in Engring. Mechanics, 1965; MBA in Mgmt., St. Mary's U., San Antonio, 1972. Registered profl. engr., Tex. With Douglas Aircraft Co., Santa Monica, Calif., 1960-62, S.W. Rsch. Inst., San Antonio, 1965-79; prof., chmn. dept. mech. and aerospace engring. Ill. Inst. Tech., Chgo., 1979-84; with Indsl. Tech. Inst., Ann Arbor, Mich., 1984-86; dir. advanced mfg. tech. Motorola Inc., Schaumburg, Ill., 1986-88; corp. v.p. Square D Co. (Schneider-N.Am.), Palatine, Ill., 1988-94; client ptnr. AT&T Solutions, AT&T, Chgo., 1995-96; mng. ptnr. Mascon Global, Ltd., Schaumburg, Ill., 1996—2002; pres. Group Francis, LLC, Georgetown, Tex., 2001—; CEO IKnowWare, LC, 2006—. Adj. prof. engring. Northwestern U., 2003—. Mem. various indsl. and acad. adv. bds. Recipient Gustas Larson award ASME and Pi Tau Sigma, 1978 Fellow ASME; mem. Soc. Mfg. Engrs., Sigma Xi, Tau Beta Pi, Pi Tau Sigma. Roman Catholic. Avocation: writing. Office Phone: 512-868-9568. Business E-Mail: phil@groupfrancis.com.

FRANCIS, PHILIP L., retail executive; BS, U. Ill.; MBA, Ind. U. Sr. leadership positions Cardinal Health, Jewel Cos.; corp. v.p. wholesale Roundy's, Pewaukee, Wis., 1988—91; pres., COO Shaw's Supermkts., E. Bridgewater, Mass., 1991-98; dir. PetSmart Inc., Phoenix, 1989—, chmn., pres., CEO, 1999—2001, chmn., CEO, 1999—. Mem. Greater Phoenix Leadership. Office: PetsMart 19601 N 27th Ave Phoenix AZ 85027*

FRANCIS, RELL GARDNER, artist, photographer, writer; b. Lake Shore, Utah, Jan. 27, 1928; s. S. Evan and Barbara (Ferguson) F.; m. Janet Oaks Francis, July 18, 1958; children: Sean Francis, Lewis Francis, Dana Francis Lepore. BA, Brigham Young U., 1954, MA, 1963; postgrad., Ill. Sch. Design, Chgo., summer 1957, Ohio State U., summer 1968, U. Utah, 1968-69. Cert. tchr. Monument designer A.H. Child & Son Monuments, Springville, Utah, 1945-54; art and English tchr. Nebo Sch. Dist., Springville, 1954-74; home study art instr. Brigham Young U., Provo, Utah, 1964-70; photo tchr. European Art Acad., Paris, summer 1966; dir. art mus. Springville Mus. Art, 1976; dir. City Spirit art Nat. Endowment for Arts, Springville City, Utah, 1974-75; owner Photo Gallery, Heritage Prints Photography, Provo, 1977-90. Cons. photography Clio, Inc., NYC, 2001, PBS (Judy Crichton) Am. 1900, Boston, NYC, 1996-97; lectr. Cyrus E. Dallin at Rockwell Mus. Exhibit, Corning, NY, 1995; cons. Cyrus E. Dallin Art Mus., Arlington, Mass., 2000; photography advisor CLIO, Inc., NYC, 2000-01; vol. docent, guest exhibitor Utah photos SLC Cultural Olympiad, 2002. Author: Cyrus E. Dallin, 1976, The Utah Photographs of George Edward Anderson, 1979, C.E. Dallin: Frontier to Fame, 2005; film prodr.: Stoneman Sheepherder, 1969, Que Bonita, 1972; contbr. articles to profl. jours.; one-person show at Provo Utilities Gallery, Provo, 1969; exhibited in group shows at Springville Mus. Art, 1982, 88, LDS Ch. Mus. Art and History, Salt Lake City, 1985, Amon Carter Mus., Ft. Worth, 1979, Brigham Young U. and Springville Mus. Art, 1974, Segnali de Fumo, Italy, 1994; retrospective exhibit of Mex. photographs and paintings, Springville Mus. Art, 1999, Peteetneet Acad. Art, Payson, Utah, 2003. Trustee Springville Mus. Art, 1958-74; environ. activist Audubon Soc., Provo, 1995—; hon. vol. mentor Slate Canyon Youth Ctr. Program, Provo, 2000. Recipient Best of Show, photography Utah State Fair, 1966, 67, Meritorious Svc. award in photography Brigham Young U., Provo, 1974, Morris Rosenblatt award Utah Hist. Quar., Salt Lake City, 1976. Mem. Utah Hist. Soc., Springville Hist. Soc. (trustee 1975-2001, 2003-06, honored as Springville's Most Notable Historian 2007). Mem. Lds Ch. Avocation: poetry. Home: 750 E Chase Ln Springville UT 84663-2053 E-mail: relljanet@msn.com.

FRANCIS, RON, professional sports team executive, retired professional hockey player; b. Sault Ste Marie, Ont., Can., Mar. 1, 1963; m. Mary Lou Francis; children: Kaitlyn, Michael, Connor. Center Hartford Whalers (now Carolina Hurricanes), 1981—91, Pitts. Penguins, 1991-98, Carolina Hurricanes, 1998—2004, Toronto Maple Leafs, 2004—05; dir player devel. Carolina Hurricanes, 2006—. Player NHL All-Star game, 1983, 85, 90, 96. Recipient Frank J. Selke Trophy, 1995, Lady Byng Trophy, 1995, 1998, 2002, King Clancy Memorial Trophy, 2002, Stanley Cup Champion, 1991, 1992. Achievements include being a member of Stanley Cup Champion Pitts. Penguins, 1991, 1992; having his number, 10, retired by Carolina Hurricanes, 2006. Office: c/o Carolina Hurricanes RBC Ctr 1400 Edwards Mill Rd Raleigh NC 27607

FRANCIS, STEVE, professional basketball player; Owner We R One Clothing; profl. basketball player Houston Rockets, 1999—2004, Orlando Magic, 2004—06, NY Knicks, 2006—07, Portland Trail Blazers, Oreg., 2007—. Named to NBA All-Star Game, 2002—06. Office: Portland Trail Blazers Rose Quarter One Center Ct Portland OR 97227

FRANCIS, TIMOTHY DUANE, chiropractor; b. Chgo., Mar. 1, 1956; s. Joseph Duane and Barbara Jane (Sigwalt) F. Student, U. Nev., 1974—80, We. Nev. C.C., 1978; BS, L.A. Coll. Chiropractic, 1982, DC magna cum laude, 1984; postgrad., Clark County C.C., 1986—; MS in Bio/Nutrition, U. Bridgeport, 1990. Diplomate Internat. Coll. Applied Kinesiology, Am. Acad. Pain Mgmt., Am. Naturopathic Med. Bd.; cert. kinesiologist, applied kinesiology tchr.; lic. chiropractor, Calif., Nev. Instr. dept. recreation and phys. edn. U. Nev., Reno, 1976-80; from tchng. asst. to lead instr. dept. principles & practice L.A. Coll. Chiropractic, 1983-85; pvt. practice Las Vegas, 1985—. Asst. instr. Internat. Coll. Applied Kinesiology, 1990, chmn. exam review com., 1993, chmn. syllabus review com., 1994; adj. faculty The Union Inst. Coll. of Undergrad. Studies, 1993; joint study participant Nat. Olympic Tng. Ctr., Beijing, China, 1990. Mem. editl. rev. bd. Alternative Medicine Rev., 1996; contbr. articles to profl. jours. including Internat. Coll. Applied Kinesiology. Charles F. Cutts scholar, 1980. Fellow Internat. Acad. Clin. Acupuncture, British Inst. Homeopathy (homeopathy diploma 1993); mem. Am. Chiropractic Assn. (couns. on sports injuries, nutrition, roentgenology, technic, and mental health), Nev. State Chiropractic Assn., Nat. Strength and Conditioning Assn., Gonsted Clin. Studies Soc., Found. for Chiropractic Edn. and Rsch., Internat. Chiropractors Assn., Internat. Coll. Applied Kinesiology, Internat. Fedn. Practitioners Natural Therapeutics, Nat. Inst. Chiropractic Rsch., Nat. Strength and Conditioning Assn., Am. Naturopathic Med. Assn., Nat. Acad. Rsch. Biochemists, Phi Beta Kappa, Phi Kappa Phi (v.p. 1979-80, Scholar of the Yr. award, 1980), Delta Signa. Republican. Roman Catholic. Avocations: Karate, weightlifting. Home: 7473 Lake Mead Blvd Las Vegas NV 89128 Office Phone: 702-221-8870.

FRANCIS, WARREN WILLIAM, retired surgeon, educator; b. NYC, Sept. 10, 1924; Grad., Princeton U., 1944; MD, Columbia U., 1948. Diplomate Am. Bd. Surgery. Intern Lenox Hill Hosp., NYC, 1948-50; resident surgery R.I. Hosp., Providence, 1952-56, surgeon, 1956-97; surg. cons. Women & Infants Hosp., 1986-97; clin. assoc. prof. surgery Brown U., 1983-97, ret., 1997. Med. officer USNR, 1950-52. Fellow ACS; mem. EVS, New Eng. Surge. Soc., NESVS.

FRANCISCO, GLEN LEIF, engineer, engineering executive; b. Little Falls, NY, Sept. 9, 1953; s. Lawrence Richard Francisco and Beatrice Wilson Love; m. Kimberly Ann Luebbert, Aug. 18, 1979 (div.); children: Melissa Jane, Grant Alan. BS in Aero./Astro Engring., Rensselaer Poly. Inst., 1975; MS in Aero./Astro Engring., MIT, 1977; MBA in Data Processing, Fla. Inst. Tech., 1984. Rsch. asst. MIT, Cambridge, 1975—77; guidance & control engr. MCDonnell Aircraft Co., St. Louis, 1977—80; sys. engr. Martin Marietta, Orlando, Fla., 1980—95; sys. engring. mgr. Tex. Instruments, Dallas, 1995—99; program mgr. Raytheon Comml. Infrared, Dallas, 1999—2004; bus./product devel. mgr. L-3 Comm. Infrared Products, Dallas, 2004—. Home: 424 Sloan Creek Pky Fairview TX 75069 Office: L3 Comm Infrared Products MS 37 13532 N Central Expy Dallas TX 75243 Office Phone: 972-528-1407. Business E-Mail: glen.francisco@L-3Com.com.

FRANCK, THOMAS MARTIN, law educator; b. Berlin, July 14, 1931; naturalized, 1977; s. Hugo and Ilse (Rosenthal) F. BA, U. B.C., 1952, LLB, 1953, LLD (hon.), 1995; LLM, Harvard U., 1954, SJD, 1956; DHL (hon.), Monterey Inst. Internat. Studies, 2003; LLD (hon.), U. Glasgow, 2004. Asst. prof. law U. Nebr., 1954-56; from assoc. prof. to prof. law NYU, 1960—2002, prof. law emeritus, 2002—, dir. Ctr. Internat. Studies, 1965—2002; judge ad hoc Internat. Ct. Justice, 2001—02. Acting dir. internat. law Carnegie Endowment Internat. Peace, 1973-75, dir., 1975-79; vis. prof. Stanford U., 1963, U. East Africa, 1964, 65, York U., 1972-73, 74-76, U. Calif., San Francisco, 2004, Georgetown U. Law Ctr., 2006; dir. rsch. UN Inst. Tng. and Rsch., 1980-82; cons. U.S. AID Dept. State, 1970-72, 85; constl. adviser govts. Tanganyika, 1963, Zanzibar, 1963, 64, Mauritius, 1965; mem. Sierra Leone Govt. Commn. Legal Edn., 1964, Nat. Liberal Adv. Coun. Can., 1952-53; lectr.in field; vis. fellow Trinity Coll., Cambridge, Eng., 1996-97. Author: Race and Nationalism, 1960, The United Nations in the Congo, 1963, East African Unity Through Law, 1965, Comparative Constitutional Process, 1968, The Structure of Impartiality, 1968, Why Federations Fail, 1968, A Free Trade Association, 1968, Word Politics, 1971, Secrecy and Foreign Policy, 1973, Resignation in Protest, 1975, Control of Sea Resources by Semi-Autonomous States, 1978, Foreign Policy by Congress, 1979, The Tethered Presidency, 1981, Human Rights in Third World Perspective, 1982, Nation Against Nation: What Happened to the U.N. Dream and What the U.S. Can Do About It, 1985, Judging the World Court, 1986, Foreign Relations and National Security Law, 1987, The Power of Legitimacy Among Nations, 1990, Political Questions/Judicial Answers, 1992, Fairness in the International Legal and Institutional System, 1993, Fairness In International Law and Institutions, 1995, The Empowered Self: Law and Society in the Age of Individualism, 1999, Recourse to Force: State Action Against Threats and Armed Attacks, 2002; co-author: U.S. Foreign Relations Law, vols. I-III, 1980-81, vols. IV & V, 1984, Foreign Relations and National Security Law, 2d edit., 1993; editor-in-chief Am. Jour. Internat. Law, 1984-93; editor: Delegating State Powers: The Effect of Treaty Regimes on Democracy and Sovereignty, 2000; co-editor: Internat. Law Decisions in Nat. Cts., 1996. Lt. Can. Army, 1953. Guggenheim fellow, 1973-74, 82-83. Mem. Inst. de Droit Internat., State Dept. Adv. Com. on Internat. Law, Can. Coun. Internat. Law, Assn. Am. Law Schs., Am. Soc. Internat. Law (pres. 1998-2000), Am. Acad. Arts and Scis., Internat. Law Assn. (v.p. U.S. br.), Coun. on Fgn. Rels. Home: 15 Charlton St New York NY 10014-4910 Office Phone: 212-998-6209.

FRANCK, WALTER ALFRED, rheumatologist, medical educator, health facility administrator; b. Shanghai, Sept. 2, 1941; s. August Albert and Hilda Sylvia (Vandamme) F.; m. Linda Ashley Callanen, June 6, 1964; children: Christopher, Patrick, Kevin, Natalee. BA, Yale U., 1960; MD, Columbia U., 1964. Intern U. Mich., Ann Arbor, 1964-65, resident in medicine, 1965-68; fellow in rheumatology Harvard U./Mass. Gen. Hosp., Boston, 1971-73; attending physician in medicine and rheumatology Mary Imogene Bassett Hosp., Cooperstown, NY, 1973—, chief of medicine, 1980—; prof. clin. medicine Columbia U., NYC, 1981—, assoc. dean Bassett Healthcare-Coll. Physicians and Surgeons, 1998—. Adj. prof. clin. medicine Rochester (N.Y.) Sch. Medicine, Albany (N.Y.) Sch. Medicine, Hanover, N.Y., SUNY, Syracuse. Contbr. numerous articles to profl. publs. Trustee, mem. fin. com. St. Mary's Ch., Cooperstown, 1991—. Maj. U.S. Army, 1968-71. Fellow ACP, Am. Coll. Rheumatology. Roman Catholic. Avocations: stamp collecting/philately, gardening, fishing, hiking. Home: 6 Lakeview Dr S Cooperstown NY 13326-3003 Office: Bassett Hosp 1 Atwell Rd Cooperstown NY 13326-1394 Home Phone: 607-547-2232; Office Phone: 607-547-3110. Business E-Mail: walter.franck@bassett.org.

FRANCKE, LINDA BIRD, journalist; b. NYC, Mar. 14, 1939; d. Samuel Curtis and Janet (King) Bird; m. G.D. Mackenzie, Jan. 12, 1961; 1 son, Andrew Mackenzie; m. Albert Francke III, Oct. 7, 1967; 2 daughters: Caitlin, Tapp. Student, Bradford Jr. Coll., 1958, New Sch. for Social Rsch., 1963—65. Copywriter Young & Rubicam, Inc., NYC, 1960-63, Ogilvy & Mather, Inc., NYC, 1965-67; contbg. editor N.Y. Mag., NYC, 1968-72, 80—; gen. editor Newsweek Mag., NYC, 1972-77; columnist N.Y. Times, 1977—; TV news commentator Spl. Edit., 1978-79. Dir. New Directions; juror Am. Book Awards, 1981; Co-chmn. Writer's Resource Center, Southampton, N.Y. Contbr. (works to anthologies including) The N.Y. Spy, 1967, The Power Game, 1970, Running Against the Machine, 1969, Women: A Book for Men, 1979, Hers: Through Women's Eyes, 1985, America Firsthand, Vol. II: From Reconstruction to the Present, 1994; author: The Ambivalence of Abortion, 1978, Growing Up Divorced, 1983, Ground Zero: The Gender Wars in the Military, 1997; collaborator: First Lady from Plains, 1984, Ferraro: My Story, 1985, A Woman of Egypt, 1987, Daughter of Destiny, 1989, Signature Life, 1998, Life So Far, 2000, On Faith, 2002, On The Road With Francis of Assisi: A Timeless Journey Through Umbria and Tuscany, and Beyond, 2005. Mem. Women's Commn. for Refugee Women and Children, Internat. Rescue Com. Inc.; chmn. East End Choice; candidate N.Y. State Assembly, 2d Dist., 1990; del. to Dem. Nat. Conv., 1992; bd. dirs. Bridgehampton Child Care & Recreational Ctr., Inc., The Retreat. Recipient award Cannes Film Festival, 1969, Nat. Clarion award, 1994; finalist Helen Bernstein Book award Excellence in Journalism, 1998. Mem. Authors Guild, Women's Media Group N.Y.C., Eastville Hist. Soc., Women Mil. Aviators, Inc. E-mail: linda@hamptons.com.

FRANCKE, REND RAHIM, former ambassador; b. Baghdad, Iraq, 1949; arrived in U.S., 1981, naturalized, 1987; d. Mahdi Rahim; m. Frederic B. Francke. MA in English, U. Cambridge; MA in French Lit., Sorbonne.

Co-founder The Iraqi Found., Washington, 1991—2003, dir., 1991—2003; amb. Iraq Washington, 2003—06. Co-author: The Arab Shi'a: Forgotten Muslims, 2000. Office: The Iraq Found 1012 14th St NW Ste 1110 Washington DC 20005

FRANCKE, UTA, geneticist, educator; b. Wiesbaden, Germany, Sept. 9, 1942; arrived in U.S., 1969; d. Kurt and Gertrud Muller; m. Bertold Richard Francke, May 27, 1967 (div. 1982); m. Heinz Furthmayr, July 27, 1986. MD, U. Munich, Fed. Republic Germany, 1967; MS, Yale U., 1985. Diplomate Am. Bd. Pediatrics, Am. Bd. Med. Genetics (bd. dirs. 1981-84). Asst. prof. U. Calif., San Diego, 1973—78; assoc. prof. Yale U., New Haven, 1978—85, prof., 1985—88; prof. genetics Stanford (Calif.) U., 1989—. Investigator Howard Hughes Med. Inst., Stanford, 1989—2000, mem. sci. rev. bd., Bethesda, Md., 1986—88; mem. mammalian genetics study sect. NIH, Bethesda, 1990—94. Profl. advisor March of Dimes Birth Defects Found., White Plains, NY, 1990, Marfan Assn., Port Washington, NY, 1991. Mem.: Am. Soc. Human Genetics (pres. 1999, bd. dirs. Rockville, Md. chpt. 1981—84), Soc. for Inherited Metabolic Disorders, Soc. for Pediatric Rsch., Human Genome Orgn., Inst. Medicine of NAS (assoc.). Avocation: piloting. Office: Stanford U Med Sch Beckman Ctr Stanford CA 94305-5323 Office Phone: 650-725-8089. Business E-Mail: ufrancke@stanford.edu.

FRANCO, ADOLFO ALBERTO, former federal agency administrator; b. Cardenas, Matazanas, Cuba, Jan. 23, 1956; came to U.S., 1961; s. Adolfo M. and Miriam (Mesa) F. BA in History, U. No. Iowa, 1978, MA in History, 1980; JD cum laude, Creighton U., 1983. Bar: D.C. 1984, Mo. 1983. Atty. Shughart, Thomson & Kilroy, Kansas City, Mo., 1983-84, Cole & Corelte, P.A., Washington, 1984-85; dep. gen. counsel Inter-Am. Found., Arlington, Va., 1985-93, gen. counsel, 1993—99, pres., 1999—2000; asst. adminstr. Bur. Latin Am. & the Caribbean US Agy. Internat. Devel., Washington, 2002—07.*

FRANCO, CARLO DIAZ, surgeon, anatomist, anesthesiologist; b. Valparaiso, Chile, Nov. 9, 1956; came to U.S., 1985; s. Ismael Segundo and Aida Rosa (Franco-Huerta) Diaz-Labarca; m. Jennifer Ann Leepard, Mar. 31, 1989 (div. May 1993). MD, U. Valparaiso, Chile, 1981. Instr. anatomy Sch. of Medicine Univ. Valparaiso, Chile, 1982; surgery resident U. Valparaiso, Chile, 1982-85, asst. prof. anatomy, surgery, 1983—89; vis. prof. anatomy Med. Coll. of Ohio, Toledo, 1985-86, 88-89; surgeon, pvt. practice Valparaiso U. Hosp., Chile, 1986-89; surgery resident Sinai Hosp., Detroit, 1990-91, anesthesiology resident, 1991-94; chmn. orthopedic anesthesia Cook County Hosp., Chgo., 1994—; asst. prof. anesthesiology Rush Med. Coll., Chgo., 1997—2004, assoc. prof. anesthesiology and anatomy, 2004—. Contbr. articles to profl. jours. Grantee WHO, 1985-86, Ednl. Commn. for Foreign Med. Grads., 1988-89. Fellow AMA, Am. Soc. Anesthesiologists, Latin Am. Soc. Regional Anesthesia. Avocations: reading, writing, travel, tennis, ice skating. Home: 419 W Grand Ave # J Chicago IL 60610-4265 Office: Cook Co Hosp Dept Anesthesia 1901 W Harrison St Dept Chicago IL 60612-3785 Office Phone: 312-864-3217. Personal E-mail: carlofra@aol.com.

FRANCO, JAMES, actor; b. Palo Alto, Calif., Apr. 19, 1978; s. Doug and Betsy Franco. Owner Rabbit Bandini Productions. Actor: (TV series) Freaks and Geeks, 1999; (films) Never Been Kissed, 1999, Whatever It Takes, 2000, At Any Cost, 2000, If Tomorrow Comes, 2000, Some Body, 2001, James Dean, 2001, Blind Spot, 2001, Spider-Man, 2002, Deuces Wild, 2002, City by the Sea, 2002, Sonny, 2002, Mean People Suck, 2003, The Car Kid, 2003, Spider-Man 2, 2004, The Great Raid, 2005, Fool's Gold, 2005, Tristan & Isolde, 2006, Annapolis, 2006, The Wicker Man, 2006, Flyboys, 2006, Good Times Max, 2007, An American Crime, 2007, Finishing the Game, 2007, Camille, 2007, Spider-Man 3, 2007; exec. prodr., dir., writer: The Ape, 2004. Office: Miles Levy-James/Levy/Jacobson Mgmt 3500 W Olive Ave Ste 920 Burbank CA 91505*

FRANCO, OMAR, government agency administrator; b. Miami, Fla., Oct. 11, 1965; s. Israel and Gloria (Santamaria) F.; m. Adria Elena Sierra, Aug. 16, 1997; children: Alyssa Nicole and Andrew Joseph (twins). AA, Miami-Dade C.C., 1985; BA in English and Bus., Fla. State U., 1988; postgrad., Fla. Internat. U., 2002—. Registered legis. lobbyist, Notary Pub. Dist. legis. asst. Rep. Art Simon, Miami, 1993-94; campaign mgr. Annie Betancourt Re-election Campaign, Miami, 1996; dist. legis. asst. Rep. Annie Betancourt, Miami, 1994-96; dist. sr. legis. asst. Sen. Mario Diaz-Balart, Miami, 1996-98; field office dir. Fla. Med. Assn., Tallahassee, 1998-99; dir. govt. rels. Sch. Medicine, U. Miami, 1999—2001, asst. v.p. govtl. rels., 2001—03; chief of staff Congressman Mario Diaz-Balart, Washington, 2003—07; prin. Petrizzo Strategic Group, Washington, 2007—. Pub. policy and advocacy com. U. Miami Mailman Ctr., 2000—02; mem. Miami-Dade Alliance for Aging, 2003. Mem. Leadership Miami; mem. Hispanic Leadership Tng. Program Cuban Am. Nat. Coun., 1996; participant Call Us Essential, Call Us the Coll. initiative Miami-Dade Coll., 2003; mem. Nat. Hispanic Working Group, Bush-Cheney, 2004; mem. sr. adv. bd. Rep. Nat. Hispanic Assembly of Va., 2007—; mem. bd. dirs. Kendall Fedn. Homeowner's Assn., Miami, 1996—2000; v.p. Kendall Lakes Master Condominium Assn., Miami, 1998—2001; mem. steering com. Nat. Multiple Sclerosis Soc., Miami, 1998—99. Recipient Leadership award Nat. Multiple Sclerosis Soc., 1997. Mem. Am. Polit. Sci. Assn., Acad. Polit. Sci., Fla. Polit. Sci. Assn., Hispanic Lobbying Assn., Fla. State Soc., Rep. Associated for Mutual Support, NALEO (Fla. conf. host com.), Pi Sigma Alpha, Delta Sigma Pi, Sigma Phi Epsilon. Home: 12823 Dogwood Hills Lane Fairfax VA 22033 Office: Petrizzo Strategic Group 601 13th St NW Ste 370 S Washington DC 20005 Home Phone: 703-988-0206; Office Phone: 202-347-8787. E-mail: omar.franco@mail.house.gov, ofranco@petrizzostratebic.com.

FRANCO, VICTOR, theoretical physics educator; b. NYC, Dec. 15, 1937; s. Isaac and Regina (Ferezy) F.; m. Jieying Zong, Sept. 12, 1983; children: Zachary M., Anna L., Eugene R. BS, NYU, 1958; MA, Harvard U., 1959, PhD, 1964. Research assoc. MIT, Cambridge, 1963-65, Los Alamos Sci. Lab., 1965-67, Lawrence Radiation Lab., Berkeley, Calif., 1967-69; assoc. prof. Bklyn. Coll., 1969-72, prof., 1973—. Guest sci. Internat. Centre for Theoretical Physics, Trieste, 1970, 75; vis. staff mem. Los Alamos Nat. Lab., 1969-75; vis. physicist Lawrence Berkeley Lab., 1974; fgn. collaborator Centre d'Etudes Nucleaires, Saclay, France, 1975-76, 86; vis. sci. U. Trondheim, Norway, 1980, U. Alta., Can., 1982, U. Karlsruhe, Germany, 1985; vis. scholar U. Wash., Seattle, 1980; sr. rsch. assoc. Harvard U. Cambridge, 1983-84; NAS exch. scholar Inst. High Energy Physics, Beijing, China, 1984; guest prof. New Sch. Social Rsch., N.Y.C., 1988, 89; cons. in the field 1973—. Contbr. numerous articles to sci. jours. Recipient various fellowships and research grants Fellow Am. Phys. Soc.; mem. Sigma Xi Office: Brooklyn College Physics Dept Brooklyn NY 11210 Office Phone: 718-951-5000 2856. E-mail: vfranco@brooklyn.cuny.edu.

FRANCOEUR, CHRISTINA, special education educator; b. Springfield, Mass., Dec. 24, 1951; d. John Harry and Santa Martha (Pescetta) Malmborg; m. William John Weckerly; children: Lida Marie Powell, Danel Susan Eitel. BA, Westfield State Coll., 1998, MEd, 2000; cert. in Advanced Grad. Studies, Our Lady of the Elms, 2004. Spl. edn. tchr. Paper Mill Elem. Sch., Westfield, Mass., 1998—. With USAF. Mem.: Phi Kappa Phi. Roman Catholic. Avocations: snow shoeing, cross country skiing, reading, swimming, aerobics. E-mail: cwec@comcast.net.

FRANCOEUR, SHEILA T., state representative; b. Lowell, Mass., Feb. 18, 1938; m. Ronald Francoeur; two children. BA, Fla. State U., 1971. Banker, ret. 1993; ret., 1993; mem. dist. 15 N.H. Ho. of Reps., 1996—. Mem., chmn. econ. devel. com., City of Hampton; mem. vice-chmn. policy bldg. study com.; mem. mcpl. budget com.; spkr. Pro Tem, 2003-04. Bd. dirs. Leadership Seacoast; dir. Rockingham Econ. Development Corp.; chmn. Commerce Com., 2005. Mem. Rotary (v.p., bd. dirs.), AAUW (treas., bd. dirs.). Roman Catholic. Home: 88 Kings Hwy Hampton NH 03842-4317 Office: NH State Legis State House Concord NH 03301 E-mail: sheila.francoeur@leg.state.nh.us.

FRANCOIS, FRANCIS BERNARD, retired professional society administrator, lawyer, transportation consultant; b. Barnum, Iowa, Jan. 21, 1934; s. Rudolph John and Irene Frances (McDonough) F.; m. Eileen M. Schmelzer, Feb. 6, 1960; children: Joseph, Marie, Michael, Monica, Susan. BS, Iowa State U.; LL.B., George Washington U. Bar: Md. 1960, U.S. Patent and Trademark Office. Chief judge Orphan's Ct. Prince George's County, Upper Marlboro, Md., 1962-66; commr. Prince George's County, Upper Marlboro, Md., 1966-71, councilman, 1971-80; exec. dir. Am. Assn. State Hwy. and Transp. Ofcls., Washington, 1980-99; retired; chmn. Md. Transp. Commn., 2002—03. Adv. com. Ctr. Transp. Studies, MIT, 1983-99; mem. adv. panel White House Intergovtl. Sci. and Engring. Tech., 1976-80; mem. Washington Suburban Transit Commn., 1978-80, chmn., 1979; dir. Washington Met. Area Transit Authority, 1978-80; exec. com. Transp. Rsch. Bd., 1980-99, Strategic Hwy. Rsch. Program, 1986-92; mem. permanent internat. commn. Permanent Internat. Assn. Rd. Congresses, 1990-99; bd. dirs. Internat. Rd. Fedn., 1991-99, Nat. Ctr. for Asphalt Tech., 1991-99, Intelligent Transp. Soc. Am., 1991—, chmn., 1992-93; chmn. Md. Transp. Commn., 2002-03, lectr. in field. Contbr. articles to profl. jours. Mem. adv. coun. Nat. Cmty. Energy Mgmt. Ctr., 1981-82; mem. local govt. energy policy adv. com. Dept. of Energy, 1979-80; vice chmn. Md. Potomac Water Authority, 1970-80; air quality control adv. coun. State of Md., 1975-80; chmn. Water Resources Planning Bd., 1975-77; mem. Gov.'s Interstate Water Quality Planning Com., 1973-74; v.p. Md. Com. for Fair Representation, 1962; counselor Washington Career Inst., 1963; bd. dirs. Bowie Jaycees, Bowie Fine Arts Soc., Bowie YMCA; trustee Md. Easter Seal Soc., Prince George's United Way, Md. Soc. Crippled Children and Adults. Recipient Cmty. Svc. award Nat. Capital chpt. ASCE, 1980, Cmty. Svc. award Bowie Jaycees, 1980, Cmty. Svc. award Cedar Heights Civic Assn., 1978, Profl. Achievement on Engring. award Iowa State U., 1984, W.N. Carey Jr. Disting. Svc. award Transp. Rsch. Bd., 1990; named Washingtonian of Yr. Washingtonian Mag., 1973; Theodore M. Matson Meml. award, Am. Assn. State Hwy. and Transp. Ofcls., Am. Rd. and Transp. Builders Assn., Fed. Hwy. Adminstrn., Am. Hwy. Users Alliance, Inst. Transp. Engrs., Matson Meml. Assocs., and Transp. Rsch. Bd., 1993; Pioneer award Conf. Minority Transp. Ofcls., 1995, Chi Epsilon, Nat. Civil Engring Honor Soc., 1995, Anson Marston Alumni medal for achievements in engring. Iowa State U., 2003, Frank Turner medal Transp. Rsch. Bd., 2007. Mem. Nat. Assn. Counties (pres. 1979-80), Nat. Assn. Regional Coun. (pres. 1972-73), Washington Met. Coun. Govts. (dir. 1966-80, pres. 1971), Cmty. Assns. Inst. (dir. 1975-80, pres. 1979-80), Cosmos Club, K.C., Chi Epsilon. Democrat. Roman Catholic. Home and Office: 2512 Q St NW Washington DC 20007 E-mail: francis@francois.org.

FRANCOIS, WILLIAM ARMAND, lawyer; b. Chgo., May 31, 1942; s. George Albert and Evelyn Marie (Smith) F.; m. Barbara Ann Sala, Aug. 21, 1965; children: Nicole Suzanne, Robert William. BA, DePaul U., 1964, JD, 1967. Bar: Ill. 1967. Pvt. practice, Lyons, Ill., 1967-68; with Am. Nat. Can Group, Inc., Chgo., 1970, sec., 1974, v.p., 1978, sr. v.p., gen. counsel, sec., 1999-2000; dep. gen. counsel N.Am. Pechiney Group, 1996-99; pvt. practice Lake Forest, Ill., 2000—. Served to capt. US Army, 1968—70. Mem. ABA, Ill. Bar Assn., Chgo. Bar Assn., Soc. Corp. Secs. and Governance Profls., Am. Corp. Counsel Assn.

FRANCONA, TERRY JON, professional baseball manager; b. Aberdeen, SD, Apr. 22, 1959; s. Tito F.; m. Jacque Lang, Jan. 9, 1982; children: Nick, Alyssa, Leah, Jamie. Student, U. Ariz. First baseman/outfielder maj. league baseball Montreal Expos, 1981—85, Chgo. Cubs, 1986, Cin. Reds, 1987, Cleve. Indians, 1988, Milw. Brewers, 1989—90; hitting instr. Sarasota, Gulf Coast Rookie League Chgo. White Sox orgn., 1991; mgr. S. Bend, 1992; coach Grand Canyon, Ariz. Fall League, 1992; mgr. Birmingham AA, 1993-95, Dominican Winter League, 1995-96, Phila. Phillies, 1996—2000; special asst., baseball ops. Cleve. Indians, 2001; bench coach Tex. Rangers, 2002, Oakland A's, 2003; mgr. Boston Red Sox, 2003—. Recipient So. League Title, 1993, Minor League Mgr. of Yr., So. League, 1993, Minor League Mgr. of Yr., Baseball Am., 1993; named Top Managerial Prospect among minor league mgrs. Baseball Am., 1994. Achievements include coaching World Series Champion Boston Red Sox, 2004; coaching Am. League All-Start Team, 2005. Avocation: golf. Mailing: c/o Boston Red Sox 4 Yawkey Way Boston MA 02215-3496 Fax: (215) 389-3050.

FRANCUCH, PAUL CHARLES, broadcast journalist; b. Highland Park, Mich., June 26, 1950; s. Charles and Anna (Protasevich) F. BA, Wayne State U., 1972; MA, U. Mich., 1973. From midwest corr. to London bur. chief Voice of Am., Chgo., 1980—96, London bur. chief, 1996—99; sci. engring. editor U. Ill., Chgo., 2001—. Mem. Phi Beta Kappa. Avocations: bicycling, photography, amateur astronomy. Office: 601 S Morgan St MC 288 Chicago IL 60607-7113 Home Phone: 312-867-3947; Office Phone: 312-996-3457. E-mail: francuch@uic.edu.

FRANDSEN, RICHARD A., lawyer; b. 1944; BA, JD, U. Ill. Sr. counsel. Com. on Energy and Commerce, US Ho. of Reps, Washington. Office: Committe on Energy and Commerce 2125 Rayburn HOB Washington DC 20515 E-mail: dick.frandsen@mail.house.gov.

FRANGOS, SPIROS G., medical educator; b. NYC, Apr. 21, 1970; s. George and Jeanne Frangos; m. Rosalia Danilatou, July 10, 2004; 1 child, Ioanna Leonora. BA in Chemistry, NYU, 1991; MD, Downstate Coll., NY, 1996; MPH, Yale U., New Haven, Conn., 2000. Lic. surgeon Am. Bd. Surgery, 2004. Surgery residency Yale U. Sch. Medicine, 1996—2003, trauma & surg. critical care fellowship, 2003—04; asst. prof. surgery NYU Sch. Medicine, 2004—. Personal E-mail: spiros_frangos@yahoo.com.

FRANK, ALAN I W, manufacturing executive; b. Pitts., Mar. 6, 1932; s. Robert and Cecelia Frank; children: Darcy Frank Mackay, Kimberly Frank Shaw. AB cum laude, Harvard U., 1954; LLB, Columbia U., 1960. Bar: NY 1961, Pa. 1982. Pres. Nat. Petroleum Corp., 1954-69; pres., chmn. bd. AIWF Corp., 1962—. Gen. chmn. $200 million campaign Pitts. area, Columbia U., NYC, 1968-70, nat. devel. bd., 1974-84; mem. Rensselaer coun. Rensselaer Poly. Inst., 1974-83; com. mem., com. chmn. Harvard Coll., 1961-2000; trustee Pitts. History and Landmarks Found., 1996-2003. Patentee in field. Served with Counter Intelligence Corps, Spl. Agt. US Army, 1955-57. Mem. NY Bar, Pa. Bar, Mid Ocean Club (Bermuda). Address: 96 E Woodland Rd Pittsburgh PA 15232-2861

FRANK, BARBARA BALIS, gastroenterologist, educator; b. Reading, Pa., Jan. 11, 1937; d. Irvin and Ruth Helen (Knoblauch) B.; m. Leonard Arnold Frank, Aug. 17, 1958; children: Michael Scott, Bradford Allan. BA magna cum laude, Smith Coll., 1958; MD, U. Pa., 1962. Diplomate Am. Bd. Internal Medicine and Gastroenterology. Intern and fellow in gastroenterology Hosp. U. Pa., Phila., 1962—64, instr. internal medicine, 1966—69; resident internal medicine Bryn Mawr (Pa.) Hosp., 1964-66; dir. divsn. gastroenterology Crozer-Chester Med. Ctr., Chester, 1968—89, attending gastroenterologist, 1968—94; clin. asst. prof. medicine Hahnemann U., Phila., 1973-75, clin. assoc. prof., 1975—85; clin. prof. Drexel U. Coll. Medicine, Phila., 1985—. Cons. Sacred Heart Hosp., Chester, Pa., 1974-94; mem. sci. adv. com. Nat. Found. Ileitis and Colitis, Phila., 1980-85; mem. gastroenterology-urology devices panel, FDA, 1988-90, chmn., 1990-92, cons. 1993-94; mem. gastrointestinal drugs adv. com. FDA, 1995-99, cons., 2000—; mem. Physician Payment Rev. Commn., Consensus Panel for Evaluation and Mgmt. Svcs., 1990; rep. for gastroenterology carrier adv. com. Pa. Medicare, 1993-2005; v.p. N.Am. Congresso Panamericano de Endoscopia, 1993-95, 99-2001. Assoc. editor MKSAP in gastroenterology and hepatology 2; contbr. articles to profl. jours. Honoree Barbara D. Frank Endoscopic Learning Ctr. Drexel U. Coll. Medicine, Phila., 2007. Recipient History of Medicine prize U. Pa. Sch. Medicine, 1962, Legion of Honor award Chapel of Four Chaplains, Phila., 1978; rsch. grantee U. Pa., 1961-62. Fellow ACP, Coll. Physicians Phila., Am. Coll. Gastroenterology (ad hoc com. on women in gastroenterology 1989—, gov. ea. Pa. 1992-96, 2003—, regional councillor, bd. govs. 1994-96, chmn. com. for ICD-9-CM revision 1986-89, mem. govt. rels. com. 1987-88, sci. exhibits com. 1985-86, ann. sci. selection com. 1984-85, 90-91, nominating com. 1988-89, ednl. affairs com. 1992-2001, Sr. Govs. award 2006), Am. Soc. Gastrointestinal Endoscopy (councillor, governing bd. dirs. 1986-90, 92-94, pres. 1991-92, Disting. Educator award 2005); mem. AMA, Am. Gastroenterol. Assn. (patient care com. 1986-88, tng. adn edn. com. 1989-90, abstract selection com. 199, nominating com. 1986-87, program evaluation com. 1981-85, mem. pub. policy com. 1992-93, mem. clin. svcs. task force 1994-95, chmn. nominating com. 1995-96, others, Disting. Educator award 2005) Am. Assn. Study Liver Disease, Am. Liver Found., Internat. Assn. for Study of the Liver, Pa. Med. Soc., Phila. GI Tng. Group (pres. 1987-93), Phila. Gastrointestinal Rsch. Forum, Delaware County Med. Soc., Delaware Valley Soc. Gastrointestinal Endoscopy (pres. 1984-86, councillor, governing bd. dirs. 1986-88), Pa. Soc. Gastroenterology councillor for Phila. 1982-84, 87-91, 2001—, governing bd. dirs.), Israel Med. Assn., Bockus Internat. Soc. of Gastroenterology (pres. elect 2005—), Alpha Omega Alpha, Sigma Xi, Alpha Phi, Kappa Psi, Phi Beta Kappa Del. Valley (gov. coun. 1991-93, 98— v.p. 1993-95, pres. 1995-97, 98—, gov. coun. 2000—). Democrat. Jewish. Avocations: sketching, dance. Office: Fl 5 MS 913 219 N Broad St Philadelphia PA 19107

FRANK, BARNEY, congressman; b. Bayonne, NJ, Mar. 31, 1940; s. Samuel and Elsie (Golush) F. AB, Harvard U., 1962, JD, 1977. Exec. asst. to mayor City of Boston, 1968-71; adminstrv. asst. to US Congressman Michael F. Harrington, 1971-72; mem. Mass. Ho. Reps., 1972-80, US Congress from 4th Mass. dist., 1981—, ranking minority mem. fin. services com., chmn. fin. services com., 2007—; lectr. Harvard U. JFK Sch. Gov., 1978—80. Teaching fellow govt. Harvard U., 1963-67, asst. to dir. Inst. Politics John F. Kennedy Sch. Govt., 1966-67, fellow Inst. Politics, 1971. Democrat. Office: US Ho Reps 2252 Rayburn Ho Office Bldg Washington DC 20515-2104*

FRANK, BARRY H., lawyer; b. Nov. 19, 1938; s. David and Rose (Pearl) F.; married: Caryl Frank; children: Toby L., S. Kenneth, Gary A. BS, Pa. State U., 1960; LLB, Temple U., 1963. Bar: Pa. 1964. Staff atty. IRS, Phila., 1963-66; tax mgr. Ernst & Whinney, Phila., 1966-74; exec. v.p., gen. counsel N.F.I. Industries, Inc., Vineland, N.J., 1974-75; ptnr. Pechner, Dorman, Wolffe, Rounick & Cabot, Phila., 1975-87, Mesirov Gelman, 1987—2000, Schnader, Harrison, Segal & Lewis, LLP, Phila., 2000—03, Pelino & Lentz, PC, Phila., 2003—. Co-author: Alimony, Child Support and Counsel Fees; contbr. more than 60 articles to profl. jours. Mem. ABA, AICPA, Phila. Bar Assn., Pa. Inst. CPAs. Republican. Jewish. Office: Pelino & Lentz PC One Liberty Pl 1650 Market St Philadelphia PA 19103-7393 Office Phone: 215-246-3103. E-mail: bhfrank@pelino.com.

FRANK, CHARLES RAPHAEL, JR., financial consultant, director; b. Pitts., May 15, 1937; s. Charles Raphael and Lucille (Briscoe) M.; m. Susan Patricia Backman, Mar. 9, 1963 (div. June 1976); children: Elizabeth Grace, Stephen Raphael; m. Eleanor Sebastian, July 19, 1976; children: Paul Sebastian, Philip Sebastian; stepchildren: Joyce Oxman, Alan Oxman. BS in Math., Rensselaer Poly. Inst., 1959; MA in Econs., Princeton U., 1961, PhD in Econs., 1963. Sr. rsch. fellow East African Inst. Social Rsch. Makerere U. Coll., Kampala, Uganda, 1963-65; asst. prof. econ. Yale U., New Haven, 1965-67; assoc. prof. econ. and internat. affairs Princeton U., NJ, 1967-70, prof. NJ, 1970-74; assoc. dir. rsch. program econ. devel. Woodrow Wilson Sch., 1967-70, dir., 1970-74; sr. fellow Brookings Inst., 1972-74; mem. policy planning staff US Dept. State, 1974-77, dep. asst. sec. state for econ. and social affairs, 1977-78; v.p. Salomon Bros. Inc., 1978-87; pres. Frank & Co. Inc., 1987-88; v.p. project fin. GE Capital Corp., Stamford, Conn., 1988-97; 1st v.p. European Bank for Reconstruction and Devel., London, 1997-2001. Bd. dirs. Ctrl. and Eastern European Media Enterprises, Mittal Steel Romania; ops. rsch. analyst US Steel, 1960-61; rsch. adv. com. AID, 1971-75; investment com. Darby Ctrl. and Ea. European Mezzanine Fund, 2005—; adv. com. Sigma-Bleyner Fund IV, 2006—. Author: Prodn. Theory and Indivisible Commodities, 1969, The Sugar Industry in East Africa, 1965, (with Brian Van Arkadie) Econ. Accounting and Develop. Planning, 2d edit., 1969, Debt and the Terms of Aid, 1970, Stats. and Econometrics, 1971, Am. Jobs and Trade with the Develop. Countries, 1973, Fgn. Exchange Regimes and Econ. Develop., The Case of South Korea, 1975, Fgn. Trade and Domestic Adjustment, 1976, Income Distribution and Econ. Growth in the Less Developed Countries, 1977. Mem. Coun. Fgn. Rels.

FRANK, DENNIS, psychotherapist, educator; b. Cherry Point, NC, Apr. 17, 1954; s. Charlotte Dotzauer and Robert Frank; children: Maximillian, Alexander. MS, U. Wis., Milw., 1997. Psychotherapist Ravenswood Clinic, Inc., Milw., 1997—2002; area supr. ATTIC Correctional Svcs. Inc., Milw., 1999—2001, also bd. dirs.; psychotherapist St. Mary's Hosp., 2001—; ad hoc prof. Concordia U. Grad Sch. Instr. Upper Iowa U., 2002—. Com. mem. The Benedict Ctr., Milw., 2000. Specialist Army, Germany, 1971-74. Mem. ACA, Am. Correctional Assn., Internat. Assn. of Addictions and Offender Counselors, Internat. Cmty. Corrections Assn.

FRANK, DIETER, retired chemicals executive; b. Erfurt, Thuringia, Germany, May 21, 1930; came to U.S., 1975; s. Karl Hermann and Luise (Metz) F.; m. Edith Anna Laufer, July 19, 1957; children: Martin, Susanne, Beate. DEng, Tech. U., Berlin, 1963. Rsch. chemist Glanzstoff A.G., Obernburg, Federal Republic of Germany, 1965-69, sect. head, 1969-71; assoc. dir. AKZO Corp. Rsch., Obernburg, Federal Republic of Germany, 1971-75; dir. rsch. ARMAK (AKZO), Chgo., 1975-76; v.p. rsch. AKZO Chems., Chgo., 1976-90, ret., 1990; tech. cons., 1991—96. Mem. indsl. adv. bd. U. Fla., Gainsville, 1987-90. Contbr. to Ullman Ency., 1985, 90, also articles on organic chemistry; patentee chemicals. County vice chmn. Social Dem. Party of Germany, Obernburg, 1968; pres. Soccer Club, Elsenfeld, Federal Republic of Germany, 1974, 75; chmn. bd. dirs. Fine Arts Found. Schleusingen, 2000-03. Recipient G.E. Meade award, Sugar Industry Technologists, 1986. Mem. AAAS, Indsl. Rsch. Inst. (rep. 1979-90, bd. editors 1981-83). Avocations: woodworking, jazz player. Home and Office: An der Hauptstr 15 98553 Schleusingen-Gethles Germany Home Phone: 036841-47650. Personal E-mail: DFrankGeth@aol.com.

FRANK, EDGAR GERALD, retired finance company executive; b. Cin., May 15, 1931; s. Carl F. and Marcella M. F.; m. Joy Hueber, Oct. 30, 1954; children: Thomas, Phillip, Angela, Walter. BBA, U. Cin., 1955. Acct. Wm. S. Merrell Co., Cin., 1960-61; asst. sec. Emery Industries, Cin., 1961-66; fin. v.p. Samuel Moore & Co., Aurora, Ohio, 1966-79; v.p. fin. Telex Corp., Tulsa, 1979-88, ret., 1988. Served with USN, 1955-58. Mem. AICPA, Fin. Execs. Inst.

FRANK, EDWARD DAVID, II, history educator; b. Boston, June 7, 1951; s. Howard Alvin and Sally (Bernkopf) F.; m. Susan Gibson Lea, Dec. 13, 1997; children: William Howard Day, Edward Morgan Day; 1 stepchild: Eleanor Talbot West. JD, NYU, 1976; BA in History, Yale U., 1973; MA in Internat. Rels., U. Pa., 1984. Assoc. Sherman & Sterling, NYC, 1976-79, Sullivan & Worcester, Boston, 1979-81; chief counsel Bur. Profl. and Occupl. Affairs Commonwealth of Pa., Harrisburg, Pa., 1982-83; internat. polit. risk cons. Bus. Environment Risk Info., Washington, 1985-86; history tchr. The Agnes Irwin Sch., Rosemont, Pa., 1985—97, chair history, 1997—. Spl. asst. to pres. Barnes Found., Merion, Penn., 1989-90. Bd. dir. Phila. Area Multicultural Resource Ctr., Bryn Mawr, Pa., 1990—; chair 25th Reunion of Yale Class of 1973, New Haven, Conn., 1993-98; trustee Lincoln U., 1985-91, Agnes Irwin Sch., Rosemont, 1992-95, pres. Cum Laude Soc., 1991-. Mem. Assn. Yale U. Alumni (bd. govs. 1972-73, sec. Class of 73, 1972-78). Home: 843 Parkes Run Ln Villanova PA 19085 Office: Agnes Irwin Sch Ithan Ave & Conestoga Rd Bryn Mawr PA 19010 Office Phone: 610-525-8400. Personal E-mail: wigsfrank@comcast.net.

FRANK, ELIZABETH, writer, educator; b. LA, Sept. 14, 1945; d. Melvin G. and Anne R. Frank; 1 child, Anne Louise Buchwald. Student, Bennington Coll.; BA, U. Calif., Berkeley, 1967, MA, 1969, PhD, 1973. Prof. modern langs. and lit. Bard Coll., Annandale-on-Hudson, NY, 1982—, faculty Ctr. Curatorial Studies, Joseph E. Harry prof. modern langs. and lit. Author: Jackson Pollock, 1983, Louise Bogan: A Portrait, 1985 (Pulitzer prize for biography, 86), Esteban Vicente, 1995, Cheat and Charmer, 2004; contbr. articles to profl. jours. Fellow, Ford Found., 1967—72, Temple U., 1977, The Newbery Libr., 1977, Am. Coun. Learned Socs., 1977, NEH, 1978. Office: Joy Harris Lit Agy 156 5th Ave Ste 617 New York NY 10010-7002 also: Bard Coll Dept Lang & Lit Annandale On Hudson NY 12504

FRANK, FREDERICK, investment banker; b. Salt Lake City, May 31, 1932; s. Simon and Suzanne (Seller) F.; m. Mary Ann Nahum (div. 1979); children: Jenny Ann, Laura Kim, Frederick S.; m. Mary Catherine Tanner. BA, Yale U., New Haven, Conn., 1954; MBA, Stanford U., Calif., 1958. Chartered fin. analyst. Mng. dir. Smith Barney & Co., NYC, 1958-69, Lehman Bros., NYC, 1969-85, sr. mng. dir., 1985-95, vice chmn., 1995—. Bd. dirs. Pharm. Product Devel., Wilmington, NC, AXS, Berkeley, Calif., Landec Corp.; chmn. bd. dirs. Epix Pharms. Trustee Irvington Inst. of Immunological Rsch.; with Nat. Genetics Found., NYC, 1985—; trustee Hotchkiss Sch., Lakeville, Conn.; adv. dir. Yale U. Sch. Mgmt., Harvard Sch. Pub. Health, Cambridge, Mass., Johns Hopkins Bloomberg Sch. Pub. Health, Balt. With US Army, 1954—56. Mem.: Chartered Fin. Analysts, NY Soc. Security Analysts. Avocations: skiing, tennis, running. Home: 109 E 91st St New York NY 10128-1601 Office: Lehman Bros 745 7th Ave New York NY 10019-0001 Business E-Mail: ffrank@lehman.com.

FRANK, GEORGE ANDREW, lawyer; b. Budapest, Hungary, Apr. 6, 1938; arrived in U.S., 1957, naturalized, 1962; s. Alex and Ilona (Weiss) F.; m. Carole Shames, Feb. 14, 1979; children: Cheryl, Charles. BS in Chemistry with high distinction, Colo. State U., Fort Collins, 1960; PhD in Organic Chemistry, MIT, 1965; JD cum laude, Temple U., Phila., 1977. Bar: Pa. 1977, US Dist. Ct. (ea. dist.) Pa. 1977, DC 1980, US Ct. Appeals (fed. cir.) 1982, US Supreme Ct. 1984, US Patent and Trademark Office, 1978. Sr. chemist Rohm & Haas Co., Phila., 1965-69; lab. head Borden Chem., Phila., 1969-73; sr. scientist Thiokol Corp., Trenton, NJ, 1973-74; counsel Du Pont Corp., Wilmington, Del., 1974-85, sr. counsel, 1986-92, corp. counsel, 1992-2001, intellectual property law group leader, 2000-2001; of counsel, chair licensing and tech. transfer practice group Drinker Biddle & Reath LLP, Philadelphia, 2001—. External adv. com. Colo. State U. Coll. Natural Scis., 1996—; mem. intellectual property adv. com. Pa. Bar Inst., 2002--. Contbr. articles to profl. jours; patentee in field. Recipient Merck award, Merck & Co., 1960; fellow, NIH, 1963—65; grantee Sun Oil Co. grantee, 1964. Mem. ABA (chair divsn. biotech. 1993-94, coun. 1994-98, chair chem. practice com. 1998-2000, chair divsn. biotech. and chem. practice 2000-02, chair divsn. profl. practice and sect. rels. 2002-04, chair lic. com. 2004-06, chair divsn. IP-related issues, 2006-), Phila. Patent Lawyers Assn. (chair bioscis. com. 1983-87, bd. govs. 1987-92, pres. 1992-93), Am. Intellectual Property Law Assn. (chair task force 1986), Benjamin Franklin Am. Inn of Cts. (v.p. 1996-97, pres. 1997-98). Republican. Avocations: tennis, squash, travel, books, opera. Home: 520 Lindy Ln Bala Cynwyd PA 19004-1331 Office: Drinker Biddle & Reath LLP 1 Logan Square 18th & Cherry St Philadelphia PA 19103 Home Phone: 610-668-8567; Office Phone: 215-988-2822. Business E-Mail: frankga@dbr.com.

FRANK, GERALD WENDEL, advocate, journalist; b. Portland, Oreg., Sept. 21, 1923; s. Aaron and Ruth (Rosenfeld) Frank. Student, Stanford U., Calif., 1941-43, Loyola U., LA, 1946-47; BA with honors, Cambridge U., 1948, MA, 1953; D Bus. Adminstrn. (hon.), Greenville Coll., Ill., 1971; LLD (hon.), Pacific U., Forest Grove, Oreg., 1983. Mgr. Meier & Frank Co., Salem, Oreg., 1955-65; v.p. Meier & Frank Co., Ltd., 1948-65; also bd. dirs.; pres. Gerry's Frankly Speaking, Salem, Oreg., 1996—; co-owner Gerry Frank's Konditorei, Inc., Salem, Oreg., 1982—. Commentator/reporter morning news shows Sta. KPTV, Portland, 1993—2001, Sta. KATU-AM N.W., 2002—05; mgmt. adv. bd. Aequitas Capital, 2003—; bd. dirs. AAA Oreg./Idaho; columnist The Oregonian. Author: Where to Find It, Buy It, Eat It in New York, 14th edit., 1980—, Where to Find It, Buy It, Eat It in New York, 15th edit., 2007—, Joan and Gerry's Little Black Book of Shopping Secrets, 1991, Friday Surprise, 1995; sr. corr.: N.W. Reports, 1992—96. Active Found. Infantile Paralysis, Arthritis and Rheumatism Found., Nat. Coun., Boy Scouts Am., Travelers Aid Soc., Nat. Mcpl. League, Nat. Retail Merchants Assn., Am. Heart Soc., Portland C. of C., Salem Area C. of C.; active Sunshine divsn. Portland Police Res.; active Portland Area Coun., Cascade Area Coun., Cascade Area Pacific Coun., Portland Rose Festival Assn., Jr. Achievement, Salem Pub. Libr. Found., Portland United Fund, Marion-Polk Counties United Way, Salem Gen. Hosp., Citizens' Conf. for Govtl. Coop., Gov.'s Econ. Devel. Commn., Oreg. Retail Distbrs. Inst., Oreg. Rsch. Assn., Salem 4-H Club, Willamette River Days, Salem YWCA, Grad. Inst. Sci. and Tech., Portland Met. Futures Unltd., Inc., Oreg. Coast Aquarium, 1990—, Oreg. Symphony Soc.; chair Oreg. State Police Found., 2002—; bd. trustees LWV; hon. chair Marion Polk Food Share Capital Campaign, 2003—; chair Salvation Army, 2005—; gen. chmn. Mark O. Hatfield for U.S. Sen., 1966, 1972, 1978, 1984, 1990; mgmt. com. U.S. Senate, 1978; chief of staff Sen. Mark O. Hatfield, 1973—92; active Culver Commn. on Reorgn. U.S. Senate, 1975—76; trustee Lorene Sails Higgins Charitable Trust, 1993—2000; exec. com. U.S. Com. for UNICEF, 1990—99; exec. com., Ray and Joan Kroc initiative com. Salvation Army, chair Kroceater com. Oreg., 2004—; bd. trustees Willamette U.; active Marion-Salem Bldg. Study Com.; emeritus trustee Oreg. High Desert Mus.; exec. com. Salem Art Assn., Parry Ctr. Children, St. Vincent Hosp. and Med. Ctr., Oreg. Health Scis. U., OMSI, chair, dir., 1996—97; bd. dirs., exec. com. AAA Oreg./Idaho; active Miss Oreg. Scholarship Program; chmn. Oreg. Tourism Commn., 1996—2001, Oreg. Ind. Coll. Found., 2000. With field aty. US Army, 1943—46, ETO. Named Oreg. Premier Citizen, 2000; recipient numerous awards including Silver Beaver, Boy Scouts Am., 1963, Reginald H. Vincent trophy, United Good Neighbor of the Yr., 1980, Brotherhood Nat. Conf. Christians and Jews, Portland, 1984, Gov.'s Gold award, 2004; Tom Lawson McCall fellow, Pacific U., 1987. Mem.: Rotary (Paul Harris fellow 1986), Elks, Am. Legion. Avocations: travel, gourmet dining. Home: 3250 Crestview Dr S Salem OR 97302-5959 Office: Gerry's Frankly Speaking Inc 2601 25th St SE Ste 500 Salem OR 97302-1287 also: PO Box 2225 Salem OR 97308-2225 Office Phone: 503-585-8411. E-mail: gerry@teleport.com.

FRANK, HOSEA (ZE FRANK), web video blogger; b. Mar. 31, 1972; Weblog creator, host zefrank.com, 2003—; host, video blog The Show, 2006—07. Adj. prof. SUNY, Purchase, 2003, Parsons Sch. Design, 2004—; artist-in-residence Microsoft MSN Divsn., 2004. Featured in (media) Economist, BusinessWeek, Newsweek, Honolulu Star Bulletin, Kans. City Star, Wall St. Jour., Guardian (UK), NY Times, others. Named Best Personal Website (zefrank.com), People's Voice award (Webby), 2002; named one of 50 Coolest Websites, Time mag., 2005, Top 25 Web Celebs, Forbes mag., 2007; recipient Experimental Category award, FlashForward Film Fest., 2005. Home: Brooklyn NY E-mail: ze@zefrank.com.*

FRANK, HOWARD, dean, information technology executive; b. NYC, June 4, 1941; s. Herman and Tina (Sander) F.; m. Jane Steinberg, Apr. 23, 1965; children: David, Laura, Erica. BSEE, U. Miami, 1962; MS, Northwesten U., 1964; PhD, Northwestern U., 1965. Asst. prof. U. Calif.-Berkeley, 1965-68, assoc. prof., 1969; exec. v.p. Network Analysis Corp., Glen Cove, NY, 1969, pres., 1970-81, Contel Info. Systems Inc., Great Neck, NY, 1982-85, Howard Frank Assocs., 1985—; chmn. Network Mgmt., Inc., 1987—91; dir. Def. Adv. Rsch. Project Agy.'s Info. Tech. Office; pres., CEO Contel Info. Sys. (sub. Contel Corp.); pres., CEO, founder Network Analysis Corp.; prof. mgmt. scis. Smith Sch., 1997—; dean Robert H. Smith Sch. Bus. U. Md., 1997—. Bd. dirs. Contel Corp.; vis. cons. Exec. Office Pres. U.S., 1968; founder, chmn., CEO Network Mgmt. Inc., Fairfax, Va., 1986-91; spkr. bus. and profl. meetings; adj. prof. decision scis. Wharton Sch.; assoc. prof. electrical engring. and computer scis. U. (Berkeley) California. Author: Communications, Transmission and Transportation Networks, 1971; contbr. over 190 articles and chpts. in books on tech. and mgmt. of tech.; mem. 7 editl. bds. NASA fellow, 1963-65; Gen. Motors fellow, 1958-62 Fellow IEEE (Leonard G. Abraham 1969, Eric Sumner award 1999), SEI Ctr. Advanced Studies in Mgmt. (sr. fellow, mem. bd. dirs.); mem. AAAS, AACSB, Mid-Atlantic Assn. Colls. and Bus. Adminstrn. (pres), Ops. Research Soc., Ams. Internat. Acad. Mgmt. (vice chancellor), Carnegie Mellon's Heinz Sch. (mem. adv. bd.), Global Tech. and Mgmt. Consortium (mem. exec. com.), Macklin Inst. Mont. Coll. (bd. dirs.), Nat. Inst. Stds. and Tech.'s Advanced Tech. Program (fed. adv. com.), Nat. Acad. Engring., N.Y. Acad. Scis. Office: Robert H Smith Sch Bus U Md 2410 Van Munching Hall College Park MD 20742-1815 Business E-Mail: hfrank@rhsmith.umd.edu.

FRANK, JACOB, lawyer; b. Albany, Apr. 4, 1936; s. Isidore and Sara F.; m. Yoelith Frank, Aug. 26, 1936; children: Eytan, Michael, Adam, Orly. BEE, Rensselaer Poly. Inst., 1957; LLB, Am. U., 1963; postgrad., George Washington U. Coll. Law, 1964-67, NYU Law Sch., 1969-73. Bar: D.C. 1963, Mass. 1979, Va. 2001, U.S. Patent Office. Of counsel Alliance Law Group, Tysons Corner, Va., 2000—, Harrity & Snyder, Fairfax, Va. Home: 17040 Thousand Oaks Dr Haymarket VA 20169 Office Phone: 703-848-1720. Personal E-mail: jyfrank8@aol.com. Business E-Mail: jfrank@alliancelawgroup.com, jfrank@harritysnyder.com.

FRANK, JAMES S., automotive executive; b. Chgo., 1942; m. Karen Frank; 3 children. BS Phi Beta Kappa, Dartmouth Coll.; MBA, Stanford U. With ZF, Inc., Ill., 1965, Wheels, Inc., Des Plaines, Ill., 1965; pres. Four Wheels, Inc., Des Plaines, Ill., 1965; pres., CEO Frank Consol. Enterprises, Des Plaines, Ill., 1967—, Wheels (subs. Frank Consol. Enterprises), Des Plaines, Ill., 1974—. Trustee U. of Chgo., 1995. Pres. Michael Reese Med. Rsch. Inst. Coun. Jr. Bd.; bd. trustees U. Chgo. Hosps., U. Chgo.; bd. overseers Thayer Engring. Sch. Dartmouth Coll. Mem.: Am. Automobile Leasing Assn. (past pres. and chair, bd. dir., chair fed. gtax and legis. com., past chair industry com., dir. 2003—). Office: Frank Consol Enterprises 666 Garland Pl Des Plaines IL 60016-4725

FRANK, JOACHIM, structural biologist, educator, biophysicist; b. Germany; Diploma in Physics, U. Munich; PhD in Biophysics, Tech. U., Munich, 1970. Dir. lab. computational biology and macromolecular imaging Wadsworth Ctr., Albany, NY, Disting. scientist structural biology. Investigator Howard Hughes Med. Inst., 1998—; prof. biology SUNY, Albany; adj. prof. biochemistry and molecular biophysics Columbia U., NYC; rsch. prof. cell biology NYU Med. Sch. Author: 5 books; contbr. 200 articles to sci. jours. Fellow: Am. Acad. Arts Scis., Biophys. Soc. (Elizabeth Roberts Cole award 1993), AAAS; mem.: NAS. Office: Wadsworth Ctr D 350 Empire State Plz Albany NY 12201

FRANK, JOHN LEROY, commissioner, lawyer, educator; b. Eau Claire, Wis., Mar. 13, 1952; s. George LeRoy and Frances Elaine (Torgerson) F. BS summa cum laude, U. Wis., Eau Claire, 1974; JD cum laude, U. Wis., Madison, 1977. Bar: Wis. 1977, U.S. Dist. Ct. (we. dist.) Wis. 1977, U.S. Supreme Ct. 1982. Instr. law U. Wis., Madison, 1976-77; assoc. Garvey, Anderson, Kelly & Ryberg, S.C., Eau Claire, 1977-81; legis dir., counsel Congressman Steve Gunderson, Washington, 1981-85, chief of staff, counsel, 1985-89; staff coord. 92 Group, Washington, 1987-89; instr. Chippewa Valley Tech. Coll., 1989-93, 97—, dir. paralegal program, 1992—93, 1997—2001, 2003—04, chair dept. behavioral sci. and civic effectiveness, 2003—07; pvt. law practice, 1990—93, 1997—2005; counsel, minority cons. House Subcom. on Livestock, Washington, Wis., 1993-95; counsel Congressman Steve Gunderson, Washington, 1993-97; dep. minority counsel House Com. on Agr., Washington, 1993-95, dep. chief counsel, 1995-97; commr. West Ctrl. Wis. Regional Planning Commn., Eau Claire, 1998—. Pol. analyst, commentator WEAU-TV, Eau Claire, Wis., 1998—; mem. Bush-Cheney Transition Adv. Com., 2001; vis. prof. U. Wis., Eau Claire, 2002-03, U. Wis., Stout, 2006—. Mem.: Assn. Career and Tech. Edn. (mem. legis. com. 2003—07, mem. re-orgn. com. 2005—07, Region III award of merit 2003, Region III Career and Tech. Edn. Tchr. of Yr. 2006), Wis. Bar Assn. (mem. paralegal task force 1998—2005), U. Wis. Alumni Assn. (Disting. Achievement award 2001), Wis. Assn. for Career and Tech. Edn. (legis. com. chair 2000—01, bd. dirs. 2000—04, strategic planning com. chair 2001—02, pres. 2002—03, conf. com. chair 2003—04, nominations com. chair 2004—05, Hambrecht award 2005, Wis. Career and Tech. Edn. Tchr. of Yr. 2006), The Presto Found. (bd. dirs. 1992—93, v.p. 1992—93, v.p 2000—, bd. dirs. 2000—), Phi Gamma Delta (Durrance award 1978), Phi Delta Phi. Address: 2113 Meadow Ln Eau Claire WI 54701-7965

FRANK, JOHN V., foundation administrator; b. Cleve., Oct. 14, 1936; s. Paul A. and Frances (Halbert) Frank. Student, Babson Coll., 1956-57; BBA, U. Miami, Fla., 1960. Mgmt. trainee Nat. City Bank, Cleve., 1960-62; investment analyst First Nat. Bank, Akron, Ohio, 1962-70, asst. trust officer, 1970-73, trust officer, 1973-80, v.p., trust officer, 1980-81; pres. Summit Capital Mgmt. Co., Akron, 1982-99. Nat. coun. mem. Norman Rockwell Mus., 2002—04, trustee, 2004—; treas. Fairlawn Heights Assn., Inc., Akron, 1971—2002, trustee, 2004—; pres. Ohio Ballet, 1973—74; trustee Burton D. Morgan Found., Akron, 1976—, Howland Meml. Fund, Akron, 1974—, Akron Art Mus., 1976—83, pres., 1979—81; trustee Akron City Hosp. Found., 1980—83, 1992, Summa Health Sys. Found., 1992—, treas., chmn. fin. com., 2003—05; treas., trustee Rectory Sch., 1999—, chmn. exec. com., 2001—04, pres., 2006—; mem. Akron Emergency Med. Adv. Bd., 1986—, Coun. Founds. Com. Legis. and Regulations, 1990—94, Akron Charter Rev. Commn., 1980, 1990, 2000; bd. overseers Blossom Music Ctr., 1996—99; trustee Akron Rural Cemetery, 1994—, v.p., 1997—2006, pres., 2006—; pres., trustee Akron Civil War Meml. Soc., 1996—; found. pres. Friends of Glendale, 2003—; trustee Our Lady of Elms Sch., 2002—07, chair fin. com., 2002—06, treas., 2003—06; councilman City of Akron, 1978—98; 50th anniversary com. UN Grace Cathedral Ch., San Francisco, 1993—95, St. Paul's Episc. Ch.; nat. steering com. Coll. Wooster, 1992—96. 1st lt. USAR, 1963—69. Named to Fashion Hall of Fame, Kent State U., 2006. Mem.: Cleve. Soc. Security Analysts, Hillsboro Club (Hillsboro Beach, Fla.), Portage Country Club. Republican. Episcopalian. Avocation: art collecting. Office: Burton D Morgan Found 22 Aurora St Hudson OH 44236 Office Phone: 330-655-1633.

FRANK, KAREN DENISE, aerospace engineer; b. Tokyo, Dec. 21, 1956; (parents Am. citizens); children: Daniel Joseph, David Michael. BS in Aerospace Engring., U. Tex., 1978; MS in Systems Engring., U. Houston, 1985. Sr. engr. Lockheed Engr. and Mgmt. Svcs., Houston, 1978-86; internat. space sta. GN&C mgr. NASA, Houston, 1983—84, aerospace engr. Johnson Space Ctr., 1986-93, head navigation sect., 1993-97, chief Guidance, Navigation and Control Devel. Test Br., 1997—. Vol. Clear Lake Emergency Med. Corps, Houston, 1979-90. Recipient Youth Appreciation award Dallas Optimist Club, 1972. Fellow AIAA (assoc., treas. Houston sect. 1983-84, vice chairperson 1984-85, chairperson 1986-87); mem. Alpha Chi, Tau Beta Pi, Sigma Gamma Tau. Office: NASA/Johnson Space Ctr Mail Code Eg #2 Houston TX 77058 E-mail: karen.d.frank@nasa.gov.

FRANK, KAREN SUSANNA, lawyer; b. New Haven, Nov. 30, 1951; d. John Paul and Lorraine Weiss Frank; 1 child, Samuel John. BA, Conn. Coll., New London, 1973; JD, U. Calif., San Francisco, 1987. Dir. new ventures KQED-TV, San Francisco, 1979—84; sr. counsel Pillsbury Madison & Sutro, San Francisco, 1987—96; shareholder Legal Strategies Group, Emeryville, Calif., 1996—2004; dir. Howard Rice Nemerovksi Canaday Falk & Rabkin, San Francisco, 2004—. Bd. dirs. Legal Cmty. Against Violence, San Francisco, 2004—. Mem.: Copyright Soc. USA (pres-elect 2006—). Office: Howard Rice Nemerovski Canady Falk and R 3 Embarcadero Ctr 7th Fl San Francisco CA 94610 Office Phone: 415-434-1600.

FRANK, LARRY JAMES, library director; b. Detroit, Oct. 9, 1943; s. George A. and Marjorie J. (McConkey) Frank; m. Bonnie L. Bonsky; children: Alyssa Ann(dec.) , Nathan D. BA magna cum laude, We. Mich. U., 1976, MA with honors, 1977; AMLS, U. Mich., 1979; cert. pub. adm. advanced mgmt. program, Miami U., Oxford, Ohio, 1983; cert. edn., U. Wis., 1996. Exec. dir. Amos Meml. Pub. Libr., Sidney, Ohio, 1981—85, Boyd County Pub. Libr., Ashland, Ky., 1986—95, St. Clair County Libr., Port Huron, Mich., 1995—99, Onondaga County Pub. Libr., Syracuse, NY, 1999—2001, Hinsdale Pub. Libr., Ill., 2001—03, Knox County Librs., Mus. and Cultural Svcs., Knoxville, Tenn., 2003—. Cons./tchr., missionary The Lang. Inst., Japan Luth. Ch., Tokyo and Niigata, Japan, 1968—71; cons. in libr. design and orgn. Port Huron, 1996—98. Author: (novel) The Arius Scrolls, 2004, (anthology) Sensual Rhythms of Appalachia, 1985, numerous poems; contbr. articles to profl. jours. Bd. dirs. Ky. Coun. on Econ Edn., Ashland, 1986-95; mem. chronic disease steering com. U. Cin. Children's Hosp., Ashland, 1987-90; mem. bd. visitors U. Tenn. Named Boss of Yr., Jaycees, Ashland, Libr. of Yr., NY Times, 2006; U. Mich. scholar, Ann Arbor, 1978-79. Mem.: PLA, ACLU, ALA, ASPA. Avocations: writing, drawing, hiking, design, painting. Office Phone: 865-215-8703. E-mail: lawf1009@yahoo.com.

FRANK, LAURA JEAN, computer scientist; b. New Rochelle, NY, May 21, 1945; d. James Florian and Erma (Guttag) F. BA, U. Vt., Burlington, 1967; MBA, Iona Coll., New Rochelle, 1971; postgrad., China Inst., NYC, Polytechnic Inst., White Plains, NY; Assoc. Masters, George Washington U., Washington, DC, 2001. Cert. project mgmt. profl. Project Mgmt. Inst., 2002. With Equitable Life Assurance Soc., NYC, 1967-79, project leader, 1978-79; sr. planning specialist PHH Relocation, Wilton, Conn., 1979-80, project mgr., 1980-83, sys. mgr., 1983-88, mgr. office tech., 1988-91; founding prof. Homequity U., Wilton, Conn., 1985-91; sys. cons. LJF Assocs., Stamford, Conn., 1991-95; sys. mgr. Fiberlux, Purchase, NY, 1994-98; pjt mgr. Synapse Group, Stamford, 1998—. Bd. dirs. Tri-State Trainers. Editor and bd. dirs.: newspaper Stamford First Nighter; contbr. articles to profl. jours. Mem. PMI Cmty. Impact Team. Mem. Stamford Hist. Soc., Women in Mgmt., Friends of Stamford Symphony, Literacy Vols. of Am. Office: 225 High Ridge Rd Stamford CT 06905 E-mail: lfrank@synapsemail.com.

FRANK, LAWRENCE, professional basketball coach; b. Teaneck, NJ, Aug. 23, 1970; m. Susan Frank; children: Dillon Grace, Caitlin Elizabeth. BS in Edn., Ind. U., 1992; MS in Edn. Adminstrn., Marquette U. Staff asst. Marquette U., 1992; asst. coach U. Tenn., 1994—97, Vancouver Grizzlies, 1997—2000, NJ Nets, East Rutherford, 2000—04, head coach, 2004—. Achievements include leading the Nets to the Atlantic Divsn. Championship, 2006; set NBA record for most consecutive wins (13) by a head coach at the beginning of his career, 2004. Office: NJ Nets 390 Murray Hill Pky East Rutherford NJ 07073*

FRANK, LILLIAN GORMAN, human resources executive, management consultant; b. NYC, July 4, 1953; d. Helmuth H. and Ida (Malitsch) Degen; m. Stephen E. Frank, Feb. 10, 2001. BA in Psychology, Lehman Coll., CUNY, 1975; MA in Indsl. Psychology, Case Western Res. U., 1978, PhD in indsl. Psychology, 1979; MBA in Corp. Fin., U. So. Calif., 1986. Econ. benefits asst. Girl Scouts U.S.A., NYC, 1971—75; psychologist Pers. Rsch. Svcs., Cleve., 1975—79; cons. psychologist Pers. Rsch. & Devel. Corp., Cleve., 1977—78; mgr. pers. rsch. 1st Interstate Bank, LA, 1979—82, v.p., mgr. human resource planning and devel., 1982—85; v.p., mgr. human resource planning and exec. devel. 1st Interstate Bancorp, LA, 1985—86; exec. v.p., human resources dir. First Interstate Bank of Calif., 1986—90; exec. v.p. human resources First Interstate Bancorp, 1990—96; sr. v.p. human resources Edison Internat., Rosemead, Calif., 1996—2000; prin. Frank Insights, LA, 2000—05. Trustee Autry Mus. Western Heritage, 2001—05; bd. dirs. INROADS/So. Calif., 1986—2005, YMCA of Met. L.A., 2002—05, Nev. Women's Fund, 2005—. Mem. APA, Soc. for Psychologists in Mgmt. (bd. dirs. 1993-97), Orgn. for Women Execs., Soc. for Human Resources Mgmt., Nev. Womens Fund. Home and Office: 5865 Strasbourg Ct Reno NV 89511 Business E-Mail: lillian@avantwireless.com.

FRANK, LINDA MARIA, science educator; b. NYC, Feb. 17, 1941; d. Felix G. and Angeline A. Frank; 1 child, Michael Santangelo, Jr. BS in Edn., St. John's U., NYC, 1961; MS in Edn., St. John's U., 1964. Cert. tchr. sci., sch. adminstr. N.Y. Sci. tchr. Seaford Schs., Seaford, NY, 1965—96, sci. chair, 1991—96; adj. prof. Hofstra U., NY, 1996—; sci. edn. cons. BOCES, NY, 1997—2003. Vol. Fire Island Lighthouse, Fire Island, NY, 2004—, Ctrl. Park, NYC, 2002—. Named Tchr. of the Yr., Seaford H.S., 1990; recipient award for encouraging women in sci. and tech. edn., AAUW, 1995. Mem.: Nat. Sci. Tchrs. Assn., L.I. Crosscountry Ski Club (pres. 2005—06). Avocations: cross country skiing, ice skating, kayaking.

FRANK, LLOYD, lawyer, director, retired chemicals executive; b. NYC, Aug. 9, 1925; m. Beatrice Silverstein, Dec. 26, 1954; children: Margaret Lois, Frederick. BA, Oberlin Coll., 1947; JD, Cornell U., 1950. Bar: N.Y. 1950, U.S. Supreme Ct. 1973. Lawyer, NYC, 1950—95; sec., dir. Grow Group, Inc., NYC, 1964-95; sr. ptnr., exec. com., chmn. corp. dept. Parker Chapin LLP, NYC, 1985—2000; sr. ptnr. Jenkens Gilchrist Parker Chapin, LLP, NYC, 2001—04, of counsel, 2004, Troutman Sanders, LLP, 2005—. Bd. dirs. Volt Info. Scis. Inc., (NYSE) N.Y.C., Madison Industries, Inc., N.Y.C., Dryclean, USA, Inc., Miami, Fla., AMEX, Pub. Art Fund, Inc., N.Y.C., Park Electrochem. Corp., (NYSE) Melville, N.Y., Internat. Longevity Ctr. U.S.A. Ltd., N.Y.C., Kulite Semicondr., Inc., Leonia, N.J.; sec. Esquire Radio & Electronics, Inc., Bklyn.; lectr. Am. Mgmt. Assn., 1967—77, Probe Internat., Inc., 1975-77, Corp. Seminars, Inc., 1968-71. Mem. ABA (com. negotiated acquisitions), Assn. Bar City of N.Y. (com. on securities law). Home: 25 Central Park W Apt 17Q New York NY 10023-7211 Office: Troutman Sanders LLP 405 Lexington Ave New York NY 10174-0002 Office Phone: 212-704-6187. Business E-Mail: Lloyd.frank@troutmansanders.com.

FRANK, MARTIN, physiologist, educator, medical association administrator; b. Chgo., Oct. 22, 1947; s. Edward D. and Ann (Horwitz) F.; m. Cheryl Lynn Motel, Aug. 19, 1970; children: Beth Susan, Eric Lawrence. AB (Evans scholar), U. Ill., 1969, MS, 1971, PhD, 1973. USPHS predoctoral research trainee U. Ill., 1971-73; research assoc. Mich. Cancer Found., Detroit, 1973-74; dept. pharmacology Mich. State U., 1974-75; assoc. prof. physiology George Washington U., 1980—. Exec. sec. physiology study sect. divsn. rsch. grants NIH, Bethesda, Md., 1978—85; exec. dir. Am. Physiol. Soc., Bethesda, 1985—; pres., treas., bd. dirs. Commn. on Profls. in Sci. and Tech., 1986—2000; mem. internat. adv. panel Galileo Found., 1990—93; mem. life scis. subcom. NASA Space Sci. and Applications Adv. Com., 1991—94; coord. Washington Prins. Coalition for Free Access to Sci., 2004—. Editor Physiologist, 1985—; contbr. articles to profl. jours. Vice pres., bd. dirs. Bennington Community Assn., Gaithersburg, Md., 1976-78, 80-81, mem. Gaithersburg City Planning Commn., 1982-85. Recipient Disting. Alumni award dept. molecular and integrative physiology U. Ill., Urbana, 2001, Presdl. award 2003; grantee Nations' Capitol Affiliate Am. Heart Assn.,1975-78, NIH, NSF. Mem. AAAS, Am. Physiol. Soc., Am. Soc. Assn. Execs., Coalition Engring Scientific Soc. Execs. Office: Am Physiol Soc 9650 Rockville Pike Bethesda MD 20814-3998 Office Phone: 301-634-7118. E-mail: mfrank@the-aps.org.

FRANK, MARY LOU BRYANT, psychologist, educator; b. Denver, Nov. 27, 1952; d. W. D. and Blanche (Dean) Bryant; m. Kenneth Kerry Frank, Sept. 9, 1973; children: Kari Lou, Kendra Leah. BA, Colo. State U., 1974, MEd, 1983, MS, 1986, PhD, 1989. Tchr. Cherry Creek Schs., Littleton, Colo., 1974—80; grad. dir. career devel. Colo. State U., Ft. Collins, 1980—86; intern U. Del., Newark, 1987—88; psychologist Ariz. State U., Tempe, 1988—93; assoc., lead prof. psychology Clinch Valley Coll. U. Va., Wise, 1992—96, asst. acad. dean, 1993—95; head psychology dept., prof. North Ga. Coll. and State U., Dahlonega, 1996—2001; dean undergrad. and univ. studies, dean univ. coll., prof. psychology Kennesaw (Ga.) State U., 2001—06; assoc. v.p. for acad. affairs, prof. psychology Gainesville State Coll., Ga., 2006—. Chmn. bd. regents adv. com. Psychology, 2000—01; instr. Colo. State U., Ft. Collins, 1981—82, counselor, 1984—85, Ft. Collins, 1986—87; spkr. in field; cons. Nat. Resource Ctr. for 1st Coll. Yr. Author: (program manual) Career Development, 1986; contbr. book chpts. on eating disorders and existential psychotherapy, 1996, 1998, 1999, 2002; reviewer: Buros Mental Measurements Yearbook. Bd. dirs. Ct. Apptd. Spl. Advocates, 2000—, Enotah Legis. Dist., Helping Teens Succeed, 2006—, Possible Woman Found.; mem. Youth Adv. Coun. Lumpkin County, 2000—02; adv. bd. mem. Chatahoochee Tech. Coll., 2004—; v.p. Ga. Women's Inst., 2006—. Mem.: ACA, AAUP, APA, Atlanta Women's Network (adv. bd. 2004—), Atlanta Women's Alliance (mem. exec. com. 2004—), Ga. ACE Network (mem. exec. com. 2001—), Ga. Assn. Women Higher Edn. (pres. 2001—04), Am. Assn. State Colls. and Univs., Southeastern Psychol. Assn. (chair undergrad. rsch. 1996—2000), Am. Assn. Higher Edn., Am. Counselor Edn. and Supv., Am. Assn. Counseling and Devel., Odeka, Phi Beta Kappa, Psi Chi (Ga. Woman of the Yr. com. 1999—, vice chair 2003—, documentary project), Pi Kappa Delta, Phi Kappa Phi (Internat. Woman's Day program com. 2003, planning com. so. women in pub. svc. conf. 2003—04, Promotion of Excellence grantee 2002—03). Avocations: music, hiking, reading. Office: Gainesville State Coll Office Academic Affairs PO Box 1358 Gainesville GA 30503 Office Phone: 678-717-3835. Business E-Mail: mlfrank@gsc.edu.

FRANK, MICHAEL J., neuroscientist, educator; b. Montreal, Canada, Nov. 22, 1974; arrived in US, 1998; s. Daniel E. and Hallie S. Frank. BSc, Queen's U., Kingston, Can., 1997; MS, U. Colo., Boulder, 2000, PhD, 2004. Postdoctoral fellow U. Colo., Boulder, 2004—05; asst. prof. U. Ariz., Tucson, 2006—. Contbr. articles to profl. jours. Grantee, Nat. Inst. Drug Abuse, 2007. Mem.: Cognitive Neuroscience Soc., Soc. Neuroscience. Achievements include development of computer model for understanding roles of neurochemicals in learning and decision making; research in levels of brain dopamine determining whether humans learn more from positive or negative outcomes of their decisions; medications affecting cognitive function in Parkinson's disease and attention deficit disorder. Office: Univ Arizona 1503 E Univ Blvd Tucson AZ 85721 Office Phone: 520-626-4787. Office Fax: 520-621-9306.

FRANK, MICHAEL M., physician; b. Bklyn., Feb. 28, 1937; s. Robert and Helen (Prakin) F.; m. Ruth Sybil Pudolsky, Nov. 5, 1961; children: Robert E., Abigail B., Brice S.H. AB, U. Wis., 1956; MD, Harvard U., 1960. Intern Boston City Hosp., 1960-61; resident in pediatrics Johns Hopkins Hosp., 1961-62, 64-65; vis. scientist Nat. Inst. Med. Research, London, 1965-66; with NIH, 1967-90; chief lab. of clin. investigation, clin. dir. Nat. Inst. Allergy and Infectious Diseases, Bethesda, Md., 1977-90; prof. Duke U. Med. Ctr., Durham, NC, 1990—, chmn.Ddept. Pediatrics, 1990—2004. Mem. ACP, Assn. Am. Physicians, Am. Soc. Clin. Investigation, Soc. Pediatric Rsch., Am. Pediatric Soc., Infectious Diseases Soc., Am. Acad. Allergy, Am. Acad. Pediatrics. Office: Duke U Med Ctr PO Box 3556 Durham NC 27710 Home Phone: 919-489-1964; Office Phone: 919-684-4626. Business E-Mail: frank007@mc.duke.edu.

FRANK, MICHAEL M., lawyer; b. NYC, Aug. 4, 1939; BS, Wash. U., 1961, JD, 1964. Bar: Mo. 1965, U.S. Dist. Ct. Mo. (Ea. Dist.) 1965. Former mcpl. judge, state prosecutor; former instr. St. Louis Met. Police Acad.; state prosecutor Cir. Atty.'s Office, St. Louis; ptnr. Frank & Juengel Attys. At Law PC, St. Louis. Lectr. in field; mem. Fed. Hate Crimes Task Force; mem. legal adv. bd. Anti Defamation League; bd. dirs. Mo. Prison Arts Bd. Mem.: ABA (past chmn.), NACDL (life), Mo. Mcpl. Judges Assn. (past pres.), St. Louis Met. Mcpl. Judges Assn. (past pres.), Mo. Assn. Criminal Def. Lawyers, Mo. Bar Assn., Bar Assn. Met. St. Louis. Office: Frank & Juengel Attys at Law 7777 Bonhomme Ave Ste 1601 Saint Louis MO 63105 Office Phone: 314-721-4403, 314-725-7777. Office Fax: 314-721-4377. E-mail: mfrank@primary.net.

FRANK, MICHAEL VICTOR, risk assessment engineer; b. NYC, Sept. 22, 1947; s. David and Bernice (Abrams) F.; m. Jane Griminger, Dec. 21, 1969; children: Jeffrey, Heidi, Heather. BS, UCLA, 1969, PhD, 1978; MS, Carnegie-Mellon U., Pitts., 1972. Registered profl. engr., Calif.; cert. mgmt. cons., cert. hazard and operability study leader. Engr. Westinghouse Electric Corp., Pitts., 1970-72, So. Calif. Edison, LA, 1972-74; lectr. U. Calif., Santa Barbara, 1976-77; task leader Gen. Atomics, San Diego, 1977-81; sr. exec. engr. NUS Corp., San Diego, 1981-85; with Mgmt. Analysis Co., San Diego, 1985-86; sr. cons. PLG, Newport Beach, Calif., 1986-89; pres. Safety Factor Assocs., Inc., Encinitas, Calif., 1989—2006; supr. Bechtel SAIC LLC, Las Vegas, 2006—, supr. safety and reliability analyses Yucca Mountain project, 2006—. Tech. dir. risk and reliability studies of NASA facilities, space and launch vehicles, internat. space sta., stratospheric obs. for infrared astronomy, space nuc. power systems, terrestrial nuc. power, nuc. waste, nuc. fuel fabrication faciliites; former risk mgmt. cons. US Interagy. Nuc. Safety Rev. Panel, NASA Hdqs., Ames Rsch. Ctr., Japan Aerospace Exploration Agy.; lectr. on risk assessment; mem. tech. program com. probabilistic safety assessment and mgmt. confs. Contbr. more than 90 articles to Reliability Engring. and System Safey, Risk Analysis, Nuc. Engring and Design, Nuc. Tech., ASME, European Safety and Reliability Soc., Am. Nuc. Soc., others; author: Choosing Safety: A Guide to Using Probabilistic Risk Assessment and Decision Analysis in Complex, High Consequence Systems, 2007. Mem.: IEEE (past pres. San Diego chpt. Reliability Soc.), Internat. Assn. Advancement Space Safety, Nuc. Technology. Avocations: running, skiing, hiking. E-mail: riskexpert@smileglobal.com.

FRANK, PETER SOLOMON, art historian, curator, critic; b. NYC, July 3, 1950; s. Reuven and Bernice (Kaplow) F. BA in Art History, Columbia U., 1972, MA in Art History, 1974. Art critic SoHo Weekly News, NYC, 1973-76; chief art critic Village Voice, NYC, 1977-79; art critic, columnist L.A. Weekly, 1988—; critic Long Beach Press-Telegram, 1993-96; L.A. corr. Contemporanea, 1989-91; curatorial assoc. Ind. Curators Inc., NYC and Washington, 1974—; co-curator Documenta VI, Kassel, W. Ger., 1976-77; assoc. editor Nat. Arts Guide, Chgo., 1979-81, Art Express, NYC, 1980-81; curator Exxon Nat. Exhbn. of Am. Artists, Guggenheim Mus., NYC, 1980-81, Dokumenta, Kassel, Germany, 1981; art critic Diversion mag., 1983-90; former editor Visions Art Quarterly; columnist Angeleno mag. Mem. faculty New Sch. for Social Rsch., 1974, Pratt Inst., 1975-76, Columbia U. Sch. Arts, 1978, Claremont Grad. Sch., 1989, 92-94, 95-97, U. Calif., Irvine, 1988-90, Calif. State U., Fullerton, 1990-91, U. Calif., Santa Barbara, 1994, Tyler Sch. Art; Am. curatorial advisor Documenta 8, 1986-87; organizer numerous theme and survey shows; co-curator "On Ramps: Moments of Transition in California Art", Pasadena Mus., California Art and "Fluxus Film and Video", Museo Reina Sofia, Madrid. Author: The Travelogues, 1982, Something Else Press: An Annotated Bibliography, 1983; co-author: New, Used and Improved: Art in the '80s, 1987; assoc. editor Tracks mag., 1974-76; editor Re Dact, 1983-85, contbg. editor Art Economist, 1981-84; contbr. articles to art periodicals including ARTnews and Art on Paper; writer on intermedia and Fluxus artists, many catalogues to one person and group exhbns.; edited Ken Friedman:Events for Jaap Rietmann, Inc. Nat. Endowment for Arts art critics travel fellow, 1978; critics project fellow, 1981; Royal Norwegian Ministry of Fgn. Affairs Fluxus rsch. fellow, 1987. Mem. Internat. Assn. Art Critics (v.p.), Coll. Art Assn., Internationale Künstlers Gremium Home: PO Box 24a36 Los Angeles CA 90024-1036 Office: LA Weekly PO Box 4315 Los Angeles CA 90078

FRANK, RICHARD ASHER, lawyer, health products executive; b. Omaha, Nov. 4, 1936; s. Alexander David and Sarah R. (Katz) F.; m. Susan Marie Kling; children: Brian, Hilary, Alexander, Nicholas. AB, Harvard U., 1958, JD, 1962. Bar: DC 1962, US Supreme Ct. Asst. legal advisor U.S. State Dept., Washington, 1962-69; dir. Ctr. Law and Social Policy, Washington, 1970-77; adminstr. NOAA, Washington, 1977-81; ptnr. Wald, Harkrader, Ross, Washington, 1981-87; pres. Population Svcs. Internat., Washington, 1987—. Adj. prof. Georgetown Law Sch., 1988—. Editor: The Constitution and the Conduct of Foreign Policy, 1976; contbr. articles to profl. jours. 1st lt. US Army, 1959—66. Mem.: Coun. Fgn. Rels. Avocations: sailing, tennis. Home: 3405 Lowell St NW Washington DC 20016-5024 Office: Population Svcs Internat 1120 19th St NW Washington DC 20036-3605 Office Phone: 202-785-0072. Business E-Mail: rfrank@psi.org.

FRANK, RICHARD CALHOUN, architect; b. Louisville, May 17, 1930; s. William George and Helen (Calhoun) F.; children: Richard, Scott, Elizabeth, William, Jennifer, Philip. BArch, U. Mich., 1953. Assoc. archtl. firms, Lansing, Mich., 1953-61; pres. Frank & Stein Assocs., Inc., Lansing, 1961-70; prin. Johnson, Johnson & Roy, Ann Arbor, 1971-75; pres. Preservation/Urban Design/Inc., Ann Arbor and Washington, 1975-84; pvt. practice Saline and Gregory, Mich., 1985—2004; pres. Frank, McCormick & Khalak, LLC, 2004—. Ind. contractor C.S. Mott Found., 1999-2000. Life trustee Hist. Soc. Mich. Fellow AIA (gold medal Mich. 1992); mem. Nat. Trust for Historic Preservation (trustee emeritus), Victorian Soc. Am. (v.p.). Home: 1408 Joliet Pl Detroit MI 48207 Office: 28 W Adams Detroit MI 48226 Home Phone: 313-567-7377; Office Phone: 313-234-8700. Personal E-mail: rcffaia@comcast.net. Business E-Mail: rcfrank@fmkdetroit.com.

FRANK, RICHARD G., healthcare educator; b. Boston, Apr. 27, 1952; BA in Econs., Bard Coll., 1974; PhD in Econs., Boston U., 1982. Prof. dept. health econs. Harvard Med. Sch., Boston, 1994-99, Margaret T. Morris prof. health econs., 1999—. Rsch. assoc. Nat. Bur. Econ. Rsch., Cambridge, Mass. and N.Y.C., 1987—. Office: Harvard Med Sch Dept Health Care Policy 180 Longwood Ave Boston MA 02115-5821

FRANK, RICHARD SANFORD, retired magazine editor; b. Paterson, NJ, July 28, 1931; s. David and Shirley (Dwoskin) F.; m. Margaret Schwartz, June 30, 1957 (dec. Apr. 2001); children: Daniel, Peter. BA, Syracuse U., 1953; MA, U. Chgo., 1956. Reporter Balt. Evening Sun, 1957-64, Phila. Bull., 1965-71; asst. to mayor City of Balt., 1964-65; reporter Nat. Jour., Washington, 1971-72, editor, 1972-76, editor-in-chief, 1976-97. Served with U.S. Army, 1953-55. Mem. Am. Soc. Mag. Editors Home: 5111 Wessling Ln Bethesda MD 20814-1232 Personal E-mail: richard.s.frank@verizon.net.

FRANK, ROBERT ALLEN, media consultant; b. Albany, NY, Sept. 26, 1932; s. Edward and Marian (Kostelanetz) Frank; m. Cynthia Tull, Aug. 1984; children: David, Chelsea, Alison. BA, Colby Coll., 1954; MBA, Amos Tuck Sch. Bus. Adminstrn., Dartmouth Coll., 1958. Cost control adminstr. ABC-TV, NYC, 1958-59; corp. auditor CBS, Inc., NYC, 1959-60, TV sales svc. account exec., 1961, account exec. radio network sales, 1962-69; exec. v.p., co-founder SFM Media Corp., NYC, 1969—97, pres. Media Svc. divsn., 1981—97; pres., CEO, SFM Media LLC, NYC, 1998-2000; vice-chmn. Media Planning Group USA, NYC, 2001—02; pvt. cons., 2003—04. Radio-TV cons. Nat. Kidney Fund, 1974; trustee Nat. Child Labor Com., 1984—96, vice chmn., 1994—96; trustee Myasthenia Gravis Found., 1984—93; bd. dirs. Judge Rotenberg Edn. Ctr., 2004—, bd. dirs. libr. programs, 2006—; active radio TV for various polit. campaigns Robert Kennedy for Senator, 1964, Richard Nixon for Pres., 1972, Ford for Pres., 1976, Bush for Pres., 1980, Reagan for Pres., 1980, Du Pont for Pres., 1988; mem. leadership coun. Nat. Rep. Congl. Com., Rep. Nat. Com., Pres.'s Club, 1984—88; mem. Citizens Rep. Pres. Com., 1984—88; mem. Inner Cir. Rep. Nat. Senatorial Com., 1985—88. Served to capt. USAF, 1954—56. Recipient Lifetime Achievement award, Media Week, 2001. Mem.: Internat. Radio-TV Soc., Amos Tuck Alumni Assn. N.Y. (pres. 1976—77, bd. dirs. 1979), Dartmouth Club (N.Y.C.), Pi Gamma Mu. Home: 35 Lounsbury Rd Ridgefield CT 06877-4710 Office: Conn Mktg 12 Godfrey Pl Wilton CT 06897

FRANK, ROBERT J., lawyer; b. NYC, July 27, 1924; BEE, Cornell U., 1949; MEE, Polytechnic Inst., NY, 1955; JD, Brooklyn Law Sch., 1959. Bar: NY 1960, US Dist. Ct., NY (So. & Ea. Dist.) 1968, Va. 1972, US Ct. of Customs and Patent Appeals 1974, DC 1978, US Dist. Ct., DC 1979, US Ct. of Appeals, Federal Circuit 1982, US Supreme Ct. 1984, US Ct. of Appeals, DC Circuit 1984, US Patent and Trademark Office. Engnr., 1954—; ptnr., technology div. Venable LLP, Washington. Mem.: IEEE, ABA, Am. Intellectual Property Law Assn., Va. State Bar Assn., DC Bar Assn. Office: Venable LLP 575 7th St NW Washington DC 20004 Office Phone: 202-344-4013. Office Fax: 202-344-8300. Business E-Mail: rjfrank@venable.com.

FRANK, ROBERT LOUIS, lawyer; b. Balt., Mar. 26, 1958; s. Louis Jr. and Beryl (Oppenheimer) F.; children: Robert Louis Jr., Michael David, Cameron Alexander, Victoria Rochelle. BSEE, Duke U., 1980; JD, U. Md., 1983. Bar: Md. 1983. Assoc. Belsky & Akman, Towson, Md., 1984-85; pvt. practice Reisterstown, Md., 1985; ptnr. Blitz Frank & Blitz, Owings Mills, Md., 1986-92, Needle, Montague & Frank, P.C., 1992-94; mem. Md. Ho. Dels., Annapolis, 1994-98; pvt. practice, 1994—2005; pres. Liberty Showcase Theatre, 2004—05. Vice-chair sci. and tech. subcom.; prof. Villa Julie Coll., 2005—. Pres. Pikesville (Md.) Recreation Parks Bd., 1988, Pikesville Baseball, 1984-86; pres. Reisterstown, Owings Mills C. of C., 1991; bd. dirs. Soldier's Delight Conservation, Inc. Mem. ABA, Md. State Bar Assn. (bd. govs. 1987-88, chmn. gen. practice sect. 1987-88), Balt. County Bar Assn., Balt. City Bar Assn., Psi Upsilon (scholarship 1978). Democrat. Home: 15 Sunnyking Dr Reisterstown MD 21136-6143

FRANK, ROBERTA, literature educator; b. NYC, Nov. 9, 1941; d. Norman Berton and Doris F.; m. Walter André Goffart, Dec. 31, 1977. BA, NYU, 1962; MA, Harvard U., 1964, PhD, 1968. Asst. prof. U. Toronto, 1968-73, assoc. prof., 1973-78, prof. English, 1978-2000, Univ. prof., 1995-2000, dir. grad studies dept. English, 1980-85, dir. Ctr. for Medieval Studies, 1994-99; Douglas Tracy Smith prof. English Yale U., 2000—. Mem. bus. bd. U. Toronto Press. Author: Old Norse Court Poetry, 1978, also articles; co-editor: Computers and Old English Concordances, 1970, A Plan for the Dictionary of Old English, 1973; gen. editor: Toronto Old English Series, 1976-2003; publs. of Dictionary of Old English, 1984-2003. Recipient Guggenheim award, 1985, Bowdoin prize in humanities Harvard U., 1968. Fellow Medieval Acad. Am. (councillor 1981-84, pres. 2006-07, Elliott prize 1972), Royal Soc. Can.; mem. MLA (mem. Old English exec. com. 1974-78, 95-99), Internat. Soc. Anglo-Saxonists (co-founder, pres. 1985-87). Office: Yale U Dept English New Haven CT 06520-8302 Home: 21 Temple Ct New Haven CT 06511 Office Phone: 203-432-2238. Business E-Mail: roberta.frank@yale.edu.

FRANK, RONALD EDWARD, marketing educator; b. Chgo., Sept. 15, 1933; s. Raymond and Ethel (Lundquist) F.; m. Iris Donner, June 18, 1958; children: Linda, Lauren, Kimberly. BSBA, Northwestern U., 1955, MBA, 1957; PhD, U. Chgo., 1960. Instr. bus. statistics Northwestern U., Evanston, Ill., 1956-57; asst. prof. bus. adminstrn. Harvard U., Boston, 1960-63, Stanford U., 1963-65; assoc. prof. mktg. Wharton Sch., U. Pa., 1965-68, prof., 1968-84, chmn. dept. mktg., 1971-74, vice dean, dir. rsch. and PhD programs, 1974-76, assoc. dean, 1981-83; dean, prof. mktg. Krannert Grad. Sch. Mgmt., Purdue U., 1984-89; dean, Asa Griggs Candler prof. mktg. Goizueta Bus. Sch. Emory U., Atlanta, 1989-98, dean, Asa Griggs Candler prof. mktg. emeritus, 1998-99; mktg. cons., 1999—; pres. Singapore Mgmt. U., 2001—04. Bd. dirs. Lafayette (Ind.) Life Ins. Co., The MAC Group, Home Hosp., Lafayette; cornerstone rsch. cons. to industry; mem. strategic issues com. Am. Assembly Collegiate Schs. of Bus., 1988-92, chmn. audit com., 1993-94, mem. strategic planning and ops. com,. 1994-95; chmn. Orgn. for the Future Task Force, 1996-97; trustee U. Singapore, 2000-01; chmn. strategic issues adv. com. Singapore Mgmt. U., 2004—. Author: (with Massy and Kuehn) Quantitative Techniques in Marketing Analysis, 1962, (with Matthews, Buzzell and Levitt) Marketing: an Introductory Analysis, 1964, (with William Massy) Computer Programs for the Analysis of Consumer Panel Data, 1964, An Econometric Approach to a Marketing Decision Model, 1971, (with Paul Green) Manager's Guide to Marketing Research, 1967, Quantative Methods in Marketing, 1967, (with Massy and Lodahl) Purchasing Behavior and Personal Attributes, 1968, (with Massy and Wind) Market Segmentation, 1972, (with Marshall Greenberg) Audience Segmentation Analysis for Public Television Program Development, Evaluation and Promotion, 1976, The Public's Use of Television, 1980, Audiences for Public Television, 1982. Bd. dirs., fin. com. Home Hosp. of Lafayette, 1985-89; bd. dirs. The Washington Campus, 1984-89, 95-98. Recipient pub. TV rsch. grants John and Mary R. Markle Found., 1975-82. Mem. Am. Mktg. Assn. (dir. 1968-70, v.p. mktg. edn. 1972-73), Inst. Mgmt. Sci., Assn. Consumer Rsch. Office Phone: 404-321-6655. Business E-Mail: ref@bus.emory.edu.

FRANK, RONALD WILLIAM, lawyer; b. Greensburg, Pa., Mar. 11, 1947; s. William John and Louise (Mautino) F.; m. Marsha Ann Kolesar, Aug. 30, 1969. BSChemE, Carnegie Mellon U., 1969; JD, Duke U., 1972. Bar: Pa. 1972. Ptnr. Buchanan Ingersoll P.C., Pitts., 1972-93, Babst, Calland, Clements & Zomnir, P.C., Pitts., 1993-99, Reed Smith LLP, Pitts., 2000—. Sec. Akers Nat. Roll Co.; chmn. PaintStar Paintball LLC. Contbr. articles to profl. jours. Chmn. nat. fund raising com., Carnegie-Mellon U., Pitts., 1983-88, bd. advisors Sch. Engring. and Sci., Carnegie Mellon U.; mem. bd. visitors sch. law Duke U., Durham, N.C. Mem. ABA, Pa. Bar Assn. (chmn. Internat. and Comparative law sect. 1992—), Allegheny County Bar Assn., Internat. Bar Assn., Duquesne Club, Shannopin Country Club. Avocations: golf, skiing, computers, amateur radio. Home: 1675 Gloucester Ct Sewickley PA 15143-8518 Office: Reed Smith 435 6th Ave Pittsburgh PA 15219-1886 Office Phone: 412-288-4044. Business E-Mail: rfrank@reedsmith.com.

FRANK, SISTER RUTH M., principal, educator; d. Walter A. Frank and Ruth Snyder. BS in Edn., Marylhurst U., Lake Oswego, Oreg., 1963; BA in Edn., U. San Francisco, 1983; postgrad., U. Notre Dame, 1990. Joined Sisters of St. Mary of Oreg., Roman Cath. Ch., 1956. Tchr., prin. Sacred Heart-Tillamook, Oreg., 1950—79; tchr. St. Marys, Stayton, Oreg., 1977—79; prin. St. Mary's Stayton, Oreg., 1987—90; tchr., prin. Archbishop Howard, Portland, Oreg., 1988—90; tchr. Holy Cross Sch., Portland, Oreg., 1991—98, prin., 1998—. Mem. accreditation teams, Oreg., 1998—2005; lectr. U. Portland, Oreg.; mem. Archbishop's coun., Portland, Oreg.; bd. trustees De La Salle North Cath. H.S. Mem.: IRA, ASCD, NCEA. Avocations: walking, music, watching sports, sewing. Home: 4595 SW 148th Ave Beaverton OR 97007 Office Fax: 503-286-5006. E-mail: rfrank@arohdpdx.org.

FRANK, STEVEN NEIL, chemist; b. Red Oak, Iowa, Feb. 15, 1947; s. Robert Joseph and Joyce (Erickson) F.; m. Carol Bert Femmer, Jan. 4, 1975. BS, Colo. State U., 1969; PhD, Calif. Inst. Tech., 1974. Sr. mem. tech. staff, solar energy project Tex. Instruments, Dallas, mgr. fuel cell devel., 1980-83, mgr. charge coupled imagers, 1983-86, mgr. wafer fabrication, focal plane array, 1986-88, mfg. mgr., focal plane array, 1988-90, mgr. focal plane array assembly and testing, 1990-91, mgr. uncooled IR imaging, 1990-99; chief engr. Raytheon Comml. Infared, Dallas, 1999—2002, chief tech. officer, 2002—04; v.p., chief tech. officer L-3 Comm. Infrared Products, 2004—. Presenter in field. Author: (with others) Laboratory Techniques in Electro-Analytical Chem, 1996; referee Jour. Applied Physics, 1977—, Jour. Phys. Chemistry, 1977—; contbr. articles to profl. jours. Robert A. Welch fellow U. Tex., 1974-77. Mem. AAAS, Am. Chem. Soc., Electrochem. Soc. Achievements include patents in field. Home: 471 Hackberry Dr Mc Kinney TX 75069-1569 Home Phone: 972-562-1989; Office Phone: 972-528-1389. E-mail: steven.frank@l-3com.com.

FRANK, STUART, cardiologist; b. NYC, Dec. 25, 1934; s. Henry and Kitty (Sternberg) F.; m. Nanchen O'Brien, Aug. 1976 (div. Feb. 1980); children: Rachel Arthur, Sebastian Noah; m. Amber Barnhart, June 22, 1982; children: Amelia Elizabeth, Abigail Kitty, Jessica Cole. BS in Chemistry, MIT, 1956; MD, NYU, 1960. Diplomate Am. Bd. Internal Medicine, Am. Bd. Cardiovascular Disease. Intern and resident in internal medicine Yale U. New Haven Hosp., 1960-64; postdoctoral fellow Inst. Cardiology, London, 1964-65, Nat. Heart Inst., Bethesda, Md., 1965-67; chief cardiology Kaiser Permanente Med. Ctr., San Francisco, 1967-77; assoc. prof. dept. medicine So. Ill. U., Springfield, 1977-86, chief div. cardiology, 1977-90, asst. chmn. dept. medicine, 1981-88, prof. dept. medicine, 1986—, dean of students, 1990-95. Author: The People's Handbook of Medical Care, 1972; contbr. numerous articles to profl. jours. Recipient Nellie Westerman prize Am. Fedn. Clin. Research, 1986. Fellow ACP, Am. Coll. Cardiology, Am. Coll. Chest Physicians, Am. Heart Assn.

(council clin. cardiology), Laennec Soc. Office: So Ill Univ Medicine Dept Cardiology PO Box 19636 Springfield IL 62794-9636 Home Phone: 217-546-5446; Office Phone: 217-545-0185.

FRANK, TERRENCE DOOLEY, diversified financial services company executive, director; b. St. Louis, Mo., Feb. 6, 1960; s. William Adolph and Cornelia Dooley Frank; children: Cornelia Dooley, Julie Elise, Terrence O'Brien. BA, Loyola U., 1983. Investment exec. Smith Barney, Clayton, Mo., 1986—95; v.p. PaineWebber, Clayton, 1995—2001; mng. dir. Century Securities, St Louis, 2001—. Bd. alderman Frontenac City, Frontenac, 1988—92. Conservative. Roman Catholic. Avocations: travel, golf. Home: 2 Country Fair Ln Saint Louis MO 63141 Office: Century Securities Associates Inc 501 N Broadway Saint Louis MO 63102 Home Phone: 314-497-2597; Office Phone: 314-342-2891.

FRANK, THEODORE DAVID, lawyer; b. Bklyn., Apr. 1, 1941; s. Paul and Bessie Frank; m. Louise Quinby Gorrell, Oct. 19, 1969; children: Carolyn Quinby Judge, Rachel Jackson. BS in Math., Rensselaer Polytech. Inst., 1963; LLB, U. Tex., 1966; LLM, Harvard U., 1969. Bar: Tex. 1966, D.C. 1969, U.S. Ct. Appeals (fed. cir. and 2d cir.) 1977, U.S. Ct. Appeals (5th and 9th cir.) 1980, U.S. Ct. Appeals (3rd cir. and 11th cir.) 1981, U.S. Ct. Appeals (D.C. cir.) 1970, U.S. Supreme Ct. 1978. Law clk. to Hon. Walter P. Gewin U.S. Cir. Ct., 5th cir., Tuscaloosa, Ala., 1966-67; faculty asst. for Ames Competition Harvard Law Sch., Cambridge, Mass., 1967-69; assoc. Arent, Fox, Kintner, Plotkin & Kahn, Washington, 1969-75, ptnr., 1976-97, Arnold & Porter LLP, Washington, 1997—2006, sr. council, 2007—. Hearing com. bd. profl. responsibility DC Bar, 1997-2003; co-chmn. Nat. Telecomms. Moot Ct. Com., 1999-2001. Chmn. zoning and tax coms. Springfield Civic Assn., Bethesda, Md., 1989—98. Mem. ABA, Fed. Comm. Bar Assn. (exec. com. 1996-98, co-chmn. profl. responsiblity com. 2001-03). Jewish. Avocations: woodworking, bike riding. Office: Arnold & Porter LLP 555 12th St NW Washington DC 20004-1206 Home Phone: 301-320-5505; Office Phone: 202-942-5790. Business E-Mail: theodore_frank@aporter.com.

FRANK, THOMAS, construction executive, management and design executive; b. Salt Lake City, Nov. 23, 1937; s. Simon and Suzanne (Seller) F. BFA, U. Utah, Provo, 1963. Lic. contractor Utah. Owner Thomas Frank Designers & Specifiers, Salt Lake City, 1962—; owner, pres. OmmiComputer West, Salt Lake City. Bd. dirs. Electronic Learning, Inc., Electronic Learning, Inc.; instr. design, textiles and drafting LDS Jr. Coll., Salt Lake City, 1963-86; lectr. on interior design for jr. and high schs. Bus. & Industry Coop. Edn. Program; profl. adviser interior design curriculum devel. program U. Utah; inter-profl. adv. coun. Utah State Bldg. Bd.; mem. adv. bd. Art Inst., Salt Lake City, 2007; cons., lectr., presenter in field. Contbr. articles to profl. publs. Exec. v.p. Salt Lake Art Ctr., 1977-80; spl. advisor Children's Ctr.; co-chmn. spl. events Utah divsn. Am. Cancer Soc., 1978; adv. bd. mem. Inst. of Art, Salt Lake, 2007. Recipient awards U. Utah, 1962, Utah Designers Craftsman Guild, 1962, State Fair Fine Arts, 1962, Recognition award Gov. Mrs. Scott Matheson, 1980, Honor award Utah Soc. AIA, 1980. Fellow Am. Soc. Interior Designers (bd. dir. Intermountain chpt. 2004-05); mem. N.Am. Autocadd Users Group, Nat. Kitchen and Bath Assn. (pres. mountain states chpt. west 1991-92), Am. Soc. Interior Designers (nat. long-range planning com. 1985-87, nat. comms. area coord. 1985, nat. membership devel. com. 1986-87, nat. regional dir. 1991-92, nat. edn. com. 1981, nat. chmn. energy conservation 1980-82, nat. chpt. pres.' orientation task force 1980, nat. bd. dir. 1977-82, chmn. regional indsl. rels. 1977-78, numerous other offices, numerous awards), AID (sec. Utah 1969-71, bd. govs. 1970-74, Utah pres. 1973-75), Nat. Coun. Interior Design Quantification. Avocations: tennis, skiing, art collecting. Home: 2360 Oakhill Dr Salt Lake City UT 84121-1520 Office: Thomas Frank Designers 3369 Highland Dr Salt Lake City UT 84106-3356 Office Phone: 801-484-1021. E-mail: tfdesigns@att.net.

FRANK, WILLIAM FIELDING, computer company executive, consultant; b. NYC, Oct. 27, 1944; s. Karl Frederick and Margaret Ruth (Denisson) F.; m. Linda Carol Hainfield, Dec. 20, 1965 (div. 1972); children: Aaron, Tobin. BA, Middlebury Coll., 1966; MA, U. Chgo., 1969; PhD, U. Pa., 1976. Assoc. prof. Oreg. State U., Corvallis, 1969-79; mem. tech. staff Bell Labs., Whippany, NJ, 1979-81; pres. Enterprise Engring. Assts. Inc., Warren, Vt., 1982-99; founder, chief scientist Cmty. Integration Tech., Manchester by the Sea, Mass., 1999—; with XTG, 2005—. Assoc. prof. MIT, Cambridge, 1981-85; cons. Citibank, 1982—, AT&T, 1984, N.Y. Times, 1985, Bank of Am., 1985, State of Calif., 1986—, Digital Equipment Corp., 1987-89, Soviet Ministry of Trade, 1990, Bankers Trust, 1991, Fidelity Investments, 1993—, Reuters, 1996, Ameritech, 1996, NEC, 1998—, U.S. chief delegate Internat. Stnds. Orgn., 1999—; tech. adv. bd. LIMITrader, 2000—, Bank of N.Y., 2000—. Contbr. articles to profl. jours. Rsch. grantee NSF, 1971, 77, NEH, 1976, 81. Mem. Assn. for Computing Machinery, Computer Soc. IEEE. Republican. Congregationalist. Achievements include pioneering of object-oriented enterprise modelling, client role modelling and research in business rule driven software design. Home and Office: XTG 363 7th Ave 11th Fl New York NY 10001

FRANK, WILLIAM P., lawyer; b. NYC, 1941; AB, Georgetown U., 1963; JD, Fordham U., 1966. Bar: NY 1967. Assoc. Skadden, Arps, Slate, Meagher & Flom LLP, NYC, head NYC office, 1992, nat. legal practice ptnr. for litigation, 1994—, serves on Policy Com. Exec. sec., planning and program com. Judicial Conference of the Court of Appeals for the Second Circuit, 1981—88; frequent panelist on seminars sponsored by Practising Law Institute, ABA, Glasser, ALI/ABA Law Journal Seminars-Press and NY Bar Assn. Bd. trustees Fordham U., 1988—; bd. dirs. Georgetown U., 1991—, bd. regents, 1988—94, bd. regents chmn., 1991—94; bd. dirs. Gregorian U. Found., 1994—. Mem.: ABA (chmn. class action and derivatives suits com. 1982—87, mem. class action improvements spl. com. 1982—87, mem. com. on jud. conf. 1988—92, mem. standing com. Judicial Selection, Tenure, Compensation 1993—95, chmn. com. 1995), Practicing Law Inst. (trustee 2002—), Fed. Bar. Coun. (mem. com. 2nd cir. Ct. of Appeals 1988—94, trustee 1989—99). Office: Skadden Arps Slate Meagher & Flom LLP 4 Times Sq Fl 24 New York NY 10036-6595 Office Phone: 212-735-2400. Office Fax: 917-777-2400. Business E-Mail: wfrank@skadden.com.

FRANK, ZE See FRANK, HOSEA

FRANKE, BRENT DOUGLAS, real estate/insurance executive; b. Milw., Feb. 13, 1949; s. Herbert Carl and Margaret A. (Custer) F. Assoc. Equitable/Stefaniak Realty, Brookfield, Wis., 1985-89, Prudential Life Ins. Co., 1989-90; agt. Nat. Guardian Life Ins. Co., Menomonee Falls, Wis., 1987-89. Owner Poplar Creek Enterprises Inc., 1989—, Opus IV Ltd., Brookfield, 1989— (formerly Poplar Creek Ltd.); State of Wis. regional mgr. Builder Profile Mag., 1991-94; illustrated parts list writer Briggs and Stratton Corp., Wauwatosa, Wis., 1994—. With USNR, 1970-76. Mem. Grad. Realtors Inst. Avocations: skiing, photography, reading, computers, home remodeling. Home and Office: 2126 N Wauwatosa Ave Wauwatosa WI 53213-1731 Office Phone: 414-259-5486. Personal E-mail: franke.brent@basco.com.

FRANKE, JACK EMIL, foreign language educator; b. Pine Bluff, Ark., July 8, 1965; s. Ernest Rudolph and Charlotte (Harris) F.; m. Lyudmila Veniaminovna Vagun, Aug. 30, 1996; 1 child, Maria. BA, U. Tex., 1987; MA, Monterey Inst. Internat. Studies, 1992; PhD, St. Petersburg U., Russia, 1995. Interpreter/at-sea rep. Marine Resource Corp., Seattle, 1988-90; tng. specialist-Russian Def. Lang. Inst., Monterey, Calif., 1990-94, prof. Russian, 2001—; computer-aided lang. instrn. dir. Dept. Fgn. Langs. George C. Marshall Ctr., Garmisch-Partenkirchen, Germany, 1994-97; asst. dean Def. Lang. Inst., 2007—. Pres. Ganbaru Yudanshakai, Monterey, 1997—2001, Monterey, 2005—; chmn. acad. adv. coun. Def. Lang. Inst., 2002—04. Co-author: Russian Topical Reader, 1992; (CD-ROM) Basic Military Language Course-Russian, 1993, The Big Silver Book of Russian Verbs, 2004, Streetwise Russian, Streetwise Chinese. Pres. acad. adv. coun. Def. Lang. Inst. Fgn. Lang. Ctr., 2002—04. With US Army, 1983—85. Named Disting. Alumnus, U. Tex., 2005, Exemplary Educator, Smart Tech Corp., 2005; recipient Campus Tech. Innovator award, Syllabus Mag., 2005. Mem. DAV, Am. Legion, U.S. Judo Fedn., Computer-Aided Lang. Instrn. Consortium, Am. Coun. on Tchg. Fgn. Langs., Phi Sigma Iota. Republican. Russian Orthodox. Avocations: Judo, travel. Office: Def Lang Inst PO Box 5818 Monterey CA 93944-0818 Fax: 831-373-2782. Personal E-mail: drfranke@yahoo.com.

FRANKE, JOHN CHARLES, retired human resources executive; b. Rochester, Minn., June 21, 1937; s. John Paul and Sophie (Thorson) F.; m. Marlys Jean Nordin, Jun 4, 1960 (div. Dec. 1978); children: John Richard, Gregory Wayne; m. Lois Ann Monnin Jones, Dec. 22, 1979; step child, Timothy Jones. BBA, U. Minn., Mpls., 1959, MA in Indsl. Rels., 1968. Life cert. sr. profl. in human resources; cert. Zenger-Miller facilitator. Rsch. asst. U. Minn. Indsl. Rels. Ctr., Mpls., 1960-61; group pers. dir. Mead Johnson & Co., Evansville, Ind., 1961-69; dir. pers. Charles F. Kettering Found., Dayton, Ohio, 1969-72; v.p. pers. Assoc. Mortgage Cos., Inc., Washington, 1972-74; founder, prin. Johns Assocs., Inc., Fairfax, Va., 1974-77; div. dir. human rels. TRW Motor Div., Dayton, 1977-82; dir. human resources Miami Valley Pub. Co., Dayton, 1983-84; dir. pers. Sverdrup Tech., Inc., 1984-85; v.p., dir. human resources Sverdrup Corp., St. Louis, 1986-93; dir. human resources, svc. contracts divsn. Calspan Corp., Tullahoma, Tenn., 1993-96. Adj. prof. Wright State U., Dayton, 1982-83, vis. asst. prof., 1983-84; cons., adj. prof. U. Evansville, Ind., 1964-67; conf. spkr. Profl. Svcs. Mgmt. Assn., Washington, 1986; seminar spkr. Profl. Women in Architecture/Engring., Phoenix, 1988. Bd. dirs. Fairfax Little League, Va., 1975-76; v.p. exec. com. Fairfax Police Youth Club, Inc., 1974-77; bd. dirs. Inroads of St. Louis, Inc., 1988-93; active Tullahoma Regional Planning Commn. and Bd. Zoning Appeals, 1994-96; active Sheriff's Law Enforcement Acad., 2006; citizen mem. employment eligibility panel Manatee County Sheriff's Dept., 2007. Named Disting. Alumnus, Tech. H.S., 2001. Mem. Soc. Human Resource Mgmt., Am. Mgmt. Assn., Human Resource Mgmt. Assn. Greater St. Louis (bd. dirs. 1990-93), Highland Rim Human Resource Mgmt. Assn. (treas. exec. com. 1985, pres. 1994, chair exec. com. 1994, exec. com. 1995), Tenn. State Coun., Soc. Human Resource Mgmt. (sec.-treas. 1995), St. Louis Area Health Care Buyers Coalition (adv. bd. 1992), Franklin/Coffee County Health Care Coalition (v.p. 1985), Imperial Lakes Condominium I Assn (pres. 2002, treas 2003), Master Assn. (sec./treas. 2001, v.p./sec. 2003), Condominium Assn., (v.p 2004, pres. 2005) Rotary, Lakewood Country Club. Republican. Avocations: photography, classic films, music, genealogy. Personal E-mail: eknarf@tampabay.rr.com.

FRANKE, LOUISE ANNA, early childhood educator, farmland manager; b. Belleville, Ill., Nov. 23, 1947; d. Ralph John Scherer and Jeanette (Givenrod) Russell; m. Dennis Franke, Mar. 7, 1965 (div. Dec. 1981); children: Michael, Keith. Student, Belleville Coll., 1987-97, Pacific Oaks Coll., 1992, Kaskaskia Coll., 1994. Tchrs. aide My Friends Presch., Mascoutah, Ill., 1983—88; head tchr. St. Martin of Tours Child Devel. Ctr., Mascoutah, Ill., 1988—2000, asst. dir., tchr., 1998—2000, ret., 2000. Contbr. articles to profl. jour. Mem. Presidents Club, Rep. Nat. Com., 2003. Recipient Key to the City Gladstone (Ill.) Bd.Edn., 1976, Presdl. award PTA of Gladstone, 1972-76, Lifetime Achievement award St. Martin of Tours Ch., 1996, Pastorial award St. Martin of Tours Ch., 1997; nominee Golden Apple award Outstanding Tchr. St. Clair County, 1997. Mem. Nat. Assn. Edn. Young Children (life), Nat. Reyes Syndrome Assn. (area coord. Ill. 1997), Mascoutah C. of C., Order of the Ea. Star, Century Club McKendree Coll. Republican. Avocations: soil conservation, real estate development, travel, continuing education. Home and Office: 11602 Renth Rd New Baden IL 62265-2114

FRANKE, WAYNE THOMAS, retired government affairs director, consultant; b. San Angelo, Tex., June 23, 1950; s. Bernard Raymond and Henrietta Elizabeth (Kozelsky) Franke; m. Regina Gale Franke; 1 child, Mauri Jane stepchildren: Colton, Christina. BBA in Gen. Bus., Angelo State U., San Angelo, Tex., 1972. Adminstrv. clk. Gen. Telephone Co. S.W., San Angelo, 1968—72, comm. cons. Irving, Tex., 1972—75, asst. govt. affairs mgr. San Angelo, 1975—78, mgr. govt. affairs Austin, Tex., 1979—86, dir. govt. affairs, 1986—98; owner MJWT Cons., Austin, 1998—; majority owner DOBWEST L.P.; ptnr. Bus. Ptnrs. Ltd., Austin, BGWT, LLC. Mem. legis. affairs com. Tex. Indsl. Devel. Coun., College Station, 1977—84, chmn., Austin, 1981—83, mem. energy and awards coms., 1978—79; mem. US Spkr. Jim Wright's Diplomatic Mission to Moscow, 1987. Fundraiser Boy Scouts Am., Austin, 1987-88, Austin Performing Arts Ctr., 1998-2000; loaned exec. Tarrant County United Way, 1973-74; issues mgmt. adv. coun. North Tex. Commn., Dallas, 1985-87; program chmn. John Ben Shepperd Leadership Forum, Odessa, Tex., 1986, chmn., Austin, 1987, John Ben Shepperd Alumni Forum, 1988; mem. John Ben Shepperd Governing Bd., 1990-91, chmn. fin., 1990-91, fin. com. 1990-92, adv. bd., 1991-93, vice-chmn. John Ben Shepperd Found., 1997-98, chmn., 1998-99, bd. dirs., 1997—; corp. co-chmn. drive United Cerebral Palsy Assn., Austin area, 1990-96; mem. Hays Country Oaks Archtl. Control & Protection Com., 1993-96; steering com., fundraising Travis County Assn. Retarded Citizens; trustee West Tex. Boy's Ranch Found., 1995-2005, treas. exec. com., 1999-2001, chmn. 2001-02; chmn. Tex. Statehood Sesquicentennial Program, 1996; bd. dirs. Angelo State U. Ex-Students Assn., 1999-2005, Hays CISD Edn. Found., 2005—, Angelo State U. Found., 2006—; mem. task force Schs. and Coms. Offering Positive Experiences, Hays ISD, 2003-05; mem. pastoral coun. St. Paul's Cath. Ch., 2006—. Recipient External Team Excellence award GTE, 1992-93, Strive for Excellence award, 1992; named Lobbyist of the Year for GTE Corp., 1987, 91, 1989 Disting. Alumnus, Angelo State U.; Wayne Franke Day proclaimed by San Angelo, Tex. City Council Oct. 14, 1989, one of ten Rising Stars of Tex., Tex. Bus. mag., 1988. Mem.: KC (recorder 2003), Lewisville/San Angelo C. of C. (amb. 1974—77, Amb. of Yr. 1975, 1976), Bus. Ins. Consumers Assn. (exec. com. 1990—95), West Tex. C. of C. (state affairs com., legis. adv. coun.), Homeowners Assn., Tex. Self-Ins. Assn. (co-chair legis. com. 1993), Tex. Taxpayers and Rsch. Assn. (state affairs com. 1985—97), Tex. Assn. Bus. and C. of C. (chmn. state affairs com. 1977—79, bd. dirs. Austin chpt. 1985—88, vice chmn. 1987, statewide state affairs com.), Austin Economic Club, St. Paul's Cath. Ch. (vision com. 2001—02, co-chair 2005 St. Paul's parish festival), Optimists (sec. Irving chpt. 1973—74, v.p. youth work 1974—75, pres. 1975, bd. dirs. San Angelo chpt. 1977, lt. gov. North Tex. dist. 1978—79, Stars of Tex Rodeo-Art Com. 2004—05). Roman Catholic. Avocations: golf, rock work, fishing, tree trimming, camping.

FRANKE, WILLIAM AUGUSTUS, investor; b. Bryan, Tex., Apr. 15, 1937; s. Louis John and Frances (Hanna) F.; m. Carolyn Diane Franke; children: Catherine Anne, Paige Estelle, Brian Hanna, David Parker, Rebecca. BA, Stanford U., 1959, LLB, 1961. Bar: Wash. 1961. With MacGillivray, Jones, Clark & Schiffner, Spokane, 1962-69; ptnr. S.W. Forest Industries, Phoenix, 1970-86; CEO S.W. Forest Industries (merged with Stone Container Corp.), Phoenix, 1978—87; pres., owner Franke & Co., Inc., Phoenix, 1987—; chmn., CEO Am. West Holdings, Corp., Phoenix, 1992—2001; mng. ptnr. Newbridge L.Am., LLP, 1996—, Indigo Ptnrs. LLC, 2001—. Chmn. bd., CEO Am. West Airlines, Inc., Phoenix, 1994—2001; bd. dirs. Phelps Dodge Corp.; mng. ptnr. Newbridge Latin Am. LLP; pres., CEO Indigo Ptnrs. LLC; chmn. Tiger Airways PTE. Ltd., WIZZ Air, Hungary. Served to capt. U.S. Army, 1961-62. Mem. ABA, Wash. Bar Assn., Chief Execs. Orgn., Paradise Valley Country Club. Episcopalian. Office: 2525 E Camelback Rd Ste 800 Phoenix AZ 85016-4230

FRANKEL, ADAM B., lawyer; b. NYC, 1968; m. Stephanie Frankel; 2 children. BA Econ., Brown U., 1989; JD, Stanford Law Sch., 1993. Clerk US Dist. Judge Anna Diggs Taylor, Mich. Ea. Dist.; corp. transaction atty. Simpson Thacher & Bartlett, 1995—99, Ford Motor Co., 1999—2003; founder in-house legal dept., atty. Genesee & Wyoming, 2003—06; sr. mng. dir., gen. counsel, 2006—. Mem. bd. dirs. Picis, Inc. Avocations: reading, tennis. Office: Evercore Partners Inc 55 E 52nd St New York NY 10055 Office Phone: 212-857-3100. Office Fax: 212-857-3101.*

FRANKEL, ANDREW JOEL, management consultant, information scientist; b. NYC, Oct. 7, 1945; s. Lazar Hirsch and Estelle Rose (Fuchs) F.; m. Marilyn Judith Marcus, Dec. 24, 1967; children: Jennifer Lauren, Jonathan Matthew. BSChemE, N.J. Inst. Tech., 1968; M of Engring., NYU, 1970; postgrad. in fin., U. Hartford, 1971-72. Cert.: CompTIA (A-plus cert.), Dell (DCSE). Physicist ABB Combustion Engring., Windsor, Conn., 1970-76, lead engr., 1976-77; nat. dir. nuc. non-proliferation programs Oak Ridge (Tenn.) Nat. Lab., 1977-78; mgr. mkt. intelligence dept. NAC Internat., Inc., Atlanta, 1978-80, gen. mgr., dir. Fuel-Trac divsn., 1980-86; mgr. mktg. info. systems Martin Marietta Energy Systems, Inc., Oak Ridge, 1986-89, mgr. info. resources, 1989-91; mgr. fin. and strategic planning Martin Marietta Utility Svcs., Inc., Oak Ridge, 1991-94; ops. cons. Lockheed Martin Utility Svcs. Inc., Bethesda, Md., 1994-97; sr. mgr. info. tech., bus. proc. re-engring Universal Scheduling Co., Bala Cynwyd, Pa., 1997-98; prin. AJF Consulting Solutions, Paducah, Ky., 1998-2000; interim v.p., dir. software devel. VR2Ltrade.net, Inc., Orlando, Fla., 2000; prin., indsl. cons. and sys. practice Am. Mgmt. Systems, Inc., Fairfax, Va., 2000—01; ind. cons. Orlando, 2001—05, Atlanta, 2006—. Contbr. articles to profl. jours. U.S. del. Internat. Nuc. Fuel Cycle Evaluation, Washington, 1977-78; nat. security cons. White House, Washington, 1977-78; nuc. safety advisor Conn. Gov.'s Office, Hartford, 1975-77. NSF fellow, 1968-70. Mem. Am. Nuc. Soc. (sec. Conn. chpt. 1976-77), Tau Beta Pi (v.p. N.Y.C. Met. chpt. 1969, pres. 1970), Omega Chi Epsilon. Republican. Methodist. Achievements include research in nuclear power, nuclear safety, nuclear arms control, nuclear non-proliferation, business process re-engineering and ERP software solutions; privatization of U.S. government uranium enrichment program. Address: 21011 Gardner Dr Alpharetta GA 30004-2164 Business E-Mail: afrankel@ajfconsulting.com.

FRANKEL, CARL ABBOTT, ophthalmologist; b. NYC, Dec. 21, 1954; s. Howard Jay and Marilyn Shinske Frankel; m. Sharon Riva Drucker, Aug. 31, 1980; children: Rachel, Jodi, Lauren. BA, U. Va., Charlottesville, 1976; MD, Ea. Va. Med. Sch., Norfolk, 1980. Asst. prof. ophthalmology Hershey Med. Ctr., Pa. State U., Pa., 1985—92; ophthalmologist pvt. practice, Harrisburg, Pa., 1992—. Fellow: Am. Coll. Surgeons, Am. Bd. Ophthalmology. Avocations: skiing, scuba diving, sailing. Office: 1800 Linglestown Rd Ste 200 Harrisburg PA 17110

FRANKEL, CHARLES JAMES, III, banker; b. Charlottesville, Va., Feb. 14, 1944; s. Charles James II and Gladys (Birmingham) F.; m. Dawn Marie Hornung, Oct. 23, 1964; 1 child, Kimberly Mavourneen Student, U. Va., 1961—65; BS, Fla. Atlantic U., 1966, MEd, 1967. Asst. v.p. Wachovia Bank & Trust Co., Winston-Salem, NC, 1967—74; exec. v.p. Sun Bank/So. Fla., Nat. Assn., Ft. Lauderdale, 1974—85; pres. Pan Am. Bank of Broward, Ft. Lauderdale, 1985—86; sr. v.p. and dir. pvt. banking, ea. U.S. and internat. Nations Bank, Ft. Lauderdale, 1989—91; with Fla. pvt. banking, 1986—88, 1992—93; mng. dir., bd. dirs. U.S. Trust Co. Fla., Boca Raton, 1993—2003, divsn. pres., 2003—06; pres., dir. Cypress Trust Co., 2006—. Pvt. lending com. Robert Morris Assocs., Phila., 1990-93; spkr. in field Pres. Greater Ft. Lauderdale Touchdown Club, 1981; chmn. Blockbuster Bowl, Ft. Lauderdale, 1992; bd. dirs. Ft. Lauderdale Beach Redevel. Bd., 1991, Greater Ft. Lauderdale C. of C. Found., 1992, Ft. Lauderdale Parks and Recreation Bd., 1992-96, Fla. Atlantic U. Found., Gulf Stream (Fla.) Civic Assn., Golden Bell Found.; active Va. Student Aid Found., U. Va. Nat. Campaign Com., nat. leadership gifts coun. 1996-2000, 2005—; lay eucharistic min. All Saints Episcopal Ch., 1994-98; chalice bearer, lector St. Paul's Episcopal Ch., 1998-2001; vestryman, lector, usher Bethesda-by-the Sea Episcopal Ch., treas. 2007-; bd. dirs. Bethesda Meml. Hosp. Found., chmn. investment com., 2003-04, mem. investment com., 2005—; mem. archtl. rev. bd. Town of Gulf Stream, 1999—, vice chmn. archtl. rev. bd., 2006—; bd. trustees Gulf Stream Sch., 2005—. Recipient Disting. Am. award Nat. Football Found., Brian Piccolo chpt., 1991; named Cystic Fibrosis Leading Man of Palm Beach County, 2002 Mem. Am. Bankers Assn. (pvt. banking exec. com. 1991-92), Jr. Achievement (bd. advisors 1988-91), Lauderdale Yacht Club (bd. govs. 1984-88), Tower Club (bd. dirs. 1985-93), Boca Raton C. of C. (bd. dirs., treas. 2000-01, vice chmn. 2002-03, chair-elect 2003-04, chmn. 2004-05), Lago Mar Beach Club, Boca Raton Hist. Soc. (bd. dirs. 1995-2001, bd. advisors 2001—), Scuttlebutt Club, Sunshine Football Classic (trustee, exec. com., 1992-2001), Gulf Stream Bath and Tennis Club (bd. govs., past pres.), Hundred Club of Palm Beach County, Farmington Country Club Episcopalian. Avocations: tennis, arts. Office: 218 Royal Palm Way Palm Beach FL 33480 Office Phone: 561-820-2004. Business E-Mail: charles.frankel@cypresscapitalgroup.com.

FRANKEL, DIANE, former museum institute administrator; b. NYC, Nov. 13, 1942; d. Harry and Frances Bejosa; m. Charles Louis Frankel, July 10, 1966; children: Alexander, Matthew. BA in Psychology, U. Calif., Berkeley, 1964; MA in Museum Edn., George Washington U., 1976. Cert. in Mus. Mgmt. Outreach educator U. Botswana, Lesotho and Swaziland, 1974-75; assoc. dir. edn. San Francisco Mus. Modern Art, 1976-80; dir. Ctr. for Mus. Studies John F. Kennedy U., Orinda, Calif., 1980-85, assoc. dean Sch. Liberal and Profl. Arts, 1980-85, dean Sch. Liberal and Profl. Arts, 1985-86; exec. dir. Bay Area Discovery Mus., Sausalito, Calif., 1986-93; dir. Inst. Mus. Svcs., Washington, 1993—99; program dir. for children, youth & families James Irvine Found., San Francisco, 1999—2003; co-chair One City One Book: San Francisco Reads, 2005—. Chair Career Day, ArtTable, San Francisco, 1989, 92, chair Washington chpt., 1995-96. Co-founder Wise-Up support group for women candidates, San Francisco; mem. vis. com. Getty Info. Inst., 1997-99, Blue Ribbon commn. Nat. Mus. Am. History, 2001-02. Named to Centennial Honor Roll, Am. Assn. Museums, 2006. Mem. Assn. Youth Museums (coun. 1991), Am. Assn. Museums (chair Women Dirs. Breakfast 1992, 93). Avocations: reading, travel, hiking.*

FRANKEL, ERNST GABRIEL, shipping and aviation business executive, educator; b. Beuthen, Germany, Oct. 17, 1923; came to U.S., 1959, naturalized, 1964. s. Siegfried Samuel and Martha (Blumenthal) F.; m. Inna Kordonsky, Sept. 9, 1990; 1 child, Michael. BS, London U., 1948; MS in Marine-Mech. Engring., MIT, 1960; MBA, Boston U., 1979, D of Bus. Adminstrn., 1986; PhD in Econs., U. Wales, 1985. Chief engr. ZimNav Co., Haifa, Israel, 1950-59; asst. prof. MIT, Cambridge, Mass., 1960-64, assoc. prof., 1964-65, mem. faculty, 1970—, prof. marine systems, 1970—, prof. mgmt. Sloan Sch., 1993—; chief divsn. operation analysis maritime adminstrn. Dept. of Commerce, 1965-66; tech. dir. Litton Industries, Beverly Hills, Calif., 1966-70. Pres. E.G. Frankel, Inc., Boston, 1969—; port, shipping and aviation advisor World Bank, 1982-89; sr. advisor on ports to sec. gen. Internat. Maritime Orgn., 1987-98; chmn. Am. Pres. Lines, Inc., 1997-2000; bd. dirs. Am. Eagle Tankers, 2003-, Am. Pres. Lines Inc., APL Inc., 1992-2002; mem. bd. advisors Panama Canal Authority; advisor Maritime Port Authority of Singapore, 1997-02. Author: Ocean Transportation, 1973, Regulation and Policies of American Shipping, 1982, Management and Operations of American Shipping, 1982, Systems Reliability and Risk Analysis, 1984, Port Planning and Development, 1986, The World Shipping Industry-Economic Transition, 1987, Project Management, 1989, Management of Technological Change, 1989, In Pursuit of Technological Excellence, 1993, Ocean Environmental Management, 1994, America's Institutional Dilemma, 1998, Managing Development, 2005, Challenging American Leadership, 2006. Served with Royal Navy, 1942-45. Recipient Gold medal Brit. Govt., 1956. Mem. Soc. Naval Architects and Marine Engrs., Ops. Rsch. Am., The Inst. of Man Scis., Marine Engrs., Internat. Assn. Maritime Economists (pres. 2003—). Home: 283 Buckminster Rd Brookline MA 02445-5841 Office Phone: 617-253-6763. Business E-Mail: efrankel@mit.edu.

FRANKEL, FRANCINE RUTH, political science professor; b. NYC, Aug. 31, 1935; d. William and Dora (Tuchschneider) Goldberg; m. Douglas Vernon Verney, Nov. 28, 1975. BA, CCNY, 1956; MA, Johns Hopkins U., 1958; PhD, U. Chgo., 1965. Asst. prof. U. Pa., Phila., 1965-70, assoc. prof., 1970-79, prof., 1979—, prof. South Asian studies, 1978—, Madan Lal Sobt prof. study contemporary India, 2004—06, dir. Ctr. Advanced Study of India, 1992—2006. Vis. fellow Ctr. of Internat. Studies, Princeton (NJ) U., 1969-73; resident scholar Bellagio Study and Conf. Ctr., 1975; vis. mem. Inst. Advanced Study, 1976; mem.-at-large Commn. Internat. Rels., Nat. Acad. Scis., 1973-79; mem. del. South Asian specialists to China, 1986; founding mem. U. Pa. Inst. for Advanced Study of India, New Delhi, 1995—. Author: India's Political Economy, 1947-2004, 2d edit., 2005, India's Political Economy, 1947-1977, The Gradual Revolution, 1978, Chinese edit., 1990, India's Green Revolution, 1971; editor, contbr. Dominance and State Power in Modern India, Decline of a Social Order, 2 vols., 1989-90, Bridging the Non-Proliferation Gap: India and the United States, 1995, Transforming India, Social and Political Dynamics of Democracy, 2000, The India-China Relationship: What the United States Needs to Know, 2004; contbr. articles on India's polit. economy, fgn. policy to profl. jours. Grantee Am. Inst. Indian Studies, 1979-80, Smithsonian Instn., 1983-86, Social Sci. Rsch. Coun., 1989-91; Woodrow Wilson fellow, 1997-98, Scholar in Residence Woodrow Wilson Internat. Ctr. for Scholars, 2006-07. Mem. Am. Polit. Sci. Assn., Assn. Asian Studies, Coun. Fgn. Rels. Home: 104 Pine St Philadelphia PA 19106-4312 Office: U Pa Dept Polit Sci 217 Stiteler Hall Philadelphia PA 19104 E-mail: ffrankel@sas.upenn.edu.

FRANKEL, JAMES BURTON, retired lawyer; b. Chgo., Feb. 25, 1924; s. Louis and Thelma (Cohn) F.; m. Louise Untermyer, Jan. 22, 1956; children: Nina, Sara, Simon. Student, U. Chgo., 1940-42; BS, U.S. Naval Acad., 1945; LLB, Yale U., 1952; MPA, Harvard U., 1990. Bar: Calif. 1953. Mem. Steinhart, Goldberg, Feigenbaum & Ladar, San Francisco, 1954-72; of counsel Cooper, White & Cooper, San Francisco, 1972-97; ret., 2000. Sr. fellow, lectr. in law Yale U., 1971—72; lectr. Stanford U. Law Sch., 1973—75; vis. prof. U. Calif. Law Sch., 1975—76, lectr., 1992—2000, U. San Francisco Law Sch., 1994—2000; adj. asst. prof. Hastings Coll. Law, 1996—2000. Pres. Coun. Civic Unity of San Francisco Bay Area, 1964-66; chmn. San Francisco Citizens Charter Revision Com., 1968-70; mem. San Francisco Pub. Schs. Commn., 1975-76; trustee Natural Resources Def. Coun., 1972-77, 79-92, staff atty., 1977-79, hon. trustee, 1992—; chmn. San Francisco Citizens Energy Policy Adv. Com., 1981-82. Mem. ABA, Calif. Bar Assn.

FRANKEL, JENNIE LOUISE, writer, composer, playwright; b. Chgo., Aug. 7, 1949; Student, Roosevelt U., 1968, U. Hawaii, 1969-71, Golden West Law Sch., 1976. Fashion model, singer/actor in TV commls., 1967—81; performer Comedy Store and the Improvisation, LA, 1977—79. Co-author: You'll Never Make Love in this Town Again, 1996 (NY Times Bestseller), Unfinished Lives, 1996, Tales From The Casting Couch, 1996; composer network TV theme songs, 1998-99, Youth at the Greek, 1999, Heartwalk LA Theme; columnist. Active USO Vietnam Tour, 1968; bd. govs. Hollywood Scriptwriting Inst.; judge Cable Ace Awards, 1987—96. Mem. The Recording Acad. Grammys, Acad. TV Arts & Scis. (blue ribbon panel judge Emmys), Acad. Country Music, LA Women in Music (bd. dirs. 1991-92), Circumnavigators Club Avocation: comedy.

FRANKEL, KENNETH M., lawyer; b. NYC, Apr. 22, 1948; BS, U. Pa., 1970; JD with honors, George Washington U., 1973. Bar: Va. 1973, DC 1981, lic.: US Supreme Ct. 1979, US Ct. Appeals (Fed. Cir.) 1982, US Dist. Ct. (Ea. Dist.) Va. 1995. Law clk. to Hon. George Willi US Ct. of Claims, 1973—74; trial atty. US Justice Dept, Antitrust Divsn.; ptnr. Finnegan, Henderson, Farabow, Garrett & Dunner LLP, Reston, Va., leader intellectual property specialties practice group. Bd. dir. DC Computer Law Forum, 1987—92, pres., 1988—89. Mem.: ABA (Litig. Sect., Antitrust Sect., Patent & Trademark & Copy Law Sect.), Va. State Bar, Am. Intellectual Property Law Assn. (chmn. antitrust law com. 2001—03). Office: Finnegan Henderson Farabow Garrett & Dunner LLP Two Freedom Sq 11955 Freedom Dr Reston VA 20190-5675 Office Phone: 571-203-2700. Office Fax: 202-408-4400. Business E-Mail: kenneth.frankel@finnegan.com.

FRANKEL, MARTIN RICHARD, statistician, educator, consultant; b. Wash., June 16, 1943; s. Lester R. and Vera B. Frankel; m. Jean L. Kaiser, Mar. 24, 1970; children: Jennifer, Margaux. BA, U. N.C., 1965; MA, U. Mich., 1967, PhD, 1971. Asst. prof. stats., assoc. prof. U. Chgo., 1971—76; prof. stats and computer info. sys. Baruch Coll. CUNY, 1977—, assoc. chair, 1995—. Tech. dir. Nat. Opinion Rsch. Ctr. U. Chgo., 1972—96; sr. statis. scientist Abt Assocs., Cambridge, Mass., 1996—; chmn. Quality Rsch. Coun. Nat. Rsch. Found., 1988—, cons. statis. methods and quality control, 1965—; mem. panel occupl. and health stats., com. nat. stats. Nat. Rsch. Coun. NAS, 1985—87. Author: Inference from Survey Samples: An Empirical Investigation, 1971; co-author: SEPP: Sampling Error Program Package, 1972, Total Survey Error: Applications to Improve Health Surveys, 1979; mem. editl. bd. Pub. Opinion Quar., Ency. Statis. Scis., Sociol. Rsch. and Methods; contbr. articles to profl. jours. Fellow: Internat. Statis. Inst., Royal Statis. Soc., Am. Statis. Assn. (chmn. census adv. com. 1981, chmn. sect. survey rsch. methods 1975—76, editl. bd. jour.); mem.: Market Rsch. Coun. (pres. 1995—96), Am. Assn. Pub. Opinion Rsch. (chmn. stds. com.). Home: 14 Patricia Ln Cos Cob CT 06807-1734 Office: Baruch Coll 17 Lexington Ave New York NY 10010-5518 Business E-Mail: martin_frankel@baruch.cuny.edu.

FRANKEL, MARY ANN (KATE FRANKEL), librarian, teacher; b. San Francisco, Feb. 24, 1926; d. Samuel Joseph Spear and Julie Bernice (Calio) Le Pla; m. Benjamin Adam Frankel, June 14, 1950; children— Daniel Adam, Rachel Lynn. B.A., U. Calif.-Berkeley, 1949, cert. in teaching, 1951, M.L.S., 1965. Librarian, San Leandro Pub. Sch., Calif., 1965, Richmond Schs., Calif., 1965-67; librarian Berkeley Schs., Calif., 1967-78, tchr. English, 1978-82, field librarian, 1982-87. Editor: Storyline 1988—. Chmn. PTA Council Study Elem. Libraries, Berkeley, 1964-65; docent Calif. Acad. Scis., 1988—. Mem. East Bay Reading Assn., ALA, LWV (co-chmn. nat. security study 1984-85), San Francisco Recorder Soc., Storytelling Assn. Alta Calif.(bd. dirs., storyteller). Avocations: early music; participant in recorder groups.

FRANKEL, MAX, retired journalist; b. Gera, Germany, Apr. 3, 1930; came to U.S., 1940, naturalized, 1948; s. Jacob A. and Mary (Katz) F.; m. Tobia Brown, June 19, 1956 (dec. Mar. 1987); children: David M., Margot S., Jonathan M.; m. Joyce Purnick, Dec. 11, 1988. AB, Columbia, 1952, MA in Polit. Sci, 1953. Mem. staff N.Y. Times, NYC, 1952-94, chief Washington corr., 1968-73, Sunday editor, 1973-76, editl. pages editor, 1977-86, exec. editor, 1986-94; ret., 1995. Columnist N.Y. Times mag., 1995-2000. Served with AUS, 1953-55. Recipient Pulitzer prize for internat. reporting, 1973 Office: 15 West 67 St New York NY 10023-6226 E-mail: maxmaxnyt@yahoo.com.

FRANKEL, RICHARD WILLIAM, retired vending company executive; b. Newark, Nov. 8, 1923; s. Charles and Helen Katherine (Kussy) Frankel; m. Betty Sophia Schwartz (dec.); children: Martha F. Stern, Barbara A. Wedler, Edward H.; m. Doreen Gordon. BS, U. Mich., Ann Arbor, 1947. Registered profl. engr. Engr. Mich. Bell Tel., Detroit, 1948—55, sr. statis., 1956; CEO R&B Stamp Vending Svc., Farmington, Mich., 1957—99; ret., 1999. Mem. charter commn. City of Farmington Hills; bd. dirs. Farmington Hills Bd. Edn., 1968; mem. bd. mgmr. fund raising Farmington YMCA, 1968—80. 1st lt. Signal Corps US Army, 1944—47, PTO, 1st lt. Signal Corps US Army, 1950—52. Mem.: Mich. Nature Assn., Am. Contract Bridge League, Mich. Bot. Club. Democrat. Avocation: bridge. Home: 5801 Miller Way E Bloomfield Hills MI 48301

FRANKEL, SHERMAN, physicist, educator; b. NYC, Nov. 15, 1922; s. Harry and Rose F.; m. Ruzena Bajcsy, Oct. 22, 1981; 1 son by previous marriage, Walter. BA, Bklyn. Coll., 1943; MS, U. Ill., 1947, PhD, 1949. Mem. staff radiation lab. MIT, 1943-46; instr. U. Pa., Phila., 1950-52, asst. prof. physics, 1952-56, assoc. prof., 1956-60, prof., 1960—. Vis. scientist Niels Bohr Inst., Denmark, 1968, C.E.R.N. Geneva, 1975, C.E.N. de Saclay, France, 1979; guest fellow Stanford U. Ctr. for Internat. Security Arms Control, 1987; guest scholar Brookings Inst., 1987; Security Progrm sr. fellow MIT, 1998-2004; vis. prof. bioengrig. U. Calif., Berkeley, 2002-04 Assoc. editor Rev. of Sci. Instruments, 1952-53. Guggenheim fellow, 1957, 79 Fellow Am. Phys. Soc.; mem. N.Y. Acad. Sci., Sigma Xi, Pi Mu Epsilon. Home: 2320 Delancey Pl Philadelphia PA 19103-6407 Office: U Pa Physics Dept 33d and Walnut Sts Philadelphia PA 19104 Office Phone: 215-898-8146. Business E-Mail: frankel@physics.upenn.edu.

FRANKEL, TERRIE MAXINE, writer, composer, playwright; b. Chgo., Aug. 7, 1949; Student, Roosevelt U., 1968, U. Hawaii, 1971, U. Hong Kong, 1979—80. Entertainer USO, Viet Nam, 1968; performer Comedy Store, Improvisation, others, 1969-79. Fashion model TV Commercials, 1967—81. Co-author: You'll Never Make Love in this Town Again, 1996 (N.Y. Times Best Seller List), Unfinished Lives, 1996; author, editor: Tales from the Casting Couch, 1996, theme song Youth at the Greek, 1998-99,Heartwlk L.A. Theme, 1999; columnist Fabulous Boomer Babes, 1999, sr. editor: The Industry Mag., 2000. Judge, comedy Cable Ace Award, 1988—96. Mem. Prodrs. Guild Am. (bd. dirs., sr. editor POV mag. 1990-2001), Hollywood Script Writing Inst. (bd. govs.), Authors Guild, Rec. Acad., Circumnavigators Club. Avocation: speaking Cantonese and Mandarin Chinese.

FRANKEN, AL (ALAN STUART FRANKEN), comedian, writer, actor; b. NYC, May 21, 1952; s. Joe and Phoebe Franken; m. Franni Bryson, 1975; children: Thomasin, Joe BA in Polit. Sci., Harvard U., 1973. Stand-up comic, Mpls. Network commentator for presdl. campaigns Comedy Ctrl., 1992, fellow, Harvard U. Kennedy School of Government, Shorenstein Center on the Press, Politics, and Public Policy, 2003. Actor: (films) Tunnel Vision, 1976, Trading Places, 1983, One More Saturday Night, 1986, When A Man Loves A Woman, 1994, Stuart Save His Family, 1995, The Definite Maybe, 1997, The Manchurian Candidate, 2004; (TV films) The Rutles: All You Need Is Cash, 1978; (TV miniseries) From the Earth to the Moon, 1998, (TV appearances) 3rd Rock from the Sun, 1996, Dr. Katz, Professional Therapist, 1997, Clerks, 2000; writer, actor (TV series) Saturday Night Live, NBC-TV, 1973—95 (Emmy awards (with others) best writing in comedy series, 1976, 1989), Lateline, 1998; author: I'm Good Enough, I'm Smart Enough, and Doggone It, People Like Me, 1992, Rush Limbaugh Is a Big Fat Idiot and Other Observations, 1996, Why Not Me? The Inside Story of the Making and Unmaking of the Franken Presidency, 1999, Oh, the Things I Know! A Guide to Success, or, Failing That, Happiness, 2002, Lies and the Lying Liars Who Tell Them: A Fair and Balanced Look at the Right, 2003, The Truth (with Jokes), 2005; author, actor (screenplays) Stuart Saves His Family, 1995, co-author, exec. prodr. When a Man Loves a Woman, 1994, host with Katherine Lanpher (radio) The O' Franken Factor, (now The Al Franken Show) Air America Radio, 2004—07. Emmy award (with others) for best writing in a comedy, The Paul Simon Special, 1977, Grammy award for best spoken comedy album, Rush Limbaugh Is a Big Fat Idiot, 1997. Democrat. Office: c/o Creative Artists Agy 9830 Wilshire Blvd Beverly Hills CA 90210

FRANKENBERGER, BERTRAM, JR., investor, consultant; b. New Haven, Jan. 24, 1933; s. Bertram and Thelma (Wisan) F.; m. Marjorie Green, Dec. 20, 1953 (dec. June 1997); children: Linda Sue Reason, Wendy Beth Goldstein; m. Harriet Feldman Newman, July 26, 1998. BS cum laude, U. Conn., 1954. CPA, Conn. Auditor Haskins & Sells, New Haven, 1956-61; ptnr. Weinstein & Timm CPAs, New Haven, 1961-70, Deloitte Haskins & Sells, New Haven, 1970-76; U.S. ptnr in charge mergers and acquisitions exec. office NYC, 1976-85; dir. Sheffield Mgmt. Co., NYC, 1985-99, Sheffield Investments, Inc., NYC, 1985-96, Lafayette Am. Bank & Trust, Hamden, 1985-96. Treas. Human Rels. Area Files, New Haven, 1963-70, 86—, assoc. sec., 1985—; cons., New Haven, 1985-94, Boynton Beach, Fla., 1994—; chmn. bd. Chargar Corp., Hamden, Conn., 1980—, Graham-Worldtek Travel, New Haven, 1985-2001; lectr. in field. Contbr. articles to profl. publs., chpt. to book. Pres., dir. Camp Laurelwood, Madison, Conn., 1970-72; pres., trustee Congregation Mishkan Israel, Hamden, Conn., 1974-76; bd. trustees Union Am. Hebrew Congregations, NYC, 1976-84; treas. Religion in Am. Life, NYC, 1983-89, dir., 1983-94. Capt. USAF, 1954-56. Recipient Pres.'s award New Haven Jaycees, 1960; Pres.'s award Camp Laurelwood, 1969. Mem. AICPA, Conn. Soc. CPAs, Hunters Run Golf and Racquet Club (Boynton Beach), Okemo Valley Golf Club. Avocations: skiing, golf, tennis, stamp collecting/philately.

FRANKENBERGER, JANE ROSSING, agricultural engineer; b. Northfield, Minn., Jan. 18, 1958; d. Thomas D. and Dorothy A. (Rosen) R.; m. James Rossing Frankenberger, July 22, 1995. BA in Physics and Religion, St. Olaf Coll., Northfield, 1979; MS in Agrl. Engring., U. Minn., St. Paul, 1984; PhD in Agrl. and Biol. Engring., Cornell U., 1996. Physics and math. tchr. Mennonite Ctrl. Com., Zaire, 1979-82; agrl. devel. specialist Evang. Luth. Chs. in Am., Senegal, 1985-90; asst. prof. Purdue U., 1996-00, assoc. prof., 2001—. Claire Boothe Luce fellow Luce Found.-Cornell U., 1990. Mem.: Alpha Epsilon, Phi Kappa Phi, Gamma Sigma Delta, Phi Beta Kappa. Home: 2640 Newman Rd West Lafayette IN 47906-4530 Office: Purdue U Agrl and Biol Engring 225 S University St West Lafayette IN 47907 Office Phone: 765-494-1194. E-mail: frankenb@purdue.edu.

FRANKENHEIM, SAMUEL, retired lawyer; b. NYC, Dec. 20, 1932; s. Samuel and Mary Emma (Ward) F.; m. Nina Barbara Mennerich, Sept. 2, 1960; children: Robert Mennerich, John Frederick. BA, Cornell U., 1954, LLB, 1959. Bar: N.Y. 1959, Mass. 1976. Law clk. N.Y. Ct. Appeals, 1959-61; assoc. Shearman & Sterling, attys., NYC, 1961-68, ptnr., 1968-69; sr. v.p., dir. Damon Corp., Needham Heights, Mass., 1969-78; sr. v.p., gen. counsel mem. Office of Chmn. Gen. Cinema Corp., Chestnut Hill, Mass., 1979-92; counsel Ropes & Gray, Boston, 1992-2000. Mem. corp. Ptnrs. Healthcare Sys., Inc., 1999—2004. Bd. govs. Newell Health Care Sys., 1983—93; trustee Wang Ctr. for Performing Arts, Boston, 1987—97, Huntington Theatre Co., Boston, 1993—2002, overseer, 2002—04; chmn. bd. Internat. Alliance of First Night Celebrations, 1994—99, treas., 1999—2000; overseer Newton-Wellesley Hosp., Newton, Mass., 1973—85, pres., 1980—82; overseer Wang Ctr. for Performing Arts, Boston, 1985—87; assoc. First Night, Inc., 1988, chmn. bd., 1991—93. 1st lt. USAF, 1955—57. Home: 115 Shornecliffe Rd Newton MA 02458-2420 E-mail: sfrankenheim@msn.com.

FRANKENSTEIN, JOHN, international management educator, consultant; b. San Francisco, Jan. 27, 1940; s. Alfred Victor and Sylvia (Lent) F.; m. Veronica M.C. Li, July 1, 1967; children: Karen, Paul, William. BA, Stanford U., 1961; MA, San Francisco State U., 1967; Diploma, Johns Hopkins S.A.I.S., Bologna, Italy, 1975; PhD, MIT, 1983. Lectr. U. Hawaii, Honolulu, 1967-68; US fgn. service officer USIA, Senegal, Belgium, Taiwan, Hong Kong, Italy, France, 1968-77; lectr. U. Mass., Boston, 1980-81; assoc. prof. Am. Grad. Sch. Internat. Mgmt., Glendale, Ariz., 1982-90; sr. lectr. internat. mgmt. U. Hong Kong, 1991—97; vis. lectr. politics Copenhagen U., 1997; vis. prof. Asia Rsch. Ctr., Copenhagen Bus. Sch., 1997—99; project dir. US-China Edn. Found., NYC, 2000—02; adj. faculty dept. polit. sci. Columbia U., 2002—03; vis. assoc. prof. dept. economics Brooklyn Coll., CUNY, 2002—; faculty Ctr. Global Affairs, NYU, 2005—. Vis. prof. Inst. for Internat. Studies and Tng., Japan, 1987, U. Internat. Bus. and Econs., Beijing, 1984, 88; cons., lectr. Hong Kong, China, Vietman. Contbr. articles to profl. jours. With USN, 1961-64, Philippines, Vietnam.

FRANKENTHALER, HELEN, artist; b. NYC, Dec. 12, 1928; d. Alfred and Martha (Lowenstein) F.; m. Robert Motherwell, Apr. 5, 1958 (div.); m. Stephen DuBrul, June 1994. BA, Bennington Coll., 1949; LHD (hon.), Skidmore Coll., 1969, Hofstra U., 1991; DFA (hon.), Smith Coll., 1973, Moore Coll. Art, 1974, Bard Coll., 1976, NYU, 1979; DFA, Phila. Coll. Art, 1980, Williams Coll., 1980; DFA (hon.), Marymount Manhattan Coll., 1989, Adelphi U., 1989, Washington U., St. Louis, 1989; DArt, Radcliffe Coll., 1978, Amherst Coll., 1979; DArt (hon.), Harvard U., 1980; DFA (hon.), Yale U., 1981, Brandeis U., 1982, U. Hartford, 1983, Syracuse U., 1985, Dartmouth Coll., 1994, Parsons Sch. Design, 1996, U. Pa., 1996, R.I. Sch. Design, 1996, Tufts U., 1998. Tchr., lectr. Yale U., 1966, 67, 70, Hunter Coll., 1970, Princeton U., 1971, Cooper Union, N.Y.C., 1972, Washington U. Sch. Fine Arts, 1972, Skidmore Coll., 1973, Swathmore Coll., 1974, Drew U., 1975, Harvard, 1976, Radcliffe Coll., 1976, Bard Coll., 1977, Detroit Inst. Arts, 1977, NYU, U. Pa., Sch. Visual Arts, Goucher Coll., Wash. U., Yale Grad. Sch., U. Ariz., 1978, Graphic Arts Council N.Y., 1979, Harvard U., 1980, Phila. Coll., 1980, Williams Coll., 1980, Yale U., 1981, Brandeis U., 1982, U. of Hartford, 1983, Syracuse U., 1985, Sante Fe Inst. Fine Arts, 1986, 90, 91; U.S. rep. Venice Biennale, 1966, lectr. in field. One-woman shows include, Tibor de Nagy Gallery, N.Y.C., 1951-58, Andre Emmerich Gallery, N.Y.C., 1959-73, 75, 77, 78, 79, 81, 82, 83, 84, 86, 87, 89, 90, 91, 92, 93, Jewish Mus., N.Y., 1960, Everett Ellin Gallery, Los Angeles, 1961, Galerie Lawrence, Paris, 1961, 63, Bennington Coll., 1962, 78, Galleria dell'Ariete, Milan, 1962, Kasmin Gallery, London, 1964, David Mirvish Gallery, Toronto, 1965, 71, 73, 75, Gertrude Kasle Gallery, Detroit, 1967, Nicholas Wilder Gallery, Los Angeles, 1967, Andre Emmerich Gallery, Zurich, 1974, 80, Swarthmore (Pa.) Coll., 1974, Solomon R. Guggenheim Mus., N.Y.C., 1975, Corcoran Gallery Art, Washington, 1975, Seattle Art Mus., 1975, Mus. Fine Arts, Houston, 1975, 85, 86, Ace Gallery, Vancouver, B.C., Can., 1975, Rosa Esman Gallery, N.Y.C., 1975, 83, 89, 3d Internat. Contemporary Art Fair, Paris, 1976, 81, retrospective Whitney Mus. Am. Art, 1969, Whitechapel Gallery, London, Eng., 1969, Kongress-Halle, Berlin, Kunstverein, Hannover, 1969, Heath Gallery, Atlanta, 1971, Galerie Godard Lefort, Montreal, 1971, Fendrick Gallery, Washington, 1972, 79, John Berggruen Gallery, San Francisco, 1972, 79, 82, Portland (Oreg.) Art Mus., 1972, Waddington Galleries II, London, 1973, 74, Janie C. Lee Gallery, Dallas, 1973, Houston, 1975, 76, 78, 80, 82, Met. Mus. Art, N.Y.C., 1973, Gallery Diane Gilson, Seattle, 1976, Greenberg Gallery, St. Louis, 1977, Galerie Wentzel, Hamburg, Germany, 1977, Jacksonville (Fla.) Art Mus., 1977-78, Knoedler Gallery, London, 1978, 81, 83, USIA exhbn., 1978-79, Atkins Mus. Fine Art, William Rockhill Nelson Gallery Art, Kansas City, Mo., 1978, 80, Saginaw Art Mus., Mich., 1980, Gimpel and Hanover and Andre Emerich Galleries, Zurich, 1980, Gallery Ulysses, Vienna, 1980, Knoedler Gallery, London, 1981, 83, Buschlen/Mowalt Fine Arts, Vancouver, 1989, Mus. Modern Art, N.Y.C., 1989, Douglas Drake Gallery, N.Y.C., 1989, Mizografia Gallery, L.A., 1989, Gerald Peters Gallery, Santa Fe, 1990, Kukje Gallery, Seoul, Korea, 1991, Assn. Am. Artists, N.Y.C., 1992, Knoedler & Co., N.Y.C., 1992, 94, 95, 96, 97, Nat. Gallery Art, Washington, 1993, San Diego Mus. Art, 1993, Mus. Fine Arts, Boston, 1994, Contemporary Arts Ctr., Cin., 1994, Meredith Long and Co., Houston, 1994, 95, 96, 97, Dennos Mus. Ctr. Northwestern Mich. Coll., Travers City, 1995, Tyler Graphics Ltd., Mt. Kisco, N.Y., 1995, Bobbie Greenfield Gallery, Santa Monica, Calif., 1995, Meyerovich Gallery, San Francisco, 1995, Greg Kucera Gallery, Seattle, 1995, Gallery One, Toronto, Canada, 1995, 97, Ace Contemporary Exhbns., L.A., 1996, Tasenda Gallery, L.A., 1997, Remba Gallery, West Hollywood, Calif., 1997, Thomas Segal Gallery, Balt., 1997, numerous others; exhibited in group shows including, Whitney Mus., 1958, 71, 75-79, 82, 89, Carnegie Internat., Pitts., 1955, 58, 61, 64, Columbus Gallery Fine Arts, 1960, Guggenheim Mus., 1961, 76, 80, 82, Seattle World's Fair, 1962, Art Inst. Chgo., 1963, 69, 72, 76, 77, 82, 83, San Francisco Mus. Art, 1963, 68, Krannert Mus., U. Ill., 1959, 63, 65, 67, 80, Washington Gallery Modern Art, 1963, Pa. Acad. Fine Arts, 1963, 68, 76, N.Y. World's Fair, 1964, Am. Fedn. Arts Circulating Exhbn., 1964, U. Austin Art Mus., 1964, Rose Art Mus. Circulating Exhbn., 1964, Detroit Inst. Arts, 1965, 67, 73, 77, U. Mich. Mus. Art, 1965, Md. Inst., 1966, Norfolk Mus. Arts and Scis., 1966, Venice Biennale, 1966, Smithsonian Instn., 1966, Expo '67, Montreal, 1967, Washington Gallery Modern Art, 1967, Ga. Mus. Art, Athens, 1967, U. Okla. Mus. Art, Norman, 1968, Philbrook Art Center, Tulsa, 1968, Cin. Mus., 1968, U. Calif. at San Diego, 1968, Mus. Modern Art, N.Y.C., 1969, 75, 76, 80, 82, Met. Mus., N.Y.C., 1969-70, 76, 79, 81, Va. Mus., Richmond, 1970, 74, 87, Balt. Mus. Art, 1970, 76, 89, Boston U., 1970, Boston Mus. Fine Arts, 1972, 82, 90, Des Moines Art Center, 1973, Mus. Fine Arts, Houston, 1974, 82, Smith Coll. Mus. Art, Northampton, Mass., 1974, El Instituto de Cultura Puertorriquena, San Juan, 1974, Basil (Switzerland) Art Fair, 1974, 76, Finch Coll. Mus. Art, N.Y.C., 1974, S.I. Mus., 1975, Denver Art Mus., 1975, Visual Arts Mus., N.Y.C., 1975, 76, Mus. Modern Art, Belgrade Yugoslavia, 1976, Chrysler Mus., Norfolk, Va., 1976, Everson Mus., Syaracuse, N.Y., Galleria d'Arts Moderna, Rome, 1976, Grey Art Gallery, N.Y.C., 1976-78, 81, Bklyn Mus., 1976-77, 82, Edmonton Art Gallery, Alta., Can., 1977, 78, Albright-Knox Mus., Buffalo, 1978, Fogg Art Mus., Harvard U., 1978, 83, Art Gallery Ont., 1979, Hirshorn Mus. and Sculpture Garden, Washington, 1980, Phoenix Art Mus., 1980, Nat. Gallery Art, Washington, 1981, Tate Gallery, London, 1981, Walker Art Ctr., Mpls., 1981, Milw. Art Mus., 1982, Mus. Fine Arts, Boston, 1982, Whitney Mus. Am. Art , N.Y., 1982, St. Louis Art Mus., 1982, High Mus. Art, Atlanta, 1989, Nelson-Atkins Mus. Art, Kansas City, Nat. Gallery Can., 1990, Williams Coll. Mus. Art, Williamstown, Mass., 1991, Aldrich Mus. Contemporary Art, Ridgefield, Conn., 1992, Mus. Modern Art, Mexico City, 1992, Yokohama Mus. Art, Japan, 1992, Marugame Inokuma-Genichiro Mus. Contemp. Art, 1992, Mus. Modern Art, Wakayama, 1992, Tokushima Modern Art Mus., Japan, 1992, Hokkaido Obihiro Mus. Art, 1993, Whitney Mus. Am. Art, Stamford, Conn., 1993, Gallery One, Toronto, Can., 1994; represented in permanent collections, Bklyn. Mus., Met. Mus. Art N.Y. , Solomon R. Guggenheim Mus., NYU, Mus. Modern Art, Albright-Knox Art Gallery, Buffalo, Whitney Mus., N.Y.C., U. Mich., High Mus., Atlanta, Milw. Art Inst., Wadsworth Atheneum, Hartford, Newark Mus., Yale U. Art Gallery, U. Nebr. Art Gallery, Carnegie Inst., Pitts., Detroit Inst. Art, Balt. Mus. Art, Univ. Mus., Berkeley, Calif., Bennington (Vt.) Coll., Art Inst. Chgo., Cin. Art Mus., Cleve. Mus. Art, Columbus Gallery Fine Arts, Honolulu Acad. Arts, Contemporary Arts Assn., Houston, Pasadena Art Mus., William Rockhill Nelson Gallery Art, Kans. City, Kans., Kans. City Art Inst., Atkins

Mus. Fine Arts, Kans. City, Kans., City Art Mus., St. Louis, Mus. Art, R.I. Sch. Design, Providence, San Francisco Mus. Art, Everson Mus., Syracuse, N.Y., Smithsonian Instn., Walker Art Inst., Mpls., Washington Gallery Modern Art, Wichita Art Mus., Brown Gallery Art, Nat. Gallery Victoria, Melbourne, Australia, Australian Nat. Gallery, Canberra, Victoria and Albert Mus., London, Eng., Tokyo Mus., Ulster Mus., Belfast, No. Ireland, Elvehjem Art Center, U. Wis., Israel Mus.-Instituto Nacional de Bellas Artes, Phila. Mus. Art, Phoenix Art Mus., Corcoran Gallery Art, Boston Mus. Fine Arts, Springfield (Mass.) Mus. Fine Arts, Witte Mus., San Antonio, Abbott Hall Art Gallery, Kendal, Eng., Mus. Contemporary Art, Nagaoka, Japan, Guggenheim Mus., N.Y.C., 1984, others; was subject of film Frankenthaler: Toward a New Climate, 1978. Trustee Bennington Coll., 1967—. Fellow Calhoun Coll., Yale U., 1968—; recipient 1st prize for painting Paris Biennale, 1959, Gold medal Pa. Acad. Fine Arts, 1968, Great Ladies award Fordham U., Thomas Moore Coll., 1969, Spirit of Achievement award Albert Einstein Coll. Medicine, 1970, Gold medal Commune of Catania, III Biennale della Grafica d'Arte, Florence, Italy, 1972, Garrett award 70th Am. Exhbn., Art Inst. Chgo., 1972, Creative Arts award Nat. Women's div. Am. Jewish Congress, 1974, Art and Humanities award Yale Women's Forum, 1976, Extraordinary Woman of Achievement award NCCJ, 1978, Alumni award Bennington Coll., 1979, N.Y.C. Mayor's award, 1986, Lifetime Achievement award Coll. Art Assn., 1994, Lotos medal of merit, 1994, Artist of Yr. award, 1995, Jerusalem prize, 1999, Lifetime Achievement award, 1999. Mem. NEA, Am. Acad. (vice-chancelor 1991), Am. Acad. Arts and Scis., Nat. Coun. Arts, Nat. Inst. Arts and Letters. Office: M Knoedler & Co Inc 19 E 70th St New York NY 10021-4907

FRANKFORT, LEW, consumer products company executive; b. Bronx, NY, Mar. 19, 1946; m. Bobbie Frankfort; children: Tamara, Alana, Sam. BA in Polit. Sci., Hunter Coll., 1967; MBA in Mktg., Columbia U., 1969. Commr. Agy. for Child Development NYC, 1973—79; v.p. New Bus. Devel. Coach Inc., 1979—85; pres. Coach Sara Lee Corp., 1985—95, exec. v.p. Sara Lee Personal Products, 1991—94, CEO Sara Lee Accessories, 1991—94, pres., CEO Sara Lee Champion, Intimates & Accessories group, 1994—95, sr. v.p., 1994—2000, chmn., CEO Coach, 1995—2000; chmn., CEO Coach Inc., 2000—. Bd. dir. Teach for Am.; mem. bd. overseers Columbia Univ. Bus. Sch. Office: Coach Inc 516 W 34th St New York NY 10001-1394*

FRANKFURT, HARRY GORDON, philosophy professor; b. May 29, 1929; m. Joan Gilbert; children: Jennifer, Katherine. BA, Johns Hopkins Univ., 1949, PhD, 1954. Asst. prof. Ohio State Univ., 1956—62; assoc. prof., philosophy SUNY, Binghamton, 1962—63; rsch. assoc. Rockefeller Univ., 1963—64, assoc. prof., philosophy, 1964—69, prof., 1969—76, chair, philosophy group, 1966—73; prof. Yale Univ., 1976—90, chair, philosophy dept., 1978—87; prof., philosophy Princeton Univ., 1990—2002, prof. emeritus, 2002—, Romanell-Phi Beta Kappa prof. philosophy, 1999—2000. Vis. prof. Univ. Calif., Riverside, 2000. Editor: Leibniz: A Collection of Critical Essays, 1972; author: (nonfiction) Demons, Dreamers & Madmen: The Defense of Reason in Descartes' Meditations, 1970, The Importance of What We Care About, 1988, Necessity, Volition & Love, 1999, On Bullshit, 2005 (Publishers Weekly Bestseller hardcover nonfiction list, 2005, No. 1 NY Times Bestseller list, 2005). With US Army, 1954—56. Grantee Nat. Endowment for Humanities fellowship, Guggenheim fellowship. Fellow: AAAS. Office: 109 Marx Hall Princeton Univ Princeton NJ 08544 Office Phone: 609-258-4296. Business E-Mail: fraharg@princeton.edu.

FRANK-KAMENETSKII, MAXIM D., biomedical engineer; b. Nizhniy Novgorod, Russia, Aug. 7, 1941; arrived in US, 1993; s. David A. and Elena E. (Fridman) F.; m. Alla D. Voskoboinik, Jan. 7, 1961 (dec. 1985); 1 child, Michael. MS, Moscow Phys. & Tech. Inst., 1964, PhD, 1967; DSc, Inst. Chem. Physics Moscow, 1972. Jr. scientist Kurchatov Inst. Atomic Engery, Moscow, 1967-72, sr. scientist, 1972-78; head lab. Inst. Molecular Genetics, Moscow, 1979-89, head. dept., 1989-93; prof. Boston U., 1993—. Disting. vis. prof. U. Ala., Birmingham, 1989, Ohio State U., Columbus, 1991-92. Author: Unraveling DNA, 1993, 97. Avocation: tennis. Office: Boston U Dept Advanced Biotechnology 36 Cummington St Boston MA 02215-2427 Office Phone: 617-353-8498. Business E-Mail: mfk@bu.edu.

FRANKL, SPENCER NELSON, dean, dentist; b. Phila., Nov. 19, 1933; s. Louis and Vera F.; m. Rhoda Lee, June 12, 1955; children: Elizabeth Ann, Catherine Susan. D.D.S., Temple U., 1958; postgrad., Children's Hosp. D.C., 1958-59; MS, Tufts U., 1961. Asst. prof. dentistry Tufts U., 1961-64; asso. prof. Boston U., 1964-67, prof., 1967—, chmn. dept. dentistry, 1964-67, asst. dean, 1970-73, asso. dean, 1973—; dean Boston Univ. Sch. of Dental Medicine, 1977—; dep. dir. Boston U. Med. Ctr., 1980—. Chief pedodontics Boston U. Med. Center U. Hosp., 1964; head pediatric dentistry Beth Israel Hosp., 1964; chief dental service Joseph P. Kennedy Jr. Meml. Hosp., Brighton, Mass., 1968— Contbr. articles to profl. jours. Fellow Am. Coll. Dentists, Internat. Coll. Dentists, Am. Acad. Pediatric Dentistry; mem. APHA, ADA, Am. Soc. Dentistry for Children, Mass. Soc. Dentistry for Children (past pres.), Internat. Assn. for Dental Rsch., Am. Bd. Pedodontics (examiner). Office: 100 E Newton St G-317 Boston MA 02118-2308 Business E-Mail: sfrankl@bu.edu.

FRANKL, WILLIAM STEWART, cardiologist, educator; b. Phila., July 15, 1928; s. Louis and Vera (Simkin) Frankl; m. Razelle Sherr, June 17, 1951; children: Victor S.(dec.) , Brian A. BA in Biology, Temple U., 1951, MD, 1955, MS in Medicine, 1961. Diplomate Am. Bd. Internal Medicine, Am. Bd. Cardiovasc. Disease. Intern Buffalo Gen. Hosp., 1955—56; resident in medicine Temple U., Phila., 1956—57, 1959—61; faculty Temple U. Sch. Medicine, 1962—68, dir. EKG sect. dept. cardiology, 1966—68, dir. cardiac care unit, 1967—68; prof. medicine, dir. divsn. cardiology Med. Coll. Pa., Phila., 1970—79; prof. medicine, assoc. dir. cardiology divsn. Thomas Jefferson U., Phila., 1979—84; physician-in-chief Springfield Hosp., Mass., 1968—70; prof. medicine, co-dir. William Likoff Cardiovasc. Inst. Hahnemann U., Phila., 1984—86, dir. William Likoff Cardiovasc. Inst., dir. divsn. cardiology, 1986—92, Thomas J. Vischer Prof. medicine, chmn. dept. medicine, 1987—92; prof. medicine, dir. cardiovasc. regional programs Allegheny U. of Health Scis., 1992—98; dir. cardiovasc. regional programs Allegheny U. Hosps., 1992—98; v.p. cardiovasc. program devel. Allegheny U. Hosps. Sys., 1995—98; prof. medicine cardiology divsn. dept. medicine Temple U. Sch. Medicine, 1998—2000. Cons. cardiology Phila. VA Hosp., 1970—79; Fogarty Sr. Internat. fellow Cardiothoracic Inst., U. London, 1978—79; clin. prof. medicine Temple U. Sch. Medicine, 2000—. Contbr. articles to profl. jours. Capt. M.C. US Army, 1957—59. Recipient Golden Apple award, Temple U. Sch. Medicine, 1967, award, Med. Coll. Pa., 1972, Lindback award for Disting. Tchg., 1975; Cardiovasc. Rsch. fellow, U. Pa., 1961—62. Fellow: ACP, Coun. Clin. Cardiology of Am. Heart Assn. (coun. arteriosclerosis), Am. Coll. Clin. Pharmacology (regent 1980—85, 1993—98), Phila. Coll. Physicians, Am. Coll. Cardiology (gov. eastern Pa. 1986—89); mem.: AAAS, AAUP, Philadelphia County Med. Soc. (pres. 1993—94, 1st dist. trustee to Pa. Med. Soc. bd. trustees 1998—2001), Am. Soc. Clin. Pharmacology and Exptl. Therapeutics, Am. Heart Assn. (bd. govs. S.E. Pa. chpt. 1972—84, pres. 1976, Pa. affiliate pres. 1984—85), Assn. Am. Med. Colls., Am. Fedn. Clin. Rsch., N.Y. Acad. Scis. Home and Office: 536 Moreno Rd Wynnewood PA 19096-1121 Office Phone: 610-649-5947. Personal E-mail: bfrankl@comcast.net. *The essence of humanity and being human is caring. When one cares, life takes on a new dimension and provides one the ability to transcend the thin veneer which separates human and animal.*

FRANKLE, DIANE HOLT, lawyer; BA, Coll. of Wooster, 1975; JD magna cum laude, Georgetown Univ., 1979. Bar: DC 1979, Md. 1980, Calif. 1985. Law clk. Judge R. Dorsey Watkins, US Dist Ct. (Md. Dist.), 1979—81; assoc. Ginsburg, Feldman & Bress, Washington, 1981—84; ptnr., co-chmn., mergers and acquisitions practice group DLA Piper Rudnick Gray Cary, East Palo Alto, Calif. Faculty mem. ABA Nat. Inst., 1997—, Practising Law Inst., 1995—. Editor (in chief): Guide to Calif. Securities Law Practice, 2004; contbr. articles to profl. jours. Mem. adv. bd. Corp. Counsel Inst., Georgetown Univ., 2003—04; mem. Cmty. Working group, Opportunity Ctr., Palo Alto, Calif. Named a No. Calif. Super Lawyer, San Francisco mag. Mem.: ABA (co-chmn. task force on pub. co. acquisitions 1995—, com. corp. laws, com. negotiated acquisitions), State Bar Calif., Phi Beta Kappa. Office: DLA Piper Rudnick Gray Cary 2000 University Ave East Palo Alto CA 94303 Office Phone: 650-833-2026. Office Fax: 650-833-2001. Business E-Mail: diane.frankle@dlapiper.com.

FRANKLIN, ARETHA LOUISE, singer; b. Memphis, Mar. 25, 1942; d. Clarence L. and Barbara (Siggers) Franklin; m. Ted White, 1961 (div. 1969); children: Clarence, Edward, Kecalf, Teddy; m. Glynn Turman, Apr. 11, 1978 (div. 1984); 3 stepchildren. MusD (hon.), U. Pa., 2007. First record at age 12, rec. artist with Columbia Records, N.Y.C., 1961, then with Atlantic records, now with Arista Records; singer: (albums) Aretha, 1961, Electrifying, Tender Moving and Swinging, 1962, Laughing on the Outside, 1963, Unforgettable, Songs of Faith, Running Out of Fools, 1964, Yeah, 1965, Soul Sister, 1966, Queen of Soul, Take It Like You Give It, Lee Cross, Greatest Hits, I Never Loved a Man, Once in a Lifetime, Aretha Arrives, 1967, Lady Soul, Greatest Hits, Vol. 2, Best of Aretha Franklin, Live at Paris Olympia, Aretha Now, 1968, Soul 69, Today I Sing the Blues, Soft and Beautiful, Aretha Gold's, Satisfaction, I Say a Little Prayer, 1969, This Girl's in Love with You, Spirit in the Dark, Don't Play that Song, 1970, Live at the Fillmore West, Young Gifted and Black, Aretha's Greatest Hits, 1971, Amazing Grace, 1972, Hey Hey Now, Firest 12 Sides, 1973, Let Me Into Your Life, 1974, With Every Thing I Feel in Me, You, 1975, Sparkle, Ten Years of Gold, 1976, Sweet Passion, 1977, Almighty Fire, Star Collection, 1978, La Diva, 1979, Aretha, 1980, Who's Zoomin' Who, 1985, One Lord, One Faith, One Baptism, 1987, Aretha Sings the Blues, 1965, 85, Lady Soul, 1988, Through the Storm, 1989, What You See is What You Sweat, 1991, Jazz to Soul, 1992, Aretha After Hours, Chain of Fools, 1993, Unforgettable: A Tribute to Dinah Washington, 1995, Love Songs, 1997, The Delta Meets Detroit, A Rose Is Still A Rose, 1998, Amazing Grace, 1999, The Queen in Waiting: The Columbia Years 1960-1965, 2002, So Damn Happy, 2003; actress (films) Blues Brothers, 1980, Shindig! Presents Soul, Shindig! Presents Groovy Gals, 1991, History of Rock 'N' Roll, 1995, Blues Brothers 2000, 1998, (TV films) Bob Hope on Campus, 1975, Aretha Franklin: The Queen of Soul, 1988, (TV miniseries) Motown 40: The Music Is Forever, 1998; performer (Showtime prodn.): Aretha, 1986; performer: (concert tours) in U.S. and Europe; performer: at Pres. Carter's Inauguration, 1977, at Pres. Clinton's Inauguration, 1992. Named Top Female Vocalist, 1967, Number One Female Singer 16th Internat., Jazz Critics Poll, 1968; named one of Greatest Rock 'n' Roll Artists of All Time, Rolling Stone mag.; named to Hollywood Walk of Fame, 1979, Rock and Roll Hall of Fame, 1987; recipient Grammy award for best female rhythm and blues vocal, 1967—74, 1981, 1985, 1987, for best rhythm and blues rec., 1988, for best soul gospel performance, 1972, for best rhythm and blues duo vocal (with George Michael), 1987, Am. Music award, 1984, Grammy Legend award, 1991, Kennedy Center Honor, 1994, 1994, Presdl. Medal of Freedom, The White House, 2005, Grammy Award for Best Traditional R&B Vocal Performance (A House is Not a Home), 2006. Achievements include first woman admitted in Rock & Roll Hall of Fame.

FRANKLIN, BARBARA HACKMAN, former government official; b. Lancaster, Pa., Mar. 19, 1940; d. Arthur A. and Mayme M. (Haller) Hackman; m. Wallace Barnes, 1986. BA with distinction, Pa. State U., 1962; MBA, Harvard U., 1964. Mgr. environ. analysis Singer Co., NYC, 1964—68; asst. v.p. Citibank, NYC, 1969—71; White House staff asst. to the Pres. for recruiting women to govt. Washington, 1971—73; commr. U.S. Consumer Product Safety Commn., Washington, 1973—79, vice chair, 1973—74, 1977—78; sr. fellow, dir. govt. and bus. program Wharton Sch. U. Pa., Phila., 1980—88; pres., CEO Franklin Assocs., Washington, 1984—92; U.S. sec. commerce Dept. Commerce, Washington, 1992—93; pres., CEO Barbara Franklin Enterprises, Washington, 1995—; commentator Nightly Bus. Report, 1997—. Mem. Pres.'s Adv. Com. for Trade Policy and Negotiations, 1982—86, 1991—92; chair task force on tax reform, 1985—86; mem. NAFTA task force Pres.'s Adv. Com. for Trade Policy and Negotiations, 1991—92; alt. Rep. and public del. 44th session UN Gen. Assembly, 1989—90; mem. cons. panel U.S. Comptroller Gen., 1984—92, 1994—98; bd. dirs. Aetna, Inc., 1979—92, 1993—, GenVec, Inc., 2002—, Dow Chem. Co., 1980—92, 1993—, MedImmune, Inc., 1995—, Washington Mutual Investors Fund, 2005—. Trustee Pa. State U., 1976—82; bd. regents U. Hartford, 1986—88; bd. advisors Harvard Bus. Sch., 1998—2003, 2006—; co-chmn. nat. fin. com. George Bush for Pres., 1987—88, George W. Bush for Pres., 1999—2000. Named Dir. Yr., NACD, 2000, Outstanding Dir., Outstanding Dir. Exch., 2003; named one of 50 Most Influential Corp. Dirs., Am. Mgmt. Assn., 1990; recipient Disting. Alumni award, Pa. State U., 1972, John J. McCloy award for audit excellence, 1992, Alumni Achievement award, Harvard Bus. Sch., 2004. Mem.: U.S. China Bus. Coun. (vice-chair, dir.), Nat. Com. U.S.-China Rels. (dir.), Coun. Fgn. Rels. (dir.), Nat. Assn. Corp. Dir. (Blue Ribbon Commn., CEO evaluation 1994, Blue Ribbon Commn., audit effectiveness 1999, co-chair Blue Ribbon Commn., exec. compensation 2003), Atlantic Coun. (dir.), Internat. Women's Forum (founding mem.), Nat. Symphony Orch. (dir.), Heritage Found. (chair Asian studies adv. coun.), Econ. Club NY (chmn.). Avocations: exercise, hiking, reading, painting. Office: 2600 Virginia Ave NW Ste 506 Washington DC 20037-1905 Office Phone: 202-337-9100.

FRANKLIN, BLAKE TIMOTHY, lawyer; b. San Mateo, Calif., Sept. 28, 1942; s. Harvey James and Marie Agnes (Leane) F. AB, Dartmouth Coll., 1963; JD, Harvard U., 1966. Bar: Calif. 1966, D.C. 1969, U.S. Supreme Ct. 1970, N.Y. 1976. AID contractor Peace Corps; vis. prof. comml. law U. Costa Rica, San Jose, 1966-68; assoc. Coudert Bros., Washington, 1969-74, ptnr. NYC, 1975-83, Gibson Dunn & Crutcher, NYC, 1983—. Bd. dirs. Union Theol. Sem., N.Y., 1996-2004, 06-, Nat. Law Ctr. for Inter-Am. Free Trade, Tucson, GLSEN, N.Y., Bolivian-Am. C. of C., Andean Resources, S.A. Chancellor of vestry St. Michael's Ch., N.Y.C., 1987-93; trustee Aids Svc. Found. of Orange County, Calif., 1994-97; St. Hilda's and St. Hugh's Sch., N.Y.C., 1988-92; mem. bd. gov.'s USO, 1987-90. Mem. ABA, Inter-Am. Bar Assn., Am. Soc. Internat. Law, Assn. of Bar of City of N.Y. Episcopalian. Office: Gibson Dunn & Crutcher 200 Park Ave New York NY 10166-0193 Business E-Mail: bfranklin@gibsondunn.com.

FRANKLIN, BONNIE GAIL, actress; b. Santa Monica, Calif., Jan. 6, 1944; d. Samuel Benjamin and Claire (Hersch) F. BA, UCLA, 1966. Mem. regional theatres in, N.Y., Mass., Ohio, Maine, N.H., Conn., Pa., 1972-99. Stage appearances include Your Own Thing, San Francisco, L.A., N.Y.C., 1968, Dames At Sea, 1969, Applause, N.Y.C., 1970-72 (Aegis Theatre Club award 1970, Theatre Club award 1970, Outer Critics Circle award 1960-70, Tony nomination), Happy Birthday and Other Humiliations, N.Y., 1987, Frankie & Johnny in the Clair de Lune, 1988, Grace & Glorie, 1996; tv appearances include One Day At A Time, 1975-84. Mem. AFTRA, SAG, Actors Equity Assn., Dirs. Guild Am. Democrat. Jewish. *To avoid criticism: say nothing, do nothing, be nothing.*

FRANKLIN, BRINLEY, library director; BA, U. Md., College Park, 1975, MLS, 1978; MBA, George Washington U., 1985. Head libr., rsch. asst. Coopers and Lybrand, Washington, 1976—79; head libr., dir. info. svcs. KPMG Peat Marwick, Washington, 1979—84, sr. cons., 1982—87, mgr., 1987—90; assoc. dir. adminstrv. svcs. U. Conn. Librs., Storrs, 1990—96, assoc. dir., 1996—98, dir. libr. svcs., 1999—2001, vice provost, dir. univ. librs., 2002—. Consulting assoc. KPMG/Bearing Point, 1990—, Jim Vitale and Assocs., Denver, 2001—, Maximus, Inc., Northbrook, Ill., 2003—. Contbr. articles to profl. jours. Mem.: ALA, Internat. Fedn. of Libr. Assoc., Assn. Coll. and Rsch. Libraries, Assn. Rsch. Librs., New England Libr. and Info. Network, Nat. Ctr. for Edn. Statistics, Boston Libr. Consortium, Beta Phi Mu. Office: U Conn Librs Homer Babbidge Libr 369 Fairfield Rd Storrs Mansfield CT 06269-2005 Office Phone: 860-486-0497. Office Fax: 860-486-0584. E-mail: brinley.franklin@uconn.edu.*

FRANKLIN, BRUCE WALTER, lawyer; b. Ellendale, ND, Feb. 26, 1936; s. Wallace Henry and Frances (Webb) F.; m. Kristy Ann Jones, Feb. 7, 1944; children: Kevin, Monica, Taylor. Student, U. Mich., 1954-56; LLB, Detroit Coll. Law, 1962. Bar: Mich. 1963. Sole practice, Troy, Mich., 1962-90; mng. ptnr. Franklin, Bigler, Berry & Johnston, P.C., Troy, Mich., 1991-98, Franklin & Davis, Troy, 1998—. Bd. dirs. Wachovia Bank, Newnan Bank; pres., CEO Landward III Devel. Corp. (Arbor Springs Plantation). Past chmn. Mich. Young Reps., United Meth. Retirement Cmtys.; bd. dirs. Peachtree Hosp., Wesley Woods. Served with U.S. Army. Office: Landward III 215 Arbor Shores N Newnan GA 30265 E-mail: bwfranklin@yahoo.com.

FRANKLIN, CARL, director; b. Richmond, Calif., Apr. 11, 1949; m. Jesse Beaton, 2000. Student, U. Calif., Berkeley; M in directing, Am. Film Inst. Dir. (films) One False Move, 1992, Devil in a Blue Dress, 1995, One True Thing, 1998, High Crimes, 2002, Out of Time, 2003, (TV) Laurel Avenue, 1993, Partners, 1999, The Riches, 2007; appeared in TV series Caribe, 1975, The Fantastic Journey, 1977, McClain's Law, 1981-82, also TV episodes; writer Devil in a Blue Dress, 1995; actor (films) Five on the Black Hand Side, 1973, Punk, 1986, Eye of the Eagle 2: Inside the Enemy, 1989, Eye of the Eagle 3, 1990, Full Fathom Five, 1990, In the Heat of Passion, 1992, (TV) It Couldn't Happen to a Nicer Guy, 1974, Centennial, 1978, The Legend of the Golden Gun, 1979, One Cooks, the Other Doesn't, 1983, Too Good to Be True, 1988, Steel Magnolias, 1990. Avocation: poetry.*

FRANKLIN, CHARLES E., manufacturing executive; b. Birmingham, Ala., July 17, 1938; BS in Mech. Engring, Ga. Inst. Tech., 1961; MS in Aeronautical-Mech. Engring., Air Force Inst. Tech., 1967. Ret. as lt. gen. USAF, 1996; v.p. quality and mission success Lockheed Martin, Nashua, NH, v.p. programs and mission success; v.p. gen. mgr. electronic systems' air and missile def. Raytheon Co., Tewksbury, Mass., 1998, pres. integrated def. systems bus., v.p. evaluation team Waltham, Mass., 2003—. Office: Raytheon Co 870 Winter St Waltham MA 02451

FRANKLIN, DARLENE KAY, elementary school educator; b. Klamath Falls, Oreg., Oct. 24, 1948; d. Elbert Lee Beck, Sr. and Nellie Jesse Herron; m. Donald Keith Knapp (div.); children: Scottie Vance, Monica Faye; m. Duane Dale Franklin, Feb. 12, 1988. Student in Hons. Colloquial Program, So. Oreg. State Coll., 1967—68, BSc, 1971, MSc, 1983. Tchr. elem. sch. Eagle Point Sch. Dist., Oreg., 1982—91, Scappoose Sch. Dist., Oreg., 1991—, dir. space sci. program, 2003. Mem. adv. bd. Oregonian Newspaper, Portland, Oreg., 1994—; unit team leader Scappoose Sch. Dist., 2003—05; mem. coun. Regional Uniserv, Gearhart, Oreg., 1994—99. Mem. com. Art Faire, 1992—. Named Regional Tchr. of Yr., Portland C. of C., 2000, Outstanding Tchr. Field Study Rsch., Forestry Dept., Jacksonville, Fla., 2003. Mem.: NEA, Oreg. Reading Assn., Oreg. Edn. Assn. Avocations: theater, painting, music, dance. Home: 1470 Kings Hwy Medford OR 97501 Office Phone: 503-543-7112.

FRANKLIN, EDWARD WARD, international investment consultant, lawyer, actor; b. NYC, Sept. 23, 1926; s. Albert Ward and Edith (Meyers) F.; m. Joan Rice, Aug. 25, 1956; children— Caroline, Melissa, Edward Ward. AB magna cum laude, Harvard U., 1947, LLB, 1950. Bar: N.Y. 1951. Assoc. Cadwalader, Wickersham & Taft, NYC, 1950-56; gen. counsel N.Y. Air Brake Co., 1956-67, v.p. internat. and legal, 1962-67; v.p., gen. counsel Gen. Signal Corp., NYC, 1967-80, sec., 1969-80, sr. v.p., 1980-83, vice chmn., 1983-85. Chmn. bd. Hamworthy Hydraulics, Ltd., Poole, Eng.; dir. Holborn Internat. Portfolio Mgrs., Ptnrs. Fund, Inc., Pacus Ventures Ltd., Chase NBW Bank. Life gov., trustee N.Y. Presbyn. Hosp., Trinity Episcopal Schs. Corp.; chmn. bd. trustees Gracie Square Hosp., N.Y.C. Mem. AEA, SAG, AFTRA, Assn. Bar City of N.Y., The Players, Knickerbocker Club, Harvard Club (N.Y.C.), Misquamicut Club (Watch Hill, R.I.), Phi Beta Kappa.

FRANKLIN, GENE FARTHING, engineering educator, consultant; b. Banner Elk, NC, July 25, 1927; s. Burnie D. and Delia (Farthing) F.; m. Gertrude Stritch, Jan. 1952; children: David M., Carole Lea. BSEE, Ga. Inst. Tech., 1950; MSEE, MIT, 1952; DEngSc, Columbia U., 1955. Asst. prof. Columbia U., NYC, 1955-57; prof. elec. engring. Stanford (Calif.) U., 1957-95, prof. emeritus, 1995—. Cons. IBM, Rochester, Minn., 1982-94. Author: Sampled-Data Control, 1958, Digital Control, 1980, 3d edit., 1997, Feedback Control, 1986, 5th edit., 2006. With USN, 1945—47. Recipient Edn. award Am. Automatic Control Coun., 1985, Bellman Award, 2005. Fellow IEEE (life), Control Soc. of IEEE (Bode lectr. 1994). Democrat. Avocations: travel, writing. Office: Stanford U Dept Elec Engring 252 Packard Bldg Stanford CA 94305 Business E-Mail: franklin@ee.stanford.edu.

FRANKLIN, J. RICHARD, principal; b. Milan, Mo., July 15, 1934; m. Joyce Ann Fishback; children: James, Elizabeth. BS, Truman State U., 1956; MA, U. Mo., 1963; postgrad., Ctrl. Mo. State U., 1972—. Prin. Ft. Osage HS, Independence, Mo., 1964—87. State rep. dist. 53 Mo. Ho. of Reps., 1989-2002, mem. edn. com., 2000-02, retirement com., 1992-93, banking com., chair appropRations, 1994-96; chmn. budget com., 1997-2000. Mem. State Hist. Soc. Mo. (pres.), Masons, Shriners. Address: 1829 S Aztec Avenue Independence MO 64057

FRANKLIN, JAMES BURKE, lawyer; b. Statesboro, Ga., Mar. 11, 1938; s. Sam J. and Eva Claire (Burke) Franklin; m. Fay Foy Smith, Mar. 20, 1976; children: Julie Foy, Rebecca Claire. BS, Ga. Inst. Tech.; JD, U. Ga. Bar: Ga. 1963, U.S. Dist. Ct. (so., mid., and no. dists.), U.S. Ct. Appeals (11th cir.). Ptnr. Allen, Edenfield, Brown & Franklin (formerly Allen & Edenfield), 1969—74; founding ptnr. Franklin, Taulbee, Rushing, Snipes and Marsh, P.C., and predecessor firms, Statesboro, Ga., 1974—. Magistrate U.S. Dist. Ct. (so. dist.) Ga., 1979—81; chmn. Devel. Authority Bulloch County. Pres. Bulloch County (Ga.) C. of C. Lt. US Army, 1964—66. Named Designated Ga. Super Lawyer, 2005, 2006; recipient Amicus Curiae Award, Ga. Supreme Ct., 2005, Disting. Svc. Scroll, U. Ga. Law Sch., 2005. Mem.: State Bar Ga. (pres. 2001—02), Rotary Club (Statesboro) (pres.). Methodist. Office: 12 Siebald St PO Box 327 Statesboro GA 30458 Home Phone: 912-764-4506; Office Phone: 912-764-9055. Business E-Mail: jfranklin@ftrsm.com.

FRANKLIN, JAMIE, curator, consultant; b. Kirkland, Wash., May 25, 1980; s. Paul Michael and Sheryll Renee Franklin. MA, Williams Coll., Williamstown, Mass., 2005. Curator collections Bennington Mus., Vt., 2005—. Office: Bennington Museum 75 W Main St Bennington VT 05201 Home Phone: 206-799-7898; Office Phone: 802-477-1571. Business E-Mail: jfranklin@benningtonmuseum.org.

FRANKLIN, JASON EDWARD, advocate, researcher; b. Santa Ana, Calif., Nov. 7, 1979; s. Wayne and Susan Franklin. BA in Polit. Comm., George Wash. U., Washington, 2002; MS in Urban Policy and Nonprofit Mgmt., New Sch. U., NYC, 2004; PhD in Pub. Adminstrn., NYU, NYC, 2002. Youth devel. cons. Oreg. Commn. Children and Families, Salem, 1997; pres., owner Youth Involved! Cons., Portland, 1997—99; vol. staff White Ho. Office Nat. AIDS Policy, 1999; dir. rsch., adminstrn. 21st Century Sch. Fund, Washington, 2000—04; founding prin. Iam LLC, NYC, 2003—04; dir. policy, planning Lower Manhattan Cultural Coun., NYC, 2005; coord. Next Generation Leadership Network, NYC, 2005—. White ho. rep. World AIDS Day Adv. Coun., Am. Assn. World Health, Washington, 1999—2000; founding dir. Oreg. Students Supporting Edn., Portland, 1996—98; founding chair Multnomah Youth Commn., Portland, 1996—97; co-chair Resource Generation, NYC, 2006—06; dir. North Star Fund, NYC, 2006. Recipient Bronze medal, Nat. Prudential Spirit Cmty., 1998. Mem.: Coun. Founds., Emerging Practitioners Philanthropy, Ams. Arts, Assn. Rsch. Nonprofit Orgns. and Voluntary Action, Am. Polit. Sci. Assn., Delta Lamda Phi. Independent. Avocations: travel, cooking. Office: New York University 295 Lafayette Street 2nd Floor New York NY 10012 Home Phone: 202-549-1316; Office Phone: 212-992-9875. Personal E-mail: franklinjason@hotmail.com.

FRANKLIN, JERRY FOREST, forest ecologist, educator; b. Waldport, Oreg., Oct. 27, 1936; m. Phyllis C.; children: James Lyman, Lewis Forest, Virginia Sandalee, Heather Ann. BS in Forest Mgmt., Oreg. State U., 1959, MS in Forest Mgmt. and Stats., 1961; PhD in Botany and Soils, Wash. State U., 1966; LLD (hon.), Simon Fraser U., Burnaby, BC, 2001. Rsch. forester USDA Forest Svc. Pacific N.W. Rsch. Sta., Corvallis, Oreg., 1959—75, chief plant ecologist, 1975—91; dir. Ecosystem Studies Program NSF, Washington, 1973-75; prof. dept. botany and plant pathology & dept. forest sciences Oreg. State U., Corvallis, 1975—92; prof. ecosystem analysis U. Wash., Seattle, 1986—; dir. Wind River Canopy Crane Rsch. Facility, 1993—. Contbr. articles to Landscape Ecology, BioSci., Forest Watch, Ecol. Applications, others. Named Conservationist of Yr., Pacific Rivers Coun., 1992; recipient Superior Svc. Award, USDA, 1970, 1986, Disting. Scientist Award, N.W. Sci. Assn., 1971, Arthur S. Flemming Award for outstanding young person in Fed. govt., 1972, Barrington Moore Award, Soc. Am. Foresters, 1986, Olaus & Margaret Murie Award, The Wilderness Soc., 1988, Howard Vollum Award, Reed Coll., Portland, 1992, George Melendez Wright Award for Excellence, George Wright Soc., 1992, Philip C. Hamm Award, Monsanto Agrl. Co. & U. Minn. Coll. Agrl., Food and Environ. Sciences, 1995, William B. Greeley Award, Am. Forests Assn., 1996, Heinz Award for the Environment, 2005; Charles Bullard Fellow for Forest Rsch., Harvard U., 1985—86. Fellow: AAAS; mem.: Internat. Assn. Landscape Ecology (Leadership in Action Award, US chpt. 2001), Soc. Conservation Biology (LaRoe Award 2004), Brit. Ecol. Soc., Am. Inst. Biol. Sciences, Ecol. Soc. Am. (pres. 1993—94). Office: U Wash Coll Forest Resources Campus Box 352100 Seattle WA 98195-2100 Office Phone: 206-543-2138. Office Fax: 206-543-7295. Business E-Mail: jff@u.washington.edu.

FRANKLIN, JOHN See SALAPATEK, JOHN

FRANKLIN, JOHN HOPE, historian, writer; b. Rentiesville, Okla., Jan. 2, 1915; s. Buck Colbert and Mollie (Parker) Franklin; m. Aurelia E. Whittington, June 11, 1940; 1 child, John Whittington. AB, Fisk U., 1935; AM, Harvard, 1936, PhD, 1941; degree (hon.), Morgan State Coll., Va. State Coll., Lincoln U., Pa., Cambridge U., Drake U., Mich. State U., U. Ill., Carnegie-Mellon U., Columbia U., Columbia Coll., Chgo., Loyola U., Bklyn. Coll., Bard Coll., Boston Coll., Brown U., Tuskegee Inst., Grand Valley Coll., Marquette U., Lincoln Coll., Ill., Princeton U., Hamline U., Fisk U., RI Coll., Dickinson Coll., Howard U., U. Md., U. Notre Dame, Tulsa U., Morehouse Coll., Miami U., Johnson C. Smith U., Lake Forest Coll., Tougaloo Coll., Union Coll., Northwestern U., Whittier Coll., U. Mass., U. Mich., Seattle U., U. Toledo, Yale U., LI U., Catholic U. Am., Tulane U., Temple U., Kalamazoo Coll., Washington U., St. Louis, Trinity Coll., Conn., Ariz. State U., SUNY, Albany, No. Mich. U., U. Utah, Coll. New Rochelle, George Washington U., Governors State U., Harvard U., U. Pa., Ripon Coll., Atlanta U., Wayne State U., U. NC, Dillard U., Manhattan Coll., Roosevelt U., NC Central U., Ind. State U., St. Olaf Coll., Emory U., U. Miami, U. Conn., U. NC, Brandeis U., Wake Forest U., Wilkes Coll., Queen's Coll., NY, Wilmington Coll., U. NC, Greensboro, Queens Coll., Charlotte, NC, Ill. State U., Bates Coll., Williams Coll., U. South, U. NC, Am. U., Furman U., Georgetown U., Tufts U., Elizabeth City State U., Shaw U., San Francisco U., Washington Lee U., Columbia Coll., Chgo., Lincoln Meml. U., Elmira Coll., Lane Coll., Bethune-Cookman Coll., Amherst Coll., U. Cin., Dartmouth Coll., U. Ky., Duke U., San Francisco State U., York Coll., Northeastern U., Occidental Coll., U. Akron, U. Vermont, Bennett Coll., San Diego U., Pa. State U., Tex. A&M U., Pomona Coll., U. San Diego, U. Vt., U. Akron, U. NC, Pembroke, SC State U., U. DC, Wesleyan U., 2006, Lafayette Coll., 2006. Prof. hist. St. Augustine's Coll., 1939—43, NC Coll., Durham, 1943—47, Howard U., 1947—56; chmn. dept. hist. Bklyn. Coll., 1956—64; prof. Am. hist. U. Chgo., 1964—82, chmn. dept. hist., 1967—70, John Matthews Manly Disting. Svc. prof., 1969—82; James B. Duke prof. hist. Duke U., 1982—85, prof. emeritus, 1985—; prof. legal hist. Duke U. Law Sch., 1985—92. Pitt. prof. Am. hist. and instns. Cambridge U., 1962—63; vis. prof. Harvard U., U. Wis., Cornell U., Salzburg Seminar, U. Hawaii, U. Calif.; chmn. bd. fgn. scholarships, 1966—69, Nat. Coun. Humanities, 1976—79; trustee Nat. Humanities Ctr., 1980—91, chmn. adv. bd. to pres.'s initiative on race, 1997—98; Fulbright prof., Australia, 1960; lectr. in field; chmn. adv. bd. Nat. Pk. Svc. Author: The Free Negro in North Carolina, 1790-1860, 1943, The Militant South, 1800-1861, 1956, Reconstruction: After the Civil War, 1961, The Emancipation Proclamation, 1963, A Southern Odyssey: Travelers in the Antebellum North, 1976, Racial Equality in America, 1976, George Washington Williams, A Biography, 1985, Race and History: Selected Essays, 1938-1988, 1990, The Color Line: Legacy for the 21st Century, 1993, Mirror to America: The Autobiography of John Hope Franklin, 2005; co-author (with Alfred A. Moss): From Slavery to Freedom: A History of African Americans, 1947, 9th edit., 2007; co-author: (with John W. Caughey & Ernest R. May) Land of the Free: A History of the United States, 1966; co-author: (with Loren Schweninger) Runaway Slaves: Rebels on the Plantation, 1999, In Search of the Promised Land: A Slave Family in the Old South, 2005; editor: Civil War Diary of James T. Ayers, 1947, A Fool's Errand by Albion Tourgee, 1961, Army Life in a Black Regiment by Thomas Higginson, 1962, Color and Race, 1968, Reminiscences of an Active Life by John R. Lynch, 1970; co-editor (with others): Illustrated History of Black Americans, 1970; co-editor: (with August Meier) Black Leaders in the Twentieth Century, 1982; co-editor: (with Abraham Eisenstadt) Harlan Davidson's American History Series; co-editor: (with Genna Rae McNeil) African Americans and the Living Constitution, 1995; co-editor: (with John Whittington Franklin) My Life and An Era: The Autobiography of Buck Colbert Franklin, 1997; mem. editl. bd.: Am. Scholar, 1972—76, 1994—; subject of (documentaries) First Person Singular: John Hope Franklin, PBS, 1997. Trustee Chgo. Symphony, 1976—80, Fisk U., 1947—80; bd. dirs. Salzburg Seminar, Mus. Sci. and Industry, 1968—80, DuSable Mus., 1970—. Named one of 100 Most Influential Black Ama., Ebony mag., 2006; named to Okla. Hall of Fame, 1978, Okla. Historians Hall of Fame, 1996, The Ebony Power 150, Ebony mag., 2007; recipient Cleanth Brooks medal, Fellowship So. Writers, 1989, Gold medal, Ency. Britannica, 1990, Caldwell medal, NC Coun. on Humanities, 1992—93, Charles Frankel medal, 1993, Bruce Catton award, Soc. Am. Historians, 1994, award, Cosmos Club, 1994, Spingarn medal, NAACP, 1995, Presdl. Medal of Freedom, 1995, Peggy V. Helmerich Disting. Author award, 1997, Smithson Bicentennial medal, 1997, Lincoln prize, 2000, Harold Washington Lit. award, 2000, Gold medal award, Am. Acad. Arts and Letters, 2002, Disting. Author award, Bergen County, 2002, Arthur Schlesinger Jr. Lifetime Hist. award, 2002, John F. Kennedy award, Mass. Hist. Soc., 2005, Benjamin Franklin medal, 2006, Robert F. Kennedy award, 2006, Lifetime Achievement award, Indigo Found., 2006, John W. Kluge prize for Study of Humanity, 2006; fellow Edward Austin fellow, 1937—39, Guggenheim fellow, 1950—51, 1973—74, Pres.'s fellow, Brown U., 1952—53, Ctr. Advanced Study in Behavioral Sci., 1973—74, Sr. Mellon fellow. Fellow: Am. Acad. Arts and Scis.; mem.: AAUP, Am. Philos. Soc. (Jefferson medal 1993, Benjamin Franklin medal 2006), Am. Studies Assn. (past pres.), Assn. for Study Negro Life and Hist., Orgn. Am. Historians (pres. 1974—75), So. Hist. Assn. (pres. 1970—71), Am. Hist. Assn. (pres. 1978—79), Phi Alpha Theta, Phi Beta Kappa (senate 1966—82, pres. 1973—76, Sidney Hook award 1994). Office Phone: 919-489-7513.

FRANKLIN, JON DANIEL, writer, journalist, educator; b. Enid, Okla., Jan. 12, 1942; s. Benjamin Max and Wilma Irene (Winburn) F.; m. Nancy Sue Creevan, Dec. 12, 1959 (div. 1976, dec. 1987); children: Teresa June, Catherine Cay; m. Lynn Irene Scheidhauer, May 20, 1988. BS with high honors, U. Md., 1970; LHD (hon.), U. Md., Balt. County, 1981, Coll. Notre Dame, Balt., 1982. With USN, 1959-67; reporter/editor Prince Georges (Md.) Post, 1967-70; sci. and feature writer Balt. Evening Sun, 1970-85; assoc. prof. U. Md. Coll. Journalism, 1985-88, prof., 1988-89; prof., chmn. dept. journalism Oreg. State U., Corvallis, 1989-91; prof. creative writing, dir. U. Oreg., Eugene, 1991-98; sci. writer, spl. assignments editor Raleigh News and Observer, Raleigh, NC, 1998-2001; Philip Merrill prof. journalism U. Md., College Park, 2001—. Author: Shocktrauma, 1980, Not Quite a Miracle, 1983, Guinea Pig Doctors, 1984, Writing for Story, 1986, The Molecules of the Mind, 1987. pub.: *Bylines*, WriterL. Recipient James T. Grady medal Am. Chem. Soc., 1975, Pulitzer prize for feature writing, 1979, Pulitzer prize for explanatory journalism, 1985, Carringer award Nat. Mental Health Assn., 1984, Penney-Mo. Spl. award for health reporting, 1985; named to Newspaper Hall of Fame, Md.-Del.-D.C. Press Assn.,also Feature Writers Hall of Fame, 2002. Mem. Nat. Assn. Sci. Writers (bd. dirs.), Soc Profl. Journalists, Authors Guild. Home: PO Box 206 Sunderland MD 20689-0206 E-mail: jonfrank@nasw.org.

FRANKLIN, JONATHAN S., lawyer; b. 1964; AB, Harvard Coll., 1986; JD, Yale Law Sch., 1990. Bar: US Supreme Ct., US Ct. Appeals (2nd cir.) DC, US Ct. Appeals (3rd cir.) DC, US Ct. Appeals (4th cir.) DC, US Ct. Appeals (6th cir.) DC, US Ct. Appeals (8th cir.) DC, US Ct. Appeals (9th cir.) DC, US Ct. Appeals (10th cir.) DC, US Ct. Appeals (Fed. cir.) DC, US Dist. Ct. (dist. DC). Law clk. US Ct. Appeals (3rd cir.); ptnr. Hogan & Hartson LLP, Fulbright & Jaworski LLP, Washington, 2006—. Named to Chambers USA, 2006. Mem.: Edward Coke Am. Appellate Inn of Ct. (Barrister mem.). Office: Fulbright & Jaworski LLP Market Sq 801 Pennsylvania Ave NW Washington DC 20004-2623 Office Phone: 202-662-0200. Office Fax: 202-662-4643.*

FRANKLIN, JUDE ERIC, electronics executive; b. St. Marys, Pa., Aug. 3, 1943; s. William Nelson and Elizabeth (Kronenwetter) F.; m. Mary Frances Bizot, Sept. 17, 1966; children: Pamela Mary, Erik Jude. BEE, Cath. U., 1965, MEE, 1968, PhDEE, 1980. Program mgr. Chesapeake Instrument Corp. (now divsn. of GE), Shadyside, Md., 1966-75; v.p. MAR, Inc., Rockville, 1975—81; mgr. Navy Artifical Intelligence Ctr. Naval Rsch. Lab., Washington, 1981-85; sr. v.p. tech. div. Planning Rsch. Corp., McLean, Va., 1985-87, sr. v.p., 1987—92, chief tech. officer and v.p., 1991—2003; tech. dir. Raytheon Network Centric Sys. Command and Control, Arlington, 2003—. Bd. dirs. Am. Univ., Washington Juvenile Diabetes Found. Contbr. to Artifical Intelligence Ency., 1987; also articles to profl. jours. V.p. Prince Mont Swim League; vol. U.S. Swimming Referee and Starter; PRC team leader Juvenile Diabetes Found., 1995. Recipient Meritorious Svc. award Armed Forces Comm. and Electronics Assn., 1988, Fed. "100" award Fed. Computer News, 1992, Best Paper of Yr. award Signal Mag., 1995 Fellow AIAA (assoc.), Washington Acad. Sci.; mem. IEEE (sr., guest editor Expert Mag., 1989), Kettering Civic Fedn. (pres. 1971-72), Sigma Xi. Democrat. Roman Catholic. Home: 7616 Carteret Rd Bethesda MD 20817-2021 Office: Ste 1700 1100 Wilson Blvd Arlington VA 22209 Personal E-mail: jude_e_franklin@raytheon.com.

FRANKLIN, JULIAN HAROLD, political science professor; b. NYC, Mar. 26, 1925; s. Jerome A. and Molly (Seidenstein) F.; m. Paula Angle, Feb. 23, 1928. BA summa cum laude, Queens Coll., 1946; MA, Columbia U., 1950, PhD, 1960. Instr. Columbia U., NYC, 1951-59, assoc. prof., 1962-68, prof., 1968-96, prof. emeritus, 1997—; vis. asst. prof. New Sch. for Social Rsch., NYC, 1959-60; asst. prof. Princeton (N.J.) U., 1960-62. Acting chmn. summer session Columbia U., 1962—, dir. grad. studies polit. theory, 1968—, dept. rep., 1971-72, 86—, dept. del. com. on instruction faculty polit. sci., 1971-73, 81-82, chmn., 1973-74, co-founder, adj. chmn. sem. on polit. and social thought; mem. adv. coun. dept. politics Princeton U., 1973-76. Author: Jean Bodin and the Sixteenth Century Revolution in the Methodology of Law and History, 1963, Constitutionalism and Resistance in the Sixteenth Century, 1969, Jean Bodin and the Rise of Absolutist Theory, 1973, rev. edit. (in French), 1993, John Locke and the Theory of Sovereignty, 1978, Animal Rights and Moral Philosophy, 2005; editor and translator: Jean Bodin on Sovereignty, 1992; editl. cons. in polit. theory Polity, 1977-79; mem. editl. bd. Polit. Theory; contbr. articles to profl. jours. Served with USAF, 1943-46. Queens Coll. scholar, 1946, Social Sci. Rsch. Coun. fellow, 1950-51, William Bayard Cutting travelling fellow, 1950-51, NEH fellow, 1975-76, 89-90, Phi Beta Kappa fellow, 1990. Mem. Conf. for Study Polit. and Social Thought. Jewish. Office: Columbia U Dept Polit Sci 116th St And Broadway New York NY 10027

FRANKLIN, KENNETH RONALD, management consultant; b. NYC, June 6, 1932; s. Lawrence and Gladys (Siegel) Franklin; m. Harriet Faye Lewis, Dec. 27, 1960; children: Gregg E., Erica G. BS, Syracuse U., 1953, MBA, 1954. Cert. mgmt. cons. Instr. Harpur Coll. Syracuse U., Vestal, NY, 1956-57; sales rep. IBM, Pitts., 1957-64; br. mgr. ABS, Pitts., 1964-66; v.p. franchising Arby's Inc., Youngstown, Ohio, 1966-70; pres. Franchise Devel. Inc., Pitts., 1970—. With Spl. Svcs., 1954-56, ETO. Mem. Inst. Mgmt. Cons., Pitts. Athletic Assn., Concorcia Club, Westmoreland C.C. Avocations: tennis, reading, travel. Office: Franchise Devel Inc 5001 Baum Blvd Ste 660 Pittsburgh PA 15213 Home Phone: 412-521-5769; Office Phone: 412-687-8484. Personal E-mail: franchise-dev@earthlink.net.

FRANKLIN, KIRK, singer; b. Fort Worth, Tex., Jan. 26, 1970; m. Tammy Collins, Jan. 20, 1996; 4 children. Choir leader Kirk Franklin & the Family, 1992, Kirk Franklin's Nu Nation, God's Property. Singer: (albums) Kirk Franklin & the Family, 1993, Kirk Franklin & the Family Christmas, 1995, Whatcha Lookin' 4, 1996 (Grammy award, Best Contemporary Soul Gospel Album), God's Property, 1997 (Grammy award, Best Choir Gospel Album), The Nu Nation Project, 1998 (Grammy award, Best Contemporary Soul Gospel Album), The Rebirth of Kirk Franklin, 2002, Hero, 2005 (Grammy award, Best Contemporary R&B Gospel Album, 2007), (songs) Imagine Me, 2005 (Grammy award, Best Gospel Song, 2007). Recipient Best Gospel Artist award, Black Entertainment TV (BET), 2006, Best Male Artist award, Christian30 Video Music Awards, 2006, Favorite Contemporary Inspirational Artist, Am. Music Awards, 2006, Image award for Gospel Artist, NAACP, 2007, Soul Train award for Best Gospel Album, 2007, Best Gospel Artist award, Black Entertainment TV (BET), 2007. Office: Fo Yo Soul Entertainment Ste 250 17120 Dallas Pkwy Dallas TX 75248 Office Phone: 972-407-9797. Office Fax: 972-407-9688. E-mail: info@FoYoSoulEntertainment.com.*

FRANKLIN, LYNNE, corporate communications specialist, writer; b. St. Paul, Aug. 24, 1957; d. Lyle John Franklin and Lois Ann (Cain) Kindseth, Thomas John Kindseth (Stepfather); m. Lawrence Anton Pecorella, Sept. 12, 1989; 1 stepchild, Lauren Pecorella. BA in Psychology and English, Coll. St. Catherine, 1979; MA, Hamline U., 1989. Residential treatment counselor St. Joseph's Home, Mpls., 1979-80; staff writer Comml. West Mag., Mpls., 1980-81; acct. exec. Edwin Neuger & Assocs., Mpls., 1981-83, Hill and Knowlton, Mpls., 1983-84; mgr. pub. rels. Gelco Corp., Eden Prarie, Minn., 1984-86; dir. fin. rels. Dunstan & Assocs., Mpls., 1986; cons. MC Assocs., Chgo., 1986-87; v.p. Fin. Rels. Bd., Chgo., 1987—; prin. Wordsmith, Glenview, Ill., 1993—; trainer SkillPath Seminars, Mission, Kans., 2004—, 2004. Trustee Lawrence Hall Youth Svcs., chairperson pub. rels. com.; former pres., v.p., sec. Skokie Valley chpt. Bus. Networking Internat., 2003—07; judge achievement awards Internat. Assn. Bus. Comm., Mpls., 1986, Publicity Club Chgo., 1992—94; presenter in fin. rels., 1990; presenter ann. report seminar Nat. Investor Rels. Inst., Chgo., 1992; presenter investor rels. survey, 2003; mktg. presenter Nat. Assn. Profl. Organizers, Chgo., 2005, World WIT Nat. Conf., Lake Geneva, Wis., 2005. Author: (novels) Second Sight, 1989. Tchr. Great Books Program, St. Paul, 1976—79, Minn. Literacy Coun., 1985—87. Recipient Ann. Report Excellence award, Fin. World Mag., 1991—98, award, MerComm-ARC Competition, 1992—2003, Nat. Assn. Investors Corp., 1994—2003, Equities Mag., 1999—2002. Mem.: Rotar (crisis comm. presenter 2007). Office: Wordsmith 2019 Glenview Rd Glenview IL 60025-2849 Business E-Mail: lynne@yourwordsmith.com.

FRANKLIN, MARC ADAM, law educator; b. Bklyn., Mar. 9, 1932; s. Louis A. and Rose (Rosenthal) Franklin; m. Ruth E. Korzenik, June 29, 1958 (dec. Dec. 2000); children: Jonathan, Alison. AB, Cornell U., 1953, LLB, 1956. Bar: N.Y. 1956. Assoc. Proskauer Rose Goetz & Mendelsohn, NYC, 1956-57; law clk to Hon. Carroll C. Hincks, New Haven, 1957-58; prof. law Stanford U., Calif., 1962-76, Frederick I. Richman prof. law, 1976—2001, emeritus, 2001—; prof. law Columbia U., 1959-62; law clk to to Earl Warren, U.S. Supreme Ct., Washington, 1958-59. Author: Biography of a Legal Dispute, 1968, Dynamics of American Law, 1968, Cases and Materials on Tort Law and Alternatives, 1971; co-author (with R.L. Rabin and M.D. Green): 8th edit., 2006; author: Mass Media Law, 1977; co-author (with D.A. Anderson and L.C.B. Lidsky): 7th edit., 2005; author: The First Amendment and the Fourth Estate, 1977; co-author (with T.B. Carter and J.B. Wright): The First Amendment and the Fourth Estate, 9th edit., 2005; author: The First Amendment and the Fifth Estate, 1986; co-author (with T.B. Carter and J.B. Wright): The First Amendment and the Fifth Estate, 6th edit., 2003. Fellow Ctr. for Advanced Study in Behavioral Scis., 1968—69; scholar Fulbright, Victoria U., 1973. Home: 999 Green St # 2005 San Francisco CA 94133 Office: Stanford U Law Sch Nathan Abbott Way Stanford CA 94305 Business E-Mail: marcf@stanford.edu.

FRANKLIN, MARGERY BODANSKY, psychology professor, researcher; b. NYC, Mar. 18, 1933; d. Oscar and Barbara (Biber) Bodansky; m. Raymond S. Franklin, Aug. 22, 1962; children— Kenneth, David AB, Swarthmore Coll., 1954; MA, Clark U., 1956, PhD, 1961. Instr. psychology Vassar Coll., Poughkeepsie, NY, 1960-62, asst. prof., 1962-64; research assoc. Bank St. Coll. Edn., NYC, 1967-72; prof. Sarah Lawrence Coll., Bronxville, NY, 1965—2002. Dir. Child Devel. Inst. Sarah Lawrence Coll., 2003—07. Co-editor: Developmental Processes: Heinz Werner's Selected Writings, 1978, Symbolic Functioning in Childhood, 1979, Child Language: A Reader, 1988, Development and the Arts: Critical Perspectives, 1994; contbr. articles to profl. jours., chpts. to books. Fellow Am. Psychol. Assn. (pres. psychology and arts divsn. 1990-91); mem. Soc. for Rsch. in Child Devel. Avocation: photography. Business E-Mail: mbf@slc.edu.

FRANKLIN, MARTIN E., consumer products company executive; BA, Univ. Pa. Chmn., CEO Benson Eyecare Corp., 1992—96, Lumen Technologies Inc., 1996—98; chmn. Bollé Inc., 1997—2000; chmn., CEO Jarden Corp., Rye, NY, 2001—. Bd. dir. Apollo Investment Corp., Kenneth Cole Productions Inc. Office: Jarden Corp Ste B-302 555 Theodore Fremd Ave Rye NY 10580*

FRANKLIN, MICHAEL HAROLD, arbitrator, lawyer, consultant; b. LA, Dec. 25, 1923; m. Betty Chernow, 1989; children from previous marriage: Barbara, John, James, Robert. AB, UCLA, 1948; LL.B., U. So. Calif., 1951. Bar: Calif. 1951. Practiced in Los Angeles, 1951-52; pvt. practice, 1951-52; atty. CBS, 1952-54, Paramount Pictures Corp., 1954-58; exec. dir. Writers Guild Am. West, Inc., 1958-78; nat. exec. dir. Dirs. Guild Am., Inc., 1978-88. Mem. Fed. Cable Adv. Commn. Served with C.E. AUS, 1942-46. Mem. Order of Coif.

FRANKLIN, PAULA ANNE, artist, writer, psychologist; b. Wheaton, Ill., Feb. 2, 1928; d. Paul Spangler and Ella Creighton (Daniels) Fowler; m. Richard Clarence Franklin, Aug. 13, 1950; children: Jan Franklin BenDor, Timothy Vickery, Edward Lee. Student, Manchester U., Eng., 1946-47; BSc in History, Northwestern U., 1949, postgrad., 1975, So. Ill. U., 1959-61; MA, W.Va. U., 1970; PhD, Union Inst., 1980; BA with honors in Art, Towson U., Md., 2003. Lic. psychologist, Md. Pres., dir. Franklinc Behavioral Sci. Cons., Balt., 1969—; human resource and orgnl. devel. faculty Johns Hopkins U., Balt., 1972—92; rsch. project dir. Social Security Adminstrn., Balt., 1973—99. Adj. faculty dept. psychology U. Balt., 1989-91. Author: (with R. Franklin) Tomorrow's Track, 1976, (with others) Disability in the U.S., 1990; editor: The Maryland Psychologist, 1994-98; contbr. articles to profl. jours. Com. mem. LWV, 1950-75; active Girl Scouts U.S., Boy Scouts Am., 1950-70. Mem. Am. Psychol. Assn., Md. Psychol. Assn. (Cert. of Recognition 1981), Internat. Assn. for Study Dreams. Unitarian Universalist. Avocations: music, theater, gardening, photography, travel. Home: 3946 Cloverhill Rd Baltimore MD 21218-1707 Office: Ste 3A 3946 Cloverhill Rd Baltimore MD 21218-1707 Office Phone: 410-235-8151. Personal E-mail: franklin@charm.net.

FRANKLIN, RICHARD MARK, lawyer; b. Chgo., Dec. 13, 1947; s. Henry W. and Gertrude (Gross) F.; m. Marguerite June Wesle, Sept. 2, 1973; children: Justin Wesley, Elizabeth Cecilia, Catherine Helena, Caroline Lucinda. BA, U. Wis., 1970; postgrad., U. Freiburg, Fed. Republic Germany, 1968-69; JD, Columbia U., 1973. Bar: Ill. 1973, U.S. Dist. Ct. (no. dist.) Ill. 1973, U.S. Ct. Appeals (7th cir.) 1973. Assoc. Baker & McKenzie, Chgo., 1973-79, Frankfurt, Fed. Republic Germany, 1979-80, ptnr. Chgo., 1980—. Mem. ABA, Ill. Bar Assn., Chgo. Bar Assn. Mem. United Ch. Christ. Avocations: music, literature, theater, outdoor activities. Home: 1161 Oakley Ave Winnetka IL 60093-1437 Office: Baker & McKenzie 1 Prudential Plz 130 E Randolph St Ste 3500 Chicago IL 60601-6342 Home Phone: 847-446-2841; Office Phone: 312-861-8860. E-mail: rmfwinn@aol.com, richard.m.franklin@bakenet.com.

FRANKLIN, ROBERT MCFARLAND, book publisher; b. Memphis, Mar. 13, 1943; s. Robert Dumont and Mary McFarland (Wilson) F.; m. Cheryl Jane Roberts, Jan. 18, 1975; children: Charles McRee, Nicholas Roberts, William Holliday. AB, Yale U., 1965. With Columbia U. Libr., NYC, 1965-66; editor to exec. editor Scarecrow Press, Metuchen, NJ, 1969-79; pres., founder McFarland & Co., Inc., Publishers, Jefferson, NC, 1979—. Pub. Jour. Info. Ethics, 1992—, Base Ball: A Jour. of Early Game, 2006—. Dir., actor Ashe County Little Theatre, Jefferson, 1980—; libr. adv. bd. Appalachian State U., 1995—. With U.S. Army, 1966-68. Recipient Gov.'s Bus. award in arts and humanities, State of N.C., 1984, 87, 97, N.C. State Arts Coun. Outstanding Vol. award 1991, Ashe County Outstanding Vol. award, 2004. Mem. ALA (pub. com. 1984-88, coun. governing body 1988-2000, pay equity com. 1991-93, intellectual freedom com. 1994-96), Am. Soc. for Psychical Rsch. (dir. 1984-88). Avocations: chess, Go, European languages and cultures, acting, canoeing. Home: 338 Cut Laurel Gap Rd Creston NC 28615-9049 Office: McFarland & Co Inc Pubs Box

611 Jefferson NC 28640-0611 Home Phone: 336-385-6002; Office Phone: 336-246-4460. Business E-Mail: rfranklin@mcfarlandpub.com.

FRANKLIN, ROBERT MICHAEL, JR., academic administrator, theology studies educator; b. Chgo., Feb. 22, 1954; m. Cheryl Goffney; children: Imani, Robert III, Julian DeShazier. Grad., Morehouse Coll., 1975; MDiv, Harvard U., 1978; PhD, U. Chgo., 1985. Protestant chaplain St. Bernard Hosp., 1981—83; dir. field edn. and instruction in religion and psychol. studies U. Chgo. Divinity Sch., 1982—84; asst. dir. ministerial studies Harvard Divinity Sch., Cambridge, Mass., 1984—85, vis. lectr. African Am. Religion, 1986—88, vis. prof., 2002; dean Black Ch. Studies Colgate Rochester Divinity Sch., NY, 1985—89; asst. prof. dir. Black Ch. Studies Candler Sch. of Theology, Emory U., Atlanta, 1989—91, presdl. disting. prof. social ethics, 2003—07; assoc. prof. ethics and society Sch. Law, Emory U., Atlanta, 1994—94, sr. fellow Ctr. for Interdisciplinary Study of Religion, 2001—07; program officer Human Rights and Social Justice Program Ford Found., NYC, 1995—97; pres. Interdenom. Theol. Ctr., Atlanta, 1997—2002, Morehouse Coll., Atlanta, 2007—. Commentator All Things Considered, Nat. Pub. Radio, 2001—; theologian in residence Chatauqua Inst., NY, 2005. Author: Another Day's Journey: Black Churches Confronting the American Crisis, Liberating Visions: Human Fulfillment and Social Justice in African American Thought, Crisis in the Village: Restoring Hope to African American Communities, 2007; cons. Steven Spielberg/DreamWorks prodn. Prince of Egypt. Bd. dirs. Congress of Nat. Black Chs., Ind. Univ. Ctr. on Philanthropy, Ga. Coun. for Humanities, Jessie Ball DuPont Fund, Joseph Lowery Inst. for Justice and Human Rights, Clark Atlanta U.; mem. adv. bd. Children's Def. Fund's Black Ch. and Cmty. Crusade. Avocations: golf, swimming. Office: Morehouse Coll Office of Pres 830 Westview Dr SW Atlanta GA 30314 Office Phone: 404-727-0756. Office Fax: 404-727-2494. E-mail: rmfrank@emory.edu.*

FRANKLIN, ROOSEVELT, minister; b. Chattanooga, Aug. 30, 1933; s. James R. and Cora Ann (Ponds) F.; m. Darnell Pinkston, Sept. 30, 1972; children: Sophia, Siemoran Dellazar. BS, Northeastern U., 1958; MA (hon.), Savannah State Coll., 1962; M. of Cybernetics, Grad. Sch. Wicca, St. Charles, Mo. Lic. metaphysician. Pastor Free For All Bapt. Ch., Greenwood, SC, 1959-61; radio min. Spiritual Ch., Aiken, SC, 1961-63; nat. lectr. United Coun. Spiritual Ch., Raleigh, NC, 1963-66; min. Holy Trinity House of God, Macon, Ga., 1966—. Youth dir. Holy Trinity Ch., Macon, 1966-72, talent coord., 1966-73; dir. Spiritual Singers, 1966—; lectr. in field; world renown authority on witchcraft and transcendental meditation; expert in clairvoyance, spiritual meditation; supporter Macon County Little League Baseball; internat. tour Prosperity Way of Living Teachings. Editor: Prosperity Way of Living. Organizer voters registration, Macon, 1977; pub. relations vol. Nat. Dem. Party, Atlanta, 1984; bd. dirs. Retired Persons Assn., 1980—. Capt. U.S. Army, 1951-54, Korea. Named extrovert promoter Music Workshop, 1979; recipient Proclamation and Key to City, Roanoke, Va., 1977, Afro Am. Heritage award Afro Am. Heritage Mus., 1987, Golden Eagle award Macon Courier, 1988, Nat. Achievers award Nat. Black Secs. Assn., 1990, Ednl. award Ptnrs. Youth Club, 1991, Golden Eagle award 500 Black Men of Am. Club, 1992, Black Achievement award Nat. Negro Achievers Assn., 1993, Humanitarian award. Gov. of Ga., 1993, Nat. Rschrs. Occult award United Spiritual Coun. Chs., 1994, Hon. Citizens award, Tuskegee, Ala., 1994, Mahogany Triumph award Am. Black Affluent Assn. Am., 1995, Cert. Recognition City of Memphis, 1995, Concerned Citizens award People in Action Club, 1996, Good Samaritan award United Youth Fellowship Club, 1997, Model Citizen's award Office of the Gov. Ga., 1997, Registered Spiritual award, Registered Psychic award and Mystic award United Spiritual Coun. Assn., 1998, Self Awareness Lecture award, Howard U., 1998, Appreciation award for continuous contbns. UNCF, 1998, Commemorative award Ga. Farmer's Assn., 1998, Activist award Boys Clubs Am., 1998, Outstanding Activities award United Fraternities Am., 1998, Presdl. Acknowledgement, Nat. Assn. Disabled Persons, 1999, Dr. of Metaphysics award, Dr. of Biblical Counseling award and Dr. of Religion award, 1999, Outstanding Citizenship award, Pilot Club, 1999, Contemporary Spkr. award, Chgo., 2000, Lectr. of Yr. award Nat. Bible Soc., Silver Raven award, 2002, Ea. Mysteries award for excellence, 2002, Order of Nostradamus, Cert. Seminar of Appreciation, 2002, Spkr. of Yr. award Spiritism, 2002, others. Mem. NAACP (life), SCLC (life), Nat. Assn. Pastoral Counselors (career specialist advisor 2000, dir. conf. on prosperity), Ednl. Media Assn. (founder 2002, counseling tax force 2001, Pursuit of Excellence award 2002), Inner Circle Congl. Aides, C. of C., Ministers Alliance (v.p. 1966—, Citizens award 1979), Ga. Black Am. Pageant (coord. 1980—, Leadership award 1982), Direct Sellers League, Smooth Ashlar (dist. dep. 1970—), Rolls-Royce Club, Woodsmen of Am., Pioneer Club, Shriners (nat. amb.), Masons (33 deg., sovereign grand gen. inspector, Grand Orator 33 deg. Scottish Rite 2002), Optimists, Kiwanis, Civitan, Elks, Nat. Lodge (treas. 1987—), Potentate of the Rosicrusicans, Sertoma, Lions, VFW (life), DAV (life), Am. Legion (life). Democrat. Avocations: martial arts, billiards. Office: Holy Trinity House of God 280 Straight St Macon GA 31204-6100

FRANKLIN, SHIRLEY CLARKE, mayor; b. Phila., May 10, 1945; d. Eugene Haywood Clarke and Ruth (Lyons) White; m. David McCoy Franklin, Feb. 5, 1972 (div. 1986); children: Kai Ayanna, Cabral Holsey, Kali Jamilla. BA, Howard U., 1968, LLD (hon.), 2002; MA, U. Pa., 1969, LLM (hon.), 2007. Contract compliance officer U.S. Dept. Labor, Washington, 1966-68; instr. social scis. Talledega Coll., 1969-71; from dir. to commr. Dept. Cultural Affairs, Atlanta, 1978-82; chief adminstrv. officer City of Atlanta, 1982-90, exec. officer for ops., 1990—2001; pvt. practice, 1997—; mayor City of Atlanta, 2002—. Trustee Atlanta Symphony Orch., 1977-81, Atlanta Found., 1980—; mem. Ga. Council for the Arts, Atlanta, 1979-82, adv. bd. Ga. Women's Polit. Caucus, Atlanta, 1982-84; chmn. expansion arts panel Nat. Endowment for the Arts, Washington, 1980-82; bd. dirs. Nat. Urban Coalition, Washington, 1980-83; dep. campaign mgr. Young for Atlanta, 1981-82; sr. v.p. external rels. Atlanta Com. Olympic Games, 1991-97; majority ptnr. Urban Environ. Solutions, LLC, 1998-. Recipient Disting. Alumni award Nat. Assn. for Equal Opportunity Higher Edn., 1983, Leadership award Atlanta chpt. NAACP, 1987, John F. Kennedy Profile in Courage Award, John F. Kennedy Libr. Found., 2005; named to Acad. Women Achievers YWCA Greater Atlanta, 1986; named one of 100 Most Influential Black Americans, Ebony mag., 2006. Mem. Nat. Forum Black Pub. Adminstrs. Clubs: Chautauqua Circle. Democrat. Avocations: gardening, travel, politics, fine arts. Office: City Hall 55 Trinity Ave SW Atlanta GA 30303-3520*

FRANKLIN, TIMOTHY A., editor; m. Alison Franklin; 2 children. BJ and Polit. Sci., Ind. U., 1982. Reporter county govt. to assoc. mng. editor Chgo. Tribune, 1982—97; v.p., editor Ind. Star, 2000, Orlando Sentinel, 2000—04; editor, sr. v.p. Balt. Sun, 2004—. Mem. bd. visitors U. Md. Sch. Journalism, 2004—; jurist Pulitzer Prizes, 2006, 07. Nominee Pulitzer prize, series state's child welfare sys., 1986; named One of the Nation's Most Influential Bus. Journalists, TJFR mag.; recipient Barney Kilgore award, Soc. Profl. Journalists. Mem.: Am. Soc. Newspaper Editors (mem. leadership com.), Fla. Soc. Newspaper Editors (co-chmn. orgn.'s pub. access com.). Office: Balt Sun PO Box 1377 501 N Calvert St Baltimore MD 21278*

FRANKLIN, WILLIAM PRICE, information technology manager; s. Billy Wayne Franklin and Kikue (Hanaoka) Johnston. Student, West Tex. State U., 1972-74; AS, Lakeland Coll., 1986; BS, Almeda U., 2005. Data processing mgr. Customized Service Co., Inc., Amarillo, Tex., 1979-81; dist. acct. Browning Ferris, Inc., 1981-84; sr. programmer Fedders Air Conditioning USA Inc., Effingham, Ill., 1986-90; systems programmer Fedders N.Am., Inc., Effingham, 1990-94; systems software mgr. Fedders Corp., Effingham, 1994-99, mgr. info. systems, 1999—2001, mgr. IS infrastructure, 2001—03, mgr. corp. IS infrastructure, 2003—07. Del. Tex. Rep. Conv., 1972. Roman Catholic. Avocations: motorcycles, music.

FRANKLYN, AUDREY POZEN, talent promoter, television personality; b. Detroit, Dec. 8, 1930; d. Sidney Pozen and Rachel (Slobasky) Franklyn. AA, LA City Coll., 1952; BA, UCLA, 1955. Dir. pub. rels., radio disc jockey Gene Norman, LA, 1957-60; owner Franklyn Agy. Pub. Rels. Firm, LA, 1960—. Ptnr. A & E Prodns. Host (TV series) The Franklyn Interview, 1977—, promoter Ella Fitzgerald, 1966—94, Pablo Records; prodr.: various commls. and talks shows for cable TV. Mem.: LA Press Club. Office: 1010 Hammond St # 312 West Hollywood CA 90069-3853 Office Phone: 323-272-6080.

FRANKOWIAK, JAMES RAYMOND, public relations executive; b. Milw., Oct. 23, 1946; s. Raymond James and Stephanie Carlene (Sztorc) F.; m. Janice Lynn Kantorski, Aug. 24, 1968; children: Jennifer Anne, Jessica Lynn. BA, Marquette U., 1970. Asst. dir. alumni rels. Marquette U., Milw., 1970-72; publicist GE News Bur., Louisville, 1972-74; acct. exec. Pub. Comm. Inc., Chgo., 1974-76, acct. supr., 1976-78, v.p., 1978-80; with pub. affairs dept. GTE Data Svcs., Tampa, Fla., 1979-80; v.p. Pub. Comm. Inc., Tampa, 1980-83, exec. v.p., 1983-87, pres., 1987—. Bd. dirs. Salvation Army, Tampa, 1990—. Mem. PRSA (accredited, dist. chair, mem. nat. hons. and awards com.).

FRANKS, BRENT J., consumer products company executive; BSBA, U. Ark., Fayetteville. Various field sales and gen. mgmt. positions Pepsi-Cola N.Am., 1982—92, gen. mgr. Capital Market Unit, 1992—95, v.p. customer devel. Gt. West Market Unit, 1995—99; v.p. foodservice SE bus. unit Pepsi Bottling Group, Inc., 1999—2000, v.p. retail sales, 2000, sr. v.p., chief customer officer N.Am., sr. v.p. global sales, chief customer officer, 2006—. Office: Pepsi Bottling Group Inc 1 Pepsi Way Somers NY 10589-2201 Office Phone: 914-767-6000.*

FRANKS, GRACIE G., elementary school educator; b. Haleyville, Ala., Aug. 7, 1952; d. Maxwell and Mary Frances (Moore) Gibbs; m. Wendell Jan Franks, Mar. 11, 1971; children: Wendell Harrison, Leslie Paige. BS, U. North Ala., 1975, MA, 1978, EdS, 1986. Cert. adminstrn., class AA. Tchr. Marion County Bd. Edn., Hamilton, Ala.; adminstr. Brilliant (Ala.) Elem. Sch.; DKG pres., 1990—92. Mem. Coun. Leaders in Ala. Schs. DKG scholar; named one of Outstanding Young Women of Am., 1983, Brilliant Alumna of Yr., 1984; named to Marion County Sports Hall of Fame; named Gracie Gibbs Franks Gymnasium and Computer Lab in her honor, 2005. Mem. NEA, PTO, ASCD, Ala. Edn. Assn., Marion County Edn. Assn., Nat. Assn. Elem. Sch. Prins., Ala. Assn. Elem. Sch. Prins., Ala. Assn. Supervision and Curriculum Devel., So. Assn. Colls. and Schs., Phi Delta Kappa, Kappa Delta Pi, Delta Kappa Gamma. Home: 13766 St Hwy 129 Brilliant AL 35548-9801 Home Phone: 205-465-2321; Office Phone: 205-465-2323. Personal E-mail: gfranksk6@yahoo.com.

FRANKS, HERBERT HOOVER, lawyer; b. Joliet, Ill., Jan. 25, 1934; s. Carol and Lottie (Dermer) F.; m. Eileen Pepper, June 22, 1957; children: David, Jack, Eli. BS, Roosevelt U., 1954; postgrad., Am. U., 1960. Bar: Ill. 1961, U.S. Dist. Ct. (no. dist.) Ill. 1961, U.S. Supreme Ct. 1967. Ptnr. Franks, Gerkin & McKenna, 1985—. Mem. Ill. Cts. Commn., 2003—; chmn. State Bank Group, 1979—, First Nat. Bank, Marengo, Ill., 1976—84, 1976—90. Bus. editor Am. U. Law Rev., 1959, 60. State pres. Young Dems. of Ill., 1970-72; trustee Hebrew Theol. Coll., Skokie, Ill., 1974—; trustee, sec. Forest Inst. Profl. Psychology, Springfield, Mo., 1979-91; chmn. Forest Hosp., Des Plaines, 1980-88. With U.S. Army, 1956-58. Mem.: Ill. Trial Lawyers (mng. bd. 1975—92, treas. 1985—87), Ill. State Bar Assn. (state pres. 2000—01), Shriners, Masons (33 deg.), Sigma Nu Phi (pres. 1980—82). Home: 19324 E Grant Hwy Marengo IL 60152-9438 Office: Franks Gerkin & McKenna 19333 E Grant Hwy Marengo IL 60152-8234 Office Phone: 815-923-2107. Business E-Mail: hfranks@fgmlaw.com.

FRANKS, HERSCHEL PICKENS, judge; b. Savannah, Tenn., May 28, 1930; s. Herschel R. Franks and Pickens Vada; m. Judy Black; 1 child, Ramona. Student, U. Tenn., U. Md.; JD, U. Tenn., Knoxville; grad., U. Nev. Bar: Tenn. 1959, US Supreme Ct. 1968. Claims atty. US Fidelity & Guaranty Co., Knoxville, Tenn., 1958; ptnr. Harris, Moon, Meacham & Franks, Chattanooga, 1959—70; chancellor 3d Chancery divsn. Hamilton County, 1970—78; judge Tenn. Ct. Appeals, 1978—, presiding judge, 2004—. Spl. justice Tenn. Supreme Ct., 1979, 1986—87, 2002—04; presiding judge Hamilton County Trial Cts., 1977—78; spl. judge Tenn. Ct. Criminal Appeals, 1990—92, commn. to study appellate cts., 1990—92. With N.G. USAF, 1949—50, with USAF, 1950—54. Mem.: ABA (Merit award), Inst. Jud. Adminstrn., Am. Judicature Soc., Chattanooga Bar Assn. (pres. 1968—69, Founds. of Freedom award 1986), Chattanooga Bar Found., Tenn. Bar Found., Tenn. Bar Assn. (Merit award 1968—69), Mountain City Club, City Farmers Club, Optimists (pres. 1965—66, Cmty. Svc. award 1971), Phi Alpha Delta. Mem. United Ch. Of Christ. Address: 540 Mccallie Ave Ste 562 Chattanooga TN 37402-2039 Home Phone: 423-886-4759; Office Phone: 423-634-6344.

FRANKS, JON MICHAEL, lawyer, mediator; b. Marshall, Tex., Sept. 26, 1941; s. Francis William and Clara Bell (Caldwell) F.; m. Sue Powers, May 23, 1987; children: Brian Alan, Michael Shawn. BA, Southwestern U., 1963; LLB, U. Tex., 1966. Bar. Tex. 1966, U.S. Dist. Ct. (no. dist.) Tex.; cert. family lawyer, Tex. Bd. of Legal Specialization. Lawyer Pettigrew and Buckley, Grand Prairie, Tex., 1966-67; pvt. practice Irving, Tex., 1967-68, 71-79, 88—; ptnr. Franks and Vice, Irving, 1968-71, Franks and Luce, Irving, 1979-88. Mem. child support and visitation guidelines com. Tex. Supreme Ct., Austin, 1989; mem. Southlake Ct. of Records Com., 1990—. Commr. Irving Planning and Zoning Bd., 1971-74; judge Mcpl. Ct., Irving, 1974-78, Southlake, Tex., 1978-88, Southlake City Coun., 1992—. Named Tex. Monthly Super Lawyer, 2003—; recipient various awards. Fellow Am. Acad. Matrimonial Lawyers; mem. ABA (family law sect.), Tex. Acad. Family Law Specialists (bd. dirs. 1988-90), North Tex. Assn. Family Law Specialists (pres. 1985-87), Tex. Bar Assn. (family law sect.), Dallas Bar Assn. (pres. family law sect. 1989), Tarrant County Family Law Assn., Am. Acad. Atty.-Mediators. Republican. Methodist. Avocations: gun collector, competition shooting. Office: 128 E Texas St Grapevine TX 76051-5307 Home Phone: 817-481-3153; Office Phone: 817-329-5573. E-mail: jonmfranks@aol.com.

FRANKS, LEWIS E., electrical and computer engineering educator, researcher; b. San Mateo, Calif., Nov. 8, 1931; s. Lloyd C. and Leora (Embree) F.; m. Mary B. Harris, June 21, 1954; children: Janet K., Jill M., Daniel J. BSEE, Oreg. State U., 1952; MSEE, Stanford U., 1953, PhD, 1957. Mem. tech. staff Bell Telephone Labs., Murray Hill, NJ, 1958-62, supr. North Andover, Mass., 1962-69; assoc. prof. U. Mass., Amherst, 1969-71, prof., 1971-96, chmn. dept elec. and computer engring., 1975-78, acting head dept. elec. and computer engring., 1991-93, prof. emeritus, 1996—. Author: Signal Theory, 1969; editor: Data Communication, 1974; contbr. over 60 articles to profl. jours. Hewlett-Packard fellow, Stanford U., 1952. Fellow IEEE; mem. NSF (program dir. networking and communications rsch., 1988-90). Office: Univ of Mass Dept of Elec & Computer Engring Amherst MA 01003 Personal E-mail: franks@ecs.umass.edu.

FRANKS, LUCINDA LAURA, journalist; b. Chgo., July 16, 1946; d. Thomas Edward and Lorraine Lois (Leavitt) F.; m. Robert M. Morgenthau, Nov. 1977; children: Joshua Franks Morgenthau, Amy Elinor Morgenthau. BA, Vassar Coll., 1968. Journalist specializing youth affairs, civil strife in No. Ireland UPI, London, 1968-73, NY Times, NYC, 1974-77; freelance writer NY Times Mag., NY Times Book Rev., Talk Mag., The Atlantic, The New Yorker, NY mag., The Nation. Vis. prof. Vassar Coll., 1977-82; Ferris prof. journalism Princeton U., 1983 Author: Waiting Out A War: The Exile of Private John Picciano, 1974, Wild Apples, 1991. Recipient Pulitizer prize for nat. reporting, 1971, NY Newspaper Writers Assn. award, 1971, Nat. Headliners award Soc. Silurians journalism award, 1976, EDI award for print journalism Easter Seals, 1999. Mem. Am. PEN Club (membership bd.), Author's League, Coun. on Fgn. Rels., Writers Rm. Inc. (past pres.). Address: 64 E 86th St New York NY 10028-1016

FRANKS, MARTIN DAVIS, broadcast executive; b. Michigan City, Ind., Sept. 27, 1950; s. R. Wendell and Alice (Barnard) F.; m. Mari J. Schleuning. BA in Politics, Princeton U., NJ, 1972. Staff asst. Dem. Senatorial Campaign Com., Washington, 1972-74; dep. chief of staff US Senator John Tunney, Washington and LA, 1975-77; chief of staff US Senator Patrick Leahy, Washington, 1977-79; nat. rsch. and issues dir. Carter/Mondale Presdl. Com., Washington, 1979-80; exec. office of pres. The White House, Washington, 1980-81; exec. dir. Dem. Congl. Campaign Com., Washington, 1981-87; v.p. Charls Walker Assocs., Washington, 1987-88, CBS Corp., Washington, 1988-94, sr. v.p., 1994—97, NYC, 1997—2000, exec. v.p. planning, policy & govt. rels., 2006—; exec. v.p. CBS TV, 2000—05; sr. v.p. Viacom, 2000—05. Office: CBS Corp 51 W 52nd St New York NY 10019-6188 Office Phone: 212-975-4321.*

FRANKS, ROBERT D. (BOB FRANKS), former congressman; b. Hackensack, NJ, Sept. 21, 1951; s. Norman A. and June Evans F. BA, Depauw U., 1973; JD, So. Methodist U., 1976. Exec. dir. People for Bateman, 1977; cons. Jim Courter for Congress Com., 1978; v.p. Med Data Inc., 1978-80; co-owner County News, 1980-83; cons. Tom Kean for Gov. Com., 1981; mem. N.J. State Assembly from 22nd Dist., Trenton, 1979-93, 103d-106th Congresses from 7th N.J. Dist., 1993-2001; mem. budget com., mem. transp. and infrastructure com.; pres. Healthcare Institute of N.J. Bd. dirs. Intrenet.; mgmt. cons. in field; founder CREO; mem. Econ. Steering Com., 1980, Com. on Energy and Nat. Resources, 1981-83, Com. on State Govt., Civil Svc., Elections, Pensions and Vet. Affairs, 1981-85, N.J. State Pension Study Commn., 1982, Com. Revenue, Finance and Appropriations, 1984-93, State and Local Expenditure and Revenue Policy Commn., 1985-93, Waste Mgmt. Planning and Recycling Com., 1990-91; chmn. Task Force to Reform Congress Redistricting Process, 1982, N.J. Coalition for Regulatory Efficiency, 1985-93, Republican Policy Com., 1990-91, N.J. State Rep. Party, 1988-93; campaign mgr. Congressman Jim Courter, 1982, Congressman Dean Gallo, 1984; assembly liaison Rep. Majority. 1985. Bd. mgrs. Children's Specialized Hosp., Mountainside, N.J., 1980; mem. long range planning com. Overlook Hosp., Summit, N.J., 1982; mem. domestic task force Hands Across Am., 1986; mem. N.J. Jaycees. Named Legislator of Yr. Nat. Rep. Legislators Assn., 1986. Republican.

FRANKS, RONALD DWYER, dean, psychiatrist, educator; b. Balt., Jan. 15, 1946; s. Wylie and H. Jeanette (Dwyer) F.; m. Vicky Ruth Vicklund; children: Aaron Matthew, Alexis Linda. Student, Albion Coll., 1964-67; MD with distinction, U. Mich., 1971. Intern Virginia Mason Hosp., Seattle, 1971-72; resident in psychiatry U. Colo. Med. Ctr., Denver, 1972-76; instr. psychiatry U. Colo. Sch. Medicine, Denver, 1976-77, asst. prof. psychiatry, 1977-83, assoc. prof., 1983-88, asst. dean student affairs, 1982-84, asst. dean student and curricular affairs, dir. inpatient svcs. dept. psychiatry, 1986-88; dean, prof. psychiatry U. Minn. Sch. Medicine, Duluth, 1988-97; v.p. health affairs East Tenn. State U., Johnson City, 1997—, dean James H. Quillen Coll. Medicine, 1997—, prof. psychiatry and behavioral scis., 1997—. Bd. dirs. Bank of Tenn., 2004—; chmn. State Health Planning and Adv. Bd., Tenn. Contbr. numerous articles to profl. jours. Mem. AMA, So. Med. Assn., Tenn. Med. Assn., Am. Psychiat. Assn., Alpha Omega Alpha. Office: Office of the Dean James H Quillen Coll Med PO Box 70694 Johnson City TN 37614-1710 Office Phone: 423-439-6315. Office Fax: 423-439-8090.

FRANKS, STEPHEN FIELD, retired judge; b. Biltmore, NC, June 12, 1930; s. Thomas Hendricks and Margaret (Field) Franks; m. Mary Elizabeth Volbeda, Apr. 28, 1962 (div. 2004); children: Stephen Bruce, Andrea Carol, Craig Thomas; m. Betty J. Causey, Nov. 21, 2004. BA, Duke U., 1952; LLB, JD, U. N.C., 1955. Bar: N.C. 1955, Calif. 1964, U.S. Supreme Ct. 1966. Dep. city atty. City Atty. Office, San Bernardino, Calif., 1964—66; counsel to mayor Mayor's Office, San Bernardino, 1966—69; legis. adv. County of San Bernardino, Sacramento, 1970—81; pvt. practice Hendersonville, NC, 1981—88; judge Dist. Ct. N.C., Hendersonville, 1988—2002; ret., 2002. Fed. aid coord. City of San Bernardino, 1966—69. Mem. San Juan Unified Sch. Dist., Sacramento, 1978—81, chmn., 1979; pres. County Bd. Edn., 1977—78; mem. Child Fatality Prevention Team, Hendersonville, NC, 2002; dir. Sacramento County Mental Health Assn., Sacramento, 1973—80, pres., 1978—79. Comdr. JAG USN, 1955—60. Fellow: ATLA; mem.: N.C. Bar Assn., Univ. Club, Elks, Rotary (bd. dirs.). Republican. Episcopalian. Avocation: hiking. Office: 514 5th Ave W Hendersonville NC 28739 Office Phone: 828-697-6238. Business E-Mail: sffranks@mchsi.com.

FRANKS, TOMMY RAY, retired military officer; b. Wynnewood, Okla., June 17, 1945; m. Cathryn Carley, Mar. 22, 1969; 1 child, Jacqueline Franks Matlock. BSBA, U. Tex., Arlington, 1971; MS in Pub. Adminstrn., Shippensburg U. Pa., 1985; grad., Armed Forces Staff Coll., U.S. Army War Coll. Commd. 2d lt. U.S. Army, 1967, advanced through grades to gen., 2000; comdr. 2d bn. 78th F.A. 1st Armored Divsn., Germany, 1981-84; dep. asst. chief staff G3 III Corps, Ft. Hood, Tex., 1985-86; comdr. div. arty. 1st Cav. Div., 1987-88, chief staff, 1988-89, asst. divsn. comdr. Operation Desert Shield-Storm, Saudi Arabia, Iraq, 1990-91; asst. comdt. U.S. Army F.A. Sch., Ft. Sill, Okla., 1991-92; dir. La. Maneuvers Task Force, Office Chief of Staff U.S. Army, Ft. Monroe, Va., 1992—94; asst. chief staff C3/J3/G3 UN and combined forces command U.S. Forces Korea, 8th U.S. Army, 1994—95; commdr. second infantry divsn., 1995-97; comdr. 3rd United States Army Ft. McPherson, Ga., 1997-2000; comdr. US Ctrl. Command, MacDill AFB, Fla., 2000—03, Operation Enduring Freedom, Afghanistan, 2001—02, Operation Iraqi Freedom, 2003. Bd. dirs. Bank Am. Corp., 2006—. Co-author (with Malcolm McConnell): (memoir) American Soldier, 2004 (Publishers Weekly Bestseller). Decorated Def. Disting. Svc. Medal, Disting. Svc. Medal with one oak leaf cluster, Legion of Merit with 3 oak leaf clusters, Bronze Star medal with V device and 4 oak leaf clusters, Purple Heart with 2 oak leaf clusters; named Knight Comdr. of the Brit. Empire, 2004, Presdl. Medal of Freedom, 2004. Office Phone: 813-839-8234. Business E-Mail: admin@tommyfranks.com.

FRANKS, TRENT, congressman; b. Uravan, Colo., June 19, 1957; m. Josephine Franks, 1980. Student, Ottawa U. Mem. Ariz. Ho. Reps., 1985—87, vice-chmn. commerce com., chmn. sub-com. on child protection and family preservation, mem. human resources com., mem. agr. com., mem. judiciary com.; head Ariz. Govs. Office for Children, 1987; exec. dir. Ariz. Family Rsch. Inst.; pres. Strategic Consulting and Liberty Petroleum Corp.; mem. U.S. Congress from 2nd Ariz. dist., 2003—. Pres. Children's Hope Scholarship Assn.; active North Phoenix Bapt. Ch. Republican. Office: US Ho Reps 1237 Longworth House Office Bldg Washington DC 20515-0302 also: Ste 200 7121 W Bell Rd Glendale AZ 85308*

FRANKSON-KENDRICK, SARAH JANE, publisher; b. Bradford, Pa., Sept. 24, 1949; d. Sophronus Ahimus and Elizabeth Jane (Sears) McCutcheon; m. James Michael Kendrick, Jr., May 22, 1982. Customer svc. rep. Laros Printing/Osceola Graphics, Bethlehem, Pa., 1972-73; assoc. editor Babcox Publs., Akron, Ohio, 1973-74, Bill Comms., Akron, Ohio, 1974-75, sr. editor, 1975-77, editor-in-chief, 1977-81; assoc. pub. Chilton

Co./ABC Pub., Chgo., 1981-83, pub., 1983-89, group pub. Radnor, Pa., 1989-93; group v.p. Cahners Bus. Info. (formerly Chilton Co.), Radnor, Pa., 1993-98; divsn. v.p. Primedia Intertec, Chgo., 1999—2001. Exec. MBA prof. Northwood U., mem. adv. coun. Mem. oper. com. Primedia Intertec. Recipient Automotive Replacement Edn. award Northwood Inst., 1983, award for young leadership and excellence Automotive Hall of Fame, 1984; bd. dirs. Automotive Hall of Fame. Mem. Automotive Found. for Aftermarket (trustee), Automotive Parts and Accessories Assn. (bd. dirs., exec. com., sec., treas., strategic planning com., edn. com., Disting Svc. award 1993), Automotive Svc. Industry Assn. (bd. dirs. automotive divsn. com.), Automotive Svc. Banyan Golf Club (Wellington, Fla.), Palm Beach Polo and Country Club (Wellington, Fla.), Winged Foot Golf Club (Mamaroneck, N.Y.). Republican.

FRANKSTON, ROBERT M., computer software executive, developer; b. Bklyn., June 14, 1949; s. Benjamin Frankenstein and Dorothy Frankston; m. Eleanor Elkin; 3 children. SB in Computer Sci. and Math., MIT, 1970, MS in Computer Sci., EE in Computer Sci., MIT, 1974. Various positions White-Weld and Co. (later became Interactive Data Corp.), Waltham, Mass., 1966-79; cons. ECD Corp., 1977—78; co-founder Software Arts, Inc., Wellesley, Mass., 1979, pres., 1979-85; individual contbr. Lotus Devel., Cambridge, Mass., 1985-90; individual contbr. on mobile and pen-based systems Slate Corp., Newton, Mass., 1990—92; individual contbr. Microsoft Corp., 1993—98. Co-founder, Student Information Processing Bd. MIT; spkr. in field. Contbr. articles to jours. Co-recipient with Daniel Bricklin, Washington award, Western Soc. Engineers, 2001; named Computer History Mus. Fellow, 2004; recipient MIT William L. Stewart award for co-founding the Student Information Processing Bd., PC Mag. Lifetime Achievement award, Esquire Mag. The Best of the New Generation, Computer Bowl MVP, MIT LCS Indsl. Achievement award, IEEE Consumer Electronics Soc. Internat. Chapters Engring. Excellence award. Fellow: Assn. Computing Machinery (Software System award). Achievements include being co-creator with Daniel Bricklin of VisiCalc, the first electronic spreadsheet in 1979; created the Lotus Express product and Fax Facilty for Lotus Notes at Lotus Development; created "IP Everywhere" at Microsoft Corp. E-mail: BobF@Frankston.com.

FRANO, ANDREW JOSEPH, lawyer, civil engineer; b. Chgo., July 14, 1953; s. Joseph Neil Frano and Lorraine Rose Patchett-Keller; children: Alaina Marie, Jacqueline Elyse. BSCE, Bradley U., Peoria, Ill., 1975, MSCE, 1976; JD, Chgo.-Kent Coll. Law, Ill. Inst. Tech., 1982. Registered profl. engr., Ill., Ind., Nebr., Wis., Minn., lic. gen. engring. constrn. contractor, Fla., Utah; bar: Ill. 1982, Nebr. 1986, Ariz. 1993, Tex. 1997, US Dist. Ct. (no. dist.) Ill. 1982, US Dist. Ct. Nebr. 1992. Soils lab. instr. and residence hall dir. Bradley U., Peoria, Ill., 1975-76; draftsman, engr. in tng. Harza Engring. Co., Chgo., 1973—76, civil engr. Soil Mechanics and Founds. I sect., geotech. dept., 1976—85; pvt. practice Chgo., 1982-85; pres. GEC Engring. Co. Inc., Chgo., 1985—86; corp. constrn. atty. Peter Kiewit Sons Inc., Omaha, 1986-92; asst. gen. counsel Harza Engring. Co., Chgo., 1992-95; owner The Law and Engring. Office of Andrew J. Frano, 1996—. Adj. asst. prof. dept. civil and archtl. engring. Ill. Inst. Tech., Chgo., 1993—98; corp. atty., civil engr. T.J. Lambrecht Constrn., Inc., Joliet, 1996—98; prin. engr. Mirza-RSV Engring., Inc., Chgo. and Schaumburg, 1998—2001, Bloom Consultants, LLC, Schaumburg, Chgo., 2001—; atty. Smetana and Avakian, Chgo., 2005—. Chmn. San. Improvement Dist. 111, Sarpy County, Nebr., 1987-92; vol. atty. Chgo. Vol. Legal Svcs., 1983-85, 2006—; bd. dirs., treas. Trails Assn. Inc., Roselle, Ill., 1983-86. Mem. ASCE, Structural Engrs. Assn. Ill. (assoc.), Tau Beta Pi, Chi Epsilon. Home: 2 N Dee Rd Unit 107 Park Ridge IL 60068-2871 Office: Bloom Consultants LLC 600 W Fulton St Ste 701 Chicago IL 60661 Office Phone: 312-876-9500. Office Fax: 312-876-9600. Business E-Mail: afrano@bloomconsultants.com. E-mail: andrewfrano@sbcglobal.net.

FRANSE, R. NELSON, lawyer; b. Clovis, N.Mex, Feb. 5, 1961; s. Roy and Jerrie Lou Franse; m. M. Marie McCulloch; 1 child, Colson Brack. BS in U. Studies, U. N. Mex., 1984, JD, 1987. Bar: N. Mex. 1987, U.S. Dist. Ct., Dist. N. Mex. 1987, U.S. Ct. Appeals, tenth cir. 1987. Ptnr. Rodey, Dickason, Sloan, Akin & Robb PA, Albuquerque, leader profl. liability sect. Rep. to ABA, Law Student Div. U. N. Mex., 1985—87. Named one of best lawyers in Am., 2003—04. Mem.: Am. Bd. Liability Atty. (diplomat with spl. competence in area of legal profl. liability), Profl. Liability Underwriting Soc., State Bar N.Mex., ABA, Albuquerque Bar Assn. Baptist. Avocations: monday morning quarterbacking, Monday morning quarterbacking. Office: Rodey Dickason Sloan Akin & Robb PA 201 Third St NW Ste 2200 PO Box 1888 Albuquerque NM 87103 Office Phone: 505-765-5900. Business E-Mail: nfranse@rodey.com.

FRANTZ, ANDREW GIBSON, endocrinologist, educator, dean; b. NYC, May 22, 1930; s. Angus Macdonald and Virginia (Kneeland) F. AB magna cum laude, Harvard U., 1951; MD, Columbia U., 1955. Intern Presbyn. Hosp., NYC, 1955-56, resident in medicine, 1956-58; fellow in endocrinology Columbia U., NYC, 1958-60, asst. prof. medicine, 1966-68, assoc. prof., 1968-73, prof., 1973—, chief divsn. endocrinology, 1971-87; chmn. admissions com., assoc. dean for admissions Columbia U. (Coll. Physicians and Surgeons), 1981—. Assoc. in medicine Harvard U., 1962-66; asst. in medicine Mass. Gen. Hosp., Boston, 1962-66; mem. staff Presbyn. Hosp., N.Y.C.; mem. med. adv. bd. Nat. Pituitary Agy., 1970-73; established investigator Am. Heart Assn., 1968-73 Contbr. articles on prolactin and other pituitary hormones and functions to med. and sci. jours.; mem. editorial bd.: Jour. Clin. Endocrinology and Metabolism, 1971-76; assoc. editor: Metabolism, 1969—. Served to lt. comdr. USNR, 1960-62. Recipient Silver Medal Coll. Physicians and Surgeons, Columbia U., 1981, Alumni Fedn. medal Columbia U., 1984, Disting. Tchr. award, Coll. Physicians and Surgeons, Columbia U., 1989. Mem. AAAS, Endocrine Soc., Assn. Am. Physicians, Am. Soc. Clin. Investigation, Internat. Soc. for Neuroendocrinology, Harvey Soc., Practitioners Soc. (pres. 1993-2000), Charaka Club, Am. Fedn. Med. Rsch., N.Y. Acad. Scis., N.Y. Acad. Medicine, Union Club, Century Assn. (N.Y.C.), P and S Alumni Assn. (pres. 1991-93), Alpha Omega Alpha. Episcopalian. Home: 1185 Park Ave New York NY 10128-1308 Office: 630 W 168th St New York NY 10032-3702 Office Phone: 212-305-3595. Business E-Mail: agf2@columbia.edu.

FRANTZ, DALE NELSON, automobile import processing company executive; b. Indpls., July 23, 1964; s. Thomas Benjamin and Joan (Phillips) F.; m. Angela Elaine Dishon, Dec. 14, 1985; 2 children. Distbr. Micro Data Base Systems, Lafayette, Ind., 1983-84; computer ops. dir. Roland's of Bloomington, Lafayette, 1984-87; named computer ops. dir. Cin. Bible Sem., Cin., 1987; regional info. tech. dir. Midwest Auto Warehousing Co., Tacomo, Wash., 1997—99, v.p., chief info. officer, chief tech. officer, 1999—. Named one of Premier 100 IT Leaders, Computerworld, 2005. Office: Auto Warehousing Co 2810 Marshall Ave Tacoma WA 98421

FRANTZ, JOHN A., physician, writer; b. Van Wert, Ohio, Feb. 18, 1923; s. George Arthur and Amy Kellogg Frantz; m. Mary H. Hodge 1946, Jan. 12, 1846; children: Caroline Smith, Winifred Hoffman children: Barbara Brown. BS, Haverford Coll., Pa., 1943; MD, U. Rochester, NY, 1946. Intern Henry Ford Hosp., Detroit, 1946—47; physician pvt. practice, Montrose, Colo., 1952—54; student health physician U. Mo., Columbia; staff physician Monroe Clinic, Wis., 1955—2006; prof. medicine Nangrahar U., Jalalabad, Afghanistan, 1968—70; vol. asst. prof. U Wis. Medicfal Sch., Madison, 1970—80. Contbr. columns in newspapers. Mem. City Planning Commn., Monroe, 2004; alderman Monroe City Coun., 1999—2005; mem. RENEW Wis., Madison, 1980; vol. US Peace Corps, Jalalabad, Afghanistan, 1968—70. Capt. USAF, 1947—49. Mem.: AMA, Nat. Assn. Sci. Writers, Am Coll. Physicians, Sierra Club (licentiate; nat. outings leader 1980—92), Phi Beta Kappa. Home: 812 22nd Ave Monroe WI 53566-1672 Office: The Monroe Clinic 515 22nd Ave Monroe WI 53566 Home Phone: 608-325-3242; Office Phone: 608-324-1912.

FRANTZ, PHARES ALBERT, architect; b. New Orleans, Nov. 1, 1923; s. Roy Florestan and Marie Lucile (O'Kelley) F.; m. Elinor Mae(McCloskey), Feb. 20, 1954; children: Ninette Marie, Colleen Marie, Melinda Marie. BArch, Tulane U., La., 1950. Registered arch., La., Miss., Tenn. Draftsman Richard Koch Arch., New Orleans, 1950-52, arch., 1952-55; assoc. Richard Koch & Samuel Wilson Jr. Archs., New Orleans, 1955-72; ptnr. Koch and Wilson, Archs., P.C., New Orleans, 1986-96. Mem. Citizens Adv. com. Studying Revisions to City Zoning Ordinance, 1969; bd. dirs. Incarnate Word Parish Sch. Bd., 1971-80, pres., 1977-80; bd. dirs. France Amerique, 1981; pres. La. Polit. Com. Design Profls., 1984. Decorated Order of St. Louis Archdiocese of New Orleans. Mem. AIA (mem. hist. resources com. 1975-83, mem. New Orleans chpt. 1950—, pres. 1969, dir. 1970-71, state preservation coord. 1982), La. Inst. Bldg. Scis. (dir. 1980), La. Archs. Assn. (pres. 1980), Constrn. Specifications Inst. (pres. New Orleans chpt. 1960), Friends of Cabildo, La. Landmarks Soc., Sons of the Revolution, Nat. Trust, Mag. St., Round Table Club (v.p. 1992-93, pres. 1994-95), Delta Tau Delta. Republican. Roman Catholic. Home: 7525 Pearl St New Orleans LA 70118-3835

FRANTZ, RAY WILLIAM, JR., retired librarian; b. Princeton, Ky., Aug. 17, 1923; s. Ray William and Marjorie (Kevil) F.; m. Doris Methvin, Aug. 26, 1951; children: Katherine Kevil, Paul William. AB, U. Nebr., 1948; MLS, U. Ill., 1949, MA, 1951, PhD in English, 1955. Dir. libr. U. Richmond, Va., 1955-60; asst. dir. Ohio State U. Libr., Columbus, 1960-62; dir. libraries U. Wyo. Libr., 1962-67; libr. U. Va. Libr., Charlottesville, 1967-93. Chmn. bd. dirs. Southeastern Libr. Network, 1975-76; vice chmn., bd. dirs. 18th Century Short-Title Catalogue, N.Am., 1985—. With inf. AUS, 1943-46. Mem. ALA, Assn. Rsch. Librs. (pres. 1977-78), Assn. Southeastern Rsch. Librs. (chmn. 1975—), Bibliog. Soc. Am., Bibliog. Soc. U. Va. (sec.-treas. 1967—).

FRANTZ, ROBERT WESLEY, lawyer; b. Long Branch, NJ, Dec. 31, 1950; BS, Rutgers U., New Brunswick, NJ, 1973; JD, Rutgers U., Newark, 1977. Bar: NJ. 1977, U.S. Dist. Ct. N.J. 1977, U.S. Ct. Appeals (4th and 10th cirs.) 1978, U.S. Ct. Appeals (6th, 7th and 8th cirs.) 1979, D.C. 1980, U.S. Ct. Appeals (9th cir.) 1980, U.S. Dist. Ct. D.C. 1981. Trial atty. U.S. Dept. Justice, Washington, 1977-80; assoc. Hamel and Park, Washington, 1980-82; asst. gen. counsel Chem. Mfrs. Assn., Washington, 1982-85; counsel, environ. protection GE, Fairfield, Conn., 1985-88, Pittsfield, Mass., 1988-89; mgr. and counsel Environ. Remediation Program, Fairfield, Conn., 1989-95; mgr., sr. counsel Environ. Ops. Program, Fairfield, 1995-98; gen. mgr., counsel GE Engines Svcs., Cin., 1998—2003; v.p. environment, health and safety Tyco Internat., Princeton, NJ, 2003—. Mem. sci. adv. bd. subcom. on risk reduction options U.S. EPA, 1996—2003. Contbr. articles to profl. publs.; editorial bd. Rutgers Law Rev., 1976. Mem. Newtown (Conn.) Charter Revision Commn., 1986-87, Glendale Planning Commn., 2000—03; bd. dirs. Environ. Law Inst., 2005—; trustee NJ Future, 2006—. Mem. ABA (exec. editor Natural Resources and Environment 1986-93, coun. mem. sect. natural resources 1993-96). Avocations: sailing, golf, skiing, bicycling, woodworking. Office: Tyco International PO Box 5260 Princeton NJ 08543-5260

FRANTZE, DAVID WAYNE, lawyer; b. Kansas City, Jan. 28, 1955; s. James W. and Margaret M. (Pursley) Frantze; m. Geri L. Sexton, July 28, 1979; children: Kevin, Lisa, Christopher, Timothy. BA, Avila U., 1976; JD, U. Mo., Kansas City, 1981. Ptnr. Stinson Morrison Hecker LLP, Kansas City, 2002—. Trustee Mid-Am. chpt. Leukemia and Lymphoma Soc., 1992—, chpt. pres., 1998—2000, nat. trustee, 2001—04, mem. exec. com., 2003—04, nat. bd. dirs., 2004—, vice chair, 2004—06, chair, 2006—; trustee Victor and Caroline Schutte Found., 2000—, U. Mo.-Kansas City Law Found., 1996—2003, exec. com., 2000—03, treas., 2000—01; mem. Civic Coun. Kansas City, 1995—, urban core com., 1996—, bd. dirs., 2001—, Kansas City Spirit, Inc., 1986—88, pres., 1988, adv. coun., 1989—2004; bd. dirs. Kansas City Neighborhood Alliance, 1987—, chmn., 1994—96; mem. Greater Downtown Devel. Authority, 2002—05; bd. counselors Avila U., 1989—2002, trustee, 2002—; bd. dirs. Econ. Devel. Corp., Kansas City, Mo., 2003—, Truman Med. Ctr. Charitable Found., 2005—. Mem.: ABA, Am. Coll. Real Estate Lawyers, Lawyers Assn. Kansas City, Kansas City Met. Bar Assn. (chmn. real estate law com. 1992), Mo. Bar Assn. Roman Catholic. Home: 11812 Central St Kansas City MO 64114-5536 Office: Stinson Morrison Hecker LLP 1201 Walnut St Ste 2600 Kansas City MO 64106-2150 Home Phone: 816-942-5697; Office Phone: 816-691-3181. Business E-Mail: dfrantze@stinsonmoheck.com.

FRANTZEN, ALLEN JOHN, English language educator; b. New Hampton, Iowa, Oct. 20, 1947; s. John Victor and Dorothy Mae (Birmingham) Frantzen. BA, Loras Coll., Dubuque, Iowa, 1969; MA, U. Va., 1973, PhD, 1976. Asst. prof. English Oberlin Coll., Ohio, 1976-78, Loyola U., Chgo., 1976-82, assoc. prof., 1983-88, prof., 1988—. Author: Literature of Penance, 1983, King Alfred, 1986, Desire for Origins, 1990, Before the Closet: Same-Sex Love from "Beowulf" to "Angels in America", 1998, Bloody Good: Chivalry, Sacrifice, and The Great War, 2003; editor: Speaking Two Languages, 1991, Troilus and Criseyde: The Poem and the Frame, 1993, (with D. Moffatt) The Work of Work, 1994, (with J. Niles) Anglo-Saxonism and the Construction of Social Identity, 1997. Pres. Edgewater Cmty. Coun., Chgo., 1984-85. With U.S. Army, 1969-72, Korea. Named Alexander von Humboldt Found. grantee, 1979, NEH fellow, 1990-91, Guggenheim Found. fellow, 1994; recipient Tempo All-Professor Team, Humanities, Chgo. Tribune, 1993, Weiss-Brown Subvention award, Newberry Libr., 2002. Office: Loyola U Lake Shore Campus Dept English 6525 N Sheridan Rd Chicago IL 60626-5385 E-mail: afrantz@luc.edu.

FRANTZEN, HENRY ARTHUR, retired investment company executive; b. Orange, NJ, Nov. 28, 1942; s. Henry and Natalie (Johnson) Frantzen; m. Julie Louise Haverty, Aug. 14, 1965; children: John Blair, Jill Marie, Eric Patrick. Student, Hamline U., 1960-62; BSBA, U. N.D., 1964. Sr. securities analyst Chem. Bank, 1968-71; adminstrv. asst. Coll. Retirement Equities Fund, 1971, asst. investment officer, 1972, investment officer, 1973, asst. v.p., 1974-76, 2d v.p., 1976, v.p., investment mgr., mem. investment com., 1976; sr. v.p., investment mgr. Tchrs. Ins. and Annuity of Am., NYC, 1980-87, Coll. Retirement Equities Fund, NYC, 1980-87; dir. SBC Portfolio Mgmt. Internat. Inc., Amsterdam, 1987-89; chmn., chief investment officer Yamaichi Capital Mgmt. Corp., 1987-89; pres. Yamaichi Funds Inc., 1987-89, chmn., 1988-89; exec. v.p., dir. equities Oppenheimer Mgmt. Corp., NYC, 1989-91; CIO, exec. v.p. Federated Global Investment Mgmt., NYC, 1995—2002. Mgr. Brown Bros Harriman & Co., 1992—95; mng. dir. Brown Bros. Harriman & Co. Investment Mgmt. Ltd., London, 1992—95; exec. v.p. Federated Global Investment Mgmt. Corp., 1995—2002, Federated Investment Mgmt. Corp., 1995—2002; chief investment officer Global Equities and Fixed Income; chmn. Frantzen Capital Mgmt., 2004—; inds. cons. Goldman Sachs & Co., 2003. Served to lt. USNR, 1964—68. Fellow: Fin. Analysts Fedn.; mem.: Naples Soc. Securities Analysts, NY Soc. Security Analysts, Alpha Kappa Psi, Sigma Nu. Republican. Avocations: sailing, golf, tennis, bodysurfing. Home: 669 Gulf Shore Blvd N Naples FL 34102 Office Phone: 813-223-6400. Business E-Mail: hfrantzen@frantzencapital.com.

FRANTZIKINAKIS, NIKOS, mathematics professor; b. Heracklion, Crete, Greece, Jan. 22, 1975; s. Olga Frantzikinaki and Emmanouil Frantzikinakis; m. Agapi Liapaki, Mar. 11, 1972; 1 child, Olga Frantzikinaki. PhD, Stanford U., Calif., 2002. Chowla rsch. asst. prof. Pa. State U., University Park, 2002—05; asst. prof. U. Memphis, 2006. Fellow, Stanford U., 1996—2002. Mem.: Inst. Advanced Studies, Am. Math. Soc. Achievements include research in ergodic theory and applications to combinatorics. Home: 7806 Grove Lake Ct Germantown TN 38138 Home Phone: 901-251-1030. Home Fax: 509-277-1030. Personal E-mail: frantzikinakis@gmail.com.

FRANZ, CHARLES NORMAN, engineer; b. Ann Arbor, Mich., Aug. 11, 1953; s. Norman Charles and C. E. Franz; m. Frances Higuchi Franz, May 22, 1983; 1 child, Stephen. BAEE, U. BC, 1979; MSEE, U. So. Calif., 1981, PhD in Elec. Engring. Comm. Svcs., 1989. Staff doctroal fellow Hughes Aircraft Co., 1979—89; prin. engr. KREMS Radar Facility, Kwajalein Atoll, Marshall Islands, 1989—99; mem. tech. staff MIT, Lincoln Lab., Kavai, Hawaii, 1999—2003; sr. enbr. SAIC, Honolulu, 2003—. Mem.: IEEE. Avocations: skiing, guitar, weightlifting, exercise, church. Home: 4993 Kolohala St Honolulu HI 96816 Office Phone: 808-551-2517. Personal E-mail: franzc001@hawaii.rr.com.

FRANZ, DENNIS, actor; b. Chgo., Oct. 28, 1944; Stage appearances include: Bleacher Bums, 1978, Brothers, 1983; films include: The Fury, 1978, Remember My Name, 1978, Stony Island, 1978, A Wedding, 1978, A Perfect Couple, 1979, Dressed to Kill, 1980, Popeye, 1980, Blow Out, 1981, Psycho II, 1983, Body Double, 1984, A Fine Mess, 1986, The Package, 1989, Die-Hard 2, 1990, The Player, 1992, American Buffalo, 1996, City of Angels, 1998; TV appearances include: (series) Chicago Story, 1982, Hill Street Blues, (as "Bad Sal" Benedetto) 1982-83 (as Lieutenant Norman Buntz) 1987-88, Bay City Blues, 1983, Beverly Hills Buntz, 1987-88, Nasty Boys, 1990, NYPD Blue, 1993—2005 (Emmy award 1994) (movies) Deadly Messages, 1985, Kiss Shot, 1989, Moment of Truth: Caught in the Crossfire, 1994, Texas Justice, 1995, Buddy Fatso, 1998. Recipient Emmy awards, 1996, 97, 99, SAG awards, 1995, 97, Golden Globes, 1995, Q awards, 1994, 96-99, Star on Walk of Fame, 1999. Office: Paradigm Talent Agency 10100 Santa Monica Blvd Fl 25 Los Angeles CA 90067-4003

FRANZ, ELIZABETH, actress; b. Akron, Ohio, June 18, 1941; Actress with Broadway credits in: Death of a Salesman, The Cripple of Inishmaan, Brighton Beach Memoirs (Tony and Drama Desk nominations), Broadway Bound, Uncle Vanya, Getting Married, The Cemetery Club, The Octette Bridge Club, The Cherry Orchard, Mornings at Seven, 2002; off-Broadway credits include: Sister Mary Ignatius (Obie award, Drama Desk nomination), Minutes from the Blue Route, The Comedy of Errors, Howard Katz, 2007; regional credits include: Eleanor of Aquataine in The Lion in Winter (Cleve.), Amanda in The Glass Menagerie, Dividing the Estate (Great Lakes), A View From the Bridge, Woman in Mind (Berkshire Theatre Festival), Dolly in The Matchmaker, Agnes of God, Hamlet, Buried Child, The Wicked Witch in The Wizard of Oz, Miss Haversham in Great Expectations, The Bird Sanctuary, 2005; appeared in numerous TV series and movies including: Roseanne, Sister, A Town's Revenge (Emmy nomination), Notes for My Daughter, Nothing Personal, Shameful Secrets, Face of a Stranger, Dottie, The Rise and Rise of Daniel Rocket, Love and Other Sorrows, A Girl Thing, Death of a Salesman (Emmy nomination, 2000), Gilmore Girls, 2001, Judging Amy, 2001; film credits include: Sabrina, 1995, The Substance of Fire, 1996, The Pallbearer, 1996, Thinner, 1996, Twisted, 1997, Jacknife, 1989, Secret of My Success, 1987, School Ties, 1992 Winner 1999 Tony award for featured actress in Death of a Salesman, also Drama Desk award, Outer Critics Circle award.*

FRANZ, FRANK ANDREW, academic administrator, physicist, educator; b. Phila., Sept. 16, 1937; s. Russell Ernest and Edna (Keller) F.; m. Judy Rosenbaum, July 11, 1959; 1 child, Eric Douglas. BS in Physics, Lafayette Coll., 1959; MS in Physics, U. Ill., 1961, PhD in Physics, 1964. Research assoc. U. Ill., Urbana, 1964-65; asst. prof. physics Ind. U., Bloomington, 1967-70, assoc. prof., 1970-74, prof., 1974-85, assoc. dean Coll. Arts and Scis., 1974-77, dean faculties, 1977-82; prof. physics, provost, v.p. academic affairs and research W.Va. U., Morgantown, 1985-91; prof. physics, pres. U. Ala., Huntsville, 1991—2007. Guest scientist Swiss Fed. Inst. Tech., Zurich, 1965-67, U. Munich, 1978. Contbr. articles to profl. jours. NSF fellow, 1965-67, Alfred P. Sloan fellow, 1968-70. Fellow AAAS, Am. Phys. Soc.; mem. AAUP (pres. Bloomington, Ind. chpt. 1972-73), Am. Assn. Physics Tchrs., Sigma Xi, Phi Kappa Phi. Avocation: tennis. Office: U Ala in Huntsville Office of the President Huntsville AL 35899-0001

FRANZ, JENNIFER DANTON, public opinion and marketing researcher; b. Oakland, Calif., Oct. 31, 1949; d. Joseph Periam and Lois (King) Danton; m. William Edwin Behnk, July 30, 1978. BA, Antioch Coll. West, 1973; MA, Stanford U., 1974; PhD, U. Calif., Berkeley, 1991. Cert. Community Coll. Student Personnel Worker, Calif., Community Coll. Supr., Calif. Cons. Alum Rock Union Elem. Sch. Dist., San Jose, Calif., 1973-75; rsch. asst. Far West Lab. for Ednl. Rsch. and Devel., San Francisco, 1974-75; project dir. Hartnell Coll., Salinas, Calif., 1975-77; project dir. Chancellor's Office Calif. Community Colls., Sacramento, 1978-80; pres., owner J.D. Franz Rsch., Sacramento, 1981—. Topic expert Nat. Mktg. Summit, 1995; adj. asst. prof. Golden Gate U., 1982—; instr. mktg. cert. program U. Calif. at Davis Extension, 1990—; lectr. Calif. State U., Sacramento, 1995—; instr. U. Calif.-Berkeley Ext., 1997—. Contbr. numerous articles to profl. jours. Mem. small bus. adv. com. Calif. Senate, Sacramento, 1986-92; bd. dirs. Jr. Achievement Sacramento, 1989-91, Episc. Cmty. Svcs. Sacramento, 1991-92; bd. dirs. Sacramento (Calif.) Philharmonic Orch., 2002—, v.p., 2003—. Recipient various rsch., svc. awards. Mem. Am. Mktg. Assn., Am. Assn. Pub. Opinion Rsch. (bd. dirs. Pacific Coast chpt., 2002—, sec., 2003-04, treas, 2004—), Am. Ednl. Rsch. Assn. (editor 1984-86, mem. div. H evaluation steering com. 1984-85, polit. edn. spl. interest group, survey rsch. spl. interest group, judge div. H awards competition 1984, program reviewer 1982—), Mktg. Rsch. Assn., Sacramento Met. C. of C. (bd. dirs. 1990-93, state govt. affairs, local govt. affairs, pub. rels. coms. 1985—), Sacramento Valley Mktg. Assn. (bd. dirs. 1987-94, pres. 1993-94). Democrat. Episcopalian. Avocations: playing piano, swimming, reading, playing organ, tennis. Office: JD Franz Rsch 1900 Point West Way Ste 276 Sacramento CA 95815 Home Phone: 916-283-6142.

FRANZ, JOHN E., bio-organic chemist, researcher; b. Springfield, Ill., Dec. 21, 1929; m. Elinor Theilken, Aug. 18, 1951; children: Judith, Mary, John, Gary. BS, U. Ill., 1951; PhD, U. Minn., 1955. Sr. research chemist Monsanto Agrl. Co., St. Louis, 1955—60, research group leader, 1960—63, fellow, 1963—75, sr. fellow, 1975—80, disting. fellow, 1980—90; ret., 1991. Co-author: Glyphosate: A Unique Global Herbicide, 1997; contbr. articles to sci. publs. Named to Nat. Inventors Hall of Fame, 2007; recipient Indsl. Rsch. Mag. award, 1977, Indsl. Rsch. Inst. Achievement award, Washington, 1985, J.F. Queeny award, Monsanto Co., 1981, Inventor of Yr. award, St. Louis Bar Assn., 1986, Nat. Medal of Tech., Washington, 1987, Outstanding Achievement award, U. Minn., 1988, The Mo. award, Gov. of Mo., 1988, Perkin medal, 1990. Mem.: Am. Chem. Soc. (Carother's award Del. sect. 1989). Achievements include discovery of the glyphosate class of herbicides while searching for product that would be effective against perennial and annual weeds, thus the invention of the marketed product called Round-up; hold over 840 US and Foreign patents.

FRANZ, JUDY R., physics professor; BA in Physics, Cornell U., 1959; MS in Physics, U. Ill., 1961, PhD in Physics, 1965. Rsch. physicist IBM

Rsch. Lab., Zurich, Switzerland, 1965-67; asst. prof. dept. physics Ind. U., 1968-74, assoc. prof., 1974-79, prof., 1979-87; prof. dept. physics W.Va. U., 1987-91, U. Ala., 1994—; exec. officer Am. Phys. Soc., 1994—. Vis. prof. Tech. U. Munich, 1978-79, Cornell U., 1985-86, 88, 90; assoc. dean coll. arts and scis. Ind. U., 1980-82; mem. coun. on materials sci. Dept. of Energy, 1997-2002; mem. rev. com. for materials sci and tech. divsn. Los Alamos Nat. Lab., 1999-2002; sec. gen. Internat. Union Pure & Applied Physics, 2002—, assoc. sec. gen., 1999-2002; mem. U.S. Commn. for UNESCO, 2005— Mem. editorial bd. Am. Jour. Physics, 1985-88; contbr. numerous articles to profl. jours. Mem. divsn. materials rsch. adv. com. NSF, 1986-89, mem. divsn. undergrad. edn. adv. com., 1991-93. Humboldt rsch. fellow Munich, 1978-79; recipient Distinguished Service Citation awd., Am. Assn. of Physics Teachers, 1993, Disting. Alumni award Coll. Eng., U. Ill., Urbana-Champaign, 1997. Fellow AAAS (coun. 1995-98), Am. Phys. Soc. (various coms. and offices, chair exec. com. divsn. condensed matter physics 1993-94), Assn. Women in Sci.; mem. Am. Assn. Physics Tchrs. (pres. 1990-91), Am. Inst. Physics (various coms., gov. bd. 1994—, exec. com. 1996-00), Coun. Sci. Soc. Pres. (exec. bd. 1990), Phi Beta Kappa, Sigma Xi (pres. local chpt. 1981-82). Avocations: hiking, reading. Business E-Mail: franz@aps.org.

FRANZ, (IRIS) VIVIAN, dean, director; b. Cin., Nov. 17, 1923; d. Edgar George Krueger and Vivian Agnes Mohn; m. Robert Vernon Franz (dec. 1981); children: Leslie Totis, Darryl Bayer(dec.) , Linda(dec.) , Kathleen Alexander. BS in Elem. Edn., Miami U., 1966, MEd in Diagnostic and Remedial Edn., 1968, PhD in Ednl. Adminstrn., Higher Edn., Pers., Curriculum, Psychology, 1972. Tchr. remedial reading Clermont Northeastern Dist., Batavia, Ohio, 1961—64, tchr. elem., 1964—66, tchr. adult basic edn., 1965—66, cons. reading, 1971—73; adminstrv. asst. reading ctr. Miami U., Oxford, Ohio, 1967—69, supr. student tchrs., 1969—70, instr., 1970—71; dir. coop. project State Dept. Edn., Miami U., 1973—75; dean program and instrn. So. State C.C., 1975—81; owner Lamplighter Ednl. Resource Ctr., Terrace Park, Ohio, 1983—2004, dir., 1983—. Recipient Adult Basic Edn. Panel of Experts Cert. of Appreciation, OH Dept. Edn., 1981. Home: PO Box 106 550 Ibold Rd Miamiville OH 45147

FRANZ, WILLIAM MATHEW, lawyer; s. William Mathew Franz; m. Lisa Serafin, July 6, 1996; children: Kelli Jane, Ashley, William Mathew. BA in Polit. Sci., SUNY, New Paltz, 1985; JD, Nova Southeastern U., Davie, Fla., 1989. Sr. assoc. Weiss and Handler P. A., Boca Raton, Fla., 1990—2004; ptnr. Toral, Gracia, Pinyero and Franz P.A., Ft. Lauderdale, Fla., 2007—. Goodwin fellow, Nova Law Sch., 1988. Mem.: Broward County Bar Assn., Fla. Bar Assn. (assoc.). Avocations: golf, sport fishing. Home and Office: Toral Garcia Piniyero and Franz 4780 Davie Rd Fort Lauderdale FL 33314 Home Phone: 954-455-4220; Office Phone: 954-455-4220, 954-703-2960. Office Fax: 954-455-6590. Business E-Mail: wfranz@torallaw.com.

FRANZE, LAURA MARIE, lawyer; b. Pitts., Apr. 20, 1956; d. Catherine Franze; m. Kenneth Charles Morton, Aug.13, 1977; 1 child, Irena Everly Morton. BA summa cum laude, Thiel Coll., 1976; JD, Duke U. Law Sch., 1979. Bar: Ohio 1979, Tex. 1982, Ohio 1990, N.Mex. 1990, US Ct. Appeals (no., so. and we. dists.) Tex.; cert. labor and employment law Tex. Bd. Legal Specialization 1984. Atty. Smith & Schnacke, Dayton, Ohio, 1979-81, Gardere & Wynne, Dallas, 1981-93, McKenna & Cuneo, Dallas, 1993-95, Akin, Strauss, Hauer & Feld, Dallas, 1995—, now ptnr., chair labor and employment practice group and mem. mgmt. com. Counsel Coalition of Responsible Employers; commentator (TV show) Ask a Lawyer. Sr. editor Texas Employment Law (2 vol.), 1998. Vice chair legal/ethical task force Dallas AIDS Commn., 1988. Recipient 40 under 40 award Dallas Bus. Jour., 1993, Top Practitioner, Texas Lawyer 2001, One of Best Lawyers in Dallas, D Mag. 1997, 2001, One of Best Labor & Employment Lawyers, Corporate Counsel Mag. 2002. Fellow Tex. Bar Found. Dallas Bar Found.; mem. Dallas Bar Assn., ABA, Dallas Employment Law Sect. (coun., officer 1993—), Dallas Area Labor and Employment Law Group (pres. 1986-87), State Bar Tex. (advanced labor law com. 1993—). Office: Akin Gump Strauss Hauer & Feld LLP 1700 Pacific Ave Ste 4100 Dallas TX 75201-4675 Office Phone: 214-969-2779. Business E-Mail: lfranze@akingump.com.

FRANZE, ROBERT DENNIS, social studies educator; b. Beloit, Wis., July 24, 1956; s. Mary Jo and Roger Dennis Franze; m. Nanette Joan Zumpft, Aug. 18, 1979; children: Alyssa Johanna, Erik Demmler. BA, Carroll Coll., Wis., 1974—78; MA, Marquette U., Milw., 1984. Cert. Secondary Edn. Wis. Dept. of Pub. Instrn., 1979. Tchr. Waukesha Pub. Schs., Waukesha, Wis., 1979—. Advanced placement U.S. history exam reader Ednl. Testing Svc., Princeton, NJ, 2004—. Mem. Southminster Presbyn. Ch., Waukesha, Wis., 1987—. Mem.: Nat. Coun. for Social Studies. Presbyterian. Home: 315 S Hartwell Ave Waukesha WI 53186 Office: Waukesha South HS 401 E Roberta Ave Waukesha WI 53186 Home Phone: 262-548-0101; Office Phone: 262-970-3755. Personal E-mail: bfranze@waukesha.k12.wi.us.

FRANZEN, BYRON T. (JOHN FRANZEN), media specialist; b. Britton, SD, Apr. 16, 1946; s. Harold G. and Marian E. (Swenson) F. BA in English and Philosophy, Concordia Coll., 1968; MA in English, McGill U., Montreal, Que., Can., 1971. Press sec. McGovern for Pres. Campaign, NH, Ill., Oreg., NY, 1971-72; pub. rels. and press. sec. various orgns., Washington, Ala., 1973-74, NY, 1973—74; legis. aide Hon. Michael Harrington U.S. Ho. Reps., Washington, 1975-76; mgr. Panetta for Congress Campaign, Calif., 1976; chief staff Hon. Leon Panetta U.S. Ho. Reps., Washington, 1977-78; pres., prin. Franzen & Co., Washington, 1979—. Lectr. U.S. Info. Agy., various countries, 1988—. Designer Harriman Comm. Ctr., Nat. Dem. Hdqs., Washington, 1982-85; works represented in permanent collection Smithsonian Mus. Am. History. Founding chmn. R.A. Overbeck Capitol Hill History Project; bd. dirs. Capitol Hill Cmty. Found. Recipient Excellence award Internat. TV Assn., 1985, Silver award Houston Internat. Film Festival, 1987, Gold award, 1988, Nat. Telly award, 1987, 93, 98, 99, Nat. Silver Microphone award, 1987, 94, 97, 2001, Addy award, 1987, Vision award, 1992, 95, 2000. Mem. Am. Assn. Polit. Cons. (bd. dirs. 1991—2005, Pollie award 1986, 88, 94, 2000). Avocations: architecture, art, antiques, history. Office: Franzen & Co 908 Massachusetts Ave Washington DC 20002-6002

FRANZEN, JANICE MARGUERITE GOSNELL, magazine editor; b. LaCrosse, Wis. d. Wray Towson and Anna Gosnell; m. Ralph Oscar Franzen, 1964. BS cum laude, Wis. State U., LaCrosse; MRE, No. Bapt. Theol. Sem. Dir. Christian Writers Inst., 1950—63, dir. studies, 1964-86; fiction editor Christian Life Mag., Wheaton, Ill., 1950-63, woman's editor, 1964-72, exec. editor, 1972-86; mem. editorial bd. Creation House, Wheaton, 1972-86. Speaker writers confs. Author: Christian Writers Handbook, 1960, 61, The Adventure of Interviewing, 1989; editor: Christian Author, 1949-54, Christian Writer and Editor, 1955-63; compiler, contbr.: The Successful Writers and Editors Guidebook, 1977; contbr. articles to various mags. Sec., bd. dirs. Christian Life Missions, Lake Mary, Fla., 1971-95; bd. dirs. Ralph O. Franzen Charitable Found., 1990—, Wesley Luehring Found., 2000—. Home: 140 Windsor Park Dr Apt E201 Carol Stream IL 60188-5314

FRANZEN, JONATHAN, writer; b. Western Springs, Ill., Aug. 17, 1959; s. Earl T. and Irene Franzen; m. Valerie Cornell, Oct. 2, 1982 (div.). BA, Swarthmore Coll., 1981. Rsch. asst. earth and planetary scis. Harvard U., 1983—87; contbg. writer New Yorker. Author: The Twenty-Seventh City, 1988 (Whiting Writers' award), Strong Motion, 1992, The Corrections, 2001 (Nat. Book award for fiction Nat. Book Found.), How To Be Alone: Essays, 2002, (memoir) The Discomfort Zone, 2006. Recipient Am. Acad. Berlin prize, 2000; fellow, Guggenheim Found., 1996. Office: Farrar Straus and Giroux Publicity Dept 19 Union Square West New York NY 10003*

FRANZEN, ULRICH J., architect; b. Rhineland, Germany, Jan. 15, 1921; s. Erik and Elizabeth (Hellersberg) F.; m. Joan Cummings, May, 1942 (div. 1962); children— Peter, David, April; m. Josephine Laura Hughes, Sept. 2, 1980 BFA, Williams Coll., 1942, LHD (hon.), 1972; MArch, Harvard U., 1949. Designer I.M. Pei & Ptnrs., NYC, 1950-55; head Ulrich Franzen & Assocs., NYC, 1955—. Vis. critic, prof. Washington U., St. Louis, 1960-61, Yale U., New Haven, 1962-69, 79, 80, 81, Harvard U., Cambridge, Mass., 1961, Columbia U., N.Y.C., 1983, 84; chmn. Archtl. Bd. Rev., Rye, N.Y., 1960-62; mem. Cin. Archtl. Bd. Rev., 1964-66 Prin. works include Alley Theatre, 1968 (AIA honor 1970), Agronomy Bldg., 1970 (AIA honor 1971), Christensen Hall, 1970 (AIA honor 1972), Harlem Sch. of Arts, 1982, Hunter Coll. N.Y.C., 1983, Philip Morris World Hdqrs., 1984, Whitney Mus. Br., 1984, Champion Internat. World Hdqrs. with Whitney Mus. Br., 1985. With U.S. Army, 1943-45. Decorated Bronze Star, Croix de Guerre Avec Palme, Belgium; recipient Bruner prize Inst. Arts and Letters, N.Y.C. Fellow AIA (Thomas Jefferson award); mem. AIA (gold medal N.Y. chpt.), Archtl. League N.Y. (pres. 1968-70, bd. dirs. 1962—), N.Y.C. Landmarks Preservation Commn. (commr. 1992-96), Century Assn. Home: 27 Lamy Dr Santa Fe NM 87506-6907 Office Phone: 505-984-8065.

FRANZKE, RICHARD ALBERT, lawyer; b. Lewistown, Mont., Mar. 7, 1935; s. Arthur A. and Senta (Clark) F.; divorced; children: Mark, Jean, Robert. BA in Polit. Sci., Willamette U., 1958, JD with honors, 1960. Bar: Oreg. 1960, U.S. Dist. Ct. Oreg., 1960, U.S. Supreme Ct., 1961. Ptnr. Stoel, Rives, Portland, 1960—. Bd. dirs., chmn. various coms. Assn. Gen. Contractors Am., Portland, 1972-79; mem. com. on legis. affairs Assn. Builders & Contractors, Portland, 1983—. Author: A Study of the Construct by Contract Issue, 1979. Mem. Gov.'s Task Force on Reform of Worker's Compensation, Salem, Oreg., 1980-81; atty. gen.'s com. on Pub. Contracting. Recipient SIR award Assn. Gen. Contractors, 1979, Nat. Winner Outstanding Oral Argument award U.S. Moot Ct., 1959. Mem. ABA (sect. pub. contract law), Oreg. Bar (law sch. liaison, com. on practice and procedure specialization), Multnomah County Bar Assn. Republican. Avocations: antique autos, antique furniture, boating. Home: 14980 SW 133rd Ave Tigard OR 97224-1646 Office: Stoel Rives 900 SW 5th Ave Ste 2300 Portland OR 97204-1229 E-mail: franzkehill@comcast.com.

FRANZONE, ERIC SCOTT, psychologist; b. Bklyn., Feb. 21, 1967; s. Robert Anthony and Barbara Adeline Franzone; m. Rosita Betancourt Franzone, Aug. 6, 1995; children: Sarah, Katherine, Hannah. BSc, Franciscan U. of Steubenville, 1989; MSc, St. John's U., 1994; PhD, Forkauf Grad. Sch. Psychology, 2001. Sch. psychologist NYC Bd. Edn., 1993—2006. Contbr. articles to profl. jour. Mem.: Nat. Assn. of Sch. Psychologists. Republican. Roman Catholic. Home: 376 Raymondskill Rd Milford PA 18337 Office: NYC Dept Edn 715 Ocean Terr Staten Island NY 10303

FRAPPIER, PEARL PETERS, retired bookkeeper; b. Woonsocket, RI, Mar. 27, 1928; d. Frank and Angele (VanMaldeghem) Peters; m. Dollard Zenon Frappier, Apr. 2, 1956 (dec. Dec. 20, 1972). Bookkeeper McCarthy Dry Goods Co., Woonsocket, 1945—56; ret., 1956. Mem. Rep. Nat. Com., 2004; gov. vol. during WWII; vol. JFK presdl. campaign, 1961; charter mem. Bush-Cheney presdl. campaign, 2004. Recipient Appreciation award, St. Francis Ho., 1996, 1997, Pearl Day award, 2004, Lifetime Opportunity award, RI Assn. Facilities & Svcs. for Aging, 1996. Mem.: The Smithsonian Inst. (assoc.), Nat. Mil. Family Assn., U.S. Holocaust Meml. Mus., Humane Soc. US, Father Paul Wattson, SA Heritage Soc., Soclumac Club, R.I. Hon. Soc. Republican. Roman Catholic. Avocations: philanthropy, travel, antiques, theater, reading. Home: 223 Burnside Ave Woonsocket RI 02895-2188

FRASCA, GABRIEL, chef; Cook Hamersley's Bistro, Boston, 1994, Chez Henri, Cambridge, 1996, St. Hubertus, Italy, Danube, NYC; apprenticeship L'abbaye de Saint Croix, 1997; chef Aquitaine Bis, Boston, 2001; chef de cuisine Radius, Boston; exec. chef Spire, Boston, 2003—; co-exec. chef Straight Wharf Restaurant, Nantucket, 2006—. Named 2001 Rising Star, The Improper Bostonian, Best Chef, Up and Coming, Boston Mag., 2003; named one of Boston's Rising Stars, StarChefs.com, 2006.

FRASCH, ALBERTO CARLOS C., molecular genetics educator; b. District Capital, Argentina, Jan. 26, 1949; s. Emilio Carlos Frasch and Haydee Norma Borghello; m. Alcira Graciela Colombo, Sept. 22, 1977; children: Federico German, Carolina Andrea. Bachellor, Urquiza, Buenos Aires, 1966; dentist, U. Buenos Aires, 1971, PhD, 1977. Fellow Nat. Rsch. Coun., Buenos Aires, 1973-78, rschr., 1981—; fellow WHO, Amsterdam, Netherlands, 1979-80; prof. U. Buenos Aires, 1986. Com. mem., chmn. WHO, Geneva, 1983; chmn. sci. com. Nat. Rsch. Coun., Buenos Aires, 1986-89; head molecular biology lab. Inst. Biochemistry Rsch., 1986-1996; chair steering com. on chagas disease Special Prog. for Rsch. and Tng. in Tropical Diseases/WHO, 1990-1993, co-chair com. on parasite genomes, 1994-; v.p. Tecnologia Genética, Buenos Aires, 1992; dir. Biotechnol. Rsch. Inst., Buenos Aires, 1994-; internat. rsch. scholar Howard Hughes Med. Inst., 1997-. Contbr. articles to profl. jours. Recipient Luis L. Leloir award Fundacion Campomar, 1993, award in biology Third World Acad. Scis., 2000, Guggenheim fellowship, 2001, merit diploma in cytology and molecular biology Konex Found., Argentina, 2003. Mem.: NAS (assoc.). Avocations: antiques, handicrafts, nature. Office: Inst de Investigation Antonio Machado 151 1405 District Capital Argentina

FRASCH, RONALD L., retail executive; m. Georgia Hobaica, 2002. Started retail career Bloomingdale's, 1970; joined Bonwit Teller, 1976—78, Saks Fifth Avenue Enterprises, 1978, divisional merchandise manager; sr. v.p., general merchandise mgr. cosmetics, women's shoes and accessories Neiman Marcus, 1984—86, sr. v.p., general merchandise mgr. women's apparel, 1986—94; pres., CEO Escada USA, Hasbrouck Heights, NJ, 1994—96; pres. GFT USA, 1996—2000; head ready to wear Neiman Marcus Group, Inc., chmn., CEO, Bergdorf Goodman NYC, 2000—04; div. merchandise mgr. Saks Fifth Avenue Enterprises, NYC, vice chmn., 2004—07, chief merchant, 2004—07, pres., 2007—, chief merchandising officer, 2007—. Bd. dir. Crocs, Inc., 2006—. Office: Saks Fifth Avenue Enterprises 12 E 49th St New York NY 10017*

FRASE, KATHARINE, information technology executive; b. Washington; Grad., Bryn Mawr Coll., 1979; PhD in Materials Sci. and Engring., U. Pa., 1983. With Interconnect Products Group IBM Corp., 1986—, dir. packaging applications and design, 2001—02, dir. devel., 2002—03, v.p. worldwide packaging and test IBM Microelectronics, 2003—05, v.p. tech., 2005—06, v.p. software strategy, 2006—. Chair NRC Visiting Com., NIST Lab. of Materials Sci.; chmn. Nat. Materials Adv. Bd.; bd. dirs. Internat. Electronics Mfg. Initiative. Contbr. articles to profl. jours. Mem.: NAE, IBM Acad. Tech. (tech. coun. mem. 2000—02). Office: IBM Corp 1133 Westchester Ave White Plains NY 10604 Office Phone: 914-766-3448. Business E-Mail: frase@us.ibm.com.

FRASE, RICHARD S., law educator; BA, Haverford Coll., 1967; JD, U. Chgo., 1970. Bar: Ill. 1970, Minn. 1977. Law clk. to L. Swygert, Chief Judge US Ct. Appeals 7th Cir., Chgo., 1970-71; rsch. assoc. U. Chgo. Law Sch., 1971—72, 1974—77; assoc. atty. Sidley & Austin, 1972—74; assoc. prof. law U. Minn. Law Sch., Mpls., 1977-81, prof. law, 1981-91, Davis prof. law, 1988-89, Berger prof. law, 1991—. Adv. bd. Fed. Sentencing Reporter, 1994—. Co-author: (textook) Criminal Justice System, 1980, (practice treatise) Minnesota Misdemeanors, 1982, 3d edit., 1999; author: (practice treatise) Criminal Evidence, 1985; co-author: (fgn. code translation) French Code of Criminal Procedure, 1988; co-editor: Encyclopedia of Crime and Justice, 2d edit., 2001, Sentencing and Sanctions in Western Countries, 2001; mem. U. Chgo. Law Rev. Mem. Am. Law Inst., Phi Beta Kappa. Republican. Office: U Minn Law Sch 229 19th Ave S Minneapolis MN 55455-0400 Business E-Mail: frase001@umn.edu.

FRASER, ALEXANDER G., research scientist; BSc, Bristol U.; PhD in Computing Sci., Cambridge U. Asst. dir. rsch. Cambridge U.; with AT&T Bell Labs., 1969—96, mem. tech. staff, 1969—77, dept. head Computer Sys. Rsch., 1977—82, dir. Computing Sci. Rsch. Ctr., 1982—87, exec. dir. Info. Sci. Rsch, 1987—94, assoc. v.p. Info. Sci. Rsch., 1994—96; v.p. rsch. AT&T Labs., 1996—98, founder AT&T Labs Rsch., 1996, chief scientist, 1998—2002; founder, pres., chmn. bd. Fraser Rsch., Princeton, NJ, 2002—. Contbr. articles to profl. jours. Past adv. bd. mem. Columbia U., Rutgers U., U. Tex. Recipient Koji Kobayashi Computers and Comms. Award, 1989, Sigcomm Award, 1992. Fellow: IEEE (Richard W. Hamming Medal 2001), British Computer Soc. (coun. mem.); mem.: NAE, Nat. Rsch. Coun. Office: Fraser Rsch 182 Nassau St #301 Princeton NJ 08542 Home: 62 Carriage House Rd Bernardsville NJ 07924 Home Phone: 908-776-5247; Office Phone: 609-479-7337. E-mail: eafibkube@fraserresearch.org.

FRASER, ALEXANDER PAUL, lawyer; b. Ottawa, Ont., Can., May 26, 1968; arrived in U.S., 1968; s. John Gabriel Fraser and Leila Hanson; m. Kristin Ruth-Katherine Pearson, Mar. 21, 1970; children: Caroline, Paul, Elaine. BS, U. Wis., 1990, MBA in Fin., Investments and Banking, 1991; JD, NYU, 1994. Ptnr. Michael Best & Friedrich LLP, Milw., 1994—. Bd. dirs. Skylight Opera Theatre, Milw., 2001—, United Performing Arts Found., Milw., 2002—; bd. dirs., past pres. First Stage Children's Theatre, Milw., 2001—; pres. bd. dirs. Nat. Assn. Health Edn. Ctrs., Milw., 2001—; bd. dirs., past chmn. Milw. Youth Arts Ctr., 2004—. Mem.: Rotary. Office: Michael Best & Friedrich LLP 100 E Wisconsin Ave Milwaukee WI 53202 Business E-Mail: apfraser@michaelbest.com.

FRASER, BRENDAN, actor; b. Indpls., Dec. 3, 1968; m. Afton Smith, Sept. 27, 1998; children: Griffin Arthur, Holden Fletcher. BFA, Cornish Coll. Arts, Seattle. Actor: (films) Dogfight, 1991, Encino Man, 1992, School Ties, 1992, Twenty Bucks, 1993, Son in Law, 1993, Younger and Younger, 1993, With Honors, 1994, In the Army Now, 1994, Airheads, 1994, The Scout, 1994, The Passion of Darkly Noon, 1995, Balto (voice), 1995, Now and Then, 1995, Kids in the Hall: Brain Candy, 1996, Mrs. Winterbourne, 1996, Glory Daze, 1996, George of the Jungle, 1997, Still Breathing, 1998, Gods and Monsters, 1998, Sinbad: Beyond the Veil of Mists (voice), 1999, Ringside, 1999, Monkey Bone, 1999, Blast from the Past, 1999, The Mummy, 1999, Dudley Do-Right, 1999, Bedazzled, 2000, The Mummy Returns, 2001, The Quiet American, 2002, Looney Tunes: Back in Action, 2003, Revenge of the Mummy: The Ride, 2004, Crash, 2004 (recipient, Outstanding Performance by a Cast in a Motion Picture, 2006), Beach Bunny, 2005. Office: William Morris Agy 151 El Camino Dr Beverly Hills CA 90212

FRASER, CASSANDRA LYNNE, chemist, educator; b. Norfolk, Va., Nov. 11, 1962; d. John Robert and Norma Jean Fraser. BA, Kalamazoo Coll., 1984; MTS, Harvard Div. Sch., 1988; PhD, U. Chgo., 1993. NIH postdoctoral fellow Calif. Inst. Tech., Pasadena, 1993—95; asst. prof. chemistry U. Va., Charlottesville, 1995—2001, assoc. prof. chemistry, 2001—05, Cavaliers' Disting. Tchg. Prof., 2004—06, prof. chemistry, 2005—. Gene and drug delivery study sect. mem. NIH, 2004—. Mem. editl. adv. bd.: Macromolecules, 2003—05. Recipient CAREER Award, NSF, 1998, Young Prof. award, Dupont, 1999, Pres. Early Career award Scientists and Engineers (PECASE), White House, NSF, 1999, Rsch. fellow award, Alfred P. Sloan Found., 1999, Non-tenured Faculty award, 3M Corp., 2001, Mead Hon. Faculty, U. Va Alumni Assn., 2002—03, Recognition Leadership and Svc., P.U.M.P.K.I.N. Soc., U. Va., 2003, Women's Leadership award, Lantern Soc., U. Va., 2004, Nat. Assoc. award, Nat. Acads., 2004; Radcliffe Inst. Advanced Studies fellow, Harvard U., 2006—. Mem.: AAAS, Am. Chem. Soc., Phi Beta Kappa. Achievements include leadership and design of interdisciplinary programs, Science, Careers and Society Forum, Color: Across the Spectrum, Biomaterials Workshop, Designing Matter Common Course, Mentoring students; design and synthesis of polymeric metal complexes, a new class of bio-inspired materials combining polymer and inorganic chemistry fields, related to biomedicine, nanoscience, and other fields; first woman in the history of the University of Virginia to receive tenure and promotion to full professor in the chemistry department. Avocations: writing, athletics, collaborative projects, cultural exchange, visual arts and design. Office: U Va Dept Chemistry McCormick Rd PO Box 400319 Charlottesville VA 22904-4319 Home Phone: 434-825-3484; Office Phone: 434-924-7998. Business E-Mail: fraser@virginia.edu.

FRASER, CATRIONA TRAFFORD, art gallery director, photographer; b. Reading, Eng., Jan. 8, 1972; arrived in U.S., 1992; d. Nigel Trafford Fraser and Christine Ilsley; m. Florencio Lennox Campello, Jan. 7, 1995; 1 child, Callum Fraser-Sharp. Diploma, Plymouth Coll. Arts and Design, Devon, Eng., 1988—89; graduated, Wallingford Sch., Oxfordshire, England, 1988. Asst. photographer trainee Reading Evening Post, Reading, England, 1987; founder Cairn Photography, Fettercairn, Scotland, 1991; dir. Fraser Gallery, Washington, 1996—, Bethesda, Md., 2002—. Founder Secondsight, 2003—; dir. Bethesda Fine Arts Festival; chair Trawick Art Prize, Bethesda Painting Awards. Photographer Dunnottar Castle, 1992 (1st prize No. Va. Fine Arts Festival, 1995), Kinnaird Castle, 1992 (1st prize No. Va. Fine Arts Festival, 1994), Glamis Castle, 1992 (1st place 6th Ann. Roseville Photography Competition, Calif., 1993), Fleur No. II, 1992 (Best of Show 17th Ann. Internat. Photo Competition Ark., 1993); exhibitions include Nat. Art. Competition, 1996, Castlegait Gallery, Scotland, 1992, Sacramento Fine Arts Ctr., 1992, New Image Gallery, Va., 1992, Carnegie Mus., Pitts., 1992, St. Helena Art League, Calif., 1993, Brusque Mus., Santa Caterina Brazil, 1993, Art League Gallery, Va., 1994, 1995, Va. Commonwealth U., 1995, Eklektikos Gallery, Washington DC, 1996, Fraser Gallery, Washington DC, 1996, 1997, 1999, 2000, 2002, Infrared Gallery, Chgo., 1998, Bruce Gallery, Edinboro Coll., Pa., 2001, Am. Ctr. Physics, Md., 2004. Adv. panel Bethesda Art and Entertainment; adv. bd. Washington Sch. of Photography. Recipient Honor Award, 42d Ann. Boardwalk Internat. Arts Festival, 1998, Best of Show, Ann. Edzell Scottish Art Invitational, Paul Ostaseski Meml. Award, Roanoke Art Festival, 1998, Merit Award, Spring Stockley Gardens Art Festival, Va., 1995, 20th Ann. Princess Anne Art Show, Va., second place, 37th Ann. Northern Calif. Art Festival, 26th Ann. Otero Mus. Nat. Exhbn., Colo., Waynesboro Fall Arts Festival, Va., 1997, 1996, Bel Air Festival Arts, Md., 1994, Fall Stockley Gardens Art Festival, Va., 1995, Bellgrade Art Festival, Va., 1995, 1997, Judge's Award, 1994. Mem.: Art Dealers Assn. Greater Washington, Bethesda C. of C. Office: Fraser Gallery 7700 Wisconsin Ave Ste E Bethesda MD 20814 Office Phone: 301-718-9651. Office Fax: 301-718-9652. Business E-Mail: catriona@thefrasergallery.com.

FRASER, DAVID WILLIAM, epidemiologist; b. Abington, Pa., May 10, 1944; s. Grant Clippinger and Ella Finlaw (Ayars) F.; m. Barbara Josephine Gaines, June 25, 1966; children: Evan Grant, Leigh Robertson. BA, Haverford Coll., Pa., 1965, DSc (hon.), 1991; MD, Harvard U., 1969; ScD (hon.), Moravian Coll., 1987. Diplomate Am. Bd. Internal Medicine. Intern in internal medicine U. Pa. Hosp., Phila., 1969-70, resident, 1970-71, chief resident in internal medicine, 1973-74, fellow in infectious diseases, 1974-75; commd. officer USPHS, 1971-73, 75-82; chief spl. pathogens br., bacterial diseases divsn. Bur. Epidemiology, Ctr. Disease Control, USPHS, Atlanta, 1975-80, med. epidemiologist, asst. dir. bacterial diseases divsn.,

1981-82; pres. Swarthmore (Pa.) Coll., 1982-91; head dept. social welfare Secretariat of His Highness Aga Khan, Gouvieux, France, 1991-95; cons. in internat. health and edn., 1996, 2000—; exec. dir. INCLEN, Inc., 1996-2000; rsch. assoc. Asian sect. U. Pa. Mus. Archaeology and Anthropology, 1999—; rsch. assoc. The Textile Mus., Washington, 2004—. Adj. prof. medicine U. Pa. Sch. Medicine, 1983-91, adj. prof. epidemiology, 1997—. Author: A Guide to Weft Twining and Related Structures with Interacting Wefts, 1989, (with Barbara G. Fraser) Mantles of Merit: Chin Textiles from Myanmar, India and Bangladesh, 2005; editl. bd. Annals of Internal Medicine, 1991-94; contbr. articles to profl. med. and textile jours. Bd. mgrs. Haverford Coll., 1980-83; bd. advisors Educators for Social Responsibility, 1986-91; chmn. bd. Consortium on Financing Higher Edn., 1986-87; trustee The Textile Mus., Washington, 1986-2003, v.p., 1990-91, 96, pres., 1997-2003; bd. dirs. Albert G. Oliver Found., 1985-91; sci. adv. bd. Ctr. for Infectious Diseases, 1989-91; mem. immunization practices adv. com. Ctrs. for Disease Control, 1988-92; mem. com. to visit med. sch. and sch. dental medicine Harvard U., 1988-94; costume and textile com. Phila. Mus. Art, 1988-91. Recipient Meritorious Svc. medal USPHS, 1978, John Scott award City of Phila., 1986, R.L. Shep Book award Textile Soc. Am., 2006; co-recipient Ancient and Modern prize Hali, Cornucopia, and Oriental Art, 2005, Millia Davenport Publ. award Costume Soc. Am., 2006; Clementine Cope fellow Haverford Coll., 1965, Daland fellow Am. Philos. Soc., 1974. Fellow ACP (Richard and Hinda Rosenthal Found. award 1979), Infectious Diseases Soc. Am., Am. Coll. Epidemiology; mem. Am. Epidemiol. Soc., Aesculapian Club, Founders Club (Haverford Coll.). Home and Office: 907 N Pennsylvania Ave Yardley PA 19067-2023 Home Phone: 215-295-2016; Office Phone: 215-295-2016. E-mail: dwffraser@earthlink.net.

FRASER, DONALD C., engineering executive, educator; b. NYC, Apr. 20, 1941; s. Donald Fraser and Anna Thurston; children: Lynn, Eric. S.B., MIT, Cambridge, 1962, MS, 1963, Sc.D., 1967. Tech. staff MIT Instrumentation Lab., Cambridge, Mass., 1967-69; divsn. leader C.S. Draper Lab., Inc., Cambridge, 1969-81, v.p. tech. ops., 1981-88, exec. v.p., 1988-90; dep. dir. operational test and evaluation Office Sec. Def., Washington, 1990-91; prin. deputy under sec. def. for acquisition Office Sec. of Def., Washington, 1991-93; vis. prof. Stanford U., Calif., 1970-71; lectr. MIT Aero/Astro Dept., Cambridge, 1972-91; founder, dir. Ctr. Photonics prof. engring. and physics Boston U., 1993—2006. Active Air Force Studies Bd. Com. Advanced Avionics, 1979-83; chmn. Air Force Studies Bd. Com. Fault Isolation, 1982-85; active USAF Aero Systems Divsn. Adv. Group, 1984-90; mem. NASA Adv. Coun. Space Systems and Tech. Adv. Com., 1982-91, U.S. Army Sci. Bd., 1987-90, NRC Aeronautics and Space Engring. Bd., 1995-2001; mem. adv. coun. NASA, 2002-05; bd. dirs. DRS Techs., Aurora Flight Scis., Ctr. for Tech. Commercialization. Assoc. editor AIAA Jour. Spacecraft and Rockets, 1970-72, editor-in-chief, 1974-78; founder, editor-in-chief AIAA Jour. Guidance, Control and Dynamics, 1977-91. Recipient Def. Disting. Svc. medal, Navy League Roosevelt Gold Medal for Tech., NASA Pub. Svc. medal. Fellow AAAS, AIAA (hon., bd. dirs. New Eng. sect. 1973-75, publs. com. 1973-74); mem. NAE, Tau Beta Pi, Sigma Xi, Sigma Gamma Tau. Avocations: flying, hiking, skiing, bicycling. Address: 50 Battery St #308 Boston MA 02109

FRASER, DONALD MACKAY, retired mayor, congressman; b. Mpls., Feb. 20, 1924; s. Everett and Lois (MacKay) F.; m. Arvonne Skelton, June 30, 1950; children: Thomas Skelton, Mary MacKay, John DuFrene, Lois MacKay (dec.), Anne T. (dec.), Jean Skelton. BA cum laude, U. Minn., 1944, LLB, 1948. Bar: Minn. 1948. Ptnr. Lindquist, Fraser & Magnuson (and predecessors), 1948-62; Minn. State senator, 1954-62; sec. Senate Liberal Caucus, 1955-62; mem. 88th-95th Congresses from 5th Dist. Minn., mem. fgn. affairs com., chmn. subcom. on internat. orgn., mem. budget com.; mayor City of Mpls., 1980-93; mem. study and rev. com. Dem. Caucus; mem. Commn. on Role and Future Presdl. Primaries, 1976; adj. prof. law and pub. affairs U. Minn., Mpls. Vice chmn., dir. Mpls. Citizens Com. on Pub. Edn., 1950-54; Sec. Minn. del. Democratic Nat. Conv., 1960; chmn. Minn. Citizens for Kennedy, 1960; mem. platform com. Dem. Nat. Conv., 1964, mem. rules com., 1972, 76; vice chmn. Com. Dem. Selection Presdl. Nominees, 1968; chmn. Democratic Study Group Congress, 1969-71, Commn. on Party Structure and Del. Selection Dem. Party, 1971-72; 1st Am. co-chmn. Anglo-Am. Parliamentary Conf. on Africa, 1964; mem. U.S. del. 7th spl. session and 30th session UN Gen. Assembly, 1975; Congl. adviser to U.S. del. to UN Conf. on Disarmament, 1967-73, to U.S. del. to 3d Law of Sea Conf., 1972, to UN Commn. on Human Rights, 1974; cons. on families HUD, 1994. Chair health com. U.S. Conf. Mayors; bd. dirs. Mpls. United Way, 1986-93, Twin Cities Rise!, 1994—2002, Connect/U.S.-Russia, 1994—, Greater Mpls. Coun. Chs., 2000—03; co-chair Ctr. for Internat. Policy, 1976-94, Early Care and Edn. Fin. Commn., 1999-2002; co-founder, chair Dem. Farmer-Labor Edn. Found.; pres. S.E. Mpls. Coun. on Learning, 2003-05; co-chair, bd. dirs. Ready 4K, 2001-; mem. Mpls. Charter Commn., 1997-2004; initiated numerous youth programs such as Transitional Work Internship Program, Youth Work Internship Program, Neighborhood Early Learning Ctrs., Youth Coordinating Bd., Youth Trust. Lt. (j.g.) USNR, 1944-46. Recipient 1st Minn. Internat. Human Rights award, 1985, Disting. Svc. award Mpls. United Way, 1992; fellow Kennedy Sch., spring 1994. Mem. Mpls. Fgn. Policy Assn. (pres. 1952-53), Citizens League Greater Mpls. (sec. 1951-54), Minn. Bar Assn., Hennepin County Bar Assn., Ams. for Dem. Action (nat. chmn. 1973-76), Dem. Conf. (nat. chmn. 1976-78), U. Minn. Law Alumni Assn. (dir. 1958-61), Univ. Dist. Improvement Assn. (pres. 1950-52), Nat. League of Cities (2d v.p. 1991, 1st v.p. 1992, pres. 1993), Minn. Advocates for Human Rights (co-founder, bd. dirs. 1983-92, 2000-03), League of Minn. Cities (bd. dirs. 1991-93, co-chmn. Ready 4K 2005—). Democrat. Personal E-mail: dfled@goldengate.net.

FRASER, JOHN WAYNE, insurance executive, consultant, underwriter; b. Ashland, Ala., Jan. 19, 1944; s. Elliott Nathaniel and Maurice Jennette (Glenn) F.; m. Diana Louise Renn, Jan. 20, 1963; children: Christine Celeste, Sean Elliott AA Bus. Adminstrn., St. Petersburg Jr. Coll., 1969; BA honors, U. South Fla., 1974. Dir. mfg. svcs. Milton Roy Co., St. Petersburg, Fla., 1965—74; sales rep. Fla. Forms Co., Tampa, 1975—76, Graphic Bus. Sys., St. Petersburg, 1976—79; dist. mgr. Blue Cross/Blue Shield Fla., St. Petersburg, 1979—86; sr. v.p. Wittner Cos., 1986—98; pres. Advocate Cons., Inc., Clearwater, Fla., 1998—2003; v.p. Wallace, Welch and Willingham, Inc., 2003—. Mem. editl. bd., monthly contbr. COBRA Advisory, 1997-02 Former mem. Internat. Found. Employee Benefit Welfare Plans; pres. Benefit One of Am., Inc., 1997-98; mem. pension coun. Tampa (Fla.) Bay, 1999-2005. With U.S. Army, 1962 Mem. Fla. West Coast Employee Benefit Coun. (bd. dirs. 1994-2004, pres. 2002-03), Nat. Assn. Health Underwriters (trustee West Coast chpt. 1988-98, pres. 1992-93), Fla. Assn. Health Underwriters (bd. dirs. 1992-93, 1st v.p. 1993-94, pres. 1994-95), Ctrl. Pinellas Jaycees (treas. 1975, v.p. 1976), Suncoast Investors Club (pres. 1996-), U. South Fla. Alumni Assn Unitarian-Universalist. Avocations: photography, sailing. Office: 300 First Ave So Fifth Fl Saint Petersburg FL 33701 Personal E-mail: jfraser2@tampabay.rr.com.

FRASER, MALCOLM CAVANAGH, mayor; b. Englewood, NJ, Nov. 26, 1929; s. Stanley and Helen L. (Cavanagh) F.; m. Joan Marie Iversen, May 1, 1954; children: Gordon, David, Stephen, Janice, Bruce, Andrew. Mech. Engr., Stevens Inst. Tech., 1951, Alexander Hamilton Inst., 1958. Mcpl. ofcl. elected cert. Rutgers U., 1997. Mktg. engr. Ingersoll-Rand Co., NYC, 1951—60, internat. coord., 1960—66, mgr. govt. ops. Painted Post, NY, 1967—75, gen. mgr. European Ops. The Hague, Netherlands, 1975—80, gen. mgr. for oil industry Houston, 1980—82, dispute resolution and corp./customer polit. coms. mgr., 1981—90; internat. mgr. IR Compression Svcs., Houston, 1983—86; gas engine product mgr. Dresser-Rand Co., Painted Post, 1986—90; ret., 1990. Mayor Borough Cape May Point, NJ, 1992—; mem. coastal area facilities and residential act com. N.J. Dept. Environ. Protection, 1998—2000, mem. SMART growth com., 2002—04; mem. pub. works com. State of N.J., 2004—; del. N.J. Citizens Tax Assembly, 2003—04. Author: The Charmed Circle, 1986. Pres. YMCA Men's Svc. Club, Westfield, N.J., 1967; residential co-chair United Fund, Westfield, 1967; treas. troop com. Boy Scouts Am., Corning, N.Y., 1968-72; ch. vestryman, Corning, 1971-74; bd. dirs. YMCA, Corning, 1967-75, pres. 1970-73; mem. Am. Sch. Bd. The Hague, Netherlands, 1978-80; bd. dirs. Taxpayers Assn., Cape May Point, 1988-92, pres. 1990-92; trustee Hist. St. Peters-by-the-Sea Ch., Cape May Point, 1990—. Cpl. U.S. Army, 1954-56 Recipient Excellence in Cmty. Svc. award DAR, Cape May County, 1997, Outstanding Leadership award N.J. Mayor's Assn., Dunellen, 1998, Lifetime Achievement award Cape May Point Taxpayers Assn., 2001; award established in his name N.J. Rural Water Assn., Tuckerton, N.J., 1999, Strathmore Recognition for Leadership in Profession, 2006-07. Mem. ASME, N.J. Rural Water Assn. (pres. 1995-98, bd. dirs. 1994-2000), N.J. State League of Municipalities (bd. dirs. 1995-2007, econ. devel. com. 2003-), Cape May County League of Municipalities (v.p., pres. 1996-98), N.J. Conf. Mayors (bd. dirs., legis. com. 2002-, v.p. 2005-) Episcopalian. Avocations: baseball, history. Home: PO Box 323 Cape May Point NJ 08212-0323 Office: Borough of Cape May Point PO Box 490 215 Lighthouse Ave Cape May Point NJ 08212 Office Phone: 609-884-2080. Personal E-mail: joan.fraser/@verizon.net.

FRASER, ROBERT BURCHMORE, lawyer; b. Newton, Mass., Aug. 13, 1928; s. Alfred Alexander and Helen Louise (Comiskey) F.; m. Mary-Ann Jackson, Sept. 7, 1963; children: Melanie, Jennifer Amy, Matthew John. AB, Harvard U., 1949, LLB, 1952, LLM, 1955. Bar: Mass. Assoc. Goodwin Procter LLP, Boston, 1955-63, ptnr., 1964-97, chmn., 1984-97. Spl. advisor to Mayor of Boston and Boston Police Commr., 1996-2006. Mem. Mass. Gov.'s Jud. Nominating Commn., 1979-82; mem. adv. com. Mass. Commr. Revenue, 1979-82; chmn. adv. com. Mass. Housing Fin. Agy, 1979-83; chmn. Boston Pub. Health Commn., 1996-97; chmn. Vol. Lawyers for Arts of Mass., 1990-97; bd. dirs. Greater Boston YMCA, 1981-87, Boston Pvt. Industry Coun., 1988-99, Citywide Ednl. Coalition, 1988-2000, Boston Against Drugs, 1988-93, chmn. 1990-93, Boston Ptnrs. in Edn., 1989-99, Am. Student Assistance Corp., 1989-97, Greater Boston C. of C., 1993—, Jobs for Mass., 1993-98, Boston Pub. Libr. Found., 1992-2000, Boston Mgmt. Consortium, 1994-2001, NCCJ, 1994-2002, chmn. 1997-99, Mass. Bus. Alliance Edn., 1995—, Ctr. for Collaborative Edn., 1998-99, The Med. Found., 1995-99, MassInc., 1996—; trustee New Eng. Conservatory Music, 1982-2001, Boston Plan for Excellence in Pub. Schs., 1987-99, chmn., 1992-95, Boston Adult Literacy Fund, 1989-96; trustee Lesley Coll., 1992-96; overseer Boston Lyric Opera, 1994-99; chmn. Boston Music Edn. Collaborative, 1999-2001; chmn. Arts & Bus. Coun. Greater Boston, 2000-05. Mem. ABA, Mass. Bar Assn., Boston Bar Assn., Harvard Mus. Assn. Harvard Club (Boston.). Home: 90 Allandale St Jamaica Plain MA 02130-3442 Office: Goodwin Procter Exchange Pl Boston MA 02109-2803 Office Phone: 617-570-1234. Personal E-mail: fraserrb@comcast.net.

FRASER, RUTH HODGES, city clerk; b. Roanoke, Va., Jan. 15, 1931; d. James Elpherson and Ruth Elizabeth (Morgan) Hodges; m. Leon Menaclus Smith, June 18, 1978 (dec.); children: Dorothy Ruth Smith Swift, Marvis Frances Smith Mills; m. Donald Fraser. Student, Potomac State Coll., 1949-51; cert. mcpl. clk., Old Dominion U., 1982. Cert. mcpl. clk. Va. Legal sec. Commonwealth Atty., Woodstock, Va., 1952-54; adminstrv. asst. Nelson Oil Corp., Mt. Jackson, Va., 1954-56; exec. sec., office mgr. Tidewater Va. Devel. Co., Norfolk, Va., 1956-72; from corp. sec. to purchasing agt. Nepratex Industries, Virginia Beach, Va., 1972-77; realtor, life agt. Real Estate/Ins., 1977—; city clk. City of Virginia Beach, 1978—. Sec.-treas. Hospice Virginia Beach, 1981—86; liaison, coord. Mayor's Sister City Commn., 1993—; mem. IIMC Acad. Advanced Edn., 1984—87, 1987—; founder Z House shelter for battered spouses; state coord. Sister Cities Internat., 2005—, parliamentarian bd. dirs., 2006. Named Ky. Col., 1993, W.Va. Mountaineer, 1993; recipient Quills award, IIMC Acad. Advanced Edn., 1991, Hon. Recognition Julian F. Hirst award for Disting. Svc., 1994. Mem.: Va. Mcpl. Clks. Assn. (pres. 1982—84, master mcpl. clk. 2000—, treas. 2002, Clk. of the Yr. 1987), Lifelong Acad. Advanced Edn., Intenrat. Mcpl. Clks. (bd. dirs. 1986—89, chair internat. com. 1989—91, chair year 2000 planning com. 1998—), Pilot Club (officer 1960—72), Shriners, Daus. of Nile (mem. gen. grand chpt. credentials com. 2006—), Order Eastern Star (worthy matron Westminster chpt. #99 1966—67, worthy grand matron grand chpt. Va. 1993—94, worthy matron Westminster chpt. #99 2004—05), Zonta Internat. (bd. dirs. 1983—90). Avocations: crafts, bicycling, ice skating, travel. Home: 1153 Belvoir Ln Virginia Beach VA 23464-6766 Office: City of Virginia Beach Room 281 City Hall Virginia Beach VA 23456

FRASER, WILLIAM M., III, career military officer; BS, Tex. A&M U., 1974; MS, U. No. Colo., 1980; grad., Marine Corps Command and Staff Coll., 1983, Armed Forces Staff Coll., 1985, Air War Coll., 1991. Advanced through ranks to lt. gen. USAF, 2005; B-52H aircraft comdr. 46th bomb squadron, Grand Forks AFB, ND, 1981—82, B-52G aircraft comdr., instr. pilot, 1982—83; chief, B-52G standardization and eval. br. 319th bomb wing, Grand Forks AFB, 1983—84; chief European single integrated operational plan tactics, Offutt AFB, Nebr., 1985—86; exec. officer to SAC chief of staff USAF, Offutt AFB, 1986—87; chief of staff US Strategic Command, Offutt AFB, 1998—99; chief nuc. requirements cell SHAPE, Mons, Belgium, 1987—90, spl. asst. to supreme allied comdr., 1995—97; dep. comdr. 384th ops. group USAF, McConnell AFB, Kans., 1991—93, comdr. 509th ops. group Whiteman AFB, Mo., 1993—95, vice comdr. 509th bomb wing, 1995, comdr. 28th bomb wing Ellsworth AFB, SD, 1997—98, comdr. 2d bomb wing Barksdale AFB, La., 1999—2000; dir. def. space reconnaissance program, dep. dir. military support Nat. Reconnaissance Office, Washington, 2000—02; dep. dir. nat. sys. ops. The Joint Staff, 2000—02; spl. asst. to comdr. Air Force Command and Control, Intelligence, Surveillance and Reconnaissance Ctr., Langley AFB, Va., 2004—05; dep. chief of staff warfighting integration Langley AFB, 2004—05; vice comdr. Air Combat Command USAF, Langley AFB, 2005—06; asst. to Chmn. Joint Chiefs of Staff The Pentagon, Washington, 2006—. Decorated DSM, Def. Superior Svc. Medal with two oak leaf clusters, Legion of Merit with two oak leaf clusters, Def. Meritorious Svc. Medal with oak leaf cluster, Air Force Commendation Medal with oak leaf cluster, Air Force Achievement Medal, Nat. Intelligence Medal of Achievement, Combat Readiness Medal, Nat. Def. Svc. Medal with bronze star, Armed Forces Expeditionary Medal, Global War on Terrorism Svc. Medal, Military Outstanding Vol. Svc. Medal, Gold Medal Nat. Reconnaissance Office; named T-37 Instr. Pilot of Yr.; recipient Air Force Pub. Affairs Directors Spl. Achievement Award for command support, Joseph A. Moller Award for Oustanding Wing Commander ACC. Office: US Dept Def The Pentagon Washington DC 20301

FRASER, WILLIAM NEIL, retired government agency administrator; b. Vancouver, BC, Can., May 25, 1932; s. James Herbert and Katherine Balkie (Grieve) Fraser; m. Marie Helm, Dec. 19, 1986; children from previous marriage: Gordon(dec.) , Alan, Katherine, Ian. Student, Banff Sch. Advanced Mgmt., 1967. Product mgr. Masonry, Deeks-McBride Ltd., Vancouver, 1952-68; gen. mgr. Masonry Contractors Assn. B.C., Vancouver, 1968-71; exec. dir. Can. Masonry Contractors Assn., Toronto, 1971-87; mem. Ont. Labour Rels. Bd., 1988-98, ret., 1999. With Can. Navy Res., 1953-57. Mem.: Royal Can. Mil. Inst., Inst. Assn. Execs. (past pres. Toronto chpt.), Capt. Olde 78th Fraser Highlanders, Monarchist League of Can., Royal Heraldry Soc. Can., St. Andrew's Soc. of Toronto, Clan Fraser Soc. Can. (chmn.), Scottish Studies Found. (patron, gov.), Heraldry Soc. of Scotland, Grant of Arms Can. Heraldic Authority, Clans and Scottish Socs. of Can. (past pres.). Home: 71 Charles St E Apt 1101 Toronto ON Canada M4Y 2T3 E-mail: neil.fraser@clanfraser.ca.

FRASIER, NIKKI, sales executive; b. Tulsa, Okla., Oct. 13, 1975; m. Matthew Jon Frasier, July 22, 2000; 1 child, Ashley T. BS in Internat. Bus., Okla. State U., Tulsa, 2006. Coord. internat. sales Scifit Sys., Inc., Tulsa, 2001—. Office: SCIFIT Sys Inc 5151 S 110th E Ave Tulsa OK 74146 Home Phone: 918-249-8720; Office Phone: 918-359-2054. Business E-Mail: nfrasier@scifit.com.

FRASIER, RALPH KENNEDY, lawyer, bank executive; b. Winston-Salem, NC, Sept. 16, 1938; s. LeRoy Benjamin and Kathryn O. (Kennedy) F.; m. Jeannine Quick, Aug. 1981; children: Karen D. Frasier Alston, Gail S. Frasier Cox, Ralph Kennedy Jr., Keith Lowery, Marie K. Frasier Washington, Rochelle Doar. BS, N.C. Cen. U., Durham, 1963, JD, 1965. Bar: N.C. 1965, Ohio 1976. With Wachovia Bank and Trust Co., N.A., Winston-Salem, NC, 1965—75, v.p., counsel, 1969-70; asst. counsel, v.p. parent co. Wachovia Corp., 1970-75; v.p., gen. counsel Huntington Nat. Bank, Columbus, Ohio, 1975-76, sr. v.p., 1976-83, sec., 1981-98, exec. v.p., 1983-98, cashier, 1983-98; ret. V.p. Huntington Bancshares Inc., 1976-86, gen. counsel, 1976-98, sec., 1981-98, ret.; sec., dir. Huntington Mortgage Co., Huntington State Bank, Huntington Leasing Co., Huntington Bancshares Fin. Corp., Huntington Investment Mgmt. Co., Huntington Nat. Life Ins. Co., Huntington Co., 1976-88; v.p., asst. sec. Huntington Bank N.E. Ohio, 1982-84; asst. sec. Huntington Bancshares Ky., 1985-97; sec. Huntington Trust Co., N.A., 1987-97, Huntington Bancshares Ind., Inc., 1986-97, Huntington Fin. Services Co., 1987-98; dir. The Huntington Nat. Bank, Columbus, Ohio, 1998-04; of counsel Porter Wright Morris & Arthur LLP, Columbus, 1998-06, ret.; trustee OCLC Online Computer Libr. Ctr., Inc., Dublin, Ohio, 1999—, mem. fin. com., 2000-04, mem. audit com., 2000-, chair 2002-04, exec. com., 2002—, pers. and compensation com., 2002-03; dir. ADATOM.COM, Inc., Milpitas, Calif., 1999-01, mem. compensation com., 1999-01, chair audit com., 1999-01. Bd. dirs. Family Svcs. Winston-Salem, 1966-74, sec., 1966-71, 74, v.p., 1974; chmn. Winston-Salem Transit Authority, 1974-75; bd. dirs. Rsch. for Advancement of Personalities, 1968-71, Winston-Salem Citizens for Fair Housing, 1970-74, N.C. United Community Svcs., 1970-74; treas. Forsyth County (N.C.) Citizens Com. Adequate Justice Bldg., 1968; trustee Appalachian State U., Boone, N.C., 1973-83, endowment fund, 1973-83, Columbus Drug Edn. and Prevention Fund, Inc., 1989-92; trustee, vice chmn. employment and Edn. Commn. Franklin County, 1982-85; mem. Winston-Salem Forsyth County Sch. Bd. Adv. Coun., 1973-74, Atty. Gen's Ohio Task Force Minorities in Bus., 1977-78; bd. dirs. Inroads Columbus, Inc., 1986-95, Greater Columbus Arts Coun., 1986-94, Columbus Urban League Inc., 1987-94, vice chmn., 1990-94; trustee Riverside Meth. Hosp. Found., 1989-90, Grant Med. Ctr., 1990-95, Grant/Riverside Meth. Hosps., 1995-97; trustee Ohio Health Corp., 1997-04, treas., chair fin./audit com., 2001-04, exec. com., 2002-04; dir. Cmty. Mutual Ins. Co., Cin., 1989-92, mem. audit com., 1989-92; trustee N.C. Ctrl. U., Durham, N.C., 1993-01, vice-chmn., 1993-94, chmn. 1995, chair ednl. planning and acad. affairs com., 1995-98, audit, devel. and personnel coms., 1998-01, chair audit com., 1999-01; mem. Ohio Bd. Regents, Columbus, Ohio, 1987-96, vice-chmn., 1993-95, chmn., 1995-96; trustee Nat. Jud. Coll., Reno, Nevada, 1996-02, fin. and audit com., 1997-02 treas., chair, 1999-02, Columbus Bar Found., 1998-05, fellows com. 1998-05, grants com., 1998-05; AEFC Pension Adminstrn. Com. defined benefit plan of the ABA, Am. Bar Endowment, Am. Bar Found., and Nat. Jud. Coll., Chgo, Ill., 1998-02. With AUS, 1958-64. Fellow: Ohio State Bar Found. (disting. life fellow, Ritter award 2003); mem.: ABA, NC State Bar, Columbus Bar Assn., Ohio Bar Assn., Nat. Bar Assn. Personal E-mail: rkfrasier@msn.com.

FRASSINELLI, GUIDO JOSEPH, retired aerospace engineer; b. Summit Hill, Pa., Dec. 4, 1927; s. Joseph and Maria (Grosso) F.; m. Antoinette Pauline Clemente, Sept. 26, 1953; children: Lisa, Erica, Laura, Joanne, Mark. BS, MS, MIT, 1949; MBA, Harvard U., 1956. Treas. AviDyne Rsch., Inc., Burlington, Mass., 1958—64; asst. gen. mgr. Kaman AviDyne divsn. Kaman Scis., Burlington, 1964—66; asst. dir. strategic planning N. Am. ACFT OPNS, Rockwell Internat., LA, 1966—69; from mgr. program planning to project mgr. advanced programs Rockwell Space Sys. Divsn., Downey, Calif., 1970—94, ret., 1994. CFO GO Aircraft Ltd., 1998—2000. Active Town Hall of Calif., LA, 1970-2006; treas. Ecology Devel. and Implementation Commitment Team Found., Huntington Beach, Calif., 1971-75, Peninsula Srs., 2003—; founding com. St. John Fisher Parish Coun., Rancho Palos Verdes, Calif., 1978-85. Recipient Tech. Utilization award, NASA, 1971, Astronaut Personal Achievement award, 1985. Fellow AIAA (assoc.; tech. com. on econs. 1983-87, exec. com. LA sect. 1987-91, 94-98, 2002—, adv. bd. 1999-2001), Inst. for Advancement of Engring.; mem. Sigma Xi, Tau Beta Pi. Roman Catholic. Achievements include rsch. in determination of aircraft damage limits and atomic-weapon-delivery capabilities of aircraft; development of cost models to account for advances in engineering state of art, of cost prioritization techniques for space shuttle improvements, of software to produce business plans. Home: 29521 Quailwood Dr Rancho Palos Verdes CA 90275

FRATANTONI, JOSEPH CHARLES, medical researcher, biotechnologist, hematologist; b. Bklyn., May 14, 1938; s. Joseph Edward and Providence Adeline (Bellante) F.; m. Pauline F. Jones, Jan. 30, 1965; children: David, Michael, Joan. BS in Chemistry egregia cum laude, Fordham Coll., 1959; MA in Chemistry, Harvard U., 1961; MD, Cornell U., 1965. Diplomate Am. Bd. Internal Medicine. Rsch. assoc. Sloan-Kettering Inst., NYC, 1960-61; fellow dept. pharmacology Cornell U., 1961-64; intern, resident in medicine Cornell-N.Y. Hosp., 1965-67; staff assoc. Nat. Inst. Arthritis and Metabolic Diseases NIH, 1967-69; resident in medicine Cornell-N.Y. Hosp., 1969-70, fellow in hematology dept. medicine, 1970-71; instr. in medicine Cornell U., 1970-71; asst. prof. medicine, dir. Coagulation Lab. Georgetown U., 1971-72, from clin. asst. to assoc. prof. medicine and pharmacology, 1972-85; sr. staff physician hematology svc. Clin. Ctr. NIH, 1972-74; thrombosis program dir. Nat. Heart, Lung and Blood Inst., 1974-75, chief blood diseases br., 1975-77, chief blood resources br., 1977-78; chief lab. of cellular hematology Ctr. for Biologics Evaluation and Rsch., FDA, 1978-92; from assoc. prof. to clin. prof. medicine Uniformed Svcs. U., 1976-96; dir. divsn. hematology FDA, 1992-96; v.p. biologics C.L. McIntosh and Assocs., Rockville, Md., 1996-99; v.p. med. affairs, clin. devel. Max Cyte Inc., Gaithersburg, Md., 1999—. Presenter in field. Patentee in non-invasive optical assessment of platelet viability, measurement of platelet aggregation using a microplate reader; contbr. over 100 articles to profl. jours. Served to capt. USPHS, 1967-96, ret. Recipient Spl. Citation, FDA Commr., 1988, Citation, USPHS, 1989, Meritorious Svc. medal USPHS, 1991. Fellow ACP; mem. Internat. Soc. Cellular Therapy, Am. Soc. Hematology, Am. Assn. Blood Banks (Disting. Svc. award 1998). Achievements include rsch. in hemostasis, platelet function and blood substitutes. Home: 9412 Overlea Dr Rockville MD 20850-3735 Office: MaxCyte Inc 22 Firstfield Rd Ste 250 Gaithersburg MD 20878

FRATE, DANIEL J., bank executive; B in Econs., John Carroll U., Cleve.; M in Fin., Purdue U., West Lafayette, Ind. Various credit, tech. and svc. mgmt. positions Citicorp; pres. payment systems bus., sr. consumer risk officer US Bancorp, vice chmn., mem. oper. com.; pres., COO Bank One Card Svcs., 2001—03; exec. v.p. consumer and small bus. fin. svcs. Nat. City Corp., Cleve., 2003—05, exec. v.p. retail banking, 2005—. Bd.

dirs. Vocat. Guidance Svcs., Consumer Bankers Assn. Mem. bus. adv. coun. John Carroll U. Office: Nat City Corp Nat City Ctr 1900 E Ninth St Cleveland OH 44114-3484 Office Phone: 216-222-2000.*

FRATELLO, MIKE (MICHAEL ROBERT FRATELLO), former professional basketball coach; b. Hackensack, NJ, Feb. 24, 1947; Student, Montclair State Coll., U. R.I. Asst. coach U. R.I., Kingston, 1971, James Madison U., Harrisburg, Va., 1972-75, Villanova U., Phila., 1976-78, Atlanta Hawks, 1978-82, NY Knicks, 1982-83; head coach Atlanta Hawks, 1983-90, Cleve. Cavaliers, 1993—99, Memphis Grizzlies, 2004—06; NBA color anaylst NBC Sports, 1990-93; analyst TNT, 2000—04. Named NBA Coach of Yr., 1986.*

FRATER, ROBERT WILLIAM MAYO, surgeon, educator; b. Cape Town, South Africa, Nov. 12, 1928; came to U.S., 1964, naturalized, 1974; s. Kenneth and Ethel (Barrow) F.; m. Elaine Glynn Nagle, Aug. 27, 1954; children: Hugh R., Dirk A., Phillipa. M.B., B.Chir. (Jagger Scholar, Medalist, Anatomy, Surgery, Pathology), U. Cape Town Med. Sch., 1952; MS in Surgery (Minn. Heart Assn. fellow), U. Minn., 1961. Intern medicine and surgery Groote Schuur Hosp., Cape Town, 1953; resident casualty officer Lewisham Hosp., London, 1955; fellow in gen. and thoracic surgery Mayo Clinic, Rochester, Minn., 1955-61; sr. lectr. cardiothoracic surgery U. Cape Town, 1962-64; asst. prof. surgery Albert Einstein Coll. Medicine, NYC, 1964-68, assoc. prof., 1968-72, prof. surgery, 1972—, chief cardiothoracic surgery, 1968—, acting chmn. dept. surgery, 1971-75; mem. Albert Einstein Coll. Medicine (Senate Council), 1971-74; chief cardiothoracic surgery Montefiore Hosp. and Med. Center, 1975-92; mem. staff, exec. council Bronx Mcpl. Hosp. Center, Albert Einstein Coll. Hosp., 1969—; mem. staff Lawrence Hosp., Bronxville, NY; pres. Glycar, Inc., Bronxville. Mem. organizing and sci. coms. Internat. Symposium on Cardiac Bioprosthesis, 1982, 95, 88, 91, 94, honored guest, 1985; pres. Glycar Inc.; med. dir. St. Jude Med. Inc., 2000—. Editor: Jour. Valvular Heart Disease, Replacement Cardiac Valves, New Horizons and the Future of Heart Valve Bioprostheses, 1994; mem. editl. bd. Cardiac Chronicle, Jour. Cardiac Surgery, 1987—. Mem. Concern for Dying Coun., 1982-88. Recipient award Noble Found., 1961, Bronx Coun. of the Arts Humanitarian award, 1989, Disting. Alumnus award Mayo Found, 2001; grantee NIH, 1965-70, 68-70, 74-78, 79-81, 82-84, Am. Heart Assn., 1966, 71. Fellow ACS, Royal Coll. Surgeons, Am. Coll. Cardiology, Am. Heart Assn. (exec. com. coun. on Cardiovasculary Surgery 1979-84, program com. 1979-82); mem. Am. Assn. Thoracic Surgery, Soc. Thoracic Surgeons (postgrad. edn. com. 1978, chmn. postgrad. program 1981), N.Y. Soc. Thoracic Surgery (pres. 1978), N.Y. Surg. Soc. (mem. coun. 1975-80), Thoracic Surgery Dirs. Assn. (exec. coun. 1982-85), Assn. Acad. Surgeons, Soc. Cardiothoracic Surgeon Great Britain and Ireland (hon. guest and mem. 1989), Soc. Heart Valve Disease (founder, chmn. membership com. 2001-, honored guest biennial Vancouver meeting, 2005), Bronxville Field Club (squash capt., bd. govs. 1987-90). Home: 17 Gladwin Pl Bronxville NY 10708-2201 Office: 1575 Blondell Ave Bronx NY 10461-2660 Personal E-mail: rwmfglycar@aol.com. *The good fortune to use both mind and hand in asking questions, finding answers and healing others.*

FRATESCHI, LAWRENCE JAN, economist, statistician, educator; b. Chgo., Oct. 7, 1952; s. Lawrence and Olga (Los) F. BS in Math. and Psychology, U. Ill., Chgo., 1975, MA in Econs., 1979, MS Pub. Health in Biostats. and Epidemiology, 1990, PhD in Econs., 1992. Teaching asst. dept. math, lectr. dept. info. and decision scis. U. Ill., Chgo., 1978-80, rsch. assoc. epidemiology and biostatistics Sch. Pub. Health, 1989-90; statistician Argonne Nat. Labs., Ill., 1980-81; asst. prof. econs. and stats. Coll. of DuPage, Glen Ellyn, Ill., 1981-86, assoc. prof., 1986-90, prof. econs., stats., 1990—; rsch. prof. epidemiology and biostats. Sch. Pub. Health U. Ill., Chgo., 1993—. Contbr. articles to profl. publs. Mem. Am. Econ. Assn., Am. Statis. Assn., Am. Pub. Health Assn., Soc. Epidemiologic Rsch., Midwest Econs. Assn., Ill. Econs. Assn., Ill. Pub. Health Assn., Phi Eta Sigma, Phi Kappa Phi, Delta Omega. Office: Coll of DuPage 425 22nd St Glen Ellyn IL 60137-6784 Business E-Mail: fratesch@cdnet.cod.edu.

FRATTO, TONY (SALVATORE ANTONIO), federal official; b. June 27, 1966; BA, U. Pittsburgh, 1988. V.p. govtl. affairs Pitts. Regional Alliance, Pa.; dir. community. & econ. affairs to Gov. State of Pa.; comm. dir. Senator of Pa.; pub. affairs specialist US Dept. Treasury, Washington, 2001, dir. pub. affairs, press officer for internat. affairs, dep. asst. sec. for pub. affairs, 2003—05, acting asst. sec., 2005, asst. sec., 2005—06; dep. asst. to Pres. & dep. press. sec. The White House, Washington, 2006—. Mem. President's Task Force on Puerto Rico's Status, 2005. Office: The White House 1600 Pennsylvania Ave Washington DC 20502

FRAUEN, KURT HERMAN, lawyer; b. Chgo., Feb. 3, 1925; s. Herman Ernst Martin and Martha (Schranz) F.; m. Marion E. Green, July 20, 1954; children: Rodger, Leith, Keith, Kimberly, Susan, Eric. BS, Northwestern U., 1948; JD, Yale U., 1951. Bar: Wis. 1951, U.S. Dist. Ct. (ea. dist.) Wis. 1951, U.S. Dist. Ct. (we. dist.) Wis. 1955, U.S. Ct. Appeals (7th cir.) 1955, U.S. Supreme Ct. 1982. Assoc. Quarles, Spence & Quarles, Milw., 1951-55; ptnr. Wickham, Borgelt, Skogstad & Powell, Milw., 1955-70; sr. ptnr., shareholder Borgelt, Powell, Peterson & Frauen, Milw., 1970—, pres., 1996—99. Presenter in field. Formerly chmn. bd. North Shore Congl. Ch. Lt. (j.g.) USN, WWII, 1942-46. Fellow Am. Coll. Trial Lawyers (state chmn. 1979-81); mem. ABA, Fedn. Ins. and Corp. Counsel, Internat. Assn. Def. Counsel, Wis. Bar Assn., Civil Trial Counsel Wis. Republican. Office: Borgelt Powell Peterson & Frauen 735 N Water St Ste 1500 Milwaukee WI 53202-4188 Home: 2335 N Mill Rd Oconomowoc WI 53066-5017 Home Phone: 262-646-8674; Office Phone: 414-287-9103. Business E-Mail: k.frauen@borgelt.com.

FRAULINO, PHILIP SAMUEL, telecommunications industry executive; b. Hartford, Conn., Apr. 10, 1952; BA, Upsala Coll., 1974; MA, Seton Hall U., 1977; MLS, CUNY, 1984. Sr. libr. asst. Commn. Blind and Visually Impaired N.J. Dept. Human Svcs., Newark, 1977—80; libr., libr. technician Nat. Oceanic and Atmopheric Adminstrn. U.S. Dept Commerce, Princeton, NJ, 1980—87; tech. info. specialist, telecommunication technician U.S. State Dept., Washington, 1987—. Chmn. Princeton (N.J.) Transp. Com., 1983—87. Recipient Franklin award, U.S. State Dept., 1999, 2000, Extra Mile award, 2001, 2003. Mem.: Am. Soc.Info. Sci. and Tech., Coll. English Assn., Nat. Assn. Rail Passengers. Home: 75 East Wayne Ave Apt 611 Silver Spring MD 20901 Office: US State Dept 2201 C St NW Washington DC 20520 Home Phone: 301-495-5686. E-mail: fraulinops@state.gov.

FRAUMANN, WILLARD GEORGE, lawyer; b. San Francisco, July 21, 1948; m. Anne C. Derleth, Dec. 18, 1971; children: Ellen, Robert, Sarah. AB, U. Mich., 1970; JD, Harvard U., 1973. Bar: Ill.1973 , US Dist. Ct. (no. dist.) Ill. Ptnr. Kirkland & Ellis, Chgo., 1977—. Served to lt. USNR, 1973-77. Mem.: Chgo. Humanities Festival (bd. of dir), U. Mich. Coll. of Lit., Sci. & Arts (vis. com.). Office: Kirkland & Ellis 200 E Randolph Dr Chicago IL 60601-6636 Office Phone: 312-861-2038. Office Fax: 312-861-2000. Business E-Mail: wfraumann@kirkland.com.

FRAUNFELDER, FREDERICK THEODORE, ophthalmologist, educator; b. Pasadena, Calif., Aug. 16, 1934; s. Reinhart and Freida Fraunfelder; m. Yvonne Marie Halliday, June 21, 1959; children— Yvette Marie, Helene, Nina, Frederick, Nicholas. BS, U. Oreg., 1956, MD, 1960, postgrad. (NIH postdoctoral fellow), 1962. Diplomate Am. Bd. Ophthalmology (bd. dirs. 1982-90). Intern U. Chgo., 1961; resident U. Oreg. Med. Sch., 1964-66; NIH postdoctoral fellow Wilmer Eye Inst., Johns Hopkins U., 1967; chmn. dept. ophthalmology U. Ark. Health Scis. Ctr., 78-98, prof., 1978—; prof., chmn. dept. ophthalmology Oreg. Health Scis. U. Dir. Casey Eye Inst., 1992-98, Nat. Registry Drug-Induced Ocular Side Effects, 1976—; vis. prof. ophthalmology Moorfields Eye Hosp., London, 1974. Author: Drug-Induced Ocular Side Effects and Drug Interactions, 1976, 5th edit., 2001, Current Ocular Therapy, 1985, 5th edit., 2001, Recent Advances in Ophthalmology, 8th edit., 1985; assoc. editor: Jour. Toxicology: Cutaneous and Ocular, 1984-2002; mem. editl. bd. Am. Jour. Ophthalmology, 1982-92, Ophthalmic Forum, 1983-90, Ophthalmology, 1984-89; contbr. over 200 articles on ocular toxicology or ocular cancer to med. jours. Served with U.S. Army, 1962-64. FDA grantee, 1976-86; Nat. Eye Inst. grantee, 1970-87; named Best Doc. in Am., 2005 Mem. AMA, ACS, Am. Acad. Ophthaolmology, Assn. Univ. Profs. in Ophthalmology (pres. 1976), Am. Ophthalmol. Soc., Am. Coll. Cryosurgery (pres. 1977), Assn. Research in Ophthalmology. Clubs: Lions, Elks. Home: 13 Cellini Ct Lake Oswego OR 97035-1307 Office: Casey Eye Inst 3375 SW Terwilliger Blvd Portland OR 97239-4197 Home Phone: 503-636-7229; Office Phone: 503-494-5686. Business E-Mail: fraunfel@ohsu.edu.

FRAUTSCHI, STEVEN CLARK, physicist, researcher; b. Madison, Wis., Dec. 6, 1933; s. Lowell Emil and Grace (Clark) F.; m. Mie Okamura, Feb. 16, 1967; children: Laura, Jennifer. BA, Harvard U., 1954; PhD, Stanford U., 1958. Rsch. fellow Kyoto (Japan) U., 1958-59, U. Calif.-Berkeley, 1959-61; mem. faculty Cornell U., 1961-62, Calif. Inst. Tech., Pasadena, 1962—, prof. theoretical physics, 1966—2006, exec. officer physics, 1988-97, master student houses, 1997—2002, prof. emeritus, 2006—. Vis. prof. U. Paris, Orsay, 1977-78, Pohang U. Sci. and Tech., Republic of Korea, 2007. Author: Regge Poles and S-Matrix Theory, 1963, The Mechanical Universe, 1986. Guggenheim fellow, 1971-72. Mem. Am. Phys. Soc. Achievements include research and publications on Regge poles, bootstrap theory, cosmology. Home: 1561 Crest Dr Altadena CA 91001-1838 Office: 1201 E California Blvd Pasadena CA 91125-0001

FRAUTSCHI, TIMOTHY CLARK, lawyer; b. Madison, Wis., Apr. 8, 1937; s. Lowell E. and Grace C. (Clark) F.; m. Pamela H. Hendricks, June 23, 1964; children: Schuyler, Jason; m. Susan B. Brumm, June 13, 1981; 1 child, Jacob. BA, U. Wis., 1959; LL.B., London Sch. Econs., U. Wis., 1963. Bar: Wis. 1963, U.S. Ct. Claims 1976, U.S. Tax Ct., 1976. Assoc. firm Foley & Lardner, Milw., 1963-70, ptnr., 1970—. Editor Wis. Law Rev. Co-founder Milw. Forum; pres. Lakeside Cmty. Coun., Skylight Comic Opera, Ltd., 1980—85, Present Music, Inc., 1991—98, Next Act Theatre, 2001—04, Danceworks, Inc., 2005—; bd. dirs. Am. Players Theater, Milw., Repertory Theater, Northcott Neighborhood House, United performing Arts Fund, Inc., Milw., Children's Svc. Soc., Wis. Theatre Tesseract; pres. Next Act Theatre, 1986—89, Watertower Landmark Trust, 1986—89; v.p. Frank Lloyd Wright Wis. Conservancy, 2001—; bd. dirs. St. Mary's Milw. Hosp. Found., pres., 2003—. Mem. Milw. Jr. Bar Assn. (pres. 1969-70), Milw. Bar Assn. (dir. 1971-74), Order of Coif, Phi Beta Kappa (pres. Milw. chpt. 1968-70), Phi Kappa Phi, Phi Eta Sigma Office: Foley & Lardner US Bank Ctr 777 E Wisconsin Ave Ste 3800 Milwaukee WI 53202-5367 Home Phone: 414-221-9688; Office Phone: 414-297-5737. Business E-Mail: tfrautschi@foley.com.

FRAUTSCHI, W. JEROME (JERRY FRAUTSCHI), foundation administrator, retired manufacturing executive; m. Pleasant Rowland. Former vice chmn. Webcrafters. Founder, chmn. Overture Found., 1997—. Named one of 50 Most Generous Philanthropists, BusinessWeek, 2005. Office: Overture Found 1 S Pinckney St, Ste 816 Madison WI 53703-2869

FRAYN, MICHAEL, playwright; b. London, Sept. 8, 1933; s. Thomas Allen and Violet Alice (Lawson) Frayn; m. Gillian Palmer, Feb. 18, 1960 (div. 1989); 3 children; m. Claire Tomalin, June 1993. BA, Emmanuel Coll., Cambridge U., Eng., 1957; DLitt (hon.), Cambridge U., Eng., 2001. Gen. reporter Guardian, Manchester, Eng., 1957-59, columnist, 1959-62, Observer, London, 1962-68; contbr. weekly comedy series Beyond A Joke BBC, 1972. Author: (novels) The Tin Men, 1965 (Somerset Maugham award, 1966), The Russian Interpreter, 1966 (Hawthornden prize, 1967), Towards the End of the Morning (also published as Against Entropy), 1967, A Very Private Life, 1968, Sweet Dreams, 1973, The Trick of It, 1989, A Landing on the Sun, 1991 (Book of Yr., Sunday Express), Now You Know, 1993, Headlong, 1999, Spies, 2002 (Whitbread Novel award, 2002, Commonwealth Writers prize, 2003); author: (with David Burke) Celia's Secret: An Investigation, 2000; author: (plays) The Two of Us: Four One-Act Plays for Two Players, 1970, The Sandboy, 1971, Alphabetical Order, 1975 (Evening Std. Best Comedy of Yr. award, 1975), Donkeys' Years, 1976 (Soc. West End Best Comedy of Yr. award, 1976, Laurence Olivier award best comedy, 1976), Clouds, 1976, Liberty Hall, 1977, Make or Break, 1980 (Evening Std. award best comedy of yr., 1980), Balmoral, 1988, Look, Look, 1990, Jamie on a Flying Visit and Birthday, 1990, Listen to This: Twenty One Short Plays and Sketches, 1991, Here, 1993, Now You Know, 1995, (pub. TV play) Alarms and Excursions: More Plays Than One, 1998, (Broadway plays) Noises Off, 1983 (Evening Standard Best Comedy of Yr. award, 1982, Soc. West End Theatres Best Comedy of Yr. award, 1982), 2001, Benefactors, 1985 (Evening Standard Best Comedy of Yr. award, 1984, Soc. West End Theatres Best Comedy of Yr. award, 1984, Tony award nom. best play, 1984, Lawrence Olivier Best Play award, 1984, Plays and Players Best New Play award, 1986, NY Drama Critics' Cir. award best play, 1986, BBC award best new play, 1984), Wild Honey, 1986, Copenhagen, 2000 (Evening Std. award best play of yr., 1998, Critics' Cir. award best new play, 1998, Tony award best play, 2000), Democracy, 2004 (Evening Std. award best play), (opera libretto) La Belle Vivette, 1995, (documentary films, teleplays) One Pair of Eyes, 1968, Birthday, 1969, Lawrence Sterne Lived Here, 1973, Making Faces, 1975, Imagine a City Called Berlin, 1975, Vienna: The Mask of Gold, 1977, Three Streets in the Country, 1979, The Long Straight, 1980, Great Railway Journeys of the World, 1981, Jerusalem, 1984, Magic Lantern: Prague, 1993, (TV documentary) Budapest: Written in Water, 1996, (screenplays) Clockwise, 1986, First and Last, 1989 (Emmy award), Remember Me?, 1997; translator: (plays) The Cherry Orchard by Anton Chekhov, 1978, The Fruits of Enlightenment by Leo Tolstoy, 1979, Three Sisters by Anton Chekhov, 1983, Wild Honey by Anton Chekhov, 1984, The Seagull by Anton Chekhov, 1986, Uncle Vanya by Anton Chekhov, 1987, The Sneeze by Anton Chekhov, 1988, Exchange by Yuri Trifonov, 1990; author: The Day of the Dog (articles reprinted from The Guardian), 1962, The Book of the Fub (articles reprinted from The Guardian), 1963, On the Outskirts (articles reprinted from The Observer), 1964, A Bay At Gear Street, 1967, Constructions, 1974, The Original Michael Frayn: Satirical Essays, 1983, After the Beep: Studies in the Art of Communicating with Inanimate and Semi-animate Objects, 1995, The Human Touch, 2007; editor: The Best of Beachcomber by John Bingham Morton, 1963; editor: (with Bamber Gascoigne) Timothy: The Drawings and Cartoons of Timothy Birdsall, 1964. Russian interpreter Brit. Army, 1952—54. Recipient Nat. Press Club Disting. Reporting award, Internat. Pub. Corp., 1970, Heywood Hill Lit. Prize, 2002, Golden PEN award, 2003, St. Louis Literary award, 2007, McGovern award, 2007; hon. fellow, Emmanuel Coll., Cambridge U. Mem.: Companion of Lit., Am. Acad. Arts and Scis. (fgn.), Royal Soc. Lit. Office: Greene & Heaton 37 Goldhawk Rd London W12 8QQ England

FRAZEN, MITCHELL HALE, lawyer; b. Great Lakes, Ill., Sept. 19, 1955; s. Sidney Joseph and Norma Ileane (Solomon) F.; m. Mary Elizabeth Huelsbusch, Sept. 14, 1974; children: Daniel Joseph, Christina Elizabeth. BA, U. Ill., 1977; JD, U. Mich., 1980. Bar: Ill. 1980, U.S. Dist. Ct. (no. dist.) Ill. 1980, U.S. Ct. Appeals (7th cir.) 1987, U.S. Dist. Ct. (ea. dist.) Wis. 1994, U.S. Ct. Appeals (8th cir.) 1995, U.S. Dist. Ct. (ea. dist.) Mich. 1995. Assoc. Phelan, Pope & John, Ltd., Chgo., 1980-87; shareholder Burditt & Radzius, Chartered, Chgo., 1987-98, dir., 1989-98; ptnr. Litchfield Cavo LLP, Chgo., 1998—. Arbitrator, chairperson mandatory ct.-annexed arbitration program Cook County Cir. Ct., Chgo., 1990-2004, mediator vol. mediation program, 1992—. Chair State Ct. Practices Com., 1995—; bd. dirs. Chgo. Coun. Lawyers, 1992—95. Mem.: ABA, Chgo. Bar Assn., Phi Beta Kappa, Order of Coif. Democrat. Lutheran. Home: 617 W Ruhl Rd Palatine IL 60074 Office: Litchfield Cavo LLP Ste 300 303 W Madison St Chicago IL 60606-3309 Office Phone: 312-781-6618. E-mail: frazen@litchfieldcavo.com.

FRAZER, JENDAYI ELIZABETH, federal agency administrator, former ambassador; BA political sci., Stanford U., MA internat. policy/internat. devel., PhD political sci. Fellow Coun. Foreign Relations Internat. Affairs, 1998-99; asst. prof. pub. policy, John F. Kennedy Sch. Govt. Harvard U., 1999—2001; spl. asst. to the Pres. & sr. dir. for African affairs NSC, Washington, 2001—04; US amb to South Africa US Dept. State, Pretoria, 2004—05, asst. sec. for African Affairs Washington, 2005—. Vis. fellow Ctr. Internat. Security and Arms Control, Stanford U.; rsch. assoc. Inst. Devel. Studies, U. Nairobi, Kenya; bd. dirs. African Devel. Found., 2005- Mem. Women in Internat. Soc. (exec. bd. 1998—). Office: US Dept State 2201 C St NW Rm 6234A Washington DC 20520

FRAZER, JOHN HOWARD, tennis association and retired manufacturing executive; b. Cin., June 3, 1924; s. H. Howard and Amelia (Spieth) F.; m. Joann Elizabeth McEvoy, Nov. 3, 1956; children: John Howard Jr., Victoria F. Fuller. BA, U. Cin., 1948, JD, 1950. Bar: Ohio 1950. V.p. H. Howard Frazer Co., Cin., 1950-62, pres., 1962-76; treas., dir. Cin. Transit Co., 1957-73; dir. Am. Controlled Industries, Cin., 1973-86, pres., 1974-75, exec. v.p., 1975-86; dir. Vulcan Corp., Cin., 1960-91, pres., 1975-88; sec., dir. Valley Industries, 1973-86, Colorpac, Inc., 1973-86. Chmn. U.S. Open Tennis Championships, 1993-94. Chmn. men's com. Cin. Symphony Orch., 1971-73; pres. Cincinnatus Assn., 1969-70; chmn. Western Tennis Championships, Cin., 1970-73; dir. Internat. Tennis Hall of Fame, 1979-2002, hon. dir., 2002—, exec. com. 1985-2002, chmn. internat. coun. 1996—. Served with USAAF, 1942-45. Named to, USTA/Midwest Tennis Hall of Fame, 2001, Greater Cin. Tennis Hall Fame, 2004; recipient Highest Effort award, Sigma Alpha Epsilon, 1995, Chmn.'s award, Internat. Tennis Hall of Fame, 2000, Golden Achievement award, 2003. Mem. USTA (mem. exec. com. 1975—, chmn. sanction and schedule com. 1973-86, bd. dirs. 1986-96, v.p. 1986-88, sec. 1988-90, 1st v.p. 1990-92, pres. 1993-94, chmn. nat. men's ranking com. 1971-73, long-range planning com. 1981-87, internat. com. 1999—, hon. chair 2003—), Internat. Tennis Fedn. (del. 1991-96, mem. com. mgmt. 1993-97, v.p. 1995-97, hon. life counsellor 1997—, mem. vets. com. 1996-99, chmn. vets. com. 1996-97, mem. constl. com. 1997-2003, mem. rewards and recognition com. 2000-, Svc. to Game award 1998), Lawn Tennis Clubs USA, France, Mex., Am. Footwear Industries Assn. (dir.), Rubber Mfrs. Assn. (dir.), Shoe Last Mfrs. Assn. (pres. 1978-79), Univ. Club, Cin. CC, Cin. Tennis Club, Quail Creek CC (Naples), Bay Colony Club (Naples), All-Eng. Lawn Tennis Club (Wimbledon), Royal Poinciana Golf Club (Naples). Home: 8171 Bay Colony Dr Apt 1701 Naples FL 34108-7566 Personal E-mail: joandbumpyfrazer@att.net.

FRAZER, ROBERT LEE, retired landscape architect; BS in Landscape Architecture, Tex. A&M U., 1948; MS in Agriculture, East Tex. State U., 1951. Registered landscape architect, Tex. Landscape architect, instr. vocat. horticulture San Antonio Sch. Dist., 1948-49; landscape architect, instr., head campus maintenance East Tex. State U., Commerce, 1949-54; dir. parks and recreation City of San Antonio, 1955-73; univ. landscape architect, prof. landscape architecture Tex. Tech. U., Lubbock, 1973-74; v.p., prin., dir. landscape architecture Groves Fernandez Frazer & Assocs., Inc., San Antonio, 1974-83, Fernandez Frazer White & Assocs., Inc., San Antonio, 1984-92, v.p. emeritus, 1992—. Adj. prof. U. Tex., Arlington, 1993. Contbr. articles to profl. jours. Recipient Robert H. Hugman award for devel. San Antonio River Walk, 1987, Disting. Svc. award San Antonio Conservation Soc., 1973. Fellow Am. Soc. Landscape Architects (Terry Hershey award for Excellence in Field of Recreation Parks or Tourism), Am. Inst. Park Execs., Am. Acad. for Park and Recreation Adminstrn., Tex. Recreation and Park Soc.; mem. S.W. Park and Recreation Tng. Inst. (past pres., co-organizer), Tex. Mcpl. Park and Recreation Assn. (past pres., organizer), Tex. Turfgrass Assn. (past pres., co-organizer), Nat. River Parks and Waterfront Assn. (past bd. dirs.), Nat. Recreation Assn. (past mem. nat. adv. com.). Office: Fernandez Frazer White & Assoc 11824 Radium St San Antonio TX 78216-2711 Personal E-mail: ffw@ffwinc.com.

FRAZER, VINCENT F., attorney general; b. St. Thomas, VI; m. Anne McLeish; 4 children. BA, Carthage Coll., 1980; JD, Howard U., 1984. Paralegal criminal divsn. VI Dept. Law, 1980—81; staff atty. VI Port Authority, 1984—88; pvt. practice, 1988—93; ptnr. Frazer & Williams, 1993—, mng. ptnr., 1993—2005; atty. gen. VI, 2007—. Mem. VI Pub. Defenders Adminstrn. Bd., 1999—. Sch. bd. mem. St. Thomas Calvary Christian Acad. Mem.: ABA, VI Com. Bar Examiners, Nat. Assn. Criminal Defense Lawyers, Am. Trial Lawyers Assn., VI Bar Assn. (bd. govs. 1988—89), Alpha Phi Alpha. Democrat. Office: Dept Justice GERS Complex 488-50C Kronprinsdens Gade St Thomas VI 00802 Office Phone: 340-774-5666.*

FRAZIER, A. D., JR., information technology executive, lawyer; b. Rocky Mountain, NC, June 23, 1944; s. Adolphus Drewry and Pauline (Smith) F.; m. Jeanne Reinhardt, June 10, 1966 (div. 2001); children: Jim, Carrie. AB, Univ. N.C., 1965, JD, 1968; postgrad., Harvard Bus. Sch., 1981. Bar: Ga., N.C. Mgmt. assoc., retail and corp. staff C & S Bank, Atlanta, 1969-76, dir. corp. planning, 1978-81; mgr. reorgn. of White House Exec. Office of Pres., Washington, 1976-77; sr. v.p., head corp. planning 1st Nat. Bank Chgo., 1982, head human resources, 1984, head corp. resources, 1985, exec. v.p., head N.Am. banking, 1986-91; sr. exec. v.p., COO Atlanta Com. for Olympic Games, 1991—96; exec. v.p. Invesco, 1996—97, pres., CEO, 1997—2000; chmn., CEO Chgo. Stock Exchange, 2001—02; pres., COO Caremark Rx, 2002—04; of counsel Balch & Bingham LLP, Atlanta, 2005—06; pres., CEO Danka Bus. Systems PLC, St. Petersburg, Fla., 2006—. Disting. vis. prof Bus. Young Harris Coll. Bd. dirs. Metro Atlanta C. of C. 1991-2004; Sta. WTTW-TV, Chgo., 1987-91, Neighborhood Housing Svcs., Chgo., 1983-91, Lyric Opera, Mus. Sci. and Industry, 1990-91; chmn. bd. Atlanta Symphony Orch., 1992; mem. Nat. Coun. on Humanities, 1979-81; bd. dirs., chmn. fin. com. Evanston (Ill.) Hosp., Corp., 1986-91; 1st pres. Atlanta Neighborhood Housing Svcs; chair Econ. Devel. Task Force for Maynard Jackson and Marvin Arrington; head mktg. com. Atlanta chpt. United Way, 1976; 1st chmn. Gov. Busbee's Telecommunications Commn., 1981; managed inauguration of Pres. Carter, 1976-77; headed team to reorganize White House, Exec. Office, for Pres. Carter; mem. bd. adv. Carter Ctr.; Officer USAR, 1969-73. Named one of Atlanta's Five Outstanding Young Men by Jaycees, 1976. Mem. Am. Bankers Assn., Assn. Res. City Bankers, Econ. Club Chgo., Northwestern U. Assn, ABA, N.C. Bar Assn., Atlanta Bar Assn., State Bar Ga. Democrat. Episcopalian. Office: Danka Bus Systems 11101 Roosevelt Blvd N Saint Petersburg FL 33716

FRAZIER, AMY, professional tennis player; b. St. Louis, Mo., Sept. 19, 1972; Prof. tennis player WTA Tour, 1990—. Mem. 1995 U.S. Fed. Cup Team. Named World Team Tennis MVP, 1995. Achievements include winner 7 career Singles Titles and 5 career Doubles Titles, WTA Tour; appeared in 18 consecutive U.S. Open Tournaments. Avocations: ceramics, painting, bicycling. Office: USTA 70 W Red Oak Ln White Plains NY 10604-3602

FRAZIER, BRETT W., waste management executive; V.p. Browning-Ferris Industries; with Waste Mgmt., Inc., 2000—, market area gen. mgr.

Houston Metro Area, v.p. bus. improvement processes, v.p. collections ops. support, sr. v.p. Ea. Group, 2007—. Office: Waste Mgmt Inc 448 Lincoln Hwy Fairless Hills PA 19030*

FRAZIER, CHAPMAN HOOD, literature and language professor; b. Clarksburg, W.Va., Sept. 30, 1951; s. Walter Chapman and Elizabeth Esker Frazier; m. Deborah F. Carrington, Dec. 21, 1973; children: Dylan Carrington, Caitlin Campbell. BA in English, W.Va. U., Morgantown, 1973, MA in English, 1976; MS in Reading, Longwood U., Farmville, Va., 1983; PhD in English Edn., U. Va., Charlottesville, 1994. Assoc. prof. English Southside Va. C.C., Keysville; lead tchr. English Murray H.S., Charlottesville, Va.; asst. prof. English U. Maine, Presque Isle; prof. English edn. Longwood U.; prof. middle and secondary edn. James Madison U., Harrisonburg, Va. Chair Waldort Sch. Editor: Dos Passo Rev.; guest editor: Hampden Sydney Poetry Rev. Mem.: Va. Assn. Diversity Edn., Va. Assn. Tchrs. English (pres. 2006). Office: Meml Hall James Madison Univ Harrisonburg VA Business E-Mail: fraziech@jmu.edu.

FRAZIER, CHARLES ROBINSON, writer; b. Asheville, NC, Nov. 4, 1950; s. Charles O. and Betty Frazier; m. Katherine Frazier, 1976; 1 child, Annie. BA, U. N.C., 1973; student, Appalachian State U.; PhD, U. S.C., 1986. Author: Cold Mountain, 1997 (Nat. Book award Nat. Book Found., 1997), Thirteen Moons, 2006; co-author: Adventuring in the Andes: The Sierra Club Guide to Peru, Bolivia, the Amazon Basin, and the Galapagos, 1985. Office: Amanda Urban Internat Creative Management Inc 40 West 57th St New York NY 10019

FRAZIER, CHARLES T., JR., lawyer; b. Covington, Ky., July 10, 1960; BA magna cum laude, Baylor U., Waco, Tex., 1982; MA, U. Kent, Canterbury, Eng., 1985; JD, Baylor U., 1986. Bar: Tex. 1986, US Dist. Ct. (no., ea. and we. dists. Tex.) 1986, US Ct. Appeals (5th cir.) 1992, US Supreme Ct. 1993. Shareholder Cowles & Thompson, P.C., Dallas. Named a Tex. Super Lawyer, Tex. Monthly and Law & Politics Mag., 2005; named one of Best Lawyers in Dallas, D Mag., 2005. Mem.: Patrick E. Higginbotham Am. Inn Ct. (barrister), State Bar Tex., Dallas Bar Assn., Tex. Assn. Def. Counsel, 5th Cir. Bar Assn., Def. Rsch. Inst. Office: Cowles & Thompson PC 901 Main St Ste 4000 Dallas TX 75202-3793 Office Phone: 214-672-2124. Office Fax: 214-672-2324. E-mail: cfrazier@cowlesthompson.com.*

FRAZIER, DOUGLAS BYRON, healthcare manufacturing manager; b. Danville, Va., Jan. 18, 1957; s. Calvin Luther and Frances Ann (Benbow) F.; m. Linda Camille Kane, Apr. 25, 1981; 1 child, John Byron. BS in Fin. with honors, U. Fla., 1979. Ops. analyst Whittaker Gen. Med., Miami, Fla., 1980, div. mgr., 1980-85; health care cons. Abbott Labs., Abbott Park, Ill., 1985-86, sr. health care cons., 1986-92; dir. cons. svcs. Abbott Labs, Abbott Park, Ill., 1992-93, dir. cons. and supply channel svcs., 1993-2000, dir., cons. supply channel and e-commerce svcs., 2000—03, dir. global product protection, 2004—. Mem. Chgo. Coun. Fgn. Rels., Citizens Against Govt. Waste, Abbott Labs. Better Govt. Fund. Republican. Avocations: golf, tennis. Office: Abbott Labs Bldg Apt 6B Abbott Park IL 60064

FRAZIER, ELIZABETH ANN, pediatric cardiologist; b. Pine Bluff, Ark., Dec. 16, 1954; Grad., Hendrix Coll., Conway, Ark., 1977; MD, U. Ark. Sch. Med. Sciences, 1981. Cert. Pediatrics, Pediatric Cardiology. Intern, pediatrics Ark. Children's Hosp./U. Ark. Med. Sciences, Little Rock, 1981—82, resident, pediatric, 1982—84, chief resident, pediatrics, 1984—85, head, cardiac transplantation program; fellow, pediatrics cardiology UCLA, 1985—87; assoc. prof. U. Ark. Med. Sciences, prof. Contbr. articles to profl. jours. Named one of Best Teacher of the Household Ark. Children's Hosp., 1985; recipient Heart Ball Quilt, Am. Heart Assn., 2005. Mem.: Alpha Chi Honor Soc. Office: Ark Childrens Hosp 800 Marshall Ave Little Rock AR 72202 Address: 1500 Dodson Ave Fort Smith AR 72901 Office Phone: 501-364-1479. Office Fax: 501-364-3667.*

FRAZIER, ELOISE M., minister; b. Gloversville, NY, Aug. 19, 1934; d. George T. and Sally M. Thompson; m. Robert G. Frazier, Oct. 19, 1963; children: Willie, Kevin, Charles, Denise. Lic. LPN, Bd. Certified Diploma, 1967. Dir. Christian edn. Mt. Olive Bapt. Ch., Schenectady, NY, 1988—2005; coord. payne satellite Payne Theol. Seminary, Albany, NY, 2000—05. Pres. Internat. Ministers Conf., Albany, NY, 1997—2000; coord. N.Y. Satellite Payne Seminary, ALbany, NY, 2000—05. Pres. Zonta Internat. Women's Club, Schenectady, NY, 1999—2001; chair and commr. Schenectady County Human Rights Commn., Schenectady. Recipient Woman of Achievment award, Young Women C Assn., Svc. award, Schenectady Family Health Ctr., 1996, cmty svc. award, Interfaith Cmty., 2001. Mem.: Dr. Martin L. King Commn. (chair 1995—2005), Internal. Min. (pres. 1997—2000).

FRAZIER, HENRY BOWEN, III, retired federal agency administrator; b. Bluefield, W.Va., Aug. 9, 1934; s. Henry Bowen and Margaret Beale (West) F.; m. Joan McIntosh, Dec. 30, 1959. BA with honors, U. Va., 1956; JD with honors, George Washington U., 1967; LLM in Labor Law, Georgetown U., 1969, MLT, 1985. Bar: Va. 1967, D.C. 1980, U.S. Supreme Ct. Pers. adminstr. Army Dept. Washington, 1959-63, spl. projects officer, 1963-67; dep. for civilian pers. policy and civil rights Office Sec. Army, 1967-70; chief program divsn. Fed. Labor Rels. Coun., Exec. Office Pres., 1970-71, dep. exec. dir., 1971-72, exec. dir., 1973-78; mem. Fed. Labor Rels. Authority, Washington, 1979-87, acting chmn., 1984-85; adminstrv. law judge EPA, Washington, 1987-89, chief adminstrv. law judge, 1990-94. Chmn. Employee Relations Commn., U.S. Fgn. Service, 1979-81; acting chmn. Fgn. Service Labor Relations Bd., 1984-85 With USAF, 1961-62. Mem. SAR, Fed. Adminstrv. Law Judges Conf., Jefferson Soc., U. Va. Alumni Assn. (bd. mgrs. 1980-87, nat. v.p. 1984-85, nat. pres. 1985-86), Va. Student Aid Found. (trustee 1990-97, v.p. 1995, pres. 1996), U. Va. Athletic Adv. Coun., Raven Soc. (Raven award 1996), Order of Coif, Colonnade Club (bd. govs. 1997-2000), Glenmore Country Club, Duck Woods Country Club, First Flight Soc. (bd. dirs. 2002-05, treas. 2003-05), Phi Beta Kappa, Omicron Delta Kappa, Phi Kappa Psi

FRAZIER, JO FRANCES, religious organization administrator, writer; b. Tulsa, Dec. 20, 1928; d. Joseph and Eva Mae Fulcher; m. Chester Jerome Frazier, July 19, 1950; children: David, Linda Frazier Parizo, Susan Frazier Kelly. Student, Duke U., 1946—49; BA, Tulsa U., 1950. Publicity chmn. Ventura (Calif.) County Mental Health Adv. Bd., 1978—81; adv. bd. mem. Charter Hosp. Bd. Trustees, Bakersfield, Calif., 1983—85, Desert Counseling Ctr., Bakersfield, 1983—85; founder, dir. Saints Alive Ministry, Bakersfield, 1995—. Lectr./spkr. in field. Prodr.: (films) Any One of Us, 1980, (video) Saints Alive Ministry, 1999; author: Second Chance, 1987, Saints for Today's Youth Book 1, Saint Therese of the Child Jesus, 1991, Book 2, Saints Joan of Arc and Francis of Assisi, 1995, Book 3, Saint Martin de Porres and Blessed Kareti Tekakwitha, 1999. Mem.: Audobon Soc., Nature Conservancy, World Wildlife Fund, Italian Cath. Fedn. (sec. 1984—86). Avocations: swimming, reading. Home: Carriage House Estates 8200 Westwold Dr #402 Bakersfield CA 93311

FRAZIER, JUNE MARIE, retired public relations executive; d. Elmer Charles Rowland and Theckla Eva Rockstroh; m. James Lawrence Frazier, Feb. 3, 1946; children: Wayne R., Larrilee, Scott E. BA, Ind. U., 1942; MA, Ball State U., 1975. Sec., clerk dept. pers. Bendix Aviation Corp., South Bend, Ind., 1938—42, pers. interviewer, asst. editor house publ., 1942—45, editor-in-chief, 1945—46; sec. dept. journalism Ind. U., Bloomington, 1946; tchr. h.s. Marshall County Schs., La Paz, Ind., 1946—48; mem. exec. staff Wapehani Girl Scout Coun., Daleville, Ind., 1961—85; staff writer Fairfield Glade Bull., Crossville (Tenn.) Chronicle, 1986; project dir. Battered Women, Inc., Crossville, 1987—92. Founder, first pres. Habitat for Humanity, Cumberland County, 1996, pub. rels., nominating chair, 1996—; pub. chair Am. Cancer Soc., Crossville, 1994—2006, amb. on the hill, 2002; past lay leader Fairfield Glade UM Ch.; servant ministry Fairfield Glade UN Ch., mem. chancel choir, mem. Westminster chimes. Recipient Women of Achievement award, Bus. and Profl. Women, Cumberland County, 1996, Humanitarian award, 1999, Vol. of Yr. award, Sr. Ctr., Cumberland County, 2004. Mem.: Fairfield Glade Ladies Club (svc. com. 2003—). Avocation: golf. Home: 161 Brokenwood Ln Fairfield Glade Crossville TN 38558

FRAZIER, KENNETH C., pharmaceutical executive, lawyer; b. Phila., Dec. 17, 1954; m. Andrea Frazier; 2 children. BA in Polit. Sci., Pa. State U., 1975; JD, Harvard U., 1978. Bar: Pa. 1978, U.S. Dist. Ct. (ea. dist.) Pa. 1978, U.S. Supreme Ct. 2002. Ptnr. dept. litigation Drinker Biddle & Reath, 1978—92; v.p., gen. counsel, sec. Astra Merck, 1992—94; v.p. pub. affairs Merck & Co., Inc., 1994—96, v.p. pub. affairs, asst. gen. counsel, 1997—98, v.p., dep. gen. counsel, 1999, sr. v.p., gen. counsel Whitehouse Sta., NJ, 1999—2006, exec. v.p., gen. counsel, 2006—07, exec. v.p., pres. global human health, 2007—. Bd. dirs. Cornerstone Christian Acad., Legal Svcs. N.J.; chmn. Ethics Resource Ctr.; mem. adv. bd. Law and Econ. Ctr., U. Pa.; mem. adv. bd. Health Law and Policy Ctr., Seton Hall U.; mem. adv. bd. Rand Inst. for Civil Justice, CorporateProBono.Org; mem. Corp. Exec. Bd.'s Gen. Counsel Roundtable; mem. CLO Roundtable-U.S., Coun. on Fgn. Rels. Named to Am. Law Inst. Coun., 2003. Mem.: ABA, Am. Law Inst., Pa. Bar Assn. Office: Merck and Co Inc One Merck Dr Whitehouse Station NJ 08889-0100 Office Phone: 908-423-1000.*

FRAZIER, KENNETH L., university librarian; BA in Philosophy, U. Kans.; MSLS, U. Denver. With libr. staff U. Wis., Madison, 1978—, dir. gen. Libr. System, 1992—. Mem. Madison Literary Soc.; bd. mem. and past pres. Old Market Place Neighborhood Assoc., Madison, Wis. Mem.: Scholarly Pub. and Academic Resources Coalition (founding mem.), Assn. Rsch. Libr. (bd. dir., past pres.). Office: Univ Wisconsin Library Rm 372F 728 State St Madison WI 53706 Office Phone: 608-262-2600. E-mail: kfrazier@library.wisc.edu.*

FRAZIER, LEROY See DYYON, MARIO

FRAZIER, MARIE DUNN, speech professional, public relations executive, personnel director; b. Milton, Mass., Oct. 26, 1932; d. Lawrence Daniel and Margaret Ethel (Henry) D.; m. M. Timothy Sullivan, Apr. 17, 1960 (div. 1974); 1 child, M. Timothy Dunn Sullivan; m. John Robinson Frazier, Aug. 28, 1975. BA, Emerson Coll., 1954, MA, 1958. Cert. tchr., Mass. Mng. theater dir. Peabody Playhouse, Boston, 1955-60; dir. alumni rels. Emerson Coll., Boston, 1971-73; dir. activities, personal devel. faculty Katharine Gibbs, Boston, 1974-78; dir. rsch. and devel. Aquinas Coll., Milton, Mass., 1981-82; dir. cmty. rels. Bryman Sch., Brookline, Mass., 1981-84; resource developer Quincy (Mass.) Cmty. Action, 1987-89; adjunct faculty, lead program Eastern Nazarene Coll., Quincy, Mass., 1993-98. Adv. bd. Ctr. Lifelong Learning, Curry Coll., Milton, 1977; tng. in speech comm. for Digital Corp., Am. Sci. and Engring. Co., Gen. Time and Security Corp., Children's Hosp., Milton Savs. Bank; mem. speech comm. faculty Garland Jr. Coll., Boston, 1967-70, Aquinas Coll., Newton, Mass., 1991. Developed (seminar) Reflections on Tea, 1993. Bd. dirs. ACCLAIM Arts Group, Milton, 1989, D.W. Dunn Co., Jamaica Plain, Mass., 1962-65, Milton Hist. Soc., 1990-92, Coastline Coun. for Children, 1987; mem. bd. Mayor's Commn. for Women, Quincy, 1988-2003; ambassador South Shore C. of C., Quincy, 1990—. Mem. AAUP, Zeta Phi Eta. Home: 25 Whitelawn Ave Milton MA 02186-3514

FRAZIER, WALTER RONALD, real estate investment company executive; b. Mar. 3, 1939; s. Walter and Gracie Neydene (Bowers) F.; m. Bertina Jan Simpson, May 10, 1963; children: Ronald Blake, Stephen Bertram. BSCE, Tex. A&M U., 1962, BS in Archtl. Constrn., 1962. Tech. dir. Marble Inst., Washington, 1965-68; dir. mktg. Yeonas Co., Vienna, Va., 1969-72; pres. McCarthy Co., Anaheim, Calif., 1972-76; chmn. Equity Programs Investment Corp., Falls Church, Va., 1980-85; pres., dir. Cmty. Constrn. Co., Falls Church, 1982-85; pres. Palestrina Corp., Falls Church, 1987-99; prin. The Williamson Group, 1999—. Bd. dirs. Annandale Jaycees, 1967-69, Annandale Nat. Little League, 1983-85. 1st lt. U.S. Army, 1963-65. Named as one of Outstanding Young Men of Am., U.S. Jaycees, 1973. Mem. Nat. Assn. Home Builders (bd. dirs. 1991-96), No. Va. Bldg. Industry Assn. (1st v.p., bd. dirs. 1991-95, pres. 1994), Prince William County C. of C. (pres. bd. dirs. 1989-92). Republican. Methodist. Avocations: golf, boating. Home: 4203 Elizabeth Ln Annandale VA 22003-3668 Office: Williamson Group 1313 Dolley Madison Blvd Ste 404 Mc Lean VA 22101 Personal E-mail: ron.frazier@cox.net. E-mail: sfrazier@twgemail.com.

FRAZZA, GEORGE S., lawyer; b. Paterson, NJ, Jan. 21, 1934; s. Paul T. and Myrtle Mary (Van Riper) F.; m. Marie Pollara, Sept. 17, 1955; children: Caren, Janine, Leslie, Lauren. AB, Marietta Coll., 1955; LL.B., Columbia U., 1958. Bar: NY 1959. Atty. Rogers & Wells, NYC, 1958-66, Johnson & Johnson, New Brunswick, NJ, 1966, assoc. gen. counsel, 1973, corp. sec., 1975—78, v.p., gen. counsel, 1978-97, mem. exec. com., 1987—96; of counsel Patterson Belknap Webb & Tyler LLP, NYC, 1997—. Bd. dirs. NJ Ballet, Morristown, 1983-97, Atlantic Legal Found.; bd. trustees Robert Wood Johnson Found, Princeton, NJ, 2000-. Mem. Assn. Gen. Counsel (pres. 1993-95), ABA (chair bus. law sect. 1996-97), NY State Bar Assn., Assn. of Bar of City of NY, Am. Corp. Counsel Assn., Am. Arbitration Assn. (bd. dirs.). Clubs: Roxiticus. Office: Patterson Belknap Webb & Tyler LLP 1133 Avenue of Americas New York NY 10036 Office Phone: 212-336-2621. E-mail: gsfrazza@pbwt.com.

FRAZZETTA, THOMAS HENRY, evolutionary biologist, educator; b. Rochester, NY, May 13, 1934; s. Joseph H. and Louise V. (Cross) F. BS, Cornell U., 1957; PhD, U. Wash., 1964. Instr. in zoology U. Wash., Seattle, 1963-64; assoc. in herpetology Harvard U., Cambridge, Mass., 1964-65; asst. prof. U. Ill., Urbana, 1965-71, assoc. prof., 1971-76, prof. dept. ecology, ethology, evolution, 1976—. Author: Complex Adaptations in Evolving Populations, 1975; contbr. articles to jours. Active ACLU, World Wildlife Fedn., Planned Parenthood Fedn. Am., Zero Population Growth, Amnesty Internat. NIH postdoctoral fellow, 1964; NSF research grantee, 1969, 77, 86. Mem. AAAS, Soc. Study Evolution, Am. Soc. Ichthyologists and Herpetologists, Am. Elasmobranch Soc., Soc. for Integrative and Comparative Biology. Democrat. Office: Univ Ill Dept Animal Biology 515 Morrill Hall Urbana IL 61801 Office Phone: 217-333-4199. Business E-Mail: tomfrazz@life.uiuc.edu.

FREAD, JOAN P., lawyer; b. Tacoma, Dec. 19, 1950; d. Paul D. and Anne L. Fread; m. Robert D. Diverstein, June 4, 1983; 1 child, Michael Fread. BA, Seattle U., 1972; MA, Western Wash. State U., 1974; JD, Yale U., 1977. Bar: D.C. 1977. Assoc. Mayer, Brown & Platt, Washington, 1977-83, ptnr. Wash., 1983—; faculty Math. Dept. Montgomery Coll., Germantown, Md. Mem. ABA, Women's Bar Assn. of D.C. Democrat. Roman Catholic. Office: Math Dept Montgomery Coll 20200 Observation Dr Germantown MD 20876 Office Phone: 301-353-7722. Office Fax: 301-353-7723. Business E-Mail: freaddiner@aol.com.

FREARS, STEPHEN, film director; b. Leicester, Eng., June 20, 1941; m. Anne Rothenstein, 1992; 4 children. BA in Law, Cambridge U., Eng. Lectr. in film Nat. Film Sch., Beaconsfield, U.K., 1987. Dir.: (stage) Waiting for Godot, 1964, Inadmissable Evidence, (TV) A Day Out, 1971, Match of the Day, 1972, Sunset Across the Bay, 1973, Playthings, 1975, Early Struggles, 1975, Last Summer, 1976, Cold Harbor, 1977, Three Men in a Boat, 1978, Long Distance in Formation, 1979, Going Gently, 1980, Bloody Kids, 1980, December Flower, 1984, Loving Walter, 1987, The Snapper, 1993, Fail Safe, 2000, The Deal, 2003, (films) The Burning, 1967, Gumshoe, 1972, Bloody Kids, 1979, Saigon-Year of the Cat, 1983, The Hit, 1984, My Beautiful Laundrette, 1985, Prick Up Your Ears, 1987, Sammy and Rosie Get Laid, 1987, Mr. Jolly Lives Next Door, 1987, Dangerous Liaisons, 1988, The Grifters, 1990, Hero, 1992, Mary Reilly, 1995, The Van, 1996, The Hi-Lo Country, 1998, High Fidelity, 2000, Liam, 2000, Dirty Pretty Things, 2002, Mrs. Henderson Presents, 2005, The Queen, 2006 (Runner-up award for Best Picture of the Yr., LA Film Critics Assn., 2006); actor: (TV) Unforgettable Richard Beckinsale, 2000.*

FREAS, GEORGE WILSON, II, computer scientist, consultant; b. Franklin, Ky., Oct. 27, 1955; s. George Wilson and Audrey Carolyn Freas; m. Cynthia Anne Fleming, Feb. 19, 1984 (div. Oct. 1990); 1 child, Alexander Morange. BS in Computer Sci., Western Ky. U., 1979; MS in Computer Sci., U. Ala., Huntsville, 1994. Pres. Synergistic Cons., Huntsville, 1991—; software cons. Bell South Telecom., Birmingham, Ala., 1995-98; software cons. Boeing Internat. Space Sta. Marshall Space Flight Ctr., Ala., 1999—. Adj. prof. Am. Sentinel U., Birmingham, 1997—. Author: Canny Canon, 1990; author: (software) GEN7 Desktop, 1993, LALL-LL(1), 1992. Home: PO Box 2885 Huntsville AL 35804-2885 Office: Synergistic Consultants PO Box 18888 Huntsville AL 35804-8888 E-mail: marquis@gen7.net.

FREASIER, AILEEN W., special education educator; b. Edcouch, Tex., Nov. 12, 1924; d. James Ross and Ethel Inez (Riley) Wade; m. Ben F. Freasier (dec.), Mar. 9, 1944; children: Ben. C., Doretha J. Christoph, Barbara F. Protzman, Raymond E. (dec.), John F. BS HE, Tex. A and I Coll., 1944; MEd, La. Tech. U., 1966; postgrad. 90 hours, La. Tech. U. Tchr. Margaret Roane Day Care Ctr., Ruston, La., 1965-71; tchr. spl. edn. Lincoln Parish Schs., Ruston, 1971-81; individualized edn. program facilitator La. Tng. Inst. Monroe Spl. Sch. Dist. # 1, 1981-89; ednl. diagnostician LTI Monroe SSD # 1, La., 1985-95. Citizen amb. People Conf. on Edn., Beijing, 1992, South Africa, 1995; presenter in field. Mem. editl. bd.: Jour. Correctional Edn., 1983—95, editor learning tech. sect.:, 1991—95; contbr. articles to ednl. publs. and profl. jours.; author: 5 comml. handwriting duplicating books. Treas. Ruston Mayor's Commn. on Women, 1996—; GED tutor Lincoln Parish Detention Class, 1996—. Named Spl. Sch. Dist. #1 Tchr. of Yr., 1988; recipient J.E. Wallace Wallin Educator of Handicapped award La. Fedn. CEC, 1994, Meritorious Svc. award La. Dept. Pub. Safety and Corrections, 1995, Pres.'s award La. CEC-Tech. and Media, 1997. Mem.: AAUW (state co-chair diversity task force 1993—94, state chmn. diversity com. 1994—2002, pres. North La. br. 1995—2005, state treas. 2001—03, La. Named Gift honoree AAUW Edn. Found. 1994), N.La. Am. Assn. U. Women (pres. 2004—06), Lincoln Parish Ret. Tchrs. Assn. (yearbook editor 1996—, pres. 1998—2000), Internat. Correctional Edn. Assn. (spl. edn. spl. interest group, newsletter editor 1991—94, chmn. 1994—96, editl. bd. CEA Yearbook of Correctional Edn. 1998—), CEC-Tech. and Media (treas. La. divsn. 1993—96, 2001—, Pres.'s award 1997), Nat. Soc. DAR (Long Leaf Pine chpt., regent 1997—99, constitution week chmn. 2000—), DAR (chmn. vets. patient com. 2000—), Kappa Kappa Iota (pres. Epsilon conclave 1985—87, state pres. 1991—92, nat. scholarship com. 1995—96, nat. tech. com. 1997—99, chmn. nat. tech. com. 1999—2000, pres. Epsilon conclave 1999—2000, nat. profl. devel. com. 2001—03, v.p. 2003, chmn. bylaws com. 2003—04, Eta state scholarship com. 2003—04, chmn. Eta state scholarship com. 2003—05, chmn. Loretta Doerr Achievement com. 2004—05, state scholar com. chair 2005—06, nat. scholar com. 2005—06, pres. Epsilon conclave 2005—, nat. bylaws com. 2006—07, chmn. Loretta Doerr achievement com. 2006—07, chmn. Kappa ad hoc com. Eta state campus 2007, Eta State Loretta Doerr award 1995), Phi Delta Kappa (newsletter editor 1989—93, past pres. chpt. 1994—96, newsletter editor 1997—98, treas. 2002—). Home: PO Box 1595 Ruston LA 71273-1595 Personal E-mail: aileenwf@bayou.com.

FRÉCHET, JEAN, chemistry professor; b. Chalon, France, Aug. 18, 1944; came to U.S., 1967; children: Jacques Christopher, Marc Alexander. MSc, SUNY, Syracuse, 1969, PhD, 1971, Syracuse U., 1971; Doctorate (hon.), U. Lyon, 2002, U. Ottawa, 2004. Asst. prof. chemistry U. Ottawa, Canada, 1973-78, assoc. prof. chemistry, 1978-82, prof. chemistry, 1982-87; IBM prof. chemistry Cornell U., Ithaca, NY, 1987-95, P.J. Debye chair chemistry, 1996—98; prof. chemistry U. Calif., Berkeley, 1996—, H. Rapoport chair organic chemistry, 2003—; head materials synthesis Lawrence Berkeley Nat. Lab., 1999—. Vis. scientist IBM Rsch. Lab., San Jose, Calif., 1979, 83; vice dean grad. studies and rsch. U. Ottawa, 1983-87; cons. Kodak, 1997-05, Xenoport, 2000—, Intermolecular, 2005-, Nanomix, 2006-; bd. dirs. Ont. Ctr. for Materials Rsch., Toronto, Dendritic Nanotechnologies, Inc. Contbr. numerous articles to profl. jours.; patentee in field. Recipient Internat. Union Pure and Applied Chemistry award, 1983, Polymer Soc. Japan, 1986, A.K. Doolittle award, 1986, Coop. Rsch. award Am. Chem. Soc., 1994, Applied Polymer Chem. award Am. Chem. Soc., 1996, 00, Kosar Meml. award Soc. Imaging Sci. Tech., 1999, Salute to Excellence award Am. Chem. Soc., 2001, Esselen award chemistry pub. svc., 2005, medal Macro Group UK, 2006, Arthur C. Cope award, Am. Chem. Soc., 2007; A.C. Cope scholar Am. Chem. Soc., 2001; numerous rsch. grants. Fellow AAAS; mem. NAS, NAE, Am. Acad. Arts and Scis. Avocation: oenophile. Office: U Calif Coll Chemistry 718 Latimer Berkeley CA 94720-1460 Home Phone: 510-594-1573; Office Phone: 510-643-3077.

FRECHETTE, PETER LOREN, dental products executive; b. Janesville, Wis., Aug. 15, 1937; s. Francis Michael and Gladys Jean F.; m. Patricia Jean O'Brien, June 24, 1961; children: Kathleen and Kristen (twins). BS in Econs., U. Wis., 1960; MBA, Northwestern U., 1980. Pres. Sci. Products, McGaw Park, Ill., 1975-82; pres., CEO Patterson Dental Co., Mpls., 1982—. Served with U.S. Army, 1961-63. Mem. Am. Dental Trade Assn. Office: Patterson Dental Co 1031 Mendota Heights Rd Mendota Heights MN 55120-1401 Office Phone: 651-686-1700. E-mail: pete.frechette@pattersondental.com.

FRECKELTON, SONDRA, artist; b. Dearborn, Mich., June 23, 1936; d. William and Elizabeth (Zimmerman) F.; m. W.H. Jack Beal, Sept. 3, 1955. Student, Sch. Art Inst. Chgo., 1954—56, U. Chgo., 1954—56; LittD (hon.), Hollins Coll., 1994; DFA (hon.), SUNY, Oneonta, 2007. Artist self-employed, 1958—, Tibor de Nagy Gallery, NYC, 1953—64, B.C. Holland Gallery, Chgo., 1964—67, Lo Giudice Gallery, Chgo., 1968—71, Brooke Alexander Gallery, NYC, 1975—85, 1991, Robert Schoelkopf Gallery, NYC, 1986—91, Alice Simsar Gallery, Ann Arbor, Mich., 1987—, Maxwell Davidson Gallery, NYC, 1991—98. Co-author: Dynamic Still-Lifes in Watercolor, 1983; one-person exhbns. include Robert Schoelkopf Gallery, 1986, 88, 90, John Berggruen Gallery, 1982, Brooke Alexander, Inc., 1976, 79, 80, 81, Fendrick Gallery, 1980, Allan Frumkin Gallery, Chgo., 1977, Lo Giudice Gallery, 1970, B.C. Holland Gallery, 1965, Tibor de Nagy Gallery, 1961, 63, Maxwell Davidson Gallery, 1994, Kalamazoo Inst. Arts, 1994, Huntington Mus., W.Va., 1998-99; group shows including Mt. Holyoke Coll., Yale U. Art Gallery, Art Mus. of Santa Barbara, Va. Mus. Fine Arts, 1987-88, Detroit Inst. Arts, 1991, Madison Art Ctr., Wis., 1998, Columbus Mus. Art, Ga., 1998, Detroit Inst. Arts, 2005, Gallery State U. NY Coll., Oneonta, 2006, others. Recipient Print award, Bradford Mus., 1979, Pollock-Krasner award, 2002; grantee, Grant Ingram-Merrill Found., 1960. Avocations: horticulture, gardening. Home and Office: 331 Epps Rd Oneonta NY 13820-6451 Office Phone: 607-433-2325. E-mail: freckbea@dmcom.net.

FRED, ROGERS MURRAY, III, veterinary oncologist; b. Leesburg, Va., July 22, 1955; s. Rogers Murray Jr. and Barbara Ann (Stewart) F.; m. Kimberly Edna Shepherd, Oct. 15, 1989; 1 child, Asa Hugh Shepherd. BS, Washington and Lee U., 1977; post grad., U. Ga., 1979-81; DVM, Va. Tech., 1985. Staff veterinarian Abbey Animal Hosp., Balt., 1986-89; resident in vet. oncology U. Pa., Phila., 1989-91; clin. oncologist, dept. head Red Bank Vet. Hosp. and Referral Svc., NJ, 1991—. Lectr. in vet. field. Co-author: Connective Tissues in Health and Disease, 1980; Globule Leukocyte Tumor in Cats: 6 Cases, 1993; Liposome-Encapsulated Doxorubicin (Doxil) and Doxorubicin in the Treatment of Vaccine-Associated Sarcoma in Cats, 2002. Bd. dir. Ebenezer Ch. and Cemetery Co., Bloomfield, Va., 1986—, Monmouth Hills N.J., Inc. Mem. SCV (camp comdr. 1988-90); Am. Vet. Med. Assn.; Vet. Cancer Soc.; N.J. Vet. Med. Assn.; Civil War Preservation Trust; Phi Kappa Phi; Phi Zeta. Republican. Episcopalian. Avocations: reading, walking, battlefield tours, birdwatching. Office: Red Bank Vet Hosp 210 Newman Springs Rd Red Bank NJ 07701-1465 Home: 15 Park Way Monmouth Hills Highlands NJ 07732 Office Phone: 732-747-3636.

FREDEMAN, BETTY COLEY (BETTY COLEY), retired librarian, editor; b. Corrigan, Tex., Aug. 4, 1933; d. Bennie Boyd and Louise (Long) Gilbert; m. Kenneth Coley, Jan. 27, 1951 (dec. 1991); 1 child, Carol Ann; m. William E. Fredeman, Jan. 16, 1995. BS, Sam Houston State U., 1953; MEd, East Texas State U., 1961; MLS, Tex. Women's U., 1980. With registrar's office Tex. A&M U., 1954; tchr. Mesquite (Tex.) Ind. Sch. Dist., 1957-64, elem. librarian, 1964-67, dir. cen. processing ctr., 1964-66; elem. librarian Aldine Ind. Sch. Dist., Houston, 1967-69; law librarian Fulbright and Jaworski, 1969-72; librarian Armstrong Browning Libr., Baylor U., Waco, Tex., 1972-94, ret., 1994. Editor: My Browning Family Album (Vivienne Browning), 1979, The Correspondence of Dante Gabriel Rossetti, vol. 1-, 2002-; contbr. to Studies in Robert Browning and His Circle, 1976, 82, 88, Baylor Browning Interest Series #27, Lot 931: A Reconstruction of Books, Periodicals and Ephemera from the Brownings' Library, 1981, The Browning Collections: A Reconstruction with Other Memorabilia, 1984, Journal of Pre-Raphaelite Studies No. 4, 1995, Pre-Raphaelite and Other Victorian Resources in the Armstrong Browning Library, 1995, others; book rev. editor, bibliographer Studies in Browning and His Circle, Vols. 14, 15, 16; mem. editl. bd. Baylor/Ohio edit. The Complete Works of Robert Browning. Pres. Mesquite Jr. Woman's Study Club, 1966-67; rec. sec. Florence Black Elem. PTA, 1965-67; membership chmn., v.p. Browning Inst. Mem. AAUW (past chpt., sec., pres., state historian, dist. coord., Outstanding Mem. award Waco br. 1980, named gift given to Ednl. Found. 1979), ALA (info. exchange com. Rare Books and Manuscripts Section 1988-90), Browning Inst. (dir. 1984-98), Internat. Browning Soc. (dir. 1976-85), Tex. Libr. Assn. (dist. chmn. 1979-80, publs. com. 1989-91, membership com. 1989-91), Southwestern Libr. Assn., Spl. Librs. Assn., William Morris Soc., Browning Soc. London, Baylor U. Round Table (rec. sec. 1976, publs. coord. 1977-78, pres. 1983-84), Beta Phi Mu, Delta Kappa Gamma (Zeta scholar 1977, Alpha state scholarship com. 1986-91), Epsilon Chi (treas., pres. 1992-94). Baptist. Personal E-mail: bfredeman@austin.rr.com.

FREDERICI, C. CARLETON, lawyer; b. Jan. 17, 1938; s. Cecil Carleton and Lois Alida (Selzer) F.; m. Virginia A. Gregori, Oct. 14, 1961 (div.); m. Susan A. Low, Oct. 1, 1983; children: Gloria M., Carleton J., Charles W., Seth L. Student, Iowa State U., 1956; BA, U. Iowa, 1960, JD with high distinction, 1965. Bar: Iowa 1965, N.Y. 1966, U.S. Dist. Ct. (no. dist.) Iowa 1968, U.S. Dist. Ct. (so. dist.) Iowa 1969, U.S. Supreme Ct. 1970, U.S. Ct. Appeals (8th cir.) 1970, U.S. Ct. Appeals (3d cir.) 1973. Assoc. Willkie, Farr & Gallagher, NYC, 1965-68, Shull, Marshall & Marks, Sioux City, Iowa, 1968-69, Davis, Brown, Koehn, Shors & Roberts, P.C., Des Moines, 1969-71, jr. ptnr., 1971-73, sr. ptnr., 1973-90, shareholder, 1990-95, counsel, 1996—. Spkr. Supreme Ct. Day, Law Sch. Drake U., 1973. Contbr. articles to legal publs. Vestryman St. Luke's Ch., bd. dirs., 1976-78, 82-85; mem. Polk County Rep. Cen. Com., 1969-71. 1st lt. U.S. Army, 1961-62. Mem. ABA (chmn. 8th cir. commn. on class actions and derivative suits), Iowa Bar Assn. (chmn. prison reform com., adv. mem. fed. practice commn., litigation sect. bench and bar com.), Polk County Bar Assn. (bench and bar com.), Assn. Bar City of N.Y., Am. Judicature Soc. (bd. dirs. Iowa 1990-96), Order of Coif, Wakonda Club. Office: Davis Brown Koehn Shors & Roberts PC 666 Walnut St Ste 2500 Des Moines IA 50309-3904 Home Phone: 515-255-4851; Office Phone: 515-288-2500. E-mail: ccf@lawiowa.com.

FREDERICK, EDWARD CHARLES, university official; b. Mankato, Minn., Nov. 17, 1930; s. William H. and Wanda (MacNamara) F.; m. Shirley Lunkenheimer, Aug. 16, 1951; children: Bonita Frederick Treangen (dec.), Diane Frederick Fox, Donald, Kenneth, Karen Frederick Swenson. BS in Agrl. Edn, U. Minn., 1954, MS in Dairy Husbandry, 1955, PhD in Anatomy and Physiology, 1957. Animal scientist, instr. N.W. Sch. and Expt. Sta. U. Minn., Crookston, 1958-64, supt. So. Sch. and Expt. Sta. Waseca, 1964-69, provost Tech. Coll., 1969-85, chancellor Tech. Coll., 1985-90; sr. fellow Hubert H. Humphrey Inst. Pub. Affairs, 1990-91, U. Minn. Coll. of Agr., Food and Environ. Sci., 1991—. Mem. Tech. Agrl. Edn. Study Team to Morocco, 1977. Contbr. articles on dairy physiology, mgmt., agrl. edn. and adminstrn. to tech. jours. and popular publs. Bd. dirs. Bob Hodgson Student Loan Fund, 1971-90, Minn. Agrl. Interpretive Ctr., 1978—, chair, 1994—; bd. dirs. Minn. Agri-Growth Coun., 1980—, pres. 1992—; bd. dirs. Southeastern Minn. Initiative Fund, 1986-92, v.p., 1991-92; bd. dirs. Waseca area United Way, 1988-94, pres., 1992; bd. dirs. Minn. Agriculture in the Classroom, 1993-99, pres., 1995-96. Recipient Alumni award 4-H, 1972, Good Neighbor award WCCO, 1990, Ed Frederick Day award State of Minn., 1990, Merit award Gamma Sigma Delta, 1994, Above Self award Waseca Cmty. Svc., 2002, Lifetime Leadership award Minn. Rural Ptnrs., 2002, Ground Breaker award So. Minn. Initiative Found., 2002, Lifetime Achievement award Agri-News, 2005; named to Minn. FFA Hall of Fame, 2004; finalist So. Minn. Agrl. Amb. of Yr., 2004. Mem. Am. Dairy Assn., Am. Soc. Animal Prodn., AAAS, Nat. Assn. Colls. and Tchrs. Agr. (pres. 1976-77), Am. Assn. Cmty. and Jr. Colls. (pres. Council of Two Yr. Colls. of Four Yr. Instns. 1988-90), Minn. FFA Alumni Assn. (pres. 1998-00, found. bd. trustees 2000—, chair exec. sponsor bd. 2006—), South Central Edn. Assn. (Disting. Service award 1971), Waseca Area C. of C. (dir. 1979), Foresters Club, Rotary (gov. dist. 596 1982-83), KC, Phi Kappa Phi. Roman Catholic. Home: 39031 State Highway 13 Waseca MN 56093-4212 Office: U Minn Coll Agrl Food and Env Sci Waseca MN 56093 Office Phone: 507-835-3422. Business E-Mail: frede010@umn.edu.

FREDERICK, ELIZABETH ELEANOR TATUM, watercolor artist, retired educator; b. Clovis, N.Mex., Dec. 22, 1915; d. John Hardy Tatum and Bessie Elizabeth Weathers Tatum; m. George Achias Frederick, June 7, 1937 (dec. Apr. 1991); children: Ronald W., George Douglas, Barbara Elizabeth Frederick Ewing, John Lawrence. BS in Edn., U. N.Mex., 1937, MS, 1943; postgrad., Highland U., Las Vegas, N.Mex., 1944, Ea. N.Mex. U., 1944-45. Tchr. Ctrl. H.S., Kirtland, N.Mex., 1936-37, Bellview HS, N.Mex., 1940-42, Hot Springs Jr. HS, N.Mex., 1943-45, N.Mex., 1951-53, N.Mex., 1954; ret., 1967. Exhibitions include Sierra Art Soc., Geronimo Mus., Truth or Consequences, N.Mex., 1950—91, Willamette Oaks Retirement Ctr., Eugene, Oreg., 1991—, El Paso Mus. Art, N.Mex. Art League, N.Mex. Watercolor Soc., Albuquerque, Nat. League Am. Pen Women, 1993—2007, Represented in permanent collections. Mem. Nat. League Am. Pen Women (pres. Rio Grande br. 1975-76), Sierra Art Soc. (pres. 1974-75, funding and program chmn. 1975-89), N.Mex. Watercolor Soc., Black Range Artists (sec.-treas. 1978-79). Republican. Avocations: sweepstakes, worldwide travel.

FREDERICK, JOHN, retired actor, writer; b. Norwalk, Iowa; Author: (memoir) Name Droppings on Your Head; actor: (Broadway plays) Something for the Boys, Catherine Was Great, Miracle in the Mountain, First Ms. Fraser, Destry Rides Again, Stalag 17, Annie Get Your Gun, Where's Charles; actor, actor: (Broadway plays) Take Me Along, (with USO on front lines of WWII) Ten Little Indians; (TV series) My Three Sons, Bonanza, Naked City, Death Valley Days, Wagon Train, The Restless Gun, Tales of the Texas Rangers, Undercurrent, Adventures of Wild Bill Hickok, Frontier, The Jack Benny Program, Stories of the Century, Tales of Wells Fargo, The Untouchables, Rifleman, guest starred over 65 TV series; (films) The Las Vegas Story, 1952, Ten Commandments, 1955, Once Upon a Time in the West, 1968, Shoes of the Fisherman, 1968, Colpt Rovente, 1969, La Caduta Delgli Dei, 1969, The Adventurers, 1970, Pussycat, Pussycat, I Love You, 1970, Jennifer on My Mind, 1971, Giu la testa, 1971, The Statue, 1971, Tarzan, (Pope Clemente VIII) Beatrice Cenci, and numerous others; contbr. articles to profl. jours. Active local charities. Avocation: gardening.

FREDERICK, JOHN EUGENE, science educator; b. Louisville, Ky., Nov. 22, 1949; s. June Deark (Ridgway) and John Harry Frederick. BA magna cum laude, Hanover Coll., Ind., 1971; PhD, U. Colo., Boulder, 1975. Postdoctoral scholar U. Mich., Ann Arbor, 1975—77; space scientist NASA/Goddard Space Flight Ctr., Greenbelt, Md., 1978—85; prof. atmospheric sci. U. Chgo., 1985—, assoc. dean phys. scis., 2006—. Chmn. geophys. scis. U. Chgo., 1994—97. Grantee, NSF, 1987—2004, Ctr. for Environ. Sci. US EPA, 2003—06. Mem.: Am. Geophys. Union. Achievements include research in new values for the absorbing properties of the oxygen molecule in the upper atmosphere based on balloon-borne observations of ultraviolet sunlight; measured enhanced ultraviolet radiation levels incident on Antarctica during the ozone hole; development of computational models that formed the basis of the first UV index; research in altered optical properties of clouds over urban areas associated with degraded air quality. Office: Univ Chgo 5734 S Ellis Ave Chicago IL 60637-1434 Office Phone: 773-702-3237. Business E-Mail: frederic@uchicago.edu.

FREDERICK, PAULA J., lawyer; b. Riverside, Calif., Apr. 11, 1958; d. Henry Lewis and Hattie Maude (McCollom) F. BA, Duke U., 1979; JD, Vanderbilt U., 1982. Bar: Ga. 1982, U.S. Dist. Ct. (no. dist.) Ga. 1982. Staff atty. Atlanta Legal Aid Soc., 1982-86, mng. atty., 1986-88; asst. gen. counsel State Bar of Ga., Atlanta, 1988-92, dep. gen. counsel, 1992—. Bd. dir. Ga. Legal Svcs. Found. Mem. ABA (chair standing com. on profl. discipline 2000-02, commr. Commn. on Opportunities for Minorities in the Profession 1994-96, mem. ho. of dels. 1993—, bd. gov. 2002-), Atlanta Bar Assn. (bd. dirs. 1994-96, pres. 1999-00), Ga. Assn. Black Women Attys. (pres. 1998), Ga. Assn. Women Lawyers (Kathleen Kessler award 2002). Office: State Bar of Georgia Suite 100 104 Marietta St NW Atlanta GA 30303-2702 Office Phone: 404-527-8720.*

FREDERICK, RICHARD C., emergency physician, educator; b. Champaign, Ill., Feb. 22, 1950; s. James A. and Betty L. Frederick; m. Cheryl A. Henderson, June 29, 1975; children: Luke R., Joshua C., Betty L., Grace G., Sandra V. MD, U. Ill., Chgo., 1976. Diplomate Am. Bd. Emergency Medicine, 1986. Assoc. prof. surgery U. Ill. Coll. Medicine, Peoria, 1989—. Contbr. articles to profl. jours. SWAT tactical physician Peoria County Sheriff's Dept., Ill., 2002—; elder Grace Presbyn. Ch., Peoria, 2000—. Fellow: Am. Coll. Emergency Physicians (life). Republican. Avocations: hunting, fishing, triathlons. Office: OSF Emergency Dept 530 NE Glen Oak Peoria IL 61637 Home Phone: 309-387-6577; Office Phone: 309-655-2553.

FREDERICK, ROBERT ALLEN, history professor; b. Mishawaka, Ind., Feb. 3, 1928; s. Ralph Leon and Garnet Laree (Bowles) F.; m. Mary Billington Swartz, Nov. 23, 1950 (div. Sept. 1967); children: Julia Christian, John Billington, Peter Carey; m. Saradell Carolyn Ard, Sept. 9, 1969 (div. April 1983). BA, Hanover Coll., 1950; MS in Edn., Ind. U., 1951, PhD in History, 1960. Assoc. dean students Tex. Technol. Coll., Lubbock, 1951-53; instr. history U.S. Naval Acad. Prep Sch., 1953-56; grad. asst. history Ind. U., Bloomington, 1956-58, fellow dept. history, 1958-60; assoc. prof. history Alaska Meth. U., Anchorage, 1960-66, prof. history, chmn. dept., 1966-73; exec. dir. Alaska Hist. Commn., Anchorage, 1973-80; ind. rschr./writer Alaska Hist. Soc., Anchorage, 1980-85; editor Ind. German Heritage Soc., Indpls., 1986-88; Richard Lieber rschr. Brown County Hist. Soc., Nashville, Ind., 1988-93. Dir. Alaska humanities task force NEH, 1972-73. Editor/contbr. Frontier Alaska: Historical Opportunity, 1968, Writing Alaska's History: A Guide to Research, 1974; contbr., hist. photo editor Anchorage: Star of the North, 1982; author: Alaska's Quest for Statehood: 1867-1959, 1985, Passage to Community: Creating the State-Based Alaska Humanities Forum, 1973; editor: newsletter Ind. German Heritage Soc., 1986-89. Pres. Cook Inlet Hist. Soc., Anchorage, bd. dirs., 1963-66; pres. Alaska Hist. Soc., 1968-69, bd. dirs., 1967-74; mem. nat. archives adv. bd. Nat. Archives and Records Svcs., Regions IX and X, 1974-77; chmn. Nat. Trust for Hist. Preservation, 1975-77, bd. advisors, 1969-78, advisor emeritus, 1979—; dir. A Pioneer Family in Alaska (film) U. Alaska Found., Homer, 1982. Lt. USNR, 1953-56. Ind. Heritage Rsch. grantee Ind. Humanities Coun., 1987-91. Mem. Historic Landmarks Found. Ind., Sigma Chi (life). Democrat. Avocations: hiking in wilderness, visiting natural and historical sites. Home: 1950 S Dayton St # 113N Denver CO 80247-3454 Home Phone: 303-755-5512.

FREDERICK, ROBERT GEORGE, lawyer; b. Evanston, Ill., Feb. 11, 1948; s. George D. and Lee (Miller) F.; m. Pamela Kaye Kline, June 13, 1970 (div. Sept. 1977);m. Ellen Due, June, 1950 (div. Sept. 1996); m. Marianne, Nov. 22, 2003; children: Robert, Julia, Christina. BS, No. Ill. U., 1969; JD, U. Ill., 1972. Bar: Ill. 1972, U.S. Dist. Ct. (cen. dist.) Ill. 1974, U.S. Ct. Appeals (7th cir.) 1975, U.S. Supreme Ct. 1978. Asst. states atty. Champaign County, Urbana, Ill., 1972-75, pub. defender, 1975-79; ptnr. Frederick & Hagle, Urbana, 1975—; commr. State Ill. Claims Ct., Springfield, 1984—92. Mem. ABA, Ill. State Bar Assn., Ill. Trial Lawyers Assn., Champaign County Bar Assn., Order of Coif. Republican. Methodist. Office: Frederick & Hagle 129 W Main St Urbana IL 61801-2714 Office Phone: 217-367-6092. Business E-Mail: bfrederick@frederickandhagle.com.

FREDERICK, THOMAS JAMES, lawyer; b. Grand Rapids, Mich., Oct. 6, 1956; s. Charles Murr and E. Marjorie (Loye) F. BA, Mich. State U., 1978; JD, U. Mich., 1984. Bar: Ill. 1984, U.S Dist. Ct. (no. dist.) Ill. 1984, U.S. Ct. Appeals (7th cir.) 1989, U.S. Supreme Ct., 1993. From assoc. to. ptnr. Winston & Strawn, Chgo., 1984—, chair litigation dept., 2006—. Assoc. editor: Michigan Law Review, 1982—83; editor, 1983—84. Mem. ABA, Chgo. Bar Assn., Seventh Cir. Bar Assn., Order of Coif. Office: Winston & Strawn 35 W Wacker Dr Chicago IL 60601-9706 Office Phone: 312-558-5983. Office Fax: 312-558-5700. Business E-Mail: tfrederick@winston.com.

FREDERICK, VIRGINIA FIESTER, state legislator; b. Rock Island, Ill., Dec. 24, 1916; d. John Henry and Myrtle (Montgomery) Heise; m. C. Donnan Fiester (dec. 1975); children: Sheryl Fiester Ross, Alan R., James D.; m. Kenneth Jacob Frederick, 1978 (dec.). BA, U. Iowa, 1938; postgrad., Lake Forest Coll., 1942-43, LLD, 1994, MLS, 1999. Freelance fashion designer, Lake Forest, Ill., 1952-78; pres. Mid Am. China Exch., Kenilworth, Ill., 1978-81; mem. Ill. Ho. of Reps., Springfield, 1979-95, asst. minority leader, 1990-95. Alderman first ward, Lake Forest, 1974-78; del. World Food Conf., Rome, 1974; subcom. pensions and employment Ill. Commn. on Status of Women, 1976-79; co-chair Conf. Women Legislators, 1982-85; bd. dirs. Lake Forest Coll., 1995-98, Lake Forest Symphony Guild, 1998—; city supr. City of Lake Forest, 1995-98. Named Chgo. Area Women of Achievement, Internat. Orgn. Women Execs., 1978; recipient Lottie Holman O'Neal award, 1980, Jane Addams award, 1982, Outstanding Legislator award Ill. Hosp. Assn., 1986, VFW Svc. award, 1988, Joyce Fitzgerald Meml. award, 1988, Susan B. Anthony Legislator of Yr. award, 1989, Delta Kappa Gamma award, 1991, Outstanding Legislator award, 1995, Svcs. for Srs. award, Ill. Dept. Aging, 1991, Ethics in Politics award, Rep. Womens's Club, 1992, Woman of Achievement award YWCA North Eastern Ill., 1994, Ill. Women in Govt. award, 1994, Lifetime Achievement award Equip for Equality, 1999. Mem. LWV (local pres. 1958-60, state dir. 1969-75, nat. com. 1975-76), AAUW (local pres. 1968-70, state pres. 1975-77, state dir. 1963-69, nat. com. 1967-69, Legislator of Yr. 1993), UN Assn. (bd. dirs.), Chgo. Assn. Commerce and Industry (bd. dirs.). Personal E-mail: k13v16@aol.com.

FREDERICK-MAIRS, T(HYRA) JULIE, administrative health services official; b. Islip, NY, Jan. 4, 1941; d. Manuel and Thyra C. (Thorsen) Cajiao. BA, Adelphi U., 1961; MSW, U. So. Calif., 1972, MPA, 1991. Social worker L.A. County Dept. Social Svcs., 1966-67, social work supr., 1967-70, planning cons., 1972-76; dep. to supr. 4th dist. L.A. County, 1976-80; asst. dir. L.A. County Office Alcohol Programs, 1980-90; assoc. adminstr. ELACO Health Ctrs., 1990—2003; CEO East Country Health Ctrs.; health care process improvement and change mgmt. cons., 2003—. Fellow U. So. Calif., 1988-90. Author: (with others) Youth Program Planning, 1975. Trustee LEARNS, 1992; active L.A. Child Sexual Abuse Project, Commn. for Sexual Equality, L.A. Unified Sch. Dist., Harbor Policy Cmty. Adv. Coun., L.A.; mem. Perinatal Substance Abuse Coun. L.A.; mem. ops. com. Interagy. Coun. Child Abuse and Neglect; adv. com. UCLA Alcohol Rsch. Ctr. Mem. Los Amigos de la Humanidad, DHS Latino Mgrs., Alpha Epsilon Delta, Beta Beta Beta, Bus. and Profl. Women's Club, Soroptimists (pres. L.A. Club, dir. Found. of L.A. 1986-88). Office Phone: 818-512-0083.

FREDERICKS, BEVERLY MAGNUSON, artist; b. Colorado Springs, Colo., June 14, 1928; d. Oscar Frederick and India King (Glenn) Magnuson; m. Harvey Ray Fredericks (dec.); children: Annetta Louise(dec.) , John Stafford, Jeffrey Robert. Student, Colorado Springs Fine Art Ctr., 1946—54, Antelope Valley Coll., Lancaster, Calif., 1960—61, Santa Monica City Coll., Calif., 1961—62. Receptionist Hughes Aircraft, LA, 1963—67; interior designer Gerald's Paint and Hardware, LA, 1967—69; owner, restorer, conservator Fine Art Beverly Fredericks, LA, 1980—. Lectr. in field. Editor: Art of Creating Monotypes, 1990; author: History & Heritage of Victoria County Texas, 2000; exhibitions include LA Co. Mus., Ringling Mus., Robiard Gallery, John Lane Galleries, Vega Fine Arts, Am. Inst. Fine Arts, Centennial Gallery, Warner Fine Art, one-woman shows include Riggs Galleries, Robertson Gallery, Armagost Fine Arts, Barton Galleries. Troop leader Girl Scouts Am., Colorado Springs, 1954—55; active Nat. Mus. Women in Arts, Washington, 1976. Named one of Ten Best Tchrs. on Tape, Arts Am., 1991; named to Alumni Hall of Fame, Colorado Springs HS, 1985. Fellow: Am. Inst. Fine Art (bd. dirs., treas. 1978—85); mem.: Am. Inst. for Conservation, Nat. League Am. Pen Women. Republican. Presbyterian. Avocations: genealogy, photography, dance, theater, travel. Home: 8227 Westlawn Ave Los Angeles CA 90045 Office: Fine Art Studio Beverly Fredericks 8227 Westlawn Ave Los Angeles CA 90045

FREDERICKS, HENRY JACOB, lawyer; b. St. Louis, Dec. 1, 1925; s. Henry Jacob III and Mary Elizabeth (Pieron) F.; m. Marjorie Helen Kiely, 1951 (div. 1962; dec.); children: Joseph Henry, James Andrew, Elizabeth Ann.; m. Susan Kay Brennecke, 1971 (div. 1991); 1 child, William Michael; m. Deborah Jean Rose, 1992; 1 child, Daniel Baptise Jerome. JD, St. Louis U., 1950; postgrad., Sch. Commerce and Fin., 1945-47. Bar: Mo. 1950, U.S. Dist. Ct. (ea. and so. dists.) Mo. 1951, U.S. Ct. Appeals (8th cir.) 1978, U.S. Supreme Ct. 1986. Pvt. practice, St. Louis County, 1950-80; assoc. Mark D. Eagleton, St. Louis, 1960, Goldenhersh Fredericks & Newman, St. Louis, 1961-69, Friedman and Fredericks, St. Louis, 1969-81. Chief trial atty. for cir. atty. St. Louis, 1955, 1st asst. to cir. atty. Thomas F. Eagleton, 1987, spl. asst. to cir. attys., 1960-81; asst. U.S. atty. Ea. Dist. Mo., Dept. Justice, 1981—; lectr. in field; chmn. bd. Gateway Boxing Promotions, Inc. Mem. Mo. Athletic Commn., 1974-76, boxing chmn. Mo. Athletic Commn. and AAU, 1977. Served with USAAF, 1943-46, ETO. Decorated Air medal with 4 battle stars. Mem. ABA, Mo. Bar Assn., St. Louis County Bar Assn., Am. Trial Lawyers Assn., Internat. Platform Assn., St. Louis Amateur Boxing Assn., Inc. (pres.), Delta Theta Phi. Home: 5959 Keith Pl Saint Louis MO 63109-3447 Office: 1600 S Forentwood Blvd Ste 500 Saint Louis MO 63144

FREDERICKS, IVY LINDSTROM, investment banker; BA in English and Econs., Smith Coll., Northampton, Mass., 1981; MA in Internat. Affairs, Columbia U., NYC, 1998. With Internat. Paper Co., NYC, 1981—83; analyst mergers and acquisitions dept. Kidder Peabody & Co., Inc., NYC, 1983—85, v.p. mergers and acquisitions dept., 1990—93; asst. v.p. mergers and acquisition group Drexel Burnham Lambert Inc., NYC, 1985—90; mng. dir. corp. fin. dept. KPMG Peat Marwick, NYC, 1993—95; mng. dir. Ambient Capital Group, Inc., NYC, 1996—2000; mng. dir., head corp. fin. Westminster Securities Corp., NYC, 2000—05; pres., CEO Transnat. Capital Corp., NYC, 2005—. Adj. asst. prof. sch. continuing and profl. studies NYU, 1999; lectr. in field. Vol. Fin. Svcs. Vol. Corps, Zagreb, Croatia, 1998; bd. dirs. Ctr. Bus. Ethics, St. Petersburg, Russia. Mem.: Women's Fgn. Policy Group, Fin. Women's Assn. of N.Y., Fgn. Policy Assn. Home: 30 Dusenberry Rd Bronxville NY 10708 Office: Transnational Capital Corp 420 Lexington Ave Ste 300 New York NY 10170 Office Phone: 212-453-0648.

FREDERICKS, JEANNE MARIA JUDSON, literary agent; b. Mineola, NY, Apr. 19, 1950; d. Howard William and Christina Hannah Judson; m. Wesley Charles Fredericks, Jr., May 19, 1973; children: Carolyn Anne, Wesley Charles III. BA, Mt. Holyoke Coll., South Hadley, Mass., 1972; MBA, NYU, NYC, 1979; publ. procedures course, Radcliffe Coll., Cambridge, Mass. asst. to editl. dir., subs. rights dir. Basic Books, NYC, 1972-74; asst. mng. editor Macmillan Publ. Co., NYC, 1974-76, mng. editor, 1976-78, acquisitions editor, 1978-80; editl. dir. Ziff-Davis Books, NYC, 1980-81; literary agent Susan P. Urstadt, Inc., New Canaan, Conn., 1990-96, acting dir., 1996-97; pres. Jeanne Fredericks Literary Agy., Inc., New Canaan, 1997—. Spkr. in field. Co-chair, co-founder Mothers' Group Congl. Ch., Wilton, Conn., 1984-87; bd. dirs. New Canaan H.S. Crew, 1999—2002, co-pres., 2002-03; trustee New Canaan Congregational Ch., 2001-04, mem. social action com., 2004—, chair, 2006—. Mem. Assn. Authors' Reps., Authors Guild, Inc., Phi Beta Kappa. Republican. Congregationalist. Avocations: crew, gardening, reading. Office: Jeanne Fredericks Literary Agy Inc 221 Benedict Hill Rd New Canaan CT 06840-2913 Home Phone: 203-966-8486; Office Phone: 203-972-3011.

FREDERICKS, ROBERT JOSEPH, language company executive; b. NYC, Dec. 26, 1934; s. Harold D. and Mary E. (McCarthy) F.; m. Jeanette C. Kubin, July 7, 1984. BS in Chemistry, Villanova U., 1957; MS in Chemistry, St. Joseph's Coll., Phila., 1959; PhD in Chemistry, Lehigh U., 1965. Rsch. chemist GAF Corp., Easton, Pa., 1960—67; rsch. supr. Allied Chem. Corp., Morristown, NJ, 1968—72; mgr. analytical chemistry Ethicon, Inc., Somerville, NJ, 1972—74, dir. rsch. svcs., 1974—76, assoc. dir. rsch., 1976—78; v.p. R&D, bd. dirs. Surgikos, Piscataway, NJ, 1978—79, Johnson & Johnson Dental Products Co., East Windsor, NJ, 1980—82; sr. v.p., gen. mgr., COO Biosci. Med. Products, Somerville, 1982—85; pres. Allen Transl. Svc., Morristown, NJ, 1985—. Author: X-Ray Diffraction for the Industrial Chemist, 1971; contbr. articles to profl. jours. Pres. Morris County Hist. Soc., Morristown, 1982—86, trustee,

1975—93; pres. Washington Assn. N.J., Morristown, 1988—92, 1993—99, trustee, 1983—2002, Craftsman Farms Found., 1994; mem. adv. bd. New Philharm., NJ, 1992—99, trustee NJ, 1994—98, 1st v.p. NJ, 1995—98; hon. historian Twp. of Morris, 1992—; mem. pres. adv. coun. Cath. initiatives Seton Hall U., 2006—. Lt (j.g.) USN, 1958—60. Recipient Achievement award Washington Assn., 2000, Svc. award Assumption Coll. for Sisters, 2005 Mem.: AAAS, N.Y. Acad. Scis., Am. Chem. Soc., Am. Assn. Sovereign Mil. Order of Malta (N.J. state chmn. 2003—, bd. councillors 2004—, chmn. Lourdes 2003 pilgrimage, N.J. Hospitaller), Rotary (bd. dirs. 1992—93), Morristown Club (bd. govs. 1996—, v.p. 1998, pres. 1999—2002), Morristown Field Club, Sigma Xi, Delta Epsilon Sigma. Republican. Roman Catholic. Avocations: tennis, gardening. Home: 16 Butterworth Dr Morristown NJ 07960-2625 Office Phone: 973-292-2737.

FREDERICKS, WARD ARTHUR, venture capitalist; b. Tarrytown, NY, Dec. 24, 1939; s. Arthur George and Evelyn (Smith) F.; m. Patricia A. Sexton, June 12, 1960; children: Corrine E., Lorrine L., Ward A. BS cum laude, Mich. State U., 1962, MBA, 1963, PhD. Assoc. dir. Technics Group, Grand Rapids, Mich., 1964-68; gen. mgr. logistics systems Massey-Ferguson, Inc., Toronto, Ont., Canada, 1968-69, v.p. mgmt. svcs., comptr., 1969-73, sr. v.p. fin., dir. fin. Americas, 1975—; comptr. Massey-Ferguson Ltd., Toronto, Ont., Canada, 1973-75; prin. W.B. Saunders & Co., Washington, 1962—64; sr. v.p. mktg. Massey.Ferguson, Inc., 1975-78, also pres., gen. mgr. tractor divsn., 1978-80; gen. mgr. Rockwell Graphic Sys., 1980-82; pres. Goss Co., Chgo.; v.p. ops. Rockwell Internat., Pitts., 1980-84; v.p. Fed. MOG, 1983-84; chmn. MIXTEC Group LLC, 1998—2002; also dir., chmn.; prin. Venture Assocs., 1993—. Dir. Polyfet RF, Inc., Venture Assocs., Badger Horthland, Inc., MST, Inc., Calif., Tech-Mark Group, Inc., Spectra Tech., Inc., Mixtec Group-Venture Capital, Inc., Unicorn Corp., Mixtec Food Group Calif., Mixtec Signal Tech., Harry Ferguson, Inc., M.F. Credit Corp., M.F. Credit Co. Can Ltd.; chmn. ProduceCareers.com., 2000-02. Author: (with Edward Smykay) Physical Distribution Management, 1974; author: Management Vision, 1988, Competitive Advantage in Technology Organizations, 1986, Competitive Advantage in Technology Firms, 1996; contbr. articles to profl. jours. Bd. dirs., mem. exec. com. Des Moines Symphony, 1975-79; pres. Conejo Symphony, 1988-90, Westlake Village Cultural Found., 1991, Conejo Valley Indsl. Assn., 1990, 93, Aviation CC Calif., 2001, Indian Wells Desert Symphony, 2002, bd. dirs., 2001-02; mem. exec. com. Alliance for Arts, vice chair; mem. Constn. Bicentennial Com., 1987-88, Ventura County Airport Commn., 1995-99, La Quinta Arts Found.; mem. World Affairs Coun. of Desert, pres., 2001-06, chmn. 2006—; bd. dirs. Ventura County Bus. Incubator, 1996-99, Cochella Valley Cmty. Concerts Assn., 1992-95, Coll. The Desert Found., 2002—, chmn. investment com., 2004, v.p., 2006, pres., 2007-; v.p. Com. Leaders Club, 1988, pres., 1989-90; bd. regents Calif. Luth. U., 1990-99, chmn. acad. affairs, 1992-99, exec. com., 1992-99, vice chmn., 1997-98; pres. coun. McCallun Theater, Palm Desert; mem. Pres.'s circle Coll. of Desert, Palm Desert; mem. rep. ctrl. com. State Calif., 1993-98; pres. World Affairs Coun. of Desert, 2001-06, chmn., 2006; bd. dirs. Boys and Girls Club Coachella Valley, 2003-; pres. Fredericks Found., 2002—; chmn. Westlake Village C. of C., 1990; nat. councillor World Affairs Coun., Washington, 2004—, dir., 2006—; chair investment com. COD Found., 2002—, exec. com., 2005- , v.p., 2006, pres. 2007-. Fellow Am. Transp. Assn.; mem. AAAS, IEEE, SAR, Am. Mktg. Assn., Nat. Coun. Phys. Distbn. Mgmt. (exec. com. 1974), Produce Mktg. Assn., United Fresh Fruit and Vegetable Assn., Internat. Fresh-Cut Produce Assn., Soc. Automotive Engrs., US Strategic Inst., Tech. Execs. Forum (Tech. Corridor 100 award 1989), Internat. Food Mfg. Assn., Produce Mktg. Assn., Toronto Bd. Trade, English-Speaking Union (bd. dirs. 2004-06), Westlake Village C. of C. (chmn. 1990), Old Crows, Assn. Advanced Tech. Edn., Air Force Assn., Aerospace Soc., Exptl. Aircraft Assn., Mil. Order World Wars, Conf. Air Force (Col.), Westlake Village C. of C. (chmn. bd. 1990-91), Cmty. Leaders Club, Pres.'s Club Mich. State U., Pres.'s Circle/Coll. of the Desert, English-Spkg. Union, Friends of Parliament, Old Bold Pilots Club, Indian Wells Country Club, Sherwood Country Club, St. Georges Club (UK), Aviation Country Club of Calif. (v.p. 1999, pres. 2000), Sandstone Club (Vail, Colo.), Rotary (dir. 2003—), Flying Rotarians, World Affairs Coun. (nat. bd. dir. 2007-), Beta Gamma Sigma. Lutheran. Home: 75375 Painted Desert Dr Indian Wells CA 92210 Office: 709 E Colorado Blvd Pasadena CA 91101

FREDERICKS, WESLEY CHARLES, JR., lawyer; b. NYC, Mar. 31, 1948; s. Wesley Charles and Dionysia W. (Bitsanis) F.; m. Jeanne Maria Judson, May 19, 1973; children: Carolyn Anne, Wesley Charles III. BA, Johns Hopkins U., 1970; JD, Columbia U., 1973. Bar: N.Y. 1974, Conn. 1976, U.S. Supreme Ct. 1979. Assoc. Shearman & Sterling, NYC, 1973-83; chmn. bd. Lotus Performance Cars, L.P., Norwood, N.J., 1983-87; group exec. cons. Group Lotus PLC, 1987; automotive industry cons., 1988-90; pres., CEO Mfrs. Products Co., 1990-94; counsel Gersten, Savage, Kaplowitz & Fredericks, LLP, NYC, 1994, ptnr., 1995-98, Dorsey & Whitney LLP, NYC, 1998—2006, dep. mng. ptnr., 2004—06; shareholder Heller Ehrman LLP, NYC, 2006—. Mem. Johns Hopkins U. Alumni Schs. Com. With USMC, 1968-69. Mem. ABA (chmn. bus. law sect. com. on internat. bus. law, 2004—, mem. com. on negotiated acquisitions 1997—), Weston Gun Club (Conn.), Preston Mountain Club. Republican. Congregationalist. Office: Heller Ehrman LLC 7 Times Sq New York NY 10036

FREDERICKS, WILLIAM CURTIS, lawyer; b. Washington, July 3, 1961; s. J. Wayne and Anne Curtis Fredericks; m. Ivy Lindstrom, Jan. 21, 1995; children: Charlotte Lindstrom, Thomas Curtis. BA in Polit. Sci. with high honors, Swarthmore Coll., 1983; MLitt in Internat. Rels., Oxford U., Eng., 1988; JD, Columbia U., 1988. Bar: N.Y. 1990, U.S. Dist. Ct. (so. and ea. dists.) N.Y. 1990, U.S. Ct. Appeals (2d cir.) 1991, U.S. Ct. Appeals (10th cir.) 1997, U.S. Ct. Appeals (6th cir.) 1998, U.S. Dist. Ct. Colo. 1998, U.S. Ct. Appeals (3d cir.) 2001. Law clk. hon. Robert S. Gawthrop U.S. Dist. Ct. Pa., Phila., 1988—89; assoc. Simpson Thacher & Bartlett, NYC, 1989—93, Willkie Farr & Gallagher, NYC, 1993—97, Milberg Weiss Bershad & Schulman LLP, NYC, 1997—98, ptnr., 1999—2006, Bernstein Litowitz Berger & Grossman, LLP, NYC, 2006—. Articles editor Columbia Jour. Transnational Law, 1987-88. V.p. Swarthmore Coll. Alumni Assn., 1988-90. Mem. Assn. of the Bar of the City of N.Y. (chair com. on mil. affairs and justice 1997-99, mem. com. on fed. cts., 2004-06). Democrat. Office: Bernstein Litowitz Berger & Grossman LLP 1285 Avenue of the Americas New York NY 10119

FREDERICKSEN, DICK HARTMAN, retired computer programmer; b. Great Falls, Mont., Jan. 16, 1931; s. Frederick Hartman and Helen Dickinson Fredericksen; m. Ann Bancroft, July 30, 1960 (div. Oct. 1990); children: Diane, Judith, Alice, Victor. AB, U. Chgo., 1951, postgrad., 1951-60, MS, 1968. Systems engr. IBM Corp., Chgo., 1960-64, programmer Poughkeepsie, 1965-66, programmer T.J. Watson Rsch. Ctr. Yorktown Heights, NY, 1969-90; part-time programmer Nat. Optical Astronomy Observatories, Tucson, 1990-92, ret., 1992. Nat. chmn. Young Peoples Socialist League, 1951-53; active L5 Soc./Nat. Space Soc., NY, Ariz., 1976—. Mem. Sonoran Arthropod Studies Inst., Tucson Space Soc. (v.p. 2000, sec.-treas. 2001-03), Tucson Computer Soc. Avocations: web publishing, hiking, motorcycling, wildlife photography, commentary. Home: 7351 E Speedway Blvd Apt 11G Tucson AZ 85710-1513 Personal E-mail: dhfred@dakotacom.net.

FREDERICKSON, ARMAN FREDERICK, mining executive, petroleum engineer; b. Glenboro, Man., Can., May 5, 1918; came to U.S., 1923, naturalized, 1940; s. Albert F. and Ethel M. (Wilton) F.; m. Mary Maxine Stubblefield, Sept. 23, 1943; children: Mary Christene, Clover Diane, Penny Kathlene, Kimberly Mei, Sigrid, Janice BS in Mining Engring, U. Wash., 1940; MS in Metall. Engring, Mont. Sch. Mines, 1942; Sc.D. in Geology, Mass. Inst. Tech., 1947. Registered profl. engr., Tex., Colo., Nev., Mo.; cert. petroleum geologist. Mining engr., chief geologist Cornucopia Gold Mines, Oreg., 1939-40; instr. mineral dressing Mont. Sch. Mines, 1941-42; research asst. Mass. Inst. Tech., 1942-43; prof. geology and geol. engring. Washington U., St. Louis, 1947-56; organizer, supr. geol. research Standard (Amoco) Oil and Gas Co., Tulsa, 1955-60; prof. geology, chmn. dept. earth and planetary sci., dir. oceanography U. Pitts., 1960-65; sr. v.p., dir. research, mgr. petroleum prospecting and mineral programs in U.S., Middle East, Africa, Latin Am., 1965-71; pres., chief engr. Sorbotec, Inc., Houston, 1971-74; pres. Global Survey, 1972—. V.p. Samoco (Panama) Challenger Desert Oil Corp., 1977-81; cons. in mining and petroleum exploration, 1971—; v.p. SAMOCO, Del., 1977-81; v.p. ops. CHADOIL, 1978-81, Crown Gems, Inc., Thailand; pres. Global-Thai Exploration Corp., Thailand; organizer, past chmn. clay minerals com. Nat. Acad. Sci.-NRC; organizer, econ. analyst land and real estate projects, Calif.; negotiator oil, gemstone and mining programs, U.S., Africa, Thailand, Middle and Far East, Latin Am., exploration specialist. Author tech. papers in field, hist. novels; patentee fertilizer, oil and water pollution processes and products. Served with USNR, 1943-45. Fulbright prof. Norway, 1955. Fellow Geol. Soc. Am., Mineral Soc. Am.; mem. Am. Inst. Mining, Metall. and Petroleum Engrs., Am. Assn. Petroleum Geologists, Soc. Econ. Geologists, Geochem. Soc. Am., Underwater Soc. Am. Republican. Lutheran. Home: 97 Mission Dr Petaluma CA 94952-5228 Office Phone: 707-658-0405.

FREDERICKSON, CHRISTINE MAGNUSON, reporter, researcher, editor, writer; d. George Adolf and Pauline Hazen Magnuson; m. Arthur Robb Frederickson, June 6, 1970 (dec.); children: Timothy R., Nathan B., Julie H. Attended, Kalamazoo Coll., 1964—66; BA cum laude, U. NH, 1969; MEd, Boston Coll., 1974. Staff writer Computerworld Newsweekly, Newton, Mass., 1969—71; radio events editor Antique Radio Classified, Carlisle, Mass., 1986—97; ct. reporter, ind. contractor LA, 1999—2003. New script reader Fountain Theatre, LA, 1998—2003. Author: Doña Victoria-First Lady of San Gabriel, 1998; prodr.: Southwest Museum, 1999—2000. Docent San Gabriel Mission, Calif., 1997—2006, Homestead Mus., Industry, Calif., 1998—2004. Critic fellow, Nat. Critics Inst., Waterford, Conn., 2000. Mem.: Eugene O'Neill Soc., Internat. Bonhoffer Soc., Dramatists Guild (assoc.), Calif. Mission Studies Assn., Caltech Women's Club (bulletin editor 1998—2000). Avocations: ice skating, aerobics, reading. Personal E-mail: cmfrederickson1@comcast.net.

FREDERICKSON, CHRISTOPHER JOHN, neuroscientist; b. Norman, Okla., Aug. 1, 1945; s. John Henry and Joan Munson Frederickson; m. Cathleen Jean McCartney, Apr. 30, 1995; 1 child, Isabel. AB magna cum laude, Harvard Coll., 1968; PhD, U. Chgo., 1972. Asst. prof. neurosci. Carnegie Mellon, Pitts., 1972-75, U. Tex. Dallas, Richardson, 1975-78, assoc. prof. neurosci., 1978-85, full prof. neurosci., 1985-99; CEO NeuroBio Tex, Little Elm, Tex., 1999—. Dir. biotech. MicroFab Tech., Inc., Plano, Tex., 1996—99, U. Tex. Med. Br., Galveston, 1999—2000; mem. adv. bd. Tex. A&M Biomed. Engring., College Station, 1998—99; inaugural chair NIH Zinc in Health/Zinc in the Brain/Metals in Medicine, 2002; spkr. in field. Editor: Zinc Neurobiology, 1985; contbr. articles to profl. jours.; patentee in field. Bd. mem. YMCA, Richardson, 1995. Small Bus. Innovation and Rsch. grantee NIH, Washington, 1998. Mem. Soc. for Neurosci., Soc. Photo-Optical Instrumentation Engrs., Am. Chemosensory Soc. Avocation: sailing. Office: NeuroBioTex 101 Christopher Columbus 14th Stus 14 Galveston TX 77550 E-mail: c.j.frederickson@neurobiotex.com.

FREDERICKSON, HORACE GEORGE, retired academic administrator, humanities educator; b. Twin Falls, Idaho, July 17, 1937; s. John C. and Zelpha (Richins) F.; m. Mary Williams, Mar. 14, 1958; children— Thomas, Christian, Lynne, David. BA, Brigham Young U., 1959; M.P.A., UCLA, 1961; PhD, U. So. Calif., 1967; LL.D. (hon.), Dongguk U., Korea. Intern Los Angeles County, 1960; research asst. Bur. Govtl. Research, U. Calif., Los Angeles, 1960-61; lectr. pub. adminstrn. U. So. Calif., 1962-64; lectr. govt. and politics U. Md., 1964-66; asst. prof. polit. sci. Maxwell Sch., Syracuse U., 1967-71; assoc. dir. Met. Studies Program, 1970-72, assoc. prof. polit. sci., 1971-72; fellow in higher edn. fin. adminstrn. U. N.C. System, 1972; chmn. Grad. Program, Sch. Pub. and Environ. Affairs, Ind. U., 1972-74, assoc. dean for policy and adminstrv. studies, 1973-74; dean Coll. Pub. and Community Services, prof. regional and community affairs U. Mo., Columbia, 1974-76; pres. Eastern Wash. U., Cheney, 1976-87; Edwin O. Stene Disting. prof. pub. adminstrn. U. Kans., Lawrence, 1987—; John G. Winont vis. prof. Am. Gov., fellow U. Oxford, 2003—. Author: New Public Administration, 1980, The Spirit of Public Administration, 1997; editor: Ethics and Public Administration, 1993, Public Policy and the Two States of Kansas, 1994, Ideal and Practice in Council-Manager Government, 2nd edit., 1994; editor in chief Jour. Pub. Adminstrn. Rsch. and Theory, 1991—. Haynes Found. fellow U. So. Calif., 1963-64 Mem. Am. Soc. Pub. Adminstrn. (pres.), Nat. Acad. Pub. Adminstrn. Office: U Kans 1541 Lilac Ln #318 Lawrence KS 66044-3177 Home: 8428 Meadow Ln Leawood KS 66206-1422

FREDERICKSON, PHILIP L., oil industry executive; b. Borger, Tex., 1956; BS, Tex. Tech.Univ. Gen. mgr., strategy & portfolio mgmt., upstream ConocoPhillips, Houston, 1997—98, v.p. bus. devel., 1998—2001, sr. v.p., corp. strategy & bus. devel., 2001—02, exec. v.p., commercial, 2003—06, exec. v.p. planning, strategy and corp. affairs, 2006—07, exec. v.p. tech., 2007—. Bd. dirs. Theatre Under the Stars. Mem.: Am. Inst. of Idustrial Engring. Office: Conoco Phillips 600 N Ashford Rd Houston TX 77079*

FREDMAN, HOWARD S., lawyer; b. St. Louis, Feb. 1, 1944; s. Manuel and Sydine Fredman; children: Jocelyn Bly, Amber Alexandra, Cameron Penn. BA, Princeton U., 1966; JD, Columbia U., 1969. Bar: Calif. 1970, U.S. Dist. Ct. (no. dist.) Calif. 1970, U.S. Ct. Appeals (9th cir.) 1970, U.S. Dist. Ct. (so. dist.) Calif. 1974, U.S. Dist. Ct. (ctrl. dist.) Calif. 1975, U.S. Dist. Ct. (ea. dist.) Calif. 1996, U.S. Dist. Ct. Colo. 2000. Law clk. to Hon. Milton Pollack U.S. Dist. Ct. (so. dist.) N.Y., NYC, 1969-70; assoc. McCutchen, Doyle, Brown & Enersen, San Francisco, 1970-75; counsel, sr. atty., atty. legal divsn. Atlantic Richfield Co., LA, 1975-87; assoc. Frandzel & Share, LA, 1987-90, ptnr., 1990—99; pvt. practice LA, 1999—2002; ptnr. Fredman/Lieberman LLP, LA, 2002—. Mem. faculty Practicing Law Inst., 1982, 86-88; lectr., spkr. in field. Mem. editl. adv bd. Calif. Causes of Action, 1998. Chair alumni schs. com. L.A. area Princeton U., 1992—94, chair alumni schs. com. San Fernando Valley area, 2000—; mem. com. to nominate alumni trustees Princeton Alumni Coun., 1998—2001, treas., exec. com., 2001—03, mem. strategic planning com., 1997—98, mem. at large, 2003—05. Recipient cert. of recognition, U.S. Dist. Ct. (ctrl. dist.) Calif., 2002. Mem. ABA, Assn. Bus. Trial Lawyers, Fed. Bar Assn., L.A. County Bar Assn. (chmn. antitrust sect. 1986-87, exec. com. antitrust sect. 1982—, nominating com. 1986-87, del. state bar conf. dels. 1987, 88), Beverly Hills Bar Assn. (del. to state bar conf. of dels. 2005-07, vice chair resolutions com. 2006-07), Princeton Club So. Calif. (pres. 1994-96). Democrat. Jewish. Office: Fredman/Lieberman LLP 1875 Century Park E Ste 2200 Los Angeles CA 90067-2523 Home Phone: 310-859-2775; Office Phone: 310-226-6796. Personal E-mail: hsflawyer@aol.com.

FREDMANN, MARTIN, ballet company artistic director, educator, choreographer; b. Balt., Feb. 3, 1943; s. Martin Joseph and Hilda Adele (Miller) Fredmann; m. Kaleriya Fedicheva Fredmann (div. Jan. 2, 1978); m. Patricia Renzetti, June 12, 1980. Student, Nat. Ballet Sch., Washington, 1962-64, Vaganova Sch., Leningrad, 1972. Prin. dancer The Md. Ballet, Balt., 1961-64; dancer The Pa. Ballet, Phila., 1964-65, Ballet of the Met. Opera Co., NYC, 1965-66; prin. dancer Dortmund (Fed. Republic Germany) Ballet, 1973-75, Scapino Ballet, Amsterdam, Holland, 1975-76; tchr. German Opera Ballet, West Berlin, Germany, 1979—82, Netherlands Dance Theater, 1979, Royal Swedish Ballet, 1980, San Francisco Ballet, 1981; tchr., coach Australian Ballet, 1982; tchr. Tokyo City Ballet, Hong Kong Ballet, 1985, 86, 87, London Festival Ballet, 1981-83; dir. ballet Teatro Comunale, Florence, Italy, 1984-85; artistic dir. Tampa Ballet, Fla., 1984—90, Colo. Ballet, Denver, 1987—2005. Tchr. German Opera Ballet, 1982, Ballet Rambert, London, 1983, Bat Dor summer course, Israel, 1983, Cullberg Ballet, Sweden, 1983, Hong Kong Acad. For Performing Arts, 1985—89, 1991, Tokyo City Ballet, 1985—90, Ballet West, 1990, Nat. Ballet Korea, 1991, Dance Divsn. Tsoying High Sch., Kaohsiung, Taiwan, 1992; guest lectr., tchr. Cen. Ballet China, Beijing Dancing Acad., P.L.A. Arts Coll., Beijing, 1990; tchr. Legat Sch., 1978, examiner, 80; tchr. Eglevsky Sch., NYC, 1980; asst. dir. ballet master Niavaron Cultural ctr., Tehran, Iran, 1978; tchr. Ballet Arts Sch. Carnegie Hall, NYC, 1979—81; choreographer Estonia Nat. Theatre, Russia, 1991; dir. Marin Ballet., Calif., 1981, Japan Grand Prix, 2003—. Choreographer Romeo and Juliet, 1983, Sachertorte, 1984, A Little Love, 1984, Ricordanza, 1986, Cinderella, 1986, Coppelia, 1987, The Nutcracker, 1987, Beauty and the Beast, 1988, Masquerade Suite, 1989, Silent Woods, 1989, The Last Songs, 1991, Centenial Suite, 1994. Recipient Recipient Mayor's award, Denver, 1996, Dance Mag. award, 1999, Bonfils-Stanton Found. award, 2000, Order of the Rising Sun, Gold Rays with Rosette, Govt of Japan, 2005. Mem.: Nat. Assn. Regional Ballet., Fla. State Dance Assn, Am. Guild Mus. Artists. Avocations: cooking, cook book collecting, travel, opera. Office: 836 E 17th Ave Apt 3A Denver CO 80218-1449 Home Phone: 303-837-9433; Office Phone: 303-837-9433.

FREDRICK, LARITA DENISE, science educator; b. Springfield, Mo., Sept. 27, 1954; d. Ordra Paul Pippin and Bernice Orene Kirkey, Clarence William Kirkey, Jr. (Stepfather); m. Gail L. Fredrick, Nov. 13, 1987. BS in Secondary Edn., S.W. Mo. State U., 1983, MS in Secondary Edn., 1994. Cert. tchr. Dept. of Elem. and Secondary Edn. , Mo., 1983. Tchr. sci. H.S. Springfield (Mo.) Pub. Schs., 1985—2001, curriculum coord. k-12 sci., 2001—. Adj. instr. Ozarks Tech. Coll., Springfield, 1994—2001, S.W. Mo. State U., 1996—2002, Drury U., Springfield, 2002—. Ex-offico mem. Springfield (Mo.) Pub. Schs. Found., 2002—05. Named Outstanding Young Alumni, S.W. Mo. State U., 2000; recipient Triple E Edn. award, 1998, Nat. Edn. award, Milken Family Found., 1999, Mo. Eddy award, Dept. Elem. and Secondary Edn. , Mo., 2000. Mem.: NEA, Am. Soc. Curriculum Devel., Nat. Assn. Sci. Tchrs. Office: Springfield Public Schools 940 N Jefferson Springfield MO 65802 Home Phone: 414-882-1006; Office Phone: 417-523-5556. Personal E-mail: ldenisefredrick@sbcglobal.net.

FREDRICK, LAURENCE WILLIAM, astronomer, educator; b. Stroudsburg, Pa., Aug. 27, 1927; s. Ishmeal T. and Grace (Slider) F.; m. Frances I. Schwenk, Feb. 5, 1949; children— Laura Grace, Theodore David, Rebecca Lyn BA, Swarthmore Coll., 1952, MA, 1954; PhD, U. Pa., 1959. Research asst. Sproul Obs., Swarthmore, Pa., 1952-56; research assoc. Flower and Cook Obs., Malvern, Pa., 1957-59; astronomer Lowell Obs., Flagstaff, Ariz., 1959-63; mem. faculty U. Va., Charlottesville, 1963-95, prof. astronomy, 1965-95, rsch. prof., 1995—; prof. U. Vienna, Austria, 1972-73. Cons. in field; Fulbright-Hays exch. lectr., Austria, 1972-73; assoc. astronomer European So. Obs., Munich, Fed. Republic Germany, 1982-83; vis. fellow Australian Nat. U., Canberra, 1991-92. Co-author: Astronomy, 10th edit., 1976, Descriptive Astronomy, 1978, An Introduction to Astronomy, 9th edit., 1980 Served with USN, 1945-48 Named Alumnus of Yr., Milton Hershey Sch., 1961 Mem. Am. Astron. Soc. (sec. 1969-80), Internat. Astron. Union (sec. U.S. nat. com. 1970-80), Am. Inst. Physics (bd. govs. 1969-79), Univs. for Space Research Assn. (trustee), Royal Astron. Soc., Soc. Sci. Exploration (sec. 1981-2005), Sigma Xi Home: 2602 Bennington Rd Charlottesville VA 22901-2211 Office Phone: 434-924-4905. Business E-Mail: lwf@virginia.edu.

FREDRICK, SUSAN WALKER, tax company manager; b. Painesville, Ohio, Nov. 17, 1948; d. Floyd Clayton and Margaret (Merkel) Walker; m. Stephan Douglas Fredrick, Oct. 20, 1973. BS, Mt. Union Coll., Alliance, Ohio, 1970; MS, U. Conn., 1973. Rsch. asst. Boyce Thompson Inst., Yonkers, NY, 1971-74; dir. quality control Lawley, Matusky, Skelly, Tappan, NY, 1974-75; field supr. Ecological Analysts, Middletown, NY, 1975-76; scientist Pandullo Quirk Assocs., Wayne, NJ, 1976-78; editor Bioscis. Info. Service, Phila., 1978-80; tax preparer H&R Block, Inc., Malvern, Pa., 1978-80, dist. mgr. King of Prussia and West Chester, Pa., 1980—2002, franchise dist. mgr. Easton, Md., 2002—05, Mid-Atlantic franchise dist. mgr., 2005—. Guest lectr. Temple U., 1981—86. Mem.: Nat. Assn. Underwater Instns. (ret. instr.), Pa. Soc. Enrolled Agts., Nat. Assn. Enrolled Agts, Keystone Drivers Club (West Chester, Pa.). Avocations: scuba diving, hiking, swimming. Office: 200 Bellevue Pky Ste 160 Wilmington DE 19809

FREDRICKSON, BRUCE E., orthopedist; b. Boston, Apr. 29, 1946; s. Richard and Elsie Fredrickson; m. Karen K. Jacobson, Apr. 12, 1969; children: Suzanne M., Kirsten L. MD, SUNY, Syracuse, 1972. Diplomate Am. Acad. Orthop. Surgeons, 1972. Prof. orthop. and neurol. surgery Upstate Med. U., Syracuse, NY, 1979—2006; chief sect. spine surgery VA Med. Ctr., Syracuse, 2006—. Bd. dirs. Pony Club, Syracuse, 1986—92. Lt. comdr. USN, 1977—79. Fellow: N. Am. Spine Soc. (life; treas. 1995—98, David Selby award 2002, Volvo award 1992). Office: VA Med Ctr Dept Surgery Syracuse NY 13210 Office Phone: 315-426-2636. Office Fax: 315-425-2639. Business E-Mail: bruce.fredrickson2@va.gov.

FREDRICKSON, GEORGE MARSH, history professor; b. Bristol, Conn., July 16, 1934; s. George Fredrickson and Gertrude (Marsh) F.; m. Helene Osouf, Oct. 16, 1956; children: Anne, Laurel, Thomas, Caroline. AB, Harvard U., 1956, PhD, 1964. Instr. history Harvard U., Cambridge, Mass., 1963-66; assoc. prof. history Northwestern U., Evanston, Ill., 1966-71, prof., 1971-84, William Smith Mason prof. Am. history, 1979-84; Edgar E. Robinson prof. U.S. history Stanford (Calif.) U., 1984—2002, prof. emeritus, 2002—. Fulbright prof. Moscow U., 1983, Harmsworth prof. Am. history Oxford U., 1988-89. Author: The Inner Civil War, 1965, 2d edit., 1993, The Black Image in the White Mind, 1971, 2d edit., 1987 (Anisfield-Wolf award 1972), White Supremacy, 1981 (Ralph Waldo Emerson award 1981, Merle Curti award, 1982, Pulitzer prize finalist 1982), The Arrogance of Race, 1988, Black Liberation, 1995, The Comparative Imagination, 1997, Racism: A Short History, 2002; co-author: America: Past and Present, 8th edit., 2006; editor: A Nation Divided, 1975; co-editor: Not Just Black and White, 2004. Served to lt. USN, 1957-60. Guggenheim fellow, 1967-68; NEH fellow, 1973-74; Ctr. for Advanced Studies in Behavioral Scis. fellow, 1977-78; NEH fellow, 1985-86; Ford sr. fellow DuBois Inst., Harvard U., 1993. Fellow Soc. Am. Historians, Am. Antiquarian Soc., Am. Acad. Arts and Scis.; mem. Am. Hist. Assn., Orgn. Am. Historians (pres. 1997-98), So. Hist. Assn. Home: 741 Esplanada Way Palo Alto CA 94305-1013 Office: Stanford Univ Dept History Stanford CA 94305 Business E-Mail: fredrick@stanford.edu.

FREDRICKSON, GLENN HAROLD, chemical engineering and materials educator; b. Washington, May 8, 1959; BS with honors in Chem. Engring., U. Fla., 1980; MS in Chem. Engring., Stanford U., Calif., 1981, PhD in Chem. Engring., 1984. Mem. tech. staff AT&T Bell Labs., Murray Hill, NJ, 1984-89, disting. mem. tech. staff, 1989-90; assoc. prof. dept. chem. engring. and engring. materials dept. U. Calif., Santa Barbara, 1990-91, dir. Macromolecular Sci. and Engring. Ctr., prof. dept. chem. engring. and engring. materials dept., 1991—, vice-chair chem. engring.,

1996-98, chair chem. engring., 1998—2001, founding dir. Mitsubishi Chem. Ctr. Advanced Materials, 2001—, dir. Complex Fluids Design Consortium, 2002—, assoc. dir. Materials Rsch. Lab., 2004—, Mitsubishi chem. chair functional materials, 2004—. Allan P. Colburn lectr. U. Del., 1991; George T. Piercy disting prof. chem. engring. and materials sci. U. Minn., Mpls., 1992; vis. rsch. prof. Miller Inst. U. Calif., Berkeley, 1993; lectr. in field. Contbr. articles to sci. jours.; mem. editl. bd. Jour. Polymer Sci. physics edit., 1992—, Macromolecules, 1994-96; mem. internat. editl. adv. bd. Acta Polymerica, 1992—. Exxon Tchg. fellow Stanford U., 1982-84, Alfred P. Sloan Rsch. fellow, 1992; recipient Presdl. Young Investigator award NSF, 1990, Camille and Henry Dreyfus Tchr.-Scholar award, 1991. Fellow Am. Phys. Soc. (publs. com. 1992-94, John H. Dillon medal Divsn. High Polymer Physics 1992, Polymer Physics prize 2007), AIChE, 1999 (Alpha Chi Sigma award); mem. Phi Kappa Phi, NAE. Office: Mitsubishi Chem Ctr Advanced Materials U Calif 3105 MRL Bldg Santa Barbara CA 93106-5080 Office Phone: 805-893-8308. Office Fax: 805-893-8797. E-mail: ghf@mrl.ucsb.edu.*

FREDRICKSON, L(AWRENCE) THOMAS, composer; b. Kane, Pa., Sept. 5, 1928; s. Eric Lawrence Fredrickson and Esther Linnea (Skoog) Bussell; m. Betty Jean Blessing, July 30, 1950; children: Lawrence Alan, Linda Kay, Gail Diane. MusB, Ohio Wesleyan U., 1950; MusM, U. Ill., Urbana, 1952, MusD, 1960. Jazz musician, Ill., 1952—; composer, arranger Urbana, Ill., 1952—; instr. music U. Ill., Urbana/Champaign, 1952-60, asst. prof., 1960-63, assoc. prof., 1963-67, prof., 1967-93, prof. emeritus, 1993, dir. Sch. of Music, 1970-74. Composer: Brass Quintet, Impressions, Deja Vu, Music for the Double Bass Alone; commns. include works for orch., band, chamber music, solo works; performer double bass in chamber music and jazz groups, symphony orchs. Mem. ASCAP, Am. Fedn. of Musicians. Home: 1814 Robert Dr Champaign IL 61821-6031 Personal E-mail: thomasfredrickson2@insightbb.com.

FREDRIK, BURRY, theater producer, director; b. NYC, Aug. 9, 1925; d. Fredric Kreuger and Erna Anita (Burry) Gerber; m. Gerard E. Meunier, Dec. 27, 1945 (div. 1949). Grad., Sarah Lawrence Coll., 1947. Ind. theatrical dir., producer U.S. and abroad, 1955—; lit. mgr., dir. Boston Post Road Stage Co., 1988—92; artistic dir. Fairfield County Stage Co. (formerly Boston Post Road Stage), 1992—93. Prodr.: (Broadway plays) Too Good to be True, 1964—65 (nominated Tony award, 1965), Travesties, 1976 (Tony award, 1976), An Almost Perfect Person, 1977, The Night of the Tribades, 1978, To Grandmother's House We Go, 1981, The Royal Family, 1975—76 (Drama Desk award, 1976), (off-Broadway plays) Thieves Carnival, 1955 (Spl. Tony award, 1955), Exiles, 1956 (OBIE award, 1956), Buried Child (Pulitzer prize, 1980); dir.: (nat. tours) Misalliance, 1953, Milk and Honey, 1963, Dark at the Top of the Stairs, 1958, Dear Love, 1971, To Grandmother's House We Go, 1982, (off-Broadway prodns.) The Decameron, 1961, Catholic School Girls, 1981, (Broadway prodn.) Wild and Wonderful, 1972; prodr.: (off-Broadway) Pretzels, 1974; dir.: (plays, Sad Hotel) White Barn Theatre, 2001—; (plays, Swansong), 2002—. Chmn. Weston Commn. Arts, 1997—2000; mem. fin. commn.; trustee Long Wharf Theatre, New Haven, 1998—. Recipient Disting. Adv. Arts award, State of Conn. Commn. Arts, 2001. Home and Office: 51 Hillside Rd N Weston CT 06883-1513 Office Phone: 203-227-9349. Office Fax: 203-222-9478.

FREE, HELEN MURRAY, chemist, consultant; b. Pitts., Feb. 20, 1923; d. James Summerville and Daisy (Piper) Murray; m. Alfred H. Free, Oct. 18, 1947 (dec. May 2000); children: Eric, Penny, Kurt, Jake, Bonnie, Nina. BA in Chemistry, Coll. of Wooster, Ohio, 1944, DSc (hon.), 1992; MA in Clin. Lab. Mgmt., Ctrl. Mich. U., 1978, DSc (hon.), 1993. Cert. clin. chemist Nat. Registry Cert. Chemists. Chemist Miles Labs., Elkhart, Ind., 1944—78, dir. mktg. svcs. rsch. products divsn., 1978-82; chemist, mgr., cons. Bayer HealthCare Diabetes Care, Elkhart, 1982—. Mem. adj. faculty Ind. U., South Bend, 1975—96; spkr. in field. Author (with others): (books) Urodynamics and Urinalysis in Clinical Laboratory Practice, 1972, 1976; contbr. articles to encys. and profl. jours. Bd. dirs. Nat. Inventors Hall of Fame Found.; women's chmn. Centennial of Elkhart, 1958; mem. adv. bd. Intellectual Property Sch. Law, Akron U.; indsl. adv. bd. chemistry/chem. engring. Tri-State U., Angola, Ind. Named Woman of Yr., YWCA, 1993, Kilby Found. laureate, 1996; named to Hall of Excellence, Ohio Found. Ind. Colls., 1992, Nat. Inventors Hall of Fame, 2000, Engring. and Sci. Hall of Fame, 1996; recipient Disting. Alumni award, Coll. of Wooster, 1980, award, Medi Econ. Press, 1986, Nat. Leadership award, Lab. Pub. Svc., 1994. Fellow: AAAS, Assn. Women in Sci., Royal Soc. Chemistry, Am. Inst. Chemists (co-recipient Chgo. award 1967); mem.: Nat. Com. Clin. Lab. Stds. (bd. dir.), Am. Soc. Clin. Lab. Sci. (chmn. assembly, Achievement award 1976), Soc. Chem. Industry (hon.), Assn. Clin. Scientists (diploma of honor 1992), Am. Assn. Clin. Chemistry (coun., bd. dir., nominating com. and pub. rels. com., coord. profl. affairs, nat. membership com., pres. 1990, Outstanding Contbn. award 2006), Am. Chem. Soc. (pres. 1993, bd. dir., chmn. Chemistry Week task force, bd. com. pub. affairs and pub. rels., chmn. women chemists com., internat. activities com., grants and awards com., prof. and mem. rels. com., nominating com., coun. policy pub. affairs and budget, councilor, chair Progress project, Garvan medal 1980, Svc. award local chpt. 1981, co-recipient Mosher award 1983, 1st recipient Helen M. Free Pub. Outreach award 1995, Helen M. Free award named in her honor 1995), Altrusa (pres. 1982—83, bd. dir.), Sigma Delta Epsilon (hon.), Iota Sigma Pi (hon.). Presbyterian. Achievements include patents in field. Home: 3752 E Jackson Blvd Elkhart IN 46516-5205 Office: Bayer HealthCare Diabetes Care Divsn 1025 N Michigan Ave Elkhart IN 46514 Personal E-mail: Hmfree23@aol.com. Business E-Mail: helen.free.b@bayer.com.

FREEBORN, MICHAEL D., lawyer; b. Mpls., June 30, 1946; s. Andrew W. and Verena M. (Keller) F.; m. Nancie L. Siebel, Oct. 19, 1947; children: Christopher A., Nathan M., Joel C., Paul K. BS, USAF Acad., 1968; JD, Ind. U., 1972; MBA, U. Chgo., 1975. Bar: Ill. 1972, Ind. 1972, US Ct. Appeals (3rd, 6th, 7th & DC cirs., US Supreme Ct. Assoc. to ptnr. Rooks, Pitts & Poust, Chgo., 1972-83; ptnr. Freeborn & Peters, Chgo., 1983—. Writer, lectr. in field. Assoc. editor Ind. Law Rev., 1970-71. Vice chmn. Voices for Ill. Children, 1993-2003; bd. dirs. Constnl. Rights Found. Chgo., 1996—. Chgo. Youth Ctrs., 1998-2005; chmn. citizens adv. coun. Ill. Coastal Zone Mgmt. Prog., Chgo., 1979. Capt. USAF, 1968—72. Recipient Founders Day award Ind. U. Law Sch., 1972. Mem.: Ind. Bar Assn., Ill. Bar Assn. (assembly del.), Union League, Legal. Lutheran. Avocations: scuba diving, coin collecting/numismatics, flying, racquetball. Office: Freeborn & Peters 311 S Wacker Dr Ste 3000 Chicago IL 60606 Office Phone: 312-360-6502. Office Fax: 312-360-6575. E-mail: mfreeborn@freebornpeters.com.*

FREED, CHARLES, engineering consultant, researcher; b. Budapest, Hungary, Mar. 21, 1926; came to U.S., 1949; s. Erno and Ernestine (Duschnitz) F.; m. Florence Joan Wallach, Apr. 16, 1956; children: Lisa Ernestine, Josie Anne. BEE, NYU, 1952; SM, MIT, 1954, EE, 1958. Registered profl. engr., Mass. Rsch. asst. MIT, Cambridge, Mass., 1952-55, mem. staff, 1955-58; sr. engr., dept. head Raytheon, Waltham, Mass., 1958-62; mem. staff Lincoln Lab., Lexington, Mass., 1962-78, sr. staff mem., 1978-94, cons., 1994—. Lectr. dept. elec. engring. and computer sci. MIT, Cambridge, 1969-99. Contbr. over 60 articles to profl. jours. Fellow IEEE, Mil. Sensing Symposia; mem. Tau Beta Pi, Eta Kappa Nu, Sigma Xi. Achievements include patent in field. Home: 16 Browning Ln Lincoln MA 01773-3911 Office: MIT Lincoln Lab 244 Wood St Lexington MA 02421-6426

FREED, DANIEL JOSEF, law educator; b. New York, May 12, 1927; s. Jules L. and Sara (Lobel) F.; m. Judith Darrow, June 30, 1967; children: Peter Jacob, Emily Sara;children from previous marriage: Jonathan Michael, Amy. BS, Yale U., 1948, LLB, 1951; LLD (hon.), New England Coll., 1994. Bar: N.Y. 1952, D.C. 1953, U.S. Supreme Ct. 1955; Justice of the Peace, Guilford, Vt, 2005—. Atty.-investigator, preparedness subcom., com. on armed svcs., U.S. Senate, Washington, 1951-52; assoc. Ford, Bergson, Adams & Borkland, Washington, 1952-59; sr. trial atty. antitrust divsn. U.S. Dept. Justice, Washington, 1959-64, assoc. dir. office of criminal justice, 1964—68, dir., 1968-69; prof. law and its adminstrn. Yale U., New Haven, 1969-75, clin. prof., 1975-94, clin. prof. emeritus, profl. lectr. in law, 1994—. Dir. clin. program law Yale U., 1969-72, dir. Daniel and Florence Guggenheim program in criminal justice, 1972-87, dir. criminal sentencing program, 1988-96. Co-author: (with Wald) Bail in the United States: 1964, publ.1964; editor (periodical) Fed. Sentencing Reporter, 1988—; contbr. articles to profl. jours. Trustee Vera Inst. Justice, NY, 1970—; pres. Yale Law Sch. Assn. Washington, 1968. With USN, 1945—46. Recipient Glenn R. Winters award Am. Judges Assn., 1992. Democrat. Jewish. Avocations: metal sculpture, swimming. Home: 53 Freed Rd Guilford VT 05301 Office: Yale Law Sch 127 Wall St PO Box 208215 New Haven CT 06520-8215 Office Phone: 203-432-4843. Business E-Mail: daniel.freed@yale.edu.

FREED, DAVID CLARK, artist; b. Toledo, May 23, 1936; s. J. Clark and Thelma F.; m. Mary Lichtenwald, Sept. 3, 1962; children— Aaron, Michael. BFA, Miami U., Oxford, Ohio, 1958; MFA, U. Iowa, Iowa City, 1962; postgrad., Royal Coll. Art, 1963-64. Instr. art Toledo Mus., 1964-66; prof. emeritus printmaking Va. Commonwealth U., Richmond, 1966—; instr. Central Sch. Art, London, 1969. One-man shows include Franz Bader Gallery, Washington, 1967, 70-71, 73, 76, 79, 82, Va. Mus. Fine Arts, 1977, Am. Cultural Ctr., Belgrade, 1982, Il Bisonte, Florence, Italy, 1989; retrospective exhbn. Anderson Gallery at Va. Commonwealth U., 2001; exhibited in group shows at World Print Show, San Francisco Mus. Modern Art, 35 Artists of the S.E., High Mus., Atlanta Art of Poetry, Nat. Coll. Fine Arts, Corcoran Gallery, Washington, others; represented in permanent collections Corcoran Gallery Washington, Mus. Modern Art, NYC, Nat. Mus. Am. Art, Washington, Chgo. Art Inst., Victoria and Albert Mus., govt. collections of UK, Yale U., U. of Va., NY Pub. Libr.; artist books include (with Steven Lautermilch) What Light Guides This Hand—Poems by Izumi Shikibu; (with Charles Wright) 6 Poems, 1964, Yard Journal, 1985; (with Larry Levis) Elegy with a Thimbleful of Water, 1995; (with Philip Levine) An Ordinary Morning, 1995. Fulbright grant, 1963-64; Va. Mus. fellow, 1983-84, Nattie Marie Jones fellow creative work, 1983, Theresa Pollak award Home: 1825 W Grace St Richmond VA 23220-2104 Studio: 308 S Laurel St Richmond VA 23220-6231 Business E-Mail: commenius@vcu.org.

FREED, DEBOW, academic administrator; b. Hendersonville, Tenn., Aug. 26, 1925; s. John Walter and Ella Lee (DeBow) F.; m. Catherine Carol Moore, Sept. 10, 1949; 1 child, Debow II. BS, US Mil. Acad., 1946; grad., US Inf. Sch., 1953, US Army Command and Gen. Staff Coll., 1959; MS, U. Kans., 1961; PhD, U. N.Mex., 1966; grad., US Air War Coll., 1966; LLD, Monmouth Coll., Ill., 1987; DLitt (hon.), Ohio No. U., 1999. Comdg. officer U.S. Army, 1946; comdr. 35th Inf. Japan, 1947-48; asst. to cmdr. 17th Airborne Div., 1948-49; comdr. 26th Inf., Federal Republic of Germany, 1949-51; asst. to chief U.S. Mission, Iran, and chief Middle Ea. Affairs, 1951-53; instr. The Inf. Sch., 1953-56; comdr. 32d Inf., Korea, 1956-57; instr. Command and Gen. Staff Coll., 1957-58; chief nuclear br. U.S. Atomic Energy Agy., 1961-65; chief plans divsn. US Army, Vietnam, 1966-67; prof. physics dept. U.S. Mil. Acad., 1967-69, ret., 1969; dean Mt. Union Coll., 1969-74; pres. Monmouth Coll., 1974-79, Ohio No. U., Ada, 1979—99, pres. emeritus, 1999—; pres. U. Findlay, 2003—. Chmn. Assoc. Colls. of Midwest, 1977-79, others. Author: Using Nuclear Capabilities, 1959, Pulsed Neutron Techniques, 1965; contbr. articles, revs. to profl. publs.; editor: Atomic Development Report, 1962-64. Bd. dirs. Presbyn. Coll. Union, 1974-79; trustee Ctr. Sci. and Industry, 1982—, Toledo Symphony, 1994—, Blanchard Valley Health Assn., 1999—, Blanchard Valley Health Found., 2000—; chmn., bd. trustees, COSI Endowment Found., 2001; v.p., dir. Buckeye coun. Boy Scouts Am., 1972-74, dir. Prairie coun., 1974-78. Decorated Bronze Star, (2) Legion of Merit, Legion of Honor Iran, Army Commendation medal, Air medal, Joint Svcs. Commendation medal, others; recipient various civic awards; Associated Western Univs. fellow, 1963-65; AEC fellow, 1963-65; Fgn. Policy Rsch. Inst. fellow, 1966; named Ohio Commodore, 1990. Mem. Assn. Meth. Colls. and Univs. (bd. dirs. 1979-99), Ohio Coll. Assn. (bd. dirs. 1980-84, 85-88, pres. 89-90), Ohio Found. Independent Colls. (bd. dirs. 1979-99), Am. Assn. Pres. of Colls. and Univs. (bd. dirs. 1988-99, treas. 1997-98, v.p. 1998-99), Ohio Commodores, Sixma Xi, Phi Kappa Phi, Phi Eta Sigma, Delta Theta Phi, Omicron Delta Kappa. Home: 1115 N Main St Findlay OH 45840 Office: Office of Pres U Findlay Findlay OH 45840 Office Phone: 419-434-4510. Business E-Mail: freed@findlay.edu.

FREED, EVA PRAEGER, investment advisor; b. Budapest, Hungary, Sept. 7, 1949; arrived in US, 1956, naturalized, 1961; d. Alexander and Ilona (Bar) Praeger; m. Myron C. Cohen, June 11, 1967 (dec. June 1979); children: Jayson L. Cohen, Jeffrey D. Cohen; m. Paul Steven Freed, Oct. 28, 1979; 1 child, Melissa H. BS in Psychology, Queens Coll., 1968; MS in Psychology, NYU, 1975; MBA, Oakland U., Rochester, Mich., 1987. Cert. in personal fin. planning; stockbroker, sr. advisor, Soc. Cert. Sr. Advisors, 2001. Elem. sch. tchr. NYC Schs., 1968-75; mktg. asst. Market Devel. Corp., NYC, 1976-79; mktg. cons. Mich., 1979-84; registered rep. Securian Fin. Svcs., Farmington Hills, Mich., 1989—; product mktg. Stanley Automatic Openers, Detroit, 1984-87; registered rep. Prudential Securities, Birmingham, Mich., 1987-89. Co-founder, v.p. ALS of Mich., Southfield, 1981-86, pres., 1986-88., bd. dirs., sec. 2000—; perinatal coach Cmty. Svcs., Pontiac, Mich., 1989-90. Mem. Internat. Assn. for Fin. Planning. Avocations: skiing, tennis, reading, cooking. Home Phone: 248-626-3148; Office Phone: 248-214-4494. Personal E-mail: shapsi@aol.com.

FREED, JACK HERSCHEL, chemist, educator; b. NYC, Apr. 19, 1938; s. Nathan and Pauline (Wolodarsky) F.; m. H. Renée Strauch, Mar. 25, 1961; children: Denise Elaine, Nadine Debra. BE, Yale U., 1958; MS, Columbia U., 1959, PhD, 1962. NSF fellow Cambridge U., 1962—63; asst. prof. chemistry Cornell U., Ithaca, NY, 1963—67, assoc. prof., 1967—73, prof., 1973—, Frank and Robert Laughlin prof. phys. chemistry, 2007—. Vis. prof. Tokyo U., 1969, Weizmann Inst. Sci., 1970, Aarhus U., 1974, U. Geneva, 1977, Delft U. of Tech., 1978, École Normale Supérieure, Paris, 1984—85, Hebrew U., Jerusalem, 1990, U. Padua, Italy, 1991, Yamagata U., 1998; fellow Inst. for Advanced Study, Hebrew U.; dir. Nat. Biomed. Ctr. for Advanced Electron Spin Resonance Techs., 2001—. Mem. edit. bd. Jour. Chem. Physics, 1976-78, Jour. Phys. Chemistry, 1979-83, 2004, Spl. Issue, Chem. Phys. Letters, 1988-90, Applied Magnetic Resonance, 1990—, Magnetic Resonance Rev., 1993-2000; assoc. editor Jour. Magnetic Resonance, 2006—; contbr. articles to profl. jours. Recipient Buck-Whitney award Ea. N.Y. sect. Am. Chem. Soc., 1981, Gold medal Internat. Electron Spin Resonance Soc., 1994, Irving Langmuir prize Am. Phys. Soc., 1997, Internat. Zavoisky award Zavoisky Inst. Russian Acad. Scis., 1998; named Ramsay Meml. fellow, 1962-63, A.P. Sloan Found. fellow, 1966-68, sr. Weizmann fellow, 1970, Guggenheim fellow, 1984-85, Bruker lectr. Chem. Soc. U.K., 1990, MacDowell lectr. in chemical physics, U.B.C., 1997. Fellow Am. Phys. Soc., Am. Acad. Arts and Scis.; mem. Nat. Magnetic Resonance Soc. India (hon.). Jewish. Home: 108 Homestead Cir Ithaca NY 14850-6214 Office: Cornell U Dept Chemistry Baker Lab Ithaca NY 14853-1301 Office Phone: 607-255-3647. Business E-Mail: jhf@ccmr.cornell.edu.

FREED, JOEL M., lawyer; b. Oct. 28, 1943; BA, Lehigh Univ., 1965, BSME, 1966; JD, Georgetown Univ., 1970. Bar: Va. 1970, D.C. 1970. Ptnr., Intellectual Property & Tech. group Arnold & Porter, Washington. Instr., legal methods U.S. Patent & Trademark Office, 1980—90; adj. prof. Georgetown Univ. Law Ctr. Mem.: Pi Tau Sigma, Phi Delta Phi. Office: Arnold & Porter 555 Twelfth St NW Washington DC 20004-1206 Office Phone: 202-942-6602. Office Fax: 202-942-5999. Business E-Mail: joel.freed@aporter.com.

FREED, KARL FREDERICK, chemistry professor; b. Bklyn., Sept. 25, 1942; s. Nathan and Pauline Freed; m. Gina P. Goldstein, June 14, 1964; children: Nicole Yvette, Michele Suzanne. BS, Columbia U., 1963; A.M., Harvard U., 1965, PhD, 1967. NATO postdoctoral fellow U. Manchester (Eng.), 1967-68; asst. prof. U. Chgo., 1968-73, assoc. prof., 1973-76, prof. chemistry, 1976—, dir. James Franck Inst., 1983—86, Henry G. Gale disting. svc. prof., 2006—. Bd. dirs. Telluride Sci. Rsch. Ctr., 2003—06, 2007—, Argonne Nat. Lab/U. Chgo. Joint Theory Inst. Author: Renormalization Group Theory of Macromolecules, 1987; editl. bd. Jour. Statis. Physics, 1976-78, Advances in Chem. Physics, 1985—, Computational Theoretical Polymer Sci., 1996—; adv. editor Chem. Physics, 1979-92, Chem. Revs., 1981-83, Internat. Jour. Quantum Chemistry, 1995-99; assoc. editor Jour. Chem. Physics, 1982-84; contbr. articles to profl. jours. Recipient Marlow medal Faraday div. Chem. Soc. London, 1973; recipient Pure Chemistry award Am. Chem. Soc., 1976; fellow Sloan Found., 1969-71; Guggenheim fellow, 1972-73; fellow Dreyfus Found., 1972-77 Fellow: Am. Acad. Arts and Scis., Am. Phys. Soc.; mem.: Am. Chem. Soc., Royal Soc. Chemistry. Office: U Chgo James Franck Inst 929 # 57th St CIS E231 Chicago IL 60637-1433 Business E-Mail: k-freed@uchicago.edu.

FREED, MELVYN NORRIS, retired educational association administrator, writer; b. Kansas City, Mo., Apr. 30, 1937; s. Carl and Betty (Wachtel) F.; m. Janet Lea Triplitt, Dec. 26, 1971; children: David A., Edward L. BA in Econs. with distinction, U. Mo., Kansas City, 1959; MS in Edn., So. Ill. U., Carbondale, 1962, PhD in Higher Edn., 1965. Dir. instl. rsch. Ark. State U., Jonesboro, 1965-72, v.p. for adminstrn., 1972-76, Govs. State U., University Pk., Ill., 1977-82, univ. prof., rsch. assoc., 1982-87; writer, 1987—. Co-founder, past dir. measurement and rsch. So. Ctrl. Region Edn. Lab., Little Rock; past evaluator rsch. grants U.S. Office of Edn., Washington; sustaining life mem. Evans Scholars Found., Par Club, 2002—; co-founder US River Acad. (chartered by Congress). Author: In Search of a Beginning: The Eastern Arkansas Scottish Rite Bodies, 1976; Co-author: The Educator's Desk Reference, 1989 (1 of 30 Best Reference Books 1989, Best Single Vol. Reference Book in Edn. 1989), 2d edit., 2002, Business Information Desk Reference, 1991, Patient's Desk Reference, 1994; contbr. articles to profl. jours.; editor: Handbook of Statistical Procedures and Their Computer Applications, 1991; tool inventor. Village trustee, Hazel Crest, Ill., 1997—2005; plan commr., 1988—97; adminstrv. asst. Congressman William Alexander, Washington, 1969; James E. West fellow Boy Scouts Am., v.p., bd. dirs. Calumet coun. Munster, Ind., 1978—96, 2001—06; bd. dirs. Ill. Masonic Charities Fund Com., 2004—, Bremen H.S. Dist. 228 Ednl. Found., 1998—2004, pres., 2002—04. Recipient U.S. Congl. citation, Washington, 1971, Silver Beaver award Boy Scouts Am., 1976, Disting. Svcs. award Ark. State U., 1975, Nat. Endowment award; Daniel Carter Beard Masonic Scouter award Boy Scouts Am., 2003. Mem. Masons (master 1999-2000, 2006-07), Scottish Rite (knight comdr. Ct. of Honor 1979), Shriner (Medinah), Alpha Epsilon Pi, Phi Kappa Phi, Omicron Delta Kappa. Home: 17023 Magnolia Dr Hazel Crest IL 60429-1020 E-mail: melfreed@earthlink.net.

FREED, MICHAEL J., lawyer; b. Chgo., Feb. 13, 1938; BS, U. Pa., 1959; JD, U. Chgo., 1962. Bar: Ill. 1963, DC 1963, US Dist. Ct. (no dist. Ill.) 1963, US Dist. Ct. (dist. DC) 1963, US Ct. Appeals (DC cir.) 1963, US Ct. Appeals (7th cir.) 1977, US Supreme Ct. 1983. Atty. Antitrust div., U.S. D.O.J.; prin. Much Shelist Freed Denenberg Ament & Rubenstein, Chgo., 1973—2006; founding ptnr. Freed, Kanner, London & Millen, LLC, Bannockburn, Ill., 2006—. Mem. adv. bd. Am. Antitrust Inst., Washington; bd. dir. Appleseed Found., Washington; trustee Cancer Rsch. Found., Chgo.; mem. vis. alumni com. U. Chgo. Law Sch. Mem.: ABA, Chgo. Bar Assn., Fed. Bar Assn., Assn. Trial Lawyers Am.

FREED, RICHARD (DONALD), music critic; b. Chgo., Dec. 27, 1928; s. Abraham Jay and Ann (Bernstein) F.; m. Louise Sumiko Kono, Mar. 19, 1958; 1 child, Erica Lesley. PhB, U. Chgo., 1947. Staff music critic N.Y. Times, NYC, 1965; asst. to dir. Eastman Sch. Music U. Rochester, NY, 1966-70; exec. dir. Music Critics Assn., Inc., Rockville, Md., 1974-90. Annotator, broadcast host St. Louis Symphony Orch., 1973-96; program annotator Phila. Orch., 1974-84; record critic Washington Post, 1976-84; annotator Nat. Symphony Orch., Washington, 1977—. Author: (with Peter Eliot Stone) Virtuosi, 1985 (Deems Taylor award 1986); contbg. editor Stereo Rev., 1973—99. Decorated knight 1st class Order of the Lion of Finland; recipient Deems Taylor award for concert notes, 1984, Grammy award, 1995. Democrat. Jewish. Avocations: hiking, puzzles. E-mail: priamclay@aol.com.

FREED, SHARON LOU, retired principal; b. LA, Feb. 23, 1944; d. Louis Robert Freed and Barbara Elizabeth Freed-Whitehead. BS Edn., U. So. Calif., 1965; MEd Curriculum Devel. and Instrn., Mich. State U., 1978. Cert. tchr. K-8 Calif., life credential K-12 Calif., credential tchr. K-8 Dept. Def. Dependent Schs., tchr. social studies and compensatory edn. grades 8-12 Dept. of Def. Dependent Schs., tchr. gifted and talented Dept. of Def. Dependent Schs., adminstr., Prin. elem. pre-K-8 Dept. of Def. Dependent Schs. Tchr. K-1 Amestoy Sch. L.A. Unified Sch. Dist., Gardena, 1965—68, tchr. grade 1 Amestoy Sch., 1969—70; tchr. grade 1 Chofu Elem. Sch. Dept. Def. Dependent Schs., Fuchu, Japan, 1968—69, tchr. grade 1 Darmstadt Am. Sch., 1970—73, tchr. K-2 Oberammergau Am. Sch., 1973—74, tchr. grade 3 RAF Lakenheath, England, 1974—82, tchr. compensatory edn., 1980—81, tchr. gifted and talented, 1981—82, prin. Uden Am. Sch. Netherlands, 1982—84, prin. W F. Halsey Sch. Edzell, Scotland, 1984—90, prin. Woodbridge Elem. Sch. RAF Woodbridge, England, 1990—93, prin. Feltwell Elem. Sch. England, 1993—2000. Mem. early childhood progress report task force Dept. of Def. Dependent Schs. Europe, Weisbaden, Germany, 1994—95; mem. base closure/sch. closure task force USAF and Dept. of Def. Dependent Schs., RAF Woodbridge, RAF Upper Heyford, and UK dist., 1992—93; mem. accreditation team NCA, Upper Heyford, 1990. Sponsor Cub Scouts and Boy Scouts, RAF Edzell, 1984—90, RAF Woodbridge/RAF Bentwaters, 1990—93, RAF Feltwell, 1993—2000; voting mem. base scholarship com. and Angel Pin com. RAF Woodbridge/RAF Bentwaters, 1990—93, family advocacy bd., 1990—93, installation adv. coun., 1990—93, task force on base closure, 1992—93; exec. coun. Lakenheath Sch., 1998—2000; mem. Family Advocacy Coun., RAF Lakenheath, 1993—95, Installation Adv. Coun., RAF Lakenheath; mem., spkr. Edzell Village Assn., 1984—90; participant Horringer Open Gardens for Charity, 2000—07; advisor Red Cross Vol. Bd., RAF Lakenheath, 1995—98; voting mem. Willie Johnson Scottish-American Sports Award Com., RAF Edzell/Edzell Village, 1984—90; active St. Andrew's Ch., Bredfield, 1990—93, Ch. of Scotland, Edzell, St. Leonard's Ch., Horringer, 1993—2007, fete com., 1993—95; mem., spkr. Protestant Women of the Chapel, RAF Edzell, 1987—92. Named Student Tchr. of Yr., U. So. Calif., 1965, Tchr. of Yr., Atlantic Region, Dept. of Def. Dependent Schs., 1989, Prin. of Yr. UK East, Dept. Def. Schs., 1989, 1990, 1992, 1999, Prin. of Yr. Atlantic Region, 1989—90, 1992—93, 1999—2000, Nat. Disting. Prin., Dept. Edn. and NAESP, 1989, 1999; recipient Sustained Superior Performance award, Dept. Def. Schs., 1984—2000, Cert. of Appreciation, 1993, Rear Adm. William Thomas award letter of commendation, USN Security Group Comdr., Edzell, 1985, Travis Trophy award USN letter of commendation,

Commdg. Officer, RAF Edzell, 1986, Guard award, Red Cross, 1997. Mem.: AAUW, NAESP, Bredfield Village Assn., Horringer Parish Coun. Assn., U. So. Calif. Alumni Assn., Sierra Club Carmel, Phi Delta Kappa (life). Presbyterian. Avocations: travel, reading, gardening, walking, attending the theatre. Home: 24525 Outlook Dr F21 Carmel CA 93923 also: Ashdown Cottage The Street Horringer Bury St Edmunds IP29 5SJ England Personal E-mail: slfcarmel@aol.com.

FREED, STANLEY ARTHUR, retired museum curator; b. Springfield, Ohio, Apr. 18, 1927; m. Ruth Shelley, Sept. 12, 1955. Ph.B., U. Chgo., 1949; BA, U. Calif., Berkeley, 1951, PhD, 1957. Vis. asst. prof. anthropology U. N.C., 1959-60; mem. staff Am. Mus. Natural History, NYC, 1960—, curator, chmn. dept. anthropology, 1969-76, curator, 1976-2000, retired, 2000. Adj. prof. Columbia U., 1992—; research fellow Am. Inst. Indian Studies, 1977-78 Served with AUS, 1945-46. Postdoctoral fellow Social Sci. Research Council, 1957; Postdoctoral fellow NSF, 1958 Mem. N.Y. Acad. Scis. (chmn. anthropology sect. 1974-75) Office: Am Mus Natural History Central Park W & 79th St New York NY 10024 Business E-Mail: sfreed@amnh.org.

FREED, SUSAN DIANNE, health facility administrator; d. Merle Allas and Sharon Lee Mearida; m. Michael Andrew Freed, Mar. 26, 2003; children: Kelsey Mearida, Logan, Madison. BS in Health Info. Mgmt., Ill. State U., Normal, 1999. Cert. healthcare privacy RHIA. Dir. med. records Iroquois Meml. Hosp., Watseka, Ill., 1999—2006, dir. compliance, prof. svcs., 2006—. Curriculum adv. bd. Health Info. Mgmt. Program, Normal, 2003—. Mem.: Ctrl. Ill. Health Info. Mgmt. Assn., Am. Health Info. Mgmt. Assn., Ill. Health Mgmt. Assn. Avocations: reading, movies. Home: 1461 N 1400 E Rd Roberts IL 60962 Office: Iroquois Meml Hosp 200 Fairman Ave Watseka IL 60970

FREED, WALTER EVERETT, petroleum company executive, state representative; b. Providence, Aug. 13, 1951; s. Richard Anthony and Alice Marie (Livesey) F.; m. Margery Anne Tyler, Oct. 19, 1974; children: Jonathan, Meghan, Meredith. BA, Dartmouth Coll., 1974. V.p. Johnson's Fuel Svc. Inc., Manchester, Vt., 1979-85; pres. Apollo Industries, Inc. (formerly Johnson's Fuel Svc., Inc.), Manchester, Vt., 1985—; state rep. dist. 15 Vt.; spkr. of the House, 2001—. Elected chair, freshman Rep. caucus, 1993. State chmn. Vt. Rep. Party, Montpelier, 1988-91; state rep. Vt. Gen. Assembly, 1992, 94, 96, house minority whip, 1995, house minority leader, 1997; bd. dirs. Vermont C. of C., Southern Vermont Art Center, Long Trail Sch., Manchester Little League. Former chair, Dorset sch. bd.; former dir., Bennington-Rutland Supervisory Union. Former Rep. Nat. Conv. Del. 1992, 1996, 2000. Mem. Mcpl. Corp. Com. 1993-1994, local govt. & Rules Com., 1995-1996, Fish, Wildlife, and Water Resources Com., Rules & Joint Com. 1997-1998, local govt., Rules, and Joint Rules Com., 1999-2000. Avocations: sailing, flying, skiing, tennis. Office: Apollo Industries Inc 105 N End Dr North Clarendon VT 05759-9762 also: Office of the Speaker of the House Vermont State House Montpelier VT 05633-5201

FREEDBERG, A. STONE, physician; b. Salem, Mass., May 30, 1908; s. Hyman and Rachel Leah (Freedberg) F.; m. Beatrice Gordon, Aug. 29, 1935; children: Richard Gordon, Leonard Earl. AB, Harvard U., 1929; MD, U. Chgo., Rush, 1935. Diplomate: Am. Bd. Internal Medicine (cardiology). Intern Mt. Sinai Hosp., Chgo., 1934-35, Mass. Meml. Hosp., Boston, summer 1935; resident Cook County Hosp., Chgo., 1935-36; house officer pathology R.I. Hosp., 1936-37; practice medicine, specializing in internal medicine Boston, 1946—. Asst. in medicine Beth Israel Hosp., 1938-40, jr. vis. physician, 1940-46, assoc. in med. research, 1940-50, assoc. vis. physician, 1946-48, vis. physician, 1949-63, assoc. dir. med. research, 1950-63, sr. Ziskind fellow, 1956, physician, 1964-84, acting physician-in-chief dept. medicine, 1973, dir. cardiology unit, 1964-69, bd. consultation, 1984-87, hon. bd. consultation, 1988—; research fellow medicine Med. Sch., Harvard U., 1941-42, asst. in medicine, 1942-46, instr. medicine, 1946-47, assoc. in medicine, 1947-50, asst. prof., 1950-57, assoc. prof., 1958-69, prof., 1969-74, prof. emeritus, 1974-, adminstrv. bd. faculty medicine, 1958-62; physician Harvard U. Health Svcs., 1974-2004, hon. physician emeritus, 2004—; cons., com. mem. med. div. Oak Ridge Inst. Nuclear Studies, 1955-56; spl. cons. metabolism study sect. USPHS, 1956-60; mem. sr. cons. staff Nuclear Medicine Inst., 1966-67 Mem. editorial bd.: Circulation, 1956-60, 62-67; contbr. articles profl. jours. Guggenheim fellow Oxford U., 1967-68 Fellow Am. Heart Assn. (bd. dirs.; mem. council clin. cardiology); mem. Mass. Heart Assn. (dir., past pres., com. chmn.), Am. Thyroid Assn. (v.p.), Mass., Charles River Dist. med. socs., Am. Soc. Clin. Investigation, Am. Physiol. Soc., Assn. Am. Physicians, New Eng. Cardiovascular Soc. (pres. 1971-72), Assn. Profs. Medicine. Home: 111 Perkins St Boston MA 02130-4313 Office: 275 Longwood Ave Boston MA 02115-5704 Office Phone: 617-432-1370. Personal E-mail: gordonbea@comcast.net.

FREEDBERG, DAVID ADRIAN, art historian, educator; b. Capetown, South Africa, June 1, 1948; s. William and Eleonore (Kupfer) F.; children: Hannah, William. BA, Yale U., New Haven, Conn., 1969; DPhil, Oxford U., 1973. Lectr. art Westfield Coll., U. London, 1973-76, Courtauld Inst. Art, U. London, 1976-84; prof. Barnard Coll., Columbia U., NYC, 1984-86, Columbia U., 1986—, dir. Italian Acad. Advanced Studies in Am., 2000—. Slade prof. fine art U. Oxford, 1983-84; dir. Print Quar., London, 1983—; Andrew W. Mellon prof. Nat. Gallery Art, 1996-98. Author: Dutch Landscape Prints of the Seventeenth Century, 1980, Rubens: The Life of Christ After the Passion, 1984, Iconoclasts and Their Motives, 1985, Iconoclasm and Painting in the Revolt of the Netherlands, 1566-1609, 1988, The Prints of Pieter Bruegel the Elder, 1989, The Power of Images: Studies in the History and Theory of Response, 1989, Joseph Kosuth the Play of the Unmentionable, 1992, Peter Paul Rubens: Paintings and Oil Sketches, 1995, The Eye of the Lynx: Galileo, His Friends, and the Beginnings of Modern Natural History, 2002; author: (with E. Baldini) The Paper Museum of Cassiano dal Pozzo: Citrus Fruit, 1997; author: (with A. Scott) The Paper Museum of Cassiano dal Pozzo: Fossil Woods, 2000; author: (with D. Pegler) Tue Papes Museum of Cassiano dal Pozzo: Fungi, 2006. Mem. Am. Acad. Arts and Scis., Am. Philos. Soc. Office: Columbia U Italian Acad Advanced Studes Am New York NY 10027

FREEDMAN, AARON DAVID, retired medicine and biochemistry educator, dean; b. Albany, NY, Jan. 4, 1922; s. Jacob Abraham and Pauline Rebecca (Hoffman) F.; m. Alice Maurer, Sept. 10, 1948, dec. 2001; children: Abigail, Jonathan, Jeremy; m. Virginia Weliky, Apr. 14, 2005. AB, Cornell U., 1942; MD, Albany Med. Coll., 1945; PhD, Columbia U., 1958; MA, U. Pa., 1972. Diplomate Am. Bd. Internal Medicine. Asst. prof. medicine and biochemistry Columbia U., NYC, 1958-65; clin. prof. U. Kans., Kansas City, 1965-69, chmn. dept. medicine Menorah Med. Ctr., 1965-69; prof., assoc. dean U. Pa., Phila., 1969-75, exec. dir. Grad. Hosp., 1972-75; prof. medicine Med. Sch. CUNY, 1975—2006, acting dean, 1978-79, dep. dean acad. affairs, 1990-92, emeritus prof., 2006—. Examiner N.Y. State Bd. Med. Examiners, Albany, 1962-65; cons. Touro Coll., N.Y.C., 1980; career investigator N.Y. Pub. Health Rsch. Coun., 1963-65; dir. Danciger Med. Inst., Kansas City, Mo., 1966-69. Mem. Ardsley (N.Y.) Bd. of Edn., 1962-65. Libman Fund fellow, 1951-54, USPHS fellow, 1958-60. Mem. Am. Soc. for Cell Biology, Am. Soc. Biochemistry and Molecular Biology. Jewish. Personal E-mail: anv@beyondbb.com.

FREEDMAN, ALBERT Z., publishing executive; b. Taunton, Mass. s. Frank and Bessie (Kanaber) F.; m. Esther Hilda Katz, Sept. 23, 1954 (dec.); children: Mara (dec.), Lisa Jolie Harris, Tani Josette Ruiz, Derek Justin; m. Nancy Lee Dworman, Aug. 17, 1984. Student, Boston U., 1945-46; BA, U. So. Calif., 1948; postgrad., Inst. Hautes Etudes Cinématagraphiques, Paris, 1949-50; PhD, Inst. for Advanced Study Human Sexuality, San Francisco, 1981. Radio writer, Los Angeles, NYC, 1950-52; TV writer, producer WOR-TV, NYC, 1952, NBC, CBS, 1952-58; playwright Mex., 1959-60; with KTLA, ABC-TV, LA, 1961-64; free lance writer London, 1964-66; editor Forum, Jour. Human Rels., London, 1967-75, co-pub. NYC, 1975-82; mng. dir. Penthouse Publs., London, 1970-75; v.p. Penthouse Internat., 1982—97; cons. Gen. Media, NYC, 1997—2004. Prof. Inst. for Advanced Study of Human Sexuality, bd. dirs. Mem. Am. Coll. Sexologists (diplomate, commr., bd. dirs.), Soc. Sci. Study of Sex. Home: 11 Laderman Ln Greenbrae CA 94904-2482 Personal E-mail: azurof@comcast.net.

FREEDMAN, ALFRED MORDECAI, psychiatrist, educator; b. Albany, NY, Jan. 7, 1917; s. Jacob Abraham and Pauline Rebecca (Hoffman) F.; m. Marcia Irene Kohl, Mar. 24, 1943; children: Paul Harris, Daniel Sholom. AB, Cornell U., 1937; MD, U. Minn., 1941. Diplomate Am. Bd. Psychiatry and Neurology. Intern Harlem Hosp., NYC, 1941-42; resident and fellow Bellevue Hosp., NYC, 1948-51, sr. psychiatrist, 1951-54; asst. pediatrician Babies Hosp.-Columbia, NYC, 1953-60; assoc. prof. psychiatry SUNY Downstate Med. Sch., Bklyn., 1955-60; prof., chmn. psychiatry N.Y. Med. Coll., Valhalla, 1960-89, chmn. and prof. psychiatry emeritus, 1989—. Vis. prof. Harvard Med. Sch., Boston, 1988-93; hon. prof. Hunan Med. U., China, 1993; dir. psychiatry Westchester Med. Ctr., Valhalla, 1979-89; cons. WHO, Geneva, 1984, 89—; Roche vis. prof., Australia and New Zealand, 1988; S.Y. Mak vis. prof. U. Hong Kong, 1989; mem. awards jury Anna Monika Stiftung, Dortmund, Germany, 1983-94; mem. Internat. Com. Prevention and Treatment of Depression, 1983-96; sec.-treas. Ctr. for Comprehensive Health Practice Svc., N.Y.C., 1990—adv. com. Memory Ctrs., Internat., 1997—. Sr. editor: (textbook) Comprehensive Psychiatry, 1967-80; sr. editor: Issues in Psychiatric Classification, 1986; editor-in-chief Polit. Psychology, 1981-90, Integrative Psychiatry, 1981-97; editor: Highlights of Modern Psychiatry, 2000; adv. bd. Philosophy, Psychiatry and Psychology Jour., 1990—; contbr. articles to profl. jours. Mem. N.Y. State Commn. to Evaluate Drug Laws, Albany, 1970-73; founding trustee Ctr. for Urban Edn., N.Y.C., 1965-70; dir. Upper Park Ave. Boys Club of Am., N.Y.C., 1970-80; NGO rep. UN for World Psychiat. Assn., 1985-90, NGO rep. UN for World Assn. Psychosocial Rehab., 1990—; trustee N.Y. Acad. Medicine; trustee Internat. Found. for Human Scis., Paris, 1987-97; chmn. bd. dirs. Ctr. for Comprehensive Health Practice, 2006. Recipient Henry Wismer Miller award, Manhattan Soc. Mental Health, 1964, Terence Cardinal Cooke medal, N.Y. Med. Coll., 1985, Lapinlahti medal, U. Helsinki, 1990, Wyeth Ayerst award, World Psychiat. Assn., Athens, 1989, A.M. Freedman Ann. award, Internat. Soc. for Polit. Psychology, 1990, Tom Levin award for cmty. svc., Am. Assn. Psychosocial Rehab., 1999, Alice Fordyce award for pub. svc., 2004. Fellow: Acad. Medicine et Psychiatricae Found. (founding fellow, pres. 1990—), Am. Orthopsychiat. Assn. (dir. 1962—64), Am. Coll. Neuropsychopharmacology (pres. 1972—73, coun. global psychiatry 1999), Am. Psychiat. Assn. (pres. 1971—72, ethics appeals bd. 1993—99, disting.fellow 2000, ethics appeals bd. 2003—, coun. on global psychiatry 2004—, Rush medal 1974, ann. award, Spl. Presdl. commendation 1999), Am. Psychopathol. Assn. (pres. 1973—74, Hamilton medal 1972); mem.: Inst. Victims of Trauma (trustee 1992), Assn. Advancement of Philosophy and Psychiatry (founding exec. com. 1989—), Internat. Found. Mental Health and Neuroscis. (U.S. dir., v.p. 1996—2004), Nat. Com. on Confidentiality of Health Records (pres. 1976—95), N.Y. Psychiat. Soc. (pres. 1986—87). Avocations: music, travel, gardening, sailing. Home and Office: 1148 Fifth Ave New York NY 10128-0807 Office Phone: 212-348-8661. Personal E-mail: alfredm@pipeline.com.

FREEDMAN, DAVID AMIEL, statistics educator, consultant; B.Sc., McGill U., Montreal, 1958; MA, Princeton U., 1959, PhD, 1960. Prof. stats. U. Calif.-Berkeley, 1961—, Miller prof., 1991, chmn. dept. stats., 1981-86. Cons. Bank of Can., Ottawa, 1971-72, WHO, 1973, Carnegie Commn., 1976, Dept. Energy, 1978-87, Bur. Census, 1983, 98, Dept. Justice, 1984, 89-92, 96, 2002-05, Brobeck, Phleger & Harrison, 1985-89, Skadden Arps, 1986, 2002, 05-, County of Los Angeles, 1989, Fed. Jud. Ctr., 1993. Author: Markov Chains, 1971, Brownian Motion and Diffusion, 1971, Approximating Countable Markov Chains, 1972, Mathematical Methods in Statistics, 1977, Statistics, 1978, 4th edit., 2007, Statistical Models, 2005; contbr. numerous articles to profl. publs. Recipient John J. Carty award for Advancement of Sci., NAS, 2003; fellow, Can. Coun., 1960, Sloan Found., 1964, 80. Mem.: Am. Acad. Scis. Home: 901 Alvarado Rd Berkeley CA 94705-1551 Office: U Calif-Berkeley Dept Stats Berkeley CA 94720-3860

FREEDMAN, DAVID NOEL, religious studies educator; b. NYC, May 12, 1922; s. David and Beatrice (Goodman) F.; m. Cornelia Anne Pryor, May 16, 1944; children: Meredith Anne, Nadezhda, David Micaiah, Jonathan Pryor. Student, CCNY, 1935-38; AB, UCLA, 1939; BTh, Princeton Theol. Sem., 1944; PhD, Johns Hopkins U., 1948; LittD, U. Pacific, 1973; ScD, Davis and Elkins Coll., 1974. Ordained to ministry Presbyn. Ch., 1944; supply pastor in Acme and Deming, Wash., 1944-45; tchg. fellow, then asst. instr. Johns Hopkins U., 1946-48; asst. prof., then prof. Hebrew and Old Testament lit. Western Theol. Sem., Pitts., 1948-60; prof. Pitts. Theol. Sem., 1960-61, James A. Kelso prof., 1961-64; prof. Old Testament San Francisco Theol. Sem., 1964-70, Gray prof. Hebrew exegesis, 1970-71, dean of faculty, 1966-70, acting dean of sem., 1970-71; prof. Old Testament Grad. Theol. Union, Berkeley, Calif., 1964-71; prof. dept. Nr. Ea. studies U. Mich., Ann Arbor, 1971-92, Thurnau prof. Bibl. studies, 1984-92, dir. program on studies in religion, 1971-91; prof., endowed chair in Hebrew Bibl. studies U. Calif., San Diego, 1987—, dir. religious studies program, 1989-97. Danforth vis. prof. Internat. Christian U., Tokyo, 1967; vis. prof. Hebrew U., Jerusalem, 1977, Macquarie U., NSW, Australia, 1980, U. Queensland (Australia), 1982, 84, U. Calif., San Diego, 1985-87; Green vis. prof. Tex. Christian U., Ft. Worth, 1981; dir. Albright Inst. Archeol. Rsch., 1969-70, dir., 1976-77; lectr. in field. Author: The Published Works of W.F. Albright, 1975, Pottery, Poetry and Prophecy, 1980, The Unity of the Hebrew Bible, 1991 (paperback edit., 1993), Divine Commitment and Human Obligation, 1997, Psalm 119, 1999, The Nine Commandments, 2000; co-author: (with J.D. Smart) God Has Spoken, 1949, (with F.M. Cross, Jr.) Early Hebrew Orthography, 1952, (with John M. Allegro) The People of the Dead Sea Scrolls, 1958, (with R.M. Grant) The Secret Sayings of Jesus, 1960, (with F.M. Cross, Jr.) Ancient Yahwistic Poetry, 1964, rev. edit., 1975, 97, (with M. Dothan) Ashdod I, 1967, (with L.G. Running) William F. Albright: Twentieth Century Genius, 1975, 2d edit., 1991, (with B. Mazar, G. Cornfeld) The Mountain of the Lord, 1975, (with W. Phillips) An Explorer's Life of Jesus, 1975, (with G. Cornfeld) Archaeology of the Bible: Book by Book, 1976, (with K.A. Mathews) The Paleo-Hebrew Leviticus Scroll, 1985, The Unity of the Hebrew Bible, 1991, (with D. Forbes and F. Andersen) Studies in Hebrew and Aramaic Orthography, 1992, (with Sara Mandell) The Relationship between Herodotus' History and Primary History, 1993, (with P.F. Kuhlken) What Are the Dead Sea Scrolls, and Why Do They Matter?, 2007; co-author, editor: (with F. Andersen) Anchor Bible Series Hosea, 1980, Anchor Bible Series Amos, 1989, Micah, 2000; editor: (with G.E. Wright) The Biblical Archaeologist, Reader I, 1961, (with E.F. Campbell, Jr.) The Biblical Archaeologist, Reader 2, 1964, Reader 3, 1970, Reader 4, 1983, (with W.F. Albright) The Anchor Bible, 1964—, including, Genesis, 1964, James, Peter and Jude, 1964, Jeremiah, 1965, Job, 1965, 2d edit., 1973, Proverbs and Ecclesiastes, 1965, I Chronicles, II Chronicles, Ezra-Nehemiah, 1965, Psalms I, 1966, John I, 1966, Acts of the Apostles, 1967, II Isaiah, 1968, Psalms II, 1968, John II, 1970, Psalms III, 1970, Esther, 1971, Matthew, 1971, Lamentations, 1972, 2d edit., 1992, To the Hebrews, 1972, Ephesians 1-3, 4-6, 1974, I and II Esdras, 1974, Judges, 1975, Revelation, 1975, Ruth, 1975, I Maccabees, 1976, I Corinthians, 1976, Additions, 1977, Song of Songs, 1977, Daniel, 1978, Wisdom of Solomon, 1979, I Samuel, 1980, Hosea, 1980, Luke I, 1981, Joshua, 1982, Epistles of John, 1983, II Maccabees, 1983, II Samuel, 1984, II Corinthians, 1984, Luke II, 1985, Judith, 1985, Mark, 1986, Haggai-Zechariah 1-8, 1987, Ecclesiasticus, 1987, 2 Kings, 1988, Amos, 1989, Titus, 1990, Jonah, 1990, Leviticus I, 1991, Deuteronomy I, 1991, Numbers 1-20, 1993, Romans, 1993, Jude and 2 Peter, 1993, Zechariah 9-14, 1993, Zephaniah, 1994, Colossians, 1995, Joel, 1995, James, 1995, Obadiah, 1996, Tobit, 1996, Ecclesiastes, 1997, Ezekiel 21-37, 1997, Galatians, 1997, Malachi, 1998, Acts of the Apostles, 1998, Exodus 1-18, 1999, Jeremiah 1-20, 1999, Mark 1-8, 2000, Numbers 21-36, 2000, 1 Peter, 2001, Isaiah 1-39, 2000, Thessalonians 1&2, 2000, Leviticus 17-22, 2000, Proverbs 1-9, 2000, Micah, 2000, Philemon, 2000, Timothy 1&2, 2001, Hebrews, 2001, Leviticus 23-27, 2001, Habakkuk, 2001, 1 Kings, 2001, Isaiah 40-55, 2002, Isaiah 56-66, 2003, Jeremiah 21-36, 2004, 1 Chronicles 1-9, 2004, 1 Chronicles 10-29, 2004, Jeremiah 37-52, 2004, Exodus 19-40, 2006; editor Anchor Bible Ref. Libr., Jesus Within Judaism, 1988, Archaeology of the Land of the Bible, 1990, The Tree of Life, 1990, A Marginal Jew Vol. 1, 1991, The Pentateuch, 1991, The Rise of Jewish Nationalism, 1992, History and Prophecy, 1993, Jesus and the Dead Sea Scrolls, 1993, The Birth of the Messiah, 1993, The Death of the Messiah, 2 vols., 1994, Introduction to Rabbinical Literature, 1994, A Marginal Jew, vol. 2, 1994, vol. 3, 2001, The Scepter and the Star, 1995, The Gnostic Scriptures, 1995, Reclaiming The Dead Sea Scrolls, 1995, An Introduction to the New Testament, 1997, Education in Ancient Israel, 1998, Warrior, Dancer, Seductress, Queen, 1998, A History of the Synoptic Problem, 1999, Archaeology of the Land of the Bible, vol. 2, 2001, A Marginal Jew, vol. 3, 2001, Peoples of an Almighty God, 2002, Introduction to the Gospel of John, 2003, Life After Death, 2004; editor: Eerdmans Critical Commentary, 1 and 2 Timothy, 1999, The Psalms, 2003, Bible in its World Series:The Parables of Jesus, 2000, The Rivers of Paradise, 2000, David's Secret Demons, 2001, Music in Ancient Israel/Palestine, 2002, Injustice Made Legal: Deuteronomic Law and the Plight of Widows, Strangers, and Orphans in Ancient Israel, 2002, Piety and Politics, 2003, Familiar Stranger, 2004, Chieftains of the Highland Clans, 2005; (Biblical Resource Series) Studies in Ancient Yahwistic Poetry, 1975, 1995, Ancient Israel: Its Life and Institutions, 1961, 1997, The Use of the Tenses in Hebrew, 1974, 1998, Semitic Background of The New Testament, 1997, To Advance The Gospel, 1981, 1998, Memory and Manuscript, 1961, 1998, Between Athensand Jerusalem, 2000, Pharisees, Scribes, and Sadducees, 1988, 2001, Letters to the Seven Churches of Asia, 1986, 2001, The Faith of Jesus Christ, 1983, 2002, Till the Heart Sings, 2004, What Are the Gospels?, 2004, Psalms in Israel's Worship, 2004, He That Cometh, 2005, Creation and Chaos in the Primeval Era and the Eschaton, 2006; (with J. Greenfield) New Directions in Biblical Archaeology, 1969; (with J.A. Baird) The Computer Bible, 1971, A Critical Concordance to the Synoptic Gospels, 1971, An Analytic Linguistic Concordance to the Book of Isaiah, 1971, I, II, III John: Forward and Reverse Concordance and Index, 1971, A Critical Concordance to Hosea, Amos, Micah, 1972, A Critical Concordance of Haggai, Zechariah, Malachi, 1973, A Critical Concordance to the Gospel of John, 1974, A Synoptic Concordance of Aramaic Inscriptions, 1975, A Linguistic Concordance of Ruth and Jonah, 1976, A Linguistic Concordance of Jeremiah, 1978, Syntactical and Critical Concordance of Jeremiah, 1978, Synoptic Abstract, 1978, I and II Corinthians, 1979, Zechariah, 1979, Galatians, 1980, Ephesians, 1981, Philippians, 1982, Colossians, 1983, Pastoral Epistles, 1984, 1 & 2 Thessalaians, 1985, Density Plots in Ezekiel, 1986, Exodus, 1987, Hebrews, 1988, Ruth, 1989, James, 1991, 1 & 2 Peter, 1991, 1, 2 & 3 John and Jude, 1991, Psalms, Job and Proverbs, 1992, Apocalypse, 1993, The Pentateuch, 1995, Aramaic Inscriptions, 1975, (with T. Kachel) Religion and the Academic Scene, 1975, Am. Schs. Oriental Research publs; co-editor: Scrolls from Qumran Cave I, 1972, Jesus: The Four Gospels, 1973, Palestine in Transition, 1983, The Bible and its Traditions, 1983, Pomegranates and Golden Bells, 1995; Reader's Digest editor: Atlas of the Bible, 1981, Family Guide to the Bible, 1984, Mysteries of the Bible, 1988, Who's Who in the Bible, 1994, The Bible Through the Ages, 1996, Complete Guide to the Bible, 1998; The Leningrad Codex, 1998, Untold Stories: The Bible and Ugaritic Studies in the Twentieth Century, 2001, Interpreting Discontinuity, 2004, On Human Nature, 2004; assoc. editor Jour. Bible Lit., 1952-54, editor, 1955-59; cons. editor Interpreter's Dictionary of the Bible, 1957-60, Theologisches Wörterbuch des Alten Testaments, 1970—, English Translation Theological Dictionary of the Old Testament, 1975—; editor in chief The Anchor Bible Dictionary, 6 vols., 1992, Eerdmans Dictionary of the Bible, 2000; co-editor (with W.H. Propp and Baruch Halpern) The Hebrew Bible and Its Interpreters, 1990; contbr. articles to profl. jours. Recipient prize in New Testament exegesis Princeton Theol. Sem., 1943, Carey-Thomas award for Anchor Bible, 1965, Layman's Nat. Bible Com. award, 1978, 3 awards for Anchor Bible Bibl. Archaeol. Soc., 1993; William H. Green fellow in Old Testament, 1944, William S. Rayner fellow Johns Hopkins U., 1946, 47, Guggenheim fellow, 1959, Am. Assn. Theol. Schs. fellow, 1963; Am. Coun. Learned Socs. grantee-in-aid, 1967, 76; named Disting. Faculty lectr. U. Calif., San Diego, 2002. Fellow U. Mich. Soc. Fellows (sr., chmn. 1980-82); mem. Soc. Bibl. Lit. (pres. 1975-76), Am. Oriental Soc., Am. Schs. Oriental Rsch. (v.p. 1970-82, editor bull. 1974-78, editor Bibl. Archeologist 1976-82, dir. publs. 1974-82), Archaeol. Inst. Am., Am. Acad. Religion, Bibl. Colloquium (sec.-treas. 1960-90), Bibl. Colloquium West (sec., treas. 2000—). Presbyterian. Office: U Calif San Diego Dept History 0104 9500 Gilman Dr La Jolla CA 92093-0104 Office Phone: 858-534-3542. Business E-Mail: dnfreedman@ucsd.edu.

FREEDMAN, ERIC, journalist, educator, writer; b. Brookline, Mass., Nov. 6, 1949; s. Morris and Charlotte (Nadler) Freedman; m. Mary Ann Sipher, May 24, 1974; children: Ian Sipher, Cara Sipher, Jennifer Gilmore. BA, Cornell U., Ithaca, NY, 1971; JD, NYU, 1975; MS in Resource Devel., Mich. State U., East Lansing, 2004. Bar: N.Y. 1976, Mich. 1985. Congl. aide U.S. Rep. Charles Rangel, Washington and NYC, 1971—76; reporter Knickerbocker News, Albany, NY, 1976—84, Detroit News, Lansing, Mich., 1984—95; asst. prof. Mich. State U., 1996—, asst. dean, Internat. Studies, 2005—. Fulbright sr. lectr., Uzbekistan, 2002. Author: Pioneering Michigan, 1992, On the Water, Michigan, 1992, Michigan Free, 1993, Great Lakes, Great National Forests, 1995, How to Transfer to the College of Your Choice, 2002; co-author: What to Study, 1997; contbr. articles to profl. jours.; co-editor: John F. Kennedy in His Own Words, 2005. Recipient Merit citation, Am. Judicature Soc., Journalism awards, AP, Pulitzer Prize for beat reporting, 1994. Mem.: Soc. Environ. Journalism, Assn. Edn. in Journalisma nd Mass Comm., NY State Bar Assn. (Journalism awards), State Bar Mich., Investigative Reporters and Editors (Journalism award), Ctrl. Eurasian Studies Soc. Avocations: travel, writing. Home and Office: 2698 Linden Dr East Lansing MI 48823-3814 Office Phone: 517-355-4729. Business E-Mail: freedma5@msu.edu.

FREEDMAN, GERALD M., lawyer; b. Hampton, Va., July 26, 1943; s. Henry and Arlene L.; m. Kristin King; 1 child, Eliza King. BA, Columbia U., 1964, JD, 1967. Bar: N.Y. 1968, U.S. Dist. Ct. (so. and ea. dists.) N.Y. 1970, U.S. Ct. Appeals (2d cir.) 1976. Adminstr. Columbia U., NYC, 1967-69; assoc. Kelley, Drye & Warren, NYC, 1969-71, Trubin Sillcocks Edelman & Knapp, NYC, 1971-76, ptnr., 1976-84, Morgan, Lewis & Bockius, NYC, 1984—. Ptnr. N.Y.C. Partnership, 2000—04. Contbr. articles to profl. jours. Mem. bd. Sharon Audobon, 2005-, vice-chair, 2006-. Mem.: ABA, Assn. of Bar of City of N.Y., Sharon Country Club, Univ. Club. Office: Morgan Lewis & Bockius 101 Park Ave Fl 44 New York NY 10178-0060 E-mail: gfreedman@morganlewis.com.

FREEDMAN, HELEN E., judge; b. NYC, Dec. 15, 1942; d. David Simeon and Frances (Fisher) Edelstein; m. Henry A. Freedman, June 7, 1964; children: Katherine Eleanor, Elizabeth Sarah. BA, Smith Coll., 1963; JD, NYU, 1967. Bar: N.Y. 1970, U.S. Dist. Ct. (so. and ea. dists.), U.S. Supreme Ct. 1979. Staff atty. office of gen. counsel Am. Arbitration Assn.,

NYC, 1967-69; assoc. Hubbel, Cohen & Stiefel, NYC, 1970-71, Shaw, Bernstein, Scheuer, Boyden & Sarnoff, NYC, 1971-74; law sec. Civil Ct., NYC, 1974-76; sr. atty. housing litigation bur. N.Y.C. Dept. Housing Preservation and Devel., 1976; supervising atty. Dist. Coun. 37 Legal Svcs. Plan, NYC, 1976-78; judge Civil Ct., NYC, 1979-88; acting justice Supreme Ct., NYC, 1984-88, justice, 1989-95; apptd. to appellate term 1st dept. NY Supreme Ct., NYC, 1995-99, apptd. to comml. divsn., 2000—, pres. judge mass tort litigation panel, 2002—. Co-chair State Judges Mass Tort Litigation Com.; mem. pattern jury instrns. com., Supreme Ct. Justices; adj. prof. N.Y. Law Sch., 1999, 2000, 03, 04, 06, 07; lectr. in field. Author: New York Objections, 1999, 8th revised edit., 2006; contbr. articles to profl. jours. Recipient Disting. Alumna award Smith Coll., 2000, Disting. Svc. award, Civil Ct. N.Y., 2004, Louis J. Capozzoli Gavel award N.Y. Ct. Lawyers Assn., 2005. Fellow Am. Bar Found., NY State Bar Found.; mem. ABA (chair small claims ct. com. 1986-89, bioethics com. nat. conf. spl. ct. judges, NY State Ct. del. to ann. meetings, nat. conf. spl. ct. judges, 1987-88, Spl. Cts. Conf. award 1987, 88, 93, Jud. Excellence award 1998), Nat. Assn. Women Judges, NY State Bar Assn. (del.), NY Fed. State Jud. Coun., NY Women's Bar Assn., NY State Assn. Women Judges (pres. 1995-97), Assn. of Bar of City of NY (com mem., chair com. med. malpractice, v.p. 1994-95), Judges and Lawyers Breast Cancer Alert (pres. 2001-03). Home: 150 W 96th St New York NY 10025-6469 Office: NY Supreme Ct 60 Centre New York NY 10007-1488 Office Phone: 646-386-3208.

FREEDMAN, JAY WEIL, lawyer; b. Washington, May 19, 1942; s. Walter and Maxine (Weil) F.; m. Linda Newman, Aug. 7, 1966; children: Courteney, Spencer. BA, Williams Coll., 1964; JD, Yale U., 1967. Bar: D.C. 1968, U.S. Supreme Ct. 1973. Atty. office of gen. counsel FCC, 1967-68; assoc. Freedman, Levy, Kroll & Simonds, Washington, 1968-72, ptnr., 1972-2001, Foley & Lardner LLP, Washington, 2001—, mng. ptnr. Washington office. Pres. Am. Jewish Com., Washington, 1987—89, Washington Hebrew Congregation, 1982—84; bd. dirs. Smithsonian Instn. Librs., 2001—, Georgetown Bus. Improvement Dist., 2002—06, first v.p., 2006—; bd. dirs. Heifitz Internat. Music Inst., 2003—; bd. trustees The Kreeger Mus., 2002—. Mem. ABA, D.C. Bar Assn., Woodmont Country Club (pres. 1997-99), Yale Law Sch. Alumni Assn. (exec. com. 1999-2004, sec. 2003-04), Econ. Club, Phi Delta Phi. Office: Foley & Lardner 3000 K Street NW Ste 500 Washington DC 20007 Home Phone: 301-320-2364. Business E-Mail: jfreedman@foley.com.

FREEDMAN, JENNA, library and information scientist; b. 1967; d. Mitch Freedman. MLIS, U. South Fla. Coord. reference svcs. Barnard Coll. Libr., NYC; founder Barnard Coll. Libr. Zine Collection, 2003. Contbr. articles to profl. jours. Founding mem. Radical Reference, 2004—; active in Progressive Coun. Caucus, Social Responsibilities Round Table. Named one of the Movers & Shakers, Libr. Jour., 2003. Mem.: ALA (mem. presdl. task force on better salaries, councilor, Elizabeth Futas Catalyst for Change award 2007), Assn. Coll. & Rsch. Librs. (Women's Studies sect. Significant Achievement award 2007). Achievements include initiating national Library Workers' Day, celebrated during National Library Week. Office: Barnard Coll Libr 3009 Broadway New York NY 10027 Office Phone: 212-854-4615. E-mail: jfreedman@barnard.edu.

FREEDMAN, JOEL F., lawyer; BA cum laude, Brandeis Univ., 1986; JD magna cum laude, Boston Univ., 1989. Bar: Mass. 1989. V.p. & gen. counsel Dial Call, 1994—96; ptnr. corp. dept. Ropes & Gray, Boston, 1996—, co-head venture capital & tech. practice group. Office: Ropes & Gray 1 International Pl Boston MA 02110-2624 Office Phone: 617-951-7309. Office Fax: 617-951-7050. Business E-Mail: joel.freedman@ropesgray.com.

FREEDMAN, JONATHAN BORWICK, journalist, writer, educator; b. Rochester, NY, Apr. 11, 1950; s. Marshall Arthur and Betty (Borwick) F.; children: Madigan, Nicholas; m. Isabelle Rooney, 1999; children: Genevieve, Lincoln. AB in Lit. cum laude, Columbia Coll., NYC, 1972. Reporter AP of Brazil, Sao Paulo and Rio de Janeiro, 1974-75; editorial writer The Tribune, San Diego, 1981-90; syndicated columnist Copley News Service, San Diego, 1987-89; free-lance opinion writer L.A. Times, 1990—; free-lance editorial writer N.Y. Times, 1990-91; dir. Hope Lit. Project, 1998—. Dist. vis. lectr. and adj. faculty San Diego State U., 1990—; mem. U.S.-Japan Journalists Exch. Program, Internat. Press Inst., 1985. Author, illustrator: The Man Who'd Bounce the World, 1979; author: The Editorials and Essays of Jonathan Freedman, 1988, Wall of Fame, 2000; contbg. author: Best Newspaper Writing, From Contemporary Culture, 1991, (nonfiction) From Cradle to Grave: The Human Face of Poverty in America, 1993; freelance columnist, 1979-81; dir. (TV documentary) Pedaling Hope, 1998; contbr. articles to N.Y. Times, Chgo. Tribune, San Francisco Examiner, Oakland Tribune, others. Moderator PBS, San Diego, 1988; bd. dirs. Schs. of the Future Commn., San Diego, 1987. Recipient Copley Ring of Truth award, 1983, Sigma Delta Chi award, 1983, San Diego Press Club award, 1984, Spl. citation Columbia Grad. Sch. Journalism, 1985, Disting. Writing award Am. Soc. Newspaper Editors, 1986, Pulitzer prize in Disting. Editorial Writing, 1987; Cornell Woolrich Writing fellow Columbia U., 1972, Eugene C. Pullian Editorial Writing fellow Sigma Delta Chi Found., 1986, Media fellow Hoover Instn., Stanford, Calif., 1991, Kaiser Media fellow, 1995, Peacemaker award San Diego Mediation Ctr., 1999, one of 45 Am. Heroes, Esquire mag., 1998. Mem. Soc. Profl. Journalists (Disting. Svc. award 1985, Casey medal for meritorious journalism 1994), Nat. Conf. Editl. Writers, Authors Guild, Phi Beta Kappa. Jewish. Avocations: skiing, tai chi. Office: 755 Genter St La Jolla CA 92037-5459

FREEDMAN, JOSEPH, retired sanitary and public health engineering consultant; b. Brighton, Mass., Oct. 16, 1923; s. Edwin and Fanny (Wine) Freedman; m. Emily Ann Feltman, Nov. 4, 1959 (dec. Oct. 5, 2002); 1 child, Susan Alexandra Freedman Noa. BS in Pub. Health Engring., Ga. Inst. Tech., 1943; MS in Sanitary Engring., U. NC, 1945; SM in Sanitary Engring., Harvard U., 1955; cert. in groundwater devel., U. Minn., 1959. Registered profl. engr., Mass. Sanitary engr. Holmes & Narver, Architect Engrs., Okinawa, Japan, 1946—48; chief sanitary engr. R & U divsn. Mariannas Bonins Command, Dept. of the Army, Guam, 1948—50; engr. Charles T. Main, Consulting Engrs., Boston, 1951—54; sanitary engr. Pan Am. Health Orgn., Honduras, 1955—61; advisor Govt. of Honduras, Tegucigalpa, 1955—61; chief sanitary engr., advisor to govts. US AID, La Paz, Bolivia and Asuncion, Paraguay, 1961—63; chief sanitary engr. Inter-Am. Devel. Bank, Washington, 1963—73; sr. sanitary engr. Latin Am. Caribbean region World Bank, Washington, 1973—79; water/waste advisor Ctrl. Office World Bank, Washington, 1979—86; ret., 2005. Cons. various water supply, sewage and pollution control and tourist projects World Bank, OAS, Vols. Tech. Assistance, 1989—; cons. on devel. North Coast and Bay Islands, Honduras Govt./OAS, 1986-87; cons. Arthur Young Assocs., Reorgn. and Decentralization Nat. Water and Sewer Authority, Honduras, 1987; World Bank rep. on bd. dirs. Internat. Ref. Ctr. for Cmty. Water Supply and Sanitation, The Hague, Netherlands, 1983-85 Author: Plan for the Development of the Hydraulic Resources of Honduras, 1953; asst. contbr. report Unified Devel. of the Hydraulic Resources of the Jordan River Valley, 1951-52; co-author: National Health Plan and Training Center for Government of Honduras, 1956-57, Development of National and Local Institutions for Planning, Building, Maintaining and Financing Urban and Rural Water and Sewer Programs; designer constrn. bldg. and facilities and training courses for technicians Buenos Aires Convention fellow, 1953 Fellow ASCE; mem. Inter-Am. Soc. Sanitary Engrs. (charter), World Bank 1818 Soc., Sigma Xi, Phi Eta Sigma, Phi Kappa Phi Avocation: genealogy.

FREEDMAN, JUDITH GREENBERG, retired elementary school educator, state legislator; b. Bridgeport, Conn., Mar. 11, 1939; d. Samuel Howard and Dorothy (Hoffman) G.; m. Samuel Sumner, Dec. 24, 1964; 1 child, Martha Ann. Student, Boston U., 1957—58, U. Mich., 1958—59; BS, So. Conn. State U., 1961, MS, 1972. Tchr. Hollywood (Fla.) Pub. Schs., 1961-62, White Plains (N.Y.) Pub. Schs., 1962-64, Wilton (Conn.) Pub. Schs., 1964-66, Weston (Conn.) Pub. Schs., 1966-72, 1982-84, tutor, 1977-80; owner Judith's Fancy, Westport, Conn., 1984—; mem. Dist. 26 Conn. Senate, Hartford, 1987—. Ranking mem. human svcs. com. Conn. Senate, 1987—88, ins. com., 1987—94, ranking mem. appropriations com., 1989—94, chmn. program rev. and investigation, 1992—94, chmn. commn. on innovation and productivity, 1994—95, ranking mem. edn. com., 1995—96, dep. pres. pro tem, 1995—97, 1995—2000, chair edn. com., 1998—2000, asst. minority leader, 1998—2002, co-chair edn. sub. com. appropriations, 1998—, mem. legis. mgmt. com., 1998—, mem. appropriation com., 1998—, ranking mem. higher edn. com., 2002—04; mem. exec. com. ea. region Coun. State Govts., chair program rev. and investigation, 2000—, dep. minority leader, 2000—02; edn. commn. of the states Conn. steering com., 2000—; mem. exec. com. ERCCSG, 2004—. Pres., v.p. 4th Congl. Rep. Women's Assn., 1976-80; pres. Rep. Women of Westport, 1976-79; mem. Bd. Edn., Westport, 1983-87, 89—; treas. Conn. Order Women Legislators. Mem. Order of Women Legislators (treas.), Weston Kiwanis, Fairfield County Navy Leagues. Jewish. Avocations: reading, art, golf. Home: 17 Crawford Rd Westport CT 06880-1823 Office Phone: 860-240-8826. Business E-Mail: judith.g.freedman@po.state.ct.us.

FREEDMAN, LOUIS MARTIN, dentist; b. Newark, Mar. 19, 1947; s. Morris and Sylvia (Swimmer) F.; m. Elizabeth Norine Palmer, June 17, 1978; children: Steven, Julie, Brian. Student, Emory U., 1963—66, DDS, 1970. Dentist Freedman, Freedman & Weitman DDS, P.C., Atlanta, 1970—; clin. instr. Emory U. Dental Sch., Atlanta, 1970—77. Team dentist Atlanta Hawks Basketball Team, 1971—, Atlanta Flames Hockey Team, 1979-80, Atlanta Knights Hockey Team, 1992-96, Atlanta Fire Ants Roller Hockey Team, 1994-96. Mgr. Sandy Springs Youth Sports Little League Baseball, 1979-96; head coach Sandy Springs United Meth. Ch. basketball program, 1991-96. Mem. Acad. Osseointegration, Internat. Congress Oral Implantologists, Alpha Epsilon Delta, Omicron Kappa Upsilon. Jewish. Avocations: softball, little league managing, gardening, skiing, waterskiing, swimming. Office: Freedman Freedman & Weitman 3111 Piedmont Rd NE Atlanta GA 30305-2507 Home Phone: 770-796-1091; Office Phone: 404-261-5388.

FREEDMAN, MICHAEL HARTLEY, mathematician, educator; b. LA, Apr. 21, 1951; s. Benedict and Nancy (Mars) Freedman; m. Leslie Blair Howland, Sept. 18, 1983; children: Hartley, Whitney, Jake; 1 child. PhD, Princeton U., 1973. Lectr. U. Calif., Berkeley, 1973—75; faculty mem. Inst. Advanced Study, Princeton, NJ, 1980—81, mem., 1975—76; asst. prof. U. Calif., San Diego, 1976—79, assoc. prof., 1979—80, prof., 1982—85, Charles Lee Powell chair math., 1985—; sr. rsch. scientist Microsoft Corp., 1997—. Author: Classification of Four Dimensional Spaces, 1982; author: (assoc. editor) Jour. Differntial Geometry, Math. Rsch. Letters and Topology, 1982—, Annals of Math., 1984—91, Jour. Am. Math. Soc., 1987—. Named Calif. Scientist of Yr., Calif. Mus. Assn., 1984; recipient Veblen prize, Am. Math. Soc., 1986, Fields medal, Internat. Congress of Mathematicians, 1986, Nat. medal of Sci., 1987, Humboldt Award, 1994; fellow MacArthur Found., 1984—89, Guggenheim, 1989, 1994. Mem.: NAS, N.Y. Acad. Scis., Am. Assn. Arts and Scis. Avocation: rock climbing. Office: Microsoft Rsch One Microsoft Way Redmond WA 98052 also: Univ Calif San Diego Dept Math 0112 9500 Gilman Dr La Jolla CA 92093-0112 E-mail: mfreedman@ucsd.edu.

FREEDMAN, MICHAEL LEONARD, geriatrician, educator; b. Newark, Dec. 12, 1937; s. David Hyman and Alice Ella (Zwain) F.; m. Cora Ruth Singer, June 24, 1962; children: Lawrence Andrew, Deborah Lynn. AB with honors, Colgate U., 1959; MD cum laude, Tufts U., 1963. Diplomate Am. Bd. Internal Medicine, Am. Bd. Hematology, Am. Bd. Geriatric Medicine. Intern, then resident NYU/Bellevue Med. Ctrs., 1963-65, 68-69; rsch. assoc. lab physiology to staff investigator Nat. Cancer Inst., NIH, Bethesda, Md., 1965-68; asst. prof. NYU Med. Ctr., 1969-74, assoc. prof., 1974-77, prof., 1977—, firm chief, dir. geriatrics, 1979—; Diane and Arthur Belfer prof. geriatric medicine NYU, 1987—. Cons. CBS, Inc., Bristol Meyers Corp., Kimberly-Clark Corp., Pfizer Corp., Nutrasweet Corp., Citicorp. Editor: Hematology in the Elderly, 1985; contbr. over 185 articles to profl. jours. Lt. comdr. USPHS, 1965-68. NIH rsch. grantee, 1969—; recipient Wholeness of Life award Hosp. Chaplaincy, 1988; named one of the Heroes of Bellevue, 1987. Fellow ACP, Am. Geriatrics Soc. (com. chmn. 1985—), Am. Soc. Hematology, Gerontol. Soc. Am. (com. chmn. 1984—); mem. Am. Soc. Clin. Investigation, Am. Soc. Hematology, AAAS, Am. Fed. Aging Rsch. (founder, mem. nat. adv. coun.), Alpha Omega Alpha. Democrat. Jewish. Avocations: photography, travel, tennis. Office: NYU Med Ctr 550 1st Ave New York NY 10016-6402 Office Phone: 212-263-7043.

FREEDMAN, MONROE HENRY, law educator; b. Mt. Vernon, NY, Apr. 10, 1928; s. Chauncey and Dorothea (Kornblum) F.; m. Audrey Willock, Sept. 24, 1950 (dec. 1998); children: Alice Freedman Korngold, Sarah Freedman Izquierdo, Caleb (dec. 1998), Judah. AB cum laude, Harvard U., 1951, LLB, 1954, LLM, 1956. Bar: Mass. 1954, Pa. 1957, D.C. 1960, U.S. Dist. Ct. (ea. dist. N.Y.), U.S. Ct. Appeals (D.C. cir.) 1960, U.S. Supreme Ct. 1960, U.S. Ct. Appeals (2d cir.) 1968, N.Y. 1978, U.S. Ct. Appeals (9th cir.) 1982, U.S. Ct. Appeals (11th cir.) 1986, U.S. Ct. Appeals (Fed. cir.) 1987. Assoc. Wolf, Block, Schorr & Solis-Cohen, Phila., 1956-58; ptnr. Freedman & Temple, Washington, 1969-73; dir. Stern Community Law Firm, Washington, 1970-71; prof. law George Washington U., 1958-73; dean Hofstra Law Sch., Hempstead, NY, 1973-77, prof. law, 1973—, Howard Lichtenstein Disting. prof. legal ethics, 1989—2003; Drinko-Baker & Hostetler chair in law Cleve. State U., 1992; CFO Olive Tree Mktg. Internat., 1998—2004. Faculty asst. Harvard U. Law Sch., 1954-56, instr. trial advocacy and legal ethics, 1978—; lectr. on lawyers' ethics; exec. dir. U.S. Holocaust Meml. Coun., 1980-82, gen. counsel, 1982-83, sr. adviser to chmn., 1982-87; cons. U.S. Commn. on Civil Rights, 1960-64, Neighborhood Legal Services Program, 1970; legis. cons. to Senator John L. McClellan, 1959; spl. com. on courtroom conduct N.Y.C. Bar Assn., 1972; exec. dir. Criminal Trial Inst., 1965-66; expert witness on legal ethics state and fed. ct. proceedings, U.S. Senate and House Coms., U.S. Dept. Justice, FDIC; spl. investigator Rochester Inst. Tech., 1991; reporter Am. Lawyer's Code of Conduct, 1979-81; mem. Arbitration panel U.S. Dist. Ct. (ea. dist.) N.Y., 1986—; Inaugural Wickwire lectr. Dalhousie Law Sch., N.S., 1992; lectr. S.C. Bar Found., 1993, numerous profl. confs; adv. subgroup on ethics U.S. Dist. Ct. (ea. dist.) N.Y., 1994-96; vis. prof. law Georgetown U. Law Ctr., 2007-08. Author: Contracts, 1973, Lawyers' Ethics in an Adversary System, 1975 (ABA gavel award, cert. of merit 1976), Teacher's Manual Contracts, 1978, American Lawyer's Code of Conduct, 1981, Understanding Lawyers' Ethics, 1990, (with Abbe Smith) 3d edit., 2004, (with Eric Freedman) Group Defamation and Freedom of Speech—The Relationship Between Language and Violence, 1995; columnist Cases and Controversies, Am. Lawyer Media, 1990-96, (with Supreme Ct. Justice Ruth Bader Ginsburg) Freedom, Life, & Death: Materials on Comparative Constitutional Law, 1997; mem. panel acad. contbrs. Black's Law Dictionary, 2002-03; television appearances include Donohue, CNN Money Line, CBS 60 Minutes, CNN Late Edition, Court TV, C-SPAN, O'Reilly Factor, and others; contbr. articles to profl. jours. Recipient Martin Luther King Jr. Humanitarian award, 1987, The Lehman-LaGuardia award for Civic Achievement, 1996, Alumni Outstanding Prof. award Hofstra Law Sch., 2006. Fellow Am. Bar Found. (life); mem. ABA (ethics adv. to chair criminal justice sect. 1993-95, ethics and professional responsibility com. 2005—, Michael Franck award 1998), ACLU (nat. bd. dir. 1970-80, nat. adv. coun. 1980—, spl. litigation counsel 1971-73), Am. Law Inst. (consultative group on the law governing lawyers, 1990-99, consultative group on Uniform Comml. Code art. 2 1990-2002), Soc. Am. Law Tchrs. (mem. governing bd. 1974-79, exec. com. 1976-79, chmn. com. on profl. responsibility 1974-79, 87-90), ABA (vice chmn. ethical considerations com. criminal justice sect. 1989-90, ethics advisor to chmn. criminal justice sect., 1993-96), N.Y. State Bar Assn. (com. on legal edn. and admission to bar 1988-92, criminal justice sect. com. on profl. responsibility, 1990-92, award for Dedication to Scholarship and pub. svc. 1997, Sanford D. Levy award for scholarship on profl. ethics 2005, award for edn. in criminal justice 2006), Assn. Bar City N.Y. (com. on profl. responsibility 1987-90, com. on profl. and jud. ethics 1991-92), Fed. Bar Assn. (chmn. com. on profl. disciplinary standards and procedures 1970-71), Am. Soc. Writers on Legal Subjects (mem. com. on constitution and bylaws 1999-2000), Am. Jewish Congress (nat. governing coun. 1984-86), Am. Arbitration Assn. (arbitrator, nat. panel arbitrators 1964—, cert. svc. award 1986), Nat. Network on Right to Counsel (exec. bd., exec. com. 1986-90), Nat. Com. on the Right to Counsel, Nat. Prison Project (steering com. 1970-90), Nat. Assn. Criminal Def. Lawyers (vice chmn. ethics adv. com. 1991-93, co-chmn., 1994), Am. Bd. Criminal Lawyers (hon.). Democrat. Jewish. Address: The Wyndham West 804 111 Cherry Valley Ave Garden City NY 11530 Office Phone: 516-873-6622. Business E-Mail: lawmhf@hofstra.edu.

FREEDMAN, PHILIP, internist, educator; b. London, June 25, 1926; came to U.S., 1963, naturalized, 1970; s. Myer and Mildred (Frankel) F.; m. Jean Kennis Cunningham, Dec. 21, 1954; children: Simon John, Marion Rose, Mark Alexander, Paul Daniel, Adam James. MB, BS with honors, Univ. Coll. Hosp. Med. Sch., London, 1948, MD, 1951. House surgeon Univ. Coll. Hosp., 1948, med. registrar, 1953-56, rsch. asst. professorial med. unit, 1956-57, Bilton Pollard fellow, 1957-59; sr. house physician Chase Farm Hosp., 1949; 1st asst. physician St. George's Hosp., London, 1959-60; cons. Woolwich Hosp. Group, London, Redhill Hosp. Group, Surrey, Eng., 1960-63; chief Chgo. Med. Sch. Divsn., Dept. Medicine Cook County Hosp., 1963-66; prof., chmn. dept. medicine Chgo. Med. Sch., 1967-74; dir. renal unit Cook County Hosp., Chgo., 1963-66; chmn. dept. medicine Mt. Sinai Hosp. Med. Ctr., Chgo., 1966-79; prof., sr. attending physician Rush Med. Coll., Rush-Presbyn.-St. Luke's Med. Ctr., Chgo., 1975-96; clin. prof. medicine U. Ill. Coll. Medicine, Urbana-Champaign, 1999—. Contbr. articles to profl. jours. With M.C. Brit. Army, 1951-53. Fellow ACP, Royal Coll. Physicians; mem. Ctrl. Soc. Clin. Investigation, Med. Rsch. Soc. London, Alpha Omega Alpha (faculty mem.). Home: 2304 Sandpoint Champaign IL 61822-9297 Business E-Mail: pfreedmn@uiuc.edu.

FREEDMAN, ROBERT, psychiatrist; b. St. Louis, June 8, 1946; BA, Harvard Coll., 1968; MD, Harvard Med. Sch., 1972. Diplomate Nat. Bd. Med. Examiners, 1973, Am. Bd. Psychiatry & Neurology, 1980, lic. Ill., 1976, Colo., 1978. Intern Harvard Med. Svc., Boston City Hosp., 1972—73; rsch. assoc. NIMH Lab. Neuropharmacology, St. Elizabeths Hosp., Washington, 1973—75; resident physician & rsch. fellow, dept. psychiatry U. Chgo. Hosp. & Clinics, 1975—78; dir., ward chief biol. consultation svc. & psychiat. assessment unit Boulder (Colo.) Psychiat. Inst., 1978—; staff psychiatrist VA Hosp., Denver, 1978—; asst. prof. psychiatry & pharmacology U. Colo. Health Sciences Ctr., Denver, 1978—81, assoc. prof. psychiatry & pharmacology, 1981—86, prof. psychiatry & pharmacology, 1986—, vice-chmn., dir. rsch., dept. psychiatry, 1986—2000, prof. & chmn., dept. psychiatry, 2000—, supt. Colo. Psychiat. Hosp., 2000—. Sr. fellow Eleanor Roosevelt Inst. Cancer Rsch., Denver, 1987—; vis. scientist, dept. histology & neurobiology Karolinska Inst., Stockholm, 1990—91; chmn. VA Med. Rsch. Adv. Group for Mental Health, 1997—; mem. bd. scientific coun. Nat. Inst. Drug Abuse, 1999—. Editorial bd. Schizophrenia Rsch., 1992, Biol. Psychiatry, 1997. Surgeon USPHS, 1973—75; pres. Mothers & Children's Project, 1984—99, Inst. Children's Mental Disorders, 1999—. Recipient Edward Sacher award, Columbia U., 1997, Eli Lilly award for social svc., 1998, William K. Warren award, Internat. Congress Schizophrenia Rsch., 1999. Fellow: Am. Psychiatric Assn. (chmn. task force on quantitative EEG, Falk fellow 1976); mem.: Mental Health Assn. Colo., Nat. Alliance for the Mentally Ill (svc. award 1984), Inst. Medicine, Am. Soc. Human Genetics, Soc. Neuroscience, Am. Coll. Neuropharmacology (editorial bd., program com., publ. com.), Soc. Biol. Psychiatry (editorial bd., Bennett Rsch. award 1976), Phi Beta Kappa. Office: Health Sciences Ctr Dept Psychiatry C268-71 4200 E 9th Ave Denver CO 80262 Office Phone: 303-315-8403. Office Fax: 303-315-5347. E-mail: robert.freedman@uchsc.edu.

FREEDMAN, RUSSELL BRUCE, author; b. San Francisco, Oct. 11, 1929; s. Louis Nathan and Irene (Gordon) F. BA, U. Calif., Berkeley, 1951. Newsman AP, San Francisco, 1953-56; with dept. TV publicity J. Walter Thompson Co., NYC, 1956-60; faculty New Sch. for Social Rsch., NYC, 1969-86. Author: Teenagers Who Made History, 1961, Jules Verne: Portrait of a Prophet, 1963, 2000 Years of Space Travel, 1965, Thomas Alva Edison, 1966, Scouting with Baden-Powell, 1967, Animal Architects, 1971, The First Days of Life, 1974, Growing Up Wild, 1975, Animal Fathers, 1976, Animal Games, 1976, Hanging On: How Animals Carry Their Young, 1978, Getting Born, 1978, Tooth and Claw, 1980, They Lived with the Dinosaurs, 1980, Immigrant Kids, 1980, When Winter Comes, 1981, Farm Babies, 1981, Animal Superstars, 1982, Killer Fish, 1982, Killer Snakes, 1982, Can Bears Predict Earthquakes? Unsolved Mysteries of Animal Behavior, 1982, Dinosaurs and Their Young, 1983, Children of the Wild West, 1983 (Western Heritage Wrangler award, Outstanding Western Juvenile Book award 1984), Rattlesnakes, 1984, Cowboys of the Wild West, 1985, Sharks, 1985, Holiday House: The First Fifty Years, 1985, Indian Chiefs, 1987, Abraham Lincoln: A Photobiography, 1987 (John Newbery medal 1988, Jefferson Cup award 1988), Buffalo Hunt, 1988, Franklin Delano Roosevelt, 1990 (Orbis Pictus award 1991, Jefferson Cup award 1991), The Wright Brothers: How They Invented the Airplane, 1991 (Newbery Honor Book 1992, Jefferson cup award 1992, Golden Kite award 1991), An Indian Winter, 1992 (Western Heritage Wrangler award 1993), Eleanor Roosevelt: A Life of Discovery, 1993 (Newbery Honor Book 1994, Golden Kite award 1993, Boston Globe Horn Book award 1993), Kids at Work, 1994 (Golden Kite award 1994, Jane Addams Book award 1995), The Life and Death of Crazy Horse, 1996 (Spur award Best Western Juvenile Non-fiction 1996), Out of Darkness: The Story of Louis Braille, 1997, Martha Graham: A Dancer's Life, 1998 (Golden Kite award 1998), Babe Didrikson Zaharias: The Making of a Champion, 1999, Give Me Liberty! The Story of the Declaration of Independence, 2000, In the Days of the Vaqueros: America's First True Cowboys, 2001 (Spur award Best Western Juvenile non-fiction, 2002), Confucius: The Golden Rule, 2002, In Defense of Liberty: The Story of America's Bill of Rights, 2003, The Voice that Challenged a Nation: Marion Anderson and the Struggle for Equal Rights, 2004 (Newbery Honor Book, 2005, Robert F. Sibert Internat. Book award, 2005), Children of the Great Depression, 2005 (Orbis Pictures award 2006, Golden Kite award 2006), Freedom Walkers: The Story of the Montgomery Bus Boycott, 2006, The Adventures of Marco Polo, 2006 (Golden Kite award 2007); co-author: (with James E. Morris) How Animals Learn, 1969, Animal Instincts, 1970, The Brains of Animals and Man, 1972. With M.I., U.S. Army, 1951-53; Korea. Mem. PEN, Author's Guild.

FREEDMAN, SAMUEL ORKIN, university official; b. Montreal, Que., Can., May 8, 1928; s. Abraham Orkin and Elvira (Gottheil) F.; m. Norah Lee Maizel, Aug. 28, 1955; children: David Orkin, Daniel Ari, Abraham Edward, Elizabeth Vera. B.Sc., McGill U., Montreal, 1949, MD, C.M.,

1953, D.Sc. (hon.), 1992. Intern Jewish Gen. Hosp., Montreal, 1953-54; resident in internal medicine and allergy Montreal Gen. Hosp., also Roosevelt Hosp., NYC, 1954-59; mem. faculty McGill U. Med. Faculty, 1959—, prof. medicine, physiology, 1968-2000, prof. medicine, physiology emeritus, 2000—, dean, 1977-81, vice-prin. (acad.), 1981-91; dir. Lady Davis Inst. for Med. Rsch., 1991—2000; sr. advisor Jewish Gen. Hosp., Montreal, 2000—. Vis. prof. U. London, Eng., 1973-74; dir. divsn. clin. immunology and allergy Montreal Gen. Hosp., 1967-77; bd. dirs. Nat. Cancer Inst. Can., 1979—; chmn. com. immunology and transplanatation Med. Rsch. Coun. Can., 1968-73, mem. program grants com., 1975-78. Editor: Clinical Immunology, 2d edit, 1976. Decorated Order of Can.; recipient Queen's Silver Jubilee medal, 1977; Gairdner Internat. award for outstanding med. rsch., 1978, Commemorative medal for the 125th Anniversary of the Confedn. of Can., 1992, prix Armand Frappier, 1998, prix de Que., 1998, Queen's Golden Jubilee medal, 2002, Order of Que., 2004. Fellow Royal Soc. Can., Royal Coll. Physicians and Surgeons Can., ACP, Am. Acad. Allergy; Mem. Internat. Assn. Allergology and Clin. Immunology (v.p. 1982-88); mem. Am. Soc. Clin. Investigation, Am. Assn. Immunology, Am. Thoracic Soc., Canadian Soc. Clin. Investigation. Clubs: Univ. (Montreal). Jewish. Achievements include co-discoverer of the CEA test for cancer. Home: 658 Murray Hill Ave Montreal PQ Canada H3Y 2W6 Office: Jewish Gen Hosp 3755 Cote Ste Catherine Rd Montreal PQ Canada H3T 1E2 Home Phone: 514-481-8501; Office Phone: 514-340-7571. Business E-Mail: sfreedma@ldi.jgh.mcgill.ca. E-mail: freedman@videotron.ca.

FREEDMAN, SANDRA WARSHAW, former mayor; b. Newark, Sept. 21, 1943; m. Michael J. Freedman; 3 children. BA in Govt., U. Miami, 1965. Mem. Tampa (Fla.) City Coun., 1974—, chmn., 1983-86; mayor City of Tampa, 1986-95. Author: Specialties of the House (Recipes for People on the Go!), 2002. Bd. dirs. Jewish Cmty. Ctr., Boys and Girls Clubs Greater Tampa, Hillsborough Coalition for Health, Tampa Cmty. Concert Assn., Hillsborough Edn. Found., Judeo Christian Clinic, NCCJ, Human Rights Task Force; mem. sports adv. bd. Hillsborough Community Coll., 1975-76; sec. Downtown Devel. Authority, 1977-78; bd. dirs., v.p. Fla. Gulf Coast Symphony, 1979-80; vice chmn. Met. Planning Orgn., 1981-82; corp. mem. Neighborhood Housing Service; bd. fellows U. Tampa; mem. steering com. Hillsborough County Council of Govt.'s Constituency for Children; mem. exec. bd. Tampa/Hillsborough Young Adult Forum; chmn. bd. trustees Berkeley Prep. Sch.; trustee Tampa Bay Performing Arts Ctr., Inc., Tampa Mus.; mem. ethics com. Meml. Hosp.; mem. Tampa Preservation, Inc., Tampa/Hillsborough County Youth Council, Davis Islands Civic Assn., Tampa Hist. Soc., Met. Ministries Adv. Bd., Rodeph Sholom Synagogue, Sword of Hope Guild of Am. Cancer Soc., Friends of Arts. Recipient Spessar L. Holland Meml. award Tampa Bay Com. for Good Govt., 1975-76, Human Rights award City of Tampa, 1980, award Soroptimist Internat. Tampa, 1981, Status of Women award Zonta of Tampa II, 1986, Woman of Achievement award Bus. & Profl. Women, Jewish Nat. Fund Tree of Life award, Disting. Citizen award U. South Fla., 1995, Nat. Conf. of Christian and Jews Humanitarian award, 1995; named to Fla. Home Builders Hall of Fame. Mem. Hillsborough County Bar Aux., Greater Tampa C. of C., C. of C. Com. of 100 (exec. com.), Fla. League of Cities (bd. dirs.), Tampa Urban League, Nat. Council Jewish Women, U. Miami Alumni Assn., Athena Soc., Hadassah. Office: 3435 Bayshore Blvd Apt 700 Tampa FL 33629-8827

FREEDMAN, SARAH WARSHAUER, education educator; b. Wilmington, NC, Feb. 23, 1946; d. Samuel Edward and Miriam Warshauer; m. S. Robert Freedman, Aug. 20, 1967; 1 child, Rachel Karen. BA in English, U. Pa., 1967; MA in English, U. Chgo., 1970; MA in Linguistics, Stanford U., 1976, PhD in Edn., 1977. Tchr. English Phila. Sch. Dist., 1967-68, Lower Merion H.S., 1968-69; instr. English U. N.C., Wilmington, 1970-71; instr. English and linguistics Stanford U., 1972-76; asst. and assoc. prof. English San Francisco State U., 1977-81; asst. prof. edn. U. Calif., Berkeley, 1981-83, assoc. prof. edn., 1983-89, dir. Nat. Ctr for Study of Writing and Literacy, 1985-96, prof. edn., 1989—, sr. rschr. Human Rights Ctr., 2001—. Resident Bellagio Conf. and Study Ctr., Rockefeller Found., 1997; mem. nat. task force Nat. Writing Project, 1998—. Author: Response to Student Writing, 1987, Exchanging Writing, Exchanging Cultures, Lessons in School Reform from the United States and Great Britain, 1994, (with E.R. Simons, J.S. Kalnin, A. Casareno and M-Class teams) Inside City Schools, Investigating Literacy in Multi-cultural Classrooms, 1999; editor: The Acquisition of Written Language: Response and Revision, 1985, (with A. Ball) Bakhtinian Perspectives on Language, Literacy, and Learning, 2004; contbr. chpts. to books and articles to profl. jours. Recipient Multicultural Book award Nat. Assn. Multicultural Edn., 2000, Alan Purves award, 2006; fellow Nat. Conf. Rsch. in English, 1986-, Ctr. Advanced Studies in Behavioral Scis., 1999-2000, 06-07; grantee Spencer Found. 1996-2003, Nat. Ctr. Study of Writing and Literacy, Office Ednl. Rsch. and Improvement, 1985-95, Minority Undergrad. Rsch. Program U. Calif., 1988, 89, 92, 93, US Inst. Peace, 2003-06, numerous other grants. Mem. Nat. Coun. Tchrs. English (standing com. on rsch. 1981-87, ex-officio 1987-96, Richard Meade award for Pub. Rsch. in Tchr. Edn. 1989, 94, chair bd. trustees rsch. found. 1990-93, Ed Fry book award, 1996, 2000, co-chair rsch. assembly 1999-2001, chmn. 2003-06), Am. Ednl. Rsch. Assn. (chair spl. interest group on rsch. in writing 1983-85, numerous other coms.) Office: U Calif Dept Edn Berkeley CA 94720-0001

FREEDMAN, STANLEY LEWIS, assistant principal; s. David and Diana Freedman; m. Phyllis Duchin, July 4, 1971; 1 child, Randi Beth. BA, Bethel Coll., 1965—69; MA, Newark State Coll., 1973—75. Language Arts NJ. State Dept. of Edn., 1970, Physical Education and Health NJ. State Dept. of Edn., 1970, Administration and Supervision NJ. State Dept. of Edn., 1975. Asst. prin. Rahway Bd. of Edn., 1998—, supr. of lang. arts, 1994—98, program dir. of sch. devel., 1993—94, dept. chmn., area supr., and acting asst. prin., 1977—93, tchr. of lang. arts and phys. edn., 1970—77. Secondary sch. validation team chmn. Mid. Atlantic States' Commn. on Secondary Schools, Phila., 2005—; validation team mem. Mid. Atlantic States Commn. on Secondary Schools, Phila., 1974—2004; mid. atlantic states co-internal coord. Rahway Pub. Schools, 2004—; mem. of statewide nj. mid. sch. peer leadership initiative adv. bd. NJ. State Dept. of Edn., 1993; pres., edn. assn. Rahway Pub. Schools, 1975—76. Dir.: (musical comedy) Funny Girl (First Pl. Winner of the Garden State Arts Ctr. Musical Comedy, 1972). Mem.: Rahway Edn. Assn. (licentiate; pres. 1975—76), ASCD (licentiate), NJ Principals and Supervisors Assn. (licentiate). Avocations: crossword puzzles, bridge, sports, weightlifting, dog grooming. Office: Rahway HS 1012 Madison Ave Rahway NJ 07065 Home: 140 Somerfield Rd Swedesboro NJ 08085-2504 Home Phone: 908-281-5480; Office Phone: 732-396-1080. Office Fax: 732-669-0626; Home Fax: 732-669-0626. Personal E-mail: freedmanstanley@hotmail.com. Business E-Mail: sfreedman@rahway.net.

FREEDMAN, STANLEY MARVIN, manufacturing executive; b. Frederick, Md., Aug. 26, 1923; s. Jacob Menaham and Ethel (Freiman) F.; m. Lynn Maureen Katchen, Apr. 24, 1957 (dec.); children: Rita, Lynn, Michael, Richard, Jon, Jack; m. Lottie Carnell, Dec. 31, 1994 (div.). Student, Georgetown U., 1944; AB in English, High Point Coll., 1946. Owner, operator retail bus., Bound Brook, N.J., 1949-63; dir. mktg. Franklin State Bank, Somerset, N.J., 1963-65; program dir. mktg. div. Am. Mgmt. Assn. N.Y.C., 1965-67; exec. dir. Internat. Bus. Forms Industries, Washington, 1967-69; dir. communications, dir. office machines group Bus. Equipment Mfrs. Assn., Washington, 1969-72; div. pres. Litton Industries, Hampton, Va., 1972-74, group v.p., paper, printing and forms group Virginia Beach, Va., 1974-86. Cons. bus. planning and devel; univ. lectr., 1986-91; dir. Somerset County Savs. & Loan; exec. in residence U. Wis. Grad. Sch. Bus., 1973; entrepreneur in residence U. of the Pacific, Stockton, Calif., 1996. Mem. Bound Brook Bd. Edn., 1955-63; trustee Raritan Valley Hosp., Somerset, N.J., 1960-62; chmn. Urban Devel., Bound Brook, N.J., 1963; mem. def. conversion team AID, Warsaw, Poland, 1995-96. Served with U.S. Army, 1943-46, PTO. Mem. Am. Mgmt. Assn. Home and Office: 7501 E Thompson Peak Pkwy Scottsdale AZ 85255 Personal E-mail: stanrlmrjj@msn.net, sfreedman2@cox.net.

FREEDMAN, STUART JAY, nuclear science educator; BS, U. Calif., Berkeley, 1965, MS, 1967, PhD, 1972. Rsch. asst. U. Calif., Berkeley, 1970-72, mem. faculty to Luis W. Alvarez Meml. Chair exptl. phyiscs, 1991—; instr. Princeton U., NJ, 1972-75, lectr., 1975-76; asst. prof. Stanford U., Calif., 1976-82; staff physicist Argonne Nat. Lab., Ill., 1982-87, sr. physicist, 1987-91, sr. scientist, 1991—; prof. U. Chgo. Enrico Fermi Inst., 1987-91; sr. scientist U. Calif. Berkeley/Lawrence Berkeley Nat. Lab., Calif., 1991—. Contbr. articles to profl. jours. Recipient Kraft award, 1962, T.W,. Bonner prize in nuc. physics, 2007; NDEA fellow, 1965—69, Sloan Found. fellow, 1978—82. Fellow: AAAS, Am. Acad. Arts and Scis., Am. Phys. Soc. (Tom W. Bonner prize in Nuc. Physics 2007); mem.: Nat. Acad. Sci., Tau Beta Pi, Phi Beta Kappa. Office: Dept Physics U Calif Berkeley 366 LeConte Hall Berkeley CA 94720-7300 Office Phone: 510-486-7850. E-mail: sjfreedman@lbl.gov.

FREEDMAN, WARREN, lawyer, educator, judge; b. Scranton, Pa., May 2, 1921; s. Samuel N. and Sarah S. (Spitz) F.; m. Esther Rosenbluth, May 3, 1944; children: Debbie Freedman Stiebel, Douglas, Miriam, Carmen. AB, Rutgers U., 1943; JD, Columbia U., 1949, LLD, 1949. Bar: N.Y. 1949, U.S. Dist. Ct. (ea. dist.) N.Y. 1954, U.S. Ct. Appeals (2d cir.) 1954, U.S. Supreme Ct. 1955, Conn. 1988. Prof. law Rutgers U., Newark, 1950—63; counsel Clairol, Inc., NYC; counsel, asst. sec. Bristol-Myers Squibb Co., NYC, 1953-80; prof. sociology and the law New Sch. for Social Rsch., NYC, 1959-66; hearing examiner, arbitrator; cons. in products liability; trial referee State of Conn. Am. counsel Israel Med. Assn. and Merephdi Med. Fedn. Author: Richards on the Law of Insurance, 1952, Allergy and Products Liability, 1961, Products Liability for Corporate Counsels, Controllers and Product Safety Executives, 1984, Guide for the Jewish Traveler, 1984, The Right of Privacy in the Computer Age, 1986, Prime Defenses to Negligence, 1986, Strict Liability, 1986, Res Judicata and Collateral Estoppel, 1987, Federal Statutes on Environmental Protection, 1987, Professional Sports and Antitrust, 1987, Frivolous Lawsuits and Frivolous Defenses, 1987, Foreign Plaintiffs in Products Liability Actions, 1987, Joint and Several Liability, 1987, Hazardous Waste Liability, 1987, Internat. Products Liability, 1987, Jewish Communities Around the World, 1988, Freedom of Speech on Private Property, 1988, Press and Media Access to the Criminal Courtroom, 1988, Product Liability Actions by Foreign Plaintiffs in the United States, 1988, The Privilege To Keep and Bear Arms, 1988, The Law of Insurance, 1989, The Business Tort of Fraud and Misrepresentation, 1989, The Tort of Discovery Abuse, 1989, (with Edward Greer) Toxic Tort Litigation, 1980; contbr. articles to law jours. Capt. JAGC, U.S. Army, 1944-46, PTO. Mem. ABA, Internat. Assn. Jewish Lawyers and Jurists, World Peace Through Law Ctr., Anti-Defamation League of B'nai B'rith (hon. life). Home: 13834 Sand Crane Dr Palm Beach Gardens FL 33418-1433 Home Phone: 561-776-8900.

FREEDMAN, WENDY LAUREL, astronomer, educator, director; b. Toronto, Ont., Can., July 17, 1957; arrived in US, 1984, naturalized, 1998; d. Harvey Bernard and Sonya Lynn Freedman; m. Barry F. Madore, June 23, 1985; children: Rachael, Daniel. BSc, U. Toronto, 1979, MSc, 1980, PhD in Astronomy and Astrophysics, 1984. Fellow Observatories of Carnegie Instn., Pasadena, Calif., 1984-87, staff mem., 1987—, Crawford H. Greenewalt chair dir., 2003—. Mem. Astronomy and Astrophysics adv. com., 2005—. Contbr. articles to sci. jours. Recipient Marc Aaronson Lectureship and prize, 1994, John P. McGovern award, 2000, Helen Sawyer Hogg award, 2000. Fellow Am. Acad. Arts & Scis.; mem. Am Philos. Soc. (Megellanic Premium award 2002), Am. Astron. Soc., Am. Phys. Soc., Can. Astron. Soc., Astron. Soc. of the Pacific, NAS. Office: Observatories of Carnegie Inst 813 Santa Barbara St Pasadena CA 91101 Office Phone: 626-577-1122, 626-304-0204. Business E-Mail: wendy@ociw.edu.*

FREEH, LOUIS JOSEPH, lawyer, former FBI director; b. Jersey City, Jan. 6, 1950; s. William and Beatrice Freeh; m. Marilyn A. Freeh; 6 children. AB, Rutgers U., 1971, JD, 1974; LLM in Criminal Law, NYU, 1984. Law clk. to Senator Clifford Case NJ State Senate, Trenton, 1974—75; spl. agt. FBI, NYC, 1975-80, spl. agt. supr., 1980-81; served in various position within US Atty's Office (so. dist.) NY including asst. US atty., chief organized crime unit, dep. US atty. & assoc. US atty US Dept. Justice, NYC, 1981-91; judge US Dist. Ct. (so. dist.) N.Y., NYC, 1991-93; dir. FBI, Washington, 1993—2001; sr. vice chmn., gen. counsel MBNA Corp., Wilmington, Del., 2001—06, corp. sec., ethics officer, 2001—06; pres. Freeh Group Internat., LLC, Del., 2006—. Spl. prosecutor investigating mail bombing deaths of Judge Robert Vance & Robert Robinson, US Dept. Justice, 1990, mem., Homeland Security Adv. Coun., US Dept. Homeland Security, 2007-; adj. assoc. prof. Fordham Law Sch., 1988-92, Widener Law Sch., 2003-04; bd. dirs., Bristol-Myers Squibb Co., 2005-, L-1 Identity Solutions, Inc., 2006-, Fannie Mae, 2007- Author: My FBI: Bringing Down the Mafia, Investigating Bill Clinton and Waging War on Terror, 2005. 1st lt. JAGC USAR, 1985-91. Recipient Fed. Law Enforcement Officers award, 1989, Presdl. award, Atty. Gen.'s award for Disting. Svc., US Dept. Justice, 1987, 1991. Mem. N.Y. County Lawyers Assn., Res. Officers Assn. U.S., Phi Beta Kappa. Roman Catholic.*

FREEHLING, ALLEN ISAAC, rabbi; b. Chgo., Jan. 8, 1932; s. Jerome Edward and Marion Ruth (Wilson) F.; m. Lori Golden; children: Shira Susman Cramer, David Matthew, Jonathan Andrew. Student, U. Ala., 1949-51; AB, U. Miami, Fla., 1953; B of Hebrew Letters, Hebrew Union Coll., 1965, MA, 1967, DD (hon.), 1992. Ordained rabbi, 1967. Asst. to pres. Stylaneze, Inc., 1953-54, Univ. Miami, 1954-56; exec. dir. Temple Israel, Miami, 1956-57; asst. to pres. Stevens Markets, Inc., 1957-59; acct. exec. Hank Meyer Assocs., 1959-60; exec. dir. Temple Emanu-El, Miami Beach, Fla., 1960-62; assoc. rabbi The Temple, Toledo, 1967-72; sr. rabbi Univ. Synagogue, LA, 1972—2002, rabbi emeritus, 2002—; exec. dir. City L.A. Commn. on Human Rels., 2002—. Adj. prof. Loyola-Marymount U., St. Mary's Coll.; v.p. Westside Ecumenical Coun., 1979-81; v.p. Bd. Rabbis of So. Calif., 1981-85, pres., 1985-87; mem. com. on rabbinic growth Cen. Conf. Am. Rabbis; chair Regional Synagogue Coun., 1984-86; bd. dirs., mem. several coms. and commns. Jewish Fedn. Coun.; cons. social actions Union of Am. Hebrew Congregations, mem. nat. and Pacific-S.W. region coms. on AIDS; mem. Rabbinic Cabinet, United Jewish Appeal; bd. dirs. Israel Bonds Orgn., Nat. Jewish Fund; bd. govs. Synagogue Coun. Am.; bd, dirs., newsletter editor Am. Jewish Com. Guest columnist L.A. Herald Examiner (Silver Angel award Religion in Media, 1987, 88); guest religion progs. Sta. KCBS, KABC; radio/TV host Nat. Conf. Christians and Jews. Chaplain L.A. Police Dept., 1974-86; bd. dirs., mem. exec. com., chair com. on pub. policy, chair govt. affairs com. AIDS Project L.A.; founding chair, exec. com. chmn. AIDS Interfaith Coun. So. Calif.; adv. bd. L.A. AIDS Hospice Com., Westside Children's Mus., Interreligious Info. Ctr.; apptd. mem., founding chair L.A. County Commn. on AIDS, 1987-89, chair svcs. com., 1989-91, L.A. County Commn. on Mental Health, 1992-95; AIDS-related grants proposal rev. com. Robert Wood Johnson Found., AIDS Task Force of United Way; com. on ethics, medicine and humanity Santa Monica Hosp., L.A. County Commn. on Pub. Social Svcs., 1984-86, Gateways Hosp. bd dirs., 1992-95, Jewish Big Bros., 1994—; City of L.A. Task Force on Diversity of Families, Commn. to Draft Ethics Code for L.A. City Govt.; mem. L.A. County Commn. on Juvenile Delinquency and Adult Crime, 1991—; bd. dirs. Jewish Homes for Aging of Greater L.A., NCCJ, 1989, exec. com., 2000—; chmn. com. on fed. legislation commn. on law and legislation L.A. Jewish Cmty. Rels. Com., trustee; chair Ctrl. Conf. Am. Rabbi's/Union Am. Hebrew Congregations com. on HIV AIDS, Progressive Religious Alliance, City of L.A. 1998; Vol. Restival adv. com. Internat. Conf. on Allocation of Health Resources, Washington, 1997, Vienna, 1999, Cairo, 2000; mem. exec. com., treas. sec., chair nominating com., bd. dirs. Heal the Bay; adv. com. Disability Rights Advocates; founding mem. Calif. Commn. Fair Adminstrn. Justice; hon. bd. dirs. Jewish Fedn. Western Region. Recipient Bishop Daniel Corrigan commendation Episcopal Diocese, 1987, Humanitarian award NCCJ, 1988, Social Responsibility award L.A. Urban League, 1988, Nat. Friendship award Parents and Friends of Lesbians and Gays, 1989, AIDS Hospice Found. Gene La Pietra Leadership award, 1989, Cath. Archdiocese's Serra Tribute award, 1989, Univ. Synagogue's Avodah award for Cmty. Svc., 1990, Am. Jewish Congress Tzedek award for Cmty. Leadership and Svc., 1990, Crystal Achievement award AIDS Project L.A., 1996, Planned Parenthood Disting. Svc. award, 1996, Cmty. Leadership award Beth Chayim Chadashim Congregation. Mem. Am. Jewish Congress (pres. 1977-80, 82-84), Ams. for Dem. Action, Internat. Assn. Physicians in AIDS Care (chmn. bd. dirs.), AIDS Nat. Interfaith Network (bd. dirs.), Jr. C. of C. (chair internat. rels. com.), Sigma Alpha Mu, Omnicron Delta Kappa, Phi Mu Alpha. Jewish. Office: Human Rels Commn City of LA 200 N Spring St #1625 Los Angeles CA 90012 Office Phone: 213-978-1660. Business E-Mail: rabbi.allen.freehling@lacity.org.

FREEHLING, DANIEL JOSEPH, lawyer, consultant; b. Montgomery, Ala., Nov. 13, 1950; s. Saul Irving and Grace L. BS, Huntingdon Coll., 1972; JD, U. Ala., 1975, MLS, 1977. Ref. libr., asst. to assoc. dean U. Ala. Sch. Law, Tuscaloosa, 1975-77; assoc. law libr. U. Md., Balt., 1977-79, Cornell U., Ithaca, NY, 1979-82; law libr. dir., assoc. prof. U. Maine, Portland, 1982-86; law libr. dir., assoc. prof. law Boston U., 1986-92, prof., 1992—2006, assoc. dean for adminstrn., 1993-97, assoc. dean for info. svcs., 1999—2006; dep. cons. on legal edn. and admissions to bar ABA, 2006—. Mem. steering com., law program com. Rsch. Librs. Group, 1989-91; treas. New Eng. Law Libr. Consortium, 1989-91; vice chair, chair-elect sect. on law librs. Assn. Am. Law Schs., 1990-91, chair, 1992. Recipient Boston U. Sch. Law Alumni award for disting. svc., 2006, Presdl. Cert. Merit, Am. Assn. Law Libr. Mem.: ABA (accreditation com. 1995—2001, coun. sect. legal edn. and bar admission 2002—06), Am. Assn. Law Librs. (chair acad. law librs. spl. interest sect. 1981—82, edn. com. 1982—83, membership com. 1983—84, program chair 1987—88, local arrangements co-chair 1992—93, chair mentoring and retention com. 1995—96). Home: 400 N McClurg Ct Apt 3307 Chicago IL 60611 Office: Am Bar Assn 321 N Clark St Chicago IL 60610 Home Phone: 978-887-1982; Office Phone: 312-988-6743.

FREE HOSFORD, MARY MOORE, biological and medical anthropologist; b. Paris, Tex., Mar. 6, 1933; d. Dudley Crawford and Margie Lou (Moore) Hubbard; m. Dwight Allen Free Jr., June 26, 1954 (dec.); children: Hardy (dec.), Dudley (dec.), Margery, Caroline. Student, Ward-Belmont Coll., 1951; BS, So. Meth. U., 1954, MLA, 1981, MA, 1987, PhD, 1989. Instr. So. Meth. U., Dallas, 1982-89, prof. continuing edn., 1989-90; prof. So. Meth. U., Dedman Coll., Dallas, 1990—; adj. asst. prof. dept. anthropology So. Meth. U., Dallas, 1990—. Prof. Richland C.C., Dallas, 1986; house anthropologist Baylor U. Med. Ctr., mem. adv. bd. Inst. for Study of Earth and Man, 1995, preceptor clin. edn. affiliation, 1990—, chair Class 1954 sustentation drive, organ/tissue transplantation task force, 1997; cardiothoracic transplantation team Baylor U. Med. Ctr., S.W. transplantation team Baylor U. Med. Ctr./U. Tex. Southwestern Med. Sch., 1990— (cardiothoracic transplantation award for excellence in svc., 1998); adv. bd. geriatrics Vis. Nurse Assn., Dallas, 1984-91; presenter in field anthropology, medicine, women's issues; bd. Dedman Coll. SMU Excellence in Sci. Lecture Series, Dallas Soc. SMU, Collegium de Vinci, SMU; contbr. AMA/JAMA protocol on authorship; spokesperson, adv. bd. Lisa Landry Childress Found. for Organ Donation Awareness. Author: The Private World of the Hermitage: Lifestyles of the Rich and Old in an Elite Retirement Home, 1995; contbr. numerous chpts. in sci. books, ednl. TV, and articles to Anthropology Newsletter, Am. Anthropologist, Am. Jour. Cardiology, Cahiers de Sociologie Economique et Culturelle-Ethnopsycholie, Jour. Heart Failure, Jour. Internat. Soc. Dermatology, Jour. Leadership Ctr., Baylor Health Care System, Jour. Lisa Landry Childrens Found.,; mem. editl. bd. Baylor U. Med. Ctr. Procs.; editor/contbr. Jour. Kimberly H. Courtwright and Joseph W. Summers Inst. of Metabolic Disease, BUMC, 1998; contbr. numerous articles to profl. jours. Bd. dirs. New Hearts and Lungs, Baylor Med. Ctr., 1994—, Lisa Landry Childress Found. for Organ Donor Awareness, Victims Outreach, 1997—, Isis Soc. and internat. issues com. Baylor U. Med. Ctr.; active various svc. and social orgns. Named one of Notable Women of Tex., 1984; recipient Outstanding Svc. Cardiothoracic Transplantation award Baylor U. Med. Ctr., 1998; provide Dr. Mary Moore Free Endowment for grad. study fieldwork in anthropology So. Meth. U. Fellow Am. Anthrop. Assn., Inst. for Study of Earth and Man; mem. AAAS, Internat. Soc. Heart Failure (sci. adv. bd.), Internat. Acad. Cardiology Inc. (internat. sci. adv. bd.), Internat. Congress Heart Disease (internat. sci. adv. bd.), Internat. Soc. Heart Disease (sci. adv. bd.), Soc. Heart Edn. (sci. adv. bd.), Dallas Women's Club, Dallas Petroleum Club, Brook Hollow Golf Club, Pi Beta Phi. Methodist. Achievements include development of position of house anthropologist in non-academic medical center, community medicine program; cross-cultural research on old age, women and cardiology. Home: 4356 Edmondson Ave Dallas TX 75205-2602 Office: Baylor U Med Ctr 3500 Gaston Ave Dallas TX 75246-2096

FREELAND, CHARLES, lawyer, accountant; b. Balt., July 18, 1940; s. Benjamin and Beatrice (Polakoff) Freeland; m. Beverly Klaff, July 15, 1965; children: Stephen Jason, Jennifer Jill, Gwen Nicole, Kimberly Suzanne. BS, U. Md., 1962, LLB, 1965; diploma, US Naval Justice Sch., 1966. Bar: Md. 1965, US Dist. Ct. Md. 1965, US Tax Ct., US Ct. Claims 1968, US Supreme Ct. 1969, US Ct. Appeals (4th cir.) 1974. Fin. v.p. Collins Electronics Mfg. Co.; dir. fin. planning Cellu-Craft, Inc., Stevensville, Md., 1963—65; contbr. Braun-Crystal Mfg. Co., Inc., Middle Village, NY, 1969—70, BCN Design Products, Inc., Bayshore, NY, 1969—70; asst. city solicitor City of Balt., 1972—82; pvt. practice law and acctg. Balt., 1971—93; ptnr. Kaplan, Freeland & Schwartz, Balt., 1982—86; pres. Charles Freeland, PC, Lutherville, Md., 1986—. Lt. USNR, 1965—68. Mem.: AICPA, ABA, Am. Arbitration Assn. (nat. panel 1970—), Md. Assn. CPAs, Am. Assn. Attys.-CPAs, Am. Judicature Soc., Woodholme Country Club. Democrat. Jewish. Home: PO Box 422 4 Timothys Green Ct Brooklandville MD 21022 Office: 1300 York Rd Ste 180 Lutherville MD 21093-6806 Office Phone: 410-339-7907.

FREELAND, CHRYSTIA, editor; b. Peace River, Can., Aug. 2, 1968; married; 2 children. BA history & lit., Harvard U., 1991; M in Slavonic studies, St. Anthony's Coll., Oxford U. Stringer Financial Times, Kiev, Ukraine, 1991—93; ea. Europe corr. FinancialTimes.com, 1994, Moscow bur. chief, 1995—98, UK nat. news editor, 1998—99, FT.com editor, 2001—02, editor Sat. ed., 2002—03, dep. editor, 2003—05, editor electronic svcs., 2005—06, US mng. editor, 2006—; dep. editor Globe & Mail, Toronto, 1999—2001. Author: Sale of the Century: Russia's Wild Ride from Communism to Capitalism, 2000. Named a Young Global Leader, World Econ. Forum, 2005; recipient Best Energy Submission, Bus. Journalist of the Yr. awards, 2004. Office: Financial Times 1330 Ave of Americas New York NY 10019 Office Phone: 212-641-6503.

FREELAND, PETE, aerospace transportation executive, consultant; b. Portland, Oreg., Nov. 29, 1965; s. Bill and Dori Freeland; m. Melissa Williams, Sept. 22, 2001; 1 child, Aidan; 1 child, Mitchell. BS Aerospace Engrng., U. So. Calif., 1988; MS Aeronautics, Embry Riddle Aero. U.,

1992; PhD Engring. Mgmt., Lacrosse U., 2004. Lic. Pvt. Pilot FAA, 1987, cert. Navigator USAF, 1989, Scuba Divemaster Nat. Assn. Underwater Instrs., Fla., 2000. Customer support engr., pilot Flight Dynamics, Portland, 1992—98; mgr. internat. space sta. and advanced vehicles engring. Boeing Human Spaceflight, Palmdale, Calif., 1998—2001; ctr. mgr., mech. integration and test Northrop Grumman Space Tech., Redondo Beach, Calif., 2001—04; mgr. sr. engring. Raytheon Space Systems, El Segundo, Calif., 2004—. V.p. Nat. Mgmt. Assn., Palmdale, Calif., 2000—01; chmn. Northrop Grumman Vets. Group, Redondo Beach, 2003—. Advisor, tchr. CAP, Lancaster, Calif., 1999—2001; mem. Nat. Ctr. for Men - Father's Rights, Portland, Oreg., 1994—99. Capt. USAF, 1988—92. Decorated Disting. Grad.-Top Gun USAF B-52 Crew Tng. Course; named Nat. Cadet of the Yr., CAP, 1984, Presdl. scholar, Pres. Ronald Reagan, 1984; recipient Silver Snoopy Award, NASA-Astronaut Office, Johnson Space Ctr., 2000; ROTC 4-Yr. scholarship, USAF, 1984. Mem.: AIAA (v.p. 2000—01). Achievements include development of Advanced Mfg & Test for Manned Spacecraft; Fluid dynamics experiment on space shuttle; Launch and support crew for STS-96; research in Flight test, team member on X-38 Crew Return Vehicle, support to Ansari X-Prize. Avocations: scuba diving, flying, international travel. Office: Raytheon Space Aeronautical Sys 2000 East El Segundo Blvd El Segundo CA 90245 Home: 11542 Venezia Way Porter Ranch CA 91326 Office Phone: 310-616-9217. Personal E-mail: freelandla@yahoo.com.

FREELAND, RICHARD MIDDLETON, former academic administrator, historian; b. Mountain Lakes, NJ, May 13, 1941; s. Harry Middleton and Margaret Lyons (Child) F. BA in Am. Studies, Amherst Coll., 1963; PhD in Am. Civilization, U. Pa., 1968; DHL (hon.), Amherst Coll., 1998, Am. Coll. Greece, 2000, Simmons Coll., 2006, Johnson & Wolfs U., 2006. Asst. to pres. U. Mass., Boston, 1970, asst. to chancellor, 1971-72, dir. Office of Ednl. Planning, asst. prof., 1972-74, dean Coll. Profl. Studies, 1974-79, assoc. prof., 1974-92, dean Coll. of Arts and Scis., 1982-92, prof. history, 1992; prof. history Grad. Sch. & Univ. Ctr. CUNY, 1992-96; vice chancellor for acad. affairs, pres. CUNY Rsch. Found., 1992-96; pres., prof. history Northeastern U., Boston, 1996—2006, emeritus prof., 2006—. Proposal reviewer NEH, Divsn. Rsch., 1989, Divsn. Edn. Programs, 1985, RI Bd. Higher Edn., 1987, Fund for Improvement Post Secondary Edn., 1988, Rockefeller Found., 1985, Am. U., 1988, 89, 90; cons. Am. Coun. Edn., 1994, US Dept. Edn., 1989-90, 92; dir. Boston Mus. Project. Author: The Truman Doctrine and the Origins of McCarthyism, 1972, Academia's Golden Age, 1992; reader, reviewer numerous profl. jours. Recipient Rsch. grants Ford Found., 1979-80, NEH, 1980-81, Rockefeller Found., 1988. Home Phone: 617-859-8748. Business E-Mail: r.freeland@neu.edu.

FREEMAN, ARTHUR MERRIMON, III, psychology professor, dean; b. Birmingham, Ala., Oct. 10, 1942; s. Arthur Merrimon II and Katherine (Lide) F.; m. Linda Poynter; children: Arthur M. IV, Katherin Leigh, Edward Todd. AB in Philosophy, Harvard U., Cambridge, Mass., 1963; MD, Vanderbilt U., Nashville, Tenn., 1967. Diplomate Am. Bd. Psychiatry and Neurology; lic. psychiatrist, Ala., NC, La. Asst. prof. dept. psychiatry and behavioral scis. Stanford U., Calif., 1974—77; prof., vice chmn. dept. psychiatry U. Ala., Birmingham, 1977—90; med. dir. Appalachian Hall Hosp., Asheville, NC, 1990—91; prof., chmn. dept. psychiatry La. State U. Med. Ctr., Shreveport, 1991—2003, dean, 1993—96; prof., chmn. dept. psychiatry Health Sci. Ctr. U. Tenn., Memphis, 2003—; clin. prof. psychology U. Ala., Birmingham, 2006—. Regional med. dir. divsn. mental health La. Dept. Health and Hosps., 1992-94. Author: Psychiatry for the Primary Care Physician, 1979. Bd. dirs. Vols. of Am., Shreveport, 1993-96, Shreveport Symphony, C. of C., 1993-96. Lt. comdr. M.C., USN, 1972-74. Nat. Merit scholar Harvard U., 1959-63; Biochemistry fellow Karolinska Inst., Stockholm, 1965, fellow in hepatic disease Royal Free Hosp., London, 1966, Disting. Paul Harris fellow Rotary Club. Fellow APA (Disting. life fellow, vice-chmn. fin. oversight com.), Am. Coll. Psychiatrists (Laughlin fellow 1971, bd. regents), Acad. Psychosomatic Medicine, So. Psychiat. Assn. (mem. fin. com.); mem. La. Psychiatry Med. Assn. (pres.), Royal Coll. Psychiatrists, Collegium Internat. Neuropsychopharmacologia. Home: 3536 Brookwood Rd Birmingham AL 35223 Business E-Mail: amfreeman@utmem.edu.

FREEMAN, BABA FOSTER, editor; d. Festus Finley and Beatrice Michelson Foster; m. Monroe E. Freeman Jr, 1959; 3 children. BA in Polit. Economy, Bennington Coll. Clk. office sci. pers. Nat. Acad. Sci., Washington, 1950—52; head info. svcs. sect. Ops. Evaluation Group Office of Chief Naval Ops., Washington, 1952—59; rsch. dir. New Town Publs., Reston, Va., 1980—96; dir., v.p. Fairfax area chpt. LWV, Annandale, Va., 1999—. Presenter to confs. Commr., coach Reston Soccer Assn., 1978—82; vol. Fairfax County Pub. Libr., 1976—; Centreville (Va.) dist. rep. Adv. Social Svcs. Bd., Fairfax County, 1986—97; Hunter Mill dist. rep. Human Svcs. Coun., Fairfax County, 1997—; del. ann. coun. Diocese of Va., 1986—92; dir. governing bd. Reston Cmty. Ctr., 1976—78; bd. dirs. Reston Interfaith Housing Inc., 1980—93. Mem.: LWV (bulletin editor 1967—71, mem. land use, transp., county issue coms. 1975—95, nat. del. 2000). Achievements include development of machine literature search program for USN R&D program. Office: LWV - Fairfax Area 4026 Hummer Rd Ste 214 Annandale VA 22003 Office Phone: 703-658-9150. Business E-Mail: lwvfa@ecoisp.com.

FREEMAN, BOB A., retired microbiology educator, retired dean; b. Eastland, Tex., May 7, 1926; s. Oswald Ledbetter and Osielee (Wilcox) F.; m. Rosemary David, June 4, 1960; children: Susan A., Robert D., Katherine E., Andrew W. BA, U. Tex., 1949, MA, 1950, PhD, 1954. Instr. biology Tex. A & M U., College Station, 1950-51; rsch. scientist I U. Tex., Austin, 1951-54; instr., asst. prof. U. Chgo., 1954-64; assoc. prof. U. Tenn., Memphis, 1964-66, prof., 1966-88, chmn. microbiology dept., 1970-83, vice chancellor, 1982-88, Disting. Svc. prof., 1988-96, interim dean Coll. Grad. Health Scis., 1993-96, dean, prof. emeritus, 1997—. Cons. WHO, Calcutta, India, 1968. Author: Burrows Textbook of Microbiology, 21st edit., 1979, 22d edit., 1984; mem. edit. bd. Jour. Dental Edn., 1980-83, U. Tenn. Press., 1983-2001; contbr. articles to profl. jours. Bd. dirs. Memphis Heart Gala, 1984-90. With USN, 1944-46, PTO. Grantee U.S. Army Rsch. and Devel. Command, USPHS, U.S. Dept. Agr. Mem. AAAS, Am. Soc. for Microbiology (br. councillor 1969-71), Imhotep Soc., Sigma Xi (chpt. pres. 1974-75). Republican. Methodist. Avocations: woodworking, outdoor activities. Home: 1319 E Crestwood Dr Memphis TN 38119-5000

FREEMAN, BRUCE GEORGE, fundraising consultant; b. Perth Amboy, NJ, Feb. 17, 1929; s. Benjamin George and Beatrice (Wright) F.; children: David B., Judith Ann, Mark D.; m. Marjorie V. Kler, Dec. 1983. BA, Rutgers U., 1952; MDiv, New Brunswick Theol. Sem., 1955; postgrad., Albany Med. Ctr., 1955-58, Andover Newton Theol. Ctr., 1955-58. Min. Presbyn. Ch., various locations, NY, 1955-64; asst. to pres. Buena Vista Coll., Storm Lake, Iowa, 1964-66; area dir. United Presbyn. Ch. U.S.A., 1966-67; campaign mgr. Marts & Lundy, NYC, 1967-75, also bd. dirs., v.p., 1975-80, treas., 1980-82, founder electron. screening div. Lyndhurst, NJ, 1984, pres., 1982-91, chmn., CEO, 1991-94, ret., 1994; CEO B.G.F. Assocs., 1994—. Inventor Electric Screening. Trustee East Jersey Olde Towne, Inc., Piscataway, 1980-2004, Wilson Coll. Chambersburg, Pa., 1992-2000; trustee Makassed Found. Am., Rutgers U., 1994—; bd. dirs. Nat. Orgn. on Disability, Washington, 1990. Mem. Nassau Club (bd. dirs.), Raritan Valley Country Club. Republican. Avocations: sports, art. Home: 1 Douglas Fir Ct Princeton NJ 08540 Office Phone: 609-542-0642.

FREEMAN, CAROLYN RUTH, oncologist; b. Kettering, Eng., Jan. 2, 1950; emigrated to Can., 1974, naturalized, 78; d. Ivor Thomas and Winifred Mary (Scotney) F.; m. J.C. Negrete, July 25, 1981. Student, King's Coll. London U., 1967-69; MB, BS, Westminster Med. Sch. London U., 1972. Prof., chmn. dept. radiation oncology, faculty medicine McGill U., Montreal, 1979—; radiation oncologist-in-chief McGill U. Hosps., Montreal, 1979—. Contbr. articles to med. publs. Fellow Royal Coll. Physicians (Can.); mem. Can. Assn. Radiol. Oncologists (pres. 1991-93), Am. Soc. Therapeutic Radiology and Oncology. Home: 4270 deMaisonneuve W Montreal PQ Canada H3Z 1K6 Office: 1650 Cedar Ave Montreal PQ Canada H3G 1A4 Office Phone: 514-934-8040. Business E-Mail: carolyn.freeman@muhc.mcgill.ca.

FREEMAN, CHARLES E., state supreme court justice; b. Richmond, Va., Dec. 12, 1933; m. Marylee Voelker; 1 child, Kevin. BA in Liberal Arts, Va. Union U., 1954; JD, John Marshall Law Sch., 1962, LLD (hon.), 1992. Bar: Ill. 1962. Pvt. practice, 1962—76; pvt. practice, Cook County, Chgo., 1962—76, asst. state's atty., 1964; asst. atty. Bd. Election Commrs., Chgo., 1964—65; mem. Ill. Indsl. Commn., Chgo., 1965—73, Ill. Commerce Commn., Chgo., 1973—76; judge law and chancery divsns. Cook County Cir. Ct., Chgo., 1976—86; judge Appellate Ct. Ill., 1986—90; justice Ill. Supreme Ct., 1990—, chief justice, 1997—2000. Recipient Cert. Achievement, Internat. Christian Fellowship Missions, Earl B. Dickerson award, Chgo. Bar Assn., Merit award, Habilitative Sys., Statesmanship award, Monarch Awards Found. of Alpha Kappa Alpha, Freedom award, John Marshall Law Sch. Mem.: ABA (task force opportunities minorities in jud. adminstrn. divsn., coms. opportunities minorities in profession, cert. Recognition), DuPage County Bar Assn., Cook County Bar Assn. (Kenneth E. Wilson award, Cert. Merit, Ida Platt award, Presdl. award, Jud. award), Ill. Judges' Assn., Ill. Jud. Coun. (Kenneth Wilson Meml. award, Meritorious Svc. award), Ill. State Bar Assn., Am. Judicature Soc., Am. Judges' Assn. Achievements include being first African-American to swear in a Mayor, City of Chicago, to serve on Illinois Supreme Court, 1990; being leader in case disposition by published opinion, 1988, 89.*

FREEMAN, CHAS W., JR., federal agency administrator, writer, ambassador; b. Washington, Mar. 2, 1943; divorced; 3 children; m. Margaret Van Wagenen Carpenter, 1993. BA, Yale U., 1963; JD, Harvard U., 1975. Joined Fgn. Svc., 1965, assigned to India and Taiwan; Am. interpreter for Pres. Nixon People's Republic of China, 1972; vis. fellow East Asian Legal Rsch. Ctr., Harvard U., 1974-75; dep. dir. for Taiwan affairs, dir. pub. programs, dir. plans and mgmt. U.S. Dept. State, Washington, 1975-78; dir. program coord. and devel. USIA, Washington, 1978, acting U.S. coord. for refugee affairs; dir. China affairs U.S. Dept. State, 1979; dep. chief of mission Am. Embassy, Beijing, 1981, Bangkok, 1984; prin. dep. asst. sec. state for African affairs U.S. Dept. State, Washington, 1986; amb. to Saudi Arabia Riyadh, 1989-92; asst. sec. def. The Pentagon, Washington, 1993-94; dist. fellow U.S. Inst. of Peace, Washington, 1994-95; chmn. bd. Projects Internat. Inc., Washington, 1995—. Co-chmn. U. S. China Policy Found., 1996—; vice-chmn. Atlantic Coun., 1997; bd. visitors Dept. Def. Regional Ctrs., 1998—2001; mem. U.S. Nat. Security Study Group, 1999—2001; internat. adv. bd. China Nat. Offshore Oil Co., 2004—; pres. Mid. East Policy Coun.; bd. dirs. Inst. for Def. Analyses, World Affair Coun., Washington, Assn. for Diplomatic Studies and Tng., Acad. Am. Diplomacy, C2C Holdings; mem. adv. bd. Stanley Found., 2005—, Pacific Pension Inst., 2006—; mem. bd. overseers Roger Williams U.; advisor Iraq Study Group, 2006. Author: The Diplomat's Dictionary, 1994, rev. edit., 1997, Arts of Power, 1997. Recipient Sec. Def. Meritorious Civilian Svc. award, 1991, Disting. Pub. Svc. awards, 1993-94, Sec. State Disting. Honor, 1991, Dir. Ctrl. Intelligence Shield Medallion award, 1991, First Class Order of Abd Al-Aziz award Saudi Arabian Govt., 1992. Mem.: Am. Acad. Diplomacy (bd. dirs.), Met. Club. Office: Projects Internat Inc 1800 K St NW Ste 1000 Washington DC 20006-2202 also: Mid East Policy Coun 1730 M St NW Ste 512 Washington DC 20036-4516 Office Phone: 202-333-1277. Business E-Mail: cfreeman@projectsinternational.com.

FREEMAN, CORINNE, financial analyst, retired mayor; b. NYC, Nov. 9, 1926; d. Bernard J. Hirschfeld and Sidonie (Daxe) Lichtenstein; m. Michael S. Freeman, Mar. 14, 1948; children: Michael L., Stephan J. Student, Adelphi Coll. Sch. Nursing, 1944—47. RN, N.Y., Mass. Nurse numerous hosps. in N.Y. and Mass., 1948-64; mayor St. Petersburg, Fla., 1977-85; mem. Pinellas County Sch. Bd., St. Petersburg, Fla., 1989-98, chmn., 1996-98; bd. trustees Palms of Pasadena Hosp., St. Petersburg, 1998—, dir., 1998—2004. Fin. advisor Prudential Securities, Wachovia Securities; bd. dirs. Creativity in Child Care. Chmn. Social Svc. Allocations Com., St. Petersburg, 1972-76, City Budget Rev. Com., 1973-76, Youth Svc. System, Pinellas County, 1975-76, West Coast Regional Water Supply Authority; past mem. community redevel. com. U.S. Conf. of Mayors; past pres. Fla. League Cities; past mem. Pinellas County Mayors Coun.; past mem. Nat. League of Cities Revenue and Fin. Task Force; pres. LWV, St. Petersburg, 1970-72, 75-76; trustee Fire Pension Bd., St. Petersburg, 1989-92, Bayfront Med. Ctr.; dir. Palms of Pasadena Hosp., 1999-2003; adv. com. Jr. League St. Petersburg, 1990-92. Recipient Disting. Alumni award Adelphi U. Mem. Fla. Nursing Assn. Mem.: Treasure Island Yacht and Tennis Club (bd. dirs. 2004—). Republican. Home: 2101 Pelham Rd N Saint Petersburg FL 33710-3659 Office: 100 Zndue South 400 N Saint Petersburg FL 33707-1728 Office Phone: 727-551-2303. Business E-Mail: corinne_freeman@wachoviasec.com.

FREEMAN, DAVID JOHN, lawyer; b. NYC, Aug. 9, 1948; s. John L. and Josephine F. (Wilding) F.; m. Ellen Gogolick, Dec. 29, 1974; children: Matthew, Julie. BA, Harvard U., 1970; JD, 1975. Bar: Mass. 1975, D.C. 1977, N.Y. 1982, U.S. Dist. Ct. D.C. 1981, N.Y. 1982, U.S. Dist. Ct. D.C. 1981, U.S. Dist. Ct. (so. and ea. dists.) N.Y. 1982, U.S. Ct. Appeals (D.C. cir.) 1979, U.S. Ct. Appeals (2nd cir.) 1982, U.S. Supreme Ct. 1988. Spl. asst. to U.S. Senator Frank E. Moss, 1970-72; trial atty. FTC, Washington, 1975-77; assoc. Ginsburg, Feldman & Bress, Washington, 1977-81, Holtzmann, Wise & Shepard, NYC, 1981-84; ptnr., 1984-94; ptnr., chair environ. dept. Battle Fowler, 1994-2000; chair N.Y. environ. practice group Paul, Hastings, Janofsky & Walker, NYC, 2000—. Editor-in-chief: Jour. Environ Law Practice (West), 1998-2000. Vice-chmn. edn. fund NY League Conservation Voters. Mem. ABA (environment, energy and resources sect.), Assn. Bar City of NY, Harvard Law Sch. Assn., NY State Bar Assn. (environ. law sect., co-chmn. hazardous waste/site remediation com., co-chmn. task force on brownfields/superfund reform), Nat. Brownfield Assn. (co-chmn. policy and legis. commn. NY chpt.). Office: Paul Hastings Janofsky & Walker LLP 75 E 55th St New York NY 10022-3205 Office Phone: 212-318-6555. Business E-Mail: davidfreeman@paulhastings.com.

FREEMAN, DONALD WILFORD, real estate developer, horse breeder; b. Brooksville, Fla., Sept. 25, 1929; s. Fred Maxwell and Dovie (Keef) F.; m. Ruby Jane Lewis, Feb. 25, 1956; children: Clifton Lewis, Susan Anne. BS, JD, U. Ala., 1953; LLM, NYU, 1957. CPA Ga. Acct. Ernst & Ernst, Atlanta, 1953-55; tax atty. Office Chief Counsel, US Treasury Dept., NYC, 1955-57, West Point Mfg. Co., Ga., 1957-58; treas. Ryder System, Inc., Miami, Fla., 1958-61; v.p., dir. Henderson's Portion Pak, Inc., 1961-63; pres. Biscayne Capital Corp., Miami, 1964-66; sr. assoc. Lazard Freres & Co., NYC, 1967-69; pres. James A. Ryder Corp., Miami, 1969-78; owner Kiyara Arabians, 1978—. With AUS, 1946-48, PTO. Mem.: Fla. Inst. CPAs, Beta Gamma Sigma, Phi Kappa Sigma. Episcopalian. Home: 1314 Parkside Dr Vero Beach FL 32966 Office Phone: 888-252-6990. Personal E-mail: dfins@bellsouth.net.

FREEMAN, DOUGLAS K., lawyer; AB with distinction, Stanford U., Calif., 1967; JD, UCLA, 1970; LLM in Taxation, U. San Diego, 1984. Bar: Calif. 1971, US Supreme Ct., US Tax Ct., US Dist. Ct. (9th cir.), US Ct. Mil. Appeals, cert.: State Bar Calif. (specialist in taxation). Chmn., nat. mng. ptnr. IFF Advs., LLC, Irvine, Calif.; founding ptnr. estate and charitable planning practice dept. Freeman, Freeman & Smiley, Irvine, Calif. Co-author: A Founder's Guide to Family Foundation; contbr. articles to profl. publs. Chmn. bd. trustees U. Calif. Irvine Found. Named one of Top 100 Attys., Worth, 2005—06. Mem.: Coun. Founds., Nat. Com. Planned Giving, ABA. Office: IFF Advs LLC 1920 Main St Ste 1050 Irvine CA 92614-7212 Office Phone: 494-833-1112. E-mail: doug@iffadvisors.com.

FREEMAN, EDWARD CARL, JR., music minister; b. Roanoke, Va., Feb. 18, 1936; s. Edward Carl Freeman Sr. and Alberta Frances Fringer. Student, Peabody Conservatory, 1959, MusB, 1962; student, Johns Hopkins U., 1959—61. Organist, dir. United Bapt. Ch., Balt., 1958—68; asst. organist, dir. Balt. Hebren Congregation, 1964—68; min. music River Rd. Ch., Richmond, Va., 1968—; faculty music Collegiate Sch. Girls, 1968—69, U. Richmond, 1970—73. Advisor, cons. to bd. trustees Peabody Conservatory, Balt., 1966—69, mem. alumni coun., 1983—85. Recipient Dirs. award, Peabody Inst. Johns Hopkins U., 1993, honor, Va. Gen. Assembly, 2003. Mem.: Am. Guild Organists (life). Avocations: reading, travel. Home: 2614 Southbay Dr Richmond VA 23233 Office: River Rd Ch 8000 River Rd Richmond VA 23229 Office Phone: 804-288-1131. E-mail: carlfreeman@rrcb.org.

FREEMAN, ELLEN WOOD, research professor; b. Gloversville, NY, Aug. 8, 1935; d. John D. and Marion (Spicer) W.; m. David N., June 15, 1957; children: Jonathan K., Anne C., Gregory S. AB, Smith Coll., Northampton, Mass., 1957; MSS, Bryn Mawr Coll., 1973, PhD, 1976. ACSW, Pa. Asst./assoc. rsch. prof. Dept. OB/GYN and Psychiatry Sch. of Medicine U. Pa., Phila., 1977—. Contbr. articles to profl. jours. Office: Univ Pennsylvania Dept Ob Gyn 3701 Market St Ste 820 Philadelphia PA 19104-5509 Office Phone: 215-662-3329.

FREEMAN, ERNEST ROBERT, retired engineering executive; b. Bklyn., Oct. 3, 1933; s. Nathan and Rose (Beginsky) F.; m. June Gladys Moser, June 6, 1954; children: Jesse David, Miriam Lisa, Sarah Ellen, Beth Bayla BSEE, U. Miami, Coral Gables, Fla., 1955; MEA, George Washington U., Washington, DC, 1966; ScD (hon.), London Inst., 1977. Registered profl. engr., Md., NJ. Mem. tech. staff Bell Telephone Labs., Whippany, NJ, 1959-61; mgr. engring. dept. IIT Rsch. Inst., Annapolis, Md., 1961-68; dir. engring. dept. Vertex Corp., Kensington, Md., 1968-69; pres., CEO SFA Inc., Landover, Md., 1969-91, exec. advisor, 1991-98, pres., chmn., CEO Largo, Md., 1998—2007; ret., 2007. Lectr. Am U. Ctr. for Tech. and Adminstrn.; dir. Data Range Ltd., High Wycombe, England; mem. engring. adv. bd. U. DC, Washington. Author: (with others) Electromagnetic Compatibility Design Guide, 1981; Interference Suppression Techniques for Antennas and Transmitters, 1982; contbg. editor Attorney's Guide to Engring., 1986; editor-in-chief IEEE NCAC Scanner, 1997-98. Trustee People to People Internat. With USAF, 1956—59. Recipient Bausch & Lomb award, 1951, Electro '76 Best Session award. Fellow: IEEE (life), VFW (life), Washington Acad. Sci. (life); mem.: Am. Technion Soc. (bd. dirs.), Assn. Fed. Comm. Cons. Engrs. (life), Mensa. Avocations: scuba, flying, sailing. Home: 5357 Strathmore Ave Kensington MD 20895-1160 Personal E-mail: erfreeman33@comcast.net.

FREEMAN, FRANKLIN EDWARD, JR., government agency administrator; b. Dobson, NC, May 5, 1945; s. Franklin Edward and Clara E. (Smith) F.; m. Margaret Carson McKnight, 1966 (div. 1974); children: Margaret Elizabeth, Nancy Lorrin; m. Katherine Lynn Lloyd, Aug. 12, 1978; children: Katherine Ann, Franklin Edward III, Alexander Lloyd, Mary Clare. BA, U. N.C., 1967, JD, 1970. Bar: N.C. 1970. Rsch. asst. Assoc. Justice Dan K. Moore, Raleigh, N.C., 1970-71; asst. dist. atty. 17th jud. dist. N.C. Ct. System, 1971-73; exec. sec. Jud. Coun., 1973-78; asst. dir. Adminstrv. Office of Cts., Raleigh, 1973-78, dir., 1981-93; dist. atty. 17th jud. dist. N.C. Ct. System, 1979-81; sec. N.C. Dept. Correction, Raleigh, 1993-97; chief staff Gov. James B. Hunt, Jr., 1997-99; assoc. justice N.C. Supreme Ct., 1999-2001; sr. asst. for govt. affairs Gov. of N.C., 2001—. Contbr. articles to profl. jours. Tchr. Sunday sch. Main Street United Meth. Ch., Reidsville, 1974-81, chmn. every mem. canvas, 1980, chmn. adminstrv. bd., 1981; mem. Hayes Barton Meth. Ch., Raleigh; pres. Raleigh Host Lions Club, 1994—95. Recipient Svc. award Conf. Superior Ct. Judges, Svc. award Conf. Dist. Ct. Judges, Svc. award N.C. Clks. Superior Ct. Assn., Svc. award N.C. Magistrates Assn. Mem. N.C. State Bar, N.C. Correctional Assn., Surry County Bar Assn., Rockingham County Bar Assn., 10th Dist. Bar Assn., 17th Dist. Bar Assn., State Correctional Adminstrs., Conf. State Ct. Adminstrs. (pres-elect 1992-93, bd. dirs. 1987-90, 94-95), Lions Club (pres. Raleigh Host club 1994), Delta Upsilon. Democrat. Avocations: horses, history, reading. Office: Gov's Office 20301 Mail Svc Ctr Raleigh NC 27699-0301

FREEMAN, FREDERICK ROE, lawyer; b. Arkansas City, Kans., July 11, 1914; s. Claude Kenneth Freeman and Agnes Roe; m. Joy Parman Freeman, 1936 (dec. Apr. 2004); children: Sheryl F. Matthews, F. William- (dec.). AB, Southwestern Coll., 1952; JD, U. Mo. Kans. City, 1954. Ptnr. Freeman Real Estate Ins., Arkansas City, Kans., 1936—39; sec., treas., mgr. Ark. Transp. Lines, Inc., Kansas City, Mo., 1939—45; proproetor, chmn. Freeman Acctg. and Income Tax Svc., Arkansas City, 1945—50; atty. pvt. practice, Kansas City, 1954—85, 1985—; founder, corp. officer, dir. Jones & Babson, Inc., Kans. City, Mo., 1959—85; pres., dir. Income and Retirement Security Corp., 1973—87. Mem.: ABA, Mo. Bar Assn., U.S. Supreme Ct. Bar. Home: 11809 Madison Ave Kansas City MO 64114

FREEMAN, GEORGE C., III, tobacco company executive, lawyer; b. Richmond, Va., May 28, 1963; BA with honors, U. Va., 1985; JD, Yale U., 1989. Bar: Va. 1989, U.S. Ct. of Appeals, 8th Circuit 1990, U.S. Ct. of Appeals, 4th Circuit 1991. Law clerk to Judge Richard S. Arnold U.S. Ct. of Appeals, 8th Circuit, 1989—90; law clerk to Justice Lewis F. Powell U.S. Supreme Ct., 1990—91; sec., gen. counsel Universal Corp., Richmond, Va., 2001—06, v.p., 2005—06, pres., 2006—. Bd. dirs. Delta Waterfowl Found. Mem.: ABA. Office: Universal Corp PO Box 25099 1501 N Hamilton St Richmond VA 23230*

FREEMAN, GEORGE CLEMON, JR., lawyer; b. Birmingham, Ala., Jan. 3, 1929; s. George Clemon and Annie Laura (Gill) F.; m. Anne Colston Hobson, Dec. 6, 1958; children: Anne Colston McEvoy, George Clemon III, Joseph Reid Anderson. BA magna cum laude, Vanderbilt U., 1950; LLB, Yale U., 1956. Bar: Ala. 1956, Va. 1958, D.C. 1974. Law clk. to Justice Hugo L. Black US Supreme Ct., 1956; assoc. Hunton & Williams, Richmond, Va., 1957-63, ptnr., 1963-95, sr. counsel, 1995—. Contbr. articles to profl. jours. Pres. Va. chpt. Nature Conservancy, 1962—63; counsel Va. Outdoors Recreation Study Com. Va. Legis., 1963—65; mem. sect. 301 Superfund Act Study Group Congl. Adv. Com., 1981—82; mem. Falls James Com., 1973—89; chmn. adv. coun. Energy Policy Studies Ctr. U. Va., 1981—85; chmn. legal adv. com. to Va. Commn. on Transp. in the 21st Century, 1986—87; mem. Va. Gov.'s Commn. to Study Historic Preservation, 1987—88, Va. Coun. on the Environment, 1989—91; chmn. Va. Bd. Hist. Resources, 1989—91; mem. The Atlantic Coun., 1986—95; bd. dirs. Nat. Mus. Am. History, 1997—2002; chmn. Richmond City Dem. Com., 1969—71. Lt (j.g.) USN, 1951—54. Ctr. for Pub. Resources fellow, 1990—. Fellow Am. Bar Found. (Va. state chmn. 1986-90); mem. ABA (chmn. standing com. on facilities of Law Libr. of Congress 1967-73, coordinating group on regulatory reform 1981-85, nominating com. 1984-87, chmn. civil justice coordinating com. 1990-92, sect. bus. law, sect. coun. 1976-79, chmn. ad hoc com. on Fed. Criminal Code 1979-81, chmn. program com. 1981-82, chmn. ad hoc com. on tort law reform 1986-87, sect. del. to ho. of dels. 1983-87, sec. 1987-88, vice-chmn. and ed. The Business Lawyer 1988-89, chmn.-elect 1989-90, chmn. 1990-91), Richmond Bar Assn., Va. Bar Assn., Am. Law Inst. (coun. 1980—, advisor to coun. on project on compensation and liability for product and process injuries 1986-91, advisor restatement of law, THRD, torts apportionment 1993-97, advisor restatement law THRD torts gen. prins. 1997—), Am. Judicature Soc., Country Club of Va., Knickerbocker Club, Met. Club, Phi Beta Kappa, Phi Delta Phi, Omicron Delta Kappa, Alpha Tau Omega. Democrat. Episcopalian. Avocation: gardening. Office: Hunton & Williams 951 E Byrd St Richmond VA 23219-0005 Office Phone: 804-788-8365. Business E-Mail: gfreeman@hunton.com.

FREEMAN, GILL SHERRYL, judge; b. NYC, June 24, 1949; d. Norman and Arlene Jacovitz. Student, U. Wis., 1966-68; BS in Edn. cum laude, Temple U., 1970; MEd, U. Miami, Fla., 1973, JD cum laude, 1977. Bar: Fla. 1977, US Dist. Ct. (so. dist.) Fla. 1977, US Dist. Ct. (mid. dist.) Fla. 1984, US Ct. Appeals (5th cir.) 1977. Tchr. Dade County Pub. Schs., Miami, 1970-76; assoc. Walton, Lantaff, Schroeder & Carson, Miami, 1977-82, Ruden, McClosky, Smith, Schuster & Russell, Miami, 1982—, ptnr., 1983-97; apptd. cir. ct. judge Dade County Fla., 1997—. Vice chair Fla. Supreme Ct. Gender Bias Commn., 1987—90; chair Fla. Supreme Ct. Gender Bias Study Implementation Commn., 1991—94; mem. Supreme Ct. Com. Fairness & Diversity, 1997, chair, 1999—; chmn. bd. dirs. Journey Inst., 1997—2001; chmn. jud. edn. com. Cir. Ct. Judges Conf., 2005—. Trustee Dade County Law Libr., 1996—, chair, 2001—; bd. dirs. Family Counseling Svcs. of Greater Miami, 1995—2003, Spectrum Programs, 1993—, chair, 1996—98. Master: Family Law Inns Ct.; mem.; Am. Coll. Bus. Ct. Judges, Cuban Am. Bar Assn., Fla. Assn. Women Lawyers (pres. 1984—85), Fla. Bar Assn. Avocations: alpine skiing, travel, tennis. Office: 73 W Flegler St Rm 1407 Miami FL 33130 Office Phone: 305-349-7255.

FREEMAN, HAROLD PAUL, oncologist, educator, medical center director; b. Washington, Mar. 2, 1933; s. Clyde and Lucille Freeman; m. Arti Artholian Palmer, 1957; children: Harold P. Jr., Neale P. AB in Biology, Cath. U. Am., 1954; MD, Howard U., 1958; DSc (hon.), Albany Med. Sch., 1989, Niagara U., 1989; DS (hon.), Adelphi U., 1989, Cath. U., 1990. Diplomate Am. Bd. Surgery; lic. oncologist, N.Y., Md. Rotating intern Howard U. Hosp., Washington, 1958-59, resident in gen. surgery, 1959-62, chief resident in surgery, 1963-64; resident in surgery Meml. Sloan Kettering Hosp., NYC, 1962-63, sr. resident, 1964-67; fellow in surgery Cornell U. Med. Ctr., NYC, 1965-66; asst. in surgery Columbia U., 1967-70, instr. surgery, 1970-73, asst. clin. prof., 1973-74, dir. surgery, 1974—99, Harlem Hospital Ctr., 1974—99; prof. Columbia U., 1989—; chair President's Cancer Panel, Bethesda, 1997—2000; pres., CEO, dir. surgery North General Hospital, NYC, 1999—2001; dir. Ralph Lauren Ctr. for Cancer Care and Prevention, NYC, 2003—, Ctr. to Reduce Cancer Health Disparities, Nat. Cancer Inst., 2000—. Asst. attending surgeon N.Y. Infirmary, N.Y.C., 1969-82, St. Luke's/Roosevelt Med. Ctr., N.Y.C., 1983—, Harlem Hosp. Ctr., N.Y.C., 1967-73, chmn. cancer com., 1968-73, attending surgeon, dir. surgery, 1974—; adj. attending surgeon Bklyn. Jewish Hosp., 1970-74, Meml. Sloan Kettering Hosp., 1981—; assoc. attending surgeon Presbyn. Hosp., N.Y.C., 1974—; attending surgeons Columbia Presbyn., 1998; chmn. eastern region Black Leadership Initiative on Cancer, NY State Commn. for Healthy NY. Contbr. articles to profl. jours.; presentations in field. Nat. pres. Am. Cancer Soc., 1988-89, chmn. nat. adv. com. on cancer in the socio-economically disadvantaged, 1987-88, chmn. med. and sci. exec. com., 1986-87, chmn. med. and sci. com., 1985-86, chmn. nat. adv. com. on cancer in minorities, 1984-87, pres. Harlem unit, 1983-88, med. dir.-at-large bd. dirs. 1977—, bd. dirs. N.Y.C. div., 1977—; mem. Columbia U. Comprehensive Cancer Ctr., 1987—; bd. trustees Howard U., 1994—; chmn. Pres. Cancer Panel, 1991—. Recipient Howard U. Women's Club award, 1977, Profl. award Nat. Assn. Negro Bus. and Profl. Women's Club, 1987, Disting. Lectr. award Manhattan Cen. Med. Soc., 1988, Disting. Cmty. Svc. award Mut. of Am., 1989, Susan G. Komen Breast Cancer Found. Betty Ford award, 1999, Mary Lasker Pub. Svc. award, 2000, Time, Inc. Health Lifetime Achievement award, 2000, CDC Champion of Prevention award, 2001, Jill Rose award, Breast Cancer Rsch. Found., 2002, Am. Soc. Clin. Oncology Spl. Recognition award, 2003, Susan B. Komen Breast Cancer Found. Champion of Change award, 2003, Assn. Cmty. Cancer Center's annual Achievement award, 2004, Rudin Prize award, NY Acad. Medicine, 2004; honored Susan G. Komen for the Cure Capitol Hill Champions, 2007. Fellow N.Y. Acad. Medicine, Am. Surgical Assn.; mem. ACS (exec. com. 1989—, gov. 1988—, com. on cancer, 1981—, sr. mem. commn. on cancer 1987—, chmn. pres. cancer panel 1991—, Medal of Honor), NIH (breast cancer task force 1979-84), Nat. Cancer Inst. (subcom. on cancer detection rsch. and applications 1987 -90), Soc. Surg. Oncology (exec. coun. 1987—), Nat. Med. Assn. (chmn. surg. sect. 1984-86), Inst. Medicine Nat. Acad. Sci. (elected 1997), Internat. Soc. Surgeons, N.Y. Acad. Scis., Am. Surg. Assn., Inst. of Medicine Nat. Acad. of Sci., County Med. Soc. N.Y., Alpha Omega Alpha. Office: Ralph Lauren Ctr for Cancer Care & Prevention 1919 Madison Ave New York NY 10035 also: Center to Reduce Cancer Health Disparities Nat Cancer Inst 6116 Executive Blvd Ste 602 MSC 8341 Rockville MD 20852*

FREEMAN, HARRY LYNWOOD, retired accountant; b. LA, May 5, 1920; s. Edward Church and Mildred Eaton (Noyes) F.; m. Ruth Turner, Feb. 14, 1941; children: Tracy Ruth (Mrs. Richard W. Flatow), Martin Harry. BS, UCLA, 1942. CPA, Calif. With Price Waterhouse & Co., CPAs, 1942-56, ptnr. Mexico City, 1956-73, ptnr.-in-charge Middle Americas firm, 1973-80. Chmn. auditing com. Am. Brit. Cowdray Hosp., 1962-68; bd. dirs., treas. YMCA of Mexico, 1967-73; bd. dirs. Inst. Mexicano-Norteamericano de Relaciones Culturales, 1961-69; trustee, v.p. Fallbrook Hosp. Found., 1987-90, pres., 1990-92; bd. dirs. Fallbrook Hosp. Dist., 1994-98, v.p., 1996-98. With AUS, 1944-46. Mem. AICPA, Calif. Soc. CPAs, Am. C. of C. Mex. (past pres.), Assn. Am. C. of C. in Latin Am. (past pres.), Eastridge Homeowners Assn. (bd. dirs. 2000-05), Aero Club of So. Calif., Book Club Calif. Home: 1002 Ridge Heights Dr Fallbrook CA 92028-3671

FREEMAN, HERBERT, retired computer engineering educator; b. Frankfurt, Germany, Dec. 13, 1925; came to U.S., 1938; s. Leo and Johanna (Friedmann) F.; m. Joan Sleppin, Nov. 25, 1955; children: Nancy, Susan, Robert. BSEE, Union Coll., Schenectady, NY, 1946; MSEE, Columbia U., NYC, 1948, DEngSc, 1956. Registered profl. engr., NY. Project engr. Sperry Gyroscope Co., Great Neck, NY, 1948-53, section head, 1953-57, dept. head, 1957-60; assoc. prof. computer engring. NYU, 1960-64, prof., chmn., 1965-75; prof. Rensselaer Poly. Inst., Troy, 1975-85; dir. Ctr. for Computer Aids for Indsl. Productivity Rutgers U., New Brunswick, 1985-90, prof. computer engring., 1985—2000; prof. emeritus, 2000—. Dir. Nat. Ctr. Geographic Info. and Analysis, 1988—93; pres. MapText, Inc., Plainsboro, 1998—2005. Author: Discrete-Time Systems, 1965; co-editor: Map Data Processing, 1980, Software Engineering, 1981; editor: Introduction to Computer Graphics, 1981, Machine Vision for Three-Dimensional Scenes, 1990. NSF postdoctoral fellow, 1966, Guggenheim fellow, 1972; recipient Medaglia Teresiana award U. Pavia, Italy, 1996. Fellow IEEE (Computer Pioneer award 1999), Internat. Assn. for Pattern Recognition (treas. 1982-88, pres. 1978-80, K.S. Fu award 1994); mem. Computer Soc. of IEEE (chmn. Pattern Analysis and Machine Intelligence sect. 1976-78), Internat. Fedn. Info. Processing (program chmn. 1974, Silver Core award 1974), Assn. Computing Machinery, Pattern Recognition Soc. Avocations: stamp collecting/philately, swimming. Personal E-mail: hfreeman@comcast.net. Business E-Mail: hfreeman@ieee.org.

FREEMAN, JANICE KALINA, elementary school educator; b. Laurium, Mich., Apr. 13, 1950; d. Edwin Cyril and Anna Margaret McCarty Kalina; m. Thomas Louis Freeman, Aug. 29, 1970; children: Kalina Suzanne Cover, Erik Thomas. BA magna cum laude, Humboldt State U., Arcata, Calif., 1972. Cert. clear multiple subjects tchr. Calif., 1985, supplementary authorization in social scis. Calif., 1996, Eng. lang. devel. and specially designed acad. instrn. Eng. Calif., 1999, English tchr. Calif., 2003, no child left behind K-8, Eng. 7-12. Tchr. 3d grade Dept. of Def. Dependents Schs., Ansbach, Baden-Wurttemburg, Germany, 1986—87; tchr. 6th grade Ripon Unified Sch. Dist., Calif., 1987—97, tchr. 8th grade, 1997—. Instr., dir. Outdoor Edn. program Ripon Elem. Sch., Calif., 1987—98, sch. site com., 1989—91, coach Acad. Pentathlon Team, 1995—, gate adv. bd., 1997—2004, chairperson Program Quality Rev. panel, 2001—02, site leadership team, 2002—, advisor student coun., 2005—; faculty adv. com. Ripon Unified Sch. Dist., Calif., 2006—. Instr. (commemorative quilt project) George Washington Bicentennial Quilt (Nat. prize Mt. Vernon Ladies' Assn. and A&E TV Network, 1999), founder, instr. (interactive hist. forum) Vet. Honor Day. Liaison Modesto Pregnancy Ctr., Calif., 1991—2007; campaign com. Election Campaign, Modesto, Calif., 2004—05; leader Calvary Luth. Ch. Jr. High Youth Program, Modesto, Calif., 1979—85; dir. Calvary Luth. Ch. Jr. Choir, Modesto, Calif., 1981—85, McKee Barracks Chapel Youth Choir, Crailsheim, Baden-Wurttemburg, Germany, 1985—87; mem. Modesto H.S. Booster Club, Calif., 1988—96. Recipient Cmty. Svc. Recognition award, McKee Barracks Mil. Cmty., Crailsheim, Germany, 1987, Panther Award for Svc., Modesto H.S., 1992, Tchr. award, San Joaquin A+, 2005, Class Acts Tchr. award, Modesto Bee Newspaper, 2006; Colonial Williamsburg Tchr. Inst. fellow, Calif. Dirs. Colonial Williamsburg Found., 2000. Mem.: Calif. Tchrs. Assn., Ripon Unified Dist. Tchrs. Assn., Delta Kappa Gamma. Avocations: family, travel, golf, reading, music. Office: Ripon Elem Sch 509 W Main St Ripon CA 95366 Home Phone: 209-572-0819. Business E-Mail: jfreeman@sjcoe.net.

FREEMAN, JOEL ARTHUR, author, organizational cultural change facilitator; b. Lewiston, Maine, July 24, 1954; s. Arthur Fickett and Katherine Ann (Schroeder) F.; m. Shirley Lee Burkhardt, Jan. 6, 1996; children: David Joel, Jesse Andrew, Jacob Edward, Shari Adelaide. MS in Pastoral Counseling, Loyola Coll., Balt., 1986; PhD in Pastoral Counseling, Evang. Theol. Sem., Dixon, Mo., 1991. Ordained to ministry Calvary Chapel Outreach Fellowship, 1975. Pastor Glorious Gospel Ch., Friendship, Maine, 1975-77, Balt., 1977-80, Columbia, Md., 1980-88, Stillmeadow Christian Fellowship, Balt., 1988-93; pres. Freeman Inst., Severn, Md., 1993—; founder, dir. Black Courage Found., 2003—. Chaplain NBA Washington Wizards Basketball Team, 1979-98; host radio talk show Sta. WABS, 1977-88; TV host Howard Cable Co., Ellicott City, Md., 1980-86; interviewer CBN Satellite Radio Network, 1988—; mentor, corp. chaplain The Shepherd's Guide, 1980—; chaplain Sports World Ministries, 1998—; exec. com. Jammin' Against the Darkness, 1998-2000. Author: The Doctrine of Fools, 1984, God Is Not Fair, 1987, Living with Your Conscience without Going Crazy, 1989, Kingdom Zoology, 1991, Return to Glory: The Powerful Stirring of the Black Man, 1997; co-prodr., co-writer (films) Return to Glory, 2003, exec prodr., facilitator (video presentation) A White Man's Journey into Black History, prodr., presenter (video) A White Man's Journey Into Black History, Professional Bloodsuckers: Dealing with the People Who Drain You of Your Time, Energy & Patience, (video seminar) Dealing with People Who Drive You Crazy!, If Nobody Loves You, Create the Demand, 2006. Instr. chaplain's office Johns Hopkins U., Balt., 1977-79; mem. steering com. Word Renewal Pastor's Fellowship, Balt., 1977-83, County Exec. Prayer Breakfast, Howard County, 1983-86; area coord. Washington for Jesus, 1980; co-founding dir. Black Courage Found., 2003—. Mem. Inst. in Basic Life Principles (coord. 1979-86). Republican. Office: Freeman Inst 1103 Burkhardt Ln Severn MD 21144-2800 E-mail: joel@freemaninstitute.com. *I choose to keep the eternal perspective in clear view. I want to invest my life in that which will be important one thousand years from now. Jesus Christ is the same yesterday, today and forever.*

FREEMAN, JOHN ARTHUR, theater educator; b. Ft. Benning, Ga., Nov. 11, 1951; s. Richard David and Edith Freeman; m. Margaret Mary Gray; children: Jessica Diane, Christopher David. AA in Secondary Edn., Albany Jr. Coll., Ga., 1972; BA in English Edn., Ga. Coll., 1976. English tchr., theatre dir. Baldwin HS, Milledgeville, Ga., 1977—96, Mt. de Sales Acad., Macon, Ga., 1996—99, dir. fine arts, theatre tchr., lit. coord., 2001—; English tchr. Houston County HS, Warner Robins, Ga., 1999—2001. Recipient Outstanding Educator of the Yr., Jaycees, 1983, Tchr. of Yr., Baldwin County, 1983, Dir. of Yr., GISA, 2005. Mem.: Am. Choral Dirs. Assn., Ga. Theatre Assn. (assoc.), Ednl. Theatre Assn. (assoc.), Ga. Music Educators Assn. (assoc.), Nat. Cath. Ednl. Assn., Ga. Thespian Soc. (assoc.). Office Phone: 478-751-3240.

FREEMAN, LEE ALLEN, JR., lawyer; b. Chgo., July 31, 1940; s. Lee Allen and Brena (Dietz) F.; m. Glynna Gene Weger, June 8, 1968; children: Crispin McDougal, Clark Dietz, Cassidy Bree. BA magna cum laude, Harvard U., Cambridge, Mass., 1962; JD magna cum laude, Harvard Sch. Law, Cambridge, Mass., 1965. Bar: Ill. 1966, D.C. 1966, Mont. 1986, U.S. Supreme Ct. 1969. Practiced in, Washington, 1965-68, Chgo., 1968—; law clk. to Justice Tom C. Clark, Washington, 1965-66; asst. U.S. atty., 1966-68; pres. Freeman, Freeman & Salzman, P.C., 1970—2007; mng. dir. MasterKey RAnch, Livingston, Mont.; spl. dep. atty. gen. Commonwealth of Pa., 1971—82; spl. asst. atty. gen. in Ill., Ind., W.Va., Mich., Colo., Tex.; spl. asst. corp. counsel City of Chgo., 1971-76; ptnr. Jenner & Brock, 2007—. Pres. Chgo. Lyric Opera Guild; pres. Fine Arts Music Found.; dir. Chgo. Lyric Opera, 1995—, mem. exec. com. Named Outstanding Young Citizen Chgo. Jaycees, 1976 Mem.: ABA (coun. mem. antitrust sect. 1985—87), Am. Coll. Trial Lawyers, Chgo. Inn of Ct., Std. Club. Home: 232 E Walton St Chicago IL 60611-1507 also: PO Box 1295 52 Little Mission Creek Livingston MT 59047 Office: Jenner and Block LLP 330 N Wabash Ave Chicago IL 60611 Office Phone: 312-923-2806. Business E-Mail: lfreeman@jenner.com.

FREEMAN, LEONARD MURRAY, radiologist, nuclear medicine physician, educator; b. NYC, Apr. 20, 1937; s. Joseph and Tillie (Krutman) F.; m. Marlene Carolyn Held, Apr. 28, 1967; children: Eric Lawrence, David Robert, Joy Esther. BA, N.Y. U., 1957; MD, Chgo. Med. Sch., 1961. Diplomate: Am. Bd. Radiology, Am. Bd. Nuclear Medicine. Intern Beth Israel Hosp. and Med. Center, NYC, 1961-62; resident in radiology Bronx Municipal Hosp. Center, 1962-65; mem. staff Albert Einstein Coll. Medicine, NYC, 1965—; co-dir. div. nuclear medicine Jacobi Med. Ctr., NYC, 1965-83; dir. nuclear medicine Montefiore Med. Center, NYC, 1976—; attending radiologist, 1977—; cons. nuclear medicine USPHS Hosp., SI, NY, 1967-82, St. Barnabas Hosp., Bronx, 1967—, Beth Israel Hosp. and Med. Center, 1974—, Maimonides Hosp. and Med. Center, 1974-99, Bklyn. VA Hosp., 1984—2001; asst. instr. radiology Albert Einstein Coll. Medicine, Bronx, 1964-65, instr., 1965-67, asst. prof., 1967-72, assoc. prof., 1972-77, prof., 1977—, prof. nuclear medicine, 1983—, vice chmn. dept. nuclear medicine, 1987—. Mem. adv. com. nuclear medicine program Brookhaven Nat. Labs., Upton, NY, 1972-82; examiner nuclear medicine Am. Bd. Radiology; spkr. in field. Author: Clinical Scintillation Scanning, 1969, Clinical Scintillation Imaging, 1975, Freeman and Johnson's Clinical Radionuclide Imaging, 1984; co-editor Seminars in Nuclear Medicine, 1970—, Physicians Desk Reference for Radiology and Nuclear Medicine, 1971-80, Clinical Nuclear Medicine, 2007; reviewer Jour. Nuclear Medicine, 1972—; editor Nuclear Medicine Ann., 1980-2004, Current Concepts in Diagnostic Nuclear Medicine, 1983-87, Advances in Functional Neuroimaging, 1988-90; mem. editl. bd. European Jour. Nuclear Medicine, 1979—, Jour. Nuclear Medicine and Allied Scis., 1982-96, Nuclear Medicine Communications, 1986-2002, Quar. Jour. Nuclear Medicine, 1996—; contbr. over 30 chapters to books, and over 140 articles to profl. jours. Named one of Best Doctors in Am., 1992—, Top Doctors in NY Metro Area, 1999—, Best Doctors in NY, NY Mag., 1998, 2001—03, 2007; recipient Disting. Educator award, Soc. Nuclear Medicine, 1993, Berson-Yalow award, Greater NY Chpt., Soc. Nuclear Medicine, 1997, Disting. Alumnus award, Chgo. Med. Sch., 1978. Fellow Am. Coll. Radiology, Am. Coll. Nuclear Physicians, NY Acad. Medicine (chmn. sect. nuc. medicine 2000-02); mem. Soc. Nuclear Medicine (gov. local chpt. 1973—, nat. trustee 1973-77, nat. v.p. 1977-78, nat. pres. 1979-80, chmn. pub. rels. com. 1981-91, chmn. correlative imaging cou. 1982-84, chmn. awards com. 1983-86, Disting. Edn. award 1993, Berson-Yallow award Greater NY chpt. 1997), Radiol. Soc. N.Am., Soc. Gastrointestinal Radiologists, NY State Med. Soc., New York County Med. Soc., Pan Am. Med. Assn. (hon. life), European Assn. Nuclear Medicine, LI Soc. Nuclear Med. Technologists (hon. life), Alpha Omega Alpha (hon.). Avocations: travel, golf, theater. Home: 50 Sutton Pl S New York NY 10022-4167 Office: 111 E 210th St Bronx NY 10467-2401 Home Phone: 212-688-9395; Office Phone: 718-920-6060. Business E-Mail: lfreeman@montefiore.org.

FREEMAN, LESLIE GORDON, anthropologist, educator; b. Warsaw, NY, Sept. 9, 1935; s. Leslie Gordon and Theresa Rosalie (Stanbro) F.; m. Susan Tax, Mar. 20, 1964; 1 child, Sarah Elisabeth. AB, U. Chgo., 1954, AM, 1961, PhD, 1964. Asst. prof. anthropology Tulane U., 1964-65; asst. prof. U. Chgo., 1965-70, assoc. prof., 1970-76, prof., 1976-2000, prof. emeritus, 2000—; pres. Inst. Prehistoric Investigations, Chgo., 1983—2001. Rsch. assoc. Mont. State U., Bozeman, 1992—. Author (with J. Gonzalez): Cueva Morin, 2 vols., 1971, 1973, Vida y Muerte en Cueva Morin, 1978, Le Paleolithique Inferieur et Moyen en Espagne, 1998, La Grotte d'Altamira, 2001; editor: Views of the Past, 1978; editor: (with Sol Tax) Horizons of Anthropology, 1976; editor: (with others) Altamira Revisited, 1987, Beato de Liebana, 1995, Estudio del Manuscrito del Apocalipsis de San Juan, Beato de Liebana de San Miguel de Escalada, 2000, Beato de Liebana: Obras Completas y Complementarias, vol. I (2d edit.), vol. II, 2004, Estudio del Manuscrito del Beato de Las Huelgas, 2004. Corporator Internat. Inst. Spain. With U.S. Army, 1957-59. Recipient Silver Plaque Provincial Deputation of Santander, Spain, 1973 Fellow AAAS, Am. Anthropol. Assn., Royal Anthropol. Inst.; mem. Reial Academia Catalana de Belles Arts de Sant Jordi Barcelona (corr.), Reial Academia Catalana de Bones Lletres Barcelona (corr.), Chgo. Acad. Scis. (trustee, 2d v.p. 1981-83). Office: U Chgo Dept Anthropology Haskell Hall M-306 Chicago IL 60637 Home: PO Box 369 Whitehall MT 59759

FREEMAN, LEWIS BERNARD, forensic accountant, lawyer; b. Cortland, NY, May 4, 1949; s. Lawrence Freeman and Doris Gold.; m. Eddi Ann R. Freeman, Nov. 26, 1976; children: Jaron, Abigail. BBA, U. Miami, Coral Gables, 1971; JD, 1974. Bar: Fla. Pres. Freeman & Ptnrs., Miami, 1992—; CPA Freeman, Dawson & Rosenbaum, CPAs, Miami, 1992—. Pres. Epilepsy Found. Fla., 1990-94; bd. mem. U. Miami Law Sch. Alumni, Coral Gables, 1990-98, Miami Children's Mus., 1994-97; com. Fla. Bar on CPA's, Talahassee, 1997. Named Humanitarian of Yr. EPIL Found. of Fla., Miami, 1996, Outstanding Alumnus of Yr., U. Miami, 1994, Outstanding Spkr. of Yr. Fla. Inst. CPAs, Tallahassee, 1982. Democrat. Jewish. Office: Lewis B Freeman & Ptnrs 3225 Aviation Ave Ste 501 Miami FL 33133-5232 Home Phone: 305-665-8588; Office Phone: 305-443-6622. Office Fax: 305-285-3441. Business E-Mail: lfreeman@lbfmiami.com.

FREEMAN, LOUIS S., lawyer; b. Cin., Apr. 21, 1940; s. Emanuel and Sadye (Harris) F.; m. Diane Ruth Edson, Jan. 28, 1967; children: Matthew E., James H., Jill E. BBA, U. Cin., 1963; JD, Harvard U., 1966; LLM in Taxation, NYU, 1972. Bar: Ohio 1966, N.Y. 1968, Ill. 1975. CPA. Mem. staff Coopers & Lybrand, NYC, 1966-68; assoc. Mudge, Rose, Guthrie & Alexander, NYC, 1968-74, Sonnenschein Nath & Rosenthal, Chgo., 1974-76, ptnr., 1976-97, Skadden, Arps, Slate, Meagher & Flom, Chgo., 1997—. Adj. prof. of taxation Ill. Inst. Tech., Chgo.-Kent Coll. of Law Grads. Program in Taxation, 1985-89 Mem. bds. of contbg. editors Jour. Corp. Taxation, Jour. Real Estate Taxation, Jour. Taxation of Investments; bd. advisors the M&A Tax Report, Jour. Corp. Taxation; also author articles. Fellow Am. Coll. Tax Counsel; mem. ABA (tax sect. com. on corp. tax), Chgo. Bar Assn., (chmn. exec. com. of fed. tax com. 1986-87), N.Y. Sate Bar Assn. (tax sect. exec. com. 1990-92), Am. Law Inst. (tax adv. group subchpt. C. Fed. Income Tax Project), Met. Club of Chgo. Office: Skadden Arps Slate Meagher & Flom 333 W Wacker Dr Chicago IL 60606-1220 Home Phone: 847-853-9353; Office Phone: 312-407-0650. Business E-Mail: LFreeman@skadden.com.

FREEMAN, MICHAEL BYRON, protective services official, consultant; b. San Antonio, May 11, 1962; s. Larry Steven Sr. and Jacqueline Blackwell Freeman; m. Dedra Kaye Sellers, July 4, 1986; children: Angelica Kaye, Michaela Gabrielle. Cert. fire inspector Internat. Code Coun., 1999. Fire fighter Laurel Fire Dept., Miss., 1996—99; asst. fire marshal Johnson City Fire Dept., Tenn., 1999—. Vol. Glade Vol. Fire Dept., Laurel, 1987—96. With USAR, 1987—95, Laurel, MS. Mem.: Mensa. Apostolic Pentecostal. Avocations: computers, hiking, camping. Home: 695 Princeton Rd Johnson City TN 37601 Office: Johnson City Fire Marshal's Office 333 E Maple St Johnson City TN 37601 Home Phone: 423-737-7452; Office Phone: 423-434-6181. Personal E-mail: mike@mbfreeman.net.

FREEMAN, MILTON MALCOLM ROLAND, anthropology educator; b. London, Apr. 23, 1934; arrived in Can., 1958; s. Louis and Fay (Bomberg) F.; m. Mini Christina Aodla; children: Graham, Elaine, Malcolm. BS, Reading U., Eng., 1958; postgrad., U. Coll., London, 1962-64; PhD, McGill U., 1965. Research scientist No. Affairs Dept., Ottawa, Ont., Canada, 1965-67; asst. prof. Meml. U., St. John's, Nfld., Canada, 1967-71, assoc. prof., 1971-72; dir. Inuit Land Use Study, Hamilton, Ont., Canada, 1973-75; prof. anthropology McMaster U., Hamilton, 1976-81; Henry Marshall Tory prof. U. Alta., Edmonton, Canada, 1982-99, prof. emeritus, 1999—, adj. prof. East Asian studies, 1993—99. Adj. prof. environ. studies U. Waterloo, Ont., 1977-81; sr. sci. advisor Indian and No. Affairs, Ottawa, 1979-81; sr. rsch. scholar Can. Circumpolar Inst., U. Alta., 1990—; McLean prof. Trent U., Peterborough, Can., 1995; chmn. UNESCO-MAB No. Sci. Network, 1983-88. Author: People Pollution, 1974, Cultural Anthropology of Whaling, 1989, Recovering Rights, 1992, Inuit, Whaling, and Sustainability, 1998; editor: Inuit Land Use and Occupancy Report, 1976, Procs. Internat. Symposium on Renewable Resources and the Economy of the North, 1981, Japanese Small-type Coastal Whaling, 1988, Endangered Peoples of the Arctic, 2000; co-editor: Adaptive Management of Marine Resources in the Pacific, 1991, Elephants and Whales: Resources for Whom?, 1994, Conservation Hunting: People and Wildlife in Canada's North, 2005 Bd. dirs. Sci. Inst. N.W.T., 1985-87; chmn. adv. bd. Can. Circumpolar Inst., 1990-2001; chmn. Man-Environ. Commn., Internat. Union Anthrop. and Ethnol. Scis., 1977-82. Fellow: Soc. Applied Anthropology, Arctic Inst. N.Am., Am. Anthropol. Assn.; mem.: Soc. Applied Anthropology Can. (pres. 1984—85). Office: U Alta Can Circumpolar Inst Edmonton AB Canada T6G 2E1 Home Phone: 780-439-8248; Office Phone: 780-492-4682. E-mail: milton.freeman@ualberta.ca.

FREEMAN, MORGAN, actor; b. Memphis, June 1, 1937; s. Grafton Curtis and Mayme Edna (Revere) F.; m. Jeanette Adair Bradshaw, Oct. 22, 1967 (div. 1979); m. Myrna Colley-Lee, June 16, 1984; children: Alphonse, Saifoulaye, Deena, Morgana. Student, L.A. City Coll. Actor: (stage prodns.) Niggerlover (debut), 1967, Hello Dolly (Broadway), 1967, Jungle of Cities, 1969, The Recruiting Officer, 1969, Scuba-Duba, 1969, Purlie (ANTA Theatre, N.Y.C.), 1970, Black Visions, 1972, Sisyphus and the Blue-Eyed Cyclops, 1975, Cockfight, 1977, Mighty Gents, 1978 (Clarence Derwent award, Drama Desk award, Tony award nomination), White Pelicans, 1978, Coriolanus, also Julius (N.Y. Shakespeare Festival), 1979, Mother Courage and Her Children, 1980, Othello, also All's Well That Ends Well (both Dallas Shakespeare Festival), 1982, Buck, 1983, Medea and the Doll, 1984, The Gospel at Colonus (Obie awards), (feature films) Who Says I Can't Ride a Rainbow, 1971, Brubaker, 1980, Eyewitness, 1980, Harry and Son, 1983, Teachers, 1984, Street Smart, 1987 (Acad. award nomination), Clean and Sober, 1988, Lean On Me, 1989, Johnny Handsome, 1989, Driving Miss Daisy (Golden Globe award, Acad. award nomination), 1989, Glory, 1989, The Bonfire of the Vanities, 1990, Robin Hood, 1991, Unforgiven, 1992, The Shawshank Redemption, 1994 (Acad. award nomination), Outbreak, 1995, Seven, 1995, Chain Reaction, 1996, Moll Flanders, 1996, Deep Impact 1997, Kiss The Girls, 1997, The Long Way Home, 1996, Hard Rain, 1998, Water Damage, 1999, Under Suspicion, 1999, Mutiny, 1999, Nurse Betty, 2000, Along Came a Spider, 2001, High Crimes, 2002, The Sum of All Fears, 2002, Levity, 2003, Dreamcatcher, 2003, Bruce Almighty, 2003, The Big Bounce, 2004, Million Dollar Baby, 2004 (Outstanding performance by male actor in supporting role, Screen Actors Guild award, 2005, Academy award for best actor in a supporting role, 2005), Unleashed, 2005, (voice) Batman Begins, 2005, (narrator) War of the Worlds, 2005, (narrator) March of the Penguins, 2005, An Unfinished Life, 2005, Edison, 2005, Lucky Number Slevin, 2006; actor, exec. prodr. 10 Items or Less, 2006; dir. Bopha!, 1993; regular cast (TV show) The Electric Company, 1971-77; TV films include: Hollow Image, 1979, Attica, 1980, The Marva Collins Story, 1981, The Atlanta Child Murders, 1985, Resting Place, 1986, Flight for Life, 1987, Clinton and Nadine, 1988, Mutiny, 1999; (TV mini series-voice) Slavery and the Making of America, 2005. With USAF, 1955—59, former mechanic USAF. Recipient Spencer Tracy award, UCLA, 2006.

FREEMAN, NEAL BLACKWELL, communications corporation executive; b. NYC, July 5, 1940; s. Malcolm T. and Virginia (Neal) F.; m. Jane Louise Metze, Mar. 19, 1966; children: Malcolm Trowbridge II, James Bragdon, Kathryn R. BA magna cum laude, Yale U., 1962. Asst. to pres. Washington Star Syndicate, 1965-66; assoc. producer TV show Firing Line, 1966-67; exec. editor King Features Syndicate, NYC, 1968-73; v.p., editor King Features div. Hearst Corp., 1973-76; pres. Jefferson Communications, Inc., 1976-86; chmn. bd., chief exec. officer Blackwell Corp., 1982—; dir. Intelsat, Ltd. Exec. prodr. Pub. TV; bd. dirs. Comsat Corp., BTG, Inc., Nat. Rev., Denver Nuggets Profl. Basketball Club, Colo. Avalanche Profl. Hockey Club, GRC Internat., Tutagon Med. N.Am. Mgmt.; bd. visitors Inst. on Polit. Journ alism, Georgetown U.; chmn. Washington Selection Panel Pres.'s Commn. on White House Fellows, 1998-2002, Found. Mgmt. Inst., 2000—; chmn. of agts. Yale Alumni Fund; bd. dirs. Corp. for Pub. Broadcasting, 1972-75; bd. dirs., vice-chmn. Ethics and Pub. Policy Ctr. Bd. dirs. Wolf Trap Found., 1984-90. Mem. Colony Found., Cosmos Club (Washington), Yale Club (N.Y.C.), York Country Club (Maine), Nat. Press Club, Sigma Delta Chi. Office: The Blackwell Corp PO Box 320 York ME 03909

FREEMAN, NEIL, accounting and computer consulting firm executive, owner; b. Reading, Pa., Dec. 27, 1948; s. Leroy Harold and Audrey Todd (Dornhecker) F. BS, Albright Coll., 1979; MS, Kennedy-Western U., 1987, PhD, 1988. Cert. systems profl., data processing specialist, info. system security profl. Acct. Jack W. Long & Co., Mt. Penn, Pa., 1977-78; comptroller G.P.C., Inc., Bowmansville, Pa., 1978-79; owner Neil Freeman Cons., Bowmansville, 1980-81; program mgr., sys. cons. Application Sys., Honolulu, 1981-82; instr. Chaminade U., Honolulu, 1983-96; owner Neil Freeman Cons., Kaneohe, Hawaii, 1982-96, Grand Junction, Colo., 1997—. Author: (computer software) NFC Property Management, 1984, NFC Mailing List, 1984; (book) Learning Dibol, 1984. Served with USN, 1966-68, Vietnam. Mem. Nat. Assn. Accts., Am. Inst. Cert. Computer Profls., Assn. Systems Mgmt. Office: 311 9th Ave Havre MT 59501 Office Phone: 406-265-1288. Personal E-mail: neil_freeman@netzero.net.

FREEMAN, PATRICIA ELIZABETH, multi-media specialist, educational consultant; b. El Dorado, Ark., Nov. 30, 1924; d. Herbert A. and M. Elizabeth (Pryor) Harper; m. Jack Freeman, June 15, 1949; 3 children. BA, Centenary Coll., 1943; postgrad., Fine Arts Ctr., 1942—46, Art Students League, 1944—45; BSLS, La. State U., 1946; postgrad., Calif. State U., 1959—61, U. N.Mex., 1964—74; EdS, Vanderbilt U., 1975. Libr. U. Calif., Berkeley, 1946-47; libr. Albuquerque Pub. Schs., 1964-67, ind. sch. libr. media ctr. cons., 1967—. One-woman shows include La. State Exhibit Bldg., 1948; author: Pathfinder: An Operational Guide for the School Librarian, 1975, Southeast Heights Neighborhoods of Albuquerque, 1993; compiler, editor: Elizabeth Pryor Harper's Twenty-One Southern Families, 1985; editor: SEHNA Gazette, 1988—93. Mem. task force Goals for Dallas-Environ., 1977—82; pres. Friends Sch. Librs., Dallas, 1979—83; v.p., editor S.E. Heights Neighborhood Assn., 1988—93. With USAF, 1948—49. Named honoree, AAUW Ednl. Found., 1979, 1996; recipient Vol. award for Outstanding Svc., Dallas Ind. Sch. Dist., 1978; AAUW Pub. Svc. grantee, 1980. Mem.: LWV (sec. Dallas 1982—83, editor Albuquerque 1984—86, editor Albuquerque/Bernalillo County Voters' Guide 1986, 1988, editor N.Mex. 2004—, editor Albuquerque 2005—), AAUW (bd. dirs. Dallas 1976—82, bd. dirs. Albuquerque 1983—85, dir. N.Mex, editor 1999—2005, bd. dirs. Albuquerque 2003—06, editor), ALA, N.Mex Symphony Guild, Nat. Trust Historic Preservation, Friends Pub. Libr., Colorado Springs Fine Arts Ctr., Alpha Xi Delta. Home: 612 Ridgecrest Dr SE Albuquerque NM 87108-3365

FREEMAN, PATSY L., director; b. West Columbia, Tex., Jan. 10, 1953; d. Herman Charles and Goldie Bertram; m. Jimmy R. Freeman, July 11, 1977; children: Shalene Rodgers, Michelle Caruth. A in Sociology, Coastal Bend Coll., Beeville, Tex., 1987; B in Sociology, Tex. A&M U., Corpus Christi, 1989, MS in Guidance and Counseling, 1993. Lic. profl. counselor Tex., 1998. Basic child care worker South Tex. Children's Home, Pettus, 1980—82, supr. Ind. Living Program, 1982—86, supr. Coll. Cottage Program, 1986—89, caseworker, 1989—91; case mgr. III Corpus Christi State Sch., Tex., 1991—93, case mgr. supr. Tex., 1993—95; spl. needs counselor Coastal Bend Coll., Beeville, 1995—2003, dir. fin. aid, 2003—. Named Outstanding Student of Am., 1989; named to Outstanding Women of Am., 1991. Mem.: Tex. Counseling Assn., ACA, Phi Theta Kappa Nat.Honor Alumni Assn. Republican. Baptist. Avocations: hunting, camping, ranching. Mailing: PO Box 4053 Beeville TX 78104 Office: Coastal Bend Coll 3800 Charco Rd Beeville TX 78102 Home Phone: 361-375-2320.

FREEMAN, PETER A., dean; PhD in Computer Sci., Carnegie-Mellon U., 1970. Asst. prof. to prof. info. and computer sci. U. Calif., Irvine, 1971-90; divsn. dir. Computer and Computation Rsch. NSF, 1987-89; vis. disting. prof. info. tech. George Mason U., Fairfax, Va., 1989-90; dean, Coll. Computing Ga. Inst. Tech., Atlanta, 1990—2002, John P. Imlay, Jr. Dean of Computing; asst. dir. NSF, Arlington, Va., 2002—07; dir. Washington Adv. Group, 2007—. Former Chief Info. Officer, Ga. Inst. Tech.; bd. dirs. Computing Rsch. Assn., 1988-2002; rev. com. IRS and FAA; chair vis. com. Schlumberger Austin Rsch.; cons. in field. Author: Software Perspectives: The System is the Message, 1987, Software System Principles, 1975; editor, co-editor: Software Design Techniques, Software Reusability; founding editor McGraw-Hill Series in Software Engineering and Technology; contbr. articles to profl. jours. Fellow IEEE (past chair IEEE/CS Tech. Com. on Software Engring.), AAAS, Assn. Computing Machinery. Office: Washington Adv Group 1725 Eye St NW Ste 800 Washington DC 20006 Office Phone: 202-682-0164. Business E-Mail: pfreeman@theadvisorygroup.com.

FREEMAN, RALPH CARTER, investment banker, management consultant; b. La Grange, Ga. s. Ralph Carter and Alice (Cordell) F.; m. Carole Stephens, July 31, 1957 (div. 1977); children: Carter III, Allyson (dec.), Stephens, LeAnna; m. Nancy Lynn Brown, Apr. 8, 1977. BBA, Emory U., 1959. CPA, Mont.; cert. mgmt. cons.; real estate broker, Calif. Acct., cons. Pannell Kerr Forster, Atlanta, Honolulu, 1959—72, ptnr., 1967—72; co-founder Freeman and Noll Accts. and Auditors, 1962—66; mgmt. cons. Touche Ross & Co., Honolulu, Am. Samoa, Asia, South Pacific, 1972-75; pres. FP Industries, Inc., Hawaii, Mont., Ga., Ala., 1975-85, Janas Consulting, Huntsville, Ala. and San Francisco, Calif., 1986—95; chmn. Janas Assoc., Investment Banking, U.S., China, S.E. Asia, Pasadena, Calif., 1995—. Founder Peoples Bank, LaGrange, Ga., 1966; founding investor Bank of Newnan, Ga., 1988, Profl. Bus. Bank, Pasadena, Calif., 2001—. Contbr. articles to profl. jours. and nat. trade mags. Mem. Inst. Mgmt. Cons. (cert., bd. dirs., treas. 1999-00), All Cities Resource Group, Hong Kong Assn., Calif. Capital Market Pl., Sigma Alpha Epsilon. Avocations: fishing, tennis, camping. Office: 225 S Lake Ave Ste 610 Pasadena CA 91101-3005 Office Phone: 626-432-7000. Business E-Mail: rcf@janascorp.com.

FREEMAN, RICHARD DEAN, new business start-up service company executive; b. Rushville, Ind., Nov. 27, 1928; s. Verne Crawford and Mary Phyllis (Dean) F.; m. Mary Jane Barkman, Aug. 21, 1950; children: Debra Dean, Phyllis Lynn, Richard Paul, Tom Crawford. BS in Aero. Engring., Purdue U., 1950, BS in Naval Sci. and Tactics, 1950, MS in Indsl. Mgmt., 1954. Supr. indsl. engring. Gen. Motors Corp., Warren, Ohio, 1954-58; prodn. mgr. Ramo Wooldridge div. TRW Corp., Denver, 1958-62; mgr. missile programs Hughes Aircraft Co., Los Angeles, 1962-68; v.p. E-Systems Inc., Dallas, 1968-72, Rockwell Internat. Co., Los Angeles, 1972-74; pres. Internat. Pacific Co., Newport Beach, Calif., 1974—. Sr. lectr. West Coast U., L.A., 1974-78; sec. proteus Corp., Newport Beach, 1978-80; chmn. Tech. Assocs. Corp., Newport Beach, 1984-85; chief exec. officer Equicenters, Inc., Irvine, 1988—. Author: Economation Approaches, 1958, Equator, 1984 (also film); prod. documentary film Zeros of the Pacific, 1979. Cubmaster, scoutmaster, dist. chmn. Boy Scouts Am., various locations, 1966-76; mem. librs. devel. adv. com. Purdue U., 1992, 2003; mem. restoration adv. bd. Marine Corps Air Sta., Tustin, 1994; pres. bd. trustees, elder Presbyn. Ch. Capt. USMC, 1946-58, Korea. Named Man of Yr., Sigma Alpha Tau, West Lafayette, Ind., 1971; recipient Disting. Engring. Alumnus award Purdue U., 1973, Outstanding Aerospace Engr. award Purdue U. Sch. Aeronautics and Astronautics, 1999. Mem. Am. Inst. Indsl. Engrs., Purdue U. Alumni Assn., Nat. Eagle Scout Assn. (pres. 1998), Exch. Club of Newport Harbor (pres. 1998-99), CA/NV Dist. Exch. Club (pres. 2001-2002, Exchangite of Yr. award 2002, Lifetime Achievement award 2004), Kappa Sigma (inducted into Hall of Fame 1997). Lodges: Masons (consistory 32 degree v.p.). Republican. Avocation: exploration for amelia earhart's missing aircraft. Home: 3910 Topside Ln Corona Del Mar CA 92625-1628 E-mail: interpac2000@yahoo.com.

FREEMAN, RICHARD MERRELL, retired lawyer; b. Crawfordsville, Ind., July 2, 1921; s. F. Rider and Ruth (Merrell) F.; m. Joanne Spears, Nov. 26, 1943; children: Randy, Mark, Candy, Marcia. AB, Wabash Coll., Ind., 1943; LLB, Columbia U., 1948. Bar: Tenn. 1948, Ill. 1957. Atty. TVA, Knoxville, 1948-57, dir., 1978-86; partner firm Belnap, Spencer, Hardy & Freeman, Chgo., 1957-67; v.p. law Chgo. & Northwestern Transp. Co., Chgo., 1967-78, also dir., voting trustee. Bd. dirs. TVA, 1978-86. With USNR, 1943-46. Mem.: Phi Beta Kappa. Democrat. Mem. Community Ch. Home: 5391 Drum Castle Pkwy Sarasota FL 34238

FREEMAN, ROBERT SCHOFIELD, musicologist, educator, pianist; b. Rochester, NY, Aug. 26, 1935; s. Henry Schofield and Florence Margaret (Knope) F.; m. Carol Jean Morgan, Dec. 10, 1976; children: John Frederick, Elizabeth Poon, Scott Alan Henry. AB summa cum laude, Harvard U., Cambridge, Mass., 1957; MFA, Princeton U., NJ, 1960, PhD, 1967; MusD (hon.), Hamilton Coll., 1988. Instr., asst. prof. Princeton U., 1963-68; asst. prof., assoc. prof. MIT, 1968-73; dir., prof. musicology Eastman Sch. Music, U. Rochester, 1972-96; pres. New England Conservatory, Boston, 1996-99; dean, Effie Marie Cain regents chair in fine arts Coll. Fine Arts U. Tex., Austin, 1999—2006, Susan Menefee regents prof. fine arts, 2006—. Chmn. nat. adv. bd. Ctr. for Black Music Research, Chgo., 1985-90; cons. for various Am. U.; vis. assoc. prof. Harvard U., 1972. Author: Opera Without Drama, 1981; contbr. articles to profl. jours. Trustee Conductors' Guild, China. Found. for Edn. and Culture. Harvard Sheldon fellow, 1958, Woodrow Wilson Found. fellow, 1959, Martha Baird Rockefeller Fund fellow, 1963, Fulbright fellow, 1960-62; recipient Civic medal Rochester C. of C., 1982. Mem. Am. Musicol. Soc. (chair New Eng. chpt. 1970-72, coun. mem. 1973-76), Coll. Music Soc. (coun. mem. 1973-76), Neue Bach Gesellschaft (chmn. 1977-82), Nat. Assn. Schs. Music (grad. commn. 1981-85), Harvard Music Assn., Headliner's Club of Austin, Princeton Club of NY, U. Tex. Club. Avocations: baseball, reading. Office: Coll Fine Arts U Tex at Austin Austin TX 78712 Home Phone: 512-338-4143. Personal E-mail: rf3519@aol.com. Business E-Mail: rsfreeman@mail.utexas.edu.

FREEMAN, RONALD EUGENE, environmental engineer; b. Ventura, Calif., Mar. 24, 1957; s. Ray Eugene and Ruby Louise Freeman; m. Cherry Katherine Gatlin, June 12, 1986. AA, Ventura Jr. Coll., 1977; BS in Petroleum Engring., U. Tulsa, 1982; MPA, U. Ctrl. Fla., 1997. Registered prof. engr., Fla. Assoc. engr. Kerr McGee Corp., Oklahoma City, 1982—83; consulting engr. So. Cross Exploration Co.; field rep. Vetco Offshore Inc., Ventura, Calif., 1984—88; shop forman Freeman Fishing Tools, Ojai, Calif., 1986—87; owner Miracle Ear Hearing Aid Ctr., Mobile, Ala., 1988—89; environ. specialist Volusia County Environ. Mgmt., DeLand, Fla., 1989—2001; profl. engr. Volusia County Health Dept., DeLand, 2001—. Recipient Spl. Achievement award, Fla. Dept. Environ. Protection, 2002, 2003, 2005; fellow, Centers Disease Control Environ. Pub. Health Leadership Inst., 2006—. Mem.: Nat. Environ. Health Assn., Am. Water Works Assn., Nat. Conf. Local Environ. Health Adminstrs. (trustee 2005—), Fla. Environ. Health Assn. (bd. mem. 2004—05), Fla. Environ. Health Assn. (bd. dirs. 2004—05, chmn. Halifax dist. 2004—05, Outstanding Environ. Health Prof. of the Yr., Outstanding Svc. Halifax chpt., Outstanding Chmn. award Halifax dist. 2000), Water Authority of Volusia (tech. adv. com. 2001—05), Kappa Sigma Frat. (chmn. Halifax dist. 1999—2000, v.p. 1981—82). Office: Volusia County Health Dept 1350 S Woodland Blvd Deland FL 32720 Home Phone: 386-668-8524; Office Phone: 386-736-5444. Business E-Mail: ronald_freeman@doh.state.fl.us.

FREEMAN, SANDRA DIANNE, insurance agent, educator; d. John Homer and Jacqueline Inez Walker; m. Clent L. Freeman, May 1, 1999. Grad. H.S, Muscle Shoals, Ala. Cert. ins. svc. rep. Soc. CISR, 1997. CSR, receptionist Tucker & Associates, Inc., Florence, Ala., 1992—93; debit rt. agt. Liberty Nat./Torchmark Corp., Florence, 1993—94; comml. lines CSR Tom Jones Ins. Agy., Inc., Tuscumbia, Ala., 1994—96; comml. transp. underwriter North Ala. Ins., Inc. DBA NAI, Florence, 1996—99; comml. lines CSR Tom Jones Ins. & Fin. Svcs., Inc., Tuscumbia, 1999—2003; agy. prodn. mgr. Sam Newton Ins. Agy., Inc., Lexington, Ala., 2003—. Ins. educator Ala. Ind. Ins. Agts. Assn., Birmingham, 2003—. Singer: (albums) Livin' the Dream. Spokesperson, fundraiser Shriners Hosps. for Children, 2005—07. Mem.: Ala. Ind. Ins. Agts. Assn. (CSR of Yr. 2006), Ind. Ins. Agts. and Brokers Am., Nat. Assn. Ins. Women Internat. (cert. profl. ins. woman 2003, pres. 2001—02, local assn. pres. 2003—04), Ala. Homebuilders Assn. (assoc.). Conservative. Avocations: singing, reading, gardening, fishing. Office: Sam Newton Insurance Agency Inc PO Box 310 11342 Highway 101 Lexington AL 35648-0310 Home Phone: 256-627-8653; Office Phone: 256-229-6624. Office Fax: 256-229-6655. Business E-Mail: insurlady@peoplepc.com.

FREEMAN, SCOTT M., lawyer; b. 1959; AB in Econ., Harvard Univ., 1981; JD magna cum laude, Univ. Pa., 1984. Bar: NY 1985. Ptnr. mergers and acquisitions and securities offerings Sidley Austin Brown and Wood LLP, NYC, and mem. exec. com. Mem. adv. com. Ontario Securities Commn., 1995—99. Exec. editor Univ. Pa. Law Rev., 1983—84; contbr. articles to profl. journals. Mem.: Order of Coif. Office: Sidley Austin Brown & Wood LLP 787 Seventh Ave New York NY 10019 Office Phone: 212-839-7358. Office Fax: 212-839-5599. Business E-Mail: sfreeman@sidley.com.

FREEMAN, SHAREE M., federal agency administrator; b. NY; BA, St. Lawrence U., 1976; JD, Georgetown U., 1980. Law clk. to Hon. Norma Holloway Johnson U.S. Dist. Ct. D.C., Washington; asst. dist. atty. City of Phila., 1982—84; atty., Office Solicitor Gen. US Dept. Interior, 1984—97, acting asst. Solicitor Gen. Indian Legal Activities; counsel U.S. Ho. of Reps. Internat. Rels. Com., 1997—2001; dir. Cmty. Rels. Svc. US Dept. Justice, Washington, 2001—. Trustee St. Lawrence U., 2003—. Office: US Dept Justice Bicentennial Bldg 600 E St NW Ste 6000 Washington DC 20530

FREEMAN, SIDNEY LEE, minister; b. Madison, Wis., Jan. 23, 1927; s. Jack and Gertrude (Kaifetz) F.; m. Evelyn Marie Gronberg, Feb. 3, 1950 (div. 1965); children: Lynn Claire, David Eugene, Michael John; m. Gaynell Bradley, Apr. 28, 1967. BS, U. Wis., 1947; MA, Bowling Green State U., 1949; PhD, Cornell U., 1951. Ordained to ministry Unitarian Universalist Assn., 1957. Min. Unitarian Ch. Charlotte, NC, 1957-89, min. emeritus NC, 1989—. Instr. comm. arts Ctrl. Piedmont C.C., Charlotte, part-time 1987—; chaplain Cedar Spring Hosp., Pineville, N.C., part-time 1989-98; pres. So. Unitarian Coun., Atlanta, 1953, Thomas Jefferson Unitarian Dist., Charlotte, 1963-64; lectr. Albert Schweitzer Coll., Churwalden, Switzerland, summer 1959, Starr King Sch. for Ministry, Berkeley, Calif., summer 1965. Pres. Charlotte Mental Health Assn., 1978-80; chair consulting bd. Cedar Spring Hosp., Pineville, N.C., 1993-98. Recipient Disting. Svc. award Charlotte Mental Health Assn., 1983, Part-time Faculty Excellence award Ctrl. Piedmont C.C., 2005. Mem. Unitarian Universalist Mins. Assn. (past sec.), Charlotte Area Clergy Assn. (past com.). Home: 4500 Rockford Ct Charlotte NC 28209-2924 *I try to live by the truth that sets us free, the hope that never dies, and the love that casts out fear.*

FREEMAN, STACEY VICARIO, director, model; b. Green Bay, Wis., Jan. 6, 1980; d. Anthony Earnest and Deborah Lynn Vicario; m. Jade Everett Freeman, Dec. 30, 2006. BA in English, U. Wis., Wis., 2002; MEd, Ariz. State U., Tempe, 2005. Site dir. YMCA, St. Paul, 2002—04; sr. program coord. Ariz. State U., Phoenix, 2004—; model FORD/Robert Black Agy., Scottsdale, Ariz., 2006—. Singer: (concert choir) U. Wis. Vol. YMCA, Phoenix, 2007, Habitat for Humanity, Miami, 2002, Cath. Charities, New Orleans, 2001. Cmty. Svc. scholar, 1998. Mem.: Nonprofit Congress, Nat. Honor Soc. Liberal. Avocations: travel, shopping, running, weightlifting. Home: 2208 E Flower St Phoenix AZ 85016 Office: Ariz State U 411 N Central Ave Ste 550 Phoenix AZ 85004-0690 Home Phone: 480-203-6150; Office Phone: 602-496-0188. Business E-Mail: stacey.vicario@asu.edu.

FREEMAN, STEVEN M., lawyer; BA, Yale U.; JD, Stanford U. Bar: NY 1981. Dir. legal affairs Anti-Defamation League. Author: Hate Crimes Laws: A Comprehensive Guide, 1994. Office: Anit-Defamation League 605 Third Ave New York NY 10158 Office Phone: 212-885-7743. Office Fax: 212-885-5882.*

FREEMAN, SUSAN TAX, anthropologist, educator, culinary historian; b. Chgo., May 24, 1938; d. Sol and Gertrude Tax; m. Leslie G. Freeman, Jr., Mar. 20, 1964; 1 dau., Sarah Elisabeth. BA, U. Chgo., 1958; MA, Harvard U., 1959, PhD, 1965. Asst. prof. anthropology U. Ill., Chgo., 1965-70, assoc. prof., 1970-78, prof., 1978—, prof. emerita, 1999—, chmn., 1979-82. Rsch. assoc. dept. sociology and anthropology Mont. State U., Bozeman, 1992—; panelist NEH, Council for Internat. Exchange of Scholars; mem. anthropology screening com. Fulbright-Hays Research Awards, 1975-78; mem. ad hoc com. on research in Spain Spain-U.S.A. Friendship Agreement, various yrs., 1977-84; field researcher Mex., 1959, Spain, 1962—, Japan, 1983; instr. Radcliffe Coll. Seminars on Food in History and Culture, 1998. Author: Neighbors: The Social Contract in a Castilian Hamlet, 1970, The Pasiegos: Spaniards in No Man's Land, 1979; assoc. editor: Am. Anthropologist, 1971-73, Am. Ethnologist, 1974-76; editl. bd. Gastronomica, 2000—. Fellow Inst. for the Humanities, U. Ill. Chgo., 1987-88; Wenner-Gren Found. for Anthrop. Research grantee, 1966, 83; NIMH grantee, 1967, 68-71; NEH fellowships , 1978-79, 89-90. Fellow Am. Anthrop. Assn. (nominating com. 1981-82, Centennial Adv. Commn. 1999-2002), Royal Anthrop. Inst. Gt. Britain and Ireland; mem. Soc. for Anthropology of Europe (exec. com. 1987-88), Soc. Spanish and Portuguese Hist. Studies (exec. com. 1990-92), Coun. European Studies (steering com. 1980-83), Internat. Inst. Spain (corporator, bd. dirs. 1982-87, 2000-2003), Centro Estudios Sorianos (hon.), Assn. Anthropologia Castilla y Leon (hon.). Home: PO Box 369 Whitehall MT 59759 Office: U Ill Dept Anthro M/C 027 1007 W Harrison St Chicago IL 60607-7135 Home Phone: 406-490-0866, 773-684-1110; Office Phone: 312-413-3570.

FREEMAN, THEODORE MONROE, physician; b. Orlando, Fla., Jan. 3, 1955; s. Fred Monroe and Mary Ann (Ridgeway) F.; m. Karen Bonaccorso, Aug. 11, 1978; children: Kathryn Maria, Michelle Terese, Jeannine Nicole, Jason Monroe. BS in Chemistry, Duke U., 1977; MD, U. So. Fla., 1980. Diplomate Am. Bd. Internal Medicine, Am. Bd. Allergy and Immunology. Intern Jacksonville (Fla.) U. Hosp., 1980-81; commd. capt. USAF, 1981, advanced through grades to col., resident internal medicine Keesler AFB Biloxi, Miss., 1981-83, staff physician Dyess AFB Abilene, Tex., 1983-84, fellow allergy and immunology Wilford Hall Med. Ctr., Lackland AFB San Antonio, 1984-86, fellow diagnostic lab. immunology Mass. Gen. Hosp. Boston, 1986-87, staff allergist and immunology Wilford Hall Med. Ctr., 1987-89, chmn. dept. allergy and immunology, program dir., 1989—2001. Med. dir. transplants Wilford Hall Med. Ctr., 1989-2002. Contbr. articles to profl. jours. Fellow ACP, Am. Coll. Allergy and Immunology, Am. Acad. Allergy and Immunology; mem. AMA, Soc. Air Force Physicians. Roman Catholic. Office Phone: 210-614-3923. Personal E-mail: tfree95900@aol.com. Business E-Mail: docfreeman@sanantonioallergydoc.com.

FREEMAN, THOMAS E., bank executive; Bank trainee Citibank, 1975, area mgr., regional credit mgr.; mng. dir. corp. strategy and devel. to consumer lending exec. credit officer to dir. portfolio mgmt. to corp. v.p. comml. real estate Fleet Boston Fin.; prin. KPMG; corp. exec. v.p., mem. mgmt. com. SunTrust Banks, Inc., 2006—, chief credit officer, 2006—07, chief risk officer, 2007—. Office: SunTrust Banks Inc PO Box 4418 Atlanta GA 30302-4418 Office Phone: 404-588-7711. Office Fax: 404-827-6173.*

FREEMAN, TOM M., lawyer; b. Wauwatosa, Wis., Oct. 5, 1952; s. Max and Betty J. (Zimmerman) F.; m. Judith Casper, June 23, 1974; children: Sarah Carolyn, Benjamin Robert. BA with honors, U. Wis., 1974; JD cum laude, Harvard U., 1977. Bar: Wis. 1977, Ill. 1978, Calif. 1980, US Dist. Ct. (we. dist.) Wis. 1977, US Ct. Appeals (7th cir.) 1978, US Dist. Ct. (no. dist.) Calif. 1980, US Ct. Appeals (9th cir.) 1982. Law clk. Wis. Supreme Ct., Madison, 1977-78; staff atty. US Ct. Appeals (7th cir.), Chgo., 1978-80; assoc. Brobeck, Phleger, Harrison, LLP, San Francisco, 1980-85, ptnr., 1985—2003, Morgan, Lewis & Bockius LLP, 2003—05; cons. pvt. practice, 2005—. Mem.: Phi Kappa Phi, Phi Beta Kappa. Republican. Jewish. Office: PO Box 63 Lafayette CA 94549 Home Phone: 925-284-1634; Office Phone: 925-283-4877. Business E-Mail: tfreeman@freemanlegal.net.

FREEMAN-CLARK, J. P. LADYHAWK, vicar, underwater exploration, security and transportation executive, model; b. Berkley, Calif., Feb. 21, 1951; d. Gilbert Richard Freeman (dec.) and P.M. (Ann) Raistrick (dec.); children: Jennifer Patricia (dec.), Schne F. (dec.), S. Lancelot (dec.), Simon L.G., Simone D. B., Simba Velvet, Scarlett; m. Joanne Marie Clark-Freeman. BA in English, Davis & Elkins Coll., W.Va., 1973; grad., USAF Air Weapons Controller Sch., Tyndall AFB, Fla., 1973, USAF Air Command and Staff Coll., 1982, U.S. Marine Corps Command and Staff Coll., 1982, Dept. Def. Computer Inst., 1984; M in Aviation Mgmt., Embry-Riddle Aeronautical U., Daytona Beach, Fla., 1986, postgrad., 1986; grad., USAF Air War Coll., Montgomery, Ala., 1988. Cert. EMT; ordained vicar Universal Ch., 2002. Mem. 56th spl. ops. rescue for Southeast Asia NKP Royal Thai Air Force Base, 1974, 75; chief wing radar standardization/evaluation RAF Alconbury, England, 1980-83; commdr. joint U.S. forces Operation Raleigh, 1986; support chief of staff Hdqs. NORAD, Colorado Springs, Colo., 1987-89; dep. base commdr. NATO Hdqs. Allied Forces No. Europe, Norway, 1989-91; chief airport mgmt. divsn. Whiteman AFB, Knob Noster, Mo., 1991-93; dir. spl. projects USAF Acad. Regional Hosp., Colorado Springs, 1993-94; systems performance specialist Colo. Sport & Spine Rehab., Colorado Springs, 1994-95; dir. FLEET Internat. Explorations and Svcs. Co., Colorado Springs, 1995-97; fashion model, 1996—2001; vicar, 2002—. Spl. adv. for anti and counter terrorist security design for 1994 Internat. Olympic Games, Oslo, Norway, 1989-91; designer Automated Provider Credentialing System USAF Acad. Regional Hosp., USAF Acad., Colo., 1993-94; spl. adv. comms. NATO German High Commd., 1977-80; paralyzed Vet. of Am., sr. legist. advocate. U.S. Congress for Colo., Mont. Ut. and Wyo., 2002-05; experience in 37 countries. Author numerous poems. Mem. bd. dirs. Johnson County (Mo.) United Way, 1991-93; surgery life support specialist ARC, USAF Acad. Regional Hosp., 1993-95; mem. nat. scholarship com. Red River Valley Fighter Pilots Assn., 1993-96; hosp. vol., med. technician, provider credentialing system designer, oral surgery life support system specialist. Recipient 53 awards and decorations including Defense Meritorious svc. medal with 1 oak leaf cluster, Meritorious Svc. medal with 2 oak leaf clusters, Joint Svc. Commendation medal with 1 oak leaf cluster, air force commendation medal, Armed Forces Expeditionary medal with 2 bronze stars, 2 Humanitarian Svc. medals, 2 Kuwait Liberation medals, 2 Southwest Asia medals; named Adminstrsn. Officer of Yr. USAF, 1986; named one of the six top Support Officers USAF, 1986-87; 1st woman named dir. Fleet Internat. Mem. VFW, DAV, Am. Legion, Air Force Assn., Soc. of Profl. Journalists, Assn. of Old Crows, Lambda Lambda Lambda, Alpha Phi Omega, Iota Beta Sigma. Mem. United Anglican Ch. Avocations: writing, skiing, horseback riding, painting, music. Home: 5913 Amber Station Ave Las Vegas NV 89131

FREEMARK, MICHAEL SCOTT, pediatric endocrinologist, educator; b. Phila., Dec. 10, 1950; s. Morton and Molly (Blumberg) F.; m. Anne R. Slifkin, May 8, 1979; children: Samara, Yonah. BA magna cum laude, Brandeis U., 1972; postgrad., Temple U., 1972-74; MD, Duke U., 1976. Diplomate Am. Bd. Pediatrics, subspecialty bds. pediatric endocrinology, Nat. Bd. Med. Examiners; lic. physician, N.C. From resident pediatrics to prof. Duke U. Med. Ctr., Durham, NC, 1976—2003, prof. pediats., 2003—, chief pediatric endocrine divsn., 1991—. Moderator Duke Disputation Forum, 2003—; med. dir. Pediatric Clinics, Harnett and Hoke Counties, NC, 1979-80; ad hoc reviewer human embryology and devel. study sect. NIH, 1989-90; dir. weekly endocrine and pediatric fellows rsch. seminars; lectr. in field. Mem. editl. bd.: Jour. Clin. Endocrinology and Metabolism, 1990—93, 2000—, Endocrinology, 1998—; contbr. numerous articles and abstracts to profl. jours. and chpts. to books. Bd. dirs. Durham Nursery Sch. Assn., 1983-88; chmn. People's Alliance Subcom. on Pub. Edn.; mem. Durham County Commn. Merger Issues Task Force, 1988-89; tchr. Triangle Children's Shule, Chapel Hill, N.C., Durham Co. Comm. Child Protection Team, 1994-96. Recipient NIH-Nat. Rsch. Svc. award, 1982-85, NIH Clin. Investigator award, 1985-88, Rsch. award March of Dimes, 1988-92, NIH Rsch. Career Devel. award, 1990—; March of Dimes-Basil O'Connor Starter grantee, 1985-87, Trent Found. grantee, 1984-85, NIH grantee, 1988—; USEPA fellow, 1972, USPHS fellow, 1974, 75, Fogarty fellow, Paris, 1993. Mem. Am. Fedn. Clin. Rsch., N.C. Med. Assn., Am. Acad. Pediatrics, Endocrine Soc., Lawson-Wilkins Pediatric Endocrine Soc. (chair program com. 1991-94, chair drug and therapeutics com. 1999—), Soc. for Pediatric Rsch. (coun. endocrinology, metabolism and nephrology 1991-94). Home: 1309 Oakland Ave Durham NC 27705-3243 Office: Duke Univ Med Ctr PO Box 3080 Durham NC 27710-0001 Home Phone: 919-286-4629; Office Phone: 919-681-1848. Business E-Mail: freem001@mc.duke.edu.

FREENEY, DWIGHT, professional football player; b. Hartford, CT, Feb. 19, 1980; Grad., Syracuse U., 2002. Defensive End Indianapolis Colts, 2002—. Named to NFL Pro Bowl Team, 2003—05, NFL All-Pro Team, 2005. Office: c/o Indianapolis Colts 7001 W 56th St Indianapolis IN 46254

FREENY, KATHERINE H., adult education educator, chemist, researcher; b. Camden, NJ, Apr. 19, 1928; d. Orville G. and Sarah Ide (Embery) Meland; m. Clarence L. Freeny, Oct. 6, 1978; m. John Swered (dec.); children: Lavella Freeny Nixon, Lynn Swered Sundermier, Suzanne Swered Barham, David Taffs. BA, Syracuse U., 1949; MS, U. Pa., 1958. Cert. tchr. N.J., Tex. Sec., 1950—55; rsch. chemist Glaxo Smith Kline, Phila., 1958—63; chemist Borough of Haddonfield (N.J.), 1965—74; tchr. St. Francis Acad., San Antonio, 1976—79, San Antonio Coll., 1976—79, Pub. Sch., Karnes City, Tex., 1984—92; tutor Schreiner U., Kerrville, Tex., 2003—. Tutor Tivy H.S., Kerrville, Tex., 2007—. Income tax preparer AARP, Kerrville, Tex., 1990—; mem. ch. choir Meth. Presbyn., 1940—. Mem.: Am. Volkssport Assn., MENSA. Avocations: hiking, bicycling, clogging, dance, singing. Home (Winter): 5 Loma Linda Dr Kerrville TX 78028 Home (Summer): 111 Gillis Ave Sequim WA 98382

FREER, FRED-CHRISTIAN, artist; b. Cortland, NY, Dec. 17, 1956; s. Fred Austin and Pia-Monica Freer; m. Lisa Ann Wickwar, Nov. 10, 1991; children: Forrest, Connor, Quinn. AAS in Fish and Wildlife, SUNY, Cobleskill, 1977; postgrad., U. Alaska, 1977-83, U. Hawaii, 1980. Cert. nurses asst., Alaska; cert. sport diver Nat. Assn. Underwater Instrs. Carpenter, handyman U. Alaska, Fairbanks, 1977-83; food svc. worker Fairbanks, 1984-93; cook Fairbanks Meml. Hosp., 1994-2000. One-man shows include New Horizons Gallery, Fairbanks, 1993, Gallery Julius, Schweinfurth Meml. Art Ctr., Auburn, N.Y., 1994; exhibited in group shows at Bear Gallery, Fairbanks, 1989, 90, 94, 95, 96, 98, 2002, Mus. History and Art, Anchorage, 1990, New Horizons Gallery, 1992, 93, 94, 95, 96, 98, 2001, Yukon Arts Ctr. Gallery, Whitehorse, Yukon, 2000. Active environ. orgns., Fairbanks Shakespeare Theatre, Fairbanks Children's Theatre. Named Mug Artist of Yr., KUAC TV and Radio, 1994, 2002. Mem. Fairbanks Arts Assn., Ice Art, Inc. (judge 1993—), Alaska Metal Arts Guild. Avocations: horticulture, herpetology, kick-boxing, fencing, music. Office: Full Spectrum Studio 1610 Kennedy St Fairbanks AK 99709

FREER, ROBERT ELLIOTT, JR., lawyer; b. Washington, Jan. 19, 1941; s. Robert E. and Alice (Barry) F.; m. Roberta Stapleton Renchard, Dec. 31, 1972; children: Kimberly Dunlap, R. Elliott III, Ashleigh Hamilton, Daniel Renchard. AB, Princeton U., 1963; JD, U. Va., 1966. Bar: Va. 1966, D.C. 1968, U.S. Supreme Ct. 1973. Trial atty. FTC, 1966-69, atty. advisor to chmn., asst. to gen. counsel, 1969—71; exec. asst. to gen. counsel U.S. Dept. Transp., Washington, 1971-74; Washington counsel Kimberly Clark Corp., 1974-83; staff v.p., 1975-80; corp. v.p., 1980-84; gen. counsel Roswell, Ga., 1983-84; pvt. practice Washington, 1984-2000; corp. cons., 2000—02; founder Free Enterprise Found., 2002—; spl. correspondent Charleston (S.C.) Mercury, 2005—. Mem. President's Commn. on White House Fellowships, 1985-93; pub. mem. Adminstrv. Conf. U.S., 1981-86; capt. land team President's Pvt. Sector Survey on Cost Control in Fedn. Govt., 1982-83; sec., gen. counsel U.S.-Cuba Bus. Coun., 1994-2000; vis. prof. Citadel Sch. Bus. Adminstrn., 2004-, John S. Grinalds leader in residence, 2005-06; adj. faculty Charleston Sch. Law, 2006-. Contbg. author, editor: Finding Our Roots/Facing Our Future: America in the 21st Century, 1997; contbr. columns to papers; contbr. articles to profl. jours. Founder, chmn. bd. trustees Washington Episc. Sch., 1986-94, chmn. emeritus, 1994—; chmn. bd. visitors Regent U. Sch. Law, 1995-2004; trustee Corcoran Gallery Art, 1986-93, asst. sec., chmn. bylaws com., 1990, sec., 1991; trustee, pres. and CEO Free Enterprise Found., 2002—; chmn. Lawyers for the Republic, 1988-2005; asst. gen. counsel Rep. Nat. Conv., 1988, 92, 96; mem. Parents Coun. Coll. Charleston, 1997, 2002, chmn., 2000-02. Mem. Rep. Nat. Lawyers Assn. (bd. govs. 1985-2000, gen. counsel 1985-89, vice chmn. 1988-89), Washington Met. Area Corp. Counsel Assn. (founder, pres. 1980-81, bd. dirs. 1980-84), Rotary Club Charleston. Office: Free Enterprise Found PO Box 21569 Charleston SC 29413 Business E-Mail: robert.freer@citadel.edu.

FREESE, ANDREW, neurosurgeon, educator; b. Boston, July 4, 1959; s. Ernst and Elisabeth (Bautz) F.; m. Marcia Geary, June 14, 1986; children: John Alexander, Elisabeth Marguerite, Ernst Timothy, Matthew Andrew. BA, Harvard U., 1981; MD, Harvard U., Boston, 1990; PhD, MIT, 1990. Lic. physican, Pa.; trauma cert. Rsch. assoc. NIH, Bethesda, Md., 1982-83; surg. intern U. Pa., Phila., 1990-91, neurosurgery resident, 1991-97, dir. Lab. Molecular Neurosurgery Grad. Hosp., 1994-97, mem. Inst. Human Gene Therapy, 1994—97; assoc. prof. neurosurgery, dir. neurosurgery rsch. Thomas Jefferson U., Phila., 1997—2003, vice chmn. neurosurgery, 2000—03, assoc. dir CNS Gene Therapy Ctr., 1998—2002; prof. Drexel U. Coll. Medicine, 2003—04; prof. of neurosurgery U. Minn., 2004—. Vis. scientist Wistar Inst., Phila., 1994-95; pres. Neurel, Inc., Boston, 1987-88, sci. dir., 1988-90; cons. Polykinetix, Inc., N.Y.C., 1993; exec. dir. Parkinson's Disease Gene Therapy Consortium; vice chmn. neurosurgery U. Minn., 2004-, dir. spine surgery, 2004-. Editor: Biotechnology Processing, 1988, Neurological Disorders: Novel Experimental and Therapeutic Approaches, 1992, Principles of Molecular Neurosurgery, 2005; editor spl. issue Exptl. Neurology, 1997; contbr. articles to profl. jours. Fellow Sigma Xi; mem. AMA, Internat. Brain Rsch. Orgn., Soc. Neurosci., Congress Neurol. Surgeons, Controlled Release Soc. Achievements include patents for controlling the release of drugs using drug delivery system for neurological disorders; one of the first viral vector systems to deliver genes into neurons; the demonstration of the precursor effect on brain kynurenines; gene therapy for Parkinson's disease, epilepsy, pituitary adenomas, neurogenetic disorders, and stroke. Home: 2914 Casco Poin Rd Wayzata MN 55391 Office: Dept Neurosurgery Univ of Minnesota 420 Delaware St SE Mayo Memorial Bldg Minneapolis MN 55455

FREESE, CAROLYN LEE, art educator; b. Chgo., Apr. 4, 1947; d. Allen F and Ruth M McKee; children: Jewel, Philip. BSc in Edn., No. Ill. U., 1969. Cert. tchr. Ill. Art tchr. Simmons Jr. H.S., Auroroa, Ill., 1969—72; sub. tchr. Moose Heart Sch., 1986—87; art tchr. Yorkville Dist. H.S., 1988—; contractor edn. dept. Chgo. Field Mus., 2002—. Visual art curriculum developer Yorkville Dist. 115, 1990—. Pub. artwork, Nat. History Mag., Nature, Papers in Paleontology, exhibitions include Norris Gallery, St. Charles, Ill., 2004, Ariz. Sonora Desert Mus., Ironwood Gallery, Tucson, 2004, Orleans St. Gallery, St. Charles, 2004, Sprague Gallery, Joliet, Ill., 2005, Ill. Artisans Gallery, 1998—, Anti-Cruelty Soc., Chgo., 2003, 2005, 2006, James R. Thompson Ctr. Atrium, 2004, 2005, 2006, NY State Mus., Albany, 2006; art contbr. Life over Time exhibit, Chgo. Field Mus., 2001—04. Choir and Sunday sch. tchr. Congl. Ch., 1984—99. Named Educator of the Month, Coca-Cola Co., 1995, Most Influential Educator, Yorkville HS Students, 1996, 1997, 1998, 2001, 2002, 2005, 2007, Tchr. of Yr., 2006; recipient, 2007. Mem.: Ill. Artisans Program, Guild of Natural Sci. Illustrators, Ill. Art Edn. Assn. Avocations: horseback riding, birdwatching, paleontology. Home: P O Box 259 400 Washington St Serena IL 60549 Office: Yorkville HS 797 Gamefarm Rd Yorkville IL 60560

FREESE, MELANIE LOUISE, librarian, educator; b. Mineola, NY, May 12, 1945; d. Walter Christian and Agnes Elizabeth (Jensen) F. BS in Elem. Edn., Hofstra U., 1967, MA in Elem. Edn., 1969; MLS, L.I. U., 1977. Cert. tchr., N.Y. Bibliographic searcher acquisitions dept. Adelphi U. Swirbul Libr., Garden City, NY, 1973—79, res. desk libr., 1979—83; catalog libr., assoc. prof. Hofstra U. Axinn Libr., Hempstead, NY, 1984—, asst. dean, chair libr. tech. svcs., 1998—2000, sr. cataloger, 2000—. Ch. librarian St. Peters Evang. Luth. Ch., Baldwin, N.Y., 1977—. Founder libr. Salvation Army Wayside Home and Sch. for Girls, Valley Stream, N.Y., 1993. Mem. ALA, Nassau County Libr. Assn. (corr. sec. acad. and spl. librs. divsn. 1986-88, v.p., pres.-elect 1989-90, pres. 1991), Bus. and Profl. Women's Club (pres. Nassau County chpt. 1990-92, 95-97, Woman of Yr. 1994). Republican. Avocations: needlecrafts, knitting, crocheting. Office: Hofstra U Axinn Library 1000 Fulton Ave Hempstead NY 11550-1030 Office Phone: 516-463-6423. Business E-Mail: melanie.l.freese@hofstra.edu.

FREGLY, B. J., engineering educator; s. Leo George and Shirley Joyce Fregly; m. Shirley Shek Fregly, Sept. 22, 1990; children: Christopher Daniel, Rachel Elisabeth. BSc in Mech. and Aerospace Engring. with high honors, Princeton U., 1986; MSc in Mech. Engring., Stanford U., 1987, PhD in Mech. Engring., 1993. Post-doctoral fellow U. Lyon, France, 1993—94; R&D engr. Parametric Tech. Rasna Corp., San Jose, Calif., 1995—99; asst. prof. U. Fla., Gainesville, 1999—2005, assoc. prof., 2005—, chair, grad. recruiting and admissions, dept. mech. and aerospace engring., 2005—. Exec. bd. mem., tech. group computer simulation Internat. Soc. Biomechanics, 2005—. Creator (exhibitions) Mus. Sci. and Industry, Tampa, Fl, 2005. Soccer coach Gainesville Country Day Sch., 2005—06; elder Creekside Cmty. Ch., Gainesville, 2005—. Recipient Faculty Early Career Devel. award, NSF, 2003—; Chateaubriand Post-Doctoral fellowship, French Govt., 1993—94. Mem.: ASME (mem. new directions com., bioengineering divsn. 2006—), Am. Soc. Biomechanics. Avocations: hiking, travel. Office: Univ Florida 231 MAE A Bldg Box 116250 Gainesville FL 32611 Office Phone: 352-392-8157. Office Fax: 352-392-7303. Business E-Mail: fregly@ufl.edu.

FREHM, LYNNE, painter; One-woman shows include Bruce Mus., Greenwich, Conn., 1974, Ruth Siegel Gallery, NYC, 1991, Andre Zarre Gallery, 1996, 2002, Exhibit A Gallery, 2000, exhibited in group shows at Yale U., New Haven, 1968, Fed. Courthouse, NYC Orgn. Ind. Artists, 1977, Landmark Gallery, NYC, 1978, Attitude Art Gallery, 1987, Blondies Contemporary Art, 1991—94, Allan Stone Gallery, 1995, Beatrice Conde Gallery, 1997, The Fanelli Show, OK Harris Gallery, NYC, 1998, 181st Ann.: An Invitational Exhib. Contemporary Art, Nat. Acad. Mus., NYC, 2006, prin. works include Black Sails, 1975—78, Life Mask, 1990, Secret Places, 1995—96, Night Sail, 1997, Grain of Rice, 2001—02, Ghosts Over Manhattan, 2001—02, NY Abstract Painter Interview, Biddington's Contemporary Art. Studio: 108 Wooster St Studio 3G New York NY 10012-5232

FREHNER, PATRICIA ANN, education educator, consultant; d. Arlen Joseph and Kenna Bowman Frehner. BA in Art History, U. Utah, Salt Lake City, 1981; MEd, Chapman U., Orange, Calif., 1992; MA in Edn. Adminstrn., Chapman U., 2001; PhD, Capella U., Mpls., 2004. Cert. Pub. Sch. Educator/Adminstr. State Ariz., 1992. Mid. sch. educator Cartwright Sch. Dist., Phoenix, 1992—2005; staff devel. specialist Cartwright Sch. Dist.- Estrella, Phoenix, 2005—. Ednl. cons. Frehner Consulting, Phoenix, 2004—; adj. prof. Ottawa U. Phoenix Ctr., 1995—. One-man shows include exhibition Exhibit 'A' Mask Images, The Faces of Illusion, Sumi-e and Ikebana, Masks, The Universality of Paper; author: (handbook) Training the Para-educator For the Classroom, Transitional Bilingual Guide for School Districts. Recipient Educator's Award, Wells Fargo Bank, 1997. Mem.: Nat. Assn. Bilingual Edn., Nat. Mid. Sch. Assn., Am. Fedn. Tchrs. (assoc.; Ariz. exec. v.p. 1996). Democrat-Npl. Achievements include research in Developing and implementing acitivities for connecting schools and families in the task of educating children; development of Educational series for educators working with Second Language Learners. Office: Cartwright Sch Dist- Estrella 3733 North 75th Ave Phoenix AZ 85033 Home Phone: 602-938-7365. E-mail: tfrehner@estr.cartwright.k12.az.us.

FREI, BRENT R., computer software executive; BS in Engring., Dartmouth Coll., NH, 1989, MS. Mech. engr. Motorola Corp., 1989-90; progammer analyst Microsoft Info. Tech. Group, 1991-94; dir. ONYX, 1994—, pres., sec., treas., 1995-98, pres., CEO, Chmn., 1998—.

FREI, EMIL, III, physician, educator, researcher; b. St. Louis, 1924; m. Elizabeth Smith (dec. Apr. 1986); children: Mary, Emil, Alice, Nancy, Judy; m. Adoria Smetana Brock, May 1987; stepchildren: Stephen, Francis, Peter, Vincent, John. MD, Yale U., 1948. Diplomate Am. Bd. Internal Medicine, Am. Bd. Med. Oncology. Intern St. Louis U. Hosp., 1948—49; resident in pathology Barnes Hosp., St. Louis, 1952—53; resident in internal medicine St. Louis U., 1953—54, VA Hosp., St. Louis, 1954—55; chief gen. medicine br. Nat. Cancer Inst., Bethesda, Md., 1955—65; head devel. therapeutics, assoc. dir. M.D. Anderson Hosp. and Tumor Inst., Houston, 1965—72; dir., physician-in-chief Children's Cancer Research Found. (now Dana-Farber Cancer Inst.), Boston, 1972—91; physician-in-chief emeritus Dana-Farber Cancer Inst., 1991—; prof. medicine Med. Sch. Harvard U., Boston, 1972—, Richard and Susan Smith prof. medicine, 1985, Richard and Susan Smith disting. prof. medicine, 1994—; nat. cons. in internal medicine-oncology USAF, 1968—72; mem. Eleanor Roosevelt internat. cancer fellowships com. Internat. Union Against Cancer, 1968—72; chmn. anti-neoplastic disease drug panel, drug efficacy study NAS, 1968—72; nat. cons. in internal medicine-oncology USAF. Mem. bd. sci. counselors Nat. Cancer Inst., 1986—90, mem. Presdl. Commn. for New Drugs for Cancer and AIDS, 1988—90; chmn. antitumor drug panel NAS, 1996. Lt. M.C. USNR, 1950—52. Recipient Lasker award, 1972, Lila W. Gruber award, 1979, Kettering prize, GM, 1983, Hamao Umezawa award, 1985, Armand Hammer Cancer Rsch. award, 1989, Disting. Alumnus award, NIH, 1990, Emil Frei III professorship in medicine, 1992, Morse award, 1996, Sidney Farber medal for contbns. to cancer rsch., 1998, 50th Anniversary Commemorative award, Leukemia Soc. Am., 1999, La Medaille de la Ville de Paris, 2000, Claude Jacquillat award, 2002, Pollin prize in pediatric rsch., 2003, Lifetime Achievement in Cancer Rsch., Am. Assn. Cancer Rsch., 2004. Fellow: ACP, Am. Acad. Arts and Scis.; mem.: AMA, Icon of Oncology (mem. 2003), Nat. Acad. Medicine, Inst. of Medicine, Assn. Am. Physicians, Am. Soc. Clin. Investigation, Am. Soc. Hematology, Am. Cancer Soc. (ann. Nat. award 1981), Am. Soc. Clin. Oncology (pres. 1968—69, Disting. Scientist award 1992), Am. Assn. for Cancer Rsch. (past pres., Lifetime Achievement in Cancer Rsch. award 2004). Office: Dana Farber Cancer Inst Physician in Chief emeritus D-1618 44 Binney St Boston MA 02115-6084

FREIBERG, ROBERT JERRY, engineering executive; b. Chgo., Mar. 26, 1939; s. Jerry and Mildred (Lukes) F.; m. Deanna Corrine Qualls, July 8, 1968; children: Joseph, Sean, Jamison. BS in Physics, Rensselear Poly. Inst., 1961; MS in Physics, U. Ill., 1963, PhD, 1966. Postgrad. rsch. assoc. U. Ill., Urbana, 1966-67; rsch. scientist Hughes Rsch. Labs., Malibu, Calif., 1967-69; group mgr. United Tech. Rsch. Labs., East Hartford, Conn., 1969-75; gen. mgr. United Tech. Optical Sys., West Palm Beach, Fla., 1975-79; bus. mgr. optics TRW, Redondo Beach, Calif., 1979-83; program dir. Baxter Healthcare, Inc., Irvine, Calif., 1983-86; dir. engring. and mfg. ops. Pfizer Laser Sys., Irvine, 1986-92; dir. engring. Lumonics, Inc., Camarillo, Calif., 1992-94; sr. v.p. engring. and program mgmt. View Engring., Inc., Simi Valley, Calif., 1994-97; v.p. engring. Indsl. Electronic Engrs. Inc., Van Nuys, Calif., 1997-2000; v.p. engr. Knowledge Universe, Inc., Los Gatos, Calif., 2000—02; gen. ptnr. Internat. Mktg. and Cons. Assocs., Kalispell, Mont., 2000—, sr. tech. cons., 2000—. Chmn. tech. adv. bd. Premier Laser Sys., Irvine, 1991-92; bd. dir. SurgiLight, Orlando, Fla., 2001-07; presenter in field. Contbr. numerous articles to Procs. IEEE, Laser Focus, Applied Optics, IEEE Jour. Quantum Electronics, Jour. Applied Physics, Phys. Rev., Applied Physics Letters, Bull. Am. Phys. Soc. Asst. scoutmaster Boy Scouts Am., Mission Viejo, Calif., 1989-92, varsity scoutmaster, Newbury Park, Calif., 1994-96. Fellow NSF, 1962-66. Fellow Internat. Soc. for Optical Engring. (mem. membership com. 1994-99, chmn. 1994-96); mem. IEEE, Am. Electronics Assn., Optical Soc. Am., Am. Soc. for Laser Surgery and Medicine, Nat. Ctr. Mfg. Scis. (Strategic Initiative Group com. 1995-97), Soc. Info. Displays, Sigma Xi. Achievements include numerous patents for surgical lasers, endoscopic instrumentation, medical catheters, novel optical resonators, laser devices, and diagnostic instruments. Home: 112 River View Dr Kalispell MT 59901 Personal E-mail: rjfreiberg@netscape.net.

FREIBERG, STEVEN J., diversified financial services company executive; m. Neena Freiberg; 2 children. BS in Econs., MBA. Mgmt. assoc. card products divsn. Citigroup Inc., 1980, mktg., bus. planning, mgmt. scis. and fin. positions, 1980—85, CFO, 1985—87; founding dir., CFO, chief investment officer, nat. sales dir. Citicorp Investment Svcs., 1987—92, mem. corp.-wide task force, 1992—93; mgr. distbn. Consumer Bank, 1993—95; CEO Citicorp Investment Svcs., Citicorp Ins. Group, 1995—97; mgr. strategic bus. groups credit card divsn. Citigroup Inc., 1997—2000, pres., CEO Citi Cards N. Am., 2000—05, co-CEO Global Consumer Group, 2005—, CEO N.Am. ops., 2005—. Bd. dirs. Citicorp Credit Svcs., Inc., Citicorp Investment Svcs., Citicorp Ins. Group, Citibank Trust N.A., Citibank FS.B, MasterCard, DMA, NYU Mgmt. Decision Lab., MasterCard Inc. Office: Citigroup Inc 399 Park Ave New York NY 10043*

FREIBERGER, WALTER FREDERICK, mathematics professor; b. Vienna, Feb. 20, 1924; came to U.S., 1955, naturalized, 1962. s. Felix and Irene (Tagany) F.; m. Christine Mildred Holmberg, Oct. 6, 1956; children: Christopher Allan, Andrew James, Nils H. BA, U. Melbourne, 1947, MA, 1949; PhD, U. Cambridge, Eng., 1953. Rsch. officer Aero. Rsch. Lab. Australian Dept. Supply, 1947-49, sr. sci. rsch. officer, 1953-55; tutor U. Melbourne, 1947-49, 53-55; asst. prof. divsn. applied math. Brown U., 1956-58, assoc. prof., 1958-64, prof., 1964—2002; prof. applied math., prof. cmty. health Brown U. Med. Sch., 1994—2002; prof. emeritus applied math., cmty. health Brown U., Brown Med. Sch., 2002—; dir. Computing Center Brown U., 1963-69, dir. Ctr. for Computer and Info. Scis., 1969-76, chmn. divsn. applied math., 1976-82, chmn. grad. com., 1985-88, assoc. chmn. divsn. applied math., 1988-91, chmn. univ. ctr. for statis. sci., 1991—2002, prof. applied math. (rsch.); joint appointment Brown U. Med. Sch., 1994—2002; prof. emeritus cmty. health and applied math. Brown U. and The Warren Alpert Med. Sch. of Brown U., 2002—. Fmr. lectr., cons. program in applied actuarial sci. Bryant Coll.; joint appointment as prof. cmty. health Sch. Medicine Brown U., 1994-2002; mem. fellowship selection panel NSF, Fulbright fellowship selection panel; mem. Rep. Nat. Com. Author: (with U. Grenander) A Short Course in Computational Probability and Statistics, 1971; editor: The International Dictionary of Applied Mathematics, 1960, (with others) Applications of Digital Computers, 1963, Advances in Computers, Volume 10, 1970, Statistical Computer Performance Evaluation, 1972; mng. editor: Quarterly of Applied Mathematics, 1965—; Contbr. numerous articles to profl. jours. Served with Australian Army, 1943-45. Fulbright fellow, 1955-56; Guggenheim fellow, 1962-63; grantee NSF Office Naval Rsch. NIH. Mem. Am. Math. Soc. (assoc. editor Math. Reviews 1957-62), Soc. for Indsl. and Applied Math., Am. Statis. Assn., Inst. Math. Stats., Assn. Computing

Machinery, Bristol Yacht Club, Univ. Club Providence. Republican. Anglican. Home: 24 Alumni Ave Providence RI 02906-2310 Office: Box F Brown U 182 George St Providence RI 02912-9056 Business E-Mail: Walter_Freiberger@Brown.edu.

FREIDBERG, STEPHEN ROY, neurosurgeon; b. Bklyn., Oct. 16, 1934; s. Leslie Max and Bess Bernblum; m. Helen Deorsay, May 1, 1964; children: Michael, Jonathan. AB, U. Pa., Phila., 1956; MD, Albert Einstein Coll., 1960. Intern U. Okla. Hosp., 1960-61; resident King's County Hosp., Bklyn., 1964-68; fellow Nat. Hosp. Queen's Sq., London, 1965; staff physician Lahey Clinic Med. Ctr., Burlington, Mass., 1969—, chmn. divsn. surgery, 1995—2003. Chmn. dept. neurosurgery Lahey Clinic Med. Ctr., Burlington, 1984-2005, bd. govs., 1978-2003. Contbr. articles to profl. jours. Capt. U.S. Army, 1962-64. Mem. Am. Assn. Neurol. Surgeons, Congress Neurol. Surgeons, New Eng. Neurosurg. Soc. (pres. 1981-83), Mass. Med. Soc. Jewish. Avocations: hiking, skiing. Office: Lahey Clinic Med Ctr 41 Mall Rd Burlington MA 01805-0002 Home Phone: 781-891-9164; Office Phone: 781-744-8643. Business E-Mail: stephen.r.freidberg@lahey.org.

FREIDEL, DAVID ALAN, archaeologist, anthropologist, educator; b. July 11, 1946; m. Carolyn Freidel; 2 children. BA, Harvard U., 1968, PhD, 1976. From adj. asst. prof. to prof. anthropology So. Meth. U., Dallas, 1974—, acting chair Anthropology Dept., 1999, Univ. Disting. prof. archaeology, 2003—; archeologist Selz Found. Yazuna Project, 1986—97; field rschr. Waká Archeol. Project, Peten, Guatemala, 2003—. Co-author: Cozumel: Late Maya Settlement Systems, 1984, A Forest of Kings, 1990 (Gambrinus Guiseppe Mazzotti Lit. Prize, 2001), Maya Cosmos: Three Thousand Years on the Sharman's Path, 1993; contbr. articles to profl. jours. Office: So Meth U 6425 Boaz Lane Dallas TX 75205 Office Phone: 214-768-2000. E-mail: dfreidel@mail.smu.edu.

FREIDHEIM, CYRUS F., JR., publishing and former food products executive; b. Chgo., June 14, 1935; s. Cyrus F. and Eleanor Freidheim; m. Marguerite VandenBosch; children: Marguerite Lynn, Stephen Cyrus, Scott. BSChE, U. Notre Dame, 1957; MBA, Carnegie Mellon U., 1963; Dr of Internat. Laws (hon.), Am. Grad. Sch. Internat. Mgmt., 1999. Plant mgr. Union Carbide Corp., Whiting, Ind., 1961; cons. Price Waterhouse, Chgo., 1962; fin. analyst Ford Motor Co., Dearborn, Mich., 1963-66; vice chmn. Booz, Allen & Hamilton, Chgo., 1966—2002; chmn. Chiquita Brands Internat., Inc., Cincinnati, 2002—04, CEO, 2002—04; pres., CEO Sun-Times Media Group Inc., Chgo., 2006—. Bd. dirs. HSBC Finance Corp., Inc., Allegheny Energy, Inc., The Sun Times Media Group, Inc., Virgin Am., Inc. Author: The Trillion Dollar Enterprise, 1998. Trustee Thunderbird, The Garvin Sch. Internat. Mgmt.; dir. Chgo. Coun. Global Affairs; trustee Rush U. Med. Ctr., 1981—; life trustee Chgo. Symphony Orch.; trustee Brookings Instn., 1998—; mem. adv. coun. Mendoza Sch. of Bus. U. Notre Dame, 2005—. With USN, 1957-61. Mem. Coun. Fgn. Rels., Chgo. Club, Econ. Club, Comml. Club, Racquet Club, Stanwich Club, Old Elm Club, Shoreacres Club, Lost Tree Club, The Bears Club. Office: Sun Times Media Group Inc 350 N Orleans St Chicago IL 60654 Home Phone: 561-799-6662.

FREIDHEIM, SCOTT J., investment company executive; BA, Northwestern U., 1987, MBA, 1991. With Lehman Bros. Holdings, 1991—, chief of staff to chmn. and CEO, 1996, global head corp. comm., mktg. and brand strategy, 2003—07, global head strategy, 2005—07, exec. v.p., co-chief adminstrv. officer, 2006—. Co-founder, chmn. New Leaders Group Inst. Internat. Edn.; mem. Forum of Young Global Leaders World Econ. Forum; mem. Econ. Club NY; mem. exec. adv. bd. Sponsors for Ednl. Opportunity. Office: Lehman Bros Holdings 745 Seventh Ave New York NY 10019 Office Phone: 212-526-7000.*

FREIER, ELLIOT G., lawyer; b. Huntington, NY, Apr. 2, 1961; s. Walter and Sondra J. Freier; children: Matthew V., Aaron M. BA in Econs., U. Va., 1983; JD, Yale U., 1986. Bar: Calif. 1986. Assoc. Irell & Manella LLP, LA, 1986—92, ptnr., 1993—; prin. The Roy Funds, LLC, 2005—. Adv. bd. The M&A Tax Report, 1992—96. Mem. editl. adv. bd.: Mergers and Acquisitions: The Monthly Tax Jour., 2000—03. Named to Am.'s Leading Lawyers, Chambers USA, Who's Who Legal, Best Lawyers in Am. Mem.: ABA (chmn. affiliated and related corps. com. 1996—97, tax sect.), Phi Beta Kappa. Avocations: tennis, skiing. Office: Irell & Manella LLP Ste 900 1800 Avenue of The Stars Los Angeles CA 90067 E-mail: efreier@irell.com.

FREIFELD, ALICE, history professor; d. Sal and Vera Freifeld; m. Peter Edward Bergmann, Aug. 0, 1979; children: Max Aaron Bergmann, Benjamin Zoltan Bergmann. PhD, U. Calif., Berkeley, 1992. Assoc. prof. U. Fla., Gainesville, 1994—. Author: (history book) Nationalism and the Crowd in Liberal Hungary (Barbara Jelavich Book prize, AAASS, 2001); co-editor: East Europe Reads Nietzsche. Mem.: Hungarian Studies Assn. (pres. 2006—). Office: Univ Fla Keene-Flint Hall Gainesville FL 32611 Home Phone: 352-377-7046.

FREIHEIT, CLAYTON FREDRIC, zoo director; b. Buffalo, Jan. 29, 1938; s. Clayton John and Ruth (Miller) F. Student, U. Buffalo, 1960; DHL (hon.), U. Denver, 1996. Caretaker Living Mus., Buffalo Mus. Sci., 1955-60; curator Buffalo Zool. Gardens, 1960-70; dir. Denver Zool. Gardens, 1970—. Contbr. articles to profl. jours. Named Outstanding Citizen, Buffalo Evening News, 1967 Mem. Internat. Union Dirs. Zool. Gardens, Am. Assn. Zool. Pks. and Aquariums (pres. 1967-68 Outstanding Svc. award). Home: 3855 S Monaco Pky Denver CO 80237-1271 Office: Denver Zool Gardens City Park Denver CO 80205 Business E-Mail: zoodirector@denverzoo.org.

FREILICH, DANIEL ADAM, epidemiologist; s. Theodore and Anne D. Freilich; children: Ariel Avram, Tamara Robyn Freililch, Leah Morgan, Joshua Doron. BA, Cornell U., Ithaca, NY, 1985; MD, SUNY, Bkyln., 1989. Lic. NY, 1990. Med. intern Albany Med. Ctr., NY, 1989—90; gen. med. officer USS Coronado AGF11, Pearl Harbor, Hawaii, 1990—92; internal medicine resident U. Vt., Burlington, 1992—94; pvt. practice Jeffersonville, Vt., 1994—98; infectious diseases fellow Naval Med. Ctr., San Diego, 1998—2000, infectious diseases attending, 2000—, malaria rschr. Silver Spring, Md., 2000—02, trauma medicine and bioterrorism rschr., 2002—. Infectious diseases attending Walter Reed Army Med. Ctr., Washington, 2000—; infectious and tropical diseases educator Uniformed Services U. Health Sci., Bethesda, Md., 2000—. Contbr. articles to profl. jours. Comdr. USN, 1990—97. Decorated Naval Achievement medal US Navy, Naval Commendation medal; grantee, Baxter Healthcare, 1997, Hemosol Inc., 1998, Hollis Eden Pharm., 1999, MIDRP, US Army, 2001—02, Office of Naval Rsch. and Bur. Medicine and Surgery, 2002—07, Dept. of Def. Challenge, 2005. Democrat-Npl. Avocations: skiing, travel. Office: Naval Med Rsch Ctr 503 Robert Grant Ave Silver Spring MD 20910-7500 Home Phone: 301-233-9789; Office Phone: 301-319-7152. Office Fax: 301-319-3161. Business E-Mail: freilichd@nmrc.navy.mil.

FREILICHER, JANE, artist; b. NYC, Nov. 29, 1924; d. Martin and Bertha (Niederhoffer); m. Joseph Hazan, Feb. 17, 1957; 1 dau., Elizabeth. AB, Bklyn. Coll., 1947; postgrad., Hans Hoffman Sch. Fine Arts, 1947; MA, Columbia U., 1948. Vis. lectr., critic art schs., colls. One-woman shows include Tibor de Nagy, 1952-68, 98, 2000, 02, 04, 05, 06, John Bernard Myers Gallery, 1971, Fischbach Gallery, 1975, 77, 79-80, 83, 85, 88, 90, 92, 95, Utah Mus. Fine Arts, 1979, Lafayette Coll., 1981, Kansas City Art Inst., 1983, David Heath Gallery, Atlanta, 1990, Reynolds Gallery, Richmond, Va., 1993, Nat. Acad., 2002; group exhbns. include Met. Mus. Art, 1979-80, Denver Art Mus., 1979, Pa. Acad., 1981, Am. Acad. and Inst. of Arts and Letters, 1981, 84-85, Bklyn. Mus. 1984, Yale U., 1986, Tibor de Nagy Gallery, 1992, Whitney Mus., 1955, 72, 95, Whitney Mus., Stamford, Conn., 1999, Artists Eye NAD, 2002, Women of Acad. NAD, 2003; curator Nat. Acad., 2002; represented in permanent collections Met. Mus. Art, Hirschorn Mus., Bklyn. Mus., NYU, Rose Art Mus., Whitney Mus., Cleve. Mus. Art, San Francisco Mus. Art, others; travelling retrospective in Currier Gallery Art, Parrish Mus., Contemporary Arts Mus., McNay Mus., 1986-87; illustrator Turandot and Other Poems, 1953, Paris Review, 1965, Descriptions of a Masque, 1998; work featured in Jane Freilicher by Klaus Kertess, Tom Noskovsky, John Ashbery, 2004. Recipient Eloise Spaeth award Guild Hall Mus., East Hampton, N.Y., 1991, Lifetime Achievement award Guild Hall Mus., 1996; AAUW fellow, 1974; Nat. Endowment Arts grantee, 1976; Benjamin West Clinedinst Meml. medal Artists' Fellowship, 1997. Mem. NAD (academician) (Saltus Gold medal 1987, Benjamin Altman landscape prize 1995, Edwin Palmer prize 2003), Am. Acad. Arts and Letters (Gold medal 2005).

FREILICHER, MORTON, lawyer, educator; b. NYC, June 23, 1931; s. Morris and Gertrude D. (Pedowitz) F.; m. Yseult A. Snepvangers, Dec. 3, 1972. BA, Columbia Coll., NYC, 1953, JD, 1956. Bar: N.Y. 1957. Assoc. Hartman & Craven, NYC, 1956-60, Phillips, Nizer LLP, NYC, 1960-67, ptnr., 1967-94, counsel, 1995—. Adj. prof. Law Sch. Fordham U., N.Y.C., 1982-92. Author: Estate Planning Handbook, 1970; editor-in-chief Jour. of Estate and Tax Planning for the Elderly and Disabled, 1986-91. Chmn. trusts and estates lawyers divsn. UJA Fedn., 1985; dir. The Edouard Found., 1996—. Harlan Fiske Stone scholar Columbia Law Sch., 1956. Fellow Am. Coll. Trusts and Estates Counsel; mem. ABA, N.Y. State Bar Assn., N.Y.C. Bar Assn. Avocations: hiking, exercise, reading. Home: 200 E 57th St New York NY 10022 Office: Phillips Nizer et al 666 5th Ave New York NY 10103-0001

FREIMAN, CHARLES VISVALD, retired engineering foundation administrator; b. NYC, June 17, 1932; s. John and Selma Marie (Pupurin) F.; m. Margaret Carol Messerschmidt, June 5, 1955; children: Paul, Katherine, Barbara, John. AB, Columbia Coll., 1954; BS, Columbia U., 1955, MS, 1956, EngScD, 1961. Adj. instr. NYU and U. Conn., NYC and Stamford, 1963-65; instr. in elec. engring. Columbia U., NYC, 1956-60; mgr. IBM R & D, various locations, 1960-84, IBM Computer Sci. Inst., Tokyo, 1985-87, IBM Corp. Artificial Intelligence Project Office, White Plains, NY, 1987-89; sec. IBM Acad. of Tech., Armonk, NY, 1989-90; dir. Engring. Found., NYC, 1990—98; exec. dir. United Engring. Found., NYC, 1998—2002. Program chair U.S. Com. for IFIP Congresses, 1971, 74, 77; steering com. Nat. Rsch. Coun., Japanese-English Machine Translation, Washington DC, 1989-90; v.p. JETS, Alexandria, Va., 1997—; computer engring. program evaluator Accreditation Bd. for Engring. & Tech., N.Y.C., 1988-91; lectr. in field. Editor: Information Processing '71, 1971; contbr. articles to profl. jours. and conference proceedings. Chmn. United Fund, Pleasantville, N.Y., 1962; pres., treas. Luth. Congregations, N.Y., Calif., Japan, 1961—; vice-chmn. Com. on Housing for the Elderly, Pleasantville, 1968-84. Pulitzer scholar Columbia U., N.Y.C., 1950-54; Goodrich prize Columbia U., 1952; named Man of the Yr. Emanuel Evangelical Luth. Ch., Pleasantville, 1984. Mem. IEEE (sr. mem., life), N.Y. Acad. Scis., AAAS, Assn. for Computing Machinery, Sigma Xi, Tau Beta Pi, Eta Kappa Nu. Democrat. Achievements include 10 U.S. patents and author of 25 patent publications for high performance computers and protective coding. Personal E-mail: freimans@nc.rr.com.

FREIMARK, JEFFREY PHILIP, corporate financial executive; b. Bklyn., Mar. 11, 1955; s. Benjamin and Fay (Lefton) F.; m. Hollis Joan Hauser, Aug. 27, 1978; children: Samara, Brandon. BS, U. So. Fla., 1976; MBA, NYU, 1980; JD, N.Y. Law Sch., 1984. Bar: N.J. 1985; CPA, N.J., Fla. Sr. staff acct. Abraham and Straus, Bklyn., 1976-78; internal audit dir. Stern's Dept. Store, Paramus, NJ, 1978-79; dir. acctg. Kings Super Markets, West Caldwell, NJ, 1979-82, controller, 1982-83, controller, sec., 1983-84, v.p. fin., 1985-86; sr. v.p. fin. and adminstrn., chief fin. officer, treas., dir. PXC & M Holdings Inc./Pueblo Xtra Internat. (formerly Pueblo Internat. Inc.), Pompano Beach, Fla., 1986-91, exec. v.p., chief fin. officer, sec., 1992-97; exec. v.p., CFO, sec., dir. Pueblo Xtra Internat., Inc., Pompano Beach, Fla., 1993-97, PXC&M, Inc., Pompano Beach, 1993-97; exec. v.p., CFO, chief adminstrv. officer, treas., dir. The Grand Union Co., 1997—2000, pres., CEO, CFO, 2000—01; sr. exec. v.p., CFO OfficeMax, Inc., 2001—; exec. v.p., CFO, CIO Beverly Enterprises, Inc., Fort Smith, Ariz., 2002—06; exec. v.p., CFO Intelsat, Pembroke, Bermuda, 2006—. Vol. dir. NYU Grad. Sch. Bus. Mgmt. Decision Lab., 1980-81. Mem. ABA, N.J. Bar Assn., Am. Inst. CPA's, Fla. Soc. CPA's, N.J. Soc. CPA's, Assn. MBA Execs., Fin. Execs. Inst. Republican. Jewish. Avocations: reading, tennis, golf. Office: Intelsat 2d Fl Wellesley House N 90 Pitts Bay Rd Pembroke HM 08 Bermuda Office Phone: 202-944-7222. Business E-Mail: jeff.freimark@intelstat.com.

FREIMARK, ROBERT (BOB), artist; b. Doster, Mich., Jan. 27, 1922; s. Alvin O. and Nora (Shinaver) F.; m. Mary Carvin (dec.); 1 child, Matisse Jon; m. Lillian Tihlarik (dec. 2005); 1 child, Christine Gay. B.E., U. Toledo, 1950; M.F.A., Cranbrook Acad. Art, 1951. Prof. art emeritus San Jose State U., 1964-86; W.I.C.H.E. prof. Soledad State Prison, 1967. Established artist in residence program Yosemite Nat. Park,1984-85, Fire Clay and Tile, Aromas, Calif., 1998; artist in residence Museo Regla, Cuba, 2000, Ferencsik Janos Zeneskola, L. Balaton, Hungary, 2002; panelist SECOLAS S.E. conf. Latin Am. Studies, Vera Cruz, Mex., NC U., Santa Domingo. Guest artist Harvard U., 1972-73; first Am. to make tapestries in Art Protis technique at Atelier Vlnena, Brno, Czechoslovakia.; contbr. to profl. publs.; One-man shows include Northamerican Cultural Inst., Mexico City, 1963, Minn. Inst. Arts, Toledo Mus. Art, Salpeter Gallery, Morris Gallery, NYC, Des Moines Art Ctr., Santa Barbara Mus., Moravska Mus., Czechoslovakia, Brunel U., London, Amerika Haus, Munich, Stuttgart, Regensburg, Joslyn Ctr. for Arts, Torrance, Calif, Stanford U., San Jose (Calif.) Mus. Art, Triton Mus., Santa Clara, Calif., Guatemalteco, Guatemala City, Dum Umeni Brno, CSFR, Strahov Closter, Prague, 1990, Walter Bischoff Gallery, Stuttgart, 1990, Kunstler aus den USA, Kunsthaus Ostbayern and Amerika Haus, Stuttgart, 1991, Max Planck Inst., Munich, The Gag Theatre, Prague, 1992, Haus Wiegand, Munich, 1993, San Jose State U., 1964, 1967-68, 1981, 1994, Viva!, Tokyo, 1994, Gallery Q, Sacramento, 1997, Parish Gallery, DC, 1997, 02, Barton Gallery, Sacramento, 1997, 2002-03, 05; Galeria Galiano Havana, 1998, Galerie Weber, Viechtach, Germany, 1998, Point Gall., Brno, Czech Rep., 1998, Galerie Divadlo, Uherske Hradiste, C.R., 1998, Marco Polo Galleries, Carmel, Calif., 2001, Colton Hall Mus., Monterey, Calif., 2002, Hart Galleries, Palm Desert, Calif., 2003, Morgan Hill Cmty. Cultural Ctr., 2004, Mexican Heritage Plz., San Jose, 2007, S. Mas. Quilts & Textiles, 2007; exhibited in group shows at Art Inst. Chgo., 1952, Pa. Acad. Fine Arts, 1953 (Lambert Fund prize), Detroit Inst. Arts, 1950, 56, Mich. State U., 1956 (Purchase award), N.A.D., 1956, Boston Print Symposium, 1997, Portland Art Mus., Oreg., 1997 (Purchase award), Honolulu Acad. Art, 1998, Internat. Graphic Triennial, Krakow, Poland, 1998, Internat. Small Engraving Salon, Florean Mus., Romania, Art Expo, NYC, 2000, Internat. Woodprint Assn., Kyoto, Japan, 1999, Bklyn. Mus. (Purchase award), Mus. Modern Art, Michael Stone Collection, DC, Contempo Collection, Tokyo, Havana Bienale, 2000, History San Jose, 2007, Sakata Gallery, Sacramento, 2007, others; exhbn. 50 States toured, European Mus., 1970-71; represented in collections including Pa. Acad. Fine Art, Boston Mus. Fine Arts, Fogg Mus., Butler Inst. Am. Art, Ford Motor Co., South Bend Art Assn., Joslyn Art Mus., Seattle Art Mus., Ga. Mus., Huntington Gallery, Des Moines Art Center, Smithsonian Instn., Libr. Congress, LA County Art Inst., Brit. Mus., Nat. Gallery, Prague, Birmingham (Eng.) Mus., Moravske Mus., Brno, Czechoslovakia, Bibliotheque Nationale, Paris, Harn Mus., Gainsville, Fla., Portland Mus. Art (over 500 prints), Nat. Mus., Washington, Natl. Mus. Cuba, La Habana, Nat. Mus. Costa Rica, San Jose, Nat. Mus. Egypt, Cairo, Mus. Arte Contemporaneo, Bahia Blanca, Mus. Genaro Perez, Cordoba, Mus. de Bellas Artes, Cordoba, Argentina, Mus. Guayasamin, Quito, Ecuador, Mus. Nat., Panama City, Panama, others; tapestries in pub. and pvt. collections, created tapestry representing U.S. for Olympic Games, Moscow, 1980, Parish Gallery, Washington, Triad Gallery, Seal Rock, Oreg., Haus Wiegand, Munich, Art Foundry Gallery, Sacramento, Greg Barlon Gallery, Sacramento, Hart Gallery, Palm Desert and Carmel, Calif.; prodr. video documentary: Arte Cubano (Contemporary Art and Culture in Cuba, 1999, 2000, 1st award, San Francisco Throwback Film Festival, Los Desaparecidos--The Disappeared Ones, 2003 (Freedom award Dahlonega Film Festival, also Best Documentary Short and Best of Show, Accolade Competition, Best Documentary Spl. Gold statuette, World Fest, Houston, Dirs. Citation award Black Maria Film Festival 2006, 20 Internat. Festivals); guest artist Joslyn Meml. Mus., 1961, instr. painting and drawing, Ohio U., 1955-59, artist in residence, Des Moines Art Center, 1959-63, dir., Crystal Lake Art Ctr., Frankfort, Mich., (1955-57), guest lectr.,one man show, Columbia U., 1963; guest artist Riverside Art Ctr., 1964, Agora Vienna, Austria, 1994, Museo Guayasamin, Quito, Ecuador, 2002; curated exhibit Stuttgart, 1993; founder Bob & Lil Freimark Collection Portland Art Mus.; artist in residence MuseoRegla, Cuba, 2002, Lake Balaton, Hungary, 2002; Am. corollary to Dakar Bienale, 5 works, Senegal, 2002, Art Workshop, Dakar, others; contbr. to craft and fibre publs. With Western Interstate Commn. Higher Edn., Soledad State Prison, 1967. Coxwain USN, 1939—46, Pacific. Recipient 2d award for oil Northwest Territorial exhibit, 1954, Roulet medal Toledo Mus. Art, 1957, 1st award Print Exhbn., 1958, purchase award Midwest Biennial and Northwest Printmakers, Jurors award Berkeley Art Ctr, 1996; Calif. State Coll. Sys. spl. creative leave edit. serigraphs; elected to New Talent in U.S.A., 1957; Ohio U. rsch. grantee, 1958-59, Ford Found. grantee, 1965; Western Interstate Commn. for Higher Edn. grantee, 1967, San Jose State Coll. Found. grantee, 1966, 67, 68, 69, 70, 71, 85; designated ofcl. U.S. Bicentennial Exhbn. Amerika Hausen, Fed. Republic Germany, 1976. Independent. Avocations: hunting, fishing, reading, films, cooking. Home: 539A Dougherty Ave Morgan Hill CA 95037-9241 Office: Grass Valley Studios Morgan Hill CA 95037 Personal E-mail: Bob_Freimark@hughes.net.

FREIRE, GLORIA MEDONIS, social worker; b. Pitts., Apr. 19, 1929; d. Vincent X. and Anastasia T. (Puida) Medonis; m. Luis Francis Freire, Aug. 30, 1958; children: Michael, Charles. BA in Polit. Sci. & Econs., Carlow Coll., 1950; MSSA, Case-Western Res. U., 1955; MPA, Cleve. State U., 1986; PhD, Union Inst., 1995. Teen-age dir. Merrick House, Cleve., 1955-62; group psychotherapist Cleve. Psychiat. Inst., 1966—73; lectr. sch. applied social scis. Case-Western Res. U., Cleve., 1973-75; cluster dir. Golden Age Ctrs., Cleve., 1975-76; specialist Cmty. Guidance & Human Svcs., Cleve., 1976, staff tng. & devel. coord., 1977, dir. consultation & edn., 1978-84; coord. psychiat. emergency svcs. systems Lake County Mental Health Bd., Ohio, 1984-86; adminstr. Hispanic office Cath. Social Svcs., Cleve., 1986-97; asst. prof. social work Cleve. State U., 1997—2004; owner GMF Mgmt. Cons. Svcs., Cleve., 2004—. Editor: SASS mag., Case Western Res. U. Alumni, 1973—79. Chmn. steering com. East Cmty. Task Force on Desegregation; chmn. subcoun. of Ohio Cmty. Mental Health Ctrs. Consultations and Edn.; chmn. Consultation and Edn. Coun. Cleve.; coord. Christian Formation Cmty. of St. Malachi, 1975-77, coord. liturgy commn., 1978-80, coord. social concerns com., 1982-84; mem. Diocesan Commn. on Cath. Cmty. Action, 1982-88, vice chmn., 1986-87; mem. Urban League Edn. Adv. and Task Force on Minimum Competency, 1978-80; trustee Cuyahoga County Pub. Libr., 2003—, sec., 2004, v.p., 2005, pres., 2007. Recipient Disting. Leadership award, Alumnae Assn. Carlow Coll., 1982. Mem. AAUW, NASW (task force on desegregation 1974-83, co-chmn. 1981-83, coord. polit. action com. 1977, dir. Cleve. chpt., 1975-77, sec.-treas. Ohio coun. chpts., 1975-76, steering com. Cleve. chpt. 1987-89), Acad. Cert. Social workers, Am. Soc. Pub. Adminstrn. (trustee Cleve. chpt. 1987-92, 98-2000), Am. soc. Profl. and Exec. Women, Nat. and Cuyahoga County Women's Polit. Caucus (exec. bd.), Am. Group Psychotherapy Assn., Am. Planning Assn., Coun. Social Work Edn., Union Inst. Learner Coun. Advocacy and Adv. Task Force (alt. chmn. 1991-92), Tri-State Group Psychotherapy Soc., Nat. Network Social Work Mgrs., Nat. Image Hispanic Profls. (trustee 1991-92, pres. N.E. Ohio chpt. 1992-94), Julia Burgos Ctr. (bd. dirs. 1998-99), Japan Soc. Cleve. (bd. dirs. 1996-98, exec. com. 1997-98), Japanese Am. Citizens League, Esperanza/Hispanic Edn. (adv. bd. 1998-99, exec. bd. 1999—, 1st v.p. 2004-05). Democrat. Roman Catholic. Home: 5001 Tuxedo Ave Cleveland OH 44134-1007 Office: GMF Mgmt Cons Svcs 4758 Ridge Rd 279 Cleveland OH 44144 Office Phone: 216-351-2351. Personal E-mail: l.freire@sbcglobal.net.

FREIRE, JOSE A., physicist, writer; b. Cienfuegos, Cuba, Apr. 18, 1925; arrived in U.S., 1968; s. Jose M. Freire and Maria C. Valle; m. Maria C. Paula Freire, Dec. 16, 1950; children: Maria C., Jose L., Jose A. BS, Mercy Coll.; D in Physics and Chemistry, Havana U., Cuba. Author: Application of the Mathematical, 1989, 1993, Experiment of Michelson-Morley and the Original Formula, 1994, Ether's Effect in Particles and Waves, 1997, Unification of Ether, Gravity and Electromagnetism, 1999, Gravitational Wave and Time, 2001. Mem.: Am. Assn. Physics Tchrs., Am. Legion (supporter). Republican. Roman Catholic. Home: 2356 SW 140 Pl Miami FL 33175

FREIREICH, EMIL J., hematologist, educator; b. Chgo., Mar. 16, 1927; s. David and Mary (Klein) F.; m. Haroldine Lee Cunningham, Mar. 13, 1953; children: Debra Ann, David Alan, Lindsay Gail, Thomas Jon. BS, U. Ill., 1947, MD with honors, 1949, D.Sc. (hon.), 1982. Diplomate Am. Bd. Internal Medicine. Intern Cook County (Ill.) Hosp., Chgo., 1949-50; resident in internal medicine Presbyn. Hosp., Chgo., 1950-53; rsch. assoc. in hematology Mass. Meml. Hosp., Boston, 1953-55; sr. investigator, head Leukemia Svc. USPHS, Nat. Cancer Inst., Bethesda, Md., 1955-65; prof. medicine U. Tex. System Cancer Ctr., Houston, 1965—, chief rsch. in hematology, 1965-85, head dept. devel. therapeutics, 1972-83, chmn. dept. hematology, 1983-85, dir. Adult Leukemia Rsch. Program, 1985—; prof. medicine U. Tex. Health Sci. Ctr. (Sch. Medicine), 1973—, chief divsn. oncology, 1973-81; mem. faculty Grad. Sch. Med., Health Scis. Ctr., 1965—, dir. Spl. Medical Edn. Programs, 2000—. Mem. rev. com. drug. devel. div. cancer treatment Nat. Carsin Inst., 1975-80; Ruth Harriet Ainsworth chair in devel. therapeutics, 1980—; spl. asst. dir. Nat. Cancer Inst., 1990-91. Assoc. editor Cancer, 1976— , Cancer Research, 1977-86; mem. editorial bd. Oncology News, 1975-90, Cancer Treatment Reports, 1976-80, Leukemia Research, 1976-87, Med. and Pediatric Oncology, 1974— , Leukemia 1987—; contbr. numerous articles on research in hematology and oncology to profl. jours. Recipient Albert Lasker Med. rsch. award, 1972, Charles F. Kettering prize Gen. Motors Cancer Rsch. Found., 1983, Outstanding Investigator award Nat. Cancer Inst., NIH, 1985-92, Alumnus award NIH, 1990; named Alumnus of Yr., U. Ill. Alumni Assn., 1974, Alumni Achievement award, 2000, Pollin prize Columbia U., 2003. Fellow ACP, AAAS; mem. Internat. Soc. Hematology, Am. Soc. Hematology, Am. Fedn. Clin. Research, Am. Soc. Clin. Pharmacology and Therapeutics, Am. Soc. Clin. Oncology (David A. Karnofsky award 1976, pres. 1980-81), Am. Soc. Clin. Investigators, Am. Assn. Cancer Research, Leukemia Soc. Am. (pres. Gulf Coast chpt. 1968-70, trustee 1968-70, Robert Roesler DeVilliers award 1979, grant rev. subcom. 1986-89), Tex. Med. Assn., AMA (editorial bd. jour. 1973-83), Assn. Am. Physicians, Alpha Omega Alpha. Achievements include research in therapy of human acute leukemia and leukocyte physiology. Co-developer of combination chemotherapy and the curative therapy for childhood acute lymphoblastic leukemia. Developed the first successful platelet replacement therapy. Inventor of continuous-flow cell separator. Home: 810 Monte Cello St Houston TX 77024-4515 Office: M D Anderson Cancer Ctr 1515 Holcombe Blvd Houston TX 77030-4009 Home Phone: 713-468-3728; Office Phone: 713-792-2660. Business E-Mail: efreirei@mdanderson.org. *The search for eternal physical and mental health has been at the forefront of man's striving to understand and to control his destiny. The opportunity to investigate, to discover and to apply new remedies for major human illness is a rare privilege, one of man's highest callings.*

FREISHTAT, HARVEY W., lawyer; b. Balt., Dec. 28, 1946; AB cum laude, Princeton U., 1968; JD, Harvard U., 1972. Bar: Mass. 1972. Chmn., founding ptnr. McDermott, Will & Emery LLP, Boston. Office: McDermott Will & Emery 28 State St Ste 33 Boston MA 02109-1775 Office Phone: 617-535-4050. Office Fax: 617-535-3800. Business E-Mail: hfreishtat@mwe.com.

FREITAG, CAROL WILMA, political scientist; Diploma in Dental Hygiene, Northwestern U., 1959; BA, Purdue U., Hammond, Ind., 1988. Registered dental hygienist, Ill. Pvt. practice dental hygiene Henry W. Freitag, D.D.S., Homewood, Ill., 1959-85; mem. group practice Chgo., 1970; faculty, interim dir. dental hygiene Prairie State Coll., Chgo. Heights, Ill., 1971-72; pvt. practice James J. Kreuz, D.D.S., Homewood, 1985-90. Contbr. articles to profl. jour. Chair US Constn. Bicentennial Commn., Village of Matteson, Ill., 1986-89; pres. Matteson Hist. Soc., 1987-89; panel spkr. South Suburban Heritage Assn., Homewood, 1990. Calumet rep. Bicentennial Com. Purdue U., 1988; vis. com. Northwestern Dental Sch., 1997-98; mem. centennial celebration com. Bloom Twp. HS, 2000; mem. Hist. Columbia Found. 2003—. Recipient Key to City, Village of Matteson, 1990, Svc. award Northwestern U., 1980, Good Neighbor award Village of Matteson, 1989, Outstanding Alumni 1950's Decade award Bloom Twp. H.S., 2000. Mem. Am. Dental Hygienists' Assn. (chair Ann. Session Program 1975), Ill. Dental Hygienists Assn. (pres. 1968-69, bd. dirs., Merit award 1979), G.V. Black Soc. (leader, pres. 1997-2001), Evelyn E. Maas Soc. (pres. 1989-90, bd. dirs., Merit award 1993), Northwestern Dental Sch. Alumni Assn. (bd. dirs. 1969-2001, pres. 1977-78, v.p. 1976-77, 90-93), Acad. Polit. Sci., Hist. Columbia Found., Sigma Phi Alpha, Alpha Chi. Avocation: travel. Home: 6256 Kallsen Dr Unit 1 Tinley Park IL 60477

FREITAG, FREDERICK GERALD, osteopathic physician; b. Milw., Feb. 12, 1952; s. Frederick August and Shirley June (Siewert) F.; m. Lynn Nadene Stegner, Sept. 10, 1977; children: Crescentia Adella, Abigail Amadea, Genevieve Angelica. BS in Biochemistry, U. Wis., 1974; DO, Chgo. Coll. Osteo. Medicine, 1979. Cert. in headache mgmt. Intern Brentwood Hosp., Warrensville Heights, Ohio, 1979-80, resident in family practice, 1980-81; dir., physician Twinsburg (Ohio) Family Clinic, 1981-83; assoc. prof. family medicine Coll. Osteo. Medicine, Ohio U., Warrensville Heights, 1982-83; staff Diamond Headache Clinic, Chgo., 1983-86, assoc. dir., 1986—; attending staff mem. Louis A. Weiss Meml. Hosp., Chgo., 1983-93; attending staff Columbus Hosp., 1993—2000, St. Joseph's Hosp., 2000—; clin. assoc. prof. family medicine Chgo. Med. Sch. Rosalind Franklin U. Health and Sci., 1999—. Clin. assoc. family medicine Midwestern U./Chgo. Coll. Osteo. Medicine, 1999—; sec. Diamond Headache Rsch. and Edn. Found.; vis. lectr. dept. family medicine Chgo. Coll. Osteo. Medicine, 1984-99; clin. assoc. dept. medicine Pritzker Sch. Medicine U. Chgo., 1989-93; mem. editl. bd. Headache Quar., 1991-2003; chmn. instnl. rev. bd. Louis A. Weiss Meml. Hosp., 1991-93; mem. migraine adv. coun. Abbott, 1995-2003, mem. primary care adv. coun., 1997—; mem. adv. group Glaxo Wellcome, 1996-2005; mem. migraine adv. coun. Zeneca, 1996—; mem. U.S Headache Consortium guidelines project; bd. dirs. Nat. Bd. for Cert. in Headache Mgmt., 2000—, sec.-treas., 2000-2002, v.p., 2002—; mem. Allergan Botox Internat. Adv. Com., 2002—; co-chair Primary Care Migraine Partnership, 2002—; mem. Ortho-MeNeil headache specialists adv. bd., 2003—. Coord. editor Headache Quar.; mem. editl. bd. Headache and Pain, 2003—; contbr. articles to profl. jours., chpts. to books. Bd. dirs. Nat. Headache Found., liaison standards of care com. to Am. Acad. Neurology; mem. pres. adv. bd. Concordia U., Chgo., 2006—. Fellow Am. Assn. for Study of Headache; mem. AMA, Am. Coll. Gen. Practioners in Osteo. Medicine, Am. Osteo. Assn. (chair headache coun. 2000—), Am. Soc. Clin. Pharmacology and Therapeutics (vice chmn. headache sect. 1995-96), Ill. Assn. Osteo. Physicians and Surgeons, Ill. Med. Soc., Internat. Assn. Study Pain, Am. Pain Soc., Am. Headache Soc. (chair primary care spl. interest sect. 1999-2004, mem. ethics com. 2002-04, mem. edn. com. 2002-04, co-chair practice com. 2006—), Nat. Headache Found., Chgo. Med. Soc. (spkrs. bur.), German Wine Soc. (past pres. Chgo. chpt.), U. Wis. Alumni Assn. Lutheran. Avocations: german oenophile, gardening, model railroading, home carpentry. Home: 931 Clinton Pl River Forest IL 60305-1503 Office: The Diamond Headache Clinic 467 W Deming Pl Ste 500 Chicago IL 60614-1726 Home Phone: 708-771-3214; Office Phone: 773-388-6383. Personal E-mail: dhcdoc@aol.com.

FREITAG, WOLFGANG MARTIN, retired librarian; b. Berlin, Oct. 27, 1924; came to U.S. 1955, naturalized, 1961; s. Georg and Anne Marie (Friess) F.; m. Doris Christiane Pfeil, Oct. 25, 1952; children— Thomas Martin, Tilman George Dr. Phil., U. Freiburg, W. Ger., 1949; postgrad., Harvard U., 1951-52; MS in Library Sci., Simmons Coll., Boston, 1956. Reference libr., program dir. U.S. Info. Ctr., Frankfurt, Germany, 1950-53; editor Droemer-Knaur Publ., Munich, 1953-55; cataloger Harvard Coll. Library, Cambridge, Mass., 1955-60; head librarian Gordon McKay Library, Harvard U., 1960-62; chief undergrad. library planning Stanford U., Calif., 1962-64; librarian Fine Arts Library Fogg Art Mus., Harvard U., 1964-91, sr. lectr. bibliography and art historiography, 1967-91; lectr. libr. sci. Simmons Coll., Boston, 1991-92; ret., 1992. Libr. cons. J.P. Getty Trust, L.A., 1982-83, U. Pitts, 1983, The Frick Collection, N.Y. 1984, Inst. Fine Arts, NYU, 1987; mem. vis. com. Met. Mus. Art, 1972-92; bd. vis. Sch. Info. Studies, Syracuse U., 1981-85, SUNY, Stony Brook, 1986, NYU Inst. Fine Arts, 1987. Editor: Artist Resource Manuals, Art Books: Monographs on Artists, 1985, 2d edit., 1997; cons. to pubs.; contbr. articles to profl. jours. Fulbright fellow, 1951, 68, Council Library Resources fellow, 1975. Mem. Art Libraries Soc. N.Am. (pres. 1980), Coll. Art Assn., Internat. Fedn. Library Assns. (exec. com. art librs. sect. 1985-93), Goethe Soc. New Eng., Boston Soc. Printers. Avocation: autograph collecting. Home: 43 Fair Oaks Dr Lexington MA 02421-6931 Personal E-mail: wolfgang.freitag@rcn.com.

FREITAS, ANTOINETTE JUNI, insurance company executive; b. Kansas City, Mo., Feb. 14, 1944; d. ANthony P. and Mariam L. Freitas; m. Stephen R. Krajcar, July 4, 1980. BA, Calif. State U., Long Beach, 1966; MA, U. So. Calif., 1974. CLU; ChFC. Counselor U. So. Calif., 1967-70, assoc. dir. fin. aid, 1970-75; sales agt. Equitable Life Assurance Co., 1975-79, dist. mgr. San Francisco, 1979-84; pres. Group Mktg. Svcs., Inc.; field dir. Northwesternn Mut. Life, San Francisco, 1984-86; pres. Penisula Fin. Group, Inc., 1986—; mktg. mgr. Home Life, H.L. Fin. Group, San Jose, Calif., 1986—. Registered rep. Carrilon, Investments, Securities, 1987-91. Author: A Study in Changing Youth Values, 1974. Bd. dirs. San Francisco Zoo. Soc., 1996—. Recipient various sales and mgmt. awards; mem. Million Dollar Round Table. Mem. AAUW, Nat. Assn. Life Underwriters, Women LIfe Underwriters Conf., U. So. Calif. Alumni Assn. Republican. Episcopalian. Office: Peninsula Fin Group Inc 2995 Woodside Rd Ste 400 Woodside CA 94062-2448 Office Phone: 650-529-9594. Business E-Mail: toni@peninsulafinancial.com.

FREIZER, LOUIS A., radio producer; b. NYC, Oct. 10, 1931; s. Morris and Celia (Lassersohn) F.; m. Michèle Suzanne Orban, July 6, 1968; children: Sabine, Eric. BS, U. Wis., 1953; postgrad., U. Heidelberg, Germany, 1956; MA, Columbia U., 1964, postgrad., 1966—. Corr. UPI, Madison, Wis., 1953-54; desk asst. CBS News, NYC, 1956-59, newswriter, 1959-60, Sta. WCBS, NYC, 1960-62, news editor, 1963-68, sr. news prodr., 1968-73, sr. exec. news prodr., 1973—. Adj. prof. comm. Fordham U.; lectr., cons. journalism and internat. rels. Prodr.: (pub. affairs series) Let's Find Out, 1966, International Briefing series, 1968-72. Served to 1st lt. US Army, 1954-56; capt. USAR, 1956-70. Recipient Am. Legion medal; Radio Journalism award AMA, Radio Journalism award Nat. Headliners Club, Radio Journalism Nat. award for Outstanding Newscast UPI, 1st place award for Best Regularly Scheduled Local News Program NY State AP Broadcasters Assn., spl. mention for Best One Day News Effort NY State AP Broadcasters Assn., Bene Merenti medal Fordham U.; winner German Study Program for US Journalists sponsored by Radio in the Am. Sect. of Berlin Commn. and the Radio and TV News Dirs. Found.; fellow CBS News Found. Mem. Am. Polit. Sci. Assn., Acad. Polit. Sci., Am. Acad. Polit. and Social Scis., Radio-TV News Dirs. Assn., Broadcast Pioneers, Sigma Delta Chi. Home: 196 Ave Winston Churchill 1180 Brussels Belgium Office Phone: 32 2347 3669. Personal E-mail: freizerl@aol.com.

FRELICK, ROBERT WESTCOTT, physician, consultant; b. Potsdam, NY, Feb. 27, 1920; s. H. Victor and Ruth (Scott) F.; m. Jane Hayden, Jan. 22, 1944; children: Susan, Alcy, Sally, William, Scott. AB, Union Coll., Barbourville, Ky., 1941; MD, Yale U., New Haven, Conn., 1944. Diplomate Am. Bd. Internal Medicine, Am. Bd. Medical Onocology, Am. Bd. Nuc. Medicine. Intern New Haven Hosp., 1944—45; resident Meml. Hosp., Wilmington, Del., 1947—49, Meml. Hosp. Ctr., NYC, 1949—50; pvt. practice Wilmington, 1950—82; program dir. Nat. Cancer Inst., Bethesda, Md., 1982—87; cons. Del. Divsn. Pub. Health, Wilmington, 1987—96; med. dir. South Jersey Cancer Ctr., 1995—97, cons., 1998—. Chief medicine Wilmington Med. Ctr., Del., 1965-72. Contbr. to profl. jours. Bd. CARE coun. bd. alumni, NYC then Atlanta, 1980-97; pres. Assn. Cmty. Cancer Ctrs., Rockville, Md., 1979-80. Capt. (Med. Svc. Corps.) US Army, 1944-47. Recipient Disting. Svc. award Del. Med. Soc., 1977, Outstanding Svc. to Cmty. award Assn. Cmty. Cancer Ctrs., 1987, St. George's medal Am. Cancer Soc., 1990. Fellow ACP (laureate, gov.); mem. AMA, APHA, ACS (surveyor hosp. cancer programs 1988-97), Med. Soc. Del. (chair com. ethics, pres. 1980-81), Soc. Surg. Oncology, Am. Soc. Internal Medicine, Am. Soc. Clin. Oncology, Am. Sch. Health Assns. Home: 1018 Overbrook Rd Wilmington DE 19807-2236 Office Phone: 302-655-3460. Personal E-mail: rfrelick@comcast.net.

FRELING, RICHARD ALAN, lawyer; b. NYC, June 21, 1932; s. Jack C. and Natalie Freling; children: Richard, Alexandra, Darryl, Robert, Dana. BBA in acctg. with honors, U. Tex., Austin, 1953, JD with honors, 1956. Bar: Tex. 1956, US Dist. Ct. No. Dist. Tex. 1959, US Ct. Appeals 5th Cir. 1961, US Supreme Ct. 1962. Mem. Jenkins & Gilchrist, Dallas; ptnr. Johnson & Wortley, Dallas; sr. ptnr. Hopkins & Sutter, Dallas, 1995—96; of counsel Jones, Day, Reavis & Pogue (now Jones Day), Dallas, 1996—. Mem. exec. adv. committees U. Calif. Securities Regulation Inst., 1973—; adv. bd. BNA/Tax Mgmt., 1976—. Editor-in-chief Tex. Law Rev., 1955-56; contbr. articles to legal jours. Chmn. Inst. on Oil and Gas Taxation Southwestern Legal Found. (now The Ctr. for Am. and Internat. Law), 1965—68, chmn. taxation divsn., 1968—71, rsch. fellow, 1970—, trustee, 1983—, founder, former chair Symposium on Securities Regulation; trustee St. Mark's Sch. of Tex., 1971—78, mem. exec. com., 1972—75; dir. The Greenhill Sch., 1972—80, mem. exec. com., 1972—75; gov., mem. exec. com. S.W. Outward Bound Sch., 1972—82, vice chmn., 1980—82; trustee Retina Found. of S.W., 1975—90, Pine Manor Coll., Chesnut Hill, Mass., 1982—85, Colo. Outward Bound Sch., 1982—, mem. exec. com., 1986—92; bd. dirs. Friends of Dallas Pub. Libr., 1982—87, Isthmus Inst., Dallas, 1983—89; trustee Aperture Found., 1984—90; bd. dirs. Dallas Symphony Assn., 1984—, v.p. ops., 1988—90, pres., 1990—92, chmn., 1992—94, chmn. emeritus, 1994—; exec. com., bd. trustee Ctr. for Am. and Internat. Law, 1985—; pres. Sun & Star 1996, Dallas, 1992—96; mem. governance com. and spl. projects com. Ctr. for Performing Arts, Dallas, 2006—, trustee, 2007—. Recipient Faculty Award, U. Tex. Sch. Law, 1981. Fellow Am. Coll. Tax Counsel, Tex. Bar Found.; mem. Am. Law Inst. (cons. fed. income tax project 1976—), ABA (chmn. com. corp. stockholder relationships 1979-81, mem. coun. taxation sect. 1982-85), Tex. Bar Assn., Dallas Bar Assn., Tex. Law Rev. Publications Inc., U. Tex. Sch. Law Alumni Assn. Office: Jones Day 2727 N Harwood St Dallas TX 75201 Office Phone: 214-969-4835. Business E-Mail: rfreling@jonesday.com.

FRELINGHUYSEN, RODNEY P., congressman; b. NYC, Apr. 29, 1946; s. Peter Hood Ballantine Frelinghuysen, Jr.; m. Virginia Frelinghuysen; children: Louisine, Sarah. BA, Hobart Coll., Geneva, NY, 1969; grad. student, Trinity Coll., Hartford, Conn.; degree (hon.), Drew U., 2004. State and fed. aid coord., adminstrv. asst. Morris County, 1972; mem. Morris County Bd. of Chosen Freeholders, 1974-83, dir., 1980, mem. welfare and mental health bds., human svcs. and pvt. industry couns., mem. freeholder fin. com.; mem. NJ Gen. Assembly, 1983-94, chmn. assembly appropriations com., 1988—89, 1992—94; mem. US Congress from 11th NJ dist., 1995—, mem. appropriations com., ranking mem. subcommittee on commerce, justice, sci. and related agencies. Bd. dirs. Morristown Meml. Hosp., Newark Mus., Peck Sch. With 93rd Engr. Bn. US Army, 1969—71, Vietnam. Named Legislator of Yr. NJ Assn. Mental Health Agencies, NJ Assn. Retarded Citizens; recipient Hero of the Taxpayer award Ams. for Tax Reform, Sci. Coalition's Champion of Sci. award Rutgers U. and Princeton U. Mem. Am. Legion, VFW (Legislator of Yr.). Republican. Episcopalian. Office: US Ho Reps 2442 Rayburn Ho Office Bldg Washington DC 20515-3011 Office Phone: 202-225-5034.*

FRELOW, ROBERT DEAN, retired school system administrator, writer; b. Seminole, Okla., Aug. 1, 1932; s. Jasper Wallace and Florine (Hamilton) Frelow; m. Maxine Camille Gibbs Badgett, Dec. 25, 1952 (div. May 1983); m. Rena Hersh, Sept. 8, 1983; children: Robert Jr., Frederick, Michael. BA, San Francisco State U., 1954, MA, 1960; PhD, U. Calif., Berkeley, 1970. Cert. tchr. Calif., N.Y., adminstr. Calif., N.Y. Tchr. Oakland Unified Schs., Calif., 1960—66, Berkeley Unified Schs., Calif., 1966—67, asst. to supt., 1967—70; asst. supt. Greenburgh Schs., Hartsdale, NY, 1970—75, supt. schs., 1975—90. Adj. prof. Columbia U., NYC, 1970—73, Pace U., NYC, 1974—90; coord. sch. desegregation Berkeley Schs., 1967—70; cons. sch. desegregation, 1966—90; cons. Wise Svcs., White Plains, NY, 1990—. Author: The Berkeley Plan for Desegregation, 1968, (novels) Blood Runs Deep, 2002, At the Rainbow's End, 2006; co-author (editor): I Am a Blade of Grass., 1989; contbr. articles to profl. jours. Bd. dirs. Westchester Arts Coun., White Plains, NY, 1990, Westchester Cable Commn., White PlainsWhite Plains, 1990, Calif. Synod, Presbyn. Ch., 1966, Hartsdale Kiwanis, 2003. Capt. USAF, 1954—64. Recipient Citizen of the Yr. award, Kappa Alpha Psi, 1978, 1984, Exec. Leadership award, Bus. Careers Club, Hartsdale, 1991, Dedication, Dr. Robert D. Frelow Cultural Ctr., Hartsdale, 1991, honors, Greensburgh Ctrl. Seven Ednl. Found., 2005; grantee Urban Studies grantee, U. Calif.-Berkeley, 1969. Fellow: Rotary of Am. (bd. dirs., Paul Harris award 1991); mem.: U. Calif. Alumni Assn. Democrat. Presbyterian. Avocations: writing, reading, travel, photography, theater. Home: 17 Tara Dr Pomona NY 10970 Office Phone: 845-354-7358. Personal E-mail: rdf66@aol.com.

FREMD, THEODORE J., paleontologist, regional science advisor; b. Port Chester, NY, June 21, 1952; s. Paula and Theodore John Fremd; m. Skylar JoAnn Rickabaugh, 1973. BS, The U. Alta., Edmonton, Can., 1979. Paleontologist Nat. Pk. Svc., Kimberly, Oreg., 1984—, regional sci. advisor, 2002—. Paleontologist Fossil Butte Nat. Monument, Kemmerer, Wyo., 1979—84. Dir., scientific coord. mus. exhibit Thomas Condon Paleontology Ctr. Mem.: Geol. Soc. Am., Soc. Vertebrate Paleontology (govt. laiason com. 1991—2000). Buddhism. Achievements include research in biostratigraphy of the John Day Basin; first to paleontological resource management in the NPS. Avocations: skiing, professional disc golf, backpacking, kayaking, running. Office: Nat Park Svc 32651 Hwy 19 Kimberly OR 97848 Office Phone: 541-987-2333. Personal E-mail: tfremd@uoregon.edu. Business E-Mail: ted_fremd@nps.gov.

FRENCH, ANTHONY PHILIP, physicist, educator; b. Brighton, Eng., Nov. 19, 1920; came to U.S., 1955; s. Sydney James and Elizabeth Margaret (Hart) French; m. Naomi Mary Livesay, Oct. 6, 1945 (dec. 2001); m. Dorothy Ada Jensen, Apr. 30, 2002; children: Martin Charles, Gillian Ruth. BA with honors, Cambridge U., Eng., 1942, MA, 1946, PhD, 1948; ScD (hon.), Allegheny Coll., 1989. Mem. atomic bomb projects Tube Alloys and Manhattan Project, 1942-46; scientific officer Atomic Energy Rsch. Establishment U.K., 1946—48; demonstrator, lectr. physics Cambridge U., 1948-55; fellow Pembroke Coll., 1950-55; prof. physics U. S.C., 1955-63, chmn. dept., 1956-62; vis. prof. MIT, 1962-64, prof., 1964-91, prof. emeritus, 1991—; vis. fellow Pembroke Coll., Cambridge, 1975. Chmn. Internat. Commn. on Physics Edn., 1975-81. Author: Principles of Modern Physics, 1958, Special Relativity, 1968, Newtonian Mechanics, 1971, Vibrations and Waves, 1971, (with Edwin F. Taylor) Introduction to Quantum Physics, 1978, (with M.G. Ebison) Introduction to Classical Mechanics, 1986; editor: Einstein: A Centenary Volume, 1979, Physics in a Technological World, 1988; co-editor: Niels Bohr: A Centenary Volume, 1985, Physics History from AAPT Jours. II, 1995; contbr. articles to profl. jours. Recipient Univ. medal Charles U., Prague, 1980, Bragg medal Inst. Physics, U.K., 1988, Oersted medal Am. Assn. Physics Tchrs., 1989. Fellow Am. Phys. Soc.; mem. Am. Assn. Physics Tchrs. (pres. 1985-86, Oersted medal 1989, Melba Newell Phillips award 1993), Sigma Xi, Sigma Pi Sigma. Office: Mass Inst Tech Dept Physics Rm 6C-435 Cambridge MA 02139 Business E-Mail: apfrench@mit.edu.

FRENCH, ARTHUR (ARTHUR WELLESLEY FRENCH JR.), actor, theater director; b. NYC, Feb. 22, 1949; s. Arthur Wellesley French and Ursilla Idonia Ollivierre. Ed., Brooklyn Coll. Staff mem. Dept. Social Services, NYC; mem. Negro Ensemble Co., 1967; acting tchr. Herbert Berghof Studio, NYC. Actor: (Broadway plays) Ain't Supposed to Die a Natural Death, 1973, The Iceman Cometh, 1973, All God's Chillun Got Wings, 1975, You Can't Take It With You, 1983, Design for Living, 1984, (Off-Broadway) Raisin' Hell in the Son, Two Trains Running, 2007 (Lucille Lortel award outstanding featured actor, 2007); (plays) Day of Absence, 1965, Death of a Salesman, King Lear; (films) Out of It, 1969, Dirtymouth, 1970, The Stone Killer, 1973, Blade, 1973, The Super Cops, 1974, Three Days of the Condor, 1975, Car Wash, 1976, Handle With Care, 1977, A Hero Ain't Nothin' But a Sandwich, 1978, Fingers, 1978, Hanky Panky, 1982, 'Round Midnight, 1986, Loose Cannons, 1990, Malcolm X, 1992, The Pickle, 1993, Crooklyn, 1994, Drop Squad, 1994, Ethel and Harvey, 1995, The Keeper, 1995, The Associate, 1996, The Out-of-Towners, 1999, Music of the Heart, 1999, Acts of Worship, 2001, Beautiful Kid, 2003, Blinding Goldfish, 2004, Kinsey, 2004, Bellclair Times, 2005, The Saint of Avenue B, 2006, Blood of a Champion, 2006; (TV films) You Can't Go Home Again, 1979, Hollow Image, 1979, The Gentleman Bandit, 1981, You Can't Take It With You, 1984, Dress Gray, 1986, Gryphon, 1990; dir.: (plays) Just Won't, Branches from the Same Tree, Two Bourgeois Blacks, The Village Wooing, One Last Look, Chameleon, Love You to Pieces, Strong Breed. Recipient OBIE award for sustained excellence of performance, Village Voice, 1997.*

FRENCH, CLARENCE LEVI, JR., retired shipbuilding company executive; b. New Haven, Oct. 13, 1925; s. Clarence L. Sr. and Eleanor (Curry) F.; m. Jean Sprague, June 29, 1946; children: Craig Thomas, Brian Keith, Alan Scott. BS in Naval Sci., Tufts U., 1945, BSME, 1947; ScD (hon.), Webb Inst., 1992. Registered profl. engr., Calif. Foundry engr. Bethlehem Steel Corp., 1947-56; staff engr., asst. supt. Kaiser Steel Corp., 1956-64; supervisory engr. Bechtel Corp., 1964-67; with Nat. Steel & Shipbldg. Co., San Diego, 1967-86, exec. v.p., gen. mgr., to 1977, pres., chief operating officer, 1977-84, chmn., chief exec. officer, 1984-86, outside dir., 1989-98. Past mem. maritime transp. rsch. bd. NRC. Bd. dirs. United Way, San Diego, YMCA, San Diego; past chmn., bd. dirs. Pres. Roundtable; chmn. emeritus bd. trustees Webb Inst. Lt. USN, 1943-53. Fellow Soc. Naval Architects and Marine Engrs. (hon., past pres.), Shipbuilders Council Am. (past chmn. exec. com.), ASTM, Am. Bur. Shipping; mem. Am. Soc. Naval Engrs., U.S. Naval Inst., Navy League U.S., Propeller Club U.S.

FRENCH, DONALD P., zoologist, educator; PhD, Ind. U., Bloomington. Rsch. assoc., vist. asst. prof U. Md. Ea. Shore, Princess Anne, Md., 1985—92; prof. Okla. State U., Stillwater, 1992—. Recipient Reagents Disting. Tchg. award, Okla. State Regents, 2006. Mem.: NSTA (mem. coun. 2005—07), Soc. Coll. Sci. Tchrs. (pres. 2005—07, Outstanding Undergraduate Sci. Tchr. award 2000). Office: Oklahoma State Univ Dept Zoology Stillwater OK 74078 Office Phone: 405-744-9690.

FRENCH, DOROTHY MARIE, music educator; b. Warrenton, Va., Mar. 5, 1964; d. Warren Douglass Thompson, Sr. and Iris Rebecca Thompson; m. Wayne James French; children: Megan, Samantha. BA in Music Edn., Marshall U., 1986. Music tchr. Prince William County Schs., Manassas, Va., 1986—. Pvt. music tchr., Manassas, Va., 1986—99, Gainsville, 2005—; ch. musician Haymarket Bapt. Ch., 1987—. Mem.: Am. Choral Dirs. Assn., Peadmont Music Fedn., Music Educators Nat. Conf., Nat. Fedn. Music Clubs. Bapt. Avocation: reading. Home: 7512 Melton Ct Gainesville VA 20155-1801 Office: Stage Presence Music Studio Gainesville VA 20155 Office Phone: 703-393-7608. Personal E-mail: wdfrench@verizon.net.

FRENCH, DORRIS TOWERS BRYAN, volunteer; b. Kissimmee, Fla., May 15, 1926; m. Lawrence Cornwell French, Sept. 7, 1947; children: Layne Bryan, Leyland Bradley. Student, Art Inst., Costa Rica, 1940-42; BFA, Tulane U., 1946; student, U. Mex., 1943-44. Fabric designer Wembley Co., 1945-46; designer silver and jewelry New Orleans, 1945-47; head art dept. pvt. sch., 1947. Columnist From the Mayor's Desk; editor pub. Paw Prints, 1981-93. Founder, v.p. Peoples Animal Welfare Soc., 1977-96; past art dir., coord. internat. gladiola show Garden Club, Binghamton. Mem. AAUW, Zeta Tau Alpha. Avocations: writing, art. Home: 3510 Aransas St Corpus Christi TX 78411-1302

FRENCH, ELIZABETH IRENE, biology professor, musician; b. Knoxville, Tenn., Sept. 20, 1938; d. Junius Butler and Irene Rankin (Johnston) F. MusB, U. Tenn., 1959, MS, 1962; PhD, U. Miss., 1973. Tchr. music Kingsport (Tenn.) Symphony Assn., 1962-64, Birmingham (Ala.) Schs., 1964-66; NASA trainee in biology U. Miss., Oxford, 1969-73; asst. prof. Mobile (Ala.) Coll. (name now U. Mobile), 1973-83, assoc. prof., 1983-94, prof., 1994—. Orch. contractor Am. Fedn. Musicians, 1983—; 1st violin Kingsport Symphony Orch., 1962-64, Birmingham Symphony Orch., 1964-66, Knoxville Symphony Orch., 1955-62, 66-68, Memphis Symphony Orch., 1970-73, Mobile Symphony Orch., 1974—, Pensacola Symphony Orch., Gulf Coast Symphony Orch., Mobile Symphony Players Com., 2001—; concertmaster Riviera Symphony Orch. and Chorus, Ala., 2005—. Violin recitalist Ala. Artists Series, 1978-81, Fairhope (Ala.) Concert Series, 1998. Mem. project Choctaw Nat. Wildlife Refuge, 1997-98. Named Career Woman of Yr., Gayfer's, Inc., 1985. Mem. Assn. Southeastern Biologists, Human Anatomy and Physiology Soc. (nat. com. to construct standardized test on anatomy and physiology), Wilderness Soc., Ala. Acad. Scis. (presenter 1996), Ala. Ornithol. Soc., Mobile Bay

Audubon Soc. (bd. dirs. 1997—), Costal Birding Assn., Am. Fedn. Musicians, Ala. Fedn. Music Clubs (chmn. composition contest 1986-90, historian 1991-94), Schumann Music Club (pres. 1977-79, 85-87, 94-97, 2000-03, adv. bd. 2005—). Republican. Roman Catholic. Avocations: camping, photography, birdwatching. Home: 36 Ridgeview Dr Chickasaw AL 36611-1317 Office: U Mobile PO Box 13220 Mobile AL 36663-0220

FRENCH, HENRY PIERSON, JR., retired historian, educator; b. Rochester, NY, Nov. 21, 1934; s. Henry Pierson and Genevieve Lynn (Johnson) F.; m. Beverly Anne Bauernschmidt, Aug. 22, 1959; children: Henry Pierson III, Donna Lynn (dec.), William Dean, Susan Gayle, John Douglas. AB, U. Del., Newark, 1960; MA, U. Rochester, NY, 1961, MA in Edn., 1962, EdD, 1968. Tchr. Pittsford Ctrl. HS, NY, 1962—66; field svc. assoc. U. Rochester, NY, 1962—66, assoc. lectr., 1967—68, vis. asst. prof. Coll. Edn. and East Asian Ctr., 1968—69, asst. prof. edn., 1969—70, assoc. prof. Ctr. Spl. Degree Programs, 1970—72, lectr. East Asian studies, 1972—74, sr. lectr., 1974—95, mem. dean's adv. com. Warner Grad. Sch. Edn. and Human Devel., 2006—; prof. history and polit. sci. Monroe CC SUNY, Rochester, 1964—2005; ret., 2005. Adj. asst. prof. history SUNY-Monroe C.C., 1964-67, asst. prof. history, 1967-70, assoc. prof., 1970-74, prof., 1974-2005, chief marshall, commencement, 2005, prof. emeritus history, 2005—, chmn. dept. history and polit. sci., 1979-85, chmn. retention, tenure and promotion com., 1985-2005, sabbatical leave, 1986, chair history and polit. sci. cluster in dept. anthropology, history, polit. sci. and sociology, 2001-04, coord. history and polit. sci. in dept. anthropology, history, polit. sci., sociology, 2001-04; moderator, host Disciplines Within the Social Scis. series, 1968; moderator, permanent panelist Fgn. Policy Assn. and Rochester Assn. for UN Great Decisions, 1973, 77, 78 series Channel 21 Ednl. TV, Rochester; cons., panelist Great Decisions TV series, 1982, 84; vis. prof. history, 1988-89; panelist Terrorism/Counterterrorism, WXXI radio, 2001—; prof. Canisius Coll., 1968, 69, 71, 73, 89, Dunlop Tire Corp. Japan Inst. faculty, 1989, Rochester Inst. Tech., 1969-70, spring 1977, 98, SUNY, Brockport, 1971; adj. mentor SUNY-Empire State Coll., 1976, 88-89, 1997, 2003-06; co-dir., adminstr. NDEA insts., 1965-69; bd. dirs. Rochester Assn. UN, 1972-83, 85-91, chmn. policy com., 1972-74, v.p., 1975-77, pres., 1977-78, chmn. bd., 1978-79, chmn. nominating com., 1983-84; panelist Internat. Assn. Historians Asia, 1986, 1991, chair, 1994, Bangkok, 1996; presenter in field. Contbr. articles to profl. jours. Vestryman St. Thomas Episcopal Ch., Rochester, 1965-68, Christ Episc. Ch., Pittsford, 1976-79, jr. warden, 1979-80, sr. warden, 1980-81, chmn. rector selection com., 1982; del. to diocesan Conv., 1989-91, 94-97, 2006-; 1st provisional lay dep. 1991; lay dep., 1994, 97; mem. commn. on Ordained Ministry, Episc. Diocese of Rochester, 1987-94, chmn., 1992-94; advisor Shanghai-Rochester Bishops' Visitation in U.S. and China, 1989-90, co-leader lay del. to Shanghai and China Christian Couns., China, 1992, 94, 97; coord. visit of Bishop Shen Yifan and Hong Luming to Rochester, Nov. 1-8, 1993; trustee Reynolds Libr. Bd., 1991—, pres. 2005—, Mendon Pub. Libr., 1996-97, Rochester Pub. Libr., 1992-2003, v.p., 1996-98, pres., 1998-2000; trustee Friends of Rochester Pub. Libr., 1983-2003, v.p., 1986-88, pres., 1988-91; trustee Rochester Regional Libr. Coun., 1998—; chmn. Rochester Lit. award to James Baldwin, 1986; active Edn. Adv. Bd., 1988-2005, Preferred Care HMO, 1988-2005, NY State Citizens' Com. for the Bicentennial of the French Revolution, 1988-90; Damon Benefactor Monroe C.C. Found., 2003; trustee Monroe C.C. Found., 2005—. Programs and Comparative Studies grantee, 1970; recipient SUNY Chancellor's medal for philanthropy for establishing endowed chair Henry Pierson French Sr. chair in bus. adminstrn./econs. at Monroe CC, Rochester, 1999, establish scholarship fund in polit. sci. in the name of Henry Pierson French III, Monroe CC Rochester, NY, 2002; established endowed award in history in names of Beverly and Henry Pierson French, Jr., Monroe CC, Rochester, NY, 2005. Mem. Assn. Asian Studies, Mid. Atlantic and New Eng. Conf. for Can. Studies, Torch (bd. dirs. Rochester chpt. 1973-76, 97-2005, pres. 1974-75, Silver Torch award Internat. Assn. 2001), Brighton Schs. Alumni Assn. (co-chair 1999—), Univ. Club (v.p. 1975-76, sec. 1988-90, pres.-elect 1991-92, pres. 1992-93), Genesee Valley Club, Twenty Club, Delta Tau Delta. Episcopalian. Home: 78 Smith Rd Pittsford NY 14534-9727 Personal E-mail: hpfrench@rochester.rr.com.

FRENCH, JENNIFER SUZANNE, language educator; BS in English Edn., Bob Jones U., Greenville, SC, 2002, MEd in Multi-Categorial Spl. Edn., 2002—04. English tchr. Harvest Christian Acad., Barrigada, Guam, 2004—. Awana leader Harvest Bapt. Ch., Barrigada, 2004—. Recipient Citation award, AWANA Clubs Internat., 1998. Mem.: Nat. Coun. Tchrs. English. Office: Harvest Christian Acad PO Box 23189 GMF Barrigada GU 96921 Home Phone: 671-472-7757.

FRENCH, JOHN, III, lawyer, director; b. Boston, July 12, 1932; s. John and Rhoda (Walker) F.; m. Leslie Ten Eyck, Jan. 11, 1957 (div. 1961); children: John B., Lawrence C.; m. Anne Hubbell, Jan. 9, 1965 (div. 1983); children: Daniel J., Susanna H.; m. Marina Kellen, Nov. 21, 1987. BA, Dartmouth Coll., Hanover, NH, 1955; JD, Harvard U., Cambridge, Mass., 1958. Bar: NY 1959, D.C. 1988. Assoc. Milbank, Tweed, Hadley & McCloy, NYC, 1961-68, Satterlee & Stephens, NYC, 1968-73; asst. gen. counsel Continental Group, Inc., Stamford, Conn., 1973-81; v.p., gen. counsel, sec. Peabody Internat. Corp., Stamford, Conn., 1981-82; ptnr. Appleton, Rice & Perrin, NYC, 1982-84, Beveridge and Diamond, NYC, 1985-93, counsel, 1993-99; chmn. Tudor Assocs., LLC, NYC, 1999—. Lectr. Practising Law Inst., 1979-83, Am. Law Inst., 1978; bd. dirs. Resorts Mgmt., Inc., Tudor Assocs., LLC, NYC, NY Philharmonic Soc., The Smithsonian Instn.; pres., dir. Salzburg Festival Soc., Inc. Contbr. articles to profl. jours. Trustee Hudson River Found., YMCA-YWCA Camping Svcs. Greater NY, Inc.; bd. dirs. Third St. Music Sch. Settlement House, Inc., NYC, Internat. House, Inc., NYC, Met. Opera Club, Young Concert Artists, Inc., 33 E. 70th St. Corp., Teatro alla Scala Found.; active Westchester County Planning Bd., 1974-85, NY State Environ. Bd., 1976-88. Capt. JAGC, USAF, 1958-61. Mem.: VFW, ABA, Am. Soc. Corp. Secs., Environ. Law Inst., Assn. of Bar City of N.Y. (lectr.), N.Y. State Bar Assn. (lectr.), Mayflower Descendants., Met. Opera Soc., Century Assn., Am. Legion, The Pilgrims, Knickerbocker Club, Harvard Club, River Club. Republican. Office: Tudor Assocs LLC 33 E 70th St New York NY 10021-4941 Home Phone: 212-879-2617; Office Phone: 212-585-3123. Personal E-mail: tudorassoc@aol.com.

FRENCH, JOHN DWYER, retired lawyer; b. Berkeley, Calif., June 26, 1933; s. Horton Irving and Gertrude Margery (Ritzen) F.; m. Annette Richard, 1955; m. Berna Jo Mahling, 1986. BA summa cum laude, U. Minn., 1955; postgrad, Oxford U., Eng., 1955-56; LLB magna cum laude, Harvard U., 1960. Bar: D.C. 1960, Minn. 1963. Law clk. Justice Felix Frankfurter, U.S. Supreme Ct., 1960-61; legal asst. to commr. FTC, 1961-62; assoc. Ropes & Gray, Boston, 1962-63, Faegre & Benson, Mpls., 1963-66, ptnr., 1967-75, mng. ptnr., 1975-94, chmn. mgmt. com., 1989-94; ret., 2004. Mem. adj. faculty Law Sch. U. Minn., 1965-70, mem. search com. for dean of Coll. of Liberal Arts, 1996; mem. exec. com. Lawyers Com. for Civil Rights Under Law, 1978—; co-chmn. U.S. Dist. Judge Nominating Commn., 1979; vice chmn. adv. com., mem. dir. search com., chmn. devel. office search com. Hubert Humphrey Inst., 1979-87. Contbr. numerous articles and revs. to legal jours. Chmn. or co-chmn. Minn. State Dem. Farm Labor Party Conv., 1970-90, 94, chmn. Mondale Vol. Com., 1972, treas., 1974; assoc. chmn. Minn. Dem.-Farmer-Labor Party, 1985-86; mem. Dem. Nat. Com., 1985-86; mem. Dem. Nat. Conv., 1976, 78, 80, 84, 88; trustee Twin Cities Public TV, Inc., 1980-86, mem. overseers com. to visit Harvard U. Law Sch., 1970-75, 77-82; chmn. Minn. steering com. Dukakis for Pres., 1987-88; mem. Sec. of State's Commn. on Electoral Reform, Minn., 1994; mem. Mayor's Commn. on Regulatory Reform, Mpls., 1995. With U.S. Army, 1955-56. Rotary Found. fellow, 1955-56 Mem. ABA (editorial bd. jour. 1976-79, commn. to study fed. trade 1969—), Minn. Bar Assn., Hennepin County Bar Assn., Jud. Coun. Minn., Lawyers Alliance for Nuclear Arms Control (nat. bd. dirs. 1982-84), U. Minn. Alumni Assn. (exec. com. 1985-87, v.p. 1989-91, pres. 1991-92, Vol. of Yr. award 1988), Phi Beta Kappa. Episcopalian. Office: Faegre & Benson 2200 Wells Fargo Ctr 90 S 7th St Ste 2200 Minneapolis MN 55402-3901

FRENCH, JOSEPH JORDAN, JR., lawyer; b. Shreveport, La., Jan. 3, 1931; s. Joseph Jordan and Minnie Graham (Tomlinson) F.; m. Carol Jean Wesner, Dec. 22, 1954; children: Mary French Breckeen, Joseph Jordan III, Elizabeth French Pospick, Charles Robert. BS, Washington & Lee U., 1950; LLB, U. Tex., 1956. Bar: Tex. 1956, U.S. Dist. Ct. (no. dist.) Tex. 1956, U.S. Ct. Appeals (5th cir.), U.S. Tax Ct. Staff acct. W.O. Ligon & Co., Dallas, 1950-51; assoc. Thompson & Knight, Dallas, 1956-59; ptnr., shareholder Locke Purnell Rain Harrell, Dallas, 1959-93; prin. Joe French & Assocs., P.C., Dallas, 1993—. Sec. Trinity Industries, Inc., Dallas, 1969-97, Halter Marine Group Inc., 1996-97. 2nd lt. USAF, 1951-53. Home: 4440 Fairfax Ave Dallas TX 75205-3028 Office: Joe French & Assocs PC 5956 Sherry Ln Ste 930 Dallas TX 75225 Office Phone: 214-363-9800.

FRENCH, JUDSON CULL, federal official; b. Washington, Sept. 30, 1922; s. Morrison Brady and Ethel (Haviland) Cull French; m. Julia A. McAllister, Aug. 1, 1951; 1 child, Judson Cull. BS cum laude, Am. U., 1943; MS, Harvard U., 1949, postgrad. at bus. sch., 1968; postgrad., Johns Hopkins U., 1943-44, George Washington U., 1944-45, MIT, 1951. Instr. physics Johns Hopkins U., Balt., 1943-44, George Washington U., Washington, 1944-47; sec., dir. Home Title Ins. Co., Washington, 1956-71; with Nat. Bur. Standards (now Nat. Inst. Standards and Tech.), Commerce Dept., Washington, 1948—; leader rsch. devel. projects microwave gaseous electronics Nat. Bur. Stds. Commerce Dept. (now Nat. Inst. Stds. and Tech.), Washington, 1949—64, leader rsch. devel. projects transistor devices and materials metrology, 1955—64; asst. chief electron devices sect. Nat. Bur. Standards (now Nat. Inst. Standards and Tech.), Commerce Dept., 1964-68, chief electron devices sect., 1968-73, chief electronic tech. div., 1973-78, dir. Ctr. for Electronics and Elec. Engring., 1978-91; dir. Electronics and Elec. Engring. Lab., Nat. Inst. Standards and Tech., Gaithersburg, Md., 1991-99, dir. emeritus Electronics and Elec. Engring. Lab., 1999—. Guest rschr., 2000-; pvt. cons., 2000; mem. policy bd. Optoelectronic Computing Sys. Ctr. U. Colo., 1992—; bd. dirs. Nat. Electronics Mfg. Intitiative, Inc., 1998-99; co-chmn. jt. mgmt. com., U.S.-Japan Jt. Optoelectronics Project, 1992-2002; founder NBS/NIST semicondr. metrology program, 1955. Contbr. articles to profl. jours. Recipient Silver medal for meritorious svc. Commerce Dept., 1964, Gold medal for exceptional svc., 1978, Edward Bennett Rosa award Nat. Bur. Standards, 1971, presdl. rank of Meritorious Exec., Sr. Exec. Svc., 1980, Disting. Exec., 1984, 93; Judson C. French award established in his honor Nat. Inst. Stds. and Tech., 1999. Fellow IEEE; mem. Am. Phys. Soc., Nat. Acad. Engring., Sigma Pi Sigma, Pi Delta Epsilon, Alpha Kappa Pi. Office: Nat Inst Standards and Tech Metrology Bldg Rm B358 Electronics Electrical Engr Lab Gaithersburg MD 20899

FRENCH, JULIA MCALLISTER (JUDY), environmental consultant; b. NYC, Dec. 18, 1922; d. Addams Stratton and Home' Catharine McAllister; m. Judson Cull French, Aug. 1, 1951; 1 child, Judson Cull Jr. AA, George Washington U., 1943. Photographic libr. Nat. Geog. Soc., Washington, 1943—54; freelance lectr., cons. on environ., horticulture, L.Am. and Japanese history and culture Bethesda and Rockville, Md., 1955—81; pres. Judy French Assocs., Inc., Rockville, 1982—. Cons., spkr. in field; instigator, leader environ. tours. Contbr. to profl. publs., mags., books and radio and TV programs. Mem. steering com. Potomac Valley Conservation and Recreation Coun., 1962—71; vice chmn. Montgomery County Com., Md. Environ. Trust, 1968—76, chmn., 1977—; chmn. Md. state conservation com. Nat. Capital Area Fedn. Garden Clubs, 1970; mem. planning com., exec. planning coun., solid waste symposium Nat. Bur. Stds., Gaithersburg, Md., 1971; mem. citizen's adv. com. for waste-water treatment facility Montgomery County, 1972; mem. citizen's air pollution workshop com. Rockville Environ. Coalition, 1972; del., mem. water resources citizen adv. com. Met. Washington Coun. Govts. Water Resources Planning Bd., 1973—77; mem. citizen's adv. com. on storm water mgmt. in Watts Br. Basin Dept. Environ. Protection, Rockville, 1974; legis. chmn. steering com. for a More Beautiful Montgomery County, 1977; mem. county line survey com. Md. Environ. Trust, 1978; mem. Solid Waste Energy Recovery Adv. Com., Montgomery County, 1981; mem. adv. coun. for Montgomery County U. Md. Coop. Extension Svc., 1955—81; mem. adv. com. Green Park Farm, Montgomery County, 1955—81; mem. exec. com. Mt. Vernon Coll. Alumnae Assn., 1955—81; mem. del. Interstate Commn. on Potomac River Basin to Thames/Potomac Seminars, London, 1978; chmn. Vol. Guide Svc., U.S. Nat. Arboretum, 1974—84; v.p. State of Md. People to People, 1992—95, chmn. events and programs Nat. Capital Area chpt., 1995—99. Recipient Sci. medal, Bausch and Lomb, 1941, award for exceptional achievement in pollution control activity, Md. Environ. Trust, 1972, Jean Ladson Legis. award, Nat. Capital Area Fedn. Garden Clubs, Inc., 1974, Conservation and Protection cert. of appreciation, Md. Environ. Trust, 1976, Environ. Action Leadership medal, Nat. Coun. State Garden Clubs and Sears Roebuck and Co., 1978.

FRENCH, KENNETH RONALD, finance educator; b. Franklin, NH, Mar. 10, 1954; s. Vernon Cecil and Barbara Jean (Craig) F.; m. Vickie Anne Welch, Sept. 18, 1976; children: Robert Timothy, Laura Nancy, Elizabeth Anne. BSME, Lehigh U., 1975; MBA, U. Rochester, 1978, MS in Fin., 1981, PhD in Fin., 1983. Machine design engr. Eastman Kodak, Rochester, NY, 1975-77; rsch. fellow Found. for Rsch. in Econs. and Edn., UCLA, 1982-83; asst. prof. Grad. Sch. Bus., U. Chgo., 1983-85, assoc. prof., 1985-87, prof., 1987-89, Chgo. Mercantile Exch. prof., 1989-91, Leo Melamed prof., 1991-94; Edwin J. Beinecke prof. Yale Sch. Mgmt., New Haven, 1994-98, mng. dir. Intenat. Ctr. Fin., 1994-98; NTU prof. fin. Sloan Sch. Mgmt., MIT, Cambridge, Mass., 1998—2001; Heidt prof. fin. Tuck Sch. Bus., Dartmouth, Hanover, NH, 2001—. Rsch. assoc. Nat. Bur. Econ. Rsch., Cambridge, Mass., 1989—; dir. Ctr. for Rsch. in Security Prices, Chgo., 1990-94. Contbr. numerous articles to profl. jours. Batterymarch Investment fellow, 1986; Sloan Found. grantee, 1989. Fellow: Am. Acad. Arts & Scis. Office: Tuck Sch Bus Dartmouth 100 Tuck Hall Hanover NH 03755-9000*

FRENCH, LAURENCE ARMAND, social sciences educator; b. Manchester, NH, Mar. 24, 1941; s. Gerald Everett and Juliette Teresa (Boucher) F.; m. Nancy Picthall, Feb. 13, 1971. BA cum laude, U. NH, 1968, MA, 1970, PhD, 1975; postdoctorate, SUNY, Albany, 1978; PhD, U. Nebr., 1981; MA, Western N.M. U., 1994. Diplomate Am. Bd. Forensic Medicine, Am. Bd. Forensic Examiners, Am. Bd. Psychol. Specialties in Forensic Psychology & Neuropsychology, Am. Coll. Advanced Practice Psychologists; lic. psychologist, Ariz. Instr. U. So. Maine, Portland and Gorham, 1971-72; asst. prof. Western Carolina U., Cullowhee, NC, 1972-77, U. Nebr., Lincoln, 1977-80; psychologist I NH Hosp., Concord, 1980-81; psychologist II Laconia State Sch., NH, 1981-88; sr. psychologist NH Divsn. for Children & Youth Svcs., Concord, 1988-89; prof., chair dept. social scis. Western N.Mex. U., Silver City, 1989—2003, prof. emeritus of psychology, 2003—; sr. rsch. assoc. justiceworks U. NH Inst. for Policy and Social Sci. Rsch., 2002—; prof., head dept. psychology Coll. Juvenile Justice and Psychology, Prairie View A&M U., 2003—04. Profl. adv. bd. Internat. Coll. Prescribing Psychologists; cons. NC Dept. Mental Health, 1972—77, Cherokee Indian Mental Health Program, NC, 1974—77, Nebr. Indian Commn., Lincoln, 1977—80; cons. alcohol program Lincoln Indian Ctr., 1977—80; adj. assoc. prof. U. So. Maine, 1980—84; faculty adviser Psi Chi Nat. Honor Soc. in psychology Western N.Mex. U., 1995—2003; mem. Psi Chi Rocky Mountain Regional Steering Com., 2001—02; faculty adviser Psi Chi Nat. Honor Soc. in psychology Prairie View A&M U., 2003—; vis. prof. criminal justice Grambling State U., 2006. Author: The Selective Process of Criminal Justice, 1976; author: (with Richard Crowe) Wee Wish Tree: Special Qualla Cherokee Issue, 1976; author: (with Hornbuckle) Cherokee Perspective, 1981; author: (with Letman et al.) Contemporary Issues in Corrections, 1981; author: Indians and Criminal Justice, 1982, Psychocultural Change and the American Indian, 1987, The Winds of Injustice, 1994, Counseling American Indians, 1997, The Qualla Cherokee Surviving in Two Worlds, 1998, Addictions and Native Americans, 2000, Native American Justice, 2003; author: (with Manzanarez) NAFTA & Neocolonialism, 2004; author: Legislating Indian Country. Peter Lang, 2007; spl. issue editor Quar. Jour. Ideology, Vol. II, 1987, mem. editl. bd. Jour. Police and Criminal Psychology; contbr. articles to profl. jours. Commr. Pilsbury Lake Village Dist., Webster, NH, 1985-90. With USMC, 1959-63, Badge of Honor, Republic of China, 1998. Recipient Hon. medal Rep. China, 1998, Nat. Int. Drug Abuse 1st Leadership in Rsch. award, 1999, Lifetime Achievement award N.Mex. Assn. for Addiction Profls., 2004; Dissertation Yr. fellow U. NH 1971-72, Nebr. U. System grad. faculty fellow, 1978. Fellow: APA, Am. Coll. Forensic Examiners (diplomate), Soc. Psychol. Study Social Issues, Prescribing Psychologists Register (diplomate); mem.: VFW (life), N.Mex. Alcohol and Drug Abuse Counselors Assn. (Educator of Yr. 1997), Am. Soc. Criminology (life), Nat. Assn. Alcohol and Drug Abuse Counselors (clin. issue com. 1996—98, nat. chmn.), Internat. Coll. Prescribing Psychologists Inc. (profl. adv. bd.), Nat. Assn. Sch. Psychologists, 3rd Marine Divsn. Assn. (life), Psi Chi (steering com. Rocky Mountain region 1999—2003, Regional Faculty Advisor award 2002—03), Phi Delta Kappa (treas. Rocky Mountain region 1990—91, pres. 1991—92). Office Phone: 603-862-1493. Personal E-mail: frogwnmu@yahoo.com. E-mail: Laurence_French@unh.edu.

FRENCH, LENNY SUE, elementary school educator; b. Norwich, NY, Aug. 15, 1967; d. Leonard Albert and Bette Lou Mayne; m. Matthew Scott French; 1 child, Lane Matthew; 1 child, Ethan Michael. MusB, Crane Sch. Music, 1989; MSc in edn., State U. of NY Coll. at Potsdam, 1993. Vocal, music and drama tchr. Salmon River Ctrl. Sch., Ft. Covington, NY, 1989—99, Graham Mid. Sch., 1999—2003; math and sci. educator Mendenhall Mid. Sch., Greensboro, NC, 2003—. Diversity trainer Alamance County Schools, Burlington, NC, 2000—03, suicide intervention counselor, 2000—03. Musician Wendover Hills Wesleyan Ch., Greensboro, NC, 2000—04, North Star Unitd Meth. Ch., Greensboro, 2005—; canoeing/kayaking instr. Red Cross, 1986—94. Recipient Gold award, Girl Scout, 1985, Nat. Vocal Music award, Sherburne-Earlville Ctrl. Sch., 1985. Mem.: NY State Music Sch. Assn., NC Assn. of Music Educators, NC Assn. of Educators, Sigma Alpha Iota. Avocations: swimming, scrapbooks, gardening. Office: Mendenhall Mid Sch Willoughby Blvd Greensboro NC 27408 Office Phone: 336-545-2000.

FRENCH, MARILYN, writer, critic, historian; b. NYC, Nov. 21, 1929; d. E. Charles and Isabel (Hazz) Edwards; m. Robert M. French, Jr., June 4, 1950 (div. 1967); children: Jamie, Robert. BA, Hofstra Coll., 1951, MA, 1964; PhD, Harvard U., 1972. Secretarial, clerical worker, 1946-53; lectr. Hofstra Coll., 1964-68; asst. prof. Holy Cross Coll., Worcester, Mass., 1972-76; Mellon fellow Harvard U., 1976-77; writer, lectr., 1967—. Author: (criticism) The Book as World: James Joyce's Ulysses, 1976, Shakespeare's Division of Experience, 1981, The Women's Room, 1977, The Bleeding Heart, 1980, Beyond Power: On Women, Men and Morals, 1986, Her Mother's Daughter, 1987, The War Against Women, 1992, Our Father: A Novel, 1994, My Summer with George, 1996, A Season in Hell, 1998, From Eve To Dawn: A History of Women, Vol. I-III, 2002—03, (introductions) Summer and The House of Mirth, 1981, Her Mothers, 1985, A Weave of Women, 1985. Mem. Phi Beta Kappa. E-mail: mfrench187@aol.com.

FRENCH, MARY B., editor, photographer, poet, retired literature educator; b. Dallas, July 21, 1942; d. Harry Blake and Mary Virginia (Jones) F.; m. Richard Edelin Crouch, Feb. 6, 1965; children: John, Virginia. BA, Coll. William and Mary, 1965; MA, U. Va., 1966. Columnist, reporter Va. Gazette, Williamsburg, 1961-65; mng. editor William and Mary Rev., Williamsburg, 1963-64; asst. editor Microfilm Publ., U. Va., Charlottesville, 1966-67; lectr. Am. lit. and women in lit. U. Va., Falls Church, 1968-99. Instr. English, No. Va. C.C., Annandale, 1968-69; instr. English composition George Washington U., Washington, 1970; cons. in lit. humanities project Arlington County Libr., 1976. Author: The State Site: A Guide to Legislative Procedures and Lawmakers, 1977; compiler: Women in Literature: A Bibliography, 1973; editor (with J.L. Anderson) Microfilm Edition of the Papers of R.M.T. Hunter, 1817-1887, 1966; editor Spokeswoman Mag., 1979-82, Washington Women's Rep. Newsletter, 1979-82; mng. editor Women's News Svc., 1979-82; assoc. editor Career Opportunities News, 1983-96; mng. editor Army Mag., 1984-93, editor, 1993-2002, editor in chief, 2002—; contbr. poetry to several anthologies. Com. on Status of Women, Arlington, Va., 1976, steering com. Coalition on Optimum Growth, 1970-73. Mem. MLA, AAUW (chmn. women's studies, dir. Arlington br. 1974-76, assoc. editor Grad. Women mag. 1982, mng. editor publ. 1983), the Am. News Women's Club, the Acad. of Am. Poets, the Lyon Village Citizens Assoc., Hillsboro Cmty. Assn., English-Speaking Union, Jane Austen Soc., US Congress Periodical Press Corrs.'s Assn., Nat. Trust Hist. Preservation, Preservation Soc. Loudoun County, Old House Group Loudoun County, Soc. Profl. Journalists, Am. Soc. Mag. Editors, Va. Hist. Soc., Land Trust of Va., The Nature Conservancy, Appalachian Trail Conf., Photo Comm. of the Nat. Press Club, (hon.) 101st Airborne Divsn. U.S. Army. Episcopalian. Office Phone: 703-907-2620. E-mail: mfrench@ausa.org.

FRENCH, MICHAEL BRUCE, business executive; b. Arlington, Va., Sept. 18, 1954; s. Orville Sidney and Doris (Goldberg) F.; m. Robin Ann Abenstein, Oct. 15, 1978; children: Brian Michael, Matthew Jeffrey, Sean Thornton. BA, Princeton U., 1976; M in Mgmt., Northwestern U., 1978. Brand asst., asst. brand mgr. Procter & Gamble Co., Cin., 1978—80, brand mgr., 1981—84; mktg. dir. Coca-Cola Bottling Mideast Inc. subs. P&G, Lexington, Ky., 1984—85; v.p. mktg. Coca-Cola Bottling Mideast, Inc., Lexington, 1985—87; brand mgr. Coca-Cola USA, Atlanta, 1987—89; mktg. mgr. chain accounts Coca-Cola Fountain, Atlanta, 1989, dir. channel mktg., 1989—93, dir. product definition and devel., 1993, asst. v.p. mktg. ops., 1993—94, v.p. mktg., 1994—95; dir. edn. mktg. Coca-Cola USA, Atlanta, 1995—97, dir. consumer occasions mktg., non-retail, 1997—99; dir. Coca-Cola Connection, 1999—2000; sr. cons. Monitor Co., Cambridge, Mass., 2000—02; v.p. consumer insights Brown-Forman Corp., Louisville, 2003—06, sr. v.p. consumer insights, 2006—07, sr. v.p. corp. strategy, 2007—. Mem. Rep. Party of Ga., Atlanta, 1984-99; mem. baseball steering com. U. Ky., Lexington, 1986-87; fundraising chmn. Jr. Achievement of the Bluegrass, Lexington, 1986-87; chmn. pub. awareness subcom. Gov.'s Anti-Substance Abuse Commn., Frankfort, Ky., 1986-87; divsn. coord. Coca-Cola United Way Campaign, 1996; mem. market rsch. exec. bd. Louisville Fund for Arts, 2003-07. Named to Hon. Order of Ky. Cols., 1986. Mem. Princeton Club of Ky. Avocations: golf, reading. Office: Brown Forman 850 Dixie Hwy Louisville KY 40210 Home: 316 Longview Park Pl Louisville KY 40245 Office Phone: 502-774-7554. Personal E-mail: frenchmike@msn.com. E-mail: mike_french@b-f.com.

FRENCH, MICHAEL FRANCIS, medical educator; b. La Crosse, Wis., July 25, 1948; s. Albert Frank Jr. and Kathryn Patricia (MacKoske) F.; m. Janet Alan Streeter Head, Nov. 26, 1991. BS in Edn., U. Wis., 1972. Cert. emergency med. technician. Tng. coord. emergency med. svcs. Wis. Dept. Health and Social Svcs., Madison, 1975-80, tng. dir. emergency med. svcs.,

1980-84, chief emergency med. svcs., 1984-90; co-dir. Area Health Edn. Ctrs. office Kirksville (Mo.) Coll. Osteo. Medicine, 1990—, adj. instr. family medicine and cmty. health, 1990—. Emergency med. svcs. cons., Kirksville, 1984—; founding mem. Continuing Edn. Coordinating Bd. for Emergency Med. Svcs., Inc., Kirksville, 1992. Author: (tng. curriculum) EMS Instructor Training Course-U.S. Dept. Transportation, 1985; editor newsletter, editor-in-chief publs. Nat. Assn. Emergency Med. Technicians, 1983-91; author book chpts. V.p., pres. bd. dirs. Adair County Ret. Sr. Vol. Program, Kirksville, 1992-95; com. chair, bd. dirs. Mo. Rural Opportunities Coun., 2000—. Recipient Lunda Trauma award Am. Trauma Soc., 1982, Svc. awards Nat. Coun. State EMS Tng. Coords., 1982, 83, A. Roger Fox Founders award Nat. Assn. Emergency Med. Technicians, 1989, others. Mem. ASTM, ASCD, ASTD, APHA, Nat. Rural Health Assn. (rural health policy bd. 1998—, gov. affairs com. 2000—, sec. 2005—, trustee 2005—), Mo. Rural Health Assn. (bd. dirs. 1995-96, 99—, pres.-elect 1996-97, pres. 1997-99, exec. com. 1999—), Mo. PEW Health Professions Partnership (chair exec. com. 1994-95), Mo. Pub. Health Assn. (awards chair 1996), Wis. Emergency Med. Tech. Assn., Am. Coll. Healthcare Execs. (assoc.), Nat. Orgn. Area Health Edn. Ctr. Program Dirs. (nominations com. 1996), Nat. Area Health Edn. Ctrs. Orgn. (pub. policy com. 2001—), Mensa Avocations: bicycling, reading, computer games. Office: KCOM AHEC Program 800 W Jefferson St Kirksville MO 63501-1443

FRENCH, RICHARD HARRY, hydrologic and hydraulic engineer, consultant; b. Wheeling, W.Va., Jan. 5, 1947; s. Clyde Leslie and Florence (McComb) F.; m. Darlene Gates, May, 1975; 1 child, Mercedes. BCE, Ohio State U., 1971, MS, 1972; PhD, U. Calif., Berkeley, 1975. Registered profl. engr., Calif., Nev. Asst. prof. Vanderbilt U., Nashville, 1975-79; assoc. prof. Water Resources Ctr., Desert Research Inst., Las Vegas, Nev., 1979-84, research prof. and assoc. exec. dir., 1984-86, spl. asst. to pres. for engring., 1986-87. Vis. prof. Nat. Def. Acad. Yokosuka, Japan, 1983; rsch. prof. Desert Rsch. Inst., 1987—. Author: Open-Channel Hydraulics, 1985, Hydraulic Processes on Alluvial Fans, 1987; editor: Salinity in Watercourses and Reservoirs, 1984, (series) Water Quality Modeling; editor: Proceedings of the Internat. Symposium on the Hydraulics/Hydrology of Arid Lands, San Diego, Calif., 1990, ASCE, N.Y. Bd. dirs. AquaVision, 1988-90. Recipient ASCE Arid Lands Hydraulic award, 1991; Boris A. Bakhmeteff rsch. fellow Columbia U., 1973. Mem. ASCE (pres. Nev. sect. 1989-90, bd. dirs., chmn. task com. on flood hazard analysis on alluvial fans, editor symposium on hydraulics/hydrology of arid lands), Internat. Assn. Hydraulic Rsch., Am. Water Resources Assn., Nev. Water Resources Assn. Office: Desert Rsch Inst Water Resources Ctr 755 E Flamingo Rd Las Vegas NV 89119-7363 Home: 3014 Whisper Lark St San Antonio TX 78230-3544

FRENCH, RODERICK STUART, university chancellor; b. LaGrande, Oreg., Apr. 5, 1931; s. Stuart Gautier and Laura A. (Richards) F.; m. Evelyn Fagg, 1955 (div. 1964); children: Roderick Stuart, Jr., Sarah Suzanne; m. Sally Stedman, May 8, 1965. AB, Kenyon Coll., 1954; MDiv, Episcopal Div. Sch., 1957; STM, Union Theol. Sem., 1965; PhD, George Washington U., 1971. Dir. youth dept. World Coun. Chs., Geneva, 1959-64; freelance writer Balt., Washington, 1964-67; spl. asst. office pub. affairs Peace Corps., Washington, 1967-68; assoc. dir. office exptl. programs George Washington U., Washington, 1969-78, dir., 1978-84, v.p. acad. affairs, 1984-95, dir. univ. seminars program, 1995-97; chancellor Am. U. Sharjah, United Arab Emirates, 1998—2002, chancellor emeritus, trustee, 2002—; sec. bd. dirs. AUS-USA Found., 2002—. Editor: What is Humanistic Education?, 1973, An Independent University in a Free Society, 1988; co-editor: The Public Humanities, 1984; gen. editor monograph series GW Washington Studies, 10 vols., 1974-82, A Voice for University, 1996, A Vission for a New University, 2002; contbr. articles to profl. jours. Chmn. D.C. Humanities Coun., 1979-81; v.p. Nat. Humanities Alliance, 1986-88, pres. 1988-92, exec. com., 1988-94; bd. dirs. Nat. Fed. State Humanities Councils, Washington, 1983-86, Potomac River Basin Consortium, Washington, 1981-85; bd. mgrs. Columbia Hist. Soc., Washington, 1980-84; trustee, 1st v.p. Ctr. for Advanced Study of the Americas, 1984-87, pres. 1987-88; trustee Nat. Cultural Alliance, 1990-92; sec. bd. dirs. AUS-USA Found., 2003—. Recipient Citation for Outstanding Contbn. to Cultural Life in Washington, Washington Rev., 1979, D.C. Pub. Humanities award, 1988; named Hon. Citizen, Winnipeg, Man., Can., 1961. Mem. Am. Soc. Environ. History (v.p. 1977-81), Cosmos Club, Phi Beta Kappa. Democrat.

FRENCH, STEPHANIE TAYLOR, grantmaking and philanthropy expert; b. Newark; d. William Taylor and Connie V. French; m. Amory Houghton III, Sept. 8, 1979 (div.); children: Christina French Houghton, Amory Taylor Houghton. BA, Wellesley Coll., 1972; MBA, Harvard U., 1978. Freelance on-air performer, prodr. San Francisco and Oakland radio and cable TV stas., 1973-76; dir. European Gallery, San Francisco, 1974-75; acct. exec. Young & Rubican, NYC, 1978-79; acct. supr. Rives Smith Baldwin & Carlberg, Houston, 1980-81; mgr. cultural affairs and spl. programs Philip Morris Cos. Inc., NYC, 1981-86, dir. cultural and contbns. programs, 1986-90, v.p. corp. contbn. and cultural programs bds., 1990—2001; pvt. practice NYC, 2001—05; sr. v.p. US Trust Co., 2005—. Bd. dirs. New Mus. Contemporary Art, Mus. Arts and Design, Parsons Dance Co., Miller Theatre Columbia U., PERFORMA, Works and Process, Shen Wei Dance, Bus. Com. of the Met. Mus. Art, Arts and Edn. Adv. Coun. for Harvard Grad. Sch. Edn., dance com. Juillard Sch.; apptd. mem. Gov. of NY to Empire State Arts Commn., Mayor of NYC to the NYC Econ. Devel. Corp.; bd. overseers Calif. Inst. of the Arts; adv. coun. Nat. Pub. Radio. Mem. Harvard Bus. Sch. Network of Women Alums, Wellesley Club.

FRENCH, TARENCE WADE, SR., minister; b. Indpls., Oct. 18, 1971; s. James Wayne French and Michelle Dianne Blackwell; m. Donna Marie Young, Apr. 15, 2001; children: Destini Marie Young, Tessa Iman, Alexa Seymone, Tarence Wanyai French, Jr. PhD, St. Luke Evang. Sch. of Bibl. Studies, Atlanta, 2003; ThD, United Theol. Sem., Ashland. Ind., 2004; cert. of Bibl. Mental Health, Master's Grad. Sch. of Continuing Studies, Evansville, Ind., 2003; DMin (hon.), So. Ind. Bible Coll. & Sem., Clarksville, 2004; DDIV (hon.), Mt. Carmel Inst. of Bibl. Studies, LA, 2003, The Interfaith Sch. of Theology, London, 2003, Trinitarian Ministries Sch. of Theology, Hot Springs, Ark., 2002. Cert. tchr. Nat. Assn. of Pvt. Theol. Instns., 2004. Ceo Urban Harvest Ministries, Inc., Indpls., 1998—; founding pastor Divine Revelations Christian Ctr., Inc., Indpls., 2002—; pres. Urban Harvest Bible Inst., Indpls., 2002—; instr. Crossroads Bible Inst., Grandeville, Mich., 2002—. Mem. Mt. Carmel Inst. of Bibl. Studies, LA, 2003; bishop elect Grace Valley Theol. Sem., Lubbock, Tex., 2004. Named Ky. Col., Gov. Paul E. Patton, 2003; recipient Name was placed on the Wall of Tolerance, Nat. Campaign for Tolerance, 2002. Mem.: Nat. Assn. Pvt. Theol. Instns. Office: Divine Revelations Christian Center Inc PO Box 44083 Indianapolis IN 46244-0083 Home Phone: 317-924-0826; Office Phone: 317-202-9313. Office Fax: 317-202-9506. E-mail: drtwfrench@yahoo.com.

FRENCH, TED R., multi-industry company executive; BBA, U. Ga., Athens, 1977, MBA, 1978. Cert. Textron Six Sigma Green Belt. Contr. to dir. bus. devel. Rockwell Automotive Rockwell Internat., Troy, Mich., 1978—89; v.p. corp. planning and devel. J.I. Case, Racine, Wis., 1989-92; pres. fin. svcs., CFO Case Corp., Racine, 1992-99, treas., 1992—94; pres. fin. svcs., CFO CNH Global NV, 1999—2000; exec. v.p., CFO Textron, Inc., Providence, 2000—, chmn., CEO Textron Fin. Corp. Bd. dirs. US C. of C.; mem. issuers adv. com. Std. & Poors. Mem. editl. adv. bd.: CFO Mag. Office: Textron Inc 40 Westminster St Providence RI 02903 Office Phone: 401-421-2800.*

FRENCH, VALERIE, history professor; b. Toledo, Ohio, Jan. 16, 1941; d. John Samuel and Elizabeth Harmon French; m. Donald Robert Allen (div.); children: Signe Allen Linscott, John French Allen; m. Robert Lee Beisner, Mar. 6, 1976. BA, Cornell U., 1964; MA, UCLA, 1967, PhD, 1971. From asst. to assoc. prof. history Am. U., Washington, 1972—2005, emeritus assoc. prof. history, 2005—. Assoc. dean curriculum Am. U., Washington, 1978—83, dir. summer sessions, 1986—96, chair dept. history, 2001—04. Author: Historians The Living Past, 1978, Families in Ancient Mediterranean, 2006. Pres., bd. dirs. Washington Soc. Archeol. Inst. Am., 1981—84, 1978—91. Recipient numerous grants. Mem.: Assn. Ancient Historians, Am. Philological Assn. (com. chair 1985—94), Womens Classical Caucas (co-chair com. 1988). Office: Am Univ Dept History 4400 Massachusetts Ave Washington DC 20016-8038 Business E-Mail: vfrench@american.edu.

FRENCH, WILLIAM HAROLD, retired newspaper editor; b. London, Ont., Can., Mar. 21, 1926; s. Harold Edward and Isabel (Brash) F.; m. Margaret Jean Rollo, June 23, 1951; children— Jane, Mark, Paul, Susan. BA, U. Western Ont., 1948; Nieman fellow, Harvard, 1954-55; DLitt (hon.), U. Western Ont., 1991. With The Globe and Mail, Toronto, Ont., Can., 1948-90, lit. editor, 1960-90; instr. journalism Ryerson Poly. Inst., 1955-88; asso. fellow York U., 1969-77; broadcaster Canadian Broadcasting Corp., 1964-90, ret., 1990. Cons. Can. Council, 1969— Author: A Most Unlikely Village, 1960. Recipient President's medal U. Western Ont., 1966; Nat. Newspaper award for critical writing, 1978, 79 Home: 78 N Hills Terr Don Mills ON Canada M3C 1M6

FRENIER, DIANE M., lawyer; b. Burlington, Vt., June 8, 1957; BS in mgmt. magna cum laude, Rutgers U., 1982, JD, 1986. Bar: NJ 1986. Assoc. Smith, Stratton, Wise, Heher & Brennan, Princeton, NJ, 1986—91, ptnr., 1993—2000; assoc. Hannoch Weisman, Roseland, NJ, 1991—93; ptnr. Reed Smith LLP, Princeton, NJ, 2000—, mem. exec. com. Mem.: NJ State Bar Assn., ABA (mem. bus. law sect.). Office: Reed Smith LLP Princeton Forrestal Village 136 Main St, Ste 250 Princeton NJ 08540 Office Phone: 609-514-5999. Office Fax: 609-951-0824. Business E-Mail: dfrenier@reedsmith.com.

FRENKEL, DAVID ARIE, law professor; b. Tel Aviv, Feb. 2, 1940; s. Tsvi and Esther-Sarah (Berezovsky) F.; m. Naomi Davis, June 8, 1971; children: Esther, Tsvi, Dov, Dvora, Raya. MJurisprudence, Hebrew U., 1961, LLD, 1975. Bar: Israel 1963. Pvt. practice, 1963-69, 81-89; asst., faculty of law Hebrew U., Jerusalem, 1969-72; instr., rschr. faculty of law and Inst. Legis. Rsch. & Comparative Law, Hebrew U., Jerusalem, 1972-75; dep. legal adviser Ministry of Edn. and Culture, Israel, 1974-76; dep., then legal advisor Ministry of Health, Israel, 1976-81; legal advisor Municipality of Beer-Sheva, Israel, 1990-97; prof. law dept. bus. adminstrn. Ben-Gurion U. Sch. Mgmt., Beer-Sheva, 1997—. External tchr. Hebrew U. Jerusalem, Hadassah Med. Sch., Pub. Health Sch. and Faculty of Dental Medicine, 1978-02; tutor Open U., 1993-01; external tchr. Haifa U., Health Adminstrn. br., 1982-98, Bar-Ilan U., Ashkelon br., 1982-91; from tchr. to sr. lectr. Ben-Gurion U., Beer Sheva, 1981-97, with faculty of tech. dept. industry and adminstrn. engring., 1986-97; lectr. Hadassah Cmty. Coll., Jerusalem, 1974-87; mem. ethics com. for experiments on animals, Ben-Gurion U., Beer-Sheva, 1998—; chmn. ethics com. for Soroka U. Med. Ctr., Beer-Sheva, 1997—; judge local authorities disciplinary tribunal, 1996-02; vis. prof. King's Coll. London Sch. Law, 2005. Author: Law of Cooperative Societies in Israel - Judicature and Legislation, 1966, Effect of Taxation on Registration of Rights in Land, 1972, Civil Judicature on Military and Security Matters, 1974, Law and Medicine - Military Aspects, 1985, Associations Law in Israel - The Law of not-for-profit Organizations in Israel, 2000, Partnership Law in Israel, 2002; co-author: (with G. Tedeschi) Law Citations, 1972, (with A. Kirschenbaum and N. Rakover) A Guide to the Sources of the Jewish Law, 1983, (with E. Davis) The Hebrew Amulet, 1995; co-editor Health Law in Can. Jour., 1980-87; mem. editl. bd. Medicine and Law; contbr. chpts. to books and articles to profl. jours. Fellow, WHO, 1979. Fellow Royal Soc. Health, Royal Inst. Pub. Health and Hygiene (Worthy of the City Beer-Sheva award 2004); mem. Am. Soc. Law, Medicine and Ethics, Internat. Assn. Jewish Lawyers, Soc. Medicine and Law in Israel, Internat. Dental, Ethics and Law Soc., World Assn. Med. Law, European Bus. and Ethic Network, Acad. Legal Sci. Bus., Internat. Soc. Bus., Econs., and Ethics, Athens Inst. Edn. and Rsch. Office: Ben Gurion U Sch Mgmt Dept Bus Admin PO Box 653 Be'er Sheva 84105 Israel E-mail: dfrenkel@bgu.ac.il.

FRENKEL, EUGENE PHILLIP, physician; b. Detroit, Aug. 27, 1929; s. David Eugene and Eva (Antin) Frenkel; m. Rhoda Beth Smilay, Dec. 21, 1958; children: Lisa Michelle, Peter Alan. BS, Wayne State U., 1949; MD, U. Mich., 1953. Diplomate Am. Bd. Internal Medicine (bd. govs. 1980-87, chmn. subspecialty com. hematology 1980-85), Am. Bd. Hematology, Am. Bd. Med. Oncology. Intern Wayne County Gen. Hosp., Eloise, Mich., 1953-54; resident in internal medicine Boston City Hosp., 1954-55; resident in internal medicine, then instr. U. Mich. Med. Center, 1957-62; mem. faculty U. Tex. Southwestern Med. Ctr., Dallas, 1962—, prof. internal medicine and radiology, 1969—, chief divsn. hematology-oncology, 1962-91, Patsy R. and Raymond D. Nasher Disting. chair in cancer rsch., 1990—, A. Kenneth Pye prof. in cancer rsch., 1994—; chief nuclear medicine, cons. hematology-oncology VA Med. Center, Dallas, 1962-80; Sydney and J.L. Huffines, Jr. disting. chair U. Tex. Southwestern Med. Ctr., 1998—, Elaine Dewey Sammons Disting. chair cancer rsch. in honor of Eugene P. Frenkel, MD, 2003—. Cons. com. evaluation rsch. hematology, nutrtion Nat. Inst. Arthritis and Metabolic Diseases, 1979—82; active Am. Joint Commn. Cancer, 1986—95; interim dir. divsn. hematology-oncology VA Med. Ctr., Dallas, 1995—97; dir. The Boone Pickens Fund for Cancer Rsch. and Treatment Honoring Dr. Eugene P. Frenkel, 2004—. Contbr. rsch. papers in field. Officer M.C. USAF, 1955—57. Fellow: ACP (coun. subspecialty secs. 1992—), Internat. Soc. Hematology; mem.: Internat. Assn. Study Lung Cancer, Internat. Soc. Hematology (councillor 1992—97), Am. Fedn. Clin. Rsch., Soc. Nuc. Medicine, Am. Urol. Assn., So. Soc. Clin. Investigation, Am. Soc. Clin. Investigation, Am. Soc. Biol. Chemists, Am. Assn. Cancer Edn., Am. Assn. Cancer Rsch., Assn. Am. Physicians, Am. Cancer Soc. (pres. Dallas unit 1970—71, mem. sci. adv. com. clin. investigations II-chemotherapy and hematolog 1978—82, mem. nat. clin. fellowship com. 1978—87, dir. Tex. divsn. 1978—, Emma Freeman prof. 1981—91, mem. internat. rsch. grants com. 1988—90, mem. sci. adv. coun. 1991—97), Am. Soc. Clin. Oncology (chmn. membership com. 1982—85), Am. Soc. Hematology (treas. 1976—84), Alpha Omega Alpha. Office: U Tex Southwestern Med Ctr Dallas TX 75390-8852

FRENKEL, JACOB AHARON, insurance company executive; b. Tel-Aviv, Israel, Feb. 8, 1943; came to U.S., 1967; s. Kalman H. and Lea (Zwibaum) F.; m. Niza Yair, Sept. 3, 1968; children: Orli-Miriam, Tahl-Ida. BA in Econs. and Polit. Sci, Hebrew U., Jerusalem, 1966, postgrad. (fellow), 1966-67; MA (fellow), U. Chgo., 1969, PhD in Econs. (Lilly Honor fellow), 1970. Mem. faculty Grad. Sch. Bus., U. Chgo., 1973-87, David Rockefeller prof. internat. econs., 1982-87; econ. counsellor, dir. research IMF, 1987-91; mem. faculty Tel Aviv U., 1991-96, Weisfeld prof. econs. of peace and internat. rels., 1994-96; gov. bank of Israel, Jerusalem, 1991-99; chmn. sovereign advisory group Merrill Lynch, London, 2000—04; chmn. Merrill Lynch Internat. Inc., 2000—04; chmn., global econ. strategies group Amer. Internat. Group, 2004—, vice chmn., 2004—. Mem. G-7 Coun., adv. com. of Inst. for Internat. Econs.; mem. group of 30, disting. mem. adv. com. Korea Inst. for Global Econs.; chmn. bd. govs. Inter-Am. Devel. Bank, 1995-96; co-chmn. Israeli del. to multilateral peace talks on regional econ. devels., 1991—. Author numerous books on internat. and macro econs.; editor Jour. Polit. Economy, 1973-87; contbr. numerous articles to profl. jours. Decorated gran cruz Orden de Mayo al Merito (Argentina); recipient Czech Karel Englis prize in econs. Fellow Econometric Soc.; mem. Am. Acad. Arts and Scis. (fgn. hon.), Japan Soc. Monetary Econs. (hon.), Israel Assn. Grads. in Social Scis. and Humanities (hon. pres.). Office: Amer Internat Group 70 Pine St New York NY 10270*

FRENKIEL, RICHARD HENRY, retired systems engineer, consultant; b. NYC, Mar. 4, 1943; s. Lucjan and Stephanie (Komorowska) Frenkiel; m. Annamae Mary Rollason, Dec. 28, 1963; children: Scott Thomas, Kathleen Ann. BSME, Tufts U., 1963; MS in Engring. Mechanics, Rutgers U., 1965. Tech. staff Bell Labs., Holmdel, NJ, 1963—71, supr., 1973—77, dept. head, 1977—88, R & D dir., 1988—93, ret., 1993. Vis. prof. Rutgers U., dir. strategic planning WINLAB, 1994—. Com. mem. Manalapan Twp., NJ, 1995—99, dep. mayor NJ, 1995, mayor NJ, 1999. Named N.J. Inventor of Yr., 1995; named to Hall Fame, Consumer Electronics Assn., 2004; recipient Achievement award, Indsl. Rsch. Inst., 1992, Nat. medal, Tech. U.S. Dept. of Commerce, 1994; fellow, Bell Labs., 1990. Fellow: IEEE (spkr. Outstanding Lecture Tour 1975—76, Alexander Graham Bell medal 1987); mem.: Nat. Acad. Engring. Republican. Achievements include design of first cellular telephone system in U.S; cordless telephone products; invention of Metroliner Radiotelephone System; cell splitting method; patents in field. Office: Rutgers WINLAB 671 Rt 1 South North Brunswick NJ 08854-8060 Business E-Mail: frenkiel@winlab.rutgers.edu.

FRENSLEY, SUSANNE H., history educator; BA, MEd, Vanderbilt Univ. History tchr. Stratford and Hillsboro H.Schs., 1995—. Named Tenn. Tchr. of Yr., 2007. Office: Hillsboro Comprehensive High Sch 3812 Hillsboro Pike Nashville TN 37215 Business E-Mail: susanne.frensley@mnps.org.*

FRENZEL, FRANCES JOHNSON, nurse, educator, real estate broker, poet; b. Bedford, Va., Feb. 2, 1911; d. J. James and Willie Calpernia (Markham) Johnson; m. Paul H. Frenzel, Dec. 21, 1933 (dec. 1990). RN, Wash. Adventist Hosp., Takoma Park, Md., 1932; BS, Columbia Union Coll., 1933; real estate license, Glendale CC, Calif., 1968. Cert. real estate broker. RN supr. Glendale (Calif.) Adventist Med. Ctr., 1933-34; instr. various flower show schs., Nat. Coun. State Garden Clubs, U.S. & Mex., 1951-98; flower design instr. Edinburg (Tex.) Coll., 1953. Founder, chmn. World Flower Festival L.A. Garden Club and Greater L.A. Dist. Calif. Garden Clubs, Inc., 1962-98; lectr. in many states including Hawaii. Author: Arrangements on Parade, 1950; contbr. poems to books and nat. and state mags.; contbr. photographs of flower arrangements to profl. jours. Mem. City of Glendale Beautification adv. council, 1974—, L.A. County Med. Auxiliary Glendale, 1956—, pres., 1968—69; founder The Golden Garden Angel fund, 1998; election precinct officer L.A. County, Glendale, 1956—2000. Recipient numerous Garden Club awards, 1962—, Editor's Choice award, 1999, Lifetime Beautification Achievement award, City of Glendale and Com. for a Clean and Beautiful Glendale, 2001, various other awards from organizations and Los Angeles County; named Guardian Angel, Staff Golden Gardens Mag., 2001; grantee Proton Treatment Ctr., Loma Linda (Calif.) Med. Ctr. Mem.: Internat. Soc. Poetry, L.A. County Med. Assn. Alliance (pres. Dist. IV 1968—69), L.A. Garden Club (pres. 1960—62), Judges Coun. Orange County, Judges Coun. So. Calif. (chmn. 1978—80), Internat. Soc. Poets, Ikebana Internat. (L.A. chpt.), Greater L.A. Dist. Calif. Gardens Club (dir. 1962—64), Nat. Coun. State Garden Clubs Inc. (life), Calif. Garden Clubs Inc. (life; pub. rels. chmn. 1999—, founder golden gardens angel fund for bd. 1999—, bd. dirs., Woman of Yr. 2002). Avocations: flower arranging, gardening, gourmet cooking, interior decorating.

FRERE, FABRICE G., publishing executive; b. France; With GQ Mag., NYC, 1993—98; creative dir., COO CITY Mag., NYC, 1998—; and creative dir., COO Desert Living Mag., Phoenix. Recipient Award of Excellence for Editl. Design, Am. Inst. Graphic Arts, 2005, Nat. Mag. award for Best Use of Photography, CITY Mag., Am. Soc. Mag. Editors, 2004, Nat. Mag. award for Photo Portfolio, CITY Mag., 2007. Mem.: Soc. Publication Designers. Office: CITY Mag 151 Mercer St New York NY 10012 Office Phone: 212-965-9484, 212-843-8096. Office Fax: 212-966-3329.*

FRERICHS, ERNEST SUNLEY, religious studies educator; b. S.I., Apr. 30, 1925; s. Ernest V. and Eva (Sunley) F.; m. Sarah Hazel (Cutts), Aug. 20, 1949; children: John Allen (dec.), David Sunley, Elizabeth Ann. BA, Brown U., 1948; MA, Harvard U., 1949; STB, Boston U., 1952, PhD, 1957; LHD (hon.), Hebrew Union Coll., 1992. Mem. faculty Brown U., Providence, 1953—, prof. religious studies, 1966-95, chmn. dept., 1964-70, asst. dean., 1958-59, dean grad. sch., 1976-82, program dir. in Judaic studies, 1982-95, prof. religious and Judaic studies emeritus, 1995—; exec. dir. Dorot Found., Providence, 1995—2003, pres., 2003—. Mem. Grad. and Profl. Sch. Fin. Aid Coun., 1978-82; mem. Grad. Record Exam. Bd., 1980-82; mem. com. on testing coun. Grad. Sch., 1980-82; mem. N.Am. com. Mellon Fellowship Program, 1982-92; chmn. coun. Grad. Studies in Religion, 1989-93. Region I and II selection com. Woodrow Wilson Found., 1959-69; trustee Am. Sch. Oriental Rsch., 1976-82, 93—, v.p., 1993-96; trustee Hiatt Inst., Brandeis U., 1979-82, Roger Williams Hosp., Providence, 1981-97, Palestine Endowment Fund Israel, Inc., 1999—, Albright Inst. Archeol. Rsch., Jerusalem, 1974—, pres., 1976-82; bd. dirs. Assn. Jewish Studies, 1990-98, Jewish Chautauqua Soc., 2002; acad. adv. coun. Ctr. for Jewish History, 2004—. With inf., AUS, 1943-46, ETO. Decorated Combat Infantryman's badge; recipient Disting. Alumnus Award Boston U., 1994; Beebe fellow Boston U., 1952-53; Lilly postdoctoral fellow Heidelberg U., 1962-63. Mem. Soc. Bibl. Lit. (exec. com. New Eng. coun. 1977-82); Am. Acad. Religion (pres. New Eng. 1970-71); Phi Beta Kappa (sec. Brown U. chpt. 1964-68, pres. 1975-77). Home: 229 Medway St Apt 209 Providence RI 02906 Office: Dorot Found 439 Benefit St Providence RI 02903-2934 Office Phone: 401-351-8866. E-mail: ernief@dorot.org.

FRERICHS, HERBERT DONALD, JR., lawyer; b. Bklyn., Aug. 17, 1957; s. Herbert Donald and Carol Ann (Gabrielsen) F.; m. Mary Elizabeth Cannon, Feb. 23, 1991; children: Mary Katherine, Colleen Ann. BS in Econ., U.S. Naval Acad., 1980; M in Marine Affairs, U. R.I., 1985; JD, U. Md., 1988. Assoc. Miles & Stockbridge, Balt., 1988-91, UNC Inc., Annapolis, Md., 1991; ptnr.-in-charge Downtown Balt. off. DLA Piper Rudnick Gray Cary, Balt. Lt. USN, 1980-85. Mem. ABA, Md. Bar Assn., Am. Corp. Counsel Bar Assn. Republican. Lutheran. Office: DLA Piper Rudnick Gray Cary Ste 1950 111 S Calvert St Baltimore MD 21202-6174 Office Phone: 410-580-3000. Office Fax: 410-580-3665. Business E-Mail: herbert.frerichs@piperrudnick.com.

FRERK-DEMARIA, DEBORAH, language educator; b. Jan. 31, 1955; BA, U. PR, Rio Piedras, 1977; MA in ESL, Cath. U. Ponce, PR, 1986. Cert. tchr. elem. sch. Sec. Pub. Instrn. PR, English elem. sch. Sec. Pub. Instrn. PR, English secondary sch. Sec. Pub. Instrn. PR. Tchr. elem. English Coll. Puertorriqueño de Niñas, Gusynabo, PR, 1977—78; tchr. English grade 4 Caribbean Sch. Inc., Ponce, 1978—89; tchr. ESL Dept. Def. Dependents Sch., San Juan, 1989—90, Netherlands, 1990—91; tchr. English grade 5 Singapore Am. Sch., 1994—98; tchr. Spanish Seven Hills Sch., Walnut Creek, Calif., 1999—. Contbr. to educational manuals and curriculla. Recipient On the Spot Spl. Act award, Dept. Def. Dependents Sch., Netherlands, 1991. Mem.: Am. Coun. Tchg. Fgn. Lang., Internat. Reading Assn. Home: 883 Orange Blossom Way Danville CA 94526-4960

FRESE, BRENDA S., women's college basketball coach; b. Cedar Rapids, Iowa, Apr. 30, 1970; d. Bill and Donna Frese; m. Mark Thomas, Aug. 20, 2005. BS in Comm., U. Ariz., 1993; MS in Athletic Adminstrn., Kent State U., 1995. Asst. coach Kent State U., 1994—95, Iowa State U., 1995—99; head coach Ball State U., 1999—2001, U. Minn., 2001—02, U. Md., 2002—. Named Coach of Yr., Mid-Am. Conf., 2000, Big Ten Conf., 2002, Nat. Coach of Yr., AP, 2002, NCAA, 2004. Achievements include coaching NCAA Women's Nat. Championship team, 2006. Office: U Md Dept Intercollegiate Athletics Womens Basketball 0730 Comcast Ctr Terrapin Trail College Park MD 20742-1011 Office Phone: 301-314-1747. E-mail: bfrese@umd.edu.*

FRESE, EDWARD SCHEER, JR., (TED FRESE), information technology executive, consultant; b. NYC, Oct. 17, 1944; s. Edward Scheer and Sylvana (Cerutti) F.; stepson Mary Margaret (Richardson) F.; m. Christine Ann Robinson, Oct. 27, 1979; 1 child, Edward Robinson. AB in Latin, Hamilton Coll., 1966; postgrad., NYU, 1970-72. Programmer trainee Mfr.'s Hanover Trust Co., NYC, 1969-70, systems analyst, 1970-75, officer, 1975-81; project mgr. Macmillan, Inc., NYC, 1981-84; dir. fin. systems Maxwell Macmillan Inc., NYC, 1984-89, dir. corp. info. systems, 1989-90; prin. Bremen Assocs., Inc., NYC, 1991-97; v.p. Year 2000 Cahners Bus. Info., 1997-98; v.p. Bremen Assocs., Inc., NYC, 1998—. Mem.: IEEE, Soc. Info. Mgmt., Univ. Club, New Eng. Soc. Republican. Episcopalian. Avocations: writing, swimming, sailing, music. Home: 79 North Ave Westport CT 06880-2722 Office Phone: 203-222-0264. E-mail: bremenai@aol.com.

FRESHWATER, MICHAEL FELIX, hand surgeon, educator; b. NYC, Feb. 4, 1948; s. Jack and Rhonda Freshwater. BS magna cum laude, Bklyn. Coll., 1968; MD, Yale U., 1972. Diplomate Nat. Bd. Med. Examiners, Am. Bd. Plastic Surgery. Asst. resident in surgery Yale New Haven Hosp., 1972-74; fellow in plastic surgery Med. Sch. Johns Hopkins U., Balt., 1974-77; resident, then chief resident in plastic surgery Jackson Meml. Hosp., 1977-78; Kleinert fellow hand and microsurgery Jewish Hosp., Louisville, 1979; pvt. practice medicine specializing in plastic/hand surgery Miami, Fla., 1979—; pres., dir. Miami Inst. Hand and Microsurgery, 1980—; dir. hand and microsurgery Cedars Med. Ctr., 1985—2000, chief surgery, 1988-90. Vol. prof. surgery U. Miami Sch. Medicine, 1979—; vol. faculty mem. Barry U. Sch. Podiatric Medicine and Surgery, 1989—; vis. prof. Javeriana U., Bogota, 1983—85, Centro Medico de los Andes, 1983—86; cons. Fla. Children's Med. Svc., Tallahassee, 1979—, Fla. Elks Crippled Children Soc., Orlando, 1983—, Fla. Dept. Profl. Regulation, Tallahassee, 1984—95, League Against Cancer, 1983—, Scientists Inst. Pub. Info., 1985—, USCG, Miami Beach, 1992—. Editor: U. Miami Plastic Surgery News, 2004—; mem. bd. reviewers: Plastic and Reconstructive Surgery, 1976—2004, reviewer: Jour. Plastic Reconstructive and Aesthetic Surgery, 2006—; contbr. chapters to books, articles to profl. jours. Trustee Yale U. Med. Libr., New Haven, 1972—77, 2000—06, D. R. Millard Found., 1987—; bd. dirs. V. and A. Gildred Found., 1980—86, Yale Sch. Medicine Fund, 1991—97, Campaign for Stuyvesant, 2003—; mem. nat. campaign com. Yale Sch. Medicine, 1993—97; mem. Fla. Bar Grievance Com., 1998—2001. Recipient Letter Commendation, Gov. Bob Graham, 1984; fellow Weinberger, NIH, 1974—76; scholar Jonas Salk, CUNY, 1968—72. Fellow: Internat. Coll. Surgeons; mem.: AAUP, AMA (numerous Physicians Recognition awards), Miami Assn. for Surgery of Hand (dir. 1991—), Am. Soc. Peripheral Nerve, Miami Soc. Plastic Surgeons (sec.-treas. 1987—88, v.p. 1988—89, pres. 1989—90), Royal Soc. Medicine, Internat. Soc. Reconstructive Microsurgery, Am. Soc. Reconstructive Microsurgery, Am. Burn Assn., Am. Assn. Hand Surgery, Assn. Yale Alumni in Medicine (bd. dirs. 1998—2000), Grove Isle Club (Miami), Yale Club (Miami, N.Y.), Phi Beta Kappa. Avocation: skiing. Office: 1 Datran Ctr Ste 502 Miami FL 33156-7814 Home Phone: 305-854-2011. E-mail: mff@miamihandsurgery.com.

FRESHWATER, SHAWNA MARIE, neuropsychologist, clinical psychologist, cognitive neuroscientist; b. Roseau, Minn., Aug. 10, 1964; d. Robert D. and Andrea K. Porter; children: Michaël, David. BA (magna cum laude), U. Miami, 1995; MS in Clin. Psychology, Nova Southeastern U., Ft. Lauderdale, 1996, PhD, 2000, postdoc., 2002. Lic. Psychology Fla., 2001. Behavioral medicine/health psychology trainee Behavioral Medicine Clin. Rsch. Ctr., U. Miami, 1993—95; psychology intern Cmty. Mental Health Ctr., Nova Southeastern U., Ft. Lauderdale, 1995—96, psychology intern child and adolescent traumatic stress program, 1995—96, psychology intern program for seriously emotionally disturbed, 1995—96; intern Brain Injury Rehab. Program, Ft. Lauderdale, 1996—97, Brief Psychotherapy Program, Ft. Lauderdale, 1997—98, V.A. Hosp., Miami, 1997—99, resident East Orange, NJ, 2000, Cornell Med. Ctr., NYC, 2000, N.Y. Presbyn. Hosp., NYC, 2000; postdoc. fellow, faculty rschr. dept. Neurology U. Fla., Gainesville, 2000—02; dir., pres. Neuropsychological Inst., P.A., Miami, 2002—. Author: (jour. article) Nineteenth Ann. Procs. of Soc. for Behavioral Medicine, 1998, The Clin. Neuropsychologist, 1998, Archives of Clin. Neuropsychology, 1999—2000, Jour. of Clin. Geropsychology, 2001. Mem.: Fla. Soc. Neurology, Internat. Neuropsychological Soc., Nat. Acad. Neuropschology, APA, Phi Theta Kappa, Phi Kappa Phi, Phi Beta Kappa. Office: Neuropsychological Inst PA 407 Lincoln Rd Ste 12-K Miami Beach FL 33139 Office Phone: 305-538-1585.

FRESTEDT, JOY LOUISE, research scientist, science administrator; b. Oak Park, Ill., Jan. 31, 1959; d. James Albert Machnicki and Wanda Louise (McConnaughhay) Katzman; m. Robert LeVance Frestedt, Aug. 8, 1987; 1 child, Megan Marie. BA Biology, Knox Coll., 1980; PhD Pathobiology, U. Minn., 1996. Rsch. asst. Knox Coll., 1978—80; cytogeneticist Ill. Masonic Med. Ctr., Chgo., 1980—81; med. tech., asst. scientist, rsch. scientist, lab. dir. U. Minn., Mpls., 1981—89, 1991—96; cancer rsch. scientist III, lab. dir. Roswell Park Cancer Inst., Buffalo, 1989—90; rsch. scientist, lab. dir. Mpls. Children's Med. Ctr., 1990—91; grad. fellow, safety expert, sr. scientist Sci. Mus. Minn., St. Paul, 1993—2001; rsch. scientist St. Jude Med. Inc., St. Paul, 1996—97. Adj. faculty Mpls. Cmty. Tech. Coll., 1996-99, North Hennepin CC, 1997-98, Anoka Ramsey CC, 1997-98, Rasmussen Bus. Coll., 1998-99, Medtronic/Mpls. Cmty. Tech. Coll., 1998, Normandale CC, 1999; mgr. Busulfex Clin. Devel. Orphan Med., Inc., 1999-00; med. info. scientist AstraZeneca Pharm., 2000-01; ops. mgr. clin. trials svc. Mayo Clinic, 2001-03; contract compliance auditor, 3M, 2002; mgr. regional clin. affairs Ortho Biotech Products, LP, 2002-04; v.p. sci. affairs, 2006-07; v.p. clin. affairs, exec. dir. rsch. Humanetics Corp./Minn. Applied Rsch. Ctr., 2004-06; adj. faculty Coll. St. Catherine, 2004-06; clin. rsch. orgn. liaison Medtronic, 2007—. Co-author: Writing About Science, 1997, Considering Graduate School in the Sciences, 1999; reviewer Jour. Women and Minorities in Sci. and Engring., Jour. Clin. Pharm.; contbr. articles to profl. jours. and books Mem.: Regulatory Affairs Profls. Soc. (ethics com. 2006—), Am. Coll. Clin. Pharmacology, Soc. Clin. Rsch. Profls., Am. Soc. Clin. Oncologists, Am. Assn. Pharm. Scientists (abstract reviewer for nat. meetings), Assn. Clin. Rsch. Profls. (co-chair programming com. 2005—05, editl. bd. jour. Monitor 2006—, v.p. 2007—, coord. CEU), Grad. Women in Sci. (pres. 1996—97, bd. dirs. 1999—2003, chair bd. dirs. 2002—03), Assn. Women in Sci., Sigma Xi. Home: 2708 Vernon Ave S Saint Louis Park MN 55416-1838 Personal E-mail: frest001@umn.edu. Business E-Mail: joy.l.frestedt@medtronic.com.

FRESTON, TOM (THOMAS E. FRESTON), former broadcast executive; b. NYC, Nov. 22, 1945; s. Thomas E. and Winifred (Geng) F.; m. Margaret Badali, Oct. 18, 1980; 1 child, Andrew. BA, St. Michaels Coll., 1967; MBA, NYU, 1969. Dir. mktg.- MTV MTV Networks, NYC, 1980-81, dir. mktg.- The Movie Channel, 1982-83; v.p. mktg.-MTV MTV Networks Inc., NYC, 1983-84, v.p. mktg., 1984-85, sr. v.p./gen. mgr. affiliate sales, mktg., 1985, sr. v.p./gen. mgr. MTV, VH-1, 1985-86, pres. entertainment, 1986-87, pres., CEO, 1987-89; chmn., CEO MTV Networks, NYC, 1989—2004; co-pres., co-COO Viacom Inc., NYC, 2004—06, pres., CEO, 2006. Bd. dirs. Cable Advt. Bur., N.Y.C., 1987, MTV Europe, London, 1986—, Rock 'n Roll Hall of Fame, N.Y.C., 1986—. Mem. Smithsonian com. Music in Am., 1987—; bd. dirs. Mus. Natural History; chmn. Louis Vuitton United Cancer Front, Actor Fund and Oceana, and others. Named one of 50 Most Powerful People in Hollywood, Premiere mag., 2005—06, 100 Most Influential People, Time Mag., 2006. Mem. Cable TV Adminstrn. & Mktg. Assn., Nat. Acad. Cable Programming. Avocations: photography, travel, antique rugs.

FRETWELL, ELBERT K., JR., retired university chancellor, consultant; b. NYC, Oct. 29, 1923; s. Elbert Kirtley and Jean (Hosford) F.; m. Dorrie Shearer, Aug. 25, 1951; children: Barbara Alice (Mrs. Peter Cooke), Margaret Jean (Mrs. John C. Cross), James Leonard, Katharine Louise (Mrs. Robert Saul). AB with distinction, Wesleyan U., Middletown, Conn., 1944; MA in Tchg., Harvard U., 1948; PhD, Columbia U., 1953; doctorate (hon.), Tech. U. Wroclaw, Poland, 1976; LLD (hon.), Wesleyan U., 1981; D in Pub. Svc. (hon.), U. NC, Charlotte, 1998. Stringer AP, 1942-44; staff writer ARC, 1944-45; vice consul Am. embassy, Prague, Czech Republic, 1945-47; tchr. Brookline (Mass.) Pub. Schs., 1948, Evanston (Ill.) Twp. High Sch. and Community Coll., 1948-50; adminstrv. sec. John Hay Fellowships, John Hay Whitney Found., 1951-53; asst. prof., asst. to dean Tchrs. Coll., Columbia U., 1953-56, assoc. prof., 1956; asst. commr. for higher edn. N.Y. State Dept. Edn., 1956-64; summer faculty U. Calif. at Berkeley, 1964; dean acad. devel. CUNY, NYC, 1964-67; pres. SUNY Coll. at Buffalo, 1967-78; chancellor U. N.C., Charlotte, 1979-89, chancellor emeritus, 1989—; sr. assoc. MDC Inc., 1989-91; interim pres. U. Mass. 5 Campus Sys., 1991-92. Interim pres. U. North Fla., 1998; mem. commn. higher instns. Mid. States Assn. of Schs. and Colls., 1965-71, chmn., 1973-74; trustee Carnegie Found. for Advancement Tchg., chmn., 1975-77; mem. Carnegie Coun. on Policy Studies in Higher Edn., 1973-79; bd. dirs. N.C. Transp. Mus. Found., 1996-2005; trustee Wesleyan U., 1967-70, Nichols Sch., Buffalo, 1969-78, Canisius Coll., 1969-76, Peace Coll., 1997-2003; exec. dir. com. on edn. N.Y. State Constl. Conv., 1967; vice chair N.Y. Am. Bicentennial Commn., 1975-79; mem. N.C. Med. Bd., 2001—. Bd. dirs. Charlotte (N.C.) Symphony, 1999—. Decorated Order of Cultural Merit Poland; recipient Disting. Alumnus award Wesleyan U., 1974, Tchrs. Coll., Columbia U., 1983, Boy Scouts Am. Silver Beaver award. Mem. Am. Assn. State Colls. and Univs. (pres. 1978-79), Am. Assn. for Higher Edn. (pres. 1964-65), Am. Coun. Edn. (chmn. 1980-81), N.C. Assn. Colls. and Univs. (pres. 1985-86), Nat. Rlwy. Hist. Soc., Adirondack Mountain Club, Rotary (pres. Charlotte 1994-95). Home: 3738 Cypress Club Dr Apt D411 Charlotte NC 28210-2492 Office: U NC-Charlotte 9201 University City Blvd Charlotte NC 28223-0002 Home Phone: 704-556-9963; Office Phone: 704-687-2484.

FREUD, ANTHONY PETER, opera company director; b. London, Oct. 30, 1957; arrived in USA, 2006, permanent resident, 2006; LLB with honors, U. London, 1978; postgrad., Inns of Ct. Sch. of Law, 1978—78. Theatre mgr. Sadler's Wells Theatre, 1980—84; sec., dir. opera planning Welsh Nat. Opera, Cardiff, Wales, 1984—91, gen. dir., 1994—2005; exec. prodr. Opera for Philips Classics, 1992—94; chmn. bd. Opera Europa, 2002—05; gen. dir., CEO Houston Grand Opera, 2005—. Chmn. jury Cardiff Singer of the World Competition, 1995—2005; hon. fellow Cardiff U., 2002. Vice-chmn. Opera AMERICA, 2006. Named to Order of Brit. Empire, 2006. Fellow: Royal Welsh Coll. Music and Drama (hon.). Office: Houston Grand Opera 510 Preston St Houston TX 77002 Office Phone: 713-546-0260. Office Fax: 713-247-0906. Business E-Mail: anthony_freud@houstongrandopera.org.

FREUD, LUCIAN MICHAEL, painter; b. Berlin, Dec. 8, 1922; s. Ernst and Lucie F.; m. Kathleen Garman Epstein, 1948 (dissolved 1952); 2 children; m. Caroline Maureen Blackwood (dissolved 1957). Student, Cen. Sch. Arts and Crafts, London, 1938-39, East Anglian Sch. Painting and Drawing. Tchr. Slade Sch. Art, 1948-58; vis. asst. Norwich Sch. Art, 1964-65. Exhibited in one-man shows at Lefevre Gallery, 1944, Nishimura Gallery, Tokyo, 1979, Thomas Agnew & Sons, 1983, Hirshhorn Mus. and Sculpture Garden Smithsonian Instn., Washington, 1987, Mus. Nat. d'Art Moderne, Paris, 1987-88, Hayward Gallery, London, 1988, Neue Nat. Gallery, Berlin, 1988, Scottish Nat. Gallery Modern Art, Edinburgh, Eng., 1988, The Fruitmarket Gallery, Edinburgh, 1988, Berggruen Gallery, Paris, 1990, Saatchi Collection, London, 1990, Nishimura Gallery, Tokyo, 1991, Thomas Gibson Fine Art Ltd., London, 1991, Palazzo Ruspoli, Rome, 1991, Castello Sforzesca, Milan, 1991-92, Tate Gallery, Liverpool, 1992, Queen's Gallery Buckingham Palace, 2002-03; numerous others; represented in pub. collections Tate Gallery, Nat. Portrait Gallery, Arts Coun. of Gt. Britian, Brit. Coun., Brit. Mus., Fitzwilliam Mus., Cambridge, Nat. Mus. Wales, Cardiff, Scottish Nat. Gallery Modern Art, Edinburgh, Hartlepool Art Gallery, Walker Art Gallery, Liverpool, Liverpool U., City Art Gallery, Whitworth Gallery, Art Gallery South Australia, Mus. Western Australia, Beaverbrook Art Gallery, N.B., Can., Centre Georges Pompidou, Paris, Bibliotheque Nationale, Paris, Victoria and Albert Mus., Sigmund Freud Mus., London, Centro Cultural Arte Contemporaneo, Mexico City, Nat. Gallery, Capetown, Republic South Africa, Art Inst. Chgo., Mus. Modern Art, NYC, Met. Mus. Art, Carnegie Inst., Pitts., Hirshhorn Mus., Washington, numerous others; author (collection of paintings): Lucian Freud: 1996-2000, 2005. With Brit. Navy, 1942. Named Companion of Honour, 1983; recipient Order of Merit, 1993. Mem. Am. Acad. and Inst. Arts and Letters (hon.), Am. Acad. Arts and Sciences (hon. fgn.) Address: care James Kirkman 46 Brompton Sq London SW3 2AF England

FREUDENHEIM, MILTON B., journalist; b. New Rochelle, NY, Mar. 4, 1927; s. Milton Benjamin and Lenore Patricia (Kroh) F.; m. Elizabeth Ege, Mar. 7, 1952 (dec. Dec. 30, 1996); children: Jo Louise, Susan Patricia, John Milton Otto, Tom Henry; m. Grace Glueck, Oct. 20, 2000. AB, U. Mich., 1948. Reporter Louisville Courier-Jour., Ky., 1948-49, Akron Beacon Jour., Ohio, 1949-52, Washington corr., 1953-56; UN corr. Chgo. Daily News, 1956-66, nat. and fgn. editor, 1966-69, Paris corr., 1969-77; dir. public affairs for Region V HEW, Chgo., 1978-79; copy editor, writer NY Times Week in Rev., 1979—88; bus. and health reporter NY Times, 1988—. Pres. UN Correspondents Assn., 1966, Anglo-Am. Press Assn., Paris, 1975; adv. US del. UN Ednl., Scientific & Cultural Orgn. Gen. Conf., 1978. Mem.: Sigma Delta Chi, Phi Beta Kappa. Office: NY Times 229 W 43rd St New York NY 10036-3959 Office Phone: 212-556-4656.

FREUDENTHAL, DAVE (DAVID D. FREUDENTHAL), governor; b. Thermopolis, Wyo., Oct. 12, 1950; m. Nancy Freudenthal; children: Don, Hillary, Bret, Katrina. BA, Amherst Coll., 1973; JD, U. Wyo. Coll. Law, 1980. Economist Wyo. Dept. Econ. Planning & Devel., 1973—75; state planning coord. State of Wyo., 1975—77; pvt. law practice, 1980—93; U.S. atty. for Wyo. U.S. Dept. Justice, Cheyenne, 1994—2001; gov. State of Wyo., Cheyenne, 2003—. Chmn. Wyo. State Demo. Ctrl. Com., 1981—85; mem. Wyo. Futures Project, 1984—87, Econ. Devel. & Stabilization Bd., 1985—89, Edn. Policy Implementation Coun., 1989—90, Gov. Substance Abuse and Violent crime Adv. Bd., 1994—2001. Democrat. Office: Office of Governor State Capitol 200 West 24th St Cheyenne WY 82002-0010 Office Phone: 307-777-7434. Office Fax: 307-632-3909. Business E-Mail: governor@state.wy.us.*

FREUDENTHAL, STEVEN FRANKLIN, lawyer, political organization worker; b. Thermopolis, Wyo., June 8, 1949; s. Lewis Franklin and Lucille Iola (Love) F.; m. Janet Mae Mansfield, Aug. 30, 1969 (div. Sept. 1996); children: Lynn Marie, Kristen Lee; m. Barbara A. Crofts, Jan. 1, 1998; stepchildren: Shane C., Jeanne N. BA, Trinity Coll., Hartford, Conn., 1971; JD, Vanderbilt U., 1975. Bar: Wyo. 1975, U.S. Supreme Ct. 1981. Tax acct. Conn. Gen. Life Ins. Co., Hartford, Conn., 1971-72; asst. atty. gen. Wyo. Cheyenne, 1975-77; atty. gen. Wyo., 1981-82; state planning coordinator Office Gov. Wyo., Cheyenne, 1977-78; dep. under sec. Dept. Interior, Washington, 1978-79, exec. asst. to sec., 1979-80; ptnr Sherman & Howard, Cheyenne, Wyo., 1980-81; ptnr. Freudenthal & Bonds, Cheyenne, 1983—; mem. Wyo. Ho. Reps., 1987-91. Trustee United Med. Ctr., 1990-97, pres., 1993-96; bd. dirs. Cheyenne LEADS, 1990-93; chmn. Wyo. Dem. Party, 1999-2001. Office: 123 E 17th St Cheyenne WY 82003-0387 Office Phone: 307-634-2240. Business E-Mail: steve@wyolaw.com.

FREUND, CAROL LOUISE, social services consultant; b. Mineola, NY, Feb. 21, 1933; d. Warren Edwin and Dorothy Geraldine (Gilbrech) Darnell; m. William O.H. Freund, Jr., Sept. 16, 1960; children: Carol Burnam, William O.H. III. BA, Allegheny Coll., 1954; MA, John Carroll U., 1982. Tchr. South Euclid Lyndhurst City Schs., Ohio, 1955—57; trainer Episc. Diocese of Ohio, Cleve., 1972—; exec. dir. Hitchcock Ho., Cleve., 1983—87. Mem., v.p. Children's Svcs., Cleve., 1965—75. Pres. Shaker Heights PTA, Cleve., 1975—76, Cleve. Internat. Program, 1980—83; 1st v.p. Coun. Internat. Program, Cleve., 1984—88, pres., 1988—91; mem. Roscoe Village Commn., 1990—, chair, 1992—; pres. Johnson-Humrickhouse Mus. Found., 1999—; trustee Roscoe Village Found., 1993—, pres., 1997—. Recipient cert. of recognition, Coun. Internat. Programs, 1981, Founding Trustee award, Edn. for Freedom of Choice in Ohio, 1982, Outstanding Vol. Svc. award, Cleve. Internat. Program, 1983, Vols. are the Heart of Hospice award, Ohio Hospice and Palliative Care, 2004, Blue Citation award, Allegheny Coll., 2005. Episcopalian. Avocation: flower arranging. Home: 699 High St PO Box 1240 Coshocton OH 43812-6240

FREUND, DEBORAH A., academic administrator; AB, Washington U., 1973; MPH, U. Mich., 1975, MA in Applied Econs., 1975, PhD in Econs., 1980. Rsch. asst. Washington U. Sch. Medicine, 1971—73; intern to dep. commr. for med. assistance N.Y. State Dept. Social Svcs., 1974; program asst. The Robert Wood Johnson Found., 1975—76; rsch. assoc. U. Mich., Mich., 1976—77; IPA Nat. Ctr. for Health Svcs. Rsch., Dept. Health and Human Svcs., 1977—79; core faculty mem. U. N.C., Chapel Hill, 1979—88, asst. prof., assoc. prof., 1979—88, dir. doctoral program, 1987—88; chair Sch. Pub. and Environ. Affairs Ind. U., 1987—88, dir. The Bowen Rsch. Ctr., 1989—99, assoc. dean for acad. affairs Bloomington, 1992—94, vice chancellor acad. affairs, 1994—99; vice chancellor, provost for acad. affairs Syracuse U., 1999—2006, disting. prof. pub. adminstrn. and econ. NY, 2006—. Adj. asst. prof. Duke U., 1979—84; adj. prof. Ind. U., 1988—94, U. N.C., Chapel Hill, 1988—, SUNY, 2002—. Mem. editl. bd.: PharmacoEconomics, 1993—, Health Econs., 1994—2003, Med. Care Rsch. and Rev., 1994—2003; contbr. chapters to books, articles to profl. jours. Recipient Jay S. Drotman Meml. award, 1981, The Elvehjam Meml. medal, 1990, Kershaw Rsch. award, 1991; fellow, Kellogg Found. Nat. Leadership, 1986—89. Fellow: Nat. Acad. Social Ins.; mem.: N.Y. Acad. Medicine. Home: 5213 Silver Fox Dr Jamesville NY 13078 Office: Ctr for Policy Rsch 426 Eggers Hall Syracuse Univ Syracuse NY 13244-1020*

FREUND, EMMA FRANCES, technologist; b. 1922; d. Walter R. and Mabel W. (Loveland) Ervin; m. Frederic Reinert Freund, March 4, 1953; children: Frances, Daphne, Fern, Frederic. BS, Wilson Tchrs. Coll., Washington, 1944; MS in Biology, Cath. U., Washington, 1953; MEd in Adult Edn., Va. Commonwealth U., 1988. Tchr. math and sci. DC Sch. Sys., Washington, 1944-45; technician in parasitology lab. U.S. Dept. Agr., Beltsville, Md., 1945-48; histologic technician dept. pathology Georgetown U. Med. Sch., Washington, 1948-49; clin. lab. technician Kent and Queen Anne's County Gen. Hosp., Chestertown, Md., 1949-51; histotechnologist Med. Coll. Va. Hosp., Richmond, 1951—. Cons. profl. meetings and workshops; exam. coun. Nat. Credentialing. Agy. Med. Lab. Pers. Co-author: (mini-course) Instrumentation in Cytology and Histology, 1985; editor Histo-Scope Newsletter. Asst. den leader Robert E. Lee coun. Boy Scouts Am., 1967-68, den leader, 1968-70. Mem. AAAS, NAFE, AAUW, APS, Am. Mgmt. Assn., Am. Soc. Clin. Lab. Sci. (rep. to sci. assembly histology sect. 1977-78, chmn. 1983-85, 89-96), Va. Soc. Med. Tech. (Richmond chpt. corr. sec. 1977-78, bd. dirs. 1981-82, pres. 1984-85), Va. Soc. Histotech. (pres. 1994-96), Nat. Credentialing Agy. (clin. lab. specialist in histotech., clin. lab. supr. clin. lab. dir.), NY Acad. Scis., Am. Assn. Clin. Chemistry (assoc.), Am. Soc. Clin. Pathology (assoc., cert. histology technician), Nat. Geog. Soc., Va. Govtl. Employees Assn., Nat. Soc. Histotech. (by-laws com. 1981—, C.E.U. com. 1981—, program com. regional meeting 1984, 85, 87, 97, 2000, chmn. regional meeting 1987, program chmn. state meeting 1998-99, Conv. scholarship award 1997, Clin. Chemists' Recognition award 1995, 98, 2002, 04), Am. Mus. Natural History, Smithsonian Inst., Am. Mgmt. Assn., Am. Chem. Soc., Am. Soc. Quality, Clin. Lab. Mgmt. Assn., Van Slyke Soc., Soc. Human Resource Mgmt., Nat. Soc. Hist. Preservation, Math. Assn. Am., Sigma Xi, Phi Beta Rho, Kappa Delta Pi, Phi Lambda Theta. Home: 1315 Asbury Rd Richmond VA 23229-5305

FREUND, FRED A., retired lawyer; b. NYC, June 18, 1928; s. Sidney J. and Cora (Strasser) F.; m. Rosalie Sampo, Nov. 18, 1975 (div. Apr. 1983); m. Patricia A. Gardner, Mar. 13, 1957 (div. Jan. 1967); children: Gregory G., K. Bailey AB, Columbia U., 1948, JD, 1949. Bar: N.Y. 1949, U.S. Supreme Ct. 1968. Law clk. to chief judge U.S. Dist. Ct. So. Dist. N.Y., NYC, 1949-51; assoc. Kaye, Scholer, Fierman, Hays & Handler, NYC, 1953-58, ptnr., 1959-93, ret., 1993. Donor Freund collection Chinese and Japanese wood carvings Spurlock Mus., U. Ill., Urbana-Champaign. Served to 1st lt. USAF, 1951—53. Mem. ABA, Assn. Bar City N.Y., Phi Beta Kappa Home: 1085 Park Ave Apt 4C New York NY 10128-1179 *Balancing the quest for excellence with humility and humor.*

FREUND, FREDRIC S., real estate broker and manager; b. Denver, Sept. 23, 1930; AB, Brown U., 1952. Sr. v.p. Hanford, Freund & Co., San Francisco, 1956—. Past adv. dir. Western Investment Real Estate Trust; bd. dirs. Berkeley Antibody Co.; instr. real estate mgmt. U. Calif. Ext.; guest lectr. Stanford U. Sch. Bus. Adminstrn. Commr. Calif. Senate Adv. Commn. on Cost Control in State Govt.; chair code adv. com. Bldg. Inspection Dept., San Francisco. Mem. Am. Soc. Real Estate Counselors (CRE, pres. no. Calif. 1987-88), San Francisco Assn. Realtors (pres. 1974-75, Realtor of Yr. 1975), Bldg. Owners & Mgrs. Assn. San Francisco, Realtors Nat. Mktg. Inst. (CCIM), Inst. Real Estate Mgmt. (CPM). Office: Hanford Freund & Co 47 Kearny St Ste 300 San Francisco CA 94108-5582 Home: 112 Alta St San Francisco CA 94133 Home Phone: 415-291-9309; Office Phone: 415-981-5780. Fax: 415-296-0725. E-mail: ffreund@hanfordfreund.com.

FREUND, JOHN RICHARD, former English educator; b. Chgo., Nov. 16, 1926; s. Charles Anton and Helen Mary Freund; m. Barbara Ann Krohn, Sept. 11, 1948; children: David Eric, Alaric James. BA, Miami U., Oxford, Ohio, 1949, MA, 1950; PhD, Ind. U., 1955. Asst. prof. English Western Mich. U., Kalamazoo, 1954—64; assoc. prof. English Grand Valley State Coll., Allendale, Mich., 1964—68; prof. English King's Coll., Wilkes-Barre, Pa., 1968—71, Indiana U. of Pa., 1971—90, English prof. emeritus, 1990. Supr. English Program for Disadvantaged Pre-Coll. Youth, Ind. Colls. Tng. Program, Kalamazoo, 1968; specialist, Adult Basic Edn. Tchr. Tng. Inst., Wilkes-Barre, 1971; cons. Consultant Cadre, Right to Read, State of Pa., 1977-78. Author: Broken Symmetries: A Study of Agency in Shakespeare's Plays, 1991; (with Arnold Nelson) Where Minds Meet ednl. radio series, 1963; author/performer: The Nature of Perception closed-circuit TV program, 1964 (Ohio State Award); editor: Studies in the Humanities Jour., 1972-81. With USN, 1944-46, PTO. Mem.: MLA, Pa.

Coll. English Assn., Assoc. Lit. Scholars and Critics. Democrat. Avocation: raising dogs and cats. Home: 8 Deborah Trl Fairfield PA 17320-8298 Personal E-mail: jrfreund79@earthlink.net.

FREUND, KRISTEN P., bank executive; 1 child. Student in Bus., Mich. State U.; MBA, Northwestern U. Kellogg Sch. Mgmt. With Exch. Nat. Bank; chief adminstrv. officer LaSalle Bank, grp. sr. v.p. Named one of Top 40 Under 40, Crain's Chgo. Bus., 2006. Office: LaSalle Bank Hdqs 135 S LaSalle St Chicago IL 60603*

FREUND, LAMBERT BEN, engineering educator, researcher, consultant; b. McHenry, Ill., Nov. 23, 1942; s. Bernard and Anita (Schaeffer) F.; m. Colleen Jean Hehl, Aug. 21, 1965; children: Jonathan Ben, Jeffrey Alan, Stephen Neil. BS, U. Ill., 1964, MS, 1965; PhD, Northwestern U., 1967. Postdoctoral fellow Brown U., Providence, 1967-69, asst. prof., 1969-73, assoc. prof., 1973-75, prof. engring., 1975—, Henry Ledyard Goddard prof., 1988—, chmn. div., 1979-83. Vis. prof. Stanford (Calif.) U., 1974-75, 95; cons. Aberdeen Proving Ground, U.S. Steel Corp.; vis. scholar Harvard U., 1983-84; mem.-at-large U.S. Nat. Com. for Theoretical and Applied Mechancis, NRC, 1985-97; mem. IUTAM Gen. Assembly, 1987—, treas., 1996-2004, pres. 2004—; Russell Severance Springer prof. U. Calif., Berkeley, 1995; cons. Advanced Rsch. Projects Agy. Def. Scis. Rsch. Coun.; disting. vis. scientist Jet Propulsion Lab NASA, 1994—. Author: Dynamic Fracture Mechanics, 1990, Thin Film Materials, 2004; editor in chief: ASME Jour. Applied Mechanics, 1983-88, editor Cambridge monographs on Mechanics and Applied Mathematics, 1989-2004, Jour. Mechanics and Physics of Solids, 1992-2004; assoc. editor Proc Royal Soc., 2004—, Proc Nat. Acad. Sci., 2005—; mem. editorial adv. bd. Acta Mechanica Sinica, 1990-2001; contbr. articles to tech. jours. NSF trainee, 1964-67; grantee NSF, Office Naval Rsch., Army Rsch. Office, Nat. Bur. Stads., Air Force Office Sci. Rsch., Dept. Energy; recipient Alumni Honor award Coll. Engring., U. Ill., 1996. Fellow ASME (Henry Hess award 1974, mem. applied mechanics divsn. exec. com. 1989-94, S.P. Timoshenko medal 2003), Am. Acad. Mechanics, Am. Acad. Arts and Scis., Soc. Engring. Sci. (William Prager medal 2000); mem. NAS, NAE, ASTM (George R. Irwin medal 1987). Home: 4 Connor Ln Barrington RI 02806-2750 Office: Brown U Dept Engngring Box D Providence RI 02912

FREVERT, JAMES WILMOT, retired financial planner, investment advisor; b. Richland Twp., Iowa, Dec. 19, 1922; s. Wesley Clarence and Grace Lotta (Maw) F.; m. Jean Emily Sunderlin, Feb. 12, 1949; children: Douglas James, Thomas Jeffrey, Kimberly Ann. BS in Gen. Engring., MIT, 1948. Prodn. mgr. Air Reduction Chem. Co., Calvert City, Ky., 1955-61; plant mgr. Air Products & Chems., West Palm Beach, Fla., 1961-62; pres. Young World HWD, Ft. Lauderdale, Fla., 1962-66; v.p. Shareholders Mgmt. Co., LA, 1966-73, Thomson McKinnon Secs., North Palm Beach, Fla., 1973-89, Raymond James & Assoc., West Palm Beach, Fla., 1989-91; ret. Founder, past pres. MIT Club Palm Beach County, dir., 1976—; ednl. council mem. 1977-81. Served to 1st lt. USAF, 1943-46. Mem. Palm Beach Pundits. Republican. Presbyterian. Home: 605 Universe Blvd T-602 Juno Beach FL 33408-2489 Personal E-mail: jimfrevert@comcast.net.

FREY, ANDREW LEWIS, lawyer; b. NYC, Aug. 11, 1938; s. Daniel B. and Ruth J. Frey; children: Matthew S., Alexandra S. BA with high honors, Swarthmore Coll., 1959; LLB, Columbia U., 1962. Bar: N.Y. 1962, D.C. 1966, U.S. Supreme Ct. 1972. Law clk. to judge U.S. Ct. Appeals (D.C. cir.), 1962—63; spl. counsel to Gov. U.S. V.I., 1963-65; assoc. Koteen & Burt, Washington, 1965-70; ptnr. Dutton, Gwirtzman, Zumas, Wise & Frey, Washington, 1970-72; asst. to solicitor gen. Office U.S. Solicitor Gen., Washington, 1972—73, dep. solicitor gen., 1973—86; ptnr. Mayer Brown Rowe & Maw, NYC, 1986—. Notes editor Columbia Law Rev., 1961—62. Recipient John Marshall award Dept. Justice, 1975, Disting. Svc. award Atty. Gen., 1980, Presdl. award for Meritorious Svc., 1985, Burton Legal Achievement award, 2005; named one of 100 Most US Influential Lawyers, Nat. Law Jour., 2006. Mem. Am. Law Inst., Am. Acad. Appellate Lawyers, Phi Beta Kappa. Office: Mayer Brown Rowe & Maw 1675 Broadway Fl 19 New York NY 10019-5820 Office Phone: 212-506-2635. Business E-Mail: afrey@mayerbrownrowe.com.*

FREY, CHARLES FREDERICK, surgeon, educator; b. NYC, Nov. 15, 1929; s. Charles N. and Julia (Leary) F.; m. Jane Louise Tower, July 20, 1957; children: Jane Elizabeth, Susan Ann, Charles Frederick, Robert Tower, Nancy Louise. BA, Amherst Coll., 1951; MD, Cornell U., 1955. Diplomate Am. Bd. Surgery. Intern Cornell Med. Ctr., NYC, 1955-56, asst. resident, 1956-57, 59-61, 1st asst. resident, 1962, chief resident, 1963; instr. surgery U. Mich., Ann Arbor, 1964-65, asst. prof. surgery, 1965-68, assoc. prof., 1968-72, prof., 1972-76, U. Calif., Davis, 1976—, vice. chmn. dept. surgery, 1976-81, exec. vice-chmn. dept., 1981-95, emeritus prof. surgery, vice chmn. dept. surgery, 1998—; mem. staff VA Hosp., Martinez, Calif., chief surg. service, 1976-80; attending surgeon Sutter Hosps., Sacramento. Surg. cons. U. Mich., 1966-76, VA, 1971—, Highway Safety Research Inst., 1973-76. Assoc. editor, mem. editorial bd. The Pancreas, Internat. Jour. of Pancreatology; mem. editorial bd. Western Jour. Medicine, Jour. Gastrointestinal Surgery; contbr. numerous articles to profl. jours. Served to capt. USAF, 1957-59. Fellow ACS (chief regional com. on trauma 1976-89, disaster preparedness com. 1978—, med. motion picutres com. 1981-91, allied health com. 1981-82, program com. No. Calif. chpt., 1981—, credentials com. No. Calif. chpt. 1982—, mem. bd. govs. 1989-94, gov. 1988-94, adv. com. on ambulatory surgery, chmn. ambulatory surg. care com. 1990-94, pres. No. Calif. chpt. 1995-96), Am. Assn. Surgery Trauma; mem. AMA, Calif. Med. Assn., El Dorado-Scarmento Med. Soc., Am. Fedn. Clin. Rsch., Am. Assn. Automotive Medicine (bd. dirs. 1970-74), Internat. Assn. Accident and Traffic Medicine, Am. Trauma Soc. (founding, standards devel. com. 1978—, v.p. Calif. divsn. 1979—, bd. dirs. 1980—), Calif. Trauma Soc. (trustee 1977—), Nat. Trauma Com. of ACS (chmn. membership com. 1980-84, exec. com. 1981-85), Assn. Acad. Surgery, Am. Surg. Assn., Brazilian Surg. Soc., Western Surg. Assn., Ctrl. Surg. Assn. (membership com. 1971-73), Pacific Coast Surg. Assn., Sacramento Surg. Soc. (pres. 1994), Assn. VA Surgeons (publs., program coms. 1981—), Soc. Univ. Surgeons, Soc. Surgery Alimentary Tract (constn. and by-laws com. 1969—, chmn. 1972-76, v.p. 1995-96), Internat. Assn. Pancreatology (mem. editl. bd. 1986, steering com.), Internat. Biliary Assn., Am. Gastroenterology Assn., Pancreas Club (chmn. 1975-96). Personal E-mail: cffreymd@pacbell.net.

FREY, DANIEL D., engineering educator, researcher; BS in Aeronautical Engring., Rensselaer Polytech. Inst., 1987; MS in Mech. Engring., U. Colo., 1993; PhD in Mech. Engring., MIT, 1997. Asst. prof. mech. engring. and engring. systems MIT, Cambridge, Mass., 1998—2006, Robert N. Noyce career devel. prof., 2005—, assoc. prof. mech. engring. & engring. systems, 2006—; with faculty Olin Coll., 2000—02. Decorated Joint Svc. Commendation Medal U.S. So. command USN; recipient R&D 100 award, R&D Mag., 1997, Teaching award, MIT Dept. Aeronautics & Astronautics, 2000, Everett Moore Baker Meml. award for Outstanding Undergrad. Teaching, MIT, 1999, Career award, Nat. Sci. Found., 2004, Junior Bose award for Excellence in Teaching, 2006, Joseph A. Martore Excellence in Teaching award, MIT Engring. Systems Divsn., 2007; Hughes doctoral fellow, 1995—97. Mem.: AIAA, ASME, Internat. Coun. on Systems Engring. (Best Paper award 2005), Am. Statistical Assn., Am. Soc. Engring. Edn. Achievements include research in system design methods including robust design, design of experiments, probability, manufacturing, and computational geometry. Office: MIT Bldg 3-449D 77 Massachusetts Ave Cambridge MA 02139-4307 Office Phone: 617-324-6133. Business E-Mail: danfrey@mit.edu.

FREY, DONALD NELSON, industrial engineer, educator, retired manufacturing executive; b. St. Louis, Mar. 13, 1923; m. Helen-Kay Eberley, Feb. 14, 2003; children: Donald Nelson, Judith Kingsley(dec.) , Margaret Bente, Catherine, Christopher, Elizabeth. Student, Mich. State Coll., 1940—42; BS, U. Mich., 1947, MS, 1949, PhD, 1950, DSc (hon.), 1965; DSc, U. Mo., Rolla, 1966. Instr. metall. engring. U. Mich., 1949—50, asst. prof. chem. and metall. engring., 1950—51; rsch. engr. Babcock & Wilcox Tube Co., Beaver Falls, Pa., 1951; various rsch. positions Ford Motor Co. (Ford div.), 1951—57, various engring. positions, 1958—61, product planning mgr., 1961—62, asst. gen. mgr., 1962—65, gen. mgr. original Mustang auto, 1965—68, co. v.p. for product devel., 1965—67; pres. Gen. Cable Corp., NYC, 1968—71, Bell & Howell Co., Chgo., 1973—81, chmn., CEO, 1971—88, also bd. dirs.; prof. of indsl. engring. and mgmt. sci. Northwestern U., Evanston, Ill., 1988—. Mem. exec. bd. World Bank, Washington; bd. dirs. Cin. Milacron, Clark Equipment Co., Packer Engring., My Own Meals, Hyatt Corp., Springs Industries, Quintar, 20th Century Fox Corp.; co-chair Japan study multinats. NRC, 1992—94; surveyor World Bank, Poland, 1990. Co-chmn. Gov.'s Commn. of Sci. and Industry, Ill., 1988—; exec. bd. mem. World Bank, 2003. With US Army, 1942—46. Named Young Engr. of Yr., Engring. Soc. Detroit, 1953, Outstanding Alumni, U. Mich. Coll. Engring., 1957, Outstanding Young Man of the Yr., Detroit Jr. Bd. of Commerce, 1958, Man of the Yr., Weizmann Inst., 1988; recipient Nat. medal for tech., 1990; Inaugural fellow, INFORMS, 2002. Fellow: INFORMS, AAAS; mem.: ASME, Coun. on Fgn. Rels., Detroit Engring. Soc. (pres., bd. dirs. 1962—65), Soc. Automotive Engrs. (vice chmn. Detroit 1958, Russell Springer award 1956), Nat. Acad. Engring. (mem. coun. 1972), Am. Soc. Metals, Am. Inst. Mining and Metall. Engrs. (chmn. Detroit chpt. 1954, chmn., editor Nat. Symposium on Sheet Steels 1956), Econ. Club, Saddle and Cycle Club, Chgo. Club, Hundred Club Cook County, Chgo. Commonwealth Club, Phi Delta Theta, Tau Beta Pi, Phi Kappa Phi, Sigma Xi. Achievements include established Margaret and Muir Frey Prize for innovation in engring., Northwestern Univ., 2002; Clara McKitrick Prize for Design in engring., Northwestern Univ., 2004. Home: 2758 Sheridan Rd Evanston IL 60201-1728 Office: Northwestern U 2145 Sheridan Rd Rm M237 Evanston IL 60208-0834 Home Phone: 847-869-5705; Office Phone: 847-491-3326. E-mail: d-frey@northwestern.edu.

FREY, FRANK MICHAEL, biology professor; b. Hackensack, NJ, Dec. 15, 1975; s. Frank H. and Karen E. Frey; m. Brenda L. Hall, June 27, 1998. BS in Biology, Pa. State U., 1998; PhD in Evolutionary Biology, Ind. U., 2003. From grad. fellow to rsch. assoc. Ind. U., 1998—2002, rsch. assoc., 2002—03; asst. prof. biology Colgate U., Hamilton, NY, 2003—. Dir., curator George R. Cooley Herbarium Colgate U., 2004—. Contbr. articles to profl. jours.; musician: (band) Dangerboy, 2004—. Nominee Phi Eta Sigma Prof. of Yr., Colgate U., 2005; recipient Tchg. Excellence Recognition award, Ind. U., 2000, Outstanding Instr. award, 2000, 2002. Mem.: The Soc. Econ. Botany, Soc. Study of Evolution, Bot. Soc. Am. Avocations: basketball, snowboarding. Office: Dept of Biology Colgate University 13 Oak Drive Hamilton NY 13346 Office Phone: 315-228-7871. Office Fax: 315-228-7997. Business E-Mail: ffrey@mail.colgate.edu.

FREY, FREDERICK AUGUST, geochemist, researcher, educator; b. Milw., Apr. 1, 1938; s. Frederick August and Evelyn Dorothy (Lange) F.; m. Julie Ann Golden; 1 child, Oren. BSCE, U. Wis., 1960, PhD in Chemistry, 1967. Prof. dept. earth, atmospheric and planetary scis. MIT, Cambridge, 1966—, Francqui Found. prof. Belgium, 1996-97. Assoc. editor: Geochimica et Cosmochimica Acta; contbr. more than 200 articles to profl. jours. Recipient Disting. Alumni award, U. Wis. Dept. Geology and Geophysics, 2006. Fellow Geochem. Soc., European Assn. Geochemist; mem. Geol. Soc. Am., European Union Geoscis., Am. Geophys. Union (pres. VGP sect. 2000-2002, VGP Bowen award 1986). Office: MIT Dept Earth Atmos & Plan Sci 54 1226 Cambridge MA 02139

FREY, GLENN, songwriter, vocalist, guitarist; b. Detroit, Nov. 6, 1948; Former band mem. The Mushrooms, Four of Us, The Subterraneans, Heavy Metal Kids; founding mem., guitarist, keyboardist, vocalist The Eagles, 1971—; co-founder Mission Records. Performed with Bo Diddly and Linda Ronstadt, songs include Take it Easy, solo artist (albums) No Fun Aloud, 1982, The Allnighter, 1984, Soul Searchin', 1988, Strange Weather, 1992, Glen Frey Live, 1993, Solo Collection, 1995; composer (theme song): (TV series) Miami Vice, Body by Jake, 1988; TV appearance Wiseguy, 1988; actor: (TV series) South of Sunset, 1993; (films) Jerry Maguire, 1996; musician: (albums) (with Eagles) Eagles, 1972, Desperado, 1973, On the Border, 1974, One of These Nights, 1975, Hotel California, 1976 (Grammy award for album of yr., 1977), The Long Run, 1979. Co-recipient Grammy award for Lyin' Eyes 1975, for New Kid in Town 1977; named (with Eagles) to Rock and Roll Hall of Fame, 1998.

FREY, HARLEY HARRISON, JR., retired anesthesiologist; b. Toledo, Feb. 22, 1920; s. Harley Harrison and Mina Rosina (Wiedemann) F.; m. Jane Luceia Murray, Aug. 28, 1944 (dec. 1964); children: Richard E., Martha J., Thomas C.; m. Emma Jean Hamilton, Apr. 15, 1966; 1 stepchild, Rick A. Gregory. BS, U. Toledo, 1942; MD, U. Cin., 1945. Diplomate Am. Bd. Anesthesiology. Intern Akron City Hosp., Ohio, 1946—47; fellow anesthesia U. Minn., Mpls., 1950; hon. mem. staff St. Elizabeth Hosp. Med. Ctr., Lafayette, Ind., 1950—, Lafayette Home Hosp., 1950—; ret. Bd. dir. Lafayette Symphony Orch., 1952-54; counselor, committeeman Lafayette coun. Boy Scouts Am., 1955-63; ruling elder Presbyn. Ch., 1964-67, active deacon, 1991-94; bd. dir. Lafayette Citizens Band, 1997-2000. Capt. US Army, 1947—49. Fellow Am. Coll. Anesthesiology; mem. Am. Soc. Anesthesiology (bd. dir. 1965-74), Ind. Soc. Anesthesiology (pres., bd. dir. 1961-74, Disting Svc. award 1992), Ind. State Med. Soc. (Cert. Distinction 1995), Tippecanoe County Med. soc. (pres. 1961), Rotary (bd. dir. 1992-95) Lafayette Country Club (bd. dir. 1963-65). Avocations: music, painting. Home: 1700 Lindberg Rd Apt 321 West Lafayette IN 47906-7323 Personal E-mail: hemfrey@fcconnections.com. *Personal philosophy: My philosophy of life is simple, whatever talent or wisdom I may have has been given to me by God as a gift. In any task I undertake, this gift should be used to the best of my ability, be fair, build goodwill, better friendships, exhibit truth and benefit all concerned.*

FREY, JAMES HARRISON, fundraising professional; b. Wheeling, W.Va., Sept. 2, 1950; s. Harrison Walther and Mary Waddell Frey; life ptnr. Michael Paul Hires. MusB, Oberlin Coll., Ohio, 1972, MusM in Tchg., 1973. Instr. music The Hill Sch., Pottstown, Pa., 1973—77; dir. alumni and devel. The Harvey Sch., Katonah, NY, 1977—82; dir. devel. and pub. rels. Kent Pl. Sch., Summit, NJ, 1982—86; dir. faculty patient gifts Harvard Med. Sch., Boston, 1986—91; sr. dir. major gifts U. Chgo. Med. Ctr., 1991—94; v.p. philanthropy Rush North Shore Med. Ctr., Skokie, Ill., 1994—96; v.p. devel. Chgo. Hist. Soc., 1996—99; cons., 1999—2005; sr. maj. gifts officer, dir. devel. Rush U. Med. Ctr., Chgo., 2005—. Mem. Atty. Gen.'s Charitable Adv. Coun., Chgo., 2004—; elder 4th Presbyn. Ch., Chgo., 2006—. Mem.: Assn. Fundraising Profls. Internat. (bd. dirs. 2004—, vice chair membership 2006—), Assn. Fundraising Profls. (bd. dirs. Chgo. chpt. 1997—2006, pres. bd. dirs. 2003—04, Pres.'s award 2002). Office: Rush U Med Ctr 1700 W Van Buren St Ste 250 Chicago IL 60612 Home Phone: 312-922-5414.

FREY, JOANNE ALICE TUPPER, art educator; b. Wakefield, Mass., Jan. 16, 1931; d. Arthur Andrew Tupper, Elva June Goddard, Joanne Alice Tupper; m. John Oscar Frey, June 14, 1953 (dec. Oct. 2000); children: David J., Donald A., Dale R., Alexandria Brennan. Grad. honors, Vesper George Sch. Art, Boston, 1951; student art history, NTL Art Gallery, London, 1979. Tchr. art Wishing Well Cards, Everett, Mass., 1951—54, Sarrin Studio, Wakefield, Mass., 1960—96; tchr. art oil, acrylic, and watercolor Wakefield H.S., Wakefield, 1997—. Antique and current doll authority; lectr. in field. Asst. resident dir. Boit Home for Women, Wakefield, Mass., 1996—; bd. dirs. The Hartshorne House. Mem.: Collie Fancier League of N.E., The Kosmos Club (decorator 1997—). Republican. Congregationalist. Avocations: painting, reading, walking, gardening, art history. Home: 701 Haverhill St Reading MA 01867

FREY, JULIA BLOCH, language and art educator, historian; b. Louisville, July 25, 1943; d. Oscar Edgeworth and Jean Goldthwaite (Russell) Bloch; m. Roger G. Frey, Dec. 27, 1968 (div. Mar. 1976); m. Ronald Sukenick, Mar. 9, 1992 (dec. 2004); m. Guust Nolet, Mar. 8, 2006. BA, Antioch Coll., 1966; MA, U. Tex., 1968; MPhil, Yale U., 1970, PhD, 1977. Instr. Brown U., Providence, 1972-73; chargée de cours U. Paris, 1974-75; lectr. Yale U., New Haven, 1975-76; prof. Inst. Internat. Comparative Law, U. San Diego, Paris, 1979-89, adminstrv. dir., 1989; prof. French, art history U. Colo., Boulder, 1976—2001, prof. emeritus, 2002—, dir. undergrad. studies, 1985-95, assoc. chmn. for grad. studies, 1996-97, 98-99, chmn., 1999. Guest prof. Sarah Lawrence Coll., Bronxville, N.Y., 1983; curator Toulouse-Lautrec Met. Mus. Art Denver Art Mus., 1999, Toulouse-Lautrec, Museo Vittoriano, Rome, 2003-04. Author: Toulouse-Lautrec, a life, 1994, Toulouse-Lautrec l'homme qui aimait les femmes, 1996; editor: Gustave Flaubert's La Lutte du Sacerdoce et de L'Empire (1837), 1981; contbr. articles and monographs to profl. publs., chpts. to books; translator: René. Recipient Conn. Grad. Study award, 1970-73; grantee NDEA, 1967, Brown U. Research and Travel, 1973, Boulder Arts Com., 1979, 80, Ctr. for Applied Humanities, 1985, S.W. Inst. for Research on Women, 1985-86, NEH, 1986; fellow NDEA, 1966-68, Yale U., 1968-72, Gilbert Chinard, Inst. Français de Washington, 1977, Big 12 2000, Humanities Rsch. Ctr., Australian Nat. U., 2000; Pen Ctr. USA West Lit. award for non-fiction, 1995; Finalist Nat. Book Critics Cir. award for Biography, 1994. Mem. MLA, PEN U.S.A., Coll. Art Assn., Yale Club. Unitarian Universalist. Home: 158 Herrontown Rd Princeton NJ 08540 E-mail: julia.frey@aya.yale.edu.

FREY, LOUIS, JR., lawyer, federal official; b. Jan. 11, 1934; m. Marcia Turner, 1956; children: Julie, Lynne, Louis III, Lauren, Christine. BA cum laude, Colgate U., 1955; JD, U. Mich., 1961; JD (hon.), Rollins Coll., 1977; DSc (hon.), Jones Univ., 1978. Bar: Fla. 1961, U.S. Supreme Ct. 1969, 5th, 11th Cir. Ct. of Appeals, U.S. Supreme Ct. Asst. county solictor Orange County, Fla., 1961-63; gen. counsel Fla. State Turnpike Authority, 1966-67; congressman U.S. Ho. of Reps., 1969-79, mem. interstate and fgn. commerce com., sci. and tech. com., select com. on narcotics, sub-com. on communications, sub-com. on energy research; ptnr. Lowndes, Drosdick, Doster, Kantor & Reed, P.A., Orlando, Fla., 1987—; commr. Dept. of Lottery State of Fla., 1987-88; founder Lou Frey Inst. Politics and Govt., U. Ctrl. Fla., 2002—. Del. or alternate del. to most Rep. Conv., 1968—; Rep. State Chmn. Pres. Ford, 1976—; nat. co-chmn., former mem. Congress for Reagan, 1980; nat. fin. com. Bush, 1988—92; Fla. state fin. com. Pres. Bush, 2000, 04; counsellor to sec. HUD, 2001; alumni bd. trustees Colgate U., 1973—75; leader delegations various countries Former Mems. of Congress; ofcl. observer Ukraine Election, 2004. Contbr. weekly column to Fla. newspapers; author, editor: Inside The House Former Members Reveal How the House Works, 2001 co-anchor: Fla. Roundtable Radio Show, 1998—; commentator pub. radio and TV, 1999—. Chmn. Fla. Fedn. of Young Reps., 1965-66; treas. Rep. Party Fla., mem. state exec. com., 1966-67; past chmn., mem. exec. com. Fla. Coun. on Econ. Edn., 1991—; chmn. Former Mems. Congress, 1992-94, bd. dirs., 1992—; candidate Fla. Gov., 1978-86, U.S. Senate, 1980; bd. dirs. Fla. Sports Found., 2006—. Served with USN, 1955-58, capt. Res. ret., 1978. Recipient Watchdog of Treasury award, 1970, 72, 74, 76, 78, Guardian of Small Bus. award, Disting. Service award Ams. for Constitutional Action, Man of Yr. award Fla. Assn. Broadcasters, 1977, Masada award, 1977, Hope for Congress, Life Mag., 1975, Gubernatorial appointment Fla. Sports Found., 2006-; named one of 200 Rising Leaders in US, Time Mags., 1974, Best Lawyers in Am., 2006, Fla. Super Lawyers, 2006; named to Sr. Citizen's Hall of Fame. Mem. Order of the Coif, Phi Gamma Delta, Phi Delta Phi. Lutheran. Home: 139 Genius Dr Winter Park FL 32789-5103 Office: Lowndes Drosdick Doster Kantor & Reed PA 215 N Eola Dr PO Box 2809 Orlando FL 32801-2095 Office Phone: 407-843-4600. Business E-Mail: lou.frey@lowndes-law.com.

FREY, MARTIN ALAN, lawyer, educator; b. Rochester, NY, Feb. 26, 1939; s. Morrey and Betty F.; m. Phyllis Sue Hurley, Apr. 19, 1966; 1 child, David Andrew. BS in Mech. Engring., Northwestern U., 1962; JD, Washington U., St. Louis, 1965; LLM, George Washington U., 1966. Bar: Mo. 1965, Okla. 1976, U.S. Dist. Ct. (no. dist.) Okla. 1983. Asst. prof. law Drake U., Des Moines, 1966-67; prof. law Tex. Tech. U., Lubbock, 1967-76, U. Tulsa, 1976—2001, assoc. dean, 1981-84, prof. emeritus, 2001—. Vis. prof. law U. Maine, Portland, 1974—75, Washington U., St. Louis, 1986—87, U. Ala., Tuscaloosa, 2003, Wake Forest U., 2005, Stetson U., 2005—06; adj. settlement judge US Dist Ct and US Bankruptcy Ct. (no. dist.) Okla., 1988—; reporter adv. group Civil Justice Reform Act, U.S. Dist. Ct. (no. dist) Okla., 1991—97; dir. Ctr. Dispute Resolution U. Tulsa Coll. Law, 1994—2000. Author: Alternative Methods of Dispute Resolution, 2003; co-author (with P.H. Frey): An Introduction to the Law of Contracts, 4th edit., 2007, Essentials of Contract Law, 2000; co-author: (with P.H. Frey and Sidney Swinson) An Introduction to Bankruptcy Law 5th edit., 2006; co-author: West's Bankruptcy Practice Systems, 1991; co-author: (with B. Bucholtz and M. Tatum) The Little Black Book: A Do-It Yourself Guide For Law Student Competitions, 2001; founder, advisor: Tex. Tech. Law Rev., 1967—71; contbr. articles to profl. jours. Mem.: ABA (accreditation site evaluation teams 1978—2000). Democrat. Jewish. Home: 9035 S Maplewood Ave Tulsa OK 74137-3040 Office Phone: 918-481-6278. Personal E-mail: martin_a_frey@yahoo.com.

FREY, PAUL HOWARD, chemical engineer, engineering consultants company executive; b. Gilman, Ill., Feb. 12, 1922; s. Carl Fredrick and Doretta Mary (Koritz) F.; m. Patricia Anne Leonard, Oct. 6, 1942; children: Paul H. Jr, Elizabeth Ann. BSChE, U. Ill., 1943. Registered profl. engr., Ill. Tech. advisor Manhatten Dist. (Atom Bomb Project) Union Carbide Corp., Tonawanda, N.Y., 1943-46, rsch. and devel. engr., 1946-49; project engr. Union Carbide Corp, Chgo., 1960-80, engring. mgr., 1980-86; plant engr. U.S. Reduction Co., East Chicago, Ind., 1949-54; project and sales engr. Sunbeam Corp., Chgo., 1954-58; plant mgr. Detinning Corp., Chgo., 1958-60; owner Freytone Co. Cons. Engrs., Spooner, Wis., 1986—. Leader Citizens for Improved Edn., LaGrange, Ill., 1967-69; mem. vestry St. Alban's Episc. Ch., 1993—. Mem. AIChE, Lions (Lion Tamer officer Spooner chpt., 1992—), Jaycees (Key award Hammond, Ind. 1951), Waukegan Yacht Club (bd. dirs. to commodore 1976-82), No. Ill. Venture Assn. (various officers to commodore 1974-78). Achievements include patents in field. Avocations: sailboat racing, long-distance sailing. Home and Office: N5683 Tanglewood Dr Spooner WI 54801-8480 Home Phone: 715-635-6505. E-mail: topfrey@centurytel.net.

FREY, PERRY A., biochemistry educator; b. Plain City, Ohio, Nov. 14, 1935; s. John Edward and Inez (Kramer) F.; m. Carolyn M. Scott, Feb. 11, 1961; children: Suzanne, Cynthia. BS in Chemistry, Ohio State U., 1959; PhD in Biochemistry, Brandeis U., Waltham, Mass., 1968. Teaching asst. Ohio State U., Columbus, 1959-60; chemist USPHS, Cin., 1960-64; asst. prof. chemistry Ohio State U., 1969-74, assoc. prof. chemistry, 1974-79, acad. vice chair chemistry, 1977-80, prof. chemistry, 1979-81; prof. biochemistry U. Wis., Madison, 1981—. Wellcome vis. prof. Emory U., Atlanta, 1995—96; cons. in field. Co-author: (with Abeles and Jencks) Biochemistry, 1992, (with Adrian D. Hegeman) Enzymatic Reaction Mechanisms, 2007; assoc. editor: Biochemistry, 1992—; mem. editl. bd. Bioorganic Chemistry, 1986—, Jour. Biol. Chemistry, 1983-88 Accounts

Chemistry Rsch., 2006-; contbr. articles to profl. jours. With US Army, 1954—56. Recipient Alexander von Humboldt sr. scientist award, 1995. Fellow AAAS, Am. Acad. Arts and Scis.; mem. Am. Chem. Soc. (Repligen award 2000), Am. So. Biochem. & Molecular Biology, Protein Soc., Nat. Acad. Scis. (life). Avocations: travel, reading, hiking. Home: 209 Eddy St Madison WI 53705-4423 Office: U Wis Dept Biochemistry 1710 University Ave Madison WI 53726 Office Phone: 608-262-0055. Business E-Mail: frey@biochem.wisc.edu.

FREY, SHARON ELIZABETH, internist, adult infectious disease physician; b. Bethlehem, Pa., Sept. 30, 1952; MD, Marshall U. Sch. Medicine, Huntington, W.Va., 1985. Cert. internal medicine, adult infectious diseases. Resident, internal medicine SUNY Upstate Med. Univ., Syracuse, 1985—88, fellow, 1988—89; fellow, infectious diseases St. Louis Univ. Hosp., Mo., 1989—90, hosp. appt. Mo.; prof. internal medicine, divsn. infectious diseases St. Louis Univ. Sch. Medicine, Mo. Prin. investigator for oral salmonella vector, hepatitis A, hepatitis B, hepatitis C, and CMV protocols; prin. investigator in the evaluation of vaccines to counter bioterrorism/biowarfare including smallpox vaccine trials St. Louis Univ. Sch. Medicine; clin. supr., HIV Vaccine Trials Unit St. Louis Univ. Office: St Louis Univ Health Sciences Ctr 3691 Rutger Ste 100 Saint Louis MO 63110-2515 Office Phone: 314-977-6333.

FREY, SUSAN M., information specialist; d. Anthony T. and Martha M. Frey. BA, SUNY-Stony Brook, 1983; MS, L.I. U., 1986; MLS, Ind. U., 2002. Info. svcs. libr. Ind. U.-Purdue U., Ft. Wayne, 1991—99; asst. libr. dir. Ind. Inst. Tech., Ft. Wayne, 2000—01; info. specialist DePuy Orthopaedics, Warsaw, Ind., 2001—05; asst. prof. Ind. State U., 2006—. Adj. lectr. Ind. U.-Purdue U., 2002; presenter in field. Contbr. articles to scholarly jours. Mem.: ALA, Am. Soc. Info. Sci. and Tech., Assn. Computing Machinery. Office: Indiana State Univ Cunningham Memorial Libr 650 Sycamore St Terre Haute IN 47809 Home Phone: 812-237-2579. Office Fax: 574-371-4984. Business E-Mail: sfrey@isugw.indstate.edu.

FREY, WILLIAM H., demographer, educator; b. Allentown, Pa., June 21, 1947; s. Elwood H. and Loretta C. Frey. BS, Ursinus Coll., Collegeville, Pa., 1969; PhD, Brown U., Providence, 1974. Sociology lectr. Rutgers U., New Brunswick, NJ, 1973-74; rsch. assoc. Ctr. for Studies in Demography and Ecology U. Wash., Seattle, 1974-75; project dir., assoc. Ctr. for Demography and Ecology U. Wis., Madison, 1975-81; rsch. prof. Population Studies Ctr. U. Mich., Ann Arbor, 1981—98, 2000—; prof. sociology SUNY, Albany, 1998-2001; sr. fellow Milken Inst., Santa Monica, Calif., 1998—2006, Brookings Instn., 2007—. Vis. rsch. scholar Internat. Inst. Applied Sys. Analysis, Laxenburg, Austria, 1980-81; vis. fellow Brooking Instn., Washington, 2003-07; Andrew W. Mellon vis. scholar Popular Ref. Bur., Washington, 1988-89; cons. US Census Bur., Population Divsn., Washington, 2000-03; dir. ednl. devel. Pub. Data Queries, Inc., Ann Arbor, Mich., 1998-2005; pres. Frey-First Demographic Networks Inc., Ann Arbor, 1999- Author: America by the Numbers: A Fieldguide to the U.S. Population, 2001, Regional and Population Growth and Decline in the U.S., 1988; contbr. articles to profl. jours. including Am. Sociol. Rev., Population and Devel. Rev., among others. Grantee Population Ref. Bur., 1998-2002, Nat. Inst. Aging, 1994-2000, Nat. Inst. child Health and Human Devel. Ctr. for Population Rsch., 1982-87, 1994-2000, 2004—, NSF, 1996—, Russell Sage Found., 1992-93, Child Trends, Inc., 1995, others; vis. fellow Brookings Inst., 2003— Fellow Urban Land Inst.; mem. Am. Sociol. Assn. (chair com. on nat. statistics 1997-99), Population Assn. Am. (com. on population stats. 1995—), Internat. Union for the Sci. Study Population Avocations: bicycling, hiking, website creation. Office: The Univ Michigan 426 Thompson St Ann Arbor MI 48104-2321 Office Phone: 888-257-7244. Fax: 888-257-7244. Business E-Mail: billf@umich.edu. E-mail: bill.frey@usa.net.

FREYD, JENNIFER JOY, psychology professor; b. Providence, Oct. 16, 1957; d. Peter John and Pamela (Parker) F.; m. John Q. Johnson, June 9, 1984; children: Theodore, Philip, Alexandra. BA in Anthropology magna cum laude, U. Pa., Phila., 1979; PhD in Psychology, Stanford U., Calif., 1983. Asst. prof. psychology Cornell U., 1983-87, mem. faculty coun. reps., 1986-87; assoc. prof. psychology U. Oreg., Eugene, 1987-92, mem. exec. com. Inst. Cognitive and Decision Scis., 1991—94, prof., 1992—, mem. dean's adv. com., 1990-91, 92-93, mem. exec. com. Ctr. for the Study of Women in Soc., 1991-93, mem. child care com., 1987-89, 90-91, mem. instnl. rev. bd., 2002—05, dir. undergrad. studies dept. psychology, 2004—, mem. exec. com. dept. psychology, 2006—. Author: Betrayal Trauma: The Logic of Forgetting Childhood Abuse, 1996 (Disting. Publ. award Assn. of Women in Psychology 1997, Pierre Janet award Internat. Soc. for Study Dissociation 1997), Spanish edit., 2003; co-editor: (with A.P. De Prince) Trauma and Cognitive Science: A Meeting of Minds, Science, and Human Experience, 2001; mem. editl. bd. Jour. Exptl. Psychology: Learning, Memory, and Cognition, 1989-91, Gestalt Theory, 1985—, Jour. of Aggression, Maltreatment, and Trauma, 1997—, Jour. of Psychopathology and Behavioral Assessment, 2001-03, Jour. Trauma Practice, 2003—, Jour. of Trauma and Dissociation, 1999-2005, assoc. editor, 2004, editor, 2005—; guest reviewer Am. Jour. Psychology, Am. Psychologist, others; contbr. over 100 articles to profl. jours. including Sci. Mag. Grad. fellowship NSF, 1979-82, Univ. fellowship Stanford U., 1982-83, Presdl. Young Investigator award NSF, 1985-90, IBM Faculty Devel. award, 1985-87, fellowship Ctr. for Advanced Study in the Behavioral Scis., 1989-90, John Simon Meml. fellowship Guggenheim Found., 1989-90, Rsch. Scientist Devel. award NIMH, 1989-94, Pierre Janet award Internat. Soc. Study of Dissociation, 1997, 05, Psychologist-Scientist of Yr. award Lane County Psychologists Assn., 2006. Fellow AAAS, APA (liaison divsn. 35 to sci. directorate 1998-2000, liaison divsn. 56 to sci. dir. 2006-, chair sci. com. trauma psychology divsn. 2006—), Am. Psychol. Soc., Psychonomic Soc.; mem. Internat. Soc. Study of Traumatic Stress, Sigma Xi. Office: Dept Psychology 1227 U Oreg Eugene OR 97403-1227 Office Phone: 541-346-4950. Business E-Mail: jjf@dynamic.uoregon.edu.

FREYD, WILLIAM PATTINSON, not-for-profit fundraiser, director; b. Chgo., Apr. 1, 1933; s. Paul Robert Freyd and Pauline Margaret (Pattinson) Gardiner; m. Diane Marie Carlson, May 19, 1984. BS in Fgn. Svc., Georgetown U., 1960. Field rep. Georgetown U., Washington, 1965-67; campaign dir. Tamblyn and Brown, NYC, 1967-70; dir. devel. St. George's Ch., NYC, 1971; assoc. Browning Assocs., Newark, 1972-73; regional v.p. C.W. Shaver Co., NYC, 1973-74; founder IDC, Henderson, Nev., 1974—. Founder, treas., prodr. SFS Entertainment, 2005. Prodr.: A Chorus Line, 2005; prodr.: Cabaret, 2006; prodr.: Best Little Whorehouse in Texas, 2006. Bd. dirs. Nev. Symphony Orch., 1994-99, NJ Symphony Orch., 1991-94, Las Vegas Philharm., 2004, exec. com., 2005, pres., 2006; bd. dirs. Nev. Opera Theater, 2004; apptd. Nev. Charitable Solicitation Task Force, 1994, pres.'s circle adv. coun. U.S. Naval Acad., 2003. Mem. SAG, Assn. Fundraising Profls. (nat. treas. 1980-81, pres. NY chpt. 1974-76, cert. 1982), Am. Assn. Fund Raising Counsel (sec. 1984-86, designated Sage 2000), World Fund Raising Coun. (bd. dirs. 1995-99, treas. 1998-99), Georgetown U. (regional club coun.), NY Yacht Club, Union League Club NY, Masons, Nassau Club, Circumnavigators Club. Achievements include invention of Phone Mail program. Office: IDC IDC Ctr 2500 Paseo Verde Pky Henderson NV 89074 Personal E-mail: wfreyd@aol.com. E-mail: wfreyd@goidc.com.

FREYER, CHARLES C., lawyer; b. Phila., Mar. 3, 1947; AB, Princeton U., 1969; JD, Yale U., 1972. Bar: Pa. 1972, U.S. Ct. Mil. Appeals 1973, N.Y. 1990. Ptnr. Saul, Ewing, Remick & Saul, Phila.; chief administrv. officer , gen. counsel. SCP Ptnrs., Waye. Mem. bd. Young Scholars Charter Sch. Lt. colonel Judge Adv. Gen's Corps. US Army, 1969—94. Mem. ABA, Pa. Bar Assn., N.Y. State Bar Assn., Assn. Comml. Fin. Attys., Princeton U. Alumni Assn. Office: SCP Ptnrs 1200 Liberty Ridge Dr Ste 300 Wayne PA 19087 Office Phone: 610-995-2900. Office Fax: 610-975-9546.

FREYER, DANA HARTMAN, lawyer; b. Pitts., Apr. 17, 1944; m. Bruce M. Freyer, Dec. 21, 1969. Student, L' Institut De Hautes Etudes Internationales, Geneva, 1963-64; BA, Conn. Coll., 1965; postgrad., Columbia U., 1968, JD, 1971. Bar: NY 1972, Ill. 1974, US Dist. Ct. (no. dist.) Ill. 1974, US Ct. Appeals (7th cir.) 1976, US Supreme Ct. 1977, US Dist. Ct. (so. dist.) NY 1978, US Dist. Ct. (ea. dist.) NY 1981, US Ct. Appeals (2d cir.) 1982. Staff atty. Legal Aid Soc. Westchester County, Mt. Vernon, NY, 1971-72; assoc. Friedman & Koven, Chgo., 1973-77, Skadden, Arps, Slate, Meagher & Flom, LLP, NYC, 1977-88; spl. counsel Skadden, Arps, Slate, Meagher & Flom, NYC, 1988-93, ptnr., arbitration and alternative dispute resolution, 1994—, mem. internat. arbitration group, head corp. compliance practice. Pres. Westchester Legal Services, Inc., White Plains, NY, 1985-87, bd. dirs., 1978-98; US Coun. for Internat. Bus. Arbitration Com.; adv. bd. World Arbitration and Mediation Report; mem. Coun. on Fgn. Rels.; lectr. in the field; leader in dispute resolution, Practical Law Company's Global Counsel Dispute Resolution Handbook, 2003-04. Contbr. articles to profl. publs.; author and co-author (articles in profl. jours. and publs.), mem. adv. bd. Bur. of Nat. Affairs' Alternative Dispute Resolution Report, 1987—90, Am. Arbitration Assn. Dispute Resolution Jour., 1996—, World Arbitration and Mediation Report, 1990—. Bd. legal advisors Legal Momentum, 2002—. Named one of World's Leading Expert in Commercial Arbitration, Euromoney, 50 Top Women Litigators in Am., Nat. Law Jour. Fellow Chartered Inst. Arbitrators, Coll. Comml. Arbitrators; mem. ABA, Bar Assn. City of NY, Internat. Bar Assn., adv. and spl. coms. on Alternative Dispute Resolution, Internat. Bar Assn.; co-chair and co-founder, Global Partnership for Afghanistan, 2002-; arbitrator, mem. corp. coun. com. and law com., Am. Arbitration Assn. Office: Skadden Arps Slate Meagher & Flom LLP 4 Times Sq New York NY 10036 Office Phone: 212-735-2506. Office Fax: 917-777-2506. Business E-Mail: dfreyer@skadden.com.

FREYER, TONY ALLAN, historian, educator; b. Indpls., Dec. 28, 1947; s. Robert Albert Freyer and Ida Marie Hadley; m. Marjorie Faller, Aug. 12, 1976; 1 child, Allan. AB in History, San Diego State U., 1970; MA in History, Ind. U., Bloomington, 1972, PhD of History, 1975. Lectr. in law Ind. U. Sch. of Law, Bloomington, 1974—75; asst. to assoc. prof. hist. U. Ark., Little Rock, 1976—81; asst. to full prof. hist. & law U. Ala., Tuscaloosa, 1981—90, Univ. rsch. prof. hist. & law, 1990—. Vis. prof. econ. hist London Sch. of Econ., London, 1986; vis. prof. constl. hist. UCLA, 1987; bus. hist. rev. editl. bd. Harvard Bus. Sch., Boston, 1985—. Author: Producers Versus Capitalists Rights: Constitutional Conflict in Antebellum America, 1994, Regulating Big Business: Antitrust in Great Britian and America, 1880 to 1990, 1992, Hugo L. Black and the Dilemma of American Liberalism, 1990, The Little Rock Crisis, 1984, Harmony & Dissonance: The Swift & Erie Cases in American Federalism, 1981, Forums of Order: The Federal Courts and Business in American History, 1979, Antitrust and Global Capitalism, 1930-2004, 2006, Little Rock on Trial Cooper v. Aaron and School Desegregation, 2007; co-author (with Timothy Dixon): Democracy and Judicial Independence: Federal Courts in Alabama, 1820-1994, 1995; editor: Defending Constitutional Rights: Frank M. Johnson, 2001; contbr. chapters to books, articles to encyclopedias, to profl. jour.; rev. (70 books to profl. jour.). PFC USMC Res., 1970—72. Recipient Burnam Disting. Faculty award, Univ. Ala., 1991, Martin Luther King. Jr. Lectr., Vanderbilt U., 1991, Abe Fellow-Japan, Ctr. for Global Partnership, 1995—96; grantee Nat. Endowment for the Humanities, Summer Stipends, 1978, 1985, Rsch. Grants Com., U. Ala., 1983, 1985, Jud. Conf. of the US, Com. on the Bicentennial of the Constn. Summer Rsch. Grant, 1991, Ark. Endowment for the Humanities Rsch. Grants, 1978, 1980, 1981; Earhart Found. Fellowships, 1982, 1985, 1994—95, 2002—03, postdoctral fellow, Project '87, 1980, Hagley Mus. and Libr. Fellowship, 1979—80, Newcomer Fellowship, Harvard Bus. Sch., 1975—76, Charles Warren Fellowship, Harvard U., 1981—82, Fulbright Sr. Scholar award, UK, 1986, Australia, 1993, Fulbright Disting. Chair Am. Studies, Warsaw Univ., Poland, 2000. Mem.: Ogrn. of Am. Hist., Am. Soc. for Legal Hist., Am. Hist. Assn., Phi Beta Kappa. Independent. Christian Sci. Avocations: travel, reading, execrise. Office: Univ Ala Sch Law Box 870382 Tuscaloosa AL 35487 Business E-Mail: tfreyer@law.ua.edu.

FREYERMUTH, CLIFFORD L., structural engineering consultant; BS in Civil Engring., State U. Iowa, 1956, MS in Structural Engring., 1958. Registered structural engr., Ariz. Consulting engr. structural design Ned L. Ashton, 1955-57; grad. teaching asst. structural mechanics State U. Iowa, 1957-58; with bridge divsn. Ariz. State Hwy. Dept., 1958-64; with Portland Cement Assn., Chgo., Skokie, Ill., 1964-71; dir. post-tensioning divsn. Prestessed Concrete Inst., 1971-76; mgr. Post-Tensioning Inst., 1976-88; pres. Clifford L. Freyermuth, Inc., 1988—. Mem. cable-stayed bridges com. Post-Tensioning Inst, editor various publs.; prin. investigator Nat. Coop. Hwy Rsch. Project, Washington, 1988. Contbr. articles to profl. jours. Recipient Martin P. Korn award Prestressed Concrete Inst., 1969, George C. Zollman award Precast/Prestressed Concrete Inst., 1999. Fellow Am. Concrete Inst. (prestressed concrete com., standard bldg. code com., bd. dirs. 1991—, Henry C. Turner medal 1992, Arthur R. Anderson award 2004); mem. ASCE (prestressed concrete com.), Structural Engrs. Assn. Ariz., Chi Epsilon. Office: Clifford L Freyermuth Inc 9201 N 25th Ave Ste 150B Phoenix AZ 85021-2721 Personal E-mail: asbi@earthlink.net.

FREYERMUTH, VIRGINIA KAREN, art educator; BFA cum laude, Boston U., 1973, MFA, 1975; edn. cert., Suffolk U., 1975; PhD in Interdisciplinary Studies, Art Edn., Union Inst. and U., 2003. Cert. art tchr., Mass. Grad. asst. Boston U., Mass., 1973-75; art tchr. Quincy Pub. Sch., Mass., 1975-76, Plymouth Pub. Sch., Mass., 1976-78, 83-85; painting tchr. Brockton Fuller Mus. Art, Mass., 1978-79; art coord. grades K-12 Duxbury Pub. Sch., Mass., 1985-99; vis. lectr. art edn. U. Mass., Dartmouth, Mass., 1999—2004; pres. Virginia K. Freyermuth, Inc., Carver, Mass., 2004—. Art reviewer Patriot Ledger, Quincy, 1975-85; dir. Freyermuth Fine Arts Ctr., Plymouth, 1990-94; mem. adv. coun. Mass. Field Ctr. Tchg. & Learning, 1993-96; tchr. in electronic residence MCET, Cambridge, 1993-95; instr. art Massasoit C.C., Brockton, 1991-92; dir. Helen Bumpus Gallery, Inc., Duxbury, 1992-94; forum tchr. Goals 2000 U.S. Dept. Edn., 1994—, internat. space camp, 1994; master tchr. Connecting Oceans Acad., ECHO Project, New Bedford, Mass, 2004-07. Columnist Learning for Life, 1994. Mem. commn. on common core of learning Mass. Dept. Edn., 1993-94; bd. dirs. Mass. Alliance for Arts Edn., 1994-95. Named Mass. Tchr. of Yr., Mass. Dept. Edn., 1994, Nat. Outstanding Visual Art Tchr., Walt Disney and McDonald's, 1995, 1995-96 Profiled in Disney Channel. Mem. Mass. Art Edn. Assn., Nat. Art Edn. Assn., Tchr. Leadership Acad. Mass. (bd. dirs., founding fellow), Lucretia Crocker Acad. of Tchg. Fellows (bd. dirs.). Personal E-mail: virginiafreyermuth@yahoo.com.

FREYMAN, THOMAS C., pharmaceutical executive; b. Evanston, Ill., Sept. 8, 1954; B in Accountancy, U. Ill.; M in Mgmt., Northwestern U. CPA. Formerly acct. Ernst & Whinney, Chgo.; with Abbott Labs., Abbott Park, Ill., 1979—, fin. dir. European distbn. ctr. Netherlands, 1984—87, divsn. contr. corp. materials mgmt., 1987—88, treas. internat. divsn., 1988—91, v.p., treas., 1991—99, v.p., contr. hosp. products divsn., 1999—2001, sr. v.p. fin., CFO, 2001—04, exec. v.p. fin., CFO, 2004—. Bd. dirs. Vista Health, Chgo. Bot. Garden. Mem.: Econ. Club Chgo. Office: Abbott Labs 100 Abbott Park Rd Abbott Park IL 60064-6400*

FREYRE, ANGELA MARIANA, lawyer; b. Havana, Cuba, Sept. 18, 1954; BA, Wellesley Coll., 1976; D.E.J.G. Mention Assez Bien, Univ. Paris, France, 1978; JD, LLM, Georgetown Univ., 1980. Bar: NY 1984. Ptnr. prin. Latin Am. practice Coudert Bros. LLP, NYC. Trustee NY Studio Sch. Drawing, Painting & Sculpture, 1984—, LongHouse Reserve Ltd., 2000—; mem. City of NY Conflicts of Interest Bd. Fulbright scholar. Mem.: Assn. Bar City of NY. Office: Coudert Bros LLP 1114 Ave of the Americas New York NY 10036 Office Phone: 212-626-4487. Office Fax: 212-626-4120. Business E-Mail: freyrea@coudert.com.

FREYRE, FABIO, publishing executive; m. Amy Leighton Thomas, Aug. 25, 1984; 2 children. BA, Hamilton Coll., 1983. Assoc. pub., advtsg. sales dir. Sports Illustrated Time Inc., New York, 1996-99, pub. Sports Illustrated mag., 1999—2003, group v.p., corp. sales & mktg., 2003—05; CEO Latina Media Ventures LLC, NYC, 2005—. Office: Latina Media Ventures LLC Ste 700 1500 Broadway New York NY 10036 Office Phone: 212-642-0200. Office Fax: 917-777-0860.

FREYSSINIER NOVA, JEAN PAUL, engineering research professor; arrived in US, 1999; s. Jose Freyssinier and Silvia Nova; m. Minerva Alonso; 1 child, Isabelle Freyssinier. BSEE, Nat. Autonomous U., Mexico, 1993; MS in Lighting, Rensselaer Poly. Inst., Troy, NY, 2001. Cert. lighting, Nat. Coun. Qualification Lighting Professions, 1998. Ptnr., sys. mgr. Genertek, SA de CV, Mexico City, 1993—95; prin., owner Octavo Arte, Mexico City, 1995—99; from rsch. grad. asst. to lighting design specialist Lighting Rsch. Ctr., Rensselaer Poly. Inst., 1999—2005; rsch. asst. prof., Lighting Rsch. Ctr. Rensselaer Poly. Inst., 2005—. Recipient Internat. Illumination Design award, 2003, Walsh-Weston award, Soc. Light and Lighting, 2005; scholar, Lightcontrol, 2000. Mem.: Illuminating Engring. Soc. N.Am. (sec. student chpt. 1992—95, mem. various coms. 1992—95, Southwestern Region Best of Show Mex., Students Lighting Design award 1994, 1995), Soc. Light and Lighting U.K. (Walsh-Weston award 2005), Assn. Energy Engrs., Instn. Lighting Engrs. U.K. (assoc.). Achievements include design of over fifty high-end commercial, residential, institutional, and historic building projects; research in energy efficiency, advanced lighting technologies, technology transfer, human factors, lighting design, and education; patents pending for a novel technique to significantly improve the efficiency of white light-emmitting diodes. Office: Lighting Research Center 21 Union Street Troy NY 12180 Office Phone: 518-687-7100. Business E-Mail: freysj@rpi.edu.

FREYTAG, SHARON NELSON, lawyer; b. May 11, 1943; d. John Seldon and Ruth Marie (Herbel) Nelson; children: Kurt David, Hillary Lee. BS with highest distinction, U. Kans., Lawrence, 1965; MA, U. Mich., 1966; JD cum laude, So. Meth. U., 1981. Bar: Tex. 1981, US Dist. Ct. (no. dist.) Tex. 1981, US Dist. Ct. (so. dist.) Tex. 2001, US Ct. Appeals (5th cir.) 1982, US Ct. Appeals (8th cir.) 2001, US Ct. Appeals (fed. cir.) 2002, US Ct. Claims 2004, US Supreme Ct. 1993. Tchr. English, Gaithersburg (Md.) H.S., 1966—70; instr. English, Eastfield Coll., 1974-78; law clk. U.S. Dist. Ct. (no. dist.) Tex., 1981-82, U.S. Ct. Appeals (5th cir.), 1982; ptnr., chmn. appellate practice sect. Haynes and Boone, Dallas, 1983—. Vis. prof. law So. Meth. U., 1985-86. Editor-in-chief Southwestern Law Jour., 1980-81; contbr. articles to profl. jours. Dir. devel. bd. U. Tex. at Dallas; bd. dirs. Ctr. Brain Health. Named Tex. Super Lawyer, 2003, 2004, 2005, 2006; named one of 50 Women Tex. Super Lawyers, 2003, 2004, 2005, Best Lawyers in Am., 2005, 2006, 2007; recipient John Marshall Constl. Law award, Baird Cmty. Spirit award, 1995; Woodrow Wilson fellow. Mem. ABA (mem. exec. com. and long range planning com., former chmn. program com., chair-elect coun. appellate lawyers, chmn. task force appellate advocacy), Fed. Bar Assn. (co-chmn. appellate practice and adv. sect. 1990-91), State Bar Tex. (bd. dir., exec. com. 1997-01, appellate coun. 1995-98), Dallas Bar Assn. (appellate sect.), Higginbotham Inn of Ct. (former barrister), Order of Coif, Phi Beta Kappa. Lutheran. Office: Haynes & Boone 901 Main Ste 3100 Dallas TX 75202 Home Phone: 972-960-7740; Office Phone: 214-651-5586. Business E-Mail: sharon.freytag@haynesboone.com.

FREZZA, ELDO E., surgeon, educator; s. Giovanni and Rosa Frezza; m. Patrizia Costa; children: Edoardo, Gianmarco. MD, Padua U., Italy, 1989. Diplomate Am. Bd. Surgery, 2003. Asst. prof. U. Pitts., 2002—03; prof. Tex. Tech U. Health Scis. Ctr., Lubbock, Tex., 2003—, chief gen. surgery, 2003—. Named to Guide to America's Top Surgeons, Consumer's Rsch. Coun. Am., 2006; recipient Neely Treadwell Cancer Investigator award, S.W. Cancer Ctr., Lubbock, Tex., 2004, Rsch. Presdl. ward, Tex. Tech U. Health Scis. Ctr., 2006; fellow, SAGES, 2003. Mem.: AMA, ACS, Italian Bd. Surgery, Southeastern Soc. Surgery, Soc. Am. Gastrointestinal Endoscopic Surgeons, Assn. Academic Surgery, Am. Soc. Bariatric Surgery (life). Avocations: journalism, basketball. Office: Texas Tech University Health Sciences Ct 3502 9th Street; Suite 380 Lubbock TX 79415 Home Phone: 806-785-2120; Office Phone: 806-743-4666. Office Fax: 806-743-4670. Business E-Mail: eldo.frezza@ttuhsc.edu.

FRI, ROBERT WHEELER, retired museum director; b. Kansas City, Kans., Nov. 16, 1935; s. Homer O. and Cora Ruth (Wheeler) F.; m. Jean Landon, Jan. 16, 1965; children— Perry, Sean, Kirk. BA, Rice U., 1957; MBA, Harvard U., 1959. Assoc. McKinsey & Co., Washington, 1963-68, prin., 1968-71, 73-75; dep. adminstr. EPA, Washington, 1971-73, acting adminstr., 1973; dep. adminstr. ERDA, Washington, 1975-77, acting adminstr., 1977; head U.S. del. to IAEA, Washington, 1977; pres. Energy Transition Corp., 1978-86, Resources for the Future, 1986-95; dir. Nat. Mus. Natural History, 1996-2001. Bd. dirs. Am. Electric Power Co., Sci. Svc., Inc., Electric Power Rsch. Inst.; mem. Nat. Petroleum Coun. Lt. USNR, 1959-62. Baker scholar. Mem. Phi Beta Kappa, Sigma Xi. Republican. Presbyterian.

FRIAS, JAIME LUIS, retired pediatrician, educator; b. Concepcion, Chile, Mar. 20, 1933; came to U.S., 1970; s. Luis Humberto and Olga Ana (Fernandez) F.; m. Jacqueline May Steel, Apr. 8, 1961; children: Jaime Arturo, Juan Pablo, Patricio Andres, Maria Josefina. MD, U. Chile, 1959. Diplomate Am. Bd. Pediatrics, Am. Bd. Human Genetics. Intern Hospital Regional, Concepcion, 1958-59; resident in pediatrics Calvo Mackenna Hosp., Santiago, Chile, 1960-62; clin. genetics and dysmorphology fellow U. Wis., Madison, 1965-66, U. Wash., Seattle, 1966-67; asst. prof. pediatrics U. Concepcion, 1967-69, U. Fla. Coll. Medicine, Gainesville, 1970-74, assoc. prof., 1974-77, prof., 1977-86, chief divsn. genetics, 1977-86, chmn. med. sch. admissions com., 1983-86; prof., chmn. dept. pediatrics U. Nebr. Med. Ctr., 1986—91; prof. pediatrics U. South Fla. Coll. Medicine, Tampa, 1991—2004, chmn. dept. pediatrics, 1991-99, dir. Birth Defects Ctr., 1999—2004, emeritus prof., 2004—; vis. scientist Nat. Ctr. for Birth Defects and Devel. Disabilities, CDC, Atlanta, 2004—. Chmn. Com. for Protection of Human Subjects, 1975-78; chmn. Fla. Com. on Prevention Devel. Disabilities, 1979-82, chmn. infant hearing screening adv. coun., 1982-86; cons. Spanish Collaborative Project on Congenital Malformation, Madrid, 1983—. Contbr. chpts. to books, articles to profl. jours. Trustee All Children's Hosp., 1991-99, Ronald McDonald Charities Tampa Bay, 1999-2001; exec. com. Assn. Med. Sch. Pediat. Dept. Chmn., 1993-96; steering com. Nat. Folic Acid Coun., 1999-2003. Named Tchr. of Yr., U. Fla. Coll. Medicine, 1978-79, Lewis A. Barness Endowed Chair Pediatrics, 1994-99. Mem. ACP (affiliate; W.K. Kellogg fellow 1965-67), Am. Acad. Pediatrics (com. genetics 1995-2002), Am. Pediatric Soc., Am. Soc. Human Genetics, Assn. Clin. Scientists, Smoke Rise Golf and Country Club. Democrat. Roman Catholic. Office: MS E-86 1600 Clifton Rd Atlanta GA 30333 Personal E-mail: jlfrias@comcast.net. Business E-Mail: jfrias@cdc.gov.

FRIAS, SHIRLEE N., elementary school educator; b. Albuquerque, Jan. 27, 1969; d. Fred and Jackie Arellano; m. Don A. Frias, Nov. 5, 1994; children: Zacharie Ty, Alexis Sheree. B in Bus., N.Mex State U., 1991; MBA, N.Mex Highland U., 2001. Cert. extra ordinary min. Queen of Heaven Parish; lic. elem. tchr. United Way liaison Intel Corp., Rio Rancho, N.Mex., 1995—2001; tchr. Queen of Heaven Sch., Albuquerque, 2002—, founder Summer Sch. Acad., 2003—. Cubmaster Cub Scouts, 2002—; vacation bible sch. instr. St. Thomas Aquinas Ch., 1998—; pastoral com. mem. Queen of Heaven Parish, 2003—, liturgy com. mem., 2004—, mem. Guadulupanas, 2005, vacation bible sch. coord., 2005, creator, coord. cheer squad, 2005—. Recipient Marian medal, Queen of Heaven Parish, 1980, Pope Puis VI Nat. award, Nat. Cath. Com. on Scouting, 2004—05. Mem.: DECA (sec. 1989, pres. 1990—91), Am. Mktg. Assn. (v.p. 1990—91), Veterans of Fgn. Wars Post 401 Ladies Aux. (nat. home chair 1998—2004, jr. v.p. 2001—02, cmty. svc. 2001—02, patriotic instr. 2001—03, Americanism chair 2001—03, dist. 2 nat. home chair 2002—03, sr. v.p. 2003—04, chair nat. home for children state 2003, dist. 2 cmty. svc. 2003—04, dist. 2 jr. v.p. 2003—04, dist. 2 sr. v.p. 2004—05, dist. 2 pres. 2005—, Nat. Recognition of Achievement for nat. home for children, Second Pl. Dept. N.Mex. Chairperson, First Pl. Dept. N.Mex. Chairperson), Delta Zeta Alumnae, Delta Mu Delta. Democrat. Roman Catholic. Office: Queen of Heaven Sch 5303 Phoenix Ave NE Albuquerque NM 87110 Personal E-mail: ztf@aol.com.

FRIBERG, GEORGE JOSEPH, electronics company executive, entrepreneur; m. Mary Seymour; children: Fane George, Felicia Lynn Friberg Clark. BSME, U. N.Mex., 1962, MBA, 1982, postgrad. Sales engr. Honeywell, LA, 1962-64; liaison engr. ACF Industries, Albuquerque, 1964-66; quality assurance mgr. data sys. divsn. Gulton Industries Inc., Albuquerque, 1966-72, mgr. mfg. Femco divsn. Irwin (Pa.), High Point (N.C.), 1972-77, v.p. mfg. data sys. divsn. Albuquerque, 1977-86; pres., CEO Tetra Corp., Albuquerque, 1986-92, also bd. dirs.; pres., CEO Laguna Industries Inc., Albuquerque, 1992-96; sr. dir. Tech. Ventures Corp., Albuquerque, 1996—. Adj. prof. U. N.Mex. Mgmt. Tech., 1998—2005; bd. dir. Noonday, Inc. Mem. editl. bd. N.Mex. Bus. Jour., 1989— Mem. N.Mex. R&D Gross Receipts Task Force, 1988-89; mem. Econ. Forum of Albuquerque; bd. dir. Technet, 1983-97, pres., 1983-84, 88-89; bd. dir. Lovelace Insts., 1988-99, U. N.Mex. R.O. Anderson Bus. Sch. Found., 1988-92, N.Mex. Bus. Innovation Ctr., 1986-92, U. N.Mex. Found., 1999—, N.Mex. Golden Apple Found., 1998-2007, pres., 2003—04; mem. coun. trustees Lovelace Respiratory Rsch. Insts., 1999-, chmn, 2004-; bd. dir. N.Mex. Natural History Mus. Found., 1999-2005, sec. 2002-05; bd. dir. N.Mex. First, 2001—05, United Way, N.Mex., 2001-02, Samaritan Counseling Found., 2007-; grad. Leadership N.Mex., 1998; mem. mech. engrng. adv. coun. U. N.Mex., 1999— Inducted Anderson Sch. of Bus. Hall of Fame, 1996, U. N.Mex. Athletic Hall of Honor, 2003; recipient Zia award U. N.Mex., 1998, Regents medal U. N.Mex., 1998, Lockheed Martin Nova award, 1998, Albuquerque High Harrington award, 2000; named to All-Time Football Team Albuquerque HS, 2001, Albuquerque HS Hall of Fame, 2004. Mem. Albuquerque C. of C. (bd. dirs. 1985-92, polit. action com. 1983-84, chair Buy N.Mex. chpt. 1986-87, vice chmn. econ. affairs planning coun. 1987—, chmn. bd. 1990-91), N.Mex. Alumni Lettermen's Club, U. N.Mex. Alumni Assn. (bd. dirs. 1995-2001, pres.-elect 1997, pres. 1997-98, chair legis. com. 2000-) Home: 13234 Sunset Canyon Dr NE Albuquerque NM 87111-4220 Business E-Mail: george.j.friberg@lmco.com.

FRIBOURG, PAUL J., grain company executive; BA, Amherst Coll.; Advanced Mgmt. degree, Harvard U. 1994exec. v.p., group pres. commodity mktg. Continental Grain Co., NYC, 1990; CEO Conti Group Cos (formerly Continental Grain Co), NYC, 1994—97, 1997—. Dir. Loews, Inc., Premium Standard Farms, Inc., Vivendi Universal, SA, Wyndham Internat., Inc. Office: Continental Grain Co 277 Park Ave Fl 49 New York NY 10172-0003

FRIBOURGH, JAMES HENRY, retired university administrator; b. Sioux City, Iowa, June 10, 1926; s. Johan Gunder and Edith Katherine (James) F.; m. Cairdenia Minge, Jan. 29, 1955; children: Cynthia Kaye, Rebecca Jo, Abbie Lynn. Student, Morningside Coll., 1944-47; BA, MA, U. Iowa, 1949, PhD, 1957; LHD (hon.), DHL (hon.), Morningside Coll., 1989. Instr. Little Rock Jr. Coll., 1949—56; assoc. prof. biology Little Rock U., 1957—60, prof., chmn. life scis. divsn., 1960—69; vice chancellor U. Ark., Little Rock, 1969—72, interim chancellor, 1972—73, exec. vice chancellor acad. affairs, 1973—82, interim chancellor, exec. vice chancellor acad. affairs, 1982, provost, exec. vice chancellor, 1983—, disting. prof., 1984—94, disting. prof. emeritus, 1994—. Cons. in field; assoc. Marine Biol. Lab., Woods Hole, Mass. Contbr. articles to profl. jours. Mem. Ark. Gov.'s Com. on Sci. and Tech., 1969-71; bd. dirs., mem. nat. adv. bd. Nat. Back Found., 1979; vice chmn. NCCJ, 1981-82; div. rep. United Way of Pulaski County, 1980-82; bd. dirs. Ark. Dance Theatre, Little Rock, 1980-82; vestryman Good Shepherd Episcopal Ch.; del. Episcopal Diocese of Ark.; fellow Ark. Mus. Sci. and History, 1987. Fribourgh Hall named in his honor, U. Ark., Little Rock, 1994; NSF fellow History of Sci. Inst., 1959-60. Fellow AAAS, Coll. Preceptors (London), Am. Inst. Fishery Rsch. Biologists, Ark. Mus. Sci. and History; mem. Am. Fisheries Soc. (chmn. com. on internationalism cert. fisheries scientist), AAUP (pres. Ark. conf.), Electron Microscopy Soc. Am., Am. Soc. Swedish Engrs. (corr. mem.), Ark. Acad. Sci. (pres. 1966), Ark. Dean's Assn. (pres. 1982), Am. Assn. State Colls. and Univs., Am. Swedish Inst., Swedish Club (Chgo.), Rotary (Paul Harris fellow), Vasa Order Am. Lodge, Sigma Xi, Phi Kappa Phi. Clubs: Swedish, Vasa Order Am. Lodges: Rotary (Paul Harris fellow). Democrat. Office: U Ark 33rd and University Ave Little Rock AR 72204 Business E-Mail: jhfribourgh@ualr.edu.

FRICK, BENJAMIN CHARLES, lawyer; b. Overbrook, Pa., Feb. 23, 1960; s. Sidney Wanning and Marie Pauline Frick; m. Stephanie Ann Sears, June 1, 1991; children: Sarah Marie, Anna Elizabeth, Charles Andrew. BA, Cornell U., 1982; JD, U. Richmond, 1985; LLM in Taxation, Villanova U., 1994. Bar: Pa. 1985. Clk. to Hon. John B. Hannum US dist. ct., 1984; trust officer Provident Nat. Bank, Phila., 1985-89; sole practice Bryn Mawr, Pa., 1989—. Deacon, elder, treas. Ardmore (Pa.) Presbyn. Ch.; bd. dirs. Civil War and Underground R.R. Mus. Phila., 2004—. Mem.: ABA, Phila. Bar Assn., Pa. Bar Assn., Soc. of Cin., Mil. Order Loyal Legion US (sec. 1993—95, v.p. 1995—97, comdr. 1997—99, judge adv.-in-chief 1997—2001, nat. v.p. 2001—05, comdr.-in-chief 2005—), St. Andrew's Soc. Phila., Soc. Colonial Wars (bd. dirs. Pa. chpt. 1999—, sec. 2004—07, v.p. 2007—), Soc. Mayflower Descs., S.R. (bd. dirs. Pa. Soc. 1987—2003, sec. 1991—95, treas. 1995—97, v.p. 1997—), Colonial Soc. Pa. (treas. 2000—03, v.p. 2003—06, pres. 2006—), The Union League, The Phila. Club, Athenaeum Phila., Alpha Delta Phi, Phi Alpha Delta. Republican. Presbyterian. Office: Bldg 2 Ste 309 919 Conestoga Rd Bryn Mawr PA 19010-1353

FRICK, DAVID RHOADS, lawyer, retired insurance company executive; b. Ft. Wayne, Ind., June 28, 1944; s. Walter Henry and Margery Ellen (Rhoads) F.; m. Ann Gray Shane, June 19, 1965; children: Thomas Rhoads, Amy Gray. BA magna cum laude, Ind. U., 1966; JD cum laude, Harvard U., 1969; HHD, Butler U., 1987, U. Indpls., 1997. Bar: Ill. 1969, D.C. 1971, U.S. Ct. Appeals (D.C. cir.) 1971, Ind. 1972, U.S. Supreme Ct. 1976. Assoc. Mayer, Brown & Platt, Chgo., 1969-72, Baker & Daniels, Indpls., 1972-76; dep. mayor City of Indpls., 1977-82; ptnr. Baker & Daniels, Indpls., 1982—95; exec. v.p., chief legal & adminstrv. officer Anthem Inc. (now WellPoint Inc.), Indpls., 1995—2005. Bd. dirs. Artistic Media Ptnrs., Inc., Indpls., Nat. Bank Indpls., Statewide Mobility Ptnrs., LLC, GS&J Investments, LLC, My Health Care Mgr., LLC. Bd. dirs., exec. com. 500 Festival Assocs., 1983-86, Commn. for Downtown, 1977-89, Greater Indpls. Progress Com., 1982-89, Indpls. Econ. Devel. Corp., 1984; bd. dirs. Ind. U. Coll. Arts and Scis. 1974-77, Pres. 1976, Indpls. Ctr. Advanced Rsch., Inc., 1987-90, Ind. Sports Corp., 1979-91, Indpls. Conv. and Visitors Assn., 1982-2000; mem. Ind. Gen. Assembly Local Govt. Study Com., 1978-81, State Ind. Commn. Enterprising Zones, 1981-82; trustee Eiteljorg Mus., 1988-91; chmn., trustee Brebeuf Prep. Sch., 1986-92, U. Indpls., 1990—98; treas., bd. mgrs. Marion County Capital Improvement Bd., 1982-92; adv. bd. Ind. U., 1986—, Purdue U., 1986—; chmn. Ind. Organizing Com. NCAA Final Four, 1987—; trustee, exec. com. Christian Theol. Sem., 1984-95. Recipient Sagamore of the Wabash award Gov. Ind., 1979-80, C.L. Whistler award Greater Indpls. Progress Com., 1984, L.A. Conrad award Ind. Soc. Assn. Exec., 1990, Pres. Medal Brebeuf Prep. Sch., 1992, Michael A. Carroll Award for Cmty. Involvement, Indpls. Bus. Jour., 1996; named Bus. Leader of 2005, Ind. C. of C. Mem. Indpls. C. of C. (bd. dirs. 1987-2005, exec. com. 1987-2005). Republican. Methodist. Avocations: jogging, hiking, reading.

FRICK, IVAN EUGENE, retired academic administrator, educational consultant; b. New Providence, Pa., May 19, 1928; s. Charles George and Lillie Jane (Miller) F.; m. Ruth Hudson, July 16, 1950; children: David Alan, Daniel Eugene, Susan Marie. AB, Findlay Coll., Ohio, 1949; B.D., Lancaster Theol. Sem., 1952; S.T.M., Oberlin Coll., 1955; PhD, Columbia U., 1959; L.H.D. (hon.), Findlay Coll., 1976. Mem. faculty Findlay Coll., 1953-71, asst. to pres., 1963-64, pres., 1964-71, Elmhurst (Ill.) Coll., 1971-94, pres. emeritus, 1994—; cons. Ivan E. Frick, Cons. in Higher Edn., Willow Street, Pa., 1994—. Vice chmn. Fedn. Ind. Ill. Colls. and Univs., 1979-81, chmn., 1983-85; pres., chmn. exec. com. Associated. Colls. of Ill., 1991-93; chmn. West Suburban Regional Acad. Consortium, 1991-92. Mem. Am. Coun. on Edn. Commn. on Govtl. Rels., 1986-89; bd. dirs. United Cmty. Fund Findlay, 1965-71, Lizzadro Mus. Lapidary Art, Elmhurst, Elmhurst YMCA, 1971-84; mem. found. bd. Ray Graham Assn. for People With Disabilities, 1995-2000; chmn. non-pub. adv. com. Ill. Bd. Higher Edn., 1990-94. Danforth Found. fellow, 1959, Paul Harris fellow, 1988; recipient Disting. Alumnus award Findlay Coll., 1964, Outstanding Young Man award U.S. Jr. C. of C., 1964 Mem. Econ. Club Chgo. Business E-Mail: ifrick@elmhurst.edu. *Mentors have played a significant role in my life; these mentors have been teachers, older friends, father figures and administrative colleagues. They have supported, challenged and stimulated me and sometimes they have presented an opposite view or role model against which I have reacted. In all, they have helped me immeasurably.*

FRICK, OSCAR LIONEL, pediatrician, educator; b. NYC, Mar. 12, 1923; s. Oscar and Elizabeth (Ringger) F.; m. Mary Hubbard, Sept. 2, 1954. AB, Cornell U., 1944, MD, 1946; M.Med. Sci., U. Pa., 1960; PhD, Stanford U., 1964. Diplomate: Am. Bd. Allergy and Immunology (chmn. 1967-72). Intern Babies Hosp., Columbia Coll. Physicians and Surgeons, NYC, 1946-47; resident Children's Hosp., Buffalo, 1950-51; pvt. practice medicine specializing in pediatrics Huntington, NY, 1951-58; fellow in allergy and immunology Royal Victoria Hosp., Montreal, Que., Canada, 1958-59; fellow in allergy U. Calif.-San Francisco, 1959-60, asst. prof. pediatrics, 1964-67, assoc. prof., 1967-72, prof., 1972—, dir. allergy tng. program, 1964—; fellow immunology Inst. d'Immunobiologie, Hosp. Broussais, Paris, 1960-62. Contbr. articles papers to profl. publs. Served with M.C., USNR, 1947-49. Mem. Am. Assn. Immunologists, Am. Acad. Pediatrics (chmn. allergy sect. 1971-72, Bret Ratner award 1982), Am. Acad. Allergy (exec. com. 1972— , pres. 1977-78), Internat. Assn. Allergology and Clin. Immunology (exec. com. 1970-73, sec. gen. 1985—), Am. Pediatric Soc. Clubs: Masons. Home: 370 Parnassus Ave San Francisco CA 94117-3609

FRICKE, MARTIN PAUL, science company executive; b. Franklin, Pa., May 18, 1937; s. Frank Albert and Pauline Jane (Wentz) F.; m. Barbara Ann Blanton, Jan. 3, 1959. BS, Drexel U., Phila., 1961; MS, U. Minn., 1964, PhD, 1967. Program mgr., group leader Gen. Atomics, San Diego, 1968-73; program mgr., divsn. mgr. Sci. Applications Internat. Corp., La Jolla, Calif., 1973-77, v.p., 1977-80, corp. v.p., 1980-84; sr. v.p. Systems Group, The Titan Corp., San Diego, Calif., 1984-87, exec. v.p. Techs Group, 1987-89, sr. v.p. corp. ops., 1989-93; program adminstr. San Diego Supercomputer Ctr., 1995-97; ind. cons., 1997—. Mem. cross sect. evaluation working group, Upton, L.I., N.Y., 1970-73, U.S. Nuclear Data Com., Washington, 1970-73. Contbr. articles to profl. jours. Recipient postdoctoral fellowship U. Mich., Ann Arbor, 1967-68, scholarship Pa. Indsl. Chem. Co., 1956-60; grad. fellow Oak Ridge (Tenn.) Assoc. Univs., 1964-67. Fellow Am. Phys. Soc. (panel on pub. affairs 1982-84); mem. Phi Kappa Phi. Roman Catholic. Achievements include first measurements and theoretical analysis of certain polarization phenomena in nucleon-nucleus inelastic scattering. Home and Office: 14929 Caminito Ladera Del Mar CA 92014 Home Phone: 858-755-0976. Personal E-mail: mfricke@adelphia.net.

FRICKE, RICHARD JOHN, lawyer; b. Ithaca, NY, Apr. 17, 1945; s. Richard I. and Jeanne L. (Hines) F.; m. Carol A. Borelli, June 17, 1967 (div. 1990); children: Laura, Richard, Amanda; m. Penny Yrizarry, Dec. 29, 1990 (div. 1999); children: Stephanie, Matthew, Tyler. BA, Cornell U., 1967, JD, 1970. Bar: Conn. 1970. Assoc. Gregory & Adams, Wilton, Conn., 1970—73; ptnr. Crehan & Fricke, Ridgefield, Conn., 1973—90; gen. counsel Connex Internat. Inc.; corp. counsel, pres. Safe Alternatives Corp. of Am., Inc.; pres., gen. counsel, dir. T.F.I. Industries, Inc.; gen. counsel, dir. Gold Mustache Pub. Corp., Inc.; sec., dir. DXTC.COM, Inc.; dir. Village Bank & Trust Co.; town atty. Town of Ridgefield, 1973—81. Bd. dirs. Gold Mustache Pub. Corp., Inc.; mem. Closing Mgmt. Svcs. LLC. Co-patentee low reactive pressure foam, polyurethane foam for cellulostic products. Bd. dirs. Ridgefield Cmty. Ctr., Ridgefield Montessori, Ridgefield Cmty. Kindergarten; founder, pres. Ridgefield Lacross League; constable Town of Wilton, Conn.; mem. Conn. Bar Commn. on Women, 1976; mem.bership chmn. Cornell U. Class of 1967. Mem. ABA, Conn. Bar Assn., Danbury Bar Assn. Democrat. Roman Catholic. Address: 35 Old Ridgefield Rd Apt 1 Wilton CT 06897-3013 Office Phone: 203-834-1115. Office Fax: 203-834-2140. Personal E-mail: rickfricke@aol.com.

FRICKLAS, MICHAEL DAVID, lawyer, broadcast executive; b. Somerville, NJ, Jan. 9, 1960; s. Richard L. and Anita (Alper) F.; children: Shanna E., Jaimee G., Gabriella S., Genevieve H.; m. Donna J. Astion, Jan. 14, 1996. BSEE, U. Colo., 1981; JD magna cum laude, Boston U., 1984. Bar: Calif. 1987, Colo. 1990, N.Y. 1993. Assoc. Ware & Freidenrich, Palo Alto, Calif., 1984-87, Shearman & Sterling, NY, San Francisco, 1987-90; v.p., gen. counsel Minorco (USA) Inc., Denver, 1990-93; sr. v.p., dep. gen. counsel, mem. ops. com. Viacom, Inc., NYC, 1993-98, sr. v.p., gen. counsel, sec., 1998-2000, exec. v.p., gen. counsel, sec., 2000—. Bd. dirs. Nat. Chamber Litigation Ctr. Trustee, sec. Jazz at Lincoln Ctr., 1995—, Am. Jewish Com., N.Y. chpt., 1998—; mem. bd. visitors Boston U. Sch. Law, 1997; bd. dirs. Nat. Chamber Legal Ctr., Legal Aid Soc. NY Mem. ABA (exec. com. of gen. counsel com.), Assn. Gen. Counsel, Assn. Bar City NY(chair gen. counsel com.). Office: Viacom Inc 1515 Broadway New York NY 10036-8901

FRICKS, ERNEST EUGENE, management consultant; b. Knoxville, Tenn., Jan. 16, 1948; s. Ernest E. Fricks and Barbara (Clark) Griffey; m. Dorothy Stanton; children: Natalie, Karen. AB, BSME, Rutgers U., 1970; MS, Pa. State U., 1974; grad., Air War Coll., 1986, U. Pa. Wharton Sch. Exec. Mgmt, 1988. Lead engr. Pub. Svc. Electric & Gas Co., Newark, 1972—76, Stone & Webster Engrng. Corp., Cherry Hill, NJ, 1976—78, mgr. licensing, 1978—79, bus. devel., 1979—85, mgr. govt. mktg., 1985—90, project mgr., 1990—2002; adj. lectr. ethics Rutgers U., New Brunswick, NJ, 2001; pres. Ernest E. Fricks, LLC, 2002—; sr. v.p. Integrated Strategic Resources LLC, Camden, NJ, 2003—. Cons. Office Sec. of Navy, 1975. Author: The Thermodynamic Effect in Developed Cavitation in Freon 113, 1974; profl. ethics reviewer Jour. Engrng. Mgmt., 2001—, mem. peer rev. panel Jour. Mil. History. Chair energy and environ. commn. So. NJ Devel. Coun.; trustee Camden County Hist. Soc., 1988—92; chair NJ KT Edn. Found., 2003—06; mem. Phila. Vietnam Meml. Adv. Bd., 2006—. Lt. col. USAFR, 1970—92. Named Outstanding Augmentee Officer, Mil. Airlift Command, 1977. Fellow: ASME (chmn. tech. and soc. divsn. 1996—98, Tech. Interests Activities award 1998), Soc. Am. Mil. Engrs. (life; pres. Phila. chpt. 1994—95), Royal Philatelic Soc. (London); mem.: Royal Aero. Soc. U.K., Newcomen Soc. (vice chmn. NJ 1992—94, 1996—99), Rutgers Engrng. Soc. (pres. 1976—77, sec. 1998—99, treas. 2001—04), Rutgers Alumni Assn. (chmn. budget and audit coms. 1999—), Rutgers U. Alumni Fedn. (treas. 1985—86, univ. sen. 1986—88, Meritorious Svc. award 2003), Am. Philatelic Soc. (v.p. 1977—80, Luff award 2007), Rutgers Club, Collectors Club (NYC), Masons (grand gov. York Rite Coll. N.J. 2002—06, past master, past grand sec. Royal Arch, past grand high priest, Order Purple Cross 2001, 33d degree). Office: Integrated Strategic Resources LLC 200 Federal St Ste 230 Camden NJ 08103 also: Integrated Strategic Resources LLC 224 W 35th St Ste 1006 New York NY 10001-2507 Office Phone: 609-254-6264. Business E-Mail: gfricks@isrllc.us.

FRIDAY, ELBERT WALTER, JR., federal agency administrator, meteorologist; b. DeQueen, Ark., July 13, 1939; s. Elbert Walter and Mary Elizabeth (Ward) F.; m. Karen Ann Hauschild, Nov. 14, 1959; children: Kristine Ann, Kelly Sue. BS in Engrng. Physics, U. Okla., Norman, 1961, MS in Meteorology, 1967, PhD in Meteorology, 1969. Commd. 2d lt. USAF, 1961, advanced through ranks to Col., 1961—81, weather officer, 1961-81, served Vietnam, 1972—73, dir. environ. and life scis., Dept. Def., 1978-81, ret., 1981; dep. dir. Nat. Weather Svc., Silver Spring, Md., 1981-87, dir., 1987-97; asst. adminstr. Office Oceanic and Atmospheric Rsch., Silver Spring, 1997-98; dir. NAS, 1998—2002; Weather News prof. applied meteorology U. Okla., 2002—05, prof. emeritus. Mem. com. on low level wind shear NAS, Washington, 1985-86; U.S. permanent rep. to UN World Meteorol. Orgn., 1988-98, mem. exec. coun., 1988-98; adj. prof. U. Okla., 1998; bd. dirs. Atmospheric Sci. and Climate, NRC, NAS, 1998-2002. Contbr. articles to prof. jours. Elder Calvary Christian Ch., Burke, Va., 1985-89, 2002—, trustee, 1989-93, chmn. bd., 1998-2002. Decorated Bronze Star; recipient Superior Svc. medal Dept. Def., 1981, Presdl. Rank award, 1988, Disting. Achievement award U. Okla., 1992, Fed. Exec. of Yr. award Fed. Exec. Inst. Alumni Assn., 1993. Fellow Am. Meteorol. Soc. (councilor 1988-90, pres. 2003, Cleve. Abbe award 1997); mem. AAAS, Nat. Weather Assn., Sigma Xi. Office Phone: 703-643-0796. Business E-Mail: joefriday@ou.edu.

FRIDAY, GILBERT ANTHONY, JR., pediatrician; b. Pitts., Apr. 16, 1930; s. Gilbert Anthony and Susan Dorothy (Kumer) F.; m. Christina Cecilia McShane, Sept. 12, 1959; children: Martin, Peter, Martha, Timothy, Amy, Anne, Robert. BS, Bucknell U., 1952; MD, Temple U., 1956. Diplomate Nat. Bd. Med. Examiners. Rotating intern Phila. Gen. Hosp., 1956-57; pediatric resident Children's Hosp. of Phila., 1960-62, Children's Hosp. of Pitts., 1962-63, asst. med. dir. ops., 1963-66, preceptorship in allergy/immunology, 1962-67; clin. instr. to asst. prof. U. Pitts., 1963-87, clin. assoc. prof., 1987, prof. pediatrics, 1987—2001, clin. prof., 2001—. Chmn. bd. dirs. Pa. Blue Shield, Camp Hill, 1992-96. Contbr. articles to profl. jours., chpts. to books. Lt. comdr. USN MC, 1956-66. Wyeth Pediatric scholar. Fellow Am. Coll. Allergy, Asthma, and Immunology, Am. Acad. Allery, Asthma, and Immunology, Am. Acad. Pediats.; mem. AMA, Allegheny County Med. Soc. (pres. 1987), Pa. Med. Soc., Pa. Allergy Soc. (pres. 1975), Alpha Omega Alpha. Republican. Roman Catholic. Avocations: boating, fishing. Home: 1901 Highgate Rd Pittsburgh PA 15241-2210 Office Phone: 412-788-1900. Personal E-mail: friday1901@aol.com.

FRIDAY, KATHERINE ORWOLL, artist; b. Granite Falls, Minn., Dec. 3, 1917; d. Melvin Sylvester and Anna Elizabeth (Hustvedt) Orwoll; m. Erling Bjarne Struxness, May 8, 1943 (div. 1961); children: John Eric Struxness, Mimi Ann McNicholas, Mari Struxness; m. George Edward Friday, Apr. 12, 1969 (dec. Jan. 1997). Student, U. Minn., Mpls., 1935-36, 40-41, Frederick Mizen Sch. of Art, Chgo., 1941. Designer, illustrator Josten's, Owatonna, Minn., 1936-39, 42-43; layout artist Tempo Inc., Chgo., 1941-42, Vogue-wright Studios, Chgo., 1943-44; layout, illustration Allan D Parson Advt. Agy., Chgo., 1945, Ad-Art, Wichita, Kans., 1952-54, 63; indsl. designer Harold W. Darr Assoc., Mpls., 1959-61; layout, illustration Lydiard Assoc., Mpls., 1961—62; owner Skyline Studio, Mpls., 1962—66; layout, illustration Comm. Cons., Wilmington, Del., 1971; freelance illustrator, med. illustration dept. pathology U. Chgo., Chgo., 1946-48; freelance illustrator Hutchinson, Kans., 1948—52, 1954—58; art dir. SPF Adv., Intermedia, Mpls., 1966-69, Arne Westerman Adv., Portland, Oreg., 1970-71, Battle Advt., Wyncote, Pa., 1971-72; creative dir., owner A'La Carte Advt./Art, Bellevue, Wash., 1973-77; graphic illustration Courseware, Moffat Field, Mountain View, Calif., 1978, Quantic, Los Altos, Calif., 1979—; ret., 1982. Curator, judge internat. miniature art exhibit Festival of the Arts, Lake Oswego, Oreg., 2002. Exhibitions include Westminster Gallery, London, 1995, Hobart, Tasmania, 2000, Internat. Miniature Exhbn., Smithsonian Mus., Washington, 2004, Portland Art Mus. Rental Gallery, Palace, Stockholm, Sweden, Hillsboro Cultural Ctr., 2007, Represented in permanent collections Internat. Miniature Exhbn., Smithsonian, Washington. Recipient Best of Show award, Internat. Miniature Art Show, Kirkland, Wash., 1997, 4th pl., 1999, 3d pl., 2001. Mem.: N.W. Artists' Support Group, Main St. Art Soc. (Best of show, 1st pl. and 2d pl. awards 2002, Best of Show, 1st pl. oil, 1st pl. watercolor 2003, 3d pl. 2004, Best of Show, 1st pl. portrait, 1st place floral 2005, Best of Show, Merit award, 1st and 2d pl. awards), Painters Showcase (Grand award 1999, Judges Choice award 2000—02), Oreg. Colored Pencil Soc. (2d pl. N.W. Regional show 2000—02), Watercolor Soc. Oreg. (Achievement award 1998, 2002), Cider Painters of Am. (award of excellence 1992—94, still life award 1995, portrait award 1995, award of excellence 1997, portrait award 1998, Pres. award 1999, award of excellence 2001, Pres. award 2002, 1st pl. in floral 2007, signature mem., 1st. pl. in floral 1993), Ga. Miniature Artists Soc. (2d pl. and 3d pl. 1990, 1st pl. 1991, 1994, Merit award 1997), Miniature Art Soc. Fla. (1st pl. 1989—90, 2d pl. 1994—95, 1st pl. 1997—98, 2d pl. 1999, 1st pl. 2002—03), Miniature Artists of Am. (hon. signature), Colored Pencil Soc. Am., N.W. Watercolor Soc. (assoc.), Miniature Painters, Sculptors, Gravers Soc. (assoc. 3d pl. 1990, 1st pl. 1996, 1st of show 1998, 2d and 3d pl. 1999, Grumbacher gold award, 2d pl. 2001, Best of Show award). Avocations: painting, drawing, reading, music.

FRIDELL, JONATHAN AARON, transplant surgeon; b. Montreal, Quebec, Canada, Jan. 2, 1970; s. Joe and Betty Fridell; m. Jennifer Ellen Schwartz, Nov. 9, 1997. MDCM in Gen. Surgery, McGill U., Montreal, Quebec, Canada; MSc, McGill U., Montreal, Quebec. Lic. Am. Bd. of Surgery, 2002, Royal Coll. of Physicians and Surgeons of Can., 2000. Transplant surgeon Ind. U. Sch. of Medicine, Indpls., 2002—. Dir. of pancreas transplantation Ind. U. Sch. of Medicine, Indpls., 2003—. Office: Ind U Sch Medicine Room 4258 550 N University Blvd Indianapolis IN 46202 Office Phone: 317-274-4370. Office Fax: 317-278-3268. E-mail: jfridell@iupui.edu.

FRIDERES, STEFFANI ANNE, art educator; b. Pullman, Wash., Oct. 15, 1965; d. James Stephen and Carol Anne Frideres; m. Michael Lee Jones, Oct. 7, 2004; m. Robert B. Chapman (div. 1990). BFA, U. Calgary, Alberta, Can., 1989; MFA, Wash. State U., Pullman, 1990. Instr. art Photographic Ctr., Seattle, 1991—95; dir. art New Gallery, Calgary, Alberta, 1996—97; graphic designer U. Calgary; prof. art Tomball Coll., Tex., 2002—. Adj.

prof. U. Calgary, 1998—2000. Mem.: Houston Ctr. Photography, Coll. Art assn., Soc. Photographic Educators. Avocations: art, reading, yoga, gardening. Office: Tomball Coll Hwy 249 Tomball Pky Tomball TX 78355 Business E-Mail: steffani.a.frideres@nhmccd.edu.

FRIDLEY-HEREFORD, VIVIAN SUZANNE, secondary school educator; d. Nimrod Darrell Fridley and Gloria Jean Hereford; children: Dawna L. Daniel, Phillip M. Daniel, Courtenay S. Graham. BA, Marshall U., 1975, MA, 1982; EdD, U. Houston, 2005. Nat. bd. cert. Nat. Bd. Profl. Tchg. Stds. Tchr. Point Pleasant (W.Va.) Jr. High, Mason County Bd. Edn., 1977—91, Klein Oak HS, Klein Ind. Sch. Dist., Spring, Tex., 1994—2001, Branch Crossing Jr. High, Conre Ind. Sch. Dist., The Woodlands, Tex., 2001—02, The Woodlands HS, Conroe Ind. Sch. Dist., 2002, Carnegie Vanguard HS, Houston Ind. Sch. Dist., 2004—. Presenter, cadre mem. Tex. Edn. Agy. Ctr. for Educator Devel. in the Fine Arts, San Antonio, 1999—; com. mem. tech. applications curriculum and assessment Region IV Edn. Svc. Ctr., Houston, 2001; amb. for tchg. stds. Nat. Bd. Profl. Tchg. Stds., China, 2001; cons. Conroe (Tex.) Ind. Sch. Dist., 2001, 04; com. mem. Test Comparability Study for State Bd. Edn., Austin, Tex., 2004; co-founder, mem. Tex. Coalition for Nat. Bd. for Profl. Tchg. Stds.; adj. lectr. U. Houston. Mem.: Am. Ednl. Rsch. Assn., Pi Lambda Delta, Kappa Delta Pi, Phi Kappa Phi. Avocations: travel, backpacking, reading. Office Phone: 713-556-8808. Personal E-mail: vivianfh@sbcglobal.net.

FRIDOVICH, IRWIN, biochemistry professor; b. NYC, Aug. 2, 1929; s. Louis and Sylvia (Appelbaum) F.; m. Mollie Finkel; children: Sharon E., Judith L. BS, CCNY, 1951; postgrad., Cornell U. Med. Coll., 1951-52; PhD, Duke U., 1955; doctorate (hon.), U. Rene Descartes, Paris, 1980. Instr. biochemistry Duke U., Durham, N.C., 1956-58, assoc., 1958—; vis. research assoc. Harvard U., Cambridge, Mass., 1961-62; asst. prof. biochemistry Duke U., 1961-66, assoc. prof., 1966-71, prof., 1971—, James B. Duke prof., 1976—, emeritus, 1996—. Mem. study sect. Am. Cancer Soc., mem. adv. com. biochemistry and chem. carcinogenesis Mem. editorial bd. Jour. Biol. Chemistry, Biochemica Biophysica Acta, Archives of Biochemistry and Biophysics, Biochem. Jour., Bioinorganic Chemistry, Biochemistry, Biochem. Pharmacology, Analytical Biochemistry; contbr. articles to sci. jours. Recipient Founders' award Chem. Industry Inst. Toxicology, 1980, Sr. Passano award Passano Found., 1987, Herty award Ga. sect. Am. Chem. Soc., 1980, Research Career Devel. award NIH, 1959-69, Cressy A. Morrison award N.Y. Acad. Sci., 1984, Townsend Harris medal City U. N.Y., 1990; co-recipient Cresson medal, Franklin Inst., 1997, City of Medicine award, Durham, N.C., 1998, Anlyan Lifetime Achievement award Duke Med. Ctr., 1998. Mem. NAS, Am. Acad. Arts and Scis., Am. Soc. Biol. Chemists (pres. 1982), N.C. Acad. Scis., Oxygen Soc. (pres. 1990), Soc. for Free Radical Rsch. Internat., (pres. 1992), Phi Beta Kappa, Sigma Xi Home: 3517 Courtland Dr Durham NC 27707-5134 Office: Duke U Med Center PO Box 3711 Durham NC 27710-0001 Office Phone: 919-689-5122. E-mail: fridovich@biochem.duke.edu.

FRIDSON, MARTIN STEVEN, finance company executive; b. Highland Park, Mich., Sept. 4, 1952; s. Harry Yale and Mariann (Rodd) F.; m. Elaine Rochelle Sisman, June 14, 1981; children: Arielle Amanda, Daniel Wolfe. BA cum laude in History, Harvard U., 1974; MBA, Harvard U., Boston, 1976. CFA. Trader Mitchell, Hutchins Inc., NYC, 1976-77; asst. v.p. Scandinavian Securities Corp., NYC, 1977-79; v.p. Paine Webber Jackson & Curtis, Inc., NYC, 1980-81, Salomon Bros., Inc., NYC, 1981-84; prin. Morgan Stanley & Co., Inc., NYC, 1984-89; mng. dir. Merrill Lynch & Co., Inc., NYC, 1989—2002; CEO FridsonVision LLC, NYC, 2002—. Cons. bd. govs. Fed. Res.; mem. Harvard Com. on Univ. Resources, 2002—. Author: High Yield Bonds, 1989, Financial Statement Analysis, 1991, Investment Illusions, 1993, It Was a Very Good Year, 1998, How to Be a Billionaire, 2000, Unwarranted Intrusions, 2006; co-editor, The Yearbook of Fixed Income Investing, 1996, editor, Extraordinary Popular Delusions and the Madness of Crowds and Confusión de Confusiones, 1996; contbr. articles to profl. jours.; author light verse pub. in Playbill, N.Y. Times, Wall St. Jour., Graham and Dodd Scroll for Excellence in Financial Writing, 1994; mem. editl. bd. Fin. Analysts Jour., 1989—, CFA Digest, 1991—, Fin. Mgmt., 1993-99, Jour. Fin. Statement Analysis, 1995-98. Participation chmn. Harvard Coll. Fund, Class of 1974, 1991-2004, mem. spl. gifts com., 1992—; trustee The Intersch. Orch. of N.Y., N.Y.C., 1992—; v.p. Jane St. Block Assn., N.Y.C., 1979; bd. dirs. Candlewood Landing Condominium Assn., 1991-2004; adv. coun. Salomon Ctr., NYU, 1991-97; mem. exec. com. wall st. divsn. United Jewish Appeal Fedn., 2000—. Mem. Fixed Income Analysts Soc. (pres. 1984-85, named to Hall of Fame 2000), Harvard Bus. Sch. Club (v.p. 1983-84), N.Y. Soc. Security Analysts (bd. dirs. 2001-03, Vol.-of-Yr. award 1991-92), Fin. Mgmt. Assn. (practitioner dir. 1994-96, Outstanding Fin. Exec. award 2002), Inst. Chartered Fin. Analysts (trustee 1997-98), Assn. for Investment Mgmt. and Rsch. (bd. govs. 1997-2001), Harvard Club of N.Y., New Milford Racquet and Swim Club. Democrat. Jewish. Avocations: tennis, theater, opera. Home: 440 W End Ave Apt 10A New York NY 10024-5358 Office: FridsonVision LLC 54 W 21st St Ste 1007 New York NY 10010 Home Phone: 212-496-9101; Office Phone: 212-937-0975. Business E-Mail: martin_fridson_ab74@post.harvard.edu.

FRIEBERT, ROBERT HOWARD, lawyer; b. Milw., Aug. 24, 1938; s. Lewis and Erna F.; m. Susan Frances Sweed, Aug. 11, 1968; children: Jonathan, Ellen, Leslie. BBA, LLB, U. Wis., 1962. Bar: Wis. 1962, U.S. Dist. Ct. (we. dist.) Wis. 1962, U.S. Ct. Appeals (7th cir.) 1964, U.S. Supreme Ct. 1967, U.S. Dist. Ct. (ea. dist.) Wis. 1968, U.S. Ct. Appeals (9th cir.) 1977, U.S. Ct. Appeals (D.C. cir.) 1998. Asst. U.S. atty. U.S. Justice Dept., Madison, Wis., 1962-64; assoc. LaFollette, Sinykin, Doyle & Abrahamson, Madison, Wis., 1964-66; state pub. defender Wis. Supreme Ct., Madison, 1966-68; assoc. Shellow, Shellow & Coffey, Milw., 1968-71; ptnr. Friebert, Finerty & St. John, Milw., 1971—. Treas. campaign fund Wis. Gov. Pat Lucey, 1971; co-chmn. Pres. Carter Re-election Campaign, Wis., 1980, Gary Hart Campaign for Pres., Wis., 1984; chmn. Al Gore Campaign for Pres., Wis., 1988; trustee Med. Coll. Wis., 1993—. Recipient Human Rels. award, Am. Jewish Com., Milw., 1996. Fellow Am Acad. Appellate Lawyers; mem. Wis. Bar Assn. Office: Friebert Finerty & St John 330 E Kilbourn Ave Ste 1250 Milwaukee WI 53202-3158 E-mail: rhf@ffsj.com.

FRIED, BRUCE MERLIN, lawyer; b. Coral Gables, Fla., Sept. 10, 1949; BA, U. Fla., 1971, JD, 1974. Bar: Fla. 1975, DC 1981. With Fla. Legal Services, 1975-81, Nat. Sr. Citizens Law Ctr., 1981-86; exec. dir. Nat. Health Care Campaign, 1986-90; exec. v.p. The Wexler Group, 1990-94; chief coord. Clinton/Gore Campaign's Health Care Adv. Group, 1992; v.p. fed. affairs FHP Internat. Corp., 1994-95; dir. Ctr. for Health Plans and Providers, Health Care Financing Adminstrn. US Dept. Health and Human Services, Balt., 1995—98; ptnr. Shaw Pittman, Washington, 1998—2003, Sonnenschein Nath & Rosenthal, Washington, 2003—. Counsel Am. Acad. Ophthalmology, Calif. Assn. Physician Groups. Mem. bd. United Cerebral Palsy; nat. adv. com. Berman Bioethics Inst. Johns Hopkins U.; chair adv. com. Dept. Health Policy George Washington U. Office: Sonnenschein Nath & Rosenthal Ste 600, E Tower 1301 K St NW Washington DC 20005 Office Phone: 202-408-9159. Office Fax: 202-408-6399. Business E-Mail: bfried@sonnenschein.com.

FRIED, BURTON THEODORE, lawyer; b. NYC, Feb. 26, 1940; s. Meyer S. and Minnie (Grossberg) F.; m. Gail K. Morgenstern, July 25, 1964; children: Marsha, Howard, Shari. BS, NYU, 1961; LL.B., Bklyn. Law Sch., 1964. Bar: N.Y. 1964, U.S. Dist. Ct. (ea. and so. dists.) N.Y. 1971. Assoc. atty. H. Bermack, NYC, 1964-66, I. Towbis, NYC, 1966-68; gen. counsel Medispas, Inc., NYC, 1968-72; real estate counsel Michael Industries, Inc., NYC, 1972-74, exec. v.p., gen. counsel and sec., 1974-86, The LVI Group, Inc., NYC, 1982-85, vice chmn., gen. counsel, dir., 1985-91; pres. The LVI Group Inc., NYC, 1991-93; pres., CEO LVI Svcs. Inc., NYC, 1986—2006, chmn., 2006—. Trustee Optometric Ctr. N.Y., 1993-99. Vice chmn. sch. bd. Forest Hills Jewish Ctr. Religious Sch., N.Y., 1983-84, chmn. sch. bd., 1984-85, trustee, 1985-88. Mem.: K.P. (Chancellor comdr. 1972-73). Office: LVI Svcs Inc 877 Post Rd E Ste 4 Westport CT 06880

FRIED, CHARLES, law educator; b. Prague, Czechoslovakia, Apr. 15, 1935; arrived in US, 1941, naturalized, 1948; s. Anthony and Marta (Winterstein) F.; m. Anne Sumerscale, June 13, 1959; children: Gregory, Antonia. AB, Princeton U., 1956; BA, Oxford U., Eng., 1958, MA, 1961; LLB, Columbia U., 1960; LLD (hon.), New Eng. Sch. of Law, 1987, Pepperdine U., 1994, Suffolk U., 1996. Bar: DC 1961, Mass. 1966. Law clk. to Hon. John M. Harlan U.S. Supreme Ct., Washington, 1960; from asst. prof. to prof. law Harvard U., Cambridge, Mass., 1961-85, Carter prof. gen. jurisprudence, 1981-85, 89-95, Carter prof. emeritus, disting. lectr. Law Sch., 1995-99, Beneficial prof. law, 1999—; assoc. justice Supreme Jud. Ct. Mass., Boston, 1995-99. Spl. cons. Treasury Dept., 1961—62; cons. White House Office Policy Devel., Washington, 1982, Dept. Transp., Washington, 1981—82, Dept. Justice, 1983; solicitor gen. U.S., 1985—89. Author: An Anatomy of Values, 1970, Medical Experimentation: Personal Integrity and Social Policy, 1974, Right and Wrong, 1978, Contract as Promise: A Theory of Contractual Obligation, 1981, Order and Law: Arguing the Reagan Revolution, 1991, (with David Rosenberg) Making Tort Law: What Should Be Done and Who Should Do It, 2003, Saying What The Law Is: The Constitution in The Supreme Court, 2004, Modern Liberty, 2006; contbr. legal and philos. jours. Guggenheim fellow, 1971—72. Fellow Am. Acad. Arts and Scis.; mem. Inst. Medicine, Am. Law Inst., Phi Beta Kappa. Office Phone: 617-495-4636. Business E-Mail: fried@law.harvard.edu.

FRIED, DANIEL, federal agency administrator, former ambassador; b. Sept. 19, 1952; m. Olga Karpiw; children: Hannah, Sophie. BA in History magna cum laude, Cornell U., 1974; MA, Columbia U., 1977. Fgn. svc. officer, 1977—2000; jr. officer East-West Trade office Econ. Bus. Bur. State Dept., 1977-79; with Consulate Gen. Office, Leningrad, 1980-81; polit. officer U.S. Embassy, Belgrade, 1982-85; reg. affairs officer Soviet Desk State Dept., Washington, 1985-87; Polish desk officer US Dept. State, Washington, 1987-89, polit. counselor Warsaw, 1990-93; dir. European affairs NSC, Washington, 1993-95, spl. asst. to pres., sr. dir. ctrl. and Ea. Europe, 1995—; amb. to Poland US Dept. State, Warsaw, 1997—2000, prin. dep. spl. advisor to the Sec. of State for the new ind. states, 2000—01; spl. asst. to Pres. The White House, Washington, 2005; sr. dir. European and Eurasian affairs Nat. Security Coun., 2001—05; asst. sec European & Eurasian Affairs US Dept. State, Washington, 2005—. Office: US Dept State Harry S Truman Bldg 2201 C St NW Rm 6226 Washington DC 20520

FRIED, DONALD DAVID, lawyer; b. NYC, Feb. 28, 1936; s. Fred and Sylvia (Falk) F.; m. Joan Hilbert, Sept. 15, 1963; children: Neil, Derek. BA, CCNY, 1956; JD, Harvard U., 1959. Bar: NY 1959. Assoc. Conboy, Hewitt, O'Brien & Boardman, NYC, 1960-68, ptnr., 1968-86, Hunton & Williams, NYC, 1986-88, 92-96; sr. counsel, 1996—; v.p., sec., assoc. gen. counsel Philip Morris Cos., Inc., NYC, 1988-91. Home: 37 W 12th St New York NY 10011-8502 Office: Hunton & Williams 200 Park Ave New York NY 10166-0091 Office Phone: 212-309-1038. Business E-Mail: dfried@hunton.com.

FRIED, JASON, software development company executive; Co-founder, pres. 37Signals LLC, 1999—. Named one of Young Innovators Under 35, MIT Tech. Rev., 2006, Top 40 Under 40, Crain's Chgo. Bus., 2006. Office: 37Signals LLC 400 N May St #301 Chicago IL 60622*

FRIED, JEFFREY MICHAEL, health care administrator; b. Kansas City, Mo., Apr. 9, 1953; s. Harvey J. and SuEllen (Weissman) F.; m. Rosalyn Sue Matz Student, Drake U., 1971—73; BGS, U. Kans., 1975; MHA, Washington U., St. Louis, 1979. Adminstrv. asst. Rsch. Med. Ctr., Kansas City, Mo., 1979—80; asst. to pres. Rsch. Health Svcs., Kansas City, 1980—81; asst. v.p. Sinai Hosp. Balt., 1981—83, Lancaster Gen. Hosp., Pa., 1983—85, v.p., COO, 1985—86; pres. Lancaster Gen. Svcs. Corp., 1986—88; sr. v.p. Lancaster Gen. Hosp., 1989—91, COO, 1992—94; pres., CEO Beebe Med. Ctr., Lewes, Del., 1994—. Pres., bd. dirs. Lancaster Med. Equipment, Barge Ganse Vena Care; sec., bd. dirs. Preferred Health Care, Lancaster; bd. dirs. Lancaster Diagnostic Imaging, Inc., Del. Nat. Bank; v.p., bd. dirs., pres. Welsh Mountain Med. and Dental Ctr., Lancaster, 1989—94; mng. ptnr. Roherstown Imaging Assocs., Lancaster, 1986-94; part-time faculty dept. health adminstrn. and devel. Pa. State U., 1988-94, Coll. of St. Francis, 1988-94; mem. bus. adv. coun. Goodwill Industries, 1989-94; asst. prof. Lebanon Valley Coll., 1994—; mem. MBA program adv. bd. Wilmington Coll., 1996—; adj. faculty Wilmington Coll. Grad. Bus. Program, 1996— Mem. Leadership Lancaster, 1987-88; pres. bd. dirs. Lancaster chpt. Nat. Commn. for Prevention of Child Abuse, 1986-89; treas., bd. dirs. Lancaster Jewish Fedn., 1986-89; bd. dirs. Lancaster Jewish Cmty. Ctr., 1989-94, bd. dirs. Temple Shaarai Shomayim, Clinic for Spl. Children, 1991-94, Pa. Acad. Music, 1994-96, Del. Hospice, 1996-99, Rehoboth Art League, 1996-2000, Lewes C. of C., Dewey Beach Lions Club, Slam Dunk to the Beach, Am. Heart Assn Recipient Grassroots Leadership award, Del. Healthcare Assn., 2006, Top Leadership Team award, Health Leaders Mag., 2006. Fellow: Am. Coll. Healthcare Execs. (com. on ethics 1991—93, credentials com. 1995—98, Del. Regents award 2006, Sr. Level Healthcare Exec. award 2006); mem.: Am. Hosp. Assn. (ho. of dels. 1998—2000), Assn. Del. Hosps. (bd. dirs.), Lancaster County Bus. Group on Health (legis. com. 1992—94), Ctrl. Pa. Health Care Adminstrs., Young Pres. Orgn., World Pres. Orgn., Lewes C. of C. (v.p. 2001—03, pres. 2003—), Dewey Beach Lions Club. Jewish. Avocations: tennis, jogging, cooking, reading. Home: 17 Patriots Way Rehoboth Beach DE 19971-1057 Office: Beebe Med Ctr 424 Savannah Rd Lewes DE 19958-1490 Office Phone: 302-645-3537. Business E-Mail: jfried@bbmc.org.

FRIED, JOHN H., chemist; b. Leipzig, Germany, Oct. 7, 1929; s. Abraham and Frieda F.; m. Heléne Gellen, June 26, 1955; children: David, Linda, Deborah. AB, Cornell U., 1951, PhD, 1955. Steroid chemist, research assoc. Merck and Co., Rahway, NJ, 1956-64; with Syntex Research, Palo Alto, Calif., 1964-92, dir. inst. organic chemistry, 1967-74, exec. v.p., 1974-76, pres., 1976-92; sr. v.p. Syntex Corp., 1981-86, vice chmn., 1986-92; dir. Corvas Internat., Inc., 1992-99, chmn., 1997-99. Chmn. Alexion Pharms., Inc., 1992-2002; pres. Fried & Co., Inc., 1992—. Mem. Am. Chem. Soc. Office: 20 Faxon Forest Atherton CA 94027-4067

FRIED, L. RICHARD, JR., lawyer; b. NYC, Apr. 3, 1941; s. L. Richard and Jane (Kent) Wick F.; married Susan Fried; 1 child, Paula Suzanne. BS, U. Ariz., 1963, JD, 1966. Bar: Ariz. 1966, Hawaii 1968, U.S. Dist. Ct. No. Mariana Islands 1978, U.S. Ct. Claims 1978, U.S. Ct. Internat. Trade 1977, U.S. Tax Ct. 1977, U.S. Ct. Appeals (9th cir.) 1969, U.S. Supreme Ct. 1977. Assoc. Case, Kay & Lynch, Honolulu, 1967-72; ptnr., pres. Cronin, Fried, Sekiya, Kekina & Fairbanks, Honolulu, 1974—. Lawyer rep. 9th Cir. Jud. Conf., Hawaii, 1991-93, 2001. Bd. mem. Shriner's Hosp., Hawaii Theatre. Mem. ABA, Assn. Trial Lawyers Am. (nat. committeeman 1980-82), Am. Bd. Trial Advocates (v.p. 1986-94), Hawaii Trial Lawyers Assn. (pres. 1981-82, 84—, Hawaii Trial Lawyer of Yr. 1994), Hawaii State Bar Assn. (bd. dirs. 1995-97), Ariz. State Bar Assn., Hawaii Acad. Plaintiffs Attys. (bd. dirs. 1994-96), Consumer Lawyers Hawaii (pres.-elect 2001, pres. 2002-), Exch. of Honolulu Club, U. Hawaii Angels. Episcopalian. Office: Cronin Fried Sekiya Kekina & Fairbanks 841 Bishop St Ste 600 Honolulu HI 96813-3962 Office Phone: 808-524-1433. Business E-Mail: rfried@croninfried.com.

FRIED, MARTIN L., lawyer; b. Neptune, NJ, Jan. 28, 1944; Atty. Goldstein Bershad Fried & Lieberman, PC, Southfield, Mich., 1985—. Office: Goldstein Bershad Fried & Lieberman PC 4000 Town Ctr Ste 1200 Southfield MI 48075 Office Phone: 248-355-5300.

FRIED, MICHAEL D., mathematician, educator; b. Buffalo, Sept. 25, 1942; s. Gerald and Mary Margaret Fried; m. Karen L Townsend, Dec. 30, 2000; m. Aulikki Kilpela, Dec. 1, 1979 (div. Mar. 1, 1991); m. Dorothy Graff, Oct. 21, 1964 (div. Apr. 4, 1976); children: David, Carlotta, Hector, Talvi, Jennifer Oliver. BS, Mich. State U., 1961; PhD in Math., U. Mich., Ann Arbor, 1967. Elec. engr. Allied Rsch. Assocs., Boston, 1961—62; engr. Bell Aerosystems, Boston, 1962—64; vis. rschr. Inst. Advanced Study, Princeton, NJ, 1967—69; from asst. prof. to prof. math. SUNY, Stony Brook, NY, 1969—74; prof. math. U. Calif., Irvine, 1974—. Vis. prof. math. Helsinki U., Helsinki, Finland, 1982—83, Tel Aviv U., 1976—77, MIT, Boston, 1972—73, U. Mich., Ann Arbor, 1972—73, Hebrew U., Jerusalem, 1987—88, 1992—93, Erlangen U., Erlangen, Germany, 1994—95, Inst. Exptl. Math., Essen, Germany, 1995—96. Contbr. articles to profl. jours. Fellow, Alfred P. Sloan Found., 1972—74, Fullbright Found., 1982—83, Humboldt Found., 1994—96; Lady Davis fellowship, Hebrew U., 1988—89. Achievements include research in first description of the precise polynomials usable for cryptography; the galois stratification procedure for the theory of finite fields; conjecture and classification of exceptional polynomials over finite fields; invention of modular towers, a translation between the inverse galois problem and the strong torsion conjecture on abelian varieties. Home: 3547 Prestwick Rd Billings MT 59101 Office: Dept Math Mont State U Billings MT 59101 Office Phone: 406-672-8472. Personal E-mail: mfried@math.uci.edu.

FRIED, RICHARD L., lawyer; b. NYC, June 5, 1958; BS, Cornell Univ., 1980; JD cum laude, NYU, 1983. Bar: NY 1984. Co-adminstrv. ptnr., structured fin. practice area Stroock & Stroock & Lavan LLP, NYC. Frequent lectr. in field. Mem.: Order of Coif. Office: Stroock & Stroock & Lavan LLP 180 Maiden Ln New York NY 10038-4982 Office Phone: 212-806-6047. Office Fax: 212-806-6006. Business E-Mail: rfried@stroock.com.

FRIED, SAMUEL P., lawyer; b. Bklyn., Aug. 16, 1951; s. Zoltan and Helen (Katina) F.; m. Gigi Panush, Dec. 27, 1981; children: Eva M., Orly Z., Jacob J., Molly R., Susanna R. AB, Washington U., St. Louis, 1971; JD, Boston U., 1974, LLM, 1997. Bar: Mass. 1974, Ill. 1983, Mich. 1989; ordained rabbi, 1971. Assoc. Warner & Stackpole, Boston, 1974-77; staff atty. The Bendix Corp., Southfield, Mich., 1977-79, sr. atty., 1979-80, asst. treas., 1980-81; v.p., corp. counsel Clevite Industries, Inc., Glenview, Ill., 1981-83, v.p., sec., gen. counsel, 1983-87; v.p., sec. gen. counsel Exide Corp., Troy, Mich., 1987-91; v.p., gen. counsel The Limited Inc., 1991-99, sr. v.p., gen. counsel, sec., 1999—. Editor: Psychosurgery, 1974. Mem. ABA, Am. Corp. Counsel Assn., Mich. Gen. Counsels Assn., Phi Beta Kappa. Jewish. Avocations: music, reading. Office: The Limited Inc PO Box 16000 3 Limited Pkwy Columbus OH 43230-1467

FRIED, VANCE HOYT, entrepreneur, educator; b. Mangum, Okla., Apr. 17, 1952; s. David Daniel and Elsie Elizabeth (Moreau) F.; m. Nancy Jane Petree, oct. 3, 1982; children: Regan, David. BS in Fin., Okla. State U., 1973, postgrad., 1986-87; JD, U. Mich., 1976. Atty., Stillwater, Okla., 1976-79, Wheatley & Fried, Stillwater, 1979-81; v.p., dir. and founding shareholder Red Eagle Exploration, Oklahoma City, 1981-84; v.p., corp. fin. Houchin, Adamson & Co., Oklahoma City, 1984-86; asst. to Brattain prof. Okla. State U., Stillwater, 1987—, dir. Entrepreneurship Ctr., 1994-99, 2004—05. Fin. and strategic cons. Vance H. Fried, Ltd., Stillwater, 1987—; mem. applied sci. and tech. com. Okla. Futures, Oklahoma City, 1996. Editl. bd.: Entrepreneurship Theory and Practice, Waco, Tex., 1991-2004, Jour. Pvt. Equity, NY, 2002—; contbr. articles to academic and profl. jours. Sec., dir. Sheltered Workshop, Stillwater, Okla., 1996-99. Grantee Coleman Found., Chgo., 1998, Okla. Capital Investments Bd., 1988, 91, 98. Mem. Acad. mgmt., Okla. Investment Forum, Okla. Venture Forum (edn. com. 1991-98), Okla. Acad. (task force chair 1994). Republican. Achievements include research on venture capital industry, management of venture capital-backed companies and corporate goverance; design of university-based programs to promote technology and social entrepreneurship. Office: Okla State U Spears Sch Bus Stillwater OK 74078-0001 Business E-Mail: vance.fried@okstate.edu.

FRIED, WENDY B., obstetrician, gynecologist; b. Queens, NY, Dec. 10, 1965; d. Norman and Helene Fried; m. Gerald Oginski, Aug. 7, 1988; children: Joseph, Shari, Mia, David. BS in Biology, SUNY, Stonybrook, 1986; MD, Albert Einstein Coll. Medicine, Bronx, 1991. Ob-gyn. pvt. practice, New Hyde Pk., NY, 1995—. Fellow: Am. Coll. Surgeons, Am. Coll. Ob-gyn. Office: 31111 New Hyde Pk Rd New Hyde Park NY 11040

FRIEDBERG, AARON LOUIS, political science professor; b. Pitts., Apr. 16, 1956; s. Simeon Adlow and Joan Libby (Brest) F.; m. Adrienne Louise Sirken, June 19, 1988; children: Eli, Gideon. BA, Harvard U., 1978, MA, PhD, Harvard U., 1986. Asst. prof. polit. sci. Princeton (N.J.) U., 1987-93, assoc. prof. polit. sci., 1993-99, prof. polit. sci., 1999—; dep. asst. for nat. security affairs Office of the Vice Pres., Washington, 2003—05. Author: The Weary Titan, 1988 (Edgar Furniss award, Mershon Ctr., Ohio U., 1989), In the Shadow of the Garrison State; contbr. articles to pofl. jours. Fellow Ctr. for Internat. Affairs, Harvard U. 1987, Woodrow Wilson Ctr., Smithsonian Inst., 1989, Norwegian Nobel Inst., 1998, Library of Congress, 2001; recipient Helen Dwight Reid award Am. Polit. Sci. Assn., 1986. Mem.: Inst. for Strategic Studies, Coun. Fgn. Rels. Home: 19 Maple St Princeton NJ 08540

FRIEDBERG, BARRY SEWELL, investment banker; b. Atlantic City, Jan. 4, 1941; s. Herbert and Mildred (Salit) F.; m. Charlotte A. Moss, Oct. 10, 1985; children: Benjamin, James. BA, Princeton U., 1962. Trainee Chem. Bank, NYC, 1963-64; with A.G. Becker, NYC, 1964-84, mgr. mergers and acquisitions dept., 1980-83, mng. dir., 1974-84, mgr. investment banking div., 1984; mng. dir. Merrill Lynch & Co., NYC, 1984—; mgr. investment banking div. Merrill Lynch Pierce Fenner & Smith Inc., NYC, 1985-93, chmn. investment banking divsn., 1993—2003; exec. v.p., mem. exec. com. Merrill Lynch & Co., Inc., 1990—2003; pres. Friedberg-Milstein, 2003—. Bd. dirs. N.Y.C. Ballet Co., 1988—96, 1997—, chmn., 2003—; bd. dirs. Boys Harbor, Inc., Lincoln Ctr. Performing Arts, 2003—, American Hosp. Paris Found., 1998—2002. Mem. Princeton Club, Econs. Club (mem. coun. fgn. rels.). Office: FriedbergMilstein 6 E 43d St New York NY 10017 Office Phone: 212-850-4134. Business E-Mail: bfriedberg@friedbergmilstein.com.

FRIEDBERG, ERROL CLIVE, pathology educator, researcher; b. Johannesburg, Oct. 2, 1937; s. Edward and Rena (Berman) F.; children: Malcolm, Andrew, Jonathan, Lawrence. BSc, Witwatersrand U., Johannesburg, 1957, MB BCh, 1961. Intern King Edward VIII Hosp./U. Natal, Durban, South Africa, 1962; resident pathologist Witwatersrand U., 1963-64, Cleve. Met. Gen. Hosp., 1965; postdoctoral fellow dept. biochemistry Case Western Res. U., Cleve., 1966-68; rsch. investigator divsn. nuclear medicine Walter Reed Army Inst. Rsch., Washington, 1969-70; asst. prof. pathology Stanford U., Calif., 1971-77, assoc. prof. pathology Calif., 1977-84, prof. pathology Calif., 1984-90; prof., chair dept. pathology U.

Tex. Southwestern Med. Ctr., Dallas, 1990—, Senator Betty and Dr. Andy Andujar chair pathology, 1990-93, Senator Betty and Dr. Andy Andujar disting. chair pathology, 1993—. Co-organizer symposia and confs. in field. Editor or co-editor: DNA Repair Mechanisms, 1978, DNA Repair: A Laboratory Manual of Research Procedures, Vol. 1, 1981, vol. 2, 1983, vol. 3, 1988, Cellular Responses to DNA Damage, 1983, Scientific American Reader: Cancer Biology, 1985, Mechanisms and Consequences of DNA Damage Processing, 1988; author: DNA Repair, 1984; editor-in-chief:; author: Cancer Answers: Encouraging Answers to 25 Questions You Were Always Afraid to Ask, 1992, 1993, Correcting the Blueprint of Life, 1997, The Writing Life of James D. Watson, 2005, From Rags to Riches, 2007; author: (with others) DNA Repair and Mutagenesis, 1995, 2006, Sydney Brenner: My Life in Science, 2001; contbr. numerous articles to profl. publs. Recipient Rsch. Career Devel. award USPHS, 1974-79, Merit award USPHS, 1988—, Rous-Whipple award Am. Soc. Investigative Pathology, 2000, Lila Gruber Honor award Am. Acad. Dermatology, 2007; fellow Andrew W. Mellon Found., 1973-76; scholar Joshua Macy Jr. Found., 1978-79. Fellow: Royal Coll. Pathology; mem.: Am. Acad. Microbiology. Office: U Tex Southwestern Med Ctr Dept Path 5323 Harry Hines Blvd Dallas TX 75390-7208 Office Phone: 214-648-4020. Business E-Mail: errol.friedberg@southwestern.edu.

FRIEDEL, JACQUES, retired physics professor; b. Paris, Feb. 11, 1921; s. Edmond and Jeanne (Bersier) F.; m. Mary Horder, June 2, 1952; children: Jean, Paul. Degree in Engring., Ecole Polytechnique, Paris, 1946; postgrad., Ecole des Mines, 1948; PhD, U. Paris., 1954; PhD in Physics., U. Bristol, Eng., 1952; doctorat (hon.), Ecole Polytechnique, Lausanne, Bristol U., Geneva U., Zagreb U., Cambridge U. Engr. Ecole des Mines, Paris, 1948-56; prof. physics U. Paris, 1956-89, ret., 1989. Pres. Cons. Scientifique France Telecom Paris, 1991-98, Obs. Nat. la Lectr., 1994-2001; pres. Comite Consultatif de la Rsch. Sci. Tech., 1979-81. Author: Dislocations, 1956, 64, Graine de Mandarin, 1994; contbr. articles to profl. jours. With French Cavalry, 1944. Decorated grand officer Legion of Honor, comdr. Order Nat. Merit; recipient Gold medals CNRS, Ste. Française Metallurgie Paris, Acta Metallurgica, prize Holweck French Soc. Physics and Inst. of Physics, Dannie Heineman prize Acad. Göttingen, von Hippel and Italgas awards. Mem. Acad. des Scis. (past pres.), Swedish Royal Acad. Scis. (hon.), Royal Soc. London (hon.), Am. Acad. Arts and Scis. (hon.), Leopoldina (hon.), Inst. Physics London (hon.), Am. Phys. Soc. (hon.), Nat. Acad. Sci. (hon.), Royal Belgian Acad. Sci. (hon.), Brazilian Acad. Sci. (hons.), European Phys. Soc. (past pres.), Max Planck Gesellschaft (hon.). Home: 2 rue Jean-Francois Gerbillon 75006 Paris France Office: Physique des Solides U Paris Sud 91405 Orsay France

FRIEDEL, JIM, air transportation executive; B in Econs., Princeton U., NJ. Cons. Mercer Mgmt. Consulting, Washington; various positions in corp. fin., passenger reservations and passenger mktg. NW Airlines Corp., 1991—97, head sales and mktg. NW Airlines Cargo, 1997—99, pres. NW Airlines Cargo, 1999—, sr. v.p. Pacific, 2005—. Office: NW Airlines Corp 2700 Lone Oak Pky Eagan MN 55121 Office Phone: 612-726-2111.*

FRIEDEL, ROBERT OLIVER, physician; b. Corona, NY, Aug. 4, 1936; s. August W. and Denise G. (D'Aoust) F.; m. Susanne Weber, June 30, 1961; children: Christine, Scott, Karin, Linda. BS, Duke U., 1958, MD, 1964. Diplomate: Am. Bd. Psychiatry and Neurology. Intern Duke U. Med. Ctr., Durham, NC, 1964-65, resident in psychiatry, 1967-70, asst. prof. psychiatry and pharmacology dept. psychiatry, 1970-73, assoc. prof. psychiatry and asst. prof. pharmacology, 1973-74; assoc. prof. psychiatry and pharmacology U. Wash. Sch. Medicine, Seattle, 1974-77, dir. div. psychopharmacology, 1974-77, vice chmn., dir. clin. services dept. psychiatry and behavioral scis., 1975-77; prof., chmn. dept. psychiatry Med. Coll. Va.-Va. Commonwealth U., Richmond, 1977-84; prof., chmn. dept. psychiatry, exec. dir. Mental Health Rsch. Inst. U. Mich., Ann Arbor, 1984-85; v.p. psychiat. medicine and rsch. Charter Med. Corp., Macon, Ga., 1985-90, psychiatrist in chief, 1987-90, sr. v.p. clin. svcs. and rsch., 1990, physician in chief, 1990, also bd. dirs.; prof., chmn. dept. psychiatry U. Ala., Birmingham, 1992-2001; disting. clin. prof., dept. psychiatry Va. Commonwealth U., Richmond, 2001—. Mem. sci. adv. bd. Nat. Edn. Alliance for Borderline Personality Disorder. Author: Borderline Personality Disorder Demystified, 2004, www.bpdemystified.com, 2007, (with others) Behavioral Science: A Selective View, 1972; editor (with L.R. Baxter) Current Psychiatric Diagnosis and Treatment, 1999, (with D. Evans) Current Psychiatry Reports and Current Psychosis and Therapeutic Reports; mem. editl. bd. Jour. Clin. Psychopharmacology, Hosp. and Cmty. Psychiatry, 1986-92; contbr. book chpts. and articles. Bd. dirs. Nat. Mental Health Assn., 1987-92. Served to lt. comdr. USPHS, 1965-67. Fellow Am. Psychiat. Assn. (disting. life); mem. AMA, Am. Coll. Psychiatrists, Soc. Biol. Psychiatry, Med. Soc. Va., Am. Coll. Neuropsychopharmacology (life), Alpha Omega Alpha. Home: 13722 Hickory Nut Point Midlothian VA 23112 Office Phone: 804-744-5261. E-mail: rofriedel@aol.com.

FRIEDEN, CARL, biochemist, educator; b. New Rochelle, NY, Dec. 31, 1928; s. Alexander and Evelyn (Gutman) F.; m. Sari Ann Schneider, Dec. 20, 1953; children: Amy, Eric, Karen. BA, Carleton Coll., 1951; PhD, U. Wis., 1955. Mem. faculty biochemistry and molecular biophysics Washington U., St. Louis, 1957—, prof. biol. chemistry, 1963—, interim dept. head, 1986—89, 1996—2000, Alumni Endowed prof., 1994-2000, dir. med. scientist tng. program, 1986-91, Wittcoff prof., head, 2000—05. Mem. NIH study sect., biochemistry, 1969-74, cellular molecular basis of disease, 1992-96. Mem. editorial bd.: Jour. Biol. Chemistry, 1963-68, 75-80, Archives Biochemistry and Biophysics, 1973-79, Biochemistry, 1975—. Protein Sci., 1992-96, 2007—. Fellow AAAS, Am. Acad. Arts and Scis.; mem. Nat. Acad. Sci., Am. Soc. Biochemistry and Molecular Biology, Am. Chem. Soc. (St. Louis award 1976), Am. Soc. Cell Biology, Biophys. Soc., Protein Soc. (Anfinsen award, 2007), Sigma Xi. Research, publs. on mechanism of enzyme action including correlation of protein structure to catalytic function, protein folding, devel., application of kinetic theory with respect to enzymes; properties of actin. Home: 7452 Wellington Way Saint Louis MO 63105-2926 E-mail: frieden@biochem.wustl.edu.

FRIEDEN, CLIFFORD E., lawyer; b. LA, Mar. 8, 1949; s. Sidney S. and Norma (Stern) Frieden; m. Dinah S. Baumring, June 20, 1971; children: Jamie, Kari, Curtis. BA, UCLA, 1971; JD, U. Calif., Berkeley, 1974. Bar: Calif. 1974, US Dist. Ct. (so. dist.) Calif. 1974, US Dist. Ct. (ctrl. dist.) Calif. 1977. Ptnr. Rutan & Tucker, Costa Mesa, Calif., 1974—. Dir. Nat. Football Found. and Coll. Hall of Fame, Orange County, Calif., 2005—; mem. Orange County chpt. ARC, 1995—2001. Mem.: Orange County Bar Assn. (del. state conv. 1983—95, chair judiciary com. 1987—88, bd. dirs. 1989—91), Phi Beta Kappa, Order of Coif. Avocation: sports. Office: Rutan and Tucker PO Box 1950 611 Anton Blvd Ste 1400 Costa Mesa CA 92626-1931 Office Phone: 714-641-5100. Business E-Mail: cfrieden@rutan.com.

FRIEDEN, FAITH JOY, obstetrician; b. NYC, Sept. 15, 1960; MD, Mt. Sinai Sch. Medicine, 1984. Diplomate Am. Bd. Ob-Gyn., Am. Bd. Maternal and Fetal Medicine. Resident in ob-gyn. Beth Israel Med. Ctr., NYC, 1984—88, attending physician, 1990—93; fellow in maternal fetal medicine Bellevue Hosp./NYU, NYC, 1988—90; perinatology dir. maternal-fetal medicine Englewood (N.J.) Hosp. and Med. Ctr., 1993—, chief ob-gyn., 2001—. Mem. faculty Mt. Sinai Sch. Medicine, NYC, 1991—. Named one of Top Drs. in N.Y. Metro Area, Castle Connolly, 1999—2006, Top Drs., N.J. Monthly Mag. Office: Englewood Hosp and Med Ctr 350 Engle St Englewood NJ 07631 Office Phone: 201-894-3669.

FRIEDEN, THOMAS R., city health department administrator, epidemiologist; b. NYC, Dec. 7, 1960; BA, Oberlin Coll., 1982; MD, MPH, Columbia U., 1986. Diplomate in internal medicine and infectious diseases Am. Bd. Internal Medicine. Resident in medicine Columbia Presbyn. Hosp., NYC, 1986-89; fellow in infectious disease Yale U., New Haven, 1989-90; med. epidemiologist Ctr. for Disease Control/NYC Dept. Health & Mental Hygiene, NYC, 1990-92, dir. Bur. Tuberculosis Control, asst. commr., 1992-96; med. officer Ctr. for Disease Control/WHO, New Delhi, 1996—2001; commr. NYC Dept. Health & Mental Hygiene, NYC, 2002—. Contbr. chpts. to books, articles to profl. jours. Office: NYC Dept Health & Mental Hygiene 125 Worth Street New York NY 10013*

FRIEDENBERG, DANIEL MEYER, investor, writer; b. Mt. Vernon, NY, Feb. 24, 1923; s. Samuel and Rose Abravanel (Klein) F.; m. Maria del Carmen Joy, May 1, 1956 (div. June 1964); children: Samuel Clark, Danielle Joy; m. June Meredith Daniels, Apr. 12, 1965 (div. May 1986); children: Jay Daniels, Bertrand Russell. BS, U. Pa., 1943. With John-Platt Enterprises, Inc., NYC, 1947—, pres., 1957—. Curator coins and medals Jewish Mus., N.Y.C., 1960-83, emeritus, 1983—; guest lectr. Columbia U., N.Y.C., Yale U., New Haven, Swarthmore Coll., Hebrew U., Jerusalem. Author: Great Jewish Portraits in Metal, 1963, Jewish Medals from the Renaissance to the Fall of Napoleon, 1970, Jewish Mint Masters & Medalists, 1976, Medieval Jewish Seals from Europe, 1987, Life, Liberty and the Pursuit of Land, 1992, Sold to the Highest Bidder: The Presidency from Dwight D. Eisenhower to George W. Bush, 2002; contbr. articles to profl. jours. Exec. dir. N.Y. County Liberal Party, 1945; sec. Young Dems., N.Y.C., 1952. Served with AUS, 1943-44. Recipient spl. achievement award Loeb Mag., 1962, Loeb Newspaper, 1965, Heath Lit. award for disting. numismatic achievement, 1969, Nat. Jewish Book award, 1988, 3d prize Nat. Libr. Poetry, 1997. Fellow Am. Numismatic Soc. (life); mem. Am. Numismatic Assn. Office: 55 Central Park W New York NY 10023-6003 Home: PO Box 767 Greenwich CT 06836-0767

FRIEDENBERG, RICHARD MYRON, radiologist, physician, educator; b. NYC, May 6, 1926; s. Charles and Dorothy (Steg) F.; m. Gloria Geshwind, Jan. 22, 1950; children: Lisa, Peter, Amy. AB, Columbia, 1946; MD, L.I. Coll. Medicine, 1949. Diplomate: Am. Bd. Radiology. Intern in medicine Maimonides Hosp., Bklyn., 1949-50; resident in radiology Bellevue Hosp., NYC, 1950-51, Nat. Cancer fellow, 1951-52; fellow radiology Columbia-Presbyn. Hosp., 1952-53; cons. radiologist 3d Air Force, London, Eng., 1953-55; asst. prof. radiology Albert Einstein Coll. Medicine, 1955-66, assoc. clin. prof. radiology, 1966-68; dir., chmn. dept. radiology Bronx Lebanon Hosp. Center, 1957-68; prof., chmn. dept. radiology N.Y. Med. Coll., 1968-80; prof., chmn. dept. radiol. scis. U. Calif., Irvine, 1980—92, emeritus prof. radiol. scis., 1992—. Dir. radiology Flower Fifth Ave. Hosp., Met. Hosp. Ctr., Bird S. Coler Hosp., NYC, Westchester County Med. Ctr., 1968—80. Author: (with Charles Ney) Radiographic Atlas of the Genitourinary System, 1966, 2d edit., 1981; Contbr. (with Charles Ney) articles to profl. jours. Fellow Am. Coll. Radiology, N.Y. Acad. Medicine; mem. Assn. Univ. Radiologists, Radiol. Soc. N.Am., Am. Roentgen Ray Soc., N.Y. Acad. Scis., Assn. Am. Med. Colls., AMA, Soc. Chairmen Acad. Radiology Depts. (past pres.), N.Y. Roentgen Soc. (past pres.), Orange CTY Radiology Soc. (past pres.). Home: 18961 Castlegate Ln Santa Ana CA 92705-2801 Office: U Calif Dept Radiology Irvine CA 92697-0001 Office Phone: 714-456-5303. Business E-Mail: rmfriede@uci.edu.

FRIEDENSOHN, HENRY, retired physician; b. Antwerp, Belgium, May 6, 1929; s. Solomon Friedensohn and Zisla Kobandwitch; m. Bernice Putter, Sept. 15, 1962; children: Jeffrey, Stephanie Deltufo. BS, LI U., Bklyn., 1952; MD, U. Utrecht, Netherlands, 1958, U. Pitts., 1960. Lic. NJ, 1961, Fla., 2007, diplomate Am. Bd. Family Practice, 1991. Intern Morristown Meml. Hosp. NJ, 1960—61; family practice physician Lake Hiawatha, NJ, 1962—81, Halladale, Fla., 1992—2006; physician Humana HMO, Delray Beach, Fla., 1982—92; ret., 2006. Bd. trustees Riverside Hosp., Boonton, 1982—84; lectr. holocaust documentation and edn., 2006. Cpl. US Army, 1952—54, Germany. Recipient Med. Comm. award, Glaxo Pharms., 2002, Donner of Yr., Hosptalized Vets. Am., 1999, 2006. Avocations: reading, tennis, swimming.

FRIEDER, GIDEON, computer scientist, educator; b. Zvolen, Czechoslovakia, Sept. 30, 1937; arrived in US, 1975; m. Dalia Bogler, Apr. 3, 1960; children— Ophir, Tally, Gony B.Sc., Israel Inst. Tech., Haifa, Israel, 1959, M.Sc., 1961, D.Sc., 1967. Staff mem. Israel Dept. Def. Research and Devel., Haifa, Israel, 1959-68, dir. computer sci., 1968-70; staff mem. IBM Sci. Ctr., Haifa, Israel, 1973-75; assoc. prof., then prof., chmn. SUNY, Buffalo, 1975-81; prof., chmn. dept. elec. engring. and computer sci. U. Mich., Ann Arbor, 1981-86; dean sch. computer info. science Syracuse (N.Y.) U., 1987-92; dean Sch. Engring. and Applied Sci., A. James Clark prof. George Washington U., 1992-97, A. James Clark chair, prof. engring., applied scis., 1997—. Cons. various industries; chief architect computers Nanodata Corp., Buffalo, 1976-80; expert witness patent and copyright cases; lectr. Contbr. articles to profl. jours.; patentee in field of computers, memory and orgn. Mem. Assn. Computing Machinery, IEEE Computer Soc. Office: 707 22d St Washington DC 20052 Office Phone: 202-994-8884. Business E-Mail: gfrieder@gwu.edu.

FRIEDHEIM, JAN V., educational association administrator; b. Corpus Christi, Tex., Oct. 20, 1935; d. Roy Lee Conyers and Bertha Victoria (Ostrom) Hamm; m. John R. Eisenhour, Nov. 22, 1962 (div. 1983); m. Stephen B. Friedheim, Sept. 1, 1984; children: Neenah, Stephen II, Robert. BS, U. Tex., 1957; PhD (hon.), Constantinian U., Malta, 1994. Chmn. bd. Exec. Secretarial Sch., Dallas, 1960—2001; ptnr. Edn. Sys. and Solutions, 2001—. Vice-chmn. Tex. Vocat.Adv. Bd., Austin, 1979-86; mem. adv. com. Dept. Edn., Washington, 1980-84; commr. So. Assn. Colls. and Schs. Commn. on Occupl. Edn. Instns., 1994-97; adv. com. State Postsecondary Rev. Entity, 1994; bd. dirs. Tex. Assn. Pvt. Schs., Career Coll. and Schs. of Tex.; commr. Coun. on Occupl. Edn., 1995-2001. Bd. dirs. Career Colls. and Schs. of Tex., 1995—. Named Disting. Evaluator, Accrediting Coun. Ind. Coll. Schs., 1999. Mem. Career Coll. Assn. (bd. dirs. 1999—), Assn. Ind. Colls. and Schs. (chmn. bd. dirs. 1980-81, commn. 1978-79, commr. 1974-79, Disting. Mem. 1974, 81, Mem. of Yr. 1979), Southwestern Assn. Pvt. Schs. (pres. 1982), Metroplex Assn. Pvt. Schs. (pres. 1989-90, 92-93), So. Assn. Colls. and Schs. (trustee 1981-85, commn. on occupational edn. instns. 1994-97), Tex. Assn. Pvt. Schs. (bd. dirs. 1992—), Career Colls. and Schs. Tex. (bd. dirs. 1995—, chmn.-elect 1998, chmn. 1999). Home: 6450 Patrick Dr Dallas TX 75214-2444 Office Phone: 214-827-5403. Personal E-mail: jfriedheim@aol.com.

FRIEDHEIM, JERRY WARDEN, museum consultant; b. Joplin, Mo., Oct. 7, 1934; s. Volmer Havens and Billie Alice (Warden) F.; m. Shirley Margarette Beavers, Oct. 17, 1956 (dec. Sept. 15, 2003); children: Daniel Volmer, Cynthia Diane, Thomas Eric; m. Jacqueline Wade Grant, April 24, 2004. BJ, U. Mo., 1956, AM, 1962. Reporter, editor, editorial writer Neosho (Mo.) Daily News, Joplin (Mo.) Globe, Columbia Missourian, 1956-61; instr. journalism U. Mo., Columbia, 1961-62; aide to Congressman Durward Hall from Mo., Washington, 1962-63; legis. asst., pres. sec., exec. asst. to U.S. Senator John Tower from Tex., Washington, 1963-69; dep. asst. Sec. Def. for Pub. Affairs, U.S. Dept. Def., Washington, 1969-72; asst. Sec. Def. for Pub. Affairs, Washington, 1973-74; v.p. pub. and govt. affairs AMTRAK, 1974-75; exec. v.p., gen. mgr. Am. Newspaper Pubs. Assn. and ANPA Found., Washington, 1975-87, pres., 1987-91; pub. Presstime mag., 1980-90; v.p. pub. affairs The Freedom Forum, Arlington, Va., 1991-95; exec. dir. The Freedom Forum Newseum, 1991-93; dep. dir. The Newseum, Arlington, Va., 1995-97, mem. adv. com., 1998—. Bd. dirs. World Press Freedom Com; past chmn. Nat. Press Found. Author: Where are the Voters, 1968. Capt. AUS, 1956-58. Congl. fellow Am. Polit. Sci. Assn.; recipient Disting. Svc. medal Dept. Def., 1972, 74. Home: 46865 Grissom St Sterling VA 20165-3575

FRIEDHEIM, STEPHEN BAILEY, educational consultant; b. Joplin, Mo., Nov. 13, 1934; s. Robert Wray and Virginia Grace (Bailey) F.; m. Jan V. Eisenhour, Sept. 1, 1984; children: Neenah Marie, Stephen Bailey II, Robert William. BA, U. Ark., 1956; DBA (hon.), Johnson and Wales U., Providence, 1978; DAM (hon.), Ctrl. New Eng. Coll., Worcester, Mass., 1984. Announcer Sta. KBRS, Springdale, Ark., 1956-57; newsman Sta. KFSB, Joplin, 1957; dir. pub. rels. Am. Pers. and Guidance Assn., Washington, 1961-66; exec. v.p. Am. Soc. Med. Tech., Houston, 1966-76; pres. Assn. Ind. Colls. and Schs., Washington, 1976-84; sr. v.p. Campbell Comm., Bethesda, Md., Dallas, 1984-90, King Edn. Svcs., 1984-89; pres. ESS Coll. Bus. (formerly Exec. Secretarial Sch.), Dallas, 1984-2001; prin. Edn. Solutions for Students LLC, 1991—2001; founder Edn. Systems & Solutions, LLC, 2001—; v.p. pub. rels. Coll. Am. Svsc., Inc. Cons. Profl. Scs., Internat., 1980-82, South-Western Pub. Co., 1984-88, Career Com Corp., 1984-91, Richard D. Irwin, Inc., Paradigm Pub., 1999, Masters Inst., 1997, Johnson & Wales U., 2002-06, Coll. Am., 2002—, KD Studio Actors Conservatory, 2002-05, Vatterott Colls., 2003-05; task force on transfer credit Coun. on Postsecondary Accreditation, 1977-78; mem. Nat. Task Force on Image of the Sec., 1980-97; pres. Am. Edn. Alliance, 1988-90; founder, mng. dir. EdVerify, 1998-2000. Editor: The Lead Generation, 1984—90, Tex. Times, 1994—2004. Bd. dirs. St. Aidan's Sch., Alexandria, Va., 1979-82, Trinity River Arts Ctr., 2002-06; trustee Dollars for Scholars, 1982-84; vestry man Ascension Ch., Houston, 1973-76, sr. warden, 1976; narrator Minn. Symphony Orch., 1972; founding mem. local county workforce devel. bd. Dallas County, 1996-2001, chmn., vice-chmn., bd. dirs., 1999, chmn., 2000; bd. dirs., exec. com. Tex. Discovery Gardens, 2000-01; vice-chmn. Workforce Leadership Tex., 2000-01. With U.S. Army, 1957-61. Recipient Freedoms Found. award, 1960, 62, Broadcasting award Am. Legion Aux., 1963. Fellow Australasian Coll. Bio-med. Scientists; mem. Am. Soc. Assn. Execs. (cert.), Nat. Assn. Trade and Tech. Schs. (Outstanding Svc. award 1984), Assn. Ind. Colls. and Schs. (Disting. Svc. award 1991), Washington Soc. Assn. Execs., Work Force Commn. Creative Svc. (1st pl. award 1990, 91), Southwestern Assn. Ind. Colls. and Schs. (bd. dirs. 1985-92, pres. 1989-91), Met. Assn. Career Schs. (bd. dirs. 1985-86, pres. 1999), Assn. Ind. Colls. and Schs. (treas. 1985-89, bd. dirs. 1985-91, chmn. bd. 1990-91), Career Coll. Assn. (bd. dirs. 1991-9, 1st chmn. bd. 1991-94, past chmn. bd. 1994-95), Nat. Ct. Reporters Assn. (strategic alliance com. for edn. 1994-95), Nat. Alliance of Bus. (bus. adv. com. 1994-2000, S.W. regional bd. dirs. 1996-98), Career Tng. Found. (bd. dirs. 1992-95, trustee 1995—2000), Am. Assn. Higher Edn., Am. Vocat. Assn., Nat. Bus. Edn. Assn., Nat. Assn. Workforce Bds. (bd. dirs. 2000-01), Am. Vocat. Assn., Nat. Assn. Execs., Nat. Assn. Concerned Vets., Career Coll. Assn., Career Colls. and Schs. of Tex. (bd. dirs. 2000-04), U.S. C. of C. (edn., employment and tng. com. 1980-92, adv. bd. 1991-95), Ctr. Workforce Preparation and Quality Edn. Home: 6450 Patrick Dr Dallas TX 75214-2444 Office Phone: 214-827-5403. Personal E-mail: sfriedheim@aol.com.

FRIEDKIN, THOMAS H., automotive executive; b. 1925; Dir. Pacific Southwest Airlines, San Diego, 1946-87; with Gulf States Toyota, Inc., Houston, 1969—, now chmn. bd. dirs., CEO. Named one of Forbes' Richest Americans, 2006. Office: Gulf States Toyota Inc 7701 Wilshire Place Dr Houston TX 77040-5399

FRIEDLAENDER, GARY ELLIOTT, orthopedist, educator; b. Detroit, May 15, 1945; s. Alex Seymour and Eileen Adrianne (Berman) Friedlaender; m. Linda Beth Krohner, Mar. 16, 1969; children: Eron Yael, Ari Seth. BS, U. Mich., 1967, MD, 1969; MA (hon.), Yale U., 1984. Diplomate Am. Bd. Orthop. Surgery. Intern, then resident in surgery U. Mich., Ann Arbor, 1969-71; resident in orthop. Yale New Haven Hosp., 1971-74; fellow in musculoskeletal oncology Mass. Gen. Hosp., Boston, 1983; dir. tissue bank Naval Med. Rsch. Inst., Bethesda, Md., 1974-76; instr. surgery Yale U., New Haven, 1974, asst. prof., 1976-79, assoc. prof., 1979-84, prof., chief orthop., 1984-86, prof. chmn. dept. orthop. and rehab., 1986—, Wayne O. Southwick prof. of orthop. and rehab., 1997—. Mem. orthop. and musculoskeletal study sect. NIH, 1986—89, mem. nat. adv. bd. arthritis and musculoskeletal and skin diseases, 1991—95, chmn., 1993—95; mem. blood products adv. com. FDA, 1995—97; mem. adv. coun. Nat. Inst. Arthritis and Musculoskeletal and Skin Diseases, 1998—2001. Mem. bd. cons. editors: Jour. Bone and Joint Surgery, 1981—89, mem. bd. assoc. editors: Clin. Orthop. and Related Rsch., 1986—97, dep. editor:, 1997—, mem. bd. assoc. editors: Modern Medicine, 1988—; editor: Rheumatology Digest, 1986—95; mem. editl. bd.: Transplantation Scis., 1991—, Jour. Cancer, 1994—; contbr. articles to profl. jours. Served to lt. comdr. USN, 1974—76. Recipient Outstanding Rsch. award, Kappa Delta, 1982, Nicholas Andry award for Outstanding Orthoped. Rsch., 1995. Fellow: ACS, Am. Acad. Orthop. Surgeons (chmn. com. biol. implants 1987—93, chmn. com. rsch. 1999—2002, bd. dir. 1999—2002, chmn. com. academic advocacy 2001—, chair musculoskeletal splty. soc. 2001—02); mem.: NIH (orthop. and musculoskeletal study sect. 1986—89, mem. nat. adv. bd. arthritis and musculoskeletal and skin diseases 1991—95, chmn. 1993—95), AMA, Acad. Orthop. Soc. (pres. 1995—96, chmn. com. rsch. 1999—2002), Assn. Bone and Joint Surgeons (pres. 2001—02), Am. Orthop. Assn., Am. Soc. Transplant Surgeons, Soc. for Surg. Oncology, Am. Coun. on Transplantation (pres. 1983—85), Musculoskeletal Tumor Soc., Transplantation Soc., Orthop. Rsch. Soc. (pres. 1994—95), Am. Assn. Tissue Banks (pres. 1983—85, Disting. Svc. award 1996), Alpha Omega Alpha. Jewish. Home: 15 Old Still Rd Woodbridge CT 06525-1101 Office: Yale U Dept Orthopedics and Rehab PO Box 208071 New Haven CT 06520-8071 Office Phone: 203-737-5660. Business E-Mail: gary.friedlaender@yale.edu.

FRIEDLAND, BERNARD, electrical engineer, educator; b. Bklyn., May 25, 1930; s. Irving and Beckle (Kissen) Friedland; m. Zita Isa Silverman, Aug. 16, 1959; children: Barbara, Irene, Shelly. AB, Columbia U., 1952, BSEE, 1953, MSEE, 1954, PhD, 1957. Registered profl. engr., Calif. Instr. Columbia U., NYC, 1953-57, asst. prof., 1957-61; head control lab. Melpar, Inc., Watertown, Mass., 1961-62; prin. scientist Kearfott Guidance and Navigation Corp. (formerly The Singer Co.), Little Falls, NJ, 1962-90; disting. prof. NJ Inst. Tech., Newark, 1990—. Adj. prof. Columbia U., 1965—72, NYU, NYC, 1970—73, Poly. U. (formerly Poly. Inst. NY), Bklyn., 1974—90; Lady Davis vis. prof. Technion (Israel Inst. Tech.), 1996—97. Co-author: Principles of Linear Networks, 1961, Linear Systems, 1965; author: Control System Design, 1986, Advanced Control System Design, 1996; contbr. articles to profl. jours. Chmn. Hilary Sch., Newark, 1965. Named to Hall of Fame, Bklyn. Tech. HS, 1998. Fellow: IEEE (various offices, disting. mem., 3d millennium medal), ASME (various offices, Oldenburger medal 1982), AIAA (assoc.; assoc. editor jour.). Democrat. Jewish. Avocations: skiing, swimming, tennis, reading, sculpting. Office: NJ Inst Tech Dept Elec and Computer Engring Newark NJ 07102 Business E-Mail: bf@njit.edu.

FRIEDLAND, MICHAEL LAWRENCE, dean, medical educator; b. Aug. 30, 1942; BS, Bklyn. Coll., 1963; MD, SUNY, Bklyn., 1967. Asst. prof. medicine, dir. hematology/oncology Brown U./Miriam Hosp., Providence, 1973-81; assoc. prof. medicine Med. Coll. Pa., 1981-82; prof. clin. medicine, sr. assoc. dean clin. affairs NY Med. Coll., 1982-87, chmn. dept. medicine, prof. clin. medicine, 1987-92; dean Binghamton Clin. Campus SUNY, Syracuse, 1992-97; v.p.affiliated programs SUNY Health Sci. Ctr., Syracuse, 1993-95; interim exec. v.p. for acad. affairs/dean medicine Tex. A&M U. Sys. Health Sci. Ctr., College Station, Tex., 1997-99; dean of medicine U. Mo. Kansas City, 1999—2001; dean ea. divsn. W.Va. U. Health Scis Ctr., Martinsburg, 2001—04; prof. biomed. sci., v.p. med. prograsm Fla. Atlantic U., Boca Raton, 2004—, dean Charles E. Schmidt Coll. Biomed. Sci., 2006—. Mem. Medicare Coverage Adv. Com.; v.p. med. programs. Co-author: (abstract) IME 21st Ann. Session, 1996, (sect. of book) The Chemotherapy Source Book, 1996; contbr. over 50 articles to profl. jours. Bd. dirs. Brazos Valley chpt. Am. Lung Assn., Bryan, Tex., 1998. Mem. AMA (governing coun. sect. on med. schs., chair sect. on med. schs. 2002-04), Mo. State Med. Assn. (coun. on med. edn.). Office: Florida Atlantic Univ Biomed Sci 777 Glades Road PO Box 3091 Boca Raton FL 33431-0991 Home Phone: 561-964-4477; Office Phone: 561-297-2219. Business E-Mail: michael.friedland@fau.edu.

FRIEDLAND, ROBERT M., mining executive; married; 3 children. B, Reed Coll. Founder, exec. chmn. Ivanhoe Mines Ltd.; co-chmn., controlling shareholder Ivanhoe Nickel & Platinum Ltd. (Ivanplats); chmn. Ivanhoe Capital Corp.; dep. chmn., controlling shareholder Ivanhoe Energy, co-chmn. subs. Sunwing Energy. Named Developer of Yr., Prospectors' and Developers' Assn. Can., 1996; named one of 400 Richest Ams., Forbes mag., 2006; recipient Investor Envoy of Yr. award, Govt. Mongolia, 2002, 2003. Office: Ivanhoe Mines Ltd World Trade Ctr 999 Canada Pl Ste 654 Vancouver BC Canada V6C 3E1

FRIEDLANDER, CHARLES DOUGLAS (CHUCK FRIEDLANDER), aerospace scientist, consultant; b. NYC, Oct. 5, 1928; s. Murray L. and Jeane (Sottosanti) F.; m. Diane Mary Hutchins, May 12, 1951; children: Karen Diane, Lauren Patrice, Joan Elyse. BS, U.S. Mil. Acad. West Point, 1950; exec. mgmt. program, NASA, 1965; grad., Command and Staff Coll. Ext. USAF, 1965, Air War Coll. Ext. USAF, 1966. Commd. 2d lt. U.S. Army, 1950, advanced 1st lt., officer inf. Republic of Korea, 1950-51, UN Forces Trieste Trieste, Italy, 1953—54, resigned, 1954; chief astronaut support office NASA, Cape Canaveral, Fla., 1963-67; space cons. CBS News, Cape Canaveral, Fla., 1967-69; exec. asst. The White House, Nat. Aeronautics and Space Coun., Washington, 1969—72. V.p. bd. dirs. Internat. Aerospace Hall of Fame, San Diego; space program cons., various cos., Boca Raton, Fla., 1967-69; mem. staff First Postwar Fgn. Ministers Conf., Berlin, 1954; radio/TV cons. space program. Author: Buying & Selling Land for Profit, 1961, Last Man at Hungnam Beach, 1952, To Bravely Go.West Point Astronauts, 2007. V.p. West Point Soc., Cape Canaveral, Fla., 1964. Served to lt. col. USAFR, maj. USAR. Decorated Bronze Star V, Combat Inf. badge; co-recipient Emmy award CBS TV Apollo Moon Landing, 1960; recipient medal of honor N.Y.C., 1951. Mem. Explorer's Club, West Point Soc., Chosin Few Survivors Korea, NASA Alumni League, Nat. Space Soc, Missile Space and Range Pioneers. Avocations: fishing, travel.

FRIEDLANDER, EDWARD JAY, journalist, educator; b. Portland, Maine, Apr. 24, 1945; s. Otto and Marguerite Evelyn (Smith) Friedlander; m. Roberta Kay Burford, July 12, 1975; 1 child, Erika Anne. BS, U. Wyo., 1967; MA, U. Denver, 1970; EdD, U. No. Colo., 1973. Reporter Denver Post, 1967-68, USIA, Washington, 1968-69; publicist Universal Pictures, NYC, 1969-70; mag. editor Daily Times-Call, Longmont, Colo., 1970-71; media coord. Centaurus HS, Lafayette, Colo., 1972-73; asst. prof. mass communication Ctrl. Mo. State U., Warrensburg, 1973-75; from asst. prof. to assoc. prof. dept. journalism U. Ark., Little Rock, 1975—81, prof., 1981-95, chairperson dept. journalism, 1988-95; dir., prof. U. South Fla. Sch. Mass Comm., Tampa, 1995—. Cons. Bur. Indian Affairs, Washington, 1979, Ark. Press Assn., Little Rock, 1980—85; cons., editor FCC, Washington, 1979—81; adminstr. Waldo Proffitt award, 1998—. Author: (book) Excellence in Reporting, 1987, Feature Writing for Newspapers and Magazines, 1988, Feature Writing for Newspapers and Magazines, 5th edit., 2004, Modern Mass Media, 1990, Modern Mass Media, 2d rev. edit., 1994, Medios de Comunicación Social, 1992. German Acad. Exch. Svc. fellow, Bonn, 1982, European Acad. fellow, Berlin, 1984. Mem.: Soc. Profl. Journalists (officer exec. bd. Ark. profl. chpt. 1986—89, v.p. 1989—91, pres. 1991—92, officer exec. bd. Ark. profl. chpt. 1992—94), Assn. Schs. Journalism and Mass Comm. (exec. com. 1997—2000, 2003—04), Assn. Edn. Journalism and Mass Comm., Kappa Tau Alpha. Office: U South Fla Sch Mass Comms CIS # 1040 4202 E Fowler Ave Tampa FL 33620-7800

FRIEDLANDER, EDWARD ROBERT, pathologist; b. Evanston, Ill., Jan. 9, 1952; s. Robert and Joanne (Hiscox) F. AB, Brown U., 1973; MD, Northwestern U., Chgo., 1977. Diplomate Am. Bd. Pathology. Pathologist, Kansas City, 1988—; chmn. dept. pathology Univ. of Health Scis. Lectr. in field; operator free disease info. svcs. online. Author: (booklets) Christian Perspectives on Evolution, 1985, William Blake's Visions, 1986. Foster parent Juvenile Corrections, Johnson City, Tenn., 1984-85; bd. dirs. Tenn. Assn. Vols. Criminal Justice, 1983-86; prison vol. Yoke Fellow, Winston Salem, 1982-83. Fellow Coll. Am. Pathologists, Am. Soc. Clin. Pathologists, Lambda Chi Alpha. Home: 7909 Tauromee Ave Kansas City KS 66112-2639 Office: 1750 Independence Ave Kansas City MO 64106-1453

FRIEDLANDER, GERHART, nuclear chemist; b. Munich, July 28, 1916; came to U.S., 1936, naturalized, 1943; s. Max O. and Bella (Forchheimer) F.; m. Gertrude Maas, Feb. 6, 1941 (dec. 1966); children: Ruth Ann F. Huart, Joan Claire F. Hurley; m. Barbara Strongin, 1983. BS, U. Calif., Berkeley, 1939, PhD, 1942; D (hon.), Clark U., 1991, U. Mainz, Germany, 1992. Instr. U. Idaho, Moscow, 1942-43; staff Los Alamos Sci. Lab., 1943-46; research assoc. Gen. Electric Co. Research Lab., Schenectady, 1946-48; vis. lectr. Washington U., St. Louis, 1948; chemist Brookhaven Nat. Lab., Upton, N.Y., 1948-52, sr. chemist, 1952-81, 89-91, cons., 1981-89, 91-93, chmn. chemistry dept., 1968-77. Chmn. Gordon Rsch. Conf. on Nuclear Chemistry, 1954. Author: (with J.W. Kennedy) Introduction to Radiochemistry, 1949, Nuclear and Radiochemistry, 1955, (with J.M. Miller), 1964, (with E.S. Macias), 1981; editor-in-chief Sci. Spectra, 1993-2000; editor Radiochimica Acta, 1972-73; assoc. editor Ann. Rev. Nuc. Sci., 1958-67; contbr. articles to profl. jours. Recipient Alexander von Humboldt award Institut für Kernchemie, Mainz, Fed. Republic of Germany, 1978-79, 87, 92, 93. Fellow AAAS; mem. Hungarian Acad. Scis. (hon.), Nat. Acad. Sci., Am. Acad. Arts and Scis., Am. Chem. Soc. (chmn. divsn. nuclear chemistry and tech. 1967, award for nuclear applications in chemistry 1967). Achievements include research in chemical effects of nuclear transformations, properties of radioactive isotopes, mechanisms of nuclear reactions, especially those induced by protons of very high energies; solar neutrino detection; cluster impact phenomena. Home: 22 St Charles Pl South Setauket NY 11720 E-mail: gfriedlander2@msn.com.

FRIEDLANDER, JOHN BENJAMIN, mathematician, educator; b. Toronto, Canada, Oct. 4, 1941; s. Daniel Theodore and Beatrice Adele (Axler) Friedlander; m. Cherryl Lynne Thompson, Sept. 1, 1974; children: Jonathan, Diana, Amanda, Keith. BSc, U. Toronto, 1965; MA, U. Waterloo, Ont., Can., 1966; PhD, Pa. State U., 1972. Asst. to A. Selberg, Inst. Advanced Study, Princeton, NJ, 1972-73, mem. Sch. Math, 1973-74, 83-84, 95-96, 99-2000, 2004; lectr., dept. math MIT, Cambridge, 1974-76; vis. prof. Scuola Normale Superiore, Pisa, Italy, 1976-77; from asst. prof. to assoc. prof. U. Toronto, 1977—82, prof. math, 1982—, chair dept. math., 1987-91; lectr. U. Ill., Urbana, 1979-80; rsch. prof. Math Sci. Rsch. Inst., Berkeley, Calif., 1991-92. Mem. grant selection com. Nat. Scis. and Engring. Rsch. Coun. Can., 1991—94; lectr. ICM, 1994; mem. sci. adv. bd. Banff Internat. Rsch. Sta., 2003—06, Field Inst. Rsch. Math. Sci., 1996—2000, Pacific Inst. Math. Scis., 2005—; math. convenor Royal Soc. Can., 1990—93; mem. gen. assembly Internat. Math. Union, 1994; lectr. in field. Mem. editl. bd.: Expositiones Mathematicae, Internat. Jour. Number Theory; contbr. articles to profl. jours. Recipient CRM Fields prize, 2002; Acad. Sci. fellow, Royal Soc. Can., 1988—, Killam Rsch. fellow, 2003—05. Mem.: Can. Math. Soc. (Jeffery-Williams prize lectr. 1999), Am. Math. Soc. Avocations: bridge, chess, sailing, barbecue. Home: 22 Stonemanse Ct Scarborough ON Canada M1G 3V3 Office: U Toronto Dept Math Toronto ON Canada M5S 3G3 also: Scarborough Coll Computer and Math Sci Scarborough ON Canada M1C 1A4 Office Phone: 416-287-7241. Office Fax: 416-978-4107. Business E-Mail: frdlndr@math.toronto.edu.

FRIEDLANDER, LEE N., photographer; b. Aberdeen, Wash., 1934; m. Maria D. Friedlander; children: Eric, Anna. Photographer Atlantic Records, NYC, 1956; tchr. UCLA, U. Minn., Rice U. One-man shows include George Eastman House, Rochester, 1963, The Desert Seen, Janet Borden Gallery, 1996, Self-Composed, 1997, At Work, Mus. Contemporary Photography, Chgo., 2005, Modern Mus. Art, 2005, exhibited in group shows at New Documents, Modern Mus. Art, NYC, 1967, Viewing Olmsted, Equitable Gallery, NYC, 1997, The Passions, James Cohan Gallery, 2001, book, American Monuments, 1967, The Desert Seen, Letters to the People, Self Portrait, American Musicians, Little Screens, Kitaj, Lee Friedlander, 2000, Represented in permanent collections Janet Borden, Inc., NY, Fraenkel Gallery, San Francisco. Recipient Friends of Photography award, 1980, MacDowell Medal Lifetime Achievement in Arts, 1986, John D. Catherine T. MacArthur Found. award, John D. Catherine T. MacArthur Found., 1990, Hasselblad Internat. award, 2005; fellow Guggenheim, 1960, 1962, Nat. Endowment Arts, 1972.

FRIEDLANDER, MICHAEL WULF, physicist, researcher; b. Cape Town, South Africa, Nov. 15, 1928; came to U.S., 1956; m. Jessica R. Friedlander; 2 children. BS in Physics, U. Cape Town, 1948, MS with 1st class honors, 1950; PhD in Physics, Bristol U., Eng., 1955. Jr. lectr. U. Cape Town, 1950-52; rsch. assoc. U. Bristol, 1954-56; asst. prof. physics Washington U., St. Louis, 1956-61, assoc. prof., 1961-67, prof., 1967—. Author: The Conduct of Science, 1972, Astronomy: From Stonehenge to Quasars, 1985, Cosmic Rays, 1989, At the Fringes of Science, 1995, A Thin Cosmic Rain, 2000; contbr. articles to Ency. Brit. and profl. jours. Guggenheim Found. fellow, vis. prof. Imperial Coll., London, 1962-63. Mem. AAUP (2d v.p. 1978-80, mem. nat. coun. 1975-78, 86-89), AAAS, Am. Phys. Soc., Am. Astron. Soc., History of Sci. Soc. Achievements include research in elementary particles, cosmic rays, infrared astronomy, and gamma ray astronomy. Office: Washington U Dept Physics One Brookings Dr Saint Louis MO 63130

FRIEDLANDER, ROBERT MAX, neurosurgeon; b. Caracas, Venezuela, Nov. 22, 1965; came to U.S., 1983; s. Isaac and Maria (Falchuk) F. BA, Brandeis U., 1987, MA biochemistry, 1987; MD, Harvard Med. Sch., 1991. Intern in surgery Mass. Gen. Hosp., Boston, 1991-92, resident in neurosurgery, 1992—97; assoc. dir. cerebrovascular surgery Brigham and Women's Hosp., Boston, dir. neurapoptosis lab.; asst. prof. in neurosurgery Harvard Med. Sch., Brigham and Women's Hospital, Boston, 1988—, instr. in neurological surgery, 1998, Harvard Med. Sch.l, Massachusetts Gen. Hospital, Boston, 1997—98; asst. prof. surgery Harvard Med. Sch., Boston, 2000—; assoc. neurosurgeon Brigham & Women's Hospital, 1998—, Children's Hospital, 1998—; asst. in neurosurgery Mass. Gen. Hospital, 1997—98. Prin. investigator clin. trials Mass. Gen. Hosp., Boston, 1993—; Trauma Bd. Mem., Brigham and Women's Hospital, 1999—; Co-chmn. Hosting Com., Congress of Neurological Surgeons nat. meeting, 1999. Vol. Hispanic Friendly Visitor Brigham & Womens Hosp., Boston, 1988-89, career advice/shadow program Brandeis U., Waltham, Mass., 1992—. Dr. Paul Dudley White fellow Harvard Med. Sch., 1989, Howard Hughes Med. Inst. Summer fellow, 1988; recipient neurosurg. resident rsch. award Cerebrovascular Joint Sect., Sect. on Cerebrovascular Surgery, Am. Assn. Neurol. Surgeons and Congress Neurol. Surgeons, 1994, award nat. meeting, 1996. Mem. Am. Assn. Nuerol. Surgeons, Congress of Neurol. Surgeons, Phi Beta Kappa. Avocations: stamp collecting/philately, wine collecting, travel. Office: Brigham and Women's Hosp Dept Neurosurgery 75 Francis St Boston MA 02115 Home: 112 Dudley St Brookline MA 02445-5937 Office Phone: 617-732-7676. Business E-Mail: rfriedlander@partners.org.*

FRIEDLANDER, SHEILA FALLON, dermatologist, educator; d. Regis Joseph and Mary Monahan Fallon; m. Martin Friedlander, Sept. 30, 1978; children: David Fallon, Mollie SarahHenni, Jeffrey Fallon, Michael Fallon, Henni Maura. BA, U. Chgo., 1975, MD, 1979. Diplomate Am. Bd. Pediat., 1984, Am. Bd. Dermatology, 1990. Chair bioethics com. Children's Hosp., San Diego, 2002—07, dir. fellowship tng. program, divsn. pediat. dermatology, 2004—, sect. chief dermatology, 2005—. Clin. prof. pediat. and medicine U. Calif., Sch. Medicine, San Diego, 2001—. Contbr. articles to profl. jours. Named one of Best Doctors in Am., 2004—, 2000 Notable Am. Women, 2005—; recipient Outstanding Tchg. award, U. Calif., Dept Pediat., San Diego, 1997, Best Doctors in San Diego, San Diego County Med. Soc., 2003, 2004, 2006; Skaggs Clin. Rsch. scholar, Scripps Rsch. Inst., 2001. Mem.: Dermatology Found., Am. Acad. Pediat., Soc. Pediat. Dermatology, Am. Acad. Dermatology (mem. ethics com. 2005—07). Office: Children's Specialists #602 8010 Frost St San Diego CA 92123 Home Phone: 858-775-3038; Office Phone: 858-576-1700 ext. 4269. Office Fax: 858-966-4040.

FRIEDMAN, ALAN JACOB, educational association administrator, former museum director; b. Bklyn., Nov. 15, 1942; s. George and Eleanor (Goldberger) F.; m. Mickey Thompson, Dec. 26, 1966. BS in Physics, Ga. Inst. Tech., 1964; PhD in Physics, Fla. State U., 1970. Research asst. Ga. Inst. Tech., Atlanta, 1960-64, Fla. State U., Tallahassee, 1964-69; asst. prof. Hiram (Ohio) Coll., 1969-74; dir. astronomy and physics Lawrence Hall of Sci. U. Calif., Berkeley, 1973-84; conseiller scientifique Cite des Scis. et de l'Industrie, Paris, 1982-84; dir. & CEO NY Hall of Sci., Corona, 1984—2006; apptd. to Nat. Assessment Governing Bd., 2006—. Vis. asst. prof. Am. studies and English Temple U., Phila, 1975; research fellow English dept. U. Calif., Berkeley, 1972-73; vis. lectr. English dept. San Francisco State U., 1974-75. Co-author: Planetarium Educator's Workshop Guide, 1980, Einstein as Myth and Muse, 1985, Planetarium Activities for Student Success, 12 vols., 1993; mem. editorial bd. Jour. Modern Lit. Younger Humanist fellow NEH, 1972-73; recipient Disting. Service award Mid-Atlantic Planetarium Soc., 1982, Merit award Astron. Assn. No. Calif., 1983, AAAS award for pub. understanding of sci. and tech., 1996; named to Centennial Honor Roll, Am. Assn. Museums, 2006. Fellow AAAS, Internat. Planetarium Soc. (Svc. award 1990); mem. Am. Assn. Physics Tchrs., Internat. Planetarium Soc. (pres. 1985-86), Assn. Sci.-Tech. Ctrs. (bd. dirs. 1989-97), Phi Beta Kappa. Office: Nat Assessment Governing Bd Ste 825 800 N Capitol St NW Washington DC 20002-4233*

FRIEDMAN, ALAN ROY, lawyer; b. NYC, Mar. 18, 1953; s. Oscar B. and Helen (Rosenkrantz) F.; m. Maya Memling, Sept. 3, 1978; 1 child, Charles. AB, Hamilton Coll., 1973; JD, Yale U., 1976. Law clk. to Hon. M. Joseph Blumenfeld U.S. Dist. Ct., Hartford, 1976-77; assoc. Kramer Levin Naftalis & Frankel LLP, NYC, 1977-84, ptnr., 1984—. Office: Kramer Levin Naftalis & Frankel LLP 1177 Ave of the Americas New York NY 10036 Office Phone: 212-715-9100. E-mail: afriedman@kramerlevin.com.

FRIEDMAN, ALAN WARREN, humanities educator; b. Bklyn., June 8, 1939; s. Leon and Anne (Markowitz) F.; m. Elizabeth Butler Cullingford, Nov. 22, 1985; children: Eric Lawrence, Scot Bradley, Lorraine Eve, Daniel Butler. Student, U. Edinburgh, Scotland, 1960-61; BA, Queens Coll., 1961; MA, NYU, 1962; PhD, U. Rochester, 1966. Grad. teaching asst. U. Rochester, 1963-64; from instr. English to prof. U. Tex., Austin, 1964—, dir. honors program, 1972-76, chmn. faculty senate, 1987-89, endowed prof., 2001—. Sr. Fulbright prof. U. Lancaster, Eng., 1977-78, Univ. Coll., Galway, Ireland, 1995; exch. prof. Universite Paul Valery, Montpellier, France, 1985, U. Paris, Sorbonne, 2000. Author: Lawrence Durrell and the Alexandria Quartet, 1970, Multivalence: The Moral Quality of Form in the Modern Novel, 1978, William Faulkner, 1984, Fictional Death and the Modernist Enterprise, 1995, Beckett in Black and Red: The Translations for Nancy Cunard's "Negro", 2000, Party Pieces: Oral Storytelling and Social Performance in Joyce and Beckett, 2007; editor books; contbr. essays and revs. to profl. jours. Chair Dem. Precinct Com.; del. state convs.; founder, 1st pres. Neighborhood Assn., Austin, 1973-74; bd. dirs. Peace Edn. Ctr., Hillel Found., Austin Hospice, Frontline Theatre Co. Recipient Fulbright Rsch. award, 1984—85, 1995, Travel award, France, 1990; fellow, NEH, 1970—71. Mem. MLA (del. assembly 1977-79, 82-84, 94-96, exec. com. divsn. on 20th century English lit. 1992-96), AAUP (pres. U. Tex. chpt. 1979-84, nat. coun. 1989-92, nat. exec. com. 1991-92, chair com. governance 1992-95), Tex. Higher Edn. Coord. Bd. (chair faculty adv. com. 1992-95), Tex. Assn. Coll. Tchrs., Nat. Collegiate Honors Coun., Fulbright Alumni Assn. (pres. ctrl. Tex. chpt.), Omicron Delta Kappa. Democrat. Jewish. Office: Univ Tex Dept English 1 Univ Sta B5000 Austin TX 78712 Home Phone: 512-472-0741; Office Phone: 512-471-4991.

FRIEDMAN, ALEXANDER STEPHEN, foundation administrator, investment banker; BA in Politics, Princeton U., NJ; MBA, Columbia U., NYC, JD, 1997. Small-claims ct. and family mediator, NYC; White House fellow US Dept. Def., 1998—99, asst. to sec. for spl. projects; head corp. devel. Medarex; mergers and acquisitions specialist, co-head fin. sponsor group Lazard Freres & Co.; CFO Bill & Melinda Gates Found., Seattle, 2007—. Co-founder Adventa.com; founder, pres. Accelerated Clin.; founder 21st Century Roundtable; cons. Harvard Ctr. Internat. Devel. Founder Climb for the Cure, 1993; bd. mem. Lower Manhattan Cultural Coun., NetAid. Mem.: Coun. Fgn. Rels. Office: Bill & Melinda Gates Found PO Box 23350 Seattle WA 98102 Office Phone: 206-709-3100.*

FRIEDMAN, ANDREW MITCHELL, director housing and neighborhood preservation; b. NYC, Jan. 29, 1950; BA, Antioch U., 1972; MS, U. Wis., 1984. Asst. dir. ARC, Green Bay, Wis., 1982-86; analyst City of Virginia Beach, Va., 1986-89, housing devel. adminstr., 1989-93, dir. housing and neighborhood preservation, 1993—. Mem. allocations com. United Way of South Hampton Roads, Norfolk; past pres. Va. Assn. Housing and Cmty. Devel. Ofcls. Office: City of Virginia Beach Mcpl Ctr Bldg 18A Virginia Beach VA 23456 Office Phone: 757-426-5752. E-mail: afriedma@vbgov.com.

FRIEDMAN, ARNOLD BERNARD, retired pediatrician; b. Cleve., May 13, 1927; s. Harry and Sally Friedman; m. Sally Louise Schwartz, June 21, 1953; children: Joel, Barbara, Howard, Judy, Stuart. BS, Western Res. U., Cleve., 1949; MD, Ohio State U., Columbus, 1953. Cert. Am. Bd. Pediat. Pediat. resident Rainbow Babies Children's Hosp., Cleve., 1953—54, 1954—55, chief resident pediats., 1955—56; chief pediat. Mt. Sinai Hosp., Cleve., 1971—76, cief pediat. outpatient, 1976—98; ret., 1998. Clin. prof. pediat. Case Western Res. U., Cleve., clin. prof. emeritus, 2005; dir. ambulatory pediat. Mt. Sinai Med. Ctr., Cleve., dir. dept. pediat.; pres. No. Ohio Pediat. Soc., Cleve., Ohio chpt. Am. Acad. Pediat. Sgt. US Army, 1946—47, PTO. Home: 27020 Cedar Rd #416 Beachwood OH 44122

FRIEDMAN, ARTHUR DANIEL, electrical engineer, computer scientist, investment company executive, educator; b. Bronx, NY, Apr. 24, 1940; s. Henry and Yetta Friedman; m. Barbara Bernstein, Mar. 31, 1968; children: Michael Kenneth, Steven David. BA, Columbia U., 1961, BS, 1962, MEE, 1963, PhD, 1965. Tech. staff Bell Labs., Murray Hill, NJ, 1965-72; assoc. prof. elec. engring. and computer sci. U. So. Calif., LA, 1972-77; prof. George Washington U., Washington, 1977-97, dept. chmn., 1980-84, prof. emeritus, 1997—. Vis. prof. U. Calif., San Diego, 1999, 2002-04, mem. Chancellor's Assocs., 1999-2005; chmn. bd., co-founder Computer Sci. Press (acquired by WH Freeman Co.), Rockville, Md., 1974-88, co-editor-in-chief, 1988-89; co-founder, pres. investment mgmt. co. ABF Enterprises, 1988—, Friedman Family Found. Inc., ABF Capital Mgmt.; founder, pres. Market Mavens, 1998-2001; gen. ptnr. Potomac Ptnrs. LP, 1991; mem. Aztec Venture Networks, 2000-01, Tech Coast Angels, 1999-2001; mem. TIE 2002-03; mem. adv. com. on elec. engring. San Diego State U., 2003—, mem. adv. com. dept. elec. engring., mem. adv. bd. Entrepreneurial Soc. Author: (with Premanchandra Menon) Fault Detection in Digital Circuits, 1971, Theory and Design of Switching Circuits, 1975, Russian trans., Logical Design of Digital Systems, 1975 (translated into Russian, 1978), Fundamentals of Logic Design and Switching Theory, 1986; (with Melvin Breuer) Diagnosis of Digital Systems, 1976; (with Miron Abramovici and Melvin Breuer) Digital System Testing and Testable Design, 1990, 2d edit., 1995, Chinese trans., 2006. Judge San Diego (Calif.) Sci. and Engring. Fair San Diego State U., judge venture challenge competition, 2002—06; pres. Friedman Family Found. Fellow IEEE. Avocations: reading, swimming, travel, writing, cooking. Home: 4969 Beauchamp Court San Diego CA 92130-2742

FRIEDMAN, AVNER, mathematician, educator; b. Petah-Tikva, Israel, Nov. 19, 1932; arrived in U.S., 1956; s. Moshe and Hanna (Rosenthal) Friedman; m. Lillia Lynn, June 7, 1959; children: Alissa, Joel, Naomi, Tamara. MSc, Hebrew U., Jerusalem, 1954, PhD, 1956. Prof. math. Northwestern U., Evanston, Ill., 1962—85; prof. Purdue U., West Lafayette, Ind., 1985—87, dir. Ctr. Applied Math., 1985—87; prof. math., dir. Inst. Math. and Its Applications U. Minn., Mpls., 1987-97, dir. Minn. Ctr. for Indsl. Math., 1994—2002; prof. Ohio State U., Columbus, 2002—; dir. Math. Bioscis. Inst., 2002—. Author: Generalized Functions and Partial Differential Equations, 1963, Partial Differential Equations of Parabolic Type, 1964, Partial Differential Equations, 1969, Foundations of Modern Analysis, 1970, Advanced Calculus, 1971, Differential Games, 1971, Stochastic Differential Equations and Applications, Vol. 1, 1975, Vol. 2, 1976, Variational Principle's and Free Boundary Problems, 1983, Mathematics in Industrial Problems, 10 vols., 1988—98; author: (with D.S. Ross) Mathematical Models in Photographic Science, 2001; contbr. articles to profl. jours. Recipient Creativity award, NSF, 1983—85, 1990—92; fellow, Sloan Found., 1962—65, Guggenheim, 1966—67. Mem.: NAS, AAAS, Soc. Math. Bioscis. (pres. 2007—), Soc. Indsl. Applied Math. (pres. 1993, 1994, chair bd. math. scis. 1994—97), Am. Math. Soc. Office: Ohio State U Math Dept 231 18th Ave Columbus OH 43210 Home Phone: 614-771-8932; Office Phone: 614-292-5296. Business E-Mail: afriedman@mbi.osu.edu.

FRIEDMAN, BART, lawyer; b. NYC, Dec. 5, 1944; s. Philip and Florence (Beckerman) F.; m. Wendy Alpern Stein, Jan. 11, 1986; children: Benjamin Alpern, Jacob Stein. AB, L.I. U., 1966; JD, Harvard U., 1969. Bar: N.Y. 1970, Mass. 1972. Rsch. fellow Harvard U. Bus. Sch., Cambridge, Mass., 1969-70; assoc. Cahill, Gordon & Reindel LLP, NYC, 1970-72, 77-80, ptnr., 1980—; spl. counsel SEC, Washington, 1974-75, asst. dir., 1975-77. Bd. dirs. Calif. Inst. for the Arts, Sanford Bernstein Mut. Funds, Allied World Assurance Holdings, dep. chmn., 2006—. Mem. Ind. Task Force on Post-Conflict Iraq, 2003—; vis. com. Harvard U. Grad. Sch. Edn., 1995—2001, com. on univ. resources, 1996—2003; trustee Juilliard Sch., 1988—2001, vice chmn., 1994—2001; coun. fgn. rels. Brookings Inst., 1995—, trustee, 1997—, joint task force on resources for fgn. affairs, ind. task force on non-lethal weapons; del. NATO Hdqrs. and Field, 1998, 2003, del. to Libya, 2005; adv. bd. Remarque Inst. NYU, 1997—2002, Internat. Inst. for Strategic Studies, 2000—; bd. dirs. Lincoln Ctr. for Performing Arts, 2002—, trustee, mem. exec. com., 2002—; coun. fgn. rels. Bretton Woods Com., 2003—, Econ. Club; mem. oversight com. Milton Acad. Mountain Sch., 2004—; dir. Sanford Bernstein Family of Mutual Funds, 2005—, Inst. Internat. Edn., 2007—. Mem. Assn. Bar City of N.Y., Coun. Fgn. Rels., Explorers Club, The River Club, Links Club,

The Tuxedo Club, Century Assn., The Met. Club (Washington), Waccabuc Club. Office: Cahill Gordon & Reindel LLP 80 Pine St Fl 17 New York NY 10005-1790 Home Phone: 212-996-4710; Office Phone: 212-701-3304. E-mail: bfriedman@cahill.com.

FRIEDMAN, BARTON ROBERT, language educator; b. Bklyn., Feb. 5, 1935; s. Abraham Isaac and Mazie Diana (Cooper) F.; m. Sheila Lynn Siegel, June 22, 1958; children— Arnold, Jonathan, Daniel, Esther. BA, Cornell U., 1956, PhD (univ. dissertation fellow), 1964; MA, U. Conn., 1958. Instr. Bowdoin Coll., Brunswick, Maine, 1961-63; from instr. to prof. English lit. U. Wis., Madison, 1963-78; prof. English lit. Cleve. State U., 1978-97, chmn. dept. English, 1978-87, prof. emeritus, 1997—. Visitor Psychoanalytic Inst. Cleve. Author: Adventures in the Deeps of the Mind: The Cuchulain Cycle of W.B. Yeats, 1977, You Can't Tell the Players, 1979, Fabricating History: English Writers on the French Revolution, 1988 (Nancy Dasher award for best scholarly book by mem. Coll. English Assn. Ohio 1989); mem. editl. bd. Irish Renaissance Ann., 1980-84, Lit. Monographs, 1970-76. Recipient William Kiekhofer Teaching Excellence award U. Wis., 1967, Disting. Scholar award Cleve. State U., 1990. Mem. MLA, Am. Com. Irish Studies, Coll. English Assn. Ohio (bd. govs. 1980-81), Soc. Lit. and Sci. (bibliographer Bibliography of Lit. and Sci. in Configurations 1996-98), Phi Kappa Phi. Jewish. Home: 2916 E Overlook Rd Cleveland OH 44118-2434 Office: Cleve State Univ Dept English Cleveland OH 44115 Personal E-mail: sheilalf@sbcglobal.net.

FRIEDMAN, BENJAMIN MORTON, economics professor; b. Louisville, Aug. 5, 1944; s. Norbert and Eva (Lipsky) Friedman; m. Barbara Allan Cook, Dec. 17, 1972; children: John Norton, Jeffrey Allan. AB summa cum laude, Harvard U., 1966, AM, 1969, PhD, 1971; MSc King's Coll., Cambridge U., 1970. Economist Morgan Stanley & Co., NYC, 1971-72; asst. prof. econs. Harvard U., Cambridge, Mass., 1972-76, assoc. prof., 1976-80, prof., 1980-89, William Joseph Maier prof. polit. economy, 1989—, chmn. dept. of econs., 1991-94. Dir. fin. markets and monetary econs. Nat. Bur. Econ. Rsch., Cambridge, 1977—93; bd. dirs. Pvt. Export Funding Corp., Ency. Brit., Inc. Author: Economic Stabilization Policy, 1975, Monetary Policy in the United States, 1981, Day of Reckoning, 1988, The Moral Consequences of Economic Growth, 2005; co-author: Does Debt Management Matter?, 1992; editor: New Challenges to the Role of Profits, 1978, The Changing Roles of Debt and Equity in Financing U.S. Capital Formation, 1982, Corporate Capital Structures in the United States, 1985, Financing Corporate Capital Formation, 1986, Handbook on Monetary Economics, 1990; assoc. editor: Jour. Monetary Econs., 1977—95. Trustee Coll. Retirement Equities Fund, NYC, 1978—82, Standish Mellon Investment, 1989—; dir. Nat. Coun. Econ. Edn., 2006—, Am. Friends Cambridge U., 1994—2000. Recipient David Horowitz prize, Bank Israel, 1982, George S. Eccles prize, Columbia U., 1989, John R. Commons award, Omicron Delta Epsilon, 2005; Marshall scholar, Cambridge U., 1966—68, Soc. Fellows Jr. fellow, Harvard U., 1968—71. Mem.: Am. Econ. Assn., Brookings Panel Econ. Activity, Coun. Fgn. Rels., Harvard Club (N.Y.C.). Home: 74 Sparks St Cambridge MA 02138-2238 Office: Harvard U 127 Littauer Center Cambridge MA 02138

FRIEDMAN, BERNARD ALVIN, federal judge; b. Detroit, Sept. 23, 1943; s. David and Rae (Garber) F.; m. Rozanne Golston, Aug. 16, 1970; children: Matthew, Megan. Student, Detroit Inst. Tech., 1962-65; JD, Detroit Coll. Law, 1968. Bar: Mich. 1968, Fla. 1968, US Dist. Ct. (ea. dist.) Mich. 1968, US Ct. Mil. Appeals 1972. Asst. prosecutor Wayne County, Detroit, 1968-71; ptnr. Harrison & Friedman, Southfield, Mich., 1971-78, Lippitt, Harrison, Friedman & Whitefield, Southfield, 1978-82; judge Mich. Dist. Ct. 48th dist., Bloomfield Hills, 1982-88, US Dist. Ct. (ea. dist.) Mich., Detroit, 1988—, chief judge, 2005—. Lt. US Army, 1967-74. Recipient Disting. Service award Oakland County Bar Assn., 1986. Mem.: Oakland County Bar Assn., Mich. Bar Assn. Avocation: running. Office: US Dist Ct US Courthouse Rm 238 231 W Lafayette Blvd Detroit MI 48226-2700

FRIEDMAN, B(ERNARD) H(ARPER), writer; b. NYC, July 27, 1926; s. Leonard and Madeline Friedman; m. Abby Noselson, Mar. 6, 1948; children: Jackson, Daisy. BA, Cornell U., 1948. With Cross & Brown Co., 1949-50; v.p., dir. Uris Bldgs. Corp., NYC, 1950-63; lectr. creative writing Cornell U., 1966-67; staff cons., dir. Fine Arts Work Ctr., Provincetown, Mass., 1968-82. Mem. adv. coun. Cornell U. Coll. Arts and Scis., 1968—83, Herbert F. Johnson Mus., 1972—87. Author: (novels) Circles, 1962, (reprinted as I Need to Love), 1963, Yarborough, 1964, Whispers, 1972, Museum, 1974, Almost A Life, 1975, The Polygamist, 1981, (short stories) Coming Close, 1982, Between the Flags, 1990, Swimming Laps, 1999, (biographies) Jackson Pollock: Energy Made Visible, 1972, Alfonso Ossorio, 1973; author: (with Flora Miller Biddle) Gertrude Vanderbilt Whitney, 1978; author: (memoir) Tripping, 2006, (plays) In Search of Luigi Pirandello, 1983, (revised as My Small Self), 1998, The Critic, 1986, Beauty Business, 1987, Heart of a Boy, 1993, Married Moments, 1999—2006, Eros and Psyche, 2000; author: (with M. Benderoth) (screenplay) Heart of a Boy, 1997; editor: School of New York, 1959, Give My Regards to Eighth Street: Collected Writings of Morton Feldman, 2001; mem. adv. bd. Cornell Rev., 1977—79; contbr. articles to mags., anthologies and reference vols. Trustee Am. Fedn. Arts, 1958—64, Whitney Mus. Am. Art, 1961—, Broida Mus., 1983—86. With USNR, 1944—46. Recipient awards for short stories including Nelson Algren award, 1983; fellow, Camargo Found., 1991. Mem.: PEN, Dramatists Guild, Authors Guild, Century Assn. (N.Y.C.). Home and Office: 439 E 51st St New York NY 10022-6473 Office Phone: 212-755-5723. Personal E-mail: friedmanbhf@aol.com.

FRIEDMAN, CAITLIN, public relations executive; married; 2 children. Segment prodr. TV Food Network; account exec. Kratz & Co. Pub. Relations; publicity mgr. cookbook program Broadway Books; founder Caitlin Friedman Comm., 1999; cofounder (with Kimberly Yorio) YC Media. Co-author (with Kimberly Yorio): The Girl's Guide to Being the Boss (Without Being a Bitch): Valuable Lessons, Smart Suggestions and True Stories for Succeeding as the Chick-in-Charge, 2006 (Quills award business The Quills Literacy Found., 2006). Avocations: reading, tennis, dining out. Office: YC Media Ste 310 547 West 27th St New York NY 10001 Office Phone: 212-609-5009 ext. 1. Office Fax: 212-684-0059.

FRIEDMAN, DANIEL MORTIMER, federal judge; b. NYC, Feb. 8, 1916; s. Henry Michael F. and Julia Freedman Friedman; m. Leah Lipson, Jan. 16, 1955 (dec. Dec. 1969); m. Elizabeth Ellis, Oct. 19, 1975 (dec. June 2002). AB, Columbia U., 1937, LLB, 1940. Bar: N.Y. 1941. Practice law, NYC, 1940—42; with SEC, Washington, 1942—51, Justice Dept., Washington, 1951—59, asst. to solicitor gen., 1959—62, 2d asst. to solicitor gen., 1962—68, 1st dep. solicitor gen., 1968—78; chief judge US Ct. Claims, Washington, 1978; judge US Ct. Appeals (Fed. cir.), Washington, 1982—89, sr. judge, 1989—. With US Army, 1942—46. Recipient Exceptional Svc. award, Atty. Gen., 1969. Office: US Ct Appeals Federal Circuit 717 Madison Pl NW Washington DC 20439-0002*

FRIEDMAN, DEBBIE, singer, songwriter, religious studies educator; b. 1952; With New Reform Congregation, LA, 1984—87; former dir. Chalutzim Hebrew prog. Olin-Sang-Ruby Union Inst., Oconomowac, Wis., co-founder, co-leader Hava Nashira songleading & music workshop, 1992—. Singer: (albums) Sing Unto God, 1972, In the Beginning, 1994, Renewal of Spirit, 1997, You Shall Be a Blessing, 1997, The Journey Continues, 1997, Shirim al Galgalim: Songs on Wheels, 1998, Live at Carnegie Hall, 1999, It's You, 1999, The Alef Bet, 2001, The Water in the Well, 2001, Live at the Del, 2002, Worlds of Your Dreams, 2002, Shanah Tovah, 2002, Light These Lights, 2004, One People, 2006. Recipient Steven S. Wise Jewish Edn. award, Bennett H. Walzer Meml. Judaic Arts award, 1992, 1994, Covenant Found. award, Crown Family Found. & Jewish Edn. Svc. N.Am., 1996, Woman of Valor award, Jewish Fund for Justice, 1997, Myrtle Wreath award, Nassau region of Hadassah, 1997, US/Israel Women to Women award, 2000, Jewish Cultural Achievement in Performing Arts award, Nat. Found. Jewish Culture, 2002, Sherut L'Am award, Kalsman Inst. Hebrew Union Coll.-Jewish Inst. Religion, 2005, Heritage award, 1st Ann. Jewish Music Awards, 2005, Burning Bush award, University Women of U. Judaism, 2006. Mem.: Am. Conf. Cantors (hon.), Nat. Fedn. Temple Youth (hon. life). Jewish. Office: c/o Golden Land Concerts & Connections Ste 605 45 E 33rd St New York NY 10016 also: c/o Sounds Write Prodns Inc PO Box 601084 San Diego CA 92160-1084 Office Phone: 212-683-7816. Office Fax: 212-213-2033. E-mail: concerts@goldenland.com.

FRIEDMAN, DENNIS J., lawyer; b. Sept. 28, 1944; BS, U. Pa., 1966; JD, Georgetown U., 1969. Bar: NY 1970. Mem. Morrison & Foerster, NYC; now ptnr. corp. transactions practice group Gibson Dunn & Crutcher LLP, NYC. Articles editor: Georgetown Law Rev., 1968-69. Office: Gibson Dunn & Crutcher 47th Fl 200 Park Ave New York NY 10166-0193 Office Phone: 212-468-8000, 212-351-3900. Office Fax 212-351-6201. Business E-Mail: dfriedman@gibsondunn.com.

FRIEDMAN, ELI A., nephrologist, educator; b. NYC, Apr. 9, 1933; s. Israel and Ida (Gutman) F.; widowed; children: Amy Louise, Rebecca Alicia, Sara Jo. BS, Bklyn. Coll., 1953; MD, SUNY Downstate Med. Center, 1957; DSc (hon.), Maduri Kamaraj U., India, 1985, L.I. U., 1991. Intern in medicine Harvard Med. Sch., 1957-58; resident in medicine Peter Bent Brigham Hosp., Boston, 1960-61; Am. Heart Assn. rsch. fellow Harvard U., 1958-60; mem. faculty, chief divsn. renal disease Downstate Med. Ctr., Bklyn., 1963—; prof. Health Sci. Ctr. SUNY, Bklyn., 1972—, Disting. Tchg. prof., 1992—, dep. chair dept. medicine, 2003—, chair instnl. rev. bd., 2002—. Bd. dirs. Am. Bur. Med. Aid to China, 1979—, Cleve. Found., 1979—, Bklyn. Neprhology Found., 1978—; Kasperzak lectr. Cleve. Clinic, 1998; Alpha Omega Alpha lectr. SUNY Health Sci. Ctr., Bklyn., 1999; Conrad Pirani lectr. Columbia Coll. Physician and Surgeons, 2000; Helen and Payne Whitney lectr. N. Shore Univ. Hosp., 2001; excellence in dialysis participant, Karachi, Pakistan, 00; mem. faculty masters in nephrology U. Naples, Italy, 2001; rsch. grants coun. reviewer Nat. Natural Sci. Found. of China, 2001; George E. Schreiner lectr. Canisus Coll., Buffalo, 2003; vis. prof. Vanderbilt U., 2002. Author: Acute Renal Failure, 1973, Strategy in Renal Failure, 1978, Diabetic Renal-retinal Syndrome, 1980, Diabetic Renal-retinal Syndrome 3 Therapy, 1986, Diabetic Nephropathy, 1986, Diabetic Renal-retinal Syndrome 4: Management Strategy, 1987; editor: Journal of Diabetic Complications, 1986—. Adv. bd. Nat. Kidney Found. Singapore, 1999. Lt. comdr. USPHS, 1961-63. Named one of Best Drs. in N.Y., N.Y. Mag., 2000—02, 2004, Am.'s Top Drs., 2001, 2002, Best Doctors in Am., 2003; recipient Hoenig award, Nat. Kidney Found., 1986, Silver medal, U. Bologna, 1988, Disting. Svc. to Black Kidney patients award, Howard U., 1989, Physicians award, Am. Assn. Kidney Patients, 1989, Alumni medal, SUNY Downstate Med. Coll., William Dock Master Tchr. award, Alumni Assn. SUNY Health Scis. Ctr., 1992, Recognition award, N.Y. Regional Transplant Program, 1994, Nat. Torchbearer award, Am. Kidney Fund, 1995, Excellence medal, 1996, award, Juvenile Diabetes Found., Bklyn., 1995, Medal of Excellence award, 1996, Torchbearer award, Organ Transplantation and Kidney Disease, 1998, Internat. Torchbearer award, India, 1998, Samuel L. Kountz award, Howard U., 1999, Peter Lundin award, Am. Assn. Kidney Patients, 2001, alumni award in nephrology, Downstate Med. Ctr., 2002, Excellence in Postgrad. Tchg., 2002, Lifetime Achievement award, Alumni Assn. Downstate Med. Ctr., 2007, Internat. Soc. Hemodialysis, 2005, Belding Scribner Lifetime Achievement award, 2006; grantee, NIH, Am. Kidney Fund, N.Y. State Kidney Disease Inst., USPHS, N.Y. Kidney Found. Fellow Explorers Club (1st prize photo competition 1995), Royal Coll. Physicians (hon.); mem. ACP (Master 1996), Am. Soc. Nephrology, Internat. Soc. Nephrology, Am. Soc. Artificial Internal Organs (pres. 1987—, editor Transactions 1985—), Am. Soc. Immunology, Transplantation Soc., Assn. Am. Physicians, Internat. Soc. Artificial Organs (pres. 1986), Italian Soc. Nephrology (hon.), Royal Soc. Medicine Belgium (corrs. mem.), German Soc. Clin. Nephrology (hon., Nils Alwall medal 2003), Internat. Soc. Geriatric Nephrology (pres. 2005). Home: 1049 E 17th St Brooklyn NY 11230-4412 Office: 450 Clarkson Ave Brooklyn NY 11203-2056 Office Phone: 718-270-1584. Personal E-mail: elifriedmn@aol.com. *Achievement is as much a function of unswerving persistence, which is a learned behavior pattern, as it is of intellectual endowment, over which we have no control. Effective individuals, though often very bright, have learned to stick with it even after initial or repetitive failure. All of us lose some or even most of the time indicating the need to extract maximal joy from our wins no matter how infrequent the event.*

FRIEDMAN, EUGENE STUART, lawyer; b. NYC, Apr. 5, 1941; s. Abe and Etta (Fischer) F.; m. Karin L. Mehlem, Feb. 3, 1968; children: Gabrielle, Douglas, Jason. AB, NYU, 1961; LLB, Columbia U., 1964. Bar: N.Y. 1965, U.S. Supreme Ct. 1979. Atty. NLRB, San Francisco, 1965-67; assoc., ptnr. Cohen, Weiss & Simon, NYC, 1968-86; sr. ptnr. Friedman & Wolf, NYC, 1987—. Lectr. Ill. Inst. Continuing Legal Edn., Chgo., 1982-84, NYU Conf. Labor & Practicing Law Inst., N.Y.C., 1983-85; adv. bd. for labor and employment law ctr. NYU Law Sch. Contbr. articles to profl. jours. Active N.Y. State Task Force Plant Closings, N.Y.C., 1984. With USN, 1964-65. Mem. NY State Bar Assn., Assn. of Bar of City of NY (chmn. labor and employment law com. 1987-90), Am. Arbitration Assn. (law com.), NY Gov.-Elect Spitzer Transition Team (labor policy adv. com. 2006). Democrat. Jewish. Avocation: scuba diving. Home: 277 W End Ave New York NY 10023-2604 Office: Friedman & Wolf 1500 Broadway Ste 2300 New York NY 10036-4056

FRIEDMAN, FRANCES, public relations executive; b. NYC, Apr. 8, 1928; d. Aaron and Bertha (Itzkowitz) Fallick; m. Clifford Jerome Friedman, June 17, 1950; children— Kenneth Lee, Jeffrey Bennett. BBA, CCNY, 1948. Dir. pub. rels. Melia Internat., Madrid, NYC, 1971-73; sr. v.p. Lobsenz-Stevens, NYC, 1973-75; exec. v.p. Howard Rubenstein Assocs., NYC, 1975-83; pres., prin. Frances Friedman Assocs., NYC, 1983-84; pres., chmn. bd. dirs. GCI Group Inc., NYC, 1984-91, pub. rels. and editl. cons., 1991-93; mng. dir. L.V. Power & Assoc., Inc., 1993-97; pub. rels. cons. NYC, 1997—. Media cons. White Ho. on Women's Issues, 1995; participant in Vital Voices Confs., Hillary Clinton's program for women in emerging democracies, 1996; feature writer Kenttribune.com, 2003—. Bd. dirs. United Nations Assn. (NW Ct. chpt.), 2003, Morris-Jumel Mansion, 1999-2001, Contemporary Guidance Svcs, 1999, 2001, City Coll. Fund, N.Y.C., 1970-79; mem. adv. bd. League for Parent Edn., N.Y.C., 1961-65; editor South Shore Democratic Newsletter, North Bellmore, N.Y., 1958-61, press sec. N.Y. State Assembly candidate, 1965, N.Y. State Congl. candidate, 1968; officer Manhasset Dem. Club, N.Y., 1965-69; mem. adv. com. N.Y.C. Coun. candidate, 1985. U. New Haven Bartels fellow, 1993. Mem. Pub. Rels. Soc. Am., Women in Comm. (Matrix award for pub. rels. 1989), The Counselors Acad., Pride and Alarm, City Club N.Y. Democrat. Jewish. Home: 30 Appalachian Rd Kent CT 06757-1009 Personal E-mail: ffried2078@aol.com.

FRIEDMAN, GARY, plastic surgeon; BS, MD, Ohio State U. Intern Mt. Zion Hosp., San Francisco; gen. surgery resident Marquette U., Milw.; plastic surgery resident St. Francis Hosp., San Francisco, clin. instr., 1973—98; pvt. practice San Francisco, 1973—. Mem.: AMA (Physician Recognition award in Continuing Med. Edn.), San Francisco Med. Soc., Calif. Soc. Plastic Surgeons, Calif. Med. Assn., Am. Soc. Aesthetic Plastic Surgery, Am. Soc. Plastic & Reconstructive Surgeons. Office: 525 Spruce St San Francisco CA 94118 Office Phone: 415-221-3300. Office Fax: 415-221-1831. E-mail: gdf@sf-plasticsurgeon.com.*

FRIEDMAN, GARY DAVID, epidemiologist; b. Cleve., Mar. 8, 1934; s. Howard N. and Cema C. F.; m. Ruth Helen Schleien, June 22, 1958; children: Emily, Justin, Richard. Student, Antioch Coll., 1951-53; BS in Biol. Sci., U. Chgo., 1956, MD with honors, 1959; MS in Biostats., Harvard Sch. Pub. Health, 1965. Diplomate Am. Bd. Internal Medicine. Intern, resident Harvard Med. Svcs., Boston City Hosp., 1959-61; 2d yr. resident Univ. Hosps. Cleve., 1961-62; med. officer heart disease epidemiology study Nat. Heart Inst., Framingham, Mass., 1962-66; chief epidemiology unit, field and tng. sta., heart disease ctrl. program USPHS, San Francisco, 1966-68; sr. epidemiologist divsn. rsch. Kaiser Permanente Med. Care Program, Oakland, Calif., 1968-76, asst. dir. epidemiology and biostats., 1976-91, dir., 1991-98, sr. investigator, 1998-99, adj. investigator, 1999—; cons. prof. Dept. Health Rsch. and Policy Stanford U. Sch. Medicine, 1998—. Rsch. fellow, then rsch. assoc. preventive medicine Harvard Med. Sch., 1962-66; lectr. dept. biomed. and environ. health scis., sch. pub. health U. Calif. Berkeley, 1968-95; lectr. epidemiology and biostats. U. Calif. Sch. Medicine, San Francisco, 1980-2000, asst. clin. prof. 1967-75, assoc. clin. prof., 1975-92 depts. medicine and family and cmty. medicine; US-USSR working group sudden cardiac death NHLBI, 1975-82, com. on epidemiology and veterans follow-up studies Nat. Rsch. Coun., 1980-85, subcom. on twins, 1980-94, epidemiology and disease ctrl. study sect. NIH, 1982-86, US Preventive Svcs. Task Force, 1984-88, scientific rev. panel on toxic air contaminants State of Calif., 1988—, adv. com. Merck Found./Soc. Epidemiol. Rsch., Clin. Epidemiology Fellowships, 1990-94; sr. advisor expert panel on preventive svcs. USPHS, 1991-96; mem. instl. rev. bd. Kaiser Permamente, 1997—. Author: Primer of Epidemiology, 1974, 5th edit. 2004; assoc. editor, then editor Am. Jour. Epidemiology, 1988-96, 99—; mem. editl. bd. HMO Practice, 1991-98, Jour. Med. Screening, 1997—; contbr. over 300 articles to profl. jours., chpts. to books; composer: Autumn for oboe and piano (First prize Composers Today Competition Music Tchrs. Assn. Calif. 1999), Fugue for Four Winds (Second prize Music Tchrs. Assn. Calif. 2000). Oboist San Francisco Civic Symphony, 1990—, Symphony Parnassus, 1994-2004, Bohemian Club Band, 1994—, Coll. Marin Orch., 2004—; bd. dirs. Chamber Musicians No. Calif., Oakland, 1991-98. Sr. surgeon USPHS, 1962-68. Recipient Roche award for Outstanding Performance as Med. Student; Merit grantee Nat. Cancer Inst., 1987, Outstanding Investigator grantee, 1989, 94; named to Disting. Alumni Hall of Fame Cleve. Heights High Sch., 1991. Fellow Am. Heart Assn. (chmn. com. on criteria and methods 1969-71, chmn. program com. 1973-76, coun. epidemiol.), Am. Coll. Physicians; mem. APHA, Am. Epidemiol. Soc. (mem. com. 1982-86, pres. 1999-2000), Am. Soc. Preventive Oncology, Internat. Epidemiol. Assn., Soc. Epidemiologic Rsch. (exec. com. 1998-2001), Med. Biol. Alumni Assn. U. Chgo. (Disting. Svc. award 2000), Phi Beta Kappa, Alpha Omega Alpha, Delta Omega. Achievements include research on cancer, cardiovascular disease, gallbladder disease, effects of smoking, alcohol and medicinal drugs, evaluation of health screening tests. Office: Stanford U Sch Medicine Dept Health Rsch and Policy Redwood Bldg Rm T210 Stanford CA 94305-5405 E-mail: gdf@stanford.edu.

FRIEDMAN, GEORGE, lawyer; b. Bronx, NY, Apr. 18, 1934; m. Vivian Friedman; children: Anthony, Paul. BA, U. Vt., 1956; LLB, NYU, 1959. Bar: NY 1960, US Dist. Ct. So. & Ea. Districts NY 1960. Assoc. Kronish & Lieb, 1959—64; gen. practitioner pvt. practice, 1964—94; mem. NY State Assembly, 1977—94; justice NY State Supreme Court 12th Jud. Dist., 1995—2002; ptnr. Wilson, Elser, Moskowitz, Edelman & Dicker LLP, NYC. Bronx Dem. County Leader, 1986—94; mem. Dem. Nat. Com., 1988—94; commr. NY State Commn. of Investigation, 2002—; mem. Commn. to Promote Pub. Confidence in Jud. Elections, 2003—04. Mem.: Assn. Supreme Ct. Justices of the City of NY, NY State Assn. Supreme Ct. Justices. Office: Wilson Elser Moskowitz Edelman & Dicker LLP 23rd Fl 150 E 42nd St New York NY 10017-5639 Office Phone: 212-490-3000 ext. 2666. Office Fax: 212-490-3038. Business E-Mail: friedmang@wemed.com. E-mail: george.friedman@wilsonelser.com.

FRIEDMAN, GEORGE JERRY, aerospace engineering executive; b. NYC, Mar. 22, 1928; s. Sander and Ruth (Oberlander) F.; m. Ruthanne Goldstein, Sept. 7, 1953; children— Sanford, Gary, David BS, U. Calif.-Berkeley, 1949; MS, UCLA, 1956, PhD, 1967. Registered profl. mech. engr., controls engr., Calif. Mech. engring. assoc. Dept. Water and Power, Los Angeles, 1949-56; devel. engr. Servo Mechanisms, Hawthorne, Calif., 1956-60; v.p. Northrop Corp., Los Angeles, 1960-94; exec. v.p., rsch. dir. Space Studies Inst., Princeton, NJ, 1994—. Mem. indsl. adv. group NATO, Brussels, 1977-78; guest lectr. UCLA, 1983—, Calif. State U., Northridge, 1983—, dir. trust fund, 1984-89; cons. to sci. adv. bd. USAF, Washington, 1985—, bd. govs. Aerospace and Elec. Sys. Soc., L.A., 1985—, v.p. publs., 1999-2001; adj. prof. U. So. Calif., L.A., 1994—; pres. Internat. Coun. on Sys. Engring., 1994, fellow 1998. Contbr. articles to profl. jours. Served as pfc. U.S. Army, 1950-52 Recipient Engring. Excellence award San Fernando Valley Engring. Council, 1983 Fellow IEEE (Baker award 1970), AIAA (assoc.; chmn. planetary def. subcom. 1995-97); mem. Am. Def. Preparedness Assn. (exec. com., preparedness award 1985). Democrat. Jewish. Home and Office: 5084 Gloria Ave Encino CA 91436-1529 E-mail: gfriedma@usc.edu.

FRIEDMAN, GERALD MANFRED, geologist, educator; b. Berlin, July 23, 1921; came to US, 1946, naturalized, 1950; s. Martin and Frieda (Cohn) F.; m. Sue Tyler Theilheimer, June 27, 1948; children: Judith Fay Friedman Rosen, Sharon Mira Friedman Azaria, Devorah Paula Friedman Zweibach, Eva Jane Friedman Scholle, Wendy Tamar Friedman Spanier. BSc, U. London, 1945, DSc, 1977; MA, Columbia U., 1950, PhD, 1952; DSc (hon.), U. Heidelberg, Fed. Republic Germany, 1986. Agrl. laborer, England, 1938-39; baker, 1940-42; internee Brit. Army, 1940; lectr. Chelsea Coll., London, 1944-45; analytical chemist J. Lyons & Co., 1945—46, E.R. Squibb & Sons (now Bristol-Myers Squibb), New Brunswick, 1946—49; asst. geology Columbia U., 1950; temp. geologist NY State Geol. Survey, 1950; from instr. to asst. prof. geology U. Cin., 1950-54; cons. geologist Sault Ste. Marie, Ont., Canada, 1954-56; from sr. rsch. scientist to supr. sedimentary geology rsch. Pan Am. Petroleum Corp. (now BP) and Amoco Corp., 1956-64; Fulbright vis. prof. geology Hebrew U., Jerusalem, 1964; prof. geology Rensselaer Poly. Inst., 1964-84, prof. emeritus, 1984—; prof. geology Bklyn. Coll., 1984—88, Disting. prof. geology, 1988—2004, Disting. prof. geology emeritus, 2004, grad. dep., 2000—02; prof. earth and environ. sci. Grad. Sch. CUNY, 1984—88, disting. prof. earth and environ. sci., 1988—2004, disting. prof. emeritus, 2004—, dep. exec. officer, 1992-94; pres. Gerry Exploration Inc., 1982-88. Rsch. sci. Hudson Labs., Columbia, 1965-69, rsch. assoc. dept. geology Lamont Geol. Obs., 1968-73; vis. prof. U. Heidelberg, 1967; cons. sci. Inst. Petroleum Rsch. and Geophysics, Israel, 1967-71; lectr. Oil & Gas Cons. Internat., 1968-98; pres. Northeastern Sci. Found. Inc., 1979—; vis. scientist Geol. Survey of Israel, 1970-73, 78; mem. Com. Sci. Soc. Pres., 1974-76; Gerald M. Friedman fellow Inst. Earth Sci., Hebrew U., Israel, 1990—; vis. prof. Martin-Luther-Univ., Halle-Wittenberg, Germany, 1998. Co-author: Principles of Sedimentology (Outstanding Acad. Books, Choice, 1978/79), 1978, Exploration for Carbonate Petroleum Reservoirs, 1982, Exercises in Sedimentology, 1982, Principles of Sedimentary Deposits: Stratigraphy and Sedimentology, 1992, Gas-Storage Assessment For New York State Principles and Practices, 2002, Discoveries of the 20th Century, 2005, SaxaLoquntur (Rocks Speak): The Life and Times of the Geologist, 2006; pub. Northeastern Environ. Sci., 1982-90; editor: Jour. Sedimentary Petrology (now Jour. Sedimentary Rsch.), 1964-70 (Best Paper award 1961, hon. mention 1964, 66, Twenhofel medal 1997),

Northeastern Geology (now Northeastern Geology and Environ. Sci.), 1979—, Earth Sci. History, 1982-93, Carbonates and Evaporites, 1986—, 10th Internat. Congress on Sedimentology, 1978, Oil Industry History, 1999-2003; sect. co-editor: Chem. Abstracts (Mineral. and Geol. Chemistry), 1962-69, abstractor, 1952-69; editl. bd. Jour. Geol. Edn., 1951-55, Sedimentary Rsch., 1967-95, Israel Jour. Earth Sci., 1971-76, Coral Reef Newsletter, 1973-75, Jour. Geology, 1977—, GeoJour., 1977-83, Facies, 1987—2004; mng. editor Sedimentology for Earth Sci. Revs., 1992-2005; contbg. co-editor: Carbonate Sedimentology in Central Europe, 1968, Hypersaline Ecosystems: The Gavish Sabkha, 1985, editor, contbr.: Depositional Environments in Carbonate Rocks, 1969; co-editor: Modern Carbonate Environments, 1983, Lecture Notes in Earth Sci., 1985—; founding editor: Earth Sci. History, 1982, hon. life mem.; contbr. articles to profl. jour.; patentee in field. Phys. edn. com., judo instr. Tulsa YMCA, 1958-64, chmn. awards com., 1962-64; adviser, instr. Judo Club, Rensselaer Poly. Inst., 1964-84; bd. dirs. Troy Jewish Cmty. Coun., 1966-72, 74-77; v.p. Temple Beth El, 1986-89, pres., 1989-91, bd. dir., 1965-76; bd. dirs. Leo Baeck Inst., NYC, 1986-2005; v.p., chmn. pub. com. Drake Well Found., 1998-2003, v.p., 2002—. Recipient award for devoted svc. Tulsa YMCA, 1963, Hon. West Virginian award, 1998, Hollis D. Hedberg award in energy Inst. for the Study Earth and Man, So. Meth. U., 2004, Disting. Svc. award SEPM, 2004; named hon. alumnus dept. geology Bklyn. Coll., 1989; grantee Office Naval Rsch., AEC, Dept. Energy, Petroleum Rsch. Fund, NY Gas Assn., NY State Energy Rsch. and Devel. Authority. Fellow: AAAS (councillor 1979—80), Soc. Econ. Geologists, N.Y. Acad. Sci. (vice chair geol. sci. sect. 1993—94, chmn. 1994—96, chair geol. sci. sect. 1997—2001), Geol. Assn. Can., Geol. Soc. London (life, chartered geologist, hon. fellow 1996), Mineral Soc. Am. (nominating com. fellows 1967—69, awards com. 1977—78), Mineral Soc. Gt. Britain, Geol. Soc. Am. (sr. chmn. sect. program com. 1969, publ. com. 1980—82, chmn. overseas pub. rels. com. internat. divsn. 1996—97, chair history geology divsn. 1999—2000, chair history geology awards com. 2000—01, Mary Rabbit History Geology award 2005, Lawrence L. Sloss Sedimentary Geology award 2006); mem.: Kodokan, Cin. Mineral Soc., N.Y. State Mus.-N.Y. State Geol. Survey (James Hall medal 1997), N.Y. State Geol. Assn. (pres. 1978—79, bd. dirs. 1979—84), Geosci. Info. Soc. (mem. membership com. 1983—85), Assn. Earth Sci. Editors (v.p. 1970—71, pres. 1971—72, Outstanding Editorial Pub. Contributions Award 1993), Nat. Assn. Geosci. Tchr. (nat. treas. 1951—55, assoc. editor Jour. of Geosci. Edn. 1953—55, pres. Okla 1962—63, pres. Ea. sect. 1983—84, Disting. Svc. Award 2001), Serbian Yugoslavian Geol. Soc., Internat. Assn. Sedimentologists (v.p. 1971—75, pres. 1975—78), Geologists' Assn., Am. Geol. Inst. (governing bd. 1971—72, 1974—75, Legendary Geoscientist 2005), New Eng. Intercollegiate Geol. Conf., Capital Dist. Geologists Assn. (chmn. program 1966—73), Hudson-Mohawk Profl. Geologists Assn. (bd. dirs. 1995—2001, chmn. program com. 1997—2001), Paleontol. Soc., Soc. for Sedimentary Rsch. (sect. pres. pro tem 1966—67, sect. pres. 1967—68, nat. pres. 1974—75, Best Paper award Gulf Coast sect. 1974, Disting. Svc. award 2004), Am. Assn. Petroleum Geologists (chmn. carbonate rock com. 1965—69, rsch. com. 1965—71, chmn. Persian Gulf liaison com. 1968—70, marine geology com. 1970—74, Disting. lectr. 1972—73, adv. coun. 1974—75, rsch. com. 1976—82, ho. of dels. 1977—80, sec. treas. 1980—81, alt. del. 1980—83, sect. pres 1982—83, vis. geologists program com. 1982—85, membership com. 1982—87, div. profl. affairs rep. from Eastern sect. 1983—84, com. on convs. 1984—85, nat. v.p. 1984—85, ho. of dels. 1984—87, chmn. sect. awards com. 1989—92, nat. hon. mem. 1990, ho. of dels. 1991—93, alt. del. 1993—98, sect. chmn. tech. program com. 1994—95, chair standing com. hist. petroleum geology 2000—01, ho. of dels. 2002—05, 2003—, John T. Galey Meml. Award medal 1993, Disting. Educator award 1996, Nat. Disting. Svc. award 1998, Sidney Powers Meml. award 2000, Divsn. Environ. Scis. Tchg. award 2001, award for excellence and dedication in tchg. environ. geology 2001), History of the Earth Sci. Soc. (hon.; co-founder 1981), Geol. Soc. Israel (hon.), Indian Assn. Sedimentologists (hon.; mem. governing coun. 1978—82), Geol. Vereinigung, Deutsche Geol. Gesellschaft, Soc. Venezolana Historia Geociencias (corr.), Soc. Venezolana Historia Geociencias (corr.; internat. corr. mem.), Am. Chem. Soc. (group leader 1962—63), Am. Inst. Profl. Geologists (cert.), Russian Acad. Nat. Sci. US sect. (Kapitsa Gold medal of honor 1996), Empire State Judo Assn., Okla. Judo Fedn. (pres 1959—60, v.p. 1961—64), Amateur Athletic Union (judo com. 1963), U.S. Judo Fedn. (San Dan, cert. judo tchr.), Honorable Ky. Cols., Sigma Xi, Sigma Gamma Epsilon (nat. pres. 1982—86, 1999—2005). Home: 32 24th St Troy NY 12180-1915 Business E-Mail: gmfriedman@thesciencefoundation.com.

FRIEDMAN, GREGORY H., energy administrator; BBA, Temple U.; MBA, Fairleigh Dickinson U. Sr. auditor U.S. Army Audit Agy., 1968-74; dep. dir. Office of Contingency Planning, FEA, Washington, 1974-80, assoc. dir. Gasoline Rationing Implementation Office, 1980-82; with Office of Insp. Gen. Dept. of Energy, Washington, 1982—, dep. asst. insp. gen. for audit ops., 1985-94, dep. insp. gen. for audit svcs., 1994-97, prin. dep. insp. gen., 1997-98, acting insp. gen., 1998, insp. gen., 1998—. Guest lectr. audit matters and govtl. affairs Princeton U., George Washington U. Office: Dept of Energy Insp Gen 1000 Independence Ave SW Washington DC 20585-0002

FRIEDMAN, HAROLD EDWARD, lawyer; b. Cleve., Apr. 7, 1934; s. Joseph and Mary (Schreibman) F.; m. Nancy Schweid, Aug. 20, 1961; children: Deborah, Jay, Susan. BS, Ohio State U., 1956; LL.B., Case Western Res U., 1959. Bar: Ohio 1960. Practiced in, Cleve., since 1960; ptnr. Simon, Haiman, Gutfeld, Friedman & Jacobs, 1967-80, Ulmer & Berne, 1981—; chair real property practice group. Sec., trustee Harry K. and Emma R. Fox Charitable Found.; pres. Jewish Vocat. Svcs., Cleve.; pres. Internat. Assn. Jewish Vocat. Svcs.; pres. Cleve. Hillel Found.; vice chmn. endowment fund Jewish Cmty. Fedn. Cleve., bd. dirs.; pres. Metro Health Found.; bd. dirs. Bur. Jewish Edn., Jewish Convalescence and Rehab. Ctr., Big Bros. Greater Cleve., Jewish Cmty. Fedn. Cleve., Jewish Family Svc. Assn., YES, Inc., Bellefaire/Jewish Children's Bur. Recipient Kane Leadership award Jewish Community Fedn. Cleve., 1974 Mem. ABA, Ohio Bar Assn., Cleve. Bar Assn., Oakwood Country Club. Home: 23149 Laureldale Rd Cleveland OH 44122-2101 also: 1660 W 2nd St Cleveland OH 44113-1454 Office Phone: 216-583-7130, 216-583-7130. Personal E-mail: hedwfried@aol.com. Business E-Mail: hfriedman@ulmer.com.

FRIEDMAN, HARVEY MICHAEL, infectious diseases educator; b. Montreal, May 29, 1944; came to U.S., 1971; s. Sidney and Sybil (Garfinkle) F.; m. Cynthia Diane Mickey, Apr. 12, 1980; children: Lisa, Steven, Julie. BS, McGill U., 1965, MD, 1969. Cert. in internal medicine 1975, in infectious diseases 1976. Intern, resident Jewish Gen. Hosp., Montreal, 1969-71; fellow in virology Wistar Inst., Phila., 1971-73; fellow in infectious disease U. Pa. Hosp., Phila., 1973-75; asst. prof., assoc. prof. Med. Sch. U. Pa., Phila., 1975-91, prof. Med. Sch., 1991—. Med. dir. Clin. Virology Lab. Children's Hosp., Phila., 1975—96; chief infectious diseases U. Pa., 1990—, dir. Penn-Botswana Program, 2001—. Contbr. numerous papers and book chpts. Grantee NIH, Found., 1978—. Fellow: Infectious Disease Soc. Am.; mem.: AAAS, Am. Clin. and Climatological Assn., Assn. Am. Physicians, Am. Soc. Clin. Investigation. Achievements include description of novel mechanisms used by herpes simplex virus glycoproteins that favor virus escape from immune attack. Office: U Pa Med Sch 502 Johnson Pavilion Philadelphia PA 19104-6073

FRIEDMAN, HOWARD W., retired real estate company executive; b. Bklyn., Aug. 21, 1925; s. Harry and Bertha (Wang) F.; m. Lee Hazan, Mar. 22, 1952; children: Ira, Debra, Patti, Jane. BBA, CCNY, 1945. CPA, N.Y. Treas. Amrep Corp., NYC, 1961-68, pres., 1968-77, chmn., chief exec. officer, 1980-91, cons., 1992-94. Mem. N.Y. State Soc. CPAs. Jewish.

FRIEDMAN, IRA HUGH, surgeon; b. NYC, July 17, 1933; s. Leonard Seymour and Ruth (Binder) F.; m. Erika Berger, Oct. 22, 1961; children: Richard Lawrence, Joanne Beth BA, NYU, 1953, MD, 1957. Diplomate Am. Bd. Surgery, Nat. Bd. Med. Examiners. Intern, resident in surgery Beth Isreal Med. Ctr., NYC, 1957-59, 61-63; surg. resident Bellevue Hosp., NYC, 1959-60; practice medicine specializing in surgery NYC, 1963—. Attending surgeon Beth Israel Med. Ctr., pres. med. bd., 1981-82; assoc. clin. prof. surgery Albert Einstein Coll. Medicine; med. adv. to N.Y.C. dir. SSS, 1968. Contbr. articles to profl. jours. Bd. dirs. Union Orthodox Jewish Congregations Am., Am. Com. for Shaare Zedek Hosp. of Jerusalem, Yeshiva Sha-alvim, Israel; pres. P'Tach; co-chmn. bd. dirs. Yeshiva Chofetz Chaim, N.Y.C. Recipient Koach award Israel Bond Orgn., 1977; N.Y. Heart Assn. fellow, 1960-61 Fellow ACS (elected gov. 1996), Am. Coll. Gastroenterology, Am. Soc. Colon and Rectal Surgeons, Royal Soc. Medicine; mem. AMA, N.Y. Acad. Medicine, N.Y. Surg. Soc., Soc. Surgery of Alimentary Tract, Soc. Am. Gastrointestinal Endoscopic Surgeons, Am. Gastroent. Assn., Am. Soc. Gen. Surgeons, Am. Hernia Soc., Am. Soc. Breast Surgeons, N.Y. Gastroent. Assn., N.Y. Cancer Soc., N.Y. Soc. Colon and Rectal Surgeons, Collegium Internationale Chirugiae Digestive, N.Y. State Med. Assn., N.Y. County Med. Assn. Home: 1175 Park Ave New York NY 10128-1211

FRIEDMAN, J. ROGER, publisher; b. NYC, Oct. 26, 1933; s. Arnold Darcy and Judith (Scheinberg) F.; m. Patricia Mosle, Dec. 1, 1962; children: Amanda, Randall. BA in English, Williams Coll., 1955. Salesman Chain Store Age, Drug Edits., NYC, 1957—81; founder, sales mgr. Discount Store News, NYC, 1961—63, publ. dir., 1963—65; v.p. sales Lebhar-Friedman, Inc., NYC, 1965—68, exec. v.p., 1968—70, pres., 1970—; sec. Chain Store Guide, NYC, 1970—; pres. Dowden Health Media, Inc., 2006—; dir. Ediciones y Estudios, Madrid. Bd. dirs. Upper Pecos Assn., N.Mex., 1971, pres., 1997—; bd. dirs. Students in Free Enterprise, Am. Bus. Press; trustee, chmn. Bus. Press Ednl. Found., McElvain Oil & Gas Co., audit com.; hon. trustee Temple Rodeph Shalom, N.Y.C., 1987. Mem. Lotos (pres. 1983-87), Williams (N.Y.C.) (pres. 1991-95, hon. bd.). Office: Lebhar-Friedman Inc 425 Park Ave New York NY 10022-3549 Office Phone: 212-756-5000.

FRIEDMAN, JAMES DENNIS, lawyer; b. Dubuque, Iowa, Jan. 11, 1947; s. Elmer J. and Rosemary Catherine (Stillmunks) F.; children: Scott, Ryan, Andrea, Sean. AB in Polit. Sci., Marquette U., 1969; JD, U. Notre Dame, 1972. Bar: Wis. 1972, U.S. Ct. Appeals (D.C. cir.) 1973, U.S. Ct. Appeals (7th cir.) 1976, U.S. Supreme Ct. 1978, U.S. Ct. Appeals (6th cir.) 1989, Ill. 1996, U.S. Tax Ct. 1997. Pvt. practice, Milw., 1972—81; ptnr. Quarles & Brady, LLP, Milw., 1981—. Presenter in field; mem. legis. coun. spl. study com. on regulation of fin. instns. State of Wis., 1986-87; bd. dirs. Concours Motors, Inc., Wis. Equal Justice Fund, Inc., pres., 2007—; mem. Wis. Dept. Fin. Instns. task force on fin. competitiveness 2005, State of Wis., 2000; mem., vice chair State of Wis. Supreme Ct., Office of Lawyer Regulation Preliminary Rev. Com., 2000-07; mem. Gov.'s Adv. Coun. on Jud. Selection of the State of Wis., Ozaukee County, 2002. Mng. editor: Notre Dame Law Rev., 1971—72; contbr. articles to profl. jours. Alderman 4th and 7th dists. Mequon, Wis., 1979-85, pres. common coun., 1980-82, bd. ethics 1996-98, 2000—, chair blue ribbon visioning com. 1998-99; bd. dirs. Weyenrg, Pub. Libr. Found. Inc., 1983—, pres., 1984—; bd. dirs. Ptnrs. Advancing Values in Edn. Inc., 1987—, Wis. Law Found., 1998—, pres., 2007—; bd. visitors Marquette U. Ctr. for Study of Entrepreneurship, Milw., 1987-95; bd. dirs. Ozaukee Family Svcs., 1983-99, sec., 1993-98; bd. dirs. Notre Dame Club of Milw., 1984-88, sec., 1978, v.p., 1986-88; bd. dirs. Marquette Club of Milw., 1987-88; chair attys. unit United Way Fund Dr. Greater Milw., 1987. Named Outstanding Sr., Coll. Liberal Arts, Marquette U., 1969, Wis. Leader in the Law, Wis. Law Jour., 2006, Wis. Super Lawyer Law & Politics, 2006, 07. Life fellow Wis. Law Found., Am. Bar Found.; mem. ABA (banking law com. sect. bus. law), State Bar Wis. (chair bd. govs. 1999-2000, chair exec. com. 1999-2000, fin. com. 1997-98, strategic planning task force 1997-98, leadership devel. com. 2004-07, bd. govs. 1996-2000, exec. com. 1998-2000, internat. transactions sect. bd. dirs. 1984-99, sec. and chair-elect 1988-89, chair 1989-90, del. to ABA Ho. of Dels. 1980-82, standing com. on adminstrn. justice and judiciary 1979-81, legal edn. and bar admissions com. 1984-89, com. on minority lawyers 1992-99, chmn. 1997-1999, bd. dirs. young lawyers divsn. 1978-82, chmn. bar admission stds. and requirements com. 1979, So. Regional chair capital fund campaign 1998-99), Milw. Bar Assn., Wis. Acad. Trial Lawyers (bd. dirs. 1980-82), Wis. Bankers Assn., Milw. Country Club. Roman Catholic. Avocations: tennis, golf. Office: Quarles & Brady LLP 411 E Wisconsin Ave Ste 2040 Milwaukee WI 53202-4497 Office Phone: 414-277-5735. Business E-Mail: jdf@quarles.com.

FRIEDMAN, JAMES MOSS, lawyer; b. Cleve., Aug. 1, 1941; s. Senor I. and Rose L. (Moskowitz) F.; m. Ruth E. Aidlin, Aug. 2, 1964; children: Laura M., Seth M. AB, Dartmouth Coll., 1963; JD, Harvard U., 1966. Bar: Ohio 1966, U.S. Ct. Appeals (6th cir.) 1966, U.S. Dist. Ct. (no. dist.) Ohio 1967. Law clk. U.S. Ct. Appeals, 6th Cir., 1966-67; assoc. Gottfried, Ginsberg, Guren & Merritt, Cleve., 1967-71; chief staff Ohio Gov. John J. Gilligan, Columbus, 1971-72; ptnr. Guren, Merritt, Feibel, Sogg & Cohen, Cleve., 1972-84, Benesch, Friedlander, Coplan & Aronoff, Cleve., 1984—. Chmn. Ohio Civil Rights Commn., 1972-74; dir. Overseas Pvt. Investment Corp., Washington, 1978-82; spl. counsel Ohio Atty. Gen., Cleve., 1983-94. Co-author: The Silent Alliance, 1984. Mem. Am. Jewish Com., 1981—; vice chmn. nat. fin. coun. Dem. Nat. Com., 1975—85; pres. Fedn. for Cmty. Planning, Cleve., 1989—92; bd. dirs. United Way Svcs., Cleve., 1989—92, Cuyahoga C.C. Found., 1989—95, Citizens League Greater Cleve., 1989—95, v.p., 1993—95; pres. Fairmount Temple, 1993—96; pres. Cleve. chpt. Am. Jewish Com., 1991—93; mem. nat. bd. trustees Union for Reform Judaism, 1991—, mem. exec. com., 1997—. Jewish. Office: Benesch Friedlander 200 Public Sq Ste 2300 Cleveland OH 44114-2378

FRIEDMAN, JAMES WINSTEIN, economist, educator; b. Cleve., Sept. 25, 1936; s. Theodore and Gertrude (Winstein) F.; m. Marcia Sherman, Aug. 11, 1957; children: Nancy Elizabeth, Robert U. Student, MIT, 1954-56; BA, U. Mich., 1959; MA, Yale U., 1960, PhD, 1963; doctorate (hon.), U. Paris, 2004. Instr., then asst. prof. econs. Yale U., 1963-68; assoc. prof. U. Rochester (N.Y.), 1968-72, prof. econs., 1972-83; prof. Va. Poly Inst., Blacksburg, 1983-85; Kenan prof. U. N.C., Chapel Hill, 1985-2001, Kenan prof. emeritus, 2001—. Mem. rsch. staff Cowles Found., 1963-68, asst. dir., 1964-66; vis. prof. U. Bielefeld, Fed. Republic Germany, 1976, 87-88, Hebrew U., Jerusalem, 1979, Cath. U. Louvain, Belgium, 1987, 91, 99, U. Paris, 1991, 93, 2000, U. Alicante, Spain, 1992, U. Kobe, Japan, 1994. Author: Oligopoly and the Theory of Games, 1977, The Theory of Oligopoly, 1983, Game Theory with Applications to Economics, 1986, 2d edit., 1990; co-author: An Experiment in Noncooperative Oligopoly, 1979; editor: Problems of Coordination in Economic Activity, 1994; assoc. editor Japanese Econ. Rev., 1994—2005, Regional Sci. and Urban Econs., 1997-2005, Games and Econ. Behavior, 1998—2005; contbr. articles to profl. jours. Fellow Econometric Soc. (assoc. editor jour. 1975-81), Game Theory Soc. Avocations: cooking, reading.

FRIEDMAN, JANE, publishing executive; BA in English, NYU, 1967. Joined Random House, 1968, with publicity dept., exec. v.p. Knopf Pub. Group, pub. Vintage Books, founder, pres. Random House Audio, exec. v.p. Random House Inc., mem. exec. com.; pres., CEO HarperCollins, NYC, 1997—. Co-chair pub. divsn., vice chair entertainment, media and comms. divsn. UJA; mem. Am. adv. com. Jerusalem Internat. Book Fair; chmn. bd. dirs., adv. com. Assn. Am. Pubs.; bd. dirs. Poets and Writers; adv. com. Literacy Ptnrs., Yale U. Press. Named Person of Yr., LMP, 1999, Person of Yr., Publishers Weekly, 2006; named one of 200 Women Legends, Leaders and Trailblazers, Vanity Fair, 1998, N.Y.'s 100 Most Influential Women in Bus., Crain's N.Y. Bus., 1999, Am.'s 100 Most Important Women, Ladies Home Jour., 1999, 101 Most Important People in Entertainment, Entertainment Weekly, 1999—2002, 50 Women to Watch, Wall St. Jour., 2006; recipient Matrix award, Women Who Change the World, 2001. Office: HarperCollins 10 E 53rd St New York NY 10022-5299*

FRIEDMAN, JARED, realtor; b. Ariz. BSBA in Fin., No. Ariz. U., Flagstaff, 1999, BSBA in Mgmt., 2000—00. Gri Nat. Assn. Realtors, Ariz., 2006. Realtor West USA Realty, Scottsdale, Ariz., 2003—06, Global Network Homes, Scottsdale, 2006—. Mem.: Mensa (life). Avocations: travel, climbing, photography. Personal E-mail: jaredfriedman@hotmail.com.

FRIEDMAN, JEFFREY J., lawyer; b. Perth Amboy, NJ, Aug. 14, 1956; BA, Franklin & Marshall Coll., 1978; JD cum laude, Villanova U., 1981. Bar: NY 1982, NJ 1982, US Ct. Appeals, 2nd and 3rd Cir., US Dist. Ct., NJ, US Dist. Ct., Ea. Dist. Mich., US Dist. Ct., Ea. and So Dist. NY, US Supreme Ct. Ptnr., mem. Bankruptcy, Reorganization and Creditors' Rights Practice Katten Muchin Zavis Rosenman, NYC. Mem.: ABA, Assn. Bar of City NY, NY State Bar Assn. Office: Katten Muchin Zavis Rosenman 575 Madison Ave New York NY 10022 Office Phone: 212-940-7035. Office Fax: 212-940-7109. E-mail: jeff.friedman@kmzr.com.

FRIEDMAN, JEFFREY M., medical researcher, educator; b. Orlando, Fla. BS in Biology, Rensselaer Poly. Inst.; MD, Union U. Albany Med. Coll.; PhD in Molecular Biology, Rockefeller U., 1986. Resident Albany Med. Ctr. Hosp.; investigator Howard Hughes Med. Inst., 1986—; with faculty Rockefeller U., NYC, 1986—, Marilyn M. Simpson prof., dir. Starr Ctr. Human Genetics. Contbr. articles to profl. jours. Recipient Bristol-Myers Squibb award, Gairdner award, Gairdner Found., 2005. Mem.: NAS (Jessie Stevenson Kovalenko medal 2007), Inst. Medicine. Achievements include discovery of Leptin, a hormone derived from fat cells; research in the causes and treatment options for obesity. Office: Rockefeller Univ 1230 York Ave New York NY 10021 Office Phone: 212-327-8086. E-mail: friedj@rockefeller.edu.*

FRIEDMAN, JEFFREY ROBERT, psychiatrist, educator; b. Mpls., May 26, 1956; s. Harry Samuel and Gertrude (Rotenberg) F.; m. Laura Jean Weisblatt, July 14, 1985; children: Gabrielle Eve, Daniel Adam. BA, Yale U., 1978; MD, U. Chgo., 1982. Diplomate Am. Bd. Psychiatry and Neurology. Intern in medicine Mt. Auburn Hosp., Cambridge, Mass., 1982-83; intern in neurology Mass. Gen. Hosp., Boston, 1982-83; resident in psychiatry McLean Hosp., Belmont, Mass., 1983-86, asst. psychiatrist, 1986-88, asst. clin. psychiatrist, 1988—; instr. psychiatry Harvard U. Med. Sch., Boston, 1986-88, clin. instr., 1988—99, asst. clin. prof. psychiatry, 2000—, psychiatrist Harvard Community Health Plan, 1988-96; assoc. residency dir. Harvard Longwood Psychiatry Residency, Boston, 1995-99; psychiatrist Harvard Pilgrim Health Care, Boston, 1996-97, Harvard Vanguard Med. Assoc., Boston, 1997—2000; faculty Boston Psychoanalytic Soc. and Inst., 2005—, Boston Inst. Psychotherapy, 2005—. Candidate Boston Psychoanalytic Soc. and Inst., 1986-97; grad. analyst Boston Psychoanalytic Soc. and Inst. Recipient Paul Howard award McLean Hosp., 1986; Group for Advancement Psychiatry Ginsburg fellow, 1984-86. Mem. Am. Psychiat. Assn., Boston Psychoanalytic Soc. and Inst., Am. Bd. Geriatric Psychiatry, Am. Bd. Forensic Psychiatry, Am. Psychoanlytic Assn., Am. Acad. Psychiatry and Law. Avocations: tennis, cross country skiing. Office: 875 Massachusetts Ave Ste 51 Cambridge MA 02139-3015

FRIEDMAN, JEROME ISAAC, physics professor, researcher; b. Chgo., Mar. 28, 1930; married, 1956; 4 children. AB, U. Chgo., 1950, MS, 1953, PhD in Physics, 1956. Research assoc. in physics U. Chgo., 1956—57; research assoc. in physics Stanford U., Calif., 1957—60; from asst. prof. to assoc. prof. MIT, Cambridge, 1960—67, prof. physics, 1967—, dir. lab. nuclear sci., 1980—83, head dept. physics, 1983—88, William A. Collidge prof., 1988—90, inst. prof., 1990—. Recipient Nobel prize in Physics, 1990. Fellow: AAAS, Am. Phys. Soc. (co-recipient W.H.K. Panofsky prize 1989); mem.: NAS, Am. Acad. Arts and Scis. Achievements include first to conduct investigations concerning deep inelastic scattering of electrons on protons and bound neutrons, which have been of essential importance for the development of quark model in particle physics. Office: MIT Room 24-512/Dept Physics 77 Massachusetts Ave Cambridge MA 02139-4307

FRIEDMAN, JOAN M., retired accountant, educator; b. NYC, Nov. 30, 1949; d. Alvin E. and Pesselle Gail (Rothenberg) F.; m. Charles E. Blair III, Sept. 20, 1992. AB magna cum laude, Harvard U., 1971; MA, Courtauld Inst., U. London, 1973; MS with honors, Columbia U., 1974; MAS, U. Ill., 1993. CPA, Ill. Asst. research librarian Beinecke Library, New Haven, 1974-75; asst. research librarian Yale Ctr. for Brit. Art, New Haven, 1975-76, curator of rare books, 1976-90; computer cons., teaching asst. dept. accountancy U. Ill., Champaign, 1990-95; vis. asst. prof. acctg. Ill. Wesleyan U., Bloomington, Ill., 1995-99, asst. prof. acctg., 1999—2006; ret., 2006. Cons. Johns Hopkins U., Balt., 1983; tchr. Sch. Library Service Columbia U., 1983-88, Sysop WordPerfect Users Forum on CompuServe, 1987-2000, Sysop, Tapcis Forum on CompuServe, 1988-95. Author: Color Printing in England, 1978; contbr. articles in field Recipient student achievement award Fedn. Schs. Accountancy, 1993; Nat. Merit scholar Harvard U., 1967; Moss Accountancy fellow U. Ill. 1990. Mem. Bibliog. Soc. Am. (coun. 1982-86, sec. 1986-88), Am. Printing History Assn., Phi Beta Kappa, Beta Phi Mu. Clubs: Grolier. Jewish. Avocations: microcomputers, bicycling, amateur radio. Personal E-mail: joanf@concentric.net.

FRIEDMAN, JOHN MAXWELL, JR., lawyer; b. NYC, Oct. 31, 1944; s. John M. and Jane (Blum) F.; m. Laurie Suzanne Nevin, July 8, 1973 (div. 1988); children: David, Michael; m. Judith Zuckerman, Mar. 5, 1989; 1 child, Julia. AB, Princeton U., 1966; MA, U. Sussex, Brighton, Eng., 1967; JD, U. Chgo., 1970. Bar: N.Y. 1971, U.S. Ct. Appeals (2d cir.) 1971, U.S. Dist. Ct. (so. and ea. dist.) N.Y. 1972, U.S. Supreme Ct. 1974. Assoc. Dewey Ballantine, NYC, 1970-78, ptnr., 1978-96. Home: 80 Rocky Mountain Rd Roxbury CT 06783-1623

FRIEDMAN, K. BRUCE, lawyer; b. Buffalo, Jan. 1, 1929; s. Bennett and Florence Ruth (Israel) Friedman; m. Lois G. Rosoff, June 15, 1986. AB, Harvard U., Cambridge, Mass., 1950; LLB, Yale U., New Haven, Conn., 1953. Bar: NY 1955, DC 1956, Calif. 1958. Atty. CAB, Washington, 1955—57; pvt. practice San Francisco, 1958—; mem. Zang, Friedman & Damir, 1969—78, Cotton, Seligman & Ray, 1978—79, Friedman, McCubbin, Spalding, Bilter, Roosevelt, & Montgomery, San Francisco, 1980—. Pres. Econ. Roundtable San Francisco, 1964; lectr. law U. Calif., Berkley, 1966—76. Trustee World Affairs Coun. No. Calif., San Francisco, 1970—76; pres. San Francisco Estate Planning Coun., 1973—74; bd. dirs. Am. Coll. Trust and Estate Counsel Found., 2000—06; bd. dirs. San Francisco chpt. Am. Jewish Com., 1960—76; regional dir. No. Calif. Harvard Alumni Assn., 1981—84. With US Army, 1953—55. Fellow: Am. Bar Found., Am. Coll. Trust and Estate Counsel; mem.: ABA, U. Calif. San Francisco Found., San Francisco Com. Fgn. Rels., Am. Law Inst., Internat. Acad. Estate and Trust Law (treas. 1996—2006), San Francisco Bar Assn., State Bar Calif., Harvard Club San Francisco (pres. 1976—78), Commonwealth Club Calif., Calif. Tennis Club, Univ. Club, Rotary. Jewish. Office: Friedman McCubbin Spalding Bilter Roosevelt & Montgomery 425 California St Ste 2500 San Francisco CA 94104-2207 Business E-Mail: kbrucefriedman@fomlaw.com.

FRIEDMAN, KENNI, health facility administrator, councilman; BA, UCLA, 1963, MBA, 1964. Councilwoman City of Modesto, Calif., 1991-99, vice mayor, 2000—; mem. bd. Sutter-affiliated Meml. Hosps. Assn., Sacramento, chmn. bd., 1993-95; bd. dirs. Sutter Health Inc., Sacramento. Bd. dirs. Sutter Gould Med. Found., Modesto; active League Calif. Cities, United Way Sanislaus County, Modesto Symphony Assn.; former mem. state bd. dirs. and nat. bd. dirs. LWV; mem. policy bd. San Juaquin Valley Unified Air Pollution Control Dist. Mem. Modesto C. of C. (bd. dirs.).

FRIEDMAN, KENT PARKS, nuclear medicine physician, educator; b. Cleve., Jan. 22, 1974; s. Robert Friedman. MD, U. Conn., Farmington, 1996—2001. Lic. dr. Am. Bd. Nuc. Medicine, 2004. Asst. prof. radiology NYU Sch. Medicine, NYC, 2005—. Home Phone: 212-867-0737. Business E-Mail: kent.friedman@med.nyu.edu.

FRIEDMAN, KINKY (RICHARD FRIEDMAN), writer, musician; b. Chgo., Nov. 1944; s. Tom and Min Friedman. Grad., Univ. Tex., Austin. Vol. Peace Corps, Borneo, 1967; songwriter, 1964—; novelist, 1986—; columnist Tex. Monthly Mag., 2001—; independent candidate, gov. State of Tex., 2005—. Performer (with Texas Jewboys Band): (albums) Sold American, 1973, Kinky Friedman, 1974; performer: (solo) Live from the Lone Star Cafe, 1982, Under the Double Ego, 1983, Old Testaments and New Revelations, 1992, Lasso from El Paso, 1993, From One Good American to Another, 1995, Pearls in the Snow, 1998, Classic Snatches from Europe, 2000; author: Greenwich Killing Time, 1986, A Case of Lone Star, 1987, When the Cat's Away, 1988, Frequent Flyer, 1989, Musical Chairs, 1991, Elvis, Jesus and Coca-Cola, 1993, Armadillos and Old Lace, 1994, Roadkill, 1997, Blast from the Past, 1998, Spanking Watson, 1999, The Mile High Club, 2000, Kinky Friedman's Guide to Texas Etiquette, 2001, Meanwhile, Back at the Ranch, 2002, Kill Two Birds and Get Stoned, 2003, The Great Psychedelic Armadillo Picnic, 2004, Prisoner of Vandam Street, 2004, 'Scuse Me While I Whip This Out: Reflections on Country Singers, Presidents and Other Troublemakers, 2004, Ten Little New Yorkers, 2005, Texas Hold 'Em: How I was Born in a Manger, Died in the Saddle, and Came Back as a Horny Toad, 2005, Cowboy Logic: The Wit and Wisdom of Kinky Friedman (and Some of His Friends), 2006, The Christmas Pig: A Fable, 2006. Founder Utopia Animal Rescue Ranch. Jewish. Office: 2100 Northland Dr Austin TX 78756 Address: c/o David Vigliano Assoc Ste 809 584 Broadway New York NY 10012 E-mail: kfcs@kinkyfriedman.com.*

FRIEDMAN, LAWRENCE M., law educator; b. Chgo., Apr. 2, 1930; s. I. M. and Ethel (Shapiro) F.; m. Leah Feigenbaum, Mar. 27, 1955; children: Jane, Amy. AB, U. Chgo., 1948, JD, 1951, LLM, 1953; LLD (hon.), U. Puget Sound, 1977, CUNY, 1989, U. Lund, Sweden, 1993, John Marshall Law Sch., 1995, U. Macerata, Italy, 1998, U. Milan, 2006. Mem. faculty St. Louis U., 1957-61, U. Wis., 1961-68; prof. law Stanford U., 1968—, Marion Rice Kirkwood prof., 1976—; David Stouffer Meml. lectr. Rutgers U. Law Sch., 1969; Sibley lectr. U. Ga. Law Sch., 1976; Wayne Morse lectr. U. Oreg., 1985; Childress meml. lectr. St. Louis U., 1987. Jefferson Meml. lectr. U. Calif., 1994; Higgins vis. prof. Lewis and Clark U., 1998; Tucker lectr. Washington and Lee U., 2000, Charter lectr. U. Ga, 2004; Johnson lectr. Vanderbilt U., 2005. Author: Contract Law in America, 1965, Government and Slum Housing, 1968, A History of American Law, 1973, 3d edit., 2005, The Legal System: A Social Science Perspective, 1975, Law and Society: An Introduction, 1977, American Law, 1984, Total Justice, 1985, Your Time Will Come, 1985, The Republic of Choice, 1990, Crime and Punishment in American History, 1993, The Horizontal Society, 1999, Law in America: A Short History, 2002, American Law in The 20th Century, 2002, Private Lives: Families, Individuals, and The Law, 2004; author: (with Robert V. Percival) The Roots of Justice, 1981; author: (with Stewart Macaulay and Elizabeth Mertz) Law in Action, 2007; co-editor (with Stewart Macaulay): Law and the Behavioral Sciences, 1969, 2d edit., 1977; co-editor: (with Stewart Macaulay and John Stookey) Law and Society: Readings on the Social Study of Law, 1995; co-editor: (with Harry N. Scheiber) American Law and the Constitutional Order, 1978; co-editor: Legal Culture and the Legal Profession, 1996; co-editor: (with George Fisher) The Crime Conundrum, 1997; co-editor: (with Rogelio Prerz-Perdomo) Legal Culture in the Age of Globalization: Latin America and Mediterranean Europe, 2003; contbr. articles to profl. jours. Served with U.S. Army, 1953-54. Recipient Triennial award Order of Coif, 1976, Willard Hurst prize, 1982, Harry Kalven prize, 1992, Silver Gavel award ABA, 1994, Rsch. award Am. Bar. Found., 2000-01; Ctr. for Advanced Study in Behavioral Sci. fellow, 1974-75, Inst. Advanced Study fellow, Berlin, 1985. Mem. Law and Soc. Assn. (pres. 1979-81), Am. Acad. Arts and Scis., Am. Soc. for Legal History (v.p. 1987-89, pres. 1990-91), Soc. Am. Historians, Rsch. Com. Sociology of Law (hon. life, pres. 2003-06). Home: 724 Frenchmans Rd Palo Alto CA 94305-1005 Office: Stanford U Law Sch Nathan Abbott Way Stanford CA 94305-9991 Business E-Mail: lmf@stanford.edu.

FRIEDMAN, LAWRENCE MILTON, lawyer, finance company executive; b. Chgo., Apr. 2, 1945; s. Armin C. and Mildred Friedman; m. Linda M. Friedman, June 25, 1967; children: Benjamin J., David K. BA, U. Ill., 1966; JD, Ohio State U., 1969. Bar: Ill. 1970, U.S. Tax Ct. 1970; CPA, Md., Ill. Ptnr. Coopers & Lybrand, Chgo., 1969-85, Lord, Bissell & Brook LLP, Chgo., 1985—2006, of counsel, 2006—; pres. Puritan Fin. Corp., Chgo., 2006—. Adj. prof. law IIT Chgo. Kent Coll. Law, Chgo., 1990-2000; mem. adv. bd. Hartford Inst. Ins. Tax, 1995-2000; spkr. on mergers, aquisitions, fin. svcs. industries, and taxation. Mem. adv. bd. Ins. Tax Rev., 1987—; contbr. articles to law jours. Sec.-treas., dir. North Shore Performing Arts Ctr. Found. in Skokie, Ill., 1993-97; vice chmn., dir. Jewish Fedn. Met. Chgo., 1992-99. Mem. ABA, Chgo. Fed. Tax Forum. Office: Lord Bissell & Brook LLP 111 S Wacker Dr Chicago IL 60606-4410 Office Phone: 312-443-1835.

FRIEDMAN, LOUIS FRANK, lawyer; b. Balt., May 26, 1941; s. Dave Sylvan and Miriam (Sugarman) F.; m. Phyllis Cole, Dec. 25, 1968; 1 son, Samuel. BS, U. Md., 1963, JD, 1965; LL.M. in Taxation, Georgetown U., 1968. Bar: Md. 1965. Since practiced in, Balt.; ptnr. firm Friedman & Friedman, 1965—. Prof. taxation U. Balt. Sch. Bus., 1975-88. Pres. 9400 Ocean Hwy. Condominium, Ocean City, Md., 1976; chmn. young lawyers div. Asso. Jewish Charities, 1975-76; bd. dirs. Carson Scholars Fund, Sinai Hosp., Balt., Life Bridge Health. Mem. Md. Bar Assn. (tax counsel 1977-79), Masons (counsel Masonic Charities Md. Inc. 1987—), Amicable Club, Order of Coif, Phi Alpha Delta. Jewish. Home: 19 Hambleton Ct Baltimore MD 21208-3333 Office: Merc Bank Bldg 409 Washington Ave Baltimore MD 21204-4920

FRIEDMAN, MARLA LEE, human resources specialist, marketing professional; b. Chgo., May 26, 1953; d. Martin P. and Charlotte K. (Beilenson) F. BSc in Commerce, DePaul U., Chgo., 1977; MBA with honors, Roosevelt U., Chgo., 1985. Gen. mgr., adminstr. Chgo. Ctr. for Devel. Learning, Inc., Ill., 1975—77; dist. health claims adminstrn. analyst Washington Nat. Ins. Co., Evanston, Ill., 1977—80; unit coord. computer resource liaison Luth. Gen. Hosp., Pk. Ridge, Ill., 1980—99; pres., owner Dancing By Candlelight, 1995—; media & investor rels. prof. IPA, Buffalo Grove, Ill., 2000—01; dir. mktg. programs Samples & Surveys, Northbrook, Ill., 2001; acting dir. mktg. & publ. rels. Penworthy Ctrl., Glenview, Ill., 2002—03; mgr. client devel., staffing coord. All Help Health Svcs. Agy., Chgo., 2004—. Mem. associated writing programs George Mason U. Contbr. prose poem Chips Off the Writer's Block, 1992, columnist, 1994; contbr. poem Guided By Voices Anthology, 1998, Best Poets of the 20th Century, 2000, Best Poets of 2000, 2000, Sound of Poetry, 2001; author short stories, children's stories, novels and articles. Recipient Editors Choice award N.Am. Poetry Open Competition, 1998, awards for nonfiction articles. Fellow Life Mgmt. Soc. (cert. fin. scis.); mem. NAFE, Acad. Am. Poets. Avocations: drama, music, creative cookery. Office: All Help Health Svcs Inc 2910 W Peterson Ave Ste 1 Chicago IL 60659 Personal E-mail: beyondpg2@yahoo.com.

FRIEDMAN, MARTIN, museum director, arts adviser; b. Pitts., Sept. 23, 1925; s. Israel and Etta (Louik) F.; m. Mildred Shenberg, Sept. 3, 1949; children: Lise, Ceil, Zoe. Student, U. Pa., 1943-45; BA, U. Wash., 1947; MA, UCLA, 1949; postgrad., Columbia, 1956-57, U. Minn., 1958-60, LHD (hon.), 1990, Bates Coll., 1983; DFA (hon.), Macalester Coll., 1983; LHD (hon.), Md. Inst., 1983; DFA (hon.), Hamline U., 1987, Phila. Coll. of Art and Design, 1989. Instr. art, curriculum cons. L.A. City Schs., 1949-56; instr. art U. Calif. Extension, LA, 1950-51; fellow Bklyn. Mus., 1956-57; grantee Belgian-Am. Ednl. Found., Brussels, 1957-58; fellow Am. art U. Minn., 1959-60; curator Walker Art Center, Mpls., 1958-60, dir., 1961-90, dir. emeritus, 1990—. Mem. mus. adv. con. NEA, 1973-78, adv. coun. internat. exhbns., 1987-91, Nat. Coun. Arts, 1978-84, Smithsonian Coun., 1988-93; adv. Am. Ctr. Paris, 1990-92, Fed. Art Com. Internat. Exhbns., 1987-91; adviser art program Hall Family Found., Kansas City, 1991—, Nat. Gallery Art, Washington, 1991-92, Nelson Atkins Mus. Art, Kansas City, Mo., 1991—, contemporary art Va. Mus. Fine Arts, Richmond, 1992-93; guest curator Landscape as Metaphor exhbn. Denver Art Mus., 1992-94, Columbus Mus. Art, 1992-94; Am. fine arts commr. São Paulo Bienal, 1963; mem. Nat. Collection Fine Arts Commn., Washington, Commn. on Founds. and Pvt. Philanthropy; hon. mem. commn. Nat. Mus. Am. Art, Washington; mem. adv. bd. on environ. planning Bur. Reclamation, Washington, 1965-69; art adv. com. Japan House Gallery, N.Y.C., 1999-2000; adviser Ind. Curators, Inc., N.Y. Author numerous catalogues on internat. contemporary art, also books, articles; dir. numerous mus. exhbns. Trustee Spring Hill Found. , Minn., 1970—81, Am. Fedn. Arts, 1972—85, Socrates Sculpture Pk., NY, 2000—02; mem. Internat. Mus. Com., Washington, 1976—78; mem. vis. com. J. Paul Getty Mus., Malibu, Calif., 1990—95. Ford Found. fellow, 1961-62; artist fellow Aspen Inst. Humanistic Studies, 1980, Intellectual Interchange fellow, Tokyo, 1982, Japan Found. fellow, 1991; Asian Cultural Coun. grantee, 1995; recipient Disting. Svc. award Mid-Am. Coll. Art Assn., 1987, Nat. Medal of Arts, White House, 1990, Lifetime Achievement award Internat. Sculpture Ctr., 1999; named to Centennial Honor Roll, Am. Assn. Museums, 2006; decorated officer Arts et Lettres (France); honoree DIA Ctr. for the Arts, 1997. Mem. Coll. Art Assn., Assn. Art Mus. Dirs. (pres. 1978-79, trustee 1979-81, citation for disting. svc. 1990). E-mail: mlfnyc@mindspring.com.*

FRIEDMAN, MARTIN BURTON, retired chemicals executive; b. NYC, June 21, 1927; s. William L. and Ella (Holstein) F.; m. Rita Fleischman, Mar. 19, 1950; children— Jay Edward, Ellen Jane. Student, Mt. St. Mary's Coll., 1943-44, Cornell U., 1944-45; BA, Pa. State U., 1949; PhD, Wiltshire U., 2004. Mgr. advt. and promotion chems. group Sun Chem. Corp., NYC, 1949-54; mgr. advt. and promotion textile chems. dept. Am. Cyanamid Co., NYC, 1954-58, mgr. advt. and promotion, organic chems. div., 1958-60, gen. merchandising mgr., mgr. fibers div., 1961-64, dir. sales, 1964-65, dir. mktg., 1965-69, asst. gen. mgr. fibers div., 1969-72; v.p. IRC Fibers Co. (subs.), 1969-72; exec. v.p. Formica Corp., Cin., 1972-73, pres., 1973-80; pres. fibers div. Am. Cyanamid, 1980-84, corp. v.p., 1984-90. Chmn. bd. 4th Dist. Fed. Res. Bank, Cin.; adj. prof. Ramapo Coll., 1990-98; chmn. Mgmt. Decision Lab., NYU Grad. Sch. Bus., 1990-98. Author: The Leadership Myth; contbr. articles to textile and tech. publs. Served with USNR, 1945-46. Mem. Am. Chem. Soc., Am. Assn. Textile Chemists and Colorists. Clubs: Chemists (N.Y.C.). Home: 6 Sundance Dr Wayne NJ 07470 Personal E-mail: friedmanm@prodigy.net. *Integrity should permeate every discussion of every facet of leadership. Integrity is the basic quality to be sought in consideration of any person's qualifications for assuming a position of trust and responsibility.*

FRIEDMAN, MARVIN ROSS, lawyer; b. Mpls., July 13, 1941; s. H. W. and Katherine F.; widowed; children: Natasha E., Chloe J. BBA, U. Miami, 1966, JD, 1969. Bar: Fla. 1969. Pvt. practice, Coral Gables, Fla., 1970—. Founder Diabetes Rsch. Found.; hon. trustee Lowe Art Mus, Mus. Contemporary Art, Wolfsonian Mus., F.I.U. Art Mus.; Tri-county v.p. Miami City Ballet; hon. trustee Friends of the Libr., Met. Opera, NYC, Mus. Modern Art, NYC, Whitney Mus., NYC, Guggenheim Mus., NY, Miami Art Mus. Mem.: ABA, ATLA, Am. Coll. Barristers, Million Dollar Advocates Forum, Dade County Trial Lawyers Assn., Fla. Acad. Trial Lawyers, Coral Gables Bar Assn., Dade County Bar Assn., Fla. Bar, English Speaking Union, Guild Hall, East Hampton (NY) Tennis Club, Fisher Island Club. Office: Friedman & Friedman 2600 S Douglas Rd Ste 1011 Coral Gables FL 33134-6142 Office Phone: 305-446-6485. Business E-Mail: marvinross@friedmantriallawyers.com.

FRIEDMAN, MARY KATHLEEN, secondary school educator; d. John S. and Catherine M. Kelly; m. Matthew L. Friedman, July 13, 1997; 1 child, Talia Cealleigh. BA, U. Colo., Boulder, 1988. Cert. secondary social studies tchr. Colo., 2000, single subject tchr. Calif., 2005. Social studies tchr. Westlake Jr. H.S., Broomfield, Colo., 1990—94; history tchr. Horizon H.S., Brighton, Colo., 1994—97; substitute tchr. St. Joseph Sch. Dist., St. Joseph, Mo., 1998—99, Elwood Sch. Dist., Kans., 1999; history tchr., chmn. dept. SJ H.S., Carmichael, Calif., 2000—. Text book reviewer Jewish Fedn. Sacramento, 2005—; participant Holocaust Teachers Program, Israel, 1995, NSF Summer Inst., Boulder, 1994; presenter in field. Author: (poetry) The Kinetic Energy of Kosher Krishnas. Vol. Chevre Kadish Sacramento, 1999—2002; sec. bd. dirs. Twin Spires Inc., St. Joseph, 1998—99; bd. dirs. Samaritan Ctr., St. Joseph, 1998—99. Named Paul Harris fellow, Rotary Internat., 2006; recipient Innovative Classroom award, Adams County Five Star Sch. Dist., 1993. Avocation: travel. Office: Jesuit HS 1200 Jacob Lane Carmichael CA 95608 Home Phone: 916-726-2424; Office Phone: 916-482-6060. Personal E-mail: friedcat@yahoo.com. Business E-Mail: friedmanm@jhssac.org.

FRIEDMAN, MAX, lawyer; b. Paris, July 10, 1953; came to U.S., 1954; BA summa cum laude, Columbia U., 1974; JD, Yale U., 1977. Bar: N.Y. 1978, U.S. Dist. Ct. (ea. & so. dists.) N.Y. 1978. Law clk. to Hon. Irving R. Kaufman, U.S. Ct. Appeals (2nd Cir.), 1977-78; assoc. Paul, Weiss, Rifkind, Wharton & Garrison, NYC, 1978-83; ptnr. Patterson, Belknap, Webb & Tyler, NYC, 1984-91, Winthrop, Stimson, Putnam & Roberts, NYC, 1991—2001; ptnr., real estate, chair, pro-bono com. Pillsbury Winthrop LLP, NYC, 2001—05; ptnr., real estate Pillsbury Winthrop Shaw Pittman LLP, NYC, 2005—06; ptnr., dir. real estate group Goulston & Storrs LLP, NYC, 2006—. Adj. prof. Cardozo Sch. Law, N.Y.C., 1988-94. Luce scholar Nat. U. Singapore, 1979-80. Office: Goulston & Storrs LLP 750 Third Ave 22nd Fl New York NY 10017 E-mail: mfriedman@goulstonstorrs.com.

FRIEDMAN, MERTON HIRSCH, retired psychologist, educator; b. Boston, Apr. 12, 1925; s. Isadore and Frances (Ponack) F.; m. Judith Lee Freeman, Nov. 27, 1955; 1 child, Eric Lund. BS, Coll. William and Mary, 1945; MA, U. Pa., 1947; PhD, U. Ill., 1952. Lic. psychologist, N.J., Mass. Psychology intern Conn. Valley Hosp., Middletown, 1947—48; postdoctoral intern Dept. VA Mental Health Clinic, Phila., 1952—53; staff psychologist Dept. VA Med. Ctr., Boston, 1953—59, chief psychology svc. Providence, 1959—62; chief psychologist Cmty. Mental Health Ctr., Brookline, Mass., 1962—64; dir. clin. svcs. Jewish Vocat. Svc., Milw., 1966—67; clin. assoc. prof. psychiatry U. Medicine and Dentistry N.J., 1968—92; chief psychology svc. Dept. VA Med. Ctr., East Orange, NJ, 1967—96; ret., 1996. Vis. lectr. Fulbright program Lund U., Sweden, 1964-66. Contbr. articles to profl. jours. USPHS Rsch. fellow, NIMH, U. Ill., 1951—52. Fellow Am. Orthopsychiat. Assn.; mem. APA, Mass. Psychol. Assn., N.J. Psychol. Assn., Sigma Xi (U. Ill. chpt.). Democrat. Jewish. Avocations: piano, hiking, stamp collecting/philately, classical music. Home: 79 Falcon Rd Livingston NJ 07039-4414

FRIEDMAN, MICHAEL, pharmaceutical executive; BA, Bklyn. Coll.; MBA, U. Conn. Various pos., including v.p. mktg. and COO pneumatic fastening systems divsn. Hilti, Inc.; v.p., asst. to pres. and chmn. Purdue Pharma, Stamford, Conn., 1985—88, group v.p., 1988—99, exec. v.p., COO, 1999—2002, pres., CEO, 2003—. Office: Purdue PHrma 1 Stamford Forum Stamford CT 06901

FRIEDMAN, MICHAEL, surgeon; BA, Yeshiva U., NY, 1968; MD, U. Ill. Chicago Sch. of Medicine, 1972. Cert. Am. Bd. of Otolaryngology, 1977. Intern Ill. Masonic Med. Ctr., 1972—73; surgery residency U. Ill., Chicago, 1973—74, otolaryngology-head and neck surgery residency, 1974—77; otolaryngologist-head and neck surgeon Ill. Masonic Med. Ctr., 1977—; dir. head and neck training U. Ill., 1980—95; med. dir. Advanced Ctr. for Specialty Care, Ill. Masonic Med. Ctr., 1980—; otolaryngologist-head and neck surgeon Rush-Presbyterian-St. Luke's Med. Ctr., 1991—, Grant Hosp., 1991—. Editor-in-chief Operative Techniques in Otolaryngology—Head & Neck Surgery; assoc. prof., chmn. head and neck surgery, dept. of otolaryngology and bronchoesophagology Rush Med. Coll., 1991—95, prof., chmn. head and neck surgery, dept. of otolaryngology and bronchoesophagology, 1995—. Published more than 150 scientific articles; co-author 28 book chapters or textbooks. Named a Top Doctor, Chicago Mag., 2001; named one of Top Doctors, Castle Connolly Med. Guide, 2001. Mem.: AMA, Am. Rhinologic Soc., Internat. Assn. of Phonosurgeons, Am. Broncho-Esophagological Assn., Am. Soc. for Head and Neck Surgery, Am. Coll. of Surgeons, Chicago Laryngological and Otological Soc., Am. Acad. of Otolaryngology-Head and Neck Surgery, Chicago Med. Soc., Am. Sleep Disorders Assn., Clinical Sleep Soc. Office: 30 N Michigan Ave Chicago IL 60602

FRIEDMAN, MILDRED, architecture educator, design educator, curator; b. LA, July 25, 1929; d. Nathaniel and Hortense (Weinsveig) Shenberg; m. Martin Friedman; children: Lise, Ceil, Zoe. BA, UCLA, 1951, MA, 1952; DFA (hon.), Mpls. Coll. Art, 1984; DFA, Hamlin U., 1987. Instr. design L.A. City Coll., 1952-54; archtl. designer Cerny Assocs., Mpls., 1957-69; design curator Walker Art Ctr., Mpls., 1970-90; freelance cons. NYC, 1990—. Mem. arch. and design panel Nat. Endowment Arts, 1975—78, mem. policy panel design arts, 1979—82, mem. presdl. design awards jury, 1991; mem. vis. com. Sch. Arch. and Planning MIT, 1985—88; mem. vis. com. Grad. Sch. Design Harvard U., 1994—; bd. dirs. Internat. Design Conf., Aspen, 1989—91, Chgo. Inst. Arch. and Urbanism, 1990—93, Nat. Inst. Archtl. Edn., 1993—; mem. deisgn jury Am. Acad. Rome, 1991; gueest instr. UCLA, 1992; mem. jury to select architect for Whitehall Ferry Terminal, NYC, 1992; vis. instr. Harvard U., 1993; cons. Battery Park City Authority, NYC; guest curator Bklyn. Mus., 1992—2002; guest curator for Frank Gehry retrospective exhbn. Solomon R. Guggenheim Mus., NYC, 2001; guest curator for Vital Forms exhbn. Bklyn. Mus. Art, 2001—02. Author, editor: Gehry Talks, 1999; editor Design Quar., 1970-91, numerous catalogues; participating author for catalogue on the work of Jack Lenor Larson, Mus. Arts & Design, 2004. Recipient Outstanding Achievement award YWCA, 1984, Outstanding Svc. award U. Minn., 1991; fellow Intellectual Interchange program Japan Soc., 1982, Chrysler Design award, 2002; grantee Nat. Endowment Arts, 1992-93, Graham Found. for Advanced Studies in Fine Arts, 1997; recipient Graham Found grant for Design Quar. Anthology. Mem. AIA (hon., nat. awards jury 1981, 87, bd. dirs. Minn. chpt. 1984-86, Inst. Honors 1994). Office Phone: 212-647-1118.

FRIEDMAN, MILES, trade association and financial services company executive, university lecturer; b. NYC, Apr. 18, 1950; s. Sol and Rose (Schenkerman) F.; m. Susan Liles, Apr. 26, 1975; children: David Andrew, Diana Leigh. BA in Pub. Affairs, George Washington U., 1971, MA in Polit. Sci., 1972, PhD candidate in Polit. Sci., 1976. Dep. commr. pub. works Town of Ramapo, Suffern, NY, 1971; grad. teaching fellow George Washington U., Washington, 1972-75; sr. assoc. Lazar Mgmt. Group, Washington, 1976-77; dir. legis. and policy Nat. Council Urban Econ. Devel., Washington, 1977-80; pres., CEO Nat. Assn. State Devel. Agys., Washington, 1980—. Founder, instr. trade specialist tng. program, Phoenix, 1980—, founder, instr. fgn. investment tng. program, 1988-96; instr. Fgn. Svc. Inst., U.S. and Fgn. Comml. Svc. Inst., Georgetown U., Washington, 1991, U. N.C. Basic Econ. Devel. Inst., Chapel Hill, 1984-85; cons. Pres.' Drug Abuse Prevention Office, Washington, 1972; lectr. George Washington U., Washington, 1975-77. Mem. editl. bd., contbg. editor Econ. Devel. Rev., 1991—; contbg. author to several books, directory; contbr. articles to profl. jours. including Wall St. Jour, Area Devel. mag., Export Today mag., others. Mem bd. dirs., sec./treas. Pub. Sector Devel. Found., Washington, 1983—; pres. Am. Devel. Fin., Inc., 1986-95, also bd. dirs.; liaison subcom. Pres.'s Export Council, Washington, 1981-82; Pinewood Forest Council Owners, 1977-78; chmn. Washington Symposium Higher Edn., 1970-71; pres. Coles Little League, 1997-98; chmn. Prince William County Econ. Devel. Coun., 1998—; bd. dirs. Friends of Brentsville Courthouse Hist. Ctr., 1998—. Recipient Pres.'s E award for Excellence in Export Svc., NASDA, 1993. S. C. of C., Am. Soc. Assn. Execs., Nat. Assn. Execs., Tau Kappa Epsilon, Delta Phi Epsilon, Lambda Alpha.

FRIEDMAN, MONROE, psychologist, educator, consultant, editor, writer; b. NYC, Oct. 16, 1934; s. Isadore and Pearl Friedman; m. Rita Joyce Shaffer, Sept. 2, 1956; children: Ethan, Mark, Jordan. BS, Bklyn. Coll., 1956; PhD, U. Tenn., 1959. Human factors scientist Sys. Devel. Corp., Santa Monica, Calif., 1959—64; prof. Ea. Mich. U., Ypsilanti, 1964—, dir. Contemporary Issues Ctr., 1970—79; editl. cons. Greenwood Press, 1991—92, Prentice Hall, 1991—92. Vis. prof. Tilburg (The Netherlands) U., 1982—83, U. Leuven, Belgium, 1990—91; cons. Pres.'s Com. on Consumer Interests, Washington, 1966, Consumer Interests Found., Washington, 1972—73, NSF, Washington, 1973—74, U.S. Gen. Acctg. Office, Washington, 1973—74, FTC, Washington, 1976—77, ACLU Found., NY, 2001—02; bd. dirs. Consumer Interest Rsch. Inst., Washington; reviewer consumer edn. lit. Fed. Res. Bd., Washington, 2004—; sr. peer counselor Ctr. for Healthy Aging, Santa Monica, Calif., 2007—; mem. insight panel NY Times, 2006—; presenter in field. Author: A Brand New Language, 1991, Consumer Boycotts, 1999 (Outstanding Academic Title of Yr., Assn. for Coll. and Rsch. Librs. 2000); editor: Jour. Consumer Affairs, 1980-84; co-editor: Frontier of Research in the Consumer Interest, 1988; issue editor Jour. Social Issues, 1991, Jour. Am. Culture, 2007; mem. editl. bd. Jour. Consumer Affairs, 1984-93, 98—, Jour. Consumer Rsch., 1973-77, 1982-85, Jour. Am. Culture, 2004—, Jour. Popular Culture, 2005-, Jour. Interdisciplinary 20th Century Studies, 2005-, Jour. Consumer Policy, 1976—, Jour. Pub. Policy and Mktg., 2006—; contbr. over 100 articles to profl. jours. Pres. Am. Coun. Consumer Interests, 1989—90; mem. exec. coun. Emeritus Coll., Santa Monica, Calif., 2005—. Rsch. grantee AARP Andrus Found., 1990, 92, Mich. Coun. for Humanities, 1975; Congl. fellow Am. Polit. Sci. Assn., 1966-67; Nat. Inst. Aging postdoc. fellow U. Mich., 1988-89; recipient Disting. Faculty award Mich. Bd. Regents, 1983, Bronze prize for ednl. films Internat. Film Festival Berlin, 1975. Fellow APA (divsn. Population and Environ. Psychology, divsn. Tchg. of Psychology, divsn. Internat. Psychology, mem. program rev. com. 2007, divsn. Media Psychology and divsn. Adult Devel. and Aging), Am. Psychol. Soc.

(charter), Am. Assn. Applied and Preventive Psychology (charter), Am. Coun. on Consumer Interests (disting., Applied Consumer Econs. award, 1991, 97), Soc. for Consumer Psychology, Soc. for the Psychol. Study of Social Issues, Soc. for Psychology of Aesthetics, Creativity, and the Arts, Soc. for the Study of Peace, Conflict and Violence; mem. Internat. Assn. for Rsch. in Econ. Psychology (U.S. rep. bd. trustees 1982—, sci. com., 2001, 02,), Internat. Assn. Applied Psychology (U.S. rep. bd. trustees econ. psychology divsn. 1988—, sci. com., 1998), Found. Soc. Consumer Affairs Profls. (chair rsch. agenda com. 1984-87, trustee). Home and Office: 855 10th St Ste 301 Santa Monica CA 90403 Office Phone: 310-656-4943. Business E-Mail: mfriedman@emich.edu.

FRIEDMAN, MORTON LEE, retired lawyer; b. Aberdeen, SD, Aug. 4, 1932; s. Philip and Rebecca (Feinstein) F.; m. Marcine Lichter, Dec. 20, 1955; children— Mark, Philip, Jeffrey. Student, U. Mich., 1950-53; AB, Stanford U., 1954, LL.B., 1956. Bar: Calif. bar 1956. Mem. firm Kimble, Thomas, Snell, Jamison & Russell, Fresno, 1957, Busick & Busick, Sacramento, 1957-59; sr. ptnr. firm Friedman, Collard & Poswall (name now Friedman, Collard & Panneton), Sacramento, 1959—2006, ret., 2006. Lectr. various law schs. and seminars; mem. Calif. Bd. Continuing Edn. Pres. Mosaic Law Congregation, 1977-80, 97-99; v.p. Sacramento Jewish Fedn., 1980-82; chmn. Sacramento campaign United Jewish Appeal, 1981; bd. dirs., former nat. v.p. Am. Israel Pub. Affairs Com.; mem. bd. Calif. State U. Inst., 1995-99; bd. dirs. Nat. Bd. AntiDefamation League. 1st lt. USAF, 1956. Recipient Sacramento Businessman of Yr. award Sacramento Met. C. of C., 1991, Best Lawyers in Am. award, Outstanding Philanthropists award Nat. Soc. Fund Raising Execs., 1999, Sacramentan of Yr., 2006, Sacramento C. of C.; Fulbright candidate Stanford Law Sch., 1956. Fellow Am. Coll. Trial Lawyers; mem. ABA, ATLA, Calif. Bar Assn., Sacramento County Bar Assn. (pres. 1976, Lawyer of Yr. 1999), Calif. Trial Lawyers Assn. (v.p. 1973-75), Capitol City Lawyers Club (past pres.), Am. Bd. Trial Advocates (adv., pres. 1977, Calif. Trial Lawyer of Yr. 1988, SCALE award 2002), West Sacramento C. of C. (dir.), Order of Coif. Democrat. Home: 1620 McClaren Dr Carmichael CA 95608-5936 Office: Friedman Collard & Panneton 7750 College Town Dr Ste 500 Sacramento CA 95826-2386 Office Phone: 916-381-9011.

FRIEDMAN, MYLES IVAN, education educator; b. Chgo., Apr. 5, 1924; s. Max Edward and Ethel (Goldman) F.; m. Betty Ann McDowell, July 4, 1978; children: Gregg Alan, Myles Ivan Jr. MA, U. Chgo., 1957, PhD, 1959. Real estate, home builder, 1946-58; asst. prof. edn. Northwestern U., 1958-60, assoc. prof., 1960-64; chaired prof. edn. U. S.C., 1964—99; vis. prof. U. Calif., Berkeley, summer 1968. Cons. in field; dir. Head Start Evaluation and Rsch. Ctr.; dir. rsch. Regional Edn. Lab., Carolinas and Va.; pres. Inst. for Evidence-Based Decision-Making in Edn., 1995—. Author: Rational Behavior, 1975, Teaching Reading and Thinking Skills, 1979; sr. author: Improving Teacher Education, 1979, Human Nature and Predictability, 1981, Teaching Higher Order Thinking Skills to Gifted Students, 1983, The Psychology of Human Control, 1991, Taking Control: Vitalizing Education, 1993, Improving the Quality of Life, 1997, Handbook on Effective Instructional Strategies, 1998, Ensuring Student Success, 2000, Educators' Handbook on Effective Testing, 2003, No School Left Behind, 2005, Effective Instruction, 2006, Developing Teaching Effectiveness, 2007; contbr. articles to profl. jours. Served with USAAF, 1942-46. Mem. APA. Home: 1709 Seay Ct Columbia SC 29206-3117

FRIEDMAN, PAUL JAY, retired radiologist; b. NYC, Jan. 20, 1937; s. Louis Alexander and Rose (Solomon) Friedman; m. Elisabeth Clare Richardson, June 18, 1960; children: Elizabeth Ruth Coley, Deborah Anne Yeager, Matthew Alexander Xu-Friedman, Rachel Clare Lentz. BS, U. Wis., 1955; postgrad., Oxford U., Eng., 1957—58; MD, Yale U., 1960. Diplomate Am. Bd Radiology. Intern Einstein Med. Sch., NYC, 1960-61; resident in radiology Columbia-Presbyn. Hosp., NYC, 1961-64; from asst. prof. to assoc. prof. U. Calif. San Diego Med. Sch., 1968-75, prof. radiology, 1975-2001, prof. emeritus, 2001—, from assoc. dean to dean acad. affairs, 1982-95. Cons. VA Hosp., 1971—2001; vis. scholar Inst. Med./NAS, AAMC, 1988—89; mem. adv. com. rsch. integrity HHS, 1991—93; cons. 26th, 27th, and 28th edit. Stedman's Med. Dictionary; specialist in chest radiology, rsch. ethics, acad. pers. issues; bd. dirs. Am. Coun. Edn., 1996—97. Mem. editl. bd. Investigative Radiology, 1976—87, Am. Jour. Roentgenology, 1986—88; contbr. articles to profl. jours. Bd. dirs. La Jolla Symphony Assn., 1987—92. Lt. cmdr. MC USNR, 1964—66. Markle scholar acad. medicine, 1969—74, Picker Found. Advanced Acad. fellow and scholar, 1966—69. Fellow: Am. Coll. Radiology, Am. Coll. Chest Physicians; mem.: Roentgen Ray Soc. (emeritus), Radiol. Soc. N.Am. (emeritus), Assn. Univ. Radiologists (emeritus), Internat. Soc. Magnetic Resonance Medicine (emeritus), Assn. Am. Med. Colls. (disting. svc. mem.), Fleischner Soc. (pres. 1994—95), Phi Beta Kappa, Alpha Omega Alpha. Avocations: singing, computers, gardening. Home: 5644 Soledad Rd La Jolla CA 92037-7048 Office: U Calif Sch Medicine Dept Radiology 200 W Arbor Dr San Diego CA 92103-8756 Office Phone: 619-543-5206. Business E-Mail: pfriedman@ucsd.edu.

FRIEDMAN, PAUL M., dermatologist; b. Memphis, Sept. 28, 1970; MD, U. Tenn., Memphis, 1996. Bd. Cert. Dermatology Am. Bd. Dermatology, 2000. Dir. laser surgery DermSurgery Laser Ctr., Houston, 2000—. Named one of Houston's Top Drs., H Tex. Mag., 2005, 2006. Mem.: Am. Soc. Laser Medicine and Surgery, Am. Soc. Dermatologic Surgery, Am. Acad. Dermatology. Office: DermSurgery Laser Ctr 7515 Main St Ste 210 Houston TX 77030 Office Phone: 713-791-9966.

FRIEDMAN, PAUL RICHARD, lawyer; b. Washington, Mar. 25, 1944; s. Herbert and Gertrude (Miller) F.; m. Ronna Lee Beck; children: Mali, Luke, Jed. BA, Princeton U., 1965; MA, Trinity Coll., Cambridge U., Eng., 1967; JD, Yale U., 1970; postgrad., Balt./D.C. Inst. Psychoanalysis, 1971—78. Bar: D.C. 1972, U.S. Ct. Appeals (D.C. cir.) 1972, U.S. Ct. Appeals (3d cir.) 1984, U.S. Ct. Appeals (4th cir.) 1979, U.S Supreme Ct. 1975. Law clk. to Hon. J. Skelly Wright U.S. Ct. Appeals (D.C. cir.), Washington, 1970-71; fellow Ctr. for Law and Social Policy, Washington, 1971-72; dir. Bazelon Ctr. (formerly known as Mental Health Law Project), Washington, 1972—81; mng. ptnr. Ennis, Friedman, Bersoff and Ewing, Washington, 1981-88; pvt. practice Washington, 1988—93, 1996—2001; dep. assoc. atty. gen. Dept. of Justice, Washington, 1993-96; of counsel Shea and Gardner, 2002—04, Goodwin Procter LLP, 2004—. Ct.-apptd. mediator and early neutral evaluator, 1988-89; chmn. Practicing Law Inst. Nat. Seminars on Legal Rights of Mentally Disabled Persons, 1979-80; coord. task panel on legal and ethical issues Pres.'s Commn. on Mental Health, 1977-78; mem. adv. com. on procedures U.S. Ct. Appeals (D.C. cir.) 1977-78; mem. steering com. Ctr. for Y2K & Soc., 1998-2000. Author: The Rights of Mentally Retarded Persons - An American Civil Liberties Handbook, 1976; editor: Legal Rights of Mentally Disabled Persons, 3 vols., 1979; note and comment editor Yale Law Jour., 1969-70, bd. editors 1967-69; contbr. articles to profl. publs. Trustee The Green Door, 1977-83. Nat. Merit scholar, Univ. scholar; Woodrow Wilson fellow, Keasbey fellow. Mem. ABA (mem. comm. on mentally disabled 1981-82), D.C. Bar, Am. Psychoanalytic Assn. (affiliate), Phi Beta Kappa. Avocations: tennis and other racquet sports, computers, photography. Office Phone: 202-346-4305. E-mail: pfriedman@goodwinprocter.com.

FRIEDMAN, PAULA SOPKIN, literature educator; b. Chgo., Jan. 18, 1947; d. George and Thelma Sopkin; m. John L. Friedman, Sept. 9; children: Mack, Kate Flanagan. BA in English with honors, U. Chgo., 1970, MA in English with honors, 1971. Lectr. So. Conn. State Coll., New Haven, 1972—74, Alverno Coll., Milw., 1977—94; instr. Cardinal Stritch Coll., Milw., 1977—81, asst. prof. English, 1981—. Bd. dirs. Friends of Milw. Pub. Libr., 1995—2003. Recipient Tng. Excellence and Campus Leadership award, Cardinal Stritch U., 1998, Martin Luther King Jr. and Peacemaker award, 2002. Mem.: Nat. Coun. Tchrs. English. Jewish. Avocations: reading, travel, gardening, exercise. Office: Cardinal Stritch U 6801 N Yates Rd Milwaukee WI 53217 Office Phone: 414-410-4539.

FRIEDMAN, PENNY, lawyer, not-for-profit developer; b. Cleve., Dec. 24, 1951; d. Harold Emanuel and Ruth (Resnick) Friedman; children: Rachel, Leah. AB in Econs. with high honors, U. Mich., 1973, JD cum laude, 1977. Bar: Ohio 1977. Atty. Taft, Stettinius & Hollister, Cin., 1977-80; v.p. property devel. Gt. Am. Broadcasting Co. (formerly Taft Broadcasting Co.), Cin., 1980-88; real estate portfolio mgr. Bartlett & Co., Cin., 1988-98; pres. BeneFactors, LLC, 1998—2007; COO Interact for Change, 2007—. Mem. Cin. Downtown Progress Com., 1991—95, mem. exec. com., 1993—95; v.p. Cin. chpt. Am. Jewish Com., 1992—96, pres., 1996—98, mem. exec. com., 1990—; v.p. Leadership Cin. Alumni Assn., 1987—89; chmn. Family Svc. Cin. Area, 1991—92, pres., 1988—90, 1985—88, trustee, 1979—93, trustee emeritus, 1993—; vice-chmn. Cin. Devel. Fund, 1989—95; vice chmn. Devel. Corp. Cin., 1990—92, trustee, 1989—92, Cin. Arts Assn., 1992—, mem. exec. com., 1994—; trustee Downtown Cin., Inc., 1998—2004, Cin. Psychoanalytic Inst., 1994—2002, Wellness Cmty., 1999—2002; vice chair, trustee KnowledgeWorks Found., 1999—2002, treas., 2002—, chair fin. and investment com., 2002—; trustee Found. Family Svc., 2000—, v.p., 2002—06, pres., 2006—; trustee Greater Cin. Arts and Edn. Ctr., 1999—, mem. exec. com., 2005—; trustee Project Grad. Cin., 2003—; bd. dirs. Cin. Ctr. for Devel. Disorders, 1979—85, Seven Hills Neighborhood Houses, 1981—86. Mem.: Cin. Bar Assn., Phi Beta Kappa. Office: InterAct for Change 3805 Edwards Rd Ste 500 Cincinnati OH 45209 Personal E-mail: psoul@aol.com. Business E-Mail: pfriedman@interactforchange.org.

FRIEDMAN, RALPH DAVID, lawyer; b. Phila., June 14, 1942; s. Albert H. and Reba (Goldstein) F.; m. Sandra Scott, July 11, 1965; children: Jennifer Amy, Susanne Jill. BSBA, Pa. State U., 1963; JD, Temple U., 1967. Bar: Pa. 1967, U.S. Dist. Ct. (ea. dist.) Pa. 1967, U.S. Tax Ct. 1978. Former jud. law clk. to presiding judge Ct. Common Pleas, Phila., 1968-70; ptnr. Friedman & Friedman, Jenkintown, Pa., 1970-98, 1998—. Bd. dirs., chmn. Chase Savs. and Loan Assn., Phila.; bd. dirs. Fred Waring Enterprises, Inc., Del. Water Gap. Author: (pamphlet) What You Should Know About Real Estate, 1978; contbr. articles to publs. Ward leader Cheltenham Twp. Regular Rep. Orgn., Glenside, Pa., 1987-92. Paul Harris fellow Rotary. Mem. Pa. Bar Assn., Rotary (pres. Elkins Park, Pa. club 1982-83, pres. 1989-90), Gundaker Found., Montgomery County Bar Assn., Rydal Country Club, Philmont Country Club. Republican. Jewish. Avocations: golf, fountain pen collecting, tennis, o gauge model trains. Office: Friedman & Friedman Ste 534 The Pavilion Jenkintown PA 19076 Office Phone: 215-572-7600. Business E-Mail: rdf@rdflaw.com.

FRIEDMAN, RICHARD EVERETT, curator, art appraiser; b. Cleve., Nov. 24, 1942; s. Harry Martin and Miriam (Zavelson) F. BS, Columbia U., 1966, MA, 1968; PhD, Yale U., 1974; MLS, Kent State U., Ohio, 1984; PhD, U. Chgo. Asst. curator Met. Mus. Art, NYC, 1968-72; curator Phillips Collection, Washington, 1972-75; pres. Fine Arts Appraisal, Inc., Cleve., 1975-85; collection mgr. U. Akron, Ohio, 1984-86; head librarian Auburn (Ala.) U. Architecture Library, 1986-89; pres. Fine Art Appraisals, Akron, Ohio, 1989—2001. Assoc. prof. Cath. U., Washington, 1973-75. Author: (book) Hundertwasser, 1975. Trustee Cleve. Modern Dance Assn., 1979-84; life fellow Met. Mus. Art; life. mem. Cleve. Mus. Art. Fellow Soc. Archtl. Historians; mem. Irish Georgian Hist. Soc. Clubs: St. Juan de Luz Club (France), Columbia U. Club (NYC), Chantaco Golf and Tennis (Biarritz, France), Villa les Orchidees (Marrakes, Morocco), Chiberta Golf and Tennis Club. Home: Champs Fleuris Boul D'Augusta 64200 Biarritz France

FRIEDMAN, ROBERT BARRY, neurosurgeon; b. Bklyn., Dec. 28, 1953; s. Roy and Bernice (Berger) Friedman. BA, SUNY, Stony Brook, 1975; MD, SUNY Health Sci. Ctr., Bklyn., 1980. Diplomate Am. Bd. Neurol. Surgery. Gen. med. officer Indian Health Svc. USPHS, Sacaton, Ariz., 1981—82; neurosurgeon USAF, Wright Patterson AFB, Ohio, 1989—91, South Broward Neurosurg. Assn., Pembroke Pines, Fla., 1991—95, Cleve. Clinic Fla., Ft. Lauderdale, 1995—97, Spectrum Neurosurg. Specialists, Marietta, Ga., 1997—98, Henry Neurosurg. Specialists, P.C., Stockbridge, Ga., 1998—. Med. staff fellow NIH, Bethesda, Md., 1986—88. Contbr. articles to profl. jours. Maj. USAF, 1988—91. Recipient Neuroscience award, U. Pitts., 1989. Fellow: ACS; mem.: AMA, Fla. Med. Assn., So. Med. Assn., Congress Neurol. Surgeons, Am. Assn. Neurol. Surgeons. Libertarian. Avocations: private pilot, computers, photography. Home: 602 Redbud Ln Stockbridge GA 30281 Office: care Henry Neurosurg Specialists 150 Eagle Spring Ct Stockbridge GA 30281-7350 Office Phone: 770-506-3303. Personal E-mail: robert3018@msn.com.

FRIEDMAN, ROBERT GLENN, film company executive; b. 1950; s. Stuart S. and Sonia K. Friedman; m. Shari Ann Bernstein, July 17, 2004. With Warner Brothers, 1970—89, pres. worldwide advt. and publicity, 1989—96; vice chmn. Paramount Motion Picture Group, LA, 1997—2005; COO Paramount Pictures, LA, 2002—05; CEO Summit Entertainment L.L.C., 2007—. Office: Summit Entertainment LLC 1630 Stewart St Santa Monica CA 90404

FRIEDMAN, ROBERT LAURENCE, investment company executive; b. Mt. Vernon, NY, Mar. 19, 1943; s. Alvin S. and Frances (Feinsod) F.; m. Barbara Lander, Dec. 25, 1964; children: Lisa, Andrew. AB, Columbia Coll., 1964; JD, U. Pa., 1967. Bar: NY 1968. Assoc. Simpson, Thacher & Bartlett, NYC, 1967—74, ptnr., 1974—99; sr. mng. dir. The Blackstone Group LP, NYC, 1999, chief adminstrv. officer, chief legal officer, 2003—. Bd. dir. Axis Capital Holdings, Northwest Airlines, TRW Automotive Holdings Corp. Office: The Blackstone Group LP 345 Park Ave Fl 31 New York NY 10154-0004

FRIEDMAN, ROBERT LEE, film company executive; s. Edward A. and Claire (Seidenberg) F.; m. Marlene Saltz; children: Marc, Lisa. Sales Universal Pictures, NYC, 1948-52, 54-59; exec. v.p., distbn. & mktg. United Artists Corp., NYC, 1959-79; pres., distbn. Columbia Pictures, Burbank, Calif., 1979-82; pres. AMC Entertainment Internat., LA, 1984-92, pres. motion picture group, 1992-99; pres. RLF Entertainment, Beverly Hills, Calif., 1999—; CEO, pres. Stereo Vision Entertainment, Beverly Hills, 2000—. Radio announcer The Bob Friedman Hour, 1952-54; cons. RLF Prodns., Beverly Hills, Calif., 1982-84; sr. entertainment advisor, cons. Chanin Capital Ptnrs.; mem. bd. advisors Smart Video Tech.; ptnr. Media Entertainment Group LLC; bd. adv. MCorp and Roar Entertainment. Exec. prodr., appeared in film 9 Deaths of the Ninja, 1984; appeared in film Stardust Memories, 1980; prodr. film Girls Gone Wild. Bd. dirs., chmn. Entertainment Industry com. Century City C. of C., LA, 1988—; chmn. Will Rogers Hosp., 1980-81, also bd. dirs.; bd. dirs. Dare Am.; mem. vision fund The Lighthouse for the Blind. With US Army, 1952—54. Named Man of Yr. NY State Nat. Assn. Theatre Owners, 1981, Va., Md., Washington DC Assn. Theatre Owners, 1980. Mem. Acad. Motion Picture Arts & Scis. (bd. dirs. endowment fund, 1979—), Variety Club Am. (LA), Motion Picture Pioneers Am., Motion Picture Assocs. Found. (pres. 1970-73), LA-Century City C. of C. (Citizen of Yr., 1994) Avocations: photography, movies, tennis, exercise. Office: RLF Entertainment 2216 Summitridge Dr Beverly Hills CA 90210-1526 Personal E-mail: rlfblz@aol.com.

FRIEDMAN, ROBERT SIDNEY, political science professor; b. Balt., Mar. 1, 1927; s. Harry N. and Eva (Cohen) F.; m. Renee Cohen, Aug. 11, 1953 (dec. Oct. 4, 2002); children: Helene, David. BA, Johns Hopkins U., Balt., 1948; MA, U. Ill., Champaign-Urbana, 1950, PhD, 1953. Rsch. asst. Bur. Govt. Rsch., Md., 1953-55; instr. govt. and politics U. Md., 1955-56; from instr. to assoc. prof. govt. La. State U., 1956-61; rsch. assoc. Inst. Pub. Adminstrn., U. Mich., 1961-67, acting dir., 1967-68; assoc. prof. polit. sci. U. Mich., 1961-66, prof., 1966-68; prof., head dept. polit. sci. Pa. State U., 1968-78; dir. Center for Study Sci. Policy, Inst. for Policy Research and Evaluation, 1978-88, dir. policy analysis program, 1991-94; prof. emeritus, 1994—. Cons. in field. Co-author: Local Government in Maryland, 1955, Government in Metropolitan New Orleans, 1959, Political Leadership and the School Desegration Crisis in New Orleans, 1963; author: The Michigan Constitutional Convention and Administrative Organization: A Case Study in the Politics of Constitution-Making, 1971; contbg. author: Politics in the American States, 1965, 5th edit., 1990; contbr. articles to profl. jours. Bd. dirs. Pa. Civil Liberties Union, 1969-72; mem. State College (Pa.) Zoning Hearing Bd., 1976-79; chmn. study com. State College Mcpl. Govt., 1991-93; active State College Planning Commn., 1996-99; safety adv. bd. Three Mile Island-2 Cleanup, 1981-89; Pa. bd. Common Cause, 1998-2004; pres. Friends of Schlow Meml. Libr., 1999-2002, trustee, 2002-06. With AUS, 1945-46. Recipient McKay Donkin award for disting. svc., 1980. Mem. Am. Polit. Sci. Assn. Home: 4100 Massachusetts Ave NW Apt LT-08 Washington DC 20016 E-mail: learitas@cs.com.

FRIEDMAN, ROGER JAY, plastic surgeon; b. Washington, Sept. 16, 1952; Grad. in Architecture, Washington U., St. Louis, Mo.; MD, George Washington U. Sch. Medicine, 1978. Cert. Am. Bd. Plastic Surgeons. Intern, gen. surgery U. Mich., Ann Arbor, Mich., resident, plastic reconstructive surgery, 1979—81, resident, 1981—84; resident, hand and microsurgery Ralph K. Davies Med. Ctr., San Francisco, 1982; fellow, cosmetic and breast surgery Plastic Surgery Ctr., Honolulu, 1983; hosp. appointment Suburban Hosp., Bethesda, Md., Holy Cross Hosp., Md., Shady Grove Advent Hosp., Md., Sibley Hosp., Washington; clin. instr. George Washington U., Washington, Georgetown U.; office practice, 1984—. Chmn., sub-sect. plastic surgery Suburban Hosp., Bethesda, Md., 1997—2000; spkr. in field. Mem.: Am. Soc. Aesthetic Plastic Surgery, Am. Soc. Plastic Surgery, Alpha Omega Alpha. Office: Plastic Surgery Inst Washington 11210 Old Georgetown Rd North Bethesda MD 20852 Office Phone: 301-881-7770.*

FRIEDMAN, ROSELYN L., lawyer, mediator; b. Cleve., Dec. 9, 1942; d. Charles and Lillian Edith (Zalzneck) Friedman. BS, U. Pitts., 1964; MA, Case Western Res. U., Cleve., 1967; JD cum laude, Loyola U., Chgo., 1977. Bar: Ill. 1977, US Dist. Ct. (no. dist.) Ill. 1977. Mem. legal dept. No. Trust Co., Chgo., 1977-79; assoc. Rudnick & Wolfe, Chgo., 1979-84, ptnr., 1984-95, Sachnoff & Weaver, Ltd., Chgo., 1995—2006, ptnr., chmn. dept. estates and trusts, 2002—05; chief adminstrv. officer investment svcs. Joseph Freed and Assocs., Palatine, Ill., 2006—. Mem. Loyola U., Chgo. law rev.; mem. profl. adv. com. Chgo. Jewish Fedn., chmn., 1999-2001; mem. profl. adv. com. Chgo. Cmty. Trust, 2001-. Trustee Jewish Women's Found., 1997—2001; mediator Ctr. for Conflict Resolution, 2000—. Fellow Am. Coll. Trust and Estate Counsel; mem. ABA, Am. Jewish Congress (gov. coun. Midwest region 1995-97), Chgo. Bar Assn. (cert. appreciation continuing legal edn. program 1984, chmn. trust law com. 1989-90), Chgo. Estate Planning Coun. (program com. 1992-94, 98-2000, membership com. 1997-98, bd. dirs. 2001-2003), spkr. Ill. Inst. CLE, Chgo. Fin. Exch. (bd. dirs. 1995-97, sec. 1996-97). Office: Joseph Freed and Assoc 30 W Monroe 5th Fl Chicago IL 60603

FRIEDMAN, ROZANNE GOLSTON, psychotherapist; b. Richmond, Va., Jan. 30, 1947; d. Richard Jerome and Evelyn Myrna (Abady) Golston; m. Bernard A. Friedman, Aug. 16, 1970; children: Matthew Aaron, Megan Jane Strain. Attended, Stephens Coll., Columbia, Mo., 1965—66; BS, Ohio State U., Columbus, 1969; MA, U. Detroit Mercy, 1987. Lic. psychologist Mich., 1988. Tchr. K-8 Columbus Bd. Edn., 1969; tchr. Alexandria Bd. Edn., Va., 1969—70, Detroit Bd. Edn., 1970—71, Temple Israel, West Bloomfield, Mich., 1980—84; psychotherapist Farmington Hills, Mich., 1987—. Dir. Jud. Campaign, Bloomfield Hills, Mich., 1982. Mem.: Mich. Assn. Profl. Psychologists, Phi Psi. Office: 32255 Northwestern Hwy # 252 Farmington Hills MI 48334 Home Phone: 248-661-4900; Office Phone: 248-539-9250. Office Fax: 313-234-5356.

FRIEDMAN, SAM, editor; Editor-in-chief Property and Casualty/Risk and Benefit Mgmt. Edit. Nat. Underwriter, Hoboken, NJ; columnist Nat. Edn. Dept. NY Times. Office: NY Times 229 W 43rd St New York NY 10036 also: Nat Underwriter 33-41 Newark St Hoboken NJ 07030 Office Phone: 201-526-1237, 212-556-4122. Office Fax: 201-526-1260, 212-556-3758. E-mail: sfriedman@nuco.com.

FRIEDMAN, SAMUEL SELIG, lawyer; b. NYC, July 25, 1935; s. Nathan and Anne M. (Sobel) F.; m. Maxine E. Goldfarb, Jan. 7, 1961; 1 child, Alison J. BS, MIT, 1956; MBA, U. Pa., 1959; LLB, Columbia U., 1965. Bar: NY 1965, US Dist. Ct. (so. and ea. dists.) NY 1967, US Supreme Ct. 1984. Assoc. Lord, Day & Lord, NYC, 1965-72; ptnr., mem. exec. com. Lord Day & Lord, Barrett Smith and predecessor firm, NYC, 1972-94; ptnr. Morgan, Lewis & Bockius LLP, NYC, 1994—2004. Vice chmn., dir., mem. exec. com. Times Square Bus. Improvement Dist., 1992-95. 1st lt. US Army, 1959-62. Mem. ABA, NY State Bar Assn., Assn. Bar City NY, MIT Club NY, Penn Club, Phi Delta Phi. Avocations: travel, wine, sports. Office: 400 West End Ave New York NY 10024-5751 Office Phone: 212-724-7859.

FRIEDMAN, SANDRA L., pediatrician; d. William W. and Geraldine Friedman; m. Terry A. Patinkin, Apr. 21, 1985; children: Jonathan A. Patinkin, Zachary W. Patinkin. MS, U. Mich., Ann Arbor, 1975; MD, Northwestern U. Med. Sch., Chgo., 1980; MPH, Harvard Sch. Pub. Health, Boston, 1995. Cert. pediatrician Am. Bd. Pediat., 1986, neurodevel. disabilities Am. Bd. Pediat., 2001, devel. behavioral pediats. Am. Bd. Pediat., 2002. Dir. pediat. tng., leadership edn. neurodevel. disabilities Children's Hosp., Inst. Cmty. Inclusion, Boston, 1994—; program dir., neurodevel. disabilities Children's Hosp. Harvard, 2003—. Med. dir. Seven Hills, CECC, Groton, Mass., 1994—. Adv. com. mem. Perkins Sch., 2005. Recipient Phi Beta Kappa, U. of Illinoise, 1971, James Scholar, U. of Ill., 1960-1971, Intern of the Yr., James Scholar, U. of Ill., 1969-1971, Intern of the Yr., Dept of Pediat., Stanford Univ Med. Ctr., 1981, Cert. of Appreciation, Am. Assn. on Mental Retardation, 2000; scholar Rehab. Services Adminstrn. Traineeship, U. of Mich., 1971-1972, 1971-1972. Fellow: Am. Assn. Mental Retardation (pres., medicine divsn. 1998—2000), Am. Acad. Pediat.; mem.: Soc. Devel. Pediat. (bd. mem. 2003—05), Child Neurology Soc., Am. Assn. Intellectual & Devel. Disabilities (chair prevention com.), Phi Beta Kappa. Office: Children's Hospital Boston 300 Longwood Ave Boston MA 02115 Home Phone: 617-332-3752; Office Phone: 617-355-6513.

FRIEDMAN, SHELLY ARNOLD, cosmetic surgeon; b. Providence, Jan. 1, 1949; s. Saul and Estelle (Moverman) F.; m. Andrea Leslie Falchook, Aug. 30, 1975; children: Bethany Erin, Kimberly Rebecca, Brent David, Jennifer Ashley. BA, Providence Coll., 1971; DO, Mich. State U., 1982. Diplomate Nat. Bd. Med. Examiners, Am. Bd. Dermatology. Intern Pontiac (Mich.) Hosp., 1982-83, resident in dermatology, 1983-86; assoc. clin. prof. dept. internal medicine Mich. State U., 1984—89, adj. clin. prof., 1989—; med. dir. Inst. Cosmetic Dermatology, Scottsdale, Ariz., 1986—. Pres. Am. Bd. Hair Restoration Surgery. Contbr. articles to profl. jours. Mem. B'nai B'rith Men's Coun., 1973, Jewish Welfare Fund, 1973. Am. Physicians fellow for medicine, 1982. Mem. AMA, Am. Osteo. Assn., Am. Assn. Cosmetic Surgeons, Am. Acad. Cosmetic Surgery, Internat. Soc. Dermatologic Surgery, Internat. Acad. Cosmetic Surgery, Am. Acad. Dermatology, Am. Soc. Dermatologic Surgery, Frat. Order Police, Sigma

Sigma Phi. Jewish. Avocations: Karate, horseback riding. Office: Scottsdale Inst Cosmetic Dermatology 5828 N 7th St Phoenix AZ 85014 Office Phone: 480-970-0300. Personal E-mail: haredoc@aol.com.

FRIEDMAN, STEPHEN, federal official, former diversified financial services executive; m. Barbara Friedman. BA, Cornell U.; JD, Columbia U. With Goldman, Sachs & Co., 1966—94, ptnr., 1973—92, co-chmn. NYC, 1990—92, chmn., sr. ptnr., 1992—94; sr. prin. Marsh & McLennan Capital, Inc., 1998—2002; asst. to the Pres. for econ. policy The White House, Washington, 2002—04; dir. The Nat. Econ. Coun., Washington, 2002—04. Mem. Fgn. Intelligence Advisory Bd., 1993—95, chmn., 2005—; chmn. emeritus bd. trustees Columbia U.; chmn. fin. com. Memorial Sloan-Kettering Cancer Ctr.; chmn. exec. com. Brookings Instn.; bd. dirs. The Goldman Sachs, Group Inc. (formerly Goldman, Sachs & Co.), 2002—. Office: Goldman Sachs & Co 85 Broad St New York NY 10004-2456

FRIEDMAN, STEPHEN J., lawyer; b. Mar. 19, 1938; s. A.E. Robert and Janice Clara (Miller) F.; m. Fredrica L. Schwab, June 25, 1961; children: Vanessa V., Alexander S. AB magna cum laude, Princeton U., 1959; LLB magna cum laude, Harvard U., 1962. Bar: N.Y. 1962, D.C. 1982. Law clk. to justice William J. Brennan Jr. U.S. Supreme Ct., 1963-64; spl. asst. to maritime adminstr. Maritime Adminstrn., Dept. Commerce, 1964-65; assoc. Debevoise & Plimpton, NYC, 1965-70, ptnr., 1970—77, 1981—86, 1993—2004; dep. asst. sec. for capital markets policy Dept. Treasury, Washington, 1977-79; commr. SEC, 1980-81; exec. v.p., gen. counsel E.F. Hutton Group Inc., NYC, 1986-88, Equitable Life Assurance Soc., NYC, 1988-93; dean Sch. Law, Pace U., 2004—. Lectr. law Columbia U., NYC, 1974—77, 1982—85; bd. dirs. N.Y. Stock Exchange, Regulation, Inc., Refco, Inc. Author: An Affair With Freedom, the Opinions and Speeches of William J. Brennan, Jr., 1967; contbr. articles on legal and policy aspects of fin. inst. to profl. jours. Active Coun. on Fgn. Rels.; chmn. emeritus Am. Ballet Theatre, NYC; trustee Practising Law Inst.; mem. bd. govs. NASD, 1991-94, Chgo. Bd. Options Exch., 1982-88; trustee Support Found. Asian U. for Women. With USAR, 1962-68. Mem. ABA, Assn. of Bar of the City of NY (chmn. com. on securities regulation), Univ. Club, Lotos Club. Office: Pace U 1 Pace Plz 18th Fl New York NY 10038 Business E-Mail: sfriedman@pace.edu.

FRIEDMAN, SUE TYLER, technical publications executive; b. Nürnberg, Germany, Feb. 28, 1925; came to U.S., 1938; d. William and Ann (Federlein) Tyler (Theilheimer); m. Gerald Manfred Friedman, June 27, 1948; children: Judith Fay Friedman Rosen, Sharon Mira Friedman Azaria, Devora Paula Friedman Zweibach, Eva Jane Friedman Scholle, Wendy Tamar Friedman Spanier. Student, Beth Israel Sch. Nursing, 1941—43. Exec. dir. Ventures and Publs. Gerald M. Friedman, 1964—90; owner Tyler Publs., Watervliet and Troy, NY, 1979—86; treas., dir. Northeastern Sci. Found., Inc., Troy, 1979—; treas. Gerry Exploration, Inc., Troy, 1982—88; office mgr. Rensselaer Ctr. Applied Geology, Troy, 1983—. Pres. Pioneer Women/Na'amat, Tulsa, 1961-64, treas., Jerusalem, Israel, 1964, pres., Albany, N.Y., 1968-70; bd. dirs. Temple Beth-El, 1975-, dir. Hebrew Sch., 1965-80; mem. social program com. Internat. Sedimentological. Congress, 1979. Recipient Disting. Svc. award Temple Beth-El, 1991, Scroll of Honor, State of Israel Bonds, 1981; named Hon. Alumna Dept. Geology Bklyn. Coll. at CUNY, 1989; Sue Tyler Friedman medal named for history of geology award Geol. Soc. London, 1988. Mem. Geology Alumni Assn. (hon.). Achievements include Gerald M. and Sue T. Friedman Distinguised Service award named in honor at the history of geology division of the Geological Society of America. Avocation: world travel. Office: Northeastern Sci Found Inc Rensselaer Ctr Applied Geology PO Box 746 Troy NY 12181-0746 Personal E-mail: gmfriedman@nycap.rr.com. Business E-Mail: nest@thescienceffoundation.com.

FRIEDMAN, SYDNEY M., anatomist, educator, medical researcher; b. Montreal, Que., Can., Feb. 17, 1916; s. Jacob and Minnie (Signer) F.; m. Constance Livingstone, Sept. 23, 1940. B.Sc., McGill U., Montreal, Can., 1938, MD, C.M., 1940, M.Sc., 1941, PhD, 1946. Med. licentiate, Que. Teaching fellow anatomy McGill U., Montreal, Que., Can., 1940-42, asst. prof. anatomy, 1944-48, assoc. prof. anatomy, 1948-50; prof., head dept. anatomy U. B.C., Vancouver, Can., 1950-81, prof. anatomy, 1981-85, prof. emeritus, 1985—. Mem. panel on shock Def. Research Bd., Ottawa, Can., 1955-57; sci. subcom. Can. Heart Found., 1962-66, Am. Heart Assn., 1966-68, B.C. Heart Found., Vancouver, founding mem. Author: Visual Anatomy, 1950, 2d edit., 1970; contbr. more than 200 articles to profl. publs. Served as flight lt. RCAF, 1943-44. Recipient Premier award for rsch. in aging CIBA Found., 1955, Outstanding Svc. award Heart Found. Can., 1981, Disting. Achievement award Can. Hypertension Soc., 1987; Commemorative medal 125th Anniversary Can. Confedn.; Pfizer travel fellow Clin. Rsch. Inst., Montreal, 1971. Fellow AAAS, Royal Soc. Can., Coun. High Blood Pressure Rsch.; mem. Am. Anatomical Assn. (exec. com. 1970-74), Can. Assn. Anatomists (pres. 1965-66, J.C.B. Grant award 1982), Internat. Soc. Hypertension, Am. Physiol. Soc., Royal Vancouver Yacht Club, Vancouver Club, Alpha Omega Alpha. Avocation: painting. Home: 4916 Chancellor Blvd Vancouver BC Canada V6T 1E1

FRIEDMAN, THOMAS LOREN, foreign correspondent, writer; b. Mpls., July 20, 1953; s. Harold Abraham and Margaret (Phillips) F.; m. Ann Louise Bucksbaum, Nov. 23, 1978, 2 children. BA in Mediterranean Studies, Brandeis U., 1975; M.Phil. in Modern Middle East Studies, St. Anthony's Coll., Oxford U., 1978. Staff corr. UPI, London, 1978-79, Middle East corr. Beirut, 1979-81; reporter Bus. Day. sect. NY Times, NYC, 1981-82, Beirut bur. chief, 1982-84, Jerusalem bur. chief, 1984-89, chief diplomatic corr. Washington, 1989—95, fgn. affairs columnist, 1995—. Bd. dir. Pulitzer Prize, 2005—. Author: From Beirut to Jerusalem, 1989 (Nat Book Award, 1989), The Lexus and the Olive Branch, 2000 (Overseas Press Club award, 2000), Longitudes and Attitudes: The World in the Age of Terrorism, 2002, The World Is Flat: A Brief History of the Twenty-First Century, 2005 (NY Times Bestseller list, 2005, Publishers Weekly Bestseller list, 2005, Fin. Times, Goldman Sachs Bus. Book of Yr. award, 2005). Recipient Pulitzer prize, 1983, 1988, 2002, George Polk award L.I. U., 1982, Livingston award Livingston Found., 1983, Overseas Press Club award, 1980, Overseas Press Club award for lifetime achievement, 2004, Robert D. Heinl Jr. Meml. award Marine Corps History, 1985, Page 1 award NY Newspaper Guild, 1984, Order Brit. Empire (OBE), 2004. Jewish. Office: NY Times 1627 I St NW Washington DC 20006

FRIEDMAN, TULLY MICHAEL, finance company executive; b. Chgo., Jan. 9, 1942; s. Louis P. and Dorothy G. Friedman; m. Elise Woolsey Dorsey; children: Albert Evans Walker (dec.), Abigail Fay, Alexander Louis, Allegra Woolsey. AB, Stanford U., Calif., 1962; JD, Harvard U., Cambridge, Mass., 1965. Bar: Calif. 1965, Ill. 1967. With Charles Percy for Senator Com., Chgo., 1966; assoc. Sidley & Austin, Chgo., 1967-70; corp. fin. assoc. Salomon Bros., NYC, 1970-71, v.p., dir. West Coast corp. fin. San Francisco, 1972-79, gen. ptnr., 1979-81, mng. dir., 1981-84; founding ptnr. Hellman & Friedman, San Francisco, 1984-97; chmn., CEO Friedman, Fleischer & Lowe, LLC, San Francisco, 1997—. Bd. dirs. Clorox Co., Mattel, Inc., Kool Smiles Holding Co. Trustee, treas. Am. Enterprise Inst., 1988—; dir. Telluride Cmty. Found., 2001-. Home Phone: 415-441-1071. Business E-Mail: tfriedman@fflpartners.com.

FRIEDMAN, WALKER C., lawyer; b. Ft. Worth, Sept. 24, 1952; s. Bayard H. and Cornelia (Cheney) Friedman; m. Joan Elizabeth Pearson; children: Dillon, Chase, Paige. BA, U. Tex., 1974; JD, So. Meth. U., 1977. Bar: Tex. 1977, US Dist. Ct. No. Dist. Tex., US Ct. Appeals 5th Cir. Assoc., then shareholder Law, Snakard & Gambill, Ft. Worth, 1977-93; shareholder Friedman, Suder & Cooke (formerly Friedman, Young & Suder), Ft. Worth, 1993—. Chmn. exec. com. Ft. Worth Transp. Authority, 1993-99; trustee Mary Potishman Lard Trust; bd. trustees Amon Carter Mus. Mem. ABA, Tex. Bar Assn., Tarrant County Bar Assn., Tarrant County Civil Trial Lawyers Assn. (pres. 1990), Tex. Bar Found., Tarrant County Bar Found., Ft. Worth Inn of Ct., Exch. Club, Ft. Worth Club. Office: Friedman Suder & Cooke Tindall Sq Warehouse No 1 Ste 200 604 E 4th St Fort Worth TX 76102 Office Phone: 817-334-0400. Office Fax: 817-334-0401.

FRIEDMAN, WILBUR HARVEY, lawyer; b. NYC, May 2, 1907; s. Isador Peter and Zara (Sloat) F.; m. Frances Margolis, May 21, 1943. AB, Columbia U., 1927, LLB, 1930. Bar: N.Y. 1931. Law sec. U.S. Supreme Ct. Justice Harlan F. Stone, 1930-31; staff atty. Office of U.S. Solicitor Gen., 1931-32; mem. firm Proskauer Rose Goetz & Mendelsohn (now Proskauer Rose LLP), NYC, 1932-40; ptnr. Proskauer, Rose, Goetz, & Mendelsohn, NYC, 1940—. Lectr. Inst. on Fed. Taxation, NYU, 1943-65, lectr. Sch. Gen. Edn., 1955-60; bd. dirs., sec. Lawrence M. Gelb Found.; bd. dirs. Cancer Rsch. Inst., 1983-99; chmn. exec. com. bd. visitors Law Sch., Columbia U., 1977-91. Contbr. articles to profl. jours. Chmn. bd. overseers Edith C. Blum Art Inst. at Bard Coll., 1985-93; mem. Rockefeller U. Coun., 1986—; mem. med. ctr. adv. bd. N.Y. Hosp.-Cornell Med. Ctr., 1986—. Mem. ABA (mem. ho. dels. 1978-87), N.Y. State Bar Assn. (mem. exec. com. sect. taxation 1968-76), Assn. of Bar of City of N.Y. (chmn. com. on mgmt. and operation of profl. practice 1981-85), N.Y. County Lawyers Assn. (pres. 1975-77, mem. exec. com. 1977-79, chmn. com. on taxation 1948-54, chmn. com. on group ins. 1960-74, chmn. spl. com. on consumer agreements 1977-83), Lotos Club, Princeton U. Club, Phi Beta Kappa, Phi Beta Kappa Assocs., Tau Delta Phi. Home: 1016 5th Ave Apt 2D New York NY 10028-0132 Office: Proskauer Rose LLP 1585 Broadway Rm 2016 New York NY 10036-8299 E-mail: wfriedman@proskauer.com.

FRIEDMANN, E(MERICH) IMRE, biologist, educator; b. Budapest, Hungary, Dec. 20, 1921; arrived in U.S., 1965; s. Hugo and Gisella (Singer) Friedmann; m. Roseli Ocampo, July 22, 1974; 1 child, Daphna. BS Sch. Agriculture, Hungary, 1943, MS Sch. Agriculture, 1944, postgrad. U. Debrecen, 1948; PhD in Botany, Zoology, U. Vienna, 1951. Instr., lectr. Hebrew U., Jerusalem, 1952-66; assoc. prof. Queens U., Kingston, Ont., Canada, 1967-68, Fla. State U., Tallahassee, 1968-76, prof., 1976—2001, Robert Lawton Disting. prof., 1991—2001, dir. Polar Desert Rsch. Ctr., 1985—2001; sr. NRC rsch. fellow NASA Ames Rsch. Ctr., Moffett Field, Calif., 2001—; vis. prof. U. Wash., Seattle, 2005—. Concurrent prof. Nanjing U., People's Republic of China, 1987—; vis. prof. Fla. State U., Tallahassee, 1966-67, U. Vienna, 1975, U. Wash., 2005-; disting. sr. vis. scientist Jet Propulsion Lab., 1999-2000. Editor Antarctic Microbiology, 1993; contbr. articles to profl. jours. Recipient Congl. Antarctic Svc. medal NSF, 1979, Alexander von Humboldt award, 1987, resolution of commendation Gov. of Fla., 1978, Bergey's medal Bergey's Manual Trust, 2001. Fellow: AAAS, Am. Acad. Microbiology, Am. Soc. Microbiology (Procter and Gamble award in environ. microbiology 1998), Royal Microsci. Soc., Linnean Soc. London, Exploreres Club; mem.: Internat. Soc. Study of Origins of Life, Soc. Phycol. France, Hungarian Algological Soc. (hon.), Internat. Phycol. Soc., Am. Phycol. Soc. (award of Excellence 2002), Indian Phycol. Soc., Brit. Phycol. Soc., Hungarian Acad. Scis. (fgn.). Jewish. Achievements include co-discovery of micro-organisms (cryptoendolithic lichens) living in Antarctic rocks, 1976; discovery of fossil bacteria in the Martian meteorite ALH 84001, 2001. Office: Space Sci Divsn 245-3 NASA Ames Rsch Ctr Moffett Field CA 94035 Home: 225 4th Ave Apt B-503 Kirkland WA 98033 Home Phone: 425-827-8724; Office Phone: 425-827-8724. Business E-Mail: ifriedmann@mail.arc.nasa.gov.

FRIEDMANN, PATRICIA ANN, writer; b. New Orleans, Oct. 29, 1946; d. Werner and Marjorie Sybil (Cahn) F.; m. Robert E. Skinner, Mar. 17, 1979 (div. Nov. 1996); children: Esme Roberson, Werner Friedmann II; m. Edward G. Muchmore, Nov. 11, 1999. AB, Smith Coll., 1968; MEd, Temple Univ., 1970; ABD, Univ. Denver, 1975. Reviewer, contbr. Publishers Weekly, Brightleaf, Times-Picayune, Oxford Am., Speakeasy, New Orleans Review, Horn Gallery, 1993—; fiction workshop facilitator, New Orleans, 1994—99; writer-in-residence Tulane U., 2001; spkr. in field. Author: Too Smart to Be Rich, 1988, The Exact Image of Mother, 1991, Eleanor Rushing, 1999 (Barnes & Noble Discover Gt. New Writers selection, Borders Original Voices selection), Odds, 2000, Secondhand Smoke, 2002 (Book Sense 76 selection), Side Effects, 2006, A Little Bit Ruined, 2007, (plays) The Accidental Jew as part of Native Tongues, 1994, Lovely Rita as part of Native Tongues, 2000; contbg. author: The New Great American Writers Cookbook, 2003, Christmas Stories from Louisiana, 2002, My New Orleans, 2006, Intersections, 2006, New Orleans Noir, 2007. Mem. Authors Guild, PEN Am. Ctr Home: 8330 Sycamore Pl New Orleans LA 70118-2941 E-mail: afreelunch@aol.com.

FRIEDMANN, PAUL, surgeon, educator, research and development company executive; b. Vienna, Dec. 2, 1933; immigrated, 1938; naturalized, 1944. s. Erich and Rochelle (Behar) F.; m. Janee Armstrong, Apr. 24, 1962; children: Pamela, Cynthia. BA, U. Pa., 1955; MD, Harvard U., 1959; MBA, U. Mass., 2000. Diplomate, Am. Bd. Surgery (Vascular Surgery). Chmn. dept. surgery Baystate Med. Ctr., Springfield, Mass., 1971-98, sr. v.p. acad. affairs, 1996—2005; exec. dir. Pioneer Valley Life Scis. Rsch. Inst., Springfield, 2005—. Prof. surgery Tufts U. Sch. Medicine, Boston, 1985—, chmn. ad interim dept. surgery, 1996-2001; mem. residency rev. com., 1985-91, chmn., 1989-91; chmn. RRC Coun., Accreditation Coun. for Grad. Med. Edn., 1989-91, mem., 1994-2000, dean's prof. in biomed. innovation Isenberg Sch. Mgmt., U. Mass., Amherst, 2006-. Contbr. articles to profl. jours. Pres. Springfield Symphony Orch., 1999—2001, bd. chmn., 2001—03. Capt. USAF, 1961—63. Fellow ACS (bd. govs. 1978-84, 94—, vice chmn., 1998-99, pres. Mass. chpt. 1987, exec. com. bd. govs. 1996-99, adv. coun. for gen. surgery 1996-2003, chmn. 2001-03); mem. Am. Surg. Assn., Assn. Program Dirs. in Surgery (sec. 1985-87, pres. 1987-89), Coun. Med. Specialty Socs. (bd. dirs., sec. 1995-96, pres. elect 1996-97, pres. 1997-98), New Eng. Soc. Vascular Surgery (recorder 1989-90, pres.-elect 1990-91, pres. 1991-92), New Eng. Surg. Soc. (treas. 1991-95, pres.-elect 1995-96, pres. 1996-97), Accreditation Coun. for Grad. Med. Edn. (exec. com. 1995—, chmn. designate 1997-98, chmn. 1998-2000, John C. Gienapp award Contbns. Grad. Med. Edn. 2003). Office: Baystate Med Ctr 3601 Chestnut St Springfield MA 01199-1001 Personal E-mail: p.friedmann@comcast.net.

FRIEDMANN, PERETZ PETER, aerospace engineer, educator; arrived in US, 1969, naturalized, 1977; s. Mauritius and Elisabeth Friedmann; m. Esther Sarfati. DSc, MIT, Cambridge, 1972. Research asst. dept. aeronautics and astronautics MIT, Cambridge, 1969-72; asst. prof. mech. and aerospace engring. dept. UCLA, 1972-77, assoc. prof., 1977-80, prof., 1980-98, chmn. dept. mech. and aerospace engring. Los Angeles, 1988-91; François-Xavier Bagnoud prof. aerospace engring. dept. U. Mich., Ann Arbor, 1999—. Editor in chief Vertica-Internat. Jour. Rotocraft and Powered Lift Aircraft, 1980-90; contbr. numerous articles to profl. jours. Grantee NASA, Air Force Office Sci. Rsch., US Army Rsch. Office, NSF. Fellow AIAA (recipient Structures, Structural Dynamics and Materials award 1996, Structures, Structural Dynamics and Materials Lectr. award 97), Am. Helicopter Soc. (Fellow award 2004); mem. ASME (Structures and Materials award 1984, Spirit of St. Louis medal 2003, ASME/Boeing Structures and Materials award 2004). Office: U Mich Aerospace Engring Dept 3001 FXB Bldg Ann Arbor MI 48109-2140 Office Phone: 734-763-2354. Business E-Mail: peretzf@umich.edu.

FRIEDMANN, THEODORE, physician; b. Vienna, June 16, 1935; s. Eric and Rochelle (Behar) Friedmann; m. Ingrid Anna Stromberg, Jan. 3, 1965; children: Eric, Carl. BA, U. Pa., 1956, MD, 1960, MA, 1994. Diplomate Nat. Bd. Med. Examiners. Staff scientist NIH, Bethesda, Md., 1965-68; from asst. to full prof. pediatrics U. Calif. San Diego, La Jolla, 1970—, prof. pediatrics, dir. gene therapy, bd. dirs. Newton Abraham vis. prof., fellow Lincoln Coll., U. Oxford, England, 1994; mem. Congrl. Biomed. Ethics Adv. Com., U.S. Congress, Washington, 1988—92, Exptl. Virology Study Sect./NIH, 1986—90; Muriel Jeannette Whitehill chair biomed. ethics U. Calif., San Diego, 1989—; mem. com. on human cloning State of Calif., 2000—; mem. com. on medicine, health & rsch. IOC, World Anti Doping Agy., 2000—; mem. Recombinant DNA Adv. Bd./NIH, 1998—, chmn., 2002—. Author: (monograph) Gene Therapy: Fact and Fiction, 1993; editor: (book series) Molecular Genetic Medicine, 1989—; patentee in gene therapy. Recipient H.C. Jacobeaus prize, Nordic Rsch. Com., Sweden, 1995, Cross of Honor for Sci. and the Arts, Austria, 1996. Mem.: AAAS (chmn. adv. com. germ line gene therapy 1995—), NIH (chmn. DNA adv. com. 2001—). Avocation: music. E-mail: tfriedmann@ucsd.edu.

FRIEDRICH, DABNEY LANGHORNE, lawyer, commissioner; BA in Econs., Trinity U., 1988; diploma in Legal Studies, Oxford U., 1989; JD, Yale U., 1992. Law clk. to judge Thomas F. Hogan US Dist Ct., DC, 1992—94; assoc. Latham & Watkins, San Diego, 1994—95; asst. US Atty. So. Dist. Calif., San Diego, 1995—97, Ea. Dist. Va., Alexandria, Va., 1998—2002; counsel to chmn. Orrin G. Hatch US Senate Judiciary Com., 2002—03; assoc. counsel White House, Washington, 2003—06; commr. US Sentencing Commn., 2006—. Office: US Sentencing Commn 1 Columbus Cir NE Washington DC 20002-8002 Office Phone: 202-502-4500.*

FRIEDRICH, GUSTAV WILLIAM, dean, communications educator; b. Hastings, Nebr., Mar. 2, 1941; s. Edwin August and Ellen Marie (Meyer) Friedrich; m. Erena Rae Bakeberg, Aug. 4, 1962; 1 child, Bruce Gregory. AA, Concordia Coll., 1961; BA summa cum laude, U. Minn., 1964; MA, U. Kans., 1967, PhD with honors, 1968. 7th grade tchr. St. John's Sch., Young America, Minn., 1961-62; asst. instr., asst. debate coach U. Kans., Lawrence, 1964-68; asst. prof. Dept. Comm. Purdue U., West Lafayette, Ind., 1968—73, assoc. prof., 1973—77; prof., chair Speech Comm. Dept. U. Nebr., Lincoln, 1977-82, prof. Ctr. for Curriculum and Instruction, 1979—82; prof. U. Okla., Norman, 1982—98, chair Comm. Dept., 1982—88, faculty adminstrv. fellow Office of Sr. V.P. and Provost, 1993—95, presdl. prof., 1998; prof., dean Sch. Comm., Info. and Libr. Studies, Rutgers U., New Brunswick, NJ, 1998—. Vis. prof. U. Nebr.-Lincoln, 1997; cons. in field. Author: Classroom Communication, 1976, Public Communication, 1983; editor: Education in Classroom Communication, 1981; author, editor Teaching Communication, 1990. Mem.: Ctrl. State Comm. Assn. (exec. sec. 1975—77, pres. 1980, Outstanding Young Tchr. award 1970), Internat. Communication Assn. (bd. dirs. 1983—85), Speech Comm. Assn. (pres. 1988—89, Golden Anniversary award 1974). Democrat. Avocations: running, racquetball, bluegrass music. Office: Sch Comm, Info and Libr Sci Rutgers U 4 Huntington St New Brunswick NJ 08901 Office Phone: 732-932-7500. Office Fax: 732-932-6916. E-mail: gusf@scils.rutgers.edu.*

FRIEDRICHS, TERENCE PAUL, special education educator; b. West St. Paul, Minn., Jan. 9, 1956; s. Eugene Nicholas and Bernadine Cecilia Friedrichs. BS in Edn. magna cum laude, U. Mo., Columbia, 1976; MA in Spl. Edn., U. St. Thomas, St. Paul, 1979, EdD in Critical Pedagogy, 2005; PhD in Gifted and Spl. Edn., U. Va., Charlottesville, 1990. Cert. social studies tchr., learning disabilities tchr., elem. and secondary prin., supt. Minn. Spl. edn. tchr., dir. St. Mary's Schs., Sleepy Eye, Minn., 1981—84; asst. prof. U. Maine, Farmington, 1990; spl. edn. prof. SUNY, Geneseo, NY, 1991—92, Winona State U., Minn., 1992—93; spl. edn. tchr. Bloomington Pub. Schs., Minn., 1995—96, Mpls. Pub. Schs., 1996—98; gifted and spl. edn. dir. Lee Edn. Ctr., Mendota Heights, Minn., 1998—2005; founder, dir. Friedrichs Edn., Mendota Heights, 2006—. Cons., presenter in field. Author: Distinguishing Characteristics of Gifted Students with Disabilities, 2001, monographs in field; contbr. articles to profl. publs. Organizer Outfront Minn., Mpls., 1993; vol. Interdenominational Soup Kitchen, Charlottesville, 1987—88; mem. AIDS Task Force, Cath. Diocese of Richmond, Va., 1988; del. precinct, county, congl. dist. and state levels Democratic-Farmer-Labor Party, St. Paul, 1974—2006, mem. state ctrl. com., 2006—, mem. Stonewall caucus, 2006—; founder, dir. AIDS ministry Cath. Ch. of Incarnation, Charlottesville, 1988. Mem.: Assn. Gifted, Coun. Exceptional Children, Nat. Assn. Gifted Children, Minn. Coun. Gifted and Talented, Kappa Delta Pi, Phi Delta Kappa. Avocations: reading, music, travel. Office: Friedrichs Edn 750 S Plaza Dr # 203 Mendota Heights MN 55120

FRIEL, BRIAN (BERNARD PATRICK FRIEL), author; b. Omagh, County Tyrone, No. Ireland, Jan. 9, 1929; s. Patrick and Christina (MacLoone) F.; m. Anne Morrison, Dec. 27, 1955; children: Paddy, Mary, Judy, Sally, David. Student, St. Columb's Coll., 1941-46; BA, St. Patrick's Coll., Maynooth, Ireland, 1948; postgrad., St. Joseph's Tchrs. Tng. Coll., Belfast, Ireland, 1949-50; Litt.D. (hon.), Dominican Coll., Chgo., Nat. U. Ireland, New U. Ulster, Trinity Coll., Dublin, Ireland, Georgetown U. Tchr. various schs., Derry City, No. Ireland, 1950-60; freelance writer, 1960—; with Tyrone Guthrie Theatre, 1963; co-founder Field Day Theatre Co., Derry, No. Ireland, 1980. Author: (short stories) A Saucer of Larks, 1964, The Gold in the Sea, 1966, The Diviner: Brian Friel's Best Short Stories, 1983, (plays) This Doubtful Paradise, 1960, The Enemy Within, 1962, The Blind Mice, 1963, Philadelphia, Here I Come!, 1964, The Loves of Cass McGuire, 1966, Lovers, 1967, Crystal and Fox, 1968, The Mundy Scheme, 1969, The Gentle Island, 1971, The Freedom of the City, 1972, Volunteers, 1975, Living Quarters, 1977, Faith Healer, 1979, Aristocrats, 1979 (London Evening Standard Best Play award 1988, Best Fgn. Play award N.Y. Drama Critics Circle 1989), Translations, 1980 (Christopher Ewart-Biggs Meml. prize Brit. Theatre Assn. 1981, Plays and Players Best New Play award 1981), American Welcome, 1980, The Communication Cord, 1982, Making History, 1988, Dancing at Lughnasa, 1990 (Tony Best Play award 1992), Wonderful Tennessee, 1993, Molly Sweeney, 1994, Give Me Your Answer, Do!, 1997, The Yalta Game, 2001, Two Plays After, 2002; translator: Three Sisters (Anton Chekhov), 1981, Uncle Vanya, 1998, Two Plays After, 2002, Performances, 2003, Fathers and Sons (Ivan Turgenev), The Home Place, 2005; (screenplay) Philadelphia, Here I Come!, 1970; (version) A Month in the Country, Performances, 2003; editor: The Last of the Name; contbr. short stories to New Yorker. Mem. Irish Senate, 1987. Recipient Macauley fellow Irish Arts Coun., 1963; hon. fellow U. Coll., Dublin; named to Theatre Hall of Fame, 2007. Fellow Royal Soc. Literature; mem. Nat. Assn. Irish Artists, Am. Acad. Arts and Letters. Office: Drumaweir House Greencastle Donegal Ireland

FRIEL, DANIEL DENWOOD, SR., manufacturing executive; b. Queenstown, Md., Aug. 11, 1920; s. Samuel Edward Whiting and Martha Washington (Reynolds) F.; m. Helen June Hennessy, May 1, 1943; children: Barbara Friel Holme, Martha Friel Wilson, Patricia , Daniel D. Jr. BChemE, Johns Hopkins U., 1942. Supr. optical instruments Manhattan Project, U. Chgo., 1943-45; dir. applied physics E.I. du Pont, Wilmington, Del., 1945-61, mgr. investments, 1961-69, dir. electronic products, 1974-77, dir. instrument products, 1977-82; pres. Holotron Corp., Wilmington, 1969-71; pres., chmn. Edgecraft Corp., Wilmington, 1983-91, chmn. bd., chief exec. officer Avondale, Pa., 1991—. Chmn. Mt. Cuba Astron. Obs., Wilmington, 1960—. Co-author: Process Instruments and Control, 1960; contbr. articles to profl. jours. Trustee Tatnall Sch., Wilmington, 1967-74. Mem. Phys. Soc. Am., Optical Soc. Am., Instrument Soc. Am., Ams. for Competitive Enterprise System (bd. dirs.), Tau Beta Pi. Achievements include patents for radiation measurement, instruments, and household appliances; invention of radiation detection and analysis devices. Office: Edgecraft Corp 825 Southwood Rd Avondale PA 19311-9765

FRIELING, GERALD HARVEY, JR., specialty steel company executive; b. Kansas City, Mo., Apr. 29, 1930; s. Gerald Harvey and Mary Ann (Coons) F.; m. Joan Lee Bigham, June 14, 1952; children: John, Robert, Nancy. BS in Mech. Engring., U. Kans., 1951. Application engr. Westinghouse Elec. Corp., Pitts., 1951-53; mfg. mgr. Madison-Faessler Tool Co., Moberly, Mo., 1956-60; gen. mgr. wire and tubing Tex. Instruments Inc., Attleboro, Mass., 1960-69; v.p. Air Products & Chems. Co., Allentown, Pa., 1969-79; pres., chief exec. officer, chmn. bd. Nat. Standard Co., Niles, Mich., 1979-89, retired. CEO Tokheim Corp., 1990—91, chmn. bd., 1990—96, vice chmn., 1997—2000; bd. dirs., lead dir. Superior Metal Products, 2002—06; bd. dirs. Mossberg Printing Co., CTS; pres. Frieling & Assocs.; instr. Brown U., 1965—68; adj. prof. U. Notre Dame, Mendoza Sch. Bus., 1990—; mem. adv. bd. U. Kans. Sch. Engring., 1983—96. Author; patentee in field. Served to lt. USNR, 1953-56, Korea. Recipient Wire Assn. medal, 1966, Disting. Engring. Service award U. Kans., 1986. Mem.: Union League (Chgo.), Signal Point Country, Summit. Presbyterian. E-mail: nordict6@aol.com.

FRIELING, SCOTT R., lawyer; b. Mich., Feb. 12, 1973; BBA, U. Tex., Austin, 1996, M of Pub. Affairs, 1996, JD, 1999. Bar: Tex. 1999, US Dist. Ct. (no. and ea. dists. Tex.). Atty. toxic tort litig. sect. Baron & Budd, P.C., Dallas, 1999—. Named a Rising Star, Tex. Super Lawyers mag., 2006. Mem.: Dallas Trial Lawyers Assn., Dallas Bar Assn., Assn. Trial Lawyers of Am. Avocation: golf. Office: Baron & Budd PC 3102 Oak Lawn Ave Ste 1100 Dallas TX 75219 Office Phone: 214-521-3605.*

FRIEND, EDWARD MALCOLM, III, lawyer, educator; b. Birmingham, Ala., Oct. 12, 1946; s. Edward M. Jr. and Hermione Frances (Curjel) F. BA in History, U. Ala., 1968, JD, 1971. Bar: Ala. 1971. Shareholder Sirote and Permutt, P.C., Birmingham, Ala., 1971—, pres., 1991-93. Chmn. Birmingham Area C. of C., 1990-91; chmn. dist. bd. dirs. Colonial Bank Ala., Birmingham, 1985-2000; vice chair Colonial Bank Ctrl. Dist., 2000—; exec. in residence, asst. prof. U. Ala., Birmingham, 1994—, chmn. adv. bd. Sch. Bus., 2003-05. Chmn. Birmingham Area chpt. ARC, 1987-88; chmn. bd. NCCJ, 1983, nat. bd., 1981-88; pres. coun. U. Ala., Birmingham, 1980-94, Birmingham Jewish Fedn., 1984-89, United Way Ctrl. Ala., 1984-99, chmn., 1993-94, gen. campaign chmn., 1989; bd. dirs. Childrens Hosp. Ala., 1986-2005; exec. com. Ala. Symphony Assn., 1980-82, bd. dirs., 1982-85, Birmingham Festival Arts, 1978-88, pres., 1984-85, chmn., 1985-86; mem. nat. leadership coun. United Way Am.; pres. Big Bros./Big Sisters Greater Birmingham, 1980, chmn., 1981-83; trustee St. Vincent's Hosp., 1982-86, v.p., 1984-86, Ala. Sch. Fine Arts Found., 1985-91; trustee Cmty. Found. of Greater Birmingham, 2002—; chmn. Leadership Ala., 1993; bd. dirs. Boy Scouts Am., 1996-2005. Recipient Brotherhood award Nat. Conf. Christians and Jews, 1987; named to Ala. Acad. of Honor; named Lawyer of Yr., Birmingham Legal Secretarial Assn., 1976, Outstanding Alumnus, U. Ala. Sch. Law, 1984, Hon. Outstanding Alumnus, Sch. Bus., U. Ala., 2005. Mem. Nat. Health Lawyers Assn. (bd. dirs. 1992-95), Farrah Law Soc. (chmn. 1982-84), (hon.) U. Ala. Birmingham Alumnus. Office: Sirote and Permutt PC 2311 Highland Ave South Birmingham AL 35205-4004 Office Phone: 205-930-5116, 205-934-8854. Business E-Mail: efriend@sirote.com.

FRIEND, HAROLD CHARLES, neurologist; b. Chgo., Nov. 28, 1946; s. Leonard Nathan and Sharlee (Friedman) F.; children: Reed, Chad. BA, U. Tex., 1968, MD, 1972. Diplomate Am. Bd. Neurology. Resident Upstate Med. Ctr., Syracuse, NY, 1972-73, Albert Einstein Coll. Medicine, Bronx, NY, 1973-75; mem. staff Boca Raton Cmty. Hosp., Fla., 1975—; pres. Neurosci. Ctr., Boca Raton, Fla., 1984—; rsch. prof. dept. brain sci. Fla. Atlantic U., Boca Raton, 2002—05, co-dir. neurosci. and neurobehavior, 2004—07, clin. dir. neurosci. and neurobehavior, 2007—, clin. prof. biomed. scis., 2004—07, adj. clin. prof. biomed. scis., 2007—. Spl. expert witness Fla. Agy. for Health Care Adminstrn.; expert med. advisor divsn. workers compensation Fla. Dept. Labor and Employment Security, 1994-2003; pres. Puget Sound Yellow Taxi, Inc., 1994-95. Author: Territorial Marking, 1968, Bell's Palsy, 1975, Transient Global Amnesia, 1977. Exec. bd., v.p. Gulfstream coun. Boy Scouts Am., 1988—93, pres. coun., area IV v.p., 1993—95, area I v.p., 1990—92, area IV pres., 1995—98, so. region exec. bd., 1993—, internat. scouting com., 1998—, chmn. direct svc. com., 1999—2004, nat. adv. coun., 2000—; treas. Interam. Scout Found., 2001—07, pres., 2003—05; exec. bd. Palm Beach County agy. rels. com. United Way, 1992—95, allocation com., 1990—92; bd. dirs. Raton Children's Mus., 1989—92. Recipient Order of Arrow Vigil Honor award Boy Scouts Am., 1983, Dist. Merit award, 1987, Silver Beaver award, 1990, Disting. Commr. award, 1991, Disting. Eagle Scout, 1997, Silver Antelope award, 1997; James West fellow, 1993, 1910 Soc., 1998, Baden Powell fellow, 2000. Fellow: Am. Acad. Neurology; mem.: Am. Headache Soc., Fla. Med. Assn., Fla. Soc. Neurology, NY Acad. Sci. (life), So. Clin. Neurol. Soc., Am. Soc. Neuroimaging (cert.), Internat. Fellowship Scouting Rotarians (N.Am. sect. chmn. 1995—96, internat. sec. 1996—98, internat. vice chair 1998—99, internat. chair 1999—2002, internat. commr. 2002—05, internat. v.p. human resources 2007—, Silver Wheel award 2002), Rotary Internat. Fellowship Running and Fitness Rotarians (internat. chmn. 1992—98, internat. treas. 1998—99, internat. sec. 1999—2001, internat. chair 2003—06), Boca Raton Road Runners Club (pres. 1992—93), Rotary (bd. dir., pres. Boca Raton Club dist. world fellowship chmn. 1992—94, dist. found. chmn. 1994, gov.'s rep. 1994—95, chmn. dist. conf. 1995, gov.'s rep. 1996—97, dist. gov. 1998—99, chmn. coll. gov. 1999—2000, zone coord. Children at Risk 2000—01, cmty. svc. task force 2001—02, fellowship com. 2004—05, Dist. Found. Svc. award 1992, Pres. Salute Commendation 1993, featured on cover of The Rotarian 2003, Paul Harris fellow), Sierra Club (life), Phi Beta Kappa, Alpha Phi Omega, Theta Xi, Phi Kappa Phi. Avocation: marathons. Office: 1500 NW 10th Ave Ste 105 Boca Raton FL 33486-1344

FRIEND, STEPHEN H., biotechnology company executive; BA in Philosophy, Ind. U., MD, PhD in Biochemistry. Faculty Mass. Gen. Hosp., Boston, 1990—95, Harvard Med. Sch., Cambridge, Mass., 1987—95; co-founder, co-dir. Seattle Project Fred Hutchinson Cancer Rsch. Ctr., 1995—2000, vis. scientist, then head dept. molecular pharmacology, 1994—2000; pres. Inpharmatics, Kirkland, Wash., 1996—. Office: 401 Terry Ave N Seattle WA 98109-5234

FRIEND, THEODORE WOOD, III, foundation executive, historian, writer; b. Pitts., Aug. 27, 1931; s. Theodore Wood and Jessica (Holton) F.; m. Elizabeth Groesbeck Pierson, Feb. 20, 1960 (dec.); children: Theodore Porter, Pierson, Elizabeth Robinson. BA, Williams Coll., 1953, LLD (hon.), 1978; PhD, Yale U., 1958. Mem. faculty SUNY, Buffalo, 1959-73, prof. history, 1966-73; pres. Swarthmore (Pa.) Coll., 1973-82; trustee Eisenhower Fellowships, 1982—, pres., 1984—96. C.V. Starr disting. vis. prof. S.E. Asia studies Johns Hopkins U. Sch. Advanced Internat. Studies, 2004; bd. dirs. Metanexus Inst. on Religion and Sci, 2001—. Author: Between Two Empires, The Ordeal of the Philippines, 1929-46, 65 (Bancroft prize in history 1966), The Blue Eyed Enemy: Japan Against the West in Java and Luzon, 1942-45, 88, Indonesian Destinies, 2003; (novel) Family Laundry, 1986; editor: Religion and Religiosity in the Philippines and Indonesia, 2006. Dir. Phila. Savings Fund Soc., 1975-90; mem. Truman Scholarships Selection Panel, Pa., NJ, Del., 1993-2005, chmn., 1997-2005; bd. advisors U.S.-Indonesia Soc., 2000—; adv. com. Sabre Found., 2005—. Fulbright grant, Philippines, 1957-59; Internat. Rels. fellow Rockefeller Found., 1961-62, Postdoctoral fellow Nat. Def. Fgn. Lang., 1966-67, Guggenheim fellow, Indonesia, Philippines, Japan, 1967-68; fellow Woodrow Wilson Internat. Ctr., 1983-84, Bellagio Ctr. for Artists and Scholars fellow, 1988; recipient Dwight D. Eisenhower medal, 1997; finalist US Open Squash Championship, 75+ divsn., 2007. Mem. Coun. on Fgn. Rels., Am. Hist. Assn., Soc. Historians Am. Fgn. Rels., Asia Soc., Phila. Com. on Fgn. Rels. (chmn. 1985-2000), Fgn. Policy Rsch. Inst. (sr. fellow), Phila. Club, Franklin Inn Club, Phi Beta Kappa. Presbyterian. Achievements include being a nationally ranked sr. squash player, 1983-93, 97—. Home: 264 S Radnor Chester Rd Villanova PA 19085-1306

FRIEND, WILLIAM BENEDICT, bishop; b. Miami, Oct. 22, 1931; s. William Eugene and Elizabeth F. Student, U. Miami, 1949—52; cert. in philosophy, St. Mary's Coll., St. Mary, Ky., 1955; cert. of ordination, Mt. St. Mary's Sem., Emmittsburg, Md., 1959; MA in Edn., Cath. U. Am., 1965; LLD, St. Leo Coll., 1986. Ordained priest Roman Cath. Ch., 1959. Parish priest, educator, counselor, adminstr., 1959—68; ednl. rsch. adminstr. U. Notre Dame, Ind., 1968—71; vicar for edn., supt. schs. Diocese of Mobile, Ala., 1971—76, chancellor adminstrn., vicar for edn., 1976—79; aux. bishop Diocese of Alexandria-Shreveport, Shreveport, La., 1979—83, diocesan bishop Alexandria, 1983—86, first bishop Shreveport, La., 1986—2006, bishop emeritus, 2007—. Mem. Nat. Conf. Cath. Bishops, 1979; chmn. Campaign for Human Devel., 1980—93; mem. sci. and human values com. Commn. of Bishops and Scholars, 1983—86, chmn., 1986—92, cons., 1993—2006, sec., USCCB, 2000—04; mem. Pontifical Coun. for Culture. Editor handbooks and study guides for Cath. edn; editor: (with Ford and Daues) Evangelizing the Cultures in A.D. 2000, 1990; co-editor (with J. Anderson): The Culture of Bible Belt Catholics, 1995; contbr. articles on Cath. edn., Cath. ch. leadership and mgmt., theol. reflections to profl. publs. Bd. dirs., v.p. S.E. Regional Hispanic Ctr., Miami, 1986—; trustee Notre Dame Sem., 1976—2006, St. Joseph Coll. Sem., New Orleans, 1979—2006; bd. councillors Shreveport Bossier Cmty. Renewal; chmn. bd. Ctr. for Applied Rsch. in the Apostolate, 1997—2004; mem. adv. bd. The John J. Reilly Ctr. Sci., Tech. and Values U. Notre Dame, 2000—04; bd. dirs. La. Interchurch Conf., La. Catholic Conf., 1979—2006. Decorated Order of Fleur de Lis K.C., knight comdr. with star Knights of Holy Sepulchre of Jerusalem; recipient Presdl. award, Nat. Cath. Ednl. Assn., 1978, O'Neil D'Amour award, Nat. Assn. Bds. Edn., 1982, NCCJ Brotherhood and Humanitarian award, 1987, Human Rels. Coun. award, 2000, Harry Blake award, 2004. Mem.: World Futures Soc., NY Acad. Scis., Cath. Acad. Sci. USA, Am. Acad. Religion, KC (former state chaplain La. coun.). Roman Catholic. Avocations: hiking, art, music, reading.

FRIENDLY, DAVID T., film executive, producer; b. NYC, May 1, 1956; s. Fred W. and Dorothy Friendly; m. Priscilla Nedd-Friendly; 1 child. BA in Journalism, Northwestern U., 1978. Reporter, corr. Newsweek mag., NYC, LA, 1978-86; sr. v.p. motion pictures Imagine Films Entertainment, LA, 1987—91, pres. prodn., 1991; pres. Davis Entertainment, 1994; co-founder Deep River Prodns., 2000—. Columnist: First Look, LA Times, 1985—87; developer, supr.: (films) The Burbs, 1988; The Dream Team, 1988; Opportunity Knocks, 1989; Kindergarten Cop, 1990; exec. prodr.: My Girl, 1991, For Love or Money, 1993, My Girl 2, 1994, Greedy, 1994, The Chamber, 1996, Digging to China, 1998; prodr.: Courage Under Fire, 1996, Daylight, 1996, Out to Sea, 1997, Dr. Doolittle, 1998, Here on Earth, 2000, Big Momma's House, 2000, Laws of Attraction, 2004, The Honeymooners, 2005, Big Momma's House 2, 2006, Little Miss Sunshine, 2006 (Darryl F. Zanuck Prodr. of Yr. award in Theatrical Motion Pictures, Prodrs. Guild of Am., 2007). Bd. dirs. US-Ireland Alliance. Avocations: golf, tennis, music. Office: Deep River Prodns Ste 350 100 N Crescent Dr Beverly Hills CA 90210*

FRIES, JAMES A., academic administrator; BS in Chem. Edn., U. SD, 1965; MS in Phys. Chem., U. Iowa, 1968, PhD in Phys. Chem., 1969. Tchg. and rsch. asst. U. Iowa; prof. chemistry Northern State Coll., 1969—78, sr. devel. officer, asst. to pres./dir. devel., 1978—85; acting pres. and v.p. adminstrn. SD State U., 1985—86; pres., CEO Coll. Santa Fe, 1986—2000, pres. emeritus; interim pres. N.Mex. Highlands U., Las Vegas, N.Mex., 2001—02, pres., 2007—; exec. dir. GROW Santa Fe Cmty. Coll. V.p. Santa Fe Econ. Devel., Santa Fe Chamber of Commerce; co-chair Higher Edn. Transition Team, 2002. Mem. bd. dirs. Golden Apple Found.; mem. Coun. Ind. Colleges and Universities on N.Mex.; involved with Santa Fe Symphony. Office: New Mexico Highlands University Office of President Box 9000 Las Vegas NM 87701 Office Phone: 505-454-3269. Office Fax: 505-454-3069.

FRIES, JAMES FRANKLIN, internal medicine educator; b. Normal, Ill., Aug. 25, 1938; s. Albert Charles and Orpha (Hair) F.; m. Sarah Elizabeth Tilton, Aug. 27, 1960; children: Elizabeth Ann, Gregory James. AB, Stanford U., 1960; MD, Johns Hopkins U., 1964. Diplomate Am. Bd. Internal Medicine. Intern Johns Hopkins Hosp., Balt., 1964-65, resident in medicine, 1965-66, fellow connective tissue disease divsn., 1966-68; resident in medicine Stanford (Calif.) U. Sch. Medicine, 1968-69, instr. in medicine, 1969-71, asst. prof. medicine, 1971-77, assoc. prof. medicine, 1978-93, prof. medicine, 1993—. Dir. Arthritis, Rheumatism, Aging Med. Info. Sys., Stanford, 1975—; chmn. bd. dirs. Fries Found., Menlo Park, Calif.; chmn. Healthtrac, Inc., 1984-2001; exec. com. The Health Project, 1992—. Author: Take Care of Yourself, 1975, 2004, Prognosis, 1981, Living Well, 1997, 1999, 2004, Taking Care of Your Child, 2005, The Arthritis Helpbook, 2005, Arthritis, 2005; mem. editl. bd. Jour. Rheumatology, Jour. Clin. Rheumatology. Named Best Med. Specialist in U.S., Town and Country mag., 1984, Best Dr. in U.S., Good Housekeeping mag., 1991, Rsch. Hero, Arthritis Found., 2001; named one of Best Drs. in Am., Woodward-White, 1995; recipient C. Everett Koop Nat. Health award, 1994. Master Am. Coll. Rheumatology (Clin. Rsch. award 2005); fellow ACP, Am. Coll. Med. Info. Avocations: skiing, running, expedition mountain climbing. Home: 135 Farm Rd Woodside CA 94062-1210 Office: Stanford U Sch Medicine 1000 Welch Rd Ste 203 Palo Alto CA 94304-1808 Home Phone: 650-851-8995; Office Phone: 650-723-6003. Business E-Mail: jff@stanford.edu.

FRIES, MICHAEL T., communications executive; BA, Wesleyan Univ.; MBA, Columbia Univ. Mgmt. positions with UnitedGlobalCom, 1990—95, head Asia Pacific ops., 1995—98, pres., COO, 1998—2004, pres., CEO, 2004—05, Liberty Global Inc., Englewood, Colo., 2005—. Mem. Colo. Gov. Commn. on Sci. & Tech. Mem.: Young Presidents' Org. Office: Liberty Global Inc 12300 Liberty Blvd Englewood CO 80112*

FRIESE, GEORGE RALPH, retail executive; b. Chgo., Feb. 15, 1936; s. George R. and Marie D. (Pilz) F.; m. Patricia J. Brown, Aug. 24, 1957; children: Christine Carol, Kurt Michael. BA, Monmouth Coll., 1956; JD, Chgo. Kent Coll. Law, 1960. Bar: Ill. 1961, U.S. Dist. Ct. Ill. (no. dist.) 1961, U.S. Supreme Ct. 1965. Asst. gen. counsel, v.p. Banner Mut. Ins. Cos., Chgo., 1959-63; ptnr. Madsen & Friese, Park Ridge, Ill., 1963-68; corp. counsel, sec. SCOA Industries, Inc., Columbus, Ohio, 1968-71, v.p. legal, sec., 1971-81, pres., 1981-85; vice chmn., dir. Hills Dept. Stores Inc., Canton, Mass., 1986—95. Propr. Portsmouth (N.H.) Athenaeum, 1993—. Bd. dirs. Columbus Symphony Orch., Greater Columbus Art Coun.; chmn., trustee New Eng. Red Cross; trustee Boy Scouts Am., Columbus, 1981-86, Boston Lyric Opera, 1988-95, Strawbery Banke Mus., 1994—, treas., 1996-98; mem., trustee Greater Piscataqua Cmty. Found., 1995—, vice chmn., 1998-2000, chmn., 2000, City of Portsmouth Cultural Commn., 2004- Mem. ABA, Ill. Bar Assn., Columbus Athletic Club, Lotus Club (N.Y.), Tau Kappa Epsilon, Phi Delta Phi. Unitarian Universalist. Home and Office: PO Box 690 New Castle NH 03854-0690

FRIESE, ROBERT CHARLES, lawyer; b. Chgo., Apr. 29, 1943; s. Earl Matthew and Laura Barbara (Mayer) F.; m. Chandra Ullom; children: Matthew Robert, Mark Earl, Laura Moore. AB in Internat. Rels., Stanford U., 1964; JD, Northwestern U., 1970. Bar: Calif. 1972. Dir. Tutor Applied Linguistics Ctr., Geneva, 1964-66; atty. Bronson, Bronson & McKinnon, San Francisco, 1970-71, SEC, San Francisco, 1971-75; ptnr. Shartsis, Friese & Ginsburg, San Francisco, 1975—. Pres., bd. dirs. Custom Diversification Fund Mgmt., Inc., 1993—; dir.-co-founder Internat. Plant Rsch. Inst., Inc., San Carlos, Calif., 1978-86 Chmn. bd. suprs. Task Force on Noise Control, 1972-78; chmn. San Franciscans for Cleaner City, 1977; exec. dir. Nob Hill Neighbors, 1972-81; bd. dirs. Nob Hill Assn., 1976-78, Palace Fine Arts, 1992-94, San Francisco Beautiful, 1986—, pres., 1988-2000; chmn. Citizens Adv. Com. for Embarcadero Project, 1991-98; mem. major gifts com. Stanford U.; bd. dirs. Presidio Heights Neighborhood Assn., 1993—, pres., 1996-98; bd. dirs. Inst. of Range and the American Mustang, 1990—, Worldwatch Inst., 2005, chmn. nominating com., 2006—. Mem. ABA (co-chmn., sec. enforcement subcom., litigation sect., 2005-), Assn. Bus. Trial Lawyers (bd. dirs.), Calif. Bar Assn., Bar Assn. San Francisco (bd. dirs. 1982-85, chmn. bus. litigation com. 1978-79, chmn. state ct. civil litigation com. 1983-90, new courthouse com. 1993-95), Assn. SEC Alumni (bd. dirs. 1995—, pres. 2005-07), Lawyers Club of San Francisco, Mensa, Calif. Hist. Soc., Commonwealth Club, Swiss-Am. Friendship League (chmn. 1971-79). Office: Shartsis Friese LLP 1 Maritime Plz Fl 18 San Francisco CA 94111-3404 Home Phone: 415-773-7244. Business E-Mail: rfriese@sflaw.com.

FRIESECKE, RAYMOND FRANCIS, health company executive, director; b. Mar. 12, 1937; s. Bernhard P. K. and Josephine (De Tomi) F. BS in Chemistry, Boston Coll., 1959; MSCE, MIT, 1961. Product specialist Dewey & Almy Chem. divsn. W. R. Grace & Co., Inc., Cambridge, Mass., 1963-66; market planning specialist USM Corp., Boston, 1966-71; mgmt. cons. Boston, 1971-74; dir. planning and devel. Schweitzer divsn. Kimberly-Clark Corp., Lee, Mass., 1974-78; v.p. corp. planning Butler Automatic, Inc., Canton, Mass., 1978-80; pres. Butler-Europe Inc., Greenwich and Munich, Conn., Germany, 1980; v.p. mktg. and planning Butler Greenwich Inc., 1980-81; pres. Strategic Mgmt. Assocs., San Rafael, Calif., 1981-96; chmn. Beyond Health Corp., 1994—, Health-E-America Found., 2000—. Bd. dirs. Better Physiology, Ltd., 2000-05; corp. clk., v.p. Bldg. R&D, Inc., Cambridge, 1966-68. Host, prodr. Beyond Health Show, Sta. KEST, San Francisco, 1994—98, WWNN, 1995—, Sta. KBZS, 1998—2001, Stas. WRPT and WSRO, 1999—2001; host, prodr. KYCY, 2001—05; host, prodr. KRLA, KSBN, KFNX, 2003—05, KNTS, 2005—, KKNT, 2006—; pub.: Beyond Health News, 1995—; author: Management by Relative Product Quality, 1982, The New Way to Manage, 1983, Never Be Sick Again, 2002, Never Be Fat Again, 2007; contbr. articles to profl. jours. State chmn. Citizens for Fair Taxation, 1972-73; state co-chmn. Mass. Young Reps., 1967-69; chmn. Ward 7 Rep. Com., Cambridge, 1968-70; vice-chmn. Cambridge Rep. City Com., 1966-68; bd. dirs. Kentfield Rehab. Hosp. Found., 1986-88, chmn., 1988-91; Rep. candidate Mass. Ho. of Reps., 1964, 66; pres. Marin Rep. Coun., 1986-91; chmn. Calif. Acad., 1986-88; sec. Navy League Marin Coun., 1984-91, v.p., 1994-2000; bd. dirs. The Marin Ballet, 1996-98; bd. dirs. Insts. for Behavioral Physiology, Seattle, 1999-2000; nat. chmn. Project to End Disease, 2005—. 1st lt. U.S. Army, 1961-63. Named Businessman of Yr., Bus. Adv. Coun., 2006. Mem. NRA, Nat. Health Fedn., Am. Chem. Soc., Physicians Com. for Responsible Medicine, Marin Philos. Soc. (v.p. 1991-92), Ctr. for Sci. in Pub. Interest, Health Medicine Forum, Assn. of Am. Physicians and Surgeons, Orthomolecular Health Medicine Soc., The World Affairs Coun., Am. Holistic Health Assn. Office: 777 Grand Ave Ste 205 San Rafael CA 94901-3509

FRIESEN, DAVID DOUGLAS, musician, music educator, composer; b. Tacoma, Wash., May 6, 1942; s. Benjamin Wilfred and Clara Friesen; m. Kirsten Pedersen, May 16, 1964; children: David, Scott Benjamin, Tobin, Jenelle Dunkin. Panelist Nat. Endowment For The Arts, Washington, 1983—; dir. music clinic/workshops Thomastik-Infeld, Vienna, 1997—. Musician: (book) Departure; musician: (composer) (short film score) Creation (Acad. Award nominee, 1988); musician: (book) Years Through Time, (record) Through The Listening Glass (Voted in L.A. Times as one of the 10 best jazz records of the decade, 1981), (CD) Four to Go (One of the 5 best jazz recordings for 1996 Jazz Times Mag., 1996), The Name of a Woman (One of the 5 best jazz recordings for 2002 Jazz Times Mag., 2002), (performance) Solo Bass Concert (Most outstanding jazz artist Monterey Jazz Festival 1977, 1977), (short film score) To Try Again And Succeed (Acad. Award nominee, 1981). Nominee Best Jazz Bassist, Am. Jazz Awards, 1997; named, Down Beat Jazz Mag., 1979; named one of Ten Most Outstanding Jazz Artists, Swing Jour. Jazz Mag. (Japan), 1980; Jazz Performance grant, Nat. Endowment For the Arts, 1984, 1988, 1992. Mem.: Musicians Union. Achievements include design of Helped design original instrument.Hemage Bass. Small bass with a stand. Played same manner as acoustic bass but , much smaller fingerboard scale. Cherry wood body, ebony fingerboard, maple neck; Recorded 70 records/CD's as a leader/co-leader, over 150 recordings as a sideman; Toured as a leader throughout the United States playing concerts and over 20 other countries in the world; One of the pioneers of Solo Bass Concerts since 1972; Over 300 original compositions recorded. Avocations: wine collector, fishing, walking, films, travel. Office: Color Pool Music 1005 NE 78th Ave Portland OR 97213 Home Phone: 503-330-5999; Office Phone: 503-330-5999. Office Fax: 503-254-3510; Home Fax: 503-254-3510. Personal E-mail: cpm@davidfriesen.net.

FRIESEN, ORIS DEWAYNE, software engineer, historian; b. York, Nebr., Jan. 4, 1940; s. Harry H. and Malita Wanda (Ratzlaff) F.; m. Carey Lea Burbank, May 28, 1964; children: Isabelle Anne, Aric Alan. BS, U. Ariz., 1964, MA, 1966; PhD, Ariz. State U., 1982. Computer sys. analyst Computer Scis. Corp., Richland, Wash., 1967-69; computer sys. designer GE, Phoenix, 1969-70; database sys. designer Honeywell Info. Systems, Phoenix, 1970-84, engring. fellow, database mgmt., 1984-90, Bull Worldwide Info. Sys., Phoenix, 1990-99; rsch. prof. computer sci. and engring. Ariz. State U., 1999—2001; cons. in field, 2002—. Adj. prof. engring. Ariz. State U., Tempe, 1984—, rsch. prof., 1999-2001; adj. faculty in info. assurance, cyber forensics, software quality engring., digital visual literacy Mesa C.C., 2002—; vice chmn. database stds. Am. Nat. Stds. Inst., Washington, 1980-85; rapporteur, database stds. Internat. Stds. Orgn., Geneva, 1984-85; gen. chmn. Internat. Conf. on Deductive and Object-Oriented Databases, Scottsdale, Ariz., 1991-94; treas. Steering Com. for Internat. Conf. on Deductive and Object-Oriented Databases, 1997-2000; mem. steering com. Advanced Info. and Comms. Infrastructure Found. Group of Ariz. Gov.'s Strategic Partnership for Econ. Devel., 1994-95; mem. indsl. coun. Coll. Engring., No. Ariz. U., Flagstaff, 1995-99; charter mem. Ariz. Telecomms. Info. Coun., Adv. Bd. to Ariz. Telecomms. Policy Office, Found. Group of Ariz. Gov.'s Strategic Partnership for Econ. Devel., 1995—; Ariz. rep. for N.Am. Free Trade Assn., Telecomms. Stds. Subcom. of Office of US Trade Reps., 1994-96; charter mem., vice chair Ariz. Learning Tech. Partnership, 1996—; mem. bd. dirs. ACTC Technologies, Inc., Calgary, Alta., Can., 1996-98; chmn., mgr. wireless fidelity (WiFi) security for first-responders project Ariz. Telecomms. and Info. Coun., 1999—; charter bd. dirs. GELIA Global E-Learning Assn., 2000—; dir. eLearning Sys. for Ariz. Tchrs. and Students, 2006-. Author: China Reporting: An Oral History of American Journalism in the 1930s-1940s, 1987; editor Procs. of Phoenix Conf. on Computers and Comms., 1987; contbr. articles to profl. jours. Mem. Phoenix Futures Forum, 1988-91; mem., officer North Tatum Cmty. Homeowners Assn., Phoenix, 1985-88; mem. steering com. for advanced info. comm. Infrastructure Found. of Ariz. Gov.'s Strategic Partnership for Econ. Devel., 1994-96. Mem. IEEE (sr., gen. chmn. Phoenix Conf. on Computers and Communications 1990-91, vice-chmn. Globecom 97 Conf., 1995-97), Assn. for Computing Machinery, Assn. Asian Studies, Am. Hist. Assn., Orgn. Am. Historians. Democrat. Avocation: chinese language. Office: Future Info Techs 5136 E Le Marche Ave Scottsdale AZ 85254-1667

FRIGARD, MONIQUE DENISE, journalist; d. Louis Theodore and Miriam Claudia Frigard. AA, Laney Coll., 1997; BA, San Francisco State U., 2001. Cmty. editor, author newsmakers and youth spotlight columns focusing on local citizens Las Vegas Rev.-Jour., 2003—. Guest reader to second graders Crestwood-Edison Elem. Sch. Editor: Laney Tower Newspaper; designer: newspaper layout (1st place on-the-spot layout for a tabloid newspaper, Journalism Assn. Cmty. Colls., 1995). Recipient Humanitarian award, Nev. Reading Week, cert. appreciation, 2004. Liberal. Avocations: reading, writing, gardening, movies, swimming. Office: Las Vegas Review Jour 1111 W Bonanza Rd Las Vegas NV 89125 Home Phone: 702-205-4054. Office Fax: 702-383-4676. Business E-Mail: mfrigard@reviewjournal.com.

FRIGERIO, CHARLES STRAITH, lawyer; b. Detroit, Mar. 8, 1957; s. Louie John and LaVern (Straith) F.; m. Annette Angela Russo, Oct. 18, 1985; 1 child, Charles Anthony. BA, St. Mary's U., 1979, JD, 1982. Bar: Tex. 1982, U.S. Ct. Appeals (5th cir.) 1987, U.S. Supreme Ct. 1987; cert. in personal injury trial law. Pros. atty. City Attys. Office, San Antonio, 1982-84; trial atty. City Atty's. Office, San Antonio, 1984—; litigation chief and chief prosecutor City Atty.'s Office, San Antonio, 1995; pvt. practice law enforcement litigation San Antonio, 1995—. Mem. Dem. Nat. Com., San Antonio, 1976; asst. mgr. local campaigns, San Antonio, 1976-84. Mem.: ABA, Cath. Lawyers Assn., Nat. Bd. Trial Advocacy, San Antono Bar Assn., Fed. Bar Assn., Tex. Bar Assn., Delta Epsilon Sigma. Democrat. Roman Catholic. Home: 317 Cleveland Ct San Antonio TX 78209-5862 Office: Riverview Towers 111 Soledad St Ste 840 San Antonio TX 78205-2219 Office Phone: 210-271-7877.

FRIGO, JAMES PETER PAUL, industrial hardware company executive; b. Iron Mountain, Mich., Jan. 11, 1942; s. Louis and Giustina (Carollo) F.; m. Patricia Mary Nellen, June 21, 1969; children: Christine, Catherine, P.J. Ortiz, Pamela Aks, Steven, Sandy. BBA, U. Miami, 1966. Sales rep. Great Dane Trailers, Miami, 1966—67, Foster Inc., Miami, 1968, Lawson Products Inc., Miami, 1968—; pres. Jim Frigo Inc., Miami, 1972—. Asst. scoutmaster Troop 314 Boy Scouts Am. Mem.: KC. Republican. Roman Catholic. Office: Jim Frigo Inc 7420 SW 175th St Miami FL 33157-6313 Office Phone: 305-235-4121. Personal E-mail: jimfrigo@aol.com.

FRIMMER, PAUL NORMAN, lawyer; b. NYC, June 8, 1945; s. William and Irene (Alper) F.; m. Carol S. Zucker, June 9, 1968; children: Tracey, Scott. BS, Queens Coll., NYC, 1966; JD cum laude, Fordham U., 1969. Bar: N.Y. 1969, Calif. 1971. Assoc. Stroock and Stroock, and Lavan, NYC, 1969-71; ptnr. Irell and Manella, LA, 1971—. Panelist Calif. Continuing Edn. of Bar, 1972, co-chmn. various sects. 73, 75, 76, 80, 86; instr. advanced profl. program U. So. Calif., 1977-80; lectr. 6th and 14th Insts. Estate Planning U. Miami Law Ctr., 1972, 80, Practicing Law Inst.-ABA programs, 1973-91, 31st Inst. Fed. Taxation U. So. Calif., 1979, other bar assn. groups on estate planning, probate, taxation, charitable giving and community property. Contbr. numerous articles to profl. jours. Nat. trustee, asst. sec. Leukemia Soc. Am., Inc., 1976-86, 91—, trustee, chmn. planned giving com. L.A. chpt., chpt. pres., 1973-86; trustee L.A. Children's Mus., 1982-86. Fellow Am. Coll. Trust and Estate Counsel, Internat. Acad. Probate and Trust Law; mem. ABA (real property, probate and trust law sect. com. charitable giving, trusts and founds., chmn. disclaimer task force), Calif. Bar Assn. Avocations: tennis, skiing. Office: Irell & Manella 1800 Avenue Of The Stars Los Angeles CA 90067-4276

FRIOU, PHILLIP J. (JACK FRIOU), insurance company executive; b. Columbus, Ga., June 26, 1949; s. Phillip John Friou and Janet Ouillette Rosenberg; m. Karen June Knowles, Jan. 10, 1978 (div. Oct. 1980); m. Connie Renee Peters, Dec. 11, 1982; children: Carrie Renee, Catherine Emily. AB in Polit. Sci., U. Ga., 1971; postgraduate student, Columbus Coll., 1977. Mktg. adminstr. Am. Family Life Assurance Co., Columbus, Ga., 1973-75, dept. mgr. policy holder svc., 1975-76, v.p. mktg. comptr., 1976-78, v.p. external affairs, 1978-82, v.p. compliance, 1982-86, sr. v.p., 1989—, pres. Aflac NY, 1990—94, sr. v.p. mktg. and agy. devel., 1995—97, sr. v.p. govtl. rels., 1997—; exec. v.p. adminstrn., bd. dirs. Communicorp, Columbus, Ga., 1986-88, pres., COO, bd. dirs., 1988-89. Bd. mem. Employers Coun. Flexible Compensation. Mem. adv. com. Jed Harris for Ga. House of Reps. campaign, Columbus, 1990. Served in US Army, 1971—73. Mem. Leadership Columbus, Employers Coun. Flexible Compensation, Am. Soc. Health Underwriters, Albany C. of C. Episcopalian. Avocations: golf, skiing, yardwork, reading. Office: Am Family Life Assurance Co 1932 Wynnton Rd Columbus GA 31999 Office Phone: 706-323-3431.*

FRISBEE, DON CALVIN, retired utilities executive; b. San Francisco, Dec. 13, 1923; s. Ira Nobles and Helen (Sheets) F.; m. Emilie Ford, Feb. 5, 1947; children: Ann, Robert, Peter, Dean. BA, Pomona Coll., 1947; MBA, Harvard U., 1949. Sr. investment analyst, asst. cashier investment analysis dept. 1st Interstate Bank Oreg., N.A., Portland, 1949-52; treas. PacifiCorp, Portland, 1958-60, then v.p., exec. v.p., pres., 1966-73, chief exec. officer, 1973-89, chmn., 1973-94; chmn. emeritus PacifiCorp., Portland, 1994-97. Bd. dirs. Wells Fargo Bank. Trustee Reed Coll.; former trustee Safari Game Search Found., High Desert Mus.; mem. cabinet Columbia Pacific coun. Boy Scouts Am.; founder Oreg. chpt. Am. Leadership Forum. 1st lt. AUS, 1943-46. Mem. Arlington Club, Univ. Club Multnomah Athletic Club, City Club. Home Fax: 503-224-1199.

FRISBIE, CHARLES, lawyer; b. Kansas City, Mo., June 1, 1939; s. A.C. Jr. and Florence (Waddell) F.; m. Julia Louise Ross, June 28, 1969; children: Ross Waddell, Andrew James Louis. AB, Princeton U., 1961; JD, U. Mich., 1964. Bar: Mo. 1964, U.S. Supreme Ct. 1968. Assoc. Lathrop Righter Gordon & Parker, Kansas City, Mo., 1964-70; ptnr. Lathrop & Norquist, Kansas City, Mo., 1971-94; mem. Lathrop & Gage L.C., Kansas City, Mo., 1994—. Lt. USAFR, 1964—70. Mem. ABA, Mo. Bar Assn. (chmn. internat. law com. 1995-97), Kansas City Country Club (sec., bd. dirs. 1981-84). Republican. Episcopalian. Avocations: golf, reading. Home: 808 Romany Rd Kansas City MO 64113-2013 Office: Lathrop & Gage LC 2345 Grand Blvd Ste 2600 Kansas City MO 64108-2617 Home Phone: 816-444-4998; Office Phone: 816-292-2000.

FRISBIE, CURTIS LYNN, JR., lawyer; b. Greenville, Miss., Sept. 13, 1943; s. Curtis Lynn and Edith L. (Brantley) F.; m. Gena F. Johnson, May 30, 1965; children: Curtis L. III, Mark A. BSBA, U. Ala., 1966; JD, St. Mary's U., San Antonio, 1971. Bar: Tex. 1971, US Dist. Ct. (no. dist.), Ga. 1974, US Dist. Ct. (no. dist.), Tex. 1978, US Dist. Ct. (we. dist.), Tex. 1985, US Dist. Ct. (ea. and so. dists.), Tex. 1986, US Dist. Ct. (ea. dist.), Wis. 1986, US Tax Ct. 1986, US Ct. Appeals (5th cir.), 1975, US Ct. Appeals (10th cir.) 1982, US Ct. Appeals (8th cir.) 1987, US Supreme Ct. 1977, US Ct. Appeals (3rd cir.) 2006. Trial atty. Antitrust divsn. U.S. Dept. Justice, Atlanta, 1971-73; assoc. King & Spalding, Atlanta, 1974-77; ptnr. Gardere Wynne Sewell LLP (formerly Gardere & Wynne LLP), Dallas, 1978—. Assoc. editor St. Mary's Law Jour., 1970-71. Bd. dirs. Tex. Hist. Found., 2002—. Capt. USMC, 1966-69, Vietnam. Named Tex. Superlawyers in Antitrust, Tex. Monthly, 2003—06, Outdoorsman of Yr., Beretea Gallery, 2005; named one of Best Lawyers in Dallas, D Mag., 2003—06; named to Am.'s Leading Bus. Lawyers in Antitrust, Chambers & Ptnrs., 2004—06. Fellow Tex. Bar Found. (life), Dallas Bar Assn. (life); mem. ABA (antitrust and bus. law sect.), Tex. Bar Assn. (antitrust sect., mem. coun. 1995—, vice chair, chair elect 2000-01, chair 2001-02), Dallas Bar Assn. (pres. antitrust and trade regulation sect. 1993), Coll. State Bar Tex., Phi Alpha Delta. Avocations: scuba diving, fishing, hunting. Home: 5605 Palomar Ln Dallas TX 75229-6417 Office: Gardere Wynne Sewell LLP Thanksgiving Tower 1601 Elm St Ste 3000 Dallas TX 75201-4761 Office Phone: 214-999-4757. Business E-Mail: cfrisbie@gardere.com.

FRISBY, HERBERT RUSSELL, lawyer; b. Balt., Dec. 28, 1950; m. June J. Frisby; children: Herbert R. III, James T. BA in Polit. Sci./Internat. Rels., Swarthmore Coll., 1972; JD, Yale U., 1975. Bar: Md. 1975, DC 1979. Asst. gen. counsel Md. Atty. Gen.'s Office, Balt., 1978-79; atty.-advisor FCC, Washington, 1979-80, legal asst., 1980-83; sr. atty. Weil, Gotshal & Manges, Washington, 1983-86; prin. Melnicove, Kaufman, Weiner & Smouse, PA, Washington, 1986-89; ptnr. Venable, Baetjer & Howard, Balt., 1989-95; chmn. Md. Pub. Svc. Commn., Balt., 1995-98; pres. Competitive Telecomm. Assn., Washington, 1998—2004; CEO CompTel/ASCENT Alliance (merged with Assoc. Communications Enterprises), 2004—05; interim CEO CompTel/ALTS, Washington, 2005; ptnr. Kirkpatrick & Lockhart Nicholson Graham, 2005—. Mem. NARUC Comms. Com., Washington, 1995-98. Bd. dirs. United Way of Ctrl. Md., Balt., 1989-97; v.p. Balt. Mus. Art, 1993-95. Recipient Charles Hamilton Houston award Minority Bus. Enterprise Legal Def. and Edn. Fund, 1989, Disting. Alumnus award Fund for Ednl. Excellence, 1991; named to Balt. City Coll. Hall of Fame, 1989. Fellow Md. Bar Found.; mem. ABA (budget officer adminstrv. law sect. 1995-98). Home Phone: 410-997-3786; Office Phone: 202-778-9415. Business E-Mail: rfrisby@klng.com.

FRISBY, JAMES CURTIS, retired agricultural engineering educator; b. Bethany, Mo., Oct. 22, 1930; s. Jackson Carey and Gladys (Selby) F.; m. Hazel M. Kallenbach, Dec. 20, 1969. BS in Edn., U. Mo., 1952, BSAE, 1956; MS, Iowa State U., 1963, PhD, 1965. Registered profl. engr., Mo. Classroom instr., tech. writer, market analyst Caterpillar Tractor Co., Peoria, Ill., 1956-60; acting mgr. farm services dept. Iowa State U., Ames, 1961-63, instr., 1963-65; asst. prof. agrl. engring. U. Mo., Columbia, 1966-69, assoc. prof., 1969-74, prof., 1974-96, chmn. agrl. engring., 1989-94; prof. emeritus, 1996—; ret. Served to 1st lt. U.S. Army, 1952-54. Recipient award of merit Gamma Sigma Delta, 1976; recipient cert. of appreciation U. Mo. Coll. Engring., 1983, 87. Mem.: NSPE, Am. Soc. Agrl. Engrs. (Mem. of Yr. Mo. sect. 1995, Spl. Svc. award MidCtrl. Conf. 1996), Nat. Assn. Colls. and Tchrs. Agr. (Tchg. award of merit 1994), Am. Soc. Engring. Edn., Am. Soc. Agrl. Engrs. (chmn. mid-ctrl. region 1982—83, dir. mid-ctrl. region 1984—86), Mo. Soc. Profl. Engrs. (pres. ctrl. chpt. 1995—96), Kiwanis Internat. Mem. Ch. of Christ. Home: 1805 Bluff Pointe Dr Columbia MO 65201-6287 Personal E-mail: jchmf@juno.com.

FRISCH, HARRY DAVID, lawyer, consultant, investment company executive; b. NYC, June 5, 1954; s. Isaac and Regina (Rottenberg) Frisch; m. Sherry Beth Bannerman, 1992; children: Rachel Michele, Michael Elliot. BS, CCNY, 1976; postgrad., Rutgers U., 1976—77; JD, Pace U., 1980. Bar: N.Y. 1981, U.S. Dist. Ct. (so. and ea. dists.) N.Y. 1981, U.S. Ct. Appeals (2d cir.) 1984, U.S. Supreme Ct. 1986, U.S. Ct. Appeals (5th cir.) 1987. Law clk. Shearson Hayden Stone, Inc., NYC, 1977-80; assoc. gen. counsel Shearson Loeb Rhoades, Inc., NYC, 1980-82; asst. v.p., asst. corp. sec., assoc. gen. counsel Shearson/Am. Express, Inc., NYC, 1982-85; v.p., sr. litigator, assoc. gen. counsel Shearson Lehman Bros., Inc., NYC, 1985-88; 1st v.p., sr. litigator, assoc. gen. counsel Shearson Lehman Hutton, Inc., NYC, 1988-90, Shearson Lehman Bros., Inc., NYC, 1990-93; 1st v.p., sr. litigator, asst. gen. counsel Smith Barney Shearson Inc., NYC, 1993-94; asst. gen. counsel Gruntal & Co. Inc., NYC, 1994-97, Gruntal & Co., L.L.C., NYC, 1997-99; spl. counsel Lubiner & Schmidt, NYC, 1999; sr. v.p., compliance mgr. Datek Online Holdings Corp., Jersey City, 1999—2002, Ameritrade Holding Corp., 2002—03; sr. counsel, cons. Merrill Lynch, NYC, 2003—. Contbr. articles to profl. jours. Mem.: ABA, Fed. Bar Coun., N.Y. County Lawyers Assn., Assn. Bar City of N.Y., N.Y. State Bar Assn. Democrat. Jewish. Home: 2 Waterview Dr Ossining NY 10562-1639 Office: Merrill Lynch Litigation Dept 222 Broadway 13th Fl New York NY 10038 Office Phone: 212-670-0375. E-mail: harry_frisch@ml.com.

FRISCH, HARRY LLOYD, chemist, educator; b. Vienna, Nov. 13, 1928; s. Jacob J. and Clara F. (Spondre) F.; children— Benjamin, Michael. BA, Williams Coll., 1947; PhD, Poly. Inst. Bklyn., 1952. Research asso. physics Syracuse U., 1952-54; instr. U. So. Calif., 1954-55, asst. prof., 1955-56; mem. tech. staff Bell Telephone Labs., Inc., Murray Hill, NJ, 1956-67; prof. chemistry SUNY, Albany, 1967-78, disting. prof. chemistry, 1978—. Assoc. dean Coll. Arts and Sci., 1969-71; vis. assoc. prof. physics Yeshiva U., 1963-65, Inst. Study Metals, U. Chgo., 1960; asst. to dean Belfer Grad. Sch. Yeshiva U., 1963-65; cons. in field. Editor: (with J. Lebowitz) The Equilibrium Theory of Classical Fluids, 1964, (with Z. Salsburg) Simple Dense Fluids, 1968; assoc. editor: Jour. Chem. Physics, 1964-66, Jour. Statis. Physics, 1970-75; mem. editorial bd.: Jour. Phys. Chemistry, 1976-80, Jour. Polymer Sci. (Physics edit.), 1976— , Jour. Membrane Sci, 1976-80, Jour. Colloid and Interface Sci., 1978-81, Jour. Adhesion, 1970-75; contbr. articles to profl. jours. NSF grantee, 1968—; recipient Botis Pregel award NY Acad. Scis., 1973, Sr. U.S. Scientist Humboldt award, 1987-89. Fellow Am. Phys. Soc.; mem. Am. Chem. Soc. (G.S. Whitby award rubber div. 1995, Joel Henry Hildebrand Award in the Theoretical & Experminetal Chemistry of Liquids, 2000), Royal Belgian Acad. Sci. (assoc. fgn. mem.), Cosmos Club, Williams Club, Sigma Xi. Democrat. Jewish. Office: Dept of Chemistry SUNYA 1400 Washington Ave Albany NY 12222-0100 Office Phone: 518-442-2586. Business E-Mail: hlf04@albany.edu.

FRISCH, IVAN THOMAS, academic administrator, educator, computer and communications company executive; b. Budapest, Hungary, Sept. 21, 1937; came to U.S., 1939, naturalized, 1941; s. Laszlo and Rose (Balog) F.; m. Vivian Scelzo, June 6, 1962; children: Brian, Bruce. BS, MS, Columbia U., 1958, PhD, 1962. Asst. prof. elec. engring. and computer sci. U. Calif., Berkeley, 1962-65, assoc. prof., 1965-69; Ford Found. resident engring. practice Bell Labs., Holmdel, NJ, 1965-66; founding mem. Network Analysis Corp., Great Neck, NY, 1969—, sr. v.p., 1971—, gen. mgr., 1978-85; v.p. Contel Bus. Networks, 1985-87; dir. Ctr. on Advanced Tech. in Telecommunications, prof. Polytech. U., Bklyn., 1989—, provost, 1992—94, exec. v.p., provost, 1994—. Adj. prof. computer sci. SUNY, Stony Brook, 1975—, Columbia U., NYC, 1977—; cons. in field. Author: (with Howard Frank) Communication, Transmission and Transportation Networks, 1971; Founding editor-in-chief: Networks, 1971—; contbr. articles to profl. publs. Guggenheim fellow, 1969. Fellow IEEE (Eric E. Sumner award 1999, 3d Millenium award 2000); mem. NAE, N.Y. Acad. Scis., Cable TV Assn. Am., Phi Beta Kappa, Tau Beta Pi, Eta Kappa Nu. Office: Poly U Six Metrotech Ctr Rm JB-555 Brooklyn NY 11201-2907

FRISCH, JOSEPH, mechanical engineer, educator, consultant; b. Vienna, Apr. 21, 1921; came to U.S., 1940, naturalized, 1946; s. Abraham and Rachel (Lieberman) F.; m. Joan S. Frisch, May 26, 1962; children— Nora Theresa, Erich Martin, Jonathan David BSME, Duke U., 1946; MS, U. Calif., 1950. Registered profl. engr., Calif. Mem. faculty U. Calif.-Berkeley, 1947—, asst. prof. mech. engring., 1951-57, assoc. prof. mech. engring., 1957—, prof. mech. engring., 1963—, asst. dir. Inst. Engring. Rsch., 1961-63, chmn. div. mech. design, 1966-70, assoc. dean, 1972-75. Cons. to indsl. and govtl. labs. Contbr. articles to profl. jours. Fellow ASME (life); mem. Phi Beta Kappa, Sigma Xi, Tau Beta Pi, Pi Tau Sigma Clubs: U. Calif.-Berkeley Faculty. Office: U Calif Dept Mech Engring Berkeley CA 94720-1740 Home Phone: 510-841-9673; Office Phone: 510-642-3740. Business E-Mail: frisch@berkeley.edu.

FRISCH, ROSE EPSTEIN, population sciences researcher; b. NYC, July 7, 1918; m. David H. Frisch; children: Henry J., Ruth Frisch Dealy. BA, Smith Coll., 1939; MA, Columbia U., 1940; PhD, U. Wis., 1943. Assoc. prof. population scis. Harvard U., Cambridge, Mass., 1984-92, assoc. prof. emerita, 1992—2006. Author: Female Fertility and the Body Fat Connection, 2002, paperback edit., 2004; contbr. articles to profl. jours. Recipient Disting. Prof. Emeritus Merit award, Harvard Sch. Pub. Health, 2005; John Simon Guggenheim Meml. fellow, 1975—76. Fellow: Am. Acad. Arts and Scis.; mem.: AAAS, Sigma Xi (nat. lectr. 1989—90). Office: Harvard U Ctr Population Studies 9 Bow St Cambridge MA 02138-5103 Office Phone: 617-495-3013. Business E-Mail: rfrisch@hsph.harvard.edu.

FRISCH, SIDNEY, JR., lawyer, real estate and insurance broker; b. Evanston, Ill., Oct. 25, 1940; m. Deborah A. King, Aug. 27, 1988; children: Lauren, Michelle. BS in Fin., U. Ill., 1962, JD, 1965. Bar: Ill. 1966, US Dist. Ct. (no. dist.) Ill. 1966, US Ct. Appeals (7th cir.) 1968, Colo. 1977, US Dist. Ct. (mid. dist.) Ga. 1974, US Supreme Ct. 1986. V.p., gen. counsel Weber-Stephen Products Co., Palatine, Ill., 1966—, Kroeschell, Inc., Chgo., 1966—; pres. Frisch & Frisch, Chartered, Chgo., 1977—; v.p. Ontario Indemnity Group SPC, Grand Cayman. Lectr. seminars in field; mem. sec. of state's adv. com. to revise Ill. Bus. Corp. Act, 1984. Author: Illinois Mechanic's Liens, 1972; Attorney's Guide to Negotiation, 1979. Asst. editor Ill. Law Forum, U. Ill. Coll. Law, 1964, 65; mem. editl. com. Illinois Business Corp. Act Annotated, 1978. Assoc. bd. mem. U. Chgo. Cancer Rsch. Found., 1982, v.p. 1984. Served to lt. USNR, 1962-69. Recipient cert. of appreciation Ill. Inst. for Continuing Legal Edn., 1983. Mem. ABA, Ill. Bar Assn., Chgo. Bar Assn. (chmn. corp. law com. 1983-84, cert. of appreciation 1978, 83), Order of Coif. Clubs: Deans (U. Ill. Coll. Law). Office Phone: 312-666-7080.

FRISCHLING, CARL, lawyer; b. NYC, Feb. 21, 1937; s. Irving and Anna (Klein) F.; m. Adele Frischling, June 21, 1959; children: William, James, Edward. BA, Columbia U., 1958, JD, 1962, MBA, 1963. Bar: N.Y. 1963, U.S. Dist. Ct. N.Y. 1968. Atty. Am. Stock Exchange, NYC, 1963-65; asst. to chmn. Investors Funding, NYC, 1965-67; exec. v.p. and gen. counsel Am. Gen. Capital Mgmt., NYC, 1968-76; ptnr. Alexander Green, NYC, 1976-79; sr. ptnr. Spengler Carlson Gubar Brodsky Frischling, NYC, 1979-92; ptnr. Reid & Priest, NYC, 1992-94, Kramer Levin, NYC, 1994—. Bd. dirs. AIM Mut. Funds, Houston, Cortland Funds. Office: Kramer Levin 1177 6th Ave New York NY 10036 Office Phone: 212-715-7520. Business E-Mail: cfrischling@kramerlevin.com.

FRISCHWASSER, HEINZ FELIX See RA'ANAN, URI

FRISCO, LOUIS JOSEPH, retired electronics executive, electrical engineer; b. Patchogue, NY, Aug. 21, 1923; s. Anthony Michael and Rose Katherine (Lotito) F.; m. Verona May Kindig, Aug. 20, 1950 (dec.); children: Richard Samuel (dec.), Charles Francis. BSEE, Johns Hopkins U., 1949, MSEE, 1952. Dielectrics lab. dir. Johns Hopkins U., Balt., 1950-64; dielectrics program mgr. GE, Schenectady, N.Y., 1964-65; various tech. and ops. mgmt. positions Raychem Corp., Menlo Park, Calif., 1965-79, dir. corp. product rev., 1979-83, gen. mgr. Wire and Cable div., 1983-89, tech. dir. Electronics Sector, 1989-90. Chmn. Conf. on Elec. Insulation, NAS/NRC, 1963-65; U.S. del. tech. com. TC-15 Internat. Electrotech. Commn., 1963-65, 79-82. Editor Digest of Lit. on Dielectrics, NAS/NRC, 1959, 60.; contbr. numerous articles to profl. jours. Fellow IEEE; mem. ASTM, Electrochem. Soc. (chmn. insulation div. 1957-59, bd. dirs. 1957-59, insulation div. editor jour. 1961-64), Tau Beta Pi, Sigma Xi. Roman Catholic.

FRISHMAN, WILLIAM HOWARD, cardiologist, educator, department chairman, cardiovascular pharmacologist, gerontologist; b. NYC, Nov. 9, 1946; s. Aaron and Frances (Fishel) F.; m. Esther Rose Sandowsky, Mar. 11, 1971; children: Sheryl Renée, Amy Helene, Michael Aaron. BA, MD, Boston U., 1969. Diplomate Am. Bd. Internal Medicine, Am. Bd. Cardiovascular Medicine, Am. Bd. Critical Care Medicine, Am. Bd. Clin. Pharmacology, Am. Bd. Geriatrics, Am. Bd. Med. Mgmt. Intern Montefiore Hosp., Bronx, NY, 1969—70, resident in medicine, 1970—71, Bronx Mcpl. and Einstein Hosps., 1971—72; fellow in cardiology N.Y. Hosp.-Cornell U. Med. Coll., NYC, 1972—74, instr., 1974—76; dir. noninvasive cardiac labs. Einstein Hosp. and Montefiore Hosp., 1976—80, dir. cardiology svc., 1980—82, chief medicine, 1982—91; prof. medicine and epidemiology, assoc. chmn. dept. medicine Albert Einstein Coll. Medicine Yeshiva U., Bronx, 1991—97; prof. medicine and pharmacology, chmn. dept. medicine N.Y. Med. Coll., Valhalla, 1997—; chief of medicine Westchester Med. Ctr., Valhalla, NY, 1997—. Expert cons. cardiorenal divsn. FDA, Bethesda, Md., 1987-97; panel mem. US Pharmacopeia Conv., Rockville, Md., 1990-2000. Author: (med. book) Clinical Pharmacology of the Beta Blocking Drugs, 1980, 2nd edit., 1984, Management of Lipid Disorders, 1992; co-author: Calcium Channel Antagonists in Cardiovascular Disease, 1984, Therapy of Angina Pectoris, 1986, Current Cardiovascular Drugs, 1994, 4th edit., 2005, Beta-3 Adrenergic Agonism, 1995, Cardiovascular Pharmacotherapeutics, 1997, 2nd edit., 2003, Manual of Cardiovascular Pharmacotherapeutics, 1998, 2nd edit., 2004, Hypertension: A Clinical Guide, 2001, Complementary and Integrative Therapies for Cardiovascular Disease, 2005, Cardiovascular Regeneration and Stem Cell Therapy, 2007, Hypertension - A Clinical Guide, 2007; editor: Year Book of Medicine: Heart Disease, 1998—2003, Cardiology in Rev., Am. Jour. Medicine (supplements); contbr. chapters to books and articles to profl. jours. Mem. fiscal affairs com. Village of Scarsdale, N.Y., 1991—. Lt. col. M.C., U.S. Army, 1969-90. Named to Boston Collegium of Disting. Alumni, Boston U., 1988, Disting. Alumnus sch. medicine, 1994; teaching scholar Am. Heart Assn., 1979-82; preventive cardiology acad. award Nat. Heart, Lung and Blood Inst., 1980-85; recipient Disting. Tchr. award AAMC-AOA, 1997, Med. Humanism award AAMC, 2001. Master: ACP; fellow: Am. Coll. Chest Physicians, Am. Coll. Cardiology (bd. govs. 1987—91, pres. N.Y. State chpt. 1991); mem.: N.Y. Cardiology Soc. (pres. 1996—97), Assn. Profs. Medicine, Am. Soc. for Clin. Rsch., Am. Soc. for Clin. Pharmacology and Therapeutics (McKeen Cattell award 1990), Scarsdale Town and Village Club, Alpha Omega Alpha (regional councilor, bd. dirs.). Jewish. Avocation: reading. Home: 7 White Birch Ln Scarsdale NY 10583-7634 Office: Munger Pavilion NY Med Coll Valhalla NY 10595 Home Phone: 914-723-1030; Office Phone: 914-594-4383.

FRISINA, ROBERT DANA, neuroscientist, educator; b. Evanston, Ill., Sept. 11, 1955; s. Robert and Louise (Boaz) Frisina; m. Susan Taylor Frisina, July 31, 1982; children: Laurin Taylor, Taylor Robert. AB in Exptl. Psychology summa cum laude, Hamilton Coll., 1977; PhD in Neurosci., Syracuse U., 1983. Rsch. asst. Hamilton Coll., Clinton, NY, 1977; Root fellow in sci. Inst. Sensory Rsch., Syracuse (NY) U., 1977-78, NSF grad. fellow, 1978-81, grad. rsch. assoc., 1981-83; NIH rsch. fellow Ctr. Brain Rsch. U. Rochester, 1983-85; asst. prof. physiology and otolaryngology U. Rochester, 1985-91, assoc. prof. surgery, neurobiology and anatomy, 1991-99, prof. surgery, neurobiology, anatomy, and biomed. engring., 1999—, dir. rsch. otolaryngology, 1988-92, assoc. chmn. otolaryngology, 1992—; v.p. and founder Auditory Sys. Technologies, Inc., Pittsford, 1989-98. Charter mem. adv. bd. Internat. Ctr. Hearing, Speech Rsch., 1988—2002, assoc. dir., 2002—; chmn. study sect. NIH, 2000—02; adj. assoc. prof. comm. sci. Nat. Tech. Inst. Deaf, Rochester, NY, 1993—2004, prof. comm. scis., 2004—; adj. prof. comm. scis. U. Buffalo, 1998—; disting. rsch. prof. Rochester (N.Y.) Inst. Tech., 2003—. Dir. vols. Hamilton Coll. Aspect Marcy Psychiat. Ctr., NY, 1974—77. Recipient 1st award in Communicative Disorders, NIH, 1988—94. Fellow: Acoustical Soc. Am. (assoc. editor jour. 1996—99), Am. Acad. Otolaryngology, Head, Neck Surgery; mem.: Acoustical Soc. Found. (charter, bd. dirs. 1996—, gen. sec., chief fin. officer 1998—2006), Am. Speech, Hearing, Lang. Assn., Soc. Neurosci., Assn. Rsch. Otolaryngology, Psi Chi, Sigma Xi, Phi Beta Kappa. Roman Cath. Achievements include patents for for a noise suppression electronic circuit for enhancing speech in the presence of background noise; a hearing aid circuit which can be custom fit to a patient's hearing loss using laser trimming. Office: U Rochester Med Ctr Otolaryngology Dept Rochester NY 14642-8629 Office Phone: 585-275-8130, Business E-Mail: robert_frisina@urmc.rochester.edu.

FRISKEY, EDWIN ROBERT, JR., former military specialist; b. Manhasset, NY, Feb. 16, 1981; s. Edwin Robert and Jane Elizabeth Friskey; m. Lisa Marie Kasyjanski, July 21, 2005. Infantryman US Army, Schofield Barracks, Hawaii, 2003—06. Decorated Army Svc. ribbon, Nat. Def. Svc. medal, Purple Heart, Army Commendation medal, Global War Terrorism Expeditionary medal, Global War on Terrorism Svc. medal, Combat Infantryman badge, Overseas Svc. ribbon, Army Good Conduct medal, Army Commendation medal. Mem.: Mil. Order Purple Heart (life). Home Phone: 518-947-6763.

FRISSORA, MARK P., automobile rental and leasing company executive; b. Aug. 4, 1955; BA, Ohio State U., 1977; postgrad., U. Pa., Thunderbird Internat. Sch. Mgmt. With lighting bus. group GE, 1977-87; various mgmt. positions Philips Lighting co., 1987-91; v.p. N.Am. mktg., sales and distbn. Aeroquip-Vickers Corp., 1991-96; v.p. original equipment sales and engring. Walker Mfg., 1996; sr. v.p., gen. mgr. original equipment bus.-program mgmt. Tenneco Automotive, Lake Forest, Ill., 1996-99, pres., CEO, 1999—2006, chmn., 2000—06; pres., CEO Hertz Global Holdings, Park Ridge, NJ, 2006—. Mem. The Bus. Roundtable; supplier's adv. coun. Nissan Motor Co.; automotive bd. gov. World Econ. Forum; bd. dir. NCR Corp., FMC Corp.; bd. dirs. Hertz Corp., 2006—. Mem.: Motor & Equipment Mfr. Assn. (bd. dir.), Automotive Original Equipment Mfr., Soc. Automotive Engrs. Office: Hertz Corp 225 Brae Blvd Park Ridge NJ 07656*

FRIST, BILL (WILLIAM HARRISON FRIST), retired senator, thoracic surgeon; b. Nashville, Feb. 22, 1952; m. Karyn McLaughlin Frist, 1982; children: Harrison, Jonathan, Bryan. AB in health care policy, Princeton U. Woodrow Wilson Sch. Pub. and Internat. Affairs, 1974; MD, Harvard U., 1978. Resident Mass. Gen. Hosp. Stanford U., 1978-83, rsch. fellow in surgery, 1983—84; chief registrar CT Surgery Southampton Gen. Hosp., Eng., 1983; chief resident CT Surgery Mass. Gen. Hosp. Stanford U., 1984-85; chief resident CT Surgery, sr. fellow cardiac transplant svc. Stanford U. Med. Ctr., 1985-86; founder, surgeon Vanderbilt Transplant Med. Ctr., 1986—, asst. prof. surgery, 1986-93, dir. heart and lung transplantation, 1986-93; founder, surgical dir. Vanderbilt Multi-Organ Transplant Ctr., 1989-93; US Senator from Tenn., 1995—2007; majority leader, 2003—07. Mem. fin. com., US Senate health, edn., labor & pensions com., rules & adminstrn. com.; mem. Nat. Bipartisan Comm. on Future of Medicaire, 1998-99; vice chair Alliance for Health Reform, 1995; Chmn. Tenn. Medicaid Task Force, 1992-93; bd. dirs. Sergeant York Historical Assn., YMCA Found. Met. Nasville; bd. regents Smithsonian Inst.; bd. trustees Princeton U.; vis. prof., Woodrow Wilson Sch. Pub. Internat. Affairs, Princeton U., 2007- Author: Transplant: A Heart Surgeon's Account of the Life-and-death Dramas of the New Medicine, 1989, When Every Moment Counts: What You Need to Know About Bioterrorism from the Senate's Only Doctor, 2002; co-author (with J. Lee Annis): Tennessee Senators, 1911-2001: Portraits of Leadership in a Century of Change, 1999; co-author: (with Shirley Wilson) Good People Beget Good People: A Genealogy of the Frist Family, 2003; editor (with J. Harold Helderman): Grand Rounds in Transplantation, 1995. Bd. regents Smithsonian Inst., Washington; bd. trustees Princeton U.; bd. dirs. Sergeant York Hist. Assn., YMCA Found. Met. Nashville. Named one of most influential people, TIME mag., 2005; recipient Taxpayer's Hero award, Coun. for Citizens Against Govt. Waste, 1997, Taxpayer's Friend award, Nat. Taxpayer's Union, 1998, Champion of Sci. award, Sci. Coalition, 1999, Hero of the Taxpayer, Americans for Tax Reform, 2000, Disting. Bd. Dir. award, Healthcare Fin. Mgmt. Assn., 2002, Nat. Leadership award, The Nat. Ctr. for Leadership, 2002, Excellence in Immunization award, Nat. Partnership for Immunization, 2002, Congl. Champion award, YMCA, 2003, IRI Freedom award, Internat. Rep. Inst., 2003, James Madison award, Am. Whig-Cliosophic Soc., 2003, Woodrow Wilson award, Princeton U., 2003, Lifetime Achievement award, Nat. Minority Health Month, 2003. Mem. Alpha Omega Alpha, Am. Coll. Chest Physicians, Am. Coll. Surgeons, AMA, Tenn. Med. Assn., Am. Soc. Transplant Surgeons, Assn. Acad. Surgery, Internat. Soc. Heart & Lung Transplantation, Middle Tenn. Heart Assn. (pres.), Soc. Thoracic Surgeons, So. Thoracic Surgical Assn., Tenn. Transplant Soc., United Way De Tocqueville Soc. Republican. Presbyn.

FRIST, THOMAS FEARN, JR., hospital management company executive; b. Nashville, Aug. 12, 1938; s. Thomas Fearn and Dorothy (Cate) Frist; m. Patricia Champion, Dec. 22, 1961; children: Trisha, Thomas Fearn III, Bill. BS, Vanderbilt U., 1961; MD, Washington U., 1966. Exec. v.p. Hosp. Corp. Am. (HCA), Nashville, 1968—77, pres., COO, 1977—82, pres., CEO, 1982—85, chmn., 1985—95; vice chmn. Columbia/ Hosp. Corp. Am. Healthcare Corp., Nashville, 1994—97; chmn., CEO Hosp. Corp. Am. Healthcare Corp., Nashville, 1995—2001; chmn. The Frist Found., Nashville. Bd. dirs. Columbia Healthcare. Past v.p. Vanderbilt Bd. Trust; past chair bd. governors United Way of Am. Named Disting. Alumnus, Vanderbilt U., 2002; named one of Forbes Richest Americans, 2006. Fellow: Am. Coll. Healthcare Execs. (hon.); mem.: Bus. Coun., Bus. Roundtable, Belle Meade Country Club. Presbyterian. Avocations: running, tennis, skiing, flying. Office: Frist Foundation 3100 W End Ave Ste 1200 Nashville TN 37203-1348

FRISTOE, MACALYNE, speech pathology/audiology services professional, psychologist, educator, writer; b. Nashville, Mar. 14, 1931; d. George Miller and Brownie Appleton Watkins; m. James Houston Fristoe, June 4, 1953 (div. Nov. 1964); children: James Houston Jr., Andrew McLean; m. John Leiper Freeman, Jr., Jan. 20, 1966 (div. Oct. 1973). BA cum laude, Vanderbilt U., 1953, MS, 1960, PhD, 1972. Lic. speech pathologist, Ind. Health Prof. Bur. Speech clinician East Tenn. Hearing & Speech Ctr., Knoxville, Tenn., 1953—54; speech clinician, speech pathologist Bill Wilkerson Hearing & Speech Ctr., Nashville, 1955—60, asst. dir. speech clinic, 1964—67; instr. speech pathology Sch. Medicine Vanderbilt U., Nashville, 1960, 1964—67, instr. psychology, 1971—72, asst. prof., 1972—74; dir. lang. intervention study project Ctr. Devel. & Learning Disorders Med. Ctr., U. Ala., Birmingham, 1974—76; asst. prof. to assoc. prof. dept. biocomm. U. Ala., Birmingham, 1974—76; dir. speech clinic Purdue U., West Lafayette, Ind., 1976—79, assoc. prof. to prof. dept. audiology & speech scis., 1976—96, dir. grad. programs dept. audiology and speech scis., 1986—90, 1992—96, assoc. dept. head audiology and speech scis., 1993—96, assoc. prof. to prof. dept psychol. scis., 1982—96, prof. emerita, 1996—. Speech clinician Nashville-Davidson County Schs., Nashville, 1955—57; cons. Vanderbilt Hosp., 1957—60, L.B. Wallace Devel. Ctr., Decatur, Ala., 1974—78; rsch. NIH-NIAMDD kidney disease contract Vanderbilt Med. Ctr., 1971—74; mem. adv. bd. Ind. Resource Ctr. for Autism, Ind. U., Bloomington, 1986—94, Steer Speech and Hearing Clinics, Purdue U., 2000—02; reviewer NIH, Bethesda, Md., 1990—96; sci. reviewer Nat. Inst. Neurological and Commn. Disorders and Stroke, NIH, Nat. Inst. Child Health and Human Devel., Nat. Inst. Deafness and Commn. Disorders, Sensory Disorders and Lang. Study sect. NIH, NSF, March of Dimes, Purdue U.; spkr. in field. Assoc. editor Jour. Childhood Comm. Disorders, 1975-78, reviewer, 1978-82; mem. pub. bd. CEC Divsn. Children with Comm. Disorders, 1977-79; editl. cons. Jour. Speech and Hearing Disorders, 1977-79, 1982—, Mental Retardation, 1977-80, Augmentative and Alternative Comm.; cons. editor Am. Jour. Mental Deficiency, 1979-83; reviewer Jour. Applied Rsch. in Mental Retardation; contbr. numerous articles to profl. jours.; co-author, developer: Filmstrip Articulation Test, 1966, Goldman-Fristoe Test of Articulation, 1969, Goldman-Fristoe-Woodcock Test of Auditory Discrimination, 1970, Goldman-Fristoe-Woodcock Auditory Skills Test Battery, 1975, Goldman-Fristoe Test of Articulation 2, 2000; author: Language Intervention Systems for the Retarded, 1975; editor: (book) Four Language Intervention Systems, 1977. Recipient Women in Rsch. award Kennedy Inst. Johns Hopkins U., Balt., 1976; scholar Vanderbilt U., 1952-53; fellow Nat. Def. Edn. Act., 1969; traineeship U. Miami, 1956, Columbia U., 1966, Vanderbilt U., 1969-70, 1970-71. Fellow APA, Am. Speech Lang. Hearing Assn. (cert. clin. competence in speech pathology), Am. Assn. Mental Retardation (v.p. comm. disorders 1985-86, pres. comm. disorders divsn. 1986-87); mem. Nat. Coun. Comm. Disorders (rep.), Phi Beta Kappa, Sigma Xi.

FRISWOLD, FRED RAVNDAL, manufacturing executive; b. Mpls., Jan. 21, 1937; s. Ingolf Oliver and Derrice Ernestine (Anderson) F.; m. C. Marie Martin, Sept. 14, 1957; children— Cynthia, Steven, Barry, Michelle (dec.), Benjamin. BBA with distinction in Fin, U. Minn., 1958. Chartered fin. analyst. With J.M. Dain & Co. (now Dain, Rauscher, Inc.), Mpls., 1958—90; exec. v.p. Dain, Bosworth, Inc., 1976-82, pres., CEO, 1982-90, cons., 1990-92; CEO Tonka Equipment Co., Plymouth, Minn., 1992—. Chmn. bd. U. Gateway Corp., UMF Investment Advisors; U. Minn. Found.; mem. bd. advisors Otologics L.L.C. Bd. dirs. Met. Mpls. YMCA, Mpls. Rotary Found. Mem. Twin City Soc. Security Analysts, Wildwood Lodge, Mpls. Rotary (pres. 1997-98). Methodist. Office: Tonka Equipment Co 13305 Water Tower Cir Plymouth MN 55441-3803 Home: 5925 Tamarac Ave Edina MN 55436

FRITCH, JOHN KENNETH, civilian military employee; s. Kenneth Reifsynder and Eleanor Louise Fritch. BA, Ind. U. Pa., 1970. Cert. life cycle logistics level III US Dept. Army, program mfmt. level I US Dept. Army. Army materiel command intern New Cumberland Army Depot, Pa., 1970—72; inventory mgmt. specialist Comms. Electronics Command, Ft. Monmouth, NJ, 1972—76; supply sys. analyst Comms. Electronic Command, Ft. Monmouth, NJ, 1976—77; supply mgmt. officer US Mil. Cmty. Activity, Augsburg, Germany, 1978—80; supply sys. analyst 200th Theater Army Materiel Mgmt. Ctr., Zweibruecken, Germany, 1980—87; real property maintenance acct. supply staff officer Hdqrs. US Army Europe and 7th Army, Dep. Chief of Staff Engr., Heidelberg, Germany, 1987—92; logistics mgmt. specialist Project Mgt. Battle Command, Ft. Monmouth, 1992—. Mem. US Power Squadron, NJ, 2003—. Recipient cert. commendation, 200th Theater Army Materiel Mgmt. Ctr., 1985, Performance award, Project Mgt. Battle Command, 1998—2005, Comndr.'s award for civilian svc., Program Exec. Office Commands, Control and Comms. Tactical, Dept. Army, 2002, Spl. Act award, Project Mgt. Battle Command, 2006. Mem.: Mensa, US Chess Fedn. (life), Shrewsbury Sailing and Yacht Club. Avocation: sailing. Home: 2 Lakeview Terr Apt B Eatontown NJ 07724 Office: Project Mgr Battle Command Fort Monmouth NJ 07703

FRITH, DOUGLAS KYLE, retired lawyer; b. Henry County, Va., Sept. 2, 1931; s. Jacob and Sally Ada (Nunn) F.; m. Ella Margaret Tuck, Sept. 10, 1960; children: Margaret Frith Ringers, Susan Elaine Frith. AB, Roanoke Coll., 1952; JD, Washington and Lee U., 1957. Bar: Va. 1957. Pvt. practice, 1957-58; assoc. Taylor & Young, Martinsville, Va., 1957-58; ptnr. Young, Kiser & Frith, 1960-71, Frith, Gardner & Gardner, 1973-78; pres. Douglas K. Frith & Assocs., P.C., Martinsville, 1979-99; ret., 1999. Bd. dirs. Frith Constrn. Co., Inc., Frith Equipment Corp.; substitute judge 21st Gen. Dist. Ct., 21st Juvenile and Domestic Relations Dist. Ct., 1969-80. Chmn. March of Dimes, 1960, Brotherhood Week, 1960; capt. profl. div. United Fund, 1971. With U.S. Army, 1952-54. Mem. ABA, Am. Bd. Trial Advocates, Va. Bar Assn., Martinsville-Henry County Bar Assn. (pres. 1970-71), Va. Trial Lawyers Assn. (dis. v.p. 1970-71, del. at large 1971-77), Kiwanis. Republican. Baptist. Address: 1409 Whittle Rd Martinsville VA 24112 Personal E-mail: dougfrith@earthlink.net.

FRITSCHE, CLAUDIA, diplomat, ambassador; Personal sec. Liechtenstein Head Gov., 1970-74, Dep. Head Gov., Liechtenstein, 1974-78; diplomatic collaborator Office of Fgn. Affairs, Liechtenstein, 1978-90; dep. Permanent Rep. to Coun. of Europe, Strasbourg, France, 1983-90; first sec. Liechtenstein Embassy, Berne, Switzerland, 1987-89, first sec., chargée d'affaires Vienna, 1989; permanent rep. of Liechtenstein UN, NYC, 1990—2002; Liechtenstein amb. to U.S. Washington, 2002—. Head Liechtenstein Nat. Com. on Equality between Women and Men, 1987-90; sec. Liechtenstein parliamentary del. to the Coun. of Europe, parliamentary del. to the European Free Trade Assn. Office: Embassy of Liechtenstein 888 17th St NW Ste 1250 Washington DC 20006 Office Phone: 202-331-0590. Business E-Mail: tamara.brunhart@was.rep.llv.li.

FRITTS, EDWARD O., broadcasting association executive; b. Cape Girardeau, Mo., Feb. 21, 1941; m. Martha Dale; children: Kimberley, Timothy, Jennifer. Grad., U. Miss. Pres. Nat. Assn. Broadcasters, Washington, 1982—2005, cons., 2005—. Past chmn. joint bd. Nat. Assn. Broadcasters; vice chair US Dept. State Internat. Media Fund. Cons. U.S. C. of C. Assns. Com.; chair media adv. com. U.S. Bicentennial Commn.; vice chmn. White House Pvt. Sector Initiatives Bd., 1985—88; mem. individual investors adv. com. N.Y. Stock Exch.; active Nat. Mus. Women in the Arts; dir. advt. coun., former trustee Mus. TV and Radio; active Wolf Trap Found., Arlington Hosp. Found.; bd. dirs. Nat. Commn. Against Drunk Driving, Partnership for a Drug-Free Am., Ctrs. for Disease Control's Bus. Responds to AIDS program. Recipient Silver Mike award, U. Miss. Mem.: Sigma Alpha Epsilon (Highest Effort award). Avocation: golf. Office: Nat Assn Broadcasters 1771 N St NW Ste 200 Washington DC 20036-2812

FRITTS, HAROLD CLARK, botanist, educator; b. Rochester, NY, Dec. 17, 1928; s. Edwin Coulthard and Ava Lee (Washburn) Fritts; m. Barbara Smith, June 11, 1955 (dec.); children: Marcia L., Paul T.; m. Miriam Colson, July 19, 1982. AB, Oberlin Coll., Ohio, 1951; MS, Ohio State U., 1953, PhD in Botany, 1956. Asst. prof. botany Eastern Ill. U., Charleston, 1956-60; asst. prof. dendrochronology U. Ariz., Tucson, 1960-64, assoc., 1964-69, prof., 1969-92, emeritus, 1992—; adj. prof. in rsch. Desert Rsch. Inst., U. Nev. Vis. scientist CSIRO forest products divsn., Melbourne, Australia, 1996; owner Dendro-Power, Tucson, 1992—; dir., founder Internat. Tree-Ring Data Bank, 1975-90; NSF faculty, mem. Task Group 3 adv. com. on paleoclimatology, Climate Dynamics Program, 1978-79; lectr. NATO Advanced Study Inst. on Climatic Variability, Sicily, 1980; vis. dir. U. Wyo. Summer Sci. Camp, summer 1956; mem. U. Ariz. del. to People's Republic of China, 1976; participant Nat. Def. U., 1978-79; mem. organizing group internat. conf. on dendroclimatology, Eng., 1980. Author: Tree Rings and Climate, 1976, reprinted 2001, Reconstructing Large-Scale Climate Patterns from Tree-Ring Data, 1991; mem. editorial adv. bd. Quaternary Rsch., 1977-82; contbr. articles to profl. jours. Mem. local sch. bd., 1971-72. Recipient Dendrochronological award of Appreciation Sci. Cmty., Lund, Sweden, 1990, award for appreciation and recognition of outstanding contbns. to dendroclimatology Tree Rings and Climate-Sharpening the Focus, Tucson, 2004; Grad. fellow Ohio State U., 1954-56, NSF fellow Oreg. Inst. Marine Biology, summer 1957, Guggenheim fellow, 1968-69; grantee NSF 1971-87, U. Calif. Lawrence Livermore Lab., 1978-79, State of Calif., 1979-80, 85-86. Fellow: AAAS; mem.: Am. Meteorol. Soc. (Outstanding Achievement in Bioclimatology award 1982), Am. Inst. Biol. Scis., Ecol. Soc. Am. (editl. bd. 1964—66, chmn. paleoecology sect. 1984, coun. rep.), Am. Assn. Quaternary Environ. (coun. 1978—82, adv. com. paleonclimatology), Tree Ring Soc. (exec. com. 2000—01, mem.-at-large exec. bd., Lifetime Achievement award 7th Internat. Conf. Dendrochronology, Beijing 2006). Avocation: photography. Home and Office: 5703 N Lady Ln Tucson AZ 85704-3905 Business E-Mail: hfritts@ltrr.arizona.edu.

FRITTS, HARRY WASHINGTON, JR., internist, educator; b. Rockwood, Tenn., Oct. 4, 1921; s. Harry Washington and Hyder (Smith) F.; m. Helen Dyer Goodwin, Aug. 25, 1949; children: John Goodwin, Benjamin Carroll, Patricia Louise. Student, Vanderbilt U., 1941; BS, Mass. Inst. Tech., 1943; MD, Boston U., 1951. Diplomate: Am. Bd. Internal Medicine (mem.). Mem. research staff MIT, 1946-47; intern, then resident Univ. Hosp., Boston, 1951-53; vis. fellow Columbia Coll. Physicians and Surgeons, 1953-56, mem. faculty, 1956-73, prof. medicine, 1967-73, Dickinson W. Richards prof. medicine, 1972-73; prof., chmn. dept. medicine Sch. Medicine, State U. N.Y. at Stony Brook, 1973-87, Edmund D. Pellegrino prof. medicine, 1986-87. William Harris vis. prof. Nat. Med. Sch. Taiwan, 1987-88; vis. physician Bellevue Hosp., 1957-68, Presbyn. Hosp., N.Y.C., 1961-73; vis. physician, cons. Manhattan VA Hosp., 1957-68; vis. prof. U. London, 1982; bd. dirs., adv. council research N.Y. Heart Assn.; mem. sci. council Parker Francis Found.; mem. physiology study sect., mem. cardiovascular tng. com. USPHS; mem. council Nat. Heart, Lung and Blood Inst. Author: On Leading a Clinical Department, 1997; assoc. editor: Jour. Clin. Investigation; mem. editl. bd.: Am. Rev. Respiratory Diseases; contbr. articles to profl. jours. Served to lt. (j.g.) USNR, 1943-46. Guggenheim fellow, 1959-60 Fellow ACP; mem. Am. Physiol. Soc., Am. Soc. Clin. Investigation, Assn. Am. Physicians, Am. Clin. and Climatol. Soc., Alpha Omega Alpha. Home: 79 Bevin Rd Northport NY 11768-1133 Office: SUNY at Stony Brook Dept Medicine Stony Brook NY 11794-0001 Personal E-mail: hwfritts@aol.com.

FRITZ, DIANE P., controller; d. James H. and Diane H. Fritz. BS in Acctg., Coll. William and Mary, Williamsburg, Va., 2002. CPA Va. Auditor Deloitte, McLean, Va., 2001—04; sr. acct. NII Holdings, Reston, Va., 2004—05; contr., asst. contr. Rosetta Stone, Harrisonburg, Va., 2005—. Vol. Vol. Farm, Woodstock, Va., 2006. Named RA Active Programmer of Yr., William and Mary, RA of the Month, Va. Mem.: AICPA. Office: Rosetta Stone 135 W Market St Harrisonburg VA 22801

FRITZ, EDWARD LANE, dentist; b. Evansville, Ind., Dec. 15, 1932; s. Edward E. and Virginia B. (Lane) F.; m. Bettye J. Samples, July 31, 1954; children: Mary Ann, Sarah Jane. AB, Ind. U., 1954, DDS, 1957; BS, U. Evansville, 1975, MBA, 1978. Pvt. practice dentistry, Evansville, 1959-99; ret.; pres., chmn. bd. Health Resources, Inc., 1986-99, chmn. bd., 1986—. Corp. bd. dirs. Va. Corp., Evansville, 1962-72, Dynatron, Inc., 1980-87; bd. dir. S.W. Ind. Oral Health Found. Editor: The Bulletin of the Am. Assn. of Dental Examiners, 1981-85. Capt. U.S. Army, 1957-59. Named Disting. Alumnus Ind. U. Sch. Dentistry, 1991. Fellow Am. Coll. Dentists (ethics achievement award 2004), Acad. Gen. Dentistry, Acad. Dentistry Internat., Internat. Coll. Dentists; mem. ADA (continuing edn. com. 1981-83, cons./evaluator 1980), Ind. Dental Assn. (trustee 1983-91, Disting. Svc. award 1996), Vanderburgh County Dental Soc. (pres. 1967, various offices), First Dist. Dental Soc. (pres. 1976-77, various offices), Am. Assn. Dental Examiners (pres. 1989, various offices), Ind. Bd. Dental Examiners (pres. 1982-83, sec. 1980-82), Acad. Operative Dentistry, Internat./Am. Assn. Dental Rsch., Am. Assn. Dental Editors, Acad. Gen. Dentistry, Pierre Fauchard Acad., Sagamores of the Wabash, Ky. Col., Phi Kappa Phi. Home: 12200 Edgewater Dr Evansville IN 47720-8169 E-mail: ebfritz@evansville.net.

FRITZ, JAMES SHERWOOD, chemist, educator; b. Decatur, Ill., July 20, 1924; s. William Lawrence and Leora Mae (Troster) F.; m. Helen Joan Houck, Apr. 26, 1949 (dec. Oct. 1987); children— Barbara Lisa, Julie Ann, Laurel Joan, Margaret Ellen; m. Miriam Simons Reeves, July 15, 1989. BS, James Millikin U., 1945; MS, U. Ill., 1946, PhD, 1948. Asst. prof. chemistry Wayne State U., Detroit, 1948-51; asst. prof. Iowa State U., Ames, 1951-55, assoc. prof., 1955-60, prof., 1960-90, disting. prof., 1990—. Author: Acid Base Titrations in Nonaqueous Solvents, 1973, An Analytical Solid-Phase Extraction, 1999; co-author: Quantitative Analytical Chemistry, Ion Chromatography, 1982, 3d edit., 2000, Solid Phase Extraction, 1999; contbr. articles to profl. jours. Recipient Minn. Chromatography Forum award, 1987, Dal Nogare award in chromatography, 1991. Mem. Am. Chem. Soc. (award in chromatography 1976, award in analytical chemistry 1985) Methodist. Avocations: tennis, collecting wall hangings. Office: Iowa State U 322 Wilhelm Ames IA 50011-0001 Office Phone: 515-294-5987.

FRITZ, JEAN GUTTERY, writer; b. Hankow, People's Republic China, Nov. 16, 1915; d. Arthur Minton and Myrtle (Chaney) Guttery; m. Michael Fritz, Nov. 1, 1941; children: David, Andrea. BA, Wheaton Coll., Norton, Mass., 1937, LittD (hon.), 1987, Washington and Jefferson Coll., 1982. Rsch. asst. Dobbs Ferry (N.Y.) Libr., 1937—41, children's libr., 1955—57; founder, instr. Jean Fritz Writers' Workshops, Katonah, NY, 1962—70; tchr. Bd. Co-operative Ednl. Svc., Westchester County, NY, 1971—73; faculty mem. Appalachian State U., Boone, NC, 1980—82. Author: Fish Head, 1954, The Late Spring, 1957, The Animals of Doctor Schweitzer, 1958, The Cabin Faced West, 1958, How to Read a Rabbit, 1958, Brady, 1960, I, Adam, 1963, Magic to Burn, 1964, Early Thunder, 1967, George Washington's Breakfast, 1969, Cast for a Revolution, 1972, And Then What Happened, Paul Revere?, 1973, Why Don't You Get a Horse, Sam Adams?, 1974, Where Was Patrick Henry on the 29th of May?, 1975, Who's that Stepping on Plymouth Rock?, 1975, Will You Sign Here, John Hancock?, 1976, The Secret Diary of Jeb and Abigail, 1976, What's the Big Idea, Ben Franklin?, 1976, Can't You Make Them Behave, King George?, 1977, Brendon the Navigator, 1979, Stonewall, 1979, Where Do You Think You're Going, Christopher Columbus?, 1980, The Man Who Loved Books, 1981, Traitor: The Case of Benedict Arnold, 1981, The Good Giants and the Bad Pukwudgies, 1981, Homesick: My Own Story, 1982 (Am. Book award 1983, Child Study Book award 1983, Honor Book, Newberry Medal Book 1983), China Homecoming, 1985, The Double Life of Pocahontas, 1983 (Boston Globe/Horn Book award 1984), Make Way for Sam Houston, 1986 (Western Writers award 1987), Shh! We're Writing the Constitution, 1987, China's Long March, 1988, The Great Little Madison, 1989, Bully for You, Teddy Roosevelt!, 1991, Around the World in 100 Years, 1994, Harriet Beecher Stowe and the Beecher Preachers, 1994, You Want Women to Vote, Lizzie Stanton?, 1995, Why Not, Lafayette?, 1999, Leonardo's Horse, 2001, The Lost Colony of Roanoke, 2002. Recipient Christopher award Cath. Library Assn., 1982, Regina Medal Cath. Library Assn., 1985, Laura Ingalls Wilder award ALA, 1986, Nat. Humanities medal, 2003. Home: 50 Bellewood Ave Dobbs Ferry NY 10522-2302

FRITZ, JIM, professional sports team executive; m. Donna Fritz; children: Zachary, Nicole. grad. in Acctg., M in Acctg., Fla. State U. With Hotel Mgmt. Assocs., PricewaterhouseCoopers; positions including contr., dir. and v.p. fin. and chief of staff Orlando Magic, 1994—2004, exec. v.p. bus. ops., 2004—06, CFO, 2006—. Treas. bd. trustees United Arts Ctrl. Fla. Office: Orlando Magic 8701 Maitland Summit Blvd Orlando FL 32810*

FRITZ, KRISTINE RAE, retired secondary school educator; b. Monroe, Wis. BS in Phys. Edn., U. Wis., LaCrosse, 1970; MS in Phys. Edn., U. N.C., Greensboro, 1978. Softball and fencing program coord. Mequon (Wis.) Recreation Dept., 1970; phys. edn., health and English tchr. Horace Jr. H.S., 1970—81; phys. edn. and health tchr. Sheboygan (Wis.) South H.S., 1982—2004; emeritus tchr. Sheboygan Early Learning Ctr., 2004—05; basketball and volleyball coach, 1972—89; girls track coach, 1972—2004; active early childhood phys. activity pilot program SASD. Mem. dist. wide curriculum and evaluation coms., 1978—2004; mem. sch. effectiveness team, 1991—94; sch. evaluation consortium evaluator, 1988—93; inbound/outbound coach Sport for Understanding, 1991—96. Contbr. articles to profl. jours. Active Sheboygan (Wis.) Spkrs. Bur., 1987—95, Women Reaching Women. Recipient Nat. H.S. Coaches award for girls track, 1987, Lifetime award, Woman's Sports Advocates of Wis., 2003. Mem.: AAHPERD (Midwest Dist. Tchr. of Yr. 1995, Pathfinder award 1997, chair 2003—04, Midwest Dist. Honor award 2006), NEA,

Sheboygan Edn. Assn., Wis. Assn. Health, Phys. Edn., Recreation and Dance (life; pres.-elect 1998—99, pres. 1999—2000, Phys. Edn. Tchr. Yr. 1993). Home: 1841 N 26th St Sheboygan WI 53081-2008

FRITZ, RENE EUGENE, JR., manufacturing executive; b. Prineville, Oreg., Feb. 24, 1943; s. Rene and Ruth Pauline (Munson) Fritz; m. Sharyn Ann Fife, June 27, 1964; children: Rene Scott, Lanz Eugene, Shay Steven, Case McGarrett. BSBA, Oreg. State U., 1965. Sales mgr. Renal Corp., Albany, Oreg., 1965-66, Albany Machine and Supply, 1965-66; pres. Albany Internat. Industries Inc., 1966-85, Wood Yield Tech. Corp., 1972-85, Albany Internat. DISC, 1972-85, Automation Controls Internat. Inc., 1975-85; co-founder, chmn. Albany Titanium Inc., 1981-89; prin. Torwest Capital, 1989; founder, pres. WY Tech. Corp., 1984-89, R. Fritz & Assocs., 1987-89; prin., owner Engaging Media, Inc., 2006—. Pres. Chief Execs. Forum, 1989—, Fritz Grup, Inc., 1989—; fin. planner, investment banker M&A, Vancouver, Wash., 1991—; chmn. Stormwater Treatment LLC, CSF Treatment Sys., NTP, Wilsonville, Oreg., 1999—, Dentamax, Inc., Vancouver, 1999—, Human Capital Oreg./Wash., Vancouver, 1999—, MindNautilus, Inc., Portland, 2000—, Engaging Media, Inc., Rustic Canyon Entertainment, Inc. Patentee computer controlled machinery. Pres. Oreg. World Trade Coun., 1982—; trustee US Naval Acad. Found., Annapolis, Md., 1988—2004. Mem.: Forest Products Rsch. Soc., Young Pres. Orgn., Oreg. State Alumni, Elks, Rotary. Presbyterian.

FRITZ, ROGER JAY, management consultant; b. Browntown, Wis., July 18, 1928; s. Delmar M. and Ruth M. (Sandley) F.; m. Kathryn Louise Goddard, Oct. 13, 1951; children: Nancy Goddard, Susan Marie. BA in Polit. Sci, Monmouth Coll., Ill., 1950; MS in Speech, U. Wis., 1952, PhD in Ednl. Counseling, 1956. Asst. dean men, asst. prof. Purdue U., 1953-56; mgr. pub. relations Cummins Engine Co.; also sec. Cummins Engine Found., 1956-59; sec. John Deere Found.; also mem. pub. relations staff Deere & Co., 1959-65, dir. mgmt. devel. and personnel research; also dir. John Deere Found., 1965-69; pres. Willamette U., 1969-72, Orgn. Devel. Cons., Naperville, Ill., 1972—. Bd. dirs. Intelligent Electronics, Inc., List Processing Co., Todays Computers Bus. Ctrs., Entre Computer Ctrs., Inc., Natural Golf, Inc., Quote Me, Optionize, Envisionworks, Inc. Author: A Handbook for Resident Counselors, 1952, The Argumentation of William Jennings Bryan and Clarence Darrow in the Tennesee Evolution Trial, 1952, How Freshmen Change, 1956, The Power of Professional Purpose, 1974, MBO Goes to College, 1975, Practical Management by Objectives, 1976, What Managers Need to Know-A Practical Guide for Management Development, 1978, Performance Based Management, 1980, Productivity and Results, 1981, People Compatibility System, 1983, Rate Yourself as a Manager, 1985, You're in Charge, 1986, Personal Performance Contracts: The Key to Job Success, 1986, Nobody Gets Rich Working for Somebody Else, 1987, Rate Your Executive Potential, 1987, The Inside Advantage, 1987, If They Can-You Can, 1988, Be Your Own Boss, 1988, Managing a Successful Team, 1989, Management Ideas That Work, 1989, Developing A Positive Attitude, 1990, The Entrepreneurial Family, 1991, Think Like a Manager, 1991, How to Export, 1992, How to Get Rich Working for Yourself, 1992, Sleep Disorders-America's Hidden Nightmare, 1993, The Sales Manager's High Performance Guide, 1993, How to Manage Your Boss, 1994, A Team of Eagles, 1994, The Small Business Troubleshooter, 1995, The Field Guide for Bosss Types.And How to Deal With Them, 1996, An Idea-A-Day For Promotable People, 1996, Crime Crisis: Bold New Ideas to Fit Punishment with Crimes, 1997, Wars of Succession, 1997, One Step Ahead: The Unused Keys to Success, 1998, Bounce Back and Win, 1999, Fast Track-How to Gain Momentum and Keep It, 1999, Attitude Makes The Difference, 2000, Beyond Commitment: The Skills All Leaders Need, 2000, Family Ties and Business Binds, 2000, Magnet People: Their Secrets and How To Learn From Them, 2001, Little Things-Big Results, 2002, How To Make Your Boss Your Ally and Advocate, 2002, Building Your Legacy--One Decision at a Time, 2002, 100 Ways to Bring Out Your Best, 2003, After You-Can Humble People Prevail?, 2004, Sharpen Your Competitive Edge, 2004, Nothing Ventured, Nothing Gained, 2005, Who Cares--Are You a Giver, Taker or Watcher, 2006, The Power of Positive Attitude, 2006, Self Management Equals Sales Success, 2007, Why Stop Now?-Resisting the Temptation to Retreat, 2007, The Challenge of Change, 2007; also articles, papers; columnnist Entrepreneur mag., New Bus. Opportunity mag., 1989, Benefits and Compensation Solutions Mag., Bus. Start Ups Mag., Bus. Ledger, 2004; mgmt. editor Communication Briefings Newsletter, 1989. Mem. com. preparation coll. tchrs. Ill. Bd. Higher Edn., 1965-67, mem. com. med. edn., 1967-68; edn. com. N.A.M., 1967-69; mem. Iowa-Ill. Indsl. Devel. Group, 1964-69; council contbr. Nat. Indsl. Conf. Bd., 1960-65, council devel., edn. and tng., 1966-69; adv. com. solicitations Nat. Better Bus. Bur., 1964-69; v.p. Oreg. Ind. Colls. Assn., 1969-72; mem. Pres. Johnson's Citizens Adv. Bd. on Youth Opportunity, 1968-69, Gov.'s Personnel Grievance Panel, Ill., 1974-77; trustee Monmouth Coll., 1957-69, chmn., 1961-69; trustee Oreg. Colls. Found., 1969-72, Ind. Coll. Funds Am., N.Y.C., 1972, Internat. Coll. Commerce and Econs., Tokyo, 1970-72, U. Chgo. Cancer Research Found., 1973-78. Recipient Achievement award, Monmouth Coll., 2002. Mem. Phi Eta Sigma, Omicron Delta Kappa, Tau Kappa Epsilon, Phi Alpha Theta, Sigma Tau Delta, Pi Kappa Delta. Clubs: Naperville (Ill.) Country. Republican. Methodist. Home: 1113 N Loomis St Naperville IL 60563-2745 Office: 1240 Iroquois Dr Naperville IL 60563-8536 Office Phone: 630-420-7673. Office Fax: 630-420-7835. Personal E-mail: rfritz3800@aol.com.

FRITZ, TERRENCE LEE, investment banker, strategic consultant; b. Ft. Dodge, Iowa, Mar. 10, 1943; s. George and Julia Evelyn (Katnik) F.; m. Pam Fritz; children: Erich, Kevin, Tanya. BS in Indsl. Engring., Iowa State U., 1967. Registered profl. engr., Colo. Mfg. system analyst Martin-Marietta, Denver, 1967-68; system fin. analyst N.Am. Philips, Denver, 1968-69; mgmt. cons. Denver, 1970-74; exec. dir. Met. Transit Authority-Iowa Dept. Transp., Des Moines, 1974-78; sr. v.p. mktg., strategic planning Holiday Inns, Trailways, Dallas, 1978-80; pres. Strategic Actions, Dallas, 1984-88; regional dir. capital markets group Grant Thornton, Dallas, 1988-90; pres. Capital Mkts. Group, Inc., Dallas, 1990—. Mem. adv. bd. So. Meth. U., 1981-84, local adv. bd. Dallas Fed. Res., 1982-84; advisor transp. rsch. bd. NAS, 1980. Bd. dirs. Dallas-Ft. Worth Adv. bd., 1980-84; cons. Dallas-Ft. Worth Transp. Authority, 1980; mem. Gov.'s Com. on Tech., Austin, 1982-83; Dallas rep. U.S. President's Carribean Initiatives Program to Jamaica, Costa Rica, 1981-83; exec. dir. Japan-Tex. Conf., 1981-84; mem. adv. bd. So. Meth. U. Cox Sch. Bus., 1981-84. Mem. Dallas C. of C. (pres., chief exec. officer 1980-84). Avocations: skiing, sailing, wine collecting. Office: Capital Markets Group Inc Ste 300 2911 Turtle Creek Blvd Dallas TX 75219-6243 Office Phone: 214-219-9096. Personal E-mail: tlfritz@att.net.

FRITZ, THOMAS VINCENT, business executive; b. Pitts., July 6, 1934; s. Zeno and Mary M. (Briley) F.; m. Barbara L. Jacob, Jan. 31, 1959; children: William T., James Z., Juliann W. BBA in Acctg. cum laude, U. Pitts., 1960; JD, Duquesne U., 1964; LLM, NYU, 1966; Advanced Mgmt. Program, Harvard Bus. Sch., 1975. Bar: Pa. 1964, U.S. Supreme Ct. 1969; CPA, Pa. 1962. Ptnr. Ernst & Young (formerly Arthur Young & Co.), Pitts., NYC, Washington, 1970, national mng. ptnr., vice chmn., 1977-89, vice chmn., 1989-92; pres., CEO, bd. dirs. Pvt. Sector Coun., Inc., Washington, 1992-2000; pres. Thomas V. Fritz & Assocs., Washington, 2000—. Adj. prof. Sch. Law Duquesne U., Pitts., 1966-79; adv. dirs. Pvt. Sector Coun., Washington, 1983-2004; bd. dirs. Innovative Sys., Inc.; chmn. Alliance for Free Enterprise, Washington, 1987-89. Editor Duquesne U. Law Rev., 1963-64. Active Century Club, Duquesne U.; bd. dirs. Evermay Comty. Assn., pres., 1994-96; bd. dirs. McLean Citizens Assn., 1994-97; co-chmn. U. Pitts. Katz Campaign 3d Century, 1988-91. With US Army, 1955—57, with USAR, 1957—63. Recipient Gorley award, 1964, Disting. Alumni award U. Pitts., 1981, Advancement Info. Tech. award, 1988, Federal 100 Info. Tech. award, 1997. Mem. AICPA, ACBA, Pa. Inst. CPAs, Duquesne Club, Met. Club, Rolling Rock Club, Avenel Club, Beta Gamma Sigma, Beta Alpha Psi. Office: 6303 Long Meadow Rd Mc Lean VA 22101-2314

FRITZE, SHEILA KAY, retired librarian; b. Belleville, Ill., Oct. 31, 1949; d. Orel Emil and Louise Elizabeth (Zimmerman) Boos; m. James Ronald Fritze, June 17, 1972; children: Elizabeth Ann, Julia Louise. AA, Belleville Area Coll., 1969; BS, U. Ill., 1971, MS, 1972. Librarian, Wellington Community Sch. Dist. (Ill.), 1972-74, Crescent City Pub. Library, 1975-82, Eagle Valley Elem. Sch. (Colo.), 1983-2002, Montrose H.S., 2002-05. Pres. Eagle Valley Elem. sch. PTA, 1987-88; Sunday sch. supt. 1st Luth. Ch. of Gypsum, Colo., 1986-91; capt. Eagle Squadron of CAP, 1989-92; treas. Eagle Valley High Sch. Booster Club, 1991-93, pres., 1993-94; bd. dirs. Montrose Regional Libr. Dist., 2006. Named Dist. Clubwoman of Yr., 8th Dist. Ill. Jr. Woman's Club, 1980. Mem. Colo. Assn. Librs., Friends of the Libr., Beta Phi Mu, Kappa Delta Phi, Delta Kappa Gamma (pres. Alpha Chi chpt. 1998-2000, sec. Chi chpt. 2004-06, treas. Chi chpt. 2006). Republican. Lutheran. Home and Office: 8195 E 128th Pl Thornton CO 80602 E-mail: sheila.fritze@gmail.com.

FRITZE, STEVEN L., service industry executive; b. St. Paul, Apr. 1954; m. Susie Fritze. B, MBA, U. Minn. With IBM; v.p., contr. Ecolab, St. Paul, 2000—01, sr. v.p. fin., contr., 2001—02, sr. v.p., CFO, 2002—04, exec. v.p., CFO, 2004—. Bd. mem. Habitat for Humanity Twin Cities, Am. Pub. Media Group, Minn. Pub. Radio. Office: Ecolab 370 Wabasha St N Saint Paul MN 55102 Office Phone: 651-293-2401. Office Fax: 651-225-3022. E-mail: steve.fritze@ecolab.com.

FRITZHAND, IRVIN DICK, psychologist; b. Bklyn., Aug. 2, 1936; s. Philip and Hannah Frances (Arbeit) Fritzhand; m. Sheila Wynn Block, June 23, 1963; children: Alan, Aaron, Jason. BS, CUNY, Bklyn., 1959; MS, CUNY, NYC, 1962; PhD, Hofstra U., 1974. Lic. psychologist NY, state cert. sch. psychologist NY; workers compensation bd. cert. authorization. Psychol. examiner NYU, NYC, 1963; grad. tchg. asst. La. State U., Baton Rouge, 1963-64; psychologist children's unit Kings Park Psychiat. Ctr., NY, 1964-71, supervising psychologist children's unit, 1971-73, treatment team leader, 1973-76, treatment svc. chief, 1983-95; pvt. practice psychology Smithtown, NY, 1975—2003; chief treatment svc. Central Islip Psychiat. Ctr., NY, 1976-83. Cons. psychologist Advanced Ctr. Psychotherapy, Hempstead, NY, 1966—72; panel psychologist NY Bur. Disability Determination, 1977—2003; adj. supr. grad. psychology dept. Hofstra U., Hempstead, 1971—75. Mem. editl. bd. Jour. Psychiat. Treatment and Evaluation, 1980—81. Mem.: APA, Am. Acad. Behavioral Medicine (diplomate in behavioral medicine 1980), Internat. Acad. Profl. Counseling and Psychotherapy (diplomate in psychotherapy 1983), Obsessive-Compulsive Found., Am. Profl. Soc. Abuse Children, Coun. Nat. Register Health Svc. Providers Psychology, Assn. Advancement Behavior Therapy, Suffolk County Psychol. Assn., NY State Psychol. Assn., Ea. Psychol. Assn. Jewish. Avocations: swimming, bicycling, gardening, travel, chess. Home and Office: 46 Hofstra Dr Smithtown NY 11787-2019 Personal E-mail: DFritzPhD@mac.com.

FRITZSCHE, HELLMUT, physics professor; b. Berlin, Feb. 20, 1927; arrived in US, 1952; s. Carl Hellmut and Anna (Jordan) F.; m. Sybille Charlotte Lauffer, July 5, 1952; children: Peter Andreas, Thomas Alexander, Susanne Charlotte, Katharina Sabine. Diploma in Physics, U. Göttingen, Fed. Republic Germany, 1952; PhD in Physics, Purdue U., 1954, DSc (hon.), 1988. Instr. physics Purdue U., Lafayette, Ind., 1954-55, asst. prof., 1955-56, U. Chgo., 1957-61, assoc. prof., 1961-63, prof., 1963-96, dir. Materials Rsch. Lab., 1973-77, chmn. dept., 1977-86, Louis Block prof. physics, 1989-96. V.p. Energy Conversion Devices, Inc., Rochester Hills, Mich.; bd. dirs. United Solar Systems Corp.; mem. adv. com. Ency. Britannica, 1969—96. Editor: 13 sci. books; assoc. editor Jour. Applied Physics, 1975-80; regional editor Jour. Non-Crystalline Solids, 1987-96; contbr. 280 articles to profl. jours.; patentee in field. Named hon. prof. Shanghai Inst. Ceramics, 1985, Nanjing U., 1987, Beijing U. Astronautics, 1988. Fellow AAAS, Am. Physical Soc. (Oliver Buckley Condensed Matter Physics prize 1989), N.Y. Acad. Scis. (chmn. divsn. condensed matter physics 1979-80). Avocations: the violin, sailing, skiing. Home: 3140 E Camino Juan Paisano Tucson AZ 85718-4206 Office: United Solas Ovonic 1100 W Maple Rd Troy MI 48084 Office Phone: 800-528-0617. Personal E-mail: hellmutf@aol.com.

FRIZELL, SAMUEL, law educator; b. Buena Vista, Colo., Aug. 30, 1933; s. Franklin Guy and Ruth Wilma (Noel) F.; m. Donna Mae Knowlton, Dec. 26, 1955 (div. June 1973); children: Franklin Guy III, LaVerne Anne; m. Linda Moncure, Jul. 3, 1973 (div. June 1996); m. Jeannette Graham, Jan. 1997. AA cum laude, Ft. Lewis Coll., 1957; BA cum laude, Adams State Coll., 1959, EdM, 1960; JD, Hastings U. Calif., 1964. Bar: Calif. 1965. Assoc. atty. McCutcheon, Black, Verleger & Shea, Calif., LA, 1964-67; atty. Law Offices Samuel Frizell, Santa Ana, Calif., 1967-82; adj. prof. Cerritos Coll., Norwalk, Calif., 1977-81, Western State U., Fullerton, Calif., 1982-84, assoc. prof., 1984-90, prof., 1990-98, prof. emeritus, 1998—; cons. Law Offices Samuel Frizell, Mira Loma, Calif., 1982-98. Author: Frizell's Torts Tips, 1992; contbr. articles to profl. jours.; editor law jour. Mem. Main St. Adv. Panel, Garden Grove, Calif., 1975-76; judge pro-tem Orange County Superior Ct., Santa Ana, 1979-80; chair, com. atty. advertising Orange County Bar Assn., 1975; bd. dirs. Orange County Trial Lawyers Assn., 1972-75; adv. panel to legal assts. Cerritos Coll., Norwalk, 1982-86; mem. pub. safety com. Town of Mancos, 2002-03. Fellow Soc. Antiquaries; mem. Order of the Coif. Avocations: history, reloading and target shooting, saddle making. Office: Western State U 1111 N State College Blvd Fullerton CA 92831-3000 Personal E-mail: SJFrizell@peoplepc.com.

FRIZZELL, GREGORY KENT, federal judge; b. Wichita, Kans., Dec. 13, 1956; s. D. Kent and Shirley Elaine (Piatt) F.; m. Kelly Susan Nash, Mar. 9, 1991; children: Benjamin Newcomb, Hannah Kirsten, Robert Nash, David Gregory, Elizabeth Piatt, Jubilee Kathryn. BA, U. Tulsa, 1981; JD, U. Mich., 1984. Bar: Okla. 1985, U.S. Dist. Ct. (no., ea. and we. dists.) Okla. 1985, U.S. Ct. Appeals (10th cir.) 1985, U.S. Supreme Ct. 1990. Jud. clk. to judge US Dist. Ct. (No. dist.) Okla., Tulsa, 1984-86; pvt. practice Tulsa, 1986-95; gen. counsel Okla. Tax Commn., 1995-97; dist. judge Tulsa County, 1997—2005, presiding judge elect, 2004—05, presiding judge, 2006—07; judge US Dist. Ct. (No. dist.) Okla., Tulsa, 2007—. Counsel bd. dirs. Tulsa Speech and Hearing Assn., 1987-95, pres., 1994-95. Mem. Okla. Bar Assn., Rotary, Federalist Soc. Office: US Dist Ct No Okla 333 W 4th St Tulsa OK 74103 Office Phone: 918-699-4780. Office Fax: 918-699-4785.

FROBERG, BRENT MALCOLM, classics educator; b. Balt., Apr. 8, 1943; s. Lawrence Oscar and Ruth Louise (Lindner) F.; m. M. Gail Galloway, Feb. 27, 1970. BA, Ind. U., 1964, MA, 1965; PhD, Ohio State U., 1972. Instr. U. Tenn., Knoxville, 1968-69; asst. prof. U. S.D., Vermillion, 1970-74, assoc. prof., 1974-96. Cons. Nat. Mythology Exam, Nat. Greek Exam; lectr. in field. Editor: (newsletter) Nuntius, 1978-96; writer Nat. Greek Exam., ATTIC, Level I, 1998-2000. Pres. Friends of the Libr., Vermillion, 1995-97, sec., 1997-99 Mem. Am. Philol. Assn. (award for excellence in tchg. 1994), Am. Classical League, Vergilian Soc. (membership chmn. 1990-94), Classical Assn. Mid. West & South (Ovatio award 1985, chair Manson Stewart scholarship com. 1998), Eta Sigma Phi (exec. sec. 1978-96, hon. life trustee). Avocations: crossword puzzles, travel. E-mail: Brent_Froberg@baylor.edu.

FROEHLICH, FRITZ EDGAR, communications educator, telecommunications scientist; b. Worms am Rhine, Hesse, Germany, Nov. 12, 1925; arrived in U.S., 1938; s. Julius and Ida (Heilborn) Froehlich; m. Eileen Karch, Dec. 25, 1949; children: Laurence Alan, Georgine K. Froehlich Scharff, Philip Marc. BS in Physics magna cum laude, Syracuse U., 1950, MS in Physics, 1952, PhD in Physics, 1955. Rsch. asst. Syracuse (N.Y.) U., 1950-54; asst. instr. Utica (N.Y.) Coll., 1952-54; with AT&T Bell Labs., 1954-87, tech. staff Whippany, NJ, 1954-56, supr. data transmission divsn. Murray Hill, NJ, 1956-63, head data theory dept. Holmdel, NJ, 1963—68, head telecom. and data sys. dept., 1968—83; head univ. rels. AT&T Info. Sys. and Comm., Lincroft, NJ, 1983—87; prof. telecom. U. Pitts., 1987—2002. Mem. adv. bd. Ctr. Info. and Comm. Scis. Ball State U., Muncie, Ind., 1987—93; nat. telecom. adv. coun. U. Pitts., 1992—95. Editor-in-chief: Ency. Telecom., 1988—2000, sr. editor: IEEE Trans. Comm., 1988—94; contbr. articles to profl. jours. Trustee Congl. B'nai Israel, Rumson, NJ, 1970—84, v.p. congregation, 1974—76; bd. dirs. Isles of Tamarac Homeowners Assn., 1992—2001, pres., 2001—02. With US Army, 1944—46. Named Ann. Fritz Froehlich award in his honor, U. Pitts. Sch. Info. Sci., 1992—; recipient Hon. Alumnus award, Pitts. U., 1992. Fellow: IEEE (life; mem. data com., trans. sys. com. 1960—95, chmn. N.J. Coast sect. 1970, chmn. comms. terminal com. 1981—84, mem. multimedia, svcs. and terminals com. 1981—89, mem. awards bd. 1992—95), Comm. Soc. IEEE; mem.: Jewish War Vets. (vice comdr. Post 519 2005—06), Phi Beta Kappa, Pi Mu Epsilon, Sigma Xi Sigma (pres. Syracuse U. chpt. 1949). Achievements include patents in field; development of first telephone data set and modem; first telephone for electronic authorization of retail credit card purchases. Home: 9419 Astor Gardens Ct Apt 106 Parkland FL 33076 Office Phone: 954-341-4077. E-mail: fefroehlich@att.net.

FROEHLICH, HAROLD VERNON, judge, retired congressman; b. Appleton, Wis., May 12, 1932; s. Vernon W. and Lillian F.; m. Sharon F. Ross, Nov. 20, 1970; children: Jeffrey Scott, Michael Ross. BBA, U. Wis., 1959, LLB, 1962. Bar: Wis. 1962. Staff acct. Ruschlien & Stortreon, CPAs, Madison, Wis., 1958-62; practiced in Appleton, 1962-81; judge Circuit Ct., 1981—; dep. chief judge 8th Jud. Dist. Wis., 1983-85, spl. dep. chief judge, 1985-88, chief judge, 1988-94; sec. Wis. Judicial Conf., 1991-97; mem. Wis. Ho. of Reps., 1963-73, speaker, 1967-71, minority floor leader, 1971-73; mem. 93d Congress from 8th Dist., Wis.; v.p. Black Creek Improvement Corp., 1967—2003, Outagamie County Family Ct. Commn., 1975-78. Chmn. Com. Chief Judges, 1992—94; chief adminstrn. judge Outagamie County, 1983—88, 1994—2006, 2007—. Rep. precinct committeeman 19th ward, Appleton, 1956-62; chmn. Outagamie County Rep. Statutory Com., 1958-62; sec. Assembly Rep. Caucus, 1965-66; bd. regents Fox Valley Luth. H.S., Appleton, 1990-93; bd. dirs. Fox Valley Luth. H.S. Found., 1967—, v.p., 2002-06, pres. 2006—. With USN, 1951-55. Mem. ABA, Am. Judges Assn. (bd. govs. 1997-99, asst. treas. 1998-99, treas. 1999—), Wis. Bar Assn., Outagamie County Bar Assns., Am. Legion, VFW (judge adv. 1963-75, 82-99), Assn. Trial Judges in Wis. (sec. 1984-91, pres. 1991-2000), Midwest Coun. State Govts. (vice chmn. 1968-69, chmn. 1969-70), Coun. State Govts. (nat. exec. com. 1970-72), Phi Alpha Delta. Office: 410 S Walnut St Appleton WI 54911-5920 Office Phone: 920-832-5602. Business E-Mail: harold.froehlich@wicourts.gov.

FROELICH, BEVERLY LORRAINE, foundation administrator; b. Vancouver, BC, Can., Oct. 23, 1948; arrived in U.S., 1968; d. Kenneth Martin and Ethel Pulham; m. Eugene Leonard Froelich, Dec. 26, 1971; children: Craig, Grant. Cert. in fundraising, U. So. Calif., 1986; profl. designation in pub. rels., UCLA, 1987. Cert. in fundraising exec. Contract analyst Universal Studios, Calif., 1968-71; exec. dir. Olive View UCLA Med. Ctr. Found., Sylmar, 1987—. Pres. Beverly Froelich Pub. Rels., Sherman Oaks, Calif., 1988—90; prin. Tracy Susman & Co., Sherman Oaks, 1986—88. Co-author: (programs) Overcoming Chronic Arthritis Pain, 1989. Contbg. writer hosp. earthquake preparedness guidelines Hosp. Coun. So. Calif., 1991; founder San Fernando Valley br. Arthritis Found., Encino, 1983, pres., 1983—87, mem. mktg. com. Recipient Nat. Vol. Svc. award, Arthritis Found., 1991, Marilyn Magaram award for Cmty. Svc., 1997. Mem.: Assn. Fundraising Profls. (pres. San Fernando Valley chpt., Fundraising Profl. of Yr. 2000), Valley Industry and Commerce Assn. (bd. dirs. health care com.), UCLA Alumni Assn. Avocations: hockey, music. Office: Olive View Med Ctr Found Cottage J2 14445 Olive View Dr Sylmar CA 91342-1437 Home Phone: 818-501-8215. E-mail: ovinfo@earthlink.net.

FROEMMING, HERBERT DEAN, retired retail executive; b. Alexandria, Minn., Aug. 19, 1936; s. Herbert Edward and Bertha Anna (Hink) F.; m. Mary Louise Gapinski, Sept. 2, 1961; children— Mark, Traci, Scott. BBA, U. Minn., 1959; MBA, U. Mo. CPA, Minn. Fin. exec. The Kroger Co., various locations, 1960-69; exec. v.p. E.F. MacDonald Shopping Bag, LA, 1969-73; also dir.; v.p., treas., dir. Western Auto Supply Co., Kansas City, Mo., 1973-78; sr. corp. v.p., controller Gamble-Skogmo Co., Mpls., 1978-80; exec. v.p. Red Owl Food Stores, Inc., 1980-84; v.p. Sullivan Assocs., Inc., 1985-88; sr. v.p.-adminstr., chief fin. officer Braun's Fashions Inc., Plymouth, Minn., 1989-94, pres., COO, 1994-97, vice chmn., 1997-98; chmn., CEO Millennium Plastics Tech., LLC, El Paso, Tex., 1999-2000. Served with AUS, 1955-57. Home: 104 Coventry Ln Edina MN 55435-5634

FROESEL, DAVID W., JR., medical products executive; Corp. contr. Mallinckrodt Medical Inc., 1989—93; v.p. fin. & adminstrn. Mallinckrodt Veterinary Inc., 1993—96; sr. v.p., CFO Omnicare Inc., Covington, Ky., 1996—. Office: Omnicare Inc 1600 Rivercenter II Covington KY 41011*

FROHLICH, ANTHONY WILLIAM, lawyer, judge; b. Covington, Ky., Dec. 8, 1954; s. Kenneth Raymond and Joan Jude (Laake) F.; m. Candace Powell Robbins, May 31, 1975; children: Kenneth Zane, Matthew Andrew. BS, No. Ky. U., Highland Heights, 1976, JD, 1980. Bar: Ky. 1980, U.S. Dist. Ct. (ea. dist.) Ky. 1981, U.S. Supreme Ct. Staff atty. Boone County (Ky.) Child Support Program, 1980-97; city atty. City of Walton, 1980-89; master commr. Boone County Cir. Ct., Burlington, Ky., 1989—2004; asst. commonwealth atty. 54th Jud. Dist., Burlington, Ky., 1984-89; ptnr. Mathis, Dallas & Frohlich, Florence, Ky., 1980-96, Law Office of Anthony W. Frohlich, Florence, Ky., 1996—2004; cir. judge 54th Jud. Cir., Burlington, 2004—06, chief cir. judge, 2006—. Pres. Soccer Tech., Union, Ky., 1994. Bd. dirs. No. Ky. Soccer Club, Florence, 1994; state coach Ky. Youth Soccer, 1994-96; coaching dir. Ky. Olympic Devel. Program Dist. One, Florence, 1992-94; soccer coach DHL USA men's nat. team, 2000-01; mem. Union Town Plan Steering Com., 1999; bd. dirs. Greater Cin. Consumer Credit Counseling, 1999-2002; nominating chmn. Boy Scouts Am., 1999-2007; steering com. Boone County Parks and Recreation, 2000—; bd. govs. Salmon P. Chase, pres., 2007—. Named Coach of Yr., No. Ky. Soccer Club, 1992, Alumnus of Yr., No. Ky. U., 2005; recipient Meritorious Svc. award, Boys Scouts Am., 2003, Award of Merit for svc. and leadership, 2004. Mem. Ky. Bar Assn. (house of dels., life fellow, Cle award 2004, Donated Legal Svcs. award 1995, 97, 00, 01, 02), Boone County Bar Assn. (treas. 1980). Roman Catholic. Avocations: coaching soccer, basketball, hunting. Home: 9253 Old Union Rd Union KY 41091-9470 Office: Boone County Justice Ctr Rogers Ln Burlington KY 41005 Personal E-mail: toncan@fuse.net. Business E-Mail: anthonyfrohlich@mail.kycourts.net.

FROHLICH, EDWARD DAVID, medical educator; b. NYC, Sept. 10, 1931; s. William and May (Zneimer) F.; m. Sherry Linda Fine, Nov. 1, 1959; children: Marjorie, Bruce, Lara. BA, Washington and Jefferson Coll., 1952; MD, U. Md., 1956; MS, Northwestern U., 1963; DSc (hon.), U. Buenos Aires, 2001. Diplomate Am. Bd. Internal Medicine. Intern, resident D.C. Gen. Hosp., 1956-58; resident Georgetown U. Hosp., Washington,

1958—60; clin. investigator VA Rsch. Hosp., Chgo., 1962-64; assoc. in medicine Northwestern U., 1963-64; staff mem. rsch. divsn. Cleve. Clinic, 1964-69; prof. medicine, physiology and biophysics U. Okla., Oklahoma City, 1969-76, George Lynn Cross rsch. prof., 1975-76; prof. medicine and physiology La. State U., 1976—; clin. prof. medicine, adj. prof. pharmacology Tulane U., 1976—; mem. staff, v.p. edn. and rsch. Alton Ochsner Med. Found., 1976—86, v.p. acad. affairs, 1986—89, disting. scientist, 1986—. Cons. in field. Editor: Pathophysiology-Altered Regulatory Mechanisms in Disease, 1972, 1976, 1984, Rypins' Medical Licensure Examinations, 13th - 18th edits., 1981—2001, Rypins' Intensive Revs., 13 vols., 1996, Take Heart, 1990, Hypertension: Evaluation and Treatment, 1998; editor-in-chief: Jour. Lab. and Clin. Medicine, 1973—76, Hypertension, 1994—2002; mem. editl. bd. (jours.) Am. Jour. Cardiology, 1982—91, Circulation, 1978—91, Archives of Internal Medicine, 1978—88, Modern Medicine, 1980—2000, Jour. Hypertension, 1994—2003; assoc. editor: Am. Jour. Physiology, Heart Circulation; contbr. chapters to books, articles to profl. jours. Capt. U.S. Army, 1960-62. Recipient Honors Achievement award, Angiology Rsch. Found., 1964, Ann. award, So. Med. Assn., 1971, Janice M. Pfeffer Disting. Lectureship, Internat. Soc. Heart Rsch., 2005, William Harvey award, Am. Soc. Hypertension, 2007; rsch. fellow, Georgetown U. Hosp., 1958—59. Master: ACP (laureate 1996); fellow: AAAS, Coun. High Blood Pressure Rsch. (exec. com. 1972—75, 1981—85, vice chmn. 1986—88, chmn. 1989—91), Am. Coll. Cardiology (gov. La. chpt. 1988—91, bd. trustees La. chpt. 1991—92, 1996—2000, Disting. Scientist award 2005), Royal Coll. Physicians and Surgeons Glasgow (hon.); mem.: Am. Soc. Hypertension (William Harvey award 2007), Polish Acad. Arts Sci. (faculty medicine), Columbian Soc. Cardiology, Peruvian Soc. Cardiology, Assn. Am. Physicians, Am. Soc. Clin. Investigations, So. Soc. Clin. Rsch., Ctrl. Soc. Clin. Rsch., Am. Soc. Nephrology, Am. Physiol. Soc., Am. Soc. Clin. Pharmacology and Therapeutics (past pres.), Am. Soc. Pharmacology and Exptl. Therapeutics, Am. Soc. Clin. Investigation, Soc. Geriat. Cardiology (pres. 2000—01), Inter-Am. Soc. Hypertension (Lifetime Achievement award 1999), Am. Heart Assn. (dir. La. chpt. 1979—83, chmn. Coun. High Blood Pressure Rsch. 1988—91, award of merit 1986, Lifetime Achievement award 1994, Okamoto Internat. award 1994), Internat. Soc. Hypertension (sci. coun. 1974—84, treas. 1980—82, v.p. 1982—84, Astra award 2000), Alpha Kappa Alpha, Phi Sigma, Chi Epsilon Mu. Office: Ochsner Clinic Found 1516 Jefferson Hwy New Orleans LA 70121-2429 Office Phone: 504-842-3700. Business E-Mail: efrohlich@ochsner.org.

FROHNA, JOHN G., pediatrician; m. Alice Zion. BS, U. Wis., Madison, 1986, MD, 1990; MPH, U. Mich., Ann Arbor, 1995. Diplomate Am. Bd. Pediat., Am. Bd. Internal Medicine. Dir. med. pediat. residency program U. Mich., Ann Arbor, Mich., 1997—. Office: Univ Michigan 3116 Taubman Box 0368 Ann Arbor MI 48109-0368 Office Phone: 734-936-4385.

FROHNMAYER, DAVID BRADEN, academic administrator; b. Medford, Oreg., July 9, 1940; s. Otto J. and MarAbel (Braden) F.; m. Lynn Diane Johnson, Dec. 30, 1970; children: Kirsten (dec.), Mark, Kathryn (dec.), Jonathan, Amy. AB magna cum laude, Harvard U., 1962; BA, Oxford U., Eng., 1964, MA (Rhodes scholar), 1971; JD, U. Calif., Berkeley, 1967; LLD (hon.), Willamette U., 1988; D Pub. Svc. (hon.), U. Portland, 1989. Bar: Calif. 1967, US Dist. Ct. (no. dist.) Calif. 1967, Oreg. 1971, US Dist. Ct. Oreg. 1971, US Supreme Ct. 1981. Assoc. Pillsbury, Madison & Sutro, San Francisco, 1967-69; asst. to sec. Dept. HEW, 1969-70; prof. law U. Oreg., 1971-81, spl. asst. to univ. pres., 1971-79; atty. gen. State of Oreg., 1981-91; dean Sch. Law U. Oreg., 1992-94, pres., 1994—. Chmn. Conf. Western Attys. Gen., 1985-86; chmn. Am. Coun. Edn. Govtl. Rels. commn, 1996-98; bd. dirs. Umpqua Holding Co. Mem. Oreg. Ho. of Reps, 1975-81; mem. coun. pub. reps. NIH, 1999-00; bd. dirs. Fred Hutchinson Cancer Rsch. Ctr., 1994-00, Nat. Marrow Donor Program, 1987-99, Fanconi Anemia Rsch. Fund, Inc., Ford Family Found., 2004-, Assn. Am. U., 2004-; active Oreg. Progress Bd., 1991-04. Fellow Am. Acad. Arts and Scis.; mem. ABA (Ross essay winner 1980), Oreg. Bar Assn., Calif. Bar Assn., Nat. Assn. Attys. Gen. (pres. 1987, Wyman award 1987), Round Table Eugene, Order of Coif, Phi Beta Kappa, Rotary. Republican. Presbyterian. Home: 2315 McMorran St Eugene OR 97403-1750 Office: U Oreg Johnson Hall Office Pres Eugene OR 97403 Office Phone: 541-346-3036. Business E-Mail: pres@uoregon.edu.

FROHNMAYER, JOHN EDWARD, lawyer, writer; b. Medford, Oreg., June 1, 1942; s. Otto J. and MarAbel (Braden) F.; m. Leah Thorpe, June 10, 1967; children: Jason Otto, Jonathan Aaron. BA in Am. History, Stanford U., 1964; MA in Christian Ethics, U. Chgo., 1969; JD, U. Oreg., 1972. Bar: Oreg. 1972, Mont. 1995. Assoc. Johnson, Harrang & Mercer, Eugene, Oreg., 1972-75; ptnr. Tonkon, Torp, Galen, Marmaduke & Booth, Portland, Oreg., 1975-89; 5th chmn. Nat. Endowment for the Arts, Washington, 1989-92; writer, lectr. on art, ethics and politics, 1992—; pvt. practice Oreg., 1972-89, Bozeman, Mont., 1995—2005. Mem. Oreg. Arts Commn., 1978-85, chmn., 1980-84; bd. dirs. Internat. Sculpture Symposium, eugene, 1974; chmn. screening com. Oreg. State Capitol Bldg., 1977; affiliate prof. liberal arts Oreg. STate U., 2004—. Author: Leaving Town Alive, 1993, Out of Tune: Listening to The First Amendment, 1994; editor-in-chief Oreg. Law Rev., 1971-72; singer; appeared in recital, oratorio, mus. comedy and various other mus. prodns. Trustee Holladay Park Pla.; founding mem. chamber choir Novum Cantorum; bd. dirs. Chamber Music Northwest, Western States Arts Found.; mem. Nat. Endowment for the Arts Opera-Mus. Theater, 1982, 83. With USN, 1966-69. Active USNR, 1966—69, Vietnam. Sr. fellow Freedom Forum, 1993; recipient People for the Am. Way Ann. 1st Amendment award, 1992, Oreg. Gov. Arts award, 1993, Intellectual Freedom award Mont. Libr. Assn., 1997, Citation of Merit Mu Phi Epsilon, 1998, Lifetime Achievement award World Arts Fedn., 2006. Fellow Am. Leadership Forum; mem. ABA (com. comml. trans. litig.), Oreg. State Bar Assn. (chmn. bar com. domestic law 1975-76, procedure and practice com. 1984-85), Multnomah County Bar Assn., City Club Portland (program com.), Sta. L. Rowing Club (sec.), Corvallis Rowing Club, Order of the Coif (legal hon. 1972). Avocations: rowing, singing. Home and Office: 1335 SW Timian St Corvallis OR 97333 Business E-Mail: john.frohnmayer@oregonstate.edu.

FROHOCK, FRED MANUEL, political science professor; b. Perry, Fla., Feb. 7, 1937; s. Fred Clifton and Marie Antonia (Domenech) F.; m. Val Jean Derrick, Sept. 7, 1963; children— Katherine Renee, Christina Marie BA, U. Fla., 1960, MA, 1961; PhD, U. N.C., 1966. Asst. prof. polit. sci. Syracuse U., NY, 1965-68, assoc. prof. NY, 1968-74, prof. NY, 1974—, chmn. dept. polit. sci. NY, 1985-89, prof. Florence program Italy, 1969-70, prof., chmn. Madrid program, 1972-74, prof., chmn. London Politics Seminar, 1984—; prof., chmn. dept. polit. sci. U. Miami, 2005—. Author: Nature of Political Inquiry, 1967, Normative Political Theory, 1974, Public Policy, 1979, Abortion: A Case Study in Law and Morals, 1983, Special Care: Medical Decisions at the Beginning of Life, 1986, Rational Association, 1987, Healing Powers, 1992, Public Reason: Mediated Authority in the Liberal State, 1999, Lives of the Psychics: The Shared Worlds of Science and Mysticism, 2000, Bounded Divinities: Sacred Discourses in Pluralist Democracies, 2006; contbr. numerous articles to profl. jours. Social Sci. Research Council fellow, 1964-65, 67-68; NEH summer fellow, 1988. Democrat. Roman Catholic. Avocations: golf, watching baseball. Home: 516 Savona Ave Coral Gables FL 33146 Office: U miami Polit Sci Dept Coral Gables FL 33124 Office Phone: 315-284-8362. Business E-Mail: f.frohock@miami.edu.

FROLIK, LAWRENCE ANTON, lawyer, educator, consultant; b. Lincoln, Nebr., Jan. 10, 1944; s. Elvin F. and Rita K. (Haley) F.; m. Ellen M. Doyle, Sept. 25, 1973; children: Winnefred, Cornelius. BA with distinction, U. Nebr., 1966; JD cum laude, Harvard U., 1969, LLM cum laude, 1972. Asst. prof. U. Pitts., 1975-78, assoc. prof., 1978-81, prof., 1981—. Bd. dirs. Kendal Corp. Author: Loss and Damage, 1987, Fed. Tax Aspects of Injury, 1993; co-author: Pa. Elder Law Manual, 1988, Advising the Elderly and Disabled Client, 1991, Elderly and the Law: Cases and Materials, 1991;; 4th edit., 2007, Elder Law in a Nutshell, 1995, 4th edit., 2006, Aging and the Law: An Interdisciplinary Reader, 1999, Law of Employer Pension and Welfare Benefits, 2004, The Law of Later-Life Health Care and Decision Making, 2006; editor -in-chief NAELA Journal, 2006—. Exec. com. Gruter Inst. Law and Behavioral Rsch., Pa. AARP exec. coun., 2002—, Pa. Coun. on Aging, 2003-05. Capt. U.S. Army, 1969-71. Capt. US Army, 1969—71. Fellow Am. Bar Found., Am. Coll. Trust and Estate Counsel; mem. Phi Beta Kappa. Home: 4345 Schenley Farms Ter Pittsburgh PA 15213-1206 Office: U Pitts Sch Law 3900 Forbes Ave. Pittsburgh PA 15260 Office Phone: 412-648-1363. Business E-Mail: frolik@law.pitt.edu.

FROMAN, SANDRA SUE, lawyer; b. San Francisco, June 15, 1949; d. Jay and Beatrice Froman. AB with honors, Stanford U., 1971; JD, Harvard U., 1974. Bar: Calif. 1974, U.S. Dist. Ct. (cen. dist.) Calif. 1974, U.S. Dist. Ct. (so. dist.) Calif. 1976, U.S. Dist. Ct. (no. dist.) Calif., U.S. Ct. Claims 1979, U.S. Tax Ct. 1984, Ariz. 1985, U.S. Dist. Ct. Ariz. 1985, U.S. Ct. Appeals (9th cir.) 1986, U.S. Supreme Ct. 1986. Assoc. Loeb & Loeb, LA, 1974-80, ptnr., 1981-84; assoc. Bilby & Schoenhair, P.C., Tucson, 1985, shareholder, 1986-89; ptnr. Snell & Wilmer, Tucson, 1989-99. Vis. asst. prof. law U. Santa Clara, Calif., 1983-85; mem. Pima County Commn. on Trial Ct. Appointments, 1996-98. Trustee NRA Civil Rights Def. Fund, 1992-98, NRA Found., pres. 1997-2000; bd. dirs. NRA, 1992-2005, pres. 2005-. Mem. Ariz. Bar Found. (pres. 1996—), Nat. 4-H Shooting Sports Found. (pres. 2002-04), Wildlife for Tomorrow Found. (pres. 1999-02). Office: Ste 140 200 W Magee Rd Tucson AZ 85704-6492 Address: NRA 11250 Waples Mill Rd Fairfax VA 22030

FROMER, KEVIN, federal agency administrator; BA. Staff asst. Office of Rep. Harold Rogers Ho. of Reps., Washington, 1982—85, legis. dir., 1985—88, chief of staff, 1993—2002; asst. to ranking minority mem. com. on appropriations, commerce, justice, state judiciary subcom. Ho. of Reps., Washington, 1988—92, asst. to spkr. for policy, budget and appropriations office of spkr., 2002—05, asst. sec. treasury for legis. affairs, 2005—. Office: US Dept Treasury 1500 Pennsylvania Ave NW Rm 3134 Washington DC 20220 Office Phone: 202-622-1900. Office Fax: 202-622-0534.

FROMM, ELI, engineering educator; b. Niedaltdorf, Germany, May 7, 1939; s. Siegfried and Helen (Lucas) F.; m. Dorothy Mildred Gold, Dec. 23, 1962; children: Stephen Arthur, Larry Brian, Richard Michael. BSEE, Drexel U., 1962, MSE, 1964; PhD, Jefferson Med. Coll., 1967. Engr. missile and space div. GE Co., Phila., 1962; engr. Applied Physics Lab. E.I. DuPont Co., Wilmington, Del., 1963; from asst. prof. to prof. biomed. sci. Drexel U., Phila., 1967-80, prof. elec. and computer engring., 1980-97, acting head dept. biol. sci., 1984-85, asst. head dept. elec. and computer engring., 1987-89, assoc. dean. Coll. Engring., 1988-89, interim dean, 1989-90, vice provost for rsch. and grad. studies, 1990-96, v.p. ednl. R&D, 1996-99, dir. Ctr. for Ednl. Rsch., 1999—, Roy A. Brothers Univ. prof. elec. and computer engring., 1997—. Mem. staff, congl. fellow com. sci. and tech. U.S. Ho. of Reps., 1980-81; program dir. NSF, Washington, 1983-84; vis. scientist Legis. Rsch. Office Pa. Ho. Reps., Harrisburg, 1986-87. Contbr. over 60 articles to profl. jours. Recipient Centennial medal Drexel U., 1992, Bernard M. Gordon prize for innovation in engring. and tech. edn. Nat. Acad. Engring., 2002, Fellow award, Internat. Engring. Consortium, 2003; Spl. fellow NIH, 1964-67; grantee NIH, 1969-78, NSF, 1969-71, 79, 84, 88-2004, 2006-. Fellow IEEE (bd. dirs. 1983-84, mem. coms., Centennial medal 1984), Nat. Acad. Engring., Am. Inst. Med. and Biologic Engring., Am. Soc. Engring. Edn. (Centennial medal 1993); mem. Sigma Xi. Jewish. Office: Drexel U Elec and Computer Engring Dept 32nd and Chestnut St Philadelphia PA 19104 Office Phone: 215-895-2201. Business E-Mail: fromm@drexel.edu.

FROMM, ERWIN FREDERICK, retired insurance company executive; b. Kalamazoo, Oct. 24, 1933; s. Erwin Carl and Charlotte Elizabeth (Wilson) F. Student, U. Mich., 1951-52, Flint Jr. Coll., 1952-53; BA, Kalamazoo Coll., 1959; postgrad., Ill. State U., 1970-72. CPCU, CLU; cert. nursing home adminstr. Underwriter State Farm Ins., 1959-72; cons. Met. Property & Liability Ins. Co., Warwick, R.I., 1972-73, dir. underwriting and policyholders svcs., 1973, asst. v.p., 1973-74, v.p., 1974—. Sr. v.p. Royal Ins. Co., Charlotte, N.C., 1979-90; ret., 1990; nursing home exec. Royal Crest Health Care Ctr., Inc., 1990-92; pres. Royal Monarch Cons., Inc., 1990—; past chmn. All Industry Ins. Com. for Arson Control; chmn. Nat. Coun. on Compensation Ins.; past chmn. Comml. Lines Com. Ins. Svc. Office; past mem. adv. com. underwriting program Ins. Inst. Am.; cert. long term care ombudsman, 1998—. Past mem. adv. coun. Bus. Sch., U. R.I.; past bd. dirs. Charlotte Symphony; bd. dirs. N.C. Ins. Edn.; mem. Calif. Sr. Legisature, 2000—, mem. adv. coun. on aging; bd. dirs. Calif. Found. on Aging; bd. dirs. Compulsive Gambling Inst. Mem. CPCU Assn. (Calif. chpt.), CLU Assn. (Calif. chpt.), Masons, Shriners. Lutheran. Home and Office: 73 Colgate Drive Rancho Mirage CA 92270 E-mail: pssstca@aol.com.

FROMM, JEFFERY BERNARD, lawyer; b. Washington, Oct. 9, 1947; s. Seymour Morris and Frances Sylvia (Goldstein) F.; m. Mary Ellen Sommer, Sept. 11, 1971; children: Aaron M., David P. BS in Elec. Engring., BA in Physics, U. Pa., 1970; JD magna cum laude, Widener U., 1981. Bar: Pa. 1982, Calif. 1982, U.S. Ct. Appeals (9th and fed. cirs.) 1982, Colo. 1988. Patent atty. Hewlett-Packard Co., Palo Alto, Calif., 1981-83, sr. patent atty., 1983-85, mng. patent counsel Andover, Mass., 1985-87, sr. mng. counsel intellectual property Ft. Collins, Colo., 1987—2002; pvt. intellectual property legal practice, 2002—03; atty. Drinker, Biddle and Reath LLP, 2003—06; v.p., dept. gen. counsel, dir. intellectual property Hewlett-Packard Co., Palo Alto, Calif., 2006—. Asst. scoutmaster Boy Scouts Am., Ft. Collins, 1988-96; asst. coach-umpire Little League, Andover and San Jose, Calif., 1983-87. Mem. IEEE, ABA, Am. Intellectual Property Law Assn., Assn. Corp. Patent Counsel, Am. Corp. Counsel, Intellectual Property Owners (bd. dirs.), Pa. Bar Assn., Calif. Bar Assn., Colo. Bar Assn., Phi Delta Phi. Avocations: skiing, golf. Office: Hewlett-Packard Co 3000 Hanover St MS 1051 Palo Alto CA 94304 Office Phone: 650-857-2472. Business E-Mail: jeff.fromm@hp.com.

FROMM, JOSEPH, retired editor, foreign correspondent, foreign affairs consultant; b. South Bend, Ind., Jan. 6, 1920; s. Michael M. and Ethel (Mentzel) F.; divorced; children: Margot, Lisa; 1 stepchild, Erik. Student, U. Chgo., 1937-38, Northwestern U., 1938-39. Reporter S. Bend Tribune, 1935-37, Southtown Economist, Chgo., 1937-39; writer UP, Chgo., 1939-40; radio news bur. chief AP, Chgo., 1940-42; mng. editor air edit. Chgo. Sun, 1942; fgn. corr. U.S. News and World Report, 1946-74, dep. editor Washington, 1974-79, asst. editor, 1979-85, contbg. editor, 1985-88. Cons. to think tanks, U.S. Dept. Def., Nat. Security Coun., CIA, Joint Warfare Analysis Ctr.; lectr. on strategy and internat. rels.; mem. tech. adv. com. Ctr. Naval Analysis. Am. field svc. Brit. Army, 1943—44, commd. capt. Indian Army, 1945. Decorated Order Brit. Empire. Fellow Johns Hopkins Fgn. Policy Inst., Internat. Inst. Strategic Studies (founding mem. 1958, mem. governing coun. 1975-92); mem. Washington Inst. Fgn. Affairs, Coun. on Fgn. Rels., Midatlantic Club, Fgn. Corr. Club Japan (pres. 1950), Assn. Am. Corrs. in London (pres. 1967), Fgn. Press Assn. London (dir. 1972-74), Arms Control Assn., Cosmos Club Washington, Pilgrims Soc. Gt. Brit. Personal E-mail: joefromm@aol.com.

FROMM, JOSEPH L., financial consultant; b. May 22, 1930; s. Charles and Elizabeth Fromm; m. Beverly C. Booth, June 18, 1960; children: Charles, Laurence, Kenneth, Lisa, Brian. AB cum laude, Princeton U., 1953; MBA, Harvard U., 1958. Rsch. asst. Harvard Bus. Sch., 1959; asst. to pres. Gen. Electronics Labs., Cambridge, Mass., 1960-62; with Chrysler Corp., Highland Park, Mich., 1963-68; treas. Marantette & Co., Detroit, 1969; asst. treas. Am. Motors Corp., Southfield, Mich., 1970-87; pres. Fiduciary Advisors, Inc., Grosse Pointe, Mich., 1988—. Dir. pension asset mgmt. Eastern Airlines, Miami, Fla., 1988-92; instr. U. Detroit Evening Divsn., 1964-65. Councilman City of Grosse Pointe Farms, 1973-86, mayor, 1986-91; trustee, treas. Bon Secours Hosp., Bon Secours Home Med., Inc., Bon Secours Pharmacy, 1975-2004; prists pension bd. Archdiocese of Detroit, 2003—; trustee St. John Sr. Svcs., 2003—. With AUS, 1954-56. Mem. Country Club of Detroit, Sr. Men's Club Grosse Pointe (pres. 1996-97). Republican. Roman Catholic. Office: Fiduciary Advisors Inc 316 Belanger Ave Grosse Pointe Farms MI 48236-3302 Personal E-mail: fromm@comcast.net.

FROMM, RONALD A., apparel executive; m. Cheryl Fromm; children: Dawn, Dana. BS in Acctg., U. Wis., MBA. Former v.p. Heath Corp.; dir. fin. Famous Footwear divsn. Brown Shoe, Madison, Wis., 1986-88, v.p., 1988-90, v.p., CFO, 1990-92, exec. v.p., then pres. Brown Shoe Co. divsn., 1992—98, pres. St. Louis, 1999—2006, chmn., CEO, 1999—. Bd. dirs. Footwear Distributors and Retailers of Am., Fashion Footwear Assn. N.Y., Two/Ten Footwear Industry charitable found. Office: Brown Shoe 8300 Maryland Ave Saint Louis MO 63105*

FROMMER, ARTHUR, editor-in-chief, travel writer; JD, Yale U. Bar: NY. Editor-in-chief Arthur Frommer's BUDGET TRAVEL. Faculty mem. Soc. Am. Travel Writers Inst., 1998, 2005; radio show host United Stations Network. Author: GI's Guide to traveling Europe, Europe on $5 a Day, 1956, Arthur Frommer's Branson!, 1995; co-author: Arthur Frommer's New World of Travel; author: of numerous other travel guidebooks. Trustee NY Cmty. Svc. Soc.; chairperson Friends of RSVP, Inc. Mem.: NY Bar Assn. Office: Arthur Frommer's Budget Travel 530 7th Ave New York NY 10018 Office Phone: 646-695-6700.*

FROMMER, LAWRENCE JULIAN, retired travel company executive; b. Trenton, NJ, Sept. 8, 1917; s. Samuel Alexander Frommer and Fannie Cohen; m. Yolande Irene Foisy, Aug. 22, 1975. BA in Journalism, Ind. U., 1939, MS in Bus. Adminstrn., 1942. Cert. travel counselor. Writer Radio Sta. WOWO, Ft. Wayne, Ind., 1943—44, Radio Sta. WKRC, Cin., 1944—45, Radio Sta. WOL, Washington, 1945—53; travel agy. exec. Frommer Travel Svc., Washington, 1958—91; travel writer Washingtonian Mag., 1969—82, Asta Agy. Mgmt., NYC, Washington, 1973—95; travel and restaurant writer Crystal City Mag., Arlington, Va., 1990—2004. Travel agy. adv. bd. State Maine, Augusta, 1980, Am. Express, NYC, 1983—90, Access Am., NYC, 1985—88; radio host Travel Talk, Wash., 1970—84. Contbr. articles to profl. jours. Pres. Louis D. Brandeis Zionist Dist., Washington, 1958—59, Skal Club Travel Execs., Washington, 1975—76; trustee Inst. Cert. Travel Agts., Wellesly, Mass., 1968—90; vol. Animal Welfare League Alexandria, Alexandria Symphony Orch., Va., US Holocaust Mus., Alexandria Homeless Shelter. Named Travel Agt. of Yr., Am. Soc. Travel Agts., Washington, 1985. Fellow: Louis D. Brandeis Zionist Dist. (life; pres.), Skal Club Washington (pres.). Avocations: music, theater, sports, volunteer work. Home: Apt 505 5902 Mount Eagle Dr Alexandria VA 22303-2516 Personal E-mail: yonlarry@erols.com.

FROMMER, WILLIAM S., lawyer; b. Bklyn., Sept. 27, 1942; s. Herbert S. and Molly S. Frommer; m. Karen Beagle, July 31, 1966; 1 child, Hillary. BEE, Cornell U., 1965; JD, Am. U., 1969. Bar: NY 1970, U.S. Patent Office 1970, U.S. Ct. Customs and Patent Appeals 1975, U.S. Ct. Appeals (fed. cir.) 1982, U.S. Supreme Ct. 1985. Assoc. Marn & Jangarathis, NYC, 1969—73, Curtis, Morris & Safford, P.C., NYC, 1973—76, ptnr., 1976—97; founding ptnr. Frommer, Lawrence & Haug, NYC, 1997—. Lectr. NY Intellectual Propery Law Assn., Practicing Law Inst. Mem. Am. U. Law Rev., 1967—69; contbr. articles to profl. jours. Mem.: ABA, Am. Intellectual Property Law Assn., Practicing Law Inst., Internat. Bar Assn., Internat. Patent and Trademark Assn., NY State Bar Assn., NY Intellectual Property Law Assn. Office: 745 5th Ave New York NY 10151-0099 Office Phone: 212-588-0800.

FRONDUTI, JOHN S., lawyer; b. Pitts., Aug. 18, 1972; BBA, U. Notre Dame, 1994; JD, U. Cin. Coll. Law, 1997. Bar: NY 1998, Ohio 2003. Assoc. Pillsbury, Winthrop LLP, NYC; ptnr. Keating, Muething & Klekamp PLL, Cin. Named one of Ohio's Rising Stars, Super Lawyers, 2006. Mem.: Cin. Bar Assn. Office: Keating Muething & Klekamp PLL One E Fourth St Ste 1400 Cincinnati OH 45202 Office Phone: 513-579-6400. Office Fax: 513-579-6457.

FRONE, MICHAEL R., psychologist, researcher; s. S. Henry and MaryAnn Frone; m. Joan Stockman. BA, SUNY at Buffalo, 1981, PhD, 1991. Pers. rsch. analyst IBM, North Tarrytown, NY, 1985; rsch. assoc. prof. dept. psychology SUNY at Buffalo, 1991—, sr. rsch. scientist Rsch. Inst. on Addictions, 1986—. Associate editor (journal) Journal of Occupational Health Psychology; author (editor): Psychology of Workplace Safety; editor: Handbook of Work Stress; contbr. articles numerous articles to profl. jours., chapters to books. Named Top 100 Fed. Grantees, SUNY at Buffalo, 2002; grantee, NIH: Nat. Inst. on Alcohol Abuse and Alcoholism grantee, 2000—04, Scientist Devel. award, NIH: Nat. Inst. on Alcohol Abuse and Alcoholism, 1994—2000; scholar Pre-doctoral Rsch. traineeship, SUNY at Buffalo and NIH: Nat. Inst. of Mental Health, 1981—84. Mem.: So. Mgmt. Assn., Soc. for Personality and Social Psychology, Soc. for Indsl. and Orgnl. Psychology, APA, Acad. of Mgmt. Achievements include research in developing a conceptual model of the work-family interface in 1992 and expanded it in 1997. This research has been highly cited and has influenced research on work-family conflict and facilitation; development of a model of employee substance use and productivity. Avocation: scuba diving. Office: SUNY-Buffalo 1021 Main St Buffalo NY 14203

FRONTZ, LESLIE KAY, art educator; b. Cleve., Aug. 23, 1950; d. James W. and Mary K. Robinson; BA in Psychology, cum laude, Muskingum Coll., New Concord, Ohio, 1972; MA in Edn., Va. Poly. Inst. State U., Blacksburg, 1976; BS in Art, summa cum laude, So. Oreg. State U., Ashland, 1981; MFA in Studio Arts, U. NC, Greensboro, 1986. Studio artist Frontz Studio, Lexington, NC, 1986—; adj. faculty art history Front Range CC, Ft. Collins, Colo., 1989—90; adj. faculty art Davidson County CC, 1995—96, 2006—07; instr. art Wash. State CC, Marietta, Ohio, 1991—92, SW Elem. Sch., 1997—2003. Mem., bd. of directors Ohio Watercolor Soc., Ohio, 1993—94. Exhibitions include Smithsonian Instn., Washington, 1987, Loveland Mus. and Gallery Co., 1990, Davidson County Mus. Art, NC, 1997, Salem Coll. Fine Arts Ctr., 2003, Landfall Found., 2003, So. Watercolor Soc., 2006—07, Soc. Women Artists, London, 2005—07; contbr. articles to profl. jours. Vol. asst. exhbns. Loveland Mus. and Gallery, Colo., 1988—90, Davidson County Hist. Mus., Lexington, NC, 2003; mem. exec. bd. Lexington Herb Guild, NC, 1996—2005. Recipient Best of Show, Nat. Art Mart, Colo., 1990, Excellence award, Ohio Watercolor Soc., 1992, Mason award, Batavia Nat. Exhbn., N.Y., 1993, Best of Show, Comer Mus. Art, Ala., 1995, Canson award, Cultural Arts Ctr., Glen Allen, Va., 2006; fellow profiled in, U.S. Art, 1989; Holderness fellow, U. N.C., Greensboro, 1985—86. Mem.: Soc. Women Artists (signature mem., HRH Princess Michael of Kent Watercolor award 2007), Southern Watercolor Soc. (signature mem., Georg Shook Meml. award 2007), Plein Air Carolina (founding mem.). Presbyterian. Avocations: genealogical and historical research, gardening, travel. Office: Frontz Studio 296 Peace Haven Dr Lexington NC 27292 Home Phone: 336-357-5974; Office Phone: 336-357-5974. Business E-Mail: hlfrontz@lexcominc.net.

FROOM, DAVID, composer, music educator; b. Calif., 1951; Student, U. Calif., Berkeley, U. So. Calif., Columbia U.; studies with, Chen Wen-chung, Mario Davidovsky, Alexander Goehr, William Kraft. Tchr. Baruch Coll., U. Utah, Peabody Conservatory; prof. music St. Mary's Coll., Md., 1989—. Bd. dirs. N.Y. New Music Ensemble. Composer: music performed by numerous ensembles. Recipient commn., Fromm and Koussevitsky Found., Friedheim Awards 1st Prize, Kennedy Ctr., 3 Individual Artist award, State of Md.; Charles Ives scholar, fellow, John Simon Guggenheim Meml. Found., 2003, Tanglewood Music Festival, Wellesley Composers Conf., MacDowell Colony, grant, NEA, Fulbright grant, Cambridge U. Mem.: League of Composers/ISCM (mem. nat. adv. bd.). Office: St Mary's Coll Md 18952 E Fisher Rd Saint Marys City MD 20686-3001

FROOMAN, THOMAS E., lawyer; b. 1967; m. Susan Frooman; 2 children. BSBA, Citadel, 1989; JD, Salmon P. Chase Coll. of Law, 1994. Atty. Keating, Muething & Klekamp, Cincinnati, 1997—2001; v.p., gen. counsel, sec. Cintas Corp., 2001—. Office: Cintas Corp PO Box 625737 6800 Cintas Blvd Cincinnati OH 45262-5737 Office Phone: 513-754-3584. Business E-Mail: froomant@cintas.com.

FROSCH, ROBERT ALAN, retired automobile manufacturing executive, physicist; b. NYC, May 22, 1928; s. Herman Louis and Rose (Bernfeld) Frosch; m. Jessica Rachael Denerstein, Dec. 22, 1957; 1 child, Margery Ellen; 1 child, Elizabeth Ann. AB, Columbia U., 1947, A.M., 1949, PhD, 1952; DEng (hon.), U. Miami, 1982, Mich. Technol. U., 1983. Scientist Hudson Labs. Columbia U., 1951—53, asst. dir. theoretical divsn., 1953—54, assoc. dir., 1954—56, dir., 1956—63; dir. nuclear test detection Advanced Rsch. Projects Agy., Office Sec. Def., 1963—65; dep. dir. Advanced Rsch. Projects Agy., 1965—66; asst. sec. navy for rsch. and devel. Washington, 1966—73; asst. exec. dir. UN Environment Programme, 1973—75; assoc. dir. for applied oceanography Woods Hole (Mass.) Oceanographic Instn., 1975—77; adminstr. NASA, Washington, 1977—81; pres. Am. Assn. Engring. Socs., NYC, 1981—82; v.p. in charge Research Labs. Gen. Motors Corp., Warren, Mich., 1982—93; sr. rsch. fellow Ctr. for Sci. and Internat. Affairs John F. Kennedy Sch. Govt., Harvard U., Cambridge, Mass., 1993—. Chmn. U.S. del. to Intergovtl. Oceanographic Commn. meetings UNESCO, Paris, 1967, Paris, 70. Contbr. numerous sci. and tech. articles to profl. jours. Recipient Arthur S. Flemming award, 1966, NASA Disting. Svc. award, 1981, IRI medal Indsl. Rsch. Inst., 1996, Founders medal, IEEE Found. Fellow: IEEE, AIAA, NAE (sr.), AAAS, Am. Astronautical Soc. (John F. Kennedy Astronautics award 1981), Acoustical Soc. Am.; mem.: Royal Acad. Engring. (U.K., fgn.), Engring. Soc. Detroit, Soc. Automotive Engrs., Soc. Naval Architects and Marine Engrs., Am. Phys. Soc., Marine Tech. Soc., Soc. Exploration Geophysicists (spl. commendation 1981), Am. Acad. Arts and Scis., Seismol. Soc. Am., Am. Geophys. Union. Office: Harvard U John F Kennedy Sch Govt BCSIA 79 JFK St Cambridge MA 02138-5801 Personal E-mail: rfrosch522@aol.com. Business E-Mail: robert_frosch@harvard.edu.

FROSH, BRIAN ESTEN, lawyer, state senator; b. Washington, Oct. 8, 1946; s. Stanley Benjamin and Judith Lee (Wirkman) F.; m. Marcy Masters, Nov. 19, 1984; children: Elena, Alexandra. Student, U. Stockholm, 1966-67; BA, Wesleyan U., 1968; JD, Columbia U., 1971. Legis. asst. Sen. Harrison Williams U.S. Senate, Washington, 1972-76; ptnr. Kass, Skalet & Frosh, Washington, 1976-79, Bingaman, Davenport & Lovejoy, Santa Fe, 1979-81; pvt. practice Bethesda, Md., 1981—96; ptnr. Karp, Frosh, Lapidus, Wigodsky and Norwind, Washington, 1996—; del. Md. Gen. Assembly, Annapolis, 1987-95, chmn. Montgomery County House del., 1991-93; state senator Md. State Senate, 1995—, dep. majority leader, 2001—02, chmn. jud. procs. com., 2003—; mem. gov.'s task force on energy Md. Gen. Assembly, Annapolis, 1989-94; chmn. environ. subcom. Econ. and Environ. Affairs Com., 1995—2002; mem. Chesapeake Bay Commn., 1995—; chmn. Chesapeake Bay Commn., 2001. Legis. acts include Md. Recycling Act, Newspaper Recycling Act, Oil Spills Bill, Bay Protection and Oil Exploration, also others; bd. dirs. State Nat. Bank Md. Bd. dirs. Hebrew Home Greater Washington, 1986-95, Jewish Cmty. Ctr. Greater Washington, 1983-89; mem. Montgomery County Charter Rev. Commn., 1983-86; nat. adv. commn. SBA, 1981-82. Recipient cert. of merit Montgomery County Common Cause Md., 1991, Clean Air award Sierra Club, 1991, Conservationist of Yr. award, 1989, Lawmaker of Yr. award Am. Lung Assn. Md., 1991, Outstanding Svc. award Am. Heart Assn. Md., John Kabler award Md. League Conservation Voters, 2003. Mem. Md. State Bar Assn. (Leadership and Outstanding Svc. award 2001), Wesleyan U. Alumni Assn. (exec. com. 1986-89). Address: Miller Senate Office Bldg 2E 11 Bladen St Annapolis MD 21401 Office: Ste 800W 7315 Wisconsin Ave Bethesda MD 20814-3217 Office Phone: 301-652-2888, 301-652-2888. Business E-Mail: brian.frosh@senate.state.md.us.

FROSS, ROGER RAYMOND, lawyer; b. Rockford, Ill., Mar. 8, 1940; s. Hollis H. and Dorothy (George) F.; m. Madelon R. Rose, Feb. 14, 1970; 1 child, Oliver. AB, DePauw U., 1962; JD, U. Chgo., 1965. Bar: Ill. 1965. Assoc. Norman and Billick, Chgo., 1965-70; ptnr. Lord, Bissell & Brook, Chgo., 1970—, mng. pntr., 1982-87. Bd. dirs. Hyde Park Bank and Trust Co., Chgo., 1975—; pres. Hyde-Park-Kenwood Devel. Corp., 1998—. Bd. dirs. Hyde Park Neighborhood Club, Chgo., 1970—, pres. 1972-73; bd. dirs., mem. exec. com. South East Chgo. Commn., 1978—; mem. Community Conservation Council, Chgo., 1980-99; bd. dirs., sec. Chgo. Metro History Fair, 1991—; bd. dirs. The Joyce Found., 1991—. Lab. Sch. U. Chgo., 1991-94, Citizens Com. of the Juvenile Ct., 1973-96. Rector schlor DePauw U., Greencastle, Ind., 1958-62. Mem. ABA, Ill. Bar Assn., Chgo. Bar Assn. (chmn. com. juvenile delinquents 1972).

FROST, A. CORWIN, architect, consultant; b. Bronxville, NY, Nov. 18, 1934; s. Frederick George Jr. and Gwendolyn Belle (Corwin) F.; m. Rosalie Randolph Halsey, Sept. 26, 1959; children: Frederick Halsey, Anne Randolph. AB, Princeton U., 1956; BS, R.I. Sch. Design, 1959. Registered architect, N.Y., other states. Designer, draftsman Harrison & Abramovitz, NYC, 1959-60; project architect Frederick G. Frost Jr. and Assocs., NYC, 1960-63, assoc., 1963-68; ptnr. Frost Assocs., NYC, 1968-78; assoc. dir. archtl. and engring. services CBS Inc., NYC, 1978-80, dir. planning and design, 1980-86, dir. facilities engring., 1986-88; prin. Frost Assocs. Cons., Bronxville, NY, 1988—; dep. dir. dept. design, cons. and mgmt. CUNY, 1992-95; cons. Newark Pub. Schs., 1995—. Chmn. Bronxville Planning Bd., 1990-2004; trustee Coun. for Arts in Westchester, White Plains, NY, 1972-81, pres. 1974-75; trustee, RI Sch. Design, 1989-99, 2000-2006, hon. trustee, 2006—, Westchester County Hist. Soc., 1998-2004; trustee, mem. exec. com. Westchester Preservation League, 1989-98; mem. Bronxville Adult Sch., 1982-88, Bronxville Planning Commn., 1977-80. Mem. AIA (exec. com. N.Y. chpt. 1974-76, ethics com. 1978-80, corp. architects com. 1980-82, fin. com. 1981-87), Princeton Club, Bronxville Field Club (pres. 1992-96). Home and Office: Frost Assoc Cons 11 Sunset Ave Bronxville NY 10708-2208 Personal E-mail: fiberarch@earthlink.net.

FROST, DAN R., history professor, department chairman; b. Wamego, Kans., July 19, 1961; s. Raymond Lyle Frost and Alene Geneva Bellman; m. Annick Rita Guilmot, May 17, 1996; 1 child, Margot Guilmot. BA in History, Calif. State U., Fullerton, 1979—84, MA in History, 1985—88; PhD in History, La. State U., Baton Rouge, 1988—94. Assoc. prof. history Dillard U., New Orleans, 2001—, chair dept. history, 2002—. Sec. faculty coun. Dillard U., 2004—05. Author: (books) Thinking Confederates: Academia and the Idea of Progress in the New South, The LSU College of Engineering, Vol. 2: Problems and Progress, 1909-1970; co-author with Kou K. Nelson (book) LSU College of Engineering, Vol. 1: Origins and Establishment, 1860-1908; contbr. articles to profl. jours. Recipient Disting. Rsch. award, Divsn. Social Scis., Dillard U., 2000—01. Mem.: La. Hist. Assn. (assoc.), So. Hist. Assn. (assoc.). Independent. Episc. Office: Dillard Univ 2601 Gentilly Blvd New Orleans LA 70122 Home Phone: 225-673-5460. Business E-Mail: dfrost@dillard.edu.

FROST, DAVID, retired biology professor, medical editor, consultant; b. Bklyn., Dec. 19, 1925; s. Charles and Regina (Sad) Feivlowitz; m. Ruthann Steinberg, Dec. 24, 1946; children: Michael Joseph, Jane Alice. BS, CCNY, 1945, MED, 1949; MS, NYU, 1952, PhD, 1960. Instr. in biology CCNY, 1946-49; instr. in sci. Rhodes Sch., NYC, 1949-52; asst. prof. biology Rutgers U., Newark, 1952-59, adj. prof. biology New Brunswick, 1960-78; sci. editor Squibb Inst. for Med. Rsch., Princeton, 1959-75; pvt. practice Plainfield, NJ, 1975—2002, Olmstedville, NY, 1975—2002; ret., 2002. Pres. N.J. SANE, 1964-65; co-chmn. Plainfield Joint Def. Com., 1970-85; newsletter editor Cen. Jersey/Masaya, Nicaragua Friendship Cities Project, 1985-97. Mem. Coun. Sci. Editors (pres. 1982-83), Schroon Lake Assn. (v.p., 1980—, pres. 1997-2007). Office: 1229 E 7th St Plainfield NJ 07062-1907 Home: 1637 Hoffman Rd Olmstedville NY 12857-2436 Office Phone: 908-755-3286.

FROST, EDMUND BOWEN, lawyer; b. Pueblo, Colo., Dec. 5, 1942; s. Hildreth and Doris (Bowen) F.; m. Molly Spitzer, 1966; children: Julia A., Elizabeth E., Edmund N., Luette S. BA, Dartmouth Coll., 1964; JD magna cum laude, U. Mich., 1967. Bar: Colo. 1967, D.C. 1970, U.S. Supreme Ct. 1980. Assoc. Steptoe & Johnson, Washington, 1969-75; chief legal advisor to commr. ICC, Washington, 1975-76; asst. dir. for gen. litigation Bur. Competition, FTC, Washington, 1976-77; v.p., gen. counsel Chem. Mfrs. Assn., Washington, 1978-82; ptnr. Kirland & Ellis, Washington, 1982-88, Davis, Graham & Stubbs, Washington, 1988-94; sr. v.p. and gen. counsel Clean Sites, Inc., Alexandria, Va., 1994-99; shareholder, dir. Leonard Frost Levin Van Court & Marsh, PC, 1998—; bd. dirs., chmn., bd. environ., health and safety com. Philip Svcs. Co., 2000—03; gen. ptnr. Frost Bros. Resources, LLLP, 2004—. Contbr. articles to profl. jours. Participant pub. policy dialogs on environ. issues Keystone (Colo.) Ctr., 1980—; guest artisan Washington Nat. Cathedral, 1997—; bd. dirs. Cmty. Coun. for the Homeless at Friendship Place, DC, exec. com., 1992—, co-pres. 2002-04; pres., bd. dirs. Vincent Palumbo Ctr. for Stonecarving and Indsl. Arts, Inc., 2001-; pres., bd. dirs., exec. com. Congl. Summer Assembly, Frankfort, Mich., 2005—. Capt. U.S. Army, 1967-69. Recipient Benjamin E. Cooper award for exceptional vol. leadership, Cmty. Coun. for the Homeless at Friendship Place, DC, 2004. Mem. Cosmos Club Washington. Avocations: sculpture and stone carving, skiing, mountain climbing, tuba and euphonium. Home: 3309 35th St NW Washington DC 20016-3141 Home Phone: 202-362-6788; Office Phone: 202-223-2500. Business E-Mail: ebfrost@leonardfrost.com.

FROST, ELIZABETH ANN MCARTHUR, physician; b. Glasgow, Scotland, Oct. 29, 1938; arrived in US, 1963; d. Robert Thomas and Annie M. (Ross) F.; m. Wallace Capobianco, Sept. 4, 1965 (dec. May 1988); children: Garrett, Ross, Christopher, Neil. MBChB, U. Glasgow, 1961. Diplomate Am. Bd. Anesthesiology, Royal Coll. Ob-Gyn., London. Intern in surgery Royal Infirmary, Glasgow, 1961-62; intern in medicine Victoria Infirmary, Glasgow, 1962; intern in obstetrics Royal Maternity Hosp., Glasgow, 1962-63; resident in internal medicine Englewood (N.J.) Hosp., 1963-64; resident in anesthesiology N.Y. Hosp., NYC, 1964-66; instr. in anesthesiology Albert Einstein Coll. Medicine, Bronx, NY, 1966-68, asst. prof. to assoc. prof., 1968-81, prof. anesthesiology, 1981-91, mem. dept. history of medicine, 1973-91; prof. dept. anesthesiology N.Y. Med. Coll., Valhalla, 1992-99; clin. prof. dept. anesthesiology Mt. Sinai Med. Ctr., NYC, 2000—; attending anesthesiology VA Bronx, 2000—04. Book reviewer New Eng. Jour. of Medicine, 1983—; editor Preanesthetic Assessment, Anesthesiology News, 1984—, Gen. Surgery News, 1991; author/contbr. books; contbr. articles to profl. jours. Mem. N.Y. State Soc. Anesthesiologists, Am. Soc. of Anesthesiologists, Assn. of Univ. Anesthesiologists, Soc. of Neurosurg. Anesthesia and Neurologic Supportive Care, Am. Assn. of Neurol. Surgeons, Anesthesia History Assn. Home: 2 Pondview West Purchase NY 10577 Office Phone: 212-241-7467. Personal E-mail: elzfrost@aol.com.

FROST, ELLEN LOUISE, political economist; b. Boston, Apr. 26, 1945; d. Horace Wier and Mildred (Kip) F.; m. William F. Pedersen, Jr., Feb. 2, 1974; 1 son by previous marriage, Jai Kumar Ojha; children: Mark Francis Pedersen, Claire Ellen Pedersen. BA magna cum laude, Radcliffe Coll., 1966; MA, Fletcher Sch. Law and Diplomacy, 1967; PhD, Harvard U., 1972. Teaching fellow, instr. Harvard U., Wellesley Coll., 1969-71; legis. asst. Office of Senator Alan Cranston, Washington, 1972-74; fgn. affairs officer Dept. Treasury, Washington, 1974-77; dep. dir. Office of Internat. Trade Policy and Negotiations, 1977; dep. asst. sec. of def. for internat. econ. and tech. affairs Dept. Def., Washington, 1977-81; dir. govt. programs Westinghouse Electric Corp., Washington, 1981-88; corp. dir., internat. affairs United Techs. Corp., Washington, 1988-91; sr. fellow Inst. for Internat. Econs., Washington, 1992-93, 95-98, vis. fellow, 1998—; counselor to U.S. Trade Rep., Washington, 1993-95. Author: For Richer, For Poorer: The New U.S.-Japan Relationship, 1987, Transatlantic Trade: A Strategic Agenda, 1997; co-editor: The Global Century, 2001. Trustee Aspen Inst. Berlin, 1990—92. NSF trainee, 1967—69. Mem. Internat. Inst. Strategic Studies, Coun. Fgn. Rels., Phi Beta Kappa.

FROST, EVERETT LLOYD, academic administrator, anthropologist; b. Salt Lake City, Oct. 17, 1942; s. Henry Hoag Jr. and Ruth Salome (Smith) F.; m. Janet Owens, Mar. 26, 1967; children: Noreen Karyn, Joyce Lida. BA in Anthropology, U. Utah, 1965; PhD in Anthropology, U. Oreg., 1970. Field rschr. in cultural anthropology, Taveuni, Fiji, 1968-69; asst. prof. in anthropology Ea. N.Mex. U., Portales, 1970-74, assoc. prof., 1974-76, asst. dean Coll. Liberal Arts and Scis., 1976-78, dean acad. affairs and grad. studies, 1978-80, v.p. for planning and analysis, dean rsch., 1980-91, dean grad. studies, 1983-88, pres., 1991-2001, pres. emeritus, prof. anthropology emeritus, 2001—. Cons., evaluator N. Ctrl. Assn. Accreditation Agy. for Higher Edn., 1989-93—, mem. rev. bd., 1993-95—; commr., past pres. Western Interstate Commn. for Higher Edn., 1993-; pres. Lone Star Athletic Conf. Pres.'s Commn., 1992-93. Chmn. N.Mex. Humanities Coun., 1980-88; mem. N.Mex. Gov.'s Commn. on Higher Edn., 1983-86; mem. exec. bd. N.Mex. First, 1987-92, chmn. rsch. com., 1989-91, exec. bd. emeritus, 1992-; bd. dirs. Roosevelt Gen. Hosp., Portales, 1989-92; pres. bd. dirs. San Juan County Mus. Assn., Farmington, 1979-82; vice chair Portales Pub. Schs. Facilities Com., 1990-91. NDEA fellow, 1969-70; grantee NEW, 1979-80, NSF, 1968-69, Fiji Forbes, Ltd., 1975-76, others. Fellow Am. Anthropol. Assn., Am. Assn. Higher Edn., Soc. Coll. and Univ. Planning, Assn. Social Anthropologists Oceania, Anthrop. Soc. Wash., Sch. Am. Rsch., Western Assn. Grad. Deans, Current Anthropology (assoc.) Polynesian Soc., Phi Kappa Phi. Office: Ea NMex Univ Dept Anthropolog Sta 3 Portales NM 88130 Office Phone: 505-562-2883. Business E-Mail: everett.frost@enmu.edu.

FROST, HELEN MARIE, writer; b. Brookings, SD, Mar. 4, 1949; d. Reuben Bernhard and Jean Elizabeth (Timmons) F.; m. Chad Lawrence Thompson, July 23, 1983; 1 child, Glen Andrew Thompson; 1 stepchild, Lloyd Samuel Thompson. BS, Syracuse U., 1971; MAT, Ind. U., 1994. Cert. in elem. edn., Alaska, Ind., Mass. Tchr. Kilquhanity House Sch., Castle Douglas, Scotland, 1976-78; prin., tchr. Telida (Alaska) Sch., 1981-84; tchr. White Cliff Sch., Ketchikan, Alaska, 1990-91; tchr. English, dir. Writing Ctr. Ind. U./Purdue U., Ft. Wayne, 1996-97. Cons. numerous schs. and orgns., 1990—. Author: Skin of a Fish, Bones of a Bird, 1993, When I Whisper, Nobody Listens, 2001, Spinning Through the Universe, 2004, Keesha's House, 2003 (ALA award, 2004), The Braid, 2006. Poetry tchr. program for at-risk youth Ft. Wayne Dance Collective, 1995—2006. Mem. Soc. Children's Book Writers and Illustrators, Tchrs. and Writers Collaborative, Poetry Soc. Am. (Robert Winner award 1992, Mary Carolyn Davies award 1993), Acad. Am. poets, Writers Ctr. Ind. Avocations: crosscountry skiing, gardening, raising and releasing monarch butterflies. Home and Office: 6108 Old Brook Dr Fort Wayne IN 46835-2438 Office Phone: 260-485-1785. E-mail: helenfrost@comcast.net.

FROST, JAMES ARTHUR, former university president; b. Manchester, Eng., May 15, 1918; arrived in US, 1926, naturalized, 1942; s. Harry Arthur and Janet (Wilson) F.; m. Elsie Mae Lorenz, Sept. 14, 1942 (dec.); children: Roger Arthur (dec.), Janet Linda Frost Naleski, Elise Anita Frost Alair. BA, Columbia U., 1940, MA, 1941, PhD, 1949; LLD, So. Conn. State U., 1993. Tchr. Am. history Nutley HS, NJ, 1946-47; instr. SUNY Coll.-Oneonta, 1947-49, asst. to pres., 1949-52, dean, 1952-64; assoc. provost acad. planning Ctrl. Adminstrn., SUNY, 1964-65, exec. dean for four yr. colls., 1965-68, vice chancellor for univ. colls., 1968-72; exec. dir. Conn. State Colls., 1972-83; pres. Conn. State U., 1983-85, pres. emeritus, 1985—, cancellor emeritus, 2007; instr. Am. history Columbia U., summers, 1947-48; Smith-Mundt prof. Am. history U. Ceylon, 1959-60. Mem. com. on rsch. and devel. Coll. Entrance Exam. Bd., 1973-76; mem. adv. bd. Conn. Rev., 1972-76; mem. commn. on higher edn. Mid. States Assn. Colls. and Secondary Schs., 1966-72; founding mem. Nat. Coun. Heads of Systems of Pub. Higher Edn., 1976-85, pres., 1979-80, now hon. mem. Author: Life on the Upper Susquehanna, 1783-1860, 1951, (with David M. Ellis, Harold Syrett, Harry J. Carman) A Short History of New York State, 1957, 2d edit., 1967, (with David M. Ellis and William B. Fink) New York: The Empire State, 1961, 5th edit., 1980, (with R.A. Brown, D.M. Ellis, William B. Fink) A History of the United States: The Evolution of a Free People, 1967, 2d edit., 1969, The Establishment of the Connecticut State University, 1965-85, Notes and Reminiscences, 1991, The Country Club of Farmington, Connecticut, 1892-1995, 1996, Life with Elsie, 2007; mem. editl. bd. SUNY Press, 1964-72; contbr. articles on history and edn. to mags. Trustee Conn. State U. Found., Inc., 1984—, bd. dirs., 1983—, treas., 1986—95, pres., 1995—98, treas., 1998—2003, chmn. investment com., 1995—2003; trustee Robinson Sch., Hartford, 1973—77; sponsor Soc. Columbia Scholars, 1997—. Maj. US Army, 1941—46, lt. col. USAFR. Rockefeller grantee, 1959. Fellow NY State Hist. Assn.; mem. Country Club of Farmington, Conn. Congregationalist. Home: 17 Neal Dr Simsbury CT 06070-2801 Office: Conn State U 39 Woodland St Hartford CT 06105-2337

FROST, JERRY WILLIAM, religious studies educator, history professor, retired library director, researcher; b. Muncie, Ind., Mar. 17, 1940; s. J. Thomas and Margaret Esther (Meredith) F.; m. Susan Vanderlyn Kohler; 1 son, James. BA, DePauw U., Greencastle, Ind., 1962; postgrad., Yale Div. Sch., 1962-63; MA, U. Wis.-Madison, 1965, PhD, 1968. Instr. Vassar Coll., 1967-68, asst. prof. history, 1968-73; assoc. prof. religion Swarthmore Coll., 1973—, prof. religion, 1980—, Howard M. and Charles F. Jenkins prof. of Quaker history and rsch., 1981—2002, sr. rsch. scholar, 2003—05, 2005—. Author: The Quaker Family in Colonial America, 1973, Connecticut Education in Revolutionary Era, 1974, A Perfect Freedom: Religious Liberty in Pennsylvania, 1990, A History of Christian, Jewish, Muslim, Hindu, and Buddhist Perspectives on War and Peace, 2004; co-author: The Quakers, 1988, Christianity: A Social and Cultural History, 1998; editor: The Keithian Controversy in Early Pennsylvania, 1980, Quaker Origins of Antislavery, 1981, Records and Recollections of James Jenkins, 1984, Seeking the Light: Essays in Quaker History, 1987; editor Pa. Mag. of History and Biography, 1981-86; contbr. articles to profl. publs. Bd. dirs. Friends Hist. Assn., 1973—. John Carter Brown Libr. fellow, 1970, Eugene M. Lang fellow, 1980-81, 97, Phila. Ctr. fellow, 1986; U.S. Inst. of Peace grantee, 1992. Mem. Soc. Of Friends. Address: Swarthmore Coll Friends Hist Libr Swarthmore PA 19081

FROST, JOHN ELLIOTT, minerals company executive; b. Winchester, Mass., May 20, 1924; s. Elliott Putnam and Hazel Lavera (Carley) F.; m. Carolyn Catlin, July 12, 1945 (div. 1969); children: John Crocker, Jeffrey Putnam, Teresa Baird, Virginia Nicholl; m. Martha Hicks, June 6, 1969 (div. 1984); m. Catherine Kearns, July 27, 1985 (dec. Jan. 1997); m. Betty Nelson, Sept. 12, 1997. BS, Stanford U., 1949, MS, 1950, PhD, 1965. Geologist Asarco, Salt Lake City, 1951-54; chief geologist, surface mines supt., gen. mgr. Philippine Iron Mines Inc., Larap, Camarines Norte, 1954-60; chief geologist Duval Corp. (Pennzoil Corp.), Tucson, 1961-67; minerals exploration mgr. Exxon Corp., Houston, 1967-71; divsn. minerals mgr. Esso Eastern Inc., 1971-80; sr. v.p. div. Exxon Minerals Co., Houston, 1980-86; pres. Exxon Minerals Internat., Houston, 1980-86, Frost Minerals Internat., Houston, 1986—; v.p. Kalahari Resources, 1996—. Chmn. real estate com. UnitedEngring. Trustees, NYC, 1986—89, v.p., 1989—91, pres., 1991—93, bd. dirs., Azco Mining. Mem. adv. bd. Earth Scis., Stanford (Calif.) U., 1983-85; pres. SEG Found., 1984, bd. dirs., 1981-84, 94-98. Served to 1st lt. USAAF, 1943-45, PTO. Fellow Geol. Soc. Am., Soc. Econ. Geologists (pres. 1989-90, councilor 1982-84, program com., chmn. nominating com. 1982); mem. AIME (chmn. edn. com. Soc. Mining Engrs. 1971, Am. Inst. Profl. Geologists (cert. profl. geologist); Charles F. Rand medal 1984, Disting. Mem. award 1984, Disting. Svc. award 1991, named to Legion of Honor 2001), Australian Inst. Mining and Metallurgy, Sigma Xi. Republican. Home and Office: 602 Sandy Port St Houston TX 77079-2419 Fax: 281-496-3638. Personal E-mail: frost-min@msn.com.

FROST, MARTIN, III, (JONAS MARTIN FROST III), lawyer, former congressman; b. Glendale, Calif., Jan. 1, 1942; s. Jack and Doris (Marwil) Frost; children: Alanna, Mariel, Camille. BA in History, U. Mo., 1964, BA in Journalism, 1964; JD, Georgetown U., 1970. Bar: Tex. 1970. Law clk. to Hon. Sarah T. Hughes U.S. Dist. Ct. (No. dist.) Tex., Dallas, 1970-71; legal commentator Sta. KERA-TV, Dallas, 1971-72; assoc. Carrington, Coleman, Sloman & Blumenthal, Dallas, 1972—73; ptnr. Barber & Frost, Dallas, 1974—77; atty. Law Office of Martin Frost, Dallas, 1977—78; mem. 96th-108th Congresses from 24th Tex. dist., Washington, 1979—2005, Select Com. on Homeland Security; shareholder Polsinelli Shalton Welte Suelthaus PC, Washington, 2006—. Del. Dem. Commn. on Congl. Mailing Stds. Nat. Conv., 1976, 84, 88, 92, 96; coord. North Tex. Carter-Mondale Campaign, 1976; chmn. Dem. Caucus 1999-2003; Tex. del. chmn. Dem. Nat. Conv., mem. rules com.; del. Dem. Nat. Conv., 2000. USAR, 1966—72. Democrat. Office: Polsinelli Shalton Welte Suelthaus PC 555 12th St NW Washington DC 20004-1200 Office Phone: 202-626-8314. Personal E-mail: martinfrost@comcast.net.

FROST, ORCUTT WILLIAM, historian, educator; b. Cloquet, Minn., June 3, 1926; s. Orcutt William and Agnes Harriet Frost; m. Mary Denison Bills, June 22, 1954; children: Carol, William, Susan, Robert. BA co-salutatorian, U. Ill., Champaign-Urbana, 1949, MA, 1950, PhD, 1954. Assoc. prof. Willamette U., Salem, Oreg., 1954—63; prof. English Alaska Meth. U., Anchorage, 1963—76; prof. humanities Alaska Pacific U., Anchorage, 1977—91, prof. emeritus, 1991. Acad. dean Alaska Meth. U., Anchorage, 1963—71, 1975—76; exchange prof. Nagoya Gakuin U., Nagoya, Japan, 1969—70; mem. bd. dirs. Alaska Humanities Forum, Anchorage, 1978—84; dir. Bering-Chirikov Conf. Alaska Pacific U., Anchorage, 1991. Author: (Book) Joaquin Miller, 1967, Bering: The Russian Discovery of America, 2003; editor (and co-translator): G. W. Steller Journal of Voyage with Bering, 1988 (Alaskan Historian of Yr., 1989); author: (book) Young Hearn, 1958, Children of the Levee, 1957. V.p. Anchorage Native Welcome Ctr., Alaska, 1964—66; pres. Coun. of Chs., Salem, Oreg., 1958—60; bd. dirs. Alaska Lung Assn., Anchorage, 1975—76. Sgt. US Army, 1944—46, Philippines, Japan. Mem.: Soc. for the History of Discoveries, Phi Beta Kappa. Presbyterian. Achievements include research in the history of Russian America from 1741 to 1867. Avocation: tennis. Home: 1130 Skyline Dr Medford OR 97504-8586

FROST, PHILLIP, pharmaceutical executive, dermatologist; BA, Univ. Pa., 1957; MD, Albert Einstein Coll., Bronx, NY, 1961. Chmn. dept. of dermatology Mt. Sinai Med. Center, Miami, Fla., 1972—90; chmn. Key Pharms., Miami, Fla., 1972—86; pres. Ivax Corp., Miami, Fla., 1991—95, founder, chmn., CEO, 1987—2006; interim CEO ImClone Systems Inc., NYC, 2005—06, exec. v.p., chief scientific officer, 2006—; vice-chmn. Teva Pharmaceutical Industries Ltd., 2006—. Chmn. IVAX Diagnostics, Inc.; bd. dir. Northrop Grumman Corp., Continucare Corp., Castle Brands Inc., Cellular Tech. Svcs.; co-vice-chmn. bd. governors Am. Stock Exchange; bd. dir. Ladenburg Thalmann Fin. Svcs., 2001—02, 2004—, chmn., 2006—. Mem. bd. regents Smithsonian Inst.; trustee Scripps Rsch. Inst.; trustee, past chmn. Univ. of Miami. Named one of Forbes' Richest Americans, 2006. Office: Ivax Corp 4400 Biscayne Blvd Miami FL 33137-3212

FROST, RICHARD W., manufacturing executive; BS, La. State Univ.; MBA, Northwestern State Univ., La. V.p. & op. mgr. S.D. Warren Co., 1992—96; v.p. timberlands & procurement Louisiana Pacific Corp., Nashville, 1996—2002, exec. v.p., 2002—04, CEO, 2004—. Past chmn. Forest Products Assn.; bd. mem. Am. Forest & Paper Assn., Forest Products Assn. Canada. Office: Louisiana Pacific Corp 414 Union St Nashville TN 37219*

FROST, RICK, manufacturing executive; BS in Gen. Studies, La. State Univ., BS Indsl. Forest Mgmt.; MBA, Northwestern State Univ., La. With Boise Cascade, La., SD Warren Co.; exec. v.p., Commodity Products, Procurement and Engring La.-Pacific Corp., 1996—2004, chmn., CEO, 2004—. Chmn. Forest Resources Assn., 2004—06; bd. dir. La.-Pacific Corp., Forest Products Assn. Canada, Am. Forest and Paper Assn. Office: Louisiana-Pacific Corp Ste 2000 414 Union St Nashville TN 37219

FROST, RITA KENTON, special education and education educator; d. George Nelson Kenton, Sr. and Elouise Bennett Kenton; m. Thaddeus William Frost, May 18, 1996; children: Timothy William, Ryan Kristopher. MEd in Spl. Edn., Wilmington Coll., Dover, Del., 2005. Cert. elem. tchr. grades 1-8 Dept. Edn. State of Del., 1996, elem. edn.grades K-6 Dept. Edn. State of Del., 2004, tchr. early childhood/primary K-4 Dept. Edn. State of Del., 1996, exceptional children - LD, SED, MH elem. Dept. Edn. State of Del., 2003, tchr. early childhood spl. edn. Dept. Edn. State of Del., 2002. Substitute tchr. grades k-8 Milford Sch. Dist., 1995—96; early childhood spl. needs educator Nurses'N Kids, Milford, 1996—97, The Wishing Well Ctr., Dover, Del., 1997—99; primary spl. edn. tchr. Caesar Rodney Sch. Dist., Camden, Del., 1999—. Adj. instr. MEd elem. divsn. Wilmington Coll., Dover and Georgetown, 2005—; primary spl. edn. tchr. Sch. Improvement Plan Com., Camden, 2006—, Mentor for Del. New Tchr. Mentoring Program, Camden, 2006—07. Nominee, Disney Tchr. Awards; named Maj. George S. Welch Bldg. Tchr. of Yr., 2006—07; Assistive Tech. grantee, Helen F. Graham Grants Program, 2002—03. Home Phone: 302-393-1358.

FROST, ROBERT EDWIN, chemistry professor; b. Gowanda, NY, Feb. 1, 1932; s. Sidney Mauthe and Mary Theresa (Bollinger) F.; m. Janice Ruth Young, May 31, 1958; children— Elizabeth Ann, Nancy Lynn, Barbara Jean. BS, Allegheny Coll., 1953; A.M., Harvard, 1955, PhD, 1957. Research chemist B.F. Goodrich Research Center, Brecksville, Ohio, 1957-61; assoc. prof. SUNY at Albany, 1961-64, prof. chemistry, 1964-95, prof. emeritus, 1995. Kettering vis. lectr. U. Ill., Urbana, 1965-66 Mem. Am. Chem. Soc., Phi Beta Kappa, Sigma Xi. Home: 329 W Highland Dr Schenectady NY 12303-5751

FROST, S. DAVID, retired naval officer; b. Southard, Okla., Apr. 21, 1930; s. Chester William and Martha Leah (Weber) F.; m. Dolores Marie Radja, Oct. 17, 1953; children: Kathleen D., David J., Karen T., Mary C. BS, US Naval Acad., Anapolis, Md., 1953; MBA, Stanford U., Calif., 1961; student, Naval War Coll., 1964-65. Commd. officer USN, 1953, advanced through grades to rear adm., 1977; jr. officer USS Henrico, 1953-55; with Navy Fin. Center, Cleve., 1956-58; supply officer USS Rankin, 1958-59; asst. planning officer Navy Ordnance Supply Office, Mechanicsburg, Pa., 1961- 64; with Navy Fleet Material Support Office, 1965-68; supply officer USS America, 1968-70; exec. asst. asst. sec. def. (comptroller) Washington, 1970-74; exec. officer Naval Supply Center, Norfolk, Va., 1974-75; comdg. officer Navy Supply Corps Sch., Athens, Ga., 1975-77; dep. comdr. plans, policy and systems devel. Navy Dept., Washington, 1977-78; dep. comptroller of the Navy, 1978-80, 81-83; comptroller, 1980-81; staff dir. for mgmt. Bd. Govs. FRS, 1983-99; ret., 1999. Pres. Civic League, Virginia Beach, Va., 1969; bd. dirs. N.E. Ga. coun. Boy Scouts Am., 1976-77; bd. dirs. Brent Soc., 1986-92, pres., 1990-91; pres. Oakton Optimist Club, 1986-87, 92-93. Decorated Disting. Service Medal, Legion Merit, Vietnamese Gallantry cross. Mem.: Athens C. of C., Optimists Club, Knights of Malta, Rotary, Phi Delta Theta. Roman Catholic. Home: 10870 Meadow Pond Ln Oakton VA 22124-1446 Personal E-mail: ddfrost1@verizon.net. *My life, both personal and professional, has been guided by allegiance to three primary areas: family, Christian faith, and the nation.*

FROST, SUE EMMONS, art educator; d. Gerald and Louise Emmons; BS, Stephen F. Austin U., Tex., 1974, M in Secondary Edn., 1975. Tchr. Jacksonville Mid. and HS, Tex., 1976—2001, Lakeview HS, Garland, Tex., 2001—04, Sachse HS, Garland, Tex., 2004—07. Art club sponsor. Recipient Outstanding Tchr. award, Lakeview H.S., 2002—03. Mem.: Tex. Art Tchrs. Assn. Avocations: watercolorist, beach goer, travel.

FROST, SUSAN BETH, theater producer; b. South Kingston, RI, Nov. 1, 1955; d. Cyril E. and Martha (Smith) F.; m. Daniel Francis Renn III, Feb. 16, 1991; 1 child, Martha Hope Renn. B in Theater, Smith Coll., 1977. Freelance theatrical mgr., NYC, 1977-84; assoc. prodr. Goodspeed Opera House, East Haddam, Conn., 1985—2005. Chair panel NEA/New Am. Works, Washington, 1991-93; awards panelist Loewe Award/New Dramatists, N.Y.C., 1994, 95; mem. com. Smith Coll./Theatre Alumni, N.Y.C., 1985—, Alliance Music Theatre, N.Y.C., 1991—. Office: Goodspeed Opera House PO Box A East Haddam CT 06423-0281

FROST, WILLIAM LEE, foundation executive; b. Larchmont, NY, Nov. 5, 1926; s. Charles and Eva (Rodman) F.; m. Judith Spivak, Oct. 18, 1952 (dec. 1961); children— Rebecca, Hannah; m. Susan Lasersohn, June 16, 1966; children— Abigail, Robert BA, Harvard U., 1947, M.P.A., 1958; LL.B., Yale U., 1951. Assoc. Sherman & Goldring, NYC, 1951-52; fgn. svc. officer Dept. State, Washington, 1952-59; pvt. practice law NYC, 1959—. Exec. Lucius N. Littauer Found., N.Y.C., 1978— , pres., 1985—. Contbr. articles to profl. publs. Mem. Pub. Health Coun. State of N.Y., 1975-96; trustee Collegiate Sch., N.Y.C., 1980-94, Radcliffe Coll., Cambridge, Mass., 1985-89, the Brearley Sch., N.Y.C., 1977-80; chmn. bd. dirs. Jewish Telegraphic Agy., N.Y.C., 1989-93, N.Y. Heart Assn., 1985-87; chair N.Y. State Archives Partnership Trust, 1994-97, Yale Law Sch. Fund, 1994-98. With USN, 1945-46, PTO. Hon. curator of Judaica, Harvard Coll. Libr., 1985-96. Mem. Assn. of Bar of City of N.Y., N.Y. County Bar Assn., N.Y. State Bar Assn., Harvard Alumni Assn. (bd. dirs. 1985), Harvard Club, Yale Club. Avocation: walking. Office: Lucius N Littauer Found 60 E 42nd St Ste 4600 New York NY 10165-2999

FROSTIC, FREDERICK LEE, strategic planning and defense policy consultant; b. Detroit; s. Frederick Ralph and Harriet Julia (Stroh) F.; children by previous marriage: Melinda Ann, Frederick Hollis; m. Dianne Kathleen Hughes, May 24, 2003. BS, USAF Acad., 1963; MS in Engring., U. Mich., 1971. Comml. pilot. Fighter pilot USAF, 1963-89, asst. prof. engring. sci., 1971-74, vice comdr. 50th Tactical Fighter Wing Hahn Air Base, Germany, 1984-87, comdr. Northeast Air Def. Sector Griffiss AFB, NY, 1987-89; sr. engr., assoc. programming dir. RAND, Santa Monica, Calif., 1989-94; dept. asst. sec. def. Dept. Def., Washington, 1994-97; prin. Booz, Allen & Hamilton, Inc., McLean, Va., 1997—. Mem. Long Range Airpower Panel, 1998—. Author: The New Calculus, 1994. Named Outstanding Young Man Am., 1970. Democrat. Presbyterian. Avocations: sports, reading. Home: 1357 Heritage Oak Way Reston VA 20194 Office: Allen & Hamilton Inc 8283 Greensboro Dr Mc Lean VA 22102-3802 Office Phone: 703-517-0503. E-mail: frostic_fred@bah.com, fredfrostic@aol.com.

FROST-KNAPPMAN, (LINDA) ELIZABETH, publishing executive, editor, writer; b. Washington, Oct. 1, 1943; d. Edward Laurie and Lorena (Ameter) Frost; m. Edward William Knappman, Nov. 6, 1965; 1 child, Amanda. BA, George Washington U., 1965; postgrad., U. Wis., 1966, NYU, 1966. Editor Natural History Press, NYC, 1967-69, William Collins and Sons, London, 1970-71; sr. editor Doubleday and Co., NYC, 1972-80, William Morrow and Co., Inc., NYC, 1980-82; founder, pres. New Eng. Pub. Assocs. Inc., Chester, Conn., 1982—. Lectr. New Eng. colls. and univs. Author: The World Almanac of Presidential Quotations, 1993, The ABC-CLIO Companion to Women's Progress in America, 1994 (Outstanding Acad. Book-Reference of Yr. award ALA), The Quotable Lawyer, 1986, 1998, Women Suffrage in America: An Eyewitness History, 1992, Courtroom Dramas, 3 vols., 1997; gen. editor: (CD-ROM) American Journey: Women in America, 1994, Women's Rights on Trial, 1998. Mem. Authors Guild. Avocations: knitting, tennis, travel, reading. Office: New Eng Pub Assocs Inc PO Box 361 Chester CT 06412-0005 Home Phone: 860-345-4976; Office Phone: 860-345-7323. E-mail: elizabeth@nepa.com.

FROTHINGHAM, THOMAS ELIOT, pediatrician; b. Boston, June 21, 1926; s. Channing and Clara Morgan (Rotch) F.; m. Phyllis Mary Steiner, June 12, 1954 (div. 1983); children: Phyllis Eliot, Thomas Dean, Benjamin Rotch, David Griffith; m. Barbara Mathis, Dec. 28, 1987 (div. 2002). Student, Harvard U., Cambridge, Mass., 1944-46, MD, 1951. Intern Bellevue Hosp., NYC, 1951-52; resident, rsch. fellow in infectious diseases Children's Hosp., Boston, 1955-59; asst. prof. epidemiology Tulane U. Med. Sch., 1959—60; assoc. mem. Pub. Health Rsch. Inst., City of N.Y., 1960-61; asst. prof., then assoc. prof. tropical pub. health Sch. Pub. Health Harvard U., 1961-69; pediatrician Corvallis Clinic, Oreg., 1969-73; prof. pediat., family and cmty. medicine Duke U. Med. Ctr., 1973-94, prof. emeritus, 1994—. Contbr. articles to profl. jours. Co-founder Ctr. for Child and Family Health, N.C., 1996—. With USNR, 1944-46, 52-55. Mem. Am. Soc. Tropical Medicine and Hygiene, Am. Acad. Pediatrics. Office: Ctr for Child and Family Health Ste 908 411 W Chapel Hill St Durham NC 27701 Home: 2701 Pickett Rd Apt 2023 Durham NC 27705 Personal E-mail: tefro@mindspring.com.

FROULA, JAMES DEWAYNE, honor society administrator; b. Oak Park, Ill., May 1945; s. James Clarence and Helen Barbara F.; m. Barbara Jean Leftwich, 1968; children: James Matthew, Anna Katherine. BSME, U. Tenn., 1967, MS, 1968. Lic. profl. engr., Tenn. Engr. IBM Corp., Lexington, Ky., 1970-74, engring. mgr. Boulder, Colo., 1974-82; exec. dir., sec.-treas., editor Tau Beta Pi, Knoxville, Tenn., 1982—; pres. Assn. Coll. Honor Socs., 1991-93. Editor: The Bent of Tau Beta Pi, 1982—; patentee magnetic brush roll. 1st lt. U.S. Army, 1968-70, Vietnam. Decorated Bronze Star; fellow NSF, 1967-68. Mem. ASME, NSPE (bd. dirs. Knoxville chpt. 1988-94, Outstanding Engr. 1994), Coun. Engring. and Sci. Soc. Execs., Tenn. Soc. Profl. Engrs. (chair divsn. profl. engrs. in edn. practice 1993-96), Am. Assn. Engring. Socs. (awards com. 1997-2000). Roman Catholic. Avocations: mountain climbing, hiking. Office: Tau Beta Pi PO Box 2697 Knoxville TN 37901-2697

FROWNER, BYRON, retired electrical engineer, researcher; b. Washington, May 12, 1937; s. Benjamin Franklin and Mary Magdalene Frowner; children: Blair, Ian, Sydny, Emanuel. BSEE, CUNY, 1959. Gen. engr. US Navy, Bklyn., 1959—69; asst. elec. engr. NYC Transit Authority, Bklyn., 1970—78, Dept. Environ. Protection, NYC, 1980—84; sr. project mgr. Health & Hosps. Corp., NYC, 1985—91; sr. constrn. engr. NY Power Authority, White Plains, 1994—2002; ret. Author: Special Relativity: Einstein's Error, 1994. Mem.: AAAS, NY Acad. Scis. Avocations: history, sports. Personal E-mail: bfrowner@aol.com.

FRUCHER, MEYER S. (SANDY FRUCHER), stock exchange executive; BS in Govt., Columbia U.; MPA, John F. Kennedy Sch. Govt., Harvard U. Chief labor negotiator State of NY, 1978—83; pres. and CEO Battery Park Authority, NYC, 1984—88; exec. v.p. devel. Olympia and York (now World Fin. Properties, Inc.), 1988—96; chmn., CEO Phila. Stock Exch., 1998—. Mgmt. cons. Chmn. bd. Mass. Mus. Contemporary Art. Mem.: Saratoga Performing Arts Ctr. Office: Phila Stock Exch 1900 Market St Philadelphia PA 19103*

FRUCHTERMAN, JAMES ROBERT, JR., computer company executive, not-for-profit executive; b. Washington, May 1, 1959; s. James R. Sr. and Ellen Patricia (Fallon) F.; m. Virginia Belwood, Aug. 11, 1984; children: James David, Richard Andrew, Katherine Elizabeth. BS in Engring., Calif. Inst. Tech., Pasadena, 1980, MS in Applied Physics, 1980; doctoral studies, Stanford U., Calif., 1980—81. Co-founder, v.p. Calera Recognition Systems, Inc. (formerly Palantir Corp.), Santa Clara, Calif., 1982—89; v.p. mktg. The Palantir Corp., Santa Clara, Calif., 1987-89; co-founder, CFO RAF Tech., Inc., Redmond, Wash., 1989—2004; chmn. Arkenstone, Inc., Moffett Field, Calif., 1989-2000; chmn., CEO, pres. Benetech Initiative, Palo Alto, Calif., 2000—. Dir. Cmty. Tech. Found. Calif., 2007-; chief elec. engr. 1st pvt. US launch vehicle venture. Mem. fed. adv. com. on telecomm. access, 1996-97; mem. Electronic and Info. Tech. Access Fed. Adv. Comm., 1998-99; social dir. Enterprise Alliance, 2000—; mem. adv. com. Rehab. Engring. Rsch. Ctr. on Telecomm. Access, U. Wis./Gallaudet U., 2001—. Recipient Access award, Am. Found. Blind, Robert S. Bray award, Am. Coun. Blind; fellow, MacArthur Found., 2006. Mem.: AIAA, AAAS, IEEE, Assn. Computing Machinery. Achievements include development of the most accurate optical character recognition technology in the world, and of leading reading machine for the blind and people with reading disabilities. Office: Benetech Initiative 480 California Ave Ste 201 Palo Alto CA 94306-1609

FRUDAKIS, ANTHONY PARKER, sculptor, educator; b. Bellow Falls, VT, July 30, 1953; s. Evangelos and Virginia Frudakis. Student, Duke U., 1972—73; cert. of completion, Pa. Acad. Fine Arts, 1976; MFA, U. Pa., 1992. Tchr. Fashion Inst. NY, NYC, 1982, Atlantic CC, Mays Landing, NJ, 1990—91; assoc. prof. Hillsdale Coll., Mich., 1991—; owner Frudakis Studio, 1976—. Tchr. Frudakis Acad. Fine Arts, Phila., 1976, Frudakis Studio, 1976—, Fashion Inst. Tech., N.Y.C., 1982, Atlantic C.C., Mays Landing, N.J., 1990-91; assoc. prof. Hillsdale (Mich.) Coll., 1991—. One-person shows include Ocean City (N.J.) Cultural Ctr., 1992, Sturgis (Mich.) Civic Ctr., 1992, Hillsdale Coll, 1999, Flatlanders Blissfield, Mich., 2004; exhibited in group shows NAD, N.Y.C., 1988, 91, 2003, Allied Artists Am., N.Y.C., 1982, Renaissance Gallery, Phila., 1988, Gloucester County Coll., Deptford, N.J., 1989, Grand Cen. Art Gallery, N.Y.C., 1990, 92, Toledo (Ohio) Art Mus., 1994, Nat. Scultpure Soc. N.Y., N.Y.C., 1997, Hillsdale Coll., 1997, 2001; represented in permanent collections Brookgreen (S.C.) Gardens Mus.; commd. Atlantic County Libr., Hammanton, N.J., 1983, Bally's Hotel, Atlantic City, N.J., 1986, Cape May Ct. House, N.J., 1989, Athens Sq., N.Y.C., 1993, Hillsdale Coll., 1992, 95 (Bronze award), St. Catherine's, Concord, Mich., 1996, St. Anthony's, Hillsdale, 1996, Adrian, Mich., 1998, St. Mary's Cathedral, Saginaw, Mich., 1999, East Lansing, Mich., 2000; featured in publs. including Masters of American Sculpture, N.Y. Art Review, Sculpture. Recipient Stewardson prize Pa. Acad. Fine Arts, 1974, 1st prize for sculpture N.J. State Juried Art Show, 1979, M.B. Hexter award Allied Artists of Am., 1982, L. Miselman prize Nat. Sculpture Soc., 1986, Gloria medal, 1983, Gold medal, 1982, Lantz award, 1978, Best Portrait award, 1977, Daniel Chester French award; Dolfinger MacMahon tuition scholar Pa. Acad. Fine Arts, 1973; NSS tuition scholar Pa. Acad. Fine Arts, 1974; Harold Bache Found. traveling grantee, 1975. Fellow NAD (Artist Fund prize 1991), Nat. Sculpture Soc. Office: Hillsdale College 33 East College Hillsdale MI 49242 Studio: 115 Cold Spring Cir Hillsdale MI 49242-1540 Home Phone: 517-437-9668; Office Phone: 517-437-7571. E-mail: tonyfrudakis@comcast.net.

FRUDAKIS, EVANGELOS WILLIAM, sculptor; b. Rains, Utah, May 13, 1921; s. William and Christina (Legerakis) F.; children— Anthony, Jennifer; m. Gerd Hesness, 1982 Student, Greenwich Work Shop, NYC, 1935-39, Beaux Arts Inst. Design, 1940-41, Pa. Acad. Fine Arts, 1941-42, 45-49, Am. Acad. in Rome, 1950-52. Founder, instr. Frudakis Acad. Fine Arts, Phila., 1976-90. One-man shows include Atlantic City Art Center, 1956, 61, Woodmere Art Gallery, 1957, 62, Phila. Art Alliance, 1958, Pa. Acad. Fine Arts, 1962, Briarcliff Coll. Mus. Art, 1975, numerous group shows, 1940—, including, Pa. Acad. Fine Arts anns., N.A.D. anns., Am. Acad. in Rome, Audubon Artists, Phila. Mus. Art, Allied Artists Am., Nat. Arts Club, Pennsylvania Treasures show, Gov.'s Mansion, 1982; represented in permanent collections Pa. Acad. Fine Arts, Lehigh Valley Art Alliance, Woodmere Art Gallery, also pvt. collections; tchr., demonstrator sculpture, Nat. Acad. Design, N.Y.C., 1969-76, sculptor John F. Kennedy meml. monument Atlantic City Conv. Hall, 1964, Statesmen in Medicine Awards; portrait works Brian Brewer Blades, 1969, Melvin R. Laird, 1970, Barnes Woodhall, 1971, Aharon Katzir and Ephraim Katzir for Weizmann Inst., Israel, 1978, Dr. William Feinbloom, Pa. Coll. Optometry, 1989, Stephen E. Hyde, Trump Castle, Atlantic City, 1990; coins and medals Ted Shawn and Ruth St. Denis medal, Jacobs Pillow, Mass., Gemini Space Flights Nat. Commemorative Soc, 1966, Dacron medallion, Dupont, Wilmington, Del., Capt. James Cook medal, Hawaii Festival, Dolly Madison coin, medal Société Commemorative de Femmes Celebres, 1967, Joseph Brant coin, Internat. Fraternal Commemorat Soc., 1968, Paul Lawrence Dunbar medal, Am. Negro Commemorative Soc., 1969, St. Damasus I medal, Cath. Commemorative Soc., Life of Christ series 12 coin medals, 1968-70, Alfred the Great medal, Britannia Commemorative Soc., 1970, Prince of Peace medal, Cath. Commemorative Soc., Scapular medal, Cath. Art Guild, 1970, St. John the 4th Apostle 12 Apostle series, Cath. Commemorative Medal Soc., 1970, John Quincy Adams and Lillian Wald medals, Hall of Fame for Great Ams., 1971, Brian Brewer Blades award medal Statesmen in Medicine, 1970, Richardson Dilworth Meml. Plaque, Phila., 1978, Deng Xioping Portrait Medal, 1979, Fishing Bear fountain, Phila. Zool. Gardens., The Signer, Independence Nat. Hist. Park, Phila., 1982, Naiad Fountain, Phila. Civic Ctr., 1982, Statue of Liberty Greek Relief, Ellis Island, 1986; Welcome Fountain, The Ritten House, Phila., 1989, The Minute Man, Nat. Guard Bld., Washington, 1991, 9' Minute Man, Nat. Guard Readiness Ctr., Arlington, Va., 1995, Reaching Fountain, Brookgreen Gardens, S.C., 1997; mem. coins and medals Art Commn., Atlantic City, Served with AUS, World War II, ETO. Decorated Bronze Battle Star (3); recipient 2 1st prizes Greenwich Work Shop 1939, Beaux Art Inst. 1941, 1st Julian B. Slevin prize Pa. Acad. Fine Arts 1941, Stimson prize 1947, Stewardson prize 1947, Cresson European scholarship 1947, spl. citation achievement 1948, 1st hon. mention fellowship 1948, Fellowship gold medal 1949, 55, 56, Henry Scheidt Meml. scholarship 1949, 1st hon. mention Prix de Rome 1942, Prix de Rome 1950, 51, Helen Foster Barnett prize N.A.D. 1948, Thomas R. Proctor prize 1957, Eben Demarest Trust Fund prize 1949, Louis Comfort Tiffany scholarship 1949, Sculpture House award Allied Artists Am. 1959, best portrait sculpture award Nat. Sculpture Soc.-Nat. Art Club 1961, John Gregory award Nat. Sculpture Soc. 1963, Nat. Fountain Competition award Little Rock 1965, Elizabeth N. Watrous gold medal N.A.D., N.Y.C. 1968, Dessie Greer prize N.A.D., N.Y.C. 1970, Artists Fund prize 1975, 77, 90, Therese and Edwin H. Richards prize Nat. Sculpture Soc., N.Y. 1972, Gold medal 1972, Francis Keally prize 1974, Herbert Adams Meml. medal 1976), N.S.S. Meiselman prize, 1981; gold medal NAD, 1984 N.A. Fellow Pa. Acad. Fine Arts, Am. Acad. in Rome, Nat. Sculpture Soc. (council), founding mem. Acad. Scis. Phila.; mem. Allied Artists Am.; hon. men. Am. Inst. Commemorative Art. Address: 312 Valley Dr Kerrville TX 78028-3910 Office Phone: 830-895-4137. Personal E-mail: gareth@ktc.com.

FRUDAKIS, ZENOS ANTONIOS, sculptor, artist; b. San Francisco, July 7, 1951; s. Vasili and Kassiani (Alexis) F. Student, Pa. Acad. Fine Arts, Phila., 1973-76; BFA, U. Pa., 1982, MFA, 1983. Co-adj. prof. sculpture and drawing Rutgers U., 1984-85, 1993. Guest lectr. anatomy and sculpture Med. Coll. Pa., Phila., 1986-87; invited artist Utsukushi-Ga-Hara Open Air Mus., Japan, 1990. Exhibitions include Nat. Sculpture Soc., 1979—97, Allied Artists Am., N.Y.C., 1980—81, NAD, 1980, 1984, 1986, 1990, 1997, Pa. Acad. Fine Arts, 1981, Inst. Contemporary Art, Phila., 1981—83, Rutgers U., 1984—86; sculptor (numerous commd. works including) Air Force Meml., Arlington, Va., Richard Tufts, Payne Stewart, Pinehurst, N.C., Frank Rizzo, Richardson Dilworth, Phila., Freedom, GSK, 16th Vine Sts, Phila., Ga. Gov. Ellis Arnall, Atlanta, Elephant Fountain, Burlington, N.J., 1993, Mike Schmidt, Steve Carlton, Richie Ashburn, Robin Roberts for Citizens Bank Pk. Recipient Hakone award, Rodin Grand prize Hakone Open Air Mus., Japan, 1990; inducted into Bobby Jones and Arnold Palmer, Ga. Golf Hall of Fame; devel. grantee Nat. Endowment for Arts, 1985, USIA travelling grantee, 1988-89. Fellow Nat. Sculpture Soc. (bd. dirs. 1988—, Art-in-Architecture award 1990, editor pro-tem Nat. Sculpture Rev. 1991-2002); mem. NAD (acad.), Academia Internat. per L'Unita della Cultura (Rome, academician), Lotos Club. Office Phone: 215-884-9433. Personal E-mail: rofrudakis@aol.com.

FRUE, WILLIAM CALHOUN, lawyer; b. Pontiac, Mich., Dec. 29, 1934; s. William Calhoun and Evelyn Laura Frue; m. Eloise Saunders, June 22, 1956 (div. Dec. 1989); m. Jane Torres Fletcher, Dec. 30, 1989; children: William C. III, John C., Michael C., Victoria. BA, Washington & Lee U., 1956; LLB, U. N.C., 1960. Bar: N.C. 1960, U.S. Dist. Ct. (we. dist.) N.C. 1961, U.S. Tax Ct. 1968, U.S. Ct. Appeals (4th cir.) 1988. Rsch. asst. Inst. of Govt., Chapel Hill, NC, 1958-60; assoc. Wright & Shuford, Asheville, NC, 1961-69; ptnr. Shuford, Frue & Sluder, Asheville, 1969-72, Shuford, Frue & Best, Asheville, 1973-84, The Frue Law Firm, Asheville, 1984—. Editor Popular Govt. mag., 1958-60. Chmn. Asheville Police Retirement Fund, 1973-83, Morehead Scholarship Selectincom., 1965-90, Asheville Planning and Zoning Commn., 1982-92. Mem. N.C. Bar Assn., Buncombe County Bar Assn., (sec., v.p. 1978-92), Trout Unl d. (N.C. coun. 1965). Democrat. Episcopalian. Avocations: fishing, camping. Office Phone: 828-258-0570.

FRUEH, DEBORAH K.A. (DEBI FRUEH), artist, poet; b. St. Louis, Nov. 24, 1951; d. Louis J. and Dorothy M. Frueh. AA, St. Louis Coll., 1971; student, Fontbonne Coll. Art, St. Louis, 1971—72, St. Louis U., 1972. Profl. portraitist, Wickliffe, Ky., 1972—. Lectr. Paducah Art Guild, Ky., 1973; sculpture tchr. Paducah C.C., U. Ky., 1977—79. Author numerous poems; one-woman shows include Florissant Valley Art Gallery, St. Louis, 1970, Evansville Mus. Arts and Sci., Ind., 1973, Paducah Art Guild/Gallery, 1973, Paducah C.C., 1974, Peoples First Nat. Bank and Trust Co., Paducah, 1974, Spring Arts Show, 1975—76, Arts Coun., 1979, Represented in permanent collections Chester Meml. Hosp., Ill., Carmin Miranda Mus., Rio de Janeiro, Cairo Marine Svc., Ill., Huffman Towing Co., Clayton, Mo., Okie Moore Diving Co., St. Louis, Wis. Barge Lines, Cassville, Office of Congressman Ed Whitfield, Paducah, Paducah C.C., The White House, Washington. Fundraiser St. Mary's, Paducah, 2000—05,

Yeiser Art Ctr., Paducah, 2001, 2005. Recipient Riverview Gardens Best in Art award, 1969, Duchess of Paducah award for excellence, 1976, Spl. award for creativity, Gamblin Artists Colors Co., 2003. Mem.: Am. Soc. Portrait Artists, Nat. Mus. Women in the Arts. Avocations: reading, gardening. Home: 1985 Deerfield Rd Wickliffe KY 42087 Office Phone: 270-335-3728.

FRUEHWALD, KRISTIN GAIL, lawyer; b. Sidney, Nebr., May 15, 1946; d. Chris U. and Mary E. (Boles) Bitner; m. Michael R. Fruehwald, Feb. 23, 1980; children: Laurel Elizabeth, Amy Marie. BS with highest distinction in History, U. Nebr., 1968; JD summa cum laude, Ind. U., 1975. Bar: Ind. 1975, U.S. Dist. Ct. (so. dist.) Ind. 1975. Assoc. Barnes & Thornburg, Indpls., 1975-81, ptnr., 1982—. Spkr. in field. Contbr. articles to profl. jours. Trustee The Orchard Sch., 1993—99, chmn., 1997—98, bd. govs., 2005—; bd. dirs. Indpls. Parks Found., 1995—2000, Arts Ind., 1994—98, Ind. Continuing Legal Edn. Forum, 1993—2001, pres., 2000—01; bd. dirs. Riley Children's Found., 1995—; treas. James Whitcomb Riley Meml. Assn., 2000—; bd. dirs. Planned Giving Group Ind., Fedn. Cmty. Defenders, Inc., 1993—99, pres., 1999—2001; bd. dirs. Ind. affiliate Am. Heart Assn., 1977—81, vice chmn. Marion County chpt., 1981; bd. trustees Ctrl. Ind. Land Trust, 2005—. Fellow: ABA (chmn. distributable net income subcom 1985—91, real property, probate and trust sect.), Ind. State Bar Assn. (chmn. probate, trust and real property sects. 1987—88, mem. ho. of dels. 1987—, bd. mgrs. 1989—90, treas. 1996—97, chair ho. of dels. 1998—99, pres. 2001—02, mem. sect. taxation), Ind. Bar Found. (bd. dirs. 2003—, bd. govs. 2004—), Am. Coll. Trust and Estate Counsel (chmn. Ind. state laws com. 1992—95); mem.: Indpls. Légal Aid Soc. (bd. trustees 2006—), Indpls. Bar Found. (bd. dirs. 1992—, chmn. 1997—99), Ind. Code Study Commn., Internat. Assn. Fin. Planners, Indpls. Estate Planning Coun., Indpls. Bar Assn. (chmn. estate planning and adminstrn. sect. 1982—83, chmn. long range fin. planning com. 1988—89, pres. 1993). Office: Barnes & Thornburg 11 S Meridian St Indianapolis IN 46204-3535 Office Phone: 317-231-7245. Business E-Mail: kris.fruewald@btlaw.com.

FRUG, GERALD E., law educator; b. 1939; AB, U. Calif.-Berkeley, 1960; JD, Harvard U., 1963. Bar: Calif. 1964, N.Y. 1969. Frank Knox fellow London Sch. Econs., 1963-64; law clk. to chief justice Supreme Ct. Calif., 1964-65; assoc. Heller, Ehrman, White & McAuliffe, San Francisco, 1965-66; spl. asst. to chmn. EEOC, 1966-69; assoc. Cravath, Swaine & Moore, NYC, 1969-70; gen. counsel Health Services Adminstrn., NYC, 1970-72, 1st dep. adminstr., 1972-73, adminstr., 1973-74; assoc. prof. U. Pa. Law Sch., Phila., 1974-78, prof., 1978-81, Harvard U. Law Sch., 1981-94, Samuel R. Rosenthal prof. law, 1994-2000, Louis D. Brandeis prof., 2000—. Mem. Phi Beta Kappa. Office: Law Sch Harvard U Cambridge MA 02138

FRÜHBECK DE BURGOS, RAFAEL, conductor; b. Burgos, Spain, Sept. 15, 1933; s. Guillermo and Estefania (Ochs) Frühbeck de Burgos; m. Maria Carmen Martinez, Dec. 21, 1959; children: Rafael, Gema. Attended, Bilbao Conservatory, Madrid Conservatory, HS for Music, Munich; student, U. Munich, Richard Strauss Price, 1958, U. Madrid; D (hon.), U. Navarra, Pamplona, Spain, 1994, U. Burgos, 1998. Chief condr. Mcpl. Orch., Bilbao, Spain, 1958—62, Nat. Orch., Madrid, 1962—78, gen. music dir. Dusseldorf Symphony, Germany, 1966—71, music dir. Montreal Symphony, Can., 1974—76, Vienna Symphony, Austria, 1991—96, Deutsche Oper, Berlin, 1992—97, Rundfunk Symphony Orch. Berlin, 1994—2000, RAI Nat. Symphony Orch., Turin, Italy, 2001—, chief condr. Dresden Philharm. Orch., Germany, 2004—, prin. guest condr. Nat. Symphony, Washington, 1980—90, Yomiuri Nippon Symphony Orch., Tokyo, 1980—90, Dresden Philharm. Orch., 2003—04, hon. condr. Yomiuri Nippon Symphony Orch., Tokyo, 1991, Nat. Orch., Madrid, 1998. Decorated Encomienda Orden de Alfonso X El Sabio (Spain), Gran Cruz Orden del Merito Civil (Spain); recipient Prize of Musical Interpretation, Larios CEOE, Madrid, 1992, Ehrenmedaille in Gold, Burgermeister, Vienna, 1995, State of Vienna, Austria, 2000, Gold medal to the Civil Merit of Austria, 1996, Gold medal, Internat. Gustav Mahler Soc., Vienna, 1996, Fundacion Guerrero prize of Spanish Music, Madrid, 1996, Big Cross to the Civil Merit, Republic of Germany, Berlin, 2001, Gold medal to the Labour Merit, Madrid, 2004. Mem.: Real Acad. de Bellas Artes de San Fernando (Madrid). Office: care Musiespaña José Marañón 10 E-28010 Madrid Spain also: care Harold Holt Ltd 122 Wigmore St London W1H ODJ England Office: Columbia Artists Management Llc 1790 Broadway # 6 New York NY 10019-1412

FRUITMAN, FREDERICK HOWARD, investment banker; b. Toronto, Oct. 8, 1950; s. Herbert Lance and Libby (Kamin) Fruitman; m. Marlin Sue Potash, Nov. 21, 1981 (div. Dec. 1996); children: Laura, Hilary; m. Susan Beth Levinsohn, Apr. 19, 1998; 1 child, Charles. SB, MIT, 1972; BA, Oxford U., Eng., 1974, MA, 1981; LLB, U. Toronto, 1976; MBA, Harvard U., 1981. Assoc. Davies, Ward & Beck, Toronto, 1976-77, Merrill Lynch White Weld Capital Markets Group, NYC, 1978-79; cons. Bain & Co., Boston, 1981-82; v.p. Investors in Industry Corp., Boston, 1982-84; assoc. E.M. Warburg, Pincus & Co. Inc., NYC, 1984-86; sr. v.p. The Stuart James Co. Inc., NYC, 1986-89; mng. dir. Loeb Ptnrs. Corp., NYC, 1990—. Mem. Law Soc. Upper Can., Can. Soc. of N.Y., Harvard Club (N.Y.C), Tuxedo Club. Office: Loeb Ptnrs Corp 61 Broadway New York NY 10006-2701

FRUMKIN, JOSEPH B., lawyer; b. Phila., May 5, 1958; s. Abe H. and Ceal S. (Brogan) F.; m. Debra A. Mayer, Aug. 13, 1982; 1 child, Alexandra. AB, Georgetown U., 1980; JD magna cum laude, U. Pa., 1985. Bar: NY 1986. Exec. asst. Sen. John Heinz, Washington, 1980-82; assoc. Sullivan & Cromwell, NYC, 1985-89; investment banker Merrill Lynch & Co., NYC, 1990; assoc. Sullivan & Cromwell, NYC, 1991-93, ptnr., 1994—. Office: Sullivan & Cromwell 125 Broad St New York NY 10004-2498 Office Phone: 212-558-4101. Office Fax: 212-558-3588.

FRUMKIN, SIMON, political organization worker, writer; b. Kaunas, Lithuania, Nov. 5, 1930; came to U.S., 1949; s. Nicholas and Zila (Oster) F.; m. Rhoda Hirsch, June 1953 (div. 1978); children: Michael Alan, Larry Martin; m. Kathy Elizabeth Hoopes, June 22, 1981 (dec. 1994); m. Ella Zousman, Dec. 11, 1995. BA, NYU, 1953; MA in History, Calif. State U., Northridge, 1964. Pres., chief exec. officer Universal Drapery Fabrics, Inc., Los Angeles, 1953-87; chmn. Southern Calif. Council for Soviet Jews, Studio City, 1969—. Lectr. Simon Wiesenthal Ctr. for Holocaust Studies, Los Angeles, 1980—; chmn. Union of Councils for Soviet Jews, 1972-73. Columnist Heritage, numerous other So. Calif. newspapers, 1980—; corr. to columnist Panorama, U.S.A. Russian Lang., 1985—; contbr. articles to newspapers. Pres. Media Analysis Found., Los Angeles, 1988; chmn. Ams. for Peace and Justice, 1972-74; mem. Pres.' Senatorial Inner Circle, U.S. Senatorial Club. Honored by Calif. Govt., Los Angeles City Council, Los Angeles Office of City Atty., numerous Jewish orgns. Mem. Assn. Soviet Jewish Emigre's (pres. 1987—), Zionist Orgn. Am., Am. Israel Polit. Action Com., Russian Republican Club, Mensa. Avocations: writing, photography, skiing, exercise. Home and Office: 3755 Goodland Ave Studio City CA 91604-2313 Office Phone: 818-769-8862. E-mail: esfrumkin@roadrunner.com.

FRUSCIANTE, JOHN ANTHONY, musician; b. NYC, Mar. 5, 1970; Guitarist Red Hot Chili Peppers, 1988—92, 1998—. Musician: (albums) Niandra Ladies & Usually Just a T-Shirt, 1995, Smile From the Streets You Hold, 1997, To Record Only Water for Ten Days, 2001, Shadows Collide with People, 2004, The Will to Death, 2004, Inside of Emptiness, 2004, A Sphere in the Heart of Silence, 2004, Curtains, 2004, (with Red Hot Chili Peppers) Mother's Milk, 1989, Blood Sugar Sex Magik, 1991, Californication, 1999, By the Way, 2002, Live in Hyde Park, 2004, Stadium Arcadium, 2006 (Best Album, MTV Europe Music Awards, 2006, Best Rock Album, Best Ltd. Edit. Package, Grammy awards, 2007), (songs) Dani California, 2006 (MTV Video Music award for best Art Direction, 2006, Best Rock Vocal Performance, Best Rock Song, Grammy awards, 2007). Co-recipient Favorite Band, Duo or Group, Am. Music Awards, 2006. Office: c/o Q Prime 131 S 11th St Nashville TN 37206 Office Phone: 615-258-1050. Office Fax: 615-258-1040. E-mail: info@qprime.com.*

FRUTH, ROMAN MARTIN, piano technician, musician; b. St. Cloud, Minn, Jan. 30, 1938; s. Martin Hubert and Frances Traut Fruth. Student, St. John's U., Collegeville, Minn., 1955—57; BA, Williams Coll., Williamstown, Mass., 1964; postgrad., Sam Houston State U., Huntsville, Tex., 1968—69. Dir., organist St. Mary's Ch., Victoria, Tex., 1964—73, Our Lady of Lourdes Ch., Victoria, 1964—74, Triumphant Luth. Ch., San Antonio, 1987—93, St. Joseph's Downtown Ch., San Antonio, 1993—; dir., tchr. St. Paul's Ch., San Antonio, 1974—76; piano technician Alamo Music Ctr., San Antonio, 1976—2005. Composer: responsorial psalms for Cath. liturgy, 1970—, CD music for 19-note scale. Mem.: Piano Technicians Guild (registered technician, pres. 1988—89, treas. 1996—), Am. Guild Organists. Home: 5143 Grovehill San Antonio TX 78228

FRY, BLAKE EDWARD, academic administrator; s. Blake and Karen Fry; m. Fry Cupp, July 28, 2001; children: Abigail, Liam. BA in Polit. Sci., Wichita State U., Kans., 1994; MA in Higher Edn. Adminstrn., U. Mo., Kansas City, 1997; MBA, Avila U., Kans. City, 2002. Coord. student activities & residence life Avila U., Kans. City, 1997—99, dir. student activities, Marian Ctr., 1999—2000; dir. campus life U. Ctrl. Okla., Edmond, 2001—05; dean student devel. & campus diversity U. Wis., River Falls, 2005—07, spl. asst. to chancellor, 2007—. Commn. student involvement, Greek affairs com. chair Am. Coll. Pers. Assn., DC, 2003—04. Mem. spkrs. bur. Ctr. Victims Torture, Mpls., 2006—07; relay for life team capt. Am. Cancer Soc., River Falls, 2006—07. Grantee Rsch. grant, Wis. Campus Compact, 2006; Robert & Maxine Kamm Disting. Grad. fellowship, Okla. State U., 2004. Mem.: Nat. Assn. Presdl. Assts. Higher Edn., Lion's Club, Phi Kappa Phi, Golden Key, Mensa, Sigma Alpha Epsilon (life). Libertarian. Buddhist. Office: Univ Wis 410 S Third S River Falls WI 54022 Office Fax: 715-425-3534; Home Fax: 715-425-3534. Personal E-mail: blakefry@yahoo.com. Business E-Mail: blake.fry@uwrf.edu.

FRY, CHARLES GEORGE, theologian, educator; b. Piqua, Ohio, Aug. 15, 1936; s. Sylvan Jack and Lena Freda (Ehle) F. BA, Capital U., 1958; MA, Ohio State U., 1961, PhD, 1965; BD, Evang. Luth. Theol. Sem., 1962, MDiv, 1977; DMin, Winebrenner Theol. Sem., 1978; DD, Cranmer Sem., 2001; MST, Holy Trinity Coll. and Sem., 2002, M in Religious Edn., 2003, D in Religious Edn., 2004; DLitt (hon.), Triune Hall, 2005. Ordained to ministry Luth. Ch. USA, 1963; diplomate Am. Psychotherapy Assn., bd. cert. psychotherapist, 2007; designated master therapist, 2005. Pastor St. Mark's Luth. Ch. and Martin Luther Luth. Ch., Columbus, Ohio, 1961-62, 63-66; instr. Wittenberg U., 1962-63, 71-72, Capital U., 1963-75, asst. prof. history and religion, 1966-69, assoc. prof., 1969-75; theologian-in-residence North Cmty. Luth. Ch., Columbus, 1971-73; assoc. prof. hist. theology, dir. missions edn. Concordia Theol. Sem., Ft. Wayne, Ind., 1975-84; sr. minister First Congl. Ch., Detroit, 1984-85; Protestant chaplain St. Francis Coll., Fort Wayne, 1982-92; prof. philosophy and theology Luth. Coll. of Health Professions, Ft. Wayne, 1992-98, U. St. Francis, Ft. Wayne, 1998-99, Winebrenner Theol. Sem., U. Findlay, Ohio, 1999—. Interim min. Arbor Grove Congl. Ch., Jackson, Mich., 1980, hon. min. emeritus 1996, First Presbyn. Ch., Huntington, Ind., 1988-89, St. Luke's Luth. Ch., Ft. Wayne, 1989-90, Mt. Pleasant Luth. Ch., 1990-91, St. Mark's Luth. Ch., 1990-91, Mt. Zion Luth. Ch., Ft. Wayne, 1991-93; interim min. Cmty. Christian Ch., New Carlisle, Ind., 1993-94, First Luth. Ch., Stryker, Ohio, 1994-95, Zion Luth. Ch., West Jefferson, Ohio, 1994-97, 98-2000, Agape Congl. Ch., Bowling Green, Ohio, 1997-98; interim min. Fairfield Parish, Lancaster, Ohio, 2000—; vis. prof. Damavand Coll., Tehran, 1973-74, Ref. Bible Coll., 1975-80, Concordia Luth. Sem. at Brock U., 1977, 79, Grad. Sch. Christian Ministry, Huntington (Ind.) Coll., 1986-89, Wheaton Coll., 1987-88; vis. scholar Al Ain U., United Arab Emirates, 1987; theologian-in-residence, tchg. theologian Queentown Luth. Ch., Singapore, 1991, 99-2000, 02; adj. faculty history Ind. U./Purdue U., Ft. Wayne, 1982-98, Winebrenner Theol. Sem., Findlay, Ohio, 1992, 99—, Holy Trinity Coll. and Sem., 1999—, Tung Ling Bible Coll., Singapore, 2000, 02, North Tenn. Bible Inst., 1998—; magister U. Antigua, 2007—; pastor-in-residence Wittenberg U., Springfield, Ohio, 1992, Deaconess Cmty. Evang. Luth. Ch. Am., Phila., 1993. Author books including Age of Lutheran Orthodoxy, 1979, Lutheranism in America, 1979, Islam, 1980, 2d edit. 1982, The Way, The Truth, The Life, 1982, Great Asian Religions, 1984, Francis: A Call to Conversion, 1988, Brit. edit., 1990, The Middle East: A History, 1988, Congregationalists and Evolution: Asa Gray and Louis Agassiz, 1989, Pioneering a Theology of Evolution: Washington Gladden and Pierre Teilhard de Chardin, 1989, Avicenna's Philosophy of Education: An Introduction, 1990, Explorations in Protestant Theology, 1992, Life's Little Lessons, 1997, Kant's Three Questions, 1997, Four Little Words, 1997, Goethe: Life and Truth, 2001, Washington Gladden as a Preacher of the Social Gospel, 1882-1918, 2003, Berthold von Schenk, 2003, Matthias Loy, 2005, Teaching the Bible in Tehran, 2005, Lively Stone, 2006, others; co-prodr. Global Perspectives, IPFW-TV, Ft. Wayne, 1987-97. Bd. dirs. Luth. Liturgical Renewal, 1983-90, 94-2000, pres., 1999-2000; v.p. Internat. Luth. Fellowship, 1995-98, pres., 1998-2001, 03-2004, presiding bishop, 2004-06, presiding bishop emeritus, 2006—; consecrated bishop, so. region Internat. Luth. Fellowship, 1996; assoc. St. Augustine's Fellowship, 1996—; bd. dirs. Zwemer Inst., Ft. Wayne, Ind., 1997-2003, Christ Cath. Ch., Springfield, Mo., 2005—; curate Soc. for the Cure of Souls, 2005—; trustee Winebrenner Theol. Sem., 2005-06 Recipient Praestantia award Capital U., 1970, Concordia Hist. Inst. citation, 1977, 2006, Archbishop Robert Leighton award Nat. Anglican Ch., 1997, Tchg. Excellence award Hancock County, Ohio, 2004; named Ky. Col., 1999; rsch. grantee Regional Coun. for Internat. Edn, 1969; Joseph J. Malone postdoctoral fellow Egypt, 1986, Malone postdoctoral fellow, United Arab Emirates, 1987. Fellow Brit. Interplanetary Soc., Am. Psychotherapy Assn., Coll. Pastoral Counseling (diplomate), Am. Assn. Integrated Medicine (diplomate, bd. coll. pastoral counseling 2001—), Oxford Soc. Scholars; mem. Am. Hist. Assn., Am. Coll. Counselors (clin. mem. 2005, sec. 2006—), Am. Acad. Religion, Mid. East Inst. Gen. Soc. War of 1812 (compatriot 1994—, chaplain Ohio chpt. 1996—, chaplain gen. 2001—, pres. 2005—), Soc. for the Care of Souls (curate 2005—), German Soc. Md., Mil. and Hospitaller Order of St. Lazarus of Jerusalem (chaplain 2000—), Phi Alpha Theta. Democrat. Home: 158 W Union St Circleville OH 43113-1965 Office: 950 N Main St Findlay OH 45840-4416 Office Phone: 419-434-4200.

FRY, CLARENCE HERBERT, retired retail executive; b. Pottstown, Pa., June 27, 1926; s. Clarence H. and Rosa B. (Savage) F.; m. Barbara Ruth McGuire, Aug. 28, 1950(dec. Jan. 16, 2003); children: James Nathan, David Andrew, Joel Timothy, Ann Elizabeth. BS magna cum laude, Syracuse U., 1950. CPA, Pa. Accountant Peat, Marwick, Mitchell & Co., Phila., 1950-56, supr., 1956-60, mgr., 1960-69; controller Acme Markets, Inc., Phila., 1969-73; chief acctg. officer Am. Stores Group Svcs., Inc., Phila., 1974-78, contr., 1974-75, v.p., 1975-78; v.p., contr. Am. Stores Co., Wilmington, Del., 1979—80, Acme Markets, Inc. subs. Am. Stores Co., Phila., 1980-83, sr. v.p., treas., contr., 1983-87; sr. v.p. fin. Am. Superstores Inc. subs. Am. Stores Co., Wilmington, 1987-89; ret., 1990. Mem. food merchandisers LIFO adv. com. Food Mktg. Inst., 1975-82. Author: Easttown: Old in History, Young in Spirit, 1704-2004, 2004. Mem. Easttown Twp. Tricentennial Com., 2001—04; bd. dirs. Tredyffrin Historic Preservation Trust, 2003—. With 69th Inf. Div. AUS, 1944-46. Mem. AICPA, Pa. Inst. CPAs, Chester County Hist. Soc., Tredyffrin-Easttown History Club (pres. 1992-95, editor quar. 1996-2003). Presbyterian. Avocations: history, motorsports. Home: 519 Daventry Rd Berwyn PA 19312-1740

FRY, DEREK A., finance company executive; Mgmt. positions Nat. Westminster Bank, London, 1961—76, Bank of Montreal, 1976—88, sr. v.p. elect. banking, 1988—95, sr. v.p. customer svc., 1995—96; pres., Visa Canada Visa Internat., Foster City, Calif., 1996—. Chmn. Interac, 1988—94; past chmn., vice-chmn. MasterCard Assn. Canada. Mailing: Visa Internat PO Box 8999 San Francisco CA 94128-8999 Office: Visa Internat 900 Metro Ctr Blvd Foster City CA 94404*

FRY, DONALD LEWIS, physiologist, educator; b. Des Moines, Dec. 29, 1924; s. Clair V. and Maudie (Long) F.; children: Donald Stewart, Ronald Sinclair, Heather Elise, Laurel Virginia. MD, Harvard U., 1949. Rsch. fellow Univ Minn Hosp., Mpls., 1952-53; sr. asst. surgeon gen. NIH, Bethesda, Md., 1953-56, surgeon, 1956-57, sr. surgeon, 1957-61, med. dir., 1961-80; prof. Ohio State U., Columbus, 1980—2004, prof. emeritus, 2004. Contbr. numerous articles and papers on physiology and biophysics of pulmonary mechanics, blood vascular interface, transvascular mass transport and the genesis of atherosclerosis to profl. jours., books. Mem. Am. Soc. Clin. Investigation. Mailing: PO Box 340187 Columbus OH 43234-0187 Business E-Mail: fry.1@osu.edu.

FRY, ELIZABETH H. W., lawyer; b. Willimantic, Conn., Mar. 31, 1951; AB, Yale U., 1973; JD cum laude, Fordham U., 1978. Bar: Conn. 1978, N.Y. 1979. Ptnr., co-leader Individual Client Svc. practice Pillsbury Winthrop Shaw Pittman, NYC. Assoc. editor Fordham Law Review, 1977-78. Mem.: NY State Bar Assn., Assn. Bar City of NY. Office: Pillsbury Winthrop Shaw Pittman 1540 Broadway New York NY 10036 Office Phone: 212-858-1520. Office Fax: 212-858-1500. Business E-Mail: elizabeth.fry@pillsburylaw.com.

FRY, HEDY, Member of Parliament; 3 children. MD, Royal Coll. Surgeons, Dublin, Ireland, 1968. Pvt. practice; mem., sec. of state (multiculturalism) (status of women) Can. Parliament/Vancouver Ctr., Ottawa, 1996—2002; chair B.C. Caucus, 2002—; mem. spl. com. on non-med. use of drugs, mem. standing com. on health, standing com. on justice and human rights Can. Parliament, Ottawa, Canada, 2002. Dr. Hirsh Rosenfeld Disting. Lectr. in family medicine McGill U., 1994; featured on Doctor-Doctor, CBC TV series, 1985-89. Mem. editl. bd. Med. Post. Mem. com. Royal Commn. on Reproductive Technologies.dn. Learning for Living Adv. Bd.; mem. Mayor's Spl. Com. on Urban Natives; bd. dirs. St. George's sch., 1989-91; adv. bd. B.C. Physicians Against Nuclear War; co-chair Liberal Party Health and Social Issues sect., Aylmer Conf., 1992, mem. Leader's Nat. Task Force on Women, 1992-93; parliamentary sec. Min. of Health, 1993-96, mem. task force on reform of social security sys., 1994, standing com. on health, 1994, subcom. on AIDS, mem. caucus com. on social policy. Recipient Cmty. Svc. award Commonwealth Caribbean Club, 1991, Black Achievement award, 1994, Congress of Black Women award, 1994. Mem. B.C. Fedn. Med. Women (pres. 1977), Vancouver Women's Network, Vancouver Med. Assn. (pres. 1988-89), B.C. Med. Assn. (pres. 1990-91, chief negotiator 1991-93), Can. Med. Assn. (chair obstetrics task force 1986-87, chair multiculturalism com. 1992-93), Coun. of Healthcare and Promotion (B.C. rep. 1984-92). Avocations: travel, gardening, reading.

FRY, JOHN, magazine editor; b. Montreal, Jan. 22, 1930; s. J. Stevenson and Beatrice (Pratt) F.; m. Marlies Strillinger, Feb. 19, 1965; children—Leslie, William, Nicole. Student, Lower Can. Coll., Montreal, 1936-47; BA, McGill U., 1951. Writer Forster McGuire & Co. Ltd., Montreal, 1951-57; assoc. editor to mng. editor Am. Metal Market, 1957-63; editor-in-chief Ski mag., NYC, 1964-74, editl. dir., 1975-79, Ski Bus., 1964-79, 92—, Golf mag., 1968-71, 77-79, Outdoor Life, 1975-79, Cross Country Ski mag., 1975—; dir. publs. devel. Times Mirror Mags., 1979-83; editl. and publs. cons., 1983—; founding editor Snow Country mag., 1987-98; editor for new mag. devel. N.Y. Times mag. group, NYC, 1995-97. Mem. World Cup com. Internat. Ski Fedn., 1970-75. Author: (with Phil and Steve Mahre) No Hill Too Fast, 1985, The Story of Modern Skiing, 2006. Bd. dirs. Beaver Dam Sanctuary, Chawkers Found. (Canada). Recipient Lifetime Achievement award Internat. Skiing History Assn., 1996; named to U.S. Nat. Ski Hall of Fame, 1995. Mem.: Internat. Skiing History Assn. (bd. dirs. 1995—, pres. 2001—04), Overseas Press Club of Am. Achievements include being the founder of the National Standard Ski Race and the Nations Cup of Alpine Skiing. Office: 23 E Lake Dr Katonah NY 10536-3501 E-mail: snowfry@worldnet.att.net.

FRY, JOHN ANDERSON, academic administrator; m. Cara Fry; children: Mia, Nathaniel, Phoebe. BA in Am. Civilization, Lafayette Coll., 1982; MBA, NYU, 1986; postgrad., U. Pa. Staff acct. Peat, Marwick, Mitchell & co., NYC, 1982—84; adj. instr. NYU Stern Sch. Bus., NYC, 1985, Hunter Coll. CUNY, NYC, 1990; cons. KPMG Peat Marwick, NYC, 1984—86, sr. cons., 1986—88, mgr., 1988—89, sr. mgr., 1989—91; mng. assoc. Coopers & Lybrand, NYC, 1991—93, ptnr., 1993, ptnr.-in-charge, 1994—95; exec. v.p. U. Pa., Phila., 1995—2002; pres. Franklin & Marshall Coll., Lancaster, Pa., 2002—. Sr. fellow Inst. for Rsch. on Higher Edn. U. Pa.; pres., CEO Penn to Bus.; bd. dirs. Sovereign Bancorp, Ban Franklin Tech. Ptnrs.; trustee Del. Investments; mem., pres. coun. NCAA Divsn. III. Bd. dirs., mem. exec. com. Phila. Indsl. Devel. Corp.; trustee Morris Arboretum; bd. dirs., vice chmn. Univ. City Sci. Ctr.; founding mem., chmn. bd. dirs. Univ. City Dist.; trustee Pa. Acad. Fine Arts, Lafayette Coll.; bd. dirs., exec. com. Greater Phila. C. of C.; bd. trustee Fulton Opera House; chmn. James St. Improvement Dist.; bd. dirs. Greater Phila. Tourism and Mktg. Corp.; bd. dir. Lancaster Alliance, Lancaster Gen. Hosp., Lancaster County Conv. Ctr.; bd. trustee Lancaster Country Day Sch. Office: Office of the Pres Franklin & Marshall Coll PO Box 3003 Lancaster PA 17604 Office Phone: 717-291-3971. E-mail: john.fry@fandm.edu.*

FRY, JOHN C., electronics executive; s. Charles; m. Ramune Ambrozaitis. BS in Math, Santa Clara Univ. Founder, CEO Fry's Electronics Inc., San Jose, Calif., 1985—; gen. ptnr. San Jose SaberCats, 1994—. Office: Frys Electronics Inc 600 E Brokaw Rd San Jose CA 95112-1006

FRY, LOWELL LAWRENCE, JR., minister; b. Wichita, Kans., July 13, 1956; s. Lowell Lawrence and Dorothy May (Baum) F.; m. Lucinda Marie Howrey, June 5, 1976; children: Jason Matthew, Lynelle Renee, Travis Tyler. Student, Butler Community Coll., El Dorado, Kans., 1974-75; BSL, Ozark Bible Coll., Joplin, Mo., 1979; MA, Cin. Bible Sem., 1997. Ordained to ministry, Christian Chs./Chs. of Christ, 1978. Min. Rose Hill (Kans.) Christian Ch., 1976-83; assoc. min. Western Hills Christian Ch., Lawton, Okla., 1983-86, sr. min., 1986-94, O'Fallon (Mo.) Christian Ch., 1994-97; founding minister Vision Christian Ch., Foristell, 2001—. Bd. dirs. S.W. Evangelizing Assn., Lawton, 1986-94; co-dir. Shepherd's Voice Ministries, Lawton, 1989-94; supervisory com. Okla. Christian Conv., Stillwater, 1988-90; area registration chmn. N. Am. Christian Conv., Cin., 1989-90. Recipient Pentecost Speech award, Ozark Bible Coll., 1976; named Outstanding Young Minister, N. Am. Christian Coun., 1989. Mem. Am. Bus. Club (bd. dirs. 1989-90). Republican. Home: 1821 Queen Anne Ct Wentzville MO 63385-2753 Office: PO Box 209 Foristell MO 63348 Office Phone: 636-327-6728.

FRY, MORTON HARRISON, II, lawyer; b. NYC, May 15, 1946; s. George Thomas Clark and Louise Magdalen (Cronin) Fry; m. Patricia Laylin Coffin, May 29, 1971. AB, Princeton U., 1968; JD, Yale U., 1971. Bar: N.Y. 1973, U.S. Ct. Mil. Appeals 1973, U.S. Dist. Ct. (so. and ea. dists.) N.Y. 1975, U.S. Ct. Appeals (2d cir.) 1975. Assoc. Cravath, Swaine & Moore, NYC, 1971-72, 75-79; dep. gen. counsel Columbia Pictures Industries, Inc., NYC, 1979-81; v.p., gen. counsel Warner Home Video Inc., NYC, 1982-83; exec. v.p. Warner Electronic Home Svcs., NYC, 1983-84; sr. counsel corp. and new techs. Warner Comms. Inc., NYC, 1984-85; pres., CEO, bd. dirs. The Congress Video Group, Inc., 1985-87; pres., cons. Fry Assocs., 1987-89; ptnr. Marshall, Morris, Bomser & Fry, NYC, 1990-94, Rubin, Bailin, Ortoli, Mayer, Baker & Fry, NYC, 1995-2000; of counsel Stairs, Dillenbeck & Finley, NYC, 2000—06, Meier, Franzino & Scher, NYC, 2006—. Active Dem. Nat. Fin. Com. Capt. USMC, 1966—75. Democrat. Congregationalist. Home: 235 E 18th St New York NY 10003 Office Phone: 212-759-9770. E-mail: frylaw@mindspring.com.

FRY, RICHARD E., architectural firm executive; BArch, U. Mich. Registered arch. Mich., Minn., Colo.; cert. Nat. Coun. Archtl. Registered Bds. Pres., prin.-in-charge Fry & Ptnrs. Archs., Inc., Aspen, Col. and Ann Arbor, Mich., 1970—. Adj. prof. U. Mich. Coll. Archtl. and Urban Planning; archtl. instr. Washtenaw C.C.; rep. Mich. archs. Nat. AIA Bd., Washington. Prin. works include U. Mich. Vis. Ctr., No. Brewery Office Bldg., Ann Arbor, Mich. League-U. Mich., Ann Arbor Art Assn., U. Mich. Dental Sch. Sindecuse Mus., We. Mich. U. Bookstore, Burns Park Elem. Sch., Ann Arbor Ctrl. Fire Sta., Heydon Wash. St. Properties, Ann Arbor, pvt. residences, others. Past mem. Ann Arbor Planning Commn.; bd. dirs. Bldg. Bd. Appeals; mem. art acquisition com. Washtenaw C.C. Fellow AIA (pres. Mich. chpt., chmn. design awards & recognition com. Mich. chpt., chmn. design retreat com. Mich. chpt., chmn. mid-summer conf. Mich. chpt., regional dir. Mich. chpt., pres. Huron Valley chpt.). Office: Fry & Partners Architects Inc 121 S Main St Ste 7 Chelsea MI 48118-1548

FRY, VIRGINIA MILNE, artist, poet; b. Mpls., June 14, 1929; d. Stewart James and Cora Woodward Milne; m. Donald Lewis Fry, Sept. 13, 1947 (div. Feb. 0, 1992); children: Donald Stewart, Ronald Sinclair, Heather Fry Raymond, Laurel Fry Erickson. MA, Am. U., Washington, DC, 1980; Grad. in Tech. Illustration, Columbia Tech. Inst., Arlington, Va., 1969. Tech. illustrator Dames & Moore Environ. Engring. Cons., Bethesda, Md., 1973—. Author: (book of poems and prints) Things Done Alone, (book of poetry) Best Poems of 1988, (poetry in mag.) The Podium, 2007, Slipstream, 2007, (poems) Centres of Expression; Exhibited in group shows at The Ohio State Fair Profl. Divsn., The West Annapolis Gallery, Annapolis, Md., St. John's Coll., The Columbus Mus. Art, The Copley Soc., Boston, The Columbus Art League Exhbns., The Columbus Cultural Art Ctr., one-woman shows include The Zanesville Art Ctr., Mount Carmel Hosp. East, Columbus, Capital U., Franklin U., The Canal House Gallery, Washington, DC, The Cosmos Club, Washington, The Online Computerized Libr. Ctr., Dublin, Ohio, Maplewood Gallery, Bethesda, Md., 2005, First Presbyn. Ch., Annapolis. Leader Girl Scouts Am., Bethesda, Md., 1962—63; rec. studio narrator Md. Libr. Blind, Balt., 1992—2003; ICU vol. Ohio State U. Hosp., Columbus, 1980—85; vol. Shelter Homeless, Annapolis, Md., 2001—02, Anne Arundel Literacy Coun.; pres. Ohio State U. Women's Club Poetry Group, Columbus, 1985—92. Recipient 3d Pl. award, Internat. Libr. of Poetry. Mem.: AAUW, Acad. of Am. Poets, Annapolis Chorale, The Annapolis Kiwanis Club (pres. 1997—98, Disting. 1998). Presbyterian. Avocations: chorale soprano, tutoring, art judge. Home: 129 Bay Shore Ave Annapolis MD 21403 Personal E-mail: gfkitty@aol.com.

FRYBURGER, VERNON RAY, JR., advertising executive, finance educator; b. Cin., June 9, 1918; s. Vernon Ray and Florence Rose (Steding) F.; m. Marjorie Anne Clarke, June 19, 1948; 1 dau., Candace. BS in Bus. Adminstrn., Miami U., Oxford, Ohio, 1939; PhD in Econs., U. Ill., 1950. Salesman U.S. Printing & Lithograph Co., 1940-41; instr. mktg. Miami U., 1941-43; assoc. rsch. dir. Nat. Assn. Broadcasters, 1946; asst. prof. journalism U. Ill., 1947-53; faculty Northwestern U., 1953-86, prof. advt. and mktg., chmn. dept. advt., 1959-84, ednl. dir. Inst. Advanced Advt. Studies, 1963-85, prof. emeritus, 1986—; nat. assoc. dean Am. Acad. Advt., 1964-65, nat. dean, 1965-66, chmn. bd.; cons. to bus., 1954—; adviser Advt. Ednl. Found., 1972-84. Vis. prof. U. Hawaii, 1965; cons. advt. U.S. Army, 1983-91. Author: (with C.H. Sandage and K. Rotzoll) Advertising Theory and Practice, 12th edit., 1989, (with Boyd and Westfall) Cases in Advertising Management, 1964; editor: (with C.H. Sandage) The Role of Advertising, 1960. Bd. dirs. Lake Forest Library. Served to lt., submarines USNR, 1943-46, PTO. Mem. Am. Mktg. Assn., Internat. Advt. Assn., Assn. Edn. Journalism, Beta Gamma Sigma, Kappa Tau Alpha, Delta Tau Delta, Delta Sigma Pi, Artus. Presbyterian. Home: 1921 Shore Acres Dr Lake Bluff IL 60044-1342

FRYE, CHANNING, professional basketball player; b. White Plains, NY, May 17, 1983; s. Thomas, Karen. Graduated, Ariz. Univ., 2005. Basketball player NY Knicks, 2005—. Vol. Knicks Summer Basketball Camp, 2005. Named to First Team All-Pac 10, 2004—05.

FRYE, CLAYTON WESLEY, JR., finance company executive; b. LA, May 18, 1930; s. Clayton Wesley Sr. and Mary Virginia (Briggs) F.; m. Dorothy Rumsfeld, Jan. 14, 1957; children: Carolyn Frye Halloran (dec.), Diane Frye Tanner. AB, Stanford U., 1953, MBA, 1959. Pres. Sutter Hill Devel. Co., Palo Alto, Calif., 1962-69; gen. ptnr. Johnson & Frye Investment Co., San Antonio, 1970-73; sr. assoc. Laurance S. Rockefeller, NYC, 1973—2004; executor Estate of Laurance S. Rockefeller, NYC, 2004—. Ptnr. Rockefeller & Assocs. Realty, L.P., San Francisco, 1990-99, Pacific Property Svcs., San Francisco, 1984-98; bd. dirs. Col. Williamsburg (Va.) Co., Woodstock Resort Corp., Vt., chmn.; dir. Tejon Ranch Co., L.A., 1975-98, Rockefeller Ctr. Inc., 1976-81, Times Mirror Co., L.A., 1988-2000, King Ranch, Inc., Tex., 1996-2000. Trustee Hist. Hudson Valley, Tarrytown, N.Y.; trustee, chmn. Jackson Hole Preserve, Inc., Woodstock Found., White House Hist. Assn., bd. dirs.; vice-chmn., former trustee South St. Seaport Mus., N.Y.C.; vice-chmn., bd. dirs. Rockresorts, Inc., N.Y.C., 1973-87; bd. overseers Hoover Inst., 2004— Office: 30 Rockefeller Plz Rm 5600 New York NY 10112-0002

FRYE, L. THOMAS, curator; b. 1938; With Oakland Mus. of Calif., 1965—, chief history curator emeritus; ret., 1996. Dir. Calif. Gold Rush Sesquicentennial Project. Co-editor: Ideas & Images: Developing Interpretive History Exhibits, 1991; project dir. (exhibitions) Gold Rush! California's Untold Stories, 1997, co-curator Gold Fever! The Lure & Legacy of the California Gold Rush, 1998. Named to Centennial Honor Roll, Am. Assn. Museums, 2006; recipient Dir.'s Chair award, Western Museums Assn., 1999. Office: Oakland Mus Calif 1000 Oak St at 10th St Oakland CA 94607 Office Phone: 510-238-3842. Office Fax: 510-238-6579. E-mail: history@museumca.org.*

FRYE, RICHARD ARTHUR, judge; b. Akron, Ohio, Sept. 3, 1948; s. Virgil Arthur and Margaret (Mullen) F.; children: Kathleen, Emily, Abigail. BA, Wittenberg U., 1970; JD, Ohio State U., 1973. Bar: Ohio 1973, U.S. Dist. Ct. (so. dist.) Ohio 1974, U.S. Ct. Appeals (6th cir.) 1978, U.S. Supreme Ct. 1980, U.S. Ct. Appeals (fed. cir.) 1987, U.S. Ct. Appeals (9th cir.) 1998, U.S. Dist. Ct. (no. dist.) Ohio, 2003. Ptnr. Chester, Willcox & Saxbe LLP, Columbus, 1996—2005; judge Franklin County Ct. Common Pleas, 2005—. Co-author: Ohio Eminent Domain Practice, 1977, Personal Injury Litigation in Ohio, 1985. Bd. dirs. Am. Heart Assn., Franklin County, Ohio, 1985-87, J. Ashburn Youth Ctr., 1996-2000; bd. dirs. Legal Aid Soc. Columbus, 1996-2004, pres., 2003-2004; chmn. adv. com. on local rules U.S. Dist. Ct. for So. Dist. Ohio, 1990-2004; chmn. com. to rev. reporting of opinions Supreme Ct. of Ohio, 2000-03; life mem. 6th Circuit. Jud. Conf. Fellow Am. Coll. Trial Lawyers, Columbus Bar Found., Ohio State Bar Found.; mem. Fed. Bar Assn. (pres. Columbus chpt. 1991), Am. Bd. Trial Advocates. Methodist. Office: Common Pleas Ct 369 S High Street Court Rm 8A Columbus OH 43215 Office Phone: 614-462-6281. Business E-Mail: Richard_Frye@fccourts.org.

FRYE, ROLAND MUSHAT, JR., lawyer; b. Princeton, NJ, Feb. 8, 1950; s. Roland Mushat and Jean (Steiner) F.; m. Susan Marie Pettey, Jan. 23, 1988. AB cum laude, Princeton U., 1972; JD, Cornell U., 1975. Bar: Pa. 1975, DC 1978, US Ct. Appeals (3rd cir.), 1975, US Ct. Appeals (DC cir.) 1991, US Supreme Ct. 1991. Litigation assoc. White and Williams, Phila., 1975-77; litigation atty. US Dept. Energy, Washington, 1977-79, asst. solicitor, 1979-80; presiding officer Fed. Energy Regulatory Commn., Washington, 1980-83, chief presiding officer, 1983-85, supervisory atty., 1985-88, adv. atty., 1988-91; energy atty. Pepper, Hamilton & Scheetz, Washington, 1991-92; sr. atty. Office Commn. Appellate Adjudication US Nuclear Regulatory Commn., Washington, 1992—. Mediator Ctr. for Cmty. Justice, DC Superior Ct., 1984-86. Editor Cornell Law Rev., 1974-75; mem. edtl. bd. Sidwell Friends Sch. Alumni Mag., 1994-2003; contbr. articles to profl. jours. Mem. schs. and ann. giving coms. Princeton U., Washington and Phila., 1978-91; arbitrator Better Bus. Bur. Greater Washington, 1983-86, Phila. Ct. Common Pleas, 1975-77; mem. Sidwell Friends Sch. Parents Assn., treas. 2001-03. Capt. USAR. Recipient Outstanding Young Man Am. award US Jaycees, 1979, Meritorious Svc. award US NRC, 2004. Mem. ABA, DC Bar Assn. (fee arbitration panel 1983-89, com. on alt. dispute resolution 1983-87), Fed. Bar Assn., Fed. Energy Bar Assn. (adminstrv. practice com. 1991-92), Sidwell Friends Sch. Alumni Assn. (exec. com. 1985-93, 94-2003, v.p. 1987-89, pres. 1989-93, Newmyer award), Soc. Cin., Mayflower Soc., St. Andrews Soc., Prettyman-Leventhal Am. Inn of Ct. (barrister 1989-92, master 1992-99, exec. com. 1992-99, program chmn. 1993-95, counsellor 1995-96, pres.-elect 1996-97, pres. 1997-98, nat. mem. 1999—), Cosmos Club. Presbyterian. Avocations: trout fishing, singing, travel. Home: 220 N Royal St Alexandria VA 22314-3329 Office: US Nuclear Regulatory Commn 11555 Rockville Pike Rockville MD 20852-2739 Home Phone: 703-548-8209; Office Phone: 301-415-3505. Personal E-mail: rmf@nrc.gov.

FRYE, WILBUR WAYNE, retired soil science educator, researcher, administrator; b. Finger, Tenn., Aug. 6, 1933; s. Alfred D. and Lela E. (Rouse) F.; m. Martha Hoskins, Apr. 20, 1957; children: Thomas W., John D. BS, U. Tenn., 1961, MS, 1964; PhD, Va. Tech, 1969. Cert. profl. soil scientist, cert. crop advisor. Air traffic controller FAA, Memphis, 1957-58; instr. Tenn. Tech. U., Cookeville, 1963-74; asst. prof. U. Ky., Lexington, 1975-78, assoc. prof., 1978-84, prof., 1984-2000, prof. emeritus, 2000—; exec. dir. Office Consumer and Environ. Protection, Ky. Dept. Agr. Contbr. numerous articles to profl. jours. and chpts. to books; editor books. Chmn. troop commn. Boy Scouts Am., Lexington, 1976-81; chmn. adminstrv. bd. Trinity Hill United Meth. Ch., Lexington, 1977-79; lay del. to Ky. Conf. United Meth. Ch., 1994-96; mem. First United Meth. Ch., Lexington, 2003-. Staff sgt. USAF, 1953—57. Recipient Sci. Faculty Fellowship award NSF, 1967, Master Tchr. award Gamma Sigma Delta, 1978, Great Tchr. award U. Ky. Alumni Assn., 1980, Pres.'s Citation Soil & Water Conservation Soc., 1976, 78; named Danforth Assoc., 1981. Fellow Soil and Water Conservation Soc. (bd. dir. 1975-79), Soil Sci. Soc. Am. (bd. dir. 1989-90, assoc. editor Jour. 1990-93, Soil Sci. Edn. award 1995), Am. Soc. Agronomy (Agronomic Resident Edn. award 1995); mem. Coun. Agrl. Sci. and Tech. (life, bd. dir. 1991-99), Assn. Am. Feed Control Ofcls. (life, bd. dir. 1995-97), Assn. Am. Plant Food Control Ofcls. (life), Lexington Lions Club Melvin Jones Fellow (chmn. program com. 2002-2004, Member of Yr. award, 2004), Gamma Sigma Delta (Ky. chpt. pres. 1989-90, Disting. Svc. award 2006). Methodist. Avocations: gardening, woodworking, stone-working, home improvement. Office: Ky Dept Agr 107 Corporate Dr Frankfort KY 40601 Personal E-mail: wilburfrye@gmail.com. Business E-Mail: wilbur.frye@ky.gov.

FRYE-MOQUIN, MARSHA MARIE, social worker; b. Tecumseh, Mich., Aug. 1, 1950; d. Jesse Roberts Gray and Evelyn Marie Binns Wade; children: Dawn M. Savidge Tourkin, James M. Savidge Jr., David R. Frye. AS, Monroe County CC, Monroe, Mich., 1976; ADN, U. Vt., 1988; BA in Sociology, North Adams State Coll., Mass., 1992; MSW, SUNY, Albany, 1994. Cert. clin. hypnotherapist; social worker Mass., lic. ind. cert. social worker Mass.; cert. case mgmt. Sales clk./cashier Woolworth's Dept. Store, Burlington, Vt.; clk., typist New Eng. Tel., Burlington, 1978-80; unit sec. Prince Georges Hosp., Cheverly, Md., 1969-72, Fairfax Hosp., Falls Church, Va., 1972-73; nurses aide Burlington Convalescent Ctr., 1976-77; EEG technician Med. Ctr. Vt., Burlington, 1980-88; lab. technician U. Vt., Burlington, 1987-88; staff nurse Berkshire Med. Ctr., Pittsfield, Mass., 1988-90, charge nurse, 1989-90; intern Women's Svcs. Ctr./Battered Women's Shelter, Pittsfield, Mass., 1991, No. Berkshire Health and Human Svcs. Coalition, North Adams, 1992, Hillcrest Ednl. Ctr., Lenox, Mass., 1992-93, Dept. Vet. Affairs Med. Ctr., Northampton, Mass., 1993-94; med. social worker Fairview Hosp., Great Barrington, Mass., 1994—, dir. mgmt., social svcs., patient adv., 1995—; nurse, med. social worker Vis. Nurses Assn. No. Berkshire, Williamstown, Mass., 1991-95. Faculty Mildred Elley Sch., Inc., 2001—02. Former mem. adv. bd. United Cerebral Palsy Assn. Berkshire County, Inc. Named to Sigma Theta Tau Honor Soc. Nursing, 2006; recipient Clin. Excellence award, Vt. State Nurses Assn., cert. of honor for vol. svc., Women's Svc. Ctr., 1991, cert. of appreciation, No. Berkshire Health and Human Svcs. Coalition, 1991. Mem.: NASW, New Eng. Sociol. Assn., Sigma Theta Tau, Alpha Chi. Avocations: concerts, theater, movies. Home: Apt 1 9 Prescott Lane Great Barrington MA 01230 Office Phone: 413-528-0790 ext 9636. Business E-Mail: mmoquin@bhs1.org.

FRYER, APPLETON, sales executive, diplomat; b. Buffalo, Feb. 25, 1927; s. Livingston and Catherine (Appleton) F.; m. Angeline Dudley Kenefick, May 16, 1953; children: Appleton, Daniel Kenefick, Robert Livingston, Catherine Appleton AB cum laude, Princeton U., 1950. Head interpreter Hewitt-Robins, Inc., Buffalo, 1950—51; with advt. dept. Buffalo Evening News, 1953—55; field rep. advt. Ketchum, MacLeod & Grove, Inc., 1955—56; pres. Duo-Fast We. N.Y., Inc., Buffalo, 1956—84; pub. Buffalo Bus. Jour., 1984—86; travel cons. Pieper Travel Bur., 1990; hon. consul gen. Japan, Buffalo, 1979—2002. Task force Inner Harbor Erie Canal, Buffalo, 2000—06; co-chmn. Erie County Bi-centennial Commn., 1976. Dep. sheriff Erie County, N.Y., 1954-68; adv. bd. Children's Hosp. Buffalo; mem. Cmty. Welfare Coun. Buffalo and Erie county; co-chmn. corp. divsn. Episcopal Charities, 1988, chmn. devel. com., 1989; mem. bd. Erie County Sesquicentennial Commn., 1970-71, 74-76, chmn. devel. com., 1988-89; adv. City Buffalo Environ. Mgmt. Commn., 1973-75; trustee Theodore Roosevelt Inaugural Nat. Hist. Site Found., 1969-87; bd. dirs. Zool. Soc. Buffalo, 1972-78, Buffalo Fine Arts Acad., Albright-Knox Art Gallery, 1973-76; chmn. Buffalo-Kanazawa Sister Cities Com., 1978-79; pres. Arboretum Met. Buffalo, 1977-78; mem. Pan Am. Centennial com., 1998-2002; bd. dirs. Maud Gordon Holmes Arboretum, 1974-88, pres., 1976-78; mem. Buffalo Landmark and Preservation Bd., 1978-87, Erie County Preservation Adv. Bd., 1978-82; mem. coun. Charles Burchfield Ctr., 1974-92, Ctrl. Erie deanery Diocese We. N.Y., 1970, Young Life on Niagra Frontier, 1971-72; mem. Erie Canal Heritage Corridor Com., 2001-05; chmn. planning com. Venture in Mission, 1979, campaign exec. com., 1979-80; chmn. N.Y. State sect. ann. giving Princeton U., 1979-82, We. N.Y. ann. giving regional com., 1978-79, nat. ann. giving com.; exec. dir. Landmark Soc. Niagara Frontier, 1998-2004, pres., 2005—; adv. bd. Erie County Cultural Resources, 1986-92, Concerned Ecumenical Ministry (West Side), 1986-98; chmn. devel. com. Crane Cutting Ctr., 1987-90; comdr. Lorenzo Burrows post Am. Legion, 1988-89; mem. N.Y. State com. Bicentennial French Revolution, 1988-90; historian We. N.Y. Commandery Naval Order U.S., 1991-99, vice comdr., 1999-2001, comdr., 2003-2005; patients' rep. Buffalo Gen. Hosp., 1996—; mem. New Millennium Group We. N.Y., Martin House Restoration Corp.; Eucharistic min. Diocese We. N.Y., 2004—, vestryman, lic. lay reader, warden. With USNR, 1945-46, to 1st lt. AUS, 1951-52 Recipient Key to City of Buffalo, Mayor Anthony Masiello, 1996, Long and Dedicated Svc. award, Buffalo-Kanazawa Sister City Com., 1997, Order of the Sacred Treasure, Gold Ray with ribbon, Govt. of Japan, 2002. Mem.: SAR (Buffalo chpt. v.p. 1993—94, pres. 1995—96), Buffalo Soc. Natural Scis., Am. Assn. Mus. (trustee 1978—81), Bi-Nat. Bridge Task Force (Peace Bridge), Old Ft. Niagara Assn. (dir. 1980—90), Buffalo and Erie County Hist. Soc. (bd. mgrs. 1969—2005, v.p. 1977—82, pres. 1982—84), Soc. Colonial Wars, Buffalo Area C. of C. (Buffalo Beautiful com.), Navy League U.S., Mil. Order Fgn. Wars U.S., Niagra Frontier Indsl. Distbrs. Assn., Soc. Mayflower Descendants (regent Buffalo colony 1961—65), Holland Soc. N.Y. (pres. Niagra Frontier br. 1969—79), Landmark Soc. Niagara Frontier (pres. 1963—73, exec. dir. 1998—2004, pres. 2004—, Outstanding award 1979, Landmarker award 2000, Appleton Fryer Founder award 2003), Order Colonial Lords of Manors, Princeton U. Alumni Assn. (chmn. schs. com. We. N.Y. area 1974—77), Canal Soc. N.Y. State, Porcupine Club (gov. 1969—73), U. Cottage Club, Nassau Club, Saturn Club (vice dean 1963, 1986, dean 1990), Princeton Club of We. NY (pres. 1960), Princeton Club NY, Rotary (internat. svc. com. 1978—90, bd. dirs. 1983—86), Masons. Episcolpalian (warden, lic. lay reader, Eucharistic min.). Home: 85 Windsor Ave Buffalo NY 14209-1018

FRYER, THOMAS WAITT, JR., writer; b. Martinsville, Va., Oct. 6, 1936; s. Thomas Waitt and Wilma Pauline (Harp) F.; m. Mary Margaret Allshouse, Jan. 5, 1980; children— Laura Elizabeth, Matthew Thomas, John Anderson. AA, Mars Hill Coll., 1956; BA, Wayland Coll., 1958; MA (Ford Found. fellow), Vanderbilt U., 1959; PhD (Kellogg Found. fellow), U. Calif., Berkeley, 1968. Instr. in English Daytona Beach Jr. Coll., 1959-61; assoc. dean instrn. Chabot Coll., 1965-67; v.p., chief campus adminstr. Miami-Dade C.C., 1967-73; chancellor Peralta Colls., 1973-78; chancellor, dist. supt. Foothill-De Anza C.C. Dist., 1978-92; vice chmn. bd. dirs. Am. Coun. on Edn., 1979-80. Vis. prof. U. Calif. at Berkeley, 1988-92; pres. Fla. Assn. Community Colls., 1971-73. Chmn. WASC Accred Com. for Community and Jr. Colls., 1984-86; pres. chief exec. officers Calif. Community Colls., 1986-87; trustee, bd. chair Fla. C.C. Jacksonville, 1999-2003. Recipient Communication and Leadership award Toastermasters Internat., 1977, selected a Young Leader of Acad., 1978; named one of Most Effective Coll. Pres. in Nation Exxon Edn. Found., 1986, one of 50 best community coll. CEO's by U. Tex., Austin, 1988. Mem. Nat. Soc. Study Edn., Am. Assn. Higher Edn. (dir. 1975-78), Assn. for Study of Higher Edn., Phi Delta Kappa. Clubs: Commonwealth of Calif., Rotary. Office Phone: 925-947-5878. Personal E-mail: tomfryer@juno.com.

FRYKENBERG, ROBERT ERIC, historian, educator; b. India, June 8, 1930; s. Carl Eric and Doris Marie (Skoglund) F.; m. Carol Addington, July 1, 1952; children: Ann Denise Lewis, Brian Robert, Craig Michael. BA, Bethel Coll., Minn., 1951; MA, U. Minn., 1953; MDiv, Bethel Theol. Sem., 1955; PhD, London U., 1961. Rsch. asst. U. Calif., Berkeley, 1955-57; instr. Oakland (Calif.) Jr. Coll., 1957-58; Ford and Carnegie rsch. and tchg. fellow U. Chgo., 1961-62; mem. faculty U. Wis., Madison, 1962—97, prof. history and S. Asian studies, 1971-97, emeritus prof. history and S. Asian studies, 1997—, chmn. dept., dir. Ctr. S. Asian Studies, 1970-73. Vis. prof. U. Hawaii, summer 1968; Radhakrishnan Meml. lectr. Oxford U., 1998; dir. Pew India Rsch. Advancement Projects, 1994-01. Author: Guntur District, 1788-1848: A History of Local Influence and Central Authority in South India, 1965, History and Belief: The Foundations of Historical Understanding, 1996; editor: Land Control and Social Structure in Indian History, 1969, 77, Land Tenure and Peasant in South Asia: An Anthology of Recent Research, 1977, Studies of South India, 1985, Delhi Through the Ages, 1986, 93, Christians and Missionaries in India: Cross-Cultural Communication since 1500, 2003, Tirunelveli's Evangelical Christians: Two Centuries of Family Traditions, 2003, Pandita Ramabai's America, 2003; co-editor: Studies in the History of Christian Missions series, 1997—, co-gen. editor (with B. Stanley), 2000—; co-editor: Christians, Cultural Interactions, and India's Religious Traditions, 2002; contbr. articles to revs. and profl. publs. Trustee Am. Inst. Indian Studies, 1971-81; dir. summer seminar NEH, 1976. Fellow Rockefeller Found., 1958-61, 1988, Am. Coun. Learned Socs.-Social Sci. Rsch. Coun. 1962-63, 67, 73-74, 83-84, 88-89, Guggenheim Found., 1968-69, HEW Fulbright Hays sr. fellow, 1965-66, NEH, 1975, Wis. Inst. Rsch. Humanities, 1975, Wilson Ctr., 1986, 91-92, Pew Found., 1997. Fellow Royal Hist. Soc., Royal Asiatic Soc.; mem. Internat. Conf. and Seminars, Soc. S. Indian Studies (pres. 1968-70, 82-84), Am. Hist. Assn. (pres. Conf. Faith and History 1970-72), Assn. Asian Studies, Inst. Hist. Studies India, Inst. Asian Studies India, Assn. S. Asian Studies Australia, Inst. Advanced Christian Studies (dir. 1979-83, 87-91, 98-2002, pres. 1981-83) Office: Univ Wis Humanities Bldg 455 N Park St Madison WI 53706 Business E-Mail: refryken@wisc.edu.

FRYMAN, VIRGIL THOMAS, JR., lawyer; b. Maysville, Ky., Apr. 9, 1940; s. Virgil Thomas and Elizabeth Louis (Marshall) F. AB cum laude, Harvard U., 1962, LLB, 1966. Bar: N.Y. 1967, U.S. Ct. Appeals (2d cir.) 1967, U.S. Dist. Ct. (so. and ea. dists.) N.Y. 1968, U.S. Supreme Ct. 1970, U.S. Ct. Appeals (6th cir.) 1988,U.S. Ct. Appeals (11th cir.) 2002, U.S. Dist. Ct. (ea. and we. dists.) Ky. 1988. Assoc. Cravath, Swaine & Moore, NYC, 1966-73; asst. U.S. atty. U.S. Dist. Ct. (so. dist.) N.Y., NYC, 1973-78; assoc. gen. counsel Price Waterhouse, NYC, 1978-86; staff counsel select com. to investigate covert arms transactions with Iran, U.S. Ho. Reps., 1987; mem. Greenebaum, Doll & McDonald PLLC, Lexington, Ky., 1988—2006. Contbr. to Proving Federal Crimes, 6th edit., 1976. Mem. ABA, Assn. Bar City of N.Y., Ky. Bar Assn., Fayette County Bar Assn., Harvard Club, Idle hour Country Club. Democrat. Episcopalian. Home: Fed Hill Washington KY 41096-0173 Office: Greenebaum Doll & McDonald PLLC 300 W Vine St Ste 1100 Lexington KY 40507-1665 Office Phone: 859-288-4615. E-mail: vtf@gdm.com.

FRYMER, MURRY, writer, film and theater critic; b. Toronto, Ont., Can., Apr. 24, 1934; came to U.S., 1945; s. Dave and Sylvia (Spinrod) F.; m. Barbara Lois Grown, Sept. 4, 1966; children: Paul, Benjamin, Carrie. BA, U. Mich., 1956; student, Columbia U., 1958; MA, NYU, 1964. Editor Town Crier, Westport, Conn., 1962-63, Tribune, Levittown, N.Y., 1963-64; viewpoints editor, critic Newsday, LI, N.Y., 1964-72; asst. mng. editor Rochester Democrat & Chronicle, N.Y., 1972-75; Sunday and feature editor Cleve. Plain Dealer, 1975-77; editor Sunday Mag. Boston Herald Am., 1977-79; film and TV critic San Jose Mercury News, Calif., 1979-83, theater critic, 1983—, columnist, 1983—, San Jose Mag., 2000—. Instr. San Jose State U., Cleve. State U., judge Emmy awards NATAS, 1968; co-founder, sr. writer TheColumnists.com.; staff mem. Pulitzer Prize, 1990. Author: They are Coming for My Mattress, 1999; author, dir. musical revue Four by Night, N.Y.C., 1963; author (play) Danse Marriage, 1955 (Hopwood prize 1955); author, dir. 6th U.S. Army show A Dozen and One, 1958. Served with U.S. Army, 1956-58. Recipient Best Columnist/Critic award Calif. Publishers Assn., 1993; named Best Columnist, Peninsula Calif. Press Club, 1993, 2003, 05. E-mail: mfrymer@yahoo.com.

FRYREAR, DONALD WILLIAM, agricultural engineer, researcher; b. Haxtun, Colo., Dec. 8, 1936; s. William Alfred and Majorie (Adams) F.; m. Sherry Janice Watson, Sept. 16, 1956; children: Debra Lou, Kenneth William. BSAE, Colo. State U., 1959; MSAE, Kans. State U., 1962.

Registered profl. engr., Tex. Engr. USDA-Agrl. Rsch. Svc., Akron, Colo., 1959-60, Manhattan, Kans., 1960-62, rsch. engr. Temple, Tex., 1962-65, rsch. leader Big Spring, Tex., 1965-97. Erosion cons. UNESCO, Medmine, Tunisia, 1983, Pretoria, South Africa, 1985; project leader for devel. of Revised Wind Erosion Equation. Contbr. articles to profl. jours. Recipient Appreciation award Howard Coll., 1977; Soil Conservation Soc. Am. fellow, 1982. Mem. Am. Soc. Agrl. Engrs. (assoc. editor 1974, SW Dirs. citation 1996), Soil and Water Conservation Soc. (charter pres. 1972), Am. Soc. Agronomy (state pres. 1977), N.Y. Acad. Sci. Baptist. Achievements include development of graded furrow concept for controlling water erosion, techniques for analyzing field erosion data; design and construction of five wind tunnels; design of first field equipment for measuring wind erosion. Office: Custon Products and Cons 7204 S Service Rd Big Spring TX 79720-0546 E-mail: dfryrear@crcom.net.

FRYT, MONTE STANISLAUS, petroleum company executive, speaker, advisor; b. Jackson, Mich., Aug. 3, 1949; s. Marion S. and Dorothy A. (Fischman) F.; m. Pollyanna Hayes, May 26, 1990. BS in Aerospace Engring., U. Colo., Boulder, 1971; MBA in Mgmt., U. Colo., Denver, 1988. Field engr. Schlumberger Well Svcs., Bakersfield, Calif., 1971-75, computer R & D engr. Houston, 1975-77, account devel. engr. LA, 1977-78, dist. mgr. Abilene, Tex., 1978-80, Williston, N.D., 1980-81; v.p. ops. Logmate Svcs. Inc., Calgary, Canada, 1981-84; pres. Fryt Petroleum Inc., Denver, 1984-91; mgr. petrophysics Am. Hunter Exploration, Ltd., Denver, 1991-92; prin. Reservoir Evaluations Group, Denver, 1992-99; ptnr., mgr. Monteray Energy LLC, Denver, 1994-98; mgr. tech. Anschutz Exploration Corp., 1995—2003; cons. Worldwide Petroleum Engring & Geol., 2003—04; dir. tech. Direct Detection Experts (DDX) Corp., Denver, 2004—. Mem. Colo. Rep. Com., 1990—, Rep. Nat. Com., Colo. Rep. Leadership Program, 1992-93; mem. exec. com. Colo. Rep. Bus. Coalition, 1993-2002, vice-chmn., 1996-97, chmn., 1997-99. Mem. Am. Assn. Petroleum Geologists, Soc. Petroleum Engrs., Rocky Mountain Assn. Geologists, Rockies Venture Club. Roman Catholic. Avocations: mountain climbing, skiing, reading, Tae Kwon Do. Home: 7400 S Curtice Ct Littleton CO 80120-3951 Home Phone: 303-324-9598. Personal E-mail: sillymoon@comcast.net.

FRYXELL, DAVID ALLEN, publishing executive; b. Sioux Falls, SD, Mar. 8, 1956; s. Donald Raymond and Lucy (Dickinson) F.; m. Lisa Duaine Forman, June 16, 1978; 1 child, Courtney Elizabeth. BA, Augustana Coll., 1978. Assoc.-sr. editor TWA Ambassador, St. Paul, 1978-80, mng. editor, 1980-81; sr. editor Horizon, Tuscaloosa, Ala., 1981-82; circuit writer Telegraph Herald, Dubuque, Iowa, 1982-85; contbg. editor Horizon mag., 1982-85; dir. publs., exec. editor Pitt mag. U. Pitts., 1985-90; editl. dir. Quad/Creative Group Milwaukee Mag., 1991-92; exec. features editor, dir. new ventures St. Paul Pioneer Press, 1992-95, sr. editor technology and new ventures, 1995-96; sr. editor bus. and tech., 1996; exec. producer Twin Cities Sidewalk Microsoft Corp., 1996-98; mag. editl. dir. F & W Publs., Cin., 1998—2001, editor-in-chief, 2001—03; editor, pub. Desert Exposure, 2003—; pub. Gila Books, 2005—; pres. Continental Divide Pub. LLC, 2005—. Chief judge mags. Golden Quill awards, Pitts., 1980; nonfiction columnist Writer's Digest, 1994—2006; faculty Maui Writers Conf., 2000—, dir., 2006—. Author: Double-Parked on Main Street, 1988, How to Write Fast While Writing Well, 1992, Elements of Article Writing: Structure and Flow, 1996, Write Faster, Write Better, 2004, The Best in Health & Nutrition, 2007; editor: Family Tree Mag., 2000-03, Comair Navigator Mag., 2001-02, Tufts University Guide to Healthy Living, 2004-05; mng. editor Tufts Health and Nutrition Letter, 2004—; contbr. articles to mags. including Travel & Leisure, Playboy, Passages, AAA World, Savvy, Online Access, Diversion, Easy Living, Readers Digest, Link Up, others. Chief writer Anderson for Pres. Com., Minn., 1978. Recipient Merit award for editing, Chgo. Art Dir. Club, 1981, 2d award master columnist, Iowa Newspaper Assn., 1983, 2d award best feature writing, 1983, 2d award best series, 1983, Periodicals Improvement award, Coun. for Advancement and Support of Edn., 1987, 1990, 1991, Top Ten Mag. award, 1990, 1991, Articles of Yr. award, 1990, Institutional Relations Publications award, 1991, Periodical Special Issues award, 1991, Periodical Resource Mgmt. award, 1990, 1991, Golden Triangle award, Internat. Assn. Bus. Communicators, 1997, 1989, Best Special Pub. award, 1988, Matrix award, Women in Comm., 1990, Hon. Mention, 1990, 1991, Gen. Excellence award, City and Regional Mgr. Assn., 1992, Special Sect. award, 1992, Commentary award, 1992, Investigative Writing award, 1992, 2d Gen. Excellence award, Mo. Lifestyle awards, 1994, 1995, Notable Essays of Yr., Best Am. Essays, 2004, 2005. Mem.: Augustana Alumni Assn. (Decades of Leadership award 1978), Augustana Coll. Fellows, Blue Key. Democrat. Unitarian Universalist. Office: PO Box 191 Silver City NM 88062 Home Phone: 505-538-4374; Office Phone: 505-538-4374. Business E-Mail: editor@desertexposure.com.

FRYXELL, GRETA ALBRECHT, marine botany educator, oceanographer; b. Princeton, Ill., Nov. 21, 1926; d. Arthur Joseph and Esther (Andreen) Albrecht; m. Paul A. Fryxell, Aug. 23, 1947; children: Karl Joseph, Joan Esther, Glen Edward. BA, Augustana Coll., 1948; MEd, Tex. A&M U., 1969, PhD, 1975. Tchr. math and sci. jr. high schs., Iowa, 1948-52; research asst. Tex. A&M U., College Station, 1968-71, research scientist, 1971-80, asst. prof. oceanography, 1980-83, assoc. prof., 1983-86, prof., 1986-94, prof. emeritus, 1994—; adj. prof. botany U. Tex., Austin, 1993—. Vis. scientist U. Oslo, 1971; chmn. adv. commn. Provasoli-Guillard Ctr. for Culture Marine Phytoplankton, Bigelow Lab, Maine, 1985-87; hon. curator NY Bot. Garden, 1992-2000; courtesy prof. U. Oreg., 1994-2000; sr. rsch. scientist U. Tex. Marine Sci. Inst., 1996-2003. Editor: Survival Strategies of the Algae, 1983; contbr. articles to profl. jours. Recipient Outstanding Woman award Brazos County, College Station, 1979, Outstanding Achievement award Augustana Coll., Rock Island, Ill., 1980; Faculty Disting. Achievement award in rsch. Tex. A&M U., 1991, Geoscis. and Earth Resources Adv. Coun. medal, 1993; grantee NSF. Fellow: AAAS; mem.: ACLU, Oceanographic Soc., Tex. Assn. Coll. Tchrs., Internat. Diatom Soc. (coun. 1986—92), Am. Soc. Plant Taxonomists, Internat. Phycol. Soc., Brit. Phycol. Soc., Phycol. Soc. Am. (editl. bd. 1976—79, 1982—85, chair Prescott award com. 1991, award of Excellence in Phycology 1996). Democrat. Unitarian-Universalist. Office: U Tex Sch Biol Scis Sect Integrative Biology Austin TX 78712 Mailing: 650 Harrison Ave Claremont CA 91711

FTHENAKIS, EMANUEL JOHN, aerospace transportation and communications executive; b. Greece, Jan. 30, 1928; came to U.S., 1952, naturalized, 1956; s. John and Evanthia F.; m. Hermione Jane Coates, 1972; children: John, Basil. Diploma mech. and elec. engring., Tech. U. Athens, 1951; MS in Elec. Engring., Columbia U., 1954; postgrad., U. Pa., 1961-62. Mem. tech. staff Bell Tel. Labs., 1952-57; dir. engring. missile and space div. G.E., Phila., 1957-61; v.p., gen. mgr. space and re-entry div. Philco-Ford Co., Palo Alto, Calif., 1961-69; pres. ITT Aerospace Co., LA, 1969-70; chmn. Am. Satellite Corp., Germantown, Md., 1971-85; v.p. Fairchild Industries, Germantown, 1971-80, sr. v.p., 1980-84, exec. v.p., 1984, pres., CEO Chantilly, Va., 1985—86, chmn., CEO, 1986—91; pres., COO Fairchild Corp., Chantilly, 1990-91; chmn., CEO CEF Corp., Potomac, Md., 1991—. Adj. prof. U. Md., 1981-84; mem. Pres.'s Nat. Security Telecomms. Adv. Coun., 1982-91; chmn., CEO, Olympic Airways, 1993. Author: A Manual of Satellite Communications, 1984; patentee in field. Mem. bd. visitors Coll. Engring., U. Md., 1980-05; bd. dirs. U. Md. Found., 1989-; bd. dirs. Challenger Ctr. for Space Sci. and Edn., 1988-96, chmn. bd., 1994-96; trustee Univs. Rsch. Assn., Inc., 1990—. Named Man of Yr., Electronic & Aerospace Systems Conf., 1982 Fellow IEEE; mem. AIAA (assoc.), The George Town Club. Greek Orthodox. Office: PO Box 59708 Potomac MD 20859-9708 Personal E-mail: efthe@aol.com.

FTHENAKIS, VASILIS, chemical engineer, consultant, educator; b. Chania, Crete, Greece, July 21, 1951; arrived in US, 1976, naturalized, 1986; s. Menelaos and Antonia Korkidis; m. Christina Georgakopoulos, Feb. 6, 1982; children: Antonia, Menelaos. Diploma in Chemistry, U. Athens, 1975; MS in Chem. Engring., Columbia U., 1978; PhD in Fluid Dynamics & Atmospheric Sci., NYU, 1991. Rsch. analyst Columbia U., NYC, project engr.; sr. chem. engr. Brookhaven Nat. Lab., Upton, NY, 1980—2002, head Nat. Photovoltaic Environ. Health and Safety Ctr., 2002—; prof. earth and environ. engring., dir. Ctr. for Life Cycle Analysis, Columbia U., 2006—. Cons. Exxon Mobil, Dow Chemical, 3M Corp., Amoco Oil, others; founder EnviroConsultants Inc., Upton, NY, 1991; chmn. confs.; adj. prof. environ. engring., chem. engring. CCNY, 1992-96, Columbia U., 1993—; expert witness on chem. process safety and environ. cases, 1997—; cons. in field. Author: Prevention and Control of Accidental Releases of Hazardous Gases, 1993; editor Fossil Energy and the Environ. newsletter, 1991-93; mem. editl. bd. Progress in Photovoltaics, 1996-, Jour. Loss Prevention, 1998-; contbr. over 200 articles to profl. jours., chpts. to books. Recipient Sci. Excellence award, EENS, 2002, 2005, Tech. Excellence award, AIMC, 2006. Fellow AIChE, Internat. Energy Found.; mem. Ctr. Chem. Process Safety (panel experts), Semiconductor Safety Assn, Am. Meteorol. Soc., Am. Chem. Soc. Home: 9 Lucille Ln Dix Hills NY 11746-5848 Office: Brookhaven Nat Lab Energy and Scis Tech Dept Ctr Bldg 475B Upton NY 11973 also: Columbia U Earth and Environ Engring 926 Mudd Engring Bldg 500 W 120th St New York NY 10027 Home Phone: 631-427-3028; Office Phone: 631-344-2830. E-mail: vmf@bnl.gov, vmfs@columbia.edu.

FU, CARY T., electronics executive; MS accounting, U. of Houston. CPA. Controller Intermedics, 1983—86; asst. sec. Benchmark Electronics, 1988—90, sec., 1990—96, treas., 1986—96, bd. dir., 1986—88, 1990—, exec. v.p, Financial Administration, 1990—92, exec. v.p., 1990—2001, pres., COO, 2001—04, pres., CEO, 2004—. Office: c/o Benchmark Electronics 3000 Technology Dr Angleton TX 77515*

FU, GREGORY CHUNG-WEI, chemistry educator; SB, MIT, 1985; PhD, Harvard U., 1991. Asst. prof. Chemistry Mass. Inst. Tech., Cambridge. Contbr. articles to profl. jours. including J. Am. Chem. Soc., J. Org. Chem. Recipient Arthur C. Cope Scholar award, 1998-99. Fellow: Am. Acad. Arts & Scis. Office: Chemistry Dept Dreyfus Bldg MIT 77 Massachusetts Ave Cambridge MA 02139-4301*

FU, JOSHUA S., environmental engineer, educator, research scientist; s. Chuan-Ven and Show-Ron Fu; m. Rachel J. C. Chen; 1 child, Katherine S. PhD, NC State U., Raleigh, 2000. Sr. sys. application scientist Lockheed Martin Corp., Research Triangle Park, NC, 1999—2000; rsch. asst. prof. U. Tenn., Knoxville, 2000—. Hon. prof. Chinese Rsch. Acad. Environ. Scis., Beijing, 2005—. Contbr. articles to profl. jours. Recipient Hon. professorship, Chinese Acad. Environ. Sciences, 2005, Lightening award, Lockheed Martin Corp., 1999. Mem.: Am. Geophys. Union, Air and Waste Management Assn., Assn. of Environ. Engring. and Sci. Profs., Chi Epsilon Soc. (hon.). Achievements include development of cost-effective air pollution control strategies. Office: U Tenn 59 Perkins Hall Knoxville TN 37996-2010 Home Phone: 865-671-1654; Office Phone: 865-974-2629. Office Fax: 865-974-2669. Personal E-mail: dssaqm@gmail.com. Business E-Mail: jsfu@utk.edu.

FU, LEE-LUENG, oceanographer; b. Taipei, Republic of China, Oct. 10, 1950; s. Yi-Chin and Er-Lan (Chen) F.; m. Cecilia C. Liu, Mar. 26, 1977; 1 child, Christine. BS, Nat. Taiwan U., Taipei, 1972; PhD, MIT, 1980. Postdoctoral assoc. MIT, Cambridge, Mass., 1980; mem. tech. staff Jet Propulsion Lab., Pasadena, Calif., 1981-85, tech. group supr., Topex/Poseidon, 1986-93, project scientist, 1988—, lead scientist/ocean scis., 1994, sr. rsch. scientist, 1994. Chmn. Jason sci. working team NASA, Washington, 1988—; vis. prof. Ocean U. Qingdao, China, 2002. Editor: Satellite Altimetry and Earth Sciences, 2001; contbr. articles to profl. publs. Recipient Laurels award Aviation Week and Space Tech., 1993, CNES medal French Space Agy., 1994, Exceptional Scientific Achievement medal NASA, 1996, Outstanding Leadership Medal, 2004, Space Sys. Team award, Am. Inst. Aeronautics and Astronautics, 2006. Fellow: Am. Meteorol. Soc. (Editor's award 2005, Verner E. Suomi award 2002), Am. Geophys. Union; mem.: Oceanography Soc. Office: Jet Propulsion Lab MS 300-323 4800 Oak Grove Dr Pasadena CA 91109-8001 Business E-Mail: llf@pacific.jpl.nasa.gov.

FU, MICHAEL C., management science educator; s. Yuen-Sun and Ruth H. Fu; m. Fan Chen, June 24, 1989; children: Lara, David. SB, SM, MIT, 1985; MS, PhD, Harvard U., 1989. Prof. U. Md., College Park, 1989—. Author: Conditional Monte Carlo: Gradient Estimation and Optimization Applications, 1997, Simulation-based Algorithms for Markov Decision Processes, 2007; editor Perspectives in Operations Research, 2006, Advances in Mathematical Finance, 2007. Recipient Ops. Rsch. Divsn. award Inst. for Indsl. Engr., 1999, Best Paper award, 1998; Outstanding Systems Engring. Faculty award Inst. for Systems Rsch., 2002; Distinguished Scholar-Tchr. U. of Md., 2004-2005. Mem. IEEE, Inst. Ops. Rsch. and Mgmt. Sci. (Outstanding Pub. award 1998), Am. Math. Soc., Math. Assn. Am. Office: U Md Van Munching Hall College Park MD 20742-1871

FU, WEINONG, electrical engineer; arrived in US, 2001; 1 child, Xiao. BEE, Hefei U. Tech., China, 1982; MEng in Elec. Engring., Shanghai U. Tech., 1989; PhD, Hong Kong Poly. U., 1999. Asst. engr. Shanghai Elec. Apparatus Rsch. Inst., 1982—86; lectr. Shanghai U., 1989—94; rsch. assoc. Hong Kong Poly. U., 1994—2000; vis. rschr. Nat. U. Singapore, 2000—01; R&D engr. Ansoft Corp., Pitts., 2001—. Contbr. articles to profl. publs. Achievements include research in theory and application of electromagnetic field computation and electric device design and control. Office: Ansoft Corp 225 West Station Square Dr Ste 200 Pittsburgh PA 15219 Office Phone: 412-261-3200 ext. 270. Personal E-mail: weinongfu@yahoo.com. Business E-Mail: wfu@ansoft.com.

FU, YAN CINDY, psychologist; permanent resident, US, 1996; B in Psychology, Beijing Normal U., 1990; MA in Cognitive Psychology, CUNY, Bklyn., 1993; MEd, U. Mass., Boston, 1996, CAGS, 1997. Lic. ednl. psychologist Calif., 2002. Sch. psychologist Walnut Valley Unified Sch. Dist., Calif., 1997—; lic. ednl. psychologist Calif., 2002—. Sch. bd. mem. Loving Savior Luth. Ch. & Sch., Chino Hills, Calif., 2005—06. Mem.: NASP, Calif. Assn. Sch. Psychologists, Internat. Sch. Psychologist Assn. (licentiate). Achievements include bridge building between US and China and efforts to bring the character education concept/character champions framework into China. Personal E-mail: cindy@impmi.com. Business E-Mail: yfu@walnutvalley.k12.ca.us.

FU, ZHENGHONG ALEX, medical educator; s. Xiuheng Fu and Xiaoping Wu; m. Nan Wang, Dec. 18, 2002; 1 child, Helen Jiani. MS, U. NC, Chapel Hill, 2002, PhD, 2005. Rsch. asst. U. NC, 2000—03; asst. staff Cleve. Clinic, 2005—; asst. prof. Case Western Res. U., Cleve., 2006—. Contbr. articles to profl. jours., chapters to books. Recipient Best Podium Presentation award, ISPOR 10th Ann. Internat. Meeting, 2005; fellow, GlaxoSmithKline, Rsch. Triangle Pk., NC, 2003—05; grantee, NIH/Nat. Libr. Medicine, 2003, NIH/NIDDK, 2003; scholar, U. NC, 2000. Mem.: Am. Econ. Assn., Soc. Med. Decision Making (mem. sci. rev. com. 2006—), Internat. Soc. Pharmacoeconomics and Outcomes Rsch. (mem. rsch. rev. com. 2005—, judge podium and poster sessions 2006—). Office: Cleve Clinic 9500 Euclid Ave/Wb-4 Cleveland OH 44195 Home Phone: 919-360-2061; Office Phone: 216-445-7745. Office Fax: 216-445-2781. E-mail: fuz@ccf.org.

FUCHS, ALFRED HERMAN, psychologist, educator; b. Englewood, NJ, Nov. 29, 1932; s. Herman and Wilhemine Katharine (Dieling) F.; m. Phyllis Elizabeth Rocke, Aug. 27, 1955; children: Christopher Frederick, Jeffrey Alfred, Lisa Marie, Eric William. AB, Rutgers U., 1954; MA, Ohio U., 1958; PhD, Ohio State U., 1960. Psychologist, scientist Gen. Dynamics/Electric Boat Co., 1961-62; asst. prof. psychology Bowdoin Coll., Brunswick, Maine, 1962-66, assoc. prof., 1966-72, prof., 1972-98, prof. emeritus, 1998—, chmn. dept., 1965-75, 94-97, dean faculty, 1975-91. Summer research participant NSF, 1963, 64 History and dictionary editor, Am. Jour. Psychology, 2007—; Contbr. articles to profl. jours. NSF grantee, 1963-64, 64-65 Fellow APA (pres.-elect divsn. 26 1997-98, pres. 1998-99); mem. History of Sci. Soc., Internat. Soc. History Behavioral Scis., Sigma Xi. Democrat. Home: 5 Longfellow Ave Brunswick ME 04011-2535 Office: Bowdoin Coll Dept Psychology 6900 College Station Brunswick ME 04011

FUCHS, ELAINE V., molecular biologist, educator; b. Hinsdale, Ill., May 5, 1950; m. David T. Hansen, Sept. 10, 1988. BS in Chemistry with highest distinction, U. Ill., Urbana, 1972; PhD in Biochemistry, Princeton U., 1977; PhD (hon.), Mt. Sinai U., 2003. Postdoctoral fellow dept. biology MIT, 1977-80; from asst. prof. to prof. U. Chgo., 1980—89, prof. Dept. Molecular Genetics and Cell Biology, 1989—2002; investigator Howard Hughes Med. Inst., 1988—; Rebecca C. Lancefield prof. mammalian cell biology and devel. Rockefeller U., NYC, 2002—. Assoc. editor Jour. Cell Biology, 1993—; contbr. 225 articles to profl. jours. Recipient Bensely award Am. Assn. Anatomists, 1988, Searle Scholar award Chgo. Cmty. Trust, 1981-84, Presdl. Young Investigator award NSF, 1984-89, NIH Merit award, 1993, 98, Wm. Montagna award Soc. Investigative Dermatology, 1995, Keith Porter Lecture award Am. Soc. Cell Biology, 1996, Sr. Woman Achievement award, 1997, Cartwright award 2001, Richard Lounsbery award, 2001, Novartis award, 2003, Dickson prize, 2004. Fellow Am. Acad. Arts and Scis., Am. Assn. Microbiology, IOM, Am. Soc. Cell Biology (past pres.), Harvey Soc., Am. Philos. Soc., NY Acad. Sci., Phi Beta Kappa. Office: Rockefeller U Lab Mammalian Cell Biology and Devel 1230 York Ave Box 300 New York NY 10021

FUCHS, ELINOR, theater critic, playwright, educator; b. Cleve., Jan. 23, 1933; d. Joseph Fuchs and Lillian Kessler; m. Michael Oakes Finkelstein, May 3, 1962 (div. 1984); children: Claire Oakes Finkelstein, Katherine Eban Finkelstein. BA summa cum laude, Radcliffe Coll., 1955; MA, Hunter Coll., 1975; MPhil, CUNY Grad. Ctr., 1976; PhD in Theatre CUNY Grad. Ctr., 1995. Rsch. dir. Sextant Prodns.-ABC, NYC, 1960-61; prodr.-writer Channel 13/WNET, NYC, 1962-63; adj. lectr. SUNY-Stony Brook, 1975, 82; lit. mgr.-dramaturg Chelsea Theater Ctr., NYC, 1978-79; staff theater critic Soho News, NYC, 1979-82; contbg. critic Village Voice, NYC, 1982—; dramaturg Women's Interart Theatre, NYC, 1984-85; cons. Nat. Endowment for Arts, Washington, 1982-83; mem. Plays-in-Process selection com. Theatre Comm. Group, NYC, 1983-84; lectr. Freie U., Berlin; prof. dramaturgy and dramatic lit. Yale Sch. Drama, 1998-, vis. lectr. 1994-97. Sr. lectr. dept. theatre Emory U., 1987-90; vis. prof. English NYU, 1990; vis. assoc. prof. English and Women's Studies Harvard U., 1995; adj. assoc. prof. Columbia U. Sch. Arts, 1992-98, adj. prof. theatre, 1998-01; adj. prof. English and Comparative Lit. Columbia U., 1998. Author play/book: (with Joyce Antler) Year One of the Empire, 1973 (produced Odyssey Theatre, L.A. 1980, Drama-Logue Critics' award in playwriting Best Play 1980, Critic's award Outstanding Achievement in Theater); contbr. numerous articles to periodicals, including N.Y. Times, Am. Theatre, Comparative Drama, Modern Drama, Theatre Communications, Vogue, Drama Rev., Performing Arts Jour.; co-editor spl. issues on Am. Theatre Alternatives théâtrales, Brussels, Nos. 9 and 10; Les américains par eux-mêmes, 1982; editor: Plays of the Holocaust, An International Anthology, 1987; author: (with others) Apocalypse Culture, 1987, Strindberg's Dramaturgy, 1988, Sacred Theatre, 1989, From Word to Image: The New Theatre in Germany and the United States, 1991, Making an Exit: A Mother-Daughter Drama with Alzheimer's, Machine Tools and Laughter, 2005; sr. contbr.: Am. Theatre, 1990-93; contbr.: The Village Voice, 1982-92; author: The Death of Character: Perspectives on Theater After Modernism (George Jean Nathan award dramatic criticism 1997, Hon. Mention, Callaway award Best Book in Drama and Theatre, 1996-97, Outstanding Acad. Book 1996); guest editor, contbr.: The Apocalyptic Century, 1999; co-editor, contbr.: (with Una Chaudhuri) Land/Scape/Theater, 2002 (Athe Excellence in Editing award 2003). V.p. Performing Artists for Nuclear Disarmament, NYC, 1981-83 Fellow MacDowell Colony, Peterborough, NH, 1982; Rockefeller fellow in humanities, 1984-85, in age studies Ctr. Twentieth Century Studies U. Wis.-Milw., 1995-96; fellow Bunting Inst. Radcliffe Coll., 1985-86; recipient Swedish Inst. Study award, Stockholm, 1981. Mem. exec. coun. Ibsen Soc. Am., 1993-01; artistic advisor Fund New Am. Plays, the Kennedy Ctr., 1992-98; mem. adv. bd. Bunting Inst., 1998-01. Mem. PEN, Assn. Theater in Higher Edn., Am. Soc. Theater Rsch., Phi Beta Kappa. Democrat. Office: Yale Sch Drama Yale Repertory Theatre PO Box 208244 New Haven CT 06520-8244

FUCHS, JEROME HERBERT, management consultant; b. N.Y.C., Jan. 7, 1922; s. Berthold and Fannie (Neuschotz) F.; m. Eleanor May DeRoo, May 26, 1945; children: Jerome S. Taylor, Susan Fuchs Decker, Sandra Fuchs Lombino. BS in Mktg. with honors, Syracuse U., 1950, MBA, 1951. Systems and methods analyst Carrier Corp., 1951-52; supr. systems and methods Lukens Steel, Coatesville, Pa., 1952-54; mgr. systems and methods PennWalt Co., Phila., 1955-57, mgr. systems and methods and office svcs. Amax, Inc., Greenwich, Conn., 1958-60; exec. asst. to pres. Rockbestos Wire & Cable Co., 1960-61; v.p. mfg. United Aircraft Products, Dayton, Ohio, 1970-71; exec. v.p. Bus. Supplies Corp. Am., N.Y.C., 1972; sr. ptnr. Fuchs Assocs., East Meadow, N.Y., 1960—2001; indsl. rsch. asst., Syracuse (N.Y.) U., 1949-51; adj. prof. Syracuse U., 1950-52, John Hopkins U., Balt., 1953-54, Drexel, Phila., 1955-57, Queens Coll., N.Y.C., 1963-65, SUNY, Stony Brook, 1987-91, Hofstra U., 1988—. Author: Making the Most of Management Consulting Services, 1975; Managment Consultants in Action, 1975; Computerized Cost Control Systems, 1976; Computerized Inventory Control Systems, 1977; Administering the Quality Control Function, 1979, The Prentice-Hall Illustrated Handbook of Advanced Manufacturing Methods, 1988. Served as 2nd lt. AC, U.S. Army, 1943-46. Mem. Soc. Profl. Mgmt. Cons. (charter, pres. 1977-79), Inst. Mgmt. Cons. (cert., founding mem.), Sigma Iota Epsilon. Home and Office: 1612 Salisbury Park Dr East Meadow NY 11554-5522 Office Phone: 516-542-0266.

FUCHS, LAWRENCE HOWARD, federal official, educator; b. NYC, Jan. 29, 1927; s. Alfred F. and Frances S. (Scheiber) Fuchs; m. Betty Corcoran, Sept. 12, 1970; 1 adopted child, Carole Hoovenchildren from previous marriage: Janet Pearl, Frances Sarah, Naomi Ruth stepchildren: Michael Hooven, Fred Hooven, John Hooven. BA, N.Y. U., 1950; PhD, Harvard U., 1955; DHL (hon.), Brandeis U., 2002. Tchg. fellow Harvard U., Cambridge, Mass., 1950-51; mem. faculty Brandeis U., Waltham, Mass., 1952—2002, chmn. dept. politics, 1959-60, dean faculty, 1960-61, prof. Am. civilization and politics, chmn. dept. Am. studies, 1970-86. Dir. Peace Corps, Philippines, 1961—63; exec. dir. US Select Commn. Immigration and Refugee Policy, 1979—81; vice chmn. US Commn. Immigration Reform, 1992—97; part-time radio-TV news commentator Stas. WCRB and WGBH, Boston, 1951—59. Author: The Political Behavior of American Jews, 1955, Hawaii Pono: A Political and Ethnic History, 1961, John F. Kennedy and American Catholicism, 1967, Those Peculiar Americans: Peace Corps and American National Character, 1967, American Ethnic Politics, 1968, Family Matters, 1972, The American Kaleidoscope: Race, Ethnicity and the Civic Culture, 1990, Beyond Patriarchy: Jewish Fathers and Families, 2000. Former mem. nat. adv. coun. Mex. Am. Legal

Def. and Edn. Fund; mem. Mass. Congress Racial Equality; mem. exec. coun. Am. Jewish Hist. Soc.; former vice chmn. Facing History & Ourselves; 1st chmn. Commonwealth Svc. Corps Commn.; former chmn. exec. com. sch. and soc. program Edn. Devel. Ctr., Inc.; founding pres. Self-Devel. Group, Inc.; former mem. nat. adv. bd. com. law and social action Am. Jewish Congress. With USNR, 1945—47. Recipient Decade Humanity award, Facing History and Ourselves, John Carroll Centennial award, John Hope Franklin award, 1991, Theodore Saloutos award, 1991, Carey McWilliams award, 1992; grantee, Social Scis. Rsch. Coun., East-West Ctr., Rockefeller Found., Ford Found., Exxon Found., Jaffe Found., Sloan Found.; Woodrow Wilson fellow. Mem.: Phi Beta Kappa. Home: 202 Del Pond Drive Canton MA 02021

FUCHS, MARK, lawyer; BS in Biology, Lewis and Clark Coll., Portland, Oreg.; MBA, Portland State U.; JD, Willamette U. Bar: Oreg. Former litig. atty., corp. bds., ins. cos. and product mfr. Bullivant Houser Bailey; corp. atty. Louisiana Pacific Co., 2001—03, gen. counsel, 2003—, v.p., 2007—. Office: Louisiana Pacific Ste 2000 414 Union St Nashville TN 37219

FUCHS, NANCY E., lawyer; BA summa cum laude, U. Pa., 1978; JD, NYU, 1981. Bar: NY 1981. Ptnr. corp. and fin. dept. Kaye Scholer LLP, NYC. Office: Kaye Scholer LLP 425 Park Ave New York NY 10022 Office Phone: 212-836-8565. E-mail: nfuchs@kayescholer.com.

FUCHS, OLIVIA ANNE MORRIS, lawyer; b. Louisville, May 2, 1949; d. H.H. Morris Jr. and Betty Jean Wills Saltkill. BA, U. Louisville, 1977; JD cum laude, 1980. Bar: Ky. 1980, Ind. 1987, U.S. Dist. Ct. (we. dist.) Ky. 1985, U.S. Tax. Ct. 1987. Assoc. Brown, Todd & Heyburn, Louisville, 1981-87; mem. Conliffe, Sandmann & Sullivan PLLC, Louisville, 1987-97; pvt. practice Louisville, 1997—. Notes editor Jour. Family Law, 1979-80. Vol. advocate R.A.P.E. Relief Ctr. YWCA, Louisville, 1981—87. Mem. ABA, Ind. Bar Assn., Ky. Bar Assn., Louisville Bar Assn. (probate sect. chmn. 1990, profl. responsibility com., com. chmn. 1988), U. Louisville Law Alumni Coun. (bd. dirs., pres. 1997-98), Exec. Club Louisville (pres. 1996-97), Citizens for Better Judges, Phi Alpha Delta. Democrat. Presbyterian. Office: Ky Home Life Bldg 239 S 5th St Ste 1700 Louisville KY 40202-3248 Office Phone: 502-587-7700.

FUCHS, OWEN GEORGE, chemist; b. Austin, Tex., June 22, 1951; s. Emil George and Hazel June (Johnson) F.; children from previous marriage: Ginny Lynn, William Oberholz, Owen George; m. Caroline S. Crook, Dec. 15, 1990; children: Evan Ashbey, Lindsey Nicole, Allison Mae. AA, Lee Jr. Coll., 1970, AS, 1973; BS, U. Houston, 1972. Chemist, Merichem Co., Houston, 1972-73; lab. mgr. Superintendence Co., Inc., Houston, 1973-78; dir. labs. and hydrocarbon research Chas. Martin Internat., Pasadena, Tex., 1978-79; pres., chief exec. officer Alpha-Omega Labs., Inc., Houston, Tex., 1979-88; bd. dirs. A.O.L. Inc., Houston, 1988—; pres., chief exec. officer Owen G. Fuchs & Assocs., Houston, 1988—, Texas City Testing Inc., 1989—, Environ. Testing Enterprises, Inc., 1991—, La. Testing Labs., Inc., 1992—. Mem. ASTM, NRA, Am. Chem. Soc. Home: PO Box 613 Highlands TX 77562-0613 Office: PO Box 3921 Texas City TX 77592-3921

FUCHS, ROLAND JOHN, geography educator, academic administrator; b. Yonkers, NY, Jan. 15, 1933; s. Alois L. and Elizabeth (Weigand) F.; m. Gaynell Ruth McAuliffe, June 15, 1957; children: Peter K., Christopher K., Andrew K. BA, Columbia U., 1954, postgrad., 1956—57, Moscow State U., 1960—61; MA, Clark U., 1957, PhD, 1959, DSc (hon.), 1995. Asst. prof. to prof. emeritus U. Hawaii, Honolulu, 1958—, chmn. dept. geography, 1964-86, asst. dean to assoc. dean Coll. Arts and Scis., 1965-67, dir. Asian Studies Lang. and Area Ctr., 1965-67, adj. rsch. assoc. East West Ctr., 1980—, spl. asst. to pres., 1986; vice rector UN U., Tokyo, 1987-94; dir. Internat. Start Secretariat, 1994—. Vis. prof. Clark U., 1963-64, Nat. Taiwan U., 1974; bd. internat. orgns. and programs NAS, 1976-81, chmn., 1980-81, bd. sci. and tech. in devel., 1980-85; mem. U.S. Nat. Commn. for Pacific Basin Econ. Coop., 1985-87; sr. advisor UN U., 1986; chmn. adv. com. UN U. Inst. for Environ. and Human Security. Author, editor: Geographical Perspectives on the Soviet Union, 1974, Theoretical Problems of Geography, 1977, Population Distribution Policies in Development Planning, 1981, Urbanization and Urban Policies in the Pacific-Asia Region, 1987, Megacities: The Challenge of the Urban Future, 1994, Global-Regional Linkages in the Earth System, 2002; asst. editor Econ. Geography, 1963-64; mem. editl. adv. com. Soviet Geography: Rev. and Translation, 1966-85, Geoforum, 1988-96, African Urban Quar., 1987, Global Environ. Change, 1990-2000, Asian Geographer, 1991-98, Internat. Jour. Environmental Pollution, 1994—. Ford Found. fellow, 1956-57; Fulbright Rsch. scholar, 1966-67. Mem. Assn. Am. Geographers, Am. Geophys. Union, Internat. Geog. Union (v.p. 1980-84, 1st v.p. 1984-88, pres. 1988-92, past pres. 1992-96), Assn. Am. Geographers (Hon. award 1982), Am. Assn. Advancement of Slavic Studies (bd. dirs. 1976-81), Pacific Sci. Assn. (mem. coun. 1978—, mem. exec. com. 1986-99, sec. gen-treas. 1991-99), Acad. Europaea (elected fgn. mem.). Home: 1200 N Nash St Arlington VA 22209-3616 Office Phone: 202-462-2213. Business E-Mail: rfuchs@agu.org.

FUCHS, VICTOR ROBERT, economist, educator; b. NYC, Jan. 31, 1924; s. Alfred and Frances Sarah (Scheiber) Fuchs; m. Beverly (Beck), Aug. 29, 1948; children: Nancy, Frederic, Paula, Kenneth. BS, N.Y. Univ., 1947; MA, Columbia Univ., 1951, PhD, 1955. Internat. fur broker, 1946—50; lectr. Columbia Univ., NYC, 1953—54, instr., 1954—55, asst. prof. econ., 1955—59; assoc. prof. econ. N.Y. Univ., NYC, 1959—60; program assoc. Ford Found. Program in econ., devel. , and adminstrn., 1960—62; mem. sr. rsch staff Nat. Bur. Econ. Rsch., 1962—; prof. econ. Grad. Ctr. City Univ. of N.Y., NYC, 1968—74; prof. cmty. medicine Mt. Sinai Sch. Medicine, 1968-74; v.p. rsch. Nat. Bur. Econ. Rsch., 1968—78; prof. econ. Stanford U. , Stanford Med. Sch., 1974—95; Henry J. Kaiser Jr. prof. Stanford U. , Stanford Med. Sch., 1988—95, prof. emeritus, 1995—. Author: The Economics of the Fur Industry, 1957; co-author (with Aaron Warner): Concepts and Cases in Econ. Analysis, 1958; author: Changes in the Location of Mfg. in the U.S. Since 1929, 1962, The Svc. Economy, 1968, Prodn. and Productivity in the Svc. Industries, 1969, Policy Issues and Rsch. Opportunities in Indsl. Orgn., 1972, Essays on the Economics of Health and Med. Care, 1972, Who Shall Live? Health, Economics, and Social Choice, 1975; co-author (with Joseph Newhouse): The Economics of Physician and Patient Behavior, 1978; author: Economic Aspects of Health, 1982, How We Live, 1983, The Health Economy, 1986, Women's Quest for Econ. Equality, 1988, The Future of Health Policy, 1993, Individual and Social Responsibility: Child Care Edn., Med. Care, and Long-term Care in Am., 1996, Who Shall Live? Health, Economics and Social Choice, expanded edit., 1998; contbr. articles to profl. jour. Served in USAF, 1943—46. Fellow: Am. Econ. Assn. (disting., pres. 1995), Am. Acad. Arts and Sci.; mem.: Am. Philos. Soc. (John R. Commons award), Am. Inst. Medicine of NAS, Beta Gamma Sigma, Sigma Xi. Home: 796 Cedro Way Stanford CA 94305-1032 Office: NBER 30 Alta Rd Stanford CA 94305-8006 Office Phone: 650-326-7639.

FUCHS, W. KENT, engineering educator; b. Elk City, Okla., Nov. 3, 1954; BS, Duke U., 1977; MDiv, Trinity Evang. Div. Sch., 1984; PhD, U. Ill., 1985. Asst. prof. U. Ill., Urbana, 1985-89, assoc. prof., 1989-93, prof., 1993-96; Disting. prof., head Sch. Elec. and Computer Engring., Purdue U., West Lafayette, Ind., 1996—2002; dean engring. Cornell U., Ithaca, NY, 2002—. Contbr. numerous articles to profl. jours. Scholar, U. Ill., 1991. Fellow IEEE, Assn. for Computing Machinery. Office: Cornell U Coll Engring 242 Carpenter Hall Ithaca NY 14853-2201 Office Phone: 607-255-9679. E-mail: engineering_dean@cornell.edu.

FUDGE, ANN MARIE, former advertising executive; b. Washington, Apr. 23, 1951; d. Malcolm R. and Bettye (Lewis) Brown; m. Richard E. Fudge, Feb. 27, 1971; children: Richard Jr., Kevin. BA, Simmons Coll., 1973; MBA, Harvard U., 1977; DHL (hon.), Adelphi U., 1995, Howard U., 1998, Simmons Coll., 1998, Marymount Coll., 1999. Manpower specialist GE, Bridgeport, Conn., 1973-75; mktg. asst. Gen. Mills, Mpls., 1977-78, asst. product mgr., 1978-80, product mgr., 1980-83, mktg. dir., 1983-86; assoc. dir., strategic planning Gen. Foods, White Plains, NY, 1986-87, mktg. dir., 1987-89, v.p. mktg. and devel., 1989-91, exec. v.p., gen. mgr., 1991-94; exec. v.p. Kraft Foods, 1994-97; pres. Maxwell House Coffee Co., White Plains, NY, 1994-97, Maxwell House Coffee and Post Cereal, Tarrytown, NY, 1997—2001; chmn., CEO Young & Rubicam, Inc., NYC, 2003—05, Y&R Brands, NYC, 2003—06. Bd. dirs. GE, Marriott Internat.; trustee Am. Grad. Sch. Internat. Mgmt., Brookings Instn. Bd. dirs. Women's Econ. Devel. Corp., St. Paul, 1984-86; chair allocations panel United Way, Mpls., 1983-86; vol. Big Sisters/Big Bros., Fairfield County, Conn., 1988-90; bd. govs. Boys and Girls Clubs Am.; trustee Rockefeller Found., 2006-. Recipient Leadership award YWCA, Mpls., 1980, Black Achievers award Harlem YMCA, 1988, Candace award Nat. Coalition of 100 Black Women, 1991-92, Corp. Women's Network award, 1994, She Knows Where She's Going award Girls, Inc., 1994, Alumni Achievement award Harvard Bus. Sch., 1998; named Woman of Yr., Glamour Mag., 1995, Ad Woman of Yr., Advt. Women of N.Y., 1995, Sara Lee Frontrunner award, 1999, one of 50 Most Powerful Women in Am. Bus., Fortune mag.; one of 100 Most Influential Black Americans, Ebony mag., 2006. Mem. Exec. Leadership Coun. (pres. 1994-96, Achievement award 2000), Com. of 200, NY Women's Forum, Coun. on Fgn. Rels.*

FUENTEALBA, VICTOR WILLIAM, professional society administrator; b. Balt., Sept. 1, 1922; s. Manuel Lagos and Antonia (Lengler) F.; m. Viola J. Henderson, Jan. 26, 1952; children: Victoria, Mary Lee, Donna Jean, Patricia. Student, Loyola Coll., 1946—47; JD, U. Md., 1950. Bar: Md. 1950, U.S. Supreme Ct. 1950. V.p. Musicians Union Met. Balt., 1951-53, sec., treas., 1953-58, pres., 1958-78; mem. internat. exec. bd. Am. Fedn. Musicians, NYC, 1967-70, v.p., 1970-78, pres., 1978-87, pres. emeritus, 1987—. Bd. dirs. Hearing and Speech Agy., Balt., 1973-78; mem. Pres.' Com. on Employment of Handicapped; adv. coun. Ctr. Labor and Indsl. Rels. of N.Y. Inst. Tech., Assn. Concert Bands, Van Cliburn Internat. Piano Competition; chmn. bd. Nat. Music Coun.; v.p. Muscular Dystrophy Assn.; adv. bd. Music Industry Educators Assn.; judge Adv. Gen. Vets. Fgn. Wars of U.S., 2001-02. Served with inf. U.S. Army, WW II. Decorated Purple Heart. Mem. Md. State Bar Assn. (chmn. sr. lawyers sect. 2006—), Delta Theta Phi. Democrat. Roman Catholic. Home: 4501 Arabia Ave Baltimore MD 21214-3306 Office: 805 Court Sq Bldg 200 E Lexington St Baltimore MD 21202-3530 Office Phone: 410-539-5115. Personal E-mail: victorlagos@aol.com.

FUENTES, BEATRIZ PASTOR, language educator, department chairman; M. SVSU, Saginaw, Mich., 1994. Spanish tchr. Ctrl. Intermediate, Midland, Mich., H.H. Dow HS, Midland; fgn. lang. dep. head Bainbridge Island HS, Wash., 2005—. Presenter in field. Named Tchr. Innovator of Yr., Midland Pub. Schs., 1994; recipient Diversity Edn. award, 2001, Contbn. award, Mich. Improving Langs. Instrn. for Tchrs. and Students, 2002; grantee, Kalamazoo Coll., Mich., 2003; Diversity grantee, Midland Pub. Schs., 2002, 2004. Mem.: ACTFL.

FUENTES, BRIAN CHRISTOPHER, professional baseball player; b. Merced, Calif., Aug. 9, 1975; m. Barbara Fuentes; 1 child, Giovanni Paolo. Grad., Merced Jr. Coll., 1996. Draft pick Seattle Mariners, 1995, pitcher, 2001, Colo. Rockies, 2001—. Named to Nat. League All-Star Team, Maj. League Baseball, 2005—07. Mailing: Colo Rockies Coors Field 2001 Blake St Denver CO 80205-2000*

FUENTES, CARLOS, writer, retired ambassador; b. Panama City, Panama, Nov. 11, 1928; s. Rafael Fuentes Boettiger and Berta Macías Rivas; m. Rita Macedo, 1959 (div. 1969); 1 dau., Cecilia; m. Sylvia Lemus, 1973; children: Carlos (dec. 1999), Natasha (dec. 2005). Degree, U. Mex., Institut des Hautes Etudes Internationales, Geneva; degree (hon.), Columbia Coll., Chgo. State U., Cambridge U., Essex U., Harvard U., Dartmouth Coll., Bard Coll., New Sch., Georgetown U., Washington U., St. Louis, Brown U., Berlin U., UCLA. Mem. Mexican del. ILO, Geneva, 1950-52; asst. chief press sect. Mexican Ministry Fgn. Affairs, 1954; asst. dir. cultural dissemination U. Mex., 1955-56; head dept. cultural rels. Mexican Ministry Fgn. Affairs, 1957-59; fellow Woodrow Wilson Internat. Ctr. for Scholars, Washington, 1974; Mexican ambassador to France, 1975-77; prof. English and romance langs. U. Pa., 1978-83; prof. comparative lit. Harvard U., 1984-86, Robert F. Kennedy prof., 1987-89; prof.-at-large Brown U., Providence, 1995—. Norman Maccoll lectr. Cambridge U., 1977, Simon Bolivar prof., 1986-87; Virgina Gildersleeve prof. Barnard Coll., 1977; Henry L. Tinker lectr. Columbia U., 1978; pres. Modern Humanities Rsch. Assn., 1989—; founder Iberoamerican Forum, 2000—. Author: Los días enmascarados, 1954, La región más transparente, 1958 (pub. as Where the Air Is Clear, 1960), Las buenas conciencias, 1959 (pub. as The Good Conscience, 1961), Aura, 1962, La muerte del Artemio Cruz, 1962 (pub. as The Death of Artemio Cruz, 1964), The Argument of Latin America: Words for North Americans, 1963, Cantar de ciegos, 1964, Zona sagrada, 1967 (pub. as Holy Places, 1972), Cambio de piel, 1967 (pub. as A Change of Skin, 1968; Biblioteca Breve prize Barcelona 1967), Paris: la revolución de mayo, 1968, La nueva novela hispanoamericana, 1969, Cumpleaños, 1969, El mundo de Jose Luis Cuevas, 1969, Casa con dos puertas, 1970, Tiempo mexicano, 1971, Cuerpos y ofrendas, 1972, Chac Mool y otros cuentos, 1973, Terra Nostra, 1975 (Rómulo Gallegos prize Venezuela 1977), Cervantes: o, La crítica de la lectura, 1976 (pub. as Don Quixote: or, The Critique of Reading, 1976), La cabeza de la hidra, 1978 (pub. as The Hydra Head, 1978), Una familia lejana, 1980 (pub. as Distant Relations, 1982), Agua quemada, 1981 (pub. as Burnt Water, 1981), High Noon in Latin America, 1983, 84, El gringo viejo, 1985 (pub. as The Old Gringo, 1986; LA Times Book award nomination 1986, Rubén Darío prize 1988, Italo-Latino Americano Instituto prize 1988), Latin America: At War with the Past, 1985, Cristóbal Nonato, 1987 (pub. as Christopher Unborn, 1989), Gabriel García Marquez and the Invention of America, 1987, Myself with Others: Selected Essays, 1988, Constancia, y otras novelas para vírgenes, 1989 (pub. as Constancia and Other Stories for Virgins, 1990), La campaña, 1990 (pub. as The Campaign, 1991), Valiente Mundo Nuevo, 1991, The Buried Mirror: Reflections on Spain and on the New World, 1992, Witnesses of Time, 1992, Return to Mexico: Journeys Beyond the Mask, 1992, El Naranjo, 1993 (pub. as The Orange Tree, 1993), Geografia de la Novela, 1993, Diana the Goddess Who Hunts Alone, 1995, The Crystal Frontier, 1995, La Edad del Tiempo, 1994—, A New Time for Mexico, 1994, Por un Progreso Incluyente, 1997, Retratos en el Tiempo, 1998, (with Carlos Fuentes Lemus) Los Anos con Laura Díaz, 1999 (pub. as The Years with Laura Díaz, 2002); Inez, 2000, Los cinco soles de Mexico, 2001, La silla del águila (pub. as The Eagle's Throne, 2005), 2003, Inquieta Compañía, 2004, Viendo Visiones, 2004, Todas la Familias Felices, 2006; (plays) Todos los gatos son pardos, 1970, El tuerto es rey, 1970, Los reinos originarios, 1971, Orquídeas a la luz de la luna, 1982 (pub. as Orchids in the Moonlight, 1982; Mexican Nat. award for lit. 1984); screenwriter: (films) Pedro Paramo, 1966, Tiempo de morir, 1966, Los Caifanes, 1967, (TV series) The Buried Mirror, 1991; contbr. to mag. and newspapers including Los Angeles Times, NY Times, Newsweek; editor: Revista Mexicana de Literatura, 1954-58, El Espectador, 1959-61, Siempre, 1960—, Política, 1960—. Trustee NY Pub. Libr.; mem. Mexican Nat. Commn. Human Rights, 1991—; pres. Iberoamerican Inst., Berlin, 2004; bd. dirs. Alfonso Reyes Chair, 1998. Recipient Centro Mexicano de Escritores fellowship, 1956-57, Xavier Villaurrutia prize (Mex.), 1975, Alfonso Reyes prize (Mex.), 1979, Miguel de Cervantes Lit. prize Spanish Ministry of Culture, 1987, Medal of Honor for Lit., Nat. Arts Club, NYC, 1988, Rector's medal U. Chile, 1991, Casita Maria medal, 1991, UCLA medal, 1993, Order of Merit (Chile), 1992, French Legion of Honor, 1992, Menèndez Pelayo Internat. award U. Santander, 1992, Picasso medal UNESCO, 1994, Principe de Asturias prize, 1994, Premio Grinzane-Cavour, 1994; named hon. citizen Santiago de Chile, 1993, Buenos Aires, 1993, Veracruz, 1993, Order of the So. Cross award Brazil, 1997, French Order of Merit, 1998, Latin Civilization prize French and Brazilian Acad., 1999, Mexican Senate award, 2000, Delaware Commonwealth award, 2002, Pablo Neruda Centennial medal (Chile), 2004, Galileo prize Florence, 2005, Arzobispo San Clemente prize Coll. Students, Santiago de Compostela, Spain, 2005, Blue Metropolis prize Montreal, 2005, Franklin Delano Roosevelt Freedom of Speech and Expression award Franklin and Eleanor Roosevelt Inst., Middleburg, Holland, 2006, Am. Acad. Achievement award, 2006, Keys to City of Los Angeles, 2006. Mem. Am. Acad. and Inst. Arts and Letters, Nat. Coll. Mex., Inst. Nat. Strategy (bd. dir.). Achievements include founder (with Gabriel García Márquez) Julio Cortázar chair University of Guadalajara, Mexico; founder Alfonso Reyes chair ITM, Monterrey, Mexico.*

FUENTES, JULIO M., federal judge; b. Humacao, PR, 1946; BA, So. Ill. U., 1971; MA, NYU, 1972; JD, SUNY, Buffalo, 1975; MA, Rutgers U., 1993. Private practice, Newark, 1975—81; judge Newark Mcpl. Ct., NJ, 1979—87, NJ Superior Ct., 1987—2000, US Ct. Appeals (3rd cir.), 2000—. Mem. ABA; Essex County Bar Assn.; Nat. Hispanic Bar Assn.; NJ Bar Assn.; NJ Hispanic Bar Assn. 1st lt. US Army, 1966—69 USAR, 1969—72. Office: US Ct Appeals 3rdCir M L King Jr Fed Bldg & Cthse 50 Walnut St Rm 5032 Newark NJ 07102*

FUENTES, MARTHA AYERS, playwright; b. Ashland, Ala., Dec. 21, 1923; d. William Herny and Elizabeth (Dye) Ayers; m. Manuel Solomon Fuentes, Apr. 11, 1943. BA in English, U. South Fla., 1969. Lectr., instr. workshops on drama, writing for TV. Author: The Rebel, 1970, Mama Don't Make Me Go To College, My Head Hurts, 1963, Two Characters in Search of An Agreement, 1970, A Cherry Blossom for Miss Chrysanthemum; contbr. articles to local, regional and nat. newspapers, feature articles to nat. mags.; author TV plays and feature articles for children and young adults. Mem. Nat. Rep. Senatorial Com., Rep. Pres. Task Force, Rep. Nat. Com., Rep. Party, Fla. Recipient George Sergel drama award U. Chgo., 1969. Mem. AAUW, NAFE, S.E. Playwrights Project, The Alliance of Resident Theatres, Stageworks, Authors Guild, Dramatists Guild, Romance Writers Am., Southeastern Writers Assn., Fla. Studio Theatre, United Daus. Confederacy. Roman Catholic. Avocations: reading, theater, travel. Home and Office: 102 3rd St Belleair Beach FL 33786-3211 Office Phone: 727-596-5393. E-mail: fuentesbellbck@aol.com.

FUENTEZ, TANIA MICHELE, journalist; b. Manhattan, Nov. 21, 1966; d. C. Pedro Alvarez Carr and E. Kay (Samuels) Queally. BA in Comm. and Rhetorical Studies, Marquette U., 1991; MA in Mass Media Comm., U. Akron, 1996. Asst. rschr. V.I. Legislature, St. Thomas, 1991; reporter V.I. Daily News, St. Thomas, 1993-95; instr. news writing U. Akron, Ohio, 1995-96; copy editor The Akron Beacon Jour., 1997-2000; newswoman AP, Atlanta, 2000—03, nat. desk editor NYC, 2003—05, copy desk supr. graphics, 2006—. Adv. bd. diversity com. V.I. Daily News, 1993-95, Contbr. articles to profl. jours. Bd. dirs. U.S. V.I. League of Women Voters, 1994-95; mem. Am. Cancer Soc., 1993-95, mem. St. Thomas Arts Coun., 1992-95. Recipient Cmty. Svc. award Pan African Support Group, 1995; scholar John S. Knight Meml. Fund, 1996, U. Akron, 1995-96. Mem. Soc. Profl. Journalists, Nat. Assn. Hispanic Journalists, Nat. Assn. Black Journalists, Comm. Workers Am.-AFL-CIO, News Media Guild, Local 31222. Roman Catholic. Avocations: writing, travel, photography, hiking, cooking. Office: The AP 450 W 33d St New York NY 10001 Office Phone: 212-621-1500. Business E-Mail: tfuentez@ap.org.

FUER-DAVIS, BEVERLY JEAN, retired elementary school educator; b. LA, Jan. 3, 1940; d. George Harold Jr. and Lucille May (Jones) Davis; m. John Anthony Fuer, Oct. 21, 1972 (dec. 1996); m. Chester B. Davis, 2002. BA, UCLA, 1961; MEd, U. Ariz., 1981. Tchr. 5th grade L.A. City Schs., 1961-62; tchr. 6th grade San Luis Obispo (Calif.) City Schs., 1962-63, LaMesa-Spring Valley Sch. Dist., LaMesa, Calif., 1963-67, gifted edn. specialist, 1967-71; middle sch. tchr. Continental Sch. Dist., Green Valley, Ariz., 1971—2002, ret., 2002. Supt.'s designee; cons. No. Ariz. U. Ideanet Spanish program; dist. rep. Tucson-Pima Arts Coun. Named Dist. Tchr. of Yr., 1988; recipient youth activities recognition award Optimist Club, 1978, Delta Kappa Gamma Soc. State Achievment award, 1990, Am. History Tchr. award Madera chpt. DAR, 1992. Mem. ASCD, NEA, Ariz. Edn. Assn., AAUW, Continental Edn. Assn. (pres. 1986-87, 97-98, 2001-02), Delta Kappa Gamma (state pres. 1993-95), Continental Sch. Dist. Ednl. Found. (bd. dirs. 1993-), Greater Green Valley Arts Coun. (v.p. 2003-), The Animal League of Green Valley (pres. 2005-). Democrat. Home: 211 E Calle Herboso Green Valley AZ 85614-4114 Personal E-mail: bjeandf@aol.com.

FUERSTENAU, DOUGLAS WINSTON, mineral engineering educator; b. Hazel, SD, Dec. 6, 1928; s. Erwin Arnold and Hazel Fuerstenau; m. Margaret Ann Pellett, Aug. 29, 1953; children: Linda(dec.) , Lucy, Sarah, Stephen. BS, S.D. Sch. Mines and Tech., 1949; MS, Mont. Sch. Mines, 1950; ScD, MIT, 1953; Mineral Engr., Mont. Coll. Mineral Sci. and Tech., 1968; doctorate (hon.), U. Liege, Belgium, 1989; DTech (hon.), Lulea U. Tech., Sweden, 2001. Asst. prof. mineral engring. MIT, 1953-56; sect. leader, metals research lab. Union Carbide Metals Co., Niagara Falls, NY, 1956-58; mgr. mineral engring. lab Kaiser Aluminum & Chem. Corp., Permanente, Calif., 1958-59; assoc. prof. metallurgy U. Calif., Berkeley, 1959-62, prof. metallurgy, 1962-86, P. Malozemoff prof. of mineral engring., 1987-93, prof. grad. sch., 1994—, Miller rsch. prof., 1969-70, chmn. dept. materials sci. and mineral engring., 1970-78; hon. prof. Huainan Inst. Tech., 2000—. Guest prof. Imperial Coll. London, 1966, U. Karlsruhe, Germany, 1973, Tech. U. Clausthal, Germany, 1984; mem. Nat. Mineral Bd., 1975—78; Am. rep. Internat. Mineral Processing Congress Com., 1978—97; mem. adv. bd. Korea Inst. for Interfacial Sci. and Engring., 1992—97. Editor: Froth Flotation-50th Anniversary Vol., 1962; co-editor-in-chief: Internat. Jour. Mineral Processing, 1974—98, hon. editor-in-chief:, 1998—, adv. editor: Elsevier Monograph Series on Advances in Mineral Processing, 1975—99, chmn. editl. bd. for the Ams.: KONA-Particle Tech., 1997—; contbr. articles to profl. jours. Trustee SD Sch. Mines Found., 1997—. Named Douglas W. Fuerstenau professorship at S.D. Sch. of Mines and Tech., 1998; named to S.D. Hall of Fame, 2005; recipient Guy E. March Silver medal, SD Sch. Mines, 1979, Disting. Alumnus award, 2002, Alexander von Humboldt Sr. Am. Scientist award, Germany, 1984, Frank F. Aplan award, Engring. Found., 1990, Lifetime Achievement award, Internat. Mineral Processing Congress, 1995; Rsch. fellow, Japan Soc. Promotion Sci., 1993, Consiglio Nationalle delle Ricerche, Italy, 1995. Fellow: Indian Nat. Acad. Engring. (fgn.), Australian Acad. Tech. Scis. and Engring. (fgn.); mem.: AIChE (Particle Tech. Forum Lifetime Achievement award 2006), NAE, Russian Fedn. Acad. Natural Scis. (fgn. mem.), Am. Chem. Soc., Soc. Mining Engrs. (bd. dirs. 1968—71, Disting. mem.), Am. Inst. Mining and Metall. Engrs. (chmn. mineral processing divsn. 1967, Robert Lansing Hardy gold medal 1957, Rossiter W. Raymond award 1961, Robert H. Richards award 1975, Antoine M. Gaudin award 1978, Mineral Industry Edn. award 1983, Henry Krumb disting. lectr. 1989, hon. 1989), The Berkeley Fellows, Sigma Xi, Theta Tau. Congregationalist. Home: 1440 Le Roy Ave Berkeley CA 94708-1912 Office Phone: 510-642-3826. Business E-Mail: dwfuerst@berkeley.edu.

FUERSTENAU, M(AURICE) C(LARK), metallurgical engineer; b. Watertown, SD, June 6, 1933; m. 1953; 4 children. BS, S.D. Sch. Mines & Tech., 1955; MS, MIT, 1957, ScD in Metallurgy, 1961. Rsch. engr. N. Mex. Bur Mines, Socorro, 1961—63; from asst. prof. to assoc. prof. Colo. Sch. Mines, 1963-68; from assoc. prof. to prof. U. Utah, 1968-70; prof., dept. head S.D. Sch. Mines & Tech., 1970-87, interim v.p., 1987-88, acting head mech. enging., 1994-96; prof. U. Nev., Reno, 1988—2005, prof. emeritus, 2005—. Contbr. articles to profl. jours. Named to SD Hall of Fame, 2006; recipient Frank F. Aplan award, United Engring. Found., 2000. Mem. Nat. Acad Engrs., Am. Inst. Mining (v.p. 1983, Robert H. Richards award 1982, Mineral Industry Edn. award 1989), Soc. Mining Engrs. (pres. 1982, Arthur F. Taggart award 1978, Antoine M. Gaudin award 1979). Office: Univ Nevada Dept Chem & Metall Engring Reno NV 89557-0001 Home Phone: 775-333-9134; Office Phone: 775-784-4310. Business E-Mail: mcf@unr.edu.

FUERSTNER, FIONA MARGARET ANNE, ballet company executive, educator; b. Rio de Janeiro, Apr. 24, 1936; d. Paul G. and Agnes Ethel (Stothard) F.; m. Dane LaFontsee, June 7, 1969 (div. 1992); 1 child, Liana Marie. Studied with San Francisco Ballet, Royal Ballet (London), Ballet Rambert (London) Ballet Theatre Sch. (N.Y.C.), Sch. Am. Ballet (N.Y.C.). With corps de ballet San Francisco Ballet, 1952-55, soloist, 1955-58, prin. dancer, 1958-62; toured with Walter Terry's Am. Dances, 1962-63; prin. dancer Les Grands Ballets Can., Montreal, 1963-64, Am. Choreographer's Co. of N.Y., 1964, Pa. Ballet, 1965—74, ballet mistress, instr. co. class, apprentice class, 1974-77, ballet mistress, instr. co. class, 1977—86; ballet mistress Nashville Ballet, 1986-87, ballet mistress, asst. to artistic dir., 1987-91; ballet mistress Milw. Ballet, 1990-95, asst. to artistic dir. ballet mistress, 1995—2003. Guest dancer Ballet Concerto, Miami, 1967, 68, Erie Civic Ballet, 1969; guest instr. Marsha Woody Dance Acad., Beaumont, Tex., 1974, U. Louisville, 1977-78, co. class San Francisco Ballet, 1985, Tenn. Assn. Dance Nashville Conf., 1988, So. Regional Workshop Chgo., Nat. Assn. Dance Masters in Nashville, 1989, BalletMet, 1991, Memphis Classical Ballet, 1992, 97, 99, Nashville Ballet, 1992; guest ballet mistress BalletMet, 1993; faculty tchr. Sch. of Pa. Ballet, 1977-78, 78-86; organized concert group, ballet mistress, dancer Pa. Ballet, 1971; mem. dance panel Nat. Found. Advancement in the Arts, 1995-98; master tchr. South Eastern Regional Ballet Assn. Festival, 1998, Nat. Found. for Advancement in the Arts, 1999, 2001, 2005; guest tchr. Ind. U. Ballet Dept., 2000, Western Mich. U., 2002, faculty tchr. DanceWorks Studio 1661, Milw., 2005, 06, 07, master tchr. Dancenter North, Libertyville, Ill., 2005, 06; master tchr. USDAN Ctr. for the Creative and Performing Arts, Wheatley Heights, NY, 2004—; vis. asst. prof. dance Wright State U., 2004; dance panelist Midwest Regional, Nat. Found. for Advancement in the Arts, 2001, 2002; guest faculty Indpls. Sch. Ballet, 2007. Staged Allegro Brillante, Sch. Pa. Ballet Student Showcase, 1986, Nashville Ballet, 1988, Madrigalesco, Pacific NW Ballet, 1981, (parts) Nutcracker, Nashville Ballet, 1989, Carmina Burana (Butler), Milw. Ballet, 1989, Scotch Symphony, Pa. Ballet, 1993, Carmina Burana, Alberta Ballet, 1993, Concerto Barocco, Ballet Omaha, 1994, Ballet Met, 1995, Serenade, Milw. Ballet Sch., 1994, 95, 96, Serenade, Milw. Ballet, 1998-99, Serenade, Western Mich. U., 1999-2000, Concerto Barocco, The Four Temperaments for Milw. Ballet, 1999-2000, Allegro Brillante for Milw. Ballet, 2000-01, (excerpts) Who Cares?, Western Mich. U., 2003, Serenade, Wright State U., 2004. Office Phone: 414-254-4086. Personal E-mail: fionafio@sbcglobal.net.

FUERTH, GLENN J., lawyer; b. NYC, Jan. 11, 1953; BA, George Washington U., 1975; JD, Fordham U., 1978. Bar: NY 1979, US Dist. Ct. So. Dist. NY, US Dist. Ct. Ea. Dist. NY, US Ct. Appeals 2nd Cir., US Ct. Appeals 3rd Cir. Ptnr. Wilson, Elser, Moskowitz, Edelman & Dicker LLP, NYC. Mem.: Assn. Trial Lawyers of Am., NY State Bar Assn. (trial law sect., ins. sect.). Office: Wilson Elser Moskowitz Edelman & Dicker LLP 23rd Fl 150 E 42nd St New York NY 10017-5639 Office Phone: 212-490-3000 ext. 2369. Office Fax: 212-490-3038. Business E-Mail: fuerthg@wemed.com.

FUESS, BILLINGS SIBLEY, JR., advertising executive; b. NYC, Mar. 11, 1928; s. Billings Sibley and Lucile (McNeill) F.; m. Doris Vannoy, July 19, 1952; children: Billings Sibley III, Doris Jr., Frederick, Lucile. AB in Journalism, U. N.C., 1949. Analyst Gallup & Robinson, Princeton, NJ, 1952-53; writer Kenyon & Eckhardt, NYC, 1953-59, Batten, Barton, Durstine & Osborn, NYC, 1959-65; creative dir. Ogilvy & Mather, NYC, 1965-89; pres. Billings S. Fuess Advt., Summit, NJ, 1989—. Mem. selection com. N.C. Advt. Hall of Fame award. Author, editor: How to Use the Power of the Printed Word, 1985. Mem. N.Y. Philharmonic Vol. Coun., 1976—. Stephen E. Kelly award Mag. Pubs. Assn., N.Y.C., 1983, Recipient Grand award Internat. Film and Television Festival N.Y., 1984, Gold award Art Dirs. Club N.J., numerous top industry awards; elected to N.C. Advt. Hall of Fame, U. N.C., Chapel Hill, 1995. Mem.: Art Dirs. Club NJ (treas. 1997—2004). Home: 19 Highland Dr Summit NJ 07901-3108

FUFUKA, NATIKA NJERI YAA, retail executive; b. Cleve., Feb. 21, 1952; d. Russell and Mindoro Reed. AA, AAB, Cuyahoga CC, Cleve., 1973; BA, Mich. State U., 1975; postgrad., Cleve. State U. Asst. pers. dir. May Co., Cleve., 1975—78; merchandiser J.C. Penney, Cleve., 1978—80; sports mgr. Joseph Hornes, Cleve., 1980—81; fashion buyer Higbee, Cleve., 1981—86; exec. v.p. Mindoro & Assocs., 1982—; merchandise exec. Fashion Bug, Euclid, Ohio, 1986—92; pres., CEO Mindy's Return to Fashion, Cleve., 1993—. Vice chmn. Joint Com. on Medicaid Provider Impact for State of Ohio, 1992; mem. Mayor's Census Task Force, Cuyahoga County Women Bus. Enterprise Adv. Coun., Cleve. Female Bus. Enterprise Adv. Coun.; pub. affairs com. Greater Cleve. Growth Assn.; active Displaced/Single Parent Homemakers Adv. Coun., Cuyahoga Cmty. Coun., Cuyahoga Hills Boys Adv. Coun., Black Aspiration Week Celebrationcom. Cleve. State U., 1990; cmty. rels. coun. Cleve. Job Corp., 1996; African Am. com. Cleve. Found., 1996; nat. nomination com. Outstanding Young Woman of Am., 1998, Outstanding Young Man of Am., 1998; chmn. Centralized Resource Referral Svc. Panel United Way, 1993l; mem. Gen. Assembly, 1993—, United Way Appeal Com., 1996, leadership devel. program; asst. dir. Project Vote, 1983-84; bd. dirs. Ohio Youth Adv. Coun., 1988-90; mem. Mayor Census Task Force, 1989-90; adv. coun. Displaced Single Parent Homemakers, Cuyahoga County Women Bus. Enterprises, Cleve. Female Bus. Enterprise; active Citizen League, Cleve. Mus. Art, Playhouse Square Found., Women in Apptd. Office Project, Planned Parenthood Greater Cleve., WCPN Radio.; bd. dirs. Ohio Youth Adv. Coun., Women Cmty. Found., 1993—, Career Beginning Program Bd., 1993—, Nat. Ctr. Non-Profit; mem. Nat. Coun. Christians and Jews, 1996 Recipient Jesse Jackson Voter Registration award, 1984, Leadership award, United Way, 1991, Cert. Appreciation award, 1998, 2001, Vol. Leadership recognition, City of Cleve., 1991, Cmty. Rels. Coun. Svc. award, Cleve. Job Corps., 1998; Ford Found. scholar, 1975. Mem. NAFE, Nat. Nominating Bd. Outstanding Ams., Assn. MBA Execs., Black Profl. Assn., Nat. Assn. Negro Bus./Profl. Women, Am. Profl. Exec. Women, Am. Women Bus. Assn., Nat. Assn. Black Female Entrepreneurs, Severance Merchant Mall Orgn., Op. Big Vote, Nat. Coun. Negro Women, Nat. Polit. Congress Black Women (nat. founder mem., founder mem. Ohio state chpt.), Nat. Hook-Up, 100 Black Women Coalition, Black Congl. Caucus Braintrust, Small Minority Bus. Braintrust, Corp. Braintrust, Nat. Non-Profit Bds., Black Women Agenda, Black Women Roundtable, Black Focus (pres. bd. trustees), 21st Congl. Dist. Caucus (exec. bd. mem., chair bus. women com., certs. of appreciation for outstanding svc. 1985, 86), Urban League Greater Cleve., Op. Push of Greater Cleve. (bd. dirs.), Project Vote (asst. dir., Voter Registration award 1984), Midwest Vote Project, Women Vote Project, WomenSpace, United Black Fund, Greater East Cleve. Dem. Club, Minority Women Polit. Action Com., LWV, Cuyahoga Women Polit. Caucus, Ohio Pub. Interest Campaign, Ohio Rainbow Coalition, Ohio Dem. Women Com., Network Together, Black Elected Dem. Ofcls. Ohio, Cleve. City Club, 16th Dist. Club, Project M.O.V.E, Kinsman Youth Devel. Program and Scholarship Cmty. Liasion Democrat. Pentecostal. Avocations: collecting African art, golf. Office: One Chagrin Highlands 2000 Auburn Drive Ste 200 Beachwood OH 44122 Personal E-mail: mindorohgcom@yahoo.com.

FUGATE-WILCOX, TERY, artist; b. Kalamazoo; Represented in permanent collections Solomon R. Guggenheim Mus., N.Y.C., Australia Nat. Gallery, Canberra, Mus. Modern Art, N.Y.C., Western Mich. U., J. Hood Wright Park, N.Y.C., J. Patrick Lannan Found. Mus., Palm Beach, Fla., Nat. Shopping Ctrs., Harrisburg, Pa., Prudential Ins. Co., Newark, Damson Oil Co., N.Y.C., N.Y.C. Dept. Parks and Recreations, Princess Gloria von Thurn and Taxis, Regensburg, Germany; sculpture located 7th Ave and Waverly, N.Y.C., City Wall, Lafayette, Houston, N.Y.C., Holland Tunnel Entrance, N.Y.C., 40-ft. sculpture Riverside Dr. and Jay Hoodwright Park, N.Y.C., 30-ft. self-watering sculpture The Prudential Gateway 4, Newark. Named laureate Nat. Endowment for Arts. *Actual art includes in its statement the long-suppressed dimension of time, in the context of the naturally occurring changes that are part of the life of any material and make it part of the life of the work of art incorporating that material.*

FUGAZY, WILLIAM DENIS, transportation company executive; Grad., Fordham U., Cornell U., Columbia U. Midshipmen's Sch. Chmn. Fugazy Franchise Internat. Corp., NYC, 1947—. Founder, master-host All-Am. Collegiate Golf Found., chmn. ann. tournament A Day with the All-Ams., Palm Springs, Calif.; founder John V. Mara Meml. Fund for Cancer Rsch. St. Vincent's Hosp., N.Y.C., Cath. Youth Orgn. Summer Camps Program, Silver Shield Found. Scholarship Fund; chmn. Nat. Ethnic Coalition Orgns., N.Y. Yankee Homecoming Dinner, N.Y. Giants Football Luncheon, N.Y. Statue of Liberty Centennial Commn., Ellis Island Medals of Honor Selection Com.; pres. Coalition Italo-Am. Assns.; active Columbus Citizens Com.; apptd. to Westway Commn., Nat. Svcs. Bd. City of N.Y., Mayor's Immigration Coalition, 1997, Westway Commn., Nat Svcs. Bd.; bd. dirs., mem. exec. com. Police Athletic League, Cath. Youth Assn.; bd. instrnl. TV Archdiocese of N.Y.; chmn. The Forum Club, N.Y. State Trooper Found., N.Y. Statue of Liberty Centennial Commn.; named hon. fire commr., N.Y.C.; vice-chmn. U.S. Holocaust Meml. Coun.; hon. chmn. Dr. Martin Luther King Jr. Nat. Holiday Celebration Ambassadorial Reception and Program. Lt. Comdr. USN Seals, WWII. Decorated knight Equestrian Order Holy Sepulchre, Knight of the Grand Cross; recipient Meritorious award Pres. of Italy; co-recipient Congl. Gold Medal of Honor U.S. Congress, Gold medal Armenian Ch. U.S., 1986, Honor medal; named Sportsman of Yr. Cath. Youth Orgn. of Archdiocese N.Y., N.Y. Athletic Club, B'nai B'rith, 1983, Man of Yr. ITV-TV of Archdiocese N.Y., N.Y.C. Police Dept., 1984, Westchester County, 1985, Archbishop of N.Y., 1986, Angel Guardians, 1988, Italian Welfare League, N.Y. Baseball Fedn., St. Jude's Children's Rsch. Hosp., Disting. Citizen of Yr., N.Y. Conf. Italian-Am. Legislators, 1992, New Yorker of Yr. award Bowling Green Assn., 1993; recipient Congl. Ellis Island Medal of Honor, B'nai B'rith Sportsman of Yr. Citizen's award N.Y. State Br. Sons of Italy, 1983, Man of Yr. award Angel Guardians, 1988, Most Outstanding Role Model award Italian Am. Student Assn., 1989, Humanitarian award Coun. for Unity, N.Y. Industry award St. Mary's Hosp. for Children, 1990, Lifeline award Cooley's Anemia Found., 1991, Edward Corsi award LaGuardia Meml. House, 1992, Tree of Life award Jewish Nat. Fund, 1993, Donald C. Platten award We Care About N.Y., 1994, Humanitarian medal of honor Tara Cir., Inc., 1995; honored Italian Am. Club of No. Westchester, 1988, Cerebral Palsy of Westchester, 1988, Grand Lodge of State of N.Y., 1988, Columbian Lawyers Assn. Nassau County, 1989, Columbus Day Soc. of Harrison (Grand Master Parade), 1989, Ancient Order of Hibernians, 1995, Cath. Mus. Am., 1995, Order of Sons of Italy in Am., 1997, Am. Inst. Stress, 1997; others. Mem. Sons of Italy (co-recipient Citizen's award N.Y. State br. 1983), Coalition of Italo-Am. Assn., Golf Coaches Assn. Am. (hon.), The Forum Club (founder). Office: Fugazy International 232 Madison Ave Rm 900 New York NY 10016-2901

FUGETT, ROBERTA LYNN, special education educator; b. Dayton, Ohio, July 18, 1957; d. Ray Walton and Bertha Collinsworth; m. Jerry Winston Fugett, July 31, 1993; children: Sarah Elizabeth, Nathaniel Lee Whitt. BA in Edn., Morehead State U., Ky., 1995, MA in Edn., 2002. Cert. tchr. exceptional children, grades K-12 Ky., 1996, thcr. social studies grades 5-8 Ky., 1996. Spl. edn. resource classroom tchr. Powell County Schs., Clay City, Ky., 1996—97; tchr. spl. edn. Rowan County Schs., Morehead, 1997—2002; lectr. Morehead State U., 2002—07. Tchr. grade 5 Elliott County Schs., Sandy Hook, Ky., 2002—03; mid. sch. collaboration tchr. Clark County Schs., Winchester, 2003—05; online instr. Tchr. Edn. Inst., Winter Park, Fla., 2003—06; tchr. English Menifee County High Sch., Frenchburg, Ky., 2005—06; substitute tchr. Bath County Schs., Owingsville, 2006—07, Morgan County Schs., West Liberty, 2006—07, Wolfe County Schs., Campton, 2006—07. Author: (poetry) Betrayal (Best Poets of Yr., 2006). Brownie troop leader Girl Scouts Wilderness Rd. Coun., Lexington, Ky., 2005—. Recipient Outstanding Undergrad. in Spl. Edn., Morehead State U., 1996. Mem.: Ky. Edn. Assn., Phi Kappa Phi. Christian. Avocations: reading, writing poetry. Personal E-mail: rfugett@mrtc.com.

FUGGI, GRETCHEN MILLER, education educator; b. Westerly, RI, Aug. 26, 1938; d. John Louis and Harriet (Scheid) M.; m. William Joseph Fuggi, Aug. 15, 1960; children: Gretchen, Juliann, John, Kristen. BS, So. Conn. State U., New Haven, 1960, MS, 1969, 6th yr. diploma, 1991, 6th yr. Ednl. Leadership diploma, 1994. Reading cons. Washington Magnet Sch., West Haven, Conn., 1974—; adj. prof. So. Conn. State U., New Haven, 1988—. Pres. Cath. Charity League of Greater New Haven, 1989-90; bd. dirs. New Haven Symphony Aux., 1992—. Named Tchr. of Yr., West Haven Fedn. Tchrs., 1998-99. Mem. AAUP, Internat. Reading Assn., Conn. Reading Assn., Stonington Hist. Soc. of Conn., Delta Kappa Gamma Soc. Internat., Grad. Club New Haven. Roman Catholic. Home: 19 Westview Rd North Haven CT 06473-2013 E-mail: Fuggi@juno.com.

FUGLESANG, CHRISTER, astronaut; b. Stockholm, Mar. 18, 1957; arrived in U.S., 1996; m. Elisabeth Walldie; 3 children. MSc in Engring. Physics, Royal Inst. Tech., Sweden, 1981; PhD in Exptl. Particle Physics, U. Stockholm, 1987; PhD (hon.), Umea U., Sweden, 1999. Fellow European Rsch. Ctr. Particle Physics (CERN), Geneva, 1988—89, sr. fellow, head of particle identification subdetector, 1989—91; with Manne Siegbahn Inst. Physics, Stockholm, 1990—92; with astronaut corp. European Space Agy., Cologne, Germany, 1992—96; mission specialist NASA, Houston, 1996—. Instr. in math. Royal Inst. Tech., 1980—92; with Euromir 95 mission European Space Agy., 1993, crew mem. 2 Euromir 95 mission, 95; crew mem. STS-116 Mission (Discovery), 2006. Achievements include being the first Swedish person in space in 2006. Avocations: sports, sailing, skiing, frisbee, reading. Office: Astronaut Office CB NASA Johnson Space Center Houston TX 77058*

FUHRMAN, SUSAN H., academic administrator, education educator, researcher; BA in history with highest honors, Northwestern U., 1965, MA in history, 1966; PhD in polit. sci. and edn., Columbia U., 1977. Prof. of edn. policy Eagleton Inst. of Polit. at Rutgers U., 1989—95; prof., dept. of pub. policy Edward J. Bloustein Sch. of Planning and Pub. Policy, Rutgers U., 1994—95; dean grad sch. edn. U. Penn, 1995—2006, George & Diane Weiss prof. edn.; pres. Tchrs. Coll., Columbia U., NYC, 2006—. Bd. mem. Carnegie Found. for the Advancement of Tchg.; founder and chmn. Consortium for Policy Rsch. in Edn. (CPRE), 1985—; former co-chair Nat. Adv. Panel for the Third Internat. Math and Sci. Study; bd. dirs. Nat. Coalition on Asia and Internat. Studies in the Schs. Editor: From the Capitol to the Classroom: Standards-Based Reform in the States, One Hundredth Yearbook of the National Society for the Study of Education, 2001, Designing Coherent Education Policy: Improving the System, 1993; co-editor (with Jennifer O'Day): Rewards and Reform: Creating Educational Incentives that Work, 1996; contbr. articles to profl. jours. Achievements include research in standards-based state education reform, state local relationships, state differential treatment of districts, federalism in education, incentives and systemic reform, legislatures and education policy. Office: Tchrs Coll Columbia U 525 W 120th St New York NY 10027 Office Phone: 212-678-3131. E-mail: susanf@itc.edu.

FUHRMANN, CHARLES J., II, financial consultant, educator; b. Seattle, Feb. 21, 1945; s. Carl I. and Darlene (Reynolds) F.; m. Eugenie A. Livanos, June 24, 1967 (div. 1982); children: Katharine Reynolds, Alexandra Livanos; m. Martha M. Harris, Oct. 17, 1987; children: Arianna Taylor, Charles J. III. AB summa cum laude, Harvard Coll., 1967, MBA with honors, 1969. Sr. v.p. White Weld & Co., Inc., NYC, 1969-78; mng. dir. Merrill Lynch Capital Markets, NYC, 1978-91; pres., CEO 50-Off Stores, Inc., 1996-97, Lot$Off Corp., 1997-99. Chmn. bd. dirs. Lot$Off Corp., 1997-99; chmn. Healthy Pl. Co., Inc., 1999—, Texace Ltd., 2001-2003. Vestry, St. James' Episcopal Ch., N.Y.C., 1979-84, treas. 1981-84; bd. trustees San Antonio Mus. Art, 1994-97, San Antonio Mus. Assn., 1993-95, The Witte Mus., 1994—, San Antonio Pub. Libr. Found., 1995-99; bd. dirs. The Sunshine Cottage, 1993-97, Children's Rehab. Ctr., 1996-99, Charity Ball Assn., 2003-05. Mem. River Club (N.Y.C.), Delphic Club (Cambridge, Mass.), Country and Yacht Clubs (Prout's Neck, Maine), San Antonio Country Club, Argyle Club, Majestic Club (chmn. 1994-96), Order of the Alamo. Home: 110 Wyckham Rise San Antonio TX 78209 Office Phone: 210-601-9021. E-mail: cjf2mhf@swbell.net.

FUHRMANN, EMILE FREDERICK, architect; b. Goodbee, La., Aug. 22, 1911; s. Emile Frederick Fuhrmann and Agnes Hilgner; m. Caroline Joan Steele, Nov. 10, 1943; children: Wayne Emil, Carolyn Joan. B in Arch., Tulane U., New Orleans, 1934, M in Arch., 2003, attended courses in Civil Engring., 1933. Registered arch. 1939, lic. La., 1947. Draftsman, checker, inspector Arch. & Engring. Offices, New Orleans, 1934—36; chief draftsman Orleans Parish Levee Bd., Lake Front Development and Lake Vista Subdivision, 1936—37; state arch. supr. Nat. Youth Adminstrn., New Orleans, 1937—39; arch. rep., supr. Landry & Mathis, Arch., Hattiesburg, Miss., 1939—41; work coord., chief estimator Gen. Contracts Defense Projects, La., 1943—44; found. rsch. Substrata Engrs., Whitehall, 1945—46; pvt. practice Metairie, 1946—54; with Stone Brothers Arch. Engrs., New Orleans, 1954—66; pvt. practice La., 1966—68; asst. dir. construction Jefferson Parish Sch. Bd., Gretna, La., 1968—72; arch. assoc. Frank Jackson & Assoc. Cons. Engrs., New Orleans, 1973—82. Assoc. New Orleans Art Assn., 1965; cert. fallout ctr. analyst FEMA, New Orleans, 1967. ARA Affiliate Pelican Rifle Club, New Orleans, 1929—36; vol. Elmeer Fire Co., Metairie, La., 1946. Pvt. US Army, 1941—43, Fla. Recipient Contributing Inmeasurably to Rsch. and Progress of Profession award, Am. Arch. Found., 1955. Fellow: Am. Registered Arch.; mem.: AIA, Guild for Religious Arch., Gargoyle-Honorary Arch. Soc., La. Arch. Assn., Intertel, Am. Mensa, Tau Sigma Delta, Sigma Phi Delta. Avocations: reading, carving. Home: 4 Oaklawn Dr Metairie LA 70005-3408

FUHS, G. WOLFGANG (GEORG WOLFGANG FUHS), environmental research manager; b. Cologne, Germany, May 19, 1932; came to U.S., 1964; s. Friedrich Karl and Lisette I. (Stayen) F.; children: Lisette Fuhs Mallary, H. Georg, Dagmar Ariane Serota. Diploma in biology, D in Nat. Scis., U. Bonn, Germany, 1956; postdoctoral, Tech. U. Delft, The Netherlands, 1956-57. Sci. employee dept. botany U. Frankfurt, Germany, 1957-58; research assoc. dept. hygiene U. Bonn Sch. Medicine, 1958-63; fellow dept. genetics U. Cologne, 1963-64; sr., prin. rsch. scientist divsn. labs. and rsch. N.Y. State Dept. Health, Albany, 1964—72, dir. environ. health labs., 1973—85; chief divsn. labs. Calif. Dept. Health Svcs., Berkeley, 1985—89; rsch. scientist Calif./EPA Dept. Toxic Substances Control Lab., 1989—93, mgr. technology evaluation, 1993—2000; ret., 2000. Vis. prof. U. Wis., Milw., 1973; rsch. assoc. U. Minn. Sch. Pub. Health, Mpls., 1970-74; adj. prof. dept. biology SUNY, Albany, 1984-86; mem. expert. com. on human health effects of Great Lakes water quality U.S./Can. Internat. Joint Commn., 1978-88; tech. adv. com. San Francisco Estuary Project, 1987-92; mem. Calif. Environ. Technol. Partnership, Calif. Comparative Risk Project, 1993-94. Contbr. articles to profl. jours. (Inst. Sci. Info. award 1969); mem. editorial bd. Jour. Phycology, 1972-74, Limnology and Oceanography, 1973-76, Microbial Ecology, 1974-89. Mem. AAAS, Am. Soc. Microbiol. (past chmn. Eastern N.Y. br.), Internat. Assn. Theoretical Applied Limnology. Home: 1021 Columbia Pl Davis CA 95616-2315

FUITEN, HELEN LORRAINE, small business owner; b. Grafton, ND, Nov. 13, 1923; d. Yat Wong and Anna Marie Schmitt; m. Robert Lester Fuiten, Mar. 15, 1947 (dec. Oct. 31, 2002); 1 child, Roderick L. Student, OReg. State Coll., Corvallis, 1943. Artist Photo Art Comml. Studios, Portland, Oreg., 1940—46; sec., bookkeeper Reo Oreg. Sales, Portland, 1942—43; draftsman engring. dept. Oreg. Ship Yard, Portland, 1943—46; pers. sec. St. Vincent Hosp., Portland, 1946—47; owner, ptnr. Forest Grove Plumbing, Oreg., 1948—50, Fuiten's Plumbing and Heating Co., Forest Grove, 1952—97, Fuiten Mech. Inc., Forest Grove, 1997—. Ptnr., owner R H & R Properties, Forest Grove, 1954—; owner, mgr. ladies' retail clothing store, Forest Grove, 1981—93. Office: Fuiten Mech Inc 1832 Pacific Ave Forest Grove OR 97116

FUJIMARA, MAKOTA, painter; b. Boston, 1960; BA cum laude, Bucknell U., 1983; MFA, Toyko Nat. U. of Fine Arts and Music, 1989. Mem. Nat. Coun. on Arts, Nat. Endowment for Arts, 2003—. Exhibitions include Contemporary Nihonga Exhbit, Comtemporary Mus. Toyko, 1998, One Hundred Years of Nihonga, Toyko Nat. Univ of Fine Arts and Music Mus., 2000, Like a Prayer, Tryon Ctr. Visual Arts, 2003, Considering Peace, Sato Mus., 2003, one-man shows include Gravity and Grace, Bellas Artes, 2002, Columbines, Gallery at Matsuya Ginza, 2002, Four Quartets, Kristen Frederickson Contemporary, 2003, Golden Pines, Dillon Gallery, 2003, The Still Point, Takashimaya Gallery, 2003—04, exhibited in group shows at Art as Prayer, Cooper Union Gallery, 2001, TriBeCa Temporary Exhibits, 2001, WATERwalks, Ise Cultural Found., 2002, The Return of Beauty, Kristen Frederickson Gallery, 2002, The WRONG Exhbit, Birmingham, England, 2003, Represented in permanent collections Contemporary Mus. Tokyo, Nerima Mus. Art, Oxford House, Sato Mus., St. Louis Art Mus., Tamaya Collection, Toyko Nat. U. of Fine Arts and Music, Yamaguchi Prefecture Mus. Office: Nat Endowment for Arts 1100 Pennsylvania Ave, NW Washington DC 20506 Office Phone: 202-682-5400. E-mail: fujimura@jamny.org.

FUJIMOTO, JAMES G., electrical engineering educator; b. Chgo., Sept. 28, 1957; s. Harold H. and Jane S. (Sakoda) F.; m. Carla Helen Millhauser. BSEE, MIT, 1979, MSEE, 1981, PhD, 1984. Rsch. scientist MIT, Cambridge, 1984—85, asst. prof. elec. engring., 1985-88, assoc. prof., 1988-94, prof., 1994—. Vis. lectr. Harvard Med. Sch., Boston, 1987-91; cons. MIT Lincoln Lab., Lexington, Mass., 1985-96; adj. prof. ophthalmology Tufts U., 1994-; principle investigator MIT Rsch. Lab. Electronics. Contbr. articles sci. jours. Recipient Presdl. Young Investigator award NSF, 1986, AT&T New Research Fund Award, 1987, William Baker award NAS, 1990, Award for Initiatives in Rsch., NAS, 1990, traveling lectr. award Lasers and Electro-Optics Soc., 1990, Discover Mag. award for Tech. Innovation, 1999, Rank prize in optoelectronics, 2001. Fellow IEEE, NAE, AAAS; mem. Optical Soc. Am., Am. Phys. Soc., NAS Office: MIT Rm 36-361 77 Mass Ave Cambridge MA 02139

FUJINAMI, ROBERT SHIN, neurology educator; b. Salt Lake City, Dec. 8, 1949; BA, U. Utah, 1972; PhD, Northwestern U., Chgo., 1977. Instr. microbiology and immunology Northwestern U., Chgo., 1973-76; rsch. fellow immunopathology Scripps Clinic and Rsch. Found., La Jolla, Calif., 1977-80, rsch. assoc. immunopathology, 1980-81, asst. mem., asst. prof. dept. immunology, 1981-85, vis. investigator dept. immunology, 1985-89; vis. investigator dept. neuropharmacology divsn. virology Scripps Rsch. Inst. (formerly Scripps Clinic and Rsch. Found.), La Jolla, 1989-90; rsch. immunopathologist dept. pathology U. Calif., San Diego, 1980-82, assoc. prof. pathology, 1985-90; prof. neurology U. Utah, Salt Lake City, 1990—, adj. prof. dept. pathology divsn. cell biology and immunology, 1991—. Mem. Weber immunology adv. com., dept. pathology U. Utah, Salt Lake City, 1991—, mem. neurosci. steering com., 1992-96, mem. biosafety com., 1992-96, chmn., 1994-96, chmn. safety com., dept. neurology, 1993—, chmn. promotion, retention and tenure com., 1993-96, mem. univ. promotions and tenure adv. com., 1995-98, chair oversight com. Fluorescence Activated Cell Sorter (FACS) Sch. Medicine, 1996-99, mem. univ. rsch. com., 1999—2004, disting. rsch. award subcom., 1999—2001, senate task force on RPT procedures, 1999—2000, adv. com. core facilities Huntsman Cancer Inst., 1999—2000, dir. grad. studies pathology PhD program, 1999—2002, chmn. tenured faculty rev. com., dept. neurology, 1999—2000. Contbr. chpts. to books, 160 articles to profl. jours. Recipient New Investigator award NIH, 1981-83; NIH scholar, 1989-96. Fellow AAAS; mem. Nat. Multiple Sclerosis Soc. (bd. dirs. Utah chpt. 1992-99—, Hary M. Weaver Neurosci. award 1982-86). Office: U Utah Dept Neurology 30 N 1900 E 3R330 SOM Salt Lake City UT 84132-0001 Home Phone: 801-582-8002; Office Phone: 801-585-3305. Business E-Mail: Robert.Fujimami@hsc.utah.edu.

FUJINO, MICHIMASA, aeronautical engineer; s. Michio and Kuniko Fujino; m. Yukiko Fujino, July 14, 1986. BS, Tokyo U., 1984. Chief engr. Honda R&D Americas, Inc., Greensboro, NC, 1995—98, chief project engr., 1998—2005, v.p., 2005—. Mem.: AIAA. Achievements include leading the design and development of the HondaJet, which is the world's most fuel-efficient business jet. Office: Honda R&D Americas Inc 6423B Bryan Blvd Greensboro NC 27409 Home Phone: 336-558-6710; Office Phone: 336-662-0849. Office Fax: 336-662-0852. Business E-Mail: mfujino@oh.hra.com.

FUJIOKA, JO ANN OTA, educational association administrator, consultant; b. Bellflower, Calif., Apr. 30, 1939; d. Richard Masayoshi and Lillian Chiyono (Ihara) Ota; m. Arthur Fujioka, Feb. 19, 1961; 1 child, Dana Kay. BSN, U. Colo., 1961, MSN, 1970; PhD, Colo. State U., 1987. RN; cert. adminstr., supt., spl. edn. dir., sch. nurse, vocat. edn. adminstr., instr. Nurse pub. health, psychiat. Denver Gen. Hosp., Denver Vis. Nurse Svc., 1961—71; sch. nurse Jefferson County Sch. Dist., Golden, Colo., 1971—76, mgr. prog., supr. sch. health prog., 1976-79, mgr. spl. edn. and related svcs., adminstr. elem. bldg., 1979—95; cons. Fujioka Cons., Denver, 1995—. Cons. Ctrl. Kans. Bd. Coop. Ednl. Svcs., Salina, 1992, Denver Children's Home, 1996, Colo. Assn. Family and Children's Agencies, 1997, Colo. Mediation Project, 1998. Contbr. articles to profl. jours. Vice chmn. bd. dirs. Creative Exch., 1997—99, chmn. bd. dirs., 1999—2001, mem. adv. bd., 2002—03; mem. edn. adv. com. PBS, 2001—; mem. Cross Cultural Dialogue, 2001—; hon. bd. dirs. Colo. Women's Hall of Fame, 2002—. Mem.: AAUW, NOW, Jefferson County Adminstrs. Assn., Colo. Sch. Health Coun. (pres. 1978—80), U. Colo. Health Scis. Ctr. Srs. Assn. (chpt. pres. 1992—94, Internat. Dist. IV project grant dir. 1993, fall conf. chair 1993—2005, Internat. Dist. IV project grant dir. 1999, internat. coord. for ethical leadership project 2000—, bd. dirs. 2000—), Am. Assn. Sch. Execs., Alliance Profl. Cons. (exec. bd.), Japanese Am. Nat. Mus., Phi Delta Kappa (Jefferson County) (internat. del. 1993, area coord. 1996—2001, internat. v.p. bd. dirs. 2001—03, dist. IV project grant dir. 2003, internat. pres. elect 2003—05, internat. pres. 2005—, internat. centennial com. 2005—, chair Dave Sanders Meml Scholarship com. 2001—, Douglas County Chpt. award 1999, Denver U. Chpt. Svc. award 1999, Jefferson County Chpt. Svc. award 2001, Jefferson County Chpt. Leadership award 2003, George H. Reavis Assoc. 2003, dist. IV project grant dir. 2003, mem. centennial com. 2005—). Democrat. Buddhist. Avocations: crossword puzzles, jigsaw puzzles, crocheting, tai chi, reading. Home and Office: 540 S Forest St #K Denver CO 80246-8164 Home Phone: 303-333-1258; Office Phone: 303-377-6641. E-mail: fujicons@aol.com.*

FUJITA, JAMES HIROSHI, history educator; b. Honolulu, July 24, 1958; s. George Hideo and Teruko (Miyano) F. BA, U. Hawaii, 1980, MA, 1983. Grad. asst. U. Hawaii at Manoa, Honolulu, 1980-85, lectr. history, 1986—97, Kapiolani C.C., Honolulu, 1987-97; adj. staff Hawaii Pacific U., Honolulu, 1998—. Lectr. Elderhostel Program, Honolulu, 1992; instr. Leeward C.C., 1997—; adj. staff Chaminade U., Honolulu, 1998—. Recipient Outstanding Lectr. award, Leeward CC, 2000. Mem. NEA, World History Assn., U. Hawaii Profl. Assembly, Phi Alpha Theta. Office: Leeward Cmty Coll Arts and Humanities 96-045 Ala Ike Pearl City HI 96782-3393 Business E-Mail: fujitaja@hawaii.edu.

FUJIWARA, HIDEJI, chemist, researcher; b. Tamano, Okayama, Japan, Nov. 19, 1943; s. Motoyoshi and Sumiko Fujiwara; m. Mieko Ogawa, Apr. 29, 1978; children: Kenichiro, Mikiko Kay. BS, Sci. U. Tokyo, 1967; MS, Stevens Inst. Tech., 1969, PhD, 1974. Postdoctoral fellow Stevens Inst. Tech., 1974-75, rsch. scientist, 1975-77; rschr. Exxon br. Tao Nenryo Kogyo KK, Saitam, Japan, 1962-67; sr. rsch. chemist (specialist) Monsanto Co., St. Louis, 1977-87, assoc., full sci. fellow, 1987-2000; sci. fellow Pharmacia Co., Chesterfield, Mo., 2000—. Contbr. articles to sci. jours., includinfg Jour. Agrl. Food Chemistry, Chem. and Engring. News. Trustee Bethany Bapt. Ch., 1990—. Schering postdoctoral fellow Stevens Inst. Tech., 1975-76. Em. Am. Chem. Soc., Am. Soc. for Mass Spectrometry, N.Y. Acad. Scis., St. Louis Japan Soc., Toastmasters (treas. Life Scis. chpt. 1999-2000), Sigma Xi. Office: Pharmacia Co 700 Chesterfield Pky Chesterfield MO 63017 Fax: 636-737-7099. E-mail: hideji.fujiwara@pharmacia.com.

FUKATA, MASAYUKI, gastroenterologist, hematologist; b. Kawagoeshi, Saitamaken, Japan, Jan. 23, 1969; s. Hiroji and Kyoko Fukata; m. Yuko Mitsuboshi, Oct. 23; children: Yuki, Mai, Masahiro. BS, Jikei Pre-Med. Sch., Tokyo, 1987; MD, Jikei U. Sch. Medicine, Tokyo, 1994, PhD, 2003. Cert. internal medicine specialist Japanese Soc. Internal Medicine, 1997. Intern, resident in internal medicine Jikei U. Hosp., Nishishinbashi, Tokyo, 1994—96; gastroenterology fellow Jikei U. Daisan Hosp., Komae, Tokyo, 1996—98; clin. instr. divsn. gastroenterology and hepatology Jikei U. Hosp., 1998—2003; post doctoral fellow Cedars-Sinai Med. Ctr., LA, 2003—04, Mt. Sinai Sch. Medicine, NYC, 2003—06, asst. prof. medicine divsn. gastoenterology, 2007—. Contbr. articles to profl. jours., chapters to books. Recipient Young Investigator award, Japan Soc. Histochemistry and Cytochemistry, 2002, Career Devel. award, Crohn's and Colitis Found. Am., 2006; Rsch. grant, Japanese Ednl. Ministry, 2003, Astrazeneca, 2003, Rsch. fellow, Uehara Meml. Found., 2005. Avocations: camping, fishing, music, movies, travel. Office: Mount Sinai Sch Medicine One Gustave L Levy PO Box1069 New York NY 10029 Home Phone: 203-661-7110; Office Phone: 212-659-8363.

FUKATSU, TANEFUSA, retired classicist, educator; b. Toyota, Aichi, Japan, Apr. 23, 1923; s. Kingo and Shizu (Noba) F.; m. Michiko Kato, Jan. 17, 1954 (dec. 1981); children: Tomonao, Arikata. BA, Tokyo U., 1951. Tchr. Chinese classics Musashi High Sch., Tokyo, 1957-89; asst. prof. Chinese classics Musashi U., Tokyo, 1971-74, prof. Chinese classics, 1974-85; retired, 1989—. Lectr. Chinese classics Nisho-Gakusha U., Tokyo, 1967-93, guest prof., 1993—. Author: Juzi Tongbian Jingdianshiwen, 1978, Lunyu Xidu, 1990, Laozi Xidu, 1994, Thought and Life of the Ancient Chinese-Mirror-, 1996, Japanese Culture and Chinese Culture-White Chrysanthemum and Yellow Chrysanthemum, 1997, Studies on the Latent Thought in Chinese Characters and Poetry, 1997, Chinese Thought and Culture, 1998, Studies of the Book of Laozi, 1999, Thought and Life of the Ancient Chinese-Cock-, 1999, Thought and Life of the Ancient Chinese—The Source and Course of the Thought of "The Book of Laozi", 2000. Mem. Nippon-Chugoku-Gakkai, Shibunkai (dir. 1990-93, councilor 1993—). Home: 86-1-501 Konya-Cho Saiwai-Ku Kawasaki-Shi Kanagawa 212-0026 Japan

FUKE, DAWN C., clinical pharmacy specialist; d. Milton Y and Karen S Fuke; m. Robert B Passmore, Apr. 19, 2003. BS in Pharmacy, Oreg. State U., Corvallis, 1999; PharmD, Oreg. State U./Oreg. Health and Sci. U., Portland, 2001. Cert. pharmacotherapy specialist Bd. of Pharm. Specialties, 2004. Long term care staff pharmacist NCS Healthcare, Portland, 1999—2000; inpatient staff pharmacist Providence St. Vincent Med. Ctr., Portland, 2000—02; primary care pharmacy splty. resident Providence Med. Group, Portland, 2001—02, clin. pharmacy specialist in primary care, 2002—. Lectr. in field. Contbr. articles to profl. jours. Mem.: Rho Chi, Am. Soc. of Health Systems Pharmacists, Am. Coll. of Clin. Pharmacy, Oreg. Soc. of Health Systems Pharmacists (no. chpt. chair 2003—05, Bd. of Directors Award 2004, 2005). Office Phone: 503-513-2142.

FUKUDA, ATSUO, physicist, materials science researcher, educator; b. Tokyo, Feb. 5, 1937; s. Katsuyuki and Kimiko (Maekawa) F.; m. Kyoko Omachi, Mar. 30, 1965; children: Mitsuhiro, Mitsunori. BSc, Tokyo Kyoiku U., 1960, MSc, 1962, DSc, 1965. Rsch. asst. U. Tokyo Inst. for Solid State Physics, Tokyo, 1965-69; vis. scientist Argonne Nat. Lab. Solid State Sci. Divsn., Argonne, Ill., 1969-71, U. Stuttgart II Physikalisches Inst., Germany, 1971-72; assoc. prof. Nagasaki U. Faculty Liberal Arts, Japan, 1973-75, Tokyo Inst. Tech. Faculty of Engring., 1975—85, prof., 1985—97, emeritus prof., 1997—; prof. faculty textile sci. and tech. Shinshu U., 1997—2002; prof. Trinity Coll. U. Dublin, 2002—04; vis. prof. Trinity Coll. U Dublin; prof. Tokyo Denki U., 2004—07. Pub. mgr. Japanese Jour. Applied Physics, Tokyo, 1987-89; dir. Ctr. for Rsch. Coop. and Info. Exch., Tokyo Inst. Tech., 1992-94. Co-author: (with Hideo Takezoe) Structure and Properties of Ferroelectric Liquid Crystals, 1990; editor, author: Future Liquid Crystal Display and Its Materials--Ferroelectric and Antiferroelectric Liquid Crystals, 1992; guest editor (with others) Conf. Procs. Ferroelectrics, 1993. Recipient Outstanding Paper award 9th Internat. Display Rsch. Conf., Kyoto, 1989, spl. recognition award Soc. Info. Display, 1997. Mem. Japan Soc. Applied Physics (mng. dir. 1985-87, A award Tokyo br. 1990), Phys. Soc. Japan, Internat. Liquid Crystal Soc. (hon. 2002-, pres. 1996-2000, mem. non-exec. bd. 1990-94). Avocation: hiking. Personal E-mail: afukuda@seagreen.ocn.ne.jp.

FUKUDA, KEIJI, epidemiologist; b. Japan, Aug. 22, 1955; BA, Oberlin Coll., Ohio; MD, U. Vermont Coll. Medicine, Burlington, 1984; MPH in Epidemiology, U. Calif. Berkeley, 1989. Resident, internal medicine Mt. Zion Hosp., San Francisco, 1984—87, chief resident, internal medicine, 1987—88; clin. instructor U. Calif., San Francisco, 1989—90; with Nat. Ctr. Infectious Disease, Divsn. Viral Rickettsial Disease, 1990; clin. asst. prof., dept. cmty. and preventive medicine Emory U. Sch. Medicine, Atlanta, 1993; joined as epidemic intelligence officer Ctr. for Disease Control and Prevention, 1990, epidemiology sect. chief, influenza branch, 1996; global influenza program coord., dept. epidemic and pandemic alert and response WHO. Vis. prof., dept. pub. health Osaka City U. Contbr. to numerous published research studies, book chapters and reviews on infectious diseases. Comdr. US Pub. Health Svc., Commd. Corps. Mem.: Commn. Corps Officers Assn., Am. Coll. Physicians. Achievements include being responsible for national influenza surveillance in the US; and led the CDC field teams that investigated the outbreak of avian influenza A (H5N1) in 1997 and influenza A (H9N2) in 1999 cases in Hong Kong; worked in China and Hong Kong in 2003 on SARS; worked in Vietnam in 2004 to assist the WHO efforts to investigate and control H5N1.

FUKUDA, NOBUO, chef; b. Tokyo, 1959; With Yamakasa, Phoenix; sushi chef Hapa, Scottsdale, Ariz.; co-owner, chef Sea Saw, Scottsdale, Ariz. Named Best New Chef, Food & Wine Mag., 2003, Best Chef: Southwest, James Beard Found., 2007. Office: Sea Saw 7133 E Stetson Dr Scottsdale AZ 85251 Office Phone: 480-481-9463. Office Fax: 480-946-3055.*

FUKUI, HATSUAKI, retired electrical engineer, art historian; b. Yokohama, Japan, Dec. 14, 1927; came to U.S., 1962, naturalized, 1973; s. Ushinosuke and Yoshi (Saito) F.; m. Atsuko Inamoto, Apr. 1, 1954 (dec. 1973); children: Mayumi, Naoki; m. Kiku Kato, Dec. 12, 1975. Diploma, Miyakojima Tech. Coll. (now Osaka City U.), 1949; BS, Sci. U. Tokyo; D.Eng., Osaka U., 1961. Rsch. assoc. Osaka City U., 1949-54; engr. Shimada Phys. and Chem. Indsl. Co., Tokyo, 1954-55; sr. engr. to mgr. semi-condr. divsn. Sony Corp. (formerly Tokyo Tsushin Kogyo KK), Tokyo, 1955-61; mgr. engring. div. Sony Corp., 1961-62; mem. tech. staff Bell Telephone Labs., Murray Hill, NJ, 1962-69, supr., 1969-73; v.p. Sony Corp. Am., NYC, 1973; asst. to chmn. Sony Corp., Tokyo, 1973; staff mem. Bell Labs., Murray Hill, NJ, 1973-81, supr., 1981-83, Lucent Techs. (formerly AT&T Bell Labs.), 1984-89. Lectr. Tokyo Met. U. (part-time), 1962 Author: Esaki Diodes, 1963, Solid-State FM Receivers, 1968; contbr. to: Semiconductors Handbook, 1963, GaAs FET Principles and Technologies, 1982; editor: Low-Noise Microwave Transistors and Amplifiers, 1981; contbr. articles to profl. jours.; patentee in field. Fellow IEEE (life; standardization com. 1976-82, edit. bd. IEEE Transactions on Microwave Theory and Techniques 1980-90, com. on U.S. competitiveness 1988-90); mem. Inst. Electronics, Info. and Comm. Engrs. Japan (Inada award 1959), IEEE Comms. Soc., IEEE Electron Devices Soc., IEEE Lasers and Electro-Optics Soc., IEEE Microwave Theory and Techniques Soc. (Microwave prize 1980, Pioneer award 1990), Electromagnetics Acad., Japan Soc. Applied Physics, Inst. TV Engrs. Japan (tech. steering com. 1973-74), Medieval Acad. Am., Assn. Art History, Am. Assn. Museums, Gakushikai, Internat. House Japan. Home: 53 Drum Hill Dr Summit NJ 07901-3141 also: 1-21-16-802 Nakane Meguro Tokyo 152-0031 Japan Personal E-mail: hfukui@ieee.org, hf07901@aol.com.

FUKUI, YOSHIO, biology professor; b. Shinagawa, Tokyo, Japan, Jan. 4, 1942; came to U.S., 1985; s. Shizuo and Momoko Fukui; m. Yumiko Fukui, Mar. 12, 1978; children: Ibuki, Maya. BA, Internat. Christian U., 1966; MS, Osaka U., Japan, 1969, PhD, 1972. Rsch. assoc. prof. Osaka U., 1972-74, asst. prof., 1974-77; rsch. assoc. Princeton (N.J.) U., 1977-78; assoc. prof. Osaka U., 1978-85; vis. assoc. prof. Northwestern U., Chgo., 1985-89, assoc. prof. cell, molecular, structural biology (tenured), 1989—, courtesy prof. mech. engr. Evanston, 2005. Prof. cell molecular biology, Yamada exch. scientist Yamada Sci. Found., Osaka, 1978; Yoshida exch. visitor Yoshida Chem. Found., Tokyo, 1983; nat. rsch. coun. assoc. in mech. engring., 2007. Contbr. articles to profl. jours. including Nature, Proc. Nat. Acad. Sci. Jour. Cell Biology, Internat. Rev. Cytology, others. Recipient Matsunaga Rsch. award Matsunaga Meml. Found., Tokyo, 1976; rsch. grantee NIH, 1988—. Mem. Cooperation of Marine Biol. Lab. (Woods Hole, Mass.), Am. Soc. for Cell Biology, Soc. Advancement of Sci., N.Y. Acad. Scis. (elected), Japan Soc. for Cell Biologist (Tokyo). Office: Northwestern Med Sch 303 E Chicago Ave Chicago IL 60611-3008 Business E-Mail: y-fukui@northwestern.edu.

FUKUMOTO, LESLIE SATSUKI, lawyer; b. LA, Mar. 10, 1955; parents: Robert Fukumoto and Florence Teruko Kodama Kuroda. BA, U. Hawaii, 1977; JD, William S. Richard Sch. Law, 1980. Bar: Hawaii 1980, U.S. Dist. Ct. Hawaii 1980, U.S. Ct. Appeals (9th cir.) 1981. Dep. pub. defender State of Hawaii, Honolulu, 1980-81; assoc. Pyun, Kim & Okimoto, 1981-83; ptnr. Pyun, Okimoto & Fukumoto, 1983-84; sole practice, 1984-85; ptnr. Fukumoto & Wong, 1985-93, Tanaka & Fukumoto, 1993-94; prin. Fukumoto Law Corp., 1994—. Bd. dirs. Ichiyo Enterprises, Inc., Honolulu, Trans-Asia Corp., T&Y Kodama, Ltd. Assoc. editor U. Hawaii Law Rev., 1979-80. Mem. ATLA, Honolulu Club. Office: 841 Bishop St Ste 1711 Honolulu HI 96813-3924 Office Phone: 808-537-4541. E-mail: fukulaw@mail.com.

FUKUSHIMA, KATSUYA, chef; Studied Math. and Art, U. Md.; attended, L'Academie de Cuisine. Chef Jaleo, Kaz Sushi Bistro, Cashion's Eat Place, Verbena, NYC, el Bulli, Roses, Spain; head chef Café Atlantico, Washington, 2002—. Featured in Washington Post, Washingtonian, Wine Spectator, Food Arts, Fretz Kitchen, Meet the Chef series, Smithsonian Resident Associates. Named one of Washington DC's Rising Stars, StarChefs.com, 2006. Office: Cafe Atlantico 405 8th St NW Washington DC 20004 Office Phone: 202-393-0812. Office Fax: 202-393-0555.*

FUKUSHIMA, KIYOHIKO, economist; b. Nishinomiya, Hyogoken, Japan, Dec. 6, 1944; s. Tohta and Yasuko Fukushima; m. Chizuko Yamauchi, Nov. 2, 1970; children: Izumi, Nobuhiko. BA in Econs., Hitotsubashi U., Tokyo, 1967, MA, 1969. Econ. corr. Mainichi Shinbun, Tokyo, 1969-77; sr. economist Nomura Rsch. Inst., Tokyo, 1978-80; guest scholar Brookings Instn., Washington, 1980-81; sr. economist Nomura Rsch. Inst., NYC, 1981-83, gen. mgr. Washington, 1983-86, dep. dir. econ. rsch. Tokyo, 1986-89, dir. policy rsch. dept., 1989-92, gen. mgr., sr. economist, 1992-94, chief economist, 1996—, chief economist Tokyo hdqrs., 2002—04; pres. Nomura Rsch. Inst. Europe, Ltd., 1999—2002; profl. lectr. sch. advanced internat. studies Johns Hopkins U., Washington, 1994-96; prof. econ. policy Rikkyo U., Tokyo, 2005—. Vis. fellow Princeton (NJ) U., 1976—77. Author: Regionalism and Foreign Direct Investment, 1993, The Age of the Pacific, 1994. Recipient Takahashi Kamekichi award Toyo Keizai Pubs., Inc., 1984, Okita Saburo award Econ. Planning Agy., 1995. Mem. Inst. Internat. Strategic Studies (Japan com. 1992—), Policy Rsch. Com. Avocations: athletics, jogging, movies. Home: 5 20 Higashi 4 Chome Kunitachi shi Tokyo 186-0002 Japan

FULCHINO, STEPHEN A., State Librarian; State libr. Mass. State Libr., Boston. Treas. Playwrights' Platform, Boston. Mem.: Boston Libr. Consortium (mem. bd. dirs.). Office: George Fingold Library State House Rm 341 24 Beacon St Boston MA 02133 Office Phone: 617-727-2592. Office Fax: 617-727-9730. Business E-Mail: Library.Director@state.ma.us.*

FULCO, ARMAND JOHN, biochemist; b. LA, Apr. 3, 1932; s. Herman J. and Clelia Marie (DeFeo) F.; m. Virginia Loy Hungerford, June 18, 1955 (div. July 1985); children: William James (dec.), Lisa Marie, Linda Susan, Suzanne Yvonne; m. Doris V.N. Goodman, Nov. 29, 1987. BS in Chemistry, UCLA, 1957, PhD in Physiol. Chemistry, 1960. NIH postdoctoral fellow Lipid Labs. UCLA, 1960—61; NIH rsch. fellow dept. chemistry Harvard U., Cambridge, Mass., 1961—63; biochemist, prin. investigator Lab. Nuc. Medicine and Radiation Biology, UCLA, 1963—80; asst. prof. dept. biol. chemistry David Geffen Sch. Medicine, UCLA, 1965—70, assoc. prof., 1970—76, prof., 1976—2003, prof. emeritus recalled, 2003, prin. investigator lab. biomed. and environ. scis., 1981—93; prin. investigator lab. structural biology/molecular med. UCLA-Dept. of Energy, 1993—95. Cons. biochemist VA, Los Angeles, 1968-79; mem. UCLA Molecular Biology Inst., 1991—; co-dir. Lipid-Hormone Core Lab., UCLA, 1989-96; mem. Jonsson Comprehensive Cancer Ctr. UCLA, 1994—. Author: (with J.F. Mead) The Unsaturated and Polyunsaturated Fatty Acids in Health and Disease, 1976; contbr. chpts. in books, articles to sci. jours. Served with US Army, 1952-54. Mem. AAAS, Am. Chem. Soc., Am. Soc. Biol. Chemistry and Molecular Biology, Am. Soc. Microbiology, Internat. Soc. for Study of Xenobiotics, Harvard Chemists Assn., Sigma Xi. Office: UCLA David Geffen Sch Medicine Dept Biol Chemistry PO Box 951737 Los Angeles CA 90095-1737 Office Phone: 310-825-8750. Office Fax: 310-206-5272. Business E-Mail: fulco@mednet.ucla.edu.

FULD, RICHARD SEVERIN, JR., (DICK FULD), investment banking executive; b. NYC, Apr. 26, 1946; s. Richard Severin and Elizabeth (Schwab) Fuld; m. Kathleen Ann Bailey, Sept. 24, 1978; children: Jacqueline, Christine, Richard S. III. BA, U. Colo., 1969; MBA, NYU Stern Sch. Bus., 1973. Joined Lehman Bros., NYC, 1969, mng. dir., 1969-84; vice chmn. Shearson Lehman (merger Shearson and Lehman Bros.), NYC, 1984-90; pres., co-CEO Shearson Lehman Bros. Inc., NYC, 1990—93; pres., COO Lehman Bros. Holdings, Inc., NYC, 1993—94, CEO, 1993—, chmn., 1994—. Mem. PSA Govt. and Fed. Agy. Securities Com.; dir. Fed. Res. Bank NY; mem. exec. com. Partnership for NYC. Trustee Mt. Sinai Med. Ctr., NYC, Middlebury Coll.; former chmn. Mt. Sinai Children's Ctr. Found., mem. exec. com.; bd. dirs. Ronald McDonald House Named one of Top 200 Collectors, ARTnews, 2006, 400 Richest Ams., Forbes mag., 2006. Mem.: Bus. Coun., Bus. Roundtable. Avocations: squash, photography, collects works on paper, especially postwar and contemporary. Office: Lehman Brothers Holdings Inc 745 Seventh Ave New York NY 10019*

FULDA, MICHAEL, political scientist, educator, space policy researcher; b. Liverpool, Eng., Apr. 21, 1939; came to U.S., 1962, naturalized, 1966; s. Boris and Catherine (Von Dehn) F.; m. Rosa Bongiorno, July 19, 1970; children: Robert, George. Student, Polytechnique, Grenoble, France, 1956-57, Tech. U., West Berlin, Germany, 1957-58, Karl Eberhardt U., Tubingen, Germany, 1963-66; MA, Am. U., 1968, PhD in Internat. Studies, 1970. Ballroom dance coor., 2001—; prof. polit. sci. Fairmont State U., W.Va., 1971—. Vis. prof. Bauman Moscow State Tech. U., 2002; internat. rels. specialist NASA, Washington, 1979. Author: Oil and International Relations, 1979; (with others) United States Space Policy, 1985; contbr. articles to profl. jours. Bd. dirs. Fairmont Chamber Music Soc., 1983—; W.Va. state com. chmn., dir. space policy Nat. Unity Campaign for John Anderson, 1980; mem. nat. adv. com. John Glenn Presdl. Com., 1984, space policy group Dukakis/Bentsen Com., 1988; dist. advancement com. Boy Scouts Am.; active psychol. ops. Vets. Assn. With U.S. Army, 1962-66. Fellow NASA Marshall Ctr., Huntsville, Ala., 1977, Langley Ctr., Hampton, Va., 1976, Woodrow Wilson Found., 1969-70; grantee Humanities Found. W.Va., 1978-80, NASA W.Va. Space Grant Consortium, 1991-2004; named del. to Aerospace States Assn. by Gov. of W.Va., 2001 Fellow AIAA (assoc.), Brit. Interplanetary Soc.; mem. Nat. Space Soc. (dir. 1991-93, 2002-04), German Assn. for Luft and Raumfamrt, Soc. Espacial Mexicana, Nat. Space Club, Assn. Argentina Tech. Space, Inst. for Social Sci. Study of Space (pres. 1988—), Fairmont Elks Lodge (edn. com.). Avocations: physical fitness, weightlifting, tango, ballroom dancing. Home: 503 Vista Oaks Dr Fairmont WV 26554 Office Phone: 304-367-4674. Business E-Mail: mfulda@fairmontstate.edu.

FULFER, MATRONA PENNY, retired school librarian, educator, columnist; b. Freeport, Ill., Aug. 9, 1944; m. Darrell Ascher Fulfer, Nov. 14, 1965; children: Shane, Athena, Mahrya. BS in Edn., Ill. State U., 1965. Libr. Lena-Winslow HS, Ill., 1965—67, Bemidji State U., Minn., 1967—70, New Glarus HS, Wis., 1970—73; elem. libr. Durand Elem., Ill., 1990—2004, 6th grade tchr., 2004—05, 5th grade tchr., 2005—06. Advisor Young Authors, Durand, Ill., 1990—, Acad. Bowl, Durand, Ill., 1995—2001. Columnist: weekly newspaper, 1980—. Mem. Ladies of the Philoptochos Greek Orthodox Ch., Rockford, Ill. Avocations: reading, writing, gardening. Home: 10215 Walnut Grove Rd Davis IL 61019

FULGONI, GIAN MARC, Internet company executive; b. Crickhowell, Brecon, England, Jan. 24, 1948; came to U.S., 1970; s. Romeo and Maria F. BSc in Physics (with honors), Manchester U., 1969; MA in Mktg., Lancaster U., 1970. Exec. v.p. Mgmt. Sci. Assocs., Inc., Pitts., 1970-81; pres. Info. Resources, Inc., Chgo., 1981-89, CEO, 1986-98, vice chmn., 1989-90, chmn., 1991-95, bd. dirs.; chmn., co-founder comScore Networks, Inc., Reston, Va., 1999—. Bd. dirs. Platinum Tech., Inc. Mem. Young Pres. Orgn. Named Ill. Entrepreneur of the Yr.; recipient Wall Street Transcript award. Mem. Am. Mktg. Assn. Avocations: scuba diving; jogging; skiing. Office: comScore Networks Inc 11465 Sunset Hills Rd Ste 200 Reston VA 20190 Office Phone: 203-438-2000. Office Fax: 203-438-2051.*

FULKER, EDMUND NORMAN, management consultant; b. Pittsfield, Mass., June 14, 1927; s. Herbert Ernest Creal Fulker and Albina Archambault; m. Jeanette Ruth Fletcher, July 31, 1948; children: Pamela J. Fulker Leonard, Glen Herbert. BS, Purdue U., 1951, MS in Psychology, 1952; EdD in Adult Edn., Am. U., 1970. Lic. psychologist, D.C. Instr. Purdue U., Indpls., 1952-54; tng. officer USAF Hdqrs., Pentagon, Washington, 1954-57, Hdqrs. USDA, Washington, 1957-59; asst. dir. USDA Grad. Sch., Washington, 1959-80, dir., 1980-85; cons. The World Bank, Washington, 1987-99. Adj. faculty Am. U., Washington, George Washington U., Ctrl. Mich. U., Nat. Cheng Chi U., Taiwan; pres. Washington chpt. ASPA, 1977-78, nat. coun. mem., 1979-81. Contbr. articles to profl. jours. Mgmt. cons. U. Mich., Taipei, Taiwan, 1963, Ford Found., New Delhi, India, Nepal, 1970-71, Ohio State U., Ankara, Turkey, 1993, Egypt Gen. Petroleum Co., Cairo, 1996-99. With USNR, 1945-47. Recipient Outstanding Pub. Adminstr. award ASPA, Washington, 1984. Mem. ASTD (pres. chpt. 1964-65, Outstanding Trainer award 1963), Royal Palm Yacht Club (Ft. Myers, Fla.). Avocations: boating, golf, travel. Home: 15240 Sam Snead Ln Fort Myers FL 33917-3260 Personal E-mail: edfulker@aol.com.

FULKERSON, RICHARD J., state agency administrator; BA in Bus. Adminstrn., Chadron State Coll., 1974; postgraduate student, U. Nebr., Omaha, 1981—83, cert. in Bus. Computing, 1986. Nat. accreditation fed. thrift regulator. Mgr. Chgo. Lumber Co., Omaha, 1977—82; v.p., contr. Midwest Fed. Savs. and Loan Assn., Nebraska City, Nebr., 1983—86; asst. dir. Fed. Home Loan Bank Topeka, 1986—89, Office Thrift Supervision, Overland Park, Kans., 1989—95; dir. exams. Colo. Divsn. Banking, Denver, 1995—96; Colo. State Bank commr. Dept. Regulatory Agys., Denver, 1996—. Office: Divsn Banking Colo Dept Regulatory Agys 1560 Broadway Ste 975 Denver CO 80202 Office Phone: 303-894-7575. Office Fax: 303-894-7570. E-mail: banking@dora.state.co.us.

FULKERSON, WILLIAM, hospital administrator, pulmonologist; b. Charlotte, NC, Sept. 8, 1951; Grad., U. N.C., Chapel Hill, 1973; MD, U. N.C., 1977; grad., Duke U. Intern Vanderbilt U. Hosp., Nashville, 1977—78, resident internal medicine, 1978—81, fellow pulmonary disease, 1981—83; asst. prof. medicine Duke U. Sch. Medicine, 1983—90, assoc. prof., 1990—95, prof., 1995—, vice chmn. dept. medicine, 1997—98, chief pulmonary and critical care medicine, 1997—99, exec. med. officer Private Diagnostic Clinic PLLC, 1997—99; chief med. officer Duke U. Hosp., 2000—, v.p., CEO, 2002—. Contbr. articles to profl. jours., chapters to books. Fellow: Soc. Critical Care Medicine, Am. Coll. Chest Physicians; mem.: Am. Thoracic Soc., ACP. Office: Duke Univ 14209 Hosp S Box 3708 Med Ctr Durham NC 27710

FULKERSON, WILLIAM MEASEY, JR., college president; b. Moberly, Mo., Oct. 18, 1940; s. William Measey and Edna Frances (Pendleton) F.; m. Grace Carolyn Wisdom, May 26, 1962; children: Carl Franklin, Carolyn Sue. BA, William Jewell Coll., 1962; MA, Temple U., 1964; PhD, Mich. State U., 1969. Asst. to assoc. prof. Calif. State U., Fresno, 1981—; asst. to pres. Calif. State U.-Fresno, 1971-73; assoc. exec. dir. Am. Assn. State Colls., Washington, 1973-77; acad. v.p. Phillips U., Enid, Okla., 1977-81; pres. Adams State Coll., Alamosa, Colo., 1981-94, State Colls. in Colo., 1994—. Interim pres. Met. State Coll., Denver, 1987-88, Western State Coll., 1996. Author: Planning for Financial Exigency, 1973; contbr. articles to profl. jours. Commr. North Ctrl. Assn., Chgo., 1980—; bd. dirs. Acad. Collective Bargaining Info. Svc., Washington, 1976, Office for Advancement Pub. Negro Colls., Atlanta, 1973-77, Colo. Endowment for Humanities, 1988-2000, pres., 1998-99. Named Disting. Alumni William Jewell Coll., 1982, Outstanding Alumnus Mich. State U. Coll. Comm., Arts & Scis., 1987. Mem. Am. Assn. State Colls. and Univs. (parliamentarian, bd. dirs. 1992-94), Am. Coun. on Edn. (bd. dirs.), Assn. Pub. Coll.s and Univs. Pres.s (pres. 1994-95), Nat. Assn. Sys. Heads, Alamosa C. of C. (dir., pres. 1984 Citizen Yr. award), Rotary. Office: State Colleges in Colorado Ste 1200 1380 Lawrence St Denver CO 80204-2059

FULKS, ROBERT GRADY, computer company executive; b. Kansas City, Mo., Apr. 8, 1936; s. Hilburne Grady and Dora Elouise (Johnson) Fulks; children: Stephanie, Scott Grady. BSEE, MIT, 1958, MSEE, 1959. Engr., chief engr., v.p. engring and product mktg. GenRad, Inc. (formerly Gen. Radio Co.), Concord, Mass., 1959—73; pres. Micro Sys., Inc., 1973—75, Omnicomp, Inc., Phoenix, 1975—80; gen. mgr. advanced tech. divsn. GenRad, Inc. (formerly Omnicomp, Inc.), Phoenix, 1980—86, v.p. parent co.; v.p. engring. Telesis Sys. Corp., Chelmsford, Mass., 1986—87; v.p., gen. mgr. PCB CAD divsn. Valid Logic Sys., 1987—89, group v.p. product divsn., 1989—91; v.p. Cadence Design Sys., Chelmsford, 1992—. Bd. dirs. Cirrus Sigma Ltd., Fareham, England, Texcon Corp., Phoenix, Custon Data Mgmt., Inc., Phoenix, Markwood, Inc., Phoenix, Office Tech. Ltd., Boston. Contbr. articles to profl. jours. Mem.: IEEE, Assn. Computing Machinery, Concord C. of C. (former bd. dirs., chmn. fin. com.), Sigma Xi. Achievements include patents in field. Office: 270 Billerica Rd Chelmsford MA 01824-4140

FULLENWEIDER, DONN CHARLES, lawyer; b. Milw., Jan. 25, 1935; s. Russell Charles and Anne Mae (Murphy) F.; m. Wendy Lattimer; 1 child, Keith Rabon. BS, U. Houston, 1957, JD, 1958. Bar: Tex. bar 1958; Cert. in family law and civil trials Tex. Bd. Legal Specialization. Assoc. Fred Parks, Houston, 1958-65; partner Haynes & Fullenweider, Houston, 1965-89; pvt. practice, Houston, 1989-93; ptnr. Fullenweider and Wardell L.L.P., 1993-97, The Fullenweider Firm, 1997—. Adj. assoc. prof. law U. Houston Bates Coll. Law, 1972-74 Mem. 43d Joint Civilian Orientation Conf., 1973; mem. Tex. Bd. Legal Specialization, 1977-98. Recipient Emison award Tex. Acad. Family Specialists, 1993. Fellow Am. Bar Found., Houston Bar Found., Tex. Bar Found. (dir. 1973-76), Am. Acad. Matrimonial Lawyers (pres. Tex. chpt. 1979-81, bd. dirs. 1981-84, treas. 1985-88, pres.-elect 1988-89, pres. 1990-91); mem. ABA, Am. Bd. Trial Advoacy (advocate), Houston Bar Assn. (treas. 1961-62, 2d v.p. 1962-63, dir. 1971, 73, 1st v.p. 1970-73, Outstanding Svc. award 1974), Am. Coll. Family Trial Lawyers (diplomate 1994—), State Bar Tex. (dir. 1973-76, chmn. bd. 1975-76, exec. com. 1976-77, chmn. litigation sect. 1979-81), Am. Trial Lawyers Assn., Houston Trial Lawyers Assn. (v.p. 1971), River Oaks Country Club, Sigma Chi, Phi Delta Phi. Home: 5555 Del Monte Dr Apt 2402 Houston TX 77056 Office: 4265 San Felipe St Ste 1400 Houston TX 77027-2999 Office Phone: 713-624-4100. E-mail: donn012535@aol.com.

FULLER, ANNE ELIZABETH HAVENS, English language and literature educator, consultant; b. Pomona, Calif., Jan. 20, 1932; d. Paul Swain and Lorraine Elizabeth (Hamilton) Havens; m. Martin Emil Fuller, II, June 17, 1961; children: Katharine Hamilton, Peter David Takashi. AB, Mount Holyoke Coll., 1953; BA (Fulbright scholar), Somerville Coll., Oxford U., 1955, MA, 1959; PhD (Univ. fellow), Yale U., 1958. Instr. English, Mount Holyoke Coll., 1957-59; instr. Pomona Coll., 1959-61; asst. prof. U. Fla., Gainesville, 1961-63; lectr. U. Denver, 1964-68, 71-73; assoc. prof., chmn. center for lang. and lit. Prescott (Ariz.) Coll., 1968-70; tchr. Colo. Rocky Mountain Sch., 1970-71; dean of faculty Scripps Coll., Claremont, Calif., 1973-80, prof. English, 1973-80; spl. asst. to pres., sec. to corp. Claremont U. Center, 1981-83; v.p. for acad. affairs Austin Coll., Sherman, Tex., 1982-84, faculty mem., 1984-96. Mem. SW dist. Rhodes Scholar Selection Com., 1975-83 Bd. dirs. Am. Council on Edn., 1979-81. Mem. Assn. Am. Colls. (dir. 1977-81, chmn. 1980-81), Am. Conf. Acad. Deans (dir. 1976-79), Commn. on Women in Higher Edn., Am. Assn. Higher Edn., Modern Lang. Assn. Am. Democrat. Episcopalian. Home: 11304 Pinos Altos Ave NE Albuquerque NM 87111-5701 E-mail: ahmefu@comcast.net.

FULLER, BETTY STAMPS, music educator; b. Prentiss, Miss., Feb. 19, 1938; d. Henry Buford and Genevieve (Bozeman) Stamps; m. Allan Riggs Fuller, Dec. 19, 1957 (dec. May 1987); children: Melodie, Valerie. Attended, Miss. Coll., 1958; BA, McNeese State U., 1983; post grad., Loyola U., 1985. Music tchr. Bearss Acad., Jackson, Miss., 1969—73, Episcopal Day Sch., Lake Charles, La., 1975—85, Our Lady's Sch., Sulpher, 1985—. Mentor tchr. Alliance for Cath. Edn., Notre Dame U., Notre Dame, Ind., 2000—01. Coord. youth orch. Miss. Coll., Clinton, Miss., 1967—72; bd. mem. Lake Charles (La.) Symphony Orch., 1975—77. Named Citizen of the Day, KLOU Radio Station, Lake Charles, 1975, Tchr. of Yr., KC Coun., 1994; Fine Arts grant, La. Divsn. of Arts, 1994—95, Arts and Humanities Coun. SW La., 1996. Mem.: Nat. Cath. Edn. Assn. Episcopalian. Avocations: production of musical plays, visual arts, historical preservation, environmental activities. Home: 2715 Roxton St Sulphur LA 70663

FULLER, BONNIE, editor-in-chief; b. Toronto, Canada; m. Michael Fuller; 4 children. BA in History, U. of Toronto, 1977. Fashion reporter Toronto Star, 1978; sportswear editor Women's Wear Daily; editor-in-chief Flare mag., Canada, 1982, YM, NYC, 1989—94; founding editor Marie Claire, 1994—96; dep. editor Cosmopolitan, 1996—97; editor-in-chief Cosmopolitan Hearst Mags., NYC, 1997—98; editor-in-chief Glamour, Conde Nast, 1998—2001; editor US Weekly, 2002—03; exec. v.p. Am. Media Inc., NYC, 2003—, chief editl. dir., 2003—. Author: From Geek to Oh My Goodness, 2003, The Joys of Much Too Much: Go for the Big Life--The Great Career, The Perfect Guy, and Everything Else You've Ever Wanted, 2006. Named Editor of Yr., Ad Age Mag. (twice); recipient Spotlight award, Amnesty Internat., 2000. Office: American Media Inc 1 Park Ave New York NY 10016

FULLER, CYNTHIA L., biologist, researcher; d. James A. and Kathy J. DeYoung; m. Jason A. Fuller, Aug. 16, 2003. BS, Grand Valley State U., Allendale, Mich., 2000; PhD, Western Mich. U., Kalamazoo, 2006. Grad. rsch. fellow, dept. biology Western Mich. U., Kalamazoo, 2001—06; postdoctoral rsch. fellow, neurology dept. U. Mich., Ann Arbor, 2006—. Contbr. articles to profl. jours. Fellow, NIH, 2006—07. Mem.: Soc. Neuroscience, Assn. Chemoreception Sci. Business E-Mail: cyntfull@umich.edu.

FULLER, DALE L., software security company executive; V.p., gen. mgr. portable computer divsn. NEC Technologies, Inc.; gen. mgr., v.p. powerbook divsn. Apple Computer, Inc.; pres., CEO WhoWhere? Inc.; dir. Software and Info. Industry Assn.; interim pres., CEO Borland Software Corp., 1999—2000, pres., CEO, 2000—05; interim CEO, pres. McAfee, Inc., 2005—. Office: McAfee Inc 3965 Freedom Cir Santa Clara CA 95054 Office Phone: 972-963-8000.*

FULLER, DAVID OTIS, JR., lawyer; b. Grand Rapids, Mich., May 28, 1939; s. David Otis and Virginia Chapin (Emery) F.; m. Isabelle Patrice Gigout, July 5, 1968; children: Thomas Andrew, Christian Scott, Pierre Emery, Margaret Isabelle. BA, Wheaton Coll., 1961; JD, Harvard U., 1964; postgrad., George Washington U., 1963, U. Paris, 1966. Bar: Mich., 1964, N.Y., 1967, U.S. Supreme Ct., 1968. Law clk. U.S. Ho. of Reps. Judiciary Com., 1963; assoc. Amberg, Law & Fallon, Grand Rapids, 1964-65; asst. dist. atty. N.Y. County, 1966-72, law sec. to justice, 1972-73; corp. atty. Pan Am. World Airways, Inc., 1973-74; dep. gen. counsel Reader's Digest Assn., Inc., 1974-84; pvt. practice N.Y.C., 1984-87; ptnr. Baker, Nelson & Williams, NYC, 1987-94, Bosworth, Gray & Fuller, Bronxville, N.Y., 1994—; justice Tuckahoe Village, N.Y., 1986—. Lectr. ABA, Practicing Law Inst., Bronx C.C. Editor: Harvard Jour. on Legislation, 1962-64; contbr. articles to profl. jours. Warden Episc. Ch., 1991-97. Maj. NY Guard, 2001—07. Mem.: ABA, Fed. Bar Coun., Westchester County Magistrates Assn. (pres. 1993—94), Westchester County Bar Assn., NY State Magistrates Assn. (pres. 2006—07), Am. Arbitration Assn. (arbitrator 1983—96), Assn. Bar City NY (comms. law com. 1984—87), NY State Bar Assn. (chmn. privacy com. 1982—84), Bras Coupé Fishing Club Quebec, Harvard Club NYC. Republican. Episcopalian. Avocations: coin collecting/numismatics, fishing, racquet sports, skiing. Office: Bosworth Gray & Fuller 116 Kraft Ave Bronxville NY 10708-3810 Office Phone: 914-337-3626. Personal E-mail: dofjr@aol.com.

FULLER, DAVID RANDALL, retired music educator; b. Newton, Mass., May 1, 1927; s. Joseph Cheever and Ruth Randall (Brodhead) Fuller. AB, Harvard U., Cambridge, Mass., 1949, AM, 1951, PhD, 1965. Instr. music Robert Coll., Istanbul, Turkey, 1950—53, Bradford Jr. Coll., Haverhill, Mass., 1953—54; asst. prof. music Dartmouth Coll., Hanover, NH, 1954—57; prof. music SUNY, Buffalo, 1963—98, prof. emeritus, 1998—. Author (with Bruce Gustafson): (book) A Catalogue of French Harpsichord Music 1688-1780, 1990; contbr. 105 articled to music dictionaries, 42 articles and reviews in profl. jours., 9 chapters to books. With USN, 1945—46. Fellow, NEH, 1976—77; Paine Travelling fellow, Harvard U., France, 1960—61. Mem.: Am. Bach Soc., Soc. Seventeenth-Century Music, Am. Guild Organists, Am. Musicological Soc. Avocation: pre-war boats and cars.

FULLER, EDWIN DANIEL, hotel executive; b. Richmond, Va., Mar. 15, 1945; s. Ben Swint and Evelyn (Beal) F. Student, Wake Forest U., 1965; BSBA, Boston U., 1968; postgrad., Harvard Sch. Bus., 1987. Security officer Pinkerton Inc., Boston, 1965-68; sales dir. Twin Bridges Marriott Hotel, Arlington, Va., 1972-73; nat. sales mgr. Marriott Hotels & Resorts, NYC, 1973-76, dir. nat. and internat. Marriott sales Washington, 1976-78, v.p. Marriott Hotels mktg., 1978-82, gen. mgr. Hempstead, NY, 1982-83, Marriott Copley Pl., Boston, 1983-85; v.p. ops. Midwest region Marriott Corp., Rosemont, Ill., 1985-89, v.p. ops. Western and Pacific regions Santa Ana, Calif., 1989-90; sr. v.p., mng. dir. Marriott Hotels & Resorts-Internat., Washington, 1990-93; exec. v.p., mng. dir. internat. lodging Marriott Lodging Internat., Washington, 1994-97, pres., mng. dir., 1997—. Chmn. bd. dir. SNR Reservation Sys., Zurich, Switzerland, 1979-81; bd. dirs. Boston U. Hotel Sch., 1984—, Barnby Books, Barnaby Books, Honolulu, 1997—; treas. MEI Pacific Honolulu, 1985—, chmn. Pres. Boston U. Gen. Alumni Assn., 1993-1996, v.p., 1990-93; v.p. Boston U. Sch. Mgmt. Alumni Bd., 1985—; adv. bd. Boston U. Hospitality Mgmt. Sch., 1985—; trustee Boston U., exec. com. bd. trustees, 1994—, dir., Prince of Whales Hotel Environ. Orgn., 1995, chmn., dir. Internat. bd. of United Way, trustee; overseer Boston U., 2007. Capt. U.S. Army, 1968-72, Vietnam. Decorated Bronze Star, Army Commendation medal. Mem. Boston U. Alumni Coun. (v.p.), Harvard Sch. Bus. Advanced Mgmt. Program (fund agt.), Sigma Alpha Epsilon, Delta Sigma Pi. Republican. Avocations: real estate, travel, golf, history. Home: 25362 Derbyhill Dr Laguna Hills CA 92653 Office: Marriott Hotels & Resorts Dept 921 19 1 Marriott Dr Washington DC 20058-0001 Office Phone: 301-380-8990. Business E-Mail: ed.fuller@marriott.com.

FULLER, FRANK ROBERT, political scientist, director; b. Savannah, Ga., Nov. 13, 1977; s. Robert Arthur Fuller and Brenda Lois Marino-Fuller; life ptnr. Ying-Chu Chen; life ptnr. JoAnna Grace Johnston; 1 child, Joseph Robert. AA in Liberal Arts, Young Harris Coll., Ga., 1998; BA in Politics, Oglethorpe U., Atlanta, 2000; MS in Internat. Affairs, Ga. Inst. Tech., Atlanta, 2001. Coop. learning cert. Ga. Inst. Tech., 2001, urban leadership cert. Oglethorpe U., 2000. Grad. rsch. asst. Ga. Tech Rsch. Inst., 2000—01, Inst. Sustainable Tech. and Devel., Ga. Tech. Rsch. Inst., 2001—02; electronics sales assoc. OfficeMax, Mentor, Ohio and Best Buy, Kennesaw, Ga., 2002—03; grad. rsch. asst. criminal justice dept. Ga. State U., Atlanta, 2003—07; IDN program dir. LeadAmerica, Washington, 2006—. Cert. referee and coach Internat. Taekwondo Fedn., Harleysville, Ga., 2007; referee various Taekwondo tournaments, Atlanta; martial arts instr. Ga. Tech. Recreation Ctr., Ho Shin Do Martial Arts, Atlanta, 1994—2005; DJ WJTL, WREK, WRAS, Atlanta, 1999—; substitute tchr. Marietta City Schs., Ga., 1999—; piano composer and performer Grape Leaf Grill, Marietta, Ga., 2006—07. Composer: (piano composition) Lost Memories, Still Dreaming; actor: (film) Werebum; author: (conference paper in political science) Challenges to the Competitive Technology Sector in Japan; actor: (martial arts action/sci-fi film) Forever; editor: Subcontracting Peace: The Challenges of NGO Peacebuilding, 2005. Vol. Make-a-Wish Found., Cleve., 2002, Atlanta, 2005; campaign vol. Gingrey Congress, Marietta, Ga., 2006; vol. Habitat for Humanity, Marietta, Ga., 1999; mem. parish workshops St. Joseph Cath. Ch., Marietta, 1999. HOPE scholar, U. Sys. Ga., 1996—2000, Governor's Honors scholar, 1998—2000, Faculty, Transfer and Christian scholar, Young Harris Coll., Oglethorpe U., 1996—2000, Fellowship grantee, Ford Found., 2002. Mem.: Am. Polit. Sci. Assn., Chancellor's List, MENSA, Koreja Do Christian Martial Arts, Japan-America Soc. Ga. (assoc.). Republican. Roman Catholic. Achievements include 4th degree black belt, Ho Shin Do; research in east Asian politics. Avocations: martial arts, piano, japanese animation, films. Home and Office: 263 Bristol Ln Marietta GA 30066 Home Phone: 770-429-8363. E-mail: frankiefuller@gmail.com.

FULLER, GERALD G., engineering educator; b. Washington, DC, Apr. 7, 1953; BS, U. Calgary, 1975; MS, Calif. Inst. Tech., 1977, PhD in Chem. Engring., 1980. Lab. asst. ATCO Rsch. and Devel., Calgary, Alberta, 1972; gas plant operator Imperial Oil Ltd., Edmonton, 1973; asst. engr. Shell Can. Ltd., Calgary, 1974; asst. prof. chem. engring. Stanford U., 1980—85, assoc. prof., 1985—90, prof. Dept. Chem. Engring., 1990—, chmn. Dept. Chem. Engring., 1996—2001. Vis. scientist Center de Recherches sur les Macromolecules, Strasbourg, France, 1980, At&T Bell Labs., Murray Hill, NJ, 1987, Katholieke Universiteit, Leuven, Belgium, 1989, E.P.F.L., Lausanne, Switzerland, 1992; vis. assoc. prof. Ecole des Mines de Paris, Nice, France, 1994, U. Strasbourg, 1996; vis. prof. Dept. Mech. Engring. Kings Coll., London, 1999—2004; Holtz lectr. Dept Chem. Engring. Johns Hopkins U., 2003; Pearson lectr. U. Calif., Santa Barbara, 2004; Julian C. Smith lectureship Cornell U., 2004. Author: Optical Rheometry of Complex Fluids, 1995; co-author: Scientifically Yours, 1995; editl. bd. mem. J. Polymer Science: Polymer Physics, 2003—; contbr. articles to profl. jours. Fellow: Am. Physical Soc.; mem.: NAE, Soc. Rheology (chair Tech. Com. 1995, v.p. 1997—99, pres. 1999—2001, past pres. 2001—03, Bingham Medal Award 1997). Office: Stanford U Dept Chem Engring Keck Sci Bldg, Rm 183 381 N S Mall Stanford CA 94305-5025 Office Phone: 650-723-9243. E-mail: ggf@stanford.edu.

FULLER, JACK WILLIAM, writer, retired publishing executive; b. Chgo., Oct. 12, 1946; s. Ernest Brady and Dorothy Voss (Tegge) Fuller; m. Debra Moskovits; children: Timothy, Katherine. BS, Northwestern U., 1968; JD, Yale U., 1973. Bar: Ill. 1974. Reporter Chgo. Tribune, 1973—75, Washington corr., 1977—78, editl. writer, 1978—79, dep. editl. page editor, 1979—82, editl. page editor, 1982—87, exec. editor, 1987—89, v.p. and editor, 1989—93, pres., CEO, 1993—97, pub., 1994—97; pres. Tribune Pub. Co., 1997—2004; dir. Torstar Corp., 2004—. Spl. asst. to atty. gen. U.S. Dept. Justice, Washington, 1975—77. Author: Convergence, 1982 (Cliff Dwellers award, 1983), Fragments, 1984 (Friends of Am. Writers award, 1985), Mass, 1985, Our Fathers' Shadows, 1987, Legends' End, 1990, News Values, 1996, The Best of Jackson Payne, 2000. Mem. Pulitzer Prize Bd., 1991—2000; trustee U. Chgo.; dir. MacArthur Found. With US Army, 1969—70, Vietnam corr., Pacific Stars and Stripes. Recipient Gavel award, ABA, 1979, Pulitzer prize for editl. writing, 1986, Excellence in Arts award, Vietnam Vets Am., 1993. Fellow: Am. Acad. Arts and Scis.; mem.: Inter-Am. Press Assn. (pres. 2003—04).

FULLER, JAMES CHESTER EEDY, retired chemical company executive; b. Toronto, June 5, 1927; came to U.S., 1968; s. James Clifford and Marion Winifred (Eedy) F.; m. Doris Shirley Johnson, June 16, 1951 (dec. June 1992); children— Hilary, John; m. Shirley Patricia Honeyman, Feb. 8, 1993. BSA., U. Toronto, 1948; MBA, U. Western Ont., 1955. Sales and mktg. ofcl. Uniroyal Chem. Co., Man. and Ont., Can., 1948-53, 55-64; with Akzo Chemicals and affiliates, 1964-90; gen. mgr. Armour Indsl. Chems., Toronto, 1964-68, nat. sales mgr., asst. to pres., internat. dir. Chgo., 1968-70; mng. dir. Armour-Hess Ltd., Harrogate, Yorkshire, Eng., 1970-73; exec. v.p. Akzo Chemie Am., Chgo., 1973-74, pres., 1975-87; exec. v.p. Akzo Chemicals B.V., Amersfoort, The Netherlands, 1988-90. Mem. Chem. Inst. Can. Home: 403-2605 Windsor Rd Victoria BC V8S 5H9 Canada E-mail: jfuller@vicsurf.com.

FULLER, JAMES WILLIAM, financial planner; b. Rochester, Ind., Apr. 3, 1940; s. Raymond S. and Mildred (Osteimeier) F.; children: Kristen Anne, Glen William. AA, San Bernardino Coll., Calif., 1960; BS, San Jose State U., Calif., 1962; MBA, Calif. State U., 1967. V.p. Dean Witter, San Francisco, 1967-71, Shields & Co., San Francisco, 1971-74; dir. fin. programs SRI Internat., Menlo Park, Calif., 1974-77; sr. v.p. N.Y. Stock Exch., NYC, 1977-81, Charles Schwab & Co., San Fransico, 1981-85; pres. Bull & Bear Corp., NYC, 1985-87; dir. Bridge Info. Systems, San Fransico, 1987—. Chmn. bd. dirs. Pacific Rsch. Inst., 1992—. Active San Francisco Rep. Party, Calif. State Rep. Party; dir. Securities Industry Protection Corp., Washington, 1981—87, Global Econ. Action Inst., NYC, 1989—2000; trustee U. Calif., Santa Cruz. Mem. The Family Club (San Francisco), Olympic Club (San Francisco), Jonathon Club (LA), Univ. Club (NYC), The Lincoln Club (San Francisco), Polit. Com. for Econ. Growth, Newcomen Soc., World Affairs Coun., Coun. on Fgn. Rels. (San Francisco com.), Commonwealth Club. Republican. Presbyterian. Avocations: tennis, politics, public affairs. Home: 2584 Filbert St San Francisco CA 94123-3318 Office Phone: 415-977-1500. Personal E-mail: jamesfuller1@gmail.com.

FULLER, JOHN WILLIAMS, economics professor; b. Phoenix, Nov. 8, 1940; s. John W. and Myrtle Arabella (Parr) F.; m. Annette Cunkle, June 16, 1962 (dec. 1977); m. Kathy J. Fait, Feb. 17, 1980; children: Helen, Douglas, Andrew, Elizabeth. AB, San Diego State U., 1962; PhD, Wash. State U., Pullman, 1968. Chief econ. analysis Wis. Dept. Transp., Madison, 1968-74, dir. environ. and policy analysis, 1974-76; hwy. commr. State Of Wis., 1976-77; deputy exec dir. Nat. Transp. Policy Study Commn., Washington, 1977-79; prof. econs., urban and regional planning and geography U. Iowa, Iowa City, 1979—, chair grad. program in urban and regional planning, 1996-99; cons. Bur. Transp. Stats., Washington, 1993—2001. Cons. Fed. Hwy. Adminstrn., Washington, 1980-82, legis. coun. Iowa Gen. Assembly, Des Moines, 1980-91; dir. Legis. Extended Assistance Group, Iowa City, 1979-2001. Contbr. articles to profl. jours. Mem., vice chair Johnson County Broadband Telecom. Commn., 1982-88; chmn. Zoning Bd. Adjustment, Johnson County, 1987-92; mem. West Branch Zoning Bd. of Adjustment, 1993-2003, West Branch Hist. Preservation Commn., 2002-, sec. 2005; trustee West Branch Libr., 1995-2001, pres. 1997-2001. Recipient Fulbright award, Venezuela, 1985. Mem.

Transp. Rsch. Bd., Am. Assn. RR Supts., Am. Soc. Transp. and Logistics, Assn. Am. Geographers, Nat. Assn. Environ. Profls., Am. Econ. Assn., Am. Planning Assn., Transp. Rsch. Forum, Am. Inst. Cert. Planners. Congregationalist. Office: U Iowa 344 Jessup Hall Iowa City IA 52242-1316 Business E-Mail: john-w-fuller@uiowa.edu.

FULLER, KATHRYN SCOTT, former environmental services administrator; b. NYC, July 8, 1946; d. Delbert Orison and Carol Scott (Gilbert) F.; m. Stephen Paul Doyle, May 29, 1977; children: Sarah Elizabeth Taylor, Michael Stephen Doyle, Matthew Scott Doyle. BA English, Am. Lit., Brown U., 1968, LHD (hon.), 1992; JD with honors, U. Tex., 1976; postgrad., U. Md., 1980-82; DSci. (hon.), Wheaton Coll., 1990; LLD (hon.), Knox Coll., 1992. Bar: Tex. 1977, D.C. 1979. Rsch. asst. Yale U., New Haven, 1968-69, Am. Chem. Soc., 1970-71, Harvard U. Mus. Comparative Zoology, Cambridge, Mass., 1971-73; law clerk Dewey, Ballantine, Bushby, Palmer & Wood and Vinson & Elkins, NYC, Houston, 1974-76, U.S. Dist. Ct. (so. dist.), Tex., 1976-77; atty., advisor Office Legal Counsel Dept. Justice, Washington, 1977-79, atty. Wildlife and Marine Resources sect., 1979-80, chief Wildlife and Marine Resources sect., 1981-82; exec. v.p., dir. Traffic USA, pub. policy, gen. counsel World Wildlife Fund, Washington, 1982-89, pres., CEO, 1989—2005. Contbr. articles to profl. jours.; bd. dirs. Alcoa Inc., 2002—, Student Conservation Assn., Fondo Mexicano para la Conservacion de la Naturaleza; mem. World Bank Adv. Com. on Sustainable Devel. Bd. trustees Ford Found., Brown U. Recipient William Rogers Outstanding Grad. award Brown U., 1990, UN Environment Programme Global 500 award, 1990; Named outstanding woman law student Tex. scholar, 1975. Mem. State Tex. Bar, D.C. Bar, Coun. Fgn. Rels., Zonta Internat. (hon.). Avocations: squash, trekking, scuba diving, gardening, fishing.

FULLER, KATHY J., special education educator, consultant, researcher; b. Lamar, Colo., Oct. 24, 1957; d. Alfred L. and Leona M. Fuller; 1 child, Samantha Devon Blake. MA, Calif. State U. Northridge, 1993; PhD in Psychol. Studies of Edn., UCLA, 2004. Tchg. cert. edn. specialist mild to moderate disabilities. Prof. UCLA ext., 1999—, Pacific Oaks Coll., Pasadena, Calif., 2002—; cons. L.A. County of Edn., 2002—. Tchr. Pasadena Unified Sch. Dist., Calif., 1992—94; tchr., full inclusion specialist LA Unified Sch. Dist., 1994—2000; prof. Calif. State U., LA, 1999—2002, adj. prof., 1997—; owner Teacher Talk, 2003—; presenter in field. Musician: (singer) New Life - Kora Music for the 21st Century (Prince Diabate CD); poet Helpless Hoping (Editor's Choice award); contbg. author: Rescued Tails, 2005; contbr. articles to profl. jours. Pet therapist Love on 4 Paws, LA, 2002; edn. dir. Beagles & Buddies, Orange County Cavy Haven; vol. pet therapist Vitas Hospice, 2006—, Ronald McDonald Houses. Recipient 1st place Edn. award, 2001, 2d place Behavioral/Social Scis. award, 2002; grantee Nat. Rsch. grant, Nat. Assn. Alternative Cert., 1999—. Mem.: Nat. Assn. Alternative Edn., Am. Ednl. Rsch. Assn., Coun. for Exceptional Children (assoc.), Phi Lambda Theta. Achievements include design of Fuller-Blake Academic Inventory. Avocations: swimming, sailing, surfing, scuba diving, painting. Home: 790 Monterey Rd South Pasadena CA 91030 Office Phone: 626-685-2532. Personal E-mail: kfullerbla@aol.com.

FULLER, KENNETH D., lawyer; b. Russellville, Ala., July 27, 1932; BS, U. North Tex., 1954; LLB, So. Meth. U., Dallas, 1962. Bar: Tex. 1962. Ptnr. Koons, Fuller, Vanden Eykel & Robertson, P.C., Dallas. Recipient Sam Emison Award for Meritorious Contbn. Family Law, Tex. Acad. Family Law Specialists, 1985. Fellow: Am. Acad. Matrimonial Lawyers; mem.: Dallas Trial Lawyers Assn., Tex. Trial Lawyers Assn., State Bar Tex. (chmn. Legis. Sub-Committee 1980—85, chmn. Family Law Coun. 1983—85, chmn. Supreme Ct. Adv. Commn. 1987—93, bd. editors Family Law Practice Manual 1987—, mem. Com. Drafting Patterned Jury Charges in Family Law Cases 1987—, named to Hall of Legends), ABA, Garland County Bar Assn., Dallas Bar Assn. (chmn. Family Law Sect. 1980). Office: Koons Fuller Vanden Eykel & Robertson PC 2311 Cedar Springs Rd Ste 300 Dallas TX 75201 Office Phone: 214-871-2727. Office Fax: 214-871-0196. E-mail: Ken@koonsfuller.com.

FULLER, KEVIN RICE, lawyer; b. Santa Ana, Calif., Nov. 16, 1958; s. Kenneth D. and Judith (Rice) F.; m. Sharla S. Neill, Nov. 10, 2002; children: Hudson McGregor Fuller, Cody N. Fuller, Casey John Fuller. BS in Econs., Tex. A&M U., 1981; JD, Baylor U., 1984. Bar: Tex. 1984. Ptnr. Koons, Fuller, Vanden Eykel & Robertson (formerly Koons, Fuller & Vanden Eykel), Dallas, 1984—. Contbr. articles to profl. jours. Bd. dirs. Dallas Child Guidance Clinic, 1990-96. Mem. Dallas Bar Assn. (chair family law sect. 1987). Avocation: horses. Office: Koons Fuller Vanden Eykel & Robertson 2311 Cedar Springs Rd Ste 300 Dallas TX 75201-1899 Office Phone: 214-871-2727. Office Fax: 214-871-0196. E-mail: kevin@koonsfuller.com.*

FULLER, MARGARET TATNALL, biomedical researcher; BA summa cum laude in Physics, Brandeis U., 1974; PhD in Microbiol., MIT, 1980. Jane Coffin Childs postdoctoral fellow devel. genetics Ind. U., 1980—83; asst. prof. dept. molecular, cellular and devel. biology U. Colo., Boulder, 1983—89, assoc. prof., 1989—90; assoc. prof. depts. devel. biology and genetics Stanford U. Sch. Medicine, Calif., 1990—2000, Reed-Hodgson prof. human biology, prof. genetics, 2000—. Mary Ingraham Bunting fellow Radcliffe Coll., 1994—95; mem. sci. adv. bd. Searle Scholars Prog., 2002—; chair devel. biology Sch. Medicine Stanford U., 2003—, mem. Comprehensive Cancer Ctr. Contbr. articles to profl. jours.; assoc. editor: Genetics, 1989—94, mem. editl. bd.: Molecular Biology of the Cell, 1994. Recipient Dr. Joseph Garrison Parker prize, 1974, Jr. Faculty Rsch. award, Am. Cancer Soc., 1983—86, Scholar in Cancer Rsch. award, 1994—95, Searle Scholars award, 1985—88; grantee Pre-doctoral Nat. Rsch. Svc. award, NIH, 1976—79. Fellow: Am. Acad. Arts & Scis. Achievements include patents in field. Office: Dept Devel Biology Stanford U Beckman B300 5329 Stanford CA 94305-5329 E-mail: fuller@cmgm.stanford.edu.

FULLER, MAXINE COMPTON, retired secondary school educator; b. Tiny, Va., Aug. 23, 1921; d. Perry and Lillie (Sutherland) Compton; m. David Thompson Fuller Jr., 1946 (dec. Mar. 1975); children: Davine Miller, Patricia Machen, Shirley Allen, Dorothy Brunson, David Thompson III BS, Longwood Coll., 1943; MA, U. Ala., 1966; AA in Edn., U. Ala., Birmingham, 1980. Receptionist Goodyear Tire and Rubber Co., Richmond, Va., 1943, office mgr. trainee Selma, Ala., 1943-44; office mgr. Goodyear Service, Bessemer, Ala., 1944-46; sec., ops. mgr. Birmingham So. Coll., 1966; tchr. Manpower-Bessemer State Tech. Coll., 1966-68, McAdory H.S., 1968-71; bus. edn. coord. Hueytown (Ala.) H.S., 1971-88; ret. Hueytown H.S., 1988. Vis. com. mem. So. Assn. Secondary Schs. and Colls., 1980, 84. Sunday sch. tchr. Pleasant Ridge Bapt. Ch., Hueytown, 1962-88, pers. com., 1980-83; mem. Hueytown High PTA, 1986-87; liaison officer Adopt-A-Sch. program Hueytown High/Lloyd Noland Hosp., 1987-88; chmn. bus. edn. dept. Hueytown H.S., 1971-88. Mem. NEA, Nat. Ret. Tchrs. Assn., Ala. Edn. Retirees Assn, Bibb County Edn. Retirees Assn (sec. 2002-06), former mem. Echo Study Club (pres. 1987-88, sec. 1991-92), former mem. Culture Club of Hueytown (pres. 1994-96), Longwood Coll. Alumni Assn., former mem., Alpha Delta Kappa (corr. sec. XI chpt. 1982-84), Delta Kappa Gamma (treas. Gamma Lambda chpt. 1976-80). Baptist.

FULLER, MELVIN STUART, botany educator; b. Livermore Falls, Maine, May 5, 1931; s. George Raymond and Hilda Gordon (Pike) F.; m. Barbara Paul Newman, Apr. 2, 1955; children: Erica Ann, Scott Eliot, Amy Elizabeth. BS, U. Maine, 1953; MS, U. Nebr., 1955; PhD, U. Calif., 1959; Master's ad eundum, Brown U., 1963. Instr. Brown U., 1959, asst. prof., 1960-63, assoc. prof., 1963-64; asst. prof. U. Calif., 1964-65, assoc. prof., 1965-68; prof. botany U. Ga., 1968—, head dept., 1968-73, 86-89, univ. prof., 1990—; vis. agrl. rsch. biologist Sandoz Ltd., Basel, Switzerland, 1983; vis. rsch. prof. U. Uppsala, Sweden, 1985, 86; adj. prof. botany U. Maine, 1992—; emeritus univ. prof. and emeritus prof. botany U. Ga., 1995—. Mem. editorial bd. for publs. in biology McGraw Hill; sec. 2d Internat. Mycol. Congress; organizer Fifth Internat. Fungus Spore Meeting, 1991. Author: The Science of Botany, 1962, Lower Fungi in the Laboratory, 1978, Zoosporic Fungi in Teach. and Research, 1987. Bd. dirs. DaPonte String Quartet, 2002—06. Fellow British Mycological Soc.; mem. Bot. Soc. Am., Mycol. Soc. Am. (counselor 1966-68, 70-72, pres. 1975, Disting. Mycologist Award, 1992), Soc. Study of Growth and Devel., Am. Phythopath. Soc., Gulf of Maine Found. (pres. 1997-99). Achievements include research on growth and development of aquatic fungi, ultrastructure, mechanism of action of fungicides. Home: 1202-1 Hummingibrd Ln Wilmington NC 28411 Personal E-mail: msfuller1@gmail.com.

FULLER, MICHAEL B., communications executive; BS in Engring., U.S. Mil. Acad., West Point, NY; MBA, U. Kans., Lawrence. Fin. analyst, corp. staff United Telecommunicatoin, 1974, various ops., mktg. and strategic planning pos., asst. v.p.-planning for telephone ops., 1981—83, various key mgmt. pos. in long-distance bus., 1983—88, v.p.-planning, ISACOMM, 1983—84, sr. v.p.-adminstrn. and plannig for US Telecom, 1985—86; pres. Southeast divsn. US Sprint, Atlanta, 1986—87, sr. v.p.-planning devel. and internat. svcs., 1987—88, exec. v.p.-staff, 1988—89; pres., United Telephone of the Northwest, Local Telecomm. Divsn. Sprint Corp., 1989—96, pres. and COO, Local Telecomm. Divsn., 1996—. Office: 6200 Sprint Pkwy Overland Park KS 66251

FULLER, MILLARD DEAN, foundation administrator, lawyer; b. Lanett, Ala., Jan. 3, 1935; s. Render and Estin (Cook) F.; m. Linda Caldwell; children: Christopher, Kimberly, Faith, Georgia. BS in Econs., Auburn U., 1957; LLB, U. Ala., 1960; LHD (hon.), Ea. Coll., Pa., 1985, Ottawa U., 1987, Susquehanna U., 1989; D Pub. Svcs. (hon.), DePauw U., 1988; HHD (hon.), Coll. of Wooster, 1989, Wake Forest U., 1990, Mercer U., 1990, Westminster Coll., 1990, Whitworth Coll., 1990, Dallas Bapt. U., 1994, Lynchburg Coll., 1992, North Park Coll., 1992, Tech. U. Nova Scotia, 1992, U. North Ala., 1994, Providence Coll., 1994, Presbyn. Coll., Clinton, SC, 1995, Bluffton Coll., 1995, Elon Coll., 1995, Nova Southeastern U., 1996; HHD (hon.), U. Ala., 2004. Bar: Ala. 1960, Ga. 1972. Co-founder Fuller and Dees Mktg. Group, Inc., Montgomery, Ala., 1960, pres., 1960-65; ptnr. Fuller and Dees (law firm), Montgomery, 1960-65; devel. dir. Tougaloo (Miss.) Coll., 1966-68; dir. Koinonia Ptnrs., Inc. (developer various bus. ops. for Koinonia Christian community), Americus, Ga., 1968-72; dir. devel. Ch. of Christ, Zaire, Equator region Africa, 1973-76, initiator housing project for low-income families, Mbandaka, Zaire Equator region Africa; founder, CEO Habitat Humanity Internat., Inc., Americus, 1976—2005; founder, pres. The Fuller Ctr. Housing, Inc., 2005—. Author: Bokotola, 1977, Love in the Mortar Joints, 1980, No More Shacks!, 1986, The Excitement is Building, 1990, Theology of the Hammer, 1994, A Simple, Decent Place to Live, 1995, More than Houses, 2000, Building Materials for Life, vol. I, 2002, vol. II, 2004, vol. III, 2007. Adv. com. Albert Schweitzer Fellowship of Am., 1992. Lt. U.S. Army, 1960. Recipient Outstanding Achievement award Coun. State Housing Agys., 1986, Clarence Jordan Exemplary Chistiran Svc. award So. Bapt. Theol. Sem., 1986, Dr. Marting Luther King, Jr. Humanitarian award, 1987, Disting. chrisitan Svc. in Social Welfare award N.Am. Assn. christians in Social Work, 1988, Internat. Humanity Svc. award Am. Overseas Assn. ARC, 1989, Pub. Svc. Achievement award Common Cause, 1989, M. Justin Herman Meml. award Nat. Assn. Housing and Devel. Ofcls., 1989, The Temple award for Creative Altruism, 1990, Joseph C. Wilson award Rochester Assn. for the UN, 1990, Amicus Certus award Luth. Social Svcs. Ill., Martin Luther Jr. Humanitarian award Ga. State Holiday Commn., 1992, Profl. Achievement award Partnership Affordable Housing, 1993, Harry S. Truman Pub. Svc. award City of Independence, 1994, The McConnell award Truett-McConnell Coll., Ga., 1995, Faithful Servant award Nat. Assn. of Evangelicals, 1996, Spirit of Ga. award, 1996; named Builder of Yr. Profl. Bldr. mag., 1995, Nat. Housing Hall of Fame, 1996, Presdl. Medal of Freedom, 1996, Jefferson award 1999. Mem. Ala. Bar Assn., Ga. Bar Assn. Baptist. Avocations: reading, walking. Office Phone: 229-924-2900. Business E-Mail: fuller35@hotmail.com, mfuller@fullercenter.org.

FULLER, RENEE NUNI, psychologist, educational publisher; b. Mannheim, Germany, Apr. 14, 1929; arrived in U.S., 1938; d. Eric Woldemar and Fridel Gronau (Henning) Stoetzner; widowed. Student, Swarthmore Coll., Pa., 1947—49; BA, Hunter Coll., 1951; MA, Columbia U., 1953; PhD, NYU, 1963. Rsch. scientist Letchworth Village NY State Dept. Mental Hygiene, Thiells, 1961—67; project dir. S.I. (N.Y.) Soc. Mental Health, 1967—68; chief psychol. svcs. Rosewood Hosp. Ctr., Owings Mills, Md., 1968-75; pres. Ball-Stick-Bird Publs. Inc., Williamstown, Mass., 1975—. Author: In Search of the IQ Correlation, 1977, (reading series) Ball-Stick-Bird; contbr. articles to profl. jours. Recipient Disting. Achievement award, Fairleigh-Dickinson U., N.J., 1979. Fellow: Am. Psychol. Soc.; mem.: APA, Soc. for Rsch. in Child Devel. Office: Ball Stick Bird Publs Inc PO Box 429 Williamstown MA 01267 Business E-Mail: info@ballstickbird.com.

FULLER, ROBERT FERREY, retired lawyer, investor; b. St. Paul, Aug. 11, 1929; s. Robert Garfield and Gwendolen (Ferrey) F.; m. Marcelle McIntosh, June 6, 1953 (div. 1984); children: Julie, Gordon McIntosh; m. Sheila Nolan Mensing, May 25, 1985; stepchildren: Andrew Mensing, Allison Mensing. AB magna cum laude, Harvard, 1950, JD, 1953. Bar: N.Y. 1956, Conn. 1988, U.S. Dist. Ct. (so. and ea. dists.) N.Y. 1960, U.S. Ct. Appeals (D.C. cir.) 1988, U.S. Ct. Internat. Trade 1988. Assoc. Patterson, Belknap & Webb, NYC, 1955-66; sec., gen. counsel Reuben H. Donnelley Corp., NYC, 1966-68; mng. dir. R.H. Donnelley Internat. Ltd., London, Eng., 1970-73; asst. sec., internat. counsel Am. Can Co., Greenwich, Conn., 1973-86; asst. sec., asst. gen. counsel Am. Can Co. (name changed to Am. Can Packaging Inc. 1986), Greenwich, Conn., 1986-87; ptnr. Bentley, Mosher & Babson, Stamford and Greenwich, Conn., 1987-89, of counsel, 1990-92. Underwriting mem. Lloyd's, 1977-97. Active Rep. Town Meeting, Greenwich, 1986-96. Served to lt. (j.g.) USCGR, 1953-55; lt. comdr. Res. ret. Mem. Harvard Club N.Y.C., Greenwich Country Club, Loxahatchee Club. Republican. Presbyterian. Avocations: golf, shotgun sports, reading, genealogy. E-mail: higun1@aol.com.

FULLER, ROBERT KENNETH, architect, urban designer; b. Denver, Oct. 6, 1942; s. Kenneth Roller and Gertrude Ailene (Heid) F.; m. Virginia Louise Elkin, Aug. 23, 1969; children: Kimberly Kirsten, Kelsey Christa. BArch, U. Colo., 1967; MArch and Urban Design, Washington U., St. Louis, 1974. Registered profl. arch., Colo. Archtl. designer Fuller & Fuller, Denver, Marvin Hatami Assocs., 1968-69; architect, planner Urban Research and Design Ctr., St. Louis, 1970-72; urban designer Victor Gruen & Assocs., 1973-75; prin. Fuller & Fuller Assocs., Denver, 1975—. Past pres. Denver East Ctrl. Civic Assn., Country Club Hist. Dist.; bd. dirs. Cherry Creek Steering Com., Cherry Creek Found.; pres. Horizon Adventures, Inc.; permanent sec.-treas. Archtl. Edn. Found., AIA Colo. Sgt. USMCR, 1964-70. Mem.: AIA (past pres. Denver chpt.), Rocky Mountain Vintage Racing Assn., Colo. Arlberg Club (past pres.), Delta Phi Delta, Phi Gamma Delta. Home: 2244 E 4th Ave Denver CO 80206-4107 Office: 3320 E 2nd Ave Denver CO 80206-5302 Office Phone: 303-333-3320.

FULLER, SAMUEL ASHBY, retired lawyer, mining executive; b. Indpls., Sept. 2, 1924; s. John L.H. and Mary (Ashby) F.; m. Betty Winn Hamilton, June 10, 1948; children— Mary Cheryl Fuller Hargrove, Karen E. Fuller Wolfe, Deborah R. BS in Gen. Engring, U. Cin., 1946, JD, 1947; cert. fin. planner, Coll. for Fin. Planning, 1989. Bar: Ohio 1948, Ind. 1951, Fla. 1984. Cleve. claims rep. Mfrs. and Mchts. Indemnity Co., 1947-48; claims supr. Indemnity Ins. Co. N.Am., 1948-50; with firm Stewart, Irwin, Gilliom, Fuller & Meyer (formerly Murray, Mannon, Fairchild & Stewart), Indpls., 1950-85, Lewis Kappes Fuller & Eads (name changed to Lewis & Kappes), Indpls., 1985-89, 1990—2000; pres., dir. Irsugo Consol. Mines, Ltd., 1953-80; ret., 2000. Dir. Ind. Pub. Health Found., Inc., 1972-84; staff instr. Purdue U. Life Ins. and Mktg. Inst., 1954-61; instr. Am. Coll. Life Underwriters, Indpls., 1964-74; mem. Ind. State Bd. Law Examiners, 1984-96, treas. 1987-88. Bd. dirs. Southwest Social Centre, Inc., 1965-70; mem. Brookshire Homeowner's Assn., pres. 1973; pres., dir. Westminster Village North, Inc., 1981-89. Fellow: Am. Coll. Trust and Estate Counsel, Indpls. Bar Found.; mem.: Internat. Assn. Ins. Counsel Rsch. Inst., Fla. Bar, 7th Cir. Bar Assn., Ind. State Bar Assn. (bd. mgrs. 1986—88), English Speaking Union, Ind. Pioneers Soc., Ctr. Ind. Bridge Assn. (pres. 1969), Lincoln Hills Golf Club, Mil. Order Loyal Legion US (recorder 1970—76, comdr. 1977—80), Masons, Beta Theta Pi. Republican. Roman Catholic. Personal E-mail: samuel105@verizon.net.

FULLER, SAMUEL R., construction executive; BA in Acctg., U. Oreg.; MBA in Fin., U. Tex., Arlington. CPA. Auditor KPMG Peat Marwick; sr. v.p., dir. internal audit Tex. Am. Bancshares/Team Bank, 1979-91; with D.R. Horton, Inc., Ft. Worth, 1991—, contr., 1995—2000, exec. v.p., CFO, treas., bd. dirs., 2000—03, sr. exec. v.p., 2003—. Office: DR Horton Inc DR Horton Tower 301 Commerce St Ste 500 Fort Worth TX 76102-4178*

FULLER, SANDRA VIVIAN, oil and gas industry executive; BBA in Petroleum Land Mgmt., The U. Tex., Austin, Tex., 1981; BS in Med. Tech., The U. Tex., Tyler, Tex., 1996. Ind. petroleum landman Benchmark Petroleum, Gordonville, Tex., 1981—. Literary critique, cons. Schlumberger Oilfield Glossary, 2006. Mem.: Fort Worth Assn. Profl. Landmen, Dallas Assn. Petroleum Landmen, Am. Assn. Profl. Landmen. Home Phone: 903-523-4488; Office Phone: 940-523-4488.

FULLER, S(HERI) MARCE, energy executive; BSEE, U. Ala.; MS in Power System Engring., Union Coll. Student engr. Ala. Power (subs. The So. Co.), 1980-83; engr. power system engring. dept. GE, 1983-85; electric system planning engr. Ala. Power (subs. The So. Co.), 1985-87; sr. fin. analyst corp. finance So. Co. Svcs., 1987-89, prin. strategic planning, asst. to pres., 1989-91; bus. devel. mgr. So. Electric (subs. The So. Co.), 1991; v.p. domestic bus. devel. So. Electric, 1994-96, sr. v.p. domestic ops., 1996; pres., CEO Mirant Corp., Atlanta, 1999—2005. Bd. dirs. Curtiss-Wright Corp., Earthlink; chairperson electricity adv. bd. U.S. Dept. Energy; mem. bd. councilors The Carter Ctr.; mem. Pres. Internat. Bd. Advisors, Philippines. Trustee Atlanta Internat. Sch. Office: Curtiss-Wright Corp Bd Directors 4 Becker Farm Rd Roseland NJ 07068

FULLER, SIMON, music company executive, television producer; b. Hastings, England, May 17, 1960; With Chrysalis Music Ltd., 1981—85; founder, CEO 19 Entertainment Ltd., London, 1985—; dir. Popworld Ltd., 2000—, CKX, Inc., 2005—. Exec. prodr.: (films) Spice World, 1997, S Club Seeing Double, 2003, From Justin to Kelly, 2003; (TV series) S Club 7 in Miami, 1999; (films) S Club 7 in LA, 2000; (TV series) Pop Idol, 2001—03, S Club 7 in Hollywood, 2001, Am. Idol: The Search for a Superstar, 2002—, Viva S Club, 2002, All Am. Girl, 2003; co-exec. prodr. Am. Juniors, 2003; exec. prodr.: (TV series) I Dream, 2004, So You Think You Can Dance, 2005—; (TV films) S Club 7 in New Zealand, 2000, S Club 7; Artistic Differences, 2000; (TV series) Search for the Next Great Am. Band, 2008. Named one of The World's Most Influential People, Time mag., 2007. Office: 19 Entertainment Ltd 33 Ransomes Dock 35-37 Parkgate Rd London SW11 4NP England*

FULLER, THEODORE, retired insurance executive; b. Yonkers, NY, Dec. 7, 1918; s. Clarence Wendel and Mary Edgar (Denniston) F. AB cum laude, Princeton U., NJ, 1941; LLB, Columbia U., NYC, 1948. Bar: N.Y. 1948. With Savs. Bank Life Ins. Fund, NYC, 1948-83, exec. v.p., 1964-65, pres., 1965-83. Former mem. N.Y. State Adv. Bd. Life Ins.; cons. Svc. Corps Ret. Execs. Comdr. USNR, World War II, Korea. Mem. Assn. of Bar of City of N.Y., Princeton Club, Univ. Glee Club, Indian Harbor Yacht Club, Retired Men's Assn. (former pres.), Ea. Packard Club, Antique Automobile Club Am., Classic Car Club Am. (former bd. dirs.), Rolls Royce Owners Club, Pierce Arrow Club, Sound Investments Club. Home: 12 Comly Ave Greenwich CT 06831-4934

FULLER, WAYNE ARTHUR, statistics educator; b. Corning, Iowa, June 15, 1931; s. Loren Boyd and Elva Gladys (Darrah) F.; m. Evelyn Rose Steinford, Dec. 22, 1956; children: Douglas W., Bret E. BS, Iowa State U., 1955, MS, 1957, PhD, 1959. Asst. prof. Iowa State U., Ames, 1959-62, assoc. prof., 1962-66, prof., 1966-83, disting. prof. stats., 1983—2001, disting. prof. emeritus, 2001—. Cons. Doane Mktg. Rsch., Inc., St. Louis. Author: Introduction to Statistical Time Series, 1976, 2nd ed. 1996, Measurement Error Models, 1987; also articles. Served as cpl. U.S. Army, 1952-54 Fellow Am. Statis. Assn. (v.p. 1991-93), Inst. Math Stats., Econometric Soc.; mem. Internat. Statis. Inst., Royal Statis. Soc. Home: 3013 Briggs Cir Ames IA 50010-4705 Office: Iowa State U Statis Lab 221 Snedecor Hall Ames IA 50010 Home Phone: 515-232-1146; Office Phone: 515-294-9773. Business E-Mail: waf@iastate.edu.

FULLER, WILLIAM SIDNEY, lawyer; b. Auburn, Ala., Aug. 9, 1931; s. William Melton and Ernestine (Torbert) F.; m. Joyce Jeffrey, Nov. 5, 1953; children: Jeffrey Melton, Barbara Rush. BS, Auburn U., 1953; LLB, U. Ala., 1956, JD, 1969. Bar: Ala. 1956. Student asst. to dean U. Ala. Law Sch., 1954—55; law clk. to U.S. dist. judge, Montgomery, Ala., 1956—57; practice law Andalusia, 1957—; chmn. bd. So. Nat. Corp.; former city atty. City of Andalusia. Dir., sec. Covington County Bank; chmn. bd. So. Nat. Corp.; lectr. Southeastern Trial Inst.; mem. grievance com. Ala. State Bar, 1968-71, mem. bd. commrs., 1979-81; mem. law and contemporary affairs adv. coun. Auburn U. Author: Personal Injury Treatises. Mem. ABA, Ala., Covington County bar assns., Am. Trial Lawyers Assn., Am. Bd. Trial Advocates, Ala. Plaintiff Lawyers Assn., Ala. Trial Lawyers Assn. (pres. 1968), Phi Delta Phi, Kappa Alpha, Alpha Phi Omega. Presbyterian (elder, trustee, past chmn. bd. deacons Sunday sch. tchr.). Club: Andalusia (dir., pres. 1972), Topsl Beach and Racket (Destin, Fla.). Home: 100 S Ridge Rd Andalusia AL 36421-4214 Office: 28 S Court Sq Andalusia AL 36420-3918

FULLERTON, ANN ELIZABETH, retired biology educator; b. Wilmington, Del., Apr. 13, 1925; d. Albert George and Blanche Elizabeth Fullerton. BA magna cum laude, We. Md. Coll., Westminster, Md., 1947; MSc, Syracuse U., NY, 1959. Tchr. biology Bethesda-Chevy Chase HS, Md., 1947—58, North Shore HS, Glen Head, NY, 1959—80, ret., 1980. Mem. secondary schs. evaluating com. Mid. Atlantic States Assn., NYC, 1968, Port Chester, NY, 74. Named Tchr. of Yr., NY Soc. Profl. Engrs., 1974, NY State Tchjrs. of Yr., 1975; grantee, NSF, 1957, 1959, 1968, 1971. Mem.: NY State United Tchrs., North Nassau Ret. Tchrs. Assn. (life), NY State Ret. Tchrs. Assn. (life), Nat. Assn. Biology Tchrs. (life), Edn. Philanthropic Orgn. Internat., Philanthropic Internat. (coll. rep. historian local chpt. 2006), Delta Kappa Gamma (Delta chpt. internat. mem.). Avocations: travel, gardening, reading. Home: 2014 Kirkwood Hwy Wilmington DE 19805-4922

FULLERTON, DENISE S.S., lawyer; married; 2 children. Grad. with honors, Gustavus Adolphus Coll., 1993, William Mitchell Coll. Law, 1998. Bar: Minn. 1998, US Dist. Ct. (dist. Minn.). Ptnr. Ramsay & DeVore, P.A., Roseville, Minn. Contbr. articles to profl. publs. Named a Rising Star, Minn. Super Lawyers mag., 2006. Mem.: Minn. State Bar Assn., Ramsey

County Bar Assn., Hennepin County Bar Assn., Minn. Trial Lawyers Assn. (mem. no-fault com. 2001—, mem. bd. govs. 2003—, mem. exec. com. 2005, chair women lawyers sect.), Minn. Women Lawyers. Office: Ramsay & DeVore PA Rosedale Towers Ste 450 1700 W Hwy 36 Roseville MN 55113 Office Phone: 651-604-0000. E-mail: dfullerton@ramsaydevore.com.*

FULLERTON, DEREK PAUL, public health service officer; b. Winchester, Mass., Mar. 25, 1975; s. Paul F. and Linda M. Fullerton; m. Heather I. Scott, Oct. 20, 2001. BS in Environ. Sci., U. NH, Durham, 1997. Civil engr. City of Gloucester, Mass., 1997—99; sr. civil engr. Town of Lexington, Mass., 1999—2003, dir. pub. health, 2004—. Mem. conservation commn. Town of Wilmington, Mass., 1998—2001, mem. water and sewer adv. bd., 1999. Recipient Cert. of Recognition for Contbns. to Pub. Health, Boston U., Sch. Pub. Health, 2006. Mem.: Mass. Health Officers Assn., Nat. Environ. Health Assn. Achievements include patents pending for decorative vent for septic system. Avocations: golf, fly fishing, boating, basketball. Home: 28 Park Ave Middleton MA 01949 Office: Town of Lexington Health Dept 1625 Massachusetts Ave Lexington MA 02420

FULLERTON, DOROTHY MALLAN, artist, modeling agency executive; b. Ancon, C.Z., May 6, 1938; d. Daniel Harrington and Dorothy (Heintzelman) Mallan; m. Geoge Latimer Fullerton, May 31, 1957 (div. 1979); children: Daphne, Stuart, Nicholas. Student, Women's Christian Coll., Madras, India, 1956, Corcoran Art Sch., 1960; Cours de Civilization certificate, Sorbonne, Paris, 1971, Ecole du Louvre, 1972. RN, Calif. Antique dealer, Paris, 1970-73, antique sales rep., Heritage Place, San Francisco, 1979-81; fashion model Model Mgmt., Ford, N.Y., Brebner, San Francisco, 1980-85, talent dir., model mgmt., San Francisco, 1983-85, Grimmé Agy, San Francisco, 1987. One man shows include Rehobeth Art League, Del., 1965, Boston Visual Artists, Union, Mass., 1976, Artist Co-op, 1984, Castlebury Gallery, Arlington, Tex.; group shows include Leahy Hosp., Boston, 1976, Chez Henri, Warren, Vt., 1977, Artist Co-op of San Francisco, 1980-85; represented in permanent collections Schueler, Boston, Latham, France, Frapier, France, McNally, Zena Jones, Ruth Assawa, Bea Kribs, San Francisco; also pvt. collections. Mem. Artist Cooperative Gallery (mem. bd.), San Francisco Women Artist Gallery, Artist Cooperative Gallery (pres. 1982), Jr. League San Francisco, Nat. Mus. Women in Arts. Republican. Episcopalian. Avocations: music; fishing; hiking; traveling. Home: 145 Connecticut St San Francisco CA 94107-2414 Office: 45 Castro St Ste 100 San Francisco CA 94114-1010

FULLERTON, R. DONALD, banker; b. June 7, 1931; married. BA, U. Toronto, 1953. With Can. Bank of Commerce, Vancouver, 1953—, exec. v.p., chief gen. mgr., 1973, dir. of bank, 1974—, pres., COO, 1976, chmn., CEO, 1984, ret. chmn., CEO, 1992, chmn. exec. com., 1992-99, ret. dir., 2004. Bd. dirs. Husky Energy, 3 Italia S.p. Avocations: skiing, golf. Office: CIBC Commerce Ct N Toronto ON Canada M5L 1A2 E-mail: rd.fullerton@cibc.com.

FULLERTON, ROBERT VICTOR, lawyer; b. Lakewood, Ohio, Mar. 30, 1918; s. Victor G. and Gertrude H. (Horsley) F.; m. Frances Riebel Aug. 23, 1941 (dec. Mar. 1989); children: Susan Anne, Thomas George; m. Margaret Paver Van Voorhis, Feb., 1991. BS in Bus., Miami U., Oxford, Ohio, 1939; LL.B., JD, Case Western Res. U., 1941. Bar: Ohio 1941, Calif. 1945, U.S. Dist. Ct. (ctrl. dist.) Calif. 1945, U.S. Dist. Ct. (so. dist.) Calif. 1974, U.S. Ct. Appeals (9th cir.) 1974, U.S. Tax Ct. 1952, U.S. Supreme Ct. 1974. Spl. agt. FBI, 1941-46; dep. dist. atty. San Bernardino County (Calif.), 1946; asst. dist. atty., 1946-47; individual practice law San Bernardino, 1947—. Chmn. San Bernardino County U.S. Savs. Bond Com. Dept. Treasury, 1963— Pres. United Fund, San Bernardino, 1961-62; trustee Found. for Calif. State U., San Bernardino, 1981—, v.p., 1986—; bd. dirs. Inland Action, 1974-90; trustee Inland Area Symphony Assn., 1983—, v.p. endowments, 1986; bd. dirs. Estate Planning Coun. San Bernadino County, 1984-92, pres., 1990-91; chmn. planning divsn. United Cmty. Svcs., San Bernardino, 1966-69; mem. adv. bd. Auto. Club So. Calif., 1969-80. Recipient Citizens of Yr. award San Bernardion Realtors, 1967. Mem. ABA, State Bar Calif. (asst. sec. San Bernardino County 1953-56, conf. coord. com. on fed. rules 1954-57), Am. Judicature Soc., Air Force Assn. (pres. local chpt. 1969-70), San Bernardino C. of C. (pres. 1968-69), Kiwanis (pres. local club 1959-60), Arrowhead Country. Republican. Home: 3255 Valencia Ave San Bernardino CA 92404-2418 Office: 215 N D St San Bernardino CA 92401-1733 E-mail: rfullerton@inlandbusinesslaw.com.

FULLMAN, ROBERT LOUIS, metallurgy consultant; b. Sewickley, Pa., Sept. 13, 1922; m. Doris Hite; children: Janice, Grant. BEng, Yale U., 1943, DEng in Metallurgy, 1950. Instr. metallurgy New Haven YMCA Jr. Coll., 1947-48; rsch. assoc. GE, 1948-55, mgr. materials and processes studies, 1955-59, mgr. metal studies, 1960-63, mgr. fuel cell studies, 1964-65, mgr. properties br., 1965-68, mgr. planning & resources, material sci. & engring., 1969-72, metallurgist R & D Ctr., 1972-83; cons., 1983—. Vis. lectr. Rensselaer Polytech. Inst., 1951-56, adj. prof., 1956-65; sec.-treas. bd. govs. Acta Metallurgica, 1965-96, treas., 1997-2000. Recipient J. Herbert Holloman award Acta Metallurgica, 1995. Fellow Am. Soc. Metals (Geisler Meml. award 1955), Am. Inst. Mining, Metallurgy & Petroleum Engrs. Achievements include research on deformation of metals; interfacial energies in solids; crystal growth; origin of microstructures; recrystallization and grain growth; relationships between microstructure and properties of metals. Home: 1710 Jamaica Way Apt 206 Punta Gorda FL 33950-5175 E-mail: rlfullman@aol.com.

FULLMER, DANIEL WARREN, former psychologist, educator; b. Spoon River, Ill., Dec. 12, 1922; s. Daniel Floyd and Sarah Louisa (Essex) F.; m. Janet Satomi Saito, June 1980; children: Daniel William, Mark Warren. BS, Western Ill. U., 1947, MS, 1952; PhD, U. Denver, 1955. Post-doctoral intern psychiat. div. U. Oreg. Med. Sch., 1958-61; mem. faculty U. Oreg., 1955-66; prof. psychology Oreg. System of Higher Edn., 1958-66; faculty Coll. Edn. U. Hawaii, Honolulu, 1966-95, retired, 1995, prof. emeritus, 1974—; pvt. practice psychol. counseling. Cons. psychologist Grambling State U., 1960-81; founder Free-Family Counseling Ctrs., Portland, Oreg., 1959-66, Honolulu, 1966-74; co-founder Child and Family Counseling Ctr., Waianae, Oahu, Hawaii, Kilohana United Meth. Ch., Oahu, 1992, v.p., sec., 1992; pres. Human Resources Devel. Ctr., Inc., 1974—; chmn. Hawaii State Bd. to License Psychologists, 1973-78. Author: Counseling: Group Theory & System, 2d. edit., 1978, The Family Therapy Dictionary Text, 1991, MANABU, Diagnosis and Treatment of a Japanese Boy with a Visual Anomaly, 1991; co-author: Principles of Guidance, 2d. edit., 1977; author (counselor/cons. training manuals) Counseling: Content and Process, 1964, Family Consultation Therapy, 1968, The School Counselor-Consultant, 1972, Family Therapy as the Rites of Passage, 1998; editor: Bulletin, Oreg. Coop Testing Service, 1955-57, Hawaii P&G Jour., 1970-76; assoc. editor: Educational Perspectives, U. Hawaii Coll. Edn. Served with USNR, 1944-46. Recipient Francis E. Clark award Hawaii Pers. Guidance Assn., 1972, Thomas Jefferson award for Outstanding Pub. Svc., 1993; named Hall of Fame Grambling State U., 1987. Mem. Am. Psychol. Assn., Am. Counseling Assn. (Nancy C. Wimmer award 1963), Masons. Methodist. Office: 1750 Kalakaua Ave Apt 809 Honolulu HI 96826-3725 Office Phone: 808-942-2072. *I grew up along Spoon River. The people of Spoon River had a principle of life: Improve on what you are. The purpose is to be able to help others help themselves. From here, it is like stepping into a river of life; the deeper you got, the stronger the current. Then, suddenly, here you are nearing the delta. Just ahead lies a beautiful ocean.*

FULLMER, STEVEN MARK, engineering executive; b. San Francisco, Mar. 15, 1956; s. Thomas Patrick and Patricia Ann (Carroll-Boyd) Fullmer; m. Rhonda Lynnette Bush, Nov. 8, 1992; children: Wesley Stevenson, Sierra Marin. BA in Chemistry, Willamette U., 1978, BA in Biology, 1978; MBA, Ariz. State U., 1993. Cert. project mgmt. profl. PMI. Sr. engr., project leader Honeywell Large Computer Products, Phoenix, 1981—86; bank officer, cons., infosecurity cons. First Interstate Bank/Wells Fargo Bank, Phoenix, 1987—96; project mgr. Wells Fargo Bank, 1996; sr. engr. AG Comm. Sys./ Lucent Technologies, Phoenix, 1996—2005; pres. Blue Sphere Solutions, 2005—. Cons. J. A. Boyd & Assoc., San Francisco, 1985—96, ImaginInc. Consulting, Phoenix, 1985—. Mem. exec. bd. Grand Canyon coun. Boy Scouts Am., scoutmaster, 1983—88, cubmaster, 2003—05, commr., 1988—92, dist. chmn., 1995—96; founder, lt. comdr. Maricopa County Sheriff's Adj. Posse, 1982—93; pres. Heard Mus. Coun., 1995—96; dept. head, lead Liberty Wildlife. Recipient Order of Merit, Boy Scouts Am., 1988, Nat. Disting. Commr. award, 1991, Silver Beaver award, 1994. Mem.: Internat. Inst. Bus. Analysis, Am. Inst. Cert. Computer Profls. (cert. data processor 1985), Mensa, Knights Cross (Sovereign Order of St. Stanislas), KC (membership dir. 1988), SAR, Beta Gamma Sigma, Sigma Iota Epsilon, Alpha Chi Sigma, Kappa Sigma (asst. dist. grand master 2001—, commr. 2006—07), Phi Eta Sigma, Phi Lambda Upsilon. Republican. Roman Catholic. Avocations: American Indian history, science fiction, scuba diving, hiking, camping. Office: Blue Sphere Solutions LLC 1019 W Kaler Dr Phoenix AZ 85021 Office Phone: 602-206-9625. Business E-Mail: steven@bluespheresoln.com.

FULMER, ASHLEE SUSAN, forensic specialist; d. John Riley and Janice Fulmer. BA in Criminology and Criminal Justice, U. Md., College Park, 1998; M in Forensic Sci., George Washington U., DC, 2003. Lab. technician I Fairfax Identity Labs., Va., 2000—00, lab. technician II, 2000—01; forensic DNA analyst I Bode Tech., Lorton, Va., 2001—03, forensic DNA analyst II, 2003—05, forensic DNA analyst III, 2005—05, supr. forensic casework, 2005—, sr. forensic DNA analyst I, 2006—. Mem.: Am. Acad. Forensic Scis. (assoc.). Office: Bode Technology 10430 Furnace Rd Suite 107 Lorton VA 22079 Home Phone: 703-867-6380; Office Phone: 703-646-9747. Business E-Mail: ashlee.fulmer@bodetech.com.

FULMER, DEBORAH LEE, education educator, oncological nurse; b. Harrisburg, Pa., July 25, 1957; d. Donald Richard Petrovic and Nancy Lee Gruber. ADN, Harrisburg Area CC, Pa., 1991; B in nursing, Graceland U., Lamoni, Iowa, 1998; MS in Biology, Millersville U., Pa., 2001; PhD student, Touro U., San Francisco, 2003—. RN Am. Nursing Assn., Pa., 1991, cert. Oncology Nurse, Am. Nursing Assn., 1995. Oncology nurse Polyclinic Med. Ctr., Harrisburg, Pa., 1991—2000; pediatric nurse Pediataric Svc. of Am., Harrisburg, Pa., 1999—; instr. biology Harrisburg Area CC, 2004—. Vol. AIDS Cmty. Alliance, Harrisburg, 1999—2006. Prodr.: (pub. awareness presentation) Rebuilding Education: Afghanistan, (ednl. presentation) Landmines - A Day At The ICRC Rehabilitation Clinic In Afghanistan. Del. Global Exch./Afghans 4 Tomorrow, San Francisco, 2003; project coord. Cultural Embrace, Austin, 2006. Mem.: ARC (vol. 2004—06), Internat. Soc. Nursing (assoc.). Avocations: victorian gardening, travel. Home: 3024 Orchard Ln Middletown PA 17057 Office: Pediatric Svcs of America Prince St Harrisburg PA 17109 Home Phone: 717-948-5172; Office Phone: 717-540-1051. Personal E-mail: dfulm_2000@yahoo.com.

FULMER, DOUGLAS ALAN, political scientist, consultant, journalist; b. Akron, Ohio, June 12, 1959; s. Gordon Lozier and Marjorie Helen (Glandorf) F.; m. Alice Marie Fry, Aug. 16, 1980 (div. Aug. 16, 1982). BA, Mt. Union Coll., Alliance, Ohio, 1981; MA, Syracuse U., 1982. Dir. state and local affairs Coalition for Scenic Beauty, Washington, 1987-89; internat. field coord. Nat. Space Soc., Washington, 1989-91; exec. dir. Com. To Preserve Assateague Island, Towson, Md., 1991; sr. assoc. Phil Noble and Assocs., Towson, 1991-92; pres. Douglas Fulmer and Assocs., Hermitage, Tenn., 1993—; freelance journalist Hermitage, Tenn., 1990—. Contbr. articles to periodicals, newspapers, mags., and Web sites. Vol. numerous polit. campaigns, 1972-80; mem. campaign staff numerous polit. campaigns, 1982-86; field rep. Am. Fedn. State, County and Mcpl. Employees, Indpls., 1986; campaign cons. Md. State Tchrs. Assn., Annapolis, Md., 1986; field rep. Am. Fedn. State, Jersey City, 1985; dir. del. selection George McGovern for Pres., Washington, 1984; field dir. Lane Evans for Congress, Rock Island, Ill., 1984; field coord. Elain Lytel for Congress, Syracuse, 1982. Office: 51 Fawn Creek Pass Nashville TN 37214-4502 E-mail: Dougfulmer@bellsouth.net.

FULMER, HUGH SCOTT, physician, educator; b. Syracuse, NY, June 18, 1928; s. Herbert C. and Emily (Price) F.; m. Zola M. Jones, July 12, 1952; children: James, Kim, Scott. AB, Syracuse U., 1948; MD, SUNY-Syracuse, 1951; M.P.H., Harvard U., 1961. Intern R.I. Hosp., 1951-52; resident internal medicine SUNY-Syracuse, 1954-57; fellow pulmonary medicine SUNY, Syracuse, 1957-58; asst. dir., rsch. assoc. Navajo-Cornell Field Health Research Project, 1958-60; instr. pub. health and preventive medicine Cornell U. Coll. Medicine, 1958-60; asst. prof. community medicine U. Ky. Coll. Medicine, 1960-64, assoc. prof., 1964-66, prof., 1966-68, dir. sr. med. student internat. cross-cultural program, 1964-68, dir. preventive medicine residency program, 1964-68; tech. cons. health Peace Corps, Malaysia, 1968-69; prof., chmn. dept. community and family medicine U. Mass. Med. Sch., 1969-77, assoc. dean clin. edn. and primary care, 1975-79, chief sect. gen. medicine, dept. medicine, 1979—83; dir. ambulatory and community svcs. Carney Hosp., Boston, 1983-88, dir. community-oriented primary care program, 1988-93, dir. preventive medicine residency, 1988-93; exec. dir. Ctr. for Cmty. Responsive Care, Boston, 1992—2000, dir. preventive medicine residency & COPC fellowship program, 1992—2002. Adj. prof. socio-med. scis., cmty. medicine and pub. health Boston U. Sch. Medicine and Pub. Health, 1983—96; adj. prof. family and internal medicine SUNY, Syracuse, 2005—. Served with M.C., USAF, 1952-54. Mem. AMA, APHA, Mass. Med. Soc., Assn. Tchrs. Preventive Medicine (past pres., Outstanding Tchr. award 1993), Am. Assn. Pub. Health Physician, Am. Coll. Preventive Medicine (bd. regents 1988-94), Harvard Sch. Pub. Health Alumni Assn. (pres. 1974-76). Achievements include research on educational initiatives to merge medicine and public health in response to community needs. Home: 61 Cherlyn Dr Northborough MA 01532-1135 Business E-Mail: hsfulmer@massmed.org.

FULMER, PHILLIP, university football coach; b. Winchester, Tenn., Sept. 1, 1950; m. Vicky Morey; children: Phillip Jr., Courtney, Brittany, Allison. BA, U. Tenn., 1972. Offensive line coach Wichita (Kans.) State U., 1974, 77-78, linebacker coach, 1975-76; asst. football coach Vanderbilt U., Nashville, 1979; grad. asst. U. Tenn., Nashville, 1972, defensive coord. freshman team, 1973, asst. coach, 1980-91, head coach, 1992—. Head coach East-West Shrine Game, 1998; coach Fla. Citrus Bowl, 1993, Orange Bowl, 1997. Led U. Tenn. Vols. to Southeastern Conf. championship, 1997; named, Nat. and SEC Coach of Year, 1998; recipient, Brotherhood/Sisterhood award from Nat. Conf.for Cmty. and Justice, 2000, State Farm Eddie Robinson Coach of Distinction award, 2000. Mem. Am. Football Coaches Assn. (trustee 1996—, mem. Hall of Fame com., I-A coaches legis. issues com., Kodak Region 2 Coach of Yr. award 1993). Office: Head Football Coach Univ Tenn PO Box 15016 Knoxville TN 37901-5016*

FULMER, VINCENT ANTHONY, retired college president; b. Alliance, Ohio, Oct. 23, 1927; s. Anthony and Catherine (Long) F.; m. Mary Alma Pineau, Dec. 27, 1950; children: Kevan, Kristine, David, Amy, Charles, Alma Leigh. AB cum laude, Miami U., Oxford, Ohio, 1949; postgrad., Harvard U., 1950; S.M., MIT, 1963; LL.D., Suffolk U., 1971; D.Sc., Fla. Inst. Tech., 1982; Ed.D., Hawthorne Coll., 1988. Mem. staff MIT, 1951-86, exec. asst. office chmn., 1960-63, v.p., 1963-73, sec. inst., 1963-85; v.p. adminstrn. William Underwood Co., 1973-75; sec. MIT Corp., 1979—85; v.p., dir. Video Optics Corp., Waltham, Mass., 1985-86; pres. Hawthorne Coll., Antrim, NH, 1986-88, pres. emeritus, 1988—. Bd. dirs. Barbour Stockwell, Inc., Control Air, Inc., Fiberspar Corp.; instr. econs. Williams Coll., 1952. Contbr. chapters to books and mags. Bd. dirs. Planning Office for Urban Affairs, Archdiocese of Boston, 1968-93; trustee Suffolk U., 1972—, chmn., 1976-81; trustee Hawthorne Coll., 1982-92, chmn., 1985-92; corporator New Eng. Coll. Optometry, 1985-87, trustee, 1987-93; bd. dirs. Sml. Bus. High Tech. Inst., Washington, 1982—; mem. exec. com. MIT Enterprise Forum, 1978—, vice-chmn. 1992-93; chmn. Tech. Capital Network, 1990-95, chmn. emeritus, 2005—. With USNR, 1944-46. Mem. Am. Econ. Assn., AAAS, Ops. Rsch. Soc. Am., Inst. Mgmt. Scis., Phi Beta Kappa, Sigma Chi, Omicron Delta Kappa. *While individuals may address themselves exclusively to high personal attainments within the existing framework of our institutions, or devote prodigious efforts to improve or restructure those institutions, in the end it is our lifetime example that counts more heavily than all else.*

FULOP, LASZLO G., architect; arrived in U.S., 1957; s. Pal Fulop Fülöp and Mária-Irma Rózsa; m. Sue Ellen Wilson, Feb. 10, 1962 (div. Nov. 1985); children: Angela, Paul, Zsuzsa; m. Agnes Maria Sylvester, Dec. 30, 1988. Student, U. Vienna; BArch, U. Minn., 1963. Registered architect, Minn., Wis. NCARB draftsman and designer Horty, Elving & Assocs., Mpls., 1963—66; designer, project mgr., and assoc. Baker Assocs., Inc., Mpls., 1966—70; mgr. design and planning Minn. State U. Sys., St. Paul, 1970—75; dir. planning U. Minn., Mpls., 1975—83; dir. planning and constrn. U. Wis., Madison, 1983—89; pres. L.G. Fulop Archs. and Planners, Mpls., 1991—. Adj. instr. N. Hennepin C.C., Brooklyn Park, Minn., 1969—76; mem. long range regional river devel. and acquisition com. City of Mpls., 1976—77; coord. joint pub. works com. Madison City-U. Wis.-Madison, 1984—89, mem. ad-hoc S. Campus planning com., 1987—89, mem. liaison com., 1988—89; ex officio mem. campus planning com. U. Wis.-Madison, 1983—90; mem. Univ. Hill Farms Archtl. Control Com., 1983—90, Univ. Rsch. Pk. Design Rev. Bd., 1983—90. Co-author: The Hurricanes are Coming, 1996, author short stories, poems; contbr. articles to profl. jours. Mem. Town Planning Commn., Baytown, Minn., 1975—83; vol. host. Spl. Olympics, Mpls., 1991; apptd. mem. Convocation Ctr. Com., 1986—88; pres. Minn.-Hungarians, 1976—78, mem. cultural exhibit com., 1990—2005, sec., 1991—2005; chair pub. rels. com. cultural exhibit com., 1996—2005; pres. Communion Hungarian Friends, 1999—2002; mem. exec. com. Hungarian Am. Coalition, Washington, 1996—, bd. dirs., 1996—2004. With forced mil. labor div., 1954—55, Communist Hungary. Mem.: Soc. Coll. and Univ. Planning, Minn. Half-Arabian Horse Assn. (bd. dirs. 1980—81, pres. 1981—83, regional del. IAHA nat. conv. 1983, 1985). Independent. Avocations: writing, history, tennis, stamp collecting/philately. Office: LG Fulop Architects and Planners 6650 Vernon Ave S Minneapolis MN 55436 Office Phone: 952-930-0043. Business E-Mail: laszlofulop@mn.rr.com.

FULSHER, ALLAN ARTHUR, lawyer; b. Portland, Oreg., July 5, 1952; s. Rémy Walter and Barbara Lee (French) F.; m. Karen Louise Schmid, Dec. 28, 1974 (dec. Sept. 1990); children: Brian Rémy, Louise Katherine, Elizabeth Alane. BA in Biology, U. Oreg., 1974, BA in Econs., 1976; JD, U. of Pacific, 1979. Bar: Oreg. 1979, Calif. 1980, U.S. Dist. Ct. Oreg. 1980, U.S. Dist. Ct. (ea. dist.) Calif. 1981, U.S. Ct. Appeals (9th cir.) 1982, U.S. Dist. Ct. (no. dist.) Calif. 1985, U.S. Dist. Ct. (so. dist.) Calif. 1986. Assoc. Law Offices of Jacques B. Nichols PC, Portland, 1979-82, Ragen, Roberts, O'Scannlain, Robertson & Neill, Portland, 1982-83; shareholder Bauer, Hermann, Fountain & Rhoades PC, Portland, 1983-87, v.p., 1984-87; shareholder, v.p. Fulsher and Weatherhead PC, Portland, 1987-88, pres., 1988—2001; gen. counsel Peregrine Holdings, Ltd., Beaverton, Oreg., 1993-97, Peregrine Capital, Inc., Beaverton, 1993-2000; mgr. Stamford Bridge, LLC, 1995—; gen. counsel Makad Corp., Vancouver, Wash., 2000—. Pres., mgr. ProSoccer, LLC, Tigard, Oreg., 1998-01; gen. counsel World Indoor Soccer League, LLC, Dallas, 1998-00; v.p., gen. counsel US Ethanol, LLC, 2006-. Republican. Roman Catholic. Avocations: basketball, automobile racing and restoration, coaching youth and adult sports. Office: Stamford Bridge LLC PO Box 92096 Portland OR 97292-2096 Personal E-mail: allanfulsher@gmail.com.

FULTON, AMY LOU, artist, former realtor; b. Edmonds, Wash., July 19, 1969; d. James Edward Palm and Charlee Theresa Pond; m. David Dean Fulton, June 29, 1991; 1 child, Kent Alex. Student, Rockwell Inst., 2004; student in Fashion Merchandising, Shoreline C.C., 1988; student in Acctg., Edmonds CC, Wash., 1990; degree as Dental Asst., Harcourt Learning, Scranton, Pa., 2002. Cert. dental asst. Scranton, PA, 2002; fashion merchandising Shoreline C.C., 1990, lic. realtor Calif. Dept. Real Estate, 2004. Title clk. Barrier Jaguar-Porsche-Audi, Bellevue, Wash., 1998—2000; realtor Coldwell Banker-Dunnigan Co, Elk Grove, Calif., 2004. Pvt. artist and designer; illustrator Bedrock Pub. Co. Author: Mischievous Guido, 2003. Preschool Bible class tchr. North Seattle Ch. of Christ, 1991—2004; tchr. children's bible class Folsom (Calif.) Point Ch. Christ, Folsom, Calif., 2005—. Grantee, Pell Grant, 1987. Republican. Avocations: painting, horseback riding, skiing, travel, gardening. Home Phone: 916-684-9554; Office Phone: 916-714-2400. Office Fax: 916-714-2424. Personal E-mail: amyfulton1@aol.com.

FULTON, CONCHETTA WHITE, pharmacist, educator; adopted d. John Bernard and Marian Fisher Stevenson; m. Bryan Leon Fulton, Sept. 5, 1992; 1 child, Kyle. PharmD, Xavier U. La., New Orleans, 1997. Registered pharmacist La. Pharmacist Broadmoor Drugstore, New Orleans, 1985—89, Walgreens, New Orleans, 1990—98; coll. of pharmacy faculty Xavier U. La., 1999—. Cons. Novartis Pharmaceuticals. Founding pres. GNO-ABO Charitable and Ednl. Found., Inc., New Orleans, 2000—06; corr. sec. Jack & Jill of Am., New Orleans. Recipient Lawrence Ferring Faculty award, Pharmacy Student Body Assn., 2003. Mem.: Am. Assn. Colls. Pharmacy, Nat. Coun. Negro Women, Am. Pharmacists Assn., Nat. Pharm. Assn. (life), Alpha Kappa Alpha (life; chmn. south ctrl. regional heritage com. 2006—, pres. Alpha Beta chpt., South Ctrl. Region coror of Yr. 2004). Home Phone: 504-899-3564; Office Phone: 504-520-7402. Office Fax: 504-520-7971. Business E-Mail: cwfulton@xula.edu.

FULTON, DANIEL S., corporate real estate executive; BA in Econs., Miami U., Ohio, 1970; MBA, U. Wash., 1976; grad. exec. program, Stanford U., 2001. Former officer USN Supply Corps; mem. investment evaluation dept. Weyerhaeuser Co., 1976—78; planning mgr. Weyerhaeuser Real Estate Co., 1978—79; investment mgr. Weyerhaeuser Venture Co., 1978—87; CEO Cornerstone Columbia Devel. Co., 1987—88; pres., CEO Weyerhaeuser Realty Investors, 1988—98, Weyerhaeuser Venture Co., 1998—2001, Weyerhaeuser Real Estate Co., 2001—. Former officer USN Supply Corps; mem. investment evaluation dept. Weyerhaeuser Co., mem. sr. mgmt. team, 2003—; planning mgr. Weyerhaeuser Real Estate Co., 1978—79, pres., CEO, 2001—; investment mgr. Weyerhaeuser Venture Co., 1979—87, pres., CEO, 1998—2001; CEO Cornerstone Columbia Devel. Co., 1987—88; pres., CEO Weyerhaeuser Realty Investors, 1988—98. Bd. dirs. United Way of King County; mem. adv. bd. U. Wash. Bus. Sch.; bd. govs. Lambda Alpha Internat. Land Econs. Soc., High Prodn. Homebuilder Coun. of Nat. Assn. Homebuilders. Office: Weyerhaeuser Co 33663 Weyerhaeuser Way S Federal Way WA 98063-9777*

FULTON, IRA, construction executive; b. Tempe, Ariz., 1931; s. David and Myrtie Fulton; m. Mary Lou Fulton. Salesman Nat. Cash Register; regional ops. mgr. Dana Brothers Signal Oil and Gas; founder Nat.

Retailer's Corp., Computer Audit; pres., CEO Fulton Homes, 1975—; owner Eagleson's Big & Tall, 1976—95. Named one of 50 Most Generous Philanthropists, BusinessWeek, 2005. Office: Fulton Homes 9140 S Kyrene Ste 202 Tempe AZ 85284

FULTON, KENNETH RAY, professional association administrator; b. Cleve., Dec. 22, 1948; BS in Social Scis., U. Md., 1973; MS in Mgmt., Am. U., 1977. Mem. staff Nat. Acad. Scis., Washington, 1971-80, dir. membership, 1980-84, spl. asst. to pres., 1984-93; exec. dir. Acad. Scis., Washington, 1993—. Mgr. membership and program activities Nat. Acad. Scis.; organizer numerous sci. confs. and symposia, art exhibitions and cultural programs; mem. U.S. delegation to Codex Alimentarius Commn. UN, 1977-80. Publisher Proceedings of the Nat. Acad. Scis. With U.S. Navy. Mem. AAAS, Internat. Coun. for Sci. (com. on dissemination of sci. info.), Am. Soc. Assn. Execs., Soc. Scholarly Publishers. Office: Nat Acad Scis 500 Fifth St NW Washington DC 20001 Business E-Mail: kfulton@nas.edu.

FULTON, MICHAEL L., optical company executive, researcher; s. Kenneth F. and Carolyn B. Fulton; m. Alehea H. Fulton, Dec. 5, 1987; 1 child, Amira B. BS in Chemistry, Sonoma State U., Rhonert Park, Calif., 1977, MA in English, 1984. Prin. engr. Rockwell Sci. Ctr., Thousand Oaks, Calif., 2000—03; pres. Ion Beam Optics Inc., Thousand Oaks, 2003—. Process engr. Optical Coating Lab. Inc, Santa Rosa, Calif., 1973—89; dir. r&d PSI Max Optics Inc, Auburn, Calif., 1989—90; rsch. scientist Boeing High Tech. Ctr., Bellvue, Wash., 1990—93; r&d specialist Avimo Electro-Optics Pte. Ltd., Singapore, 1993—97; dir. r&d ZC&R Coatings for Optics Inc., Torrance, Calif., 1997—2000. Recipient Distinguish Alumni award, Sonoma State U., 2006. Mem.: Optical Soc. Am., Soc. Vacuum Coaters, Internat. Soc. Optical Engring. Achievements include first to pioneer ion assisted deposition technology that is now used through out the optics industry; made first narrow band pass filters using hard oxide coatings; Unique deposition processes that converts metals to dielectric materials now used throughout the optics industry; research in wide range of energetic processes to produce some of the most advanced optical coatings in the world; invention of ion-assisted filtered cathodic arc deposition technology; patents for Filtered Cathodic Arc Depostion System now used in the computer hard drive industry; development of filter cathodic arc technology in conjuction with Lawrence Berkeley National Laboratory for deposting optical coatings in space; laser damage resistant coatings for laser fusion mirrors; ultra violet protection coatings on silicone fresnel lenses used in advanced space solar power applications; optical coatings for military night vision systems for pilots. Office: Ion Beam Optics Inc 2060 E Ave de Los Arboles #D243 Thousand Oaks CA 91362 Office Phone: 805-277-9464.

FULTON, ROBERT LESTER, sociology educator; b. Toronto, Ont., Can., Nov. 30, 1926; s. Edgar John and Mary Grace (Ouderkirk) F.; m. Patricia Alma Brown, July 29, 1948 (div.); children: David, Richard; m. Julie Ann Rockman, June 13, 1964; 1 son, Regan. AB cum laude, U. Ill., 1951; MA, U. Toronto, 1953; PhD, Wayne State U., 1959. Instr. U. Wis., 1957-58; asst. prof. sociology Calif. State U., LA, 1958-65, prof. sociology, 1965-66, U. Minn., Mpls., 1966-97; dir. Ctr. for Death Edn. and Rsch., 1969-97. Vis. prof. U. Minn., 1963-65, U. Osmania, India, 1967, St. Christopher's Hospice, London, 1975, Radium Hemmet, Stockholm, 1975, U. Calif.-Irvine, 1975, U. Calif.-San Diego, 1978, 79, U. Calif.-San Francisco, 1986, U. Vt., 1983, 84, 86, 88, 89, 92, St. Luke's Coll., Tokyo, 1985, U. Cape Town, 1993, Rikkyo U., Tokyo, 1993, Nankai U., Tianjin, China, 1995. Author: Death and Identity, 1965, 3rd rev. edit., 1993; Education and Social Crisis, 1967, Death, Grief and Bereavement: Bibliography 1845-1975, 1977, Death and Dying: Challenge and Change, 1978; assoc. editor Omega, 1970-73. With Royal Can. Navy, 1944. Fellow Am. Sociol. Assn.; mem. Internat. Workgroup on Death, Dying and Bereavement, Soc. Thanatologie de la Langue Française. Home: 139 Nina St Saint Paul MN 55102-2129 Office Phone: 651-292-0716. Business E-Mail: fulto001@umn.edu.

FULTON, THOMAS, theoretical physicist, educator; b. Budapest, Hungary, Nov. 19, 1927; came to U.S., 1941; s. Michael and Irene (Weisz) F.; m. Babette Pilzer, June 14, 1952; children: Ruth Carol, Judith Pamela. BA, Harvard U., 1950, MA, 1951, PhD, 1954. Prof. emeritus Johns Hopkins U., Balt., 2000—; Frank B. Jewett Found. postdoctoral fellow Inst. Advanced Studies, Princeton, NJ, 1954-55; NSF postdoctoral fellow Princeton, NJ, 1955-56; from asst. prof. to assoc. prof. physics Johns Hopkins U., Balt., 1956-64, prof., 1964-2000. Rsch. cons. and vis. scientist numerous orgns., 1954—. Author: (with others) Resonances in Strong Interaction Physics, 1963; assoc. editor Jour. Math. Physics, 1968-71; contbr. over 100 articles to profl. jours. Bd. dirs. Shriver Hall Concert Series, Balt., 1981-91. With U.S. Army, 1946-47. John Simon Guggenheim Found. fellow, U. Vienna, 1964-65, Fulbright sr. rsch. fellow, 1964-65; prin. investigator rsch. grantee NSF, Johns Hopkins U., 1960-92. Fellow Am. Phys. Soc.; mem. Archeol. Inst. Am., Sigma Xi. Home: 5600 Roxbury Pl Baltimore MD 21209-4502 Office: Johns Hopkins U Dept Physics And Astro Baltimore MD 21218 Office Phone: 410-516-7363.

FULTON, WILLIAM, mathematics professor; b. Aug. 29, 1939; BA, Brown U., 1961; PhD, Princeton U., 1966. Instr. Princeton (N.J.) U., 1965-66; from instr. to asst. prof. Brandeis U., 1966-69; assoc. prof. Brown U., 1970-75, prof., 1975-87, U. Chgo., 1987-98, Charles L. Hutchinson Disting. Svc. prof., 1995-98; Keeler prof. math. U. Mich., Ann Arbor, 1998—. Vis. asst. prof. Princeton U., 1969-70; vis. prof. U. Genoa, 1969, Aarhus U., 1976-77, Orsay, 1987; vis. mem. Inst. des Hautes Etudes Scis., 1981, Inst. Advanced Study, 1981-82, 94, Math. Scis. Rsch. Inst., 1992-93, Ctr. Advanced Study, Oslo, 1994; Erlander prof. Mittag-Leffler Inst., 1996-97; lectr. in field. Author: Intersection Theory, 1984, Introduction to Intersection Theory in Algebraic Geometry, 1984, Introduction to Toric Varieties, 1993, Algebraic Topology, 1995, Young Tableaux, 1997; (with R. MacPherson) A Categorical Framework for the Study of Singular Spaces, 1981; (wih S. Lang) Riemann-Roch Algebra, 1985, (with J. Harris) Representation Theory; a first course, 1991; (with S. Bloch and I. Dolgachev, editors) Proceedings of the US-USSR Symposium in Algebraic Geometry, Univ. of Chicago, June-July, 1989, 1991; assoc. editor Duke Math. Jour., 1984-93, Jour. Algebraic Geometry, 1992-93; editor Jour. Am. Math. Soc., 1993-99, mng. editor, 1995-98; mem. editl. bd. Cambridge Studies in Advanced Math., 1994—, Chgo. Lectures in Math., 1994-98. Grantee NSF, 1976—, Sloan Found., 1981-82; Guggenheim fellow, 1980-81; named Erlander prof. Swedish Sci. Found., 1996-97. Mem.: NAS, AAAS, Royal Swedish Acad. Sci.

FULTZ, PHILIP NATHANIEL, management analyst; b. NYC, Jan. 29, 1943; s. Otis and Sara Love (Gibbs) F.; m. Anita Neu, Nov. 8, 1998. AA in Bus., Coll. of the Desert, 1980; BA in Mgmt., U. Redlands, 1980, MA in Mgmt., 1982. Enlisted USMC, 1967, advanced through grades to capt., 1972, served in various locations, 1964-78, resigned commn., 1978; CETA coord. County of San Bernardino, Yucca Valley, Calif., 1978-85; mgmt. analyst Advanced Technology, Inc., Twentynine Palms, Calif., 1985-88; spl. transit analyst Omintrans, San Bernardino, Calif., 1988-89; tech. analyst Atlantic Rsch. Corp. (formerly Calculon Corp.), Twentynine Palms, Calif., 1988—; mgmt. analyst Marine Corps Base, Twentynine Palms, Calif., 1991—. Adj. assoc. prof. mgmt. Chapman U., Orange, Calif., 1992—. Founding dir. Unity Home Battered Women's Shelter, Joshua Tree, Calif., 1982, Morongo Basin Adult Literacy; bd. dirs. Twentynine Palms Water Dist., 1991-95; bd. trustess Copper Mountain C.C., 1999, 2003, trustee, 1999—. Mem. Rotary (sec. Joshua Tree chpt. 1983-85). Republican. Home: 73477 Desert Trail Dr Twentynine Palms CA 92277-2218 Home Phone: 760-367-9639; Office Phone: 760-830-6218. Personal E-mail: 4anita_phil2@verizon.net. Business E-Mail: philip.fultz@usmc.mil.

FULWEILER, HOWARD WELLS, language professional; b. Media, Pa., Aug. 26, 1932; s. Howard Wells and Mary Louise (Boyles) F.; m. Sally Starr Nichols, Dec. 28, 1953; children— Peter, John, Mary, Ann. Grad., Kent Sch., 1950; BA, U. S.D., 1954, MA, 1957; PhD, U. N.C., 1960. Teaching fellow U. S.D., 1956-57; teaching fellow U. N.C., 1957-59, 59-60; asst. prof. U. Mo. at Columbia, 1960-64, assoc. prof., 1964-70, prof. English, 1970—2000, chmn. dept., 1967-71, prof. emeritus, 2000—. Author: Letters from the Darkling Plain, 1972, Here a Captive Heart Busted, 1993; contbr. articles profl. jours. Served to lt. AUS, 1954-56. Mem. AAUP, Modern Lang. Assn. Am. Democrat. Episcopalian. Home: 601 S Greenwood Ave Columbia MO 65203-2768 Business E-Mail: fulweilerh@missouri.edu.

FULWILER, ROBERT NEAL, oil industry executive; b. Belton, Tex., Nov. 5, 1937; s. Charles Calvin and Luella (Smith) F.; m. Sylvia Jean Marshall, Dec. 26, 1959; 1 child, Roger Neal. AA, Temple Jr. Coll., 1959; BBA, U. Tex., 1961. Statis. asst. Tex. Eastern Transmission Corp., Houston, 1961-62; adminstrv. asst. subs. LaGloria Oil & Gas, Houston, 1969-76, v.p., 1976; exec. v.p. La Jet, Inc., Houston, 1976-81, pres., 1981-82; chmn. bd. dirs. EnJet Inc., 1982-88; chief exec. officer Trend Energy, Houston, 1989—. Bd. dirs. BFC Assocs., Inc. Author: Competition and Growth in American Energy Markets, 1947-1985, 1968. Mem. Aspen Found., Colo. Mem. Knights of Momus., Aspen Inst. (assoc.), Houston Mus. Fine Arts, Galveston Tex. Country Club. Republican. Mem. Ch. of Christ. Office: Trend Energy 5100 Westheimer Rd Ste 200 Houston TX 77056-5597 Home Phone: 713-626-4376. Personal E-mail: trendenergy@sbcglobal.net.

FUNDERBURK, DAVID BRITTON, retired congressman, ambassador, consultant; b. Langley Field, Va., Apr. 28, 1944; married; 2 children. BA, Wake Forest Coll., 1966; MA, Wake Forest U., 1967; PhD, U. S.C., 1974. Instr. Wingate (NC) Coll., 1967—69, U. SC, Columbia, 1969—70; assoc. prof. history Hardin-Simmons U., Abilene, Tex., 1972—78; prof. history Campbell U., Buies Creek, NC, 1978—81, 1985—86; U.S. amb. to Romania Bucharest, 1981—85; cons. U.S. Dept. Edn., 1987—88; mem. Nat. Edn. Com. on Internat. Ednl. Programs, 1987—90, 104th Congress from 2nd N.C. dist., Washington, 1994—96. Candidate for U.S. Senate from N.C., 1986; exec. dir. Conservatives for Freedom Polit. Action Com., 1988-94; chmn. Internat. Romanian Relief Fund, 1990-94; mem. U.S. Congress, 1994-96; hon. consul gen. Albania for N.C. Republican. Office: 130 Sandhurst Pl Southern Pines NC 28387 E-mail: ambromdf@aol.com.

FUNDERBURK, RAYMOND, judge; b. Phila., Mar. 2, 1944; s. Walter and Inez (Prince) F. AA, Olive-Harvey Coll., 1972; BA, U. Ill., 1974; MPA, Roosevelt U., 1975; JD, U. Ill., 1978. Bar: Ill. 1979, U.S. Dist. Ct. (no. dist.) Ill. 1979, U.S. Ct. Appeals (7th and fed. cirs.) 1983, U.S. Supreme Ct. 1983. Staff atty. Cook County Legal Assistance, Harvey, Ill., 1978-80, mng. atty., 1980-82; assoc. O. Kenneth Thomas Ltd., Harvey, 1982-83, Jones, Ware & Grenard, Chgo., 1983-88, Earl L. Neal and Assocs., Chgo., 1988-93; judge Cir. Ct. of Cook County, Chgo., Ill., 1993—. Bd. dirs. Cook County Legal Assistance Found., Oak Park, Ill., chmn. 1985-87; active legal adv. bd. Thornton Community Coll., South Holland, Ill., 1982—, Aunt Martha's Service, Park Forest, Ill., 1981-83. Chmn. Zoning Bd. of Appeals, Park Forest, 1988-99, Housing Bd. of Appeals, Park Forest, 1988-99, Equal Employment Opportunity Bd., Park Forest, 1988-99, Housing Rev. Bd., Park Forest, 1988-99; bd. dirs. Park Forest Pub. Library, 1982. Served with U.S. Army, 1965-67. Recipient Cert. of Appreciation Aunt Martha's Youth Svc., 1980, Thornton C.C., 1985, Wendell Phillips H.S., 1985, South Suburban YMCA, 1986, 1987, City Ptnr. award U. Ill. Chgo., 1995; named Disting. Grad., U. Ill. Coll. of Law, 1998-99, Olive-Harvey Jr. Coll., 2001. Mem. ABA, Chgo. Bar Assn., Cook County Bar Assn., Ill. Jud. Coun., Ill. Judges Assn., Phi Alpha Delta, Alpha Phi Alpha. Democrat. Avocations: running, chess, tennis. Office: Cir Ct Cook County Ill Rm 2600 Richard J Daley Ctr Dearborn & Randolph Sts Chicago IL 60602

FUNG, JOHN JULIAN, transplant surgeon, immunologist; b. Bethlehem, Pa., July 9, 1956; s. Sui-An and Shu-Nung (Wu) F.; m. Beth Ann Loftus, 1986; children: Justin, Lauren, Brendan, Shannon. BS, Johns Hopkins U., 1975; PhD, U. Chgo., 1980, MD, 1982. Diplomate Am. Bd. Surgery. Gen. surg. resident U. Rochester, NY, 1982-84; chief resident, transplant fellow U. Pitts., 1984-86; chief resident U. Rochester, 1986-88, dir. histocompatibility, 1987-88; from asst. surgery to prof. U. Pitts., 1989—99, prof. surgery, 1999—2004; chmn. Dept. Gen. Surgery Cleve. Clinic, 2004—. Mem. sci. adv. bd. Astella Healthcare Bd. dirs. Family House, Pitts., 1993-2004, Nat. Kidney Found., 1994—2004, Lt. col. USAR, 1987-2003, Desert Storm. Recipient Sci. Rsch. award Ortho Biotech, 1988, Outstanding Abstract award Transplant Soc., 1990, Nat. Kidney Found. award, 1994, Vectors Man of Yr. in Sci., 1997, award Am. Liver Found., 1997, Novartis Clin. Investigator award Am. Soc. Transplantation, 2004. Fellow ACS; mem. AMA, Am. Soc. Transplant Surgeons, Am. Assn. Study Liver Diseases (Liver Transplant Achievement award 2006), Internat. Soc. Liver Transplantation (councilor 1993, pres. 1997-99), Am. Surg. Assn., Transplant Soc. (councilor 2004—). Presbyterian. Achievements include use of OKT3 with Cyclosporine in treatment of rejection; use of FK506 in organ transplantation; clinical attempts at baboon to human transplantation. Home: 65 Winding River Trail Chagrin Falls OH 44022 Office: Dept Gen Surgery Cleveland Clin Found 9500 Euclid Ave A80 Cleveland OH 44195 Home Phone: 440-893-0746; Office Phone: 216-444-3776. Business E-Mail: fungj@ccf.org.

FUNG, MAXWELL ALEXANDER, medical educator; b. Sacramento, Mar. 1, 1967; BA, Stanford U., Calif., 1989; MD, U. Calif., San Francisco, 1993. Asst. prof. U. Conn., Farmington, 1998—2002; assoc. prof. U. Calif., Sacramento, 2006—. Dir. U. Calif. Davis Dermatopathology Svc., Sacramento, 2003—. Finalist Boothe prize excellence in writing, Stanford U., 1986; recipient Faculty Tchg. award, U. Calif., Davis, Dept. Dermatology, 2003, 2006, U. Calif., Davis, Dept. Pathology and Lab. Medicine, 2006. Mem.: Alpha Omega Alpha. Office: Univ Calif Davis 3301 C St Ste 1300 Sacramento CA 95816 Office Phone: 916-734-6373. Office Fax: 916-442-5702. E-mail: maxwell.fung@ucdmc.ucdavis.edu.

FUNG, ROSALINE LEE, language educator; b. China, May 14, 1944; came to U.S., 1963; d. Frank Kwok-Wai and Teresa Wai-Hing (Cheung) Lee; m. Stephen Ying-Chung Fung, Aug. 23, 1968. BA, Briar Cliff Coll., 1966; MA, Idaho State U., 1968. Instr. Highland C.C., Freeport, Ill., 1968-69, Merced (Calif.) Coll., 1969-70; tchr. Linden (Calif.) High Sch., 1970-84; prof. San Joaquin Delta Coll., Stockton, Calif., 1984—. Cons. in field. Author: (textbooks) ESL Writing Manual, 1992, Patterns for Success, 4 vols., 1997, Basic Composition, 1997, Writing Essays, 1998, Writing Paragraphs, 1999. Coord. cultural exch. San Joaquin Delta Coll., 1995, 96, 98. Mem. NEA, Calif. Tchrs. Assn. Avocations: reading, writing, concerts, theater, surfing the net. Office: San Joaquin Delta Coll 5151 Pacific Ave Stockton CA 95207-6304 Home Phone: 510-658-6665; Office Phone: 209-954-5252. E-mail: rfung@deltacollege.edu.

FUNG, SHUN CHONG, retired chemical engineer; BS in Chem. Engring., U. Calif., Berkeley, 1965; MS, U. Ill. Urbana-Champaign, 1967, PhD in Chem. Engring., 1969. Retired sr. rsch. assoc. ExxonMobil Rsch. and Engring. Co., Bridgewater, NJ. Contbr. articles to sci. jours. Recipient Indsl. Innovation awards, Am. Chem. Soc., 2002. Mem.: NAE. Achievements include patents in field. Mailing: 855 Papen Rd Bridgewater NJ 08807*

FUNG, VICTOR K. (VICTOR FUNG KWOK KING), consumer products trading company executive; b. Hong Kong; married; 3 children. BEE, MEE, MIT; PhD in Bus. Economics, Harvard U.; LLD (hon.), U. Hong Kong, 1997. With Citibank NY; prof. Harvard U., 1969—73; mgr. Li & Fung Grp., Kowloon, Hong Kong, 1973—77, mng. dir., export trading bus., 1977—81, group mng. dir., 1981—89, group chmn., 1989; group non-executive chmn., chmn. nomination com. and risk mgmt. com. Li & Fung, Ltd., Kowloon, Hong Kong. Founder, shareholder Transpac; independent non-executive dir. Bank of China (Hong Kong) Ltd., PCCW Ltd., Baosteel Grp. Corp., Orient Overseas Internat. Ltd., 1996—, Sun Hung Kai Properties Ltd., 1999—, BOC Hong Kong Ltd. & BOCHK, 2003—, mem. audit com. and remuneration com.; former mem. internat. adv. panel CapitaLand Ltd., Singapore, independent non-executive dir., 2005—; dir. Hong Kong Telecom; chmn. Hong Kong Airport Authority, 1999—, Prudential Asia Investments Ltd., Hong Kong, Prumerica Fin. Asia Ltd.; mem. Chinese People's polit. Consultative Conf.; mem. exec. com. Commn. on Strategic Development; mem. Judicial Officers Recommendation Com., Hong Kong Govt.; chmn. Hong Kong Trade Development Coun., 1991—2000; Hong Kong representative APEC Bus. Adv. Coun., 1996—2003; past mem. preparatory com. Hong Kong Spl. Adminstrv. Region; hon. prof. Renmin U.; spkr. in field. Chmn. Hong Kong Univ. Coun., Greater Pearl River Delta Bus. Coun., Hong Kong-Japan Bus. Co-operation Com.; past chmn. Hong Kong Gen. C. of C.; mem. adv. bd. Sch. Economics and Mgmt., Tsinghua U. Named Commander of the Order of the British Empire (CBE), 1993, Hong Kong Leader of Yr., 1998; named one of 50 Asian Leaders Leading the region out of economic crisis, Business Week, Forbes' Richest Americans, 2006; recipient Harvard medal for Outstanding Svc., 2001, Gold Bauhinia Star for Disting. Svc. to the Cmty., Hong Kong Govt., 2003. Mem.: Hong Kong Exporter's Assn. Office: Li & Fung Ltd LiFung Tower 11th Fl 888 Cheung Sha Wan Rd Kowloon Hong Kong

FUNG, YUAN-CHENG BERTRAM, bioengineering educator, writer; b. Yuhong, Changchow, Kiangsu, China, Sept. 15, 1919; arrived in U.S., 1945, naturalized, 1957; s. Chung-Kwang and Lien (Hu) F.; m. Luna Hsien-Shih Yu, Dec. 22, 1949; children: Conrad Antung, Brenda Pingsi. BS, Nat. Ctrl. U., Chungking, China, 1941, MS, 1943, DSc (hon.), 2002; PhD, Calif. Inst. Tech., 1948; DSc (hon.), Hong Kong U. Sci. and Tech., 1992, Drexel U., 2001, Sichuan U., 2002, Nat. Cheng Kung U., 2003, Northwestern U., 2004. Rsch. fellow Bur. Aero. Rsch. China, 1943-45; rsch. asst., then rsch. fellow Calif. Inst. Tech., 1946-51, mem. faculty, 1951-66, prof. aerospace, 1959-66; prof. bioengring. and applied mechanics U. Calif., San Diego, 1966—2000, prof. emeritus bioengineering, 2000—. Cons. aerospace indsl. firms, 1949—; hon. prof. 15 univs., China; hon. chair World Coun. Biomechanics, 1998. Author: The Theory of Aeroelasticity, 1955, 69, 93, Foundations of Solid Mechanics, 1965, A First Course in Continuum Mechanics, 1969, 77, 93, Biomechanics, 1972, Biomechanics: Mechanical Properties of Living Tissues, 1980, 1993, Biodynamics: Circulation, 1984, Biomechanics: Circulation, 1996, Biomechanics: Motion, Flow, Stress and Growth, 1990, Selected Works on Biomechanics and Aeroelasticity by Y.C. Fung, 1997, Classical and Computational Solid Mechanics, 2001, Introduction to Bioengineering, 2001; also papers; editor Jour. Biorheology, Jour. Biomech. Engring. Hon. bd. trustees Chongqing U.; hon. chair, bd. trustees Nanjing U., China. Recipient Achievement award Chinese Inst. Engrs., 1965, 68, 93, Lifetime Achievement award of Asian Ams. in Engring., 2004, Landis award Microcirculatory Soc., 1975, Poiseuille medal Internat. Soc. Biorheology, 1986, Engr. of Yr. award San Diego Engring. Soc., 1986, von Karman medal ASCE, 1976, ALZA award Biomed. Engring. Soc., 1989, Borelli award Am. Soc. Biomechanics, 1992, US Nat. Medal of Sci., 2000.; Guggenheim fellow, 1958-59. Fellow AIAA, ASME (hon., Lissner award 1978, Centennial medal 1978, Worcester Reed Warner medal 1984, Timoshenko medal 1991, Melville medal 1994); mem. Japan Soc. Mech. Engrs. (Bioengring. award 1995), NAS, NAE(Founders award, 1998, Fritz J. and Dolores H. Russ prize, 2007), Inst. Medicine, Soc. Engring. Sci., Microcirculatory Soc., Am. Physiol. Soc., Nat. Heart Assn., Acad. Sinica, Chinese Acad. Scis. (fgn. mem.), Basic Sci. Coun., Sigma Xi. Achievements include contributing to tissue engineering for the treatment of burns and other severe tissue injuries and the development of engineered blood vessels. Office: U Calif Dept Bioengring 9500 Gilman Dr La Jolla CA 92093-0412

FUNG-CHEN-PEN, EMMA TALAUNA SOLAITA, librarian, director; b. Pago Pago, Am. Samoa, Sept. 4, 1951; d. Talauna and Ema (Tauoa) S.; m. Su'a oelu T. Fung-Chen-Pen, Nov 1, 1971; children: John Kevin, Juliet Ruth, Jacqueline Josie, Jennifer Lorna, Jonathan Emosi. AA Gen. Edn., Am. Samoa C. C., 1973, AS Libr. Studies, 1974; BA, Brigham Young U., Honolulu, 1977; MS in Librarianship, U. Hawaii, 1979. Libr. clerk Libr. Svcs., Pago Pago, 1971-74, libr. technician, 1974-76, libr. II, 1976-79, program dir., 1980—. Sec. Seventh Day Adventist Leone (Am. Samoa) Ch., 1990-94; dir. Seventh Day Adventist Leone Pathfinder, 1993—; pres. Parent-Tchr. Assn.-Sch., 2000-; active SDA Sch. Bd., 1991-98, mem. exec. bd. Samoa Mission, 1999-; mem. libr. bd. Feleti Barstow Pub., 2000-; mem. Samoa bd. dirs., coun. Read to Me, 1998-; mem. TV ministry bd. Leone SDA Ch., 1999-. Avocations: volleyball, reading, walking. Home: PO Box 1952 Pago Pago AS 96799-1952 Office: Am Samoa-Office of Lib Svcs PO Box 1329 Pago Pago AS 96799-1329

FUNK, CARLA JEAN, library association director; b. Wheeling, W.Va., Sept. 21, 1946; d. David H. and Jean (Duffy) Belt. BA in Psychology, Northwestern U., 1968; MLS, Ind. U., 1973; MBA, U. Chgo., 1985. Libr. adult svcs. Northbrook (Ill.) Pub. Libr., 1973-77; dir. Warren-Newport Pub. Libr. Dist., Gurnee, Ill., 1977-80; cons. Suburban Libr. Sys., Burr Ridge, Ill., 1980-83; dir. automation and tech. svcs., med. student svcs. AMA, Chgo., 1983-92; exec. dir. Med. Libr. Assn., Chgo., 1992—. Adj. faculty Dominican U., 1986—2000. Contbr. articles to profl. jours. Mem. Internat. Fedn. Libr. Assns. and Insts. (treas., mgmt. libr. assn. sec.), Am. Soc. Assn. Execs. (cert. assn. exec.), Assn. Forum of Chicagoland, Beta Phi Mu, Delta Zeta. Office: 65 E Wacker Pl Ste 1900 Chicago IL 60601-7246 Business E-Mail: funk@mlahq.org.

FUNK, CYRIL REED, JR., agronomist, educator; b. Richmond, Utah, Sept. 20, 1928; s. Cyril Reed and Hazel Marie (Jensen) F.; m. Donna Gwen Buttars, Feb. 2, 1951; children: Bonnie Arlene, David Christopher, Carol Jean. BS (Scholarship A 1955), Utah State U., 1952, MS, 1955; PhD, Rutgers U., 1961; DAgr (hon.), Utah State U., 1994. Mem. faculty Rutgers U., New Brunswick, NJ, 1956—, rsch. prof. turfgrass breeding plant biology and pathology dept., 1969—, also instr. grad. faculty. Author, patentee in field. Served to 1st lt. AUS, 1952-54. Recipient Green Sect. award U.S. Golf Assn., 1980, Achievement award Lawn Inst., 1977; named to Hall of Disting. Alumni, Rutgers U. Fellow Crop Sci. Soc. Am., Am. Soc. Agronomy (research award N.E. sect. 1979); mem. AAAS (fellow 1992), Am. Sod Producers Assn. (hon.), Golf Course Supts. Assn. (hon. mem.; Disting. Service award 1979), Internat. Turfgrass Soc., N.J. Turfgrass Assn. (Achievement award 1976, Hall of Fame award 1984), N.J. Golf Course Supts. Assn. (hon.), N.J. Acad. Scis., Sigma Xi, Phi Kappa Phi, Acad. Scis. Uzbekistan (hon.), Acad. Agrl. Scis. Kyrgyzstan (hon.). Mem. Lds Ch. Achievements include developing numerous turfgrasses. Home: 4 Delaware Dr East Brunswick NJ 08816-3255 Office: Rutgers U Cook Coll New Brunswick NJ 08901 Office Phone: 732-932-9480. Personal E-mail: reedonna1@comcast.net.

FUNK, DAVID ALBERT, retired law educator; b. Wooster, Ohio, Apr. 22, 1927; s. Daniel Coyle and Elizabeth Mary (Reese) F.; children— Beverly Joan, Susan Elizabeth, John Ross, Carolyn Louise; m. Sandra Nadine Henselmeier, Oct. 2, 1976 Student, U. Mo., 1945—46, Harvard Coll., 1946; BA in Econs., Coll. of Wooster, 1949; MA, Ohio State U., 1968; JD, Case Western Res. U., 1951, LLM, 1972, Columbia U., 1973. Bar: Ohio 1951, U.S. Dist. Ct. (no. dist.) Ohio 1962, U.S. Tax Ct. 1963, U.S. Ct. Appeals (6th cir.) 1970, U.S. Supreme Ct. 1971. Ptnr. Funk, Funk & Eberhart, Wooster, Ohio, 1951-72; assoc. prof. law Ind. U. Sch. Law, Indpls., 1973-76, prof., 1976-97, prof. emeritus, 1997—. Vis. lectr. Coll. of Wooster, 1962-63; dir. Juridical Sci. Inst., Indpls., 1982—. Author: Oriental Jurisprudence, 1974, Group Dynamic Law, 1982; (with others) Rechtsgeschichte und Rechtssoziologie, 1985, Group Dynamic Law: Exposition and Practice, 1988; contbr. articles to profl. jours. Chmn. bd. trustees Wayne County Law Library Assn., 1956-71; mem. Permanent Jud. Commn., Synod of Ohio, United Presbyn. Ch. in the U.S., 1968. Served to seaman 1st class USNR, 1945-46 Harlan Fiske Stone fellow Columbia U., 1973; recipient Am. Jurisprudence award in Comparative Law, Case Western Res. U., 1970 Mem. Assn. Am. Law Schs. (sec. comparative law sect. 1977-79, chmn. law and religion sect. 1977-81, sec.-treas. law and social sci. sect. 1983-86), Pi Sigma Alpha. Republican. Home: 6208 N Delaware St Indianapolis IN 46220-1824

FUNK, EDITH KAY, retired minister, psychotherapist, social worker; b. Durham, Feb. 19, 1944; d. Clinton M. and M. Josephine Frick; m. Francis Lee Funk, Sept. 3, 1967; 1 child, Aaron Lee. B in Music Edn., Kans. State Tchrs. Coll., Emporia, 1966, MusM, 1968; MDiv, St. Paul Sch. Theology, Kansas City, Mo., 1984; MSW, Kans. U., Lawrence, 1995. Ordained minister Kans. Ea. Ann. Conf. United Meth. Clergy, 1983; LCSW State of Kans., 1997. Music tchr. Osage City Pub. Schs., Kans., 1969—72, Shawnee Mission Pub. Schs., Kans., 1972—74; pastor United Meth. Ch., various locations, Kans., 1984—90; chaplain Topeka State Hosp., 1990—93, The Menninger Clinic, Houston, 2002—05; ret., 2005; preaching assoc. pastor 1st United Meth. Ch., Topeka, 1993—96; psychotherapist Woodridge Counseling Svc., Topeka, 1996—2003. Named Outstanding Young Educator, Osage City Jaycees, 1972; recipient Kimbrill award Excellence in Biblical Studies, St. Paul, 1983; grantee Ministry grant, St. Paul Sch. of Theology, 1984. Mem.: Kans. E. Conf. United Meth. Ch. (Elder 1983—). Democrat. Avocations: weaving, needlecrafts, gardening, cooking, woodcarving.

FUNK, JEANNE B., psychology professor; d. June H. and M. Lawrence Brockmyer; m. Max O. Funk, Aug. 28, 1971; children: Jenna B., Theodore M. BA, Bucknell U., Pa., 1971; PhD, U. N.C., Chapel Hill, 1975. Lic. psychologist Ohio State Bd. of Psychology, 1978. Prof. psychology U. Toledo, 2001—06, Disting. prof. psychology, 2006—. Invited spkr. Computer Games Designer's Assn., Long Beach, Calif., 1998, U. Chgo. Cultural Policy Ctr., 2001, King Faisal Rsch. Hosp., Riyadh, Saudi Arabia, 2001, Riyadh, 02, Internat. Soc. for Rsch. on Aggression, Montreal, Canada, 2002; invited expert Markle Found., Children and Interactive Media, Austin, Tex., 1999, Freedom Forum, Vanderbilt U., Nashville, 2000; invited participant APA Advocacy Workshop, Washington, 2000, Video Game Tech. and Medicine Conf., LA, 2004; invited testimony US Senate, Washington, 2000; dir. doctoral tng. program in clin. psychology U. Toledo, 2001—05; vis. prof. U. Ark. Med. Ctr., Little Rock, 2006. Cons. United Way Women's Initiative, Toledo, 2005, Cullen Ctr. of The Toledo Hosp., 2003; mem. Joint Hosp. Child Protection Team, Toledo, 1979—99; chair Toledo Healthy Tomorrows, The Toledo Hosp., 1994—96. Recipient Outstanding Faculty Rsch. award, U. Toledo, 2005. Mem.: APA, N.Y. Acad. Scis., Nat. Register of Health Svc. Providers in Psychology, Am. Soc. of Clin. Hypnosis, Internat. Soc. for Rsch. on Aggression, Soc. for Rsch. in Child Devel., Bucknell U. Mortar Bd., Sigma Xi, Psi Chi, Phi Beta Kappa. Achievements include research in Children And Violent Video Games And Desensitization. Avocations: gardening, travel. Office: Univ Toledo MS 948 2801 W Bancroft Toledo OH 43606 Office Phone: 419-530-4392. Office Fax: 419-530-8479. E-mail: jeanne.funk@utoledo.edu.

FUNK, MICHAEL S., food products executive; Pres. Mountain People's Warehouse, 1976—2001; co-founder, bd. dir. United Natural Foods Inc., Dayville, Conn., 1996—, exec. v.p., 1996, pres., 1996—99, vice-chmn., 1996—2002, CEO, 1999—2002, chmn., 2003, pres., CEO, 2005—. Bd. dir. Organic Ctr., Frontier Natural Products, Traditional Medicinal Tea Co. Office: United Natural Foods 260 Lake Rd Dayville CT 06241*

FUNK, WILLIAM HENRY, retired environmental engineering educator; b. Ephraim, Utah, June 10, 1933; s. William George and Henrietta (Hackwell) F.; m. Ruth Sherry Mellor, Sept. 19, 1964 (dec.); 1 dau., Cynthia Lynn; m. Lynn Bridget Robson, Mar. 30, 1996. BS in Biol. Sci, U. Utah, 1955, MS in Zoology, 1963, PhD in Limnology, 1966. Tchr. sci., math. Salt Lake City Schs., 1957-60; research asst. U. Utah, Salt Lake City, 1961-63; head sci. dept. N.W. Jr. High Sch., Salt Lake City, 1961-63; mem. faculty Wash. State U., Pullman, 1966-99, assoc. prof. environ. engring., 1971-75, prof., 1975-99, chmn. environ. sci./regional planning program, 1979-81; dir. Environ. Research Center, 1980-83, State of Wash. Water Research Ctr., 1981-99; ret., 1999. Cons. U.S. Army C.E., Walla Walla, Wash., 1970—74, Harstad Engrs., Seattle, 1971—72, Boise Cascade Corp., Seattle, 1971—72, Wash. Dept. Ecology, Olympia, 1971—72, ORB Corp., Renton, Wash., 1972—73, U.S. Civil Svc., Seattle, Chgo., 1972—74; mem. High Level Nuclear Waste Bd., Wash., 1986—89, Wash. 2010 Com., 1989, Pure Water 2000 Steering Com., 1990; co-dir. Inst. Resource Mgmt.; co-founder Terrene Inst., Washington, 1991, pres., 1993—2002. Contbr. articles to profl. jours. Capt. USNR, 1955—76. Grantee NSF Summer Inst., 1961, U.S. Army C.E., 1970-74, 94-96, 97-98, Office Water Resources Rsch., 1971-72, 73-76, EPA, 1980-83, 93-94, 95-96, U.S. Geol. Survey, 1983-94, 95-96, 97-98, 99-00, Nat. Parks Svc., 1985-87, Colville Confederated Tribes, 1990-92, Nez Pierce Tribe, 1992-95, Wash. Conservation Commn., 1992-95, Clearwater Co., 1992-93, Idaho Dept. Environ. Quality, 1995-96, U.S. Bur. Reclamation, 1995-98; USPHS fellow, 1963; recipient Pres.'s Disting. Faculty award Wash. State U., 1984. Mem. Naval Res. Officers Assn. (chpt. pres. 1969), N.Am. Lake Mgmt. Soc. (pres. 1984-85, Secchi Disk award 1988), Pacific N.W. Pollution Control Assn. (editor 1969-77, pres.-elect 1982-83, pres. 1983-84), Water Pollution Control Fedn. (Arthur S. Bedell award Pacific N.W. assn. 1976, nat. bd. dirs. 1978-81, bd. dirs. Rsch. Found. 1990-92), Nat. Assn. Water Inst. Dirs. (chair 1985-87, bd. dirs. univ. council on water resources 1986-89), Wash. Lakes Protection Assn. (co-founder 1986, Friend of Lakes award 1999), Am. Water Resources Assn. (v.p. Wash. sect. 1988), Am. Soc. Limnology and Oceanography, Am. Micros. Soc., N.W. Sci. Assn., North Am. Lake Mgmt. Soc. (co-founder 1972), Sigma Xi, Phi Sigma. Achievements include research in water pollution control and lake restoration. Home: 202 W 200 South Manti UT 84642-1309 Personal E-mail: wfwhf@mail.manti.com.

FUNKHOUSER, DAVID EDWARD, lawyer; b. Ft. Madison, Iowa, Nov. 11, 1941; s. Floyd Franklin and Nellie Mae (Short) F.; m. Michaela Irene Lannon, June 28, 1969; children: Stacy Skye, Shelby Kathleen, David Edward III. BBA, U. Iowa, 1964, JD, 1967. Bar: Iowa 1967, US Dist. Ct. (no. and cen. dists.) Iowa 1968, US Supreme Ct. 1979. Law clk. Iowa Supreme Ct., Des Moines, 1967-68; ptnr. Brown, Kinsey & Funkhouser & Lander PLC, Mason City, Iowa, 1968—. CLE commr. Iowa Supreme Ct., Des Moines, 1979-83; mem. Iowa Jud. Qualification Commn., 1992—. Commr. Civil Service Commn., Mason City, Iowa, 1972-86; pres., bd. trustees Mason City Pub. Library, 1974-86. Fellow Am. Coll. Trial Lawyers, Am. Bar Found., Iowa Acad. Trial Lawyers (bd. dirs. 1984-86, v.p. 1987, pres. 1988); mem. Iowa State Bar Assn. (bd. govs. 1984-86, v.p. 1986, pres.-elect 1987-88, pres. 1988-89), Am. Bd. Trial Advocates; ABA (bd. govs., 2005-) Democrat. Roman Catholic. Avocations: hunting, skiing, conservation. Home: 231 Lakeview Dr Mason City IA 50401-1619 Office: Brown Kinsey Funkhouser & Lander 214 N Adams Ave PO Box 679 Mason City IA 50402-0679

FUNKOUSER, MARK, mayor; b. New Brighton, Pa., Oct. 4, 1949; BA in Polit. Sci., Thiel Coll., 1971; MSW, W. Va. U., 1976; MBA, Tenn. State U., 1985; PhD in Pub. Administration, U. Mo.-Kansas City. Cert. legal auditor. Head performance audit group divsn. of state audit State of Tenn., 1978-88; city auditor City of Kansas City, 1988—2006, mayor, 2006—. Former adjunct prof. Park U., U. Mo., U. Kans. Editor: Local Govt. Auditing Quarterly; contbr. articles to profl. jours. Office: City Hall 414 E 12th St Kansas City MO 64106*

FUNSETH, ROBERT LLOYD ERIC MARTIN, international consultant, retired diplomat; b. International Falls, Minn., May 10, 1926; s. Martin Emmanuel and Agnes Evangeline (Guibault) F.; m. Marilyn Ann Schuelke, Mar. 23, 1957; 1 child, Eric Christian. BA, Hobart Coll., 1948, postgrad., 1950-51, Cornell U., 1950-51, Sch. Advanced Internat. Studies, Johns Hopkins U., 1951-52; MS, George Washington U., 1969; LL.D, Hobart and William Smith Colls., 1978. Editor Coachella Desert Barnacle, Calif., 1948; mng. editor Anaheim Gazette, Calif., 1948-50; corr. AP, 1950; resident tutor Hobart Coll., 1950-51; info. officer U.S. Mut. Security Agy., 1952-53; editor USIA, 1953-54; joined U.S. Fgn. Service, 1954; advanced to rank of minister-counselor Career Sr. Fgn. Service; vice consul Tehran, Tabriz, Azerbaijan and Kurdistan, Iran, 1954-56; 3d sec. Am. embassy, Beirut, 1957-59; UN polit. affairs officer Dept. State, 1959-61; Am. consul (Bordeaux), France, 1961-64; Portuguese desk officer Dept. State, Washington, 1964-66; mem. U.S. del. 20th UN Gen. Assembly, 1965; dep. dir. Iberian affairs Dept. State, 1966-68; assigned to Nat. War Coll., 1968-69; dir. mgmt. U.S. diplomatic and consular posts Dept. State, Mex. and Central Am., 1969-70, coordinator Cuban affairs, 1970-72, sr. fgn. service insp., 1972-73; counselor Am. embassy, Ottawa, Ont., Can., 1973-74; dep. dept. spokesman and dir. office of press relations Dept. State, Washington, 1974-75, dept. spokesman and spl. asst. to sec. of state for press relations, 1975-77, dir. office No. European affairs, 1977-82, dep. asst. sec. for refugee resettlement, 1982-83, sr. dep. asst. sec. Bur. Refugee Programs, 1983-91, cons., 1991—; trustee, former pres. Diplomatic and Consular Officers Ret.-Bacon House Found., Washington. Detailed to U.S. Falkland Island Peace Mission to London and Buenos Aires, 1982; vis. disting. alumni scholar in residence Hobart and William Smith Colls., 1978, Nat. Cathedral Assn.; vis. fellow Woodrow Wilson Found., Princeton, NJ; lectr. Am. studies U. Tabriz, 1955—56; mem. U.S. Del. NATO Ministerial Meeting, Ottawa, 1976—89, Brussels, 1976—89, Oslo, 1976—89, former Pres. Ford's state visit to Philippines, 1975, U.S. China Ministerial Consultations, Beijing, OECD, Paris, SALT, Moscow, U.S.-So. Africa Initiative, Nairobi, Dar es Salam, Lusaka, Kinshasa, Monrovia, Dakar, UN Trade and Devel. Conf., Kenya, OAS Ministerial Meeting, Santiago, Chile, econ. summit Pres. Ford Puerto Rico, 1976, 1st U.S. South African Ministerial meeting, Grafenau, Germany, U.S.-Iran Joint Commn., Tehran, U.S. Bilateral Ministerial Consultations with Afghanistan and Pakistan, Inauguration Mexican Pres. Lopez-Portillo, 1976; head U.S. dels. U.S.-Vietnamese Refugee Consultations, Geneva, 1982—90; head U.S. del. U.S.-Vietnamese negotiations, Resettlement Vietnamese Polit. Prisoners, Hanoi, Vietnam, 1988, Hanoi, 89, 2d internat. conf. Indochinese Refugees, Geneva, 1989. U.S. observer Internat. Cath. Migration Commn. Conf., Vatican City, 1990; bd. dirs. Episcopal Ch. Presiding Bishop's Fund for World Relief; mem. peace commn. Episcopal Diocese of Washington. Lt. (j.g.) USNR, 1943—46, PTO. Recipient Outstanding Service commendation Am. Forces Spl. Command, Middle East, 1958, Disting. and Superior Honor Group awards Dept. State, 1959, 61, 70, Superior Honor award Dept. State, 1977, Sesquicentennial award Hobart Coll., 1972, Presdl. honor awards Sr. Fgn. Svc., 1986, 88, 91, Disting. Honor award Dept. State, 1989, Resolutions of Commendation Calif. State Senate, 1989, 91, Wilbur Carr disting. svc. award Dept. State, 1991, medal of excellence Hobart Coll. Alumni Assn., 1997, Hero of the Vietnamese Polit. Prisoners award Fedn. U.S. Assns. Vietnamese Polit. Prisoners, 1999. Mem.: Johns Hopkins Alumni Assn. (exec. coun. 1968—70), Diplomatic and Consular Officers Ret. (bd. govs. 1999—, v.p. 2001—03, pres. 2003—05, sec., pres. Dacor-Bacon House Found., hon. trustee for life Dacor Bacon House Found. 2005—), Assn. Diplomatic Studies (hon. gov. for life Dacor, Inc. 2005—), Am. Fgn. Svc. Assn., USN Meml. Found., Ebenezer Sch. N.Y. Alumni Assn., George Washington U. Alumni Assn., Hobart Coll. Alumni Assn. (medal of excellence 1997, Disting. Svc. Alumni award 1998), Sch. Advanced Internat. Studies Alumni Assn. (mem. adv. coun. 1969, 1970, pres.), Nat. War Coll. Alumni Assn., West Seneca (N.Y.) Hist. Soc., Mil. Order of Carabao (Disting. Svc. award 2005), Phi Delta Journalism Soc., Phi Sigma Kappa. Office Phone: 202-682-0500 x10. Personal E-mail: dacor@dacorbacon.org.

FUOCO, PHILIP STEPHEN, lawyer; b. Riverside, NJ, Oct. 28, 1946; s. Francis and Mary Helen Fuoco; m. Carol Freeman, June 7, 1969; 1 child. BA in Philosophy, U. Notre Dame, Ind., 1968; JD, Villanova U., Pa., 1971. Bar: NJ 1972, US Dist. Ct. NJ 1972, Pa. 1973, US Dist. Ct. (ea. dist.) Pa. 1975, US Ct. Appeals (3d cir.) 1977, US Supreme Ct. 1980; cert. criminal trial atty. NJ Supreme Ct. Trial atty. civil rights divsn. US Dept. Justice, Washington, 1971—75; asst. US atty. US Dist. Ct. (ea. dist.) Pa., Phila., 1975; pvt. practice Haddonfield, NJ, 1975—. Adj. prof. law Rutgers U., Camden, 1997-2000. Contbr. articles to profl. jours. and law revs. Mem. Haddonfield Environ. Commn., 1991—93; apptd. mem. com. on model jury charges-criminal NJ Supreme Ct., 1996—2002, apptd. mem. dist. IV ethics com., 1997—2001, apptd. mem. com. on character, 2001—05, apptd. mem. dist. IV fee disputes com., 2005—, vice chair, 2006; mem. steering com. First Night Haddonfield, 1999; bd. dirs. Steininger Ctr., 1990—92, Haddonfield Zoning Bd., 1984—88. Named NJ Super Lawyer, NJ Monthly Mag., 2007; named one of Top Attorneys of South Jersey, South Jersey Mag., 2003; recipient Stivale d'Italia award, Italian Tribune, Newark, 2003, NJ Super Lawyer, NJ Monthly Mag., 2005; fellow, NEH, 1978. Mem. ABA, ACLU, Nat. Assn. Dist. Attys., Nat. Assn. Criminal Def. Lawyers, Camden County Bar Assn. (trustee 1986-89), NJ Bar Assn., Lions (Haddonfield pres. 1986-87). Office: 24 Wilkins Place Haddonfield NJ 08033-2406 Office Phone: 856-354-1100.

FUQUA, CHARLES JOHN, retired classicist; b. Paris, Oct. 5, 1935; (parents Am. citizens); s. John Howe and Gillian Elynor (Quennell) F.; m. Mary Louise Morse, Aug. 26, 1961; children— Andrew Morse, David Reed, Gillian Quennell. BA magna cum laude, Princeton, 1957; MA, Cornell U., 1961, PhD, 1964. Instr. classics Dartmouth Coll., Hanover, NH, 1964, asst. prof., 1965-66; assoc. prof. classics, chmn. dept. classics Williams Coll., Williamstown, Mass., 1966-72, Garfield prof. ancient langs., chmn. dept. classics, 1972-86; ret., 2003. Mem. adv. council Am. Acad. in Rome, 1966, chmn. exec. com., 74. Served to lt. (j.g.) USNR, 1957-60. Mem.: Vergilian Soc., Classical Assn. Mass., Classical Assn. New Eng., Am. Philol. Assn., Phi Beta Kappa, Phi Kappa Phi. Home: 96 Grandview Dr Williamstown MA 01267-2528 Personal E-mail: charles.fuqua@verizon.net.

FURASH, EDWARD ELLIOTT, investment company executive, banker, educator, writer, theater producer; b. Boston, Oct. 31, 1934; s. Moses Harry Furash and Sara (Jacobs) Dorfman; m. Elizabeth Louise Wilson, Jan. 2, 1959; children: Jennifer Lee, Jonathan Wilson, James Shortlidge. AB magna cum laude, Harvard Coll., 1956; MBA, U. Pa., 1958; postgrad., Harvard Bus. Sch., Boston, 1959-67. Rsch. asst. Harvard Grad. Sch. Bus., Boston, 1958-59; asst. editor Harvard Bus. Review, Boston, 1959-62; instr. bus. adminstrn. Harvard Grad. Sch. Bus., Boston, 1961-62; sec. com. on space Am. Acad. Arts & Scis., Boston, 1962-64; sr. staff assoc., bus. mgr. Arthur D. Little, Inc., Cambridge, Mass., 1964-67; v.p. mktg. Nat. Shawmut Bank Boston, 1967-72, sr. v.p. mktg., 1972-74; sr. v.p. corp. planning Shawmut Corp. Boston, 1972-78; mng. dir. Golembe Assocs., Washington, 1978-80; chmn. Furash & Co., Washington, 1980-98; vice chmn. dir. Headway Corp. Resources, Inc., NYC, 1995-98; CEO Furash Holdings, Washington, 1994-2000; chmn. Monument Fin. Group, Alexandria, Va., 1999—, Effinity Fin. Corp., Alexandria, 1999—2003, Treasury Bank, 2000—03; pres., CEO City First Bank DC, Washington, 2005—. Bd. dirs. Inova Alexandria Hosp. Found., Pa. Bus. Bank, City First Bank, Washington, Online Resources; interviewed on TV ABC, CBS, CNBC, PBS; lectr. Williams Sch. of Banking, 1974—78, Am. Inst. Banking, 1968—98, Stonier Sch. Banking, 1994, 95. Gen. editor: Technology Space & Soc.; contbr. (newspapers, mags.) including Wall St. Jour., Bus. Week, Bankers Mag., Am. Banker, RMA Jour. Credit and Risk Mgmt., and many others; contbr. to profl. jours. Chmn. appropriations com. Town of Lexington, Mass., 1967-78; participant Lexington Town Meetings, 1969-78; trustee The Carroll Sch., Lincoln, Mass., 1976—. Shell Oil Found. fellow U. Pa., 1957-58. Mem. Am. Assn. Bank Dirs. (bd. dirs. 1998—), Cosmos Club, City Club Washington, Harvard Club, Belle Haven Country Club, Beta Gamma Sigma. Republican. Office: City First Bank 1432 U St NW Washington DC 20009 Office Phone: 202-243-7106. Business E-Mail: efurash@cityfirstbank.com.

FURBACHER, STEPHEN A., energy executive; BSME, Valparaiso U. Design engr. Chevron, Richmond, Calif., 1973-81, staff analyst Bakersfield, Calif., 1981-83, mgr. refinery, 1983-92; v.p., gen. mgr. natural gas bus. unit Chevron U.S.A. Prodn. Co., 1992, pres. Warren Petroleum Co., 1992-96; sr. v.p., pres. COO Midstream Svcs. Dynegy, Inc., Houston, 1996—2005, pres., COO, 2005—. Bd. dirs. Southeast Tex. Jr. Achievement. Mem. Gas Processors Assn. (exec. com.), Natural Gas Supply Assn. (steering com.). Office: Dynegy Inc 1000 Louisiana St Ste 5800 Houston TX 77002-5006*

FURBUSH, DAVID MALCOLM, lawyer; b. Palo Alto, Calif., Mar. 25, 1954; s. Malcolm Harvey and Margaret (McKittrick) F. BA, Harvard U., 1975, JD, 1978. Bar: Calif. 1978, U.S. Dist. Ct. (no. dist.) Calif. 1978, U.S. Ct. Appeals (9th cir.) 1987, U.S. Supreme Ct. 1990. Assoc. Chickering & Gregory, San Francisco, 1978-81, Brobeck, Phleger & Harrison, San Francisco, 1981-85, ptnr. Palo Alto, Calif., 1985—2003, O'Meleny & Myers, LLP, Menlo Park, Calif., 2003—. Office: Pillsbury Winthrop Shaw Pittman LLP 2475 Hanover St Palo Alto CA 94304 Office Phone: 650-233-4623. Office Fax: 650-233-4545. Business E-Mail: david.furbush@pillsburylaw.com.

FURCAL, RAFAEL, professional baseball player; b. Loma de Cabrera, Dominica Republic, Aug. 24, 1978; Short stop Atlanta Braves, 2000—05, Los Angeles Dodgers, 2005—. Recipient NL Rookie Yr. award, MLB, 2000. Office: Los Angeles Dodgers 1000 Elysian Park Ave Los Angeles CA 90012

FURCHGOTT, ROBERT FRANCIS, pharmacologist, educator; b. Charleston, SC, June 4, 1916; married, 1941; 3 children. BS, U. N.C., 1937; PhD in Biochemistry, Northwestern U., 1940; DM (hon.), Autonomous U. Madrid, 1984, U. Lund, 1984; DSc (hon.), U. N.C., 1989, U. Ghent, 1995; degree (hon.), Mt. Sinai Med. Sch., 1995, Ohio State U., 1996, Med. U. S.C., 1997, Med. Coll. Ohio, 1997, Northwestern U., 1998, U. Coll., London, 1998, Washington U., 2001, Charles U., Prague, 2003. Rsch. fellow medicine Med. Coll. Cornell U., 1940—43, rsch. assoc., 1943—47, instr. physiology, 1943—48, asst. prof. med. biochemistry, 1947—49; from asst. prof. to assoc. prof. pharmacology Med. Sch. Wash. U., 1949—56; chmn. dept. pharmacology SUNY Coll. Med. (now SUNY Health Sci. Ctr.), Bklyn., 1956—82; prof. dept. pharmacology SUNY Health Sci. Ctr., Bklyn., 1956—88, Disting. prof., 1988—89, disting. emeritus prof. pharmacology, 1990—. Mem. pharmacol. tng. com. USPHS, 1961—64, mem. pharmacotoxicol. rev. com., 1965—68; Commonwealth fellow, 1962—63; vis. prof. U. Geneva, 1962—63, U. Calif., San Diego, 1971—72, Med. U. S.C., 1980, UCLA, 1980; adj. prof. pharmacology, Sch. Medicine U. Miami, 1988—2001; disting. vis. prof. Med. Univ. South Carolina, 2001. Recipient rsch. achievement award, Am. Heart Assn., 1990, Bristol-Myers Squibb award for achievement in cardiovasc. rsch., 1991, Gairdner Found. Internat. award, 1991, medal, N.Y. Acad. Medicine, 1992, Roussel Uclaf prize for rsch. in cell communication and signalling, 1993, Wellcome Gold medal, Brit. Pharmacology Soc., 1995, ASPET award for exptl. therapeutics, 1996, Gregory Pincus award for rsch., 1996, Albert Lasker award for basic med. rsch., Lasker Found., 1996, Lucian award, 1997, Nobel prize for Medicine, 1998. Mem.: NAS, AAAS, Harvey Soc., Am. Soc. Pharmacology and Exptl. Therapeutics (pres. 1971—72, Goodman and Gilman award 1984), Am. Soc. Biochemistry, Am. Chem. Soc., Am. Acad. Arts and Scis., Polish Physiol. Soc. (hon.), Sigma Xi. Office: SUNY Health Sci Ctr Dept of Pharmacology 450 Clarkson Ave Box 29 Brooklyn NY 11203-2056

FURCHTGOTT-ROTH, HAROLD WILKES, economist, consultant; b. Knoxville, Tenn., Dec. 13, 1956; s. Ernest and Mary A. (Wilkes) Furchtgott; m. Diana Elizabeth Roth, June 21, 1983; children: Leon Adam, Francesca Cecily, Jeremy Bernard, Godfrey Eugene, Theodore Raphael, Richard Abraham. SB, MIT, 1978; PhD, Stanford U., 1986. Rsch. fellow Brookings Instn., Washington, 1983-84; rsch. analyst Ctr. for Naval Analyses, Alexandria, Va., 1984-88; sr. economist Economists Inc., Washington, 1988-95; chief economist U.S. House Commerce Com., 1995-97; mem. FCC, 1997—2001; vis. fellow Am. Enterprise Inst., 2001—03; pres. Furchtgott-Roth Econ. Enterprises, 2003—. Co-founder Oneida Broadband; bd. dirs. MRV Comm.; chmn. bd. Telecomm. Policy Rsch. Conf. Mem. Am. Econ. Assn., Econometric Soc. Home: 2705 Daniel Rd Chevy Chase MD 20815 Office: 1200 New Hampshire Ave Washington DC 20036 Office Phone: 202-776-2032. Business E-Mail: hfr@furchtgott-roth.com.

FURCON, JOHN EDWARD, management and organizational consultant; b. Mar. 17, 1942; s. John F. and Lottie F.; children: Juliana, Annalisa, Diana BA, DePaul U., 1963, MA, 1965; MBA, U. Chgo., 1970. With Human Resources Ctr. Chgo. U., 1963-81, project dir., 1966-70, rsch. psychologist, divsn. dir., 1970-81; with orgn. change practice Harbridge House, Inc., Northbrook, Ill., 1981—93, v.p., 1987-93; ptnr. human resource adv. group Coopers & Lybrand, 1993-98; ptnr. Global Human Resource Solutions PricewaterhouseCoopers LLP, 1998—2001, prin., 2001—; regional practice leader, human resource mgmt. cons. Buck Cons., Chgo., 2002—. Faculty Traffic Inst., Northwestern U., 1969-84, DePaul U. Sch. for New Learning, 1974-82, Ctr. Pub. Safety Northwestern U., 2004—; cons., lectr. in field. Contbr. articles to profl. jours. Active parents bd. Marquette U., 1988-89. Served to lt. AUS, 1963-65. Mem. Soc. Indsl. and Orgnl. Psychology, Indsl. Psychology Assn. Chgo. (chmn. 1973-75), Internat. Assn. Chiefs of Police, Chgo. Coun. Global Affairs (formerly known as Chgo. Coun. Fgn. Rels.), World Future Soc., Human Resource Mgmt. Assn. Chgo. Office: Buck Consultants One N Dearborn St Chicago IL 60602 Office Phone: 312-846-3650. Business E-Mail: john.furcon@buckconsultants.com.

FUREY, RAYMOND JOSEPH, lawyer; b. Rockville Ctr., NY, June 17, 1946; s. Raymond J. and Florence (Caparelli) F.; m. Laura DeVenoge, Nov. 23, 1974; children: Marie, Michael. BA, Rutgers U., 1968; JD, Ind. U., 1971. Bar: N.Y. 1972, Fla. 1980; bd. cert. by Nat. Bd. Trial Advocacy in Personal Injury Litigation. Atty. Law Offices of James Rogan, Mineola, N.Y., 1972-73; ptnr. J.M. Furey & R.J. Furey, 1973-88; pvt. practice, Mitchel Field, 1988—. Mem. 10th Judicial Dist. Grievance Com.; bd. dir. Nassau County Bar Assn. Named one of Best Lawyers in Am., 2005—07,

MY Area's Best Lawyers, 2005—07. Mem. Fla. Bar Assn., N.Y. State Bar Assn., N.Y. Trial Lawyers Assn., Am. Hosp. Lawyers Assn., Nassau Suffolk Trial Lawyers Assn (chmn.). Office: Furey Kerley Walsh Matera Cinquemani 2174 Jackson Ave Seaford NY 11783-2608 Office Phone: 516-409-6200. Business E-Mail: rfurey@fureykerley.com.

FUREY, ROGER P., lawyer; b. Washington, May 30, 1954; BS, George Mason U., 1979; JD, U. Va., 1983. Bar: DC 1983, Va. 1984, US Dist. Ct., Ea. Dist. Va., US Dist. Ct., DC, US Dist. Ct., Md., US Ct. Appeals, 4th, 6th, 9th and DC Cirs., US Ct. Appeals, Fed. Cir., Va. Supreme Ct. Ptnr. Katten Muchin Zavis Rosenman, Washington, DC. Mem.: Va. Bar Assn., Internat. Trademark Assn., Internat. C. of C., DC Bar Assn. Office: Katten Muchin Zavis Rosenman East Lobby, Ste 700 1025 Thomas Jefferson St, NW Washington DC 20007 Office Phone: 202-625-3630. Office Fax: 202-339-8268. E-mail: roger.furey@kmzr.com.

FURGASON, ROBERT ROY, academic administrator, director, retired engineering educator; b. Spokane, Wash., Aug. 2, 1935; s. Roy Elliott and Margaret (O'Halloran) F.; m. Gloria L. Althouse, June 14, 1964; children: Steven Scott, Brian Alan. BSChemE, U. Idaho, 1956, MSCE, 1958; PhD in Chem. Engring., Northwestern U., 1961; postdoctoral, U. Wis., 1961. Registered profl. engr., Idaho. Design engr. Phillips Petroleum Co., Bartlesville, Okla., 1956; rsch. engr. Martin Marietta Co., Denver, 1958; instr. chem. engring. U. Idaho, Moscow, 1957-59, asst. prof., 1961-63, assoc. prof., 1963-67, acting head dept. chem. engring., 1964-65, chmn. dept. chem. engring., 1965-74, prof., 1967-84, dean Coll. Engring., 1974-78, v.p. acad. affairs and rsch., 1978-84; prof., vice chancellor acad. affairs U. Nebr., Lincoln, 1984-90; prof., pres. Tex A&M U.-Corpus Christi, 1990—2004; dir. Harte Rsch. Inst. TAMU CC, 2005—. NSF advisor scientists and engrs. in econ. devel. program Escuela Politecnica Nacional, Quito, Ecuador, 1973-74, 76; proposal reviewer NSF, 1965-84; program reviewer Clearwater Econ. Devel. Assn., 1978-84; mem. long-range planning commn. Idaho State Bd. Edn., 1978-80, Gov.'s Com. Faculty Salary Equity, 1980, State of Idaho Energy Policy Bd., 1980-84, adv. com. Northwest Power Policy Coun., 1982-84, engring. accreditation commn. Accreditation Bd. Engring. and Tech., 1981-96, exec. bd., 1984-89, vice chmn., 1985-87, chmn., 1988-89, bd. dirs., 1989-95, fellow, 1990, pres., 1993-94; bd. dirs. Hanover Cos., Am. Bank; trustee Driscoll Hosp. Foundn., 2002—. Contbr. articles to profl. jours. Chmn. Idaho-Ecuador Ptnrs. of Ams., 1975-77; commr. Moscow Parks and Recreation Commn., 1977-81; mem. charter revision commn. City of Lincoln, 1989-90; chair Nebr. Energy Mgmt. Plan Adv. Com., 1989-90; mem. chem. engring. vis. com. Colo. Sch. Mines, 1989-99; exec. adv. bd. Coastal Bend United Way, 1991-93; bd. dirs. S.W. Moscow Cmty. Assn., 1977-84, Am. Festival Ballet, 1978-80, Lincoln Cancer Ctr., 1988-90, Tex. Econ. Edn. Commn., 1991-2001, Ada Wilson Children's Rehab. Ctr., 1993-96, Tex. State Aquarium, 1994—; adv. bd. Sta. KEDT-TV, Sta. KEDT-FM. Recipient Pub. Svc. award Idaho State Libr. Assn., 1978, Phillip Carrol Nat. award Soc. Advanced Mgmt., 1996, Grinter award Accreditation Bd. Engring. and Tech., 1996, Baldwin award Corpus Christi C. of C., 2000, Humanitarian award, NCCJ, 2002; named Citizen of Yr. Kappa Sigma, 1980, Newsmaker of the Yr., Corpus Christi Caller-Times, 1997, Newsmaker of the Decade, 2000; CASE Chief Exec. Leadership award, 2001; Walter P. Murphy fellow. Fellow AIChE (chmn. nat. tech. sessions 1967, sec. dept. heads forum 1971-72, chmn. 1981, nat. vis. lectr. 1977-79, edn. and accreditation com. 1981-92, chair 1989-91, accreditation visitation group 1977—); mem. Am. Soc. Engring. Edn. (Pacific Northwest coord. effective tchg. 1962-64, bd. dirs. chem. engring. divsn. 1974-77, Centennial medal 1993), Idaho Soc. Profl. Engrs. (No. Idaho chpt. pres. 1970, state pres. 1980, Idaho's Young Engr. of Yr. 1967), Northwest Coll. and Univ. Assn. Scis. (exec. com. bd. dirs. 1976-80, 81-84, chmn. bd. dirs. 1979-80), Corpus Christi C. of C. (bd. dirs. 1990-94), Crucible Club, Wranglers Club, Lions (program chmn., corr. sec., bd. dirs.), Rotary, Sigma Xi, Phi Kappa Phi, Phi Eta Sigma, Sigma Tau. Avocations: piloting, skiing, camping, woodworking. Home: 1334 Sandpiper Dr Corpus Christi TX 78412-3818 Office: Tex A&M U Harte Rsch Inst 6300 Ocean Dr Corpus Christi TX 78412-5503 Office Phone: 361-825-2000. Business E-Mail: robert.furgason@tamucc.edu.

FURGESON, WILLIAM ROYAL, federal judge; b. Lubbock, Tex., Dec. 9, 1941; s. W. Royal and Mary Alyene (Hardwick) F.; m. Marion McElroy, Aug. 15, 1964 (div.); m. Juli Ann Bernat, July 29, 1973 (div.); children: Kelly Lynn, Houston, Joshua, Seth, Jill; m. Marcellene Malouf, July 5, 2003. BA in English, Tex. Tech Coll., 1964; JD with honors, U. Tex., 1967. Bar: Tex. 1969, U.S. Dist. Ct. (we. dist.) Tex. 1971, U.S. Ct. Appeals (5th cir.) 1974, U.S. Supreme Ct. 1976. Law clk. to presiding judge U.S. Dist. Ct. for No. Dist. Tex., 1969-70; ptnr. Kemp, Smith, Duncan & Hammond, El Paso, Tex., 1970-94; judge U.S. Dist. Ct. (we. dist.) Tex., Midland/Odessa, 1994—2003, San Antonio, 2003—. Gen. campaign chmn. El Paso United Way, 1979, 1st v.p., 1980, pres., 1981; mem. Jewish Fedn., El Paso, 1980-86; trustee Baylor U. Coll. Dentistry, 1982-86; chmn. YWCA Capital Devel. Campaign, 1986-87. Served to capt. U.S. Army, 1967-69 Decorated Bronze Star; recipient Service award Social Workers of El Paso, 1982, Faculty award U. Tex. Law Sch., 1983, Dean Leon Green award Tex. Law Review, 2001, Jurist of Yr., Tex. ABOTA, 2004. Mem. El Paso Bar Assn. (pres. 1982-83, Outstanding Young Lawyer award 1972), Am. Law Inst., U. Tex. Law Sch. Assn. (pres. 1978), U. Tex. Law Rev. Assn. (pres. 1982-83), El Paso Legal Assistance Soc. (bd. dirs. 1972-78), NCCJ (chmn. El Paso region 1980), ABA, Fed. Bar Assn. (pres. West Tex. chpt. 1987), Am. Law Inst., Tex. Bar Assn. (sec., treas., chair anti-trust and trade regulation sect. 1985-86), Am. Bar Found., Tex. Bar Found. Democrat. Jewish. Office: US Dist Ct 655 E Durango San Antonio TX 78206

FURGURSON, ERNEST BAKER, JR., (PAT FURGURSON), writer; b. Danville, Va., Aug. 29, 1929; s. Ernest Baker and Passie Durham (Ferguson) F.; m. Mary Louise Stallings (div.); children— Ernest Baker III, Elisabeth Glyn; m. Cassie Woodward Thompson, Apr. 21, 1973. Student, Averett Coll., 1948-50; AB, Columbia, 1952, MS, 1953. Reporter Danville Comml. Appeal, Sta. WDVA, 1948-51; with Roanoke (Va.) World-News, 1952, Richmond (Va.) News Leader, 1955-56; reporter, Washington corr. Balt. Sun, 1956-61, chief Moscow bur., 1961-64, White House corr., nat. polit. corr., Saigon corr., nat. affairs columnist, 1964-92, chief Washington bur., 1975-87, assoc. editor, 1987-92; syndicated by L.A. Times Syndicate, 1970-90. Author: Westmoreland: The Inevitable General, 1968, Hard Right: The Rise of Jesse Helms, 1986, Chancellorsville 1963: The Souls of the Brave, 1992, Ashes of Glory: Richmond at War, 1996, Not War But Murder: Cold Harbor 1864, 2000, Freedom Rising: Washington in the Civil War, 2004; contbg. editor Washingtonian mag., 1973-83, Mid-Atlantic Country mag., 1983-96. 1st lt. USMC, 1953-55. Mem. Gridiron Club, Cosmos Club. Home: 4812 Tilden St NW Washington DC 20016-2330

FURINO, ANTONIO, economist, educator; b. Rome; JD, U. Rome, 1955; MA, U. Houston, 1965, PhD, 1972. Asst. prof. to assoc. prof. econs. St. Edwards U., Austin, Tex., 1967—70; dir. regional analysis Alamo Area Coun. Govts., San Antonio, 1970—73; prof. econs. U. Tex., San Antonio, 1973—90, dir. Ctr. for Studies in Bus., Econs. and Human Resources, 1973—79, dir. human resource mgmt. and devel. program, 1979—82; sr. ptnr., dir. Devel. Through Applied Sci., San Antonio, 1972—; prof. econs. U. Tex. Health Sci. Ctr., San Antonio, 1985—, dir. Ctr. for Health Econs. and Policy, 1987—2006, dir. Regional Ctr. for Health Workforce Studies at Ctr. for Health Econs. and Policy, 2001—06; sr. rsch. fellow U. Tex. IC 2 Inst., Austin, 1986—; assoc. dir. Regional Ctr. for Health Workforce Studies, Ctr. for Health Econs. and Policy, 2006—. Cons. in field. Home: 16114 Robinwood Ln San Antonio TX 78248-1744 Business E-Mail: furino@uthscsa.edu.

FURLANE, MARK ELLIOTT, lawyer; b. Joliet, Ill., Aug. 2, 1949; s. Francis Emilio and Tosca (Cipriani) F.; m. Susan M. Keegan, July 4, 1987; children: Gahan Patricia, Michael Keegan. BA magna cum laude, Ctrl. Coll., 1971; JD with honors, George Washington U., 1974; MBA in Finance Specialization, U. Chgo., 1982. Bar: Ill. 1974, U.S. Dist. Ct. (no. dist.) Ill. 1979, U.S. Ct. Appeals (5th, 6th, 7th, 9th and 11th cirs.), U.S. Ct. Mil. Appeals, U.S. Supreme Ct. 2001. Ptnr. Drinker Biddle Gardner Carton, Chgo., 1979—. Bd. mem. Ctr. for Disability and Elder Law, 2000—, Chgo. Boy Choir. Capt. USMCR. Mem. FBA (labor and employment com. 1996—, trustee 1999—), Chgo. Bar Assn. (chmn. labor and employment com. 1994-95), GSB Chgo. Club. Democrat. Roman Catholic. Office: Drinker Biddle Gardner Carton 191 N Wacker Dr Chicago IL 60606-1698 Office Phone: 312-569-1332. Business E-Mail: mark.furlane@dbr.com.

FURLAUD, RICHARD MORTIMER, pharmaceutical executive; b. NYC, Apr. 15, 1923; s. Maxime Hubert and Eleanor (Mortimer) F.; children: Richard Mortimer, Eleanor Jay, Elizabeth Tamsin; m. Isabel Phelps Furlaud. Student, Institut Sillig, Villars, Switzerland; AB, Princeton U., 1944; LLB, Harvard U., 1947. Bar: NY 1949. Assoc. Root, Ballantine, Harlan, Bushby & Palmer, 1947-51; with legal dept. Olin Mathieson Chem. Corp., 1955-56, asst. to exec. v.p. for finance, 1956-57, asst. pres., 1957-59, v.p., 1959-64, gen. counsel, 1957-60, gen. mgr., v.p. internat. div., 1960-64, exec. v.p., 1964-66, now dir., 1964-94; pres., dir. E. R. Squibb & Sons, Inc., 1966-68; pres., chief exec., dir. Squibb Beech-Nut, Inc. (renamed Squibb Corp. 1971), Princeton, NJ, 1968-74; chmn., chief exec., dir. Squibb Corp. (merged with Bristol-Myers Co.), NYC, 1974-89; pres., bd. dirs. Bristol-Myers Co. (renamed Bristol-Myers Squibb Co.), NYC, 1989-91. Mem. profl. staff Ho. of Reps. Com. Ways and Means, 1954; chmn. Rockefeller U. Coun. 1st lt. JAGC U.S. Army, 1951-53. Mem. Assn. Bar City of N.Y., Coun. on Fgn. Rels., River Club. Home: 745 HiMount Rd Palm Beach FL 33480 Office: 8th Fl West 777 S Flagler Dr West Palm Beach FL 33401 Home Phone: 561-848-2267; Office Phone: 561-515-6016. Personal E-mail: ternaboutx@aol.com.

FURLONG, GEORGE MORGAN, JR., museum program director, retired military officer; b. Muskogee, Okla., Nov. 23, 1931; s. George M. and Anna (Moore) F.; m. Ryland Hagood Blakey, June 5, 1956; children: Morgan, William. BS in Naval Sci., U.S. Naval Acad., 1956; BS in Aero. Engring., U.S. Naval Postgrad. Sch., 1963. Commd. ensign U.S. Navy, 1956, advanced through grades to rear adm. (upper half), 1981; F-14 program mgr. Comdr. Naval Air Forces, U.S. Pacific Fleet, 1973-74; wing comdr. Attack Carrier Air Wing 14, USS Enterprise, 1974-75; comdg. officer USS Ponchatoula, Pearl Harbor, Hawaii, 1975-76, USS Independence, Norfolk, Va., 1977-78; chief of staff U.S. Sixth Fleet, Gaeta, Italy, 1978-80; dir. Air Warfare Systems Analysis Staff, Office Chief of Naval Ops., Washington, 1980-81; comdr. Fighter Airborne Early Warning Wing. U.S. Pacific Fleet, Naval Air Sta., Miramar, San Diego, 1981-83; dep. chief Naval Edn. and Tng., Pensacola, Fla., 1983-85; ret., 1986; exec. v.p. Naval Aviation Mus. Found., Pensacola, 1986-96; dir. devel. Bapt. Health Care Found., Pensacola, 1997—2001; cons. Naval Aviation Mus. Found., 2001—06. Deocorated Legion of Merit with gold star; recipient John Paul Jones award Nat. Navy League Assn., 1971 Home Phone: 850-475-0067; Office Phone: 850-475-0064. Personal E-mail: skipone@aol.com.

FURLONG, MARK FRANCIS, diversified financial services company executive, bank executive; b. 1957; BS in Acctg., Fin. and Bus., So. Ill. U., 1981. CPA, Mich. Sr. mgr. KPMG Peat Marwick, 1981—85; audit ptnr. Deloitte & Touche USA LLP, LA, 1985—90; first v.p. H.F. Ahmanson & Co., 1992—98; exec. v.p., CFO Old Kent Fin. Corp., 1998—2001; sr. v.p., CFO Marshall & Ilsley Corp., Milw., 2001—02, exec. v.p., CFO, 2002—04, exec. v.p., 2004—05, pres., 2005—, CEO, 2007—; pres. M&I Marshall & Ilsley Bank, 2004—07, pres., CEO, 2007—. Office: Marshall & Ilsley Corp 770 N Water St Milwaukee WI 53202*

FURLOTTI, ALEXANDER AMATO, real estate company executive, investment company executive; b. Milan, Apr. 21, 1948; came to U.S., 1957; s. Amato and Polonia Concepcion (Lopez) F.; m. Nancy Elizabeth Swift, June 27, 1976; children: Michael Alexander, Patrick Swift, Allison Nicole. BA in Econs., U. Calif. Berkeley, Berkeley, 1970; JD, UCLA, 1973. Bar: Calif. 1973, U.S. Dist. Ct. (9th cir.) 1973. Assoc. Alexander, Inman, Kravetz & Tanzer, Beverly Hills, Calif., 1973-77, ptnr., 1978-80, Kravetz & Furlotti, Century City, Calif., 1981-83; pres. Quorum Properties, LA, 1984—, Quorum Funds, LA, 2000—. Trustee Harvard-Westlake Sch., L.A., 1989-97, Yosemite Nat. Inst., San Francisco, 1990-92. Recipient Grand award Pacific Coast Bldrs. Conf., 1993, 98, Golden Nugget award, 1993, 98, Grand award Nat. Assn. Home Builders, 1993, Platinum award, 1997, Best Attached Housing award, 1998, Residential Project of Yr., 1998; finalist Pillars of Industy award Nat. Assn. Homebuilders, 2004 Mem. Am. Bar Assn., Urban Land Inst., The Beach Club, Calif. Club, Bohemian Club. Republican. Episcopalian. Personal E-mail: af@qfuds.net.

FURLOW, MACK VERNON, JR., retired chief financial officer, treasurer, financial analyst; b. Summit, Miss., Aug. 20, 1931; s. Mack Vernon and Trudie Dena (Ratcliff) F.; m. Barbara Elaine Rolfs, Mar. 20, 1954 (div. Dec. 1985); children— David Wayne, Kevin Rolfs. BS, La. State U., 1953; grad., advanced mgmt. program Harvard, 1968. Financial and systems analyst Humble Oil & Refining Co., Baton Rouge, 1957-61; asst. controller Skyland Internat. Corp., Chattanooga, 1961-65; v.p., corp. controller Blount, Inc., Montgomery, Ala., 1965-71; pres. Pipeco Steel Co., Inc., Wilmington, Del., 1971-73; sr. v.p., CFO, treas. The Hunt Corp., Indpls., 1973-96, dir., 1977-96. Asst. treas. 54th Advanced Mgmt. Program class Harvard Bus. Sch., 1968— Served to 1st lt. AUS, 1953-57. Mem. La. State U. Alumni Assn. (mem. adv. com. Montgomery chpt. 1967-71), Nat. Assn. Accts. (nat. bd. dirs. 1976-78), Fin. Execs. Internat. (nat. bd. dirs. 1994-97). Republican. Lutheran. Home: 9337 Spring Forest Dr Indianapolis IN 46260-1269 Personal E-mail: mackvf@yahoo.com. *The creation of a management climate or environment which causes people to want to excel and perform to their fullest capabilities is a far superior approach than is a management style which causes people to perform because they are constantly afraid of the consequences of failing to perform.*

FURLOW, WILLIAM LAWRENCE, retired financial consultant; b. Castroville, Tex., July 19, 1944; s. William Elmer and Mary Ellen (Griffin) F.; m. Patricia Mary Nevins, July 20, 1974; 1 child, Christopher Randolf. Student, U. Ky., Lexington, 1962-64, Santa Monica City Coll., Calif., 1966, La. Poly., 1972. Shipping clk. Coastal Dynamics Corp., Venice, Calif., 1964; sr. PC clk. Vol-Shan Mfg. Co., Culver City, Calif., 1965-68; materials coord. Hughes Aircraft, Culver City, 1969-70; PC clk. Everest & Jennings Inc., LA, 1970-72; supr. Audio Magnetics Corp., Compton, Calif., 1973-74, Am. Safety Corp., Pacoima, Calif., 1975-76; agent Combined Ins. Co. Am., Virginia Beach, Va., 1977; buyer Perma-Bilt Industries, Torrance, Calif., 1978-80; gen. mgr. Cweco, Gardena, Calif., 1980-83, Saferail Inc., Gardena, 1980-83; PC mgr. DB Products Inc., Pasadena, Calif., 1984-92; CFO Bulltek Ltd., Running Springs, Calif., 1996—2005; ret., 2005; purchasing agt. Custom Woodworker, Daytona Beach, Fla., 2006—07. Cons. in field, Ocean Springs, Miss., 2000-05; affiliate Maple Leaf Meds, Kirkland, Wash., 2003-05; owner websites. Author poems. Enumerator US Census Bur., Gulfport, Miss., 2000. Pfc USAR, 1963—69. Mem. Am. Legion, Internat. Soc. Photographers, Internat. Soc. Poets, Hist. Ocean Springs Assn., Jud. Watch, CRJ Press Assocs., Nat. Assn. Uniformed Svcs., Arthritis Found., The Sr. Citizen Assn. Am., Wounded Warrior Project. Republican. Methodist. Avocations: coin collecting/numismatics, stamp collecting/philately, writing, photography. Home: 1408 Churchill Dr Ocean Springs MS 39564 Office Phone: 228-235-8394. Personal E-mail: furlowbill@bellsouth.net.

FURMAN, ANTHONY MICHAEL, public relations executive; b. LA, Nov. 5, 1934; s. LeRoy S. and Geraldine P. Furman; m. Betty Gayle Morgan, Nov. 1, 1970; 1 child, Michael Jason. BA, Bethany Coll., W.Va., 1957; post grad., Columbia U., 1957—58. Asst. account exec. Jules Beitler, Pub. Rels., Newark, 1958; account exec. Barber & Baar Pub. Rels. Corp., NYC, 1959—60; account exec. and media dir. Sydney S. Baron & Co., Inc., 1961—66; pres. Anthony M. Furman, Inc., 1966—81; v.p. and mng. dir. sports devel. divsn. Hill & Knowlton, Inc., 1981—85; pres. Dorf and Stanton Sports Mktg., 1985—86, Anthony M. Furman, Inc., 1986—. Adj. prof. L.I. U., 1986—91; guest lectr. NYU, 1989, adj. prof., 1992—2004; bd. dir. FKP Assoc., Lake Placid, NY. Prodr.: (films) Floating Free, 1977 (Acad. award nominee, 1978). With MC US Army, 1957—58. Recipient Outstanding Alumnus award, Bethany Coll., 1987. Mem.: Pub. Rels. Soc. Am. Democrat. Jewish. Office: Ste 1501 250 W 57th St New York NY 10107 Office Phone: 212-956-5666. Business E-Mail: tony@furmansports.com.

FURMAN, DAVID STEPHEN, artist, educator; b. Seattle, Aug. 15, 1945; s. Stanley Albert and Lenore (Silverman) F.; m. Luann Lovejoy, Dec. 17, 1983. BA, U. Oreg., 1969; MFA, U. Wash., 1972. Prof. Otis/Parsons, LA, 1975, Calif. State U., LA, 1976, Colo. Mt. Coll., Vail, 1976-78, Claremont Grad. Sch., Calif., 1973—. Prof. studio arts Pitzer Coll., Claremont, 1973—, Peter and Gloriagold endowed chair, 2003—07. One-man shows include: Tortue Gallery, Santa Monica, Calif., 1985, 87, 89, 91, Elaine Horwitch Gallery, Santa Fe, 1989, Margulies Taplin Gallery, Miami, Fla., 1990, O.K. Harris Works of Art, N.Y.C., 1990, Judy Youvens Gallery, Houston, 1993, Sherry Frumkin Gallery, Santa Monica, 1996. NEA fellow, 1975, 86-87, Fulbright fellow, 1979, sr. artist fellow, 1990, NEA Vis. Artist fellow, 1996. Mem. Nat. Coun. Edn. of Ceramic Arts, Am. Crafts Coun. Office: Pitzer Coll 1050 N Mills Ave Claremont CA 91711-3908 Home: 4739 Glen Ivy St La Verne CA 91750 Office Phone: 909-607-3252. Business E-Mail: david_furman@pitzer.edu.

FURMAN, HOWARD, arbitrator, lawyer, mediator; b. Newark, Nov. 30, 1938; s. Emanuel and Lilyan (Feldman) F.; m. Elaine Sheitleman, June 12, 1960 (div. 1982); children: Deborah Toby, Naomi N'chama, David Seth; m. Janice Wheeler, Jan. 14, 1984. BA in Econs., Rutgers U., 1966; JD cum laude, Birmingham Sch. Law, 1985. Bar: Ala. 1985, U.S. Dist. Ct. (no. dist.) Ala. 1986, U.S. Dist. Ct. (so. dist.) Ala. 1996. Designer/draftsman ITT, Nutley, NJ, 1957-61; pers. mgr. Computer Products Inc., Belmar, NJ, 1962-64, Arde Engring. Co., Newark, 1964-66; econs. instr. Rutgers U., New Brunswick, NJ, 1966-74; dir. indsl. rels. Harvard Ind. Frequency Engring. Labs. Divsn., Farmingdale, NJ, 1966-74; commr. Fed. Mediation and Conciliation Svc., Birmingham, Ala., 1974-96; pvt. practice Birmingham, 1985—. Instr. bus. law Jefferson State C.C., 1989-95; instr. human resources mgmt. Nova U., 1993; prof. personal property, adminstrv. law, sales and alternative dispute resolution Birmingham Sch. Law, 1993—2005. Pres. Ocean Twp. (NJ) Police Res., 1968. Recipient ofcl. commendation Fed. Mediation and Conciliation Svc., 1979, 81-82, 88. Mem. ABA, Ala. Bar Assn., Birmingham Bar Assn., Soc. Profls. in Dispute Resolution, Fed. Soc. Labor Rels. Profls., Indsl. Rels. Rsch. Assn., Sigma Delta Kappa. Jewish. Office Phone: 205-853-8204. Personal E-mail: hfesq@bellsouth.net.

FURMAN, L. ROBERT, principal, music educator; b. Washington, Pa., Mar. 12, 1972; s. Robert Louis and Rosalie Furman; m. Tiffeni Sue Patrick, Dec. 26, 1999; 1 child, Robert Lucas. BS in Music Edn., W.Va. U., 1995; MS in Ednl. Adminstrn., Duquesne U., 2000, EdD in Leadership, 2006. Cert. tchr. music edn. k-12 W.Va. Dept. Edn., 1995, Pa. Dept. Edn., 1995, edn. aminstrn. K-12 Duquesne U., Pa. Dir. H.S. band Owings Mills H.S., Balt., 1995—97, Elizabeth Forward Sch. Dist., Pa., 1997—2000, Joshua Sch. Dist., Tex., 2000—01; mid. sch. music tchr. Pitts. Pub. Schs., 2001—03; asst. prin. Gateway Sch. Dist., Monroeville, Pa., 2003—06; prin. South Park Elem. Ctr., Pa., 2006—. Instr. percussion Baltimore Ravens Marching Band, 1995—97; dir. Western Pa. Honors Band/Pa. Music Educators Assn., Pitts., 1997—2000, dir. European tour, 1998—99. Recording, Teachable Moment, 2005. Recipient Charles Gray award Music Edn., Civic Light Orch., 2002; Music scholarship, Pa. State U., 1990. Mem.: Percussive Arts Soc., Pa. Mid. Sch. Assn., Pa. Music Educators Assn., Phi Mu Alpha Sinfonia, Kappa Delta Rho. Roman Catholic. Avocations: recording music, photography, videography, hunting, boating. Home: 174 Sylvania Dr Pittsburgh PA 15236 Office: South Park Elem Ctr 2001 Eagle Pride Ln South Park PA 15129 Home Phone: 412-714-8880. Office Fax: 412-373-5885; Home Fax: 724-745-6457. E-mail: rfurman@gatewayk12.org.

FURMAN, MARK EVAN, neuroscientist; b. Bronx, NY, Mar. 14, 1962; s. Edward and Charlotte F.; m. Beth Ann Schad, Aug. 9, 1987; children: Lauren Ashley, Jonathan Cyle. BA in Behavioral Scis./Psychology, Coll. of SI, 1984. Cert. practitioner of neuro-linguistic programming. Dir. edn. and rsch. Assoc. Schs. Music, Inc., Cooper City, Fla., 1988-97; spkr., author, human performance cons., 1990—; founder, exec. dir. Furman Rsch. Assocs., Boca Raton, Fla., 1987—; dir. edn. and rsch. The Keys to Success, Inc., Coral Springs, Fla., 1992—2000, Ozone Park, NY, 1992—2000; human performance cons. Interactive Response Techs., 2001—04; dir. behavioral scis. Burton Tng. Group, Inc., 2004—; pres. Mind Imaging Techologies, Inc., 2006—. Lectr. in field of neurosci.; founder, exec. dir. Furman Rsch. Assocs.; designer comm. program Jewish Ednl. Found. of Am., theoretical tng. model Syntonics Ednls., Switzerland; cons. Keys to Success Music Sch., NY, Century 21, Fla.; founder Internat. Soc. for Edn. Neurosci.; developer Intelligent Learning Systems, Mind Imaging, Neuroprint, Human Performance Modeling & Engineering, Decernomics; numerous others application models. Author: Mind in Motion, The Human Performance Technology for the Next Millenum, 1996; author: Jour. for the Soc. of Neuro-Linguistic Programming, 1995-2002, The Neurophysics of Human Behavior: Explorations at the Interface of Brain, Mind, Behavior and Information, 1999, (audio CD) Escaping the Mind Prison, 2006; contbg. author: Energy Psychology in Psychotherapy, 2002; contbr. articles to profl. jours. Mem.: APA (affiliate, divsn. 48, divsn. peace psychology), AAAS, Soc. for Study of Peace, Conflict and Violence, Internat. Soc. for Cognitive Neurophysics (founder). Achievements include developing intelligent learning systems (ILS); neuroprint; mind imaging; decernomics and human performance modeling and engineering; currently pioneering coordinated research and development efforts in the field of education neuroscience, studying the neurophysics of human information processing and its application to the field of human education, psychotherapy, marketing, crisis negotiation and the management sciences; advanced standard theory: Pattern-Entropy dynamics of matter and energy interaction; formerly established the interdisciplinary branch of science known as cognitive neurophysics. Home: 9559 Trivolo Pl Boca Raton FL 33434-2057 Office: Furman Rsch 9559 Trivolo Pl Boca Raton FL 33434 Personal E-mail: neuroprint@yahoo.com.

FURMAN, ROY LANCE, investment banker, theater producer; b. NYC, Apr. 19, 1939; s. Joseph M. and Frances L. (Kurlander) F.; m. Frieda Anne Bueler, Nov. 7, 1965; children: Jill Tracy, Stephanie Gail. AB, Bklyn. Coll., 1960; LL.B., Harvard U., 1963. Atty. Western Electric Co., NYC, 1964-67; v.p. Continental Tel. Supply Co., NYC, 1967-68; with Seiden & de Cuevas, Inc., NYC, 1968-73, pres., 1972-73; co-founder, pres. Furman Selz LLC, NYC, 1973-98, also bd. dirs., 1973-98; chmn., CEO Livent Inc., NYC, 1998-99; vice chmn. Furman Selz LLC, NYC, 1997-99, ING Barings, NYC, 1999—2001, Jefferies and Co., NYC, 2001—; chmn. Jefferies Capital Mgmt., NYC, 2001—. Former nat. fin. chmn. Dem. Nat. Com.; past chmn. splty. firms adv. com. N.Y. Stock Exch.; bd. dirs. Westfield Group. Prodr.: Spamalot (Tony winner), History Boys (Tony winner),Fosse (Tony winner), The Color Purple, Legally Blonde, Dirty Rotten Scoundrels, The Odd Couple, Inherit The Wind. Chmn. emeritus Film Soc. of Lincoln Ctr.; v.p. N.Y.C. Opera; vice chmn. Lincoln Ctr. for Performing Arts; past nat. chmn. Harvard Law Sch. Fund; exec. com. dean's adv. bd. Harvard Law Sch. Mem.: Core Club NYC, East Hampton Golf Club, Palm Beach Country Club (Fla.), Harmonie Club (NYC). Office: Jefferies and Co 520 Madison Ave New York NY 10022

FURMAN-MARKOWITZ, JOANNA FLORENCE, dance educator; b. Balt., Sept. 28, 1952; d. Henry John Furman and Irene Anna Russ; m. Jack Saul Markowitz, May 3, 1986; children: Jesse Michael, Jacob Alexander. BS in Clin. Psychology, Towson U., 1975. Dancer Linda Kohl & Dancers, NYC, 1984—86, Theatre Dance Ensemble, NYC, 1980—86; adminstrv. asst. Dance Theater Workshop, NYC, 1980—86; dir., choreographer Little Feet Dance Co., Monroe, NY, 1992—; dance instr. Bklyn. Coll., 1980—87; dance prof. Orange County C.C., Middletown, NY, 1986—2004; owner, dir. Orange County Sch. Dance, Monroe, 1992—. Choreographer (modern dance) Graphic Illusion, 2000, For One, 1977. Named Advisor of Yr., Orange County C.C., 1989; recipient Appreciation award. Roman Catholic. Avocations: gardening, reading, music. Office: Orange County Sch Dance 16 Lake St Monroe NY 10950 Office Phone: 845-782-2482.

FURNAS, DAVID WILLIAM, plastic surgeon, educator; b. Caldwell, Idaho, Apr. 1, 1931; s. John Doan and Esther Bradbury (Hare) F.; m. Mary Lou Heatherly, Feb. 11, 1956; children: Heather Jean, Brent David, Craig Jonathan. AB, U. Calif., Berkeley, 1952, MS, 1957, MD, 1955. Diplomate Am. Bd. Plastic Surgery, Royal Coll. Surgeons. Intern U. Calif. Hosp., San Francisco, 1955-56, asst. resident in surgery, 1956-57; asst. resident in psychiatry, NIMH fellow Langley Porter Neuropsychiat. Inst. U. Calif., San Francisco, 1959-60; resident in gen. surgery Gorgas Hosp., Panama Canal Zone, 1960-61; asst. resident in plastic surgery N.Y. Hosp., Cornell Med. Center, NYC, 1961-62; chief resident in plastic surgery Cornell U. Svc., VA Hosp., Bronx, NY, 1962-63; registrar Royal Infirmary and Affiliated Hosps., Glasgow, Scotland, 1963-64; assoc. in hand surgery U. Iowa, 1964-68, sr. resident, faculty assoc. in surgery, 1964-65, asst. prof. surgery, 1966-68, assoc. prof., 1968-69; assoc. prof. surgery, chief div. plastic surgery U. Calif., Irvine, 1969-74, prof., chief div. plastic surgery, 1974-80, clin. prof., chief div. plastic surgery, 1980-99, clin. prof. plastic surgery, 1999—2002, emeritus prof. plastic surgery, 2002—. Surgeon East Africa Flying Drs. Svc., African Med. and Rsch. Found., Nairobi, Kenya, 1972-73; plastic surgeon S.S. Hope, Nicaragua, 1966, Sri Lanka, 1968; mem. Balakbayan med. mission Mindanao and Sulu, The Philippines, 1980-82; overseas vis. prof. plastic surgery Ednl. Found., 1994; Godrej vis. prof. Assn. Plastic Surgeons of India, 2000; keynote spkr. Pan African Assn. Plastic Surgeons, 2000; dir. Am. Bd. Plastic Surgeons, 1979-85; trustee Royal Coll. Surgeons Found., 1995-2002. Contbr. chpts. to textbooks, articles to profl. jours.; author, editor 5 textbooks; mem. editl. bd. Jour. Hand Surgery, Annals of Plastic Surgery, Jour. Craniofacial Surgery; reviewer Plastic and Reconstructive Surgery. Expedition leader Flag 171 Skull Surgeons of the Kisii Tribe Explorer's Club, Kenya, expedition leader Flag 44 Skull Surgeons of the Marakwet Tribe, 1987; bd. govs. Bowers Mus. Cultural Art, 2000—02. Capt. M.C. USAF, 1957—59, col. M.C. USAR, 1989—92. Recipient Golden Apple award U. Calif.-Irvine Sch. Medicine, 1980, Kaiser-Permanente award U. Calif.-Irvine Sch. Medicine, 1981, Humanitarian Svc. award Black Med. Students, U. Calif. Irvine, 1987, Sr. Rsch. award Plastic Surgery Ednl. Found., 1987, Cert. of Spl. Recognition, U.S. Congress, 1998; named Orange County Press Club Headliner of Yr., 1982, Physician of the Year, Orange County Med. Assn., 1998, Alumnus of Yr. U. Calif. San Francisco Alumni Assn., 2005. Fellow ACS, Royal Coll. Surgeons Can., Royal Soc. Medicine, Explorers Club (chmn. So. Calif. chpt. 2001-02), Royal Geog. Soc.; mem. AMA (Disting. Svc. award 2002), Calif. Med. Assn., Orange County Med. Assn. (Physician of Yr. 1998), Am. Soc. Plastic Surgery (bd. dirs. 1970-73), Am. Soc. Reconstructive Microsurgery, Soc. Head and Neck Surgery, Am. Cleft Palate Assn., Am. Soc. Surgery of Hand, Soc. Univ. Surgeons, Am. Assn. Plastic Surgeons (trustee 1983-86, treas. 1988-91, v.p. 1993-94, pres.-elect 1994, pres. 1995, Godrej vis. prof. 2000), British Assn. Plastic Surgeons (hon.), Am. Soc. Craniofacial Surgery, Am. Soc. Aesthetic Plastic Surgery, Am. Soc. Maxillofacial Surgeons, Assn. Acad. Chairmen Plastic Surgery (bd. dirs. 1986-89), Assn. Surgeons East Africa, Assn. Plastic and Reconstructive Surgeons So. Africa (hon.), Pacific Coast Surg. Assn., Internat. Soc. Aesthetic Plastic Surgery, Internat. Soc. Reconstructive Microsurgery, Internat. Soc. Craniomaxillofacial Surgery, Pan African Assn. Neurol. Sci., African Med. and Rsch. Found. (bd. dirs. U.S.A. 1987-2002, team leader Reconstruct! mission for victims of Am. Embassy bombing, Nairobi, Kenya, 1999), Muthaiga Club, Ctr. Club, Club 33, Univ. Club, Phi Beta Kappa, Alpha Omega Alpha. Personal E-mail: daktari1@cox.net. *A crisis, at the outset, usually augurs nothing but ill. In the long run, however, my crises have more often than not marked a new course for my life, which is more fulfilling, and more exciting than anything in the past. Yes, a bit of good luck is needed, but the special feature of a crisis is that you are suddenly cut off from past patterns, habits, and interdependencies. Along with the distress and pain is freedom! Freedom to build again, with a new foundation and modern structure, using wisdom you didn't have the last time you built.*

FURNIER, VINCENT DAMON See COOPER, ALICE

FURR, QUINT EUGENE, marketing executive; b. Concord, N.C., Sept. 21, 1921; s. Walter Luther and Mary (Barnhardt) F.; m. Helen Wilson, Dec. 30, 1961; children: Tiffany Grantham, Quentin, Robert; stepchildren: Pamela Erickson, Erik Erickson. Grad. Belmont Abbey Coll., BA, U. N.C., Chapel Hill, 1943, postgrad. Law Sch., 1946-47. Promotion rep. Sears, Roebuck & Co., Atlanta and Greensboro, N.C., 1947-49; nat. advt. and sales promotion mgr. Western Auto Supply Co., Kansas City, Mo., 1949-61; regional mgr. J.F. Pritchard Co., Charlotte, N.C., 1961-63; gen. mgr. Hogan Rose Advt., High Point, N.C., 1963-65; regional mgr. Top Value Enterprises, Washington, 1965-67; v.p. corp. mktg. Textilease Corp., Beltsville, Md., 1967-85; v.p. sales and mktg. Am. Directory Service Agy., Bethesda, Md., 1985-88; Marketing Consultant, 1988—. Lt. USNR, World War II, Korea. Recipient Mktg. award Textile Leasing Industry, 1970-74. Mem. Sales and Mktg. Execs. Internat., Inst. Indsl. Laundries (past chmn. mktg. com.), Am. Legion, VFW, Pi Kappa Alpha. Roman Catholic. Club: AD (Washington). Lodges: Moose, Elks. Home and Office: 32 Obsidian Dr Chambersburg PA 17201-8207

FURSE, ELIZABETH, retired congressman, small business owner; b. Nairobi, Kenya, 1936; came to U.S., 1958, naturalized, 1972; children: Amanda Briggs, John Briggs; m. John Platt. BA, Evergreen State Coll., 1974; postgrad., U. Wash., Northwestern U., Lewis and Clark Coll. Dir. Western Wash. Indian program Am. Friends Svc. Com, 1975-77; coord. Restoration program for Native Am. Tribes Oreg. Legal Svc., 1980-86; co-owner Helvetia Vineyards, Hillsboro, Oreg.; mem. 103rd-105th Congresses from 1st Oreg. dist., 1993-98, mem. commerce com. Exec. dir. Inst. for Tribal Govt., Portland State U. Co-founder Oreg. Peace Inst., 1985. also: Inst Tribal Govt PO Box 751 Portland OR 97207 Home: 7414 SW Miles Pl Portland OR 97219-3028

FURST, ALEX JULIAN, thoracic and cardiovascular surgeon; b. Augusta, Ga., Aug. 21, 1938; m. George Alex and Ann (Segall) F.; m. Elayne Kobrin, Aug. 11, 1962; children: James Andrew, Jeffrey Michael, Joseph Robert. Student, U. Fla., 1963; MD, U. Miami, 1967. Intern U. Miami Hosp., 1967-68, resident, 1968-72, clin. instr. dept. surgery, 1974-91; chief resident in thoracic and cardiovascular surgery Emory U. Hosp., Atlanta, 1972-73, sr. surg. registrar of thoracic unit, 1972-73, Hosp. for Sick Children, London, 1973-74; practice medicine specializing in thoracic and cardiovascular surgery Miami, Fla.; clin. assoc. prof. surgery and cardiology, chief surg. svc. Miami VA Med. Ctr., 1991—2003, clin. prof., surgery and medicine, chief of surgery; chief surgeon West Palm Beach Med. Ctr., Va., 2000—02; sr. cons. dept. surgery U. Miami Sch. Medicine, 2005—. Chief thoracic surgery, pres. med. staff Mercy Hosp.; mem. staff Bapt. Hosp., South Miami Hosp., Doctor's Hosp. (all Miami), North Ridge Gen. Hosp., Ft. Lauderdale; program dir. cardiothoracic surgery U. Miami Sch. of Medicine, 1998-2000. Fellow ACS, Am. Coll. Cardiology, Am. Coll. Chest Physicians; mem. Dade County Med. Assn., Fla. Med. Assn., Heart Assn. Greater Miami, Soc. Thoracic Surgeons, So. Thoracic Surg. Assn. Home: 8802 Arvida Dr Miami FL 33156-2302 Office Phone: 305-575-3157.

FURST, E. KENNETH, accountant; b. Oct. 11, 1946; BS in Econs., U. Pa., 1968, MS in Acctg., 1969. CPA, N.J. V.p. fin. Sea-Land Corp., Edison, NJ, 1971—89; CFO, dir., owner Toledo, Peoria & We. Railway, Ill., 1989—96; CFO, v.p. Golden Eagle Network, Bethel, Conn., 1996—97; owner E. Kenneth Furst, CPA, Short Hills, NJ, 1982—; v.p. RBC Dain Ranscler, Florham Park, 1988—2006, Ryan Beck & Co., 2006—. Chair U. Pa. Secondary Sch. Com., Essex County. Mem. N.J. Soc. CPA (trustee 1997-2000, pres. Essex chpt. 1995-96), Ct. Apptd. Spl. Adv. (trustee 2000-2005, treas. 2000-03), U. Pa. Club Metro. N.J. (pres. 1995-96, trustee 1971—). Office Phone: 973-549-4097. E-mail: furstk@att.net, kenneth.furst@ryanbeck.com.

FURST, ERIC JONATHAN, physician, surgeon; b. NYC, Dec. 11, 1957; s. Robert Irving and Selmo Barbara Furst; m. Ann Louise Sterling, May 29, 1984; children: Julie, Nicole. BS in Zoology, U. Mass., Amherst, 1980, MS in Pub. Health, 1982; MD, Baylor U., Houston, 1986. Diplomate Am. Bd. Otolaryn. Surgery. Attending physician/surgeon Falls Church Med. Ctr., Va., 1992—95; pvt. practice Springfield, Va., 1995—. Bd. dirs. Congl. Schs. Va., Falls Church, 1993—. Named one of Washington's Top Drs., Washington Mag., 2002, 2005. Fellow: Va. Soc. Otolaryngology, No. Va. Med. Soc., Am. Acad. Otolaryngology. Avocations: jazz, piano, golf, tennis, scuba diving. Office: 5504 Back Lick Rd Springfield VA 22151

FURTADO, NELLY KIM, vocalist; b. Victoria, BC, Can., Dec. 2, 1978; d. Maria Manuela and Antonio Jose Furtado; 1 child, Nevis. Signed to Dreamworks Records, 1999—2005, Geffen Records, 2005—. Singer: (albums) Whoa Nelly!, 2000, Folklore, 2003, Loose, 2006 (Album of Yr., Pop Album of Yr., Juno awards, 2007), (songs) I'm Like a Bird, 2000 (Juno award for Best Single, 2001, Grammy award for Best Female Pop Performance, 2002), Turn Off the Light, 2000, Promiscuous, 2006 (Choice Song of the Summer and Choice V Cast Music Artist, Teen Choice Awards, 2006, Billboard Pop 100 Single of Yr., 2006, Single of Yr., Juno awards, 2007); background vocals: albums Phrenology (The Roots), 2002, vocals: albums Bunkka (Oakenfold), 2002. Recipient 4 Juno awards: Best Single, Best New Solo Artist, Best Prodr., Best Songwriter, 2001, World's Best Pop/Rock Artist, World Music Awards, 2007, Internat. Female Solo Artist, BRIT Awards, 2007, 5 awards, including Fan Choice award and Artist of Yr., Juno Awards, 2007. Office: c/o Chris Smith Mgmt Inc 5th Fl 21 Camden St Toronto ON M5V 1V2 Canada Office Phone: 416-362-7771. Office Fax: 416-362-6648. E-mail: info@ChrisSmithManagement.com.

FURTH, FREDERICK PAUL, lawyer; b. West Harvey, Ill., Apr. 12, 1934; s. Fred P. and Mamie (Stelmach) F.; children: Darby, Ben Anthony, Megan Louise; m. Peggy Wollerman, July 19, 1986. Student, Drake U., 1952-53; BA, U. Mich., 1956, JD, 1959; postgrad., U. Berlin, 1959, U. Munich, Fed. Republic Germany, 1960. Bar: Mich. 1959, N.Y. 1961, D.C. 1965, U.S. Supreme Ct. 1965, Calif. 1966. Assoc. Cahill, Gordon, Reindel & Ohl, NYC, 1960-64; with Kellogg Co., Battle Creek, Mich., 1964-65; assoc. Joseph L. Alioto, San Francisco, 1965-66; sr. ptnr. The Furth Firm LLP, San Francisco, 1966—. Bd. dirs. Robert Half Internat.; chmn., propr. Chalk Hill Winery. Trustee, chmn. bd. Furth Family Found., San Francisco; bd. dirs. Franklin and Eleanor Roosevelt Inst., 1996—, The Ctr. for Democracy, Washington; chmn. Internat. Jud. Conf., Strasbourg, France, 1992-. Mem. ABA, Internat. Bar Assn., N.Y. Bar Assn., San Francisco Bar Assn., State Bar Calif., Assn. of Bar of City of N.Y., St. Francis Yacht Club, Olympic Club. Office: Furth Firm LLP 225 Bush St 15th Flr San Francisco CA 94104 E-mail: fpfurth@aol.com.

FURTH, JOHN JACOB, molecular biologist, educator, pathologist; b. Phila., Jan. 25, 1929; s. Jacob and Olga (Berthauer) F.; m. Mary Autry, June 24, 1959; children: Karen, Susan, Robin. BA, Cornell U., 1950; student, Yale Law Sch., 1950-51; MD, Duke U., 1958; MA, U. Pa., 1972. Intern Bellevue Hosp., NYC, 1958-59; resident in pathology NYU Sch. Medicine, NYC, 1959-60, postdoctoral fellow dept. microbiology, 1960-62; mem. faculty dept. pathology U. Pa. Med. Sch., Phila., 1962—, prof., 1978—2001, emeritus prof., 2001—. Contbr. articles to profl. jours. Bd. dirs., chmn. hist. sites com. Darby Creek Valley Assn., 1984-96, 1st v.p. 1997—; bd. dirs., founder Friends of the Swedish Cabin (constructed circa 1654), Upper Darby, Pa., 1987, pres. 2002—03; bd. dirs. Fair Housing Coun. of Suburban Phila., 1995-97, 2d dist. leader Upper Darby Democratic Party, 1994—2002, chmn., 2002—; candidate for Congress, 7th Dist. Pa. 2d lt. Q.M.C., U.S. Army, 1951-53. Recipient Hoffman LaRoche award, 1958; Eleanor Roosevelt fellow, 1977-78. Mem. AAAS, Am. Soc. Biol. Chemists and Molecular Biologists, Am. Assn. Cancer Rsch., Am. Assn. Pathologists. Democrat. Mem. Soc. Of Friends. Achievements include codiscovery of RNA polymerase. Home: 43 Roselawn Ave Lansdowne PA 19050-2317 Office: U Pa Sch Medicine Dept Pathology and Lab Med Philadelphia PA 19104-6082 E-mail: jjfurth@mail.med.upenn.edu.

FURTH, KAREN J., artist; BA in Am. History, U. Pa., 1983; MA in Photography, NYU, 1988. Photographer Smithsonian Instn., 1989—94; freelance photographer, 1994—; tchr., cons. Ctr. Urban Cmty. Svcs. The Times Sq., 1994—2002; tchr. Internat. Ctr. Photography at The Point, NYC, 1998—2005; adj. tchr. photography Eugene Lang Coll. New Sch. Social Rsch., 1999—2005. Artist-in-residence Creative Ctr. NYC Hosp., 2003—06; presenter in field. One-woman shows include 494 Gallery, NYC, 1991—92, 1994, Pulse Art Gallery, 1997, exhibited in group shows at 494 Gallery, 1991—92, Synchronicity Space, N.Y.C., 1995, Sullivan County Mus., 1995, Pulse Art Gallery, 1996, Golin/Harris, 1998, 2002, at A.I.R., 2004, others, curatorial projects include, The Times Sq. Photography Project, Met. Transp. Authority, 1999, Represented in permanent collections J.P. Morgan, Mt. Sinai Hosp., others; contbr. articles to profl. jours. Recipient Gilbert Graphic Paper award, 1993; fellow Open Soc. Inst. Individual Project fellow, Soros Found., 1997; Faculty scholar, U. Pa., 1979—83, Internat. Outreach grante, 1993—94. Personal E-mail: karen@karenfurth.com.

FURTH, YVONNE, advertising executive; BS in Mktg., Georgetown U., postgrad., DePaul U. Asst. account exec. Draft Worldwide, 1981—88, gen. mgr., 1988—92, pres. of Chicago office, 1992—96, pres. & COO US operations, 1996—2001, pres., COO Chgo., 2002—06, pres., CEO, 2006—. Adv. coun. mem. Smithsonian Nat. Postal Mus., 2003. Named Direct Mktg. Women of Yr., Chgo. Chpt. of Women in Direct Mktg. Internat., 2003, Advertising Woman of Yr., Chgo. Advertising Fedn. and the Women's Advertising Club Chgo., 2005; named one of Advertising Working Mother of Yr., Working Mother Mag., 2004. Mem.: Chgo. Assn. Direct Mktg., Direct Mktg. Assn. Office: Draft Chicago 633 N St Clair St Chicago IL 60611*

FURUBOTN, EIRIK GRUNDTVIG, economics professor; b. NYC, Apr. 18, 1923; s. Konrad Martin and Caroline (Grundtvig) F.; m. Florence Birkby Duckworth; children: Karin Florence, Erik Grundtvig, Kristian George BA, Brown U., 1948; MA, Columbia U., 1950, PhD, 1959. Instr. Wesleyan U., Middletown, Conn., 1953-55; asst. prof. Lafayette Coll., Easton, Pa., 1958-60; assoc. prof. Emory U., Atlanta, 1960-63; prof. SUNY, Binghamton, 1963-67, Tex. A&M U., College Station, 1967-82; James L. West prof. econs. U. Tex., Arlington, 1982-96; rsch. fellow pvt. enterprise rsch. ctr. Tex. A&M U., College Station, 1996—. Com. mem. Tex. A&M Univ. Press, College Station, 1974-82; co-dir. Ctr. for Study of New Instl. Econs., U. Saarland, W.Ger., 1986—; mem. bd. advs. Utrecht Sch. Econs., Utrecht U., Netherlands, 2002. Co-author: (with R. Richter) Neue Institutionen Okonomik, 1996, The Evolution of Modern Demand Theory, 1972; co-editor: The Economics of Property Rights, 1974, The New Institutional Economics: An Assessment, 1991, Institutions and Economic Theory, 1997, 2nd edit., 2005, also Russian, German and Chinese transls.; mem. editl. bd. Applied Econs., London, 1971-72; mem. bd. editors So. Econ. Jour., 1979-81, Zeitschrift für die gesamte Staatswissenschaft, 1984—; contbr. articles to profl. jours. Trustee Allen Acad., Bryan, Tex., 1974-76; mem. adv. coun. Polit. Economy Rsch. Ctr., Bozeman, Mont., 1984-92; mem. nat. adv. bd. Nat. Ctr. for Privatization, Wichita, Kans., 1985-95. Cpl. U.S. Army, 1942-46, ETO. Francis Wayland scholar Brown U., 1948; named Honorarprofessor für Volkswirtschaftslehre U. Saarland, Fed. Republic of Germany. Mem. Am. Econ. Assn., So. Econ. Assn. (exec. com. 1975-77), Kürschners Deutscher Gelehrten-Kalender, Phi Beta Kappa, Omicron Delta Epsilon, Beta Gamma Sigma, Omega Rho. Republican. Episcopalian. Avocations: antiques, travel. Home: 750 N Rosemary Dr Bryan TX 77802-4307 Office: Tex A&M U Pvt Enterprise Rsch Ctr PO Box 3327 College Station TX 77841-3327 Office Phone: 979-845-7722. Business E-Mail: perc@tamu.edu.

FURUTA, SOICHI, poet, art consultant, educator; b. LA, July 1, 1927; s. Junzo Furuta and Yae Kitahara; m. Misao Yokota, Nov. 2, 1958; 1 child, Yoshiya. BA cum laude, UCLA, 1954. Ptr. Triad Design Co., Inc., NYC, 1957-59; sr. design dir. Francis Blod Design Assoc., NYC, 1959-64; prin., owner Stuart Gunn and Furuta Inc., NYC, 1964-85; curatorial dir. Urban Art Rsch. Ctr., NYC, 1988; adj. prof. lit. St. Andrews Coll., Laurinburg, NC, 1988—. Adj. assoc. prof. art H. Lehman Coll. of CUNY, N.Y.C., 1968-78; adv. bd. Asian Am. Art Ctr., N.Y.C., 1988—. Author: Montefeltro the Hawk Nose, 1989 (Pulitzer nominee 1989), Pierando/Pieroing, 1996; translator: Chieko's Sky, 1978. Active Poetry Project St. Mark's Ch., 1985—. With U.S. Army, 1955-56. Recipient graphic design awards N.Y.C., 1957-85. Mem. The Acad. Am. Poets, Haiku Soc. N.Y. (Haiku award 1980, pres. 1980-82). Avocations: music appreciation, travel, reading. Home: 130 Plantation Trce Woodstock GA 30188-2273

FURY, MICHAEL ANDREW, materials scientist, research and development company executive; s. Andrew Ferdinand and Elizabeth Blanche Fury; m. Beate Boultinghouse, Oct. 11, 1998. BS in Chemistry, Iowa State U., Ames, 1973; PhD, U. Ill. Sr. mgr. engring. IBM Corp., East Fishkill, NY, 1978—94; dir. rsch. Rippey Corp., El Dorado Hills, Calif., 1994—95; global industry mgr. Rodel, Inc., Newark, Del., 1995—97; dir. process integration AlliedSignal Electronic Materials, Sunnyvale, Calif., 1997—99; sr. mgr. Silterra, Kulim, Malaysia, 1999—2000; v.p. R&D and engring. DuPont EKC Tech., Inc., Hayward, Calif., 2000—06; prin., owner InterCrossIP Mgmt. LLC, San Francisco, 2006—. Contbr. chapters to books, 100 articles to profl. jours. Trustee, planning bd. Village of Fishkill, NY, 1988—93. Mem.: AAAS, IEEE, Minerals, Metals and Materials Soc., Electrochem. Soc., Materials Rsch. Soc., Internat. Soc. Optical Engring. Achievements include first to early development and implementation of CMP; 14 patents in field. Office: InterCrossIP Mgmt LLC One Embarcadero Ctr Ste 1140 San Francisco CA 94111 Office Phone: 415-395-6945. Business E-Mail: mf@hultquistcapital.com.

FURYK, JIM (JAMES MICHAEL FURYK), professional golfer; b. West Chester, Pa., May 12, 1970; m. Tabitha Furyk; children: Caleigh Lynn, Tanner James. Grad. in Gen. Bus., U. Ariz., 1992. Profl. golfer PGA, 1992—. Mem. Ryder Cup team, 1997, 99, 2002, 04, Presidents Cup team, 1998, 2000, 03, World Cup team, 2003. Winner Nike Miss. Gulf Coast Classic, 1993, Las Vegas Internat., 1995, United Airlines Hawaiian Open, 1996, Argentine Open, 1997, Las Vegas Invitational, 1998, Fred Meyer Challenge, 1998, Doral-Ryder Open, 2000, Mercedes Championship, 2000, Memorial Tournament, 2002, US Open Championship, 2003, Buick Open, 2003, Western Open, 2005, Wachovia Championship, 2006, Canadian Open, 2006, 07, Nedbank Golf Challenge, 2006; 2d pl. Meml. Tournament, 1997, The Tour Championship, 1997. Avocation: sports. Office: c/o PGA America Box 109601 100 Ave of Champions Palm Beach Gardens FL 33410*

FURZE, EDWARD WILLIAM, fundraising consultant; b. Syracuse, NY, Jan. 7, 1938; s. John T. and Marion Joy (Gieselman) F.; m. Joanne M. Sojewicz, Aug. 4, 1962 (div. 1992); children: David John, Jeffrey Paul, Daniel Edward. BS in History, LeMoyne Coll., 1961. Exec. dir. agy. ops. United Way Cen. N.Y., Syracuse, 1965-70; exec. dir. Community Found., Syracuse, 1968-70; dir. devel. and community rels. LeMoyne Coll., Syracuse, 1970-83; v.p. Mt. St. Mary's Coll., Emmittsburg, Md., 1983-85; sr. devel. officer Pa. State U., Harrisburg, 1985-87, Fairleigh Dickinson U., Rutherford, N.J., 1987-90; exec. dir. for found., asst. v.p. devel. Gen. Hosp. Ctr., Passaic, N.J., 1990-92; fundraising cons. Ketchum, Inc., Pitts., 1992—; resource devel. dir. Boys and Girls Club of Syracuse, N.Y., 1995-97. Cons. Cyo-Brighton Family Ctr., Syracuse, 1972-73, Christ the King Retreat House, Syracuse, 1972-95, 2003, Vol. Ctr., Newark, 1990-91, Ketchum, Inc., Pitts., 1989-90; trustee St. Camillus Extended Care, Syracuse, 1972-83. Alt. del. Rep. Nat. Conv., Detroit, 1980. Mem.: Nat. Soc. Fundraising Execs., Pub. Rels. Soc. Am., Rotary (pres. 1991). Home: 429 Westcott St Syracuse NY 13210-2109

FUSARO, PETER C., environmental scientist, consultant; b. NYC, Oct. 18, 1950; s. Dominick Richard and Pauline Fusaro; m. Carmen Jane Cook, Jan. 28, 2006; 1 child, Laura Doris. BA, Carnegie-Mellon U., Pitts., 1972; MA, Tufts U., Medford, Mass., 1979. Policy analyst U.S. Dept. Energy, Washington, 1975—81; fin. analyst D.R. Fusaro & Co., NYC, 1982—85; policy analyst N.Y.C. Mayor's Office, 1985—87; prin. analyst Petroleos de Venezuela, NYC, 1988—89; energy mgr. Energy Info. Ltd., NYC, 1989—91; chmn. Global Change Assocs., NYC, 1991—. Adv. bd. Energy Forum, NYC, 1992—2004; founder Wall St. Green Trading Summit; spkr. on environ. issues. Author: What Went Wrong at Enron, 2002 (NY Times bestseller). Advisor Green Ground 0, NYC, 2004—05. Mem.: Internat. Assn. Energy Econs. (coun. mem. 1998—2002), Chgo. Climate Exch. (mkts. com. 2003—06), Energy Inst. London. Avocations: travel, writing. Office: Global Change Associates 2576 Broadway PMB 385 New York NY 10025 Office Phone: 212-316-0223.

FUSARO, RAMON MICHAEL, dermatologist, preventive medicine physician, researcher; b. Bklyn., Mar. 6, 1927; s. Angelo and Ida (Pucci) F.; m. Lavonne Johnsen, Nov. 6, 1971; children: Lisa Ann, Toni Ann; stepsons: Jeff, Scott. BA, U. Minn., 1949, BS, 1951, MD, 1953, MS, 1958, PhD, 1965. Diplomate Am. Bd. Dermatology. Intern Mpls. Gen. Hosp., 1953-54, resident in dermatology, 1954—57; from instr. to assoc. prof. U. Minn., 1957-70, dir. outpatient dermatology clinic, 1962-70; prof., chmn. dept. dermatology U. Nebr. Med. Center, Omaha, 1970-82; prof. dermatology sect. dept. internal medicine U. Nebr. Med. Ctr., Omaha, 1982—, acting chief sect. dermatology, 1991-94; prof., chmn. dept. dermatology Creighton U., Omaha, 1975-87; prof. dermatology dept. internal medicine Creighton U. Sch. Medicine, Omaha, 1983-89; prof. Creighton U., Omaha, 1989—; dir. dermatology residency program Creighton/Nebr. Univs. Health Found., 1975-83; prof. dept. pub. health and preventive medicine Hereditary Cancer Inst., Creighton U., 1984—. Adj. prof. coll. pharmacy dept. pharmaceutical scis. Creighton U., 2007—. Contbr. more than 300 articles to profl. publs., chpts. to books. With USN, 1944-46. Mem. Am. Acad. Dermatology, Sigma Xi. Home: 908 Beaver Lake Blvd Plattsmouth NE 68048-4500 Office: 984360 Nebr Med Ctr Omaha NE 68198-4360 also: Creighton U Med Sch Nixon-Lied Bldg Dept Prev Med 2500 California Plz Omaha NE 68178-0403 Personal E-mail: rfusaro@unmc.edu. Business E-Mail: rmfusaro@creighton.edu.

FUSCO, ANDREW G., lawyer; b. Punxsutawney, Pa., Jan. 11, 1948; s. Albert G. and Virginia N. (Whitesell) F.; m. Deborah K. Lucas; children: Matthew, Geoffrey, David. BS in Bus. Adminstrn. and Fin., W.Va. U., 1970, JD, 1973. Bar: W.Va. 1973, US Ct. Appeals (4th cir.) 1974, US Supreme Ct. 1977, US Ct. Appeals (fed. cir.) 1985, US Tax Ct. 1995, US Ct. Appeals (9th cir.), 2003. Pvt. practice, Morgantown, W.Va., 1973-85; prin. Fusco & Newbraugh, L.C., Morgantown, 1985-98, The Fusco Legal Group, L.C., Morgantown, 1998-2001; mem. Eckert Seamans Cherin & Mellott, LLC, 2001—. Pros. atty. Monongalia County, W.Va., 1977—81; instr. Coll. Bus. and Econs., Law Ctr., W.Va. U., 1975—76, W.Va. U. Sch. Journalism, 1997—2003. Author: Antitrust Law (West Virginia Practice Handbook), 1991; editor, contbg. author: Twenty Feet From Glory (John R. Goodwin), 1970, Business Law (John R. Goodwin), 1972, Beyond Baker Street (Michael Harrison), 1976; gen. editor Baker Street Irregulars Manuscript Series, 2006—. Bd. dirs. W.Va. Career Colls., 1971-76; profl. adv. bd. Childbirth and Parent Edn. Assn., 1975-82, Rape and Domestic Violence Info. Ctr., 1977-81; mem. W.Va. Sec. State's Tribunal on Election Reform, 1977-81; chmn. Monongalia County Drug Edn. Task Force, 1978-80; bd. advisors Nat. Smokers Alliance, 1998-99; vis. com. W.Va. U. Coll. Law, 2000-03. Recipient Am. Jurisprudence award Bancroft-Whitney Publ. Co., 1971; named Outstanding Young Man of Morgantown, 1979. Mem. ABA (bus. torts, civil RICO com., antitrust law sect.), Monongalia County Bar Assn., Am. Judicature Soc., W.Va. Bar Assn., Baker St. Irregulars of NY, Sherlock Holmes Soc. London, Bootmakers of Toronto, Baker St. Irregulars Trust (trustee), Nat. Dist. Attys. Assn., Sons of Italy, W.Va. Law Sch. Assn., Monongalia Arts Ctr. (pres., treas., vice-chmn., trustee). Democrat. Roman Catholic. Home: 2054 Iron Bridge Cir Morgantown WV 26508 Office: Eckert Seamans Cherin & Mellott 2400 Cranberry Sq Morgantown WV 26508-9209 Home Phone: 304-594-2412; Office Phone: 304-594-1000. Office Fax: 304-594-1181. Business E-Mail: afusco@eckertseamans.com.

FUSCO, AURILLA MARIE, director; d. Delmar A. and Catherine F. (Bryan) Thibodeau; m. John A. Fusco; 1 child, Craig L. Jr. BS in Paralegal/Govt. Bus., U. Md., 1986; MPA, Troy State U., 1990; EJD, Concord Sch. Law, 2007. Staff asst. to Sen. George J. Mitchell U.S. Senate, Washington, 1981—85, staff asst. to Sen. Albert Gore, Jr. Nashville, 1985—86, staff asst, office mgr. subcom. on children, families, drugs and alcoholism, 1987; program analyst, adminstrv. officer Dept. of Army, Germany, 1987—91; dir. child care River Valley Child Devel., Huntington, W.Va., 1992—97; exec. dir. Child Advocates of Blair County, Altoona, Pa., 1998—2001; regional mr. capital gifts Bucknell U., Lewisburg, Pa., 2001—04; dir. devel. Main Campus Librs. Georgetown U., Washington, 2004—06; assoc. dir. devel. Georgetown U. Law Ctr., 2006—. Presenter Nat. Assn. for Edn. of Young Children; cons. W.Va. Welfare Reform Coalition, 1996—98; v.p. Mongrel Mgmt., LLC, Altoona, Pa., 2000—. Co-chair Children's Issues Advocates, W.Va., 1997—98; pres. Jr. League, Huntington, 1997—98; sustainer adviser Jr. League Williamsport, 2003—04; mem. devel. com. Heurich House Found.; mem. parents com. Bishop Ireton H.S. Hockey Team. Mem.: Sunrise Rotary. Office: Georgetown U Law Ctr 600 NJ Ave NW Washington DC 20001

FUSCO, GEORGE MATTHEW, retired military officer, engineer; b. Southington, Conn., June 28, 1932; s. Angelo and Florance Fusco; m. Elizabeth Ann Binkowski (dec.); children: Angelo, George, Mary, Frank; m. Cynthia Stanish, Oct. 1, 2005. Diploma, Command Gen. Staff Coll., Ft. Levenworth, Kans., 1988. Advanced through grades to brig. gen. US Army, 1948, command various units, 1948—92; facilities engr. Custom Hardwood, Middletown, Conn., 2004—. Republican. Roman Catholic. Avocations: hunting, fishing. Home: 155-91 Redstone Hill Rd Bristol CT 06010 Office: Custom Hardwood Flooring 234 Middle St Middletown CT 06457

FUSCO, JO ELLEN, music educator; b. S.I., NY, Sept. 2, 1956; d. Vincent Albert and Josephine Evelyn (Juliano) Fusco. BA in Music Edn., Wagner Coll., SI, NY, 1978; MS in Spl. Edn., Coll. SI, 1999. Pvt. instrumental tchr., SI, NY, 1973—; account rep. European Am. Bank & Trust, NYC, 1978—89; tchr. spl. edn. Pub. Sch. 25, SI, 1995; tchr. music Pub. Sch. 39, 1995—96, Pub. Schs. 3, 18, 32 and 39, 1996—2001, Pub. Schs. 30, 41 and 20, 2001—02, Pub. Sch. 30, 2001—. Mem. United Fedn. Tchrs. Consultative Coun., SI, NY, 2003—, United Fedn. Tchrs. Unity Steering Com., 2003—. Exhibitions include Forum- U.S. and Can., AIA Students, 1985, KINSA, S.I., 1983 (Black and White Photo award). Saxophonist Big Apple Corp Band, 2001—; top fundraiser Am. Diabetes Assn. Tour de Cure, SI, 2004; participant MS Soc. Bikeathon, 1989, Susan G. Komen Breast Ctr. Race for the Cure Walk, 2002; vol. City Harvest Food Drive, 2001, 2002; guitarist and vocalist St. Clare's Cath. Ch., SI, 1974—83, Holy Child Cath. Ch., 1983—85. Recipient First place state accordion competition, N.Y. State Accordion Assn., 1973, 11th place nat. accordion competition, Nat. Accordion Assn., 1973. Democrat. Roman Catholic. Avocations: music, travel, bicycling, theater, fine dining. Home: 99 Mid Loop Rd Staten Island NY 10308 Office: PS 30 200 Wardwell Ave Staten Island NY 10314 Personal E-mail: jofus2000666@cs.com.

FUSCO, RICHARD, English literature educator; b. Phila., Apr. 27, 1952; BA, U. Pa., 1973, MA, 1974, U. Miss., 1982; PhD, Duke U., 1990. Instr. English St. Joseph's U., Phila., 1988-91, asst. prof. English, 1997—2003, assoc. prof. English, 2003—. Author: Maupassant and the American Short Story: The Influence of Form at the Turn of the Century, 1994, (pamphlet) Fin de millénaire: Poe's Legacy for the Detective Story, 1993; contbr. articles to profl. jours. Served as intelligence officer U.S. Navy, 1975-79. Mem. MLA. Home: 2237 S 23rd St Philadelphia PA 19145-3321 Office: Dept English St Joseph's U 5600 City Ave Philadelphia PA 19131-1308 Office Phone: 610-660-1887. Business E-Mail: fusco@sju.edu.

FUSELIER, HAROLD ANTHONY, JR., urologist, director, educator; b. Abbeville, La., Dec. 1, 1942; s. Harold Anthony and May Elizabeth (Fowler) F.; m. Ann Valentino, May 17, 1968; children: Harold Anthony III, F. Scott, J. Prentice, Mims Michael. BS, La. State U., Baton Rouge, 1964; MD, La. State U., New Orleans, 1967. Diplomate Am. Bd. Urology. Internship Charity Hosp., New Orleans, 1967-68; residency urology Alton Ochsner Medical Found., 1970-74; mem. dept. urology Ochsner Clinic Found., New Orleans, 1974—, chmn. dept. urology, 1989—2002; med. dir. surgery Ochsner Found. Hosp., New Orleans, 1990—2006; clin. prof. urology Tulane U. Med. Ctr., New Orleans, 1988—, La. State U. Med. Ctr., New Orleans, 1990—. Program dir. La. State U./Ochsner Urology Tng. Program, 1991-2005. Contbr. articles to profl. jours. Capt. USAF, 1968-70. Fellow ACS; mem. Am. Urol. Assn., Soc. Internat. d'Urologie, Soc. for Study of Impotence, Soc. Univ. Urologists. Roman Catholic. Avocations: golf, hunting, fishing. Office: Ochsner Clinic 1514 Jefferson Hwy New Orleans LA 70121-2483 Office Phone: 504-842-4084. Business E-Mail: hfuselier@ochsner.org.

FUSSELL, KAREN MARIE, social worker, protective services official; b. Detroit, June 24, 1957; d. Jefferson E. and Bessie E. (Sullivan) Fussell; m. Paul Joseph Wolfe (div.). BS in Social Work, Western Ky. U., Bowling Green, 1980. LCSW 2007; cert. seaman USN, Orlando, Fla., 1983, massage technician Health Enrichment Ctr., Lapeer, Mich., 1991, in handgun safety Mich. State Police, 1994. Geriatric social worker Dearborn Heights Healthcare Ctr. Heartland, Mich., 1976—; customer svc. rep. Rich's Dept. Store, Atlanta, 1980—83; enumerator US Bur. Census, Dearborn, 1990; security police Battle Creek Vets. Adminstr. Med. Ctr., Mich., 1991—, Detroit, 1991—. Group counselor Real Life Day Camp, Dearborn Heights, 1979; intern Bur. Social Svcs., Bowling Green, 1980; project cons. Wayne County Cmty. Mental Health Agy., Detroit, 2005—. Mem. Women's Aux. Vol. Emergency Svc., 1986—, sgt.-at-arms. E-3 USN, 1983—90. Mem.: Cambrid, Am. Massage Therapy Assn., Nat. Assn. Social Workers, Disabled Am. Vet. Commander's Club, Sabana Seca Players Club, Am. Legion, VFW. Avocations: walking, swimming, scuba diving, bicycling. Office: Detroit VAMC 4646 John R Rd Detroit MI 48201

FUSSELL, PAUL, writer, literature educator; b. Pasadena, Calif., Mar. 22, 1924; s. Paul and Wilhma Wilson (Sill) F.; m. Betty Ellen Harper, June 17, 1949 (div. 1987); children: Rosalind, Samuel; m. Harriette Rhawn Behringer, Apr. 11, 1987. BA, Pomona Coll., Calif., 1947, LittD (hon.), 1981; MA, Harvard U., 1949, PhD, 1952; MA (hon.), U. Pa., 1983; LittD (hon.), Monmouth U., NJ, 1985. Instr. English Conn. Coll., 1951-55; mem. faculty Rutgers U., 1955—, John DeWitt prof. English lit., 1976-83; Donald T. Regan prof. English lit. U. Pa., Phila., 1983-94, prof. emeritus, 1994—. Cons. editor Random House, 1963-64; lectr. Am. univs., 1965—; vis. prof. Kings Coll., London, 1990-92. Author: The Rhetorical World of Augustan Humanism, 1965, Poetic Meter and Poetic Form, 1965, rev., 1979, Samuel Johnson and The Life of Writing, 1971, The Great War and Modern Memory (Nat. Book Critics Circle award 1975, Nat. Book award 1976), Abroad: British Literary Traveling Between the Wars, 1980, The Boy Scout Handbook & Other Observations, 1982, Class: A Guide through the American Status System, 1983, Thank God for the Atom Bomb & Other Essays, 1988, Wartime: Understanding and Behavior in the Second World War, 1989; BAD: or The Dumbing of America, 1991, The Anti-Egoist: Kingsley Amis, Man of Letters, 1994, Doing Battle: The Making of a Skeptic, 1996, Uniforms: Why We Are What We Wear, 2002, The Boys Crusade, 2003; contbg. editor Harper's, 1979-83, The New Republic, 1979-85. Served with AUS, 1943-46. Decorated Purple Heart, Bronze Star; recipient James D. Phelan award Phelan Found., 1964; Lindback Found. award, 1971; Ralph Waldo Emerson award Phi Beta Kappa, 1976; sr. fellow NEH, 1973-74; Guggenheim fellow, 1977-78; Rockefeller Found. fellow, 1983-84 Fellow Royal Soc. Lit., Soc. Am. Historians; mem. MLA, Acad. Lit. Studies. Home: 2020 Walnut St 4H Philadelphia PA 19103-5635

FUSSNER, F. SMITH, history professor, retired rancher; b. Cin., Sept. 21, 1920; s. Hugo Amor Fussner and Grace Elizabeth Smith; m. Jane Spencer, Mar. 13, 1943 (dec. Sept. 6, 1990); children: Jonathan Hugh, Sara Elizabeth Gay. BS magna cum laude, Harvard U., 1942, MA, 1947, PhD, 1951. Mem. faculty Reed Coll., Portland, Oreg., 1950—. Author: The Historical Revolution, 1962, 1976, Tudor History and the Historians, 1962, 1970, Time's Silent Stealth, A Tribute to Jane, 1984; editor: William Camden's Discourse Concerning the Prerogative of the Crown, Glimpses of Wheeler County's History, 1975. Sgt. US Army, 1943—45, ETO. Recipient fin. award, Am. Philos. Soc.; grantee, 1962; Fulbright grantee, 1964—65. Mem.: VFW, NRA (life), Humane Soc. of US. Home: 45534 Hwy 207 S Spray OR 97874

FUSTÉ, JOSÉ ANTONIO, federal judge; b. San Juan, Nov. 3, 1943; BBA, U. P.R., San Juan, 1965, LLB cum laude, 1968. Ptnr. Jimenez & Fuste, Hato Rey, P.R., 1968-85; judge US Dist. Ct. P.R., San Juan, 1985—, chief judge, 2004. Prof. U. P.R., 1975—85, 1996—2002. Office: US Courthouse CH-133 150 Ave Carlos Chardon San Juan PR 00918-1758 Office Phone: 787-772-3120.

FUSTER, VALENTIN, cardiologist, educator; b. Barcelona, Jan. 20, 1943; s. Joaquin and Pilar Fuster; m. Angela-Maria Guals, Sept. 3, 1968; children: Pablo, Silvia. Baccaluarate, Colegio Jesuitas, Barcelona, 1961; MD, Barcelona U., 1967; granted several honorary degrees. Diplomate Am. Bd. Internal Medicine (mem. com. subsplty. bd. cardiovas. disease), Am. Bd. Cardiology. Intern Hosp. Clinico, Barcelona, 1967-68; rsch. fellow, cardiology U. Edinburgh, Scotland, 1968-71; resident, medicine and cardiovasc. diseases Mayo Grad. Sch. Medicine, Rochester, Minn., 1971-74; asst. prof. medicine Mayo Med. Sch., Rochester, 1974-77, assoc. prof. medicine, 1978-81, assoc. prof. pediat., 1980—, prof. medicine and cardiovasc. diseases, 1981-82; Mallinckrodt prof. medicine Harvard Med. Sch., 1991—94; chief cardiology unit Mass. Gen. Hosp., 1991—94; chief, divsn. cardiology, Mt. Sinai Sch. Medicine, NY, 1981—91, Arthur A. and Hilda M. Master prof. medicine NY, 1982—91, dir., Zena & Michael A. Wiener Cardiovasc. Inst. and Marie-Josée & Henry R. Kravis Ctr, for Cardiovascular Health NY, 1994—, Richard Gorlin, MD/Heart Rsch. Found. prof. NY. Mem. cardiology adv. com. NIH; mem. com. Am. Bd. Cardiology; hon. lectr. numerous orgns.; mem. adv. coun. Nat. Heart, Lung and Blood Insts., 1997, strategic planning com. Stanley J. Sanroff Endowment for Cardiovasc. Sci., 2002-04; former chmn., Fellowship Tng. Directors Program, Am. Coll. Cardiology; mem. scientific adv. bd. Vasogen, Inc. Mem. editl. bd. Am. Jour. Cardiology, 1982, Arteriosclerosis, 1982, Jour. The Am. Coll. Cardiology, 1987, Circulation, 1988, consulting editor, 1992, circulation rsch. consulting editor, 1997; editor-in-chief Nature Jour. that focuses on Cardiovasc. Medicine, 2004-; lead editor (textbook) The Heart, Atherothrombosis and Coronary Artery Disease; contbr. several articles to profl. jours. Recipient 30 rsch. and tchg. awards including Andres Gruntzig Scientific award European Soc. Cardiology, 1992, Disting. Scientist award Am. Coll. Cardiology, 1993, Disting. Conner Lectr. award Am. Heart Assn., 1993, Principe de Asturias award for sci. and tech. U. Asturias in conjunction with Royal Family of Spain, 1996, Andreas Gruntzig award Internat. Soc. Interventionalists, 2002, Disting. Researcher award, Interamerican Soc. Cardiology, 2005; named Disting. Scientist, AHA/ASA, 2003; named to European Acad. Yuste; named one of Medical Marvels, New York Mag., 2006. Fellow Am. Coll. Cardiology (chair tng. dirs. com. 1997, Disting. Scientist award, Disting. Bishop Lectr. award 1994, Disting. Svc. award 2000, chair cardiology tng. and workforce com., 2000-03), Royal Coll. Physicians; mem. Am. Heart Assn. (chmn. pub. com., bd. dirs. 1994, pres.-elect 1997, pres. 1998-99, Disting. Achievement award 1997, James B. Herrick Achievement award, Coun. Clin. Cardiology, 2001, Lewis A. Connor Meml. award, Gold Heart award, 2003, Disting. Scientist award), Am. Soc. Clin. Investigations, Assn. Am. Physicians, European Soc. Clin. Investigation, Brit. Cardiac Soc. (corr.), European Soc. Cardiology (U.S. bd. dirs. and Industry), World Heart Fedn. (pres-elect 2003-04, pres. 2005-06), Fundacion Centro Nacional de Investigaciones Cardiovasculares Carlos III (pres. scientific adv. and external evaluation com.), Inst. Medicine. Achievements include contributing first hand to the launching of the new forum for young investigators of the AMA. Office: Mt Sinai Med Ctr 1 Gustave L Levy Pl # 1030 New York NY 10029-6500 also: Cardiovascular Medicine Assocs 5 E 98th St 3rd Fl New York NY 10029 Office Phone: 212-241-7911. Office Fax: 212-423-9488. Business E-Mail: valentin.fuster@mssm.edu.*

FUSTER BERLINGERI, JAIME B., judge; b. Guayama, PR, Jan. 12, 1941; s. Jaime L. and Maria Luisa (Berlingeri) Fuster; m. Mary Jo Fuster, Dec. 19, 1966; children: Maria Luisa, Jaime. BA, Notre Dame U., 1962; JD, U. P.R., 1965; LLM, Columbia U., 1966; SJD, Harvard U., 1974; LLD (hon.), Temple U., 1985. Bar: P.R. 1966. Prof. law U. PR, 1966—73, 1978—80; dean Law Sch. U. PR., 1974—78; project dir. Study on Legal Profession of P.R. Ctr. Social Rsch., 1970—73; ednl. cons. Office of Cts. Adminstrn. Govt. of PR, 1978—80; dep. asst. atty. gen. U.S. Dept. Justice, Washington, 1980—81; pres. Cath. U. PR, 1981—84; mem. Congress from PR, Washington, 1984—92; resident commr. Commonwealth of PR, 1984—92; assoc. justice PR Supreme Ct., 1992—. Cons., lectr. in field. Author: Political and Civil Rights in Puerto Rico, 1968, The Duties of Citizens, 1973, The Lawyers of Puerto Rico: A Sociological Study, 1974, Law and Problems of Elderly People, 1978; editor-in-chief: U. P.R. Law Rev., 1964—65; contbr. chapters to books, articles to profl. jours. Named One of Outstanding Young Men of Am., U.S. Jr. C. of C., 1978. Mem.: Interam. Bar Found. (bd. dirs. 1975—79), Assn. Am. Colls. (adv. bd. 1980—84). Democrat. Roman Catholic. Avocation: tennis. Office: PO Box 2392 San Juan PR 00902-2392 Office Phone: 787-723-0856. Business E-Mail: jaimefb@tribunales.gobierno.pr.*

FUTAMI, NORMAN, lawyer; b. Hermosa Beach, Calif., Jan. 5, 1960; arrived in Japan, 1993; s. Akimasa and Reiko (Nobe) F.; m. Jean Kiyoko Kashiwabara, July 11, 1987; 1 child, Gregory Minoru. BA, Yale U., New Haven, Conn., 1981; JD, Harvard U., Cambridge, Mass., 1984. Bar: Calif. 1984, Japan 1993. Assoc. Paul, Hastings, Janofsky & Walker LLP, LA, 1984-92, ptnr. Tokyo, 1988—90, 1993—95, LA, 1990—93, 1995—, vice chmn. mgmt.-L.A. Office. Office: Paul Hastings Janofsky & Walker LLP 515 S Flower St Los Angeles CA 90071-2228 Office Phone: 213-683-6321. Office Fax: 213-627-0705. Business E-Mail: normanfutami@paulhastings.com.

FUTCH, MICHAEL, lawyer, construction executive; b. Monroe, La., Sept. 7, 1947; BSCE, So. U., 1970; MSCE, U. Calif., Berkeley, 1975; JD, Cornell U., 1981. Cert. engr., Calif., 1975. Structural engr. Western Div. Naval Facilities Engring. Command, San Bruno, Calif., 1972—76; sr. structural engr. Parsons Brinckerhoff, San Francisco, 1976—78; assoc. Cox, Castle & Nicholson, Los Angeles; gen. counsel, sec. Kasler Corp., San Bernadino, 1983—86; v.p., gen counsel Penhall Internat., 1986—88; of counsel Robinson & Pearman, 1988—96; v.p., gen. counsel Granite Construction Inc., 1996—. Sgt. US Army, 1970—72. Mem.: ABA, Am. Soc. Corp. Secs., Am. Corp. Counsel Assn., Nat. Bar Assn. Office: Granite Construction Inc 585 W Beach St PO Box 50085 Watsonville CA 95077-5805 Office Phone: 831-761-4708.

FUTEY, BOHDAN A., federal judge; b. 1939; BA, Case Western Res. U., 1962, MA, 1964; JD, Cleve. State U., 1968. Ptnr. Futey & Rakowsky, Cleve., 1968-72; chief asst. police prosecutor Cleve., 1972-74; exec. asst. to Mayor City of Cleve., 1974-75; ptnr. Bazarko, Futey and Oryshkewych, Cleve., 1975-84; chmn. US Fgn. Claims Settlement Commn., 1984-87; judge US Ct. Fed. Claims, Washington, 1987—2002, sr. judge, 2002—. Mem. ABA, Parma Bar Assn., Ukrainian Am. Bar Assn., Cleve. Bar Assn., DC Bar Assn. Office: US Ct Fed Claims 717 Madison Pl NW Ste 603 Washington DC 20439-0002*

FUTRELL, ALVIN, director; BSE in Phys. Edn., MSE in Phys. Edn., Henderson State U.; EdS in Ednl. Adminstrn., Ark. State U.; EdD in Secondary Edn., Ball State U., 1987. Prof. dept. secondary edn. Henderson State U., Arkadelphia, Ark., 1975—88, dir. tchr. admissions and field experiences, 1988—99, asst. to pres. for diversity, 1999—. Mem.: S.W. Ednl. Lab. (bd. mem. 2003—). Office: Henderson State Univ WO 311 1100 Henderson St Arkadelphia AR 71999-0001

FUTRELL, JOHN WILLIAM, environmental agency executive, lawyer; b. Alexandria, La., July 6, 1935; s. J.W. and Sarah Ruth (Hitesman) F.; m. Iva Macdonald, Aug. 13, 1966; children: Sarah, Daniel. BA, Tulane U., 1957; postgrad., Free U. Berlin, 1958; LLB, Columbia U., 1965. Bar: La. 1966. Atty. Lemle & Kelleher, New Orleans, 1966-71; prof. law U. Ala., 1971-74, U. Ga., 1974-80; pres. Environ. Law Inst., Washington, 1980—2003, Sustainable Devel. Law Assocs., Arlington, Va., 2003—. Lectr. USIA, Japan and India, 1978, Austria, 1979, Sweden, Germany, U.K. and Ireland, 1980, Argentina, 1988, Brazil, 1991, 92, 2004, Mex., 1992, Germany and Chile, 1993, India, 1997, 2000; Woodrow Wilson fellow Smithsonian Instn., Washington, 1978-80. Co-author: Sustainable Environmental Law, 1993. Del. UN Conf. on Water, 1977, White House Conf. Inflation, 1974. Capt. USMC, 1957-62. Recipient Chair's award, Natural Resources Coun. Am., 2005; scholar, Fulbright, 1958. Mem.: ABA (Disting. Achievement award 2004), Am. Law Inst., Sierra Club (nat. bd. dirs. 1971—81, pres. 1977—78, hon. v.p. 2002—), Cosmos Club, Marines' Meml. Club, Phi Beta Kappa, Order of Coif. Office: Sustainable Devel Law Assocs 4600 7th St N Arlington VA 22203 Office Phone: 703-522-0247. E-mail: sdla2003@aol.com.

FUTRELL, STEVEN, psychologist; s. Murline and Cecil Brooks (Stepfather). BS, NE La. U., Monroe, 1987; PsychD, Forest Inst. Profl. Psychology, Springfield, Mo., 1998. Lic. psychologist La., 2001, NY, 2005. Supervising psychologist State of La., Pineville and Hammond, 2001—03, Mental Health Mgmt., Montgomery, Ala., 2003—05; consulting psychologist Indsl. Med. Assocs., Albany, NY, 2005—. Mem.: Internat. Soc. for Mental Health Online, Mensa.

FUTTER, ELLEN VICTORIA, museum administrator; b. NYC, Sept. 21, 1949; d. Victor and Joan Babette (Feinberg) F.; children: Anne Victoria, Elizabeth Jane. Student, U. Wis., 1967-69; AB magna cum laude, Barnard Coll., 1971; JD, Columbia U., 1974, LLD (hon.), 1984, Hamilton Coll., 1985, NY Law Sch.; DHL (hon.), Amherst Coll., Hofstra U., 1994, CCNY, 1996, LI City Coll., 1995, Yale U., 2000; DL, Columbia U.; degree (hon.), Skidmore Coll., 2003, Williams Coll., 2004. Bar: NY 1975. Assoc. Milbank, Tweed, Hadley & McCloy, NYC, 1974-80; acting pres. Barnard Coll., NYC, 1980-81, pres., 1981-93, Am. Mus. Natural History, NYC, 1993—. Bd. dirs. Am. Internat. Group, JP Morgan Chase, Consol. Edison NY; overseer Meml. Sloan Kettering Cancer Ctr., NYC; trustee Am. Mus. Natural History Recipient L. Sachar award Brandeis U., Elizabeth Cutter Morrow, Distinction medal Barnard Coll., Excellence medal Columbia U., Gold medal award Nat. Inst. Social Scis., Legacy Conservation award Theodore Roosevelt Sanctuary, Visionary award New Vision in Pub. Sch., Alexander Hamilton award Manhattan Inst. Policy Rsch., 2002. Fellow Am. Acad. Arts and Scis.; mem. ABA, N.Y. State Bar Assn., Assn. Bar City N.Y., Nat. Inst. Social Scis., Coun. Fgn. Rels., Cosmopolitan Club, Century Club, Econ. Club NY, Phi Beta Kappa. Office: Am Mus Natural History Central Park West at 79th New York NY 10024

FUTTERMAN, DAN, actor, scriptwriter; b. Silver Spring, Md., June 8, 1967; m. Anya Epstein, Sept. 23, 2000; 1 child, Sylvie. Grad., Columbia U., 1989. Actor: (TV films) Daughters of Privilege, 1991, Class of '61, 1993, Tracey Takes on New York, 1993, Thicker Than Blood, 1998, When Trumpets Fade, 1998, Gerald L'Ecuyer, 2004; (films) The Fisher King, 1991, Passed Away, 1992, Big Girls Don't Cry.They Get Even, 1992, The Birdcage, 1996, Breathing Room, 1996, Far Harbor, 1996, Shooting Fish, 1997, 1999, 1998, Urbania, 2000, Enough, 2002; (TV series) Another World, 1992, Judging Amy, 1999—2001, 2004—05; guest appearances: New York News, 1995; guest appearances (TV series) Caroline in the City, 1997; guest appearances: (TV series) Homicide, 1999; Sex and the City, 1999; Will & Grace, 2003; guest appearances (TV series) Related, 2005; writer, prodr.: (films) Capote, 2005 (Best Screenplay, Boston Society Film Critics award, 2005, Best Screenplay, Independent Spirit award, 2006). Office: Gersh Agency 232 N Canon Dr Ste 201 Beverly Hills CA 90210*

FUTTERMAN, RONALD L., lawyer; b. Chgo., Mar. 5, 1943; s. Sol and Edythe (Greenberg) F.; m. Pamela Ann Hayes, June 5, 1966; children: Elizabeth, Samantha. BBA, U. Wis., Madison, 1964; JD, Northwestern U., 1967. Bar: Ill. 1967, U.S. Dist. Ct. (no. dist.) Ill. 1967, U.S. Ct. Appeals (7th cir.) 1975, U.S. Ct. Appeals (D.C. cir.) 1977, U.S. Supreme Ct. 1984. Atty. anti-trust divsn. U.S. Dept. Justice, Chgo., 1967-73; assoc. Pressman & Hartunian, Chgo., 1973-78, ptnr., 1978-82, Hartunian, Futterman & Howard, Chartered, Chgo., 1982-91, Futterman & Howard, Chartered, Chgo., 1991—2006, Futterman, Howard, Watkins, Wylie & Ashley Chartered, Chgo., 2006—. Instr. law and psychology Adler Sch. Profl. Psychology, Chgo., 1999-2003. Active Ill. Sch. Dist. 113 Polit. Caucus, Deerfield,

1976-78, chmn. publicity, 1977-78; pres. South Park Elem. Sch. PTO, Deerfield, 1980-81. Mem. ABA, Chgo. Bar Assn., Chgo. Coun. Lawyers (v.p. 1983-84, bd. govs. 1984-88) Office: Futterman Howard Watkins Wylie & Ashley Chartered 122 S Michigan Ave Ste 1850 Chicago IL 60603-6199 Office Phone: 312-427-3600. Business E-Mail: rfutterman@futtermanhoward.com.

FUTUYMA, DOUGLAS JOEL, ecology educator; b. New York, Apr. 24, 1942; s. Joseph and Eleanor (Haessler) F. BS, Cornell U., 1963; MS, U. Mich., 1966, PhD, 1969. Asst. prof. SUNY, Stony Brook, 1969-76, assoc. prof., 1976-83, prof. ecology and evolution, 1983—. Author: Evolutionary Biology, 1979, 2d edit., 1986, Science on Trial: The Case for Evolution, 1983, 2d edit., 1995; co-editor: Coevolution, 1983, Oxford Surveys in Evolutinary Biology Vol. 7, 1991, Vol. 8, 1992, Vol. 9, 1993; editor Evolution, 1981-83; assoc. editor Ann. Review of Ecology and Systematics, 1992—. Fellow J. S. Guggenheim Meml. Found., 1992; rsch. grantee NSF, 1974—. Mem. Soc. for Study of Evolution (pres. 1987), Am. Inst. Biol. Scis. (bd. dirs. 1995), Am. Soc. Naturalists (pres. 1994), NAS. Office: State Univ New York Dept Ecology And Evolution Stony Brook NY 11794-0001

FUZESI, STEPHEN, JR., lawyer, communications executive; b. Budapest, Hungary, Aug. 3, 1948; naturalized, US, 1963; s. Stephen Sr and Marta Fuzesi; m. Nancy J Steinhardt, Apr. 5, 1975; children: Stephen Joseph, Timothy Roger. AB, Princeton U., 1970; JD, U. Pa., 1974. Bar: NY 1975, DC 1982. Atty. Davis, Polk & Wardwell, NYC, 1974-82; ptnr./of counsel Reid & Riege, PC, Hartford, Conn., 1982-83; 1st. sr. v.p., gen. counsel and sec. Am. Savings Bank, FSB, NYC, 1984-87; sr. v.p., gen. counsel, sec. Stamford Capital Group, Inc., 1987-90; of counsel White & Case, NYC, 1990-94; v.p., sec., chief counsel Newsweek, NYC, 1994—. Contbr. articles to profl jours, newspapers. Mem. Coun. Fgn. Rels., 1976—81, Am. Coun. Germany, 1977—80, Greenwich Bd. Edn., 1987—91, Greenwich Dem. Town Com., 1985—94; candidate 36th dist. Conn. State Senate, 1986; trustee Greenwich Round Hill Cmty. Ch., 2003—07; bd. dirs. Greenwich Soccer Assn., 1989—94, Media Law Resource Ctr., 2004—. Recipient Keedy Law Rev. award, U. Pa. Law Sch., 1974. Mem.: Mag. Pubs. Assn. (legal affairs comt 1994—, chmn bus affairs subcommittee 1995—99), Assn. Bar City N.Y. (comt int human rights 1979—81, banking law comt 1987—90, com. on comm. and media law 1995—99, 2002—). Office: Newsweek 251 W 57th St New York NY 10019-1802 Business E-Mail: sfuzesi@newsweek.com.

FYE, W. BRUCE, III, cardiologist; b. Meadville, Pa., Sept. 25, 1946; s. W. Bruce Jr. and Anne Elizabeth (Schreck) F.; m. Lois Eileen Baker, May 10, 1969; children: Katherine Anne, Elizabeth Jane. AB, Johns Hopkins U., 1968, MD, 1972, MA in Med. History, 1978. Diplomate Am. Bd. Internal Medicine, Am. Bd. Cardiovascular Diseases. Intern N.Y. Hosp.—Cornell Med. Ctr., NYC, 1972-73, asst. resident, 1973-74, sr. asst. resident, 1974-75, fellow cardiology, 1975; fellow in cardiology Johns Hopkins U. Sch. Medicine, Balt., 1975-77, postdoctoral fellow in med. history, 1976-78, instr. in medicine, 1977-78; dir. cardiographics lab. Marshfield (Wis.) Clinic, 1978-99, chmn. dept. cardiology, 1981-99, dir. noninvasive cardiology, 1999; assoc. prof. medicine Med. Coll. Wis., Milw., 1988-99; prof. medicine and history medicine Mayo Clin. Coll. of Medicine, Rochester, Minn., 2000—. Vice chief of staff St. Joseph's Hosp., Marshfield, 1989-99, exec. com., bd. dirs., 1994-97; clin. prof. medicine, adj. prof. history medicine U. Wis., Madison, 1990—; sr. assoc. cons. Mayo Clinic, Rochester, 2000, cons., 2001—; dir. Mayo Clinic Ctr. for the History of Medicine, 2006—. Author: The Development of American Physiology, 1987; editor: William Osler's Collected Papers on the Cardiovascular System, 1985, Classic Papers on Coronary Thrombosis and Myocardial Infarction, 1991; editor-in-chief: Classics of Cardiology Library, 1985—; author: American Cardiology; The History of a Specialty and Its College, 1996; mem. editl. bd. Marshfield Med. Bull., 1985-95, Am. Jour. Cardiology, 1990—, Clin. Cardiology, 1994—; co-editor (with J. Willis Hurst, Richard Conti, W. Bruce Fye): Profiles in Cardiology, 2003. Named to Soc. Scholars, Johns Hopkins U., 2005. Fellow Am. Coll. Cardiology (chmn. libr. com. 1991, historian 1991—, gov. Wis. chpt. 1993-96, steering com. bd. govs., 1994—, nominating com., 1994-96, chair govt. rels. com. 1996-99, trustee 1997—, v.p. 1999—, pres. 2002—); mem. State Med. Soc. Wis. (alt. del. 1990-94), Am. Hist. Assn., Am. Osler Soc. (pres. 1988-89), Am. Heart Assn. (exec. com. coun. on clin. cardiology 1991-97, chmn. membership com. coun. on clin. cardiology 1994-97, chair credentials com. coun. on clin. cardiology 1994-97), Inst. for Study of Cardiovasc. Medicine (bd. dirs. 1994—), Am. Assn. History of Medicine (program chair 1987, v.p. 2006-), Found. Advances in Medicine and Sci., Johns Hopkins Soc. Scholars, Phi Beta Kappa, Alpha Omega Alpha, Grolier Club. Presbyterian. Avocation: collecting and selling antiquarian medical books. Home: 1533 Seasons Ln SW Rochester MN 55902 Office: Mayo Clinic Coll of Medicine 200 1st St SW Rochester MN 55905-0002 Office Phone: 507-266-4130. Business E-Mail: fye.bruce@mayo.edu.

FYFE, ALISTAIR IAN, cardiologist, scientist, educator; b. Hobart, Tasmania, Australia, Sept. 5, 1960; came to U.S., 1991; s. Ian John and Merrill Millicent (Faragher) F.; married Michelle Lee Fenner; children: Alexander Jonathan, Calista Madison, Ethan Alexander. B of Med. Sci., U. Tasmania, 1980, B of Med. Sci. with honors, 1981, MBBS, 1984; PhD in Molecular Biology, UCLA, 1995. Diplomate Am. Bd. Internal Medicine and Cardiovasc. Disease. Intern Royal Hobart Hosp., 1985-86; resident in internal medicine U. B.C., Vancouver, Can., 1986-89; cardiology fellow U. Toronto, Ont., Can., 1989-91; cardiac rsch. fellow UCLA, 1991-95, asst. prof. medicine and cardiology, 1995-99, dir. Ctr. for Cholesterol and Lipid Mgmt., 1995-98, assoc. mem. Molecular Biology Inst., 1996-98; cardiologist Heart Place, Dallas, 1999—2000, Dallas Heart Group, 2000—04; founder Cardiac Assocs. Dallas, 2004—; dir. primary and secondary cardiac prevention Med. City, Dallas, 2004—. Author: (with others) Progress in Pediatric Cardiology, 1993; contbr. articles to profl. jours. Recipient Fellowship Clinician Scientist award Med. Rsch. Coun., Can., 1992. Fellow Royal Coll. Physicians Can., Am. Coll. Cardiology, Coun. Arterial Sclerosis; mem. Internat. Heart Transplant Soc., Am. Heart Assn. (fellow arteriosclerosis coun., reviewer 1993—, Young Investigator award, 1993, 95), Am. Soc. Clin. Investigation, Am. Diabetes Assn. Achievements include first demonstration of genetic modification of solid organ transplants. Office: Cardiac Assocs Dallas 7777 Forest Ln Ste C 655 Dallas TX 75230-2500 Office Phone: 972-566-8474. Business E-Mail: afyfe@cadmd.com.

FYFE, STEVEN TREY, otolaryngologist; b. Amarillo, Tex., Aug. 22, 1956; s. Raymond Edwin and Sara Stevens Fyfe; m. Cary Namron Young; children: Taylor, Jack. BA with honors, U. Tex., Austin, 1981; MD, Baylor Coll. Medicine, Houston, 1984. Pvt. practice Austin Ear, Nose & Throat Clinic, Austin, Tex., 1993—. Mem.: AMA, Am. Acad. Otolaryngology, Tex. Med. Assn. Office: Austin Ear Nose Throat Clinic Ste 320 3705 Med Pkwy Austin TX 78705-1023 Home: 3002 Willowood Cir Austin TX 78703 Office Phone: 512-454-0392.

FYFE, WILLIAM SEFTON, geochemist, educator; b. New Zealand, June 4, 1927; s. Colin Alexander and Isabella Fyfe; m. Patricia Walker, Feb. 27, 1981; children: Christopher, Catherine, Stefan. BSc, U. Otago, New Zealand, 1948, MS, 1949, PhD, 1952; DSc (hon.), Meml. U., Lisbon, Portugal, 1989-90, Lakehead U., 1992, Guelph U., 1994, St. Mary's U., Otago, New Zealand, 1994, Otago U., New Zealand, 1995, U. Western Ont., 1995. Prof. chemistry in, N.Z., 1955-58; prof. geology U. Calif., Berkeley, 1958-66; research prof. Manchester U. and Imperial Coll., London, 1966-72; chmn. dept. geology Western Ont. U., 1972-84, prof. dept. geology, 1984-92, prof. emeritus dept. earth sci., 1992—, dean faculty sci., 1986-90. Decorated companion Order of Can.; Commemorative medal (New Zealand), Commemorative medal (Canada); recipient Logan medal Geol. Assn. Can., Arthur Holmes medal European Union of Geoscis., Can. Gold medal for Sci. and Engring., 1991; Guggenheim fellow, 1964, 83; named hon. prof. U. Beijing. Fellow Geol. Soc. London (hon.; Wollaston medal 2000), Royal Soc. London, Geol. Soc. Am. (hon. life, Day medal), Mineral Soc. Am. (Roebling medal); mem. AAAS (chmn. geology geography sect. 2000—), Internat. Union Geoscis. (pres. 1992-96, Grand Cross Ordem Nacional do Merito Cientifico, Brazil, 1996), Nat. Sci. and Engring. Rsch. Coun. Can., Royal Soc. Can., Acad. Sci. Brazil, Brit. Chem. Soc., Russian Acad. Sci., Indian Acad. Sci., Chinese Acad. Sci. Home: 1197 Richmond London ON Canada N6A 3L3 Office: U Western Ont Dept Earth Scis London ON Canada N6A 5B7 Office Phone: 519-661-3180. Office Fax: 519-661-2179. Business E-Mail: pjfyfe@uwo.ca.

FYLER, CARL JOHN, retired dentist; b. Spearville, Kans., May 14, 1921; s. John Henry and Helen Elsie (Parthie) Fyler; m. Marquerite E. Burris, Feb. 14, 1946. DDS, U. Mo., Kansas City, 1950. Practice dentistry, Topeka, Kans., 1950-92; ret., 1992. Author: Staying Alive. Maj. USAF, 1942—46, ETO. Decorated Disting. Flying Cross, Silver star; recipient French Legion of Honor, 2006. Mem.: ADA, 8th Air Force Hist. Soc. (bd. dirs. 1989—92, heavy bomb group), Internat. Fedn. Dentists, Shawnee County Dental Assn., Kans. Dental Assn., Kans. Ex-Prisoners of War (mem. Gov.'s adv. com. 1978—86), Am. Ex-Prisoners of War (nat. dir. 1974—85, nat. jr. vice comdr. 1984—85), Am. Vets., D.A.V., Am. Legion, Disting. Flying Cross Soc., Mil. Order World Wars (pres. Topeka chpt. 1996—), 303d H.B.G. Assn. Republican. Presbyterian. Avocations: flying, lapidary, rock hunting. Home: 300 SW Yorkshire Rd Topeka KS 66606-2260

FYLER, JOHN MORGAN, language educator; b. Chgo., Sept. 17, 1943; s. Earl Harris and Harriet (Morgan) F.; m. Julia Ann Genster, Aug. 5, 1978; children: Amanda, Lucy. AB, Dartmouth Coll., 1965; MA, U. Calif., Berkeley, 1967, PhD, 1972. Asst. prof. Tufts U., Medford, Mass., 1972-78, assoc. prof., 1978-88, prof., 1988—. Lectr. Bread Loaf Sch. English, 1995—. Author: Chaucer and Ovid, 1979, Language and the Declining World in Chaucer, Dante, and Jean de Meun, 2007; contbg. editor: Riverside Chaucer, 1986. ACLS fellow, 1975-76, Guggenheim fellow, 1982-83, Camargo Found. fellow, 2002; fellow Clare Hall, U. Cambridge, 2003. Home: 126 Central St Concord MA 01742-2911 Office: Dept English Tufts U Medford MA 02155 Office Phone: 617-627-2379. E-mail: john.fyler@tufts.edu.

GAA, WILLY C., ambassador; LLB, U. Philippines, 1970; LLM, NYU, 1985. Consul gen. Philippine Consulate Gen., NYC, 1997—99; asst. sec. Office Asian and Pacific Affairs Dept. Fgn. Affairs Republic of Philippines, 1999—2002; amb. to Australia, Nauru, Tuvalu, Vanuatu Embassy of Philippines, Australia, 2002—03, amb. E. and P. China, 2003—06; consul gen. Philippine Consulate Gen., LA, 2006; amb. to U.S., 2006—. Office: Philippine Embassy 1600 Massachusetts Ave NW Washington DC 20036 Office Phone: 202-467-9300. Office Fax: 202-467-9417.

GAAL, JOHN, lawyer; b. Flushing, NY, Oct. 10, 1952; s. Stephen Alfred and Marjorie (Lappin) G.; m. Barbara Jeanne Zacher, Aug. 5, 1973; children: Bryan A., Adam C., Benjamin Z. BA cum laude, U. Notre Dame, 1974, JD magna cum laude, 1977. Bar: N.Y. 1978, U.S. Ct. Appeals (D.C. cir.) 1978, U.S. Dist. Ct. (no. dist.) N.Y. 1979, U.S. Supreme Ct. 1986. Law clk. to judge U.S. Ct. Appeals (D.C. cir.), Washington, 1977-78; assoc. Bond, Schoeneck & King, Syracuse, NY, 1978-85, ptnr., 1986—. Bd. dirs. Legal Svcs. of Ctrl. N.Y., Syracuse, 1981-87, 94-2000, pres. 1999-2000—; adj. prof. Sch. of Mgmt., Syracuse U., 1989-92, Coll. of Law, 2001. Editor: Senior Citizens Handbook, 1988; contbg. author: Public Sector Labor and Employment Law, 1988; mem. editl. bd. Jour. Coll. and Univ. Law, 1998—, co-chair, 2000-02; columnist The Bus. Jour., 1998-2000; mem. bd. advs. N.Y. Employment Law Practice Newsletter, 2001-04; contbr. articles to profl. publs. Bd. dirs. Transitional Living Svcs., 2001—07, Dunbar Assn., 2003—, Crouse Health Hosp. Found., 2005—. Fellow Am. Bar Found., Am. Coll. Labor and Employment Lawyers (Best Lawyers in Am.); mem. ABA (labor and employment law sect.), N.Y. State Bar Assn. (exec. com. labor and employment law sect., chair young lawyer sect. 1989-90, spl. com. on AIDS and the law 1988, spl. com. on mandatory pro bono svc. 1989, ho. of dels. 1987-89, 90-91, co-chair com. ethics 1999—). Democrat. Roman Catholic. Home: 8006 Austrian Pine Cir Manlius NY 13104- Office: Bond Schoeneck & King 1 Lincoln Ctr Fl 18 Syracuse NY 13202-1324 Office Phone: 315-218-8288. Business E-Mail: jgaal@bsk.com.

GAAR, NORMAN EDWARD, lawyer, former state senator; b. Kansas City, Mo., Sept. 29, 1929; s. William Edward and Lola Eugene (McKain) G.; children: Anne, James, William, John; m. Marilyn A. Wiegraffe, Apr. 12, 1986. Student, Baker U., 1947-49; AB, U. Mich., 1955, JD, 1956. Bar: Mo. 1957, Kans. 1962, U.S. Supreme Ct. 1969. Assoc. Stinson, Mag, Thomson, McEvers & Fizzell, Kansas City, 1956-59; ptnr. Stinson, Mag & Fizzell, Kansas City, 1959-79; mng. ptnr. Gaar & Bell, Kansas City, St. Louis, Overland Park, Wichita, Kans., 1979-87; ptnr. Burke, Williams, Sorensen & Gaar, Overland Park, Kans., L.A., Camarillo, Fresno, Costa Mesa, Calif., 1987-96; shareholder McDowell, Rice, Smith & Gaar, Overland Park, 1996—2004; ptnr. Gaar Buxbaum & Roth, Overland Park, 2005—. Mem. Kans. Senate, 1965-84, majority leader, 1976-80; faculty N.Y. Practising Law Inst., 1969-74; adv. dir. Panel Pubs., Inc., N.Y.C.; chmn. Lone Summit Bank, Lake Lotawana, Mo., 2004—. Mcpl. judge City of Westwood, Kans., 1959-63, mayor, 1963-65. With USN, 1949-53. Decorated Air medal (3); named State of Kans. Disting. Citizen, 1962. Fellow Am. Coll. Bd. Coun.; mem. ABA, Kans. Bar Assn., Mo. Bar Assn., Am. Radio Relay League, Nat. Assn. Bond Lawyers, Calif. Assn. Bond Lawyers (charter), Russian-Am. Internat. Studies Assn. (dir. 2000—), Flying Midshipmen Assn., Assn. Naval Aviators, Tailhook Assn., Antique Airplane Assn., Exptl. Aircraft Assn. (dir. Kansas City chpt.), People to People. Republican. Episcopalian. Office: 7101 College Blvd Ste 250 40 Executive Hills Overland Park KS 66210-1891 Home: 11126 Brookwood Ave Leawood KS 66211-3092 Office Phone: 913-338-2150. Business E-Mail: ngaar@gbrattorneys.com.

GAARDER, MARIE, speech pathologist; b. New Britain, Conn., July 19, 1935; d. Nicholas and Clara (Sangeloty) Sarris; m. Kenneth R. Gaarder, Dec. 8, 1962; children: Jason, Galen. BS, U. Ill., 1957; postgrad., U. Md., 1962-63; postgrad. Our Lady of Lake U., Grad. Sch. Social Work, San Antonio, 1976-77. Founder speech therapy program Flossmoor (Ill.) Sch. Dist. 161, 1957-59; speech pathologist Prince George's County (Md.) Bd. Edn., 1959-65, Sidwell Friend's Sch., Washington, 1966-67, St. Maurice Sch. for Learning Disabilities, Potomac, Md., 1968-69; pvt. practice speech therapy Chevy Chase, Md., 1967—; adminstrv. officer Gaarder Med. Corp., Chevy Chase, 1977—. Pres., Prince George's chpt. Coun. for Exceptional Children, 1963-64; mem. Florence Crittenton Circle, 1966-69, Hospitality and Info. Svc. for Diplomats, 1967—; chmn. activities com. Jr. Teens, 1979-80; chmn. publicity YWCA Internat. Fair, 1977-79, chmn. entertainment, 1983, chmn., 1987-88; mem. internat. com. Woman's Nat. Dem. Club; co-chmn. Adv. Com. for Quality Integrated Edn. in Montgomery County, 1977-78; bd. dirs. D.C. br. YWCA, 1981-82, Washington Ctr.; chmn. oral history 65th Birthday Town of Chevy Chase; chmn. Mid-Atlantic regional adv. bd. Am. Found. for the Blind, 1984-85; founding mem. exec. bd. internat. adv. com. Very Spl. Arts, 1990-93; victim asst., ct. accompaniment, Divsn. Health & Human Svcs., Md., 2004-. Recipient Appreciation cert. Opera Guild San Antonio, 1977, Outstanding and Dedicated Svc. to 1987 Internat. Fair Plaque YWCA of the Nat. Capital Area, Nat. Svc. Registry award, 1990, Disting. Svc. in Profession citation, Appreciation cert. Internat. Tng. in Communication, 1994. Mem. Am. Speech, Lang. and Hearing Assn. (advanced cert.), Md. Speech, Lang. and Hearing Assn., Meridian Internat. Ctr., Salvation Army Women's Aux., World Affairs Coun. Washington, Soc. Internat. Devel., Asia Soc., Soc. Preservation Greek Heritage, Capitol Spkrs. Club (sec. chpt. III 1983-84), Zeta Phi Eta. Greek Orthodox. Home and Office: 4221 Oakridge Ln Bethesda MD 20815-6058 Office Phone: 301-656-0379. Personal E-mail: mariespeech@hotmail.com.

GABARRA, CARIN LESLIE, professional soccer player, professional soccer coach; b. East Orange, NJ, Jan. 9, 1965; m. Jim Gabarra. Degree in bus. mgmt., U. Calif., Santa Barbara, 1987. Mem. U.S. Nat. Women's Soccer Team, 1987—96; head coach, women's soccer Westmont Coll., 1987—88; assist. coach, women's Soccer Harvard U., Boston, 1988—93; head coach, women's soccer Navy, 1993—. Mem. U.S. Olympic World Festival team, 1986—89; mem. women's soccer U.S. Naval Acad., 1993. Named U.S. Soccer's Female Athlete of Yr., 1987, 1992; named to, U. Calif.-Santa Barbara Athletic Hall of Fame; recipient Golden Ball, FIFA Women's World Championship, China, 1991, gold medal, Atlanta Summer Olympic Games, 1996. Achievements include ranked as 3d-leading goal scorer in U.S. women's history; mem. CONCACAF Championship team, 1993, 94. Office: c/o US Soccer Fedn 1801 S Prairie Ave # 1811 Chicago IL 60616-1319

GABAY, DONALD, lawyer; b. Bklyn., Apr. 1935; s. Harry I. and Rachel Gabay. BBA, CCNY, 1956; LLB, Bklyn. Law Sch., 1961. Bar: N.Y. 1962. Pvt. practice law, NYC, 1962-75; chief counsel N.Y. State Assembly Com. on Ins., Albany, 1975-78; 1st dep. supt. N.Y. State Ins. Dept., NYC, 1978-84; ptnr. Stroock & Stroock & Lavan, LLP, NYC, 1984—. Pres. Ins. Fedn. N.Y., 1994-98, 99-2005, chmn. With US Army, 1956—58. Named Ins. Man of Yr., Ind. Ins. Brokers Assn., 1973; recipient Pub. Svc. award Bklyn. Ins. Brokers Assn., 1977, ann. achievement award Coun. Ins. Brokers, 1981, Outstanding Achievement award CCNY Alumni Assn., 1981, Pub. Svc. award Ind. Ins. Agts. Assn., 1984, Torch of Liberty award ins. divsn. Anti-Defamation League, 1984, Lifetime Achievement award, Coun. Ins. Brokers Greater NY, 2007. Office: Stroock Stroock & Lavan LLP 180 Maiden Ln New York NY 10038-4925 Office Phone: 212-806-5541. Business E-Mail: dgabay@stroock.com.

GABAY, ELEONORA V., mechanical engineer, educator; b. Leningrad, Russia, Apr. 20, 1938; arrived in US, 1991; d. Victor N. and Antonina V. Gabay; m. Natan A. Kogan, May 27, 1961; 1 child, Leon N. Kogan. BSME, U. Cinema Engring., St. Petersburg, 1959, MSME with honors, 1961. Author: (tchrs.' tool) FeedBack Cards (Diploma of All-Union contest on instrnl. tools, 1986), (instrnl. tool) Hands-on COLORIDE workbooks, 1999. Coord. Russian Leadership Com., Edison, NJ, 2001—03. Achievements include patents for Workbook with movable colored tabs. Home: 1412 Stone Ridge Cir Helmetta NJ 08828 Office Phone: 732-605-0956. Personal E-mail: nevka@comcast.net.

GABAY, JANIS T., literature and language educator; b. Honolulu, 1953; BA, San Diego State Univ., 1972, MA, 1978. Tchr. English lang. Junipero Serra High Sch., San Diego, 1980—; advanced placement English tchr., staff developer Preuss Sch., Univ. Calif. San Diego. Reg. dir. Calif. Lit. Project. Recipient Nat. Tchr. of Yr. award, 1990. Office: The Preuss Sch UCSD 9500 Gilman Dr La Jolla CA 92093-0536 Business E-Mail: jgabay@ucsd.edu.*

GABBANA, STEFANO, fashion designer; b. Milan, Nov. 14, 1962; Studied graphic design. Asst. in an atellier in Milan, 1980—82; cons. in field, 1982; co-owner Dolce & Gabbana, Milan, 1982—. First collection established in 1986; first boutique opened in Japan in 1989; established first men's collection and opened first women's boutique in Milan in 1990; co-designer La Maglie di Dolce & Gabbana (knitwear), 1986, Dolce & Gabbana Beachwear, 1989, L'intimo di Dolce & Gabbana (lingerie), 1989, Complice line for the Genny Group in Milan, 1990, scarves, ties, beachwear, perfume, and accessories added in 1992; D&G (diffusion), manufactured by Ittierra S.p.A., 1994, jeans, 1995, Basic women's line, Dolce & Gabbana Occhialli, 1996; co-author with Domenico Dolce (book) Dolce & Gabbana: Animal, 1998; co-author with Domenico Dolce and Eve Claxton (book) Hollywood, 2003; recorded Compact Disc. Recipient Woolmark award, 1990. Office: Dolce & Gabbana Via Santa Cecilia 7 20122 Milan Italy Office Phone: 02 79 50 15 or 79 50 16. Office Fax: 02 78 44 36.*

GABBARD, DOUGLAS, II, (JAMES GABBARD), judge; b. Lindsay, Okla., Mar. 27, 1952; s. James Douglas and Mona Dean (Dodd) G.; m. Connie Sue Mace, Dec. 30, 1977 (div. Feb. 1979); m. Robyn Marie Kohlhaas, June 18, 1981 (div. July 2005); children: Resa Marie, David Ryan, James Douglas III, Michael Drew, Zachary; m. Pethi C. Hayes, July 23, 2005. BS, Okla. U., 1974, JD, 1977; grad., Nat. Jud. Coll., 1987, U. Kans. Law Orgnl. Econs., 1997. Bar: Okla. 1978. Ptnr. Stubblefeild & Gabbard, Atoka, Okla., 1978; sole practice Atoka, 1979; asst. dist. atty. State of Okla., Atoka, 1979-82, 1st asst. dist. atty. Atoka, Durant and Coalgate, 1982-85; dist. judge 25th Jud. Dist. State of Okla., 1985—2005; presiding judge South East Adminstrn. Dist., Okla., 1992—2005, State Ct. Tax Review, Okla., 1992—2005; judge Divsn. IV Okla. Ct. Civil Appeals, 2005—, presiding judge Divsn. IV, 2006—. Presiding judge of emergency panel of State Ct. Criminal Appeals, State Ct. on Judiciary Trial divsn., 1997-04, vice-presiding judge 2003-04, appellate divsn. 2005-06; mem. Supreme Ct. Com. on Civil Jury Instructions, 2002—; dir. Okla. Trial Judges Assn., 1996-2005; mcpl. judge City of Atoka, 1978-79; chmn. Chickasaw Nation Ethics Commn., 2003—. Mem. Bryan County/Durant Arbitration Com., 1984; negotiator Bryan Meml. Hosp. Bd., Durant, 1984-85. Nominated to Okla. Supreme Ct., State Jud. Nominating Commn., 2004. Mem. Okla. Bar Assn. (legal ethics com. 1988-90, jud. adminstrv. com. 1988-90, resolutions com., 1998, long range planning com., bench and bar com. 1999), Okla. Jud. Conf., Am. Judges Assn., Masons. Democrat. Methodist. Avocations: painting, carpentry, reading. Office: Okla Ct Civil Appeals Ste 601 440 South Houston Tulsa OK 74127 Home: 415 N Hill Atoka OK 74525 Office Phone: 918-581-2711. Personal E-mail: doug.gabbard@oscn.net.

GABBARD, GLEN OWENS, psychiatrist, psychotherapist; b. Charleston, Ill., Aug. 8, 1949; s. Earnest Glendon and Lucina Mildred (Paquet) G.; children: Matthew, Abigail, Amanda, Allison; m. Joyce Eileen Davidson, June 14, 1985. BS, Eastern Ill. U., 1972; MD, Rush Med. Coll., 1975; degree in psychoanalytic tng., Topeka Inst. for Psychoanalysis, 1984. Diplomate Am. Bd. Psychiatry and Neurology. Resident in psychiatry Menninger Sch. Psychiatry, Topeka, 1975-78, mem. faculty, 1978—; staff psychiatrist C.F. Menninger Hosp., Topeka, 1978-83, sect. chief, 1984-89. Med. dir., 1989-94; tng. analyst Topeka Inst. for Psychoanalysis, 1989-2001, dir., 1996-2001; v.p. for adult svcs. Menninger Clinic, 1991-94; clin. prof. psychiatry U. Kans. Med. Sch., 1991-2001; Callaway Disting. prof. Menninger Clinic and Karl Menninger Sch. Psychiatry, 1994-2001; prof. psychiatry Baylor Coll. Medicine, 2001—, Brown Found. chair psychoanalysis, 2003—. Author: With the Eyes of the Mind, 1984, Psychiatry and the Cinema, 1987, 2d edit., 1999, Medical Marriages, 1988, Sexual Exploitation in Professional Relationships, 1989, Psychodynamic Psychiatry in Clinical Practice, 1990, Portuguese transl., 1992, Italian transl., 1992, 2d edit., 1994, Korean transl., 1996, Japanese transl., 1997, 4th edit., 2005, Treatments of Psychiatric Disorders: the DSM-IV Edition, 1995; meml. editl. bd. Am. Jour. Psychiatry, Am. Psychiat. Press; joint editor-in-chief Internat. Jour. Psychoanalysis; contbr. articles to profl. jours. V.p. Topeka Civic Theatre, 1981-82, pres. 1982-83, bd. dirs. 1981-83. Named one of

Outstanding Young Men in Am. U.S. Jaycees, 1984. Mem. AAAS, Am. Psychoanalytic Assn. (assoc. editor jour., mem. editl. bd.), Am. Psychiat. Assn. (Falk fellow 1976, Edward A. Strecker award 1994, Disting. Psychiatrist lectr. 1995, C. Charles Burlingame award 1997, Mary S. Sigourney award 2000, Disting. Svc. award 2002, Adolf Meyer award 2004), Sch. Psychotherapy Rsch., Menninger Sch. Psychiatry Alumni Assn. (pres. 1982-83), Alpha Omega Alpha. Avocations: theater, music. Home: 1290 Jimmy Phillips Blvd Angleton TX 77515 Office: Dept Psychiatry Baylor Coll Medicine One Baylor Plz MS 350 Houston TX 77030 Office Phone: 713-798-6397. Business E-Mail: ggabbard@bcm.tmc.edu.

GABBE, STEVEN GLENN, dean, educator, obstetrician, gynecologist; b. Newark, Dec. 1, 1944; s. Charles Paul and Marcia May Gabbe; m. Jessica Gabbe, June 26, 1966 (div. 1980); children: Amanda, Daniel; m. Patricia Temple, July 26, 1981. BA, Princeton U., 1965; MD, Cornell U., 1969; MA (hon.), U. Pa., 1983. Diplomate Am. Bd. Ob-Gyn (examiner 1980-01), Am. Bd. Maternal-Fetal Medicine (examiner 1979-01). Intern in medicine N.Y. Hosp., NYC, 1969-70; rsch. fellow reproductive medicine Boston Hosp. for Women, 1970-71, resident in ob-gyn, 1972-74; rsch. fellow in biol. chemistry Harvard Med. Sch., Boston, 1970-71, clin. fellow ob-gyn., 1972-74; asst. prof. ob-gyn U. So. Calif., LA, 1975-77; assoc. prof. U. Colo. Sch. Medicine, Denver, 1977-78; assoc. prof. ob-gyn. and pediatrics U. Pa. Sch. Medicine, Phila., 1978-87, prof. radiology, 1987; mem. staff Hosp. of U. Pa., Phila., 1978-87, dir. Jerrold R. Golding divsn. fetal medicine, 1978-87, mem. med. bd. and numerous coms., 1984-87; prof. U. Pa. Sch. Nursing, Phila., 1982-87; prof., chmn. dept. ob-gyn Ohio State U. Coll. Medicine, Columbus, 1987-96; prof., chmn. dept. ob/gyn. U. Wash. Sch. Medicine, Seattle, 1996—2001; dir. Jerrold R. Golding divsn. fetal medicine Hosp. of U. Pa., Phila., 1978-87, mem. med. bd. and numerous coms., 1984-87; dean Sch. of Medicine Vanderbilt U., Nashville, 2001—. Vis. prof. ob-gyn King's Coll. Hosp., London, 1985-86; dir. maternal and infant care program Phila. Dept. Health, Disease Prevention and Health Promotion, 1982-87; mem. maternal and infant care adv. coun. Dept. Pub. Health, Phila., 1983-87; mem. subcom. on pregnancy and weight gain NRC, NAS, 1981; mem. internat. sci. bd. Reproductive Toxicology Ctr., 1984—; bd. dirs., med. adv. bd. Diabetes Treatment Ctrs. Am., 1984, others; mem. Coun. Univ Chairs of Ob-Gyn., 1996—; chair Maternal Fetal Medicine Rsch. Network Nat. Inst. Child and Human Devel. Author: Clinical Obstetrics and Gynecology: Diabetes and Pregnancy, 1985, Clinical Obstetrics and Gynecology: Obstetric Ultrasound Update, 1988; (with J.R. Niebyl and J.L. Simpson) Obstetrics: Normal and Problem Pregnancies, 1986, 4th edit., 2002; contbr. numerous articles to profl. jours. and chpts. to books; editor in chief Am. Jour. Perinatology, 1983—87; mem. numerous editl. bds. Mem. Pa. Diabetes Task Force, 1981-87, Ohio Diabetes Task Force, 1987—; bd. dirs. UNITE, Jeanes Hosp., 1980-87. Recipient Sr. Resident's award for Excellence in Tng., L.A. County Women's Hosp., 1976, Disting. Tchr. award from Graduating Class, U. Wash., 1999; grantee Juvenile Diabetes Found., 1981, HHS, 1984, 1985, Diabetes Treatment Ctrs. Am., 1986. Fellow Am. Coll. Obstetricians and Gynecologists (mem. Prolog self assessment program task force 1981-82, chmn. 1986, mem. Prolog subcom. 1986—); mem. Am. Gynecol. and Obstet. Soc., Am. Inst. Ultrasound in Medicine, Perinatal Rsch. Soc., Soc. Gynecologic Investigation, Soc. Perinatal Obstetricians (v.p. 1986, pres. 1987-88, bd. dirs. 1983-88, chmn. credentials, constn. and by-laws com. 1983-87), Am. Diabetes Assn. (mem. nat. rsch. bd. 1981-83, chmn. coun. on diabetes in pregnancy 1985, com. on food and nutrition 1976-80), Juvenile Diabetes Found. (mem. med. sci. rev. com., med. sci. adv. bd. 1981-83), Phila. Neonatal Soc., Obstet. Soc. Phila. (program chmn. 1986-87), Phila. Perinatal Soc. (pres. 1982-84), Columbus Ob-Gyn Soc., Pa. Diabetes Acad. (acad. steering com. 1986—, editl. rev. com. 1986—), Union League (Phila.), Phi Beta Kappa, Alpha Omega Alpha. Avocations: sports, running. Office: Vanderbilt U Sch Medicine Office of Dean D-3300 MCN 21st Ave South at Garland Ave Nashville TN 37232 Office Phone: 615-322-5191. Office Fax: 615-343-7286. E-mail: steven.gabbe@vanderbilt.edu.

GABBOUR, ISKANDAR, city and regional planning educator; b. Mansura, Egypt, Feb. 6, 1929; s. Iskandar Gabbour and Mathilde Louli; m. Amy Surur, Feb. 4, 1956; children: May, Tamer, Rami. B.Arch. with honors, Cairo U., 1953; M.Arch., M.C.P., U. Pa., 1963, PhD, 1967. Arch., chief designer Devel. & Popular Housing Co., Cairo, 1954-61; rschr. assoc. U. Pa., Phila., 1966-67; prof. city and regional planning U. Montreal, Que., Canada, 1967-97, vice dean acad. affairs, faculty environ. design, 1993—97, hon. prof. Que., 1997—, interim chmn. dept. landscape architecture Que., 2000—02. Cons. UN Ctr. for Human Settlements, Nairobi, Kenya, 1985; vol. advisor Tech. Studies and Devel. Office, Abidjan, Ivory Coast, 1998. Contbr. numerous articles to profl. jours. Mem. Am. Planning Assn. (charter), Am. Inst. Cert. Planners (charter), Can. Inst. Planners, Royal Archtl. Inst. Can., Assn. Collegiate Schs. Planning, Order Urbanists of Que. Home: 5510 Ashdale Ave Montreal PQ Canada H4W 3G4 Fax: (514) 484-8245. E-mail: iskandar.gabbour@umontreal.ca.

GABEL, CONNIE, chemist, educator; b. Green Bank, W.Va. d. William Ashby and Marie Lowry; m. Richard Gabel; children: Greg, Keith, Debbie. BS in Chemistry magna cum laude, James Madison U., Harrisonburg, Va.; MA in Ednl. Adminstrn. summa cum laude, U. Colo., 1984, PhD in Ednl. Leadership and Innovation, 2001. Tchg. asst. U. Wis., Madison, 1969-70, specialist endocrinology, 1970-71; tchr. Dept. Def. Schs., Tokyo, 1972-74, Poudre R-1 Schs., Ft. Collins, Colo., 1975-78, Boulder Valley Schs., 1985-87, 96-98, intern asst. prin., 1984-85; intern supt. Jefferson County Schs., Golden, Colo., 1992; tchr. Mapleton Pub. Schs., Thornton, Colo., 1992-95; internat. studies Egyptian program Regis U., Denver, 1994; instr. chemistry Colo. Sch. Mines, 1995-98; dean students Horizon HS, Thornton, Colo., 1995-96; project 2061 coord. dept. chemistry/edn. U. Colo., Denver, 1998-2000; instr. St. Mary's Acad., Englewood, Colo., 2000—03, Met. State Coll. Tchr. Edn. and Chemistry, Denver, 2004—. Cons. sch. fin. Colo. Dept. Edn., Denver, 1984; rschr. AMC Cancer Rsch. Ctr., Denver, 1993, Colo. U. Med. Ctr., Denver, 1994; display tech. Boulder-Chemistry Rsch., 1995. Charter mem., pres. Friends Louisville (Colo.) Libr., 1985—; charter mem. Nat. Women's History Mus.; charter mem., pres., v.p. Coal Creek Rep. Women, Louisville, 1987—; sec., mem. Boulder County Reps., 1988—98, precinct chair; mem. Nat. Rep. Women, Washington, 1987—; sec. Dist. 17 Colo. Senate, Dist. 13 Colo. Ho., 1993—2002; mem. Colo. Fedn. Rep. Women, 1987—, Colo. Rep. Ctrl. Com. Mem.: AAUW, AAAS, ASCD, NY Acad. Sci., Math., Engring. and Sci. Achievement (mem. state level adv. bd. 1992—96, dir., advisor 1992—97), Colo. Chemistry Tchrs. Assn., Colo.-Wyo. Acad. Sci., Colo. Assn. Sci. Tchrs., Nat. Soc. Study Edn., Nat. Assn. Rsch. Sci. Tchg., Am. Chem. Soc. (chair elect Colo. local sect. 2007), Nat. Assn. Sci. Tchrs., Am. Ednl. Rsch. Assn., Phi Delta Kappa. Avocations: reading, hiking, gardening. Business E-Mail: cgabel@mscd.edu.

GABEL, GEORGE DESAUSSURE, JR., lawyer; b. Jacksonville, Fla., Feb. 14, 1940; s. George DeSaussure and Juanita (Brittain) G.; m. Judith Kay Adams, July 21, 1962; children: Laura Gabel Hartman, Meredith Gabel Harris. AB, Davidson Coll., 1961; JD, U. Fla., 1964. Bar: Fla. 1964, D.C. 1972. With Toole, Taylor, Moseley, Gabel & Milton, Jacksonville, Fla., 1966—74, Gabel & Hair (formerly Wahl & Gabel), Jacksonville, 1974—98; ptnr. Holland & Knight, Jacksonville, 1998—2001, exec. ptnr., 2002—06, dep. sect. leader litigation sect., 2007—. Mem. Fla. Jud. Nominating Commn., 4th cir., 1982-86.; delegate to the Comit-é Maritime Internat. Conferences in Sydney, Australia, Antwerp, Belgium, and Singapore; mem. exec. coun., World Affairs Coun., 2001-. Pres. Willing Hands, Inc., 1971-72; chmn. N.E. Fla. March of Dimes, 1974-75; mem. budget com. United Way, 1972-74, chmn. rev. com., 1976; bd. dirs. Ctrl. and So. brs. YMCA, 1973-79, Camp Immokalee, 1982-86; elder Riverside Presbyn. Ch., 1970-77, 80-86, 90-92, 97-2003, clk. session, 1975-76, 85-86, trustee, 1988-91; pres. Riverside Presbyn. Day Sch., 1977-79; chmn. Nat. Eagle Scout Assn., 1974-75; pres. Boy Scouts Am., North Fla. Coun. 1993-96, silver Beaver award, 1978; trustee Davidson Coll., 1984-95; Norwegian Consul for N.E. Fla., 1989-2002; pres. Jacksonville Consular Corps, 1992-93, 1996-2002; mem. nat. adv. bd. Tulane Admiralty Law Inst., 2001—. Capt. U.S. Army, 1964-66. Named Internat. Person of Yr., Jacksonville Regional C. of C., 2002. Fellow Am. Coll. Trial Lawyers, Am. Bar Found.; mem. ABA (chmn. admiralty and maritime law com., 1980-81. chmn. media law and defamation torts com. 1988-89. tort and ins. practice sect.), Am. Counsel Assn. (bd. dirs. 1980-82, pres. 1992-93), Maritime Law Assn. U.S. (bd. dirs. 1994-97), Assn. Average Adjusters (U.S.) (overseas subscriber-London), Fla. Bar (chmn. grievance com. 1973-75, chmn. admiralty law com. 1978-89, chmn. media and comms. law com. 1990-91), Southeastern Admiralty law Inst. (bd. govs. 1973-75), Duval County Legal Aid Assn. (bd. dirs. 1971-74, 81-84), Am. Inn of Ct. (master of bench, sec.-treas. 1990-95), Rotary of Jacksonville (bd. dirs. 1982-84, 88-89, pres. 87-88), World Affairs Coun. of Jacksonville (exec. com. 2001—), Jacksonville Regional C. of C. (bd. dirs. 2005—, internat. chair), DC Bar, Chester Bedell Inn of Ct. (master of bench), U.S. Dist. Ct. for Middle Dist. Fla. (fed. rules adv. com., 1993-96), Libel Def. Resource Ctr. (mem. def. counsel sect.). Democrat. Office: Holland & Knight LLP 50 N Laura St Ste 3900 Jacksonville FL 32202-3622 Office Phone: 904-353-2000, 904-798-7360. E-mail: ggabel@hklaw.com.

GABEL, KATHERINE, retired academic administrator; b. Rochester, NY, Apr. 9, 1938; d. M. Wren and Esther (Conger) G.; m. Seth Devore Strickland, June 24, 1961 (div. 1965). AB, Smith Coll., Northampton, Mass., 1959; MSW, Simmons Coll., 1961; PhD, Syracuse U., 1967; JD, Union U., 1970; bus. program, Stanford U., 1984. Psychol. social worker Cen. Island Mental Health Ctr., Uniondale, NY, 1961-62; psychol. social worker, supt. Ga. State Tng. Sch. for Girls, Atlanta, 1962-64; cons. N.Y. State Crime Control Coun., Albany, 1968-70; faculty Ariz. State U., Tempe, 1972-76; supt. Ariz. Dept. of Corrections, Phoenix, 1970-76; dean, prof. Smith Coll., 1976-85; pres. Pacific Oaks Coll. and Children's Sch., Pasadena, Calif., 1985-98; western region v.p. Casey Family Program, Pasadena, 1998—2001; pvt. practice, 2001—. Advisor, del. UN, Geneva, 1977; mem. So. Calif. Youth Authority, 1986-91; west region dir. Lambda LegalDef. Fund, LA, 2003— Editor: Master Teacher and Supervisor in Clinical Social Work, 1982; author report Legal Issues of Female Inmates, 1981, model for rsch. Diversion program Female Inmates, 1984, Children of Incarcerated Parents, 1995. Vice chair United Way, Northampton, 1982-83; chair Mayor's Task Force, Northampton, 1981. Mem. Nat. Assn. Social Work, Acad. Cert. Social Workers, Nat. Assn. Edn. Young Children, Western Assn. Schs. and Colls., Pasadena C. of C., Athenaeum, Pasadena Rotary Club. Democrat. Presbyterian. Avocation: collecting south west Indian art, aviary. Personal E-mail: gabelk@prodigy.net.

GABEL, RONALD GLEN, telecommunications executive; b. Allentown, Pa., Nov. 22, 1937; s. Glen Harry and Mary (Oberlin) G.; m. Claire A. Hollern (div.); children: Debra K., Jeffrey A., Stacy L.; m. Elaine M. Petro, Sept. 29, 1988. Student, Pa. State U., 1957-58. Cert. elec. and electronic mfg. engr. Design draftsman Mack Trucks Inc., Allentown, 1958-62, Bell Telephone Labs., Allentown, 1962-66; indsl. engr. Western Electric, Allentown, 1966-84; sr. engr. AT&T, Allentown, 1984-95, Lucent Technologies, Allentown, 1995-97. Cons. expert Man at Arms Mag.; gen. chmn. Engrs.' Week Joint Planning Coun., Lehigh Valley, 1981; cost reduction coord. Western Elec. Allentown Works, 1982-86; Western Electric Speakers Bureau, 1972-83; adminstr. Tel. Pioneers Am., Allentown, 1987-94. Co-author: Work Simplification by Motion Economy Handbook, 1982; coord. Western Elec. Allentown Works Indsl. Engring. newsletter, 1973-85. Advisor Lehigh County Dept. Human Svcs., 1989—93; solicitor United Way, 1974, 1982, 1989, 1990; dir. Lehigh County Hist. Soc., 1999—2000; v.p. Jacobsburg Hist. Soc., 1999—2000, pres., 2000—01; dir. Lehigh County Mus. Commn., 1977—81; sec. devel. and prodn. com. Lehigh County Bicentennial Commn., 1977; pres. Indian Guides Allentown YMCA, 1972, v.p., 1971; treas. Jacobsburg Hist. Soc., 2003—; sec. ch. coun. St. James Luth. Ch., 1964—67; advisor St. James Luther League, 1964—67. Mem.: Am. Inst. Indsl. Engrs. (pres. 1976—77, editor nat. mfg. sys. divsn. newsletter 1979—80, dir. Lehigh Valley chpt. 1983, Outstanding Svc. award 1978, 5 nat. awards for profl. soc. newsletters 1971—75), Internat. Inst. Indsl. Engrs., Ky. Rifle Found. (pres. 2001—03), Forks of Del. Weapons Assn., Tex. Gun Collectors Assn., Pa. Antique Gun Collectors Assn. (bd. dirs. 1996—97, v.p. 1998—99, sec.-treas. 1999—, editor Bugle newsletter 2001—), Ducks Unltd., Am. Soc. Arms Collectors (bd. dirs. 1988—91, v.p. 1991—94, pres. 1994—95), Ky. Rifle Assn. (newsletter editor 1974—), NRA (life), U.S. Power Squadrons (dist. lt. D-5 1991—95), Delhigh Power Squadron (comdr. 1990—91, pres. past comdr. club 2000—01), Nat. Soc. Pershing Rifles, Pa. Antiques Appraisers Assn., Ky. Rifle Assn. (pres. 1972—73), Mercedes Benz Club (v.p. N.E. Pa. sect. 2002—03), Shriners, KT, Upper Lehigh Lions (pres. club 1987—88, treas. 1998—, pres. Past Pres. Club 2000, sec.-treas. Past Pres. Club 2003—06), Rajh Temple, Internat. Order DeMolay. Republican. Avocation: antique firearms. Personal E-mail: rggabel@ptd.net.

GABELLI, MARIO J., diversified financial services company executive; 4 children. Grad. summa cum laude, Fordham U., 1965; MBA, Columbia U., 1967. Founder Gabelli Funds LLC, 1977—; chmn., CEO, chief investment officer Gabelli Asset Mgmt. Inc., 1999—; CEO, chmn. Lynch Corp., 1986—2001, vice chmn., 2001—; chmn. Lynch Interactive Corp., 1999—2002, CEO, dir., 1999—. Gov. Am. Stock Exchange. Trustee Winston Churchill Found.; mem., bd. overseers Columbia U. Grad Sch. Bus.; bd. trustees Fairfield U., Roger Williams U.; bd. dirs. Bruce Mus.; trustee E.L. Wiegand Found., Reno; chmn., patron's com. Immaculate Conception Sch., Bronx, NY. Recipient Columbus Citizens Found. Award, 1994, Ellis Island Medal of Hon. for Bus. Leaders, 1996, Cavaliere, Italian Legions of Merit. Office: Gabelli Funds Inc One Corporate Center Rye NY 10580-1430

GABELNICK, HENRY LEWIS, medical research administrator; b. Boston, May 10, 1940; s. Murray and Lillian G.; m. Faith Schectman, June 17, 1962; children: Deborah Anne, Tamar Miriam; m. Judith Andai, Mar. 15, 2003. BS, MIT, 1961, MS, 1962; PhD, Princeton U., 1966. Sr. chem. engr. Monsanto Co., Springfield, Mass., 1966-68; biomed. engr. NIH, Bethesda, Md., 1968-1986; dir. extramural rsch. CONRAD Program Ea. Va. Med. Sch., Arlington, 1986-89, dep. dir. CONRAD Program, 1989-90, dir. CONRAD Program, 1990—. Tech. expert UN Devel. Program, Haifa, Israel, 1973; tech. advisor WHO, Geneva, 1977—; pres. Reprodn. Rsch. Inst., 1997—2001; mem. adv. panel on contraception Internat. Fedn. Ob-gyns., 1998—; mem. adv. coun. dept. chem. engring. Princeton U., 2004—; bd. dirs. Alliance for Microbicide Devel.; founding bd. mem. Internat. Partnership for Microbicides, sec., 2002—06. Editor: Rheology of Biological Systems, 1973, Drug Delivery Systems, 1976, Heterosexual Transmission of AIDS, 1990, Barrier Contraceptives, 1993, Biology, Pharmacology, and Clinical Applications of Androgens, 1996. Recipient Lifetime Achievement award, 5th Internat. Symposium on AIDS, India, 2005. Fellow Textile Resch. Inst.; mem. APHA, N.Y. Acad. Scis., Am. Chem. Soc., Controlled Release Soc., Soc. for Reproductive Care (bd. dirs. 2000—, v.p. 2001-02, pres. 2002—), Assn. Reproductive Health Profls., Indian Soc. Study Reprodn. and Fertility (life), Global Health Coun., Cosmos Club, Sigma Xi. Avocation: nature photography. Home: 6315 Swords Way Bethesda MD 20817 Office Phone: 703-276-3904. Personal E-mail: hgabelnick@alum.mit.edu. Business E-Mail: hgabelnick@conrad.org.

GABER, ROBERT, psychologist; b. NYC, Nov. 5, 1923; s. William and Freda (Harris) Gaber; m. Heidi Walters, Apr. 3, 1967 (div. Jan. 5, 1976); 1 child, Nathan. BA, NYU, 1949, MA, 1951; PhD, Columbia Pacific U., San Rafael, Calif., 1982. Psychotherapist Nat. Hosp. Speech Disorders, NYC, 1954-57; psychologist Indsl. Home for the Blind, NYC, 1957-58; sch. psychologist Roosevelt Sch., Stamford, Conn., 1958-60; sr. clin. psychologist N.Y. State Dept. Mental Hygiene, Thiells, 1960-64; staff psychologist N.Y. Med. Coll., NYC, 1965-66; cons. psychologist Salvation Army, Phila., 1971-72; psychologist Md. Dept. Mental Hygiene, 1975-76, Dept. Corrections, Balt., 1979-80; CEO Axxiom De-Stress Ctrs., Balt., 1980—; dir. Ctr. Stress Rsch., Norristown, Pa., 1994—. Dir. mental health, nursery divsn. Dept. Welfare, NYC, 1953—56; cons. Gov., Pa. Dept. Corrections, 1971, Family Crisis Ctr. Balt., 1973—74. Author: (book) The Experience of Enlightenment, 1980, Federal Prisoners' Attitudes Toward Crime and Confinement, 1982, Personality Traits and Behaviorisms of a Well-Adjusted Person, 1993, What Kind of Person is the Drug Addict?, 1996, The Psychodynamics of Self-Hypnosis, 1998, The SEEP Factors in Crime, 1999, (booklet) Comprehensive Therapy Questionnaire, 1978; contbr. articles to profl. jours. With USAF, 1942—46, PTO. Mem.: AAAS, APA. Democrat. Avocations: golf, horseback riding, skiing, water-skiing, tennis. Office Phone: 484-250-2161.

GABERINO, JOHN ANTHONY, JR., lawyer; b. Tulsa, Aug. 6, 1941; s. John A Sr and Elizabeth (McCafferty) Gaberino; m. Marjory Ann Diamond, Aug. 21, 1965; children: Christina M, Megan E, Courtney L, John A III, Kathleen A. AB cum laude, Georgetown U., Washington, DC, 1963, JD, 1966. Bar: Okla 1966, US Dist Ct (no & we dists) Okla, US Ct Appeals (10th cir) 1968, US Tax Ct 1968, US Supreme Ct 1994. Assoc. Huffman, Arrington & Kihle, Tulsa, 1968-75; ptnr. Arrington, Kihle, Gaberino & Dunn, Tulsa, 1975-87, also bd. dirs., 1987-97; sr. v.p., gen. counsel ONEOK, Inc., 1998—2006; shareholder Gable & Gotwals, 2006—. Counsel, bd dirs St Francis Health Sys, Inc, Tulsa, Okla., 1989—97. Chmn. Law Ctr. Alumni Bd. Georgetown U., 1990—92, bd. govs., 1990—2004, chair, 2000—02, bd. dirs., 2000—02; pres. Georgetown U. Club Okla; past chmn. Georgetown U. AAP Okla.; bd. regents Georgetown U., 2002—04; past chmn. Christ the King Bd. Edn.; past pres. bd. trustees Monte Cassino Sch.; past chmn. bd. trustees Monte Cassino Sch. Endowment Fund; bd. dirs. W.K. Warren Found, Tulsa Pub. Schs. Found., Tulsa Area United Way, 2000—, campaign chmn., vice chmn., 2005, chmn. bd. dirs., 2006; bd. dirs. Operation Aware Inc., 1987—95, chmn. bd. dirs., 2006; bd. dirs. The Salvation Army-Tulsa Region, 2002—04. Capt US Army, 1966—68. Recipient John Carroll Medal, Georgetown Univ, 1993. Mem.: NCCJ (bd. dirs. Tulsa chpt. pres. 1993—95, Ann. Dinner honoree 2003), Okla. Fellows of the Am. Bar Found. (chair 2000—01), Tulsa County Bar Found (bd. dirs. 1993—99, pres. 1994), Tulsa Bar Asn (sec. 1988, chmn. constn. and bylaws com., bd. dirs. 1989, 1991—94, pres. 1993), Okla Bar Asn (mem. bd. govs. 1990—92, 1995, v.p. 1995, mem. bd. govs. 1997—99, pres. 1998), Metropolitan Tulsa CofC (bd. dirs. 1996—, chair 2001, CEO 2006), Southern Hills Country Club (mem. bd. govs. 1990—95, 1st v.p. 1991—93, pres. 1994), Knights Holy Sepulchre (chair Tulsa Diocese rev. bd. 2002—, hon. soc. Cath ch.), Phi Beta Kappa. Republican. Roman Catholic. Avocation: golf. Office: Gable & Gotwals 100 W 5th St Ste 1100 Tulsa OK 74103-4217 Office Phone: 918-595-4868. Business E-Mail: jgaberino@gablelaw.com.

GABERMAN, HARRY, retired lawyer; b. Springfield, Mass., May 6, 1913; s. Nathan and Elizabeth (Binder) G.; m. Ingeborg Luise Gruda, Sept. 24, 1953; children: Claudia, Natalie Razzook, Victor Lucius. JD, George Washington U., 1941; LLM, Cath. U. Am., 1954. Bar: D.C. 1942. Priorities analyst War Prodn. Bd., 1942, asst. indsl. and indsl. analyst, 1943-45; asst. chief industry control sect., legal and intercorp. rels. analyst U.S. Mil. Govt. and U.S. High Commn. for Germany, Berlin, Frankfurt, Bonn; atty.-investigator, atty-advisor; indsl. specialist, bus. economist U.S. Mil. Govt. and U.S. High Commn. for Germany, Berlin, Frankfurt, Bonn, 1945—53; asst. legal advisor, attache, dep. U.S. agt. Italian-U.S. Conciliation Commn., Am. Embassy, Rome, 1953; pvt. practice Washington, 1953-55; intelligence analyst Army Transp. Intelligence Agy., Gravelly Point, Va., 1955-56; supervisory atty.-advisor, atty.-advisor Air Force Sys. Command, Andrews AFB, Md., 1956-75; ret. Asst. to U.S. mem. Four-power liquidation of German War Potential Com., Berlin, 1946; chief deconcentration br. U.S. High Commn., Frankfurt, 1949; acting dep. U.S. mem. law com. Allied Kommandatura, Berlin, 1951; U.S. mem. 3-power Film Reorgn. Com., Bonn, 1949-50. Contbr. articles to profl. jours. Recipient Profl. Achievement award George Washington U. Law Assn., 1983. Mem. Fed. Bar Assn. (dep. coun. and com. coord. 1982, coun. and com. coord. 14 substantive law couns. containing 83 constituent coms. 1983, chmn. coun. on govt. contracts 1970-75, 80-81, chmn. internat. procurement com. 1977-79, dep. chmn. sect. on internat. law and its newsletter editor 1984-97, dep. chmn. sect. on internat. law and its newsletter contbg. editor 1998-99, found. advisor 1996-2000; numerous Disting. Svc. and other awards), D.C. Bar Assn. (chmn. govt. contracts com. 1964-66), Diplomatic and Consular Officers Ret. (charter mem., DACOR House), Am. Fgn. Svcs. Assn., Air Force Assn. Avocations: walking, reading, listening to classic and semi-classic music.

GABLE, CARL IRWIN, writer, investor, retired lawyer; b. Charleston, SC, Aug. 7, 1939; s. Carl Irwin and Charlotte Belle (Kersey) G.; m. Sarah Alice Bogle, June 6, 1964; children: Ashley Grinnell, Carl Irwin III, James Kersey. BA, Harvard U., 1961; JD, Harvard, 1964. Bar: Ga. 1964, D.C. 1976. Assoc. Kilpatrick & Cody, Atlanta, 1964-70, ptnr., 1970-84; pres. Interface Inc., Atlanta, 1984-85; vice chmn. Intermet Corp., Atlanta, 1985-90, also bd. dirs.; of counsel Booth, Owens & Jospin, 1992—96, Troutman Sanders L.L.P., Atlanta, 1996-98. Pres. Boglewood Corp., Kiev, Ukraine, 1993-96; bd. dirs. Interface, Inc. Contbr. articles to profl. jours.; author: Murano Magic, 2004; co-author (Sarah B. Gable): Palladian Days, 2005. Bd. dirs. Atlanta Coun. Internat. Visitors, Inc., 1987-93, Atlanta Opera, Inc., 1980-2002, Michael Carlos Mus. Emory U., 1994-2003; bd. dirs. Spoleto Festival USA, Inc., 1993-99, treas., 1993-95; founder, chmn. Atlanta Opera Endowment, Inc., 1986-2000; pres. Ctr. for Palladian Studies in Am., Inc., 2006-. Fellow Am. Coll. Investment Counsel; mem. ABA., Capital City Club. Achievements include invention of interlocking modular carpet. Avocation: Italian studies.

GABLE, KAREN ELAINE, retired healthcare educator; b. Des Moines, Nov. 12, 1939; d. John E. and Mabel I. (Davis) Clay; m. Robert W. Gable, Jr., Feb. 4, 1961; children: Susan Kay, Barbara Lynne, R. J. Kent. AS, 1969; BS in Edn., Ind. U., Indpls., 1976, MS in Edn., 1979, EdD, 1985. Registered dental hygienist Ind. U., cert. dental asst. Ind. U. From clin. instr. dental hygiene program Sch. Dentistry to assoc. prof. Ind. U., Indpls., 1976—94, assoc. prof. Sch. Health and Rehab. Scis., 1994—2006, program dir., 1994—2006, chair dept. health sci., 2002—06, prof. emerita, 2006—. Contbr. articles to profl. jours. Recipient Disting. Dental Hygiene Alumna award, Ind. U. Sch. Dentistry. Mem.: ACTE/Health Occupations Edn. (mem. policy bd. 2002—), Ind. Career and Tech. Edn. Assn. (Outstanding Svc. awards), Ind. Dental Hygienists Assn. (sec.), Ind. Health Careers Assn. (pres.-elect, pres.), Health Occupations, Supvs. and Tchr. Educators Coun. (treas., pres.), Sigma Phi Alpha.

GABLE, ROBERT ELLEDY, real estate investment company executive; b. NYC, Feb. 20, 1934; s. Gilbert E. and Paulina (Stearns) G.; m. Emily Brinton Thompson, July 5, 1958; children: James, Elizabeth, John. BS, Stanford U., 1956. With The Stearns Co. Ltd. (formerly Stearns Coal & Lumber Co. Inc.), Lexington, Ky., 1958-60, sec., 1960-70, treas., 1961-62, v.p., 1962-70, chmn. bd., 1970—, pres., dir., 1975-78. Past chmn. bd., dir. Ky. & Tenn. Railway, Stearns, Ky.; past chmn. bd. Lumber King Inc., Stearns; past dir., audit com. Kuhn's Big K Stores Corp., Nashville,

1979-81; dir. emeritus Blue Cross and Blue Shield Ky.; past dir. Bank of McCreary County. Bd. dirs. Lexington Conv. and Tourist Bur., 1982—85, Frazier Rehab. Found., Inc., Louisville, 1982—84, Headley-Whitney Mus., Lexington, 1985—90; pres., CEO Kentuckians for Fair Redistricting, Inc., 2001—03; chmn. Ky. Arts Coun., 2004—05; Rep. candidate for U.S. Senate from Ky., 1972; Ky. co-chmn. Fin. Com. for Re-election of Pres., 1972; mem. Rep. Nat. Com., 1986—94, mem. budget com., 1989, Rep. Nat. Fin. Com., 1971—76; Rep. state fin. chmn., 1973—75, 1986; mem. Ky. Rep. Ctrl. Com., 1974—94, 2004—; state chmn. Rep. Party Ky., 1986—94; Rep. nominee for gov. Ky., 1975, 1995; mem. nat. leadership coun. Rep. Exch. Satellite Network, Nashville, 1993—95; candidate for gov. Ky.; former mem. missions bd. Episcopal Diocese of Lexington; mem. bd. founders Nat. Coun. Econ. Edn. (formerly Joint Coun. Econ. Edn.), NYC, 1982—2000; mem. Nat. Com. for Performing Arts, John F. Kennedy Ctr. for Performing Arts, Washington, 1993—2004, pres., CEO, 1993—97; commr. Ky. Dept. Parks, 1967—70; mem. pub. lands com. Interstate Oil Compact Commn., 1968—70; mem. adv. com. Ky. Ednl. TV, 1971—75; former mem. Breaks Interstate Park Commn.; past pres., past dir. McCreary County Indsl. Devel. Corp.; former trustee Stearns Recreational Assn., Inc.; mem. S.E. regional adv. com. Nat. Pk. Svc., 1973—78, sec., 1977—78; former bd. dirs. Ky. Mountain Laurel Festival Assn., v.p., 1974—75; mem. McCreary County Air Bd., 1967—81; mem. adv. bd. U. Ky. for Somerset Cmty. Coll., 1965—73; trustee George Peabody Coll. for Tchrs., Nashville, 1970—79, mem. exec. com., 1976—79, chmn. bd., 1979; former trustee Capital Day Sch., Frankfort, Ky.; bd. dirs., past chmn., past pres., founder Ky. Coun. on Econ. Edn., Inc.; trustee Ky. State U. Found., 1979—82, Vanderbilt U., Nashville, 1979—87, mem. budget com.; bd. trustees Ky. Better Roads Coun., Inc., vice chmn., 1976—79; bd. trustees Epworth Assembly, Ludington, Mich., 1995—2001, treas., 1995—2000, pres., 2000—01; founding bd. Lexington Fund for the Arts, 1984—86; mem. So. Assn. of Rep. State Chmn., 1987—94; apptd. Pres. Adv. Com. Arts, 1992—93; bd. dirs., exec. com. Ky. Ctr. for the Arts, 2004—. Served to lt. (j.g.) USNR, 1956—58. Named Ky. Col., Mr. Coal of Ky., 1970. Mem. Ky. Coal Assn. (dir. 1972-86, exec. com. 1974-78, sec. 1979-86), Ky. C. of C. (regional v.p., 1971-72, 76-80, exec. com. 1971-72, 76-80, dir. 1971-80, fin. com. 1978-79), Lexington C. of C. (dir. 1982, 84-87), Frankfort Country Club, Keeneland Club, Lexington Club, Bluegrass Auto Club (former bd. dirs.), River Valley Club, Capitol Hill Club, Coral Beach Club, Tau Beta Pi, Alpha Kappa Lambda (past chpt. pres.). Home: 1715 Stonehaven Dr Frankfort KY 40601-8624 Office: 200 W Vine St Ste 600 Lexington KY 40507-1616

GABLER, ELIZABETH BRAND, film company executive; m. Lee Gabler. Agent motion picture literary dept. ICM; creative exec. Columbia Pictures; v.p. prodn. United Artists; with 20th Century Fox, Beverly Hills, Calif., 1988—, exec. v.p. prodn.; pres. Fox 2000 Pictures, 1999—. Mem. adv. bd. Ctr. Film, TV and New Media U. Calif., Santa Barbara. Named one of 100 Most Powerful Women in Entertainment, Hollywood Reporter, 2004, 2005, 2006. Office: 20th Century Fox PO Box 900 Beverly Hills CA 90213-0900*

GABLIK, SUZI, art educator, writer; b. NYC, Sept. 26, 1934; d. Anthony Julius and Geraldine (Schwartz) G. BA, Hunter Coll., 1955. Vis. prof. art Sydney Coll. Arts, 1980, U. of the South, Sewanee, Tenn., 1982, 84, U. Calif., Santa Barbara, 1985, 86, 88, Va. Commonwealth U., Richmond, 1987, Va. Tech., Blacksburg, 1990, U. Colo., Boulder, 1990. Endowed lectr. U. Victoria, B.C., 1983, Colo. Coll., 1983, U. Santa Barbara, 1985, Va. Tech., 1989. Author: Magritte, 1979, Has Modernism Failed?, 1984, The Reenchantment of Art, 1991, Conversations Before the End of Time, 1995, Living the Magical Life, 2002. Recipient Lifetime Achievement award, Women's Caucus for Art, 2003. Home: 3271 Deer Run Rd Blacksburg VA 24060-9075 E-mail: suzi@swva.net.

GABOR-HOTCHKISS, MAGDA, research scientist, librarian; b. Paris, Mar. 21, 1934; arrived in U.S., 1967; adopted d. Andor and Olga (Halpern) Gabor; m. Rollin D. Hotchkiss, May 21, 1967 (dec. Dec. 2004). D of Natural Scis. summa cum laude, Eotvos Lorand Sci. U., 1963. Intern Plant Physiology Humboldt U., Berlin, 1957—58; rsch. asst., rsch. assoc. Inst. Genetics Hungarian Acad. Scis., Budapest, 1959—67; rsch. assoc. Rockefeller U., NYC, 1967—82; asst., assoc. libr. Hancock Shaker Village Mus., Pittsfield, Mass., 1985—94, coord. libr. collections, 1995—99, vol. libr., archivist, 2000—. Postdoctoral Bacterial Genetics, Animal Viruses Cold Spring Harbor Lab. of Quantitative Biology, NY, 1965; guest investigator Rockefeller U., NYC, 1964—66; mem. adv. bd. We. Mass. Libr. Assn., Hadley, 1996—97; adj. asst. prof. biology SUNY, Albany, NY, 1982—2002, multilingual contbg. indexer for film/lit. index, Film and TV Document Ctr., 1985—94. Author, compiler: Guide to Hancock Shaker Village Library Collections, 2001—03, annotator, editor: The Shaker Image, 1994; contbr. chpts. to sci. books, articles to sci. jours. Vol. libr. Berkshire Mus., Pittsfield, 1998—; tutor ESL Lit. Vols. Am., Pittsfield, 2001—04. Mem.: N.Y. Acad. Scis., Genetics Soc. Am., Sigma Xi. Achievements include discovery of entry of various forms of purified DNAs into bacterial cells of pneumococcus progresses in a linear fashion; recombination patterns of induced bacterial diploids (via protoplast fusion in Bacillus subtilis) follow the classical mechanism found in eucaryotic cells. Avocations: reading, photography, yoga, languages.

GABORIAU, HENRI P., plastic surgeon; b. Paris, Aug. 14, 1964; arrived in US, 1989; s. Henri and Paule Marie-Louise Gaboriau. BS, Nova U., Ft. Lauderdale, Fla., 1991; MD, Tulane U., New Orleans, 1994. Intern Henri-Mondor Hosp., Paris XII U. Med. Sch., Creteil, France, 1992, Tulane U. Med. Sch., 1994—95, resident, 1995—99; plastic surgeon Sammamish Ctr. Facial Plastic and Reconstuctive Surgery, Wash. Fellow, U. Wash., Seattle, 1999—2000. Office: Sammamish Ctr Facial Plastic Surgery 22840 NE 8th St #103 Sammamish WA 98074

GABOVITCH, STEVEN ALAN, lawyer, accountant; b. Newton, Mass., Feb. 7, 1953; s. William and Annette (Richman) Gabovitch; m. Rhonda Merle Kitover, Aug. 6, 1978; children: Daniel J., Lindsey D. BS in Acctg., Boston Coll., 1975, JD, 1978; LLM in Taxation, Boston U., 1982. CPA Mass.; bar: Mass. 1978, RI 1979, US Dist. Ct. RI 1979, US Tax Ct. 1980, US Ct. Appeals (1st cir.) 1980, US Dist. Ct. Mass. 1981, US Ct. Appeals (fed. cir.) 1982, US Supreme Ct. 1983. Tax specialist Peat, Marwick, Mitchell & Co., Providence, 1978-80; prin. William Gabovitch & Co., Boston, 1980-97; pvt. practice Stoughton, Mass., 1998—. Lectr. bankruptcy taxation. Contbr. articles to profl. jours. Mem.: Boston Bar Assn., Mass. Bar Assn., RI Bar Assn., Beta Gamma Sigma. Office: 378 Page St 3 Deerfield Corp Ctr Stoughton MA 02072 E-mail: steve@gabovitch.com.

GABOW, PATRICIA ANNE, internist, health facility executive; b. Starke, Fla., Jan. 8, 1944; m. Harold N. Gabow, June 21, 1971; children: Tenaya Louise, Aaron Patrick. BA in Biology, Seton Hill Coll., 1965; MD, U. Pa. Sch. Medicine, 1969. Diplomate Am. Bd. Internal Medicine, Am. Bd. Nephrology, Nat. Bd. Med. Examiners; lic. Colo. Internship in medicine Hosp. of U. of Pa., 1969-70; residency in internal medicine Harbor Gen. Hosp., 1970-71; renal fellowship San Francisco Gen. Hosp. and Hosp. of U. Pa., 1971-72, 72-73; instr. medicine divsn. renal diseases, asst. prof. U. Colo. Health Scis. Ctr., 1973-74, 74-79, assoc. prof. medicine divsn. renal diseases, prof., 1979-87; chief renal disease, clin. dir. dept. medicine Denver Gen. Hosp., 1973-81, 76-81, dir. med. svcs., 1981-91; CEO, med. dir. Denver Health and Hosps., 1992—. Intensive care com. Denver Gen. Hosp., 1976-81, med. records com., 1979-80, ind. rev. com., 1978-81, continuing med. edn. com., 1981-83, animal care com., 1979-83; student adv. com. U. Colo. Health Scis. Ctr., 1982-87, faculty senate, 1985, 86, internship adv. com., 1977-92; exec. com. Denver Gen. Hosp., 1981—, chmn. health resources com., 1988-90, chmn. pathology search com., 1989, chmn. faculty practice plan steering com., 1990-92. Mem. editorial bd. EMERGINDEX, 1983-93, Am. Jour. of Kidney Disease, 1984-96, Western Jour. of Medicine, 1987-98, Annals of Internal Medicine, 1988-91, Jour. of the Am. Soc. of Nephrology, 1990-97; contbr. numerous articles, revs. and editorials to profl. publs., chpts. to books. Mem. Mayor's Safe City Task Force, 1993; mem. sci. adv. bd. Polycystic Kidney Rsch. Found., 1984-96, chmn., 1991; mem. sci. adv. bd. Nat. Kidney Found., 1991-94; mem. Nat. Pub. Health and Hosps. Inst. Bd., 1993-2001, 03—. Recipient Sullivan award for Highest Acad. Average in Graduating Class, Seton Hill Coll., 1965, Pa. State Senatorial scholarship, 1961-65, Kaiser Permanente award for Excellence in Tchg., 1976, Ann. award to Outstanding Woman Physician, 1982, Kaiser Permanente Nominee for Excellence in Tchg. award, 1983, Seton Hill Coll. Disting. Alumna Leadership award, 1990, Florence Rena Sabin award U. Colo., 2000, Nathan Davis award AMA, 2000, Good Housekeeping Women in Govt. award, 2002; named one of The Best Doctors in Am., 1994-95, 2002; grantee Bonfils Found., 1985-86, NIH, 1985-90, 91-96, 96-00, W.K. Kellogg Found., 1997—, AHRQ, 2000-03; named to Colo. Women's Hall of Fame, 2004, One of the Top 25 Women in Healthcare, 2005, 100 Most Influential People in Healthcare in Modern Healthcare, Women Who Make a Difference International Women's Forum, 2005. Mem. Denver Med. Soc., Colo. Med. Soc., Am. Fedn. Clin. Rsch., Am. Physiol. Soc., Polycystic Kidney Disease Rsch. Found. (sci. advisor 1984-96), Western Assn. Physicians, Nat. Kidney Found. (sci. adv. bd. 1987-91), Women's Forum of Colo., Inc., Assn. Am. Physicians. Roman Catholic. Office: Denver Health 660 Bannock St Denver CO 80204-4506 Address: Denver Health 777 Bannock St Denver CO 80204

GABRIEL, DIANE AUGUSTA, artist, educator; b. NYC, Sept. 12, 1947; d. Herbert N. and Jean L. (Wertheimer) Gabriel; m. Mark A. Stoler, Aug. 11, 1991; 1 child, Eben Gabriel Cahan. BA, Goddard Coll., Plainfield, Vt., 1976. Designer/owner Diane Gabriel Fiber Arts, Vt., 1977—93; instr. Firehouse Ctr. for the Arts, Vt., 1999; lectr. Helen Day Art Ctr., Stowe, Vt., 2000, Burlington City Arts, Vt., 2000; instr. Studio 250/Print Making Studio, Burlington, 2001, C.C. of Vt., 2003—. Founding mem. 215 Coll. Gallery, Burlington, 2005—; juried artist Vt. Arts Coun., Montepelier, 2005—. One and two person shows, The Doll Anstadt Gallery, Burlington, 1999, The Grannis Gallery, 2002, Lorraine B. Goode Gallery, 2002 (Barbara Smail award, 2003). Fellow, Vt. Studio Ctr., Johnson, 2006. Mem.: Mus. Women in the Arts. Home: 43 Prospect Hill Burlington VT 05401 Personal E-mail: dgabriel1@mac.com.

GABRIEL, DONALD ALBERT, real estate company executive; s. Cecelia Mary Gabriel; m. Catherine Mary Guttenberger; 1 child, Barbara Anne. AA, Balt. City CC, 1957—59; BS, U. Md., College Park, 1959—62; JD, U. Balt., 1968—72; PhD, Calif. Coast U., Santa Anna, 1976—78. Cert. in aging Johns Hopkins U., 2003; in mgmt. Towson U., 1978, in meeting adminstrn. Goucher Coll., 1994, in mktg. Goucher Coll., 1996, in profl. fundraising Goucher Coll., 1997, in non-profit orgns. Goucher Coll., 1998, hist. studies Goucher Coll., 2000, environ. studies Johns Hopkins U., 2001. Pres. Ivy League Fin. Svcs., Balt., 1972—; chief real estate appraiser Balt. County Govt., Towson, 1989—. Bd. mem. Inst. ND, 1992—98, Essex CC, Md., 1997—2005, Balt. City CC, 1998—2005, Mosaic Cmty. Svcs., Towson, 1999—2005, Balto. Co. Ethics Review Panel Bd, 1999—2005, St. Elizabeth Sch., Balt., 2002—05. E-4 US Coast Guard, 1962—68, Balt. Recipient Alumnai Hall Fame, Balt. City CC, 2003. Mem.: Appraisal Inst. (pres. Md. chpt. 2002—03), Am. Soc. Appraisers (pres. Md. chpt. 1990—91). Office: Balt County Govt 111 W Chesapeake Ave Baltimore MD 21204

GABRIEL, DONALD EUGENE, science educator; b. Brush, Colo., May 24, 1944; s. Max and Vera Ellen (Coleman) G.; m. Evonne Kay Asheim, Sept. 27, 1964; children: Shawn Lee, Dawn Kay. AA, Northeastern Jr. Coll., Sterling, Colo., 1964; BA, Colo. State Coll., 1967; MA, U. No. Colo., 1972. Cert. secondary chemistry tchr. Tchr. sci. and math. Brush (Colo.) H.S., 1967—. Adv. bd. mem. Colo. Sci. and Engring. Fair, Fort Collins, 1980—; ea. zone chairperson Colo.-Wyo. Jr. Acad. Sci., Fort Morgan, Colo., 1980—; co-dir. Morgan-Washington BiCounty Sci. Fair, Fort Morgan, 1975—. Contbr. articles to profl. jours. Pres. South Platte Valley BOCES, Fort Morgan, 1993-99, v.p., 1991-93; Eagle Scout reviewer Boy Scouts Am., Fort Morgan, 1990—; sec., treas. Brush Pub. Schs., 1995-99. Grantee Tandy Corp., 1989, Joslin Needhams Found., 1990; recipient Presdl. award NSF, 1994; named Milken Nat. Educator, Milken Found., 1991, Tandy Tech. Scholars Outstanding Tchr., 1994-95, Pub. Svc. Co. of Colo. Classroom Connection awards, 1993-99, S. Platte Valley Bd. of Coop. Ednl. Svcs. grants, 1995-98. Mem. Nat. Sci. Tchrs. Assn. (Presdl. award 1994), Colo. Assn. Sci. Tchrs. (regional dir. 1993-96, Outstanding Tchr. 1990). Republican. Lutheran. Avocations: arrowhead hunting, rock hounding. Home: 26137 MCR S 2 Brush CO 80723 Office: Brush HS PO Box 585 Brush CO 80723-0585

GABRIEL, EBERHARD JOHN, lawyer, bank executive; b. Bucharest, Romania, Mar. 22, 1942; arrived in US, 1952, naturalized, 1955; s. William and Margaret (Eberhart) Krzyzewski; m. Janice Josephine Jedrzejewski, Aug. 21, 1965; children: John, Stephanie, Christopher. BA in English, St. Joseph's Coll. of Ind., 1963; JD, Georgetown U., 1966. Bar: Md. 1966, U.S. Supreme Ct. 1972, Minn. 1993. Staff atty. Fgn. Claims Settlement Commn., Washington, 1966-68; sr. v.p., gen. counsel Govt. Employees Fin. Corp., Denver, 1968-87; pres., CEO MNC Am. Indsl. Banks, Denver, 1987-89; v.p., asst. gen. counsel and chief compliance officer ITT Consumer Fin. Corp., Mpls., 1989-94; pvt. practice Mpls., 1994-95; coun. Comml. Credit Co., Balt., 1995-99; sr. v.p., gen. counsel Citibank USA, Wilmington, Del., 1995—2002; assoc. gen. counsel CitiFin., Balt., 2002—04; sr. v.p., gen. counsel Citicorp Trust Bank, Irving, Tex., 2004—. Fellow St. Joseph's Coll.; sec., treas. Indsl. Bank Savs. Guaranty Corp., Colo., 1973—83, pres., 1983—87; lectr. advanced mgmt. program Am. Fin. Svcs. Assn., 1974—81, 1985, 87, mem. law com., 1978—89, bd. dirs., 1988—89. Bd. dirs. Jeffco/Lakewood (Colo.) C. of C., 1974—80, 1982—86, chmn., 1984—85; mem. Jefferson County DA Adult Diversion Coun., 1985—89; mem. adv. coun. Colo. Office Regulatory Reform, Colo. Dept. Regulatory Agys., 1984—89; chmn. Lakewood on Parade, 1980; vice chmn. fin. divsn. United Way Metro Denver, 1982; trustee Lakewood Polit. Action com., 1978—89, chmn., 1986—87. Mem.: Am. Counsel Assn., Phi Alpha Delta. Roman Catholic. Office: Citicorp Trust Bank 9113 Gardenia Dr Denton TX 76207 Office Phone: 469-220-4094. Personal E-mail: gabelex@aol.com. Business E-Mail: eberhard.j.gabriel@citigroup.com.

GABRIEL, JEANETTE HANISEE, curator, art historian; b. Long Beach, Calif., Jan. 12, 1940; d. William Edward and Lorena Lester; m. Robert Maxwell Hanisee, Sept. 28, 1973 (div. 1986); children: Robb Andrew Hanisee, Michele Alpoente Hanisee, Leigh Mathilde Hanisee, Caleb Joseph Hanisee, Patricia Lorena Hanisee, Molly Beverly Hanisee; m. Angelo Julius Gabriel, Oct. 1, 1992. BS, MS, Calif. State U., Northridge, 1978; MA, U. Calif., Santa Barbara, 1988. Instr. Ventura Coll., Calif., 1979—81; dir., founder Adoptions Unltd., Ontario, Calif., 1981—83; curator L.A. County Mus. Art, 1988—92, Gilbert Collection, London, 1994—2002; dir. art collections Gilbert Found.; pvt. practice, 2003—. Author: The Gilbert Collection Micromosaics, 2000, The Gilbert Collection Hardstones; co-author: By Judgement of the Eye: The Varya and Hans Cohn Collection at the Los Angeles County Museum of Art, 1991, The World of Jade, 1992; contbr. articles to profl. jours Mem. Internat. Churchill Soc., Churchill Ctr. (founder, Clementine Churchill assoc. 1998), Reform Club London Avocations: antiques, writing. Personal E-mail: jeanettegabriel@aol.com.

GABRIEL, JUDITH A., bodywork therapist, educator, writer; b. Reading, Pa., July 14, 1949; d. Daniel Jacob and Alma Geraldine (Wengel) Tobias; m. Cleon Jay Hertzog, Oct. 5, 1974 (div. 1987). BS, Kutztown U., 1971, MEd, 1977; cert. massage therapist, Pa. Sch. Muscle Therapy, Phila., 1989; further tng., U.S. and Sweden. Cert. tchr. Pa., bodywork therapist. Tchr. Hamburg (Pa.) Area Sch. Dist., 1971-96; bodywork therapist, owner, operator Judith Gabriel Integrational Bodywork, Reading, Pa., 1989—; Rebirther (breathwork counseling) Reading, Pa., 1988—. Presenter WIOV Radio, 1997; asst. Patrick Collard's Internat. Apprenticeship, 1997, 98, 99; prodr. concert A Tribute to John Denver: The Man and His Music, Kempton, Pa., 2000; prodr. A Tribute to John Denver: The Man and His Music concert, Kempton, Pa., 2001; organizer Hibernia County Park, Pa., 2002; pres., CEO, The John Denver Meml. Found., Inc.; presenter Tuly's Conf. for Women, Reading, Pa., 2003; prodr., pres./CEO John Denver Meml. Found., Inc.; prodr. concert A Tribute to John Denver: The Man and His Music, Hibernia County Park, Pa., 2002; presenter Tulip Conf. for Women, Reading, Pa., 2003. Choir singer various chs., Reading; stress mgmt. demonstrator Berks Advocates Against Violence, Reading, 1997. Recipient Corp. Achiever award, Multiple Sclerosis Found., 2002. Mem.: Berks C. of C., Assoc. Bodyworkers and Massage Profls. (cert. massage therapist, cert. bodywork therapist). Avocations: reading, walking, singing, meditation, travel.

GABRIEL, MICHAEL, psychology professor; b. Phila., May 5, 1940; s. Michael and Josephine (Alesio) G.; m. Linda Prinz, June, 1967 (div.); 1 child, Joseph Michael; m. Sonda S. Walsh, 1984. AB in Psychology, St. Joseph's Coll., 1962; MA, U. Wis., 1965, PhD, 1967. Asst. prof. Pomona Coll., Claremont, Calif., 1967—70; staff psychologist Pacific State Hosp., Pomona, Calif., 1968-70; NIMH sr. postdoctoral fellow U. Calif.-Irvine, 1970-72; asst. prof. U. Tex.-Austin, 1973-77, assoc. prof., 1977-82; prof. psychology U. Ill., Urbana, 1982—2004, appointee Ctr. for Advanced Study, 1990-91, prof. emeritus dept. psychology and Beckman Inst., 2004. Area chmn. Biol. Psychology Program, U. Tex., Austin, 1979-82; mem. rev. panel in behavioral and neural scis. NSF, 1988-91, prin. investigator database system for neuronal pattern analysis project, 1992—, ad hoc mem. biopsychology rev. panel, 1997-98; faculty Beckman Inst., U. Ill., Urbana, 1989—; chmn. Neuronal Pattern Analysis Group, Beckman Inst., mem. neuroinformatics rev. panel, NIH, 2000-. Co-editor: (with J. Moore) Learning and Computational Neuroscience: Foundations of Adaptive Networks, 1989, (with B. Vogt) Neurobiology of Cingulate Cortex and Limbic Thalamus, 1993; mem. editl. bd. Neural Plasticity, Neurobiology of Learning and Memory. Grantee NIMH, 1978-88, 1998-2002, NIH, 1988-2003, Air Force Office Sci. Rsch., 1988-91, NSF, 1992-2003, NIDA, 1996-2001. Fellow Am. Psychol. Soc., Internat. Behavioral Neurosci. Soc.; mem. Sigma Chi. pioneered methods for multi-site recording and analysis of neuronal activity during learning in behaving animal subjects; identification of key elements of the neural circuitry for avoidance learning; made major breakthroughs in understanding neural circuitry for contextual facilitation of memory retrieval; documentation of specific functional brain changes resulting from exposure to cocaine in utero. Office: Beckman Inst Univ Ill Urbana IL 61801-2325 Business E-Mail: mgabriel@uiuc.edu.

GABRIEL, MORDECAI LIONEL, biologist, educator; b. NYC, Mar. 18, 1918; s. Joseph and Bertha (Fram) G.; m. Elinor Rosenstein, Nov. 11, 1945; children— Alisa, Jessica. AB, Yeshiva U., 1938; MA, Columbia, 1938, PhD, 1944. Instr. genetics U. Conn., 1943-45; mem. faculty Bklyn. Coll., 1945—, prof. biology, 1963—, chmn. dept., 1965-71; dean Bklyn. Coll. (Sch. Sci.), 1971-76, acting v.p. for acad. affairs, 1981-82; assoc. provost Bklyn. Coll., 1982-88, assoc. provost emeritus, 1988—. Vis. prof. Columbia, 1956; Fulbright lectr., vis. prof. U. Tel Aviv, 1959-60; mem. Marine Biol. Lab., Woods Hole, Mass., 1950— Author: (with S. Fogel) Great Experiments in Biology, 1956. Ford Found. faculty fellow, 1955-56 Fellow AAAS; mem. Am. Soc. Zoologists, Am. Assn. Anatomists, N.Y. Acad. Scis., Soc. Study Evolution, Vertebrate Paleont. Soc., AAUP (pres. Bklyn. Coll. chpt. 1964-66), Phi Beta Kappa, Sigma Xi. Home: 120 Old Mill Rd Great Neck NY 11023-1936

GABRIEL, PETER PAUL, business educator; b. Halle, Germany, July 11, 1929; s. Paul and Eva Wernecke G.; m. Linea Elizabeth Larson, Sept. 9, 1950; children: Paul Lawrence, John Peter, Kathryn Anne, Christina Eva. MBA, Harvard U., 1962, DBA, 1965. Various adminstrv. positions, Germany, France, S. Am., 1948-60; assoc. McKinsey & Co., NYC, 1966-69, ptnr., 1969-73; prof. of mgmt. dean Sch. of Mgmt. Boston U., 1972-76; prof. bus. adminstrn. U. Ulm, Germany, 1989-92. Contbr. articles and essays to publs. in field of internat. bus. and investment Recipient G.M. Loeb award for Disting. Writing in Bus. and Fin., U. Conn., 1967, Horace G. Crockett award McKinsey & Co., N.Y., 1966. Home: 240 Beldingville Rd Ashfield MA 01330

GABRIEL, RONALD SAMUEL, child neurologist; b. Monterey, Calif., Mar. 19, 1937; s. Philip Louis and Theresa Shaheen Gabriel; children: Philip Louis III, Paula Shaheen, Matthew William. BA with honors, Yale U., 1959; MD, Boston U., 1963. Diplomate Am. Bd. Psychiatry and Neurology (examiner 1978-88), Am. Bd. Pediatrics. Intern, resident in pediatrics Los Angeles County Gen. Hosp., 1963-66; fellow in neurology and pediatric neurology UCLA med. ctr., 1966-68, 70-71; head physician, cons. Calif. Children's Svcs., 1970—; clin. prof. neurology/pediatrics UCLA Sch. Medicine, 1971—, dir. pediat. neurology/outpatient, 1971-76. Cons. Regional Ctr.-Calif., 1971—; vis. prof. Prince of Wales, Royal Children's Hosp., Sydney and Melbourne, Australia, 1978; mem. expert panel L.A. Superior Ct., 1992—; founding and mng. gen. ptnr. Med. Imaging of So. Calif., L.A., 1980-94; mng. dir. GFA Cattle and Farm Co. Author: The 410 Shotgun, 2000, Diary of a Mountain Hunter, 2000; contbr.: Textbook of Child Neurology, 1974, 4 edits., 1990, Difficult Diagnoses in Pediatrics, 1990, Founders of Child Neurology, 1990. Mng. dir. GFF Natural History Mus. Maj. U.S. Army, 1968-70. Spl. fellow Nat. Inst. Neurol. Disease/Stroke, 1966-68, 70-71. Fellow Am. Acad. Pediatrics, Am. Acad. Neurology; mem. Calif. Med. Assn. (mem. sci. adv. panel 1987-94, chmn. sci. adv. com. 1989-90). Roman Catholic. Avocations: writing, mountain climbing, hunting. Office: Neurology-Pediat Neurology Assocs 2080 Century Park E Ste 203 Los Angeles CA 90067-2005 Fax: (310) 277-9285.

GABRIEL, STUART A., real estate professor, director; PhD in Econs., U. Calif., Berkeley. Asst. prof. Dept. Econs. Ben-Gurion U. of Negev, Israel, 1982—85; rsch. assoc. Jacob Blaustein Inst. Desert Rsch., Israel, 1982—85; vis. asst. prof. U. Calif., Berkeley, 1986—86; staff economist Div. Rsch. and Statistics, Bd. Govs. of Fed. Reserve Sys., Washington, 1986—90; assoc. prof. Dept. Fin. and Bus. Econs. Marshall Sch. Bus., U. So. Calif., 1990—94, prof., 1994—2007, dep. dean. academic programs, 1997—99, dir., Lusk chair real estate Lusk Ctr. for Real Estate; Arden realty chair, prof. fin., dir. Richard S. Ziman Ctr. for Real Estate UCLA, 2007—. Vis. scholar Fed. Reserve Bank of San Francisco. Office: Richard S Ziman Ctr for Real Estate UCLA Anderson Sch Mgmt 110 Westwood Plaza, Gold Hall, Ste B100 Los Angeles CA 90095-1481 Office Phone: 310-206-9424. Office Fax: 304-267-5391. E-mail: ziman.center@anderson.ucla.edu.*

GABRIEL, TRIP (BERTRAM GABRIEL III), editor; s. Bertram and Helen Gabriel; m. Alice Elizabeth Simon, June 29, 1985. BA, Middlebury Coll. Fashion editor NY Times; editor Sunday Styles of the Times; now style editor NY Times. Contbr. NY Times, Rolling Stone, Outside, 1985—. Office: NY Times Style Desk 229 W 43rd St New York NY 10036

GABRIELSE, GERALD, physics professor; BS with honors, Calvin Coll., Grand Rapids, Mich., 1973; MS, U. Chgo., 1975, PhD, 1980. Rsch.

assoc. U. Wash., Seattle, 1978—82, Chaim Weizmann postdoctoral fellow, 1979—82, rsch. asst. prof., 1982—85, asst. prof., 1985—86, assoc. prof., 1986—87; prof. physics Harvard U., Cambridge, Mass., 1987—, George Vasmer Leverett prof. physics, 2003—. Scientist in residence Lexington Christian Acad., 1995—96; cons. Intermagnetics Gen. Corpn., 1995, PolyChip, Inc., 1999; chair physics dept. Harvard U., 2000—03. Contbr. articles to sci. jours. Vice chair bd. dirs. North Shore Christian Sch., 1994—95; bd. trustees Calvin Coll., 1995—2000, chair edn. com., 1998—2000; bd. trustees Trinity Christian Coll., 2003—06. Recipient Alexander von Humboldt Rsch. award, Germany, 2005. Fellow: Am. Phys. Soc. (Davisson-Germer prize 2002); mem.: NAS. Office: Physics Dept Harvard U 17 Oxford St Cambridge MA 02138 Office Phone: 617-495-4381. E-mail: gabrielse@hussle.harvard.edu.*

GABRIELSON, CHARLES, publishing executive; Various mgt. pos. Gannett Co., Inc., 1971—84; formerly advert. dir. Bambergers Co., NY; mkt. sales dir. Advert. Age , 1986—89; exec. V.P., USA Weekend Gannett Co., Inc., 1989—96, pub. USA Weekend, 1996—. Office: Gannett Co Inc 535 Madison Ave Fl 21 New York NY 10022-4212

GABRILOVE, JACQUES LESTER, physician; b. NYC, Sept. 21, 1917; s. Benjamin and Pauline (Levine) G.; m. Hilda R. Weiss, May 19, 1946 (dec.); children: Sandra Leslie Saltzman, Janice Lynn Gabrilove Dirzulaitis. BS magna cum laude, CCNY, 1936; MD Alpha Omega Alpha prize, NYU, 1940. Diplomate Am. Bd. Internal Medicine. Intern Mt. Sinai Hosp., NYC, 1940-41, rotating intern, 1941-43, vol. radiology, 1943, resident medicine, 1943-44, Blumenthal fellow medicine, 1946-48, research asst. medicine, 1949-51, asst. attending physician, 1952-60, assoc. attending physician, 1960-68, attending physician, 1969—. Clin. prof. medicine Mt. Sinai Sch. Medicine, 1969-82, chief endocrine clinic, 1969-92, Baumritter prof., 1982-90, Baumritter prof. emeritus, 1990—, prof., 1995—, cting dir. divsn. endocrinology, 1985, assoc. dir. divsn., 1986-2005, dir. endocrine fellowship program, 1986—; Libman fellow in medicine Yale U., 1945; clin. asst. prof. SUNY Coll. Medicine, N.Y.C., 1957-59, clin. assoc. prof., 1959-66, clin. prof., 1966-69, professorial lectr., 1969—; cons. endocrinology VA Hosp., East Orange, N.J., 1958-66, Elizabeth A. Horton Hosp., Middletown, N.Y., 1961—, VA Hosp., Bronx, N.Y., 1969—, Norwalk (Conn.) Hosp., 1974—, Elmhurst (N.Y.) City Hosp., St. Francis Hosp., Port Jervis, N.Y.; mem. panel on metabolic and rheumatoid diseases U.S. Pharmacopeia, 1956; mem. spl. com. on rsch. tng. grants in diabetes, endocrinology and metabolism NIH, 1976-79, mem. com. on diabetes rsch. and tng. ctrs., 1977-79; Saltzman lectr. Mt. Sinai Hosp., Cleve., 1974; cons. Jour. Urology, 1984-89. Mem. editl. bd. Mt. Sinai Jour.; contbr. chpts. to books, articles to profl. jours. Trustee, v.p. area Jewish synagogue. Recipient Globus prize Mt. Sinai Jour., Townsend Harris medal CCNY Alumni Assn., 1998; J. Lester Gabrilove award established in his honor, 1988; Hilda and J. Lester Gabrilove MD Divsn. Endocrinology, Diabetes and Bone Disease named in his honor, 2007; named to Hall of Fame Alumni Assn. Townsend Harris H.S. Fellow ACP, Am. Coll. Endocrinology (Disting. Clin. Endocrinologist award 1996, Festschrift in his honor on 80th birthday, Hilda and J. Lester Gabrilove MD divsn. endocrinology, diabetes and bone disease named in his honor 2007, Ann. J. Lester Gabrilove MD lectureship named in his honor 2007), N.Y. Acad. Medicine, Phi Beta Kappa; mem. AMA, AAAS, Am. Assn. Clin. Endocrinologists (Disting. Clin. Endocrinologist award 1996), Am. Diabetes Assn., Harvey Soc., Endocrine Soc., Royal Soc. Medicine, Pan Am. Med. Assn. (v.p. N.Am. endocrinology), Peruvian Endocrine Soc. (hon.), N.Y. Acad. Scis., N.Y. County Med. Soc., N.Y. Diabetes Assn., Mt. Sinai Alumni Assn. (pres. 1970, Jacobi medallion 1973), Lotos Club (bd. dirs.), Alpha Omega Alpha. Achievements include research in delineaton of hyperfunctioning and hypofunctioning endocrine disorders of the adrenal cortex and gonads; mechanism of gynecomastia; medical treatment of thyrotoxicosis; medical treatment of benign prostatic hyperplasia; pathogenesis of the polycystic ovary syndrome. Home: 25 E 86th St New York NY 10028-0553 Office Phone: 212-241-5907. Business E-Mail: lester.gabrilove@mssm.edu.

GABRILOVICH, DMITRY I., immunologist, educator; b. Minsk, Belarus, May 24, 1961; s. Isaak and Galina Gabrilovich; m. Yulia Nefedova, Aug. 16, 2002; children: Jacob, Sofia, Alyssa, Lev. MD, Kabardino-Blakarian State U., Nalchik, Russia, 1984; PhD, Ctrl. Inst. Epidemiology, Moscow, 1989. Rsch. asst. prof. Vanderbilt U., Nashville, 1997—98; asst. prof. pathology Loyola U., Chgo., 1999—2000; assoc. prof. interdisciplinary oncology U. South Fla., Tampa, 2000—05, prof. interdisciplinary oncology and molecular medicine, 2005—. Editor several rsch. monographs; contbr. more than 100 articles to profl. jours. Named Scientist of Yr., H. Lee Moffitt Cancer Ctr., 2006; grantee, NIH, 1999—; Rsch. grantee, Am. Cancer Soc., 1999—, Dept. Def., 2000, Myeloma Rsch. Found., 2005—07, Cancer Treatment Rsch. Found., 2006. Mem.: Am. Assn. Immunologists, Am. Cancer Soc. Office: H Lee Moffitt Cancer Ctr MRC 2067 12902 Magnolia Dr Tampa FL 33612 Office Phone: 813-903-6863.

GAD, LANCE STEWART, investment advisor, lawyer, private investor; s. Martin Harold and Claire (Entner) G.; m. Helen Alexandra Grevey, Jan. 14, 1972 (div. 1978); m. Janiece Lee Feiden, Feb. 14, 1987. BA cum laude, SUNY, Stony Brook, 1967; JD, Cornell U., 1970, MBA, 1971; LLM in Taxation, NYU, 1975. Assoc. Spear & Hill, NYC, 1971-72, Wien, Malkin & Bettex, NYC, 1972-74; mgr. Wheelabrator-Frye, NYC, 1974-75, Citicorp, NYC, 1975-86, Citibank N.A., NYC, 1975-77, asst. v.p., 1977-79, v.p., 1979-86; v.p., gen. counsel and sec. Citicorp Services, Inc., NYC, 1980-85; v.p. Citicorp Investment Bank, NYC, 1985-86; investment advisor WR Family Assocs., NYC, 1986-90, Am. Securities Corp., NYC, 1986-90; chmn., mng. dir., chief investment officer Greenfield Hill Capital Mgmt., 1991—; chmn., pres., treas., dir. The Lance and Janiece Gad Found., Inc., 1987—; special advisor OC Fin. Inc., 2006—. Deans spl. leadership com. Cornell Law Sch., 2000—; chmn. 2005 Reunion Campaign Cornell Law Sch. Class of 1970; co-pres. family coun. Jewish Home for the Elderly, 2001—04. Mem. NY State Bar Assn., Cornell Law Assn., Johnson Sch. Mgmt. Alumni Assn., NY U. Grad. Law Alumni Assn., Cornell Club NY (founding mem.). Office: 1250 Fence Row Dr Fairfield CT 06824 also: 6 Peter Cooper Rd Apt 8F New York NY 10010-6709 also: 14 N Hollow Dr East Hampton NY 11937 Office Phone: 203-259-5291. Business E-Mail: lancegad@optonline.net.

GADAGKAR, RAGHAVENDRA, ecologist, educator, entomologist; b. India, June 28, 1953; married; 1 child. BSc with honors in Zoology, Bangalore U., 1972, MSc in Zoology; PhD in Molecular Biology, Indian Inst. Sci., Bangalore, 1979. Rsch. officer Indian Inst. Sci. Ctr. Theoretical Studies, Bangalore, 1979—80, rsch. assoc., 1980—83, sr. rsch. fellow, 1983—84, assoc. mem., 1987—; lectr. Indian Inst. Sci. Ctr. Ecol. Scis., 1984—87, asst. prof., 1987—91, assoc. prof., 1991—97, prof., 1997—; chmn. Indian Inst. Sci. Ctr. Contemporary Studies. Short-term fellow Smithsonian Tropical Rsch. Inst., Panama, 1980—81; vis. scholar dept. entomology U. Kans., Lawrence, 1982; chmn. Indian Inst. Sci. Ctr. Ecol. Scis., 1992—2002; hon. prof. Behavioural Ecology Lab. Jawaharlal Nehru Ctr. for Advanced Sci. Rsch. Evolutionary and Organismal Biology Unit, Bangalore; hon. sr. fellow Jawaharlal Nehru Ctr. for Advanced Sci. Rsch., 1993—98, hon. prof. Indian Inst. Sci. campus, 1998—2005; sec. Indian Acad. Scis., 1995—2000; vis. faculty mem. Manipal Acad. Higher Edn., 1997—; Schering fellow Inst. Advanced Study, Berlin, 2000—01, guest of the rektor, 2001—02, non-resident permanent fellow, 2002—; v.p. Indian Nat. Sci. Acad., New Delhi, 2003—05; disting. vis. scholar U. Pretoria, South Africa, 2003; mem. Indian delegation Inter-acad. Panel and Internat. Coun. for Sci., China, 2005; internat. lectr. Mem. editl. bd.: Jour. Genetics, 1984—, Jour. Biosciences, 1991—, Insectes Sociaux, 1991—, Jour. Bombay Natural Hist. Soc., 1993—, Current Sci., 1994—, Ecotropica, 1995—97, Jour. Parasitology and Applied Animal Biology, 1997—, Mathematical Modelling and Analysis of Complex Systems, 2001—, Jour. Ethology, 2002—, mem. editl. adv. bd.: Israel Jour. Zoology, 1992—98, Ecol. Rsch., 1996—, mem. planning grp.: Jour. Sci. Edn., 1995, assoc. editor: Resonance, 1996—2001; editor, 2002—04; spl. corr. Down to Earth, 1996—; subject editor: Biotropica, 2003—04, mem. bd. reviewing editors: Science, 2003—, mem. publ. adv. bd.: Indian Nat. Sci. Acad., 2003—05; contbr. articles to sci. jours. Recipient Dr. A. Krishna Murthy award for the best paper, Soc. of Biol. Chemists, 1982, cert. of appreciation as a young scientist, Lion's Club Internat., 1987, Saraswathi Narayanan award in biol. scis., 1990—91, Prof. T.N. Anathakrishnan award, 1990—91, B.M. Birla sci. prize in biology, 1991, Shanti Swarup Bhatnagar award in biol. scis., 1993, Swami Pranavananda Saraswathi award in environ. sci. and ecology, 2002, Vasvik award, 2002, Rustum Choksi award for excellence in rsch. for sci., 2004; grantee Homi Bhabha fellowship, 1992—94, B.P. Pal Nat. Environ. fellowship on biodiversity, Indian Ministry of Environ. and Forests, 1995—97. Fellow: Third World Acad. Scis. (Award in biology 1999), Indian Acad. Entomology, Nat. Acad. Scis., India (U.S. Srivastava Meml. Lecture award), Indian Nat. Sci. Acad. (Young Scientist medal in animal scis. 1985), Indian Acad. Scis. (Young Assoc. 1984); mem.: Indian Soc. Devel. Biologists, AAAS, Indian Sci. Congress Assn., Nat. Inst. Ecology, Jaipur, Indian Complex Systems Soc., Am. Soc. Naturalists, Internat. Soc. Behavioral Ecology, Bangalore Bee Keepers Assn., Assn. for Tropical Biology, Ctr. for Sci. and Environment, Internat. Soc. Hymenopterists, Karnataka Assn. for Advancement of Sci. (Young Scientist award in biol. scis. 1984), Bombay Natural Hist. Soc., Ethological Soc. India, Internat. Union for Study of Social Insects, Indian chpt., Internat. Union for Study of Social Insects, North Am. sect., Animal Behaviour Soc., NAS, Sigma Xi. Office: Ctr Ecol Scis Indian Inst Sci Bangalore 560 012 India

GADDES, RICHARD, opera company director; b. Wallsend, Northumberland, Eng., May 23, 1942; s. Thomas and Emilie Jane (Rickard) G. L.T.C.L. in piano, L.T.C.L. for sch. music; G.T.C.L., Trinity Coll. Music, London, 1964; D. Mus. Arts (hon.), St. Louis Conservatory, 1983; D.F.A. (hon.), U. Mo.-St. Louis, 1984; D.Arts (hon.), Webster U., 1986. Founder, mgr. Wigmore Hall Lunchtime Concerts, 1965; dir. Christopher Hunt and Richard Gaddes Artists Mgmt., London, 1965-66; bookings mgr. Artists Internat. Mgmt., London, 1967-69; artistic adminstr. Santa Fe Opera, 1969—75, assoc. gen. dir., 1995—2000, gen. dir., 2000—, Opera Theatre of St. Louis, 1975-85, life bd. dirs., 1985—. Bd. dirs., emeritus mem. Grand Ctr., Inc., 1988—, pres., 1988-95; bd. dirs. William Matheus Sullivan Found. Mem. bd. advisors Royal Oak Found.; bd. dirs. Pulitzer Found. for the Arts. Recipient Lamplighter award, 1982, Mo. Arts award, 1983, St. Louis award, 1983, Human Relations award Jewish-Am. Com., St. Louis, 1985, Nat. Inst. for Music Theatre award, 1986, Cultural Achievement award Young Audiences, 1987. Office: Santa Fe Opera PO Box 2408 Santa Fe NM 87504-2408 E-mail: director@santafeopera.org.*

GADDIS, JOHN LEWIS, history professor; b. Cotulla, Tex., Apr. 2, 1941; m. Toni Dorfman. BA, U. Tex., 1963, MA, 1965, PhD, 1968. Asst. prof. Ind. U. S.E., Jeffersonville, 1968-69; asst. prof. history Ohio U., Athens, 1969-71, assoc. prof., 1971-76, prof., 1976-83, disting. prof. history, 1983-97, dir. Contemporary History Inst., 1987-93; Robert Lovett prof. history Yale U., New Haven, 1997—. Vis. prof. Naval War Coll., 1975-77; Bicentennial prof. Am. history, U. Helsinki, 1980-81; vis. prof. politics Princeton U., 1987; Harmsworth prof. Am. History Oxford U., 1992-93, Eastman prof., 2000-01. Author: The United States and the Origins of the Cold War, 1941-47, 1972, Russia, the Soviet Union, and the United States: An Interpretive History, 1978, 2d edit., 1990, Strategies of Containment: A Critical Appraisal of Postwar American National Security Policy, 1982, 2d edit., 2005, The Long Peace: Inquiries into the History of the Cold War, 1987, The United States and the End of the Cold War, 1992, We Now Know: Rethinking Cold War History, 1997; The Landscape of History: How Historians Map the Past, 2002, Surprise, Security, and the American Experience, 2004, The Cold War: A New History, 2005. Fellow Woodrow Wilson Ctr., 1995-96; recipient Bancroft prize, 1973, Stuart L. Bernath prize, 1973, Nat. Hist. Soc. prize, 1973, Nat. Humanities medal, 2005, Harry S. Truman Book prize, 2006. Mem. Am. Hist. Assn., Orgn. Am. Historians, Soc. for Historians of Am. Fgn. Rels., Coun. on Fgn. Rels.

GADDIS ROSE, MARILYN, literature educator, translator; b. Fayette, Mo., Apr. 2, 1930; d. Merrill Elmer and Florence Georgia (Lyon) Gaddis; m. James Leo Rose, Dec. 23, 1956 (div. 1966); m. Stephen David Ross, Nov. 16, 1968 (div. Sept. 2005); 1 child, David Gaddis Ross. BA, Central Meth. Coll., 1952; MA, U. S.C., Columbia, 1954-55; PhD, U. Mo., 1958; LHD, Ctrl. Meth. Coll., 1987. Instr. Stephens Coll., Columbia, Mo., 1958-68; assoc. prof. Ind. U., Bloomington, 1968; prof. comparative lit. SUNY, Binghamton, 1968—, disting. svc. prof., 1991—, dir. translation program, 1973—2002. Translator: (book) Axel, 1970, 1986, Eve of the Future Eden, 1981, Lui: A View of Him, 1986, Adrienne Mesurat, 1991, Volupté, The Sensual Man, 1995, Translation Horizon, 1996, Translation and Literary Criticism, 1998, Beyond the Western Tradition, 2000; editor, contbr.: book Translation Spectrum, 1981; editor: Translation Perspectives, (jour.) Women Writers in Translation, 1983—; contbr. articles to profl. jours. Fulbright fellow, U. Lyon, France, 1953—54, Humanities Rsch. Centre Sr. fellow, Australian Nat. U., 1977. Mem.: MLA (del. assembly 1974—78, pres. N.E. sect. 1975—76, del. assembly 1984—87, exec. coun. 2004—), Am. Translators Assn. (bd. dirs. 1986—88, mng. editor series 1986—96, endowed lectr. 1998—, Spl. Svc. award 1983, 1995, Alexander Gode award 1988), Am. Lit. Translators (sec.-treas. 1981—83), PEN N.Y. Home: Apt 508 5 Riverside Dr Binghamton NY 13905-4644 Office Phone: 607-777-6726. Business E-Mail: mgrose@binghamton.edu.

GADDY, JAMES LEOMA, chemical engineer, educator; b. Jacksonville, Fla., Aug. 16, 1932; s. Leoma Ithama and Mary Elizabeth (Edwards) Gaddy; m. Betty Maricella, Sept. 7, 1952; children: James, Teresa. BSChemE, La. Poly. U., 1955; MSChemE, U. Ark., 1968; PhDChemE, U. Tenn., 1972. Registered prof engr, Ark. Process engr. Ethyl Corp., Baton Rouge, 1955-60; project mgr., engring. supr. Ark.-La. Gas, Shreveport, La., 1960-66; assoc. prof. chem engring. U. Mo., Rolla, 1972-79, prof., dir. rsch. ctr., 1979-80; prof., head chem. engring. U. Ark., Fayetteville, 1980-88, disting. prof., 1988-91, emeritus disting. prof., 1991—. Pres Bioengineering Resources, Fayetteville, 1984—; consult to 15 orgns; teacher numerous short courses in chemical eng for indust; adminr research contracts various cos; vis. prof. Swiss Fed. Inst. Tech. Zurich, 1978. Mem ed bd: Biomass and Biofuels, Chemical Eng R&D; contbr. to numerous presentations and publs. Mem.: AAAS, AIChE (mem speakers bur), Am Soc Eng Educ, Am Chemical Soc, Omega Chi Epsilon, Alpha Chi Sigma, Tau Beta Pi (Eminent Eng 1976). Baptist. Office: Bioengring Resources 1650 Emmaus Rd Fayetteville AR 72701-7283 Home: 3781 N Sassafras Hill Rd Fayetteville AR 72703 Home Phone: 479-443-4145. Personal E-mail: jlgaddy@aol.com.

GADDY, SHEILA MAE, application developer, geriatrics nurse, writer, volunteer; b. Albany, NY, June 5, 1951; d. Charles Milton and Gladys Lee (Byncom) Gaddy; m. Wayne Douglas Benson Sr. (div.); children: Steven Durrell, Wayne Douglas Benson Jr., Lanissa Ramona Benson. AAS, Hudson Valley C.C., Troy, NY, 1991. LPN, Albany Manpower Tng. Ctr., 1974. Lic. practical nurse Albany Vets. Hosp., 1974—75, Physicians Hosp., Queens, NY, 1975—79; I.V. tech. Albany Med. Ctr., Albany, NY, 1980—82; lic. practical nurse Acad. Infirmary, Albany, NY, 1983—84, Albany V.A. Hosp., Albany, NY, 1985—89; programmer analyst Mt. Sinai Med. Ctr., NYC, 1991—97; lic. practical nurse Julie Blair Rehab., Albany, NY, 1999—2000, Albany Co. Nursing Home, NY, 2000—. Author: (poetry) Life's Experiences & Challenges in Poetry, 2004, My God Help Me, 1998 (Golden Poetry award, 1988). Vol. Tsehaya Dance Sch., Albany, NY, 2000; founder, pres. Odyssey Lady's Club, 1999—. Mem.: Internat. Masons & Order Ea. Star (fin. sec. 1999—2004, treas., youth matron, worthy matron 2002—03). Democrat. Avocations: sewing, reading, piano, poetry, youth volunteer. Home: 1949 Western Ave Albany NY 12203

GADDY, SIDNEY WARREN, government agency administrator; b. Waynesville, Mo., Feb. 20, 1950; s. Joseph Harrison and Elmeta Bernadene Gaddy; m. Elizabeth Karen Dobry, Aug. 30, 1968; 1 child, Kristina Marie Smith. BS, U. Mo., Rolla, 1971; MA, Webster U., St. Louis, 1979. Cert. rsch. development Assn. Sys. Mgmt., Army Logistics Mgmt. Coll., 1989, sys. planning rsch. development & engring. Army Aquisition Corps, 1995, program mgmt. Army Aquisition Corps., 1996. Commd. 2lt. U.S. Army Res., 1971, advanced through grades to lt. col., 1993, air def. arty. officer Ft. Bliss, Germany, 1971—82, civil svc. engr. Huntsville, Ala., 1982—94, dep. project mgr. patriot missile sys. Lower Tier Project Office, 1994—2004, ret., 2004; prin. rsch. info. scientist U. Ala., Huntsville, 2004—. Certifying ofcl. Army Aquisition Corps., Huntsville, 2000—05. Vol. musician Cahaba Shrine Band, Huntsville, 1986—94; bugler, reader Sons of Union Veterans, Huntsville. Capt. US Army, 1971—82, US, Germany, Korea. Decorated Army Commendation medal US Army, Meritorious Svc. medal; recipient Superior Civilian Svc. award, 1996, Commander's award for civilian svc., 1999, Value Enging. award, Dept. Def., 1999, Achievement medal for civilian svc., US Army, 1999, Meritorious Civilian Svc. award, 2004, Decoration for Exceptional Civilian Svc., Sec. of Army, 2005; scholar ROTC Scholarship, U.S. Army, 1969. Fellow: Soc. Antiquaries of Scotland; mem.: Res. Officers Assn. (life), Air Def. Arty. Assn. (life), Inst. Indsl. Engrs. (sr.), Clan Scott Soc. (regional commr. 2000—06), Heraldry Soc. Scotland, VFW (life), Sons of Union Veterans of Civil War (life), Ancient Order St. Barbara, Hon. Order St. Barbara, SAR, Mil. Order of Loyal Legion of US. Protestant. Avocations: music, skeet shooting, golf, history.

GADE, MARVIN FRANCIS, retired paper company executive; b. Clinton, Iowa, Nov. 10, 1924; s. Bernhardt Henry and Anna Mae (Jessen) G.; m. Lorraine F. McDonald, Dec. 2, 1944 (dec.); children: Michael David, Patricia Ann Gade Conn, Steven Dennis, Laura Jean Gade Quattlebaum, Mary Kay Gade Brock, Karen Lynn Gade Murphy, Jeffrey Scott; m. Carmell M. Clayton, July 16, 1994. BS in Engring., U. Iowa, Iowa City, 1952; postgrad. exec. program, UCLA, 1960—61. Process instrumentation engr. Standards Brands Co., Clinton, 1946-50; with Kimberly-Clark Corp. (hdqrs.), Neenah, Wis., 1952-88, sr. v.p., group exec., 1974-77, exec. v.p. Coosa Pines, Ala., 1977-88; also dir. Kimberly-Clark Corp.; pres. Kimberly Clark Health Care, Paper and Spltys. Cos., 1981-88, vice chmn. bd., 1983-88. Dir. First Bank of Childersburg, Ala. Bd. dirs. Calif. Water Quality Control Bd., 1964-67, S.C. Tech. Edn. Bd., 1968-70; bd. dirs., sec. Children's Harbor, Alexander City, Ala.; chmn. bd. adv. com. St. Jude's Hosp., Fullerton, Calif., 1962-67; trustee Fulton County Ga. Hosp. Authority, Northside Hosp., Oglethorpe U., Atlanta, Wesley Woods Hosp., Atlanta, Woodruff Art Alliance; bd. visitors Emory U., Atlanta. Served as aviator USNR, 1943-46. Home: The Brittany # 705 4021 Gulf Shore Blvd N Naples FL 34103-2232 *In my lifetime of managing operations and administration I never met a "small" person - just small jobs.*

GAD-EL-HAK, MOHAMED, aerospace and mechanical engineering educator, researcher; b. Tanta, El-Gharbia, Egypt, Feb. 11, 1945; came to U.S., 1968; s. Mohamed Gadelhak and Samira (Hosni) Ibrahim; m. Dilek Karaca, July 19, 1976; children: Kamal, Yasemin. BSc in Mech. Engring. summa cum laude, Ain Shams U., Cairo, 1966; PhD in Fluid Mechanics, Johns Hopkins U., 1973. Instr. Ain Shams U., Cairo, 1966-68; postdoctoral fellow Johns Hopkins U., Balt., 1973, U. So. Calif., LA, 1973-74; asst. prof. engring. sci. & systems U. Va., Charlottesville, 1974-76; program mgr. Flow Rsch. Co., Seattle, 1976-86; prof. aerospace & mech. engring. U. Notre Dame, Ind., 1986—2002; Inez Caudill prof. bioengring., chmn. mech. engring. Va. Commonwealth U., Richmond, 2002—. Cons. USN, Washington, 1990-91, UN, N.Y.C., 1991, many others; lectr. in field. Author: Flow Control: Passive, Active, and Reactive Flow Management, 2000; assoc. tech. editor AIAA Jour., 1988-91; assoc. editor Applied Mechanics Revs., 1988—; contbg. editor: Springer Verlag's Lecture Notes in Engineering, 1988—; reviewer Jour. Fluid Mechanics, Physics of Fluids, AIAA Jour., Jour. of Aircraft, many others; editor: Advances in Fluid Mechanics Measurements, 1989, Frontiers in Experimental Fluid Mechanics, 1989, Flow Control: Fundamentals and Practices, 1998, The CRC MEMS Handbook, 2002, 2006, Transition and Turbulence Control, 2006, Large-Scale Disasters: Prediction, Control and Mitigration, 2006; contbr. numerous articles to profl. jours. Recipient Alexander von Humboldt prize, 1999; Whitehead fellow Johns Hopkins U., Balt, 1968-73; Freeman scholar, 1998; professeur invité Univ. de Grenoble, France, 1991-92; sr. guest NATO, Paris, 1991, USN Disting. Faculty fellow, 1993; professeur exceptionnel univ. de Poitiers, France, 1994; rsch. grantee USN, 1976-80, USCG, 1976-78, NASA-Ames, 1981, NASA-Langley, 1985-87, 86, ONR, 1981-85, AFOSR, 1982-85, 85, Boeing Co., 1984, NSF, 1986, 95, Flow Industries, Inc., 1986-88, Cortana Corp., 1989-90, ONR, 1991, DARPA, 1991, Bourse de Haut Niveau Ministere de la Recherche et de la Technologie, Paris, 1991-92, NATO, 1991-92, others. Fellow AIAA, Am. Acad. Mechanics, ASME, Am. Phys. Soc. Achievements include patents on method and apparatus for controlling bound vortices in the vicinity of lifting surfaces, for reducing turbulent skin friction, for controlling turbulent boundary layers, for micropumping. Office: Va Commonwealth U PO Box 843015 Richmond VA 23284-3015 Home Phone: 804-794-2742; Office Phone: 804-828-3576. Business E-Mail: gadelhak@vcu.edu.

GADEN, ELMER LEWIS, retired engineering educator; b. Bklyn., Sept. 26, 1923; s. Elmer Lewis and Gertrude Estelle (McClellan) G.; m. Jennifer Marie Soley, Mar. 28, 1964; children: David Andrew, Paul Alexander; 1 dau. by previous marriage, Barbara Joan. BS, Columbia U., 1944, MS, 1947, PhD, 1949; DEngring (hon.), Rensselaer Poly., 1987. Rsch. engr. Pfizer Inc., 1948-49; mem. faculty Columbia, 1949-74, prof. chem. engring., 1958-74, chmn. dept., 1960-69, 71-74; dean Coll. Engring. Math. and Bus. Adminstrn., U. Vt., Burlington, 1975-79; Wills Johnson prof. chem. engring. U. Va., Charlottesville, 1979—94, prof. emeritus, 1994—, chmn. dept., 1985—88. Founding editor: Biotech. and Bioengring. Jour., 1959-83. Served with USNR, 1943-46. Mem.: AIChE, NAE, Am. Chem. Soc. Home: 3400 Rodman Dr Charlottesville VA 22901-9450 Personal E-mail: jgaden@earthlink.net.

GADEPALLI, VIJAYA L., mathematics educator; b. Hyderabad, India, May 22, 1953; d. Satyanarayana and Krishnaveni Kondubhotla; m. Venkateswararao Gadepalli, July 31, 1974; children: Pallavi, Mallika. BS, Osmania U., Hyderabad, India, 1969; B of Edn., Dev. Ahulya U., Indore, India, 1985. Tchr. math. St. Xavier H.S., Mhow, India, Choith Ramy H.S., Indore, India, Crerec Pub. Sch., Hyderabad, India, Atomic Energy Ctrl. Sch., Bombay, Air Force Pub. Sch., Nagpur, India, Avondale Mid. Sch., Atlanta, Balt. Pub. Schs., West Side H.S., Newark. Mem.: Newark Tchrs. Union, Nat. Coun. Tchrs. Math., Newark Assn. Math. Educators. Home: 31 Mirebrook Rd #169X Edison NJ 08820 Office: West Side High Sch 403 S Orange Ave Newark NJ 07103

GADIESH, ORIT, management consulting executive; b. Haifa, Israel, Jan. 31; BA in psychology summa cum laude, Hebrew U., Israel, 1973; MBA, Harvard Bus. Sch., 1977. Asst. to dep. chief of staff Israeli Army; asst. prof. Hebrew U., Israel; with Bain & Co., Boston, 1977—, head Boston office, 1991—93, chmn., 1993—. Bd. dir. Peres Inst. for Peace, Israel, WPP, World Econ. Forum; coun. mem. Harvard Bus. Sch., Kellogg Sch., Haute Ecole Commerciale, France; bd. mem. Fed. Reserve Bank of New Eng.

Named one of 100 Most Powerful Women in World, Forbes mag., 2005—06; recipient Disting. Leadership award, IDC U., 2000, Alumni Achievement award, Harvard Bus. Sch., 2000. Mem.: Coun. Fgn. Rels.

GADOMSKI, ROBERT EUGENE, consulting and retired gas industry executive; b. Chgo., Mar. 24, 1947; s. Chester and Adeline (Carpinelli) G.; m. Susan Freed, Aug. 12, 1972; children: Stephen, Andrew, Elizabeth. BS, Purdue U., 1969, MS in Indsl. Adminstrn., 1970, D (hon.) of Engring., 2001, PhD (hon.), 2001; grad. advanced mgmt. program, Harvard U., 1990. Bus. mgr. indsl. chems. div. Air Products and Chems., Inc., Allentown, Pa., 1974-77, gen. sales mgr. indsl. chems. div., 1977-78, asst. gen. mgr. indsl. chems. div., 1978-81, mgr. chems. group mfg. div., 1981-83, gen. mgr. chems. group mfg. div., 1983-84, v.p., gen. mgr. chems. group mfg. div., 1984-86, v.p., gen. mgr. indsl. chems. div., 1986-88, v.p., gen. mgr. process systems group, 1988-90, mgmt. com., 1988—96, group v.p. process systems group, 1990-92, group v.p. chems. group, 1992-96, exec. v.p., mem. corp. exec. com., 1996—2004, exec. v.p. chems., Asia and Latin Am., 1998-99, exec. v.p. gases and equipment, 1999—2004; mng. dir. Napowan Assocs., LLC Bus. Consulting, 2004—. Bd. dirs. Reeb Millwork, Quality Distbn., Inc.; Halsey vis. prof. U. Va., 2006. Chmn. March of Dimes Walkathon, Allentown, 1985; v.p. Minsi Trails coun. Boy Scouts Am., 1998—99, 2002—03; bd. dirs. South Whitehall Planning Commn., Allentown, 1984—89, Lehigh Valley United Way, Allentown, 1991—94, 1999—2000, Kemerer Mus. Decorative Arts, 1991—94, St. Luke's Hosp., Bethelehem, Pa., 1994—99, Hist. Bethlehem Partnership, 1993—2002, Phila. Acad. Scis., 1999—2002, Nat. Assn. Mfg., 1999—2000. Named Disting. Alumnus, Krannert Sch. Mgmt., Purdue U., 1988, Sch. Engring., 1992. Mem. AIChE; mem. Nat. Petroleum Refiners Assn. (bd. dirs. 1986-93), Internat. Oxygen Mfrs. Assn. (bd. dirs. 2000-03), Mfrs. Alliance/MAPI (trustee 2000-03), Pa. Bus. Roundtable (exec. com. 2001-03). Roman Catholic. Avocations: golf, fine dining. Office Phone: 610-745-0659. Business E-Mail: gadomsre@cs.com.

GADRE, ANIL, information technology executive; BSEE, Stanford U., Calif.; M of Mgmt., Northwestern U. With Hewlett-Packard, Apollo Computer; v.p. software mktg. Sun Microsystems, Inc., gen. mgr. Solaris group, v.p. North Am. field mktg., v.p. product mktg., exec. v.p., chief mktg. officer. Office: Sun Microsystems Inc 4150 Network Cir Santa Clara CA 95054 Office Phone: 650-960-1300.*

GADSBY, ROBIN EDWARD, chemicals executive; b. St. Leonards on Sea, Eng., Mar. 22, 1939; arrived in U.S., 1977, naturalized, 1988; s. John Ernest and Emily Louisa (Burt) G.; m. Olwyn Diane Bowen, Aug. 5, 1961 (div. 1981); children: Tricia Clare, Tracey Carolyn; m. Margaret Alice Fuessel, Dec. 29, 1983 (div. Dec. 15, 2004) MA in Natural Scis., Cambridge U., Eng., 1960, MEng, 1961; MBA, U. Chgo., 1982. CFA. Chem. engr. ICI Billingham (Eng.) div., 1961-62, corp. planner, 1962-65; plant mgr. ICI PLC Agrl. div., Heysham, Eng., 1965-67, chem. engring. mgr. Billingham, 1967-70, process tech. mgr., 1970-76, research group mgr., 1976-77; pres. Katalco Corp., Oak Brook, Ill., 1978-83; gen. mgr. Rubicon Chems. Inc., Wilmington, Del., 1984-86; pres. polyurethanes group div. ICI Ams., Inc., Wilmington, 1986-90, pres. chems. and polymers group, 1990-97. Chmn. Cempra Pharms. Inc. Mem. AIChE, Am. Chem. Soc., CFA Inst., Inst. Chem. Engrs. (U.K. editl. bd. 1976-77), Internat. Isocynates Inst. (pres. 1990-91), N.Y. Acad. Scis., Fin. Analysts Soc. Phila., Lely Resort and Country Club, (Fla.), Beta Gamma Sigma. Home and Office: PO Box 630 West Chester PA 19381-0630

GADSDEN, JAMES IRVIN, ambassador; b. Charleston, SC, Mar. 12, 1948; BA cum laude, Harvard U., 1970; MA in East Asian Studies, Stanford U., 1972; postgrad., Princeton U., 1984. Various positions to counselor for econ. affairs U.S. Embassy, Paris, 1989—93, dep. chief of mission Budapest, 1994—97; dep. asst. sec. of state for European Affairs U.S. Dept. of State, 1997—2001; spl. negotiator for agrl. biotechnology Bur. for Econ. and Bus. Affairs, Washington, 2001—01; US amb. to Iceland, 2002—05.

GADUS, PEG, pastoral associate; d. Frank O'Brien and Katherine Alexander; children: Thomas J., Timothy J., Katherine M., Kevin M. BS in Edn., Calumet Coll., Whiting, Ind., 1976; cert., Liturgical Inst., St. Anselmo, Rome, Italy, 1999. Cert. lay minister Archdiocese Chgo., 1996, bereavement minister Cath. Cemeteries, 2001. Tchr. elem. sch. Joliet (Ill.) Diocese, 1955—57, Rockford (Ill.) Diocese, 1957—59, Archdiocese Chgo., 1959—2003, dir. religious edn., 1992—. With mktg. St. Florian Sch., Chgo., 2003—05, saramental preparation coord. Roman Catholic. Office: St Florian 13145 Houston Ave Chicago IL 60633

GAEDE, JAMES ERNEST, physician, educator; b. Calgary, Alta., Can., July 2, 1953; s. John Ernest and Florence Eleanor (Hilmer) G.; married, Dec. 23, 1994; children: Graham, Jason, Nikki, Mary Frances, Sydney, Camille. BA, Augustana Coll., 1975, MA, 1976; MD, U. S.D., 1980. Diplomate Am. Bd. Family Practice. Staff physician Queen of Peace, Mitchell, SD, 1983—2001, chief of staff, 1988, med. dir., 1988-89, St. Joe's Med. Assn., Howard, SD, 1988—2000, Women's Health Clinic, Mitchell, SD, 1983—2000; assoc. prof. U. S.D. Sch. Medicine; 2005med. dir. Desert Regional Med. Ctr., Palm Springs, Calif., 2001—05; med. dir. Tenet Home Health, 2005; CEO Physiogard LLC, 2005—. Presenter U.S. Senate, Washington, 1991; med. dir. Cave South Home Health, 2005, Sleep Disorders of Palm Springs, 2005 Contbr. articles to profl. jours. Bd. dirs. Dakota Weslayan U., Mitchell, 1986-89, Dakota Mental Health, Mitchell, 1988-90; mem. Commn. 2000 S.D., Sioux Falls, 1988-00; pub. health officer City of Mitchell, 1983-01. Named one of Top 100 Family Physicians in U.S., Consumer Rsch. Coun., Washington, Top 70 Drs. in 35 Specialties, Caste Connolly Med. Ltd. Fellow Am. Acad. Family Practice (Active Tchrs. award 1984—); mem. AMA, Calif. Acad. Family Practice, S.D. Assn. Family Practice, S.D. State Med. Assn. (del. 1983-2000, sec. 1998-99, v.p. 1999, pres. 2000), Calif. State Med. Assn., Mitchell C. of C., Mayo Alumni Assn., Doctors Mayo Soc. Avocations: sailing, music, auto restoration. Home: 2525 N Farrell Dr Palm Springs CA 92262-2601 Office: 555 Tachevah Ste 2E-101 Palm Springs CA 92262 Office Phone: 760-218-7662.

GAEDE, ROBERT MATTHEW, music educator; b. El Centro, Calif., Mar. 27, 1970; s. Robert Francis and Helen Bonita (Thiessen) Gaede; m. Mandy Gaede; 1 child, Tory. BA in Music Edn., Tabor Coll., Hillsboro, Kans., 1993; MusM, No. Ariz. U., Flagstaff, 2001. Cert. Profl. Clear Single Subject Tchg. Calif. Comm. Tchr. Credentialing. Music tchr. Unified Sch. Dist. 398, Peabody, Kans., 1993—95; fine arts creative music tchr. El Centro (Calif.) Elem. Sch. Dist., 1995—2003; fine arts choral music tchr. Ctrl. Union HS, El Centro, 2003—; part time lectr. San Diego State U. Imperial Valley Campus, Calexico, Calif., 2003—. Choir dir. Imperial Valley Choral Soc., El Centro, Calif., 2003—06. Musician: Living on the Edge. Worship leader Christ Cmty. Ch., El Centro, 2001. Mem.: Gideons Internat. (assoc.), Am. Choral Dirs. Assn. (assoc.), Music Educators Nat. Conf. (assoc.). Avocations: travel, four wheeling, skiing. Home: 250 S Waterman Ave B El Centro CA 92243 Office: Ctrl Union HS 1001 Brighton Ave El Centro CA 92243 Home Phone: 760-352-1617; Office Phone: 760-336-4300. Office Fax: 760-353-3570.

GAELENS, ALBERT ROBERT, retired director, educational administrator, priest; b. Rochester, NY, Oct. 3, 1932; s. Gaston and Adrienne (Dhont) G. BA, U. Toronto, Ont., Can., 1955; MEd, U. Rochester, 1958; STB, U. St. Michael's, Toronto, 1961; MA, Cath. U. Am., 1967. Joined Congregation St. Basil., Roman Cath. Ch., 1950, ordained priest, 1960. Tchr. Aquinas Inst., Rochester, 1955—57, 1961—62, 1969—70, dean students, 1962-64, vice prin., 1964-66, prin., 1970-77, 1995—97; tchr. Assumption HS, Windsor, Ont., Canada, 1967-69, St. Thomas HS, Houston, 1977—78, asst. prin., 1978-82, dir. guidance, 1982-87, prin., 1987—94, mem. found. bd., 1982—94, dir. alumni rels., 2000—07; prin. St. Pius X High Sch., Alburquerque, 1998—2000. Sch. rep. Coll. Bd., 1980—87; religious rep. Diocesan Priest Coun., 1975-77; mem. Basilian Fathers High Sch. Com., 1970-77, 87-94; mem. adv. bd. Dewey-Ridge br. Community Savs. Bank, 1972-75. Bd. dir. U. St. Thomas, Houston, 1988-94 sch. leader United Way, Houston, 1987-89; mem. Project Hope, 1971-72, Rochester Civic Music Assn., 1971-77, Urban League Rochester, 1972-77, Maplewood Neighborhood Assn., 1975-77; chaplain Camp Massawepie, Boy Scouts Am., N.Y., 1962, 63, dist. chmn. Otetiana coun., 1974-75; chmn. Longhorn dist. nominating com., 1977 Recipient Disting. Svc. award Tex. Assn. Student Couns., 1986, award Inroads of Houston, Inc., 1986, Nat. Leadership award Soc. Disting. Am. High Sch. Students, 1988, Meritorious Svc. award Aquinas Inst., Rochester, NY, 2006. Mem. ASCD, Nat. Cath. Edn. Assn., Nat. Assn. Secondary Sch. Prins., Tex. Assn. Secondary Sch. Prins., Basilian High Sch. Prins. Assn. (chmn. 1989-91), Tex. Assn. Coll. Admission Counselors, Tex. ASCD, Tex. Pers. and Guidance Assn., Houston Pers. and Guidance Assn., Phi Delta Kappa (program com. 1971-72, dist. del. 1972-73). Avocations: gardening, walking, travel. Home and Office: St Thomas High Sch 4500 Memorial Dr Houston TX 77007-7332

GAENGLER, PETER WOLFGANG, dentist, researcher; b. Meissen, Saxony, Germany, Oct. 30, 1941; s. Wolfgang Ernst-Otto and Dorothea Friedericke (Moebius) G.; m. Sabine Gertrud Ahlborn, Nov. 6, 1970; children: Felix Peter, Beate Petra. Stomatology Diploma, Faculty of Dental Medicine, Leningrad, Russia, 1965; DrMedDent, Sch. Dental Medicine, Dresden, Germany, 1967, PhD, 1974; DHC (hon.), Semmelweis U., Budapest, 2004. Diplomate in dentistry. Dentistry Community Hosp., Wittenberg, Germany, 1965-66; asst. prof. Sch. Dental Medicine, Dresden, 1966-75, prof., chmn. Erfurt, Germany, 1975-92, Faculty of Dental Medicine, Witten/Herdecke, Germany, 1992—, dean, 1992—2006; bd. dirs. U. Witten/Herdecke, 1995—2002, mem. exec. bd., 2002—06. V.p. for rsch. U. Witten/Herdecke, 2003—05; mem. joint working group FDI/WHO, Geneva, 1979, 2005. Author: Lehrbuch der Konservierenden Zahnheilkunde, 4th edit., 2005; editor Medizin aktuell, 1975-90; mem. editl. bd. European Jour. Dental Edn., 2000—, Jour. Oral Rehab., 2001-05, Ceska Stomatologie, 2005— Recipient Humboldt medal Ministry Higher Edn., Berlin, 1978; grantee in field. Mem.: Internat. Assn. for Dental Rsch. (com. on membership and recruitment 1989—93, mem. publs. com. 2002—05), Assn. Dental Edn. Europe (exec. com. 1997—2001), Assn. Stomatology (v.p. 1988—90, Philip-Pfaff medal 1988), Assn. Conservative Dentistry (pres. 1978—87), Hungarian Assn. Dentistry (hon. Semmelweis medal 1993), Polish Assn. Dentistry (hon.). Avocations: literature, sailing, skiing. Home: Waldweg 9 D-58313 Herdecke Germany Office: U Witten/Herdecke Faculty Dental Medicine D-58448 Witten Germany Office Phone: 0049-2302-926-664. E-mail: peter.gaengler@uni-wh.de.

GAER, MICHAEL IRA, financial planner; b. Englewood, NJ, Sept. 27, 1968; s. Arthur and Linda Gaer; m. Jayne A Macognone, Mar. 30, 2001; children: Joseph Vincent, Brandon Logan. BBA, U. of Miami, 1986—90. Cert. CFP Bd. of Standards, Inc., 2003. Pres. Gaer Fin. Group, Inc., Rochelle Park, NJ, 1998—. Honoray chmn. nat. Rep. Congl. Com. Bus. Adv. Coun., Washington, 2001. Mem.: Fin. Planning Assn. Office: Gaer Financial Group Inc 5 West Passaic St Rochelle Park NJ 07662 Home Phone: 201-291-2337; Office Phone: 201-291-2337.

GAETA, ROSEMARIE, psychotherapist; b. Bklyn., Apr. 15, 1947; d. James and Rose (Scorcia) G. BS, Fordham U., 1968, MSW, 1970. Diplomate NASW; lic. clin. social worker, NY; bd. cert. clin. social worker, Am. Bd. Examiners, 1988. Pvt. clin. practice, SI, 1973—. Co-founder Psychoanalytic Consortium, 1991, mem. nat. membership com. psychoanalysis in clin. social work, 1980—, first pres. nat. membership com. psychoanalysis in clin. social work, 1991—93. Bd. mem. Accreditation Council for Psychoanalytic Edn., 2004—. Recipient Disting. Practitioner, Nat. Acad. Practice in Social Work. Mem. NY State Soc. Clin. Social Work Psychotherapists (diplomate, chair state com. on psychoanalysis 1987-91), Inst. Psychoanalytic Tng. and Rsch., Internat. Psychoanalytical Assn. Office: 416 Crown Ave Staten Island NY 10312-2828 Home Phone: 718-356-8809; Office Phone: 718-356-8881. Personal E-mail: rosemariegaeta@aol.com.

GAFF, BRIAN MICHAEL, lawyer; b. Boston, Mar. 14, 1962; s. Gilbert Gerard and Josephine Claire (Franklin) G. BSEE magna cum laude, U. Mich., Ann Arbor, 1983, MSEE, 1984; JD magna cum laude, Suffolk U., Boston, 1998. Bar: Mass. 1999, Calif. 1999, NY 2005, NH 2005, US Dist. Ct. Mass. 1999, US Dist. Ct. NH 2005, US Ct. Appeals (1st cir.) 1999, US Ct. Appeals (fed. cir.) 1999, US Patent Office 1999, US Dist. Ct. (no. dist.) Calif. 2000, US Dist. Ct. (ea., ctrl. and so. dists.) Calif. 2004, US Ct. Appeals (9th cir.) 1999, US Supreme Ct., 2002, US Dist. Ct. (ea. dist.) Tex. 2006; registered profl. engr., Mass., Calif., NH, NY. Engr. GTE Communications Products Corp., Westborough, Mass., 1984; mem. tech. staff Draper Lab., Cambridge, Mass., 1984-88; engring. specialist GPT Stromberg-Carlson, Lake Mary, Fla., 1989-90; safety mgr. imaging sys. divsn. Hewlett-Packard Healthcare Solutions Group, Andover, Mass., 1990-2000; pvt. practice, 1999; assoc. Testa, Hurwitz & Thibeault, LLP, Boston, 2000—05, Edwards Angell Palmer & Dodge, LLP, Boston, 2005—. Founder, prin. Solid-State Cons., Swampscott, Mass., 1983—, SSC Constrn., Swampscott, 1991—. Mem. IEEE (sr.), NSPE, ABA, Los Angeles County Bar Assn., Am. Phys. Soc., Am. Vacuum Soc., Am. Intellectual Property Law Assn., Mensa, Mass. Soc. Profl. Engrs., Mass. Bar Assn., NH Trial Lawyers Assn., Boston Patent Law Assn., Essex County Bar Assn., Boston Bar Assn., NH Bar Assn. Republican. Roman Catholic. Avocation: photography. Home: PO Box 166 Swampscott MA 01907-0266 Office: Edwards Angell Palmer Dodge LLP 111 Huntington Ave Boston MA 02199-7613 Office Phone: 617-439-4444. Business E-Mail: bgaff@sscco.com.

GAFFIN, DAVID MORRIS, meteorologist, researcher; b. Fayetteville, Tenn., May 16, 1968; s. Morris Chadwick and Marilyn Hallberg Gaffin. BA, U. Tenn., Knoxville, 1990; MS, Tex. A&M U., Coll. Sta., 1993. Meteorologist intern Nat. Weather Svc., Memphis, 1994—98, gen. forecaster Morristown, Tenn., 1998—2001, sr. forecaster, 2002—. Tchg. asst. Tex. A&M U., College Station, 1991—92, asst. to state climatologist, 1992—93. Contbr. articles to profl. jours. Trail guide Sommers Canoe Base Boy Scouts Am., Ely, Minn., 1986, aquatics camp counselor Wichita Falls, Tex., 1987—91; cir. giving leader United Way, Morristown, 1999—; rsch. ptnr. Am. Diabetes Assn., Washington, 2004—. Recipient Eagle Scout, Boy Scouts Am., 1983; Band scholar, U. Tenn., 1986—90. Mem.: Nat. Weather Assn., Am. Meteorology Soc. (v.p. Smoky Mountain chpt. 2003—05, pres. Smoky Mountain chpt. 2006—07). Avocations: golf, tennis, music, canoeing, hiking. Personal E-mail: david_gaffin@yahoo.com.

GAFFNEY, DONALD LEE, lawyer; b. Dallas, July 7, 1952; s. Leroy H. and Myriam (Brazeal) G.; m. Debby Dunn, May 31, 1974; children: Brian, Colin, Caitlin. BA, Austin Coll., 1974; JD, U. Tex., 1977. Bar: Ariz. 1979, U.S. Ct. Appeals (9th cir.) 1979, U.S. Ct. Appeals (10th cir.) 1984, U.S. Supreme Ct. 1984. Ptnr. Streich & Lang, Phoenix, 1977-89, Snell & Wilmer L.L.P., Phoenix, 1988—; consumer privacy ombudsman US Bankruptcy Ct. Ariz., 2006—. Adj. prof. Ariz. State U. Law Sch., Tempe, 1983-84; dean's council U. Tex. Law Sch., 2005—; atty. rep. 9th Cir. Ct. Appeals Judicial Conf. Co-author: Bankruptcy, 1987; note comment and book review editor: Tex. Law Review 1976-77; contbr. to profl. jours. Mem. Gov.'s Task Force Ctrl. Ariz. Project, 1993. Austin scholar. Mem. ABA, Am. Arbitration Assn. (com. panel), Comml. Law League of Am. (bankruptcy com. 1980-84), State Bar Ariz. (chmn. bankruptcy sect., 1982-84, com. on bankruptcy rules 1979-81, uniform comml. code com. 1980—) , Phi Delta Phi. Democrat. Presbyterian. Office: Snell & Wilmer LLP 1 Arizona Ctr Phoenix AZ 85004-0001

GAFFNEY, ELIZABETH MALLORY, editor, writer, literature educator, translator; b. NYC, Dec. 22, 1966; d. Richard Waring and Ann Walker Gaffney; m. Alexis David Boro, July 15, 1995; 1 child, Lucy Waring Gaffneyboro. BA, Vassar Coll., 1988; MFA, Bklyn. Coll., 1997. Mem. editl. staff The Paris Rev., NYC, 1988—93, mng. editor, 1993—95, editor-at-large, 1995—2004, adv. editor, 2004—05; editor-at-large A Public Space, 2006—. Writing tchr. NYU, NYC, 1997—2006, The New Sch., NYC, 2007. Author: (novels) Metropolis, 2005, short stories; translator: The Pollen Room, 1998, Invisible Woman, 2000, The Arbogast Case, 2003. Resident/fellow, MacDowell Colony, Peterborough, NH, 1996, 1997, Blue Mountain Ctr., NY, 1999, Yaddo, Saratoga Springs, NY, 2000, 2001, 2004. Mem.: PEN, Phi Beta Kappa. Democrat. Avocations: hiking, kayaking, bicycling, camping. Office: c/o Darhansoff Verrill Feldman 236 West 26th St Ste 802 New York NY 10001

GAFFNEY, JOHN T., lawyer; b. Poughkeepsie, NY, May 10, 1960; BA, George Washington Univ., 1982; MBA, JD, NYU, 1986. Bar: NY 1987. Assoc. Cravath Swaine & Moore LLP, NYC, 1986—93, ptnr., corp., 1993—. Mem.: NY State Bar Assn., Assn. of Bar of City of NY. Office: Cravath Swaine & Moore LLP Worldwide Plz 825 Eighth Ave New York NY 10019-7475 Office Phone: 212-474-1122. Office Fax: 212-474-3700. Business E-Mail: jgaffney@cravath.com.

GAFFNEY, JOSEPH M., lawyer; b. 1944; BCS in Acctg., Seattle U., 1967; JD, U. Calif., 1972; LLM in Tax., NYU, 1975. Bar: Wash. 1972. Atty., tax, bus., estate planning Dorsey & Whitney LLP, 2000—03, ptnr.-in-charge, Seattle, tax, estate planning group Seattle, 2003—, mem., mgmt. com.; and officer & dir. Dorsey & Whitney Trust Co. Bd. trustees Seattle Univ., Wash. Edn. Found., Wash. Assn. Ind. Coll. & Univ., Nesholm Family Found., 1989—. Bd. trustees Arts Fund, Seattle; adv. bd. Elder-Health Northwest. Named a Super Lawyer, Wash. Law & Politics; recipient Disting. Alumni award, Seattle Univ., 1991. Fellow: Am. Coll. Trust & Estate Counsel; mem.: King Co. Bar Assn., Wash. State Bar Assn., Seattle Estate Planning Coun., Order of Coif. Office: Dorsey & Whitney LLP Ste 3400 US Bank Ctr 1420 Fifth Ave Seattle WA 98101-4010 Office Phone: 206-903-5448. Office Fax: 206-903-8820. Business E-Mail: gaffney.joe@dorsey.com.

GAFFNEY, MARK WILLIAM, lawyer; b. Spokane, Wash., July 3, 1951; s. William Joseph and Anne Veronica (McGovern) G.; m. Jean Elizabeth O'Leary, Oct. 8, 1988. BA, U. Notre Dame, 1973; JD, George Washington U., 1976. Bar: Wash. 1976, N.Y. 1982, D.C. 1984, Conn. 1984. Law clk. antitrust divsn. U.S. Dept. Justice, Washington, 1974-76; trial atty. NYC, 1976-81; assoc. Solin & Breindel, P.C., NYC, 1982-83; ptnr. Chapman, Moran & Gaffney, Stamford, Conn., 1984-85; of counsel Kaplan & Kilsheimer, NYC, 1985-93; corp. counsel Sta. WLNY-TV, Inc., Melville, NY, 1993-95; atty. Bellavia Gentile & Assocs. LLP, Mineola, NY, 2004—. Recipient Spl. Achievement award U.S. Dept. Justice, 1978, 79. Mem. ABA, Assn. of Bar of City of N.Y., Conn. Bar Assn., N.Y. Athletic Club. Republican. Roman Catholic. Home and Office: 1395 Roosevelt Ave Pelham NY 10803-3605 Office Phone: 914-738-6897. Personal E-mail: markgaffney@verizon.net.

GAFFNEY, PAUL GOLDEN, II, academic administrator, retired military officer; b. Attleboro, Mass., May 30, 1946; s. Paul G. and Elfrieda L. (Piepenstock) G.; m. Linda L. Myers; 1 child, Crista L. BS, U.S. Naval Acad., 1968; MS in Engring., Cath. U. Am., 1969; grad. with highest distinction, Naval War Coll., Newport, RI, 1979; MBA, Jacksonville U., 1986, LHD (hon.), 2002, U. S.C.; doctorate (hon.), Jacksonville U., 2002, U. S.C., 2002, Catholic U. of Am., 2003. Commd. ensign USN, 1968, advanced through grades to vice adm., 1994, ops. officer USS Whipporwill Sasebo, Japan, 1969-71, advisor Vietnamese Combat Hydrog. Survey Team Vietnam, 1971-72, ocean svcs. officer Fleet Weather Cen. Rota, Spain, 1972-75, exec. asst. Office of Oceanographer Alexandria, Va., 1975-78, rsch. fellow Naval War Coll Ctr. Advanced Rsch. Newport, RI, 1978-78, comdg. officer Oceanographic Unit 4 Indonesia, 1979-80, dir. Arctic and Earth Scis. Rsch. Office Naval Rsch. Arlington, Va., 1980-81; mil. asst. internat. security affairs to Asst. Sec. Def. Washington, 1981-83; comdg. office Oceanography Command Facility USN, Jacksonville, Fla., 1983-86, dir. resources Office of Oceanographer Washington, 1986-89, asst. chief, Office Chief of Naval Rsch. Arlington, Va., 1989-91, comdg. officer Naval Rsch. Lab. Washington, 1991-94, comdr. Naval Meteorology and Oceanography Command Stennis Space Ctr., Miss., 1994-97, chief naval rsch. and naval test/evaluation/tech. requirements for the Navy Staff, dep. comdt. USMC for sci. and tech. Arlington, Va., 1996-2000; pres. Nat. Def. U., Washington, 2000—03; commr. U.S. Commn. Ocean Policy, 2000—04; pres. Monmouth U., West Long Branch, NJ, 2003—. Bd. dirs. Diamond Offshore Drilling Inc., Meridian Health Sys.; grad. rsch. asst. Cath. U. Am., Washington, 1968—69. Mem. policy com. Jour. Def. Rsch., 1989-91. Acad. adv. bd. NATO Def. Coll., Rome, 2001—04, U.S. Inst. of Peace, 2000—03; bd. dirs. Marymount U., 2000—03, Fla. State U. Rsch. Found., Jacksonville U., 2002—03, Jacksonville (Fla.) U., 2002—03. Decorated DSM, Legion of Merit with three gold stars, Bronze Star with V; recipient Middendorf prize Naval War Coll., 1979. Fellow Am. Meteorol. Soc., Explorer's Club; mem. Naval Acad. Alumni Assn., Sigma Xi. Roman Catholic. Avocations: running, track and field and cross country announcing and officiating. Office: Office of the Pres Monmouth U 400 Cedar Ave West Long Branch NJ 07764-1898 Business E-Mail: president@monmouth.edu.

GAFFNEY, THOMAS, retired banker; b. San Francisco, Sept. 22, 1915; s. John and Hannah (Doherty) G.; m. Claire Bastian, Dec. 15, 1945. Cert., Am. Inst. Banking, 1940. Bank insp. Bank of Am., 1935-50; asst. cashier First Nat. Trust and Savs. Assn., Santa Barbara, Calif., 1950-51; asst. cashier, asst sec. Oakland Central Bank, Calif., 1951-53; chief insp. Transamerica Corp., San Francisco, 1953-55; v.p., auditor First Western Bank, San Francisco, 1955-61; v.p. New First Western Bank, Los Angeles, 1961-74; v.p. and auditor Lloyds Bank Calif., Los Angeles, 1974-80; ret., 1980. Pres. Golden Gate chpt. Bank Adminstrn Inst., San Francisco, 1961, nat. bd. dirs., 1965-67, gen. chmn. conv., L.A., 1967, speaker bank convs., nationwide; chmn. crime deterrant com. Calif. Bankers Assn., 1977-79; banking cons., 1980—. Ad hoc com. to study and recommend controls on all city depts. City of LA, 1977—. Mem.: Elks (bd. dir. Locker Room 67 club San Francisco 1960). Personal E-mail: ewolfram@cox.net.

GAFFNEY, THOMAS EDWARD, physician; b. East St. Louis, Ill., Nov. 5, 1930; s. John V. and Leola (Heisner) G.; m. Edith Ann Heitholt, June 12, 1954; children— John, David, Michael. AB, U. Mo., 1951, MS, 1953; MD, U. Cin., 1957. Intern Harvard Med. Service of Boston City Hosp., 1957-58; resident medicine Mass. Gen. Hosp., 1958-59; instr. pharmacology, asst. medicine U. Cin., 1959-60; clin. assoc. Nat. Heart Inst., 1960-62; assoc. prof. pharmacology U. Cin., 1962-67, asst. prof. medicine, 1962, dir. div. clin. pharmacology, 1962-72, prof. pharmacology, 1967-72, prof. medicine, 1969-72; prof., chmn. dept. pharmacology, prof. medicine Med. U. S.C., 1972-90, disting. prof., 1986-90; vis. scientist Merck Sharp & Dohme Rsch. Labs., Rahway, NJ, 1989-93; vol. clinician Buncombe County Health Ctr., 1998—2004; clin. prof. medicine U. S.C. Sch. Medicine, Columbia, 2004—. Cardiovascular panel NAS Drug Efficacy Study, 1967-70; pharmacology and exptl. therapeutics study sect. Nat. Heart Inst., 1967-69; med. adv. bd. Coun. High Blood Pressure Rsch., 1969—; mem.

Coun. on Basic Scis. of Am. Heart Assn., 1969—, cardiovascular A study sect., 1972; program rev. com. pharmacology and toxicology Nat. Inst. Gen. Med. Scis., 1971-75, chmn. 1973-75; mem. tech. adv. bd. S.C. Rsch. Authority, 1986-89 Mem. editorial bd. Jour. Pharmacology and Exptl. Therapeutics, 1965-77, Ann. Rev. Pharmacology and Toxicology, 1986-91. Served with USPHS, 1960-62. Recipient Rsch. Career devel. award Nat. Heart Inst., 1962, 67, 72; Myrtle Wreath award for research Hadassah, 1980; Sr. Rsch. fellow NIH, 1989. Mem. Am. Fedn. Clin. Rsch., Am. Soc. Pharmacology and Exptl. Therapeutics, Ctrl. Soc. Clin. Rsch., Am. Soc. Clin. Investigation, Alpha Omega Alpha. Home: 1342 Sanford Dr Columbia SC 29206 Personal E-mail: tegaff@worldnet.att.net.

GAFFNEY, THOMAS FRANCIS, private investor; b. Rockford, Ill., Aug. 29, 1945; s. Francis William and Catherine Zeta (Haeberle) G.; m. Donna Lee Gottfried, Apr. 17, 1971; 1 child, Cory. BA, Brown U., 1967; MBA, U. Chgo., 1969. CPA Ill. Fin. cons. Duff and Phelps, Inc., Chgo., 1969-70; dir. adminstrn. Masury-Columbia Co. subs. Alberto-Culver Co., Melrose Park, Ill., 1970-75; exec. v.p., dir. Guardian Industries Corp., Northville, Mich., 1975-87; chmn. bd. The Oxford Investment Group, Bloomfield Hills, Mich., 1985-90; chmn. bd., CEO Automotive Plastic Techs., Inc., Sterling Heights, Mich., 1990-92; chmn. Ashland Products, Inc., Chgo., 1992-95; mng. dir. Raymond James Captial, Inc., St. Petersburg, Fla., 1997—2002. Bd. dirs. Amerus Decorated chevalier de L'Orde Grand Ducal de le Couronne de Chene (Luxembourg). Mem.: AICPA. Home: 2091 Oceanview Dr Tierra Verde FL 33715-2512 Home Phone: 727-867-3102; Office Phone: 727-866-8729. Personal E-mail: gaffneyd@aol.com. Business E-Mail: tom@andersongroup.biz.

GAFFORD, MARY MAY GRIMES, retired humanities educator; b. Paris, Tex., Jan. 4, 1936; d. Benjamin Earl and Mary Elizabeth (Perfect) Grimes; m. Frank Hall Gafford, Dec. 31, 1958 (dec. May 2003); children: Michelle Marguerite, Georgette Marie. BA in English and Social Studies, North Tex. State U., Denton, 1957, MA in English, Spanish and History, 1958; postgrad., U. Nev., 1970. Tchr. English Alpine Pub. Schs., Tex., 1959-61; tchr. English and history Houston Sch. Dist., 1957-58; tchr. English and Spanish Grapevine Sch. Dist., Tex., 1958-59, Amarillo Sch. Dist., Tex., 1962-65; tchr. English, Spanish and Journalism Fabens Schs., Tex., 1965-67; tchr. English and Spanish Flagstaff Schs., Ariz., 1967-68, Mesa County Schs., Grand Junction, Colo., 1968-71; tchr. English Clark County Schs., Las Vegas, Nev., 1976—2004; ret., 2004. Editor: Ethnic Etchings, 1990-93 (award of Excellence 1991, 92); co-editor: Skirts That Swept the Desert Floor. Vol. Am. Cancer Soc., Las Vegas, 1974—, Very Spl. Arts Festival, 1990—92, youth health fair Nev. Bus. Svcs., Las Vegas, 1989; mem. Nev. Symphony Guild; chair Christopher Columbus Quincentennial, 1990—; publicist Nev. Women's History Project, 1998—2002, 1st v.p. so. region, state sec., 2004—, state sec., 2003—; cultural chair Roy Martin Mid. Sch., 2000—03; charter mem. Desert Arts Nev., Inc., publicist, 2005—07; publicist, mem. publicity com. Super Summer Theatre, 2005—07; vol. So. Nev. Dems., Las Vegas, 1980; bd. dirs., hospitality chair Summer Theatre, 2003—06; cultural arts bd. State Pks., 1990—2001. Named Outstanding Woman of Las Vegas, Las Vegas Mus., Outstanding Vol., Dept. Vet. Affairs; recipient Nat. Def. Edn. Act award, U. Alaska, Fairbanks, 1966, Spanish Inst. Calif. Luth. Coll., Thousand Oaks, 1968, Las Vegas Centennial award, Wall of Women, 2005, Pin recognition 25 yrs. svc., Super Summer Theatre Bd. Mem.: AAUW (pres. 1976—77, life chair teen-age pregnancy study group chpt. 1983—92, chair coupon clippers 1984—93), DAR (Francisco Garcés chpt., vice-regent 1983—90, regent 1990—92, chair Christopher Columbus Quincentennial 1990—, chair WWII 50th Anniversary Commemoration 1992—, chair US Constn. week 1992—, Nev. state chair com. Am. Indians 2004—, Nev. state nominating com. 2006, Sarah Winnemucca award for svc. 2003), Soc. Nev. Tchrs. English, Clark County Classroom Tchrs., Daus. Confederacy (So. Nev. charter mem., v.p.), Cameo Soc., Nev. Soc. Descs. Mayflower (lt. gov. 1997—, state sec. 2002—), Sons and Daus. Pilgrims So. Nev. (charter mem., state sec. 2003—), Las Vegas Towne Club, Las Vegas Mesquite Club (chmn. donations for cmty. 2007, ednl. interest chair 2007), Paradise Dem. Club, Pilot Club (pres. 1989—90, hospitality chair 1993). Methodist. Avocations: numismatics, antiques, creative writing, collecting Native American artifacts. Home: 5713 Balzar Ave Las Vegas NV 89108-3184

GAFFORD, RONALD J., construction executive; B in Bldg. Constrn., Tex. A&M U., 1972; cert. Advanced Mgmt. Program, Harvard U., 1987. Devel. and constrn. ptnr. Trammel Crow Co., Atlanta; project mgr. Henry C. Beck Co., Dallas; pres. Austin Industries, Inc., Dallas, 1996—2001, pres., CEO, 2001—. Former chmn., vice chmn. Austin Comml., Inc., Austin Bridge & Road, Inc., Austin Indsl., Inc. Active mem. Dallas Together Forum, Nat. Real Estate Adv. Coun. Trust for Pub. Land; elder Preston Hollow Presbyn. Ch., 1991—; bd. dirs. Dallas Citizens Coun., Dallas Symphony Assn., Trinity Industries, Interfaith Housing Coalition, Lakehill Prep. Sch.; former bd. dirs. Assoc. Gen. Contractors of Am., Dallas chpt. and Tex. Bldg. br., Real Estate Coun., North Tex. Pub. Broadcasting, Vis. Nurses Assn., Greater Dallas C. of C. Office: Austin Industries Inc 3535 Travis St Ste 300 Dallas TX 75204-1466

GAGE, BEAU, artist; b. Rye, NY, Dec. 3, 1945; d. John Alden and Frances (Johnston) G.; m. Glenn A. Osterhout, May 24,1980. BA, St. John's Coll., Santa Fe and Annapolis, Md., 1971; student, Internat. Ctr. Photography, NYC, 1981-82, 82-83, Art Students League NY, 1983-87, The Sculpture Ctr. Sch., NYC, 1985-87, Nat. Acad. Design, 1988-89. Staff asst. to the pres. The White House, Washington, 1972-73; key accounts mgr. Sterling Drug, Inc., Montvale, NJ, 1975-79. Works exhibited at Internat. Ctr. Photography, 1981-83, Art Students League, 1984-87, The Sculpture Ctr., 1985-87, Westbeth Gallery, NYC, 1984, 86, Sotheby's Auction House, 1990, others; permanent pub. sculpture Jacksonville Jaguars, Inc.; permanent exhbn. Jacksonville Mus. Sci. & History. Supporter, guild mem. Martha Graham Dance Co., NYC, 1989—; canopy assoc. Rainforest Alliance, 2000—; mem. adv. bd. Buglisi/Foreman Dance Co., NYC, 2001—; leader Perlman Music Program, NYC, 2001—. Fellow Mus. Modern Art; mem. Met. Mus. Art, Internat. Ctr. Photography, Orgn. Ind. Artists, The Nature Conservancy, Mass. Soc. Mayflower Descendants, Poets House (NYC). Avocations: astronomy, sailing, yoga. Home: 320 E 46th St Apt 34E New York NY 10017-3039 Mailing: PO Box 882 Shelter Island Heights NY 11965 Personal E-mail: beau7gage@aol.com.

GAGE, EDWIN C., III, (SKIP GAGE), travel and marketing services executive; b. Evanston, Ill., Nov. 1, 1940; s. Edwin Cutting and Margaret (Stackhouse) G.; m. Barbara Ann Carlson, June 26, 1965; children—Geoff, Scott, Christine, Richard BS in Bus. Adminstrn., Northwestern U., 1963, MS in Journalism, 1965. Account exec. Foote, Cone and Belding, 1965-68, dir. mktg. devel. & rsch., 1968-70; v.p. direct mktg. Carlson Mktg. Group of Carlson Cos., Mpls., 1970-75, exec. v.p., 1975-77, pres., 1977-83, also bd. dirs.; exec. v.p., COO Carlson Cos. Inc., Mpls., 1983, pres., CEO, 1984-89, pres., chief exec. officer, 1989-91; now chmn., CEO Gage Marketing Group, Mpls. Bd. dirs. Gage Mktg. Group, Carlson Holdings Inc., Carlson Real Estate, Carlson Real Estate Co., Inc., Supervalu Stores Inc., Fingerhut Cos., Kellogg adv. bd. Northwestern U., Minn. Coun. Quality, Mpls. Inst. Arts. Lt. USN. Mem. Young Pres. Orgn., Minn. Execs. Orgn. Avocations: music, tennis, golf, hunting, fishing. Office: Gage Marketing Group 10000 Highway 55 Ste 100 Minneapolis MN 55441-6365

GAGE, FRED H., neuroscientist, educator; BS, U. Fla.; PhD, Johns Hopkins U., Balt. Assoc. prof. dept. histology U. Lund, Sweden; prof. dept. neuroscience U. Calif., San Diego; prof. Lab. Genetics Salk Inst. Biol. Studies, San Diego, 1995—. Contbr. articles to profl. jours. Recipient MERIT award, NIH, Decade of the Brain medal, Neurosciences award, Pew Found., Neuroscience Rsch. award, Bristol-Myers Squibb, 1987, IPSEN prize, Neuronal Plasticity, 1990, Charles A. Dana award, Pioneering Achievements in Health and Edn., 1993, Christopher Reeve Rsch. medal, 1997, Max Planck Rsch. prize, 1999, Robert J. and Claire Pasarow Found. award, 1999, Award, Med. Rsch., MetLife, 2002, Klaus Joachim Zulch prize, Max Planck Soc., 2003; grantee Predoctoral fellowship, NIMH. Fellow: NAS Inst. Medicine, Am. Acad. Arts & Sci., NAS; mem.: Soc. Neuroscience (pres. 2001). Achievements include first successful strategies to stimulate recovery of function following brain and spinal cord injuries. Office: Salk Inst Biol Studies PO Box 85800 San Diego CA 92186-5800 E-mail: gage@salk.edu.

GAGE, GASTON HEMPHILL, lawyer; b. Charlotte, NC, June 16, 1930; s. Lucius Gaston and Margaret (White) G.; m. Jane Basinger, July 11, 1959; children: Gaston Hemphill Jr., John Robert, Stephen Matheson. BA, Duke U., 1953; LLB, U. N.C., 1958. Bar: N.C. 1958, U.S. Ct. Appeals (4th cir.) 1964, U.S. Ct. Appeals (7th and fed. cirs.) 1983, U.S. Supreme Ct. 1965, U.S. Ct. Fed. Claims. Ptnr. Grier, Parker, Poe, Thompson, Bernstein, Gage & Preston, Charlotte, 1964-84, Parker, Poe, Thompson, Bernstein, Gage & Preston, Charlotte, 1984-90, Parker, Poe, Adams & Bernstein, Charlotte, 1990—. Dir. Elon Homes for Children, Elon Coll., N.C., 1986—, vice chair, 1995-96, chair, 1996-97; pres. Boys Town of N.C., Charlotte, 1974-78, A.G. Jr. High PTA, Charlotte, 1974-75, Mecklenburg Kiwanis, Charlotte, 1968; sec., ofcl. bd. Myers Park United Meth. Ch., Charlotte, 1970-72; trustee Oak Ridge Mil. Acad., 2001—. Mem. ABA, N.C. Bar Assn., N.C. State Bar Assn., Mecklenburg County Bar Assn., Kiwanis (lt. gov. Carolinas dist. 1995-96). Methodist. Home: 324 Lockley Dr Charlotte NC 28207-2330 Office: Parker Poe Adams & Bernstein 401 S Tryon St Ste 3000 Charlotte NC 28202

GAGE, JOHN, labor union administrator; b. 1946; m. Patti McGowan. BA, Wheeling Jesuit U., 1968. Profl. baseball player Balt. Orioles, 1968—69; with Liberty Mut. Ins. Co.; disability examiner Social Security Adminstrn., 1974—82; 2nd v.p. Am. Fedn. Govt. Employees, exec. v.p., pres. Balt., 1985—2003, nat. pres. Washington, 2003—. Editor: Newsletter, Local 1923. Trustee Nat. Labor Coll. Office: Am Fedn Govt Employees 80 F St NW Washington DC 20001*

GAGE, LARRY S., lawyer; b. Hollywood, Calif., Aug. 9, 1947; BA cum laude, Harvard Coll., Cambridge, Mass., 1986; JD, Columbia U., NYC, 1972. Bar: DC 1973. Counsel U.S. Senate Subcommittee on Employment, Poverty and Migratory Labor, 1973—75; staff dir. U.S. Senate Subcommittee on Alcoholism and Drug Abuse, 1975—77; dep. asst. sec. Health Legis., U.S. Dept. of Health and Human Services, 1978—81; ptnr. Powell, Goldstein, Frazer & Murphy LLP, Washington, dir. health practice grp. Named one of Washington's Legal Elite, Smart CEO Mag., 2005, 100 Most Influential Lawyers, Nat. Law Jour., 2006. Mem.: U. HealthSystem Consortium (governing bd. 1998—), Nat. Assn. of Pub. Hospitals and Health Systems (pres. 1981—), Am. Health Lawyers Assn., Am. Internat. Health Alliance (bd. dirs. 1992—, chmn. 2000—). Office: Powell Goldstein LLP 901 New York Ave, NW Third Floor Washington DC 20001-4413

GAGE, NATHANIEL LEES, retired psychologist, educator; b. Union City, NJ, Aug. 1, 1917; s. Hyman and Rose (Lees) Gewirtz; m. Margaret Elizabeth Burrows, June 27, 1942 (dec. Jan. 2006); children: Elizabeth, Thomas Burrows, Sarah, Anne. Student, CCNY, 1934—36; AB magna cum laude, U. Minn., 1938; PhD, Purdue U., 1947, LittD (hon.), 1979; PhD (hon.), U. Liège, 2001. Rsch. asst. Coll. Entrance Bd., Princeton, NJ, 1939; asst. prof. Purdue U., West Lafayette, Ind., 1947-48, U. Ill., Urbana, 1948—52, assoc. prof., 1952—56, prof., 1956—62, Stanford U., Calif., 1962—79, Margaret Jacks prof., 1979—87, prof. emeritus, 1987—. Sachs vis. prof. Tchrs. Coll., Columbia U., 1977; lectr. U. Hamburg, 1978, Taipei, 1989, Madrid, 1992, U. Ill., 1994, numerous others; vis. fellow Brasenose Coll., Oxford U., 1983; vis. prof. NYU, 1959, Harvard U., 1984, SUNY, Albany, 1988; mem. rsch. adv. com. Am. Coun. Edn., 1967-73, chmn., 1972-73; mem. Nat. Adv. Com. on Edn. Labs, 1966-69; cons. Internat. Inst. Ednl. Planning, Paris, 1973-74; chmn. exec. bd. Stanford Ctr. Rsch. and Devel. in Tchg., 1968-76, founding co-dir., 1965-68; also dir. program on teaching effectiveness Ctr. for Ednl. Rsch., Stanford, 1972-83; vis. scholar, chmn. planning conf. on studies in teaching Nat. Inst. Edn., 1974; chmn. project coun. internat. classroom environ. study Internat. Assn. for Evaluation of Ednl. Achievement, 1979-81; Fulbright lectr., Brazil, 1985; mem. final selection com. Spencer Found. Dissertation Yr. Fellowships, 1987, 88; participant U. S. Dept. Edn. Conf. on School-Linked Comprehensive Svcs. for Children and Families, 1994. Author: Teacher Effectiveness and Teacher Education, 1972, Scientific Basis of the Art of Teaching, 1978, Hard Gains in the Soft Sciences: The Case of Pedagogy, 1985; co-author: Educational Measurement and Evaluation, 1943, 2d edit., 1955, A Practical Introduction to Measurement and Evaluation, 1960, 2d edit., 1965, Educational Psychology, 1975, 6th edit., 1998; editor: Handbook of Research on Teaching, 1963, Mandated Evaluation of Educators, 1973, Psychology of Teaching Methods, 1976; founding editor Teaching and Teacher Education: An Internat. Jour. Rsch. and Studies, 1983-86; co-editor: Readings in the Social Psychology of Education, 1963; cons. editor Jour. Ednl. Psychology, numerous other jours. Served with USAAF, 1943-45. Recipient Creative Leadership award NYU Sch. Edn., 1980, Outstanding Writing award Am. Assn. Colls. Tchr. Edn., 1986, Disting. Alumnus award Purdue U., 1994, Rsch. and Dissemination Program award Am. Fedn. Tchrs., 2000; fellow Ctr. for Advanced Study in Behavioral Scis., 1965-66, 87-88, USPHS, 1965-66, Guggenheim fellow, 1976-77. Fellow APA (pres. divsn. ednl. psychology 1961-62, Thorndike award 1986), Assn. for Psychol. Sci. (charter fellow); mem. Am. Ednl. Rsch. Assn. (pres. 1963-64, Disting. Contbns. award 1988), Nat. Soc. Study Edn. (bd. dirs. 1970-80, chmn. 1972, 74, 78), Nat. Acad. Edn., Fulbright Assn., Phi Beta Kappa, Sigma Xi, Phi Delta Kappa (award for meritorious contbns. to edn. 1981). Home and Office: 65 Pearce Mitchell Pl Stanford CA 94305 Office Phone: 650-725-7387. Business E-Mail: nlgage@stanford.edu.

GAGE, PATRICK (LEONARD PATRICK GAGE), biotechnology & pharmaceutical industry consultant; b. Endicott, NY, May 4, 1942; s. Leonard Augustine and Mary Margaret (O'Brien) G.; m. Nancy Virginia Graffius, Aug. 7, 1965 (div. Mar. 1985); children: Darren, Cynthia; m. Evelyn Anne Devine, June 29, 1985 (separated Aug. 2006); children: Christopher, Devin. BS, MIT, 1964; PhD, U. Chgo., 1969. NIH postdoctoral fellow Carnegie Inst., Washington, 1969—71; mem. dept. cell biology Roche Inst. Molecular Biology, 1971—80, dir. dept. molecular genetics Nutley, NJ, 1981—83, v.p. biol. R&D, 1983—84; v.p. exploratory rsch. Hoffmann-La Roche Inc., Nutley, NJ, 1984—89; exec. v.p. Genetics Inst., Inc., Cambridge, Mass., 1989—93, COO, 1993—97, pres., 1997—98, Wyeth Rsch., Collegeville, Pa., 1998—2002; sr. v.p. sci. and tech. Wyeth, 2001—02. Chmn. Dublin Molecular Medicine Ctr., 2002—04, Adnexus Therapeutics (also known as Compound Therapeutics), 2003—, Acceleron Pharma, 2004—06, Neose Tech., Inc., 2006—, POL BioPHarma, 2007—; advisor Functional Genetics; life sci. adv. bd. Warburg Pincus; bd. dirs. Biotech. Inst., Alvine Pharm., Immune Control, Inc.; venture ptnr. Flagship Venture, Cambridge, Mass. Mem. vis. com. divsn. biol. sci. U. Chgo.; bd. dirs. Phila. Orch. Avocations: skiing, golf. Home Phone: 610-667-3107; Office Phone: 610-460-4020. E-mail: patrickgage@comcast.net.

GAGGINI, JOHN EDMUND, lawyer; b. Chgo., Dec. 17, 1949; BA cum laude, Knox Coll., 1971; MS, Ohio U., 1972, JD magna cum laude, 1975; LLM, NYU, 1976. Bar: Ill. 1975, D.C. 1977; CPA, Ill. Law clk. to Hon. Shiro Kashiwa U.S. Ct. Claims, 1976-77; ptnr. McDermott, Will & Emery, Chgo. Adj. prof. law Chgo.-Kent Coll. Law, 1987—. Mem. ABA, Ill. State Bar Assn., Chgo. Bar Assn. (chmn. state and local tax com. 1986-87), Phi Kappa Phi, Phi Beta Kappa, Beta Alpha Psi, Phi Gamma Mu, Phi Alpha Delta. Office: McDermott Will & Emery 227 W Monroe St Ste 4700 Chicago IL 60606-5096 Home Phone: 708-424-1804; Office Phone: 312-984-7533.

GAGGIOLI, RICHARD ARNOLD, mechanical engineering educator; b. Highwood, Ill., Dec. 3, 1934; s. Gustavo and Constantina Lucille (Mordini) G.; m. Anita Catherine Sage, Nov. 9, 1957; children: Catherine Anne, Michael James, Daniel Richard, Edward Thomas, Mary Esther. BME, Northwestern U., Evanston, Ill., 1957, MS (NSF fellow), 1958; PhD (Gen. Electric, NSF fellow), U. Wis., 1961. Registered profl. engr., Wis., 1965. Coop. student engr. Abbott Labs. (pharms.), North Chicago, Ill., 1954-58; asst. prof. mech. engring. U. Wis., Madison, 1962-66, assoc. prof., 1966-69; prof., chmn. dept. mech. engring. Marquette U., Milw., 1969-72, prof., 1969—81, 1990—2001, rsch. prof., 2002—; dean engring. and architecture Cath. U. Am., Washington, 1981-84; prof. mech. engring. U. Mass., Lowell, 1985-89. Mem. U.S. Army Math. Rsch. Ctr., Madison, 1964-66; NSF-Soc. Indsl. and Applied Math. vis. lectr., 1969-72, engring. cons., 1970—. Author: (with E.F. Obert) Thermo-dynamics, 1963; editor: Thermodynamics-Second Law Analysis, Vol. 1, 1980, Vol. 2, 1983, Analysis of Energy Systems, 1985, Computer-Aided Engineering of Energy Systems, 1986; (with M.J. Moran) Analysis and Design of Advanced Energy Systems: Fundamentals, 1987; (with G. Tsatsaronis) Fundamentals of Thermodynamics and Energy Analysis, 1990; (with G.M. Reistad) Thermodynamics and Energy Systems: Fundamentals, 1991, (with R.F. Boehm et al.) Thermodynamics and the Design of Energy Systems, 1992; hon. editor Internat. Jour. Applied Thermodynamics, 1998-2004; contbr. articles to profl. jours. Chmn. bd. trustees Montrose Sch., Westwood, Mass., 1987-89. Recipient Emil H. Steiger Meml. Tchg. award U. Wis., 1965, Pere Marquette award Marquette U., 1976, Best Paper award Am. Chem. Soc. Chem. Tech. jour. 1977; NSF postdoctoral fellow chem. engring. U. Wis., 1961-62; vis. fellow Battelle Meml. Inst., 1968-69; invited lectr., Rome, 1987, 95, Shanghai, 1986, Dalian, 1986, Beijing 1986, 89, 97, Abu Dhabi, 1988, Zaragoza 1993, Florence, 1989, 2003, Athens, 1991, Istanbul, 1995, Bucharest, 1997, Nancy, 1997, Krakow, 1994, 98, Tokyo, 1999, Padova, 2007, others. Fellow ASME (life; James Harry Potter gold medal 1988, advanced energy sys. divsn. best paper award 1991, E.F. Obert best paper award 2000); mem. AIChE, Summit Edn. Assn. (sec., trustee 1993—), Sigma Xi, Pi Tau Sigma, Tau Beta Pi. Roman Catholic. Office: Marquette U Dept Mech Engring Milwaukee WI 53201-1881 Home: W2202 Wilmers Grove Rd East Troy WI 53120 Office Phone: 414-430-5240. Business E-Mail: richard.gaggioli@marquette.edu.

GAGHAN, STEPHEN, scriptwriter, film director; b. Louisville, Ky., May 6, 1965; m. Minnie Mortimer, May 19, 2007; 1 child. Actor: (films) Alfie, 2004; writer: (TV series) New York Undercover, 1994; American Gothic, 1995; The Practice, 1997; NYPD Blue, 1997; (films) Rules of Engagement, 2000; Traffic, 2000 (Acad. award for best adapted screenplay, 2001); The Alamo, 2004; Havoc, 2005; dir., prodr. Abandon, 2002; Syriana, 2005 (Best Adapted Screenplay, Nat. Bd. Review, 2005, Edgar Allan Poe award for motion picture screenplay, Mystery Writers Am., 2006); writer, prodr.: (TV series) Sleepwalkers, 1997; actor: (TV appearances) Entourage, 2007. Recipient Best Adapted Screenplay award, Nat. Bd. Rev., 2005. Office: William Morris Agy One William Morris Pl Beverly Hills CA 90212*

GAGIN, LAWRENCE VINCENT, ceramics engineer, consultant; b. Sterling, Ill., Oct. 19, 1918; s. Charles Francis and Lillian Ella Gagin; m. Marion Winifred Buffinger, May 28, 1942; children: Jean, Paula, Lawrence, Mary, James. BS in Engring., U. Ill., Champaign-Urbana, 1942. Registered profl. ceramic engr., Nat. Inst. Ceramic Engring. Rsch. engr. Libbey Glass Co., Toledo, 1946—48; asst. dir. glass tech. Kimble Glass Co., Toledo, 1948—54; chief ceramic engr. Glass Fibers, Inc., Toledo, 1954—58; mgr. rsch. Johns-Manville Fiber Glass, Toledo, 1958—76, Denver, 1976—82; tech. cons. in field, 1982—. Instr. chem. engring. night sch. U. Toledo, 1950—52; vis. scientist Elem. and H.S., 1989—98. Contbr. articles to profl. publs. Vol. exec. Internat. Exec. Svc. Corp., Bangkok, 1989; chmn. planning and zoning Town of Columbine Valley, Colo., 1979—84; scoring observer Internat. Golf Tournament, 1986—2002. Capt. Corps Engrs. US Army, 1942—46, ETO. Fellow: Am. Ceramic Soc.; mem.: ASTM (glass and glass products coms. 1970—82, mortars for masonry com. 1974—82, resource recovery 1978—82, cons. engr. 1982—2006, C14-91 std. ref. materials 1968—82), Nat. Inst. Ceramic Engrs., Columbine Country Club. Republican. Roman Catholic. Achievements include development of Dyna Quartz pure silica fiber insulation for Boeing Dyna-Soar, first vehicle designed to return from space; patents for low lead television glass; low viscosity glass for glass fibers; superior durability, easily fiberized glass; high temperature glass for fibers; fiber die pad for extruding hot metals; fluroine free glass for fiber glass insulations; alkali resistant glass for reinforcing cement; low viscosity glass for air attenuating glass fibers; development of manufacturing process for TV cathode ray tubes; patents for lead free glass for TV bulbs; improved glass for fibers for reinforcing plastics; high temperature resistant silaceous compounds and method for producing; development of manufacturing processes for TV cathode ray tubes. Avocations: golf, woodworking, photography, gardening. Home: 18 Wedge Way Columbine Valley CO 80123 Personal E-mail: LVGglassman@aol.com.

GAGLIANI, WILLIAM DENNIS, school librarian; s. Gilbert Dario and Albertina Gagliani; life ptnr. Janis M. Radziun. BA, U. Wis., Milw., 1986, BA in English and Geol. Sci., 1982. Lectr. dept. English U. Wis., Milw., 1987—88; stacks supr. Marquette U. Meml. Libr., Milw., 1988—. Author: Thin Hung the Web, To Flutter in Memories, Icewall, Until Hell Calls Our Names (Darrell award Memphis Sci.Fiction Assn., 1999), Kiss a Bubba Good Mornin', A Knight of Swords, Carried on the Wind, Only Spectres Still Have Pity, Kneel at the Shrine, If She Promised You Heaven, Port of Call, Lead Me Into Temptation, We Were Like Lions, Starbird, Dark Places, Underground, The Serpent Said, The Great Belzoni and the Monster of Goa, Of A Feather, Stand by Your Zombie, The Great Belzoni and the Gait of Anubis; author: (with David Benton) Mood Elevator; author: (novels) Wolf's Trap, 2003 (Bram Stoker award finalist, 2004), 2006; editor: (literary magazine) Square One, 1984—89. Recipient 3d prize, Sci. Fiction Writers of Earth, 1989, 2d prize, 1993, 1994. Mem.: Internat. Thriller Writers, Horror Writers Assn. (Bram Stoker award additions com. mem. 2003—, acting sec. 2006, membership chair 2006). Avocations: weapons collecting, progressive rock music. Home: PO Box 214 Oak Creek WI 53154 Personal E-mail: wdg@williamdgagliani.com, tarkusp@execpc.com.

GAGLIARDI, RAYMOND ALFRED, physician; b. New Haven, Nov. 20, 1922; s. Carl Albert and Carmela (Esposito) G.; m. Patricia DeTuncq, Apr. 6, 1946; children: Laura E. Quigley, John Bell. BS, Yale U., 1943, MD, 1945. Pvt. practice radiology, Pontiac, Mich., 1951-92; chmn. dept. radiology St. Joseph Mercy Hosp., Pontiac, 1976-91, chmn. emeritus, 1991—. Clin. faculty radiology Wayne Univ. Sch. of Medicine, 1951—92. Author: The Golf Story: An Anecdotal History of Golf, 1999, Reflections and Recollections, 2000; editor-in-chief History of the Radiological Sciences, 1995; contbr. articles to profl. jours. Capt. U.S. Army, 1946-48; PTO. Fellow Am. Coll Radiology; mem. Am. Roentgen Ray Soc. (pres. 1987-88, Gold Medal award 1989, Hartman medal 1995, Centennial lectr. 2000), Mich. Radiol. Soc. (pres. 1972), Mich. Med. Soc. (Disting. Svc. award 1988), Oakland Hills Country Club, Royal Palm Yacht and Country Club (past commodore 1994), Heathers Club. Republican. Avocation: golf. Home: 789 Upper Scotsborough Way Bloomfield Hills MI 48304-3827 Address: 2100 Queen Palm Rd Boca Raton FL 33432 Home Phone: 248-332-2102. Personal E-mail: raygagliardi@bellsouth.net.

GAGLIARDI, UGO OSCAR, systems software architect, educator; b. Naples, Italy, July 23, 1931; came to U.S., 1956; s. Edgardo and Lina (Valenzuela) G.; m. Anna Josephine Italiano, July 7, 1954 (div. May 1972); children: Oscar Marco, Alex Piero. Diploma in Math. and Physics, U. Naples, Italy, 1951; DEng in Elec. Engring., U. Naples, 1954. Chief scientist U.S. Air Force, Hanscom AFB, Mass., 1965-66; rsch. fellow Harvard U., Cambridge, Mass., 1966—67, lectr., 1967—74, prof. practice computer engring., 1974-83, Gordon McKay prof. practice computer engring., 1983—2000; v.p. tech. ops. Interactive Scis., Inc., Braintree, Mass., 1968-70; dir. engring. Honeywell Info. Systems, Waltham, Mass., 1970-75; pres. Gen. Systems Group, Salem, NH, 1975—; chmn. Ctr. for Software Tech., Inc., 1982-99; vis. prof. Harvard Grad. Sch. Design, 2000—. Mem. NAS rsch. coun. panel Nat. Computer Systems Lab. (formerly Inst. Computer Scis. and Tech.), Nat. Inst. Standards and Tech. (formerly Nat. Bur. Standards), 1985-91, chmn., 1988-91. Fulbright scholar Columbia U., 1955-56. Office: Harvard U 335 Gund Hall 48 Quincy St Cambridge MA 02138 Address: General Systems Group 280 Perry Oliver Rd Wells ME 04090-6937 Home Phone: 207-646-9119; Office Phone: 207-646-9694. Personal E-mail: uog@focus.com. Business E-Mail: uog@deas.harvard.edu.

GAGNÉ, DOREEN FRANCES, nurse practitioner, educator; b. Altoona, Pa., Jan. 9, 1960; d. Arch Leon and Kim (Youngja) Gunnett; m. Philip Bast Gagné, Sept. 4, 1984; children: Philip Alexander, Laura Elizabeth. BS in Nursing, Pa. State U., State College, 1981; MS in Nursing, U. Md., Balt., 2002. Cert. family nurse practitioner, Am. Nurses Credentialing Ctr., 2002, Am. Nurses Credentialing Ctr., 2006, otorhinolaryngology nurse, Soc. Otorhinolaryngology/Head and Neck Nurses, 2004. Clin. staff nurse pediatric oncology/transplant Children's Hosp., Phila., 1981-85, Johns Hopkins Hosp. Children's Ctr., Balt., 1985-89; nursing educator Anne Arundel Med. Ctr., Annapolis, Md., 1998—2002; ENT nurse practitioner Office of Drs. Gehris, Jordan, Day and Assocs., Balt., 2002—. Nursing instr., vis. lectr. Anne Arundel CC, Arnold, Md., 1998—2002; nursing educator, clin. staff nurse Greater Balt. Washington Med. Ctr., Glen Burnie, Md., 1998—2002; grad. tchg. asst. U. Md. Sch. Nursing, 1999—2001. Co-chair cmty. and project rsch. Jr. League Annapolis (Md.), 1992. Mem. Social Register Assn., Sigma Theta Tau. Republican. Avocations: skiing, running, aerobics. Home: 21 Windward Dr Severna Park MD 21146-2442 Office: Anne Arundel C C Allied Health Bldg Arnold MD 21012 Office Phone: 410-879-9100. Business E-Mail: dgagne@drsgehrisjordandayandassociates.com.

GAGNE, ERIC, professional baseball player; b. Montreal, Can., Jan. 7, 1976; Pitcher LA Dodgers, 1999—2006, Tex. Rangers, 2006—07, Boston Red Sox, 2007—. Named Rolaids Relief Man, Nat. League, 2003, 2004; named to All Star Team, 2002, 2003, 2004; recipient Cy Young award, Nat. League, 2003, Espy Award for Record Breaking Performance, ESPN, 2004. Achievements include holding MLB record of 84 consecutive saves. Office: Boston Red Sox 4 Yawkey Way Boston MA 02215-3496*

GAGNÉ, SIMON, professional hockey player, Olympic athlete; b. Ste-Foy, Que., Can., Feb. 29, 1980; Left wing Phila. Flyers, 1999—. Mem. Team Can., Olympic Games, Salt Lake City, 2002, Torino, Italy, 06, Team Can., Word Cup of Hockey, 2004. Named to NHL All-Rookie Team, 2000, NHL All-Star Game, 2001. Achievements include being a member of gold medal Canadian Hockey team, Salt Lake City Olympic Games, 2002; being a member of World Cup Champion Team Canada, 2004. Office: c/o Phila Flyers 3601 S Broad St Philadelphia PA 19148 also: Can Hockey Assn Father David Bauer Arena 2424 University Dr NW Calgary AB T2N 3Y9 Canada

GAGNON, CRAIG WILLIAM, lawyer; b. St. Cloud, Minn., Dec. 19, 1940; s. Marvin Sylvester and Signa Gunhild (Johnson) G.; children: Nicole, Jeffrey, Camille; m. Pam Peglow, Nov. 8, 1980; children: Claire, Jillian, Jane. BA, U. Minn., 1964; JD magna cum laude, William Mitchell Coll. Law, 1968. Bar: Minn. 1968, U.S. Dist. Ct. Minn. 1968, U.S. Tax Ct. 1972, U.S. Supreme Ct. 1970. Ptnr. Oppenheimer, Wolff & Donnelly, Mpls., 1968—. Chmn. bd. Equity Bank; bd. dirs. XOX Corp., First Fla. Bank. Trustee William Mitchell Coll. Law, St. Paul. 1989—, chmn. bd., 1999-2000. Named Alumnus of Notable Achievement, U. Minn. Fellow Am. Coll. Trial Lawyers; mem. Metro Breakfast Club (pres. 1993), Am. Bd. Trial Advocates (assoc.), Am. Law Inst. Avocations: hunting, fishing, golf. Home: 4807 Sunnyside Rd Edina MN 55424-1109 Office: Oppenheimer Wolff & Donnelly 45 S 7th St Ste 3400 Minneapolis MN 55402-1609 E-mail: cgagnon@oppenheimer.com.

GAGNON, ROBERT, application developer; b. Chelsea, Mass., Oct. 6, 1951; s. Francis Ovid Gagnon and Evelyn Mildred Muollo. BS, U. Mass., Boston, 1973. Report designer/programmer Bay Cove Human Svcs., Boston, 1985—. Owner 1728 Software Sys., Revere, Mass., 1999—. Mem.: Am. Mensa. Personal E-mail: wolf@1728.com.

GAGNON, STEWART WALTER, lawyer; b. Beaumont, Tex., Jan. 29, 1949; s. Stewart Paul and Helen Anne (Payne) G.; m. Lynn Bass, July 29, 1972; children— Ashley Lynn, Jason Stewart. Student, Trinity U., 1967-69; B.A., U. Houston, 1971; J.D., S. Tex. Coll. Law, 1974. Bar: Tex. 1974 , U.S. Dist. Ct. (so. dist.) Tex. 1975, U.S. Ct. Apls. (5th cir.) 1975, U.S. Supreme Ct. 1976. Assoc. firm Fulbright & Jaworski, Houston, 1974-83, participating assoc., 1983—87, ptnr., 1987—, and head, family law dept.; mem. family & law coun. State Bar of Tex., 1990—, Supreme Ct. Commn. on Child Support Guidelines; master/referee Harris County Dist. Cts., Houston, 1977—. Asst. scoutmaster Boy Scouts Am., Troop 642, Houston, 1970—; mem. State Dem. Exec. Com., Tex., 1984-90; mem. Houston Found. Bd. Pub. Trust, 1982-90; lectr. Spring Branch Ind. Sch. Dist., 1976—; mem., bd. dirs. Sam Houston Area coun. Boy Scouts Am. Recipient Award of Merit, Boy Scouts Am., 1982, Silver Beaver award, 1983, Dan R. Price award for Outstanding Contbns. to Family Law in the State of Tex., 1994. Fellow Am. Acad. Matrimonial Lawyers; mem. Houston Bar Assn., Tex. Bar Assn. (dist. 4 com. on admissions), Gulf Coast Family Law Specialists Assn. (dir., pres. 1986—), Tex. Acad. Family Law Lawyers (v.p., pres. 1988), Gulf Coast Legal Found. (bd. dirs., pres. 1991), Houston Volunteer Lawyers Program, 1987-88; Presbyterian. Office: Fulbright & Jaworski LLP 1301 McKinney St Houston TX 77010-3031 Office Phone: 713-651-5151. Office Fax: 716-651-5246. Business E-Mail: sgagnon@fulbright.com.

GAGNON BLODGETT, MICHELLE DAWN, psychologist; b. West Palm Beach, Fla., Jan. 30, 1965; BA, Fla. Internat. U., Miami, 1992; Psy.D., Nova Southeastern U., Davie-Ft. Lauderdale, Fla., 1998. Lic. clin. psychologist Fla. Dept. of Profl. Regulation, 1999. Dir., rsch. grant (trauma & long-term care) Phila. Geriatric Inst., 1999—2000; dir. of geriatric inst. and clin. faculty Ctr. for Psychol. Studies Nova Southeastern U., Davie-Ft. Lauderdale, Fla., 2000—05, coord. of geriatric svcs. health professions divsn., clin. faculty Coll. of Medicine, 2005—. Contbr. articles to profl. jours. Founding mem. NSU Suicide Prevention Team, NSU Interdisciplinary Balance and Fall Prevention Clinic, Broward County Coalition for Optimal Behavioral Health and Aging; bd. dirs. Silver Impact Ctr., Lauderdale, Fla., 2001—06; mem. Broward Coalition for Optimal Behavioral Health and Aging, Ft. Lauderdale, 2001—06. Fellow Geropsychology fellow, Phila. Geriatric Ctr., 1998—99. Mem.: Gerontol. Soc. of Am. (assoc.), APA (assoc.). Achievements include development of a standard mental capacity clinical evaluation for Adult Protective Services & provide training. Avocations: yoga, travel, art, gardening, bicycling. Office: Nova Southeastern University 3200 S University Dr Fort Lauderdale FL 33328 Home Phone: 561-795-3403. Personal E-mail: mgagnon123@aol.com. Business E-Mail: gagnonmi@nova.edu.

GAGOSIAN, LARRY, art dealer; b. LA, 1945; Founder, owner Gagosian Gallery, NYC, Chelsea, NY, Beverly Hills, Calif., London, 2000; established King's Cross Gallery, London, 2004; represents Andy Warhol estate; co-founder (with Peter M. Brant) Contemporary Art Holding Corp., Tex., 1990, pres., dir. Tex., 1990—. Named World's Greatest Art Businessman, Art Review mag., 2004. Office: care Gagosian Gallery Inc 980 Madison Ave New York NY 10021-1848 also: Gagosian Gallery 6-24 Britannia St London WC1X 9JD England

GAGOSIAN, ROBERT B., chemist, educator; b. Medford, Mass., Sept. 17, 1944; m. Susan Gagosian; children: Travis, Alex. SB in Chemistry, MIT, 1966; PhD in Organic Chemistry, Columbia U., 1970; degree (hon.), LI Univ., 2000, Northeastern U., 2000. Asst. scientist Woods Hole Oceanog. Instn., Mass., 1972-76, assoc. scientist, 1976-82, sr. scientist, 1982—, chmn. dept. chemistry, 1982-87, assoc. dir. rsch., 1987-92, sr. assoc. dir., dir. rsch., 1992-93, acting dir., 1993, dir., 1994, pres., dir., 2002. Vis. lectr. dept. geology and geophysics Yale U., 1975, cons., lectr. in field; mem. numerous vis. coms. and rsch. panels NSF, Office Naval Rsch., univs. and rsch. orgns. in U.S. and fgn. countries; mem. corp. Bermuda Biol. Sta. for Rsch., Sea Edn. Assn. Contbr. chpts. to books, articles to profl. jours. Vis. scholar U. Wash., 1983, Australian Inst. Marine Scis., 1983; vis. fellow Australian Nat. U., 1983; William Evans fellow, U. Otago, Dunedin, New Zealand, 1987. Mem. Am. Chem. Soc., AAAS, Geochem. Soc. Am., Am. Geophys. Union, European Assn. Organic Geochemists, Sigma Xi. Office: Pres & Dirs Office WHOI Mail Stop 40A Woods Hole MA 02543 Office Phone: 508-289-2502. Office Fax: 508-457-2190. E-mail: prose@whoi.edu.

GAHAGAN, THOMAS GAIL, obstetrician, gynecologist; b. Brush Valley, Pa., Apr. 14, 1938; s. Ben D. and Zula C. (Brown) G.; m. Mary A. Miller, Dec. 23, 1960; children: David, Diane, Kevin, Keith. BA, Washington and Jefferson Coll., 1960; MD, U. Pa., Phila., 1964. Diplomate Am. Bd. Ob/Gyn. Intern U. Ky., Lexington, 1964-65, resident in ob/gyn., 1965-68; group practice Dr. Jones and Kelch P.A., Newark, Ohio, 1970-71, Naples (Fla.) Ob/Gyn., 1971-85; pvt. practice Naples, 1985-99; ret., 1999. Capt. USAF, 1968-70. Fellow ACOG, Fla. Ob-Gyn. Soc.; mem. AMA, Am. Cancer Soc. (life, bd. dirs. Collier unit 1973-93, bd. dirs. Fla. div. 1976-91, pres. 1986-87, St. George medal 1990), Fla. Med. Assn., Collier County Med. Soc. (exec. com. 1989-94, pres.-elect 1991-92, pres. 1992-93). Republican. Presbyterian. Avocations: scuba diving, flying, golf, skiing, fishing. *The secret to my enjoyment of life has been keeping my priorities in order.*

GAHALA, ESTELLA MARIE, writer, consultant; b. Alva, Okla., Mar. 28, 1929; d. Ivan Grant Crouse and Margaret Estella Beck; m. Dale Lowell Lange, Apr. 18, 1998; m. John W. Gahala, Nov. 27, 1964 (dec. Aug. 1, 1989). BA magna cum laude, Wichita State U., Kans., 1953; MA, Middlebury Coll., Vt., 1963; PhD, Northwestern U., 1980. Tchr. Highland Pk. HS, Topeka, 1953—57, Amarillo HS, Tex., 1957—60, Glenbrook North HS, Northbrook, Ill., 1960—64; dept. chmn. Evanston Township HS, Ill., 1964—73; dir. curriculum Lyons Township HS, LaGrange, Ill., 1973—84; author, cons. Scott Foresman Pub., Glenview, Ill., 1984—94, McDougal Littell Pub., Boston, 1994—. Pres. Gahala Assocs., Pk. Ridge, Ill., 1980—96. Author: Son et Sens, 1984, Dis-moi, 1993, En Español, 2004, Avancemos, 2007; contbr. articles to profl. jours. Vol. Albuquerque (N.Mex.) Mus. Art, 1987—2003, Presbyn. Hospice Care, Albuquerque, 1991—2007; vol. working with homeless and abused women; mem. ch. counsel First United Meth. Ch. Named Chevalier Palmes Académiques, French Ministry Edn., 1975. Mem.: Am. Assn. Tchrs. French (chpt. pres. 1970—72, mem. exec. coun. 1976—81), Am. Coun. Fgn. Langs. Democrat. Avocations: art, genealogy. Home and Office: 2315 Madre Drive NE Albuquerque NM 87112 Personal E-mail: egahala@aol.com.

GAIBER, LAWRENCE JAY, financial company executive; b. Chgo., Mar. 20, 1960; s. Sy Bertrym and Mildred (Dickler) G. BS in Econ., U. Pa., 1982. Mgmt. intern Eisai Co. Ltd, Tokyo, 1980; dept. mgr. Anglo Am. Corp., Johannesburg, Republic of South Africa, 1982-84; pres. Sandton Fin. Group, LA, 1984—, Swellendam Fin. Group, Studio City, Calif., 1984—, also bd. dirs. Bd. dirs. Lawrand Ltd, Satellite Telecommunication, Inst. Cellular Nutritional Immunology, Introlagater, Gaiber, Introlagater, L.A. Greetings; chmn. Mechanics Express Inc. Contbr. articles to profl. jours and mags. Mem. South Africa Found., Johannesburg, 1984—, Town Hall Calif., 1986; bd. dirs. Brentwood Arts Coun.; vice chmn. western region 1986 Pres.' dinner Rep. Nat. Com., Washington. Recipient Most Active Vol. award S. African Inst. Internat. Affairs, 1983; honoree for contbns. to aspiring entrepreneurial women Mayor Tom Bradley's Office and Nat. Network of Hispanic Women, L.A., 1986. Mem. L.A. Venture Assn., L.A. C. of C., L.A. Jr. C. of C., Van Nuys C. of C., L.A. County Rep. Lincoln Club, L.A. County Young Reps., Brentwood Rep. Club (pres. 1984—). Clubs: Wharton Bus. Sch., Calif. Yacht. Avocation: world travel.

GAIHA, VISHNU DAS, cardiologist; b. New Delhi, May 2, 1945; arrived in U.S., 1969; MBBS, All India Inst. Med. Scis., 1968. Diplomate Am. Bd. Internal Medicine, Am. Bd. Cardiology, bd. cert. Am. Bd. Interventional Cardiology, 2002. Intern Albert Einstein Med. Ctr., Phila., 1969-70; resident internal medicine Northwestern U. Med. Ctr., Chgo., 1970-72; fellow cardiologist U. Mich. Hosps., Ann Arbor, 1972-74; attending physician active cons. St. Francis Hosp., Evanston, Ill., 1974—. Attending physician, cons. Swedish Covenant Hosp., Rush N. Shore Hosp., 1974—, Evanston Hosp., 2000—. Fellow Am. Coll. Cardiologists (cert.), Am. Coll. Chest Physicians, Soc. Internat. Cardiology. Office: 800 Austin St Ste 602 Evanston IL 60202-3446 Office Phone: 847-491-1977. Office Fax: 847-491-0949. Personal E-mail: vgaiha100@hotmail.com.

GAILEY, CHAN, JR., (THOMAS CHANDLER GAILEY), college football coach; b. Gainesville, Ga., Jan. 5, 1952; m. Laurie Gailey; 2 children. BS in Phys. Edn., U. Fla., 1974. Grad. asst. U. Fla., 1974-75; defensive backfield coach Troy State U., 1976-79, head coach, 1983-84; defensive backfield coach Air Force, 1979-82; asst. coach Denver Broncos, NFL, 1989-90, offensive coord., wide receivers coach, 1989-90; head coach Birmingham Fire, WFL, 1991-92, Samford U., 1993; wide receivers coach Pitts. Steelers, NFL, 1994-95, offensive coord., 1996-98; coach Dallas Cowboys, 1998-99; offensive coord. Miami Dolphins, 2000—01; head coach Ga. Tech., 2002—. Office: Georgia Tech Athletic Assn 150 Bobby Dodd Way NW Atlanta GA 30332-0455*

GAILIUS, GILBERT KEISTUTIS, manufacturing executive; b. Boston, June 21, 1931; s. Joseph B. and Mary K. Gailius; m. Lillian P. Romanskis, Sept. 6, 1954; children: Gregory, Laura, Louise, Gilbert, Linda, Gary. BS in Bus. Adminstrn., Suffolk U., 1958; MBA, Boston Coll., 1962. Plant controller, staff asst. corp. controller Continental Group, NYC, 1954-66; v.p. fin. Foster Grant Co., Inc., Leominster, Mass., 1966-77, Midland Glass Co., Cliffwood, NJ, 1977-78, Am. Biltrite Inc., Wellesley Hills, Mass., 1978—99, v.p. strategic planning, 2001, now bd. dirs. Served with U.S. Army, 1952-54. Mem. Fin. Execs. Inst. Office: Am Biltrite Inc 57 River St Wellesley MA 02481-2013

GAILLARD, GEORGE SIDAY, III, architect; b. Miami, Fla., Apr. 24, 1941; s. George Siday and Sarah Margaret (Crawford) G.; m. Charlalee Bailey, 1965 (div. 1969); m. Sylvia Gayle Bridgewater, July 18, 1977; 1 child, Barron Matthew. BS, Ga. Inst. Tech., 1965; postgrad., Ga. State U. Registered architect Ga. Sole propr. Fox Magnanimus, Atlanta, 1971—78, Gaillard & Assocs., Atlanta, 1978—81, 1983—2004; mgr. design dept. Deca Inc., Miami, 1982, ret., 2004; prin., owner GIII Enterprises, 2005—. Sculpture exhibited in group shows at Piedmont Arts Festival, 1971, 73. Cubmaster Cub Scouts Am., Stone Mountain, Ga., 1988-89. With USMCR, 1962-68. Mem. AIA (chmn. liaison com. So. Coll. Tech. Atlanta chpt. 1989-90), Huguenot Soc. SC, Clan Lindsay Assn. U.S.A. Inc. (Ga. rep. 1989-95, elected coun. 2006), St. Andrew's Soc. Atlanta (bd. dirs. 1996-98, interim v.p. 2002), Clan Gunn Soc. N.Am. Avocations: reading, camping, constructing and competing with blackpowder rifles.

GAILLARD, MARY KATHARINE, physicist, educator; b. New Brunswick, NJ, Apr. 1, 1939; d. Philip Lee and Marion Catharine (Wiedemayer) Ralph; children: Alain, Dominique, Bruno. BA, Hollins Coll., Va., 1960; MA, Columbia U., 1961; Dr du Troiseme Cycle, U. Paris, Orsay, France, 1964, Dr-es-Sciences d'Etat, 1968. With Ctr. Nat. Rsch. Sci., Orsay and Annecy-le-Vieux, France, 1964-84, head rsch. Orsay, 1973-80, Annecy-le-Vieux, 1979-80, dir. rsch., 1980-84; prof. physics, sr. faculty staff Lawrence Berkeley lab. U. Calif., Berkeley, 1981—. Morris Loeb lectr. Harvard U., Cambridge, Mass., 1980; Chancellor's Disting. lectr., U. Calif., Berkeley, 1981; Warner-Lambert lectr. U. Mich., Ann Arbor, 1984; vis. scientist Fermi Nat. Accelerator Lab., Batavia, Ill., 1973-74, Inst. for Advanced Studies, Santa Barbara, Calif., 1984, U. Calif., Santa Barbara, 1985; group leader L.A.P.P., Theory Group, France, 1979-81, Theory Physics div. LBL, Berkeley, 1985-87; sci. dir. Les Houches (France) Summer Sch., 1981; cons., mem. adv. panels U.S. Dept. Energy, Washington; cons. Nat. Sci. Bd., 1996-97, 2002, bd. dirs., 1997-2002. Co-editor: Weak Interactions, 1977, Gauge Theories in High Energy Physics, 1983; contr. articles to profl. jours. Recipient Thibaux prize U. Lyons (France) Acad. Art and Sci., 1977, E.O. Lawrence award, 1988, J.J. Sakurai prize for theoretical particle physics, APS, 1993; Guggenheim fellow, 1989-90. Fellow Am. Acad. Arts and Scis., Am. Phys. Soc. (mem. various coms., chair com. on women, J.J. Saburai prize 1993); mem. AAAS, NAS, Am. Philos. Soc. Office: U Calif Dept Physics Berkeley CA 94720-0001

GAILLARD, THEODORE LEE, JR., literature and language educator, writer; b. NYC, Feb. 6, 1939; s. Theodore Lee and Patricia Coffin (Lindsay) G.; m. Elena Love, June 23, 1962 (div. July 1979); children: Gregory Lindsay, Jennifer Love; m. Ann Elizabeth Schwarberg, July 9, 1985. AB, Yale U., 1961; AM, Middlebury Coll., Vt., 1970. Asst. promotion mgr. Time-Life Internat., NYC, 1961-64; history/English instr. Athens (Greece) Coll., 1964-65; tchr. English, crew coach St. Mark's Sch., Southboro, Mass., 1965-73; head upper sch., chair English dept. The Hockaday Sch., Dallas, 1973-88; dean faculty Brunswick Sch., Greenwich, Conn., 1988-89; acad. dean Lake Forest (Ill.) Acad., 1989-94; freelance writer Phila., 1994—; tchr. English Agnes Irwin Sch., Rosemont, Pa., 1996-97; sr. product mktg. specialist Kulick & Soffa Industries, Willow Grove, Pa., 1998; dir. comm. U. Pa. Law Sch., Phila., 1999; tchr. French, Latin, English Wm. Penn Charter Sch., Phila., 1999—2000; contbr. Straus Military Reform Project, Ctr. Def. Info, Washington, 2005—. Cons. Armed Forces Jour. Internat., McLean, Va., 1996-03, ITV-West, Bristol, UK, 2005; advanced placement reader in English, Ednl. Testing Svc., Princeton, NJ, 1972-81. Contbr. over 100 articles to profl. jours. and newspapers. Cpl. USMCR, 1961-67. Recipient Am. Spirit Honor medal Citizens Com. for Army, Navy and Air Force, 1962, Outstanding Tchr. award U. Chgo., 1993; named in his honor Hockaday Sch. English Dept. Office, 2006; English Speaking Union fellow, 1956-57. Mem. U.S. Naval Inst., Nature Conservancy, Natural Resources Def. Coun., Fedn. Am. Scientists, Phila. Mus. Art, Franklin Inn Club, Phi Beta Kappa. Episcopalian. Avocations: photography, writing, hiking, reading. Home: 755 Manatawna Ave Philadelphia PA 19128-1020

GAINER, RONALD LEE, lawyer; b. Lansing, Mich., Aug. 7, 1934; s. Asher Leroy and Gladys Irene (Harvey) G.; m. Alice Louise Sherwood, June 15, 1957; children— Gregory Sherwood, Geoffrey Scott. BA magna cum laude, Mich. State U., 1956; JD, U. Mich., 1959. Bar: N.Y. 1960, D.C. 1963, U.S. Supreme Ct. 1963. Atty. appellate sect., criminal div. Dept. Justice, Washington, 1963-69, dep. chief legis. and spl. projects, 1969-73, chief legis. and spl. projects, 1973-75, dir. Office of Policy and Planning, 1975-77; dep. asst. atty. gen. Office for Improvements in Adminstrn. of Justice, 1977-81, Office of Legal Policy, 1981-83, dep. assoc. atty. gen., 1984-85, assoc. dep. atty. gen., 1985-86, dep. assoc. atty. gen., 1986-89; ptnr. Gainer, Rient and Hotis (and successor Gainer and Rient), Washington, 1990—2002; consulting atty. on internat. criminal fraud, 2003—. U.S. expert mem. UN Com. on Crime Prevention and Control, 1979-92; designated mem. U.S. Sentencing Commn., 1985-88; bd. dirs., mem. adv. com. Internat. Ctr. Criminal Law Reform and Criminal Justice Policy, 1992—; dir. fed. criminal code reform project Dept. Justice, 1970-84. Mem. editl. bd. Criminal Law Forum, 1989—; contbr. articles to nat. and internat. profl. jours. Served to capt. U.S. Army, 1960-63. Recipient Disting. Svc. award U.S. Atty. Gen., 1973; Guggenheim fellow Yale Law Sch., 1974-75. Mem. Am. Law Inst., Internat. Soc. Reform Criminal Law (bd. dirs., mem. mgmt. com., 1989—), Internat. Assn. Prosecutors, DC Bar Assn., Cosmos Club. Home: 3000 N Monroe St Arlington VA 22207-5371 Office Phone: 202-408-8000. E-mail: rlg@gainer.us.

GAINES, BOYD, actor; b. Atlanta, May 11, 1953; Diploma, Julliard Sch. Performances include (stage) Spring Awakening, 1978, Oliver Oliver, 1984, The Double Bass, 1985, The Heidi Chronicles, 1988, Philadelphia, Here I Come!, 1988, The Show Off, 1992, She Loves Me, 1993 (Antoinette Perry award for leading actor in a musical 1994), Company, 1995, Cabaret, 1999, Contact, 2000, Anything Goes, 2002, Short Talks on the Universe, 2002, Twelve Angry Men, 2004, Journey's End, 2007 (Outer Critics Cir. award outstanding featured actor in a play, 2007, Drama Desk award outstanding featured actor in a play, 2007), (film) Fame, 1980, Porky's, 1982, The Sure Thing, 1985, Heartbreak Ridge, 1986, Call Me, 1988, Ray's Male Heterosexual Dance Hall, 1988, The Grass Harp, 1995, I'm Not Rappaport, 1996, (TV) One Day at a Time, 1981-84, Evergreen, 1985, Remington Steele, 1985, LA Law, 1986, Hotel, 1984, 1985, & 1986, Spenser: For Hire, 1988, Pigeon Feathers, 1988, The Days and Nights of Molly Dodd, 1989, Piece of Cake, 1990, A Woman Named Jackie, 1991, Anything But Love, 1992, Murder She Wrote, 1992, Law & Order, 1993, 1995, & 1997, Frasier, 1994, Caroline in the City, 1997, Remember WENN, 1997, The Education of Max Bickford, 2001 & 2002, 100 Centre Street, 2001 & 2002, Queens Supreme, 2003; reader for audio books.*

GAINES, BRENDA J., retired financial services company executive; b. Chgo., July 22, 1949; d. Clarence and DeLouise Gaines. BA, U. Ill., 1970; MA, Roosevelt U., 1976. Spl. asst. to regional adminstr then dep. regional adminstr. US Dept. Housing & Urban Devel., Chgo.; commr. Housing Authority City of Chgo., dep. chief staff to Mayor Harold Washington, 1985—87; advanced through co. in govt. and cmty. rels. to sr. v.p. residential lending Citigroup, Inc., Chgo., 1988—92; sr. v.p. Diners Club N.Am. (subsidiary of Citigroup), Chgo., 1992—99, pres., 1999—2004. Mem. Diners Club Internat. Global bd.; bd. dirs. CNA Financial, Nicor, Inc., Tenet Healthcare Corp., Office Depot, Inc, Fannie Mae, 2006—. Named Volunteer of the Yr., Boys & Girls Club Chgo., 1999; named one of 50 Most Powerful Black Executives in Am., Fortune, 2002, Chicago's 100 Most Influential Women, Crain's Chicago Business, 2004; recipient Black Achievers in Industry award, 1995, Pioneer award, Urban Bankers Forum, 1996, Woman of Achievement award, Anti-Defamation League, Otto Wirth award, Roosevelt U., 2000.

GAINES, ERNEST JAMES, author; b. Oscar, La., Jan. 15, 1933; s. Manuel and Adrienne J. (Colar) G., m. Dianne Saulney BA, San Francisco State Coll., 1957; LHD (hon.), Denison U., 1980, Brown U., 1985, Bard Coll., 1985, Whittier Coll., 1986, La. State U., 1987. Prof. English and resident writer U. Southwestern La., Lafayette, 1983—. Writer in residence Denison U., 1971, Stanford U., 1981, Whittier Coll., 1986, currently at Univ. Southwestern La.; vis. prof. Whittier Coll., 1983. Author: Catherine

Carmier, 1964, Of Love and Dust, 1967, Bloodline, 1968, The Autobiography of Miss Jane Pittman, 1971, A Long Day in November, 1971, In My Father's House, 1978, A Gathering of Old Men, 1983, A Lesson Before Dying, 1993 (Nat. Book award for fiction 1994), Mozart and Leadbelly: Stories and Essays, 2005. Wallace Stenger fellow Stanford U, 1957; Rockefeller grantee, 1970; Guggenheim fellow, 1971, John D. and Catherine T. MacArthur fellow, 1993; recipient Joseph Henry Jackson award San Francisco Found. for "Comeback", 1959, Nat. Endowment for the Arts award, 1967, Black Academy Arts and Letters award, 1972, La. Library Assn. award, 1972; San Francisco Arts Commn. award for excellence of achievement in lit., 1983, Amer. Academy of Arts and Letters lit. award, 1987. also: U of Southwestern LA Dept of English PO Box 44691 Lafayette LA 70504-0001 Home: PO Box 81 Oscar LA 70762-0081

GAINES, FRANCIS PENDLETON, III, judge; b. Lexington, Va., Sept. 24, 1944; s. Francis Pendleton Jr. and Dorothy Ruth (Bloomhardt) G.; m. Mary Chilton, Dec. 19, 1967 (div. Aug. 1992); children: Elizabeth Chilton, Edmund Pendleton, Andrew Cavett. Grad., Woodberry Forest Sch., Va., 1962; BA in Hist., U. Ariz., 1967; LLB, U. Va., 1969. Bar: U.S. Dist. Ct. (Ariz.) 1969, Ariz. 1969, U.S. Ct. Appeals (9th cir.) 1972, U.S. Supreme Ct. 1975. Assoc. Evans, Kitchel & Jenckes, Phoenix, 1969-75, ptnr., 1975-89, Fennemore Craig, Phoenix, 1989-99; judge Superior Ct. of Ariz., Phoenix, 1999—; assoc. presiding civil judge Maricopa County Superior Ct., 2001—05, Maricopa County Complex Civil Litigation Ct., 2003—. Panel arbitrators N.Y. Stock Exch., 1984-99, NASD, 1984-99; judge pro tem Ariz. Ct. Appeals, 1994-95, 2006-07, Maricopa County (Ariz.) Superior Ct., 1994-99; mem. State Bar Disciplinary Hearing Com., 1991-94, chair, 1995-97; mem. nat. litig. panel U. Va. Sch. Law; mem. Ariz. Commn. on Judicial Performance Review, 2001—; lectr. and panelist CLE programs. Author: Punitive Damages-A Railroad Trial Lawyers Guide, 1985. Chmn. bd. govs. All Saints' Episcopal Day Sch., Phoenix, 1990—91; sr. warden All Saints' Episcopal Ch., 1994—97, parish chancellor, 1997—99, diversity preceptor, 1999—2003; standing com. Episcopal Diocese of Ariz., 1997—2001. Named one of 500 Leading Judges in Am., Lawdragon mag., 2006; recipient Outstanding Alumnus award, U. Az., 2002. Fellow: Ariz. Bar Found., Am. Bar Found.; mem.: ABA, Am. Coll. Bus. and Comml. Ct. Judges, Nat. Conf. State Trial Judges (coms. on jury mgmt. and bus. and comml. cts.), Securities Industry Assn., Nat. Assn. R.R. Trial Counsel (exec. com. Pacific Region, v.p. 1997—98), Maricopa County Bar Assn., State Bar Ariz. (civil practice and procedure com. 2000—, professionalism course oversight com. 2001—), U. Ariz. Pres.'s Club, Univ. Club. Republican. Episcopalian. Office: Superior Ct Ariz 201 W Jefferson St Phoenix AZ 85003-2205 Home Phone: 602-943-6219; Office Phone: 602-506-3940. Business E-Mail: pgaines@superiorcourt.maricopa.gov.

GAINES, IRVING DAVID, lawyer; b. Milw., Oct. 14, 1923; s. Harry and Anna (Finkelman) Ginsburg; m. Ruth Rudolph, May 22, 1947 (dec. Apr. 5, 1979); children: Jeffrey S., Howard R., Mindy S. Gaines Pearce; m. Lois Conen, Nov. 25, 1979 (div. Sept. 2005). BA, U. Wis., Madison, 1943; JD, 1947; postgrad., U. Pa., 1943-44. Bar: Wis. 1947, U.S. Dist. Ct. (ea. dist.) Wis. 1947, U.S. Supreme Ct. 1954, U.S. Ct. Appeals (7th cir.) 1954, U.S. Dist. Ct. (we. dist.) Wis. 1970, Fla. 1971, U.S. Dist. Ct. (so. dist.) Fla. 1972, U.S. Dist. Ct. (mid. dist.) Fla. 1976, U.S. Ct. Appeals (11th cir.) 1981. Pvt. practice, Milw., 1947—72; ptnr. Gaines & Saichek, S.C. (and predecessor firm), Milw., 1972-78; sr. ptnr. Gaines Law Offices, S.C., Milw., 1979—. Arbitrator N.Y. Stock Exch., 1988—, Nat. Assn. Securities Dealers, 1988—, Am. Stock Exch., 1988—; mediator Wis. Ct. of Appeals, Dist. I. Contbr. articles to profl. jours. Bd. vis. U. Wis. Law Sch., 1987—96, Milw. County Cir. Ct. Commn., 1997—2005. With US Army, 1943—46. Mem.: ATLA (state committeeman 1981—83, lectr.), ABA (com. current lit. on real property law, com. law and medicine negligence sect., various coms. title ins. litig. and real estate), Bar Assn. U.S. Ea. Dist. of Wis., Am. Arbitration Assn. (arbitrator 1966—, nat. panel arbitrators), Milw. Bar Assn. (exec. com. 1974—77, cts. com., econs. of law com., past chmn. unauthorized practice of law com., past chmn. negligence sect., lectr. programs, seminars, bench-bar com., appellate bench bar com.-civil), Wis. Acad. Trial Lawyers (pres. 1958—59, 1970—71, lectr.), 7th Fed. Cir. Bar Assn., State Bar Assn. Wis. (bd. govs. 1982—85, publs. com. 1982—91, past com. ethics, rsch. planning and earlier settlement coms., lectr. CLE seminars, convs., dist. com. state bd. lawyer regulation 2003—), Fla. Bar Assn. (bd. editors Fla. Bar Jour. 1972—84). Office: 312 E Wisconsin Ave Ste 208 Milwaukee WI 53202-4305 Home: 1600 W Green Tree Rd Apt 218 Milwaukee WI 53209 Home Phone: 414-352-5575; Office Phone: 414-271-1938.

GAINES, JAMES EDWIN, JR., retired librarian; b. Dalton, Ga., Feb. 21, 1938; s. James Edwin and Olivia (McCarty) Gaines; m. Sally Martin, Nov. 27, 1965 (div. May 1985); children: Thomas Martin, Robin Jeannette, Steven McCarty; m. Elizabeth Hood, July 28, 1990. AB, Emory U., 1961, MLS, 1964; PhD, Fla. State U., 1977. Tchr. English Marist Coll. H.S., Atlanta, 1961-62; grad. library asst. Emory U., Atlanta, 1962-64; asst. to head of pub. services U. Cin., 1964-65; asst. cataloger Antioch Coll., Yellow Springs, Ohio, 1965-68; dir. library Birmingham-So. Coll., Birmingham, Ala., 1968-74; head librarian Va. Mil. Inst., Lexington, 1976-93; ret., 1994. Contbr. Mem. Com. on Fgn. Rels., Charlottesville, Va., 1982—91; sec. ARC, Rockbridge County, Va., 1993—98, Rockbridge Disability Svcs. Bd., 1993—; v.p. Rockbridge Area Transp. Sys., 2005—. Mem.: ALA, Va. Libr. Assn. (chmn. coll. and univ. sect. 1979—80), So. Assn. Colls. and Schs. (vis. committeeman 1979—89), Kiwanis (sec. 1985—92, 1999—2001, v.p. 2001—02, pres. 2002—03, sec. 2003—04, 2006—07). Democrat. Presbyterian. Home: 9 Edmondson Ave Lexington VA 24450-1903 E-mail: jegaines@rockbridge.net.

GAINES, JERRY LEE, retired secondary school educator; b. Seminole, Okla., Feb. 18, 1940; s. Frank Gaines and Jane M. (Crowe) Gring; m. Lorraine Louise Paulson, Oct. 7, 1961; children: Paul Martin, Mark Edwin. AA, Pasadena City Coll., 1960; BA, Calif. State U., LA, 1964; MA, Calif. State U., Long Beach, 1969. Tchr. bus. Rolling Hills High Sch., Rolling Hills Estates, Calif., 1965-91, Palos Verdes Peninsula High Sch., Rolling Hills Estates, 1991—2002. Coord. driver edn. Palos Verdes Peninsula Unified Sch. Dist., Palos Verdes Estates, Calif., 1970-91, mentor tchr., 1984-93. Co-author driver edn. workbook; contbr. articles to traffic safety publs. Chmn. San Pedro (Calif.) Citizens Adv. Com., 1985-88; pres. South Shores Homeowners Assn., San Pedro, 1986-90, 95-96, San Pedro and Peninsula Homeowners Coalition, 1990-93; commr. City of L.A. Charter Reform Commn., 1997-99, City of L.A. Planning Commn., 2000-02; County of L.A. Workforce Investment Bd., 2002—; bd. dirs. South Bay Credit Union, 1997—. With USN, 1960-62. Mem. NEA, Calif. Tchrs. Assn., Nat. Bus. Edn. Assn., Calif. Bus. Edn. Assn., Am. Driver and Traffic Safety Edn. Assn. (bd. dirs. 1982-88), Calif. Assn. Safety Edn. (pres. 1982-83, 1998-2000), Elks, Lions, Phi Delta Kappa. Avocations: travel, model railroading. Home: 2101 W 37th St San Pedro CA 90732-4707 Personal E-mail: jgaines852@aol.com.

GAINES, LA DONNA ADRIAN See SUMMER, DONNA

GAINES, MARY S., library director; B, Fla. A&M U., Tallahassee; MLS, Fla. State U., Tallahassee. With St. Petersburg Pub. Libr. Sys., Fla., 1985—, dir. Mem.: ALA, Pinellas Pub. Libr. Coop. (mem. libr. dir.'s adv. coun.), Tampa Bay Libr. Consortium (bd. dirs.), Nat. Forum Black Pub. Adminstrs., Fla. Libr. Assn. Office: St Petersburg Pub Libr Sys 280 5th St N Saint Petersburg FL 33701 Office Phone: 727-893-7736.

GAINES, RUTH ANN, secondary school educator; BA in Drama and Speech, Clarke Coll.; MA in Dramatic Art, U. Calif., Santa Barbara. Tchr. drama East High Sch., Des Moines, 1971—. Host Classroom Connection Cable TV; former TV/radio prodr., talk show host TCI of Ctrl. Iowa, WHO; diversity facilitator Heartland Area Edn. Agy., Des Moines, 1979—; instr. speech and drama Des Moines Area C.C., 1971—. Bd. dirs. Very Spl. Arts, Hospice of Ctrl. Iowa, Westminster Ho.; former bd. dirs. YWCA of Greater Des Moines, Polk County Mental Health Assn., Drama Workshop, Des Moines Tutoring Ctr.; vice chair City Wide Strategic Plan, 1994-95; state senate candidate, 1994; racial justice coord. YWCA, 1992-93; chair Cross Cultural Rels., Des Moines Area Religious Coun., 1988-89; dir. religious edn. St. Ambrose Cathedral, 1981-83; grad. Leadership Iowa Class of 1997. Recipient Wal-Mart Tchr. of Yr., 1998, Iowa Tchr. of Yr., 1998, Angel in Adoption award, 1999, Friends of Iowa Civil Rights Commn. Tchr. of Yr. award, 2000, U. Iowa's Phyllis M. Yeager Commitment to Diversity award, 2001, I'll Make Me a World in Iowa Heritage Legacy, 2002, Des Moines Bus. Records' Woman of Influence, 2002, USA Today's All USA Tchr. Recognition 3d Team, 2002; grad. Greater Des Moines Leadership Inst., 2002; inducted into Nat. Tchr. Hall of Fame, 2003. Mem. Iowa Edn. Assn., Des Moines Edn. Assn., Delta Kappa Gamma, Phi Delta Kappa, Delta Sigma Theta, Delta Kappa Pi. Home: 3501 Oxford St Des Moines IA 50313-4562 Office: East High Sch 815 E 13th St Des Moines IA 50316-3499

GAINES, WEAVER HENDERSON, lawyer; b. Ft. Meade, SD, Aug. 31, 1943; s. Weaver Henderson and Bertha Louise (Harris) G. AB in Philosophy, Dartmouth Coll., 1965; LLB, U. Va., 1968. Bar: N.Y. 1969, Pa. 1979, U.S. Dist. Ct. (so. dist.) N.Y. 1973, U.S. Dist. Ct. (ea. dist.) N.Y. 1975, U.S. Ct. Appeals (2d cir.) 1975. Assoc. Dewey, Ballantine, Bushby, Palmer & Wood, NYC, 1970-79; sr. staff counsel INA Corp., Phila., 1979; asst. gen. counsel, sec. Thyssen-Bornemisza Inc., NYC, 1979-82, v.p. strategic projects, 1982-85; v.p., dep. gen. counsel Mut. of N.Y., NYC, 1985-86, sr. v.p., gen. counsel, 1986-90, exec. v.p., gen. counsel, 1990-92; pres. Unified Mgmt. Corp., 1989-90; chmn. Ixion Biotechnology, Inc., Alachua, Fla., 1993—2007, CEO, 1993—2002; v.p., mng. dir. Americas Biotech Distributor, LLC, 2005—. Bd. dirs. Unified Fin. Svcs., Inc., Voyetra Turtle Beach, Inc., Americas Biotech Distributor, LLC, EccoArray, Inc., BIO Fla. Inc., Fla. Rsch. Consortium, Inc., Eagle Pines Acad.; vis. prof. Sch. Law U. Va., 2003—; adv. coun. Keck Grad. Inst. Life Scis. Bd. dirs. N.Y. Lawyers for Nixon, 1972; sr. advisor Bush/Quayle '92. Capt. U.S. Army, 1968-70, Vietnam. Decorated Bronze Star. Mem. ABA, Assn. Bar City N.Y., N.Y. Athletic Club, Haile Plantation Golf and Country Club. Republican. Episcopalian. Office: Americas Biotech Distributors LLC 13709 Progress Blvd Box 28 Alachua FL 32615-9495 Office Phone: 386-462-3961. Personal E-mail: weaver.gaines@worldnet.att.net. Business E-Mail: weaver.gaines@americasbiotech.com.

GAINES-PAGE, RENA L., science educator; d. Llyod William Gaines and Jo-Dee Petre; m. David H. Page III, Apr. 19, 1987. BS in Phys. Anthropology, U. Calif., Davis, 1986. Cert. tchng. credential Calif. Secondary tchr. Wilson HS, LA, 1989—91; seconday tchr. Huntington Pk. (Calif.) HS, 1991—. Sci. dept. chairperson Huntington Pk. HS, 2003—05, sci. dept. coord., 2005—. Mem.: Calif. Tchg. Assn. Office: Huntington Park HS 6020 Miles Ave Huntington Park CA 90255 Home Phone: 562-924-7730; Office Phone: 323-583-3333.

GAINETDINOV, RAUL RADIKOVICH, pharmacologist, researcher; b. Mishkino, Bashkiria, Russia, Sept. 1, 1964; s. Radik Akhmetovich Gainetdinov and Lilia Masgutovna Gainetdinova; m. Tatyana Dmitirevna Sotnikova; 1 child, Bulat Raulevich. MD, 2-nd Moscow Med. Inst., Russia, 1988; PhD, Inst. of Pharmacology, Moscow, 1992. Sr. rschr. Inst. of Pharmacology, Moscow, 1994—2004; asst. rsch. prof. Duke U., Durham, NC, 2000—06, assoc. rsch. prof., 2006—. Contbr. chapters to books, articles to profl. jours. Recipient Young Investigator award, Internat. Soc. Neurochemistry, 1993, Investigator award, Tourette Syndrome Inc., 1997, Michael J. Fox Parkinson's Rsch., 2005, 2006. Mem.: NY Acad. Sci., European Behavioral Pharmacology Soc., Soc. for Neurosci. Achievements include development of novel pharmacotherapies for schizophrenia, ADHD; patents pending in field; research in cocaine abuse, Parkinson's disease, schizophrenia. Avocations: chess, fishing. Office: Duke Univ CARL Bldg Rm 487 Research Dr Durham NC 27710 Office Fax: 919-681-8641. Business E-Mail: r.gainetdinov@cellbio.duke.edu.

GAINEY, BOB (ROBERT MICHAEL), professional sports team executive, retired professional hockey player; b. Peterborough, Ont., Can., Dec. 13, 1953; m. Cathy Collins (dec. June 21, 1995); children: Anna, Laura, Colleen. Hockey player Montreal Canadiens, 1973-89; coach, player Les Ecureuils, Epinal, France; head coach, gen. mgr. Minn. North Stars, 1990-96; head coach Dallas Stars, 1993—96, v.p., gen. mgr., 1996—2001, cons., 2002; exec. v.p., gen. mgr. Montreal Canadiens, 2003—, interim head coach, 2006. Recipient Frank J. Selke award as Best Defensive Forward, 1977-78, 78-79, 79-80; Conn Smythe trophy as Most Valuable Player Nat. Hockey League Playoffs, 1978-79; elected to Hockey Hall of Fame, 1992. Office: Montreal Canadiens 1275 St Antoine St West Montreal PQ Canada H3C 5L2

GAINEY, LILAH LEIGH, librarian; b. Lubbock, Tex., Nov. 15, 1950; d. Will Allison and Bertha Beatrice G. B. Music. Edn., Lubbock Christian Coll., 1974; M.Ed., Tex. Tech. U., 1980; M.L.S., Sam Houston State U., 1982. Tchr. Crosbyton Elem. Sch. (Tex.), 1974-78; tchr.Levelland (Tex.) Pub. Schs., 1979-80; grad. teaching asst. Sch. Library Sci., Huntsville, Tex., 1981-82; librarian Abilene Christian U., 1982-95, Ea. N.Mex. U., 1996—. Mem. com. svc. computer and tech. Ea. N.Mex. U., 1997—, scholarship com., 2003—, campus devel. staff com., 2005—, leadership program, 2004-05, profl. senate, 2005—; svc. adv. com. Amigos Lib. Svc., 2000-01; chmn. libr. consortium Llano Estacado Info. Access Network, 1999—; chmn. Reading is Fundamental, 2001-03; coord. Meals on Wheels, 2000—. Contbr. articles to profl. jours. Mem. ALA (Jr. Mems. Roundtable, publicity chmn. 1985-87), Tex. Library Assn. (dist. 1 sec. 1983-84, pres. 1986-87)), Sam Houston Library Sch. Alumni Assn. (v.p. 1982-83, pres. 1983-84) AAUW, Ea. N.Mex. U. Women (pres. 2005—), N.Mex. Libr. Assn. (membership com., presenter), Delta Kappa Gamma. Home Phone: 505-760-0672; Office Phone: 505-562-2640. Business E-Mail: lilah.gainey@enmu.edu.

GAINOR, THOMAS EDWARD, bank executive; b. St. Paul, Oct. 13, 1933; s. Joseph Paul and Teresa Cecilia (Whelan) G.; m. Janan Rose Nolan, Aug. 8, 1964; children: Mary, Michael, John, Daniel. BS, Marquette U., 1955; postgrad., Rutgers U., 1965-67, Stanford U. Exec. Program, 1977; PhD in Internat. Rels. and Diplomacy (hon.), Am. Grad. Sch. Internat. Rels. and Diplomacy, Paris, 1999. With Fed. Res. Bank of Mpls., 1958-93, asst. v.p., 1967-72, v.p., 1972-75, sr. v.p. ops., 1975-78, 1st v.p., COO, 1978-93. Bd. dirs. Am. Bancorp., 1994-96. Bd. dirs. Mpls. United Way, 1974-83, v.p., 1974-77; bd. dirs. Vis. Nurse Svc., 1967-75, pres., 1971-72; trustee Visitation Sch., 1983-89, v.p., 1985, chmn., 1986-88; mem. Commn. Archdiocesan Programs, 1983-89, chmn., 1986-87; trustee St. Joseph's Ch., 1985—; trustee St. Thomas Acad., 1989-98, chmn., 1992-98; bd. dirs. St. John Vianney Sem., 1986-2002, Cath. Charities, 1990-96; pres. Cath. Cmty. Found., 1994-2001, sec., 2002-03; internat. adv. coun. Am. Grad. Sch. Internat. Rels. and Diplomacy, Paris, 1997—; bd. dirs. Total Life Care Ctrs., 1998—, v.p., 1999-2001, pres., 2002-04. Served as officer USNR, 1955-58. Mem.: Naval Res. Assn., Marquette U. Alumni Assn., Stanford Alumni Assn., Six o'Clock Club (pres. 1982). Roman Catholic. E-mail: tjgainor@aol.com.

GAINSBOROUGH, JENNI, advocate; Grad., U. London; MBA, Pepperdine U., Malibu, Calif. Staff assoc. Pub. Adminstrn. Svc.; pub. policy coord. ACLU Nat. Prison Project; prog. assoc. with Campaign for an Effective Crime Policy to sr. policy analyst The Sentencing Project, Washington; dir. Washington office Penal Reform Internat., 2002; policy and prog. assoc. Nat. Juvenile Justice Network. Contbr. articles to profl. publs. Office: Nat Juvenile Justice Network at the Coalition for Juvenile Justice 1710 Rhode Island Ave NY 10th Fl Washington DC 20036 Office Phone: 202-467-0864. Office Fax: 202-887-0738. E-mail: gainsborough@juvjustice.org.*

GAINSBURG, ROY ELLIS, publishing executive; b. Bklyn., May 1, 1932; s. Herbert Harry Gainsburg and Etta (Stein) Kornfeld; m. Vicki Bloye, July 12, 1957; children: Julie, Jeanne. AB, Brown U., 1954; LLB, Harvard U., 1957. Bar: NY 1957. From assoc. to ptnr. Szold & Brandwen, NYC, 1957-87; exec. v.p. St. Martin's Press Inc., NYC, 1987, pres., 1987-97, part-time v.p. adminstrn., 1997—. V.p. adminstrn. Holtzbrinck Pubs. and Tor Books; bd. dirs., exec. v.p. Macmillan Acad. Pub., Inc. Bd. dirs. The Partnership for the Homeless, NYC, 1997—2006, chair, 2001—04. Democrat. Home: 157 Ralston Ave South Orange NJ 07079-2344 Office: Holtzbrinck Pubs 175 5th Ave New York NY 10010-7848 Home Phone: 973-763-0445; Office Phone: 646-307-5478. Personal E-mail: rgainsburg@verizon.net. Business E-Mail: roy.gainsburg@hbpub.com.

GAISER, ROBERT RAYMOND, obstetric anesthesiologist, educator; b. Pt. Pleasant, New Jersey, Sept. 18, 1962; s. Alfred and Eleanor Gaiser; m. Randi Berkowitz, Aug. 13, 1992; children: Matthew Thomas, Kimberly Beth. MD, Columbia U., NYC, 1984—88. Diplomate in anesthesiology Am. Bd. of Anesthesiology, 1993. Prof. of anesthesia and critical care U. of Pa., Phila., 2007—. Den leader Boy Scouts of Am., Mt. Laurel, NJ, 2001—04; Sunday sch. tchr. Recipient Tchr. of the Yr., Dept. of Anesthesia, 1993, 1996, Lindback Award for Edn., 1997, Outstanding Clin. Tchr., Graduating Med. Students, 1999—2000, Tchr. of the Yr., Dept. of Anesthesia, 2000, Internat. Anesthesia Rsch. Soc. Award, 2004. Mem.: Soc. of Obstetric Anesthesia (assoc.), John Morgan Honor Soc. (assoc.). Achievements include research in multiple publications concerning obstetric anesthesia. Home: 8 Edinburgh Ln Mount Laurel NJ 08054 Office: Univ of Pa 3400 Spruce St Philadelphia PA 19104 Office Phone: 215-662-3773. Office Fax: 215-615-3898. Business E-Mail: gaiserr@uphs.upenn.edu.

GAISSER, JULIA HAIG, classics educator; b. Cripple Creek, Colo., Jan. 12, 1941; d. Henry Wolseley and Gertrude Alice (Lent) Haig; m. Thomas Korff Gaisser, Dec. 29, 1964; 1 child, Thomas Wolseley. AB, Brown U., 1962; MA, Harvard U., 1966; PhD, U. Edinburgh, Scotland, 1966. Asst. prof. Newton Coll., Mass., 1966-69, Swarthmore Coll., Pa., 1970-72, Bklyn. Coll., Bklyn., 1973-75; assoc. prof. dept. Latin Bryn Mawr Coll., Pa., 1975-84, prof., 1984—2006, rsch. prof., 2006—. Martin Classical lectr. Oberlin Coll., 2000. Author: Catullus and his Renaissance Readers, 1993, Pierio Valeriano On the Ill Fortune of Learned Men, 1999, Catullus in English, 2001; editor Bryn Mawr Latin Commentaries, 1983—. Mem. Mid-East sel. com. Marshall Scholarships, Washington, 1975-89, chmn., 1984-89; mem. mng. com. Intercollegiate Ctr. for Classical Studies in Rome, Stanford, Calif., 1984-92, chmn., 1988-92. Decorated MBE; named Marshall scholar, U. Edinburgh, 1962—64, Phi Beta Kappa Vis. scholar, 1996—97, ACLS Travel grantee, 1985, fellow, ACLS, 1989—90, NEH sr. fellow, 1985—86, 1993—94, 1999; recipient NEH summer stipend, 1977, rsch. grantee, Am. Philos. Soc., 1980, 1993. Mem. Am. Philol. Assn. (dir. 1985-88, pres. 2000), Renaissance Soc. Am., Internat. Neo Latin Soc., Am. Philos. Soc. Office: Bryn Mawr Coll Dept Latin Bryn Mawr PA 19010 Business E-Mail: jgaisser@brynmawr.edu.

GAITHER, EDMUND BARRY, museum director, curator; b. Great Falls, SC, 1944; BA, Morehouse Coll.; attended, Ga. State U.; MFA, Brown U., 1968; LHD (hon.), Northeastern U., 1984, Framingham State Coll., 1993; DFA (hon.), RI Coll., 1994. Lectr. Spelman Coll., 1968—69, Mass. Coll. Art, 1970—71, Wellesley Coll., 1971—74, Harvard Coll., 1972—75; dir. & curator Mus. of the Nat. Ctr. of Afro-Am. Artists, Boston, 1969—; spl. cons. Mus. Fine Arts, Boston, 1969—. Vis. prof. Afro-Am. studies Boston U., 1971—83; mem. summer faculty U. Minn. Arts Leadership Inst., 1989; mem. George W. Bush's adv. bd. on Historically Black Colls. & Univs.; panel chmn. Expansion Arts Divsn, Nat. Endowment for the Arts, 1980—83. Recipient MassArt award, Mass. Coll. Art, 1988, J. Eugene Grigsby award, Nat. Art Educators Assn. Com. on Minority Concerns, 1989, Men of Vision award, Mus. Afro-Am. History, 1992, 20th Ann. award, Fondo del Sol Visual Arts Ctr., 1993, citation for contbn. to the arts, Mass. Ho. Reps., 1997, Commonwealth award for Organizational Leadership, State of Mass., 1997, Unity award, Northeastern U. John D. O'Bryant African Am. Studies Inst., 1998. Mem.: Am. Assn. Museums (Commn. on Museums for a New Century 1984, Commn. on Equity & Excellence 1986, Commn. on Museums & Cmtys. 2000, named to Centennial Honor Roll 2006), Assn. for African Am. Museums (co-founder 1968, first pres.). Office: NCAAA 300 Walnut Ave Boston MA 02119 also: Mus Fine Arts Ave of the Arts 465 Huntington Ave Boston MA 02115-5597 Office Phone: 617-442-8614. E-mail: bgaither@mfa.org.*

GAITHER, GEORGE MANNEY, marketing consultant; b. Mineola, NY, Sept. 21, 1930; s. Roscoe Bradley and Frances Bullitt (Williams) G.; m. Dorothy Wineman Streater, Apr. 4, 1953; children: Neal, George, Anne, Emee, Bruce. B in Journalism, U. Mo., 1952. From gen. mgr. to pres. Internat. Rsch. Assocs., Inc., NYC, 1955-71; pres., founder Gaither Internat., Inc., Stamford, Conn., 1971-96; cons. GMG Cons., Winchester, Va., 1997—. Lt. U.S. Army, 1952-55, Korea. Mem. Market Rsch. Coun. Republican. Avocation: writing. Home: 2628 Windwood Dr Winchester VA 22601-6418 Home Phone: 540-662-5696; Office Phone: 540-723-6892. E-mail: gmg@visuallink.com.

GAITHER, JAMES C., lawyer; b. Oakland, Calif., Sept. 3, 1937; s. Horace Rowan Jr. and Charlotte Cameron (Castle) G.; m. Susan Good, Apr. 30, 1960; children: James Jr., Whitaker, Reed, Kendra. BA in Econs., Princeton U., 1959; JD, Stanford U., 1964. Bar: Calif. 1964, U.S. Dist. Ct. D.C. 1965, U.S. Dist. Ct. (no. dist.) Calif. 1965, U.S. Ct. Appeals (D.C. cir., 7th cir., 9th cir.), 1965, U.S. Supreme Ct. Law clk. to chief justice Earl Warren, Washington, 1964-65; spl. asst. to asst. atty. gen. John W. Douglas, Washington, 1965-66; staff asst. Pres. Lyndon B. Johnson, Washington, 1966-69; atty. Cooley Godward Kronish LLP, San Francisco, 1969-71, ptnr., 1971—2000, mng. ptnr., 1984-90, sr. counsel, 2000—; mng. dir. Sutter Hill Ventures, 2000—. Cons. to sec. HEW, 1977, chmn. ethics adv. bd., 1977—80; bd. dirs. Kineto, Milpitas, Calif., nVidia Corp., Santa Clara, Satmetrix, Foster City, Calif., Hewlett Found., SeeSaw Networks, San Francisco; chair Carnegie Endowment for Internat. Peace; former trustee The RAND Corp. Editor: Stanford Law Rev., 1963—64. Former pres. bd. trustees, Stanford (Calif.) U.; mem. exec. com. bd. vis. Sch. Law Stanford U.; former chmn. bd. trustees Branson Sch., Ross, Calif., Ctr. for Biotech. Rsch. San Francisco; past trustee Family Svc. Agy. San Francisco, St. Stephens Parish Day Sch., Belvedere, Calif., The Scripps Rsch. Inst.; past trustee, chmn. protem Marin Cmty. Found, Marin County, Calif.; past pres. bd. trustees Marin County Day Sch., Corte Madera; past pres. bd. trustees Marin Ednl. Found., San Rafael; past treas., trustee Rosenberg Found.; past v.p., trustee, vice chmn. San Francisco Devel. Fund; past chmn. Dean's Adv. Coun. Stanford Law Sch., chmn. capital campaign; Inst. Capt. USMC, 1959-61. Recipient Disting. Pub. Svc. award HEW, 1977, Stanford Assocs. award Stanford U., 1989, 97; named Entrepreneur of Yr. Harvard Bus. Sch., 1979. Fellow Am. Acad. Arts and Scis.; mem. ABA, Calif. Bar Assn., San Francisco Bar Assn., Order of Coif, Phi Delta Phi (province 12). Democrat. Presbyn. Avocations: tennis, hiking, camping, fishing, photography. Office: Sutter Hill Ventures 755 Page Mill Rd # A-200 Palo Alto CA 94304

GAITHER, JOHN FRANCIS, accountant, consultant; b. Louisville, Oct. 26, 1918; s. Thomas R. and Marice F. Gaither; m. Marjilee Schaeffer, Nov. 26, 1942 (dec.); children: John Francis Jr., James M.; m. Catherine W. Cox, June 18, 2002. BCS, U. Notre Dame, 1941. CPA, Ind., Ky., Ill. Controller Evansville div. Whirlpool Corp., Ind., 1946-56; cons. Gaither, Rutherford & Co., CPAs, 1954-93; city contr., dep. mayor City of Evansville, 1972-76. Lectr., seminar leader and cons. in health care industry; legis. contact Am. Hosp. Assn., AICPA. Author: Financial Management of Medical Laboratories; contbr. articles to profl. jours. Past pres. Buffalo Trace coun. Boy Scouts Am.; mem. adv. com. Ind. Vocat. Rehab.; past trustee Brescia U., St. Benedicts Convent; past mem. regional cmty. adv. coun. Ind. U. Med. Sch.; past chmn. community adv. coun. Evansville Ctr. Med. Edn.; past chmn. Ind. Select Com. Ednl. Fin., past chmn. Ind. Utility and Energy Regulation Adv. Commn.; vice chmn. Ind. Health Facilities Fin. Authority; dir., officer Nat. Coun. Health Facilities Fin. Authorities; past mem. Ind. Transp. Coordinating Bd.; past Gov.'s rep. Ind. Hosp. Rate Rev. Commn.; past officer YMCA, Cancer Soc., Serra Club. Officer USNR, 1941-46. Recipient various awards Boy Scouts Am., other civic groups. Mem. AICPA, Ind. Assn. CPAs, Ill. Assn. CPAs, Ky. Assn. CPAs, Evansville Assn. CPAs, Inst. Mgmt. Accts. (past pres. Evansville), Ind. Assn. Cities and Towns Controllers Div. (past pres.), Ind. Soc. Chgo. (v.p.), SAR, Soc. J. Gaither Descendants Found. (pres.), Internat. Soc. Descendants of Charlemagne, First Families of Va., Evansville Country Club, Rotary Internat. Republican. Home: 730 S Colony Rd Evansville IN 47714-0636 Personal E-mail: johng730@aol.com.

GAITHER, JOHN FRANCIS, JR., lawyer, health products executive; b. Evansville, Ind., Mar. 31, 1949; s. John F. and Marjilee G.; m. Christine Luby, Nov. 26, 1971; children: John F. III, Maria Theresa. BA in Acctg., U. Notre Dame, 1971, JD, 1974. Bar: Ind. 1974, Ill. 1975, U.S. Ct. Appeals (7th cir.) 1975, U.S. Ct. Mil. Appeals 1977. CPA, Ind. Law clk. to Hon. Wilbur F. Pell, Jr. Ct. of Appeals 7th Cir., Chgo., 1974-76; assoc. atty. Bell, Boyd & Lloyd, Chgo., 1979-82; sr. atty. Baxter Healthcare Corp., Deerfield, Ill., 1982-83, asst. sec., sr. atty., 1983-84, asst. sec., asst. gen. counsel, 1984-85; sec., assoc. gen. counsel Baxter Internat. Inc., Deerfield, 1985-87, sec., dep. gen. counsel, 1987-91; v.p. law/devel. Baxter Diagnostics Inc., Deerfield, 1991-92; v.p. law, strategic planning Baxter Global Businesses, Deerfield, 1992-93; dep. gen. counsel, v.p. strategic planning Baxter Internat. Inc., Deerfield, 1993-94, corp. v.p., corp. devel., 1994-2001; v.p., sec., gen. counsel Global Healthcare Exch., LLC, Westminster, Colo., 2001—03; sr. v.p., sec., gen. counsel NeighborCare, Inc., Baltimore, Md., 2003—. Editor-in-chief Notre Dame Lawyer, 1973-74; contbr. articles to profl. jours. Lt. comdr. USNR, 1976-79. Mem. ABA, Ill. Bar Assn., Ind. Bar Assn., Chgo. Bar Assn., Ind. Assn. CPAs. Avocations: sailing, skiing. Office: Neighborcare 7 E Lee St Baltimore MD 21202-6000 Home Phone: 847-615-9680; Office Phone: 410-528-7404. E-mail: john.gaither@neighborcare.com.

GAITHER, WILLIAM SAMUEL, civil engineering executive, consultant; b. Lafayette, Ind., Dec. 3, 1932; s. William Marcius and Susan Frances (Kirkpatrick) G.; m. Robin Cornwall McGraw, Aug. 1, 1959; 1 dau., Sarah Curwen. Student, Purdue U., 1950—51; BS in Civil Engring, Rose Poly. Inst., 1956; M. Sci. Engring. (Arthur Le Grand Doty fellow), Princeton, 1962, MA (Ford Found. fellow), 1963, PhD (Ford Found. fellow), 1964. Registered profl. engr., Del., Penn. Engr. Dravo Corp. (marine constrn.), Pitts., 1956-60; supt. Myer Corp., Neenah, Wis., 1960-61; supervising engr., pipeline divsn. Bechtel Corp., San Francisco, 1965-67; assoc. prof. coastal engring. dept. U. Fla. at Gainesville, 1964-65; mem. faculty U. Del. at Newark, 1967-84, assoc. prof. civil engring., 1967-70, prof. civil engring., 1970; prof., dean U. Del. at Newark (Coll. Marine Studies), 1970-84, also dir. sea grant coll. program; pres., prof., trustee Drexel U., Phila., 1984-87, Weston Inst., West Chester, Pa., 1988-93; Inner City Consortium, Inc., 1993-94; owner Gaither & Assocs., Tucson, 1993—. Trustee Mut. Assurance Co., 1985-96; mem. marine bd. NRC, 1975-81; chmn. Gov.'s Oil Transp. Study Com., 1971-73; mem. Gov.'s Task Force Marine and Coastal Affairs, 1970-72, Gov.'s Coun. Sci. and Tech., Del., 1970-72; bd. dirs. Roy F. Weston, Inc., 1974-91, vice chmn., 1988-91; bd. dirs. Phila. Electric Co., 1985-89; mem. ocean affairs adv. com. U.S. Dept. State; mem. Commn. on the Future, Rose-Hulman Inst. Tech., 1991-93; mem. Cyberfab.net. LLC, 1999—. Chmn. adv. coun. dept. civil engring. Princeton U., 1973-84; bd. dirs. University City Sci. Ctr., 1984-93, Penjurdel Coun., 1984-2000, Ednl. Found. of Chester County, 1989-92; pres., dir. Soc. John Gaither Desc., Inc., 1984-87; port warden Phila. Maritime Mus., 1987-93; founding dir., sec. Internat. Consciousness Rsch. Labs., 1996—; vestryman Ch. St. Andrew and St. Monica, 1987-93, chmn. fin. com. 1991-96; bd. dirs., mem. exec. com. Phila. H.S. Acads., Inc., 1988-93; chmn. bd. govs. Environ. Tech. Acad., 1988-93; prin. sponsor Delaware Valley Sci. Fairs, 1990-93. Pvt. U.S. Army, 1953. Recipient Disting. Achievement award Rose Poly. Inst., 1975, Disting. citizenship award News Jour. Papers, Del., 1975, Norman Sollenberger award Princeton U., 1983; named to Lambda Chi Alpha Alumni Hall of Fame, 1996; named hon. citizen of Lewes, Del., 1980. Fellow: ASCE (chmn. offshore policy com. 1979—84); mem.: Nat. Water Rsch. Inst. (rsch.adv. bd. 1991—2002), Acad. Sci. Phila. (bd. dirs. 1989—92), Sea Grant Program Instns. (pres. 1973—74), Del. Acad. Scis. (pres. 1971—72), Ariz. Sr. Acad., Cosmos Club. Home and Office: 7719 S Galileo Ln Tucson AZ 85747-9605 Office Phone: 520-647-7267. E-mail: gaitherws@cox.net.

GAJARSA, ARTHUR J., judge; b. Norcia, Italy, Mar. 1, 1941; arrived in U.S., 1949; m. Melanie E. Gajarsa. BSEE, Rensselaer Polytech. Inst, 1962; JD, Georgetown U., 1967; MA in Econs., Cath. U., 1968. Bar: US Patent Office 1963, DC 1968, US Dist. Ct. DC 1968, US Ct. Appeals (DC cir.) 1968, Conn. 1969, US Supreme Ct. 1971, DC Superior Ct. 1972, US Ct. Appeals (DC cir.) 1972, US Ct. Appeals (9th cir.) 1974, US Dist. Ct. (no. dist.) N.Y. 1980. Patent examiner US Patent Office, Dept. Commerce, 1962—63; patent adviser USAF, Dept. Def., 1963—64, Cushman, Darby & Cushman, 1964—67; law clk. to Judge Joseph C. McGarraghy US Dist. Ct. (DC), Washington, 1967—68; atty. office gen. counsel Aetna Life and Casualty Co., 1968—69; spl. counsel, asst. to commr. Indian affairs Bur. Indian Affairs, Dept. Interior, 1969—71; assoc. Duncan and Brown, 1971—72; ptnr. Gajarsa, Liss & Sterenbuch, 1972—78, Gajarsa, Liss & Conroy, 1978—80, Wender, Murase & White, 1980—86; ptnr., officer Joseph, Gajarsa, McDermott & Reiner, P.C., 1987—97; judge US. Ct. Appeals (Fed. cir.), Washington, 1997—. Contbr. articles to profl. jours. Trustee Rensselaer Neuman Found., 1973—, Found. Improving Understanding of Arts, 1982—96, Outward Bound, 1987—96, Rensselaer Polytech. Inst., 1994—; gov. John Carroll Soc., 1992—99; regent Georgetown U., 1995—2000, bd. dirs., 2000—. Recipient Sun and Balance medal, Rensselaer Polytech. Inst., 1990, Rensselaer Key Alumni award, 1992, Albert Demers Fox award, 1999, Gigi Pieri award, Camp Hale Assn., 1992, 125th Anniversary medal, Georgetown U. Law Ctr., 1995, Order of Commendatore, Republic of Italy, 1995, Alumni Fellows award, Rensselaer Alumni Assn., 1996, Paul Dean award, Georgetown U., 1999. Mem.: Am. Judicature Assn., DC Bar Assn., Nat. Italian Am. Found. (bd. dirs. 1976—99, gen. counsel 1976—89, pres. 1989—92, vice-chair 1993—96), Fed. Cir. Bar Assn. Office: US Ct Appeals Fed Cir 717 Madison Pl NW Washington DC 20439-0002*

GAJL-PECZALSKA, KAZIMIERA J., retired surgeon, pathologist, educator; b. Warsaw, Nov. 15, 1925; came to U.S., 1970; d. Kazimierz Gajl and Anna Janina (Gervais) Gajl; widowed; children: Kazimierz Peczalski, Andrew Peczalski. Student, Jagiellonian Univ., Cracov, Poland, 1945-47; MD, Warsaw U., Poland, 1951, PhD in Immunopathology, 1964. Diplomate Polish Bd. Pediatrics, Polish Bd. Anatomic Pathology, Am. Bd. Pathology. Attending pediatrician Children's Hosp. for Infectious Diseases, Warsaw, Poland, 1953-58, head, pathology lab., 1958-65; adj. prof. Postgrad. Med. Sch., Warsaw, Poland, 1965-70; fellow U. Minn., Mpls., 1970-72, asst. prof. dept. pathology, 1972-75, assoc. prof. dept. pathology, 1975-79, prof. dept. pathology, 1979-00, dir. immunophenotyping and flow lab., 1974-00, dir. cytology dept. pathology, 1976-95; ret., 2000. Author chpts. to book; contbr. of numerous papers to profl. jours. Fellow WHO, Paris, 1959, London, 1962, Paris, 1967, U.S. Pub. Health Svcs. fellow, 1968-69; recipient Scientific Com. award Polish Ministry of Health and Social Welfare, 1964. Mem. Am. Soc. Experimental Pathology, Am. Soc. Cytology, Internat. Acad. Pathology, British Soc. Pediatric Pathology, Polish Soc. Pathology, Polish Soc Pediatricians. Roman Catholic. Avocations: music, skiing.

GAJRAJ, NOOR, anesthesiologist, educator; b. London, United Kingdom, Nov. 4, 1959; s. Harold and Mary Gajraj; m. Serena Wang, May 26, 2002; 1 child, Gavin. MD, King's Coll., London, 1978—83; fellow of royal coll. anaesthetists, King's Coll., 1978—83. Cert. Bd. cert. anesthesiology, pain mgmt., hospice and palliative care medicine, and addiction medicine. Assoc. prof. U. Tex. Southwestern Med. Ctr., Dallas, 1996—2004. Author more than 100 scientific articles. Fellow: Royal Coll. Anesthesiologists. Office: Baylor Ctr for Pain Mgmt 5575 warren Pkwy 220 Frisco TX 75034 Office Phone: 214-618-3686. E-mail: noorgajraj@aol.com.

GAL, SUSAN, anthropologist, educator; PhD, Univ. Calif., Berkeley, 1976. Mae & Sidney G. Metzl disting. svc. prof., anthropology, linguistics, social sci. Univ. Chgo. Co-author (with Gail Kligman): The Politics of Gender After Socialism, 2002 (Heldt Prize, Am. Assn. Advancement of Slavic Studies). Grantee John Simon Guggenheim Found. Fellowship, 2002—03. Fellow: Collegium Budapest, Am. Acad. Arts & Scis.; mem.: Soc. Linguistic Anthropology (pres. 1999—2002). Office: Anthropology Univ Chgo 1126 East 59th St Chicago IL 60637 Office Phone: 773-702-7701. Office Fax: 773-702-4503. Business E-Mail: s-gal@uchicago.edu.

GALAGAN, CAROL ANNE, special education educator; b. Vancouver, Wash., Dec. 26, 1963; d. John Michael and Madeline Galagan. AA, Bakersfield C.C., Bakersfieled, Calif., 1984; BA Liberal Studies, Calif. State U., Bakersfield, Calif., 1987. Calif. Asst. Tech. Project (CTAP) Levels I & II Kern County Supt. of Schools, 2003; Multiple Subject Tchg. Credential with Crosscultural Language & Academic Devel. Calif. Commn. on Tchr. Credentialing, 1999, Edn. Specialist Instruction Credential Calif. Commn. on Tchr. Credentialing, 2004, Crisis Prevention Inst. (CPI) Non-violent tng. Panama-Buena Vista Union Sch. Dist., 2005, cert. CPR Panama-Buena Vista Union Sch. Dist., 2005. Sub. tchr. Panama-Buena Vista Union Sch. Dist., Bakersfield, Calif., 1997—99; tchr., resource specialist Panama-Union Sch. Dist., Bakersfield, Calif., 1999—. Safety compliance coord. Freymiller Trucking, Bakersfield, Calif., Okla. City, 1991—97; english tchr. Ednl. Svcs. Exhchange with China, Tangshan City, China, 1991; student study team coord./facilitator Panama-Buena Vista Union Sch. Dist.: Panama Sch., Leo B. Hart Sch., Bakersfield, Calif., 2002—; sci. fair com. Panama-Buena Vista Union Sch. Dist., Leo B. Hart Sch., Bakersfield, Calif., 2005—06. Mem. talent show com. Leo B. Hart Sch., Bakersfield, Calif., 2004—06; team leader, coord. Mission to Mexico, All Saints Episcopal Ch., 1999, 2000, 2003; vol. Spl. Olympics, 2003, 2004; vestry, sr. warden, jr. warden, vestryman All Saints Episcopal Ch., Bakersfield, Calif., 1998—2002, vestryman, 2006—, youth dir./leader Bakersfield, Calif., 1997—2004, hearts and hands ministry leader, 2004—; vestry mem. Episcopal Ch. of the Resurrection, Oklahoma City, 1997; lay eucharistic min. All Saints Episcopal Ch., 2005—; del. San Joaquin Diocesan Convention, All Saints Episc. Ch., Bakersfield, Calif., 1991—93, 1997—99, 2001—02, 2005—. Mem.: Coun. for Exceptional Children (membership chair, local u. chpt. 2002—03). R-Consevative. Episcopalian. Avocations: counted cross stitch, reading. Home Phone: 661-663-8128. Personal E-mail: cgalagan@bak.rr.com.

GALAINENA, M. DAVID, lawyer; b. Cleve., Nov. 9, 1957; BA magna cum laude, Tulane U., 1980; JD, U. Notre Dame, 1983. Bar: Ill. 1983. Ptnr. Winston & Strawn LLP, Chgo., 1995—, mem. exec. com. Mem.: Phi Beta Kappa. Office: Winston & Strawn LLP 35 W Wacker Dr Chicago IL 60601-9703 Office Phone: 312-558-7442. Office Fax: 312-558-5700. E-mail: dgalainena@winston.com.

GALAMBOS, JOHN THOMAS, internist, medical educator; b. Budapest, Hungary, Oct. 29, 1921; came to U.S., 1947; m. Eva G. Cohn; children: Sharon Tobae Galambos McDuff, John Douglas, Michael Robert. BS, U. Ga., 1948; MD, Emory U., 1952. Diplomate Nat. Bd. Med. Examiners, Am. Bd. Internal Medicine, Am. Bd. Gastroenterology. Intern Barnes Hosp., St. Louis, 1952-53; resident U. Chgo. Clinics, 1953-55; dir. gastroenterology teaching program Emory U. Sch. Medicine, Atlanta, 1957-92, dir. gastroenterology labs., 1958-92, dir. div. digestive diseases, 1966-92. Dir. Gastroenterology Clinic Grady Hosp., Atlanta, 1957-92; mem. adv. bd. Nat. Inst. Digestive Diseases, NIH, Washington, 1985-88 Author: Cirrhosis, 1979, Digestive Diseases, 1983; author or co-author 36 book chpts.; contbr. 165 articles to profl. jours. Fellow ACP, Am. Coll. Gastroenterology (pres. 1975), Am. Gastroenterol. Assn., Am. Assn. for Study Liver Diseases, Internat. Assn. for Study Liver Diseases, Alpha Omega Alpha. Republican. Jewish. Avocation: sailing. Office: 95 Collier Rd NW Ste 4075 Atlanta GA 30309-1751 Office Phone: 770-804-0492. Personal E-mail: jgalambos@myway.com.

GALAMBOS, THEODORE VICTOR, civil engineer, educator; b. Budapest, Hungary, Apr. 17, 1929; s. Paul and Magdalena (Potzner) G.; m. Barbara Ann Asp, June 25, 1957; children: Paul, Ruth, Ronald, John. BSCE, U. ND, 1953, MSCE, 1954; PhD in CE, Lehigh U., 1959; Dr. honoris causa, Tech. U., Budapest, 1982; PhD (hon.), U. ND, 1998; DSc (hon.), U. Minn., 2001. Registered profl. engr. Minn., Mo. From asst. to assoc. prof. civil engring. Lehigh U., Bethlehem, Pa., 1959-65; prof. Washington U., St. Louis, 1965-81, head dept., 1970-78; prof. U. Minn., Mpls., 1981-96, emeritus prof., 1997—. Cons. engr. Steel Joist Inst., Myrtle Beach, S.C., 1965-2003; vis. prof. U.S. Mil. Acad., West Point, 1990. Author, co-author 4 books in field; editor 1 book; contbr. over 100 articles to profl. jours. Served with U.S. Army, 1954-56. Recipient T.R. Higgins award Am. Inst. Steel Constrn., 1981. Mem. ASCE (hon., Norman medal 1983, Shortridge Hardesty award 1988, E.E. Howard award 1992, OPAL award 2002, Walter P. Moore award 2004, Nathan M. Newmark medal 2004), NAE, Internat. Assn. Bridge and Structural Engrs. Democrat. Baptist. Avocation: photography. Home: 4375 Wooddale Ave Minneapolis MN 55424-1060 Office: U Minn Civil Engring Dept Minneapolis MN 55455 Business E-Mail: galam001@umn.edu.

GALAN, LEONIDEZ VINDOLLO, architect; b. Poblacion, Phillipines, Aug. 8, 1948; s. Juan Garcia Galan and Maria Victoria (Vergara) Vindollo; m. Adoracion Cipriaso Galan; children: John Patrick C., Denise Victoria. BS in Architecture, Calumpit Inst., Philippines; BS in Arch., Far Ea. U., 1965; MS in Archtl. Tech., Columbia U., 1973. Structural detailer Le Messuer Assoc. Engrs., St. Louis, 1968—69; arch. designer Port Authority N.Y. & N.J., 1969—85, task leader arch., 1985—. Cons. various cos.; pres. John Dendor Realty Corp.; asst. prof. arch. design NYU, NYC; asst. prof. Angeles Tech. Author: World Trade Center Book at Tenants Development, 1985. With US Army, 1965—68, Vietnam. Mem.: Illuminating Engring. Soc., Foreign Policy Assn., Constrn. Specification Inst., Am. Inst. Architects, Colonial Williamsburg, Nat. Trust Hist. Preservation, Lions (bde. dirs.). Roman Catholic. Avocations: tennis, bowling, swimming, dance, boxing. Office: Port Authority NY & NJ One World Trade Ctr Rm 1933 New York NY 10048

GALANDIUK, SUSAN, colon and rectal surgeon, educator; b. NYC, Mar. 6, 1957; d. Joseph and Dora (Neu) G.; m. Hiram C. Polk Jr., Dec. 22, 1991. BS cum laude, SUNY, Albany, 1976; MD summa cum laude, Julius Maximilians U., Wuerzburg, Germany, 1982. Diplomate Am. Bd. Surgery, Am. Bd. Colon and Rectal Surgery. Surg. intern Chirurgische Univ. Klinik, Julius Maximilians U., Wuerzburg, Germany, 1982-83, Cleve. Clinic Found., 1983-84, surg. resident, 1984-88; Price fellow in surg. rsch., dept. surgery U. Louisville, 1988-89, colon and rectal surgery fellow dept. surgery, 1989-90, instr. dept. surgery, 1990-91, asst. prof. dept. surgery, 1991-96, assoc. prof., 1996-2001, program dir. sect. colon and rectal surgery, 1999—, prof., 2001—; dir. Price Inst. Surg. Rsch., 2001—. Presenter in field. Editl. bd. Digestive Surgery, Mayor Clin. Procs., Diseases Colon Rectum, Archives of Surgery; contbr. chpts. to books, articles to profl. jours. Chmn. fund raising com. ARC, Louisville, 1993, 1995—97, bd. dirs., 1997—2000, chmn. bd., 2001—03; bd. mem. Fund for the Arts, 1996—2003; chair med. adv. com. Ky. chpt. Crohn's and Colitis Found. Am., Louisville, 1993—97, 1999—2003. William E. Lower Fellow Thesis prize, Clinic Found., Cleve., 1986. Fellow ACS, AAUP, Am. Soc. Colon and Rectal Surgeons (mem. chmn. rsch. found. young rschrs. com. 1996—, mem. program com. 1994-96, trustee rsch. found., 2001—, membership com., 2000—); mem. AMA, Am. Med. Women's Assn., Am. Soc. Microbiology, Assn. Acad. Surgery, Assn. Women Surgeons, Collegium Internat. Chirurgiae Digestivae, Jefferson County Med. Soc., Ky. Med. Assn. (mem. cancer com.), Louisville Surg. Soc. (pres. 2005), Hiram C. Polk Jr. Surg. Soc., Ohio Valley Soc. Colon and Rectal Surgeons, Priestly Soc., Soc. Surgery of Alimentary Tract, Soc. Am. Gastrointestinal Endoscopic Surgeons, Soc. Surg. Oncology (mem. corp. rels. and issues, govt. affairs coms.), Southea. Surg. Congress (councillor 1997-99), Surg. Infection Soc., Soc. Univ. Surgeons, Am. Soc. Gastrointestinal Endoscopists, Ctrl. Surg. Assn., Western Surg. Assn., Am. Gastroent. Assn., So. Surg. Assn., Am. Gastroenterol. Assn., Am. Soc. Human Genetics, Am. Soc. Clin. Oncology, Assn. Program Dirs. in Colon & Rectal Surgery, Soc. Pelvic Surgeons, Surg. Biol. Club I., Am. Surg. Assn. Greek Catholic. Office: U Louisville Dept Surgery 550 S Jackson St Louisville KY 40202-1622 Office Phone: 502-583-8303.

GALANIS, JOHN WILLIAM, lawyer; b. Milw., May 9, 1937; s. William and Angeline (Koroniou) G.; m. Patricia Caro, Nov. 29, 1969; children: Lia Galanis Economou, William, Charles, John. BBA cum laude, U. Wis., 1959; JD, U. Mich., 1963; postgrad. (Ford Found. grantee), London Sch. Econs., 1964. Bar: Wis. 1965; CPA, Wis. Assoc. firm Whyte & Hirschboeck S.C., Milw., 1964-68; sr. v.p., gen. counsel, sec. MGIC Investment Corp. and Mortgage Guaranty Ins. Corp., Milw., 1968-88; ptnr. Galanis, Pollack, Jacobs & Johnson, S.C., Milw., 1988—. Assoc. editor: Mich. Law Rev, 1962-63. Bd. visitors Law Sch. U. Mich., Sch. Bus. U. Wis.; past chmn. Milw. Found.; bd. dir., past pres. Milw. Boys' and Girls' Club; pres. Family Svc. Milw. Recipient Disting. Svc. award Internat. Inst., Hope Chest award Nat. MS Soc., Disting. Alumni award Milw. Boys' Club, Disting. Svc. award Milw. Civic Alliance Club, 1989, Ellis Island Medal of Honor, 2005. Mem.: ABA, Order of Coif, Milw. Bar Assn., Wis. Bar Assn., Am. Hellenic Ednl. and Progressive Assn. (past dist. gov.), Blue Mound Golf and Country Club, Milw. Athletic Club. Greek Orthodox. Home: 1200 Woodlawn Cir Elm Grove WI 53122-1639 Office: Galanis Pollack Jacobs & Johnson 2 Plaza East Ste 560 330 E Kilbourn Milwaukee WI 53202 Home Phone: 262-784-5664; Office Phone: 414-271-5400. Business E-Mail: jwg@jpjlaw.com.

GALANTE, GUSTAVO E., plastic surgeon; b. Buenos Aires, Apr. 23, 1959; BA summa cum laude, Wabash Coll., 1981; MD, Ind. U., 1985. Cert. Nat. Bd. Med. Examiners, Am. Bd. Plastic Surgery. Internship gen. surgery Loyola U. Med. Ctr., Maywood, Ill., 1985—86, resident plastic surgery, 1986—91; fellow Inst. for Aesthetic & Reconstructive Surgery, Nashville, 1991; pvt. practice Schererville and Valparaiso, Ind., 1992—. Active staff Cmty. Hosp., Munster, Ind., 1992, St. Anthony Med. Ctr., Crown Point, Ind., 1993, Ill. Surg. & Med. Ctr., Munster, 1994; with St. Margaret Mercy Health Care Ctr. Recipient Physicians Recognition award in continuing med. edn., AMA, 1995—2001. Fellow: Ohio Valley Soc. Plastic and Reconstructive Surgery, Am. Soc. Laser Medicine and Surgery, Am. Coll. Surgeons; mem.: Am. Soc. Plastic Surgeons, Phi Beta Kappa, Alpha Omega Alpha. Avocations: music, reading, running, swimming, bicycling. Office: 322 Indianapolis Blvd Ste 103 Schererville IN 46375 also: 1700 Pointe Dr Valparaiso IN 46384 Office Phone: 219-322-3131, 800-721-3244.*

GALANTE, JANE HOHFELD, musician, historian; b. San Francisco, Feb. 14, 1924; d. Edward and Lillian (Devendorf) Hohfeld; m. Clement Galante, Dec. 26, 1956; children: Edward Elio, John Clement. AB, Vassar Coll., 1944; MA, U. Calif., Berkeley, 1949. Instr. U. Calif. Ext., Berkeley, 1948—51, Mills Coll., Oakland, Calif., 1951—54. Founder, dir. Composers' Forum of San Francisco, 1946-56. Music editor Berkeley, A Jour. Modern Culture, 1944-52; concert pianist German tours for USIS, 1952-54; Young Audience Concerts, San Francisco, 1963-70; mem. Lyra Chamber Music Ensemble, 1980-90; transl.: Darius Milhaud (Paul Collaer) including revised and edited catalog Milhaud's Compositions, 1988, Darius Milhaud: Interviews with Claude Rostand, 2002. Trustee Morrison Chamber Music Ctr., San Francisco State U., 1956—; hon. trustee San Francisco Conservatory Music, 1970-99; co-founder San Francisco Friends of Chamber Music, 1999. Decorated chevalier de l'ordre des arts et des lettres; recipient Disting. Svc. award Chamber Music Am., 1992, Pres.'s medal San Francisco State U., 1998. Mem.: Am. Fedn. Musicians.

GALANTE, JORGE OSVALDO, orthopedic surgeon, educator; b. Buenos Aires, Dec. 18, 1934; arrived in U.S., 1958; m. Sofija Kabliauskas; 1 child, Charles. BA, Colegio Nacional de Buenos Aires, 1952; MD, U. Buenos Aires, 1958; DMSc, U. Goteborg, Sweden, 1967. Diplomate Am. Bd. Orthopedic Surgery. Resident in orthopaedics U. Ill., Chgo., 1960-64; assoc. investigator bioengineering lab. U. Goteborg, 1964-67; asst. prof. orthopedic surgery U. Ill. Med. Ctr., Chgo., 1967-70, assoc. prof., 1970-72; lect. in orthopedics U. Ill. Abraham Lincoln Sch. Medicine, Chgo., 1972—; adj. rsch. prof. U. Ill. Circle, Chgo., 1972—, mem. graduate faculty, 1974—; prof., chmn. dept. orthopedic surgery Rush-Presbyn.-St. Luke's Med. Ctr., Chgo., 1972-94; prof. anatomy Rush Med. Coll., Chgo., 1977—; dir. Rush Arthritis and Orthopedic Inst., 1994—. Assoc. prof. exptl. orthopedics U. Goteborg, 1969—. Contbr. articles to profl. jours. Recipient Kappa Delta award Am. Acad. Orthopedic Surgery, 1970, Clemson (S.C.) U. award, 1975, Steindler award Orthopedic Rsch. Soc., 1990, Zimmer award for Disting. Achievement in Orthopedic Rsch. Bristol-Myers Squibb, 1996, Shands award Orthop. Rsch. Soc., 2006. Office: Rush-Presbyn-St Luke's Med Ctr 1725 W Harrison Chicago IL 60612-3833 Office Phone: 312-432-2344.

GALANTE, JOSEPH A., bishop; b. Philadelphia, Pa., July 2, 1938; BA, St. Charles Seminary, Phila.; JCD, Lateran U., Rome; MA in Spiritual Theology, U. St. Thomas, Rome. Ordained priest Roman Cath. Ch. 1964, bishop 1992. Asst. pastor Our Lady of Consolation Parish, 1964—65, St. John of the Cross, Roslyn, 1965; Bishop's sec., Diocesan Master of Ceremonies Diocese of Brownsville, Tex., 1968—72, vicar for religious, Diocesan newspaper editor, 1969—72; asst. vicar for religious Archdiocese of Phila., 1972—79; resident Good Shepherd Parish, 1972—73; defender of The Bond Archdiocesan Tribunal, Phila., 1972—74; chaplain Catholic Home for Girls, St. Vincent's Residence, 1972—81; prof. Canon Law St. Charles Seminary, 1974—77, Mary Immaculate Seminary, Northampton, Pa., 1975—78; vicar for religious Archdiocese of Phila., 1979—87; chaplain Convent of the Handmaids of the Sacred Heart, Haverford, Pa., 1981—87; undersec. Congregation for Institutes of Consecrated Life & Societies of Apostolic Life, Rome, 1987—92; aux. bishop Diocese of San

Antonio, 1992—94; bishop Diocese of Beaumont, Tex., 1994—99; coadjutor bishop Diocese of Dallas, 2000—04; bishop Diocese of Camden, NJ, 2004—. Pres. Nat. Conf. for Vicars of Religious, 1976—80; spkr. in field. Religious affairs com. Canon Law Soc. Office: Diocese of Camden PO Box 708 631 Market St Camden NJ 08101

GALANTE, THOMAS W., library director; married; 2 children. BBA, St. Bonaventure U., NY; MBA, Hofstra U., Hempstead, NY; MLS, Queens Coll., CUNY, 2004. Bus. mgr. Queens Borough Pub. Libr., 1987—95, asst. libr. dir., 1995—99, dep. libr. dir. fin. and adminstrn., 1999—2003, interim dir., 2003—05, dir., 2005—. Bd. trustees, chair tech. com. Wilton Libr. Assn., Conn. Office: The Ctrl Libr 89-11 Merrick Blvd Jamaica NY 11432 Office Phone: 718-990-0700. E-mail: thomas.w.galante@queenslibrary.org.*

GALANTER, EUGENE, psychologist, educator; b. Phila., Oct. 27, 1924; s. Max and Sarah (Honigman) G.; m. Patricia Anderson, Dec. 22, 1962; children: Alicia, Gabrielle, Michelle. AB, Swarthmore Coll., 1950; A.M., U. Pa., 1951, PhD, 1953. From instr. to prof. psychology U. Pa., 1952-62; sr. rsch. fellow Harvard U., 1955—57, Ctr. Advanced Study Behavioral Scis., 1958-59; chmn. dept. psychology U. Wash., 1962-64, prof., 1964-66; Joseph Klingenstein vis. prof. social psychology Columbia U., NYC, 1966-67, prof. psychology, 1967—2007, prof. emeritus, 2007—. Cons. NIH, NSF, also to industry; mem. Coun. for Biology in Human Affairs; chmn. commn. on biology, learning and behavior Salk Inst.; founder Children's Computer Sch., 1980, sold to CompuServe, 1984; founder, chmn. bd. dirs. Children's Progress Inc., 1999—. Author: Plans and Structure of Behavior, 1960, 2d edit., 1986, CD edit., 2005, New Directions in Psychology, 1962, Textbook of Elementary Psychology, 1966, Kids & Computers: The Parents' Microcomputer Handbook, 1983, Kids & Computers: Elementary Programming for Kids in BASIC, 1983, Kids & Computers: Advanced Programming Handbook, 1984; editor: Handbook of Mathematical Psychology, 3 vols., 1963-64, Readings in Mathematical Psychology, 2 vols., 1963-65, Psych Tech Notes, 1988, version 2.1, 1994. Served with AUS, 1943-46. Decorated Bronze Star, Croix de Guerre with Palm France. Fellow AAAS, APA, Acoustical Soc. Am., N.Y. Acad. Scis.; mem. Eastern Psychol. Assn., Assn. Aviation Psychologists (pres. 1970-71), Human Factors Soc., Internat. Soc. for Psychophysics, Sigma Xi (past chpt. pres.). Achievements include patent in field. Office: Children's Progress Inc 108 W 39th St #1305 New York NY 10018 Office Phone: 212-730-0905 ext. 203.

GALANTER, MARC, psychiatrist, educator; b. NYC, Sept. 17, 1941; s. Jacob and Ada (Simms) G. BA, Columbia U., 1963; MD, Albert Einstein Coll. Medicine, 1967. Diplomate Am. Bd. Psychiatry and Neurology with added qualifications in addiction psychiatry; cert. Am. Soc. Addiction Medicine. Intern UCLA Hosp., 1967-68; resident in psychiatry Albert Einstein Coll. Medicine-Bronx Mcpl. Hosp. Ctr., 1968-71, fellow in community psychiatry, 1972-73, clin. instr., 1972-74, dir. Drug and Alcohol Cons. Service, 1972-75, career tchr. drug abuse and alcoholism Nat. Inst. on Alcohol Abuse and Alcoholism, Nat. Inst. Drug Abuse, 1973-76, asst. prof., 1974-78, dir. div. alcoholism and drug abuse, 1975-87, assoc. prof., 1978-83, prof. dept. psychiatry, 1983-87; prof. psychiatry, dir. div. alcoholism and drug abuse NYU Sch. Med., 1987—; dir. addiction divsn., rsch. scientist Collaborating Ctr. WHO, 1987-98, dep. dir. Collaborating Ctr., 1998—. Clin. assoc. Lab. Clin. Psychopharmacology, NIMH, Washington, 1970-72; instr. psychiatry residency program St. Elizabeth's Hosp.; presenter at profl. confs. U.S., Can., Thailand, Germany, Japan, India, Kenya and Italy; chmn. Nat. Conf. on Alcohol and Drug Abuse Edn., 1977; program chmn. Internat. Conf. Med. Edn. in Alcohol and Drug Abuse, WHO and Assn. Med. Edn. and Rsch. in Substance Abuse, 1982, founder, pres., 1976-77; dir. Lab. Alcoholism and Drug Abuse WHO. Editor: Ofcl. Sci. Procs. of Nat. Coun. on Alcoholism, 1978-80, Alcohol and Drug Abuse in Medical Education, 1980, (book series) Currents in Alcoholism, 1979, 80, 81, Recent Developments in Alcoholism; mem. editl. bd. Am. Jour. Drug and Alcohol Abuse, 1978—; assoc. editor jour. Alcoholism Clin. and Exptl. Rsch., Am. Jour. of Addictions, 1979, Jour. Substance Abuse Treatment, 1995—; co-editor: Advances in the Psychosocial Treatment of Alcoholism, 1984; editor-in-chief Substance Abuse Jour., 1978—; author: Cults: Faith, Health and Coercion, 1989, 2nd edit., 1999, Network Therapy for Alcohol and Drug and Abuse, 1993, 2nd edit., 1999, Spirituality and the Healthy Mind, 2005. Recipient Psychopharmacology award Am. Psychol. Assn., 1972; Career Tchr. award in drug abuse and alcoholism NIMN, 1973-77, Organon Tchg. awad Am. Psychiat. Assn., 1999; ann. Book award Commonwealth Fund, 1978-82, Macarthur medal Assn. Med. Edn. and Rsch., 1994. Fellow Am. Psychiat. Assn. (life, chmn. panel on alcoholism, nat. task force on psychiat. treatment 1983—, mem. task force on cults 1977-80, mem. com. on alcoholism, chmn. com. on addiction edn. 1992—, chmn. com. on religion 1985-90, Gold Achievement award 1993, bd. dirs. pub. group 1998--, Seymour Vastermark Edn. awrd 2002), Am. Soc. on Addiction Medicine (bd. dirs. 1986—, 2002—, sec. 1995-97, pres. elect 1997-99, pres. 1999-2001); mem. AAAS, Internat. Soc. Addiction Medicine (bd. dirs. 1999—), Am. Bd. Psychiatry and Neurology (vice chair com. on added qualifications in addiction psychiatry 1992-98), Rsch. Soc. on Alcoholism (sec. 1983-85), N.Y. State Task Force on Dual Psychiat. and Addictive Disorders (task force chmn. 1986-89, 93), N.Y. Psychiat. Soc., Am. Acad. Addiction Psychiatrists (v.p. 1987-89, pres. 1991-93, bd. dirs. 1986—, Founders award 2004), Nat. Inst. Alcohol Abuse and Alcoholism (Nat. Adv. Coun. 1997—). Office: Div Alcoholism & Drug Abuse NYU School of Medicine 550 First Avenue New York NY 10016 Office Phone: 212-887-4093, 212-263-6960. Business E-Mail: marcgalanter@nyu.edu.

GALANTI, RICHARD A., wholesale business executive; BS, U. Pa. Wharton Sch.; MBA, Stanford U. Grad. Sch. Bus., Calif., 1982. Assoc. Donaldson Lufkin & Jenrette Securities Corp., 1978—84; v.p. fin. Costco Wholesale, Corp., Issaquah, Wash., 1984—85, sr. v.p., treas., CFO, 1985—93, exec. v.p., CFO, 1993—, dir., 1995—. Office: Costco Wholesale 999 Lake Dr Ste 200 Issaquah WA 98027-5367*

GALANTOWICZ, MARK EDWARD, cardiothoracic surgeon; s. Richard and Deena Galantowicz; m. Barbara Boogh, Nov. 26, 1983; children: Maarten Louis, Nicholas Richard, Tess Erin, Derrick Kristian. Student, Middlebury Coll., 1978—80; BA, U. Pa., 1982; MD, Cornell U., NYC, 1987. Cert. in thoracic and cardiac surgery Am. Bd. Thoracic Surgery, 1993, Am. Bd. Surgery, 1994, Am. Bd. Thoracic Surgery, 1996, lic. Ohio, NY, Fla., Del., Md. Gen. surgery resident Columbia-Presbyn. Med. Ctr., NYC, 1987—93, cardiothoracic surgery fellow, 1993—95, dir. cardiopulmonary transplantation divsn. cardiothoracic surgery, 1995—99, pediat. cardiothoracic surgery fellow, 1995—96, dir. pediat. heart transplantation divsn. cardiothoracic surgery, 1997—99; asst. surgeon divsn. cardiothoracic surgery Columbia Presbyn. Med. Ctr., 1995—96, asst. attending divsn. cardiothoracic surgery, 1996—99; instr. surgery Columbia U., NYC, 1995—96, asst. prof. surgery, 1996—99; chief dept. cardiothoracic surgery Arnold Palmer Hosp. for Children and Women, Orlando, Fla., 1999—2002, Columbus Children's Hosp., Ohio, 2002—, co-dir. Heart Ctr., 2002—, dir. congenital cardiopulmonary transplant program, 2003—; assoc. prof. surgery Ohio State U., Columbus, 2002—. Academic chief resident Columbia-Presbyn. Med. Ctr., 1992—93; chmn. exec. com. Nemours Cardiac Ctr., Orlando, Fla., 1999—2002; presenter in field. Jour. reviewer, mem. editl. bd.: Circulation, Jour. Thoracic and Cardiovascular Surgery, Annals of Thoracic Surgery; contbr. articles to profl. jours., chapters to books. Founder, med. dir. Forum's Children's Found.; founding bd. dir. Heartcare Internat., Heart Trust Pediat. Heart Surgery Mission Trips, Guatemala, 1994, 1995, 1996, 1997, 1998, 2000, 2003, 2004, 2006, Dominican Republic, 2000, 2001, 2002, 2003, 2004, Peru, 2004, China, 2004, 2005, Kenya, 2005; mem. procurement med. adv. bd. Lifeline of Ohio. Lt. col. med. corps USAR. Recipient Blakemore Rsch. Prize, Columbia U. Coll. Physicians & Surgeons, 1989—91, 1990, 1991, 1993, Resident Rsch. Competition award, 1992, Claire Lucille Pace Humanitarian award, 1996, Ellis Island Medal of Honor, Congl. Record, 1999; vis. scholar in Congenital Cardiac Anatomy, U. Leiden, Holland, 1995; Charles Edison Pediat. Rsch. fellowship, Columbia U. Coll. Physicians & Surgeons, 1988—90. Mem.: ACS, Lifeline of Ohio Procurement Med. Adv. Bd., World Soc. Pediat. and Congenital Heart Surgery (founding mem.), Soc. Thoracic Surgeons, NY State Thoracic Organ Transplant Consortium, Internat. Soc. Heart & Lung Transplantation, Internat. Soc. Adult Congenital Cardiac Disease, Columbus Med. Review Club. Office: Columbus Children's Hosp 700 Childrens Dr Ste ED620 Columbus OH 43205 Office Phone: 614-722-3103. Office Fax: 614-722-3111. Business E-Mail: galantm@chi.osu.edu.

GALASK, RUDOLPH PETER, obstetrician, gynecologist; b. Ft. Dodge, Iowa, Dec. 23, 1935; s. Peter Otto and Adeline Amelia (Maranesi) G.; m. Gloria Jean Vasti, June 19, 1965 BS, Drake U., 1959; MD, U. Iowa, 1964, MS, 1967. Diplomate Am. Bd. Obstetrics and Gynecology. Research fellow in microbiology U. Iowa, Iowa City, 1965-67, resident in ob-gyn., 1967-70, asst. prof., 1970-74, asst. prof. microbiology, 1973-74, assoc. prof. obstetrics and gynecology microbiology, 1974-78, prof., 1978—, chmn. exec. com. Coll. Medicine, 1992-93, prof. dermatology, 1999—2006, prof. emeritus, 2006—. Cons. in field. Editor: Infectious Diseases in the Female Patient, 1986-89; contbr. numerous articles to profl. jours. Served to staff sgt. USNG, 1954—64. Recipient I.D.S.O.G./Ortho McNeil award, A.P.G.O. Excellence in Tchg. award, 1997, I.D.S.O.G. Founders award, 2004; named one of Ams. Top Drs., 2000, Ams. Top OB/GYN, 2002, Ams. Top Drs. for cancer, 2005; numerous grants to study the efficacy of various antibiotics and chemotherapeutics. Fellow Am. Gynecol. and Obstet. Soc., Am. Coll. Obstetricians and Gynecologists, Infectious Disease Am.; mem. AAAS, Cen. Assn. for Obstetricians and Gynecologists, Infectious Disease Soc. for Ob-Gyn. (pres. 1982-84, founding mem.), Soc. Gynecol. Investigation (coun. 1987-90), Queens Gynecol. Soc. (hon.), Tex. Assn. Obstetricians and Gynecologists (hon.), Am. Soc. Microbiology, Izaac Walton League, Ducks Unltd. Club (sponsor), Sigma Xi. Roman Catholic. Office: U Iowa Hosps Dept Ob Gyn Iowa City IA 52242 Personal E-mail: rudolph-galast@aol.com. Business E-Mail: rudolph-galast@uiowa.edu. *Power is a perception that lasts a moment but respect is a legacy that lasts forever.*

GALASSO, FRANCIS SALVATORE, materials scientist; b. Monson, Mass., Apr. 26, 1931; s. Paul and Rubino (Cirillo) G.; m. Lois E. Wood; children: Cynthia Egolf, Gary Galasso. BS, U. Mass., 1953; MS, U. Conn., 1957, PhD, 1960. Prin. scientist United Techs. Rsch. Ctr., East Hartford, Conn., 1974-77, sr. material scientist, 1977-85, mgr., 1985-91; owner Galasso Tech. Assocs., Manchester, Conn., 1991—; chief materials United Techs. Rsch. Ctr., East Hartford, Conn., 1960-74. Mem. adv. bd. Chem. Rubber Co., 1971—; cons. in space experiments NASA, Huntsville, Ala., 1971-77; vis. prof. U. Conn., Storrs, 1985—. Author 6 books; contbr. articles to profl. jours. patentee in field. Coach Manchester Little League, 1960-75, v.p., 1970-84, pres., 1984=88, mem. bd. govs. adv. com. on accreditation, 1988-90. 1st lt. USAF, 1953-55. Fellow Am. Ceramic Soc.; mem. AIME, Am. Chem. Soc., Am. Legion, Army-Navy Club. Democrat. Roman Catholic. Office: 13 Green Manor Rd Manchester CT 06040-3342 E-mail: locyngar@aol.com.

GALATAS, RUTH ANN, musician, publishing executive, educator; b. New Orleans, La., June 29, 1958; d. Robert I. and Shirley A. Galatas; m. Rick Sands. BFA, La. Tech., 1980; MFA, U. Fla., 1982; MusD, U. Miami, 1989. Tchr. Miami Dade C.C., Miami, 1994—98; prin., owner Rim Sky Pub., Miami, 1998—. US. liaison Lloyd's of London Music Found., 1990—94; chmn. Frank Angelo Music Fund, 1998—. Musician: (albums) Exhalation of The Soul, 1999, A More Gentle Time, 2001, My Fav Things, 2006; prodr.: (album) Juba Live, 1996, (edit prodr.) At Last, 2002 (Grammy award, 2002). Mem.: Nat. Music Tchrs. Assn. (v.p. 1996), Phi Mu, Sigma Alpha Iota. Methodist. Avocations: swimming, art collecting, miniatures. Office: Rim Sky Pub PO Box 558025 Miami FL 33255 Business E-Mail: rgalatas@bellsouth.net.

GALATI, FRANK JOSEPH, stage and opera director, educator, screen writer, actor; b. Highland Park, Ill., Nov. 29, 1943; s. Frank Joseph and Virginia Frances (Cassel) G. BS, Northwestern U., 1965, MA, 1966, PhD, 1971. Asst. prof. speech U. South Fla., Tampa, 1965-67; instr. interpretation Northwestern U., Evanston, Ill., 1970-71, assoc. prof., 1973-83, prof. performance studies, 1983—; instr. theater Roosevelt U., Chgo., 1971-72; instr. acting Goodman Sch. Drama, Chgo., 1971-72; assoc. dir. Goodman Theatre, 1986—; dir. Chgo. Opera Theater, 1976; mem. Steppenwolf Theatre Co., 1986—. Dir.: (Broadway plays) The Grapes of Wrath, 1990 (Tony award best direction of a play, 1990, Tony award best play, 1990, Drama Desk award outstanding dir. of a play, 1990), The Glass Menagerie, 1994, Ragtime, 1998—2000 (Dora Mavor award), Seussical, 2000, The Pirate Queen, 2007, (regional theatre) You Can't Take It With You, 1985, Aunt Dan and Lemon, 1987, Born Yesterday, 1987, The Grapes of Wrath, 1988, Earthly Possessions, 1991, As I Lay Dying, 1995, Everyman (A Moral Play), 1995, Morning Star, 1999, Valparaiso, 2000, The Drawer Boy, 2001, Talking With Studs, 2001, The Royal Family, 2002, Homebody/Kabul, 2003, after the quake, 2005, Love Repeating: A Musical of Gertrude Stein, 2005, The Mother of Us All, The Merry Wives of Windsor, Summer and Smoke, Albert Herring, The Good Soldier Schweik, The Visit, The Government Inspector, She Always Said, Pablo, A Funny Thing Happened on the Way to the Forum, Passion Play, The Winter's Tale, Cry, The Beloved Country, The Good Person of Setzuan, Melanctha; (Operas) A View from the Bridge, Pelleas and Mellisande, La Traviata, Tosca, The Voyage of Edgar Allen Poe; screenwriter The Accidental Tourist. Recipient Tchr. of Year award U. South Fla., 1967, Joseph Jefferson Best New Play award Chgo., 1973, Jefferson award for best actor, 1980, Jefferson award for best dir. Drama Desk, 1986-88; Acad. award nomination for best screenplay Accidental Tourist N.Y. Outer Circle Critics, 1989, 2 Antoinette Perry awards for Grapes of Wrath, 1990. Mem. Actors Equity Assn., Speech Communication Assn. Office: Northwestern U Theater Interpretation Ctr 1979 S Campus Dr Evanston IL 60208-0824 Home: 2990 Emathla St Miami FL 33133-3223*

GALATI, NESTORE, materials engineer, researcher; b. Scorrano, Italy, Oct. 16, 1973; s. Raffaele Galati and Michela Rosaria Siciliano; m. Silvia Valentina Rocca Camasca, July 30, 2005. BSc in Material Engring., U. Lecce, Italy, 1999, PhD in Civil Engring., 2003; MS in Engring. Mechanics, U. Mo., Rolla, 2002. Registered profl. engr., Ordine degli Ingegneri, Lecce, Italy, 2000, engr. in tng., Ohio, 2002. Rsch. engr. U. Mo., Rolla, 2003—; cons. Coforce Internat., Rolla, 2003—. Cons. Monte Dei Paschi Di Siena Bank, Lecce, 1999—2000. Contbr. articles to profl. jours. Supporter Children Internat., Kansas City, Mo., 2006, Mo. Fraternal Order of Police, St. Louis. Scholar, Italian Min. Edn., 1994—99, 2000—03, U. Mo., Rolla, 2001—02. Mem.: Assn.Italiana Compositi (assoc.), The Masonry Soc. (assoc.), Am. Concrete Inst. (assoc.), ASCE (assoc.). Achievements include patents pending for enhanced smart-FRP material having embedded optical fiber for Brillouin strain sensing; flood monitoring device for low water bridges; research in in situ load testing of Bridge A6358 (Part 1) and Bridges A6101 and A6102 (Part 2); structural assessment of I-70 Blanchette Bridge; design, construction, laboratory and field testing of bridge on the Arnault Branch, Washington County, Missouri; blast testing and research on bridge at the Tenza Viaduct; development and field testing of FRP composite bridge decks comprising guard rail system for Bridge 1480230, Greene County, Missouri; strengthening of rural bridges using rapid-installation FRP technology; FRP strengthening of large-size concrete columns; assessment of bridge technologies through field testing. Home: 1705 N Olive St Apt 3 Rolla MO 65401 Office: U Mo-Rolla 218 Engring Rsch Lab Rolla MO 65401 Home Phone: 573-426-4893; Office Phone: 573-341-6223. Office Fax: 573-341-6215. Business E-Mail: galati@umr.edu.

GALATIANOS, GUS A., computer company executive, consultant, real estate developer, educator; b. Hermoupolis, Siros, Greece, Jan. 18, 1947; came to U.S., 1973; s. Athanassios Constantine and Despina Athanassios (Stefanou) G.; m. Katerina E. Saridis, Sept. 29, 1974; children: Athanassios, Deborah. BSEE, N.Y. Inst. Tech., 1974; MSEE, Columbia U., 1977; MS in Computer Sci., Stevens Inst. Tech., 1977; PhD in Computer Sci., Poly. U., NYC, 1986. Mgr. ops. Solomos Bus. Machines, Athens, Greece, 1970-73; computer cons. Univ. Computer Ctrs., NYC, 1973-77; tech. dir. Computer Dynamics Corp., NYC, 1977-79; assoc. prof., chmn. dept. computer sci. SUNY, Old Westbury, 1979-93, prof., 1993-2000, chmn. dept. computer sic., 1995-98; mgr. fin. systems Singer/Electronic Systems Divsn., Little Falls, NJ, 1984—87; pres. Advanced Computer Cons. Internat., NYC, 1988—2004, ACCI Properties, Inc., NYC, 1988—. Cons. in field. Author: Principles of Software Engineering, 1986, Principles of Database Systems, 1986; contbr. articles to profl. jours. Active Statue of Liberty Found. Inc., N.Y.C., 1984, Nat. Fedn. Blind, Balt., 1988, Rep. Presdl. Task Force, Washington, 1984—, Greater Whitestone Taxpayers Civic Assn., N.Y.C., 1984—. Served with Greek Air Force, 1965-67. Republican. Greek Orthodox. Avocations: music, hunting, travel, reading. Home: 17-24 Parsons Blvd Whitestone NY 11357-3041 Office: SUNY 160 Havemeyer St Brooklyn NY 11211 Office Phone: 718-344-1147, Personal E-mail: accidrg@aol.com.

GALATZ, HENRY FRANCIS, lawyer; b. NYC, Feb. 5, 1947; s. Julius D. and Dorothy (Kirschen) G.; children: Benjamin Chase, Brandon Kyle. BA, U. Ariz., 1970, MEd, MA with honors, 1973; JD, U. the Pacific, 1979. Bar: Ill. 1981, U.S. Ct. Appeals (7th cir.) 1981, U.S. Dist. Ct. (no. dist.) Ill. 1982, U.S. Dist. Ct. (ea. dist.) Mich. 1982, U.S. Ct. Appeals (6th cir.) 1982, U.S. Dist. Ct. (ea. dist.) Mo. 1985, U.S. Supreme Ct. 1985, U.S. Dist. Ct. Mont. 1986, U.S. Dist. Ct. (we. dist.) Tex. 1987, U.S. Dist. Ct. (no. dist.) Calif. 1992, U.S. Dist. Ct. Nebr. 1993, U.S. Dist. Ct. (no. dist.) Ohio 1997, U.S. Ct. Appeals (11th cir.) 2000; cert. coach and referee U.S. Soccer Fedn. Cons. labor rels. Phoenix Closures, Chgo., 1974-75, Galatz Elec. Corp., Las Vegas, Nev., 1975-80; labor counsel W.W. Grainger, Inc., Skokie, Ill., 1980—; pvt. practice Flossmoor, Ill., 1981—. Hearing officer Ill. State Bd. Edn., Chgo., 1982—: atty. Chgo. Legal Svcs. Found., 1983—, Ill. Inst. for Dispute Resolution, 1992—; mem. com. Employment Law Inst., Northwestern U., Evanston, Ill.; adv. coun. H-F Bus. Ptnr., 2000; mem. pres. counsel McGeorge Sch. Law, 2001-. Pres., coach Homewood-Flossmoor (Ill.) Soccer Club, 1985—, Intercollegiate Varsity Athletics (soccer and lacrosse); co-chair soccer Ill. Prairie State Games, 1992; pres. P.O.P.S. Homewood-Flossmoor H.S., 1996—; mem. bd. edn., pers. chairperson Homewood-Flossmoor H.S., 1998—, mem. improvement coun., 2001; coord, soccer official Spl. Olympics, 2005—. Recipient Judge Mason Rothwell Award, 1979, Cert. of Merit Chgo. Legal Svcs. Found., 1983. Mem. ABA, ATLA, Am. Corp. Counsel Assn. (labor and employment sect.), Ill. Bar Assn., Chgo. Bar Assn., Am. Arbitrators Assn. (arbitrator), Am. Judicature Soc., Ill. Trial Lawyers Assn., North Shore (Ill.) Labor Counsel Assn., Phi Delta Phi, Alpha Epsilon Pi. Democrat. Jewish. Avocations: soccer, lacrosse. Home: PO Box 374 Flossmoor IL 60422-0374 Office: W W Grainger Inc 100 Grainger Pkwy Lake Forest IL 60045-5201

GALATZER-LEVY, ROBERT MILTON, psychiatrist; b. NYC, July 26, 1944; s. Milton and Helen Nadine (Class) Levy; m. Susan Jeanne Galatzer, June 22, 1974; children: Daniel, Isaac, Benjamin, David, Emma. BA, NYU, 1964, MS, 1965; MD, Washington U., St. Louis, 1971. Resident in psychiatry U. Chgo., 1971-74, fellow in child psychiatry, 1973-74; candidate Inst. for Psychoanalysis, 1975-81; lectr. psychiatry U. Chgo., 1974—; pvt. practice specializing in psychiatry Chgo., 1974—; faculty Chgo. Inst. for Psychoanalysis, 1976—. Cons. Ill. Dept. Mental Health, Manteno, 1974-76, Skokie pub. schs., 1976-79. Author: (with B. Cohler) The Essential Other: A Developmental Psychology of the Self, 1993, (with H. Bachrachetal) Does Psychoanalysis Work, 1999, (with B. Cohler) The Course of Gay and Lesbian Life, 2000, (with L. Kraus) The Scientific Basis of Child Custody Decisions, 2001; contbr. articles to profl. jours. Trustee Jewish Family and Cmty. Svcs., Chgo., 1988-97. Mem. Am. Psychoanalytic Assn., Am. Soc. Adolescent Psychiatry, Chgo. Soc. Adolescent Psychiatry (pres. 1987-88), Chgo. Psychoanalytic Soc. (sec. 1991-94), Am. Soc. Child Adolescent Psychiatry. Democrat. Jewish. Avocation: Tae Kwon Do. Office: 122 S Michigan Ave Chicago IL 60603-6191 Office Phone: 312-922-5077. Business E-Mail: gala@uchicago.edu.

GALBRAITH, JAMES MARSHALL, lawyer, corporate executive; b. Iowa City, Oct. 4, 1942; s. John Semple and Laura (Huddleston) G.; m. Margaret Rodi, Aug. 19, 1966; children: Margaret Laura, Katherine Lou, Robert James. BA, Pomona Coll., 1964; JD, Stanford U., 1967. Bar: Calif. 1968. Assoc. Gibson, Dunn & Crutcher, Los Angeles, 1967-68; ptnr. Rodi, Pollock, Pettker, Galbraith & Cahill, Los Angeles, 1968-84, of counsel, 1984—2003; pres. Bell Helmets Internat., Inc., 1980-84; ptnr. Palm Properties Co., 1979—2001. Pres., dir. Van de Kamp's Bakers, Inc., 1984—87; ptnr. Huntington Hotel Assocs., San Marino, 1986—95; pres. Crestmont Investments, LLC, 1991—. Author: In the Name of the People, 1977, The Money Tree, 1982, Fear of Failure, 1993, Patient Power, 1995; mem. bd. editors Stanford Law Rev., 1965-67. Trustee Pomona Coll., 1987-89, trustee emeritus, 1989—; trustee, mem. exec. com. Childrens Hosp. L.A., 1986-91, hon. trustee, 1991—; mem. Soc. of Fellows, Huntington Libr. Art Gallery and Bot. Gardens, 1982—; mem. Young Pres. Orgn., 1979-93. Mem. State Bar Calif., Phi Beta Kappa. Clubs: California (L.A.), Valley Hunt (Pasadena). Episcopalian. Home: 1640 Oak Grove Ave San Marino CA 91108-1109 Office: 2600 Mission St San Marino CA 91108-1676

GALBRAITH, MARIAN, elementary school educator; Tchr. West Side Mid. Sch., Reading and Lang. Arts Dept., Groton, Conn., 1991—, various U., 1986—96; with Conn. State Dept. Edn., Fist Assessment Devel. Lab. Served various com. State Dept. Edn., 1986—93. Bd. dirs. Nat. Edn. Assn., 1993—99. Finalist Nat. Tchr. of Yr., 2002. Mem.: Groton Edn. Assn. PAC (treas. 2007). Office: West Side Mid Sch Reading and Lang Arts Dept 250 Brandegee Ave Groton CT 06340*

GALBRAITH, PETER WOODARD, former ambassador; b. Boston, Dec. 31, 1950; s. John Kenneth and Catherine (Atwater) G.; m. Tone Rand Bringa; children: Eamon Andrew, Liv Catherine. AB, Harvard U., 1973; MA, Oxford U., 1975. Prof. Windham Coll., Putney, Vt., 1975-78; profl. staff mem. U.S. Senate Com. on Fgn. Rels., 1979-93; US amb. to Croatia US Dept. State, Zagreb, 1993—98; U.S. negotiator Z-4 Croatia Peace Process, 1994-95; co-mediator Eastern Slavonia Peace Negotiations, 1995; prof. nat. security strategy Nat. War Coll., 1998—99, 2001—03; dir. polit., constitutional & electoral affairs UN Transitional Adminstrn. (UNTAET), East Timor, 2000—01; sr. diplomatic fellow Ctr. for Arms Control & Non-Proliferation, Washington, 2003—. Mem. U.S. delegation to 35th UN Gen. Assembly, 1980, 10th and 11th UN Environment Program Governing Coun., 1982, 83; chmn. Vt. Dem. State Com., 1977-79. Author: Civil War in Iraq, 1991, Kurdistan in the Time of Saddam Hussein, 1991, The End of Iraq: How American Incompetence Created a War Wuthout End, 2006; co-author: (with Chris Van Hollen) Chemical Weapon Use in Kurdistan: Iraq's Final Offensive, 1988, (with Michelle Maynard) The Ethnic Cleansing of Bosnia-Herzegovina, 1992. Recipient Sitari-i-Quaid-i-Azam award Pakistan, 1989. Office: Center for Arms Control & Non-Proliferation 322 Fourth St NE Washington DC 20002

GALBRAITH, ROBERT LYELL, JR., lawyer; b. Rochester, NY, May 18, 1960; s. Robert Lyell and Barbara Williams Galbraith; m. Debra Lee Dastyck, June 25, 1985; children: Taylor, Mary. BA, Hamilton Coll., 1982; JD, U. Buffalo, 1986. Bar: N.Y. 1987, U.S. Dist. Ct. (we. dist.) N.Y. 1987. Assoc. Osborn, Reed, VandeVate & Burke, Rochester, N.Y., 1986-88, Saperston & Day, P.C., Rochester, 1989-92, ptnr., 1992-98, chmn. R.E. practice group, 1994-98; ptnr. Davidson, Fink, Cook, Kelly & Galbraith LLP., Rochester, 1998—, mng. ptnr., 2001—. Mem. nat. atty. adv. bd. Citifin. Mortgage Co.; adv. bd. mem. Ticor/Chgo. Title Ins. Co., Rochester, 1991—; assoc. mem. N.Y. State Econ. Devel. Coun., Rochester, 1991-2000; adv. bd. dirs. Rochester Binding and Finishing, Rochester, 1993-96. Bd. mem., pres. Mental Health Assn., Rochester, 1991-2000; coach Brighton (N.Y.) Town Soccer, 1996-2001. Named Vol. of the Yr., Mental Health Assn., Rochester, 1995, one of 40 under 40 Rochester Bus. Jour., 1996. Mem. N.Y. State Bar Assn. (exec. com. for young lawyers sect., liason to real property exec. 1992-97), Monroe County Bar Assn. (real estate sect., pres. 1992-2000). Avocations: skiing, reading, soccer, football. Office: Davidson Fink Cook Kelly & Galbraith LLP 28 E Main St Ste 900 Rochester NY 14614-1916 E-mail: rgalbraith@dfckg.com.

GALBRAITH, RUTH LEGG, retired dean, home economist; b. Lecompte, La., Nov. 5, 1923; d. Byron S. and Dora Ruth (Lindley) Legg; m. Harry W. Galbraith, June 16, 1950; 1 son, Allan Legg. BS, Purdue U., 1945, PhD, 1950. Chemist E.I. duPont de Nemours, Waynesboro, Va., 1945-46; textile chemist Gen. Electric Co., Bridgeport, Conn., 1946-47; teaching asst. Purdue U., 1947-48, research fellow, 1948-50; prof. textiles and clothing U. Tenn., Knoxville, 1950-55; asso. prof. U. Ill., Urbana, 1956-64, prof., 1964-70, chmn. textiles and clothing div., 1962-70; prof., head consumer affairs dept. Auburn (Ala.) U., 1970-73; dean Sch. Home Econs., head home econs. research, 1973-85. Mem. task force on quality of living Dept. Agr., 1967-68; mem. nat. adv. com. Flammable Fabrics Act, 1971-73; mem. U.S. Dept. Agr. Com. of Nine, 1981-83, chmn., 1983 Mem. editl. bd.: Rsch. Jour. Home Econs., 1973-77, chmn. policy bd., 1978-80; contbr. articles to profl. jours. Recipient Disting. Alumni award Purdue U., 1970 Fellow Am. Inst. Chemists; mem. Am. Home Econs. Assn. (chmn. agy. mem. unit 1975-76, chmn. research sect. 1978-80, Outstanding Home Economist award 1984), Ala. Home Econs. Assn. (pres. 1983-84), Am. Assn. Textile Chemists and Colorists, Am. Chem. Soc., ASTM (3d v.p. com. D-13 textiles 1975-79), Assn. Adminstrs. Home Econs., Nat. Council Adminstrs. Home Econs., AAUW, Sigma Xi, Omicron Nu, Phi Kappa Phi, Delta Kappa Gamma. Home: 368 Singleton St Auburn AL 36830-6317

GALBRAITH, WILLIAM BRUCE, internist, educator; b. Romeo, Mich., Oct. 21, 1930; s. Bruce McKenzie and Helen Athelene (Stringham) G.; m. Jo Anne Fetterly Ames, June 27, 1953; children: Elise, Susan, Scott. BS, Ariz. State U., 1953; MD, George Washington U., 1957. Diplomate Am. Bd. Internal Medicine. Internship Good Samaritan Hosp., Phoenix, 1957-58; residency U. Iowa Hosps. and Clinics, Iowa City, 1958-61; instr. internal medicine U. Iowa Coll. Medicine, Iowa City, 1961-63, asst. prof., 1963-65, dir. gen. medicine tng. program, 1994-96, assoc. internal medicine, 1994-95; prof. clin. internal medicine U. Iowa, Iowa City, 1995-97, prof. emeritus, 1998—; owner Internists P.C., Cedar Rapids, Iowa, 1965-93, pres., 1986-93. Bd. dirs. Am. Bd. Internal Medicine, Phila., 1992-96. Trustee Mercy Med. Ctr., Cedar Rapids, 1997—, Meth-Wick Cmty., 1999—, chair, 2005-2007; founding chmn. Cmty. Health Free Clinic, Cedar Rapids, 2002-06. Fellow ACP/ASIM (gov. for Iowa 1979-83, Laureate award 1988, Master 1997); mem. Alpha Omega Alpha. Avocation: fly fishing. Personal E-mail: WGalbra66@aol.com.

GALBUT, MARTIN RICHARD, lawyer; b. Miami Beach, Fla., June 27, 1946; s. Paul A. and Ethel (Kolnick) G.; m. Cynthia Ann Slaughter, June 4, 1972; children: Keith Richard, Lindsay Anne. BS in Speech, Northwestern U., 1968, JD cum laude, 1971. Bar: Ariz. 1972, US Dist. Ct. Ariz. 1972, US Ct. Appeals (9th cir.) 1972. Assoc. Brown, Vlassis & Bain PA, Phoenix, 1971-75; founder, ptnr. McLoone, Theobald & Galbut PC, Phoenix, 1975-86; of counsel Furth, Fahrner, Bluemle & Mason, 1986-89; founder Galbut & Hunter, PC, Phoenix, 1989—. Presenter guest Law Talk cable TV; former judge pro tem Maricopa County Superior Ct.; lectr. comml. real estate litigation, arbitration, mediation, securites, antitrust and intellectual property law Lorman Bus. Seminars. Contbr. articles to profl. jours. Chmn., Ariz. State Air Pollution Control Hearing Bd., 1984-89; active Govs. Task Force on Urban Air Quality, 1986, City Phoenix Environ. Quality Commn., 1987-88; bd. dirs. Men's Art Coun. Phoenix Art Mus., Scottsdale Artists Sch.; bd. dirs., founder Ariz. Asthma Found. Clarion de Witt Hardy scholar, Kosmeryl scholar; Russel Sage grantee. Mem. Ariz. State Bar Assn. (sect. antitrust bus. litigation securities law), Am. Arbitration Assn. (arbitrator), Maricola County Bar Assn., Can. Ariz. Bus. Coun., Nat. Assn. Securities Dealers (arbitrator, trainer and lectr.), Nat. Arbitration Forum. Jewish. Avocations: painting, collecting antiques and fine art, international travel. Office: Galbut & Hunter PC 2425 E Camelback Rd Ste 1020 Phoenix AZ 85016-4216 Office Phone: 602-955-1455. Business E-Mail: mgalbut@galbuthunter.com.

GALDA, DWIGHT WILLIAM, finance company executive; b. Bklyn., Dec. 19, 1942; s. Fred C. and Audrey D. G.; children: Cynthia A., Gregory J.; m. Suzanne Galda, May 20, 2004. BA, Widener U., 1964; MBA, Tex. Christian U., 2000; MPA, MS, U. Tex., 2002. ChFC; registered Prin. and Nat. Panel Arbitration. Rep. United Svcs. Planning Assn. and Ind. Rsch. Agy., Ft. Worth, 1983-86; dist. exec. USPA and IRA, Ft. Worth, 1986-92, regional exec., 1992-96; prin. Carefree (Ariz.) Capital Mgmt. and Rsch., Carefree, Ariz., 1997—. Ind. cons. Dwight W. Galda Consultancy, 1985-, adj. econ. and mgmt. prof. Western Internat. U., 2003-. Contbr. articles profl. jours.; creator U.S. Army Opposing Force Program, 1976. Lt. col. U.S. Army, 1964-82; Army attache U.S. Embassy, Cambodia, 1973-75. Recipient Pace award Dept. of Army, 1976, 77, Legion of Merit, Bronze star with V and 2 oak leaf clusters, Meritorious Svc. medal 4 oak leaf clusters, air medal with V and 4 oak leaf clusters, Vietnamese Cross of Gallantry with Silver star, Cambodian Nat. Def. Svc. medal. Fellow Chartered Fin. Analysts Inst.; mem. Phoenix Chartered Fin. Analysts Soc. Episcopalian. Avocations: running, chamber music, travel. Office Phone: 480-213-9663. E-mail: dgalda@att.net.

GALDAMEZ, RICARDO, internist; b. Suchitoto, Cuzcatlan, El Salvador, June 29, 1952; came to U.S., 1984; s. Santiago Galdamez and Maria Angela Monge; m. Elsa Ramos, Dec. 17, 1977; children: Emma, Ana, Martha. MD, U. El Salvador, 1982. Diplomate Am. Bd. Internal Medicine, Am. Bd. Forensic Medicine. Rotating intern (surgery, internal medicine, pediat., etc.) various hosps., El Salvador, 1979-81; pub. health dir. Ahuachapan, El Salvador, 1981-82; dir. health care Self-Help Group, El Salvador, 1982-84; resident in internal medicine Woodhull Hosp., Bklyn., 1987-91, physician, 1991—, Montefiore Rickers Island Health Svcs., Queens, 1993-96; internist Elmhurst Hosp., Queens, 1997-98. Union del. Doctors Coun., N.Y., 1995—. Fellow AMA, Interam. Coll. Physician, Surgeon; mem. ACP, Am. Soc. Internal Medicine, Rosicrucian Order. Avocations: parapsychology, mystic work. Home: 5602 137th St Flushing NY 11355-5034 Office: 5602 137th St Flushing NY 11355-5034

GALE, FOURNIER JOSEPH, III, lawyer; b. Mobile, Ala., Aug. 3, 1944; s. Fournier J. Jr. and Clara (Beckham) G.; m. Louise Smith, Aug. 7, 1965; children: Carolyn, Jeanette. BA, U. Ala., 1966, JD, 1969; postgrad., Oxford U., summer 1968. Bar: Ala. 1969. From assoc. to ptnr. Cabaniss, Johnston, Gardner, Dumas & O'Neal, Birmingham, Ala., 1969-84; ptnr. Maynard, Cooper & Gale, PC, Birmingham, 1984—. Bd. dirs. McWane, Inc., Birmingham; gen. counsel, bd. dirs. Bus. Coun. Ala., Birmingham, 1977—; bd. dirs., So. Rsch. Inst.; mem. Ala. Permanent Study Commn. on Judiciary, 1977-83; mem. Jefferson County Jud. Nominating Commn., 1993-2000; chmn. Ala. Commn. on Higher Edn., 1998-2003; spl. counsel to Gov. of Ala., 1999-2002. Mem. Leadership Birmingham, 1986-87; pres. U. Ala. Law Sch. Found., 1987-89. Mem. ABA (standing com. on environ. law, standing com. on fed. judiciary), Birmingham Bar Assn. (pres. 1989), Ala. Young Lawyers Assn. (pres. 1976-77), Am. Judicature Soc. (bd. dirs. 1980-85), Jud. Conf. Ala., Am. Bar Found., Ala. State Bar (pres. 2006-07), Kiwanis. Roman Catholic. Office: Maynard Cooper & Gale PC 2400 Amsouth Harbert Plz Birmingham AL 35203-2600 Office Phone: 205-254-1000. Business E-Mail: bgale@maynardcooper.com.

GALE, JAMES L., lawyer; b. Alexander City, Ala., Aug. 20, 1947; s. Richard J. Gale and Mattie R. Gale; m. Darlene Floyd, June 5, 1971; children: James L. Jr., Brian Patterson. BA, Eckerd Coll., 1969; JD magna cum laude, U. Ga., 1974. Bar: Ga. 1974, N.C. 1974, Fla. 1989. Law clk. U.S. Dist. Ct. (ea. dist.) N.C., Raleigh, 1974-76; ptnr. Smith Moore LLP, Raleigh, 1976—. Mem. ABA, Def. Rsch. Inst., N.C. Bar Assn. Office: Smith Moore LLP 2800 Hanover Sq 2 Raleigh NC 27601 Home: 7336 Fontana Ridge Ln Raleigh NC 27613-1469 Home Phone: 919-571-0538; Office Phone: 919-755-8700. Business E-Mail: jim.gale@southmooreshu.com, jimgale@smithmoorelaw.com.

GALE, JOHN A., state official; b. Omaha, Oct. 30, 1940; s. John C. Gale, Jr. and Faye Gale; m. Carol Gale; children: David, Elaine, Steve. BA in Govt. Internat. Rels., Carleton Coll., Northfield, Minn., 1962; JD in Govt. Internat. Rels., U. Chgo. Law Sch., Northfield, Minn., 1965. With legal dept. No. Natural Gas Co., Omaha, 1965—68; legis. asst. to Senator Roman Hruska US Senate, Washington, 1968; asst. US atty. US Dept. Justice, Omaha, 1970, Lincoln, Nebr., 1971; pvt. practice atty., 1971—2000; sec. state State of Nebr., Lincoln, 2000—. Chmn. Nebr. State Rep. Party, 1986. Republican. Office: Office Sec of State State Capitol Ste 2300 Lincoln NE 68509 Office Phone: 402-471-2554. Business E-Mail: receptionist@sos.ne.gov.*

GALE, JOHN QUENTIN, lawyer; b. Hartford, Conn., June 16, 1951; s. John J. and Doris A. (Boissoneault) G.; m. Tracy Thompson, Sept. 23, 1978; children: Adrienne Hope, Calabria T., Aurelia D., Nathaniel J. BSEE, U. Pa., 1973; JD, U. Conn., 1977. Bar: Conn. 1977, U.S. Dist. Ct. 1978. Engr. GE, Valley Force, Pa., 1972-74; staff atty., corp. counsel City of Hartford, 1977; ptnr. Calvocoressi & Gale, Hartford, 1977—2000, Gale & Kowalyshyn, LLC, 2000—. Bd. dirs. New Horizons, Inc., pres., 1998-2000; bd. dirs. Conn. Vision Svcs., Inc., Immanuel House, Inc., Silver Svc., Inc., Peace Train Found., Inc. Founder, editor Professional Discipline Digest, 1991. Trustee Bloomfield (Conn.) United Meth. Ch., 1991—, Hartford Pub. H.S. Alumni Assn., 1998--; founder, trustee Noah Webster Sch. Alumni Assn., 1998--; treas. Hartford Dem. Town Com., 1994-2002. Recipient Salutation for Improving City award Hartford Courant Columnist-Tom Condon, 1993. Mem. Conn. Bar Assn. (mem. profl. discipline com. 1987—, chmn. profl. discipline com. 1994—), Greater Hartford C. of C. (govt. affairs com. 1988-93), Lions Club (dir. 1980—), Phi Delta Phi (hon.). Avocations: recreational sports, bluegrass mandolin, 1941 oldsmobile, golf, 1897 house. Office: Gale & Kowalyshyn LLC 363 Main St Fl 4 Hartford CT 06106-1845 Office Phone: 860-522-8296. Business E-Mail: jgale@lawlordsofhartford.com.

GALE, JOSEPH H., federal judge; b. Smithfield, Va., 1953; s. Robert Whitfield and Charlotte H. G. AB, Princeton U., 1976; JD, U. Va., 1980. Atty. Dewey, Ballantine, Bushby, Palmer & Wood, NYC, Washington, 1980-83, Dickstein, Shapiro & Morin, Washington, 1983-84; legis. counsel Senator Daniel P. Moynihan, Washington, 1985-88; adminstrv. asst. and tax counsel Hon. Daniel P. Moynihan, Washington, 1989, chief counsel, 1990-92; chief tax counsel Senate Fin. Com., Washington, 1993-94, minority chief of staff, 1995; judge US Tax Ct., Washington, 1996—. Dillard fellow U. Va. Mem.: ABA. Office: US Tax Court 400 2nd St NW Washington DC 20217-0002*

GALE, NEIL JAN, Internet company executive, computer scientist, consultant; b. Chgo., Jan. 12, 1960; s. Jack and Adele Gale. AA in Computer Sci., Wright Coll., 1980; D of Bus. Mgmt. (hon.), London Inst. Applied Rsch., 1993; diploma, Academia Argentina de Diplomacia, 1994; diploma (hon.), Institut Des Affaires Internationales, Paris, 1994; D of Bus. Mgmt. (hon.), World Acad., Monchengladbach, Germany, 1994. Mgr. Gen. Fin. Co., Chgo., 1980-84; mktg. mgr. Midland Fin. Co., Chgo., 1984-85; mktg. dir. Diamond Mortgage Corp., Chgo., 1985-86; sr. fin. analyst McKay Mazda-Nissan, Evanston, Ill., 1987-88; pres., CEO, Nat. Consumer Credit Cons., Chgo., 1988—; webmaster Everything Internet (merger with Millenium Techs. Inc. 1998), Naperville, Ill., 1996-98; pres. DrGale.com, Carol Stream, Ill., 1998—. Hon. prof. bus. mgmt. Inst. des Hautes Etudes Econs. et Sociales, Brussels, 1993; hon. prof. fin. Australian Inst. Coordinated Rsch., 1994; mem. adv. coun. Internat. Biog. Ctr., Cambridge, Eng.; mem. bd. govs., Continental gov. Am. Biog. Inst., 1990—, mem. rsch. bd. advisors, 1989—; notary pub. Ill., 1986-90; bd. dirs., amb. Ill. affiliate U.S. Woman's C. of C., 2002—; bd. dirs. U.S. Dept. of Peace Coaliton, 2003—. Contbr. articles to profl. jours. First aid chmn. Walk with Israel, 1977; notary pub., Ill., 1986-90; mem. computer com. Village of Hanover Park, Ill., 1997-2000; mem. bd. advisors U.S. Women's C. of C., 2002-. Decorated Knight of Order of San Ciriaco; recipient Bus. in Urban Environment award Chgo. Bd. Edn. and Ill. Bell Tel. Co., 1978, Outstanding Achievement award Chgo. Pub. Libr., 1979. Mem. Auto Credit (hon.), Friendship Cir. Club (treas. 1976-78). Avocation: collecting antique Chicago postcards and books. Home and Office: DrGale dot com PMB 208 780 W Army Trail Rd Carol Stream IL 60188-9297 Home Phone: 630-736-9558; Office Phone: 800-736-1036. Personal E-mail: drgale@drgale.com. Business E-Mail: info@drgale.com.

GALE, ROBERT L., retired educational association administrator, consultant; b. St. Cloud, Minn., Jan. 13, 1927; s. John Henry and Helen (Andrews) G.; m. Barbara Carr Davis, Oct. 19, 1951; children: Jennifer Gale Dunkin, Robert L. Gale, Jr., Morgan Andrews. USN V-12 program, U.S. Naval Acad., 1944—45; BA, Carleton Coll., 1948; DHL, U. N.C., 1989. Editor-in-chief Maco Mag. Corp., NYC, 1954—57; v.p. Carleton Coll., Northfield, Minn., 1957—63; dir. recruiting Peace Corps, Washington, 1963—65; dir. pub. affairs EEOC, Washington, 1965—66; chmn., CEO Gale Assocs., Washington, 1966—74; pres. Assn. Governing Bds. Univs. and Colls., Washington, 1974—92, pres. emeritus, 1992—. Bd. trustees Carleton Coll., Northfield, 1972-2002; bd. dirs. Nat. Peace Corps Assn., Washington, BoardSource, Washington, Nat. Exec. Svcs. Corps, N.Y.C., CARE, Inc., Atlanta, 1982-96, U. Pretoria Fund. Chmn. bd. Nat. Peace Garden Monument, Washington, 1995—. With USN, 1944-45. Democrat. Episcopalian. Avocations: tennis, travel, volunteering. Home: 33381 Coleman Gale Ln Bethany Beach DE 19930-9801 Personal E-mail: bob1barb1@aol.com.

GALE, ROBERT LEE, retired literature educator, critic; b. Des Moines, Dec. 27, 1919; s. Erie Lee and Miriam (Fisher) G.; m. Maureen Dowd, Nov. 18, 1944; children: John Lee, James Dowd, Christine Ann. BA, Dartmouth Coll., 1942; MA, Columbia U., 1947, PhD, 1952. Lectr. Columbia U., NYC, 1947-48; instr. U. Del., Newark, 1949-52; asst. prof. U. Miss., Oxford, 1952-56, assoc. prof., 1956-59; asst. prof. U. Pitts., 1959-60, assoc. prof., 1960-65, prof. Am. lit., 1965-87; ret., 1987. Fulbright prof. Inst. Univ. Orientale, Naples, Italy, 1956-58, U. Helsinki, Finland, 1975. Author: Thomas Crawford, 1964, The Caught Image: Figurative Language in Henry James, 1964, Richard Henry Dana, Jr., 1969, Francis Parkman, 1973, Plots and Characters in Mark Twain, 1973, John Hay, 1978, Luke Short, 1981, Will Henry, 1984, Louis L'Amour, 1985, rev. edit., 1992, A Henry James Encyclopedia, 1989, Matt Braun, 1990, A Nathaniel Hawthorne Encyclopedia, 1991, The Gay Nineties: A Cultural Dictionary of the 1890s in the U.S., 1992, A Cultural Encyclopedia of the American 1850s, 1993, A Herman Melville Encyclopedia, 1995, An F. Scott Fitzgerald Encyclopedia, 1998, A Sarah Orne Jewett Companion, 1999, A Dashiell Hammett Companion, 2000, An Ambrose Bierce Companion, 2001, A Lafcadio Hearn Companion, 2002, A Ross Macdonald Companion, 2002, A Mickey Spillane Companion, 2003, A Henry Wadsworth Longfellow Companion, 2003, An Edwin Arlington Robinson Encyclopedia, 2006, Characters and Plots in the Fiction of Graham Greene, 2006; contbr. articles to profl. jours., chpts. to books, revs. Served with U.S. Army, 1942-46, ETO. Mem. MLA, Phi Beta Kappa. Home: 131 Techview Ter Pittsburgh PA 15213-3820 Office Phone: 412-683-7872.

GALE, STANLEY WILLIAM, psychiatrist; b. Mpls., Apr. 30, 1947; s. Harvey and Florence G.; children: Shawna, Greg. BS, Yale U., 1970, JD, 1974, MD, 1975. Asst. psychiatrist N.Y. Hosp., NYC, 1975-78; pvt. practice Providence, 1978—. Mem. staff Butler Hosp., Providence, Miriam Hosp., Providence, R.I. Hosp., Providence. Mem. Am. Psychiat. Assn. Office Phone: 401-831-7756.

GALE, STEPHEN C., surgeon, educator; b. Canton, Ill., Dec. 19, 1969; s. John and Judith Gale; children: Nicholas Edward, Jacob Tyler. BS in Biology, U. Ill., Urbana-Champaign, 1988—92; MD, U. Ill., Chgo., 1992—96. Diplomate general surgery Am. Bd. Surgery, 2004, surgical critical care Am. Bd. Surgery, 2006. Resident general surgery U. Ariz. Coll. Medicine, Tucson, 1996—2003; fellow trauma/critical care U. Pa. Coll. Medicine, Phila., 2003—05; asst. prof. surgery Tulane U. Sch. Medicine, New Orleans, 2005—06, U. Tex. Med. Sch., Houston, 2006—. Fellow: ACS (assoc.). Office: Univ Tex Med Sch 6431 Fannin Houston TX 77030 Home Phone: 856-404-3994. Personal E-mail: scgalemd@yahoo.com.

GALEA, SANDRO, epidemiologist; b. Sliema, Malta, Apr. 24, 1971; s. Emidio and Mary Carmen Galea; m. Margaret Elizabeth Kruk. MD, U. Toronto, 1994; MPH, Harvard U., 2000; DrPH, Columbia U., 2003. Cert. Can. Coll. Family Physicians Grant Cert. 1997. Family med. resident McMaster U. Family Med. No., Thunder Bay, Canada, 1994—96; emergency med. resident U. Toronto, Ont., Canada, 1996—97; physician Geraldton Dist. Hosp., Geraldton, Ont., Canada, 1996—98, Medecins Sans Frontieres, Galkayo, Somalia, 1998—99; med. epidemiologist N.Y. Acad. Medicine, NYC, 2000—05, associate dir. Ctr. for Urban Epidemiologic Studies, 2002—05; asst. prof. epidemiology Columbia U., NYC, 2003—05; assoc. prof. epidemiology U. Mich., Ann Arbor, 2005—. Assoc. editor Journ. Urban Health, 2004—. Contbr. chapters to books, articles to profl. jours., 2002. President Professional Association of Internes and Residents of Ontario, Toronto, Ontario, Canada, 1995—96. Recipient Mosby Book award, U. Toronto, 1991, George & Nora Elwin Book award, 1991, Armando & Nicolina Pavone Outstanding Achievement award, 1991, Mary L. Cassidy award, 1992, Med. Soc. Honour award, 1994, Coll. Family Physicians of Can./Prof. Assoc. of Interns and Residents of Ontario Nat. Resident Rsch. award, Can. Coll. of Family Physicians, 1996, John & Kathleen Gorman Pub. Health Humanitarian award, Columbia U., 2002, Investigator Travel award, NIH, 2004, William Farr award in Epidemiology, Columbia U., 2004. Mem.: APHA, Ont. Med. Assn., Can. Med. Assn., Can. Coll. Family Physicians, Am. Acad. Advancement Sciences, Royal Inst. Pub. Health, Am. Acad. Family Physicians, Pub. Health Assn. NY, Am. Coll. Epidemiology, Soc. Epidemiol. Rsch. Office: Ctr for Social Epidemiology & Population Health U Mich Sch Pub Health 1214 S Univ Rm 243 Ann Arbor MI 48104 E-mail: sgalea@umich.edu.

GALEF, SANDRA RISK, state legislator, educator; b. LaCrosse, Wis., May 7, 1940; d. William P. and Christine Risk; m. Steven Allen Galef, Mar. 30, 1963 (dec.); children: Gregory Todd, Gwendolyn. BS, Purdue U., 1962; MS in Edn., U. Va., 1965. Tchr. Albemarle Schs., Charlottesville, Va., 1962-65, Scarsdale (N.Y.) Schs., 1965-67; mem. Westchester County Bd. Legislators, 1980-93, minority leader, 1984-93; mem. N.Y. State Assembly, Dist. 90, 1993—, former chair com. on librs. and ednl. tech. Bd. dirs. Children's Hosp. Found., 1998-2006, Bethel Nursing Home, 1999—2003; bd. dirs. United Way No. Westchester, 1973—, pres., 1979-80, v.p., 1975-79; trustee Ossining (N.Y.) Pub. Libr., 1975-80, Briarcliff (N.Y.) Nursery Sch., 1974-76, Metro. NY Libr. Coun., 2007—; pres. chpt. LWV, 1973-75; chair Ossining Youth Employment Svc., 1977-80, Assembly Com. on Real Property Taxation; bd. dirs Day Care Coun. Westchester, 1976-79; pub. affairs chair Jr. League Westchester-on-Hudson, Tarrytown, 1978-80, mem. tng. com., 1980-85; mem. adv. bd. Children's Village, Dobbs Ferry, N.Y., 1984—, Interfaith Coun. for Action, Ossining, 1983—; mem. Ossining Upward Bound Substance Abuse Coun., 1984—, Ossining Restoration Com., 1975-77; mem. nominating com. White Plains chpt. ARC, 1985-86; bd. dirs. Phelps Meml. Hosp. Ctr., Vis. Nurse Svcs. Westchester; found. bd. U. Va. Carry Sch. Edn., 2005—. Recipient Harold J. Marshall award United Way No. Westchester, 1981. Mem. N.Y. Assn. Counties (v.p. 1984-85, pres. 1985, mem. steering com. 1989-92, Legislator of Yr. 1993), Westchester Mcpl. Planning Fedn. (bd. dirs. 1982—), Westchester 2000 (mem. task force 1985), Ossining C. of C. Avocations: gardening, sewing, crafts, decorating. Office: 2 Church St Ossining NY 10562-4802 Office Phone: 914-941-1111. Business E-Mail: galefs@assembly.state.ny.us.

GALEL, SUSAN ALPERT, transfusion medicine physician; MD, Harvard U., 1979. Diplomate Am. Bd. Pediat., Am. Bd. Pediatric Hematology/Oncology. Dir. clin. ops. Stanford Med. Sch. Blood Ctr., Palo Alto, Calif., 1987—. Office: Stanford Med Sch Blood Ctr 3373 Hillview Ave Palo Alto CA 94304

GALEMA, JOSEPH M., music director; b. Lafayette, Ind., Sept. 30, 1954; s. Joseph Martin Galema, Sr. and Lois Mae Galema. BA, Calvin Coll., 1976; MusM, U. Mich., 1978, D Musical Arts, 1982. Asst. organist Christ Ch. Grosse Pointe, Grosse Pointe Farms, Mich., 1978—81; organist First English Evang. Luth. Ch., Grosse Pointe, 1981—82; asst. for adminstrn. and music USAF Acad., USAF Academy, Colo., 1982—84, assoc. music dir., 1984—89, sr. music dir., acad. organist, 1989—. Musician: (recital) Am. Inst. Organbuilders 27th Nat. Conv., Organ Hist. Soc. Nat. Conv., Region VI Am. Guild Organists Conv., Assn. anglican Musican Conf., 2005, (arranger) NBA All-Star Game Nat. Anthem, 2005, Rose Bowl Pre-Game Music, 2006, (service organist) 73rd Nat. Episcopal Conv. Eucharist; contbr. articles to profl. jours.; musician: (recs.) From Age to Age with the Denver Brass, 2007, Stellar Brass Fireworks for Brass and Organ, 2006. Named to, Outstanding Young Men Am., 1985; recipient Palmer Christian award, U. Mich., 1987. Mem.: Am. Guild Organists, Organ Hist. Soc., Assn. Anglican Musicians. Episcopalian. Avocations: travel, reading. Home: 2672 Hatch Cir Colorado Springs CO 80918-6020 Office: Cadet Chapel Ste 100 2348 Sijan Dr U S A F Academy CO 80840-8280 Home Phone: 719-590-1628; Office Phone: 719-333-7846. Personal E-mail: joegalema@aol.com. Business E-Mail: joseph.galema@usafa.edu.

GALEN, ALBERT JOHN, retired lawyer; b. Helena, Mont., May 24, 1928; s. James Albert and Catherine Louise Galen; m. Sheila J. Sullivan (dec.); children: Sheila M., John M., Kimberly A., James A.; m. Margaret R. Hanley, June 22, 2002. BA in Bus. and law, U. Mont., 1950, JD, 1952; LLM, U. So. Calif., 1960. Bar: Mont. 1952, Calif. 1952. Ptnr. Holley & Galen, LA, 1952—92; executor Estate of Levinson, LA, 1992—99; ret., 1999. 1st lt. USAF, 1954—56. Mem.: Mont. CPA Soc. Republican. Roman Catholic. Home: 3511 E Cortez St West Covina CA 91791

GALES, SAMUEL JOEL, retired civilian military employee, counselor; b. Dublin, Miss., June 14, 1930; s. James McNary McNeil and Alice Francis (Smith) Broadus-Gales; m. Martha Ann Jackson (div. Jan. 1978); children: Samuel II (dec.), Martha Diane Townsend, Katherine Roselein, Karlmann Von, Carolyn B., Elizabeth Angelica McCain. BA, Chapman Univ., 1981, MS, 1987. Ordained Eucharist minister, Episcopal Ch., 1985; cert. tchr., Calif.; registered parliamentarian. Enlisted U.S. Army, 1948, advanced through grades to master 1st sgt., 1969, ret., 1976; tchr. Monterey (Calif.) Unified Sch. Dist., 1981-82; civilian U.S. Army Directorate of Logistics, Ft. Ord, Calif., 1982-93; collateral EEOC counselor Dept. Def., U.S. Army, 1987-93; instr. AARP Driver Safety Program, 2001—. Peer counselor, 1982-84. Active Family Svc. Agy., Monterey, 1979-85; rep. Episc. Soc. for Ministry on Aging, Carmel, Calif., 1980-86, Task Force on Aging, Carmel, 1983-87, vestryman, 1982-85, 91-94; ombudsman Monterey County Long-Term Care Program, Calif. Dept. for the Aging, 1993-97; vol. guide Monterey Bay Aquarium Found., 1994—, vol. docent Bay Net, Ctr. for Marine Conservation, Monterey Bay Nat. Marine Sanctuary, 1997-2003. Decorated Air medal. Mem.: Am. Inst. Parliamentarians (registered parliamentarian), Am. Legion (post comdr. 1973—74), Nat. Assn. Parliamentarians (pres. 2000—01, pres. Pi Gamma unit Calif. State Assn. 2000—01), Nat. Assn. Ret. Fed. Employees (pres. chpt. 579 1999—2000), Calif. State Assn. Parliamentarians (dir. Pacific area 2005—07), Toastmasters (pres. Monterey chpt. 2006—07), Forty and Eight (chef-de-gare 1979, 1980), Comdr.'s Club Calif. (pres. Outpost 28 1981—82), Monterey Chess Club. Republican. Avocation: classical music. Home: PO Box 919 1617 Lowell St Seaside CA 93955-3811 Office Phone: 831-394-4520. Personal E-mail: samuelg875@aol.com.

GALESI, DEBORAH LEE, artist; b. Paterson, NJ, Oct. 08; d. John Michael Galesi and Ethel Marchitti; m. Samuel Peace Eagle Dolphin, Oct. 3, 1997. BFA, U. Colo.; studied with, Raymond Whyte and Gene Scarpentoni, NY, Benjamin Long, Florence; MA, Villa Schifanoia/Inst. Florence. One-woman shows include Lo Sprone, Florence, Italy, 1983, Spinetti Gallery, Florence, 1985, Benvenuti Gallery, Venice, 1986, Salaria Gallery, Spoleto, 1987, Lo Spirale, Prato, Italy, 1988, Traghetto Gallery, Venice, 1987, Monteserrat Gallery, NYC, 2005; group show Amsterdam Whitney Gallery, NYC, 2005-06; works exhibited at U. Colo., Boulder, 1980, NY Gallery, NYC, 1981, NJ Gallery, 1981, U. Avignon, France, 1981, Sieve Art Expo, Pontassieve, Italy, 1984, Cenacolo Gallery, Florence, 1985, Modigliani Gallery, Milan, 1990, Art Expo, Verona, 1990, Palazzo Congressi, Salsomaggiore, 1995, Palazzo, Florence, 1996, Montserrat Gallery NY, 1997; represented in permanent collections Montserrat Gallery Chelsey, NYC; contbr. articles to profl. jours. Vol. Natural Resource Def. Coun., Washington, Pacific Whale Found., Hawaii, Ctr. for Marine Conservation, Washington, WWF, Greenpeace. Nat. Art Ctr. award, NY, 1978, others; recipient Stewardess of Ctr. of Light and Harmony award, Sierra Club. Mem. Ptnrs. of Destiny. Avocations: scuba diving, rollerblading, chinese painting, piano, ballet. Office: PMB 523 PO Box 959 Kihei HI 96753-0959

GALFAS, TIMOTHY, II, wholesale distribution executive; b. Atlanta, Sept. 28, 1943; s. Timothy and Louise (Cooledge) G.; m. Jytte Holst Malling, June 1, 1974; children: Kara Erika, Vikki Luise, Erin Kristiana. Student, French Inst. of Athens, Greece, 1959—60, Columbia U., NYC, 1961. Editor, prodr. Galfas Prodns., Inc., NYC, 1961-71, writer, prodr. Allendale, NJ, 1977-78; prof. Gilead Coll., NYC, 1967-77; pres. Delamotte-Turner Internat., Atlanta, 1978-82; dir. franchise ops. Mighty Distbg. Sys., Inc., Atlanta, 1982-91; pres., dir. Ctr. for Bus. Regeneration, Atlanta, 1991—; v.p., dir. Total Car Franchising Corp., Atlanta, 1991-94, pres., CEO Norcross, Ga., 1994-98; pres., CEO, chmn. bd. dirs. Colors in Europe, Inc., Norcross, 1997—98; v.p. franchise devel. Philly Franchising Co., Atlanta, 1998-99; pres. franchise ops. divsn. Aero Colours, Inc., Atlanta, 1999-2001; COO Isthmos, Inc., Atlanta, 2001—02; pres., CEO Maximum Recon, Inc., Atlanta, 2002, CEO, 2002—; CEO, bd. dirs. Restcon Devel. Ltd., Atlanta, 2003—05; CEO, chmn. bd. Automotive Resources Internat., Inc., Houston, 2005—06; COO, bd. dirs. Insular Corp., Balt., 2006—, ASAP Walls, Balt., 2006—. Bd. dirs. Carworks Inc., Decatur, Ga.; pres. bd. dirs. Ultimate Appearance Franchising Inc., Atlanta, 2002. Author: Creating and Managing a Distributing System, 1990, Take a Brave New Look at Your Business, 1990, Corporate Takeovers and Assorted Love Songs, 1991, Regenerating the Franchise System, 1993, Akhnaton Waits Alone, 2000, To Touch the Leper, 2002, rev. edit., 2005, What Every Business Owner Better Know, 2006; pub. newsletter Regenerator, author 365 radio scripts. Active Friends of Zoo, Atlanta, 1987. Recipient Best Editing of TV Comml. award N.Y. Art Dirs. Club, 1967; named Best Dir., Peachtree Players, 1980, 83, Achievement of Vision award Colors on Parade Franchise Adv. Coun., 1995, Franchiser of Yr., S.E. Franchise Forum and Kennesaw State U., 1998, Trailblazer award, 2005, Franchiser of Yr. Am. Assn. Franchises & Dealers, 2006. Mem. Am. Mgmt. Assn., Southeast Franchise Forum, Internat. Franchise Assn., Am. Assn. Franchises and Dealers (stds. com. 2002—, bd. dirs. 2006—). Avocations: lego, concert violin, poetry. Home: 6038 Maryjo Ln Norcross GA 30093-2015 Fax: 770-923-0873. Personal E-mail: tgalfas2@yahoo.com.

GALIARDO, CHRISTOPHER JAMES FRANCIS, language educator, political organization worker; b. Denver City, Tex., Oct. 14, 1980; s. James Anthony Galiardo and Juliana Powers Tragasz, Ronald Wayne Tragasz (Stepfather). BA, Dartmouth Coll., Hanover, NH, 2006—06; cert. in Chinese, Beijing Normal U., 2004; cert. in indigenous law, Universidad Panamericana, Mexico City; cert. in Arabic, Ctr. Maghrib Studies, Tunis, Tunisia, 2007; postgrad., U. Oxford, Eng., 2007. Cert. Office 2007 Microsoft, 2007. Mag. exec. editor Legion of Christ, Bad Muenstereifel, Germany, 1999—2002; pub. rels. dir. Tucker Found., Hanover, 2002—06; field rep. gt. lakes region Leadership Inst., Alexandria, Va., 2006; CEO, pres. Ivy League Tutors, Schaumburg, Ill., 2006—07; Arabic fellow Dept. of State, Tunis, 2007—. English instr. Beijing Normal U., 2004; rschr. The White House, Washington, 2004; cons. Kay Bailey Hutchison for Gov. exploratory com., Washington, 2005; youth moblzn. cons. Dave McSweeney for Congress, Palatine, Ill., 2006. Contbr. articles to profl. jours.; discovery a new nth-root estimation method in mathematics. Vol. Habitat for Humanity, Washington, 2004. Recipient Carpe Diem Humanitarian award, Carpe Diem Found. Ill., 2002—05; scholar, Dartmouth Coll., 2002—06; Nat. AP scholar, Coll. Bd., 1999, NROTC scholar, MIT, 1999, Nat. Merit scholar, 1999, Honors scholar, U. Chgo., 1999, Frank Corsaro scholar, Nat. Italian Am. Found., 2002, Starting Bloc Leaders fellow, 2005. Mem.: KC (4th degree), Phi Beta Kappa. Republican. Roman Catholic. Avocations: running, mountain climbing, scuba diving, white-water rafting. Home Phone: 224-213-0934.

GALIETTE, BRAD W., entrepreneur; b. 1985; Student, Yale Coll., 2004—. Founder & CEO PolariStar LLC, Essex, Conn., 2003—. Named one of Best Entrepreneurs Under 25, Bus. Week, 2006. Mem.: Yale Entrepreneurial Soc. (v.p.). Office: PolariStar LLC 3 Teal Lane Essex CT 06426-1046 Home Phone: 203-436-0683; Office Phone: 860-575-4984. Office Fax: 860-767-0508.

GALINAT, WALTON CLARENCE, research scientist; b. Manchester, Conn., Dec. 9, 1923; m. Elizabeth Ruth Warren, 1945; children: David W., Alice R. BS with honors, U. Conn., 1949; MS, U. Wis., 1951, PhD, 1953. Asst. in genetics Conn. Agrl. Experiment Sta., 1946-50; asst. in agronomy Wis. Agrl. Experimenbt Sta., 1950-53; rsch. fellow, rsch. assoc. Bussey Inst. Harvard U., 1953-64; assoc. prof. Waltham Field Sta. U. Mass., 1964-68, prof. Suburban Experiment Sta., 1968-90, prof. emeritus plant and soil scis., 1990—. With USCG, 1943-46. Recipient Disting. Econ. Botanist award Soc. Econ. Botany, 1994; Disting. Lifetime Achievement in Sci. and Art award U. Mass., 2001. Fellow AAAS. Office: Suburban Experiment Sta U Mass 240 Beaver St Waltham MA 02452-8096 Home Phone: 617-969-6523; Office Phone: 781-891-0650 x36.

GALINSKY, DENNIS LEE, radiation oncologist, educator; b. Des Moines, Sept. 16, 1948; s. Sam and Joyce Geraldine (Givant) G.; m. Daryl Lee Goldstein, Nov. 9, 1975; children: Dana Lauren, David Lawrence. BS, Drake U., 1970; MD, U. Iowa, 1974. Diplomate Am. Bd. Radiology. Intern U. Ariz., Tucson, 1974-75, resident in radiation oncology, 1975-77, U. Minn., Mpls., 1977-78; assoc. attending physician Evanston (Ill.) Hosp., 1978-80; dir. radiation oncology Copley Meml. Hosp., Aurora, Ill., 1980-89, U. Ill. Hosp., Chgo., 1991-93, DuPage Oncology Ctr., Winfield, Ill., 1993; assoc. prof. Rush U., Chgo., 1994—, 1994—; pvt. practice, Chgo., 1978. Clin. assoc. Northwestern U., Evanston, 1978-80; co-dir. rev. course Osler Inst., Lisle, Ill., 1991; presenter Internat. Congress Radiology, 1989, European Soc. Radiation Oncology, 1990. Contbr. articles to med. jours. Bd. dirs. Congregation Beth Shalom, Naperville, Ill., 1984-85; mem. Dist. 27 Sch. Bd., Northbrook, Ill., 1990—. Grantee NSF, 1968; recipient gold medal Am. Coll. Radiation Oncology, 2003. Fellow: Am. Coll. Radiation Oncology (vice chmn. 1991—92); mem.: AMA (del. 1996—), Chgo. Met. Area Radiation Oncology Soc. (pres. 1987—88), Beta Beta Beta. Avocations: golf, coin collecting/numismatics. Office: Nuclear Oncology SC 6929 Ogden Ave Berwyn IL 60402-3649

GALINSKY, GOTTHARD KARL, classicist, educator; b. Strassburg, Alsace, Feb. 7, 1942; came to U.S., 1961, naturalized, 1971; s. Hans Karl and Edith (Margenburg) G.; children Robert Charles, John Anthony. BA, Bowdoin Coll., 1963; MA, Princeton U., 1965, PhD, 1966. Instr. classics Princeton U., 1965-66; mem. faculty U. Tex., Austin, 1966—, prof. classics, 1972—, chmn. dept., 1974-90, Armstrong Centennial prof., 1985-91, Cailloux Centennial prof., 1991—, Disting. tchg. prof., 1999—, chmn. grad. assembly, 1977-79, chmn. faculty senate, 1981-82. Dir. summer seminars NEH, 1975, 76, 83-85, 97, 02, 05, 07; dir. residential seminar, 1977-78, dir. Collaborative Sch. Project, 1987-89, cons., 1976-78, 80-98; classicist-in-residence Am. Acad. Rome, 1972-73, vis. scholar, 1991; mem. adv. coun. Classical Sch., 1967—, chmn., 1982-85, mem. classical jury, 1970-71; lectr. U.S.-U.K. Edn. Commn., 1973; regional chmn. Mellon Humanities Fellowships, 1982-90; nat. lectr. Phi Beta Kappa, 1989-90; vis. Mellon prof. Tulane U., 1995; vis. prof. U. Nacional de La Plata, 1997; vis. prof. Gutenberg U. Mainz, Germany, 1998, Inst. Advanced Study, Princeton, 2000, U. Tex. Inst. for the Humanities, 2001. Author: Aeneas, Sicily and Rome, 1969, Tibulli Carmina, 1971, The Herakles Theme, 1972, Perspectives of Roman Poetry, 1974, Ovid's Metamorphoses, 1975, The Interpretation of Roman Poetry, 1992, Classical and Modern Interactions, 1992, Augustan Culture, 1996, Cambridge Companion to the Age of Augustus, 2005; mem. editl. bd. Classical World, 1973-76, Vergilius, 1973—, Classical Jour., 1991-98, Auster, 1996—. Mem. Leadership Austin, 1983-84. Fellow Am. Coun. Learned Socs., 1968-69, Fulbright fellow, 1972-73, Guggenheim fellow, 1972-73, NEH fellow, 1993-94; recipient Teaching Excellence award U. Tex., 1970, 76, 99, Robert W. Hamilton Author award U. Tex., 1997; Humboldt Found. sr. rsch. award, 1993, reinvitation award, 1998. Mem. Am. Philol. Assn. (Teaching Excellence award 1979, dir. 1980-83), Archaeol. Inst. Am., Classical Assn. Midwest and South (pres. 1980-81), Vergilian Soc. Am. (trustee 1972-76, v.p. 1976-77), Assn. Depts. Fgn. Langs. (exec. com. 1980-83, pres. 1983) Home: 4508 Edgemont Dr Austin TX 78731-5224 Office: U Tex Dept Classics Austin TX 78712-0308 Office Phone: 512-471-8504. Business E-Mail: galinsky@mail.utexas.edu.

GALKIN, SAMUEL BERNARD, orthodontist; b. Newark, Feb. 9, 1933; s. Saul J. and Mollie (Kleinberg) G.; m. Gail Beth Elkin, Feb. 26, 1972; children: Scott David, Seth Paul. Student, U. Conn., 1951-54; DDS, Temple U., 1958; MS in Histology, U. Ill., 1963, cert. grad. orthodontics, 1963; cert. in craniomandibular disorders, U. Medicine and Dentistry of N.J., 1989. Diplomate Am. Bd. Orthodontics. Group practice orthodontics, Woodbridge, NJ, 1963—; staff orthodontist J.F.K. Community Hosp., Edison, NJ, 1966—, with cleft palate com., 1971—, dir. dental dept., 1979—; staff Woodbridge Health Ctr., 1967—, with dental adv. com., 1971—; dir. dept. dentistry John F. Kennedy Med. Ctr., Edison, 1979-81; staff orthodontist Perth Amboy (N.J.) Gen. Hosp., 1986—, dir. dept. dentistry, 1990—; staff orthodontist Rahway Hosp., NJ, 1986—. Asst. prof. orthodontics N.J. Coll. Medicine and Dentistry, Jersey City, 1963-73; mem. panel physicians N.J. Crippled Children Program, 1971—; dentist Woodbridge Twp. Sch., 1989—. Chmn., Woodbridge Twp. Debutante Ball, 1970; bd. dirs. Woodbridge Twp. YMCA. Lt. Dental Corps, USN, 1958-61. Mem. ADA, Mid. Atlantic Soc. Orthodontists (chmn. clinics 1969-72), N.J. Dental Soc., Middlesex County Dental Soc., Am. Soc. Dentistry for Children, Am. Assn. Orthodontists, Am. Lingual Orthodontic Assn. (charter), Am. Assn. Dental Schs., Am. Acad. Head, Neck, Facial Pain and TMJ Orthopedics, N.E. Craniomandibular Soc., N.J. Craniomandibular soc. (charter), Am. Acad. Orofacial Pain, Am. Acad. Oral Medicine, Alpha Omega (chpt. v.p. 1969—), Omicron Kappa Upsilon. Home: 3 Dorset Rd Colonia NJ 07067-3101 Office: 711 Amboy Ave Woodbridge NJ 07095-3139 Office Phone: 732-750-2600.

GALL, ERIC PAPINEAU, internist, educator; b. Boston, May 24, 1940; s. Edward Alfred and Phyllis Hortense (Rivard) G.; m. Katherine Theiss, Apr. 20, 1968; children: Gretchen Theiss Gall, Michael Edward. AB, U. Pa., 1962, MD, 1966. Cert. Am. Bd. Internal Medicine, 1972, in rheumatology Am. Bd. Internal Medicine, 1974. Asst. instr. U. Pa., Phila., 1970-71, post doctoral trainee, fellow, 1971-73; asst. prof. U. Ariz., Tucson, 1973-78, assoc. prof., 1978-83, prof. internal medicine, 1983-94, prof. surgery, 1983-94, prof. family/community medicine, 1983-94, chief rheumatology allergy and immunology, 1983-93, dir. arthritis ctr., 1986-94; prof. medicine Rosalind Franklin Univ. Medicine & Sci., The Chgo. Med. Sch., North Chicago, Ill., 1994—, prof. microbiology and immunology, 1994—, chmn. dept. medicine, 1994—, chief rheumatology divsn., 1994-98, 2005—, assoc. dean clin. affairs, 1996-97, dir. metabolic bone unit, 1998—2007; prof. medicine Scholl Coll. Pediat. Medicine, 2007—. Author, editor: Rheumatoid Arthritis: Illustrated Guide to Path DX and Management of Rheumatoid Arthritis, 1988, Rheumatic Disease: Rehabilitation and Management, 1984, Primary Care, 1984; editor Clin. Care in The Rhematic Diseases, 1996; contbr. numerous articles to profl. jours. Chmn. med. and scientific com. Arthritis Found., Tucson, 1979-81; mem. Ill. Partnership for Arthritis; chair profl. edn. task force Ill. Dept. Pub. Health, 2001—. Major M.C. US Army, 1968—70. Decorated Bronze Star; recipient Addie Thomas Nat. Svc. award Arthritis Found., 1988. Master: ACP (coun. Ill. chpt. 1995—, Laureate award 2002), Chgo. Inst. Medicine, Am. Coll. Rheumatology (founding chair ednl. materials com. 1986—96, edn. coun. 1991—96, bd. dirs. 1992—95, chmn. rehab. sect. 1992—95); mem.: AMA (rep. sect. on med. schs. 1995—2002), Lake County Med. Soc. (treas. 1998—99, sec. 2000—, pres. 2002—03), Ill. Med. Soc. (del. 2002—07), Assn. Profs. Medicine, Arthritis Found. (nat. vice chmn. 1982—83, chmn. profl. edn. com. 1996—2001, trustee Greater Chgo. chpt. 1997—, bd. dirs. 1997—, exec. com. 1998—, treas. 2003—06, sr. vice chmn. 2006—07, chmn. 2008—, blue ribbon com. on quality of life), Ctrl. Soc. Clin. Investigation, Inst. Medicine of Chgo., Am. Fedn. Clin. Rsch., Am. Assn. Med. Colls., Arthritis Health Professions Assn. (nat. pres. 1982—83, Star award 2005), Alpha Epsilon Delta, Alpha Omega Alpha (counselor Chgo. Med. Sch. chpt. 1995—, regional counselor 1998—2004, nat. bd. dirs. 2006—), Sigma Xi. Roman Catholic. Avocation: photography. Office: The Chgo Med Sch Dept Medicine 3333 Green Bay Rd North Chicago IL 60064-3037 Office Phone: 847-578-8644. Business E-Mail: eric.gall@rosalindfranklin.edu. *Academic medicine provides the ideal opportunity to help patients, help touch and shape the lives of hundreds of students and trainees, and to add to the fund of knowledge in one's world.*

GALL, JOHN RYAN, lawyer; b. San Francisco, 1945; BA, Miami U., 1967; JD, Ohio State U., 1970. Bar: Ohio 1971. Ptnr. Squire, Sanders & Dempsey, Columbus, Ohio. Office: Squire Sanders & Dempsey 1300 Huntington Ctr 41 S High St Columbus OH 43215-6101 Office Phone: 614-365-2806. Business E-Mail: jgall@ssd.com.

GALL, JOSEPH GRAFTON, biologist, researcher, educator; b. Washington, Apr. 14, 1928; s. John Christian and Elsie (Rosenberger) G.; m. Dolores Marie Hogge, Sept. 17, 1955 (div. 1982); children: Lawrence, Barbara.; m. Diane Marie Dwyer, July 17, 1982. BS, Yale, 1949, PhD, 1952. Faculty U. Minn., 1952-63, prof., 1963; prof. biology and molecular biophysics Yale, 1963-83; staff dept. embryology Carnegie Instn., Balt., 1983—, Am. Cancer Soc. prof. developmental genetics, 1984—. Mem. cell biology study sect. NIH, 1963-67, chmn., 1972-75; chmn. bd. sci. counselors Nat. Inst. Child Health and Human Devel., NIH, 1986-90; mem. Yale Corp., 1989-95. Contbr. articles profl. jours. Recipient E.B. Wilson award Am. Soc. Cell Biology, 1983, Wilbur Cross medal Yale U., 1988, V.D. Mattia award Roche Inst. Molecular Biology, 1989, Purkinje medal Czech Acad. Scis., 1999, Albert Lasker Spl. Achievement in Med. Sci. award, Lasker Found., 2006. Mem. AAAS (Mentor award for lifetime achievement 1996), Am. Soc. Cell Biology (pres. 1967-68), Genetics Soc. Am., Nat. Acad. Scis., Am. Acad. Arts and Scis., Am. Philos. Soc., Accademia Nazionale dei Lincei, Soc. Developmental Biology (pres. 1984-85, Lifetime Achievement award 2004). Home: 107 Bellemore Rd Baltimore MD 21210-1314 Office: Carnegie Instn Dept Embryology 3520 San Martin Dr Baltimore MD 21218 Office Phone: 410-246-3017. E-mail: gall@ciwemb.edu.

GALL, MARY SHEILA, former federal agency administrator; 2 children. BA, Rosary Hill Coll., 1971; MS in Edn., Old Dominion U., 1998. Staff mem. various mems. of Senate and Ho. of Reps., 1971-79; sr. legis. analyst study com. Ho. of Reps., 1980-81; dep. domestic policy adviser Office of V.P. of U.S., 1981-86; counselor to dir. U.S. Office Pers. Mgmt., 1986-89; asst. sec. human devel. svcs. HHS, Washington, 1989-91; commr. U.S. Consumer Product Safety Commn., Washington, 1991—2004. Chair Pres.'s Task Force on Adoption, 1987-89. Dir. rsch. George Bush for Pres. campaign, 1979-80; mem. Reagan-Bush Presdl. campaign and transition team, 1980-81; tchr. Sunday sch. Republican.

GALL, MEREDITH (MARK) DAMIEN, retired education educator, writer; b. New Britain, Conn., Feb. 18, 1942; s. Theodore A. and Ray G.; m. Joyce Pershing, June 12, 1968; 1 child, Jonathan. AB, EdM, Harvard U., 1963; PhD, U. Calif., Berkeley, 1968. Sr. research assoc. Far West Lab. for Ednl. Research and Devel., San Francisco, 1968-75; assoc. prof. edn. U. Oreg., Eugene, 1975-79, prof., 1980—2005, dept. head for tchr. edn., 2002—05; ret., 2005. Author: Handbook for Evaluating and Selecting Curriculum Materials, 1981; author: (with K.A. Acheson) Techniques in the Clinical Supervision of Teachers, 5th edit., 2002; author: (with J.P. Gall) Making the Grade, 1993; author: (with W.R. Borg and J.P. Gall) Educational Research: An Introduction, 8th edit., 2007; author: (with J.P. Gall, D.R. Jacobsen, and T.L. Bullock) Tools for Learning: A Guide to Teaching Study Skills, 1990; author: (with W.R. Borg and J.P. Gall) Applying Educational Research, 5th edit., 2005; author: Clinical Supervision and Teacher Development, 5th edit., 2003; editor (with B.A. Ward): Critical Issues in Educational Psychology, 1974; cons. editor: Jour. Rsch. in Rural Edn., Forum for Reading, Elem. Sch. Jour. Grantee, USPH, 1963—64. Fellow Am. Psychol. Assn.; mem. ASCD, Am. Ednl. Research Assn., Oreg. Ednl. Research Assn. (pres. 1985-86), Phi Delta Kappa (Dist. I Meritorious award 1978). Home: 4810 Mahalo Dr Eugene OR 97405-4609 Business E-Mail: mgall@uoregon.edu.

GALL, STANLEY ADOLPH, immunologist, researcher; b. Bismarck, ND, May 31, 1936; s. Adolph and Wilma Thelma (Nickisch) G.; m. Florence Marie Ketterling, Aug. 17, 1958; children: Stanley, Kathryn Louise, Mark Allan, Thomas Andrew. BA, U. Minn., 1958, MD, 1962. Diplomate Am. Bd. Ob-Gyn. Intern U. Oreg. Hosp., Portland, 1962-63; resident in ob-gyn U. Minn. Hosp., Mpls., 1963-66; asst. prof. ob-gyn U. Miami, Fla., 1968-73; assoc. prof. ob-gyn Duke U. Med. Ctr., Durham, NC, 1973-78, prof., 1968—, dir. divsn. perinatal medicine; prof. ob-gyn, assoc. head dept. ob-gyn U. Ill. Coll. Medicine, 1985-89; prof. U. Louisville, 1989—, chmn. dept. ob-gyn., 1989—2000. Contbr. articles to profl. jours. Capt. M.C., U.S. Army, 1966-68. Fellow ACOG (liaison to ACIP); mem. AMA, Soc. Gynecol. Oncology, Soc. Gynecol. Investigations, Infectious Diseases Soc. Ob-Gyn, Soc. Maternal Fetal Medicine. Episcopalian. Office: U Louisville Dept Ob-Gyn 550 S Jackson St Louisville KY 40202-1622 Office Phone: 502-561-7447. Business E-Mail: sagall@louisville.edu.

GALLAGER, ROBERT GRAY, electrical engineering educator; b. Phila., May 29, 1931; s. Jacob Boon and May (Gray) G.; m. Ruth Atwood, Oct. 19, 1957 (div. July 1981); children: Douglas, Ann, Rebecca; m. Marie Tarnowski, July 18, 1981. BEE, U. Pa., 1953; MEE, MIT, 1957, ScD, 1960. Mem. tech. staff Bell Telephone Labs., Murray Hill, NJ, 1953-54; rsch. asst. MIT, Cambridge, Mass., 1956-60, asst. prof., 1960-64, assoc. prof., 1964-67, prof., 1967—. Co-dir. Lab. Info. and Decision Systems, 1986-96; chmn. adv. com. NSF Div. on Networking and Comm. Rsch. and Infrastructure, Washington, 1989-92; mem. adv. coun. Elec. Engring. Dept., U. Pa., 1991-93; chair adv. com. Elec. Engring. Dept., The Technion, Haifa, Israel, 1999. Author: Information Theory and Reliable Communication, 1968, Discrete Stochastic Processes, 1995; co-author Data Networks, 1987, 2d edit. 1992; patentee in field. Recipient Gold medal Moore Sch., U. Pa., 1973, Harvey prize The Technion, 1999, Eduard Rhein Basic Rsch. award, 2002; Guggenheim fellow, 1978, Marconi fellow, 2003. Fellow IEEE (Baker prize 1966, Medal of Honor 1990); mem. AAAS, NAS, NAE, Infor. theory Soc. of IEEE (bd. govs. 1965-72, 79-88, pres. 1971, Shannon Award 1983). Avocations: piano, skiing. Home: 13 Strawberry Cove Gloucester MA 01930-4128 Office: MIT Dept Elec Eng/Comp Sci Rm 32-D628 Cambridge MA 02139 Business E-Mail: gallager@mit.edu.

GALLAGHER, ANNE PORTER, communications executive; b. Coral Gables, Fla., Mar. 16, 1950; d. William Moring and Anne (Jewett) Porter; m. Matthew Philip Gallagher, Jr., July 31, 1976 (div. July 1998); children: Jacqueline Anne, Kevin Sharkey. BA in Edn., Stetson U., 1972. Tchr. elem. schs., Atlanta, 1972-74; sales rep. Xerox Corp., Atlanta, 1974-76, Rosslyn, Va., 1976-81, No. Telecom Inc., Vienna, Va., 1981-84, account exec., 1984-85, sales dir., 1985-91, mktg. dir., 1995-96; v.p. Fed. Pub. Sector Timeplex Fed. Sys., Inc., Fairfax, Va., 1995-96; bus. devel. dir. Informix Software, Vienna, 1996-97; sr. v.p. Tricor Industries Inc., Alexandria, Va., 1997-98; sr. v.p. fed. sys. Metromedia Fiber Network, McLean, Va., 1999—2002; sr. v.p. bus. devel. Source1 Techs., Arlington, Va., 2002—04; pres. AG Consulting LLC, Alexandria, Va., 2004—. Mem. Pi Beta Phi. Episcopalian. Avocations: running, working out. Home: 4643 Kirkland Pl Alexandria VA 22311-4949 Office Phone: 703-626-9466. Business E-Mail: APGallaghe@aol.com.

GALLAGHER, ARTHUR J., academic administrator; BA in English, Fairfield U., MEd. Assoc. dean student life Brown U., dir. student life; v.p. student affairs Johnson & Wales, Providence, 1999—2003, pres. Charlotte, 2003—. Mem. Leadership RI Class of 2002, Leadership Charlotte Class of 2003; bd. mem. United Way of Ctrl. Carolinas, Arts & Sci. Coun., Charlotte Ctr. City Partners, Charlotte C. of C. Office: Johnson & Wales U 801 W Trade St Charlotte NC 28202 Office Phone: 980-598-1011.*

GALLAGHER, BRIAN, editor; b. 1949; Employed The Jour. News, Westchester County, 1971—80, Gannett News Svc., Washington, 1980—83, mng. editor, 1983—86; employed USA Today, McLean, Va., 1986—91, editl. writer, 1991—99, editl. page editor, 1999—2002, 2004—, exec. editor, 2002—04. Office: USA Today Editor of the Editl Page 7950 Jones Branch Dr Mc Lean VA 22102 Office Phone: 703-854-3400.

GALLAGHER, BRIAN JOHN, lawyer; b. Bklyn., Oct. 24, 1939; s. John Joseph and Margaret R. Gallagher; m. Mary Loughney, Sept. 10, 1966; children: Amanda, Ian. BS, Fairfield U., 1961; JD, Fordham U., 1964; postgrad., NYU Law Sch., 1969-70. Bar: N.Y. 1965, U.S. Dist. Ct. (so. dist.) N.Y. 1967, U.S. Ct. Appeals (2d cir.) 1971, U.S. Dist. Ct. (ea. dist.) N.Y. 1974, U.S. Ct. Appeals (11th cir.) 1982, U.S. Ct. Appeals (D.C. cir.) 1986. Asst. U.S. Atty. So. Dist. N.Y., 1967-71; ptnr. Kronish, Lieb, Weiner & Hellman, LLP, NYC, 1976—. Mayor Village of Pelham Manor, N.Y., 1995-97, trustee, 1989-95. Mem. ABA, N.Y. State Bar Assn., Assn. Bar City N.Y., Fed. Bar Coun., Larchmont (N.Y.) Yacht Club, Williams Club, N.Y. Athletic Club. Office: 1114 Avenue Of The Americas New York NY 10036-7703 E-mail: bgallagher@klwhHp.com.

GALLAGHER, BYRON PATRICK, JR., lawyer; b. Bay City, Mich., Feb. 29, 1964; s. Byron Patrick and Ethel Jean (Gebowski) G.; m. Michelle Francis Burdick, May 21, 1994; children: Byron Patrick III, Grace Katherine. AB, Kenyon Coll., Gambier, Ohio, 1986; JD, Washington U., St. Louis, 1989. Bar: Mich. 1989, U.S. Dist. Ct. (we. dist.) Mich. 1990, U.S. Dist. Ct. (ea. dist.) Mich. 1995, U.S. Tax Ct. 2003. Ptnr. Gallagher Duby, PLC, Lansing, 1998—2003; founder The Gallagher Law Firm, PLC, Lansing, 2004—, mem. exec. com., mem. audit com. Bd. dirs., initial incorporator Summit Cmty. Bank. Bd. dirs. Ingham County Social Svc. Bd., Mason, Mich., 1991-92, Ingham County Commn., Mason, 1993-97, Mich. Underground Storage Tank Fin. Assurance Authority, 1996-2002; dir. State Bldg. Authority, 2002—; Rep. cand. Mich. State Senate, 1998. Mem. Ingham County Bar Assn. (bd. dirs. 1996-99, bench bar com. 2000—), County Club of Lansing, Mich. Athletic Club. Republican. Avocations: flying, golf. Home: 951 Walbridge Dr East Lansing MI 48823 Office: The Gallagher Law Firm PLC 2408 Lake Lansing Rd Lansing MI 48912

GALLAGHER, DONALD, physician; b. Santa Maria, Calif., Apr. 22, 1933; s. Donald MacKormac Sr. and Rebecca Mossman Gallagher; m. Nancy Joan Schwind, June 13, 1959; children: Margaret, Patricia, Timothy, James. BS cum laude, U. Notre Dame, Ind., 1955; MD, Loyola U., Chgo., 1959. Diplomate Am. Bd. Family Practice. Rotating intern LA County Gen. Hosp., 1959—60; pvt. practice Marshall-Putnam Clinic, Grandville, Ill., 1962—91; physician St. Margaret's Hosp., Spring Valley, Ill., 1991—. Med. advisor Spring Valley Nursing Ctr., 1979—92, Prairieland Home Health, Spring Valley, 2004—06. Author: (biographical event) A Little Boy ad Pearl Harbor - 12/7/41, 1995. Death investigator Putnam County, Ill., 1983—92. Capt. Med. Corps US Army, 1960—62. Decorated Cert. Appreciation. Mem.: AMA, Bureau County Med. Soc. (sec. 1972—82), Ill. Med. Soc., Am. Legion. Roman Catholic. Avocations: reading, golf, swimming. Home: 4 Westminster Dr Spring Valley IL 61362 Office: St Margaret's Hosp 600 E 1st St Spring Valley IL 61362

GALLAGHER, EDWARD PETER, foundation executive; b. San Francisco, Mar. 23, 1951; s. Edward Owen and Virginia Anne (Scully) G. BA, U. Calif., 1976; MBA, Columbia U., 1982. Dir. comm. Wolf Trap Farm Pk. for Performing Arts, Vienna, Va., 1977; program mgr. Smithsonian Instn., Washington, 1977-79; sr. program mgr. Smithsonian Inst., Washington, 1979-81; dir. membership Mus. Modern Art, NYC, 1983-90, dir. devel., 1986-87; dir. NAD, NYC, 1990-96; pres. Am.-Scandinavian Found., NYC, 1996—; also trustee. Cons. Cooper Hewitt Mus., N.Y.C., 1982-83; Yorkville Common Pantry, N.Y.C.; knight 1st class Norwegian Royal Order of Merit. Mem. Internat Commn. Mus., Am. Assn. Mus.

GALLAGHER, ELLEN, artist; b. Providence, 1965; Student, Sch. Mus. Fine Arts, Boston, 1992, Skowhegan Sch. Art, 1993, Oberlin Coll. One-woman shows include Akin Gallery, Boston, 1992, Mario Diacono Gallery, 1994, Mary Boone Gallery, N.Y., 1996, Anthony d'Offay Gallery, London, 1996, Gagosian Gallery, 1998, Ikon Gallery, Birmingham, 1998, Galerie Max Hetzler, Berlin, 1999, Anthony d'Offay Gallery, London, 2000, Watery Ecstatic, ICA, Boston, 2001, Ellen Gallagher: Preserve, Drawing Ctr., NYC, 2002, Currents 88, St. Louis Art Mus., 2003, Murmur, Galerie Max Hetzler, Berlin, 2003, Orbus, Fruitmarker Galley, Edinburgh, 2004, deLuxe, Whitney Mus. Am. Art, NYC, 2005, Fluidity of Time, Mus. Contemporary Art, Chgo., 2005—06, exhibited in group shows at Brandeis U., Waltham, 1993, Mus. Fine Arts, Boston, 1993, Inst. Contemporary Art, 1994, 1996, Mus. Fine Arts, 1995, Whitney Mus. Am. Art, N.Y., 1995, Whitechapel Art Gallery, London, 1996, Mario Diacono Gallery, Boston, 1997, De Beyerd Ctr. Contemporary Art, Breda, The Netherlands, 1998, others, Represented in permanent collections Mus. Modern Art, N.Y., Whitney Mus. Art, Met Mus. Art, Guggenheim Mus., Mus. Fine Art, Boston, Mus. Contemporary Art, L.A., Denver Mus. Art, Moderna Museet, Stockholm; featured in numerous articles and revs. Recipient Am. Acad. award, Art; Ann. Gund fellow, 1993, Provincetown Fine Arts Work Ctr. fellow, 1995, Joan Mitchell fellow, 1997. Office: Gagosian Gallery 555 W 24th St New York NY 10011

GALLAGHER, EUGENE BENNETT, sociologist, medical educator; b. Lancaster, Pa., Mar. 25, 1929; s. Joseph and Dorothy (Bennett) G.; m. Carol Thompson, Dec. 22, 1951 (div. July 1975); children: David Travis, Robert Thompson; m. Marilyn Milne, Aug. 20, 1977. BS, Lehigh U., 1949; MA, Harvard U., 1954, PhD, 1958. Lectr. Boston U., 1960-62; prof. U. Ky., Lexington, 1962—2003. Vis. prof. Bristol (Eng.) U., 1969-70, King Faisal U., Damman, Saudi Arabia, 1979-80, United Arab Emirates U., Al Ain, 1990, 97; rschr. NIH, Bethesda, Md., 1975-76. Author, editor: Patienthood in the Mental Hospital, 1964, Infants, Mothers and Doctors, 1977, Health and Health Care in Developing Countries, 1993, Global Perspectives on Health Care, 1995, Culture, Society, and Illness, 1996, Toward a Global Sociology of Health and Medicine, 2001. Fellow Am. Coun. Learned Socs., Washington, 1950; recipient Fulbright Rsch. award, 1996-97. Fellow: Am. Sociol. Assn.; mem.: Internat. Sociol. Assn. (pres. rsch. com. 1994—2002). Democrat. Office: U Ky Dept Behavioral Sci Lexington KY 40536-0001 Office Phone: 440-774-4497. E-mail: gallagher@oberlin.net.

GALLAGHER, GARY W(AYNE), educational services executive; b. Ponca City, Okla., May 13, 1954; s. Linden B. and Lenna J. (Greenshields) Wilson; m. Carole B. Stewart, May 1, 1979 (div. Mar. 1994); children: Heather, Danielle; m. Jani B. Viljoen, Aug. 5, 1998; children: Trevor, Derek, Stephen. BA in Polit. Sci., Okla. State U., 1975, L.Am. Area Studies cert., 1975, MS in Curriculum Studies, 1995, Supt. and Prin. Adminstrv. cert., 1995, postgrad., 1995—. Tchr. Ponca City Pub. Schs., Okla., 1987—88; instr. transitional sch. and work program for seriously emotionally disturbed children Am. Legion Children's Home, Ponca City, 1988—89; instr. social scis. Olive Pub. Schs., 1989—90; instr. social scis. and tech. applications Ponca City Pub. Schs., 1990—98; founder, curriculum theorist Advanced Academics, Ponca City, 1999—2001; dir. comml. mktg. Okla. ops. Applied Techs. divsn. Sci. Rsch. Corp., 2002—03; dir. bus. devel. Applied Marine Tech., Inc., Ponca City, 2003—06; dir. facilities Okla. State U., 2006—. Gov.'s Commendation for Volunteerism, 1993, 94; named Okla. Tech. Tchr. of the Yr., Tech. and Learning Mag., 1990. Mem. ASCD, NAESP, Am. Assn. Sch. Adminstrs., Nat. Assn. Secondary Sch. Prins., Internat. Internet Learning Assn., Internat. Soc. Tech. in Edn., Nat. Coun. Social Studies (instrnl. media/tech. com.), Am. Ednl. Rsch. Assn., Nat. Youth Leadership Coun., Okla. Alliance for Geog. Edn., Internat. Assn. Sch. Bus. Ofcls., Okla. Coun. Social Studies, Okla. Hist. Soc., Assn. Ednl. Comm. and Tech., Assn. Childhood Edn. Home: 1813 E Hartford Ave Ponca City OK 74604-2521 Office Phone: 580-762-2684. Personal E-mail: gwg@cableone.net. Business E-Mail: ggallagher@okstate-uml.org.

GALLAGHER, GERALD RAPHAEL, venture capitalist; b. Easton, Pa., Mar. 17, 1941; s. Gerald R. and Marjorie A. G.; m. Ellen Anne Mullane, Aug. 8, 1964; children: Ann Patrice, Gerald Patrick, Megan Ann. BS in Aero. Engring., Princeton U., 1963; MBA (Exec. Club Chgo. fellow 1969), U. Chgo., 1969. Dir. strategic planning Metro-Goldwyn-Mayer, NYC, 1969; v.p. Donaldson, Lufkin & Jenrette, NYC, 1969-77; from v.p. to sr. v.p. planning and control Dayton Hudson Corp., Mpls., 1977-79; exec. v.p., chief adminstrv. officer subs. Mervyn's, Hayward, Calif., vice chmn., chief adminstrv. officer, 1979-85, vice chmn., chief adminstrv. office parent co., 1985-87, also dir.; gen. ptnr. Oak Investment Ptnrs., Mpls., 1987—. Bd. dirs. Cheddar's eStyle, Lucy Activewear, Ulta, XIOtech, Potbelly. With USN, 1963—67. Mem. N.Y. Soc. Security Analysts, Mpls. Club, Interlachen Country Club, Beta Gamma Sigma. Roman Catholic. Office: Oak Investment Ptnrs 4550 Wells Fargo Ctr 90 S 7th St Minneapolis MN 55402-3903 Office Phone: 612-339-9322. E-mail: jerry@oakvc.com.

GALLAGHER, J. PATRICK, JR., insurance company executive; b. Chgo., 1952; Degree, Cornell U., 1974. From v.p. ops. to pres. Arthur J. Gallagher & Co., Itasca, Ill., 1985—90, pres., 1990—, CEO, 1995—, bd. dir. Trustee Am. Inst. CPCU. Office: Arthur J Gallagher & Co Two Pierce Place Itasca IL 60143

GALLAGHER, JAMES C., lawyer; b. Lyndonville, Vt., June 16, 1945; BA, Tufts U., 1967; JD, Cornell U., 1971. Bar: Vt. 1971, US Dist. Ct. (Dist. Vt.) 1972, US Ct. Appeals (2d Cir.) 1977, US Supreme Ct. 1984, NH 1986, US Dist. Ct. (Dist. NH) 1986, US Dist. Ct. (No. Dist. NY) 1986. Dir. Downs Rachlin & Martin P.C., St. Johnsbury, Vt. Bd. dirs. Lyndon Inst., pres. bd. trustees, 1994—2003; trustee Vt. Legal Aid, Lyndon State Coll. Found. Editor Cornell Law Review, 1970-71. Mem. ABA, NH Bar Assn., Vt. Bar Assn. (treas. 1999, pres.-elect 2004, pres. 2005), Def. Rsch. Inst., Am. Bd. Trial Advocates. Office: Downs Rachlin & Martin PC PO Box 99 90 Prospect St Saint Johnsbury VT 05819-0099 Office Phone: 802-473-4208. Office Fax: 802-748-4394. E-mail: jgallagher@drm.com.*

GALLAGHER, M. CATHERINE, English literature educator; b. Denver, Feb. 16, 1945; d. John Martin and Mary Catherine Sullivan; m. Martin Evan Jay, July 6, 1974; children: Margaret Shana, Rebecca Erin. BA, U. Calif., Berkeley, 1972, MA, 1974, PhD, 1979. Asst. prof. U. Denver, 1979-80, U. Calif., Berkeley, 1980-84, assoc. prof., 1984-90, prof., 1990—. Author: The Industrial Reformation of English Fiction, 1985, Nobody's Story, 1994, The Body Economic, 2005; co-author: The Making of the Modern Body, 1987, Practicing New Historicism, 2000; editor Representation, 1983—. Guggenheim fellow Guggenheim Found., 1989; fellow NEH, 1990, ACLS, 1990, Mem. MLA (del. assembly mem. 1985-86, exec. com. lit. criticism divsn. 1991-94), Am. Acad. Arts and Scis., Acad. Lit. Studies, Brit. Studies Assn., The Dickens Soc. Office: U Calif Dept English Berkeley CA 94720-0001 Business E-Mail: cgall@berkeley.edu.

GALLAGHER, MARTIN JOSEPH, neurologist, neuroscientist; s. George Vincent and Gertrude Mary Gallagher; m. Nancy Gail Henis, June 11, 1995. BS in Chemistry, U. Notre Dame, 1989; MD, Wash. U., St. Louis, 1997, PhD in Molecular Biophysics, 1997. Cert. Am. Bd. Psychiatry and Neurology (specialty in clin. neurophysiology), epilepsy monitoring Am. Bd. Clin. Neurophysiology. Vis. scholar Harvard U. Sch. Medicine, Boston, 1992—96; intern in internal medicine Wash. U. Sch. Medicine, St. Louis, 1997—98, resident in neurology, 1998—2001, epilepsy fellow, 2001—02, instr. dept. neurology; asst. prof. dept. neurology, divsn. epilepsy Vanderbilt U. Sch. Medicine, Nashville, 2002—. Recipient Young Investigator award, Am. Epilepsy Soc., 2003, Early Career Physician Scientist award, Am. Epilepsy Soc., Milken Family Found., 2005. Office: Vanderbilt U Med Ctr 465 21st Ave S 6140 MRBIII Nashville TN 37232 Office Phone: 615-322-5979. Office Fax: 615-322-5517.

GALLAGHER, MICHAEL DAVID, lawyer, former federal agency administrator; b. 1964; BA, U. Calif. Berkeley; JD, U. Calif. LA. Bar: Wash. Adminstrv. asst. & chief of staff to Congressman Rick White US Congress, Washington, 1995—97; mng. dir. govt. rels. AirTouch Comm., Inc., Bellevue, Wash., 1998—2000; staff v.p. state pub. policy Verizon Wireless, Bellevue, Wash., 2000—01; dep. asst. sec. comm. & info. Nat. Telecom. & Info. Adminstrn. US Dept. Commerce, Washington, 2001—03, acting asst. sec., 2003, asst. sec., 2003—06; dep. chief of staff for policy & counselor to sec. U.S. Dept. Commerce, Washington, 2003; sr. assoc. Perkins Coie LLP, Seattle, 1989—94, of counsel, govt. rels. practice chair, 1997—98, ptnr., chmn. Comm. & Govt. Rels. Group Washington, 2006—. Pres. Cellular Carriers Assn. Calif., 2000. Recipient Spirit of Innovation award, Telecom. Industry Assn., 2005, Leadership in Govt. award, Wireless Comm. Assn., 2006, Redfield award, 2006. Office: Perkins Coie LLP 607 Fourteenth St NW Washington DC 20005 E-mail: MGallagher@perkinscoie.com.

GALLAGHER, MICHAEL L., lawyer; b. LeMars, Iowa, Apr. 14, 1944; BA, Ariz. State U., 1966, JD, 1970. Bar: Ariz. 1970. Maj. league scout N.Y. Mets, 1967—70; atty. Snell & Wilmer, Phoenix, 1970—78, Gallagher & Kennedy, Phoenix, 1978—. Judge pro tem Maricopa County Superior Ct., 1979, Ariz. Ct. Appeals, 1985; Amerco, U-Haul; bd. dirs. Ariz. Pub. Svc. Co., Omaha World Herald Co., Pinnacle West Capital Corp. Chmn. gov.'s adv. com. profl. football, 1981-87, mayor's adv. com. profl. sports, 1984-91; bd. dirs. Maricopa County Sports Authority, 1989; bd. visitors law sch. Ariz. State U., 1979; dir. Valley of the Sun YMCA, chmn., 1995; trustee Peter Kiewit Found. Fellow Internat. Acad. Trial Lawyers. Office: Gallagher & Kennedy PA 2575 E Camelback Rd Phoenix AZ 85016-9225 Home Phone: 602-277-9462; Office Phone: 602-530-8000. Business E-Mail: mlg@gknet.com.

GALLAGHER, MICHAEL ROBERT, retired consumer products company executive; b. Cedar Rapids, Iowa, Jan. 21, 1946; s. John Robert and Mabel Helen (Slaymaker) Gallagher; m. Linda Katherine Nebb, Oct. 25, 1975; children: Megan Elizabeth, John William, Edward Michael. BS, U. Calif., Berkeley, 1967, MBA, 1968. Brand mgr. Procter & Gamble Co., Cin., 1968-72; various positions Clorox Co., Oakland, Calif., 1972-77; pres., gen. mgr. Clorox Can., Vancouver, B.C., advt. mgr. household products div., 1980-81, gen. mgr. household products div., 1982-84; pres. consumer products div. Lehn & Fink/Sterling Drug, Montvale, NJ, 1984-85; sr. v.p. Lehn & Fink Products, Montvale, NJ, 1985-87, exec. v.p., 1987-88; pres., chief exec. officer L&F Products Inc. (formerly Lehn & Fink), Montvale, NJ, 1989-95; pres., CEO Reckitt & Colman Inc., Montvale, 1995; CEO Playtex Products Inc., Westport, Conn., 1995—2004, ret., 2004. Bd. dir. Allergan. Vice chmn. United Way Bergen County, NJ, 1985—87, bd. dirs. NJ, 1989—96, chmn. bd. dirs. NJ, 1993—95, chmn. Golden Ball NJ, 1990; sports chmn. Cancer Care Am., 1989; mem. exec. coun. Boy Scouts Am., Bergen County, 1990—95; bd. dirs. Haas Sch. Bus., U. Calif., Berkeley, 2002—; trustee St. Luke's Sch., 1998—2005. Mem.: Assn. Sales and Mktg. Cos. (bd. dirs. 2001—04), Grocery Mfrs. Assn. (bd. dirs. 1997—2004), Soap and Detergent Assn. (bd. dirs. 1992—95).

GALLAGHER, PATRICK FRANCIS XAVIER, public relations executive; b. Cleve., Feb. 9, 1952; s. Patrick Francis and Eileen (Brennan) G.; m. Anne Platek, May 3, 1980; children: Molly Anne, Kate Louise. Student, Holy Cross Coll., Worcester, Mass., 1970-72; BA, U. Pa., 1974; MBA, Cleve. State U., 1991. Accredited in pub. rels. Staff editor Penton Pub. Co., Cleve., 1975-80, editor, 1980-83; mgr. corp. communications Leaseway Transp. Corp., Cleve., 1983-84, dir. pub. rels., 1984-85; sr. account exec. Edward Howard, Cleve., 1985-89, v.p., 1990-94, sr. v.p., 1994—. Past-pres. Project LEARN, Cleve.; bd. trustees Great Lakes Theater Festival, Cleve. Mem. Pub. Rels. Soc. Am., Nat. Investor Rels. Inst. (past pres. Cleve.-No. Ohio chpt.2001-03), CFA Soc. Cleve. Office: Edward Howard 16th Fl 1100 Superior Ave Cleveland OH 44114-2518

GALLAGHER, PATRICK J., lawyer; BA, Hamline U., 1991; JD cum laude, William Mitchell Coll. Law, 1999. Bar: Minn. 1999, US Dist. Ct. (dist. Minn.) 2000. Sr. assoc. intellectual property & tech. dept. Fulbright & Jaworski, L.L.P., Mpls. Adj. prof. trademark litig. William Mitchell Coll. Law. Contbr. articles to profl. publs.; editor-in-chief: William Mitchell Law Rev. Vol. 25, 1998—99; editor: INTA Bull. Named a Rising Star, Minn. Super Lawyers mag., 2006. Mem.: Minn. Intellectual Property Law Assn., Internat. Trademark Assn. (mem. bull. com.), Minn. State Bar Assn., St. Paul Young Lacrosse Club (pres.). Office: Fulbright & Jaworski LLP 2100 IDS Ctr 80 S 8th St Minneapolis MN 55402 Office Phone: 612-321-2812. E-mail: pgallagher@fulbright.com.*

GALLAGHER, RICHARD SIDNEY, lawyer; b. Minot, ND, May 10, 1942; s. J.W.S. and Esther T. (Tappon) G.; m. Ann Rylands Larson, June 24, 1972; children: Elizabeth, Catherine. BSBA, Northwestern U., 1964; JD, Harvard U., 1967. Ptnr. Foley & Lardner LLP, Milw., 1967—, chmn. tax and individual planning dept., 1995—2006. Bd. dirs. Badger Meter Found., Milw. Bd. chmn. Milw. Youth Symphony Orchs., Milw., 1980-82, Milw. County Performing. Arts Ctr., Milw., 1986-91; dir. Curative Rehab. Ctr., Milw., 1988-93, United Performing Arts Fund, 1991-99, Blood Ctr. S.E. Wis., Milw. Youth Arts Ctr.; pres. Donors Forum of Wis., 1997-2000. Lt. comdr., USN, 1967-69, Vietnam. Fellow Am. Coll. Tax Counsel, Am. Coll. Trust & Estate Coun., Am. Law Inst.; mem. ABA (chmn. exempt orgns. com., sect. of taxation 1989-91, governing coun. sect. taxation, 2005-, chmn. com. adminstrn. trusts & estates, sect. probate & trust law 1996-98). Office: Foley & Lardner LLP US Bank Ctr 777 E Wisconsin Ave Milwaukee WI 53202 Business E-Mail: rgallagher@foley.com.

GALLAGHER, SCOTT FARRELL, surgeon, researcher; s. Farrell John and Mary Jean Gallagher; m. Linda S. Boyer, Sept. 19, 1998; 1 child, Mitchell Scott. BA, Ohio Wesleyan U., 1993; MD, Ohio State U., 1997. Diplomate Am. Bd. Surgery, 2004. Intern U. South Fla. Health, Tampa, 1997—98, resident, 1998—2001, chief resident, 2001—02, asst. prof. surgery, 2004—, jr. faculty fellow in surg. endocrinology, 2005; advanced GI and Bariatric Surgery Fellow U. South Fla. Coll. Medicine, Tampa, 2002—04. Assoc. dir. bariatric surgery divsn. gen. surgery U. South Fla., Tampa, 2005—. Contbr. chapters to books, articles to profl. jours. Eagle Scout; pres. Epsilon Chpt. Housing Corp., Delaware, Ohio, 2004—06; bd. dirs. Delaware, Ohio, 2004—06. Recipient Chrysler Leadership award, Army Reserve Scholar-Athlete award. Mem.: AMA, Assn. for Acad. Surgery, Soc. for Surgery of the Alimentary Tract, Soc. for Am. Gastrointestinal and Endoscopic Surgery, Am. Soc. Bariatric Surgery, Tampa Bay Surg. Soc., Soc. for Laparoendoscopic Surgeons, ACS Candidate & Assoc. Soc. (assoc.), The Pancreas Club, Ohio State Alumni Assn., Alpha Sigma Phi Frat. (life Delta Beta Xi award 2001). Roman Catholic. Avocations: travel, piano. Office: c/o Tampa Gen Hosp USF Health Ste F145 2 Columbia Dr Tampa FL 33606 Home Phone: 813-963-7558; Office Phone: 813-844-7540. Office Fax: 813-844-1920. Business E-Mail: sgallagh@health.usf.edu.

GALLAGHER, TERRENCE VINCENT, editor; b. Phila., Nov. 22, 1946; s. Harold John and Marie Elizabeth (Kershaw) G.; m. Eileen Rose Small, Dec. 26, 1971; children: Sean Terrence, Elizabeth I. BS in Journalism, Temple U., 1971. With Chilton Co., Radnor, Pa., 1971-94; asst. editor Product Design and Devel. mag, 1971-73; mng. editor Internat. Product Digest, 1973-74; editor-in-chief Instrument and Apparatus News mag., 1974-84, Hardware Age mag., 1984-94, Decorative Products World, 1989-94, Outdoor Power Equipment Mag, 1989-94, Garden Supply Retailer mag., 1989-94; editorial dir. Chilton's Home and Yard Care Group, 1989-94; chmn. editorial bd. Chilton Co., 1980-83; contbg. editor Tennis U.S.A., 1974-75; pres. Gallagher Communications, 1994—. Served to 1st lt. U.S. Army, 1966-69, Vietnam. Decorated Bronze Star with 2 V devices; Vietnamese Cross of Gallantry. Home: 141 Chaps Ln West Chester PA 19382 Office Phone: 610-399-5211. E-mail: tvg315@aol.com.

GALLAGHER, THOMAS C., diversified manufacturing executive; b. 1948; With SP Richards Co., 1983, Genuine Parts Co., 1963—, exec. v.p., 1989-90, pres., COO, dir., 1990—2004, pres., CEO, dir., 2004—05, chmn., pres., CEO, 2005—. Bd. dir. Oxford Industries, STI Classic Funds. Office: Genuine Parts Co 2999 Circle 75 Pkwy NW Atlanta GA 30339-3050*

GALLAGHER, WILLIAM T., lawyer, manufacturing executive; b. 1954; BA, LaSalle U., 1976; JD, Temple U., 1984. Bar: Pa. 1984, US Ct. Appeals (3rd cir.) 1985, US Dist. Ct. (ea. dist. Pa.) 1985. V.p. Crown Holdings Inc., Phila., sec., gen. counsel. Office: Crown Holdings One Crown Way Philadelphia PA 19154 Office Phone: 215-698-5383. Office Fax: 215-698-2604.*

GALLAHER, FREDERICK BLAKE, emergency mgmt. specialist; b. Socorro, N.Mex., Jan. 10, 1947; s. Frederick Eugene Gallaher and Letha Evelyn Morris; children: Justin Blake, Patrick James. Student, U. Okla., Norman, 1973; BA in Theology, San Jose Christian Coll., 1974; MPA, U. N.Mex., Albuquerque, 1988; MPH, Harvard U., Cambridge, Mass., 1995. LPN, emerg. room mgr. U. N.Mex. Hosp., Albuquerque, 1975-77, 78-79; health facility surveyor State of N.Mex. Health and Environ. Dept., Santa Fe, 1979-82, state tng. coord. emergency med. svcs., 1988-90; adminstrv. intern City of Albuquerque/Office of the Mayor, 1985-86; dir. admissions, LPN Ladera and Montebello Nursing Homes, Albuquerque, 1987-88; adminstr. Ctr. for Disaster Medicine U. N.Mex. Sch. Medicine, Albuquerque, 1990-93; dir. tng. Brewster Ambulance Co., Boston, 1993-94; spl. forces med. specialist, instr. US Army, 1975-94; project mgr. Human Survival Program Harvard U., Cambridge, Mass., 1994-95; pres. High Desert Cons., Santa Fe, 1995—96; dir. Health Facility Compliance Health Dept., Santa Fe, 1996—2001; CEO Gallaher Cons., 2001—02, Pecos Valley Med. Ctr., Inc., 2003—05; pres. Policy and Orgnl. Consulting, Inc., Pecos, N.Mex., 2002—05; fin. analyst Merrill Lynch, Inc., Pecos, N.Mex., 2006; dir. emergency and disaster mgmt. Miracopa Integrated Health Sys., Phoenix, 2007—. Presenter in field. Contbr. articles to profl. publs.; author: A Medical Handbook for Disaster and Refugee Operations, U. N.Mex., 1993. Mem. Nat. Coun. State EMS Tng. Coords. (chmn. practical exam com. 1989-90), Nat. Disaster Med. Sys., Spl. Forces Assn. (decade), Mensa, Am. Coll. Healthcare Exec., Pi Alpha Alpha.

GALLAND, LEO, internist, researcher; b. Bombay, Mar. 7, 1943; came to U.S., 1948; s. H. William and Rachel (Zakkai) G.; m. Christine Oelz, Sept. 29, 1974; children: Nicole, Jefferson, Jonathan, Christopher, Jordan. AB, Harvard U., 1964; MD, NYU, 1968. Diplomate Am. Bd. Internal Medicine. Resident in medicine NYU-Bellevue Med. Ctr., NYC, 1968-72; instr. Albert Einstein Coll. Medicine, Yeshiva U., NYC, 1972-73; asst. prof. SUNY Med. Ctr., Stony Brook, 1973-77; pvt. practice Winsted (Conn.) Hosp., 1977-82; dir. rsch. Gesell Inst., New Haven, 1982-85; pvt. practice, NYC, 1985—. Asst. prof. U. Conn. Health Ctr., Farmington, 1977-85; sr. rsch. cons. Gt. Smokies Diagnostic Lab., Asheville, N.C., 1990-97; dir. Found. for Integrated Medicine, 1997—. Author: Superimmunity for Kids, 1988, The Four Pillars of Healing, 1997, The Fat Resistance Diet, 2005; also numerous articles on nutrition and infectious diseases. Recipient

Harold Harper award Am. Coll. Advancement in Medicine, 1989, Linus Pauling award Inst. Functional Medicine, 2000, Clinician award Nat. Nutritional Foods Assn., 2004. Fellow ACP, Am. Coll. Nutrition. Avocations: travel, skiing, surfing. Home: 142 5th Ave New York NY 10011-4312 Office: 156 Fifth Ave #817 New York NY 10011 Office Phone: 212-772-3077. Business E-Mail: drgalland@nutritionworkshop.com.

GALLANT, BRAD (KEITH BRADOC GALLANT), lawyer; m. Joanna Waley-Cohen; children: Isabel, Kit. BA with honors, Cambridge U., Eng., 1975, MA, 1979; JD cum laude, U. Conn. Sch. Law, 1978; LLM, U. London, 1979. Bar: Conn. 1978. Ptnr. Day, Berry & Howard, LLP, New Haven; ptnr. individual clients dept. Day Pitney, LLP (following merger of Day, Berry & Howard, LLP and Pitney Hardin, LLP), New Haven, 2007—. Contbr. articles to profl. jours. Bd. dirs. Ctr. Medicare Advocacy; pres. bd. dirs. New Haven Free Pub. Libr. Named a Conn. Super Lawyer, 2006, 2007; named Citizen of Yr., Conn. Probate Cts., 1994; named one of Top 100 Attys., Worth mag., 2005—06, Top 10 Conn. Lawyers, Conn. Mag., 2006. Fellow: Am. Coll. Trust and Estate Counsel (mem. fiduciary litig. and elder law coms., rep. to Nat. Guardianship Network), Conn. Bar Found. (life); mem.: Nat. Acad. Elder Law Attys., Conn. Bar Assn. (chair estates & probate sect., mem. exec. com. of elder law sect., mem. animal law com.). Office: Day Pitney LLP 1 Audubon St New Haven CT 06511 Office Phone: 203-752-5025. Office Fax: 203-752-5001. E-mail: bgallant@daypitney.com.*

GALLANT, STEPHEN LAURIE, librarian; b. Balt., July 14, 1953; s. Thomas F. and Myra Gallant; m. Jennifer Jung, Apr. 23, 1983. MusB, U. Cin., 1975; MS in Libr. Sci., Case Western Res. U., 1976. Audio-visual asst. Cuyahoga County Pub. Libr., Cleve., 1978—80, libr. adult and young adult svcs. South Euclid, Ohio, 1980—89, libr. adult svcs. Beachwood, Ohio, 1989—97, regional reference specialist Mayfield Village, Ohio, 1997—. Presenter at chpt. confs. Ohio Libr. Coun., 2001; presenter at staff day Dayton and Montgomery County Pub. Libr., Dayton, 2001; spkr., writer on current awareness resources in libr. and info. sci. Mem.: Am. Soc. for Info. Sci. and Tech. (chair No. Ohio chpt. 2000—03), Nat. Space Soc., Cuyahoga Astron. Assn. Avocations: piano playing, computer programming, astronomy. Home Phone: 440-892-7934. Personal E-mail: slgallant@gmail.com. Business E-Mail: sgallant@cuyahogalibrary.org.

GALLARDO, HENRIETTA CASTELLANOS, writer; b. San Antonio, July 16, 1934; d. Francisco Garcia and Elisa Duarte (Moreno) Castellanos; m. Albert Joseph Gallardo, Aug. 19, 1965; children: Frank Cantu, Roger Cantu (dec.), Gloria Michelle. Cert., Draughn's Bus. Coll., San Antonio, 1952. Sec. Kelly Air Force Base, San Antonio, 1952-53; exec. sec. U. Tex., Dallas, 1974-82; interior decorator Plano, Tex., 1983-85; writer. Author: Tangled Web of Destiny, 1992, Marsh & Co., 1993, Everyday Heroes, 2002. Democrat. Roman Catholic. Avocations: photography, travel, reading, charity work. Home: 2212 Parkhaven Dr Plano TX 75075-2013 E-mail: hgallardo@comcast.net.

GALLARDO, MIGUEL E., psychologist; b. San Antonio, July 5, 1974; s. Frank Epsinoza and Evangelina Robles Gallardo. BS, Tex. Christian U., 1996; D of Psychology, Calif. Sch. Profl. Psychology, 2001. Cert. trainer Stanford U., 2003. Dir. sexual offenders program Santa Anita Family Svcs., 1998—2001; intern UCLA Counseling Ctr., LA, 2000—01; staff psychologist, lectr. Counseling Ctr., Dept. Social Ecology U. Calif., Irvine, 2001—04. Asst. prof. grad. sch. edn. and psychology Pepperdine U., 2003—05; mem. adv. bd. Am. Sch. Profl. Psychology, Argosy U., 2004—; mem. exec. coun. Nat. Inst. Multicultural Competence, Nat. Planning and Implementation Com., 2004—. Contbr. articles to profl. jours. Mem.: APA (chair program com. ind. practitioners 2004—05, mem. early career psychologists com. 2005—, Campus Rep. Yr. award 1999), Nat. Latino Behavioral Health Assn., Orange County Psychol. Assn. (bd. dirs. 2003—), Calif. Latino Psychol. Assn. (pres. 2004—), Nat. Latino Psychol. Assn. (chair chpt. devel. com. 2004—), Calif. Psychol. Assn. (chair pubs. com. 2002—05, chair diversity com. 2005—, Bronze Psi award 2000). Roman Catholic. Avocations: running, golf, basketball, movies. Office: Pepperdine U 18111 Von Karman Ave Ste 209 Irvine CA 92612

GALLARDO, SANDRA SILVANA, television producer, actress; b. Bronx, Jan. 13, 1947; d. Edward Francis and Grace (Mallory) G.; m. Gerald O'Connor, Jan. 21, 1968 (div. 1978); m. Billy Burrows, Sept. 21, 1985. Student, HB Studio, NYC, 1964—72, CCNY, 1964—66. CEO Gallardo Studios, North Hollywood, Calif., 1980—; pres. Camellia Prodns., Studio City, Calif., 1987—. Guest spkr. IRS, Hollywood, Calif., 1990. Prodr., dir., writer The Acting Class, 1988, Fading to Zero--a docudrama, 2007; author: The Winning, 1998, Acting for Success, 1999, 2d edit., 2005 (Academic World Star); co-author (films) Sammy and Friends, 2007; actress (film) Solar Crisis, The Windwalker, Death Wish II, Out of the Dark, The Tin Angel; (TV) Prison Stories: Women on the Inside, Calendar Girl Murders, The People vs. Inez Garcia, Days of Our Lives, NYPD Blue, Lou Grant, ER, Babylon 5, Providence, Strong Medicine, Golden Girls, Ressurection Blvd., Kingpin, Children of Times Square, Hill St. Blues, Silence of the Heart; appeared on stage in American Mosaic; writer, prodr. (films) The Anger, 2006, The Tin Angel, 2006. Recipient Bronze Star halo So. Calif. Motion Picture Coun., 1985, Golden Eagle award Nosotros, 1989. Mem. SAG (guest spkr. 1988-96), Am. Fedn. TV Arts Scis., Am. TV Arts & Scis., Equity. Avocations: writing, paddle tennis, hiking, museums. Office: Camellia Prodns PO Box 545 Paris KY 40361 Office Phone: 661-607-9649. Personal E-mail: sgalla2222@aol.com.

GALLAS, MARTIN HANS, librarian; b. Berlin, Nov. 23, 1947; came to U.S., 1953; s. Ernst Gallas and Kate Lesser; m. Myoung Ok Lee, Dec. 23, 1977; children: Monica, Matthew. AA, Springfield Coll., Ill., 1971; AB, U. Ill., 1973, MLS, 1974. Reference libr. Starved Rock Libr. Sys., Ottawa, Ill., 1979—81; libr. dir. Springfield Coll., Ill., 1974—79, Oakland City U., Ind., 1981—86, Ill. Coll., Jacksonville, 1986—. Translator: German letters from Swiss Settlers in Lewis County, Tennessee. With U.S. Army, 1965-68. Avocation: shortwave radio. Office: Ill Coll Schewe Libr 1101 W College Ave Jacksonville IL 62650-2212 Office Phone: 217-245-3020. Business E-Mail: gallas@ic.edu.

GALLAS, PHILIP S., lawyer; b. Kansas City, Mo., July 23, 1953; AB, Wash. U., 1975; JD, Am. U., 1978. Bar: DC 1978, US Ct. Internat. Trade 1982, US Ct. Appeals Fed. Cir. 1982. With Classification and Value Divsn., Office of Regulations and Rulings US Customs Svc., 1978—80; Antidumping Order Compliance Divsn., Internat. Trade Adminstrn. US Dept. Commerce, 1980—84; assoc. Grunfeld, Desiderio, Lebowitz, & Silverman, Washington, 1984—96, of counsel, 1996—98; ptnr. Sandler, Travis & Rosenberg, PA, Washington, 1998—2004, head internat. trade practice; ptnr. Sonnenschein Nath & Rosenthal LLP, Washington, 2004—07; counsel Vorys, Sater, Seymour & Pease LLP, Washington, 2007—. Mem.: Washington Customs Brokers and Freight Forwarders Assn., Customs and Internat. Trade Bar Assn. Office: Vorys Sater Seymour & Pease LLP 1828 L St NW Ste 1111 Washington DC 20036 Office Phone: 202-467-8887. Office Fax: 202-533-9016. Business E-Mail: psgallas@vssp.com.*

GALLASPY, DIXIE, interior designer, innkeeper; b. Franklinton, La., Dec. 12, 1934; d. Fred Whithurst and Camille Gardner Yates; m. John Norman Gallaspy, June 14, 1958; children: John Whithurst, Gardener Weeks, Leland Redding. BA in Interior Design, Tex. Woman's U., 1957; floral degree, Tex. A&M Coll., 1985. Cert. interior designer, La. Dir. interior design Mullers Dept. Store, Lake Charles, La., 1958-60; draftsperson Gabriel & Reames AIA, Lake Charles, 1960-61; owner Dixie's Designs & Flowers, Bogalusa, La., 1962—; interior design dir. Gulf State Theatre, New Orleans, 1978-84, United Artists Cinemas, Dallas, 1979-80, Alfalfa Video Stores, Hammond, La., 1986-91; owner Smoky Creek Plantation Bed and Breakfast Inn, Bogalusa. Chairperson United Way of Bogalusa, 1983, Meth. Ch. Pasonage, 1972—; tchr. New Day Sunday Sch. Meth. Ch., 1972—; mem. Bogalusa Civic League, 1995—, M.A.S.H. Ladies Mardi Gras Riding Group, 1985—; vol. Rest Haven Nursing Home, 1969—; bd. dirs. Washington Parish Fair Assn., 1983-86; foun. and dir. Smoky Creek Summer Sch. for Girls, Bogolusa, 1985—. Named Woman of Yr. Bus. and Profl. Women's Club, 1977, Citizen of Yr. Bogalusa Daily News, 1983, First Queen Magic City Carnival Assn., 1981. Mem. Am. Soc. of Interior Designers (bd. dirs. La. chpt. 1975-80). Republican. Avocations: aerobic dance, organ and piano, gardening, floral arranging, reading. Home: 1737 Gaylord Dr Bogalusa LA 70427-4056 Office: Smoky Creek Plantation 1500 Youngs Rd Bogalusa LA 70427-4040 Fax: 504-735-1550.

GALLE, JEFFREY WAYNE, literature and language professor, department chairman; m. Jo Kuhn Galle. BA in English, La. Tech. U., Ruston, 1977, MA in English, 1979; PhD in English, La. State. U., Baton Rouge, 1991. Instr. English U. La., Monroe, 1988—92, asst. prof., 1992—98, assoc. prof., 1998—2003, head English dept., 1998—, prof. English, 2003—. Sec. adv. bd. La. Assn. Coll. Composition, 1991—94; presenter Modern Lang. Conf., New Orleans, 2001, Fifth Internat. Marlowe Conf., Cambridge, England, 2003. Contbr. articles and revs. to profl. jours. Named to Scott Endowed Professorship Tchg. Excellence, U. La. Monroe, 1996—99; recipient Coll. Liberal Arts Tchg. award, 1994—95. Mem.: Modern Lang. Assn., South Ctrl. Renaissance Soc., Marlowe Soc. Am. Avocations: jogging, antiques, tennis. Office: U La at Monroe Monroe LA 71209 Office Phone: 318-342-1485. Office Fax: 318-342-1491. Business E-Mail: galle@ulm.edu.

GALLEGLY, ELTON WILLIAM, congressman; b. Huntington Park, Calif., Mar. 7, 1944; m. Janice Shrader; four children. Student, Calif. State U., LA, 1962—63. Businessman, real estate broker, Simi Valley, Calif., from 1968; mem. Simi Valley City Coun., 1979; mayor City of Simi Valley, 1980-86; mem. US Congress from 21st (now 24th) Calif. dist., 1986—; chmn. internat. rels. subcom. internat. terrorism; judiciary com.; resources com.; select com. intelligence. Mem. Congl. Human Rights Caucus, Congl. Fire Svcs. Caucus, Congl. Task Force on Tobacco and Health, Congl. Task Force on Alzheimers Disease, other congl. caucuses include Automotive, Fight and Control Methamphetamine, Friends of Animals, Wine caucus, Diabetes caucus, Fairness caucus, House Renewable Energy and Energy Efficiency caucus, Older Ams. caucus; chmn. Task Force on Urban Search and Rescue; past vice-chmn., chmn. Ventura County Assn. govts., Calif. Bd. dirs. Moorpark Coll. Found. Republican. Office: US Ho Reps 2427 Rayburn Hob Washington DC 20515-0524*

GALLEGOS, LARRY DUAYNE, lawyer; b. Cheverly, Md., Mar. 23, 1951; s. Belarmino R. and Helen (Schlotthauer) G.; m. Claudia M. King, Oct. 1, 1994; 1 child, Will Adam. BS summa cum laude, U. Puget Sound, 1978; JD, Harvard U., 1981. Bar: Colo. 1981, U.S. Dist. Ct. Colo. 1981, U.S. Tax Ct. 1989. Assoc. Pendleton & Sabian, Denver, 1981-83, O'Connor & Hannan, Denver, 1983-86, ptnr., 1986-89, Rossi & Judd, P.C., Denver, 1989-92, Berliner Zisser Walter & Gallegos, P.C., Denver, 1992—2003, Gallegos & Assocs., P.C., 2003—. Served with U.S. Army (ARCOM), 1972—74. Mem. Colo. Bar Assn., P.O.E.T.S., Colo. Trial Lawyers Assn., Denver Bar Assn., U.S. Golf Assn. Avocations: tennis, golf. Office: Gallegos & Assocs PC 7720 E Belleview Ave Ste B-350 Greenwood Village CO 80111 Office Phone: 303-539-4495. Business E-Mail: lgallegos@revealmail.com.

GALLEGOS, MARY ELLEN, education educator, department chairman; b. Raton, N.Mex., Dec. 4, 1949; d. Joe I. and Mary F. Martinez; m. Manuel F. Gallegos, Sept. 23, 1972; children: Manuel R., Jonathan, Stephanie. BS in Math, Econ., Western N.Mex. U., Silver City, 1971; post grad., Calif. Luth. U., 1972—73. Tchr. Bakersfield Pub. Schs., Calif., 1971—72, Archdiocese Santa Fe, Albuquerque, 1972—73, Santa Fe Pub. Schs., 1973—74; assoc. prof., dept. chair Santa Fe CC, 1984—. Bd. mem. Loretto Tutor Team, Pastoral Counseling Group. Vol. Hospice, Boy Scouts Am. Mem.: N.Mex. Assn. Two Yr. Coll. (del. 2000—02, sec. 2002—04, treas. 2004—06). Office: Santa Fe Cmty Coll 6401 Richards Ave Santa Fe NM 87509

GALLEGOS, VERNON DAVID, theater educator; b. Pomona, Calif., June 4, 1960; s. Ernest Elias Gallegos and Gallegos May Helen. BA, UCLA, 1996; MA, Calif. State U., LA, 1999. Instr. dance Dupree Dance Acad., LA, 1987—90, Moro-Landis Studios, Studio City, Calif., 1990—94, Cavoline Culture Studios, Ryoguku, Sumida-Ku, Japan, 1992—92, On Stage, Hamburg, Germany, 1994—94, Calif. State U., LA, 2000—00, Chaffey Çoll., Rancho Cucamonga, Calif., 2000—04, Calif. State Summer Sch. Arts, Valencia, 2003; prof. dance, theatre Foothill De Anza Coll., Cupertino, Calif., 2004—. Mem.: De Anza Coll. (senator 2006), Actor's Equity Assn., Screen Actor's Guild. Office: De Anza College 21250 Stevens Creek Blvd Cupertino CA 95014 Home Phone: 408-396-2225; Office Phone: 408-864-8506. Personal E-mail: m95578@aol.com. E-mail: gallegosvernon@fhda.edu.

GALLEHER, GAY, psychologist; b. Delaware, Ohio, Nov. 3, 1946; d. Richard Adair Galleher and Ellen Jean Huntsberger; m. Charles Frost Gould III (div.). MS in Learning Disabilities, Med. Sci. Sch. U. Pacific, San Francisco, 1976; MA in Psychology, Pacific Grad. Sch. Profl. Psychology, Palo Alto, 1983, PhD, 1987. Bd. cert. diplomate in clin. psychology Am. Bd. Profl. Psychology, lic. psychologist Maine. Pvt. practice clin. psychologist Gay Galleher PhD, Kentfield, Calif., 1990—2000; clin. psychologist USAF, Lakenheath, England, 2001, Maine Gen. Med. Ctr., Waterville, 2002—04; pvt. practice clin. psychologist Gay Galleher PhD, ABPP, Bath, 2004—. Contbr. articles to profl. jours. Mem.: Am. Bd. Profl. Psychology, Nat. Register Health Svc. Providers, San Francisco Psychotherapy Rsch. Group. Democrat. Congregationalist. Avocations: painting, gardening, interior decorating, old house renovation. Home: 579 Berrys Mill West Bath ME 04530 Office: One Lincoln St Ste 4 Bath ME 04530 Office Phone: 207-443-4334.

GALLERANO, ANDREW JOHN, lawyer; b. Houston, Dec. 2, 1941; s. Andrew H. and Victoria J. (LaNasa) G.; m. Evelyn Cornelius, June 6, 1964; children: Kelly Lynn, Wendy Michelle. BA, U. Tex., Austin, 1964; JD, South Tex. Coll. Law, 1968. Bar: Tex. 1968, U.S. Supreme Ct. 1973. Asst. atty. gen., Tex., 1968-71; regional atty. Montgomery Ward & Co., 1971-72; v.p. Foley's, div. Federated Dept. Stores Inc., 1972-79; v.p., gen. counsel, sec. Nat. Convenience Stores Inc., Houston, 1979-89, sr. v.p., gen. counsel, sec., 1989-96; ptnr. Baker, Boldt & Gallerano, Dripping Springs, Tex., 1996-2000; v.p., gen. counsel K.C. Engring., Inc., Austin, Tex., 2000—03, DuBois, Bryant, Campbell & Schwartz, Austin, 2003—. Adj. prof. South Tex. Coll. Law, 1973-75; mem. adv. coun. U. Tex. Coll. Bus., 1993-98. Pres. S. Tex. Hosp. Fin. Agy., 1979—; mem. devel. bd. U. Tex. Health Sci. Ctr., Houston, 1978-93; bd. dirs. YMCA, 1973-86, 90-92, Assn. Cmty. TV, 1974-80; chmn. bd. trustees Star of Hope Mission, 1990-96. Mem. Tex. Bar Assn. (grievance com. 1986-89), U. Tex. Ex-Students Assn., Houston Retail Mchts. Assn. (bd. dirs. 1973—, pres. 1976-78), Tax Rsch. Assn. (bd. dirs. 1975-92). Office: DuBois Bryant Campbell & Schwartz 700 Lavaca Ste 1300 Austin TX 78701 Office Phone: 512-457-8000.

GALLIAN, JOSEPH ANTHONY, mathematics professor; b. New Kennington, Pa., Jan. 5, 1942; s. Joseph Anthony Gallian and Alvira Helen (Gardner) Strauss; m. Charlene Toy, May 29, 1965; children: William, Ronald, Kristin. BA, Slippery Rock State U., 1966; MA, U. Kans., 1968; PhD, Notre Dame U., 1971. Vis. asst. prof. Notre Dame (Ind.) U., 1971-72; asst. prof. U. Minn., Duluth, 1972-76, assoc. prof., 1976-80, prof., 1980—. Nat. coord. Math. Awareness Month, 2003; adv. bd. Math. Horizons, 1993—. Author: Contemporary Abstract Algebra, 1986, 6th edit., 2006, For All Practical Purposes, 6th edit., 2003, 7th edit., 2006, Principles and Practices of Mathematics, 1997; editor: American Mathematical Society, 2000; assoc. editor Math. Mag., 1981-85, Am. Math. Monthly, 1992-2007, MAA OnLine, 1997—. Named Prof. of Yr., Case and Carnegie Found. Minn., 2002; fellow, Coun. Undergrad. Rsch., 2002. Mem.: Math. Assn. Am. (2d v.p. 2002—03, pres. 2007—, Trevor Evans award 1996, Deborah and Franklin Tepper Haimo award 1993, Allendoerfer award 1977). Home: 1522 Triggs Ave Duluth MN 55811-2742 Office: U Minn Dept Math and Stats Solon Campus Ctr 140 1049 Univ Dr Duluth MN 55812-3000

GALLIAN, RUSSELL JOSEPH, lawyer; b. San Mateo, Calif., Apr. 24, 1948; m. Pauline G. Davis, Sept. 29, 2000; children: Lisa, Cherie, Joseph, Russell, Yvette, Jason, Ryan, Jennifer. BS, U. San Francisco, 1969, JD with honors, 1974. CPA Calif.; bar: Calif. 1974, Utah 1975, US Ct. Appeals (10th cir.) 1975, US Supreme Ct. 1990. Staff acct. Arthur Andersen & Co., CPAs, San Francisco, 1969-71; treas., contr. N.Am. Reassurance Life Svc. Co., Palo Alto, Calif., 1972-74; assoc. VanCott Bagley Cornwell & McCarthy, Salt Lake City, 1975-77; sr. ptnr. Gallian Wilcox, Welker & Olsen, LC, St. George, Utah, 1977—. Chmn. Tooele Planning Commn., Utah, 1978—80; atty. City of Tooele, 1978—80, Town of Ivins, Utah, 1982—2000, Town of Sprindgdale, Utah, 1987—90, Town of Virgin, 1995—2000, 2002—07, City of Santa Clara, 2001—; commr. Washington County, 1993—96; chmn. Washington County Econ. Devel. Coun., 1993—96; bd. dirs. Dixie Ctr., 1993—96; mem. Habitat Conservation Plan Steering Com., 1993—99; atty. Town of Rockville, 1987—. Mem. ABA, Utah State Bar Assn., Tooele County Bar Assn. (pres. 1978-79), So. Utah Bar Assn. (pres. 1986-87). Republican. Mem. Lds Ch. Office: Gallian Wilcox Welker & Olsen, LLC 59 S 100 E Saint George UT 84770-3422 Office Phone: 435-628-1682. Business E-Mail: carma@gwwo.com.

GALLIGAN, JAMES, retired guidance counselor; b. Rockaway, NY, May 13, 1947; s. Kenneth Joseph and Zelina Theresa Galligan. B in Math Edn., King's Coll., Wilkes-Barre, Pa.; MA in Guidance & Counseling, Trinity Coll., DC, 1976—86. Cert. tchr. Md. State Bd. Edn., 1973, in math. and counseling Md. State Bd. Edn., 2006. Math. tchr. Chopticon HS St. Mary's County Bd. Edn., Morganza, Md., 1983—88, counselor Leonardtown Mid. Sch. Leonardtown, Md., 1988—; ret. Field hockey coach Chopticon HS, 1980—. Mem.: Md. State Counselor's Assn. Independent. Roman Cath. Avocations: baseball card collecting, coin collecting, stamp collecting/philately. Home: 44654 Scarlet Oak Ct California MD 20619 Home Phone: 301-863-6577. Personal E-mail: friartuck12@juno.com.

GALLIGAN, THOMAS C., JR., law educator; AB, Stanford U., 1977; JD, Seattle U., 1981; LLM, Columbia U., 1986. With Lane Powell Moss & Miller, Seattle; prof. law Paul Hebert Law Ctr. La. State U., Dale E. Bennett prof. law, 1997, exec. dir. La. Jud. Coll., 1996-98; prof. law U. Tenn., Knoxville, 1998—, Elvin E. Overton Disting. prof. law, 2002—, dean, 1998. Spkr. legal topics various groups, 1987—. Co-author: Legislation and Jurisprudence on Maritime Personal Injury Law, 1997, Louisiana Tort Law, 1996, 2004, Personal Injury in Admiralty, 2000, Admiralty in a Nutshell, 4th edit., 2000, Tort Law: Cases, Materials on Maritime Law, 2003; contbr. articles to profl. jours. Recipient John Minor Wisdom award for Acad. Excellence in Legal Scholarship, Tulane Law Rev., 1996—97. Office: U Tenn 279 Law Complex George C Taylor Wing 1505 W Cumberland Ave Ste 278 Knoxville TN 37996-0001 Office Phone: 865-974-2521. Fax: 423-974-6595. Business E-Mail: tgalliga@utk.edu. E-mail: galligan@libra.law.uth.edu.

GALLIN, JOHN I., medical researcher; b. NYC, Mar. 25, 1943; s. Nathaniel Mitchel and Helen (Cohen) G.; m. Elaine Barbara Klimerman, June 23, 1966; children: Alice Jennifer, Michael Louis. BA cum laude, Amherst Coll., 1965, ScD honoris causa, 1988; MD, Cornell U. Med. Sch., 1969. Diplomate Nat. Bd. Med. Examiners. Intern medicine Bellevue Hosp., NYC, 1969-70, asst. resident, 1970-71; teaching asst., instr. in medicine NYU Sch. Medicine, 1970-74, 74-81; clin. assoc. lab. clin. investigation Nat. Inst. Allergy and Infectious Diseases, NIH, Bethesda, Md., 1971-74, sr. investigator lab. clin. investigation, 1975-91, dir. div. intramural rsch., 1985-94, chief lab. of host defenses, 1991—2003; dir. NIH Clin. Ctr., 1994—; assoc. dir. clin. rsch. NIH, 1994—2005. Asst. surgeon gen., rear adm. USPHS ret.; guest lectr. and spkr. in field. Editor: Principles and Practice of Clinical Research, 2002; co-editor: Inflammation, Basic Principles and Clinical Correlates, 1988, 3d edit., 1999; contbr. numerous articles to profl. jours. mem. editl. bd. various profl. jours. Recipient Rsch. award Am. Fedn. for Clin. Rsch., 1984, Squibb award Infectious Diseases Soc. Am., 1987, Disting. Svc. medal USPHS, 1992, Physician Exec. of Yr. award USPHS, 2001, Sec. Disting. Svc. award U.S. Dept. HHS, 2006. Fellow ACP (Richard and Hinda Rosenthal Found. award 2006), Infectious Diseases Soc. Am.; mem. Inst. Medicine of NAS, Assn. Am. Physicians, Am. Soc. for Clin. Investigation, Am. Clin. and Climatological Assn., Am. Fedn. for Med. Rsch., Internat. Immunocompromised Host Soc. (pres. 1992-94), Am. Assn. Immunologists, Soc. for Leukocyte Biology (Marie T. Bonazinga award 2002). Office: NIH Bldg 10/2C 146 10 Center Dr MSC 1504 Bethesda MD 20892-1504 Office Phone: 301-496-4114. Business E-Mail: jig@nih.gov.

GALLIS, JOHN NICHOLAS, retired military officer, executive leadership training consultant; b. Pitts., Dec. 18, 1944; s. John Vincent Glade (dec.) and Sylvia Delores (Rizzo) Friedman (dec.); m. Carole Campbell, June 17, 1967; children: J. Christopher, Robin Noel. AS in Edn., No. Va. C.C., 1975; BS in Healthcare Adminstrn., George Washington U., 1977; MPA, Pa. State U., 1980. Enlisted USN, 1962, advanced through grades to capt., 1995; outpatient svcs. officer Submarine Med. Ctr., New London, Conn., 1974-76; patient adminstrn. officer Naval Hosp., Phila., 1977-80; officer-in-charge Naval Med. Clinic, Willow Grove, Pa., 1980-82; hosp. corpsman/dental technician rating assignment officer Bur. Naval Pers., Arlington, Va., 1982-85; dir. for adminstrn. Naval Hosp., Phila., Va., 1985-88; dir. leadership course Naval Sch. Health Scis., Bethesda, Md., 1988-91; adj. faculty leadership dept. U.S. Naval Acad.; assignment officer Med. Svc. Corps, Arlington, Va., 1991-93; exec. officer Naval Acad. Med. Clinic, Annapolis, Md., 1993-96; leadership and splty. tng. Naval Sch. Health Scis., Bethesda, 1996-98; cons., instr. Navy Medicine Ctr. Orgnl. Devel., Bethesda, 1999-2000; adj. faculty Nat. Fire Acad., Emmitsburg, Md., 2000—. Recipient Meritorious Svc. medal (3 awards), Navy Achievement medal, Navy Commendation medal (5 awards), Submarine Svc. badge. Fellow (life) Am. Coll. Healthcare Execs. Republican. Roman Catholic. Avocations: teaching, workshop. Home: 727 Suellen Dr King Of Prussia PA 19406 also: 3 Dewey Dr Annapolis MD 21401 E-mail: gallis@starpower.net.

GALLIVAN, JOHN WILLIAM, retired publishing executive; b. Salt Lake City, June 28, 1915; s. Daniel and Frances (Wilson) G.; m. Grace Mary Ivers, June 30, 1938 (dec.); children: Gay, John W. Jr., Michael D., Timothy. BA, U. Notre Dame, 1937. With Salt Lake Tribune, 1937—, promotion mgr., 1942-48, asst. pub., 1948-60, pub., 1960-84; pres. Kearns-Tribune Corp., 1960-86, chmn. bd., 1984-99; dir., exec. com. Tele-Communications, Inc., 1989-2000, ret., 2000—. Pres. Silver King Mining Co., 1960-97. Pres. Utah Symphony, 1964-65. Mem. Sigma Delta Chi, Bohemian Club (San Francisco). Clubs: Nat. Press (Washington); Alta (Salt Lake City), Salt Lake Country (Salt Lake City), Rotary (Salt Lake City). Home and Office: 1665 White Pine Canyon Rd Park City UT 84060 Personal E-mail: jwgallivan@comcast.net.

GALLO, ANTHONY ERNEST, playwright, economist; b. Vandergrift, Pa., Feb. 3, 1939; s. Dominic and Sara (Raso) G.; divorced; 1 child, Thomas Augustus. BA, Coll. William and Mary, 1961; MBA, U. Pa., 1963; postgrad., U. Pitts., 1966-70. Investment analyst Pitts. Nat. Bank, 1963-66; instr. mktg. and stats. Duquesne U., Pitts., 1964-69; instr. mktg. U. Pitts., 1965-69; instr. money and banking St. Vincent Coll., Latrobe, Pa., 1966-69; asst. prof. econs. Allegheny C.C., Pitts., 1966-70; econ. cons. SBA, Washington, 1967—; bus. economist Bur. Econ. Analysis/U.S. Dept. Commerce, Washington, 1970-71; sr. economist Econ. Rsch. Svc./USDA, Washington, 1971-2000. Propr. Capitol Hill Victorian Restorations, Washington, 1970-90. Econs. editor U.S. Food Mktg. Rev., 1984-2001; contbr. 300 articles to profl. and govt. jours.; writer (plays) Eugenio, 2002, Margherita, 2003, Death, (opera librettos) Eugenio, 2003, Margherita, 2003, Solomon, 2005; librettist, lyricist. Mem. Capitol Hill Restoration Soc., Washington, 1972—, mem. endowment bd., 1999; mem Capitol Hill Garden Club, Washington, 1972—; commr. Vandergrift Mcpl. Authority, 1965-67; pres. Civic League, Vandergrift, 1965-70; mem. governing coun., endowment bd. Holy Rosary Ch. With U.S. Army, 1963. Named Outstanding Civic Leader, Jaycees, Vandergrift, 1967. Mem. Cosmos Club (endowment advisor 1996—2001), Arts Club Washington (endowment bd. 1996-99), John Carroll Soc., Red Circle, U.S. Food Distbn. Rsch. Soc. (bd. dirs. 1994-97), Wharton Sch. Club (bd. dirs. 1991—), Italian Cultural Soc. (bd. dirs. 1994-97), Playwright's Forum, Writers Ctr., Charter Theatre, Dramatists Guild, Am. Composers Forum, Am. Music Ctr. Women in Film, Wash. Screenwriter's Group, Washington Area League Arts. Roman Catholic. Avocations: reading, gardening, swimming, dance, historic preservation, bridge. Home: PO Box 15414 Washington DC 20003-0414 Office Phone: 202-544-6973. Personal E-mail: agallo2368@verizon.net.

GALLO, DAVID, scenic designer; Scenic designer (Broadway Shows) Hughie, 1996, Jackie, 1997—98, A View From the Bridge, 1997—98, More to Love, 1998, Little Me, 1998—99, You're a Good Man, Charlie Brown, 1999, The Lion in Winter, 1999, Voices in the Dark, 1999, Epic Proportions, 1999, King Hedley II, 2001, The Smell of the Kill, 2002, Thoroughly Modern Millie, 2002—04, Dance of the Vampires, 2002—03, Ma Rainey's Black Bottom, 2003, Drowning Crow, 2004, Gem of the Ocean, 2004—05, The Drowsy Chaperone, 2006— (Drama Desk award outstanding set design of a musical, 2006, Tony Award, best scenic design of a musical, 2006, Outer Critics Cir. award, outstanding set design, 2006), asst. scenic designer Titanic, 1997—99, scenic designer (Off-Broadway) Bunny Bunny (Drama Desk award outstanding set design of a play, 1997), The Wild Party, Jitney (Drama Desk award outstanding set design of a play, 2000, Lucille Lortel award, 2001), Wonder of the World, Jar the Floor, Machinal, Blue Man Group, designer 135th Ringling Bros. Barnum and Bailey Circus, (nat. tour) Dora the Explorer, Blues Clues, Clifford the Big Red Dog. Recipient Obie for Sustained Excellence in Set Design, 2000. Office: David Gallo and Assocs 630 Ninth Ave, Ste 1205 New York NY 10036 also: Marquis Theatre 1535 Broadway New York NY 10036 Office Phone: 212-664-1341.

GALLO, DONALD ROBERT, retired literature educator; b. Paterson, NJ, June 1, 1938; s. Sergio and Thelma Mae (Lowe) G.; m. C.J. Bott, Feb. 14, 1997; 1 child, Brian Keith; 1 stepchild, Christian Perrett. BA in English, Hope Coll., 1960; MAT in English Edn., Oberlin Coll., 1961; PhD in English Edn., Syracuse U., 1968. English tchr. Bedford Jr. High Sch., Westport, Conn., 1961-65; rsch. assoc. Syracuse (N.Y.) U., 1965-67; from asst. prof. to assoc. prof. edn. U. Colo., Denver, 1968-72; reading specialist Golden Jr. High Sch., Jefferson County Pub. Schs., Colo., 1972-73; prof. English Cen. Conn. State U., New Britain, 1973-97. Instr. composition Onondaga C. C., Syracuse, 1967; vis. faculty grad. liberal studies program Wesleyan U., 1983; staff writer reading assessment Nat. Assessment Ednl. Progress, Denver, 1972-73; speaker in field; cons. to schs. and librs. Mem. editl. bd. Nat. Coun. Tchrs. English, 1985-88; compiler, editor: Speaking for Ourselves, 1990, Speaking for Ourselves, Too, 1993; editor: Connections: Short Stories by Outstanding Writers for Young Adults, 1989, Visions: Nineteen Short Stories by Outstanding Writers for Young Adults, 1987, Center Stage: One-Act Plays for Teenage Readers and Actors, 1990, Sixteen: Short Stories by Outstanding Writers for Young Adults, 1984, Books for You, 1985, Authors' Insights: Turning Teenagers into Readers and Writers, 1992, Short Circuits: Thirteen Shocking Stories by Outstanding Writers for Young Adults, 1992, Within Reach: Ten Stories, 1993, Join In: Multiethnic Short Stories by Outstanding Writers for Young Adults, 1993, Ultimate Sports: Short Stories by Outstanding Writers for Young Adults, 1995, No Easy Answers: Short Stories About Teenagers Making Tough Choices, 1997, Time Capsule: Short Stories About Teenagers Throughout the Twentieth Century, 1999, On The Fringe, 2001, Destination Unexpected, 2003, First Crossing: Stories About Teen Immigrants, 2004, What Are You Afraid Of? Stories about Phobias, 2006; author: Presenting Richard Peck, 1989, Bookmark Reading Program, Seventh and Eighth Grade Texts and Workbooks, 1979, Heath Middle Level Literature, 1995; co-author: (with Sarah K. Herz) From Hinton to Hamlet: Building Bridges Between Young Adult Literature and the Classics, 1996, rev. and expanded, 2005; interviewer of authors for Authors4Teens.com website. Recipient Disting. Svc. award Conn. Coun. Tchrs. English, 1989, ALAN award Assembly on Lit. for Adolescents of the Nat. Coun. Tchrs. English, 1992, Cert. of Merit award Cath. Libr. Assn., 1995, Ted Hipple Svc. award ALAN, 2001. Mem. Nat. Coun. Tchrs. English, Assembly on Lit. for Adolescents, Ohio Coun. Tchrs. English Lang. Arts (named an Outstanding English Lang. Arts Educator 2003), Soc. Children's Book Writers and Illustrators, Authors Guild. Avocations: gardening, cooking, travel, photography. Address: 34540 Sherbrook Park Dr Solon OH 44139-2046 Personal E-mail: gallodon@sbcglobal.net.

GALLO, JOAN ROSENBERG, lawyer; b. Newark, Apr. 28, 1940; BA in Psychology, Boston U., Mass., 1965; postgrad., We. Md. Coll., Westminster, 1966—67; postgrad, We. Grad. Sch. Psychology, 1966—67; JD magna cum laude, U. Santa Clara, 1975. Bar: Calif. 1975. Assoc. with Cynthia Mertens U, Santa Clara, Calif., 1975-76; sr. law clk. US Dist. Ct., Calif., 1976-78; assoc. Decker and Collins, San Jose, Calif., 1978-79; from dep. city atty. to city atty. City of San Jose, 1979-2000; ptnr. Terra Law LLP, San Jose, 2000—02, Realty Law, LLP, San Jose, 2002—03; of counsel Hopkins & Carley, 2004—. Mem.: Psi Chi. Office: Hopkins & Carley 70 S First St San Jose CA 95113 Office Phone: 408-286-9800. Business E-Mail: jgallo@hopkinscarley.com.

GALLO, JON JOSEPH, lawyer; b. Santa Monica, Calif., Apr. 19, 1942; s. Philip S. and Josephine (Sarazan) G.; m. Jo Ann Broome, June 13, 1964 (div. 1984); children: Valerie Ann, Donald Philip; m. Eileen Florence, July 4, 1985; 1 child, Kevin Jon. BA, Occidental Coll., 1964; JD, UCLA, 1967. Bar: Calif. 1968, U.S. Ct. Appeals (9th cir.) 1968, U.S. Tax Ct. 1969. Assoc. Greenberg, Glusker, Fields, Claman & Machtinger, LA, 1967-75, ptnr., 1975—. Bd. dirs. USC Probate and Trust Conf., L.A., 1980—; bd. dirs. UCLA Estate Planning Inst., chmn. 1992—99. Contbr. articles to profl. jours. Fellow Am. Coll. Trust and Estate Counsel; mem. ABA (chair generation skipping taxation com. 1992-95, co-chair life ins. com. 1995-2000, chair psychol. and emotional issues of estate planning 2001—), Internat. Acad. Estate and Trust Law, Assn. for Advanced Life Underwriting (assoc.). Avocation: photography. Office: Greenberg Glusker Fields Claman & Machtinger LLP Ste 2100 1900 Avenue Of The Stars Los Angeles CA 90067-4502

GALLO, JOSEPH E., vintner; b. 1941; Various positions E&J Gallo Winery, South San Francisco, 1962—, now co-pres. & CEO. Office: E & J Gallo Winery 600 Yosemite Blvd Modesto CA 95354

GALLO, KENNETH A., lawyer; b. Ridgewood, NJ, Nov. 16, 1956; BA, U. Ga., 1978; JD, U. Ga. Sch. Law, 1982. Bar: DC, US Dist. Ct. DC, US Ct. Appeals, DC Cir. 1983, US Ct. Appeals, Fed. Cir. 2000, US Ct. Appeals, 2nd Cir. 2001, US Ct. Appeals, 11th Cir. 2002. Ptnr. Paul Weiss Rifkind Wharton & Garrison LLP; notes editor Ga. Law Review, 1981—82; law clerk Hon. George L. Hart, Jr., US Dist. Ct. for the Dist. of Columbia, 1982—83; ptnr. Paul, Weiss, Rifkind, Wharton & Garrison LLP. Named one of The Nation's Top Litigators, Nat. Law Jour., 2007. Mem.: ABA. Office: Paul Weiss Rifkind Wharton & Garrison LLP 1615 L St NW Ste 1300 Washington DC 20036-5694 Office Phone: 202-223-7356. Office Fax: 202-223-7456. E-mail: kgallo@paulweiss.com.*

GALLO, MARTHA J., diversified financial services company executive; married; 1 child. BS in Acctg., Cornell U., MBA. Tech. and ops. trainee J.P. Morgan Chase & Co., 1981, contr. tech. and ops., 1989, mng. dir., 1992—, co-head tech., 1993—96, CEO Credit Risk Bus., 1996, chief auditor, 1998. Co-pres. Battery Park City Neighbors and Parents' Assn., NYC. Office: JP Morgan Chase & Co 270 Park Ave New York NY 10017-2070 E-mail: gallo_m@jpmorgan.com.

GALLO, PENNY HOWE, lawyer; b. Fresno, Dec. 29, 1945; BA Hist., U Calif., 1967; JD, Harvard U., 1970. Bar: DC 1970, Calif. 1973. With Ware & Friedenrich P.C., Palo Alto; ptnr. DLA Piper, East Palo Alto, Calif. Mem. Western Pension Conf., Harvard U Com. on U Resources; founding dir. Silicon Valley Employee Benefits Assn.; dir., pres. Combined Training Equestrian Team Alliance, Woodside, Calif.; founding bd. mem., past pres. Menlo Park Atherton Edn. Found. Named Super Lawyers, Law & Politics and San Francisco mag. Mem. ABA (sect. taxation employee benefits com. 1982), State Bar Calif., Palo Atlo Bar Assn., Phi Beta Kappa. Office: DLA Piper 2000 University Ave Palo Alto CA 94303 Office Phone: 650-833-2064. Office Fax: 650-833-2001. Business E-Mail: greg.gallo@dlapiper.com.

GALLO, ROBERT CHARLES, research scientist; b. Waterbury, Conn., Mar. 23, 1937; s. Francis Anton Gallo, Louise Mary (Ciancuilli) Gallo; m. Mary Jane Hayes, July 1, 1961; children: Robert, Marcus, Caroline. BA in biology, Providence Coll., 1959, DSc (hon.), 1974; MD, Jefferson Med. Coll., 1963; 27 hon. degrees. Intern, resident medicine U. Chgo., 1963-65; clin. assoc. med. br. Nat. Cancer Inst. NIH, Bethesda, Md., 1965-68, sr. investigator human tumor cell biology br., 1968-69, head sect. cellular control mechanisms, 1969-72, chief lab. tumor cell biology, 1972—95; founder, dir. Inst. Human Virology, U. Md., Balt., 1996—, dir. Basic Sciences Divsn.; prof. Medicine, Microbiology and Immunology, Sch. Medicine U. Md., Balt. Adj. prof. genetics George Washington U.; adj. prof. biology Johns Hopkins U., Balt., hon. prof. biology, 1985—; hon. prof. medicine Karolinska Inst., Stockholm, 1998—; US rep. to world com. Internat. Comparative Leukemia and Lymphoma Assn., 1981—; mem. bd. govs. Franco Am. AIDS Found., 1987, World AIDS Found., 1987; sr. cons. HIV/AIDS China CDC, 2005—. Author: (book) Virus Hunting, 1991; author: (or co-author) more than 1,100 sci. papers. With USPHS, 1965—68. Named to Inventor's Hall of Fame, 2004; recipient Dameshek award, Am. Hematol. Soc., 1974, CIBA-GIEGY award in biomed. sci., 1977, 1988, Superior Svc. award, USPHS, 1978, Meritorious Svc. medal, 1983, DSM, 1984, First F. Stohlman lecture award, Am. Soc. Hematol., 1979, Albert Lasker award for basic biomed. rsch., 1982, 1986, Abraham White award in biochem., George Washington U., 1983, First Otto Herz award for cancer rsch., Tel Aviv U., 1982, Griffuel prize, Assn. for Cancer Rsch., France, 1983, GM award in cancer rsch., 1984, Gruber prize, Am. Soc. Investigative Dermatology, 1984, Lucy Wortham prize in cancer rsch., Am. Soc. for Surg. Oncology, 1984, Gold medal, Am. Cancer Soc., 1984, Berla Internat Sci. prize, India, 1985, Hammer prize for cancer rsch., 1985, Gairdner prize for biomed. rsch., Can., 1987, spl. award, Am. Soc. Infectious Disease, 1986, Gold Plate award, Am. Acad. Achievement, 1987, Lions Humanitarian award, 1987, Japan prize in sci. and tech., 1988, Ciba Corning award, 1993, 1st Dale McFarlin award for rsch., Internat. Soc. Human Retrovirology, 1994, 1st Gustav Embden award, U. Frankfurt, 1996, Pomesa award, 1996, 1st award, Internat. Soc. Blood Transfusion, 1997, Nomura prize for AIDS and Cancer Rsch, Japan, 1998, Warren Alpert prize, Harvard U., 1998, Paul Erlich award, Germany, 1999, Hero in Medicine award, Can, 2000, Frank Annunzio sci. award, Washington, 2000, Prince Asturias prize, Spain, 2000, 1st award, Ireland C. of C. and USA, 2001, Seminal contbrns. to field of Human Retrovirology award, Internat. Soc. HTLV, 2001, award, Internat. Retrovirology Assn., 2001, World Health award, Pres. M. Gorbachev Found., 2001, Austria, 2001, Archimedes prize in sci., Italy, 2003, Lifetime Achievement award, Sons of Italy, 2004, Ellis Island Medal of Honor, 2005, Tevi Comet-Wallerstein prize, Bar-Ilan U., Israel, 2005, Servero Ochoa award, 2006, Gold Mercury award, 2006. Mem.: AAAS, NAS, Fedn. for Advanced Edn. in Scis., Am. Fedn. Clin. Rsch., Am. Soc. Microbiology, Am. Assn. Cancer Rsch., Biochem. Soc., Am. Microbiology Soc., Am. Soc. Biol. Chemists, Am. Soc. Clin.Investigation, Internat Soc. Hematology, Inst. Medicine, Royal Acad. Medicine of Spain (hon.), Royal Soc. Medicine (hon.), Royal Soc. Physicians of Scotland (hon.), Royal Soc. Medicine Belgium (sr.), Alpha Omega Alpha. Achievements include discovery of AIDS virus; research in viruses, AIDS and leukemia; discovery of the first and second human retroviruses and Interleukin-2 (IL-2); development of HIV blood test; discovery of human herpes virus-6. Office: 725 W Lombard St Ste S307 Baltimore MD 21201-1009 Office Phone: 410-706-8614. Business E-Mail: gallo@umbi.umd.edu.

GALLO, WILLIAM VICTOR, cartoonist; b. NYC, Dec. 28, 1922; s. Francisco and Henrietta (Caballero) G.; m. Dolores Rodriguez, Mar. 13, 1950; children: Gregory, William. With N.Y. Daily News, 1941—, sports cartoonist, sports columnist, 1960—, assoc. sports editor, 1984—. One-man show, Spectrum Fine Arts Gallery, N.Y.C., 1981; works represented in permanent collection, Baseball Hall of Fame, Cooperstown, N.Y., Syracuse U. archives. Served with USMC, 1942-45. Named best sports cartoonist, Nat. Cartoonist Soc., 1969—73, 1984—86; named to Yonkers Hall of Fame, 1984, Westchester Hall of Fame, 1984, Boxing Hall of Fame, Canostota, N.Y., 2001; recipient 19 Page One awards, N.Y. Newspaper Guild, 1965—86, Elzie Segar award, 1976, Alumni Achievement award, Sch. Visual Arts, 1977, Power of Printing award, 1977, Long and Meritorious award, The Baseball Writers of Am., 2004. Mem. N.Y. Boxing Writers (pres.), Nat. Cartoonists Soc. (pres., Milt Caniff Lifetime Achievement award 1999), Baseball Writers, Profl. Football Writers, Turf Writers, N.Y. Press Assn., (award 1986), Soc. Silurians, Soc. Illustrators. Home: 1 Mayflower Dr Yonkers NY 10710-3801 Office: NY Daily News 450 W 33rd St New York NY 10001-2603 Home Phone: 914-779-6734. *Everything has to start with a dream. First the dream, and then the chasing of it. I pity the person who doesn't own a dream.*

GALLOGLY, JAMES LAWRENCE, oil industry executive, lawyer; b. St. Johns, N.F., Can., Sept. 1, 1952; came to U.S., 1955; s. Tommy M. and Margery L. (Abbas) G.; m. Janet Marie Ostermiller, June 3, 1974; children: Kelly, Kasey, Kimberly. BA in Psychology, U. Colo., 1974; JD, U. Okla., 1977. Bar: Colo. 1978, Okla. 1980, U.S. Ct. Appeals (5th and 11th cirs.) 1983, Tex. 1987. Assoc. Calkins, Kramer, Grimshaw & Harring, Denver, 1978-80; atty. Phillips Petroleum Co., Bartlesville, Okla., 1980-84, legal dir. Stavanger, Norway, 1984-87, regional chief atty. Odessa, Tex., 1987-91, mgr. bus. svcs. N.Am. exploration and prodn. divsn. Bellaire, Tex., 1991-92, fin. mgr. N.Am. exploration and prodn. divsn., 1992-93, mgr. Ekofisk II, Norway, 1993-94, v.p. N.Am. prodn. divsn. Bellaire, Tex., 1995, v.p. plastics, 1997, sr. v.p. chemicals, 1999; pres., CEO Chevron Phillips Chem. Co. LLC, 2000; exec. v.p. refining, mktg., supply and transportation ConocoPhillips, Houston, 2006—. Republican. Roman Catholic. Office: ConocoPhillips PO Box 2197 Houston TX 77252-2197*

GALLOP, JANE (JANE ANNE GALLOP), women's studies educator, writer; b. Duluth, Minn., May 4, 1952; d. Melvin Gordon and Eudice Zelda (Titch) G.; children: Max Blau Gallop, Ruby Gallop Blau. BA, Cornell U., 1972, PhD, 1976. Lectr. French Gettysburg (Pa.) Coll., 1976; asst. prof. Miami U., Oxford, Ohio, 1977-81, assoc. prof., 1981-85; prof. women's studies Rice U., Houston, 1985-87, Autrey prof., 1987-90; prof. English U. Wis., Milw., 1990-92, Disting. prof., 1992—. NEH vis. prof. Emory U., Atlanta, 1984-85; Hill vis. prof. U. Minn., Mpls., 1987; dir. seminar for coll. tchrs. NEH, Milw., 1985, 88; instr. Sch. of Criticism and Theory, Dartmouth Coll., 1991; vis. disting. prof. Johns Hopkins U., Balt., 2006. Author: Intersections, 1981, The Daughter's Seduction, 1982, Reading Lacan, 1985, Thinking Through the Body, 1988, Around 1981, 1992, Feminist Accused of Sexual Harassment, 1997, Anecdotal Theory, 2002, Living with His Camera, 2003; editor: Pedagogy, 1995, Polemic, 2004. Guggenheim fellow, 1983-84. Mem. MLA. Office: Dept English Univ Wis - Milw PO Box 413 Milwaukee WI 53201-0413 Home Phone: 414-332-0232. Business E-Mail: jg@uwm.edu.

GALLOP, SOPHRONIA LANGSTON, elementary school educator; b. Portsmouth, Va., Feb. 9, 1948; d. Morris Alexander and Neva Crawford Langston; m. Willie E. Gallop, Jr., Jan. 1, 1969; children: Willie E. III, Langston L. B of Edn., Norfolk State U., Va., 1972; MEd, Va. State U., Petersberg, 1978. Tchr. New Haven Bd. Edn., 1972—. Presenter in field. Pres. Nat. Coun. Negro Women, Bridgeport, Conn., 1986—89; treas. Links, Inc., Milford, Conn., 1997—. Avocations: reading, writing, crocheting. Home: 3 Fowler Terr Milford CT 06460

GALLOPOULOS, GREGORY STRATIS, lawyer; b. Detroit, Oct. 8, 1959; s. Nicholas E. and Mary Frances Gallopoulos; m. Christa L. Gallopoulos. AB with highest distinction, U. Mich., 1981, JD magna cum laude, 1984. Bar: Ill. 1984, US Dist. Ct. No. Dist. Ill. 1984, Supreme Ct. Ill. 1984, US Dist. Ct. Ea. Dist. Mich. 1988, US Ct. Appeals 7th Cir. 1990, US Supreme Ct. 1992, US Tax Ct. 1995, US Ct. Fed. Claims 1995, US Ct. Appeals 9th Cir. 1996, US Ct. Appeals Fed. Cir. 2001. Assoc. Jenner & Block LLP, Chgo., 1984-91, ptnr., 1992—, firm co-chair tax controversy practice, firm mng. ptnr., 2005—. Author: Preserving Error for Appeal in Illinois, 1990, Why Do We Work?, 2006. Mem. ABA, 7th Cir. Bar Assn., Ill. State Bar Assn., Chgo. Bar Assn., Order of Coif, Phi Beta Kappa. Presbyterian. Office: Jenner & Block LLP 330 N Wabash Chicago IL 60611 Office Phone: 312-923-2754. Office Fax: 312-840-7754. Business E-Mail: ggallopoulos@jenner.com.

GALLOPS, R. WAYNE, music educator; s. Janice Lee Carroll; m. Donna L. Luttrull, Nov. 30, 1986; children: Daniel, Lauren. AA, Hillsborough C.C., Tampa, 1982; MusB, U. Tampa, 1984; MusM, Fla. State U., Tallahassee, 1986; PhD, U. South Fla., Tampa, 2005. Cert. ednl. leadership Nova Southeastern U., 1995. Dir. bands Pierce Jr. H.S., Tampa, 1985—87, Hillsborough H.S., Tampa, 1987—89, H.B. Plant H.S., Tampa, 1989—97; dir. instrumental music Howard Blake H.S. for the Performing Arts, Tampa, 1997—2001; dir. bands, prof. music edn. Radford U., Va., 2004—. Vis. prof. music U. Tampa. Home Phone: 540-362-7038; Office Phone: 540-831-5177.

GALLOWAY, DAVID CRAIG, chemist; b. Augusta, Ga., Feb. 13, 1956; s. Craig Coleman Galloway and Wanda Louise Price. BS in Chemistry, Tenn. Wesleyan Coll., Athens, 1978; MS in Organic Chemistry, Western Carolina U., Cullowhee, NC, 1984; postgrad., Middle Tenn. State U., Murfreesboro, 2002—03. Chemistry instr. Tri-County C.C., Murphy, NC, 1984—86; rsch. chemist Morgantown Energy, W.Va., 1986—87; analytical chemist Bur. Alcohol, Tobacco, Firearms and Explosives, Rockville, Md., 1987—89; chemistry instr. Robeson C.C., Lumberton, NC, 1989—90, Chatham Coll., Pitts., 1990—91; chemist Stuart-Ironsides, Inc., Verona, Pa., 1991; analytical chemist Consumer Product Safety Commn., Rockville, Md., 1991—92; chemist Unimin Corp., Spruce Pine, NC, 1995—96; chemistry tchg. asst. U. Tex.-Dallas, Richardson, 1997—98; chemist Artech Testing, Chantilly, Va., 1999; sci. tchr. Sinai Acad., Bklyn., 2000; chemistry tchg. asst. Middle Tenn. State U., Murfreesboro, 2002—03; analytical chemist Tenn. Valley Authority, Muscle Shoals, Ala., 2004—05. Alternative energy cons., Hayesville, NC, 2002—. Active Dem. Party, Clay County, NC, 2004—. Mem.: Am. Chem. Soc. (Outstanding Sr. in Chemistry award 1978), Alpha Chi. Democrat. Methodist. Avocation: genealogy. Home: 918 Jarrett Rd Hayesville NC 28904 Personal E-mail: dcgalloway1956@hotmail.com.

GALLOWAY, EILENE MARIE, space and astronautics consultant; b. Kansas City, Mo., May 4, 1906; d. Joseph Locke and Lottie Rose (Harris) Slack; m. George Barnes Galloway, Dec. 23, 1924; children: David Barnes, Jonathan Fuller. Student, Washington U., St. Louis, 1923—25; AB, Swarthmore Coll., 1928, LLD (hon.), 1997; postgrad., Am. U., 1937—38, postgrad., 1943; LLD (hon.), Lake Forest Coll., 1990. Tchr. polit. sci. Swarthmore Coll., 1928-30; editor Student Svc., Washington, 1931; staff mem. edn. div. Fed. Emergency Relief Adminstrn., 1934-35; asst. chief info. sect. div. spl. info Library of Congress, 1941-43; editor abstracts Legis. Reference Svc., 1943-51, nat. def. analyst, 1951-57, specialist in nat. def., 1957-66; sr. specialist internat. rels. (nat. security) Congl. Rsch. Svc., 1966-75, cons. internat. space activities, 1975—2006; ret.; hon. dir. Internat. Inst. Space Law, 2006—. Staff mem. Senate Fgn. Rels. Com., 1947; profl. staff mem. U.S. group Interparliamentary Union, 1958-66; cons. Senate Armed Svcs. Com., 1953-74, Ford Found., 1958; spl. cons. Spl. Senate Com. on Space and Astronautics, 1958; spl. cons. to Senate Com. on Aero. and Space Sci., 1958-77; cons. to Senate Com. on Commerce, Sci. and Transp., 1977-82; chmn. com. edn. and recreation Washington, 1937-38; forum leader, 1976-79; guest Soviet Acad. Sci., 1982, adult edn. U.S. Office Edn., 1938; mem. Internat. Inst. Space Law of Internat. Astronautical Fedn., 1958—, U.S. bd. dirs., v.p., 1967-79, hon. dir., 1979—, Fedn. ofcl. observer at sessions UN Com. on Peaceful Uses Outer Space and legal sub-com., 1970-94, com. for rels. with internat. orgns., 1979—; space law and sociology com. Am. Rocket Soc., 1959-62; adv. panel Office Gen. Counsel, NASA, 1971; adviser outer space del. U.S. Mission to UN Working Group on Direct Broadcast Satellites, 1973-75; observer UN Conf. Exploration and Peaceful Uses of Outer Space, Vienna, 1982; lectr. NAS, 1972, U.S. CSC, Exec. Seminar Ctr., Oak Ridge, 1973-78; ednl. counselor Purdue U., 1974; lectr. Inst. Air and Space Law McGill U., 1975, Inter Am. Def. Coll., 1977-78, U. Akron, 1984, 91; mem. panel on solar power for satellites and U.S. space policy Office Tech. Assessment, 1979-80, 82-86, cons., 1982; cons. COMSAT, 1983, FCC Commn. on U.S. Telecomm. Policy, 1983-87; spkr. internat. space law UN, N.Y.C., 1995; mem. NASA Nat. Adv. Com. on Internat. Space Sta., 1996-99, NASA Spaceflight Adv. com., 2000-03, UN seminar Space Futures and Human Security, Alpbach, Austria, 1997, chmn. Session in Internat. Astronautical Fed. Congress Concepts of Space Law, 1997; active European Space Agy. Internat. Lunar Workshop, 1994, 97; chair UN Workshop UNISPACE III Space Treaties: Strengths and Needs, Vienna, Austria, 1999; invited spkr. UN Com. Peaceful Uses of Outer Space and Internat. Astronautical Fedn., Paris, 2007. Author: Atomic Power: Issues Before Congress, 1946; author: (with Bernard Brodie) The Atomic Bomb and the Armed Services, 1947; author: History of United States Military Policy on Reserve Forces, 1775-1957, 1957, The Community of Law and Science, 1958, United Nations Ad hoc Committee on Peaceful Uses of Outer Space, 1959, Space Policy Guidelines, 2003, Space Law for the Moon-Mars Program, 2004; contbr. articles to profl. jours. Pres. Theodore Von Karman Meml. Found., 1973-84; mem. alumni council Swarthmore Coll., 1976-79; mem. organizing com., author symposium on Conditions Essential For Maintaining Outer Space for Peaceful Uses, Peace Palace, Netherlands, 1984; bd. advisers Student for Exploration and Devel. of Space, 1984—. Rockefeller Found. scholar-in-residence, Bellagio, Italy,

1976; elected to Coun. of Advanced Internat. Studies, Argentina, 1985, Uruguyan Centro de Investigacion y Difusion Aeronautica-Expacial, 1985; recipient Andrew G. Haley gold medal Internat. Inst. Space Law, 1968, Disting. Svc. award Libr. Congress, 1975, NASA Gold Medal for Pub. Svc., 1984, USAF Space Command plaque, 1984, Internat. Acad. Astronautics' Theodore Von. Karman award, 1986, Women in Aerospace Lifetime Achievment award Internat. Inst. Space Law, 1989, Leadership award NASA Johnson Space Ctr., 1997, NASA award for contbns. to internat. space sta., 1999, Cologne U. Inst. Air and Space Law and German Aerospace Ctr. award, 2003, Contbns. to Preserve Outer Space award UN Office Outer Space Affairs, NASA, Inst. Air and Space Law, Germany, Can. Space Agy., McGill U., 2006; Wilton Park fellow, Eng., 1968; Eilene M. Galloway award established by Internat. Inst. Space Law, 2000; honored Annals Vol. award Galloway NASA Adv. Com. on Internat. Space Sta., Internat. Inst. Space Laws, The Netherlands, 2006, UN Offices for Outer Space Affairs, NASA, Inst. Air and Space Law, U.S. Congress, Can. Space Agy., McGill U. Inst. Air and Space Law, 2006; dedication Informational Workshops on Policy and Law on Moon, Mars and Celestial Bodies, Montreal, 2006, Proceedings Internat. Space Law, Valencia, Spain, 2006; Eilene M. Galloway Symposium on Critical Issues in Space Law, Washington, 2006. Fellow: AIAA (hon.; tech. com. on legal aspects of aeros. and astronautics 1980—84, internat. activities com. 1985—, European space agy. internat. lunar workshop 1994, Pub. Policy award 2002, Pub. Svc. award and medal 2003), Internat. Acad. Astronautics (trustee emeritus, Social Scis. award 1999, Moot Ct. Best Brief award 2002), Am. Astronautical Soc. (John F. Kennedy Astronautics award 1999); mem.: Internat. Inst. Space Law, Nat. Aeronautic Assn. (Katharine Wright award 2003, 2003), Internat. Law Assn., LWV (chmn. study groups housing, welfare in DC 1937—38, mem. tech. com. on law and sociology task force on legal aspects 1979—), World Peace Through Law Ctr., Lamar Soc. Internat. Law, Am. Soc. Internat. Law, Kappa Alpha Theta, Phi Beta Kappa.

GALLOWAY, GERALD EDWARD, JR., civil engineer, educator; b. Mobile, Ala., Nov. 27, 1935; s. Gerald Edward and Jane Shirley Galloway; m. Diane Messinger; children: Laura Chadwell, Gerald E. III, Kevin T., Hillary Davis, John, Gregory. BS, U.S. Mil. Acad., 1974-77; MS, Princeton U., 1962; MPA, Pa. State U., 1974; M in Milit. Art and Sci., U.S. Army Command and Staff Coll., 1968; PhD, U. N.C., 1979. Commd. 2d lt. U.S. Army, 1957, advanced through grades to brig. gen., 1990; dist. engr. Vicksburg Dist. Corps of Engr., Miss., 1974-77; rsch. scientist water resources U. N.C., Chapel Hill, 1977-79; prof., deputy, then head dept. geography and computer sci. U.S. Mil. Acad., West Point, NY, 1979-89, chief staff, dep. post commdr., 1987-88, prof., head dept. geography and environ. engring., 1989-90, dean acad. bd., 1990; spl. asst. to commdr. in chief U.S. Army Europe, Heidelberg, Germany, 1985-86; Glenn L. Martin Inst. prof. engring. U. Md., College Park. Cons. U.S. Army C.E., Washington, 1981, U.S. Water Resources Coun., Washington, 1980-82; exec. dir. Interagy. Floodplain Mgmt. Rev. Com., Exec. Office of Pres., 1994; v.p. Enterprise Engring. Group, Titan Corp. Author: Assessing Man's Impact on Wetlands, 1978, Ex-Post Evaluation of Water Resources Development, 1980; co-editor: A Bibliography of Military Geography, vols. I-!V; contbr. articles to profl. jours. Mem. Miss. River Commn., 1988—. Fellow Am. Soc. Mil. Engrs. (chmn. com. 1989—); mem. NAE, Hudson River Environ. Soc. (bd. dirs.), Soc. Am. Mil. Engrs. (Bliss medal 1992), Am. Geog. Soc. (councilor 1990—), Univs. Coun. on Water Resources (pres. 1989-90), Assn. Am. Geographers (pres. mid. states 1985-86), Permanent Internat. Assn. Navigation Congress, Phi Kappa Phi. Roman Catholic. Home: 1267 S Oakcrest Rd Arlington VA 22202-2229 Office: Dept Civil & Environ Engring U Md 1173 Glenn L Martin Hall College Park MD 20742 Office Phone: 301-405-1341. Office Fax: 301-405-2585. E-mail: gegallo@umd.edu.

GALLOWAY, HOYT WILSON, library director; b. Blue Ridge, Ga., May 16, 1946; s. Hoyt Wilson Sr. and Mary Ruth (Smith) G.; m. Lydia Vermeer Sugihara, June 27, 1987; children: Patrick Sugihara Galloway, Lawton Richard Metcalfe III. AA, Prince George's Coll., 1969; BA, U. Md., 1971; MLS, U. South Fla., 1978. Tchr. Maricopa County, Phoenix, 1978-79; med. rsch. dir. Nat. Med. Adv. Svc., Bethesda, Md., 1979-80; br. libr. Ft. Amador, Panama Canal Zone, 1980-81; tech. info specialist Army Tropic Test Ctr., Panama Canal Zone, 1981-84; systems libr. Walter Reed Army Med. Ctr., Washington, 1984-87, med. libr. dir., 1987-2001; dir. Info. Resources Ctr. U.S. Customs and Border Protection, Washington, 2001—. Treas. D.C. Health Scis. Info. Network, Washington, 1988-89, pres., 1990-91; mem. fed. libr. info. ctr. com., fedlink adv. coun. Libr. of Congress, Washington, 1994—. Editor (bibliography) Medical Research Publications, vol. 1, 1990, vol II, 1993, (bibliography) Army Tropic Test Ctr. Publs., 1984. 2nd infantry divsn. US Army, 1966—68. Recipient Cert. of Appreciation, Libr. Congress, 2006. Mem.: Internat. Fedn. Libr. Assns., ALA, Am. Soc. Info. Sci., Spl. Libr. Assn., Med. Libr. Assn. Independent. Episcopalian. Avocations: swimming, scuba diving, hiking, reading. Home: 3939 Sunflower Cir Bowie MD 20721-2466 Office: Info Resources Ctr US Customs & Border Protection Ste 2.4 1300 Pennsylvania Ave NW Washington DC 20229 Home Phone: 301-464-1961; Office Phone: 202-344-3303. Personal E-mail: hoyt.galloway@gmail.com. Business E-Mail: hoyt.galloway@dhs.gov.

GALLOWAY, JAMES MALCOLM, cardiologist; b. San Mateo, Calif., May 24, 1953; s. Ellison and Doris Galloway; m. Edie Galloway; children: Kate, Brooke, Kelly, Dillon. BS, Va. Commonwealth U., 1978; MD, Med. Coll. Va., 1982. Diplomate Am. Bd. Internal Medicine with subspecialty in cardiovascular disease. Resident in internal medicine U. Vt., Burlington, 1982-85; internist Keams Canyon (Ariz.) PHS Hosp., 1985-88; clin. dir. Whiteriver (Ariz.) PHS Hosp., 1988-90; cardiology fellow U. Ariz., Tucson, 1990-93, dir. Native Am. cardiology program, 1993—2003, asst. prof. clin. medicine, 1993—2004; clin. asst. prof. pub. health Ctr. for Native Am. Health, Tucson, 1997—2004, clin. assoc. prof. medicine, 2003—, assoc. prof. clin. medicine, 2004—, assoc. prof. pub. health, 2003—. Co-investigator Strong Heart Study, 1995—; prin. investigator White Mountain Heart Study, 1995—; gov. USPHS Am. Coll. Cardiologist. Contbr. articles to profl. jours. Capt. USPHS, 1997—. Named Outstanding Clinician of Yr., Nat. Clin. Dirs., IHS, 1997, Physician of Yr., USPHS, 2005; named one of Best Doctors in Am., 2002; recipient Salsbury award for outstanding contbns. to healthcare for people of Ariz., 2001. Fellow ACP, Am. Coll. Cardiology, Am. Coll. Chest Physicians; mem. Am. Heart Assn.-Ariz. Affiliate (bd. dirs. 1993-97), Phi Kappa Phi, Alpha Omega Alpha. Office: Native Am Cardiology/Univ Ariz 1501 N Campbell Ave PO Box 245037 Tucson AZ 85724 Office Phone: 928-214-3920. E-mail: galloway@u.arizona.edu.*

GALLOWAY, JANICE, writer, editor; b. Kilwinning, Scotland, Dec. 2, 1956; d. James and Janet (McBride) G.; 1 child, James Alexander Galloway McNaught. MA, Glasgow U., 1978. Tchr. Strathclyde Regional Coun., Ayrshire, Scotland, 1980-90. Music critic. Editor: The Scotsman and Orange Short Story Collection, 2005; editor: (with Hamish Whyte) New Writing Scotland, 1990, 1991, 1992; author: The Trick is to Keep Breathing, 1990, Foreign Parts, 1994, Where You Find It, 1996, Clara, 2002 (Saltire book of yr., 2002), Boy Book See, 2002; editor: The Scotsman & Orange Short Story Collection, 2005; author (with sculptor Anne Bevan): +Rosengarten, 2004; librettist (with sculptor Anne Bevan): Operas Pipelines, librettist (with composer Sally Beamish): Operas Monster. Recipient Mind/Allan Lane prize, 1990, Cosmopolitan/Perrier award, 1991, E.M. Forster award in lit. Am. Acad. Arts and Letters, 1994, McVitie's prize for Scottish Writer of the Yr., 1994, Saltire prize, 2002; Times Literary Supplement Rsch. fellow Brit. Libr., 1999. Office: care Jonathan Cape 20 Vauxhall Bridge Rd London SW1 6RB England also: care Derek Johns AP Watt Agy 20 John St London WCIN 2DR England E-mail: sarah@galloway.itol.org.

GALLOWAY, KENNETH FRANKLIN, engineering educator; b. Columbia, Tenn., Apr. 11, 1941; s. Benjamin F. and Carrie (Dowell) G.; m. Dorothy Elise Lamar; children: Kenneth Jr., Carole A. BA, Vanderbilt U., 1962; PhD, U. S.C., 1966. Rsch. assoc. Ind. U., Bloomington, 1966-67, asst. prof., 1967-72, assoc. prof., 1972; rsch. physicist Naval Weapons Support Ctr., Crane, Ind., 1972-74; tech. staff Nat. Bur. Standards, Gaithersurg, Md., 1974-77, chief sect., 1977-79, chief divsn., 1980-86; prof. elect. engring. U. Md., 1980-86; prof., dept. head elect. and computer engring. U. Ariz., Tucson, 1986-96; dean engring., prof. elec. engring. Vanderbilt U., Nashville, 1996—. Contbr. articles to profl. jours. Sci. and Tech. fellow U.S. Dept. Commerce, 1979-80. Fellow IEEE (gen. chmn. Nuc. and Space Radiation Effects Conf. 1985, v.p. Nuc. and Plasma Sci. Soc. 1990, chmn. radiation effects com. 1991-94, chmn. engring. rsch. and devel. policy com. 1994, gen. chmn. Internat. Electron Devices Meeting 1997), AAAS, Am. Phys. Soc.; mem. Am. Soc. Engring. Edn., Sigma Xi, Eta Kappa Nu, Tau Beta Pi. Office: Vanderbilt U Sch Engring VU Sta B 351826 Nashville TN 37235-1826 Office Phone: 615-322-0720. Business E-Mail: kenneth.f.galloway@vanderbilt.edu.

GALLOWAY, MARIANNE THÉRÈSE, performing company executive; b. Garden City, NY, Oct. 17, 1976; m. Steven Donald Galloway, June 21, 2003. Diploma, Manhattan Sch. music Prep, NYC, 1992—94; student, New World Sch. of Arts, Miami, 1995—96; BA in English & Theater, U. Fla., 1998—2000. Broadcast prodn. coord. The Richards Group, Dallas, 2000—02; mktg. dir. Plano Repertory Theatre, 2002—03; gen. mgr. Shakespeare Festival of Dallas, 2004; founding artistic dir. Risk Theater Initiative, Dallas, 2002—. Councilwoman, artistic adv. coun. Shakespeare Festival of Dallas, 2004—; master planning com., samuell grand pk. City of Dallas, 2004—; master builders, dirs. panel Bath House Cultural Ctr., 2004; panelist, creating new theater Collin County CC, Plano, 2004; pres. Dallas Theater League, 2006—; founder artistic dir. Dirs. Lab Southwest, 2006—. Dir.: (theater prodns.) Waiting for Godot, 2003 (Leon Rabin award for Best Dir./Best Play, 2004), Rosencrantz & Guildenstern Are Dead, 2004, Marisol, 2006, Much Ado About Nothing, 2006, Angels in America, 2006, Shadowlands, 2007, Lawrence and Halloman, 2007, All of the Above, 2007; asst. dir. Open Window, 2005. Hotline operator trainer Parkland Rape Crisis Ctr., 2004; vol. recruiter Muscular Dystrophy Assn., Dallas, 2003—04; mem. Lincoln Ctr. Theater Dir. Lab., 2005—06. Recipient Top 10 Prodns., Dallas Morning News, 2003, Metroplex Column award, Dallas, 2003, 2006; Prodn. grant, City of Dallas Office Cultural Affairs, 2005. Mem.: Sons of Hermann Hall, Soc. Stage Dirs. and Choreographers (assoc.). Libertarian. Buddhist. Avocations: reading, equestrian eventing, properties designer, youth mentor. Office: Risk Theater Initiative Inc Adminstrv Offices 2120 Winslow Dr Plano TX 75023 Office Phone: 214-529-0896.

GALLOWAY, PATRICIA DENESE, civil engineer; b. Lexington, Ky., June 14, 1957; d. Howard John and Maudine Lou (Jones) Frisby; m. Kris Richard Nielsen, Mar. 16, 1987. BS in Civil Engring., Purdue U., 1978; MBA, NY Inst. Tech., 1984; PhD in Civil Engring., Kochi U. Tech., Japan, 2005. Registered profl. engr. Ky., NY, NJ, Ariz., Wis., Wyo., Fla., Wash., Colo., Pa., Man., Can., Australia. Project engr., insp. CH2M Hill, Milw., 1978-79, master program scheduler, 1979-81; sr. cons. Nielsen-Wurster Group, NYC, 1981-83, sr. engr., 1983-84, v.p., 1984-85, prin., exec. v.p., 1985-99, pres., 1999-2000, CEO, pres., 2001—04, CEO, 2004—. Lectr. Columbia U., U. Wis.-Madison; vis. prof. Kochi U. Tech.; presenter to numerous orgns; ptnr. Unionville Vineyards, Ringoes, NJ; pres. Unionville Ranch, L.L.C., Wash.; chief exec. Nielsen-Wurster Asia Pacific, Melbourne, Australia, 2001—, bd. dirs., mem. adv. bd. Contbr. articles to profl. jours. Named one of Top 10 Women in Constrn., Engring. New Record, 1986, one of Top 10 Women, Glamour Mag., 1987, 88, White House fellow regional finalist, 1990, Ky. Col., Gov. Patten, Sts. of Ky., 2002; named to Lafayette H.S. Hall of Fame, 2001; recipient Nat. Leadership Coun. Capital award, 1990, Engr. of Yr. award Mercer County Profl. Engrs., 1990, Nat. Leadership award Profl. Women in Constrn., 1995, Fed. Infrature Design award Whitehouse Commn., 1999, Upward Mobility award Soc. Women Engrs., 2003, Tribute to Women in Industry award, YWCA, 2004; named Disting. Engring. Alumnus, Purdue U., 1992, Celebration of Women, NAE, 2000. Fellow ASCE (instr. constrn. claims course, bd. chair task com. on women in civil engring. 1998—2000, internat. dir., bd. dirs. 1992-95, chmn. membership com. 2001—, pres.-elect 2003—, pres., bd. dirs. 2004 (1st woman); mem. NSF (dir. engring. 2004-), YWCA (Tribute to Women award), Am. Assn. Engring Socs., Nat. Soc. Professional Engrs., Am. Arbitration Assn., Professional Women in Construction, The Acad. Experts, UK, The Inst. Engrs., Australian Fellow, Soc. Women Engrs. (pres. Wis. chpt. 1980, pres. NY chpt. 1982, Disting. New Engr. 1980, Mobility award 2003-), Project Mgmt. Inst. (dir. pub. bd.), Am. Assn. Cost Engrs., Am. Nuclear Soc., Garden State Wine Growers Assn. (pres. 1990-92), Somerset County C. of C. (most outstanding woman in bus. and industry 1987), Purdue Engring. Alumni Assn. (bd. dirs., 1975-2001), Toastmasters, Sigma Kappa (fin. com. 1993-97), Tau Beta Pi. Republican. Methodist. Avocations: scuba diving, cross country skiing, hiking, horseback riding, wine making. Office: Nielsen-Wurster Group 719 Second Ave Ste 700 Seattle WA 98104 Office Phone: 509-857-2235. Office Fax: 609-497-3412. Personal E-mail: patnwg@aol.com.

GALLOWAY, WILLIAM JEFFERSON, retired foreign service officer; b. Throckmorton, Tex., Oct. 21, 1922; s. James Thomas and Ottis Virgil (Marrs) G.; m. Elizabeth Alice Cox, June 3, 1950; children— Jeff, Mary Elizabeth. BS, Tex. A&M U., 1943. Fgn. affairs officer Dept. State, 1948-50; spl. asst. to U.S. ambassador to NATO, London, Paris, 1950-53; spl. asst. to counselor Dept. State, 1953-56, 1st sec. Vienna, 1956-59, spl. asst. to dir. gen. fgn. service Washington, 1959-64; assigned Nat. War Coll., 1964-65; 1st sec., counselor polit. affairs Am. embassy, London, Eng., 1965-74; exec. asst. to under sec. state Dept. State, Washington, 1974-80, cons., 1980—. Served to capt. AUS, 1943-48. Home: The Jefferson 900 N Taylor St Apt 723 Arlington VA 22203 Personal E-mail: wmjgallo@aol.com.

GALLUCCI-BREITHAUPT, ADRIANNE, psychologist, social worker; b. Bridgeport, Conn., Nov. 17, 1959; d. Helen Mary and Alfred Joseph Gallucci; m. Mark Breithaupt, May 11, 2002. BA, Boston U., 1977—81, MSW, 1994—96; D of psychology, Mass. Sch. of Profl. Psychology, 1997—2002. Lic. psychologist Ariz., 2004, Md., 2004. Supr. Shawmut Bank, Boston, 1982—86; product mgr. Fidelity Investments, 1986—91; asst. v.p. Putnam Investments, 1991—94; crisis clinician Tri-City Mental Health, Lynn, Mass., 1996—97, Boston Emergency Services, 1997—99; psychotherapist Children's Charter, Inc., Waltham, Mass., 1998—99; rsch. cons. The Oak Group, Wellesley, Mass., 1999—2000; sr. psychologist No. Va. Mental Health Inst., Falls Church, Va., 2003—04; psychology cons. Arizona state, Phoenix, 2005—. Mem.: Am. Psychology Assn. Liberal. Avocations: travel, amatuer aquarist, tennis, painting. Home Phone: 602-870-3060.

GALLUP, JOHN GARDINER, retired paper company executive; b. Bridgeport, Conn., Oct. 31, 1927; s. Prentiss Brownell and Evelyn (Crocker) G.; m. Paula Burgee, June 10, 1951; children: Susan, Paula, Bruce. AB, Dartmouth Coll., 1949; William Pynchon hon. degree in Humanics, Springfield Coll., 1998. Dept. mgr. J.B. White Co., Greenville, SC, 1951, Castner Knott Dept. Store, Nashville, 1951-52; asst. store mgr. A.T. Gallup, Inc., Holyoke, Mass., 1952-55; with Strathmore Paper Co., Westfield, Mass., 1955-92, prodn. mgr., 1968-70, pres., div. mgr., 1970-92. Dir. Bank of New Eng.-West, Springfield, Mass.; chmn. Mass. Ventures, Inc. Mem. George Bush Campaign Com., 1979; chmn. Baystate Med. Ctr.r, Springfield, 1979-82; chmn. Baystate Health Systems, Inc., 1982-83; bd. dirs. Jr. Achievement Western Mass., 1979; trustee Springfield Coll., 1979-91; chmn. Valley 2,000; trustee Cmty. Found. We. Mass., Plan for Progress, Beveridge Found; commr. Mass. Commn. Jud. Conduct; trustee St. Andrew's Ch. Longmeadow, Econ. Devel. Coun. We. Mass.; bd. dirs. Willie Ross Sch. for Deaf, Reed's Landing. Served with USMC, 1945-47. Mem. Boston Paper Trade Assn. (pres. 1979), Am. Paper Inst. (exec. com. cover and text paper group 1979-91), Greater Springfield C. of C. (vice chmn. 1985-88, chmn. 1988-91, vol. econ. devel.), Vis. Nurses Assn. (bd. dir.), Corp. for Bus., Work and Learning (bd. dir.), Cmty. Svc. Learning (bd. dir.), World Affairs Coun. (bd. dir.), Springfield Orch. Assn. (pres.), Associated Industries Mass. (hon. dir.), Century Club, Colony Club (Springfield). Episcopalian. Home and Office: 64 Cambridge Cir Longmeadow MA 01106-2828 Personal E-mail: jggcamb@comcast.net.

GALLUP, PATRICIA, computer company executive; Grad., U. Conn., 1979. Chmn. PC Connection, Inc., Milford, Mass., 1982—, CEO, 2002—, pres., 2003—. Named Entrepreneur of Yr., Ernst & Young, 1998, 2003, N.H. High Tech. Coun., 2003; named one of Top 50 Women Bus. Owners in U.S., Working Woman, 2000—03. Office: PC Connection Inc Rt 101A 730 Milford Rd Merrimack NH 03054-4631*

GALLUZZO, JAY A., lawyer; b. 1974; BA magna cum laude, U. Pa., 1996; JD, Columbia U., 1999. Bar: NY 2000. Law clk. to Hon. Charles L. Brieant So. Dist. NY, 1997—99; assoc. Skadden, Arps, Slate, Meagher & Flom, LLP, 2000—03; sr. v.p., gen. counsel, sec. Warnaco Group, Inc., NYC, 2003—. Office: Warnaco Group Inc 501 Seventh Ave New York NY 10018 Office Phone: 212-287-8282. Office Fax: 212-287-8275. Business E-Mail: jgalluzzo@warnaco.com.

GALOWICH, RONALD HOWARD, real estate company executive, venture capitalist, pilot; b. Peoria, Ill., Feb. 18, 1936; s. Louis J. and Leah (Kahn) G.; m. Eleanor Bernstein, June 16, 1957 (div. Aug., 1977); children: Jeffrey, Robert, Pamela; m. Susan E. Loggans, Sept. 11, 1977 (div. Apr. 1988); m. Linda L. Kroupa, Oct. 18, 2000. BS in Commerce and Law, U. Ill., 1957, JD, 1959. Bar: Ill. 1959, U.S. Supreme Ct. 1963. Pres. Twin Oaks-Burr Oaks Realty, Joliet, Ill., 1961-81; ptnr. Galowich & Galowich, Joliet, Ill., 1960-81; dir. real estate ops. Pritzker & Pritzker, Chgo., 1981-90; chmn. Madison Realty Group, Inc., Chgo., 1985—, Madison Group Holdings, Inc., Chgo., 1990—; founder, chmn. Initiate Sys., Inc. (formerly Madison Info. Technologies, Inc.), Chgo., 1994—. Co-founder, dir. First Health Group Corp. (formerly Health Care Compare Corp.), Downers Grove, Ill., 1982—2005; commr. Ill. Supreme Ct., 1968-70. Chmn. devel. com. Joliet Greater YMCA, 2002—06; bd. dirs. Athletes Against Drugs, 1992—; mem. leadership com. Cancer Inst., Rush U. Med. Ctr., Chgo., 1993—; bd. visitors U. Ill. Coll. Law, 1996—, pres., 1998—2000. Fellow Am. Judicature Soc., Ill. Bar Found.; mem. ABA, Ill. Bar Assn., Urban Land Inst., Chgo. Bar Assn. Jewish. Home: 1248 N Astor St Chicago IL 60610-2308 Office: Madison Group Holdings Inc 200 W Madison St Ste 2300 Chicago IL 60606-3416 Personal E-mail: rhgalo@ix.netcom.com. Business E-Mail: rgalowich@initiatesystems.com.

GALSTON, ARTHUR WILLIAM, biology professor; b. NYC, Apr. 21, 1920; s. Hyman and Freda (Zaks) G.; m. Dale Judith Kuntz, June 27, 1941; children: William Arthur, Beth Dale. BS, Cornell U., 1940; MS, U. Ill., 1942, PhD, 1943. Rsch. plant physiologist emergency rubber project Calif. Inst. Tech., 1943-44, sr. rsch. fellow, 1947-50, assoc. prof. biology, 1951-55; instr. Yale U., 1946-47, prof. plant physiology, 1955-65, prof. biology, 1965-72, Eaton prof. botany, 1973-90, emeritus prof., 1990, dir. div. biol. scis., 1965-66, ret., chmn. dept. botany, 1961-62, chmn. dept. biology, 1985-88, lectr. in polit. sci., 2003—05. Cons. ctrl. rsch. dept. E.I. duPont de Nemours & Co., 1956-78, Plant Resources Venture Funds, 1983-89, NASA, 1988-94; mem. divsn. biology and agr. NRC, 1963-66, 85-88, mem. com. on space biology and medicine, 1983-86; Einstein prof. Faculty Agr. Hebrew U., Jerusalem, 1980; vis. scientist Plant Breeding Inst., Cambridge, Eng., 1983; vis. fellow Wolfson Coll., Cambridge U., 1983; vis. scholar Riken Inst., Japan, 1988-89. Author: Life of the Green Plant, 1961; author: (with Peter J. Davies and Ruth L. Satter) 3d edit., 1980; Principles of Plant Physiology, 1952; author (with James Bonner): Control Mechanisms in Plant Development, 1970; author: Daily Life in People's China, 1973, Green Wisdom, 1981, Life Processes in Plants, 1994; editor: New Dimensions in Bioethics, 2001, Expanding Horizons in Bioethics, 2005; mem. editl. adv. bd. World Book Science Year, 1976—78, Pesticide Physiology and Biochemistry, 1978—88, Plant Growth Regulation, 1983—93, Chem. Engring. News, 1977—78, Environment, 1979—83; contbr. sci. articles. Served as ensign USNR, 1944-46; mil. govt. Okinawa. Guggenheim fellow Stockholm, Paris, Sheffield, Eng., 1950-51; Fulbright fellow Canberra, Australia, 1960-61; Sci. Faculty fellow NSF, London, 1967-68. Fellow AAAS (chmn. com. on meetings 1956-59, life mem.), Am. Soc. Plant Physiologists (sec. 1955-57, v.p. 1957-58, pres. 1963-64); mem. Internat. Assn. Plant Physiology (sec.-treas. 1961-67), Bot. Soc. Am. (editl. bd. 1959-61, 72-76, pres. 1967-68), Fedn. Am. Scientists (coun. 1973-76), Am. Soc. Biochemists, Molecular Biol., Am. Soc. Photobiology, Am. Inst. Biol. Scis., Am. Acad. Arts & Scis., Sigma Xi. Office: Molecular Cellular & Devel Dept Biology Yale U New Haven CT 06520-8103 Home: 200 Leeder Hill Dr Apt 410 Hamden CT 06517-2749 Office Phone: 203-432-3509. Business E-Mail: arthur.galston@yale.edu.

GALSTON, WILLIAM ARTHUR, political scientist, educator; b. Bklyn., Jan. 17, 1946; s. Arthur William and Dale Judith (Kuntz) G.; m. Miriam, Sept. 15, 1968; 1 child, Ezra Moses. BA, Cornell U., 1967; MA, U. Chgo., 1969, PhD, 1973. Asst. prof. dept. govt. U. Tex., Austin, 1973-80, assoc. prof. dept. govt., 1980-82; issues dir. Mondale Pres. Campaign, Washington, 1982-84; dir. econ. and social programs Roosevelt Ctr. Am. Policy Studies, Washington, 1985-88; prof. sch. pub. affairs U. Md., College Park, Md., 1988—2005, Saul I. Stern Prof. Civic Engagement, dir. Inst. Philosophy and Pub. Policy, interim dean, Md. Sch. Pub. Policy; dep. asst. to pres. domestic policy The White House, Washington, 1993—95; sr. fellow Governance Studies Program The Brookings Instn., Washington, 2006—. Vis. fellow Instn. Social and Policy Studies, Yale U., 1980-81; cons. Temple for Gov. Campaign, 1982; mem. adv. bd. Ford/Aspen-Wye Rural Econ. Policy Project, 1989-92; mem. selection com. rural policy fellowships Woodrow Wilson Nat. Fellowship Found., 1989-91; cons. and spkr. in field. Author: Kant and the Problem of History, 1975, Justice and the Human Good, 1980, A Tough Row to Hoe: The 1985 Farm Bill and Beyond, 1985, Liberal Purposes, 1991 (Spitz prize 1993), Rural Development in the United States, 1995, Liberal Pluralism, 2002, The Practice of Liberal Pluralism, 2004, Public Matters, 2005; editor Virtue, 1992, Philosophical Dimensions of Public Policy, 2002; mem. editl. bd. Ethics, 1991—, Nomos, 1991—, Prospectives on Politics, 2002-; contbr. numerous articles to profl. jours. Advisor Gore for Pres. Campaign, Washington, 1988, 2000; chief speechwriter John Anderson Nat. Unity Campaign, Washington, 1980; mem. working group on bicentennial bill of rights Wilson Ctr., 1990-91. Sgt. USMC, 1969-70. Fellow Danforth Found., 1967-68, NEH, 1980-81, Woodrow Wilson Ctr., 1991-92. Mem. Am. Polit. Scis. Assn. (program chmn. normative polit. theory sect. 1992), Am. Acad. Arts and Scis., Conf. Study Polit. Thought, Am. Soc. Polit. and Legal Philosophy (program chmn. ann. mtng. 1989), Phi Beta Kappa.

Democrat. Jewish. Home: 5616 Durbin Rd Bethesda MD 20814-1014 Office: The Brookings Instn 1775 Massachusetts Ave NW Washington DC 20038 Office Phone: 202-797-2979. Business E-Mail: wgalston@brookings.edu.

GALTON, STEPHEN HAROLD, lawyer; b. Tulare, Calif., Dec. 23, 1937; s. Harold Parker and Marie Rose (Tuck) Galton; m. Grace Marilyn Shaw, Aug. 15, 1964; children: Mark(dec.) , Bradley, Jeremy, Elisabeth. BS, U. So. Calif., 1966, JD, 1969. Bar: Calif. 1970, U.S. Ct. Appeals (9th cir.) 1973, U.S. Dist. Ct. (no. dist.) Calif. 1973, U.S. Dist. Ct. (cen. dist.) Calif. 1970, U.S. Dist. Ct. (ea. and so. dists.) Calif. 1973. Assoc. Martin & Flandrick, San Marino, Calif., 1970-71, ptnr., 1971-72; assoc. Booth, Mitchell, Strange & Smith, LA, 1973-77, ptnr., 1978-85; sr. ptnr. Galton & Helm, LA, 1986—. Contbr. articles to profl. jours. Named Super Lawyer, LA Mag., 2005. Mem. ABA (litigation, tort, ins. sects.), Am. Bd. Trial Advs., Calif. State Bar Assn. (del. 1974-81, chair fed. cts. com.), Wilshire Bar Assn. (pres. 1986-87), Los Angeles County Bar Assn. (trustee 1987-89). Episcopalian. Office: Galton & Helm 500 S Grand Ave Ste 1200 Los Angeles CA 90071-2624 Office Phone: 213-629-8800. Business E-Mail: sgalton@galtonhelm.com. E-mail: sgalton@charter.net.

GALUPPO, LYNN T., lawyer; b. Calif., Aug. 1973; BA, Pepperdine U., Malibu, Calif., 1995, JD cum laude, 1999. Bar: Calif. 1999. Student extern US Securities and Exch. Commn., LA, 1998, extern, 1998; summer assoc. FNA Milberg, Weiss, Bershad, Heines & Lerach, San Diego, 1998; assoc. Stroock & Stroock & Lavan LLP, LA, 1999—2004, Cox, Castle & Nicholson, LLP, Irvine, Calif., 2004—. Contbr. articles to profl. jours. Office: Cox Castle & Nicholson LLP 19800 MacArthur Blvd Ste #500 Irvine CA 92612 Home Phone: 949-515-3745; Office Phone: 949-476-2111. Business E-Mail: lgaluppo@coxcastle.com.

GALVÁN, GARY, small business owner, educator; s. Geronimo Joe Galván and Joan Lorraine Hutton; m. Tammy Lou Galván, Oct. 31, 1990; children: LaTisha Marie Galván-Vreeland, Geddy Rowe. B in Mus. Jazz Performance, Rowan U., Glassboro, NJ, 1993; MA in Music Edn., U. Ctrl. Fla., Orlando, Fla., 2001; PhD in Musicology, U. Fla., Gainesville, Fla., 2007. Registered respiratory therapist Nat. Bd. Respiratory Care, 1988, pulmonary function technologist Nat. Bd. Respiratory Care, 1997, lic. neonatal perinatal specialist Nat. Bd. Respiratory Care, 1998. Prin., owner Galvanized Media, Sewell, NJ, 1992—. Preservationist galvanized media digital archive Free Libr. Phila., 2006—; adj. faculty La Salle U., Phila., 2006—. Mem.: ASCAP, Guitar Found. Am., Music Libr. Assn. (Carol June Bradley award 2007), Soc. Am. Music, Coll. Music Soc. (Outstanding Student Paper award So. chpt. 2006), Am. Musicological Soc., Phila. Mus. Art. Achievements include research in WPA music copying project; Henry Cowell; Edwin A. Fleisher collection of orchestral music. Avocations: photography, filmmaking. Home: PO Box 507 Sewell NJ 08080-0507 Office: La Salle Univ 1900 W Olney Ave Philadelphia PA 19141 Home Phone: 1 (352) 514-5574. Personal E-mail: ggalvan@musician.org. Business E-Mail: galvan@lasalle.edu.

GALVIN, ANTHONY J., auditor; b. Ill. Degree in fin., Depaul U., Chgo. Sr. auditor Daimler Chrysler, Lisle, Ill., 2001—. Mem.: Mensa (life). Home Phone: 630-258-9256. Personal E-mail: ajgone2003@yahoo.com.

GALVIN, CHARLES O'NEILL, retired law educator; b. Wilmington, NC, Sept. 29, 1919; s. George Patrick and Marie (O'Neill) G.; m. Margaret Edna Gillespie, June 29, 1946; children: Katherine Marie, George Patrick, Paul Edward, Charles O'Neill, Elizabeth Genevieve. BSc, So. Meth. U., Dallas, 1940, LLD, 2005; MBA, Northwestern U., Evanston, Ill., 1941, JD, 1947; SJD, Harvard U., Cambridge, Mass., 1961; LLD, Capital U., Columbus, Ohio, 1990. Bar: Ill. 1947, Tex. 1948, US Dist. Ct. (no. dist.) Tex. 1948, US Tax Ct. 1949; CPA, Tex. Pvt. practice, Dallas, 1947-52; from asst. to assoc. prof. So. Meth. U., Dallas, 1952-55, prof., 1955-82, dean Sch. Law, 1963-78; Centennial prof. law Vanderbilt U., Nashville, 1983-90, Centennial prof. emeritus, 1990—, exec. in residence, 1990-93; of counsel Haynes and Boone, LLP, Dallas, 1994—2007; ret. Thayer tchg. fellow Harvard U., 1956-57; vis. prof. U. Mich., 1957, Duke U., 1979, Pepperdine U., 1980; Raymond Rice Disting. vis. prof. U. Kans., 1990; adj. prof. law U. Tex., 1995-97; Disting. prof. law emeritus So. Meth. U., 1996—; trustee Am. Tax Policy Inst., 1992-97. Author: Estate Planning Manual, 1987; tax editor Oil and Gas Reporter; co-editor: Texas Will Manual, 1972—2006. Chmn. Dallas County Cmty. Action, Dallas 1970-72; pres. Cath. Found., Dallas, 1963-67; trustee Cath. Charities Trust. Served to lt. comdr. USNR, 1942-46. Recipient Disting. Alumnus award So. Meth. U., 1984, Alumnus Merit award Northwestern U., Chgo., 1993, John Rogers award Southwestern Legal Found., Dallas, 1997, McGill award Cath. Found., 1997. Fellow Am. Bar. Found., Tex. Bar Found. (Outstanding Fifty Yr. Lawyer award 2004), Dallas Bar Found.; mem. AICPA, ABA, Tex. Bar Assn., Dallas Bar Assn., Am. Law Inst. (life), Am. Judicature Soc., Tex. Soc. CPAs, Order of Coif, Am. Tax Policy Inst., U.S. Supreme Ct. Soc. (trustee), Tex. Supreme Ct. Soc. (trustee), Serra Club, KC, Knights of Holy Sepulchre, Phi Delta Theta, Beta Gamma Sigma. Roman Catholic. Home: 4240 Twin Post Rd Dallas TX 75244-6741 Home Phone: 972-392-2719. Personal E-mail: cogalvin@swbell.com.

GALVIN, JOHN ROGERS, retired army officer, law educator; b. Wakefield, Mass., May 13, 1929; s. John James and Mary Josephine (Rogers) G.; m. Virginia Lee Brennan, June 5, 1961; children: Mary Jo, Elizabeth Ann, Kathleen Mary, Erin Elizabeth. BS, U.S. Mil. Acad., 1954; MA, Columbia U., 1962; postgrad., U. Pa., 1964-65; grad., Command and Gen. Staff Coll., 1966. Commd. 2d lt. U.S. Army, 1954, advanced through grades to gen.; mil. asst. to Supreme Allied Comdr. Europe, 1974-75; comdr. DISCOM, chief of staff 3d Infantry div., Germany, 1975-78; asst. div. comdr. 8th Infantry div., 1978-80; comdg. gen. 24th Infantry div., Ft. Stewart, Ga., 1981-83, also post comdr.; comdg. gen. VII U.S. Corps, Stuttgart, Fed. Republic Germany, 1983-85; comdr. in chief U.S. So. Command, Quarry Heights, Panama, 1985-87; supreme allied comdr. Europe, comdr.-in-chief U.S. European Command, 1987-92; ret., 1992; Olin disting. prof. nat. security studies U.S. Mil. Acad., West Point, NY, 1992-93; disting. vis. policy analyst The Mershon Ctr., Ohio State U., 1994-95; dean Fletcher Sch. Law and Diplomacy, Tufts U., Boston, 1995-2000; dean emeritus, 2000—. Author: The Minute Men, 1967, Air Assault, 1969, Three Men of Boston, 1976. Former bd. dirs. Wesleyan Coll. Fletcher Sch. of Law and Diplomacy fellow, 1972-73; decorated Silver Star, Legion of Merit, DFC, Bronze Star. Mem. Ctr. for Creative Leadership (past bd. govs.), Seligman (bd. dirs.), Am. Coun. on Germany (chmn. emeritus bd. dirs.), Inst. for Def. Analyses (trustee, 1995-2002). Roman Catholic. Home: 2714 Lake Jodeco Cir Jonesboro GA 30236-5329

GALVIN, KATHLEEN MALONE, communications educator; b. NYC, Feb. 9, 1943; d. James Robert and Helen M. (Sullivan) G.; m. Charles A. Wilkinson, June 19,1973; children: Matthew, Katherine, Kara. BS, Fordham U., Bronx, NY, 1964; MA, Northwestern U., Evanston, Ill., 1965-80, PhD, 1968. Tchr. Evanston (Ill.) Township High Sch., 1967-72; asst. prof. Northwestern U., Evanston, 1968-73, assoc. prof., 1973-78, prof., 1978—, assoc. dean, 1988-2001. Presenter workshops in field. Author: Listening by Doing, 1986, multiple articles and chpts. family communication; sr. author: Family Communication, 7th edit., 2007; co-author: Person to Person, 5th edit., 1996, Basics of Speech, 4th edit., 2004; co-editor: Making Connections, 4th edit., 2006, Communication Works!, 2000; developer, instr. 26-video series on Family Communication (PBS Adult Satellite Sys.). Office: Northwestern U Comm Studies Dept 2240 N Campus Dr Evanston IL 60208-3545 Business E-Mail: k-galvin@northwestern.edu.

GALVIN, KERRY A., lawyer, chemicals executive; b. Greenville, SC, Jan. 27, 1961; BS cum laude in Fgn. Svc., Georgetown U., 1983; JD cum laude, U. Mich., 1986. Bar: Tex. 1986. Assoc. Mayor Day & Caldwell, Houston; fin. counsel legal dept. Lyondell Chem. Co., Houston, 1990, assoc. gen. counsel, sec., 1998, assoc. gen. counsel internat. legal affairs Maidenhead, England, v.p., gen. counsel, sec. Houston, 2000—02, sr. v.p., gen. counsel, sec., 2002—. Office: Lyondell Chem Co 1221 McKinney St Ste 700 Houston TX 77010*

GALVIN, MATTHEW REPPERT, psychiatry educator; b. Seattle, July 24, 1950; s. Ralph B. and Virginia (Reppert) G.; children: Joseph, Sarah, Erin; m. Margaret Gaffney. AB with honors, Ind. U., 1975, MD, 1979. Diplomate Am. Bd. Adolescent Psychiatry, Am. Bd. Psychiatry and Neurology. Asst. prof. Ind. U. Med. Ctr., Indpls., 1984-95, clin. assoc. prof., 1995—. Staff psychiatrist Larue Carter Meml. Hosp., Indpls., 1984-88, assoc. dir. youth svcs., 1988, acting dir., 1988-90; child psychiatrist Riley Child Psychiatry Svcs., Indpls., 1990-98, Pleasant Run Children's Home, 1998-2001, St. Vincent Stress Ctr., 2001-06, Children's Bur. Inc., 2001—, Ind. Sch. for the Blind, 2003—; vol. faculty Riley Child Psychiatry and Ind. U. Med. Ethics Program. Author: Ignatius Finds Help, A Story about Psychotherapy, 1988, Otto Learns About Medicine, 1988, 3d edit., 2001, A Story About Grown-ups Helping Children, 1988, Clouds and Clocks, A Story for Children Who Soil, 1989, 2 edit., 2007, The Otters of Conscience-Berg, 2005, Carlotta Learns About Her Medicine, 2005, 2d edit., 2007, Grandma Grady's Grade-A Gray Day, 2007; co-author: Sometimes Y, A Story for Families with Gender Identity Issues, 1993, The Conscience Celebration, 1998, Right vs. Wrong: Raising a Child with a Conscience, 2000, Rachel and the Seven Bridges of Conscience-Berg, 2002, A Guide to Conscience, 2007; editorial staff Conscience Works; contbr. articles to profl. jours. With M.C., U.S. Army, 1970-73, Vietnam. Fellow Am. Psychiat. Assn.; mem. Am. Acad. Child Adolescent Psychiatry, Am. Soc. Adolescent Psychiatry, Nat. Alliance Against Mental Illness (affiliate), Ind. Coun. Child and Adolescent Psychiatry (treas. Indpls. chpt. 1986-89, pres. elect 1989-90, pres. 1990-91). Office Phone: 317-844-0055.

GALVIN, MICHAEL JOHN, JR., lawyer; b. Winona, Minn., July 8, 1930; s. Michael John Sr. and Margaret Elizabeth (O'Donohue) G.; m. Frances Dennis Culligan, Sept. 7, 1957; children: Sean, Kevin, Kathleen, Nora, Mary, Margaret, Patricia. BA, U. St. Thomas, 1952; LLB, U. Minn., 1957. Bar: Minn. 1957, U.S. Dist. Ct. Minn. 1957, U.S. Supreme Ct. 1961. With sales and svc. Badger Machine Co., Winona, 1950-56; mgr. Oaks Hotel Inc., Winona, 1950-56; ptnr. Briggs & Morgan, P.A., St. Paul, 1957—. Pres. St. Paul Winter Carnival Assn., 1970; sec. St. Paul Area C. of C., 1968-71; trustee U. St. Thomas, 1978-85, Coll. St. Catherine, St. Paul, 1999—; nat. chmn. U. Minn. Law Sch. Ptnrs. in Excellence Program, 2000-01; chmn. Indianhead Coun. Boy Scouts Am., 2003—; bd. dirs. Maritime Heritage Soc., 2005—. Lt. USAF, 1952-54, USAFR, 1954-60. Named Boss of Yr., St. Paul Jaycees, 1990, Disting. Cmty. Builder, Can. Govt., 2007; named an Oustanding Young Man, City St. Paul, 1964; recipient Disting. Alumnus award, U. St. Thomas, 1983, U. Minn. Law Sch., 2001, Great Living St. Paulite award, St. Paul Area C. of C., 2000, Eugene and Mary Frey Cmty. award, Cretin-Derham Hall Schs., 2000, Monsignor James Lavin award, U. St. Thomas, 2003. Mem. ABA (labor and employment law sect., Leonard Linquist award 2007), Minn. Bar Assn. (treas. 1991-93, pres.-elect 1993, pres. 1994-95, chair labor and employment law sect. 1984), Ramsey County Bar Assn. (exec. coun. 1965-68, 83-86, pres. 1984-85), Minn. Vol. Attys. Corp. (pres. 1993-94), Univ. Club (pres. 1962), Minn. Club (pres. 1971), St. Paul Athletic Club (pres. 1986), St. Paul Area C. of C. (bd. dirs. 1995—, chmn. 1997-98). Republican. Roman Catholic. Office: Briggs & Morgan 2200 1st Nat Bank Bldg Saint Paul MN 55101 Office Phone: 651-808-6553. Business E-Mail: mgalvin@briggs.com.

GALVIN, PATRICK, state official; m. Alyse Galvin; 4 children. B in Visual Arts and Quantitative Econ., U. Calif. San Diego; JD, U. San Diego; MBA, San Diego State U. Atty. pvt. practice; dir. Divsn. Governmental Coord., Ala.; petroleum land mgr. Alaska Dept. Nat. Resources Divsn. Oil and Gas; commr. Alaska Dept. Revenue, 2006—. Office: Alaska Dept Revenue PO Box 110400 333 W Willoughby 11th Fl SOB Juneau AK 99811-0400*

GALVIN, ROBERT W., electronics executive; b. Marshfield, Wis., Oct. 9, 1922; Student, U. Notre Dame, U. Chgo.; LLD, Quincy Coll.; LLD (hon.), St. Ambrose Coll., DePaul U., Ariz. State U. With Motorola, Inc., Chgo., 1940—48, exec. v.p., 1948—56, former pres., 1956, chmn. bd., 1964—90, CEO, 1964—86, chmn. exec. com., 1990—2001, also dir.; ret., 2003; chmn. bd. Semantech Inc., Austin, Tex. Author: America's Founding Secret: What the Scottish Enlightment Taught our Founding Fathers, 2002. Past mem. Pres.'s Commn. on Internat. Trade and Investment.; chmn. industry policy adv. com. U.S. Trade Rep.; active Pres.'s Pvt. Sector Survey; chmn. Pres.'s Adv. Coun. on Pvt. Sector Initiatives, Ill. Inst. Tech., U. Notre Dame; bd. dirs. Jr. Achievement, Chgo. With Signal Corps US Army, WWII. Named Decision Maker of Yr., Chgo. Assn. Commerce and Industry-Am. Statis. Assn., 1973; named one of Forbes' Richest Americans, 2006; recipient Nat. medal, Tech. U.S. Dept. Commerce Tech. Adminstrn., 1991, Sword of Loyola award, Loyola U., Chgo., Washington award, Western Soc. Engrs., 1984, Vannevar Bush award, NSF, 2005. Mem.: Nat. Bus. Hall of Fame, Electronic Industries Assn. (pres. 1966, bd. dirs., Medal of Honor 1970, Golden Omega award 1981). Office: Motorola Inc 1303 E Algonquin Rd Schaumburg IL 60196-1079

GALVIN, WALTER J., electrical equipment manufacturing executive; Controller, Ridge Tool subs. Emerson Electric Co., 1973—78, asst. v.p. investor rels., 1978—81, v.p. fin., US electric motors divsn. to exec. v.p. fin., adminstrn., 1981—84, v.p. fin., analysis sys. to sr. v.p. controller, 1984—93, CFO St. Louis, 1993—2000, exec. v.p., CFO, 2000—04, sr. exec. v.p., CFO, 2004—. Office: Emerson Electric Co PO Box 4100 Saint Louis MO 63136-8506*

GALVIN, WILLIAM FRANCIS, state official; b. Brighton, Mass., Sept. 17, 1950; m. Eileen Galvin; 1 child, Bridget. Grad. cum laude, Boston Coll., 1972; JD, Suffolk U. Law Sch., 1975. Bar: Mass., Fed. Aide Gov.'s Coun., 1972; mem. Mass. Ho. Reps., 1975-91, vice-chmn. Congl. Redistricting Com., 1981-83, chmn. Govt. Regulations Com., 1983-91; sec. state Commonwealth of Mass., Boston, 1995—. Mem.: Nat. Assn. Secs. State. Democrat. Office: Office Sec of State State House Room 337 Boston MA 02133-1000 Office Phone: 617-727-7030. E-mail: cis@sec.state.ma.us.*

GALVIS, CAMILO ANDRES, real estate company executive, researcher; b. Bogota, Colombia, Dec. 6, 1976; m. Maria Claudia Pena, Jan. 22, 2002; 1 child, Emma. Degree in Economics, U. Sydney, Australia, 1999, U. Los Andes, Bogota, 2000; MS in Ops. Rsch., Columbia U., NYC, 2006. Cert. economist Colombian Soc. Economists, 2000. Integrated tech. specialist IBM, Bogota, 2001; dir. info. Fortune Internat., Miami, Fla., 2001—. Cons. Real Estate Optima, NYC, 2006—. Donor Christian Children's Fund, Richmond, Va., 2006—07. Mem.: Inst. Ops. Rsch. Mgmt. Scis. (assoc.), Math. Programming Soc. (assoc.). Achievements include research in optimal static and dynamic pricing of multi-unit real estate developments; price/earnings ratio to identify over speculative real estate markets; positive correlation matrix analysis to identify correctness of price composition in multi-unit pre construction developments; patents pending for SQL powered online public database for searching and indexing unrelated user content which is subsequently analysed and unified.

GALWANKAR, SAGAR CHANDRAMOHAN, public health service officer; s. Chandramohan Galwankar; m. Dhanashree Kelkar. MBBS, DNB, MPH, Bharati Vidyapeeth Med. Coll., Pune. Internat. advisor Internat. Ctr. Health and Human Advancement, Chgo.; global emergency med. scis. specialist U. South Fla., Tampa, 2004—. Asst. prof. U. South Fla. Coll. Pub. Health, Tampa, 2002—04. Editor in chief: Jour. Gen. Medicine (Award for Recognition for Contributions to the 55 Yr. old Indian Practitioner Jour., 2001). Mem.: Am. Assn. Physicians Indian Origin (mem. com. 2005—). Achievements include development of INDUS-EM model for academic development of emergency and trauma sciences in India. Office: U South Fla Bruce B Downs Blvd Tampa FL 33612 Home Phone: 813-349-6532.

GALWAY, SIR JAMES, flutist; b. Belfast, Northern Ireland, Dec. 8, 1939; s. James Galway and Ethel Stewart (Clarke) G.; m. 1965 (div.), 1 child; m. Anna Christine Renggli, 1972 (div.), 3 children; m. Jeanne Cinnante, 1984. Student, Royal Coll. Music, Guildhall Sch. Music, London, Conservatoire National Superieur de Musique, Paris; MA (hon.), Open U., Eng., 1979; MusD (hon.), Queen's U., Belfast, 1979, New Eng. Conservatory Music, 1980. Prin. guest conductor London Mozart Players. Flutist, Wind Band of Royal Shakespeare Theatre, Sadler's Wells Orch., 1960-65, Royal Opera House Orch., BBC Symphony Orch.; prin. flutist London Symphony Orch., 1966, Royal Philharm. Orch., 1967-69; prin. solo flutist Berlin Philharm. Orch., 1969-75; internat. solo performer and condr., 1975-; U.S. debut, 1978; U.S. performances with Nat. Symphony Orch., NY Philharmonic, Houston Symphony Orch., San Diego Symphony, Cinn. Pops Orch. Boston Symphany Orch., 2004-2005; recordings include works of C.P.E. Bach, J.S. Bach, Beethoven, Corigliano, Danzi, Dvorak, Feld, Franck, Mozart, Quantz, Prokofiev, Nielsen, Reinecke, Rodrigo, Stamitz, Telemann, Vivaldi, Khachaturian; recordings include Annie's Song, The Classical James Galway, The Concerto Collection, Dances for the Flute, The Enchanted Forest: Melodies from Japan, Galway at the Movies, Greatest Hits Vol 1, Vol. 2, Vol. 3, James Galway and the Chieftains In Ireland, Galway at 50: A Portrait of James Galway, Winter's Crossing, 1998, James Galway Plays Lowell Liebermann, 1998, 60 Years, 60 Flute Masterpieces, Vols. 1-4, 1999, A Song of Home: An American Musical Journey, 2002, A Windham Hill Wedding Album, 2003, Andrea Immer Presents: Chardonnay, Shellfish, & Schubert, 2003, Best Classics 100, 2004, Quiet on the Set: James Galway at the Movies, 2004, numerous others; author: James Galway: An Autobiography, 1978, Flute, 1982, James Galway's Music in Time, 1983, Masterclass, 1987, others; several TV appearances including The Tonight Show, Good Morning America, CBS This Morning, Live with Regis and Kathie Lee, Sesame Street, Live from Lincoln Center. Pres. Flutewise (vol. nonprofit ogrn.). Decorated officer Order Brit. Empire, 1977; recipient Grand Prix du Disque, 1976, Order of the British Empire award, 1979; Record of Yr. awards Cash Box and Billboard mags., Pres. Merit award Recording Acad., 2004; named Musician of Yr., Musical Am., 1997; knighted 2001. Fellow Royal Coll. Music, Birmingham Schs. Music. Avocations: swimming, walking, films, theater, computers. Office: Galway Mgmt Benzeholzstrasse 11 6045 Meggen Switzerland

GALWAY, RICHARD E., JR., state supreme court justice; b. Manchester, NH, 1944; m. Anita Galway; 2 children. BA, U. N.H., 1966; Fulbright scholar, U. Leeds, England, 1966—67; JD, Boston U. Law Sch., 1970. Bar: N.H. 1970. Atty. worker's compensation law Devine, Millimet & Branch, Manchester, NH, 1970—95; judge NH Superior Ct., 1995—2004; justice NH Supreme Ct., 2004—. Author: Worker's Compensation Law in New Hampshire, 1990, New Hampshire Worker's Compensation Manual, 2nd Edition, 1993. Mem.: ABA, Nashua Bar Assn., N.H. Bar Assn. (pres. 1981—82). Office: NH Supreme Ct 2 Noble Dr Concord NH 03301*

GAMACHE, CLAUDETTE THERESA, artist, nurse; b. Fall River, Mass., Dec. 9, 1941; d. Raymond Alfred Cote and Yvette Marguerite Lavigne; m. Peter Paul Gamache, May 23, 1964; children: Daniel, Raymond, Christopher. Diploma, St. Anne's Nursing Sch., Fall River, Mass., 1962; BFA, U. Hartford, West Hartford, Conn., 1984; MA, Lesley U., Cambridge, Mass., 1985. RN Mass., NY, Calif., Conn., Maine, NH; registered Am. Art Therapy Bd. RN Mt. Sinai Hosp., Hartford, Conn., 1984—86; expressive therapist Elmcrest Psychiat. Hosp., Portland, Conn., 1986—87; nurse clinician/expressive therapist, adolescent partial program New Britain Gen. Hosp., 1987—89; hospice nurse VNA Group, Hartford, 1989—93; hospice mgr. Portsmouth Visiting Nurses, NH, 1994—97; artist Claudette Gamache Gallery, Bath, Maine, 1997—. Pastel painting tchr. Heartwood Coll. Art, Kennebunk, Maine, 2000—02, Chocolate Ch. Art Ctr., Bath, 2003; vis. art tchr. Wells Mid. Sch., 2000; ind. pastel painting tchr., Bath, 2004—; spkr. in field of hospice nursing, 1990—97. Pastel painting, Reflection, 2001, Retreat, 2004, exhibitions include Internat. Pastel Soc., Raleigh, NC, 2005, pub. in various profl. jours. Mem.: Am. Art Therapy Assn., Pastel Painters Maine (v.p. 2006, pres. 2007), Pastel Soc. Am. Avocations: writing, astrology, piano, shaman drumming. Office Phone: 207-443-9978. Personal E-mail: claudettegamache@yahoo.com.

GAMACHE, R. DONALD, retired business development executive; b. Fall River, Mass., Aug. 30, 1935; s. Armand Wilfred and Imelda (Gagnon) G.; m. Kathleen Florence Smith, Nov. 22, 1958; children: Mariette (dec.), Nanette Estes, Lisette Becker (dec.). BS, St. Peter's Coll., 1958. Account exec. Harold Shore Assocs., NYC, 1965-67; v.p. Van Dyck Corp., Southport, Conn., 1967-69; pres. Shippan Corp., Stamford, Conn., 1969, INNOTECH. Corp., Trumbull, Conn., 1969-86, chmn., 1985-94; ret., 1994. Contbg. author Handbook for Creative and Innovative Managers, 1988, New Directions in Creative and Innovative Management, 1988; author: The Creativity Infusion, 1989; contbr. numerous articles to profl. jours. Formerly active Sea Island Habitat for Humanity, Charleston Symphony Orch., SC, United Way Upper Valley, Lebanon, NH; bd. dirs. Enfield Village Assn.; pres., bd. dirs. Lower Shaker Village Bds. Avocations: music, baking, gardening. Home: 6 Simple Gifts Ln Enfield NH 03748-3557 Personal E-mail: peperegama@aol.com.

GAMALDO, CHARLENE EDIE, medical educator; BA, U. Va., Charlottesvile, 1993; MD, George Wash. U., Washington, 2000. Diplomate Am. Bd. Sleep Medicine, 2006. Resident U. NC, Chapel Hill, 2001—04; asst. prof. neurology dept. Johns Hopkins U., Balt., 2006—, clin. instr. pulmonary and critical care divsn., 2006—. Fellow, Johns Hopkins U., 2004—06. Office: Johns Hopkins Hosp 5501 Hopkins Bayview Cir Baltimore MD 21224 Office Phone: 410-550-1044. Office Fax: 410-550-3364. E-mail: cgamald1@jhmi.edu.

GAMBA, SANDRO, chef; b. Neufchâteau, France, 1970; Commis de cuisine Le Pre Catelan, Paris, 1988—89, Le Moulin de Mougins, Provence, France, 1989—90; chef de partie Le Jamin, Paris, 1990—92, Louis XV Hotel, Monte Carlo, 1993—96; chef de cuisine La Cabro d'Or, Les-Baux-Provence, France, 1996—98; exec. chef Lespinasse, Washington, 1998—2000, NoMI, Park Hyatt, Chgo., 2000—. Nominee Best Chef: Midwest, James Beard Found., 2005; named one of Best New Chefs, Food & Wine mag., 2001. Office: NoMI 800 N Michigan Ave Chicago IL 60611 Office Phone: 312-239-4030.*

GAMBARDELLA, THOMAS M., lawyer; b. Jamaica, NY, Mar. 28, 1954; BA magna cum laude, St. John's U., 1976, JD, 1979. Bar: NY 1980, US Dist. Ct. Ea., So., & No. Districts NY, US Ct. Appeals 2nd Cir. Ptnr. Wilson, Elser, Moskowitz, Edelman & Dicker LLP, White Plains, NY, co-chmn. firm profl. liability practice team. Mem.: ABA, NY State Bar Assn. Office: Wilson Elser Moskowitz Edelman & Dicker LLP 3 Gannett Dr White Plains NY 10604 Office Phone: 914-323-7000 ext. 4523. Office Fax: 914-323-7001. Business E-Mail: gambardellat@wemed.com.

GAMBATESA, DONALD ANTHONY, federal agency administrator; Grad., John Carroll U., 1969, Nat. Exec. Inst. FBI. Various leadership positions including spl. agent in charge US Secret Svc., Washington; spl. agent in charge spl. investigations divsn. office inspector gen. US Agy. Internat. Devel.; dep. dir. US Marshals Svc., 2001—06; inspector gen. US Agy. Internat. Devel., 2006—. Inspector gen. Millennium Challenge Corp., African Devel. Found., Inter-Am. Found., Overseas Pvt. Investment Corp. Former officer USN. Mem.: Nat. Exec. Inst. Assocs., Internat. Assn. of Chiefs of Police. Office: US Agy Internat Devel 1300 Pennsylvania Ave NW Washington DC 20523 Office Phone: 202-712-1150.

GAMBEE, ROBERT RANKIN, investment banker; b. NYC, Aug. 26, 1942; s. Sumner and Eleanor Elizabeth (Brown) G.; m. Elizabeth Gregory Heard, 1991; children: Robert Gregory, Claire Elizabeth Fay. Grad., Phillips Exeter Acad.; AB, Princeton U., 1964; MBA, Harvard U., 1966. Assoc. corp. fin. White, Weld & Co., NYC, 1966-71, v.p., 1971-73, Schroder Capital Corp. affiliate J Henry Schoder Wagg-London, NYC, 1973-78, Atlantic Capital Corp. affiliate Deutsche Bank AG, Frankfurt, Germany, 1978-84; 1st v.p. Deutsche Bank Securities Inc., 1985-91, dir., 1992—. Prin. N.Y. Stock Exch., 1971—, Nat. Assn. Securities Dealers, 1971—; v.p. Apollo, Atlas, Hercules, Hermes, Mercury, Olympus, Orion, Pegasus, Taurus, Titan and Zeus Instl. Investments, Inc., 1984-92; COO, sec. Germany Fund, Inc., 1986—, The New Germany Fund, Inc., 1990—, The Future Germany Fund, Inc, 1990-95, The Ctrl. European Equity Fund, Inc., 1995—; v.p., sec. Deutsche Funds Inc., 1997-2000, Deutsche Bank Investment Mgmt. Inc., 1995—; dir. Deutsche Bank AG and Bankers Trust Co., 1999—, Deutsche Bank Securities, Inc., 2002—. Author, photographer: Nantucket Island, 1973, rev. edit., 1974, 81, paper edit., 1978, 87, 89, color edits., 1986, 88, 98, Manhattan Seascape: Waterside Views Around New York, 1975, Exeter Impressions (intro. by Nathaniel Benchley), 1980, Princeton in Color (intro by Robert F. Goheen), 1987, paperback edit., 1988, 2d rev. edit., 1993, 98, A Wall Street Christmas, 1989, rev. edit., 1990, Nantucket in Color, 1992, 94, 96, paperback edit., 1996, Wall Street-Financial Capital, 1999, Nantucket Impressions, 2001. Trustee Dwight-Englewood Sch., 1978-85, Elizabeth Morrow Sch., 1990—, Rye (N.Y.) Art Ctr., 1993—, Rye Presbyn. Ch., 1998-2001. Mem. Soc. Colonial Wars, Princeton Alumni Assn. Nantucket (v.p., sec.), Princeton Club N.Y. (gov.), Nantucket Yacht Club, Univ. Club. Republican. Presbyterian. Home: Wendover Rd Rye NY 10580 Office Phone: 212-289-9393. Personal E-mail: bobgambee@aol.com.

GAMBET, DANIEL G(EORGE), academic administrator, minister; b. June 9, 1929; Student, DeSales Hall Sch. Theology, 1953-57; AB in Latin and Greek, Niagara U., 1954; MA in Latin and Greek, Cath. U. Am., 1957; PhD in Classical Studies, U. Pa., 1963, postgrad. in higher edn. adminstrn, 1964; LHD (hon.), Lehigh U., 1986; HHD (hon.), Moravian Coll., 1988; DD (hon.), Lafayette Coll., 1994, Muhlenberg Coll., 1999. Ordained priest Roman Catholic Ch. (Order of Oblates of St. Francis de Sales), 1957; tchr. Latin Father Judge High Sch., Phila., 1957-58; dean of men. instr. Latin, French and German Salesianum Sch., Wilmington, Del., 1958-61; instr. history Oblate Coll., Childs, Md., 1962-64, St. Mary's Coll., Wilmington, 1962-64; acad. dean, instr. Latin and history Allentown Coll. of St. Francis de Sales, 1965-70, v.p., acad. dean, instr. Latin, 1970-72, v.p., 1972-78, pres., 1978—99, pres. emeritus, 1999—. Provincial Eastern Province Oblates of St. Francis de Sales, 1972-78; mem. Allentown Diocesan Bd. Edn., 1978-81, chmn., 1968-70, 79-81; pres. bd. trustees DeSales Hall Sch. Theology, 1972-77; pres. bd. dirs. Salesianum Sch., 1972-77; chmn. vis. com. dept. classica Lehigh U., 1977-85; mem. instl. survey com. Commn. for Ind. Colls. and Univs. in Pa., 1977-81, chmn. instl. survey com., 1980-81, exec. com., 1980-89; exec. com. Found. Ind. Colls., 1984—; chmn. vis. com. for religious studies Lehigh U., 1985-94; bd. dirs. Pa. Power and Light Co. Trustee Allentown Coll. of St. Francis de Sales, 1972-99; bd. dirs. Better Bus. Bur. of Ea. Pa., 1978, United Way of Lehigh County, 1979-88, Health East Inc., 1987-91, Moravian Acad., 1991-98, Ben Franklin Mfrs. Resource Ctr., 1994-97, Lehigh Valley Cmty. Fedn., 1996—; exec. com. Minsi Trails coun. Boy Scouts Am., 1980; trustee Valley Youth House, 1991-97; vice-chmn. bd. dirs. Lehigh Valley Hosp. Ctr., 1983-88. Mem. Pa. Assn. Colls. and Univs. (bd. dirs. 1994-99), Lehigh Valley Assn. Ind. Colls. (bd. dirs. 1978-99, chmn. 1980-81), Ctr. for Agile Pa. Edn. (chair bd. dirs. 1996-99), Assn. Governing Bds. Univs. and Colls., Allentown-Lehigh County C. of C. Home and Office: DeSales U Office of the Pres Emeritus 2755 Station Ave Center Valley PA 18034-9568 Office Phone: 610-282-4135. Business E-Mail: daniel.gambet@desales.edu.

GAMBINO, RICHARD JOSEPH, materials engineer, educator; b. NYC, May 17, 1935; BA, U. Conn., 1957; MS, Polytech Inst. N.Y., 1976. Phys. sci. U.S. Army Signal Rsch. Lab., Ft. Monmouth, NJ, 1958—60; metallurgist Pratt & Whitney Aircraft divsn. United Aircraft Corp., 1960—61; rsch. staff mem. T.J. Watson Rsch. Ctr., IBM, Yorktown Heights, NY, 1961—93; prof., lab. dir. SUNY, Stony Brook, 1993—. Pres. MesoScribe Technologies, Inc., 2002—. Recipient Nat. Medal of Tech., 1995. Fellow: IEEE; mem.: NAE, IEEE Magnetic Soc., Nat. Acad. Engring., Materials Rsch. Soc., Am. Vacuum Soc. (thin film divsn. bd.), Tau Beta Pi, Sigma Xi. Home: 148 Sycamore Cir Stony Brook NY 11790-3161 Office: Dept Material Scis & Engng State U NY 107 Engineering Bldg Stony Brook NY 11794-2275 Office Phone: 631-444-6455. Business E-Mail: rgambino@mesoscribe.com.

GAMBINO, S(ALVATORE) RAYMOND, lab administrator, educator; b. NYC, Oct. 13, 1926; s. Salvatore Benedict and Rose (Ragona) G.; m. Madeline Russo, Apr. 5, 1953; children: Catherine Rose Garroni, Stephen Raymond. BS, Antioch Coll., 1948; MD, U. Rochester, 1952. Diplomate Am. Bd. Pathology. Dir. labs. Englewood Hosp., NJ, 1961—68; prof. pathology Columbia U., NYC, 1968—82; dir. chemistry labs. Presbyn. Hosp., NYC, 1968—77; dir. labs. St. Luke's-Roosevelt Hosp., 1978—82; chief med. officer, exec. v.p. MetPath, Inc., Teterboro, NJ, 1983—94, exec. v.p., chief med. officer emeritus, 1994—. Adj. prof. pathology Columbia U., N.Y.C., 1983—; mem. Corning (N.Y.) Mgmt. Group, 1984-94; bd. dirs. Ciba-Corning, 1988-94. Co-author: Beyond Normality, 1975; editor: (newsletter) Lab Report for Physicians, 1979-98. Mem. Englewood Cliffs (N.J.) Sch. Bd., 1966-69. Served with USN, 1945-46. Mem. Am. Soc. Clin. Pathologists (editor check sample program 1968-93), Alpha Omega Alpha. Roman Catholic. Avocations: walking, writing, travel. Office: Quest Diagnostics Inc 1300 E Newport Ctr Dr Deerfield Beach FL 33442 E-mail: doclab@aol.com.

GAMBLE, CAHTINA ROBYNE, elementary school educator; b. Troy, NY, Jan. 26, 1973; d. John Robert and Sandra Dale Gamble. BA in Music Edn., Social Sci., U. Stonybrook, NY, 1997; M in Elem. Edn., Wilmington Coll., 2004. Cert. cosmetologist N.Y., Md., Del. Kindergarten tchr. Prime-Time Daycare and Develop. Ctr., Troy, NY, 1990—94; residential skills instr. Adults and Children with Learning Disabilities of Bethpage, NY, 1998; tchr. Delcastle Vocational Tech. H.S., Wilmington, Del., 1999—2001; mental health technician The Devereux Found., Malvern, Pa., 2002—03; 4th grade tchr. Highlands Elem. Sch., Wilmington, 2002—04; tchr. NY City Dept of Edn., Bklyn., 2006—. Mentor Jr. Achievement Inc., Newark, 2004—06; dance instr. Bethel Bapt. Ch. Youth Dept., 2005—. Youth mentor vol. Bethel Bapt. Ch., 2005—. Mem.: Wind and Fire Ministries. Avocations: singing, dance, music, writing poetry. Home: 200 8th St Troy NY 12180 Office: NYC Dept Edn PS 243 1580 Dean St Brooklyn NY 11213

GAMBLE, DESIRATA, artist, poet; b. Wilkesboro, NC; d. Robert Lee and Mary Etta Gamble; m. David Bullins, Feb. 14; 1 child, Zoe Bullins. AA with honors, Surry C.C., Dobson, NC, 1983; BA in Psychology, U. N.C., Wilmington, 1985, BA in Studio Arts, 2001; postgrad., U. Ga., 1985—87. Ordained to ministry Apostolic Ch. Proofreader Joan S. Northrop, Wilmington, 1984—85; artist U. N.C., Wilmington, NC, 1996—2002; artist transp. MerleFest, Wilkesboro, NC, 1994—2005, 2006—07; prof. arts in art Buxton U., England, 2003; with Apollo Apostilic Svcs., 2005—. One-woman shows include The Morning Dew, Winston-Salem, NC, 1997—98, 2005, Claude Howell Gallery, Wilmington, 1998, 1999, The Deluxe, Wilmington, NC, 1998—99, 2006, The Beanstalk, Boone, NC, 1999—2001, Daughtry's Old Books, Wilmington, 2003, 2004, 2005, 2006, 2007, 2007, William Vance Nichols/Wilkes Art Gallery, Wilkesboro, NC, 2003, Nth Degree, Boone, 2006, The Space, Greensboro, NC, 2006; artist, poet: Sights of the Wind, Her White Hair Peeps and We Heard the Music for Miles, 1985 (Book award for poetry U. N.C. Wilmington); Represented in permanent collections Daniel Hall, Wilkes C.C., Wilkesboro, NC, River Valley Animal Foods, Harmony, NC; author: numerous poems. Named State-wide Hon. Mention for the Lyricist, A Violet Letter from Frannie, 2005, State-wide winner for the Lyricist, Wall of Words, 2007. Mem.: AAUW, Assn. Rsch. and Enlightenment, Smithsonian Inst., Acad. Am. Poets, Nature Conservancy, Southeastern Ctr. for Contemporary Art, Ala. State Poetry Soc. Personal E-mail: gambled1@excite.com.

GAMBLE, E. JAMES, lawyer, accountant; b. Duluth, Minn., June 1, 1929; s. Edward James and Modesta Caroline (Reichert) G.; m. Lois Kennedy, Apr. 3, 1954; children: John M., Martha M., Paul F. AB, U. Mich., 1950, JD, 1953. Bar: Mich. 1953, D.C. 1980; CPA, Mich. Tax acct. Ernst & Ernst, Detroit, 1957-59; assoc. Dykema, Gossett, Spencer, Goodnow & Trigg, Detroit, 1959-67; ptnr. Dykema Gossett, Detroit, 1967-94, Gamble, Rosenberger & Joswick LLP, Bloomfield Hills, 1994—2006, Gamble & Joswick LLP, Bloomfield Hills, 2006—. Adj. prof. law Wayne State U., Detroit, 1964-79; adj. lectr. law U. Mich., Ann Arbor, 1979-81, 93; co-reporter, prin. draftsman Uniform Principal and Income Act (1997); mem. adv. com. Restatement of the Law, 3rd, Property, Wills and Other Donative Transfers, Restatement of the Law, 3rd, Trusts; counsel Mich. State Bd. Accountancy, Lansing, 1973-77. Author: (handbook) The Revised Uniform Principal and Income Act, 1966; contbr. articles to profl. jours. Trustee Rehab. Inst., Inc., Detroit, 1961-84, chmn. bd. trustees, 1974-77; bd. dirs., sec. Jr. Achievement Southeastern Mich., 1973-86; trustee Walsh Coll. Accountancy and Bus. Adminstrn., Troy, Mich., 1975-87, Alma (Mich.) Coll., 1981-91; mem. Fin. and Estate Planning Coun. Detroit, bd. dirs., 1969-76, pres., 1975. Lt. USN, 1953-57. Recipient Bronze Leadership award Jr. Achievement, Inc., 1985 Fellow Am. Coll. Tax Counsel, Am. Coll. Trust and Estate Counsel (bd. regents 1988—, chmn. estate and gift tax com. 1989-92, pres. 1998-99), Academician, Internat. Acad. Estate and Trust Law (exec. coun. 2001-04), Am. Bar Found. (life), Mich. State Bar Found.; mem. ABA (mem. spl. com. on profl. rels. with AICPA 1968-70), Mich. Bar Assn. (mem. various coms.), Detroit Bar Assn. (chmn. taxation com. 1968-74), Detroit Bar Assn. Found. (trustee, treas. 1973-79), Birmingham Athletic Club, Leland Country Club. Presbyterian.

GAMBLE, GEOFFREY, academic administrator; Degree in English, Fresno State Coll., 1965, M Linguistics, 1971; PhD Linguistics, U. Calif., Berkeley, 1975. Cert. specialist in Native Am. linguistics. Chair, anthropology chair Washington State U., dir. mus. anthropology, dir. summer session, interim vice provost, vice provost; provost, sr. v.p. U. Vt.; pres. Mont. State U.-Bozeman, 2000—. Grantee Nat. Endowment of Arts, Nat. Endowment for Humanities. Office: Mont State U-Bozeman 211 Montana Hall Bozeman MT 59717-2420*

GAMBLE, MICHAEL F., human resources generalist; BA in Mktg. and Comms., Bowling Green State U., Ohio, 1985. Cert. blackbelt Sigma Six, 2000, mediation 2000, profl. human resources Soc. Human Resource Mgmt. Ops. supr. and labor rels. specialist Ryder Distbn. Resources, Cleve., 1987—89; ter. mgr. employee rels. Norrell Svcs., Cleve., 1990—94; employee rels. mgr. Charter One Bank, 1995—97; human resources and union rels. mgr. Gen. Electric Quartz, Inc., Willoughby, 1997—2000; corp. human resources mgr. Werner Co., Greenville, Pa., 2000—01; human resources officer Nat. City Bank, Cleve., 1994—95, v. p. human resources, 2001—03; dir. human resources Revlon, Oxford, NC, 2004—. Bd. mem. Cuyahoga County Workforce Devel. Mem.: Soc. Human Resource Mgmt. Home: 354 Amherst Creek Dr Wake Forest NC 27587-9202 Office Phone: 919-603-2592. Business E-Mail: michael.gamble@revlon.com.

GAMBLE, RAYMOND WESLEY, retired marriage and family therapist, clergyman; b. East Orange, NJ, Feb. 11, 1933; s. Kenneth Nelson and Lillian Clare (Apgar) G.; m. Margaret Gamble, Sept. 11, 1954 (div. 1964); children: Karen F., Roy B.; m. Penelope Louise Hansen, Nov. 19, 1979; 1 child, Wesley B. BA, Houghton Coll., NY, 1956; MDiv, Union Theol. Sem., Richmond, Va., 1960; postgrad., Yale U., New Haven, 1967; D Ministry, Columbia Theol. Sem., Decatur, Ga., 1990. Ordained to ministry Presbyn. Ch., 1960. Student chaplain Va. State Penitentiary, 1958-60; asst. pastor Immanuel Presbyn. Ch., Lake Park, Fla., 1960-62; founder, pastor Westminster Presbyn. Ch., Palm Beach Gardens, Fla., 1962-67; exec. dir. Mental Health Assn. Palm Beach County, West Palm Beach, 1967-73; pvt. practice marriage and family therapy, West Palm Beach, Stuart, Fla., 1973—; founder, sr. pastor Palm City Presbyn. Ch., Fla., 1984—2003; interim minister Indian River Presbyn. Ch., Ft. Pierce, Fla., 2005. Guest instr. Indian River Community Coll., 1978; cons., chaplain Lake Hosp., Lake Worth, Fla., 1973-75; chaplain Savannas Hosp., Port St. Lucie, Fla., 1986—2004; program dir., aftercare counselor narcotic addict rehab. program NIMH, West Palm Beach, 1969-73. Active numerous drug abuse rehab. programs, Palm Beach County; past mem. Com. for Mental Health Edn.; active Presbytery Tropical Fla., 1960—; past mem. ch.-coll. coun. Montreat Coll., 1988-96; past bd. dirs. Alcohol and Drug Abuse Coun. Palm Beach County, North County Drug Abuse Bd., Boca Raton (Fla.) Drug Abuse Found.; past pres. Drug Abuse Rehab. Team, Inc. Mem. Am. Assn. for Marriage and Family Therapy (clin.). Avocations: sport fishing, horticulture. Home and Office: 288 NE Alice St # 101S Jensen Beach FL 34957-6006

GAMBLE, THEODORE ROBERT, JR., investment banker; b. St. Louis, Sept. 18, 1953; s. Theodore Robert and Rispah Adele (Dowse) Gamble; m. Susan Lee Stupin, Mar. 3, 1984. AB, Princeton U., 1975; MArch, Harvard U., 1977, MBA, 1979. Assoc. Morgan Stanley & Co., Inc., NYC, 1979-84, v.p., 1984-86, prin., 1986-87; pres. Prescott Group Inc., NYC, 1987—, mng. dir., 1999—, Transwestern Comml. Svcs., LLC, NYC, 1999—2002. Mem. bus. com., mem. vis. com. Met. Mus. Art; bd. dirs., exec. v.p. Greater N.Y. coun. Boy Scouts Am.; bd. dirs. N.Y. Hist. Soc., Coll. Arms Found.; mem. vis. com. Mary Inst. St. Louis Country Day Sch.; mem. vestry St. Thomas Ch., NYC; co-chmn. adv. com. real estate devel., chmn. vis. com. Grad. Sch. Design Harvard U.; vice chancellor, bd. govs. Am. Soc. Order St. John of Jerusalem. Mem.: Young Mortgage Bankers Assn., Real Estate Bd. NY, Internat. Assn. Corp. Real Estate Execs., Assn. Fgn. Investors Real Estate, Nat. Assn. Real Estate Investment Trusts, Urban Land Inst. (mem. comml. and retail devel. coun., mem. internat. com.), Internat. Coun. Shopping Ctrs., The Pilgrims, Gulf Stream Bath and Tennis Club (Fla.), Coral Beach and Tennis Club (Bermuda), City Club (Miami), Harvard Club (NYC, Boston), Princeton Club (bd. govs., mem. exec. com., pres.), Doubles Club, Brook Club, Links Club, Knickerbocker Club, Univ Club, Racquet and Tennis Club, River Club. Republican. Episcopalian. Home: 860 UN Plaza New York NY 10017 Office: The Prescott Group Inc 666 Fifth Ave 27th Fl New York NY 10103 Personal E-mail: trgamblejr@msn.com. Business E-Mail: trgamblejr@prescott-group.com.

GAMBLE, VANESSA NORTHINGTON, historian, healthcare educator, bioethicist; b. May 20, 1953; BA, Hampshire Coll., 1974; MD, U. Pa., 1983, PhD, 1987. Resident U. Mass. Med. Ctr.; visiting scholar Harvard U. Sch. Pub. Health; assoc. prof. family & comty. medicine U. Mass.; asst. prof. history of medicine, science and family medicine U. Wis., Madison, 1989-93, assoc. prof., 1994—2000; dir. Ctr. for the Study of Race and Ethnicity in Medicine U. Wis. Sch. of Medicine, Madison, 1996—2000; v.p. Div. Comty. & Minority Programs Assn. Am. Med. Colleges, 2000—02; assoc. prof. health policy & mgmt. Johns Hopkins Bloomberg Sch. Pub. Health, 2002—04; dir. Nat. Ctr. Bioethics in Rsch. & Health Care Tuskegee U., 2004—, prof. bioethics & health care, 2004—. Adv. bd. Nat. Ctr. Primary Care Morehouse Sch. Medicine; adv. bd. Ctr. Study of Health Disparities Tex. A&M U.; adv. com. Soros Reproductive Health & Rights Fellowship; bd. trustees Ctr. for the Advancement of Health. Health commentator The Tavis Smiley Show, NPR; author: The Black Community Hospital: Contemporary Dilemmas in Historical Perspective, 1989, Germs Have No Color Line: Blacks & American Medicine 1900-1940, 1989, Making a Place for Ourselves: The Black Hospital Movement, 1920-1945, 1995 (Choice mag. Outstanding Academic Book). Chairwoman Tuskegee Syphilis Study Legacy Com., 1996—97. Mem.: Inst. Medicine.

GAMBOLI, MICHAEL A., lawyer; s. Anthony and Kate Gamboli; m. Jane Patzwall, Aug. 5, 1989; children: Caitlin, Erin, James. BS, Bucknell U., 1986; JD, Boston U., 1991. Ptnr. Partridge Snow & Hahn, Providence, 1991—. Office: Partridge Snow & Hahn 180 S Main St Providence RI 02903 Office Phone: 401-861-8200. Business E-Mail: mag@psh.com.

GAMBON, MICHAEL JOHN, actor; b. Dublin, Oct. 19, 1940; s. Edward and Mary Gambon; m. Anne Miller, 1962. Student, St. Aloysius Sch. for Boys, London. Engring. apprentice, 7 yrs.; with Edwards/MacLiammoir Theatre Co., Dublin, Ireland, 1962, Nat. Theatre, Old Vic., 1963-67, Birmingham Rep. and other provincial theatres, 1967-69. Performances include: (with regional theatres) Othello, Macbeth, Coriolanus; Aldwych, 1970-71, Norman Conquests, 1974, Otherwise Engaged, 1976, Just Between Ourselves, 1977, Alice's Boys, 1978, King Lear and Anthony and Cleopatra, 1982-83, Old Times, 1985, Galileo, 1980 (recipient Best Actor award, London Theatre Critics'), Betrayal, 1980, Tales from Hollywood, 1980, Chorus of Disapproval, 1985 (Olivier award, Best Comedy Performance), Tons of Money, 1986, A View form the Bridge, 1987, A Small Family Business, 1987; numerous film and TV appearances including The Singing Detective, 1986 (BAFTA award, Best Actor), The Storyteller: Greek Myths, 1990, Wives and Daughters, 1999, Angels in America, 2003, (films) Sleepy Hollow, 1999, Harry Potter and the Prisoner of Azkaban, 2004, Being Julia, 2004, Sky Captain and the World of Tomorrow, 2004, The Life Aquatic with Steve Zissou, 2004, Harry Potter and the Goblet of Fire, 2005, The Omen, 2006, Amazing Grace, 2006, The Good Shepherd, 2006. Avocations: flying, gun collecting, clock making. Office: care Larry Dalzell Assocs 126 Kennington Park Rd London SE11 4D England*

GAMBONE, JOSEPH CHARLES, medical educator, consultant; children: Lynn Anne, Joseph Charles. DO, Phila. Coll. of Osteo. Medicine, Pa., 1974; Master's of Pub. Health, MPH, UCLA, 1997—99. Diplomate Am. Bd. of Obstetrics and Gynecology, 1982, Am. Bd. Ob-Gyn, Reproductive Endocrinology and Infertility, 1984. Prof. emeritus David Geffen Sch. of Medicine, UCLA, 1986—; clin. prof. of obstetrics and gynecology Western U. of Health Scis., Pomona, Calif., 2006—. Healthcare cons. Decision-Works, Durango, Colo., 1999—. Editor: (textbook) Essentials of Obstetrics and Gynecology. Capt. USNR, 1966—2003. Achievements include mountain named in his honor, Gambone Peak, Antarctica. Office: Western Univ of Health Scis Pomona CA Home Phone: 970-375-6429. Personal E-mail: jgambone@ucla.edu. Business E-Mail: jgambone@westernu.edu.

GAMBONE, VICTOR, JR., internist, geriatrician; b. Phila., Aug. 28, 1949; s. Victor Emmanuel and Eleanor Joyce (Porambo) G. BS, Pa. State U., 1971, MD, 1975. Diplomate Am. Bd. Quality Assurance and Utilization Rev. Physicians, Am. Bd. Internal and Geriatric Medicine; cert. med. dir. in long term care. Intern, resident in internal medicine U. South Fla., Tampa, 1975-78, practice medicine internal medicine and geriatrics Dunedin, Fla., 1978—; med. dir. Evercare (United Health Group), Oldsmar, Fla., 1996—; project coord. Fla. Med. Quality Assurance, Inc., Tampa, 2000—. Med. dir. Hospice Care, Inc., Pinellas County, 1982—86; chmn. dept. internal medicine Mease Health Care, Dunedin, Fla., 1989; med. dir. Stratford Ct. Health Ctr., Palm Harbor, Fla., 1991—, St. Mark Village, 1993—, Mease Continuing Care, Dunedin, Fla., 1993—, Largo Health Care Ctr., 1999—2007, Spanish Gardens Nursing Ctr., Dunedin, Fla., 1994—98, East Bay Nursing Ctr., 1996—2005, Sylvan Health Ctr., 1996—2002, Manor Care Nursing Ctr., Dunedin, Fla., 1996—2001, Bayview Nursing Pavillion, Clearwater, 1996—99, Arbors of Safety Harbor, 1997—98, Mariner Health Belleair, 1997—98, Sabal Palms Health Care Ctr., Largo, Fla., 1997—99, Morton Plant Rehab. Ctr., 1998—2000, Drew Village Rehab. and Nursing Ctr., Clearwater, Fla., 1998—99, Oak Manor Village, Largo, Fla., 1999, Encore Sr. Village, Clearwater, Fla., 1999—2004. Author: Post Operative Recall of Intra-Operative Events, 1975 (rsch. award U. Miami Med. Sch.). Fellow: ACP; mem.: AMA, Fla. Med. Assn., Fla. Geriatrics Soc., Fla. Med. Dirs. Assn. (pres. 2003—05), Am. Geriatrics Soc., Am. Med. Dirs. Assn. Office: Evercare 601 Brooker Creek Blvd Oldsmar FL 34677 Office Phone: 727-799-5041. E-mail: Victor.Gambone@verizon.net.

GAMBRELL, DAVID HENRY, lawyer; b. Atlanta, Dec. 20, 1929; s. E. Smythe and Kathleen (Hagood) G.; m. Luck Coleman Flanders, Oct. 16, 1953; children: Luck Coleman, David Henry, Alice Kathleen Hagood, Mary Latimer. BS, Davidson Coll., 1949; JD cum laude, Harvard U., 1952. Bar: Ga. 1951. Pvt. practice, Atlanta, 1952-54, 56—; teaching fellow Harvard Law Sch., 1954-55; ptnr. firm Gambrell & Stolz, LLP, 1963—2007; sr. counsel Baker, Donelson, Bearman, Caldwell & Berkowits, PC, 2007—. U.S. senator from Ga. to succeed Richard B. Russell Coms. on Banking and Space, 1971-72. Bd. editors: Am. Bar Assn. Jour, 1969-70. Chmn. Ga. Gov.'s Com. on Postsecondary Edn., 1978-79; bd. dirs. Nat. Legal Aid and Defender Assn., 1965-69; chmn. Dem. Party of Ga., 1970-71; trustee Ga. Legal History Found., 1996—, Lawyers Found. of Ga., 1997-2003; bd. dirs. Buckhead Coalition, Inc., 2003—. Mem. ABA (ho. of dels. 1975), Atlanta Bar Assn. (pres. 1965-66, Leadership award 2007), State Bar Ga. (pres. 1967-68, Disting. Svc. award 2002), Lawyers Club Atlanta, Ga. C. of C. (bd. dirs. 1989-92), N.C. Soc. Cin., Ga. Hist. Soc. (bd. curators 1999-2001), Met. Club Washington, Piedmont Driving Club, Commerce Club, Capital City Club, Peachtree Golf Club, Sigma Alpha Epsilon, Omicron Delta Kappa. Democrat. Presbyterian. Home: 3205 Arden Rd NW Atlanta GA 30305-1918 Office: Gambrell & Stolz LLP 3414 Peachtree Rd NE #1600 Atlanta GA 30326-1164 Office Phone: 404-577-6000. E-mail: dgambrell@gambrell.com.

GAMBRELL, JAMES BRUTON, III, lawyer, educator; b. Rochester, Minn., Jan. 17, 1926; s. James Bruton Gambrell and Martha Judson Corley; m. Helen Jeanette Roddy, Aug. 12, 1950; children: Jamey, Gretchen, James Bruton IV. BS in Mech. Engring, U. Tex., 1949; MA in Econs, Columbia U., 1950; LL.B., N.Y. U., 1957. Bar: D.C. 1957, Okla. 1958, Calif. 1961, N.Y. 1967, Tex. 1976. Mem. staff Tex. Legis. Coun., Austin, 1950; instr. econs. Baylor U., Waco, Tex., 1950-51; mem. tech. staff (engr.) Bell Tel. Labs., Murray Hill, NJ, 1951-53, mem. patent staff NYC, 1953-57; admitted to practice before U.S. Patent Office, 1954; asst. patent atty. Well Surveys, Inc., Tulsa, 1957-59; assoc. Townsend & Townsend, San Francisco, 1959-61; spl. asst. to commr. patents, dir. office legis. planning U.S. Patent Office, Washington, 1961-63; ptnr. Fowler, Knobbe & Gambrell, Santa Ana, Calif., 1963-66; prof. law NYU, NYC, 1966-76, patent counsel, 1967-76; prof. law U. Houston, 1976-82; ptnr. Pravel, Gambrell, Hewitt, Kimball & Krieger, Houston, 1976-92, Gambrell, Wilson & Hamilton,

Austin, Tex., 1993-95, Akin, Gump, Strauss, Hauer & Feld L.L.P., Austin, Tex., 1995-2000; vis. prof. law U. Tex., Austin, 2000—. Cons. to Practicing Law Inst., N.Y.C., 1966-71, cons. to Commn. Revision Fed. Ct. Appellate System, 1974, Energy and Rsch. Adminstrn., 1976; commr. patents Patent Adv. Com., 1968-72. Author: Patent Law Perspectives, 2d edit., 6 vols., 1970-88; editor: Orange County Bar Bull., 1965-66; mem. adv. bd.: Patent, Trademark and Copyright Jour., 1972-86, 94—. Lt. (j.g.) USNR, 1943-46. Mem. ABA, Tex. Bar Assn., Am. Intellectual Property Law Assn. (bd. mgrs. 1977-80), Intellectual Property Panel of Experts, Am. Arbitration Assn., Ctr. for Pub. Resources. Home: PO Box 584 Hunt TX 78024-0854 Office: Roddy Tree Ranch 820 State Hwy 39 Hunt TX 78024 Office Phone: 830-367-5137. E-mail: jim@gambrell.org.

GAMBRELL, LUCK FLANDERS, corporate financial executive; b. Jan. 17, 1930; d. William Henry and Mattie Moring (Mitchell) Flanders; m. David Henry Gambrell, Oct. 16, 1953; children: Luck G. Davidson, David Henry, Alice Kathleen, Mary G. Rolinson. Grad., St. Mary's Coll., Raleigh, NC, 1948; AB, Duke U., Durham, NC, 1950; diplome d'etudes françaises, L'Institut de Touraine, Tours, France, 1951. Chmn. bd. dirs. LFG Co., 1960—. Mem. State Bd. Pub. Safety, 1981—90, Chpt. Nat. Cathedral, Washington, 1981—85, World Svc. Coun. YWCA, 1965—; chmn. bd. dirs. Student Aid Found., Atlanta, 1992—99; life mem. bd. councilors Carter Ctr., Emory U.; mem. bd. advisors Emory U., Atlanta, 2001—04; coun. mem. Presbytery Greater Atlanta, 1988; elder First Presbyn. Ch., Atlanta; bd. dirs. Atlanta Symphony Orch., 1982—85. Recipient East Ga. Coll. Student Ctr. named in her honor, Swainsboro, Ga., 2002. Mem.: Atlanta Jr. League, Alpha Delta Pi.

GAMBRELL, MICHAEL R., chemicals executive; BSChemE, Rose-Hulman Inst. Tech., Terre Haute, Ind. Chem. engr. rsch. and devel. Dow Chem. Co., Midland, Mich., 1976, mfg. and engring. positions, 1979—88, bus. dir. N.Am. Chlor-Alkali assets bus., 1989, gen. mgr. plastic lined pipe bus., 1992, v.p. ops. L.Am., 1994, corp. dir. tech. ctrs. and global process engring., 1996, global bus. dir. Chlor-Alkali assets bus., 1998, bus. v.p. EDC/VCM & ECU Mgmt., 2000, bus. v.p. Chlor-Vinyl bus., 2003, sr. v.p. chems. and intermediates, 2003, mem. Office of the Chief Exec., 2004—, exec. v.p. basic plastics and chems. portfolio, 2005—. Chmn. bd. dirs. Chlorine Chemistry Coun.; chmn. governing coun. World Chlorine Coun. Office: Dow Chem Co 2030 Dow Ctr Midland MI 48674

GAMBRELL, SARAH BELK, retail executive; b. Charlotte, NC, Apr. 12, 1918; d. William Henry and Mary (Irwin) Belk; m. Charles Glenn Gambrell (dec.); 1 child, Sarah Belk Gambrell Knight. BA, Sweet Briar Coll., 1939; D in Humanities (hon.), Erskine Coll., 1970, U. N.C., Asheville, 1986, Furman U., 1997, Johnson C. Smith U., 2003. Dir. Belk Inc., Charlotte, 1947—2005, dir. emeritus, 2005—. Adv. bd. Erskine Coll. and Sem., Union PSCE, Opera Carolina; trustee Queens U., Charlotte; nat. bd. asset mgmt. and devel. com. YWCA, dir. emeritus, 2007—; hon. trustee Cancer Rsch. Inst.; hon. trustee emeritus Princeton Theol. Sem., NJ; trustee emeritus Furman U., Charlotte Mus. of History; bd. dirs. Parkinson's Disease Found., NYC, NC Cmty. Found., Raleigh, Charlotte Philharmonic Orch., NC Transp. Mus., Spencer, Hist. Rosedale, Charlotte, YWCA of Ctrl. Carolinas; hon. bd. dirs. YWCA, NYC. Recipient Algernon Sydney Sullivan award, Queens U., Charlotte, N.C., Univ. award, U. N.C. Chapel Hill, 1993, Woman of Achievement award, YWCA Charlotte, Mary Elizabeth Francis award, Florence Crittenton Svcs. Mem.: DAR, Fashion Group, Inc. (N.Y.C.), Jr. League Charlotte, Nat. Soc. Colonial Dames. Home: 300 Cherokee Rd Charlotte NC 28207-1908 Office: Belk Inc 2801 W Tyvola Rd Charlotte NC 28217-4500 also: 6100 Fairview Rd Ste 640 Charlotte NC 28210

GAMER, CARLTON EDWIN, composer, music educator; b. Chgo., Feb. 13, 1929; s. Carl Wesley Gamer and Alice Clara Michael; m. Eleanor Everett; 1 child, Michael. MusB, Northwestern U., 1950; MusM, Boston U., 1951. Instr. The Colo. Coll., Colorado Springs, 1954—60, asst. prof., 1960—66, assoc. prof., 1966—74, prof., 1974—94, prof. emeritus, 1994—; vis. lectr., vis. prof. Princeton U., NJ, 1974, 1981, sr. fellow coun. of humanities, 1976—76; vis. prof. U. Mich., Ann Arbor, 1982—82. Adv. coun., dept. music Princeton U., 1987—93; jour. editl. bd. Perspectives of New Music, 1972—. Composer: (instrumental music) Fantasy for Flute, Clarinet and Piano, Organum, Duetude, String Quartet, Fanovar, Sonata for Violin and Piano, New Beginnings, Piano Raga Music, Sonata Breve, From the Gardens of the West, (orchestral music) Arkhe, (vocal music) Aria da Capo, Rilke Songs, Li Po Songs, Choros, There is a Spirit, Star in Clay; contbr. articles to profl. jours. Vice-chmn. Pikes Peak Justice & Peace Commn., Colorado Springs, Colo., 2001—04. Fellow Asia Soc. Fellowship, 1962-1963, MacDowell Colony Fellowship, 1976. Mem.: Am. Music Ctr., Soc. Music Theory, Soc. Composers, Inc. Mem. Soc. Of Friends. Avocations: travel, fitness, languages. Home Phone: 719-475-2188.

GAMET, DONALD MAX, appliance company executive; b. Mapleton, Kans., Feb. 21, 1916; s. Carl Adolph and Pearl May (McClanahan) G.; m. L. Pauline Fleming, Apr. 14, 1938 (dec. Dec. 1981); children: Merilyn Kay Gamet Paris, Carleton Lenoir, Kathy Lynn Gamet Stephenson; m. Marilyn Lang, Jan. 15, 1983. BBA, Ft. Hays State Coll., 1938; MBA, U. Kans., 1939, JD, 1942. CPA, Mo. Staff acct. Arthur Andersen & Co., Kansas City, Mo., 1942-46, mgr., 1946-54, ptnr., 1954-78, mng. ptnr. Kansas City office, 1956-70, vice chmn. tax practices Chgo., 1970-77, sr. ptnr., 1977-78; cons. Kansas City, 1978-84; v.p.-treas. Chgo. Pacific Corp. (merged with Maytag 1989), 1984-85, exec. v.p. fin., 1985-87, spl. cons. to chief exec. officer, 1987-89, ret., 1989. Bd. dirs. ANUHCO, Inc., Overland Park, Kans. Pres., chmn. bd. dirs. Heart Am. United Funds, Met. Kansas City, 1967-68, chmn. spl. reorgn. study com., 1980-84; mem. adv. bd. Salvation Army Kansas City, 1982-84; mem. personnel com. Village United Presbyn. Ch., 1982-84; pres., bd. dirs. Estate Planning Coun. Kans., 1962-63, Minority Supplier's Devel. Coun. Kansas City, 1983-84; bd. dirs., mem. exec. com., treas. Civic Coun. Kansas City, 1967-70; bd. dirs., chmn. long range planning com. Geriatric Resources Corp. Kansas City, 1982-84; bd. dirs. Metro Kansas City C. of C., 1962-70, pres., 1969-70; bd. dirs. Kansas City Indsl. Found., 1968-70, Jr. Achievement Kansas City, 1960-65. Named Boss of Yr., Met. Kansas City Jaycees, 1962; recipient Alumni Achievement award Ft. Hays State Coll., 1969. Mem. AICPA, Kansas City Club. Republican. Home: 12921 Riggs Rd Apt 102 Shawnee Mission KS 66209

GAMMON, JAMES ALAN, lawyer; b. Keokuk, Iowa, Jan. 30, 1934; s. Tench Temme and Helen Dolores Gammon; m. Joanne Mott, Aug. 31, 1957; children— Daniel, Thomas, Matthew, Kelly, Timothy. BS in Commerce cum laude, U. Notre Dame, 1956; JD, Georgetown U., 1959. Bar: D.C. 1959. Assoc. McGrath & McGrath, Washington, 1959-62; ptnr. Molnar & Gammon, Washington, 1962-72; pvt. practice Washington, 1972—76; ptnr. Gammon & Tierney, Washington, 1976, Gammon & Grange, Washington, 1977-89, of counsel, 1989—; pres. Gammon Media Brokers Inc., Washington, 1981—; chmn. Gammon Media Brokers, LLC, Phoenix, 1998—. Mem. Fed. Comms. Bar Assn., Christian Legal Soc., Nat. Assn. Media Brokers (pres. 1989-91). Republican. Avocation: body building. Office: 8280 Greensboro Dr Fl 7 Mc Lean VA 22102-3807 Office Phone: 301-332-0940. E-mail: jag@gg-law.com.

GAMMON, MALCOLM ERNEST, SR., surveying and engineering executive; b. Chattanooga, Tenn., Sept. 7, 1947; s. George A. and Frances Helen (Conway) G.; m. Glenna Dee Shirk, June 5, 1971; children: Malcolm Ernest Jr., Christopher Brian. BS, Miss. State U., 1970. Ops. mgr. Pyburn & Odom, Inc., Baton Rouge, 1970-84; chief exec. officer, prin. owner Hydro Cons., Inc., Baton Rouge, 1984—. Tech. contbr. (textbook) 4567 Review Questions for Surveyors, 11th edit., 1985, Elementary Surveying, 8th edit., 1989. State chmn. La. Trig Star Program, Baton Rouge, 1988-89; mem. adv. bd. La. Math. Coalition. Fellow Am. Congress on Surveying and Mapping (dir., cert. hydrographer, bd. dirs. 1998-2003, hydrographer cert. bd.); mem. Am. Congress on Surveying and Mapping Hydrograher Cert. Bd.; mem. La. Soc. Profl. Surveyors (registered, pres. 1990), Miss. Assn. Profl. Surveyors (registered), Nat. Soc. Profl. Surveyors , Ark. Soc. Profl. Surveyors (registered), Ala. Profl. Land Surveyors (registered). Home: 19021 Saint Clare Dr Baton Rouge LA 70810-7979 Office: Hydro Cons Inc 10275 Siegen Ln Baton Rouge LA 70810-4926 Home Phone: 225-756-4848; Office Phone: 225-766-4422. Business E-Mail: egammon@hydroconsultants.com.

GAMMON, SAMUEL RHEA, III, retired association executive, former ambassador; b. Tex., Jan. 22, 1924; m. Mary Renwick. BA, Tex. A. and M. U., 1946; A.M., Princeton U., 1948, PhD, 1953. Instr. Emory U., 1952-54; joined Fgn. Service, Dept. State, 1954; served in Milan and Palermo, Italy, 1954-58; with Dept. of State, 1959-63; detailed fgn. affairs aide to Vice Pres. Lyndon Johnson, 1963; consul gen. Asmara, Ethiopia, 1964-67; counselor for polit. affairs Rome, 1967-70; detailed USIA dep. asst. dir. for W. Europe, 1970-71; exec. asst. to undersec., 1971-73; dep. exec. sec. State Dept., 1973-75; minister counselor Am. Embassy, Paris, 1975-78; ambassador to Mauritius Port Louis, 1978-80; exec. dir. Am. Hist. Assn., 1981-94, ret., 1994. Pres. Nat. Humanities Alliance, 1986-88; bd. dirs. Consortium Social Sci. Assns., 1981-94, Truman Libr. and Inst., 1982-94, Assn. for Diplomatic Studies, 1986—, Charlottesville Com. on Fgn. Rels., 2006-. Served to Capt. AUS, 1943-46, 1950-52. Mem. Am. Fgn. Svc. Protective Assn. (bd. dirs. 1991-2005, chmn. 1992-2005).

GAMMONS, PETER, columnist, commentator; b. Boston, Apr. 9, 1945; s. Edward Babson and Betty (Allen) G.; m. Gloria Fay Trowbridge, Aug. 24, 1968. BA, U. N.C., 1969. Writer, columnist Boston Globe, 1969-86; sr. writer Sports Illustrated, 1982-90; Major League Baseball studio analyst ESPN, 1988—, columnist, 1990—. Contbr. articles to numerous newspapers; author: (book) Beyond the Sixth Game. Named to Major League Baseball Hall of Fame. Home: 36 Glen Rd Brookline MA 02445-7721 Office: ESPN Sports Television ESPN Plaza Bristol CT 06010-1099

GAMPEL, ELAINE SUSAN, investment company executive, consultant; b. New Haven, Apr. 12, 1950; d. Stanley Irwin and Marion (Levine) G.; m. Alan Joseph Tedeschi, Sept. 9, 1984; children: Zachary Joseph Gampel Tedeschi, Matthew Samuel Gampel Tedeschi. BS in Spl. Edn., Boston U., 1972; MS in Counseling, So. Conn. State U., New Haven, 1975; cert. investment mgmt. analyst, Wharton Sch. Bus., 1990. Spl. edn. tchr. Ansonia (Conn.) Pub. Schs., 1972-77; v.p., investment mgmt. cons. Paine Webber Inc., Denver, 1977-89; v.p. investments Dean Witter Reynolds, Denver, 1989-93, 1st v.p. investments, sr. cons., 1993-2000, sr. v.p. investments, sr. cons., 2000—, wealth advisor, 2002—. Bd. dirs. United Cerebral Palsy of Denver, 1984-93; outside editl. bd. Denver Post, 1991-94; chair investment com. Women's Found. Colo., Denver, 1995-97, treas. 1998, 99, chair bd. trustees, 2002; elected mem. Women's Forum of Colo., 2002; cmty. bd. Denver Nuggets, 1992-95; bd. dirs. Project PAVE, 2003—, Judith Ann Griese Found., 2004-05, Jewish Family Svc., 2006—; mem. investment com. Jewish Family Svc., 2005—. Recipient Women Leaders of Excellence award, Colo. Women's Leadership Coalition, 2003, Women of Distinction award, Miletti coun. Girl Scouts US, 2004. Mem. Investment Mgmt. Cons. Assn. (membership com., cert. com. 1990—), Denver Soc. Security Analysts. Avocations: tennis, running, biking. Office: Morgan Stanley 370 17th St Ste 5100 Denver CO 80202-5651 Office Phone: 303-595-2080. E-mail: elaine.gampel@morganstanley.com.

GAMROTH, ARTHUR PAUL, small business owner; b. Independence, Wis., Jan. 1, 1930; s. George Dominic and Frances Kathleen (Sylla) G.; m. Arline Hellen Leipski, Feb. 14, 1953; children: Shawne HCF, Bradley Paul, Todd Arthur, Timothy Curtis, Gary Mac. Diploma, Milw. Area Tech. Ctr., 1950. Mechanic Bonded Heating, Elm Grove, Wis., 1949-55; real estate salesman Anchor Realty, Waukesha, Wis., 1959-70; v.p. Ablenc, Inc., Waukesha, Wis., 1967—; pres. Energy Mgmt. of Wis., Waukesha, 1977—. Cons. E.M.O.W., Waukesha, 1977—. Designer Sophisticated Mcpl. Recycling Facility with composting capabilities; patentee biomass burner. Lobbyist RDF, Wis., 1987—. With U.S. Army, 1950-52, Korea. Recipient Spl. Recognition award U. Wis., 1986. Mem. Am. Contract Bridge League, Waukesha Bridge Club Am., Eagles. Lodges: Eagles. Republican. E-mail: ablene@yahoo.com, artgmrth1@aol.com.

GAMSON, JOSHUA PAUL, sociology educator, writer; b. Ann Arbor, Mich., Nov. 16, 1962; s. William Anthony and Zelda (Finkelstein) G. BA, Swarthmore Coll., 1985; MA, U. Calif., Berkeley, 1988, PhD, 1992. Asst. editor Moment Mag., Boston, 1985-86; tchr. h.s. The Cambridge Sch., Weston, Mass., 1986-87; instr. U. Calif., Berkeley, 1992, lectr., 1993; asst. prof. Yale U., New Haven, 1993—98, assoc. prof., 1998—2002, U. San Francisco, 2002—. Author: Claims to Fame: Celebrity in Contemporary America, 1994, Freaks Talk Back: Tabloid Talk Shows and Sexual Nonconformity, 1998, Fabulous Sylvester, 2005; contbr. articles to profl. jours. Activist, media coord. Act Up/San Francisco, 1988-90. Spencer fellow Woodrow Wilson Nat. Fellowship Found., 1991-92, Regents-Intern fellow U. Calif., 1987-92, program on non-profit orgns. fellow Yale U., 1994. Mem. Am. Sociol. Assn. (coun. mem. coun. on stats. of lesbians, gays and bisexuals in sociology 1995—, Fund for the Advancement of the Discipline award 1995), Ea. Sociol. Assn. Office: Univ San Francisco 2130 Fulton Street San Francisco CA 94117

GAMST, FREDERICK CHARLES, social anthropologist; b. NYC, May 24, 1936; s. Rangvald Julius and Aida (Durante) G.; m. Marilou Swanson, Jan. 28, 1961; 1 child, Nicole Christina. AA, Pasadena City Coll., 1959; AB, UCLA, 1961; PhD, U. Calif., Berkeley, 1967. Instr. anthropology Rice U., Houston, 1966-67, asst. prof., 1967-71, assoc. prof., 1971-75; prof. dept. anthropology U. Mass., Boston, 1975—2001, chmn. dept. anthropology, 1975-78, assoc. provost for grad. studies, 1978-83, prof. emeritus, 2001—. Cons. in social rels., human factors and ops. to R.R. industry, 1970—; acting dir. Houston Inter-Univ. African Studies Program, 1969-71, Behavioral Sci. Grad. Program, Rice U., 1974-75; mem. Joint Internat. Observer Group (for observation of Ethiopian elections), 1992; mem. com. on human factors for railroads and other fixed guideway transp. sys. Transp. Rsch. Bd., 1999—; adj. prof. anthroplogy U. Wyo., 2001—. Author: Travel and Research in Northwestern Ethiopia, 1965, The Qemant: A Pagan-Hebraic Peasantry of Ethiopia, 1969, Peasants in Complex Society, 1974, The Hoghead: An Industrial Ethnology of the Locomotive Engineer, 1980, Highballing with Flimsies: Working under Train Orders, 1990; editor: Studies in Cultural Anthropology, 1975, Letters from the United States of North America on Internal Improvements, Steam Navigation, Banking, Etc., 1990, Anthropology Quar., Golden Anniversary Spl. Issue on Indsl. Ethnology, 1977, (with Edward Norbeck) Ideas of Culture: Sources and Uses, 1976, Meanings of Work: Consideration for the Twenty-First Century, 1995, Early American Railroads: Franz Anton Ritter von Gerstner's Die Innern Communicationen (1842-1843), 2 vols., 1997, (video documentary) T-Time: The History of Mass Transit in Boston, 1984; contbr. articles and revs. to profl. publs., chpts. to books. Adv. com Quincy Quarries Hist. Site, Met. Dist. Commn. Mass., 1987—2001; bd. dirs. Cheyenne Depot Found., 2002—. N.Y. State Regents scholar 1954-58, UCLA scholar 1959-60, Haynes Found. scholar 1960-61; Woodrow Wilson Nat. fellow 1961-62, Ford Found. Fgn. Area fellow 1962-63, Social Sci. Rsch. Coun. and ACLS Fgn. Area fellow 1963-66; Rice U. rsch. grantee 1967, NSF grantee 1970-72, NIMH grantee 1972-74, others. Fellow AAAS, Am. Anthrop. Assn. (Conrad Arensberg award 1995, Festschrift Session honoring life's work 2002), Soc. Applied Anthropology, Royal Anthrop. Inst. Gt. Britain and Ireland; mem. Sci. Rsch. Soc., Ry. and Locomotive Hist. Soc. (dir., editor 4 vol. Franz Anton Ritter von Gerstner project 1988-), Labor and Employment Rels. Assn., Soc. for History Tech., Lexington Group in Transp. History, Internat. Assn. Railway Operating Officers, Am. Assn. R.R. Supts., Soc. Anthrop. Work (pres. 1984-87, bd. dirs. 1987-90), Internat. Union Anthrop. and Ethnol. Scis. (chmn. curriculum com. Commn. Study of Peace 1983-86), Assn. for Study Lang. in Prehistory (bd. dirs. 1988-), Mass. Tchrs. Assn. (mem. exec. com. Faculty Staff Union 1996-2001), Cheyenne Mus. Depot Mus. Found. (bd. dirs. 2002-, sec. bd. dirs. 2003-04). Home: 5419 Ridge Rd Cheyenne WY 82009-4527 Office: U Mass Dept Anthropology Harbor Campus Boston MA 02125-3393 Office Phone: 617-287-6850. Personal E-mail: fcgamst@aol.com.

GAN, CHENNY QUAN, musician, educator, artist; b. Nanning, Guangxi Province, China, May 11, 1981; arrived in U.S., 1989, naturalized, 2006; d. Haiyan Gan and Grace Gang Wang. BA with honors in Studio Art and Music, Wesleyan Coll., 2002; MusM in Piano Performance, U. N.C., 2004, MM in Accompanying, 2005. One-woman shows include Fort Valley State U. Pettigrew Ctr., Wesleyan Coll., 2000, exhibited in group shows at Winter Arts Festival, Macon, Ga., 2002, Macon Mus. Arts and Scis., 2006, Greensboro Ctr. for Visual Arts. Recipient First Pl. award, Warner Robins Art Assn., 1998, Concerto Competition prize, U. N.C., 2003; Adele Marcus Found. scholar, Wintergreen Music Festival, 2003, Pierce Talent scholar in the Fine Arts, Wesleyan Coll., 1998—2002, Grad. Keyboard scholar, Atlanta Music Club, 2002. Mem.: Mus. Contemporary Art L.A., Weatherspoon Mus., Ga. Music Educators Assn. (winner all state piano auditions 2001), Greensboro Music Tchrs. Assn. (winner young artists competition 2004), Music Tchrs. Nat. Assn., Soc. Ethnomusicology, Coll. Music Soc. (presenter), Am. Musicol. Soc. (Minority Travel scholar 2003), Greensboro Chinese Assn., Phi Kappa Phi (life Grad. fellow 2002). Daoist-Buddhist. Achievements include research in Chinese music notation; Daoist ritual music; the Trobairitz; Gyorgy Ligeti's piano etudes; Zemlinsky's opera Der Kreidekreis and Orientalism; Buddhist temples in Greensboro N.C; speaking English, Mandarin Chinese and German. Avocations: swimming, travel, languages, philosophy, singing. Home Phone: 323-733-6384. Personal E-mail: chenny@iname.com.

GAN, JIANBANG, agricultural studies educator, economist; s. Darui Gan and Xiujiao Cai; m. Hong Liu; children: Steven L., Eric L., David W. BS, Fujian Agr. and Forestry U., 1982; MS, Iowa State U., 1988, PhD, 1990. Postdoctoral rsch. assoc. Iowa State U., Ames, 1991—92; faculty mem. Tuskegee U., 1992—2001, coord. for internat. project devel., 1992—2001, coord. forest resources program, 1998—2001; assoc. prof. Tex. A&M U., College Station, 2001—. Adj. prof. Fujian Agr. and Forestry U., Fuzhou, 2005—; mem. exec. adv. bd., cons. AdventGX, College Station, 2004—; mem. nat. grant rev. panels NSF, USDA; peer grant reviewer NSF, NRC, USDA, McGraw Hill, various sci. jours.; guest assoc. editor Forest Sci.; co-chmn. conf. rsch. roundtable China-US Rels.: Trade, Diplomacy and Rsch., Beijing, 2005; lectr. in field. Assoc. editor: Can. Jour. Forest Rsch.; contbr. articles to profl. jours., ency. Recipient Faculty Outstanding Performance award in Tchg., Tuskegee U., 1997; grantee, Biomass R & D Initiative, 2005—, Joint Fire Sci. Program, 2005—, USDA, 1997—; vis. scholar Grad. scholar, Fujian Overseas Chinese Scholarship Found. Mem.: Tex. Forestry Assn., So. Forest Economics Workers, Soc. Am. Foresters, Xi Sigma Pi, Gamma Sigma Delta (chpt. treas. 1994—96), Sigma Xi. Achievements include research in climate change, bioenergy, trade and the environment, socially disadvantaged forestland owners; natural resource management, economics and policy in China, Senegal, Tanzania, Thailand and The Philippines. Office: Texas A&M U 305 Horticulture/Forest Science Building College Station TX 77843-2138 Home Phone: 979-690-8688; Office Phone: 979-862-4392. Business E-Mail: j-gan@tamu.edu.

GAN, JUIS, interior designer; Diploma in Interior Design, Modern Inst. of Interior Design, Kuala Lumpur, Malaysia, 1996; BFA in Interior Design, Calif. State U., Long Beach, 2006. Freelance designer, Calif., 2001—. Visionary architect The World's First Underwater Museum. Recipient Gold Award Winner, 11th Nat. Furniture Design Competition, 1999, Hon. Mention, IPA Internat. Photography Awards, 2003, Cert. of Merit, Media Art Awards, 2004, 1st Pl. Winner, IPA Internat. Photography Awards, 2004, Hon. Mention, Black and White Spider Awards, 2004, 3rd Pl. Winner, ASID Student Interior Design Competition, ASID, 2005; 1st Pl. Winner, EDPA Found., 2005, DAAG Scholarship Winner, Dramatic Allied Arts Guild, 2005, 2d Pl. Winner, IESLA, 2005. Independent Thinkers. Avocations: photography, filmmaking, sculpting. Home Phone: 714-925-2505. Personal E-mail: chiasso_usa@hotmail.com.

GAN, YONG XUE, materials engineer, educator; b. Gongan, China, May 2, 1965; arrived in US, 1995, naturalized, 2007; s. Xing Ji Gan and Fu Lan Yang; m. Feng Hong Wang, Sept. 2, 1991; children: Bo Jian, Ryan Neil, Jeremy Brian. BS, Hunan U., Changsha, China, 1984; MS, Beihang U., Beijing, China, 1987, D in Engring., 1992; MPhil, Columbia U., NYC, 2004, PhD, 2005. EIT Ala., 2005. Grad. rsch. asst. Beihang U., 1984—87, asst. prof., 1987—92, assoc. prof., 1993—94; vis. rsch. scholar Auburn U., Ala., 1995—97; rsch. assoc. Tuskegee U., Ala., 1997—2002; grad. tchg. asst. Columbia U., 2002—03, grad. rsch. asst., 2003—05; asst. prof. The Cooper Union, NYC, 2005—. Contbr. articles to profl. jours. Durbin grantee, The Cooper Union, 2007. Mem.: ASME. Home: 109-05 72nd Ave Apt 4J Forest Hills NY 11375 Office: The Cooper Union 51 Astor Pl New York NY 10003 Home Phone: +1-646-573-5286; Office Phone: +1-212-353-4310. Office Fax: +1-212-353-4341. Personal E-mail: yongxuegan@yahoo.com. Business E-Mail: gan@cooper.edu.

GANAI, SABHA, surgeon, researcher; b. Royal Oak, Mich., Apr. 23, 1976; d. Zulqarnain Ganai and Mussarat Abidi. BS in Biomed. Engring., U. So. Calif., LA, 1997, MD, 2001; PhD in Molecular and Cellular Biology, U. Mass., Amherst, 2007. Lic. Mass. Bd. of Registration in Medicine, 2004, cert. advanced trauma life support instr. ACS, 2003. Surg. resident Baystate Med. Ctr., Springfield, Mass., 2001—. Contbr. articles to profl. jours. Recipient Significance in Rsch. award, Baystate Med. Ctr., 2006. Mem.: AAAS, ACS (assoc.), Assn. for Acad. Surgery, USC Salerni Collegium, Am. Med. Soc., Soc. of Am. Gastrointestinal Endoscopic Surgeons (assoc.), Airplane Owners and Pilots Assn., Tau Beta Pi Engring. Honor Soc. Islam. Avocations: aviation, writing, arts, guitar, herpetology. Office: Baystate Med Ctr 759 Chestnut St Springfield MA 01199 Office Phone: 413-794-5165. E-mail: sabha.ganai@bhs.org.

GANAS, PERRY SPIROS, physicist; b. Brisbane, Australia, June 20, 1937; came to U.S., 1968, naturalized, 1975; s. Arthur and Lula (Grivas) G. BS, U. Queensland, Australia, 1961; PhD, U. Sydney, 1968. Tchg. fellow U. Sydney, 1967; postdoctoral rsch. assoc., instr. U. Fla., 1968-70, vis. asst. rsch. prof., 1972, vis. assoc. rsch. prof., 1978, vis. assoc. prof. physics, 1979—80, 1981; prof. physics Calif. State U., LA, 1970—2001, emeritus prof., 2001—. Adj. faculty U. So. Calif., 1985-86, East L.A. Coll., 1988-2004; vis. prof. physics UCLA, summer 1987, 91, 92; referee Astrophys. Jour., Astron. and Astrophysics. Contbr. articles to profl. jours. Mem. AAUP, Congress of Faculty Assns., Am. Phys. Soc., Sigma Xi. Home: 11790 Radio Dr Los Angeles CA 90064-3615 Office: Calif State U Physics Dept Los Angeles CA 90032 Office Phone: 323-343-2121. Business E-Mail: pganas@calstatela.edu.

GANAWAY, GEORGE KENNETH, psychiatrist, psychoanalyst, educator, researcher; b. Davenport, Iowa, Mar. 22, 1946; s. Kenneth Joseph and Elizabeth Earl Ganaway; m. Elzada Lawson, Dec. 27, 1969; children: Heather, Erin. BS in Clin. Psychology, Duke U., 1968; MD, Emory U., 1973; grad., Emory Psychoanalytic Inst., 2001. Diplomate Am. Bd. Psychiatry and Neurology; lic. physician, Ga. Resident in psychiatry Emory Affiliated Hosps., Atlanta, 1973-76; pvt. practice in gen. adult and adolescent psychiatry Atlanta, 1976—; regional med. advisor Social Security Disability Program, 1997—; pvt. practice psychoanalysis, 2001—; founder, program dir. Ridgeview Ctr. for Dissociative Disorders, Smyrna, Ga., 1987-96; med. cons. dissociative disorders Ridgeview Inst., 1996—2006; asst. prof. psychiatry Emory U. Sch. Medicine, Atlanta, 1976-80, clin. asst. prof. psychiatry, 1981—, Morehouse Sch. Medicine, Atlanta, 1990—; tchg. faculty Emory Psychoanalytic Inst., 1997—, assoc. tchg. analyst, 2002—. Psychiat. cons. Disability Adjudication br. Social Security Adminstrn., Atlanta, part-time, 1980-87, Douglas County Mental Health Clinic, Douglasville, 1977-81, South Cobb Mental Health Ctr., Austell, Ga., 1978-80, Atlanta Depression Clinic of Ctr. Metabolic Studies, 1976-77, others; ann. chmn. S.E. Regional Conf. Dissociative Disorders, 1987-96; med. staff Ridgeview Inst., 1976-98, courtesy staff, 1999-2006. Asst. editor Dissociation: Progress in Dissociative Disorders, 1988-98; assoc. editor Internat. Jour. Clin. and Exptl. Hypnosis, 1995-96; mem. editl. adv. bd. Insight mag.; editl. reviewer Am. Jour. Psychiatry, Child Abuse and Neglect: The Internat. Jour., Jour. Psychology and Theology, Jour. Nervous and Mental Disease, Dissociation: Progress in the Dissociative Disorders; contbr. articles to profl. jours., chpts. to textbooks of psychiatry. Sci. adv. bd. False Memory Syndrome Found., 1992—. Fellow: Am. Psychiat. Assn. (Disting. fellow), Internat. Soc. for Study of Dissociation (task force on stds. of practice 1991—96); mem.: Internat. Psychoanalytical Assn., Atlanta Psychoanalytic Soc. (chair sci. program com. 2001—03, pres.-elect 2003—05, pres. 2005—07), Ga. Psychiat. Physicians Assn., So. Med. Assn., Am. Psychoanalytic Assn. Avocation: collecting maritime antiques. Office: D-201 5064 Roswell Rd NE Ste 201D Atlanta GA 30342-2266 Office Phone: 404-252-4525. Business E-Mail: gganawa@emory.edu.

GAND, GALE, chef, restaurateur; b. Chgo. married; 1 child. Student, La Varenne, Paris. With Strathallen Hotel, Rochester, NY, Jam's, NYC, Carlos' Restaurant, Chgo., 1987; pastry chef Gotham Bar & Grill, NYC, Pump Room, Chgo., 1987, Stapleford Park, Leicestershire, England, Charlie Trotter's, Chgo., 1993; co-owner Trio, Chgo., 1993—95, Brasserie T, Northfield, 1995—2001, Vanilla Bean Bakery, Chgo., 1996—98; co-owner, exec. pastry chef Tru, Chgo., 1999—. Chef's coun. Chefs for Humanity. Host (TV series) Sweet Dreams, Food Network, 2000—; co-author (with Rick Tramonto, Julia Moskin): (cookbooks) American Brasserie, 1997 (finalist Julia Child Cookbook Awards); co-author: Butter Sugar Flour Eggs: Whimsical, Irresistible Desserts, 1999 (nominee James Beard award in baking and desserts category); co-author: (with Julia Moskin) Gale Gand's Just a Bite, 2001, Gale Gand's Short and Sweet, 2004; co-author: (with Rick Tramonto, Mary Goodbody) Tru: A Cookbook from the Legendary Chicago Restaurant, 2004. Named Top Pastry Chef of Yr., Best of Best Awards, Bon Appetit, 2001; named one of Top 10 Best New Chefs, Food & Wine, 1994, Chicago's 100 Most Influential Women, Crain's Chicago Bus., 2004; recipient Robert Mondavi award for culinary excellence, 1994, James Beard Found. award for outstanding pastry chef, 2001, Outstanding Svc. award, James Beard Found., 2007. Mem.: Culinary Coun., Marshall Field's. Mailing: Tru Restaurant 676 N St Clair St Chicago IL 60611 Office Phone: 312-202-0001.*

GANDARA, DAVID RAYMOND, internist, oncologist, educator; b. Tyler, Tex., 1947; MD, U. Tex. Med. Br., Galveston, 1973. Intern Madigan Med. Ctr., Tacoma, 1973-74, resident internal medicine, 1974-76; fellow hematology-oncology Letterman Army Med. Ctr., San Francisco, 1976-78; assoc. dir. clin. rsch. U. Calif. Davis Cancer Ctr.; prof. medicine, hematology/oncology U. Calif. Davis Med. Ctr. Named one of Top Cancer Specialists for Women, Good Housekeeping mag., 1999, Sacramento's Best Doctors, Sacramento mag., Solano mag., 2005. Fellow ACP; mem. IASLC, MASCC, Am. Soc. Clin. Oncology (past sec.-treas.), Am. Soc. Hematology, Am. Assn. for Cancer Rsch., Southwest Oncology Group (chmn. lung com.). Office: U Calif Davis Cancer Ctr Hematology-Oncology 4501 X St Ste 3016 Sacramento CA 95817 Office Phone: 800-282-3284. Business E-Mail: david.gandara@ucdmc.ucdavis.edu.*

GANDER, JOHN EDWARD, biochemistry educator; b. Roundup, Mont., Mar. 9, 1925; s. Loren Dwight and Blanche Lenore (Mackay) G.; m. Dorothy Alice Hoffman, Jan. 1, 1951; children: Sharon Lee, Peggy Corinne, Linda Kay. BS in Agr, Mont. State U., 1950; MS in Biochemistry, U. Minn., 1954, PhD, 1956. Asst. prof. chemistry Mont. State U., Bozeman, 1955-58; asst. prof. agrl. biochemistry Ohio State U., Columbus, 1958—62, assoc. prof., 1962—64; with U. Minn., St. Paul, 1964—68, assoc. prof. biochemistry, 1968—84; prof., chmn. dept. microbiology and cell sci. U. Fla., 1984-89, prof., 1989-97, prof. emeritus, 1997—; guest scientist Los Alamos Nat. Lab., 2001—. Mem. external site visit rev. teams for Dept. Energy, USDA, NIH, 1979-93. Contbr. chpts. to books, articles to profl. jours. and encys. Served with USAAF, 1943-46. Recipient Research Career award NIH, 1966-71; research grantee USPHS, 1960-69, 74-87; research grantee NSF, 1957-75, 80-84 Mem. AAAS, Am. Soc. Biochemistry and Molecular Biology, Am. Chem. Soc., Am. Soc. Microbiology, Masons. Presbyterian. Home: 4219 Rancho Grande Pl NW Albuquerque NM 87120-5337 Personal E-mail: jgander12@comcast.net.

GANDHI, HAREN S., chemical engineer; b. Calcutta, India, May 2, 1941; m. Yellow Gandhi; 2 children. BSc in Chem. Engring., U. Bombay, 1963; MSc in Chem. Engring., U. Detroit, 1967, D in Chem. Engring., 1971. With Ford Motor Co., Dearborn, Mich., 1967—, rsch. engr., 1967, various rsch. engring. and staff scientist positions, mgr. dept. chem. engring. Ford Rsch. Lab., head emission and fuel economy core team, 1997, Ford tech. fellow. Mem. adv. com. Ministries of Industry and Environment. Contbr. numerous articles to profl. jours. Named Chem. Engr. of Yr., AIChE, 1984; recipient Nat. Medal Tech., US Dept. Commerce, 2002, Crompton Lanchester Medal, Instn. Mech. Engrs., 1988—89, Tech. Innovation award, Discover Mag., 1990, Exxon award Excellence in Catalysis, Nat. Assn. Sci. and Tech., 1994, Partnership New Generation of Vehicles Medal, 1997. Mem. NAE. Achievements include more than 40 U.S. patents; development of the monolithic three-way catalyst; pioneering research in catalysts for alternative fuels, oxygen components in three-way catalysts, poisoning of automotive catalysts, and novel catalyst formulation strategies. Office: 20000 Rotunda Dr Rm 3437 Dearborn MI 48124-3958

GANDHI, NATWAR M., city manager; BCom, LLB, U. Bombay; MBA, Atlanta U.; doctorate in Acctg., La. State U. Asst. prof. acctg. U. Pitts. Grad. Sch. Bus., 1973—76; adj. prof. MBA programs AM. U., Georgetown U., U. Md., 1976—98; spl. asst. to Gov. Jim Florio NJ, 1991; assoc. dir. tax policy and adminstrn. U.S. Gen. Acctg. Office (GAO); dep. CFO Office for Tax and Revenue, 1997—2000; CFO Washington, 2000—. Bd. dirs. Washington Convention Ctr. Authority, Nat. Capital Revitalization Corp., DC Sports and Entertainment Commn., Anacostia Waterfront Corp. Named Washingtonian of Yr., Washingtonian mag., 2006; recipient Meritorious Leadership award, Morris & Gwendolyn Cafritz Found., President's award, Gr. Washington Soc. of CPAs, 2000, Impact award, DC C. of C., 2005, Achievement of Yr. award, Assn. Govt. Accountants, 1999, 2000, Disting. Local Govt. Leadership award, 2007. Fellow: Nat. Acad. Pub. Adminstrn.; mem.: Met. Club Washington DC. Office: Office of CFO 1350 Pennsylvania Ave NW Rm 203 Washington DC 20004 Office Phone: 202-727-2476. Office Fax: 202-727-1643.*

GANDHI, OM PARKASH, electrical engineer; b. Multan, Pakistan, Sept. 23, 1934; came to U.S., 1967, naturalized, 1975; s. Gopal Das and Devi Bai (Patney) G.; m. Santosh Nayar, Oct. 28, 1963; children: Rajesh Timmy, Monica, Lena. BS with honors, Delhi U., India, 1952; MSE, U. Mich., 1957, Sc.D., 1961. Rsch. specialist Philco Corp., Blue Bell, Pa., 1960-62; asst. dir. Cen. Electronics Engring. Rsch. Inst., Pilani, Rajasthan, India, 1962-65, dep. dir., 1965-67; prof. elec. engring., rsch. prof. bioengring. U. Utah, Salt Lake City, 1967—, chmn. elec. engring., 1992-2000. Cons. U.S. Army Med. R&D Command, Washington, 1973-77; cons. to microwave and telecom. industry and govtl. health and safety orgns.; mem. Commns. B and K, Internation Union Radio Sci.; mem. study sect. on diagnostic radiology NIH, 1978-81. Author: Microwave Engineering and Applications, 1981; editor: Engineering in Medicine and Biology mag., 1987, Electromagnetic Biointeraction, 1989, Biological Effects and Medical Applications of Electromagnetic Energy, 1990; contbr. over 200 articles to profl. jours. Recipient Disting. Rsch. award U. Utah, 1979-80. Microwave Pioneer award IEEE-MTT Soc., 2001, Gov.'s medal for sci. and tech. State of Utah, 2002; grantee NSF, NIH, EPA, USAF, U.S. Army, USN, N.Y. State Dept. Health, others. Fellow IEEE (editor spl. issue Procs. IEEE 1980, co-chmn. com. on RF safety stds. 1988-97, Tech. Achievement award Utah sect. 1975, Utah Engr. of Yr. 1995), Am. Inst. for Med. and Biol. Engring.; mem. Electromagnetics Acad., Bioelectromagnetics Soc. (bd. dirs. 1979-82, 87-90, v.p., pres. 1991-94, d'Arsonval award 1995). Office: Univ Utah Dept Elec Engring 3280 Merrill Engring Salt Lake City UT 84112 Office Phone: 801-581-7743. Business E-Mail: gandhi@ece.utah.edu.

GANDHI, SANDIP R., pharmacist; b. Balasinor, Gujarat, India, Nov. 10, 1957; s. Rasiklal Mojilal and Pushpaben Rasiklal Gandhi. BPharm, KMK Coll. Pharmacy, Mumbai, India, 1979; PharmM, U. OK, 1983. Lic. RPH Calif. Apprentice Burroulihs Welcme, Mumbai, India, 1980—81; libr. asst. OU HSC Libr., OKC, 1982—83. Mem. United Food Comml. Worker's Union, 1987—.

GANDHI, SHAAN-CHIRAG C., biochemistry and chemistry scholar; s. Shaan and Kalpana G. BS in Biochemistry, Chemistry, Case Western Reserve Univ., 2007; MSc. student in Integrated Immunology, Oxford Univ., 2007—. Recipient Cancer Training award, Nat. Cancer Inst. of NIH, 2004; Rhodes Scholar. Achievements include receiving rsch. grants from Mem. Sloan-Kettering and NIH; being med. vol. in India and Guyana. Avocation: badminton.*

GANDHI, TARAK, computer engineer; s. Lalit and Rajni Gandhi; m. Vaishali Amin. BTech in Computer Sci. and Engring., Indian Inst. Tech., Bombay, 1991; PhD, Pa. State U., University Park, 2000. Grad. rsch. asst. Pa. State U., 1993—99; vision software engr. Adept Tech. Inc., City of Industry, Calif., 2000—02; postgrad. rschr. U. Calif. San Diego, La Jolla, 2002—06, asst. project scientist, 2006—. Contbr. articles to profl. jours. Recipient Best Rsch. Asst. award, Pa. State U., 1999. Mem.: IEEE. Achievements include generation of dynamic panoramic surround map from a moving vehicle using a pair of omnidirectional cameras; detection of independently moving objects from omnidirectional camera mounted on moving vehicle using parametric ego-motion compensation algorithm; development of panoramic appearance map for reidentification of persons moving between non-overlapping scenes covered by multiple cameras; research in algorithm for calibration of a reconfigurable array of omnidirectional cameras. Office: 9500 Gilman Dr MC 0434 La Jolla CA 92093 Personal E-mail: tarakgandhi@hotmail.com. Business E-Mail: tgandhi@ucsd.edu.

GANDOLF, RAYMOND L., media correspondent; b. Norwalk, Ohio, Apr. 2, 1930; s. Raymond L. Gandolf and Rose (Brenner) Gandolf Neller; m. Blanche Haywood Cholet, Oct. 13, 1956; children— Alexandra, Jessica, Victoria, Amanda, Susanna BS in Speech, Northwestern U., 1951. Actor, 1951-62; writer, producer WCBS-TV, NYC, 1963-65; writer, corr. CBS News, NYC, 1965-82; corr. ABC News-Sports, NYC, 1982-92, host Our World, 1986-87. Panel mem. Dictionary of Contemporary Usage, 1985 Recipient Peabody award U. Ga., 1980, Dupont award Columbia U., 1981, Emmy award, 1987. Mem. AFTRA, Writers Guild Am.

GANDOLFINI, JAMES, actor; b. Westwood, NJ, Sept. 18, 1961; m. Marcy Wudarski, 1999 (div. 2002); 1 child. BA in Comm., Rutgers U., 1983. Actor: (films) A Stranger Among Us, 1992, Mr. Wonderful, 1993, Italian Movie, 1993, True Romance, 1993, Money for Nothing, 1993, Angie, 1994, Terminal Velocity, 1994, Le Nouveau Monde, 1995, Crimson Tide, 1995, Get Shorty, 1995, The Juror, 1995, Night Falls on Manhattan, 1997, She's So Lovely, 1997, Perdita Durango, 1997, Fallen, 1998, The Mighty, 1998, A Civil Action, 1998, Wild Flowers, 1999, 8MM, 1999, A Whole New Day, 1999, The Mexican, 2001, The Man Who Wasn't There, 2001, The Last Castle, 2001, Surviving Christmas, 2004, Stories of Lost Souls, 2005, Romance & Cigarettes, 2005, Lonely Hearts, 2006, All the King's Men, 2006, Club Soda, 2006; (TV films) 12 Angry Men, 1997; (TV series) Gun, 1997, The Sopranos, 1999—2007 (Emmy award best actor drama, 2000, 2001, 2003, Golden Globe best actor drama, 2000, Screen Actors Guild award best actor drama, 2000, 2003, TV Critics Assoc. award, 1999, 2000, 2001); (Broadway plays) A Streetcar Named Desire; led Mardi Gras parade, New Orleans, 2007. Named one of Top 20 Entertainers of 2001, E!; recipient Joe DiMaggio award, Xaverian HS, 2005. Office: c/o United Talent Agy 9560 Wilshire Blvd Ste 500 Beverly Hills CA 90212

GANDSEY, LOUIS JOHN, petroleum and environmental consultant; b. Greybull, Wyo., May 19, 1921; s. John Wellington and Leonora (McLaughlin) G.; m. Mary Louise Alviso, Nov. 10, 1945; children: Mary M., Catherine K., John P., Michael J., Laurie A. AA, Compton Jr. Coll., 1941; BS, U. Calif., Berkeley, 1943; M in Engring., UCLA, 1958. Registered profl. engr., Calif. With Richfield Oil Corp., LA, 1943-65, process engr., foreman, mfg. coord., 1943-61, project leader process computer control, 1961-63, light oil per. supt., 1963-64, refinery supt., 1964-65; mgr. planning Richfield div. Atlantic Richfield Co., LA, 1966-68, mgr. evaluation products div., 1968-69, gen. mgr. supply and transp. Chgo., 1969-71, mgr. planning and mgmt. sci. NYC, 1971, mgr. supply and transp. LA, 1971-72, mgr. coordination and supply, 1972-75, mgr. domestic crude, 1975-77; v.p. refining Lunday-Thagard Oil Co., South Gate, Calif., 1977-82; petroleum cons. World Oil Corp., LA, 1982-85; gen. petroleum cons., 1986—. Instr. chem. and petroleum tech. L.A. Harbor Coll., 1960-65; cons. on oil crops, Austria, 1991; U.S. del. in environ. affairs to Joint Inter-Govtl. Com. for Environ. Protection, USSR, 1991, asphalt tech. to Joint Inter-Govtl. Com. for Highway Design CWS, 1992; U.S. del. Econ. and Environ. Affairs, Portugal, Spain, 1994, Hist. & Econ. Affairs, Mexico, 1995, Basque Country, Spain, 1996. Contbr. articles to profl. jours. Served with C.E., AUS, 1944-45. Mem. AICE, Am. Chem. Soc., Calif. Soc. Profl. Engrs. Home: 2340 Neal Spring Rd Templeton CA 93465-8413 Personal E-mail: marjon@tcsn.net.

GANDY, GERALD LARMON, rehabilitation counseling educator, psychologist, writer; b. Thomasville, Ga., Feb. 9, 1941; s. Larmon Brinkley and Ruby Wylene (Vickers) G.; m. Patricia Kay Haltiwanger, Jan. 22, 1966. BA, Fla. State U., 1963; MA, U. S.C., 1968, PhD, 1971. Lic. profl. counselor, Va.; lic. clin. psychologist, Va.; nat. cert. rehab. counselor; nat. cert. counselor; nat. registered psychologist; cert. profl. qualification in psychology Assn. of State and Provincial Psychology Bds. Profl. counselor U. S.C. Counseling Ctr., Columbia, 1968-70; counseling psychologist VA Regional Office, Columbia, 1970-75, chief counseling psychologist, 1974-75; ind. cons., prof. emeritus Med. Coll. Va., Va. Commonwealth U., Richmond, 1996—, prof., program dir., 1975-95. Chair nat. com. on undergrad. rehab. edn. Nat. Coun. on Rehab. Edn., 1984-89; mem. numerous state and govt. adv. coms., 1970—; cons. in field. Author: Mental Health Rehabilitation, 1995; co-author: Rehabilitation and Disability, 1990; co-author/editor: Rehabilitation Counseling and Services, 1987, Counseling in the Rehabilitation Process, 1999; co-editor: International Rehabilitation, 1980, 89; contbr. numerous articles to profl. jours. Faculty pres. Sch. of Community and Pub. Affairs, VA Commonwealth U., 1989-93. Capt. U.S. Army, 1963-66. Recipient Disting. Svc. award Sch. of Community and Pub. Affairs, 1988, School and U. Leadership award, 1993. Fellow Internat. Acad. of Behavioral Medicine, Counseling and Psychotherapy (diplomate); mem. APA, ACA, World Fedn. for Mental Health, Phi Kappa Phi. Home and Office: Highland Springs 300 Southern Ct Richmond VA 23075-1519 Office Phone: 804-737-6089. Business E-Mail: ggandy@vcu.org.

GANDY, H. CONWAY, retired judge, state official; b. Washington, Nov. 3, 1934; s. Hoke and Anne B. (Conway) G.; m. Carol Anderson, Aug. 29, 1965; children: Jennifer, Constance, Margaret. BA, Colo. State U., 1962; JD, U. Denver, 1968. Bar: Colo. 1969, U.S. Dist. Ct. Colo. 1969. Pvt. practice, Ft. Collins, Colo., 1969-81; adminstrv. law judge divsn. adminstrv. hearings State of Colo., Denver, 1981-99. Bd. dirs. Foothills-Gateway Rehab. Ctr., 1970-80, Colo. State Bd. Dental Examiners, 1976-81; Dem. candidate for Colo. Senate, 1974, dist. atty., 1976; trustee Internat. Bluegrass Music Assn. Trust Fund, 1990—; pres. Colo. chpt. Nat. Assn. Adminstrv. Law Judges, 1985-86. With USN, 1954-58. Mem. Sertoma (Centurion award 1973, Tribune award 1975, Senator award 1977, 79, sec. Honor club 1977-78, pres. Ft. Collins club 1978-79, pres. Front Range club 1988-89). Home: 724 Winchester Dr Fort Collins CO 80526-2636 Personal E-mail: hcgcag@comcast.net.

GANDY, JAMES THOMAS, meteorologist, entrepreneur; b. Memphis, Tenn., Nov. 25, 1952; s. Thomas Marion and Sible Christaline (McBride) G.; m. Ann Cuppia, Apr. 12, 1986. BS, Fla. State U., 1974; postgrad., U. S.C. Meteorologist Sta. WREG-TV (CBS affiliate), Memphis, 1975-77; staff meteorologist Sta. KTVY-TV (NBC affiliate), Oklahoma City, 1977-82; dir. ops. Weather Data, Inc., Wichita, Kans., 1982-84; meteorologist Kans. State Network (NBC affiliate), Wichita, 1982-84; chief meteorologist Sta. WIS-TV (NBC affiliate), Columbia, SC, 1984-98; pres. JAG Corp. of S.C. dba Cartoon Connection, 1997—; cons. meteorologist Gannett TV, Arlington, Va., 1998—; writer, cons. The State Newspaper, Columbia, SC, 1999—. Guest lectr. U. S.C., Columbia, 1991, 95, 98; writer, cons. The State Newspaper, Columbia, S.C., 1999—. Named Best TV Weather Forecaster, The State Newspaper, Columbia, S.C., 1993, Best TV Weather Personality, Columbia Met. Mag., 1994, 95, 96, 97, 98. Mem. AAAS, Am. Meteorol. Soc. (TV Seal of Approval 1985, Memphis chpt. sec. 1976-77, chmn. 1977, Ctrl. Okla. chpt. sec.-treas. 1979, 82, pres. 1980, Palmetto chpt. v.p. 1988-89, 97-98, pres. 1989-90, 98-99), Nat. Weather Assn., Planetry Soc. (charter mem.), N.Y. Acad. Scis., Order Internat. Fellowship (charter). Home and Office: 507 Old Woodlands Rd Columbia SC 29209-2024

GANDY, SAM, neurologist, neuroscientist, educator; b. Chesterfield, SC, Nov. 3, 1956; s. Sam Evans Gandy and Millie Frances King; m. Michelle E. Ehrlich, Feb. 7, 1987. BS in Chemistry summa cum laude, Charleston So. U., SC, 1976; MD, PhD in Molecular and Cellular Biology, Med. U. SC, 1982. Diplomate Am. Bd. Psychiatry and Neurology. Intern dept. medicine Presbyn. Hosp., NYC, 1982—83; vis. clin. fellow Coll. Physicians and Surgeons Columbia U., Columbia-Presbyn. Med. Ctr., NYC, 1982—83; resident and clin. assoc. neurology NY Hosp.-Cornell Med. Ctr., NYC, 1983—86; rsch. assoc. lab. molecular and cellular neuroscience Rockefeller U., NYC, 1986—91, asst. prof. lab. molecular and cellular neuroscience, 1991—92; asst. prof., lab. dir., asst. attending neurologist dept. neurology and neuroscience NY Hosp.-Cornell Med. Ctr., NYC, 1992—93, assoc. prof., lab. dir., assoc. attending neurologist dept. neurology and neuroscience, 1993—97; rsch. scientist Nathan S. Kline Rsch. Inst. Psychiat. Rsch. and prof. psychiatry and cell biology NYU Sch. Medicine, Orangeburg and NYC, 1997—2001; dir. Farber Inst. Neurosciences and prof. dept. neurology dept. biochemistry and molecular biology Thomas Jefferson U., Phila., 2001—07; prof. neurology and psychiatry Mt. Sinai Sch. Medicine, NYC, 2007—, Sinai prof. Alzheimer's rsch., 2007—. Ad hoc site visit mem. Nat. Inst. Neurol. Diseases and Stroke, 1993; dir. molecular basis of human neurol. diseases Cold Spring Harbor Labs, 1996—; adj. prof. Rockefeller U., NYC, 1997—; vis. disting. prof. U. We. Australia, Perth, 1999—2000; eminent scholar Ga. Rsch. Alliance, 2007—. Assoc. editor Alzheimer's Disease and Associated Disorders, 2003, cons. editor Jour. Clin. Investigation, 2003, mem. editl. adv. bd. Alzheimer's Disease and Associated Disorders, 1992—, Neurodegenerative Diseases, 2003; contbr. articles to numerous profl. jours.; reviewer in field, investigator in field. Fellow, Huntington's Disease Found., 1986—87, Glorney-Raisbeck fellow, NY Acad. Medicine, 1986—87. Mem.: Am. Fedn. Aging Rsch. (mem. nat. sci. adv. coun. 1995, mem. rsch. com. 1996—2001), Fisher Found. Alzheimer's (chair sci. adv. bd. 2001—03), Alzheimer's Assn. (chair nat. med. and sci. adv. coun. 2005—), Rotary (chair CART grant award com. 2000—05). Home: 616 S American St Philadelphia PA 19147 Office: Dept Neurology Mt Sinai Sch Medicine Annenberg Bldg Rm 14 60 1 Gustave L Levy Pl Box 1137 New York NY 10029 Personal E-mail: samgandy@earthlink.net.

GANEK, DAVID KENT, investor; s. Howard L. and Judie Ganek; m. Danielle DiGiacomo, Oct. 13, 1990; children: Harrison, Nicholas. Grad., Franklin & Marshall Coll., 1985. Risk arbitrage trader Donaldson Lufkin & Jenrette, NYC; ptnr. SAC Capital Advisors LLC, Stamford, Conn.; co-founder, prin. Level Global Investors LP, Greenwich, Conn., 2003—. Named one of Top 200 Collectors, ARTnews mag., 2004, 2006, Top Billionaire Art Collectors, Forbes Mag., 2005. Avocation: Collector contemporary art & photography. Office: Level Global Investors LP 537 Steamboat Rd Greenwich CT 06830*

GANEM, BRUCE, chemistry educator; b. Boston, Feb. 7, 1948; s. Emil J. and Arlene C. Ganem; m. Beth Carlson, June 20, 1987. BA, Harvard U., 1969; PhD, Columbia U., 1972-73. Postdoctoral fellow Stanford U., 1973-74; asst. prof. chemistry Cornell U., Ithaca, NY, 1974-79, assoc. prof., 1979-80, prof., 1980-93, Franz and Elisabeth Roessler prof. chemistry, 1993—, J. Thomas Clark prof. entreprenurship, chmn. dept. chemistry, 1993—. Cons. Purdue Pharma, 1993-94, Parke-Davis, 1996—, Genencor Internat., 1992-94, Cordis Corp., 1993—, Magainin Pharm., 1996—, Ciba-Geigy Corp., 1978—; mem. sci. adv. bd. LeukoSite, Inc., 1994—; chief scientific officer KensaGroup, LLC; developer of The World of Chemistry, 1991, created Chemistry 404, Entrepreneurship in Chemical Enterprise, Cornell U.; scientific advisor in field; lectr. in field. Asst. editor Chemtracts, 1989—; mem. adv. bd. Jour. Organic Chemistry, 1987-91; cons. editor VCH Pubs., 1987—; contbg. editor Cornell Mag., 1992—; N.Am. exec. editor Tetrahedron Letters; mem. editl. bd. Canadian Journal of Chemistry, Ency. Analytical Chemistry; consulting chemistry editor 1999 Encarta World English Dictionary; contbr. articles to profl. jours.; patentee in field. Recipient Arthur C. Cope Scholar award, 1996, Nat. Catalyst award, Chem. Manufacturers Assn., 1999. Mem. Am. Chem. Soc.(award for creative invention, 2007), Chem. Soc. London. Office: Cornell U Coll Arts and Sciences Dept Chemistry 330 Baker Lab Ithaca NY 14853 Office Phone: 607-255-7360. Office Fax: 607-255-6318. Business E-Mail: bg18@cornell.edu.*

GANEM, DONALD E., immunologist; AB, MA, Harvard U., 1972, MD, 1977. Asst. prof. microbiollogy, immunology and medicine U. Calif., San Francisco, 1982—88, assoc. prof. microbiology and medicine, 1988—90, prof. microbiology and medicine, 1990—, vice-chair, Dept. Microbiology & Immunology, 1995—; assoc. investigator Howard Hughes Med. Inst., San Francisco, 1991—94, investigator, 1995—. Recipient Soma Weiss award for med. student rsch., Harvard Med. Sch., 1975, Leon Resnick prize for rsch., 1977, Kaiser award for excellence in basic sci. tchr., 1986, Acad. Senate Tchg. award, U. Calif., 1986, 2d Yr. Students' Tchg. award for small group tchg., 1986, 2d Yr. Students' Tchg. award for excellence in lecturing, 1987, 1989, 1991; scholar Harkness scholar, Harvard Med. Sch., 1972. Fellow: Am. Acad. Arts and Scis.; mem.: Am. Soc. Clin. Investigation (v.p.

1997), Assn. Am. Physicians, Inst. of Medicine (life), Am. Acad. Microbiology, Alpha Omega Alpha. Office: UCSF Box 0552 San Francisco CA 94143-0552 Office Phone: 415-476-2826. Office Fax: 415-476-0939. E-mail: ganem@cgl.ucsf.edu.

GANETZKY, BARRY S., geneticist, science educator; PhD, U. Wash., 1976. Postdoctoral rschr. Calif. Inst. Tech., 1976—79; faculty to prof. genetics and med. genetics U. Wis., Madison, 1979—, Steenbock prof. biol. scis. Bd. dirs. Joint Steering Com. Pub. Policy. Contbr. articles to sci. jours.; adv. bd.: Jour. Neurogenetics. Recipient Career Devel. award, NIH, McKnight Neuroscience Devel. award, 1991—93; grantee Klingenstein fellowship in neurosciences, 1987. Fellow: AAAS; mem.: Genetics Soc. Am. (pres.), NAS. Achievements include discovering the importance of the Golgi apparatus in the development of Drosophila. Office: 4120 Genetics Biotechnology Ctr 425 Henry Mall Madison WI 53706 E-mail: ganetzky@wisc.edu.

GANG, JEANNE, architect; b. 1964; BS with honors in Arch., U. Ill., Urbana-Champaign, 1986; MArch with distinction, Harvard U., 1993. Registered arch., Ill. With Office Met. Architecture/Rem Koolhaas, Rotterdam, Netherlands; sr. designer Booth Hansen Archs., Chgo.; founder, prin. Studio Gang Archs., Chgo., 1997—. Adj. assoc. prof. Ill. Inst. Tech., Chgo.; facilitator Archeworks. Prin. works include Starlight Theatre at Rock Valley Coll., Rockford, Ill., Chinese-Am. Cmty. Ctr., Chgo., Marble Curtain, Masonry Variations Exhbn., Washington. Named one of 25 Women to Watch, Crain's Chgo. Bus., 2007. Mem.: AIA. Office: Studio Gang Archs 1212 N Ashland Ave Ste 212 Chicago IL 60622 Office Phone: 773-384-1212. Office Fax: 773-384-0231. E-mail: jgang@studiogang.net.*

GANG, ROBERT C., lawyer; b. Huntington, WVa., Jan. 19, 1948; AB in history, Princeton Univ., 1969; JD, Univ. Va., 1972. Bar: RI 1972, Mass. 1985, Fla. 1986, US Dist. Ct. (RI dist.) 1973. Shareholder, co-chair nat. public fin. practice Greenberg Traurig LLP, Miami. Dir. Fla. Grand Opera. Mem.: Fla. Bar Assn., Nat. Assn. Bond Lawyers. Office: Greenberg Traurig LLP 1221 Brickell Ave Miami FL 33131 Office Phone: 302-579-0886. Office Fax: 305-961-5886. Business E-Mail: gangr@gtlaw.com.

GANGEMI, COLUMBUS RUDOLPH, JR., lawyer, educator; b. Phila., Aug. 6, 1947; BA, Villanova U., 1969, JD, 1973; doctoral fellow, Temple U., 1970. Bar: Ill., U.S. Dist. Ct. Ill. (no. dist.), U.S. Supreme Ct., U.S. Ct. Appeals (1st, 3rd, 5th-8th, 10th, 11th cir.). Assoc. to mng. ptnr. Winston & Strawn LLP, Chgo., 1973—, nat. head labor and employment rels. practice, mem. exec. com. Spl. Ill. asst. atty. gen. 1991-94; adj. prof. Ill. Benedictine Coll., Lisle, Ill., 1988-1995; instr. Nat. Inst. Trial Advocacy Northwestern U.; mem. labor and employee rels. com. Chgo. Assn. Commerce and Industry, 1979-90. Contbr. articles to profl. jours. Bd. dirs. Ill. State C. of C.; v.p., bd. dirs. Easter Seal Soc. Chgo., 1983-89. Fellow Coll. Labor and Employment Lawyers; mem. ABA (nat. labor rels. bd. practice com. 1976-), Chgo. Bar Assn. Republican. Office: Winston & Strawn LLP 35 W Wacker Dr Chicago IL 60601-9703 Office Phone: 312-558-5811. Office Fax: 312-558-5700. E-mail: cgangemi@winston.com.

GANGL, KENNETH R., automotive executive; Grad., U. Ill., Urbana-Champaign, 1967. Pres. CNH Capital Am. LLC; pres., CEO Case Credit Corp.; v.p. fin. svcs. PACCAR, Bellevue, Wash., 1999—2005, sr. v.p., 2005—; bd. dirs. PACCAR Fin. Corp. Mem. bus. adv. coun. U. Ill. Urbana-Champaign. Office: PACCAR PO Box 1518 Bellevue WA 98009*

GANGOPADHYAY, ABHIJIT, geophysicist; s. Mihir Kumar and Asha Gangopadhyay; m. Cutie Vahali, Nov. 26, 2004; 1 child, Sana Vahali. BSc with honors, U. Calcutta, 1996; MSc in Tech., Indian Sch. Mines, Dhanbad, India, 1999; MS, U. S.C., Columbia, 2001, PhD, 2005. Rsch. asst. geol. sci. U. S.C., Columbia, 1999—2005, instrnl. asst., coord. geol. sci., 1999—2005; fellow U. Tex., Inst. Geophysics, Austin, 2006—. Editl. adv. bd. mem.: Sci. Jour. Internat., 2006—; contbr. articles to profl. jours. Mem.: European Assn. Geoscientists and Engrs. (reviewer 2006—), Seismol. Soc. Am. (co-convener ea. sect. 2002), Geol. Soc. Am., Am. Geophys. Union, Soc. Exploration Geophysicists (assoc.; reviewer 2006—). Office: Univ Tex Inst Geophysics 10100 Burnet Rd JJ Pickle Research Campus Bldg 196 Austin TX 78758 Home Phone: 512-965-8497; Office Phone: 512-471-0388. Office Fax: 512-471-8844. Personal E-mail: abhijit29208@gmail.com. Business E-Mail: abhijit@ig.utexas.edu.

GANGOPADHYAY, ARUP, research scientist; s. Amal Kumar and Shanti Gangopadhyay; m. Gopa Banerjee, Dec. 5, 1986; children: Payel, Moynakh. B Tech., Bengal Engring. Coll., Shibpur, India, 1979; M Tech., Indian Inst. Tech., Kanpur, 1982; PhD, U. Minn., Mpls., 1985. Postdoctoral rschr. Northwestern U., Evanston, Ill., 1985—88; guest scientist NIST, Gaithersburg, Md., 1988—89; tech. expert Ford Rsch. and Advanced Engring., Dearborn, Mich., 1989—2003, tech. leader, 2003—. Contbr. articles to profl. jours. Pres. Bichitra Inc, Bloomfield Hills, Mich., 2004—05. Recipient Disting. award, Bichitra Inc., 2005, Tech. Achievement award, Ford Motor Co., Edmond E. Bisson award, Tribology Trans., 2004, Best Written Contbn. award, Jour. Engring. Tribology, 2004. Fellow: Soc. Tribologists and Lubrication Engrs. (bd. dirs. Detroit sect. 1996—, mem. ann. meeting program com. 2003—, Disting. Svc. award 1999); mem.: ASME (mem. awards and honors com. 2000—03), Bichitra Inc. Achievements include patents for 5 innovations in the area of friction, wear and lubrication. Office Phone: 313-322-6986.

GANGSTAD, JOHN ERIK, lawyer; b. New Brunswick, NJ, May 16, 1948; s. Edward Otis and Ruth Margaret (Fletcher) G.; m. Cynthia Diane Coffman, July 5, 1974; children: Allison, Erik, Amy. BA, U. Tex., 1970, JD, 1974. Bar: Tex. 1974, U.S. Dist. Ct. (no. dist.) Tex. 1974. Assoc. Turner, Hitchins, McInnery, Webb & Hartnett, Dallas, 1974-76, ptnr., 1977-81, Brown McCarroll & Oaks Hartline, L.L.P., Austin, Tex., 1982-2000, Bickerstaff, Heath et al., Austin, 2000—. Partnership com. State Bar Tex., 1981-98. Bd. dir. Found. for the Homeless, Austin, 1988—. With USNG. Mem. ABA, Tex. Bar Assn., Order of Coif. Presbyterian. Avocations: golf, reading. Home: 7924 Cobblestone Dr Austin TX 78735 Office: Bickerstaff Heath et al 816 Congress Ave Ste 1700 Austin TX 78701-2443 Home Phone: 512-291-2868; Office Phone: 512-404-7827. E-mail: jgangstad@bickerstaff.com.

GANGULY, ANANDA ROOP, business management educator; b. Calcutta, India, Oct. 19, 1963; came to U.S., 1988; s. Purna Nanda and Kalyani Ganguly; m. Dianne Hammes, July 4, 2003. B Comm. with honors, U. Calcutta, 1985; PhD, U. Pitts., 1995. Part-time lectr. U. Pitts., 1991-95; lectr. U. Ill., Champaign/Urbana, 1995, asst. prof., 1995—2004; assurance rsch. fellow Assurance and Adv. Svcs. Ctr., KPMG LLP, 1999-2000; vis. asst. prof. Purdue U., 2004—. Mem., cons. Round Table Group, 1997—; session chair, conf. organizer in field; ad-hoc reviewer Am. Acct. Assn., Acctg. Rev., Contemporary Acctg. Rsch., Mgmt. Sci., 1996—; faculty advisor undergrad. case-study competitions Deloitte and Touche, 1995—; cons. new accountancy curriculum devel. and implementation Nanyang Tech. U., Singapore, 2000-01. Contbr. articles to profl. jours. Mem. focus groups Deloitte Touche Tohmatsu, Pitts., 1994; faculty mentor summer rsch. opportunities program for minority students U. Ill., 1997, 99, 2002. Grantee/fellow Case Devel., 1993, Arthur Andersen & Co. Found., 1994, U. Pitts., 1996, U. Ill., 1997, Caterpillar Inc., 1998. Mem. Am. Acctg. Assn. (doctoral consortium fellow 1994), Am. Econ. Assn., Soc. for Computational Econs., Soc. for Judgment and Decision Making, Mensa. Avocations: creative writing, computers, chess, photography, target shooting. Home Phone: 765-464-8368; Office Phone: 765-494-0701. E-mail: argangul@purdue.edu, aadro2@aol.com.

GANGWAL, RAKESH, air transportation executive; b. Calcutta, India, July 25, 1953; arrived in U.S., 1977, permanent resident; s. K. P. and C. D. Gangwal; m. Shobha Agarwal, Mar. 16, 1983. ME, Indian Inst. Tech., 1975; MBA, U. Pa., 1979. With cen. planning dept. Philips India Ltd., Calcutta, 1975-77; fin. analyst Ford Motor Co., Dearborn, Mich., 1979-80; assoc. Booz, Allen & Hamilton, Chgo., 1980-84; mgr. strategic planning United Airlines, Chgo., 1984-85, dir. flight bus. plans, 1985-86, v.p. flight adminstrn., 1986-87, v.p. revenue mgmt., 1987-94; exec. v.p. planning and devel. Air France, 1994-96; pres., COO U.S. Airways Group Inc., Arlington, Va., 1996—98, pres., CEO, 1998—2001; chmn., pres., CEO Worldspan Technologies Inc., Atlanta, 2003—. Bd. dir. Petsmart Inc., OfficeMax Inc. Office: Worldspan Technologies 3000 Galleria Pkwy NW Atlanta GA 30339*

GANGWISCH, JAMES EDWARD, social worker, researcher; b. South Bend, Ind., Sept. 22, 1963; s. Robert Lee Roy and Edna May Gangwisch. MBA, Ohio State U., Columbus, 1993; MSW, U. Mich., Ann Arbor, 1995; PhD, Columbia U., NYC, 2003. Diplomate clin. social worker NASW; LCSW NY; lic. marriage and family therapist Mich., cert. alcoholism and substance abuse counselor NY. Zone mgr. Lincoln-Mercury divsn. Ford Motor Co., Detroit, 1989—95; psychotherapist St. John Health Sys., Detroit, 1996—99; postdoc. fellow Columbia U., 2003—06; asst. prof. Columbia U. Coll. P&S, 2006—. Nat. Rsch. Svc. awardee, NIMH, 1999—. Mem.: N.Am. Assn. for Study of Obesity. Achievements include research in short sleep duration as a risk factor for obesity and hypertension. Office: Columbia Univ Rm 5211 Mailbox # 2 1051 Riverside Dr New York NY 10032 Home: 120 Haven Ave Apt 46 New York NY 10032 Office Phone: 212-543-4289. Office Fax: 212-543-6176.

GANIS, SIDNEY, film company executive, producer; b. Jan. 8, 1940; Sr. v.p. Lucasfilm; pres. worldwide mktg. Paramount Pictures, pres. motion picture group; various positions including pres. worldwide mktg. Columbia/TriStar Motion Pictures; vice chmn. Columbia Pictures. Founder Out of the Blue Entertainment. Actor: (films) All the President's Men, 1976, Little Nicky, 2000, Anger Management, 2003, Montgomery West and the Wings of Death, 2003, Click, 2006; actor, prodr.: Mr. Deeds, 2002; Akeelah and the Bee, 2006; exec. prodr.: (TV films) Great Movie Stunts: Raiders of the Lost Ark, 1981, The Making of Raiders of the Lost Ark, 1981, The Making of Indiana Jones and the Temple of Doom, 1984; prodr.: (films) Deuce Bigalow: Male Gigolo, 1999, Big Daddy, 1999, The Master of Disguise, 2002. Mem.: Acad. Motion Picture Arts and Scis. (bd. govs. 1973—77, 1979—81, 1992—, pres. 2005—). Office: Acad Motion Picture Arts and Scis 8949 Wilshire Blvd Beverly Hills CA 90211-1972

GANLEY, CHARLES JAMES, federal agency administrator, internist; b. Oct. 25, 1954; BS in Chemistry, U. Pitts.; MD, Hahnemann Univ. Med. Coll., Phila., 1981. Cert. Internal Medicine, 1984. Resident tng., internal medicine Hahnemann Hosp.; fulfilled Pub. Health Svc. obligation; fellowship, clin. pharmacology Cornell U. Med. Ctr.; med. reviewer, divsn. cardio-renal drug products FDA, Md., 1989, med. team leader, Divsn. Cardio-Renal Drug Products Md., dir., Over-the-Counter Drug Products (reorganized into the Office of Nonprescription Drug Products) Md., 1999—2005, dir., Office of Nonprescription Drug Products) Md., 2005—. Office: Office Nonprescription Products Ctr for Drug Evaluation and Rsch FDA 10903 New Hampshire Ave WO22 Silver Spring MD 20903

GANLEY, OSWALD HAROLD, retired director; b. Amsterdam, The Netherlands, Jan. 28, 1929; came to U.S., 1947, naturalized, 1952; s. Eric Harold and Emily (Auerbach) G.; m. Gladys Dickens, Sept. 3, 1950; children: Robert C., Delia A. AB, Hope Coll., 1950; MS, PhD, U. Mich., 1953; MPA, Harvard U., 1965. Cert. physician asst. Rsch. asst. Walter Reed Inst., 1953-55; rsch. assoc. Merck Inst. Therapeutic Rsch., Rahway, NJ, 1955-60; asst. dir. internat. rels. Merck, Sharp and Dohme Rsch. Labs., Rahway, 1960-64; head tech. div. Bur. Internat. Sci. and Tech. Affairs, State Dept., 1965-66, head European affairs, 1966-69; sci. attaché Am. Embassy, Rome and Bucharest, 1969-73; dir. Soviet and Eastern European sci. and tech. affairs State Dept., Washington, 1973-75; diplomatic advisor to sci. adv. to pres. Washington, 1973-78; dep. asst. sec. for tech. affairs State Dept., Washington, 1975-78; rsch. assoc. John F. Kennedy Sch. Govt. Harvard U., Cambridge, Mass., 1978-80, lectr. pub. policy, 1980—94; exec. dir. Harvard Program Info. Resources Policy, 1980-94; physician assoc. in cardiology Med. Ctr. Duke U., Durham, 1997—2000, ret., 2000. With The Healing Place of Wake County Clinics, 2001—; prin. investigator rsch. N.C. Physicians Health Program, 2002—, bd. dir., 2002—; lectr. in field. Author: To Inform or to Control?, 1982, 2d edit., 1989, The Global Political Impact of VCRs, 1987; contbr. articles to sci. jours. Bd. dirs. Jaycees, 1958-60, Am. Hosp., Rome, Fulbright Commn., 1970-73, Ctr. Info. Policy Rsch., 1992—; dir. pub. rels. CD, Plainfield, N.J., 1962-64. Served with AUS, 1953-55, USPHS Res., 1956-84. Sci. and Pub. Policy fellow Harvard U., 1964-65 Fellow Am. Acad. Physician Assts., Am. Acad. Microbiology; mem. Am. Physiol. Soc., Am. Soc. Microbiology, Assn. Mil. Surgeons, N.C. Med. Soc., Sigma Xi. Clubs: Circolo Catoniere Tevereremo (Rome); Cosmos; Harvard (N.Y.C.). Home: 408 N Estes Dr Chapel Hill NC 27514-7629 Office Phone: 919-838-9800.

GANN, PAMELA BROOKS, academic administrator; b. 1948; BA, U. NC, 1970; JD, Duke U., 1973. Bar: Ga. 1973, NC 1974. Assoc. King & Spalding, Atlanta, 1973; 1975assoc. Robinson, Bradshaw & Hinson, P.A., Charlotte, 1974; asst. prof. Duke U. Sch. Law, Durham, 1975—78, assoc. prof., 1978—80, prof., 1980—99, dean, 1988—99; pres. Claremont McKenna Coll., Claremont, Calif., 1999—. Vis. asst. prof. U. Mich. Law Sch., 1977; vis. assoc. prof. U. Va., 1980 Author: (with D. Kahn) Corporate Taxation and Taxation of Partnerships and Partners, 1979, 83, 89; article editor Duke Law Jour. Mem. Am. Law Inst., Coun. Fgn. Rels., Order of Coif, Phi Beta Kappa Office: Claremont McKenna Coll Office Pres 500 E 9th St Claremont CA 91711-5903 Office Phone: 909-621-8111. Business E-Mail: pamela.gann@cmc.edu.

GANNON, SISTER ANN IDA, retired philosophy educator; b. Chgo., 1915; d. George and Hanna (Murphy) G. AB, Clarke Coll., 1941; A.M., Loyola U., Chgo., 1948, LL.D., 1970; PhD, St. Louis U., 1952; Litt.D., DePaul U., 1972; L.H.D., Lincoln Coll., 1965, Columbia Coll., 1969, Luther Coll., 1969; LHD, Augustana Coll., 1969; L.H.D., Marycrest Coll., 1972, Ursuline Coll., 1972, Spertus Coll. Judaica, 1974, Holy Cross Coll., 1974, Rosary Coll., 1975, St. Ambrose Coll., 1975, St. Leo Coll., 1976, Mt. St. Joseph Coll., 1976, Stritch Coll., 1976; LHD, Stonehill Coll., 1976, Elmhurst Coll., 1977, Manchester Coll., 1977, Marymount Coll., 1977; L.H.D., Governor's State U., 1979; LHD, Seattle U., 1981, St. Michael's Coll., 1984, Nazareth Coll., 1985, Holy Family Coll., 1986, Keller Grad. Sch. Mgmt., Our Lady of Holy Cross Coll., New Orleans, 1988. Mem. Sisters of Charity, B.V.M.; tchr. English St. Mary's High Sch., Chgo., 1941-47; residence, study abroad, 1951; chmn. philosophy dept. Mundelein Coll., 1951-57, pres., trustee, 1957—75, prof. philosophy, 1975-85, emeritus faculty, 1987—, archivist, 1986—. Contbr. articles philos. jours. Mem. adv. bd. Sec. Navy, 1975—80, Chgo. Police Bd., 1979—89; bd. dirs. Am. Coun. on Edn., 1971—75, chmn., 1974—75; nat. bd. dirs. Girl Scouts USA, 1966—74, nat. adv., 1976—85; trustee St. Louis U., 1974—87, Ursuline Coll., 1978—92, Cath. Theol. Union, 1983—89, DeVry, Inc., 1987—98, Duquesne U., 1989—91, Montay Coll., 1993—95, Mundelein Coll., 1957—75; bd. dirs. Newberry Libr., 1976—, WTTW Pub. TV, 1976—, Parkside Human Svcs. Corp., 1983—89. Recipient Laetare medal, 1975, LaSallian award, 1975, Aquinas award, 1976, Chgo. Assn. Commerce and Industry award, 1976, Hesburgh award, 1982, Woman of Distinction award Nat. Conf. Women Student Leaders, 1985, Outstanding Svc. award Coun. Ind. Colls., 1989, Woman of History award for edn. AAUW, 1989; named One of 100 Oustanding Chgo. Women, Culture in Action, 1994, Alpha Sigma Nu, 1996. Mem. Am. Cath. Philos. Assn. (exec. coun. 1953-56), Assn. Am. Colls. (bd. dirs. 1965-70, chmn. 1969-70), Religious Edn. Assn. Am. (pres. 1973, chmn. bd. 1975-78), North Cen. Assn. (commn. on colls. and univs. 1971-78, chmn. exec. bd. 1975-77, bd. dirs.), Assn. Governing Bds. Colls. and Univs. (bd. dirs. 1979-88, hon. bd. dirs. 1989-92). Home: Wright Hall 6364 N Sheridan Rd Chicago IL 60660-1726 Office: Gannon Ctr Piper Hall 6525 N Sheridan Rd Chicago IL 60626-5344 Office Phone: 773-508-8450. Business E-Mail: aganno2@luc.edu.

GANNON, JOHN SEXTON, lawyer, management consultant, arbitrator, mediator; b. East Orange, NJ, Apr. 7, 1927; s. John Joseph and Agnes (Sexton) G.; m. Diane Ditchy, Aug. 11, 1951; children: Mary Catherine, John, Lanie Elizabeth, James. BA, U. Mich., 1951; JD, Wayne State U., Detroit, 1961. Bar: Mich. 1962, Tenn. 1971, U.S. Ct. Appeals (6th cir.) 1977, U.S. Dist. Ct. (mid. dist.) Tenn. 1989; Rule 31 approved mediator Tenn. Supreme Ct. Labor negotiator, mgr. employee rels. Chrysler Corp., Highland Park, Mich., 1951-61; labor counsel, mgr. employee rels. Ex-Cell-O Corp., Highland Park, 1961-65; assoc. Constangy & Powell, Atlanta, 1966; v.p. employee rels., labor counsel Werthan Industries, Nashville, 1967-80; ptnr. Dearborn & Ewing, Nashville, 1980-90; pvt. practice Nashville, 1991—. Mem. adj. faculty Owens Sch., Vanderbilt U., Nashville, 1975—85; instr. Soc. Human Resource Mgmt. Profl. cert. program Mid. Tenn. State U., 1993—2000; pres. Employee Rels. Svcs., Nashville, 1987—; chair bd. dirs. Elk Brand Mfg. Co. Inc., Nashville, 2002—. Contbr. articles to profl. jours. Mem. Birmingham (Mich.) Bd. Zoning Appeals, 1963-66; mem. Human Rels. Commn., Nashville, 1979-89; chmn. Tenn. Citizens for Ct. Modernization, Nashville, 1979-80; chmn. Pvt. Industry Coun., Nashville, 1986-95. With USN, 1945-47. Mem. ABA, FBA (former chmn. sr. lawyers divsn. mediation and arbitration com.), Tenn. Bar Assn., Nashville Bar Assn., Nat. Orgn. Social Security Claimants Reps., Am. Arbitration Assn. (panel employment mediators and arbitrators), Indsl. Rels. Rsch. Assn., Hillwood Country Club, Kiwanis. Home: 216 Jackson Blvd Nashville TN 37205-3300 Home Phone: 615-292-1179; Office Phone: 615-386-7003. Personal E-mail: jg216@msn.com.

GANOE, CHARLES STRATFORD, banker, consultant; b. Abington, Pa., July 16, 1929; s. Robert L. and Leonette (Rehfuss) G.; m. Frances-Sue Williams, Apr. 2, 1960; children: F. Hemsley Hughes, Alice Ryden. BA, Princeton U., 1951; MBA, U. Pa., 1952. With Fidelity Bank (now Wachovia Bank), Phila., 1952—, asst. treas., 1956—60, asst. v.p., 1960—61, v.p., 1961—66, sr. v.p., 1966—69, exec. v.p., 1969—75, sr. exec. v.p., dir., 1975—79; exec. v.p. N.Y. Bank for Savs., NYC, 1979—82; sr. v.p. Am. Express Internat. Banking Corp., NYC, 1982—84, 1st Am. Bank of N.Y., NYC, 1984—91; mng. dir. FMS Group inc., Blue Bell, Pa., 1991—94; pres. Ganoe Assocs., LLC, Princeton, NJ, 1995—. V.p. Co. for Investing Abroad (became Fidelity Internat. Corp., merged into Fidelity Internat. Bank 1972), 1963-65, pres., bd. dir., 1965-72; bd. dir., chmn. exec. com. Fidelity Internat. Bank, N.Y.C., 1970-79; mem. adv. com. Export-Import Bank U.S., 1973-74. Co-author: Offshore Lending by U.S. Commercial Banks; contbr. articles to profl. jours. Class agt. Class of 1951 Princeton U., 1954-56, treas., 1956-61, v.p., 1981-85, pres., 1985-86; bd. dirs. Phila. Coun. for Internat. Visitors, 1963-69, chmn., 1969-73; mem. Phila. Dist. Export Coun., 1966-75. Mem. Bankers Assn. for Fgn. Trade (bd. dirs. 1969—, v.p. 1971-72, exec. v.p. 1972-73, pres. 1973-74), Robert Morris Assocs. (now RMA-Risk Mgmt. Assocs.)(past pres. Phila. chpt., Duning Meml. awards 1962, 65, 68), Greater Phila. C. of C. (sec. 1960-64, treas. 1960-70, bd. dirs. 1960-73, mem. adminstrv. com.), Wharton Grad. Sch. Alumni Assn. (past pres.), Coun. Fgn. Rels., Merion Cricket Club (Haverford, Pa.), Princeton Club (N.Y.C.), Princeton (N.J.) Elm Club, Ausable Club (St. Huberts, N.Y.), Delta Psi. Home: 23 Constitution Hl W Princeton NJ 08540-6752 Office: Ganoe Assocs 475 Wall St Princeton NJ 08540-1509 Home Phone: 609-924-3745; Office Phone: 609-497-4740. E-mail: cganoe@erols.com.

GANONG, WILLIAM F(RANCIS), physiologist, educator; b. Northampton, Mass., July 6, 1924; s. William Francis and Anna (Hobbet) G.; m. Ruth Jackson, Feb. 22, 1948; children: William Francis III, Susan B., Anna H., James E. AB cum laude, Harvard U., 1945, MD magna cum laude, 1949; DSc (hon.), Med. Coll. Ohio, 1995, Ohio State U., 2003. Intern, jr. asst. resident in medicine Peter Bent Brigham Hosp., Boston, 1949-51, asst. in medicine and surgery, 1952-55; research fellow medicine and surgery Harvard U., 1952-55; asst. prof. physiology U. Calif., San Francisco, 1955-60, assoc. prof., 1960-64, prof., 1964-82, Jack D. and Deloris Lange prof., 1982-91, Lange prof. emeritus, 1991—, faculty research lectr., 1968, vice chmn. dept., 1963-68, chmn., 1970-87. Cons. Calif. Dept. Mental Hygiene. Author: Review of Medical Physiology, 22nd edit., 2005, Physiology: A Study Guide, 3d edit., 1989; editor: (with L. Martini) Neuroendocrinology, vol. I, 1966, vol. II, 1967, Frontiers in Neuroendocrinology, 1969, 71, 73, 76, 78, 80, 82, 84, 86, 88; editor (with S. McPhee) Pathophysiology of Disease, 5th edit., 2006; editor-in-chief Neuroendocrinology, 1979-84; co-editor Frontiers in Neuroendocrinology, 1990-2002. Served with U.S. Army, 1943-46; served to capt. M.C. 1951-52. Recipient Boylston Med. Soc. prize Harvard U., 1949, A.A. Berthold medal, 1985, Lifetime Achievement award High Blood Pressure Rsch. Coun., Am. Heart Assn., 1995; named Disting. Svc. mem. Am. Assn. Med. Colls., 1988. Fellow: AAAS; mem.: Soc. for Neurosci., Internat. Brain Rsch. Orgn., Chilean Endocrine Soc. (corr.), Endocrine Soc. (Disting. Educator award 2002), Soc. Exptl. Biology and Medicine (councillor 1989—93), Am. Soc. for Gravitational and Space Biology (bd. dirs. 1984—87), Assn. Chairmen Depts. Physiology (pres. 1976—77), Am. Physiol. Soc. (pres. 1977—78), Internat. Soc. Neuroendocrinology (hon.; v.p. 1976—80). Home: 710 Hillside Ave Albany CA 94706-1022 Office: U Calif Dept Physiology San Francisco CA 94143

GANS, BRUCE MERRILL, physiatrist, educator, health facility administrator; b. NYC, Jan. 15, 1947; s. Murray and Bessie Jean (Schnitzer) G.; m. Linda Sharon Aberbach, June 22, 1969; children: Rebecca, Jeremy. BSEE, Union Coll., Schenectady, 1968; MS, BMEE, MD, U. Pa., 1972; MS, U. Wash., 1976. Diplomate Am. Bd. Phys. Medicine and Rehab. (bd. dirs.). Intern Phila. Gen. Hosp., 1972-73; resident in phys. medicine and rehab. U. Wash., 1973-76, instr. Seattle, 1976-78; from asst. prof. to prof., chair dept. phys. medicine/rehab. Tufts U. Sch. Medicine, Boston, 1978-88; physiatrist-in-chief New Eng. Med. Ctr., Boston, 1978-88; pres. Rehab. Inst. Mich., Detroit, 1989-99; chair dept. phys. medicine and rehab. Wayne State U. Sch. Medicine, Detroit, 1989-99; sr. v.p. Detroit Med. Ctr., 1989-99, North Shore-Long Island Jewish Health Sys., 1999—2001; chair dept. phys. medicine and rehab. L.I. Jewish Med. Ctr., Parker Jewish Inst., North Shore U. Hosp., 1999—2001; exec. v.p., chief med. officer Kessler Rehab. Corp., West Orange, 2001—03; chief med. officer Kessler Inst. for Rehab., West Orange. Bd. dirs. Greenery Rehab. Group, Inc., Newton, Mass., 1988-93. Editor: Principles and Practice of Rehabilitation Medicine, 4th edit., 2004; editl. bd.: Jour. Head Trauma Rehab., 1988—92. Trustee Met. Ctr. for High Tech., Detroit, 1989-94; bd. dirs. Health and Retirement Properties Trust, 1995-99, Five Star Quality Care, Inc., 2002—. Fellow Am. Acad. Phys. Medicine and Rehab. (bd. dirs., pres. 2004); mem. Am. Hosp. Assn. (chair governing coun. sect. for rehab. 1992), Assn. Acad. Physiatrists (pres. 1993), Am. Rehab. Assn. (bd. dirs. 1995-97), Am. Med. Rehab. Providers Assn. (bd. dirs. 1997—). Avocations: computers, reading, video. Office: Kessler Inst Rehab 1199 Pleasant Valley Way West Orange NJ 07052 Home Phone: 973-665-0885; Office Phone: 973-324-3658. E-mail: bgans@kessler-rehab.com.

GANS, EUGENE HOWARD, cosmetic and pharmaceutical company executive, consultant; b. Dec. 17, 1929; married, 1953; 2 children. BS, Columbia U., 1951, MS, 1953; PhD, U. Wis., 1956. Lab. asst. Columbia

U., 1951—53; sr. scientist group leader Hoffman-LaRoche, Inc., NJ, 1956—60; head new product devel. sect. Vick Div. R&D Labs. Richardson-Merrell, NY, 1960—64, asst. dir. devel. NY, 1964—67, dir. NY, 1967—71; dir. rsch. Vicks Personal Care div. Richardson-Vicks div. Proctor-Gamble, Shelton, Conn., 1972—76, v.p., dir. R&D, 1976—87; pres. Hastings Assocs., Westport, Conn., 1987—, Lincoln Techs., Westport, 1989—. Chmn. proprietary drug task group FDA, 1976—86; chmn. sci. adv. com. Cosmetic, Toiletry and Fragrance Assn., Washington, 1984—86; chmn. Consumer Health Products Assn. task group FDA, 1996—2003; chmn. ctrl. rsch. Medicis Pharm. Co., Phoenix, 1992—2002, sr. advisor, 2002—. Mem.: Soc. Investigative Dermatology, Am. Acad. Dermatology, Am. Chem. Soc., Am. Pharm. Assn., Sigma Xi. Address: 5101 N Casa Blanca Dr #223 Scottsdale AZ 85253-6988 Office Phone: 203-221-2023, 203-221-2023. E-mail: egans48845@aol.com.

GANS, HERBERT J., sociologist, educator; b. Cologne, Germany, May 7, 1927; arrived in US, 1940, naturalized, 1945; s. Carl M. and Elise (Plaut) Gans; m. Louise Gruner, Mar. 19, 1967; 1 child, David. PhB, U. Chgo., 1947, MA, 1950; PhD, U. Pa., 1957, DSc (hon.), 2003. Planner pvt. and pub. planning agys., Chgo. and Washington, 1950—53; from lectr. to assoc. prof. urban studies and planning U. Pa., 1953—64; from asso. prof. to adj. prof. sociology Tchrs. Coll., Columbia, also sr. staff scientist Center Urban Edn., 1964—69; prof. sociology and planning MIT, also MIT-Harvard Joint Ctr. for Urban Studies, 1969—71; prof. sociology, Ford Found. Urban chair Columbia U., 1971—, Robert S. Lynd prof. sociology, 1985—. Film critic Social Policy mag., 1971—78; sr. fellow Gannett Ctr. Media Studies, 1985—86, Media Studies Ctr., 1996—97; vis. scholar Russell Sage Found., 1989—90; cons. Ford Found., HEW, Nat. Adv. Commn. Civil Disorders. Author: The Urban Villagers, 1962, 2d edit., 1982, The Levittowners, 1967, 1982, People and Plans, 1968, More Equality, 1973, Popular Culture and High Culture, 1974, rev. edit., 1999, Deciding What's News, 1979, 25th Anniversary edit., 2004, Middle American Individualism, 1988, 1991, People, Plans and Policies, 1991, 2d edit., 1994, The War Against the Poor, 1995, 1996, Making Sense of America, 1999, Democracy and the News, 2003; co-editor: On the Making of Americans, 1979; editor: Sociology in America, 1990; adv. editor Jour. Am. Inst. Planners, 1965—75, Jour. Contemporary Ethnography, 1971—, Am. Jour. Sociology, 1972—74, Society, 1971—76, Social Policy, 1971—, Pub. Opinion Quar., 1972—86, Jour. Comm., 1974—91, Jour. Ethnic and Racial Studies, 1977—89, 1995—2003, Internat. Ency. Comm., 1984—88, The Am. Sociologist, 1991—95, Georgetown Jour. Fighting Poverty, 1992—, Critical Studies in Mass Comm., 1992—96, Rose Monograph Series, 1998—, Qualitative Sociology, 1998—2001. Bd. dirs. Ams. for Dem. Action, 1969—75, Met. Action Inst. (formerly Suburban Action Inst.), 1974—85, Human Serve Inst., 1987—, Workers Def. League, 1992—, Working Today, 1995—, Rsch. Coun. Jt. Project Equality, 1996—, Nat. Jobs for All Coalition, 1996. With US Army, 1945—46. Recipient Excelsior award, SUNY, Albany, 1987, award for disting. contbn. to media and media studies, Freedom Forum Media Studies Ctr., 1995; Guggenheim fellow, 1977—78, Rsch. fellow, German Marshall Fund, 1984. Fellow: Am. Acad. Arts and Scis.; mem.: Sociol. Rsch. Assn., Ea. Sociol. Soc. (pres. 1972, Merit award 1995), German Sociol. Assn. (hon.), Am. Sociol. Assn. (exec. coun. 1968—71, pres. 1988, Lynd award for Lifetime Contbn. to Rsch. Cmty. and Urban Sociology sect. 1992, Pub. Understanding Sociology award 1999, Disting. Career award Internat. Migration Sect. 2004, Career of Disting. Scholarship award 2006). Office: Columbia U 413 Fayerweather Hall New York NY 10027 Home Phone: 212-662-2031. Business E-Mail: hjg1@columbia.edu.

GANSCHINIETZ, DEEPA, elementary school educator; b. India; B in Elem. Edn., Univ. Kans.; M. in Children's Lit., Reading, Ohio State Univ. Tchr., 1991—, Columbus Pub. Sch. Dist, Ohio, 1994—, Olde Orchard Elem. Sch. Named Ohio Tchr. of Yr., 2006; recipient The I CAN Learn-NEA Found. Awards for Tchg., 2005. Mem.: Columbus Edn. Assn., Ohio Edn. Assn. Office: Olde Orchard Elem Sch 800 McNaughten Rd Columbus OH 43213

GANSKE, J. GREG, former congressman, plastic surgeon; b. New Hampton, Iowa, Mar. 31, 1949; s. Victor Wilber and Mary Jo (O'Donnell) G.; m. Corrine Mikkelson, 1976; children: Ingrid, Briget, Karl. BA, U. Iowa, 1972, MD, 1976. Diplomate Am. Bd. Plastic Surgery, Am. Bd. Surgery. Intern U. Colo. Med. Ctr., Denver, 1976-78; resident in gen. surgery U. Oreg. Health Sci. Ctr., Portland, 1978-81, chief resident in gen. surgery, 1981-82; resident in plastic surgery Harvard Med. Sch., Boston, 1982-84; chief resident plastic surgery Brigham and Women's Hosp. and Children's Hosp., 1983-84; pvt. practice Des Moines, 1984-94; mem. U.S. Congress from 4th Iowa dist., Washington, 1994—2002; mem. energy and commerce com. Staff Iowa Luth. Hosp., Iowa Meth. Med. Ctr., Mercy Hosp. Med. Ctr. Lt. col. M.C., USAR, 1984—. Fellow ACS, Am. Soc. Plastic and Reconstructive Surgeons; mem. AMA, Am. Assn. Plastic Surgeons, Iowa Med. Soc., Iowa Soc. Plastic and Reconstructive Surgeons, Am. Assn. Hand Surgery, Am. Soc. Surgery Hand, Am. Cleft Palate-Craniofacial Assn. Republican. Roman Catholic. Office Phone: 515-265-4414.

GANSLER, DOUGLAS F., state attorney general, former prosecutor; b. Summit, NJ, Oct. 30, 1962; s. Jacques and Alison Gansler; m. Laura Leedy; children: Sam, Will. BA cum laude, Yale U.; JD, U. Va. Sch. Law, 1989. Bar: Md. Assoc. Howrey & Simon, 1990—92; asst. US atty. Dist. Md. US Dept. Justice, 1992—98; of counsel Coburn & Schertler, 1998; state's atty. Montgomery County, Md., 1999—2007; atty. gen. State of Md., Annapolis, 2007—. Mem. Montgomery County Commn. Aging; co-chair NAACP Criminal Justice Com. Bd. dirs. Jewish Cmty. Ctr. Greater Washington, Jewish Found. Grp. Homes, Most Valuable Kids, Teen Ct. Recipient Champion of Children award, Victims' Rights Found., 2000, Hero award, MADD, 2002. Mem.: DC Bar Assn., Md. Bar Assn. Democrat. Office: Office of Atty Gen 200 St Paul Pl Baltimore MD 21202*

GANSLER, JACQUES SINGLETON, public policy educator; b. Newark, Nov. 21, 1934; BE, Yale U., 1956; MSEE, Northea. U., 1959; MA in Polit. Econ., New Sch. for Social Rsch., 1972; PhD in Econs., Am. U., 1978. Engring. mgr. Raytheon Corp., 1956-62; program mgr. Singer Corp., 1962-70; v.p. ITT Corp., 1970-72; dep. asst. def. sec. U.S. Govt., 1972-77; exec. v.p, dir. TASC, Inc., 1977-97; undersec. of def. for acquisition, tech. and logistics U.S. Govt., 1997—2001; prof., Robert C. Lipitz chair Sch. Pub. Affairs, U Md., 2001—. Vis. scholar at Kennedy Sch. of Govt. Harvard U., 1984-97; hon. prof., Indsl. Coll. of Armed Forces; vis. prof. U. Va. Author: The Defense Industry, 1980, Affording Defense, 1989, Defense Conversion: Transforming the Arsenal of Democracy, 1995; contbr. author to 22 books on nat. security, rsch. and devel. mgmt, and pub. adminstr.; contbr. articles to profl. jours. Office: U Md Sch Pub Affairs Van Munching Hall College Park MD 20742-0001 Office Phone: 301-405-4794. Business E-Mail: jgansler@umd.edu.

GANSLER, ROBERT, professional soccer coach; b. Mucsi, Hungary, July 1, 1941; came to U.S., 1952; m. Nancy Gansler; children: Robert, MIchael, Peter, Daniel. Grad., Marquette U., 1964. Coach Univ. Wis., Milwaukee, 1984—88, US Under-19 Men's Soccer Team, 1979—82, US Under-20 Men's Soccer Team, 1987—89, Milwaukee Rampage, 1996—98; head coach US Men's Soccer Team, 1989—91, Kansas City Wizards/MLS, 1999—. Named Coach of Year, Major League Soccer, 2000. Office: Kansas City Wizards 2 Arrowhead Dr Kansas City MO 64129

GANT, DONALD ROSS, investment banker; b. Long Branch, NJ, Oct. 5, 1928; s. Raymond LeRoy and Evelyn (Ross) G.; m. Jane Harriet Taylor, Sept. 12, 1953; children: Laura R., Christopher T., Sarah R., Alison A. BS, U. Pa., 1952; MBA, Harvard U., 1954. Assoc. Goldman, Sachs & Co., NYC, 1954-64, ptnr., 1965-90, ltd. ptnr., 1990-99, sr. dir., 1999—. Bd. dirs. Diebold, Inc., Canton, Ohio, Stride Rite Corp., Lexington, Mass.; mem. vis. com. Harvard Bus. Sch., 1991—97. Served with U.S. Army, 1946-48. Republican. Presbyterian. Home: PO Box 83 New Vernon NJ 07976-0083 Office: Goldman Sachs & Co 85 Broad St New York NY 10004-2456 E-mail: don10285@cs.com.

GANT, NORMAN FERRELL, JR., obstetrician, gynecologist, educator; b. Wichita Falls, Tex., Feb. 16, 1939; s. Norman Ferrell and Eleanor (Taylor) Gant. BA, North Tex. State U., Denton, 1962; MD, U. Tex., 1964. Diplomate Am. Bd. Ob-Gyn. (exec. dir.). Intern Parkland Meml. Hosp., Dallas, 1964—65, resident, 1965—68; mem. faculty U. Tex. Southwestern Med. Sch., Dallas, 1968—, prof. obstetrics and gynecology, 1976—, chmn. dept., 1977—83. Bd. dirs. Am. Bd. Ob-Gyn., Inc., 1993—; v.p. Internat. Soc. for Study of Hypertension in Pregnancy, 1992—94. Co-author: Williams Obstetrics; editor, sec./treas. Clin. Jour. of Hypertension; contbr. articles to med. jours. Recipient Outstanding Alumnus award, U. North Tex., 1998. Fellow: Am. Coll. Ob-Gyn., Royal Coll. Ob-Gyn.; mem.: Inst. Medicine, Southwestern Gyn. Assembly (pres. 1993), Am. Bd. Ob-Gyn. (maternal-fetal medicine, examiner for ob-gyn. and maternal-fetal medicine bds., mem. exec. com., credentials com.), Dallas-Ft. Worth Obstet. and Gynecol. Soc., Tex. Assn. Ob-Gyns., Dallas County Med. Assns., Soc. Gynecol. Investigation (pres. 1991). Address: Am Bd Ob-Gyn 2915 Vine St Dallas TX 75204-1045 Office Phone: 214-871-1619. Business E-Mail: ccash@abog.org.

GANTER, SUSAN LYNN, foundation administrator, retired mathematics professor; b. Waynesboro, Va., Jan. 29, 1964; d. Dorrance Lynn and Gertrude M. (Kirschner) G. B.Music Edn., BS in Math. Sci., So. Meth. U., Dallas, 1986; MA in Math., U. Calif., Santa Barbara, 1988; PhD in Math. Edn., U. Calif., 1990. Grad. math. instr. U. Calif., Santa Barbara, 1986-88; math. instr. Santa Barbara City Coll., 1988-90; asst. prof. math. Western Wash. U., Bellingham, 1990; dir. for program for promotion of inst. change Am. Assn. for Higher Edn.; math. sci. faculty Worcester Polytechnic Inst.; assoc. prof., math. sci. Clemson U., SC, 1999—2004; exec. dir. Assn. of Women in Sci., Washington, 2004—. Contbr. articles to profl. jours. Santa Barbara City Coll. faculty enrichment grantee, 1990, U. Calif.-Santa Barbara grantee, 1989. Mem. Nat. Coun. Tchrs. Math., Math. Assn. Am., Am. Math. Soc., Wash. Math. Coun., Soc. for Indsl. and Applied Math., Western Wash. U. Collegiate Chorale, Music Acad. of the West Opera, Kappa Mu Epsilon, Kappa Delta Pi, Mu Phi Epsilon. Roman Catholic. Avocations: singing, hiking, swimming. Office: Assn for Women in Sci Ste 650 1200 New York Av NW Washington DC 20005

GANTT, EDWIN ELRAY, psychology professor; b. Idaho Falls, Idaho, Sept. 8, 1965; s. Raymond Edwin and Lucy Elvira Gantt; m. Anita Lerene Wages; children: Jared Michael, Mark Soren, Benjamin Taylor, Stephen Joseph. BS, Brigham Young U., Provo, Utah, 1993; MA, Duquesne U., Pitts., 1994, PhD, 1998. Cert. level 4 coach USA Hockey, 2007. Asst. prof. Brigham Young U., 1998—2004, assoc. prof., 2004—. Contbr. articles to profl. jours. R-Consevative. Mem. Lds Ch. Avocation: ice hockey. Office: Brigham Young Univ 1086 SWKT Provo UT 84602 Office Phone: 801-422-9785. Business E-Mail: ed_gantt@byu.edu.

GANTT, HARVEY B., architect, former mayor; b. Charleston, SC, Jan. 14, 1943; m. Lucinda Brawley; four children. Student, Iowa State U., Ames, 1960-62; BArch, Clemson U., SC, 1965; MA in City Planning, MIT, Cambridge, 1970. Lectr. U. NC, Chapel Hill, 1970-72; vis. critic Clemson U., 1972-73; mem. Charlotte City Coun., NC, 1975-79; mayor pro tem City of Charlotte, 1981-83, mayor, 1983-91; chmn. Nat. Capital Planning Commn.; prin. Gantt Huberman Archs., Charlotte. Life mem. NAACP; bd. dirs. 100 Black Men of Charlotte, Ctrl. Piedmont Coll. Found., Am. Archtl. Found.; former bd. dirs. YMCA, Afro-Am. Cultural Ctr., Found. for the Carolinas, Charlotte C. of C., Urban League, United Negro Coll. Fund; choir mem. Friendship Bapt., former bd. trustees. Named Citizen of Yr., Charlotte chpt. NAACP, 1975, 84. Fellow AIA; mem. Am. Planning Assn., NC Design Found. Avocations: tennis, reading. Office: Gantt Huberman Archs 500 N Tryon St Charlotte NC 28202 Office Phone: 704-334-6436. Office Fax: 704-342-9639.*

GANTZ, BRUCE JAY, otolaryngologist, educator; b. NYC, May 18, 1946; m. Mary Katherine DeJong; children: Ellen Katherine, Jessica Rose, Jay Alexander. BS in Gen. Sci., U. Iowa, 1968, MD, 1974, MS in Otolaryngology, 1980; fellow neurotology, U. Zürich, Zurich, 1981-82. Asst. prof. dept otolaryngology U. Iowa Coll. Medicine, Iowa City, 1980-84, assoc. prof., 1984-87, prof., 1987—; interim head dept. otolaryngology head & neck surgery U. Iowa Hosps. & Clinics, Iowa City, 1993-95, head dept. otolaryngology head & neck surgery, 1995—. Mem. adv. bd. Deafness Research Found. Sci., 1988—. Mem. editl. bd. Am. Jour. Otology, Laryngoscope, Skull Base Surgery, Operative Techniques in Otolaryngology-Head and Neck Surgery, Anales De Otolarnolaringologica Mexicana, Annals Otolaryngology, Rhinology and Laryngology; contbr. articles to profl. jours. Recipient Tchr.-Investigator Devel. award Pub. Health Svc., 1981-86, Program Project award NIH, 1985—; clin. rsch. ctr. grantee NIDCD, 1990, 95. Mem.: AMA, NAS Inst. Medicine, Collegium Oto-Rhino-Laryngologicum Amictuae Sacrum, Am. Otological Soc., Am. Neurotology Soc. (v.p. 1994—96, pres.-elect 1996—97, pres. 1997—98), Soc. Univ. Otolaryngologists, Am. Acad. Otolaryngology-Head and Neck Surgery, Deafness Rsch. Found. (state chmn. 1985—), Assn. Rsch. in otolaryngology (pres. 1995). Office: U Iowa Hosps & Clinics 200 Hawkins Dr Iowa City IA 52242-1078 Office Phone: 319-356-2173.

GANTZ, CARROLL MELVIN, industrial design consultant, consumer product designer; b. Sellersville, Pa., Sept. 9, 1931; s. Melvin Charles G. and Leona Alberta (Hornberger) Barner; m. Lorraine Sachs, Mar. 5, 1955; children: Erika Christine, Mitchell Allen. B.F.A., Carnegie Mellon U., 1953. Head indsl. design Hoover Co., North Canton, Ohio, 1956-72; mgr. indsl. design Black & Decker, Inc., Towson, Md., 1972-81, dir. indsl. design household products group Shelton, Conn., 1981-86; prof., head dept. design Carnegie Mellon U., Pitts., 1987—92; established Carroll Gantz Design, 1992; designer canal boat St. Helena II, Canal Fulton, Ohio, 1967-70; dir. Am. Canal Soc., York, Pa., 1974-79. Author: Design Chronicles. Significant Mass Produced Products of the 20th Century, 2005. Bd. dirs. Stark County Hist. Soc., 1970. Served with Nat. Security Agy. U.S. Army, 1953-56. Recipient Design award Indsl. Designers Inst., 1961, Indsl. Design Excellance award, 1995; Brashear scholar, 1949. Fellow Indsl. Designers Soc. Am. (pres. 1979-80, chmn. bd. 1981-82); mem. SAR, Omicron Delta Kappa, Tau Sigma Delta Republican. Achievements include patents for original Black & Decker Dustbuster, 1978; 28 others.

GANTZ, DAVID ALFRED, lawyer, academic administrator; b. Columbus, Ohio, July 30, 1942; s. Harry Samuel and Edwina G.; m. Susan Beare, Aug. 26, 1967 (div. Feb. 1989); children: Stephen David, Julie Lorraine; m. Catherine Fagan, Mar. 28, 1992. AB, Harvard U., 1964; JD, Stanford U., 1967, M in Jud. Sci., 1970. Bar: Ohio 1967, D.C. 1971, U.S. Ct. Internat. Trade 1983, U.S. Ct. Appeals (9th cir.) 1972, U.S. Supreme Ct. 1972. Asst. prof. law U. Costa Rica, San Jose, 1967-69; law clk. U.S. Ct. Appeals, San Francisco, 1969-70; asst. legal advisor U.S. Dept. State, Washington, 1970-77; ptnr. Cole & Corrette, Washington, 1977-83, Oppenheimer Wolff & Donnelly, Washington, 1983-90, Reid & Priest, Washington, 1990-93, of counsel, 1993-97, Dorsey & Whitney, 1997-99; Samuel M. Fegtly prof. law, dir. inter trade law program U. Ariz. Coll. Law, Tucson, 1993—; assoc. dir. Nat. Law Ctr. for Inter-Am. Free Trade, 1993—. Panelist US-Can. Free Trade Agreement, 1989-92, NAFTA, 1994-2007; judge OAS Adminstrv. Tribunal, 1987-95; adj. prof. Georgetown U. Law Ctr., 1982-93; vis. prof. law George Washington U., 2003-04. Contbr. articles to profl. jours. Pres. Potomac River Sports Found., 1992-94. Mem. ABA, Am. Soc. Internat. Law, Potomac Boat Club (Washington, bd. dirs. 1986-93). Office: Ariz James E Rogers Coll Law 1201 E Speedway Blvd Tucson AZ 85721 Home Phone: 520-319-1859; Office Phone: 520-621-1801. Business E-Mail: gantz@law.arizona.edu.

GANTZER, MARY LOU, medical products executive; d. Richard John and Mary Jane (Capistrant) G. B in Chemistry, U. Minn., 1972, MS, 1976; PhD in Chemistry, U. Va., 1980. Instr., postdoctoral fellow dept. chemistry U. Va., Charlottesville, 1980—81; rsch. scientist diagnostics divsn. Miles, Inc., Elkhart, Ind., 1981—84, sr. rsch. scientist, 1984—86, staff scientist, 1986—87, supr. R&D, 1987—91, project mgr., 1991—98, coord. clin. and outcomes rsch., 1996—98; dir. clin. and sci. affairs Dade Behring, Inc., Newark, Del., 1998—2004, v.p., clin. and sci. affairs, 2004—. Mem. Women in Mgmt. del. to People's Republic of China, 1988; bd. dirs. Clin. and Lab. Stds. Inst. (formerly Nat. Comm. for Clin. Lab. Stds.), 2003-. Contbr. articles to chemistry jours.; patentee in field. Mem. Am. Assn. Clin. Chemistry (chmn. Chgo. sect. 1988, chair long range planning com. 1993-95, bd. editors Clin. Chem. News 1993-95, pres. 2002, Chmn.'s award 1988), Am. Heart Assn. (profl. mem.), Soc. Chest Pain Ctrs. Roman Catholic. Avocation: needlecrafts. Office: Dade Behring Inc (MS709) PO Box 6101 Newark DE 19714-6101

GANULIN, JUDY, public relations professional; b. Chgo., May 2, 1937; d. Alvin and Sadie (Reingold) Landis; m. James Ganulin, June 23, 1957; children: Stacy Ganulin Clark, Amy Ganulin Lowenstein. BA in Journalism, U. Calif., Berkeley, 1958. Copywriter-sec. Joe Connor Advt., Berkeley, 1958; exec. sec. Prescolite Mfg. Co., Berkeley, 1958-59; info. officer Office of Consumer Counsel, Sacramento, 1959-61; pub. rels. positions various polit. campaigns, Fresno, Calif., 1966; adminstrv. asst., editor, mktg. Valley Pubs., Fresno, 1971-80; staff asst. to county supr. Bd. Suprs., Fresno, 1980-82; field rep. Assemblyman Bruce Bronzan, Fresno, 1982-84; prin. Judy Ganulin Pub. Rels., Fresno, 1984—. Speaker new bus. workshop SBA/Svc. Corps Ret. Execs., Fresno, 1990—. Active Hadassah, Fresno, 1975—; pres. Temple Beth Israel Sisterhood, Fresno, 1976; panelist campaign workshop Nat. Women's Polit. Caucus, Fresno, 1994, 2001, publicity chmn. ctrl. Caifl. chpt., 1999—2000; mem. C. of C. Art and Wine Festival Com., 1999—2000, Juvenile Justice Ctr. Task Force, 2001, Valley Women's Polit. Fund; bd. dirs. Temple Beth Israel, Fresno, 1972—75, Planned Parenthood Ctrl. Calif., Fresno, 1986—91, Empty Bowls, Sr. Companion Program. Mem. Pub. Rels. Soc. Am. (accredited pub. rels. practitioner, pres. Fresno/Ctrl. Valley chpt. 1994), Am. Mktg. Assn. (pres. ctrl. Calif. chpt. 1987-88), Calif. Press Women, Fresno Advt. Fedn., Fresno Comm. Network (v.p., pres. 1991-93), Fresno C. of C. (mem. mktg. com. 1988-), Fresno Comm. Network (formerly Pub. Rels. Roundtable). Democrat. Avocations: travel, reading, cooking. Office: Judy Ganulin Pub Rels 1117 W San Jose Ave Fresno CA 93711-3112 Home Phone: 559-227-5122; Office Phone: 559-222-7411. Personal E-mail: jganulin@comcast.net.

GANZ, DAVID L., lawyer; b. NYC, July 28, 1951; s. Daniel M. and Beverlee (Kaufman) G.; m. Barbara Bondanza, Nov. 3, 1974 (div. 1978); m. Sharon Ruth Lamnin, Oct. 30, 1981 (div. 1996); children: Scott Harry, Elyse Toby, Pamela Rebecca; m. Kathleen Ann Gotsch, Dec. 28, 1996. BS in Fgn. Svc., Georgetown U., Washington, 1973; JD, St. John's U., Jamaica, NY, 1976. Bar: N.Y. 1977, D.C. 1980, N.J. 1985; cert. mediator U.S. Dist. Ct. (N.J.). Assoc. Regan, Dorsey & De Riso, Flushing, N.Y., 1977-79; ptnr. Durst & Ganz, NYC, 1979-80; mng. ptnr. Ganz, Hollinger & Towe, NYC, 1981-98, Ganz & Hollinger, NYC, 1999—. Exec. com. Industry Coun. Tangible Assets, Washington, 1983—, bd. dirs.; pres. World Mint Coun., 1993-95; cons. in field. Author: A Critical Guide to the Anthologies of African Literature, 1973, A Legal and Legislative History of 31 USC Sec 342d-324i, 1976, The World of Coin Collecting, 1980, 3d edit., 1998, The 90 Second Lawyer, 1996, The 90 Second Lawyer's Guide to Selling Real Estate, 1997, How to Get an Instant Mortgage, 1997, Planning Your Rare Coin Retirement, 1998, Guide Commemorative Coin Values, 1999, Official Guide to America's State Quarters, 2000, rev. edit., 2002; corr. Numis. News Weekly, 1969-73, 96—, asst. editor, 1973-74, spl. corr., 1974-75, columnist, 1969-76, 96—; contbg. editor, columnist COINage Mag., 1974—; columnist Coin World, 1974-96, COINS Mag., 1973-83; contbr. articles to profl. jours. Presdl. appointee Annual Assay Commn., 1974; bd. dirs. Georgetown Libr. Assocs., Washington, 1982-2005, Bialystoker Home and Infirmary for the Aged, NYC, 2001-06, Care Plus N.J. Inc., 2003—; active N.Y. County Draft Bd., 1984, Bergen County, NJ, 1985-2005, vice chair, 1996-2005; mem. Citizens Commemorative Coin Adv. Com. U.S. Treas., 1993-96; sec., mem. Zoning and Adjustment Bd., Fair Lawn, NJ, 1988-92, chmn., 1993-97; elected mem. Dem. County Com. Bergen County, 1988-96, borough coun. Borough of Fair Lawn, 1998—2006, mayor, 1999—2006, Bergen County freeholder, 2003—, vice-chmn., 2005-06; atty. Zoning Bd. Adjustment, Paramus, 2002-03, Rent Leveling Bd., Hoboken, NJ, 2005-06. Decorated Order of St. Agatha (Republic of San Marino) Fellow Am. Numis. Soc. (life); mem. Am. Numis. Assn. (life, legis. coun. 1978-81, 83-95, elected bd. govs. 1985-95, v.p. 1991-93, pres. 1993-95), Assn. of Bar of City of N.Y. (com. on state legis. 1987-90), N.Y. State Bar Assn. (mem. civil practice com., chmn. subcom. 1978-84), Profl. Numis. Guild Inc. affiliated mem. 1989—, gen. coun. 1981-92), Am. Soc. Internat. Law, Nat. Assn. Coin and Precious Metals Dealers (asoc. mem., gen. coun. 1981-85), Flushing Lawyers Club (pres. 1982-83). Democrat. Jewish. Avocation: coin collecting/numismatics. Office: Ganz & Hollinger PC 1394 3rd Ave New York NY 10021-0404 Office Phone: 212-517-5500. Personal E-mail: davidlganz@aol.com.

GANZ, HOWARD LAURENCE, lawyer; b. NYC, Apr. 3, 1942; s. Myron and Beatrice (W.) Ganz; children: Beth, David. BA, Colgate U., 1963; LLB, Columbia U., 1966. Bar: N.Y. 1966, U.S. Dist. Ct. (so. dist.) N.Y. 1968, U.S. Dist. Ct. (ea. dist.) N.Y. 1969, U.S. Dist. Ct. (no. dist.) Calif. 1984, U.S. Ct. Appeals (3rd cir.) 1974, U.S. Ct. Appeals (4th cir.) 1985, U.S. Dist. Ct. (9th cir.) 1984, U.S. Dist. Ct. (D.C. cir.) 1986, U.S. Supreme Ct. 1986. Law clk. to Hon. Marvin E. Frankel U.S. Dist. Ct., NYC, 1966-68; assoc., ptnr. Proskauer Rose LLP, NYC, 1968—, mem. exec. com., 1990—93, co-chmn. Labor and Employment Law Dept., 2004—; co-chmn. Sports Law Group, 2000—. Articles editor: Columbia Law Rev. Named One of 100 Best Lawyers in NY NY Mag., 1995, 2005, Best Lawyers in Am., 1987-2006, Am.'s Leading Lawyers for Bus., Chambers USA, 2004-2006, Best Lawyers in NY mag., 2005, 07, 500 Leading Lawyers in Am., Lawdragon, 2005-06. Fellow Coll. Labor and Employment Lawyers; mem. Fed. Bar Coun., NY State Bar Assn., NY County Lawyers Assn., Assn. of Bar of City of NY (chair com. on sports law 2003-2005). Office: Proskauer Rose LLP 1585 Broadway New York NY 10036-8299 Home Phone: 212-734-3009; Office Phone: 212-969-3035. Office Fax: 212-969-2900. Business E-Mail: hganz@proskauer.com.

GANZ, LOWELL, scriptwriter, television producer; b. NYC, Aug. 31, 1948; s. Irving and Jean (Farber) G.; m. Jeanne Russo, Dec. 26, 1976; 3 children. Student, Queens Coll., NYC. Adj. prof.grad. film screenwriting USC. TV work includes: story editor The Odd Couple, ABC, 1972-74, producer Happy Days, ABC, 1975, 79-81, Laverne & Shirley, ABC, 1976-78, exec. producer Busting Loose, 1978-79, Joanie Loves Chachi (also dir.), 1982, all Paramount TV, (with Babaloo Mandel) Makin' It, ABC, 1979, Gung Ho, ABC, 1986, Knight and Daye, NBC, 1986, A League of Their Own, CBS, 1993, (pilots) Herndon, NBC, 1983, Take Five, CBS, 1987, Channel 99, CBS, 1987, Hiller and Diller, 1997; dir. TV series The Bad News Bears, 1979; screenwriter: (with Babaloo Mandel) Night Shift, 1982, Splash (Nat. Film Critics Screenplay of Yr. award),

1984, Spies Like Us, 1985, Gung Ho, 1986, Vibes, 1988, Parenthood, 1989, City Slickers, 1991, A League of Their Own, 1992, Mr. Saturday Night, 1992, Greedy, 1994, (with Dan Aykroyd and Babaloo Mandel), City Slickers II: The Legend of Curly's Gold, 1994, Forget Paris, 1995, Multiplicity, 1996, Father's Day, 1997, Edtv, 1999, Where the Heart Is, 2000, Robots, 2005, Fever Pitch, 2005.

GANZ, MARY KEOHAN, lawyer; b. Weymouth, Mass., Nov. 17, 1954; d. Francis and Margaret (Quinn) Keohan; m. Alan H. Ganz, Sept. 7, 1980. BA magna cum laude, Emmanuel Coll., 1976; JD, Suffolk U., 1979. Bar: Mass. 1979, U.S. Dist. Ct. Mass. 1979, N.H. 1981, U.S. Dist. Ct. N.H. 1981. Pvt. practice, Seabrook, NH, 1981—. Bd. dirs. My Greatest Dream Inc., Seabrook, 1985—, N.H. Child and Family Svc., 2004—, Newburyport 5 Corp.; corporator Anna Jaques Hosp., 2002—, Newburyport Five Cent Savs. Bank, 2004—; chmn. N.H. Child and Family Svc., 2005—. Mem.: ABA, Seacoast Vis. Nurses Assn. (bd. dirs. 1994—2001, sec. 1997—98, v.p. 1998—99, pres. 1999—2001), Seabrook Bus. and Profl. Assn. (pres. 1986—87), Rockingham County Bar Assn., N.H. Bar Assn., Kappa Gamma Pi, Phi Delta Phi. Roman Catholic. Office: 779 Lafayette Rd Seabrook NH 03874-4215

GANZ, PATRICIA ANNE, medical educator, physician; b. LA, Mar. 23, 1948; d. Raymond W. and Ida (Shrier) Conn; m. Tomas Ganz, Aug. 16, 1970; children: David, Rebecca. BA magna cum laude, Harvard-Radcliffe, 1969; MD, UCLA, 1973. Diplomate Am. Bd. Internal Medicine, Am. Bd. Med. Oncology. Post doctoral tng., internal medicine and med. oncology UCLA Med. Ctr.; chief resident in medicine med. ctr. UCLA Sch. Medicine, 1977-78, from asst. to assoc. prof. medicine San Fernando Valley program, 1978-90, prof., 1990-92, prof. health svcs. and medicine, schs. medicine and pub. health, 1990—. Dir. divsn. cancer prevention and control rsch. Jonsson Comprehensive Cancer Ctr., LA, 1993-; clin. rsch. prof., Am. Cancer Soc., 1999-, researcher, Breast Cancer Rsch. Found.; mem. bd. scientific advisors Nat. Cancer Inst.; onvolvement of clin. trials, with leadership roles in Southwest Oncology Group and Nat. Surgical Adjuvant Breast and Bowel Project; founding mem. Nat. Coalition for Cancer Surviorship. Assoc. editor Journal Clin. Oncology, Journal of National Cancer Inst., mem. editl. group Cochrane Breast Cancer Group; contbr. articles to profl. jours. Named Susan G. Komen Prof. of Surviorship. A medical oncologist who has spent the past 20 years doing systematic research on the health-related quality of life impact of cancer and its treatment; has contributed to the understanding of how women adjust to the diagnosis of breast cancer, including its effects on their physical, emotional, social, and sexual well-being. Office: UCLA Divsn Cancer Prevention PO Box 951772 Los Angeles CA 90095-1772 Office Phone: 310-206-1404. Office Fax: 310-206-3566. Business E-Mail: pganz@ucla.edu.*

GANZI, VICTOR FREDERICK, publishing executive; b. NYC, Feb. 14, 1947; s. Walter John and Gertrude (Meyer) G.; m. Patricia Frances Martin, July 10, 1971; children: Danielle Martin, Victoria Louise. BS, Fordham U., 1968; JD, Harvard U., 1971; LLM in Taxation, NYU, 1981. Bar: NY 1973, U.S. Dist. Ct. (so. and ea. dists.) NY 1975, US Ct. Appeals (2d cir.) 1975, US Tax Ct. 1975; CPA, Colo. Tax acct. Touche Ross & Co., Denver, 1971-73; assoc. Rogers & Wells, NYC, 1973-78, ptnr., 1978-86; mng. ptnr. Rogers & Wells (now Clifford Chance Rogers & Wells), 1986-90; v.p., sec., gen. counsel Hearst Corp., NYC, 1990—92, CFO, chief legal officer, sr. v.p., 1992—97; pres. Hearst Books/Bus. Pub. Group, 1995—99; exec. v.p Hearst Corp, NYC, 1997—2002; also COO Hearst Corp., NYC, 1998—2002, pres., CEO, 2002—. Bd. dirs. Palm Mgmt. Corp., NYC, PGA Tour, Inc., ESPN, NYC, IMI Sys. Inc., N.Y.C, NYC, Econ. Devel. Corp., Olsten Corp.; mem. Coun. future of Law Sch., NYU Sch. Law; chmn. Hearst Argyle TV, 2003—; spkr. in field. Bd. dirs. William Randolph Hearst Found., Hearst Found.; trustee Whitney Mus. Am. Art. Mem. ABA, AICPA, Colo. Soc. CPAs, Sky Club, Cherry Valley Club (Garden City, NY). Office: Hearst 250 W 55th St New York NY 10019-5201*

GAO, DAYONG, science educator; b. Shanghai, Mar. 11, 1959; PhD, Concordia U., Montreal, Can., 1990. Prof. U. Ky., Lexington, 1998—2004, U. Wash., Seattle, 2004—. Office: Univ Washington ME Bdg Seattle WA 98195 Office Phone: 206-543-1411. Office Fax: 206-685-8047. Business E-Mail: dayong@u.washington.edu.

GAON, SIMON A., artist, painter; b. NYC, 1943; Studied with Aurthur Bressler, Roosevelet Sch., Stamford, Conn., 1959—60. Represented in permanent collections Mus. City NYC, NY Hist. Soc., NYC, West Valley Art Mus., Surprise, Ariz., Yeshiva U. Mus., NYC, France Loisirs, Paris, Art Student's League, NYC, White and Case, Millenium Hotel, NY, Carrot Capital LLC, one-man shows include Stern Bros. Gallery, NYC, 1965, Art Students Leage, 1968, Gallery Des Ambassadeurs, Paris, 1974, Nicolas Roerich Mus., NYC, 1986, Ingber Gallery, 1988, Gallery Peter Fischinger, Stuttgart, Germany, 1990, Gallery Rose, Hamburg, Germany, 1990, 1999, 2005, Gallery Le Chainon Manquant, Paris, 1991, France Loisirs Corp. Offices, 1991; Frank Bustamante Gallery, NYC, 1992, Susan Conway Gallery, 1995, Gallery Peter Fischinger, Stuttgart, 1995, Gallery Rubens, Smedjebacken, Sweden, 1999, Yeshiva U. Mus., NYC, 2001, Ludvika Konsthall, Sweden, 2002, West Valley Art. Mus., Surprise, 2004, Famira Gallery, Sylt, Germany, 2004, 2006, Nabi Gallery, NYC, 2005, Berlin Capital Club, 2007, others, exhibited in group shows at Loeb Ctr., NYC, 1969, Subjectivist Gallery, 1975, Brotherhood Synagogue, 1978, Adelphi U., Garden City, NY, 1981, Parish Art Mus., Southampton, NY, 1982, Pace U., Westchester, NY, 1982, Lever Ho. Gallery, NYC, 1982—87, NY Inst. Tech., 1985, Helander Gallery, NYC, 1990, Gallery Rose, 1990, Graham Modern, 1992, Elizabeth Harris Gallery, 1994, ACA Galleries, 1995, Peter Findlay Gallery, 1995—2004, 2006, Mangel Gallery, Phila., 1997, Nabi Gallery, Sag Harbor, NY, 1997, 1999, 2001, NYC, 2006, Gallery Bristol Myers Squibb, Princeton, NJ, 2002, 2004, Lizan-Tops, Easthampton, NY, 2002, NY Hist. Soc., 2003, Schlessinger Gallery, NYC, 2003, Handsel Gallery, Santa Fe, N.Mex., Hudson, NY, 2004, Spanierman Gallery, East Hampton, NY, 2005, Gallery North, Setauket, NY, 2006, Valley Ho. Gallery, Dallas, 2006, Butler Fine Art Gallery, East Hampton, 2007, Acme Gallery, Boston, 2007. Scholar, Art Students League, NYC, 1962—63, 1965; Edward G. McDowell Traveling scholar, 1966. Home and Studio: 425 Riverside Dr #154 New York NY 10025

GARABEDIAN, PAUL ROESEL, mathematics professor; b. Cin., Aug. 2, 1927; s. Carl A. and Margaret (Roesel) G.; m. Gladys Rappaport, Oct. 22, 1949 (div. 1963); m. Lynnel Marg, Dec. 31, 1966; children: Emily, Catherine. AB, Brown U., 1946; A.M., Harvard U., 1947, PhD, 1948. Asst. prof. math. U. Calif.-Berkeley, 1949-50; asst. prof. Stanford U., Calif., 1950-52, assoc. prof., 1952-56, prof., 1956-59; prof. math. Courant Inst., NYU, 1959—; dir. Courant Math. and Computing Lab. Dept. Energy, 1972—78, dir. divsn. computational fluid dynamics, 1978—. Mem. editl. bd. Internat. Jour. Computational Fluid Dynamics, Applicable Analysis, Internat. Jour. Computational and Applied Math.; contbr. articles to profl. jours. NRC fellow, 1948-49, Sloan Found. fellow, 1961-63, Guggenheim fellow, 1966, 81-82, Fairchild Disting. scholar Calif. Inst. Tech., 1975; recipient Pub. Service Group Achievement award NASA, 1976, Boris Pregal award N.Y. Acad. Scis., 1980. Fellow Am. Phys. Soc.; mem. NAS (Applied Math. and Numerical Analysis prize 1998), Am. Acad. Arts and Scis., Am. Math. Soc. (Birkhoff prize 1983), Soc. Indsl. and Applied Math. (von Karman prize 1989). Home: 60 E 8th St Apt 9K New York NY 10003-2101 Office: NYU 251 Mercer St New York NY 10012-1110 Office Phone: 212-998-3237. Business E-Mail: garabedi@cims.nyu.edu.

GARAGIOLA, JOE, JR., baseball team executive; m. Noel Garagiola; children: Meredith, Valerie, Natalie, Christopher. BA cum laude, U. Notre Dame, 1972; JD, Georgetown U., 1975. Bar: Ariz., Calif., N.Y. Gen. counsel, asst. to pres. N.Y. Yankees, NYC; ptnr. Gallagher and Kennedy, Phoenix, 1982—; chmn. bd. dirs. Phoenix Met. Sports Found., 1985-87; v.p., gen. mgr. Ariz. Diamondbacks (profl. baseball expansion team), 1995—. Vice chmn. Gov.'s Cactus League Task Force, Phoenix; mem. Mayor's profl. baseball com.; chmn. Maricopa County (Ariz.) Sports Authority, Ariz. Baseball Commn. Bd. dirs. Am. West Airlines Ednl. Found., Phoenix Meml. Hosp. Recipient Inst. Human Rels. award, Am. Jewish Com., 1998. Office: c/o Ariz Diamondbacks 401 E Jefferson St Phoenix AZ 85004-2438

GARAMENDI, JOHN R., lieutenant governor, former state legislator; b. Mokelumne Hill, Calif., 1945; m. Patricia Wilkinson; 6 children. BA in Bus., U. Calif.-Berkeley; MBA, Harvard Bus. Sch. Rancher nr. Sacramento County; former mem. Calif. Assembly, 1974—76; senator Calif. State Senate, 1976—91; chmn. revenue and taxation Joint Com. on Sci. and Tech.; insurance commr. State of Calif., 1991—94, 2002—06; dep. sec. Dept. Interior, 1995—98; ptnr. Yucaipa Companies, 1998; lt. gov. State of Calif., 2007—. Chair Joint Com. on Sci. and Tech., Senate Health and Welfare Com., Senate Revenue and Taxation Com. Vol. US Peace Corps, Ethiopia, 1966—68. Democrat. Office: Lieutenant Governor State Capitol Rm 1114 Sacramento CA 95814 Office Phone: 916-445-8994.*

GARANZINI, MICHAEL J., academic administrator, priest; b. St. Louis; BA in Psychology, St. Louis U., 1971; MA in Am. Civilization, NYU, 1978; MDiv, Weston Sch. Theology, 1980; STM in Moral Devel., U. Calif., Berkeley, 1981, PhD in Psychology and Religion, 1986. Part-time faculty mem. U. San Francisco, 1984—86, asst. prof. dept. psychology, 1986—88, asst. prof. dept. ednl. psychology Sch. Edn., 1986—88; assoc. prof. edn. St. Louis U., 1988—98, acting v.p. student devel., 1991—92, asst. acad. v.p., 1992—93, acting acad. v.p., 1993—94, acad. v.p., 1994—98; vis. prof. counseling Fordham U., 1998—99; spl. asst. to the pres., acting chair dept. psychology Georgetown U., 1999—2001; pres. Loyola U., Chgo., 2001—. Vis. prof. psychology and family studies grad. divsn. Gregorian U., 1986, 88. Author: The Attachment Cycle: An Object Relations Approach to the Healing Ministries, 1987, Child-Centered Schools: An Educator's Guide to Family Dysfunction, 1995; contbr. articles to profl. jours. Office: Loyola Univ Chgo Office of the Pres 820 N Michigan Ave Chicago IL 60611 Office Phone: 312-915-6400. E-mail: mgaranz@luc.edu.

GARAUFIS, NICHOLAS G., federal judge; b. Paterson, NJ, Sept. 28, 1948; married. AB, Columbia Coll., 1969; JD, Columbia U., 1974. Assoc. Chadbourne & Parke LLP, 1974-75; asst. atty. gen. State of NY, 1975-78; pvt. practice Queens, NY, 1978-86; counsel to Hon. Claire Shulma Office Pres. of Borough of Queens, NYC, 1986-95; chief counsel FAA, Washington, 1995-2000; judge US Dist. Ct. (ea. dist.) NY, Bklyn., 2000—. Office: US Dist Ct Ea Dist NY 225 Cadman Plz E Brooklyn NY 11201 Office Phone: 718-613-2540.

GARAVANI, VALENTINO See VALENTINO

GARBACZ, GREGORY A., lawyer; b. Columbus, Ind., May 21, 1967; s. Gerald G. and Jane Elizabeth (Snyder) Garbacz; m. Lauren Krause, Sept. 17, 1995; children: Luke, Matthew, Juliet Grace. BA in Govt. and Law, Lafayette Coll., Easton, Pa., 1989; JD, Wash. and Lee U., Lexington, Va., 1993. Shareholder, COO Klinedinst PC, San Diego, 1993—2002, mng. shareholder LA, 2002—05, COO, 2006—. Contbr. articles to profl. jours. Office: Klinedinst PC 777 S Figueroa Ste 4700 Los Angeles CA 90017-3584 also: Klinedinst PC 501 W Broadway San Diego CA 92101 Business E-Mail: ggarbacz@klinedinstlaw.com.

GARBAJOSA (CHAPARRO), JORGE, professional basketball player; b. Madrid, Dec. 19, 1977; Forward Tau Vitoria, Spain, 1996—2000, Benetton Treviso, Italy, 2000—04, Spanish ACB League Unicaja Malaga, 2004—06, Toronto Raptors, Ont., Canada, 2006—. Mem. Spanish Olympic Team, 2000, 04. Named Player of Yr., Eurobasket.com, 2003, Spanish Cup Finals MVP, 2005, 2006; named to All-Euroleague First Team, Eurobasket.com, 2003, NBA All-Rookie First Team, 2007. Achievements include winning two Spanish National Cups, 1999, 2005, one Spanish National Championship, two Italian National Cups, 2003, 04, two Italian National Championships, two Italian Supercups, 2001, 02, one Saporta Cup and a Spanish Junior Championship. Mailing: Toronto Raptors 40 Bay St Toronto ON M5J 2X2 Canada*

GARBARINI, WILLIAM NICHOLAS, pharmaceutical executive; b. Somerville, NJ, Oct. 24, 1969; s. William Nicholas and Janet L. Garbarini; m. Maureen Elizabeth Murphy, June 10, 1995; children: Dana Marie, William Nicholas. BS in Econs., Coll. N.J., 1992; MBA in Pharm. Studies, Fairleigh Dickinson U., 2002. Profl. sales rep. Glaxo SmithKline, Research Triangle Park, NC, 1993—96; account supr. Lowe Healthcare Worldwide, NYC, 1996—98; product mgr. Key Pharmaceuticals Schering-Plough Corp., Kenilworth, NJ, 1998—2000; dir. client svcs. Caresoft, Inc., Sunnyvale, Calif., 2000—01; exec. dir. sales and mktg. Ferring Pharms. Inc., Suffern, NY, 2001—. Named Premier Performer, Burroughs Wellcome Co., 1994—95; named to Ferring Excellence Club, 2003, 2005, 2006; recipient Dir. Leading Change award, Burroughs Wellcome Co., 1995. Mem.: Delta Mu Delta, Phi Kappa Psi (chpt. pres. 1991—92). Roman Catholic. Avocations: music, baseball, golf, woodworking. Home: 421 Manor Ave Cranford NJ 07016 Office: Ferring Pharmaceuticals Inc 4 Gatehall Dr 3rd Fl Parsippany NJ 07054 Home Phone: 908-931-0646; Office Phone: 973-796-1640. Office Fax: 973-796-1711. Business E-Mail: william.garbarini@ferring.com.

GARBER, AARON MATTHEW, performing company executive, music director; b. Harrisonburg, Va., Apr. 9, 1973; BA in Music, Bridgewater Coll., 1995; MusM in Choral Conducting, U. Tenn., 2000. Dir. music coll. Luth. Ch., Salem, Va., 2000—; artistic dir. Salem Choral Soc., 2001—. Composer: (mass) Mass for Peace, (oratorio) Job, Mary, (choral) Stabat Mater (Ramond W. Brock Student Composition Contest, 2001). Mem.: Jefferson Choral Soc. (artistic dir.), Rotary. Office Phone: 540-389-4963.

GARBER, ALAN MICHAEL, internist, educator, economist; s. Harry Garber; m. Anne Yahanda, Oct. 9, 1988. AB in Econs. summa cum laude, Harvard Coll., 1976, AM in Econs., 1977, PhD in Econs., 1982; MD, Stanford U., 1983. Diplomate Am. Bd. Internal Medicine. Cons. Inst. Medicine, Washington, 1979-80; clin. fellow Med. Sch. Harvard U., Boston, 1983-86, rsch. fellow John F. Kennedy Sch. Govt. Cambridge, Mass., 1986; staff physician VA Palo Alto Health Care System, Calif., 1986—; rsch. assoc. Nat. Bur. Econ. Rsch., Palo Alto, Calif., 1986—, dir. health care program Cambridge, 1990—; asst. prof. Stanford U., Calif., 1986-93, assoc. prof., 1993-98, dir. Ctr. Health Policy/Ctr. Primary Care and Outcomes Rsch., 1997—, prof. medicine, 1998—, Henry J. Kaiser jr. prof., endowed chair; contractor Office Tech. Assessment, Washington, 1987-88, 89-92. Chair Medicare Coverage Adv. Com., 2005—; mem. Nat. Adv. Coun. Aging, 2004—. Grad. fellow NSF, 1976, Henry J. Kaiser faculty fellow Kaiser Found., 1989-92. Fellow ACP, Acad. Health; mem. Inst. Medicine of NAS, Soc. Med. Decision Making (trustee 1989-91), Am. Econ. Assn., Am. Fedn. Clin. Rsch. (nat. councillor 1991-96), Soc. Gen. Internal Medicine, Am. Soc. for Clin. Investigation, Assn. Am. Physicians, Internat. Health Econs. Assn. Office: Primary Care Outcomes Rsch Ctr Health Policy 117 Encina Commons Stanford CA 94305-6019 Business E-Mail: garber@stanford.edu.

GARBER, DONALD, Major League Soccer commissioner; b. 1960; married; 2 children. BA Business, Journalism, State University of New York, College at Oneonta. Marketing mgr. NFL Properties, 1984—88, dir., marketing, 1988—90, v.p., business development and special events, 1990—96; pres. NFL International, 1996—99; commissioner Major League Soccer, 1999—. Mem.: National Soccer Hall of Fame Board of Trustees, United States Soccer Foundation, United States Soccer Federation Executive Committee. Office: c/o MLS 110 E 42nd st 10th Fl New York NY 10017

GARBER, HELEN KOLIKOW, photographer, artist; b. Bklyn., Aug. 9, 1954; d. Alex and Geraldine (Rubin) Kolikow; m. Stuart Garber, Aug. 12, 1979. BS, SUNY, New Paltz, 1976. Cover and 45 interior photographs in Parents at Last, 1998; photography work has appeared in Photo Dist. News, B&W Mag., Focus Mag., Am. Photo, Popular Photography, NY Times, NY Mag., LA Times, Travel Holiday; one-woman shows include Santa Monica Mus. Flying, 1990, Paul Kopeikin Gallery, LA, Samuel Dorsky Mus. Art, New Paltz, NY, 2007; represented in permanent collection at Bklyn. Mus. Art, Portland (Oreg.) Art Mus., Mus. City NY, Yale U., Peter Palmquist Archives, Gearge Eastman House Internat. Mus. Film and Photography, NY, Samuel Dorsky Mus. Art, New Paltz; author: Venice Beach, California Carnivale, 2005. Avocation: travel. Office Phone: 310-392-4272. Business E-Mail: mail@helenkgarber.com.

GARBER, JEFFREY RICHARD, endocrinologist; b. Bklyn., Nov. 25, 1949; s. Aaron and Mae Garber; m. Sheri Leiman, May 30, 1974; children: Benjamin, Solomon. AB, Cornell U., Ithaca, NY, 1971; MD, SUNY, Stony Brook, 1974. Diplomate Am. Bd. Internal Medicine, Am. Bd. Endocrinology. Chief endocrinology Harvard Vanguard Med. Assocs., Boston, 1981—; clin. asst. prof. Harvard Med. Sch. Author: The Harvard Medical School Guide to Overcoming Thyroid Problems, 2005. Mem. med. adv. coun. Thyroid Found. Am., Boston. Recipient physician recognition award, Harvard Cmty. Health Plan, 1985, 1988; Peabody Clin. fellow, Harvard Med. Sch., 1981—84. Fellow: Am. Coll. Endocrinology (trustee); mem.: ACP, Am. Thyroid Assn. (mem. exec. coun. 2000—04), Am. Assn. Clin. Endocrinology (bd. dirs. 1999—2005, sec./treas. 2005—06, v.p. 2007—). Office: Harvard Vanguard Med Assoc 133 Brookline Ave Boston MA 02215

GARBER, MARGARET MARY, elementary school educator; b. Wilkes Barre, Pa., June 19, 1926; d. Gilbert Thomas Steever and Margaret Mary Thomas; m. Henry M. Garber, June 26, 1949; children: Kim Garber Lifton, Joan Garber Hossler, Tobin Henry. BS in Phys. Edn., West Chester U., Pa., 1948. 1st grade tchr. Donegal Sch. Dist., Maytown, Pa., 1965—92. Sec. Elizabethtown Hist. Soc., Pa., 2003—05; vice regent DAR, Columbia, Pa., 2003—05; mem. Rep. Com. Home: 1032 S Mount Joy St Elizabethtown PA 17022 Personal E-mail: mgarber705@aol.com.

GARBER, NICHOLAS JACK, civil engineer, educator; b. Freetown, Sierra Leone, Apr. 13, 1936; came to U.S., 1980; s. Nicholas Abisodun and Rosamond Marian (John) G.; m. Ada Mary Smith, Mar. 31, 1962; children: Alison, Valerie, Elaine. BSc in Civil Engring., U. London, 1961; MS, Carnegie-Mellon U., 1969, PhD, 1971. Chartered engr., Eng.; reg. profl. engr., Va. Engr. Jenkins, Porter & Bingham Consulting Engrs., London, 1961-62, Rendall, Palmer & Tritton consulting Engrs., London, 1962-63, Scott & Wilson Kirkpatrick Consulting Engrs., London, 1963-64; exec. engr. Min. Work, Freetown, Sierra Leone, 1964-67; asst. prof. SUNY, Buffalo, 1970-72; lectr. to sr. lectr. U. Sierra Leone, Freetown, 1972-74, 74-76, assoc. prof., dean faculty of engring., 1976-80; vis. assoc. prof. U. Va., Charlottesville, 1980-81, assoc. prof., 1981-91, prof., 1991—, chmn. dept. civil engring., 1996—. Design engr. Consulting Engr., London, 1961-62; ptnr., dir. Techsult & Co., Freetown, 1972—; chmn. com. Transp. Rsch. Bd., Washington, 1989-95. Co-author: Traffic & Highway ENgineering, 2d rev. edit., 1999; contbr. articles to Transp. Rsch. Record. Mem. bd. dirs. Workshop V, Charlottesville, 1985-89. Recipient TRB D. Grant Mickle award, 1996. Mem. NAE, Sojourner Kilwinning Lodge (founding, Master's award 1996). Episcopalian. Achievements include development of a statistical sampling method for traffic counts, procedure for controlling speeds at highway work zones. Home: 104 Woodhurst Ct Charlottesville VA 22901-2236 Home Phone: 434-295-2745; Office Phone: 434-924-6366. E-mail: njg@virginia.edu.

GARBER, PAUL WILLIAM, lawyer; b. Boston, Nov. 16, 1934; s. Rubin Elias and Sarah Rose Garber. AB in Medieval History magna cum laude, Harvard Coll., 1956, JD, 1961; diploma in Command and Staff, U.S. Naval War Coll., 1967, diploma in Naval Warfare, 1970. Registered Land Court Title Examiner, 1966. Atty. Garber and Garber, Esqs., Boston, 1961—, pres.; consul. Consulate of Chile, Boston, 1974—. Author: (with Philip C. Garber) The Political Constitution of Chile-An English Translation, 1981, The Political Constitutiuon of Chile, 2005; contbr. articles to profl. jours. Pres. Constn. Chpt. Naval Res. Assoc., 1973-75, Navy Chpt. 5 Res. Officers Assn., 1979, First Region Naval Res. Assn., 1980, exec. v.p. 1971-72, Club Chileno, hon. pres., 1974-80, dir. Alumni Assoc., West End House, 1963-99, Scholarship Com., 1976-99, bd. dirs. Eastern Mass. chpt. Navy League U.S., 1976-85; judge Adv. Mass. Bay Coun., NLUS, 1985-99, dir. emeritus, 1999—; trustee USS Constitution Mus., 2003—. Capt. USNR, 1956-86. Decorated Navy Achievement medal USN, knight comdr. and grand officer Order Bernardo O'Higgins (Chile), officer Order of Naval Merit (Chile). Mem.: Naval War Coll. Found. (life), Surface Warfare Assn. (life), USS Constn. Mus. (life), Navy League U.S. (life), Medieval Acad. Am. (life), USN Inst. (life), Mil. Officers Assn. Am. (life), Boston Athenaeum (life), Caleuche Club Litoral Valparaiso, Wardroom Club, Harvard Club of Boston. Avocations: gardening, reading. Office: Consulate of Chile 1 Bernardo O'Higgins Cir Brighton MA 02135 Office Phone: 617-232-0416. E-mail: conchile.org@comcast.net.

GARBER, PHILIP ROBERT, academic administrator, researcher; s. Robert Thomas and Patricia Sparr (Graziano) Garber. PhD, U. Chgo., 1997. Dir. assessment Nat. Louis U., Chgo., 1998—; dir. rsch. Rsch. Pros, Inc., Chgo., 1999—2002. Democrat. Achievements include research in cognitive devel. Office: Nat Louis University 122 S Michigan Ave Chicago IL 60603 Office Phone: 312-261-3028. Business E-Mail: pgarber@nl.edu.

GARBER, ROBERT EDWARD, lawyer, insurance company executive; b. NYC, Jan. 4, 1949; s. Edward Robert and Estelle (Rosenberg) G.; m. Mary Ellen Roche, Jan. 17, 1981; 1 child, Edward Thomas AB, Princeton U., 1970; JD, Columbia U., 1973. Bar: N.Y. 1974. Law clk. U.S. Dist. Ct. (so. dist.), NYC, 1973-75; assoc. Debevoise, Plimpton, Lyons & Gates, NYC, 1976-79; assoc. counsel, v.p. Irving Trust, NYC, 1979-82, sr. v.p., 1982-87; gen. counsel Irving Bank Corp. and Irving Trust Co., NYC, 1987-89; sr. v.p., dep. gen. counsel Equitable Life Assurance Soc. U.S., NYC, 1989-93; sr. v.p., gen. counsel Equitable Cos., Inc. and Equitable Life Assurance Soc. U.S., 1993-94, exec. v.p., gen. counsel, 1994-99; exec. v.p., chief legal officer Equitable Life Assurance Soc. U.S., 1999—2001; exec. v.p., gen. counsel AXA Fin., Inc., 1999—2001. Served to capt. USAR, 1970-78 Home: 45 Sturgis Rd Bronxville NY 10708-5012

GARBER, SAMUEL B., lawyer, retail executive; b. Chgo., Aug. 16, 1934; s. Morris and Yetta G.; m. Marietta C. Bratta; children: Debra Lee, Diane Lori. JD, U. Ill., 1958; MBA, U. Chgo., 1968. Bar: Ill. 1958. Ptnr. Brown, Dashow and Langluttig, Chgo., 1960-62; corp. counsel Walgreen Co., 1962-69; gen. counsel, exec. asst. to the pres. Carlyle & Co., 1969-73; dir. legal affairs Stop & Shop Co., Inc., 1973-74; v.p., gen. counsel Goldblatt Bros., Inc., 1974-76; v.p., sec., gen. counsel, dir. Evans, Inc., 1976-99, pres., CEO, 1999-2000; prof. mgmt. DePaul U., 1975—; prin.

The Garber Group, Bus. Cons. and Turnaround Management Firm, Chgo., 2000—. Adj. prof. bus. law Grad. Sch. Bus., U. Chgo., 1993-2005; arbitrator NY Stock Exch., 1996, Chgo. Merc. Exch., 1996, Am. Stock Exch., 1997, Nat. Futures Assn., 1997; columnist Garber's Gurus, Tribune Media Svcs., 1999-2001. With US Army, 1958-60. Mem. ABA, NYSE (arbitrator 1996—), Am. Arbitration Assn. (arbitrator 1993, mediator 1994—), Internat. Coun. of Shopping Ctrs., Turnaround Mgmt. Assn., Beta Gamma Sigma. Home: 2626 N Lakeview Ave Chicago IL 60614-1809 Office: DePaul U 1 E Jackson Blvd Ste 7010 Chicago IL 60604-2287 Business E-Mail: thegarbergroup@yahoo.com, sgarber@depaul.edu.

GARBER, VICTOR, stage and film actor; b. London, Ont., Can., Mar. 16, 1949; Actor: (films) Liberace: Behind the Music, 1988, Light Sleeper, 1991, Sleepless in Seattle, 1993, Life with Mikey, 1993, Mixed Nuts, 1994, First Wives Club, 1996, Titanic, 1997, How Stella Got Her Groove Back, 1998, External Affairs, 1999, Legally Blonde, 2001, Tuck Everlasting, 2002, Home Room, 2002; (TV films) Life with Judy Garland: Me and My Shadows, 2001 (Emmy nominee); (TV series) Alias, 2001—06 (Emmy nominee, 2002), (TV appearances) Days and Nights of Molly Dodd, 1987, I'll Fly Away, 1991, E.N.G. intermittently, Kung Fu: The Legend Continues, 1992, Law and Order, 1990, Frasier, 1993 (Emmy nominee), Outer Limits, 1996, Invisible Child, 1999, The Music Man, 2002, Will & Grace, 2004; (Broadway plays) Deathtrap, 1978 (Tony nominee), Sweeney Todd, 1979 (Tony nominee), Little Me, 1982 (Tony nominee), Lend Me A Tenor, 1989 (Tony nominee), revival of Damn Yankees, 1994 (Tony nominee), Art, 1998, Of Thee I Sing, 2006, (Off-Broadway) Assassins, Love Letters, Wenceslas Square, Ghost; (plays) Present Laughter, 2007.*

GARBER, WILLIAM MACY See MACY, BILL

GARBIN, ALBENO PATRICK, sociology educator; b. Girard, Ill., June 20, 1932; s. Cipriano and Angelina (Sommavillia) G.; m. Carol Townsend Nichols, Sept. 3, 1969; children: Angela Marie, Tina Ann, A. Patrick, Carol Anne. AB, Blackburn Coll., 1956; MA, La. State U., 1959, PhD, 1963. Instr., asst. prof. sociology U. Omaha, 1961-64; asst. prof. Fla. State U., Tallahassee, 1964-66; assoc. prof., specialist occupation edn. Ohio State U., Columbus, 1966-68; prof. sociology U. Ga., Athens, 1968-97, prof. emeritus, 1997—. Served in US Army, 1954—56. Recipient rsch. award Am. Personnel and Guidance Assn., 1977, Excellence in Undergrad. Tchg. award U. Ga., 1978, meritorious svc. award Ga. Soc. Assn., 1991. Mem. Am. Sociol. Assn., So. Sociol. Soc., Ga. Sociol. Assn. (v.p. 1984-85, pres. 1986-87). Democrat. Roman Catholic. Avocations: gardening, photography. Home: 85 Timberland Trail Arnoldsville GA 30619-2216 Office: U Ga Dept Sociology Athens GA 30602 Office Phone: 706-542-3218. Business E-Mail: algarbin@arches.uga.edu. *Hard work is a requisite, but luck can be very helpful! A loving wife and family make it all worthwhile.*

GARBIS, MARVIN JOSEPH, judge; b. Balt., June 14, 1936; s. Samuel and Adele E. (Warshaw) G.; children: Kendall Rose, Jason Anders, Kerri Jill. BES., Johns Hopkins U., 1958; JD, Harvard U., 1961; LLM, Georgetown U., 1962. Bar: D.C. 1961, Md. 1962. Trial atty. Tax Div., Dept. Justice, Washington, 1962-67; sole practice Balt., 1967-71; ptnr. Garbis, Marvel & Junghans, Balt., 1971-86, Melnicove, Kaufman, Weiner, Smouse & Garbis, Balt., 1986-88, Johnson & Gibbs, Washington, 1988-89; judge U.S. Dist. Ct. Md., 1989—. Lectr. U. Md. Law Sch., 1970-85, NYU Fed. Tax Inst., 1970, 74, 79, 87-88; adj. prof. Georgetown U. Law Sch., 1978-80, U. Balt. Law Sch., 1982—; adviser on tax procedure study, jud. com. U.S. Senate, 1969-70; mem. adv. commr. to commr. IRS, 1982; mem. adv. coun. U.S. Claims Ct., 1982—; mem. Md. Inst. for Continuing Profl. Edn. for Lawyers, 1978-80, pres., 1980-82; vis. scholar Fed. Ct. of Australia, 1998. Author: (with Frome) Procedures in Federal Tax Controversy, 1968, (with Schwait) Tax Refund Litigation, 1971, Tax Court Practice, 1974, (with Struntz) Cases and Materials on Federal Tax Procedure, Civil and Criminal, 1981, (with Junghans and Struntz) Federal Tax Litigation, 1985, (with Struntz and Rubin) Cases and Materials on Tax Procedure and Tax Fraud, 2d edit., 1987, (with Rubin and Morgan) Cases and Material on Tax Procedure and Tax Fraud, 3d edit., 1991; contbr. articles to profl. jours. Recipient Jules Ritholz Meml. Merit award, 1996; E. Barrett Prettyman fellow, Georgetown Law Sch., 1961—62. Mem. Fed. Bar Assn. (pres. Balt. chpt. 1972-73, nat. vice chmn. tax com. 1974-76), Md. Bar Assn. (chmn. tax sect. 1970-71, chmn. continuing legal edn. 1973-80), ABA (chmn. ct. procedure com., tax sect. 1975-77), Balt. Bar Assn. (bd. govs. 1974-79), Fed. Cir. Bar Assn. (bd. dirs. 1985—). Am. Law Inst., Md. Inst. Continuing Profl. Education Lawyers (pres. 1981-82) judge. Office: US Dist Ct 101 W Lombard St Ste 530 Baltimore MD 21201-2605 Business E-Mail: judge_garbis@mdd.uscourts.gov.

GARBRANDT, GAIL ELAINE, political science professor, consultant; b. Dover, Ohio, Oct. 10, 1955; d. Floyd Madison Grewell and Mary Catherine Sica; children: John Paul Marino, Vanessa Marie Marino. BA, Kent State U., Ohio, 1992; MA, U. Akron, Ohio, 1995. Pres. and CEO Citi-Energy Ops., Dover, Ohio, 1983—91; campaign coord. Senator Robert L. Burch, 1992—94; adj. prof. Stark State Coll., Canton, 1996—98, Malone Coll., 1998—2005, Mount Union Coll., Alliance, 1998—, Walsh U., N. Canton, 1998—; intern coord. and nat. campaign trainer Ray C. Bliss Inst. U. Akron, 2000—. Mem. adv. bd. Ctr. Women in Pub. Svc., Cleve., Canadian Studies U. Akron, North Am. Free Trade Agreement Program Ctr., Washington. Author: NWPC Campaign Training, 2005; contbr. articles to profl. jours. Vol. Main Street, New Philadelphia, Ohio, 2005—06, Tuscarawas County Hospice, 2005—06; mem. exec. com. Tuscarawas County Dem. Party, New Philadelphia, 2003—06; mem. think tank Ohio Dem. Party, Columbus, 2006. Named a Ky. Col., Gov. Ky., 2002, Woman of Worth, Worth Corp., Ltd., 2003; recipient Pioneer award, Mortar Bd., 2003, Woman of Excellence award, Women's Network, Inc., 2007. Mem.: Soc. Cath. Social Scientists, Am. Acad. Polit. Cons. (bd. mem. 2005—, pres. midwest chpt. 2004—06), Nat. Women's Polit. Caucus (bd. mem. 2005—). Roman Catholic. Office: U Akron Olin Hall Rm 224A Akron OH 44325-0002 Office Phone: 330-972-5182.

GARBUS, MARTIN SOLOMON, lawyer; b. Bklyn., Aug. 8, 1934; s. Solomon and Anna (Washinsky) G.; m. Sarina Tang, June 24, 1995; children from previous marriage: Cassandra, Elizabeth. BA, Hunter Coll., 1955; JD, NYU, 1959. Bar: NY 1960, US Supreme Ct. 1962, US Ct. Appeals (2nd, 3rd and 5th cirs.) 1970, US Tax Ct. 1975. Mem. faculty Columbia U., NYC, 1968-78, Yale U., New Haven, 1969; ptnr. Frankfurt, Garbus, Klein & Selz, NYC, 1978—2002, Davis & Gilbert, LLP, NYC, 2003—. Assoc. dir. Civil Liberties Union, 1967-69; faculty mem., Columbia U., 1968, Yale U. 1978; lectr. Stanford Law Sch., Harvard Law Sch., Practising Law Inst. on criminal, civil, libel, comm. law and trial techniques, 1960-84; apptd. adv. to Chinese team on creation of intellectual property laws Chinese Govt., 2004; instr. Tsinghua U. Beijing; spkr. in field. Author: Ready for the Defense, 1969, Traitors and Heroes, 1987, Tough Talk: How I Fought For Writers, Comics, Bigots, and the American Way, 1998, Courting Disaster: The Supreme Court and the Unmaking of America Law, 2002, The Next 25 Years: The New Supreme Court and What it Means for Americans, 2007; TV appearances include: 60 Minutes, Dateline, Good Morning America, Charlie Rose Show; commentator: NBC, ABC, CBS, PBS, CNN, Fox News Channel, Court TV; contbr. numerous articles to law revs. and to NY Times, Washington Post, LA Times, and others. Mem. Mayor's Select Com. on Criminal Justice, Criminal Law, 1972-75, Internat. Law, 1976-78. Named one of Top 10 Litigators, Nat. Law Jour., Best Lawyers in NY, NY Mag. Mem. ABA, ACLU (bd. dirs. 1986-89), Bar Assn. NYC (mem. comm. and medial law com.) Achievements include representing well-known authors, publishers, actors, playwrights, directors, producers, and motion picture studios; selected as a consultant on media and communications by Canada, England, Australia, the former Soviet Union, Czechoslovakia, Poland, China, and Hungary. Office: Davis & Gilbert LLP 1740 Broadway New York NY 10019 Office Phone: 212-468-4883. Office Fax: 212-468-4888. E-mail: mgarbus@dglaw.com.

GARCHIK, LEAH LIEBERMAN, journalist; b. Bklyn., May 2, 1945; d. Arthur Louis and Mildred (Steinberg) Lieberman; m. Jerome Marcus Garchik, Aug. 11, 1968; children— Samuel, Jacob BA, Bklyn. Coll., 1966. Editorial asst. San Francisco Chronicle, 1972-79, writer, editor, 1979-83, editor This World, 1983-84, columnist, 1984—; also author numerous book and movie reviews, features and profiles. Author: San Francisco; the City's Sights and Secrets, 1995; panelist (radio quiz show) Minds Over Matter; contbr. articles to mags. Vice pres. Golden Gate Kindergarten Assn., San Francisco, 1978; pres. Performing Arts Workshop, San Francisco, 1977-79; bd. dirs. Home Away From Homelessness, 1994-99. Recipient 1st prize Nat. Soc. Newspaper Columnists, 1992. Mem. Newspaper Guild. Democrat. Jewish. Home: 156 Baker St San Francisco CA 94117-2111 Office: San Francisco Chronicle 901 Mission St San Francisco CA 94103-2905 Home Phone: 415-626-0993. Business E-Mail: lgarchik@sfchronicle.com.

GARCIA, ADOLFO RAMON, lawyer, director; b. Havana, Cuba, Nov. 5, 1948; arrived in US, 1961; s. Adolfo Damian and Luz I. (Garcia) G.; m. Elizabeth Ensor, July 17, 1971; children: Andrew, Laurence. AB magna cum laude, Harvard U., 1971; JD, Georgetown U., 1974. Bar: N.Y. 1975, Mass. 1981. Assoc. Cahill Gordon & Reindel, NYC, 1974-79, Choate, Hall & Stewart, Boston, 1979-82; sr. ptnr. McDermott, Will & Emery, Boston, 1982—2003; ptnr., co-head internat. practice group Ropes & Gray, Boston, 2003—. Former bd. dirs. Certified Oil Co., Carboclor Industrias Quimicas S.A., Sol Petrolgo, S.A., Boston, Healthcare Assocs., Inc. Co-chmn. legal affairs com., bd. dirs. Internat. Bus. Ctr. New Eng. Inc., Boston, 1983-87; past chmn. and pres., bd. dirs. Boston Ctr. for Internat. Visitors, 1981-86; active Mass. Internat. Trade Coun., Boston, 1984-86; v.p., dir. New Eng.-Latin Am. Bus. Coun; v.p. & dir. New England-Latin Am. Bus. Council. Mem. Internat. Bar Assn., Boston Bar Assn. (co-chmn. pvt. internat. law sect. 1982-86, co-chair internat. law sect. 2005-), InterAm. Bar Assn., Essex County Club, Manchester (Mass.) Yacht Club, Union Club, Singing Beach Club, Everglades Club. Republican. Home: October Hill Prides Crossing MA 01965 Home Phone: 508-932-4211; Office Phone: 617-951-7468. Office Fax: 617-951-7050. Business E-Mail: agarcia@ropesgray.com.

GARCIA, ANDREW BERNARD, chemical engineer; b. Las Cruces, N.Mex., Apr. 22, 1949; s. Rudolf A. and Margaret (Rivera) Garcia; m. Katherine D. Montano, July 5, 1974 (dec. Aug. 1996); children: Lauren, Alexandra; m. Elaine Rose Richards, Nov. 29, 2002. BS in Chem. Engring. with honors, N.Mex. State U., Las Cruces, 1972; MBA, St. Mary's Coll., Moraga, Calif., 1979; postgrad., U. Calif., Berkeley, 1994. Registered environ. assessor; cert. hazardous materials mgr. Design engr. Gen. Electric Co., San Jose, Calif., 1972-75; chem. engr. Chevron Chem. Co., Richmond, Calif., 1975-78; supr. Chevron Corp., San Francisco, 1978-80; supply product mgr. Chevron USA Inc., Walnut Creek, Calif., 1980-89; project mgr. Chevron Land & Devel. Co., San Francisco, 1989-93; environ. project mgr. Alameda County, Oakland, Calif., 1993-95; environ. support mgr. Computer Scis. Corp., Edwards AFB, Calif., 1995-99; due diligence coordinator Greenberg Farrow Architecture, Inc., 2000; site project mgr. Knight Piesold, 2000-2001; sr. engr., project mgr. MACTEC, LA, 2001—05; sr. engr. Premier Environ./Premo, LA, 2005—07; prin. engr. Brown and Caldwell, 2007—. Park and recreation commr. City of Martinez, Calif., 1984-89; mem. citizens adv. bd. City of Martinez, 1989-91, former faithful navigator Knights of Columbus. Mem.: Project Mgmt. Inst., AIChE. Roman Catholic. Achievements include being an expert on the site cleanup and due diligence. Home: 28420 Rock Canyon Dr Santa Clarita CA 91390 Office: Brown and Caldwell 11111 Santa Monica Blvd Ste 750 Los Angeles CA 90025 Personal E-mail: garciaA1@aol.com.

GARCIA, ANDY, actor; b. Havana, Cuba, Apr. 12, 1956; m. Marivi Lorido Garcia, 1982; children: Dominik, Daniella, Alessandra, Andres. Student, Fla. Internat. U.; DFA (hon.), St. John's Univ., 2000. Actor: (films) Guaguasi, 1979, Blue Skies Again, 1983, The Mean Season, 1985, 8 Million Ways to Die, 1986, The Untouchables, 1987, Stand and Deliver, 1987, American Roulette, 1988, Black Rain, 1989, Internal Affairs, 1990, The Godfather III, 1990 (Oscar nominee best supporting actor, 1999, Golden Globe nominee, 1999), Dead Again, 1991, Hero, 1992, Jennifer 8, 1992, When a Man Loves a Woman, 1994, Steal Big Steal Little, 1995, Things to Do in Denver When You're Dead, 1996, Night Falls on Manhattan, 1997, The Disappearance of Garcia Lorca, 1997, Hoodlum, 1997, Desperate Measures, 1999 (ALMA award, 1997), Lakeboat, 1999, Ocean's 11, 2001 (Outstanding Supporting Actor in a Motion Picture, Nat. Coun. of La Raza, ALMA award American Latino Media Arts 2002), Confidence, 2002, Blackout, 2003, Twisted, 2004, Modigliani, 2004, Lazarus Child, 2004, Ocean's Twelve, 2004, Smokin' Aces, 2006, Ocean's Thirteen, 2007; actor, prodr.: (TV) Swing Vote, 1999, (film) Just the Ticket, 1999, The Man From Elysian Fields, 2002, The Unsaid, 2002; dir., prodr.: (films) Cachao, Like His Rhythm There Is No Other, Cachao.Goza Mi Mambo Cubano; actor, dir.: (film) The Lost City, 2005; music prodr.: (album) Cachao Master Sessions, vol. I (Grammy award 1994), Cachao Master Sessions, Vol. II (Grammy nominee 1995), Just the Ticket soundtrack, 4 songs for Steal Big, Steal Little soundtrack, Cachao-Cuba Linda, 2000(nominated for Latin Grammy, 2000, Grammy, 2001), For Love or Country: The Arturo Sandoval Story soundtrack, 2000, Cachao-Anora Si, 2003. Recipient Harvard Univ. Found. award, Star on Hollywood Walk of Fame, Hispanic Heritage award for Arts, Father of Yr. award Father's Day Coun., ALMA award, PRISM award, Spirit of Hope award, 2001, Oscar de la Hoys Found. Champion award, 2000, Palm Springs Film Festival Desert Palm award, 2002, Imagen Found. Creative Achievement award, 2002, LA's BEST Focus on Family award, 2002, RP Internat. Film Artist of Vision award, Anthony Quinn award for Excellence in Motion Pictures, Nat. Coun. of La Raza, ALMA award (American Latino Media Arts), 2006; named Nat. Assn. of Theater Oweners Star of Yr.; nominated for Oscar and Golden Globe for Godfather III,. Office: Paradigm Talent Agency 500 5th Ave Fl 37 New York NY 10110-3799*

GARCIA, ASTRID J., newspaper executive; b. Caguas, Puerto Rico, Sept. 6, 1950; m. Robert Gillespie; children: Robert, Richard. BA with distinction, Barnard Coll., 1972; JD, Bklyn. Law Sch., 1980. Bar: N.Y. 1980. Dir., lighting designer various theatres, NYC, 1972-74; equal employment opportunity specialist Gen. Svcs. Adminstrn. Fed. Govt., Region II, NYC, 1974-76; paralegal So. Dist. N.Y. U.S. Atty.'s Office, NYC, 1976-80; atty. Puerto Rican Legal Def. and Edn. Fund, NYC, 1980-81, NLRB, NYC and Hartford, Conn., 1981-85; mgr. employee rels. dept. human resources The Hartford Courant, 1985-87; asst. dir. human resources The Miami (Fla.) Herald, 1987-90; v.p., dir. employee rels. St. Paul Pioneer Press, 1990-94; sr. v.p. human resources and labor, dir. labor rels. Jour. Comm., Milw., 1994-97; sr. v.p. ops. Milw. Jour. Sentinel, 1997—. Mem. N.Y. Bar Assn. Office: Milw Jour Sentinel PO Box 661 Milwaukee WI 53201-0661 Home: 10 Claudia Cir Media PA 19063-1012

GARCIA, BEATRICE MAUDE, social worker, director; b. Boston, Jan. 18, 1929; d. George Louis and Beatrice Lawrence (White) Joughin; m. Edward P. Black, June 4, 1950 (dec.); children: Victoria, Edward, Barbara; m. Marvin Victor Aquirre, May 10, 1956 (div.); children: Deborah (dec.), Michael; m. Peter Charles Garcia, Aug. 13, 1961. BA in Anthopology with honors and distinction, Sonoma State U., 1971; MA in Anthropology, San Francisco State U., 1979; postgrad., Sonoma State U., 1982—. Coord. Boyle Heights Coalition, LA, 1953-55; dir. Truman Boyd Housing Assn., Long Beach, Calif., 1961-63; med. records supr. Crestview Hosp., Petaluma, Calif., 1979-81; investigator, ombudsman Sonoma County Ombudsman, Santa Rosa, Calif., 1984—88; dir. sr. svcs. Ctrl. YMCA, San Francisco, 1988-90; dir. case mgmt. East Valley Sr. Ctr., North Hollywood, Calif., 1994-98, regional mgr. Region VIII, long term care ombudsman LA, 2001—06; field coord. Health Ins. Counseling and Advocacy Program Lake and Mendocino Counties, 2006—. Sec. Red Banks Oaks Assn., 1998—, Dem. Club High Desert, 1999—; exec. dir. Big Bros./Big Sisters Lake County, 2007—; organizer campaigns Dem. Orgn., Santa Maria, Calif., 1964, Vallejo, Calif., 1968. Mem. AAUW (sec. Antelope Valley chpt. 1999—), No. Calif. Manx Assn. (adminstrv. 1999—). Democrat. Episcopalian. Avocations: reading, travel, antiques. Home: Box 221 9885 Lee Barr Rd Lower Lake CA 95457 Personal E-mail: pbgarcia29@mchsi.com.

GARCIA, EDUARDO, neurologist, consultant; b. Montreal, Mar. 3, 1968; s. Eduardo Garcia Flores and Adriana Almaguer; m. Claudia Lavin, June 13, 1998; children: Sebastian, Valeria, Emilia Alexandra. MD, U. Monterrey, Mex., 1997. Diplomate Am. Bd. Psychiatry and Neurology. Intern Boston VA Med. Ctr., 1998—99; neurology resident Boston Med. Ctr., 1999—2002; fellow clin. neurophysiology/epilepsy Cleve. Clinic Found., Ohio, 2002—03; cons. neurologist So. NH Med. Ctr., Nashua, 2003—06, Newton-Wellesley Hosp., Newton, Mass., 2006—. Guest lectr. Boston U. Sch. of Medicine. Contbr. articles and abstracts to profl. jours. Guest lectr. Nat. Headache Found., Nashua, NH. Mem.: N.H. Med. Soc. (assoc.), Mass. Med. Soc. (assoc.), Am. Clin. Neurophysiology Soc. (assoc.), Am. Epilepsy Soc. (assoc.), Am. Acad. of Neurology (assoc.). Avocations: skiing, swimming. Office: Newton-Wellesley Neurol Assocs Green Bldg 2000 Washington St Ste 567 Newton MA Office Phone: 617-928-1500. Personal E-mail: egarcia6@partners.org.

GARCIA, ERNEST G., audiologist, technologist; s. Silvano Garcia and Thomasa Gastelum; m. Paula M. Kulina; children: Monica M. Neal, Amanda N. Snell. BS, Ariz. State U., Tempe, 1970, MS, 1975. Cert. surg. technologist Assn. Oper. Rm. Technologists, 1974, lic. dispensing audiologist Ariz. Dept. Health Svcs., 2007. Clin. audiologist, surg. technologist Phoenix Ear, Nose & Throat Med. Group, 1970—89, office mgr., 1976—80; owner, operator West Valley Hearing Svcs., Phoenix, 1972—89; instr. audiology Phoenix CC, 1978—80; bldg. mgr. Palo Verde Med. Ctr., Phoenix, 1980—89; sr. clin. audiologist, surg. technologist Ariz. Physicians Ctr., Phoenix, 1989—2000, Entegrity Ear, Nose & Throat Specialists, Phoenix, 2000—. Pres. Assn. Oper. Rm. Technicians, Phoenix, 1977. Founder Garcia-Gastelum Family Scholarship Lowell Elem. Sch., Phoenix, 2000—. Served with Ariz. N.G., 1970—76. Mem.: Assn. Oper. Technologists (assoc.), Am. Acad. Otolaryngologists-Head and Neck Surgeons (assoc. Presdl. citation 1996). Unitarian Universalist. Avocations: travel, birding, hiking, fishing, skiing. Office: Entegrity Ear Nose & Throat Specialists 11208 N Tatum Blvd Ste 275 Phoenix AZ 85028-3091 Office Phone: 602-494-5090.

GARCIA, F. CHRIS, academic administrator, political scientist, educator; b. Albuquerque, Apr. 15, 1940; s. Flaviano P. and Crucita A. Garcia; m. Sandra D. Garcia; children: Elaine L., Tanya C. BA, U. N.Mex., 1961, MA in Govt., 1964; PhD in Polit. Sci., U. Calif., Davis, 1972. Prof. U. N.Mex., Albuquerque, 1970—, dean arts coll., 1980—87, acad. v.p., 1987—90, provost, 1993, 1998—2000, pres., 2002—03, disting. prof., 2005—; founder Zia Rsch. Assocs., Inc., Albuquerque, 1973-94, also chmn. bd. dirs. Cons.-evaluator North Ctrl. Assn. Higher Learning Commn., 1994-06; bd. dirs. Think N.Mex., 2005—. Author: Political Socialization of Chicano Children, 1973, La Causa Politica, 1974, The Chicano Political Experience, 1977, State and Local Government in New Mexico, 1979, New Mexico Government, 1976, 81, 94, Latinos and the Political System, 1988, Latino Voices, 1992, Pursuing Power, 1997, Governing New Mexico, 2006. Charter rev. com. City of Albuquerque, 1999, Albuquerque goals commn., 1985—87; bd. dirs. Nat. Hispanic Cultural Ctr., 2002—04. With N.Mex. Air N.G., 1957—63, hon. comdr., 2005—. Recipient Disting. Svc. award, Am. Polit. Sci. Assn., 2001. Mem. Western Polit. Sci. Assn. (pres. 1977-78), Am. Polit. Sci. Assn. (v.p. 1994-95, exec. coun. 1984-86, sec. 1992-93, Disting. Svc. award 2001), Am. Assn. Pub. Opinion Rsch., Coun. Colls. of Arts and Sci. (bd. dirs. 1982-85), Nat. Assn. State Univs. and Land Grant Colls. (coun. acad. affairs 1987-90, exec. com. 1989), Western Social Sci. Assn. (exec. coun. 1973-76), Phi Beta Kappa, Phi Kappa Phi, Gold Key. Home: 1409 Snowdrop Pl NE Albuquerque NM 87112-6331 Office: U N Mex Polt Sci Dept Social Scis Bldg 2053 Albuquerque NM 87131-1121 Home Phone: 505-292-3301; Office Phone: 505-277-5217. Business E-Mail: cgarcia@unm.edu.

GARCIA, HENRY FRANK, supply and project management consultant; b. San Antonio, Aug. 29, 1943; s. Henry V. and Lucia (Dominguez) G.; m. Rose Lozano, Feb. 28, 1970; children: John Henry, Rebecca. BA in Psychology, St. Mary's U., San Antonio, 1969, MA in Econs., 1974. Cert. purchasing mgr., Tex. Buyer purchasing Southwest Rsch. Inst., San Antonio, 1967, asst. mgr. purchasing, 1970—74, mgr. purchasing, 1974—78, asst. dir. materials mgmt., 1978—80, dir. corp. travel, 1980—87, dir. materials mgmt., 1980—87; dir. fin. and adminstrn. Ctr. for Nuc. Waste Regulatory Analyses, San Antonio, 1987—2003; ret., 2003; cons., trainer Asentrene. Instr. U. Tex., San Antonio, 1976-77; instr. materials mgmt. and econs., San Antonio Coll., 1975-83; instr. econs. St. Marys U., San Antonio, 1976-81; adj. prof. econs. Webster U., San Antonio, 1980—. Contbr. articles to profl. jours. Chmn. San Antonio Regional Minority Purchasing Council, 1983. Mem. Nat. Purchasing Inst. (pres. 1979-80, Outstanding Svc. award 1986), Nat. Assn. Purchasing Mgmt. (cert., v.p. dist. II 1987-89, Pro-D Man of Yr. award 1985, Congrove Outstanding Mem. award 1991, President's award 1994, J. Shipman Gold Medal award 1998), Purchasing Mgmt. Assn. San Antonio (pres. 1981-82, Conway L. Holmes award 1984, James H. Lieberman award 2000), Nat. Bus. Travel Assn. (v.p. 1985-86), Nat. Assn. Bus. Economists (pres. local chpt. 1978), Project Mgmt. Inst. (pres. 2005-06). Democrat. Roman Catholic. Office: Asentrene PO Box 782474 San Antonio TX 78278-2474 Office Phone: 210-493-1971. Personal E-mail: hfgarcia@asentrene.com.

GARCIA, HUMBERTO SIGIFREDO, former prosecutor, lawyer; b. Harlingen, Tex., June 7, 1944; s. Porfirio and Margarita (Herrera) G.; m. Lana Cheryl Caswell, Aug. 9, 1975. BA, Lamar U., 1974; JD, U. Tex., 1977. Bar: Tex. 1978, U.S. Dist. Ct. (ea. dist.) Tex. 1978, U.S. Dist. Ct. (so. dist.) Tex. 1979, U.S. Ct. Appeals (5th cir.) 1979, U.S. Supreme Ct. 1982. Ptnr. Mehaffy, Garcia & Bradford, Beaumont, Tex., 1977-83; asst. US atty. (ea. dist.) US Dept. Justice, 1983—2002, US atty. Puerto Rico dist., 2002—06. Instr. Lamar U., Beaumont, 1980-83; bd. dirs. Western State Bank, Denton, Tex. Served to capt. USMC, 1968-71. Mem. Fed. Bar Assn., Tex. Bar Assn, Kappa Sigma. Republican. Presbyterian. Avocations: long distance running, fishing, photography, cars, golf. Home Phone: 787-724-8017; Office Phone: 787-766-5656. E-mail: h.garcia@usdoj.gov.*

GARCIA, JEFF (JEFFREY JASON GARCIA), professional football player; b. Gilroy, Calif., Feb. 24, 1970; s. Bob and Linda Garcia; m. Carmela DeCesare. Postgrad in bus. & mktg., San Jose State U. Quarterback Calgary Stampede CFL, 1994—99, San Francisco 49ers, 1999—2003, Cleve. Browns, 2004, Detroit Lions, 2005—06, Phila. Eagles, 2006—07, Tampa Bay Buccaneers, 2007—. Named NFL All-Pro, 2001—03; named to Nat. Football Conf. Pro-Bowl Team, 2000—02; recipient Jeff Nicklin Meml. Trophy, Can. Football League, 1997. Achievements include becoming one of seven NFL QBs to throw 30-plus TDs in consecutive years. Office: Tampa Bay Buccaneers 1 Buccaneer Pl Tampa FL 33607*

GARCIA, JOHN, psychologist, educator; b. Santa Rosa, Calif., June 12, 1917; married; 3 children. BA, U. Calif., Berkeley, 1948, MA, 1949, PhD, 1965. Teaching asst. U. Calif., Berkeley, 1949-51; psychologist U.S. Naval Radiol. Def. Lab., San Francisco, 1951-58; tchr. biol. sci. Oakland (Calif.) Pub. Schs., 1958-59; asst. prof. psychology Calif. State Coll., Long Beach, 1959-65; assoc. biologist, neurosurg. svc. Mass. Gen. Hosp., Boston, 1965-68; prof. psychology, chmn. psychobiology program SUNY, Stony Brook, 1968-71, chmn. dept., 1971-72; prof. U. Utah, Salt Lake City, 1972-73; prof. psychology and psychiatry UCLA, 1973-87, emeritus prof. psychology and psychiatry, 1987—. Author (edited by Stuart Ellins): John Garcia: Life of a Neuroethologist and History of Conditioned Taste Aversion, 2007. Recipient Lifetime Achievement award for neurosci., Soc. for Neurosci., 1998. Fellow Soc. Exptl. Psychologists (Howard Crosby Warren medal 1978); mem. AAAS, APA (Disting. Sci. Contbn. award 1979), Nat. Acad. Scis., Am. Psychol. Soc. (William James fellow), N.Y. Acad. Scis., Western Psychol. Assn. (pres. 1991—), Phi BEta Kappa, Sigma Xi. Address: PO Box 1217 La Conner WA 98257

GARCIA, JORGE, actor; b. Omaha, Neb., Apr. 28, 1973; Student, UCLA. Actor: (films) Raven's Ridge, 1997, Tomorrow by Midnight, 1999, King of the Open Mic's, 2000, The Slow and Cautious, 2002, Happily Ever After, 2004, Our Time is Up, 2004, The Good Humor Man, 2005, Little Athens, 2005, Deck the Halls, 2006; (TV films) Columbo Likes the Nightlife, 2003; (TV series) Becker, 2003—04, Lost, 2004— (Outstanding Performance by an Ensemble in a Drama Series, Screen Actors Guild award, 2006, Outstanding Supporting Actor in a TV Series, Nat. Coun. La Raza ALMA award (Am. Latin Media Arts), 2006); numerous TV series guest appearances.

GARCIA, JULIA THERESA, secondary school educator; b. NYC, Aug. 30, 1923; d. Ignatius Colletti-Riena and Julia Pendeleur; m. Frank Leonard Garcia, May 26, 1949 (dec. Aug. 1995); children: Julia, Frank, Annette. BA, Hunter Coll., 1951; MA, Columbia U., 1956. Cert. tchr. chemistry N.Y., asst. prin. supervision phys. scis. N.Y. Tchr. gen. sci. Alfred E. Smith Jr. H.S. Bd. Edn. N.Y.C., tchr. chemistry Alfred E. Smith H.S., asst. prin. supervision phys. scis. Alfred E. Smith H.S., prin. summer sch. Alfred E. Smith H.S. Bd. examiner sci. and math. Bd. Edn. N.Y.C., 1984—89. Active Diabetic Assn. Recipient Dedicated Svc. Children award, NYC, 1989. Mem.: Am. Assn. Scientists, Phi Delta Kappa, N.Y.C. Acad. Sci.

GARCIA, JULIET VILLARREAL, academic administrator; m. Oscar E. Garcia; two children. BA in Speech, English, U. of Houston, 1970, MA in Speech, English, 1972; PhD in Communications & Linguistics, U. of Texas Austin, 1976. Teaching asst. U. of Houston, 1970—72; Instr. Pan American Univ. at Edinburg, 1972; teaching asst. U. of Texas Austin, 1974—76; adj. prof. Pan American U. Brownsville, 1977—79; instr. Tex. Southmost Coll., 1972—74, 1976—81, dir. TSC Self-Study, 1979—81, dean, arts and sciences, 1981—86, pres., 1986—92, U. Tex. at Brownsville, Tex. Southmost Coll., 1992—. Bd. dirs. Fed. Res. of Dallas/San Antonio br. of Tex. Commerce Bancshares Inc.; past bd. dirs. Am. Coun. Edn., chmn. bd. dirs. 1995. Bd. dirs. Carnegie Found. for Advancement of Teaching, Pub. Welfare Foun.; vice-chair adv. com. on Fin. Aid; appointed mem. White House Initiative on Ednl. Excellence for Hispanic-Ams. Named Woman of Distinction Nat. Conf. of Coll. Women Student Leaders, 1995, one of most influential Hispanics Hispanic Bus. Mag. Office: U Tex & Tex Southmost Coll Office of Pres 80 Fort Brown St Brownsville TX 78520-4956

GARCIA, JUNE MARIE, librarian; b. Bryn Mawr, Pa., Sept. 12, 1947; d. Roland Ernest and Marion Brill (Hummel) Traynor; m. Teodosio Garcia, July 17, 1928; children: Gretchen, Adrian. BA, Douglass Coll., 1969; MLS, Rutgers U., 1970. Reference libr. New Brunswick (N.J.) Pub. Libr., 1970-72, Plainfield (N.J.) Pub. Libr., 1972-75; br. mgr. Phoenix Pub. Libr., 1975-80, extension svcs. adminstr., 1980-93; dir. San Antonio Pub. Libr., 1993-99; CEO, CARL Corp., Denver, 1999-2001; v.p., chief amb. TLC/CARL, Denver, 2001—02; mng. ptnr. Dubberly Garcia Assocs., 2002—, E-Learn Librs., Inc., Nashville and Denver, 2004—. Recipient Productivity Innovator award, City of Phoenix, 1981. Mem. ALA (life, coun. 1986-90, 93-2001, pres. Pub. Libr. Assn. 1991-92, new stds. task force 1983-87, goals, guidelines and stds. com. 1986-90, chairperson 1987-90, resource allocation com. 1998-99), Freedom to Read Found. (bd. dirs.), Ariz. State Libr. Assn. (pres. 1984-85, Libr. of Yr. award 1986, Pres.'s award 1990), Pub. Libr. Internat. Network (exec. dir.), Beta Phi Mu. Office: 1195 S Harrison St Denver CO 80210 Home Phone: 303-757-7420; Office Phone: 303-757-7420. Business E-Mail: jgarcia@dubberlygarcia.com.

GARCIA, LUIS F., photographer; b. Nogales, Ariz., Sept. 28, 1963; s. Francisco and Amanda E. Garcia; children: Vania, Fernando. BA, Our Lady of the Lake U., San Antonio, 1988. Press Photographer Am. Image Press, Wash., D.C., 1988, Profl. Photographer N.Y. Inst. of Photography, 2000, Master Photographer Internat. Freelance Photographers Assn., 2002. Photography calendar, China: Portraits of a Timeless land, photography, Climb Against the Odds/ Breast Cancer Fund, 2003, photography book, Ranchos de Sonora, 2006. Cons. Breast Cancer Fund, San Francisco, 2000—03. Recipient Star award for Creativity, Leadership, and Collaboration, United Way of Silicon Valley, Vida award for Outstanding Svc. Office Phone: 858-549-7170. E-mail: ranchosdesonora@yahoo.com.

GARCIA, MARC ANTHONY, diplomat; b. Bklyn., June 1962; s. Carlos Antonio and Yolande (Price) G.; m. Shegurah Rolle; 1 child, Christina Chanel. BA, Hampton Inst., 1984; postgrad., SUNY, Albany, 1986, Cen. Mich. U., 1991. Legis. aide N.Y. State Assembly, Albany, 1984-85; commd. 2d lt. U.S. Army, 1982; advanced through grades to lt. col. USAR; officer UN Hqrs. Secretariate, NYC, 1985; program monitor N.Y. state exec. dept. USAR, N.Y. Army N.G., NY, 1985—86; spl. agt. N.Y. field office U.S. Dept. of State, NYC, 1987-89, 1998—2002; attaché fgn. svc. U.S. Dept. State, Washington, 1986—. Cons. Garcia, Garcia and Peoples, Ltd., Ft. Greene, N.Y., 1989—; officer of Provost Marshall, Ft. Buchanan, P.R., 1993; observer Olympics, Seoul, Korea, 1988, Atlanta, 1996; detail agt. U.S. Presdl. Inaugural, 1988; mem. Presdl. Security Adv. Unit, Haitian govt., 1994. Author: (monograph) Caribbean Basin Initiative, 1984; contbr. articles to crime prevention series. Advocate Nat. Orgnl. for Victims Assistance, Washington, 1986—; county committeeman Kings County Com., 1984-86; assoc. Am. Mus. Natural History, Bklyn., 1985; inspector N.Y. Bd. Elections, 1984-85; catechist Archdiocese of Bklyn., 1980; Am. Security Coun. Found. Ednl. grantee Va. Army N.G., 1981, 95. Mem. NAAACP, VFW (mem.-at-large), DAV (life), Am. Fgn. Svc. Assn., Mil. Police Regtl. Assn. (mem.-at-large), Mil. Civil Affairs Regtl. Assn. (mem.-at-large), Am. Polit. Sci. Assn., Nat. Org. Black Law Enforcement Execs. (assoc.), Assn. MBA Execs. (mem.-at-large), Joint Ctr. for Polit. Studies (assoc.), Fed. Law Enforcement Officers Assn. (spl. agt.), Res. Officer Assn., Hampton Inst. Alumni Assn. (booster 1984-89), Blacks in Govt. Fgn. Affairs (Washington chpt.), Fraternity, Inc. (life), Ft. Hamilton Officers Club, Ft. Monroe NCO Club (asst. mgr. 1982), Masons Scottish Rite, Prince Hall Affiliates, Am. Legion, Alpha Phi Alpha (past chmn. internat. bros. affairs). Democrat. Roman Catholic. Avocation: radio telephone operator. Home: 19701 E Country Club Dr Aventura FL 33180 E-mail: marc.garcia@us.army.mil.

GARCIA, MARCELO HORACIO, engineering educator, consultant; b. Cordoba, Argentina, Apr. 22, 1959; came to U.S., 1983; s. Juan Carlos Jose and Beatriz Alba Garcia; m. Estela Beti Rodriguez-Canga, May 17, 1984; children: Blas Ignacio, Emma Paina. Diploma in Engring., U. Litoral, Santa Fe, Argentina, 1982; MS in Civil Engring., U. Minn., Mpls., 1985; PhD in Civil Engring., 1989. Registered profl. engr., Argentina. Tech. asst. Agua y Energia Electrica, Santa Fe, Argentina, 1979-85; rsch. asst. St. Anthony Falls Lab., Mpls., 1983-87; rsch. fellow, 1988-89; asst. prof. U. Ill., Urbana, 1990-96, assoc. prof., 1996—2000, prof., 2000—. Cons. Govt. Taiwan, Taipei, 1993, U.S. Army of Engrs., Vicksburg, Miss., 1993—, Electricite de France, Toulousse, 1996; tech. adv. U.S./Taiwan Sedimentation, Washington, 1992-94; vis. prof. U. Litoral, Santa Fe, Argentina, 1993—, Calif. Inst. Tech., Pasadena, 1997-; disting. lectr. Hokkaido River Disaster Prevention Inst., Japan, 1990; guest lectr. U. Essen, Germany, 1995. Author: Environmental Hydrodynamics, 1996; contbr. articles to profl. jours. Recipient Karl Emil Hilgard hydraulics prize ASCE, N.Y.C., 1996, Alvin Anderson award U. Minn., Mpls., 1989; named Disting. Vis. Prof. U. Genoa, Italy, 1993. Mem. ASCE (Walter L. Huber Rsch. prize 1998), Am. Geophys. Union, Internat. Assn. for Hydraulic Rsch., Internat. Water Resources Assn., Sigma Xi. Achievements include development of the first model for sediment mixtures transport by turbidity currents in the ocean. Office: U Ill 205 N Mathews Ave Urbana IL 61801

GARCIA, MARIA LUISA, biochemist, researcher; b. Valladolid, Spain, Oct. 9, 1953; came to U.S., 1979; d. Baldomero and Dolores (Garcia) G.; m. Gregory Kaczorowski, June 21, 1982. PhD, Autonoma U., Madrid, 1979. Sr. rsch. biochemist Merck & Co., Rahway, NJ, 1985—87, rsch. fellow, 1987—91, sr. rsch. fellow, 1991—97, sr. investigator, 1997—2003, disting. sr. investigator, 2003—. Invited speaker, presenter papers in field. Contbr. numerous articles and revs. to profl. jours.; patentee in field. Mem. AAAS, Am. Soc. Biol. Chemists, Biophys. Soc., N.Y. Acad. Sci. Home: 5 Ashbrook Dr Edison NJ 08820-4318 Office: Merck Rsch Labs PO Box 2000 Rahway NJ 07065-0900 Personal E-mail: maria_garcia@merck.com.

GARCIA, MELVA YBARRA, counseling administrator, educator; d. Estanislaso B and Ofelia M Ybarra; m. Frank Garcia, Dec. 28, 1974; children: Ruben Jesus, Luis Francisco, Ramon Estanislado. Student, San Francisco State U., 1969—72; B.A. in Sociology, Calif. State U., Hayward, 1974, MS in Counseling, 1983; PhD (hon.), U. Calif.-Berkeley, 1992. Cert. cmty. coll. counselor Calif., 1986, student pers. workers credential Calif., 1986. Dir. Chicano student counseling ctr. Wash. State U., Pullman, 1984—86; Chicano studies advisor U. of Calif., Berkeley, 1987—92; counselor/instr. Chabot Coll., Hayward, Calif., 1992—. Co-author (counseling manual) Counseling Chicanos: The Affects of Racial and Cultural Stereotype, 1985. Mem. Self-Help for the Hard of Hearing, 2001—; sponsor Children's Internat., Kansas City, Mo., 2002—; mem. La Alianza, Hayward, Calif., 1993; mentor Puente Program, Chabot Coll., 1992—; advisor Wash. State U.; ptnr. Spl. Olympics, 1995—; assoc. mem. Nat. Coun. of La Raza, Washington, 2000—. Mem.: Assn. Main United Farm Workers, So. Law Poverty Ctr., Chabot-Las Positas Faculty Assn., Faculty Assn of Calif. Cmty. Colls., Chicano/Latino Edn. Assn. (mem., 1992-present, co-chair 1998—99), NACADA. D-Liberal. Catholic. Avocations: travel, aerobics. Office: Chabot College 25555 Hesperian Blvd Hayward CA 94545 E-mail: mgarcia@chabotcollege.edu.

GARCIA, MICHAEL, Sommelier; Grad., Fordham U. With Campton Place, San Francisco, Chapeau!, San Francisco; sommelier XYZ, San Francisco. Named one of San Francisco's Rising Stars, StarChefs.com, 2007. Mem.: Ct. Master Sommeliers. Office: XYZ 181 3rd St San Francisco CA 94103 Office Phone: 415-777-5300.*

GARCIA, MICHAEL J., prosecutor, former federal agency administrator; b. 1961; BA, SUNY; MA, Coll. William & Mary; JD, Union U. Atty. Cahill Gordon & Reindel, Manhattan, NY, 1989—90; law clk. to Hon. Judith S. Kaye NY State Ct. Appeals, 1990—92; asst. US atty. (So. dist.) NY US Dept. Justice, 1992—2001; asst. sec. export enforcement US Dept. Commerce, Washington, 2001—02; commr. Immigration and Naturalization Svc. US Dept. Justice, Washington, 2002—03; asst. sec. Bur. Immigration & Customs Enforcement US Dept. Homeland Security, Washington, 2003—05; US atty (so. dist.) NY US Dept. Justice, NYC, 2005—. Office: US Attys Office One St Andrews Plz New York NY 10007*

GARCIA, NINA, publishing executive; b. Baranquilla, Columbia; m. David Conrod; 1 child, Lucas Alexander Conrod. Studied Liberal Arts, Boston U.; attended, Fashion Inst. Tech. With pub. rels. dept. Perry Ellis; asst. stylist, market editor Mirabella mag.; fashion dir. Elle mag., 2000—. Judge, critic Bravo's Project Runway. Office: c/o Elle Magazine 1633 Broadway 44th Fl New York NY 10019*

GARCIA, OFELIA, art educator, administrator; b. Havana, Cuba, Feb. 12, 1941; d. Ramon Garcia-Castro and Nieves (Gomez de Molina) Garcia. Student, Escuela de Bellas Artes, Havana, 1958-60; BA, Manhattanville Coll., 1969; MFA, Tufts U., 1972; postgrad., Duke U., 1973-75; D. Fine Arts (hon.), Atlanta Coll. Art, 1991. Asst. prof., art dept. chair, div. dir. humanities and fine arts Newton (Mass.) Coll., 1969-75; dir. studio art Boston Coll., Chestnut Hill, Mass., 1975-76; exec. dir. The Print Ctr., Phila., 1978-86; critic Pa. Acad. Fine Arts, Phila., 1982-86; pres. Atlanta Coll. Art, 1986-91; Rosemont (Pa.) Coll., 1991—95; sr. fellow Am. Coun. on Edn., 1995—97; dean, coll. arts and comm. William Paterson U., 1997—2006, prof., 2006—. Visual arts panelist State Coun. of the Arts, Pa. and N.J., 1985-86, Ga., 1990-91; mem. vis. com. dept. art and architecture Lehigh (Pa.) U., 1990-96; bd. mgrs. Haverford Coll., 1992—2004. Artist exhibitions of prints and drawings; curator, juror numerous nat. and internat. or regional art exhibitions. Nat. pres. Women's Caucus for Art, 1984-86; bd. mem. and chair, Commn. on Women in Higher Edn., Am. Coun. on Edn., 1988-91; bd. dir. Am. Coun. on Edn., 1993-96; co-chair Mayor's Commn. for Women, City Phila., 1992-97; Arts Adv. Com. Barnes Found. Bd., 1992-95; trustee Jersey City Mus., 2000—, chair, 2001—; bd. dirs. Caths. for Free Choice, 2000—, Artpride NJ, 2005—. Recipient Am. Bookbuilders prize Boston Mus. Sch., 1969, Park Found. award, 1974; Kent fellow Danforth Found., 1975-80. Fellow Soc. for Values Higher Edn.; mem. Coll. Art Assn. Am. (bd. dirs. 1986-90, bd. coms. 1986-92), Am. Assn. Mus., ArtTable, Inc. Roman Catholic. Office: William Paterson U 300 Pompton Rd Wayne NJ 07470-2152 Business E-Mail: garciao@wpunj.edu.

GARCIA, OSCAR NICOLAS, computer science educator; b. Havana, Cuba, Sept. 10, 1936; s. Oscar Vicente and Leonor (Hernandez) G.; m. Diane Ford Journigan, Sept. 9, 1962; children: Flora, Virginia. BSEE, N.C. State U., Raleigh, 1961, MSEE, 1964; PhDEE, U. Md., College Park, 1969. Engr. IBM Corp., Endicott, NY, 1962-63; asst. prof. Old Dominion U., 1963-66, assoc. prof., 1969-70; research asst., instr. U. Md., 1966-69; assoc. prof. U. South Fla., Tampa, 1970-75, prof. computer sci., chmn. dept., 1975-85; prof. dept. elec. engring. and computer sci. George Washington U., Washington, 1985-95; disting. NCR prof. Wright State U., Dayton, Ohio, 1995—2003, chmn. dept. computer sci. and engring., 1995—2003; founding dean Coll. Engring. U. North Tex., Denton, 2003—. Dir. interactive sys. program in info., robotics and intelligent sys. divsn. Computer and Info. Sci. and Engring. Directorate, Intergovtl. Pers. Act, NSF, Washington, 1992-94; cons. and lectr. in field. Author: (with Y.T. Chien) Knowledge-Based Systems: Fundamentals and Tools, 1991. Fellow IEEE (bd. dirs. 1984-85, 2005—, mem. U.S. activities bd. 1984, Profl. Leadership award 1991, Richard M. Emberson award 1994), Computer Soc. of IEEE (pres. 1981-83, awards com. chmn. 2002-03, bd. govs. 2003—, sec. bd. govs. 2003-04, Richard E. Merwin Disting. Svc. award 1988, Meritorious Svc. award 1991), AAAS; mem. Assn. Computing Machinery, Am. Soc. Engring. Edn., Am. Assn. Artificial Intelligence, Sigma Xi, Eta Kappa Nu, Phi Kappa Phi, Tau Beta Pi. Office: U North Tex Coll Engring PO Box 310440 Denton TX 76203-0440 Home: 120 W El Paseo St Denton TX 76205-8590 Office Phone: 940-565-2500.

GARCIA, PAUL R., lawyer; AB in Polit. Sci. and Hispanic Studies, Vassar Coll., 1987; JD, U. Chgo., 1992. Bar: Ill. 1992, US Dist. Ct. (no. dist. Ill.). Assoc. atty. Pattishal, McAuliffe, Newbury, Hilliard & Geraldson, Chgo., 1992—94, Kirkland & Ellis, Chgo., 1994—96, ptnr., co-chair firm diversity com., 2001—; asst. US atty. US Dept. Justice, Chgo., 1996—2001. Mem.: Hispanic Nat. Bar Assn., Hispanic Lawyers Assn. Ill., Chgo. Coun. Lawyers, Internat. Trademark Assn. Office: Kirkland & Ellis 200 E Randolph Dr Chicago IL 60601-6636 Office Phone: 312-861-2327. Office Fax: 312-861-2200. E-mail: pgarcia@kirkland.com.*

GARCIA, PHILIP A., insurance company executive; B in Acctg., Grove City Coll. CPA. From corp. acct. to mgr. internal audit Erie (Pa.) Indemnity Co., 1981—88; dept. mgr. life acctg. Erie Family Life Ins. Co., 1988—93; sr. v.p., contr. Erie Cos., 1993—97; exec. v.p., CFO Erie Ins. Group, 1997—. Bd. dirs. Hamot Health Found., Hamot Med. Ctr., Warner Theatre Preservation Trust, Bayfront Eastside Task Force, Erie Arts Coun. Mem.: AICPA, Fin. Exec. Inst., Pa. Inst. CPAs. Office: Erie Ins Group 100 Erie Insurance Pl Erie PA 16530*

GARCIA, RAFAEL JORGE, retired chemical engineer; b. Havana, Cuba, July 2, 1933; came to US, 1962; s. Rafael and Martha Teresa (Suarez) G.; m. Amelia Fernandez, Feb. 23, 1958; children: Amelia Maria, Rafael Jorge Jr. BA, Columbia Coll., NYC, 1954; BSChE, La. State U., 1957; MS in Environ. Engring., Johns Hopkins U., Balt., 1975. Registered profl. engr., Ind., Ky., La., Md.; registered environ. mgr. Chem. engr. Freeport Sulphur Co., New Orleans, 1957—58; prodn. supt. Litografia Garcia Muniz, Havana, 1958—62; chem. engr. Am. Sugar Refining Co., Balt., 1962—63, House of Seagram, Balt., 1963—80, chief ecology engr. Louisville, 1981—97; cons. environ. regulatory affairs, 1998—; pres. Garcia Environ., 1997—. Mem. Am. Inst. Chem. Engrs., Instrument Soc. Am., St. Matthews Lions (pres. 1986-87). Republican. Roman Catholic. Home: 912 Lake Forest Pkwy Louisville KY 40245-5126 Personal E-mail: rj@garcia.win.net.

GARCIA, RUDOLPH, lawyer; b. Phila., June 22, 1951; s. Rudolph Sr. and Assunta Rita (Marrara) G.; m. Randi Ellen Pastor, Aug. 3, 1980; 1 child, Jonathan P. BA magna cum laude, Temple U., 1974, JD cum laude, 1977. Bar: Pa. 1977, U.S. Dist. Ct. (ea. dist.) Pa. 1977, U.S. Ct. Appeals (3d cir.) 1982, U.S. Supreme Ct. 1982. Assoc. Wright, Thistle & Gibbons, Phila., 1977-78, Saul Ewing LLP, Phila., 1978-84, ptnr., 1984—2005; shareholder Buchanan Ingersoll & Rooney, PC, 2005—. Judge pro tem Phila. Ct. Common Pleas. Fellow: Acad. Adv.; mem.: ABA (del. 2003—), Phila. Assn. Def. Counsel, Phila. Bar Assn. (chmn. local rules subcom. 1988—92, chmn. state civil com. 1999, bd. govs. 2000—02, chair fed. cts. com. 2004, bd. govs. 2004—, chair state civil litigation sect. 2005, chmn. website com. 2006—), Pa. Bar Assn., Justinian Soc. (bd. govs. 1999—, vice-chancellor 2002—06, chancellor 2006—), Phi Beta Kappa. Avocations: computers, photography, golf. Home: 235 Lloyd Ln Wynnewood PA 19096-3323 Office: Buchanan Ingersoll and Rooney PC 1835 Market St 14th Fl Philadelphia PA 19103-2985 Home Phone: 610-642-0134; Office Phone: 215-665-3843. E-mail: rudolph.garcia@bipc.com.

GARCIA, SERGIO, professional golfer; b. Castellon, Spain, Jan. 9, 1980; s. Victor Garcia. Mem. PGA Tour, 1999—; mem. European team Ryder Cup, 1999, mem. winning European team, 2002, 2004, 2006; mem. winning Spanish team Dunhill Cup, 1999, mem. Spanish team, 2000; mem. winning Continental European team Seve Trophy, 2000, mem. Continental European team, 2003; mem. Spanish team World Cup, 2001, 2004, 2005. Named Sir Henry Cotton Rookie of Yr., PGA European Tour, 1999. Achievements include winning PGA Tour events including the MasterCard Colonial, 2001, Buick Classic, 2001, 04, Mercedes Championships, 2002, EDS Byron Nelson Championship, 2004, Booz Allen Classic, 2005; winner, international events including the Catalonian Open Championship, 1997, Murphy's Irish Open, 1999, Linde German Masters, 1999, Trophee Lancome, 2001, Nedbank Golf Challenge, 2001, 03; winner, Canarias Open de Espana, 2002, Kolon Cup Korean Open, 2002, Mallorca Classic, 2004, Omega European Masters, 2005; winner, 19 amateur events; record holder as youngest Ryder Cup participant, youngest player to make cut, Turespana Open Mediterranea, 1995, youngest winner of European Amateur Championship, 1995. Avocations: soccer, computer games. Office: PGA Tour 112 PGA Tour Blvd Ponte Vedra Beach FL 32082

GARCIA, VERONICA, school system administrator; BA, MA, U. N.Mex, EdD in Edn. Leadership. Exec. dir. N.Mex Coalition of Sch. Adminstrs.; supt. Santa Fe Pub. Schs.; regional supt. Albuquerque Pub. Schs.; sec. edn. N.Mex Pub. Edn. Dept., 2003—. Named one of Top Ten Hispanic Woman in N.Mex, N.Mex Legis., 2000; recipient Educator of Yr., N.Mex Rsch. and Study Coun., 2003, Lifetime Achievement award, Hispanic Mag., 2004. Office: NMex Pub Edn Dept 300 Don Gaspar Ave Santa Fe NM 87501-2786 Office Fax: 505-827-6696. E-mail: veronica.garcia@state.nm.us.*

GARCIA-BUÑUEL, LUIS, neurologist; b. Madrid, Feb. 24, 1931; came to U.S., 1955; s. Pedro Garcia and Concepcion Buñuel; m. Virginia May Hile, June 30, 1960. BA, BS, U. Zaragoza, Spain, 1949; MD, U. Zaragoza, 1955. Diplomate Am. Bd. Psychiatry and Neurology. Resident neurology Georgetown U., Washington, 1955-59; postdoctoral fellow Washington U., St. Louis, 1959-61; asst. prof. neurology Thomas Jefferson U., Phila., 1961-67; assoc. prof. U. N.Mex., Albuquerque, 1967-72, U. Oreg. Health Scis. Ctr., Portland, 1972-84; chief neurology svc. Portland VA Med. Ctr., 1972-84; pvt. practice, Phoenix, 1984—; chief staff Carl T. Hayden VA Med. Ctr., Phoenix, 1984-96. Contbr. articles to sci. jours., including Nature, Sci., Neurology, Jour. Neurol. Sci. Lt. Spanish Air Force, 1952-55. Fellow Am. Acad. Neurology (sr. mem.), Sigma Xi. Unitarian Universalist. Avocations: painting, computer art, steel-welded sculpture. Home and Office: 128 N French Dr Prescott AZ 86303 Personal E-mail: luisgbunuel@hughes.net.

GARCIA-FEBO, LOIDA, librarian; BA in Bus. Edn., U. PR, 1996, MS in Libr. and Info. Sci., 1999; PhD candidate, LI U. Libr. Unit Libr. Svc. Blind and Disabled Jose M. Lazaro Libr., U. PR, 2000; Spanish Language Collections and Cultural Arts mgr. Queens Libr., 2000—05, asst. coord. Spl. Services, 2006—. Webmistress www.sisterama.com. Named one of the Movers & Shakers, Libr. Jour., 2007; recipient Libr. Luminary award, Queens Libr., 2004. Mem.: Assn. Caribbean Universities, Rsch. and Investigation Libraries, Assn. to Promote Libr. Services to Latinos and Spanish Speaking, Internat. Fedn. Libr. Assn., ALA. Office: Queens Library 89-11 Merrick Blvd Jamaica NY 11432 Office Phone: 718-990-0700.

GARCIA FRANCO, CARLOS ENRIQUE, thoracic surgeon; b. Madrid, June 26, 1974; s. Francisco Garcia Aguilera and Mercedes Franco Frias. MD, Complutense U. Med. Sch., 1998. Cert. Ednl. Commn. Br. Fgn. Med. Grads., 2005. Resident gen. thoracic surgery Fundacion Jimenez Diaz, Madrid, 2000—05; clin. fellow gen. thoracic surgery Mayo Clinic, Rochester, Minn., 2005—, fellow, 2005—06. Contbr. articles to profl. jours. Mem.: Spanish Soc. Pulmonology and Thoracic Surgey, European Soc. Thoracic Surgeons (assoc.). Christian. Avocations: reading, trekking, golf, skiing. Office: Mayo Clinic 200 First Street SW Rochester MN 55905 Home Phone: +34915430902; Office Phone: 507-284-2808. Home Fax: +34915439891. Personal E-mail: cgarciafranco@terra.es. Business E-Mail: garciafranco.carlos@mayo.edu.

GARCIA-GRANADOS, SERGIO EDUARDO, portfolio manager, writer, historian; b. June 11, 1942; s. Jorge and Miriam Garcia-Granados; m. Elizabeth Bentley, Apr. 3, 1973; children: Tatiana, Sybil. Law degree with honors, 1960-66, U. San Carlos, Guatemala, 1966; postgrad., U. Paris Inst. Scis. Politique, Paris, 1966-68. Bar: 1968. Rsch. assoc. Hague Acad. Internat. Law, 1969, Internat. Bur. Fiscal Documentation, Amsterdam, 1969-70; ptnr. law firm Saravia y Muñoz, Guatemala City, 1970—81; v.p. sales mgr. Merrill Lynch Capital Markets Internat., NYC, 1982-88; v.p. sales resident mgr. internat. div. Shearson Lehman Hutton, NYC, 1988—90; portfolio mgr. Lehman Bros., Miami, Fla., 1990—99; sr. portfolio mgr. UBS, Miami, 1999—. Lectr. tax problems in Central Am. Common Market, U. San Carlos, bus. orgns.,U. Landivar, Globalization of Capital Markets, Guatemalan Mgmt. Assn., 1991; bd. dirs. Miami Soc. Fin. Analysts, 1996—, Miami Symphony Orch., 2004—. Author: Academia de Geografía e Historia, Revista Anales, 1999, El Siglo de las Luces, Libre Crezca Fecunda (1729-1821), Editorial Magna Terra - Guatemala, 2005; co-author: Cuaderno de Memorias (1900-1922), Artemis-Edinter, 2000, Reminiscencias (1944-51); organizer, 1st editor loose-leaf corp. taxation in Latin Am., Amsterdam, 1970. Bd. dirs. Patronato de Bellas Artes, 1977—84, Guatemala Nat. Theatre Directorate, 1979—82, Cuban Mus. Art, 1994—2000, Miami Symphony Orch., 2004—. Mem. Colegio de Abogados, Internat. Fiscal Assn. (gen. coun. 1972-80), CFA Inst., Miami Soc. Fin. Analysts (pres. 2005—), Acad. Geografía e Historia Guatemala. Personal E-mail: sggran@aol.com.

GARCIA-LUNA-ACEVES, J.J., education educator; b. Mex. City, Mex., Oct. 20, 1955; s. Gustavo Garcia Luna Hernandez and Maria (del Socorro) Aceves de Garcia Luna; m. Patricia A. Power, Oct. 22, 1987; children: Patrick Joaquin Garcialuna, Aelxander Gustavo Garcialuna. BS in Elec. Engring., Universidad Iberoamericana, Mex. City, Mex., 1977; MS in Elec. Engring., U. of Hawaii at Manoa, Honolulu, 1980; PhD in Elec. Engring., U. of Hawaii at Manoa, 1983. Rsch. engr. SRI Internat., Menlo Park, Calif., 1983—86, sr. rsch. engr., 1986—88, acting program dir., 1988—89, dep. dir., network info. systems ctr., 1989—91, dir., network info. systems ctr., 1991—93; assoc. prof. computer engring. U. Calif., Santa Cruz, 1993—97; prof. computer engring. U. of Calif., Santa Cruz, Calif., 1997—. Cons. Rooftop Comm. Corp., Mountain View, Calif., 1997—99; prin. of protocol design Nokia, Mountain View, 1999—2003; prin. scientist Palo Alto Rsch. Ctr., Calif., 2004—. Author: (book) Multimedia Communications: Protocols and Applications; contbr. articles to profl. jours. Recipient Best Paper award, 2d IEEE Internat. Conf. on Mobile Ad-Hoc and Sensor Systems, 2005, Jack Baskin Endowed Chair of Computer Engring., U. of Calif., Santa Cruz, 2003—, Best Student Paper, IEEE Internat. Conf. on Systems, Man, and Cybernetics, 1998, Exceptional Achievement award, SRI Internat., 1985, SRI Internat. Exceptional-Achievement Award for work on adaptive routing algorithms, 1989; SRI Internat. fellow, 1982—83, CONACYT scholarship, Consejo Nacional de Ciencia y Tecnologia (CONACYT), Mex., 1978—82. Fellow: IEEE (Richard W. Hamming medal com. 1998—2000, internet tech. award com. 1999—2001); mem.: Assn. for Computing Machinery. Office: Univ of Cali Computer Engring Dept Santa Cruz CA 95064 Home Phone: 650-570-7356; Office Phone: 831-459-4153.

GARCIAPARRA, NOMAR (ANTHONY NOMAR GARCIAPARRA), professional baseball player; b. Whittier, Calif., July 23, 1973; m. Mia Hamm, Nov. 22, 2003; 2 children. Student, Ga. Tech. Shortstop Fla. St. League, Sarasota, Fla., 1994, Ea. League, Trenton, NJ, 1995, Internat. League, Pawtucket, 1996, Boston Red Sox, 1996—2004, Chicago Cubs, 2004—05; infielder LA Dodgers, 2005—. Named Am. League Rookie Player of the Yr., The Sporting News, 1997, Baseball Writers' Assn. Am., 1997, Player's Choice Am. League Outstanding Rookie, AL Batting Champion, 1999, 2000, NL Comeback Player Yr, Players Choice Awards, 2006; named to Am. League All-Star Team, 1997, 1999, 2000, 2002, 2003, Nat. League All-Star Team, 2006, Cape Cod League Hall of Fame, 2002. Achievements include being a mem. of U.S. Olympic Baseball Team, 1992; led Am. League in Batting Avg., 1999 (.357), 2000 (.372); led Am. League in Hits (209), 1997. Office: LA Dodgers 1000 Elysian Park Ave Los Angeles CA 90012

GARCIA Y CARRILLO, MARTHA XOCHITL, pharmacist; b. Austin, Tex., Dec. 7, 1919; d. Alberto Gonzalo and Guadalupe Eva (Carrillo) Garcia; m. Jerjes Jose Rodriguez, Oct. 9, 1943 (dec. 1987); children: Marie Eugenia, Jerjes Alberto, Nicanor Francisco. BS in Pharmacy, U. Tex., 1944. RPh, Tex. Retail pharmacist Ward Drug Store, Austin, Tex., 1952-57, Sommer's Drug Store, San Antonio, 1957-62, Skillern's Drug Store, Dallas, 1962-66; hosp. pharmacist Brackenridge Hosp., Austin, 1968-75; retail pharmacist Thorp Lane Pharmacy, San Marcos, Tex., 1975-77, The Pharmacy, San Marcos, 1975-79, MHMR Pharmacy, Austin, 1975-78, Ace Drug Co., Austin, 1979-82; ret. Contbg. author: The New Handbook of Texas, 1996. Recipient Citation of Achievement Tex. State Bd. Pharmacy, 1996. Mem. Am. Pharm. Assn. (emeritus mem.), Tex. Pharmacy Assn., Capitol Area Pharmacy Assn., Tex. State Hist. Assn., Ex-Students Assn. U. Tex. (life, Golden Anniversary cert. 1994). Republican. Avocations: reading, playing piano, current events, pharmacy medicine.

GARDE, JOHN CHARLES, lawyer; b. Lyndhurst, NJ, Aug. 17, 1961; s. John Charles and Jean (Shepherd) G.; m. L. Allison Ghenn, Aug. 9, 1986. BA, Drew U., 1983; JD, William and Mary, 1986. Bar: N.J. 1986, U.S. Ct. N.J. 1986, U.S. Ct. Appeals (2nd, 3rd and 7th cirs.) 1990. Law sec. to presiding judge Superior Ct Appellate div., Hackensack, N.J., 1986-87; assoc. McCarter & English, Newark, 1987-94, ptnr., 1995—. Contbr. William and Mary Law Rev. Warden St. Thomas Epis. Ch., 1987—; trustee St. Phillip's Acad., 1996-2000; trustee Diocese of Newark Episcopal Properties and Fin., 2001—, judge ecclesiastical ct., 1996-2000. Mem.: ABA, Essex County Bar Assn., N.J. State Bar Assn., Phi Beta Kappa, Order of the Coif. Republican. Episcopalian. Office: McCarter & English 100 Mulberry St Newark NJ 07102-4004 Home Phone: 973-292-1201; Office Phone: 973-622-4444. Business E-Mail: jgarde@mccarter.com.

GARDEBRING, SANDRA S., academic administrator; Grad., Luther Coll., Decorah, Iowa; JD, U. Minn. Dir. Region 5 U.S. EPA; commr. Minn. Pollution Control Agy., Minn. Dept. Human Svcs.; judge Minn. Ct. Appeals; assoc. justice Minn. Supreme Ct., 1991-98; v.p. univ. rels. U. Minn., 1998—2004; v.p. univ. advancement Calif. Polytech. State Univ., San Luis Obispo, 2004—. Bd. dirs. Nature Conservancy of Minn., Regions Hosp. Hearth Connection, Greater Mpls. Conv. and Visitors Assn. Mailing: 1055 Capistrano Ct San Luis Obispo CA 93405

GARDENHIRE, RONALD CLYDE, professional athletics manager; m. Carol Kissling Gardenhire; children: Toby, Tiffany, Tara. BA in phys. edn., U. Tex. Mgr. Class A Kenosha, 1988; bench coach Minn. Twins , 1995, 1st base coach, 1996, 3d base coach, 1998, mgr., 2002—. Named Co-mgr. of Yr., So. league, 1990, Best Managerial Prospect, Baseball Am., Best Mgr., 1989; named to Carolina League All-Star team, 1979. Office: Minn Twins 34 Kirby Puckett Pl Minneapolis MN 55415*

GARDENIER, JOHN STARK, statistician, philosopher, researcher, writer; b. Portland, Maine, Apr. 10, 1937; s. John Stark and Lucia Esther (Christensen) G.; m. Margaret Elizabeth Mann, Jan. 26, 1962 (dec. 1976); children: Brenda Anne Marshall, Patricia Suzanne Depew, Linda Marie Sievering-Albrecht, Pamela Lee Antoun; m. Turkan Emine Kumbaraci, June 18, 1977; children: George Halil Bonneval, Jason Celal Stark. BA, Yale U., 1959; MS, George Washington U., 1968, DBA, 1973. Tech. staff Computer Scis. Corp., Falls Church, Va., 1968-69; sr. analyst CONSULTEC, Rockville, Md., 1969-71; ops. rsch. analyst USCG, Washington, 1971-90; survey statistician Nat. Ctr. Health Stats., Hyattsville, Md., 1990—2003; ret., 2003. Adj. assoc. prof. George Washington U., 1980-81; prof. lectr. Am. U., Washington, 1982-84; cons. in field. Comdr. USN, ret. Recipient Silver medal U.S. Dept. Transp., 1983, Dir.'s award CDC/Nat. Ctr. for Health Stats., 2000. Mem. AAAS, Am. Statis. Assn. (com. profl. ethics 1994-96, chair com. profl. ethics 1996-99, vice chair com. reps. 2002—, rep. to AAAS sect. history and philosophy of sci. 2002—), Nat. Assn. Sci. Writers, Naval Res. Assn Avocations: music, golf. Home: 115 St Andrews Dr NE Vienna VA 22180-3660 Home Phone: 703-319-3981; Office Phone: 703-319-3981. E-mail: drgarden@verizon.net.

GARDENIER, TURKAN KUMBARACI, statistician, researcher; b. Istanbul, Turkey, Nov. 10, 1941; arrived in U.S., 1958; d. Celal and Aysel (Triandafilidu) K.; m. John Stark Gardenier, June 18, 1977; children: Pamela Lee, George HalilBonneval, Jason Celal Stark. AB, Vassar Coll., 1961; MA, Columbia U., 1962, PhD, 1966. Ops. rsch. scientist IIT Rsch. Inst., Chgo., 1966-68; asst. prof., chmn. Middle East Tech. U., Ankara, Turkey, 1968-70; vis. scientist Brookhaven Nat. Labs., Upton, L.I., NY, 1970-71; assoc. dir. Pfizer Pharms., NYC, 1971-73; asst. prof. N.Y. State Maritime Coll., Bronx, NY, 1973-78; health scientist U.S. EPA, Washington, 1978-81; assoc. prof. Am. U., Washington, 1982-84; pres. Pragmatica Corp., Vienna, Va., 1982—. Tech. cons. Analytic Services Corp., Arlington, Va., 1982-90; expert U.S. Energy Info. Adminstrn., Washington, 1982-84; statis. expert EEO, 1990—, statis. cons. Engring. Computer Optecnomics, Annapolis, Md., 1977—; cons. C.R. Cushing Co., Marine Engring., N.Y.C., 1974-77. Organizer, pub. Symposium on Data Efficiency Design; preprocessing pub. Garden-ear Math./Stat. Series for Quanititative Literacy. Corp. mem. Am. Friends of Turkey, McLean, Va., 1983-89; com. mem. World Mut. Service Com., N.Y.C., 1982—; bd. dirs., v.p. Friends of Am. BoardSchs. in Turkey, 1986-88, Am. Turkish Assn., Washington, 1988-90, Washington parents rep. Foxcroft Sch., Middleburg, Va., 1981-84. Grantee, NSF, 1980, CENTO, 1969, NIH/NCI, 1997-2000. Mem. Am. Statis. Assn. (audio-visual graphics com. 1979), Ops. Rsch. Soc. Am. (fin. com. 1980), Soc. Computer Simulation (assoc. editor jour. 1980-84), Soc. Risk Analysis (fin. com. 1980), AAAS (symposium organizer 1979-2003). Avocations: swimming, photography, music composition, multi-media training. Address: Pragmatica Corp 115 St Andrews Dr NE Vienna VA 22180-3660 Home Phone: 703-319-3981; Office Phone: 703-319-9009. E-mail: drgarden@verizon.net.

GARDIN, HERSHEL, academic administrator, dean, management consultant; s. Abraham and Ruth G.; m. Joy Beth Lewis, Oct. 10, 1972; children: Naftali M., Dov E., Miriam S., Yehudis K. BA, Wayne State U., 1969, MA, 1971, PhD, 1975, Columbia Pacific U., 1983. Instr. Wayne State U., Detroit, 1970—74; dir. psychol. svcs. Alexandrine Ho., Inc., Detroit, 1975—77; social planner IV Wayne County Dept of Substance Abuse Svcs., Detroit, 1977—79; assoc. Annis and Assocs., P.C., Bingham Farms, Mich., 1979—81; sr. rsch. analyst The Wellness Plan, Detroit, 1981—83, v.p., corp. officer, 1983—2000; v.p., dean acad. adminstrn. MJI Inst., Oak Park and West Bloomfield, Mich., 2000—. Pres. Gardin Consulting Group, LLC, Oak Park, Mich., 2000—. Contbr. articles to profl. jours., chapters to books. Rec. sec. Cong. Shomer Israel, Oak Park, Mich., 1994—2007; regional cabinet mem. Anti Defamation League Bnai Brith, Detroit, 1978—90; adv. position Caring Together interdenominational group providing health care to the elderly, Detroit, 1998—2000. Numerous grants. Mem. AAAS, Am. Pub. Health Assn., Soc. for Psychologists in Addictive Behavior. Jewish. Office: MJI 25401 Coolidge Highway Oak Park MI 48237 Office Phone: 877-281-8229. E-mail: thgardin@gardinconsulting.com.

GARDIN, JULIUS MARKUS, cardiologist, educator; b. Detroit, Jan. 14, 1949; s. Abram and Fania (Toba) G.; children: Adam Lev, Tova Michal, Margot Anne. BS with high distinction, U. Mich., 1968, MD cum laude, 1972. Diplomate Am. Bd. Internal Medicine; cert. cardiovascular diseases. Intern then resident in medicine U. Mich., Ann Arbor, 1972-75; fellow in cardiology Georgetown U., Washington, 1975-77; dir. cardiology noninvasive lab., staff cardiologist Lakeside VA Med. Ctr., Chgo., 1977-79; staff cardiologist Northwestern U., Chgo., 1977—79, asst. prof. Med. Sch., 1978—79; dir. cardiology noninvasive lab. Irvine Med. Ctr. U. Calif., Orange, 1979-2000, from asst. prof. to assoc. prof. Irvine Med. Ctr., 1979—89, prof., 1989-2000, chief cardiology Irvine, 1994-99; acting chief cardiology Long Beach (Calif.) VA Med. Ctr., 1982—84; prof. Wayne State U., Detroit, 2000—; St. John Guild disting. chmn. St. John Hosp. and Med. Ctr., Detroit, 2000—, chief div. cardiology, 2000—07, vice chmn. rsch. dept. medicine, 2007—. Co-editor: Textbook of Two-Dimensional Echocardiography, 1983, assoc. editor Preventive Cardiology, 2000, 05; assoc. editor (jour.) Update on Cardiovascular Diagnostics, 1982, Am. Jour. Cardiac Imaging, 1985-97, Jour. Am. Soc. Echocardiography, 2007—; mem. editl. bd. Archives of Internal Medicine and Chest, 1978-88, Am. Jour. Noninvasive Cardiology, 1985-95, Am. Jour. Cardiology, 1987-94, 97—, Cardiovascular Imaging, 1988—, Echocardiography, 1985—, Jour. Am. Coll. Cardiology, 1990-94, 2001-05, Am. Jour. Geriatric Cardiology, 1992—, Am. Jour. Sports Medicine, 1998-2004, Jour. Am. Soc. Echocardiography, 1992-2001; cardiovasc. area editor Jour. Clin. Ultrasound, 1989-94; contbr. articles to profl. jours. Maj. Med. Svc. Corps USAR. Grantee Am. Heart Assn., 1980-84, 99-02, Nat. Heart Lung and Blood Inst., 1988-; named one of Best Drs. in Am. Woodward White Publs., 1994-, Am.'s Top Drs. Castle Connolly Publs., 2002-. Fellow ACP, Am. Coll. Cardiology (physician workforce adv., health care reform and echocardiography coms., 1993-99, publs. com. 2007—), Am. Heart Assn. (coun. clin. cardiology, coun. epidemiology and prevention, coun. cardiovascular radiology, ACC/AHA/ACP-ASIM task force to update guidelines for mgmt. of patients with chronic stable angina 1998-99, 01-02, co-chair 2007—, Seymour Gordon Disting. Achievement award AHA Detroit chpt. 2006), Soc. Geriat. Cardiology (v.p. 1990-92, pres. 1992-93); mem. Internat. Cardiac Doppler Soc. (bd. dirs., chmn. Pan-Am. sect. 1984—, v.p. 1988-90, pres. 1990-92, exec. sec. 2006-), Am. Soc. Echocardiography (bd. dirs., treas. 1989-91, v.p. 1991-93, pres. 1993-95, chmn. nomenclature and stds. 1991-95, chmn. task force on standardized echo report 1999-02, co-chmn. writing group on vascular imaging 2001—, assoc. editor Jour. 2007—), U. Mich. Med. Ctr. Alumni Assn. (bd. govs. 1979-81), Phi Beta Kappa, Alpha Omega Alpha, Phi Delta Epsilon. Jewish. Office: St John Hosp and Med Ctr PBII Ste 470 22201 Moross Rd Detroit MI 48236 Home Phone: 248-706-2346; Office Phone: 313-343-6390. Business E-Mail: julius.gardin@stjohn.org.

GARDINER, DAVID M., biologist, educator; AB with honors, Occidental Coll., LA, 1971; PhD, Scripps Institution of Oceanography, U. Calif. San Diego, 1976. Rsch. assoc., lectr., Marine Biology, Dept. Biology Occidental Coll., LA, 1976—78, vis. asst. prof., biology, 1976—80, assoc. dir. marine sciences, 1978—80; postdoctoral tng. U. Calif. Davis, 1980—82, vis. asst. prof. zoology and develop. biology, 1980—82; asst. rsch. biologist, Develop. Biology Ctr. U. Calif. Irvine, 1982—84, course coord. , develop. and cell biology, 1995—96, assoc. rsch. biologist, Develop. Biology Ctr., 1994—2000, asst. dean for corp. rels, sch. biol. sciences, 1999—2000, rsch. biologist, dept. develop. and cell biology, Develop. Biology Ctr., 2000—. Faculty adv. bd. U. Calif. Irvine-Santa Ana Teachers Inst., 2000—; bd. dir. Orange County Sci. and Engring. Fair, 2000—. Contbr. articles to profl. jours. Mem.: AAAS, Am. Soc. for Cell Biology, Soc. for Develop. Biology. Office: Dept Develop and Cell Biology Develop Biology Ctr Univ Calif Irvine 4111 Natural Sciences II Mail Code 2305 Irvine CA 92697-2275 Office Phone: 949-824-2792. Business E-Mail: dmgardin@uci.edu.*

GARDINER, HOBART CLIVE, petroleum company executive; b. Boston, Jan. 12, 1929; m. Patricia Williams, Oct. 14, 1950. BA, Yale U., 1950; postgrad., U. Central Caracas, Venezuela. Various mgmt. positions Esso Standard Oil Co. S.A., Havana, Cuba, 1954, Panama City, Panama, 1954, San Salvador, El Salvador, 1954-56, Guatemala City, Guatemala, 1956, country mgr. San Jose, Costa Rica, 1956-57, Tegucigalpa, Honduras, Brit. Honduras, 1957-60; asst. employee rels. mgr. Esso Interamerica Inc., Coral Gables, Fla., 1960; pres., gen. mgr. Esso Standard Oil Co., S.A., San Juan, P.R., 1960-62; v.p. Internat. Petroleum Co. Ltd., Bogota, Colombia, 1962-64, ops. mgr. Talara, Peru, 1964-66; pres. Esso Std. Oil (Chile), Santiago, 1966-69; L.Am. area advisor Standard Oil Co. N.J., NYC, 1969-71; v.p. Esso Standard Oil Co. C.Am., Panama, San Salvador, El Salvador, 1971-74; gen. mgr. Esso Chile, Uruguay and Paraguay, Montevideo, Uruguay, 1974-77; pub. affairs program mgr. Exxon Corp., NYC, 1977-79; asst. gen. mgr. Esso Caribbean, Coral Gables, Fla., 1979-81; v.p. fin. and adminstrn. Internat. Exec. Svc. Corps., Stamford, Conn., 1982-84, v.p. L.Am. and Caribbean, 1984-90, exec. v.p., 1990-93, pres., CEO, 1993—2003; ret., 2003. With USMC, 1950—52. Mem.: Country Club Fairfield. Episcopalian. E-mail: hcg1@optonline.net.

GARDINER, JOHN JACOB, writer, educator, philosopher; b. Tel Aviv, Feb. 6, 1946; arrived in U.S., 1952; s. Leon and Zipora Zucker; m. Joanna Meredith Winslow, 1967 (div. 1998); children: James, Katharine. BA, U. Fla., 1967, PhD, 1973; postgrad., U. Oreg., 1978, Stanford U., 1983. Tchr., dept. chair Keystone Heights (Fla.) Sch., 1968-72; instr., asst. to v.p. acad. affairs U. Fla., Gainesville, 1973-75; asst. prof. edn. The Citadel, Charleston, SC, 1975-77; prof., dept. chair Okla. State U., Stillwater, 1979-91, Seattle U., 1991—. Assoc. in edn. Harvard U., 1985; vis. asst. prof. Fla. State U., Tallahassee, 1977-78, U. Oreg., Eugene, 1978-79; chair bd. Pacific N.W. Postdoctoral Inst., Seattle, 1995-99; bd. dir. Internat. Leadership Assn., Conflict Resolution Inst., Human Connection Inst., Ctr. for Advanced Study of Leadership, U. Md., College Park; co-founder All Russia Leadership Devel. Ctr., Novosibirsk, 1999-2000; mem. exec. com. Internat. Leadership Assn., 2001-03. Co-author: UNESCO Guide, 1991, Insights on Leadership, 1998, Building Leadership Bridges, 2003. Recipient Svc. to State award Gov. and Ho. of Reps., 1991; fellow W. K. Kellogg Found., 1972-73; grantee James McGregor Burns Leadership Acad. Ctr. for Advanced Study of Leadership, 1998. Mem. Am. Coun. Edn. (bd. dirs. Nat. Leadership Group 1985-96), Assn. Study of Higher Edn. (bd. dirs. 1983-85), Am. Ednl. Rsch. Assn. (bd. dirs. divsn. J 1983-85), Vashon Island Rotary Club (pres. 2000-01, dist. 5030 gov. 2003-04, permanent fund chair dist. 5030, 1996-2002, strategic advisor ann. program fund Zone 33, 2005—). Avocations: walking, reading, gardening, public speaking. Office: Seattle U 413 Loyola Hall Broadway and Madison Seattle WA 98122 Office Phone: 206-296-6171. Business E-Mail: gardiner@seattleu.edu.

GARDINER, KEITH MATTINSON, engineering executive, educator; b. Stockport, Eng., Mar. 30, 1933; came to U.S., 1967; s. Fred and Florence (Mattinson) G.; m. Eileen Veronica, Oct. 28, 1964 (div. 1981); children: Helen Marie, Claire Celine (dec.); m. Bernice Bult, Dec. 17, 1989. BS, Manchester U., Eng., 1953, PhD, 1957. Registered profl. engr., Calif., 1978. Sect. leader atomic power div. English Electric Co. Ltd. (UK), Leicester, Eng., 1956-59; asst. dir. F. Gardiner Ltd., Manchester, 1959-61; asst. mgr. Rolls-Royce Aero Engine divsn. Mfg. Methods Devel., Derby, Eng., 1961-66; sr. engr. IBM Corp., Eng., 1966-67, IBM Corp., US, 1967-87; prof. indsl. and sys. engring., dir. Ctr. Mfg. Sys. Engring. Lehigh U., Bethlehem, Pa., 1989—. Cons., reviewer Nat. Rsch. Coun., NSF; mem. adv. bd. Nat. Engrs. Week Future City Competition, 2000-. Editor: Systems and Technology for Advanced Manufacturing, 1983, Jour. Electronics Mfg., 1991-2003;; assoc. editor Jour. Mfg. Sys. 1984-, Jour. Mfg. Process, 1999-; author papers, tech. reports, book chpts. in field. Chmn. Lehigh Valley Engring. Coun., 1997-98; founding chmn. Green Mountain Bicycle Club, Vt., 1969. Fulbright fellow. Fellow Soc. Mfg. Engrs. (sr. mem., exec. com. 1974-91, chpt. exec. 1974-76, 89-91, internat. dir. 1992-93, 95-96, 01-02, v.p. 1999, sec./treas. 2000, Joseph A. Siegel award, 2003); mem. ASME, Fulbright Assn., Engrs. Club Lehigh Valley (chmn. 2004—); Sigma Xi (sr., pres. Lehigh U. chpt. 1997-98, 2006-07), Phi Beta Delta (pres. Beta Pi chpt. 1993-94). Avocations: bicycling, photography, backpacking, industrial archeology. Office: Lehigh U Ctr Mfg Sys Engring 200 W Packer Ave Bethlehem PA 18015-1518 Office Phone: 610-758-5070. Business E-Mail: Keith.Gardiner@Lehigh.edu, kg03@lehigh.edu. *As Shakespeare has it "Life is but a dream." and it's up to us to do the best that we can with it!.*

GARDINER, KENT A., lawyer; b. 1958; BA with honors, State U. NY, 1981; JD cum laude, Georgetown U., 1984. Bar: NY 1985, DC 1992. Trial atty. antitrust divsn. US Dept. Justice, 1984—87; ptnr. Crowell & Moring LLP, Washington, chmn., 2006—. Mem., editor Am. Criminal Law Review, 1982—84; spkr. in field. Contbr. articles to profl. jours. Office: Crowell & Moring LLP 1001 Pennsylvania Ave NW Ste 1100 Washington DC 20004-2595 Office Phone: 202-624-2578. Office Fax: 202-658-5116. E-mail: kgardiner@crowell.com.

GARDINER, LESTER RAYMOND, JR., retired lawyer; b. Salt Lake City, Aug. 20, 1931; s. Lester Raymond and Sarah Lucille (Kener) G.; m. Janet Ruth Thatcher, Apr. 11, 1955; children: Allison Gardiner Bigelow, John Alfred, Annette Gardiner Weed, Leslie Gardiner Crandall, Robert Thatcher, Lisa Gardiner West, James Raymond, Elizabeth Gardiner Smith, David William, Sarah Janet Gardiner Boyden. BS with honors, U. Utah, Salt Lake City, 1954; JD, U. Mich., Ann Arbor, 1959. Bar: Utah 1959, U.S. Dist. Ct. Utah 1959, U.S. Ct. Appeals (10th cir.) 1960. Law clk. U.S. Dist. Ct., 1959; assoc. then ptnr. Van Cott, Bagley, Cornwall & McCarthy, Salt Lake City, 1960—67; ptnr. Gardiner & Johnson, Salt Lake City, 1967—72, Christensen, Gardiner, Jensen & Evans, 1972—78, Fox, Edwards, Gardiner & Brown, Salt Lake City, 1978—87, Chapman & Cutler, 1987—89, Gardiner & Hintze, 1990—92; CEO and pres. Snowbird Ski and Summer Resort, Snowbird Corp., 1993—97; prin., mgmt. cons. Ray Gardiner Assocs., 1998—2003; ret. Reporter, mem. Utah Sup. Ct. Com. on Adoption of Uniform Rules of Evidence, 1970-73, mem. com. on revision of criminal code, 1975-78; master of the bench Am. Inn of Ct. I, 1980-90; mem. com. bar examiners Utah State Bar, 1973; instr. bus. law U. Utah, 1965-66; adj. prof. law Brigham Young U., 1984-85. Mem. Republican State Central Com. Utah, 1967-72, mem. exec. com. Utah Rep. Party, 1975-78, chmn. state convs., 1976, 77; mem. Salt Lake City Bd. Edn., 1971-72; bd. dirs. Salt Lake City Pub. Library, 1974-75; trustee Utah Sports Found., 1987-91; bd. dirs. and exec. com. Salt Lake City Visitors and Conv. Bur., 1988-91, 93-98; mem., chmn. bd. dirs. Inst. Outdoor Recreation and Tourism Utah State U., 1997-03. Served to 1st lt. USAF, 1954-56. Mem.: Utah State Bar Assn., Rotary. Mem. Lds Ch.

GARDINER, PAMELA NAN, performing company executive; m. David Edward Miller, 1974 (div. 1988); m. Anton Labuschagne, 1998 (div. 1999). BA, U. Wis.; MA, Columbia U.; JD, Case Western Res. U. Bar: Ohio 1975, Wis. 1982, Fla. 1999. Asst. trust officer Cleve. Trust Co., 1975-78; asst. dean acad. affairs Coll. Letters and Sci. U. Wis., 1978-84; exec. dir. Madison Festival of the Lakes, 1984-88, Miami City Ballet, Fla., 2000—, Gardiner & Fix LLC, Arts and Entertainment Atty., 2002—. Bd. dirs. Miami Performing Arts Ctr. Found.; mem. adv. bd. The Playground Theatre for Young Audiences. Office: Miami City Ballet 2200 Liberty Ave Miami Beach FL 33139-1641 Office Phone: 305-929-7000 ext. 1106. Business E-Mail: pamela@miamicityballet.org.

GARDINER, T(HOMAS) MICHAEL, artist; b. Seattle, Feb. 5, 1946; s. Thomas Scott Gardiner and Carolyn Virginia (Harmer) Bolin; m. Kelly Michelle Floyd, Mar. 7, 1981 (div. Dec. 1983); m. Diana Phyllis Shurtlieff Rainwater, Sept. 26, 1986; children: Rita Em, Nigel Gus. BA in Philosophy, Sulpician Sem. N.W., Kenmore, Wash., 1969; student, Cornish Inst. Arts, 1971—73. Seaman Tidewater Barge, Camas, Wash., 1969; parimutuel clk. Longacres Racetrack, Renton, Wash., 1969-92; dock worker

Sealand, Inc., Seattle, 1970. Tchr. Coyote Jr. H.S., Seattle, 1989-95, Sch. Visual Concepts, Seattle, 1990-95; tchr., vis. artist Ctrl. Wash. U., Ellensburg, 1991; installer fine art Artech, Seattle, 1999—. Represented in permanent collections Tacoma Art Mus., Ballard HS, Seattle, Microsoft Corp., Stoel Rives LLP, Stokes Lawrence PS, Seattle Water Dept., Nordstrom, Seattle City Light, Mus. of N.W. Art, LaConner, Wash., Sultan (Wash.) Sch. Dist., King County Portable Works Collection, SAFECO Ins. Co., Seattle, City of Portland Collection, 1988, Highline Sch. Dist., Seattle, U. Wash. Med. Ctr.; commns. include ARTp Metro Art Project, Seattle, interior painting Villa del Lupo restaurant, Vancouver, B.C., Can.; illustrations included in New Yorker Mag., Am. Illustration 13, Seattle Times. Recipient Best Design award Print Mag., 1985; Nat. Endowment for Arts fellow, 1989; grantee Gottlieb Found., 2007. Democrat. Roman Catholic. Home and Office: 3023 NW 63rd St Seattle WA 98107-2566 E-mail: gardiner@speakeasy.net.

GARDINO, VINCENT ANTHONY, broadcast executive; b. NYC, Sept. 19, 1953; s. Anthony John and Carmelina Mary (Boglia) Gardino. BA in History magna cum laude, St. Francis Coll. V.p. NY sales mgr., dir. spl. programming and sales Metro Radio Sales, NYC, 1976-79; acct. exec. Sta. WABC-AM Radio, NYC, 1979-81; dir. ABC Radio Network, NYC, 1981-85, ABC Direction and Entertainment Radio Networks, 1981-85; pres., COO Selcom Radio, NYC, 1985—; v.p., gen. sales mgr. Sta. WOR-AM, NYC, 1985-95; v.p. ea. sales CNBC, 1995-98; exec. dir. underwriting radio and digital media Sta. WNYC-FM, Sta. WNYC-AM, 1998—. Cons. DEI, Inc., 2001—; adj. assoc. prof. comm., arts St. Francis Coll., NY, 2003—. Mem. parish coun. St. Malachy's Ch.; trustee St. Francis Coll., 2005—; bd. dirs. Kaplan Cancer Ctr., NYU Med. Ctr. Mem.: Mus. Broadcasting, Internat. Radio and TV Soc., Columbus Citizens Found., Inc., Famija Piemonteisa, NY Athletic Club. Roman Catholic. Avocations: tennis, golf, skiing, historical autograph collecting. Office: WNYC AM/FM 1 Centre St New York NY 10007-1602 Home Phone: 212-799-8640. Business E-Mail: vgardino@wnyc.org.

GARDNER, ANNETTE LENORE, health policy researcher, political scientist; d. Murray and Donna Gardner; m. Charles Simons, June 21, 1995; children: Ian Simons, Annette. BA, Reed Coll., Portland, Oreg., 1983; MPH, U. Hawaii, Oahu, 1994, PhD, 2000. Sr. rschr. Inst. Health Policy Studies, U. Calif., San Francisco, 2000—06, academic specialist, 2006—. Chair grand rounds com. Inst. Health Policy Studies, U. Calif., San Francisco, 2005—06, chair star award com., 2007—; presenter in field. Contbr. articles to profl. jours. Vol. Peace Corps, Washington, Benin, 1983—85. Mem.: APHA (assoc.), Am. Evaluation Assn., World Future Soc. Democrat. Achievements include research in local (county) health policymaking and the role of clinic associations in representing community clinics and the medically underserved; access to healthcare. Avocations: skiing, gardening, music. Office: U Calif San Francisco 3333 California St Ste 265 San Francisco CA 94118 Home Phone: 415-933-8071; Office Phone: 415-514-1543. Office Fax: 415-476-0705. Business E-Mail: annette.gardner@ucsf.edu.

GARDNER, ARNOLD BURTON, lawyer; b. NYC, Jan. 3, 1930; s. Harry P. and Ruth G. (Gutfreund) G.; m. Sue Shaffer, Aug. 24, 1952; children— Jonathan H., Diane R. BA summa cum laude, U. Buffalo, 1950; LL.B., Harvard U., 1953. Bar: N.Y. State bar 1954. Assoc. firm Kavinoky Cook LLP (and predecessor), Buffalo, 1953—58, ptnr., 1958, sr. ptnr., 1977. Mem. Buffalo Bd. Edn., 1969-74, pres., 1971-72; mem. nat. bd. govs. Am. Jewish Com., 1972-95, nat. v.p., 1986-89; chmn. N.Y. State Ed. Dept. Task Force on Tchr. Edn. and Certification, 1975-77; trustee SUNY, 1980-99, vice chmn., 1991-95; bd. govs. Hebrew Union Coll., Jewish Inst. Religion, Cin., 1981-87; trustee N.Y. State Archives, 1994—; mem. N.Y. State Bd. Regents, 1999—. With U.S. Army, 1954-56. Recipient Cmty. Service award NCCJ, 1974, 88; named Lawyer of Yr. U. Buffalo Sch. of Law, 1994; named to Best Lawyers in Am., 1992—. Mem. N.Y. State Bar Assn.(Root Stimson award, 2006), Erie County Bar Assn., Am. Law Inst. (life), Buffalo Club. Office: Kavinoky Cook LLP 726 Exchange St Ste 800 Buffalo NY 14210 Office Phone: 716-845-6000. Business E-Mail: a.gardner@kavinokycook.com.

GARDNER, BONNIE MILNE, theater educator, playwright; b. Cleve., Oct. 17, 1954; d. Alexander Robert and Lois Chase Milne; m. Bruce Andrew Gardner, July 9, 1977; children: Jesse Milne, Elizabeth Milne. BA in Theatre, Ohio Wesleyan U., 1977; MA in Theatre, U. Akron, 1980; PhD in Theatre, Kent State U., 1985. Intern Meri Mini Players, NYC, 1975; mng. dir. Theatre on the Square, Brecksville, Ohio, 1976—79; pub. rels. dir. Fairmount Theatre of the Deaf, Cleve., 1980—81; doctoral fellow Kent State U. Sch. of Theatre, 1981—84; dir. Kent State U., Youth Enrichment Program, 1982—83; instr. U. Akron, 1984—85; prof. theatre Ohio Wesleyan U., Delaware, 1985—. Author: The Emergence of the Playwright-Director in American Theatre, 2001; contbr. articles various profl. jours.; author: (plays) produced off Broadway and regional theatres. Adv. bd. mem. Arts Edn. Ohio Dept. of Edn., 1996—2002; mem. program rev. bd. Theatre Edn. Ohio Dept. of Edn., 1998—2000; program bd. mem. Del. County Cultural Arts Ctr., Ohio, 1990—92. Individual Artist grantee, Playwrights Ohio Arts Coun., 1994. Mem.: Ohio Theatre Alliance, Ohio Alliance for Arts Edn., Assn. for Theatre in Higher Edn., Dramatists Guild. Unitarian Universalist. Office: Ohio Wesleyan U Theatre 45 Rowland Ave Delaware OH 43015

GARDNER, BRIAN E., lawyer; b. Des Moines, July 13, 1952; s. Lawrence E. and Sarah I. (Hill) G.; m. Rondi L. Veland, Aug. 7, 1976; children: Meredith Anne, Stephanie Lynn, John Clinton. BS with distinction, Iowa State U., 1974; JD with high distinction, U. Iowa, 1978. Bar: Iowa 1978, Mo. 1978, U.S. Dist. Ct. (we. dist.) Mo. 1978, Kans. 1979, U.S. Dist. Ct. Kans. 1979, U.S. Ct. Appeals (10th cir.) 1980. Assoc. Morrison, Hecker, Curtis, Kuder & Parrish, Kansas City, Mo., 1978-80, Parker & Handsaker, Nevada, Iowa, 1980-81, Morrison, Hecker, Curtis, Kuder & Parrish, Overland Park, Kans., 1981-83; ptnr. Morrison & Hecker, Kansas City, Mo., 1983—2002, mng. ptnr., 1990—93, 1996—2002; city atty. Mission Hills, Kans., 1992—2003; co-mng. ptnr. Stinson Morrison Hecker LLP, Kansas City, 2002—04; exec. v.p., gen. counsel Hallmark Cards, Inc., Kansas City, 2004—. Bd. dirs. Overland Park Conv. and Visitors Bur., 1985-97, chmn., 1988-90; dir., mem. exec. com. Johnson County C.C. Found., Overland Park, 1990—, pres., 1997-98; bd. dirs. KCPT, 1993-99, 2000—, chmn., 1997-98; active Kansas City Area Devel. Coun., 1992—, Civic Coun. Greater Kansas City, 1998—; bd. dir. Crown Media, Swope Cmty. Enterprises. Mem. Kans. Bar Assn., Kans. Assn. Def. Counsel, Kansas City Met. Bar Assn., Mo. Bar Assn., Johnson County Bar Assn., Blue Hills Country Club, Cardinal Key, Phi Beta Kappa, Phi Kappa Phi. Lutheran. Avocation: golf. Office: Hallmark Cards Inc MD 339 2501 McGee Trafficway Kansas City MO 64108 Mailing: Hallmark Cards Inc PO Box 419580 Kansas City MO 64141-6580 Office Phone: 816-274-5111. Office Fax: 816-274-5061.*

GARDNER, CAROL ANN, insurance company executive; b. Moscow, Idaho, Aug. 18, 1948; d. Hyrum Watkins Kershaw and Mildred Hanks; m. Rick D. Gardner, Aug. 31, 1967; children: Jennifer Ann Mead, Allison Weenig, Amanda Ridd, Hillary Rothey. BS, Brigham Young U., Provo, Utah, 1966—70. Lic. agent Calif. Dept. Ins., 1991; cert. long term care 2004. Account rep. Providential Home Income Plan, San Francisco, 1987—90; pres., owner LifeStyle Ins. Svcs., Inc., San Juan Capistrano, Calif., 1991—. V.p. Nat. Long Term Care Network. Contbr. articles to mags. Leadership Ch. Jesus Christ of Latter-Day Saints, San Juan Capistrano, 1975—2004. Mem.: HIAA (chmn. curriculum com. long term care profl. designation 2001—02), UNUM Provident (mem. long term care exec. cir. 1992—2003), NY Life (mem. long term care adv. group 2000—), MetLife Leadership Coun., Calif. Long Term Care Partnership Agt. Adv. Group, Nat. Long Term Care Exec. Study Coun. (com. mem. 2000—05), Soc. Actuaries (co-chmn. long term care ins. com. 2004—05), Nat. Long Term Care Network (bd. mem. 2004—05). R-Conservative. Lds Ch. Avocations: travel, reading, cooking. Office: LifeStyle Ins Svcs Inc 30448 Rancho Viejo Rd Ste 250 San Juan Capistrano CA 92675 Home Phone: 949-496-7819. Business E-Mail: cgardner@lifestyleinsurance.com.

GARDNER, CHRIS(TOPHER), securities trader, entrepreneur; b. Milw., Wis., Feb. 9, 1954; s. Bettye Jean Gardner and Thomas Turner, Freddie Triplet (Stepfather); m. Sherry Dyson (div.); 1 son with Jackie Medina Chris Jarrett Jr.; 1 daughter Jacintha. Former rsch. asst. U. Calif. San Francisco; former med. equipment salesman; intern Dean Witter Firm, 1981—82; with Bear Stearns & Co., 1983—87; founder, CEO Gardner Rich & Co. , Inc. (now Christopher Gardner Internat. Holding Co.), Chgo., 1987—. Motivational spkr. Co-author (with Quincy Troupe): (memoir) The Pursuit of Happyness, 2006 (Best Biography or Autobiography, NAACP Image awards, 2007, NY Times and Wash. Post Best-Seller, 2006); assoc. prodr. (inspired major motion picture starring Will Smith) The Pursuit of Happyness, 2006, featured on Evening News with Dan Rather, 20/20, Oprah, Today Show, The View, Entertainment Tonight, CNN, CNBC, Fox News Channel, subject of profiles in People, USA Today, AP, NY Times, Fortune, Jet, Reader's Digest, Trader Monthly, Chgo. Tribune, San Francisco Chronicle, NY Post and Milw. Journal Sentinel. Bd. dir. Nat. Ed. Found., Nat. Fatherhood Initiative; vol., donor Glide Meml. United Methodist Church, San Francisco, Cara Prog., Chgo. Served USN. Named Father of Yr., Nat. Fatherhood Initiative, 2002; recipient Peace Over Violence 2006 Humanitarian Awards-Spirit award, LA Commn. on Assaults Against Women, 2006, Friends of Africa award, Continental Africa C. of C., 2006. Office: Christopher Gardner Internat Holdings Co 401 S Financial Pl Chicago IL 60605*

GARDNER, DALE RAY, lawyer; b. Broken Arrow, Okla., May 8, 1946; s. Edward Dale and Dahlia Faye (McKeen) G.; m. Phyllis Ann Weinschrott, Dec. 27, 1969. BA in History, So. Ill. U., 1968; MA in History, St. Mary's U., San Antonio, 1975; JD, Tulsa U., 1979. Bar: Okla. 1979, Colo. 1986, Tex. 1991, U.S. Ct. Mil. Appeals 1988, U.S. Ct. Claims 1989, U.S. Dist. Ct. (no. dist.) Okla. 1981, U.S. Dist. Ct. Colo. 1986, U.S. Dist. Ct. (so. dist.) Tex. 1992, U.S. Ct. Appeals (10th cir.) 1986, U.S. Dist. Ct. (ea. dist.) Okla. 2003, U.S Supreme Ct., 2004. Pvt. practice, Sapulpa, Okla., 1979—80, 1994—2005; asst. dist. atty. child support enforcement unit 24th Dist. Oklahoma, Sapulpa, 1980-86, 94-95; pvt. practice Aurora, Colo., 1986-91, Houston, 1991-94; mng. atty. Hyatt Legal Svcs., Aurora, 1988-89; city atty. City of Sapulpa, Okla., 1996-99; ptnr. Gardner and Holdsclaw, 2005. Adj. settlement judge north program Alternate Dispute Resolution Sys. Okla. Author: Immigration Act of 1965: The Preliminary Results, 1974, Teapot Dome: Civil Legal Cases that Closed the Scandal, 1989. Mem. Child Support Enforcement, Sapulpa, 1980-86, 94-96; trustee United Way, Sapulpa, 1985, 95, subchair for attys. campaign, 2000, 2002, domestic violence counsel, Sapulpa, 1985; mem. cmty. investments strategy panel Tulsa Area United Way., 2006, 07; chmn. bd. trustees, elder, deacon 1st Presbyn. Ch., Sapulpa, 1985, elder rep. Eastern Okla. Presbyn.; bd. dirs. Inverness Village, Tulsa, 2007-. Capt. US Army, 1969—75, Vietnam, lt. col. US Army. Decorated Bronze star US Army, Legion of Merit. Mem. Okla. Bar Assn., Tex. Bar Assn., Colo. Bar Assn., Creek County Bar (pres. 2003), Gold Coat Club (pres.), Sertoma (pres. Sapulpa 1985, pres. Collumbine 1988, 90, Sertoman of Yr. 1985), Rotary Internat. (v.p. 2006, pres.-elect 2007-). Democrat. Presbyterian. Avocations: fishing, post card collecting. Home and Office: 7401 Loch Ness Cir Tulsa OK 74132-2145 Office Phone: 918-625-4016, 918-625-4016. Personal E-mail: drgardner@invernessvillage.com.

GARDNER, DAVID JOHN, communications executive, sound recording engineer; b. Binghamton, NY, Jan. 8, 1953; s. Daniel Sparrow and Anne Mae (Worthing) G.; m. Nancy Tipton Peacock, 1992; 1 child, Deborah Anne. AA, Broome CC, Binghamton, 1973; BA, Hofstra U., 1975. Prodn. control analyst IBM, Systems Mfg. Div., Endicott, N.Y., 1971-73; rec. engr. Eye-Full Films, San Francisco, 1972-78; gen. mgr. J.K. Theater Corp., Binghamton, 1975-77; rec. engr. The Image Works, Binghamton, 1977-80; audio/video engr. Sta. WBNG, Binghamton, 1977-78; media technician Nat. Sci. Found., Washington, 1978-79; tech. ops. RCA Americom Svcs., Inc., Princeton, N.J., 1980-84, supr. ops., 1984-86; mgr. network ops. ctr. GE Americom, Inc., Princeton, 1986-90, mgr. Vernon Valley tech. ops., 1990-92, mgr., customer svcs. and ops., 1992-95; dir. media svcs. Orion Atlantic, Rockville, MD, 1995-99; dir. mktg. svcs. Loral Skynet, Bedminster, NJ, 1999—2004, dir. satellite sys. engring., 2004—. Owner, pres., rec. engr. Ind. Sound, Binghamton, 1963—; co-founder, COB, bd. dirs. New Orleans Rec. Co., 1980—, Street Rhythm Prodns., Street Rhythm Records, Bklyn., 1980—. Mem. Soc. Broadcast Engrs., Soc. Motion Picture and TV Engrs. Lodges: Order of DeMolay. Episcopalian. Avocations: tennis, basketball, audio/video recording. Office: Loral Skynet 500 Hills Dr Bedminster NJ 07921-1538 Home: PO Box 205 Springtown PA 18081-0205 Business E-Mail: djg@loralskynet.com.

GARDNER, DONNA RAE (DONNA RAE DIEHL), education educator; b. Johnstown, Pa., Sept. 25, 1954; d. G. Edwin and Hilda M. (Batley) D.; m. William W. Gardner. BS in Edn., Geneva Coll., 1976; MEd, U. Pitts., 1984; EdD, U. Ga., 1997. Cert. tchr., Pa. Substitute 2d and 3d grade tchr. Portage (Pa.) Elem./Mid. Sch., 1976-77, 3d grade tchr., 1977-86, 2d grade tchr., 1986-87; from assoc. prof. to prof. Toccoa Falls Coll., Ga., 1987, prof., 1998—. Chair Curriculum Rev. Com. Accelerated Christian Edn.; asst. chair sch. tchr. edn. Toccoa Falls Coll., Ga., 2005—07, interim chair sch. tchr. edn., 2007—; spkr. in field. Editor (newsletter) Chalk Talk, Pew Pal; contbr. revs., articles to profl. publs., and ch. newsletter. Mem. choir First Alliance Ch., Toccoa, 1989-92, 96—; storyteller Stephens County Schs., Toccoa. Named 1st Lady, Toccoa Falls Coll., 2004; grantee U. Ga., 1991-92, Ga.'s Educators Profl. Devel. Mem. Internat. Reading Assn., Nat. Coun. Tchrs. English, Ga. Assn. Colls. Tchr. Edn., Ga. Assn. Ind. Colls. Tchr. Edn. Office: Toccoa Falls Coll PO Box 875 Toccoa Falls GA 30598 Office Phone: 706-886-6831. Business E-Mail: dgardner@tfc.edu.

GARDNER, ELIZABETH ANN HUNT, artist, poet, genealogist; b. Chgo., Aug. 8, 1916; d. William Luther and Elizabeth (Miller) Hunt; m. Vernon Everett Gardner, Mar. 25, 1950. Student, Wilson Tchrs. Coll., Washington, 1934-35. Art instr. Studio 6624, Falls Church, Va., 1968—. Vol. arts tchr. Anderson Orthopedic Hosp., Arlington, Va., 1958-66; flower judge, Alexandria, Va., 1965. Author: Nature-God's Realm Acknowledged, 2005; author and photographer: Accidental Surprises in Art, 2005, Spotlight on Little Mountain Garden Gems, Collection of Poetry on Current Themes Hand Illuminated, Gardens and Nurseries to Explore; photographer numerous color photographs Framed Restoration Worn Thin Keepsake Copy Salvadore Dali's Mystical Art, 2004; exhbn. Smithsonian Inst., Washington; one-woman show at Bowie Art Ctr., S.C., 1997; oil paintings, watercolors, brass rubbings included in area exhbns. including Brevard, NC, 2004; presenter recitation of original compositions including Winter Wonderland, Shut-In, Easter, Easter Haiku, 2004, Mother's Day, Father's Day, A Matter of Survival, 2005; author, compilor: Nature: God's Realm Acknowledged, 2004. Mem.: Nat. Wildlife Fedn., Cornell Lab. Ornithology, Nat. Audubon Soc., Nat. Home Gardening Club, Shillelaghs the Travel Club, Washington Figure Skating Club. Unitarian Universalist. Avocation: ornithology. Office Phone: 703-533-0999.

GARDNER, ELMER CLAUDE, academic administrator; b. Marmaduke, Ark., Jan. 16, 1925; s. O.A. Gardner and Edna (Sutton) Rowe; m. Delorese Tatum, June 17, 1945 (dec.); children: Phyllis, Rebecca, Claudia, David; m. Glenda Jacobs, Sept. 10, 2002. AA, Freed-Hardeman Coll., 1944; BS, Abilene Christian U., 1946; MA, SW Tex. State U., 1947; postgrad., George Peabody Coll., 1951; LLD (hon.), Magic Valley Christian Coll., 1962, Pepperdine U., 1969; LittD (hon.), Okla. Christian U., 1969; HHD (hon.), Morehead State U., 1973; LLD (hon.), Freed-Hardeman U., 1990. Chmn. dept. edn. and psychology Freed-Hardeman U., Henderson, Tenn., 1949-56, registrar, 1950-68, dean, 1956-69, v.p., 1969, pres., 1969-90, chancellor, 1990-92, pres. emeritus, 1992—; chancellor Ga. Christian Sch., 1993—, Crowley's Ridge Coll., 2002—. Bd. dirs. Chester County Bank, Henderson; col. on former Gov. McWherter's staff, 1988—; internat. spkr. and lectr. in field. Editor: Brigance's Sermons, 1951, Van Dyke's Sermons, 1971; contbr. numerous articles to Gospel Advocate and other publs. Former commr. Edn. Commn. of States, 1991; mem. pub. svcs. coun. Tenn. State Cert. Commn., 1988-91; past pres. Heritage Towers Bd., Henderson; past chmn. Crime Stoppers of Henderson and Chester County. Named Civitan of Yr., Civitan Internat., Henderson; named to Sch. Edn. Hall of Fame Freed-Hardeman U., 2006. Mem. Tenn. Coll. Assn. (pres. 1986-87), Chester County C. of C. (founder), Alpha Chi. Democrat. Mem. Ch. of Christ. Home and Office: 372 E Mill St Henderson TN 38340-2428

GARDNER, EMERSON N., JR., military officer; b. Chestertown, Md., Oct. 16, 1951; Grad. cum laude, Duke U., 1973; grad., Basic Sch., Def. Lang. Inst., Command and Staff Coll., Armed Forces Staff Coll., Norwegian Def. Coll. Commd. 2d lt. USMC, 1972, advanced through grades to lt. gen., 2005, helicopter pilot; White Ho. liaison officer, presdl. helicopter commd. pilot, 1980-85; commdg. officer 26th MEU, 1996-98; staff officer 9th Marine Amphibious Brigade, Okinawa, Japan, 1986-87; asst. chief of staff for ops. and logistics Allied Forces No. Europe, Kolsas, Norway and High Wycombe, England, 1993-95, High Wycombe, Eng., 1994-95; asst. dep. chief of staff aviation USMC, 1998-2000, dep. comdr. Marine Forces Atlantic, 2000—02, dir. ops. U.S. Pacific Command, 2002—04, dep. commandant for programs and resources, 2005—. Decorated Def. Superior Svc. medal., Legion of Merit with Gold star, Def. Meritorious Svc. medal, Air medal; Olmsted scholar, 1978, Germany. Office Phone: 703-614-3127. Business E-Mail: gardneren@hqmc.usmc.mil.

GARDNER, ERIC RAYMOND, lawyer; b. Derry, NH, Nov. 13, 1946; s. William Rudolph and Lois Brooks (Wilson) G.; m. Kathleen Linda Chertok, June 14, 1969 (div. Mar. 1985); children: Matthew Eric, Thomas Martin; m. Melissa Rae Hastings, Oct. 21, 1988. BA in Polit. Sci., U. N.H., 1969; JD, Boston U., 1972. Bar: N.H. 1972, Mass. 1972, U.S. Dist. Ct. Vt., 1987, U.S. Supreme Ct. 1979, Vt. 2004. Law clk. N.H. Supreme Ct., Concord, 1972-73; assoc. Goodnow, Arwe, Ayer & Prigge, Keene, N.H., 1973-76; ptnr. Goodnow, Arwe, Ayer, Prigge & Gardner, Keene, N.H., 1977-81; pvt. practice Keene, N.H., 1981—. Appointee N.H. Supreme Ct. Profl. Conduct Com., Concord, 1984—93; sr. counsel Am. Coll. Barristers. Editor Boston U. Law Rev., 1971-72. Clk., dir. Monadnock United Way, Keene, 1975-80; dir. Keene Family YMCA, 1974-82; chair Cheshire County Crimestoppers, Inc., 1997-98. Fellow N.H. Bar Found.; mem. ABA, ATLA, Am. Bd. Trial Advocates, Nat. Bd. Trial Advocacy, N.H. Trial Lawyers Assn., Million Dollar Advocates Forum, Greater Keene C. of C. (clk., dir. 1975-80). Avocations: flying, golf, tennis, skiing, travel. Office: PO Box C 372 West St Keene NH 03431-2455

GARDNER, EVERETTE SHAW, JR., information sciences educator, consultant, author; b. Osceola, Ark., Oct. 3, 1944; s. Everette Shaw and Evelyn (Fletcher) G.; m. Mary Ann Sihelnik, May 28, 1966; children: Cynthia Anne, Stacey Diane. BBA, Memphis State U., 1966; MBA, U. N.C., 1974, PhD, 1978. Commd. ensign USN, 1966, advanced through grades to comdr., 1980, ret., 1986; assoc. prof. U. Houston, 1987-88, chmn. dept. of decision and info. scis., 1988-95, prof., 1989—, dir. Ctr. Global Mfg., 1991—. Bd. dirs., Gardner Rsch., Inc., Sugar Land, Tex., pres., 1987—; cons. NASA Johnson Space Ctr., Houston, 1988-89, Shell Oil Co., Houston, Continental Airlines, Houston, 1993—, Continental Micronesia, Guam, Delta Airlines, Atlanta, 2007—, Hawaiian Airlines, Honolulu, 2000—, Texaco, Houston, Pennzoil, Houston, Arthur Andersen, Houston, Exxon Co. USA, Houston, Compaq Computers, Houston, Frito-Lay, Dallas, Southwestern Bell, Houston, Centel Comm., Houston, Sys. Evolution, Houston, Tenneco, Houston, Spring Comm., L.A., Alamo Water Refiners, San Antonio, Houston Livestock Show and Rodeo, Oil and Gas Consultants Inc., Tulsa, 1996-99, Telecheck Svcs. Inc., Houston, 1997-99, Randalls Food Markets, Inc., Houston, 1997-99, Trees Inc., Houston, 1999-2000, Tex. Industries, Inc., Houston, 2001—. Co-author: Quantitative Approaches to Management, 1993; author: (software) Autocast: Business Forecasting System, 1992, The Spreadsheet Forecaster, 1994, The Spreadsheet Quality Manager, 1993; assoc. editor Internat. Jour. of Forecasting, 1985-97, Mgmt. Sci., 1987-91, Interfaces, 1987-92; contbr. articles to profl. jours.; columnist Lotus mag., 1986-92. Bd. dirs. Women's Home Houston, 1992-97; mem. Republican Nat. Com. Mem. NRA, La. Shooting Assn., Tex. State Rifle Assn., Internat. Inst. Forecasters (pres. 1990-92, dir. 1987-94), Inst. for Ops. Rsch. and Mgmt. Scis., Operational Rsch. Soc., U.S. Naval Inst., Am. Prodn. and Inventory Control Soc. (bd. dirs. Houston chpt. 1997-98), Ret. Officers Assn., Sons. of Confederate Vets., Mus. of Confederacy Richmond Va., Confederate Meml. Hall New Orleans. Presbyterian. Avocations: competitive pistol shooting, tennis, gardening, civil war history. Office: U Houston 4800 Calhoun Rd Houston TX 77204-6021

GARDNER, GARY A., lawyer; b. Glen Cove, NY, Mar. 10, 1959; BS, US Naval Acad., 1982; JD, St. John's U., 1994. Ptnr. Wilson, Elser, Moskowitz, Edelman & Dicker LLP, NYC. Served USN, 1977—89. Recipient USN Meritorious Unit Commendation, Coast Guard Unit Commendation. Mem.: ABA (aviation law sect.), Lawyer Pilot's Bar Assn. Office: Wilson Elser Moskowitz Edelman & Dicker LLP 23rd Fl 150 E 42nd St New York NY 10017-5639 Office Phone: 212-490-3000 ext. 2770. Office Fax: 212-490-3038. Business E-Mail: gardnerg@wemed.com.

GARDNER, GEOFF, chef; m. Sarah Gardner. B, Boston U. Sch. Restaurant Mgmt. Sous chef L'Espalier restaurant, Boston; ptnr., exec. chef Sel de la Terre, Boston, 2000—. Named one of Boston's Rising Stars, StarChefs.com, 2006. Avocation: gardening. Office: Sel de la Terre 255 State St Boston MA 02109 Office Phone: 617-720-1300.*

GARDNER, GEORGE VICTOR, lawyer; b. New Castle, Pa., June 13, 1921; s. Victor Marcellus Gardner and Elsie May Cann; m. Sarah Cary Delaney; children: Katherine Graves, Sallie Cary, Margaret Dawson, Anne Armistead, John Norwood(dec.); m. Cecilia Gordon Bowdin Hill, June 2, 1990. BA, Allegheny Coll., Meadville, Pa., 1943; postgrad., Harvard Divinity Sch., Cambridge, Mass., 1943—45; JD, Case Western Res. U., Cleve., 1948; MEd, U. Va., Charlottesville, 1961. Bar: Ohio 1949, US Ct. Mil. Appeals 1953, US Ct. Appeals (DC cir.) 1958, US Ct. Appeals (4th cir.) 1961, US Ct. Appeals (4th cir.) 1961, US Ct. Appeals (7th cir.) 1963, US Ct. Appeals (6th cir.) 1964, US Ct. Appeals (8th cir.) 1966, US Ct. Appeals (1st, 2d, 3d, 5th, 9th and 10th cirs.) 1968, US Supreme Ct. 1968, US Dist. Ct. (no. dist.) Ohio 1968, US Ct. Claims 1961, DC 1973, cert.: Interstate Commerce Commn. 1950, War Claims Commn. 1950, Post Office Dept. 1973. Atty. Erie RR, Cleve., 1949—54, Chesapeake & Ohio RR, Richmond, Va., 1954—56; labor atty. Gardner & Gandal, Washington, 1956—58; ptnr. Sullivan & Beauregard, Washington, Cyrus Ching & Assocs., Washington, 1967; sr. ptnr. Gardner, Moss, Brown & Rocovich, Washington, 1982—92; cons. in conflict resolution Gardner Assocs., Washington, 1992—; sole practice Gardner Legal Consultancy, Washington, 1992—. Lectr. U. Va. Grad. Sch. Bus., Charlottesville; spkr. in field. Contbr. articles to profl. publs.; author various manuals. Mem. Nixon's Commn. on Govt. Contracts. Joined Nat. Guard US Army, 1938, advanced to rank of capt. USAR, 1960. Recipient Gold medal, Freedom Found.,

1953, 1956. Mem.: ABA. Episcopalian. Avocations: history, foreign policy, golf, tennis, bicycling. Home: 4101 Cathedral Ave Washington DC 20016 Personal E-mail: gvggvg@yahoo.com.

GARDNER, GRACE JOELY, writer, consultant, psychologist; b. Lynn, Mass., 1947; d. Joseph B. and Shirley E. (Phillips) Beatty; m. David C. Gardner, Mar. 24, 1984. BA, Simmons Coll., 1968; MEd, Boston U., 1972, EdD, 1979; PhD, Columbia Pacific U., 1984. Diplomate Am. Bd. Med. Psychotherapists (fellow), lic. psychologist Mass. Tchr. Braintree (Mass.) H.S., 1968—70; asst. prof. Quincy (Mass.) Jr. Coll., 1971—77; sr. rsch. assoc. Boston U., 1977—79; owner, mgr. Gardner Beatty Group, Rancho La Costa, Calif., 1979—; v.p. CyberHelp, Inc., Carlsbad, Calif., 1995—; pres. Self-Test Labs., Inc., 1999—; dir. human experience rsch. Rare Medium, Inc., 2001—; pres., CEO Human Factors Rsch., Inc., 2003—. Dir. human factors rsch. France Telecom R&D, 2001—03; pres., CEO Human Factors Rsch., Inc., 2003—; part-time faculty U. Calif., San Diego. Author (with David C. Gardner): Access for Windows 95, ACT 2.0 for Windows, Cruising American On-Line (2.0 and 2.5), Cruising CompuServe, Cruising Microsoft Network, Excel 5 for Mac: The Visual Learning Guide, Excel 5 for Windows: The Visual Learning Guide, Internet for Windows: The Visual Learning Guide (AOL 2.0 and 2.5 edits., Microsoft 95 edit.), Lotus 123 for Windows: The Visual Learning Guide (v4), Powerpoint for Windows 95: The Visual Learning Guide, Quicken 5 for Windows: The Visual Learning Guide, Windows 95: The Visual Learning Guide, Wind-FaxPro: The Visual Learning Guide (7.0), Word 7 for Windows 95: The Visual Learning Guide, WordPerfect 6 for DOS: The Visual Learning Guide, Words for Windows 95: The Visual Learning Guide, Dissertation Proposal Guidebook: How to Write a Research Proposal and Get It Accepted, 1979, Career and Vocational Education, 1984, Stop Stress and Aging Now, 1986, Never be Tired Again!, 1989 (Book-of-Month Club selection), Discover Internet Explorer, 1997, Discover Netscape Communicator, 1997, Windows NT 4.0 Workstation: Visual Desk Reference, 1997, Visual Guide to Installing Mandrae 7-1 on a Windows Machine, 2000, others. Home: 2844 Esturion Pl Carlsbad CA 92009-5819 Office: Human Factors Rsch Inc Ste 107-389B 3675 S Rainbow Blvd Las Vegas NV 89103 Home Phone: 760-431-2244. Personal E-mail: joelygardner@yahoo.com.

GARDNER, H. MCINTRYE (MAC GARDNER), diversified financial services company executive; BA in Religion, Dartmouth Coll., 1983. With corp. and instl. client grp. Merrill Lynch & Co., 1983—87; pres., CEO various consumer products cos., 1987—2000; pres. Hanover Assocs., Inc., 1991—94; various positions pvt. client bus. Merrill Lynch & Co., 2000—01, head ins. grp., 2001, sr. v.p. NYC, 2001—, COO global pvt. client, 2002, head Ams. region and global bank grp. Global Pvt. Client Grp.; chmn. bd. dirs. Merrill Lynch Bank U.S.A. Office: Merrill Lynch & Co 4 World Fin Ctr 250 Vesey St New York NY 10080

GARDNER, HOWARD ALAN, travel company executive, writer, editor; b. Rockford, Ill., June 24, 1920; s. Ellis Ralph and Leanor (Roseman) Gardner; m. Marjorie Ruth Klein, Sept. 29, 1945; children: Jill, Jeffrey. BA, U. Mich., 1941. With advt. dept. Chgo. Tribune, 1941-43; mgr. promotion dept. Esquire mag., 1943-46; advt. mgr. Mrs. Klein's Food Products Co., 1946-48; pres. Sales-Aide Svc. Co., 1948-56, Gardner & Stein, 1956-59, Gardner, Stein & Frank, Inc., Chgo., 1959-83, Fun-derful World, Chgo., 1983—. Mem.: Connoisseurs Internat., Nat. Geog. Soc., Am. Geog. Soc., Confrerie de la Chaine des Rotisseurs (Bailli Honoraire, grand comdr., Pres.'s medal of honor), Travel Industry Assn. Am., Mid-Am. Club, Internat. Club, Travelers' Century Club, Phi Beta Kappa. Home: 100 E Bellevue Pl Chicago IL 60611-1157 Office: Fun-derful World 100 E Bellevue Pl Chicago IL 60611-1157 Home Phone: 312-944-4061; Office Phone: 312-944-4060.

GARDNER, HOWARD EARL, psychologist, educator, writer; b. Scranton, Pa., July 11, 1943; s. Ralph and Hilde (Weilheimer) G.; m. Ellen Winner; children: Kerith, Jay, Andrew, Benjamin. AB summa cum laude, Harvard U., Cambridge, Mass., 1965, PhD, 1971; degree (hon.), Wheaton Coll., Mass., 2002, Curry Coll., Milton, Mass., 1992, New Eng. Conservatory Music, 1993, Ind. U., 1995, Moravian Coll., 1996, Cleve. Inst. Music, 1996, Salem State Coll., 1996, LI U., 1997, Macalester Coll., St. Paul, Minn., 1997, Tel-Aviv U., 1998, Princeton U., NJ, 1998, Pa. State U., State Coll., 1998, Ithaca Coll., NYC, 1999, Conn. Coll., New London, 1999, McGill U., Montreal, Quebec, Can., 1999, U. Hartford, Conn., 2000, Mass. Sch. Profl. Psychology, 2000, Nat. U. Ireland, 2001, U. Toronto, 2001, U. Urbino, Italy, 2003, East China Normal Univ., 2004, U. Valparaiso, Chile, 2006, Hanyang U., Republic of Korea, 2007. Lectr. edn. Harvard U., Cambridge, Mass., 1971-86, co-dir. Project Zero, 1972-2000, prof. edn., 1986-98—, affiliated prof. psychology, 1987—, Hobbs prof. cognition and edn., 1998—. Prof. neurology Boston U. Sch. Medicine, 1984-87, adj. prof. neurology, 1987-05; rsch. psychologist Boston VA Med. Ctr., 1978-93; hon. prof. East China Normal U., 2004; lectr. Hanyang U. Republic of Korea, 2007. Author: The Shattered Mind, 1975, Art, Mind and Brain, 1982, Frames of Mind, 1983 (Best Book award APA 1984), The Mind's New Science, 1985 (William James award 1988), To Open Minds, 1989, The Unschooled Mind, 1991, Creating Minds, 1993, Leading Minds, 1995, Extraordinary Minds, 1997, The Disciplined Mind, 1999, Intelligence Reframed, 1999, (with M. Csikszentmihalyi and W. Damon) Good Work, 2001, (with W. Fischman, B. Solomon and D. Greenspan) Making Good, 2004, Changing Minds, 2004, The Development and Education of the Mind, 2006, Multiple Intelligences: New Horizons, 2006, Howard Gardner Under Fire, 2006, Five Minds for the Future, 2007, Responsibility at Work, 2007. Bd. dir. Mus Modern Art, 2005—, Spencer Found., 2001—. Recipient Grawemeyer award in edn., 1990, Disting. Svc. medal Columbia U. Tchr.'s Coll., 1994, Pa. Gov.'s award in humanities, 1994, McGovern award Smithsonian Inst., 1998, Walker prize Boston Mus. of Sci., 1999, Samuel T. Orton award Internat. Dyslexia Assn., 1999, medal of the Pres. of Italy, 2001; MacArthur Prize fellow, 1981, Guggenheim Found. fellow, 2000; rsch. grantee numerous govtl. and pvt. founds. Fellow AAAS; mem. Am. Acad. Arts and Scis., Am. Philos. Soc., Royal Soc. Arts (Eng.), Phi Beta Kappa. Office: Harvard U Grad Sch Edn Larsen Hall Cambridge MA 02138 Business E-Mail: hgasst@pz.harvard.edu.

GARDNER, HOWARD GARRY, pediatrician, educator; b. Gary, Ind., Oct. 5, 1943; s. Oscar and Anita (Arenson) G.; m. Judith (Geen), June 21, 1986; children: Molly, Joseph. BA, Ind. U., 1965, MD, 1968. Intern, resident St. Louis U., 1969-73; pvt. practice Hinsdale (Ill.) Pediatrics, 1973-79, DuPage Pediatrics, Darien, Ill., 1979—; attending staff Hinsdale Hosp., 1973—, chmn. dept. pediatrics, 2000—02; courtesy staff Childrens Meml. Hosp., Chgo., 1988—. Clin. prof. dept. pediatrics Loyola U. Sch. of Medicine, Maywood, 1983-2002; chmn. dept. pediatrics Hinsdale Hosp., 1983-85, 2000-02; prof. clin. pediatrics Northwestern U. Med. Sch.; med. adv. bd. YMCA of the USA, Chgo., 1989-2006. Mem. editl. bd. Pediatric News, 1990—; contbr. articles to profl. jours. Co-chmn. med. adv. bd. DuPage Easter Seal Ctr., Villa Park, Ill.; past, founding mem. bd. dirs. Loyola Ronald McDonald House; co-founder, past pres. Ill. Child Passenger Safety Assn.; mem. med. adv. bd. Pathways Awareness Found.; officer, steering com. DuPage Interagy. Coun. on Early Intervention. Lt. USN, 1969-71. Recipient Outstanding Clin. Tchr. award Loyola Med. Sch., 1978, Tchr. of Yr. Hinsdale Hosp. Family Practice Residency, 1981, Chgo. Caring Physician's award Met. Chgo. Health Care Coun., 1987, Buckle Up Am.! award Ill. Coalition for Safety Belt Use, 1991, Parent and Child Edn. Soc. 20th Anniversary Achievement award, 1992, Outstanding Vol. award West Suburban United Way, 1999, Carol Sanicki Crystal Heart award Easter Seals, DuPage, 2002. Fellow Am. Acad. Pediat. (past pres. Ill. chpt., past mem. nat. nominating com., instnl. rev. bd., chmn. com. on injury and poison prevention 2007-, Pisani Pediatrician of Yr. award 1986); mem. Chgo. Pediat. Soc. (past pres., Archibald Hoyne Pediatrician of Yr. 1994), Ill. Maternal and Child Health Coalition (bd. dirs., pres., 2000-2002, Advocacy award 1996), DuPage County Med. Soc. Democrat. Jewish. Avocations: reading, skiing, photography. Office: DuPage Pediatrics 1306 Plainfield Rd Darien IL 60561-5038 E-mail: ggard4922@aol.com.

GARDNER, JAMES BAILEY, historical association administrator; b. McKenzie, Tenn., May 27, 1950; s. John Edward and Mary Amna (Bailey) G.; m. Mildred Blackburn Mussett, Jan. 5, 1974; 1 child, Joshua Blackburn. BA, Rhodes Coll., 1972; MA, Vanderbilt U., 1974, PhD, 1978. With Am. Assn. for State and Local History, Nashville, 1978-86, asst. dir. edn. div., 1984-85, dir. edn. and spl. programs, 1985-86; dep. exec. dir. Am. Hist. Assn., Washington, 1986—. Mem. historians com. Mus. of Am. Immigration Statue of Liberty Nat. Monument, 1991—; advisor history areas com. Nat. Park Svc. Adv. Bd., 1990-92; mem. Interdisciplinary Task Force, Common Agenda for History Mus., Washington, 1987-89. Author, editor: A Historical Guide to the U.S., 1986; editor Ordinary People and Everyday Life, 1983; contbr. The President and the CEA, 1984, History of Public Works in the U.S., 1776-1976, 1976. Member Tenn. Humanities Coun., 1984-86. Am. Pub. Works Assn. fellow, 1974; recipient Regional History award Nat. Soc. Colonial Dames, 1975; NEH and Rockefeller Found. fellow, 1977. Mem. Am. Hist. Assn., Orgn. Assn. Historians, Southern Hist. Assn., Am. Assn. for State and Local History (program com. 1987-90, heritage edn. com. 1990—), Nat. Coun. for Pub. History, Phi Beta Kappa. Democrat. Presbyterian. Office: Am Hist Assn 400 A St SE Washington DC 20003-3807

GARDNER, JANET PAXTON, journalist, film producer; b. Dayton, Ohio, Sept. 6, 1940; d. Edward Tytus and Mary Elizabeth (Paxton) G.; m. George Karl Debreczeny, Sept. 10, 1964 (div. Feb. 1970); 1 child, Karl Philip; m. George Edward Bradshaw Morren, Jr., Nov. 6, 1980. BFA in Art and Architecture, Cooper Union, NYC, 1965; MFA in Film Prodn., NYU, 1971; postgrad., Columbia U., NYC, 1976. Film editor, assoc. prodr. Sta. WRC-TV, NBC, Washington, 1972; asst. film editor NBC News, NYC, 1973-74; newswriter, field prodr. NewsCenter4 NBC, NYC, 1974-75; freelance film editor CBS News, NYC, 1976-79; staff reporter, feature writer The Plain Dealer, Cleve., 1979-81; edn. columnist, editor Glamour mag., NYC, 1981-82; staff writer Asbury Park Press, Neptune, N.J., 1985-86; press officer UN, 1989; owner, mgr. prodr. The Gardner Documentary Group, NYC, 1991—. Adj. faculty journalism U. Coll., Rutgers U., Newark, 1988-92, Montclair State Coll., Upper Montclair, NJ, 1992; mem. LA Times pub.-prof. exch. program, 1989. Prodr., dir., writer documentary videos The United Nations: It's More Than You Think, 1991, Vietnam: Land of the Ascending Dragon, 1993, Children of the Night & Starting Over, 1994, A World Beneath The War, 1996, Dancing Through Death: The Monkey Magic & Madness of Cambodia, 1999, Precious Cargo: Vietnamese Adoptees Come of Age, 2001, Siberian Dream, 2004, The Last Ghost of War, 2007; editor CBS News documentary film The Black Robes, 1978; prodr. Preparing To Give Birth, 1977, Choices in Childbirth, 1977, (film) Inside Ladies Home Jour., 1970; contbr. to NY Times, Phila. Inquirer, Boston Globe, Newsday, The Nation, Glamour, Working Women, New Woman, Diversion, Health Week, Indochina Newsletter, NJ Monthly, others. Co-chair peace and social order com. Religious Soc. of Friends, Princeton, N.J., 1994; participant U.S.-Indochina Reconciliation Project Del. to Vietnam, 1987, to Cambodia, 1990. Nominee Emmy award Outstanding Hist. Programming, NATAS, 1997; recipient spl. citation, Edn. Writers Assn., 1983, 2d pl. for news reporting, N.J. Press Women, 1990, 1st pl. for newspaper feature writing, 1990, cert. of merit, Media & Methods mag., 1992, Lowell Thomas award for video on Vietnam, Soc. Am. Travel Writers Found., 1993, Bronze Apple award, Nat. Edn. Film and Video Festival, 1993, Silver Apple award, 1997, Golden Eagle award, CINE, 1994, 1999, 2001, 2004, Spl. Jury award, 2001, Best Feature Reporting TV award, Soc. Profl. Journalists N.Y. chpt. Deadline Club, 1998, 2001, Bronze medal, Sigma Delta Chi, 2002, award, Chgo. Internat. Film Festival, 2002; Woolrich writing fellow, Columbia U. Sch. Gen. Studies, 1976. Mem. Soc. Profl. Journalists (juror nat. mag. awards 1985, scholastic press awards 1986, chief juror editl. writing awards 1988, recipient Best Feature Reporting TV award NY chpt. 2001), Investigative Reporters and Editors, Internat. Documentary Assn., North Jersey Press Club (2d pl. for bus. feature writing 1990, 1st pl. 1991, 1st pl. for best documentary 1992, 2d pl. for feature photography 1993), NY Women in Film and TV. Office: The Gardner Documentary Group 330 W 42d St Ste 2420 New York NY 10036-6902 Home: 118 Washington St PO Box 166 Rocky Hill NJ 08553-0166

GARDNER, JERRY LEE, financial consultant; b. Long Beach, Calif., Sept. 8, 1943; s. Don Gerard and Carol (Sorenson) G.; m. Rita Frandsen, May 29, 1969; children: Marc Don, Edward David, Victor John, Denise, Joyce, John Mackay, Michael Christopher. BA, Brigham Young U., 1971; MA, Calif. State U., Sacramento, 1973; postgrad., U. Calif., Davis, 1998-99. Account exec. duPont Glore Forgan & Co., Sacramento, 1973-74, E.F. Hutton & Co., Sacramento, 1974-84; sr. investment advisor Am. Savs., Sacramento, 1984-89; fin. cons. The Golden 1 Credit Union, Sacramento, 1989—. Leaders coun. Mass. Fin. Svcs., Boston, 1993—2006; mem. Kite & Key Club, Franklin Templeton Group, San Mateo, Calif., 1993—2006; v.p. LDS Bus. Assocs., 1992—94. Mem. Valley Choral Soc., 2006—; living history reinactor Old Sacramento Living History Assn., 2000—03; mem. Valley Choral Soc., 2000—03. With US Army, 1965—68, Vietnam. Recipient MVP award, Fin. Network Investment Corp., 1994—95, Century Club, 1996—2000, Amb. Club, 2001, Gov.'s award, 2002, Asst. VP award, XCU Capital Corp., 2004—06. Mem.: Fin. Planning Assn., United Families Internat., BYU Mgmt. Soc. (bd. dirs. 1990—). Mem. Lds Ch. Avocations: travel, history of california, violin, guitar. Office: The Golden 1 Credit Union 8945 Cal Center Dr Sacramento CA 95826-3239 E-mail: jgardner@golden1.com.

GARDNER, JOEL ROBERT, writer, historian; b. NYC, May 12, 1942; s. Stephen H. and Diana (Schneider) G.; m. Holly Alpine Phelps, July 7, 1980. BA, Tulane U., 1962; MA, UCLA, 1966. Assoc. editor The Riverdale (N.Y.) Press, 1966-68; oral historian UCLA Oral History Program, 1971-80, La. State Archives, 1980-82; asst. dir. La. Divsn. of the Arts, 1983-85; dir. Perkins Ctr. for the Arts, 1985-87; pres. Gardner Assocs., Cherry Hill, N.J., 1987—. Cons. The Pew Charitable Trusts, 1988-94, Robert Wood Johnson Found., 1991—, John D. and Catherine T. MacArthur Found., 1994—, H.B. Earhart Found., 2005—. Author: Oral History for Louisiana, 1980, 75 Years of Good Taste: A History of the Tasty Baking Company, 1990, A History of the Pew Charitable Trusts, 1991, (with others) In the Company of Writers, 1991, Neighbor Caring for Neighbor, 1996; editor: Built in Louisiana, 1985, Oral History and the Law, 1985. Bd. dirs. N.J. Com. for the Humanities, 1991-94, sec., 1993-94; pres. Trenton Cmty. Mus. Sch., 1999—2004. Mem. Oral History Assn. (bd. dirs. 1982-83), Oral History for Middle Atlantic Region (v.p. 1991-92, pres. 1992-93), Rotary (Garden State club 1998—, sec. 2005—06). Democrat. Jewish. Office: 210 E Miami Ave Cherry Hill NJ 08034

GARDNER, JOHN HOWLAND, III, neurologist; b. New Haven, Conn., Oct. 1, 1931; s. John Howland Jr. and Ruth (Huntley) G.; m. Anne Kates Larkin, Apr. 23, 1960; children: Elizabeth Larkin Gardner Milgram, Helen Douglass Gardner. Student, Harvard U., 1949-52; MD, Yale, 1956. Diplomate Am. Bd. Psychiatry and Neurology. Intern Stanford, 1956-57; asst. to assoc. resident in medicine Strong Mem. Hosp., Rochester, NY, 1957-59; resident in neurology Boston City Hosp., 1959-61; resident in neuropathology Strong Mem. Hosp., Rochester, NY, 1961-62; officer in charge in neurology USAF Hosp. Keesler AFB, Biloxi, Miss., 1962-64; asst. prof. Case Western Res. U. Sch. Med., Cleve., 1965-67; asst. clin. prof. Case Western Res. U. Sch. Medicine, Cleve., 1967-83, assoc. clin. prof., 1983-98, emeritus assoc. prof. neurology, 1998—; chief of neurology St. Luke's Hosp., Cleve., 1967-85; neurologist U. Suburban Health Care Ctr., Cleve., 1975-96. Pres. Greater Cleveland Chpt. Epilepsy Fdn. Am., 1973-75; chmn. Mediation Comm. Acad. Med. Cleveland, 1982-84. Vestryman, St. Paul's Episcopal Church, Cleveland Hts., 1980-82. Capt. USAF, 1962-64. Decorated Commendation Medal, USAF. Fellow Am. Acad. Neurology; mem. AMA, Acad. Med. Cleveland, Ohio State Med. Assn., Yale Alumni Assn. (v.p. Cleve. 1988—). Avocations: skeet shooting, photography, hunting, music, sailing.

GARDNER, JULIE, retail executive; V.p. advt. and mktg. Eckerd Corp.; sr. v.p. mktg. Kohl's Corp., exec. v.p., chief mktg. officer. Named to Retail Advt. and Mktg. Hall of Fame, Retail Advt. and Mktg. Assn., 2005. Office: Kohls Corp N56 W17000 Ridgewood Dr Menomonee Falls WI 53051-5660 Office Phone: 262-703-7000.*

GARDNER, KAREN HIGH, special education educator; b. Longview, Tex., Sept. 2, 1958; d. Lawrence Wayne and Mary Elizabeth; m. Flexton L. Gardner, Nov. 5, 1983; children: Flexton Lee, Alycia Yvonne. BS in Spl. Edn., Va. State U., 1981; MS in Secondary Edn., Old Dominion U., 2001. Cert. collegiate profl. cert. 1981. Spl. edn. tchr. Va. Beach Public Sch., 1981—, Princess Anne H.S., Va. Beach, 2001—. Dept. chair Windsor Oaks Elem., 1991—93, Corp. Landing Middle Sch., 1999—2001; mentor Va. Beach Public Sch., 1999—; coord. Ptnr. in Edn, Va. Beach, 2003—. Planning coun. Windsor Oaks Elem., 1992—93, Corp. Landing Middle Sch., 1997—99; child study team coord. Bayside Middle Sch., 1994—97; season for nonviolence sponsor Princess Anne H.S., 2003—. Recipient Human Rights award, Va. Beach Human Rights Commn., 2004. Fellow: Assn. Supervision and Curriculum Devel. Avocations: reading, bicycling, travel, chess. Home: 3545 Byrn Brae Dr Virginia Beach VA 23464 Office: Princess Anne HS 4400 Va Beach Blvd Virginia Beach VA 23462 Office Phone: 757-473-5000. Business E-Mail: khgardne@vbschools.com.

GARDNER, KERRY ANN, librarian; b. Honolulu, May 19, 1955; d. Byron Patton and Claire Gardner. BA in Polit. Sci. magna cum laude, Temple U., 1976; MA in L.Am. Studies, U. Ariz., 1983, MLS, 1990. Documents libr. FMC Corp., Chgo., 1977-78; grad. rsch. asst. U. Ariz., Tucson, 1983-86; rsch. cons., 1983-92; libr. asst. I Phoenix Pub. Libr., 1988-89; mgr. faculty resource libr., English 2d lang. U. Ariz. Ctr., 1989—90; project mgr. U. Ariz., 1990-92; mgr. faculty resource libr., English 2d lang. U. Ariz. Ctr., 1991—92; pub. svcs. libr. Bryan Wildenthal Meml. Libr., Sul Ross State U., Alpine, Tex., 1992-95; libr. dir. Am. U., Dubai, United Arab Emirates, 1995-96; literacy libr. Sterling Mcpl. Libr., Baytown, Tex., 1996-98; libr. Valle Verde campus, El Paso C.C., Tex., 1998—, co-head libr., 2001—02, head libr., 2007—. Indexer Hispanic Am. Periodicals Index, 1995; maintain GPO Access Web site, 1998—. Contbr. articles to profl. publs. Tchr. English, Literacy Vols. Am., 1991-92, 96-98. Named Libr. of Yr., Border Regional Libr. Assn., 2001; grad. scholar, U. Ariz., 1976—77, 1981—82. Mem.: NEA, ALA, Tex. C.C. Tex. Assn., Border Regional Libr. Assn. (chair publicity com. 1999—2002, chair. Libr. of the Yr. com. 2002—03), Assn. Coll. and Rsch. Librs., Tex. Libr. Assn. (legis. com. coll. and univ. librs. divsn. 1993—94), Friends El Paso Pub. Libr. (sec. 2006—07, bd. dirs. 2007—), Beta Phi Mu. Avocations: travel, birding. Office: El Paso C C Valle Verde Campus PO Box 20500 El Paso TX 79998-0500

GARDNER, MURRAY BRIGGS, pathologist, educator; b. Lafayette, Ind., Oct. 5, 1929; s. Max William and Margaret (Briggs) G.; m. Alice E. Danielson, June 20, 1961; children: Suzanna, Martin, Danielson, Andrew. BA, U. Calif., Berkeley, 1951; MD, U. Calif., San Francisco, 1954. Intern Moffitt Hosp., San Francisco, 1954-55; resident in gen. practice Sonoma County Hosp., Santa Rosa, Calif., 1957-59; resident in pathology U. Calif. hosps., San Francisco, 1959-63; faculty U. So. Calif. Sch. Medicine, Los Angeles, 1963-81, prof. pathology, 1973-81, U. Calif., Davis Sch. Medicine, 1981—, chmn. dept. pathology, 1982-90. Contbr. chpts. to books, numerous articles in field to profl. jours. Served to lt. M.C. USNR, 1957-59. Grantee NIH, 1968— Fellow AAAS; mem. Coll. Am. Pathologists, Internat. Acad. Pathology, Am. Coll. Vet. Pathologists (hon.). Home: 8313 Maxwell Ln Dixon CA 95620-9662 Office: Ctr of Comparative Medicine U Calif Davis Davis CA 95616 Business E-Mail: mbgardner@ucdavis.edu.

GARDNER, PETER JAGLOM, lawyer, publishing executive; b. NYC, 1958; s. Ralph David and Natalie (Jaglom) G.; m. Victoire Taittinger, 1984; children: Evan, Emma, Nadya, Parker. BA, Middlebury Coll., Vt., 1980; JD, Vt. Law Sch., 1999, M in Environ. Law magna cum laude, 1999; M in Intellectual Property Law, Franklin Pierce Law Ctr., 2002. Pres. Transatlantic Comml. Svcs. Corp., 1985-90; pub. Northern Centinel, Kinderhook, NY, 1991—98; pres., CEO Centinel Co., 1991—2004; pvt. practice Hanover, NH, 2004—. Rsch. fellow Vt. Law Sch., 2002—04; vis. scholar Tuck Sch., Dartmouth Coll., 2002—04; rsch. fellow Franklin Pierce Law Ctr., 2004—06. Mem. editl. bd. N.H. Bar Jour., 2002—; contbr. articles to profl. jours. Trustee Ford Sayre Meml. Ski. Coun., 2000—03; bd. overseers Hitchcock Found., 2003—. Mem.: Internat. Fedn. Intellectual Property Attys., Howe Libr. Corp., Am. Intellectual Property Law Assn., Licensing Execs. Soc. (USA and Can. chpts.), Frank Rowe Kenison Inn of Ct. (treas. 1999—2001), Vt. Bar Assn., N.Y. Bar Assn., N.H. Bar Assn. (sec. intellectual property law sect. 2002—03, vice-chmn. 2003—04, chmn. 2004—05), ABA, Overseas Press Club. Office: Peter J Gardner PLLC 30 Reservoir Rd Hanover NH 03755

GARDNER, RICHARD KENT, retired librarian, educator, editor; b. New Bedford, Mass., Dec. 7, 1928; s. Francis and Millicent Annetta (Kent) G. AB cum laude, Middlebury Coll., Vt., 1950; Dipl. Litt., U. Paris, 1954; MS in Library Sci., Western Res. U., 1955; PhD, Case Western Res. U., 1968. Asst. libr. Case Inst. Tech., 1955-57; library adviser Mich. State U. adv. group pub. adminstrn. to Govt. South Vietnam, 1957-58; libr., assoc. prof. Marietta Coll., Ohio, 1959-63; founding editor Choice: Books for Coll. Libraries, Middletown, Conn., 1963-66; lectr., assoc. prof. Case Western Res. U. Sch. Libr. Sci., 1966-69; prof. agrege Ecole de Bibliotheconomie, U. Montreal, Canada, 1969-70, dir., 1970—72, prof. titulaire, 1970—72; editor Choice: Books for Coll. Libraries, Middletown, Conn., 1972-77; prof. Grad. Sch. Library and Info. Sci. UCLA, 1977-82; prof. titulaire Ecole de Bibliotheconomie, U. Montreal, Canada, 1982—93, dir., 1982—87; ret., 1993. Internat. libr. edn. cons., 1966-93. Author: Cataloging and Classification of Books, with the Vietnamese Decimal Classification, 1958, rev. edit., 1966, Opening Day Collection, 1965, rev. edit., 1974, Education for Librarianship in France: An Historical Survey, 1968, Library Collections: Their Origin, Selection, and Development, 1981 (Blackwell award 1982), Education of Library and Information Professionals: Present and Future Prospects, 1987; also articles. Mem. Forest Press com. Lake Placid Ednl. Found., 1972-87; trustee Russell Library, Middletown, 1975-77. Served with AUS, 1951-53 Mem. ALA, Ohio Library Assn. (exec. bd. 1962-63), Can. Library Assn., Assn. Coll. and Research Libraries (Spl. Presdl. Recognition award, 2005), Music Library Assn., Ohio Coll. Assn. (v.p. librarians sect. 1962-63, pres. 1963), Corp. des Bibliothecaires professionals du Que. (adminstrv. council 1970-72), Tudor Singers Montreal (v.p. 1970-72), Assn. internat. des ecoles des scis. de l'information Home: 1890 East 107th Street #507 Cleveland OH 44106 E-mail: rkgardn@sbcglobal.net.

GARDNER, RICHARD NEWTON, diplomat, lawyer, educator; b. NYC, July 9, 1927; s. Samuel I. and Ethel (Elias) G.; m. Danielle Luzzatto, June 10, 1956; children: Nina Jessica, Anthony Laurence. AB magna cum laude, Harvard U., 1948; JD, Yale U., 1951; PhD, Oxford U., 1954. Bar: NY 1952. Corr. UP, 1946-47, AP, 1948; teaching fellow internat. legal studies Harvard Law Sch., 1953-54; with Coudert Bros., NYC, 1954-57; assoc.

prof. law Columbia U., 1957-60, prof., 1960-61, 65-66, Henry L. Moses prof. law and internat. orgn., 1967-77, 81—; sr. counsel Morgan, Lewis & Bockius, 1997—; U.S. amb. to Italy Am. Embassy, Rome, 1977-81, U.S. amb. to Spain Madrid, 1993-97. Dep. asst. sec. state internat. orgns. Dept. State, 1961-65; vis. prof. U. Istanbul, 1958, U. Rome, 1967-68; dep. U.S. rep. UN Com. on Peaceful Uses of Outer Space, 1962-65; U.S. alt. del. 19th UN Gen. Assembly; sr. adviser U.S. del. to 20th and 21st UN Gen. Assemblies; U.S. alt. del. 55th UN Gen. Assembly; rapporteur UN Com. Experts on Econ. Restructuring, 1975; mem. Pres.'s Commn. on Internat. Trade and Investment Policy, 1970-71, U.S. Adv. Com. on Law of Sea, 1971-76; cons. to sec.-gen. UN Conf. on Human Environment, 1972, UN Conf. Environment and Devel., 1992; mem. pres.'s adv. com. Trade Policy and Negotiations, 1998-2002. Author: Sterling-Dollar Diplomacy, 1956, New Directions in U.S. Foreign Economic Policy, 1959, In Pursuit of World Order, 1964, Blueprint for Peace, 1966, (with Max F. Millikan) The Global Partnership: International Agencies and Economic Development, 1968, In Pursuit of World Order, 1980, Negotiating Survival: Four Priorities after Rio, 1992, Mission Italy: On the Front Lines of the Cold War, 2005; note editor: Yale Law Jour, 1950-51. Bd. dirs. Ditchley Found., Salzburg Seminar. Served with AUS, 1945-46. Recipient Detur prize for disting. scholarship Harvard U., 1948, Arthur S. Flemming award, 1963; Harvard Club scholar, 1944, Rhodes scholar, 1951-53. Mem. ABA, UN Assn. (dir.), Assn. Bar City NY, Council Fgn. Relations, Am. Acad. Arts and Scis., Am. Philosophical Soc., Phi Beta Kappa, Order of Coif, Century Assn, Met. Club. Clubs: Century Assn. (NYC); Met. (Washington). Office: Columbia U Sch Law JG Room 824 435 W 116th St New York NY 10027-7297 Office Phone: 212-309-6942. Business E-Mail: rgardner@morganlewis.com.

GARDNER, ROBERT, financial services executive; b. Dec. 19, 1949; s. Sam and Edythe (Berman) G.; m. Barbara Paccione, Apr. 21, 1975; children: Theodore Mathew, Jessica Andrea. BA in Philosophy, Hunter Coll., 1978. Account exec. Merrill Lynch & Co., NYC, 1977-80; v.p. Lehman Bros., NYC, 1980-89; v.p. investments Prudential Securities, NYC, 1989-97, 1st v.p., retirement planning advisor, 1998—2000; 1st v.p., wealth mgmt. Smith Barney Citigroup, 2000—. Mem. Internat. Assn. Fin. Planning. Avocations: golf, reading. Office: Smith Barney 1129 Northern Blvd 3rd Fl PO Box 4210 Manhasset NY 11030-4355

GARDNER, ROBIN PIERCE, engineering educator; b. Charlotte, NC, Aug. 17, 1934; s. Robin Brem and Margaret (Pierce) G.; m. Linda Jean Gardner, Oct. 21, 1976. B.Ch.E., N.C. State U., 1956, MS, 1958; PhD, Pa. State U., 1961. Scientist Oak Ridge Inst. Nuclear Studies, 1961-63; research engr., asst. dir. measurement and controls lab. Research Triangle Inst., Research Triangle Park, NC, 1963-67; research prof. nuclear engring. and chem. engring., dir. Center Engring. Applications of Radioisotopes, N.C. State U., 1967—. Cons. Oak Ridge Inst. Nuclear Studies, Research Triangle Inst., Oak Ridge Nat. Lab., Internat. Atomic Energy Agy., NASA, AEC, TVA, Alcoa. Author: (with Ralph L. Ely, Jr.), Radioisotope Measurement Applications in Engineering, 1967; regional editor Applied Radiation and Isotopes, Jour. Fine Particle Soc., Nuc. Geophysics; contbr. articles to sci. jours. Served to 1st lt. AUS, 1956. Recipient Alcoa Found. Disting. Rsch. award N.C. State U. Sch. Engring., 1986, Alumni Disting. Grad. Professorship award, 1996, R.J. Reynolds award for excellence in tchg. and rsch., 1998; Centennial fellow Coll. Earth and Mineral Scis., Pa. State U., 1996. Fellow Am. Nuc. Soc. (Radiation Industry award isotopes and radiation divsn. 1984), Am. Nuc. Soc., Am. Soc. Engring. Edn. (Glenn Murphy award for Outstanding Nuc. Engring. 2003), Sigma Xi, Phi Kappa Phi, Phi Lambda Upsilon. Achievements include founding of a successful series of topical meetings entitled Industrial Radiation and Radioisotope Measurement Applications. Home: 3005 Randolph Dr Raleigh NC 27609-6941 Office: NC State U Ctr Engring Applications of Radioisotope Dept Nuclear Engring Raleigh NC 27695-0001 Business E-Mail: gardner@ncsu.edu.

GARDNER, RULON E., Olympic athlete; b. Afton, Wyo., Aug. 16, 1971; s. Reed and Virginia Gardner. Grad., Ricks Coll., 1991; BS in Phys. Edn., U. Nebr., 1996. Greco-Roman wrestler Olympic Games, Sydney, 2000, Athens, 2004; ret., 2004. Named USA Wrestling Greco-Roman Wrestler of Yr., 2000, Flag Bearer, Closing Ceremonies, Olympics, Sydney, 2000, Amateur Wrestling News Man of the Year, 2000, USA Wrestling Man of Yr., 2001, USOC Sportsman of Yr., 2001, James E. Sullivan Award-Amateur athlete of the year, 2001; named one of Top 100 Most Powerful in sports, Sporting News, 2000; named to Ricks Coll. Athletic Hall of Fame, 2001, Wyo. Sports Hall of Fame, Athlete of Yr., 2001; recipient Best Original Score award, USA Today's Sports, 2000, Arete award, U.S. Olympic Spirit award, 2001, ESPY award for Male U.S. Olympic Athlete of Yr., 2001, Jesse Owens award, 2001, USOC Citizenship through Sports Alliance award, 2001. Achievements include development of recognized as National Junior College Athletic Champion, 1991; recognized as National Champion, Greco-Roman, 1995, 1997, 2001; named World Cup Champion, Greco-Roman, 1996; named Pan-American Champion, 1998; named Vantaa Cup Champion, Finland, 1998; winning Senior Greco-Roman Championship Belt Series, 1998; winning Winter Classic, 1999; winning gold medal in 120kg Greco-Roman Wrestling, Sydney Olympic Games, 2000; winning gold medal, World Wrestling Championships, 2001; winning Kurt Angle Classic, 2003; winning bronze medal in 120kb Greco-Roman Wrestling, Athens Olympic games, 2004. Office: c/o USOC 1 Olympic Plaza Colorado Springs CO 80909

GARDNER, RUSSELL MENESE, lawyer; b. High Point, NC, July 14, 1920; s. Joseph Hayes and Clara Emma-Lee (Flynn) G.; m. Joyce Thresher, Mar. 7, 1946; children: Winthrop G., Page Stansbury, June Thresher. AB, Duke U., 1942, JD, 1948. Bar: Fla. 1948, U.S. Ct. Appeals (5th cir.) 1949, U.S. Tax Ct. 1949, U.S. Supreme Ct. 1985. Ptnr. McCune, Hiaasen, Crum, Gardner & Duke and predecessor firms, Ft. Lauderdale, Fla., 1948-90, Gunster, Yoakley, & Stewart, 1990—. Bd. govs. Shepard Broad Law Ctr. Nova S.E. U. Trustee Mus. of Art, Inc., Ft. Lauderdale, pres., 1964-67; bd. dirs. Stranahan House, Inc., 1981—, pres., 1983-85; bd. dirs. Ft. Lauderdale Hist. Soc., 1962—, pres. 1975-85, pres. emeritus, 1985—; mem. estate planning council Duke U. Sch. Law; bd. dirs., vice chmn. Broward Performing Arts Found., Inc., 1985—. Served to lt. USNR, 1943-49. Fellow Am. Coll. Trust and Estate Counsel; mem. ABA (real property, probate, trust sect.), Am. Judicature Soc., Fla. Bar Assn. (probate, guardianship rules com. 1978-2002, probate law com.), Broward County Bar Assn. (estate planning council), Coral Ridge Country Club, Lauderdale Yacht Club, Tower Club. Republican. Presbyterian. Office: PO Box 14636 Fort Lauderdale FL 33302-4636 E-mail: rgardner@gunster.com.

GARDNER, SHERYL PAIGE, gynecologist; b. Bremerton, Wash., Jan. 24, 1945; d. Edwin Gerald and Dorothy Elizabeth (Herman) G.; m. James Alva Beat, June 20, 1986. BA in Biology, U. Oreg., 1967, MD cum laude, 1971. Diplomate Am. Bd. Ob-Gyn. Intern L.A. County Harbor Gen. Hosp., Torrance, Calif., 1971-72, resident in ob-gyn., 1972-75; physician Group Health Assn., Washington, 1975-87; pvt. practice Mililani, Hawaii, 1987—; chmn. dept. ob-gyn. Wahiawa Gen. Hosp., 1994—. Med. staff sec. Wahiawa (Hawaii) Gen. Hosp., 1994-95. Mem. Am. Coll. Ob-Gyn., Am. Soc. Colposcopy and Cervical Pathology, N.Am. Menopause Soc., Sigma Kappa, Alpha Omega Alpha. Democrat. Office: 95-1249 Meheula Pkwy Ste 127 Mililani HI 96789-1763 Office Phone: 808-625-5277.

GARDNER, STEPHEN HENRY, lawyer; b. Dallas, Aug. 5, 1951; s. Willard Henry and Mary Frances (Brown) G.; m. Kathi Buchanan Child, Sept. 2, 1972 (div. Dec. 1977); m. Margaret Grace Bonner, Dec. 11, 1982; children: James Bonner, Mary Elizabeth. BA with honors, U. Tex., 1972, JD, 1975. Bar: Tex. 1976, N.Y. 1983, DC 2006, U.S. Supreme Ct. 1980, U.S. Ct. Appeals (2d cir.) 1984, U.S. Ct. Appeals (5th cir.) 1978, U.S. Ct. Appeals (7th cir.) 1999, U.S. Ct. Appeals (8th cir.) 1990, U.S. Ct. Appeals (9th cir.) 1993, U.S. Ct. Appeals (D.C. cir.) 1988, U.S. Dist. Ct., Ark. (ea. and we. dists.) 1986, U.S. Dist. Ct., Ill. (middle and no. dists.) 1999, US Ct. Appeals (3d cir.) 2006, U.S. Dist. Ct., N.Y. (ea. and so. dists.) 1983, U.S. Dist. Ct., Tex. (we. dist.) 1977, U.S. Dist. Ct., Tex. (no. dist.) 1984, U.S. Dist. Ct., Tex. (so. dist.) 1993, U.S. Dist. Ct., Tex. (ea. dist.) 2002. Staff atty. Legal Aid Soc. of Cen. Tex., Austin, 1975—81; students atty. U. Tex., Austin, 1982; asst. atty. gen. State of N.Y., NYC, 1982—84, State of Tex., Dallas, 1984—91; of counsel Nat. Consumer Law Ctr., 2002—06. Fellow Consumer Law Ctr., Boston, 1980-81; coun. mem. Consumer Adv. Coun. of the Fed. Res. Bd., Washington, 1986-89; dir. Litigation for Sci. Public Interest, 2004-; bd. dir. Consumers Union, 1997-2004. Contbr. articles to profl. jours. Bd. dir. Legal Svcs. of North Tex., Dallas, 1987-89. Adm. Tex. Navy. Recipient Good Old Boy award Tex. Women's Polit. Caucus, 1987, Marvin award Nat. Assn. Attys. Gen., 1988, Hall of Fame award Ctr. for Sci. in the Pub. Interest, 1991. Mem. Tex. Bar Assn., Honorable Order of Ky. Cols., N.Y. State Bar Assn., DC Bar Assn. Democrat. Home: 3230 Bryn Mawr Dr Dallas TX 75225-7645 Office: Ctr for Sci in Pub Interest 5646 Milton St Ste 211 Dallas TX 75206 Business E-Mail: sgardner@cspinet.org.

GARDNER, TIMOTHY JOSEPH, surgeon, educator; b. Phila., Dec. 6, 1938; s. Joseph Thomas and Elva (Flynn) G.; m. Nina Hooton, July 4, 1964; children: Julie, Joseph, Emily, Nicholas. BA, Georgetown Coll., 1962; MD, Georgetown U., 1966. Intern Johns Hopkins Hosp., Balt., 1966-67, asst. resident in surgery, 1967-68, 71-74, rsch. fellow cardiac surg. lab., 1970-71, chief resident, 1974-75, chief resident in cardiac surgery, 1975-76, asst. prof., 1976-80, assoc. prof., 1980-86; prof. Johns Hopkins U. Sch. Medicine, 1986-93, Hosp. U. Pa., Phila., 1993—, chief divsn. cardiothoracic surgery, 1993—; with Christiana Care Health Sys., Newark, Del., 2007—. Speaker in field; vis. prof. Royal Australasian Coll. Surgeons, Hobart, Tasmania, 1994, Royal Prince Alfred Hosp., Sydney, 1989, U. Kans. Sch. Medicine, 1984, Children's Hosp. Phila., 1981. Contbr. articles to profl. jours.; guest editl. reviewer: Jour. Thoracic and Cardiovascular Surgery, 1981-83, Circulation, 1983-91; book reviewer: Annals Thoracic Surgery, 1985-89. With U.S. Army, 1968-70. Fellow ACS, Am. Coll. Cardiology; mem. Am. Surg. Assn., Assn. for Acad. Surgery, Balt. City Med. Soc., Med. and Chirurgical Faculty Md., So. Thoracic Surg. Assn., Soc. Thoracic Surgeons, Soc. Univ. Surgeons, Am. Assn. for Thoracic Surgery, So. Surg. Assn., Am. Surg. Assn., Am. Heart Assn. (mem. coun. on cardiovasc. surgery), Am. Bd. Med. Specialists Thoracic Surgery (dir., 1995-2005, vice-chair, 2001-2003, chair, 2003-2005). Office: Christiana Care Health Sys PO Box Newark DE 19718

GARDNER, WILFORD ROBERT, physicist, researcher; b. Logan, Utah, Oct. 19, 1925; s. Robert and Nellie (Barker) G.; m. Marjorie Louise Cole, June 9, 1949; children: Patricia, Robert, Caroline. BS, Utah State U., 1949; MS, Iowa State U., 1951, PhD, 1953; DSc honoris causa (hon.), Ohio State U., 2002. Physicist U.S. Salinity Lab., Riverside, Calif., 1953-66; prof. U. Wis., Madison, 1966-80; physicist, prof., head dept. soil and water sci. U. Ariz., Tucson, 1980-87; dean coll. natural resources U. Calif., Berkeley, 1987-94, dean emeritus, 1994—; adj. prof. Utah State U., 1995—. Hon. prof. Nanjing U., China, 1984. Author: Soil Physics, 1972. Served with U.S. Army, 1943-46. Recipient Hon. Faculty award, U. Ghent, Belgium, 1972, Centennial Alumnus award, Utah State U., 1986; NSF Sr. fellow, 1959, Fulbright fellow, 1971—72, Haight travel fellow, U. East Asia, 1978, Macalaster fellow, Australia. Fellow: AAAS, Am. Soc. Agronomy; mem.: NAS, Soil Sci. Soc. Am. (pres. 1990, Rsch. award 1962), Internat. Union Soil Sci. (hon.), Internat. Soil Sci. Soc. (pres. physics commn. 1968—74). Office Phone: 801-981-9568. Personal E-mail: colegardner@comcast.net.

GARDNER, WILLIAM ALBERT, JR., pathologist, medical products executive; b. Sumter, SC, Aug. 2, 1939; s. William A. and Betty Lee (Kennedy) G.; m. Kathryn Ann Medlin, June 30, 1960; children: Mary Elizabeth, Kathryn Lee, William Dylan. BS, Wofford Coll., Spartanburg, SC, 1960; MS in Anatomy, Med. Coll. SC, Charleston, 1963, MD, 1965. Diplomate Am. Bd. Pathology, 1965, 67, 76, 81. Intern dept. pathology The Johns Hopkins Hosp., Balt., 1965-66, fellow in pathology, 1965-67, asst. resident dept. pathology, 1966—67; asst. resident dept. pathology Med. Ctr. Duke U., Durham, NC, 1967-68, instr. pathology, chief resident, 1968-69; career resident lab. svcs. VA Med. Ctr., Durham, 1967—69, chief lab. svc. Charleston, SC, 1969—76, Nashville, 1976-81; rsch. asst. in anatomy Med. U. SC, Charleston, 1961—63, tchg. asst. in anatomy, 1962—63, asst. prof. pathology, 1969-72, assoc. prof. pathology, 1972-76, vis. prof. pathology, 1976—81; prof. pathology, vice chmn. dept. pathology Sch. Medicine Vanderbilt U., Nashville, 1976-81; prof., chair dept. pathology Coll. Medicine U. South Ala., Mobile, 1981—2002, pres. health svc. found., 1988—91, Locke disting. prof. pathology Coll. Medicine, 1994—2002, assoc. dean clin. affairs, 1997—, interim dean, v.p. med. affairs Coll. Medicine, 1997—99, emeritus prof. Coll. Medicine, 2002—, asst. v.p. risk adminstrn. Coll. Medicine, 2001. Exec. dir. Am. Registry Pathology, Washington, 2002-; pres., CEO Internat. Registry Pathology, 2003-. Contbr. articles on oncology, urology, parasitology and pathology to profl. jours. Recipient Outstanding Teaching award Med. U. S.C., 1975, Disting. Alumnus award Med. U. S.C., 1988; named to Alumni Assn. Centennial Recognition list, 1992; Fulbright scholar, 1996. Fellow Am. Soc. Clin. Pathologists, Coll. Am. Pathologists (del. for govtl. pathology); mem. AMA, Internat. Acad. Pathology (v.p., chair fin. com. 1994—, internat. councillor 1994—), U.S.-Can. Acad. Pathology (v.p., pres.-elect 1993-95, pres. 1995-96, mem. fin. com. 1996—), Acad. Clin. Lab. Physicians and Scientists, Ala. Med. Assn., Assn. Pathology Chmn. (coun., pres. 1992-94), Armed Forces Inst. of Pathology (mem. sci. adv. bd. 1996—, chair sci. adv. bd., 1997—), Alpha Omega Alpha. Methodist. Office: Am Registry Pathology 14th St at Alaska Ave Washington DC 20306-6000 Business E-Mail: gardnerw@afip.osd.mil.

GARDNER, WILLIAM MICHAEL, state official; b. Manchester, NH, Oct. 26, 1948; s. William George and Mildred Irene (Claus) G.; m. Kathleen Gordon, May 21, 1978; children: William Gordon, Kathleen Meghan. BA, U. N.H., 1970; diploma, London Sch. Econs., 1972; ME, U. N.C., Greensboro, 1973; MPA, Harvard U., 1985. Mem. N.H. Ho. Reps., Concord, 1973-76; sec. state State of N.H., Concord, 1976—. Chmn. N.H. Mcpl. Records Bd., 1978—; pres. Nat. Assn. Secs. State, 1998—99. Editor: Towns Against Tyranny: Hills Borough County New Hampshire During the American Revolution 1775-83, 1976, New Hampshire: The State That Made Us a Nation, 1989; co-author: Why New Hampshire? The First-in-the-Nation Primary State, 2003. Mem. exec. com. Hillsborough County, N.H., 1973-74; chmn. Manchester Del., 1974-75; trustee Belanger-Gardner Found., Bishop's U., Can., 1985—. Democrat. Roman Catholic. Office: Office of Sec State 107 N Main St State Ho Rm 204 Concord NH 03301-3222*

GARDOM, GARDE BASIL, former lieutenant governor of British Columbia; b. Banff, Alta., Can., July 17, 1924; s. Basil and Gabrielle Gwladys (Bell) G.; m. Theresa Helen Eileen Mackenzie, Feb. 11, 1956; children: Kim Gardom Allen, Karen Gardom MacDonald, Edward, Brione Gardom MacDonald, Brita Gardom McLaughlin. BA, LLB, U. BC, Vancouver, Can., 1949; LLD (hon.), U. B.C., 2003, U. Victoria, 2004. Called to bar 1949. With Campbell, Brazier & Co., 1949; sr. ptnr. Gardom & Co., Vancouver, 1960-75; apptd. Queen's Counsel, 1975; mem. BC Legis. Assembly for Vancouver-Point Grey, 1966-87; atty. gen. BC, 1975-79; min. intergovtl. rels., 1979-86; policy cons. Office of Premier, 1986-87; agt. gen. BC, 1987-92, Europe; mem. Premier's Econ. Adv. Coun., 1988-91; lt.-gov. BC, 1995—2001; dir. Brouwer Claims Can., 2002—. Dir. Justitute Inst. BC. Hon. dir. Boys and Girls Club Vancouver; hon. chmn. Bibl. Mus. Can.; v.p. Pacific Alzheimer Rsch. Found.; former mem. adv. coun. BC Cmty. Achievement awards. Decorated Order of BC; named to BC Sports Hall of Fame, 1995; named Freeman of City of London, 1992; hon. col. BC Regiment. Mem. Can. Bar Assn., BC Law Soc., Heraldry Soc. Can., Royal United Svcs. Inst. Vancouver, Govt. House Garden Soc., Brock House Soc., Royal Commonwealth Soc., Vancouver Lawn Tennis and Badminton Club (hon. life), Union Club BC, Knight of Justice, Order St. John, Royal Overseas Club, Can. Club Vancouver (life), Vancouver Club, Phi Delta Theta. Anglican. Home Phone: 604-263-7450; Office Phone: 604-267-9507. Home Fax: 604-267-9525. E-mail: heggbg@shaw.ca.

GAREAU, JEAN L., application technology executive; BS, U. Que., Montreal, 1989; MSEE, U. Montreal, 1992. Tchr. U. Calif., San Jose, 1998—99; dir. engring. Annasoft Systems, San Diego, 1999—2001, WIDCOMM, 2001—04; pres. VidaOne, Inc., 2004—. Author: (book) Windows CE from the Ground Up; developer (fitness software) MySport-Training (SmartPhone and Pocket PC Best Software Awards 2005, Health and Fitness, 2005), (Pocket PC Mag. Awards 2004, Health and Fitness, 2004); contbr. articles to profl. jours. Mem.: IEEE. Home Phone: 858-776-1331; Office Phone: 858-618-3868.

GARELICK, MARTIN, retired transportation executive; b. Rochester, NY, May 18, 1924; s. Samuel and Esther (Gerber) G.; m. Betty J. Mann, Jan. 18, 1951. BSC.E., Purdue U., 1947. With Milw. Rd. R.R., 1947-78, asst. v.p. mktg. devel. and planning Chgo., 1973-76, v.p. ops., 1976-78; exec. v.p., chief operating officer AMTRAK, Washington, 1978-80; v.p. Wyer, Dick & Co., Chgo., 1980-82; v.p., gen. mgr. N.J. Transit Rail Ops., Newark, 1982-84; dir. Kyle Rys., Inc., Scottsdale, Ariz., 1979-97; ret., 1997. With US Army, 1943—46. Mem. Am. Soc. Traffic and Logistics, Am. Assn. R.R. Supts., Tau Epsilon Phi. Jewish. Home: 20876 Del Luna Dr Boca Raton FL 33433-1788 Personal E-mail: garelick@worldnet.att.net.

GAREN, ALAN, biophysicist, educator; b. Bklyn., May 26, 1926; m. 1959; five children. BS, U. Colo., 1945, PhD in Biophysics, 1953. Chemist Oak Ridge Nat. Lab., 1946-48; fellow Nat. Found. Infantile Paralysis, Cold Spring Harbor, NY, 1951-55; rsch. assoc. Purdue U., Lafayette, Ind., 1955-57; sr. rsch. assoc. biology dept. MIT, Cambridge, Mass., 1957-60; assoc. prof. to prof. biology dept. U. Pa., Phila., 1960-63; prof. molecular biophysics and biochemistry Yale U., New Haven, 1963—, prof. genetics, 1970—. Guggenheim fellow, 1970. Contbr. articles to sci. jours. Recipient Waksman Medal in Microbiol., 1962, William Raveis Exceptional Project award, 2006. Fellow AAAS; mem. NAS. Office: Molecular Biophysics & Biochemistry Dept Yale U 333 Cedar St PO Box 208024 New Haven CT 06520-8024 Office Phone: 203-785-2765. Office Fax: 203-785-7979. E-mail: alan.garen@yale.edu.*

GAREY, DONALD LEE, oil industry executive; b. Ft. Worth, Sept. 9, 1931; s. Leo James and Jessie (McNatt) G.; m. Elizabeth Patricia Martin, Aug. 1, 1953; children: Deborah Anne, Elizabeth Laird. BS in Geol. Engring., Tex. A&M U., College Station, 1953. Registered profl. engr., Tex. Reservoir geologist Gulf Oil Corp., 1953-54, sr. geologist, 1956-65; v.p., mng. dir. Indsl. Devel. Corp. Lea County, Hobbs, N.Mex., 1965-72, dir., 1972-86, pres., 1978-86; v.p., dir. Minerals, Inc., Hobbs, N.Mex., 1966-72, pres., dir., 1972-86, CEO, 1978-82; mng. dir. Hobbs Indsl. Found. Corp., 1965-72, dir., 1965-76; v.p. Llano, Inc., 1972-74, exec. v.p., COO, 1974-75, pres., 1975-86, CEO, also dir., 1978-82; pres., CEO Pollution Control, Inc., 1969-81. Pres. NMESCO Fuels, Inc., 1982-86; chmn., pres., CEO Estacado, Inc., 1986—, Natgas Inc., 1987—; pres. Llano Co2, Inc., 1984-86; cons. geologist, geol. engr., Hobbs, 1965-72. Chmn. Hobbs Manpower Devel. Tng. Adv. Com., 1965-72; mem. Hobbs Adv. Com. for Mental Health, 1965-67; chmn. N.Mex. Mapping Adv. Com., 1968-69; mem. Hobbs adv. bd. Salvation Army, 1967-78, chmn., 1970-72; mem. exec. bd. Conquistador coun. Boy Scouts Am., Hobbs, 1965-75; vice chmn. N.Mex. Gov's Com. for Econ. Devel., 1968-70; bd. regents Coll. Southwest, 1982-85. Capt. USAF, 1954-56. Mem. AIPG, AAPG, SPE of AIME. Home: 315 E Alto Dr Hobbs NM 88240-3905 Office: Broadmoor Tower PO Box 5587 Hobbs NM 88241-5587 Home Phone: 505-393-8683; Office Phone: 505-393-6300.

GAREY, PATRICIA MARTIN, artist; b. State College, Miss., Nov. 11, 1932; d. Verey G. Martin and Eva Myrtle Jones; m. Donald L. Garey, Aug. 1, 1953; children: Deborah Anne Garey Furst, Elizabeth Laird Garey Jones. BS in Costume Design, Tex. Women's U., 1953; MFA, Tex. Tech. U., 1973; postgrad. in art history, Two-Dimensional Studio Art, 1970-73. Prodn. mgr. Cox Advt. Agy., Roswell, N.Mex., 1958-63; art instr. Coll. of Southwest, Hobbs, N.Mex., 1967-69, 72-73, prof. art history, art appreciation, 1974-76; studio artist Hobbs, 1976—; prof. art/painting and drawing N.Mex. Jr. Coll., 1997-98. Instr. Cloudcroft Artists Sch., N.Mex., 1991; prof. drawing, painting N.Mex. Jr. Coll.; prof. art hist. Coll. of Southwest, 1999—2001; rep., drawing instr. Villa Maria Ctr. for the Arts, Perugia, Italy, 1996; apptd. commr. N.Mex. Arts Commn., 1999; artist-in-residence N.Mex. Art Commn., Santa Fe, 1975—76. Artist (one-woman shows) Sand Hills Mus., Kermit, Tex., 1968, N.Mex. Jr. Coll., Hobbs, 1969, 1985, Coll. of SW, 1974, 1979, Sangre de Cristo Arts Ctr., Puebl, 1979, U. Tex. of Permian Basin, Odessa, 1980, (exhibitions) Roswell Mus. Art, Four Women Artists of Hobbs, N.Mex., 1966, Lubbock Mcpl. Garden and Arts Ctr., 1966, Laguna Gloria Art Mus., 1968—, Southeastern N.Mex. Small Painting Exhibit, 1975 (2d pl., 1966, 2d pl. Graphics, 2d pl. Sculpture, 2d pl. Acrylics, 1st pl. Ceramics, 1st pl. Drawing, 2d pl. Painting), Americas Gallery, Taos, 1974, Blair Gallery, Santa Fe, 1976, Mus. Fine Arts, 1976, Tex. Tech. U. Grad. Show, 1977, Little Rock Art Ctr., Ark., 1978, Hills Gallery, Santa Fe, 1979, Dallas Mus. Fine Art, 1986, 1987, 1988, 1990, Beaux Arts Ball Art Auction, 1990, Okla. City Mus. Art nat. drawing competition, Little Rock Art Ctr., El Paso Sun Carnival, Tex., Govs. Gallery, State Capitol, Santa Fe, 1997, Llano Estacado Art Assn., Hobbs, N.Mex., 1999 (Best of Show, 1st pl. watercolor), (permanent collections) Home Scis. Dept., Tex. Tech. U., The Round House/State Capitol, Santa Fe, Villa Maria Ctr. for the Arts, Raimondi Collection, Perugia, Italy, State Capitol, Santa Fe, N.Mex. Jr. Coll., docent Meadows Mus. of Art So. Meth. U., Dallas, 1990, Govs. Invitiational, Govs. Gallery, 1996, 35 Clay Workers of N.Mex., artist (exhibitions) Southeastern N.Mex. Small Painting Exhibit, 1976, 1987, 1988, 1990, (represented by) Design Today, Lubbock, Tex., Sylvia Ullman Am. Crafts, Cleve.; represented by, DeLis Backdoor Gallery, N.Mex., Old Pecos Gallery, Carlsbad, N.Mex., Contemporary Arts Studio, Hobbs, N.Mex. Arts commr. State of N.Mex., 1999—2002, N.Mex. Arts Commn., 1999—2003; artistic bd. S.W. Symphony, Hobbs, 1987—99; Bd. dirs. The Bridge Breast Ctr., Dallas, 1992—93, Llano Estacado Art Assn. Recipient Best of Show award for mixed media Llano Estacado Art Assn. Regional Show, Hobbs, N.Mex., 1996, Best of Show award for ceramics, 1999, 1st pl. award for watercolor, 1999, Best of Show for oil painting, 2004, others. Mem. Delta Phi Delta, Chi Omega. Democrat. Methodist. Avocations: swimming, cooking, classical music, book collecting. Studio: 315 E Alto Dr Hobbs NM 88240-3905 also: Piney Woods Cloudcroft NM 88350 Office Phone: 505-393-8683.

GARFIELD, ERNEST, bank executive, consultant; b. Colorado River, Ariz., July 14, 1932; s. Emil and Carmen (Ybarra) G.; m. Betty Ann Redden, Apr. 18, 1953; children: Laural, Jeffery Alan. BS, U. Ariz., 1975; B of Internat. Mgmt., Am. Grad. Sch., Phoenix, 1975, M of Internat. Mgmt., 1976. Owner Garfield Ins. Agy., Tucson, 1962-70; senator State of Ariz., Phoenix, 1967-68, dep. treas., 1970-71, treas., 1971-74; commr. Ariz. Corp. Commn., Phoenix, 1974-79; chmn. United Bancorp Systems, Inc., Phoenix, 1979—, Interstate Bank Developers, Inc., Scottsdale, 1994—. Chmn. The White House Conf. on Energy, Com. on Energy Policy of Nat. Assn. Regulatory Utility Commn.; pres. Western Conf. Pub. Svc. Commns.; mem. Ad Hoc Com. on Regulatory Reform, Electric and Nuclear Energy Com., bd. dirs. East Valley Inst. Tech. Edn. Found., 2004—; chmn. Ariz. Fin. Insts. Task Force. Mem. Ariz. Kidney Found., Multiple Sclerosis Soc., Rep. Senatorial Inner Circle, 1989; mem. Pres. Bush Task Force, 1989; mem. adv. bd. St. Joseph's Hosp., Phoenix; mem. establishment com. Pima County Jr. Coll., Tucson; mem. orgn. com. Pima County Halfway House, Tucson; chmn. Ariz. Gov. Commn. on Rape Prevention, 1988, Nat. Commn. on Rape Prevention, 1990—; commr. Ariz. Gov. Commn. on Violence Against Women, 1993-03; active Ariz. Gov.'s Sexual Assault Task Force; dir. Ariz. Sexual Assault Network; bd. dirs. Ariz. Cactus-Pine coun. Girl Scouts U.S.; mem. Men Against Violence Network; chmn. Ariz. Fin. Instns. Task Force, 2007—. With U.S. Army, 1952-55. Recipient Outstanding Young Men Ariz. award, Press Club award; named to U.S. Arty. Hall of Fame, 1999. Mem.: Thunderbird Internat. Banking Inst. (mem. adv. coun. 1990—), Ariz-Mex. C. of C. Republican. Roman Catholic. Avocation: graphology. Home and Office: 8442 N 72nd Pl Scottsdale AZ 85258-2762 Home Phone: 480-348-0505; Office Phone: 480-348-0404. E-mail: egarfield@qwest.net.

GARFIELD, LESLIE JEROME, real estate executive; b. NYC, Mar. 23, 1932; s. Jack and Anne (Weinert) G.; m. Johanna Rosengarten, Sept. 28, 1960; children: Clare Louisa, Jed Herbert, Cory Alexander. BA, U. Wis., Madison, 1953; MA, Harvard U., Cambridge, Mass., 1956; MBA, Columbia U., NYC, 1958. V.p. Pease & Elliman, Inc., NYC, 1965—68, William A. White & Sons, Inc., NYC, 1968—78; pres. Leslie J. Garfield & Co., Inc., NYC, 1978—. Vice-chmn., bd. dirs. Internat. Print Ctr. Chmn. bd. dirs. NY Youth Symphony, 1986—, pres. bd. dirs., 1975-86; bd. dirs. Carnegie Hill Neighbors, N.Y.C., 1985—; coun. Chazen Mus. Art Com. prints and illustrated books Mus. Modern Art; bd. overseers Mus. Fine Arts, Boston. Mem. Real Estate Bd. N.Y. (chmn. sales brokers com. 1985-86), Century Assn., Nat. Arts Club, Grolier Club (coun.). Avocation: art. Office: Leslie J Garfield and Co 505 Park Ave New York NY 10022-9332 Personal E-mail: lesliejre@aol.com.

GARFIELD, MARTIN RICHARD, lawyer; b. NYC, Feb. 19, 1935; s. Harry and Sarah (Spielman) G.; 1 child, Robin; m. Sophia Csala, Aug. 2001. BA, Hunter Coll., 1957; JD, Bklyn. Law Sch., 1964. Bar: N.Y. 1965, U.S. Dist. Ct. (ea. and so. dists.) N.Y. 1979, U.S. Supreme Ct. 1996. Assoc. Figueroa & Madow, NYC, 1965—68, Schneider Kleinick & Weitz, NYC, 1968—70; ptnr. Breadbar Garfield & Solomon, NYC, 1970—86; sr. ptnr. Breadbar Garfield & Schmelkin, NYC, 1986—. Arbitrator Civil Ct. N.Y. County, 1986—; mgr. N.Y. State Athletic Commn., 1996—. Mem. Am. Trial Lawyers Assn., NY State Bar Assn. (torts, ins. sect.), NY Trials Lawyers Assn., Million Dollar Advocates Forum. Avocations: tennis, basketball, boxing analysis, body building. Office: Breadbar Garfield & Schmelkin 11 Park Pl Fl 10 New York NY 10007-2895 Office Phone: 212-227-8865. Personal E-mail: lawwire@aol.com.

GARFIELD, ROBERT EDWARD, journalist; b. Phila., June 20, 1955; s. Samuel M. Garfield and Nancy G. Rowen; m. Carla Patricia Cain, Dec. 16, 1977; children: Kathryn Sarah, Allison Patricia, Ida Rose; m. Milena Trobozic, Mar. 11, 2001. BA, Pa. State U., 1977. Reporter Reading Times, Pa., 1977-81, Wilmington News-Jour., Del., 1981-82; columnist USA Today, Washington, 1982-85, Crain News Svc. and Advt. Age, Washington, 1985—; corr. Nat. Pub. Radio, 1986—. Analyst ABC News, 1999-2005; co-host On the Media, Nat. Pub. Radio, 1999—. Host Ad Age Reports program Fin. News Network, 1989-91; polit. advt. analyst CBS This Morning, 1992; contbg. writer Washington Post Mag., 1985-97; corr. Here and Now, Sta. WETA-TV, 1995; contbg. editor Civilization Mag., 1996-98; contbg. columnist U.S.A. Today, 1995-98; contbr. CNBC "Power Lunch", 1996-99, Adam Smith's Money Game, 1998; author: Waking Up Screaming from the American Dream, 1997, And Now a Few Words from Me, 2003. Recipient Keystone award Pa. Newspaper Pubs. Assn., 1981, Best of Gannett award Gannett Co. Inc., 1982, journalism award Saatchi & Saatchi/Compton Advt., 1984, 85, award Am. Soc. Bus. Press Editors, 1994, Neal award Am. Bus. Press, 1996, Internat. Radio award NY Festivals, 2003, RTNDA Edward R. Murrow award, 2003, Arthur Rowse award Nat. Press Club, 2003, Peabody award U. Ga., 2005. Mem. Nat. Press Club. Jewish.

GARFIELD, WINIFRED L., nursing administrator; b. Fredericksted, St. Croix, V.I., July 28, 1941; d. Walter Antonio and Idalia Crystalia (Stephens) L.; m. Victor Conrad Garfield, June 30, 1968; children: Vilma Cecilia, Victor Conrad, Vynette Crystine, Vivicka Celeste. RN, St. Lukes Sch. Nursing, Ponce, PR, 1962; grad. anesthesiology for nurses, Harlem Hosp. Sch., 1966. RN, CRNA, AANA. Staff nurse Knud Hansen Hosp., St. Thomas, V.I., 1962-64, nurse anesthetist, 1966-70, nurse anesthetist supr., 1970-89, respiratory therapy instr., 1976-77; campus nurse U. of V.I., St. Thomas, V.I., 1979-82; first aid instr., trainer ARC, St. Thomas, V.I., 1973-80; supr. anesthesia and respiratory svc. St. Thomas Hosp., St. Thomas, V.I., 1980-89; exec. dir. V.I. Bd. of Nurse Licensure, St. Thomas, V.I., 1989—. Nurse cons. Educare Sch., Inc., 1970—, asst. dir., 1980—. Recipient Disting. Nurse Cons. award Dept. of Health Office of Commr., 1982, named Nurse of the Year V.I. Licensed Practical Nurse Assn., 1986. Mem. V.I. Nurses Assn. (v.p. 1963-64), Chi Eta Phi (historian, 1963-64), Eta Phi Beta (Alpha Chi chpt). Democrat. Roman Catholic. Avocations: reading, gardening, travel. Home: 394-140 Anas Retreat Charlotte Amalie VI 00803 Office: VI Bd of Nursing Licensure Veterans Dr Sta Charlotte Amalie VI 00803

GARFIELD-WOODBRIDGE, NANCY, writer; b. NYC; d. Solomon and Betty Silbowitz; m. George Charles Woodbridge, Apr. 20, 1980; children from previous marriage: Maurice Garfield, Joshua Garfield. BA in Lit., Bennington Coll., 1955; MS in Edn., Hofstra U., 1972, postgrad., 1973. Cert. tchr. K-8, English 7-9 N.Y. Editl. asst. Wenner Gren Found. Anthropol. Rsch., NYC, 1952—55; picture editor Forbes Mag., NYC, 1955—56; editor-in-chief The Gifted Child Mag., NYC, 1957—58; v.p. Info. Retrieval Systems, Great Neck, NY, 1958—72; rsch. assoc. to v.p. and editor N.Y. Inst. Tech., Westbury, 1972—73; dir. spl. projects Girl Scouts of USA, NYC, 1973—2000; children's author, 2000—. Spkr. v.p.'s task force on youth employment, Little Rock, 1979, gov.'s conf. on juvenile justice, Baton Rouge; presenter Edn. Commn. for the States, Denver, 1979. Author: The Tuesday Elephant, 1968, The Dancing Monkey, 1970, Juvenile Justice, 1981; contbr. articles to profl. jours. and mags. Vol. Kennedy Kenya Airlift Program, NYC, 1962, Biafran Refugee Campaign, NY-London, 1967; fundraiser Sara's Ctr. Very Spl. Arts Festival, LI to Washington. Scholar Breadloaf Writers Conf., Vt., 1967. Mem.: Acad. Am. Poets, The Author's Guild, Milford Fine Arts Coun., Soc. Children's Book Writers and Illustrators. Avocations: travel, reading, opera, painting, photography.

GARFIN, LOUIS, retired actuary; b. Mason City, Iowa, June 7, 1917; s. Sam and Etta (Larner) Garfin; m. Clarice Fagen, Apr. 11, 1943 (dec. Apr. 8, 2004); children: Eugene Arthur, Erica. Student, Mason City Jr. Coll., 1934-36; BA, State U. Iowa, 1938, MS, 1939, PhD, 1942. Instr. USAAF, Scott Field, Ill., 1942-43; instr. math. Ill. Inst. Tech., Chgo., 1943, U. Minn., 1943-44; actuary Oreg. Ins. Dept., Salem, 1946-52; assoc. actuary Pacific Mut. Life Ins. Co., Los Angeles, 1952-62, actuary, 1962-64, v.p., chief actuary, 1964-82, cons. actuary, 1982-90; ret., 1990. Bd. dirs. Calif. Health Decisions, 1989—95, chairperson, 1993—94; bd. dirs. Laguna Beach Cmty. Clinic, 1989—93; treas. Laguna Canyon Found., 1990—99, Mykonos Village, 1999—2007. Fellow: Soc. Actuaries; mem.: Am. Math. Soc., LA Actuarial Club (pres. 1959—60), Actuarial Club Pacific States (pres. 1967—68), Internat. Congress Actuaries (bd. dirs. 1977—80), Am. Acad. Actuaries (v.p. 1976—78), Sigma Xi, Phi Beta Kappa. Home: 4013 Arcadia Way Oceanside CA 92056-5139 Personal E-mail: lgarfin@cox.net.

GARFINKEL, BARRY HERBERT, lawyer; b. Bklyn., June 19, 1928; s. Abraham and Shirley (Siegel) G.; m. Gloria Lorenz, Feb. 16, 1969; children— David, James, Paul. BSS, CCNY, 1950; LLB, Yale U., 1955. Bar: N.Y. State 1955, U.S. Supreme Ct. 1959. Law clk. to Hon. Edward Weinfeld U.S. Dist. Ct., NYC, 1955-56; assoc. Skadden, Arps, Slate, Meagher & Flom, NYC, 1956-61, ptnr., 1961-2000, of counsel, 2000—. Trustee, chmn. Practising Law Inst., Law Ctr. Found. of N.Y. U. Sch. Law Aperture Found., program com. 2d. Cir. Jud. Conf. Mng. editor: Yale Law Jour. Bd. dirs., former dir. Jewish Mus., Legal Aid Soc.; former trustee N.Y. Community Trust; pres. coun. Mus. City of N.Y.; chmn. lawyers' div., spl. gifts campaign United Jewish Appeal/Fedn. Jewish Philanthropies, 1979-81; mem. print com. Whitney Mus., Com. on Rsch. Libraries N.Y. Pub. Lib. Recipient Torch of Learning award Am. Friends of Hebrew U., 1983, Brandeis Distingish. Community Svc. award Brandeis U., 1985. Fellow: Am. Bar Found., Coll. of Commercial Arbitrators, Am. Coll. Trial Lawyers; mem.: ABA, Am. Law Inst., N.Y. State Bar Assn., Assn. of Bar of City of N.Y. (exec. com., judiciary com., past chmn. fed. cts. com.), Am. Arbitration Assn., Yale (N.Y.C.), Yale Club (N.Y.C.). Home: 211 Central Park W New York NY 10024-6020 Office: Skadden Arps Slate Meagher & Flom 4 Times Sq Fl 24 New York NY 10036-6595 Office Phone: 212-735-2500. Business E-Mail: bgarf@skadden.com.

GARFINKEL, HARMON MARK, retired specialty chemicals company executive; b. Bklyn., May 20, 1933; s. Samuel and Elsie (Schwartz) G.; m. Lorraine Plawsky, Mar. 4, 1956; children: Elyse, Michelle. BA, Bklyn. Coll., 1957; PhD, Iowa State U., 1960; postgrad. program for mgmt. devel., Harvard U. Bus. Sch., 1973. Dir. bio-organic tech. Corning Inc., NY, 1973-74, dir. applied chemistry and biology, 1974-75, dir. biomed. and chem. tech., 1975-78, dir. rsch., 1978-85; v.p. R&D Engelhard Corp., Edison, NJ, 1985-95, cons., 1995—. Instr. math. Elmira Coll., 1964. Patents and publs. in field. Mem. Am. Chem. Soc., Am. Phys. Soc., Am. Inst. Chemists, Am. Ceramic Soc. Republican. Jewish. Home: 3836 Outlook Ct Jupiter FL 33477-1309 Office Phone: 561-744-2963. E-mail: Harmgarf@aol.com.

GARFINKEL, JANE E., lawyer; b. NYC, Dec. 2, 1952; d. Albert E. and Rita H. (Halpern) G.; m. Louis F. Solimine, May 20, 1979. BA, Wheaton Coll., 1974; MA, U. Mich., 1975, JD, 1979. Bar: Ohio 1980. Assoc. Smith & Schnacke, Cin., 1980-88, ptnr., 1988-89, Thompson Hine LLP, Cin., 1989—. Office: Thompson Hine LLP 312 Walnut St Ste 1400 Cincinnati OH 45202-4089 Office Phone: 513-352-6530. Business E-Mail: jane.garfinkel@thompsonhine.com.

GARFINKEL, LAWRENCE SAUL, academic administrator, educator, television producer; b. NYC, Mar. 9, 1932; s. Benjamin and Rose (Rochkind) G.; m. Adrienne Rederer, June 26, 1960; children: Andrew, Rodger, Craig. BS in Art Edn., NYU, 1953, MA in Higher Edn., 1955, postgrad. in Edn. Comm., 1975. Tchr., supr. art, prin. hs W. Hempstead Pub. Schs., NY, 1954-56, dir. related arts NY, 1957-69, dir. cmty. rels. NY, 1961-71; tchg. fellow, instr. NYU Sch. Edn.; nprof. edn. adminstrn. and comm., dir. instrnl. comm. program Hofstra U., Hempstead, NJ, 1969-76; dir. summer tv & media insts.; dir. gifted programs Sachem Pub. Schs., Lake Ronkonkoma, NY, 1978-79; dir. ednl. comm. Coll. Dentistry, Kriser Dental Ctr., NYU, 1979-91, ret.; adj. prof. dept. speech Baruch Coll., CUNY, 1980-91, Adelphi U., Stern Coll.-Yeshiva U., St. Johns U., Temple U., NY Inst. Tech.; adj. prof. dept. media arts C.W. Post-L.I. U., 1991—. Adj. assoc. prof. art dept. Nassau C.C.; cons. bd. regents N.Y. State Edn. Dept., Ctr. Urban Edn., N.Y.C. Pub.: Restorative Dentistry, 1985; illustrator: Classroom Television, 1970; illustrator N.Y. Times, John Huston Prodns., Century Theatres, Nat. Audio Visual Assn., and numerous publs.; editl. cartoonist Merrick Life; asst. prodr. WPIX-TV, programming Dumont Network; pub. Garson Assocs.; contbr. articles to profl. jours. Coord. youth edn. Mothers Against Drunk Driving, Long Island Area, 1997-99; bd. dirs. Hist. Soc. Merricks, 1983— pres., 2001-; bd. dirs. Higher Edn. Assn. TV, 1972; v.p. Health Equities, N.Y.C.; oral historian Bi Centennial Commn., 1975. Nominee, Woodrow Wilson Found.; named alt., Fulbright award; recipient Grad. Arch award medal, NYU, scholarship masters NYU, numerous awards, Nat. Com. Sch. Pub. Rels.; grad. tchg. fellow, NYU. Mem. N.Y. Acad. Sci., L.I. Art Tchrs. Assn. (pres. 1967-68), Nat. Com. Art Edn. (co-pres. 1967). Avocations: illustrating, lecturing on communications theory, arts, visual literacy, nostalgia therapy. Home and Office: Garson Assocs 172 Babylon Tpke Merrick NY 11566-4407

GARFINKEL, LEE, advertising agency executive; married; 2 children. BA, CUNY. From copywriter to exec. v.p., exec. creative dir. Levine, Huntley, Schmidt & Beaver; exec. v.p., sr. creative dir., also dir. BBDO; chief creative officer, chmn. Lowe, Lintas & Ptnrs., NYC, 1992—2001; worldwide creative chief D'Arcy Masius Benton & Bowles, 2001—03; chmn., chief creative officer DDB New York, 2003—. Stand-up comedian and musician. Named 1986 East Coast All-Star Team as Best TV Copywriter, Adweek, Creative Dir. of Yr. on 1994 Nat. Creative All-Star Team; selected ann. Forty Under Forty feature Crain's New York Bus.; named one of top three creative dirs. as well as number one copywriter in U.S., Winners mag., 1989; inducted in Am. Advt. Fedn. Hall of Achievement. Mem. One Club for Art and Copy (bd. dirs., pres. 1992-95). Avocations: song writing, collecting guitars, animated art, cars. Office: DDB New York 437 Madison Ave New York NY 10022

GARFINKLE, ELAINE MYRA, writer; b. Canton, Ohio, July 24, 1936; d. Clifford and Dora Adelman Margolis; m. Jack George Garfinkle, Dec. 27, 1959; 1 child, Marcia Lizabeth. Gen. mgr., editor, pub. Stark Jewish News, Inc., Canton, 1970—83; owner, writer, rschr. Canton Writing Svc., 1978—90; pres., treas. Marce Pubs., Inc., Canton, 1979—83; owner, rschr. Leo Rsch. unlimited, Canton, 1979—83; cmty. rels. supr. Goodwill Rehab., Canton, 1984—87; advt. exec. Cmty. Newspapers, Massillon, Ohio, 1987—91. Presenter in field. Historian, pub., compiler, author Through the Years, the Informal History of the Canton, Ohio, Area Jewish Community 1870-2006, 80 vols. Historian on Canton, Ohio PBS Spl., 1999—2006; adv. U.S. Holocaust Meml. Mus.; supporter Goodwill's Amb. of Goodwill; bd. mem., publicity chair Canton chpt. Hadassah; vol. Canton Jewish Cmty. Ctr.; mem. Cleve. Jewish Genealogy Soc.; mem., supporter Stark County Hist. Soc., McKinley Mus. Mem.: Friends of Ctr. Jewish History, Ohio Libr., Am. Friends Hebrew U., Leo Baeck Inst., Friends North Canton, YIVO Inst. Jewish Rsch., Am. Jewish Hist. Soc., Canton Jewish Cmty. Fedn. (edn. com. 1996—2006, Outstanding Svc. award 1996—2006), Internat. Jewish Women (life; past pres., treas.), Am. Heart Assn. (cmty. rels. com. 1992—96, Outstanding Svc. award 1992—96), Am. Sephardi Fedn., Nat. Geographic Soc., Hadassah (life; program presenter 2003, former edn. com. mem., bd. mem., publicity chair Canton chpt.), Anti-Defamation League, Women's League Conservative Judaism, Shaaray Torah Sisterhood (former social action chmn.). Jewish. Avocations: photography, practical psychology, music, reading, studying Jewish history.

GARFUNKEL, ART, singer, actor; b. Forest Hills, NY, Nov. 5, 1941; m. Kim Cermak, September 18, 1988; children: James Arthur, Beau. BA, Columbia, 1965, MA, 1967. Former mem. team, Simon and Garfunkel; recs. with Simon include Bridge Over Troubled Water, Sounds of Silence, Dangling Conversation, Homeward Bound, I Am a Rock, Mrs. Robinson, others; now soloist: albums as soloist include Angel Clare, 1973, Breakaway, 1975, Watermark, 1978, Fate For Breakfast (Doubt for Dessert), 1979, Scissors Cut, 1981, Simon & Garfunkel The Concert in Central Park, 1982, (with Amy Grant) The Animals' Christmas, 1986, Lefty, 1988, Garfunkel, 1989, UP Till Now, 1993, Across America, 1997, Songs from a Parent to a Child, 1997, Everything Waits to be Noticed, 2002; films include Catch-22, 1970, Carnal Knowledge, 1971, Bad Timing.A Sensual Obsession, 1980, Good to Go, 1986. Recipient Grammy awards for Mrs. Robinson, 1969; 6 Grammy awards for Bridge Over Troubled Water, 1970; inducted into Rock & Roll Hall of Fame, 1990. Address: care Mary Ellen Kirby 12182 Daugherty Dr Zionsville IN 46077-8716

GARG, ASHUTOSH, computer scientist, researcher; PhD, U. Ill., Urbana Champaign, 2003. Mem. rsch. staff Almaden Rsch. Ctr. IBM, San Jose, Calif., 2003—04; staff rsch. scientist Google Inc., Mountain View, Calif., 2004—. Author: (book) Machine Learning in Computer Vision. Recipient Best Undergrad Project award, Indian Inst. Tech., Delhi, 1997, Robert T. Chien Outstanding Rsch. award, U. Ill., Urbana Champaign, 2003; fellow, IBM Corp., 2002. Office: Google Inc 1600 Amphitheater Pkwy Mountain View CA 94043 Home Phone: 408-737-2984; Office Phone: 650-253-6175. Personal E-mail: ashu.garg@gmail.com.

GARG, UMESH, physicist, researcher; b. Bikaner, Rajasthan, India, Mar. 29, 1953; came to U.S., 1974; s. Shiv Nandan and Shakuntala (Mittal) G.; m. Anita Padhye, Dec. 28, 1980; children: Noopur Neha, Neehar Nimesh. BS, Birla Inst. Tech. and Sci., Pilani, India, 1972, MS, 1974; MA, SUNY, Stony Brook, 1975, PhD, 1978. Teaching asst. SUNY, Stony Brook, 1974-75, rsch. asst., 1975-78; rsch. assoc. Tex. A&M U., College Station, 1978-82; asst. prof. U. Notre Dame, Ind., 1982-87, assoc. prof. Ind., 1987-93; prof. U. Notre Dame (Ind.), 1994—. Cons. Tex. A&M U., 1982-83; vis. scientist Bhabha Atomic Rsch. Ctr., Bombay, India, 1985-87; vis. prof. Vrije U., Amsterdam, 1988-89. Editor: Symposium of Northeastern Accelerator Personnel, 1987. Vice pres. India Assn. Tex. A&M, College Station, 1981. Mem. Am. Phys. Soc. (program com. divsn. nuclear physics), Am. Chem. Soc., Indian Physics Assn. (pres. U.S. chpt. 1986, chmn. nominating com. 1992-95), Sigma Xi Hindu. Achievements include discovery of splitting of giant monopole resonance in deformed nuclei; superdeformation in Hg region of nuclei; the isoscalar giant dipole resonance. Office: Univ Notre Dame Physics Dept Notre Dame IN 46556 Home Phone: 574-272-2957; Office Phone: 574-631-7352. Business E-Mail: garg@nd.edu.

GARG, VIJAY KUMAR, telecommunications engineer; b. Jahangirabad, India, July 7, 1938; arrived in US, 1965; s. Reoti S. and Prem V. (Mittal) G.; m. Pushpa Bansal, May 11, 1961; children: Nina Taneja, Meena Dorr, Ravi K. Garg. BS, Banaras U., Varanasi, India, 1960; MS, U. Calif., Berkeley, 1966; PhD, Ill. Inst. Tech., Chgo., 1973. Registered profl. structral engr., Ill., profl. engr., Ill. Asst. prof. engring. U. Jodhpur, India, 1960-65; structural engr. Chgo. Bridge, Oakbrook, Ill., 1967-69; devel. engr. GMC, Lagrange, Ill., 1969-76; mgr. dynamic rsch. AAR, Chgo., 1976-84; assoc. prof. engring. U. Maine, Orono, 1984-85; dist. mem. tech. staff Bell Labs Lucent Techs., Naperville, Ill., 1985-2000, Motorola Inc., Arlington Heights, Ill., 1997; prof. elec. and computer engring. U. Ill., Chgo., 1999—2004. Vis. prof. elec. and comm. engring. U. Ill., Urbana, 1996-97; adj. prof. engring. Ill. Inst. Tech., Chgo., 1976-84. Author: Wireless and Personal Communications System, 1996, Applications of CDMA in Wireless Communications, 1997, Dynamics of Railway Vehicle System, 1984, Advanced Dynamics, 1984, Principles and Applications of GSM, 1999, CDMA IS-95 and CDMA 2000, 2000, Wireless Network Evolution-2G to 3G, 2002, Wireless Communication and Networks, 2007. Recipient NSF travel grants India, 1984, China, 1985. Fellow ASME, ASCE; mem. IEEE (sr.). Democrat. Hindu. Avocations: gardening, travel, reading, music. Home: 146 Somerset Rd Hinsdale IL 60527-5429 Office: 851 S Morgan St Chicago IL 60605-4220 Personal E-mail: garg.v@comcast.net.

GARIEPY, CAROLE JANE, writer, retired elementary school educator; b. Gardner, Mass., Dec. 1, 1937; d. Granville A. and M. Gwendolyn (Chase) Lombard; m. Gerard Beals Gariepy, Feb. 10, 1962; children: Grant, Cortland, Barton. BS in Elem. Edn., Worcester State Tchrs. Coll., Mass., 1959; MA in Counseling Psychology, Assumption Coll., Worcester, 1995. Tchr. elem. sch. Wallingford Pub. Schs., Conn., 1959—61, Barre Pub. Schs., Mass., 1961—64, tchr. remedial reading, 1968—70; docent Worcester Art Mus., Mass., 1984—92. Author: Queen Lake.A History, 1998, Quilt of America, 2002, The Spirit of Phillipston, 2007. Scout leader Boy Scouts Am., Barre, 1972—80; tchr. Sunday Sch., 1960—70. Mem.: Hist. Soc. Phillipston. Avocations: quilting, travel, hiking, snorkeling, art.

GARING, IONE DAVIS, civic worker; b. Huntsville, Ala., Jan. 8, 1930; d. Drury McNary and Ione (Thompson) Davis; m. John Seymour Garing, Apr. 26, 1952; children: John Davis, Susan Carolyn. BSc in Edn. cum laude, Ohio State U., 1951. Tchr. Columbus (Ohio) Pub. Schs., 1952-54, Upper Arlington Pub. Sch., Columbus, 1957-58; libr. Newton (Mass.) Libr., 1955; interviewer audits and surveys Elmo Roper, Boston, 1956. Adv. com. Sch. Com. on Spl. Edn., Lexington, Mass., 1979-80; adv. bd. Cary Meml. Libr., Lexington, 1989—. Elected Town Meeting mem., Lexington, 1980-2002, Lexington 2020 Vision Study, 2001; exec. bd. Lexington Dem. Com., 1987-89, mem., 1986—; del. Mass. Dem. Convs., 1986, 88, 90, 92, 94, 96, 98, 2000, 2002; exec. bd. Friends Coun. on Aging, 1986, PTA, 1965-79; vol. Meals on Wheels, 1985-89; pres. United Meth. Women, Lexington, 1973-75; bd. dir. Meth. Weekday Sch., 1971-80, chmn. bd. dir., 2004—; co-organizer 1st town-wide hazardous waste collection in U.S., Lexington, 1983; vol. Lexington Hist. Soc., 1978—; co-founder, chmn. Friends of Cary Meml. Libr. Orgn., 1990-97, bd. dirs., 1990—, co-pres. 2006—; founding mem., treas., Precint 8 Residents Assn., 1996-2005; mem. Cary Meml. Libr. Found., 2007—. Mem. LWV (pres. Lexington 1983-85), AAUW (Mass. long range planning com.), DAR (vice regent 1977-80, Mass. chmn. scholarships and loan com. 1980-83), Florence Crittenton League, Outlook Club (pres. 1985-87, chmn. scholarships com. 1990-2002), Lexington Field and Garden Club (chmn. Wednesday Workshop 1998-2000, 2d v.p. 2000-02), North Shore Rock and Mineral Club (Peabody, Mass.), Brookline Bird Club, Minute Man Nat. Pk. Assn., Alpha Chi Omega. Avocations: conservation, gardening, birdwatching, genealogy, travel. Home: 157 Cedar St Lexington MA 02421-6507

GARINGER, LOUIS DANIEL, retired religion educator; b. Johnson City, Tenn. s. Merrion X. and Hilda (Gasteiger) G.; m. Joanne Mazna, June 21, 1958. AB, U. Tenn., 1947, JD, 1949; MA in Govt, Harvard, 1957. Staff writer Christian Sci. Monitor Youth Forums, Boston, 1949-51; teaching fellow, tutor govt. Harvard, 1955-58; assoc. dir. Salzburg Seminar in Am. Studies, 1958-60; editorial writer Christian Sci. Monitor, 1965-67, religious affairs editor, 1967-71; research, 1971-72; assoc. prof. polit. sci. and religion Principia Coll., Elsah, Ill., 1973-86; dir. Found. Bibl. Research, Charlestown, NH, 1987-88. Vis. scholar Boston U. Sch. Theology, 1980, Grad. Theol. Union, Berkeley, Calif. Contbr. articles to profl. jours. Served with AUS, 1951-53. Recipient Religious Pub. Relations Council merit award, 1969; William E. Leidt award for religious reporting, 1970 Mem. Scarabbean, Pi Kappa Phi, Phi Kappa Phi, Phi Eta Sigma, Sigma Delta Pi, Phi Alpha Eta. Home: 105 Spaulding Hill Rd West Chesterfield NH 03466-3120 *Unless religion means a deep and heartfelt love for God and man expressed in very concrete and practical ways, unless it cuts to the very core of our being and radically changes our lives, it is worth little or nothing.*

GARLAND, CARL WESLEY, chemist, educator; b. Bangor, Maine, Oct. 1, 1929; s. Cecil G. and Blandena Couillard (Wadell) G.; m. Joan A. Donaghy, July 30, 1955; children: Leslie J., Andrew E. BS, U. Rochester, NYC, 1950; PhD, U. Calif.-Berkeley, 1953. Instr. chemistry U. Calif.-Berkeley, 1953; faculty MIT, 1953—, assoc. prof. chemistry, 1959-68, prof. chemistry, 1968-98; prof. emeritus, 1998—. Vis. prof. U. Calif., San Diego, 1972, U. Rome, 1974, Cath. U. Leuven, Belgium, 1977, Ben Gurion U., Israel, 1980, U. Paris, 1981, 82, U. Bordeaux, France, 1990; chmn. Gordon Rsch. Conf. Orientational Disorder in Crystals, 1984. Author: (with J.W. Nibler, D.P. Shoemaker) Experiments in Physical Chemistry, 7th edit., 2003; editor: Optics and Spectroscopy, 1960-81, Liquid Crystals, 1991-95; contbr. over 200 articles to profl. jours. A.P. Sloan fellow, 1954-60; Guggenheim fellow, 1963. Fellow Am. Acad. Arts and Sci.; mem. Am. Phys. Soc. Home: 4 Edward St Belmont MA 02478-2343 Office: MIT Rm 2-121 Cambridge MA 02139-4307 E-mail: cgarland@mit.edu, carlwgarland@aol.com.

GARLAND, CEDRIC FRANK, epidemiologist, educator; b. La Jolla, Calif., Nov. 10, 1946; s. Cedric and Eva (Caldwell) Garagliano. BA, U. So. Calif., 1967; MPH, UCLA, 1970, DrPH, 1974. Asst. prof. Johns Hopkins U., Balt., 1974-81; prof. Sch. Medicine U. Calif., La Jolla, 1981—. Contbr. chpts. to books, articles to profl. jours. Recipient Aristotle award for acad. excellence UCLA, 1974, Golden Apple award for Tchg. Excellence Johns Hopkins U., 1980, Environ. Health Coalition Disting. Svc. award, 1984, NIH Rsch. Career award, 1982. Fellow Am. Coll. Epidemiology; mem. Physicians for Social Responsibility (chmn. info. resources 1982—), Soc. Epidemiol. Rsch., Sierra Club (chmn. Save Our Shore 1982—, Disting. Achievement award 1984). Roman Catholic. Achievements include work with Dr. Frank Garland and Dr. Edward Gorham who together played a role in establishing the association between deficiency of vitamin D and calcium, and risk of intestinal, breast and ovarian cancer and melanoma; this group also played the central role in establishing that ultraviolet A is a cause of human melanoma. Office: U Calif Dept 0631C Dept Family & Preventive Medicine 9500 Gilman Dr La Jolla CA 92093-0631 Business E-Mail: cgarland@ucsd.edu.

GARLAND, DAVID WILLIAM, law and sociology educator; b. Dundee, Scotland, Aug. 7, 1955; s. David Watt and Elizabeth (Gray) G.; m. Anne Jowett, July 21, 1984; children: Kasia Jowett Garland, Amy Elizabeth Jowett Garland. LLB with first class honors, Edinburgh U., Scotland, 1977, PhD in Socio-Legal Studies, 1984; MA in Criminology, Sheffield U., Eng., 1978. Lectr. Edinburgh U., Scotland, 1979-90, reader, 1990-92, prof., 1992—97; prof. law NYU Sch. Law, NYC, 1997—, Arthur T. Vanderbilt prof. law, 2001—; also prof. sociology NYU. Vis. reader Leuven U., Belgium, 1983; Davis Fellow history dept. Princeton U., 1984-85; vis. prof. Boalt Hall Sch. Law, U. Calif., Berkeley, 1985, 88, NYU Sch. Law, 1992-93, Global law program prof., 1995-97. Author: Punishment and Welfare: A History of Penal Strategies, 1985, Punishment and Modern Society: A Study in Social Theory, 1990, The Culture of Control: Crime and Social Order in Contemporary Society, 2001; co-editor (with R. Sparks): Criminology and Social Theory, 2000. J.S. Guggenheim fellow, 2006—07. Fellow Royal Soc. Edinburgh.; mem. ACLU, Law & Soc. Assn., Am. Soc. Criminology (Sellin-Glueck Award, 1993), Amnesty Internat. British Labour Party. Avocations: reading, skiing, squash, cinema, music. Office: NYU Sch Law Vanderbilt Hall Rm 340 40 Washington Sq S New York NY 10012-1099 Office Phone: 212-998-6337. E-mail: david.garland@nyu.edu.

GARLAND, ELSIE M., counselor; BA in Human Studies, Marylhurst U., Oreg., 1991; MA in Counseling Psychology, Lewis and Clark Grad. Sch., Portland, 1995. Lic. profl. counselor, therapist. Instructional asst. Beaverton Sch. Dist., Oreg., 1981—92; juvenile ct. counselor Multnomah County Dist. Ct. Judge, Portland, 1992—. Mem.: Oreg. Counseling Assn.

GARLAND, GLORIA JEAN, lawyer; d. James Conrad and Edith Robinson Garland; m. Bruce Byers, Sept. 2, 1990. BS, U. Colo., Boulder, 1977, BA magna cum laude, 1977, JD, 1982; LLM cum laude, Free U. of Brussels, 1986. Bar: Calif. 1982. Rule of law advisor US AID, Bratislava, Slovakia, 1994—96; program dir. Internat. Ctr. for Not-for-Profit Law, Budapest, Hungary, 1997—2000; legal dir. European Roma Rights Ctr., 2000—03; cons. Coun. of Europe, Strasbourg, France, 2003—; sr. rule of law advisor US AID, Washington, 2006—. Adj. prof. Ctrl. European U., Budapest, 1998—2001. Contbg. author (book) The State of Roma Rights and Identity, 2005. Human rights del. Guatemala Human Rights Commn., Washington, 2005; dir. Women in Internat. Trade, San Francisco, 1991—93, Alameda County Legal Aid Soc., Oakland, Calif., 1991—93. Recipient Wiley Manuel Pro Bono Services award, State Bar Calif., 1992, 1993, 1994. Mem.: World Affairs Coun., Phi Delta Phi, Kappa Tau Alpha, Phi Beta Kappa. Democrat. Office: US Agency for internat Devel 1300 Pennsylvania Ave NW Washington DC 20523 Home Phone: 510-499-6413; Office Phone: 202-712-5346. Business E-Mail: ggarland@usaid.gov.

GARLAND, JAMES C., retired academic administrator; BA in Physics, Princeton U., 1964; D in Solid State Physics, Cornell U., 1969; postgrad., Cambridge U., 1969-70. Asst. prof. physics Ohio State U., 1970-75, assoc. prof. physics, 1975-80, prof., 1980-96, chair dept. physics; pres. Miami U., Oxford, Ohio, 1996—2006. Acting v.p. for rsch. and grad. studies Ohio State U., dir. materials rsch. lab., 1986-90; pres., bd. dirs. Ohio State U. Rsch. Found., 1982-83; First Fin. Bancorp; First Nat. Bank of SW Ohio. Contbr. articles to profl. jours. Recipient numerous rsch. grants; postdoctoral fellowship NSF. Fellow Am. Phys. Soc. E-mail: w8zr@arrl.net.

GARLAND, LARETTA MATTHEWS, psychologist, nursing educator; b. Jacksonville, Fla. d. Wilburn L. and Clyde-Marian (Chamberlin) Matthews; m. John B. Garland, Mar. 2, 1946; children: John Barnard, Brien Freeling, Amy-Gwin. Diploma, Fla. State Sch. Nursing, 1942; BSN, Emory U., 1950; MA, 1953; BA in Edn., U. Fla., 1951; cert. cardiovascular nurse specialty, Tex. Med. Ctr., 1965; EdD, U. Ga., 1975; postgrad. in counseling and guidance, Ga. State U., 1969; grad. cert. in gerontology, 1981. Cert. nat. counselor. Office and staff nurse, Lakeland, Fla., 1942, 45; nurse ARC, Buffalo, 1956; asst. prof. nursing Med. Coll. Ga., 1965-67; instr. Emory U., 1952-54, assoc. prof., 1967-71, prof., 1972-86, asst. to dean, prof. emeritus, 1987—. Ednl. psychologist, dir. gerontol. nurse practitioner program, 1978-80, asst. to dean, 1983-86. Author: (with Carol Bush) Coping Behavior and Nursing, 1982; contbr. articles to profl. jours. With Nurse Corps, U.S. Army, 1942-45. Decorated 2 Bronze Stars; recipient Outstanding Tchg. award Emory U. Sch. Nursing Grad. Srs., 1977, Appreciation award So. Region Constituent Leagues, Nat. League for Nursing award, 1987, Mabel Korsell award of appreciation Ga. League Nursing, 1987, Spl. Recognition award Ga. Nurses Assn., 1988, 90, Nurse of Yr. award, 1992, Appreciation award Ga. Assn. Nursing Students, 1990, Van de Vrede award Ga. League Nursing, 1993; HEW fellow, 1967-68. Mem. APA, AACD, ANA, Ga. Assn. Nursing Students (hon.), Nat. League Nursing, Bs. and Profl. Women, China Burma India VA Assn. (mem. nat. bd. 1993—), 14th Air Force Asssn. (Flying Tigers), Hump Pilots Assn., Ormond Beach Womens Club, Ormond Beach Hist. Trust, Nat. Assn. Women Vet. (steering com.), Women in Mil. Svc. Meml. Found. (charter), ARC Nurses, Panhellenic Assn., Hist. Trust, Alpha Chi Omega, Sigma Theta Tau, Kappa Delta Pi, Alpha Kappa Delta, Omicron Delta Kappa. Office: Emory U Nell Hodgson Woodruff Sch Atlanta GA 30322-0001 Office Phone: 386-677-9466.

GARLAND, MERRICK BRIAN, federal judge; AB summa cum laude, Harvard U., 1974, JD magna cum laude, 1977. Bar: DC 1979, US Dist. Ct. DC 1980, US Ct. Appeals (DC and 9th cirs.) 1980, US Ct. Appeals (4th cir.) 1983, US Ct. Appeals (10th cir.) 1996, US Supreme Ct. 1983. Law clk. to Hon. Henry J. Friendly US Ct. Appeals (2nd cir.), NYC, 1977—78; law clk. to Justice William J. Brennan Jr. US Supreme Ct., Washington, 1978—79; spl. asst. to atty. gen. US Dept. Justice, Washington, 1979—81, assoc. ind. counsel, 1987—88, asst. U.S. atty., 1989—92, dep. asst. atty. gen., criminal divsn., 1993—94, prin. assoc. dep. atty. gen., 1994—97; judge US Ct. Appeals (DC cir.), Washington, 1997—; from assoc. to ptnr. Arnold & Porter, Washington, 1981—89, ptnr., 1992—93. Lectr. Harvard U. Law Sch., 1985—86; mem. com. on jud. br. US Jud. Conf. Author: Deregulation and Judicial Review, Harvard Law Review, 1985, Antitrust and State Action, Yale Law Jour., 1987, Antitrust and Federalism, Yale Law Jour., 1987. Mem. bd. overseers Harvard U. Mem.: Am. Law Inst., Phi Beta Kappa. Office: US Court of Appeals 333 Constitution Ave NW Washington DC 20001-2866

GARLAND, RICHARD ROGER, lawyer; b. Princeton, Ill., Aug. 20, 1958; s. Louis Roger and Irene Marie (Tonozzi) Garland. BA in Polit. Sci. summa cum laude, U. South Fla., Tampa, 1979; JD with honors, U. Fla., Gainesville, 1982. Bar: Fla. 1982, US Dist. Ct. (mid. dist.) Fla. 1983, US Ct. Appeals (11th cir.) 1987, US Supreme Ct. 1988, US Ct. Appeals (fed. cir.) 1995, Fla. (cert. in appellate practice) 1995. Instr., supr. appellate advocacy U. Fla., Gainesville, 1981-82; assoc. Dickinson, O'Riorden, Gibbons, Quale, Shields & Carlton, Venice, Fla., 1983-85, Sarasota, Fla., 1986-90; ptnr., sr. atty. Dickinson & Gibbons, Sarasota, Fla., 1991—. Mem. adv. bd. Sarasota County Libr., 1999—2001; pres. parish coun. San Pedro Cath. Ch., Nort Port, Fla., 1986—92. Mem.: ABA, Sarasota County Bar Assn. (editor newsletter 1991—93, bd. dirs. 1994—95, treas. 1996—97, sec. 1996—97, v.p. 1999—99, pres.-elect 1999—2000, pres. 2000—01), Fla. Bar Assn., U. S. Fla. Alumni Assn., Sarasota County Gator Club (bd. dirs. 2001—07, v.p. 2002—03, 2006—07), Judge John M. Scheb Am. Inn of Ct. (treas. 1998—99, counselor 1999—2000, pres.-elect 2000—01, pres. 2001—02, master historian 2004—), Pi Sigma Alpha, Phi Kappa Phi. Democrat. Roman Catholic. Office: 401 N Cattlemen Rd Ste 300 Sarasota FL 34232 Office Phone: 941-366-4680. Business E-Mail: rgarland@dglawyers.com.

GARLAND, WILLIAM JAMES, nuclear engineer, educator; b. St. John's, Nfld., Can., July 26, 1948; B in Engring. Physics, McMaster U., Hamilton, Ont., Can., 1970, M in Engring. Physics, 1971, PhD in Chem. Engring., 1975. Registered profl. engr., Ont. Design engr. Ont. Hydro, Toronto, Canada, 1975-79; design specialist Atomic Energy of Can. Ltd., Mississauga, Ont., 1979-83; assoc. prof. McMaster U., 1983-97, chmn. dept. engring. physics, 1988-94, prof., 1997—; dir. McMaster Nuclear Reactor, 1994-95; acad. dir. CANTEACH, 2000—; program dr. UNENE, 2004—06, exec. dir., 2006—. Cons. System Analytics, Burlington, Ont., 1982—. Mem. Am. Nuclear Soc., Can. Nuclear Soc., Assn. Profl. Engrs. Ont. Office: McMaster U Dept Engring Physics 1280 Main St W Hamilton ON Canada L8S 4L7 Office Phone: 905-525-9140 ext. 24925. Business E-Mail: garlandw@mcmaster.ca.

GARLICK, MICHAEL, lawyer, franchise consultant; b. NYC, Oct. 20, 1944; s. Nathan S. and Gertrude (Finkel) G.; m. Judith Ann Schaufeld, May 12, 1977; children: Nathan S., Max Aaron, Jacob Abraham. BA, Lehigh U., 1966; JD, NYU, 1969. Bar: NY 1970, Fla. 1971, Calif. 1973, DC 1974, Tex. 1995, Colo. 1995, US Dist. Ct. (so. dist.) Fla. Gen. counsel Internat. House of Pancakes Fla., Miami, 1970-74, cons., 1983—; sr. ptnr. Garlick, Cohn, Darrow & Hollander, Miami, 1974-79; gen. counsel Internat. Adv. Group, Inc., Miami, 1980—; Editor Lawletter, 1981-83. Served with US Army, 1969. Mem. Forum Com. on Franchising, ABA, Dade County Bar Assn. North Miami Beach Karate (pres. 1970-80), Tai Chi Chaun Assn. (pres. 1983—), Phi Beta Kappa, Beta Alpha Psi. Office: 1515 N Federal Hwy Boca Raton FL 33432-1911 Office Phone: 808-528-2575. E-mail: lawson@aloha.com.

GARLIKOV, PATRICIA MOODIE, education educator; b. Mt. Vernon, Ill., Jan. 25, 1951; d. Stanley Thompson Moodie and Thelma Johanson Moodie; m. Richard Garlikov, July 1, 1975; children: Margaret, Lydia. BA, Birmingham-So. Coll., 1972; MAE, U. Ala., Birmingham, 1974, PhD, 1990. Cert. elem. tchr., early childhood edn. tchr., Ala. Tchr. kindergarten, 1st and 2d grades Jefferson County Schs., Birmingham, 1972-88; kindergarten tchr. Hoover (Ala.) City Schs., 1988-92; asst. prof. early childhood edn. Troy State U., Dothan, Ala., 1992-98; exceptional edn. supr. Jefferson County Bd. Edn., 1998-2000, reading specialist, 2000—03; coord. reading first Bessemer City Schs., Ala., 2003—05, coord. prof. devel. fed. programs, 2005—. Cons. Brookwood Early Childhood Ctr., Mountain Brook, Ala., 1992—; bd. dirs. Children's Fresh Air Farm, Birmingham, 1980-85, 90-93; adj. asst. prof. early childhood edn. Birmingham-So. Coll., 2000-01; grant writer Bessemer City Even Start, 2005— REading First, 2004—. Author articles. Troop leader Cahaba coun. Girl Scouts U.S., Birmingham, 1990-2000. Named to Outstanding Young Women of Am., 1983. Mem. Am. Assn. Colls. for Tchr. Edn., Over the Mountain Reading Coun. (charter, pres. 1976, 92), Ala. Reading Coun., Internat. Reading Assn., Am. Ednl. Rsch. Assn., Nat. Coun. Tchrs. of English, Bessemer Reading Coun., Phi Delta Kappa, Kappa Delta Pi. Presbyterian. Avocations: sewing, reading, ice skating, hiking, camping. Office: Bessemer City Schs 1621 5th Ave North Bessemer AL 35020 Business E-Mail: pgarlikov@bessk12.org.

GARLOUGH, WILLIAM GLENN, marketing executive; b. Syracuse, NY, Mar. 27, 1924; s. Henry James and Gladys (Killam) Garlough; m. Charlotte M. Tanzer, June 15, 1947; children: Jennifer, William, Robert. BEE, Clarkson U., 1949. With Knowlton Bros., Watertown, NY, 1949—67, mgr. mfg. svcs., 1966—67; v.p. planning, equipment systems div. Vare Corp., Englewood Cliffs, NJ, 1967—69; mgr. mktg. Valley Mould divsn. Microdot Inc., Hubbard, Ohio, 1969—79, dir. corp. devel., 1977—78; v.p. corp. devel. Am. Bldg. Maintenance Industries, San Francisco, 1979—83; pres. The Change Agts. Inc., Walnut Creek, Calif., 1983—2005, Holland, Mich., 2005—. Bd. dirs. My Chef Inc.; mem. citizens adv. com. Watertown Bd. Edn., 1957. Ruling elder Presbyn. Ch.; bd. dirs. Watertown Cmty. Chest, 1958—61. With USMCR, 1942—46. Mem.: TAPPI, Assn. Corp. Growth (pres. San Francisco chpt. 1984—85, v.p. chpts. west 1985—88), Am. Mktg. Assn., Internat. Sanitary Supply Assn., Bldg. Svc. Contractors Assn., Inst. Mgmt. Cons. (cert.), Am. Mgmt. Assn., Clarkson Alumni Assn. (Watertown sect. pres. 1955), Am. Contract Bridge League (life master), No. N.Y. Transp. Club, No. N.Y. Contract Club (pres. 1959), Marine's Meml. Club, Mensa, Lincoln League (pres. 1958), Tau Beta Pi. Office: The Change Agts LLC Ste 402 145 Columbia Ave Holland MI 49423-2978 Home Phone: 616-392-5064; Office Phone: 616-886-7370.

GARMAN, DAVID KLINE, former federal agency administrator; b. Greensboro, NC, May 29, 1957; s. Jack Donald and Jane (Holtzclaw) G. BA in Pub. Policy, Duke U., 1979; MS in Environ. Scis., Johns Hopkins U., 1998. Legis. aide to Senator Richard Stone US Senate, Washington, 1980-81, legis. asst. to Senator Frank Murkowski, 1981-85, chief of adminstrn., exec. asst., 1986-90, profl. staff mem. intelligence com., 1991-92, spl. projects dir. to Senator Frank Murkowski, 1993-94, profl. staff subcom. energy R&D, 1995—2001; asst. sec. for energy efficiency & renewable energy US Dept. Energy, Washington, 2001—05, acting under sec. energy, sci. & the environment, 2004—05, under sec for energy, sci. & the environment, 2005—07. Republican.*

GARMAN, RAY FILLMORE, occupational physician, director; s. Wynona Hudson Garman; m. Eugenie (Gigi) Virginia Moravec, Aug. 16, 1958; children: Ray Fillmore III, Scott Clayton, Andrew Seitz. AB, Johns Hopkins U., Balt., 1957; MD, George Wash. U., Washington, DC, 1961; MPH, Med Coll. Wis., Milw., 1995. Cert. in internal medicine U. Penna Grad. Sch. Medicine, Phila., 1962, Am. Bd. Internal Medicine, 1968, in pulmonary diseasese Am. Bd. Internal Medicine, 1974, in occupl. medicine Am. Bd. Preventive Medicine, 1996. Pulmonary medicine physician Guthrie Clinc/Robert Packer Hosp., Sayre, Pa., 1972—81, chief pulmonary medicine, 1981—90, med. dir., 1991—95; chief occupl. medicine and environ. health Lexington Clinic, Ky., 1995—99; med. dir. Gen. Electric Appliance Divsn., Bloomington, Ind., 1999—2000; clincal med. dir. Toyota Motor Mfg., Georgetown, Ky., 2000—04; assoc. prof., dir. occupl. med. training U. Ky., Lexington, 2004—. Sr. aviation med. examiner FAA, Lexington, 1977—; pres. Bradford County Med. Soc., Sayre, Pa., 1979—80; instr. quality process Quality Coll. (Crosby), Winter Park, Fla., 1989—90. Active Lexington Children's Mus., 1995—99; treas. Lex-Fayette Urban County Airport Bd., Lexington, 2003, sec., 2002, chmn., 2004—05; vice chair-med. Lexington Arts & Cultural Coun., 2000—04; pres. Lexington Opera Soc., 2005—, bd. dirs.; pres. Lexington Kennel Club, 2002—05; survey chair Lexington Forum, 1997—2005; bd. dirs. Planned Parenthood of the Bluegrass, 2005—, Aviation Mus. Ky., 2006—. Capt. USAF, 1963—66, Brig Gen. Res., mobilization asst. to surgeon AF material command USAF, chief flight surgeon USAF. Decorated Golden Cross of Royal Order of Phoenix King of Greece, Legion of Merit USAF. Mem.: Am. Coll. Physician Exec., Jefferson Club (Louisville), Lexington Club, Lafayette Club (membership chmn. 1999—99). Home: 1214 Richmond Rd Lexington KY 40502-1614 Office: Univ Ky Coll Pub Health 200 Washington Ave Lexington KY 40536 Home Phone: 859-268-9899; Office Phone: 859-257-5166. Business E-Mail: ray.garman@uky.edu.

GARMAN, RITA B., state supreme court justice; b. Aurora, Ill., Nov. 19, 1943; children: Sara Ellen, Andrew Gil. BS in Econs., U. Ill., 1965; JD with distinction, U. Iowa, 1968. Asst. state atty. Vermilion County, 1969—73; pvt. practice Sebat, Swanson, Banks, Lessen & Garman, 1973; assoc. cir. judge, 1974—86; cir. judge Fifth Jud. Cir., 1986—95, presiding cir. judge, 1987—95; judge Fourth Dist. Appellate Ct., 1996—2001; justice Ill. Supreme Ct., 2001—. Mem.: Ill. Judge's Assn., Vermilion County Bar Assn., Iowa Bar Assn., Ill. State Bar Assn. Office: Ill Supreme Ct 160 N LaSalle St Chicago IL 60601*

GARMANY, CATHARINE DOREMUS, astronomer; b. NYC, Mar. 6, 1946; d. Edwin and Janet (MacMaster) Doremus; children: Richard, Jeffrey. BS, Ind. U., 1966; MS, U. Va., 1968, PhD, 1971. Rsch. assoc. U. Va., Charlottesville, 1971-73; rsch. assoc. Joint Inst. for Lab Astrophys. U. Colo., Boulder, 1977-84, sr. rsch. assoc. Joint Inst. for Lab Astrophys., 1984-2000; dir. Fiske Planetarium, 1991-2000; dir. astronomy Astronomy, Oracle, Ariz., 2000—03, Nat. Optical Astronomy Observatory, 2004—. Contbr. articles to profl. jours. Recipient Annie J. Cannon award AAUW, AAS, 1976; grantee NASA, NSF. E-mail: garmany@noao.edu.

GARMEL, MARION BESS SIMON, retired arts journalist; b. El Paso, Tex., Oct. 15, 1936; d. Marcus and Frieda (Alfman) Simon; m. Raymond Lewis Garmel, Nov. 28, 1965 (dec. Feb. 1986); 1 child, Cynthia Rogers; 1 stepchild, Christine Blum. Student, U. Tex., El Paso, 1954-55; BJ, U. Tex., Austin, 1958. Exec. sec. Nat. Student Assn., Phila., 1958-59, pub. rels. dir., 1960-61; sec. World Assembly Youth, Paris, Brussels, 1959-60; dictationist Wall Street Jour., Washington, 1961; libr., staff writer Nat. Observer, Silver Spring, Md., 1961-70; art critic Indpls. News, 1971-91, editor Free Time sect., 1975-91, critic radio and TV, 1991-95; theater critic Indpls. Star and News, 1995-99, Indpls. Star, 1999—2002, ret., 2002. Mem. Nat. Fedn. Press Women (1st Place Critics award 1974), Ind. Soc. Profl. Journalists (1st place criticism 2002), Hadassah Women's Zionist Orgn. Am. (life), Woman's Press Club Ind. (1st Place Critics award 1995, 2002). Jewish. Avocations: tennis, bridge. Home: 226 E 45th St Indianapolis IN 46205-1712 E-mail: mgarmel@earthlink.net.

GARMENT, LEONARD, lawyer, author; b. Bklyn., May 11, 1924; s. John and Jennie Eckert G.; m. Grace Albert Garment, June 20, 1951 (dec. 1976); children: Ann Rebecca, Sara, Paul; m. Suzanne Rose Weaver, Jan. 1, 1980. LLB, Bklyn. Law Sch., 1949. Mem. Mudge Stern Williams & Tucker, NYC, 1949-69; counsel, asst. Pres. Richard Nixon, Washington, 1969-74; asst. Pres. Gerald Ford, Washington, 1974; counselor UN amb. Daniel P. Moynihan & William Scranton, NYC, 1975-77; U.S. rep. Commn. on Human Rights of UN Econ. and Social Coun., NYC, 1975-77; mem. Dickstein Shapiro Morin & Oshinsky, Washington, 1980-93, Mudge Rose Guthrie Alexander & Ferdon, Washington, 1993-95; of counsel Verner Liipfert Bernhard McPherson & Hand, Washington, 1998—. Author: In Search of Deep Throat: The Greatest Political Mystery of our Time, 2000, Crazy Rhythm: My Journey from Brooklyn, Jazz, and Wall Street to Nixon's White House, Watergate and Beyond., 1997. Trustee, pres. Jazz Mus. in Harlem, N.Y., 2000—; co-dir. The Willis Conover Jazz Preservation Found., Inc., Washington, 1996—; mem. Corp. of Yaddo, Saratoga Springs, 1990—. Pvt. U.S. Army, 1944. Recipient Nat. Medal of Arts, Nat. Endowment for the Arts, 2005. Mem.: The Century Assn., NY Bar Assn., DC Bar Assn., ABA. Jewish. Avocation: musician. Office: Jazz Museum in Harlem 104 E 126th St New York NY 10035 Office Phone: 212-348-8300. E-mail: lgarment@earthlink.net.

GARN, SUSAN LYNN, art educator; b. Astoria, Oreg., July 12, 1948; d. Everett Leslie and Jeanne Esther (Linquist) G. BA in Art, U. Nev., Reno, 1970; MEd in Ednl. Adminstrn. and Higher Edn., U. Nev., Las Vegas, 1990. Tchr. art Desert Sands Unified Sch. Dist., Indio, Calif., 1973-74; art. resource tchr. Trinity County Schs., Weaverville, Calif., 1974-75; multi-subject tchr., primarily in visual arts Clark County Sch. Dist., Las Vegas, 1975-80, 87—; tchr. English, reading Jordan Sch. Dist., Sandy, Utah, 1982-84; lead community sch coord. Lincoln County Sch. Dist., Newport, Oreg., 1984-87. Sole propr. Sue Garn and Kids Art, Las Vegas, 1988-98; presenter at profl. confs.; long term substitute tchr. Chemawa Indian Sch., Salem, Oreg., 1984. Work displayed at Educators as Artists exhibit, 1990, 92-93, 2001-07 Bd. dirs. Las Vegas Indian Ctr., 1996-99; rep. Native Am. Womens Assn., 2007. Named Tchr. of Yr. Nev. State PTA, 1990, Excellence in Edn., CCSD, 1991, Nev. Art Educator of Yr., 1992, South West Region Disting. Star, CCSD, 2004. Mem. Art Educators So. Nev., Nat. Art Edn. Assn. (Pacific region v.p. 1997-2000), Art Educators Nev. Avocations: german short haired pointer, weimaraner wirehaired terrier, travel, movies, art. Home: 3709 El Jardin Ave Las Vegas NV 89102-3821 Office: Biltmore Continuation HS 801 Veterans Meml Dr Las Vegas NV 89101 Office Phone: 702-799-7880 ext 3001. Personal E-mail: sgarninlv@cox.net.

GARNEAU-TSODIKOVA, SYLVIE, chemistry professor; b. Vanier, Quebec, Canada, July 8, 1973; d. Michelle Boulet and Jean Garneau; m. Oleg Vyacheslav Tsodikov, June 3, 2005. PhD, U. Alta., Edmonton, Can., 2003. Fellow Harvard Med. Sch., Boston, 2003—06; John G. Searle asst. prof. med. chemistry U. Mich., Ann Arbor, 2006—. Contbr. articles to profl. jours. Mem.: Chem. Inst. Can., Am. Chem. Soc. Achievements include research in drug discovery by using techniques from the fields of organic chemistry, molecular biology, mechanistic enzymology, and biochemistry. Office: Univ Mich 210 Washtenaw Ave Rm 4437 Ann Arbor MI 48109 Office Phone: 734-615-2736. Office Fax: 734-615-2251. Business E-Mail: sylviegt@umich.edu.

GARNER, ALBERT HEADDEN, investment banker; b. Memphis, Dec. 17, 1955; s. Jesse B. Jr. and Noella (Headden) Garner; children: Cyrus Dalton, Shelby Harris, Pleasant Noel. BS in Engring., Princeton U., 1977. Assoc. Devel. and Resources Corp., NYC, 1977-79, Lazard Freres & Co., NYC, 1979-83, v.p., 1984-88; gen. ptnr. Lazard Freres & Co. LLC, NYC, 1989-95, mng. dir., 1995—. Elder 1st Presbyn. Ch., NYC; vice chair Prospect Park Alliance. Home: 1510 Albemarle Rd Brooklyn NY 11226-4506 Office: Lazard Freres & Co LLC 30 Rockefeller Plz Fl 59 New York NY 10112-5900 Business E-Mail: al.garner@lazard.com.

GARNER, ALGEAN, II, healthcare company administrator, consultant; s. Algean and Charmaine Garner. BA in Psychology summa cum laude, Shaw U., 1993; PsyD, Ill. Sch. Profl. Psychology, 2001. Lic. clin. psychologist Ill. Psychology intern Houston Ind. Sch. Dist., 1997—98; assessment coord. Shelia Jenkins and Assocs., Houston, 1998—2000; postdoc. fellow ADAPT Counseling, Houston, 2000—02; dir. comprehensive svcs. Near North Health Svc. Corp., Chgo., 2002—06; asst. dir. health and human svcs. Village of Hoffman Estates, Ill., 2006—, dir. tng. Ill., 2006—. Bd. dirs. Houston Assn. Marriage and Family Therapists, 2001—02; presenter in field. Mem. aux. bd. Childrens Place Assn., 2005—. Mem.: APA. Avocations: cooking, health and fitness. Home Phone: 773-960-3859. Personal E-mail: agarnerii@sbcglobal.net.

GARNER, BETH L., music educator; b. Monticello, NY, Sept. 6, 1958; d. Jack R. Leshner and Florence Miller; m. David Garner, Oct. 5, 1991; children: Emily, Sarah. MusB, Crane Sch. Music, Potsdam, NY, 1980; MusM, Manhattan Sch. Music, NYC, 1982. Cert. Orff level I. Adminstrv. asst. Manhattan Sch. Music, NYC, 1982—84; tchr. music and dance accompanist the Chapin Sch., 1984—88; tchr. music Hicksville Pub. schs., 1988—. Pianist Mary Kane and Dancers, NYC, 1980—84, Trio Dolce, 1980—84, Musique du Chambre, 1984—86. Recipient Founders Day honors, Woodland Sch., Hicksville, N.Y., 1994, 2006, Scholars Dinner honors, 2003. Mem.: Lescheti Assn., Orff Schulwerk Assn., Behre Piano Assn., Nassau Music Educators Assn., PTA (hon.). Office: Hicksville Pub Schs Woodland Elem Sch Ketchams Rd Hicksville NY 11801-2099 Office Phone: 516-733-6566.

GARNER, BRYAN ANDREW, law educator, consultant, writer; b. Lubbock, Tex., Nov. 17, 1958; s. Gary Thomas and Mariellen (Griffin) G.; m. Pan Anurugsa, May 26, 1984; children: Caroline Beatrix, Alexandra Bess. BA, U. Tex., 1980, JD, 1984; LLD (hon.), Thomas M. Cooley Law Sch., 2000. Bar: Tex. 1984, U.S. Ct. Appeals (5th cir.) 1985, U.S. Dist. Ct. (no. dist.) Tex. 1986. Law clk. to judge U.S. Ct. Appeals (5th cir.), Austin, Tex., 1984-85; assoc. Carrington, Coleman, Sloman & Blumenthal, Dallas, 1985-88; dir. Tex./Oxford Ctr. for Legal Lexicography U. Tex. Sch. Law, Austin, 1988-90; adj. prof. law So. Meth. U., Dallas, 1990—. Vis. assoc. prof. law U. Tex., 1988—90; pres. LawProse, Inc., 1990—; vis. scholar U. Salzburg, 1995, 98, U. Glasgow, 1996, U. Cambridge, England, 1997; chmn. plain-lang. com. State Bar Tex., 1989—95; lectr. in field; cons. in field. Author: A Dictionary of Modern Legal Usage, 1987, A Dictionary of Modern Legal Usage, 2d edit., 1995, The Elements of Legal Style, 1991, Guidelines for Drafting and Editing Court Rules, 1996, A Dictionary of Modern American Usage, 1998, Securities Disclosure in Plain English, 1999, The Winning Bried, 1999, Legal Writing in Plain English, 2001, The Redbook: A Manual on Legal Style, 2002; editor: Scribes Jour. Legal Writing, 1989—2000, Tex, Our Texas, 1984, Black's Law Dictionary, 1996, Black's Law Dictionary, 7th edit., 1999, A Handbook of Basic Law Terms, 1999; A Handbook of Business Law Terms, 1999; editor: A Handbook of Family Law Terms, 2001; mem. editl. bd.: Tex. Law Rev., 1984; contbr. articles to profl. jours. Recipient Henry C. Lind award, Assn. Reporters Judicial Decisions, 1994, Clarity award, State Bar Mich, 1997, Outstanding Young Tex. Ex. award, 1998. Fellow: Tex. Bar Found.; mem.: ABA, Tex. Bar Assn. (chmn. plain lang. com. 1990—), Am. Law Inst. (commn. on bylaws & coun. rules 1993—94), Scribes (exec. bd. 1990—2001, pres. 1997—98), Dictionary Soc. N.Am., Am. Dialect Soc., Philos. Soc. Tex., Friars (abbot 1981—84), Bent Tree Country Club, Phi Beta Kappa. Republican. Avocation: golf. Home: 8133 Inwood Rd Dallas TX 75209-3337

GARNER, CARLENE ANN, not-for-profit fundraiser, consultant; b. Dec. 17, 1945; d. Carl A. and Ruth E. (Mathison) Timblin; m. Adelbert L. Garner, Feb. 17, 1964; children: Bruce A., Brent A. BA, U. Puget Sound, 1983. Adminstrv. dir. Balletacoma, 1984-87; exec. dir. Tacoma Symphony, 1987-95; prin. New Horizon Cons., Tacoma, 1995-98; co-owner Stewardship Devel., 1998—. Cons. Wash. PAVE, Tacoma, 1983-84. Treas. Coalition for the Devel. of the Arts, 1992-94; pres. Wilson High Sch. PTA, Tacoma, 1983-85; chmn. Tacoma Sch. Vol. Adv. Bd., 1985-87; pres. Emmanuel Luth. Ch., Tacoma, 1984-86, chmn. future steering com., 1987-93; sec.-treas. Tacoma-Narrows Conf., 1987-98; vice chmn. Tacoma Luth. Home, 1996-98; pub. mem. Wash. State Bd. Pharmacy, 1993-98. Mem. N.W. Devel. Officers Assn. (chair Tacoma/Pierce County com. 1994-96), Jr. Women's Club Tacoma (pres. 1975-76, pres. Peninsula dist. 1984-86), Gen. Fedn. Women's Club-Wash. State (treas. 1988-90, 3d v.p. 1990-92, 2d v.p. 1992-94, 1st v.p. 1994-96, pres. 1996-98, Clubwoman of Yr. 1977, Outstanding FREE chmn. Gen. Fedn. 1982), Commencement Bay Woman's Club (pres. 1990-92), Gen. Fedn. of Women's Club (bd. dirs., chair nat. conv. 1995, state pres. 1996-98, chair cmty. improvement program 1998-2000, treas. 2000—02, rec. sec. 2002-04, 2d v.p. 2004-06, 1st v.p. 2006—). Lutheran.

GARNER, CHARLES WILLIAM, retired educational administration educator, consultant; b. Pine Grove Mills, Pa., Apr. 18, 1939; s. Adam Krumrine and Blanche Ella (Gearhart) G.; m. Karyl J. Packer, Sept. 8, 1962; children: Ronald Adam, Juliet Paige. Student, U.S. Navy Electronics Airborne Sonar Sch., 1959; BS in Bus. Edn., Pa. State U., 1965, MEd in Higher Edn. Adminstrn., 1968, EdD in Vocat. Indsl. Edn., 1974. Cert. govt. fin. mgr. Adminstrv. asst. dept. psychology Pa. State U., 1965-75; asst. prof., site adminstr. March AFB, Calif. for So. Ill. U., 1975-77; asst. prof., coordinator Ft. Knox Ctr.- U. Louisville, 1977-78; assoc. prof., acting vice dean Rutgers U., Camden, NJ, 1978-79, assoc. prof. urban edn., chmn. dept. edn. Univ. Coll. New Brunswick, NJ, 1978-81, assoc. prof. vocat. tech. edn. Grad. Sch. Edn., 1981—2006, chmn. dept. vocat. tech. edn., 1982-85, assoc. prof. edn. adminstrn., 1985—2006, exec. dir. Vocat. Edn. Resource Ctr., 1983-88, dir. continuing edn., 1987-89, program chair edn. adminstrn., 1990-96, prof. emeritus, 2006—; cons. CWG Assocs., McElhattan, Pa., 1989—. Cons. CWG Assocs., McElhattan, Pa., 1989—; pres. Penn State Auto Repair, Inc., Williamsport, 1997—2000. Author: Accounting and Budgeting in Public and Nonprofit Organizations: A Manager's Guide, 1991, Financial Management of School Districts in New Jersey: For School Leaders, 1996, Education Finance for School Leaders: Strategic Planning and Administration, 2004, Chinese trans., 2006, (with R. Garner) The Service Consultant: Working in an Automotive Facility 2005, (with R. Garner) Managing Automotive Businesses: Strategic Planning, Personnel, and Finance, 2006; contbr. articles to profl. jours.; co-editor: Occupational Edn. Forum, 1979-85; editl. reader Jour. Indsl. Tchr. Edn., 1981; prodr., host talk show pilot for pub. TV, 1979; producer, host: TV tape series Rutgers U.: Current Issues in Vocat. Edn., 1979; editor edn. sect. Pub. Budgeting and Fin. Mgmt., 1995. Bd. dir., treas. Cerebral Palsy League of Union County, N.J., 1996-99. With USN, 1959-62. Grantee N.J. Dept. Edn. Divsn. Vocat. Edn., 1978-88; grantee HEW, 1979-80. Mem.: DAV (life), Spl. Needs Pers. (exec. coun. 1980—81, pres. 1981—82), Non-Commd. Officers Assn. (life), Elks (exalted ruler 1972—73). Home: PO Box 456 Mc Elhattan PA 17748 Personal E-mail: kgarner@kcnet.org. *Our influence in life is determined by the good deeds we do rather than by the emotions that we feel.*

GARNER, DANIEL C., lawyer; b. Austin, Tex., Jan. 18, 1950; BS, Tex. A&M U., 1972; JD with high honors, Tex. Tech. U., 1975. Bar: Tex. 1975. Shareholder Geary, Stahl & Spencer, Dallas, Jenkens & Gilchrist, P.C., Dallas, 1991—, firm leader fin. services practice group. Topics editor: Tex. Tech. Law Review, 1974-75. Mem. ABA, Dallas Bar Assn., Tex. State Bar Assn., Tex. Assn. Bank Counsel. Office: Jenkens & Gilchrist PC 1445 Ross Ave Ste 3200 Dallas TX 75202-2799 Office Phone: 214-855-4794. Office Fax: 214-855-4300. Business E-Mail: dgarner@jenkens.com.

GARNER, FRADLEY HAMILTON, freelance/self-employed writer, editor; b. Potsdam, NY, June 20, 1926; s. L. Hamilton and Geneva Van Bergen Garner; children: Luke, Glen, Nicholas. Pregrad, 24th Corps U., Seoul Korea, 1946; BS in Psychology, St. Lawrence U., Canton, NY, 1950; MA in Cultural Anthropology, Colgate U., Hamilton, NY, 1970; postgrad., SUNY, Potsdam, 1950, Northwestern U., Evanston, Ill., 1951. Divsnl. pub. rels. mgr. Pfizer, Inc., NYC, 1955-60; freelance writer, editor, film/video narrator Denmark, 1960—. Author: Environment Denmark, 1972, Walt Disney's Donald Duck's Fritidsbok, 1976, Greenland: Arctic Denmark, 1977, Jakobshavn/Ilulissat: A Town in Greenland, 1977, Walt Disney's The Haunted Hotel, 1978; co-founder, editor Scoot mag., 1955; assoc. editor Family Health mag., 1969; internat. editor, columnist Ecology Today, 1971-72, Environment mag., 1973-77; editor: TMI World, 1988; chief translator, copy editor: Danish Music Review., 1994-95, Katalog, the Danish Jour. Photography and Video; appeared in film The Prince of Jutland, 1994; country editor, writer Insight Guide Denmark, 2000—; covered Denmark's dogsled patrol Sirius in No. Greenland for Internat. Edits. Reader's Digest; Nordic-Tanganyika project in Dar es Salaam, Tanzania for Scanorama mag.; humor columnist, Abroad Mag., 2004-06, internat. editor, Jersey Jazz, 2005—; contbr. numerous articles to profl. jours. and gen. mags.; narrator over 500 indsl., sci. and gen. documentary films and videos; bassist Amatorsymfonikerne (Copenhagen Symphony Orch.), 1995-2005, Gladsaxe Haydn Orch., 1998—, Lungby-Taarbaek Sumforiorkester, 2007—. Bd. dirs. HOF Internat. Edn. Program, 2000—. Named Denmark amateur Runner of Yr., (Aarets Eremitageløber), 1995. Mem. Fgn. Press Assn. in Denmark. Home: Ordruphøjvej 32 DK-2920 Charlottenlund Denmark Home Phone: 45-3964-2872; Office Phone: +45-3964-1315. Office Fax: +45-3964-1315. Personal E-mail: fradgar@get2net.dk.

GARNER, HARVEY LOUIS, computer scientist, consultant, engineering educator; b. Lake, Colo., Dec. 23, 1926; s. Homa and Violet (Thuelin) Garner; m. Yvonne Lillian King, Aug. 7, 1949; children: Susan Ann, Harvey Thomas. BS, U. Denver, 1949, MS, 1951; PhD, U. Mich., 1958. Engr. with devel. MIDAC and MIDSAC computers U. Mich., 1951-55, from instr. to assoc. prof. elec. engring., 1955—63, prof., 1963-70; dir. Info. Sys. Lab., 1960-64, Sys. Engring. Lab., 1964-66, acting chmn. dept. comm. scis., 1965-67, prof. computer and comm. scis., 1967-70; prof. elec. engring. Moore Sch. Elec. Engring., 1970-86, dir., 1970-76, Microelectronics and Computer Tech. Corp., Austin, 1984-88; cons. sys. design and computer arithmetic, 1988—. Gen. chmn. Islands Applications Conf., Tokyo, 1972, 1st Nat. Computer Conf. and Exhbn., 1973. Contbr. articles to profl. jours. With USNR, 1945—46. Fellow: IEEE; mem.: AAAS, Assn. Computing Machinery (apptd. nat. lectr. 1965), Sigma Xi, Sigma Pi Sigma, Eta Kappa Nu. Achievements include development of Garner's algorithm, 1958. Home and Office: 15 Delaware XingE Delaware OH 43015

GARNER, JAY MONTGOMERY, retired military officer; b. Arcadia, Fla., Apr. 15, 1938; s. James Harley and Consuello Adelaide (Pooser) G.; m. Mary Connie Kreigh, Dec 30, 1958; 1 child, Lori Lee Gibson. BA, Fla. State U., 1962; MA, Shippensburg U., 1983; attended, Air Defense Artillery Sch., Marine Corps. Command and Staff Coll., US Army War Coll., US Army Air Defense Sch., Ft. Bliss, Tex., 1962, Defense Lang. Inst., SW br., Ft. Bliss, 1966-67, Air Defense Artillery Officer Advanced Course, US Army Air Defense Sch., 1969, Vietnam Tng. Ctr. Fgn. Svc. Inst., Dept. State, Washington, 1970-71, Marine Corps. Command and Staff Coll., Quantico, Va., 1974-75, US Army War Coll. Carlisle Barracks, Pa., 1982-83. Commd. 2d lt. US Army, 1962, advanced through grades to lt. gen., 1994, ret., 1997, asst. platoon leader to platoon leader to exec. officer, Battery C, 3d Missile Battalion, 7th Artillery, US Army Europe, 1962-64, inactive Army Nat. Guard, 1964-65, ops. officer 53d Artillery Brigade Maxwell AFB, Ala., 1965-66, asst. subsector advisor, later dep. dist. sr. advisor adv. team 38, mil. assistance command Viet Nam Vietnam, 1967-68, comdr. Battery B, 5th Battalion, 7th Artillery, US Army Air Defense Commd. Franklin Lakes, NJ, 1968, chief, programs br., logistics divsn., office mil. assistance, US Army So. Command Ft. Amador, Panama, 1969-70, dist. sr. advisor, adv. team 36, military assistance commd. Vietnam, 1971-72, S-3, then plans, tng. officer, reserve component study, later S-3, 1st Battalion, 3d Air Defense Artillery, 101st Airborne Divsn. (Airmobile) Ft. Campbell, Ky., 1972-74, staff officer, firepower divsn., requirements directorate, later asst. exec. officer, office dept. chief staff ops. Washington, 1975-78, comdr. 1st Basic Combat Tng. Battalion, tng. and doctrine command, 1978-79, comdr. 2d Battalion, 59th Air Defense Artillery, 1st Armored Division, US Army Europe, 1979-81, comdr. 108th Air Defense Artillery Brigade, 32d Army Air Defense Command, US Army Europe, 1984-86, dir. force requirements (combat support systems) office of dep. chief of staff ops. and plans Washington, 1986-88, dep. commdg. gen. US Army Air Defense Artillery Ctr., asst. commandant US Army Air Defense Artillery Sch. Ft. Bliss, 1988-90, dep. commdg. gen. V Corps. US Army Europe, 7th Army, 1990-91, commdg. gen. joint task force BRAVO Northern Iraq, 1991, asst. dep. chief staff ops. and plans force devel. Office of Dep. Chief of Staff Ops. and Plans Washington, 1992-94; commdg. gen. U.S. Army Space and Strategic Def. Command, 1994-96; asst. vice chief of staff U.S. Army, 1996-97; dir. Office of Reconstruction and Humanitarian Assistance Coalition Provisional Authority, Baghdad, Iraq, 2003. Pres. SY Tech. (now SYColeman Corp.), 1997—2004; bd. dirs. Digital Fusion, Inc., 2005—. Decorated DSM with oak leaf cluster, Def. Superior Svc. medal with oak leaf cluster, Legion of Merit with 4 oak leaf clusters, Bronze Star, Air medal, Meritorious Svc. Medal, Joint Svc. Commendation Medal, Army Commendation Medal, Combat Infantryman Badge. Democrat. Episcopalian. Avocations: health, exercise.

GARNER, JENNIFER ANNE, actress; b. Houston, Apr. 17, 1972; d. Bill and Pat Garner; m. Scott Foley, Oct. 19, 2000 (div. Mar. 30, 2003); m. Ben Affleck, June 29, 2005; 1 child, Violet Anne. BFA, Dennison U., 1994. Actor: (TV miniseries) Danielle Steele's Zoya, 1995, Dead Man's Walk, 1996; (TV films) Harvest of Fire, 1996, The Player, 1997, Rose Hill, 1997, Aftershock: Earthquake in New York, 1999; (TV series) Swift Justice, 1996, Law & Order, 1996, Spin City, 1996, Fantasy Island, 1998, The Pretender, 1999, Significant Others, 1998, The Time of Your Life, 1999—2000, Alias, 2001—06 (Emmy nominee for outstanding lead actress in a drama, 2002, 2003, 2004, 2005, Golden Globe award for best actress in a television series, 2001, Saturn award for best actress in a television series, 2003, SAG award for outstanding performance in a drama series, 2005); (films) Deconstructing Harry, 1997, Washington Square, 1997, Mr. Magoo, 1997, In Harm's Way, 1997, Nineteen Ninety-Nine, 1998, Dude, Where's My Car, 2000, Pearl Harbor, 2001, Rennie's Landing, 2001, Catch Me if You Can, 2002, Daredevil, 2003, 13 Going On 30, 2004, Elektra, 2005, Catch and Release, 2006, (voice) Charlotte's Web, 2006. Recipient People's Choice award, favorite female TV star, 2006, People's Choice award, favorite female action star, 2006.*

GARNER, JIM D., state official, lawyer; b. Coffeyville, Kans., June 14, 1963; s. Wayne W. and Carol L. Garner. AA with honors, Coffeyville C.C., 1983; BA in History with distinction, U. Kans., 1985, JD, 1988. Bar: Kans. 1988, U.S. Dist. Ct. Kans. 1988, U.S. Ct. Appeals (10th cir.) 1990, U.S. Supreme Ct. 2003. Jud. clk. for Dale E. Saffels U.S. Dist. Judge, Kans., 1988-90; atty. Hall, Levy, Lively, DeVore, Belot and Bell, Coffeyville, 1990-92; pvt. practice Coffeyville, 1992—; mem. Kans. Ho. of Reps., 1991—2003, minority leader, 1999—2003; sec. Kans. Dept. Labor, 2003—. Bd. dirs. Nat. Assn. State Workforce Agys.; mem. Program for Emerging Polit. Leaders, Darden Sch. of Bus., U. Va., 1994, Bowhay Inst. for Legis. Leadership Devel., Coun. of State Govts., U. Wis., 1995. Active cmty. co-chair, City of Coffeyville's Youth Focus Task Force, 1998; adv. com. Youth and Bus. Tng. Program; bd. dirs. Hospice Care Inc., Coffeyville, 1993-97, Pioneer chpt. ARC, 1998—2003; mem. leadership Coffeyville Class of 1995; mem. legis. adv. bd. Dem. Leadership Coun., 1999-2002; mem. bd. govs. U. Kans. Law Sch., 2000-02. Mem. Kans. Bar Assn., Order of Coif, Phi Alpha Theta, Phi Kappa Phi, Lions, Rotary. Office: 114 W 9th St Coffeyville KS 67337-5810 Home: Po Box 1184 Lawrence KS 66044-8184 Business E-Mail: jim.garner@dol.ks.gov.

GARNER, MABLE TECOLA, health facility administrator; b. Sharon, Miss., June 11, 1931; d. Annie B. (Johnson) Garner; 1 child, Wendell Orson Siggers. BA, Fisk U., 1953; MD, Meharry Med. Coll., 1959; MTH, Springhill Coll., 1996. Diplomate Am. Bd. Clin. Pathology, 1967, Am. Bd. Anatomical Pathology, 1968. Intern Meharry Med. Coll., Nashville, asst. prof. pathology, 1968; resident in pathology Hubbard Hosp./Meharry Med. Coll., Nashville, 1963—66; sr. resident anataomny clin. and pathology VA Hosp., Nashville, 1966—67; USPHS spl. postdoctoral fellow dept. biochem. hypertension rsch. Case Western Res. U., Cleve., 1969—70; dir. health cons. Fayette St. Clinic Ltd., Shaw, Miss., 1979—. Mem.: Alpha Omega Alpha. Home and Office: PO Box 798 Shaw MS 38773-0798 Office Phone: 662-754-2314.

GARNER, MARGARET, construction executive; 1 child, Margarite. BA in Bus. and econ., U. Pittsburg, 1981. Property mgr. Pittsburgh's public housing authority; recruited Detroit housing commn.; founder, pres., CEO Broadway Consolidated Companies, Inc., 1999—. Pres. Fedn. of Women Contractors, 2004—. Named one of 25 Women to Watch, Crain's Chgo. Bus., 2007; recipient Black Contractors United Mentor/Protege, 2002, Minority Small Bus. Person of the Year Award, U.S. Small Bus. Adminstrn. for the State of Ill., 2006. Mem.: UN Commn. on the Status of Women. Achievements include being the first African Am. woman ever hired by Wal-Mart to build a store. Office: Broadway Consolidated Companies Inc 400 N Noble Chicago IL 60622 Office Phone: 312-491-0330. Office Fax: 312-491-0333.*

GARNER, MARK, communications executive; b. 1965; Affiliate sales exec. MTV Networks; co-founder satellite network, South Africa; v.p., Distbn. and Field Mktg. Lifetime Networks. Named one of 40 Executives Under 40, Multichannel News, 2006. Mem.: Nat. Assn. Minorities in Cable (bd. mem.), Nat. Assn. Multi-Ethnicity in Comm. (bd. mem.). Office: Lifetime Networks 309 W 49th St New York NY 10019 Office Phone: 212-424-7304. Office Fax: 212-957-4449. Business E-Mail: mgarner@lifetimetv.com.

GARNER, MELVIN C., lawyer; b. Phila., Feb. 9, 1941; BSEE, Drexel U., 1964; MSEE, NYU, 1968; JD, Bklyn. Law Sch., 1973. Bar: N.Y. 1974, U.S. Supreme Ct. 1977, U.S. Patent and Trademark Office. Prin., procurement and litig. patent, trademark, trade secret and copyright matters Darby & Darby, NYC. Sr. editor Bklyn. Law Review; bd. mem. Nat. Inventors Hall Fame, 2001—. Named one of Am. Top Black Lawyers, Black Enterprise Mag., 2003. Mem.: ABA, Am. Intellectual Property Law Assn. Edn. Found. (v.p. 2001—02, sec. 2002—03, trustee 2003—), Am. Intellectual Property Law Assn. (vice chmn. com. on elec. and computer law 1998—99, bd. dirs. 1999—2002, second v.p. 2002—03, first v.p. 2003—04, pres. 2005—06), N.Y. Intellectual Property Law Assn. (chmn. com. on trade secret law and practice 1990—96, bd. 1997—98, sec. 1998—2000, second v.p. 2000—01, first v.p. 2001—02, pres. elect 2002—03, pres. 2003—04), Assn. Bar City of N.Y., Eta Kappa Nu. Office: Darby & Darby 805 Third Ave New York NY 10022-7513 Office Phone: 212-527-7700. Office Fax: 212-527-7701. Business E-Mail: mgarner@darbylaw.com.

GARNER, ROBBY GLEN, software research executive, roboticist; Student, Floyd Coll., 1980-81, U. Ga., 1981-84, State U. West Ga., 1986-86, 96, Kennesaw State U., 1996-97. Clk., repair technician Garner's TV, Radio Shack Dealer, 1975-81; data entry clk. Star Mfg., 1985-86; adminstr. UNIX sys. Quality Ctrl. Lab. Henkel Chems., Cedartown, Ga., 1988-91; pres. Robitron Software Rsch., Inc., 1987—; staff roboticist FringeWare, Inc., 1995—. Developer, ptnr. Data Access Corp., Miami; presenter in field. Co-prodr., performer Poe Boy Jam 85; founding mem. Flux Oersted band; featured roboticist BBC MegaLab 98 Turing Test. Lt. col. USAF. Recipient Loebner prize Cambridge Ctr. for Behavioral Studies. Achievements include creation of FRED. Address: 223 Lawson Ave Cedartown GA 30125-2320 E-mail: robitron@fringeware.com.

GARNER, ROBERT EDWARD LEE, lawyer; b. Bowling Green, Ky., Sept. 26, 1946; s. Alto Luther and Katie Mae (Sanders) G.; m. Suzanne Marie Searles, Aug. 22, 1981; children: Jessica Marie, Abigail Lee. BA, U. Ala., Tuscaloosa, 1968; JD, Harvard U., 1971. Bar: Ga. 1971, U.S. Dist. Ct. (no. dist.) Ga. 1974, U.S. Ct. Appeals (5th cir.) 1974, U.S. Ct. Appeals (11th cir.) 1981, Ala. 1982, U.S. Ct. Appeals (4th cir.) 1991, S.C. 1992. Assoc. Gambrell, Russell & Forbes, Atlanta, 1972-76, ptnr., 1976-80, Haskell, Slaughter & Young and predecessors, Birmingham, Ala., 1981-88, mng. ptnr., 1986-87, of counsel, 1988-90; gen. counsel, sec. Builders Transport, Inc., 1988-90; ptnr. Nelson, Mullins, Riley & Scarborough, Atlanta and Columbia, SC, 1991-96; mem. Haskell Slaughter Young & Rediker, LLC, Birmingham, 1996—, mng. ptnr., 2000—02. 1st lt. JAGC, USAF, 1971-72. Mem. ABA (com. on fed. regulation of securities, subcom. on disclosure matters and continuous reporting, subcom. on securities registration, ad hoc com. on pub. co. info. practices), State Bar Ga., Ala. State Bar, Birmingham Bar, S.C. Bar, U. Ala. Alumni Assn., Harvard U. Alumni Assn., Am. Soc. Corp. Secs. (mem. tech. com.), Phi Alpha Theta, Pi Sigma Alpha. Republican. Home: 284 Kings Crest Ln Pelham AL 35124-2846 Office: Haskell Slaughter Young & Rediker LLC 2001 Park Pl North Ste 1400 Birmingham AL 35203-2618 Office Phone: 205-254-1417, 205-251-1000. Business E-Mail: relg@hsy.com.

GARNER, SCOTT, communications executive; b. 1970; Positions with Nickelodeon, Children's TV Workshop; dir. rsch. Cartoon Network; exec. dir., Planning and Scheduling Disney Channel, dir. rsch., sr. v.p., Programming. Named one of 40 Executives Under 40, Multichannel News, 2006. Office: Disney Channel Worldwide 500 S Buena Vista St Burbank CA 91521-6078 Office Phone: 818-560-1000. Office Fax: 818-560-1930.

GARNER, SHIRLEY NELSON, language educator; b. Waxahachie, Tex., Aug. 8, 1935; d. Cleo and Ruby D. Nelson; m. Frank L. Garner, Nov. 24, 1972; children: Hart Phillip, Celia Ann. AB magna cum laude, U. Tex., 1957; MA, Stanford U., 1966, PhD, 1972. Instr. Stanford (Calif.) U., 1964-65, instr., asst. to dir. fresh composition, 1967-70; asst. prof. U. Minn., Mpls., 1972-76, assoc. prof., 1976-86, assoc. mem. faculty Women's Studies, 1980—86, prof., 1986—, chair Women's Studies, 1989-90, dir. Ctr. Advanced Feminist Studies, 1990-94, chair English dept., 1994—2000, assoc. dean grad. sch., 2001—. Editor: (with Personal Narratives Collective) Interpreting Women's Lives: Feminist Theory and Personal Narratives, 1989, (with Madelon Sprengnether) Shakespearean Tragedy and Gender, 1995, Antifeminism in the Academy, 1996, (with VeVe Clark, Ketu Katrak, and Margaret Higonnet) Is Feminism Dead?, 2000; editor, contbg. author: (with Clare Kahane and Madelon Sprengnether) The (M)other Tongue: Essays in Feminist Psychoanalytic Interpretation, 1985; contbg. author: Bad Shakespeare: Revaluations of the Shakespeare Canon, 1988, Seduction and Theory: Readings of Gender, Representation and Rhetoric, 1989, Shakespeare's Personality, 1989, Novel Mothering, 1991, Feminism and Psychoanalysis, Feminism and Philosophy: Essential Readings in Theory, Reinterpretation and Application, 1992, The Intimate Critique: Autobiographical Literary Criticism, 1993; founder, mem. editl. bd. Hurricane Alice, 1983-95; mem. editl. bd. Signs, 1992-95; contbr. articles, revs. to profl. jours. Recipient Horace T. Morse-Amoco award, 1982, Pres.'s award for outstanding svc., 1999, Mullen/Spector/Truax Women's Leadership award, 2007; Phillips Petroleum Found. scholar, 1953-57; Woodrow Wilson fellow, 1959-60, Sorptimists' fellow, 1965-66, 66-67; grantee U. Minn. 1974-76, 81, 87-88, Bush Sabbatical, 1984-85, Office Internat. Edn., 1988, CLA, 1981, 84-90, UROP, 1991-92; named to U. Minn. Acad. Disting. Tchrs., 1999. Mem. MLA (co-chair Marriage and the Family in Shakespeare divsn., Shakespeare sect. 1979, chair 1980-82, chair/co-chair various seminars, symposia), Nat. Women's Studies Assn., Midwest Modern Lang. Assn. (sec. Shakespeare sect. 1972, chair 1973, nominations com. 1974-77, sec. Women and Lit. sect. 1978-79, chair 1980-81, nomination com. Women and Lit. sect. 1981-84), Shakespeare Assn. Office: U Minn English Dept 207 Church St SE Minneapolis MN 55455-0134 Office Phone: 612-625-4858. Business E-Mail: sngarner@umn.edu.

GARNER, STEPHEN TRENT, meteorologist; b. Bismarck, ND, Apr. 3, 1955; s. Robert Eugene and Almeta Greathouse Garner. PhD, MIT, Cambridge, Mass., 1985. Post-doctoral fellow Nat. Ctr. for Atmospheric Rsch., Boulder, Colo., 1985—86; post-doctoral fellow meteorology dept. U. Reading, England, 1987—89; post-doctoral fellow Atmospheric and Atmospheric Scis. Program Princeton U., NJ, 1990—92; rsch. meteorologist Geophys. Fluid Dynamics Lab., Princeton, 1992—. Contbr. articles to profl. jours. Avocation: volleyball. Office: Princeton U Geophysical Fluid Dynamics Lab PO Box 308 Princeton NJ 08542 Home Phone: 609-466-8536; Office Phone: 609-452-6543. Personal E-mail: s4ephen@aol.com. Business E-Mail: steve.garner@noaa.gov.

GARNER, STEVEN C., radiologist, emergency physician; m. Anne Garner; 2 children. Grad., Chgo. Med. Sch. Diplomate Am. Bd. Radiology, Am. Bd. Emergency Physicians, cert. aviation med. examiner. Chief med. officer St. Vincent Hosp. & Med. Ctr., NY; sr. v.p. St. Vincent Cath. Med. Ctrs.; intern Brookdale Med. Ctr., Bklyn.; resident Mt. Sinai Hosp.; asst. prof. radiology N.Y. Med. Coll. Cons. N.Y.P.D; cons. U.S. customs dept. N.Y. JFK Internat. Airport, pres. med. ctr. Host (TV series) Ask The Doctor; contbr. Fox News Channel; author: column in Bklyn. (N.Y.) Tablet. Fellow: Am. Acad. Emergency Physicians; mem.: Am. Coll. of Radiology (nat. emergency radiology com.), Am. Heart Assn. (edn. com., cert. fed. aviation med. examiner). Office: 88-25 153 Rd St Jamaica NY 11432 Business E-Mail: asgarner@optonline.net.

GARNETT, DOUGLAS ACREE, financial analyst, researcher; b. Caroline, Va., Aug. 11, 1928; s. James Richard Garnett and Mary Ella Acree; m. Natalie Rebecca Davis, Nov. 4, 1953; children: Michael Keith, Susan Jeanine Garnett-Rogers. Student, Bryan Coll., Dayton, Tenn., 1947—48; grad., Am. Inst. Banking, Richmond, Va., 1969. Check processing clk. Fed. Res. Bank, Richmond, Va., 1947—52, check processing supr., 1953—77, banking supr. dir., bond acct. analyst, 1978—87. Author, editor (book) Garnett Family: Ancestors and Descendants of Joseph B. Garnett, Sr., 2000. Avocation: gardening. Home: 5431 Claridge Dr Chesterfield VA 23832-7324 Office Phone: 804-276-0400.

GARNETT, KEVIN, professional basketball player; Basketball player Minn. Timberwolves, 1995—2007, Boston Celtics, 2007—. Named MVP, NBA All-star Game, 2003, NBA MVP, 2004; named to NBA All-Rookie 2nd Team, 1995—96, All-NBA 3rd Team, 1999, USA Basketball Sr. Men's Nat. team, 1999, All-NBA 1st team, 2000, All-NBA 2nd Team, 2001, 2002, 2005, 9 NBA All-star Games, NBA All-Defensive team, 2000—05; recipient Gold medal, US Men's Olympic Basketball team, 2000, Espy Award for Best NBA Player, 2004, J. Walter Kennedy Citizenship award, NBA, 2006. Achievements include 1st NBA player to receive 3 consecutive player of the month honors; led NBA in rebounds per game (12.8), 2007. Office: Boston Celtics 226 Causeway St 4th Fl Boston MA 02114*

GARNETT, STANLEY IREDALE, II, utilities executive, lawyer; b. Petersburg, Va., Aug. 11, 1943; s. Stanley Arthur and Edith (Keirstead) G.; m. Beverly Jackson; children: Matthew S.A., Andrew F.W., Christie, Alfred. BA, Colby Coll., 1965; MBA, U. Pa., 1967; JD, NYU, 1973. Bar: N.Y. 1974. Sr. fin. analyst Standard Oil Co. of N.J., NYC, 1967-70; assoc. Milbank, Tweed, Hadley & McCloy, NYC, 1973-81; v.p.-legal and regulatory Allegheny Power Sys., Inc., NYC, 1981-90, v.p. fin., 1990-94, sr. v.p. fin., 1994-95; sr. advisor Putnam, Hayes & Bartlett, 1996-97, 98-00; exec. v.p. Fla. Progress Corp., St. Petersburg, 1997-98; ptnr. PA Consulting Group, 2000—04; prin., owner Garnett Consulting Group, Inc., 2004—. Vice chmn. Episcopal Ch. Bldg. Fund. Joseph P. Wharton scholar, 1965-67. Mem. ABA, N.Y. State Bar Assn. Republican. Episcopalian. Home: 2504 Sunset Way Saint Petersburg Beach FL 33706-4127 Home Phone: 727-360-5073. Business E-Mail: stangarnett@aol.com.

GARNETTE, CHERYL PETTY, government agency administrator; BS in Math., U. Md., MA in Measurement and Stats. With Model Secondary Sch. for Deaf; dir. tech. edn. programs Office Innovation and Improvement U.S. Dept. Edn., Washington; rsch. assoc. Applied Mgmt. Scis., Silver Spring, Md. Comm. dir. Assn. for Ednl. Comm. and Tech. Editor: (Rsch. Notes column) Jour. Ednl. Computing Rsch. Office: US Dept Edn Rm 4W230 FB-6 400 Maryland Ave SW Washington DC 20202

GARNIER, JEAN-PIERRE, pharmaceutical executive; married; three children. PhD in Pharmacology, U. Louis Pasteur, France, 1972; MBA, Stanford U., 1974. Various positions to pres. U.S. Pharms. Products Divsn. Schering-Plough Corp., 1975-89, 89-90; pres. Smithkline Beecham, Phila., 1990-93, pres. N.Am. pharm., 1993—94, chmn. pharms., 1994—95, COO, 1995—2000, CEO, 2000—01, bd. dirs., 1992—2001; CEO GlaxoSmith-Kline, 2001—. Mem. bd. dirs. United Technologies Corp., Eisenhower Exchange Fellowships, Inc. Trustee Eisenhower Exch. Fellowships, Inc.; bd. dirs. Com. to Encourage Corp. Philanthropy; former bd. dirs. Phila. Mus. of Art, Mass. Eye and Ear Hosp., others. Decorated Chevalier de la Legion d'Honneur, 1997; recipient Communicator of Yr. award Internat. Assn. Bus. Communicators, 1993, Cancer Rsch. Inst. Oliver R. Grace award for Disting. Svc. in Advancing Cancer Rsch., 1997, Marco Polo award, 2001, Humanitarian award, Sabin Vaccine Inst., 2002; recipient Fulbright Association's Lifetime Achievement Medal. Mem. Am. Soc. French Legion of Honor, United Technologies Corp. (bd. dirs.), The Acad. of Natural Scis. (emeritus trustee), Am. Found. for Pharm. Edn. (past bd. dirs.), French/Am. C. of C., others. Avocations: tennis, ping pong/table tennis, squash, golf, wind surfing. Office: GlaxoSmithKline Box 7929 One Franklin Plz Philadelphia PA 19101-7929

GARNISS, JOAN BREWSTER, musician, educator; b. Bangor, Maine, Aug. 10, 1940; d. William Ayer Brewster and Constance Miriam (Witham) Page; adopted d. Woodrow Evans Page; m. Howard Freeman Garniss, Aug. 26, 1962; children: Gretchen, Jonathan. MusB, Boston U., 1962, MusM, 1991. cert. music tchr., Music Tchr. Nat. Assn. Pvt. practice, Dover-Foxcroft, Maine, 1954-58, Hingham, Mass., 1963-65, Waltham, Mass., 1974—. Frequent adjudicator/evaluator student events, Mass.; frequent adjudicator/evaluator, NH. Musician: (albums) En blanc et noir, 2001; accompanist Wintersauce Chorale, 1984—86, Duo Con Anima, 1987—, U. Mass., Lowell, 1988—. Co-founder, pres. Waltham Band Parents, 1979-82, Waltham Music Festival, 1994-97; pres. Friends Waltham Pub. Libr., 1980-83 (bd. dir. 1980-89, 1995—); trustee Waltham Pub. Libr., 1986—, co-chmn. fundraising com., 1995-96; dir. children's choir, All Saints Ch., 1963-66; vol. Boston Pub. Sch., 1969-73; active City Coun. Citizens Com. Transp., Waltham, 1977 Mass. Cultural Affairs Coun. grantee, 1988-89. Mem. UUA/MA N.E. Dist. (human rels. chmn. 1967-70), LWV (v.p. 1979-83, pres. 1983-85, sec. 1997-2003, bd. dir., 2003—, Outstanding Mem. award 1995), Music Tchrs. Nat. Assn.(rep. East Divsn. Cmty. Outreach 1995-97, Ind. Music Tchr. Forum oversight com. 1997-99), Mass. Music Tchrs. Assn. (v.p. 1987-91, pres.-elect 1991-93, pres. 1993-97, immediate past pres. 1997-99, Tchr. of Yr. 2007), New England Piano Tchr. Assn. (co-chmn. junior recitals com. 1982-88, student master class 1988-90, dir. 1988-90, chair Ensemble Festival, 2000-05), Mass. Libr. Trustees Assn., Lexington Music Club, Mu Phi Epsilon, Pi Kappa Lambda. Avocations: needlecrafts, travel, reading. Business E-Mail: jbgarnissstudio@aol.com.

GAROFALO, DONALD R., window manufacturing executive; b. St. Paul; Sales rep. Andersen Corp., Bayport, Minn., 1965—93, v.p. bus. planning and devel., 1993—95, sr. v.p., bus. planning and devel., 1995—96, exec. v.p., COO, 1996—98, pres., 1998—2002, CEO, 1998—. Bd. Capital City Partnership, St. Paul; bd. trustees Science Mus. of Minn.; exec. com. Courage Ctr.; bd. dir. Bayport Found. Office: Andersen Corp 100 4th Ave N Bayport MN 55003-1096

GAROFALO, DOUGLAS, architectural firm executive, educator; b. Schenectady, NY, 1958; BArch, U. Notre Dame, Ind., 1981; M, Yale U., New Haven, 1987. Prin. Garofalo Archs., Chgo. Assoc. prof. U. Ill. Chgo. Sch. Architecture. Facilitator design lab. Archeworks. Recipient Young Arch. award, Archtl. League NY, 1991; fellow, Am. Inst. Architecture, 2003; grantee Skidmore, Owings & Merrill Found. Traveling Fellowship, 1987. Fellow: AIA (Young Arch. award 1995, Design award 1992). Office: Garofalo Archs 3752 N Ashland Ave Chicago IL 60613 Office Phone: 773-975-2069. Office Fax: 773-975-2069. E-mail: doug@a-node.net.

GAROFALO, JANEANE, actress, comedienne; b. Newton, NJ, Sept. 28, 1964; d. Carmine Garofalo; m. Robert Cohen, Aug. 16, 1991 (separated). BA in History and Am. Studies, Providence Coll. Co-anchor Majority Report Air America Radio, 2004—. Actress (films) Late for Dinner, 1991, That's What Women Want, 1992, Armistead Maupin's Tales of the City, 1993, Suspicious, 1994, Reality Bites, 1994, Bye Bye Love, 1995, I Shot a Man in Vegas, 1995, Coldblooded, 1995, Now and Then, 1995, Sweethearts, 1996, The Truth About Cats & Dogs, 1996, The Cable Guy, 1996, Larger Than Life, 1996, HBO 1 Hour Special, 1997, Touch, 1997, Romy and Michele's High School Reunion, 1997, Cop Land, 1997, The MatchMaker, 1997, The Thin Pink Line, 1998, Half Baked, 1998, Thick as Thieves, 1998, Permanent Midnight, 1998, Dog Park, 1998, Clay Pigeons, 1998, Can't Stop Dancing, 1999, The Minus Man, 1999, 200 Cigarettes, 1999, Dogma, 1999, Mystery Men, 1999, The Bumblebee Flies Anyway, 1999, The Cherry Picker, 2000, Steal This Movie, 2000, The Independent, 2000, The Adventures of Rocky & Bullwinkle, 2000, Titan A.E., 2000, Wet Hot American Summer, 2001, The Search for John Gissing, 2001, The Laramie Project, 2002, Martin & Orloff, 2002, Big Trouble, 2002, Manhood, 2003, Ash Tuesday, 2003, Wonderland, 2003, Nobody Knows Anything!, 2003, Junebug and Hurricane, 2004, Jiminy Glick in Lalawood, 2004, Duane Hopwood, 2005, Stay, 2005, The Wild, 2006, (TV films) Slice o' Life, 2003, Nadine in Date Land, 2005, (TV appearances) The Ben Stiller Show, 1992—93, The Larry Sanders Show, 1992—97, Saturday Night Live, 1994—95, Comedy Product, 1995, Mr. Show with Bob and David: Fantastic Newness, 1996, Ellen, 1996, Seinfeld, 1996, Home Improvement, 1997, Law & Order, 1997, The Simpsons, 1998, Felicity, 1999, Mad About You, 1999, Jimmy Kimmel Live, 2003, The King of Queens, 2004, The West Wing, 2006, King of the Hill, 2003; co-author (with Ben Stiller): Feel This Book, 2000. Office: UTA Inc 9560 Wilshire Blvd Fl 5 Beverly Hills CA 90212-2401 also: The Majority Report Air America Radio 641 Sixth Ave 4th Floor New York NY 10011

GAROIAN, CHARLES RICHARD, artist, educator; b. Fresno, Calif., Nov. 7, 1943; s. Kurken Makhtesi and Satenig Suzanne (Bezdigian) G.; m. Sherrie Elyce Alexanian, Jan. 27, 1968; children: Jason Aram, Stephanie Tamar. BA in Visual Art, Calif. State U., Fresno, 1968, MA in Visual Art, 1969; PhD in Edn., Stanford U., 1984. Art instr. and art curriculum coord. Los Altos (Calif.) High Sch., 1969-86; vis. lectr. U. Wash., Seattle, summer 1977; edn. dir. Pa. State U., Palmer Mus. of Art, University Park, 1986-90, asst. dir., 1990-91; assoc. prof. art edn. Sch. Visual Arts, Pa. State U., University Park, 1991—; dir. Sch. Visual Arts Pa. State U., University Park, 1999—. Exhibits include San Francisco Mus. Modern Art, 1974, Charles Garoian, San Jose Mus. Art, 1975, Rites of Sculpture, Berkeley Mus. Art, 1976, New Adventures: Time and Space, Wash. State U., 1982; contbr. articles to profl. jours. Bd. dirs. Cen. Pa. Festival of Arts, State College, 1988-90; chmn. Com. for Pub Sculpture, 1988-91. Named Tchr. of the Yr. Mountain View/Los Altos High Sch. Dist., 1976; Pa. Coun. on Arts grantee, 1986, 87, 88, 90, 91; recipient Creative Programming award Nat. U. Continuing Edn. Assn., 1990, 91. Mem. Nat. Art Edn. Assn., Coll. Art Assn. Fluent in Armenian. Office: School of Visual Arts Penn State University 210 Patterson Building University Park PA 16802-2502 Office Phone: 814-865-0444. Office Fax: 814-865-1158. E-mail: crg2@psu.edu.

GARON, PHILIP STEPHEN, lawyer; b. Duluth, Minn., Nov. 11, 1947; s. Lawrence and Helen (Cohen) G.; m. Phyllis Sue Ansel, Mar. 22, 1970; children: Edward B., Sara B. BA summa cum laude, U. Minn., 1969, JD summa cum laude, 1972. Bar: Minn. 1972, DC 1973, US Dist. Ct. Minn. 1974. Assoc. Covington & Burling, Washington, 1972-74, Faegre & Benson, Mpls., 1974-79, ptnr., 1980—. Mem. mgmt. com. Faegre & Benson, 1992-2004, chmn., 2001-04; mem. US Law Firm Group, 2002-, pres., 2005. Co-author: Minnesota Corporation Law & Practice, 1996, 2d edit., 2004 (Burton awards for legal writing 2001, 07). Bd. dirs. Herzl Camp, Webster, Wis., 1985-91, Beth El Synagogue, Mpls., 1989-99, v.p., 1993-96; bd. vis. U. Minn. Law Sch., 2003-, vice chair, 2007. Mem. Minn. Bar Assn. (pres. exec. coun. bus. law sect. 1996-97). Avocations: tennis, reading, bridge. Office: Faegre & Benson 2200 Wells Fargo Ctr 90 S 7th St Ste 2200 Minneapolis MN 55402-3901 Office Phone: 612-766-8101. Business E-Mail: pgaron@faegre.com.

GARON, RICHARD JOSEPH, JR., political organization worker; b. Bronxville, NY, Sept. 9, 1948; s. Richard Joseph Sr. and Jeane Helen (Schlemmer) G.; m. Karen Barclay, Jan. 15, 1972; children: Cynthia Beth, Timothy Michael. BA, Hartwick Coll., 1972; MA, NYU, 1975, PhD, 1983. Legis. asst. U.S. rep. Benjamin A. Gilman, Washington, 1977-79, adminstrv. asst. U.S. rep., 1985-89; staff cons. House Com. on Fgn. Affairs, Washington, 1983-85; staff asst. House Com. on Post Office & Civil Svc., Washington, 1979-83, dep. minority staff dir., 1989-92; Rep. chief of staff House Com. on Fgn. Affairs, Washington, 1993-95; chief of staff House Com. on Internat. Rels., Washington, 1995—2001; writer, 2001—. NYU scholar, 1976-77. Republican. Episcopalian. Home: 11526 Gunner Ct Woodbridge VA 22192-5745 E-mail: rgaron@comcast.net.

GARONZIK, SARA ELLEN, stage producer; b. Phila., Jan. 12, 1951; d. Milton and Bernice (Kohn) Garonzik. BA in Spanish cum laude, Temple U., 1972. Producing artistic dir. Phila. Theatre Co., 1982—. Bd. dirs. Arts and Bus. Coun. Greater Phila., Phila. Theatre Co., Theatre Alliance Greater Phila., Phila. Cultural Fund. Recipient prize, Sigma Delta Pi, 1972, award of Honor, Alumnae Assn. Girls HS, 1997, Pres. award, Phila. Young Playwrights, 2006. Office: Phila Theatre Co 230 S 15th St Philadelphia PA 19102 Office Phone: 215-985-1400. Business E-Mail: sgaronzik@phillytheatreco.com.

GARR, DAVID ROSS, physician, educator; b. Boston, Mass., Sept. 6, 1946; s. Fred Manuel and Ida Shuman Garr; m. Deborah Camille Williamson, Dec. 10, 1976; children: Joshua, Rebecca. BA in Chemistry, Duke U., 1968, MD, 1972. Diplomate Am. Bd. Family Medicine. Resident family practice Highland Hosp., Rochester, NY, 1972—75; med. dir. Family Medicine Group of Tooele, Utah, 1975—81; dir. learning resources family practice residency Mercy Med. Ctr., Denver, 1981—85; clinician, prof., assoc. dean cmty. medicine Med. U. S.C., Charleston, 1985—, exec. dir. SC Area Health Edn. Consortium, 2003—. Office: Med Univ SC PO Box 250814 19 Hagood Ave Ste 802 Charleston SC 29425

GARR, SALLY D., lawyer; b. Atlanta, June 10, 1952; BA magna cum laude, Ga. State U., 1977; JD cum laude, U. Ga., 1980. Bar: Ga. 1980, DC 1980, US Dist. Ct. (DC, Md., Colo., ea. Mich., no. Ill. dist), US Ct. Appeals (4th, 6th, DC cir.), US Supreme Ct. Former assoc. gen. counsel, labor & personnel Amtrak, Washington; ptnr., Employment Law, Litigation & Dispute Resolution practices, mem. mgmt. com. Patton Boggs LLP, Washington. Office: Patton Boggs LLP 2550 M St NW Washington DC 20037-1350 Office Phone: 202-457-6525. Office Fax: 202-457-6315. Business E-Mail: sgarr@pattonboggs.com.

GARR, TERI (ANN), actress; b. Lakewood, Ohio, Dec. 11, 1949; m. John O'Neil, Nov. 1993 (div. 1996); 1 adopted child, Molly. Began career as dancer performing with San Francisco Ballet at age 13; in original road show co. of West Side Story; stage appearences include One Crack Out, 1978, Broadway, 1978, Ladyhouse Blues, 1979, Night of 100 Stars II, 1985; appeared in films including Viva Las Vegas, Head, 1968, Maryjane, 1968, Moonshine War, 1970, The Conversation, 1974, Young Frankenstein, 1974, Won Ton Ton, The Dog Who Saved Hollywood, 1976, Oh God!, 1977, Close Encounters of the Third Kind, 1977, Mr. Mike's Mondo Video, 1979, The Black Stallion, 1979, Honky Tonk Freeway, 1981, The Escape Artist, 1982, Tootsie, 1982, One From the Heart, 1982, The Sting II, 1983, The Black Stallion Returns, 1983, Mr. Mom, 1983, Firstborn, 1984, After Hours, 1985, Miracles, 1987, Out Cold, 1988, Let It Ride, 1989, Short Time, 1990, Waiting for the Light, 1990, Mom and Dad Save the World, 1992, Ready to Wear, 1994, Dumb and Dumber, 1994, Michael, 1996, A Simple Wish, 1997, Changing Habits, The Definite Maybe, 1997, Kill the Man, 1999, Dick, 1999, The Sky is Falling, 2000, Life Without Dick, 2001; TV movies include Doctor Franken, 1980, Prime Suspect, 1982, The Winter of Our Discontent, 1983, To Catch a King, 1984, Intimate Strangers, 1986, Fresno, 1986, Pack of Lies, 1987, Teri Garr in Flapjack Floozie, 1988, Drive, She Said (Trying Times), 1987, Mother Goose Rock n Rhyme, Stranger in the Family, 1991, Deliver Them From Evil: The Taking of Alta View, 1992, Fugitive Nights: Danger in the Desert, 1993, Ronnie and Julie, 1996, Casper Meets Wendy, 1998, Half a Dozen Babies, 1999, A Colder Kind of Death, 2001; regular on TV series The Sonny and Cher Comedy Review, 1974, Good and Evil, 1991, Good Advice, 1994, Duckman, 1994, The Women of the House, 1995, Double Jeopardy, 1996, Nightscream, 1997, Murder Live!!, 1997; other TV appearances include Law and Order, 1976, Fresno, Late Night with David Letterman, the Frog Prince, Tales From the Crypt, Friends, 1997-98; guest appearances include Murphy Brown, 1993, Frasier, 1995, Sabrina, the Teenage Witch, 1997, ER, 1999, Felicity, 2001, Life with Bonnie, 2003; author (memoir): Speedbumps: Flooring it Through Hollywood, 2005. Office: William Morris Agy 151 S El Camino Dr Beverly Hills CA 90212-2775

GARRA, RAYMOND HAMILTON, II, marketing executive; b. Apr. 2, 1934; s. Raymond Hamilton and Dorothy (Gardner) Garra; m. Sandra Beatrice Pheasant, Dec. 27, 1962 (div. May 1970); children: Therese Helene, Raymond Hamilton III. Gen. mgr. fine paper divsn. Noland Paper Co., Inc., Buena Park, Calif., 1959—67; v.p. sales We. Lithograph Co., Inc., 1967—71; pres. L.A. Lithograph Co., 1971—73, World Sports Mktg., Inc., Miss Calif. Teenager, Inc., 1974—79, Westaire Properties, Inc., Westaire Travel and Tours, 1975—93, Teragar Mktg., 1994—, Gamra Graphics, Inc., 1996—; mgr. REMAX Resale Office Indian Palms Country Club, Indio, 2006—. Exec. bd. U. Calif., Irvine Sports Assocs.; founder Internat. Divers Festivals, 1979, West Coast Challenge Cup Yacht Regatta, 1983; participant (swimming) Nat. Sr. Olympics, 1995, 1997, 2001; mem. Rep. State Ctrl. Com., 1966—67. With USCGR, 1956—59, lt. comdr. Res. Flotilla Comdr., USCG Aux., 1990. Recipient Sports Family of Yr. award, 1975. Mem.: Balboa Bay, Bahia Corinthian Yacht, Buena Park C. of C. (sec. 1967), Mensa (founder Orange County soc. 1964), Navy League (v.p. Greater Palm Springs Coun. 2003—07, v.p.), Nat. Coronado 25 Assn. (pres. 1969—70, Yachtsman of Yr. award 1971), Desert Legionaires, Shriners (pres. El Bandito club 1992), Phi Kappa Psi (pres. Orange County Alumni Assn. 1994—2002). Home: 82361 Crosby Dr Indio CA 92201 Office Phone: 760-863-2333. E-mail: ray.garra@verizon.net.

GARRAMONE, CHARLES, plastic surgeon; MD in Osteo. Medicine, Nova-Southeastern U., Ft. Lauderdale, Fla., 1998. CEO Aesthetic Plastic Surgery Inst., PA, Sunrise, Fla., 2005—. Mem.: Am. Osteo. Assn. Office: Aesthetic Plastic Surgery Inst PA 12651 W Sunrise Blvd Ste 102 Sunrise FL 33323 Office Phone: 954-752-7842.

GARRARD, WILLIAM L., aerospace engineer, educator; BS in Mech. Engrng., U. Tex., Austin, 1962, PhD in Aerospace Engrng. and Engrng. Mechanics, 1968. Asst. prof. aerospace engrng. and mechanics U. Minn., 1967—73, assoc. prof., 1973—86, prof., 1986—. Prin. rsch. engr. Honeywell Systems and Rsch. Ctr., Mpls., 1973; assoc. dept. head aerospace engrng. and mechanics U. Minn, 1983—91, acting dept. head, 1991—92, dept. head, 1991—, dir. Minn. Space Grant Consortium, 1991—; vis. scientist CERT/ONERA, Toulouse, France, 1995. Contbr. articles to sci. jours. Recipient Ednl. Award for Excellence, US Army Soldier Systems Command, 1996. Fellow: AIAA (mem. aerodynamic decelerator tech. com. 1981—84, 1996—2003, mem. guidance and control tech. com. 1977—80, mem. edn. com. 2003—, J. Leland Atwood award 2006); mem.: Am. Soc. Engrng. Edn. Office: U Minn Dept Aerospace Engrng and Mechanics 117B Akerman Hall 110 Union St SE Minneapolis MN 55455 E-mail: garrard@aem.umn.edu.*

GARRAUX, JAMES D., lawyer, metal products executive; B magna cum laude in Polit. Sci., Duke U., Durham, NC, 1975; JD, U. Pitts., 1978. With labor arbitration sect. of corp. labor rels. dept. US Steel Corp., Pitts., 1979, mgr. labor arbitration, 1987—90, dir. labor arbitration, 1990—91, gen. mgr. labor rels., 1991—96, gen. mgr. employee rels., 1996—2000, v.p. employee rels., 2000—03, v.p. labor rels., 2003—07, gen. counsel, sr. v.p. labor rels. and environ. affairs, mem. exec. mgmt. com., 2007—. Mem. exec. com. Three Rivers Area Labor Mgmt. Com. Mem. Gov.'s Com. Econ. Devel. Through Labor-Mgmt. Partnerships; dir. SW Pa. chpt. ARC. Mem.: ABA, Pa. Bar Assn., Allegheny County Bar Assn., Tri-State Constrn. Users Assn. Office: US Steel Corp 600 Grant St Pittsburgh PA 15219-2800 Office Phone: 412-433-1121.*

GARRE, GREGORY, federal agency administrator; b. 1964; JD, George Washington Law, 1991. With Hogan & Hartson, ptnr., 2004—05; with US Solicitor Gen. Office, Washington, 2000—04; dep. US Solicitor Gen. Washington, 2005—. Named one of Litigation's Rising Stars, The Am. Lawyer, 2007. Office: US Dept Justice Robert F Kennedy Bldg 10th St & Constitution Ave NW Washington DC 20530*

GARRELICK, JOEL MARC, acoustical scientist, consultant; b. NYC, May 20, 1941; s. Samuel J. Garrelick and Phyllis Weidenbaum; m. Renee Brosell, Dec. 22, 1963; children: Kevin, Jenine, Daniel. BCE, CCNY, 1963, ME, 1965; PhD, CUNY, 1969. Lectr. CCNY, 1968-69; scientist Cambridge (Mass.) Acoustical Assocs., 1969-75, corp. scientist, 1976-97; sr. corp. scientist Cambridge Acoustical Assocs./ Anteon Corp., 1998—2002; prin. scientist Applied Phys. Sci. Inc., 2002—. Contbr. articles to profl. jours. Fellow Acoustical Soc. Am.; mem. ASME. Office: APS Inc 4 Muzzey St Lexington MA 02421 E-mail: jgarrelick@aphysci.com.

GARRELS, ANNE, news correspondent; b. July 2, 1951; m. Vint Lawrence Garrels. Grad., Harvard U., 1972. Various positions ABC News, 1975—85, Moscow bur. chief, Ctrl. Am. corr., 1984—85; State Dept. corr. NBC News, 1985—88; fgn. corr. Nat. Pub. Radio, Washington, 1988—. Author: Naked in Baghdad, 2003. Recipient Alfred I. duPont-Columbia U. award, 1992, 1996, 2007, Whitman Bassow award, Overseas Press Club, 1999, Alumnae Recognition award, Radcliffe Assn., 2002, Courage award, Internat. Women's Media Found., 2003, George K. Polk award for radio reporting, 2004; Edward R. Murrow fellow, Coun. on Fgn. Rels., 1996. Mem.: Com. to Protect Journalists (bd. mem.). Office: NPR 635 Massachusetts Ave NW Washington DC 20001-3753*

GARRELS, SHERRY ANN, lawyer; b. Chgo., Feb. 5, 1956; d. William Henry and Jacqueline Ann G.; m. Timothy Anthony Marion, Aug. 1, 1987 (div. June 1988); 1 child, William Garrels-Marion; 1 child, Georgianna Garrels-Rogers. BA, Barat Coll., 1980; certificate, Trinity Coll., 1989; JD, Western State U., 1990. Bar: Calif. 1992, US Dist. Ct. (ctrl. dist.) Calif. 1992, US Dist. Ct. (no. dist.) Calif. 1993, US Dist. Ct. (so. dist.) Calif. 1996, US Ct. Appeals (9th cir.) 1994, US Tax Ct. 1996. Pvt. practice, Huntington Beach, Calif., 1992—; judge pro tem West Justice Ctr., Westminster, Calif., 1998—. Arbitrator Nat. Panel Consumer Arbitrators, Huntington Beach, 1996, State Panel Consumer Arbitrators, Huntington Beach, 1996, Better Bus. Bureau, 1996—, US C. of C., 1996, Huntington Beach C. of C., 1996. Editor The Dictum, 1989. Active 4th of July Exec. Bd., Huntington Beach, 1996—. Mem. Assn. Trial Lawyers, LA Trial Assn., Orange County Bar Assn., St. Bonny Golf Classic (dir. 1991-97), Delta Theta Phi. Republican. Presbyterian. Avocations: swimming, golf, scuba diving. Office: 4952 Warner Ave Ste 106 Huntington Beach CA 92649 Office Phone: 714-840-3413, 714-374-0101. Office Fax: 714-846-6867. E-mail: garrelslaw@aol.com.

GARRELTS, COLBY, chef; b. 1974; m. Megan Schultz; 1 child, Madilyn. Chef American Restaurant; sous chef Stolen Grill, Kans. City; rounds man Tru, Chgo., 1999, sr. sous chef; asst. mgr. Eiffel Tower, Paris Hotel, Las Vegas; chef Aureole, Las Vegas; chef de cuisine Röckenwagner Restaurant, Santa Monica; co-owner, exec. chef Bluestem, Kans. City, 2003—, Bluestem Wine Lounge, Kans. City, 2006—. Named Top New Chef, Food & Wine Mag., 2005. Office: Bluestem 900 Westport Rd Kansas City MO 64111 Office Phone: 816-561-1101. Office Fax: 816-561-5726. Business E-Mail: colby@bluestemkc.com.*

GARRETSON, HENRY DAVID, neurosurgeon; b. Woodbury, NJ, June 8, 1929; s. O.K. and Mary Marjorie (Davis) G.; m. Marianna Schantz, July 4, 1964; children: John, Steven. BS, U. Ariz., 1950; MD, Harvard U., 1954; PhD, McGill U., 1968. Diplomate: Am. Bd. Neurol. Surgery (mem. 1981-87, vice chmn. 1985-86, chmn. 1986-87. Surg. intern Royal Victoria Hosp., Montreal, 1954-55; resident Montreal Neurol. Inst., 1959-63; asst. prof. neurosurgery McGill U., Montreal, 1966-71; prof. U. Louisville, 1971-98, prof. emeritus, 1998—, chmn. divsn. neurol. surgery, 1971-93, chmn. dept. neurol. surgery, 1993-97, assoc. dean clin. affairs Sch. Medicine, 1975-79, dir. neuroscis. programs Sch. Medicine, 1979-82. Individual practice medicine, specializing in neurosurgery, Montreal, 1963-71; with Grantham & Garretson, Louisville, 1971-90, Neurosurgery Inst. Ky., 1990-2000. Contbr. numerous articles, abstracts, editorials, presentations in field. Served with USNR, 1955-58. Fellow ACS; mem. AAAS, AMA, Am. Assn. Neurol. Surgeons (bd. dirs. 1983-85, sec. 1985-86, pres. elect 1986-87, pres. 1987-88), Am. Acad. Neurol. Surgery (pres. 1991-92), Congress Neurol. Surgeons, Ky. Neurosurg. Soc., Ky. Surg. Soc., Louisville Surg. Soc., Ky. Med. Assn., Soc. Neurol. Surgeons, Soc. U. Neurosurgeons (pres. 1983-84), So. Neurosurg. Soc. (pres. 1986-87), Jefferson County Med. Soc., Phi Beta Kappa, Phi Kappa Phi, Sigma Xi. Home: 517 Tiffany Ln Louisville KY 40207-1438 Office: Univ Louisville Dept Neurosurgery 210 E Gray St #1102 Louisville KY 40202-3907

GARRETSON, MATTHEW LEE, lawyer; b. 1970; BA, Yale U., 1997, Salmon P. Chase Coll. Law, 1997. Bar: Ohio 1998. Ptnr. Garretson Law Firm, Cin. Named one of Ohio's Rising Stars, Super Lawyers, 2006. Office: Garretson Law Firm 9545 Kenwood Rd Cincinnati OH 45245 Office Phone: 513-794-0400. Office Fax: 513-936-5186.

GARRETT, BRAD, actor, comedian; b. Woodland Hills, Calif., Apr. 14, 1960; s. Al and Barbara Gerstenfeld; m. Jill Diven, May 18, 1999 (separated); children: Maxwell Brady, Hope. Actor in films including: Jetsons: The Movie (voice), 1990, Casper (voice), 1995, Suicide Kings, 1997, George B., 1997, Postal Worker, 1998, Postal Worker, 1998, A Bug's Life (voice), 1999, Sweet and Lowdown, 1999, An Extremely Goofy Movie (voice), 2000, Facade, 2000, Stuart Little 2, 2002, The Country Bears (voice), 2002, Finding Nemo (voice), 2003, The Trailer, Garfield (voice), 2004, The Moguls, 2005, The Pacifier, 2005, Asterix and the Vikings (voice), 2006, Night at the Museum (voice), 2006, Music and Lyrics, 2007, Ratatouille (voice), 2007; TV films include: The Bears Who Saved Christmas, 1994, Don King: Only in America, 1997, Hooves of Fire (voice), 1999, Club Land, 2001, Bleacher Bums, 2002, Gleason, 2002, Legend of the Lost Tribe, 2002; TV series include: The Transformers (voice), 1984, Rock 'n' Wrestling (voice), 1985, First Impressions, 1988, Where's Waldo (voice), 1991, Eek! the Cat (voice), 1992, Biker Mice From Mars (voice), 1993, Bonkers (voice), 1993, 2 Stupid Dogs (voice), 1993, Pursuit of Happiness, 1995, Project G.e.e.K.e.R. (voice), 1996, Mighty Ducks (voice), 1996, Everybody Loves Raymond, 1996-2005 (Emmy award outstanding supporting actor comedy series, 2002, 2003, 2005), Nightmare Ned, 1997, Toonsylvania (voice), 1998, 'Til Death (also prodr.), 2006-; TV guest appearances include: Roseanne, 1991, The Fresh Prince of Bel-Air, 1994, Lois & Clark: The New Adventures of Superman, 1996, Mad About You, 1996, Seinfeld, 1996, Superman (voice), 1996, 97, Murphy Brown, 1998, The King of Queens, 1998, Batman: The Animated Series, 1992; appeared on Broadway in Chicago, 2002, The Odd Couple, 2005 & 2006.*

GARRETT, BRUCE C., materials scientist, researcher; b. Fort Knox, Ky., Nov. 18, 1951; s. Arnold C. and Nancy A. Garrett; m. Suzanne M. Kenney; children: Sean K., Elisa N. PhD, U. Calif., Berkeley, 1977. Postdoctoral rsch. specialist U. Minn., Mpls., 1977—79; rsch. scientist Battelle Columbus Labs., Ohio, 1979—80; co-founder, lead rsch. scientist Chem. Dynamics Corp., Upper Marlboro, Md., 1980—89; leader tech. group environ. molecular scis. lab. Pacific NW Nat. Lab., Richland, Wash., 1989—2003, assoc. dir. molecular interactions and transformations chem. and materials scis. divsn., 2003—05, dir. chem. and materials scis. divsn., 2005—. Fellow: AAAS (fellow 2004), Am. Phys. Soc. (sec. 2001—07, treas. 2001—07, fellow 1999); mem.: Am. Chem. Soc. Achievements include development of theoretical methods for predicting rates of chemical reactions that are important in the environment. Office: Pacific Northwest Nat Lab 902 Battelle Blvd MA K9-90 Richland WA 99352 Home Phone: 509-735-9385; Office Phone: 509-372-6344.

GARRETT, CHARLES GEOFFREY BLYTHE, physicist, consultant; b. Ashford, Kent, Eng., Sept. 15, 1925; came to U.S., 1950, naturalized, 1989; s. Charles Alfred Blythe and Laura Mary (Lotinga) G. BA in Natural Scis., Trinity Coll., Cambridge U., Eng., 1946; MA in Natural Scis., PhD in Physics, Cambridge U., 1950. Instr. physics Harvard U., 1950-52; mem. tech. staff Bell Labs., Murray Hill, NJ, 1952-54, supr., 1955-56, dept. head, 1960-69; dir. AT&T Bell Labs., Murray Hill-Morristown, NJ, 1969-87. Chmn. Gordon Conf. on non-linear optics, 1964 Author: Magnetic Cooling, 1954, Gas Lasers, 1963; contbr. articles to profl. jours.; patentee in field Named knight of Sovereign Order St. John of Jerusalem (Orthodox) Fellow: IEEE (life), Am. Phys. Soc.; mem.: Guild of Carillonneurs in N.Am. Episcopalian. Avocations: piano, harpsichord, carillon, restoring 18th century houses and older Rolls-Royce cars. Home: 1 Fithian Ln East Hampton NY 11937-2605

GARRETT, CHRISTOPHER J.R., oceanographer; BA in Math., U. Cambridge, 1965, PhD in Geophys. Fluid Dynamics, 1968. Rschr. Trinity Coll., U. Cambridge, U. Brit. Columbia Inst. Oceanography, Inst Geophysics and Planetary Physics, La Jolla, Calif.; prof. dept. oceanography Dalhousie U., Halifax, Nova Scotia, Canada, 1971—82; Lansdowne Professor of Ocean Physics sch. earth and ocean scis. and dept. physics and astronomy U. Victoria, Brit. Columbia, Canada. Contbr. articles to sci. jours. Recipient A.G. Huntsman award, Bedford Inst. Oceanography, 1982, Stommel Rsch. award, 2001. Fellow: Am. Geophys. Union; mem.: Royal Soc. Can., NAS (fgn. assoc.). Office: Sch Earth and Ocean Scis U Victoria Victoria BC V8W 2Y2 Canada E-mail: cgarrett@uvic.ca.

GARRETT, E. REID, lawyer; b. Perry, Ga., Nov. 23, 1946; AB, U. Ga., 1968; JD, Harvard U., 1973. Bar: Ga. 1973. Ptnr. Powell, Goldstein, Frazer & Murphy, Atlanta; pvt. practice Atlanta. Mem. ABA, Atlanta Bar Assn., State Bar Ga., Phi Beta Kappa Phi, Pi Sigma Alpha, Phi Kappa Phi. Office: Bldg 12 750 Hammond Dr Ste 200 Atlanta GA 30328 Office Phone: 404-843-1009. Office Fax: 404-843-2009.

GARRETT, ELIZABETH, law educator, academic administrator; b. Oklahoma City, June 30, 1963; d. Robert D. and Jane (Thompson) Garrett. BA in History with spl. distinction, U. Okla., Norman, 1985; JD, U. Va., Charlottesville, 1988. Bar: Tex. 1988, DC 1989. Law clk. to Hon. Stephen Williams US Ct. Appeals (D.C. cir.), Washington, 1988—89; law clk. to Hon. Thurgood Marshall US Supreme Ct., Washington, 1989—90; legal adviser to Hon. Howard M. Holtzman Iran-U.S. Claims Tribunal, The Hague, Netherlands, 1990—91; legal counsel, tax counsel Senator David L. Boren, Washington, 1991—93, legis. dir., tax counsel, 1993—94; vis. assoc. prof. U. Va., Charlottesville, 1994—95; asst. prof. U. Chgo. Law Sch., 1995—99, prof., 1999—2003, dep. dean, 1999—2001; vis. asst. prof. Harvard U., 1998; vis. prof. Ctrl. European U., Budapest, Hungary, 1999—2003, Interdisciplinary Ctr. Law Sch., Tel Aviv, 2001, Calif. Inst. Tech., Pasadena, 2004, U. Va., 2001, U. So. Calif. Law Sch., LA, 2002; dir. Caltech Ctr. Study Law & Politics U. So. Calif., LA, 2003—, vice provost acad. affairs, 2005—06, v.p. academic planning and budget, 2005—, Sydney M. Irma prof. pub. interest law, legal ethics and polit. Sci. Pasadena, 2005—. Bd. dir. Initiative & Referendum Inst.; articles editor U. Va. Law Rev.; mem. editl. bd. Election Law Jour. Contbr. articles to profl. jours. Vice chair nat. governing bd. Common Cause, 2006—. Fellow: Am. Bar Found.; mem.: ABA, DC Bar Assn., Tex. Bar Assn., Am. Law, Econ. Assn., Phi Beta Kappa, Mortar Bd., Order of Coif, Chi Omega. Office: Univ So Calif Rm 103 Bovard Adminstrn Bldg Los Angeles CA 90089-4019 Office Phone: 213-740-0064. Business E-Mail: vpapb@usc.edu.

GARRETT, GEORGE PALMER, JR., language educator, writer; b. Orlando, Fla., June 11, 1929; s. George Palmer and Rosalie (Toomer) G.; m. Susan Parrish Jackson, June 14, 1952; children: William, George, Rosalie. AB, Princeton U., 1952, MA, 1956, PhD, 1985; DLitt (hon.), U. South, 1995. Asst. prof. English Wesleyan U.; writer-in-residence, resident fellow in creative writing Princeton U., 1964-65; former assoc. prof. U. Va.; prof. English Hollins Coll. Va., 1967-71; prof. U. S.C., Columbia, 1971-73, Princeton U., 1974-78, U. Mich., 1979-80, 83-84; Hoyns prof. creative writing U. Va., Charlottesville, 1984—2001; prof. Bennington Coll., 1980; Coal Royalty chair U. Ala., 1994. Author: The Reverend Ghost: Poems (Poets of Today IV), 1957, King of the Mountain, 1958, The Sleeping Gypsy and Other Poems, 1958, The Finished Man, 1959, Which Ones Are the Enemy, 1961, (poems) Abraham's Knife, 1961, (stories) In the Briar Patch, 1961, (play) Sir Slob and the Princess, 1962, (stories) Cold Ground Was My Bed Last Night, 1964, (screenplays) The Young Lovers, 1964, Frankenstein Meets the Space Monster, 1965, The Playground, 1965, (novels) Do, Lord, Remember Me, 1965, For a Bitter Season, 1967, A Wreath for Garibaldi, 1969, Death of the Fox, 1971, The Magic Striptease, 1973, Welcome to the Medicine Show, Postcards/Flashcards/Snapshots, 1978, To Recollect a Cloud of Ghosts: Christmas in England 1602-03, 1979, Luck's Shining Child: Poems, 1981, The Succession: A Novel of Elizabeth and James, 1983, The Collected Poems of George Garrett, 1984, James Jones, 1984, An Evening Performance: New and Selected Short Stories, 1985, Poison Pen, 1986, Understanding Mary Lee Settle, 1988, Entered from the Sun, 1990, The Sorrows of Fat City, 1992, Whistling in the Dark, 1992, My Silk Purse and Yours, 1992, The Old Army Game, 1994, The King of Babylon Shall Not Come Against You, 1996, Days of Our Lives Lie in Fragments, 1998, Bad Man Blues, 1998, Going to See the Elephant, 2001, Southern Excursions, 2003, Double Vision, 2004, Empty Bed Blues, 2006; editor: The Girl in the Black Raincoat, 1966, The Sounder Few, 1971, Film Scripts I-IV, 1971, Craft So Hard to Learn, 1973, The Writer's Voice, 1973, Intro V, 1974, Intro 6: Life As We Know It, 1974, Intro 7: All of Us and None of You, 1975, Botteghe Obscure Reader, 1975, Intro 8: The Liar's Craft, 1977, Intro 9: Close to Home, 1978, Eric Clapton's Lover, 1990, The Wedding Cake in the Middle of the Road, 1992, Elvis in Oz, 1992, That's What I Like (About the South), 1993, The Yellow Shoe Poets, 1999, Best New Poets, 2005. Served in occupation of Trieste, Austria and Germany. Recipient Rome prize AAAL, 1958-59, Sewanee Rev. fellow poetry, 1958-59, Am. Acad. and Inst. of Letters award, 1985, T.S. Eliot award Ingersoll Found., 1990, Pen/Malamud award, 1990, Hollins Coll. medal, 1992, U. Va. Pres.'s Report award, 1992, Aiken-Taylor award, 1999, Gov.'s award Commonwealth of Va., 2000, Lifetime Achievement award Libr. Va., 2004, Cleanth Brooks medal, 2005, Carole Weinstein prize in poetry, 2006, Thomas Clayton Wolfe prize, 2006; named Cultural Laureate of Va., 1986, Poet Laureate of Va., 2000; Ford Found. grantee in drama, 1960, Nat. Found Arts grantee, 1966; Guggenheim fellow, 1974, resident fellow Bellagio Ctr., 2000. Fellow: Am. Acad. in Rome; mem.: PEN, MLA, Acad. Am. Poets, Fellowship So. Writers (vice chancellor 1988, chancellor 1993—97, Cleanth Brooks medal), Poetry Soc. Am., Writers Guild Am. East, Authors League. Democrat. Episcopalian. Home: 1845 Wayside Pl Charlottesville VA 22903-1630 Personal E-mail: gpg@virginia.edu.

GARRETT, HOWARD LEON, lawyer; b. Tampa, Fla., July 7, 1929; s. Herbert and Frances (Adams) G.; m. Marie Leonora Garcia, Dec. 10, 1950; children— Gloria Susan, Howardene Gay, Leslie Marie Garrett. A.A., U. Fla., 1947, LL.B., 1949, J.D. 1967. Bar: Fla. 1949, U.S. Dist. Ct. (so. dist.) Fla. 1950, U.S. Ct. Appeals (5th cir.) 1950, U.S. Supreme Ct. 1983; cert. cir. civil mediator. Ptnr. Sells & Garrett, 1949-53; ptnr. firm Garrett & Garrett, P.A., Tampa, Fla., 1953—; assoc. city judge, Tampa, 1965; chmn. Code Enforcement Bd., 1980-84. Author essays on alcoholism (Fla. Bar Assn. award 1983). Served with USAR, 1948-52. Mem. Lawyer-Pilot Bar Assn., Hills County Criminal Def. Lawyers, Hills County Bar Assn., Palma Ceia Golf and Country Club. Democrat. Office: Garrett & Garrett PA 3314 Henderson Blvd Ste 208 Tampa FL 33609-2934 Office Phone: 813-875-7895.

GARRETT, JOSEPH EDWARD, aerospace engineer; b. Hendersonville, NC, Mar. 4, 1943; s. Kenneth Pace and Anna Lou (Lytle) Garrett; m. Aurelia Jane Pryor, Aug. 7, 1971. BS in Aerospace Engring., N.C. State U., 1966; MS in Aerospace Engring., Ga. Inst. Tech., 1978. Registered profl. engr., Ga. Basic and fatigue loads assoc. aircraft engr. LASC-Ga. (formerly Lockheed-Ga.), Marietta, 1966—67, basic and fatigue loads structures engr., 1967—75, fatigue and fracture mechanics sr. structures engr., 1975—80, company planning, 1980—82, fracture mechanics structures engr., 1982—91, advanced structures sr. engr., 1991—96, fatigue and fracture mechanics sr. structures engr., 1996—2003, aero. engr. staff, 2003—. Loaned exec. United Way, Atlanta, 1984; chmn. individual gifts Cobb County, Marietta, 1985, chmn. adv. com., 1987—88, bd. dirs. Atlanta, 1987—88. Mem.: AIAA (life; dir. Region II 1990—96, assoc. fellow, Mem. of the Yr. Atlanta sect. 1986, Booster of the Yr. 1988, 1992, 1994—95, Sustained Svc. award 1999, life mem.), Inst. Cert. Mgrs. Lockheed Ga. Mgmt. Assn. (v.p. mem. achievmenet 1988—89, v.p. adminstrn. 1989—90, Booster of the Month 1980, 1st Lockheed-Ga. Cert. Mgr. of the yr. 1989). Republican. Baptist. Avocations: landscaping, woodworking. Home: Ste A9-342 3595 Canton Rd Marietta GA 30066-2658 Office: LASC-Ga Dept 6 E5M Zone 0441 86 S Cobb Dr Marietta GA 30063-0441 Office Phone: 770-494-7695. Personal E-mail: joegarrett@lifename.com.

GARRETT, LAURIE, journalist, global health scholar; b. LA, Sept. 8, 1951; d. Banning and Lou Ann (Pierose) G. BA in biology with honors, U. Calif., Santa Cruz, 1975; postgrad. work in dept. bacteriology and immunology, U. Calif., Berkeley; PhD (hon.), Wesleyan Ill. U., U. Mass., Lowell, 2002. Sci. reporter KPFA, Berkeley, Calif.; with Calif. Dept. Food and Agr.; freelance journalist So. Europe, E. Africa, 1979; freelance reporter, 1980-88; sci. corr. Nat. Public Radio, 1980—88; health and sci. writer Newsday, NYC, 1988—2004; sr. fellow in global health Coun. Fgn. Relations, 2004—. Vis. fellow Harvard Sch. Pub. Health, 1992-93; Editor-at-large, SEED Mag., 2003-. Author: The Coming Plague: Newly Emerging Diseases in a World Out of Balance, 1994, Betrayal of Trust: The Collapse of Global Public Health, 2000 (George C. Polk Award for Best Book, 2000, Nat. Book Critics Award finalist, 2000, Madeline Dane Ross Award, Overseas Press Club of Am., 2001, First Prize Med. Book Competition, Brit. Med. Assn., 2002); contbr. articles to periodicals including Omni, Washington Post, L.A. Times, Foreign Affairs, Vanity Fair, others; frequent guest appearances on Dateline, Jim Lehrer Newshour, ABC Nightline, The Charlie Rose Show, BBC, NPR, CNN, others; contbr. reports including Science Story (George Foster Peabody Broadcasting Award, 1977), Hard Rain: Pests, Pesticides, and People (Edwin Howard Armstrong Award in Broadcast Journalism, 1978), The VDT Controversy (Best Consumer Journalism Award, Nat. Press Club, 1982), Why Children Die in Africa (Meritorious Achievement Award in Radio, San Francisco Media Alliance, 1983, First Prize in Radio, World Hunger Alliance, 1987), AIDS in Africa (J.C. Penney/Mo. Journalism Cert. Merit, Award of Excellence, Nat. Assn. Black Journalists, 1989), Breast Cancer (Best Beat Reporter, Deadline Club N.Y., 1993, First Place Award, Soc. Silurians, 1994), AIDS in India (Bob Considine Award, Overseas Press Club of Am. 1995), Ebola (Madeleine Dane Ross Award, Overseas Press Club of Am., 1996, Pulitzer Prize in Explanatory Journalism, 1996), Crumbled Empire, Shattered Health (George C. Polk Award for Internat. Reporting, 1998), Orphans of AIDS (First Place in Internat. Reporting, NY Assn. Black Journalists, 2000). Named Times Mirror Journalist of Yr., 1996, Alumna of Yr., U. Calif., Santa Cruz, 1996, Champion of Prevention, Centers for Disease Control and Prevention, 1997; recipient Award of Excellence, Nat. Assn. Black Journalists, 1989, Spl. Citation for Outstanding Journalism, AAAS, 1995, Disting. Achievement Award, Ednl. Press Assn. of Am., 1996, Presdl. Citation, APHA, 1996, Pub. Health Hero Award, NYC Dept. Health, 2000, Victor Cohn Prize for Excellence in Med. Sci. Reporting, Coun. for the Advancement of Sci. Writing, 2000, Rsch. in Action Award, Treatment Action Group, 2002. Mem.: Nat. Assn. Sci. Writers. Achievements include Only person ever to be awarded the George Polk Award for Journalism, the George Foster Peabody Award for Broadcasting, and the Pulitzer Prize. Office: Coun Fgn Rels Harold Pratt House 58 E 68th St New York NY 10021

GARRETT, MARSHALL LEE, anesthesiologist, educator; b. Sacramento, 1951; m. Carol E. Kolbo, June 21, 1986; children: Mackenzie Lee, Lane Christian, William James. BA cum laude, U. of the South, 1972; MD, Creighton U., 1978. Diplomate Am. Bd. Anesthesiology. Intern St. Mary Med. Ctr., Long Beach, Calif., 1978—79; resident in anesthesiology U. Fla., Gainesville, 1979—81; chief fellow cardiothoracic anesthesiology Clevel. Clin. Found., 1988-89; anesthesiologist Cypress Fairbanks Med. Ctr., Houston, 1993—. Assoc. prof. U. Calif. Med. Ctr., Davis, 1983—85, Thomas Jefferson U., Phila., 1985—86. Bible Study fellow. Mem.: Harris County Med. Assn., Tex. Med. Assn., Soc. Cardiothoracic Anesthesiologists, Am. Soc. Anesthesiologists, Phi Beta Kappa.

GARRETT, MICHAEL D., utilities executive; b. 1949; Coop. edn. student Ga. Power Southern Co., 1968, various exec. positions in customer ops., regulatory affairs, fin. and external affairs Ala. Power, v.p. Birmingham divsn., exec. v.p. external affairs Ala. Power, 1998—2000, exec. v.p. customer svc. Ala. Power, 2000—01, pres., CEO, bd. dirs. Miss. Power, 2001—03, pres., CEO Ga. Power, 2004, bd. dirs. Ga. Power, 2004—, exec. v.p., 2004—. Bd. dirs. US C. of C. Office: Southern Co 30 Ivan Allen Jr Blvd NW Atlanta GA 30308 Office Phone: 404-506-5000.*

GARRETT, NANCY FALES, playwright, educator; b. Bryn Mawr, Pa., July 10, 1943; d. Haliburton and Katharine Ladd Fales; m. Jared Christopher Martin, June 8, 1963 (div. 1972); 1 child, Christian Mastrangelo Martin; m. Kent Garrett, Jan. 21, 1979; 1 child, Kabir William Richard. BA, Barnard Coll., NYC, 1965; MA, Sarah Lawrence Coll., Bronxville, NY, 1967. Playwriting tchr. St. Ann's Sch., Bklyn., 1975—; workshop leader West Kortright Ctr., East Meredith, NY, 1987—; dir. Shakespeare in the Valley, East Meredith, NY, 1988—; adj. faculty mem., English N.Y. Tech. Coll., CUNY, Bklyn., 2000—02. Vis. artist Alaska Bd. Edn., Juneau, 1985; workshop leader ITLP, Tanzania, 2007. Mem. editl. bd. St. Ann's Rev., Bklyn., 2003—; author: (novels) Payback, 1980, (plays) How They Made It, 1969, Predicates: A Dance, 1971, Passion and Garbage, 1972, Surviving Death in Three Acts, 1973, Casserole: An Illusion, 1974, Ark, 1975, Zone of Middle Dimensions, 1977, Nicole Willing, 1978, Indianhead, 1979, Playing in Local Bands, 1982, The Secret Life of Women, 1985, A Hotel Room Somewhere on 8th Avenue, 1984, Long Distance, 1983, The Puppy Show, 1987, Some Sweet Day, 1985, The Northern Kingdom, 2003 (Best Play award Downtown Urban Theater Festival, 2004), (libretto for opera) Dora, 1990, (screenplays) The Stranger, 1990, The Northern Kingdom, 2006; co-author (with Joie Lee) Farmville, 2004. Fellow, NEA, 1979, Eugene O'Neill Theater Ctr., 1982, NY Found. for the Arts, 1989. Office: 122 Ashland Pl 9J Brooklyn NY 11201

GARRETT, PAUL JAMES, financial planner; b. Chgo., Aug. 18, 1962; children: Tristan Paul, Annie. Registered rep. Inland Securities, Oak Brook, Ill., 1988-91; v.p. New Eng. Securities, Chgo., 1991-96; v.p., prin. Oak Brook Securities Corp., Oak Brook Terrace, Ill., 1996-2001; prin. Garrett Consulting, Glen Ellyn, Ill., 2001—. Republican. Avocation: musician. Office: Garrett Consulting Corp 101 W 22d St Ste 200 Lombard IL 60148 Office Phone: 630-576-5182. E-mail: paul.garrett@garrettconsulting.org.

GARRETT, REGINALD HOOKER, biology professor, researcher; b. Roanoke, Va., Sept. 24, 1939; s. William Walker and Lelia Evelyn (Blankenship) G.; m. Linda Joan Harrison, Mar. 15, 1958 (div.); children: Jeffrey David, Randal Harrison, Robert Martin; m. Catherine Leigh Touchton, June 12, 1989 (div.). BS, Johns Hopkins U., 1964, PhD, 1968. Asst. prof. biology U. Va., 1968-73, assoc. prof., 1973-82, prof., 1982—. Guest prof. U. Paul Sabatier, France, 2003; cons. in field. Author textbooks; contbr. articles to profl. jours. NIH fellow, 1964-68; Fulbright Hays fellow, 1975-76; Thomas Jefferson vis. fellow, 1983; grantee NIH, NSF Mem. Am. Soc. Biochemistry and Molecular Biology, Am. Soc. Microbiology, Am. Soc. Plant Physiology, Soc. Gen. Physiology, Sigma Xi, Phi Lambda Upsilon, Phi Sigma Office: U Va Dept Biology Gilmer Hall Charlottesville VA 22904 Home Phone: 434-293-7277; Office Phone: 434-982-5494. Business E-Mail: rhg@virginia.edu.

GARRETT, RICHARD G., lawyer; b. NYC, Oct. 16, 1948; BA magna cum laude, Emory U., 1970, JD, 1973. Bar: Ga. 1973, Fla 1979; U.S. Dist. Ct. (no. dist.) Ga. 1973, (so. dist.) Fla. 1979, U.S. Dist. Ct. (so. dist. trial bar) Fla. 1979; U.S. Ct. Appeals (5th cir.) 1974; U.S. Ct. Appeals (9th. cir., 11 cir.) 1981; U.S. Supreme Ct. 1981. Program dir., instr. rsch., writing and advocacy Emory U. Sch. Law, 1972-73; gen. counsel Greenberg, Traurig, Miami, Fla., prin. shareholder, 1978—. Past chmn. litigation dept., exec. com. bd. dirs. Greenberg, Traurig, Miami. Editor Emory Law Journal,

1972-73. Recipient 1st place and Best Brief award Region V Nat. Moot Ct. Competition, 1972. Mem. ABA, The Fla. Bar Assn., State Bar Ga., Omicron Delta Kappa, Order of the Barristers. Office: Greenberg Traurig LLP 1221 Brickell Ave Miami FL 33131-3224 Office Fax: 305-579-0717. Business E-Mail: garrettr@gtlaw.com.

GARRETT, ROBERT, investment banker, director; b. Morristown, NJ, Feb. 27, 1937; s. Harrison and Grace Dodge (Rea) G.; m. Jacqueline E. Marlas, July 10, 1965; children: Robert Jr., Johnson. AB, Princeton U., 1959; MBA, Harvard U., 1965. V.p. Smith, Barney & Co., NYC, 1965-69, Robert Garrett & Sons, NYC and Balt., 1969-71; 1st v.p. Smith, Barney, Harris Upham & Co., NYC, 1972-78; sr. v.p. Smith, Barney Real Estate Corp., NYC, 1978-84; exec. v.p. Security Capital Corp., NYC, 1978-85; pres. Robert Garrett & Sons Inc., NYC, 1986—. Pres. AdMedia Ptnrs. Inc., 1990-2005, founder, mng. dir. 2005-07, chmn. adv. bd., 2007—; bd. dirs. Mickelberry Corp., Inside Commns., Inc., United Metro Media; chmn. bd. dirs. Penn Virginia Corp. Trustee Cleveland H. Dodge Found., Abell Found., N.Y. Bot. Garden, Adirondack Mus. With AUS, 1959-63. Mem. Univ. Club of N.Y., Nantucket Yacht Club, Knickerbocker Club of N.Y. Republican. Episcopalian. Office: 444 Madison Ave New York NY 10022-6903 also: 210 E 65th Apt 16 I New York NY 10021 Office Phone: 212-759-1870.

GARRETT, ROBIN SCOTT, health facility administrator; b. Sparta, NC, Jan. 24, 1965; d. Milton William Scott, Peggie Adams Scott; m. William Earle Garrett; 1 child, Nicolas. BS in Mgmt. and Mktg. magna cum laude, U. S.C., 2004. Med. clk. WJBD VA Med. Ctr., Columbia, SC, 1986, sec., stenographer, 1986—91, civilian pay technician, 1991—95, lead civilian pay technician, 1995—97, fiscal adminstrn. supr., 1997—2000, adminstrv. officer, 2004—. Preparer strategic mgmt. plans Edward Jones Investments, Columbia, SC, 2002, Ashley Fetner Fine Art Photography, Columbia, 2002; notary pub. State of SC, Columbia, 1996—; adminstrv. mgmt. intern, VALUE, Atlanta, 2000. Named Fed. Woman of Yr., 1995; named to Nat. Dean's List, 2004; recipient CPCU Mem. Scholarship, Lanville Mengedoht, 2003, Honor Cord for Superior Academic Achievement, Darla Moore Sch. Bus., U. S.C., 2004. Mem.: Nat. Soc. Collegiate Scholars, Phi Beta Kappa, Golden Key, Beta Gamma Sigma. Baptist. Avocation: photography, travel, hiking, reading, music. Home: 101 Fox Run Dr Hopkins SC 29061-9231 Home Phone: 803-776-9711; Office Phone: 803-776-4000 ext. 6404. Personal E-mail: rgarrett@sc.rr.com.

GARRETT, SCOTT (E. SCOTT GARRETT), congressman, lawyer; b. Englewood, NJ, July 9, 1959; m. Mary Ellen Cosmas; 2 children. BA in Polit. Sci., Montclair State U., NJ, 1981; JD, Rutgers U. Sch. Law, NJ, 1984. Atty. Kelly, Gaus and Holub, Sellar, Richardson, Stuart and Chisholm, Roseland, NJ; mem. NJ Assembly from Dist. 24, 1990—2002, US Congress from 5th NJ dist., 2003—. Asst. majority leader NJ Assembly, 2000—01; mem. budget com. US Congress, mem. fin. svcs. com. Past pres. Sussex County Big Bros. Named Legislator of Yr., Bldg. Ofcls. Assn. of NJ; recipient Proactive Policy of Yr. award, NJ Bus. and Industry Assn., 1995, Conservation Legislator award, NJ Assn. Conservation Dists., State Soil Conservation Com., 2003, Hero of the Taxpayer award, Americans for Tax Reform, 2003, Tax Fighter award, Nat. Tax Limitation Com., 2004. Mem.: NJ Def. Assn., Sussex County Bar Assn., NJ Bar Assn. Republican. Protestant. Office: US House Reps 1318 Longworth Ho Office Bldg Washington DC 20515-3005 Office Phone: 202-225-4465. Office Fax: 202-225-9048.*

GARRETT, SCOTT T., medical products executive; BS in Mech. Engring., Valparaiso U.; MBA, Lake Forest Grad. Sch. Mgmt. Various positions Baxter Internat., Am. Hosp. Supply Corp.; chmn. Dade Behring, 1994—97; interim CEO Kendro Lab. Products, L.P., 2000; CEO Garrett Capital Advisors; pres., clin. diagnostic divsn. Beckman Coulter, Fullerton, Calif., 2002—03, pres., COO, 2003—05, pres., CEO, 2005—. Chmn. LifeStream Internat.; vice chmn. Kendro Lab. Products; dir. Inovision Holdings, Sunol Molecular Corp., Biotrin Holdings plc, Ability One Corp., Lake Forest Hosp. Found.; mem., adv. bd. Radius Ventures. Office: Beckman Coulter 4300 N Harbor Blvd PO Box 3100 Fullerton CA 92834-3100*

GARRETT, SPENCER, actor, writer, director; b. LA, Sept. 19, 1963; s. Richard Steve Heckenkamp and Kathleen Nolan. BA, Fordham U., NYC, 1987; student, Duke U., Durham, NC. Actor: (films) Air Force One, 1998, Ghosts of Mississippi, George of the Jungle, 1998, Albino Alligator, 1997, The Truth About Juliet, 1997, Permanent Midnight, 1998, Robbers, 2000, Lovely and Amazing, 2001, Dickie Roberts: Former Child Star, 2003, House of Sand and Fog, 2003, Thank You for Smoking, 2005, Wannabe, 2005, Valley of the Wolves: Iraq, 2006, 9 Lives of Mara, 2006, others; over 100 guest lead roles on TV series including The West Wing, Law and Order, The X-Files, The Practice, My Life and Times, Judging Amy, Star Trek Voyager, North Shore, Las Vegas, Navy NCIS: Naval Criminal Investigative Service, Cold Case, Close to Home, many others; accomplished stage actor in plays on Broadway including Roots and Wings, America's Spirit and off-Broadway including Alone Together, In The Moonlight Eddie, Gunplay. Recipient Dramalogue award for Best Actor for world premiere of Jack Heifner's Heartbreak, 1996. Mem. Actors Equity, AFTRA, SAG. Democrat. Avocations: skydiving, rockclimbing, softball, films. Home: 624 N Plymouth Blvd Apt 7 Los Angeles CA 90004-1440 E-mail: spoonsmcgee@aol.com.

GARRETT, STEVEN LURIE, physicist; b. LA, Apr. 3, 1949; s. Fred Ellis and Vivian Dorothy (Lurie) Garrett. BS in Physics, UCLA, 1970, MS in Physics, 1972, PhD in Physics, 1977. Asst. prof. Naval Postgrad. Sch., Monterey, Calif., 1981-85, assoc. prof., 1985-88, prof., 1988-95; United Techs. prof. of Acoustics Pa. State Univ., State College, Pa., 1995—. Rosen prof. Technion, Haifa, Israel, 1985; cons. in field, 1982—. Contbr. Fellow, Miller Inst. Basic Rsch. in Sci., 1978—81. Fellow: Acoustical Soc. Am. (Hunt fellow 1978, Silver Medal in Phys. Acoustics and Engring. Acoustics 1993); mem.: Soc. Audio Engrs., Sigma Xi. Achievements include patents in field. Home: PO Box 10271 State College PA 16805-0271 Office: Grad Program in Acoustics PO Box 30 State College PA 16804-0030 Home Phone: 814-235-9526; Office Phone: 814-863-6373. Business E-Mail: sxg185@psu.edu. E-mail: garrett@thermoacousticscorp.com.

GARRETT, TED EUGENE, surgeon; b. St. Louis, May 31, 1951; s. Eugene Frank and Alice Marie Garrett; m. Gayle Robbins Bodine, May 15, 1982; children: Kristin, Carter. BA, Westminster Coll., Fulton, Mo., 1973; MD, Vanderbilt U., Nashville, 1977. Bd. cert. Am. Bd. Thoracic Surgery. Resident gen. surgery Barnes Hosp., Washington U., St. Louis, 1977—82, fellow cardiothoracic surgery, 1982—84; cardiothoracic surgeon St. Btn. Mercy Med. Ctr., St. Louis, 1984—2004, St. Louis Heart Inst., 2004—. Chmn. bd. Woolsthorpe Techs., St. Louis, 2005—, Nashville, 2005—. Active Humane Soc., St. Louis; bd. mem. Westminster Coll. Alumni, Fulton, 2000—03; bd. mem., adv. bd. U. Va. Nursing Sch., Charlottesville, 2003—06. Mem.: Soc. Thoracic Surgeons, Boone Valley Golf Club, Old Warson Country Club (bd. dirs. 2003—), Alpha Omega Alpha. Presbyterian. Avocations: golf, hunting, fishing, bridge, car collecting. Office: St Louis Heart Inst 2355 Dougherty Ferry Rd Ste 310 Saint Louis MO 63122

GARRETT, THEODORE LOUIS, lawyer; b. New Britain, Conn., Sept. 4, 1943; s. Louis and Sylvia (Greenberg) G.; m. Bonnie Garrett, Nov. 27, 1968; children: Brandon, Natalie. BA, Yale Coll., 1961—65; JD, Columbia Law Sch., 1965—68. Bar: NY 1968, DC 1971, US Supreme Ct. 1973, all eleven US Cts. Appeals. Law clk. to Judge J. Joseph Smith US Ct. Appeals for 2d Circuit, 1968-69; spl. asst. to asst. atty. gen. William H. Rehnquist US Dept. Justice, Washington, 1969-70; law clk. to Chief Justice Warren E. Burger US Supreme Ct., 1970-71; assoc. Covington & Burling, Washington, 1971-76, ptnr., 1976—, co-chmn. Environ. Practice Group. Editor, prin. author: Corporate Counsel Environmental Law Guide, 1993; author: Environmental Law and the Eleventh Amendment, 2000, Downwind Ozone: Clearing the Air, 2004; co-author: Clean Air Act Desk Book, 1991; contbg. author: A Practical Guide to Environmental Law, 1987, Liability for Hazardous Waste Sites Under CERCLA, 1988, Practice Under the New Federal Sentencing Guidelines, 4th edit., 2001, Environmental Dispute Handbook, 1991, Environmental Litigation, 2d edit., 1999; editor, contbg. author: The Environmental Law Manual, 1992, RCRA Policy Documents, 1993, RCRA Practice Manual, 2d edit., 2004; contbr. articles to profl. jours. Editl. bd. Chem. Waste Lit. Reporter; environment adv. com. Columbia Law Sch.; hazardous waste com. Ctr. Pub. Resources. Named One of 100 Most Influential US Lawyers, Nat. Law Jour., 1994, 500 Leading Lawyers in Am., The Lawdragon, 2005, Global Environmental Lawyer of Yr., 2007. Mem. ABA (chair sect. environ., energy and resources 2000-01, mem. exec. com. 1995-2001, exec. bd. Environ. Lawyer, adv. bd. ABA Jour., contbg. author Trends, mem. task force on superfund reform, liaison standing com. on environ. law), DC Bar Assn. (steering com. environment, energy and natural resources sect., 1991-97, co-chair 1992-94, chair coun. on sects, 1994-95). Avocations: piano, tennis, woodworking, gardening. Office: Covington & Burling 1201 Pennsylvania Ave NW PO Box 7566 Washington DC 20044-7566 Office Phone: 202-662-5398. Office Fax: 202-778-5398. Business E-Mail: tgarrett@cov.com.

GARRETT, WENDELL, antiques appraiser, historian, editor; BA in Am. History, UCLA; MA, Winterthur Program, U. Del.; MA in Am. History, Harvard U. Worked with the Adams Papers Mass. Hist. Soc., 1959—66; asst. editor The Diary and Autobiography of John Adams (4 vols.); assoc. editor first 2 vols. of Adams Family correspondence; editor, pub. The Magazine Antiques, 1966—90; sr. v.p., Americana Sotheby's, NYC, 1990—; regular feature appraiser PBS' Antiques Roadshow. Editor: John Adams diary, 1965; author: Classic America: The Federal Style & Beyond, 1992, George Washington's Mount Vernon, 1999; co-author (with David Larkin): Victorian America: Classical Romanticisim to Gilded Opulence, 1993; author: American Home: From Colonial Simplicity to the Modern Adventure, 2001. Chmn., bd. trustees Thomas Jefferson Meml. Found., Monticello, 1987—93. Recipient Henry Francis du Pont award for Disting. Contbn. to the Am. Arts, 1994. Office: Sothebys 1334 York Ave New York NY 10021 Home: 279E 44th St Apt 18C New York NY 01001 Home Phone: 212-661-8917; Office Phone: 212-606-7137.

GARRETT, WILBUR (BILL), magazine editor; b. Kansas City, Mo., Sept. 4, 1930; s. Clay Dean and Cecil Zora (Melton) Garrett; m. Lucille Hall, Dec. 26, 1950; children: Michael Dean, Kenneth Lewis. BJ, U. Mo., 1954; LittD (hon.), U. Miami. With Nat. Geog. Mag., 1954—90, editor, 1980—90; faculty photojournalism workshop U. Mo., 1963—64, 1969—70, 1973—75, 1977—80, 1994; editor Cosmos Jour., 1995—98. Mem. XIX Olympiad Cultural Com.; bd. dirs. Congentrix Energy, Inc., Nat. Geographic Soc., 1980—90, rsch. and exploration com., 1981—90; bd. advisors Corbis Prodns., Inc., Ptnrs. for Livable Cmtys. Designer (photog. exhbn.) U.S. Pavilion, N.Y.'s World Fair, 1965, designer, prodr. (exhibitions) Nat. Geog. Soc. Exhbns. 23d, 24th, 25th Picture of Yr. Competition. Bd. govs. The Nature Conservancy, 1988—98, Am. Land Conservancy; trustee W. Eugene Smith Meml. Fund; founder, pres. La Ruta Maya Conservation Found., 1990; bd. dirs. Heritage U.S.A. With USNR, 1946—52. Decorated Order of the Quetzal Guatemala; recipient Newhouse citation, U. Syracuse, 1963, Nat. Mag. awards for Excellence, 1984, 1989, 1990, 1991, Leadership Medal, UN Environ. Programme, 1990, Chevron Environ. award, 1990, La Pluma Plata, Pres. of Mex., 1990, Rotondi award, Italy, 1998. Mem.: Cosmos Club (Washington). Avocation: winemaking. Home and Office: 209 Seneca Rd Great Falls VA 22066-1108 Personal E-mail: billgarret@aol.com.

GARRETTO, LEONARD ANTHONY, JR., insurance company executive; b. NYC, Apr. 13, 1925; s. Leonard and Evenia (Egidio) G.; m. Theresa Cennamo, Aug. 6, 1949; children: Deborah, Mark, Michael, Paula, David. BEE, Manhattan Coll., 1951. Engr. Gen. Precision Lab. Inc., Pleasantville, N.Y., 1951-53, project adminstr., 1953-55, project mgr., 1955-58, subcontracts mgr., 1958-59; adminstrv. engr. Sperry Sys. Mgmt. divsn. Sperry Rand Corp., Great Neck, N.Y., 1959-61, mgmt. svcs. adminstr., 1961-63, mgmt. svcs. mgr., 1963-65, fin. planning mgr., 1965-66, planning mgr., 1966-68, dir. adminstrn., 1968; agt. First Investors Corp., NYC, 1966-69, dist. mgr., 1969-70; gen. mgr. David Gracer Co., NYC, 1970-72; v.p. regional sales Somerset Capital Corp., NYC, 1972-75; regional dir. Wis. Nat. Life Ins. Co., Oshkosh, 1975-77, regional sales v.p. Englewood Cliffs, N.J., 1977-84, sr. regional sales v.p., 1984-86, area sales v.p. Stroudsberg, Pa., 1986-93, ret., 1993; owner Ter-Len-Co Benefits, Bushkill, Pa., 1993—. With U.S. Army, 1943-45, ETO. Democrat. Roman Catholic. Home: 94 Saw Creek Est Bushkill PA 18324-9403

GARRIGLE, WILLIAM ALOYSIUS, lawyer; b. Camden, NJ, Aug. 6, 1941; s. John Michael and Catherine Agnes (Ebeling) G.; m. Jeannette R. Regan, Aug. 15, 1965 (div.); children: Maeve Regan, Emily Way; m. Rosalind Chadwick, Feb. 17, 1984; 1 child, Susan Chadwick. BS, LaSalle U., 1963; LLB, Boston Coll., 1966. Bar: N.J. 1966, U.S. Dist. Ct. N.J., U.S. Ct. Appeals (3rd cir.) 1973, U.S. Supreme Ct., 1973; cert. civil trial atty., N.J.; cert. civil trial adv., Nat. Bd. Trial Advocacy; diplomate Am. Bd. Profl. Liability Attys. Assoc. Taylor, Bischoff, Neutze & Williams, Camden, NJ, 1966-67, Moss & Powell, 1967-70; ptnr. Garrigle and Palm, Cherry Hill, 1970—. Sr. counsel Am. Coll. Barristers. With USAR, 1959-67. Mem. ABA, N.J. State Bar Assn., Burlington County Bar Assn., Camden County Bar Assn., Internat. Assn. Def. Counsel, Def. Rsch. Inst., N.J. Def. Assn., Am. Bd. Trial Advs. (diplomate; pres. South Jersey chpt. 2001), Fedn. of Ins. and Corp. Counsel, Trial Attys. N.J., Camden County Inn of Ct. (master of the bench, chmn. 1989-96, treas. 1996-2004), Tavistock Country Club. Home: 223 E Main St Moorestown NJ 08057-2905 Office: Garrigle and Palm 1415 Route 70 E Ste 311 Cherry Hill NJ 08034-2237 Home Phone: 856-234-1230; Office Phone: 856-427-9300. Personal E-mail: garrigle@aol.com.

GARRIOTT, OWEN KAY, astronaut, scientist; b. Enid, Okla., Nov. 22, 1930; m. Evelyn Long; children by previous marriage: Randall O., Robert K., Richard A., Linda S. BSEE, U. Okla., 1953; MS, Stanford U., 1957, PhD, 1960; DSc (hon.), Phillips U., Enid, 1973. NSF fellow Cambridge (Eng.) U., Radio Research Sta., Slough, Eng., 1960-61; asst. and assoc. prof. elec. engring. Stanford U., 1961-65; astronaut, scientist Johnson Space Ctr. NASA, Houston, 1965-86, sci. pilot Skylab-3, 1973, dep. dir. Sci. and Applications Directorate, 1974-76, dir. Sci. and Applications Directorate, 1976, asst. dir. for space and life scis., 77-78, mission specialist on first Spacelab flight, 1983, project scientist Space Sta. Program, 1984-86; v.p. Space Programs Teledyne Brown Engring., Huntsville, Ala., 1988-93; co-founder Enid (Okla.) Arts and Scis. Found., 1993; adj. prof. lab. for structural biology U. Ala. in Huntsville. Served with USN, 1953-56. Recipient Disting. Svc. medal NASA, 1973, Gold medal City of Chgo., 1974, Robert J. Collier trophy, 1974, V.M. Komarov diploma Fedn. Aeronautique Internationale, 1974, Robert H. Goddard Meml. trophy, 1975; inducted into Okla. Hall of Fame, 1980, U.S. Astronaut Hall of Fame, 1997, Okla. Mil. Hall of Fame, 2000. Fellow Am. Astronautical Soc., AIAA (assoc.); mem. IEEE, Am. Geophys. Union, Assn. Space Explorers, Internat. Acad. Astronautics, Astronaut Scholarship Found. (past chmn. bd. dirs.), Sigma Xi, Tau Beta Pi, Eta Kappa Nu (eminent mem.).

GARRIQUES, RON G., computer company executive; b. 1964; B in Mechanical Engring, Boston U., 1986; MS in Engring., Stanford U.; MBA, U. Pa. Mgmt. position Bell Labs, Lucent Technologies; v.p. and gen. mgr. performance category Motorola Inc., Piscataway, NJ, 1998, v.p. and gen. mgr. program mgmt. orgn., corp. v.p. and gen. mgr. worldwide product line mgmt., sr. v.p., gen. mgr., Worldwide Product Line Mgmt., 2001—02, sr. v.p., gen. mgr. Europe, Middle East and African Region, personal communications sector, 2002—04; exec. v.p., pres., personal communications sector, 2004—05, exec. v.p., pres. mobile devices, 2005—07; pres. global consumer divsn. Dell Inc., 2007—. Bd. trustees Boston U., chmn. Alumni Coun.; bd. dirs. United Way of Lake County, Ill. Office: Dell Inc One Dell Way Round Rock TX 78682*

GARRIS, CHARLES ALEXANDER, mechanical engineer, educator; b. Pomona, Calif., Feb. 2, 1944; s. Charles Alexander and Kathleen Ann (White) Garris; m. Eugenia Dolores Cardenas, Sept. 11, 1971; children: Charles Alexander, Eugenia Catalina. B Engring., SUNY, NYC, 1965; MS, SUNY, Stony Brook, 1968, PhD, 1971. Registered profl. engr.; registered patent agt. Va. Rsch. chief mech. engr. dept. Venezuela Inst. Sci. Rsch., Caracas, 1971-73, chief mech. engring., 1976-78; rsch. assoc. MIT, Cambridge, 1973-76; prof. engring. George Washington U., Washington, 1978—; program dir. NSF. Cons. in field. Contbr. articles to engring. publs.; patentee in field. Fellow: AIAA, ASME (Thomas Edison Patent award 2006), Am. Soc. Engring. Edn., Sigma Xi, Pi Tau Sigma. Roman Catholic. Avocations: bicycling, skating, swimming. Office: George Washington U Dept of Mech and Aerospace Engring Washington DC 20052-0001 Home: 2125 Twin Mill Ln Oakton VA 22124-1022 Office Phone: 202-994-3646. Business E-Mail: garris@gwu.edu.

GARRIS, MICHAEL JACK, lawyer; b. Ann Arbor, Mich., May 24, 1954; s. Jack John and Helen (Cazepis) G. BA, U. Mich., Ann Arbor, 1976; JD, Wayne State U., Detroit, 1979. Bar: Mich. 1979, Fla. 1980, U.S. Dist. Ct. (ea. dist.) Mich. 1979. Ptnr. Garris, Garris, Garris & Garris, PC, Ann Arbor, 1979—. Named a Super Lawyer, 2006; named to Lawdragon 3000, 2006. Mem. Washtenaw County Trial Lawyers, Mich. Trial Lawyers Assn., Assn. Trial Lawyers Am., ABA. Greek Orthodox. Office: Garris Garris Garris & Garris PC 300 E Washington St Ann Arbor MI 48104-2000 Office Phone: 734-761-7282.

GARRISH, THEODORE JOHN, lawyer; b. Detroit, 1943; s. Theodore and Adella Beatrice (Kimball) Garrish; m. Joy Ann Ziegler, Aug. 4, 1967 (div. 1979); children: Theodore John, Amelia Sutter. AB, U. Mich., 1964; JD cum laude, Wayne State U., 1968. Bar: Mich. 1969, DC 1972. Trial atty. U.S. Dept. Justice, Washington, 1969-72; pub. opinion analyst Com. for Reelection of Pres., Washington, 1972; chief advt. substantiation FTC, Washington, 1973-74; asst. spl. counsel to Pres. Washington, 1974; asst. to sec. U.S. Dept. Interior, Washington, 1976, legis. counsel, 1981-82; gen. counsel Consumer Product Safety Commn., Washington, 1976-78; ptnr. Deane, Snowdon, Shutler, Garrish & Gherardi, Washington, 1978-81; gen. counsel Dept. Energy, Washington, 1983-85, asst. sec., 1985-89; fed. insp. Alaska Natural Gas Transp. Sys., 1986-89; Wash. counsel Flanagan Group, 1989-91; pres. Brewery Mgmt. Co., 1989-94, Kent Island Investment Co., 1989-91, chmn., 1991-94; mng. ptnr. Wild Gooose Brewery, 1989-91, dir., 1994-98; v.p. Hospitality Assocs., Washington, 2002—06. Mem. U.S. Adminstrv. Conf., Washington, 1976—78, Washington, 1983—85, Pres.'s Commn. Catastrophic Nuc. Accidents, 1988—90; sr. v.p. Am. Nuc. Energy Coun., 1991—94; v.p. Nuc. Energy Inst., 1994—2000; energy program mgr. Bechtel Nat., Inc., 2001—03; dep. dir. Office Civilian Radioactive Waste Mgmt., Dept. Energy, Washington, 2003—05; v.p. fed. ops. and strategic planning CH2M Hill, 2005—. Advisor Nat. Policy Forum, 1994—96; dir. Nat. Energy Resources Orgn., 1987—2001, counsel, 2001—03; asst. to group dir. Pres. Inaugural Com., 1973, dep. exec. dir., 1981; mem. adv. com. human concerns Rep. Nat. Com., 1979; del. Mich. Rep. Conv., 1966. Mem.: DC Bar Assn., Mich. Bar Assn., Fed. Bar Assn., Alpha Delta Phi. Congregationalist. Home: 103 Chesapeake Ave Annapolis MD 21403-3305 Office: 901 New York Ave NW Ste 5100 West Washington DC 20001 Home Phone: 410-280-2337; Office Phone: 202-393-2426. Personal E-mail: tedco2000@hotmail.com.

GARRISON, ARLENE ALLEN, academic administrator, engineering educator; BA in Liberal Arts, U. Tenn., 1975, PhD in Analytical Chemistry, 1981, BSEE, 1988. Instr. analytical chemistry, grad. rsch. asst. U. Tenn., Knoxville, 1975-81, rsch. assoc., 1981, sr. electonic design engr. dept. chemistry, 1985-89, rsch. asst. prof. dept. chemistry, 1989—; dir. measurement and control engring. ctr. Coll. Engring. U. Tenn., Knoxville; licensing exec. U. Tenn., Knoxville, 1998-99, dir. industry programs and tech. transfer, 1999-2000, asst. v.p., 2000—07, assoc. v.p., 2007—. Mem. NRC bd. assessment for Nat. Inst. Standards and Tech., Panel for Chem. Sci. and Tech., 1996-2001; mem. chemistry dept. alumni steering com. U. Tenn. Knoxville, 1994—; participant in NATO Advanced Study Inst. on Analytical Applications of Fourier transform infrared to Molecular and Biolog. Systems, Florence, Italy, 1980; organizer insl. spectroscopy symposium Internat. Conf. on Raman Spectroscopy, Hong Kong; co-chair Soc. Photo-Optical Instrumentation Engrs. conf. on optical methods for chem. process control, 1994; sci. bd. Iternat. Forum Process Analytical Chemistry, 1993-2002; presenter in field. Contbr. over 30 articles to profl. jours., chapters to books. Chair bd. trustees Fountain City United Meth. Ch., 1991-94; sec. Wesley Found. Bd., 1992-93; bd. dirs. Appalachian Sci. Fair, 1993-2007, WATTec, 1994-96, Discovery Ctr., 1995-98; mem. Pub. Bldg. Authority, 1995-, chair, 2000-02, Tenn. Econ. Coun. Women, 2002-. Recipient Chancellors Citation for extraordinay cmty. svc., 1993, Com. Hero Olympic Torchbearer, 1996. Mem. Soc. for Applied Spectroscopy (Meggars award 1982), Soc. of Photo Instrumentation Engrs., Coblentz Soc. (bd. mgrs. 1989-92, pres. 1997-98), Am. Chem. Soc. (sec. East Tenn. sect. 1988-90, chair-elect 1991, chair 1992, steering com. divsns. chem. edn. and analytical chemistry, chair Williams Wright award com. 1991, 92). Phi Beta Kappa, Phi Kappa Phi, Alpha Lambda Delta, Tau Beta Pi. Office: U Tenn P251 Andy Holf Tower Knoxville TN 37996-0142 Office Phone: 865-974-6410. Business E-Mail: garrison@utk.edu.

GARRISON, BARBARA JANE, chemistry professor; b. Big Rapids, Mich., Mar. 7, 1949; BS, Ariz. State U., 1971; PhD in Chemistry, U. Calif., Berkeley, 1975. Rsch. fellow in chemistry Purdue U., Lafayette, Ind., 1975-77; lectr. U. Calif., Berkeley, 1977-78; from asst. prof. to assoc. prof. Pa. State U., University Park, 1979-86, prof. chemistry, 1986—, head dept. chemistry, 1989-94, Disting. prof. chemistry, 2000—02, Shapiro prof. chemistry, 2002—. Vis. asst. prof. Purdue U., 1978-79; vis. assoc. chemistry Calif. Inst. Tech., 1985-86. Alfred P. Sloan Found. rsch. fellow, 1980. Fellow Am. Phys. Soc., Am. Vacuum Soc.; mem. Am. Chem. Soc. (Francis P. Garvan - John M. Olin medal 1994). Office: Pa State U Dept Chemistry 104 Chemistry Bldg University Park PA 16802-4615

GARRISON, CAROL Z., academic administrator; b. Upper Montclair, NJ; BA, U. N.C., Chapel Hill, 1974; MS in nursing, U. Ala., Birmingham, 1976; PhD, U. N.C., Chapel Hill, 1982. Cert. nurse practitioner, U. Ala. Birmingham, 1978. Asst. prof. nursing U. Ala., Birmingham, 1976—78, U. N.C., 1978—82; faculty U. S.C., 1982—92, prof. and chair epidemiology and biostatistics, 1992—97, assoc. provost, 1994—97, dean grad. sch., 1994—97; provost U. Louisville, 1997—2002, acting pres., 2002; pres. U. Ala., Birmingham, 2002—. Office: AB 7070 1530 3rd Ave S Birmingham AL 35294-0110

GARRISON, DAVID H., insurance company executive; JD. Head purchasing and contracting Pa. Electric Co. unit Gen. Pub. Utilities; global dir. procurement and materials Halliburton Co.; chief procurement officer Aetna, Inc.; sr. v.p. procurement USAA (United Svcs. Automobile Assn.), sr. v.p. corp. svcs., exec. v.p. corp. svcs. Office: USAA 9800 Fredericksburg Rd San Antonio TX 78288 Office Phone: 210-498-8222.*

GARRISON, ELIZABETH JANE, artist; b. Elmira, NY, Feb. 11, 1952; BFA, Ringling Sch. Art and Design, 1973; postgrad., Mansfield U., 1976—78; MS, Fla. State U., 1980. Exhibits include Mus. Contemporary Art, Netherlands, Mus. Fine Arts, St. Petersburg, Fla., Renwick Gallery, Smithsonian Inst., Washington, and others; represented in permanent collections Yale U. Art Gallery, New Haven, Conn., Kunstgewerbe Mus., Berlin, Honolulu Acad. Arts, Mus. Fine Arts, Houston Nat. Endowment Arts fellow, 1981, 88; Saltonstall Found. grantee, 1996 Home: 317 Elm St Ithaca NY 14850-3018

GARRISON, GENEVA, retired administrative assistant; b. Bowling Green, Ky., Feb. 14, 1933; d. Claude Harrison and Helen (Bohannon) Garrison; m. Marion Murphey Dare, Jr., Aug. 1955 (div. Mar. 1972); 1 child, Marcus Glenn. AAS, U. Louisville, 1975, BLS summa cum laude, 1977. Tchr. behavior disorders, learning disabilities, mentally handicapped Jefferson County Schs., Louisville, 1974—77; coord. parent edn. project U. Louisville, 1977—79; exec. sec. to dir. AHES Western Ky. U., Bowling Green, 1980, sec., asst. to dir. devel., 1980—84, exec. sec. to exec. v.p. adminstrv. affairs, 1984—87, sec. to pres., 1987—89; ret., 1989. Part-time crisis counselor LifeSkills Inc., Bowling Green, 1993—96. Author: (poetry) to profl. jours. Recipient Omicron Delta Kappa Outstanding Grad. Sr. award, U. Louisville, 1978. Mem.: AAUW, DAR, Warren County Ret. Tchrs. Assn., Ky. Ret. Tchrs. Assn., So. Appalachian Nature Photography Club, Internat. Soc. Poets, Phi Kappa Phi (scholar 1978). Avocations: photography, walking, reading, travel. Home: 733 Newman Way Bowling Green KY 42104-3810

GARRISON, GUY GRADY, librarian, educator; b. Akron, Ohio, Dec. 17, 1927; s. Grady and Emma (Dodson) G.; m. Joanne Ruth Sergeant, Mar. 22, 1964; 1 dau., Anne Olivia. BA, Baldwin-Wallace Coll., 1950; MS, Columbia U., 1954; PhD, U. Ill., 1960. Mem. staff Oak Park (Ill.) Pub. Library, 1954-58; head reader services Kansas City (Mo.) Pub. Library, 1960-62; prof., dir. library research center Grad. Sch. Library Sci., U. Ill., 1962-68; prof., dean Coll. Info. Studies, Drexel U., 1968-87, Alice B. Kroeger prof., 1987-91, dean emeritus, prof. emeritus, 1992—. Contbr. articles to profl. jours. Served with AUS, 1950-52. Mem. ALA, Assn. for Library and Info. Sci. Edn., Beta Phi Mu. Home: 731 Limehouse Rd Wayne PA 19087-2856 Personal E-mail: guy.garrison@drexel.edu.

GARRISON, GWEN E., educational researcher, consultant; d. Thomas B. and Peggy A. Garrison; life ptnr. Linda K. Hodson. BA in English cum laude, Seattle Pacific U., 1985; MA in Theology, Fuller Theol. Sem., 1992; PhD in Edn., Claremont Grad. U., 2003. Tchr. English Auburn Sch. Dist., Wash., 1986—89; mgr. Burns Espresso Co., Seattle, 1989—90; grad. academic advisor Fuller Theol. Sem., Pasadena, Calif., 1991—94, dir. academic advising, 1994—97; instl. rschr. Azusa Pacific U., Calif., 1997—98; rsch. assoc. Inst. at Indian Hill, Claremont, Calif., 1998—2001, dir. rsch. and ops., 2001—03; dir. student and applicant rsch. AAMC, Wash., 2003—. Prin. evaluator Inst. at Indian Hill, 2003—. Author: (rsch. report) The Impending Loss of Talent. Com. mem. Branford Pk. Home Owners Assn., Silver Spring, Md., 2005. Mem.: Assn. Study of Higher Edn. Independent. Christian. Avocations: dog training, hiking, music, bicycling. Home: 12006 Sawmill Ct Silver Spring MD 20902 Office: AAMC 2450 N St NW Washington DC 20037 Home Phone: 301-949-1102; Office Phone: 202-862-6186. Business E-Mail: ggarrison@aamc.org.

GARRISON, JOHN RAYMOND, organization executive; b. Bridgeton, NJ, Jan. 30, 1938; s. Raymond Wilson and Clara Ella (Moore) G.; m. Sally Anne Woodruff, Sept. 10, 1960; children: Glenn Thomas Wilson, Matthew Moore. AB, Harvard U., 1960; MPA (scholastic award), NYU, 1964. Adminstrv. asst. N.Y. State Banking Dept., 1962-63; planner N.J. Dept. Econ. Devel. and Conservation, 1963-64; sr. planner N.Y. State Office Regional Devel., 1964-66; mem. staff Gov. N.Y. State Exec. Chamber, 1966-71; program sec. Office of Lt. Gov., NY, 1971-73; dep. commr. adminstrn. N.Y. State Health Dept., 1973-75; exec. v.p. Hosp. Assn. N.Y. State, 1975-78; CEO Nat. Easter Seal Soc., 1978—90, Am. Lung Assn., NYC, 1990—2001, Cherish Our Children Internat., Shiloh, NJ, 2001—; pres. J.R. Garrison and Assocs., 2001—. Bd. dir. Internat. Union Against TB and Lung Disease, 1996—2003, World No Tobacco Day, 1999-2006, Health Care Choices, 1997—; mem. Nat. Bd. Respiratory Care, 2003—. Mem.: Harvard Club (NYC). Office: JR Garrison and Assocs PO Box 209 Shiloh NJ 08353 Home Phone: 856-392-7867; Office Phone: 856-453-1288. Personal E-mail: jrg@jrgarrison.com.

GARRISON, LINDA, retired foundation administrator; b. Lockport, NY, July 25, 1953; d. Robert Groves and Mary Jean Garrison. BS, Excelsior Coll., Albany, 1995; D (hon.), Pepperdine U., 1997; MA in Spiritual Psychology, U. Santa Monica, 2005. V.p. Headline Brokers, Secaucus, NJ, 1976-85; mgr. Forest Lawn Meml. Pks., Glendale, Calif., 1985-89; v.p. Forest Lawn Found., Glendale, Calif., 1993—98, pres., 1998—2003, ret., 2003. Dir., officer Goodwill Industries So. Calif., LA, 199-2001; dir., mem. exec. com. ARC, LA, 1993-2000; dir. Children's Bur. So. Calif., LA, 1998—, chmn. bd. 2002-05. Mem. So. Calif. Grantmakers (bd. dirs. 2000-03) Home: 8983 Whispering Pine Curve Sylvania OH 43560

GARRISON, MARK W., medical educator; s. Francis Eugene and Jane Suzanne Garrison; m. Sue R. Henry, June 23, 1963; children: Jake H., Joe R., Caylee J. PharmD, U. of Minn., Mpls., 1987. Asst. prof. of pharmacotherapy Wash. State U., Spokane, 1989—95, assoc. prof. of pharmacotherapy, 1995—, asst. dean for student svcs., 2005—; infectious diseases fellow U. Minn., 1997. Named Tchr. of Yr., Wash. State U., 2004—05, 2005—06. Mem.: Am. Soc. for Health-Sys. Pharmacists, Am. Coll. of Clin. Pharmacy, Soc. of Infectious Diseases Pharmacists, Am. Soc. for Microbiology. Office: Wash State U Coll Pharmacy PO Box 1495 Spokane WA 99210-1495 Office Phone: 509-358-7658.

GARRISON, MATTHEW MOORE, artist, educator; b. Albany, Jan. 4, 1968; s. John Raymond and Sally Woodruff Garrison; m. Qin Huang, June 11, 2005; 1 child, Tong Pu. BFA in Sculpture, RI Sch. Design, Providence, 1990; MFA in Sculpture, CUNY: Hunter Coll., NYC, 1997. Studio asst. Ellsworth Kelly Studios, Columbia County, NY, 1988—90; asst. dir. CDS Gallery, NYC, 1990—92; studio asst. Judith Shea Studios, NYC, 1993—96, Petah Coyne Studios, Bklyn., 1995—2000, Catherine Lee Studios, NYC, 1999—2001; asst. prof. digital media Albright Coll., Reading, Pa., 2001—. Rotating chair, Digital Media Dept. Albright Coll., 2002—05, vis. prof. Digital Art, 2004—; curator The Lab Gallery, NYC, 2005—. Exhibited in group shows at Kingston Gallery, Boston, 1992, 1997, CDS Gallery, NYC, 1992, San Diego Art Inst., 1993, NYU, Washington Square Galleries, NYC, 1994, 1999, Internat. Arts Ctr., Higashi Hiroshima, Japan, 1995, Spring Gallery, NYC, 1996, Yearsley Spring Gallery, Phila., 1998, Loft 51/Avril Sergeon, NYC, 1999, Gen Art, 1999, Galapagos Art and Performance Space, Bklyn., 1999, Contemporary Mus., Balt., 2000, Long Beach Island Found. Arts and Scis., NJ, 2001, Waterfront Ctr. for the Arts, Belfast, Ireland, 2003, Fish Tank Gallery, Bklyn., 2004, Albright Coll. Cult. Ctr., Reading, 2004, The Lab, Roger Smith Arts, NYC, 2005, 2006, Hunter Coll./Times Square Gallery, 2005, Yellow Bird Gallery, Newburgh, NY, 2006, one-man shows include Gallery 50, Bridgeton, NJ, 1993, exhibited in group shows at Roger Smith Arts, NYC, 2006, Piazza Cenci, Rome, 1988, one-man shows include Spring Gallery, NYC, 1996, Yearsley Spring Gallery, 1998, exhibited in group shows at Arts Under the Bridge Festival, Bklyn., 2006, Foster Gallery, U. Wis., 2006, Artist Network, Miami, Fla., 2006, 2007, Minn. Mus. Am. Art., St. Paul, 2007. Mem.: Am. Assn. Mus. Home: 199 Spring Run Lane Downingtown PA 19335 Office: Albright College 13th and Bern Streets Reading PA 19612 Home Phone: 201-362-1535. Personal E-mail: matthew@garrisonarts.com.

GARRISON, MICHAEL S., academic administrator, lawyer, educator; b. Fairmont, W.Va., Nov. 6, 1968; m. Heather Malone; children: Julia Grace, Gabriella Malone. BA cum laude, W.Va. U., 1992, JD with honors, 1996. Bar: W.Va. 1996, DC 1999, W.Va. Supreme Ct. Appeals, US Dist. Ct. (no. and so. dists.) W.Va. Adminstrv. asst. instl. advancement W.Va. U., Morgantown, 1993, guest lectr. Coll. Law, 1998—99, adj. prof. Eberly Coll. Arts and Scis., 2002—, pres.-elect, 2007, pres., 2007—; assoc. Steptoe & Johnson LLP, 1996—2001, Bowles Rice McDavid Graff & Love LLP, 1999; adj. prof. bus. U. Charleston, 1999—2000; cabinet sec. Dept. Tax and Revenue State W.Va., 2001, chief of staff, 2001—03; mng. mem. Spilman Thomas & Battle PLLC, Morgantown, W.Va., 2003—. Former chmn. W.Va. Higher Edn. Policy Commn. Named one of Ten Outstanding Young Americans, US Jaycees, 2004; scholar St. Anne's Coll., U. Oxford, 1992—93; Henry Toll Fellow, 2003. Mem.: DC Bar Assn., W.Va. Bar Assn. Office: Spilman Thomas & Battle PLLC 150 Clay St, Second Fl PO Box 615 Morgantown WV 26507-0615 also: WVa U Office of Pres PO Box 6201 Morgantown WV 26506 Office Phone: 304-291-7926. Office Fax: 304-291-7979. E-mail: mgarrison@spilmanlaw.com.*

GARRISON, RAY HARLAN, lawyer; b. Allen County, Ky., Aug. 6, 1922; s. Emmett Washington and Ollie Irene (Keen) G.; m. Eunice Anne Bolz, Oct. 7, 1961. BA, Western Ky. U., 1942; MA, U. Ky., 1944; postgrad., Northwestern U., 1945-46; JD, U. Chgo., 1949. Bar: Ky. 1951, Ill. 1962, U.S. Ct. Appeals 1962, U.S. Tax Ct. 1962, U.S. Ct. Internat. Trade 1968, U.S. Supreme Ct. 1980. Tax acct. Ky. Dept. Revenue, Frankfort, 1943, supr. escheats, 1944-45, fiscal analyst, 1945; research asst. Bur. Bus. Rsch., U. Ky., Lexington, 1943-44; research assoc. Fedn. Tax Adminstrs., Chgo., 1946-52; spl. atty. U.S. Dept. Treasury, St. Louis, 1952-57, spl. asst., 1957-59, asst. regional counsel, 1959-61; sr. counsel Internat. Harvester Co., Chgo., 1961-86; gen. tax atty. Navistar Internat. Corp., Chgo., 1986-88, cons. atty., 1989—; gen. counsel Balmoral Racing Club, Inc., Crete, Ill., 1990—. Lectr. Loyola U., Chgo., 1949-51; del. Ill. Constl. Conv., 1969-70 Contbr. articles to various publs. Mem. Ill. Racing Bd., 1975-88; mem. adv. bd. Ill. thoroughbred Breeders Fund, 1976-80; hon. mem. coun. state taxation (COST), Washington. Mem. ABA, NAM (taxation com. 1969-88), Ill. Mfrs. Assn. (taxation com. 1969-88), Motor Vehicle Mfrs. Assn. (taxation com. 1963-88), Ill. Bar Assn., Ky. Bar Assn., Chgo. Tax Club, South Suburban Geneal. and Hist. Soc. (bd. dirs. 1973-77), Ky. Hist. Soc., Mecklenburg Hist. Assn., Cumberland Valley Civil War Heritage Assn. (adv. bd.), Filson Club, Beta Gamma Sigma. Methodist. Home and Office: 848 Braemar Rd Flossmoor IL 60422-2204 Office Phone: 708-798-6681.

GARRISON, ROBERT FREDERICK, astronomer, educator; b. Aurora, Ill., May 9, 1936; s. Robert W. and Dorothy I. (Rydquist) G.; m. Ada V. Mighell, June 7, 1957 (div. 1980); children: Forest L., Alexandra, David C.; life ptnr. Susanna E. Jacob, 1982. BA in Math., Earlham Coll., 1960; Postgrad., U. Wis., 1961-62; PhD in Astronomy and Astrophysics, U. Chgo., 1966. Research assoc. Mt. Wilson and Palomar Obs., Pasadena, Calif., 1966-68; asst. prof. U. Toronto, Ont., Canada, 1968-74, assoc. prof. Ont., 1974-78, prof. astronomy Ont., 1978—2001, prof. emeritus Ont., 2001—, assoc. dir. D. Dunlap Obs. Ont.; dir. U. Toronto So. Obs., Chile, 1970-98. Bronowski lectr., 1987; Sigma Xi lectr., 1988—90. Editor: The MK Process and Stellar Classification, 1984; co-editor: The MK Process at Fifty Years: A Powerful Tool for Astrophysical Insight, 1994; subject The Garrison Festschrift, 2003; contbr. articles to profl. jours. Bd. dirs. Bruce Trail Assn., 1975—76. With USMC, 1954—56. Recipient Dean's award Lifetime Achievement as Outstanding Tchr., 2001, Queen's Golden Jubilee medal, 2003. Mem.: Royal Can. Inst. (v.p. 1991—93, pres. 1993—94), Internat. Astron. Union (pres. com. 45 on stellar classifications 1985—88), Royal Astron Soc. Can. (v.p. 1996—2000, pres. 2000—02, Svc. award 2005), Am. Assn. Variable Star Observers, Astron. Soc. Pacific, Am. Astron Soc. (Shapley lectr. 1985—), Can. Astron. Soc. (coun. 1978—81), U. Chgo. Club Can. (v.p. schs. 1982—88, pres. 1988—90). Office Phone: 416-538-3108. Business E-Mail: garrison@astro.utoronto.ca.

GARRISON, WAYNE, transportation executive; Plant mgr. J.B. Hunt Transport Svcs., Inc., Lowell, Ark., 1976, v.p. fin., 1978, exec. v.p., 1979, pres., 1982, CEO, 1987, vice-chmn., 1986—91, chmn., 1995—. Office: JB Hunt Transport Svcs Inc 615 JB Hunt Corporate Dr Lowell AR 72745*

GARRISON, WILLIAM LLOYD, retired cemetery executive, social worker; b. Ridgway, Pa., Dec. 26, 1939; s. Lloyd and Mary Rebecca (Morrow) G.; m. Mary Jo Florio, May 30, 1964 (div. Mar. 2002), m. Mary Jo L. Mlakar, Jan. 21, 2005; children: David, Mark. BA in Psychology, Ohio Wesleyan U., 1962; postgrad., Garrett Theol. Sem., 1962—63, U. Pa., 1963—64; MSW, Fla. State U., 1967; MS in Mgmt., Case Western Res. U., 1976. Caseworker Mcpl. Ct. Chgo., 1963-64, United Cerebral Palsy Assn., Phila., 1964-65; psychiat. social worker Bellefaire, Shaker Heights, Ohio, 1967-74; dir. pers. and tng. Ctr. Human Svcs., Cleve., 1974-81, dir. resource devel., 1981-83; exec. dir. Cleve. Soc. for the Blind, 1983-85, Cleve. Eye Bank, 1983-85; exec. v.p. Lake View Cemetery Assn., Cleve., 1985-87, pres., CEO, 1987—2005; v.p. Lake View Cemetery Found., Cleve., 1988—2005; interim exec. dir. Heights Youth Ctr., 2007—. Adj. prof. Sch. Applied Social Sci., Case Western Res. U., 1974-80; v.p. E.A. Mabry Inc., Akron, Ohio, 1970-2001; chmn. agri-bus. adv. com. Cleve. Pub. Schs., 1990-2005, bus. adv. directorate, 1991-97. Numerous positions including ongoing and most recently Boy Scouts Am., coun. exec. bd., 1981—, mem. nat. coun., 1989—, cubmaster, 1997—, region nominating com., 1997—, nat. cub scout com. vice chmn., 1999—2005, nat. cub scout character connections task force, 2001—07; coun., v.p. cub scouting, 2003—04, dist. chmn., 2004—06, nat. venture scout com., 2005—; pers. com. Lake Erie coun. Girl Scouts U.S., 1982—89; active Big Bros., Cleve., 1968—73; pres. Mayfield Heights Homeowners Assn., 1974—84, Cuyahoga County Reach Out Counseling Svcs., trustee, 1977—95, pres., 1991—95; mem. del. assembly United Way Svcs. of Cleve., 1987—95; trustee Alta Ho. Cmty. Ctr., 1994—2000, Ctr. for Families and Children, 1995—2002; co-founder East Cleveland Pks. Assn., 1998—, pres., 2002—06, v.p., 1998—2002, 2006—07; co-chair civic divsn. United Way Campaign, 1999—2001; founder, pres. East Cleveland Twp. Cemetery Found., 2001—; co-founder Greater Cleve. Urban Scouting Found., 2007; bd. dirs. Garfield Meml. United Meth. Ch., 1979—81, vice chair pastor/parish rels. com., 1999—2000, trustee adult guardianship svcs., 2006—. Recipient Dist. award merit, Boy Scouts Am., 1980, Silver Beaver award, 1984, Silver Antelope award, 1994, 4-Way Test award, Rotary Club Cleve., 2000, hon. mention, No. Ohio LIVE award of achievement, 1994, 2002, Whitney M. Young award, 2005; fellow, Menninger Found. Mem. NASW, Acad. Cert. Social Workers, Soc. Human Resource Mgmt., Pers. Accreditation Inst., Internat. Cemetery and Funeral Assn. (cert. cemetery exec. 1997, membership com. 1993-2000, strategic planning com. 1994-96, hist. cemetery adv. com. 1994-2004, dir. 2003-06), Ohio Assn. Cemetery Supts. and Ofcls. (exec. bd. 1992-97, v.p. 1993, pres.-elect 1994, pres. 1995-96), Greater Cleve. Cemetery Assn. (pres. 1987-90), Nat. Eagle Scout Assn., Greater Cleve. Pers. Coun., Social Agys. Employees Union (pres. 1970-73), Greater Cleve. Growth Assn., St. Luke's Hosp. Assn., Cleve. U. Cir. Inc., Am. Soc. Assn. Execs., Assn. Fundraising Profls., Cleve. Restoration Soc., Ohio Assn. Hist. Socs. and Museums, N.E. Ohio Intermus. Coun., Ohio Hist. Soc., Am. Field Svc., Cleve. Playhouse Club, Rotary (trustee Cleve. club 1993-96, v.p. 1996, pres. 1997-98, del. 88th Rotary Internat. conv. Glasgow, Scotland, 89th Indpls., 96th Chgo.), Cleve. Rotary Found. (trustee 1997-99, 2007—, v.p. 1999-2000, pres. 2000-01), Hist. Cemetery Alliance (co-founder), Internat. Fellowship of Scouting Rotarians, Univ. Club, Delta Tau Delta, Phi Mu Alpha.

GARRISON, WILLIAM LOUIS, civil engineering educator; b. Nashville, Apr. 20, 1924; s. Sidney Clarence and Sara (Elisabeth) McMurry; s. Marcia Fordyce Stanley, Aug. 31, 1938; children: Sara, Ann, Helen, Deborah, James, Jane, John. BS, Peabody Coll., 1946, MS, 1947; PhD, Northwestern U., 1950. From asst. prof. to prof. dept. geography U. Wash., Seattle, 1950-60; prof. dept. geography, civil engring. Northwestern U., Evanston, Ill., 1960-67, dir. transp. ctr., 1965-67; dir. ctr. for urban studies U. Ill., Chgo., 1967-69; Weidlein Prof. Environ. Engring. U. Pitts., 1969-73; dir. Inst. for Transp. Studies U. Calif., Berkeley, 1973-81, prof. civil engring., 1981—. Cons. U.S. Bur. Pub. Rds., Washington, 1960-68; bd. govs. Regional Sci. Rsch. Inst., Phila., 1964—; adv. com. on econs. NSF, Washington, 1958-63; panel on values of social sci. rsch. Nat. Sci. Bd., Washington, 1963-64. Author: Geographical Impact of Highway Improvements, 1960, Tomorrow's Transportation, 2000; author, editor Jour. Transp. Tech., 1985, The Transportation Experience, 2005; editor: Quantitative Geography, 1969; articles in field. Served to capt. USAF, 1943-46. Recipient Disting. award U. Coun. of Transp. Rsch. Ctrs., 1999. Mem. AAAS, ASCE, Transp. Rsch. Bd. (chmn. 1972-73, Roy C. Crum award 1973), Regional Sci. Assn. (pres. 1960), Assn. Am. Geographers (Outstanding Rsch. award 1958). Home: 10 Rancho Diablo Dr Lafayette CA 94549-2722 Office: U Calif Dept Civil Engring Berkeley CA 94720 Business E-Mail: garrison@newton.berkeley.edu.

GARRISON-FINDERUP, IVADELLE DALTON, writer, educator; b. San Pedro, Calif., Oct. 4, 1915; d. William Douglas and Olive May (Covington) Dalton; m. Fred Marion Garrison, Aug. 8, 1932 (dec. Nov. 1984); children: Douglas Lee, Vernon Russell, Nancy Jane; m. Elmer Pedersen Finderup, Apr. 8, 1994 (dec. Oct. 1997). BA, Calif. State U., Fresno, 1964; postgrad., U. Oreg., 1965, U. San Francisco, 1968. Cert. secondary tchr., Calif. Tchr. Tranquillity (Calif.) H.S., 1964-78, West Hills Coll., Coalinga, Calif., 1970-74. Lectr. in field. Author: Roots and Branches of Our Garrison Family Tree, 1988, Roots and Branches of Our Dalton Family Tree, 1989, The History of James' Fresno Ranch, 1990, 3d edit., 1993, There is a Peacock on the Roof, 1993; (with Vernon R. Garrison) William Douglas Dalton, a Biography, 1995, Sam (The Cat That Thought He Was a Boy), 1997, Amanda and Her Feathered Friends, 1997, Freddy Goes on a Trailer Outing, 1998, David Learns to Count, 1998, Laura and the Lizard: a fairy tale, 2001, A Mystery Story, 2005. Mem. Arne Nixon Ctr. Study Children's Lit., Henry Madden Libr. Mem. DAR (sec. 1987-89, regent 1989-91, regent Fresno chpt. 1999-2001, scholarship chmn. 2002, 05, nat. recognition for excellence in cmty. svc. Cert. of Award 1995), Nat. Trust for Hist. Preservation, Frazier Clan N.Am., Fresno City and County Hist. Soc. (life), Fresno Archaeology Soc. (sec. 1994), Children of the Am. Revolution (life patriot, sr. pres. 1991-97), Westerners Internat., Fresno Gem and Mineral Soc., Thora # 11 Dannebrog, Friends of the Libr. (Fresno), Chaffee Zool. Gardens of Fresno, Archaeol. Inst. Am. (San Joaquin Valley chpt., charter mem.), Fresno Met. Mus., Baker Hist. Mus. (life). Republican. Lutheran. Avocations: quilting, knitting. Office: Garrison Libr 3427 Circle Ct E Fresno CA 93703-2403

GARRISS, PHYLLIS WEYER, music educator, performer; b. Hastings, Nebr., Dec. 25, 1923; d. Frank Elmer and Mabelle Claire (Carey) Weyer; m. William Philip Garriss, Aug. 28, 1954; children: Daniel, Meredith, Margaret. AB, MusB, Hastings Coll., 1945; MusM, U. Rochester, 1948. Instr. DePauw U., Greencastle, Ind., 1948-51; assoc. prof. music Meredith Coll., Raleigh, N.C., 1951-94, assoc. prof. emerita, part-time prof., 1994—. Instr. Cannon Music Camp, Appalachian State U., Boone, N.C., 1973-98; vis. instr. Ball State U., Muncie, summers 1951, 53; dir. Lamar Stringfield Chamber Music Camp, Meredith Coll., 1980—; bd. dirs. Raleigh Symphony Orch., Raleigh Chamber Music Guild; mem. various symphonic groups as violinist, including Roanoke Symphony, Raleigh Civic Symphony, Duke U. Symphony, Tri-City Chamber Orch., Raleigh Symphony Orch., Capital Chamber Music Ensemble. Mem. Raleigh Civic Coun., 1958-60; bd. dirs. Raleigh Comty. Mus. Sch., 1993-97, N.C. Fedn. Music Clubs, 1988-96; mem. PEO. Recipient Medal of Arts, City of Raleigh Arts Commn., 1987. Mem. Am. String Tchrs. Assn. (corr. sec. 1950-54, Disting. Svc. award 1979), Music Tchrs. Nat. Assn., Music Educators Nat. Conf., Local 500 Musicians Assn. (bd. dirs. 1980—), Raleigh Music Club (pres. 1958-60, 93-95), Pi Kappa Lambda, Mu Phi Epsilon. Democrat. Presbyterian. Avocations: cooking, travel. Home: 3400 Merriman Ave Raleigh NC 27607-7004 Office: Meredith Coll 3800 Hillsborough St Raleigh NC 27607-5237 Home Phone: 919-834-7000; Office Phone: 919-760-2821. Business E-Mail: garrissp@meredith.edu.

GARRITY, VINCENT FRANCIS, JR., lawyer; b. Phila., July 26, 1937; s. Vincent Francis and Anne (Glenn) G.; m. Maryellen O'Brien, May 8, 1965; children: Vincent III, Ellen, Christopher, Elisa. AB cum laude, Coll. of Holy Cross, Worcester, Mass., 1959; LLB, Harvard U., 1962. Bar: Pa. 1963, U.S. Dist. Ct. (ea. dist.) Pa. 1963. Assoc. Duane, Morris & Heckscher, Phila., 1963-70; ptnr. Duane, Morris LLP, Phila., 1970—2002, co-chmn. bus. law dept., 1981—94, of counsel, 2003—. Disting. practitioner in residence Cornell Law Sch., 2001; adj. prof. Sch. Law Temple U., 1996—, Law Sch. U. Va., 2004; adj. prof. Sch. Law., U. Pa., 1999—; vis. prof. law faculty Eotvos Lorand U., Budapest, Hungary, 2006; presenter, panelist, lectr. in field. Contbr. numerous articles to profl. jours. With USAR, 1962—68. Mem. ABA (com. on corp laws bus. law sect. 1983-89, participant in preparation Model Bus. Corp. Act; vice chmn. 1991-95, chmn. 1995-98, com. on negotiated acquisitions), Pa. Bar Assn. (chmn. sect. corp. banking and bus. law 1981-83, vice chmn. Title 15 task force on 1988 Pa. Bus. Corp. Law 1983-2004, co-chmn. 2005—, Spl. Achievement award 1982), Am. Law Inst., Merion Golf Club (Ardmore, Pa.), Union League Phila. Roman Catholic. Home: 118 Derwen Rd Bala Cynwyd PA 19004-2710 Office Phone: 215-979-1242. Business E-Mail: garrity@duanemorris.com.

GARROTT, CARL LEE, foreign language educator; b. Indpls., Dec. 4, 1948; s. George Richard and Rosie (Diggs) G. BA, Ky. State U., 1970; MA, Tenn. State U., 1974; EdS, Western Ky. U., 1977; EdD, U. Ky., 1985; postgrad., Guadalajara U., Mex., 1999—2000, Inst. de Filologia Hispanica, 1990, 91, 93, Monteverde Inst., Costa Rica, 2002—03, U. Guanajuato, Mex., 2005. Instr. Cath. High Sch., Frankfort, Ky., 1969-70, Christian County Schs., Hopkinsville, Ky., 1974-81; prof. Chowan Coll., Murfreesboro, N.C., 1984-95; assoc. prof. Hampton U., 1995-98; prof. Va. State U., 1998—. Author: (monograph) The Thinking Man in France, 1977, (book) José Martí Poesía, Cuentos, Teatro, 2001, A systematic Approach to Teaching Intonation Patterns in French, 2003; contbr. articles to profl. jours. Donor Sci. Enrichment Scholarship, Hertford County, 1984-91, 93; founder African-Am. Forum, Franklin, Southampton, 1987—. Sgt. U.S. Army, 1971-73. Woodrow Wilson Found. fellow, 1970, U. Ky. fellow, 1970-71, 81-84; grantee Ford Found., Starr Found., Va. Found. Humanities; faculty rsch. grantee Hampton U. Mem. MLA, Am. Assn. Tchrs. Spanish and Portuguese, Am. Assn. Tchrs. French, N.E. Conf. on the Tchg. Fgn. Langs., Am. Assn. for Applied Linguistics, Coll. Lang. Assn., Afro-Latin Am. Rsch. Assn., Internat. Assn. Appllied Linguistics, County Alliance for Sci., Cmty. Concert Assn., Alpha Phi Alpha, Alpha Mu Gamma. Democrat. Baptist. Avocations: shortwave radios, internat. travel. Office: Va State Univ Dept Langs and Lit Petersburg VA 23806 Office Phone: 804-524-5168. E-mail: cgarrott@vsu.edu.

GARROW, DAVID JEFFRIES, historian, author; b. New Bedford, Mass., May 11, 1953; s. Walter and Barbara Mae (Fassett) G.; m. Virginia Darleen Opfer, Dec. 15, 2003. BA, Wesleyan U., Middletown, Conn.,

1975; MA, Duke U., 1978, PhD, 1981. Instr. polit. sci. Duke U., Durham, NC, 1978-79; vis. mem. Sch. Social Sci., Inst. Advanced Study, Princeton, NJ, 1979-80; asst. prof. polit. sci. U. N.C., Chapel Hill, 1980-84; assoc. prof. polit. sci. City Coll. N.Y., CUNY Grad. Ctr., 1984-87, prof., 1987-91. Vis. fellow Joint Ctr. Polit. Studies, Washington, 1984; sr. advisor Eyes on the Prize: Am.'s Civil Rights Yrs., PBS TV documentary broadcast, 1985-90; bd. dirs. Martin Luther King Jr. Papers Project, King Ctr., Atlanta; fellow 20th Century Fund, 1991-93; James Pinckney Harrison vis. prof. history Coll. William and Mary, 1994-95; disting. historian in residence Am. U., 1995-96, disting. Presdl. prof., Emory U., 1997—2005; sr. rsch. fellow Homerton Coll., U. Cambrige, 2005—. Author: Protest at Selma: Martin Luther King and the Voting Rights Act of 1965, 1978 (Chastain award 1979), The FBI and Martin Luther King, Jr.: From "Solo" to Memphis, 1981, Bearing the Cross: Martin Luther King, Jr. and the Southern Christian Leadership Conference, 1986 (Pulitzer Prize for Biography 1987, Robert F. Kennedy book award 1987), Liberty and Sexuality: The Right to Privacy and the Making of Roe v. Wade, 1994; editor: The Montgomery Bus Boycott and the Women Who Started It: The Memoir of JoAnn Gibson Robinson, 1987; co-editor: The Eyes on the Prize Civil Rights Reader, 1987, 91, The Forgotten Memoir of John Knox, 2002; contbr. articles to publs. and profl. jours. Recipient NEH grant, 1984-85, Ford Found. grant, 1979-80, Lyndon B. Johnson Found. grant, 1979-80, Eisenhower World Affairs Inst. grant, 1985-86. Phi Beta Kappa. Democrat. Avocations: bicycling, hiking. Office: Homerton Coll Univ Cambridge Cambridge CB2 8PH England

GARROW, EUGENE, pediatric surgeon; b. NYC, July 8, 1935; s. Elias and Sophie Garrow; m. Barbara Miller Garrow, July 8, 1990; m. Anita Arbeit Garrow (dec.); children: Philip, Celeste, Andrew. BA, NYU, NYC, 1954; MD, SUNY Downstate, Bklyn., 1958. Cert. in pediatric surgery Am. Bd. Surgery. Pediat. surgeon Children's Surgery of NJ, Jersey City, 1964—2002, SUNY Downstate, Bklyn., 2002—. Fellow: ACS, Am. Pediat. Surg. Soc., Am. Acad. Pediat. Avocations: running, bicycling. Office: SUNY Downstate Med 450 Clarkson Ave Brooklyn NY 11203 Office Phone: 718-270-1386. Business E-Mail: egarrow@downstate.edu.

GARRUTO, JOHN, counseling administrator; b. Binghamton, NY, Aug. 26, 1973; s. Michael and Kathleen Garruto; m. Denise Mero, Sept. 4, 2004. BA, SUNY, Oswego, 1995, MS, 1997. Cert. Sch. Psychologist NASP. Sch. psychologist Oswego (NY) City Sch. Dist., 1997—98, LaFayette (NY) Ctrl. Sch. Dist., 1998—99, Oswego (NY) City Sch. Dist., 1999—. Columnist Today's Sch. Psychologist, Horsham, Pa., 2004—; chmn. com. spl. edn. LaFayette (NY) Ctrl. Sch. Dist., 1998—99. Co-editor: The Ontarian. Named to Pres. List, SUNY, Fall 1994, Dean's List, Spring 1992, Fall 1993, Spring 1994. Mem.: NASP. Roman Catholic. Avocations: reading, chess, writing. Office: Frederick Leighton Elem Sch 1 Buccaneer Blvd Oswego NY 13126 Home Phone: 315-729-7248; Office Phone: 315-341-2740. Business E-Mail: jgarruto@oswego.org.

GARRUTO, JOHN ANTHONY, cosmetics executive; b. Johnson City, NY, June 18, 1952; children: James, Christopher, Catherine, Gabrielle, Sofia. BS in Chemistry, SUNY, Binghamton, 1974; AAS in Bus. Adminstrn., Broome Coll., 1976. Rsch. chemist Lander Co. Inc., Binghamton, 1974-77, rsch. dir. St. Louis, 1977-79, Olde Worlde Products, High Point, N.C., 1979-81; v.p. rsch. and devel. LaCosta Products Internat., Carlsbad, Calif., 1981-89; chief ops. officer Randall Products Internat., Carlsbad, 1989-91; pres. Dermasearch Internat., 1991-92; chief tech. officer Innovative Bioscis. Corp., Oceanside, Calif., 1992-95; v.p. rsch. Garden Botanika, Oceanside, Calif., 1995-99; pres., founder Free Radical Tech., 1999—. Cons. Trans-Atlantic Mktg., Binghamton, 1975-78; instr. cosmetic sci UCLA, 1991—, UCLA Ext.; lectr. to cosmetic industry. Patentee in field. Mem. AAAS, Soc. Cosmetic Chemists (newsletter editor 1980-81, feature editor, 2004—, publicity chmn. 1984—, edn. chmn. 1987, employment chmn. 1994—, chmn. elect 1999-2000, chmn. 2000, nat. elections com. 2001—, nominations com., 2006—, lab lorn editor, 2004—), Am. Chem. Soc., Inst. for Food Technologists (sec. beauty industry west), Pacific Tech. Exch., Fedn. Am. Scientists, N.Y. Acad. Scis., Cosmetic, Toiletry and Fragrance Assn. (sci. adv. com.).

GARRUTO, RALPH MICHAEL, biomedical anthropologist, biologist, educator; b. Binghamton, NY, Nov. 20, 1943; s. Ralph Anthony and Josephine Janet (DiMartino) G.; children: Jessica Anne, Jason Michael, John Ralph. BS, Pa. State U., 1966, MA, 1969, PhD, 1973. Postdoctoral fellow NIH, Bethesda, Md., 1972-73, staff, then sr. staff fellow, 1973-78, from rsch. biologist to supervisory rsch. biologist, 1978—2003; adj. prof. med. genetics Coll. Medicine U. South Ala., Mobile, 1982—; adj. sr. scientist biol. anthropology Pa. State U., University Park, 1985—95; prof. biomedical anthropology neuroscis. SUNY, Binghamton, 1997—, assoc. dir. Inst. Biomed. Tech., 2000—, dir. grad. program biomed. anthropology, 2002—; adj. clin. prof. pathology Upstate Med. U., Syracuse, 1998—. Participant anthropol. and biomed. fieldwork, Cambodia, China, Mariana Islands, Papua New Guinea, Peru, Philippine Islands, Western Caroline Islands, 1969—; mem., NIH rep. US Nat. Com. US Man and the Biosphere Program, 1993-95; founding mem. bd. trustees Nat. Mus. Health and Medicine Found., Washington, 1989-91; exec. sec. Commn. on Aging and the Aged, Zagreb, Yugoslavia, 1985-89; cons. WHO, 1987; chair selection com. Paul T. Baker Disting. lectr. in human biology and anthropology Pa. State U., 1986-98; Wellcome Found. lectr., vis. prof. U. Mich., Dearborn, 2001. Co-editor: Biological Anthropology and Aging: Perspectives on Human Variation over the Lifespan, 1994, Dermatoglyphics: Science in Transition, 1991; contbr. articles on neurodegenerative disorders, neurosci. and aging to profl. jours.; patentee bil. agts. Recipient Commendation for Rsch., Guam Legislature, 1987, Spl. Achievement award, 1990, Merit award NIH, 1991, Dir.'s award, 1993; Wenner-Gren Found. leadership grantee, 1986, grantee, 1993-95, NIH grant, 2003—; Alumni fellow Pa. State U., 1987. Fellow AAAS, Am. Coll. Epidemiology, Am. Dermatoglyphics Assn. (sec.-treas. 1981-82, pres. 1987-89, disting. achievement award 1995), Human Biology Assn. (pres./pres.-elect 1993-96, exec. com. 1991-93), Internat. Assn. of Human Biologists (pres. 1999-2002, Gorjanović-Krambergeri medal 1999-2000, Franz Boas Disting. Achievement award 2005), Internat. Genetic Epidemiology Soc. (founding fellow), NAS, Acad. Sci. for the Developing World; mem. Soc. for Neurosci., World Fedn. Neurology (rsch. com. on neurepidemiology). Avocations: field trialing, environmental projects. Business E-Mail: rgarruto@binghamton.edu.

GARRY, JAMES B., historian, naturalist, storyteller, writer; b. Taylor, Tex., Apr. 28, 1947; s. Mahon Barker and Grace (Dellinger) G. BS, U. Mich., 1970, MS, 1975. Part-time wilderness guide, naturalist Triangle X Ranch, Moose, Wyo., 1969-75; community organizer, media cons., tchr. Hobart St. Project, Detroit, 1974-75; media specialist, lobbyist Powder River Basin Resource Coun., Sheridan, Wyo., 1975-76; pvt. practice media and polit. cons. Big Horn, Wyo., 1976-78; video and film artist-in-residence Wyo. Coun. on the Arts/Sheridan Coll., Sheridan, 1978-80; mem. staff Great Plains Lore and Natural History, Big Horn, 1980—. Storyteller Buffalo Bill Hist. Ctr., Cody, Wyo., 1980—; tchr. Yellowstone (Wyo.) Inst., 1986—; tour study leader, rsch. collaborator Smithsonian Instn., Washington, 1984—. Co-author: Writing About Wildlife, 1974; author, editor: Buck: Stories by Lloyd Buck Bader, 1984, This Ol' Drought Ain't Broke Us Yet But We're All Bent Pretty Bad, 1992, The First Liar Never Has a Chance: Curly, Jack and Bill (and Other Characters of the Hills, Brush and Plains), 1994; storyteller in field. 2d lt. U.S. Army, 1970. Recipient Spl. Heritage award Old West Trail Found., 1983; named one of Individual Humanist of Yr., Wyo. Coun. for Humanities, 1986. Democrat. Roman Catholic. Avocation: nature. Office: Great Plains Lore and Natural History PO Box 2165 Cody WY 82414-2165 Office Phone: 307-272-5749.

GARSCADDEN, ALAN, physicist; b. Glasgow, Scotland, June 10, 1937; came to U.S., 1962; s. Andrew and Sarah Florence (Black) G.; m. Avril Margaret Thompson Garscadden, Jan. 24, 1962; children: A. Graeme, A.K. Neil, A.K. Gael, A.E. Hilary. BS (hon.), Queens U., Belfast, Ireland, 1958; PhD in Physics, 1962. Rsch. physicist Aerospace Rsch. Labs, Wright-Patterson AFB, 1962-73; lab. dir., 1973-75; rsch. physicist Aero Propulsion and Power Divsn., 1975-91; chief scientist Aero Propulsion Directorate, 1991-94, Wright Lab., 1995-97, Propulsion Directorate/Air Force Rsch. Lab., Wright-Patterson AFB, 1997—, Edwards AFB, Calif., 1997—. Adj. prof. physics Air Force Inst. Tech., Wright Patterson AFB, 1969—; trustee Ohio Aerospace Inst., 1996-98; bd. dirs. Von Karman Inst., 1997-2006. Contbr. articles to profl. jours. Commr. Planning Commn., Village of Yellow Springs, 1985-96. Decorated DSM USAF; recipient Presdl. Meritorious award, 2003; fellow, Air Force Rsch. Lab. Fellow IEEE, AIAA, Am. Phys. Soc. (Will Allis prize 2002), Inst. Physics (U.K.). Avocation: history. Office: AFRL/PR Air Force Rsch lab 1950 5th St Wright Patterson Afb OH 45433-7251 Office Phone: 937-255-2246. Business E-Mail: alan.garscadden@wpafb.af.mil.

GARSH, THOMAS BURTON, publisher; b. New Rochelle, NY, Dec. 12, 1931; s. Harry and Matilda (Smith) G.; m. Beatrice J. Schmidt; children: Carol Jean, Thomas Burton, Janice Lynn. BS, U. Md., 1955. Edn. rep. McGraw Hill Book Co., NYC, 1959-68; mktg. mgr. D.C. Heath & Co., Boston, 1969-71; dir. mktg. Economy Co., Oklahoma City, 1971-72; sr. v.p. Macmillan Pub. Co., NYC, 1972-78; pres. Am. Book Co., NYC, 1978-81; founder, pres., dir. Am. Ednl. Computer, Inc., Palo Alto, Calif., 1981-86. Founder, chmn., chief exec. officer OmnyEd Corp., Palo Alto, 1987-91; pres. Silver Burdett & Ginn divsn. of Simon and Schuster, 1991-92; dir. Fifty Plus Fitness Assn., Palo Alto, Calif. Publ. Homes and Land of Santa Clara, 1998—. Mem. county council Boy Scouts Am., 1963-65; mem. ch. council on Interracial Affairs, 1966-68, pres., 1967; vice-chmn. Madison County Democratic Party, 1967. Mem. Assn. Am. Pubs., Profl. Bookman's Assn., Omicron Delta Kappa, Sigma Alpha Epsilon. Clubs: Cazenovia Country (founder). Home: 401 Old Spanish Trl Portola Valley CA 94028 E-mail: tnb401@aol.com.

GARSON, ARNOLD HUGH, publishing executive; b. Lincoln, Nebr., May 29, 1941; s. Sam B. and Celia (Stine) Garson; m. Marilyn Grace Baird, Aug. 15, 1964; children: Scott Arnold, Christopher Baird, Gillian Grace, Megan Jane. BA, U. Nebr., 1964; MS, UCLA, 1965. Reporter Omaha World-Herald, 1965-69, Des Moines Tribune, 1969-72, city editor, 1972-75; reporter Des Moines Register, 1975-83, mng. editor, 1983-88; editor San Bernardino (Calif.) County Sun, 1988-96; pub., pres. Sioux Falls (S.D.) Argus Leader, 1996—; v.p. Gannett Pacific Newspaper Group, 2000—. Past pres. S.D. Symphony Orch.; mem. adv. bd. Neuharth Ctr. U. S.D. Recipient Pub. Svc. Reporting award, Am. Polit. Sci. Assn., 1969, Mng. Editors Sweepstakes award, Iowa AP, 1976, John Hancock award for excellence in bus. and fin. journalism, 1979, Calif.-Nev. AP award for column writing, 1995. Mem.: S.D. Newspaper Assn. (past pres.). Jewish. Home: 5 S Riverview Hts Sioux Falls SD 57105-0252 Office: Sioux Falls Argus Leader PO Box 5034 Sioux Falls SD 57117-5034

GARSON, ARTHUR, JR., dean, medical educator; b. NYC; m. Suzan Garson; 2 children. Grad., Princeton U., 1970; MD, Duke U., 1974; MPH, U. Tex., Houston, 1992. V.p. Tex. Children's Hosp.; fellow in pediat. cardiology Baylor Coll. Medicine, 1979, chief pediat. cardiology, 1988, sr. v.p., dean acad. ops., 1995; assoc. vice chancellor health affairs Duke U., 1992; dean, v.p. U. Va. Sch. Medicine, 2002—. Mem. White House Adv. Panel on Health Sys. Improvement; chair quality nat. adv. coun. Agy. Healthcare Rsch. Mem.: Assn. Acad. Health Ctrs., U. Hosps. Consortium, Assn. Am. Med. Colls. (adv. panel on healthcare delivery), Am. Coll. Cardiology (pres. 2000—01, trustee, mem. govt. rels. com., mem. quality of care com.). Office: U Va Health Sys PO Box 800793 Charlottesville VA 22908 Office Phone: 434-924-5118. E-mail: garson@virginia.edu.

GARSON, GARY WAYNE, lawyer, diversified holding company executive; b. NYC, Oct. 16, 1946; s. Norman and Pearl (Milikowski) G.; m. Bernice Susan Schumer, June 17, 1967; children: Burt M., Lauren L. BA, Queens Coll., 1967; JD, Bklyn. Law Sch., 1970. Bar: NY 1971. Assoc. Lord, Day & Lord, NYC, 1970-79; asst. gen. counsel Loews Corp., NYC, 1979-85, dep. gen. counsel, 1985—2002, v.p., 1988—2002, sr. v.p., sec., gen. counsel, 2002—. Mem. NYC Bar Assn. (com. on uniform state laws 1974-77, com. on mcpl. affairs 1978-81). Avocation: sailing. Office: Loews Corp 667 Madison Ave Fl 7 New York NY 10021-8087 Office Phone: 212-545-2932.*

GARSTANG, ROY HENRY, astrophysicist, educator; b. Southport, Eng., Sept. 18, 1925; came to U.S., 1964; s. Percy Brocklehurst and Eunice (Gledhill) G.; m. Ann Clemence Hawk, Aug. 11, 1959; children: Jennifer Katherine, Susan Veronica. BA, U. Cambridge, 1946, MA, 1950, PhD, 1954, Sc.D., 1983. Research assoc. U. Chgo., 1951-52; lectr. astronomy U. Coll., London, 1952-60; reader astronomy U. London, 1960-64, asst. dir. Obs., 1959-64; prof. astrophysics U. Colo., Boulder, 1964-94, chair faculty assembly, 1988-89, prof. emeritus, 1994—; chmn. Joint Inst. for Lab. Astrophysics, 1966-67. Cons. Nat. Bur. Standards, 1964—73, Internat. Commn. Illumination, 1990—; v.p. commn. 14 Internat. Astron. Union, 1970—73, pres., 1973—76; Erskine vis. fellow U. Canterbury, New Zealand, 1971; vis. prof. U. Calif., Santa Cruz, 1971. Editor: Observatory, 1953-60; Contbr. numerous articles to tech. jours. Recipient Excellence in Svc. award, U. Colo., 1990. Fellow Am. Phys. Soc., AAAS, Optical Soc. Am., Brit. Inst. Physics, Royal Astron. Soc.; mem. Am. Astron. Soc., Royal Soc. Scis. Liege (Belgium). Achievements include rsch. on atomic physics and astrophys. applications; calculation of atomic transition probabilities, atomic spectra in very high magnetic fields and magnetic white dwarf stars; modelling of light pollution. Home: 830 8th St Boulder CO 80302-7409 Office: U Colo Boulder CO 80309-0440 Home Phone: 303-444-3606; Office Phone: 303-492-7795. Personal E-mail: garstang@earthlink.net.

GARSTEN, JOEL JAY, gastroenterologist; b. NYC, Jan. 10, 1948; s. Richard Maxwell and Gertrude Ann (Perlberg) G.; m. Marion Susan Moscovitz, July 10, 1971; children: Bryan David, Lauren Roberta. BA in Biology, CUNY, 1968; MD, Georgetown U., 1973. Resident in internal medicine Cornell-Coop. Hosps. Program, NYC, 1973-76; fellow gastroenterology Yale Affiliated Gastroenterology Program, New Haven and Waterbury, Conn., 1976-78; gastroenterologist Gastroenterology Assocs. of Waterbury, 1978-90; physican, mng. ptnr. Digestive Disease Ctr. of Conn., 1990—; dir. sect. of gastroenterology Waterbury Hosp. Health Ctr., 1990—; assoc. dir. Yale Affiliated GI fellowship program Waterbury Hosp. and Hosp. of St. Raphael, New Haven and Waterbury, 1990-2000; clin. instr. internal medicine Yale U. Sch. Medicine, New Haven, 1978, asst. clin. prof., 1981, assoc. clin. prof., 1987—. Med. dir. Liberty Health Plan, Naugatuck, Conn., 1987-89, Physicians Health Plan, Trumbull, Conn., 1989-90, med. adv. bd., 1990-92. Contbr. articles to profl. jours. Med. adv. chmn. Crohn's and Colitis Found., WTBY Satelite, Waterbury, 1990—; resource speaker Waterbury Celiac Group, Thomaston, Conn., 1990—, Am. Cancer Soc., 1991—; prin. investigator multiple drug trials. Fellow ACP, Am. Coll. Gastroenterology; mem. Am. Soc. for Liver Disease, Conn. Soc. Internal Medicine (pres. sect. gastroenterology 1996-98), Am. Soc. Internal Medicine, Am. Gastroenterology Assn., Am. Soc. Parenteral and Enteral Nutrition, others. Achievements include introduction of home parenteral nutrition of sclerotherapy, esophageal stenting, percutaneous gastrostomy, other endoscopic techniques to Waterbury; prin. investigator in drug rsch. trials (chosen for Best Drs. in the Am.). Home: 47 Harvest Ct Cheshire CT 06410-1844 Office: Digestive Disease Ctr Conn 60 Westwood Ave Waterbury CT 06708-2460 Office Phone: 203-574-3007. Business E-Mail: jgarsten@ddcct.com.

GARTEN, DAVID BURTON, lawyer; b. Iowa City, Mar. 23, 1952; s. William B. and Linda (Laird) G.; m. Anita Wallner, Mar. 12, 1983. BA summa cum laude, honors in Econs., Yale U., 1974, JD, 1977. Bar: Ill. 1979. Law clk. to Hon. Anthony M. Kennedy U.S. Ct. Appeals (9th cir.), Sacramento, 1977-78; assoc. Kirkland & Ellis, Chgo., 1979-84, ptnr., 1984-90; v.p., gen. counsel NL Industries Inc., Houston, 1990—2004, Chevron Corp., San Ramon, Calif., 2004—. Mem. Phi Beta Kappa. Avocations: skiing, golf. Office: Chevron Corp 6001 Bollinger Canyon Rd T3046 A7 San Ramon CA 94583 Office Phone: 925-842-3232. Office Fax: 925-842-2022.

GARTEN, INA, chef; m. Jeffrey Garten. Mgmt. and budget office The White House, 1978; owner Barefoot Contessa specialty food store, 1978—96. Author: Barefoot Contessa Cookbook, 1999, Barefoot Contessa Parties!, 2001, Barefoot Contessa Family Style, 2002, Barefoot in Paris, 2004, Barefoot Contessa at Home, 2006; host Barefoot Contessa, Food Network, columnist Martha Stewart Living mag., featured in O Mag. Office: Barefoot Contessa 46 Newtown Ln East Hampton NY 11937*

GARTEN, JEFFREY E., finance educator; BA, Dartmouth Coll., 1968; MA, Johns Hopkins U., 1972, PhD, 1980. Mng. dir. Lehman Brothers and the Blackstone Group, NYC, 1979-92; undersec. commerce internat. trade Washington, 1993-95; dean Yale Sch. Mgmt., New Haven, 1995—2005, Juan Trippe prof. in practice of internat. trade, fin., and bus., 2005—. Bd. dirs. Aetna Corp., CarMax, Inc., Credit Suisse Asset Mgmt., The Conf. Bd., The Internat. Rescue Com. Author: A Cold Peace: America, Japan, Germany and the Struggle for Supremacy, 1993, The Big Ten: The Big Emerging Markets and How They Will Change Our Lives, 1997, The Mind of the CEO, 2001, The Politics of Fortune: A New Agenda for Business Leaders, 2002; editor: World View: Global Strategies for the New Economy, 2000; contbr. articles to profl. journals. Capt. U.S. Army Special Forces. Office: Yale School of Management PO Box 208200 135 Prospect St New Haven CT 06520-8200 Office Phone: 203-432-6179. E-mail: jeffrey.garten@yale.edu.

GARTEN, MORRIS L., lawyer; b. Balt., Feb. 1, 1967; BA, Franklin and Marshall Coll., 1989; JD, U. Balt., 1995. Bar: Md. 1995, DC 1998. Law clk. to Hon. Barbara Kerr Howe Balt. County, Md. Cir. Ct., 1995—96; atty. Fedder & Garten, Balt. Mem.: ABA, Md. State Bar Assn., Balt. County Bar Assn., Bar Assn. Balt. City, Franklin and Marshall Coll. Alumni Assn., Associated Jewish Cmty. Fedn. Balt. (chmn. 2000—01, pres. 2004—). Office: Fedder & Garten 36 S Charles St Ste 2300 Charles Ctr S Baltimore MD 21201 Office Phone: 410-539-2800. Office Fax: 410-659-0543. E-mail: MGarten@fedgar.com.*

GARTENBERG, SEYMOUR LEE, retired recording industry executive; b. NYC, May 27, 1931; s. Morris and Anna (Banner) G.; m. Anna Stassi, Feb. 18, 1956 (dec. Feb. 3, 1998); children: Leslie, Karen, Mark; m. Phyllis H. Hecker, Mar. 14, 1999. BBA cum laude, CCNY, 1952, LHD (hon.), 1996. Asst. contr. Finlay Straus, Inc., NYC, 1950-56; contr. Tappin's Inc., Newark, 1956; sr. v.p. Columbia House divsn. CBS, NYC, 1956-65; v.p. fin. Columbia Records divsn. CBS, NYC, 1965-67; exec. v.p. Columbia House divsn. CBS, NYC, 1967-73; pres. CBS Toys Divsn., Cranbury, NJ, 1973-78; v.p. CBS/Columbia Group, NYC, 1978—; sr. group v.p. CBS Records Group, 1979-87; exec. v.p. CBS Records Inc., 1987-91; ret., 1991. Mem.: Am. Mgmt. Assn., Inst. Mgmt. Accts., Mill Island Civic Assn. Personal E-mail: garten@optonline.net.

GARTENHAUS, SOLOMON, physicist, educator; b. Kassel, Germany, Jan. 3, 1929; came to U.S., 1937, naturalized, 1943; s. Leopolt and Hanna (Brandler) G.; m. Johanna Lore Weisz, Aug. 30, 1953; children: Michael M., Kevin M. BS, U. Pa., 1951; MS, U. Ill., 1953, PhD, 1955. Instr. Stanford U., 1955-58; faculty physics Purdue U., Lafayette, Ind., 1958—, prof., 1963—; asst. dean Grad. Sch., 1972-77, sec. of faculties, 1980—. Disting. vis. prof. USAF Acad., Colo., 1977-78; dir. Purdue-Ind. Studienprogram, U. Hamburg, W. Ger., 1979-80; cons. Lockheed, summers 1958-60; officer, dir. Advanced Research Corp., 1961-65 Author: Elements of Plasma Physics, 1964, Physics-Basic Principles, 1975; contbr. articles to profl. jours. Fellow Am. Phys. Soc.; mem. N.Y. Acad. Scis., Am. Assn. Physics Tchrs., Phi Beta Kappa, Sigma Xi. Home: 2102 S 9th St Lafayette IN 47905-2132 Office: Purdue U Dept Physics Lafayette IN 47907 E-mail: garten@physics.purdue.edu.

GARTH, LEONARD I., judge; b. Bklyn., Apr. 7, 1921; s. Frank A. and Anne F. Goldstein; m. Sarah Miriam Kaufman, Sept. 6, 1942; 1 child, Tobie Gail Garth Meisel. BA, Columbia U., 1942; postgrad., Nat. Inst. Pub. Affairs, 1942—43; LLB, Harvard U., 1952. Bar: N.J. 1952. Mem. firm Cole, Berman & Garth (and predecessors), Paterson, NJ, 1952—70; judge US Dist. Ct. for Dist. NJ, Newark, 1970—73, US Ct. Appeals (3d cir.), 1973—; lectr. Inst. Continuing Legal Edn.; lectr., coadj. mem. faculty Rutgers U. Law Sch., 1978—98, Seton Hall Law Sch., 1980—95. Mem. N.J. Bd. Bar Examiners, 1964—68; mem. com. on revision gen. and admiralty rules Fed. Dist. Ct. N.J.; former mem. com. on fin. disclosure Jud. Conf. U.S.; adv. bd. Fed. Cts. Study Com. Pres.; trustee Harvard Law Sch. Assn. N.J., 1958—63; adv. bd. Law and Soc. Major of Ramapo Coll. 1st lt. US Army, 1943—46. Mem.: FBA, ABA (N.J. fellows, appellate judges conf.), Am. Law Inst., Passaic County (N.J.) Bar Assn. (pres. 1967—68). Office: Ct Appeals ML King Jr Fed Bldg 50 Walnut St Rm 5040 Newark NJ 07102-3506 also: 20613 US Courthouse Philadelphia PA 19106 Business E-Mail: chambers_of_judge_leonard_garth@ca3.uscourts.gov.*

GARTHOFF, RAYMOND LEONARD, retired diplomat, diplomatic historian; b. Cairo, Mar. 26, 1929; parents Am. citizens; s. Arnold Alexander and Margaret Louise (Frank) G.; m. Vera Alexandrovna Vasilieva, Sept. 16, 1950; 1 child, Alexander Raymond. AB, Princeton U., 1948; MA, Yale U., 1949, PhD, 1951. Rsch. staff RAND Corp., Washington, 1950-57; estimates officer CIA, Washington, 1957-61; spl. asst for Soviet bloc polit. mil. affairs U.S. Dept. of State, Washington, 1961—68, counselor for polit.-mil. affairs US mission to NATO, 1968—70, exec. sec. US delegation to US-Soviet strategic arms talks, 1969—73, dep. dir. bur. politics-mil. affairs, 1970—73, pres. sr. seminar, 1973—74, sr. fgn. svc. inspector, 1974—77, amb. to Bulgaria, 1977—79; sr. fellow Brookings Instn., Washington, 1980-94. Author: Detente and Confrontation, 1985, rev. edit., 1994, Deterrence and Revolution in Soviet Military Doctrine, 1990, The Great Transition, 1994, Reflections on the Cuban Missile Crisis, 1987, rev. edit. 1989, A Journey through the Cold War, 2001, 11 other books; editor, co-author 90 books; contbr. over 100 articles to profl. jours. Recipient Arthur S. Flemming award Jaycees, 1965, Superior Honor award Dept. of State, 1965, Disting. Honor award, 1972, Wilbur L. Cross medal Yale U., 1992. Mem. Coun. Fgn. Rels., Soc. for Historians of Am. Fgn. Rels., Internat. Inst. for Strategic Studies, Acad. Polit. Sci., Assn. Diplomatic Studies. Home: 1901 Wyoming Ave NW Apt 14 Washington DC 20009

GARTHWAITE, GENE RALPH, historian, educator; b. Mt. Hope, Wis., July 15, 1933; s. Ralph Albert and Merle I. (Quarne) G.; div.; children: R. Andrew, Alexander, Martin. BA, St. Olaf Coll., 1955; postgrad., U Chgo., 1958-59; PhD, U. Calif., 1969; MA, Dartmouth Coll., 1987. From instr. to prof. history Dartmouth Coll., Hanover, NH, 1968-98, chair Asian studies, 1980-92, chair history dept., 1992-96, Jane & Raphael Bernstein prof. in Asian studies, 1998—. Author: Khans and Shahs, 1983, The Persians, 2004, 06; contbr. articles to profl. jours. Capt. USAF, 1955-58. Grantee Social Sci. Rsch. Coun., NEH, 1979-80, 91-93. Mem. Middle East Studies Assn. (dir. 1968—), Soc. Iranian Studies (exec. sec. 1969—), Phi Beta

Kappa. Democrat. Episcopalian. Avocation: gardening. Office: Dartmouth Coll Dept History Hanover NH 03755 Office Phone: 603-646-2594. E-mail: gene.r.garthwaite@dartmouth.edu.

GARTHWAITE, THOMAS LEONARD, medical officer; b. Port Allegany, Pa., July 8, 1947; 2 children. AB, Cornell U.; MD, Temple U., 1973. Intern Med. Coll. Wis. Affiliated Hosp., 1973—74, resident, 1974—76; with Veterans Health Adminstrn., 1976—87, chief of staff, 1987—95, dep. under sec. for health, 1995—2000, undersec. for health, 2000—02; assoc. prof., medicine Med. Coll. Wis., 1985—95, assoc. dean, 1987—95; dir., chief med. officer L.A. Co. Dept. Health Svcs., 2002—05; chief med. officer Catholic Health East, Newton Square, 2006—. Office: Catholic Health East 14 Campus Blvd Ste 300 Newtown Square PA 19073

GARTLAND, ALICE JOHNSON, artist; b. Phila., Jan. 27, 1922; d. Nelson Vincent Johnson and Alice Marie McDonald; m. Henry Joseph Gartland, Apr. 15, 1944; children: Kevin Henry, Michael Henry, Sean Henry. Student, Mary Washington Coll., 1945-46, George Washington U., 1950, Santa Fe C.C., 1971-72, Fla. C.C. With U.S. Govt., Phila., 1940—42, Petersburg, Va., 1942—44; tchr. Fla. CC, Jacksonville, 1989—91; writer, columnist Art Scene Beaches Leader Newspaper, Jacksonville, 1991—. Exhibitions include St. Augustine Art Assn., 1994, Beaches Fine Arts Guild, 1990 (1st Prize), Gainesville Fine Arts Guild, 1980, Art League, Washington, 1975, 1984, Fla. Capitol, Tallahassee, 2001, one-woman shows include Cultural Ctr., Alantic Beach, Fla., 2003—04, Art Ctr., Jacksonville Beach, Fla., 1990, 1998. Pres., founder Beaches Art Found., Jacksonville, 1990; pres. Beaches Fine Arts Guild, Jacksonville; bd. dirs., 1st v.p. Beaches Area Hist. Soc., Jacksonville, 1995-2000; bd. dirs., chmn. cultural bd. City of Atlantic Beach, Fla., 1995-2000, 03; apptd. by mayor Cultural Coun. City of Jacksonville, 2002—; bd. dirs. Beaches Fine Arts Coun., Jacksonville Beach, Fla., City Grants Com., Jacksonville, 1991, 92; cultural coun. Jacksonville, 2001—; active Atlantic Beach Pub. Arts Commn., 2005-07. Recipient Monetary award Jacksonville Comty. Found., 1994; named Beaches Arts Ctr. scholarship in her honor, 2005. Mem. Nat. Soc. Arts and Letters (pres., v.p. Fla. chpt.). Republican. Roman Catholic. Avocations: reading, gardening, painting. Home: 1140 Seminole Rd Atlantic Beach FL 32233-5505 Personal E-mail: kmgg@aol.com.

GARTLAND, JOHN JOSEPH, physician, writer; b. Phila., Nov. 16, 1918; s. John Joseph and Jane Madelyn (Lafferty) G.; m. Madelyn T. Duffy, Jan. 5, 1944; children: Lynn, Barbara, John Jr., Patricia, Mary Ellen. AB, Princeton U., 1941; MD, Jefferson Med. Coll., 1944. Diplomate Am. Bd. of Orthopaedic Surgery. Chief orthopaedic surgery Meth. Hosp., Phila., 1960-68, Lankenau Hosp., Phila., 1968-70; James Edward prof., chmn. dept. of orthopaedic surgery Jefferson Med. Coll., Thomas Jefferson U., Phila., 1970-85, dir. office departmental rev. Jefferson Med. Coll., 1986-89, univ. med. editor, 1990—. Author: Fundamentals of Orthopaedics, 1965, 4th edit., 1986, Medical Writing and Communicating, 1993; contbr. numerous articles to profl. jours. Trustee Thomas Jefferson U., 1996-2002. Served to capt. U.S. Army, 1945-47. NIH grantee, 1971-74. Fellow Am. Acad. Orthopaedic Surgeons (pres. 1979-80), Am. Orthopaedic Assn.; mem. Coun. Med. Splty. Socs. (pres. elect 1987, pres. 1988), Overbrook Golf Club (Bryn Mawr, Pa.), Alpha Omega Alpha, Sigma Xi. Democrat. Roman Catholic. Avocations: tennis, writing. Office: Thomas Jefferson U 1710 Edison Bldg 130 S 9th St Philadelphia PA 19107 Home Phone: 610-649-0995; Office Phone: 215-503-4042.

GARTMAN, DAVID MINER, cardiothoracic surgeon; b. Columbia, La. s. David Miner and Billie Marie Gartman; m. Mary Gregg, Nov. 20, 1987; children: Jackson, Lucas. BS, La. State U., Baton Rouge, 1976; MD, La. State Med. Ctr., New Orleans, 1980. Resident surgery Yale U., New Haven, 1980—86; fellow cardiac surgery U. Wash., Seattle, 1986—89, attending cardiac surgeon, 1989—90, Children's Hosp., Seattle, 1989—92, Swedish-Providence Hosp., Seattle, 1990—. Chmn. Swedish-Providence Hosp., 1995—2004; cons. Medtronic, Mpls., 1998—2004. Contbr. scientific papers, articles to profl. jours. Recipient George Sam Bell award, La. State U. Med. Ctr., 1980. Fellow: ACS; mem.: AMA, King County Med. Assn., Seattle Surg. Soc., Internat. Soc. Minimally Invasive Surgery, Soc. Thoracic Surgeons, Western Thoracic Surg. Assn., Donald Ross Soc., Alpha Omega Alpha (pres. 1979—80), Phi Kappa Phi. Avocations: motorcycling, woodworking, skiing, coaching, Karate. Office: Swedish Cardiac Surgery Ste 110 1600 W Jefferson Seattle WA 98122 Office Phone: 206-320-7300. Business E-Mail: david.gartman@sweish.org.

GARTMAN, MAX DILLON, language educator; b. Mobile, Ala., May 3, 1938; s. Noah Christopher and Edna Olga (Schwarzauer) G.; m. Marcia Ann Hubbard, Aug. 31, 1962; children: Noel Don, Polly Antoinette, Paul Dillon. AB in French and History, Samford U., Birmingham, Ala., 1960; MA in French, U. Ala., Tuscaloosa, 1962, PhD in Romance Langs., 1974; cert., U. Nice, France, 1985. NDEA fellow U. Ala., Tuscaloosa, 1960-65; prof. Romance langs. Samford U., 1965-82, head dept. fgn. langs., 1975-82; chmn. dept. fgn. langs., prof. romance langs. U. North Ala., Florence, 1982-99, dir. Ctr. for Critical Langs., 1999—2003; dir. French program, profl. French and Spanish Bryan Coll., Dayton, Tenn., 2003—05; prof. Spanish and French Chattanooga State Tech. CC, 2006—. Pres. Internat. Edn. Travel, Florence, 1982—. Editor SU Faculty Forum Ann., 1967-72; performer rec. The Holy City, 1976. Chmn. Ala. Assn. Fgn. Lang. Tchrs., 1973-74, So. Conf. Lang. Tchg., 1976; bd. dirs. Ala. Humanities Found., 1992-96. Mem. Ala. Assn. Tchrs. of French (chmn. 1995-97), Ala. Consortium for Fgn. Langs. (chmn. 1995-97, 2001-02), Rotary (Paul Harris fellow). Baptist. Avocations: tennis, music, european travel. Office: Rm 211 Humanities Bldg Chattanooga State Tech Coll 4501 Amnicola Hwy Chattanooga TN 37406-1097 Home: 3097 N Market St Dayton TN 37321-1060 Home Phone: 423-775-6867; Office Phone: 423-697-2505. Personal E-mail: mdgartman@charter.net.

GARTNER, HAROLD HENRY, III, lawyer; b. LA, June 23, 1948; s. Harold Henry Jr. and Frances Mildred (Evans) Gartner; m. Denise Helene Young, June 7, 1975 (div. 2003); children: Patrick Christopher, Matthew Alexander. Student, Pasadena City Coll., 1966-67, George Williams Coll., 1967-68, Calif. State U., Los Angeles, 1969; JD cum laude, Loyola U., Los Angeles, 1972. Bar: Calif. 1972, U.S. Dist. Ct. (ctrl. dist.) 1973, U.S. Ct. Appeals (9th cir.) 1973. Assoc. Hitt, Murray & Caffray, Long Beach, Calif., 1972; dep. city atty. City of L.A., 1972-73; assoc. Patterson, Ritner & Lockwood, LA, 1973-79; mng. ptnr. all offices Patterson, Ritner, Lockwood, Gartner & Jurich, LA, Bakersfield, and San Bernardino, Calif., 1991—2006; ret., 2006; of counsel Law Office Eugene Chittuck, Susanville, Calif., 2007—. Instr. law Ventura Coll., 1981. Recipient Am. Jurisprudence award Trusts and Equity, 1971. Mem. ABA, Am. Bd. Trial Advocates, Calif. Bar Assn., Ventura County Bar Assn., Nat. Assn. Def. Counsel, Assn. Am. Bd. Trial Advocates. Republican. Avocations: sailing, scuba diving, flying. Home: 463-515 Spears Rd Janesville CA 96114 Office: Law Offices Eugene Chittuck 100 S Lassen St Susanville CA 96130 Office Phone: 530-257-9351. Personal E-mail: hgartner@frontiernet.net. Business E-Mail: hgartner@chittucklaw.com.

GARTNER, JOSEPH CHARLES, retired systems administrator; b. Detroit, Feb. 3, 1945; s. Joseph Owen and Frances Alice (Harrington) G.; m. Marilyn Jean Kern, June 26, 1971; children: Stephanie, Jonathan, Jamie Lynn. Student, U. Mich., 1963-66; BSE, Marquette U., 1968; MBA, U. Rochester, 1979. Cert. systems profl. Constrn. engr. B.A.S.F., Wyandotte, Mich., 1966-67; systems engr. IBM Corp., Milw., 1968-70; mgr. mgmt. info. systems Borg Warner Corp., Toledo, 1970-73; dir. info. systems Donnelly Corp., Holland, Mich., 1973-75; mgr. fin. systems Bausch & Lomb, Rochester, NY, 1975-82, mgr. EDP audit, 1982-85; mgr. bus. systems Wegmans Food Markets Inc., Rochester, 1985-97; group mgr. bus. sys. Penn Traffic Co., Syracuse, NY, 1997—2007; ret., 2007. Trustee Fairport Pub. Libr., NY, 1992-2002. Mem. Assn. for Systems Mgmt. (internat. dir. 1984-87, Disting. Svc. award 1988), KC (grand knight 1985-87), Genesee Valley Dist. PTA (legis. chmn. 1985—). Home: 3139 Fox Rd Syracuse NY 13215-9744 Office Phone: 315-254-6455. Personal E-mail: gartnerjc@aol.com.

GARTNER, JOSEPH JOHN, II, obstetrician, gynecologist; b. Hackensack, NJ, Feb. 21, 1943; s. Joseph John Gartner and Hilda Hasenfuss. BA, Monmouth Coll., Ill., 1965; MS, Fairleigh Dickinson U., Teaneck, NJ, 1967; MD, Mt. Sinai Sch. Medicine, NYC, 1971. Asst. clin. instr. Fairleigh Dickinson U., 1966—77; intern Hackensack Hosp. Med. Ctr., NJ, 1971—72, resident in psychiatry, 1972—75; resident in ob-gyn. St. Joseph's Hosp. Med. Ctr., Paterson, NJ, 1975—77; assoc. dir. ob-gyn. Margaret Hague Matowitz Hosp., Jersey City, 1977—79; founder Bergen Passaic Ob-Gyn. Ctr., Wyckoff, NJ, 1979—; restauranteur, founder, CEO Metronome Hospitality Group, NYC, 1993—; pres., founder Gartner Real Estate Co., Wyckoff, 1996—. Dir. Planned Parenthood Passaic County, Paterson, NY, 1978. Mem.: Med. Soc. NJ, Bergen County Med. Soc., Beta Beta Beta. Avocation: tennis. Home: 334 W Shore Dr Wyckoff NJ 07481 Office: Bergen Passaic Ob-Gyn 258 Godwin Ave Wyckoff NJ 07481 Office Phone: 201-891-7631.

GARTNER, LAWRENCE MITCHELL, pediatrician, medical educator; b. Bklyn., Apr. 24, 1933; s. Samuel and Bertha (Brimberg) G.; m. Carol Sue Blicker, Aug. 12, 1956; children— Alex David, Madeline Hallie. AB, Columbia U., 1954; MD, Johns Hopkins U., 1958. Intern pediatrics Johns Hopkins Hosp., 1958-59; resident pediatrics Albert Einstein Coll. Medicine, 1959-60, chief resident, 1960-61, instr. pediatrics, 1962-64, asst. prof., 1964-69, assoc. prof., 1969-74, prof., 1974-80, dir. divsn. neonatology, 1967-80, dir. divsn. pediatric hepatology, 1967-80; dir. clin. research unit Rose F. Kennedy Ctr., 1972-80; attending physician Hosp. of Albert Einstein Coll. Medicine, 1967-80; prof. dept. pediatrics U. Chgo. Pritzker Sch. Medicine, 1980-98, prof. dept. obstetrics and gynecology, 1995-98, prof. emeritus pediatrics and obstetrics and gynecology, 1998—; chmn. dept. pediatrics, med. dir. Wyler Children's Hosp., U. Chgo. Med. Ctr., 1980-93. Chmn. Physicians Breastfeeding Network of Ill., 1993-98. Contbr. articles to med. jours. and textbooks. Pediatrician-of-the-Yr. award Ill. chpt. Am. Acad. Pediatrics, 1995; recipient award NIH, 1967-74; Appleton Century Crofts prize, 1956; Mosby book award, 1958. Mem. AAAS, Am. Pediatric Soc. (chmn. coun. 1989-90), Soc. Pediatric Rsch., Perinatal Rsch. Soc., Am. Assn. Study Liver Disease, Chgo. Pediatric Soc. (editor 1990-91, treas. 1992-93, sec. 1993-94, v.p. 1994-95, pres. 1995-96), Am. Acad. Pediatrics (chair breastfeeding workgroup 1994-2000, chair exec. com. sect. on breastfeeding 2000-06), N.Am. Soc. Pediatric Gastroenterology (pres. 1974-75), The Milk Club (chmn. 1994-96), Acad. Breastfeeding Medicine (founding bd. dirs. 1994-95, editor newsletter 1995-2000, v.p. 1997-98, pres., 1998-99, adv. coun. 2006—), LaLeche League Internat., Phi Beta Kappa, Alpha Omega Alpha. Personal E-mail: gart@midway.uchicago.edu.

GARTNER, MICHAEL CONSTANTIN, plastic surgeon; b. Bklyn., Aug. 7, 1964; married; 3 children. BS, Boston U.; MD, U. Medicine and Dentistry of NJ, 1993. Cert. Am. Bd. Plastic Surgeons, Am. Bd. Surgery. Intern, gen. surgery Atlantic City Med. Ctr., NJ, 1993—94; resident, plastic reconstructive surgery Monmouth Med. Ctr., Long Branch, NJ, 1994—99; fellow, hand surgery Nassau County Med. Ctr., East Meadow, NY, 1999—2001; fellow, micro surgery Thomas Jefferson U., Phila., 2001, fellow, 2001; staff mem. Centra State Med. Ctr., Freehold, NJ, Paramus Surgery Ctr., Paramus, NJ, The Valley Hosp., Ridgewood, NJ; private practice NJ. Spkr. in field. Performed charitable surgeries Healing the Children. Named one of Consumer's Rsch. Coun. Am., Guide to America's Top Plastic Surgeons, 2004—06. Fellow: Am. Coll. Surgeons; mem.: AMA, ACS (NJ Chpt.), ACS, NY Regional Soc. Plastic and Reconstructive Surgeons, Am. Soc. Plastic Surgeons. Being one of the few plastic surgeons in the country who performs scar-less breast augmentation through the bellybutton (trans-umbilical-breast augmentation), scar-less breast reduction, minimal scar facial rejuvenation and gluteus enhancement (Brazilian Butt Lift). Office: 351 Evelyn St Paramus NJ 07652 Address: 44 Monmouth Rd Eatontown NJ 07724 Office Fax: 201-265-1300.*

GARTNER, MICHAEL GAY, editor, baseball and television executive; b. Des Moines, Oct. 25, 1938; s. Carl David and Mary Marguerite (Gay) Gartner; m. Barbara Jean McCoy, May 25, 1968; children: Melissa, Christopher (dec.), Michael. BA, Carleton Coll., 1960; JD, NYU, 1969; LittD (hon.), Simpson Coll., 1984; LLD (hon.), James Madison U., 1989; LittD (hon.), Grand View Coll., 1990, Iowa Wesleyan Coll., 1997; LLD (hon.), Drake U., 2001. Bar: NY, Iowa. With Wall St. Jour., NYC, 1960—74, page one editor, 1970—74; exec. editor Des Moines Register and Tribune, 1974—76, editor, 1976—82, editl. chmn., 1982—85, v.p., 1975—76, exec. v.p., 1977, pres., COO, 1978—85; editor Courier-Jour. and Louisville Times, 1986—87; gen. news exec. Gannett Co., 1987—88; pres. NBC News, 1988—93; editor, co-owner Ames (Iowa) Daily Tribune, 1986—99; chmn., majority-owner Iowa Cubs, 1999—; chmn., co-owner New West Newspapers, 2000—06. Bd. dirs. Creative Loafing, Inc., Big Green Umbrella Assn. Syndicated columnist on lang., 1978—95, columnist USA Today, 1993—98; author: Outrage, Passion & Uncommon Sense, 2005. Chmn. Vision Iowa, 2000—05; hon. trustee Simpson Coll.; mem. Pulitzer Prize Bd., 1982—92, chmn., 1991—92; trustee Freedom Forum Newseum, Washington, Freedom Forum Diversity Inst.; bd. dirs. World Food Prize; pres. Iowa Bd. Regents, 2005—. Recipient Pulitzer prize for editl. writing, 1997; fellow, Harvard U. Inst. Politics, 1994. Mem.: Am. Soc. Newspaper Editors (pres. 1986—87), Assn. Bar City N.Y., Iowa Bar Assn., ABA, Wakonda Club. also: 366 W 11th St New York NY 10014-6225 Office: One Line Dr Des Moines IA 50309-4631 Home: 100 Market St Unit 515 Des Moines IA 50309 Business E-Mail: mgartner@iowacubs.com.

GARTNER, MIKE (MICHAEL ALFRED GARTNER), former sports association administrator, retired professional hockey player; b. Ottawa, Ont., Can., Oct. 29, 1959; married; children: Joshua, Natalie, Dylan. Right wing Washington Capitals, Landover, Md., 1979-89, Minn. North Stars, Mpls., 1989-90, NY Rangers, 1990-94, Toronto Maple Leafs, 1994-96, Phoenix Coyotes, 1996-98; pres. NHL Players Assn., Toronto, 1996—98, dir. bus. rels., 1999—2006, dir. hockey affairs, 2006—07. Player NHL All-Star game, 1980, 85, 86, 88, 90, 93. Named to Team Can. World Hockey Championships, 1981, 82, 83, All-Star MVP, 1993. Achievements include being inducted into the Hockey Hall of Fame, 2001.*

GARTNER, MURRAY, lawyer; b. NYC, Sept. 23, 1922; s. Leo and Celia G.; m. Anne Ellis Thompson, June 9, 1961; children: Marion Moreau, Thomas Murray. AB, NYU, 1942; LLB, Harvard U., 1945. Bar: N.Y. 1946, Calif. 1948. Law clk. to assoc. justice Robert H. Jackson U.S. Supreme Ct., Washington, 1945-47; assoc. Pillsbury, Madison & Sutro, San Francisco, 1947-51; lectr. law Hastings Coll. Law, San Francisco, 1948; asst. to gen. counsel U.S. rep. in Paris, Econ. Coop. Adminstrn. Mut. Security Adminstrn., 1951-53; assoc. Roosevelt, Freidin & Littauer, NYC, 1953-59; ptnr. Poletti, Freidin, Prashker & Gartner (and predecessors), NYC, 1959-85, Proskauer Rose, LLP, NYC, 1985-2000. Trustee Children's Aid Soc., 1971-2004. Office: Proskauer Rose LLP 1585 Broadway New York NY 10036-8299

GARTNER, STEVEN J., lawyer; b. Westwood, NJ, Nov. 22, 1959; BSBA, Georgetown U., 1981; JD magna cum laude, St. John's U., 1984. Bar: NY 1985, NJ 1986. Assoc. Willkie Farr & Gallagher LLP, London, 1988—90, ptnr., Corp. and Fin. Svcs. Dept. NYC. Office: Willkie Farr & Gallagher LLP 787 Seventh Ave New York NY 10019 Office Phone: 212-728-8222. E-mail: sgartner@willkie.com.

GARTON, ROBERT DEAN, state legislator; b. Chariton, Iowa, Aug. 18, 1933; s. Jesse Glenn and Ruth Irene (Wright) G.; m. Barbara Hicks, June 17, 1955; children: Bradford, Brenda. BS, Iowa State U., 1955; MS, Cornell U., 1959. Pers. rep. Cummins Engine Co., Columbus, Ind., 1959-61; owner Garton Assocs. Mgmt. Cons., Columbus, 1961-96; v.p. profl. devel. Ivy Tech. Cmty. Coll., Columbus, 1996—; mem. Ind. Senate, Indpls., 1970—2006, minority caucus chmn., 1976-78, majority caucus chmn., 1978-80, pres. pro tempore, 1980—2006. Bd. dirs. Rural Water Sys., 1969—. Mem. exec. com. Nat. Conf. State Legislatures, 1989-92; chmn. Mid-West Conf. State Legislatures, Coun. State Govts., 1984-85, mem. gov. bd., 1985-2006; chmn. Ind. Civil Rights Commn., 1969-70; mem. exec. com. Nat. Fedn. Young Reps., 1966; trustee Franklin Coll., 1998—; bd. dirs. Independent Colls. of Ind., 2001—06, State Legis. Leaders Found., 2003—06. With USMCR, 1955-57. Co-recipient William M. Bulger Excellence in State Legis. Leadership award, 1999, Legislator of Yr. award, Ind. Civil Liberties Union, 2000; named a Legislator honoree, Ind. Coalition Human Svcs., 2006; named Hon. Citizen, Iowa, 1962, winner internat. speech contest, Toastmasters, 1962, Hon. Citizen, Tenn., 1977, Small Bus. Champion, Ind. Small Bus. Coun., 1997, Pub. Servant of the Yr., Ind. Assn. Rehab. Facilities, 2000, Hon. Field Examiner, State Bd. Accts., 2005, Ind. Wildlife Legis. Conservationist of Yr., 2006; named one of 5 Outstanding Young Men in Ind., 1968; recipient Disting. Svc. award, Jr. C. of C. Columbus, 1968, Guardian Small Bus. award, Nat. Fedn. for Ind. Bus., 1990, Man of Yr., Ind. Rep. Mayor's Assn., 1991, Guardian Small Bus. award, Nat. Fedn. Ind. Bus., 1993, 1994, Lee Atwater Leadership award, Nat. Rep. Legislator Assn., 1991, Outstanding Pub. Svc. award, Podiatric Assn., 1993, United Sr. Action Legis. Leadership award, 1994, Outstanding Govt. Leader award, Apt. Assn. Ind., 1998, Freedom of Road award, ABATE of Ind., 2000, Senator of Yr. award, Ind. Primary Health Care Assn., 2001, Friend of Edn. award, N. Ctrl. Bus. Edn. Assn., 2001, Disting. Pub. Svc. award, Am. Legion, 2001, Pub. Sector award, Benjamin Harrison Medallion, 2001, Friend of Autism award, 2001, Legislator of Yr., Trial Lawyers Assn., 2003, first Virgil "Gus" Grissom Leadership award, Consulting Engrs. Ind., 2005, Lifetime Achievement award, 2005, ARC Ind., 2005, Mental Health Assn. Am., 2006, Becky Campbell Lifetime Achievement award, Johnson County Retarded Citizens, 2006, First Freedom award, Hoosier State Press Assn., 2007. Mem. Rotary, Beta Theta Pi. Office: Ivy Tech Cmty Coll PO Box 1111 Columbus IN 47202-1111 Business E-Mail: rgarton@ivytech.edu.

GARTON, THOMAS WILLIAM, lawyer; b. Ft. Dodge, Iowa, Jan. 19, 1947; s. H. Boyd and Ruth A. (Porter) G.; m. Marcia K. Hoover, June 21, 1969; children: Geoffrey, Matthew. BA, Carleton Coll., 1969; JD magna cum laude, U. Minn., 1974. Assoc. Fredrikson & Byron, PA, Mpls., 1974-80, shareholder, 1980—, chmn. corp. practice group. Adj. prof. William Mitchell Coll. Law, St. Paul, Minn., 1977-80, U. Minn. Law Sch., Mpls., 1980; bd. dirs. RS/Eden Programs; presenter continuing legal edn. seminars on tax, mergers and acquisitions, and bus. planning, 1977—. With U.S. Army, 1969-71. Mem. ABA (tax sect.), Minn. Bar Assn. (dir. tax coun. 1987-89). Office: Fredrikson & Byron PA 200 S Sixth St Ste4000 Minneapolis MN 55402-1425 Business E-Mail: tgarton@fredlaw.com.

GARTRELL, DAVID CHRISTIAN, archivist; b. Norfolk, Va., Aug. 22, 1969; s. Cecil Eugene and Wilma Goodwin Gartrell; m. Susan Leigh Garrison, June 18, 1994; 1 child, William Goodwin. BA, Va. Commonwealth U., 1992; MLIS, UCLA, 1997. Cert. archivist Acad. Cert. Archivists, 1998. Archivist, humanistic psychology archives Davidson Libr., U. Calif., 1999—2001, archivist and manuscripts curator, 2001—. Archivist, John C. Liebeskind history of pain collection Louise Darling Biomed. Libr., UCLA, 1996—98. Vestry mem., clk. Trinity Episcopal Ch., Santa Barbara, 2005—. Mem.: Jamestowne Soc., Acad. Cert. Archivists, Soc. Am. Archivists. Episcopalian. Avocation: horseback riding. Office: Spl Collections Davidson Libr U Calif Santa Barbara CA 93106-9010 Office Phone: 805-893-7912. Business E-Mail: gartrell@library.ucsb.edu.

GARTZ, ROLF F., foundation administrator; b. Bonn, Germany, Dec. 23, 1940; s. Fritz and Hildegard (Rhein) G.; m. Christel Anneliese Overgahr gen. Willebrand, Aug. 7, 1970; 1 child, Stephan. Student, Bonn and Cologne U., Germany, 1964—69; PhD in Cell Biology, Bonn U., 1969; PhD (hon.), State U. Social Scis., Moscow, 2000. Civil servant, govt. dir., Germany, 1970-90; mng. chmn. Eduard Rhein Found., Hamburg, Germany, 1990—; prof. Tech. U. MIREA, 2005—. Bd. dirs. Prof. Rhein Found., Koenigswinter, Germany, 1987—; academician Internat. Informatization Acad., 2000; hon. prof. internat. bus. sch. MIRBIS, 2003. Decorated Cross of the Order of Merit Fed. Republic of Germany; recipient Sputnik medal Russian Fedn. Cosmonautics, 2000, Highest Order of Merit, Internat. Informatization Acad., 2001. Mem. AAAS, NY Acad. Scis., Assn. German Natural Scientists and Physicians, German Soc. Cell Biology, Max Planck Soc. for Advancement of Sci., Soc. Biochemistry and Molecular Biology. Avocations: hunting, riding. Home and Office: Eduard-Rhein-Stiftung Alex von Humboldt Str 6 D-56727 Mayen Germany Office Phone: 0049-2651-77270. Office Fax: 0049-2651-1003. E-mail: rheinstiftung@t-online.de.

GARUTHARA, ROHANA K., physics professor; s. James Garuthara and Nape Withanage; m. Senani Garuthara; 1 child, Thilini. PhD, CUNY, 1980—86. Prof. physics Hofstra U., Hempstead, NY, 1990—. Charity worker, Sri Lanka, 1983. Sentinal Party. Achievements include patents for opto-electronic trigger pulse device for a streak camera; research in laser spectroscopy. Office: Hofstra Univ Physics & Astronomy Dept Hempstead NY 11550 Office Fax: 516-463-3059. Business E-Mail: phyrkg@hofstra.edu.

GARVENS, ELLEN JO, artist, educator; b. Omro, Wis., Aug. 15, 1955; d. Leonard Kenneth and Eugenia Mary (Wetter) G.; m. James Patrick Phalen, Oct. 18, 1988; children: Cole Garvens Phalen, Mason Garvens Phalen. BS in Art, U. Wis., 1979; MA, U. N. Mex., 1982, MFA, 1987. Asst. prof. of art Oberlin (Ohio) Coll., 1990-94; assoc. prof. art U. Wash., Seattle, 1994—. Artist: one person shows include: Humboldt State, 2000, Jayne H. Baum Gallery, N.Y.C., 1986, 89, 93, Wooster (Ohio) Mus. of Art, U. R.I., Kingston. Recipient Wis. Women in Arts award Madison, 1978, Fullbright Hays scholarship Internat. Comm. Agy., Washington, 1979-80; grantee, NEA, Washington, 1986, HC Powers grant, Oberlin Coll., 1991, Royalty Rsch. Fund grant, U. Wash., 1996, Artist Trust Washington State fellowship, 2000—. Home: 19518 67th Ave NE Kenmore WA 98028-3447 Office: U Wash Sch of Art PO Box 353440 Seattle WA 98195-3440 E-mail: elgarv@u.washington.edu.

GARVER, ROBERT VERNON, retired research physicist; b. Mpls., June 2, 1932; s. Walter Burdette and Daveda Margaret (Hansen) G.; m. Shirley Marie Phillips, June 15, 1957; children: Debra, Douglas, Daniel, Mary, Jennifer. BS, U. Md., 1956; M.E.A., George Washington U., 1968. Physicist Harry Diamond Labs., Washington, 1956-69, supervisory physicist, 1969-89. Program mgr. Army High Power Microwave Hardening Tech., 1982-89; cons. Weinschel Engring., Gaithersburg, Md., 1970-75; chmn. electromagnetic effects subcom. DoD VHSIC Qualification Com., 1981-89; pvt. cons., 1989-95; sr. engr. Xeta Internat. Corp., Crystal City, Va., 1990-95; cons. Envisioneering, Inc., Dahlgren, Va., 2000-05; developer Leap Flight Tech., The Garver Product Co., 2000-. Author: Microwave Diode Control Devices, 1976; inventor Microwave Diode Switch; patentee in field. Elder Presbyn. Ch., Germantown, Md., 1975. Served with

U.S. Army, 1953-54. Fellow: IEEE (editor Jour. Solid State Cirs. 1969—73, mem. nat. adminstrv. com. profl. group microwave theory and techniques); mem.: Toastmasters. Republican. Home and Office: 2393 Bear Den Rd Frederick MD 21701-9328

GARVER, THOMAS HASKELL, curator, consultant, writer; b. Duluth, Minn., Jan. 23, 1934; s. Harvie Adair and Margaret Hope (Foght) G.; m. Natasha Nicholson, Apr. 13, 1974. BA, Haverford Coll., 1956; MA, U. Minn., 1965. Asst. to dir. Krannert Art Mus., U. Ill., Urbana, 1960-62; asst. dir. fine arts dept. Seattle World's Fair, 1962, Rose Art Mus., Brandeis U., Waltham, Mass., 1962-68; dir. Newport Harbor Art Mus. (now Orange County Mus. Art), Calif., 1968-72, 77-80; curator exhbns. Fine Arts Mus. of San Francisco, 1972-77; dir. Madison (Wis.) Art Ctr., 1980-87; asst. prof. Calif. State U., 1970-71, 79-80. Curator art collection Rayovac Corp., Madison, 1985-2001; organizing curator O. Winston Link Mus., Roanoke, Va., 2001-04. Author: Twelve Photographers of the American Social Landscape, 1967, Just Before the War: Urban American from 1935-41, 1968, The Paintings of George Tooker, 1985, rev. edit., 1992, The Last Steam Railroad in America: Photographs by O. Winston Link, 1995; exhbn. catalogues including Robert Rauschenberg, 1969, Tom Wesselmann, 1971, Reginald Marsh, 1972, Joseph Raffael, Paintings From the California Years, 1977, George Herms, 1978, 83, Nathan Oliveira, 1984, George Tooker, Paintings, 1983-87, 88, Mind and Beast: Contemporary Artists and the Animal Kingdom, 1992, Flora: Contemporary Artists and the World of Flowers, 1995, Trains that Passed in the Night: The Railroad Photographs of O. Winston Link, 1998, WATER: Contemporary Artists Who Use Water as a Theme in Their Art, Gibbes Mus. of Art, Charleston, S.C., 1999. Trustee U.S.S. Mass. Meml. Commn., Fall River, 1965-68; trustee South Coast Repertory Co., Costa Mesa, Calif., 1970-72; trustee Wis. Citizens for Arts, 1985-87; steering com. Archives Am. Art, San Francisco, 1977-80; active Newport Beach Art Commn., 1978-79, Madison Com. for Arts, 1984-87. Mem. Western Assn. Art Mus. (pres. 1970-71, trustee 1970-73), Art Mus. Assn. Am. (pres. 1979-82, trustee 1979-85). Home and Office: 1962 Atwood Ave Madison WI 53704-5221 Home Phone: 608-246-3964; Office Phone: 608-246-3967. Business E-Mail: thgart@aol.com.

GARVEY, DANIEL EDWARD, foundation administrator, educator; b. Westfield, Mass., Apr. 25, 1950; s. John Henry and Ruth Marie (Long) G.; m. Barbara Nelson, Apr. 28, 1973; children: Kathryn, Connor. BA in Sociology, Worcester State Coll., 1973; MA in Social Change, Cambridge Goddard Coll., 1974; PhD in Edn., U. Colo., 1990. Dir. Upward Bound U. NH, Durham, 1974-79, assoc. dean students, 1979-88, adj. assoc. prof., 1988; exec. dir. Assn. for Exptl. Edn., Boulder, Colo., 1988-91; v.p. Am. Youth Found., Ossipee, NH, 1991; pres. Prescott Coll., 2001—. Adj. assoc. prof. Moscow State U.; dean, semeseter at sea prog., U. Pitts., mem., exec. com. AmeriCorps, trustee, Nat. Outdoor Leadership Sch., mem., bd. dirs., Project Am., Ariz. State Commn. Svc. and Volunteerism Guest editor Multi-Cultural Issues in Edn., 1992; author Management Development Directory, 1989; contbr. articles to profl. jours. Coach Youth Soccer, South Berwick, Maine; vol. Volunteers in Svc. to Am. Recipient Kurt Hahn award, 1997, Outstanding Teaching award, UNH Sch. Health Studies, 1998, Julian Smith award, 2002. Mem.: Assn. Experiential Edn. (pres., exec. dir.). Avocations: music, woodworking. Office: Prescott Coll Office of Pres 220 Grove Ave Prescott AZ 86301*

GARVEY, JOANNE MARIE, lawyer; b. Oakland, Calif., Apr. 23, 1935; d. James M. and Marian A. (Dean) Garvey. AB with honors, U. Calif., Berkeley, 1956, MA, 1957, JD, 1961. Bar: Calif. 1962. Assoc. Cavaletto, Webster, Mullen & McCaughey, Santa Barbara, Calif., 1961-63, Jordan, Keeler & Seligman, San Francisco, 1963-67, ptnr., 1968-88, Heller, Ehrman, White & McAuliffe, San Francisco, 1988—. Bd. dirs. Mex.-Am. Legal Def. and Ednl. Fund; chmn. Law in Free Soc., Continuing Edn. Bar; mem. bd. councillors U. So. Calif. Law Ctr. Recipient Paul Veazy award, YMCA, 1973, Internat. Women's Yr. award, Queen's Bench, 1975, honors, Advs. Women, 1978, CRLA award, Boalt Hall Citation award, 1998, Judge Lowell Jensen Cmty. Svc. award, 2001, Margaret Brent award, 2003, Latcham State and Local Disting. Svc. award, 2003, Lifetime Achievement award, Am. Lawyer mag., 2006. Fellow: Am. Bar Found.; mem.: ABA (gov., state del., chmn. SCLAID, chmn.delivery legal svcs., chmn. 10LTA), Calif. Women Lawyers (founder), Am. Law Inst., San Francisco Bar Assn. (pres., pres. Barristers), Calif. State Bar (v.p., gov., tax sect., del., Jud Klein award, Joanne Garvey award), Phi Beta Kappa, Order of Coif. Democrat. Roman Catholic. Home: 16 Kensington Ct Kensington CA 94707-1010 Office: 333 Bush St San Francisco CA 94104-2806 Office Phone: 415-772-6729. Business E-Mail: joanne.garvey@hellerehrman.com.

GARVEY, JOHN HUGH, dean, law educator; b. Sharon, Pa., Sept. 28, 1948; s. Cyril T. and Claudia C. (Evans) G.; m. Jeanne Barnes Walter, Aug. 30, 1975. AB, U. Notre Dame, 1970; JD, Harvard U., 1974. Bar: Ky. 1976, U.S. Supreme Ct. 1982. Law clk. to chief judge U.S. Ct. Appeals (2d cir.), NYC, 1974-75; assoc. Morrison & Foerster, San Francisco, 1975-76; asst. prof. Coll. Law U. Ky., Lexington, 1976-79, assoc. prof. Coll. Law, 1979-80, prof. Coll. Law, 1981-94; Univ. Rsch. prof. Coll. Law, 1989-90, Ashland prof., 1990-94; prof. Notre Dame Law Sch., South Bend, Ind., 1994-99; dean Boston Coll. Law Sch., Chestnut Hill, 1999—. Asst. to Solicitor Gen., U.S. Dept. Justice, Washington, 1981-84; vis. prof. law sch. U. Mich., Ann Arbor, 1985-86; chmn. constl. law sect. Assn. Am. Law Schs., Washington, 1991-93, chmn. law and religion sect., 1998-99. Author: Modern Constitutional Theory, 1989, 5th edit., 2004, The First Amendment, 1992, 2d edit., 1995, What Are Freedoms For?, 1996. Recipient Alpha Sigma Nu Jesuit Book Award, 2004; fellow Danforth Found., 1970. Mem. Am. Law Inst., Assn. Am. Law Schs. (exec. com. 2004—). Office: Boston Coll Law Sch Stuart House M307 885 Centre St Newton Center MA 02459 Office Phone: 617-552-4340. E-mail: john.garvey.1@bc.edu.*

GARVEY, RICHARD ANTHONY, retired lawyer; b. NYC, Jan. 10, 1950; s. James Joseph Garvey and Janet Mary (Mooney) Rowse. AB, Boston Coll., 1972; JD, Harvard U., 1975. Bar: N.Y. 1976. Assoc. Simpson Thacher & Bartlett, NYC, 1975-82, ptnr., 1982—93, 1997—2003, of counsel, 2003—. Mem. ABA, N.Y. State Bar Assn., Assn. Bar City N.Y., Phi Beta Kappa. Home: Apt 7D 105 Fifth Ave New York NY 10003 Office: Simpson Thacher & Bartlett 425 Lexington Ave New York NY 10017 Office Phone: 212-455-2578. Business E-Mail: rgarvey@stblaw.com.

GARVEY, TONI, library director; m. Kevin Garvey; children: Brendan, Tess. BA, Western Mich. U., 1975, MLS, 1977. Children's libr. Tucson-Pima Pub. Libr., Ariz., 1979; dep. dir. Loudoun County Pub. Libr., Leesburg, Va., 1987, dir. libr. svcs.; city libr. Phoenix Pub. Libr., 1996—; dir. Phoenix Libr. Dept., 2002—. Pres. Pub. Libr. Assn., 2002; bd. mem. Librs. for the Future. Named Libr. of Yr., Libr. Jour., 2004. Mem.: ALA. Office: Phoenix Pub Libr 1221 N Central Ave Phoenix AZ 85004 E-mail: toni.garvey@phoenix.gov.

GARVICK, KENNETH RYAN, broadcast engineer, announcer, educator; b. Akron, Ohio, Apr. 11, 1945; s. Kenneth Rodger and Dorothy Lillian G. Diploma, DeVry Inst. Tech., Chgo., 1966, Cleve. Inst., 1970, diploma, 1981. Cert. electronic technician. Electronic repairman RCA Consumer Electronics, Indpls., 1966—70; compilation technician Howard W. Sams & Co., Indpls., 1970—73; broadcast engr. Sta. WIBC/WNAP Fairbanks Broadcasting, Indpls., 1973; announcer, engr. Stas. WHYT-AM, WNON-FM, 1974—76; transmitter engr. Sta. WISH-TV, Indpls., 1976—79; instr. electronics Arsenal Tech. H.S., Indpls., 1979—82; announcer, engr. Stas. WSVL AM/FM, 1979—81; instr. various schs., Ohio, 1987—2005; announcer, engr. Sta. WMAN-AM, 1994—95. Author: Gerberich Descendants from York, PA, 1987; contbr. articles to profl. jours. With Signal Corps U.S. Army, 1966-72, Vietnam. Mem. Soc. Broadcast Engrs., Arsenal Tech., Radio Club (sec. 1979-82). Republican. Avocations: film history, amateur radio, bicycling. Address: 210 Fiftieth Ave Ter W Bradenton FL 34207-2741

GARVIN, ANDREW PAUL, computer company executive, writer; b. NYC, July 24, 1945; s. Gene G. and Nora (Sheldon) London; m. 2d Linda Gail Bernstein, Oct. 1, 1983; children: Kira, Jeffrey. BA, Yale U., 1967; MS, Columbia U., 1968. Corr. Newsweek mag., NYC, 1967-68; v.p. Four Elements, Inc., NYC, 1968-69; co-founder, pres. FIND SVP, Inc., NYC, 1970—, Info. Clearing House, Inc., NYC, 1970—2004. Author: How to Win With Information, 1983, The Art of Being Well Informed, 1996. Chmn. Nat. Info. Conf. and Expn., Washington, 1979. Mem. Info. Industry Assn. (dir. 1979-82 Product of Yr. award 1974), Assn. Info. Mgrs. (dir. 1978-82), Am. Mktg. Assn., Am. Mgmt. Assn., Spl. Libraries Assn., St. Elmo Soc. (treas. 1974-81), Young Pres.' Orgn. Office: Guideline Inc 625 Ave of the Americas New York NY 10011-2095 Business E-Mail: agarvin@guideline.com.

GARVIN, FLORENCE WARD, management consultant; b. Ft. Sam Houston, Tex., Oct. 6, 1928; d. Edward Joseph and Florence Emily (Bock) Ward; m. Sheldon R. Rappaport, Mar. 2, 1950 (div. July 1969); children: Bruce Ward, Lisa Lynn; m. Stefan J. Garvin, Oct. 3, 1981. BA, Our Lady of Lake U., San Antonio, 1949; postgrad., Trinity U., San Antonio, 1949-50. Co-founder, asst. to pres. Pathway Sch., Norristown, Pa., 1961—68; adminstrv. dir. Neurosurg. Clinic for Children, Media, Pa., 1968—70; v.p. for devel. Vanguard Schs., Haverford, Pa., 1970—72; asst. to pres. Elwyn (Pa.) Inst., 1972—75; pvt. practice Media, 1976—78; cons. employee rels. dept. E.I. DuPont de Nemours & Co., Inc., Wilmington, Del., 1978—85, sr. bus. assoc. internat. dept., 1985—89, mgr. bus. rels. devel., 1989—90, mgr. internat. human resources devel. human resources dept., 1990—94. Dir. spl. project Gabriella and Paul Rosenbaum Found., 1997—2001, bus. mgr., 2006—; mng. dir. Rose Tree media Ednl. Found., 2000—01; cons. Delaware County Office of Adult Svcs., 2003—04. Charter mem., bd. dirs. Montgomery County Mental Health Clinics, 1956-72; bd. dirs. Phila. United Fund, 1969-72; bd. mgrs., sec. Garrett-Williamson Found., 1973-81; trustee Wilmington Coll., 1979—, Curtis Inst. Music, 1985-92; devel. com. Mercy Haverford Hosp., 1994-95; policy coun. Del. County Head Start, 1994-96; pres. bd. dirs. AIDS Task Force/Phila. Cmty. Health Alternatives, 1994-96; bd. dirs. Mary Campbell Ctr., Wilmington, 1978-81, Pacific Rim Bus. Coun., 1994-96, Nationalities Svc. Ctr., 1996-98, Green Cir. Program, 1996-98, East Side Charter Sch., Wilmington, Del., 1996-98; pres. bd. dirs. Delaware County AIDS Network, 1999-2002; v.p. bd. dirs. Media Fellowship House, 2003-04; trustee Phila. Acad. Natural Scis., 2006—. Home: 2 Yarmouth Ln Media PA 19063-4327 Office Phone: 610-565-7348.

GARVIN, MICHELE M., lawyer; b. Nov. 8, 1952; BA, Coll. William & Mary, 1974; MA, Boston Coll., 1977, PhD Sociology, 1981; JD, Suffolk Univ., 1987. Bar: Mass. 1988. Assoc. to ptnr. corp. dept. Ropes & Gray, Boston, 1988—, chmn. health care practice group. Contbr. articles to profl. jours., chapters to books. Mem.: ABA, Mass. Bar Assn., Boston Bar Assn., Jackson Hole Task Force on HCCPs. Office: Ropes & Gray 1 International Pl Boston MA 02110-2624 Office Phone: 617-951-7495. Office Fax: 617-951-7050. Business E-Mail: michele.garvin@ropesgray.com.

GARVRE, FANNY P., art gallery owner; b. Racine, Wis., Apr. 3, 1927; d. August and Sarafina Pcitolka Puchinsky; m. John C. Garver, June 18, 1948; children: John C. Jr., Christian J., Sara A. BA, U. Wis., Madison, 1947, BLA, 1950. Libr. U. Wis. Med. Sch., Madison, 1950—51; dir. Jane Haslem Gallery, Madison, 1969—72; owner, dir. Fanny Garver Gallery, Madison, 1972—2000, chmn., cons., 2000—. Mem. planning com. arts Overature Ctr., Madison, 1998; show judge various schs. and mus., 1980—2000. Spl. art shows. Mem. Madison Mus. Contemporary Art, 1975—, Elveyhem Mus., Madison, 1975—, Madison Sr. Ctr., 2001—. Mem.: Blackhawk Country Club, Am. Craft Coun. Office: Fanny Garver Gallery 230 State St Madison WI 53703 Personal E-mail: fcgarver@aol.com.

GARWIN, RICHARD LAWRENCE, physicist; b. Cleve., Apr. 19, 1928; married; 3 children. BS in Physics, Case Western U., 1947, DSc (hon.), 1966; MS, U. Chgo., 1948, PhD in Physics, 1949. Instr. to asst. prof. physics U. Chgo., 1949-52; physicist T.J. Watson Ctr. IBM, Yorktown Heights, NY, 1952-65, dir. applied rsch., 1965-66, lab. dir., 1966-67, fellow, 1967-93, fellow emeritus, 1993—; Phillip D. Reed sr. fellow for sci. and tech. Coun. on Fgn. Rels., NYC, 1994—2004. Cons. Los Alamos (N.Mex.) Sci. Lab., 1950-93, Sandia Nat. Lab., 1994—, U.S. govt. on matters of military technology, arms control, etc.; mem. com. Pres.'s Sci. Adv. Com., 1962-65, 69-72, cons., 1958-62; mem. Def. Sci. Bd., 1966-69; adj. prof. physics Columbia U., 1957—; prof. pub. policy Harvard U., Cambridge, 1979-81, vis. prof. applied physics, 1974; adj. rsch. fellow, Kennedy Sch. of Govt., Harvard U.; mem. scientific adv. group to the Joint Strategic Target Planning Staff; commr. Rumsfeld Commn. to Access the Ballistic Missle Threat to the U.S.; chmn., Arms Control and Nonproliferation Adv. Bd., Dept. State, 1993-2001. Contbr. articles to profl. jours.; co-author: Nuclear Weapons and World Politics, 1977, Nuclear Power Issues and Choices, 1977, Energy: The Next Twenty Years, 1979, Science Advice to the President, 1980, Managing the Plutonium Surplus: Applications and Technical Options, 1994, Feux Folles et Champignons Nucleaires, 1997; co-author: (with Georges Charpak) Megawatts and Megatons: A Turning Point in the Nuclear Age?, 2001. Recipient Wright prize for interdisciplinary scientific achievement, 1983, Ettore Majorana-Erice Sci. for Peace award Ettore Majorana Ctr., 1991, R.V. Jones Intelligence award U.S. Govt. Fgn. Intelligence Cmty., 1996, Enrico Fermi award, 1997, Nat. Medal of Sci. award, 2002. Fellow Am. Phys. Soc.(chmn. panel on pub. affairs, 1978), IEEE, Am. Acad. Arts and Scis. (Sci. Freedom and Responsibility award 1988); mem. NAS, NAE, Inst. of Medicine, Am. Philos. Soc., Inst. for Strategic Studies (coun. 1977-85), Coun. on Fgn. Rels., Fedn. Am. Scientists (bd. dirs.), Pugwash Coun., Union of Concerned Scientists. Achievements include patents in field.

GARWOOD, JULIE, writer; b. 1946; Author: (novels for young adults) A Girl Named Summer, 1985, (as Emily Chase) What's A Girl to Do, 1985, (historical romance novels) Gentle Warrior, 1985, Rebellious Desire, 1986, Honor's Splendor, 1987, The Lion's Lady, 1988, The Bride, 1989, Guardian Angel, 1990, The Gift, 1990, The Prize, 1991, The Secret, 1992, Castles, 1993, Saving Grace, 1993, Prince Charming, 1994, For the Roses, 1995, The Wedding, 1996, One Pink Rose, One White Rose, One Red Rose, Come the Spring, 1997, The Wedding, 1998, Ransom, 1999, Heartbreaker, 2000, Mercy, 2002, Killjoy, 2002, Killjoy, 2003, Murder List, 2004 (Publishers Weekly Bestseller), Slow Burn, 2005 (Publishers Weekly Bestseller), Shadow Dance, 2006. Office: PO Box 7574 Leawood KS 66207-0574 Address: Jane Rotrosen Agy 318 East 51st St New York NY 10022*

GARWOOD, WILLIAM LOCKHART, federal judge; b. Houston, Oct. 29, 1931; s. Wilmer St. John and Ellen Burdine (Clayton) Garwood; m. Merle Castlyn Haffler, Aug. 12, 1955; children: William Lockhart, Mary Elliott. BA, Princeton U., 1952; LLB with honors, U. Tex., 1955. Bar: Tex. 1955, US Supreme Ct. 1959. Law clk. to judge US Ct. Appeals (5th cir.), 1955—56; mem. Graves, Dougherty, Hearon, Moody & Garwood (and predecessor firms), Austin, Tex., 1959—79, 1981; justice Supreme Ct. Tex., Austin, 1979—80; judge US Ct. Appeals (5th cir.), 1981—97, sr. judge, 1997—; dir. Anderson, Clayton & Co., 1976—79, 1981, exec. com., 1977—79, 1981. Mem. adv. com. on appellate rules Jud. Conf. US, 1994—2001, chair, 1997—2001. Pres. Child and Family Svc. of Austin, 1970—71, St. Andrew's Episcopal Sch., Austin, 1972; bd. dirs. Cmty. Coun. Austin and Travis County, 1968—72, Human Opportunities Corp. Austin and Travis County, 1966—70, Mental Health and Mental Retardation Ctr. Austin and Travis County, 1966—69, United Fund Austin and Travis County, 1971—73; mem. adv. bd. Salvation Army, Austin, 1972—. With US Army, 1956—59. Fellow: Tex. Bar Found. (life); mem.: Tex. Law Rev. Assn. (pres. 1990—91, dir. 1986—96), Am. Law Inst. (life), Chancellors, Phi Delta Phi, Order of Coif. Episcopalian. Office: US Ct Appeals Homer Thornberry Jud Bldg 903 San Jacinto Blvd Austin TX 78701-2394*

GARY, JAMES M., lawyer; b. Jonesboro, Ark. BA, Ouachita Bapt. Univ., 1977; JD, Univ. Ark., 1980. Bar: Ark. 1980, Tex. 1998, US Supreme Ct., Us Ct. of Appeals (5th, 8th cir.), US Dist. Ct. (no., so., ea., we. dists.) Tex., US Dist. Ct. (ea., we. dists.) Ark. Now ptnr., head, labor and employment practice group Akin Gump Strauss Hauer & Feld LLP, Austin, Tex. Editl. rev. bd. Tex. Employment Adv., Employer Resource Inst., 1999—2003, contbr. articles to profl. publications. Mem.: ABA, Fed. Bar Assn., Austin Human Resource Mgmt. Assn. (mentor), Soc. for Human Resource Mgmt., Phi Alpha Delta. Office: Akin Gump Strauss Hauer & Feld LLP Ste 2100 300 W Sixth St Austin TX 78701-2916 Office Phone: 512-499-6297. Office Fax: 512-703-1112. Business E-Mail: jgary@akingump.com.

GARY, KENNETH J., lawyer; b. NYC, May 2, 1956; BA, Brown U., 1980; JD, U. Pa., 1983. Bar: NY 1984, Pa. 1986. Atty. Kaye, Scholer, Fierman, Hays & Handler, NYC, 1983—85, Pepper, Hamilton & Scheetz, Phila., 1985—87; asst. v.p. Bell Atlantic Properties, Inc., 1988—2000; sr. v.p., gen. counsel Toll Brothers, Inc., 2000—05; exec. v.p., gen. counsel, sec. Beazer Homes USA, Inc., Atlanta, 2005—. Mem.: ABA, Pa. State Bar Assn., Phila. Bar Assn. Office: Beazer Homes USA Inc Ste 1200 1000 Abernathy Rd Atlanta GA 30328

GARY, MARC, lawyer, former telecommunications industry executive; b. Englewood, NJ, July 14, 1952; BA summa cum laude, Northwestern U., 1974; JD, Georgetown U., 1977. Bar: Va. 1977, DC 1978, US Ct. Appeals (DC cir. and 4th cir.) 1978, US Dist. Ct. (dist. DC) 1978, US Supreme Ct. 1982, US Ct. Appeals (6th cir.) 1983, US Dist. Ct. (dist. Md.) 1985, US Ct. Appeals (9th cir.) 1989. Assoc. Mayer, Brown & Platt, Washington, 1984—90, ptnr., 1984—90, 1992—2000; assoc. ind. counsel Office of Ind. Counsel, Washington, 1990—92; v.p., assoc. gen. counsel Bell South Corp., Atlanta, 2000—04, exec. v.p., gen. counsel, 2004—07. Mem. regulatory agy. task force Pres'. pvt. sector survey cost control, 1982-83. Contbr. articles to profl. jours. Bd. dirs., coun. trustees Am. Friends of Hebrew U., 1995-2000; nat. bd. dirs. United Synagogue of Conservative Judaism, 1994—; bd. dirs. DC Jewish Cmty. Ctr., 1990-2000. Named a Fellow, Am. Bar Found., 1999; named One of 10 Outstanding In-House Counsel, Corp. Counsel mag., 2002. Mem. ABA, DC Bar (pub. svc. activities com., steering com., antitrust, trade resolution and consumer affairs sect.), Va. State Bar, Washington Coun. Lawyers (bd. dirs. 1982-2000), Phi Eta Sigma.*

GARY, RICHARD DAVID, lawyer; b. Richmond, Va., Apr. 25, 1949; s. Morton Nathan and Blanche (Rudy) G.; m. Linda Levene, Aug. 6, 1972; children: Brent Ryan, Lauren Renee. AB in Econs., U. N.C., 1971; JD, U. Va., 1974. Bar: Va. 1974. From assoc. to ptnr.,r egulated industries & govt. rels. Hunton & Williams LLP, Richmond, 1974—, and mem. exec. com. Guest lectr. law Coll. William and Mary, Williamsburg, 1983-90, U. Va. Law Sch., 2004-2005; guest lectr. telecom. Va. Commonwealth U., 2004. Pres. Beth Sholom Home Ctrl. Va., Richmond, 1989-91; chmn. Beth Sholom Home Va., 1991-92, 2005—; v.p. Jewish Cmty. Fedn. Richmond, 2002—. Recipient Disting. Svc. award Beth Sholom Home Ctrl. Va., 1984. Mem. ABA (pub. utilities sect. coun. mem.), Va. State Bar (chmn. adminstrn. law sect. 1982-83), Va. Bar Assn., Fed. Comm Bar Assn., Fed. Energy Bar Assn. Avocation: sports. Office: Hunton & Williams Riverfront Plz East Twr PO Box 1535 Richmond VA 23219-1535 Home: 121 Countryside Ln Richmond VA 23229-7336 Office Phone: 804-788-8330. Office Fax: 804-788-8218. Business E-Mail: rgary@hunton.com.

GARY, STUART HUNTER, lawyer; b. Richmond, Va., Nov. 22, 1946; s. Morton Nathan and Blanche (Rudy) G.; m. Donna (Rothman), Aug. 19, 1967; children: Kenneth Asher, Robin Leigh. BA in Econ., U. Va., 1968; JD, Am. Univ., 1972. Bar: Va., 1972, D.C., 1973, U.S. Dist. Ct. (ea. dist.) Va., 1975, D.C., 1974, U.S. Tax Ct., 1976, U.S. Ct. Appeals (4th cir.), 1975, (D.C. cir.), 1974, U.S. Supreme Ct., 1976. Law clerk D.C. Ct. Appeals, Washington, 1972—73; atty. anti-trust divsn. Fed. Trade Commn., Washington, 1973—74; ptnr. Swift and Gary, Washington, 1974—75, Falcone and Gary, Fairfax, Va., 1975—81; prin. Stuart H. Gary and Assoc., McLean, Va., 1981—85, Stuart H. Gary P.C., McLean, Va., 1992—93, Goodman, Gary, and Lickstein, P.C., 1993—97, Gary and Goodman PLLC, Vienna, Va., 1997—2004, Gary and Regenhardt PLLC, Vienna, 2004—. Bd. cons. Riggs Nat. Bank Va., 1976-88. Editl. bd. Am. U. Law Rev. Washington, 1971-72. Chmn. No. Va. Heart Fund Drive, 1976; bd. dir. No. Va. Jewish Cmty. Ctr., Fairfax, Va.; co-chmn. Am. Assoc. Ben Gurion U. Washington D.C. chpt. Mem. ABA, Va., D.C. Bar Assn., Fairfax County Bar Assn., McLean Bar Assn., Am. Arbitration Assn. (panel of arbitrators). Office: Gary and Regenhardt PLLC 8500 Leesburg Pike Ste 7000 Vienna VA 22182-2498 Office Phone: 703-848-2828. Business E-Mail: wahoo@abanet.org.

GARY, WARLENE D., educational association administrator; BS in Phys. Edn. and Health, DC Tchrs. Coll.; MEd in Spl. Edn., Howard U. Tchr. Washington Pub. Schs.; with Coun. Chief State Sch. Officers, Howard U. Ctr. Study of Handicapped Children and Youth; acting exec. dir. Pres.'s Adv. Com. for Women; staff mem. NEA, Washington, 1981, mgr. intergovernmental rels., assoc. dir. govt. rels., assoc. dir. human and civil rights, mgr. parent and cmty. outreach, dir. Office Human and Civil Rights, 2002; CEO PTA, Chgo. Office: PTA 541 N Fairbanks Ct Ste 1300 Chicago IL 60611-3396 Office Phone: 312-670-6782. Office Fax: 312-670-6783.*

GARY, WILLIE E., lawyer; b. Eastman, Ga., July 12, 1947; s. Turner and Mary Ella (McNarr) G.; m. Gloria R. Gary, Aug. 25, 1978; children: Kenneth, Sekou, Ali, Kobie. BA in Bus. Administrn., Shaw U., 1971; JD, N.C. Cen. U., 1974. Bar: Fla., admitted to practice: US Dist. Ct. (So. Dist.) Fla., US Dist. Ct. (Mid. Dist.) Fla. Pvt. practice, Martin County, Fla., 1975-1976; ptnr. Gary, Williams, Parenti, Finney, Lewis, McManus, Watson, & Sperando, P.L., Stuart, Fla., Fla., 1976—. Founder MTBC Network. Chmn. bldg. fund Evergreen Bapt. Ch. of Indiantown, mem. adult choir; past pres. Young Men's Progressive Assn. of Martin County; chmn. bd. trustees Shaw U.; mem. NAACP, Urban League, Civitan Internat., Fla. Guardsmen, Inc., United Way of Martin County, Martin Mem. Hosp. Found. Coun.; contbr. to various charities. Named Role Model of Yr. Bethune-Cookman Coll., 1989, one of two Coll. Alumni of Yr. United Negro Coll. Fund, 1989; recipient Learned Hand Award, Am. Jewish Com., 1996, Golden Trumpet Award, Turner Broadcasting Co., 1997, Horatio Alger Award, Horatio Alger Soc., 1999; named one of Am.'s Top Black Lawyers, Black Enterprise Mag., 2003, 100 Most Influential Black Americans, Ebony mag., 2006. Mem. ABA, Martin County Bar Assn., St. Lucie Bar Assn., Fla. Bar Assn. (past mem. bd. govs.), Nat. Bar Assn. (past pres. Fla. chpt., Lawyer of Yr.), Fla. Acad. Trial Lawyers, Am. Trial Lawyers Assn., Million Dollar Verdict Club, Phi Alpha Delta. Office: Gary Williams & Parenti Waterside Profl Bldg 221 E Osceola St Ste 300 Stuart FL 34994-2289 also: 320 S Indian River Dr Fort Pierce FL 34950*

GARYPIE, RUDOLPH RENWICK, retired library director; b. Massapequa, NY, May 21, 1932; s. Rudolph Seigfried and Muriel Anderson Garypie; m. Barbara Mathilda Phillips, July 13, 1963; children: Robert, Catherine. BA, Hamilton Coll., 1954; MLS, U. Mich., 1956. Cert. Libr. of

Mich. Profl. asst. Wayne (Mich.) Libr., 1956-62; libr. dir. Ingham County Libr., Mason, Mich., 1962-67, Sioux City (Iowa) Pub. Libr., 1967-69, Genesee Dist. Libr., Flint, Mich., 1969-76, Oxford (Mich.) Pub. Libr., 1976-84, Garfield County Libr., New Castle, Colo., 1984-90, Marshall Dist. Libr., Mich., 1990—2005; ret., 2005. Judge Am. Film Festival, N.Y.C., 1961-62. Organizer regional libr. coop. sys. Capital Libr. Coop., Lansing, Mich., 1965, Siouxland Libr. Coop., Sioux City, 1968, Marshall Dist. Libr., 1995; founder, pres. Garfield County Literacy, Glenwood Springs, Colo., 1984-90; pres., treas. Calhoun County Literacy, Battle Creek, Mich., 1992-2001. Mem. ALA (life), Pub. Libr. Assn., Mich. Libr. Assn., Detroit Suburban Librs. Roundtable, Rotary Club (Paul Harris fellow 1998). Unitarian Universalist. Avocation: camping.

GARZA, ANTONIO O., JR., ambassador; BBA, U. Tex., Austin, 1980; JD, So. Meth. U., 1983. Counsel Garza & Garza, Brownsville, Tex.; judge Cameron County Ct., Tex., 1988—94; sec. state State of Tex., 1995-97; atty. Bracewell & Patterson, LLP, 1997—98; commr. Tex. R.R., 1998—2001; US amb. to Mex. US Dept. State, Mexico City, 2002—. Dir. pks. adv. bd. Tex. Parks and Wildlife Commn.; past mem. State Job Tng. Coord. Coun., Census Complete Count Com., US Marshall Selection Com.; conferee jud. conf., US Ct. Appeals (5th cir.), 1986.; mem. presdl. del. Fed. Elections, El Salvador, 1991; mem. del. to Poland/Hungary, Am. Coun. Young Polit. Leaders, 1993; spkr. in field. Past dir. United Way So. Cameron County; past pres. Rio Grande Valley Big Bros./Big Sisters; dir. Brownsville Adult Lit. Coun. Cameron County; active H.O.S.T. prog. Brownsville Ind. Sch. Dist.; coach soccer and jr. varsity basketball. Named one of Five Outstanding Young Texans, 1989, 1990. Office: US Embassy Paseo de la Reforma 305 06500 Colonia Cuauhtemoc Mexico Mailing: DOS Amb 8700 Mexico City Pl Washington DC 20521-8700*

GARZA, CUTBERTO, nutrition educator; b. San Diego, Tex., Aug. 26, 1947; s. Cutberto and Diamantina (Salinas) G.; m. Yolanda, Mar. 21, 1970; children: Luis-Andres, Carlos-Daniel, Ariel-Abram. BS summa cum laude, Baylor U., 1969; MD, Baylor Coll. Medicine, 1973; PhD, MIT, 1976. Asst. prof. Baylor Coll. Medicine, Houston, 1977-85, assoc. prof., 1984-86, prof., 1986-88, Cornell U. Divsn. Nutritional Sci., Ithaca, NY, 1988—2005, dir., 1988—98, 2003—05; vice-provost Cornell U., 1998-2000; dir. food nutrition program UN Univ., Cornell U., 1998—; acad. v.p., dean of faculty Boston Coll., 2005—. Chmn. Inst. Medicine Food and Nutrition Bd., Washington, 1995-2002; mem. WHO expert adv. panel on nutrition; adv. com., chmn. Nat. Dietary Guidelines, 2000. Contbr. articles to profl. jours. on normal growth of young children, Nutritional Mgmt. of Prematures, Comparison of Energy Expenditure, Energy Expenditure and Deposition. Bd. dirs. Tex. Rehab. Commn., Houston, 1985-88; mem. N.Y. State Pub. Health Coun., 1990-98. Recipient Disting. Achievement award Baylor U., 1986, Alan S. Feinstein World Hunger prize for Edn. and Rsch., Brown U., 1996, Lydia J. Roberts prize U. P.R., 1993. Mem. AAAS, NAS (nat. assoc.), Inst. of Medicine, Am. Soc. Clin. Nutrution, Am. Inst. Nutrition, Am. Pediatric Soc., Soc. Pediatric Rsch. Roman Catholic. Achievements include definition of energy requirements of infants, identification of functional outcomes of infants fed human milk or formula. Office Phone: 617-552-3260.

GARZA, DEBORAH A., federal agency administrator, lawyer; b. 1958; BA magna cum laude, No. Ill. U., 1978; JD, U. Chicago Law Sch., 1981. Bar: DC 1982. Spl. asst. Antitrust Divsn., US Dept. Justice, 1983—84, chief of staff, counselor, 1988—89; editl. chair ABA Antitrust Mag., 2001—04; ptnr. Fried, Frank, Harris, Shriver & Jacobson LLP, 2001—07; leader merger guidelines project team Internat. Competition Network, 2002; dep. asst. atty. gen for regulatory matters Antitrust Divsn., US Dept. Justice, 2007—. Named one of 100 Most Influential Lawyers, Nat. Law Jour., 2006, The 50 Most Influential Women Lawyers in Am., 2007. Office: US Dept Jusice Antitrust Divsn 950 Pennsylvania Ave NW Washington DC 20530*

GARZA, ED, former mayor; b. San Antonio; m. Anna Laura Garza. Student in bus. adminstrn., U. Tex., Austin; B in Landscape Architecture, Tex. A&M U., MS in Land Devel. With various planning, devel., real estate fin., landscape architecture, and architecture firms; dir. land planning and devel. Internat. Waterfront Group, San Antonio; elected dist. 7 rep. San Antonio City Coun.; elected mayor City of San Antonio, 2003—. Adj. prof. U. Tex., San Antonio, St. Mary's U.; v.p. N.Am. Internat. Trade Corridor Partnership (NAITCP). Mem. San Antonio Trees Bd., CEOs for Cities, Urban Land Inst.; Fannie Mae; Internat. Coun. of Shopping Ctrs.; adv. bd. Nat. League of Cities, 2000—, nominating com., 2003—; bd. advisors Nat. Assn. Latino Elected and Appointed Ofcls. (NALEO); past bd. dirs. Jefferson Neighborhood Assn., Woodlawn Lake Neighborhood Assn.; bd. dirs. Hispanic Elected Local Ofcls., 1998—, pres.; bd. dirs. San Antonio Water Sys., City Pub. Svc., Tex. Municipal League. Named one of 40 Under 40 Rising Stars, San Antonio Bus. Jour., 1996. Office: City Hall PO Box 839966 San Antonio TX 78203-3966

GARZA, EMILIO MILLER, federal judge; b. San Antonio, Aug. 1, 1947; s. Antonio Peña and Dionisia (Miller) Garza. BA, U. Notre Dame, 1969, MA, 1970; JD, U. Tex., 1976. Assoc. Clemens, Spencer, Welmaker & Finck, San Antonio, 1976—82, ptnr., 1982—87; dist. judge 225th Dist. Ct., Bexar County, San Antonio, 1987—88, US Dist. Ct. (we. dist.) Tex., San Antonio, 1988—91; judge US Ct. Appeals (5th cir.), San Antonio, 1991—. Adv. coun. U. Tex. San Antonio Coll. Fine Arts and Humanities, 1992—98; adv. bd. Phoenix Inst., 1992—; bd. advisors Hispanic Law Jour. U. Tex. at Austin Sch. Law, 1992—96; adv. com. Notre Dame Law Sch., 1998—; bd. dirs. Symphony Soc. San Antonio, 1987—89; mem. Century Club San Antonio, 1987—88. Capt. USMC, 1970—79, active duty USMC, 1970—73. Mem.: San Antonio Bar Assn., State Bar Tex. Office: 8200 I-10 W Ste 501 San Antonio TX 78230*

GARZA, ROBERTO JESUS, retired education educator; b. Hargill, Tex., Apr. 10, 1934; s. Andres and Nazaria (De La Fuente) G.; m. Idolina Alaniz, Aug. 24, 1957; children: Roberto Jesus Jr., Sylvia Lynn. BA in Psychology, Tex. A&I Coll., Kingsville, 1959, MA in Spanish, 1964; grad., postgrad., U. Tex., Austin, 1960, U. Ariz., Tucson, 1963, grad., postgrad., 1965, U. Kans., Lawrence, 1964—65, U. Wash., Seattle, 1965—66; EdD in Curriculum and Instrn., Higher Edn., Okla. State U., Stillwater, 1975. High sch. tchr. and counselor, Tex., Ill., Wyo., 1959-64; instr., chmn. dept. St. Joseph Jr. Coll., Mo., 1964-65; teaching asst. U. Wash., Seattle, 1965-66; instr., chmn. dept. S.W. Tex. Jr. Coll., Uvalde, 1966-68; prof. Spanish Sul Ross State U., Alpine, Tex., 1968-70; adminstr. Office of Equal Opportunity, Edinburg, Tex., 1970-71; NEH rsch. fellow U. Notre Dame, Ind., 1972-73; prof., chmn. dept. higher edn. U. Tex., Brownsville, 1973-96; ret., 1996. Cons. migrant edn. S.W. Lab., Austin, 1966-67; psychometrist Peace Corps, San Marcos, Tex., 1965; counselor Job Corps, San Marcos, 1966; higher edn. tchr. edn. evaluator Tex. Edn. Agy., Austin, 1980-85; mem. Tex. Edn. Agy. Accreditation Team, 1979-96; journalism scholarship com. KGBT-TV and KRGV-TV, 1979-96; mem. So. Assn. Schs. and Colls. Accreditation Team, 1990-96; cons. U.S. Dept. Edn., 1993—. Author, editor Contemporary Chicano Theatre: An Anthology, 1975. Trustee, v.p., pres. Brownsville Ind. Sch. Dist., 1985-87; mem. Cameron County Appraisal Dist., Brownsville, 1985-87, Tex. Ho. Reps. Resolution #521, 1987; assoc. dir. Reynaldo Garza Law Sch., Edinburg, 1985-87. With U.S. Army, 1954-56. Recipient recognition/appreciation award Brownsville Ind. Sch. Dist., 1987; grantee NDEA, 1963, John Hay Whitney Found., 1970-71; NEH fellow Notre Dame U., 1972-73. Mem. AAUP, So. Assn. of Colls. and Schs., Tex. Assn. Coll. Tchrs., Am. Assn. for Higher Edn., Smithsonian Assocs., Phi Delta Kappa. Democrat. Roman Catholic. Home: 2 Alvarado Ave Rancho Viejo TX 78575-9501 Personal E-mail: rrobertogarza@aol.com.

GARZARELLI, ELAINE MARIE, economist; b. Phila., Oct. 13, 1952; d. Ralph J. and Ida M. (Pierantozzi) G.; BS, NYU, 1973, MBA, 1977, Ph.D, Drexel Univ., 1992. With A.G. Becker, N.Y.C., 1973-84, v.p., economist, 1975-84, mgn. dir., 1984; ptnr., portfolio mgr. Lehman Bros. Inc., 1984-94; prin. Garzarelli Rsch. Inc., 1994—; lectr. in field. COmmentator Fox Bus. News, CNBC, PBS Nightly Bus. Report; Named Businesswoman of Yr. Fortune Mag., 1987, # 1 in Quantitative Analysis, Instl. Investor Annual Contest. Mem. Nat. Assn. Bus. Economists, Women's Fin. Assn., Am. Statis. Assn., Women's Bond Assn. Developer Sector Analysis (econometric model for predicting industry profits and stock price movements, also predicted stock market crash of 1987). Office: Garzarelli Research 534 Hudson St New York NY 10014*

GARZOLINI, JUDITH A., information technology manager; m. Michael Rusnack. BS in Textiles and Clothing, Ind. State U.; BSChemE, Wayne State U.; MBA, U. Calif., Davis. Staff Ford Motor Co., Detroit; rocket engine materials engr. AeroJet Strategic Propulsion Co.; prog. mgr. Hewlett-Packard, Boise, Idaho. Campus diversity coord. Hewlett-Packard-Purdue Tech. Recruiting Team. Co-chair logistics com. Ride Idaho Bicycle Tour, 2005. Mem.: Soc. Women Engrs. (sr.; pres. 2006—, Purdue indsl. adv. bd.). Achievements include patents in field; patents pending in field. Office: Soc Women Engrs 230 E Ohio St Ste 400 Chicago IL 60611 E-mail: president@swe.org.

GASAWAY, SHARILYN, telecommunications industry executive; B acctg., La. Tech. Univ. CPA. Positions through audit mgr. Arthur Andersen LLP, 1991—99; fin. mgmt. positions Alltel Corp., Little Rock, 1999—2002, controller, 2002—06, exec. v.p., CFO, 2006—. Office: Alltel Corp 1 Allied Dr Little Rock AR 72202-2099*

GASBARRO, PASCO, JR., lawyer; b. Providence, Apr. 3, 1944; m. Mary Alyce McNamara, May 30, 1967; children: Pasco, John A., Christopher E. AB, Brown U., Providence, 1966; JD, Boston U., 1969. Bar: R.I. 1969, U.S. Dist. Ct. R.I. 1971, Mass. 1972, U.S. Dist. Ct. Mass. 1974. Law clk. R.I. Supreme Ct., Providence, 1969-70; atty. R.I. Legal Svcs., Providence, 1970-71, New Eng. Elec., Westborough, Mass., 1971-76; counsel Narragansett Elec. Co., Providence, 1976-79; asst. gen. counsel New Eng. Elec., Westborough, 1979-83; ptnr. Hinckley, Allen & Snyder LLP, Providence, Boston, Concord, NH, 1983—. Del. White House Conf. on Small Bus., 1995; mem. adv. bd., Advanced Technol. Mfg. Ctr. Former chmn. adv. coun. R.I. Small Bus. Devel. Ctr.; mem. adv. bd. Advanced Tech. and Mfg. Ctr. Mem. ABA, R.I. Bar Assn., Brown Club of R.I. Office: Hinckley Allen & Snyder LLP 50 Kennedy Plz Ste 1500 Providence RI 02906-2319 Office Phone: 401-274-2000.

GASH, LAUREN BETH, lawyer, state legislator; b. Summit, NJ, June 11, 1960; d. Ira Arnold and Sondra Regina (Stetin) G.; m. Gregg Allen Garmisa, June 12, 1983; children: Sarah, Benjamin. BA in Psychology, Clark U., 1982; JD, Georgetown U., 1987. Bar: Ill. 1989. Projects dir. U.S. Senator Alan Dixon, Washington, 1981-83; statewide constituency coord., dir. Women for Simon, U.S. Senator Paul Simon, Chgo., 1990; aide State Rep. Grace Mary Stern, Highland Park, Ill.; atty. Prairie State Legal Svcs., Waukegan, Ill.; mem. Ill. State Ho. of Reps., chair judiciary-criminal com. Mem. women's health adv. bd. Highland Park Hosp., southeast adv. bd Coll. Lake County, JUF govt. agencies divsn. campaign cabinet, 1999, chair, Highland Park 2000 com., human needs subcom. Women in Law as 2d Career grantee; recipient Disting. Svc. award Ill. Com. for Honest Govt., 1996, Best Legis. Record Voting award Ind. Voters Ill., 1996; named Legis. of Yr. Alliance for the Mentally Ill, 1997. Mem. Ill. State Bar Assn. (mem. com. cmty. involvement), Formerly Employed Mothers at the Leading Edge (co-founder North Shore chpt.), Chgo. Women in Govt. Rels., Women Employed, Ravinia PTA (bd. dirs., polit. action chair), Com. for Interdist. Cooperation, North Shore Synagogue Beth El (social action com.) LWV (bd. dirs. Highland Park chpt., bd. dirs. Lake County chpt.). Avocations: flute, languages. also: 2052-l Stratton Bldg Springfield IL 62706-0001 Office: 1345 Forest Ave Highland Park IL 60035-3456

GASICH, WELKO ELTON, retired aerospace defense executive, management consultant; b. Cupertino, Calif., Mar. 28, 1922; s. Elija J. and Catherine (Paviso) Gasich; m. Patricia Ann Gudgel, Dec. 28, 1973; 1 child, Mark David. AB cum laude in Mech. Engring. (Bacon scholar), Stanford U., 1943, MS in Mech. Engring., 1947, cert. in fin. and econs. (Sloan exec. fellow), 1967; Aero. Engr., Calif. Inst. Tech., 1948. Aerodynamicist Douglas Aircraft Co., 1943-44, supr. aeroelastics, 1947-51; chief aero design Rand Corp., 1951-53; chief preliminary design aircraft divsn. Northrop Corp., LA, 1953-56, dir. advanced systems, 1956-61, v.p., asst. gen. mgr. tech., 1961-66, corp. v.p., gen. mgr. Northrop Ventura divsn., 1967-71, corp. v.p., gen. mgr. aircraft divsn., 1971-76, corp. v.p., group exec. aircraft group, 1976-79, sr. v.p. advanced projects, 1979-85, exec. v.p. programs, 1985-88, ret., 1988; aerospace cons. Encino, Calif., 1988—. Author: (book) 40 Years of Ferrari V-12 Engines, 1990. Chmn. adv. coun. Stanford Sch. Engring., 1981—83; past. mem. adv. coun. Stanford Grad. Sch. Bus.; chmn. United Way, 1964; chmn. Scout-O-Rama, L.A. coun. Boy Scouts Am., 1964, chmn. explorer scout exec. com., 1963—64. Served to lt. USN, 1944—46. Fellow: AIAA, Soc. Automotive Engrs.; mem.: NAE, Navy League, Stanford Grad. Sch. Bus. Alumni Assn. (pres. 1971), Bel Air Country Club, Conquistadores del Cielo Club. Republican. Achievements include patents in field. Office: 10900 Chalon Rd Los Angeles CA 90077

GASIORKIEWICZ, EUGENE ANTHONY, lawyer; b. Milw., Jan. 7, 1950; s. Eugene Constantine and Loretta Ann (Kasprzak) G.; m. Jana Jamieson, Jan. 12, 1980; children: Suzanne A., Alexei E. AB, Regis Coll., 1971; JD, U. Miss., 1974. Bar: Wis. 1974, U.S. Supreme Ct. 1986. Law clk. to presiding justice Miss. Supreme Ct., Jackson, 1974-75; assoc. Schoone, McManus & Hanson SC, Racine, Wis., 1975-79; ptnr. Hanson & Gasiorkiewicz SC, Racine, Wis., 1979-90; pres., shareholder Hanson, Gasiorkiewicz & Weber, SC, Racine, 1990-96, Hanson & Gasiorkiewicz, SC, Racine, 1997—. Lectr. labor law U. Wis., Racine, 1975-76, worker's comp., State Bar Wis., 1984-86, med. malpractice, Wis. Acad. Trial Lawyers, 1986. Mcpl. judge Village of Wind Point, Wis., 1983-85; moot ct. instr., The Prairie Sch., Racine, 1986-87. Named one of Best Lawyers in Am., Consumer Guide, 2001. Mem. State Bar Wis. (spl. ethics com. regarding trust accts. 1988-89), Assn. Trial Lawyers Am., Am. Arbitration Assn., Wis. Acad. Trial Lawyers (bd. dirs. 1999—), Nat. Bd. Trial Advocacy (cert. civil trial advocate), Racine County Bar Assn. (liaison local physicians and attys. 1990—). Roman Catholic. Avocation: tennis. Home: 3929 S Brook Rd Franksville WI 53126-9303 Office: Hanson & Gasiorkiewicz SC 2932 Northwestern Ave Racine WI 53404-2249 Office Phone: 262-632-5550. Business E-Mail: info@lawracine.com.

GASKELL, IVAN GEORGE ALEXANDER DE WEND, art museum curator, educator; b. Weston-super-Mare, Somerset, U.K., Feb. 26, 1955; came to U.S., 1991. s. William George Keith de Wend and Johanna Catharina (van Leeuwen) G.; m. Jane Susan Whitehead, May 9, 1981; 1 child, Alexander Leo Ralph de Wend. Attended, Worcester Coll., Oxford, 1973-76, Courtauld Inst. Art, London, 1976-80; MA in Modern History, Oxford U.; MA in History of Western Art, London U.; PhD in History of Art, Cambridge U. Rsch. fellow, acad. curatorial asst. Warburg Inst. London U., 1980-83; fellow Wolfson Coll. Cambridge U., 1983-91, mem. faculty architecture, history of art, 1983-91; sr. lectr. fine arts Harvard U., Cambridge, Mass., 1991—, head dept. paintings and sculpture Fogg Art Mus., 1991—, Margaret S. Winthrop curator of paintings, 1991—, sr. lectr. history, 2002—; 8. Presenter papers at numerous internat. confs., 1978—; chair seminars in field; lectr. Royal Acad., Nat. Gallery, London, Courtauld Inst. Art, 1982—. Author: The Thyssen-Bornemisza Collection: Dutch and Flemish Painting, 1990, Vermeer's Wager: Speculations on Art History, Theory and Art Museums, 2000; co-editor: The Language of Art History, 1991, Landscape, Natural Beauty and the Arts, 1993, Explanation and Value in the Arts, 1993, Nietzsche, Philosophy and The Arts, 1998, Vermeer Studies, 1998, Sketches in Clay for Projects by Gianlorenzo Bernini, 1999, Performance and Authenticity in the Arts, 1999, Politics, Aesthetics and The Arts, 2000; joint gen. editor: Cambridge Studies in Philosophy and the Arts, 1988-2000; contbr. articles, revs. to profl. jours. Mem. Coll. Art Assn., Am. Soc. for Aesthetics. Avocation: sight-seeing. Office: Harvard U Fogg Art Mus 32 Quincy St Cambridge MA 02138-3845 Home Phone: 781-862-6854; Office Phone: 617-496-4252. E-mail: ivan_gaskell@harvard.edu.

GASKELL, JUDITH ANN, law librarian; b. Littlefork, Minn., Oct. 22, 1945; d. Charles Thomas and Mabel Harriet (Armitage) G. BA, Carleton Coll., 1967; MA, U. Chgo., 1975; JD, DePaul U., 1980. Bar: Ill. 1980. Law firm libr. Sonnenschein, Carlin, Nath & Rosenthal, Chgo., 1974-76; reference libr. U. Chgo. Law Libr., Chgo., 1977-79, head pub. svcs., 1980-83; dir. law libr. DePaul U. Law Libr., Chgo., 1983—2003; law libr. U.S. Supreme Ct., Washington, 2003—. Bd. dirs. Chgo. Libr. System, pres., 1999-2001; bd. dirs. LLMC-Digital. Life bd. dirs. Shirley Heinze Land Trust, Michigan City, Ind., chair Land Strategy Com. 1997-2003. Mem. Am. Assn. Law Librs., Assn. Am. Law Schs. (chair sect. on law librs. 2001-2002), Chgo. Assn. Law Librs. (pres. 1983-84, Agnes Harvey Reid award 1990-91, 2002-03), Law Librs. Soc. D.C. Avocations: preservation and restoration of natural areas, native plant gardening. Office: 1 First St NE Washington DC 20543 Office Phone: 202-479-3037.

GASKIN, FELICIA, biochemist, educator; b. Carlisle, Pa., Jan. 17, 1943; d. Joseph A. and Wanda J. (Rakowski) G.; m. Shu Man Fu, Nov. 29, 1969; children: Kai-Ming, Kai-Mei. AB in Chemistry, Dickinson Coll., 1965; MA in Organic Chemistry, Bryn Mawr Coll., 1967; PhD in Biochemistry, U. Calif., San Francisco, 1969. Postdoctoral fellow Stanford U., Palo Alto, Calif., 1969—71; rsch. assoc. Rockefeller U., NYC, 1971—72, Columbia U., NYC, 1972—74; asst. prof., then assoc. prof. Albert Einstein Coll. Medicine, NYC, 1974—82; prof. Sch. Medicine U. Okla., Oklahoma City, 1982—88, U. Va., Charlottesville, 1988—. Mem. Okla. Med. Rsch. Found., 1982-88. Contbr. articles to profl. jours. Recipient rsch. career devel. award NIH, 1975-80; Nat. Inst. Neurol. Diseases and Stroke spl. fellow, 1972-74. Mem. AAAS, Am. Soc. Biochemistry and Molecular Biology, Soc. Neurosci. Office: U Va Sch Medicine Box 800203 Charlottesville VA 22908-0001

GASKIN, STEVEN PAUL, marketing executive, consultant; b. Annapolis, Md., Oct. 7, 1955; s. Herbert Lee and Flora Annette Gaskin; m. Barbara Coombs, Sept. 27, 1986; children: Michael Alexander, Evan Paul. MS, MIT, Cambridge, Mass., 1982. Dir. new product devel. Mgmt. Decision Sys., Inc., Waltham, Mass., 1983—89; pres. Delphi Group, Inc., Sherborn, Mass., 1993—2003; sr. cons. Applied Mktg. Sci., Inc., Waltham, 2004—. Commr. Conservation Commn., Sherborn, Mass., 1999—2007. Lt. USN, 1977—81. Recipient Best Mktg. Sci. Article award, TIMS Coll. of Mktg., 1986. Mem.: Asian Arts Soc. New England (founder, pres. 2000—), Informs. Democrat. Avocations: Asian art, bicycling, skiing, mountain climbing, scuba diving. Office: Applied Mktg Sci Inc 303 Wyman St Ste 205 Waltham MA 02451 Home Phone: 508-651-8396; Office Phone: 781-250-6311. Business E-Mail: sgaskin@ams-inc.com.

GASMAN, DANIEL E., retired history professor, writer; b. NYC, Nov. 18, 1933; s. Murray and Lillian Gasman. BA, Bklyn Coll., 1955; PhD, U. Chgo., 1969. Instr. SUNY, Stony Brook, 1960—66; instr., asst. prof. Yeshiva U., NYC, 1966—70; from asst. prof. to full prof. John Jay Coll.-CUNY, 1970—; prof. Grad. Ctr. CUNY, 1980—. Author: The Scientific Origins of National Socialism, Haeckel's Monism and the Birth of Fascist Ideology; dir.: Diétudes Ehess, 1987. Rsch. grantee, CUNY, 2001, 2003. Mem.: History of Sci. Soc. Am. Achievements include research on the German Zoologist, Ernst Haeckel, and his scientific and historical influence. Office: John Jay Coll-CUNY History Dept 445 W 59th St New York NY 10019 Home Phone: 212-874-6995; Office Phone: 212-237-8827.

GASPAR, ANNA LOUISE, retired elementary school educator, consultant; b. Chgo., May 12, 1935; d. Miklos and Klotild (Weiss) G. BS in Edn., Northwestern U., 1957. Cert. elem. tchr., Calif. Tchr. 6th grade Pacific Palisades Elem. Sch., LA, 1957-58; tchr. 1st grade Eastman St. Elem. Sch., LA, 1959, Glassell Park, LA, 1959-62, Stoner Ave. Elem. Sch., LA, 1962-67; 2nd-4th grade tchr. Brentwood Elem. Sch., LA, 1967-78; tchr. 4th and 5th grades Brockton Ave. Elem. Sch., LA, 1978-90; vol., established Swakopmund Tchrs. Resource Ctr., Peace Corps, Namibia, 1991-93; tchr. English, Atlantic Sr. Primary Sch., Swakopmund, Namibia, 1992; career info. cons. Peace Corps., 1991—; substitute tchr. Hebrew Acad./Pre-Primary, Las Vegas, 1994-2000. Mem.: Calif. State Ret. Tchrs. Assn., So. Nev. Peace Corps Assn., Peace Corps, Northwestern U. Alumni Assn. Democrat. Jewish. Avocations: world travel, playing piano, art, collecting costume dolls, folk music. Home: 2700 Hope Forest Dr Las Vegas NV 89134-7322 Personal E-mail: agasparl@cox.net.

GASPARETTI, LORENZO E., lawyer; b. Beloit, Wis., Oct. 15, 1962; m. Rita Gasparetti; 3 children. BA, U. Calif., Berkeley, 1984, JD, 1988. Bar: Calif. 1988, DC 1995. Assoc. Crosby Heafey Roach & May (combined with Reed Smith in 2003), LA, 1988—96, ptnr., 1996—2003, Reed Smith LLP, LA, 2003—, So. Calif. practice group leader litig. group. Mem.: Italian-Am. Lawyers Assn. Avocations: travel, music, photography, tennis. Office: Reed Smith LLP 355 S Grand Ave, Ste 2900 Los Angeles CA 90071 Office Phone: 213-457-8038. Office Fax: 213-457-8080. Business E-Mail: lgasparetti@reedsmith.com.

GASPARINE, BARBARA ELLEN, elementary school educator; b. New Haven, Conn., Sept. 22, 1952; d. Alfred Joseph and Mary Carmella Maiorano; m. John Michael Gasparine, May 10, 1975 (div. Jan. 8, 1999); children: John Alfred, Lauren Ann. BA, U. Bridgeport, 1974, MS Reading, 1977; Sixth Yr. in Reading and Lang. Arts, So. Conn. State U., 2001. Cert. elem. tchr. Conn., reading and lang. arts cons. Conn., intermediate adminstr. and supr. Conn. Tchr. second grade Point Beach Sch., Milford, Conn., 1975—79; tchr. pre-sch. Cabbage Hill Nursery Sch., Woodbridge, Conn., 1987—89; reading tutor and substitute tchr. Beecher Rd. Sch., Woodbridge, Conn., 1990—95, lang. arts cons. and coord., 1995—2001; lang. arts cons. Jerome Harrison Sch., North Branford, Conn., 2001—, lead tchr., 2001—. Liaison So. Conn. State U., New Haven, 2004—; presenter Early Childhood Edn. Conf., Conn., 2000—01. Judge VFW Essay Contest, North Branford, 2002; treas. Our Lady of the Assumption Ladies Guild, Woodbridge, 1990—92; fundraiser North Branford, 2003—05. Recipient Americanism Award, VFW, 2003. Mem.: Nat. Coun. Tchrs. English, Area Coop. Ednl. Svcs. Lang. Arts Coun., Internat. Reading Assn. Roman Catholic. Avocations: travel, gardening, gourmet cooking, antiquing, walking. Office: Jerome Harrison School 335 Foxon Road North Branford CT 06471 Home Phone: 203-530-7312; Office Phone: 203-484-1235. Office Fax: 203-484-1237. E-mail: bgasparine@northbranfordschools.org.

GASPAR-MARTINS, ISMAEL, Angolian diplomat, former government minister, business executive; b. Luanda, Angola, Jan. 12, 1940; s. Sebastao and Antonia (Brandao) Gaspar-M.; m. Luzia de Jesus, Sept. 27, 1968; children: Henda, Giza, Ulanga, Luziela. B in Econ., Lycoming Coll., Pa.; completed post-graduate studies in Econ., U. Mannheim, Germany, 1969; attended, receiving a diploma in econ. develop., Oxford U., 1969—71. Research officer on agricultural development policies in Africa UN Rsch. Inst. for Social Develop., Geneva, 1971—72; served with the United

Nations Conference on Trade and Development (UNCTAD), 1972—75; external and economic affairs adviser President of Angola., 1975; gov. Central Bank of Angola, 1976—77; min. fin. Gov. of Angola, 1977—82, min. external commerce, 1982—87; exec. dir. African Development Bank, Abidjan , Cote d'Ivoire, 1989—95; founding mem. and co-pres. Angola-South Africa C. of C. and Industry, 1996—; mng. dir. Gaspar Martins and Assocs. Internat. Bus. Cons.; served on Southern African Development Cmty. Task Force, World Economic Forum Summit, 1996—2000; permanent rep.-Gov. of Angola UN, NY, 2001—. Econ. cons. Min. Ext. Affairs, Luanda, 1987-89; exec. dir. Am. Devel. Bank, Abidjan, Ivory Coast, 1989-95; mng. dir. Jaspar-Marthias & Assocs., Johannesburg, 1995—. Del. Popular Assembly, 1980-87, head del. So. Africa Devel. Cmty., 1980-87. Mem. Rotary, World Econ. Forum (task force 1997—), Angola-South Africa C. of C. Industry (co-chmn. 1998—). Methodist. Avocations: gym, tennis, reading, jazz. Office: Permanent Mission of the Republic of Angola to the UN 125 E 73rd St New York NY 10021 Office Phone: 212-861-5656. Office Fax: 212-535-2850.

GASPAROVIC, JOHN J., lawyer; BA, Wayne State U., 1979; JD, Northwestern U., 1982. Atty. Jones, Day, Reavis and Pogue, Cleve.; v.p., gen. counsel Automotive Div. Guardian Industries; exec. v.p., gen. counsel Roadway Corp.; sr. v.p., gen. counsel Federal Mogul Corp.; v.p., gen. counsel, sec. BorgWarner Inc., Auburn Hills, Mich., 2007—. Mem.: ABA, Ohio Bar Assn., Mich. Bar Assn. Office: BorgWarner Inc 3850 Hamlin Rd Auburn Hills MI 48326 Office Phone: 248-754-9200.*

GASPARRINI-ETHERIDGE, CLAUDIA, publishing executive, research scientist, writer; b. Genova, Italy, Apr. 25, 1941; arrived in US, 1984, permanent resident; d. Corrado and Tina (Pizzuti) G.; m. James K. Etheridge, Oct. 15, 1998. D in Earth Scis., U. Rome, 1965. Cert. in English U. Cambridge, Eng., 1965, Pitman Inst., 1965. Sr. tech. U. Toronto, Can., 1966-67, rsch. asst., 1967-70, rsch. assoc., 1970-72; phys. scientist II Geol. Survey Can., Ottawa, 1973; rsch. scientist Nat. Inst. for Metallurgy (now Mintek), Johannesburg, 1974-75; ind. cons. Toronto, 1976; pres., owner Minmet Sci. Limited, Toronto, 1977—, Jacksonville, Fla., 1982-86, Tucson, 1986—2000, The Space Eagle Pub. Co., Inc., Toronto, Tucson, 1986—, 1987—; writer, pub., 1989—. Adviser Chinese chpt. Internat. Precious Metals Inst., 1996—2000; guest lectr. U. Heidelberg, 1990, 91, Inst. Precious Metals, Kunming, China, 1984, U. Padua, U. Florence, 1995; presenter in field; assoc. Amazon.com, 2003—. Author: Gold and Other Precious Metals-The Lure and the Trap, 1989, How to Get the Most Out of the Legal System Without Spending a Fortune, 1990, Gold and Other Precious Metals-From Ore to Market, 1993, Murder of the Mind-The Practice of Subtle Discrimination, 1993, Murder of the Mind-The Practice of Subtle Discrimination, rev. 2d edit., 1996, When You Make the Two One, 1994, When You Make the Two One, rev. 2d edit., 1996; author: (as Gloria J. Duv) How to Run a Successful Mail Order Business by Defrauding the Public, 1995; author: Deceit-The Fad of the Nineties, 1997, Gold and Other Precious Metals-Occurrence, Extration, Applications, 2000, From Darkness to Light, 2001, Mechanics-Doctors, Does the Quality of Their Assistance Justify the Fees?, 2002, Subtle Discrimination, 2003, The Enemy Within, 2003, The Wrath of the Devil, 2004; mem. bd. editors: Chinese mag. Gold Sci. and Tech., 1996—2000; contbr. articles to profl. jours. and books. Scientist Sci. by Mail Program, Boston Mus. Sci., 1991-92; mem. rsch. bd. advisors Am. Biog. Inst., Raleigh, N.C., 1990—; hon. mem. Internat. Biog. Ctr. Adv. Coun., Cambridge, Eng., 1992—. Recipient Cert. Appreciation Outstanding Svc. Internat. Precious Metals Inst., 1994; named hon. mem. organizing com. Internat. Conf. on Precious Metals, Kosice, Slovakia, 1995. Avocations: classical music, collecting books, crystals, precious and semi-precious stones, guitar, piano. Home and Office: 9880 East Sterling View Tucson AZ 85749 Office: Minmet Sci Ltd/ The Space Eagle Pub Co Inc 1210 Sheppard Ave E # 200 North York ON Canada M2K 1E3 Home Phone: 520-760-0155; Office Phone: 520-760-0155. Personal E-mail: claudiaetheridge@thespaceagle.net, claudiaetheridge@comcast.net.

GASPER, JO ANN, social services administrator, consultant; b. Providence, Sept. 25, 1946; d. Joseph Siegleman and Jeanne Van Matre Shoaf; m. Louis Clement Gasper, Sept. 21, 1974; children: Stephen Gregory, Jeanne Marie, Monica Elizabeth, Michelle Bernadette (dec.), Phyllis Anastasia, Clare Genevieve. BA, U. Dallas, 1967, MBA, 1969. Adminstrv. asst. U. Dallas, 1964-68; asst. dir. adminstrn. Britian Convalescent Ctr., Irving, Tex., 1964-68; pres. Medicare Ctrs., Inc., Dallas, 1968-69; bus. mgr., treas. U. Plano, Tex., 1969-72; ins. agt. John Hancock Ins. Co., Dallas, 1972-73; systems analyst Tex. Instrument, Richardson, 1973-75; pvt. practice acctg., bus. cons. McLean, Va., 1976-81; editor, pub. Congl. News for Women and the Family, McLean, Va., 1978-81, Register Report, McLean, Va., 1980-81; dep. asst. sec. for social services policy HHS, Washington, 1981-85; exec. dir. White House Conf. on Agys., HHS, Washington, 1982-85; dep. asst. sec. for population affairs HHS, Washington, 1985-87; policy advisor to under sec. U.S. Dept. Edn., Washington, 1987-88, cons.; pres. Franklin Pk. Assocs., 1989—; exec. dir. Nat. Assn. for Abstinence Edn., 1989-94; mgr. TSR, 1995-98. Tchr. Grapevine-Colleyville Ind. Sch. Dist., 1998-2006. Co-chmn. St. John's Refugee Resettlement Commn., Va., 1977; bd. dirs., treas. Coun. Inter-Am. Security, Washington, 1978-80; active Fairfax County Citizens Coalition for Quality Child Care, Va., 1979-80; del. White House Conf. on Families, Va., 1979-80; mem. U.S. adv. Inter-Am. Commn. on Women, OAS, 1982-85; U.S. del. XVI Pan Am. Child Congress, Washington, 1984; mem. nat. family policy adv. bd. Reagan-Bush Campaign, 1980; mem. City of Colleyville Planning and Zoning Comm., 2000-02. Recipient Eagle Forum award, 1979, Wanderer Found. award, 1980, Bronze medal HHS, 1982; named Outstanding Conservative Woman, Conservative Digest, 1980, 81 Mem. Exec. Women in Gov. (treas. 1985, sec. 1986) Roman Catholic. Office Phone: 817-498-2671. Personal E-mail: joanngasper@yahoo.com.

GASPER, RUTH EILEEN, real estate executive; b. Valparaiso, Ind., July 16, 1934; d. Reuben John and Effie (Wesner) Tenpas; m. Ralph L. Gasper, May 25, 1957. Student, Purdue U., 1952—56; BA, Govs. State U., 1982. Analyst computer sys. Leo Burnett Advt., Chgo., 1958-69; nat. adminstr. registrars Sports Car Club Am., Denver, 1977-79; pres. Ainslie Inc., Port Orange, Fla., 1982—. Mem. North River Commn. Housing Com., Chgo., 1982-83, fin. com. Mayor's Task Force on Homelessness City of Chgo. Area coord. Concerned Action party, Lansing, Ill., 1977; chief race registrar Ind. N.W. Region Sports Car Club Am., 1969-80; co-founder, Single Rm. Operators Assn., 1987-98; treas. Sand Dollar Home Owners Assn. Inc. Mem. Dolphin Beach Club Condo Assn., Fantasy Island II Condo Assn. (sec.). Avocations: sports car racing, classical music. Personal E-mail: regasper@earthlink.net.

GASPERONI, EMIL, SR., realtor, real estate developer; b. Hillsville, Pa., Nov. 13, 1926; s. Attico and Rose Mary (Sarnicola) G.; m. Ellen Jean Lias, May 28, 1955; children: Samuel Dale, Emil Attico, Jean Ellen. Diploma in real estate, U. Pitts., 1957. Owner, pres. Gasperoni Real Estate, New Castle, Pa., 1956-63, Ft. Lauderdale, Fla., 1965-86, Gasperoni Internat. Group, Longwood, Fla., 1986—. Founder, chmn. bd. Fill-R-Up Auto Wash Systems Inc., Ft. Lauderdale, 1967-72. With U.S. Army, 1945-46, ETO. Mem. Nat. Inst. Real Estate Brokers, Fla. Assn. Mortgage Brokers, Sweetwater Country Club, Lake Toxaway Country Club. Home: 1126 Brownshire Ct Longwood FL 32779 Personal E-mail: gaspgroup@aol.com. Business E-Mail: gasperoni@commercialrealtyfla.com.

GASPIN, JEFF, broadcast executive; b. Bayside, NY, Dec. 29, 1960; m. Karen Gaspin; children: Max, Ben, Samantha. B., SUNY, Binghamton, 1982; MBA, NYU. With NBC, NBC News, 1984—93; exec. v.p. programming & prodn. VH1, 1996—2001; exec. v.p. alternative series, longform, specials & program strategy NBC, 2001; pres. Bravo, 2002—04; pres. cable entertainment & cross-network strategy NBC Universal, 2004—07, pres. cable & digital content, 2007—, pres. & COO TV group, 2007—. Creator (TV series) Behind the Music, Pop-Up Video, Rock & Roll Jeopardy, Storytellers, Before They Were Rock Stars, Divas Live. Named a Rising Exec., Entertainment Weekly, 2003; recipient GE Leadership award, 2003. Office: NBC Universal 100 Universal City Plz Universal City CA 91608*

GASS, GERTRUDE ZEMON, psychologist, researcher; b. Detroit; d. David Solomon and Mary (Goldman) Zemon; m. H. Harvey Gass, June 19, 1938; children: Susan, Roger. BA, U. Mich., 1937, MSW, 1943, PhD, 1957. Lic. clin. psychologist Mich. Mem. faculty Merrill-Palmer Inst., Detroit, 1958-69, lectr., 1967; mem. faculty Advanced Behavioral Sci. Ctr., Grosse Pointe, Mich., 1969-72; pvt. practice clin. psychology Birmingham, Mich., 1972—. Adj. prof. psychology U. Detroit, 1969-75; cons. Continuum Ctr. Oakland U., Rochester, Mich., 1961-77, Traveler's Aid, Detroit, 1959-75; pres. Shapero Sch. Nursing, Detroit, 1967-72, cons. 1958-78; psychol. cons. Physician's Ins. Co. of Mich., 1988—, mgmt. Mich. Bell Telephone, 1979-82. Mem. Adv. Com Sch. Needs, 1954-56; trustee Sinai Hosp. Detroit, 1972-99; bd. dirs. Tribute Fund United Cmty. Svcs., 1955-67. Fellow Am. Assn. Marriage-Family, Am. Orthopsychiatric Assn. (v.p. 1975-76), Mich. Psychol. Assn.; mem. Am. Psychol. Assn., Psychologists Task Force (v.p. 1977-84), Mich. Inter-Profl. Assn. (pres. 1976-78), Mich. Assn. Marriage Counselors (1979-80, pres. 1979-80), Mental Health Adv. Svc., Blue Cross and Blue Shield of Mich., Phi Kappa Phi, Pi Lambda Theta. Home and Office: 6155 E Longview Dr East Lansing MI 48823

GASS, JENNIFER S., oncologist, surgeon; b. Washington, Aug. 14, 1961; d. Anthony DeWitt and Anne Jenkins Gass; m. James G. Fingleton, May 23, 1992; children: Samuel Ford Fingleton, Erin Leiser Fingleton. BS, Dickinson Coll., Carlisle, Pa., 1983; MD, U. Md., Balt., 1987. Diplomate Am. Bd. Surgery, 1993. Clin. asst. prof. med. sch. Brown U., Providence, 1994—, dir. breast fellowhip med. sch. women's oncology program women and infants hosp., 2003—, chief surgery women and infants hosp., 2005—. Fellow: ACS; mem.: Assn. Women Surgeons, Am. Soc. Breast Surgeons (mem. ethics com. 2006—07), Soc. Surg. Oncolgy (mem. fellowship dirs. com. 2003—07). Office: Program in Womens Oncology Brown Univ 101 Dudley St Providence RI 02905 Office Phone: 401-453-7540.

GASS, JOHN D., oil industry executive; b. Key Biscayne, Fla., Apr. 1952; BS in civil engring., Vanderbilt U., 1974; MS in civil engring., Tulane U., 1980. Design engr. Chevron U.S.A., New Orleans, 1974—88; ops. mgr. Amoseas Indonesia Inc., Jakarta, 1988—91; field project mgr. U.K. Alba Field Devel. project Chevron, 1991—94; profit ctr. mgr. Chevron U.S.A. Prodn. Co., Bay Marchand, La., 1994—96; mng. dir. Chevron Australia Pty Ltd., Perth, 1996—2001; mng. dir. Southern Africa strategic bus. unit Chevron, Luanda, Angola, 2001, Chevron Texaco Corp., Luanda, Angola, 2001—03, v.p. San Ramon, Calif., 2003—; pres. Chevron Texaco Global Gas, 2003—. Bd. dirs. Sasol Chevron Holdings Ltd., LG-Caltex Oil Corp. Mem.: Soc. Petroleum Engr., Am. Soc. of Civil Engr. Office: Chevron-Texaco Corp 6001 Bollinger Rd San Ramon CA 94583-2324

GASS, MANUS M., accountant, construction executive; b. Montreal, Que., Can., June 28, 1928; came to U.S., 1948, naturalized, 1953; s. Maurice and Bertha (Silverberg) G.; m. Estella L. Gass; children: Thomas Evan, Winifred Caitlyn. Student, McGill U., 1945-48; BBA cum laude, CCNY, 1953. CPA, N.Y. Pres., dir. Buitoni Foods Corp., South Hackensack, NJ, 1966-86; chief exec. officer Stavola Constrn. Inc., Tinton Falls, NJ, 1989—. Dir. Buitoni Perugina Inc., N.Y.C., Perugina Chocolates & Confections Inc., Little Ferry, N.J.; acct. Am. Jewish Tercentenary Com., 1953-54 Chmn. River Edge-Oradell United Jewish Appeal, 1964-65, 67-76; mem. Shade Tree Commn., River Edge, 1987—; bd. govs. Hackensack Med. Center. Mem. Am. Inst. C.P.A.s, N.Y. State Soc. C.P.A.s, Fin. Execs. Inst. Home: 184 Woodland Ave River Edge NJ 07661-2321

GASS, MICHELLE PETKERS, advertising executive; b. Maine; BSChemE, Worcester Poly. Inst., 1990; MBA, U. Washington, 1999. Healthcare products R & D grp. Procter & Gamble, 1990—96; category mgr. for blended beverages, mktg. Starbucks Coffee Co., 1996—2001; v.p. beverage category, Starbucks Coffee Co., 2001—04; sr. v.p. category mgmt., Starbucks Coffee Co., 2004—. Named a Woman to Watch, Advt. Age, 2007; recipient Ichabod Washburn Young Alumni for Prof. Achievement, Worcester Poly. Inst., 2005. Office: Starbucks Corp 2401 Utah Ave S Seattle WA 98134*

GASS, WILLIAM H., writer, educator; b. Fargo, ND, July 30, 1924; s. William Bernard and Claire (Sorensen) G.; m. Mary Patricia O'Kelly, 1952 (div.); children: Richard, Robert, Susan; m. Mary Alice Henderson, 1969; children: Elizabeth, Catherine. AB, Kenyon Coll., 1947, LHD (hon.), 1973, LHD (hon.), 1985, LHD (hon.), 2005; PhD, Cornell U., 1953. Instr. philosophy Coll. of Wooster, Ohio, 1950-54; asst. prof. Purdue U., Lafayette, 1954-60, assoc. prof., 1960-66, prof. philosophy, 1966-69, Washington U., St. Louis, 1969-79, David May Disting. Univ. prof. in humanities, 1979-99, prof. emeritus, 1999—; dir. Internat. Writers Center, 1990—2001. Vis. lectr. U. Ill., 1958-59; mem. Rockefeller Commn. on Humanities, 1978-80; mem. literature panel Nat. Endowment for the Arts, 1979-82. Author: Omensetter's Luck, 1966, In the Heart of the Heart of the Country, 1968, Willie Masters' Lonesome Wife, 1968, Fiction and the Figures of Life, 1970, On Being Blue, 1974, The World Within the Word, 1978, The Habitations of the Word: Essays, 1984, The Tunnel, 1995, Finding a Form, 1996, Cartesian Sonata, 1998, Reading Rilke, 1999, Tests of Time, 2002, A Temple of Texts: Essays, 2006; contbr. to periodicals including NY Rev. of Books, NY Times Book Rev., New Republic, TriQuar., Salmagundi, others. Office: 6304 Westminster Pl Saint Louis MO 63130

GASSEND, BLAISE LAURENT PATRICK, technologist, researcher; b. Nice, France, Nov. 16, 1978; s. Max Louis Aimé and Linda Margaret Gassend; m. Valérie Maimiti Leblanc, July 28, 2006. Diplome d'Ingenieur, Ecole Polytechnique, Palaiseau, France, 2001; MSc in Elec. Engring. and Computer Sci., MIT, Cambridge, 2003, PhD in Elec. Engring. and Computer Sci., 2007. Rsch. asst. MIT, 2001—. Lt. French Army, 1998—2001. Master: MIT Underwater Hockey Club (pres. 2006—07). Achievements include patents pending for physical random functions; patents for hand assembly of microfabricated components; research in fully integrated planar electrospray thruster array; secure computing platforms; space elevators. Home: 474 Cambridge St Cambridge MA 02141 Office: MIT 77 Massachusetts Ave Rm 37-438 Cambridge MA 02139 Personal E-mail: blaise@gassend.com.

GASSER, JONATHAN S., prosecutor; b. NYC, Nov. 10, 1962; BA, Brandeis U., 1979; JD, Bklyn. Law Sch., 1986. Bar: New York 1988, U.S. Dist. Ct. Asst. solicitor 5th Jud. Cir., SC, 1987—93, dep. solicitor SC, 1993—2002; asst. US atty., dep. chief violent crime section, Dist. SC US Dept. Justice, Columbia, SC, 2002—, acting US atty., 2005—06. Office: US Attys Office 1441 Main St Ste 500 Columbia SC 29201

GASSER, MICHAEL J., consumer products company executive; BA, Ohio Northern U. CPA Ohio. Internal auditor Greif, Inc., 1979—81, controller, 1981—88, v.p., finance, 1988—94, mem. bd. dir, 1991—, vice chmn., COO, 1994, chmn., CEO, 1994—.*

GASSERE, EUGENE ARTHUR, lawyer, investment company executive; b. Beaumont, Tex., Oct. 20, 1930; s. Victor Eugene and Althea June (Haight) G.; m. Mary Alice Engelhard, Aug. 4, 1956; children— Paul, John, Anne. BS, U. Wis., 1952, JD, 1956; postgrad., Oxford U., 1956-57. Bar: Wis. bar 1956. Asst. counsel Wurlitzer Co., Chgo., 1958-61, Campbell Soup Co., Camden, NJ, 1961-65; asst. to pres. Thilmany Pulp & Paper Co., Kaukauna, Wis., 1966-68; with Skyline Corp., Elkhart, Ind., 1968-92, v.p., gen. counsel, asst. sec., 1973-92, ret., 1992—. Pres., bd. dirs. Elkhart Urban League, 1972-73, Elkhart Symphony, 1975-76, Elkhart Concert Club, 1976-77. Served with U.S. Army, 1952-54. Mem. Wis. Bar Assn., Phi Mu Alpha. Home: PO Box 165 Mindoro WI 54644-0165 Office: Skyline Corp 2520 Bypass Rd Elkhart IN 46514-1584 E-mail: pelt2ridge@centurytel.net.

GASSMAN, ANDREA C., paralegal, artist; b. Freeport, Ill., May 23, 1952; d. Carl E. H. and Eldora E. (Baker) DeFrane; m. Nicholas George Spirtos, Aug. 19, 1979 (dec. Dec. 2002); m. Alan James Gassman, Dec. 26, 2003. BA in Psychology, BA in Edn. cum laude, U. Dubuque, 1973; MA in Guidance Counseling cum laude, U. Iowa, 1974; JD, Loyola U., LA, 1983; EdD in Instl. Mgmt., Pepperdine U., 1994. Cert. rape crisis counselor Calif. Tchr., counselor Kennedy HS, Cedar Rapids, Iowa, 1973-74; counselor UCLA, 1974-77; youth cons. ARC, 1977-79; dir. donor svcs. and shelter svcs. United Way, 1979-80; dir. youth svcs. Am. Heart Assn., 1980-82; pres. Comprehensive Office Sys. Tech., 1982; co-founder, corp. officer Pacific Multiple Sclerosis Rsch. Found., 1982-99; devel. dir. Junipero Serra HS, 1987-88; v.p. Compensation Strategies, 1988; office mgr. Law Office of Nicholas G. Spirtos, Pacific Palisades, Calif., 1982—93, Palm Desert, Calif., 1993—2002; pres. Tekni-query Cons., 1991—2002; account rep. Met. Life, 1996; contbr. Desert Woman Monthly, Palm Springs, Calif., 1997-99; columnist Charity Check Desert Sun Gannet Pub., 1997-99; columnist Random Acts of Kindness Profile mag., 1999—; care giver, 2000—02; law clk. Martin C. Brhel plc, 2002—04, William S. Bonnheim PLC, 2004; litigation paralegal Best Best & Krieger, Indian Wells, Calif., 2004—06; paralegal Walter Clark Legal Group, 2006, Anderholt & Turner, LLP, 2006—. Author: Not in My Wildest Dreams, 1995; co-editor, author: Cutting Edge Technician: The Future of the Community College, 1993, columnist: Freeport Jour. Std., 1968—70, Seventeen mag., 1969—70, Trumpeter, 1990—92, columnist, editor, layout: Youth News, 1977—82; columnist, editor, layout Random Acts, 1999—2000. Vol. La Quinta Cultural Arts Commn., 2003—04, commr., 2004—05; founder Vol. Income Tax Assistance, 1974; commr. City of La Quinta Cmty. Svcs., 2005—, Cmty. Affairs, 2006; mem. Smithsonian, 2000—, La Quinta Playhouse Theater, 2004—; notary pub., 1995—. Decorated Legion of Merit; named Woman of Yr., ABI, 1997; recipient medallion of recognition, Joint Chiefs of Staff U.S., 1993, Presdl. Order of Merit, 1991; grantee, Danforth Found., 1969—70. Mem.: Desert Bar Assn., Desert Palms Legal Profls. Assn., Internat. Platform Assn. (co-editor poetry anthology 1992—95, gov. 1994—2002, author poetry newsletter 1995—96), Am. Pen Women, Amnesty Internat., Lincoln Club, Kappa Delta Pi. Republican. Avocations: painting, knitting, weightlifting, gourmet cooking. Home: 53-415 Avenida Obregon La Quinta CA 92253-3438 Office: 74-770 Hwy 111 Ste 201 Indian Wells CA 92210 Office Phone: 760-674-0998 ext. 241. Business E-Mail: agassman@palmdesertlaw.com.

GASSON, JUDITH C., research scientist; m. David Kronemyer; children: Andrew, Lauren. BS in microbiology, Colo. State Coll., 1973; PhD in physiology, U. Colo., 1979; postdoctoral, Salk Inst., 1979—82. With UCLA Jonsson Comprehensive Cancer Ctr., 1983—, dir., 1995—; prof. medicine and biol. chemistry UCLA Sch. Medicine; and co-dir. UCLA Inst. Stem Cell Biology and Medicine, 2005—. Pres. Jonsson Cancer Ctr. Found., 1995—. Recipient Scholar award, Leukemia Soc. Am., 1988, Stohlman Scholar award, 1991, Women of Sci. award, UCLA, 1991, Am. Soc. Clin. Investigation award, 1994. Office: UCLA Jonsson Comprehensive Cancer Ctr 8-684 Factor Bldg 10833 Le Conte Ave Box 951781 Los Angeles CA 90095-1781

GAST, ALICE PETRY, academic administrator, chemical engineering educator; b. 1958; BS, U. So. Calif., 1980; MA, Princeton U., 1981; PhD, Princeto U., 1984. Asst. prof. dept. chem. engring. Stanford U., Calif., 1985—90, assoc. prof., 1991—95, assoc. prof., chem. by courtesy, 1992—95, prof., 1995—2001; affiliated faculty Stanford Synchotron Radiation Lab., 1994—2001; prof. chem. engring., Robert T. Haslam Chair MIT, 2001—06, v.p. rsch., assoc. provost, 2001—06; pres. Lehigh U., Bethlehem, Pa., 2006—. Chair ACS Div. Colloid and Surface Chemistry. Recipient Allan P. Colburn award, 1992, Camille and Henry Dreyfus Tchr. award, Stanford Univ., Alexander von Humboldt award, 1998. Fellow: NSF (Pres. Young Investigator award), Am. Acad. Arts and Sci.; mem.: NAS (mem. bd. chemical sci., tech. 1999—2001), AAAS (bd. mem. 2005—), NAE, Am. Chemical Soc. (Langmuir Lectr. 1995). Achievements include discovery of scientific fidings having direct impact and applications in biotech., nanotech., advanced materials; research in field supported by NSF, NASA. Office: Lehigh U Office of Pres 618 Broadhead Ave Bethlehem PA 18015*

GASTON, MARILYN HUGHES, physician, administrator, public health expert, author; b. Cin. children: Amy Marie, Damon Allen. AB in Zoology, Miami U., Oxford, Ohio, 1960; MD, U. Cin., 1964. Diplomate Am. Bd. Pediats. Intern Phila. Gen. Hosp., 1964—65; resident in pediat. Childrens Hosp. Med. Ctr., Cin., 1965—67, asst. dir. out-patient dept., 1967—68, Convalescent Hosp. for Children, Cin., 1968—69; med. dir. Lincoln Heights (Ohio) Health Ctr., 1969—72; dir. Sickle Cell screening clinic Cin. Health Dept., 1972—76; med. expert Nat. Heart, Lung & Blood Inst./NIH, Bethesda, 1976—79; commd. 2d lt. USPHS, 1979—89; dir. divsn. medicine Bur. Health Professions USPHSBur. Health Professions, Rockville, Md., 1989—90; asst. surgeon gen. dir. Primary Health Care, USPHS, Rockville, Md., 1990—2002; chief med. officer Nat. Minority Health Month, 2002; co-dir. Gaston Porter Health Improvement Ctr., Potomac, Md., 2002—. Instr. pediats. U. Cin. Coll. Medicine, 1967—68, asst. clin. prof. divsn. cmty. pediats., 1968—70, asst. prof. pediats., 1970—76, assoc. prof. pediats., 1976—77; asst. clin. prof. pediats. Cin. Tech. Coll., 1974—76, Howard U. Coll. Medicine, 1978—91, Uniformed Svcs. U. the Health Scis., 1987—; attending pediatrician Children's Hosp. Med. Ctr., 1969—76, attending pediatrician and clinician, 1969—76, dir. med. staff, 1969—76; attending pediatrician Bethesda Hosp., 1974—76; pediatrician Hosp. Albert Schweitzer Deschapelles, Haiti, 1967; presenter, lectr., spkr. in field. Author: AL Bibliography: Comprehensive Sickle Cell Centers, 1977; co-author (with C.L. Calhoun), 1981; author: Management and Therapy of Sickle Cell Disease, 1984, 1988, Prime Time: The African American Woman's Complete Guide to Midlife Health and Wellness, 2003; author: (with others) Newborn Screening for Sickle Cell Disease and Other Hemoglobinopathies, 1989; contbr. articles to profl. jours. Co-chair Nat. Sickle Cell Dirs., 1974; med. advisor Sickle Cell Awareness Group, 1971—77, State Crippled Children's Svcs., 1975—77; bd. trustees Child Health Assn., 1974—77; bd. dirs. U. Cin. Found., 1989—, George Washington U. Life Scis., 1993—, U. Md. Ctr. for Minority Rsch. External Adv. Bd., 1993—, Komen Found. for Breast Cancer, Wellesley Ctr. for Women, Nat. Black Woman's Health Project. Named Woman of the Yr. in Medicine, Harriet Tubman Black Women's Dem., 1976; named one of Outstanding Young Women in Am., 1973, Outstanding Black Women in Cin., 1974; named to Ohio Women's Hall of Fame, 1990; recipient Phyllis Wheatley award, State of Ohio, 1975, Hildrus A. Poindexter award, Pub. Health Svcs., 1990, State of Ohio Gov.'s award, 1987, Disting. Alumnae award, U. Cin., 1989, Pub. Health award, D.C. Health Care for the Homless Project, Inc., Nathan Davis award, AMA. Mem.: APHA, AAAS, Inst. of Medicine/NAS, N.Y. Acad. Scis., Am. Med. Women's Assn., Am. Pediat. Soc., Am. Soc. Hematology, Nat. Med. Assn. (Living Legend award), Nat.

Assn. Med. Minority Educators, Am. Acad. Pediats., Alpha Kappa Alpha, Sigma Delta Epsilon. Office: Gaston Porter Health Improvement Ctr 8612 Timber Hill Ln Potomac MD 20854 Home Phone: 301-983-9586; Office Phone: 301-765-1942. E-mail: gastonandporter@gastonandporter.org.

GASTON, PAUL LEE, academic administrator, language educator; b. Hattiesburg, Miss., Aug. 23, 1943; s. Paul Lee and Ruth (Gooch) Gaston; m. Eileen Margaret Higgins, June 29, 1968; children: Elizabeth, Tyler Lee(dec.). BA, S.E. La. U., 1965; MA, U. Va., 1966, PhD, 1970. Ordained min. Episcopal Ch., 1990. Prof. English So. Ill. U., Edwardsville, 1969-88, assoc. v.p., 1984-88; dean Coll. Arts and Scis. U. Tenn., Chattanooga, 1988-93; provost, exec. v.p. No. Ky. U., Highland Heights, 1993-99; provost Kent (Ohio) State U., 1999—. Author: W. D. Snodgrass, 1978, Concordance Conrad, Arrow of Gold, 1980; contbr. articles to profl. jours. Chair, bd. dirs. Ohio Learning Network, Ohio Lik. Mem.: Nat. Assn. State U. and Land Grant Colls., Assn. Specialized and Profl. Accreditors, Phi Beta Kappa. Democrat. Avocations: softball, hiking, calligraphy. Office: Kent State U Office of Provost PO Box 5190 Kent OH 44242-0001 Home Phone: 330-653-3186; Office Phone: 330-672-2220. Business E-Mail: pgaston@kent.edu.

GASTWIRTH, DONALD EDWARD, lawyer, literary agent; b. NYC, Aug. 7, 1944; s. Paul and Tillie (Scheinert) G. BA, Yale U., 1966, JD, 1974. Bar: Conn. 1979, U.S. Dist. Ct. Conn. 1981. Mem. advt. staf New Yorker mag., NYC, 1967-68; v.p. Reader's Press, New Haven, 1968-74, dir., 1968-75; exec. v.p. Mainstream TV Studio, New Haven, 1974-77, dir., 1974-79; pres. Quasar Assocs., New Haven, 1979-89; account exec. Bache Halsey Stuart Shields Inc., New Haven, 1977-79; ptnr. Gastwirth, Mc-Millan & Still, New Haven, 1981-84; pres. Don Gastwirth & Assocs. Literary Agy., New Haven, 1984—. Adj. prof. law Thomas Jefferson Sch. Law, 1996-99; lectr. in field; advisor fund raising, mem. benefit com. John Steinbeck Lit. Project, 1986-94; assoc. fellow Trumbull Coll., Yale U., 1991—. Assoc. prodr. Yankee Fishing (TV series, 1995-98); contbr. to Nat. Rev., Wall St. Jour., New Haven Register; mem. bd. advisors Yale Lit. Mag., 1987-94, Touchstone Mag., 1990-95, 98-99. Trustee Yale Ctr. for Parliamentary History, 1995-2002; bd. dirs. Chancel Opera Co. Conn., 2003-06, New Haven Downtown Soup Kitchen, 2004-06; mem. bd. advisors Endowment for Middle East Truth, 2005—. Mem.: PEN Writers Assn., ABA, Writers Guild Am., Berzelius Soc., Lambs Club, Yale Club (N.Y.), Elizabethan Club. Home and Office: 265 College St New Haven CT 06510-2420 Office Phone: 203-562-7600. Business E-Mail: donlit@snet.net.

GASTWIRTH, GLENN BARRY, medical association administrator; b. NYC, Sept. 18, 1946; s. Milton and Janette (Wasserman) G.; m. Joy Ann Binstock, Nov. 29, 1969; children: Sara Beth, Bradley Aaron. BA, Ohio State U., 1968; postgrad., NYU, 1968-69; DPM magna cum laude, NY Coll. Podiatric Medicine, NYC, 1974; LHD (hon.), Ohio Coll. Podiatric Med., 2004. Diplomate Am. Bd. Podiatric Surgery. Pvt. practice podiatry, Southgate, Mich., 1975-86, Tri-County Family Podiatrists, Pontiac, Mich., 1979-86; dir. sci. affairs Am. Podiatric Med. Assn., Bethesda, Md., 1986-92, dep. exec. dir., 1992—98, exec. dir., 1998—. Surgical residency Kern Hospital, Detroit; predoctoral fellow preventive medicine NYU Sch. of Medicine. Editor-in-chief Jour. Am. Podiatric Med. Assn., 1989—91, exec. editor, 1991—. Pres. Cold Spring Sch. PTA, Potomac, Md., 1988-90; bd. dirs. Nat. Coun. on the Aging, 1996—; chair del. coun. Nat. Voluntary Orgns. for Ind. Living for the Aging. Named a Disting. Practitioner, Nat. Acads. of Practice, 1994; named Ky. Colonel, 1998, Ark. Traveler; named to, Podiatry Mgmt. Hall of Fame, 2005; recipient Appreciation cert., NY Coll. Podiatric Med., 1998, Lifetime Achievement award, NY State Podiatric Med. Assn., 2006, Podiatry Mgmt. Mag., 2006, Disting. Svc. medallion, Fedn. Internat. Podiatrists, 2007, Disting. Svc. citation, Am. Podiatric Med. Assn.; fellow, NIH, 1968—69, NYC Dept. Pub. Health, 1970; Hon. fellowship, Soc. Chiropodists and Podiatrists, UK, 2003. Fellow Am. Coll. Foot Surgeons, Am. Coll. Podiatric Med. Rev. (sec. 1990—), Am. Coll. Foot and Ankle Surgeons, Am. Assn. Hosp. Podiatrists, Am. Coll. Podiatric Med. Review; mem. Mich. Podiatric Med. Assn. (pres. 1981-82, Legion of Merit 1982, Honor award 2001), Am. Pub. Health Assn. (sect. council mem. 1972-74), Am. Diabetes Assn., Am. Podiatric Med. Assn. (ho. of dels. 1973-74, 80-86, Disting. Svc. citation 1996), Am. Acad. Podiatric Practice Mgmt. (hon.), Am. Coll. Foot and Ankle Orthops. and Med., Am. Soc. of Assn. Execs., Am. Soc. Podiatric Execs. Avocations: running, writing. Office: Am Podiatric Med Assn 9312 Old Georgetown Rd Bethesda MD 20814-1646 Business E-Mail: gbgastwirth@apma.org.

GATCH, MILTON MCCORMICK, JR., library director, clergyman, educator; b. Cin., Nov. 22, 1932; s. Milton McCormick and Mary (Curry) G.; m. Ione Georganna White, Aug. 25, 1956; children: Ione Waite, Lucinda McCormick, George Crosby White. AB, Haverford Coll., 1953; student, U. Cin. Sch. Law, 1953-55; BD, Episc. Theol. Sch., Cambridge, Mass., 1960; MA, Yale U., 1961, PhD, 1963. Ordained priest Episc. Ch., 1961. Chaplain Wooster Sch., Danbury, Conn., 1963-64; chaplain, chair humanities dept. Shimer Coll., Mt. Carroll, Ill., 1964-67; assoc. prof. English No. Ill. U., DeKalb, 1967-68; prof. English U. Mo., Columbia, 1968-78, chair dept., 1971-74; prof. ch. history Union Theol. Sem., NYC, 1978-98, acad. dean and provost, 1978-89, dir. Burke Libr., 1990-98, emeritus, 1998—; priest-in-charge Chapel of St. James Fisherman, Well-fleet, Mass., 1976—2005. Mem. coun. Coll. of Preachers, 1992-98; vis. fellow Emmanuel Coll., Cambridge, 1991; Bonhöffer vis. prof. Humboldt U., Berlin, 1998. Author: Death: Meaning and Mortality in Christian Thought and Contemporary Culture, 1969, Loyalties and Traditions: Man and His World in Old English Literature, 1971, Preaching and Theology in Anglo-Saxon England, 1977, So Precious a Foundation: The Library of Leander van Ess, 1996, The Yeats Family and the Book, 2000, Eschatology and Christian Nurture, 2000, The Library of Leandervan Ess and the Earliest American Collections of Reformation Pamphlets, 2007; contbr. numerous articles on antiquarian, bibliographical medieval subjects. With U.S. Army, 1955-57. NEH sr. fellow, 1974-75. Fellow Soc. of Antiquaries London, Medieval Acad. Am. (del. to Am. Coun. Learned Socs. 1981-93); mem. Internat. Soc. Anglo-Saxonists (founding, mem. adv. bd. 1980-85), Am. Coun. Learned Socs. (bd. dirs. 1992-93, fin. com. 2000-), Early English Text Soc., Bibliog. Soc., Bibliog. Soc. Am., Am. Printing History Assn. (trustee 1995-99), Yale Libr. Assocs. (trustee 1999-2003, 2004—), Century Assn., Grolier Club. Democrat. Avocations: book collecting, gardening, photography. Office Phone: 212-213-6990. E-mail: mac@miltongatch.us.

GATELY, MARK DONOHUE, lawyer; b. Balt., Jan. 6, 1952; s. Bernard Patrick and Margret (Donohue) G.; m. Rosemary Connolly, Dec. 27, 1986; children: Maeve Donohue, Harry John Connolly, Fiona Anne McCourt. BA, U. Md., 1974, JD, 1977. Bar: Md. 1977, U.S. Dist. Ct. Md. 1978, U.S. Ct. Appeals (4th cir.) 1978, U.S. Ct. Appeals (D.C. cir.) 1981, D.C. 1982, U.S. Supreme Ct. 1994, U.S. Ct. Appeals (3d cir.) 1988, U.S. Dist. Ct. (D.C. cir.) 1991, U.S. Ct. Appeals (7th cir.) 1993, U.S. Court of Appeals (6th Dist.) 2005. Law clk. to Hon. C. Stanley Blair U.S. Dist. Ct. Md., Balt., 1977-78; asst. atty. gen. Office Md. Atty. Gen., Balt., 1980-81; assoc. Miles & Stockbridge, Balt., 1978-84, ptnr., 1984-2000, chair litigation dept., 1992-2000; ptnr. Hogan & Hartson, 2000—. Named Md. Super Lawyer, Balt. Mag., 2007; named to Best Lawyers in Am., Woodward, White Publ., Inc., Am.'s Leading Lawyers, Chambers USA, 2004—06. Fellow Am. Coll. Trial Lawyers, Internat. Acad. Trial Lawyers, Am. Bd. Trial Advs., Internat. Soc. Barristers; mem. Order of Coif. Office: Hogan & Hartson LLP 111 S Calvert St Ste 1600 Baltimore MD 21202 Office Phone: 410-659-2700. Business E-Mail: mdgately@hhlaw.com.

GATES, ANTONIO, professional football player; b. Detroit, June 18, 1980; Grad., Kent State U. Tight end San Diego Chargers, 2003—. Named to AFC Pro-Bowl Team, 2004—06, NFL All-Pro Team, 2005—07. Office: c/o San Diego Chargers 4020 Murphy Canyon Rd San Diego CA 92123*

GATES, BILL (WILLIAM HENRY GATES III), computer software company executive; b. Seattle, Oct. 28, 1955; s. William H. and Mary M. (Maxwell) G.; m. Melinda French, January 1, 1994; children, Jennifer Katherine, Rory John, Phoebe Adele. Grad. high sch., Seattle, 1973; student, Harvard U., 1973-75, LLD (hon.), 2007. Co-founder Traf-O-Data Co., Seattle, 1972—73, Microsoft Corp. (formerly Micro Soft), Albuquerque, 1975; gen. ptnr. Microsoft Corp., Redmond, Wash., 1975—77, pres., 1977—82, chmn. bd., 1981—, exec. v.p. development activities, 1982—83, CEO, 1981—2000, chief software architect, 2000—06; founder Corbis, 1989. Bd. dirs. ICOS Corp., 1990—, Berkshire Hathaway Inc., 2004—; spkr. Consumer Electronics Show, 2006; spkr. in field. Author: The Future, 1994, The Road Ahead, 1995 (held the No. 1 spot on the NY Times' bestseller list for seven weeks), Business at the Speed of Thought, 1999 (listed on the best-seller lists of NY Times, USA Today, Wall Street Journal and Amazon.com.). Founder William H. Gates Found., 1994—2000; co-founder Gates Learning Found. (formerly Gates Library Found.), 1997—2000, Bill and Melinda Gates Found., 2000—; pledged $900 million to fight tuberculosis, 2006; sponsor Code4Bill, a contest to identify software students in India, offering as top prize an internship with the Microsoft tech. team for a year., 2005; Bill and Melinda Gates Found. will give a $9.7 million grant to the Elizabeth Glaser Pediatric AIDS Found. to study ways to prevent HIV/AIDS transmission via breast milk, 2007. Recipient Howard Vollum award, Reed Coll., Portland, Oreg., 1984, Nat. medal Tech. U.S. Dept. Commerce Tech. Adminstrn., 1992, Hon. Knighthood, UK, 2005; named CEO of Yr., Chief Executive mag., 1994; named one of Top 200 Collectors, ARTnews Mag., 2004, 100 Most Influential People, Time mag., 2005, 06, World's Richest People, Forbes Mag., 1996-, Forbes Richest Ams. 2006, World's Billionaires, Forbes Mag., 2007, 50 Who Matter Now, CNNMoney.com Bus. 2.0, 2006; named one of three Persons of Yr., Time Mag., 2005. Avocations: Collector 19th Century Am. Art, reading, golf, bridge. Office: Microsoft Corp 1 Microsoft Way Redmond WA 98052-8300*

GATES, BRUCE CLARK, chemical engineer, educator; b. Richmond, Calif., July 5, 1940; s. George Laurence and Frances Genevieve (Wilson) G.; m. Jutta M. Reichert, July 17, 1967; children: Robert Clark, Andrea Margarete. BS, U. Calif., Berkeley, 1961; PhD in Chem. Engring., U. Wash., Seattle, 1966. Rsch. engr. Chevron Rsch. Co., Richmond, Calif., 1967-69; asst. prof. to assoc. prof. U. Del., Newark, Del., 1969-77, prof. chem. engring., 1977-85, assoc. dir. Ctr. Catalytic Sci. & Tech., 1977-81, dir. Catalytic Ctr. Sci. & Tech., 1981-88, H. Rodney Sharp prof., 1985-92; prof. chem. engring. U. Calif., Davis, 1992—2003, disting. prof., chmn. engring., 2003—. Basic energy sci. adv. com. Dept. Energy, 2004—. Author: Catalytic Chemistry, 1992; co-author: Chemistry of Catalytic Processes, 1979; co-editor: Metal Clusters in Catalysis, 1986, Surface Organometallic Chemistry, 1988, Advances in Catalysis, 1996—. Recipient Sr. Rsch. award Humboldt Found., U. Munich, 1998-99, 2002; R.W. Moutlon medal, Disting. Alumnus award, Dept. Chem. Engring., U. Wash., 2005; Pruitt award Coun. Chem. Rsch., 2006; Fulbright Rsch. grantee Inst. Phys. Chemistry U. Munich, 1966-67, 75-76, 83-84, 90-91. Mem.: NAE, AIChE (Alpha Chi Sigma award 1989, William H. Walker award 1995, R.H. Wilhelm award 2002), Catalysis Soc. N.Am. (bd. dirs. 1997—), Am. Chem. Soc. (Del. sect. award 1985, Petroleum Chemistry award 1993, G.A. Somorjai award for creative rsch. in catalysis 2004). Achievements include research in catalysis, surface chemistry and reaction kinetics, chemical reaction engineering, petroleum and petrochemical processes, catalysis by solid acids, zeolites, soluble and supported transition-metal complexes and clusters, catalytic hydroprocessing. Office: Dept Chem Engring & Materials Sci U Calif 3102 Bainer Hall Davis CA 95616 Office Phone: 530-752-3953. E-mail: bcgates@ucdavis.edu.*

GATES, GREGORY ANSEL, lawyer; b. Cortland, NY, Sept. 25, 1953; s. Herbert Ansel and Mary (O'Connor) G.; m. Margaret Anne Schell, Aug. 9, 1975; children: Ryan Mary, Connor Ansel. BA, SUNY, Oswego, 1975; JD, Albany Law Sch. Union U., 1978. Bar: N.Y. 1979, U.S. Dist. Ct. (no. dist.) N.Y. 1979, U.S. Dist. Ct. (no. dist.) Calif. 1985, U.S. Ct. Appeals (2d cir.) 1993, U.S. Supreme Ct. 1994. Assoc. Levene Gouldin and Thompson, Binghamton, NY, 1979-84, ptnr., 1984-85, Hickey, Sheehan and Gates, Binghamton, NY, 1985--. Mem. Continuing Edn. Adv. Com., Binghamton, 1982-87. Commn. of Elections Broome County Gov., Binghamton, 1984-97, town justice, 1997—; pres. Broome County Magistrates Assn., 2002-2004; dir. Broome Sports Found., 1987--; counsel Broome County Dem. Com., 1984-87. Mem. ABA, N.Y. Bar Assn., Assn. Trial Lawyers Am., Broome County Bar Assn. (dir. 1988-91). Democrat. Roman Catholic. Avocations: hockey, golf, travel. Office: Hickey Sheehan and Gates PO Box 2124 Binghamton NY 13902-2124 Office Phone: 607-723-1990.

GATES, HENRY LOUIS, JR., literature and language professor, historian; b. Keyser, W.Va., Sept. 16, 1950; s. Henry-Louis and Pauline Augusta (Coleman) G.; m. Sharon Lynn Adams, Sept. 1, 1979; children: Maude Augusta Adams, Elizabeth Helen-Claire. BA summa cum laude, Yale U., 1973; MA in English Lang. and Lit., U. Cambridge, Eng., 1979, PhD in English Lang. and Lit., 1979; degree (hon.), Dartmouth Coll., 1989, U. W.Va., 1990, U. Rochester, 1990, U. NH, 1991, Harvard U., 1991, Manhattan CC, 1992, Bryant Coll., 1992, George Washington U., 1993, Williams Coll., 1993, U. Mass., Boston, 1993, Bates Coll., 1995, Macalester Coll., 1995, Emory U., 1995, Colby Coll., 1995, Purchase Coll., 1995, Bard Coll., 1995, Bethany Coll., 1995, NYU, 1996, Haverford Coll., 1996, Nazareth Coll., 1996, U. Palacky, Czech Republic, 1996, Lawrence U., 1997, N. Ctrl. Coll., 1997, LI U., 1997, Pace U., 1998, Toronto U., 1998, Fairleigh Dickinson U., 1999, Potomac State U., 1999, Hamilton Coll., 1999, U. St. Thomas, Minn., 1999, City Coll. San Francisco, 2000, Cmty. Coll. Phila., 2000, Colgate U., 2001, U. Benin, 2001, U. Ill., Chgo., 2002, RI Sch. Design, 2002, U. Ala., 2002, Marymount Manhattan Coll., 2006, U. Pa., 2006, Washington U., St. Louis, 2006. Lectr. English and Afro-Am. studies Yale U., New Haven, 1976—79, asst. prof., 1979—84, assoc. prof., 1984—85; prof. English, comparative lit. and Africana studies Cornell U., Ithaca, NY, 1985—88, W.E.B. DuBois prof. lit., 1988—90; John Spencer Bassett prof. English and Lit. Duke U., 1990—91; W.E.B. DuBois prof. humanities, prof. English Harvard U., 1991—, chair dept. African and African Am. studies, 1991—2006, Alphonse Fletcher univ. prof., 2006—. Dir. W.E.B. DuBois Inst., 1991—; pres. Afro-Am. Acad. 1984—; mem. Pulitzer Prize Bd., 1997-, chmn., 2005-. Author: Figures in Black, 1987, Signifying Monkey, 1988, Loose Canons, 1992, Colored People: A Memoir, 1994, (with Cornel West) The Future of the Race, 1996, Thirteen Ways of Looking at a Black Man, 1997, Wonders of the African World, 1999, Africana: The Encyclopedia of the African American Experience, 1999, (with Cornel West) The African-American Century, 2000, Little Known Black History Facts, 2000, The Trials of Phillis Wheatley: America's First Poet and Her Encounters with the Founding Fathers, 2003, American Behind the Color Line: Dialogues with African Americans, 2004, Finding Oprah's Roots Finding Your Own, 2007; editor: Black is the Color of the Cosmos: Charles T. Davis's Essays on Black Literature and Culture, 1942-81, 1982, Our Nig, 1983, The Slave's Narrative, 1985, Black Literature and Literary Theory, 1985, Race, Writing, and Difference, 1986, The Classic Slave Narratives, 1987, The Souls of Black Folk, 1989, Reading Black, Reading Feminist, 1990, Bearing Witness, 1991, The Norton Anthology of African American Literature, 1996, The Dictionary of Global Culture, 1997, Hannah Crafts, The Bondwoman's Narrative, 2002; series editor: Oxford-Schomburg Library of the 19th Century Black Women, 1988; co-editor: Encarta Africana Encyclopedia, 1999 (Outstanding Contbn. to Pub., Black Caucus of Am. Libr. Assn., 2000), AFrican American Lives, 2006, The New Annotated Uncle Tom's Cabin, 2006; co-editor, mem. editl. bd. Transition, 1991—; mem. editl. bd. Black Am. Lit. Forum, 1981-86, Am. Quar., 1981, Studies in Am. Fiction, 1981, Porteus, 1984—, Diacritics, 1985—, Publs. of MLA, 1987, Critical Inquiry, 1987, Cultural Critique A/B. Trustee Whitney Mus. Am. Art; bd. dirs. NAACP Legal Def. Fund; Imagine W.Va. NY Hist. Soc. Recipient MacArthur prize MacArthur Found., 1981, Faculty prize Yale Afro-Am. Cultural Ctr., 1984, Am. Book award 1989, Anisfield-Wolfe Book award, 1989, Zora Neale Hurston prize, 1986, George Polk award for social commentary, 1993, Lillian Smith Book award, Chgo. Tribune Heartland award West Virginian of Yr. award, 1994, Nat. Humanities medal, 1998, Tchrs. Coll. Medal for Disting. Svc., Columbia U., 2000, Jefferson lectr., 2002, Rave award for Education, WIRED Mag., 2007; named one of 100 Most Influential Black Ams., Ebony mag., 2006; named to The Ebony Power 150, Ebony mag., 2007. Mem. Am. Acad. Arts and Scis., African Lit. Assn., Am. Studies Assn., MLA, Assn. for Study of Afro-Am. Life and History, Coll. Lang. Assn., PEN, Caribbean Studies Assn., Coun. on Fgn. Rels., Lincoln Ctr. Theatre (bd. dirs.), Century Club, Elizabethan Club, Phi Beta Kappa. Episcopalian. Avocations: jazz, billiards. Office: Harvard U WEB DuBois Inst for African and African Am Rsch 104 Mt Auburn St #3R Cambridge MA 02138 Office Fax: 617-495-9490.*

GATES, JAMES DAVID, retired professional society administrator; b. East Cleveland, Ohio, July 9, 1927; s. James Adelbert and Margaretta (Voigt) G.; m. Carol Marie Schreiber, June 9, 1956; children: David, Keith, Robert. AB, Hiram Coll., Ohio, 1951; MA, Columbia, 1956; EdD, George Washington U., 1975. Tchr. Maple Heights (Ohio) City Schs., 1951-61; profl. asst. Nat. Council Tchrs. Math., Reston, Va., 1961-63, exec. sec., 1963-76, exec. dir., 1976-95. Mem. faculty U. Va., 1963-66, George Washington U., 1966-75; assoc. dir. Math. Scis. Edn. Bd., Ctr. for Sci., Math., and Engring. Edn., Nat. Rsch. Coun., 1997-99. Mem. Va. Coalition Math. and Sci.; bd. dirs. MathCounts Found.; sec.-treas. Jr. Engring. Tech. Soc. Served with AUS, 1945-46. Fellow AAAS; mem. NEA, ASCD, Nat. Coun. Suprs. Math., Nat. Coun. Tchrs. Math., Math. Assn. Am., Assn. State Suprs. Math., Benjamin Banneker Assn., Assn. Math. Tchr. Educators, Am. Math. Assn. Two-Yr. Colls., Todos: Math. for All, Rotary. Home: 11303 Fieldstone Ln Reston VA 20191-3905 E-mail: jamgate@aol.com.

GATES, JONATHAN DEAN, surgeon, educator; b. Boston, Mar. 27, 1957; MD, Cornell U., 1983. Cert. in surgery, subspecialty in gen. vascular surgery, subspecialty in surg. critical care. Intern Beth Israel Hosp., Boston, 1983-84, resident in gen. surgery, 1984-89, fellow in cardiac surgery, 1989-90; fellow in vascular surgery Brigham-Women's Hosp., Boston, 1990-91, vascular assoc. surgeon, dir. trauma ctr.; chief vascular surgery West Roxbury VA Med. Ctr., Mass.; asst. prof. surgery Harvard Med. Sch., 1995—. Mass. Med. Soc. Office: Brigham and Womens Hosp Division of Trauma Burns & Critical Care 75 Francis St Dept Surgery Boston MA 02115-6106 Business E-Mail: jgates@partners.org.*

GATES, KATHERINE A., accountant, writer; b. Birmingham, Ala., May 8, 1955; d. Charles James Gates and Jacquie Katherine Kirk. Attended, Ohio State U., Columbus, 1974—77. Registered rep. NASD. Acctg. and quality rev. profl. Western So. Life, Cin., 1978—. Author: Reflective Meditation, 2002, The Power of Your Thoughts, 2002, Love, Relationships and Reflective Meditation, 2004. Vol. WCVO-Christian Radio Sta., Columbus, Ohio, 1978—85. Mem.: Mensa (sec. 1979—85, 2003—04). Avocations: hiking, swimming, cross country skiing, scuba diving. Home: 1642 Brandon Ave Cincinnati OH 45230

GATES, MAHLON EUGENE, retired research and development company executive, retired military officer; b. Tyrone, Pa., Aug. 21, 1919; s. Samuel Clayton and Elsie (Nieweg) G.; m. Esther Boone Campbell, July 4, 1972; children by previous marriage: Pamela Townley, Lawrence Alan. BS, US Mil. Acad., 1942; MS, U. Ill., 1948; postgrad., Command and Gen. Staff Coll., 1957, Army War Coll., 1962, Harvard U., Cambridge, Mass., 1965. Commd. 2d lt. U.S. Army, 1942, advanced through grades to brig. gen., 1966; area engr. Iran, Gulf Dist., 1960-61; chief, engr. br., officer Personnel Directorate, Dept. Army, 1963-64; gen. staff Dept. Army, 1964-66; comdg. gen. Cam Ranh Bay, Vietnam, 1966-67; dir. constrn. Vietnam, 1967; dir. research, devel. and engring. Army Materiel Command, Washington, 1971; ret., 1972; mgr. Nev. ops. office AEC now Dept. Energy, Las Vegas, 1972-82; sr. v.p. S.W. Rsch. Inst., San Antonio, 1982-89, ret., 1989. Leader US sci. team to N.W. Territories during recovery ops. for crashed nuclear-powered Russian satellite, 1978. Past pres. Boulder Dam Area council Boy Scouts Am.; past chmn. adv. bd. Clark County C.C. Decorated D.S.M., Legion of Merit, Bronze Star, Air medal; Army Distinguished Service Order 1st class Govt. Vietnam; Meritorious Service award; named Meritorious Exec. ERDA. Home: 1 Towers Park Ln Apt 2011 San Antonio TX 78209-6439 Personal E-mail: ink1942@aol.com. *Cherish the past; do not worship it.*

GATES, MELINDA FRENCH, foundation administrator; b. Dallas, Aug. 15, 1964; m. Bill Gates, Jan. 1, 1994; 3 children. BS in Computer Sci. and Economics, Duke U., 1986, MBA, 1987. Gen. mgr. info. products Microsoft Corp., Redmond, Wash., 1987—96; co-founder Bill & Melinda Gates Found., Seattle, 2000—. Bd. dir. drugstore.com, The Wash. Post Co., 2004—. Bd. trustee Duke U., 1996—2003; former co-chair Wash. State Gov. Commn. on Early Learning. Named one of Most Powerful Women, Forbes mag., 2005, 2006, three Persons of Yr., Time mag., 2005, 100 Most Influential People, 2006, 50 Women to Watch, Wall St. Jour., 2006. Mem.: Bilderberg Group. Roman Catholic. Office: Bill & Melinda Gates Found PO Box 23350 Seattle WA 98102*

GATES, MILO SEDGWICK, retired construction company executive; b. Omaha, Apr. 25, 1923; s. Milo Talmage and Virginia (Offutt) G.; m. Anne Phleger, Oct. 14, 1950 (dec. Apr. 1987); children: Elena Motlow, Susan Gates Suman, Virginia Lewis, Anne Symington, Milo T.; m. Robin Templeton Quist, June 18, 1988; stepchildren: Robert L. Quist, Catherine Brisbin, Sarah Mazzocco. Student, Calif. Inst. Tech., 1943-44; BS, Stanford U., 1944, MBA, 1948. With Swinerton & Walberg Co., San Francisco, 1955—, pres., 1976—, chmn., 1988-96, ret. Bd. dirs., trustee Children's Hosp. San Francisco; trustee Grace Cathedral, San Francisco; bd. dirs. Calif. Acad. Scis. Lt. (j.g.), USNR, 1944-46. Mem. Pacific-Union Club, Bohemian Club. Republican. Home: 7 Vineyard Hill Rd Woodside CA 94062-2531

GATES, MIMI GARDNER, museum director; b. Dayton, Ohio, July 30, 1942; BA, Stanford U.; MA in Oriental and Chinese studies, U. Iowa; PhD in art hist., Yale U. Curator Asian art dept. Yale U. Art Gallery, New Haven, 1975—87, dir., 1987—94; Illsley Ball Nordstrom dir. Seattle Art Mus., Wash., 1994—. Instr. Chinese art hist. and mus. studies Yale U.; faculty mem. U. Wash.; chair Fed. Indemnity panel The Nat. Endowment, 1999—2002. Contbr. Bones of Jade, Soul of Ice: The Flowering Plum in Chinese Art, 1985, co-curator Stories of Porcelain, From China to Europe, 2000, Ancient Sichuan: Treasures from a Lost Civilization, 2001. Bd. mem. Downtown Seattle Assn., YWCA. Mem.: Assn. Art Mus. Dirs. (past pres.). Office: Seattle Art Mus 100 University St Seattle WA 98101

GATES, RICHARD DANIEL, retired manufacturing executive; b. Trenton, Mo., Mar. 27, 1942; s. Daniel G. and Effie Wright (Johnson) G.; m. Jean Gates, Jan. 26, 1966; 1 child, Daniel Wright. BS, U. Mo., 1964; M.C.S., Rollins Coll., Winter Park, Fla., 1968; postgrad., Harvard U., 1976. Mgmt. assoc. Western Electric Co., NYC, 1964-66; bus. mgmt. adminstr. Martin Marietta Aerospace Co., Orlando, Fla., 1966-68, chief indsl.

engring., 1968-69; fin. analyst Martin Marietta Co., NYC, 1969-70, sr. acct., 1970-71; controller Dragon Cement Co., divsn. Martin Marietta Co., 1971-72, N.E. divsn. Martin Marietta Aggregates Co., 1972-73; asst. controller, then asst. treas. Rubbermaid, Inc., Wooster, Ohio, 1973-79, treas., 1979-80, v.p., treas., 1980-91, sr. v.p., bus. devel., investor rels. and corp. communications, 1991-98; ret., 1998. Pres. The Rubbermaid Found., Wooster. Mem. Wooster City Fin. Task Force, All Am. City Com.; chmn. Wooster Growth Assn.; active local Cub Scouts.; adviser Art Center, chmn. maj. indsl. capital campaign Boy Scouts Camp; trustee, chmn. Wayne Ctr. Arts; mem. parents' com. St. Paul's Sch., Wesleyan U. Mem. Nat. Assn. Corporate Treas., Main St. Wooster Inc. (bd. trustees), Beta Gamma Sigma, Omicron Delta Kappa. Clubs: Harvard Bus. Sch, Wooster Country (bd. dirs.). Home: 4751 Gulf Shore Blvd N 1606 Naples FL 34103 Mailing: Ste 9-470 88005 Overseas Hwy Islamorada FL 33036

GATES, ROBERT MICHAEL, secretary of defense, former academic administrator; b. Wichita, Kans., Sept. 25, 1943; s. Isabel Gates; m. Rebecca Wilkie Gates; children: Eleanor, Bradley BA, Coll. William and Mary, 1965; MA in History, Ind. U., 1966; PhD in Russian & Soviet History, Georgetown U., 1974; DHL (hon.), Coll. William and Mary, 1998. Intelligence analyst CIA, Washington, 1969—72, staff mem. of spl. asst. to dir. for strategic arms limitation, 1972—73, asst. nat. intelligence officer for strategic programs, 1973—74; staff mem. NSC, Washington, 1974—76, staff mem. Ctr. for Policy Support, 1976—77, spl. asst. to asst. to Pres. for nat. security affairs, 1977—79, dir. Strategic Evaluation Ctr., 1979—80; exec. asst. to dir. CIA, Washington, 1980—81, dir. exec. staff for dir & dep. dir., 1981—82, dep. dir. for intelligence, 1982-86, chmn. Nat. Intelligence Coun., 1983-86, acting dir., 1986-87, dep. dir., 1986-89, dir., 1991—93; asst. to Pres., dep. asst. to Pres. for nat. security affairs The White House, Washington, 1989-91; interim dean, Sch. Govt & Pub. Services Texas A&M U., College Station, Tex., 1999—2001, pres., 2002—06; sec. US Dept. Def., Washington, 2006—. Bd. dir. Fidelity Funds, NACCO Industries, Inc., Brinker Internat., Inc., Parker Drilling Co., Inc.; mem. Iraq Study Group, 2006. Author: From the Shadows: The Ultimate Insider's Story of Five Presidents and How They Won the Cold War, 1996. Nat. pres. Nat. Eagle Scout Assn. Served in USAF, 1967—69. Recipient President's Citizens medal, Nat. Intelligence Disting. Svc. medal (2), Disting. Intelligence medal (3), Nat. Security medal, Intelligence medal of merit, Arthur S. Flemming award presented annually to ten most outstanding young men and women in the Fed. Svc., Disting. Eagle Scout award, 1993 Office: US Dept Def Office Sec 1000 Defense Pentagon Washington DC 20301 Office Phone: 703-692-7100.*

GATES, STEPHEN FRYE, lawyer, oil industry executive; b. Clearwater, Fla., May 20, 1946; s. Orris Allison and Olga Betty (Frye) Gates; m. Laura Daignault, June 10, 1972. BA in Econ., Yale U., 1968; JD, MBA, Harvard U., 1972. Bar: Fla. 1972, Mass. 1973, Ill. 1977, Colo. 1986. Assoc. Choate, Hall, and Stewart, Boston, 1973-77; atty. Amoco Corp., Chgo., 1977-82, gen. atty., 1982-86; regional atty. Amoco Prodn. Co., Denver, 1987-88; asst. treas. Amoco Corp., Chgo., 1988-91, assoc. gen. counsel, corp. sec., 1991-92; v.p. Amoco Chem. Co., 1993-95; v.p., gen. counsel Amoco Corp., Chgo., 1995-98; exec. v.p., group chief of staff BP Amoco, London, 1999-2000; sr. v.p., gen. counsel, sec. FMC Corp., Chgo., 2000—01; ptnr. Mayer, Brown, Rowe and Maw, Chgo., 2002—03; sr. v.p., gen. counsel ConocoPhillips, Houston, 2003—. Bd. dirs. Nat. Legal Ctr. Pub. Interest, Washington, 1999—, Internat. Inst. for Conflict Prevention and Resolution, NYC, 2003—, Inst. Energy Law, Dallas, 2003—. Trustee Newberry Libr., Chgo., 1998—2005, Appleseed Found., 2003—; mem. adv. coun. Chgo. Schweitzer Urban Fellows Program, 1996—2000; mem. adv. bd. Chgo. Vol. Legal Svcs. Found., 1996—98; mem. Chgo. Crime Commn., 2000—03, bd. dirs., 2000—03; bd. dir. Houston (Tex.) Grand Opera, 2003—. Knox fellow, 1972—73. Fellow: Am. Bar Found., Royal Soc. Arts (London); mem.: ABA, Assn. Gen. Counsels, Yale Club, Chgo. Club, Univ. Club. Office: ConocoPhillips 600 N Dairy Ashford Houston TX 77079 Business E-Mail: steve.gates@conocophillips.com.

GATES, SYLVESTER JAMES, JR., physics professor, researcher; BSc in Physics, MIT, 1973, BSc in Math., 1973, PhD in Physics, 1977; LHD (hon.), Georgetown U., 2001. Jr. fellow Harvard Soc. Fellows, Harvard U., 1977—80; rsch. fellow Calif. Inst. Tech., 1980—82; asst. prof., applied math., math. dept. MIT, 1982—84, dir., Office Minority Edn., 1983—84; assoc. prof. physics, dept. physics & astronomy U. Md., College Park, 1984—88, prof. physics, dept. physics, 1988—, John S. Toll Prof. Physics, 1998—, dir., Ctr. for String & Particle Theory; vis. prof. physics, dept. physics & astronomy Howard U., 1990—91, prof. physics, dept. physics, 1991—93, chair, physics dept., 1991—93. Curriculum cons. Boston Sch. Com., 1982—83; external cons. Howard U., U. Adv. Evaluation Com., 1986; mem. adv. com. for physics NSF, 1988—92, fellowship panel evaluator, 1990, 91, cons., mem., theoretical physics/formal theory spl. emphasis panel, physics divsn., Directorate Math. and Phys. Sciences, 98, mem., Directorate Math. and Phys. Sciences adv. bd., 2000—03, mem., com. visitors, physics divsn., Directorate Math. and Phys. Sciences, 2003; cons. US Dept. Energy, US Dept. Def., Ednl. Testing Svc., 1991—92, 1993—94, Time-Life Books, 1991, Inst. Def. Analysts, 1992—93; vis. prof., divsn. astronomy, math. & physics Calif. Inst. Tech., 2002—04; vis. prof., physics dept. MIT, 1994; mem.-in-residence Math. Sciences Rsch. Inst., Berkeley, Calif., 1994; Martin King/Cesar Chavez/Rosa Parks vis. prof. Wayne State U., 1992; Disting. vis. prof. U. Calif., Davis, 1986; mem. adv. com. Particle Detector Rsch. Ctr., Prairie View, A&M Univ., 1992—93; mem. Physics Adv. Com, Nuclear and High Energy Particle Ctr., Hampton U., 1992—97; mem. com. visitors, physics divsn. Directorate Math. and Phys. Sciences, NSF, 1994; mem., High Energy Physics Adv. Panel Dept. Energy, 1994—97; mem., physics. edn. program initiation mtg. NRC, 1997; mem. search com. for Dir. Fermi Nat. Accelerator Lab., 96; mem., review com. Profl. Opportunity for Women in Rsch. & Edn. Prog., NSF, 1998; mem. external review com., dept. physics and astronomy U. SC, 1999; cons. to faculty physics search com. Va. Tech, 1999—2000; bd. dir. Quality Edn. for Minorities Network, 2000; mem. physics panel, com. on progress for advanced study math. and sciences in Am. HS NAS, 2000; mem. site review of the Inst. Theoretical Physics U. Calif., Santa Barbara, 2000, mem. adv. bd., Inst. Theoretical Physics, 2000—03; fellow African Sci. Inst., Oakland, Calif., 2001; patron African Inst. Math. Sciences, Cape Town, South Africa, 2002—; mem. review com., The Adv. Group Argonne Nat. Lab, 2002; mem. Nat. Task Force on Undergraduate Physics, 2000—; mem. selection com. AAAS Sci. Journal Awards, 2002; mem. AAAS Com. On Opportunities in Sci., 2002—04, US Linear Collider Steering Group, 2002—; spkr. in field. Co-author (with M.T. Grisaru, M Roček and W. Siegal): Superspace or 1001 Lessons in Supersymmetry, 1983; contbr. articles to profl. jours., chapters to books; scientific cons. (PBS documentary) Race for the SUPERCOMB, 1999. Recipient Nat. Technical Achiever of Yr., Nat. Tech. Assn., 1993, Physicist of Yr., 1993, Giants of Sci. award, Quality Edn. for Minorities Network, Washington, DC, 1999, Coll. Sci. Teacher of Yr., Washington Acad. Sciences, 1999, 2006 AAAS Award for Pub. Understanding of Sci. & Tech., Disting. Black Marylander award, Towson U., 2003; Grad. Fellowship, Nat. Fellowship Fund, 1973—77, NSF Postdoctoral Fellowship, 1981—82, First Delmos Jones Vis. Scholar, CUNY, 2002, Woodrow Wilson Teacher-as-Scholar Fellow, U. Md., 2002—03. Fellow: Nat. Soc. Black Physicists (pres. 1994—96), Am. Phys. Soc. (tech. exec. officer 1990—93, mem. com. on minorities 1993—96, exec. bd. mem. 1997—2000, gen. councillor 1997—2001, exec. com. mem. 1998—2000, mem. com. on minorities 1999—2001, First recipient Vis. Minority Lectureship award (Bouchet prize) 1994); mem.: Sigma Xi. Achievements include being the first African-American to hold an endowed chair in physics at a major research university in the US. Office: Physics Dept U Md Room 4121 Physics Building College Park MD 20742-4111 Office Phone: 301-405-6025. Office Fax: 301-314-9525. Business E-Mail: gatess@wam.umd.edu.*

GATES, VIOLA R., writer; b. St. Joseph, Mo., Oct. 13, 1931; d. Howard and Elsie (Lynch) Bennett; m. James E. Gates, May 7, 1949; children: Barbara Gates Bauguess, Nancy Gates Davis. Student, U. Denver, 1959—60; AA, U. Chgo., 1968; student, U. Colo., 1981—83. Tchr. piano pvt. practice, 1961—85, Brico Studios, Denver, 1970—82, Hamilton Mid. Sch., 1983—85, Englewood Christian, 1983—85. Author: Snow Storm, Journey to Center Place, 1996, Amanda's Gone; co-author: Winning Works, 1992. Ch. pianist, choral dir. Mem.: Denver Area Music Tchrs., Colo. State Music Tchrs. Assn., West Wind Writers, Nat. Writers Assn. (2d pl. award 1991), Brico Symphony Guild (sec.). Avocation: exploring ancient Pueblos. Home: 2149-A Hartford Way Montrose CO 81401

GATEWOOD, WILLARD BADGETT, JR., retired historian, writer; b. Pelham, NC, Feb. 23, 1931; s. Willard Badgett and Bessie Lee (Pryor) G.; m. Mary Lu Brown, Aug. 9, 1958; children: Willard Badgett III, Elizabeth Ellis. BA, Duke U., 1953, MA, 1954, PhD, 1957. Asst. prof. history East Tenn. State U., 1957-58, East Carolina U., 1958-60; assoc. prof. N.C. Wesleyan Coll., 1960-64; prof. U. Ga., 1964-70; Alumni Disting. prof. history U. Ark., 1970-98, ret., 1998, provost and chancellor, 1984-85. Author: Theodore Roosevelt and the Art of Controversy, 1970, Smoked Yankees, 1971, Black Americans and the White Man's Burden, 1975, Slave and Freeman, 1979, Free Men of Color, 1982, Aristocrats of Color, 1990, Arkansas Delta, 1993; mem. bd. editors Ga. Rev., 1968-70, Jour. Negro History, 1972-74, Ark. Hist. Quar., 1992-94. Bd. dirs. Winthrop Rockefeller Found., 1990-96. Recipient Parks Excellence in Teaching award Phi Alpha Theta, 1970, Michael Rsch. award, 1967; Outstanding Teaching award Omicron Delta Kappa, 1979, rsch. award U. Ark. Alumni Assn., 1980, Gingles award Ark. Hist. Assn., 1982, Chancellor's medal, 1994, Ledbetter prize, 1994; Truman Libr. fellow, 1963; Acad. Arts and Scis. grantee, 1962. Mem. So. Hist. Assn. (pres. 1986-87), Ark. Hist. Assn., Orgn. Am. Historians, Phi Beta Kappa. Presbyterian. Personal E-mail: wgatewood@cox.net.

GATFIELD, STEPHEN J., advertising executive; Planning dir. Saatchi & Saatchi, London; joined Leo Burnett Worldwide (divsn. of Publicis), London, 1987, head, London office, 1993—97, regional mng. dir., Asia Pacific region Hong Kong, 1997—2000, COO Chicago, 2001—03; exec. v.p. strategy and network oper. Interpublic Group, 2004—; CEO Lowe Worldwide, NYC, 2006—. Office: Lowe Worldwide 150 East 42nd St New York NY*

GATHOGO, PATRICK NDURU, geologist, researcher; arrived in U.S., 1999; s. Christine Warigia Gathiga. MS, postgrad., U. Utah, Salt Lake City, 1999—. Field geologist Koobi Fora and Kalakol Rsch. Projects, Nairobi, Kenya, 1997—2005; rsch. asst. U. Utah, Salt Lake City, 1999—2006; sr. petrologist Schlumberger, Salt Lake City, 2006—. Achievements include research in human origins and evolution in eastern Africa, part of the discovery of Kenyanthropus platyops, a new genus in the human familly. Office: U Utah Geology and Geophys Dept 135 South 1460 East Salt Lake City UT 84112 Home Phone: 801-583-0154. Business E-Mail: pgathogo@mines.utah.edu.

GATHRIGHT, JOHN BYRON, JR., colon and rectal surgeon, educator; b. Oxford, Miss., Sept. 29, 1933; s. J. Byron Sr. and Connie (Love) G.; m. Barbara Cooper, Sept. 19, 1959; children: John Byron III, Lin, John Miles, Peter C. BS, U. Miss., 1955; MD, Northwestern U., 1957. Diplomate Am. Bd. Colon and Rectal Surgery (pres. 1989-90), Am. Bd. Surgery. Intern Charity Hosp., New Orleans, 1957-58, resident in gen. surgery, 1958-62; fellow in colon & rectal surgery Alton Ochsner Med. Found., New Orleans, 1962-63; mem. staff So. Bapt. Hosp., New Orleans, 1963-69, Ochsner Found. Hosp., New Orleans, 1969-97, chmn. colon and rectal surgery dept.; clin. prof. surgery Tulane U., New Orleans, 1991—. Vis. surgeon So. La. Med. Ctr., Houma, 1977-97; trustee, exec. com., bd. dirs. Alton Ochsner Med. Found., 1980-97. Assoc. editor Diseases of the Colon and Rectum, 1977-93, Perspectives in Colon and Rectal Surgery, 1987-97, Colon and Rectal Surgery Outlook, 1987-97; mem. bd. editors Current Concepts in Gastroenterology, 1980-89. Fellow ACS (grad. edn. com. 1981-89, Am. Soc. Colon and Rectal Surgeons (pres. 1989-90), Soc. Coloproctology of Eng. and Ireland (hon.), Internat. Soc. Univ. Colon and Rectal Surgeons (sec. 1990-2002), Mex. Soc. Colon and Rectal Surgeons (hon.). Republican. Presbyterian. Avocations: boating, photography. Personal E-mail: jbeegee2@cox.net.

GATI, TOBY T., international advisor; b. Bklyn., July 27, 1946; m. Charles Gati; 2 children; 3 stepchildren. BA, Pa. State U., 1967; MA in Russian Lit., Columbia U., 1970, M in Internat. Affairs, 1972. Rsch. asst, project dir., dep. v.p., v.p., sr. v.p. UN Assn. of the U.S.A., 1972-93; spl. asst. to the pres. for nat. security affairs Nat. Security Coun., sr. dir. for Russia, Ukraine and Eurasian States, 1993; asst. sec. for intelligence and rsch. Dept. State, Washington, 1993-97; sr. internat. advisor Akin Gump Strauss Hauer & Feld LLP, Washington, 1997—. Commentator CNN Headline News and CNN; cons. ABC World Tonight, 1986, Ford Found., 1987-89, BDM Internat., 1989; mem. Coun. on Fgn Rels., Internat. Inst. for Strategic Studies. Office: Akin Gump Strauss Hauer & Feld LLP Ste 400 1333 New Hampshire Ave NW Washington DC 20036-1564 Home: 2123 O St NW Washington DC 20037-1008 Office Phone: 202-887-4422. Business E-Mail: tgati@akingump.com.

GATI, WILLIAM EUGENE, architect, educator, industrial designer; s. John and Edith Gati. Student, The Juilliard Sch. of Music, 1965-77; BS in Architecture, CCNY, 1980, BArch cum laude, 1982; MS in Urban Planning, CUNY, 1985. Registered architect, NY, NJ, Conn. Freelance designer, NYC, 1978-83; designer Urban Living, Inc., NYC, 1983-84, Robert L. Henry, Architect, NYC, 1984-86, Glass & Assocs., NYC, 1986-87; prin. architect William E. Gati, RA, AIA, NYC, 1987—; prin. Architecture Studio, NYC, 1991—; writer Home Editor Resident Publs., 1995-97. Prof. architecture N.Y. Inst. Tech., Old Westbury, 1985-89; instr. religious architecture Cooper Union, N.Y.C., 1989; instr. architecture St. John's U., N.Y.C., 1995—96; curator Fundamentals of Architecture, N.Y. Inst. Tech., 1987; vice chair, prof. Design Ctr., Queens, N.Y.; guest jury critic, lectr. in field. Archtl. designs include offices for Here's Life, N.Y.C., alterations to Calvary Bapt. Ch., N.Y.C., El Eden Ch., Bklyn., Living Word Christian Ctr., N.Y.C., All Saints Ch., Queens, N.Y.C., Dr. Aviles Med. Ctr., Queens, Tampellini Residence, Queens, Khafi Residence, Queens, expansion for Flushing Christian Sch., Queens, N.Y., Faith Assembly Ch., Queens, P.S. 68 annex, Queens, Perkovich Residence, Queens, Kaufman Residence, L.I., Cardinal Residence, Mas, Lindas Natural Kitchen, Queens, Resurrection Ch., Bklyn., Dr. Peter Chin's Med. Offices, Queens, Dr. Peter Murowski's Med. Offices, Queens, Dr. Larry Weinstein med. offices, Quantum Feet Store, Queens, Greenberg Residence, Queens, Parson Residence, Queens, Malik Residence, Queens, Benenati Residence, Queens, Mukherjee Residence, Queens, Koshe Residence, Queens; author: Solar Energy Techniques, 1979 (AIA Recognition 1979), Frank L. Wright, 1981, Theory of Modern Architecture, 1981, Boston's Pub. Space, 1985, Vacant Lots, Architectural League N.Y.C., 1987; contbg. illustrator Jonathan Friedman Creations in Space, Fundamentals of Architecture; columnist Queens AIA. Chmn. religious architecture com., organized series: Places for Worship, N.Y.C. 1990; planning bd. Kew Gardens; dir. Queens Design Ctr. Recipient Design award, Queens County Builder's Assn., 2002, 2006, Builders award, 2002. Mem. AIA (mem. religious arch. com. N.Y.C., v.p and pres. Queens chpt., head coms., bd. dirs. N.Y. State chpt.), Mcpl. Art Soc. (assoc.), Archtl. League (assoc.), CCNY Alumni Assn. (v.p. 1983-92), N.Y. Arts Group, Christian Architects Fellowship (pres.), Am. Planning Assn. Avocations: photography, chess, piano, art, saxophone. Office: 11231 84th Ave Jamaica NY 11418-1321 Home Phone: 718-849-8083; Office Phone: 718-805-2797. Personal E-mail: wgati@williamgati.com. Business E-Mail: wgati@architecturestudio.us.

GATJE, ROBERT FREDERICK, architect, writer; b. Bklyn., Nov. 27, 1927; s. Frederick Christopher and Erna Henrietta (Kelting) G.; m. Barbara Mansfield Wright, Oct. 20, 1956 (div. Aug. 1981); children: Alexandra Lord, Marianna Gatje Perrier, Margot Gatje Small. B.Arch., Cornell U., 1951; Fulbright scholar, Archtl. Assn. Sch. Architecture, London, 1951-52. Architect Gatje, Papachristou Smith (formerly Marcel Breuer Assocs.), NYC, 1953-56, assoc., 1956-87, ptnr., 1965-87, dir. Paris office, 1964-66; ptnr. Richard Meier and Ptnrs., NYC, 1987-95. Architect: Broward County Main Library, 1980; co-architect: IBM France Research Center, 1962, Ski Town, Flaine, France, 1969, IBM Mfg. Center, Boca Raton, Fla., 1969, Armstrong Rubber Co. Hdqrs, New Haven, 1969, Baldegg (Switzerland) Convent, 1972, Mundipharma GmbH Hdqrs, Limburg, Ger., 1975; author: Marcel Breuer, A Memoir, 2000. Trustee Deep Springs Coll., Calif., 1974-82, N.Y. Hall of Sci., 1985-96, N.Y. Found. for Arch., 1994-96; pres. Telluride Assn., 1953-55; bd. dirs. Franklin and Eleanor Roosevelt Inst. With C.E., AUS, 1946-47. Telluride scholar, 1947-51; Skidmore, Owings and Merrill scholar, 1950-51; recipient Clifton Beckwith Brown medal Cornell U. Coll. Architecture, 1951, Charles Goodwin Sands medal, 1951 Fellow AIA (pres. N.Y. chpt. 1975-76, Sch. medal 1951); mem. Ordre des Architectes Francais, Century Assn., Am. Arbitration Assn. Democrat. Home: 1040 5th Ave Apt 6A New York NY 10028-0137 Office Phone: 212-861-7906. E-mail: bobgatje@verizon.net.

GATLIN, JUSTIN, Olympic track and field athlete; b. Brooklyn, NY, Feb. 10, 1982; Student, U. Tenn., St. Augustine's Coll. Professional runner, 2002—; mem. U.S. Track and Field Olympic Team, Athens, 2004. Named Best Male Track and Field Athlete, ESPY awards, 2006. Achievements include being the NCAA Outdoor Champion, 100m, 200m, 2001, 2002, Indoor Champion, 60m, 200m, 2002, 60m, 2003; being the US Champion in Indoor 60m, 2003; being the World Champion in Indoor 60m, 2003; winning gold medal in 100m, Athens Olympic games, 2004.

GATLING, PATRICIA L., lawyer, commissioner; b. Jan. 16, 1957; BA, Johns Hopkins U.; JD, U. Md., 1982. Bar: NY, US Supreme Ct., US Ct. Appeals, Fed. Cir., US Dist, Ct. (ea. dist.) NY. Asst. dist. atty. Kings County Dist. Atty.'s Office, Brooklyn, 1982, first. asst. dist. atty.; spl. narcotics asst. Office of Spl. Narcotics Prosecutor; spl. asst. atty. gen. Office to Investigate the NYC Criminal Justice Sys., 1987—90; commr., chmn. NYC Commn. on Human Rights, 2002—. Sr. trainer John Jay Coll. Criminal Justice, CUNY; lectr. Dubai Police Acad., U. Iowa Sch. Law, Am. Women's Econ. Devel. Corp., Nat. Assn. Black Narcotics Agents, Practicing Law Inst. Mem.: Assn. of Bar of City of NY, Nat. Black Prosecutors Assn. (former pres.). Office: NYC Human Rights Commn 40 Rector St, 10th Fl New York NY 10006*

GATRIA, AMERICA I, retired writer; b. Havana, Cuba, Mar. 6, 1943; US, 1968; d. Jose F Gatria and Pilar T Varela. B, Havana's Inst., 1962. Clk. Citibank, NYC, 1969—70, asst. mgr., 1970—72, mgr., 1972—80, asst. v.p., 1980—90, v.p., 1990—95, sr. v.p., 1995—98; exec. dir. Dime Savings Bank, NYC, 1998—2002. Author: (book) Kristaluaght, 2004. Named Woman of the Yr., Hispanic Assn. Human Civil Rights, 1979, Hispanic Bus. Person of the Yr., State of NY, 1991. Republican. Avocations: writing, antiques, photography.

GATSAS, TED (THEODORE L. GATSAS), state legislator; b. Manchester, NH, May 22, 1950; s. Louis T. and Pauline Gatsas; m. Cassandra Gatsas. BS, U. N.H. Co-founder Staffing Network; mem. N.H. Senate from 16th Dist., Concord, 2001—, pres., 2005—, chmn. interstate coop. com., 2001—, vice chmn. energy and econ. devel. com., 2001—, mem. ways and means and wildlife and recreation coms., 2001—. Alderman, Ward 2, Manchester, N.H., 1999- Office: State House 107 N Main St Rm 302 Concord NH 03301

GATTEN, DAVID, filmmaker; b. Ann Arbor, Mich., 1971; MFA, Sch. Art Inst. Chgo., 1998. Assoc. prof., Cinema and Photography Ithaca Coll. Exhibitions include Whitney Biennial, 2002, 2006, The American Century, Whitney Mus. Am. Art, Art Inst. Chgo., San Francisco Cinémathèque, Art Gallery of Ont., Cinémathèque Française, Helsinki Film Co-Op, Mus. Contemporary Cinema, Lisbon, Millennium Film Workshop, First Person Cinema, Anthology Film Archives, Cinema Project, Chgo. Filmmakers, Views from the Avant Garde, NY Film Festival, 2005, Represented in permanent collections Whitney Mus. Am. Art, Art Inst. Chgo. Fellow Guggenheim Found., 2005. Office: 14 Verona St 4C Brooklyn NY 11231 E-mail: david.gatten@gmail.com.*

GATTI, EUGENE ANTHONY, immunologist, pediatrician; b. Camden, NJ, June 14, 1955; MD, Georgetown U., 1982. Diplomate Am. Bd. Allergy & Immunology, Am. Bd. Pediatrics. Resident pediatrics Thomas Jefferson U. Hosp., Phila., 1982-85, fellow allergy & immunology, 1985-87; immunologist West Jersey Hosp., Voorhees, NJ, 1987—, Cooper Hosp., Camden, 1987—. Mem. AMA, Am. Acad. Allergy and Immunology, Am. Acad. Pediatrics, Am. Coll. Allergy & Immunology. Home: 1135 Washington Ave Haddonfield NJ 08033 Address: 54 E Main St Marlton NJ 08053-2180 Office Phone: 856-988-0570. E-mail: eagatti@hotmail.com.

GATTI, RICHARD A., medical educator, medical geneticist; b. Hoboken, NY, Jan. 12, 1937; s. Attilio Gatti, Jr. and Esther G. Picco; m. Deborah Kerr McCurdy, Feb. 2, 2002; children from previous marriage: Pamela, Mark, Tana, Allegra, Ilana, Kaitlyn. BA, Columbia Coll., NYC, 1958; MD, St. Louis U. Sch. Medicine, 1962. Diplomate Am. Acad. Pediat., 1971. Postdoctoral fellow immunology U. Minn., Mpls., 1968—72; fellow tumor immunology Karolinska Inst., Stockholm, 1972—74; prof. pediat. UCLA, 1975—80, prof. pathology and lab. medicine, 1980—, prof. human genetics, 2006—, founder, co-dir. diagnostic molecular pathology, 1986—, disting. prof., 2004—, Rebecca Smith endowed chair, 2005—. Sci. adv. bd. ImmunoCon, Pa., 1982—2000, NeoStem, Calif., 2004—06; sci. dir. Ataxia-Telangiectasia Med. Rsch. Found., Hidden Hills, Calif., 1984—. Author 3 books; contbr. articles to profl. jours. Capt. US Army, 1966—68. Recipient Career Devel. award, NIH, Bethesda, Md., 1970—74, Lifetime Achievement award, Jeffrey Modell Found., NY, 1980, Ataxia-Telangiectasia Med. Rsch. Found., 1990; fellow John Simon Guggenheim, 1973; awardee Ralph Abercrombie Meml. Lectureship, 1999. Fellow: Am. Acad. Pediat.; mem.: Fedn. Clinical Immunology Socs., Am. Soc. Forensic Examiners, Soc. Pediat. Rsch., Am. Pediat. Soc., Am. Soc. Blood and Marrow Transplantation, Radiation Rsch. Soc., Assn. Molecular Pathology, Am. Assn. Immunologists, Am. Assn. Cancer Rsch., Robert Good Soc. (pres. 2006—), Am. Soc. Human Genetics. Achievements include patents in field; first to perform a successful bone marrow transplant; positional cloning of ATM gene. Avocation: piano. Office: Dept Pathology and Lab Medicine UCLA Sch Medicine Los Angeles CA 90095-1732 Business E-Mail: rgatti@mednet.ucla.edu.

GATTING, CARLENE J., lawyer; b. Hartford, Conn., Apr. 12, 1955; d. Charles W. and Jean A. (Murkowicz) G. BS, U. Conn., 1977; JD, Rutgers U., 1983. Counsel Skadden, Arps, Slate, Meagher & Flom, NYC, 1987—2001. Mem. ABA. Address: 26 Cow Bay Edgartown MA 02539 E-mail: cjgatting@msn.com.

GAU, GEORGE W., dean; BS, U. Ill., Urbana-Champaign, 1969, MS, 1971, PhD in fin., 1975. Asst. prof. fin. U. Okla., 1975—79; asst. to assoc. prof. U. British Columbia, 1979—88; joined faculty McCombs Sch. Bus., U. Tex., Austin, 1988, chair fin. dept., 1992—2002, founding dir. Ctr. Real Estate Fin., 1999—2002, George S. Watson Centennial prof. in real estate, J. Ludwig Mosle Centennial Meml. prof. in investments and money mgmt., Centennial chair is bus. edn. leadership, dean, 2002—. Co-editor: (book) North American Housing Markets into the Twenty-First Century, 1983; contbr. articles in acad. and profl. jour. Recipient Tchg. Excellence award, Univ. British Columbia, 1984, Adv. Coun. award for tchg. innovation, CBA Found., 1994. Fellow: Homer Hoyt Inst., Urban Land Inst.; mem.: Fin. Mgmt. Assn. (bd. dirs. 1984—86), Am. Real Estate and Urban Econ. Assn. (pres. 1986—87, Rsch. Award 1990). Office: McCombs Sch Business Univ Tex Dept Finance GSB 2-104 Austin TX 78712-1178 Office Phone: 512-471-5921. Office Fax: 512-471-7725. Business E-Mail: ggau@mail.utexas.edu.*

GAU, JENN-TERNG, engineering educator; s. Wu-I Gau and Mei-Chin Cheng; m. Jin-Meei Juang, June 25, 1993; children: Isabella Louise, Moriah Jenn. BS, Nat. Taiwan Inst. Tech., Taipei, 1990; MS, U. Mo., Rolla, 1994; PhD, Ohio State U., Columbus, 1999. With Forward Electric Co., Taipei, 1990; automation engr. Taiwan Devel. Co., Taipei, 1991—92; rsch. assoc. Ohio State U., Columbus, 1995—96; stamping engr. C3P devel./implementation/tng. and stamping engring. support, Ford Motor Co., Dearborn, Mich., 1996—2000, stamping engr. aluminum tech. dept., 2000—02; tech. staff engr. metal forming, styled surface dept., Harley-Davidson Motor Co., Wauwatosa, Wis., 2002—03; asst. prof. dept. mech. engring. No. Ill. U., DeKalb, 2004—. Mem.: ASME. Office: No Ill U Mech Engring Dept Dekalb IL 60563 Office Phone: 815-753-1261. Office Fax: 815-753-0416. Business E-Mail: gau@ceet.niu.edu.

GAUCH, EUGENE WILLIAM, JR., retired air force officer; b. Newark, Dec. 6, 1922; s. Eugene William and Wilhelmina Katrina (Beiswenger) G.; m. Beryl Merle Walker, Jan. 15, 1947 (dec. Oct. 1995); children: Kathryn A. (Mrs. Jerry T. Stansfield), Tracey L. (dec.). Enlisted as pvt. USAAF, 1942; advanced through grades to brig. gen. USAF, 1972; assigned Okinawa, World War II and Korean War; tng. and standardization officer SAC, Offutt AFB, Neb., 1955-59; ops. staff officer 72 Bombardment Wing, Ramey AFB, P.R., 1959-63; asst. exec. sec. to air staff bd. Office Vice Chief Staff Air Force, Washington, 1963-67; asst. chief staff, exec. to comdr. 7th Air Force, Vietnam, 1967-68; faculty Nat. War Coll., 1969; exec. to comdr. Hdqrs. Tactical Air Command, Langley AFB, Va., 1969-70, chief staff, 1970-72; comdr. 834th Air Div., Little Rock AFB, 1972-74; dir. automated mobility requirements DSC/Plans and Ops., Hdqrs. USAF, Washington, 1974—75; ret. USAF, 1975. Decorated Legion of Merit with 3 oak leaf clusters, D.F.C., Air medal with 4 oak leaf clusters, Air Force Commendation medal. Home: 628 Owl Way Sarasota FL 34236-1928

GAUDIERI, ALEXANDER V.J., art historian, educator, museum director; b. 1940; married; 1 child. BA, Ohio State U., 1962; diploma, Sorbonne U. Paris, 1962; postgrad., Colgate U., 1963; MBA in Internat. Fin., Am. Grad. Sch. Internat. Commerce, 1965; MA, NYU, 1976. Internat. banking officer Marine Midland Bank, NYC, 1965—71; with Sotheby Parke Bernet, 1972—; dir. Telfair Acad. Arts and Scis., Savannah, Ga., 1977—83; dir. Montreal Mus. Fine Arts, 1983—88; art historian, art cons., 2003—. Adj. prof. mus. studies program Grad. Sch. Arts and Scis., NYU; dir. Samuel F.B. Morse hist. site Locust Grove, Poughkeepsie, N.Y., 1995-96. Mem. bd. sponsors Attingham Park Program, Eng.; bd. dirs. Young Concert Artists, NYC. Barton Kyle Yount scholar. Mem. Assn. Art Mus. Dirs., Am. Assn. Mus. (accreditation commn.), Brit. Nat. Trust, Soc. Archtl. Historians. Office: PO Box 3 Palm Beach FL 33480 Office Phone: 561-832-6005. E-mail: gaudieri@bellsouth.net.

GAUDINO, MARIO, physician, pharmaceutical company executive, scientist; b. Buenos Aires, May 22, 1918; came to the U.S., 1945, naturalized, 1966; s. Nicolas M. and Maria Teresa (Ferrari) G.; m. Ann Murray, Sept. 24, 1947 (div. Jan. 1983); children: David, Brian; m. Judith A. Jenkins, May 19, 1984. BA, U. Buenos Aires, 1934, MD with hons., 1944; PhD in Physiology, NYU, 1950; student in Radioisotope Techniques, Oak Ridge Inst. Nuc. Studies, 1952. Lic. physician N.J., 1979, N.Y., 1981. Asst. Inst. Histology and Embryology, U. Buenos Aires, 1936; asst., rsch. asst. Inst. Physiology, 1937-42, chief lab. biol. physics, 1944; resident, chief resident Ramos Mejia Hosp., Buenos Aires, 1941-44; Millet and Roux fellow Argentine Assn. for Advancement Sci., 1943; asst., attending physician Inst. Semiology, Nat. Clin. Hosp., Buenos Aires, 1944-46; fellow Argentine Nat. Cultural Commn., 1945; Sauberan fellow Argentine Assn. Advancement Sci., 1946; physiol. rsch. fellow NYU, U.S. State Dept., Dazian Found. Med. Rsch., 1946-49; asst. prof. Tex. U., 1949; chmn. dept. biol. physics U. La Plata Med. Sch., Argentina, 1950-51; attending physician Ctrl. Inst. Cardiology, Buenos Aires, 1950-51; assoc. dir. med. writing and advt. Lederle Labs. divsn. Am. Cyanamid Co., NYC, 1951-52; rsch. assoc., prof. dept. surgery NYU, 1952-55, adj. assoc. prof. surgery, rsch., 1955-57; established investigator Am. Heart Assn., NYC, 1954-57; med. dir. Abbott Labs Internat. Co., Abbott Universal Ltd., Chgo., 1957-61; assoc. prof. dept. medicine Northwestern U., 1959-61; assoc. med. dir. Pfizer Internat. Inc., NYC, 1962-67; assoc. dir. advanced clin. rsch. Internat. Merck Sharp & Dohme Rsch. Labs., Rahway, N.J., 1967-70, dir., 1970-71, sr. dir. clin. rsch. internat. med. affairs area, 1971-74; dir. med. compliance drug regulatory affairs CIBA-GEIGY Pharms., Summit, NJ, 1974-80, assoc. dir. med. svcs. med. affairs dept., 1980—89, dir. med. cons. svcs., 1989—96, ind. expert, 1997—. Clin. asst. prof. medicine Cornell U., N.Y.C., 1971-77. Fellow N.Y. Acad. Scis.; mem. AMA, Internat. Soc. Nephrology, Am. Fedn. Clin. Rsch., Am. Soc. Nephrology, Am. Soc. Clin. Pharmacology and Therapeutics, Am. Physiol. Soc., Am. Acad. Clin. Toxicology, Acad. Medicine N.J., Summit Med. Soc., Soc. for Exptl. Biology and Medicine, Microcirculatory Soc., Jockey Club, Argentine Yacht Club, Univ. Club, Buenos Aires Rowing Club. Home and Office: 3 Brainerd Rd Summit NJ 07901-1410

GAUDIO, BOB, composer, musician; b. Bronx, NY, Nov. 17, 1942; m. Judy Parker. Pianist Royal Teens; founding mem., singer, keyboardist, composer The Four Seasons, 1961—; co-founder FBI Records, 1984. Composer: (songs) Short Shorts, Sherry, Big Girls Don't Cry, Walk Like a Man, Rag Doll, Bye Bye Baby, Working My Way Back to You, Can't Take My Eyes Off of You, Who Loves You, December, 1963 (Oh, What a Night), (Broadway plays) Peggy Sue Got Married, Jersey Boys, 2005 (Grammy award, Best Musical Show Album, 2007); musician: (albums) Four Seasons Greetings, 1962, Folk Nanny, 1963, Born to Wander, 1964, Rag Doll, 1964, The Four Seasons Entertain You, 1965, Working My Way Back to You, 1966, The Four Seasons' Christmas Album, 1966, Genuine Imitation Life Gazette, 1969, Half & Half, 1970, Chameleon, 1972, Who Loves You, 1975, Fallen Angel, 1975, Helicon, 1977, Reunited, 1981, Streetfighter, 1985, Hope & Glory, 1992, Dance Album, 1993, Oh What a Night, 1995. Named to Rock & Roll Hall of Fame with The Four Seasons, 1990, Songwriters' Hall of Fame, 1995.*

GAUDIO, GASTON, professional tennis player; b. Buenos Aires, Dec. 9, 1978; s. Norberto and Marisa Gaudio. Profl. tennis player ATP Tour, 1996—. Achievements include Winner of 8 singles titles: Barcelona, 2002, Mallorca, 2002, Roland Garros, 2004, Kitzbuhel, 2005, Gstaad, 2005, Estoril, 2005, Vina del Mar, 2005, Buenos Aires, 2005; Winner of 3 doubles titles. Office: c/o ATP Tour Internat Hdqs 201 ATP Tour Blvd Ponte Vedra Beach FL 32082*

GAUDIO, MAXINE DIANE, biofeedback therapist, stress management consultant; b. Stamford, Conn., Oct. 7, 1939; d. Robert Fridolin and Doris (Altstadter) Goodman; m. Arthur Sebastian Gaudio, Oct. 7, 1962; 1 child, Dante Sebastian. Ordained minister, 2002. Relaxation therapist The Biofeedback Clinic, New Canaan, Conn., 1970-73; chief EEG technologist St. Barnabas, Bronx, N.Y., 1973-75; biofeedback therapist Biofeedback Clinic, Stamford, Conn. and Winston-Salem, N.C., 1973—; clin. dir. Biofeedback Unltd. N.C., 1979—; clin. dir. Creative Mind Systems, Stamford, Conn., 1980—; tech. advisor Creative Mind Systems N.C., 1980-83; indsl. cons. major corps. U.S.A., 1976—; writer, creator stress video Hartley Prodns., Old Greenwich, Conn., 1984—; writer, creator, narrator Robert Gross Assocs., Stamford, Conn., 1984; spkr. in field. Author, narrator video: Stress, 1984, Your Secret Energy Source, 1984; writer, dir. audio/visual package Captain Mind; creator, producer Stress and Relaxation, 1986-87; author, narrator book and tapes: Creative Union, 1980; author: Land Within the Shadow, 1980. Exec. dir. Friends of Children, Darien, Conn., 1985-87; dir. spl. projects Victim Svcs. Agy., N.Y.C., spl. events 1988-91; dir. pub. info. and devel. Louise Wise Svcs., N.Y.C., 1992-93; founder, chair bd. Kids with Kids, N.Y.C., 1991—; bd. dirs. cons. Childhope, N.Y.C., 1987-89. Mem. Am. Fed Press Women, Am. Soc. EEG Technologists, Biofeedback Soc. Am., Biofeedback Soc. N.C., Internat. Platform Assn., Internat. Reiki Alliance. Avocations: swimming; fencing; flying; metaphysics; astrology; piano. Club: Conn. Press. Personal E-mail: emax3@earthlink.net.

GAUDREAU, RUSSELL A., JR., lawyer, educator; b. Weymouth, Mass., Feb. 25, 1943; s. Russell A. and Jean (Sandwen) G.; m. Elizabeth Flanagan, Dec. 26, 1966; children: Russell A. III, Seth F. BA, U. Mass., Amherst, 1965; JD cum laude, Suffolk U., 1968; LLM in Taxation, NYU, 1969. Law clk. to Hon. Harold R. Tyler, Jr., U.S. Dist Ct. (so. dist.) N.Y., 1969-70; assoc. Ropes & Gray, Boston, 1970-79, mng. ptnr. Washington, 1990-94, ptnr. tax & benefits dept. Boston, 1979—, head benefits consulting practice group. Adj. prof. law Bentley Coll., 1978-80; adj. prof. law Boston U. Law Sch., 1980—; adj. prof. law Georgetown U. Law Ctr., 1991—; frequent spkr. in field. Editor-in-Chief Suffolk U. Law Rev. Trustee Suffolk U., 2005—. Fellow: Am. Coll. Employee Benefits Counsel; mem.: ABA (tax. sect., com. employee benefits), Boston Bar Assn., DC and Boston ERISA and Tax Discussion Groups, D.C. Bar Assn., New Eng. Benefits Coun. (dir.). Office: Ropes & Gray One International Pl Boston MA 02110-2624 Home Phone: 617-367-2111; Office Phone: 617-951-7261. Office Fax: 617-951-7050. Business E-Mail: russell.gaudreau@ropesgray.com.

GAUEN, PATRICK EMIL, news correspondent; b. St. Louis, July 15, 1950; s. Louis Otto and Wilma Ellen (Rogers) G.; m. Patti Lynn Seib, Dec. 8, 1972 (div. 1992); children: Bethany, Heather; m. Karen Earhart, July 11, 1992; 1 stepchild, Christopher Stephenson. Student, So. Ill. U., 1968-70. Reporter, photographer Collinsville (Ill.) Herald, 1969-72, news editor, 1972-78; reporter St. Louis Globe-Democrat, 1978-84, mng. editor, 1984-85; reporter Ill. affairs St. Louis Post-Dispatch, 1985-89, polit. corr., 1989—, pub. safety team leader, 2000—; faculty univ. coll. Washington U., St. Louis, 1991—2001. Pub. safety reporting team leader St. Louis Post Dispatch, 2000. Recipient Outstanding Med. News Series award Ill. State Med. Soc., 1970, Best Feature Story award Suburban Newspapers Am., 1971, Best News Story award Suburban Newspapers Am., 1973, Best Spot News Story award UPI Editors Ill., 1972, Best Pub. Svc. Reporting award Ill. Press Assn., 1974, Best Feature Story award, 1975, Bar-News Media award Bar Assn. Met. St. Louis, 1987, Bob Hardy award Southern Ill. Chiefs of Police and Southwestern Law Enforcement, 1996, Terry Hughes award St. Louis chpt. Newspaper Guild, 1996, Liberty Bell award Madison County Bar Assn., 1999. Mem. Mid-Am. Press Inst. (bd. dirs. 1985—), Press Club Met. St. Louis (bd. dirs. 1985—), Investigative Reporters and Editor, Criminal Justice Journalists, FBI Citizens Acad., Sigma Delta Chi (bd. dirs. St. Louis chpt. 1985—, chpt. pres. 1985-86, 86-87). Avocations: reading, photography. Home: 30 Meadowlark Ln Highland IL 62249-3000 Office: St Louis Post Dispatch 900 N Tucker St Saint Louis MO 63101 Home Phone: 618-659-7234; Office Phone: 314-340-8154. Business E-Mail: pgauen@post-dispatch.com.

GAUGHAN, DENNIS CHARLES, lawyer; b. Buffalo, July 3, 1955; s. Charles Joseph Gaughan and Mary Lynn Rucker; m. Mary Rose DeBergalis, Sept. 22, 1989; children: Charles Joseph, Dennis Charles Jr., Joseph Rocco. BA, Syracuse U., NY, 1978; JD, NY Law Sch., 1982. Bar: NY 1984, US Dist. Ct. (we. dist.) NY 1984, US Ct. Appeals (2d cir.) 1984, US Supreme Ct. 1988, US Tax Ct. 2004. Counsel Erie County Dept. Social Svcs., Buffalo, 1984-89; pvt. practice, Hamburg, NY, 1989—. Asst. town atty. Town of Hamburg, 1995—; prosecutor Village of Blasdell, NY. Chmn. Hamburg Rep. Ctrl. Com. 1988-90. Served with USAR, 1983-89. Mem. Erie County Bar Assn., KC, Am. Legion, Am. Vets. Roman Catholic. Office: 6161 S Park Ave Hamburg NY 14075-3837 Home: 5338 Briercliff Dr Hamburg NY 14075-3440 Office Phone: 716-648-8000. Business E-Mail: dgaughan@adelphia.net, hamburglaw@gmail.com.

GAUGHAN, EUGENE FRANCIS, lawyer, retired accountant; b. Aug. 31, 1945; s. Eugene Francis and Ruth Mae (Webster) Gaughan; m. Arlene Barber, July 8, 1972 (dec. May 1981); m. Margaret Duffy, Jan. 2, 1983. AB, Coll. Holy Cross, 1967; MBA, Rutgers U., 1968; postgrad., Duke U., 1989; MME, INSEAD, France, 1990; JD, Seton Hall U., 2004. CPA NY, NJ, Conn., Fla.; bar: NY, NJ. Staff acct. Price Waterhouse LLP, NYC, 1968—70, sr. acct., 1970—72, mgr., 1972—78, sr. mgr., 1978—79, ptnr., 1979—98, PricewaterhouseCoopers, NYC, 1998—99, World Firm Coun. Ptnrs., 1987—90. Mem. supr. bd. Price Waterhouse Ea. Europe, 1991—97; trustee Lenox Hill Hosp.; bd. dirs. Manhattan Eye, Ear and Throat Hosp. Mem.: ABA, AICPA, NY County Lawyers Assn., Suffolk County Bar Assn., Assn. Bar City of NY, NY State Soc. CPAs (bd. dirs. 1986—89), NJ State Bar Assn., NY State Bar Assn., Doonbeg Golf Club, Laurel Links Country Club, KC. Roman Catholic. Home: Apt 7B 164 E 72nd St New York NY 10021-4363 also: 33 Niamogue Ln PO Box 1675 Quogue NY 11959-1675 Personal E-mail: lawefg@aol.com.

GAUL, GERALD, ophthalmologist; b. Davenport, Iowa, Nov. 18, 1959; s. Peter Joseph and Hilary Mae Gaul; 1 child, Jonathan Peter. BA in Viola Performance, New Coll., Sarasota, Fla., 1981; MD, Mayo Med. Sch., Rochester, Minn., 1985. Diplomate Am. Bd. Ophthalmology, 1991. Resident ophthalmologist Mayo Grad. Sch. Medicine, Rochester, 1985—89; opthalmologist Grand Forks Clinic, Grand Forks, ND, 1989—92; ophthalmologist ND Eye Clinic, Grand Forks, 1992—. Pres. ND Eye Clinic, Grand Forks, 2002—, ND Surgery Ctr., Grand Forks, 1997—; asst. prof. surgery sch. medicine U. ND, Grand Forks, 1989—, instr. chamber music sch. music, 2005—. Musician: Greater Grand Forks Symphony Orch., 1989—; contbr. articles to profl. jours. Named Best Dr., Best Doctors Am., 2005, 2006. Fellow: ACS, Am. Acad. Ophthalmology (pres. ND chpt. 1997—98); mem.: Am. Viola Soc., Buffalo Commons Chamber Music Soc. (pres. 1990—, founder 1990—). Avocations: bicycling, running, piano, viola. Home: 1009 Almonte Ave Grand Forks ND 58201 Office: North Dakota Eye Clinic 3035 DeMers Ave Grand Forks ND 58201 Home Phone: 218-779-5039; Office Phone: 701-775-3151. Office Fax: 701-775-3153.

GAULDIN, ROBERT L., music educator, composer; b. Vernon, Tex., Oct. 30, 1931; s. Robert L. and Lula Mae Gauldin; m. Barbara Jane Hullender, May 30, 1953; children: Elizabeth Ann, Phillip Vincent, Cecilia Jeanne, Angela Lynne. BM Composition, N. Tex. State U., Denton, 1952; MA Music Theory, Eastman Sch. of Music, Rochester, NY, 1956; PhD Music Theory, U. Rochester, 1958; DM (hon.), William Carey Coll., Hattiesburg, Miss., 1990. Prof. music William Carey Coll., Hattiesburg, Miss., 1958—63; from asst. prof. to prof. Eastman Sch. of Music, Rochester, NY, 1963—97, prof. emeritus, 1998—2005. Coord. contemporary music project Eastman Sch. of Music, Rochester, NY, 1966—68; vis. prof. music Oxford U., 1984—85; mem. rev. bd. Jour. of Music Theory Pedagogy, 1985—2000. Author: (textbook) Practical Introduction to 16th Century Counterpoint, Practical Introduction to 18th Century Counterpoint, 1988, Harmonic Practice in Tonal Music, 1997, 2004; contbr. articles to music theory jours., papers to nat. and regional convs. Cpl. US Army, 1953—56. Named to Keynote Speaker, AMS/SMT Nat. Conv., Seattle, 2004; recipient 1st prize quartet Berkshire competition, Tanglewood, Mass., 1968, Lifetime Achievement award, de Stwolinski Ctr., Kans. City, Kans., 2002. Mem.: Coll. Music Soc., Theory Soc. N.Y. State (v.p. 1981—83), Soc. for Music Theory (v.p., pres. 1988—94). Baptist. Avocations: astronomy, Southwestern Cooking, chess. Home: 379 Wellington Ave Rochester NY 14619 Office: Eastman Sch of Music 26 Gibbs St Rochester NY 14604 E-mail: Bobgauldin@aol.com.

GAULKE, MARY FLORENCE, retired library administrator; b. Johnson City, Tenn., Sept. 24, 1923; d. Gustus Thomas and Mary Belle (Bennett) Erickson; m. James Wymond Crowley, Dec. 1, 1939; 1 child, Grady; m. Bud Gaulke, Sept. 1, 1945 (dec. Jan. 1978); m. Richard Lewis McNaughton, Mar. 21, 1983 (div. 1995). BS in Home Econs., Oreg. State U., Corvallis, 1963; MS in Libr. Sci., U. Oreg., Eugene, 1968; Phd in Spl. Edn., 1970. Cert. pers. supr., std. handicapped learner Oreg. Head dep. home econs. Riddle Sch. Dist., Oreg., 1963-66; libr., cons. Douglas County Intermediate Edn. Dist., Roseburg, Oreg., 1966-67; head resident, head counselor Prometheus Project So. Oreg. coll.ect, Ashland, summers 1966-68; supr. librs. Medford Sch. Dist., Oreg., 1970-73; instr. psychology So.Oreg. Coll., Ashland, 1970-73; libr. supr. Roseburg Sch. Dist., 1974-91; resident psychologist Black Oaks Boys Sch., Medford, 1970-75. Mem. Oreg. Gov.'s Coun. Librs., 1979. Author: Vo-Ed Course for Junior High, 1965, Library Handbook, 1967, Instructions for Preparation of Cards for All Materials Cataloged for Libraries, 1971, Handbook for Training Library Aides, 1972. Coord. Laubach Lit. Workshops HS Tutors, Medford, 1972. Fellow: Internat. Biog. Assn. (life; adv. coun. 1990); mem.: ALA, Pacific N.W. Libr. Assn., Oreg. Libr. Assn., So. Oreg. Libr. Fedn. (sec. 1971—73), Am. Biog. Inst. (lifetime dep. gov. 1987—), Internat. Biog. Ctr. (hon.), Phi Delta Kappa (historian, rsch. rep.), Delta Kappa Gamma (pres. 1980—82). Democrat. Methodist. Office Phone: 210-213-8833. Personal E-mail: ggmum1@earthlink.net.

GAULT, POLLY L., utilities executive; Grad. magna cum laude, Mt. Holyoke Coll., South Hadley, Mass., 1975. Legis. asst. US Senator Richard S. Schweiker of Pa., 1977—80; staff dir. US Senate Edn., Arts and Humanities Subcommittee, 1981—87; mem. Presdl. Commn. on HIV Epidemic, 1987—88; exec. dir. Presdl. Commn. Exec., Legis. and Jud. Salaries; chief of staff Dept. Energy, 1989—93; prin. dir., exec. v.p. Wexler Group; with So. Calif. Edison subs. Edison Internat., 1997—, exec. v.p. pub. affairs, 2006—, exec. v.p. pub. affairs So. Calif. Edison subs., 2006—. Mem.: Phi Beta Kappa. Office: Edison Internat 2244 Walnut Grove Ave Rosemead CA 91770-3714*

GAULT, ROBERT MELLOR, lawyer; b. Pitts., Sept. 3, 1945; s. James Edward and Laura (Mellor) G.; m. Mary Joan Donnelly, Sept. 18, 1983; children: Sarah, Laura, Matthew. BA, Williams Coll., 1968; JD, U. Mich., 1971. Bar: US Dist. Ct. (We. Dist.) Wash. 1972, US Ct. Appeals (9th Cir.) 1972, Mass. 1973, US Dist. Ct. (Mass.) 1974, US Ct. Appeals (1st Cir.) 1974, US Supreme Ct. 1977, US Ct. Appeals (DC Cir.) 1983, US Ct. Appeals (7th Cir.) 1984. Law clk. US Dist. Ct. (We. Dist.) Wash., Seattle, 1971-73; assoc. Mintz, Levin, Cohn, Ferris, Glovsky, and Popeo, PC, Boston, 1973-78, mem., 1978—, chmn. Employment, Labor, Benefits, Sect. Former mem. adv. bd. Law Firm Resources Project. Bd. dirs. Greater Boston Legal Svcs., 1982—95, Greater Boston Food Bank, 2000—. Named Mass. Super Lawyer, Boston Mag., 2004. Office: Mintz Levin Cohn Ferris Glovsky & Popeo PC 1 Financial Ctr Fl 39 Boston MA 02111-2657 Office Phone: 617-348-1643. Office Fax: 617-542-2241. Business E-Mail: rgault@mintz.com.

GAULTIER, JEAN-PAUL, fashion designer; b. Arcueil, France, Apr. 24, 1952; Design asst. Pierre Cardin, 1970—76; launched, head designer, chmn. Jean Paul Gaultier, 1976—, launched jr. collection, 1988—, launched Gaultier Jeans collection, 1992, launched first perfume for women, 1993, launched JPG line replacing the jr. collection, 1994, launched first Haute Couture collection, 1997; launched signature fragrance Jean Paul Gaultier Le Male, 1995. Designed costumes for (film) The Cook, the Thief, His Wife, and Her Lover, 1989, Kika, 1993, La Citè des Enfants Perdus, 1995, The Fifth Element, 1997, Nearest to Heaven, 2002, Bad Education, 2004, (ballet) le Dèfile de Règime Chopinot, 1985, (music) Madonna's Blond Ambition tour and Drowned World tour, Madonna's Confessions World Tour, 2006, (TV series) Dangerous Liaisons, 2004; rec. How to Do That, 1989 (Progetto Leonardo award 1989); actor Ready to Wear, 1994, Absolutely Fabulous, 2001. Named Best Internat. Designer, Coun. Fashion Designers Am., 2000, Chevalier, Bastille Day Honours List, France, 2001; recipient Fashion Oscar award, 1987. Office: 70 Galerie Vivienne 75002 Paris France*

GAUNAURD, GUILLERMO C., physicist, researcher, engineer; b. Havana, Cuba, July 19, 1940; arrived in US, 1961, naturalized; s. Celestino Carlos and Ana Marie (Herrera) G.; m. Marlene Jane Johnson, June 10, 1967. AB in Math., Cath. U. Am., Washington, 1964; BSME, Cath. U. Am., 1966, MS, 1967, PhD in Physics/Acoustics, 1972. Cons. engr. Ocean Systems Inc. (div. Union Carbide), Arlington, Va., 1966-68; sr. cons. engr. Litton Industries Inc., College Park, Md., 1968-71; rsch. physicist, sci. and tech. materials dept. Naval Surface Warfare Ctr., White Oak and Carderock Divsns., West Bethesda, Md., 1971-2000; sr. physicist, sensors and electron devices directorate Army Rsch. Lab., Adelphi, Md., 2001—. Lectr. U. Md. Sch. Engring., College Park, 1983-92, Cath. U. Am. Sch. Engring., Wash., 1974-78 Contbr. over 400 articles to profl. sci. jours., chpts. to books and conf. procs.; patentee in field Mem. Randolph Hills Civic Com., Rockville, Md., 1971—. Recipient various publ. awards and sci. excellence medals; grantee Office Naval Rsch., 1967—; Fellow Nat. Defense Edn. Act, 1967-70. Fellow ASME, IEEE (editor IEEE Jour. Oceanic Engring. 1987—, assoc. editor IEEE Jour. Ultrasonics, Ferroelectrics and Frequency Control 1992—), SPIE, AIAA (assoc.), Acoustical Soc. Am. (various offices, assoc. editor Linear Acoustics 2002-05), Wash. Acad. Scis.; mem. Philos. Soc. Wash., Optical Soc. Am., Internat. Union Math. Physics, Am. Acad. Mechanics, Wash. Soc. Engrs., N.Y. Acad. Scis., Sigma Xi, Tau Beta Pi Avocations: photography, classical music. Home: 4807 Macon Rd Rockville MD 20852-2348 Office: Army Rsch Lab Code AMSRD-ARL-SE-RU Microwaves Br 2800 Powder Mill Rd Adelphi MD 20783-1197 Office Phone: 301-394-1357. Personal E-mail: electron20@aol.com. Business E-Mail: ggaunaurd@arl.army.mil.

GAUNCE, MICHAEL PAUL, insurance company executive; b. Paris, Ky., Oct. 17, 1949; s. Paul D. and Mary E. Gaunce; m. Annette Beauchamp Gaunce. BA, U. Ky., Lexington, 1971. Agt., mgr. Equitable Life NY, Lexington, Ky., 1972-74; agt., regional mgr. Assn. Ins. Marketers, Inc., Indpls., Cin., South Bend, Ind., 1974-77; pres., chmn. Ins. Corp. Am., Indpls., 1977—. Chmn. bd. dirs. Argent Ins. Corp., Alternative Healthcare Marketers, Inc.; bd. dirs., past chmn. Brokers Ins. Corp., bd. dirs., Brokers Ins. Agy., Ins. Corp., Agy. Mgmt. Corp.; cons. adv. bd. Blue Cross/Blue Shield, Indpls., 1982—89; mem. adv. bd. Acordia, Inc., Indpls., 1996—98; mem. adv. group Trustmaker Ins. Co., 2000; mem. adv. bd. Advantage Healthcare Solutions, Inc. Active Rep. Nat. Com.; adv. bd. Salvation Army, 2005—. Mem.: Ind. Assn. Employee Benefit Cons. (pres. 1984—88), Seymour C. of C., Franklin C. of C., Greenwood C. of C., Elks. Republican. Avocations: fishing, swimming, reading, investments, travel. Office: Ins Corp Am 500 S Polk St Ste 18-19 Greenwood IN 46143-1629

GAUNT, JANET LOIS, arbitrator, mediator; b. Lawrence, Mass., Aug. 23, 1947; d. Donald Walter and Lois (Neuhart) Bacon; children: Christopher, Andrew D. BA, Oberlin Coll., 1969; JD, Wash. U., St. Louis, 1974. Bar: Wash. 1974, U.S. Dist. Ct. (we. dist.) Wash. 1974, U.S. Ct. Appeals (9th cir.) 1978. Assoc. Davis, Wright, Todd, Riese & Jones, Seattle, 1974—80; arbitrator/mediator Seattle, 1981—. Dir. Seattle King County Labor Law Sect., 1976-77; mem. Pacific Coast Labor Law Planning Com., 1977-83; com. vice chmn. Wash. State Task Force on Gender and Justice on the Cts., 1987-89; chmn. Wash. Pub. Employment Rels. Commn., Olympia, 1989-96. Author, editor: Alternative Dispute Resolution, 1989; author: Public Sector Labor Mediation and Arbitration, Arbitration and Mediation in Washington, 2d edit., 1995. Recipient Pass the Torch award, Wash. Women Lawyers, 1999. Fellow: Coll. Labor and Employment Lawyers; mem.: Washington Women Lawyers (state co-pres. 1986), Wash. State Bar Assn., Nat. Acad. Arbitrators (dir. rsch. and edn. found. 1991—96, bd. govs. 1998—2001, v.p. 2002—04, dir. rsch. and edn. found. 2006—07). Office Phone: 206-932-7020. E-mail: j.gaunt@comcast.net.

GAUNT, KAREN KREIDER, lawyer; b. Cin., Aug. 14, 1971; BA, Denison U., 1993; JD, U. Cin. Coll. Law, 1997. Bar: Ohio 1997, US Ct. Internat. Trade 1999, US Dist. Ct. Southern Dist. Ohio 1999, US Ct. of Appeals Sixth Cir. 2003, US Dist. Ct. Eastern Dist. Mich. 2003. Ptnr. Keating Muething & Klekamp PLL, Cin. Named one of Ohio's Rising Stars, Super Lawyers, 2005, 2006; named to America's Leading Bus. Lawyers, Chambers USA, 2006. Mem.: Internat. Trademark Assn., Ohio State Bar Assn., Cin. Bar Assn. Office: Keating Muething & Klekamp PLL One E Fourth St Ste 1400 Cincinnati OH 45202 Office Phone: 513-579-6400. Office Fax: 513-579-6457.

GAUNT, MARIANNE I., university librarian; BA, Montclair State U.; MLS, Drexel U. Rsch. libr. E. I. Dupont de Nemours Co., Wilmington, Del.; head Serials Dept. Brown U. Librs.; joined Rutgers U. Librs., 1979, online reference coord. NJ, circulation libr., dir. Humanities and Social Sci. Librs., assoc. univ. libr. rsch. and undergrad. svcs., acting univ. libr., 1996—97, univ. libr., 1997—. Contbr. articles to profl. jours. Mem.: Pa. Academic Library Consortium (bd. trustees), Virtual Academic Library Environment NJ (founding chair), Assn. Rsch. Libraries (v.p., pres. elect 2006—07), PALINET (bd. dirs. 2007—), NJ Libr. Assn. (Disting. Service award Coll. and Univ. Section 2000). Office: Rutgers U Librs 169 College Ave New Brunswick NJ 08901-1163 Office Phone: 732-932-7505. E-mail: gaunt@rci.rutgers.edu.*

GAURON, PAUL R., lawyer; BA, Bowdoin Coll., 1969; JD, Harvard Univ., 1972. Bar: Mass. 1972. Ptnr., energy practice group Goodwin Procter LLP, Boston, chair, bus. law dept, mem. exec. com. Knight of Malta. Mem.: Mass. Bar Assn., Boston Bar Assn., Phi Beta Kappa. Office: Goodwin Procter LLP Exchange Pl 53 State St Boston MA 02109 Office Phone: 617-570-1484. Office Fax: 617-523-1231. Business E-Mail: pgauron@goodwinprocter.com.

GAUSAS, ROBERTA ELISABETH, oculoplastic and orbital surgeon; b. Chgo., Jan. 6, 1964; m. Allen J. Model, Jan. 11, 2003. MD, Northwestern U., Chgo., 1989. Diplomate Am. Bd. Ophthalmology. Fellow in oculoplastic surgery U. Wis., Madison, 1993—94; fellow in orbital surgery Moorfields Eye Hosp., London, 1994—95; intern McGaw Hosp., Chgo., 1989—90; resident U. Wis. Hosp. and Clinic, Madison, 1990—93; instr. U. Wis.-Madison Hosp. and Clinics, 1995—96; dir. oculoplastic and orbital surgery svc., assoc. prof. dept. ophthalmology U. Pa. Med. Sch., Phila., 1996—. Recipient Top Doc award, Phila. Mag., 2000, 2002; scholar, DAAD, German Academic Exch. Svc., 1985. Fellow: Am. Soc. Ophthalmic Plastic and Reconstructive Surgery (program chmn. ann. sci. symposium 2002, mem. exec. com. 2002—04, program chmn. ann. spring sci. symposium 2003, Merril Reeh Pathology award 1999), Am. Acad. Ophthalmology (Achievement award 2001). Avocations: travel, conservation, art. Office: Scheie Eye Inst U Pa 51 North 39th St Philadelphia PA 19104 Home Phone: 215-772-9640; Office Phone: 215-662-8652.

GAUSE, CHARLES PHILLIP, education educator; b. NYC, Feb. 23, 1966; s. Walter Timothy Gause and Ernestine LaVerne Lewis-Gause. BS, Trinity Internat. U., Miami, Fla., 1990—91; MEd in Elem. Edn., Columbia Internat. U., SC, 1991—93; MEd, U. SC, Columbia, 1994—96; PhD, Miami U., Oxford, Ohio, 1999—2001. Tchr. Richland Sch. Dist. One, Columbia, 1993—96; v.p. Florence Sch. Dist. One, SC, 1996—97; prin. Williamsburg County Pub. Schs., Kingstree, SC, 1997—99; doctoral tchg. assoc. Miami U., 1999—2001; v.p. North Coll. Hill Sch. Dist., Cin., 2001—01; asst. prof. Winthrop U., Rock Hill, SC, 2002—03, U. NC, Greensboro, 2003—. CEO Gause Ednl. Solutions, Greensboro, 2006—. Author (co-editor): (textbook) Keeping the Promise: Essays on Leadership, Democracy and Education; author: (guest editor) Jour. Sch. Leadership-Special Issue Edu-tainment; contbr. articles to profl. jours. Mem.: NAESP, NC Assn. Sch. Adminstrs., Nat. Assn. Secondary Sch. Prins., Am. Ednl. Rsch. Assn., Am. Ednl. Studies Assn. Achievements include research in black masculinity; African American educators and hip-hop; collaborative activism; same-affection loving gender identity. Avocations: hiking, travel, bicycling, white-water rafting. Home: 2523 Wheatfield Dr Greensboro NC 27405 Office: Univ NC 239 C Curry Bldg Spring Garden St Greensboro NC 27402-6170 Home Phone: 336-509-7985. Home Fax: 336-334-4737. Personal E-mail: ges1993@yahoo.com. Business E-Mail: cpgause@uncg.edu.

GAUSS, JOHN A., former federal agency administrator, retired naval officer; b. Salem, Mass. BS in Engring. and Physics, Cornell U., 1969; M of Philosophy, Naval Postgrad. Sch., 1976, PhD in Electronics Engring. Commd. ensign USN, 1969, advanced through ranks to rear adm.; various assignments to comdr. Def. Info. Systems Agy., Arlington, Va., 1994-97; dir. Allied & Fleet Requirements Divsn. Space, Info. Warfare Command & Control Directorate, Washington, 1997—2001; asst. sec. and chief info. officer for info. and tech. U.S. Dept. Veterans Affairs, Washington, 2001—03. Decorated Def. Disting. Svc. medal, Legion of Merit (3 times), Meritorious Svc. medal, Navy Achievement medal.

GAUSTAD, EDWIN SCOTT, historian, educator; b. Rowley, Iowa, Nov. 14, 1923; s. Sverre and Norma (McEachron) G.; m. Helen Virginia Morgan, Dec. 19, 1946; children: Susan, Glen Scott, Peggy Lynn. BA, Baylor U., 1947; MA, Brown U., 1948, PhD, 1951. Instr. Brown U., 1951-52, Am. Council Learned Socs. scholar in residence, 1952-53; dean Shorter Coll., 1953-57; prof. humanities U. Redlands, 1957-65; assoc. prof. history U. Calif., Riverside, 1965-67, prof., 1968-89, prof. emeritus, 1989; prof. Princeton (N.J.) Theol. Sem., 1991-92, Auburn U., 1993. Vis. prof. Baylor U., 1976, U. Calif., Santa Barbara, 1986, U. Richmond, 1987. Author: The Great Awakening in New England, 1957, New Historical Atlas of Religion in America, new edit., (with P.L. Barlow), 2001, Religious History of America, revised edit., (with Leigh E. Schmidt), 2002, Dissent in American Religion, 1973, Baptist Piety: The Last Will and Testimony of Obadiah Holmes, 1978, 2005, George Berkeley in America, 1979, Faith of Our Fathers, 1987, 2004, Liberty of Conscience: Roger Williams in America, 1991, Revival, Revolution, and Religion in Early Virginia, 1994, Sworn on the Altar of God: A Religious Biography of Thomas Jefferson, 1996, Church and State in America, 1998, 2d edit., 2003, Memoirs of the Spirit, 1999, Roger Williams: Prophet of Liberty, 2001, (with Mark Noll) Documentary History of Religion in America, 2 vols., 3d edit., 2003, Benjamin Franklin: Inventing America, 2004, Roger Williams, 2005, (with five others) Unto a Good Land, 2005. Served to 1st lt. USAAC, 1943-45. Decorated Air medal; Am. Council Learned Socs. grantee, 1952-53, 72-73; Am. Philos. Soc. grantee, 1972-73 Mem. Am. Soc. Ch. History (pres.), Orgn. Am. Historians, Phi Beta Kappa. Democrat. Baptist. E-mail: egaustad@aol.com.

GAUSTER, STEPHEN WILHELM, lawyer, corporate financial executive; b. Albuquerque, July 8, 1970; s. Wilhelm B. and Norma S. G. AB summa cum laude, Harvard Coll., 1992; AM, Harvard U., 1994; JD cum laude, Harvard Law Sch., 1997. Bar: NY 1998, U.S. Dist. Ct. (so. and ea. dists.) NY 1999, U.S. Ct. Appeals (3d cir.) 2001, DC 1999. Law clk. to Hon. Jane R. Roth, U.S. Ct. Appeals (3d cir.), Wilmington, Del., 2000—01; assoc. Cleary, Gottlieb, Steen & Hamilton, NYC, 1997—2004; v.p., corp. counsel, asst. sec. Prudential Fin., Inc., Newark, 2004—; gen. counsel, sec. Prudential Funding, LLC, 2004—; adj. prof. sch. law Rutgers U., Newark, 2006—. Editor Harvard Law Rev., 1995-97. Active Dem. Nat. Com., 1999—. Mem. ABA, N.Y. State Bar Assn. (com. on securities regulation), D.C. Bar Assn., Phi Beta Kappa. Office: Prudential Fin Inc 751 Broad St Newark NJ 07102 Home: 77 River St Hoboken NJ 07030-7715

GAUT, C. CHRISTOPHER, oil industry executive; b. 1957; BA in Engring. Sci., Dartmouth Coll.; MBA in Fin., U. Pa. Various fin. mgmt. positions Amoco Corp.; ptnr. Pacific Asset Capital; pres., COO, CFO ENSCO Internat., Inc., Dallas, 1988—2003; exec. v.p., CFO Halliburton, Houston, 2003—. Mem.: Fin. Execs. Internat., Internat. Assn. Drilling Contractors (mem. exec. com.). Office: Halliburton 5 Houston Ctr 1401 McKinney St Ste 2400 Houston TX 77010 Office Phone: 713-759-2600. E-mail: cris.gaut@halliburton.com.*

GAUTHIER, DOREEN ANN, librarian; b. Davenport, Iowa, July 18, 1941; d. Clifford H. and Dorothy H. Wildman; m. William E. Gauthier, July 18, 1989. BA, Midland Coll., Fremont. Nebr., 1972; grad. cert., U. Omaha, 1972; MA, U. South Fla., 1996. Children's libr. Keene Meml. Libr., Fremont, Nebr., 1967-77; circulation libr. Pompano Beach (Fla.) Libr., 1978-79; libr. dir. The Doreen Gauthier Lighthouse Point (Fla.) Libr., 1979—. Dir. Fla. Pub. Libr. Assn., Lakeland, 1992—98. Mem. ALA, Fla. Libr. Assn., Broward County Libr. Assn. Episcopalian. Home: 1990 NE 32nd Ct # 44 Lighthouse Point FL 33064-7684 Office: The Doreen Gauthier Lighthouse Point Library 2200 NE 38th St Ste A Lighthouse Point FL 33064-3913 Home Phone: 954-785-0042; Office Phone: 954-946-6398. Personal E-mail: gauthid22@hotmail.com. Business E-Mail: dgauthier@lighthousepointlibrary.com.

GAUTO, NELSON FERNANDO, plastic surgeon, consumer products company executive; b. Asuncion, Paraguay, Sept. 20, 1964; s. Mamerto and Maria Selva Gauto. BS in Major Biology, U. Asuncion, Paraguay, 1982; MD, Sch. Med. Scis., Paraguay, 1988. Cert. in med. scis. Ednl. Commn. Fgn. Med. Grads., 1991, plastic surgeon Royal Coll. Surgeons Can., 1999. Pres. So. Ill. Plastic Surgery, Herrin, Ill., 2001—. Aesthetic and Rejuvenation Ctr., Mt. Vernon, Ill., 2003—. Pro bono reconstructive surgeon US, overseas. Recipient Dept. of Surgery Rsch. Day award, Dalhousie U., 1999. Master: Grand Lodge Ill., Grand Lodge Mass.; fellow: Royal Coll. Surgeons Can.; mem.: AMA, Am. Soc. Aesthetic Plastic Surgery, Mass. Med. Soc., Ill. Med. Soc., Soc. Latin Am. Plastic Surgeons N.Am. (pres. 2004—), Can. Aesthetic Soc. Plastic Surgery, Am. Soc. Plastic Surgeons. Roman Catholic. Achievements include research in effect of vascular supply on bone graft healing in the canine tibial segmental osteotomy model; vascular study for breast reconstruction, and vascular delay in the canine rectus abdominis muscle flap. Avocations: travel, hiking, soccer. Office: So Ill Plastic Surgery 3307 Logan Dr Herrin IL 62948 Home Phone: 618-993-0157; Office Phone: 618-998-9600. Office Fax: 618-998-9611. Personal E-mail: nfgauto@yahoo.com.

GAUVEY, SUSAN KATHRYN, judge; b. Van Wert, Ohio, Mar. 1, 1948; d. Richard David and Asta Walburga (Frericks) G.; m. David E. Kern, May 10, 1975; children: Megan E. Gauvey-Kern, Kevin C. Gauvey-Kern, Elizabeth H. Gauvey-Kern. Student, Georgetown U., 1968-69; BA cum laude Polit. Sci., Rosary Coll, River Forest, Ill., 1970; JD, Northwestern U., 1973; postgrad. Mental Hygiene, Johns Hopkins U., 1976-77. Bar: Wash. 1974, Md. 1975. Law clerk to fed. dist. ct. judge We. Dist. Ct., Seattle, 1973-74; staff atty. Mental Health Law Project Legal Aid Bur., Balt., 1975-77, co-chief Mental Health Law Project, 1977-79; asst. atty. gen. Dept. Health and Mental Hygiene Office of Atty. Gen., Balt., 1979-81, asst. atty. gen. Civil Divsn., 1981-86, prin. counsel trial litigation, 1984-86; with litigation divsn. Venable, Baetjer and Howard L.L.P., Balt., 1986-96; magistrate judge U.S. Dist. Ct. for Md., Balt., 1996—. Contbr. articles to profl. jours. Chair bd. dirs. Marian House for Women. Mem. Nat. Assn. Women Judges, Wranglers Law Club, Lawyers' Roundtable, Sgt.'s Inn Network. Democrat. Office: US Courthouse 101 W Lombard St Baltimore MD 21201-2605 Office Phone: 410-962-4953. Business E-Mail: mdd_skgchambers@mdd.uscourts.gov.

GAVALER, JOAN SUSAN, dance educator; d. John Raymond and Judith Stohr Gavaler; m. Robert Lian Foster. BA, Coll. William and Mary, Williamsburg, Va., 1985; MA, Ohio State U., Columbus, 1987. Cert. tchg. mem. Alexander Technique Internat., 1999. Assoc. prof. dance Coll. William and Mary, Williamsburg, 1994—2007, prof. dance, 2007—. Mem. The Moving Arts Co., Columbus, 1987—90; guest artist Days of Creation, Arts for Kids, Columbus, 1987—94; artistic dir. Gavaler Danceworks, Williamsburg, 1990—; co-artistic dir. Gravity Optional Dance Co., Williamsburg, 2002—; disting. guest artist So. Dist. AAHPERD Conv., 2005. Choreographer Translations, Captured. Seeking, Nostalgia (Starry Night Again), Moment, Virus Warning, Even If You Did, Barrier, You Cannot Hear Me, Sextet # 1 With Rests, The Waiting Room, Grace, Dyslexia. Recipient Fellowship award for Excellence in Tchg., Alumni Soc., Coll. William and Mary, 2002—03; Nat. Merit scholar, Richard King Mellon, 1981—85, Project grantee, Ohio Joint Program in the Arts and Humanities, 1990, 1991, Greater Columbus Arts Coun., 1991, 1992, 1993. Mem.: Am. Dance Guild (bd. mem. 2003), Alexander Technique Internat., Phi Beta Kappa. Office: Coll William and Mary Dept Theatre Speech Dance PO Box 8795 Williamsburg VA 23187 Office Phone: 757-221-2785.

GAVENDA, J(OHN) DAVID, physicist; b. Temple, Tex., Mar. 25, 1933; s. Edward and Rose Katherine (Machalek) G.; m. Janie Louise Yeoman, Dec. 22, 1952; children— Victor Joseph, Philip Martin. Student, U. Chgo., 1950-51; BS, U. Tex., Austin, 1954, MA, 1956; PhD, Brown U., 1959. Asst. prof. physics U. Tex., Austin, 1959-62, assoc. prof., 1962-65, assoc. prof. physics and edn., 1965-67, prof., 1967-99, prof. emeritus, 1999—. Contbr. articles on physics of metals and electromagnetic wave propagation to profl. jours. Sr. rsch. fellow Inst. Study of Metals, U. Chgo., 1963, NATO sr. fellow in sci. U. Oslo, 1969. Fellow: Am. Phys. Soc., Tex. Acad. Sci.; mem.: Am. Assn. Physics Tchrs. (Robert N. Little award 1988, Disting. Svc. citation 1997), Phi Beta Kappa, Sigma Xi. Democrat. Baptist. Home: 7317 Blue Heron Cove Volente TX 78641-6140 Office: Univ Tex Dept Physics 1 University Sta C1600 Austin TX 78712-0264 Office Phone: 512-471-3201. E-mail: gavenda@physics.utexas.edu.

GAVER, FRANCES ROUSE, lawyer; b. Lexington, Ky., Mar. 13, 1929; d. Colvin P. Rouse and Elizabeth Turner Sympson; m. Donald Paul Gaver, Jan. 24, 1953; children: Elizabeth, Donald, William. BA, Wellesley Coll., 1950; MA, U. Pitts., 1968; JD, Monterey Coll. Law, Calif., 1986. Bar: Calif. 1986, U.S. Dist. Ct. (no. dist.) Calif. 1986; cert. specialist in probate, estate planing and trust law, Calif. Assoc. Hoge, Fenton, Jones & Appel, Monterey, 1986-93, Fenton & Keller, Monterey, 1993-97; ptnr. Johnson, Gaver & Leach, Monterey, 1997-99, of counsel, 2000—. Bd. dirs. Carmel (Calif.) Unified Sch. Dist., 1973-81, Monterey Coll. of Law, 1991-97, Legal Svcs. for Srs., Seaside, Calif., 1994-2000; bd. dirs. Monterey Peninsula Coll. Found., 2000-06. Mem. Monterey County Bar Assn. Avocations: playing recorder, swimming. Office: Johnson Gaver & Leach LLP 2801 Monterey Salinas Hwy Monterey CA 93940-6401 Business E-Mail: fgaver@jgllp.com.

GAVERAS, HARRY, architect; b. NYC, Feb. 9, 1971; s. Christos and Kyriaki Gaveras. BArch, Cooper Union U., 1993; MArch in Urban Design, Harvard U., 1997. Registered arch., Greece, NY. Pres. Propylaea Arch., PLLC, NYC, 2000—. Vis. critic and instr. Harvard U. Grad. Sch., 2003; vis. prof. Ctrl. Acad. Fine Arts, Beijing, 2004. Orpheus Assn. Traveling grantee, 1992. Mem.: AIA (co-chair Emerging NY Archs. com. NY chpt. 2005—, Young Archs. Forum NY regional liaison 2007—, Emerging Profls. Program of Yr. award 2006), Cooper Union Alumni (coun. mem.), Harvard Club NYC. Avocations: painting, writing, travel. Office: Propylaea Arch Atelier 795 E 135th St Bronx NY 10454 Office Phone: 718-401-9393. Personal E-mail: hgaveras@yahoo.com.

GAVIAN, PETER WOOD, securities analyst; b. Brewster, Mass., Dec. 8, 1932; s. Sarkis Peter and Ruth Millicent (Wood) G.; children: Sarah, Deborah Gavian Costolloe, Margaret Elizabeth BA, Yale U., 1954; MBA cum laude, Harvard U., 1959. Chartered fin. analyst; accredited sr. appraiser; bus. valuation; USCG master's lic. Assoc. McKinsey & Co., NYC, 1959—61; sec., treas. Greater Washington Investors, 1961—64, 1970—71; v.p. fin. NUS Corp., Washington, 1965—66; asst. to group v.p. internat. Carborundum Co., Niagara Falls, NY, 1966—68; pvt. investment banker Washington, 1968—; pres. Corp. Fin. Washington, Inc., 1976—. Expert witness in bus. valuation, 1980—; lectr. Am. U., Washington, 1978-80; ind. trustee Calvert Group Funds, Bethesda, Md., 1980—, chair investment policy com., 2003— Contbr. articles to profl. jours Vol. varsity sailing coach U.S. Naval Acad., 1981-89; vestryman St. Luke's Episcopal Ch., Annapolis, 2006—; bd. dirs. ACLU, Va., 1993-95. Lt. USN, 1954-57 Mem. Washington Soc. Investment Analysts (pres. 1978-79), Am. Soc. Appraisers (pres. Washington chpt. 1998-99), CFA Inst Avocations: ocean sailing, amateur radio. Home: 12 B3 Spa Creek Landing Annapolis MD 21403 Office Phone: 410-626-2567. Personal E-mail: petergavian@verizon.net.

GAVIN, DONALD GLENN, lawyer, educator; b. Newark, Oct. 12, 1942; s. Louis Brooks and Elizabeth (Nievert) Gavin; m. Irene Dunn, Nov. 25, 1965; children: Andrew Scott, Mitchell Bryant. BS in Econs., U. Pa., 1964, JD, 1967; LLM, George Washington U., 1972. Bar: Pa. 1967, D.C. 1972, Va. 1973. Law clk. Ct. Common Pleas, Phila., 1967—68; assoc. to ptnr. Lewis, Mitchell & Moore, Washington and Vienna, Va., 1972—74; founding ptnr. Wickwire, Gavin P.C., Washington, L.A. and Vienna, 1974—2006; shareholder Akerman Senterfitt Wickwire Gavin, 2006—. Lectr. in field. Contbr. articles to profl. jours. Nat. bd. Am. Ceramic Cir. To capt. JAG US Army, 1968—72. Recipient Outstanding Svc. award, US Ct. Federal Claims. Fellow: ABA (past nat. chmn. pub. contract law sect., past chmn. fed. grant legis., policies and remedies com., past chmn. grant coordination com., past chmn. environ. law com., mem. forum on construction industry, mem., former vice-chair tort & insurance practice sect., fidelity and surety com., legal claim divsn., past coun. mem.), Am. Bar Found., Am. Coll. Constrn. Lawyers; mem.: US Coun. Internat. Bus., Internat. Bar Assn. (construction and arbitration com.), Pa. Bar Assn., Va. Bar Assn., US Ct. Fed. Claims Com., Fed. Bar Assn. Home Phone: 703-734-3049; Office Phone: 703-790-8750. Business E-Mail: donald.gavin@akerman.com.

GAVIN, JAMES RAPHAEL, III, biochemist; b. Oviedo, Fla., Nov. 23, 1945; m. Annie Ruth Jackson, June 19, 1971; 3 children. BS in Chemistry, Livingstone Coll., Salisbury, NC, 1966; PhD in Biochemistry, Emory U., 1970; MD, Duke U., 1975. Diplomate Am. Bd. Internal Medicine, Nat. Bd. Med. Examiners. With USPHS, 1971—; staff assoc. diabetes br. NIH, Bethesda, Md., 1971-73; intern dept. pathology Duke U., Durham, N.C., 1975-76; intern dept. internal medicine Barnes Hosp., St. Louis, 1976-77, resident dept. internal medicine, 1977-78, asst. physician, 1978-85, assoc. physician, 1985-87; prof. medicine, chief diabetes sect. U. Okla. Health Scis. Ctr., Oklahoma City, 1988-89, William K. Warren prof. diabetes studies, 1989-91; sr. scientific officer Howard Hughes Med. Inst., Chevy Chase, Md., 1991—2002; pres. Morehouse Sch. Med., 2002—05; clin. prof. med., sr. adv. health affairs Emory U., 2005—; exec. v.p. clin. affairs Healing Our Village LLC, 2005—. Asst. prof. medicine Washington U., St. Louis, 1978-85, dir. RIA core lab., diabetes, rsch., tng. ctr., 1978-87, assoc. prof., 1985-87; George H. Howard, Jr. lectr. Meharry Med. Coll., 1988; Dr. Martin L. King, Jr. lectr. Washington U., 1988; Zollicofer vis. prof. U. N.C., 1990, Ralph Landes lectr., 1996; George H. Hamwi Meml. lectr. Ohio State Coll., 1991; Marty Alpern lectr. Henry Ford Hosp., 1991; Edward Hook Disting. lectr. U. Va., Charlottesville, 1994; Roerig Diabetes vis. prof. U. Hawaii Med. Ctr., Honolulu, 1995; mem. med. sci. adv. com. Juvenile Diabetes Found. Internat., 1981; mem. adv. com. minority med. faculty devel. program Robert Wood Johnson Found., 1983-93, nat. program dir., 1992, sr. program cons., 1987, nat. program dir. minority med. edn. program, 1987-93; bd. trustees, 1996; mem. adv. com. ctr. drugs biologics FDA, 1986-90; mem. Nat. Diabetes Adv. Bd., 1988-92; spl. reviewer endocrinology study sect. NIDDK, 1989-91, chmn. study sect. initiative diabetes minorities, 1991, chmn. study sect. intervention minorities diabetes, 1993, chmn. spl. rev. group prevention type 2 diabetes, 1994, chmn. investigator's working group diabetes minorities, 1995, mem. data monitoring bd. diabetes prevention program, 1995—; mem. com. increasing minority participation in health professions Inst. Medicine, Washington, 1992-94; mem. bd. overseers urban inst. Liberty Med. Ctr., Balt., 1993; mem. adv. coun. Miles Inst. Health Care Comm., 1994; chmn. diabetes adv. bd. Bayer Pharm., Inc., 1995; mem. steering com. Nat. Diabetes Edn. Program, 1995; various vis. prof. Author: (chpt.) Immunopharmacology, 1977, Introduction to Endocrine Investigation: Techniques and Concepts, 1987, Key Issues in Minority Education: Research Directions and Practical Implications, 1989; co-author: (chpt.) Advances in Human Growth Hormone Rsch., 1973; mem. editl. bd. Am. Jour. Physiology, 1982-88, Am. Jour. Med. Sci., 1989-94, Acad. Medicine, 1994—; contbr. articles to Endocrinology, Sci., Biochemistry Biophysics Rsch. Comm., Nature New Biology, Jour. Biol. Chem., Jour. Clin. Endocrinology Metabolism, Pharmacology Rev., Israel Jour. Med. Sci., Jour. Pediat., Jour. Exptl. Medicine, Metabolism, Archives Internal Medicine, Jour. Applied Physiology, Obstetrics Gynecology, Diabetes, Am. Jour. Physiology, Am. Jour. Medicine, Nephron, Diabetes Edn., Bone, Am. Jour. Nursing, Diabetologia, Brain Rsch., Acta Diobetol, Preventive Medicine, Internat. Jour. Obesity, Diabetes Forecast, Am. Clin. Climatol. Assn., Patient Care. Founder, bd. dirs. Alpha Edn. Found. Bd., St. Louis, 1988, Baxter US, 2003-, Amylin Pharmaceuticals Inc., MicroIslet Inc.; mem. Okla. State Student Loan Authority, 1989-90; bd. trustees Okla. Sch. Sci. Math. Found., 1991. Elk's scholar, 1962; recipient traineeship award NSF, 1966-70, Spl. Achiever award St. Louis Sentinel Newspaper, 1982, Disting. Alumnus award Nat. Assn. Opportunity Higher Edn., 1987, Excellence award Okla. Alliance Affirmative Action, 1988, Daniel Hale Williams award Chgo. Med. Assn., 1993, E.E. Just award Am. Soc. Cell Biology, 1995, Herbert Nickens award, Daniel Savage Meml. award; USPHS Predoc. fellow, 1970, Hastings Inst. Ethics Life Scis. fellow, 1971-75, Washington U. Sch. Medicine fellow, 1978-79; named Outstanding African Am. in Medicine, Aetna, 1993. Mem. Am. Assn. Physicians, Am. Diabetes Assn. (mem. rsch. com. St. Louis affiliate 1982-84, chmn. patient edn. com. 1982-86, v.p. 1985-86, mem. nat. com. scientific programs 1986-89, vice-chmn. 1987-88, chmn. 1988-89, pres.-elect Okla. affiliate 1989-90, pres. 1990-91, mem. nat. com. budget fin. 1989-91, nat. v.p. 1991-92, pres.-elect 1992-93, pres. 1993-94, immediate past pres. 1994-95, bd. dirs. rsch. found. 1994-95, chmn. workgroup reclassification diabetes 1995—, Outstanding Clinician

1990, Banting medal 1994), Am. Fedn. Clin. Rsch., Am. Soc. Acad. Black Surgeons, Am. Soc. Clin. Investigation, Assn. Acad. Minority Physicians, Ctrl. Soc. Clin. Rsch., Assn. Am. Physicians, So. Soc. Clin. Rsch., Endocrine Soc., Am. Clin. Climatol. Assn., Inst. Medicine, Sigma Xi, Alpha Omega Alpha, Beta Kappa Chi, Alpha Phi Alpha (life, William Alexander Cmty. Leadership award 1982), Omicron Delta Kappa, Sigma Pi Phi. Office: Healing Our Village Ste 210 10104 Senate Dr Lanham MD 20706*

GAVIN, JOHN NEAL, lawyer; b. Chgo., Aug. 31, 1946; s. John Anthony and Mary Anne (O'Donnell) G.; m. Louise A. Sunderland, June 16, 1979; children: Anne, Matthew. AB, Coll. of Holy Cross, Worcester, Mass., 1968; JD, Harvard U., 1975. Bar: Ill. 1975. Law clk. to Hon. Charles M. Merrill US Ct. Appeals (9th cir.), San Francisco, 1975-76; atty. office of legal counsel US Dept. Justice, Washington, 1976-79; ptnr. Hopkins & Sutter, Chgo., 1981-2001, Foley & Lardner LLP, Chgo., 2001—. Served to lt. USN, 1968-71. Mem. ABA, Chgo. Bar Assn. Office: Foley & Lardner LLP 321 N Clark St Chicago IL 60610 Office Phone: 312-832-4544. Business E-Mail: jgavin@foley.com.

GAVIN, MARIA, television producer, writer; s. John Anthony Gavin and Cicely Jean Evans-Wheelon. BA, U. of the Pacific, Stockton, Calif., 1985; MA, Stanford U., Palo Alto, Calif., 1987. Coordinating prodr.: Fox L.Am. Channel, 1995; segment coord. Fox News at 10 KTTV/Fox 11, 1995—97; program coord.: KTTV/Fox 11, 1995—97, assoc. prodr., segment prodr.: AXN TV, Sony/Columbia Tristar, 1998, prodr., writer, dir.: Our Family (Hispanic Telecomm. Network), 1999, LA Cityview/Channel 35, 1995—2001, Hometown TV, 2000, City TV, 1998—2006, coordinating prodr.: Kiviat Prodns., 2000, writer pledge breaks: KCET-TV, 2000—05, writer, segment prodr., dir.: 9 On the Town, Tri-Crown Prodns., 2004, prodr., dir., writer: E! Networks/Style, 2002—05, prodr., writer: City Cable, 2004—05; prodr.: Fox Reality, 2005. Vol. Children's Hosp. LA, 1996—98. Named one of Outstanding Young Women of Am., 1985; recipient Excellence in Reporting Media award, 1st pl. pub. affairs show, Am. Diabetes Assn., LA chpt., 1990, LA Area Emmy award, 2004. Mem.: NATAS, Internat. Documentary Assn., Prodrs. Guild Am., Mensa. Personal E-mail: mariagavin@verizon.net.

GAVIN, MARY ELLEN, marketing professional, consultant; b. Chgo. d. Francis Edward and Agnes Mary (Rolder) Des Enfants; m. William Francis Gavin; children: Michael James, Terence Francis. MBA, U. Palmers Green, Eng., 1999. Lic. pvt. investigator. Analyst A.C. Nielsen, Chgo.; asst. br. mgr. Borg-Warner Fin. Svc., Chgo.; asst. leasing mgr. Borg-Warner Leasing, Chgo., midwest leasing mgr.; v.p. Gen. Equipment Leasing, Chgo.; leasing mgr. Pitney Bowes Credit Corp., Chgo.; ind. rep. Gen. Elec. Mobile Radio & Tele., Chgo.; pres. Gavin Communications, Annapolis, Md.; owner Gavin & Assocs., Chantilly, Va. Adult edn. tchr. Fairfax County, 1996—, Nova C.C., 2000—. Author: And Still We Celebrate, 2001, We Celebrate the Macabre, 2002, We Celebrate Food for the Soul, 2004; editor: Post War Letter Messages From the Heart, 1997. Mem.: Sisters in Crime, The Writers of Chantilly (founder), Nat. Assn. Writers, Women in Mgmt., Gulf Coast Writers, Internat. Women's Writing Guild, Associated Writing Program George Mason Univ., Nat. Writers Assn. Republican. Roman Catholic. Home: 8250 Vineyard Ave Apt 84 Rancho Cucamonga CA 91730-8707 Home Phone: 985-727-3063. E-mail: maryellengavin@yahoo.com.

GAVIN, MARY JANE, retired medical/surgical nurse; b. Prairie Du Chien, Wis., Sept. 1, 1941; d. Frank Grant and Mary Elizabeth Wolf; m. Alfred William Gavin, Nov. 9, 1963; children: Catherine Heidi Elizabeth, Carl Alfred Eric. Student, North Cen. Coll., Naperville, Ill., 1959-61; BS, RN, U. Wis., 1964; postgrad., Deepmuscle Tng. Ltd., 1980; postgrad. in deep muscle therapy. RN, Wis. Staff nurse U. Wis. Hosps., Madison; nurse home response VA, Milw.; ret., 2006. Unit chair Badger Girls State, 1991-2005; active Wis. Am. Legion Aux.; task force for handicapped Eastside Wis. Evang. Luth. Ch., Madison, 1993 U. Wis. scholar. Mem.: Monona Grove Am. Legion Aux. (pres. Unit 429 1990—2005). Achievements include writer material that made a federal law null and void.

GAVIN, ROBERT MICHAEL, JR., educational consultant; b. Coatesville, Pa., Aug. 16, 1940; s. Robert Michael and Helen Regina (Finnegan) G.; m. Charlotte Marie Dugan, June 2, 1962; children— Anne, Patricia, Robert, Charles, Sean. BA, St. John's U., Collegeville, Minn., 1962; PhD, Iowa State U., 1966; DSc (hon.), Haverford Coll., 1986, St. John's U., 1996. Mem. faculty Haverford (Pa.) Coll., 1966-84, prof. chemistry, 1975-84, dir. computing, 1979-80, provost, dean faculty, 1980-84, interim pres., 1996-97; pres. Macalester Coll., St. Paul, 1984-96, Cran Brook Ednl. Cmty., Bloomfield Hills, Mich., 1997—2001; ret., 2001. Bd. dirs. Hartford Funds, St. John's U., Minn.; chmn. bd. Hartford Mutual Funds, 2004-. Author papers in field. Pres. Haverford Twp. Sch. Bd., 1975. Recipient Dreyfus Tchr.-Scholar award, 1973; NSF fellow, 1969-70 Democrat. Roman Catholic. Home: 751 Judd St Marine On Saint Croix MN 55047 Personal E-mail: robertgavinjr@aol.com.

GAVIOLA, KAREN Z., television director; Dir.: (TV series, episodes) NYPD Blue (3 episodes), 1999—2001, Providence (1 episode), 2002, Strong Medicine (1 episode), 2002, CSI: Miami (12 episodes), 2003—, Cold Case (2 episodes), 2004, The Inside (1 episode), 2005, CSI: NY (1 episode), 2005, Medical Investigation (1 episode), 2005, Close to Home (1 episode), 2005, Crossing Jordan (1 episode), 2006, Lost: The Whole Truth, 2006 (NAACP Image award, Dir. of a drama series, 2007), Alias (1 episode), 2006, Justice (1 episode), 2006, Bones (1 episode), 2006, Prison Break (1 episode), 2006, Lincoln Heights (1 episode), 2007; (TV series) The Unit (1 episode), 2007. Mem.: Dirs. Guild Am. Mailing: Met Talent Agy c/o Dino Carlaftes 4526 Wilshire Blvd Los Angeles CA 90010 E-mail: gavvy2000@yahoo.com.*

GAVRAS, CONSTANTIN See COSTA-GAVRAS

GAVRIL, JEAN (JEAN VAN LEEUWEN), writer; b. Glen Ridge, NJ, Dec. 26, 1937; d. Cornelius Van Leeuwen and Dorothy Elizabeth Charlton; m. Bruce David Gavril, July 7, 1968; children: David, Elizabeth BA, Syracuse U., NYC, 1959. Asst. editor TV Guide Mag., NYC, 1959—60; libr. promotion asst. Abelard-Schuman, NYC, 1960—63; from asst. editor to assoc. editor Random House, NYC, 1963—68; assoc. editor Viking Press, NYC, 1968—69; sr. editor Dial Press, NYC, 1970—73; freelance writer, 1973—. Author: Timothy's Flower, 1967, One Day in Summer, 1969, The Great Cheese Conspiracy, 1969, I Was a 98-Pound Duckling, 1972, Too Hot for Ice Cream, 1974, The Great Christmas Kidnapping Caper, 1975, Seems Like This Road Goes On Forever, 1979, Tales of Oliver Pig, 1979, More Tales of Oliver Pig, 1981, The Great Rescue Operation, 1982, Amanda Pig and her Big Brother Oliver, 1982, Benjy and the Power of Zingies, 1982, Benjy in Business, 1983, Tales of Amanda Pig, 1983, Benjy the Football Hero, 1985, More Tales of Amanda Pig, 1985, Oliver, Amanda, and Grandmother Pig, 1985, Dear Mom, You're Ruining My Life, 1989, Oliver and Amanda's Christmas, 1989, Oliver Pig at School, 1990, Amanda Pig on Her Own, 1991, Going West, 1991, The Great Summer Camp Catastrophe, 1992, Oliver and Amanda's Halloween, 1992, Emma Bean, 1993, Two Girls in Sister Dresses, 1994, Bound for Oregon, 1994, Across the Wild Dark Sea, 1995, Oliver and Amanda and the Big Snow, 1995, Blue Sky Butterfly, 1996, Touch the Sky Summer, 1997, Amanda Pig, 1997, A Fourth of July on the Plains, 1997, Amanda Pig and Her Best Friend Lollipop, 1998, The Tickle Stories, 1998, Growing Ideas, 1998, Nothing Here But Trees, 1998, The Srange Adventures of Blue Dog, 1999, Hannah of Fairfield, 1999, Hannah's Helping Hands, 1999, Hannah's Winter of Hope, 2000, Oliver and Albert: Friends Forever, 2000, Sorry, 2001, "Wait for me!" Said Maggie Mcgee, 2001, Lucy Was There, 2002, The Amazing Air Balloon, 2003, Amanda Pig and the Awful Scary Monster, 2003, The Great Googlestein Museum Mystery, 2003, Oliver the Mighty Pig, 2004, Cabin on Trouble Creek, 2004, Amanda Pig and the Really Hot Day, 2005 (Theodor Seuss Geisel Honor Book, 2006), Benny and Beautiful Baby Delilah, 2006, Oliver Pig and the Best Fort Ever, 2006, Papa and the Pioneer Quilt, 2007, Amanda Pig, First Grader, 2007. Avocations: gardening, antiques, music, tennis. Personal E-mail: jvgavril@verizon.net.

GAVRILIS, JAMES, military officer; s. Nicholas and Nancy Gavrilis. BA in Polit. Sci., Pa. State U., 1989; MA in Internat. Studies, Old Dominion U., Norfolk, Va., 2001. Lt. col., spl. forces US Army, 1985—, co. comdr. B Co., 1st Bn., 5th Spl. Forces Grp. Ft. Campbell, Ky., 2002—03, ops. officer 1st Bn., 5th Spl. Forces Grp., 2003—04; polit. military planner Joint Chiefs Staff, DC, 2005—. Adj. prof. Georgetown U., DC, 2005—. Decorated Bronze Star with Oak Leaf Cluster US Army; Internat. Affairs fellow, Coun. Fgn. Rels., 2004—05. Mem.: Acad. Polit. Sci., Inst. Study Diplomacy (assoc.), Phi Kappa Phi. Avocations: writing, scuba diving, art, running, skydiving. Office: Joint Chiefs Staff Pentagon Washington DC 20318

GAVRIN, JONATHAN ROBERT, medical educator, internist; b. NYC, Apr. 25, 1950; s. Joseph Benjamin Gavrin and Natalie Ruth Nixon, Charles Nixon (Stepfather); life ptnr. Linda Ann Valleroy; m. Margaret Ann Wheeler, Aug. 16, 1980 (div. July 0, 2003); children: Joseph David, Kathryn Lee. MD, Dartmouth Med. Sch., Hanover, NH, 1978. Cert. internal medicine Am. Bd. Internal Medicine, 1982, anesthesiology Am. Bd. Anesthesiology, 1993, pain mgmt. Am. Bd. Anesthesiology, 1994, palliative care Am. Bd. Hospice and Palliative Medicine, 2006. Dir. symptom mgmt. and palliative care U. Pa., Phila., 2003—. Clin. assoc. prof. anesthesiology and critical care U. Pa., Phila., 2003—; physician co-chair ethics com. Hosp. of U. Pa., 2005—. Editor: Palliative Care, An Issue of Anesthesiology Clinics, 2006; contbr. articles to peer-reviewed profl. jours. Med. Scientist scholar, Mass. Mut. Life Ins., 1975—78, Tchg. fellow, U. Wash. Sch. Medicine, 1996—97. Mem.: Am. Pain Soc., Am. Bd. Hospice and Palliative Medicine, Am. Soc. Anesthesiologists. Avocations: walking, hiking, bicycling, reading, travel. Home: 201 S 25th St #423 Philadelphia PA 19103-6006 Office: Hosp Univ Pa Dulles 6-Anesthesiology 3400 Spruce St Philadelphia PA 19104 Home Phone: 267-252-5311; Office Phone: 215-615-0991. Office Fax: 215-349-8863; Home Fax: 215-349-8863. Business E-Mail: gavrinj@uphs.upenn.edu.

GAVRITY, JOHN DECKER, retired insurance company executive; b. S.I., NY, Oct. 26, 1940; s. John S. and Eleanor R. (Decker) G.; m. Camille Appello, April 16, 1998; children: John, Joseph. BS, Wagner Coll., 1963. From staff to assoc. actuary U.S. Life, NYC, 1963-74; from actuary to exec. v.p., fin. actuary USLIFE Corp., NYC, 1975-97, exec. v.p., chief actuary, 1997-98; ret., 1998. Fellow Soc. Actuaries; mem. Am. Acad. Actuaries. Republican. Roman Catholic. Home: 688 New Dorp Ln Staten Island NY 10306-4933

GAWANDE, ATUL A., surgeon, writer; b. Bklyn., Nov. 5, 1965; s. Atmaram S. Gawande, Sushila Goswami Gawande; m. Kathleen Hunter Hobson; children: Walker, Hattie, Hunter. BAS, Stanford U., 1987; MA, Oxford U., 1989; MD, Harvard Med. Sch., 1995; MPH, Harvard Sch. Pub. Health, 1999. Chief social policy advisor Clinton/Gore 1992 Campaign, Little Rock, 1992—92; deputy dir. health policy Clinton/Gore Presidential Transition Team, Washington, 1992—93; intern, resident Brigham and Women's Hosp., Boston, 1995—2003, assoc. surgeon, general and endocrine surgery, 2003—, asst. dir., Ctr. for Surgery and Pub. Health, 2004—; asst. prof. dept. surgery Harvard Med. Sch., Boston, 2003—; asst. prof. dept. health policy and mgmt. Harvard Sch. Pub. Health, Boston, 2004—. Author: COMPLICATIONS: A Surgeon's Notes on an Imperfect Science, 2002; writer Notes of a Surgeon column, New England Journal Medicine, staff writer The New Yorker mag., 1998— (AAAS Sci. Journalism award, mag. reporting, 2005); contbr. articles to peer-reviewed jours. MacArthur Fellow, John D. and Catherine T. MacArthur Found., 2006. Office: Brigham and Womens Hosp 75 Francis St Boston MA 02115 also: Harvard Sch Pub Health Dept Health Policy and Mgmt Kresge Bldg Rm 400 677 Huntington Ave Boston MA 02115 Business E-Mail: agawande@hsph.harvard.edu.

GAY, CARL LLOYD, lawyer; b. Seattle, Nov. 11, 1950; s. James and Elizabeth Anne (Rogers) G.; m. Robin Ann Winston, Aug. 23, 1975; children: Patrick, Joel, Alexander, Samuel, Nora. Student, U. of Puget Sound, 1969-70; BS in Forestry cum laude, Wash. State U., 1974; JD, Willamette U., 1979. Bar: Wash. 1979, U.S. Dist. Ct. (we. dist.) Wash. 1979. With Taylor & Taylor, 1979-82, Taylor, Taylor & Gay, 1982-85; prin. Greenaway & Gay, Port Angeles, Wash., 1985-91, Greenaway, Gay & Tassie, Port Angeles, 1991-96, Greenaway, Gay & Angier, Port Angeles, 1996—2001, Greenaway, Gay & Tulloch, 2002—. Judge pro tem Clallam County, Port Angeles, 1981-85; commr. superior Ct., 1985-91; judge Juvenile Ct., 1985-87; instr. Guardian Ad Litem Program, Port Angeles, 1985—, Peoples Law Sch., 1989—. Bd. dirs. Cmty. Concert Assn., Port Angeles, 1982—85, 1994—, pres., 1984—85, 1988—89, 1999—2000; bd. dirs. Am. Heart Assn., 1987—95, Clallam County YMCA, 1987—2002, exec. com., 1995—2002; adv. com. Salvation Army, Port Angeles, 1982—; subdivsn. chmn., bd. dirs. United Way Clallam County, 1987—92; bd. dirs., pres. Friends of Libr., Port Angeles, 1983—91; trustee Fisher Cove, 1988—; advisor youth in govt. program YMCA, 1986—; chmn. long-range planning com. Port Angeles Sch. Dist.; bd. govs. Peninsula Coll. Found., 2000—; advisor United Meth. Youth Coun., 1987—95, trustee, 1989—; pres. Holy Trinity Luth. Ch., 2001—04; bd. dirs. Clallam County Pro Bono Lawyers, 1988—96. Named Clallam County Citizen of Yr., 1987; recipient Disting. Svc. award, Clallam County Pro Bono Lawyers, 1998, YMCA, 1992. Mem.: ATLA, ABA (real property, probate and trust and gen. practice sects.), Wash. State Trial Lawyers Assn., Superior Ct. Judges Assn. (com.), Nat. Coun. Juvenile and Family Ct. Judges, Clallam County Bar Assn. (pres. 1995), Wash. Bar Assn. (real property, probate, elder law and trust sects.), Kiwanis (local bd. dirs. 1982—84, pres. 1986—87, Kiwanian of Yr. 1983—84). Lutheran. Avocations: backpacking, cross country skiing, raquetball, sailing. Home: 3220 Mcdougal St Port Angeles WA 98362-6738 Office: Greenaway Gay & Tulloch 829 E 8th St Ste A Port Angeles WA 98362-6452 Office Phone: 360-452-3324. E-mail: clgay@tenforward.com.

GAY, DARRELL S., lawyer; b. Bklyn., July 20, 1955; BA, Fordham Univ., 1976; JD, Columbia Univ., 1979. Bar: NY 1982, Mass. 1980, US Dist. Ct. (so. and ea. dists. (NY) 1987, US Dist. Ct. (we. and no. dists. (NY) 1992, US Ct. Appeals (2d cir.) 2003. Atty. NLRB, 1979—84; dir. labor rels. Met. Hosp., 1984—85; mng. ptnr. DSGay Law Group PLLC, NYC; ptnr., head U.S. Labor & Employment Law practice Coudert Bros. LLP, NYC, 2003—. Commr. NY State Civil Svc. Commn., 1991—94; dir. Labor Rels. Met. Hosp. Editor (writing & rsch.): Human Rights Law Rev. Former chmn. Coalition of Black Profl. Orgns. Named one of Forty Under Forty People to Watch in the 90's, Crain's NY; Charles Evans Hughes fellow. Fellow: Am. Bar Found.; mem.: ABA, Nat. Bar Assn., Assn. Bar City of NY, Minority Corp. Counsel Assn. (found. mem.), Com. Minority Labor Attys. (found. mem.), Nat. Employment Law Coun. (found. mem., coord.). Office: Coudert Bros LLP 1114 Ave of the Americas New York NY 10036 Office Phone: 212-626-4549. Office Fax: 212-626-4120. Business E-Mail: dgay@coudert.com.

GAY, E(MIL) LAURENCE, lawyer; b. Bridgeport, Conn., Aug. 10, 1923; s. Emil Daniel and Helen Lillian (Mihalich) Gulyassy; m. Harriet A. Ripley, Aug. 2, 1952; children: Noel L., Peter C., Marguerite S., Georgette A. BS, Yale U., 1946; JD magna cum laude, Harvard U., 1949. Bar: N.Y. 1950, Conn. 1960, Calif. 1981, Hawaii 1988. Assoc. Root, Ballantine, Harlan, Bushby & Palmer, NYC, 1949—52; mem. legal staff U.S. High Commr. Germany, 1952—53; law sec. fo David W. Peck, presiding justice appellate divsn. 1st dept. N.Y. Supreme Ct., NYC, 1953—54; assoc. Debevoise, Plimpton & McLean, NYC, 1954—58; v.p., sec.-treas., gen. counsel Hewitt-Robins, Inc., Stamford, Conn., 1958—65; pres. Litton Gt. Lakes Corp., NYC, 1965—67; sr. v.p. fin. AMFAC, Inc., Honolulu, 1967—73, vice chmn., 1974—78; fin. cons. Burlingame, Calif., 1979-82; of counsel Pettit & Martin, San Francisco, 1982—88, Goodsill, Anderson, Quinn & Stifel, Honolulu, 1988—. Editor: Harvard Law Rev., 1948—49. Pres. Honolulu Symphony Soc., 1974—78; officer, dir. numerous arts and ednl. orgns.; bd. dirs. Loyola Marymount U., 1977—80, San Francisco Chamber Soloists, 1981—86, Honolulu Chamber Music Series, 1988—. 1st lt. US Army, 1943—46. Mem.: ABA, Hawaii State Bar Assn., Phi Beta Kappa. Republican. Roman Catholic. Avocations: music, literature. Home: 1159 Maunawili Rd Kailua HI 96734-4641 Office: Goodsill Anderson Quinn & Stifel 1099 Alakea St #1800 Honolulu HI 96814 Home Phone: 808-262-8491; Office Phone: 808-547-5641. Business E-Mail: egay@goodsill.com.

GAY, ESMOND PHELPS, lawyer; b. New Orleans, Sept. 15, 1952; s. Charles Fenner and Harriott (Phelps) G.; m. Marian Enochs, June 6, 1981; children: Jacqueline Elinor, Marian Phelps. AB, Princeton U., NJ, 1975; JD, Tulane U., 1979. Bar: La. 1979, US Dist. Ct. (ea. dist.) La. 1979, US Ct. Appeals (5th cir.) 1986. Assoc. Christovich & Kearney, New Orleans, 1979-84, ptnr., 1985—. Mem. ABA (ho. of dels. 2004-06, , State Bar Tex., Internat. Bar Assn., La. Bar Assn. (pres. 2000-01), New Orleans Bar Assn. (bd. dirs. 1997-99), Fed. Ins. and Corp. Counsel (chmn. maritime law com.), La. Assn. Def. Counsel (bd. dirs. 2003-05), Def. Rsch. Inst. Home: 237 Hector Ave Metairie LA 70005-4117 Office: Christovich & Kearney 601 Poydras St Ste 2300 New Orleans LA 70130-6078 E-mail: engay@christovich.com.

GAY, JOHN MARION, retired federal agency administrator, financial analyst; b. Sept. 23, 1936; s. John Henry and LolaBell (Collins) Gay; m. Rebecca Jane Gay; children: John Marion II, Dierdre, Michael, Michelle-(dec.) , Steven, Christina. BA, Tex. So. U., 1956; MSW, U. Richmond, 1968; BS, Fla. Meml. Coll., 1976; MBA, Nova U., 1977. Cert. tchr. Fla. Compensation analyst SE Banks, N.A., Miami, Fla., 1976—78; personnel job analyst Kaiser Transit Group, Miami, 1978—80; tribal adminstr. Miccosukee Indians, Everglades Nat. Park, Fla., 1980—81; tchr. Broward County Schs., Fort Lauderdale, Fla., 1981—83, Dade County Schs., Miami, 1983—84; from postal employee to postal inspector US Postal Svc., North Miami Beach, Fla., 1984—96; postal inspection svc. detail US Postal Svc. DHQ, North Miami Beach, 1996—2003; ret. Corp. coord. United Negro Coll. Fund, Dade County, Fla., 1977; bd. govs. Tuskegee Airmen Nat. Mus., chmn. fin. com., pres. Gen. Daniel "Chappie" James chpt. With USAF, 1956—59. Recipient Honor award, Alpha Kappa Mu, 1974, award, Fla. Meml. Coll. Alumni Assn., 1978; scholar Max Fleischmann, United Negro Coll. Fund, 1975. Fellow: NEA; mem.: Nat. Assn. Postal Suprs., Tuskegee Airmen, Inc. Democrat. Avocations: bowling, tennis, writing. Home: 373 NW Irma Ave Lake City FL 32055-335 Office Phone: 954-336-5236. Personal E-mail: jongay36@bellsouth.net.

GAY, LARRY KENNETH, artist, automotive executive, consultant; b. Tucson, Oct. 10, 1952; s. Alvin Arthur and Sylvia Mae Gay; m. Carol Lee Rowberry; children: Shaun Kenneth White, Allen Arthur, Todd Elton Gaytley. Student, Lexington Bapt. Coll., Ky., 1975—77, Western Bapt. Coll., Salem, 1982—84; M in Theology, Almeda U., Ind., 2006. Cert. Master Comml. Fin. Mgr., Ford Motor Credit Co., 2006; Master Sales Mgr. Ford Motor Co., 2006, Master Customer Rels. Mgr. Ford Motor Co., 2006. Newspaper pub. Bargain Express Newspaper, Libby, Mont., 1979—82; owner Western States Liquidators, Centralia, Wash., 1999—2004. Chief reserve dep. Lincoln County Mont. Sheriffs Dept, Libby, 1981—82. Represented in permanent collections C.R. Russell Mus., Gt. Falls, Mont. Adult Sunday sch. tchr. Victory Bapt. Ch., Chehalis, Wash., 1987—97. Recipient Best Show awards for artwork, Western Art Assn., 1992, 1993, 1994, 1997, 2000. Mem.: MENSA (assoc.). Conservative. Baptist. Avocations: travel, weightlifting, sculpting. Home: 1004 Spring Ln Centralia WA 98531 Office: Larry Gay Inc 1004 Spring Ln Centralia WA 98531 Home Phone: 360-736-4000; Office Phone: 360-736-4000. Office Fax: 360-736-4000.

GAY, PETER, historian, educator, writer; b. Berlin, June 20, 1923; came to U.S., 1941, naturalized, 1946; s. Morris Peter and Helga (Kohnke) G.; m. Ruth Slotkin, May 30, 1959 (dec., May 9, 2006); stepchildren: Sarah Khedouri, Sophie Glazer Cohen, Elizabeth Glazer. BA, U. Denver, 1946; MA, Columbia U., 1947, PhD, 1951; LHD (hon.), U. Denver, 1970, U. Md., 1979, Hebrew Union Coll., Cin., 1983, Clark U., 1985, Suffolk U., Boston, 1987, Tufts U., 1988; LHD (hon.), Tavistock Inst., 1999; LHD (hon.), U. Ill., 2003. Faculty Columbia U., NYC, 1947-69, prof. history, 1962-69, William R. Shepherd prof. history, 1967-69; prof. comparative European intellectual history Yale U., New Haven, 1969—, Durfee prof. history, 1970-84, Sterling prof., 1984-93, Sterling prof. emeritus, 1993—; dir. Ctr. for Scholars and Writers N.Y. Pub. Libr., 1997—. Author: The Dilemma of Democratic Socialism: Eduard Bernstein's Challenge to Marx, 1952, Voltaire's Politics: The Poet as Realist, 1959, The Party of Humanity: Essays in the French Enlightenment, 1964, A Loss of Mastery: Puritan Historians in Colonial America, 1966, The Enlightenment: An Interpretation, vol. I, The Rise of Modern Paganism, 1966, Weimar Culture: The Outsider as Insider, 1968, The Enlightenment, vol. II, The Science of Freedom, 1969, The Bridge of Criticism: Dialogues on the Enlightenment, 1970; author: (with R.K. Webb) Modern Europe, 1973; author: Style in History, 1974, Art and Act, 1976, Freud, Jews, and Other Germans, 1978, Education of the Senses, 1984, Freud for Historians, 1985, The Tender Passion, 1986, A Godless Jew: Freud, Atheism, and the Making of Psychoanalysis, 1987, Freud: A Life for Our Time, 1988, A Freud Reader, 1989, Reading Freud: Explorations and Entertainments, 1990, The Cultivation of Hatred, 1993, The Naked Heart, 1995, Pleasure Wars, 1998, My German Question: Growing Up in Nazi Berlin, 1998, Mozart, 1999, Schnitzler's Century: The Making of Middle-Class Culture, 1815-1914, 2001, Savage Reprisals, Bleak House, Madame Bovary, Buddenbrooks, 2002, Modernism, The Lure of Heresy; from Bandelaire to Beckett and Beyond, 2007. Fellow Am. Coun. Learned Soc., 1959-60, Ctr. Advanced Study Behavioral Scis., 1963-64; Guggenheim fellow, 1967-68, 77-78; Overseas fellow Churchill Coll., Cambridge, 1970-71; Rockefeller Found. fellow, 1979-80; Wissenschaftskolleg zu Berlin, 1984; recipient First Amsterdam prize in Hist. Sci., 1991. Mem. Am. Philos. Soc., Am. Inst. Arts and Letters (gold medal in history 1996), Ctr. for Scholars and Writers (dir. emeritus), N.Y. Pub. Libr., Phi Beta Kappa. Home: 270 Riverside Dr 8C New York NY 10025 E-mail: petergay@verizon.net.

GAY, ROBERT DERRIL, behavioral health consultant; b. Savannah, Ga., June 23, 1939; s. Roscoe Degomer and Mollie Ann (Jones) G. BA, Oglethorpe U., 1962; MA, Emory U., 1966, PhD, 1984. Dep. dir. Divsn. Mental Health and Mental Retardation Ga. Dept. Human Resources, Atlanta, 1975-77, asst. commr., 1977-78, dir. Divsn. Mental Health and Mental Retardation, 1978-81; dep. dir. DeKalb County Health Dept., Decatur, Ga., 1981-94; dir. DeKalb Community Mental Health, Mental Retardation and Substance Abuse Svc. Bd., Decatur, 1994—2004; ind. cons., 2004—. Vis. instr. Oglethorpe U., 1966, 67, 85-94, Emory U. Sch. Nursing, 1970; mem. Ga. Gov.'s Coun. on Devel. Disabilities, 1978-81, Ga. Gov.'s Coun. on Mental Health and Mental Retardation, 1978-81, DeKalb County Coun. on Devel. Disabilities, 1981-2004 Bd. dirs. St.

Joseph's Mercy Care Svcs., 1994-2000. Mem. Am. Sociol. Assn. So. Sociol. Soc., Ga. Sociol. Assn., Nat. Assn. State Mental Health Program Dirs. (bd. dirs. 1978-81, pres. 1990-91), Atlanta Mercy Mobile Health Program (bd. dirs. 1987-94, chair 1991-94). Home and Office: 308 Oglethorpe Dr NE Atlanta GA 30319-2772

GAY, RUDY CARLTON, JR., professional basketball player; b. Balt., Aug. 17, 1986; s. Rudy Gay, Sr. and Rae Gay. Student in Liberal Arts, U. Conn., 2004—06. Draft pick Houston Rockets, 2006; forward Memphis Grizzlies, 2006—. Mem. USA Men's Under 21 World Championship Team, 2005. Named Nat. Freshman of Yr., Sporting News, 2005, Big East Rookie of Yr., 2005, First Team All-Am., Nat. Assn. Basketball Coaches, 2006; named to All-Big East First Team, 2006, All-Nat. Assn. Basketball Coaches First Team, 2006, All-US Basketball Writers Assn. All-Dist. First Team, 2006, NBA All-Rookie First Team, 2007. Mailing: Memphis Grizzlies 191 Beale St Memphis TN 38103*

GAY, SARAH ELIZABETH, lawyer; b. Cambridge, Mass., May 24, 1950; d. Frank Smith and Jane (Spencer) Fussner; m. Kirk D. Gay; 1 child, John Russell. BA, Harvard/Radcliffe U., 1972; JD, U. Oreg., 1975. Bar: Alaska 1976, U.S. Dist. Ct. Alaska 1976, U.S. Ct. Appeals (9th cir.) 1976, U.S. Supreme Ct. 1980. Assoc. Ely, Guess & Rudd, Anchorage, 1975—77; asst. atty. gen. natural resources sect. State of Alaska, Anchorage, 1977—88, asst. atty. gen. oil spill sect., 1989—91, supr. natural resources sect., 1991—93; corp. counsel Alaska Safari, Inc., Alaska's Valhalla Lodge, Inc., Anchorage, 1993—; pvt. practice Anchorage, 1993—. Workshop leader U. Oreg. Law Sch., Eugene, 1989; chmn. Anchorage Mcpl. Airports Adv. Com., 1990-93; food safety adv. com. Dept. Environ. Conservation, State Alaska, 2000—; mem. com. Alaska Bar Examiners, 1984-2005 Mng. bd. editor U. Oreg. Law Rev., Eugene, 1975. Citizens' adv. bd. Land Conservation & Devel. Bd., Salem, Oreg., 1975. Mem.: Phi Delta Phi. Avocations: flying, sport fish lodge operator. Address: Gen Delivery Valhalla Lodge Nondalton AK 99640 Office Phone: 907-248-4235. Business E-Mail: sarah@valhallalodge.com.

GAY, WILLIAM ARTHUR, JR., thoracic surgeon; b. Richmond, Va., Jan. 16, 1936; s. William Arthur and Marion Harriette (Taylor) G.; m. Frances Louise Adkins, Dec. 17, 1960; children— William Taylor, Mason Arthur. BA, Va. Mil. Inst., 1957; MD, Duke U. Med. Sch., 1961. Resident, general surgery Duke U. Med. Ctr., Durham, NC, 1961—63, 1965—69, resident, thoracic surgery, 1969—71; clin. assoc. Nat. Heart, Lung, and Blood Inst., 1963—65; asst. prof. surgery Cornell U. Med. Coll., NYC, 1971—74, assoc., prof., 1974—78; cardiothoracic surgeon-in-chief N.Y. Hosp., 1976—84; prof., chmn. dept. surgery U. Utah Sch. Medicine, 1984—92; v.p. for health scis. U. Utah, 1990—91; thoracic surgeon Washington U. Sch. Medicine, St. Louis. Prof. surgery Sch. Medicine Washington U., St. Louis; exec. dir. Am. Bd. Thoracic Surgery. Contbr. articles to profl. jours. With USPHS, 1963—65. Recipient Career Scientist award, Irma T. Hirschl Charitable Trust, 1972. Mem. ACS, Soc. Vascular Surgery, Soc. Thoracic Surgeons, Am. Assn. Thoracic for Surgery (treas. 1989-94), Am. Surg. Assn., Soc. Univ. Surgeons (treas. 1977-80), Western Thoracic Surgical Assn., Am. Bd. Thoracic Surgeons (chmn., 1995-97, sect.-treas., 2000, exec. dir.). Office: Washington U Sch Medicine 3180 Queeny Tower 1 Barnes Jewish Hospital Plz Saint Louis MO 63110-1013 also: Am Bd Thoracic Surgery 633 N St Clair St Ste 2320 Chicago IL 60611 Office Phone: 314-747-1315, 312-202-5900. Office Fax: 314-367-8459, 312-202-5960. E-mail: gayw@wustl.edu.

GAY, WILLIAM INGALLS, veterinarian, retired health science association administrator; b. Sussex, NJ, Jan. 25, 1926; s. William David and Dorothy Julia (Ingalls) G.; m. Millicent Ruth Chapman, June 10, 1948. DVM, Cornell U., 1950; grad., Fed. Exec. Inst., 1972. Diplomate Am. Coll. Lab. Animal Medicine. Pvt. practice vet. medicine, Richmond Hill, NY, 1950-52; chief animal hosp. sect. lab. aids br. divsn. research services NIH, Bethesda, Md., 1954-63, asst. chief lab. aids br. divsn. research services, 1962-63, asst. chief animal resources br. divsn. research facilities and resources, 1964-65; program dir. comparative medicine Nat. Inst. Gen. Med. Scis., NIH, 1966-67, program adminstr. radiology and physiology tng. programs, 1966, chief research grants br., 1967-70, acting assoc. dir., 1970; assoc. dir. extramural programs Nat. Inst. Allergy and Infectious Diseases, NIH, 1970-80, dir. animal resources program, divsn. research resources, 1981-88; cons. ROW Svcs., Rockville, Md., 1989-98; pvt. practice Bethesda, Md., 1999—; ret., 2002. Mem. com. on primates Inst. Lab. Animal Resources, NRC, 1961-63, chmn. subcom. on cat standards, 1963-64, mem. standards com., 1965-66; program chmn. Internat. Symposium on Lab. Animals, 1969 Author numerous papers on expt. surgery and lab. animal research.; editor: Methods of Animal Experimentation, 7 vols. Mem. sci. adv. bd. Mark L. Morris Found., 1966-71, trustee, 1971-84; mem. grants adv. council The Seeing Eye, 1971-74. Served as Lt. Vet. Corps, AUS, Walter Reed, 1952-54. With ISPHS, 1958—. Recipient Superior Service cert. HEW, 1975, NIH Dir's. award, 1983, Superior Service award USPHS, 1987, Spl;. Recognition award Am. Assn. Accreditation Lab. Animal Sci., 2003. Mem. AVMA (sec.-treas. D.C. chpt. 1957-58, v.p. 1962, pres. 1963), AAAS, Am. Assn. Lab. Animal Sci. (dir. 1961-69, program chmn. 1962-64, exec. bd. 1963, 66, nat. pres. 1968, chmn. awards com. 1969, Griffin award 1971, pres. Washington br. 1962, chair Gala 2000 com., Lifetime Achievement award 2003), Am. Assn. Lab. Animal Sci., NIH Alumni Assn. (bd. dirs. 1994, v.p. 1995-98, pres. 1999-2002), Phi Zeta, Cosmos Club.

GAYDA, MICHAEL D., lawyer; b. Phila., Sept. 23, 1954; BS econ., U. Pa., 1976; JD, Boston U. Sch. Law, 1979. Bar: Calif. 1979, Pa. 1981. Sr. v.p., gen. counsel, sec. Premcor Inc., Old Greenwich, Conn. Mem.: State Bar Calif., Fed. Energy Bar Assn., ABA. Office: Premcor Inc 1700 E Putnam Ave Ste 400 Old Greenwich CT 06870 Office Phone: 203-698-7500. Office Fax: 203-698-7925.

GAYDOS, JOEL CARL, physician; b. Edenborn, Pa., 1942; s. Joseph and Ann G.; m. Charlotte Ann Klaus, 1965; children: Kathryn, Joseph, Steven, Jennifer. AB, W.Va. U., 1964, MD, 1968; MPH in Epidemiology, U. Pitts., 1972. Diplomate Nat. Bd. Med. Examiners, Am. Bd. Preventive Medicine. Intern Walter Reed Gen. Hosp., Washington, 1968-69, resident in gen. preventive medicine, 1972-74; commd. 2d lt. U.S. Army, 1964, advanced through grades to col.; mil. physician Med. Corps, 1968-97; dir. occupl. and environ. health U.S. Army Environ. Hygiene Agy., Aberdeen Proving Ground, Md., 1983-85; occupl. health cons., chief preventive medicine cons. divsn. Dept. of the Army Office of the Surgeon Gen., Falls Church, Va., 1985-89; assoc. prof., assoc. dean acting Uniformed Svcs. U. of the Health Scis., Bethesda, Md., 1989-93; dir. clin. preventive medicine U.S. Army Ctr. for Health Promotion and Preventive Medicine, Aberdeen Proving Ground, Md., 1994-97; dir. pub. health practices Dept. of Def. Global Emerging Infections Surveillance & Response Sys., 1997—; sr. scientist Henry M. Jackson Found., Rockville, Md., 1997—. Adj. prof. Uniformed Svcs. U. Health Scis., 1999—, adj. prof., professorial lectr. George Washington U., Washington, 2000—. Contbr. chapters to books, articles to profl. jours. Decorated Def. Superior Svc. medal, Legion of Merit. Fellow: Am. Coll. Occupl. and Environ. Medicine, Am. Coll. Preventive Medicine, Infectious Diseases Soc. Am.; mem.: AMA, Assn. Mil. Surgeons US, Am. Soc. Tropical Medicine and Hygiene. Office: Walter Reed Arm Inst Rsch Divsn Preventive Medicine 503 Robert Grant Ave Silver Spring MD 20910-7500 Business E-Mail: joel.gaydos@na.amedd.army.mil.

GAYLE, HELENE D., pediatrician, public health service officer; b. Buffalo; BS in Psychology cum laude, Columbia U., 1976; MD, U. Pa., 1981; MPH, John Hopkins U., 1981. Diplomate Am. Bd. Pediats. Intern then resident in pediats. Children's Hosp. Nat. Med. Ctr., Washington, 1981-84; epidemic intelligence svc. officer br. epidemiology divsn. nutrition Ctr. Health Promotion and Edn., 1984-86; preventive medicine resident divsn. evaluation and rsch. office internat. health program Ctrs. Disease Control Ga. State Dept. Health, 1986-87; med. epidemiologist pediats. and family studies sect., AIDS program Ctrs. Disease Control, 1987-89, acting spl. asst. minority HIV policy coordination office dep. dir. (HIV), 1988-89, asst. chief sci., 1989-90, chief internat. activity divsn. HIV/AIDS Atlanta, 1990-92, assoc. dir. Washington, 1994-96; agy. AIDS coord., chief divsn. HIV-AIDS Agy. Intl. Devel., Washington, 1992-94; dir. Nat. Ctr. HIV, Sexually Transmitted Diseases and Tb Prevention Ctrs. Disease Control, Atlanta, 1995—2001; dir. HIV, Tb, reproductive health Bill and Melinda Gates Found., 2001—06; pres., CEO Cooperative for Assistance and Relief Everywhere, Inc. (Care USA), Atlanta, 2006—. Lectr. Sch. Medicine Morehouse U., 1987—92; lectr. masters in pub. health program Emory U., Atlanta, 1989, 90, clin. asst. prof. cmty. medicine, 1996—; cons. WHO, others; bd. dir. Africa Am. inst. Global Health Coun., Internat. Ctr. Rsch. in Women, Inst. Medicine, Coun. Fgn. Rels.; adj. assoc. prof. Sch. Pub. Health U. Wash. Contbr. articles to profl. jours. Adm. USPHS. Merit scholar, 1981; recipient Henrietta and Jacob Lowenburg prize, 1981, Model Excellence award Colgate-Palmolive Co., 1992, Medal of Excellence Columbia U., 1996, Sec. Award Disting. Svc. US Dept. Health and Human Svcs., 1999, Disting. Svc. Award Nat. Med. Fellowships, 2003, Disting. Alumnus Award, John Hopkins U. Sch. Pub. Health; named Barnard Woman of Achievement Barnard Coll., 2001; named one of 50 Women to Watch, Wall St. Jour., 2006. Mem. AAS, AMA, APHA, Am. Coll. Epidemiology, Internat. AIDS Soc. (pres.), Soc. Against AIDS in Africa, Inst. Med. (coun. mem.). Office: CARE USA 151 Ellis St NE Atlanta GA 30303*

GAYLES, JOSEPH NATHAN, JR., fundraiser, chemist; b. Ala. s. Joseph Gayles; children: Jonathan, Monica Gayles Dorsey. AB summa cum laude, Dillard U., 1958, LL.D. (hon.), 1983; PhD, Brown U., 1963; postgrad., Oreg. State U., 1962-63, U. Uppsala, Sweden, 1965; D.Sc (hon.), Morehouse Sch. Medicine, 2000. Asst. prof. chemistry Oreg. State U., 1962-63; Woodrow Wilson teaching asso., asst. prof. chemistry Morehouse Coll., 1963-66, assoc. prof. chemistry, 1969-71, founding dir. med. edn. project, 1971-75, founding dir. Sch. Medicine, 1975-77, prof. Sch. Medicine, 1971-77; pres. Talladega (Ala.) Coll., 1977-83, emeritus pres., 1983; v.p., rsch. prof. medicine Morehouse Sch. Medicine, Atlanta, 1983-97; chmn., CEO Gayles and Assocs., Inc., Fund Raising Cons., 1983—; cons. v.p. Clark Atlanta U., 1996-98; v.p. advancement Sojourner Douglass Coll., 2002—05. Staff scientist, project dir. IBM Research Lab., San Jose, Calif., 1966-69 Contbr. articles to profl. jours. Bd. dirs. Woodrow Wilson Nat. Fellowship Found., 1978-98, Rotary Internat., 1991—; bd. overseers Sch. Medicine, Morehouse Coll., 1977-81; bd. dirs. Coun. for Internat. Exchange Scholars, 1979-83; mem. Gov. Wallace Commn. on Future of Ala. in Yr. 2000, 1982-83; trustee Morehouse Coll., 1976-77, Talladega Coll., 1977-83, Morehouse Sch. Medicine, 1981-83; mem. nat. adv. coun. divsn. rsch. resources NIH, 1980-85; bd. visitors MIT, 1981-88. Woodrow Wilson fellow, 1958-59; Dreyfus Found. Tchr.-scholar, 1972; recipient Tchr. of Yr. award Morehouse Coll., 1976; Alumnus of Yr. award Dillard U., 1977; Presdl. Leadership award Morehouse Sch. Medicine, 1986 Mem. Am. Phys. Soc., Am. Chem. Soc., Nat. Assn. Equal Opportunity in Higher Edn. (bd. dirs. 1979-82), Sigma Xi, Phi Beta Kappa, Alpha Phi Alpha.

GAYLIN, NED L., psychologist, educator; b. Cleve., May 2, 1935; s. Harry C. and Fay I. G.; m. Rita Atran, June 30, 1957; children: Hilarie C., Ann E., Jed J., Daniel S. BA, U. Chgo., 1956, MA, 1961, PhD, 1965. Counselor Bellefaire Children's Home, Cleve., 1953, Sonja Shankman Orthogenic Sch., Chgo., 1954-56; group worker, supr. Jewish Community Ctrs. Chgo., 1957-60; grad. rsch. asst. Com. Human Devel., U. Chgo., 1959-60; intern Inst. Juvenile Rsch., Chgo., 1960-61, staff psychologist, 1965-68; intern Counseling and Psychotherapy Rsch. Ctr., U. Chgo., 1961-63; grad. teaching asst. dept. psychology U. Chgo., 1961-63; psychol. cons. State Ill., Rockford, 1961-64; psychotherapist, cons. Counseling and Psychotherapy Rsch. Ctr., U. Chgo., 1963-65, psychol. cons., lectr., 1965; lectr. dept. social sci. S.E. Jr. Coll., Chgo., 1965-66; psychol. cons. Peace Corps, No. Ill. U., DeKalb, 1966-68; chief psychologist S.W. Suburban Mental Health Assn., LaGrange, Ill., 1966-68; psychol. cons. Virginia Frank Child Devel. Ctr., Chgo., 1966-68; child clin. rsch. psychologist NIMH, Bethesda, Md., 1968-70; lectr., cons. Washington Sch. Psychiatry, 1968-72; chmn. dept. family and community devel. Coll. Human Ecology U. Md., College Park, 1970-77, prof., dir. family therapy tng. Coll. Health and Human Performance, 1977—2003, prof. emeritus, 2003—. Mem. rsch. com. Md. Community Coordinated Child Care, 1970-75. Author: Family, Self, and Psychotherapy, 2001; contbr. articles in field to profl. jours. USPHS grantee, 1961-63; U. Chgo. fellow and scholar, 1954-56, 58-60; State Ill. edn. and tng. grantee, 1963-65 Mem. APA, Nat. Coun. on Family Rels., Am. Assn. Marriage and Family Therapy, Groves Conf. on the Family, Assn. for Devel. of Person-Centered Approach, Sigma Xi. Home: 4617 Norwood Dr Chevy Chase MD 20815-5348 Office: Univ Md 1210 Marie Mount Hall College Park MD 20742-7515 Home Phone: 301-656-4351; Office Phone: 301-405-4006. Business E-Mail: gaylin@umd.edu.

GAYLIN, WILLARD, physician, educator; b. Cleve., Feb. 23, 1925; s. Harry C. and Fay (Baumgard) Gaylin; m. Betty Schofer, June 15, 1947; children: Ellen Andrea, Jody. AB, Harvard U., 1947; MD, Western Res. U., 1951. Lic. psychiatrist N.Y. Intern Cleve. City Hosp., 1951—52; resident psychiatry Bronx VA Hosp., 1952—54; faculty Columbia Psychoanalytic Sch., 1956—, clin. prof. psychiatry, 1972—; adj. prof. psychiatry Union Theol. Sem.; adj. prof. psychiatry and law Columbia Sch. Law, 1970; founder The Hastings Ctr., Briarcliff Manor, NY, 1970—, chmn. bd., 1970—96. Author: The Meaning of Despair, 1968, In The Service of Their Country: War Resisters in Prison, 1970, Partial Justice: A Study of Bias in Sentencing, 1974, Caring, 1976; author: (with others) Doing Good: The Limits of Benevolence, 1978; author: Feelings: Our Vital Signs, 1979, The Killing of Bonnie Garland: A Question of Justice, 1982, The Rage Within: Anger in Modern Life, 1984, Rediscovering Love, 1986, Adam and Eve and Pinocchio, 1990, The Male Ego, 1992, The Perversion of Autonomy, 1996, Talk Is Not Enough: How Psychotherapy Really Works, 2000, Hatred: The Psychological Descent into Violence, 2003; contbr. articles to profl. jours. Bd. dirs. Helsinki Watch., Nat. Bd. Planned Parenthood. With USNR, 1943—45. Recipient George E. Daniels medal of Merit for contbns. to psychoanalytic medicine, 1973, Elizabeth Cutter Morrow lectureship, Smith Coll., 1970; fellow Chubb, Yale U., 1972. Fellow: Am. Psychiat. Assn.; mem.: N.Y. Psychiat. Soc., Am. Psychoanalytic Assn., Inst. Medicine NAS. Office Phone: 914-478-2712. Personal E-mail: willgaylin@gmail.com.

GAYLOR, DONALD HUGHES, surgeon, educator; b. Bklyn., Apr. 17, 1926; s. Norman Hunter and Frances (Hughes) G.; m. Joan Winifred Power, Apr. 3, 1948; children: David, Christopher, Steven, Susan, Timothy. AB, U. Rochester, 1946, MD, 1949. Diplomate Am. Bd. Surgery, Am. Bd. Thoracic Surgery. Commd. lt. (j.g.) USN, 1949, advanced through grades to capt. M.C., 1966; intern U.S. Naval Hosp., Phila., 1949-50; student flight surgeon Sch. Aviation Medicine, Pensacola, Fla., 1950-51; flight surgeon U.S. Naval Sta., Trinidad, B.W.I., 1951-53; resident gen. surgery U.S. Naval Hosp., St. Albans, NY, 1953-57; postgrad. fellow surgery Royal Victoria Hosp., McGill U., Montreal, Canada, 1957; resident thoracic surgery U.S. Naval Hosp., St. Albans, NY, 1957-59; resident cardiovascular surgery St. Francis Hosp., Roslyn, NY, 1958; staff thoracic surgeon U.S. Naval Hosp., Portsmouth, Va., 1959-64; surgeon U.S.S. Enterprise, 1964; staff thoracic surgeon U.S. Naval Hosp., Nat. Naval Med. Ctr., Bethesda, Md., 1964-65, chief thoracic and cardiovascular surgery, 1965-68; chief surgery, exec. officer U.S.S. Repose, 1968-69; exec. officer Naval Med. Sch., Bethesda, Md., 1969-72; ret., 1972; clin. assoc. surgery U. Pa. Sch. Medicine, 1976-90; prof. clin. surgery Hahnemann U. Sch. Medicine, 1986-96. Chief surgery Allentown (Pa.) Hosp., 1972-90, Sacred Heart Hosp., 1973-76, Lehigh Valley Hosp. Ctr., 1974-90. Contbr. articles to profl. jours. Fellow ACS; mem. AMA, Am. Thoracic Soc., Am. Trauma Soc. (pres. Pa. divsn. 1979-83, treas. 1985-91), Soc. Thoracic Surgeons (founding), Pa. Assn. for Thoracic Surgery, Assn. Mil. Surgeons U.S., Am. Trauma Soc. (founding mem.). Roman Catholic. Home and Office: 3761 Devonshire Rd Allentown PA 18103-9628 Personal E-mail: capdonjo@earthlink.net.

GAYNES, THOMAS EDWARD, JR., retired judge, lawyer, educator, mediator; b. NYC, Mar. 19, 1940; s. Thomas Edward and Ann Jane (Burke) B.; m. Maija Eva Kokko, Dec. 30, 1963; children: Cynthia Lynn, Barbara Ann. BBA, U. Ga., 1962; JD, Emory U., 1967, LLM, 1972, Yale U., 1973. Bar: Ga. 1968, U.S. Supreme Ct. 1971, Ct. of Mil. Appeals 1978, Fla. 1981. Dir. Legal Assistance to Inmates Program, Emory U., 1968-69; asst. dean, asst. prof. bus. law Ga. State U., 1969-72; acting regional dir. Nat. Ctr. for State Cts., Atlanta, 1973-74; prof. law and public adminstrn. Nova U. Law Ctr., Ft. Lauderdale, Fla., 1974-76, 77-81; jud. fellow U.S. Supreme Ct., 1976-77; speedy trial reporter U.S. Dist. Ct., So. Dist. Fla., 1977-81; ptnr. Peterson, Myers, Craig, Crews, Brandon & Mann, Lake Wales, Fla., 1981-87; U.S. bankruptcy judge for mid. dist. Fla. U.S. Bankruptcy Ct., Tampa, 1987—2005, chief bankruptcy judge, 2000—03; ret., 2005. State chmn., Ga., Nat. Council on Crime and Delinquency, 1971-72; legal counsel Reorgn. Study Commn. Ga., 1971-72 Author: (with W. Scott) Legal Aspects of Laboratory Medicine in Quality Assurance in Laboratory Management, 1978, Eminent Domain in Florida, 1979, Florida Mortgage Law, 1999, (with others) Supreme Court Justices, Illustrated Biographies, 1993; supplement editor Fla. Real Estate Law and Procedure, 1976; contbg. editor Norton Bankruptcy Law and Practice, 1995. Bd. dirs. F. Lee Moffitt Cancer Rsch Hosp., Tampa, 1989-94, 97—. Comdr. JAGC, USNR, 1960-80, ret. Sterling fellow Yale U. Law Sch., 1972-73; Harry J. Loman Found. rsch. fellow, 1979. Mem. Ga. Bar Assn., Fla. Bar Assn. (cert. cir. ct. and fed. ct. mediator and arbitrator), Am. Law Inst., Hillsborough Assn. Women Lawyers (bd. dirs. 2001-04), Fla. Acad. Profl. Mediators Inc., Supreme Ct. Hist. Soc., Am. Arbitration Assn., Nat. Adv. Com. for Bankruptcy, Ferguson-White Inn (pres. 1992-93, master), Omicron Delta Kappa. Office Phone: 863-221-2232. Personal E-mail: tebaynes@aol.com.

GAYNOR, JOSEPH, chemical engineer, management consultant; b. NYC, Nov. 15, 1925; s. Morris and Rebecca (Schnapper) G.; m. Elaine Bauer, Aug. 19, 1951; children: Barbara Lynne, Martin Scott, Paul David, Andrew Douglas. B in Chem. Engring., Poly. Inst., 1950; MS, Case Western Res. U., 1952, PhD, 1955. Rsch. asst. Case Inst., Cleve., 1952-55; with Gen. Engring. Labs. GE, Schenectady, NY, 1955-66, mgr. R & D sect., 1962-66; group v.p. rsch. Bell & Howell Co., 1966-72; mgr. comml. devel. group, mem. pres.' office Horizons Rsch., Inc., Cleve., 1972-73; pres. Innovative Tech. Assocs., Ventura, Calif., 1973—; mem. nat. materials adv. bd. com. NAS; chmn. conf. com. 2d internat. conf. on bus. graphics, 1979; program chmn. 1st internat. congress on advances in non-impact printing techs., 1981; mem. adv. com. 2d internat. congress on advances in non-impact printing techs., 1984; chmn. publs. com. 3rd internat. congress on advances in non-impact printing techs., 1986; chmn. internat. conf. on hard copy media, materials and processes, 1990. Editor: Electronic Imaging, 1991, Procs. Advances in Non-Impact Printing Technologies, Vol. I, 1983, Vol. II, 1988, 3 spl. issues Jour. Imaging Tech., Proc. Hard Copy Materials Media and Processes Internat. Conf., 1990; delivered invited keynote address NIP-17 Digital Printing Techs. Internat. Conf., 2001; patentee in field. Served with U.S. Army, 1944-46. Fellow AAAS, AIChE, Imaging Sci. and Tech. Soc. (sr., gen. chmn. 2nd internat. conf. on electrophotography 1973, chmn. bus. graphics tech. sect. 1976—, chmn. edn. com. L.A. chpt. 1978—), Am. Soc. Photobiology, Sigma Xi, Tau Beta Pi, Phi Lambda Upsilon, Alpha Chi Sigma. Home: 108 La Brea St Oxnard CA 93035-3928 Office: Innovative Tech Assocs 3639 Harbor Blvd Ste 203E Ventura CA 93001-4255 Office Phone: 805-650-9353. Personal E-mail: joseph.gaynor@adelphia.net.

GAYNOR, KEVIN ALLEN, lawyer; b. Cambridge, Mass., Oct. 5, 1948; s. William Joseph and Ruth Claire (Krepelka) G.; m. Cathy Thayer Cook, Oct. 20, 1973. BA, U. Conn., 1970; JD, U. Va., 1973. Bar: Conn. 1973, D.C. 1978, Conn. 1974, Md. 1978, U.S. Dist. Ct. D.C. 1978, U.S. Ct. Appeals (1st cir.) 1985, U.S. Ct. Appeals (D.C. cir.) 1978. Assoc. Thompson, Weir and Barclay, New Haven, 1973-74; atty. U.S. EPA, Washington, 1975-76; assoc. Nixon, Hargraves, Devans & Doyle, Washington, 1977-82; atty., asst. sect. chief U.S. Dept. Justice, Washington, 1983-87; ptnr. Venable, Baetjer, Howard & Civiletti, Washington, 1988-1993, Vinson & Elkins, Washington, 1993—. Adv. bd. Environ. Counselor, Chesterland, Ohio, 1989—. Co-author: Regulation of Chemical, 1982; contbr. articles to profl. jours. Sec. Rockburn Land Trust, Elkridge, Md., 1989—. Mem. ABA (vice chmn. natural resources com. 1989—), D.C. Bar Assn., Environ. Law Inst., Md. Bar Assn., Nat. Hist. Trust, Md. Conservation Found. Avocations: hiking, running, bicycling. Office: Viscon & Elkins LLP Willard Office Bldg 1455 Pennsylvania Ave NW, Ste 600 Washington DC 20004

GAYNOR, SUZANNE MARIE, healthcare executive, researcher; b. Jan. 10, 1941; d. Howard Aloyousis and Irene Marie (Dunn) Gaynor; m. John Michael Hayes, May 26, 1962 (div. 1982); children: Marguerite Hayes, Jennifer Hayes, Christopher Hayes. Diploma in nursing, Fitzgerald-Mercy Sch. Nursing, 1961; BS, Marymount U. Va., 1977, MBA, 1981; DrPH, U. Mich., 1991. RN Pa., Va. Svc. coord. Upjohn Health Care, Washington, 1972—74, tng. coord., 1974—75; health intern U.S. Senate, Washington, 1977; health analyst Am. Blood Commn., Arlington, Va., 1977—79, dir. regionalization program, 1979—83, cons., 1983; dir. regional svcs. Greater NY Blood Program, NYC, 1983—89; mem. faculty Mt. Sinai Sch. Medicine, 1989—2003; mem. interacy. tech. com. Working Group on Blood Resources and Blood Substitutes Dept. HHS, 1981—83; mem. subcom. on blood supply and blood svcs. Com. on Pub. Health N.Y. Acad. Medicine, 1984—; mem. Blood Bank Task Force Region II, Regional Comprehensive Hemophilia Treatment Ctrs.; sr. environ. health policy analyst, Office of Healthy Homes and Lead Hazard Control U.S. Dept. HUD, Washington, 2004—. Co-founder, chmn. East Harlem Asthma Working Group, Inc., NYC, 1996—; mem. East Harlem Asthma Working Group, Inc. Housing Subcom., NYC, 1998—; co-founder, chmn. CUES Asthma Working Group, NYC, 2000—; mem. Manhattan Consortium for Children with Spl. Health Car Needs, NYC, 2000—; mem. asthma working group Ctr. for Urban Epidemiol. Studies NY Acad. Medicine, 1996—; mem. com. on environ. N.Y.C. Asthma Partnership, 2001—, mem. steering com., 2000—02, chmn. com. on the environ., 2001—02; mem. pediat/child health subcom. East Harlem Cmty. Health Com., 1995—2002. Contbr. articles to profl.jours. Discussion leader Jr. Great Books, Arlington, 1974—75; bd. dirs. LWV, 1973—76, mem. bd. dirs., study com., membership com., 1971—76. Recipient Plaque for Recognition of Svc., Am. Blood Commn., 1983—83, Healthy Housing award, Indoor Environ. Health and Tech. Conf., 2003; grantee, NHLBI,SBIR, 2003—; PEW fellow, U. Mich. Grad. Sch. Pub. Health, 1986—91, Health Homes Demonstration grant, HUD, 2003—, Healthy Homes, Healthy Families grant, EPA, 2002—. Mem.: Assn. Tchrs. Preventive Medicine, APHA, NOW, NAFE, Assn. for Health Svcs. Rsch., Coun. Cmty. Blood Ctrs. (membership com.), Am. Assn. Blood Banks (dist. adv. group), Internat. AIDS Soc., Am. Soc. Law and Medicine, Delta Sigma Epsilon. Roman Catholic. Avocations: reading, travel, music, theater. Office: HUD Office Health Homes & Lead Hazard Control 451 7th St 520 Rm P-3206 Washington DC 20410

GAYTON, JOHNNY LEE, ophthalmologist, educator, recreational facility executive; b. Canton, Ga., Nov. 23, 1955; s. Elmer Eugene and Hazel Brand Gayton; children: John Christopher, Amanda Faye, Amy Renee' Hester, Mary Louise, David Allan, Stephen Lee, Elisabeth Faye, Lydia Brooke, James Lee. MD, Med. Coll. Ga., Augusta, 1979, post grad. Ophthalomology, 1979—83. Cert. Am. Bd. Ophthalmology, 1985. CEO Eyesight Assoc., Warner Robins, Ga., 1983—, DJ's GalaxyQuest, 2004—. Mentor and spkr. Alcon Corp., Fort Worth, 1993—; adj. prof. ophthalmology Mercer Med. Sch., Macon, Ga., 2006—; lectr. in field. Author: Maximizing Results, Crystal Clear Guide to Sight, Refractive Surgery for Technicians; contbr. chapters to books, articles to profl. jours. Fin. support Mus. Aviation, Warner Robins, Ga., HODAC, Inc.; chmn. WCOP Christian Radio, 1984—93. Named Spkr. of Day, Royal Hawaiian Eye Meeting, Wrestling Champion, Med. Coll. GA, 1979; recipient 3rd pl. Powerlifting (Augusta, Ga.), Powerlifting Soc., 1980, Ga. Bench Press title, Powerlifting Assn., 2006, 3d pl. Powerlifting (age 40 and up), 2006. Fellow: Soc. Excellence in Eye Care (life; bd. dir. 2000—02), Am. Coll. Eye Surgeons (life), Am. Assn. Opthalmologists (life); mem.: Internat. Refractive Surgery Club (life), Am. Soc. Cataract and Refractive Surgery (life Best Presentation 1994, 2006). Achievements include development of piggyback lens technique; first to recommend routine temporal approach cataract surgery; research in Restor lens in macular degeneration; use of endolaser for glaucoma treatment; youngest practicing ophthlamolgist at age 27. Avocations: weightlifting, travel, music, poker. Home: 111 Willow Creek Bonaire GA 31005 Office: Eyesight Assoc 216 Corder Rd Warner Robins GA 31088 Home Phone: 478-922-6897; Office Phone: 478-923-5872.

GAYVORONSKY, LUDMILA, artist, educator; b. Kharkov, Ukraine, Dec. 4, 1939; arrived in U.S., 1980; d. Pavel Nikanorovich Nikitin and m. Eva Lazarevna Skibityanskaya; m. Alexander Vitalievich Eremenko, June 9, 1996; 1 child, Gleb. Diploma in Meteorology, Hydrometeorol. Inst., Odessa, Ukraine, 1961; PhD in Geography, World Meteorol. Ctr., Moscow, 1965; BFA, Acad. Fine Art Moscow, Moscow, 1968. Engr.-climatologist Climatol. Obs., Samara, Russia, 1961—62; engr.-agrometeorologist World Meteorol. Ctr., Moscow, 1965—66; editor Inst. Tech. Info., Moscow, 1966—69, chief editor, 1969—79; instr. fine art Sts. Cosmas & Damian Human Svcs. Ctr., SI, NY, 1983—93; prof. fine art Lebanon Coll., NH, 1997—; with Libr. Art Ctr., Newport, NH, 1993—. Artist stage art constrn. for Childrens Week, Lincoln Ctr., N.Y.C., 1990, wall mural for Sinergia, Inc., N.Y.C., 1992-93, wall mural Town of Newport, N.H., 1998, backdrop panel Dicken's Fair, 1997. Named Acad. knight Acad. Verbano, Italy, 1999; recipient Gold medal Festival of Art, Moscow, 1968, Jurors prize distinction Spring art competition, Moscow, 1968, medal of honor, Ukrainian Inst. Am., NYC, 1988, cert. of appreciation USCG, Govs. Island, NY, 1989, Jurors prize distinction Sunapee art fair, NH, 1999. Mem. World Phenomenological Inst. (artist-in-residence 1997—), N.H. Art Assn., Keene Art Assn., Acad. Fine Arts. Mem. Orthodox Ch. Of Am. Home: 26 Church St Newport NH 03773-1908 Personal E-mail: ludmila.gayvoronsky@verizon.net.

GAZZANIGA, MICHAEL S., neuroscientist, psychologist; married; 6 children. AB, Dartmouth Coll., 1961; PhD, Calif. Inst. Tech., 1964; MA (hon.), Dartmouth Coll., 2000. Post-grad. fellow Calif. Inst. Tech., 1964—66, Inst. Physiology, Pisa, Italy, 1966; asst. prof. dept. psychology, U. Calif. Santa Barbara, 1967—68, assoc. prof., chmn., 1968—69; assoc. prof. NYU Grad. Sch., 1969—72, prof., 1973—78, SUNY Stony Brook, 1973—78, Cornell U. Med. Coll., 1977—88, dir. cognitive neuroscience div., neurology dept., 1977—88; pres. Cognitive Neuroscience Inst., 1982—; Andrew W. Thomson Jr. prof. psychiatry Dartmouth Med. Sch., 1988—92, dir. program in cognitive neuroscience, 1988—92; prof. U. Calif. at Davis, 1992—96, dir. Ctr. for Neuroscience, 1992—96; David T. McLaughlin Disting. Prof. Dartmouth Coll., 1996—, dir. Ctr. for Cognitive Neuroscience, 1996—, dean of faculty, 2002—. Adv. bd. Cortex Pharmaceuticals, 1988—, Children's Television Workshop, 3-2-1 Contact Extra, NYC; Mind/Body planning com. MacArthur Found.; dir. McDonnell Summer Inst. in Cognitive Neuroscience, 1989—; cons. WGBH History of Sci. program, 1996—; founding fellow Genisis, San Francisco, 1999—. Editor-in-chief emeritus: Jour. Cognitive Neuroscience; editor: Monographs in Cognitive Neuroscience; assoc. editor: Cerebral Cortex, 1990—; author: numerous books on neuroscience & psychology; contbr. scientific papers, articles to scientific journals. Adv. NAS com. on Brain & cognition, 1988, WHO, Beijing; Office of Tech. Assessment adv. bd. US Congress, 1991; founder, bd. govs. Cognitive Neuroscience Soc., 1993—; mem. President's Bioethics Coun., Washington. Recipient John Simon Guggenheim Meml. Fellowship, 1982—83, Javits Neuroscience Investigator award, 1985—92, C.U. Ariens Kappers Medal for Neuroscience, Royal Netherlands Acad. Arts & Sciences. Fellow: Am. Acad. Neurology, AAAS, Am. Physiological Soc., APA; mem.: Am. Acad. Arts & Sciences, Inst. Medicine, Am. Neurol. Assoc., Internat. Neuropsychology Group, Psychonomics Soc., Soc. for Neuroscience (elected counselor 1992—96), Soc. Exptl. Psychologists, Sigma Xi. Office: Ctr for Cognitive Neuroscience 6162 Moore Hall Dartmouth College Hanover NH 03755 Office Phone: 603-646-1182. E-mail: michael.s.gazzaniga@dartmouth.edu.

GAZZARA, BEN, actor; b. NYC, Aug. 28, 1930; s. Antonio and Angelina (Cusumano) G.; m. Louise Erickson, 1952 (div. 1956); m. Janice Rule, 1 child, Elizabeth; m. Elke Stuckmann; 1 adopted child, Danja. Student, CCNY, 1947-48, Erwin Piscator Dramatic Workshop of New Sch. for Social Research, 1948-49; mem., Actors Studio, from 1951. Actor: stage appearances include Jezebel's Husband, 1952, End As a Man, 1953, Cat on a Hot Tin Roof, 1955, Hatful of Rain, 1955, The Night Circus, 1959, Epitaph for George Dillon, 1959, Two for the Seesaw, 1960, Strange Interlude, 1963, Traveller Without Luggage, 1964, Hughie/Duet, 1974, Who's Afraid of Virginia Woolfe, 1975, Shimada, 1992, Chinese Coffee, 1994; motion pictures include The Strange One, 1957, Anatomy of Murder, 1959, Joy of Laughter, 1960, The Passionate Thief, 1960, The Young Doctors, 1961, Convicts Four, 1961, A Rage to Live, 1964, Husbands, 1969, Al Capone, 1974, High Velocity, 1976, Killing of a Chinese Bookie, 1976, Voyage of the Damned, 1976, Opening Night, 1977, Bloodline, 1978, Saint Jack, 1978, Inchon, 1979, They All Laughed, 1980, Tales of Ordinary Madness, 1981, The Girl from Trieste, 1985, The Cammorista, 1985, A Lovely Scandal, 1986, Quicker than the Eye, 1987, Roadhouse, 1989, Beyond the Ocean, 1990, And Quiet Flows the Don, 1992, Nefertiti, 1992, People across the Way, 1993, Els de Devart, 1993, Swallows Never Die in Jerusalem, 1994, Farmer and Chase, 1994, Shadow Conspiracy, 1995, Stag, 1996, The Spanish Prisoner, 1996, Buffalo 66, 1997, The Big Lebowski, 1997, Too Tired to Die, 1997, Illuminata, 1997, Happiness, 1998, Buffalo 66, 1998, Undertaker's Paradise, 1999, Blue Moon, 1999, No Man's Land, 1999, Very Mean Men, 1999, The List, 2000, Home Sweet Hoboken, 2000, Dogville, 2003, Awake and Sing!, 2006; TV series Arrest and Trial, 1963-64, Run for Your Life, 1965-68 (4 Emmy Nominations), Police Story, 1987; appeared: TV dramas including Playhouse 90, DuPont Show of the Month (Recipient Drama Critics award for role in End As a Man 1953, Theatre World award 1953, 3 nominations Antoinette Perry award, 4 Emmy nominations), An Early Frost, 1985, A Letter to Three Wives, 1985, Downpayment on Murder, 1987, People Like Us, 1990, Lies Before Kisses, 1991, Blindsided, 1993, Fatal Vows: The Alexandra O'Hara Story, 1994, Parallel Lives, 1994, Strangers, 1995, Valentine's Day, 1998, Angelo Nero (miniseries), 1998, Tesoro di Damasco (miniseries), 1998, Tre Stelle (miniseries), 1999, Brian's Song, 2001, Hysterical Blindness (Emmy award best sup. actor TV Movie, 2003), 2002; author, director, actor Ladykiller, 1996; Vicious Circle, 1997; (author) In the Moment: My Life as an Actor, 2004. Office: care J Julien 1501 Broadway New York NY 10036-5601

GE, NIEN-HUI, chemist, educator; BS, Nat. Taiwan U., Taipei, 1990, MS, 1992; PhD, U. Calif., Berkeley, 1998. Grad. rsch./tchg. asst. Nat. Taiwan U., Taipei, 1990—92, tchg. asst., 1992—93; grad. rsch./tchg. asst. U. Calif., Berkeley, 1993—98; postdoctoral rsch. fellow U. Pa., Phila., 1998—2002; asst. prof. of chemistry U. Calif., Irvine, 2002—. Treas. Western Spectroscopy Assn., Calif. Contbr. numerous articles to profl. jours. Recipient Book Coupon award, Nat. Taiwan U., 1987—90, 1st prize in chemistry, 1st Nat. Sci. Coun. Undergrad. Rsch. Competition, Taiwan, 1990, Career award, NSF, 2005—; fellow, Ednl. Ministry Taiwan, 1990—92; grantee rsch. grantee, U. Calif. Irvine, Sch. Phys. Scis., Com. on Rsch., 2003—04, U. Calif. Irvine, Coun. on Rsch., Computing and Libr. Resources, 2003—04; scholar, Taipei Journalists Club, 1987—90, Mr. Li Chung & Mrs. Li Hung Lai-Guei Found., 1989, Mr. Liou Shih-Bing Found., 1989, Mr. Tseng Chi Scholarship Found., 1989—90, Tse Hang Pu Sa Meml. Found., 1989, Mr. Wu Jung-Ya Found., 1990, Tai-Tz Constrn. Co., Taiwan, 1990, Taiwan Civic Svc. Club, 1990, Mr. Chiou Hai-Shui Found., 1990, Hsin Tung Yang Found., 1990, Mr. Tzung Juo-Jang Found., 1991; grad. student travel fellow, Am. Chem. Soc., 1997, Margaret Jorgenson Meml. fellow, Dept. Chemistry, U. Calif. Berkeley, 1997—98, grad. fellow, Am. Phys. Soc., 1997, grad. student travel grantee, U. Calif., Berkeley, 1996—2007, rsch. grantee, U. Calif. Irvine, Coun. on Rsch., Computing and Libr. Resources, 2004—05, Am. Chem. Soc. Petroleum Rsch. Fund, 2003—05, U. Calif., Cancer Rsch. Coord. Com., 2006—. Mem.: Iota Sigma Pi, Optical Soc. of Am., Am. Phys. Soc., Am. Chem. Soc. Office: University of California Irvine Department of Chemistry Irvine CA 92697-2025 Office Phone: 949-824-1263. Office Fax: 949-824-8571.

GEAKE, RAYMOND ROBERT, psychologist; b. Detroit, Oct. 26, 1936; s. Harry Nevill and Phyllis Rae (Fox) G.; m. Carol Lynne Rens, June 9, 1962; children: Roger Rens, Tamara Lynne, William Rens. BS in Spl. Edn., U. Mich., 1958, MA in Guidance and Counseling, 1959, PhD in Edn. and Psychology, 1963. Coord. child devel. rsch. Edison Inst., Dearborn, Mich., 1962-66; dir. psychology dept. Plymouth (Mich.) State Home and Tng. Sch., Mich. Dept. Mental Health, 1966-69; pvt. practice ednl. psychology Northville, Mich., 1969-72; mem. Mich. Ho. of Reps., 1973-76, Mich. Senate, 1977-98; investigator, dir. Mich. Office of Children's Ombudsman, 1999—2002; commr. Mich. Racing, 2002—04. Adj. asst. prof. edn./psychology dept. Madonna Coll., Livonia, Mich., 1984-86. Co-author: Visual Tracking, A Self-instruction Workbook for Perceptual Skills in Reading, 1962. Trustee-at-large Schoolcraft C.C., 1969-72, chmn. bd. trustees, 1971-72; vice chmn. nat. adv. com. on mental health and illness of elderly HEW, 1976-77; vice chmn. human svcs. com., assembly fed. issues Nat. Conf. State Legislatures, 1994-95. Recipient Recognition award Found. for Improvement of Justice, 1993. Fellow Mich. Psychol. Assn.; mem. NEA (life), APA, Rotary. Republican.

GEALT, MICHAEL A., environmental microbiologist, educator; b. Phila., Nov. 27, 1948; s. Edward Leonard Gealt and Lillian Rose Brenner; m. Maryjanet McNamara, Jan. 2, 1981; 1 child; m. Antonia Malandrucco, May 12, 1967 (div. 1977); 2 children. BA, Temple U., 1970; PhD, Rutgers U., 1974. Rsch. assoc. Med. Sch. Rutgers U., Piscataway, NJ, 1974-76; postdoct. assoc. Inst. Cancer Rsch., Phila., 1976-78; asst. prof. biol. scis. Drexel U., Phila., 1978-84, assoc. prof., 1984-90, prof., 1990-2000, dir. Sch. Environ. Sci., Engring. and Policy, 1994-2000; dean Sch. Engring., Math. and Sci. Purdue U. Calumet, Hammond, Ind., 2000—05, prof. biology, 2000—05, U. Ark., Little Rock, 2006—, dean Coll. Sci. and Math., 2006—. Contbr. articles to profl. jours. Grantee EPA, 1983, 85, 89, NSF, 1981, 94, 97, USAF, 2002. Mem. AAAS, Am. Soc. Microbiology (chair environ. and applied micro divsn. 1995), Am. Soc. Cell Biology, Assn. Environ. Engrs. & Science Profs., Am. Soc. Engring. Educ., Sigma Chi. Avocations: motorcycles, photography. Office: Univ Ark 2801 S University Ave Little Rock AR 72204 Office Phone: 501-569-3247. Business E-Mail: magealt@ualr.edu.

GEAN, THOMAS C., lawyer, former prosecutor; b. 1962; BA, U. Ark.; JD, Vanderbilt U. Atty. Alston and Bird, Atlanta, 1988—92, Gean, Gean and Gean, Ft. Smith, Ark., 1992—96; prosecuting atty. Sebastian County Dist. Atty.'s Office, 1997—2001; U.S. atty. western dist. Ark. U.S. Dept. Justice, 2001—04; v.p. legal dept., chief legal compliance officer Wal-Mart Corp., Bentonville, Ark., 2004—. Office: Wal-Mart Corp 702 SW 8th St Bentonville AR 72716

GEAREN, JOHN JOSEPH, lawyer; b. Wareham, Mass., Sept. 1, 1943; BA, U. Notre Dame, 1965; MA (Rhodes Scholar), Oxford U., 1967; JD, Yale U., 1970. Bar: Ill. 1972. Ptnr. Mayer, Brown & Platt, Chgo., 1970—. Democrat. Roman Catholic. Home: 179 Linden Ave Unit 2 Oak Park IL 60302-1661 Office: Mayer Brown & Platt 190 S La Salle St Ste 3100 Chicago IL 60603-3441 E-mail: jgearen@mayerbrown.com.

GEARHART, RANDALL F., healthcare educator; b. Charleroi, Pa., Mar. 25, 1971; s. Randy F. and Carol A. Gearhart; m. Kelly L. Collins, May 16, 1972; children: David A., Emma C. PhD, U. Pitts., 1999. Lic. CPR Am. Heart Assn.; cert. strength and conditioning specialist. Asst. prof. So. Ill. U., Carbondale, 1999—2003, Ashland U., Ohio, 2003—06, assoc. prof., 2006—. Invited presenter Oxford Round Table of Nutrition. Deacon 1st Christian Ch., Carbondale, 2001—03. Mem.: Nat. Strength and Conditioning Assn., Am. Coll. of Sports Medicine. Republican. Disciples Of Christ. Avocations: exercise, travel. Office: Ashland Univ 916 King Rd Ashland OH 44805 Office Fax: 419-289-5460. Business E-Mail: rgearhar@ashland.edu.

GEARON, JOHN MICHAEL, SR., (MICHAEL GEARON), professional sports team owner; b. Englewood, NJ, May 6, 1934; s. C.P. and Elizabeth (Asbury) G.; m. Patricia Smith, Jan. 1, 1960 (div.); children: Tierney, Michael, Tim; m. Mary F. Davis, Mar. 4, 1989. Gen. mgr. NBA Atlanta Hawks, 1977—79, pres., 1977—86, chmn. bd., 1986—2004; owner Gearon & Co., Atlanta, 1983; investor Atlanta Spirit, LLC (parent co. of NBA Atlanta Hawks and NHL Atlanta Thrashers). Bd. dirs. Turner Broadcasting Systems Inc. Mailing: Atlanta Spirit LLC Ste 1900 101 Marietta St NW Atlanta GA 30303 Office Phone: 404-827-3800.

GEARON, JOHN MICHAEL, JR., (MICHAEL GEARON), professional sports team owner, communications executive; married; 3 children. Student, U. Ga.; B cum laude in Interdisciplinary Studies, Ga. State U., 1989. Founder, CEO Gearon Comm. (merged with Am. Tower in 1998), 1990—98; exec. v.p. Am. Tower, Boston, 1998—2001, bd. dirs., 1998—2003; pres. Am. Tower Internat., 2000—; vice chmn. Am. Tower, 2002—; prin. Atlanta Spirit, LLC (parent co. of NBA Atlanta Hawks and NHL Atlanta Thrashers). Office: Atlanta Spirit LLC Ste 1900 101 Marietta St NW Atlanta GA 30303 E-mail: michael.gearon@americantower.com.*

GEARY, DAVID PATRICK, criminal justice educator, consultant, writer; b. Milw., May 20, 1928; s. Cornelius John and Madeline (Cushway) G.; m. Mary Ann Delavan, June 19, 1954; children: Patrick, John, Daniel, Peter BS, LaVerne U., LA, 1971; MPA, U. So. Calif., 1972; PhD, Marquette U., 1979; postgrad., U. Mich., 1980. Cert. life tchg. credential, Calif. Police officer City of Greendale, Wis., 1950—55; chief police City of Hales Corners, Wis., 1955—61, City of Salem, Oreg., 1961—65, City of Ventura, Calif., 1965—72; assoc. prof. criminal justice U. Wis., Milw., 1972—76, U. South Fla., Tampa, 1976—79, U. Nev., Reno, 1979—82, Va. Commonwealth U., Richmond, 1982—2003, pres. faculty senate, 1989, emeritus faculty, 2003—. Mem. vis. faculty Ventura Coll., 1966-72, Carthage Coll., Kenosha, Wis., 1974; cons. Commn. on Accreditation for Law Enforcement Agys., Fairfax, Va., 1990; cons. to Va. State Police, 1994, Richmond Police, 1996—; cons. to city atty. and police dept. City of Dallas, 1990; cons. to atty. gen. City of Birmingham, 1991; cons. to postal insp. U.S. Postal Svc., Washington, 1992; cons. to City of Richmond, 1996— Author: How To Deliver Death News, 1981; editor: Community Relations, 1976; also articles Gen. chmn. Arts in Justice, Anderson Gallery, Richmond, 1989. With U.S. Maritime Svc., 1944-46 Named Outstanding Young Man, U.S. Jaycees, Hales Corners, 1965; rsch. fellow U.S. Govt. Law Enforcement Assistance Adminstrn., 1976 Mem. AAUP (pres. Va. Commonwealth U. chpt. 1987, 94), Va. Assn. Criminal Justice Educators (pres. 1985-87), Va. Internat. Human Rights and Responsibilities Found., Inc. (founder 1998) Home: 7678 Yarmouth Dr Richmond VA 23225-2145 Personal E-mail: nocon2@verizon.net. *Don't let the barbarians get you. Don't let them injure your body, but more important don't let them get into your head and make you one of them.*

GEARY, HILARY R., society editor; d. J. Jeffrey Roche and Sidney B. Wood; m. John W. Geary II, Apr. 28, 1973 (dec. 1995); children: Alfred, John; m. Peter Green, 2000 (div. 2002); m. Wilbur Ross, Oct. 9, 2004. Student, Finch Coll. Society editor Quest Mag. Mem.: Southampton Rose Soc. Office: QUEST Media 920 Third Ave 6th Fl New York NY 10022 Office Phone: 646-840-3404 ext. 106. Office Fax: 646-840-3408.

GEARY, MARIE JOSEPHINE, art association administrator; b. Boston, Dec. 1, 1933; d. Vincent and Maryanne (DeAngelo) Bianco; m. John Francis Geary, Oct. 11, 1959; 1 child, John Francis Jr. Grad., Medford H.S., 1951. Registrar grad./postgrad. div. Tufts U. Sch. Dental Medicine, Boston, 1951-60; reporter, arts editor Chelmsford (Mass.) Newsweekly, 1970-82; owner, mgr. Village Sq. Art Gallery, Chelmsford, 1976-80; founder, owner A Way With Words, Chelmsford, 1980—; founder, dir. Eastcoast Quilters Alliance, Westford, Mass., 1988—. Mktg. cons. Westford Regency Inn, 1991; cons. to arts orgns. for seminar planning, curator exhibits, 1999—. Contbr. articles to profl. mags. Pub. rels. dir. New England Quilt Mus., Lowell, 1986-88; founder, pres. Chelmsford Art Soc., 1970-75; founder, bd. dirs. Chelmsford Cultural Coun., 1980-84; founder, dir. pub. rels. Chelmsford Crafters, Inc., 1976-80; publicity dir. Chelmsford Town 4th of July Celebration, 1971-74; founder Women in Bus. Conf., 1994. Mem. Am. Quilting Soc., Chelmsford Quilters (pres. 1985-89, 99-2003), New Eng. Quilters Guild (Compass editor 1985-88), Chelmsford Book Discussion Soc., Quilters Connection (Quiltations editor 1992-93, v.p. 1994-95, pres. 1995-96), Middlesex Women's Network, Women in Bus. (formed 1993, coord. 1st conf. 1994), Enterprising Women. Republican. Roman Catholic. Avocations: art, antiques, reading, economics, marketing trends. Home: 38 Amble Rd Chelmsford MA 01824-1968 Office: Eastcoast Quilters Alliance PO Box 711 Westford MA 01886-0021 E-mail: eqaquilter@aol.com.

GEARY, PATRICK JOSEPH, security and emergency planning administrator, writer; b. Milw., Mar. 6, 1957; s. David Patrick and Mary Ann (Delavan) G. BS, Va. Commonwealth U., 1984; MA, U. Richmond, 1987, U.S. Naval War Coll., 2000. Operations security cert. profl. Tech. pubis. writer Dept. Def. Security Inst., Richmond, Va., 1987—88; ops. security officer David Taylor Naval Rsch. Ctr., Bethesda, Md., 1988—91, Space and Naval Warfare Sys. Command, Arlington, Va., 1991—92; divsn. head office of security Naval Sea Sys. Command Dept. Navy, Arlington, 1992—2002; dir. office of security and continuity planning Dept. of Treasury, Washington, 2002—03; dir. office of security programs and continuity planning Naval Sea Sys. Command Dept. Navy, Washington, 2006—. Pres. Ybor City Jaycees, Tampa, Fla., 1979, Reno Jaycees, 1980-81; regional/dist. dir. Nev. Jaycees, Reno, 1981-83; co-campaign mgr. state assembly Rep. Party of Nev., Reno, 1982; senator Jaycees Internat., Coral Gables, Fla., 1983, life mem.; active West End Jaycees Richmond, 1983-98. Decorated superior civilian svc. medal Dept. Navy, 1995; recipient Charles Kulp meml. award U.S. Jaycees, 1981, Nat. Interagy. award for individual achievment in ops., 1998; Albright grad. fellow U. Richmond, 1985. Mem. NRA, KC, Nat. Def. Indsl. Assn. (life), Ops. Security Profls. Soc. (life, charter, nat. bd. dirs. 1995-2004, pres. 2000-2003), Nat. Assn. Parliamentarians, Nat. Mil. Intelligence Assn. (life), U.S. Naval War Coll. found. (alumni life), Va. Commonwealth U. Alumni Assn. (life), Pi Sigma Alpha, Alpha Phi Sigma. Roman Catholic. Avocations: water-skiing, basketball, football, parliamentary procedure, pistol shooting. Home: 7035 Devereux Circle Dr Alexandria VA 22315

GEARY, STEPHEN R., engineer, educator, engineering executive; s. Joseph F. Geary, Jr. and Ruth P. Geary; m. Holley Kay Snowden, Sept. 22, 2006. BS in Engring., Cornell U., Ithaca, NY, 1977—82, M of Engring., 1982—83, MBA, 1985—86. Cert. Prodn. & Inventory Control Mgr. Am. Prodn. & Inventory Control Soc., 1987. Mfg. engr. Emerson Electric, Milford, Conn.; mgmt. cons. PRTM, Wellesley Hills, Mass., 1986—87; various positions Teradyne Connection Systems, Nashua, NH, 1987—96, global mfg. mgr., 1996—98; svc. dir. Performance Measurement Group, Waltham, Mass., 1999—2001; v.p. Tilion, Inc., Maynard, Mass., 2001—02; ptnr. Supply Chain Visions, Stoneham, Mass., 2002—; faculty & rsch. assoc. U. Tenn. Coll. Bus. Adminstrn., Knoxville. Rsch. adv. bd. ChainLink Rsch., Cambridge, Mass. Contbg/ editor: DC Velocity, 2006—, editor-at-large: CSCMP's Supply Chain Quar., 2007—; contbr. articles and papers to profl. jours. and pubs. Mem. Town of Stoneham Fin. Bd., Mass., 1998—2002. Mem.: Coun. Supply Chain Mgmt. Profls. (assoc.). Home Phone: 781-254-5351; Office Phone: 781-254-5351. Business E-Mail: steve@scvisions.com.

GEBAUER, KURT MANFRED, management executive; b. Paterson, NJ, Dec. 12, 1951; s. Werner and Edna Julie (Harris) G.;. Cheryl Lawton, Oct. 24, 1981. BA, Burknell U., 1974. Gen. mgr. Sta. WUDO, Lewisburg, Pa., 1973-74; v.p. New Sound Assocs., Lewisburg, 1974-75; ops. mgr. Sta. WCRV, Washington, N.J., 1975-76; pres. WTS Corp., Rockaway, N.J., 1976—. Product mgr. BestWare, Inc., 1994-95, dir. internat. ops., 1995-96, mng. dir. MYOB (now MYOB US, Inc.) product line, 1996-99; internet & E strategist MYOB Global Technology, 1999-2001; personal and bus. mgr. Light, 1980-82; N. Am. tour mgr. Cleo Laine/John Dankworth, 1980-82, bus. and concert mgr., 1983-93; East Coast tour mgr. Henry Mancini, 1980-86; mgr. bus. and legal affairs Nielsen Media Rsch., 2001—; cons. Warren Broadcasting Co. (WFMV-FM), Blairstown, N.J., 1977-79, Cam Kay, Inc., 1979-84 1st Nat. Bank of Hope, N.J., 1986-88; dir. Sonoma-Hope, Inc., 1984—, Keynight Pty. Ltd., 1988-93, Consolidated Libr. Assocs., Inc., 1989-96, Distinctive Artists Mgmt., Inc., 1990-95. Sound. designer A Little Night Music, Mich. Opera Theater, 1983, Lady in Waiting, Houston Ballet, 1984, The Merry Widow, Mich. Opera Theater, 1984; prodr. DRG album Cleo at Carnegie: The 10th Anniversary Album, 1986 (Grammy award for best female jazz vocalist 1995), RCA Victor album Woman to Woman, 1989, Blues and Sentimental, 1993, Golden Records albums: Cleo Laine Live in Manhattan, 2001, Quintessential Cleo, 2001. Mem. Pi Delta Epsilon.

GEBBIA, ROBERT JAMES, tax executive; b. New Castle, Pa., Nov. 29, 1947; s. Joseph A. and Helen M. (Staransky) G.; m. Eileen A. Zuk, Oct. 2, 1971; children: Jamie, Christopher, Maria. BS, Youngstown State U., 1969; MBA, Canisius Coll., 1979. CPA Va. Tax law specialist IRS, Washington, 1972-74, IRS agt. Detroit and Buffalo, 1974-77; tax supr. Peat, Marwick, Mitchell, Buffalo, 1977-79; tax mgr. Coopers & Lybrand, Pitts., 1979-81; tax dir. UNC Resources, Falls Church, Va., 1981-85; sr. tax mgr. Occidental Petroleum, Tulsa, 1985-88; dir. taxes Carpenter Tech., Reading, Pa., 1988—. Instr. Albright Coll., Reading, 1989—; treas. Carpenter Tech. Fed. Pac, Carpenter Tech. Pa. Pac. Treas. Carpenter Tech. Pa./Fed. PAC. With U.S. Army, 1970-71, Vietnam. Decorated Bronze Star, Army Commendation medals (2). Mem. Mfrs. Alliance for Productivity and Innovation, Pa.

Chamber of Bus. and Industry, Tax Execs. Inst., Nat. Assn. Corp. Treasurers, Berks County C. of C. Roman Catholic. Avocation: tennis. Home: 217 Logan Ave Wyomissing PA 19610-2655 Personal E-mail: rjgebbia@yahoo.com.

GEBBIE, GEOFFREY, research scientist, oceanographer; PhD, MIT, Cambridge. Rsch. scientist Harvard U., Cambridge, 2004—. Contbr. articles to profl. jours. Earch Scis. fellow, NASA, 2004. Mem.: Am. Geophys. Union, Phi Beta Kappa. Achievements include research in improving predictions of El Nino for use by the international community. Office: Harvard Univ 24 Oxford St Cambridge MA 02138

GEBBIE, KRISTINE MOORE, medical educator; b. Sioux City, Iowa, June 26, 1943; d. Thomas Carson and Gladys Irene (Stewart) Moore; m. Lester N. Wright; children: Anna, Sharon, Eric. BSN, St. Olaf Coll., 1965; MSN, UCLA, 1968; DPH, U. Mich., 1995. Project dir. USPHS Tng. Grant, St. Louis, 1972—77; coord. nursing St. Louis U., 1974—76, asst. dir. nursing, 1976—78, clin. prof., 1977—78; adminstr. Oreg. Health Div., Portland, 1978—89; sec. Wash. State Dept. Health, Olympia, 1989—93; coord. Nat. AIDS Policy, Washington, 1993—94; assoc. prof. Sch. Nursing Columbia U., 1994—2007, prof., 2007—; assoc. prof. Oreg. Health Scis. U. Portland, 1980—90. Chair secretarial panel on evaluation of epidemiologic rsch. activities U.S. Dept. Energy , 1989—90; mem. Presdl. Commn. on Human Imunodeficiency Virus Epidemic, 1987—88. Author (with Deloughery and Neuman): Consultation and Community Orgn., 1971; author: (with Deloughery) Political Dynamics: Impact on Nurses, 1975; author: (with Scheer) Creative Teaching in Clinical Nursing, 1976. Bd. dirs. Lusth. Family Svcs. Oreg. and S.W. Wash., 1979—84, Oreg. Psychoanalytic Found.1, 1983—87. Recipient Disting. Alumna award, St. Olaf Coll., 1979; scholar Disting. scholar, Am. Nurses Found., 1989. Fellow: Am. Acad. Nursing; mem.: Am. Soc. Pub. Adminstrn. (Adminstrn. award II 1983), N.Am. Nursing Diagnosis Assn. (treas. 1983—84), Inst. Medicine, Am. Pub. Health Assn. (exec. bd.), Assn. State and Territorial Health Ofcls. (pres. 1984—85, exec. com. 1980—87, McCormick award 1988). Office: Columbia U Sch Nursing 630 W 168th St New York NY 10032-3702 Business E-Mail: KMG24@columbia.edu.

GEBELEIN, RICHARD STEPHEN, judge, former state attorney general; b. Upper Darby, Pa., June 8, 1946; s. Walter C. and Margaret E. (Stratton) G.; m. Anna Grace Thomason.; children: R. Zachary, Lauren E. V., Alexandra D. BS in Math., U. Pitts., 1967; JD, Villanova U., 1970. Bar: Pa. 1971, Del. 1971, U.S. Supreme Ct. 1975. Justice of peace, Kennett Twp., Pa., 1967-70; dep. atty. gen. State of Del., 1971-74, state solicitor, 1974-75, chief dep. public defender, 1975-76; ptnr. firm Wilson & Whittington, Wilmington, Del., 1976-79; atty. gen. State of Del., Wilmington, 1979-83; assoc. judge Del. Superior Ct., 1984—2005; vice chmn. Nat. Assn. Crug Ct. Profls., 2003—05; judge Ct. of Bosnia and Herzegovina Spl. War Crimes Chamber, 2005—. Adj. prof. Del. Law Sch., Widener Coll.; instr. U. Del.; mem. Del. Gov.'s Sentencing Reform Commn.; chmn. Sentencing Accountability Commn. State of Del., 1989—2004. Republican. Roman Catholic.

GEBHARD, LAVERNE ELIZABETH, retired accounting educator; b. Milw., Aug. 30, 1936; d. Frank and Helen Gebhard. BS, Marquette U., 1958, MBA, 1964. CPA, cert. internal auditor, cert. cost analyst, cert. mgmt. acct. Internal auditor Fed. Res. Bank Chgo., 1958-60; gen. acct. City Products, 1960-61; tchr. bus. Milw. Pub. Schs., 1961-65; from instr. to lectr. to sr. lectr. U. Wis., Milw., 1966-93; cons. New Berlin, Wis., 1993—. CMA exam. adminstr. ICMA-Milw. site, Montvale, N.J., 1984-97. Contbr. articles to profl. jours. Vol. advisor Milw. Hist. Soc., La Farge Learning Ctr., others. Recipient Citizen Ambassador award People to People, Inc., 1991—. Mem. Inst. Internal Auditors, Wis. Inst. CPAs (ch. bd. dirs. 1984—, mem. numerous coms., cons. 1984-86), Inst. Mgmt. Accts., Beta Gamma Sigma, Delta Pi Epsilon, Beta Alpha Psi (faculty advisor, founder). Avocations: travel, reading, tennis, continuing education, volunteer work. Home: 12685 W Bobwood Rd New Berlin WI 53151-6975 E-mail: gebhard3@netzero.com.

GEBHARDT, ROBERT CHARLES, lawyer; b. Old Forge, NY, Nov. 23, 1937; s. Charles R. and Marcelle M. (Jovet) G.; m. Carolyn A. Searle, Dec. 18, 1968 (div. June 1977); children: Carolyn G., Marcelle C.; m. Johnnie L. Watts, Aug. 29, 1988. AB, SUNY, Albany, 1961; JD, Georgetown U., 1967. Bar: N.Y. 1968, Fla. 1981. Atty. Harris, Beach & Wilcox, Rochester, NY, 1967-70; sr. v.p., gen. counsel Lincoln st Banks, Inc., Rochester, NY, 1970-81; ptnr. Goldstein, Goldman, Kessler & Underberg, Miami, 1981-84; sr. v.p. Asset Mgmt. & Disposition, Inc., Naples, Fla., 1986-89; ptnr. Gebhardt & White, P.A., Naples, 1989—95, Porter Wright, Morris & Arthur LLP, 1996—2003; pvt. practice Gebhardt Law Office, Whispering Pines, NC, 2002—. Chmn. Com. of Bank Holding Co. Attys., Rochester, 1978-81. Mem. Fla. Bar, N.Y. Bar, Collier County Bar Assn. Republican. Roman Catholic. Home: 25 Lakeview DR Whispering Pines NC 28327-9405 Office: Gebhardt Law Office 25 Lakeview Dr Carthage NC 28327 Home Phone: 910-949-0443; Office Phone: 910-638-3330. Personal E-mail: skipgebhardt@earthlink.net.

GEBHART, RONALD JOHN, infectious disease specialist, administrator; b. Ft. Worth, Tex., Apr. 10, 1945; s. Harold John and Ione Jeanette (Becker) G.; m. Suzanne Spiggle Parrish, Aug. 18, 1969; children: Skyler Parrish, Douglas Becker. BS, St. Edward's U., Austin, Tex., 1967; MD, Med. Coll. of Va., 1972. Diplomate Am. Bd. Internal Medicine, Am. Bd. Infectious Diseases. Commd. USAF, 1968, advanced through grades to lt. col., 1979, resigned, 1981; resident Wilford Hall USAF Med. Ctr., San Antonio, Tex., 1972-75; chief internal medicine USAF Hosp. Torrejon AFB, Madrid, 1975-76, USAF Hosp. RAF Lakenheath, Suffolk, Eng., 1976-79, USAF Hosp. Langley AFB, Hampton, Va., 1979-81; fellow infectious disease Med. Coll. of Va., Richmond, 1981-84; assoc. chief of staff VA Med. Ctr., Atlanta, 1984—. Cons. USAFE Surgeon Gen., 1976-79. Contbr. articles on antifungal drugs to profl. jours., 1980-90. Grantee NIH, Richmond, 1982-83. Fellow Am. Coll. Physicians; mem. Infectious Disease Soc. Am., Am. Coll. Physician Execs., Am. Fed. Clin. Rsch., Nat. Assn. VA Physician Mgrs. (pres. 1991). Episocpalian. Home: 2921 Cravey Dr NE Atlanta GA 30345-1421 Office: VA Med Ctr 1670 Clairmont Rd Decatur GA 30033-4098

GEBROSKY, NORMAN PAUL, urologist; b. Jeannette, Pa., Aug. 1, 1964; s. Robert Jackson and Margaret Elaine Gebrosky; m. Lisa Leblang Gebrosky, May 25, 1990; children: Hannah Catherine, Jacob Joseph. BS, U. Pitts., 1986, MD, 1990. Diplomate Am. Bd. Urology, 1998. Physician Dieter Sauer M.D., Inc., Greensburg, Pa., 1996—2004; ptnr. G.U., Inc., Latrobe, Pa., 2005—. Fellow, ACS, 2005. Mem.: Pa. Med. Soc., AMA, Am. Urologic Assn. Office: GU Inc 522 W Newton St Greensburg PA 15601 Office Phone: 724-838-7500. Office Fax: 724-837-6670.

GECELTER, GARY RAYMOND, gastrointestinal surgeon, researcher; b. Johannesburg, S. Afica, Aug. 18, 1958; came to U.S., 1993; s. Louis and Sybil (Win) G.; m. Jacqueline Naomi Gittleson, Jan. 29, 1986; children: Ryan J., Rachel C., Amy M. MBBCh, U. Witwatersrand, Johannesburg. Intern Johannesburg Hosp., 1982, attending surgeon, 1992-93; surg. resident U. Witwatersrand, Johannesburg, 1985-90, fellow in gastroenterology, 1990-92; asst. prof. surgery SUNY, Stony Brook, 1993-98; chief gen. surgery L.I. Jewish Hosp., New Hyde Park, NY, 1998—. Oper. rm. dir. Stony Brook U. Hosp., 1994-98, chmn. med. exec. bd., 1998 Mem. editl. bd. S. Afican Jour. Surgery, 1989-90; contbr. articles to profl. jours. Lt. S. African Med. Corps, 1983-84. Fellow ACS, Coll. Surgeons; mem. Soc. Gastrointestinal Endoscopic Surgeons. Jewish. Avocations: golf, tennis, jogging, piano. Office: LI Jewish Med Ctr 270-05 70th Ave New Hyde Park NY 11040

GECHTOFF, SONIA, artist; b. Phila., Sept. 25, 1926; d. Leonid and Etya (Freedman) G.; children: Susannah Kelly, Miles Kelly. BFA, Phila. Mus. Sch. Art, 1950. Instr. painting, drawing Calif. Sch. Fine Art, 1957-58; adj. asst. prof. art NYU, 1960—70; lectr. Queens Coll., NYC, 1970-74; assoc. prof. U. N.Mex., 1974-75. Artist-in-residence Skidmore Coll., summers 1988, 89, 90, Adelphi U., N.Y., 1991, 93; vis. artist Chgo. Art Inst., 1989; instr. master classes Nat. Acad. Fine Art, NYC, 2000—. One-woman shows include DeYoung Mus., San Francisco, 1957, Ferus Gallery, L.A., 19157, 59, Poindexter Gallery, N.Y.C., 1959, 60, Cortella Gallery, N.Y.C., 1976, 78, Gruenebaum Gallery, N.Y.C., 1979, 80, 82, 83, 85, 87, Witkin Gallery, N.Y.C., 1984, 89, Kraushaar Gallery, N.Y.C., 1990, 92, 95, Fine Arts Gallery, San Francisco, 1991, Adelphi U., 1993, Skidmore Coll., N.Y., 1995, Harrison Mus. Art, Utah, 1996, Kraushaar Gallery, NYC, 1998; group shows include Guggeneim Mus., N.Y.C., 1954, San Francisco Mus. Art, 1953-58, Brussels World's Fair, 1958, 1st Paris Biennale, 1959, Whitney Mus., N.Y.C., 1959. 60, Sao Paulo Biennale, 1961, Nat. Gallery Am. Art Smithsonian Instn., 1976, Mus. Modern Art, N.Y.C., 1977, Aldrich Mus. Contemporary Art, Ridgefield, Conn., 1981, Bennington Coll., Vt., 1985, Weatherspoon Gallery, Greensboro, 1987, Gruenebaum Gallery, 1987, The Butler Inst. of Am. Art: 56th Nat. Mid-Yr. Exhbn., Youngstown, Ohio, 1992, Santa Cruz (Calif.) Mus., 1993, Laguna Art Mus., Laguna Beach, Calif., 1996, San Francisco Mus. Modern Art, 1996, Worcester Mus. Art, Mass., 2001, San Jose Mus. Art, Calif., 2003, Whitney Mus., NYC, 2005, Pollock-Krasner House, East Hampton, NY, 2006, Menil Collection, Houston, 2006, Nat. Acad. Art Mus., NYC, 2007; represented in permanent collections, San Francisco Mus. Modern Art, Guggenheim Mus., Mus. Modern Art, Met. Mus., N.Y.C., Balt. Mus. Art, Harrison Mus. Art at Utah State U., Worcester (Mass.) Art Mus., Laguna (Calif.) Art Mus., Whitney Mus. Am. Art, NYC, San Jose Mus., Menil Collection, Houston; also pvt. and corp. collections. Ford Found. fellow Tamarind Inst., L.A., 1963; recipient Purchase awards San Francisco Mus. Art, 1955-59; grantee Esther and Adolph Gottlieb Found., 1987, Mid. Atlantic NEA, 1988, Pollock-Krasner Found., 1994, 2002, Richard Florsheim Art Fund, 1994. Mem. Nat. Acad. Design. *I have, since my early twenties, always thought of myself as a painter. As the mother of two children (now adults), I was able to work on my paintings and to develop my art continuously. My life is my work.*

GECKER, JAMES M., lawyer; b. Milw., July 1, 1947; BA, U. Calif., Berkeley, 1971; JD cum laude, U. Wis., 1974; MSIR, Loyola U., Chgo., 1984. Bar: Ga. 1974, Ill. 1976, Wis. 1977, Ohio 1978, US Ct. Appeals, 5th, 6th & 7th Cirs., US Ct. Appeals, Fed. Cir., US Dist. Ct., Ea. Dist. Mich., US Dist. Ct., No. Dist. Ill. Ptnr. Katten Muchin Zavis Rosenman, Chgo. Mem.: ABA. Office: Katten Muchin Zavis Rosenman 525 W Monroe St Chicago IL 60661 Office Phone: 312-902-5586. Office Fax: 312-577-8825. E-mail: james.gecker@kmzr.com.

GECKLE, GEORGE LEO, III, language educator; b. Danbury, Conn., Dec. 2, 1939; s. George Leo and Dorothy Marion (Hill) G.; m. Justine Virginia Carroll, Aug. 19, 1961 (dec. Nov. 26, 2002); children: George, Richard; m. Shelley A. Smith, Sept. 3, 2006. AB, Middlebury Coll., Vt., 1961; MA, U. Va., Charlottesville, 1962, PhD, 1965. Asst. prof. English U. Wis., Madison, 1965-68, U. S.C., Columbia, 1968-70, assoc. prof. English, 1970-74, prof. English, 1974—2002, dir. honors program, 1970-73, dir. English grad. studies, 1974-76, 77-78, chmn. English dept., 1978-87. Author: John Marston's Drama, 1980, Tamburlaine and Edward II: Text and Performance, 1988; editor: Twentieth Century Interpretations of Measure for Measure, 1970, Measure for Measure, Shakespeare: The Critical Tradition, 2001. Fulbright grantee sr. prof. category U. Bamberg, Fed. Republic Germany, 1984-85; recipient 1st Jo Ann Boydston Essay prize Assn. for Documentary Editing, 1995. Mem. MLA, South Atlantic MLA, Shakespeare Assn. Am., Southeastern Renaissance Conf. (pres. 1985-86). Office: U South Carolina Dept English Humanities Bldg Columbia SC 29208-0001 Home: 937 Arcadia Lakes Dr Columbia SC 29206

GECKLE, ROBERT ALAN, manufacturing executive; b. Newtown, Conn., July 12, 1944; s. George Leo and Dorothy Marion (Hill) G.; m. Katherine Bernarda Landry, July 22, 1967; children: Sarah Nicole, Robert Alan Jr. BA in Econs., Middlebury Coll., 1967; MBA in Mktg., U. Pa., 1969. Sales mgr. Branson Cleaning Equipment Co., Stamford, Conn., 1969-71, product mgr. Shelton, Conn., 1971-73, dir. mktg., 1973-75, gen. mgr., 1975-78, pres., 1978-86, Branson Ultrasonics Corp., Danbury, Conn., 1987-94; pres., CEO Scan-Code, Inc., Rocky Hill, Conn., 1994-97; pres. Fluid and Power Systems Group, Textron, Providence, 1997—2002; adv. dir. Investcorp Internat., 2002—. Bd. dirs. Fleet Pride Corp., Playpower Corp., CCC Corp., Greatwide Corp. Contbr. articles on ultrasonics to profl. jours.; patentee in field. Bd. dirs. Danbury Health Systems, 1988—, mem. fin. com.; mem. Pres.'s Club, 1988—. Mem. Conn. Bus. Industry Assn. (bd. dirs. 1991, exec. com., 1992), Ridgewood Country Club, Danbury C. of C. Republican. Roman Catholic. Avocations: golf, gardening. Office: Investcorp Internat 280 Park Ave New York NY 10017

GECKLE, TIMOTHY J., lawyer; b. 1952; m. Bernadette Geckle; children: Caroline, Noelle. BA in religion, Catholic U. Am., 1974, MA in religion, 1979; JD, U. San Francisco, 1984. Bar: 1985. Lawyer Piper & Marbury, 1985—91; corp. counsel The Ryland Group, Calabasas, Calif., 1991-95, v.p., dep. gen. counsel, 1995-97, v.p., corp. counsel, sec., 1997, sr. v.p., gen. counsel, sec., 1997—. Office: The Ryland Group Inc 24025 Pk Sorrento Ste 400 Calabasas CA 91302 Office Phone: 410-715-7000.*

GECKLER, RICHARD DELPH, retired metal products executive; b. Toledo, Nov. 4, 1918; s. Maurice T. and Edith (Payne) G.; m. Elaine Mary Campbell, June 27, 1965; 1 child, Elaine Demian; 1 child by previous marriage, Carole Faye (Mrs. Gene Hendrix). AB, DePauw U., 1939. Chem. engr. Standard Oil Co., Ind., 1939-45; with Aerojet-Gen. Corp., Calif., 1945-68, v.p., mgr. solid rocket plant, Sacramento Calif., 1956-63, corp. v.p., El Monte Calif., 1963-68; chmn. bd., chief exec. Aerojet Delft Corp., 1968-69; pres. Marquardt Co., 1972-73, Pitter Metal Products, Inc., 1972-89, J.L. Mallard Co., 1972-89, Geckler Industries, Inc., 1972—2003; ret., 2003. Asst. dir. strategic weapons Office Sec. Def., 1964-66 Recipient Meritorious Pub. Service citation Navy Dept., 1961 Fellow Am. Inst. Aeros. and Astronautics; mem. Am. Chem. Soc., Am. Math. Soc., Am. Assn. of Artificial Intelligence, The Athenaeum, Phi Beta Kappa. Home: 7450 Olivetas Ave # C245 La Jolla CA 92037-4902 E-mail: pgeckler@mac.com.

GEDDES, JOHN M., editor; BA economics, cum laude, U.R.I., 1974; MA business journalism, U. Wa., 1976. Reporter The Ansonia Evening Sentinel, 1976, AP-Dow Jones News Service, New York, 1976—78, Bonn, Germany, 1978—79; economics correspondent The Times, Bonn, Germany, 1979—80; news editor, asst. mgr., sr. editor The Wall St. Journal, 1976—93; CEO BIS Strategic Decisions, 1993—94; business, financial editor New York Times, 1994—97, deputy mgr., 1997—2003, mng. editor, 2003—. Office: c/o NY Times 229 W 43rd St New York NY 10036

GEDDES, LESLIE ALEXANDER, engineering educator, forensic engineer, physiologist; b. Scotland, May 24, 1921; s. Alexander and Helen (Humphrey) G.; m. Irene P. Bloomer; 1 child, James Alexander; m. La Nelle E. Nerger, Aug. 3, 1962. BEE, MEngring., ScD (hon.), McGill U.; PhD in Physiology, Baylor U. Med. Coll. Demonstrator in elec. engring. McGill U., 1945, research asst. dept. neurology, 1945-52; cons. elec. engring. to various indsl. firms Que., Can.; biophysicist dept. physiology Baylor Med. Coll., Houston, asst. prof. physiology, 1956-61, assoc. prof., 1961-65, prof., 1965-74; dir. Lab. of Biophysics, Tex. Inst. Rehab. and Research, Houston, 1961-65; prof. physiology Coll. Vet. Medicine, Tex. A. and M. U., College Station, 1965-74, prof. biomed. engring., 1969-74; Showalter Disting. prof. bioengring. and elec. engring. Purdue U., West Lafayette, Ind., 1974-91, Showalter Disting. prof. emeritus, 1991—. Cons. NASA Manned Spacecraft Center, Houston, 1962-64, USAF, Sch. Aerospace Medicine, Brooks AFB, 1958-65; expert witness, 1981—. Author: 22 books; cons. editor: Med. and Biol. Engring., 1969—, Med. Research Engring., 1964-74, Med. Electronics and Data, 1969—, Jour. Cardiovasc. Engring., 2004-; mem. editl. bd. Jour. Electrocardiology, 1968—, med. instr., 1974—; contbr. over 800 articles to bioengring. Mem. Soc. Free Space Floaters, 1961. With Can. Army OTC. Named 2006 Nat. Medal Tech. Laureate; recipient Ctrl. Ind. Corp. award for Commercialization, 2003—04, Corp. Vitae award, Am. Heart Assn., 2005. Fellow: IEEE (Lee De Forest award 2001, Leadership award, Edison gold medal, IEEE 3d Millennium award, World of Difference award), AAAS (Am. Heart Vital award 2005, Nat. Tech. medal 2006), Biomed. Engring. Soc., Royal Soc. Medicine, Australasian Coll. Physicists in Biology and Medicine, Am. Inst. Med. and Biol. Engring., Am. Coll. Cardiology, Nat. Acad. Forensic Engrs.; mem.: NAE, NSPE, Am. Physiol. Soc., Assn. Advancement Med. Instrumentation (Health Care Hero award 2007, Leadership award), Tex. Soc. Profl. Engrs., Radio Club Am., Phi Zeta, Tau Beta Pi, Sigma Xi. Achievements include holder 33 US patents. Home: 400 N River Rd Apt 701 West Lafayette IN 47906-3131 Office: Purdue U POTR Bldg 500 Central Dr West Lafayette IN 47907-2022 Home Phone: 765-743-1941; Office Phone: 765-494-2995. Office Fax: 765-494-1193. Business E-Mail: geddes@ecn.purdue.edu.

GEDDES, ROBERT, architect, educator; b. Phila., Dec. 7, 1923; s. Louis J. and Kay (Malmed) G.; m. Evelyn Basse, June 15, 1947; children: David, Ann. Student, Yale U., 1941—46; MArch, Harvard U., 1950; LHD, NJ Inst. Tech., 1998, CUNY, 1999. Sr. ptnr. Geddes-Brecher Qualls Cunningham (architects), Phila., 1954-89, Princeton, 1965-89; pvt. practice Robert Geddes, Arch., Princeton and NYC, 1990-99; prof. architecture and civic design U. Pa., 1951-65; prof. architecture, dean Sch. Architecture Princeton U., 1965-82, William Kenan prof., 1968-89; Henry Luce prof. architecture, urbanism and history NYU, 1989-98. Bd. dirs. Manville Corp., Butler Mfg. Co.; chmn. adv. bd. design Redevel. Authority Phila., 1959-66; bd. dirs. Citizens Council City Planning, Phila., 1961-63, Urban America, Inc.; cons. Regional Plan Assn., NY; advisor on architecture and urban design, US Delegation to UN, Habitat II Conf., Istanbul, 1996; founder, co-chmn. Princeton Future Inc., 2000—. Contbr. articles on architecture to Ency. Brit., 1974-79; editor Principles and Precedents, Process Architecture jour., 1985; prin. works include Moore Sch. Elec. Engring, U. Pa., 1958, Police Hdqrs, Phila., 1962, resident halls U. Del., 1966, U. Pa., 1967, housing projects, Westchester, Pa., Phila., Princeton, Trenton, 1966-77, U. Pa. Med. Sch. and Hosp., 1978-84, dining hall and acad. bldg., Sch. Natural Scis., 2001, Inst. for Advanced Study, Princeton, 1971, humanities and social scis. bldg., So. Ill. U., Carbondale, 1968-74, Stockton State Coll, 1971-75, Corning Downtown Renewal, NY, 1975; master plan and design Liberty State Park, NJ, 1975-77, lab. bldgs., Mobil Corp., 1981, J. B. Speed Art Mus., Louisville, 1983; Muhlenberg Coll. Libr., 1986, Center City plan, Phila., 1985-87, Hosp. U. Pa., 1987, Pub. Safety Bldg., White Plains, NY, 1985—, Franklin Inst., Phila., 1987-90, Stern Sch. Bus. NYU, 1987-93, Alexanderpolder urban design, Rotterdam, 1993; co-dir. Crosstown 116 Upper Manhattan HUD U. Partnership, 1997; editor: Cities in Our Future, 1997. Trustee NJ Future. Fellow, N.Y. Inst. for the Humanities, 1989—, Appleton Traveling fellow Harvard U., 1950-51; recipient Design awards Progressive Architecture, First Design award, 1958; 2d prize Nat. Opera House, Sydney, Australia, 1958; first prize Internat. Town Planning Competition for Expansion of Vienna, Austria, 1971, award for Excellence in Archtl. Edn. ACSA-AIA, 1984. Fellow for design AIA (dir. edn. research project 1965-67, pres. N.Y. chpt. 1997, Nat. First Honor award 1960, 77, Archtl. Firm award 1979, Gold medals Phila. chpt., Design medals Pa. Soc., medals N.J. Soc., pres. N.Y. chpt. 1997); mem. Harvard Grad. Sch. Design Alumni Assn. (past pres.). E-mail: rgeddes@earthlink.net.

GEDDIE, ROWLAND HILL, III, lawyer; b. Tuscaloosa, Ala., Jan. 7, 1954; s. Rowland Hill Jr. and Mary Martha (McGaughy) G.; m. Peggy O'Neal Emmons, Aug. 13, 1977; children: Mary Catherine, Virginia Jane. BA, U. Miss., 1976, JD, 1978. Bar: Miss. 1978, US Dist. Ct. (no. dist.) Miss. 1978, Tex. 1979, Mo. 1995. Assoc. Baker & Botts, Houston, 1978-87; assoc. gen. counsel Lower Colo. River Authority, Austin, Tex., 1987-88; sr. counsel Houston Industries Inc./Houston Lighting & Power Co., 1988-92; contract atty. Tandy Corp./TE Electronics Inc., Ft. Worth, 1993; v.p., gen. counsel, sec. O'Sullivan Industries Holdings Inc., Lamar, Mo., 1993—. Treas. Southgate Civic Club, Houston, 1991—92. Presdl. scholar US Govt., Washington, 1972. Mem.: Am. Corp. Counsel Assn., Tri-State Swim Conf. (pres. 2005—07), Barton County C. of C. (bd. dirs. 2003—, pres. 2004—05), Lamar Swim Team Assn., Inc. (pres. 2000—02), Lamar Rotary Club (v.p. 2001—02, pres. 2002—03). Methodist. Avocations: personal computers, bicycling, scuba diving, swimming, theater. Home: 1503 Gulf St Lamar MO 64759-1830 Office: O'Sullivan Industries Inc 1900 Gulf St Lamar MO 64759-1899 Business E-Mail: rowland.geddie@osullivan.com.

GEDDIE, THOMAS EDWIN, retired small business owner; b. Oct. 7, 1930; s. Nolen Dawson and Fannie (Troublefield) G.; m. Minnie Maxine Smith, Feb. 18, 1968; children: Susan, Tommy, Sherry. BS in Agr., Okla. State U., 1951; postgrad., Tex. A&M U., 1951. Owner, oper. Thomas E. Geddie Assocs., Athens, 1955—96; ret., 1996; pvt. investor. With US Army, 1952—54. Mem.: Masons (32 deg.). Presbyterian. Home and Office: 901 Clifford St Athens TX 75751-2959 Personal E-mail: tinkerg30@suddenlink.net.

GEDEON, LUCINDA HEYEL, museum director; b. Port Chester, NY, Oct. 13, 1947; d. Philip H. and Isabel (Oldham) H.; m. Francis A. Sprout, Feb. 8, 1987. BA, Calif. State U., Long Beach, 1978; MA, UCLA, 1981, PhD, 1990. Asst. curator Grunwald Ctr. UCLA, 1978-81, asst. dir. Grunwald Ctr., 1981-83, acting dir. Grunwald Ctr., 1983-85; chief curator Ariz. State U. Art Mus., Tempe, 1985-91; CEO, dir. Neuberger Mus. SUNY, Purchase, 1991—2004; dir., CEO, Vero Beach Mus. Art, Fla., 2004—. Author: (exhbn. catalogues) Tamarind: Los Angeles to Albuquerque, 1985, Fiber Concepts, 1989 (book) The Art of Leonard Lehrer, 1986; gen. editor: Melvin Edwards Sculpture: A Thirty Year Retrospective, 1993, Shared Beginnings Separate Passages: A Retrospective of the Work of Carol Anthony and Elaine Anthony, 1996, June Wayne; A Retrospective, 1997, Elizabeth Catlett Sculpture: A Fifty-Year Retrospective, 1998, Marisol, 2001, Toshiko Takaezu, 2001, Grace Hartigan, 2001, Masters of Light: Selections of American Impressionism from the Manoogian Collection, 2006, Geoge Rickey Kinetic Sculpture: A Retrospective, 2007, The Reality of Things: Trompe l'oeil in America, 2007; contbr. articles to profl. jours. Chairperson Tempe Mcpl. Arts Commn., 1989-90; bd. dirs. Balboa Art Conservation Ctr., San Diego, 1986-91, ArtTable, N.Y., 1995-98, Westchester Arts Coun., 1998-2004. Recipient Individual Arts award Westchester Arts Coun., 2002, Chancellor's award Excellence, SUNY, 2002; Edward A. Dickson History of Art fellow UCLA, 1984, Afro-Am. Studies fellow, 1984. Mem. Am. Assn. Mus., Assn. Art Mus. Dirs. Office: Vero Beach Mus Art 3001 Riverside Pk Dr Vero Beach FL 32963 Home Phone: 772-234-8041; Office Phone: 772-231-0707 ext. 113. Business E-Mail: lgedeon@vbmuseum.org.

GEDJEYAN, GAIANE DIANA (ASTVATSATRIAN), pianist, physical therapist; b. Armenia, Calif., Sept. 13, 1953; d. Jora Geoarge Astvatsatrian and Tamara Matevosyan; m. Hovhannes John Gedjeyan, June 20, 1956; children: Sarkis Astvatsatrian, Marina Astvatsatrian. Diploma in phys. therapy (hon.), Chaikovcky Sch., Yerevan. Cert. Calif., 2002. Musician, piano player, doc. phys. therapy doc., profl. instr., 1996—2003. Candidate Al Malaikah Temple, LA, 2001—03; bd. dirs., nat. v.p. G.A. & H.G. L.L.C., Glendale, Calif., 2002—03. Conservative. Achievements include invention of color cubes. Office: Magic Realty 409 S Glendale Ave Ste 200 Glendale CA 91206 Home: 1031 Grover Ave Apt A Glendale CA 91201-5032 Personal E-mail: foreverinvestmentllc@charter.net. Business E-Mail: foreverinvestmentllc@cnarter.net.

GEDWED, WILLIAM J., insurance company executive; BS, MBA, Univ. Houston. Mgmt. positions Health Markets (formerly UICI), No. Richland Hills, Tex., 1997—2001, bd. dir., 2000—, pres., CEO, 2003—, chmn., 2005—06. Dir., chmn., pres., CEO The MEGA Life and Health Insurance Co, Mid-West Nat. Life Insurance Co. of Tenn., Chesapeake Life Ins. Co., Fidelity First Ins. Co. Office: Health Markets 9151 Grapevine Hwy North Richland Hills TX 76180*

GEE, CHUCK YIM, dean; b. San Francisco, Aug. 28, 1933; s. Don Yow Elsie (Lee) G. AA, City Coll. of San Francisco, 1953; BSBA, U. Denver, 1957; MA, Mich. State U., 1958; PhD (hon.), China Acad. Chinese Cultural U., 1972; D of Pub. Svc. (hon.), U. Denver, 1991. Assoc. dir. Sch. of Hotel and Restaurant Adminstrn. U. Denver, 1958-68; cons. East West Ctr., Honolulu, 1968-74; assoc. dean and prof. Sch. of Travel Industry Mgmt. U. Hawaii, 1968-75, dean and prof. Sch. Travel Industry Mgmt., 1976-99, interim dean Coll. Bus. Adminstrn., 1998-99, dean emeritus, 2000—. Vis. prof. Sch Bus. and Commerce, Oreg. State U., 1975; hon. prof. Nankai U., Tianjin, China, 1987—, Shanghai Inst. Tourism, 1994-03, Dept. Tourism Huaqiao U., Xiamen, China, 1995—, Shanghai Normal U., 2004—, Shunde Poly. U., Guangdong, China, 2005—, Hubei Coll., 2006—; cons. Internat. Sci. and Tech. Inst., Washington, 1986-90, cons. on tourism devel., Jiaojuo, Henan Province, Xiamen City, Fujian Province, China, 2004—, Xiaogen City, Hubei Province, 2006—; trustee Pacific Asia Travel Assn. Found., San Francisco; chmn. Govs. Tourism Tng. Coun., Honolulu, 1989-92, chmn., 1992-96, chmn. industry coun. PATA, 1994-96, PATA Human Resource Devel. Coun., 1996-99, chmn. PATA Coun. on Ednl. Devel. and Certification, 2000-02; mem. State Workforce Devel. Coun., 1997-98, Pacific Asia Travel Assn. Human Resource Devel. Coun, 1996-98; acad. Inst. Cert. Travel Agts., Wellesley, Mass., 1989—; mem. Coun. on Hotel, Restaurant Edn., 1967-00, Honolulu Commn. on Fgn. Rels., 1979-98; mem. Pacific Asian Affairs Coun.; sr. acad. adv. China Tourism Assn. Cons., Inc., 1993-2000; adv. World Tourism Orgn. Internat. Tourism Edn. and Tng. Ctr., 1991-2000; external examiner sch. accountancy and bus. Nanyang Tech. U., Singapore, 1996-98; bd. dirs. ProjectonNet.com; bus. advisor Che Che NY, 2004—, Grand Cafe, Honolulu, 2004—. Author: Resort Devel. and Mgmt., 1988, 2d edit., The Story of PATA, 2d edit., co-editor, 2001; co-author: The Travel Industry, 1988, 3d edit., 1997, Profl. Travel Agency Mgmt., 1990, Internat. Hotels: Devel. and Mgmt., 1994; editor: Internat. Tourism: A Global Perspective, 1997; founding dir., Hong Kong, China, Hawaii Chamber of Commerce, 1998-; mem. adv. bd. Asian Hotelier mag., 1997-99, Get2Hawaii.com, 2001-04. Bd. dirs. Hawaii Visitors Bur., 1993-95, Kaukini Med. Ctr., Honolulu, 1986-95, 96-2005; mem. Travel and Tourism Adv. Bd., U.S. Dept. Commerce, Washington, 1982-90, Pacific Rim Found., Honolulu, 1987-93, vice-chmn. Tourism Policy Adv. Coun., Dept. Bus. and Econ. Devel., Honolulu, 1978-92; chmn. Kuakini Geriat. Care, Inc., bd. dirs., 1992-95; trustee Pata Found., 1984-95, Kuakini Health System, 1988-2003, 05—, fin. com., 2007-; mem. exec. com. Kuakini Med. Ctr., 2006—; consulting com. Beijing Inst. Tourism, 1992—; v.p. Hawaii Vision 2020, 1992-93; mem. Mayor's Task Force on Waikiki Master Plan, 1992-93; devel. bd. Miss Hawaii Scholarship Pageant, 1993—; workforce devel. coun. Hawaii Dept. of Labor and Indsl. Rels., 1996-98; bd. dirs., Cmty. Enterprises, Hawaii Dept. Edn., 1997—, Hong Kong Hawaii C. of C., 1999—; mem. Mayor's Adv. Com. on Oahu Strategic Tourism Plan, 2005-07. Served with U.S. Army, 1953-55. Named State Mgr. of Yr., Office of Gov., State of Hawaii, 1995; named one of 100 Who Made a Difference in Hawaii during 20th Century, Star Bull., 1999; recipient NOAH award, Acad. Tourism Orgns., 1987, Gov.'s Proclamation honors, Office of Gov., State of Hawaii, 1998, 1999, 2003, Dean Chuck Yim Gee Excellence in Creative Film Achievements award, China-Hawaii C. of C., 2004; grantee Chuck Yim Gee-Hawaii Scholarship Endowment established in his honor, Nat. Tourism Found., 2001; Chuck Yim Gee Tech. Learning Ctr. at U. Hawaii named in his honor, Travel Industry Mgmt. Internat., Inc. U. Hawaii Found., 2003. Mem. Acad. for Study of Tourism (emeritus), Pacific Asia Travel Assn. (hon. life Hawaii chpt., bd. dirs. 1993-96, chmn. industry coun. 1994-96, 50th Anniversary Hall of Honors, 2001, Grand award 1991, Life award 1990, Presdl. award 1986), Travel Industry Am. (Travel Industry Hall of Leaders award 1988), China Tourism Assn. (award of excellence 1992), China-Hawaii C. of C. (founding dir. 1998), Hong Kong-China-Hawaii C. of C. (bd. dirs. 1999—), Golden Key. Office: U Hawaii Sch Travel Industry Mgmt 2560 Campus Rd Honolulu HI 96822-2217 Home Phone: 808-524-5510. Business E-Mail: cgee@hawaii.edu.

GEE, DAVID E., academic administrator; BS, Muskingum Coll., 1966; MA, U. Bridgeport, 1974, Columbia U., 1969, EdD, 1988. Supt. Queensbury (N.Y.) Union Free Sch. Dist., Western Suffolk Bd. Coop. Ednl. Svcs., Dix Hills, NY, 1998—2004; asst. prof. ednl. leadership SUNY, New Paltz, NY, 2004—. Exec. com. liaison Leadership Adv. Com., Suburban Schs. Adv. Com.; mem. Am. Assn. Sch. Adminstrs./N.Y. State Resolutions Com. Mem.: N.Y. State Coun. Sch. Supts. (pres. 1999—2000), Am. Assn. Sch. Adminstrs. (pres. 2005—06, presenter, presider nat. confs., chair fin. com., mem. governance com., mem. new bldg. com., past chair suburban schs. adv. com., mem. exec. dir.'s nat. adv coun., mem. blue ribbon evaluation task force, mem. women administrators adv. com., leadership adv. com.). Office: Dept Ednl Adminstrn SUNY New Paltz Old Main Bldg 101B 1 Hawk Dr New Paltz NY 12561-2443 Office Phone: 703-528-0700, 845-257-2813. Office Fax: 703-841-1543. E-mail: geed@newpaltz.edu.*

GEE, ELWOOD GORDON, academic administrator; b. Vernal, Utah, Feb. 2, 1944; s. Elwood A. and Vera (Showalter) Gee; m. Elizabeth Dutson, Aug. 26, 1968 (dec. Dec. 1991); 1 child, Rebekah; m. Constance Bumgarner, Nov. 26, 1994. BA, U. Utah, 1968; JD, Columbia U., 1971, EdD, 1972. Asst. dean U. Utah Coll. Law, Salt Lake City, 1973—74; sr. staff asst., jud. fellow US Supreme Ct., Washington, 1974—75; prof. law, assoc. dean Brigham Young U. Law Sch., Provo, Utah, 1975—79; prof. law, dean W.Va. U. Coll. Law, Morgantown, 1979—81; pres. W.Va. U., Morgantown, 1981—85, U. Colo., Boulder, 1985—90, Ohio State U., Columbus, 1990—97, 2007—, Brown U., Providence, 1998—2000; chancellor Vanderbilt U., Nashville, 2000—07. Bd. dirs. Nabisco, Inc., Hasbro, The Limited, Dollar Gen. Corp., Massey Energy Corp., Gaylord Entertainment Co., Jason Found., Nat. Hospice Found., Kresge Found.; mem. Pres. Coun. for Imagining Am., Christopher Isherwood Found., Bus.-Higher Edn. Forum. Author: Education Law and Public Schools, 1975, Law and Public Education, 1980, Violence, Values and Justice in American Education, 1982, Fair Employment Practice, 1982. Recipient Good Guy award, Nashville Women's Polit. Caucus, 2004; fellow, W.K. Kellogg, 1971—72, Mellon fellow, 1977—78. Mem.: ABA, Adminstrv. Conf. U.S., Phi Kappa Phi, Phi Delta Kappa. Mem. Lds Ch. Office: Ohio State U Enarson Hall 154 W 12th Ave Columbus OH 43210*

GEE, GAVIN M., state agency administrator; b. Idaho; m. Libby Gee; 4 children. BA in Polit. Sci., Brigham Young U.; JD. U. Idaho Coll. Law. Securities examiner Idaho Dept. Fin., Boise, 1977—78, dep. atty. gen., 1978—81, securities bur. chief, 1981—86, fin. instns. bur. chief, 1986—95, acting dir., 1995—96, dir., 1996—. Vice chmn. Idaho Endowment Fund Investment Bd. Youth sports coach; numerous leadership positions Boy Scouts of Am., Ch. Mem.: Nat. Assn. State Credit Union Suprs. (bd. dirs. 1991—95, chmn. 1993—94, Pierre Jay award 2000), Conf. State Bank Suprs. (bd. dirs., chmn. 2002—03), Idaho State Bar Assn. (mem. corp. and securities law sect.), Fed. Fin. Instns. Exam. Coun. (chmn., mem. state liaison com. 1994—99). Avocations: mountain biking, white-water rafting, snow and water skiing, hiking, tennis. Office: Idaho Dept Fin PO Box 83720 Boise ID 83720-0031 Office Phone: 208-332-8010. E-mail: ggee@finance.idaho.gov.

GEE, ROBERT NEIL, law librarian; b. Miami, Okla., June 22, 1956; s. Robert Sanford and Nancy Ann (Neil) G. AA, Tulsa Jr. Coll., Okla., 1976; BA, U. Okla., Norman, 1978, JD, 1981; LLM, George Washington U., Washington, 1984. Bar: Okla. 1981, U.S. Suprem Ct. 1986, D.C. 1989. Legal reference specialist Library of Congress, Washington, 1984—94; asst. dir. law libr. svc., chief pub. svcs. Law Libr. of Congress, Washington, 1994. Mem. ABA (recipient Silver Key cert. 1981), Fed. Bar Assn., Am. Assn. Law Librs., Okla. Bar Assn., Am. Judicature Soc., D.C. Bar Assn., Phi Delta Phi. Avocations: reading, travel, current events.

GEEKER, NICHOLAS PETER, lawyer, judge; b. Pensacola, Fla., Dec. 15, 1944; BA in English, La. Poly. Inst., 1966; JD, Fla. State U., 1969. Bar: Fla. 1969, U.S. Dist. Ct. 1970, US. Supreme Ct., 1980. Assoc. firm Merritt & Jackson, Pensacola, 1969; law clk. U.S. Dist. Judge D.L. Middlebrooks, Tallahassee, 1970-73; asst. state atty. Fla. 1st Jud. Circuit, 1973; asst. U.S. atty. No. Dist. Fla., 1973-76, U.S. atty., 1976-82; sole practice Pensacola, Fla., 1982-85; circuit judge Fla. 1st Jud. Circuit, 1985—. Mem. Fed.-State Joint Com. on Law Enforcement. Mem. Fla. Bar Assn., Fla. Trial Lawyers Assn. (editor Newsletter 1975), Phi Delta Phi. Office: 190 Government St Pensacola FL 32501-5773 Office Phone: 850-595-4439.

GEELAN, JOHN, lawyer; BA, U. Notre Dame, 1986; JD cum laude, Am. U., 1990. Bar: NY 1991. Law clerk to Hon. A. Andrew Hauk US Dist. Ct., Ctrl. Dist. Calif., 1990—91; ptnr. Employment & Labor Law Group Kaye Scholer LLP, NYC. Recipient Thurgood Marshall Award. Mem.: Assn. Bar of City NY. Office: Kaye Scholer LLP 425 Park Ave New York NY 10022 Office Phone: 212-836-8121. E-mail: jgeelan@kayescholer.com.

GEEM, ZONG WOO, engineer; b. Seoul, Republic of Korea, May 21, 1968; s. Won Bae Geem and Whi Won Oh; m. Jeong-Yoon Choi; children: Sophia Seulgee, Michelle Misol. B of Engring., Chung Ang U., Seoul; PhD, Korea U., Seoul. Vis. scholar Va. Tech, Blacksburg, Va.; faculty rschr. U. Md., College Park, Md.; cons. WESTAT, Rockville, Md. Reviewer Engring. Optimization, Lecture Notes in Computer Sci., Jour. of Spatial Hydrology, Jour. Energy Engring.; mem. program com. Indian Internat. Conf. Artificial Intelligence, 2007. Author: Lecture Notes in Computer Science, 2005, Lecture Notes in Artificial Intelligence, 2006, Springer's Soft Computing Applications in Industry; contbr. articles to profl. jours. Dir. choir Epiphany Cath. Ch., Georgetown, DC. Mem.: ASCE, Am. Water Works Assn. Roman Catholic. Achievements include invention of harmony search algorithm meta-heuristic algorithm. Home: 729 Fallsgrove Drive 6133 Rockville MD 20850 Personal E-mail: zwgeem@gmail.com.

GEER, RONALD LAMAR, mechanical engineer, consultant, retired oil industry executive; b. West Palm Beach, Fla., Sept. 2, 1926; s. Marion Wood and Bertha (Lightfoot) G.; m. Geneva Yvonne Chappell, Dec. 24, 1951; children— Ronald Lamar, Mark Randall. B.M.E., Ga. Inst. Tech., 1951. With Shell Oil Co., 1951—, sr. staff mech. engr., head office Houston, 1969-71, cons. mech. engr., 1971-86. Mem. various govt., univ. adv. coms. Contbr. articles on petroleum drilling and prodn. to profl. jours.; patentee petroleum drilling and prodn. equipment; mem. Shell Oil Co. team recognized in Offshore Tech. Conf. Disting. Achievement award to co., 1971, for individuals, 1984. Recipient Robert Earll McConnell award Am. Inst. Mech. Engrs., 1995; named to Offshore Energy Ctr. Pioneer Engring Tech. Hall of Fame, 1999, Offshore Energy Ctr. Industry Pioneer Hall of Fame, 2002. Mem. Nat. Acad. Engring., NRC (marine bd.), Nat. Security Indsl. Assn. (petroleum panel, research and engring. adv. com.), ASME (hon.), Marine Tech. Soc., Am. Petroleum Inst., Model-A Ford Club Am., Classic T-Bird Club Internat., Thistle Class Assn., Pi Tau Sigma. Republican. Home (Summer): 430 Covered Bridge Ln # 135 Sky Valley GA 30537-2593 Home (Winter): 14723 Oak Bend Dr Houston TX 77079

GEESEMAN, ROBERT GEORGE, lawyer; b. Shreveport, La., Oct. 23, 1944; s. George Robert and Cora (Hamilton) Glasgow; m. Rosemary Monahan, Aug. 19, 1967; 1 child, Regan Glasgow. BA, Yale U., 1966; JD, U. Mich., 1969. Bar: Pa. 1969, U.S. Dist. Ct. (we. dist.) Pa. 1969, U.S. Supreme Ct. 1973, U.S. Tax Ct. 1979. Assoc. Blaxter, O'Neill, Houston & Nash, Pitts., 1969-75; ptnr. Lynch, Lynch, Carr & Kabala, Pitts., 1975-81, Lynch, Kabala & Geeseman, Pitts., 1981, Kabala & Geeseman, Pitts., 1981—2002; spl. counsel Fox, Rothschild, L.L.P., Pitts., 2002—. Lectr. tax law and employee benefits. Mem.: ABA (mem. closely held bus. com. sect. taxation, bd. editors Withdrawal Retirement and Disputes, bd. editors What You and Your Firm Should Know), Pitts. Inst. Legal Medicine, Allegheny County Bar Assn., Pa. Bar Assn., John's Island Country (Vero Beach, Fla.), Rivers Club, Mory's Club (New Haven), Phi Delta Phi. Address: Fox Rothschild LLP 625 Liberty Ave Fl 29 Pittsburgh PA 15222-3110 Office Phone: 412-391-1334.

GEFFE, PHILIP REINHOLD, electrical engineer, consultant; b. Napa, Calif., Oct. 22, 1920; s. Eugene Carl and Mary Rebecca (Woliston) G.; m. Barbara Ann Wean; children: Bethann, Philip, Timur. Student, Calif. Inst. Tech., 1947-49. Chief filter engr. Triad Transformer Corp., Venice, Calif., 1952-56; dir. engring. Hycor, Inc., Sylmar, Calif., 1957-60; sr. staff engr. Axel Electronics Inc., Jamaica, NY, 1962-65; fellow engr. Westinghouse Electric Corp., Balt., 1965-74; staff engr. Lynch Communication Systems, Inc., Reno, 1974-80, Scientific-Atlanta, Inc., Atlanta, 1980-85, K&L Microwave, Inc., Salisbury, Md., 1985-87; ind. cons., 1988—; sr. engr. PULSE divsn. Technitrol, San Diego, 1997—; ret., 2003. Cons. in field, 2001—02. Author: Simplified Modern Filter Design, 1963; contbr. articles to profl. jours.; patentee in field. Master U.S. Chess Fedn. New Windsor, N.Y., 1968 Fellow IEEE; mem. AAAS Address: 28789 Calle De La Paz Murrieta CA 92563-5790 Office Phone: 951-677-2588. E-mail: p_geffe@yahoo.com.

GEFFEN, DAVID LAWRENCE, film company and former recording company executive; b. Bklyn., Feb. 21, 1943; s. Abraham and Batya (Volovskaya) Geffen. Student, U. Tex., 1961—63, Bklyn. Coll. With William Morris Agy., NYC, 1964—68, Ashley Famous Agy., 1968; exec. v.p., agt. Creative Mgmt. Assocs., 1969; founder (with Laura Nyro) and pres. Tuna Fish Pub. Co.; pres. Geffen-Roberts, Inc., 1970—71, Asylum Records, 1970—73, Elektra-Asylum Records, 1973—76; vice-chmn. & chief asst. to chmn. Warner Bros. Pictures, 1974—75; founder, pres., chmn. Geffen Records & Geffen Film Co., LA, 1980—89; founder, pres. David Geffen Co., 1990—95; co-founder (with Jeffrey Katzenberg & Steven Spielberg) DreamWorks SKG, Universal City, Calif., 1994—, chmn., 1994—2006, co-chmn. Glendale, Calif., 2006—. Mem. faculty Yale U., 1978; apptd. Regent U. Calif., Govt. Calif., 1980—87; bd. councilors USC Sch. Cinema-TV. Prodr.: (films) Personal Best, 1982, Risky Business, 1983, After Hours, 1985, Lost in America, 1985, Little Shop of Horrors, 1986, Beetlejuice, 1988, Men Don't Leave, 1990, Interview with the Vampire, 1994; co-prodr.: (plays) Master Harold.and the Boys, 1982, Cats, 1982, Good, 1982, Dreamgirls, 1983, Social Security, 1986, Madam Butterfly, 1988 (9 Tony awards including best play); (films) Dreamgirls, 2006, (musical) Miss Saigon. Bds. dirs. Los Angeles County Art Mus. Named one of Forbes' Richest Americans, 1999—, World's Richest People, Forbes mag., 2001—, Top 200 Collectors, ARTnews Mag., 2004, 2006, 50 Most Powerful People in Hollywood, Premiere mag., 2005—06. Democrat. Avocation: Collector of Modern and Contemporary Art, especially Abstract Expressionism. Office: DreamWorks SKG 1000 Flower St Glendale CA 91201*

GEFFNER, DONNA SUE, speech pathology/audiology services professional, audiologist, educator; d. Louis and Sally (Weiner) Geffner. BA magna cum laude, Bklyn. Coll., 1967; MA, NYU, 1968, PhD (NDEA fellow), 1970; postgrad., Advanced Inst. Analytic Psychology, 1973—75; EdD (hon.), Providence Coll., 2003. Asst. prof. Lehman Coll., 1971-76; assoc. prof. dept. speech St. John's U., 1976-81, prof., 1982—. Dir. Speech and Hearing Ctr., 1976—, chmn. dept. speech comm. scis. and theater, 1983—92, developer M.A. program in speech pathology and audiology, 1984, developer Au.D audiology and doctoral consortia, 2004, dir. grad. program in speech-lang. pathology and audiology, 1992—; pvt. practice, 1980—; cons. to corp. execs.; TV prodr. and hostess NBC, 1977—78, CBS, 1978—79; mem. N.Y. State Licensure Bd., 1993—97. Issue editor: Jour. Topics Lang. Disorders, 1980; editor: ASHA monograph, 1987, Auditory Processing Disorders, 2007—; author: What Professionals Need to Know About Attention Deficit Hyperactivity Disorder, 2005, The Listening Inventory, 2005; contbr. articles to profl. jours., chapters to books. Recipient Emmy nomination for outstanding instrnl. program, 1978, award, Pres.'s Com. Employment Handicapped, Disting. Achievement award, N.Y.C. Speech-Lang.-Hearing Assn., 1994, Honors, L.I. Speech-Lang.-Hearing Assn., 1998; grantee, CUNY Rsch. Found., 1972, N.Y. State Dept. Edn., 1976—78. Fellow: Am. Speech, Lang. and Hearing Assn. (legis. councillor 1978—87, 1988—90, 1990—94, v.p. acad. affairs 1995—97, pres.-elect 1998, pres. 1999, past pres. 2000, ednl. standards bd. 1992—94); mem.: Coll. Bd. Com. on Literacy, Am. Guidance Svc. (mem. bd. advisors), Audiology Study Group N.Y., N.Y. State Speech and Hearing Assn. (pres. 1978—80, honors). Office: St John's U Speech and Hearing Ctr 8000 Utopia Pkwy Jamaica NY 11432-1343 Business E-Mail: geffnerd@stjohns.edu.

GEFKE, HENRY JEROME, lawyer; b. Milw., Aug. 4, 1930; s. Jerome Henry and Frances (Daley) G.; m. Caroline Ann Lawrence, June 25, 1955 (div. Jan. 1968); children: Brian Lawrence, David Jerome; m. Mary Clare Nuss, Aug. 28, 1976; children: Lynn Marie, James Scott. BS, Marquette U., 1952, LLB, 1954; postgrad., Ohio State U., 1955—56. Bar: Wis. 1954, Tax Ct. U.S 1969; C.P.A., Wis. Acct.-auditor John G. Conley & Co. (C.P.A.s), Milw., 1956-59; with J.I. Case Co., Racine, Wis., 1959-68, corp. sec., asst. gen. counsel, 1965-68; assoc. Maier & Mulcahy, S.C., Milw., 1968-69; prin. Mulcahy, Gefke & Wherry, S.C., Milw., 1969-73; individual practice law Milw., 1973—. Corp. officer, dir. various bus. corps. Pres., bd. dirs. Big Bros., Greater Racine, 1965-67; trustee Racine County Instns., 1960-63; bd. dirs., sec., legal counsel Racine Transitional Care, Inc., 1973-76; bd. dirs., legal counsel Our Home Found., Milw., 1979-82; bd. dirs. Racine County Mental Health Assn., 1963-67, Alliance for Mentally Ill Milw. County, 1986-88; bd. dirs., sec., legal counsel Glendale Econ. Devel. Corp., 1996—; bd. dirs. Glendale Bus. Coun., 1996-97; bd. dirs. Glendale C. of C., Inc., 1997—, treas., 1998-00, pres. 2000-02. Mem. Wis. Bar Assn., Milw. Bar Assn., Wis. Inst. CPA's, Delta Sigma Pi, Delta Theta Phi. Home and Office: 5521 N Lydell Ave Milwaukee WI 53217-5042 Home Phone: 414-964-1477; Office Phone: 414-332-1200. E-mail: hjgjdcpa@aol.com.

GEH, HANS-PETER, retired library director, consultant; b. Frankfurt am Main, Germany, Feb. 11, 1934; s. Peter and Maria Geh; m. Roswitha Dieterich, Aug. 31, 1968. MA, U. Bristol, Eng., 1963; PhD, U. Frankfurt am Main, 1963. Subject specialist City and Univ. Libr., Frankfurt am Main, 1962—69; dir. Libr. Sch., Frankfurt am Main, 1967—69, Stuttgart, Germany, 1970—80, Württemberg State Libr., Stuttgart, 1970—97, prof., 2003—. Hon. prof.; cons. UNESCO, 1971—; chmn. libr. assns. and lit. socs., Germany, 1965—. Author: Insular Policy in England before the Tudors, 1964; co-editor jours., 1965—; also articles. Trustee Bibliotheca Alexandrina, Egypt. Decorated Order of Merit (Germany). Mem. Internat. Fedn. Libr. Assns. and Instns. (pres. 1985-91); European Found. for Libr. Coop. (pres. 1991-95); hon. mem. numerous internat. libr. assns. Avocation: travel. Home: Hebbergstrasse 76/1 70794 Filderstadt Germany Office: Württemberg State Libr Konrad-Adenauer-Strasse 8 70049 Stuttgart Germany Personal E-mail: gehhp@t-online.de.

GEHA, ALEXANDER SALIM, cardiothoracic surgeon, educator; b. Beirut, June 18, 1936; arrived in US, 1963; s. Salim M. and Alice I. (Hayek) G.; m. Diane L. Redalen, Nov. 25, 1967; children— Samia, Rula, Nada BS in Biology, Am. U. Beirut, 1955, MD, 1959; MS in Surgery and Physiology, U. Minn.-Rochester, 1967; MS (privatum), Yale U., 1978. Asst. prof. U. Vt., Burlington, 1967-69; asst. prof. Washington U., St. Louis, 1969-73, assoc. prof., 1973-75, Yale U., New Haven, 1975-78, prof., chief cardiothoracic surgery, 1978-86, Case Western Res. U. and Univ. Hosp. of Cleve., 1986-98; Jay L. Ankeney prof. cardiothoracic surgery Case Western Res. U., 1994-98; pres. Univ. Cardiothoracic Surgeons, Inc., Cleve., 1986—2000; prof., chief cardiothoracic surgery U. Ill. Med. Ctr., Chgo., 1998—2007, prof. emeritus cardiothoracic surgery, 2007—; chief cardiothoracic surgery Mt. Sinai Hosp. Med. Ctr., Chgo., 2000—07. Cons. VA Hosp., West Haven, Conn., 1975-86, VA Hosp., Cleve., 1986-98, Westside VA Hosp., Chgo., 1998—, Cleve. Met. Health Med. Ctr., 1986-98, Mt. Sinai Med. Ctr., Cleve., 1990-98, Waterbury Hosp., 1976-86, Sharon Hosp., 1981-86, Michael Reese Hosp., 2002—; mem. study sect. Nat. Heart Lung and Blood Inst., 1981-85. Editor: Glenn's Thoracic and Cardio-vascular Surgery, 4th edit. 1983, 5th edit. 1991, 6th edit. 1996; editor Basic Surgery, 1984. Bd. dirs. New Haven Heart Assn., 1981-85; trustee Am. U. Beirut. Mem. AMA, Assn. Clin. Cardiac Surgery (chmn. membership com. 1978-80, sec.-treas. 1980-83, pres. 1988), Am. Heart Assn. (bd. dirs. 1981-85. councils on basic sci., cardiovascular surgery), Am. Coll. Chest Physicians (steering com. 1980-84), Am. Assn. Thoracic Surgery, Am. Coll. Cardiology, ACS (chmn. coordinating com. on edn. in thoracic surgery, chmn. 1992-95), Am. Lung Assn., Am. Physiol. Soc., Am. Surg. Assn., Assn. Acad. Surgery, Central Surg. Assn., Chgo. Inst. Medicine, European Assn. Cardiothoracic Surgery, Internat. Soc. Heart and Lung Transplantation, Internat. Soc. Cardiovascular Surgery, Lebanese Order Physicians, New Eng. Surg. Soc., Pan Am. Med. Assn., Halsted Soc., Soc. Thoracic Surgeons (govt. rels. com., manpower com., program com., edn. and resources com.), Soc. for Vascular Surgery, Soc. Univ. Surgeons, Chgo. Surg. Soc., also others. E-mail: ageha@uic.edu.

GEHAN, MARK WILLIAM, lawyer; b. St. Paul, Dec. 19, 1946; s. Mark William and Jean Elizabeth (McGee) G.; m. Lucy Lyman Harrison, Aug. 25, 1971; children: Mark Harrison, Alice McGee. BA, U. Notre Dame, 1968; JD, U. Minn., 1971. Bar: Minn., 1972; U.S. Supreme Ct., 1989. Asst. county atty. Ramsey County Atty.'s Office, St. Paul, 1972-76; prosecutor, Met. Area Dist. Urban County Attys. Bd., St. Paul, 1976-77; ptnr. Collins Buckley Sauntry & Haugh, St. Paul, 1978—. Bd. dirs. Minn. State Bd. Pub. Def., St. Paul, 1982-90. Pres. St. Paul Charter Commn., 1986-94. Mem. Minn. Bar Assn. (pres. 1998-99), Ramsey County Bar Assn. (pres. 1990-91). Avocations: scuba diving, tennis, guitar. Office: Collins Buckley Sauntry & Haugh First Nat Bank Bldg 332 Minnesota St Ste W1100 Saint Paul MN 55101-1379 Office Phone: 651-227-0611. E-mail: mgehan@cbsh.net.

GEHL, WILLIAM D., manufacturing executive; b. 1947; Bar: Wis., Fla. With The Ziegler Co., Inc., West Bend, Wis., 1978-92, sr. v.p., gen. counsel, 1985-92, exec. v.p., COO, gen. counsel, sec., 1990-92, also bd.

dirs.; dir. Gehl Co., 1987—, chmn. nominating com., mem. compensation and benefits com., pres., CEO, 1992—, also chmn. bd. dirs. Office: Gehl Co PO Box 179 143 Water St West Bend WI 53095-3400

GEHM, AMY K., lawyer; married; 2 children. JD cum laude, South Tex. Coll. Law, Houston, 1992. Cert.: Tex. Bd. Legal Specialization (family law) 2002. With Office of the Atty. Gen., Tex. Dept. Ins.; atty. Law Office of Jennifer Tull; prin. atty. Law Office of Amy K. Gehm, L.L.C., Austin, Tex. Named a Rising Star, Tex. Super Lawyers mag., 2006. Mem.: Collaborative Law Inst. Tex. Office: Law Office of Amy K Gehm LLC The Canyon at Wild Basin 115 Wild Basin Rd Ste 106 Austin TX 78746 Office Phone: 512-327-7272. E-mail: amy@amygehm.com.*

GEHRELS, NEIL (CORNELIUS A. GEHRELS), astrophysicist; b. Lake Geneva, Wis., Oct. 3, 1952; s. Tom and Aleida (de Stoppelaar) Gehrels; m. Ellen D. Williams, Apr. 5, 1980; children: Thomas W., Emily W. MusB, U. Ariz., 1976, BS with honors in Physics, 1976; PhD in Physics, Calif. Inst. Tech., Pasadena, 1982. Rsch. asst. Calif. Inst. Tech., 1976-81; rsch. assoc. NASA/Goddard Space Flight Ctr., Greenbelt, Md., 1981-83, astrophysicist, 1983—, head gamma ray and cosmic ray astrophysics br., 1995—, chief astroparticle physics lab. Project scientist Compton Gamma Ray Obs., 1991—2000; adj. prof. astronomy U. Md.; adj. prof. astronomy and astrophysics Pa. State U. Contbr. articles to sci. jours. Recipient Discover Mag. award for Technol. Innovation, 1992, NASA Outstanding Leadership medal, 1993, Randolph Lovelace award, Am. Astron. Soc., 2000, Goddard Lindsay award, 2005. Fellow: Am. Phys. Soc.; mem.: Am. Astron. Soc. (chair high energy astrophysics divsn. 1996, Bruno Rossi prize 2007). Avocation: music. Home: 8616 57th Ave Berwyn Heights MD 20740-4331 Office: Astrophysics Sci Divsn NASA/Goddard Space Flight Ctr Code 661 Astroparticle Physics Lab Greenbelt MD 20771-0001 E-mail: gehrels@milkyway.gsfc.nasa.gov.*

GEHRES, JAMES, retired lawyer; b. Akron, Ohio, July 19, 1932; s. Edwin Jacob and Cleora Mary (Yoakam) G.; m. Eleanor Agnew Mount, July 23, 1960. BS in Acctg., U. Utah, 1954; MBA, U. Calif.-Berkeley, 1959; JD, U. Denver, 1970, LLM in Taxation, 1977. Bar: Colo. 1970, U.S. Dist. Ct. Colo. 1970, U.S. Tax Ct. 1970, U.S. Supreme Ct. 1973, U.S. Ct. Appeals (10th cir.) 1978, U.S. Ct. Claims 1992. Atty. IRS, Denver, 1965-80, atty. chief counsel;s office, 1980—2002; ret., 2002. Contbr. articles to profl. jours. Treas., dir. Colo. Fourteeners Initiative. With USAF, 1955-58, capt. Res. ret. Mem. ABA, Colo. Bar Assn., AICPA, Colo. Soc. CPAs, Am. Assn. Atty.-CPAs, Am. Judicature Soc., Order of St. Ives, The Explorers Club, Am. Alpine Club, Colo. Mountain Club, Colo. Mountain Club Found. (bd. dirs., pres.), Beta Gamma Sigma, Beta Alpha Psi. Democrat. Office: 935 Pennsylvania St Denver CO 80203-3145 Business E-Mail: jimgehres@yahoo.com.

GEHRICH, LEONORA SUPPAN, artist, musician, German literature educator; arrived in US, 1963; d. Josef Cornelius and Josefine Maria Suppan; m. Heinz-Guenter Gehrich; children: Alan, Brian, Colleen. Diploma, Acad. Music, Vienna, 1958; MusM, Ind. U., 1965; PhD, Quincy U., 1988. Cert. performer Ind. U., 1965. Asst. prof. Western Ill. U., Macomb, 1965—68; artist-in residence Culver-Stockton Coll., Canton, Miss., 1968—75, Quincy U., 1977—2005. Musician, pianist (concerts), Austria, Germany, France, Italy, Poland, Hungary, Eng., Portugal, Can., Costa Rica, Mex., Holland, Czech Republic. Recipient City of Quincy Arts award, 1995. Mem.: Am. Coll. Musicians, Muddy River Opera (mem. bd. 2003), Hist. Soc. Avocations: sailing, tennis, swimming. Office: Quincy U 1800 College Ave Quincy IL 62301 Office Phone: 217-228-5460. Office Fax: 217-885-3024. Business E-Mail: ggehrich@msn.com.

GEHRIG, EDWARD HARRY, electrical engineer, consultant; b. Portland, Oreg., Oct. 31, 1925; s. Henry Oscar and Selma Victoria (Charf) G.; m. May 20, 1950; children: Cynth Ann, Nanette Lou, Timothy Alexander. BA in Physics, Reed Coll., 1948; BSEE, Stanford U., 1949; MSEE, Oreg. State U., 1951. Registered profl. engr., Oreg. Physicist AEC, 1950-52; head system planning Bonneville Power Adminstrn., Portland, 1963-72, chief transmission design, 1972-76, chief R & D, 1976-81; ind. cons. Lake Oswego, Oreg., 1982—. Participant Electric Power Rsch. Inst. and GE Project UHV; designer, distbr. for Lindal Cedar Homes, Seattle, 1987—. Patentee in field; contbr. articles to profl. jours. Chmn. Lake Grove Zoning Bd., Lake Oswego, Oreg., 1962-64; elder First Presbyn. Ch., Portland; coach basketball, soccer, Lake Grove. Sgt. U.S. Army, 1944-46, ETO. Recipient Meritorious Svc. award Dept. of Interior, 1979. Fellow IEEE. Democrat. Avocations: woodcraft, golf. Home: PO Box 2062 Lake Oswego OR 97035 Office Phone: 541-996-6895.

GEHRIG, LEO JOSEPH, retired surgeon; b. Mapleton, Minn., Apr. 25, 1918; s. Paul P. and Marcella (Hund) G.; m. Marillyn May Nelson, June 10, 1944; children: Gregory Paul, Mark Nelson. BS, U. Minn., 1942, MB, 1944, MD, 1945. Diplomate Am. Bd. Surgery, Am. Bd. Thoracic Surgery. Intern Salt Lake County Gen. Hosp., Salt Lake City, 1944—45; resident New Eng. Deaconness Hosp., Boston, 1947—50; with USPHS, 1945—70, advanced through grades to rear adm., ret., 1970, chief chest surgery unit SI, NY, 1950—52, resident, 1952—55, chief thoracic surgery Seattle, 1955—57, asst. chief divsn. hosps. Washington, 1957—59, dep. chief, 1959—60, program officer bur. med. svcs. Washington, 1960—61; med. dir. Peace Corps, Washington, 1961—62; asst. surgeon gen., dep. chief Bur. Med. Svcs., 1962—64, chief bur., 1964—65, dep. surgeon gen., 1965—68; dir. office internat. health HEW, 1968—70; assoc. dir. Washington svc. bur. Am. Hosp. Assn., 1970—72, v.p., 1972—75, sr. v.p., dir. Washington office, 1978—80. Dir. rsch. Health Rsch. Edn. Trust, 1985—89. Bd. dirs. St. Lukes Inst., Silver Spring, Md., 1988—2002. Recipient U.S. Disting. Svc. medal. Fellow ACS, Am. Coll. Thoracic Surgery; mem. AMA, APHA, Am. Heart Assn., Assn. Mil. Surgeons, USPHS Clin. Soc., Mil. Officer Assn. Am. (bd. dirs. Alexandria, Va. 1990-97), Alpha Omega Alpha. Home: 4535 Alton Pl NW Washington DC 20016-2023 Personal E-mail: ljgehrig@msn.com.

GEHRIG, MICHAEL FORD, lawyer; b. Cin., Jan. 25, 1947; s. John Richard and Mary Bonita (Ford) G.; m. Barbara Jane Rigg, June 16, 1973; children: Michael Ford, Caroline Cristina, Angela Victoria. BA, Ohio State U., 1970; JD, Chase Coll. Law, Cin., 1974. Bar: Ohio 1974, U.S. Dist. Ct. (so. dist.) Ohio 1974, U.S. Dist. Ct. (ea. dist.) Ky. 1983, U.S. Supreme Ct., 1985. Assoc. Beall, Hermanies & Bortz, Cin., 1974-76; mem. firm Gehrig & Gehrig, Cin., 1976-79, Gehrig, Parker & Baldwin, Cin., 1979-88, Fingerman, Guckenberger & Gehrig, 1988-96, Gehrig, Gelwicks & Eynon, 1996—; lectr. various legal seminars. Contbr. articles to jours., chpts. to books. Recipient book awards Chase Coll. Law, 1971, 73, 74. Mem. ABA, Ohio State Bar Assn., Cin. Bar Assn., Assn. Trial Lawyers Am. (sustaining), Am. Bd. Trial Advocates, Ohio Acad. Trial Lawyers (sustaining), Cin. Hist. Soc., English Speaking Union, Cin. Athletic Club, Univ. Club, Hyde Park Golf & Country Club, Phi Gamma Delta. Episcopalian. Office: 1140 Bartlett Bldg 36 E 4th St Ste 1140 Cincinnati OH 45202-3809

GEHRING, DAVID AUSTIN, cardiologist, physician, health facility administrator; b. Bryn Mawr, Pa., Dec. 6, 1930; s. Harry Rittenhouse and Anne Gardiner (Bozarth) G.; m. Joan Helen Lotz, June 7, 1953 (div. Aug. 1982); children: David, Paul, Peter, Sue, Barbara, Eric; m. Victoria Marie Damiano, Sept. 2, 1982 (dec. May 2000); children: Theresa, Judy Lynne, Michael Austin; m. Rose Y. Barron, May 5, 2001. BA magna cum laude, U. Pitts., 1952, MD, 1956; grad., Naples Sch. Real Estate, 2000. Diplomate Am. Bd. Internal Medicine; cert. geriatric medicine. Commd. USN, 1956, advanced through grades to lt. comdr., intern, then resident in internal medicine U.S. Naval Hosp. Phila., 1956—60, mem. staff internal medicine U.S. Naval Hosp., 1960—61, chief internal medicine heart sta. U.S. Naval Hosp. Annapolis, Md., 1961—63, resigned, 1963; cardiologist K.G.E. Med. Group, Woodbury, NJ, 1963—82; cardiologist, pres. Hobbs Cardiology, P.A., N.Mex., 1982—86; med. dir. Polk Ctr., Pa., 1986—91; physician, chief grade VA Med. Ctr., Coatesville, Pa., 1991—97, assoc. chief of staff for ambulatory care, 1993—96, chief med. svc., 1995—96, chief primary care and chief of staff, 1995—96, chief of staff, 1995—96, cardiologist, 1996—97; assoc. med. dir. for correctional med. svcs. South Jersey, 1997—98; med. dir. site South Woodstate Prison, 1997—98; clin. dir. Del. Hosp. Chronically Ill, 1998—99; clin. dir. long term care pub. health divsn. State of Del., 1998—99; physician VA Clinic, Naples, Fla., 2002—. Clin. dir. Del. Hosp. for Cronically Ill, Smyrna, 1998—99; v.p. Regent Park Villas II Assoc., Inc., Naples, Fla., 1999—2000, pres., 2000—01; realtor VIP Lodge McKee Realtors, 2000—01, VIP Lodge McKee, 2000—01; sect. chief VA Med. Ctr., Salisbury, NC, 2001—02, occupl. health physician, 2002, mem. ethics com., 2001—02, mem. hosp. disaster com., 2002, chair small pox com., 02; testing cardiologist Anthropometrics United Med. Group, Cherry Hill, NJ, 1974—82; clin. asst. prof. medicine Temple U. Hosp., Phila., 1975—82; adj. asst. prof. medicine Jefferson Meml. Coll., 1981—82; chief cardiac rehab. unit Lea Regional Hosp., Hobbs, 1982—86; chief med. svcs. 829th Sta. Hosp., USAR, Lubbock, Tex., 1984—86; cons. cardiology, Oil City, Pa., 1986—91; staff Franklin (Pa.) Regional Med. Ctr., 1986—90, Oil City Area Health Ctr., 1986—91; teaching staff St. Joseph Hosp., Lancaster, Pa., 1991—97; clin. preceptor U. Pa. Sch. Nursing, 1993—96; cons. Southeastern Vets. Ctr., Spring City, Pa., 1997—98, Providence Med. Ctr., Media, 1997—98; others; assoc. med. dir. Correctional Med. Svcs. South Jersey, 1997—98; mem. adult protective svcs. coun. State of Del., 1998—99; mem. profl. devel. com. Naples Area Bd. Realtors, 2000—01, mem. complaint rev. com., 2000—01; chair pharmacy and therapeutics com. Dept. Health and Social Svcs., State of Del., 1998—99; mem. pharmacy and therapeutics com. for VISN 6 dept. Vet. Affairs, 2001—02; cons. in field. Author: EKG Workbook, 1972, EKG Workbook I, 1978; contbr. articles to profl. jours. Project dir. 23 Greater Del. Valley Reg. Med. Program, Pa., 1971—75; mem. ACLS Inst. and affiliated faculty Pa. Heart Assn., 1986—98, bd. dirs. N.W. chpt., 1988—90; bd. dirs. Inst. Christianna Hosp., Del., 1998—99; bd. dirs. adv. com., chmn. personnel com. med. health, rehab., drugs and alcohol Venango County, Franklin Parl, Pa., 1986—90, pres., 1988—89; mem. Health Care Adv. Com. to Congressman William F. Clinger, Jr., 23d Dist., 1989—91, Naples Mus. Art, 2000—; patron Philharmonic Ctr. for Arts, 1998—, Carolina Opera, 2001—03; lector St. Joseph Ch., Oil City, 1987—91, eucharistic min., 1990—92, Swedesboro, NJ, 1992—93, Sacred Heart Ch., Mt. Ephraim, 1994—99, lector, 1998—99. Lt. col. USAR, 1983—90. Recipient Outstanding Svc. award Am. Cancer Soc. NJ, 1967, Benjamin Berkowitz award NJ Heart Assn., 1975, Nat. Def. Svc. medal, 1975, USAR Components Achievement medal, 1988, Letter of Commendation USAR, 1988, 90, Pres.'s medal of Merit, Rep. Task Force, 1984, Letter of Commendation Sec. of Vets. Affairs, 1994; Cert. of Appreciation, Sec. of State N.Mex., 1982, Venango County Commrs., 1987, 88, 89, 90, Polk Ctr. award of Merit, 1991, Spl. Contbn. award and Mgr. of Yr. award VAMC Coatesville, 1996, Spl. Contbn. award VA Med. Ctr., Salisbury, NC, 2002. Fellow ACP (life, Recognition awards 1967-70), Am. Coll. Cardiology, Am. Coll. Chest Physicians, Coll. Physicians Phila., Am. Coll. Clin. Pharmacology; mem. AMA, Am. Geriat. Soc., St. Jude Soc., Holy Name Soc., Assn. Miraculous Medal (promoter 1987—), Venango County Med. Soc. (pres. 1989-91), Assn. Mil. Surgeons, Mil. Officers Assn. Am. (life), Am. Coll. Physician Execs., Mil. Officers Club Collier County Fla. (dir.), Am. Legion, Mil. Officers Assn. SW Fla. (dir., membership chair), KC. Republican. Roman Catholic. Avocations: stamp collecting/philately, reading, walking, swimming, opera. Home: 2347 Butterfly Palm Dr Naples FL 34119 Office: VA Primary Care Clinic Ste 101 2685 Horseshoe Dr S Naples FL 34104 Office Phone: 239-659-9188. Personal E-mail: david34119@aol.com.

GEHRING, FREDERICK WILLIAM, mathematician, educator; b. Ann Arbor, Mich., Aug. 7, 1925; s. Carl E. and Hester McNeal (Reed) G.; m. Lois Caroline Bigger, Aug. 29, 1953; children: Kalle Burgess, Peter Motz. BSE in Elec. Engring., U. Mich., 1946, MA in Math, 1949; PhD (Fulbright fellow) in Math, Cambridge U., Eng., 1952, ScD, 1976; PhD (hon.), U. Helsinki, Finland, 1977, U. Jyväskylä, 1990, Norwegian U. Sci. & Technology, 1997. Benjamin Peirce instr. Harvard U., Cambridge, Mass., 1952-55; instr. math. U. Mich., Ann Arbor, 1955-56, asst. prof., 1956-59, assoc. prof., 1959-62, prof., 1962-96, T.H. Hildebrandt prof. math., 1984-96, prof. emeritus, 1996, chmn. dept. math., 1973-75, 77-84, disting. univ. prof., 1987—; hon. prof. Hunan U., Changsha, People's Republic of China, 1987. Vis. prof. Harvard U., 1964-65, Stanford U., 1964, U. Minn., 1971, Inst. Mittag-Leffler, Sweden, 1972, Mittag-Leffler, Sweden, 1990; Lars Onsager prof. Norwegian Tech. Hochschule, Norway, 1995; chair program in Geo Function Theory, Math. Scis. Rsch. Inst., Berkeley, 1986. Editor Duke Math. Jour., 1963-80, D. Van Nostrand Pub. Co., 1963-70, North Holland Pub. Co., 1970-94, Springer-Verlag, 1974-2002; editl. bd. Procs. Am. Math. Soc., 1962-65, Ind. U. Math. Jour., 1967-75, Math. Revs., 1969-75, Bull. Am. Math. Soc., 1979-85, Complex Variables, 1981—, Mich. Math. Jour., 1989-98, Annales Academiae Scientiarum Fennicae, 1996—, Conformal Geometry and Dynamics, 1997—, Computational Methods and Function Theory, 2001—; contbr. numerous articles on rsch. in pure math. to sci. jours. With USNR, 1943-46. Decorated comdr. Finnish White Rose; NSF fellow, 1959-60; Fulbright fellow, 1958-59; Guggenheim fellow, 1958-59; Sci. Rsch. Coun. sr. fellow, 1981; Humboldt fellow, 1981-84; U. Auckland Found fellow, 1985; Finnish Acad. fellow U. Helsinki, 1989. Mem. NAS, Am. Acad. Arts and Scis., Assn. Women in Math., Math. Assn. Am., Am. Math. Soc. (coun. 1969-75, 80-83, trustee 1983-93, mem. editl. bd. 1997-98, Leroy P. Steele prize for Lifetime Achievement, 2006), Inst. for Math. and Its Applications (gov. 1981-84), Swiss Math. Soc., Finnish Math. Soc., London Math. Soc., Finnish Acad. Sci., Royal Norwegian Soc. Scis. and Letters. Office Phone: 734-764-1219. Business E-Mail: fgehring@umich.edu.

GEHRING, JOHN F., food products executive; Ptnr. Ernst and Young, LLP, 1997—2001; v.p. internal audit ConAgra Foods, Inc., Omaha, 2002—03, sr. v.p., 2003—04, sr. v.p., corp. contr., 2004—, acting CFO, 2006. Office: ConAgra Foods Inc 1 ConAgra Dr Omaha NE 68102-5001 Office Phone: 402-595-4000. Office Fax: 402-595-4709.*

GEHRING, RONALD KENT, lawyer; b. Ft. Wayne, Ind., Feb. 5, 1941; s. Ronald G. and Beverly M. (Failor) G.; m. Teresa L. Eyer, June 18, 1966; children: Gregory D., Douglas K., Suzanne C. AB, Ind. U., 1963, JD, 1967. Bar: Ind. 1967, U.S. Dist. Ct. (no. and so. dists.) Ind. 1967, U.S. Ct. Appeals (7th cir.) 1975. Assoc. Peters, McHie, Enslen & Hand, Hammond, Ind., 1967-70; ptnr. Tourkow, Danehy, Crell, Hood & Gehring, Ft. Wayne, 1971-79, Grossman, Boeglin & Gehring and predecessor, Ft. Wayne, 1980-84; pvt. practice, Ft. Wayne, 1984—. Panelist Ind. Collection Law Seminar, 1982-83; atty. Ind. Dist. Luth. Ch. Bd. dirs. Concordia Cemetery Assn., 1982—83, Luth. Assn. Broadcasting, Inc. Mem. ABA, Ind. Trial Lawyers, Comml. Law League, Ind. Bar Assn., Allen County Bar Assn., Phi Delta Phi. Office: 202 W Berry St Ste 321 Fort Wayne IN 46802-2242 Office Phone: 260-422-6912. Personal E-mail: ronald.gehring@verizon.net.

GEHRING, WALTER JAKOB, biology professor, geneticist; b. Zurich, Switzerland, Mar. 20, 1939; s. Jakob and Marcelle (Rebmann) G.; m. Elisabeth Lott, Jan. 31, 1964; children: Stephan, Thomas. Diploma in Zoology, U. Zurich, 1963, PhD, 1965; PhD honoris causa, U. Torino, Italy, 2003, U. Nuevo Léon, Mex., 2003. Rsch. assoc. U. Zurich, 1963-67; postdoctoral fellow Yale U., New Haven, Conn., 1967-69, assoc. prof., 1969-72; prof. U. Basel, Switzerland, 1972—. Assoc. editor: Jour. Exptl. Zoology, Mechanisms of Devel., Trends in Genetics, Growth & Differentiation. Recipient Otto Nägeli prize Zurich, 1982, Warren Triennial prize Harvard Med. Sch., Cambridge, Mass., 1986, Dr. Albert Wander prize City of Bern, Switzerland, 1986, Charles Léopold Mayer prize Inst. of France, Paris, 1986, Louis Jeantet prize for medicine City of Geneva, 1987, Prix d'Honneur, Moet Hennessy Louis Vuitton, 1993, Newcomb Cleve. prize AAAS, 1994-1995, Otto Warburg-medaille, 1996, Paul Wintrebert prize U. Pierre and Marie Curie, 1996, March of Dimes prize Devel. Biology, 1997, Karl von Frisch prize German Zool. Soc., 2000, Kyoto prize Inamori Found., 2000, Preis der Alfred Vogt Stiftung zur Förderung der Augenheilkunde, Zürich, 2001, Premio Balzan, Fondazione Internat. Premio E. Balzan, 2003. Mem. AAAS, NAS, European Molecular Biology Orgn., European Devel. Biology Orgn., Deutsche Akademie der Naturforscher Leopoldina, Academia Europaea, Genetics Soc. Am., Internat. Soc. for Developmental Biology, Swiss Soc. for Cell Biology, Molecular Biology and Genetics, Am. Soc. for Developmental Biology, Human Genome Orgn., Royal Soc. London (fgn.), Acad. Scis. (fgn.), Sigma Xi. Avocations: birdwatching, photography. Home: Hochfeldstrasse 32 CH-4106 Therwil Switzerland Office: U Basel Biozentrum Klingelbergstrasse 70 CH-4056 Basel Switzerland E-mail: walter.gehring@unibas.ch.

GEHRINGER, RICHARD GEORGE, publishing executive; b. Newark, Oct. 31, 1949; s. George John and Constance Mary (Volz) G.; m. Phyllis Jean Salerno, Nov. 13, 1977; children: Alexandra Rane, Skyler George. BS, U. SC, 1972; MBA, St. John's U., Jamaica, NY, 1976. Cert. cash mgr.; cert. treasury profl. Mgmt. trainee Avdel Corp., Teterboro, NJ, 1972-74; purchasing analyst Resistoflex Corp., Roseland, NJ, 1974-76; staff acct. McGraw-Hill Pub. Co., Hightstown, NJ, 1976-78; fin. analyst corp. real estate McGraw-Hill Inc., NYC, 1978-79; bus. mgr., corp. real estate McGraw-Hill Inc., NYC, 1979-80; asst. contr. McGraw-Hill Book Co., NYC, 1980-81; contr. Oxford U. Press Inc., Fair Lawn, NJ, 1981-86, v.p., CFO NYC, 1986—90, Cary, NC, 1990—95, sr. v.p., CFO NYC, 1995—. Fin. advisor Pi Kappa Alpha, Columbia U., NYC, 1988-89; bd. dirs. Fin. Execs. Inst., Dickens Pen & Inc., Books Alive!. Mem. Fin. Execs. Inst., Inst. Mgmt. Accts., Treasury Mgmt. Assn., Bldg. Owners' and Mgrs.' Assn. of Greater NY, NC Citizens for Bus. and Industry, Raleigh C. of C., Assn. for Fin. Profls. Republican. Roman Catholic. Office: Oxford U Press Inc 198 Madison Ave New York NY 10016-4341 E-mail: rggehringer@aol.com.

GEHRKE, CHARLES WILLIAM, biochemistry professor; b. NYC, July 18, 1917; s. Henry Edward and Louise (Mader) G.; m. Virginia Dorothy Horcher, Dec. 25, 1941; children: Charles William (dec.), Jon Craig, Susan Gay. BA in Biochemistry, Ohio State U., 1939, BS in Edn, 1941, MS in Biochemistry and Bacteriology, 1941, PhD in Agrl. Biochemistry, 1947. Prof., head dept. chemistry Missouri Valley Coll., Marshall, Mo., 1942-49; instr. agrl. chemistry Ohio State U., Columbus, 1945-46; assoc. prof. agrl. chemistry U. Mo., Columbia, 1949-54, prof. biochemistry, 1954-87, prof. emeritus, 1987—, mgr. Expt. Sta. Chem. Labs., 1954-87, dir. interdisciplinary chromatography Mass Spectrometry Facility, 1982-87; founder, chmn. bd. dirs. Bioscis. and Tech. Internat., Inc., 1992. Founder, chmn. bd. dirs. Analytical Biochemistry Labs., Columbia, 1968-92, dir., 1992—; USA co-chmn. colloquium on A Lunar-Based Chem. Analysis Lab., 1989, 93; co-investigator lunar samples NASA, 1969-75; lectr., Russia, 1972, 74, 90, Japan, China, Taiwan, The Philippines, Hong Kong, 1982, 87, France, Germany, Eng., Norway, Sweden, Switzerland, Italy, Egypt, 1986, 89. Author: 75 Years of Chromatography--A Historical Dialogue, 1979, (book chpt.) Quantitation of Amino Acids and Amines by Chromatography, 2005, Milestones in Chromatography, 2006; author, editor: Amino Acid Analysis by Gas Chromatography, 3 vols., 1987, Chromatography and Modification of Nucleosides, 3 vols., 1990, A Lunar-Based Chemical Analysis Laboratory, 1993, A Lunar-Based Analytical Laboratory, 1997, Chromatography a Century of Discovery, 2001; mem. editl. bd. Jour. Chromatographic Sci., Jour. Chromatography; contbr. chpts. to books, more than 270 articles to sci. jours. Recipient Faculty Alumni Gold medal award U. Mo., 1975, Chromatography Meml. medal Sci. Council on Chromatography of USSR Acad. Scis., 1980, Ohio State Alumni Profl. Achievement award, 2001; Ohio State Outstanding scholar, 1996. Fellow Am. Inst. Chemists, Assn. Ofcl. Analytical Chemists (Harvey W. Wiley award 1971, chmn. Magruder standard sample subcom. 1958-79, bd. dirs., mem. editl. bd. 1979-82, pres.-elect 1983, pres. centennial yr. 1984); mem. AAAS, Am. Soc. Biol. Chemists, Am. Chem. Soc. (pres. Mo. sect. 1958-59, 78-79, Spencer award 1979, Midwest Chemist award 1986, Dal Nogare award in chromatography 1995, U. Mo. Faculty Retiree of Yr. award 1993, Nat. Am. Chem. Soc. Sci. and Tech. award 1999, Nat. Am. Chem. Soc. Chromatography award 2000), Am. Dairy Sci. Assn. (chmn. com. on protein nomenclature 1961-62), Fedn. Am. Socs. Exptl. Biology, Internat. Soc. Study of Origin of Life, N.Y. Acad. Sci., Cosmopolitan Luncheon Club (chmn. Diabetes Ctr. adv. com. 1976—), Diabetes Ctr., Sigma Xi. Home: 708 Edgewood Ave Columbia MO 65203-7410 Office Phone: 573-442-4964.

GEHRLEIN, WILLIAM VINCENT, business professor; b. Erie, Pa., June 8, 1946; s. Vincent Francis and Eunice Mae (Knauff) G.; m. Sheila Eileen Lawson, Nov. 25, 1973 (div. May 1991); m. Barbara Elaine Eller, June 29, 2001. BS in Physics, Gannon Coll., 1968; MS in Physics, Pa. State U., 1972, PhD in Bus. Adminstrn., 1975. Postdoctoral fellow Pa. State U., State College, Pa., 1975-77; asst. prof. Clarkson Coll., Potsdam, NY, 1977-78; assoc. prof. U. Del., Newark, 1978-81, prof. of bus. adminstrn., 1981-2001. Mem. editl. bd.: Social Choice and Welfare; guest editor: Spl. Issue of Annals of Opers. Rsch., 1990, 97; author: Operations Management Cases, 2003, Condorcet's Paradox, 2006; contbr. numerous articles to profl. jours.; mem. bd. assoc. editors Inst. of Indsl. Engrs., 1985. With U.S. Army, 1968-70. Fellow Ctr. for Advanced Study, U. Del., 1988; grantee NSF, 1978. Mem. Internat. Soc. for Social Choice and Welfare (exec. coun.), Opers. Rsch. Soc. of Am. Avocations: running, fishing, genealogy. Office: Dept Bus Adminstrn Univ Del Newark DE 19716 Business E-Mail: wvg@udel.edu.

GEHRY, FRANK OWEN, architect; b. Toronto, Ont., Can., Feb. 28, 1929; arrived in U.S., 1947; s. Irving and Thelma (Caplan) Gehry; m. Berta Aguilera, Sept. 11, 1975; children: Alejandro, Samuel; children: Leslie, Brina. BArch, U. So. Calif., 1954; postgrad., Harvard U., 1956—57; DFA (hon.), RI Sch. Design, 1987, Otis Art Inst. at Parsons Sch. Design, 1989; Doctorate of Visual Arts (hon.), Calif. Inst. Arts, 1987; DEng (hon.), Tech. U. Nova Scotia, 1989; HHD (hon.), Occidental Coll., 1993; doctorate (hon.), Whittier Coll., 1995, Calif. Coll. Arts and Crafts; DAgr (hon.), Southern Calif. Inst. Architecture, 1997; LLD (hon.), U. Toronto, 1998. Registered profl. architect , Calif. Designer Victor Gruen Assocs., LA, 1953—54, planning, design and project dir., 1958—61; project designer, planner Pereira & Luckman, LA, 1957—58; prin. Frank O. Gehry & Assocs. (succeeded by Gehry & Krueger, Inc., now Gehry Partners, LLP), Santa Monica, Calif., 1962—. William Bishop chair Yale U, 1979, Charlotte Davenport Professorship in Architecture, 82, 85, 1987—89, 1999; Eliot Noyes chair Harvard U., 1984; vis. scholar Fed. Inst. Tech., Zürich, Switzerland, 1996—97; vis. prof. UCLA, 1998. Prin. works include Loyola Law Sch., LA, 1978—92, Temporary Contemporary Mus., 1983, Calif. Aerospace Mus., 1984, Frances Goldwyn Regional Br. Libr., Hollywood, Calif., 1986, U.C.I. Info. and Computer Sci./Engring. Rsch. Lab. and Engring Ctr., Irvine, Calif., 1986—88, Vitra Internat. Mfg. Facility and Design Mus., Weil am Rhein, Germany, 1989, Chiat/Day Hdqs., Venice, Calif., 1991, Advanced Tech. Labs. Bldg., U. Iowa, Iowa City, 1992, U. Toledo Ctr. for Visual Arts, Toledo, Ohio, 1992, Walt Disney Concert Hall, LA, 1993, Frederick R. Weisman Art Mus., Mpls., 1993, Vitra Internat. Hdqs., Basel, Switzerland, 1994, Am. Ctr., Paris, 1994, Team Disneyland Adminstrn. Bldg., Anaheim, Calif., 1995, EMR Communication and Tech. Ctr., Bad Oeynhausen, Germany, 1995, Nationale-Nederlanden Bldg., Prague, Czech Republic, 1996, Guggenheim Mus., Bilbao, Spain, 1997, Vontz Ctr. for Molecular Studies, U. Cin., Ohio, 1999, Der Neue Zolihof, Dusseldorf, Germany, 1999, DG Bank Hdqrs., Berlin, Germany, 2000, Experience Music Project, Seattle, 2000, Bard Coll. Ctr. for the Performing Arts, Annandale-on-Hudson, NY, 2001, The Walt Disney Concert Hall, LA, 2002, Peter B. Lewis Weatherhead Sch. Mgmt. Case Western Reserve U., Cleve., 2003, Ray and Maria Stata Ctr., MIT, Cambridge, Mass., 2003, Pritzker Pavilion, Millennium Pk., Chgo., Ill., 2004, MARTa, Headford, Germany, 2005, IAC/Interactive Corp. West Coast Hdqs., L.A., Calif., 2005, Marqués de Riscal Winery, Elciego, Spain, 2006, IAC/Interactive Corp. East Coast Hdqs., NYC, 2007, and several others, selected exhbn. designs, Art Treasures of Japan, LA County Mus. Art, 1965, Assyrian Reliefs, 1966, Billy Al Bengston Retrospective, 1968, Treasures of Tutankhamen, 1978, Avant-Garde of Russia 1910-1930, 1980, Seventeen Artists in the Sixties, 1981, German Expressionist Sculpture, 1983, Degenerate Art, 1994, Exiles & Emigrés, 1997, The Art of the Motorcycle, Solomon R. Guggenheim Mus., NY, 1998, Guggenheim Mus., Bilbao, Spain, 1999; work featured in major architectural publs. including Newsweek, Time, Forbes, Economist, Vanity Fair, Art in America, Wall Street Jour., NY Times, LA Times, Washington Post, Le Monde, L'Express, El Correo and Frankfurter Allgemeine. Trustee Hereditary Disease Found., Santa Monica, Calif., 1970—. Named Hon. Consul, City of Bilbao, Spain, 1997, Chancellor, 1998; recipient Arnold W. Brunner Meml. prize in architecture, AAAL, 1983, Pritzker Architecture prize, Hyatt Found., 1989, Wolf prize in art, Wolf Found., 1992, Praemium Imperiale award, Japan Art Assn., 1992, Dorothy and Lilian Gish award, 1994, Nat. Medal of Arts, Nat. Endowment of the Arts, 1998, Friedrich Kiesler prize, Friedrich Kiesler Found., 1998, Gold medal, Royal Architectural Inst. Canada, 1998, Lotus medal of Merit, Lotos Club, 1999, Gold medal, Am. Inst. of Architects, 1999, Lifetime Achievement award, Am. for the Arts, 2000. Fellow: Am. Inst. Architects, AAAS, AAAL; mem.: Royal Acad. Arts (hon. academician 1998), Nat. Acad. Design (academician 1994), Am. Acad. Rome (trustee 1989). Office: Gehry Partners LLP 12541 Beatrice St Los Angeles CA 90066*

GEIBEL, SISTER GRACE ANN, university president; b. Sept. 17, 1937; BA in Piano and Music Edn., Carlow Coll., 1961; MA in Music Edn., U. Rochester, 1967, PhD in Music, 1975. Tchr. elem. and high schs., 1959-67; ch. musician, 1972-80; assoc. prof. and co-chmn. music dept. Carlow Coll., Pitts., 1981-82, acting acad. dean, 1982-83, dean, 1983-88, v.p. acad. affairs, 1984-88, pres., 1988—2005. Mem. adv. bd. Pitts. Symphony Soc.; bd. dir. Oakland Cath. H.S., Urban League Pitts., Penn. Econ. League. Office: Carlow Univ Office of the Pres 3333 5th Ave Pittsburgh PA 15213-3109 Business E-Mail: geibelga@carlow.edu.

GEIER, KATHLEEN T., human resources specialist; b. Akron, Ohio, Aug. 7, 1956; BS, Heidelberg Coll., 1978. Indsl. engr., various human resources positions Goodyear Tire and Rubber Co., Akron, Ohio, 1978—86; ops. mgr. Cosmoflex (subsidiary of Goodyear Tire and Rubber Co.), 1986—90, plant mgr., pres. Mt. Pleasant, Iowa, 1992—94; bus. ctr. mgr. Goodyear Tire and Rubber Co., St. Marys, Ohio, 1990—92, dir. salaried human resources end employment practices Akron, Ohio, 1994—95, dir. human resources employment practices and systems, 1995—96, dir. human resources ctrl. svcs. N.Am. bus. unites and corp. staff, 1996—99, dir. human resources Europe, Africa, Middle East region Brussels, sr. v.p. human resources Akron, 2002—. Office: Goodyear Tire and Rubber Co 1144 E Market St Akron OH 44316-0001 Office Phone: 330-796-2121. Office Fax: 330-796-2222.

GEIER, PHILIP HENRY, JR., advertising executive; b. Pontiac, Mich., Feb. 22, 1935; s. Philip Henry and Jane (Gillen) G.; m. Faith Power, children: Hope Smith, Johanna Howard. BA, Colgate U., 1957; MS, Columbia U., 1958. With McCann-Erickson, Inc., Cleve., 1958-60, NYC, 1960-68; chmn. McCann-Erickson Internat. U.K. Co., London, 1969-73; vice chmn. internat. ops. McCann Worldwide, London, 1973-75; vice chmn. internat. Interpublic Group of Cos., Inc., NYC, 1975-77, pres., chief operating officer, 1977-80, chmn., CEO, 1980—2000, chmn. emeritus, 2001—; chmn. Geier Group LLC, 2001—; sr. advisor Lazard Freres & Co. LLC. Bd. dirs. AEA Investors, Inc., Alcon, Inc., Fiduciary Trust Internat., Foot Locker, Inc., Mettler-Toledo Internat. Inc. Bd. dirs. Meml. Sloan-Kettering Cancer Ctr., Save the Children Fedn., Inc., Autism Speaks, Columbia Bus. Sch., Whitney Mus. Am. Art, Internat. Tennis Hall of Fame. Mem.: New Canaan Country Club, River Club (N.Y.C.). Address: The Geier Group 70 E 55th St New York NY 10022 Office Phone: 646-840-6721. Business E-Mail: pgeier@geiergroup.com.

GEIER, PHILIP OTTO, III, foundation executive, consultant, director, academic administrator; b. Cin., 1948; s. Philip O. Jr. and Susanne (Ernst) G.; m. Amy Yeager, Dec. 27, 1975; children: Katherine, Elizabeth, Christopher. BA in Am. Civilization with honors, Williams Coll., 1970; attended, U. Paris, 1973; MA in History, Syracuse U., 1975, PhD in Am. Studies and History, 1980. Instr. history and Am. studies Dickinson Coll., Carlisle, Pa., 1976-77; Fulbright lectr. U. Paris-Sorbonne, 1977-78; interim exec. dir. French-Am. Found., NYC, 1978-79; assoc. dir. Am. Farm Sch., Thessaloniki, Greece, 1979-82; v.p. external affairs World Learning, Brattleboro, Vt., 1982-93; pres., dir. United World Coll.-USA, Montezuma, N.Mex., 1993—2005; exec. dir. Davis United World Coll. scholars program Middlebury Coll., 2005—, spl. advisor to pres., 2005—. Bd. dirs. Monterey Inst. Internat. Studies, Pine Manor Coll., United World Coll.; chair social Svcs. and Internat. Exch. Commn. 2d U.S.-USSR Emerging Leaders Summit, Moscow and Sochi, 1990, del. to 1st Commn., Phila., 1988; mem. Coun. Fgn. Rels., Pacific Coun. on Internat. Policy, L.A. Supply Corps officer, USN, 1970-72, Vietnam. Fulbright award Fed. Republic of Germany, 1988. Avocations: international relations, outdoor recreation. Office: Middlebury Coll Davis United World Coll Scholars Progra Adirondack House Middlebury VT 05753 Office Phone: 802-443-3200. Office Fax: 802-443-3230. Business E-Mail: phil.geier@davisuwcscholars.org.

GEIGER, ALEXANDER, lawyer; b. Kosice, Czechoslovakia, May 21, 1950; came to U.S., 1965; s. Emil and Alice (Brickmann) G.; m. Helene R. Mortar, May 28, 1972; children: Theodore, Aviva. AB, Princeton U., 1972; JD, Cornell U., 1975. Bar: N.Y. 1976, U.S. Dist. Ct. (we. dist.) N.Y. 1976, U.S. Supreme Ct. 1980, U.S. Ct. Appeals (2d cir.) 1985, U.S. Tax Ct. 1986. Assoc. Nixon, Hargrave, Devans & Doyle, Rochester, N.Y., 1975-82; sr. ptnr. Geiger & Rothenberg, Rochester, 1982—. Adj. asst. prof. St. John Fisher Coll., Rochester, 1977-78. Mem. N.Y. State Bar Assn., Monroe County Bar Assn., Assn. Trial Lawyers Am., Rochester Inns of Ct. (master). Jewish. Home: 227 Brittany Ln Pittsford NY 14534 also: 30 Newport Pkwy # 3009 Jersey City NJ 07310 Office: Geiger & Rothenberg 45 Exchange Blvd Ste 800 Rochester NY 14614-2093 also: Geiger and Rothenberg 30 Vesey St 4th Fl New York NY 10007 Business E-Mail: ageiger@geigroth.com.

GEIGER, BETH C., freelance/self-employed journalist; Contbr. articles on Washington's geologic attractions to AAA Journey, Sunset mag., Current Sci. mag., others. Recipient AAAS Sci. Journalism award for children's sci. news, 2006. Mem.: NW Sci. Writers Assn.

GEIGER, DAVID E., engineer; b. Passaic, NJ, May 28, 1954; s. Gordon R and Norma B Geiger; children: Jesse David, Andrea Nicole. BEE with honors, Stevens Inst. Tech., Hoboken, NJ, 1976, MEE, 1989; cert. in bus. adminstrn., Heriot-Watt U., Scotland, 2002. Registered profl. engr., NJ. Engr. Universal Mfg., Paterson, NJ, 1976, Transistor Devices, Cedar Knolls, NJ, 1976—77; mem. tech. staff ITT Def. Commn. Divsn., Nutley, NJ, 1977—79; art dir. Hudson Studios, Totowa, NJ, 1981—83; engr. KDI Electronics, Whippany, NJ, 1983—84, Western Union Telegraph Co., Upper Saddle River, NJ, 1984—85, Merrimac Industries, West Caldwell, NJ, 1985, Con Edison of NY, 1987—2000; owner, home inspector Hip Home Inspections, 2004—. Author: Change Happens: What Direction for NNJM:, 1995 (Mensa award, 1995). Mem.: Am. Mensa Ltd. Republican. Roman Cath. Avocations: hiking, pen pals. Mailing: P O Box 3577 Wayne NJ 07474 Personal E-mail: commish456@hotmail.com.

GEIGER, HEATHER L., lawyer; BSc cum laude in Acctg., Ohio State U., Columbus, 1990, JD, 1993. CPA Accountancy Bd. Ohio, 1995; bar: Supreme Ct. Ohio 1993. Acct. Deloitte & Touche, LLP, Columbus, 1993—96; sr. counsel Am. Electric Power Svc. Corp., Columbus, 1997—, corp. sec. subsidiaries, 2004—. Sec. nuc. oversight com. Am. Electric Power Svc. Corp., 2004—; spkr. in field. Mem.: Soc. Corp. Secs. and Governance Profls. (assoc.). Office: Am Electric Power Svc Corp 1 Riverside Plz Columbus OH 43215 Home Phone: 614-855-4159; Office Phone: 614-716-3305. Business E-Mail: hlgeiger@aep.com.

GEIGER, JAMES NORMAN, lawyer; b. Mansfield, Ohio, Apr. 5, 1932; s. Ernest R. and Margaret L. (Bauman) G.; m. Paula Hunt, May 11, 1957; children: Nancy G., John W. BA, Ohio Wesleyan U., 1954; JD, Emory U., 1962, LLD, 1970. Bar: Ga. 1961, U.S. Dist. Ct. (mid. dist.) Ga. 1966, U.S. Ct. Appeals (5th and 11th cirs.) 1980, U.S. Dist. Ct. (so. dist.) Ga. 1983. Ptnr. Henderson, Kaley, Geiger, Thurmond and Marietta, Marietta, Ga., 1962—64, Nunn, Geiger and Hunt, Perry, Ga., 1964—72, Geiger & Geiger, PC and Predicessors, 1972—. Trustee Westfield (Ga.) Schs., 1970—74, bd. visitors, 2003—; mem. civilian adv. bd. Warner Robins AFB, 1976; chmn. coun. ministries Perry United Meth. Ch., 1970—71, mem. adminstrv. bd., 1968—. Capt. USAF, 1954—57. Mem.: ABA, Perry C. of C. (pres. 1976, 1990), South Ga. C. of C. (bd. dirs.), Houston County Bar Assn., Ga. Bar Assn., Perry Club Coun. (pres. 1967), Perry Kiwanis (pres. 1968, Man of Yr. 1968), Phi Sigma Alpha, Phi Delta Phi. Methodist. Home: 1910 Northside Rd Perry GA 31069-2223 Office: Geiger & Geiger 1007 Jernigan St Perry GA 31069-3325 Office Phone: 478-987-2952. Business E-Mail: geigerj@comsouth.net.

GEIGER, MARK WATSON, management educator; b. Grand Forks, ND, Aug. 22, 1949; s. Louis George and Helen Marjorie (Watson) G.; children: Harley, Uintah, Klaus. BA, Carleton Coll., 1971; MBA, U. Pa., 1975; MA, U. Mo., 2000, PhD, 2006. CPA, N.Y. Bldg. contractor Spiral Remodeling, Phila., 1976—78; mgr. EDP project Ariz. State Govt., Phoenix, 1978—81; mgr. internal audit Gulf & We. Industries, NYC, 1981—85; v.p. spl. projects Kidder, Peabody & Co., Inc., NYC, 1986—90; v.p., chief adminstrv. officer Analytical Bio-Chemistry Labs., Inc., Columbia, Mo., 1990—92; ind. mgmt. cons. Columbia, 1992—94; asst. prof. fin. William Woods U., Fulton, Mo., 1994—2002; tchg. asst. U. Mo., Columbia, 2002—04; postdoctoral fellow Minn. Population Ctr., U. Minn., Minn., 2006—. Presenter in field. Recipient Richard S. Brownlee Fund award, 1999, 2002, Nels Andrew Clevens prize, 2006, Disting. Doctoral Dissertation award, U. Mo., 2007; grantee, William Woods U., 1994, Minn. Population Ctr., 2006, 2006; Allen Cook White Jr. fellow, 2003, Frank F. and Louis I. Stephens fellow, 2004, Alfred D. Chandler grantee, 2005. Mem. AICPA, Am. Hist. Assn., So. Hist. Assn., Am. Soc. Legal History, Bus. History Conf., Econ. History Assn., Orgn. Am. Historians, Social Sci. History Assn., Wharton Club Chgo. Office: Minn Population Ctr 50 Willey Hall U Minn 225 19th Ave S Minneapolis MN 55455 Office Phone: 612-636-3486. Business E-Mail: mgeiger@umn.edu.

GEILFUSS, C. FREDERICK, II, lawyer; b. Aug. 5, 1953; BA cum laude, Williams Coll., Williamstown, Mass., 1975; MA in econs., U. Wis., 1976, JD cum laude, 1979. Bar: Wis. 1979, U.S. Ct. Appeals, seventh cir. 1979, U.S. Supreme Ct. 1982, U.S. Dist. Ct., Ea. Dist. Wis. 1983. Law clk. Hon. Judge Harlington Wood, Jr. US Ct. Appeals (7th cir.), 1979-80; atty., appellate staff Civil divsn. U.S. Dept. Justice, Washington, 1980-83; atty. Foley & Lardner LLP, Milw., 1983—88, ptnr., 1988—. Co-author: chpt. Long-Term Care Facilities: Regulation. Trustee Univ. Sch. Milw., 2002—, pres. trustees, 2004—07. Mem.: ABA, State Bar Wis., Am. Health Lawyers Assn., Wis. Psychol. Found. (chair 1999—2004), Curative Care Network (chmn. 1997—99), Milw. County War Meml. Inc., Columbia Coll. Nursing, Grand Ave. Club, Gardner Found., Milw. County Marcus Ctr. Performing Arts (chmn. 1998—2001), Order Coif. Office: Foley & Lardner LLP 777 E Wisconsin Ave Milwaukee WI 53202-5306 Office Phone: 414-271-2400. Office Fax: 414-297-4900. Business E-Mail: fgeilfuss@foley.com.

GEIMAN, J. ROBERT, lawyer; b. Evanston, Ill., Mar. 5, 1931; s. Louis H. and Nancy O'Connell-Crowe G.; m. Ann L. Fitzgerald, July 29, 1972; children: J. Robert, William Patrick, Timothy Michael. BS, Northwestern U., 1953; JD, Notre Dame U., 1956. Bar: Ill. 1956, U.S. Ct. Appeals (7th cir.) 1956, U.S. Supreme Ct. 1969. Assoc. Eckert, Peterson & Lowry, Chgo., 1956-64; ptnr. Peterson, Lowry, Rall, Barber & Ross, Chgo., 1964-70, Peterson & Ross, Chgo., 1970-96, of counsel, 1996—. Mem. com. on civil jury instructions Ill. Supreme Ct., 1979-81. Case editor Notre Dame Law Rev., 1956. Bd. advisors Cath. Charities of Archdiocese of Chgo., 1973-96. Fellow Internat. Acad. Trial Lawyers, Am. Coll. Trial Lawyers, Ill. Bar Found.; mem. ABA (aviation com., tort and ins. practice sect. 1980-90), Ill. Bar Assn. (sec. 1969-70, sec. bd. govs. 1969-71), Chgo. Bar Assn. (aviation law com. 1970-73), Bar Assn. of 7th Fed. Ct. (meetings com. 1968-70, vice chmn. membership com. 1973-75), Soc. Trial Lawyers, Cath. Lawyers Guild of Chgo. (bd. advisors 1973-96), Law Club Chgo., Chgo. Athletic Assn. (pres. 1973). Republican. Home: 4861 River Village Dr Vero Beach FL 32967-7452 Office: Peterson Ross 200 E Randolph St Ste 7200 Chicago IL 60601-7719

GEIMANN, STEVE, radio producer; m. Carol Sadler. Student, Syracuse U. Reporter Gannett Co., Binghamton, NY; with United Press Internat., Washington, 1983—94, Washington bur. chief., 1991, exec. editor & spokesman, 1992—93; sr. editor Comm. Daily, 1994—99; editor, team leader Bloomberg, Washington, 1999—2005; prodr. Bloomberg Radio, 2005—; anchor Bloomberg: The Final Word. Pres. Sigma Delta Chi Found., Indpls. Mem.: Soc. Profl. Journalists (sec.-treas. 1994—95, pres. elect 1995—96, pres. 1996—97, former chmn. ethics com., Wells Meml. Key 2001). Office: Bloomberg Radio 1399 New York Ave Washington DC 20005 Office Phone: 202-624-1960. Business E-Mail: sgeimann@bloomberg.net. E-mail: sgeimann@spj.org.

GEIRINGER, STEVE R., medical educator; b. Detroit, July 8, 1953; m. Karen A Bantel. BS, U. Mich., Ann Arbor, 1975, MD, 1979. Lic. physician Mich., 1980. Asst. prof. U. Mich., Ann Arbor, Mich., 1982—91; prof. Wayne State U., Detroit, 1991—. Author: Anatomic Localization for Needle Electromyography. Named one of Best Doctors in Am., Best Doctors, 1996—2006. Mem.: Am. Bd. PM&R (dir. 2000—, treas. 2000—), Am. Acad. PM&R (chmn. med. edn. com. 2003—). Office: Steve R Geiringer MD 36301 Warren Rd Westland MI 48185 Office Phone: 734-722-5568. Office Fax: 734-722-0742. Business E-Mail: sgrehabdoc@aol.com.

GEIS, JEROME ARTHUR, lawyer, educator; b. Shakopee, Minn., May 28, 1946; s. Arthur Adam and Emma Mary (Boegemann) G.; m. Beth Marie Bruger, Aug. 11, 1979; children: Jennifer, Jason, Joan, Janice. BA in History magna cum laude, St. John's U., Collegeville, Minn., 1968; JD cum laude, U. Notre Dame, 1973; LLM in Taxation, NYU, 1975. Bar: Minn. 1973, U.S. Dist. Ct. Minn. 1973, U.S. Tax Ct. 1973, U.S. Ct. Appeals (8th cir.) 1973. Law clk. Minn. Supreme Ct., St. Paul, 1973-74; assoc. Dudley & Smith, St. Paul, 1975-76, Briggs & Morgan P.A., St. Paul, 1976-79, chief tax dept., 1983-95. Adj. prof. tax law William Mitchell Coll. Law, St. Paul, 1976-83; adj. prof. state and local taxation U. Minn., 2001-. Columnist Minn. Law Jour., 1986-89, Bench & Bar, 1990—; editl. cons.: Sales and Use Tax Alert; former reviewer Summary Reporter: Finance and Commerce, Minnesota State Bar Assn.; corr. State Tax Notes. Bd. dirs. Western Townhouse Assn., West St. Paul, 1979, St. Matthews Cath. Ch., West St. Paul, 1981; adv. bd. Minn. Inst. of Legal Edn., 1984—2002. Served to specialist 4th class U.S. Army, 1969-71. Recipient Disting. Svc. award, MSBA Tax Sect., 1990. Fellow Am. Coll. Tax Counsel; mem. ABA, Am. Law Inst., Tax Inst. Am. (chmn. sales and use tax commn. 1988-90), Nat. Tax Assn., Am. Judicature Soc., Minn. Bar Assn. (bd. dirs. tax coun. sect. 1984-93, 94-97, 99—, chmn. 1990-91), Ramsey County Bar Assn., Minn. Taxpayers Assn. (bd. dirs. 1988—), Inst. Property Taxation, Supreme Ct. Hist. Soc., Nat. Assn. State Bar Tax Sects. (exec. com. 1993—), Citizens League, Minn. Club (bd. dirs. 1997-2000), Federalist Soc., Kiwanis (bd. dirs. 2000-02). Home: 1116 Dodd Rd Saint Paul MN 55118-1821 Office: Briggs & Morgan PA 2200 1st St N Saint Paul MN 55109-3210 Home Phone: 651-455-0298; Office Phone: 651-808-6409. Business E-Mail: jgeis@briggs.com.

GEISEL, CAMERON MEADE, JR., retired bank executive; b. Harrisburg, Pa., Oct. 7, 1937; s. Cameron Meade and Dorothy Mae G.; m. Martha L. Frohring, Sept. 3, 1977 (dec.); children: Melissa Ellen, Gregory Stuart, Andrew Frohring, Martha Bliss; m. Saskia Hessler, Sept. 8, 1991. BA, Bucknell U., Lewisburg, Pa., 1960; grad. Sch. Credit and Fin. Mgmt., Harvard U., 1970; Advanced Mgmt Program, Harvard Bus. Sch., 1985. With Phila. Nat. Bank, 1961-86, asst. v.p., then v.p., 1965-77, sr. v.p., 1977-86; ret. Bd. dirs. Hessler Properties, Inc. Trustee Lankenau Hosp. Found., Fox Chase Cancer Ctr., Morris Arboretum. 2d lt. inf. U.S. Army, 1960-61. Mem. U.S. Coun. Internat. Bus. (trustee, exec. com.), Merion Golf Club, Merion Cricket Club, Phila. Club, Royal Ashdown Forest Golf Cloub, Royal and Ancient Golf Club of St. Andrews, Honourable Co. of Edinburgh Golfers, Loblolly Pines Golf Club, Sunningdale Golf Club, Rolling Rock Club, The Everglades Club. Republican. Episcopalian. Home: 1411 Youngsford Rd Gladwyne PA 19035-1232

GEISEL, HAROLD WALTER, diplomat; b. Chgo., May 11, 1947; s. Gustav and Stefi Geisel; m. Susan L. Gordon, Oct. 2, 1983; children: Jacqueline Julie, Katherine Louise. BA in History, Johns Hopkins U., 1968; MBA, U. Va., 1970. Commd. fgn. service officer Dept. State, 1970, adminstrv. officer Washington, 1973-75; 1st sec. Am. embassy, Bern, Switzerland, 1975-78, Bamako, Mali, 1978-80; adminstrv. officer Dept. State, Washington, 1980-82; consul gen. U.S. consulate gen., Durban, South Africa, 1982-85; mem. NATO Def. Coll., Rome, 1985-86; adminstrv. counsellor Am. Embassy, Rome, 1986-88, adminstrv. minister-counsellor Bonn, 1988-92, adminstrv. minister-counselor Moscow, 1992-93; exec. asst. to under-sec. Dept. State, Washington, 1993-94, deputy inspector gen., 1994-95, dep. asst. sec. for info. mgmt., 1995-96, amb. to Mauritius, Seychelles, and Comoros, 1996-99, sr. negotiator, 1999-2000; acting dep. asst. sec. logistics mgmt. Dept. State A/LM, Washington, 2001—; head U.S. Dels. to U.S.-Chinese COCA Negotiations, 2002—04; mgmt. analyst, 2004—. Jewish. Home Phone: 301-941-1386.

GEISENDORFER, JAMES VERNON, religious writer, researcher; b. Brewster, Minn., Apr. 22, 1929; s. Victor H. and Anne B. (Johnson) G.; m. Esther Lillian Walker, Sept. 23, 1949; children: Jane, Karen, Lois. Student, Augustana Coll., 1950-51, Augsburg Coll., 1951-54, Orthodox Luth. Sem., 1954-55; BA, U. Minn., 1960; LLD, Burton Coll. and Sem., 1961. Grain buyer Pillsbury Mills, Inc., Worthington, Minn., 1947-48; acct. Boote Hatcheries, Worthington, 1949-50; night supr. Strutwear, Inc., Mpls., 1951-52; dispatcher Chgo. and North Western Ry., 1953-54; office mgr. Froedtert Malt Corp., Mpls., 1955-56, Nat. Automotive Parts Assn., 1957-60; sr. creative writer Brown & Bigelow, St. Paul, 1960-72; religious rschr., writer, 1972—. Rsch. cons. Inst. for the Study of Am. Religion; mem. panel of reference Chelston Bible Coll., New Milton, Eng. Author: (with J. Gordon Melton) A Directory of Religious Bodies in the United States, 1977, Religion in America, 1983, Religion USA, 1989; mem. editl. bd. Biog. Dictionary Am. Cult and Sect Leaders; contbr. articles to profl. jours.; cons. editor Directory of Religious Organizations in the United States, 1977. Recipient Amicus Poloniae medal Polish Ministry of Culture and Edn., 1969. Mem. AAAS, Am. Acad. Religion, Acad. Ind. Scholars, Wis. Evang. Luth. Synod Hist. Inst., Augustana Hist. Soc., Royal Anthrop. Inst., Ea. Territorial Hist. Soc. (charter), Medieval Acad. Am., Renaissance Soc. Am., George Eliot Fellowship, Wis. Acad. Scis., Arts and Letters, Aristotelian Soc. (life), Hegel Soc. Am., Sixteenth Century Studies Conf., Am. Cath. Philos. Assn., N.Am. Conf. on Brit. Studies, Internat. Soc. for Comparative Study of Civilizations, Religous Rsch. Assn., Internat. Assn. Greek Philosophy, Brit. Soc. Philosophy Religion, Inst. Interdisciplinary Rsch., League for Yiddish, Inst. for Advanced Studies in Culture, Assn. Lit. Scholars and Critics, Thomas More Law Ctr., Trinitarian Bible Soc., Chs. of God Hist. Soc., Am. Friends the Vatican Libr. Lutheran. Address: 1001 Shawano Ave Green Bay WI 54303-3020

GEISER, ELIZABETH ABLE, publishing company executive; b. Phillipsburg, NJ, Apr. 28, 1925; d. George W. and Margaret I. (Ross) G. AB magna cum laude, Hood Coll., 1947. Promotion mgr. coll. dept. Macmillan Co., NYC, 1947-54; promotion mgr. R.R. Bowker, NYC, 1954-60, sales mgr., 1960-67, dir. mktg., 1967-70, v.p., 1970-73, sr. v.p., 1973-75, sr. v.p., pub. book divsn.; adj. prof., dir. U. Denver Pub. Inst., 1976—; sr. v.p. Gale Rsch. Co., 1976-91, cons., 1991—. Cons. Excerpta Medica, Elsevier, 1976-82; lectr. pub. procedures Radcliffe Coll., 1966-75; lectr. schs. libr. sci. U. Wash., U. So. Calif.; panel mem. TV series Living Library, 1970 Editor: The Business of Book Publishing, 1985; contbr. Manual of Bookselling, 1969. Trustee Hood Coll., 1993-99. Inducted into Pub. Hall of Fame, 1988; recipient PubWest Rittenhouse award for lifetime achievement contbn. to pub. in the west, Mem. Assn. Am. Pubs. (exec. coun. prof. and scholarly pub. divsn. 1989-91, adv. coun. Frankfurt book fair 1971, sch. and libr. promotion and mktg. com. 1972-76, bd. dirs. 1982-85), ALA (pres. exhibits roundtable 1968-70, bd. dirs. exhibits roundtable 1968). Presbyterian. Home: 3329 E Bayaud Ave Denver CO 80209 Office: Pub Inst 335 E 51st St Apt 5E New York NY 10022-6765 Office Phone: 212-752-8652. E-mail: egeiser@worldnet.att.net.

GEISER, ROBERT NEIL, computer scientist; b. Cleve., Jan. 20, 1961; s. Roger Neal and Betty Lou (Keiner) G.; m. Laura Jane Burkholder, June 18, 1983; children: Jessika, Benjamin, Matthew. BS in Acctg., AS in Data Processing, U. Akron, 1982. CPA, Ohio; cert. data processor, Ohio. Acct., programmer G&S Titanium, Inc., Wooster, Ohio, 1979-83, cons., 1983-93; computer specialist, acct. Hall, Kistler & Co., Canton, Ohio, 1983-88; owner Computer Productivity Assistance, Wooster, 1988—2000; MIS dir. G&S Titanium, Inc., Wooster, 1988—2000, v.p. fin., 2000—. Group leader Appalachia Service Project Home Repair, various locations, 1984-87; mem. Grace Brethren. Mem. AICPA, Ohio Soc. CPAs (chmn. local computers in practice 1987-88, mem. statewide computers in practice panel 1987-95), Nat. Assn. Accts. (Mem. of Yr. award 1984-85), Assn. of the Inst. for Cert. of Computer Profls. Republican. Achievements include leading genetics research assistance at Beth Israel Deaconess Medical Center and Boston University School of Public Health, and others. Avocations: backpacking, studying the Bible, reading. Home: 9520 E Moreland Rd Apple Creek OH 44606-9448 Office: G&S Titanium Inc 1550 Spruce St Wooster OH 44691-4600 Office Phone: 330-263-0564. Business E-Mail: bob@gs-titanium.com.

GEISER, THOMAS CHRISTOPHER, lawyer, insurance company executive; b. Bern, Switzerland, Aug. 13, 1950; came to U.S., 1952; s. Henry Abraham and Pia Margaret (Tschudin) G.; m. Catherine Barlow Yeakle, Oct. 20, 1973 (div. Mar. 1983); m. Donna Lea Schweers, Jan. 3, 1987; 1 child, Kelsey Schweers. BA, U. Redlands, 1972; JD, U. Calif., San Francisco, 1977. Bar: Calif. 1978. Atty. Internat. Bur. Fiscal Documentation, Amsterdam, Netherlands, 1977—78; assoc., ptnr. Hanson, Bridgett, Marcus, Vlahos & Stromberg, San Francisco, 1979—85; ptnr. Epstein, Becker, Stromberg & Green, San Francisco, 1985—90, Brobeck, Phleger & Harrison, San Francisco, 1990—93; sr. v.p., gen. counsel, sec. WellPoint Health Networks Inc., Woodland Hills, Calif., 1993—96, exec. v.p., gen. counsel, sec., 1996—2005; sr. advisor Tex. Pacific Group, Santa Monica, Calif., 2006—. Mem. Am. Health Lawyers Assn., Calif. Soc. Health Care Attys., Order of Coif. Office: TPG 1733 Ocean Ave Ste 325 Santa Monica CA 90401 Office Phone: 310-656-9580. Personal E-mail: thomasgeiser@aol.com. Business E-Mail: tgeiser@northbp.com.

GEISLER, JAMES E., corporate financial executive; BA, Univ. Ky.; MBA, Univ. Va. With United Technologies, 1993—, dir. strategic planning, 1997—99, dir. investor rels., 1999—2001, dir. fin. planning & analysis, 2001—04, v.p. fin., 2004—. Office: United Technologies United Technologies Bldg Hartford CT 06101*

GEISLER, NATHAN DAVID, financial consultant; b. Kokand, Russia, Jan. 22, 1946; s. Leon and Esther (Korn) G.; m. Susan D. Starsky, 1982; 1 child, Jonathan Starsky Geisler. BA, Ohio State U., 1968; JD, U. Toledo, 1970. Asst. v.p. Merrill Lynch Pierce Fenner & Smith, Toledo, 1973-89, 1st v.p., 1989—. With USAF, 1971—73, advanced through ranks to lt. col. Ohio Air Nat. Guard, 1974—93. Avocations: golf, tennis, travel, sports cars. Home: 2600 Forestvale Rd Toledo OH 43615-2251 Office: 333 N Summit St Toledo OH 43697-9910 Office Phone: 419-259-5874. Personal E-mail: redhorse143@cs.com.

GEISLER, THOMAS MILTON, JR., law educator, lawyer; b. Orange, NJ, Jan. 16, 1943; s. Thomas M. and Helen K. (Thomas) G.; m. Sarah Ann Farrell Geisler, Aug. 6, 1977; children: Sarah C., Ann. C. AB in Math. (cum laude), Harvard Coll., Cambridge, Mass., 1965; JD, Harvard Law Sch., Cambridge, Mass., 1968. Bar: NJ, NY, Conn., U.S. Dist. Ct. (2d cir.), U.S. Supreme Ct. Asst., base legal officer U.S. Naval Submarine Base, New London, Conn., 1969-71; appellate def. counsel Naval Appellate Review Activity, Washington, 1971-72; assoc. Shearman & Sterling, NYC, 1973-80, ptnr., 1980-91; pvt. practice NYC, 1991-96, New Haven, 1994—2006; instr. legal studies program U. New Haven, 2006—; instr. math. U. Conn., 2006—. Dir., bd. dirs. Friends of Harvard Law Record, Cambridge, Mass., 1997—. Author: Am. Jour. Proof of Facts 3d, 1995—; editor: Trial Practice Newsletter, 1986—2001. Lt., USNR, 1969-72. Recipient Litigation Star ABA Litigation Sect., 1997, Navy Achievement award USN, Washington, 1971. Mem. ABA , Conn. Bar Assn., Harvard Club So. Conn. (dir.), Harvard Club NYC, Quinnipiack Club, Madison Beach Club. Presbyterian. Avocations: tennis, squash, theater, concerts. Office Phone: 203-927-1985. E-mail: t1827@aol.com.

GEISMAR, RICHARD LEE, communications executive; b. Paterson, NJ, Aug. 22, 1927; s. Sylvan and Marjorie (Leeser) G.; m. Patricia Willard, Nov. 27, 1954; children: John, Elisabeth, Nancy. B in Mgmt. Engring., Rensselaer Poly. Inst., 1949; MBA, Harvard, 1951. With DuMont TV Network, 1951-55, Metromedia, Inc. (and predecessors), NYC, 1955-69, also bd. dirs.; pres., dir. Reeves Telecom Corp., 1969-70; comm. cons. BGW Assocs., Inc., 1970-84; chmn. Broad St. Comm. Corp., 1971-84; pres. Broad St. Ventures, 1984-98; chmn. Broad St. TV, 1989-96; com. mem. Greenwich GCTV Cable, 2007—. Bd. dirs., treas. Greenwich chpt. ARC, mem. state svc. coun, 1992-96; bd. dirs., treas. Greenwich Adult Day Ctr., Inc., 1997-2005. Served with USNR, 1945-46. Mem. Riverside Yacht Club, Sigma Xi. Republican. Congregationalist. Home: 18 Hidden Brook Rd Riverside CT 06878 Personal E-mail: daddick37@aol.com.

GEISSBUHLER, STEPHAN, graphics designer; b. Zofingen, Kanton Aargau, Switzerland, Oct. 21, 1942; arrived in US, 1967; s. Theodor and Ruth (Schneider) Geissbuhler; m. Elissa Beth Feuerman, June 26, 1983; children: Alexander Charles, Benjamin Adam;children from previous marriage: Marc Phillip, Christopher Luke. MA, Sch. Design Basel, 1964. Designer J.R. Geigy A.G., Basel, Switzerland, 1964-67; assoc. prof., dept. chmn. Phila. Coll. Art, 1967-73; design cons. Murphy-Levy-Wurman Architects, Phila., 1968-71; designer/assoc. Anspach-Grossman-Portugal, Inc., NYC, 1973-75; assoc. ptnr. Chermayeff & Geismar, Inc., NYC, 1975-79, ptnr., 1979—2005, C & G Ptnrs., 2005—. Mem. faculty improvement Fed. Graphics, Washington, 1976—; vis. lectr. field. With Swiss Army, 1962—67. Recipient nat. prize applied art, Fed. Govt. Switzerland, 1966, 1967, Gold medal, NY Art Dirs. Club, 1984, Gold medal, Lifetime Achievement award, Am. Inst. Graphic Arts, 2005. Mem.: Alliance Graphique Internat. (pres. US membership 1993—2000), Group Environ. Edn., Am. Ctr. Design, Am. Inst. Graphic Arts (v.p., dir. 1980—83, pres. NY chpt. 1984—86), NY Art Dirs. Club. Methodist. Office: C & G Ptnrs Inc 116 E 16th St New York NY 10003 Home Phone: 914-478-4095; Office Phone: 212-532-4460. Business E-Mail: steff@cgpartnersllc.com.

GEISSINGER, FREDERICK WALLACE, finance company executive; b. Huntingdon, Pa., Oct. 3, 1945; s. Harry Lloyd and Elizabeth Gertrude Geissinger; m. Anne Beth Lawrenz, Feb. 14, 1970 (div.); children: Amy Elizabeth, Jacqueline Marie. AB, Dartmouth Coll., 1967; MBA, U. Chgo., 1969. Lic. in securities and real estate, N.Y.C. Corp. banking officer Chase Manhattan Bank, NYC, 1969-74, dir. corp. planning, 1974-76, asst. gen. mgr. Tokyo, 1976-80, chief staff Western Hemisphere NYC, 1980-83, budget dir., 1983-86, sr. v.p. real estate, 1986-90; exec. v.p. Daiwa Securities Am. Inc., NYC, 1990-92; prin. Geissinger and Assocs., NYC, 1993; CEO Am. Gen. Land Devel. Inc., Houston, 1994-95, Am. Gen. Mortgage and Land Devel. Inc., 1995; chmn., CEO Am. Gen. Finance, Evansville, Ind., 1995—; vice chmn., group exec. Am. Gen. Corp., Houston, 1998—. Trustee Pelham (N.Y.) Bd. Edn., 1983-86. Mem. Urban Land Inst. (coun. 1986—); Real Estate Bd. N.Y., Pelham Country club (bd. govs. 1987-92, pres. 1990-92). Republican. Presbyterian. Avocations: skiing, golf, tennis, coaching girls soccer, classical music. Office Phone: 812-468-5500.

GEIST, LORRAINE PINNELLI, music educator, director; b. Bryn Mawr, Pa., Nov. 26, 1950; d. Joseph John and Grace Beatrice Pinnelli; m. Dennis D. Geist, May 25, 1974 (dec.); children: Kristin Leigh Ledbeter, Denise Nicole, Stefanie June. BA, Ea. U. (formerly Ea. Coll.), 1972; MA, U. No. Colo., 1981. Cert. tchr. Pa., 1972, instructional II Pa., 2003. Gen. choral orch. music tchr. Moanalua Intermediate Sch., 1979—80; elem. sch. counselor Mokapu Elem. Sch. and Enchanted Lakes Elem. Sch., Kailua, Hawaii, 1981—82; music tchr. Devereux Day Sch., Malvern, Pa., 1985—86; elem. music tchr. Calvary Luth. Sch., Havertown, Pa., 1989—95; elem. gen. music tchr. St. Clement Ireneaus Sch., Phila., 1996—99, St. Thomas Apostle, Chester Heights, Pa., 1996—99, Bell Ave./Park Ln. Elem., Yeadon, Darby, Pa., 2001—04; choral music dir. Penn Wood HS, Lansdowne, Pa., 2004—. Music dir. Upper Darby Summer Stage, Pa., 1999—2001, St. Andrew's Player, Drexel Hill, Pa., 2001—04, bd. dirs., 2001—04. Sgt. at arms ladies aux. USMC, 2000. Mem.: NEA, PSEA, PMEA, Music Educator's Nat. Conf. Roman Catholic. Avocations: reading, knitting, making ornaments. Office: Penn Wood HS 100 Green Ave Lansdowne PA 19050 Office Phone: 610-284-8076. Personal E-mail: mamageist26@comcast.net, lpgeist@comcast.net. Business E-Mail: lpgeist@wpsd.k12.pa.us.

GEISTFELD, JAMES GORDON, veterinarian; b. St. James, Minn., Oct. 11, 1947; s. Victor Edgar and Viola Otille (Becker) G.; m. Barbara Jean Lane, July 22, 1972; children: Matthew James, Erin Michal. BA, St. Olaf Coll., Northfield, Minn., 1969; DVM, U. Minn., 1973; MBA, U. Evansville, 1983. Diplomate Am. Coll. Lab. Animal Medicine. Epidemiologist Ctrs. for Disease Control, Atlanta, 1973—75; postdoctoral fellow Bowman Gray Sch. Medicine, Winston-Salem, NC, 1976—77; staff veterinarian Mead Johnson Rsch. Ctr., Evansville, Ind., 1977—82; sr. rsch. scientist Bristol-Myers Co., Evansville, Ind., 1982—87; dir. lab. animal medicine and surgery Rorer Pharm. Co., Ft. Washington, Pa., 1988—90; v.p. TNT Genetics Svcs., Albany, NY, 1995—97; dir. lab. animal medicine, v.p. Taconic Ventures, Inc., Germantown, NY, 1990—2001; exec. dir. Taconic Farms, Inc., Germantown, 2002—03, v.p. sci. affairs, 2003—06, sr. v.p. sci. affairs, 2007—. Cons. Ind. State U., Terre Haute, 1982-87, U. Evansville, 1983-87, OrienTreich Found., Cold Spring-on-Hudson, NY, 1992—, SUNY, Albany, 1997—; adj. prof. U. Pa., Phila., 1989-90; mem. expert coms. NIH/ILAR; dir. Mutant Mouse Regional Resource Ctr., NIH, 2000-06; bd. dirs. La Mesa Group, McKinney, Tex.; prin. investigator govt. contracts; leader evaluation team, mem. mgmt. bd. MCI, Strasbourg, France. Contbr. articles to profl. jours. Mem. ch. coun. 3d Luth. Ch., Rhinebeck, NY, 1992-96; trustee Friends of Clermont, Germantown, 1994-96; mem. C.L. Davis Found. Recipient Hole-In-The-Shoe award, USPHS, 1975; fellow, NIH, 1975—77. Mem. AVMA, Am. Soc. Lab. Animal Practitioners, Am. Coll. Lab. Animal Medicine, Am. Assn. for Lab. Animal Sci., Am. Assn. Ind. Vets., Am. Gnotobiotic Soc., Internat. Soc. for Gnotobiology, Global Alliance Lab. Animal Standardization Coun., Am. Soc. Microbiology, Rip Van Winkle Hiking Club (leader 1991-94), Catskill 3500 Hiking Club, Sigma Xi. Lutheran. Achievements include design of a new dog run, new animal research facilities; first to report a new mouse bacterial pathogen-group B type V streptococcus; discovery of several new animal models for human disease research. Home: 288 Linden Ave Red Hook NY 12571-1032 Office: Taconic Inc One Hudson City Centre Hudson NY 12534 Office Phone: 518-697-3928. Business E-Mail: jgei@taconic.com.

GEISTFELD, RONALD ELWOOD, retired dental educator; b. St. James, Minn., Nov. 9, 1933; s. Victor E. and Viola (Becker) G.; m. Lois N. Tolzman Wilkens, June 15, 1955 (div. June 1974); m. Annette L. Swenson, Jan. 14, 1977; children: Shari, Mark, Steven, Ann, Leah, Erik. AA, Bethany Jr. Coll., 1952; BS, U. Minn., 1954, DDS, 1957. Pvt. practice dentistry, Northfield, Minn., 1959-72; clin. asst. prof. dentistry U. Minn. Sch. Dentistry, Mpls., 1969-72, assoc. prof., 1972-82, chmn. dept. operative dentistry, 1978-87, prof., 1982-97, prof. emeritus, 1997; dir. quality programs Pentegra Dental Group, Inc., 1998-2000. Dental cons. Hennepin County Med. Ctr., Mpls., 1975-96, VA Hosp., Mpls., 1977-96, VA Hosp., St. Cloud, Minn., 1978-96, Human Performance and Informatics Inst., Atama, Japan, 1990-95, K-9 Dental Sys. Quidnunc Australia Pty. Ltd., 1994-95, Metro Dental Group, Mpls., 1995-2000, The Dentists Ins. Co., 1995-99, VGM Expert Systems, 1996-98, Met. Life Ins. Co., 1996—, Pentegra Ltd., 1997-2000; mem. resource faculty for Bush faculty devel. program on excellence and diversity in teaching U. Minn., 1993-94; founder Global Network for Systematic Healthcare, 2003. Pres. PTA, Northfield, 1965, Arts Guild, Northfield, 1968; bd. dirs., chairperson Rice County Health and Sanitation Bd., Faribault, Minn., 1966-74; bd. dirs. Northfield Bd. Edn., 1969-74; pres. Roseville Luth. Ch., 1987-88. Capt. U.S. Army, 1957-59. Am. Coll. Dentists fellow, 1972; recipient Prof. of Yr. award Century Club, 1996-97. Mem. Am. Dental Assn. (chairperson operative dentistry sect. 1979-80, curriculum cons. 1981-88, grants and spl. projects request evaluator 1988-92, Am. fund for Dental Health, edit. review bd. JADA 1992-96), Minn. Dental Assn. (ethics com. 1969-76, chairperson sci. and ann. sessions com. 1984-86, spkr. house del. 1992-96, del. to ADA 1992-96, bd. dirs. 1992-96), Mpls. Dist. Dental Soc. (program chairperson 1978-79, peer rev. com. 1988-92, bd. dirs. 1979-80, 87-89, MDA del. 1989-92), Minn. Acad. Restorative Dentistry (pres. 1979-80), Minn. Acad. Gnathological Rsch. (pres. 1986-87), Am. Assn. Dental Schs. (chairperson operative dentistry sect. 1984-85, edit. rev. bd. 1984-88), Acad. Operative Dentistry (exec. council 1978-81, rsch. com. 1987-89), Am. Acad. Gold Foil Operators, Northfield C. of C. (treas. and chairperson 1968-70), Delta Sigma Delta, Omicron Kappa Upsilon (Theta chpt.). Lodges: Rotary (pres. Northfield 1972-73). Personal E-mail: RAGeist@comcast.net.

GEITHNER, PAUL HERMAN, JR., retired banker; b. Phila., June 7, 1930; s. Paul Herman and Henriette Antonine (Schuck) G.; m. Irmgard (Hagedorn), Sept. 6, 1956; children: Christina, Amy, Paul. BA cum laude, Amherst Coll., Mass., 1952; MBA with distinction, U. Pa., Phila., 1957. Sec., treas. Ellicott Machine Co., Balt., 1964—68. V.p., sr. v.p., exec. asst. to the chmn. First Va. Banks, Inc., Falls Church, 1968-85, pres., chief adminstrv. officer, 1985-95, bd. dirs., vice chmn., 1986-95; pres. First Va. Life Ins. Co., 1974-96; trustee, mem. investment com. Bridgewater Coll., Va., 1988—. Bd. dirs. Fairfax Symphony Orch., Va., 1988—2004, pres., 1991—92; sec.-treas. Fairfax Symphony Orch. Found., Va., 1999—; bd. dirs. Va. Coll. Fund, 1987—91; trustee Va. Banker Sch. Bank Mgmt., 1988—92. Lt. USNR, 1952—55. Mem. Va. Bankers Assn., (pres. 1992-93).

GEITHNER, TIMOTHY F., bank executive; b. NYC, Aug. 18, 1961; m. Carole Sonnenfeld; children: Elise, Benjamin. BA in Govt. and Asian Studies, Dartmouth Coll., 1983; MA in Internat. Econ. and East Asian Studies, Johns Hopkins Sch., 1985. With Kissinger Assoc., Inc., 1985—88; dep. asst. sec. for internat. monetary and fin. policy US Dept. Treasury, 1995—96, sr. dep. asst. sec. for internat. affairs, 1996—97, asst. sec. for internat. affairs, 1997—98, under-sec. for internat. affairs, 1998—2001; dir. policy devel. and rev. dept. Internat. Monetary Fund, 2001—03; pres., CEO Fed. Res. Bank NY, NYC, 2003—. Adv. com. Ctr. for Global Devel.; coun. mem. Fgn. Rels.; chmn. com. payment and settlement sys. Bank for Internat. Settlements. Mem.: Econ. Club N.Y. (trustee), Coun. Fgn. Rels. Office: Fed Res Bank NY 33 Liberty St New York NY 10045 Office Phone: 212-720-5000.*

GEJDENSON, SAM, former congressman; b. Eschwege, Fed. Republic of Germany, May 20, 1948; m. Betsy Henley-Cohn; children: Mia, Ari stepchildren: Juri Henley-Cohn, Jesse Henley-Cohn. AS, Mitchell Coll., 1968; BA, U. Conn., 1970. Mem. Conn. State Ho. of Reps., 1974-78; coal broker, 1978-79; legis. liaison Conn. Office Policy and Mgmt., Hartford, 1979-80; mem. U.S. Congress from 2d Conn. dist., Washington, 1981-2001; owner & founder Sam Gejdenson Internat., 2001—. Democrat. Office: Sam Gejdenson International 84 Johnson Point Rd Branford CT 06405

GEKELMAN, DIANA, dentist, dental educator, researcher; d. Edward and Margareta Gekelman; m. Jean-Sebastien El Kaim; 1 child, David Gekelman El Kaim. DDS, U. Sao Paulo, Brazil, 1993; specialization in endodontics, U. Sao Paulo, 1997, MS, 2000. Post-doctoral fellow lasers in dentistry U. Calif., San Francisco, 2000—02, asst. prof. clin. endodontics, 2002—. Presenter in field; spkr. nat. and internat. confs. Sci. reviewer (articles); contbr. articles to profl. jours. Grantee, Sao Paulo Found. Rsch., 1999—2000, Found. Sci. and Technol. Devel. Dentistry, 2000, Lares Rsch., 2001—02, Parnassus Funding, U. Calif., San Francisco Sch. Dentistry, 2004—05. Mem.: ADA, San Francisco Dental Soc., Calif. Dental Assn., Am. Assn. Endodontists, Am. Assn. Dental Rsch., Soc. Photo-Optical Instrumentation Engrs., Acad. Laser Dentistry, Internat. Assn. Dental Rsch. Office: Univ Calif San Francisco Sch Dentistry 707 Parnassus Ave San Francisco CA 94143-0758 E-mail: gekelmand@dentistry.ucsf.edu.

GELATT, CHARLES DANIEL, manufacturing executive; b. La Crosse, Wis., Jan. 4, 1918; s. Philo Madison and Clara (Johnson) G.; m. Jane Leicht, Mar. 6, 1942 (div. 1972); children: Sarah Jane Gelatt Gephart, Charles D., Philip Madison; m. Paula Jo Evans, Aug. 22, 1973 (div. 1978); m. Sue Anne Jimieson, Dec. 11, 1983. BA, MA, U. Wis., 1939. V.p. Gelatt Corp., La Crosse, 1940-52, pres., 1952-95, chmn., 1995—99; pres. No. Engraving Corp., Sparta, Wis., 1958-67, chmn., 1967-96, chmn. emeritus, 1996—; pres. N.E. Co. Ltd., 2000—. Trustee Northwestern Mut. Life Ins. Co., Milw., 1960-88, mem. exec. com., 1961-77; chmn. North Ctrl. Trust Co., La Crosse, 1989-93; mem. bd. regents U. Wis., 1947-74, pres. bd. regents, 1955-57, v.p., 1964-68, pres., 1968-69; mem. Wis. Coordinating Com. for Higher Edn., 1955-59, 64-69, chmn., 1956; chmn. Assn. Governing Bds. Univs. and Colls., Washington, 1971-72; trustee Carroll Coll., Waukesha, Wis., 1971-79, Viterbo U., La. Crosse, 1972-2002; trustee Gundersen Found., La Crosse, 1973-95. Mem. Phi Beta Kappa. Home (Summer): 30976 Old MIll Rd La Crescent MN 55947 Home (Winter): 9133 Collins Ave #3A Miami FL 33154-3118

GELB, ARTHUR, electrical and systems engineering executive; b. NYC, Sept. 20, 1937; m. Linda Lewis; children: Ronald, Caren, Laurie. BEE, CUNY, 1958; MS in Applied Math., Harvard U., 1959; ScD in Systems Engring., MIT, 1961. Engr. Aviation Gas Turbine div. Westinghouse Electric Corp., Kansas City, Mo., 1956, Am. Dist. Telegraph Co., NYC, 1957-58, Draper Lab., Cambridge, Mass., 1959; dept. mgr. Dynamics Research Corp., Stoneham, Mass., 1961-66; pres., chief exec. officer TASC (The Analytic Sciences Corp.), Reading, Mass., 1966-93, chmn., 1993-94, sr. chmn., 1994; pres. Four Sigma Corp., Lexington, Mass., 1995—. Chmn. adv. bd. Ctr. for Tech., Policy and Indsl. Devel., MIT, 1987-97; mem. MIT Corp., 1996—; mem. Lincoln Lab. Adv. Bd. Co-author: Multiple-Input Describing Fns., 1968, Applied Optimal Estimation, 1974; contbr. articles to profl. jours. Bd. dirs. Massport, Boston, 1977-85; bd. regents Higher Edn., Mass., 1989-90; mem. Higher Edn. Coord. Coun., Mass., 1990-95. Named Outstanding Young Engr. CUNY, 1969. Fellow AIAA, IEEE (bd. editors Control Systems Mag. 1981-91), AAAS; mem. Mensa. Avocations: music, tennis, golf, microcomputing, math. Office: Four Sigma Corp One Cranberry Hill Lexington MA 02421-7394

GELB, HAROLD SEYMOUR, retired manufacturing executive, entrepreneur, consultant; b. NYC, Apr. 26, 1920; s. Daniel and Fanny (Gelb) G.; m. Sylvia M. Miller, Sept. 24, 1942; children: Richard, Alan. BBA, CCNY, 1941. CPA, N.Y. With S.D. Leidesdorf & Co. (CPAs), NYC, 1943-78, mng. partner, 1969-78; sr. ptnr. Ernst & Young, NYC, 1978-82; chmn. United Indsl. Corp., NYC, 1995—2003; ret. Past vice chmn. Citizens Budget Commn., N.Y.C., now trustee emeritus; past chmn. N.Y. State Bd. Pub. Accountancy. Pres. Bronx-Lebanon Hosp. Ctr., 1977; bd. dirs., v.p. S.D. Leidesdorf Found., 1969-80; trustee Accts. Found., 1973-80, Adelphi U., 1997—; bd. overseers Albert Einstein Med. Coll., 1977-79; bd. dirs., sec. Benjamin Cardozo Law Sch., 1977-89; mem. Gov.'s Task Force, Bus. Alliance with Edn., Mayor's Com. on Taxi Regulatory Issues, 1981-82. Recipient Disting. Cmty. Svc. award Brandeis U., 1978 Mem. AICPA (coun. 1970-76), N.Y. State Soc. CPAs (past v.p., bd. dirs.), Metropolis Country Club (White Plains), Town Club (Scarsdale). Home and Office: 575 Osgood St North Andover MA 01845

GELB, JOSEPH DONALD, lawyer; b. Wilkes-Barre, Pa., Dec. 13, 1923; s. Edward and Esther (Fierman) G. m. Anne Mirman, July 3, 1955; children: Adam, Roger. Student, Pa. State Coll., 1943; BS, U. Scranton, 1950; LLB, George Washington U., 1952. Bar: D.C. 1954, Md. 1963, U.S. Supreme Ct. 1972. Adjudicator War Claims Commn., 1952—54; pvt. practice Washington and Md., 1954—69; ptnr. Gelb & Pitsenberger, Washington, 1968—74; prin. Joseph D. Gelb Chartered, Washington, 1974—80, Gelb, Abelson & Siegel, P.C., Washington, 1980—82, Gelb & Siegel, P.C., Washington, 1982—85, Joseph D. Gelb, Chartered, Washington, 1985—93, Gelb & Gelb, P.C., Washington, 1994—. Served with USAAF, 1943-46 Mem. Md. Bar Assn., D.C. Bar Assn., Bethesda Country Club, B'nai B'rith, Masons. also: 525 N Ocean Blvd Pompano Beach FL 33062-4640 Office: Gelb & Gelb PC 1120 Connecticut Ave NW Washington DC 20036-3902 Home: 5220 Pooks Hill Rd Bethesda MD 20814 Office Phone: 202-331-7227. Personal E-mail: joegelb@comcast.com. Business E-Mail: lawyers@gelbandgelb.com.

GELB, JUDITH ANNE, lawyer; b. NYC, Apr. 5, 1935; d. Joseph and Sarah (Stein) G.; m. Howard S. Vogel, June 30, 1962; 1 child, Michael S. BA, Bklyn. Coll., 1955; JD, Columbia U., 1958. Bar: N.Y. 1959, U.S. Dist. Ct. (so. and ea. dists.) N.Y. 1960, U.S. Ct. Appeals (2d cir.) 1960, U.S. Ct. Mil. Appeals 1962. Asst. to editor N.Y. Law Jour., NYC, 1958—59; confidential asst. to U.S. atty. ea dist. N.Y., Bklyn., 1959—61; assoc. Whitman & Ransom, NYC, 1961—70, ptnr., 1971—93, Whitman Breed Abbott & Morgan LLP, NYC, 1993—2000, Winston & Strawn LLP, NYC, 2000—07; counsel Allegaert Berger & Vogel LLP, NYC, 2007—. Mem.: ABA (individual rights sect., real property and trust law sect.), Assn. Bar City N.Y., N.Y. State Bar Assn. (trusts and estates com.), Fed. Bar Coun., Columbia Law Sch. Alumni Assn. (bd. dirs.), Princeton Club. Home: 169 E 69th St New York NY 10021-5163 Office: Allegaert Berger & Vogel 111 Broadway New York NY 10006 Business E-Mail: jgelb@abv.com.

GELB, LESLIE HOWARD, writer, lecturer, consultant; b. New Rochelle, NY, Mar. 4, 1937; s. Max and Dorothy (Klein) G.; m. Judith Cohen, Aug. 2, 1959; children: Adam, Caroline, Alison. AB magna cum laude in Govt. and cum laude in Philosophy, Tufts U., 1959; MA, Harvard U., 1961, PhD, 1964. Teaching fellow govt. and social scis., non-resident tutor Winthrop House, Harvard U., 1962-64, assoc. def. studies program, 1963-64; asst. prof. govt. Wesleyan U., Middletown, Conn., 1964-65; exec. asst. to US Senator Jacob K. Javits US Senate, 1966-67; dep. dir. policy planning staff US Dept. Def., Washington, 1967-68, dir. policy planning staff, 1968, acting dep. asst. sec. def. for policy planning and arms control staff, 1968-69; dir. sec. def. Vietnam task force, 1967-68; sr. fellow Brookings Instn., Washington, 1969-73; corr. NY Times, Washington, 1973-77; dir. bur. politico-mil. affairs US Dept. State, Washington, 1977-79; sr. assoc. Carnegie Endowment for Internat. Peace, 1979-81; chmn. Carnegie Endowment Panel on Future U.S. Security and Arms Control, 1980-81; nat. security corr. N.Y. Times, 1981-86, dep. editorial page editor, op-editorial page editor, 1986-90, fgn. affairs columnist, 1991-93; pres. Coun. Fgn. Rels., 1993—2003, pres. emeritus, sr. fellow bd, 2003—. Bd. dirs. certain funds advised by Salomon Bros. Asset Mgmt., certain registered investment cos. advised by Legg Mason Mutual Fund, Ctr. Partners Fund, britannica.com, The Nixon Ctr.; mem. The Trilateral Commn., 1993-2000; chmn. adv. bd. Emerging Europe Pvt. Equity Fund III. Author: The Irony of Vietnam: The System Worked, 1979, Anglo-American Relations, 1945-49, 1988; co-author: Our Own Worst Enemy: The Unmaking of American Foreign Policy, 1984; contbr. numerous articles to mags.; sr. cons. and producer "The Crisis Game," 1983 (Emmy, DuPont, Hood awards); sr. editor postwar history of U.S. "45/85," 1985 Trustee emeritus Tufts U., Carnegie Endowment for Internat. Peace; mem. adv. bd. Sch. Internat. and Pub. Affairs, Columbia U., 1997-2001; bd. dirs. James A. Baker III Inst. Pub. Policy; adv. mem. Ctr. Press, Politics and Pub. Policy, Harvard U. John F. Kennedy Sch. Govt., 1991-2001. Recipient Woodrow Wilson award, 1980, Page One award in explanatory journalism, 1985, Nat. Father of Yr. award U.S. Nat. Com. on Fathers and Mothers of Yr. Awards, 1993; mem. N.Y. Times Pulitzer Prize Winning Team, 1985. Fellow AAAS; mem. Internat. Inst. Strategic Studies, Coun. Fgn. Rels. Office: Coun Fgn Rels 58 E 68th St New York NY 10021-5953

GELB, MORRIS, chemicals executive; BSChemE, Cooper Union, 1967. With E.I. Dupontde Nemours & Co., 1969-77, Oxirane, 1977-80; mng. dir. ARCO Chem. Iberica, Barcelona, Spain, 1984; v.p., ops. and bus. mgmt.

ARCO Chem., Eng., v.p. rsch. and engring. Phila., 1986-97, sr. v.p. mfg. process devel. and engring., 1997-98, exec. v.p., COO, 1998—. Office: Lyondell Chem Co 1221 McKinney St Ste 700 Houston TX 77010*

GELB, PETER, performing company executive; b. 1953; s. Arthur and Barbara Gelb; m. Keri-Lynn Wilson; 2 children. Mgr. Vladimir Horowitz; pres. CAMI Video, 1987—93, Sony Classical, 1995—2004; gen. mgr. Met. Opera, 2005—. Prodr.: (TV special) Horowitz in London: A Royal Concert, 1982, Ozawa, 1985, Vladimir Horowitz: The Last Romantic, 1986, Aida, 1989, Tchaikovsky: 150th Birthday Gala from Leningrad, 1990, Kathleen Battle and Wynton Marsalis in Baroque Duet, 1991, A Carnegie Hall Christmas, 1991, La Fanciulla del West, 1992, Oedipus Rex, 1992, Vladimir Horowitz: A Reminiscence, 1993, Kathleen Battle at the Metropolitan Museum, 1993, Bobby McFerrin: Loosely Mozart, the New Innovators of Classical Music, 1996, Our Favorite Things: Christmas in Vienna, 2000, Recording 'The Producers': A Musical Romp with Mel Brooks, 2001 (Grammy award), The Little Prince, 2004; (TV series) Marsalis on Music, 1995 (Peabody award), Great Performances, 1995, Horowitz Plays Mozart, 1987, Jessye Norman Sings Carmen, 1988, Soldiers of Music, 1991, Voices from a Locked Room, 1995, Vangelis: Mythodea - Music for the NASA Mission, 2001 Mars Odyssey, 2001. Recipient 6 Emmy awards. Office: Metropolitan Opera 70 Lincoln Center Plaza New York NY 10023*

GELB, RICHARD MARK, lawyer; b. NYC, June 12, 1947; s. Harold Seymour and Sylvia Mildred (Miller) Gelb; m. Gail Kleven, July 29, 1973; 1 child, Daniel Kleven. BA, NYU, 1969; JD, Boston Coll., 1973. Bar: Mass. 1973, N.Y. 1975, D.C. 1975, U.S. Dist. Ct. (so. and ea. dists.) N.Y. 1975, U.S. Ct. Appeals (2d cir.) 1975, U.S. Dist. Ct. Conn. 1977, U.S. Ct. Appeals (1st cir.) 1978, U.S. Dist. Ct. Mass. 1978, U.S. Supreme Ct. 1980. Assoc. Proskauer Rose, LLP, NYC, 1975-77; ptnr. Gelb & Gelb LLP, Boston, 1987—. Contbr. articles to profl. publs. Mem. Mass. Bar Assn. (ethics com. 1991-96, civil litig. coun. 1994-96, chmn. bus. litig. com. 1992-94, assoc. editor Mass. Law Rev. 1982-87), Am. Inn of Ct. Found. (trustee 1994-98), Boston Inn of Ct. (co-pres. 1993-94), Boston Coll. Law Sch. Intellectual Property Am. Inns of Ct. (pres. 1998-2000, treas. 2001-02), Boston Coll. Law Sch. Alumni Coun. (v.p. comms. 2001-03), Suffolk U. Law Sch. Litig. Am. Inn Ct. (co-pres. 2002-05), Pi Sigma Alpha. Democrat. Jewish. Home: 60 Pine Hill Rd Swampscott MA 01907-2240 Office: Gelb & Gelb LLP 84 State St Boston MA 02109 Office Phone: 617-345-0010. Business E-Mail: rgelb@gelbgelb.com.

GELBART, LARRY, scriptwriter, television and theater producer; b. Chgo., Feb. 25, 1928; s. Harry and Frieda (Sturner) G.; m. Pat Marshall, Nov. 25, 1956; children: Gary, Paul, Adam, Becky. LittD (hon.), Union Coll., Schnectady, NY, 1986; LHD (hon.), Hofstra U., 1999. Writer: for radio series The Eddie Cantor Show, 1946, Maxwell House Coffee Time with Danny Thomas, 1946, Duffy's Tavern, 1946, Command Performance, 1946-47, Jack Carson, 1947-48, The Jack Paar Show, 1949, The Joan Davis Show, 1949, The Bob Hope Show, 1949-52; for ballet, Peter and the Wolf, 1992; for theatre My L.A., 1950, The Conquering Hero, 1960, A Funny Thing Happened on the Way to the Forum, 1962 (Tony award with Burt Shevelove best musical play 1963), Sly Fox, 1976, One, Two, Three, Four, Five, 1988, City of Angels, 1989 (Drama Desk award best book of musical 1989, Tony award best musical, best book of musical 1990, Best New Musical citation NY Drama Critics Circle 1990, Outer Critics Circle award outstanding Broadway musical, contbn. to comedy award 1990, Edgar Allan Poe award best mystery play 1990), Mastergate, 1989 (Outer Critics Circle award contbn. to comedy 1990), (co-author) Jerome Robbins' Broadway, 1989; for films The Notorious Landlady, 1962, The Thrill of It All, 1963, (also co-producer) The Wrong Box, 1966, Not With My Wife You Don't, 1966, The Chastity Belt, 1968, A Fine Pair, 1969, Oh, God, 1977 (Acad. award nomination best screenplay material from another medium 1977, Edgar Allan Poe award, Mystery Writers Am. award, Writers Guild award), Movie, Movie, 1978 (Writers Guild award, Christopher award), Neighbors, 1981, Tootsie, 1982 (Acad. Award nomination best screenplay written directly for screen 1982, LA Film Critics award, NY Film Critics award, Nat. Soc. Film Critics award), (also exec. producer) Blame It on Rio, 1984, Bedazzled, 2000; writer, prodr., co-prodr. TV shows M*A*S*H, 1972-76 (Emmy award nomination outstanding writing comedy 1972, 75, Writers Guild Am. award 1972, 74, Emmy award outstanding comedy series 1973, Emmy award nominations outstanding comedy series 1974, 75, George Foster Peabody award 1975, Humanitas award), Roll Out!, 1973-74, Karen, 1975, United States, 1980, After M*A*S*H, 1983-84 (Emmy award nomination outstanding directing comedy series 1983); TV adaptation Mastergate, 1992; writer, exec. prodr. HBO film Barbarians at the Gate, 1993 (Outstanding Made-for-TV-Movie Emmy award, Best Made-for-TV-Motion Picture award The Am. TV Awards, Program of Yr., The TV Critics Assn., Cable Ace award, Writing in a Movie or Miniseries), Weapons of Mass Distraction, 1997; Best Teleplay awd., PEN Ctr. USA West, writer TV shows The All-Star Revue, 1950-53, The Red Buttons Show, 1952-55, Honestly, Celeste!, 1954, The Patrice Munsel Show, 1954-62, Caesar's Hour, 1955-57 (Emmy award nominations best comedy writing 1955, 56, 57), The Pat Boone Chevy Showroom, 1957-60, The Danny Kaye Show, 1963 (Emmy award nomination outstanding writing comedy or variety show 1963), The Marty Feldman Comedy Machine, 1972, (TV movie) And Starring Pancho Villa as Himself, 2003, Like Jazz, A New Kind of Musical, 2003; author: Laughing Matters, 1998. Served with AUS, 1945-46. Recipient Lee Strasberg Lifetime Achievement in Arts and Sci. award, 1990, William S. Paley award for excellence in TV, Anti-Defamation League, 2001, citation for disting. svc., AMA, 2001, Valentine Davies award, Writers Guild Am., West, 2007. Mem. Dramatists Guild, Writers Guild Am. (award 1972, 74), ASCAP, Dir. Guild Am. Address: 807 N Alpine Dr Beverly Hills CA 90210-2901 E-mail: elsig@aol.com.

GELBEIN, JAY JOEL, accountant; b. Bklyn., Sept. 11, 1949; s. Leo and Sara (Eskolsky) G.; m. Marilyn Stern, Dec. 8, 1974; children: Moshe, Avi, Danielle. BS, Bklyn. Coll., 1972; MS with distinction, L.I. U., 1978. CPA, NY; cert. fin. planner; registered investment advisor. Appellate conferee IRS, NYC, 1971-79; tech. mgr. AICPA, NYC, 1979-81; pvt. practice acctg. and tax cons. Staten Island, N.Y., 1979—. Prof. bus. Kingsborough C.C., Bklyn., 1981—; lectr. in field Author: Tax-wise Investing for High Income Taxpayers, 1992, 2d edit., 1993; contbr. to The Practical Accountant, 1991; co-author: Accounting Demonstration Problems Workbook. Mem. AICPA, N.Y. State Soc. CPAs (mem. profl. svc. corp. com.), Inst. Cert. Fin. Planners. Home and Office: 13 President St Staten Island NY 10314-4119 Office Phone: 718-494-1423. Personal E-mail: jjgcpa18@aol.com.

GELBER, DON JEFFREY, lawyer; b. LA, Mar. 10, 1940; s. Oscar and Betty Sheila (Chernitsky) G.; m. Jessica Jeasun Song, May 15, 1967; children: Victoria, Jonathan, Rebecca, Robert. Student UCLA, 1957-58, Reed Coll., 1958-59; AB, Stanford U., 1961, JD, 1963. Bar: Calif. 1964, Hawaii 1964, US Dist. Ct. (cen. and no. dists. Calif.) 1964, US Dist. Ct. Hawaii 1964, US Ct. Appeals (9th cir.) 1964, US Supreme Ct. 1991. Assoc. Greenstein, Yamane & Cowan, Honolulu, 1964-67; reporter Penal Law Revision Project, Hawaii Jud. Council, Honolulu, 1967-69; assoc. H. William Burgess, Honolulu, 1969-72; ptnr. Burgess & Gelber, Honolulu, 1972-73; prin. Law Offices of Don Jeffrey Gelber, Honolulu, 1974-77; pres. Gelber, Gelber & Ingersoll, 1978-; legal counsel Hawaii State Senate Judiciary Com., 1965; adminstrv. asst. to majority floor leader Hawaii State Senate, 1966, legal counsel Edn. Com., 1967, 68; majority counsel Hawaii Ho. of Reps., 1974; spl. counsel Hawaii State Senate, 1983. Contbr. articles to legal publs. Mem. State Bar Calif., ABA (sect. bus. law), Fed. Bar Assn., Am. Bankruptcy Inst., Hawaii State Bar Assn. (sect. bankruptcy law, bd. dirs. 1991-93, pres. 1993). Clubs: Pacific, Plaza (Honolulu). Office: Gelber Gelber Ingersoll & Klevansky 745 Fort Street Mall Ste 1400 Honolulu HI 96813-3877 Office Phone: 808-524-0155.

GELBER, LOUISE C(ARP), lawyer; m. Milton Gelber (dec.); children: Jack, Bruce, Julie McCoy. BA, U. Calif., Berkeley, 1943, JD, 1944. Bar: Calif. 1945, US Dist. Ct. (so. dist.) Calif. 1945, US Supreme Ct. 1965. Pvt. practice; commr. Calif. Bd. Examiners for Nursing Home Adminstrs.; adminstr. Calif. Dept. Consumer Affairs. Spkr. local drug rehab. hosp.; mem. Vis. Nurses Bd.; commr. Calif. Adv. Cost Control to State Govt.; mem. temporary judge panel LA County; settlement officer dispute resolution svc. Pasadena Superior Ct. Mem. editorial staff U. Calif. Law Rev. Calif. nominee for State Assembly, 1992; judge pro tem Rio Hondo Mcpl. Ct.; pro bono Bd. Legal Aid; v.p. local PTA; mem., invocator Arcadia Coord. Coun.; bd. dirs. Foothill Apt. Assn., People-For People; active ARC, Community Chest, United Way, Boy Scouts Am., Girl Scouts US. Mem. ABA, Calif. Bar Assn., Foothill Bar Assn., L.A. County Bar ASsn., Pomona Valley Bar Assn., Citrus Bar Assn., Arcadia C. of C. (legis. com.), So. Calif. Women Lawyers (treas.), Pasadena C. of C., Bus. and Profl. Women Lawyers (past state legis. chmn., state legis. adv.), Order of Eastern Star, LWV, Sierra. Home and Office: 1225 Rancho Rd Arcadia CA 91006-2241 Office Phone: 626-355-1872. Personal E-mail: french.court@verizon.net.

GELBER, ROBERT CARY, law librarian; b. NYC, Dec. 21, 1951; s. Louis and Dora (Zimmerman) G.; m. Cathy Lynne Domin, Mar. 24, 1974; 1 child, Cari. BA, Pace U., 1973; MLS, Pratt Inst., 1974. Asst. cataloger N.Y. County Lawyer's Assn., NYC, 1969-74; librarian Office Spl. State Prosecutor, NYC, 1974; asst. libr. N.Y. State Appellate Div., NYC, 1974-97, sr. ct. analyst, 1997-98; prin. ct. analyst Continuing Legal Edn. Staff of Office of Ct. Admin., NYC, 1998—. Instr. legal rsch., adult edn. program Baruch Coll., SUNY, 1990-91. Mem. Law Librarians Assn. Greater N.Y.

GELBERG, LILLIAN, family medicine physician, educator; b. LA, May 14, 1955; married; 3 children. BA, UCLA, 1977; MD, Harvard U., 1981; MSPH, UCLA, 1987. Diplomate Am. Bd. Family Practice. Robert Wood Johnson Found. clin. scholar UCLA/VA, 1984-86; asst. prof. UCLA, 1987-97, assoc. prof., 1997—, George F. Kneller prof. family medicine, 2001—. Contbr. chpts. to books, articles to profl. jours. Vol., com. chair various family clinics, Venice, Calif., 1984—. Recipient CAFP 1st Rsch. Excellence award, 2001; Robert Wood Johnson Found. scholar UCLA, 1984-86, Robert Wood Johnson faculty scholar, 1995-2001. Fellow Am. Acad. Family Physicians; mem. Soc. Gen. Internal Medicine, Assn. Health Svc. Rsch. (Young Investigator award 1995, Article of the Yr. award 1997), Soc. of Tchrs. of Family Medicine, Am. Pub. Health Assn., Inst. Medicine, 2004. E-mail: gelberg@ucla.edu.

GELBERMAN, RICHARD H., orthopedist, surgeon; b. NYC, Nov. 27, 1943; MD, U. Tenn. Health Scis. Ctr., 1969. Diplomate orthopedic surgery and in hand surgery Am. Bd. Orthopaedic Surgery. Resident U. Wis., Madison, 1971—75; fellow, hand & microsurgery Duke U., 1976—77; fellow, pediat. orthopedics Boston Children's Hosp., 1985—86; prof. orthop. surgery Harvard U. Med. Sch., Boston, 1987—94; Fred. C. Reynolds prof. orthop. surgery Washington U. Sch. Medicine, St. Louis, 1995—. Mem.: Am. Bd. Orthop. Surgeons, Assn. Bone & Joint Surgeons, Orthop. Rsch. Soc., Inter-Urban Orthop. Soc., Inst. Medicine, IOS, Am. Soc. Surgery of the Hand, Am. Orthop. Assn., Am. Acad. Orthop. Surgeons (pres. 2001—02). Office: Washington U Sch Medicine Ste 11300 One Barnes Hosp Plz Saint Louis MO 63110

GELBKE, CLAUS-KONRAD, nuclear physics educator; b. Celle, Germany, May 31, 1947; came to the U.S., 1976; s. Heinz and Gertraud Gelbke; m. Brigitte Zabeschek, Apr. 6, 1973; children: Susanne, Martin. Diploma für physik, U. Heidelberg, Germany, 1970, doctor rerum naturalium, 1973. Wissenschaftlicher asst. Max-Planck-Inst für Kernphysik, Heidelberg, 1973-76; physicist Lawrence Berkeley (Calif.) Lab., 1976-77; assoc. prof. physics Mich. State U., East Lansing, 1977-81, prof. physics, 1981-87, assoc. dir. nuclear sci. Nat. Superconducting Cyclotron Lab., 1987-90, disting. prof., 1990—, dir. Nat. Superconducting Cyclotron Lab., 1992—. Summer visitor Brookhaven Nat. Lab., Upton, N.Y., 1974, U. Washington, Seattle, 1975. Alfred P. Sloan fellow, 1979-83; Scholarship Studienstiftung des Deutschen Volkes, 1971-72; Humboldt Rsch. award U.S. Scis. Fellow AAAS, Am. Physical Soc. Office: Mich State U Cyclotron Lab S Shaw Ln East Lansing MI 48824 E-mail: gelbke@nscl.msu.edu.

GELBOIN, HARRY VICTOR, biochemistry educator, researcher; b. Chgo., Dec. 21, 1929; s. Herman and Eva (Jurkowsky) Gelboin; m. Stella Bezansky, June 19, 1951; m. Marlena Maisels, Apr. 1, 1962; children: Michele Ida, Lisa Rebecca, Sharon Anna, Tamara Rachel. BA in Chemistry, U. Ill., 1951; MS in Biochemistry and Oncology, U. Wis., 1956, PhD in Biochemistry and Oncology, 1958; DSc (hon.), U. Inonu, Malatya, Turkey, 1999. Devel. chemist U.S. Rubber Co., Chgo., 1952-54; rsch. asst. McArdle Meml. Lab. for Cancer Rsch., U. Wis., 1954-58; biochemist lab. cellular pharmacology NIMH, 1958-60, biochemist lab. clin. sci., 1960-61; supervisory biochemist chemistry sect., diagnostic rsch. br. Nat. Cancer Inst., 1962-64, head chemistry sect., carcinogenesis studies br., 1964-66, chief lab. molecular carcinogenesis, div. cancer etiology, 1966—; adj. prof. Georgetown U., 1974-78. Bd. dirs. Internat. Soc. Polycyclic Aromatic Com.; keynote spkr. carcinogenesis Gordon Res. Conf., 1965; Franz Bielschowsky meml. lectr., Dunedin, New Zealand, 66; Smith Kline French hon. lectr. U. Fla., 1974, U. Mich., 1976; hon. lectr. Israel Cancer Soc. and U. Tel Aviv, Israel, 1983; keynote lectr. Internat. Conf. Carcinogenesis, Alghero, Italy, 1986; Nakasone hon. lectr. Japan Found. Promotion Sci., Tokyo and Osaka, Japan, 1989; keynote speaker U.S. organizer and co-chmn. Princess Takamatsu Cancer Symposium, Tokyo, 1990; vis. prof. Hebrew U., Jerusalem, 1985—86, 2000; plenary lectr. Glinos Found., Athens, 1996; cons. drug metabolism, toxicology and drug discovery; domestic and fgn. spkr. in field. Editor 8 profl. books; assoc. editor Cancer Rsch., 1968-79, 83-87, mem. editl. adv. bd., 1965-67; assoc. editor Biochem. Toxicology, 1984—; mem. editl. bd. Chemico-Biol. Interactions, 1969-75, Archives Biochemistry and Biophysics, 1969-76, Life Scis., 1976, Environ. Health Scis., 1976-78; contbr. and co-contbr. over 420 sci. papers to med. publs.; editor/co-editor 10 books, 8 patents. Recipient Superior Svc. award NIH, 1970, Claude Bernard award U. Montreal, 1970, New Horizons award Radiol. Soc. N.Am., 1970, Merit awards Sr. Sci. Svc. NIH, 1983, 85, EEO award NIH, 1989 Fellow: Amer. Coll. Clin. Pharmacol.; mem.: Internat. Soc. for Study Xenobiotics, Internat. Soc. for Preventive Oncology, Am. Soc. for Pharmacology and Exptl. Therapeutics, Am. Soc. Biol. Chemists, Am. Cancer Soc. (adv. com. on carcinogenesis, mem. coun. 1975—), Am. Assn. for Cancer Rsch., AAAS. Achievements include discovery of mechanism of carcinogenesis and cytochrome P450; microsomal P450 activation of chemicals to forms binding to proteins and DNA; describing the activation system for the initial stages of mutagenesis and carcinogenesis, activation for Ames mutagen detection system; development of isolation of specific inhibitory and immunoblotting monoclonal antibodies to each of human cytochrome P450 enzymes, system analyzing drug and xenobiotic metabolism for reduction of drug toxicity; drug discovery. Personal E-mail: HGG@helix.nih.gov.

GELDER, JOHN WILLIAM, lawyer; b. Buffalo, Aug. 7, 1933; s. Ray Horace and Grace Catherine (Kelly) G.; m. Martha J. Kindleberger, June 12, 1953; William R., Mark S., Cathryn J. Gelder Brooks, Carolyn G. Gelder Bird BBA, U. Mich., 1956, JD with distinction, 1959. Bar: Mich. 1960, D.C. 1981, U.S. Supreme Ct. 1982. Assoc. Miller, Canfield, Paddock and Stone, P.L.C., Detroit, 1959-68, mng. ptnr., 1975-81, 90-93, ptnr., 1968-93, prin., 1994—. Bd. dirs. Tecumseh Products Co., 1989—. Asst. editor Mich. Law Rev., 1958, 59 Trustee, officer Herrick Found., Detroit, 1989—. Mem. State Bar Mich. (coun. mem. bus. law sect. 1984-90), Order of Coif, Bloomfield Hills Country Club. Home: 30845 River Crossing St Bingham Farms MI 48025-4656 Office: Miller Canfield Paddock & Stone PLC 840 W Long Lake Rd Ste 200 Troy MI 48098-6358 E-mail: gelder@millercanfield.com.

GELEERD, JAMES D. (JAKE GELEERD), property manager; b. 1966; BS, Univ. Ill. Tax consul. Arthur Andersen & Co., Chgo., 1990—94; with Equity Group Investment, Chgo., 1994—99; pres. Sportsco Internat.; prin. Terrapin Properties. LLC, Chgo., 2002—. Appeared (TV series) Oprah Winfrey Show. Named one of 40 Under Forty, Crain's Bus. Chgo., 2005. Mem.: Young Presidents' Orgn., Sigma Alpha Mu (assoc.). Office: Terrapin Properties 5th Floor 217 N Jefferson St Chicago IL 60661 Office Phone: 312-466-1500. Office Fax: 312-466-1555.*

GELEHRTER, THOMAS DAVID, medical educator, geneticist; b. Liberec, Czechoslovakia, Mar. 11, 1936; arrived in U.S., 1939; married 1959; 2 children. BA, Oberlin Coll., 1957; MA, U. Oxford, Eng., 1959; MD, Harvard U., 1963. Intern, then asst. resident in internal medicine Mass. Gen. Hosp., Boston, 1963—65; rsch. assoc. in molecular biology NIAMD NIH, Bethesda, Md., 1965—69; fellow in med. genetics U. Wash., 1969—70; asst. prof. human genetics, internal medicine and pediatrics Sch. Medicine Yale U., 1970—73, assoc. prof., 1973—74, U. Mich., Ann Arbor, 1974—76, prof. internal medicine and human genetics, 1976—87, dir. divsn. med. genetics, 1977—87, chmn. dept. human genetics, 1987—2004, prof. human genetics and internal medicine, 1987—. Josiah Macy, Jr. Found. faculty scholar and vis. scientist Imperial Cancer Rsch. Fund Labs., London, 1979-80; vis. fellow Inst. Molecular Medicine; Keeley vis. fellow Wadham Coll., U. Oxford, Wellcome Rsch. Travel grantee, 1995. Mem. editl. bd. Jour. Biol. Chemistry, 1995-2000. Trustee Oberlin Coll., 1970-75; mem. NIH Recontinant DNA Adv. Com., 2002-05. Rhodes scholar, 1957-59. Fellow AAAS, Am. Coll. Med. Genetics; mem. Am. Soc. Human Genetics (bd. dir. 1994-96), Am. Soc. Clin. Investigation, Am. Soc. Biochemistry and Molecular Biology, Assn. Am. Physicians. Office: Univ Mich Med Sch Dept Human Genetics Box 0618 1241 Catherine St Ann Arbor MI 48109-0618 Office Phone: 734-936-2860. Business E-Mail: tdgum@umich.edu.

GELENBE, SAMI EROL, computer scientist, engineering educator; b. Istanbul, Turkey, Aug. 22, 1945; arrived in France, 1972; s. Ali Yusuf and Maria (Sacchet) G.; m. Deniz Arman, June 8, 1968; 1 child, Pamir. BSEE, Mid. East Tech. U., Turkey, 1966; MSEE, Poly. Inst. Bklyn., 1968, PhD, 1969; DSc, U. Paris, 1973; D of Engring. (hon.), U. Rome, 1996; PhD (hon.), Boğaziçi U., Istanbul, 2004; DSc (hon.), U. Liege, 2006. Asst. prof. U. Mich., Ann Arbor, 1970-72; prof. U. Liege, Belgium, 1972-79, U. Paris, 1979—. Sci. dir. Inria, Rocquencourt, France, 1973—82; sci. advisor Sec. State, Paris, 1984—86; chaired prof. Duke U., 1993—98; assoc. dean engring. U. Ctrl. Fla., 1998—2003, univ. chaired prof., 2001—03; chair tech. adv. bd. US Army Simulation and Tng. Command, 1999—2003; Dennis Gabor chair Imperial Coll., London, 2003, head of intelligent sys. and networks, chaired prof., 2003—; mem. sci. and tech. bd. Def. Tech. Ctr. on Data and Info. Fusion, Ministry of Def. U.K., 2003—. Author: (books transl. into Japanese and Korean) Analysis and Synthesis of Computer Systems, 1980, 1980, Introduction aux reseaux de files d' attente, 1982, Multiprocessor Performance, 1988, Concurrency Control in Distributed Databases, 1989, Introduction to Networks of Queues, 1999; mem. editl. bd.: Acta Info., 1978—, Performance Evaluation, 1979—, IEEE Transactions on Software Engring, 1979—92, Computer Comms., 1999—, Telecomm Systems, 1993—, Simulation Practice and Theory, 1996—, Computer Jour., Annales des Telecommunications, 2002—, Computational Mgmt. Sci., 2002—, Recherche Opérationnelle, 1994—; contbr. articles to profl. jours. Adv. com. elec. US Army, 1995, mem. tech. adv. bd. army simulation and tng. command, 1999—2003. Decorated chevalier and officer Order of Merit France, chevalier Palmes Académiques, France, comdr. Order of Merit Italy; recipient Silver Core award, IFIP, 1980, Sci. award, Parlar Found., Turkey, 1994, French Acad. Sci. award, Grand Prix France Telecom, 1996; fellow, Fulbright Found., 1966, Gordon McKay fellow, Harvard U., 1974. Fellow: IEE, ACM, IEEE (mem. editl. bd. 1985—93, rev. bd. France 1974—82, Meritorious Svc. award 1989, 1992); mem.: Academia Europaea, Eta Kappa Nu, Epsilon Pi Upsilon, Sigma Xi. Achievements include numerous patents in field; invention of first finite state models to predict the performance of memory paging algorithms, concurrently with W.F. King of IBM; proved that the FIFO paging algorithm is strictly equivalent to a random page replacement policy for the independent memory references establishing a hierarchy of memory management policies; going from random to optimal and deriving their page fault ratios in explicit form; derived first diffusion approximation for queuing systems using holding times at the boundries; thus providing for better accuracy than conventional "reflecting boundary" diffusions at light traffic, and good accuracy at heavy traffic; later applying it to the analysis of Asynchronous Transfer Mode cell traffic, leading to a patented call admission control protocol for ATM networks; published the first performance analyses of window protocols in computer networks. Avocations: history, bicycling. Office: Imperial College London SW7 2BT England Office Phone: 44-207 594 6342. E-mail: e.gelenbe@imperial.ac.uk.

GELFAND, DAVID R., lawyer; b. Bethpage, NY, 1963; BA, Vanderbilt Univ., 1984, JD, 1987. Bar: N.Y. 1988, D.C. 1990, US Dist. Ct. So. & Ea. N.Y., Ea. Dist. Wis., US Ct. Appeals Second, Fifth, Seventh & Eleventh Cir., US Supreme Ct. Assoc. Milbank Tweed Hadley & McCloy, NYC, 1987—96, ptnr. & Nat. Litigation Dept. group leader, 1996—. Editor: Vanderbilt Jour. Transnational Law. Mem.: ABA, Assn. Bar City of N.Y. (mem. Com. Judicial Adminstrn.), D.C. Bar Assn. Office: Milbank Tweed Hadley & McCloy 1 Chase Manhattan Plz New York NY 10005-1413 Office Phone: 212-530-5520. Office Fax: 212-530-5219. Business E-Mail: dgelfand@milbank.com.

GELFAND, HOWARD MICHAEL, history professor; b. New Brunswick, NJ, Dec. 20, 1967; s. Elayne Phyllis and Gerald Gelfand. PhD, U. Ariz., 2002; AB, U. Ga., 1989, MA, 1994, U. Ky., 1991. Prof. U. Ariz. Hist. Dept., Tucson, 2001—05, Ariz. State U. Hist. Dept., Tempe, Ariz., 2003, James Madison U. Hist. Dept., Harrisonburg, Va., 2005—. Analyst U. S. Air Force Air Combat Command, Hampton, Va., 1995—2000; advisor U. of Ariz. Delta Tau Delta Frat., Tucson, 1994—2006, James Madison U. Frat., Sorority Life Adv. Com., Harrisonburg, Va., 2005—06, James Madison U. Sigma Chi Frat., 2006—. Author: (book) Seachange At Annapolis: The United States Naval Academy, 1949-2000. Recipient Faculty Excellence in Tchg. award, U. Ariz., 2004, Outstanding Tchg. award, U. Ariz. Found., 2002. Jewish. Avocations: surfing, swimming, skateboarding, weightlifting. Office: U Arizona Hist Dept 215 Social Sciences Bldg Tucson AZ 85721 Home Phone: 201-214-7829; Office Phone: 520-621-1586. Personal E-mail: hgelfand@hotmail.com.

GELFAND, JEFFREY ALAN, physician, educator; b. NYC, Sept. 13, 1946; BS, U. Pa., 1967; MD, Tufts U., 1971. Bd. cert. internal medicine, 1976, infectious diseases, 1980, allergy and immunology, 1981. Intern Johns Hopkins Hosp., Balt., 1971-72, resident, 1972-73, chief resident, 1976-77; rsch. fellow NIH, Bethesda, Md., 1973-76; asst. prof. Tufts Univ. Sch. Medicine, Boston, 1977-82, assoc. prof., 1982-90, prof., 1991—; vice chmn. dept. medicine New Eng. Med. Ctr., Boston, 1991, acting chmn., 1994-95, chmn. dept. medicine, physician-in-chief, 1995-98, dr. v.p. rsch. & technology, 1998—; dean rsch. Tufts U. Sch. Medicine, Boston, 1998-99; sr. attending physician Mass. Gen. Hosp., Boston, 1999—. Dean rsch. Tufts U. Sch. Medicine, Boston, 1998-99. Contbr. articles to profl. jours. Lt. commdr. USPHS, 1973-76. Office: Mass General Hosp Ste 801 50 Staniford St Boston MA 02114-2696 Office Phone: 617-726-1796. Business E-Mail: jgelfand@partners.org.

GELFAND, LAWRENCE EMERSON, historian, educator; b. Cleve., June 20, 1926; s. Maurice Hirsch and Rachel S. (Shapiro) G.; m. Miriam J. Ifland, June 14, 1953; children: Julia M., Daniel B., Ronald S. BA, Western Res. U., 1949, MA, 1950; PhD, U. Wash., 1958. Asst. prof. history U. Hawaii, 1956-58; acting asst. prof. history U. Wash., 1958-59; asst. prof. history U. Wyo., 1959-62, U. Iowa, Iowa City, 1962-64, assoc. prof., 1964-66, prof., 1966-94, chmn. history dept., 1989-92; prof. emeritus, 1994—; vis. prof. U. Oreg., summer 1966, U. Mont., summer 1970, U. Wash., 1974. Mary Ball Washington prof. Am. History, Univ. Coll., Dublin, Ireland, 1987-88. Author: The Inquiry: American Preparations for Peace 1917-1919, 1963; contbr.; editor: A Diplomat Looks Back (Memoirs of Lewis Einstein), 1968, Essays on the History of American Foreign Relations, 1972, Herbert Hoover: The Great War and Its Aftermath 1914-1923, 1979; contbr. chapters to books, articles to profl. jours. Bd. curators State Hist. Soc. Iowa, 1970-72; mem. adv. bd. Nat. Archives for Region VI, 1968-74; chmn. Ctr. for Study Recent History of U.S., Iowa City, 1981-91; mem. rsch. and book prize com. Hoover Presdl. Libr., 1996-99. Served with AUS, 1944-46. Decorated Purple Heart; Am. Council Learned Socs. grantee in Korean studies, summer 1951; Rockefeller Found. grantee, 1964-65. Mem. Am. Hist. Assn., Orgn. Am. Historians, Soc. for Historians of Am. Fgn. Relations (v.p. 1981, pres. 1982) Home: 1 Oaknoll Ct Iowa City IA 52246-1622

GELFAND, NEAL, oil industry executive; b. Bronx, NY, Nov. 8, 1944; s. Daniel and Faye (Frank) G.; m. Jane Auerbach, Sept. 11, 1982; children: Alexandra, Laura. BS in Psychology, CCNY, 1965; MS in Indsl. Psychology, Western Mich. U., 1967; PhD in Organizational Psychology, U. Houston, 1972. Ptnr. Hay Assocs., NYC, 1972-80; sr. v.p. human resources Hess Corp., NYC, 1980—2004; pres. Pondfield Group, LLC, Naples, Fla., 2004—. Mem. APA, N.Y. Acad. Scis. Office: Pondfield Group LLC 295 Grande Way #604 Naples FL 34110 Office Phone: 914-316-7733. Business E-Mail: gelfandn@optonline.net.

GELFMAN, ROBERT WILLIAM, retired lawyer; b. NYC, Jan. 22, 1932; s. Irving and Lillian (Meltzer) G.; m. Phyllis Trustman, Dec. 18, 1955; children: Lisa Jane (Mrs. Gary S. Matthews), Peter Trustman. BS, U. Pa., 1953; LL.B., Harvard U., 1956. Bar: N.Y. 1956, Mass. 1956. Ptnr. Battle Fowler LLP, 1974—99. Dir. Graycor, Inc.; trustee Independence Savs. Bank, 1988-2004; adj. prof. Columbia U. Grad. Sch. Bus. Adminstrn., 1998-2004; past chmn. bd. dirs. Arrow Lock Corp.; mem. panel disting. neutrals CPR Inst. for Dispute Resolution. Former trustee, v.p. Jewish Bd. Guardians; past chmn. bd. Hawthorne Cedar Knolls Sch., past pres. bd. edn. Served to capt. USAF, 1957-60. Mem. Am. Law Inst., Am. Arbitration Assn. (mem. comml. dispute panel of arbitrators), ABA, Assn. Bar City N.Y., N.Y. County Lawyers Assn. Clubs: Harvard (N.Y.C.); Metropolis Country (White Plains, N.Y.). Jewish. Home: 18 West Ln Greenwich CT 06831-2632

GELLAR, SARAH MICHELLE, actress; b. NYC, Apr. 14, 1977; d. Arthur and Roselen Gellar; m. Freddy Prinze Jr., Sept. 1, 2002. Appearances include (TV movie) Invasion of Privacy, 1983, (TV series) All My Children (Daytime Emmy award for outstanding younger leading actress in a daytime drama series 1995) 1993-96, Buffy The Vampire Slayer, 1997-2003 (Saturn Award Best Genre TV Actress, 1999), (films) I Know What You Did Last Summer, 1997 (Blockbuster Entertainment award for favorite best supporting actress-horror, MTV Movie award for best breakthrough performance), Scream 2, 1997, Beverly Hills Family Robinson, 1997, Cruel Intentions, 1999, Simply Irresistable, 1999, Scooby Doo, 2002, Harvard Man, 2002, Scooby-Doo 2: Monsters Unleashed, 2004, The Grudge, 2004, Southland Tales, 2006, The Grudge 2, 2006, The Return, 2006, (voice) Happily N'Ever After, 2007, The Air I Breathe, 2007, (voice) TMNT, 2007, others, also TV commls. Avocations: Tae Kwon Do, kickboxing, gymnastics.*

GELLER, BUNNY ZELDA, poet, writer, publisher, sculptor, artist; b. NYC, May 21, 1926; d. Herman and Shirley (Shoenfeld) Juster; m. Lester Roy Geller; children: Judy Lynn, Robert Douglas, Sheryl Sue, Wayne Mitchell. Student, UCLA, 1944-46, Fla. Internat. U., 1989-97. Invited artist Pegasus Internat. Corp., N.J., 1981-85, Internat. Art Expo., N.Y., 1982-83; invited guest artist Broward County Main Lib., Ft. Lauderdale, Fla., 1988; pres. BZG Enterprises. Author: Bunny Geller Original Poetry, 1995, Destiny, 1995, Choices (poetry), 1996, The Monkey and the Parakeet (A Poetic Tale for Children), 1997, Kaleidoscope (poetry), 1997, Impressions (poetry), 1999, Bunny Geller Original Sculpture, 1985; one woman sculpture shows include Bowery Savings Bank, N.Y.C., 1978, Lynn Kottler Galleries, N.Y.C, 1978, Hollywood (Fla.) Art Mus., 1978-79, Broward County Main Libr., Fla., Hallandale Cultural Ctr., 1996; group exhbns. include All Broward Exhibit 78, Ft. Lauderdale, Fla., 1978, Old Westbury Hebrew Congregation, Westbury, N.Y., 1978, De Ligny Galleries, Ft. Lauderdale, Fla., 1979, 1983-84, Internat. Treas. Fine Art, Plainview, N.Y., 1978, 79, 80, 81, Artists Equity Assn. Hollywood (Fla.) Art Mus., 1979, Limited Edition Galleries, Bal Harbour, Fla., 1979, Temple Beth-El, Boca Raton, Fla., 1979, Expo 79, Pompano, Fla., 1979, Hilda Rindom Galleries, Hallendale, Fla, 1980, Jockey Club Art Gallery, Miami, 1980, 81, 83, 84, Gallery SO-HO 7, Ltd., Great Neck, N.Y., 1979-80, Exhibition of Fine Art Nassau Mus. of Fine Art Assn., 1985, Gallery at Turnberry, Turnberry Isle, Fla., 1980-81, Galleria Martin, Palm Beach, Fla., 1981, Contextual Fine Arts, Ft. Lauderdale, Fla., 1980-81, Art and Culture Ctr. of Hollywood (Fla.), 1981, Miami Convention Ctr., 1981, Anita Gordon Gallery, Inc., North Miami Beach, 1981, Collier Art Internat., Ltd., Westbury, N.Y., 1981, Tavistock Country Club, Haddonfield, N.J., 1982, Internat. Art Expo, N.Y.C., 1982, 83, Ohio All Arabian Show and Buckeye Sweepstakes, Columbus, 1982, West Elec. Co., Hopewell, N.J., 1982, Devon (Pa.) Arabian Horse Show, 1982, Bondstreet Art Gallery, Pitts., 1982, Blumka II Gallery, N.Y.C., 1982, Korby Gallery, Cedar Grove, N.J., 1982, Washington Internat. Horse Show, Gaithersburg, Md., 1982, Pegasus Internat. Corp., Pennington, N.J., 1981, 82, 83, 84, 85, Patricia Judith Art Gallery, Boca Raton, Fla., 1983-84, Panache Gallery, Ft. Lauderdale, Fla., 1983, The Nelson Rockefeller Collection, Inc., N.Y.C., 1983, Shorr Goodwin Gallery, N.Y.C., 1983, Carrier Found. Auxiliary, Belle Meade, N.J., 1983, First Annual Internat. Wildlife Exposition, Atlantic City, N.J., 1983, Amann Gallery, Inc., Palm Beach, Fla., 1984-85, Robert's One-of-a-Kind, Bal Harbour, Fla., 1984, Hallandale (Fla.) Pub. Lib., 1984-85, Galleria Camhi, Bar Harbor Is., Fla., 1984-85, Tatem Galleries, Ft. Lauderdale, Fla., 1984-85, Westbury (N.Y.) Meml. Lib., 1984, Trenton Country Club, 1984, Designers' Showcase 1985 Cashelmara, Glen Cove, N.Y., 1985, UN Conf., Nairobi, 1985, Hallandale Cultural Ctr., Fla., 1998; sculptures on permanent exhibits; featured in (book) Artists/USA, 1979-80, The Am. Album, Nat. Mus. Women Arts permanent collection, Washington, 1985, Art Expo N.Y. catalogue, 1982, 83, 92, Limited Collectors Edition, 1982, Town and Country mag., 1982, Gold Coast Life mag., 1983, Art in America mag., 1983-84, Sunstorm Arts Mag., 1984; represented in permanent collection Kushi Found.; Wrote words, music to song One World, 1989. Pres. Sisterhood Westbury Hebrew Congregation, Westbury, N.Y., 1967-69; judge Fine Art and Craft Show, Ft. Lauderdale, Fla., 1979-81; art adv. coun. Westbury Meml. Libr., 1990-94. Recipient 1st prize Carrier Found. Aux. 2d Ann. Arts Festival, 1983; named to Internat. Poetry Hall Fame, 1996, Merit award, Hallandale Beach, Fla., 2004; inducted into Internat. Libr. Photography, 2002. Mem. Nat. Mus. Women in the Arts (assoc.), Nat. Libr. Poetry (Editor's Choice award 1995, published in Best Poems of the 90s 1996), Internat. Soc. Poets (disting. mem. 1995, Poet of Merit 1995, semi-finalist symposium 1995, inducted into Internat. Poetry Hall of Fame 1996), Nat. Trust for Historic Preservation. Avocations: tennis, all sports, cultural events, national events, art shows. Home: 400 Diplomat Pkwy Apt 711 Hallandale Beach FL 33009

GELLER, ESTHER (BAILEY GELLER), artist; b. Boston, Oct. 26, 1921; d. Harry and Fannie (Geller) G.; m. Harold Shapero, Sept. 21, 1945; 1 child, Hannah. Diploma, Sch. Boston Mus. Fine Arts, 1943. Tchr. Boston Mus. Sch., 1943, Boris Mirski Sch., 1945-49. Art cons. Leonard Morse Hosp., Natick, Mass. One-woman shows at Boris Mirski Art Gallery, Boston, 1945-46, 49, 52, 61, Addison Gallery Am. Art, Children's Art Centre, Andover, Mass., 1953-55, Mayo Gallery, Provincetown, Mass., 1958, Marion (Mass.) Art Centre, 1966, St. Mark's Sch., Southboro, Mass., 1969, Decenter Gallery, Copenhagen, 1969, Regis Coll., Weston, Mass., 1970, Am. Acad. Gallery, Rome, 1971, Newton (Mass.) Libr., 1973, Newton Art Centre, 1978, Artworks of Wayne, Providence, 1979, Stonehill Coll., Easton, Mass., 1986; 2-person show at The Ctr. for Arts in Natick, 2001; exhibited in group shows at San Francisco Mus., Va. Mus. Art, Chgo. Art Inst., Worcester Art Mus., U. Ill., Smith Coll., Inst. Contemporary Art, DeCordova Mus., USIA traveling show, USIS circulating exhbn., Far East, Boston Mus., Regis Coll., 1984, Danforth Mus. Art, 1995, Boston Ctr. for Arts, 1997, Firehouse Artists Show, Natick, 1998, Univ. Place, Cambridge, 1999, Mass. State House, Boston, 2000, Boston U. Art Gallery, 2002, Visionary Decade Thorne-Sagendorph Art Gallery, Keene, N.H., 2003, Smiley Studio Gallery, 2006. Cabot fellow, 1949; Studios Am. Acad. fellow, 1949-50, 70-71, 75; MacDowell Colony-Yaddo fellow, 1945, 67, 69 Mem.: Arts Wayland Assn., Boston Visual Arts Union. Home: 9 Russell Cir Natick MA 01760-1223 Studio: 5 Summer St Natick MA 01760-4511

GELLER, GLENN, broadcast executive; b. Jan. 24, 1972; MA, Northwestern U. Exec. drama dept. 20th Century Fox TV, 1999; with CBS Paramount Network TV, LA, 2001—, v.p. current programming, 2004—06, sr. v.p. current programming, 2006—. Achievements include working on such shows as Judging Amy, Joan of Arcadia and CSI:Crime Scene Investigation.*

GELLER, KENNETH ALLEN, otolaryngologist; b. Bklyn., Feb. 5, 1948; MD, U. So. Calif., 1972. Cert. in otolaryngology. Intern L.A. County-U. So. Calif. Med. Ctr., LA, 1972-73; resident in gen. surgery Wadsworth VA Hosp., LA, 1973-75; resident in otolaryngology UCLA Health Scis. Ctr., LA, 1975-78; active Childrens Hosp., LA, 1978—; courtesy Huntington Meml. Hosp., 1993—. Assoc. clin. prof. U. So. Calif. Mem. ACS, Am. Acad. Otolaryngology-Head and Neck Surgery, Am. Acad. Pediatrics, Am. Bronco-Esophagological Assn., Am. Soc. Pediat. Otolaryngology. Office: Childrens Hosp Divsn Otolaryngology # 58 4650 Sunset Blvd Los Angeles CA 90027-6062 Office Phone: 323-669-2145. E-mail: kgeller@chla.usc.edu.

GELLER, KENNETH STEVEN, lawyer; b. NYC, Sept. 22, 1947; s. Edward and Sylvia R. (Tannenbaum) G.; m. Judith B. Ratner, Sept. 9, 1990; children: Eric Jonathan, Lisa Beth. BA magna cum laude, CCNY, 1968; JD magna cum laude, Harvard U., 1971. Bar: NY 1972, US Dist. Ct. (so. and ea. dists.) NY 1972, US Ct. Appeals (2d cir.) 1972, US Ct. Appeals (DC cir.) 1974, US Supreme Ct. 1975, US Ct. Appeals (10th cir.) 1976, DC 1986, US Ct. Appeals (6th cir.) 1987, US Ct. Appeals (4th cir.) 1987, US Ct. Appeals (9th cir.) 1988, US Ct. Appeals (5th and 11th cirs.) 1990, US Dist. Ct. DC 1991, US Ct. Appeals (3rd and 7th cirs.) 1991, US Ct. Appeals (Armed Forces) 1995, US Ct. Appeals (8th cir.) 1996, US Ct. Appeals (fed. cir.) 1999. Law clk. US Ct. Appeals (2d cir.), 1971-72; assoc. Nickerson, Kramer, Lowenstein, Nessen & Kamin, NYC, 1972-73; asst. spl. prosecutor Watergate Spl. Prosecution Force, Washington, 1973-75; asst. to solicitor gen. Dept. Justice, Washington, 1975-79, dep. solicitor gen., 1979-86; ptnr. Mayer, Brown, Rowe & Maw LLP (formerly Mayer, Brown & Platt), Washington, 1986—, mng. ptnr., 1995—2007, vice chmn., 2007—. Mem. adv. bd. State and Local Legal Ctrs., 1986-92; mem. adv. com. on rules U.S. Ct. Appeals for Armed Forces, 1994-2000; mem. adv. com. on procedures Ct. Appeals D.C. Cir., 2000—, chmn., 2006—. Co-author: (Stern, Gressman, Shapiro & Geller) Supreme Court Practice, 8th edit., 2002; contbg. author: Business and Commercial Litigation in Federal Courts, 1998, 2d edit., 2005; contbr. articles to profl. jours. Mem. vis. com. Harvard U. Law Sch.; trustee, chmn. publs. com. Supreme Ct. Hist. Soc. Recipient Younger Fed. Lawyer award FBA, 1981, Presdl. Disting. Exec. award. Office: Mayer Brown Rowe & Maw LLP 1909 K St NW Washington DC 20006-1152 Office Phone: 202-263-3000. E-mail: kgeller@mayerbrown.com.

GELLER, LAURENCE S., hotel executive; Grad., Ealing Tech. Coll. Dir. Grand Met. Hotels, London; sr. v.p. Holiday Inns, Inc.; exec. v.p., COO Hyatt Devel. Corp.; chmn., CEO Geller & Co., 1989—97; founder, pres., CEO, dir. Strategic Hotel Capital, LLC, Chgo., 1997—. Disting. vis. prof. Johnson & Wales U., Providence, 2001; former vice chmn. Commercial and Retail Coun. Urban Land Inst. Bd. mem., fin. com. mem. Children's Meml. Hosp.; bd. mem. NAREIT; mem. Pres. coun. Midwest Region of the US Fund for UNICEF; co-chmn. bd. trustees Churchill Centre. Recipient Horatio Alger Award, Anti-Defamation League (ADL), 2003. Mem.: Am. Jewish Com. (mem. Nat. Leadership Coun.), Chicago Olympic Com., Real Estate Roundtable, Hotel and Catering Institutional Mgmt. Assn. (N.Am. abm.), Am. Hotel and Motel Assn. (immediate past chmn. Industry Real Estate Financing Adv. Coun.). Office: Strategic Hotels & Resorts Ste 4600 77 W Wacker Chicago IL 60601*

GELLER, MARGARET JOAN, astrophysicist, educator; d. Seymour and Sarah Geller. AB, U. Calif., Bekeley, 1970; MA, Princeton U., 1972, PhD, 1975; DSc (hon.), Conn. Coll., 1995, Gustavus Adolphus Coll., 1997, U. Mass., Dartmouth, 2000. Rsch. assoc. Harvard Coll. Obs., Cambridge, Mass., 1978-80; asst. prof. Harvard U., Cambridge, 1980-83; astrophysicist Smithsonian Astrophys. Obs., Cambridge, 1983—. Goodspeed-Richardo lectr. U. Pa., 1992; Brickwedde disting. lectr. JHU, 1993; Hogg lectr. Royal Astro. Soc. Can., 1993; Bethe lectr. Cornell U., 1996; Hilldale lectr. U. Wis., 1999; disting. lectr. NSF, 2004; disting. fellow U. Calif., Irvine, Calif., 2006. Contbr. articles to profl. jours.; mem. editl. bd. Sci., 1991—94. Named Libr. Lion, N.Y. Pub. Libr., 1997; recipient Newcomb-Cleve. prize, 1989—90, Klopsteg award, Am. Assn. Physics Tchrs., 1996, ADION medal, 2003; fellow, MacArthur Found., 1990—95. Fellow: AAAS, APS; mem.: NAS (coun. mem. 2000—03), Assoc. Univs. Rsch. in Astronomy (dir.-at-large), Am. Astron Soc. (councillor), Am. Acad. Art and Scis. (coun. mem.), Internat. Astron Union, Phi Beta Kappa (senator 1998—99). Office: Smithsonian Astrophys Obs 60 Garden St Cambridge MA 02138-1516

GELLER, MARVIN ALAN, meteorology educator, researcher; b. Boston, Mar. 19, 1943; s. James and Saide (Schlager) G.; m. Lynda Louise Grafinger, June 16, 1968; children: Stephanie, Steven. BS in Applied Math., MIT, 1964, PhD in Meteorology, 1969. From asst. prof. to prof. U. Ill., Champaign-Urbana, 1969-77; prof. U. Miami, Fla., 1977-80; rsch. scientist NASA Goddard Space Flight Ctr., Greenbelt, Md., 1980-84, chief Lab. for Atmospheres, 1984-89; prof., head Inst. for Terrestrial and Planetary Atmospheres SUNY, Stony Brook, 1989-2000, dean, dir. Marine Scis. Rsch. Ctr., 1998—2002, prof. atmospheric scis., 2002—. Contbr. articles to profl. jours. Fellow Am. Meteorol. Soc., Am. Geophys. Union (pres. atmospheric scis. sect. 2000-02); mem. Sci. Com. Solar-Terrestrial Physics (pres. 2000-07), Nat. Assn. U.S. Nat. Acads. Democrat. Jewish. Avocations: golf, music. Office: SUNY-Stony Brook Msrc Stony Brook NY 11794-5000 Home: 440 Kent Ave Apt 17 Brooklyn NY 11211 Office Phone: 631-632-8686. Business E-Mail: marvin.geller@sunysb.edu.

GELLER, ROBERT JAMES, advertising executive; b. NYC, May 5, 1937; s. Jerome and Pearl (Klein) G.; m. Lois Dee Fromkin, June 9, 1968; children: Richard Evan, Stephen Laurence. BS, CCNY, 1958. Account exec. Furman, Feiner & Co., NYC, 1958-62; media supr. Interpublic Group of Cos., NYC, 1962-64; asst. media dir. Foote, Cone & Belding, NYC, 1964-69; pres. Adforce, Inc., NYC, 1970-92, Robert J. Geller & Assocs., Inc., NYC, 1993—; pres., CEO Reel Am., Inc., NYC, 2000—03; mng. dir. Charter Media, 2002—; sec.-treas., CFO, COO, Charter Digital Media Inc., 2005—. Contbr. numerous articles to profl. jours. Pres. Robert J. and Lois F. Geller Found. Mem. Assn. Nat. Advertisers (mgmt. policy com. 1980-92, corp. membership com. 1990-92), Am. Advt. Fedn. (bd. dirs., corp. membership com. 1989—, plans rev. com. 1990—, asst. sec. 1992—), Advt. Club NYC Republican. Home: 155 E 76th St New York NY 10021-2810 also: Parsonage Ln Sagaponack NY 11962 Office: Robert J Geller & Assocs Inc 708 Third Ave 29th Fl New York NY 10017 Home Phone: 212-249-0258; Office Phone: 212-351-3350. Personal E-mail: rjgeller@mindspring.com.

GELLER, SCOTT A., management consultant; married; 3 children. BA in Pub. Adminstrn. and Pre-Law, Carthage Coll., 1986; MS in Healthcare Adminstrn. and Cmty. Mental Health and Counseling, LI U., US Mil. Acad., West Point, NY, 1990; post grad., Regis U., 2005—; grad., US Army Chaplain's Ctr. and Sch. Mgr. recruit new store openings, tng. and gen. mgr. devel. Pepsi Co.; staff mem. US Military Acad., 1987—90; asst. chaplain U.S. Army, West Point, Europe, Saudi Arabia, Ft. Lewis, Wash.; field assoc., coll. liaison and mktg. instr. Gen. Motors Ednl. Programs; exec. dir. sr. assisted living and memory care Sunrise Assisted Living, Inc.; mktg. cons. and nat. acct. exec. SALEM Comm. Corp.; adminstr. cmty.-based residential facility and gen. mgr. The Harbor Campus Lakeview Properties, LLC; regional mgr. and nat. healthcare adminstr. Sunwest Mgmt. Co.; pres. small bus. devel. Cow Country Enterprises; exec. bd. mem. Fox Valley Cmty. Benefit Tree, 2007—. Adj. prof. bus. and humanities U. Phoenix, 2007—. Mem. Police and Fire Commn., 2004—; team leader Nat. Rep. Party Presdl. Re-Electon Campaign, 2004—05; mem. GLG Global Coun. Decorated Army Commendation medal with Oakleaf Cluster, Southwest Asia Svc. medal with Bronze Star, Army Achievement medal, Nat. Defense medal. Mem.: Am. Assn. Counseling and Devel., Oliver Wendell Holmes Pre-Law Soc., Gamma Kappa Alpha. Address: PO Box 151 Appleton WI 54912 Home Phone: 920-277-1614; Office Phone: 920-954-1569. Business E-Mail: scott@cowcountryenterprises.com.

GELLER, STEPHEN ARTHUR, pathologist, educator; b. Bklyn., Apr. 26, 1939; s. Sam John and Alice (Podber) G.; m. Kate Eleanor DeJong, June 24, 1962; children: David Phillip, Jennifer Lee. BA, Bklyn. Coll., 1959; MD, Howard U., 1964. Diplomate Am. Bd. Pathology, Nat. Bd. Med. Examiners. Intern Lenox Hill Hosp., NYC, 1964-65; resident in pathology Mt. Sinai Hosp., NYC, 1965-69; chief lab. Naval Hosp., Beaufort, SC, 1969-71; asst. prof. pathology Mt. Sinai Med. Ctr., NYC, 1971-75, assoc. prof., 1975-78, prof., 1978-84; chmn. dept. pathology Cedars-Sinai Med. Ctr., LA, 1984—2006, chmn. emeritus Dept. Pathology, 2006—; prof. pathology UCLA, 1984—. Co-author: Histopathology, 1989, Biopsy Interpretation of the Liver, 2004; contbr. articles to profl. jours. Recipient Excellence in Teaching award CUNY, 1974, Golden Apple tchg. award Cedars-Sinai Med. Ctr., 1986, 2000, 02, 05. Fellow Coll. Am. Pathologists, Am. Soc. Clin. Pathologists; mem. Am. Assn. Study of Liver Diseases, Hans Popper Hepatopathology Soc., Calif. Soc. Pathologists (sec. 1989-91, v.p. 1991-93, pres. 1994-96), L.A. Soc. Pathologists (v.p. 1989-91, pres. 1992), N.Y. Pathol. Soc., Alpha Omega Alpha. Democrat. Jewish. Avocations: music, photography, writing fiction. Office: Cedars Sinai Med Ctr 8700 Beverly Blvd Los Angeles CA 90048-1865 Office Phone: 310-423-6632. Business E-Mail: geller@cshs.org.

GELLER, WILLIAM ALAN, criminologist, consultant, protective services official; b. Bklyn., June 4, 1950; s. Maurice and Shirley F.E. (Scherker) G.; m. Julia Marie Arment, Oct. 1, 1978. BA, SUNY, Buffalo, 1972; JD, U. Chgo., 1975. Bar: Ill. 1975, U.S. Dist. Ct. (no. dist.) Ill. 1975. Rsch. asst. U. Chgo., 1974—75; law clk. to Hon. Walter V. Schaefer Ill. Supreme Ct., Chgo., 1975-76; exec. dir. Chgo. Law Enforcement Study Group, 1976-81; project dir. Am. Bar Found., Chgo., 1981-86; dir. Louisa May Alleycat Music, 1985—; spl. counsel Chgo. Park Dist., 1986-88; assoc. dir. Police Exec. Rsch. Forum, 1987-97; dir. Geller & Assocs. Consulting, Wilmette, Ill., 1997—. Mem. Pres. Clinton's Transition Team (U.S. Dept. Justice search team mem.), 1992-93; staff Office Presdl. Pers., Washington, 1993; commr. Wilmette Fire and Police Commn., 1985-88; co-founder Cmty. Safety Initiative, 1994; cons. Local Initiatives Support Corp., 1995—, Nat. Inst. Justice, U.S. Dept. Justice, Washington, 1980—, Office of Cmty. Oriented Policing Svcs., U.S. Dept. Justice, 1994-2002, fellow Office of Cmty. Oriented Policy Svcs., 1999-2001; dep. atty. gen., 1993-94, civil rights divsn., 2001, NYC Police Dept., 1985-88, 93, FBI, Washington, 1986-96, L.A. Police Dept., 2005, Police Found., 1986-88, NYC Met. Transp. Authority, 1991, Boston Police Dept., 2002-04, Des Moines Police Dept., 2002, Detroit Police Dept., 2003, Albuquerque Police Dept., 1997, Charlotte-Mecklenburg Police Dept., 1998, 2003—, LA Police Dept, 2005, Seattle Police Dept., 1998, Fed. Signal Corp., 1990, Chgo. Police Bd., 1991-95, St. Louis Police Dept., 1991-97, Office of the Mayor, Washington, 1992-93, St. Louis, 1997-2001, Boulware & Assocs., 1992—, U.S. Info. Agy., 1999, Burkhalter & Assocs., 1992-95, Washington Post, 1998, San Francisco Chronicle, 2005, Harvard U. Office Gen. Counsel, 1995, Ill. Criminal Justice Info. Authority, 1993; police chief exec. searcher Washington, Charlotte, NC, Detroit; rsch. adv. com. Chgo. Police Dept., 1983-86; mem. Cook County Sheriff's adv. com. on internal affairs, 1986; exec. com. Chgo. Ethics Project. Author: Split-Second Decisions: Shootings Of and By Chicago Police, 1981, Deadly Force: What We Know.A Practitioner's Desk Reference on Police-Involved Shootings in the United States, 1991, Police Violence: Understanding and Controlling Police Abuse of Force, 1996, And Justice For All, 1995, Managing Police Innovation, 1995; also many articles to profl. jours., mags., and newspapers; editor: Police Leadership in America: Crisis and Opportunity, 1985, Local Government Police Management, 1991, 2003; script cons. (TV show) L.A. Law, 1991; mem. expert adv. panel RAND Corp., 2002-03. Co-chmn. Citizens for Safety Vests, Chgo., 1982-83; adv. bd. March of Dimes Met. Chgo., 1983; bd. dirs. John Howard Assn., Chgo., 1978—99, Bus. and Profl. People for Pub. Interest, 1988—, Travel Light Theatre, Chgo., 1980-82; adv. bd. Yale U. Nat. Ctr. Children Exposed to Violence, 2000—; priority grants com. United Way Met. Chgo., 1990-92; task force on criminal justice studies, Clark-Atlanta U., 1991-95; mgr. Harvard Exec. Session on Drugs and Cmty. Policing, Cambridge, Mass., 1990-92. Recipient Richard J. Daley Police medal of honor, City of Chgo., 1983, commendation N.Y.C. Police Commr., 1986, commendation St. Louis Police Chief, 1997; grantee Nat. Inst. Justice, 1980, 84, 88, 90, 91, Chgo. Bar Found., 1980, Chgo. Cmty. Trust, 1976-80, 84, 85, Charles Stewart Mott Found., 1990, Edna McConnell Clark Found., 1998. Mem. ABA (com. on stds. for criminal justice 1983-86, prison and jail problems com. 1985-86), Internat. Assn. Chiefs Police, Police Exec. Rsch. Forum, NOBLE, Am. Soc. Criminology, Acad. Criminal Justice Scis. Home: 939 Wedgewood Dr Glenview IL 60025-4100 E-mail: wageller@aol.com.

GELLERMAN, BRUCE EDWARD, reporter; b. Bklyn., Dec. 10, 1950; s. Seymour and Florence (Waxman) G.; m. Yulia; 2 children BA, Ohio State U., 1973; postgrad., Hebrew U., 1975-76. Sr. corr. Ctr. for Investigative Journalism, Washington, 1981-82; gen. assignment reporter Nat. Pub. Radio, Washington, 1982-83, sci. reporter, 1983-85, producer, 1986-87; bus. reporter Sta. WBUR-FM Radio, Boston, 1987-88, exec. prodr., news, host Here and Now, 1988—2002; now reporter, Living on Earth Pub. Radio Internat., Boston. Pub. affairs producer Sta. WORT-FM, Madison,

Wis., 1980-82. Co-author (with Eric Sherman) Massachusetts Curiocites. Recipient Investigative award UPI, 1982, Milw. Press Club, 1983; Journalism award AAAS, 1984, Pub. Svc. award Corp. Pub. Broadcasting, 1985, 90, Ohio State U., 1990, ABA, 1991, Pub. Radio News Dirs., 1991, Lincoln Unity award, 1992, 94, Nat. Headliners award, 1993, Nat. Press Club award, 1993, Sigma Delta Chi. award, 1993, AAAS Sci. Journalism award for radio reporting, 2006; named Knight fellow U. Md., 1990, Travel fellow for the Advancement of Sci. Writing, Fulbright Scholar/Fulbright Sr. Specialist. Mem. Nat. Assn. Sci. Writers. Jewish. Avocations: skiing, hiking, bicycling, scuba diving. Office: Living on Earth 20 Holland St Ste 408 Somerville MA 02144-2749

GELLERT, GEORGE GEZA, food importing company executive; b. NYC, Apr. 15, 1938; s. Imre and Martha (Tessler) G.; m. Barbara Rubin, July 21, 1963; children— Andrew, Amy, Thomas. BS, Cornell U., 1960, MBA, 1962, LL.B., 1963. Bar: N.Y. State bar 1963. Atty. SEC, Washington, 1963-64; v.p., exec. v.p., pres. Atalanta Corp., NYC, 1966—, chmn. bd., 1978—. Chmn. U.S.-Rumanian Econ. Council; bd. dirs. Am. Importers Meat Products Group. Trustee Cornell U., 1995-99, mem. Cornell U. Council. Served to 1st lt. Office Staff Judge AUS, 1964-66. Decorated Army Commendation medal; recipient Outstanding Alumni award Cornell U., 2000, Ellis Island Nat. Medal of Honor, 2001, Ernst & Young Master Entrepreneur of the Yr. award, 2001, George Washington award Am. Hungarian Found., 2004. Mem. Am. Importers Assn. (dir., exec. com. meat product group), Am. Assn. Exporters and Importers (bd. dirs.), Met. Pres.'s Orgn. Home: PO Box 213 New Vernon NJ 07976 Office: Atalanta Corp Atalanta Plz Elizabeth NJ 07206 Office Phone: 908-351-8000. Personal E-mail: ggellert@atalanta1.com.

GELLERT, JAY M., health and medical products executive; b. Mar. 13, 1954; BA, Stanford U., 1975. Dir. health services, County of San Mateo Calif. Dept. of Health Services; sr. v.p., COO Calif. Healthcare System, 1985-88; pres., CEO Bay Pacific Health Corp., 1988-91; dir. strategic advisory engagements Shattuck Hammond Ptnrs. Inc.; pres., COO Health Systems Internat. Inc. (merged with Found. Health. Corp. in 1996), 1996—97, Health Net, Inc. (formerly Found. Health Systems), 1997—98; pres., CEO Health Net, Inc., 1998—, bd. dirs., 1999—. Chmn., admin. simplification com. Coun. Affordable Quality Healthcare; bd. dirs. Am. Assoc. Health Plans, MedUnite, Inc., Miavita, Inc. Office: Health Net Life Insurance Co 21281 Burbank Blvd Woodland Hills CA 91367-6607*

GELLERT, MICHAEL ERWIN, investment banker; b. Prague, Czechoslovakia, June 15, 1931; s. Oswald Rudolf and Grete (Petschek) G.; m. Mary Crombie, Jan. 11, 1969; children: John Matthew, Catherine Ann. BA, Harvard U., 1953; MBA, U. Pa., 1955. Exec. dir. Drexel Burnham Lambert and predecessor co., NYC, 1958-89; gen. ptnr. Windcrest Ptnr., NYC, 1967—. Bd. dirs. Seacor Holdings, NYC, Worldwide Spl. Fund N.V. Trustee Caramoor Ctr. for Mus. and Arts, Katonah, NY; chmn. bd. trustees Carnegie Instn. Washington; vice chmn. bd. trustees New Sch. U., NYC. With U.S. Army, 1955-57. Fellow: AAAS; mem.: Am. Acad. Arts and Sci. (trustee), Cosmos Club, The Field Club (Greenwich, Conn.), Penn Club (NYC), Harvard Club (NYC), Burning Tree Country Club (Greenwich). Office: Windcrest Ptnrs 122 E 42nd St New York NY 10168-0002 E-mail: mgellert@chelseacap.com.

GELLES, RICHARD JAMES, sociology and psychology professor, academic administrator; b. Newton, Mass., July 7, 1946; s. Sidney S. and Clara (Goldberg) G.; m. Judy S. Isacoff, July 4, 1971; children: Jason Charles, David Philip. AB, Bates Coll., 1968; MA, U. Rochester, 1971; PhD, U. N.H., 1973. Asst. prof. sociology U. R.I., Kingston, 1973-76, assoc. prof., 1976-81, prof., 1982-98, dean Coll. Arts and Scis., 1984-90; Joanne and Raymond Welsh chair child welfare/family violence Sch. of Social Policy and Practice, U. Pa., 1998—, dean, 2002—. Cons. Children's Hosp. Med. Ctr., Boston, 1973—98; lectr. Harvard Med. Sch., Boston, 1979-88, 95—98; rsch. dir. Louis Harris and Assocs., N.Y.C., 1981-82, cons., 1982-86; cons. Sage Pubs., Newbury Park, Calif., 1986—2004. Author: The Violent Home, 1974, Family Violence, 1979; co-author: Behind Closed Doors: Violence in the American Family, 1980, Intimate Violence, 1988, The Book of David, 1996. Mem. Am. Sociol. Assn. (chair family sect. 1985-86, recipient Disting. Contributions to Teaching award Sect. on Undergrad. Edn. 1979), Nat. Council Family Relations (chair rsch. and theory sect. 1989-91, v.p. publs. 1996-98). Jewish. Avocations: tennis, golf. Office: Sch Social Policy and Practice U Pa 3701 Locust Walk Philadelphia PA 19104-6214 Office Phone: 215-898-5541. Business E-Mail: gelles@sp2.upenn.edu.

GELLHORN, ALFRED, physician, educator; b. St. Louis, June 4, 1913; s. George and Edna (Fischel) Gellhorn; m. Olga Frederick, Aug. 4, 1939; children: Martha, Anne, Christina, Maria, Edna. Student, Amherst Coll., 1930—32, DSc (hon.), 1969; MD, Washington U., St. Louis, 1937; DSc (hon.), CCNY, 1979, SUNY, 1984, Albany Med. Coll., 1986, U. Pa., 1992. Diplomate Am. Bd. Internal Medicine. Gen. surg. tng. Barnes Hosp., St. Louis, 1937—39; gynecology trainee Passavant Meml. Hosp., Chgo., 1939—40; fellow Carnegie Instn. of Washington, Balt., 1940—43; instr., later asst. prof. physiology Coll. Physicians and Surgeons, Columbia U., NYC, 1943—45, asst., then assoc. prof. pharmacology, 1945—48, assoc. prof. clin. cancer research dept. medicine, 1948—52, assoc. prof. medicine, 1952—58, prof. medicine, 1958—68; prof. medicine and pharmacology, dean Sch. Medicine, also dir. Med. Ctr. U. Pa., Phila., 1968—73; dir. Ctr. Biomed. Edn., City Coll., v.p. for health affairs CUNY, 1974—79, emeritus, 1979—; dir. med. affairs N.Y. State Dept. Health, Albany, 1983—96; rsch. dir., cons. diamond fund fell. prgm. Aaron Diamond Post Doctoral Rsch. Fell. Prgm., 1996—. Cons. Commonwealth Fund, NY, 1979—80, Aaron Diamond Found., 1987—; vis. prof. Harvard Sch. Pub. Health, 1980—83; physician Francis Delafield Hosp., NYC, 1949—52, chief med. svc., 1952—68; vis. prof. medicine Albert Einstein Med. Sch.; dir. Inst. Cancer Rsch., Columbia; bd. regents Nat. Libr. Medicine. Mem.: ACP, Am. Soc. Biol. Chemistry, Inst. Medicine, Am. Soc. Pharm. and Exptl. Therapeutics, Am. Assn. Cancer Rsch. (pres. 1962—63), N.Y. County Med. Soc., Assn. Am. Physicians, Soc. for Clin. Investigation, Coll. Physicians Phila. Office: 90 Church St 13th Fl New York NY 10007 E-mail: axg08@health.state.ny.us.

GELLIN, GERALD ALAN, dermatologist; b. Bklyn., May 24, 1934; m. Lucille E. Gellin. AB, U. Pa., 1954; MD, NYU, 1958. Diplomate Am. Bd. Dermatology. Chief sect. dermatology VA Hosp., Bklyn., 1964-67; clin. prof. U. Calif. Med. Ctr., San Francisco, 1969—. Chief dermatology divsn. VA Hosp., Bklyn., 1963-67, San Francisco Gen. Hosp., 1969-73, Calif. Pacific Med. Ctr., 1986—2003. Contbr. articles to profl. jours. With USPHS, 1967-69. Fellow ACP. Office: 3838 California St San Francisco CA 94118-1522 Office Phone: 415-668-2400.

GELLIS, ZVI DAN, healthcare educator; PhD, U. Toronto, 1998. Asst. prof. SUNY, Albany, 1999—2005, assoc. prof., 2005—. Rsch. dir. Ctr. Mental Health and Aging, Albany, 1999—. Recipient Faculty Rsch. award, SUNY, Albany, 1999, Competitive Faculty Rsch. award, 2002, Summer Rsch. Inst. award on Aging, Nat. Inst. Aging, 2003, Behavioral Health Leadership award, St. Peter's Med. Ctr., 2004, Career Devel. award, NIMH, 2005—, R.C.T. Summer Rsch. Inst. award, 2005; grantee, John A. Hartford Found., 2002—04, NY State Office Mental Health, 2002—, NY State Coalition Aging, 2004—05, NY State Office Atty. Gen., 2004—; scholar, Hartford Found., 2002—04. Mem.: NASW, Soc. Social Work Rsch., State Soc. Aging NY, Gerontol. Assn. Am. Office: SUNY 1400 Washington Ave Albany NY 12222 Office Phone: 518-442-5152.

GELLMAN, BARTON DAVID, correspondent; b. Phila., Nov. 3, 1960; s. Stuart Bergman Gellman and Marcia (Kramer) Jacobs; m. Tracy Ellen Sivitz, Sept. 2, 1990; children: Abigail, Michael, Lily. AB, Princeton U., 1982; MLitt in Politics, Oxford U., Eng., 1988. Courthouse reporter Washington Post, Washington, 1988-90, Pentagon corr., 1990-94, Jerusalem corr. Jerusalem, 1994-97, diplomatic corr., 1998—99, spl. projects reporter, 1999—. Author: Contending with Kennan, 1984. Co-recipient Pulitzer Prize for Nat. Reporting, 2002, recipient Def. Writing award Gerald R. Ford Found., 1994, Jesse Laventhal prize Am. Soc. Newspaper Editors, 1996, Overseas Press Club award for fgn. affairs coverage, 1998, Sigma Delta Chi award, Soc. Profl. Journalists, 1999; Rhodes scholar, 1982. Mem. Coun. on Fgn. Rels. Office: Washington Post NY Bur 251 W 57th St 12th Fl New York NY 10019 Office Phone: 212-445-4999. E-mail: gellmanb@washpost.com.*

GELLMAN, GLORIA GAE SEEBURGER SCHICK, marketing professional; b. La Grange, Ill., Oct. 5, 1947; d. Robert Fred and Gloria Virginia (McQuiston) Seeburger; m. Peter Slate Schick, Sept. 25, 1978 (dec. 1980); 2 children; m. Irwin Frederick Gellman, Sept. 9, 1989; 3 children BA magna cum laude, Purdue U., 1969; student, Lee Strasberg Actors Studio; postgrad., UCLA, U. Calif. Irvine. Lic. in real estate Pa., 2006. Mem. mktg. staff Seemac, Inc. (formerly R.F. Seeburger Co.), 1970; v.p. V.I.P. Properties, Inc., Newport Beach, Calif., 1989—90, 1991; pres. Glamglo Prodns., 1997—2006, Glamglo LLC, 2006—; realtor Coldwell Banker Preferred, West Chester, Pa., 2006—. Host radio show Orange County Art Bytes, 1997-99, Sneak Previews from the Orange County Performing Arts Ctr., 1997-99; prodr. corp. videos, 2001-05. Profl. actress, singer, artist, writer; TV and radio talk show hostess, Indpls.; performer radio and TV commls.; feature writer arts and entertainment column H mag., The Grand Tour mag.; co-prodr. Fullerton: Then and Now (PBS); exec. prodr. (video) Paris Air Show, 2003, Tibet: Beyond Mystique (PBS, 2004 Emmy finalist); prodr. Art Bytes, 1998-99, The Destiny Report. Devel. officer Mission Media, Orange County Philharm. Soc., 2005-06, bd. dirs. women's com.; mem. Orange County Master Chorale, Orange County Performing Arts Ctr., v.p., treas. Crescendo chpt., Ctr. Stars, 1st v.p. membership; bd. dirs. Newport Harbor (Calif.) Art Mus., v.p. membership, mem. acquisition coun.; bd. dirs., mem. founders soc. Opera Pacific, mem. exec. com. bd. dirs.; patron Big Bros./Big Sisters Starlight Found.; mem. Visionaries Newport Harbor Mus., Designing Women of Art Inst. Soc. Calif.; past pres. Opera Pacific Guild Alliance; past pres. Spyglass Hill Philharm. Com.; v.p. Pacific Symphony Orch. League, chair endowment sect., spl. events chair; bd. dirs. Pacific Symphony Orch., v.p. cmty. affairs, vice chair vol. devel.; mem. U. Calif. Irvine Found. Bd., mem. devel. com., honors com., pub. affairs and advocacy com.; mem. social scis. dean's adv. coun. U. Calif. Irvine; chmn. adv. coun. Cold War Studies Ctr., Chapman U., Fashionables com.; chmn. numerous small and large fundraisers; mem. com. Red Cross; bd. dirs. Sta. KOCE PBS TV; bd. dirs., exec. com., nominating com., 25th anniversary com., devel. com., vice chmn. vol. devel. Pacific Symphony; fundraising cons. Mission Media Pa.; dir. devel. Mission Media Ministries, Pa., 2005 Recipient Lauds and Laurels award U. Calif., Irvine, 1994, Gellman Courtyard Sculpture honoring contbn. to Sch. of Humanities, U. Calif., Irvine, Most Outstanding Vol. award Pacific Symphony, 2002, Pacific Symphony Orch. League, 2002; finalist Emmy award, 2004 Mem. AAUW, AFTRA, SAG, Am. Acad. TV Arts and Scis., Internat. Platform Assn., Actors Equity, U. Calif. Irvine Chancellor's Club, U. Calif. Irvine Humanities Assocs. (founder, pres., bd. dirs.), Mensa, Orange County Mental Health Assn., Seneca Network, Balboa Bay Club, U. Club, Club 39, Islanders, Covergirls, Pacific Symphony Supper Club (founder), Pacific Symphony "Symphony 100" (pres., founder), Sadsbury Village Home Owners Assn. (pres. 2005-07), Western Chester County C. of C., Exton C. of C., Nat. Soc. DAR, Phila. Acad. Arts, Alpha Lambda Delta, Delta Rho Kappa, Pi Beta Ph. Republican. Home: PO Box 189 Sadsburyville PA 19369 Office Phone: 484-947-7078. Personal E-mail: glanglo@comcast.net. Business E-Mail: ggellman@cbpref.com.

GELLMAN, MARC, rabbi; m. Betty Gellman; children: Mara, Max. BA in Hebrew and Semitic Studies, U. Wisc., Madison, 1969; grad., Hebrew Union Coll.-Jewish Inst. Religion, 1971; PhD, Northwestern U., 1982. Cert. ordained Rabbi Hebrew Union Coll.-Jewish Inst. Religion, 1972. Former adj. faculty mem. Antioch Coll., Hebrew Union Coll., Seminary of Reform Judaism; prof., depts. English, Philosophy Northwestern U., Chgo.; Sr. Rabbi Temple Beth Torah, Melville, NY, 1981—. Guest lectr. Princeton U., Amherst Coll., Harvard U. Med. Sch., Mt. Sinai Hosp.; chmn. Medical Ethics Committee of the UJA Fed., NYC; mem. bioethics com. Nassau U. Med. Ctr. Author: (children's books) Does God Have a Big Toe?, 1989, God's Mailbox, 1996, Always Wear Clean Underwear and Other Ways Parents Say They Love You, 1997, And God Cried Too, 2002, Where Does God Live?, How Do You Spell God?. Named one of The Top 50 Rabbis in America, Newsweek Mag., 2007. Mem.: UJA Fedn. (chmn. Rabinnical Adv. Com.), Long Island Rabbinical Adv. Council, NY Bd. Rabbis (past pres.). Office: Temple Beth Torah 35 Bagatelle Rd Melville NY 11747 Office Phone: 631-667-7913.*

GELLMAN, SAMUEL HELMER, chemist, educator; b. Evanston, Ill., Sept. 12, 1959; AB, Harvard U., 1981; PhD, Columbia U., 1986. Postdoctoral fellow Calif. Inst. Tech., Pasadena, 1986-87; asst. prof. chemistry U. Wis., Madison, 1987-93, assoc. prof., 1993-95, prof., 1995—, Evan P. Helfaer prof., 2001—06, Ralph F. Hirschmann prof., 2005—. Contbr. articles to Jour. Am. Chem. Soc., Nature. Office Naval Rsch. young investigator, 1990; NSF presdl. young investigator, 1991; Alfred P. Sloan fellow Alfred P. Sloan Found., 1993. Fellow AAAS; mem. Am. Chem. Soc. (Arthur C. Cope scholar 1997,Ralph F. Hirschmann Award in Peptide Chemistry 2007), Am. Peptide Soc. (Vincent du Vigneaud award 2006). Office: U Wis Dept Chemistry 1101 University Ave Madison WI 53706-1322 E-mail: gellman@chem.wisc.edu.*

GELL-MANN, MURRAY, theoretical physicist, educator; b. NYC, Sept. 15, 1929; s. Arthur and Pauline (Reichstein) Gell-Mann; m. J. Margaret Dow, Apr. 19, 1955 (dec. 1981); children: Elizabeth Sarah, Nicholas Webster. BS in Physics, Yale U., 1948; PhD in Physics, MIT, 1951; ScD (hon.), Yale U., 1959, U. Chgo., 1967, U. Ill., 1968, Wesleyan U., 1968, U. Turin, Italy, 1969, U. Utah, 1970, Columbia U., 1977, Cambridge U., 1980, Oxford U., Eng., 1992, So. Ill. U., 1993; ScD in Natural Resources (hon.), U. Fla., 1994; ScD (hon.), So. Meth. U., 1999. Mem. Inst. for Advanced Study, Princeton, NJ, 1951, 1955, 1967—68; instr. U. Chgo., 1952—53, asst. prof., 1953—54, assoc. prof., 1954, prof., 1956; assoc. prof. Calif. Inst. Tech., Pasadena, 1955—56, prof., 1956—67, Robert Andrews Millikan prof. physics, 1967—93, Robert Andrews Millikan prof. emeritus, 1993—; co-chmn. sci. bd. Santa Fe Inst., 1985-2000, visitor, 1992—93, disting. fellow, 1993—. Vis. prof. MIT, 1963, CERN, Geneva, 1971—72, Geneva, 1979—80, U. N.Mex., 1995—; vis. assoc. prof. Columbia U., 1954; overseas fellow Churchill Coll., 1966; mem. Pres.'s Sci. Adv. Com., 1969—72, Pres.'s Coun. of Advisors on Sci. and Tech., 1994—2001; mem. sci. and grants com. Leakey Found., 1976—88, mem. sci. adv. com., 1988—; chmn. bd. trustees Aspen Ctr. for Physics, 1973—79; founding mem. Santa Fe Inst., 1982, bd. trustee, 1984—, chmn. bd. dir., 1984—85, co-chmn. sci. bd., 1985—2000, prof. and disting. fellow, 1993—, prof., disting. fellow, 1993—; cons. Inst. Def. Analysis, Arlington, Va., 1961—70, Rand Corp., Santa Monica, Calif., 1956; mem. physics panel NASA, 1964, Coun. Fgn. Rels., 1975—, Los Alamos Sci. Lab., N.Mex., 1956—, visitor, N.Mex., 1975, 1992—93, Lab. fellow, N.Mex., 1982—; mem. adv. bd. Network Physics, 1999—; fel. Com. for the Scientific Investigation of Claims of the Paranormal, 1985—. Author (with Y. Ne'eman): Eightfold Way, 1964; author: The Quark and the Jaguar: Adventures in the Simple and the Complex, 1994; author: (with S. Lloyd) Entropy: Interdisciplinary Applications, 2004. Citizen regent Smithsonian Instn., 1974—88; trustee Wildlife Conservation Soc., 1994—; dir. J.D. and C.T. MacArthur Found., 1979—2002, chmn., World Environ. & Resources Com., 1982—97; bd. dirs. Calif. Nature Conservancy, 1984—93, Aero Vironment, Inc., 1971—, So. Calif. Skeptics, 1985—91, Lovelace Insts., 1993—95; mem. sci. adv. com. Conservation Internat., 1993—. Co-recipient Erice "Science For Peace" prize, 1989; named to UN Environ. Program Roll of Honor for Environ. Achievement, 1988; recipient E. O. Lawrence Meml. award, AEC, 1966, Franklin medal, Franklin Inst. Phila., 1967, Rsch. Corp. award, 1969, Nobel prize in Physics, 1969, Ellis Island Family Heritage award in Sci., Statue of Liberty-Ellis Island Found., Inc., 2005, Albert Einstein medal, Albert Einstein Soc., 2005; fellow NSF postdoctoral, vis. prof., Coll. de France and U. Paris, 1959—60. Fellow: Am. Acad. Arts and Scis. (v.p. 1970—76, chmn. We. ctr. 1970—76), Am. Phys. Soc. (Dannie Heineman prize 1959); mem.: AAAS, NAS (John J. Carty medal 1968), Irish Acad. Scis., Russian Acad. Scis. (fgn. 1993—), Indian Acad. Scis. (fgn. 1985—), Pakistan Acad. Scis. (fgn. 1985—), French Phys. Soc. (hon.), Royal Soc. London (fgn. 1975—), Conservation Internat. (sci. adv. com. 1993), Am. Philos. Soc., Coun. on Fgn. Rels., Athenaeum, Century Assn., Cosmos Club, NY Explorers Club, Phi Beta Kappa, Sigma Xi (Procter Sci. Achievement prize 2004). Achievements include contributions and discoveries concerning the classification of elementary particles and their interactions. Address: Santa Fe Institute 1399 Hyde Park Rd Santa Fe NM 87501 Office Phone: 505-984-8800. Office Fax: 505-982-0565. E-mail: mgm@santafe.edu.

GELMAN, ALEXANDER, theater director, educator; b. Leningrad, Russia, Dec. 21, 1960; s. Simon and Maria Gelman; m. Jennifer Hendrix Clayton; children: Samuel Clayton, Anna Hendrix. MFA, Boston U., 1985; BFA, Birmingham So. Coll., 1982. Head of directing U. Nebr., Linclon, 1991—94, U. Utah, Salt Lake City, 1994—2001; dir. Sch. Theatre and Dance No. Ill. U., DeKalb, 2001—; producing artistic dir. Organic Theater Co., Chgo., 2006—. Dir.: (plays) Taming of the Shrew, As you Like It, Twelfth Night, Coronation of Popea, Barber of Seville, Carmen, Eugene Onegin, Turn of the Screw, Romeo and Juliet. Office: No Ill Univ Dekalb IL 60115 Home Phone: 815-895-9042; Office Phone: 815-753-8253. Business E-Mail: agelman@niu.edu.

GELMAN, ANDREW RICHARD, lawyer; b. Chgo. s. Sidney S. and Beverly Gelman; m. Amy H., 1985; children: Stephen S., Adam P., Elizabeth F. BA, U. Pa., 1967; JD, U. Va., 1970. Bar: Va. 1970, Ill. 1971. Assoc. Roan & Grossman Law Firm, Chgo., 1971-74, McBride, Baker & Coles Law Firm (now Holland & Knight LLP), Chgo., 1974-77, ptnr., 1978—. Mem. com. on character and fitness of Ill. Supreme Ct., Chgo., 1979-95. Bd. dirs. Scholarship and Guidance Assn. Youth and Family Svcs., Chgo., 1979—, Children's Meml. Rsch. Ctr. of Children's Meml. Hosp., Chgo., 1991—, vice-chair, 1998—; chmn. Med. Rsch. Inst. Coun., 1983-86, 91-92; trustee Michael Reese Hosp. and Med. Ctr., Chgo., 1987-91. Named one of Top 100 Attys., Worth mag., 2006, Best Lawyers in Am., 2007; recipient Weigle award, Chgo. Bar Found., 1980. Mem. ABA (standing com. jud. selection, tenure and compensation 1982-87, pub. understanding about the law com. 1987-91, chair probate and estate planning com. gen. practice sect. 1994-97, commn. on mental and phys. disability law 1995-97), Chgo. Bar Assn. (past chmn. divsn. probate practice com., bd. mgrs. 1978-80, chmn. young lawyers sect. 1976-77), Chgo. Estate Planning Coun., The Quadrangle Club (bd. dirs. 2005—). Office: Holland & Knight LLP 131 S Dearborn St 30th Fl Chicago IL 60603-5547 Office Phone: 312-715-5718. E-mail: andy.gelman@hklaw.com.*

GELMAN, ROCHEL, psychology professor; b. Toronto, Ont., Can., Jan. 23, 1942; came to U.S., 1963; d. Isaac and Ida (Linver) G.; m. Charles R. Gallistel, Nov. 21, 1969; 1 child, Adam BA with first class honors, U. Toronto, 1963; MA, UCLA, 1965. PhD, 1967. Asst. prof. psych. Brown U., Providence, 1967—68, U. Pa., Phila., 1968-72, assoc. prof., 1972—77, prof., 1977—89; prof. psych. UCLA, 1989—2000; prof. psych. and cognitive sci. Rutgers U., New Brunswick, NJ, 2000—. Vis. asst. prof. U. Minn. Inst. Child Devel., Mpls., 1968; vis. scholar U. Calif. Sch. Social Scis.-, Irvine, 1973—74; dir. grad. studies psych. U. Pa., 1974—81; fellow Ctr. Advanced Study Behavioral Scis., 1977—78, 1984—85; assoc. dean grad. office U. Pa. Sch. Arts and Scis., 1981—82; vis. scholar Inst. Psych., Beijing, 1982, Penn Israel Exchange, Tel Avivi, Israel, 1987; chair devel. area UCLA, 1989—94; vis. scholar psych. NYU, 1995—96; dir. training grant in devel. cognitive sci. Nat. Inst. Mental Health, 1995—99; vis. prof. Rutgers U. Ctr. Cognitive Scis., 1999; emeritas prof. psychology UCLA, 2000—. Author: The Child's Understanding of Number, 1978; co-assoc. editor Internat. Ency. Psych Devel. secs.; editl. bd. Cognitive Psych., 1977-, Substratum, 1992-, Math. Cognition, 1994-, Applied Devel. Psych., 2000-; contbr. articles to profl. pubs., chpts. to books Guggenheim fellow, 1973-74 Fellow Am. Psychol. Assn. (early career rsch. contbn. award 1976, pres. div. 7 1985-86, disting. sci. contbn. award 1995, mentor award div. 7 2003), Am. Psychol. Soc., Cognitive Sci Soc., Am. Acad. Arts Scis.; mem. Piaget Soc., Psychonomics Soc., Soc. Rsch. in Child Devel., Soc. Exptl. Psychologists, Phi Beta Kappa (foreign mem.), NAS. Office: Rutgers Ctr for Cognitive Sci Psych Bldg Addition Busch Campus 152 Frelinghuysen Rd Piscataway NJ 08854

GELMAN, SIMON, anesthesiologist, educator; b. St. Petersburg, Russia, May 26, 1936; arrived in US, 1976, naturalized, 1982; s. Isaac Gelman and Raisa Mekler; m. Maria Gelman, July 7, 1959; children: Alex, Dan Samuel. MD, First Leningrad Med. Inst., USSR, 1959; PhD, Kirov Advanced Inst. Doctors, Leningrad, USSR, 1965. Lic. specialist in anesthesiology Israel Med. Assn., 1975, diplomate Am. Bd. Anesthesiologists, 1981. Head surg. office Polyclinic, Siktivkar, Russia, 1959—61; physician, resuscitationist Ctr. Treatment Patients with Myocardial Infarction, Leningrad, 1964—65; assoc. prof. anesthesiology Kirov Advanced Tng. Inst. Doctors, 1965—73; sr. anesthesiology Eilnson Med. Ctr. Tel Aviv U., Petah Tikva, Israel, 1974—75; from assoc. prof. to prof. Sch. Medicine U. Ala., Birmingham, Ala., 1978—81, prof. Sch. Medicine, 1981—92, dir. clin. rsch. anesthesiology Sch. Medicine, 1979—84, vice chmn. rsch. in anesthesiology Sch. Medicine, 1984—89, chmn. Dept. Anesthesiology Sch. Medicine, 1989—92; chmn. Dept. Anesthesiology Brigham and Women's Hosp., Boston, 1992—2002, prof. anesthesiology, 2002—. Mem. numerous coms. U. Ala., 1985—92, Brigham and Women's Hosp., 1992—, Partners Cmty. Healthcare, Inc., Boston, 1994—2003; mem. search com. chief of anesthesia Mass. Gen. Hosp., 1993—93; mem. Am. Medico-Legal Found., 1994—; dir. Found. Anesthesia Edn. and Rsch., 1996—; chair, grant rev. com. Found. for anesthesia Edn. and Rsch., 2001—; Leroy D. Vandam and Benjamin G. Covino prof. anaesthesia Harvard U., Boston, 1992—2002, Leroy D. Vandam and Benjamin G. Covino disting. prof. anaesthesia, 2002—; Jobson vis. prof. Royal Prince Alfred Hosp. U. Sydney, 2002; lectr. in field. Editor: Anesthesia and Organ Transplantation, Anaesthesia for Major Vascular Surgery. Recipient Rsch. award, Am. Soc. Anesthesiology, 1979. Master: Alpha Omega Alpha; fellow: Australian and New Zealand Coll. Anesthesia; mem.: Acad. Anesthesia Mentors, Acad. Anesthesia Mentors (pres. 2006), Israel Soc. Anesthesiologists (hon.), Found. Anesthesia Edn. and Rsch. (chmn. grant rev. com., bd. dirs.). Jewish. Office: Brigham and Womens Hospital 75 Francis Street Boston MA 02115 Office Phone: 617-732-8280. Office Fax: 617-264-5230. Business E-Mail: sgelman@partners.org.

GELMANN, EDWARD PAUL, oncologist, educator; b. NYC, May 31, 1950; m. Connie Sommers; children: Lauren R., Elyssa R., Emily B, Jonathan S. BS magna cum laude, Yale U., 1972; MD, Stanford U., 1976. Diplomate Nat. Bd. Med. Examiners, Am. Bd. Internal Medicine. Intern then resident U. Chgo. Hosps., 1976—78; med. staf fellow Nat. Cancer Inst., Bethesda, Md., 1979—83, sr. investigator, 1983—88; adj. assoc. prof.

microbiology Georgetown U., Washington, 1986—88, prof. medicine and cell biology, 1988—2007, chief med. oncology divsn., 1988—93, chief hematology/oncology divsn., 1993—95, vice chair Dept. Medicine, 1997—98; prof. Columbia U., NYC, 2007—, chief divsn. hematology/oncology, 2007—; dep. dir. Herbert Irving Comprehensive Cancer Ctr., 2007—. Dir. urologic oncology program Lombardi Cancer Rsch. Ctr., 1990-93, dir. prostate cancer program, 1993-2007, dir. program in growth regulation of cancer, 2001-07, William M. Scholl Professorship in Oncology, 2002. Mem. editl. bd. jour. Blood, 1985-90, Cancer Rsch., 2004—; ad hoc reviewer jours.; contbr. 180 articles to profl. jours Sr. surgeon USPHS, 1978-88. Grantee Nat. Cancer Inst., 1990—. Fellow ACP; mem. AAAS, Am. Soc. Clin. Investigation, Am. Assn. Cancer Rsch., Am. Soc. Clin. Oncology. Office: Columbia U Milster Hosp 6N-435 117 Ft Washington Ave New York NY 10032 Office Phone: 202-444-7303.

GELPI, ALBERT JOSEPH, language educator, department chairman, critic; b. New Orleans, July 19, 1931; s. Albert Joseph and Alice Marie (Delaup) G.; m. Barbara Charlesworth, June 14, 1965; children: Christopher Francis Cecil, Adrienne Catherine Ardelle. AB, Loyola U., New Orleans, 1951; MA, Tulane U., 1956; PhD, Harvard U., 1962. Asst. prof. Harvard U., 1962-68; assoc. prof. Stanford U., 1968-74, prof. Am. lit., 1974-99, Wm. Robertson Coe prof. Am. lit., 1978-99, Coe prof. emeritus, 1999—, chmn. Am. studies program, 1980-83, 94-97, asso. dean grad. study and research, 1980-85, chmn. English dept., 1985-88. Author: Emily Dickinson: The Mind of the Poet, 1965, The Tenth Muse: The Psyche of the American Poet, 1975, A Coherent Splendor: The American Poetic Renaissance 1910-1950, 1987; editor: The Poet in America: 1650 to the Present, 1974, (with Barbara Charlesworth Gelpi) Adrienne Rich's Poetry, 1975, Wallace Stevens: The Poetics of Modernism, 1985, (with Barbara Charlesworth Gelpi) Adrienne Rich's Poetry and Prose, 1993, Denise Levertov: Selected Criticism, 1993, The Blood of the Poet: Selected Poems of William Everson, 1994; editor Cambridge Studies in American Literature and Culture, 1981-91, Living in Time: The Poetry of C. Day Lewis, 1998, The Wild God of the World: An Anthology of Robinson Jeffers, 2003, Wild God of Eros: A William Everson Reader, 2003, (with Robert J. Bertholf) The Letters of Robert Duncan and Denise Levertov, 2004, Robert Duncan and Denise Levertov: The Poetry of Politics, The Politics of Poetry, 2006. Served with U.S. Army, 1951-53. Guggenheim fellow, 1977-78 Mem. MLA, Am. Lit. Assn. Democrat. Roman Catholic. Home: 870 Tolman Dr Palo Alto CA 94305-1026 Office: Stanford U Dept English Stanford CA 94305

GELPI, GUSTAVO ANTONIO, federal judge; b. San Juan, 1965; BA, Brandeis U., 1987; JD, Suffolk U., 1991. Bar: PR 1992. Law clk. to Hon. Juan M. Perez-Gimenez, US Dist. Ct. PR, 1991—93, asst. pub. defender, 1993—97, magistrate judge, 2001—06, dist. judge, 2006—; asst. to atty. gen. PR Dept. Justice, 1997, dep. atty. gen. legal counsel, 1997—99; solicitor gen. Commonwealth of Puerto Rico, 1999—2000; spl. litig. counsel McConnell Valdes, 2001. Office: Clemente Ruiz-Nazario US Courthouse Office 483 150 Carlos Chardon St Hato Rey PR 00918 Office Phone: 787-772-3103.*

GELPKE, PETER HALL, science educator; b. Boston, June 10, 1955; s. Roy Franklin and Glory Michaud Gelpke. BA, U. Rochester, NY, 1978. Cert. secondary tchr. Calif. Tchr. Fairfield (Calif.) HS, 1991—, chmn. dept. sci., 2000—06. Pres. Fairfield HS Scholarship Fund, 2002—. Named Tchr. of the Yr., Fairfield HS, 2000; recipient award of Excellence, U. Calif. San Diego, 1998—99, Recognition award, U. Calif., Santa Barbara, 2006—07. Avocation: music. Office: Fairfield HS 205 E Atlantic Ave Fairfield CA 94533

GELSINGER, PATRICK P., computer company executive; married; 4 children. AS in Elec. Engring., Lincoln Tech. Inst., 1979; BEE magna cum laude, Santa Clara U., 1983; MEE, Stanford U., 1985. Various positions, including design mgr. and chief architect original i486 microprocessor & gen. mgr. Pentium Pro, IntelDX2, Intel486 microprocessor. Intel Corp., 1979—92, dir. Platform Architecture Group, mgr. CAD methodologies, key contbr. on the original i386 and i286 chip design teams, responsible Intel ProShare video conferencing and Internet comm. product line, 1992—96, leader Desktop Products Group, chief tech. officer, architecture group, v.p., gen. mgr., desktop products group, 1996—2000, chief tech. officer, computing group, 2000—01, chief tech. officer, 2001—05, sr. v.p., gen. mgr. digital enterprise group, 2005—, also adv. bd. mem. Contbr. articles to profl. publs. Holds six patents and six applications in the areas of VLSI design, computer architecture and communications. Office: Intel Corp 2200 Mission College Blvd Santa Clara CA 95052

GELSTON, PHILIP A., lawyer; b. NYC, Aug. 26, 1952; AB cum laude, Harvard Univ., 1974, JD magna cum laude, 1977. Bar: NY 1978. Law clk., Hon. John Minor Wisdom US Ct. of Appeals, 5th Cir.; assoc. Cravath Swaine & Moore, LLP, NYC, 1978—84, ptnr., corp., 1984—. Supreme Ct. note editor Harvard Law Rev. Mem.: ABA, NY State Bar Assn., Bar of Assn. of City of NY, Phi Beta Kappa. Office: Cravath Swaine & Moore LLP Worldwide Plz 825 Eighth Ave New York NY 10019-7475 Office Fax: 212-474-3700. Business E-Mail: pgelston@cravath.com.

GELTMAN, EDWARD ALAN, lawyer; b. Newark, Apr. 14, 1946; s. Donald and Muriel G.; m. Elizabeth Ann Glass, Jan. 2, 1989; children: Andrew, Jeffrey, Rachel. BA with honors, Franklin & Marshall Coll., 1968; JD with honors, George Washington U., 1971. Bar: D.C. 1971, U.S. Ct. Appeals (D.C. cir.) 1971, U.S. Supreme Ct. 1980. Trial atty. FTC, Washington, 1971-73; assoc., then ptnr. Nicholson & Carter, Washington, 1973-79; ptnr. Squire, Sanders & Dempsey, Washington, 1979—. Contbr. articles to profl. jours. Mem. ABA (antitrust sect.), Order of Coif. Office: Squire Sanders & Dempsey 1201 Pennsylvania Ave NW Washington DC 20004-2491 Office Phone: 202-626-6681. Business E-Mail: egeltman@ssd.com.

GELTZEILER, MICHAEL S., publishing executive; b. Oct. 2, 1958; BA, U. Del., 1980; MBA, NYU. Former audit mgr., regional contr., sr. v.p., CFO NCH Promotional Svcs. Dun & Bradstreet, former asst. treas.; sr. v.p., CFO Europe, Mid. East and Africa ACNielsen, Belgium, 1995—97, contr., treas., sr. v.p., CFO, The Reader's Digest Assn., Inc., Pleasantville, NY, 2001—07, pres. sch. & ednl. services, 2007—. Office: The Reader's Digest Assn Inc Reader's Digest Rd Pleasantville NY 10570*

GELTZER, ROBERT LAWRENCE, lawyer, arbitrator, mediator, retired retail executive; b. NYC, Jan. 27, 1945; s. Edward and Grace Theresa (DeFeo) G.; m. Elise Anne Lewis, Nov. 11, 1972; 1 child, Joshua Alexander. BA Biochemistry and Polit. Sci., Queens Coll., NYC, 1965; JD, George Washington U. Law Sch., 1968; postgrad. in English Lit., CCNY. Bar: N.Y., 1969, U.S. Dist. Ct. (so. and ea. dists.), U.S. Ct. Appeals (2nd cir.), U.S. Supreme Ct., U.S. Ct. Mil. Appeals. Ptnr. Tendler, Biggins & Geltzer, NYC, 1990—2002; sole practitioner, 2002—. Appointments include: Private Law Practice, 1968-71; Assoc. Atty. for Legal and Governmental Affairs for Allied Stores Corp., 1971-74; Sr. Atty. for J.C. Penney, 1974-84; Northeastern Regional Counsel, 1984-88; counsel firm Meyer, Suozzi, English & Klein, 1988-89. Admitted to N.Y. State Bar, 1969; U.S. Dist. Cts. Appeal (so. and ea. dists.) (2d cir.), 1974; U.S. Supreme Ct., 1976. Dir., Credit Specialist Program at Adelphi Univ., 1976-78; mem. ABA Bd. Govs., 1988-91, bd. program com., 1988-90, bd. ops. com., 1990-91, liaison commn. on mentally disabled, 1988-89, liaison standing com. on specialization, 1989-91, spl. com. on youth edn., 1988-91, spl. com. on pub. understanding about the law, 1988-91; House of Delegates, 1980-86, 88-93, 94-97; chair Task Force on Providing Mem. Benefits for Disabled Lawyers, 1991-93; mem. standing com. on pub. edn. about law, 1992-98; mem. Law Day Task Force, 1994-97, Nat. Conf. on Lawyers and Corp. fiduciaries, 1986-87; Standing Com. on Legal Drafting, 1979-82; Spl. Com. on Youth Edn. for Citizenship, 1982-86; chmn. Tellers Com., 1982-83; Conf. of Section Chairs, chair fiscal com., 1986-88; Annual Meeting Host Coms., mem. (1986), vice-chair, (1993); Coordinating Group on Bioethics and the Law, (1991-96); liaison to Standing Com. on Scope and Correlation of Work, 1988-91, mem. Standing Com., 1991-96, chair, 1994-95; corp. Com. of Resource Devel. coun., 1987-92; Sci. and Tech. Sect. (coun. mem. 1981-84, 91-93) sec., 1984-85, vice chair, 1985-86, chair-elect, 1986-87, chair, 1987-88; chair Nat. Conf. on Birth, Death & Law, 1987-88; Corp., Banking and Bus. Law Sect. (co-chmn. Corporate Counsel Com., mem. Consumer Fin. Svc. Commn., Long-Range Planning Com., Issues Affecting the Profession Com., Comml. Arbitration Com., 1992—), Bus. Bankruptcy Com., (1992—), Consumer Bankruptcy Com., (1992—); Individual Rights and Responsibilities Sect. (vice-chmn. Equal Protection of the Laws, mem. 1st Amendment Rights Com., 1992-97), Rights of the Elderly Com., (1992-97), Rights of Children Com., (1992-97); Economics of Law Practice Sect. (mem.); Family Law Sect. (mem.); Judicial Adminstrn. Div. (Exec. Com., Lawyers' Conf.; chair Membership Com., Jud. Compensation Com.; Litigation sect., 1st co-chair com. on corp. counsel, mem. class action com., liaison with ABA com.); co-chair Nat. Conf. on the Role of the Lawyer in the 1980s (1979-81). New York State Bar Assn. House of Delegates (1981-97); Exec. Com. At-Large Mem., (1992-95), state bar del., 1995-97, liaison to atty. and community com. juvenile justice commn., solo and small firm practitioners commn. and judicial evaluation commn.; Founder and 1st Chmn. Corp. Counsel Sect. (1981-83); chair Commn. to Provide Legal Svcs. to Middle Income Consumers (1995—); chair Unlawful Practice of Law Com. (1990-92), chair Solo and Small Firm Practitioner Task Force (1991-96); mem. Action Unit #5 pertaining to Regulatory Reform (1980-83); mem. Law Simplification Task Force (1982-88), chair Pub. Rels. Com., 1983-86; mem. AIDS and the Law Com. (1988-91); recipient Corp. Counsel of Yr. award (1989). Assn. of the Bar of the City of N.Y.: del. to N.Y. State Bar House of Delegates, 1988-92, mem. Profl. and Jud. Ethics Com. (1982-83); Sci. and Law Com. (1985-88); Children and the Law Com. (1985-88); N.Y. County Lawyers' Assn.: mem., bd. dirs. (1982-88); chmn. spl. projects com., 1992-96; mem. 75th Anniversary Steering Com. (1982-84); mem. Federal Legislation, State Legislation, Trade Regulation, and Alcoholism in the Profession committees; mem. Am. Law Inst.; life fellow Am. Bar Found. (fellow, vice chair N.Y. fellows, 1988-91, chair, 1991-96); fellow N.Y. Bar Found., ABA Young Lawyers' Div. (fellow, bd. dirs.); life mem., dir. N.Y. state chair (1979-82) of Am. Judicature Soc. Adjunct prof., Pace College. Mem. Am. Soc. for Polit. and Legal Philosophy; Am. Soc. for Legal History: General Com., Conf. on Personal Finance Law; speaker at various state and local bar assns. (Ark., Calif., Colo., Conn., Ill., Mich., N.J., N.Y., Pa., Va., W.Va. and various programs of practicing law instns. and ABA Nat. Insts.). Pro Bono General counsel for Nat. Kidney Found. (1981-91). Co-first male mem. of Nat. Assn. Women Lawyers. Bd. dirs. Fund for Justice and Edn. (1988-91), Community Action for Legal Svcs. (1988-90). Mem. Vol. Lawyers for the Arts. Past chancellor commander, past spl. dep. grand chancellor Knights of Pythias. Mem. American Jewish Com., Masons, Phi Epsilon Phi, Phi Delta Phi, George Washington U. Law Sch. Alumni Assn. Contbr. to various profl. jours. in areas of fed. and state consumer credit legislation, regulation, litigation and compliance, class action litigation, law firm mgmt., consumer, comml., gen. practice and state civil litigation issues affecting the legal profession. Fellow Am. Bar Found.; mem. Congregation Temple Emanu-El; mem. legal com., bicentennial com. Am. Jewish Com.; mem. Jewish Welfare Bd.; chair JC Penney Legal Dept.'s Ann. Blood Dr., 1979, 83; mem. Vol. Lawyers for the Arts; pro bono gen. counsel, chair legal com. Nat. Kidney Found. 1981-91. Mem. ABA (bd. govs. rep. N.Y. State 1988-91; mem. ho. of dels. 1980-86, 88-93, 95—; vice chmn. tellers com. 1981-82; chmn. 1982-83, bd. dirs. Am. Bar Retirement Assn. 1988-91, Nat. Jud. Coll. 1988-91, Fund. Justice and Edn. 1988-91; bd. govs. liaison standing com. on scope and correlation of work 1988-91, 91-96; spl. com. on youth edn. for citizenship 1982-86, mem. standing com. 82-86; commn. on public understanding about the law 1989-91; mem. steering com. on unmet legal needs of children 1996-97; chair task force on member benefits for disabled lawyers 1991-93; mem. standing com. on pub. edn. 1992-95; mem. law day working group 1994-95; chmn. fiscal com. conf. of sect. chairs 1987-89, Nat. Conf. on Birth, Death and Law, 1987-88, ann. meeting host coms. 1986, vice chair, 1993, coordinating group on bioethics and the law 1991-95; chmn. subcom. on liaison with state and local bars 1983-86; mem. young lawyers divsn., corp., banking and bus. law sect, litigation sect., sci. and tech. sect., gen. practice sect., individual rights and responsabilities sect., numerous other sects. and coms.), Am. Law Inst., Am. Judicature Soc. (life, mem. mem bership com. 1979-80, chair N.Y. State 1989-94), N.Y. State Bar Assn. (founder 1981, first chair corp. counsel sect. 1981-83, Corp. Counsel of Yr. award 1989; mem. at large exec. com. 1992-95, liaison, ho. of dels. 1981-87, 88-93, 95-97; mem. spl. com. alternat dispute resolution 1993—, numerous other coms., sects.), Assn. Bar City of N.Y., N.Y. County Lawyers' Assn., Fed. Bar Assn. Home: 115 E 87th St New York NY 10128-1136 Office Phone: 212-410-0100. Office Fax: 212-410-0400.

GELTZER, SHEILA SIMON, public relations executive; b. NYC; d. Sidney E. and Bertie (Rome) Simon; m. Howard E. Geltzer, Sept. 10, 1967; children: Jeremy Niles, Gabriel Lewis. BA, Queens Coll., 1961. With Philip Lesly Co., NYC, 1962-63, Benjamin Co., NYC, 1963-68; ptnr. Simon and Geltzer, Inc., NYC, 1968-74, Ries and Geltzer, NYC, 1974-79; pres. Geltzer and Co., Inc., NYC, 1979—2000; mng. dir., exec. prin. Publicis Dialog, NYC, 2000—. Mem. Pub. Rels. Soc. Am. (counselors acad.), Women in Comms., Women in Pub. Rels., Nat. Coun. of Women, Abingdon Theater. Business E-Mail: sgeltzer@geltzerco.com.

GELWICKS, JAMES M., retired communications educator; b. Boulder, Colo., Nov. 14, 1949; s. Melvin G. Jr. and Maryjoel Gelwicks. BA, U. Colo., 1972; MA, No. Ill. U., 1977; postgrad., Fla. State U., 1973—82. Decontamination trainee Dow Chem., Rocky Flats, Colo., 1969; rsch. cons. Tallahassee, 1975—81; adj. prof. Fla. State U., Tallahassee, 1980; asst. prof. Western State U., Gunnison, Colo., 1981—2004, emeritus asst. prof., 2005—. Gen. mgr. KWSB-FM, Gunnison, 1987—2001; chair comm. arts and sociology Western State U., 1994—97; del. People to People Speech Comm. Leaders to China and Soviet Union, 1984. Contbr. articles to profl. jours. Mayor City of Gunnison, 1993—95; pres. Colo. Mcpl. League, 1994—95; chair environ. health bd. Gunnison County, 2000—03; chair Gunnison County Dem. Party, 1985—87; Dem. state committeeman Leon County, Fla., 1980—81. Named Outstanding Sr. Debator, Colo.-Wyo. Forensics Assn., 1971, Broadcast Citizen of Yr., Colo. Broadcasters, 1994; recipient Lion award, Colo. Edn. Assn., 2002; fellow, Corp. for Pub. Broadcasting, 1973—74. Mem.: Nat. Comm. Assn. (life), Elks, Sons of Am. Legion (detachment comdr. 2004—05, nat. exec. com 2007—, Man of Yr. 2005). Avocations: fly fishing, stamp collecting/philately, hiking. Home: PO Box 539 Gunnison CO 81230 E-mail: jgelwicks@western.edu.

GEMAN, DONALD, mathematics professor; b. Chgo., Sept. 20, 1943; s. Harold Geman and Dorothy Shapiro; m. Helyette Slama, Apr. 11, 1985; 1 child, Nathanael. PhD, Northwestern U., Evanston, Ill., 1970. Disting. prof. U. Mass., Amherst, 1970—2000; prof. math. Johns Hopkins U., Balt., 2001—. Office: Johns Hopkins Univ 302A Clark Hall 3400 N Charles St Baltimore MD 21218-2686 Home Phone: 410-464-1357; Office Phone: 410-516-7678. Business E-Mail: geman@jhu.edu.

GEMERY, HENRY ALBERT, economics professor; b. Shelton, Conn., Sept. 5, 1930; s. John and Mary (Benco) G.; m. Pamela Joyce Malcolm, Aug. 30, 1958; childen: John Malcolm, Pamela Ann. BS, So. Conn. State Coll., 1952; MBA, Harvard U., 1958; PhD, U. Pa., 1967; MA hon., Colby Coll., 1977. Asst. dir. admissions Colby Coll., Waterville, Maine, 1958-61, from instr. to Pugh Family prof. econs., 1961—2001, emeritus, 2001—. Assoc. Charles Warren Ctr., Harvard U., 1989—90. Contbg. author, co-editor: The Uncommon Market, 1979, Science Technology and Environment, 1994; author: monograph Emigration from the British Isles, 1980, European Emigration to North America, 1984. Served to 1st lt., C.E. US Army, 1953—56. NDEA fellow, U. Pa., 1963—65, NIH postdoctoral fellow, 1968—69, Charles Warren fellow, Harvard U., 1982—83. Mem.: Internat. Union for Sci. Study of Population, Econ. History Assn., Cliometric Soc., Am. Econs. Assn. Home: 1185 Pond Rd Sidney ME 04330-2015 Office: Colby Coll Mayflower Hill Waterville ME 04901 Business E-Mail: hagemery@colby.edu.

GEMIGNANI, JOSEPH ADOLPH, lawyer; b. Hancock, Mich., Apr. 17, 1932; s. Baldo A. and Yolanda M.; m. Barbara A. Thomson, Sept. 5, 1953; children: Joseph, Jon. BSME, Mich. Technological U., 1953; JD, U. Mich., 1958. Bar: Wis. 1959, Mich. 1960, U.S. Dist. Ct. (ea. and we. dists.) Wis., U.S. Ct. Appeals (7th cir.), U.S. Ct. Appeals (fed. cir.). In-house counsel McGraw Edison Co., Milw., 1958-60; ptnr. Michael, Best & Friedrich, Milw., 1960—. 1st lt. USAF, 1953-55. Home: 616 E Day Ave Milwaukee WI 53217-4841 Office: Michael Best & Friedrich 100 E Wisconsin Ave Ste 3300 Milwaukee WI 53202-4108

GEMIGNANI, MICHAEL CAESAR, clergyman, retired mathematics professor; b. Balt., Feb. 23, 1938; s. Hugo J. and Dorothy G.; m. Carol A. Federico, June 30, 1962 (dec.); children: Stephen, Susan; m. Nilda B. Keller, May 18, 1985. BA, U. Rochester, 1962; MS, U. Notre Dame, 1964, PhD, 1965; JD, Ind. U., 1980. Bar: Ind. 1980, U.S. Dist. Ct. Ind. 1980, Maine 1987, U.S. Dist. Ct. Maine 1987, Tex. 1990; ordained to ministry Episcopal Ch., 1973. Asst. prof. math. SUNY, Buffalo, 1965-68; assoc. prof. Smith Coll., 1968-72; prof., chmn. dept. math. scis. Ind. U.-Purdue U., Indpls., 1972-81; dean Coll. Scis. and Humanities Ball State U., Muncie, Ind., 1981-86; dean Coll. Arts and Scis. U. Maine, Orono, 1986-88; sr. v.p., provost U. Houston-Clear Lake, 1988-91, prof. math. and computer sci., 1991-92; rector St. Paul's Episcopal Ch., Freeport, Tex., 1991—. Vicar St. Francis Episcopal Ch., Zionsville, Ind., 1974-79; pres. Met. Indpls. Campus Ministry, 1975-76, bd. dirs., 1974-81; mem. adv. bd. Ind. Office Campus Ministry, 1973-86, pres., 1983-85; chair divsn. spiritual formation Episcopal Diocese of Tex., 1997—; founder, chmn. bd. Brazosport Med. Ctr., 1999—. Author: books including Elementary Topology, 1967, 2d rev. edit., 1972, Introductory Real Analysis, 1970, Law and the Computer, 1981, Computer Law, 1985, Legal Guide for EDP Managers, 1989, To Know God: Small Group Exercises in Spiritual Formation, 2001, Spiritual Formation for Pastors Tending the Fire Within, 2002; composer; rsch., publs. in math. Mem. ABA, AAAS, Am. Math. Soc. (chmn. N.E. sect. 1970-71, chmn. Ind. sect. 1975-76), Scribes, Sigma Xi, Kappa Sigma. Business E-Mail: mgmign@hal-pc.org.

GEMMETT, ROBERT J., dean, English language educator; b. Schenectady, NY, Mar. 11, 1936; s. A James and Dorothy M. (MacFarlane) G.; m. Kendra B. Baxter, Jan 24, 1964; children: Stephen, Scott, David, Kerry. BA cum laude, Siena Coll., 1959; MA, U. Mass., 1962; PhD, Syracuse U., 1967. Instr. Clarkson U., NYC, 1964-65; assoc. prof. English SUNY, Brockport, 1965-70, prof., 1970-92, 97—, chmn. dept., 1975-79, dean humanities, 1979-82, dean letters and scis., 1982-92; prof. English, provost, v.p. for acad. affairs SUNY Coll., Buffalo, 1992-97. Author: Poets and Men of Letters, 1972, William Beckford, 1977, Beckford's Fonthill: The Rise of Romantic Icon, 2003; editor: Biographical Memoirs of Extraordinary Painters, 1969, Dreams, Waking Thoughts and Incidents, 1971, 2d edit., 2006, The Consummate Collector, 2000. 2d lt. U.S. Army, 1959. Recipient Chancellor's Excellence in Tchg. award SUNY, 1975; fellow, rsch. grantee SUNY, 1967-69, 84-85. Office: SUNY Dept English Brockport NY 14220 Office Phone: 585-395-2476. Business E-Mail: rgemmett@brockport.edu.

GEMUNDER, JOEL FRANK, healthcare company executive; b. NYC, July 15, 1939; s. Abraham and Frances (Kubrick) G.; m. Claudia Joan Hoffman (div. 1984); children: David Austin, Allison Paige. AB, CCNY, 1960; MBA, U. Chgo., 1962. Fin. analyst W. R. Grace & Co., NYC, 1962-68, v.p. splty. products group, 1968-71; v.p. Chemed Corp., Cin., 1971-77, v.p., group exec. health care group, 1977-81, exec. v.p., 1981; pres. Omnicare, Inc., Cin., 1981—, CEO, 2001—, also bd. dirs. Cin. Bd. dirs. Chemed Corp., Cin., Datacare, Inc., Roanoke, Va., Cin., The John Bunn Co., Buffalo, Xorbox Corp., Buffalo, Sequoia Pharmacy Svcs., Inc., L.A., The Veterex Corp., Troy. Mich., Medarco Corp., Troy, Bignall Dental Supply, Grand Rapids, Mich., Labtronics, Inc., Palo Alto, Calif. Mem. Cin. Council World Affairs, 1986; trustee City of Hope, Cin., 1983. Recipient Spirit of Life award City of Hope, 1983. Mem. Cin. C. of C. (aviation com. 1981). Office: Omnicare Inc 1600 RiverCenter II 100 E RiverCenter Blvd Covington KY 41011-1555*

GEN, MARTIN, protective services executive; b. Feb. 14, 1926; s. Max and Gussie (Bluestone) G.; m. Sara Tobin; children: Gilda Gen Paul, Sam Gen. Student, Syracuse U., 1946-50; BA, Pace U., 1950. Lic. pvt. detective. V.p., treas. Merlin, Inc., North Bergen, N.J., 1950-73; pres. Washmasters, Inc., North Bergen, 1950-73; pres., exec. dir., CEO Expert Investigation and Protective Industries, Inc., Kenilworth, N.J., 1974—. Pres. InterGlobal Trading, Kenilworth, N.J.; pres., exec. dir. EIP, Inc., Kenilworth, N.J., 1973-74; pres. Expert Investigation. Bd. dirs. Jewish Nat. Fund, Teaneck, N.J., 1986—, YMHA, Union, N.J., 1970, Fedn. Union County, N.J., 1970, Jewish Ednl. Ctr., Elizabeth, N.J., 1960. Served with USN, 1943-46, ETO, PTO. Named Man of Yr., YMHA, Bnai Brith. Mem. Am. Soc. Indsl. Security, Club 100. Home and Office: PO Box 195 Kenilworth NJ 07033-0195 Home Phone: 908-276-8589; Office Phone: 908-272-3344.

GENACHOWSKI, JULIUS, communications executive; b. Brookline, Mass., Aug. 19, 1962; s. Azriel Genachowski and Adele Reiss. BA magna cum laude, Columbia Coll., 1985; JD magna cum laude, Harvard U., 1991. Law clk. to Chief Judge Abner J. Mikva U.S. Ct. Appeals (D.C. cir.), Washington, 1991-92; law clk. to Justice William Brennan U.S. Supreme Ct., Washington, 1992-93, law clk. to Justice David Souter, 1993-94; counsel to chmn. FCC, Washington, 1994-95; gen. counsel, sr. v.p. bus. devel. USA Broadcasting, 1997—2000; v.p. corp. devel. Ticketmaster Online-Citysearch, Inc., 2000; sr. v.p., gen. counsel USA Networks, Inc. Interactive Corp., 2000—02, exec. v.p., gen. counsel USA Networks, Inc., 2002, chief bus. operations, 2003—06; gen. counsel General Atlantic LLC, Greenwich, Conn., 2006—. Bd. dir. JackBe.Com; bd. mem. Expedia Inc, Hotels.com, Ticketmaster. Office: General Atlantic LLC 3 Pickwick Plz Greenwich CT 06830 Office Phone: 203-629-8600. Office Fax: 203-622-8818.*

GENADER, ROBERT J., investment company executive; With Citibank; exec. v.p. Ambac Assurance, NYC, 1986—98, Ambac Financial Group Inc., NYC, 1991—98, dir., 1992—, vice chmn. Specialized Fin. Div., 1998—2000, vice chmn. Fin. Insurance Bus. Group, 2000—01, pres., COO, 2001—04, pres.; CEO, 2004—06; chmn., pres., CEO Ambac Financial group Inc., NYC, 2006—. Mem.: Assn. of Fin. Guaranty Insurors (chmn. 1994—96). Office: Ambac Fin Group One State St Plz New York NY 10004 Office Phone: 212-668-0340. Office Fax: 212-509-9190.*

GENARO, DONALD MICHAEL, industrial designer; b. Hoboken, NJ, Feb. 22, 1932; s. Gustav G. and Margaret (DeMave) G.; m. Margaret Hermes, June 23, 1956; children: Susan, Karen. BID, Pratt Inst., 1957.

Archtl. designer F.W. Fisher-Architects, NJ and NY, 1951-52; indsl. designer Henry Dreyfuss Assocs., NYC, 1957-63, assoc., 1963-68, ptnr., 1968-82, sr. ptnr., 1982-94; ret., 1994. Lectr., cons. in field. Designer of Trimline Phone; holder over 200 patents; contbr. numerous articles to profl. jours. Trustee, chmn., bd. dirs. Pascack Valley Hosp.; bd. dirs. Well Care Group, Inc. Represented in permanent collection at Mus. of Modern Art and Cooper-Hewitt (Smithsonian) Mus.; recipient Contemporary Achievement award Pratt Inst., 1970, Best Product Design 1983 Time Mag., Design award Indsl. Designers Soc. Am. and Indsl. Design Mag.; named one of 25 Best Designed Products Fortune Mag., 1977. Mem. Indsl. Designers Soc. Am.

GENBERG, IRA, lawyer; b. Newark, July 27, 1947; s. Jack and Ann (Lerman) G.; m. Rosemary Lawlor, Jan. 15, 1981; children: Jack Michael, Anne Rebecca. AB magna cum laude, Rutgers U., 1969; JD, U. Pa., 1972. Bar: Ga. 1972, D.C. 1978. Assoc. Haas, Holland, Levison & Gibert, Atlanta, 1972-75; ptnr. Stokes, Shapiro, Fussell & Genberg, Atlanta, 1975-87; ptnr., head litigation sect. Smith, Gambrell & Russell LLP, Atlanta, 1987—. Spkr. Seminar on Constrn. Litigation, Atlanta, 1985, Seminar on Constrn. Law, Atlanta, 1986; co-chmn. Seminar on Trying A Complex Constrn. Case, 1994. Contbr. articles to Constrn. Bus. Review Mag. Mem. ABA, Ga. Bar Assn., Atlanta Bar Assn., D.C. Bar Assn. Office: Smith Gambrell & Russell LLP 1230 Peachtree St NE Atlanta GA 30309-3592 Office Phone: 404-815-3638. Business E-Mail: igenberg@sgrlaw.com.

GENCO, ROBERT JOSEPH, immunologist, periodontist, educator, scientist; b. Silver Creek, NY, Oct. 31, 1938; s. Joseph A. and Santa G. Genco; children: Deborah Genco Powell, Robert M., Julie Clarke Alford. DDS cum laude, SUNY-Buffalo Sch. Dentistry, 1963; PhD in Microbiology and Immunology, U. Pa., 1967. Resident, periodontology U. Pa., 1967; asst. prof. dept. oral biology Sch. Dental Medicine SUNY, Buffalo, 1967—69, assoc. prof., 1969—72, prof., 1972—, chmn. dept. oral biology, 1977—, Disting. Univ. prof. dept. oral biology, 1990—; Disting. Univ. prof. dept. microbiology Sch. Medicine and Biomed. Scis. SUNY, Buffalo. Editor-in-chief: Jour. Periodontology, 1988—2006, Annals Periodontology; contbr. to books and publications in the field. Recipient Gold medal for Excellence in Rsch., ADA, 1991, Basic Rsch. in Oral Sci. award, Internat. Assn. for Dental Rsch., Rsch. in Periodontal Disease award, Deans medal, George Thorn award. Fellow: AAAS (chmn. dental sect 1980); mem.: NAS, Am. Assn. Immunology, Am. Acad. Periodontology, Internat. Assn. Dental Rsch. (pres. 1991—92), Inst. Medicine, Am. Assn. Dental Rsch. Achievements include patents in field. Avocations: music, sports. Office: SUNY at Buffalo Periodontal Disease Rsch Ctr 135 Foster Hall 3435 Main St Buffalo NY 14214 Address: Sch Dental Medicine U Buffalo 115 Foster Hall Buffalo NY 14214 Business E-Mail: rjgenco@buffalo.edu.

GENDELL, GERALD STANLEIGH, retired public relations executive; b. Stamford, Conn., June 14, 1929; s. Irving and Henrietta (Lund) G.; m. s. Marion F. Belvin, July 28, 1952; children: Carin Gaye, Danna Joyce, Adrian Leigh, Jeffrey Lund, David Blake, Marc Steven, Bradley Howard. BS, NYU, 1949. With Procter & Gamble Co., Cin., 1954-91, dir. community affairs and contbns., 1976-80, mgr. external affairs divsn., 1980, mgr. pub. affairs div., 1981—91, also pres., trustee Procter & Gamble Fund. Trustee Glen Manor Home, 1978-80, Queen City Housing Corp., Cin., 1981-89, Cin. Local Initiative Support Corp., The Spire Found., Jewish Fedn. So. Ariz.; vice chmn. bd. trustees Jewish Hosp. of Cin.; bd. dirs., trustee Nat. Coun. on Econ. Edn., 1985-91; mem. met. adv. coun. U. Cin.; mem. adv. coun. George Mason U. Sch. Law, 1988-91; mem. Cin. Mayor's Com. on Econ. Devel.; chmn. Found. for Pub. Affairs; mem. bd. overseers Hebrew Union Coll.; pres. Jewish Cmty. Found. of So. Ariz.; bd. dirs. Jewish Fedn. of So. Ariz., Ariz. Jewish Post. 1st lt. U.S. Army, 1950-53. Mem. Pub. Affairs Coun. Am. (bd. dirs. 1981-91, chmn. 1988-89), Greater Cin. C. of C. (vice chmn., mem. exec. com. 1981-87), Conf. Bd., Bankers Club (bd. govs. 1988-93). Personal E-mail: gendellgm@aol.com.

GENDLER, ELLEN, dermatologist; b. Bklyn., Feb. 15, 1956; BA, Wesleyan Univ.; MD, Columbia U., 1981. Diplomate Am. Bd. Dermatology. Internal med. intern Lenox Hill Hospital, NYC; resident in dermatology NYU Med. Ctr., NYC, 1982—85; pvt. practice dermatology NYC, 1985—. Clin. assoc. prof. dept. dermatology NYU Sch. Medicine, NYC, 1990—; trustee Dermatology Found.; consul., med. advisor to numerous cosmetics and health-care companies; spkr. in field. Contbr. articles to numerous profl. jours. Mem.: Am. Acad. Dermatology (assoc.; dir. cosmetics symposium). Office: 1035 Fifth Ave New York NY 10028

GENDRON, ANDREW, lawyer; b. North Brunswick, NJ, Oct. 6, 1960; s. Robert Emmett and Norma (Brunalli) G. AB, Georgetown U., 1982; JD, U. Md., 1986. Bar: DC, Md., U.S. Ct. of Appeals (3d cir.), U.S. Ct. of Appeals (4th cir.), U.S. Dist. Ct. DC, U.S. Dist. Ct. Md. Assoc. Piper & Marbury, Balt., 1986—88, Goodell, DeVries, Leech & Gray, Balt., 1988—96, ptnr., 1997—2001, Venable LLP, Balt., 2001—. Mem. ABA, Md. State Bar Assn. (People's Pro Bono award), Bar Assn. Balt. City, Md. Def. Trial Counsel, Md. Inst. Continuing Profl. Edn. Lawyers (faculty, contbg. author), Def. Rsch. Inst., Georgetown U. Alumni Assn. (fundraising chmn. class 1982, 1987-92), Georgetown Alumni Md. Club (dir. 1983-85). Democrat. Roman Catholic. Office: Venable LLP 2 Hopkins Plaza 1800 Mercantile Bank & Trust Bldg Baltimore MD 21201 Office Phone: 410-244-7439. Office Fax: 410-244-7742. Business E-Mail: agendron@venable.com.

GENDRON, GEORGE, magazine editor; With New York Mag.; editor-in-chief Boston Mag., Inc. Mag., Boston, 1983—2002; Kauffman Entrepreneur-in-Residence Clark Univ. Grad. Sch. Mgmt., Worcester, Mass., 2003—. Adv. bd. mem. Foundation Source; nat. dir. Initiatives for a Competitive Inner City.

GENDRON, MARY W., retired educator; b. Columbia, Miss., Oct. 9, 1926; d. Henry W. and Mary Elizabeth (Pace) Williamson; m. Robert Louis Gendron, Aug. 18, 1960; children: Gina, Robert John. BA, Southeastern U., Hammond, Ind., 1950; M of Edn., La. State U., 1953; postgrad., U. Fla., 1957—61. Tchr. Calcasieu Parish, Lake Charles, La., East Baton Rouge Parish, Baton Rouge; assoc. prof. U. Fla., Gainesville; tchr. Brevard County, Melbourne, Palm Bay. Sec./treas. Palm Bay H.S. Music Dept. Contbr. poetry to anthologies. Sec. La. Dept. Classroom Tchrs., treas.; deacon Meth. Ch., Palm Bay. Mem.: AAUW, NEA (life; regional dir., bd. regents Rep. La. 6th Congl. Dist.), Nat. Women's History Mus. (charter mem.), Fla. Edn. Assn. (life). Avocations: reading, swimming. Home: Apt 133 7015 Red Bug Lake Rd Oviedo FL 32765-5057

GENDRON, SUSAN ANN, school system administrator; b. Tewksbury, Mass. m. Mark Gendron; children: Stacey, Matthew. BS in Elem. and Secondary Edn., U. So. Maine, Gorham, MS in Ednl. Adminstrn. From tchr. to supt. Scarborough Pub. Schs., Maine; supt. Windham Sch. Dist., 1997—2003; commr. of edn. State of Maine, Augusta, 2003—. Mem.: Maine Sch. Supts Assn. (Disting. Educator award 2001, Supt. of Yr. award 2002). Office: Commr of Edn State House Sta #23 Augusta ME 04333 E-mail: susan.gendron@maine.gov.*

GENEGO, WILLIAM JOSEPH, lawyer; b. Albany, Mar. 27, 1950; s. William Joseph and Olga Alice (Sultan) G. BS in Bus. and Pub. Adminstrn. magna cum laude, NYU, 1972; JD, Yale U., 1975; LLM, Georgetown U., 1977. Bar: D.C. 1975, Calif. 1982, U.S. Supreme Ct. 1984, other dist. and appellate cts. Spl. asst. state's atty. Cir. and Dist. Cts. Montgomery County, Md., 1975-77; staff atty. legal intern program Georgetown U. Law Ctr., Washington, 1975-77, adj. prof., dep. dir. legal intern program, 1977-79; cons., vis. supervising atty. Yale Legal Svcs. Orgn., Law Sch. Yale U., New Haven, 1977; with Baker & Fine, Cambridge, Mass., 1980-81; asst. clin. prof. Law Ctr. U. So. Calif., LA, 1981-83, assoc. clin. prof., 1983-86, clin. prof., 1986-89, adj. prof., 1990-92; vis. prof. law Boston U., 1990, UCLA, 1991-92; pvt. practice Law Offices of William J. Genego, Santa Monica, Calif., 1990-2000; ptnr. Nasatir, Hirsch, Podberesky & Genego, Santa Monica, 2000—. Mem. practitioners' adv. group U.S. Sentencing Commn., 1989—; presenter in field. Mem. adv. bd. Criminal Practice Manual, Bur. Nat. Affairs, 1987-2000; editor Yale Law Jour., 1974-75; contbr. articles to legal publs. Bd. dirs. Nat. Network for Right to Counsel, 1986-88. Recipient Ann. Humanitarian award inmate rep. com. Fed. Correctional Instn., Danbury, Conn., 1974. Mem. NACDL (chairperson com. on rules of practice and procedure 1991—, Pres.'s award 1988), ABA (mem. ad hoc com. on U.S. Sentencing Commn. 1986—, chairperson competency com. sect. criminal justice 1983-85), Nat. Legal Aid and Defender Assn. (chairperson def. counsel competency com. 1984-87), Calif. Pub. Defenders Assn., Calif. Attys. for Criminal Justice. Office: Main St Law Bldg 2115 Main St Santa Monica CA 90405-2215

GENEL, MYRON, pediatrician, educator; b. York, Pa., Jan. 6, 1936; s. Victor and Florence (Mowitz) G.; m. Phyllis Norma Berkman, Aug. 25, 1968; children: Elizabeth, Jennifer, Abby. Grad., Moravian Coll., Bethlehem, Pa., 1957, DSc (hon.), 1995; MD, U. Pa., Phila., 1961; MA (hon.), Yale U., New Haven, Conn., 1983. Diplomate Am. Bd. Pediat. Intern Mt. Sinai Hosp., NYC, 1961—62; resident in pediat. Children's Hosp. Phila., 1962—64; trainee pediat. endocrinology Johns Hopkins Hosp., Balt., 1966—67; instr. pediat. U. Pa. Sch. Medicine, 1967—69, assoc. in pediat., 1969—71; trainee in genetics, inherited metabolic diseases Children's Hosp. Phila., 1967—69, assoc. physician, 1969—71; attending physician Yale-New Haven Hosp., 1971—; faculty Yale U. Sch. Medicine, New Haven, 1971—, dir. pediat. endocrinology, 1971—85, program dir. Children's Clin. Rsch. Ctr., 1971—86, prof., 1981—2004, prof. emeritus, 2004—, assoc. dean, 1985—2004, dir. Office Govt. and Cmty. Affairs, 1985—2004. Mem. genetic adv. bd. State of Conn., 1979—82, 1994—, mem. stem cell adv. com., 2005—; cons. subcom. investigations, oversight com. sci. and tech. US Ho. of Reps., 1982—84; mem. adv. bd. New Eng. Congenital Hypothyroidism Collaborative; cons. Hosp. St. Raphael, Milford Hosp., Norwalk Hosp., Stamford Hosp., Danbury Hosp., Greenwich Hosp.; chmn. transplant adv. com. Office of Commr. Conn. Dept. Income Maintenance, 1984—92; health policy fellowship bd. Inst. Medicine, 1989—95; clin. rsch. roundtable Inst. Medicine NRC, 2000—04; mem. fed. adv. com. nat. children's study Nat. Inst. Child Health and Devel./NIH, 2005—; mem. Sec.'s Adv. Com. on Human Rsch. Protections, 2006—. Contbr. articles to profl. jours. Bd. dirs. Rsch. America!, 1997—2000. Capt. USAR, 1964—66. Robert Wood Johnson Health Policy fellow Inst. Medicine NAS, Washington, 1982-83; recipient ann. award Conn. Campaign Against Cooley's Anemia, 1979, Ann. Comenius Alumni award Moravian Coll., 1990, Abraham Jacobi Meml. award Am. Acad. Pediat. and AMA, 1999, Joseph W. St. Geme Leadership award Fedn. Pediat. Orgns., 2004. Fellow: AAAS; mem.: AMA (med. schs. sec. 1985—, coun. on sci. affairs 1994—2001, task force on fin. grad. med. edn. 1995, alt. del. governing coun., med. schs. sec. 1995—98, task force on privacy and confidentiality 1998—99, del. 1998—2002, chair 2003—04), APHA, Assn. Patient Oriented Rsch., NY Acad. Medicine, Conn. Acad. Sci. and Engring. (coun. 2000—, v.p./pres.-elect 2006—), Soc. Pediat. Rsch. (Disting. Svc. award 2003), Endocrine Soc. (rsch. initiative com. 1995—99, legis. affairs com. 2002—), Conn. United for Rsch. Excellence (chmn. steering com. 1989—90, pres. 1990—93, chmn. bd. dirs. 1993—94), Conn. Endocrine Soc., Nat. Assn. Biomed. Rsch. (bd. dirs. 1990—93, exec. com. 1991—93), Assn. Program Dirs. (pres.-elect 1980—81, pres. 1981—82), New Haven County Med. Assn. (bd. govs. 1990—2002, 2004—), Assn. Am. Med. Colls. (adminstrv. bd. coun. acad. socs. 1987—92, chmn.-elect coun. acad. socs. 1989—91, exec. coun. 1989—92, adv. panel on rsch. 1999—2003, Disting. Svc. mem. 2005), Am. Soc. Bone and Mineral Rsch., Am. Pediat. Soc., Am. Fedn. Med. Rsch., Am. Diabetes Assn. (co-recipient Jonathan May award 1979), Am. Coll. Preventive Medicine, Am. Coll. Nutrition, Am. Assn. Clin. Endocrinologists, Am. Acad. Pediat. (task force organ transplants, com. on fed. govt. affairs), Sigma Xi. Jewish. Office: Yale Sch Med Child Health Rsch Ctr PO Box 208081 New Haven CT 06520-8081 Office Phone: 203-785-6019, 203-393-2685. Business E-Mail: myron.genel@yale.edu.

GENERAZZO, ARLENE DIAMOND, retired elementary school educator; b. Malden, Mass., June 16, 1944; d. Gordon and Minnie Stromer Diamond; m. Ronald A. Generazzo, June 25, 1978. BS, L.I. U., Bklyn., 1969; MEd, State Coll. Boston, 1974. Tchr. Town of Arlington Pub. Schs., Mass., 1969—70, City of Medford Pub. Schs., 1971—2003, cons., 2005. Scorer Mass. Test Educator Lic., 2006. Author: Looking at Olde Medford and Its Past, 1989. Com. chair Centre Club of Lynnfield, Mass., 2003—; v.p. Friendship Force of North Shore, Lynnfield, 2003—, Medford Hist. Soc., 1990—2005. Mem.: NEA, Mass. Tchrs. Assn., Royall House Assn., Peabody Hist. Soc., Lynnfield Hist. Soc. Home: 6 Herrick Rd Peabody MA 01960-4552

GENEREUX, L. JOSEPH, lawyer; b. 1952; BA in Polit. Sci., Grinnell Coll., 1974; MSc in Internat. Rels., London Sch. Econ., 1977; JD, U. Mich., 1981. Bar: Minn. 1982. Mem., mgrs. com. Dorsey & Whitney, Mpls., 1981—89, dep. mng. ptnr., chair, comml. banking practice group; chair, fin. svcs., 1989—. Staff Mich. Jour. Law Reform, 1980—81. Mem.: ABA (adv. com. law firm pro bono project 2000—), Legal Corps (pres. 2004—, bd. dirs.), Minn. State Bar Assn. (co-chair, bus. law pro bono task force 2002—03), Minn. Legal Aid Soc. (pres 2003—, bd. dir.). Office: Dorsey & Whitney LLP Ste 1500 50 S Sixth St Minneapolis MN 55402-1498 Office Phone: 612-340-2888. Office Fax: 612-340-2868. Business E-Mail: genereux.joe@dorsey.com.

GENEROUS, WILLIAM THOMAS, JR., (TOM), coach, educator; b. Pawtucket, RI, Feb. 20, 1939; s. William T. and Marjorie Myette (Smith) Generous; m. Diane B. Kowalchuck, Oct. 24, 1964; children: Michelle Elizabeth, Suzanne Felice. AB, Brown U., 1963; MA, Stanford U., 1968, PhD, 1971. Charles T. Wilson jr. tchr. of history Choate Rosemary Hall, Wallingford, Conn., 1971-97, girls squash coach, 1975-96, boys squash coach, 1996—99; coach Wallingford Jr. Squash, 1992—99; squash coach U. N.C., 1999—. History tchr. summers St. Paul's Sch., Concord, NH, 1985, 87; adj. assoc. prof. phys. edn., squash coach U. NC, adj. prof. Peace, War and Def. Author: Swords and Scales: The Development of the Uniform Code of Military Justice, 1950-69, 1973, History of Choate Rosemary Hall 1890-1990, 1997, Sweet Pea at War: A History of USS Portland, 2003. Lt. USN, 1956—67. Mem.: U.S. Squash Racquets Assn. Avocation: flute. Home: 206 Wild Oak Ln Carrboro NC 27510-4140 E-mail: tomgenerous@earthlink.net.

GENESONI, JACQUELINE, mathematics educator; BA in Math., Columbia U., NYC, 1999, MA, 2004. Cert. in tchg. NY, 2004, in sch. dist. adminstrn. NY, 2005. Math. tchr. Freeport HS, NY, 2001—, math. dept. chair, 2006—, prin. summer sch., 2006; asst. dir. Freeport Cmty Sch., 2006—. Mem.: Sch. Adminstrs. Assn. NY State, Am. Assn. Sch. Adminstrs., Kappa Delta Pi. Business E-Mail: jgenesoni@freeportschools.org.

GENEST, JACQUES, nephrologist, clinical scientist, science administrator; b. Montreal, Que., Can., May 29, 1919; s. Rosario and Annette (Girouard) G.; m. Estelle Deschamps, Oct. 3, 1953; children: Paul, Suzanne, Jacques, Marie, Helene. BA, Coll. Jean de Brebeuf, Montreal, 1937; MD, U. Montreal, 1942; LLD (hon.), Queen's U., 1966, U. Toronto, Can., 1970; DSc (hon.), Laval U., Can., 1973, Sherbrooke U., 1974, Meml. U. Nfld., 1978, McGill U., Can., 1979, U. Ottawa, 1980, St. Francis Xavier U., 1983, SUNY, Buffalo, 1984, Rockefeller U., 1986, Concordia U., Montreal, 1986, Chinese Acad. Med. Scis., 1987, U. Montpelier, France, 1989. Resident in medicine and pathology Hôtel-Dieu Hosp., Montreal, 1942-45, cons. physician in nephrology, endocrinology and internal medicine, 1952-91; rsch. fellow Johns Hopkins Hosp., Balt., 1945—48, Harvard Sch. Chemistry, Boston, 1948, Rockefeller Hosp. Med. Rsch., NYC, 1948-51; chmn. dept. medicine U. Montreal, 1962—65, prof. medicine, 1965-96; prof. exptl. medicine McGill U., Montreal, 1960-98; founder, 1st dir. Clin. Rsch. Inst. Montreal, 1965-84, adviser, 1984-94. Editor: (with Erich Koiw) Hypertension, 1972; (with Erich Koiw and Otto Kuchel) Hypertension: Physiopathology and Treatment, 1977, 83; (with Marc Cantin, Otto Kuchel, Pavel Hamet) 2d edit., 1983; author: One Ideal, One Life, 1998, L'Homme Seul, 2005. Decorated companion Order of Can., grand officer Ordre Nat. du Que.; recipient award Gairdner Found., 1963, Archambault medal Can. Assn. for Advancement Sci., 1965, Stouffer prize, 1969, Marie-Victorin Sci. prize Govt. of Que., 1977, Royal Bank award, 1980, Isaac Walton Killam award, 1986, Armand Frappier prize Govt. of Que., 1996, Patronat du Quebec prize, 1998, Grand Montrealais prize, 2000, FCAR award Govt. Que., 2001, Purkynje medal Czech Acad. Sci., 2002; named to Can. Med. Hall of Fame, 1994. Master ACP; fellow Royal Coll. Physicians and Surgeons Can. (James H. Graham award of merit 1993), Royal Soc. Can. (Flavelle medal and award 1968); mem. Assn. Am. Physicians, Am. Clin. and Climatol. Assn., Am. Heart Assn. (Disting. Scientist award 2003), Peripatetic Club. Roman Catholic. Home: 5955 Wilderton Ave PH-L6 Montreal PQ Canada H3S 2V1 Office: Inst de Recherches Cliniques 120 Pine Ave Montreal PQ Canada H2W 1R7 Business E-Mail: jacgensr@sympatico.ca.

GENÉT, BARBARA ANN, accountant, travel company executive; b. NYC, Oct. 14, 1935; d. Arthur Samuel and Louise Margaret (Scheider) G. Profl. cert. in acctg., U. Calif., La Jolla, 1995, student, 1996—; BS of Acctg., U. Phoenix, 2001; MBA, Keller Grad. Sch. Mgmt., 2003. Asst. to chmn. bd., asst. v.p. pub. rels. Brink's Inc., Chgo., 1976-78; co-owner, pres. Ask Mr. Foster, Chgo., 1982-90; with Profl. Cmty. Mgmt., Laguna Hills, Calif., 1990-92; travel counselor E.J. Brown & Assocs., San Diego, 1992-94; tchr.'s asst. U. Calif-San Diego, La Jolla, 1996—. Rep. Becker CPA-CMA Rev., San Diego, 1995—. Mem. campership cmty. coun. YMCA. Becker scholar, 1995, scholar Marks CPA Rev., 1996. Mem. Am. Soc. Woman Accts., Inst. Mgmt. Accts., Inst. Cert. Travel Agts., Order Ea. Star, Ladies of Shrine N.Am., Zonta Internat. of La Jolla (treas. 1998-2000, kids camp 2005). E-mail: barbaragenet@cox.net.

GENETSKI, CHRISTIAN S., lawyer; b. NYC, Aug. 28, 1970; BA magna cum laude, Birmingham-Southern Coll.; JD, Vanderbilt U., 1995. Bar: Ga. 1995, DC 2001. Assoc. King & Spalding, Atlanta; trial atty. Computer Crime and Intellectual Property Sect., Criminal Divsn. US Dept. Justice, Washington; assoc. Kirkland & Ellis, Washington, ptnr., 2002—03, Sonnenschein Nath & Rosenthal LLP, Washington, 2003—, vice chair Info. Security and Internet Enforcement Practice Group. Adj. prof. computer crime law Georgetown U. Law Ctr. Office: Sonnenschein Nath & Rosenthal LLP Ste 600, E Tower 1301 K St NW Washington DC 20005 Office Phone: 202-408-6463. Office Fax: 202-408-6399. Business E-Mail: cgenetski@sonnenschein.com.

GENETSKI, ROBERT JAMES, economist; b. NYC, Dec. 26, 1942; s. Alex and Helen Genetski. BS, Ea. Ill. U., 1964; MA, NYU, 1968, PhD, 1972. Tchr. English St. Procopius Acad., Lisle, Ill., 1965-66; research analyst Nat. Econ. Research Assn., NYC, 1967-68; lectr. econs. NYU, NYC, 1969-70; econ. analyst Morgan Guaranty Trust Co., NYC, 1969-71; sr. v.p., economist Harris Trust & Savs. Bank, Chgo., 1971-88; pres. Stotler Econs., Chgo., 1988-90; sr. v.p., chief economist The Chgo. Corp., 1990-91; pres. Robert Genetski & Assocs., 1991—; sr. mng. dir. Chgo. Capital, 1995-2000. Lectr. econs. NYU, 1969-70, U. Chgo., 1973; vis. prof. Wheaton Coll., Ill., 1986; census adv. com. US Dept. Commerce, 1983-86; bd. dirs. DNP Select Income Fund, Midwest Banc Holdings. Author: (with Beryl Sprinkel) Winning with Money, 1977, Taking the Voodoo out of Economics, 1986, 88, A Nation of Millionaires, 1997. Chmn. ednl. com. Sch. Bd. Dist. 25, West Chicago, Ill., 1973-79; bd. dirs. Ctrl. DuPage Health Svcs., 1988-94. Mem. Am. Statis. Assn., Am. Econ. Assn. (fin. com. 1983-), Nat. Assn. Bus. Economists (editor Newsletter 1978), Western Econ. Assn., Am. Bankers Assn. (econ. adv. com. 1980-83), U.S. C. of C. (econ. adv. com. 1985-) Office: 107 Park St Saugatuck MI 49453 Office Phone: 312-565-0112. Business E-Mail: rgenetski@classicalprinciples.com.

GENETTA, ANN H., psychologist, neuropsychologist; d. Anthony L. and Beverly S. Genetta; m. Robert E. Edinoff, Apr. 6, 1999. BA, Rutgers U., 1983; MS, Drexel U., 1989; D in Psychology, Widener U., 1996. Cert. Nat. Register of Health Svc. Providers in Psychology, lic. psychologist Pa., Del. Postdoctoral fellow Bryn Mawr Rehab. Hosp., Malvern, Pa., 1996—97; neuropsychologist Physicians of Rehab. Medicine, Harrisburg, Pa., 1998—2001; clin. neuropsychologist, mem. med. staff ChristianaCare Health Svcs., Wilmington, Del., 2002—. Med. staff affiliate Holy Spirit Hosp., Harrisburg, 2000—01; adj. faculty mem. Phila. Coll. of Osteo. Medicine, 2000—01; presenter in field. Contbr. articles to profl. jours. Mem.: APA, Nat. Acad. Neuropsychology, Del. Psychol. Assn. Avocations: hiking, travel, environmentalism. Office: ChristianaCare Health Svcs 501 West 14th St PO Box 1668 6th floor Wilmington DE 19899 Office Phone: 302-428-6692. Business E-Mail: agenetta@christianacare.org.

GENGA, JOHN MICHAEL, lawyer; b. Detroit, Apr. 28, 1962; BA, Stanford U., 1983; JD, U. Mich., 1986. Bar: Calif. 1986, U.S. Dist. Ct. (ctrl. and ea. dists.) Calif. 1987, U.S. Dist. Ct. (no. and so. dists.) Calif. 1988, U.S. Ct. Appeals (9th cir.) 1988, U.S. Supreme Ct. 1993, U.S. Ct. Appeals (10th cir.) 1997. Assoc. Jones, Day, Reavis & Pogue, LA, 1986-88, Hill Wynne Troop & Meisinger, LA, 1988-93; ptnr. Troop Steuber Pasich Reddick & Tobey, LLP, LA, 1994—2000, Paul, Hastings, Janofsky & Walker LLP, San Francisco, chmn. entertainment practice group; founder, owner Genga & Assocs., Encino, 2004—. Mem. ABA, State Bar Calif., L.A. County Bar Assn. Office: Genga & Assocs PC 15821 Ventura Blvd Ste 525 Encino CA 91436 Office Phone: 818-444-4580. Business E-Mail: jgenga@gengalaw.com.

GENGARO, CHRISTINE LEE, music educator; b. Queens, NY, May 30, 1974; d. Frank and Geraldine Gengaro; life ptnr. Jeffrey Norman Kausch. BA, MA, CUNY, 1997; PhD, U. So. Calif., LA, 2005. Mid. sch. tchr. NYC Pub. Sch. Sys., 1998—2000; adj. lectr. Pasadena City Coll., Pasadena, Calif., 2002—06, LA City Coll., 2004—06, asst. prof., 2006—. Author: (book) Notches; contbr. articles to profl. jours. Literacy tutor LA Pub. Libr., 2003—04. Finalist Am. Music Edn. Initiative award, Nat. Music Found., 2002; recipient Tchg. Excellence award, Lois Bailey Glenn, 2005. Mem.: Soc. Children's Book Writers and Illustrators, Coll. Music Soc., Am. Musicological Soc., Golden Key, Phi Beta Kappa, Pi Kappa Lambda. Catholic. Office: LA City Coll 855 N Vermont Ave Los Angeles CA 90029 Business E-Mail: gengarcl@lacitycollege.edu.

GENGLER, RICHELLE RUTH, musician, educator; b. Hoisington, Kans., Apr. 14, 1951; d. Richard Albert and Charlotte Ruth (Schepmann) Popp; m. Scott Edward Gengler, June 22, 1985; children: Shawn, Barry, Jeremy, Kristin, Jordan. AA, St. John's Coll., Winfield, Kans., 1972. Parish worker Holy Cross Luth. Ch., Memphis, 1972—73, Zion Luth. Ch., Chanute, Kans., 1973—75; sec. to divsn. atty. Exxon Co. U.S., Midland, Tex., 1980—88; sec. to dir. Cmty. Devel. Greater Hutchinson Kans. C. of C., 1975—76; pvt. piano instr. Midland, 1985—. Organist various Luth.

chs., Midland, Odessa, Tex., 1980—2000; mem. handbell choir 1st Bapt. Ch., Midland, 2001—, Sunday sch. dir., 2002—, mem. benevolence com., 2003—. Mem.: Nat. Guild Piano Tchrs. (cert.), Midland Symphony Guild (newsletter chmn. 2004—), R. E. Lee Choir Booster Club, Nat. Fedn. Jr. Music Clubs (dist. 9 chmn. 2004—, cert.), Musicians Club Midland (pres. 2003—). Republican. Avocations: swimming, singing, counted cross stitch.

GENGOR, VIRGINIA ANDERSON, financial planning executive, educator; b. Lyons, NY, May 2, 1927; d. Axel Jennings and Marie Margaret (Mack) Anderson; m. Peter Gengor, Mar. 2, 1952 (dec.); children: Peter Randall, Daniel Neal, Susan Leigh. AB, Wheaton Coll., 1949; MA, U. No. Colo., 1975, MA, 1977. Cert. fin. planner Coll. Fin. Planning. Chief hosp. intake svc. County of San Diego, 1966-77; chief Kearny Mesa Dist. Office, 1977-79, Dept. Children of Ct., 1979-81, chief child protection svcs., 1981-82; registered rep. Am. Pacific Securities, San Diego, 1982-85; registered tax preparer State of Calif., 1982—; registered rep. (prin.) Sentra Securities, 1985—; assoc. Pollock & Assocs., San Diego, 1985—86; pres. Gengor Fin. Advisors, 1986—. Cons. instr. Nat. Ctr. for Fin. Edn., San Diego, 1986-88; instr. San Diego Community Coll., 1985-88. Mem. allocations panel United Way, San Diego, 1976-79; children's cir. Child Abuse Prevention Found., 1989—; chmn. com. Child Abuse Coord. Coun., San Diego, 1979-83; pres. Friends of Casa de la Esperanza, San Diego, 1980-85, bd. dirs., 1980—; 1st v.p. The Big Sis. League, San Diego, 1985-86, pres., 1987-89. Mem. NAFE, AAUW (bd. dirs.), Fin. Planning Assn., Inland Soc. Tax Cons., Nat. Assn. Securities Dealers (registered prin.), Nat. Ctr. Fin. Edn., Am. Bus. Women's Assn., Navy League, Freedoms Found. of Valley Forge, Internat. Platform Assn. Presbyterian. Avocations: community service, travel, reading. Home: 6462 Spear St San Diego CA 92120-2929 Office: Gengor Fin Advisors 4950 Waring Rd Ste 7 San Diego CA 92120-2700 Office Phone: 619-583-8055. E-mail: vgengor@cox.net.

GENIA, JAMES MICHAEL, lawyer; b. Chgo., Sept. 16, 1964; s. Anthony Leo and Anne Louise (Hawley) Genia. BA, Augsburg Coll., 1987; JD, William Mitchell Coll. Law, 1990. Bar: Minn. 1990, U.S. Dist. Ct. Minn. 1992, U.S. Ct. Appeals (8th cir.) 1994, U.S. Supreme Ct. 1999. Jud. law clk. State of Minn., Duluth, 1990-92; dep. solicitor gen. Mille Lacs Band of Ojibwe Indians, Onamia, Minn., 1992-93, solicitor gen., 1993-99; atty. Lockridge Grindal Nauen, Mpls., 1999—2002, ptnr., 2002—. Bd. dirs. Woodlands Nat. Bank., chmn. bd. dirs.; vice chmn. bd. dirs. Anishinabe O. I. C.; lectr. Am. Indian sovereignty and treaty rights various univs., continuing edn. seminars, civic groups, 1992—; adj. prof. St. Cloud State U., 1999—. Actor: (plays) Mille Lacs Cmty. Theater, 1996—. Bd. dirs. Johnson Inst. Found., 1998—. Named Atty. of the Yr., Minn. Lawyer Newspaper, 1999; named one of Top 100 All-Time Grads., William Mitchell Coll. Law, 2000. Mem.: ATLA, Minn. State Bar, Minn. Am. Indian Bar Assn., Fed. Bar Assn., Am. Indian C. of C. (bd. dirs. 2001—), William Mitchell Coll. Law Alumni Assn. (bd. dirs. 1996—99). Avocations: softball, golf, jogging, reading, acting. Office Phone: 612-963-2186. Personal E-mail: jmgenia@yahoo.com.

GENIESER, NANCY BRANOM, radiologist; MD, Med. Coll. Pa., 1962. Diplomate Am. Bd. Radiology, Am. Bd. Diagnostic Radiololgy, Am. Bd. Pediat. Radiology. Intern Phila. Gen. Hosp., 1962—63; resident radiology NYU Hosps., NYC, 1963—65; prof. radiology NYU Med. Ctr.; staff Bellevue Hosp., NYC; cons. Manhattan VA; assoc. dean, admissions and fin. aid NYU Sch. Medicine, 2004—. Fellow Am. Coll. Radiology; mem. NYC Med. Soc., NY Radiol. Soc., NY State Radiol. Soc., Radiol. Soc. N.Am., Soc. Pediat. Rsch Office Fax: 212-263-7666.

GENIESSE, ROBERT JOHN, lawyer; b. Appleton, Wis., Sept. 16, 1929; s. Arthur John and Rhoda (Miller) G.; m. Jane Elizabeth Fletcher, June 10, 1961; children: Julia Forrest, Thomas Guy. BA magna cum laude, Williams Coll., 1951; LLB cum laude, Harvard U., 1957. Bar: N.Y. 1958, D.C. 1982. Assoc. Debevoise and Plimpton, NYC, 1957-61, 64-66, ptnr., 1966-94; asst. U.S. atty. So. Dist. N.Y., 1962-63, chief appellate atty., 1963-64. Editor Harvard Law Rev., 1955-57. Bd. dirs. Legal Action Ctr., N.Y., 1973-78, Environ. Def. Fund, 1974-82; trustee Williams Coll., 1974-87; trustee World Monuments Fund, 1993—, sec., gen. counsel, 1995—; trustee Nat. Bldg. Mus., 1994-00; trustee Sterling and Francine Clark Art Inst., Williamstown, Mass., 1974-01, pres., 1987-98; trustee Ringling Mus. Art, Sarasota, Fla., 2001—. 1st lt. Inf. U.S. Army, 1952-54. Mem. N.Y. State Bar Assn., D.C. Bar Assn., Soc. Alumni of Williams Coll. (pres. 1973-74), Phi Beta Kappa. Home: PO Box 516 Boca Grande FL 33921-0516 also: 2101 Connecticut Ave NW Apt 61 Washington DC 20008-1757 Office: Devevoise & Plimpton 555 13th St NW Ste 1100E Washington DC 20004-1163

GENINI, RONALD WALTER, retired history educator, historian; b. Oakland, Calif., Dec. 5, 1946; s. William Angelo and Irma Lea (Gays) G.; m. Roberta Mae Tucker, Dec. 20, 1969; children: Thomas, Justin, Nicholas. BA, U. San Francisco, 1968, MA, 1969. Cert. secondary edn. tchr., Calif.; adminstrv. svcs. credential. Tchr. Ctrl. Unified Sch. Dist., Fresno, Calif., 1970—2004, ret., 2004—. Judge State History Day, Sacramento, 1986-94; mem. U.S. history exam. devel. team Golden State, San Diego, 1989-93; securer placement of state-registered landmarks; guest appearance History Channel program "UFO Hotspots,", Jan. 2003; guest contbr. Time Line Films, 2006. Author: Romualdo Pacheco, 1985, Darn Right It's Butch, 1994, Theda Bara, 1996; editl. asst. The Invincible Quest, 2007; contbr. articles to profl. jours.; cited as authority on Theda Bara by Ency. Brit. Online Am. Women in History, 1999, also on Romualdo Pacheco by Biog. Directory of Am. Congress. Bd. dirs. Fresno Area 6 Neighborhood Coun., 1973-74, Fresno City and County Hist. Soc., 1975-78, St. Anthony's sch. bd., Fresno, 1980-84; active Good Company Players, Fresno, 2000-01. Named one of Outstanding Young Educators Am., Fresno Jaycees, 1978; recipient recognition for Tchr. Cares award Calif. State Assembly and Fresno City Coun., 1996. Mem.: Mt. Vernon Ladies Assn., Calif. Ret. Tchrs. Assn., Smithsonian Inst., Carmel Bach Festival, Utah Shakespeare Festival, San Joaquin Pkwy. and Conservation Trust, Arte de Americas. Democrat. Roman Catholic. Avocations: writing history, motion picture scriptwriting, commercial acting. Home: 1486 W Menlo Ave Fresno CA 93711-1305 E-mail: r_genini@yahoo.com.

GENIS, SEAN A., philosophy, politics and economics scholar; b. Conn., 1985; s. Vincent and Roxana G. BS in Physics, US Naval Acad., Annapolis, 2007; student in Philosophy, Politics, Econ., Oxford Univ., 2007—. Named a Trident Scholar; Rhodes Scholar. Achievements include conducting rsch. on techniques for acoustic detection of landmines; Eagle Scout. Avocation: bicycling.*

GENKIN, BARRY HOWARD, lawyer; b. Phila., Aug. 8, 1949; s. Paul and Pearl (Rosenfeld) G.; m. Marian (Block), Aug. 15, 1975; children: Matthew Todd, Kimberly Beth. BS (hon.), Pa. State U., 1971; JD (hon.), U. Balt., 1974; LLM in Taxation, Georgetown U., 1977. Bar: Pa. 1975, Wash. 1977, N.Y. 1995. Spl. counsel divsn. corp. fin. SEC, Washington, 1975—79; assoc. Blank Rome LLP, Phila., 1979—83, ptnr., 1983—, co-chmn. bus. and corp. dept., 1988—93, mem. mgmt. com., distribution com., 1997—, chmn., budget com., 1996—, mem. exec. com., finance ptnr., 2001—. Pres. bd. dirs. Smeal Bus. Sch., Pa. State U., 2003-05; lectr. in field. Contbr. U. Balt. Law Rev., 1991—. Mem.: ABA, Pa. Bar Assn., Ace Country Club (bd. trustees); Omicron Delta Kappa, Heuisler Honor Soc. Office: Blank Rome LLP One Logan Sq Philadelphia PA 19103 Office Phone: 215-569-5514. Office Fax: 215-832-5514. Business E-Mail: genkin@blankrome.com.

GENKINS, GABRIEL, physician; b. Berlin, Mar. 20, 1928; came to U.S., 1940, naturalized, 1945; s. Arkady and Tamara (Schlesinger) G.; children: Karen Lee Genkins Fairbank, Steven M., Amy E. BS, NYU, 1949, MD, 1952. Diplomate Am. Bd. Internal Medicine, Am. Bd. Cardiology. Intern, resident Mt. Sinai Hosp., NYC, 1952-57; practice medicine specializing cardiology NYC; chief myasthenia gravis clinic rsch. labs. Mt. Sinai Med. Ctr., NYC, 1972—, clin. prof. medicine, 1973—; attending physician cardiology Mt. Sinai Hosp., NYC, 1973—; mem. nat. med. adv. bd. Myasthenia Gravis Found., 1956—, v.p. bd. dirs., 1973—. Contbr. articles to profl. jours., chpts. to books. Served with airborne inf., U.S. Army, 1945-46. Democrat. Home Phone: 718-268-5412; Office Phone: 718-268-5412. Office Fax: 718-268-5412. Business E-Mail: ggenkins@nyc.rr.com.

GENN, NANCY, artist; b. San Francisco; d. Morley P. and Ruth W. Thompson; m. Vernon Chathburton Genn; children: Cynthia, Sarah, Peter. Student, San Francisco Art Inst., U. Calif., Berkeley. Lectr. on art and papermaking Am. Ctrs. in Osaka, Japan, Nagoya, Japan, Kyoto, Japan, 1979-80; guest lectr. various univs. and art mus. in U.S., 1975—; vis. artist Am. Acad. in Rome, 1989, 94, 2001. One-woman shows include, De Young Mus., San Francisco, 1955, 63, Gumps Gallery, San Francisco, 1955, 57, 59, San Francisco Mus. Art, 1961, U. Calif., Santa Cruz, 1966-68, Richmond Art Center, 1970, Calif., Oakland Mus., 1971, Linda/Farris Gallery, Seattle, 1974, 76, 78, 81, LA Inst. Contemporary Art, 1976, Susan Caldwell Gallery, NYC, 1976-77, 79, 81, Nina Freudenheim Gallery, Buffalo, 1977, 81, Annely Juda Fine Art, London, 1978, Inoue Gallery, Tokyo, 1980, Toni Birckhead Gallery, Cin., 1982, Kala Inst. Gallery, Berkeley, Calif., 1983, Ivory/Kimpton Gallery, San Francisco, 1984, 86, Eve Mannes Gallery, Atlanta, 1985, Richard Iri Gallery, LA, 1990, Harcourts Modern and Contemporary Art, San Francisco, 1991, 93, 96, Am. Assn. Advancement of Sci., Washington, 1994, Anne Reed Gallery, Ketchum, Id., 1995, Michael Petronko Gallery, NY, 1997, Mills Coll. Art Mus., Oakland, Calif., 1999, Takada Gallery, San Francisco, 1999-00, 03, Ulivi Gallery, Prato, Italy, 2002, Fresno Art Mus., Calif., 2003, Bolinas Mus., Calif., 2003, Inst. Italiano di Cultura, Chgo., LA, 2004, Inst. Italiano Di Cultura/Chgo. Art Inst., Flatfile Galleries, Chgo., 2005; group exhbns. include San Francisco Mus. Art, 1971, Aldrich Mus., Ridgefield, Conn., 1972-73, Santa Barbara Mus., Calif., 1974-75, Oakland Mus. Art, 1975, Susan Caldwell, Inc., NYC, 1974-75, Mus. Modern Art, NYC, 1976, traveling exhbn. Arts Coun. Gt. Britain, 1983-84, Inst. Contemporary Arts, Boston, 1977, J.J.Brookings Gallery, San Francisco, 1997, Portland Art Mus., Oreg., 1997—, Takada Gallery, San Francisco, 1999-00, Leighton Glalery, Blue Hill, Maine, 2005; represented in permanent collections Frederick Weisman Art Mus., U. Minn., Mpls., NYC Pub. Lib., Mus. Modern Art, NYC, NY Pub. Libr., Achenback Found., Palace of the Legion of Honour, San Francisco, Albright-Knox Art Gallery, Buffalo, Libr. of Congress, Washington, Nat. Mus. for Am. Art, Washington, LA County Mus. Art, Art Mus. U. Calif., Berkeley, McCrory Corp., NYC, Mus. Art, Auckland, NZ, Aldrich Mus., Ridgefield, Conn., (collection) Bklyn. Mus., (collection) U. Tex., El Paso, Internat. Ctr. Aesthetic Rsch., Torino, Italy, Cin. Art Mus., San Francisco Mus. Modern Art, Oakland Art Mus., LA County Mus., City of San Francisco Hall of Justice, Harris Bank, Chgo., Chase Manhattan Bank, NYC, Modern Art Gallery of Ascoli Piceno, Italy, Mills Coll. Art Mus., Oakland, Calif., Mills Coll. Art, Oakland, Calif., various mfg. cos., also numerous pvt. collections; commd. works include, Bronze lectern and 5 bronze sculptures for chancel table, 1st Unitarian Ch., Berkeley, Calif., 1961, 64, bronze fountain, Cowell Coll., U. Calif., Santa Cruz, bronze menorah, Temple Beth Am, Los Altos Hills, Calif., 17, murals and 2 bronze fountain sculptures, Sterling Vineyards, Calistoga, Calif., fountain sculpture, Expo 1974, Spokane, Wash; vis. artist Am. Acad., Rome, 1989. U.S./Japan Creative Arts fellow, 1978-79; recipient Ellen Branston award, 1952; Phelan award De Young Mus., 1963; honor award HUD, 1968 Home: 1515 La Loma Ave Berkeley CA 94708-2033 Office Phone: 510-849-4366.

GENNARI, F(RANK) JOHN, medical educator; b. Jersey City, May 18, 1937; s. Frank and Amelia (Sargia) G.; m. Emily Hewson Michie, Sept. 15, 1958; children: John Hewson, Jennifer Meade, Amelia Sargia. BS cum laude, Yale U., 1959, MD, 1963. Diplomate Am. Bd. Internal Medicine, Am. Bd. Nephrology. Intern U. Va. Hosp., Charlottesville, 1963—64, resident in medicine, 1964—66; fellow in nephrology Tufts-New Eng. Med., Boston, 1968—71; asst. prof. Sch. Medicine Tufts U., Boston, 1971—75, assoc. prof. Sch. Medicine, 1975—79; prof. Coll. Medicine U. Vt., Burlington, 1979—, Robert F. and Genevieve B. Patrick prof. medicine Coll. Medicine, 2000—, dir. nephrology Coll. Medicine, 1979—2002, assoc. chair dept. medicine Coll. Medicine, 1987—92, 1996—, interim chair dept. medicine Coll. Medicine Burlington, 1993. Mem. Nephrology bd. Am. Bd. Internal Medicine, 1994-2000. Co-author: Acid-Base, 1981, Acid-Base Disorders, 1987; editor Medical Mgmt. of Kidney and Electrolyte Disorders, 2001; sr. editor Acid-Base Disorders and Their Treatments, 2005; contbr. articles to profl. publs., chpts. to books. Mem. exec. com. Vt. Heart Assn., 1982-85; mem. exec. com. Vt. Kidney Assn., 1980—, pres., 1984-86; mem. merit rev. bd. VA, Washington, 1989-92. Capt. Med. Corps, USAF, 1966-68. Grantee NIH, 1971-91, Fogarty Internat., 1991. Fellow ACP; mem. Am. Fedn. Clin. Rsch., Am. Soc. Clin. Investigation, Am. Soc. Nephrology, Am. Physiol. Soc., Internat. Soc. Nephrology. Democrat. Avocations: skiing, hiking. Office: UHC Campus Fletcher Allen Health Care Rehab 2319 Burlington VT 05401

GENNARO, ROCCO JOSEPH, philosopher, educator; b. NYC, Oct. 13, 1963; m. Deidra Lynn York, May 19, 1990; children: Olivia Anne, Joseph Rocco. PhD, Syracuse U., NY, 1991. Asst./assoc. prof. philosophy Ind. State U., Terre Haute, 1995—2005, prof. philosophy, 2005—, interim chair philosophy dept. Presenter in field. Author: A Dialogue on Ethical Issues of Life and Death, Consciousness and Self-Consciousness, Mind and Brain: A Dialogue on the Mind-Body Problem; author, editor: Higher-Order Theories of Consciousness, author, co-editor: New Essays on the Rationalists, Philosophy of Mind area editor: Internet Encyclopedia Philosophy, 2005—; contbr. chapters to books, articles to profl. jours. Active Cmty. Theater of Terre Haute, 2000—01. Fellow Summer Seminar Participant, Nat. Endowment for the Humanities, 1995; Rsch. Com. grantee, Ind. State U., 2003. Mem.: Assn. for the Sci. Study of Consciousness, Soc. for Philosophy and Psychology, Coun. for Secular Humanism (assoc.), Am. Philos. Assn. (life). Office: Indiana State University Root Hall A-138F Terre Haute IN 47809 Office Phone: 812-237-3103. Office Fax: 812-237-2982. Business E-Mail: rocco@indstate.edu.

GENNETT, TIMOTHY, academic administrator; b. Richmond, Ind., July 25, 1951; s. Henry and Barbara Milda (Collignon) G.; m. Sharon Gail Cox, Mar. 5, 1976 (dec. Feb. 2005). BS in Chemistry, Purdue U., 1973, MS in Indsl. Adminstrn., 1974, MSEd, 1984. Lic. amateur radio operator. Sales engr. Gulf Oil Corp., San Antonio, 1975-77; asst. mgr. residence halls Purdue U., West Lafayette, Ind., 1977-82, mgr. residence halls, 1982-90, asst. dir. residence halls, 1990-95, dir. facilities housing and food svcs., 1995—2003. Bd. dirs. Gennett Graphics, Lafayette, Ind.; presenter in field. Contbr. articles to profl. jours. Damage assessement coord. ARC, Tippecanoe County, Ind., 1998-2000. Named Vol. of Yr. Disaster Svsc. ARC, 1996 Mem. Assn. Higher Edn. Cable TV Adminstrs. (bd. dirs. 2000-04), Tippecanoe Amateur Radio Assn. (sec. 1995-97), Soc. Cable TV Engrs. Office: Purdue U 1225 3d St West Lafayette IN 47906-4205

GENOVA, JOSEPH STEVEN, lawyer; b. Red Bank, NJ, Nov. 12, 1952; s. M. Leonard and Margaret (Coons) G.; m. Janet Scott, May 18, 1974 (div. Dec. 1980); m. Diane Melisano Genova, Jan. 15, 1983; children: Anthony Robert, Matthew Edward. BA, Dartmouth Coll., 1974; JD, Yale U., 1977. Bar: N.Y. 1978, U.S. Dist. Ct. (no., so. and ea. dists.) N.Y., Calif. 1993. Assoc. Milbank, Tweed, Hadley & McCloy, NYC, 1977-85, ptnr., 1986—. Ct. appointed arbitrator U.S. Dist. Ct. (ea. dist.) N.Y., 1986—; mediator U.S. Dist. Ct. (so. dist.) N.Y., 1992—. Bd. dirs. Legal Aid Soc., N.Y.C., 1995-2000; N.Y. Lawyers Pub. Interest, 1997—, Legal Svcs. N.Y.C., 2001—; apptd. N.Y. Chief Judge Pro Bono Review Com. (1990-94), Legal Svcs. Project., 1997-2000 Fellow Am. Bar Found., N.Y. Bar Found.; mem. ABA (Pro Bono Pub. award 1992, William Reece Smith award 1996, ABA Commn. on Iolta 1996-99), Assn. Bar City N.Y. (com. on housing and urban devel. 1982-85, com. on judiciary 1988-91, vice chmn. 1990-91, frequent interim mem., com. pro bono legal svcs., 1993-99, project on homelesness 2001—), N.Y. State Bar Assn. (com. on legal aid 1980—), chmn. 1986-91, pres.'s com. on access to justice 1990—, co-chmn. 1990-99, mem. task force on law guardian sys. 1989-99, mem. special com. future profession, 1998-2000), Fed. Bar Coun. (com. on 2d cir. cts. 1988-98, com. pub. svc. responsibility 1991—, chmn. 1994-2000, trustee 1998—2004, mem. 1st dept. disciplinary com. 2005-). Roman Catholic. Avocations: fishing, skiing. Office: Milbank Tweed Hadley & McCloy 1 Chase Manhattan Plz Fl 47 New York NY 10005-1413 Office Phone: 212-530-5532. Business E-Mail: jgenova@milbank.com.

GENOVESE, FRANCIS CHARLES (FRANK), economist, educator, editor-in-chief, writer; b. Toronto, Ont., Can., Feb. 16, 1921; came to U.S., 1946, naturalized, 1960; s. Francis A. and Florence M. (Ferguson) G.; m. Candace Eleanor Moorhouse, June 17, 1944; children: Margaret, Steven, Jeremy, Michael, Anne. BA, U. Toronto, 1942, MA, 1946; PhD, U. Wis., 1953. Mem. faculty Babson Coll., Babson Park, Mass., 1955—87, dean Grad. Sch., 1962-73, prof. econs., 1962-87, prof. emeritus, 1987—; pres. Pleiad Corp., 1974-76. Advisor Ctrl. Bank Jordan, 1975; vis. prof. NYU, 1960-62; vis. faculty Brown U. Grad. Sch. Banking, 1962-64, Wellesley Coll., 1962; pres. Am. Jour. Econs. & Sociology, Inc., 1997-99. Editor: Lombard Street; editor in chief Am. Jour. Econs. and Sociology, 1989-97; dir. Babson-Bernays Competition, 1976; contbr. articles to profl. jours., newspapers. Active Dem. Town Com., 1978—; Nelson small bus. task force Ea. Boston Cmty. Devel. Corp., 1964-66; bd. dirs. Mass. Higher Edn. Loan Corp., 1978-81, Schalkenbach Found., 1983-99; corp. mem. Mass. Goodwill Industries, 1973-86; chmn. Am. adv. com. Mrs. Helena Kaushik Coll., 1999—. With Can. Army, 1944-45. Fellow, U. Wis., 1946—47. Mem. Am. Econ. Assn., Am. Fin. Assn., Can. Econ. Assn., Harvard Faculty Club. Unitarian Universalist. Home: 18 Massasoit Rd Wellesley MA 02481-2411 Office: Babson Coll Faculty Babson Park MA 02481-0310 Office Phone: 781-235-1200. Office Fax: 781-239-6465. Business E-Mail: genovese@babson.edu.

GENOWAYS, HUGH HOWARD, systematic biologist, educator; b. Scottsbluff, Nebr., Dec. 24, 1940; s. Theodore Thompson and Sarah Louise (Beales) G.; m. Joyce Elaine Cox, July 28, 1963; children: Margaret Louise, Theodore Howard. AB, Hastings Coll., 1963; postgrad., U. Western Australia, 1964; PhD, U. Kans., 1971. Curator Mus. of Tex. Tech U., Lubbock, 1972-76, lectr. Mus. Sci. Program, 1974-76; curator Carnegie Mus. Natural History, Pitts., 1976-86; dir. U. Nebr. State Mus., Lincoln, 1986-94; chair mus. studies program U. Nebr., 1989—95, 1997—2004, prof. state mus., 1986—2004, prof. mus. studies, 1989—2004, prof. natural resource scis., 1997—2003, prof. phased retirement program, 2003—06, prof. emeritus state mus., 2006—. Author, editor:(with Michael A. Mares) Mammalian Biology in South America, 1982, (with Marion A. Burgwin) Natural History of the Dog, 1984; (with Mary R. Dawson) contbns. in Vertebrate Paleontology, 1984, Species of Special Concern in Pennsylvania, 1985, Current Mammalogy, 1987, 90, (with James H. Brown), Biology of the Heteromyidae, 1993, (with Carolyn Rose and Catherine Hawks) Storage of Natural History Collections: A Preventive Conservation Approach, 1996, (with Robert J. Baker) Mammalogy: A Memorial Volume Honoring Dr. J. Knox Jones, Jr., 1996, (with Ted Genoways) A Perfect Picture of Hell: Eyewitness Accounts by Civil War Prisoners from the 12th Iowa, 2001, (with Lynne M. Ireland) Museum Administration: An Introduction, 2003, (with J.R. Baker J.W. Bickham and C.J. Phillips) Bats of Jamaica, 2005, Museum Philosophy for Twenty-first Century, 2006; founding editor: Collections: A Journal for Museum and Archives Professionals, 2003-06 (Best New Jour. any catagory 2004). Packmaster Allegheny Trails coun. Boy Scouts Am., 1981—83, asst. scoutmaster, 1983—86. Co-recipient Acad. Freedom Coalition Nebr. award, 2004; grantee Fulbright Found., 1964, NSF, 1977-86, R.K. Mellon Found., 1981-86, Smithsonian Fgn. Currency Program, 1983-84, Inst. Mus. Svcs., 1989-96, Nebr. Game and Park Commn., 2001-05. Mem. Am. Soc. Mammalogists (pres. 1984-86, C. Hart Merriam award 1987, editor Spl. Pubs. 1995-96, historian 1997—, elected hon. mem. 2002, Hartley H. T. Jackson award 2004), Internat. Theriological Congress (steering com. 1985-2004), Southwestern Assn. Naturalists (pres. 1984-85, trustee 2003--), Am. Assn. Mus., Nebr. Mus. Assn. (pres. 1990-92, 1st Hugh H. Genoways Achievement award 1994, sec. 1997-2000), Assn. Systematics Collections (bd. dirs. 1993-94), Nat. Inst. for Conservation Cultural Property (bd. dirs. 1993-94), Sociedad Argentina para Estudio Mamiferos, Lincoln Attractions and Mus. Assn. (chair 1987-94), Soc. Systematic Biologists, Rotary (bd. dirs. Lincoln N.E. club 1990-92). Office: U Nebr-Lincoln State Mus W436 Nebraska Hall Lincoln NE 68588-0514 Business E-Mail: hgenoways1@unl.edu.

GENRICH, MARK L., corporate communications director; b. Buffalo, Aug. 28, 1943; m. Allison Forbes, 1967; children: Audrey, Liza, Colby. BA, Bucknell U., 1966. Editl. writer Palladium-Item, Richmond, Ind., 1970; writing exec. Bruce Eberle & Assocs., Inc., Vienna, Va., 1975-77; dep. editor editl. pgs. Phoenix Gazette, 1977-96; editl. writer, columnist The Ariz. Republic, Phoenix, 1996-98; dir. Warne Ctr. Goldwater Inst., Phoenix, 1998-2000; pub. rels. dir. Qwest Comm. Internat., Inc., 2000—02; dir. Ariz. Affairs, 2002—, U. Club. Ariz. Voice Crime Victims, 2006—. Participant U.S. Army War Coll., Carlisle, Pa., U.S. Naval War Coll., Newport, R.I.; participant arms control, disarmament programs including Space & Arms talks, Geneva; chmn. New Tech. Com., Journalism in Edn. Com.; mem. various coms. Creator, host cable TV program focus on polit. figures; regional editor The Masthead. Grantee European Cmty. Visitor Programme, 1993; recipient highest honors editl. writing, newspaper design Ariz., Western Region; highest honor Maricopa County Bar Assn.; Hoover Inst. media fellow, 1985. Mem. Nat. Conf. Editl. Writers (bd. dirs., included vol. Editl. Excellence), First Amendment Cong. (bd. dirs.), Soc. Profl. Journalists/Sigma Delta Chi, ABA (com. prisons, sentencing). Home: 130 W Pine Valley Dr Phoenix AZ 85023-5283 Office: Qwest Comm Internat Inc 4041 N Central Ave 11th Fl Phoenix AZ 85012

GENS, RALPH SAMUEL, electrical engineering consultant; b. Berlin, Nov. 25, 1924; s. Alexander and Renata Gens; m. Ida L. Mattson; children: Marilyn R., David A. BS in Elec. Engring., Oreg. State U., 1949. Registered profl. engr., Oreg. Engr. Bonneville Power Adminstrn., Portland, Oreg., 1949-80, chief, system engr., 1966-74, mgr. planning, research and devel., 1974-77, chief engr., asst. adminstr. for engring and constrn., 1977-80; cons. Portland, 1980—. Advisor NSF, 1971-76; mem. adv. com. Project UHV, 1968-79; mem. Electricity Commn. of Papua, New Guinea, 1981-88; chmn. energy rsch. adv. bd. U.S. Dept. Energy, 1984-85, mem., 1985-89; chmn. planning coordination com. of Western Systems Coordinating Coun., 1975-76. Contbr. articles to profl. jours.; patentee in field. Served as sgt. U.S. Army, 1943-46, PTO. Recipient Disting. Service award Dept. Interior, 1978. Fellow IEEE (chmn. surge protective devices com. 1971, chmn. Portland sect. 1968, William M. Harbishaw award 1984, Centennial medal 1984, medal for engring. excellence 2003); mem. NAE, Internat. Conf. Large High Voltage Electric Systems (U.S. v.p. 1979-80, chmn. study com. system analysis and technique 1986-92, Atwood award 1990, Internat. honorary mem., 1992), Electric Power Rsch. Inst. (rsch. adv. com. 1977-80), Tau Beta Pi, Sigma Tau, Eta Kappa Nu, Pi Mu Epsilon.

GENSER, JARED MATTHEW, lawyer; b. New Haven, Conn., June 17, 1972; s. Sander Gary and Lyne Taylor Genser; m. Lisa Joy Noik, June 1, 2003. BS, Cornell U., 1995; MA in Pub. Policy, Harvard U., 1998; JD, U. Mich., 2001. Bar: Md. 2001, D.C. 2002, lic.: Law Soc. UK (solicitor England and Wales) 2005. Assoc. McKinsey & Co., Washington, 2001—03, DLA Piper US LLP, Washington, 2003—. Vis. fellow Nat. Endowment for Democracy, 2006—. Pres. Freedom Now, Bethesda, 2001—. Named Pro Bono Lawyer of Yr., DLA Piper US LLP, 2005, 2006; recipient John F. Kennedy Meml. award, Cornell U., 1995, Jane L. Mixer Social Justice award, U. Mich. Law Sch., 2001, Rising Star award, Harvard U. John F. Kennedy Sch. of Govt., 2002; Raoul Wallenberg scholar, Hebrew U., Jerusalem, 1995—96. Mem.: Am. Soc. Internat. Law. Home Phone: 301-897-4771; Office Phone: 202-302-4049. Personal E-mail: jmg11@cornell.edu.

GENSHAFT, JUDY LYNN, academic administrator, psychologist, educator; b. Canton, Ohio, Jan. 7, 1948; d. Arthur I. and Leona (Caghan) G. BA, U. Wis., 1969; MA, Kent State U., 1973, PhD, 1975. Lic. psychologist, Ohio. Sch. psychologist Canton City Schs., Ohio, 1972-75; asst. prof. Ohio State U., 1976-81, assoc. prof., asst. chmn., 1981-85, prof., 1985—92, asst. chair, 1985-86, chair, 1987—92, presdl. intern, acting assoc. provost, 1986-87; dean Sch. Edn. SUNY, Albany, 1992-95, interim v.p. for acad. affairs, 1995-97, provost, v.p. acad. affairs, 1997-2000; pres. U. South Fla., Tampa, 2000—. Psychiat. social worker Canton Mental Health Clinic, 1970-72; vis. prof. U. British Columbia, Vancouver, Can., 1976-81. Contbr. numerous articles and book chpts. to profl. publ. Mem. Ballet Met., Columbus, 1986; cons. League Against Child Abuse, Columbus, 1978—, Bur. Vocat. Edn., Columbus, 1980—; mem. adv. bd. Support for Talented Students, Columbus, 1985—; bd dirs. H. Lee Moffitt Cancer Ctr. and Rsch. Inst., Fla. High-Tech Corridor, Greater Tampa Bay C. of C., Tampa Bay Partnership, Coun. of 100 (chair-designate). Nat. Rsch. grantee, 1984-85; recipient Kathryn Schoen Endowment award, 1986, Huelsman award, 1988, Hon. award Ohio Dept. Edn., 1984, Disting. Affirmative Action award, 1991, Leadership award Nat. Sch. Devel. Coun., Shirley A. Ryals award, Prevent Blindness, 2003. Mem. Am. Psychol. Assn., Nat. Assn. Sch. Psychologist, (sec. 1983-85, Presl. award 1982, 85, 87), Am. Assn. Counseling and Devel., Internat. Assn. Sch. Psychologists, Ohio Sch. Psychologist Assn. (ethics chmn. 1985-86), Sigma Xi. Avocations: sports, reading. Office: U South Fla Office of Pres 4202 E Fowler Ave, ADM241 Tampa FL 33620-6150 Office Phone: 813-974-2791.

GENSLER, M. ARTHUR, JR., architect; b. NYC, July 12, 1935; s. M. Arthur and Gertrude (Wilson) G.; m. Drucilla Cortell, Sept. 7, 1957; children— David, Robert, Kenneth, Douglas BA in Architecture, Cornell U., 1957. Lic. architect, 38 states. Jr. designer Shreve, Lamb & Harmon, NYC, 1958-59; project mgr. Norman & Dawbarn, Kingston, Jamaica, 1959-60, Albert Sigal & Assocs., NYC and San Francisco, 1961-63, Wurster, Bernardi & Emmons, San Francisco, 1963-65; pres., founder Gensler & Assocs., Architects, San Francisco, 1966—, now chmn. Mem. adv. council, mem. bldgs. and properties com. Coll. Architecture, Cornell U., Ithaca, N.Y., 1981-83. Co-author: A Rational Approach to Office Planning. Bd. dirs. World Coll. West, Petaluma, Calif., 1984-87; bd. overseers U. Calif., San Francisco; trustee World Affairs Coun., 1990—. Wity C.E., U.S. Army, 1958. Recipient Charles Goodwin Sands award Cornell U. Coll. Architecture, 1958; named charter mem. Interior Design mag. Hall of Fame, Cornell Enterpeneurs of Yr., 1995. Fellow AIA, Internat. Interior Design Assn.; mem. Inst. Bus. Designers (Star award 1992), San Francisco Planning and Urban Rsch. Assn., Bldg. Mgrs. and Owners Assn., Bay Area Coun., Urban Land Inst., San Francisco C. of C. (bd. dirs. 1984-86, 94—), Bohemian Club, Univ. Club, Bankers Club, Presidio Club. Republican. Congregationalist. Office: 2 Harrison St Ste 400 San Francisco CA 94105

GENSON, EDWARD MARVIN, lawyer; b. Chgo., June 30, 1941; BA, Northwestern U., 1962, JD, 1965. Bar: Ill. 1965. Ptnr. Genson & Gillespie, Chgo. Mem. Gov.'s Commn. on Criminal Legis. Bd. dirs. Ill. Historic Preservation Agy. Mem.: Nat. Assn. Criminal Def. Lawyers, Ill. Bar Assn., Chgo. Bar Assn., Ill. Attorneys for Criminal Justice, Internat. Acad. Trial Lawyers, John Howard Assn. Office: Genson & Gillespie 53 W Jackson Ste 1420 Chicago IL 60604*

GENT, ALAN NEVILLE, physicist, researcher; b. Leicester, Eng., Nov. 11, 1927; came to U.S., 1961, naturalized, 1972; s. Harry Neville and Gladys (Hoyle) G.; m. Jean Margaret Wolstenholme, Sept. 1, 1949; children: Martin Paul Neville, Patrick Michael, Andrew John; m. Ginger Lee, Sept. 4, 1997. BS, U. London, 1946, BS in Physics, 1949, PhD in Sci., 1955; DHC, U. Haute-Alsace, France, 1997; DSc (hon.), De Montfort U., Eng., 1998. Lab. asst. John Bull Rubber Co., Leicester, Eng., 1944-45; research physicist Brit. (now Malaysian) Rubber Producers' Research Assn., 1949-61; prof. polymer physics U. Akron, Ohio, 1961-88, Dr. Harold A. Morton prof. polymer physics and polymer engring., 1988-94; prof. emeritus, 1994—; dean grad. studies and research U. Akron, 1978-86. Vis. prof. dept. materials Queen Mary Coll., U. London, 1969-70; vis. prof. dept. chem. engring. McGill U., 1983; Hill vis. prof. U. Minn., 1985; cons. Goodyear Tire & Rubber Co., 1963-2002, Gen. Motors, 1973-87. Contbr. articles to profl. publs. Served with Brit. Army, 1947-49. Recipient Mobay award, Cellular Plastics divsn. Soc. of Plastics Industry, 1963, Colwyn medal Plastics and Rubber Inst. Gt. Brit., 1978, Adhesives award Com. F-11, ASTM, 1979, Internat. Rsch. award Soc. Plastics Engrs., 1980, Whitby award Rubber Chem. divsn. Am. Chem. Soc., 1987, Pub. Svc. medal NASA, 1988, Charles Goodyear medal Rubber Chem. divsn. Am. Chem. Soc., 1990; installed Ohio Sci. Tech. and Industry Hall of Fame, 1993. Mem. NAE, Soc. of Rheology (pres. 1981-83, Bingham medal 1975), Adhesion Soc. (pres. 1978-80, 3M award 1987, Pres.'s award 1997), Am. Phys. Soc. (chmn. divsn. high polymer physics 1977-78, High Polymer Physics prize 1996). Democrat. Office: U Akron Inst Polymer Science Akron OH 44325-3909 Office Phone: 330-972-7505. Business E-Mail: gent@uakron.edu.

GENTER, JOHN ROBERT, grocery industry executive; b. Huntsville, Ala., Oct. 16, 1957; s. John C. and Madge (McDaniel) G.; m. Margaret F. MacNaughton, Sept. 5, 1981; children: John Thomas, Lois Katharine. BS in Mktg. and Bus. cum laude, U. Ala., 1980. Sales rep. Food divsn. Procter & Gamble, Cin., 1980-81, dist. field rep., 1981, unit mgr., 1982-84; divsn. trade devel. mgr., regional mgr. Frito-Lay, Inc., Dallas, 1984-85; field mktg. mgr. vintage divsn. E&J Gallo Winery, Modesto (Calif.), Tampa, 1985, state mgr., 1986, divsn. mgr., 1986-91, region mgr. chain div., 1992-95; dir. mktg. Purity Wholesale Grocers, Boca Raton, Fla., 1995-96; bus. mgr. Acosta Sales Co., Tampa, 1996-97; divsn. mgr. Sutter Home Winery, Tampa, 1998-99, gen. sales mgr. South, 1999—2000, trainer sales mgmt., 1999-2000; S.E. regional sales mgr. Banfi Vintners, Old Brookville, NY, 2000—03; East Coast mgr. PuraFilter, Las Vegas, 2003—04, nat. sales mgr., 2004—. Trainer Sales Mgmt. Tng. Sch. Procter & Gamble, Cin., 1982-83, Sales Devel. Program Frito-Lay, Dallas, 1984-85. Author: (with others) E&J Gallo Field Marketing Manual, 1986. Mem. vestry St. John's Ch., Tampa, 1998-2001, active Father's Ministry, chmn. Every Mem.; youth soccer, basketball coach YMCA; trustee patrons St. John's Sch., sec., treas. sch. bd., 2003— Recipient Coach of Yr. award Tampa Tribune. Mem. U. Ala. Alumni Assn., Soc. de Vinum Honoratus, Beta Gamma Sigma. Republican. Episcopalian. Home and Office: 559 Ladrone Ave Tampa FL 33606-4036 Office Phone: 813-250-9247. E-mail: jrgenter@aol.com.

GENTILCORE, EILEEN MARIE BELSITO, principal; b. Glen Cove, NY; d. Samuel Francis and Nellie Theresa (McKenna) Belsito; m. James Matthew Gentilcore, Aug. 4, 1951; children: Kevin, John, Scott BS Edn., SUNY, Potsdam; MS Edn., Hofstra U., 1968, profl. diploma, 1976, EdD, 1979. Tchr. first grade Sea Cliff Sch., NY, 1951—52; founder, pre-K German Elementary Schs., Munich, 1952—53; tchr. first grade Peekskill Schs., NY, 1953—54; tchr. second grade Syosset Sch., NY, 1954—55, reading cons., 1970—84, head tchr., 1974—84, prin., 1985—96; ret., 1996. Bicentennial adv. bd. Syosset Cmty., 1976; adv. bd. Telicare, Uniondale, N.Y., 1978-80; mem. children immunized against polio, Med. Mission to India, 2004; mem. Gift of Life med. mission, Shanghai, Beijing and Hong Kong, 2003; cons. in field. Author: Developmental Learning, 1979 Organizer med. team to Honduras, 1998; coord. Internat. World Literacy, 2004—05, Rotary World Health and Hunger, 2006—; mem. Nassau County Graffiti Task Force, 1994—. Named Woman of Distinction, N.Y. State Senate, 1998, 2003, Town Oyster Bay, 2004; recipient Jenkins award N.Y. State PTA, 1968, Hon. Life, 1976, Pius X award Rockville Ctr. Diocese, 1985, Disting. Svc. award, N.Y. State PTA Dist., 1996, Teddy Roosevelt Achievement award, 1999, Syosset-Woodbury Rep. Club and Senator Carl Marcellino Achievement award, 1999, Literary Scholarship award, 2006-07, C. of C. Cmty. Svc. award, 2007, Disting. Svc. award, Rd. Found., 2007; grantee Karla Project, 1998, Queens Coun. Boy Scouts Am., 2003; N.Y. State PTA fellow, 1971-73, Hofstra fellow, 1971; lit. scholarship named after N.Y. State Sen. Liberty award, 2006. Mem.: Profl. and Bus. Women (Rotary Internat. world literacy coord. 2005—06), Syosset Prins. (pres. 1992), Rotary Internat. (pres. Syosset-Woodbury 1993—95, gov. aide 1995, med. mission to Russia dist. 7250 1995, launched Operation Mitch, Honduras 1996, Gift of Life pres., vocat. dir. dist. 7250 1996—97, med. mission to Honduras 1997, 1st woman dist. gov. dist. 7250 1998—99, children at risk task force 2000—, conf. chair Zone 32 2000—, coord. Internat. Avoidable Blindness task force 2002—, mem. internat. task force children at risk 2003—04, coord. literary task force zone 32 2003—04, coord. literacy task force zone 32 2003—, chair centennial com. dist 7250 2003—, coun. on legis. del. 2004, asst. gen. world coord. literacy task force 2004—, coord lit. gen. world 2005, strategic planning com. 2005—, coord. world health and hunger 2006—, Rotary Internat. world health and hunger coord. 2006—08, coord. Internat. Children at Risk task force, v.p., presenter, Paul Harris fellow 1995, N.Y. State Senate Woman of Distinction 1998, Internat. Achievement award 1999, Outstanding Svc. award 1999, Abe Gordon V.P. Outstanding Svc. award 2000, Achievement award 2000, Disting. Past Dist. Gov. award Zone 32 2002, R.I. Internat. Found. Meritorious Svc. citation 2002, Internat. Global award 2002, Svc. Above Self award 2003, Lifetime Achievement award 2004—, Internat. Lit. award 2005, 4 Aves. Svc. citation 2006, Disting. Svc. award 2006, 2007), Kappa Delta Pi, Alpha Sigma Omicron. Roman Catholic. Avocations: swimming, writing, reading, gardening. Office Fax: 516-921-0206. Personal E-mail: genheart@optonline.net.

GENTILE, ANTHONY, coal company executive; b. Aguila, Italy, Nov. 1, 1920; s. Gregorio and Antonieta (Duronio) G.; m. Nina Angela Discipio, Mar. 4, 1943; children: Robert Henry, Anita Marie, Rita Ann, Thomas Gregory. Student, Youngstown Coll., 1939-42; LH (hon.), U. Steubenville, 1977; DHL (hon.), 1988. Co-owner Pike Inn-Restaurant, Bloomingdale, OH, 1946-52; asst. to owner Huberta Coal Co., Steubenville, OH, 1952-55; gen. mgr. Half Moon Coal Co., Weirton, W.Va., 1955-57, Ohio River Collieries Co., Columbus, OH, 1957-59, pres., 1959—; Lafferty Coal Mining Co., Eastern Ohio Coal Co., 1959—; vice pres. Big Mountain Coals Inc., Prente, WV, 1962—. Chmn. bd., 1962—; pres. Bither Mining Co. W.Va.; v.p. N & G Constrn., Bannock Land Co.; chmn., pres. Bannock Coal Co., Lafferty, Ohio, 1985-88, chmn., 1988—; chmn. bd. dirs. Mining and Reclamation Council Am., Washington; bd. dirs. Union Bank, Steubenville. Mem. 1st Ohio Trade Commn. to Europe, 1965; mem. adv. bd. St. John Med. Ctr., Steubenville; trustee Coll. Steubenville, Ohio Valley Hosp., past chmn., Steubenville. Served to 1st lt. AUS, 1942-45, capt. Decorated Purple Heart, Silver Star; recipient Citizen of Yr. awd. Wintersville, C. of C., 1976, Conservation award for Ohio River Collieries Gov. Ohio., 1977, Humanitarian award Jeffersonian Lodge, Jefferson County, Ohio, 1977, Visionary award Jefferson County, 1999, Macedonia Visionary award AHA, 1999, Commodore award Gov. of Ohio, 1965; honoree Ohio Cancer Rsch. Assocs., 2000; inductee Upper Ohio Valley Lou Holtz Hall of Fame, 2000. Mem. Am. Mining Congress (mem. adv. council coal divsn. 1965). Home: 4 Normandy Dr Wintersville OH 43953-3800 Office: Ohio River Collieries Co PO Box 128 Bannock OH 43972-0128

GENTILE, DOMINIC P., lawyer; b. Chgo., Mar. 25, 1946; BS, DePaul U., 1968, JD, 1972. Bar: Ill. 1972, U.S. Supreme Ct. 1975, Nev. 1979. Pvt. practice Dominic P. Gentile, Ltd., Las Vegas. Adj. prof. law U. Nev., Las Vegas, mem. law sch. adv. com.; assoc. dean. nat. coll. criminal def. U. Houston, 1977—78; with faculty Yeshiva U.; guest faculty Harvard Law Sch., Cambridge, Mass.; spkr. in field. Author: various publications. Mem.: First Amendment Lawyers Assn., Libel Def. Resource Ctr., Nat. Assn. Criminal Def. Lawyers, Ill. State Bar Assn., State Bar Nev. (mem. bd. govs. 1991—96). Office: Dominic P Gentile Ltd 3960 Howard Hughes Pky Las Vegas NV 89109 Office Phone: 702-386-0066. Office Fax: 702-382-9309.*

GENTILE, ROBERT A., assistant principal; b. Bklyn., Dec. 16, 1966; s. Robert F. and Connie F. Gentile; m. Lucy Gentile, July 19, 1991; children: Joseph A., Marica C. BA in History, Bklyn. Coll. CUNY, 1989; MS in Social Sci., LI U., Bklyn., 1996; cert. in Secondary Adminstrn, Coll. St. Rose, Albany, NY, 2001. Tchr. social studies New Utrecht HS, Bklyn., 1990—2002, asst. prin., 2002—. Volleyball coach New Utrecht HS, 1993—96, head football coach, 1996—2000. With US Coast Guard Res., 1989—96. Recipient John Bunzel Meml. award, Assn. Tchrs. Social Studies, NY State Social Studies Suprs. Assn., 2004. Mem.: NYC Social Studies Suprs. Assn. (v.p. 2006—), NY State Social Studies Suprs. Assn. Office: New Utrecht HS 1601 80th St Brooklyn NY 11214 Office Phone: 718-232-2500 451. Business E-Mail: rgentil@schools.nyc.gov.

GENTILE SACHS, VALERIE ANN, lawyer; b. Cleve., Aug. 4, 1955; d. John Charles and Doreen Phyllis (Neale) G. B.L.S., Bowling Green U., 1977; J.D., Case Western Res. U., 1981. Bar: Ohio 1981. Summer assoc. Arter & Hadden, Cleve., 1980, assoc., 1981-83; sec. Royal Petroleum Properties, Inc., Cleve., 1982-83; assoc. Baker & Hostetler, Cleve., M.A. Hanna Co., v.p., gen. counsel, sec. RELTEC Corp., 1997-2000; v.p., gen. counsel, Marconi Comm., Inc., 2000-01; exec. v.p., gen. counsel, 2001-02, gen. counsel, chief legal officer Marconi PLC, London, 2002-03; exec. v.p., gen. counsel, sec. Jo-Ann Stores, Inc., 2003-05; v.p., sec., gen. counsel OM Group Inc., 2005-; Editor: Case Western Res. U. Law Rev., 1980-81, assoc. editor, 1979-80; assoc. editor Case Western Res. U. Jour. Internat. Law, 1978-79. Mem. Cleve. Citizens League, 1982-84; trustee Forest Hills Housing Corp., Cleve., 1982-84; mem. fgn. trade policy com. Cleve. World Trade Assn., 1982—. Mem. ABA, Ohio State Bar Assn., Cleve. Bar Assn., Alpha Epsilon Delta, Beta Beta Beta, Alpha Lambda Delta. Office: OM Group Inc 127 Public Sq Cleveland OH 44114 Office Phone: 330-656-2600 2156. Office Fax: 330-463-6675.

GENTINE, LEE MICHAEL, marketing professional; b. Plymouth, Wis., Feb. 18, 1952; s. Leonard ALvin and Dolores Ann (Becker) G.; m. Debra Ann Suemnicht, Dec. 29, 1973 (div. Nov. 2003); children: Amanda, Joshua, Jonathan. BBA, U. Notre Dame, 1974; MBA, DePaul U., 1977. Acct. Hurdman & Cranston, Chgo., 1974-75; sales rep. Sargento Cheese Inc., Plymouth, 1975-78, mktg. mgr., 1978-81, sr. v.p. mktg., 1981-84, exec. v.p. mktg., 1984-89, pres. consumer products divsn., 1989-97; mng. ptnr. Dairyland Investors Group LLP, Plymouth, Wis., 1997—; ptnr. Vintage Neighborhood LLC, 2004—. Adv. bd. Kaytee Products Inc., Chilton, Wis., 1994-98; bd. dirs. Sargento Foods Inc. Bd. dirs. Plymouth Softball Assn., 1980—; pres. Plymouth Indsl. Devel. Corp., 1981-85, Parish Coun., 1989-90; chmn. Plymouth Advancement Com., 1992-96, pres., 1992-2002; mem. adv. bd. St. Nicholas Hosp., 1998—; pres. Quit Qui Oc Athletic Alliance, Inc., 1999—; vice chmn. Elkhart Lake Tourism Commn., 1998-2004. Named One of 100 Best and Brightest Advt. Execs., Advt. Age, 1986. Mem. Am. Mktg. Assn., Sheboygan County C. of C. (bd. dirs. 1987-89), Beta Gamma Sigma. Roman Catholic. Avocations: softball, golf, home rehabilitation. Home: PO Box 467 Plymouth WI 53073-0467

GENTLE, KENNETH WILLIAM, physicist; b. Oak Park, Ill., Oct. 27, 1940; s. William and Cathryn Mary (Spence) G. BS, MIT, 1962, PhD, 1966. Asst. prof. dept. physics U. Tex., Austin, 1966-69, assoc. prof., 1970-75, prof. physics, 1976—, chair dept. physics, 1997-2001. Sloan fellow, 1973-75 Fellow Am. Phys. Soc. Home: 212 Buckeye Trl Austin TX 78746-4420 Office: Univ Tex Dept Physics Austin TX 78712 Home Phone: 512-327-1732; Office Phone: 512-471-7581. Business E-Mail: k.gentle@mail.utexas.edu.

GENTNER, PAUL LEFOE, architect, consultant; b. Seattle, Feb. 24, 1944; s. Edward George and Opal Eloise (Davis) G.; m. Glenda Frank Hoy, May 25, 1975; 1 stepchild, Robert Michael Hurd. AA in Architecture, Anne Arundel C.C., Arnold, Md., 1970; BS in Engring., Century U., 1984. Registered arch., Md., Va. Project rep. RTKL Assocs., Inc., Balt., 1970-73; staff architect James R. Grieves Assocs., Balt., 1973-77; sr. engr. Morrison-Knudsen (MKSAC), Columbia, Md., 1977-79, staff engr. Saudi Arabia, 1979-81; planning mgr. Morrison-Knudsen Internat. Inc., Barranquilla, Colombia, S.Am., 1981-86; staff architect RTKL Assocs., Inc., Balt., 1986-92; specifications writer Sverdrup Cpr., Arlington, Va., 1992-93; mgr. specifications Daniel, Mann, Johnson, & Mendenhall, Balt., 1993-95, Arlington, Va., 1995-96; cons. Marriott Internat., Washington, 1996-98; sr. project mgr., arch. and constrn. design mgmt. Marriott Internat. Corp., Washington, 1998—. With USNR, 1965-68, Vietnam; Persian Gulf, 1990-91. Mem. AIA, Constrn. Specifications Inst. (cert. constrn. specifier, bd. dirs. Balt. chpt. 1991-92, 1st v.p. 1993-94, pres. 1994-95), Soc. Am. Mil. Engrs., Bricklayers (local # 1). Home: 2028 Park Ave Baltimore MD 21217-4816 Office: Marriott Internat Dept 70/104-03 Marriott Dr Washington DC 20058 Office Phone: 301-380-5018. Personal E-mail: pgentarch@comcast.net. Business E-Mail: paul.gentner@marriott.com.

GENTRY, ALBERTA ELIZABETH, elementary school educator; b. Richter, Kans., Feb. 18, 1925; d. John Charles and Dessie Lorena (Duvall) Briles; m. Kenneth Neil Gentry, June 1, 1947; children: Michal Neil, Alan Dale, Elisa Ann. BE, Emporia U., Kans., 1975. Cert. tchr., Kans. Tchr. Chippewa Rural Sch., Ottawa, Kans., 1943-44; prin., tchr. Pomona (Kans.) Grade Sch., 1944-47, tchr., 1960-61, Silverlake Rural Sch., Pomona, 1947-48, Hawkins Rural Sch., Ottawa, 1948-49, Davy Rural Sch., Ottawa, 1950-53, Eugene Field Sch., Ottawa, 1953-54, Centropolis Grade Sch., Ottawa, 1964, Appanoose Elem. Sch., Pomona, 1964-90, ret., 1990. Trainer student tchr., 1985-86. Author: Proven Ideas for Classroom Teachers, 1988. Project leader, supporter 4-H, Franklin County, Kans., 1963-67; den mother Boy Scouts Am., Ottawa, 1955-66; dir. Bible sch., tchr. Trinity Meth. Ch., Ottawa, 1955-70, supt., 1955-66, mem. choir, 1947—. Named to Kans. Tchrs. Hall of Fame, 1991. Mem. NEA, Kans. Tchrs. Assn., Kans. Edn. Assn., Alpha Delta Kappa (sec. 1988-90). Republican. Methodist. Avocations: bird watching, arts and crafts, flower gardening, music, genealogy. Home: 1057 Hwy K68 Pomona KS 66076-9070

GENTRY, BERN LEON, SR., management consultant; b. Goldsboro, NC, Sept. 9, 1941; s. Theodore Alfonso and Ruth Ester (Taylor) G.; m. Jane A. Price, Nov. 11, 1965; children: Michelle Lorraine, Bern Leon. Student, Rutgers U., 1959-61, Temple U., 1961-63, Cornell U., 1966-67, U. Okla., 1971. Tax acct. IRS, Phila., 1965-66; collection mgr., credit mgr., appliance store mgr., soft goods mdse. mgr. Sears, Roebuck & Co., Phila., 1966-71; program mgr., dir. nat. urban affairs U.S. Jr. C. of C., 1971-73, cons., 1973—; pres. Together, Inc., Tulsa, 1971—. Contbr. articles to profl. jours. Mem. nat. adv. bd. Boys Clubs Am., 1971—; mem. nat. Black alliance for grad. level edn. U. Mich.; past pres., bd. dirs. Tulsa Econ. Opportunity Task Force; pres. Community Service Agy.; bd. dirs. Jr. Achievement. Recipient award of accomplishment Sears Staff Sch., 1967; award of appreciation Black Peoples Unity Movement Econ. Devel. Corp., 1971; George Washington Honor medal Freedoms Found., 1974, 76; Keys to cities of Roanoke, Va.; Keys to cities of Baton Rouge, La.; Keys to cities of New Orleans; named Outstanding Young Man Camden, 1970; Outstanding Chpt. Pres. N.J. Jaycees; Outstanding Jaycee. Mem. Nat. Urban League, NAACP, Am. Mgmt. Assn., Nat. Assn. Human Rights Workers, Assn. Black Found. Execs., Nat. Assn. Pub. Relations Execs., Nat. Civil Service League, Nat. Assn. Community Devel., Nat. Assn. Vol. Services Coordinator, Camden Jaycees (pres. 1970-71), Tulsa Met. C. of C. Office: Together Inc PO Box 52528 802 E 6th St Tulsa OK 74120-3610

GENTRY, DONALD WILLIAM, engineering executive, mining engineer; b. St. Louis, Jan. 18, 1943; s. William Henry and Roberta Elizabeth (Bardelmeier) G.; m. Sheila Carol Schuepbach, Aug. 21, 1965; children: Tara Cassandre, Chad Ryan. BSE., U. Ill., 1965; MS, U. Nev., 1967; PhD, U. Ariz., 1972, DEng (hon.), 2002. From asst. prof. mining engring. to prof. Colo. Sch. Mines, Golden, 1972—78, prof. mining engring., 1978—2003, dean undergrad. studies, 1983—90, dean engring. and undergrad. studies, 2001, head dept. mining engring., 1995-98; pres., CEO Terra Nova Resources, Golden, 1990—2004; pres., CEO, bd. dirs. PolyMet Mining Corp., Golden, 1998—2003. Bd. dirs. Gryphon Gold Corp., 2005—, Constellation Copper Corp., 2006—. Contbr. articles to profl. jours. Mem. Soc. Mining Engrs. of AIME (pres. 1993), AIME (dir. Colo. sect. 1982-83, Krumb lectr. 1987, pres. 1996, Mineral Industry Edn. award 1991, Daniel C. Jackling award 1998), Nat. Acad. Engring. (elected 1996). Republican. Lutheran. Personal E-mail: dwgentry@cox.net.

GENTRY, JAMES WILLIAM, retired state agency administrator; b. Danville, Ill., Aug. 14, 1926; s. Carl Lloyd and Leone (Isham) G.; m. Dorothie Shirley Hechtlinger, Mar. 18, 1967; 1 stepdau., Susan Mushkin. AB, Fresno State Coll., 1948; MJ, U. Calif., Berkeley, 1956. Field rep. Congressman B.W. Gearhart, Fresno, Calif., 1948, Assemblyman Wm. W. Hansen, Fresno, 1950, sec., 1953-56; exec. asst. Calif. Pharm. Assn., LA, 1956-69; asst. adminstr., dir. pub. info. So. Calif. Comprehensive Health Planning Coun., 1969-71, acting adminstr., 1971-72, exec. sec., 1972-73, Calif. Adv. Health Coun., 1973-85, fed. cons., 1986-88. Editor, pub. Calif. Pharmacy Jour., L.A., 1956-69; pub. rels. dir. PAID Prescriptions, 1963-64; dir. pub. info. Comprehensive Health Planning coun., LA County, 1969; fed. cons. Calif. Health Care Commn., 1973-75; acting pub. info. officer Calif. Office Statewide Health Planning and Devel., 1978-79, interim dir., 1983; mem. L.A. Civil Svc. Police Interview Bd., 1967-72, Calif. Health Planning Law Revision Commn.; asst. sgt.-at-arms Calif. State Assembly, 1950; exec. sec. Calif. Assembly Interim Com. on Livestock and Dairies, 1954-56; adv. bd. Am. Security Coun.; former mem. Calif. Bldg. Safety Bd. Editor: Better Health, 1963-67, Orientation Conf. Comprehensive Health Planning, 1969, commentary, 1969-71, Program and Funding, 1972, Substance Abuse, 1972; editl. adv. Pharm. Svcs. for Nursing Homes: A Procedural manual, 1966. Active Fresno County Rep. Ctrl. Com., 1950; charter mem. Rep. Presdl. Task Force. Col. AUS, 1949-85, Korea, 1950-53. Decorated Legion of Merit, Bronze Star medal, Commendation Ribon with metal Pendant; recipient pub. awards Western Soc. Bus. Publs. Assn., 1964-67. Mem. Am. Assn. Comprehensive Health Planning, Pub. Rels. Soc. Am., Allied Drug Travelers So. Calif., L.A. Press Club, Mil. Police Assn., Mil. Officers Assn. Am., Res. Officers Assn. (life), Assn. US Army, US Senatorial Club, The Victory Svcs. Club of London, Pi Gamma Mu, Phi Alpha Delta, Sigma Delta Chi. Home: 1603 Patriots Colony Dr Williamsburg VA 23188-1341

GENTRY, MACK A., lawyer; b. Knoxville, Tenn., July 18, 1944; s. Edgar C. and Elizabeth (Cates) G.; m. Cheryl T. Gentry; children: Tucker J., Carter L., Cates E. BSBA, U. Tenn., 1966, JD, 1968; LLM in Taxation,

NYU, 1976. Bar: Tenn. 1969, Colo. 2001, US Dist. Ct. (ea. dist.) Tenn. 1983, US Tax Ct. 1972, US Claims Ct. 1983, US Ct. Appeals (6th cir.) 1985, US Ct. Appeals (fed. cir.) 1986. Assoc. Kramer, Johnson, Rayson, Greenwood & McVeigh, Knoxville, 1972—75; founder Gentry, Tipton & McLemore, P.C., Knoxville, 1976, pres., 1976—2000; pvt. practice law Knoxville, 2000—. Trustee Tenn. Fed. Tax Inst.; bd. dirs. U. Tenn. Coll. Law Alumni Adv. Coun. Mem. Tenn. Bar Assn., Knoxville Bar Assn. (chmn. tax sect. 1978-79), Beta Alpha Psi, Phi Delta Phi (v.p. 1966). Office: 900 S Gay St Ste 2300 Knoxville TN 37902

GENTRY, ROBERT VANCE, physicist, researcher, writer; b. Chattanooga, July 9, 1933; s. Vance Ault and Sara Frances (Northington) G.; m. Patricia Ann Gentry, Jan. 20, 1953; children: Patricia Lynn, Michael Vance, David Wayne. BS in Physics, U. Fla., 1955, MS, 1956; D.Sc. (hon.), Columbia Union Coll., Takoma Park, Md., 1977. Nuclear engr. Gen. Dynamics Co., Ft. Worth, 1956-58; sr. engr. Martin Co., Orlando, Fla., 1958-59; instr. math. U. Fla., Gainesville, 1959-61, Walla Walla (Wash.) Coll., 1961-62; instr. physics Ga. Inst. Tech., 1962-64; research physicist Archeol. Research Found., Atlanta, 1965-66; mem. faculty Columbia Union Coll., 1966-84, assoc. prof. physics, 1977-84; cons. physicist, 1984-86; research physicist Earth Sci. Assocs., Knoxville, Tenn., 1986—; pres. The Orion Found., 1997—. Guest scientist chemistry div. Oak Ridge Nat. Lab., 1969-82, 89; hon. asst. res. prof. physics U. Tenn.-Knoxville, 1982-83. Author: Creation's Tiny Mystery, 1986, 1986, 4th edit., 2003; chief rschr.: (video) Fingerprints of Creation (Telly award, 1993); The Young Age of the Earth, 1994; Center of the Universe, 2006; contbr. articles to profl. jours. Grantee NSF, 1962, 1971-77, NASA, 1970-72. Mem. AAAS, Am. Phys. Soc., Am. Geophys. Union, N.Y. Acad. Scis., Sigma Xi (assoc.). Seventh-day Adventist. Achievements include discovery of polonium radiohalos in granites, a new model of the universe to explain the Hubble redshift relation and the 2.7K Cosmic Blackbody Radiation without the use of spacetime expansion. Home: PO Box 12067 Knoxville TN 37912-0067 Office Phone: 865-947-4726. Personal E-mail: esa@halos.com. *To recognize that success in any field is not the result of chance or destiny but instead the reward of faithfully developing those talents endowed by the Creator provides the highest possible incentive for achieving that station in life for which each individual is uniquely fitted.*

GENTRY, SHIRLEY, music educator, writer; b. Trenton, NJ, Dec. 3, 1934; d. Howard E. and Wyvonne Robinson Gentry; m. David Lyman (div.). MusB in Edn., Ctrl. Meth. U., Fayette, Mo., 1957. Cert. tchr. Mo., 1960, Wash., 1965. Tchr. music Richland Schs., Wash., 1963—68; tchr. elem. sch. Hawaii Schs., Oahu, 1968—69; tchr. music Chariton Schs., Iowa, 1969—73, Tehran Am. Schs., Iran, 1973—76; with Chariton Phone Co., 1979—84; ret., 1984. Author: A Christmas In Rime, 2003, From the Pen of a Poetess, 2003, Posy Unsung, 2004. Sec. Dem. Party, Chariten, 1991—93. Scholar, Ctrl. Meth. U., 1953. Mem.: AARP, Mensa (contbr. mag. 1982—), Phi Kappa Theta. Democrat. Baptist. Avocations: piano, writing, poetry, crossword puzzles. Home: 511 Main 11 Trenton MO 64683

GENTRY, WARREN MILLER, investment company executive; b. Manville, Wyo., Oct. 3, 1921; s. William George and Ina Ella (Miller) G.; m. Billie Jean Axline, Aug. 15, 1948; children: Edward, Thomas, Bradley. AA, Curtiss Wright Tech. Inst., 1940; BA with distinction, Ariz. State U., Tempe, 1950, MA, 1955. Tchr. Miami H.S., Ariz., 1950—53; art supply salesman Elquest & Son, Phoenix, 1953—55; tchr. Phoenix Union H.S. Dist., 1955—63; from asst. prof. to prof. humanities Glendale C.C., Ariz., 1963—83, founding dir. art collection, 1983—. Founding chmn. dept. art, Glendale C.C., 1963-68; owner, operator Gentry Gallery, Scottsdale, Ariz., 1984-90; co-owner, operator Gentry Enterprises, Scottsdale, 1990—; cons. art silk screen U.S. Army, Ft. Huachuca, Ariz. One-man shows Phoenix Art Mus., 1954, Sombrero Playhouse, 1955, Phoenix Coll., 1963; group shows include De Young Mus., San Francisco, 1956, Artists U.S.A., Wynnewood, Pa., 1970-71; author: Gentry-Axline Families, History, Genealogy, 2004, AX from Arizona to No Man's Land WWI, 2006 1st chmn. Scottsdale Beautification Com., 1960s; mem. first Scottsdale Fine Arts Com., 1960s; mem. West Coast Air Tng. Command, 1941-43. Recipient Painting awards Ariz. State Fair, 1950s, Purchase award Valley Bank Sister City, Orange, France, 1958. Mem. Humanities Coun. We. Colls. and Univs., Masons. Republican. Office: PO Box 4082 Scottsdale AZ 85261-4082

GENTY, PHILIP, law educator; BA, Colorado Coll., 1977; JD, NYU, 1980. Atty. Prisoners' Legal Svcs., NY, NYC Dept. Housing, Preservation and Develop., Bedford-Stuyvesant Cmty. Legal Svcs. Corp.; faculty mem. Brooklyn Law Sch., 1987; clin. prof. Columbia U. Law Sch., 1989—. Mem. adv. group Fed. Resource Ctr. for Children of Prisoners. Office: Columbia Law Sch 435 W 116th St New York NY 10027 Office Phone: 212-854-3250. Office Fax: 212-854-3699. E-mail: pgenty@law.columbia.edu.

GENTZSCH, WOLFGANG, grid computing and networking service company executive; With Max Planck Inst. Physics, Germany, Siemens, Germany; head, computational fluid dynamics and supercomputing German Agency for Aerospace and Aeronautics, DLR; prof. mat. and computer sci. U. Applied Sciences, Regensburg, Germany, 1985—2000; cons. for many computing companies such as, IBM, Cray Computers and Digital Equipment Corp., 1985—2000; founder Genias Software (also called the Ctr. for Numerically Intensive Applications and Supercomputing), 1990—99; also founder of Genias Parallel Computing, Genias Benelux, Genias Internet, and Genias Graphics; founder Gridware (predecessor of Genias Software), 1999—2000; joined (with acquisition of Gridware) Sun Microsystems, Inc., 2000—04, sr. engring. dir. for grid computing, 2000—04; mng. dir. MCNC Grid Computing & Networking Svcs., Research Triangle Park, NC, 2004—. Spkr. in the field; adj. prof. Duke U., NC State U., U. NC, Charlotte. Author of 150 articles about computer science, numerical algorithms, engring. applications, and grid computing. Responsible for Sun Microsystem's grid computing vision, strategy and technology development. Gridware's technology became the foundation for the Sun Grid Engine, the world's leading distributed resource management software no used in over 10,000 departmental and enterprise grids worldwide. Office: MCNC Grid Computing & Networking Svcs PO Box 12889 3021 Cornwallis Rd Research Triangle Park NC 27709-2889 E-mail: wgentzsh@mcnc.org.

GENZEN, GARY CARL, minister; b. Cleve., Feb. 18, 1944; s. Carl Henry and Lydia Caroline (Fobel) G.; m. Harriet Frieda Kretzschmar, June 28, 1969; children: David Carl, Jonathan Robert. BA, Valparaiso U., Ind., 1966; BD, Concordia Sem., 1970, MDiv, 1973; D Ministry, Internat. Sem., Plymouth, Fla., 1980. Ordained to ministry Luth. Ch.-Mo. Synod, 1970. Pastor Christ Luth. Ch., Southwick, Mass., 1970-77, Zion Luth. Ch., Lorain, Ohio, 1977—98, Bethany Luth. Ch., Leesburg, Fla., 1998—. Pres. Greater Southwick Clergy Assn., 1973, 75; counselor Ohio Dist. Cir., 1993-98. Author: Pastor, 1990; book reviewer Sharing the Practice, Concordia Theol. Quar.; contbr. articles to profl. jours. Mem. Westfield (Mass.) Area Mental Health and Retardation Bd., 1975-77; bd. trustees Luth. Home, Westlake, Ohio, 1993-98. Mem. Greater Leesburg Ministerial Assn., Acad. Parish Clergy, Am. Acad. Ministry, Clergy Assn., Acad. Parish Clergy. Office: 1334 Griffin Rd Leesburg FL 34748-3559 Home Phone: 352-314-0514; Office Phone: 352-787-7275. Personal E-mail: ggenzen@comcast.net.

GEOFFRION, ARTHUR MINOT, management scientist; b. NYC, Sept. 19, 1937; s. Arthur Joseph and Dorothy Arline (Senter) Geoffrion; m. Helen Mathilda Hamer, Dec. 22, 1962; children: Susan, Deborah. BME, Cornell U., 1960, M in Indsl. Engring., 1961; PhD, Stanford U., 1965; Dr.rer.pol. in Econ. and Social Scis. honoris causa, RWTH Aachen U., 2005. Asst. prof. in ops.rsch. UCLA, 1965-67, assoc. prof., 1968-70, prof. Grad. Sch. Mgmt., 1971-97; chair in mgmt. James A. Collins, 1998—. Bd. dirs. Insight, Inc. Author: Perspectives on Optimization, 1972; contbr. chapters to books, articles to profl. jours. Recipient Sys. Sci. prize, NATO, 1976, Harold Larnder Meml. prize, Can. Operational Rsch. Soc., 2002; fellow, Internat. Acad. Mgmt., 1996; Faculty Rsch. fellow, Ford Found., 1967—68, Rsch. grantee, 1969—72, NSF, 1968—91, Office Naval Rsch., 1972—90. Mem.: NAE, Inst. Ops. Rsch. and Mgmt. Scis. (pres. 1997, George E. Kimball medal 2000, fellow 2002), Ops. Rsch. Soc. Am., Inst. Mgmt. Scis. (pres. 1981—82, Disting. Svc. medal 1992), Omega Rho (hon.). Achievements include research in optimization theory (parametric concave programming, integer programming, multi-criterion optimation, large-scale, decompostion, duality theory); optimization applications to logistics, production, finance; aggregation; foundations of modeling; analytical methods for e-business. Home: 322 24th St Santa Monica CA 90402-2518 Office: The UCLA Anderson Sch Mgmt Box 951481 Los Angeles CA 90095-1481

GEOFFROY, GREGORY L., academic administrator, educator; b. Honolulu, July 8, 1946; s. Glenn Gaylord and Lucille Lavaughn (Lewis) G.; m. Kathleen Carothers, Apr. 17, 1971; children: Susan, Janet, David, Michael. BS in Chemistry, U. Louisville, 1968; PhD in Chemistry, Calif. Inst. Tech., 1974. Asst. prof. dept. chemistry Pa. State U., University Park, 1974-78, assoc. prof. dept. chemistry, 1978-82, prof. dept. chemistry, 1982-88, head dept. chemistry, 1988-89, dean Eberly Coll. Sci., 1989-97; provost, sr. v.p. acad. affairs U. Md., 1997; pres. Iowa State U., 2001—. Bd. dirs. Assn. Advancement Res. Astro., Washington; cons. Union Carbide Corp., South Charleston, W.Va., 1984-95, ARCO Chem., Newtown Square, Pa., 1988-92. Author: Organometallic Photochemistry, 1979; contbr. articles to profl. jours. Recipient Tchr.-Scholar award Camille & Henry Dreyfus Found., 1978, fellowship John Simon Guggenheim Found., 1982. Fellow AAAS; mem. Am. Chem. Soc. (chair inorganic chemistry divsn. 1990). Avocations: mountain biking, skiing. Office: 1750 Beardshear Hall Ames IA 50011 Home Phone: 515-294-7152; Office Phone: 515-294-2042. Business E-Mail: president@iastate.edu.

GEOGA, DOUGLAS GERARD, real estate developer, lawyer; b. Detroit, Aug. 13, 1955; s. Christ and Virginia M. (Juras) G. AB, Harvard U., 1977, JD, 1980. Bar: Mich. 1980., Ill. 1984. Assoc. Miller, Canfield, Paddock and Stone, Detroit, 1980-83; devel. counsel Hyatt Devel. Corp., Chgo., 1983-85, gen. counsel, 1985-86, v.p., gen. counsel, 1986-88, sr. v.p., 1988-89, exec. v.p., 1989-94; pres. Hyatt Hotels Corp., Chgo., 1994—2000, Hospitality Investment Fund LLC, 2000—05, Global Hyatt Corp., 2003—06; dir. Unitrin, Inc., Chgo., 2002—06; hospitality investment and advisory cons. Geoga Group LLC, 2006—. Mem. Industry Real Estate Financing Adv. Coun.; bd. dirs. Unitrin Corp., 2000—. Bd. dirs. United Way of LaGrange (Ill.), United Way of Surburban Chgo.; mem. strategic planning com. United Way/Crusade of Mercy. Mem. ABA, Am. Hotel & Motel Assn. (trustee Ednl. Inst., chmn. govtl. affairs com.), U.S. Nat. Travel Orgn. (bd. dirs.), Travel Industry Assn. (past mem. travel and tourism govt. affairs coun.), Travel Bus. Roundtable, Urban Land Inst. (assoc.). Democrat. Roman Catholic. Office: Unitrin Inc 1 E Wacker Dr Chicago IL 60601 Office Phone: 312-661-4600.*

GEOGHEGAN, PATRICIA, lawyer; b. Bayonne, NJ, Sept. 9, 1947; d. Frank and Rita (Mihok) G. BA, Mich. State U., 1969; MA, Yale U., 1972, JD, 1974; LLM, NYU, 1982. Bar: N.Y. 1975. Assoc. Cravath, Swaine & Moore, NYC, 1974-82, ptnr., 1982—. Mem. ABA, N.Y. State Bar Assn., Assn. of Bar of City of N.Y. Office: Cravath Swaine & Moore Worldwide Plz Fl 45 825 8th Ave New York NY 10019-7416 Office Phone: 212-474-1584. Office Fax: 212-474-3700. Business E-Mail: pgeoghegan@cravath.com.

GEOPPINGER, JEFFREY D., lawyer; b. Sept. 11, 1975; BA, Boston Coll., 1998; JD, U. Cin. Coll. Law, 2001. Bar: Ohio 2001, US Ct. of Appeals Fifth Cir., US Dist. Ct. Northern Dist. Ohio, US Dist. Ct. Southern Dist. Ohio, US Dist. Ct. Southern Dist. Tex. Assoc. Ulmer & Berne LLP, Cin. Named one of Ohio's Rising Stars, Super Lawyers, 2006. Mem.: Am. Inn of Courts, Cin. Bar Assn., Ohio State Bar Assn., ABA, North Avondale Neighborhood Assn., Boston Coll. Alumni Club. Office: Ulmer & Berne LLP 600 Vine St Ste 2800 Cincinnati OH 45202 Office Phone: 513-762-6249. Office Fax: 513-698-5001.

GEORGANAS, NICOLAS D., electrical engineering educator, academic administrator; b. Athens, Greece, June 15, 1943; s. Demetrios N. and Athanasia (Kotsovou) G.; m. Jacynthe Savard, June 17, 1972; children: Nikita, Emmanuel. Diploma in Engring., Nat. Tech. U. Athens, 1966; PhD summa cum laude, U. Ottawa, Ont., Can., 1970; Doctorate (hon.), Tech. U. Daermstadt, Germany, 2004. Registered profl. engr., Ont. Lectr., elec. engring. U. Ottawa, 1970-71, asst. prof., 1971-76, assoc. prof., 1976-80, prof., 1980—, chmn., 1981-84, dean engring., 1986-93, assoc. v.p. rsch., 2005—. Vis. prof. IBM, LaGaude, France, 1977-78, INRIA/Bull-Transac, Paris, 1984-85, Bell-No. Rsch., Ottawa, 1993-94, CRC, Ottawa, 1997. Author: Queueing Networks—Exact Computational Algorithms: A Unified Theory by Decomposition and Aggregation, 1989; contbr. over 100 articles to profl. jours., more than 200 conf. articles. Recipient Killam Prize for Engring., Can. Coun. for Arts, 2002, IBM Pioneer of Computing in Can. award, 2005, Can. award in telecom. rsch., 2006, Order of Can., 2007. Fellow IEEE (Computer medal, 2007), Can. Acad. Engring., Royal Soc. Can.(Thomas W. Eadie medal, 1999), Engring. Inst. Home: 1915 Montereau Ave Gloucester ON Canada Office: U Ottawa 550 Cumberland Ottawa ON Canada K1N 6N5 Home Phone: 613-837-7966; Office Phone: 613-562-5800 ext. 5270. Personal E-mail: n.georganas@ieee.org.

GEORGE, ALBERT RICHARD, mechanical and aerospace engineer, educator; m. Carol Mae Frerichs; children: Albert Frederick, David Kovtoun, Amy Margaret. BSE., Princeton U., 1959, MA, 1961, PhD, 1964. Asst. prof. Cornell U., 1969-77, prof., 1977—, John F. Carr prof. mech. engring., 1992—, asst. dir. mech. and aerospace engring. dept., 1972-77; dir. mech. and aero. engring., 1977-87; dir. mfg. engring. and productivity program Cornell U., 1991—, dir. Ctr. Mfg. Enterprise, 1993—; head sect. BMW AG Automobile Mfrs., Fed. Republic of Germany, 1987-88; NRC sr. research assoc. NASA Ames Research Ctr., 1988; scholar-in-residence Harley-Davidson Motor Co., 1996—97; dir. systems engring. Cornell U., 1999—2002. Mem. Univ. Grants Com., Hong Kong, 1991-02; vis. sr. fellow U. Southampton, Eng., 1971-72; cons. in field. Contbr. articles to profl. jours. Mem. AIAA (fellow), ASME, Soc. Automotive Engrs., Am. Helicopter Soc. Congregationalist. Office: Cornell U 100 Rhodes Hall Ithaca NY 14853-3801 Home: 315 Savage Farm Dr Ithaca NY 14850-6503 Home Phone: 607-257-4118; Office Phone: 607-255-6254. E-mail: arg2@cornell.edu.

GEORGE, ALEXANDER ANDREW, lawyer; b. Missoula, Mont., Apr. 26, 1938; s. Andrew Miltiadin and Eleni (Efstathiou) G.; m. Penelope Mitchell, Sept. 29, 1968; children: Andrew A., Stephen A. BBA honors, U. Mont., 1960, JD, 1962; postgrad., John Marshall U., 1964-66. Bar: Mont. 1962, U.S. Ct. Mil. Appeals 1964, U.S. Tax Ct. 1970. Sole practice, Missoula, 1966—. Mem. adv. com. U. Mont. Tax Inst., 1973-76; adj. lectr. U. Montana Law Sch. Corp. Taxation. Pres. Missoula Civic Symphony, 1973; nat. dir. Assn. Urban and Cmty. Symphony Orch., 1974, Mont. Eye Endowment Found.; pres. Greek Orthodox Ch., 1978, 91. Served to capt. JAG U.S. Army, 1962-66. Recipient Jaycee Disting. Svc. award, 1973. Mem.: Mont. Soc. CPA, Mont. Law Found. (treas. 1986—92), Western Mont. Bar Assn. (pres. 1971, lifetime achievement award 1998), State Bar Mont. (pres. 1981), Glacier-Waterton Internat. Peace Pk. Assn. (bd. dirs. 1999—2002), Ahepa (pres. 1967, state gov. 1968), Rotary (pres. 1972, state chmn. found. 1977, membership com. chmn. 1978), Sigma Nu (alumni trustee 1966—71), Alpha Kappa Psi, Phi Delta Phi. Home: 4 Greenbrier Ct Missoula MT 59802-3342 Office: 210 N Higgins Ave Ste 234 Missoula MT 59802-4497 Home Phone: 406-728-3785; Office Phone: 406-728-4310. Business E-Mail: georgelaw@in-tch.com.

GEORGE, ALFRED L., JR., medical educator, researcher; b. Batavia, NY, June 14, 1956; BA in Chemistry, Coll. of Wooster, Ohio, 1978; MD, U. Rochester, 1982. Diplomate Am. Bd. Internal Medicine, Am. Bd. Nephrology. Intern and resident in internal medicine Vanderbilt U. Hosps., Nashville, 1982—86; chief resident in medicine St. Thomas Hosp., Nashville, 1985—86; instr. medicine Vanderbilt U. Sch. Medicine, Nashville, 1985—86, asst. prof. dept. medicine nephrology and pharmacology, 1992—95; assoc. prof. medicine and pharmacology Vanderbilt U., Nashville, 1995—; postdoctoral fellow in clin. nephrology renal-elctrolyte sectl dept. medicine Hosp. of U. Pa., Phila., 1986—87; rsch. fellow dept. medicine and dept. biochemistry and biophysics U. Pa., Phila., 1988—91, rsch. assoc. dept. medicine and Inst. Neurol. Scis., 1991—92. Vis. postdoctoral fellow Inst. Suisse de Recherches Experimentales sur le Cancer, Lausanne, Switzerland, 1987—88. Mem. editl. bd.: Am. Jour. Physiology, 1996—, jour. reviewer: Neuron, —, Nature Genetics, —, Jour. Membrane Biology, —; Jour. Biol. Chemistry, —; jour. reviewer: Kidney Internat., —, Jour. Physiology, —. Mem.: AAAS, Biophys. Soc., Am. Heart Assn. (mem. coun. on kidney disease, established investigator award 1996), Am. Soc. Nephrology.

GEORGE, ARTHUR CHARLES, lawyer; b. Boston, Dec. 9, 1954; s. Charles Arthur and Diana Kanavos George; m. Soteria Liousas, May 22, 1983; children: Charles Arthur, Peter Arthur, Elizabeth Diana. BSBA, Boston U., 1976; JD, New Eng. Sch. Law, 1979. Bar: Mass. 1980, U.S. Dist. Ct. Mass. 1981, U.S. Ct. Appeals (1st cir.) 1981. Lawyer Arthur C. George, Esq., Randolph, Mass., 1980-86; ptnr. George & George, Stoughton, 1987—. Town counsel Town of Holbrook, Mass., 1986—; mem. Rep. Town Com., Holbrook, 1988—, chmn., 1990-2000, 2004—; co-leader Adventurer's 4-H Club, Holbrook, 1988—; trustee Bridgewater State Coll., 1999—, sec., 2005-07; chmn. Holbrook Rep. Town Com., 2004—; mem. adv. bd. Greek Inst. Recipient Cert. of Appreciation, Mass. Chpt. Black Rep. Coun., citation Mass. State Senate, 1995, Salute to Excellence award U. Mass. Ext. and Mass. 4-H Found., 1998, Lucem Diffundo Plate award Mayor of New Bedford, 2001. Mem. Mass. Bar Assn., Bar Assn. Norfolk County (coun. mem. 2004-07), Ripon Soc. (nat. sec. 1992-94), Holbrook Sportsmen's Club. Avocations: research and policy, political speechwriting, chess, baseball. Office: 1st Fl 10 Cabot Pl Fl 1 Stoughton MA 02072-4600 Office Phone: 781-341-4430.

GEORGE, ARTHUR L., electronics executive; BSEE, So. U., Baton Rouge, 1983; M in Engring. Mgmt., So. Meth. U., Dallas, 1990. Test engr. logic operation Tex. Instruments, Inc., Dallas, 1984, mgr. High-Performance Linear bus. unit, v.p., 2003, sr. v.p., mgr. High-Performance Analog bus. unit, 2006—. Office: Tex Instruments Inc PO Box 660199 Dallas TX 75266-0199 Office Phone: 972-995-2011. Office Fax: 972-995-4360.*

GEORGE, BARBARA M., theater educator, department chairman, actor, director; b. Tahlequah, Okla., Dec. 29, 1950; d. Benjamin B. and J. Louise George; m. Sheldon E. Morton, Mar. 31, 2005. BA in speech and theatre, Northeastern State U., Okla., 1971; MA in theatre, North Tex. State U., Denton, 1974, EdD in comms., 1976. Tchg. fellow in speech North Tex. State U., Denton, Tex., 1971—76; theatre instr. La. State U., Eunice, 1976—77; asst. prof. theatre Bacone Coll., Muskogee, Okla., 1977—80; actor self-employed, NYC, 1980—2002; mng. dir. Hill Country Cmty. Theatre, Horseshoe Bay, Tex., 1997—99; bus. mgr., edn. dir. Players Guild, Canton, Ohio, 1999—2001; chair fine arts, instr. theatre NEO A&M Coll., Miami, Okla., 2002—. Staff Tex. Gov. Ann Richards, Austin, 1991—95. Mem.: Okla. Speech Theater Comm. Assn. Democrat. Avocation: gardening. Home: 4 E St SW Miami OK 74354 Office: NEO A&M Coll 200 I St NE Miami OK 74354 Personal E-mail: barbara.george@cableone.net.

GEORGE, BOYD LEE, consumer products company executive; b. 1942; BBA, U. Notre Dame, 1963; LLB, U. Va., 1966. With Merchants Distbrs., Inc., 1969-72, v.p., 1972-76, pres., COO, 1976-83, chmn. bd., 1983—; chmn., CEO Alex Lee, Hickory, NC, 1992—, pres., 1992—95. Bd. dir. CommScope. Treas. bd. trustees Lenoir Rhyne Coll. Capt. USMC, 1966—69. Office: Alex Lee PO Box 800 120 4th St Dr Hickory NC 28603

GEORGE, CYNTHIA COULTER, lawyer; b. Conn., June 11, 1953; 2 children. BA, Cornell U., Ithaca, NY, 1975; JD, Loyola U., 1978. Bar: Conn. 1978. Atty. Cummings & Lockwood, 1978—87, ptnr., 1987; atty. Schoonmaker, George & Colin, P.C., Greenwich, Conn. Contbr. articles to profl. publs. Named one of Best Lawyers in Am., 2004—07, Top 100 Attys., Worth mag., 2005, Top 50 Super Lawyers and Top 25 Super Lawyers, Conn. Mag. Fellow: Am. Acad. Matrimonial Lawyers (counsel nat. chpt. 1996, pres. Conn. chpt. 1998—99, bd. govs.); mem.: ABA (fin. officer family law sect. 1997—98, 1999—2000). Office: Schoonmaker George & Colin PC PO Box 5059 81 Holly Hill Ln Greenwich CT 06831-5059 Office Phone: 203-862-5010. Office Fax: 203-862-5099. Business E-Mail: cgeorge@sgcfamlaw.com.

GEORGE, DEVERAL D., editor, journalist, advertising consultant; b. Dallas, Nov. 23, 1939; s. Jack Weldon and Lleen Lelia (Hume) G. Student, U. Tex., 1958-61; BA, North Tex. State U., 1964; P.BA, U. Houston, 1974. Copywriter advt. agys., Houston, Dallas, 1964-70; free lance journalist, 1970-73, 75-76; copy and creative dir. Schey Advt., Houston, 1973, Bruce Advt., Houston, 1973-75; editor-in-chief, v.p. Bus. and Energy Internat., Houston, 1976-80; editor Ultra mag., 1980-81; freelance journalist Houston, 1981-83, 84-85; editor Saudi Bus. Mag.; cons. Saudi Research and Mktg. Inc., Houston, Washington, and Jeddah, Saudi Arabia, 1983-84; writer, advt. cons. Dale Carnegie & Assocs., Garden City (NY) and Houston, 1985-90; mng. editor internat. Offshore Mag., Houston, 1991-97; editor Schlumberger Oilfield Rev., 1997-98, Oil and Gas Online, Vertical Net, Horsham, Pa., 1998-2001, Houston, 1998-2001; owner, mng. editor Oil and Gas Internat., Houston, 2001—. Author: Cathedrals of Mexico, and Other Poems, 1963, The Erratic Pilgramage, 1973, The Whole World Cookbook, 1976, The Offshore Atlas, 1995; screenplays: The Monument, 1980, Armageddon, 1981; television series Treasure Hunt, 1984; editor: Worldwide Directory of Petroleum Ministries and National Oil Companies, 1995; mem. editl. bd. Xi'an Petroleum Inst., China. Del., Democratic Conv., 1972; mem. Houston Outdoor Group. Mem. ACLU, Am. Assn. Petroleum Geologists, Soc. Exploration Geophysicists, Geophys. Soc. Houston, Soc. Internat. Devel., N.Am. Congress on Latin Am., Amnesty Internat., Internat. Platform Assn., Ctr. for Study of Dem. Instns., Asia Soc., World Expeditionary Assn., Soc. Profl. Journalists-Sigma Delta Chi, Houston Press Club. Clubs: Houston Press. Home: 8310 Braesdale Ln Houston TX 77071-1228 Office: PO Box 710046 Houston TX 77071-1030

GEORGE, DILEEP, electrical engineer; BEE, Indian Inst. Tech., Bombay; MEE, Stanford U., PhD in Elec. Engring. Prin. engr. in several communications related start-up companies; grad. rsch. fellow Redwood Neuroscience Inst., 2003; co-founder, prin. architect Numenta, Inc., Menlo Park, Calif., 2005—. Achievements include patents pending in field; Numenta Inc. is creating a new pattern recognition software called Hierarchical Temporal Memory modeled on the human brain's neocortex. Office: Numenta Inc 1010 El Camino Real Ste 380 Menlo Park CA 94025 Office Phone: 650-321-8282. Office Fax: 650-321-8585.

GEORGE, DONALD, opera and concert singer; b. Pittsburg, Calif., Sept. 13, 1957; s. George and Norma (Trezza) Smith; Evelyn M. Edwards, Nov. 12, 1956; two children. BA, Southeastern La. U., 1977; MMus, La. State U., 1978.

GEORGE, DONALD WARNER, online columnist and editor, freelance writer; b. Middlebury, Conn., June 24, 1953; s. Lloyd Foster and Vivian (Minor) G.; m. Kuniko Ninomiya, Apr. 24, 1982; children: Jennifer Ayako, Jeremy Naoki. BA, Princeton U., 1975; MA, Hollins Coll., Va., 1977. Tchg. fellow Athens (Greece) Coll., 1975-76, Internat. Christian U., Tokyo, 1977-79; TV talk show host Japan Broadcasting Corp., Tokyo, 1977-79; freelance writer, 1980-81; travel writer San Francisco Examiner, 1981-82, sr. editor Calif. Living mag., 1982-85, sr. editor Image mag., 1985-87, travel editor, 1987-95; cyber columnist, Global Network Navigator American Online, Berkeley, Calif., 1995-96; editor Salon Wanderlust Online Travel Mag., 1997-2000; global travel editor Lonely Planet Publs., 2001—. Editor: Wanderlust: Real-Life Tales of Adventure and Romance, 2000, A House Somewhere: Tales of Life Abroad, 2002, The Kindness of Strangers, 2003 (Best Travel Book of 2003, Ind. Publishers Assn., Bronze Medal in best travel book competition, Soc. Am.Travel Writers, 2003), By the Seat of My Pants: Humorous Tales of Travel & Misadventure, 2005; co-author (with Amy Greimann Carlson): Travelers' Tales: Japan, 2005. Recipient gold award Pacific Asia Travel Assn., 1987-94, 2001. Mem. Soc. Am. Travel Writers (Lowell Thomas award 1987-94, 2002). Office: Lonely Planet 150 Linden St Oakland CA 94607 E-mail: dgeorge@lonelyplanet.com.

GEORGE, EDDIE (EDWARD NATHAN GEORGE), former professional football player; b. Phila., Sept. 24, 1973; s. Donna George; m. Tamara George; 2 children. BS in Landscape Architecture, Ohio State U., 1996. Running back Tenn. Titans (formerly Tenn. Oilers), 1996—2004, Dallas Cowboys, 2004; ptnr., co-owner The Edge Group; founder, co-owner Eddie's Sports Grill. Co-founder Visions With Infinite Possibilities Found., 2000—. Named NFL Rookie of Yr., 1996, NFL Pro Bowl, 1997—2000; recipient Maxwell award, 1995, Heisman trophy, 1995. Office: PO Box 150283 Nashville TN 37215

GEORGE, ELIZABETH (SUSAN ELIZABETH GEORGE), writer; b. Warren, Ohio, 1949; Student, Foothill Cmty. Coll.; graduate, Univ. Calif., Riverside; M in counseling, psychology, Univ. Calif., Fullerton; DHL (hon.), Calif. State U. English tchr. Mater Dei H.S., Santa Ana, Calif., 1974-75, El Toro (Calif.) H.S., 1975-87; creative writing tchr. Coastline Coll., Costa Mesa, Calif., 1988—92, Irvine (Calif.) Coll., 1989, U. Calif., Irvine, 1990. Author: A Great Deliverance, 1989 (Anthony award, Agatha award, 1989, Le Grand Prix de Litterature Policiere, 1990), Payment in Blood, 1989, Well Schooled in Murder, 1990 (MIMI award, Germany), A Suitable Vengeance, 1991, For the Sake of Elena, 1992, Missing Joseph, 1993, Playing for the Ashes, 1994, In the Presence of the Enemy, 1996, Deception on His Mind, 1997, In Pursuit of the Proper Sinner, 1999, A Traitor to Memory, 2001, Remember, I'll Always Love You, 2001, I, Richard, 2002, A Place of Hiding, 2003, Write Away, 2004, A Moment on the Edge, 2004, With No One as Witness, 2005 (Publishers Weekly bestseller list), What Came Before He Shot Her, 2006 (Publishers Weekly bestseller list.) Named Orange County Tchr. of Yr. Mailing: c/o Trident Media fl 36 41 Madison Ave New York NY 10010*

GEORGE, EMERY EDWARD, foreign language and studies educator, writer; b. Budapest, Hungary, May 8, 1933; came to U.S., 1946, naturalized, 1954; AB, U. Mich., 1955, MA, 1959; postgrad., Fed. Rep. Germany, 1961-62; PhD, U. Mich., 1964. Instr. U. Ill., Champaign-Urbana, 1964-65, asst. prof. German, 1965-66, U. Mich., Ann Arbor, 1966-69, assoc. prof., 1969-75, prof., 1975-88, prof. emeritus, 1988—, faculty program in comparative lit., 1969—, faculty program Center for Russian and East European Studies, 1975—. Author: Hölderlin's Ars Poetica, 1973, Mountainwild: Poems, 1974, Black Jesus, 1974, A Gift of Nerve: Poems, 1966-77, 1978, Kate's Death, 1980, The Poetry of Miklós Radnóti: A Comparative Study, 1986, The Boy and the Monarch, 1987, Voiceprints, 1987; (essay) The Allegory of Spandau, 1990 (Kenyon Rev. 2d ann. nonfiction award 1991), Hölderlin and the Golden Chain of Homer, 1992, Blackbird: Poems on the World and Work of Franz Kafka, 1993, Valse Triste: Songs and Ballads, 1997, Hölderlin's Hymn Der Einzige, 1999, Compass Card: One Hundred Villanelles, 2000, Iphigenie in Manhattan: A Play in Five Acts, 2001, Iphigenie in Czestochowa: A Play in Five Acts, 2001, Orest: A Play in Five Acts, 2001, Iphigenie in Auschwitz: A Play in Five Acts, 2001; editor: Friedrich Hölderlin: An Early Modern, 1972, (with L.T. Frank) Husbanding the Golden Grain, 1973, Contemporary East European Poetry: An Anthology, 1983, expanded, 1993, (with D. E. Sattler) Friedrich Hölderlin, Homburger Folioheft (Frankfurter Hölderlin-Ausgabe, Supplement III), 1986, 93; also transls.; contbr. poetry, non-fiction prose, transls., articles, revs. to scholarly jours., lit. publs.; founding editor Mich. Germanic Studies; assoc. editor Russian Lit. Triquar.; mem. editl. bd. advisors Germano-Slavica, 1973-77; editl. bd. Mich. Monographs in the Humanities, 1979—, (yearbook) Cross Currents, 1986—. Served with M.I. U.S. Army, 1957-58. Recipient Avery and Jule Hopwood award in poetry U. Mich., 1960; Ottendorfer Meml. fellow, 1961; Am. Council Learned Socs. Publs. award, 1964; Rackham Publ. award U. Mich., 1973, 80; Hungarian PEN Research and Travel grant, 1979; IREX Exchange fellow to Hungary, 1981, Deutsche Forschungsgemeinschaft research and travel grantee, 1986. Fellow: Internat. Acad. Poets; mem.: MLA, Assn. Literary Scholars and Critics, Hungarian Writers Assn., Hungarian Acad. Scis., Shelley Soc. NY, Poetry Soc. Am., Hölderlin-Gesellschaft. Home: 16 Buckingham Ave Trenton NJ 08618-3312 Home Phone: 609-984-8375; Office Phone: 609-984-8375. E-mail: eegeorge@hotmail.com. *Listen carefully to language, to words; try to write each day. Make no separation between writing and scholarship, between old and new literature. Monitor the eternal present. Try to achieve newness, a sense of experiment from within.*

GEORGE, FRANCIS EUGENE CARDINAL, cardinal; b. Chgo., Jan. 16, 1937; Ordained priest Roman Cath. Ch., 1963. Provincial ctrl. region Oblates of Mary Immaculate, 1973—74, vicar gen., 1974—86; bishop Diocese of Yakima, Wash., 1990—96; archbishop Archdiocese of Portland, Oreg., 1996—97, Archdiocese of Chgo., 1997—; created cardinal, 1998. Chancellor Cath. Ch. Ext. U. St. Mary of Lake, 1997; mem. Congregation Divine Worship, Discipline of Sacraments, Congregation for Oriental Chs., 2001—, Congregation Insts., Consecrated Life, Socs. Apostolic Life, Pontifical Commn. for Cultural Heritage of Ch., 1999—, Pontifical Coun. Cor Unum, 1998, Congregation Evangelization of Peoples, Pontifical Coun. for Culture, 2004—; v.p. US Conf. Cath. Bishops, 2004—. Mem.: Coll. Cardinals. Roman Catholic. Office: Archdiocese of Chgo Pastoral Ctr PO Box 1979 Chicago IL 60690-1979 Office Phone: 312-751-8230.

GEORGE, FRANK WADE, small business owner, antiquarian book dealer; b. Austin, Tex., Aug. 22, 1918; s. Frank Wade and Rosa Scott (Slaughter) W.; m. Marjorie Ann Miller, Dec. 27, 1948 (div. Jan. 1955); children; Frank Wade III, Gregory Scott, Barbara Lee; m. Martha Jeanne Wagner, Feb. 8, 1964 (dec. 1996); m. Wenona Thoma, 1996. Student, Tex. Sch. Fine Arts, 1936-41, Mexico City Coll., 1947; BJ, U. Tex., 1948. Office mgr. Tex. Sch. Fine Arts, 1936-41; mgr. Austin Symphony Orch., 1946-48, Erie (Pa.) Philharmonic Orch., 1948-49, Birmingham (Ala.) Symphony Orch., 1949-50, Ala. Pops Orch., Birmingham, 1955-62, Town and Gown Theatre, Birmingham, 1962-65; pres. Birmingham Opera Co., 1973-75; owner Books! By George, Birmingham, 1981—. Co-founder Margo George Fashion Prodns., 1951, Hanna Antiques, 1981; participant Antiquarian Book Seminar, U. Denver, 1986. Pres. Rockwood Plantation Condominium Assn., 2001—; treas. Greater Birmingham Arts Alliance, 1971—75, Birmingham Opera Guild, 1971—74, So. Regional Opera, 1981—84; trustee Birmingham Symphony Assn., 1973—75; chmn. artist hospitality Arts Hall of Fame, Birmingham, 1974; judge nat. coun. auditions Met. Opera Assn., 1981; docent Birmingham Mus. Art, 1980—82. With USAF, 1941—45. Mem. Gideons Internat. (pres. 1980-83), Allegro Mus. Club (v.p. 1993-94), Ala. Symphonic Assn. (dir. speakers bur. 1995), Rockwood Plantation Condominium Assn. (pres. 2001—). Avocations: lay preaching, public speaking, reading, writing, travel. Home: 1851 Rockwood Rd Birmingham AL 35216-1425 Office: Books! By George 2424 7th Ave S Birmingham AL 35233-3318 Office Phone: 205-323-6036. Business E-Mail: booksbygeorge@aol.com.

GEORGE, GAY, lawyer; b. Hollywood, Calif., Mar. 3, 1955; d. Wallace Erby and Audrey Eva Elizabeth George. BS, Calif. Poly. U., 1977; MBA, U. Wyo., 1993, JD, 2001. Bar: Wyo. 2001. Peace Corps vol. U.S. Govt., Apia, Western Samoa, 1979—80; quality assurance mgr. Arnott's Biscuits, Auckland, New Zealand, 1981—88; R&D mgr. ETA Foods, Ltd., Auckland, 1988—99; tech. writer G&G Enterprises, Laramie, Wyo., 1991—98; law clk. to Hon. Barton R. Voigt Wyo. Supreme Ct., Cheyenne, 2001—03; corp. counsel Blue Cross Blue Shield Wyo., Cheyenne, 2003—. Contbr. chapters to books. Avocations: reading, films, theater, camping, backpacking. Office Phone: 307-432-2914. Business E-Mail: ggeorge77@earthlink.net.

GEORGE, GERALD WILLIAM, writer; b. Caldwell, Kans., Aug. 4, 1938; s. Chester Dale and Mildred M. (Jolitz) G.; m. Patricia Rae Woolsey, Sept. 23, 1961 (div. 1989); children: Brian William, Roxane Elizabeth; m. Carol Maryan Bell, Sept. 18, 1993 BA, U. Wichita, 1960; MA, Yale U., 1962. Instr. Bethany Coll., Lindsborg, Kans., 1962; reporter Salina (Kans.) Jour., 1962-64; staff writer The Nat. Observer, Washington, 1964-67; editl. assoc. Woodrow Wilson Nat. Fellowship Found., Princeton, NJ, 1967-68; spl. asst. to chmn. NEH, Washington, 1969-70; free-lance writer Washington, Netherlands, 1971-73; mng. editor book series Am. Assn. State and Local History, Nashville, 1973-78, dir., 1978-87, mem. steering com. endowment campaign, 1999—2001; free-lance writer, cons. to hist. orgns. Arlington, Va., 1987-90; exec. dir. Nat. Hist. Publs. and Records Commn., 1990-94; program devel. officer Coun. on Libr. Resources, Washington, 1995; exec. dir. Nat. Hist. Publs. and Records Commn., Washington, 1995-97; dir. commns. Nat. Archives and Records Adminstrn., College Park, Md., 1997-2000; spl. projects assoc. Coun. on Libr. and Info. Resources, Washington, 2000—03, ret., 2003. Author: Visiting History, Arguments Over Museums and Historic Sites, 1990, Imitations of Indonesia and Other Poems, 1997; co-author: Starting Right: A Basic Guide to Museum Planning, 1986, rev. edit., 2004; mng. editor: The States and the Nation; mem. editl. bd.: Ency. of the Am. West; co-editor Digital Library Development, the View From Kanazawa, 2006; contbr. articles to profl. jours. and mags Woodrow Wilson fellow, 1960-61 Mem. Am. Assn. State and Local History, Nat. Trust Hist. Preservation, Kans. State Hist. Soc., Hist. Soc. Machias

GEORGE, HARDY, curator; b. Tyler, Tex. s. Hardy and Anestelle George. BA in History, Tex. Christian U., Ft. Worth; MA in Art History, U. Calif., LA; PhD in Art History, Courtauld Inst. Art, London. Asst. prof. Georgetown U., DC, 1969—71; assoc. prof. Temple U., Phila., 1971—73, Concordia U., Montreal, Canada, 1973—97; vis. prof. U. Coll. London, 1998—99; chief curator Okla. City Mus. Art, 1999—. Contbr. chapters to books, articles to profl. jours. Vol. Florence Flood Opera del Duomo, Italy, 1968. Office: Okla City Mus Art 415 Couch Dr Oklahoma City OK 73102

GEORGE, JAMES EDWARD, accountant; b. Mt. George, Ark., May 22, 1943; m. Corliss Ann, Sept. 3, 1965. BA in Acctg., U. Ark., Little Rock, 1967; MS in Logistics, Air Force Inst. Tech., 1979; grad., Air Command and Staff Coll. of USAF, 1987, USAF Air War Coll., 1992. CPA, Ark. Commd. 2d lt. USAF, 1967, advanced through grades to capt.; commdr. Field Tng. Detachment, Mt. Clemens, Mich., Kadena AFB, Japan and Kunsan AFB, Korea, 1967-73; supr. maintenance Field Maintenance Squadron, Craig AFB, Ala., 1973-75; flightline br. chief Royal AFB, Bentwater, Eng., 1976-77; officer in charge quality control Tactical Fighter Wing, Royal AFB, Bentwater, 1977-78; left active duty USAFR, 1978, advanced through grades to lt. col., 1988, ret., 1994; pub. utility auditor Ark. Pub. Svc. Commn., Little Rock, 1979-98; exec. dir. Ark. State Bd. Pub. Accountancy, Little Rock, 1998—2003. Lectr. pub. utility income taxes and depreciation ea. utility rate Nat. Assn. Regulatory Utility Commrs., 1984—85; adj. faculty U. Ark., Fayetteville, 1997—2003, Webster U., 1998—. Bd. dirs. Brockington Rd. Ch. of the Nazarene, 1989—94, 1998—2002, 2004—05. Mem. AICPA (infol retrieval com. 1987-90), Ark. Soc. CPAs (pres. Ctrl. Ark. chpt. 1992-93, 95-96, chmn. membership com. 1991-93, bd. dirs. 1994-97, exec. com. 1996-97, chmn. public rels. com. 1997-03, 05—, pub. rels. com. 2003-04, Outstanding Ark. CPA in Industry and Bus. award 1995), Toastmasters (pres. Uptown chpt. 1985, Able Toastmaster award 1988), Officers Club (bd. dirs. Kadena AFB, Okinawa, 1971-72), Nat. Assn. Investment Clubs (dir. ctrl. Ark. chpt. 2006-). Home: 6631 Gap Point Cir Sherwood AR 72120-4052

GEORGE, JEAN CRAIGHEAD, author, illustrator; b. Washington, July 2, 1919; d. Frank Cooper and Carolyn (Johnson) Craighead; m. John L. George, Jan. 28, 1944 (div. Jan. 1964); children: Twig George Pittenger, John Craighead, Thomas Lothar. BA, Pa. State U., 1941. Reporter Washington Post, 1943-44; artist Pageant mag., 1945; reporter United Features, 1945-46; roving editor Reader's Digest, 1966-80; continuing edn. tchr. Chappaqua, NY, 1960-68. Author, illustrator: My Side of the Mountain, 1959, Summer of the Falcon, 1962, Gull Number 737, 1964, The Thirteen Moons, 1967-69, Coyote in Manhattan, 1968, River Rats, Inc., 1968, Who Really Killed Cock Robin, 1972, Julie of the Wolves, 1972, American Walk Book, 1978, Cry of the Crow, 1980, Journey Inward, 1982, The Talking Earth, 1983, One Day in the Alpine Tundra, 1984, How to Talk to Your Animals, 1985, One Day in the Prairie, 1986, Water Sky, 1987, (mus.) One Day in the Woods, 1988, The Shark Beneath the Reef, 1989, On the Far Side of the Mountain, 1990, One Day in the Tropical Rain Forest, 1990, The Missing 'Gator of Gumbo Limbo, 1992, The Fire Bug Connection, 1993, The First Thanksgiving, 1993, Dear Rebecca, Winter Is Here, 1993, Animals Who Have Won Our Hearts, 1994, Julie, 1994, To Climb a Waterfall, 1995, Acorn Pancakes & Dandelion Salad, 1995, There's an Owl in the Shower, 1995, Everglades, 1995, The Case of the Missing Cutthroat Trout, 1996, The Tarantula in My Purse, 1996, Look to the North, A Wolf Pup Diary, 1997, Julie's Wolf Pack, 1997, Arctic Son, 1997, Rhino Romp, 1998, Giraffe Trouble, 1998, Dear Katie, the Volcano Is a Girl, 1998, Survival Filmstrips, 1984, (film) My Side of the Mountain, 1965, Nature Filmstrips, 1978-80, One Day in the Woods Musical for Children (music by Chris Kubie), 1997, Elephant Walk, 1998, Gorilla Gang, 1999, Morning, Noon and Night, 1999, Frightful's Mountain, 1999, Snow Bear, 1999, How to Talk to Your Dog, 2000, How to Talk to Your Cat, 2000, Nutik, the Wolf Pup, 2001, Nutik & Amaroq Play Ball, 2001, Tree Castle Island, 2002, Cliff Hanger, 2002, Frightful's Daughter, 2002, Fire Storm, 2003, Charlie's Raven, 2004, Snowboard Twist, 2004, (musical) Julie of the Wolves, 2004, Luck, 2005, DVD Storyteller, 2005, The Wolves Are Back, 2007. Recipient Aurianne award, 1957, Newbery Honor Book award, 1961, medal, 1973, Hans Christian Andersen Honor List award, 1964, Pa. State Woman of Yr. award, 1968, World Book award, 1971, Kerlan award, 1982, U. So. Miss. award, 1986, Washington Irving award, 1991, 92, Knickerbocker award, 1991, Washington Post Children's Book Guild award, 1998, Empire State award, 1998, runner-up Lamplighter award, 2002, Regina medal Cath. Libr. Assn., Literary Lights award for children's lifetime work Boston Pub. Libr., 2003, Ludington award Am. Paperback Assn., 2004, Lamplighter Hon. Book, 2005, Roger Caras award, 2007. Address: 20 William Pl Chappaqua NY 10514-3114 E-mail: jeangeorgemail@aol.com.

GEORGE, JENNIFER M., management professor, psychology professor; BA, Wesleyan U., 1977; MBA, NYU, 1979, MPh, 1986, PhD, 1987. Asst. prof. Tex. A.&M. U., 1987—92, assoc. prof. dept. mgmt., 1992—97, prof. dept. mgmt., 1997—99; Mary Gibbs Jones prof. mgmt. and psychology Rice U., Houston, 1999—.

GEORGE, JOEY RUSSELL, lawyer; b. Bklyn., Oct. 8, 1963; s. Jonas and Celeste Dorothy (Russell) G. BA, Howard U., 1985; JD, Harvard U., 1988. Bar: N.Y. 1989, Conn. 1989, U.S. Dist. Ct. (so. and ea. dists.) N.Y. 1989, U.S. Supreme Ct. 1992. Asst. prosecutor Queens County Dist. Atty., Kew Gardens, NY, 1988-90; asst. gen. counsel Exec. Office of the Pres., Office Mgmt. and Budget, Washington, 1990-91; assoc. dir. for policy The White House, Washington, 1991-93; assoc. Kramer, Levin, Naftalis, Nessen, Kamin & Frankel, NYC, 1993—94; chief staff, chief counsel com. govt. reform subcom. on govt. efficiency, fin. mgmt. and intergovtl. rels. U.S. Ho. Reps., Washington, 1995—2002; inspector gen. US Corp. for Nat. and Cmty. Svc., Washington, 2002—04; inspector gen. for tax adminstrn. US Dept. Treasury, Washington, 2004—. Trustee Howard U., Washington, 1984-85; big brother Big Bros. Am. Cambridge, Mass., 1986-96; bd. advisers City Harvest, 1993-95. Mem. ABA (vice chmn. govt. ops. com., adminstrv. law sect. 1997-99), Ripon Soc. (pres. Harvard chpt. 1986-87, nat. v.p. 1987-88, bd. dirs. ednl. fund 1989-97, pres. ednl. fund 1993-97), Harvard Club, Univ. Club, Rotary Club of Washington D.C., Phi Beta Kappa, Pi Sigma Alpha, Phi Alpha Theta. Republican. Episcopalian.

GEORGE, JOHN ANTHONY, health corporation executive; b. New Kensington, Pa., July 11, 1948; s. Moses and Veronica (Raymond) George; m. Leah Diane George, Oct. 30, 1971 (div. 1992); m. Carolyn D. Dozier, Sept. 22, 2000. BS, Duquesne U., Pitts., 1970; MBA, U. Pitts., 1973; MS in Taxation, Robert Morris Coll., Pitts. CFP. Asst. adminstr. mental health and mental retardation program Western Psychiat. Inst. and Clinic, Pitts., 1971-72; adminstrv. dir. Latrobe Area Hosp., Pa., 1973-76; asst. dir. Presbyn. U. Hosp., Pitts., 1976-80; owner, prin. George-Anstey Food Distbg. Corp., Pitts., 1978-81; mgmt. cons. Arthur Young & Co., Pitts., 1980-82; exec. dir. Ea. Allegheny County Health Corp., 1982-85; pres. Alpha Health Network, 1985-88; pres., bd. dirs. Intergroup Svc. Corp., 1988—; mng. ptnr. Med. Benefit Svc., 1991—. Bd. mgrs. Health Coalition Ptnrs.; lectr. in field. Contbr. articles to profl. jours. Mem.: Am. Assn. Prepared Provider Orgns., Am. Coll. Health Care Execs. Roman Catholic. Home: 5121 Ellsworth Ave Pittsburgh PA 15232-1419 Office: 401 Shady Ave Suite B108 Pittsburgh PA 15206-4450 Business E-Mail: jgeorge@igs-ppo.com.

GEORGE, JOHN MARTIN, JR., lawyer; b. Normal, Ill., Dec. 17, 1947; s. John and Ada George; m. Judy Ann Watts; children: Sarah, Michael. AB with high honors, U. Ill., 1970, AM, 1971; PhD, Columbia U., 1976; JD cum laude, Harvard U., 1982. Bar: Mass. 1982, U.S. Dist. Ct. Mass. 1983, Ill. 1984, U.S. Dist. Ct. (no. dist.) Ill. 1984, U.S. Ct. Appeals (11th cir.) 1987, U.S. Ct. Appeals (9th cir.) 1988, U.S. Ct. Appeals (7th cir.) 1992, U.S. Ct. Appeals (3d cir.) 2000, U.S. Ct. Appeals (6th cir.) 2005. Assoc. Hill & Barlow, Boston, 1982-84, Sidley & Austin (now Sidley, Austin LLP), Chgo., 1984-89; ptnr. Sidley Austin LLP, 1989—. Editor Harvard U. Law Rev., 1980-82. Sr. warden Trinity Ch., 1998-2000. Named Ill. Super Lawyer, 2006; named to Hall of Fame, Unity H.S., 2005. Fellow Am. Bar Found.; mem. ABA, Chgo. Bar Assn., Leading Lawyers Network, Mid-Day Club, Phi Beta Kappa. Democrat. Episcopalian. Office: Sidley Austin LLP One South Dearborn St Chicago IL 60603 Office Phone: 312-853-7550. E-mail: jgeorge@sidley.com.

GEORGE, KIRANRAJ, electrical engineer, researcher; MSc, Bharathiar U., India, 1999; MS, Wright State U., Dayton, Ohio, 2000, postgrad., 2002—06. Grad. trainee Kochi Refineries, Ltd, India, 1999—2000; grad. tchg. asst. mgmt. sci. and info. systems dept. Wright State U., 2000—03, grad. project asst., 2003—05, rschr., 2003—; asst. prof. Calif. State U., 2007—. Contbr. articles to profl. jours. Active mem. Wrigtt State Cath. Assn., Dayton, 2000—. Recipient Chair's Spl. recognition for excellence in tchg. mgmt. sci. and info. systems dept., Wright State U., 2002, Chair's Spl. recognition for contbns. mgmt. sci. and info. systems dept., 2003, Dean's award for outstanding grad. student, 2006; DAGSI scholar, 2003—06, PhD engrng. scholar, 2006. Mem.: IEEE (assoc.), IEEE Internat. Microwave Soc. Achievements include research in automation and implementation of Configurable 2D LFSR for SoC BIST applications; hardware implementation of Electronic Warfare (EW) Receiver-On-a-Chip (ROC); design and implementation architecture of 2.5 giga-sample per second (GSPS) receiver-on-a-chip (ROC).

GEORGE, LILA GENE PLOWE KENNEDY, music educator; b. Sioux City, Iowa, Sept. 25, 1918; d. Eugene Preston Plowe and Lila Mazo Pickel; m. Richard Painter George; children: Eugenia, Richard Jr. BA in English and French, U. Okla., 1939, MusB in Theory, 1940; postgrad., Northwestern U., 1950, Columbia U., 1963—65; pvt. piano study with Egon Petri, Silvio Scionti & Edward Steuermann; pvt. composition study with Nadia Boulanger, Fontainebleau, France, 1971—78. Pvt. piano tchr., Oklahoma City, 1938—42, Talara, Peru, 1947—54, Houston, 1954—60, 1970—, Pelham Manor, NY, 1960—65. Soloist Oklahoma City Little Symphony, 1939, Houston Symphony, 1957; judge piano competitions Nat. Guild Piano Tchrs., Tex. State Music Tchrs. Recipient Houston Alumnae Music Leadership award, Sigma Alpha Iota, 2005. Mem.: Houston Tuesday Musical Club (pres. 1960), European Piano Tchrs. Assn., Am. Music Ctr. (composer), Sigma Alpha Iota (Music Leadership award Houston (Tex.) Alumnus chpt. 2005). Episcopalian. Avocation: genealogy. Home: 701 N Rusk Wharton TX 77488

GEORGE, MELVIN DOUGLAS, retired university president; b. Washington, Feb. 13, 1936; s. Douglas Elmer and Catherine Evelyn (McNelly) G.; m. Meta Jane Barghusen, Aug. 17, 1958; children— Elizabeth Anne, Margaret Susan BA, Northwestern U., 1956; PhD, Princeton U., 1959. From asst. to assoc. prof. math. U. Mo., Columbia, 1960-67, prof., assoc. dean, 1967-70, v.p. acad. affairs, 1975-85; dean Coll. Arts and Scis. U. Nebr., Lincoln, 1970-75; pres. St. Olaf Coll., Northfield, Minn., 1985-94, pres. emeritus, 1994—; v.p. instnl. rels. U. Minn., Mpls., 1994-96; prof. math. emeritus U. Mo., Columbia, 1996—, interim pres., 1996-97, pres. emeritus, 1997—. Contbr. articles to profl. jours. Recipient Robert W. Martin award for Acad. Freedom, Mo. conf. AAUP, 1985 Mem. Am. Math. Soc., Math. Assn. Am. Lutheran. Avocations: music, swimming. Home: 1509 W Rollins Rd Columbia MO 65203-2378

GEORGE, NICHOLAS, lawyer, entrepreneur; b. Seattle, July 11, 1952; s. Harry and Mary (Courounes) G.; children: Harry Nicholas, James Michael. BA in Polit. Sci. cum laude, Whitman Coll., 1974; MBA in Mktg. and Corp. Planning, U. Chgo., 1979; JD, U. Puget Sound, 1989. Bar: Wash. 1991, U.S. Dist. Ct. (we. dist.) Wash. 1991, U.S. Ct. Appeals (9th cir.) 1991, U.S. Tax Ct. 1992, U.S. Dist. Ct. (ea. dist.) Wash. 1994, U.S. Supreme Ct. 1994. Fin. cons. Pacific Western Investment Co., Lynnwood, Wash., 1975-77; planning dir. Clinton Capital Ventures, Seattle, 1979-81; corp. planning mgr. Tacoma Boatbldg., 1981-83; pres. MegaProf Investors, Bellevue, Wash., 1983-89; practice trial-settlement law bus., Seattle, 1989—. Free-lance coll. counselor, Seattle, 1980—. Author: Legitimacy in Government: Ideal, Goal, or Myth? 1974. Bd. auditor St. Demetrios Greek Orthodox Ch., Seattle, 1982-83; bd. dirs. Hellenic Golfers Assn., Seattle,

1981-83. Mem. ABA, Assn. Trial Lawyers Am., Wash. State Bar Assn., Wash. Assn. Criminal Def. Lawyers, Wash. State Trial Lawyers Assn., Fed. Bar Assn., Nat. Assn. Criminal Def. Lawyers, Tacoma-Pierce County Bar Assn., Seattle-King County Bar Assn., Wash. Defender Assn., Wash. State Hist. Soc., Am. Inst. Archeol., Phi Alpha Delta. Greek Orthodox. Avocations: weightlifting, travel, football coaching, writing. Home: 5007 80th St SW Lakewood WA 98499-4077 Office: 1919 N Pearl St Ste A2 Tacoma WA 98406 Office Phone: 253-272-7181. Business E-Mail: ngeorge@legalpaladin.com.

GEORGE, OAKIE LEE, mechanic; b. Canton, Ohio, May 7, 1966; s. Dale Lee George and Linda Lou Knox; m. Cindra Sue Wensel, Mar. 5, 1988; 1 child, Brian Keith Wensel; m. Mary Beth Stammer, Apr. 24, 1993 (div. Dec. 21, 2001); children: Emilee Ann, Tricha Dawn Robinson, Lane Stephan, Thomas Anthoy; m. Cindra Sue Wensel, July 12, 2002. Grad., United Local HS, Hanoverton, Ohio. Mechanic, wrecker operator US Army, Ft. Lewis, Wash., 1984—91; mechanic Bauer Truck Repair, Appleton, Wis., 1992—94, Kimberly-Clark, Neenah, Wis., 1994—95, Foreway Express, Appleton, Wis., 1995—96, Waste Mgmt., Kaukauna, Wis., 1996—98; equipment operator City of Appleton, 1998—2003; mechanic, wrecker operator 3670th Maint. Co., Clackamas, Oreg., 2004—06; engine rebuilder CECOM/OSMS, Clackamas, 2006—. With N.G. US Army, 1994—2007. Mem.: VFW. Home: 3374 SE Woodward St Portland OR 97202 Office: CECON OSMS 10101 SE Clackamas Rd Clackamas OR 97015 Home Phone: 503-232-7710.

GEORGE, PAUL G., finance company executive; b. Pasadena, Calif., May 25, 1951; BA magna cum laude in Polit. Sci. and Econs., Occidental Coll., LA; JD, UCLA. With Meserve, Mumper & Hughes, LA; head human resources Pacific SW Airlines, Inc., San Diego; sr. v.p. human resources United Airlines; mem. interim mgmt. team Waste Mgmt. Inc.; sr. exec. v.p., head human resources Wachovia Corp., Charlotte, NC, 2001—05; exec. v.p. human resources Fed. Home Loan Mortgage Corp., 2005—. Active Habitat for Humanity. Mem.: Fin. Svcs. Human Resources Exec. Forum. Office: Fed Home Loan Mortgage Corp 8200 Jones Branch Dr Mc Lean VA 22102-3110 Office Phone: 703-903-2000.*

GEORGE, PAUL M., law librarian, director; b. 1952; AB magna cum laude, with high distinction in History, U. Ill., Urbana-Champaign, 1974; JD, Duke U., 1977; MLS, U. Ill., Urbana-Champaign, 1985. Bar: Ill. 1977. Atty. Land of Lincoln Legal Assistance Found., Champaign, Ill., 1977—84; reference libr. U. Southern Calif. Law Libr., 1985—88, head, pub. services, 1988—91, asst. dir., pub. services, 1991—94; assoc. libr., rsch. services Harvard U. Law Sch. Libr., 1994—2002, acting libr., 1999—2000; dir. Biddle Law Libr. and adj. law prof. U. Pa. Law Sch., Phila., 2002—. Mem.: So. Calif. Assn. Law Libraries (pres. 1994), Ill. State Bar, Am. Assn. Law Libraries, Phi Kappa Phi, Phi Beta Kappa. Office: U Pa Law Sch Biddle Law Libr 3400 Chestnut St Rm T-209 Philadelphia PA 19104-3406 Office Phone: 215-898-7488. Office Fax: 215-898-6619. Business E-Mail: pmgeorge@law.upenn.edu.

GEORGE, PETER JAMES, economist, educator; b. Toronto, Sept. 12, 1941; s. Ralph Langlois and Kathleen May (Larder) G.; m. Gwendolyn Jean Scharf, Oct. 19, 1962 (dec. Mar. 1997); children— Michael James, Katherine Jane; m. Allison Mary Barrett, July 31, 1998. BA with honors, U. Toronto, 1962, MA, 1963, PhD, 1967; DU (hon.), U. Ottawa, 1995; D Hon. C. (hon.), Lviv Nat. Poly U., 2001; DLitt (hon.), Nipissing U., 2002; LLD (hon.), U. Toronto, 2005. Lectr. McMaster U., 1965-67, asst. prof., 1967-71, assoc. prof., 1971-80, prof. econs., 1980—, assoc. dean grad. studies, 1974-79, dean social scis., 1980-89, pres., vice chancellor, 1995—; spl. lectr. U. Toronto, 1967; vis. lectr. U. Cambridge, 1974; economist Govt. of Ont., 1963; project mgr. Tanzania Tourist Corp., 1970-71; pres. Coun. Ont. Univs., Toronto, 1991-95; hon. prof. Beijing U. Sci. and Tech., 1998, Dongguan U. Tech., 2006. Author: Government Subsidies and the Construction of the Canadian Pacific Railway, 1981, The Emergence of Industrial America: Strategic Factors in American Economic Growth Since 1870, 1982; Appointed to Ont. Coun. on Univ. Affairs, 1987-91. Decorated Order of Can., 1999; recipient Commemorative medal 125th Anniversary Confedn. of Can., 1993; recipient The Queen's Golden Jubilee medal, 2002. Mem. Can. Econs. Assn., Can. Hist. Assn., Am. Econ. Assn., Econ. History Assn., Econ. History Soc. Office: McMaster U Office Pres GH-238 1280 Main St W Hamilton ON Canada L8S 4L8 Home Phone: 905-648-2522; Office Phone: 905-525-9140 ext. 24340. Business E-Mail: presdnt@mcmaster.ca, pgeorge@mcmaster.ca.

GEORGE, RONALD M., state supreme court chief justice; b. LA, Mar. 11, 1940; AB, Princeton U., 1961; JD, Stanford U., 1964. Bar: Calif. 1965. Dep. atty. gen. Calif. Dept. Justice, 1965-72; judge L.A. Mcpl. Ct., L.A. County, 1972-77, Superior Ct. Calif., L.A. County, 1977-87, supervising judge criminal divsn., 1983-84; assoc. justice 2d dist., divsn. 4 Calif. Ct. Appeal, LA, 1987-91; assoc. justice Calif. Supreme Ct., San Francisco, 1991-96, chief justice, 1996—. Named Trial Judge of the Yr., L.A. Metropolitan News, 1983, Appellate Justice of the Yr., L.A. Trial Lawyers Assn., 1991, Person of the Yr., L.A. Metropolitan News, 1996; recipient St. Thomas More Medallion award, St. Thomas More Law Honor Soc., 1997, Judge Learned Hand award, 2000, Found. of the State Bar's Justice award, 2000, William H. Rehnquist award for Judicial Excellence, 2002, James Madison Freedom of Information award, Soc. of Professional Journalists, 2003, George Moscone award for Outstanding Public Service, Consumer Attorneys of L.A., 2003, William O. Douglas award, 2004. Mem. Calif. Judges Assn. (pres. 1982-83), Conf. Chief Justices (pres. 2003-04). Avocations: hiking, skiing, running. Office: Calif Supreme Court 350 McAllister St Fl 5 San Francisco CA 94102-4797 Office Phone: 415-865-7060.

GEORGE, RUSSELL LLOYD, lawyer, former state legislator; b. Rifle, Colo., May 28, 1946; s. Walter Mallory and Eleanora (Michel) G.; m. Neal Ellen Moore, Nov. 24, 1972; children: Russell, Charles, Thomas, Andrew. BS in Econs., Colo. State U., 1968; JD, Harvard Law Sch., 1971. Bar: Colo 1972, Mont. 1975. Shareholder Stuver & George, P.C., Rifle, 1976—; dir. Co. Div. Wildlife, Denver, 2000—04; exec. dir. Colo. Dept. of Natural Resources, Denver, 2004—. State rep. dist. 57 Colo. Gen. Assembly, 1993—, speaker of the House, Colo Gen.Assembly. Named Legislator of Yr., by Associated Press capitol reporter, 1994, 1996; recipient Boettcher Scholar, 1968. Fellow Colo. Bar Found.; mem. Colo. Bar Assn., Rotary Internat., Masonic Lodge. Republican. Methodist. Office: Colo Dept of Natural Resources 1313 Sherman St Rm 718 Denver CO 80203 Office Phone: 303-866-3311. Office Fax: 303-866-2115.

GEORGE, SARAH B., museum director; Dir. Utah Mus. of Natural History, Salt Lake City. Office: Utah Mus Natural History U Utah 1390 E Pres Cir Salt Lake City UT 84112 E-mail: sgeorge@umnh.utah.edu.

GEORGE, THOMAS, artist; b. NYC, July 1, 1918; s. Rube and Irma (Seeman) Goldberg; m. Laverene Burton, July 16, 1951; children: John R., Geoffrey T. Beorge. BA, Dartmouth Coll., Hanover, NH, 1940. Vis. artist U. Tex., 1978; artist-in-residence Darmouth Coll., 1979. One-man shows include Feragil Gallery, NYC, 1951, 1953, Korman Gallery, 1954, Dartmouth Coll., 1965, 1979, 1990, Contemporaries Gallery, NYC, 1956, Bridgestone Mus., Tokyo, 1957, Betty Parsons Gallery, NYC, 1959, 1963, 1965, 1966, 1968, 1970, 1972, 1974, 1976, 1978, 1981, Reid Gallery, London, 1962, 1964, Del. Mus., 1971, 1976, Henie-Onstad Art Mus., Oslo, 1971, Princeton U. Art Mus., 1975, Nat. Gallery, Oslo, 1980, Maxwell Davidson Gallery, NYC, 1983, 1985, 1988, 1990, Riis Gallery, Oslo, 1982, 1984, 1986, 1988, 1990, Hood Art Mus., Dartmouth Coll., 1990, Snyder Fine Art, NYC, 1991, 1993, 1996, Julian Hartnoll Gallery, London, 1993, Williams Gallery, Princeton, 1997, 1999, Mercer County Coll., NJ, 2002, Rider U. Art Gallery, 2006, exhibitions include retospective NJ State Mus., 1987, Princeton U. Art Mus., 2005, exhibitions include Rider U. Art Gallery, 2006, exhibited in group shows at Met. Mus. Art, NYC, Am. Fedn. Arts, Mus. Modern Art, NYC, Whitney Mus. Ann., Carnegie Internat., Pitts., Pa. Acad., Japan Internat. Biennial Art, Tokyo, White House, Lausanne Mus., Switxerland, Lawrenceville Sch., NJ, 2007, Represented in permanent collections Whitney Mus., Mus. Modern Art, NYC, Bklyn. Mus., Tate Gallery, London, Nat. Coll Fine Arts, Smithsonian Instn., Washington, Chase Manhattan Coll., NYC, Libr. of Congress, Bridgestone Mus., Hood Art Mus., Dartmouth Coll., Lausanne Mus. Art, Mus. Fine Arts, Houston, U. Calif. Art Mus., Berkeley, Santa Barbara Mus. Fine Arts, Okla. Art Ctr., U. Calif. Mus., Santa Clara, Yale U. Art Gallery, Flint Inst., Mich., NJ State Mus., Rose Art Mus., Brandeis U., Heine-Onstad Art Mus., San Francisco Mus. Art, Del. Art Mus., Nat. Gallery, Oslo, Princeton Art Mus., Inst. Advanced Study, Princeton, numerous corps., commn., Olympic Games poster, 1974. With USNR, 1942—45. Recipient Purchase prize, Bklyn. Mus., 1955, Ford Found., 1961, Whitney Mus. Ann. Am. Painting, 1962, N.J. State Mus., 1971, Presdl. medal, Dartmouth Coll., 1991, Princeton Arts Coun. award, 1992, 2000; fellow, Edward MacDowell Colony; Rockefeller Found. grantee, 1957. Address: 1087 The Great Rd Princeton NJ 08540-4801 Office Phone: 609-924-7316. *A good artist must work hard all his life. He must know his craft and, most important of all, he must feel deeply about something in life.*

GEORGE, THOMAS FREDERICK, academic administrator; b. Phila., Mar. 18, 1947; s. Emmanuel John and Veronica Mather (Hansel) G.; m. Barbara Carol Harbach, Apr. 25, 1970. BA in Chemistry and Math., Gettysburg Coll., Pa., 1967; MS in Chemistry, Yale U., 1968, PhD, 1970. Rsch. assoc. MIT, 1970; postdoctoral fellow U. Calif., Berkeley, 1971; mem. faculty U. Rochester, NY, 1972-85, prof. chemistry, 1977-85; dean Faculty Natural Sci. and Math., prof. chemistry and physics SUNY-Buffalo, 1985-91; provost, acad. v.p., prof. chemistry and physics Wash. State U., Pullman, 1991-96; chancellor, prof. chemistry and physics U. Wis., Stevens Point, 1996—2003, U. Missouri, St. Louis, 2003—; Disting. vis. lectr. dept. chemistry U. Tex., Austin, 1978; lectr. NATO Advanced Study Inst., Cambridge, England, 1979; Disting. speaker dept. chemistry U. Utah, 1980; Disting. lectr. Air Force Weapons Lab., Kirtland AFB, N.Mex., 1980; mem. com. recommendations U.S. Army Basic Sci. Research, 1978-81; lectr. NATO Summer Sch. on Interfaces under Photon Irradiation, Maratea, Italy, 1986; organizer NSF workshop on theoretical aspects of laser radiation and its interaction with atomic and molecular systems Rochester, NY, 1977; vice chmn. 6th Internat. Conf. Molecular Energy Transfer, Rodez, France, 1979; chmn. Gordon Rsch. Conf. Molecular Energy Transfer, Wolfeboro, NH, 1981. Adj. rsch. prof. physics Korea U., Seoul, 1994-99, vis. prof. physics, 1994-03; Dow lectr. polymer sci. U. Detroit Mercy, 1996; program com. Internat. Conf. on Lasers, San Francisco, 1981-83, ACS Symposium on Recent Advances in Surface Sci., Rochester sect., 1982, Internat. Laser Sci. Conf., Dallas, 1985, external rev. com. for chemistry Gettysburg Coll., 1984, awards com. ACS Procter and Gamble student prizes in chemistry, 1982-83, Free-electron Laser peer rev. panel Am. Inst. Biol. Sci. Med., alt., bd. trustees alt. Calspan-UB Rsch. Ctr., 1989-91; organiser APS Symposium on Laser-Induced Molecular Excitation/Photofragmentation, NY, 1987; co-organizer ACS Symposium on Phys. Chemistry High-Temp. Supercondrs., LA, 1988, MRS Symposium on High-Temperature Superconductors, Alfred, NY, 1988; chmn. SPIE Symposium on Photochemistry in Thin Films, LA, 1989; internat. program adv. com. Internat. Sch. Lasers and Applications, Sayanogorsk, East Siberia, USSR, 1989; lectr. chemistry at cutting edge Smithsonian Instn./Am. Chem. Soc., Washington, 1990; Musselman lectr. Gettysburg Coll., 1999; Disting. lectr. Korean Acad. Sci. and Tech., 2003; internat. adv. com. Xth Vavilov Conf. Nonlinear Optics, Novosibirsk, USSR, 1990; Am. coord. NSF Info. Exchange Seminar for U.S.-Japan Program of Cooperation in Photoconversion and Photosynthesis, Honolulu, 1990; program com. Optical Soc. Am. Topical Meeting on Radiative Processes and Dephasing in Semiconductors, Coeur d'Alene, Idaho, 1998; sci. com. Sixth Brijuni Internat. Conf. on Interdisciplinary Topics in Physics and Chemistry, Brijuni Isles, Croatia, 1998; super-regional steering com. Wis. Econ. Summit, 2000; exec. bd. NY State Inst. on Superconductivity, 1990-91; mem. ONT/ASEE rev. panel for Engring. Edn. postdoctoral fellowship program, 1990; rev panel rsch. experiences for undergrads of sci. and tech. rsch. ctrs., NSF, 1989, rev. panel grad. res. traineeships NSF, 1992; cons., lectr. in field Co-author: (with Blackwell) Notes in Classical and Quantum Physics, 1990, (with Kluwer) Fundamentals in Chemical Physics, 1998; (with Nova) Phase Conjugation in a Layer on Nonlinear Materials, 2005; editor: Photochemistry in Thin Films, 1989; co-editor Internat. Jour. Theoretical Physics, Group Theory, and Nonlinear Optics, 1999—; co-editor: Chemistry of High-Temperature Superconductors, Vol. I, 1987, vol. II, 1988, ACS Symposium Series, (with World Scientific) Computational Studies of New Materials, 1999, (with Wiley) Optics of Nanostructured Materials, 2001, (with Resarch Signpost) Modern Topics in Chemical Physics, 2001, (with Springer) Molecular Buidling Blocks ofr Nanotechnology, 2007; editor-at-large Marcel Dekker, 1989; feature editor Jour. of Optical Soc. of Am.,1987, Spectrochimica Acta, 1987, Optical Engring., 1980; mem. editl. bd. Molecular Physics, 1984-90, Jour. Cluster Sci., 1989-97, Jour. Quantum Nonlinear Phenomena, 1991-96, Nova Jour. Theoretical Physics, 1996-97; mem. adv. bd. Jour. Phys. Chemistry, 1980-84; mem. adv. editl. bd. Chem. Physics Letters, 1979-81, Chem. Materials, 1989; contbr. over 665 articles to profl. jours. and chpts. to books. Tchr., scholar Camille and Henry Dreyfus Found., 1975-85; bd. mgrs. Buffalo Mus. Sci., 1986-92; exec. bd. NY State Inst. on Superconductivity, 1990-91; canvassing com. ACS; external rev. com. for chemistry Gettysburg Coll., 1984; mem. NEASC site visit team Boston U., ten-yr. accreditation, 1989; bd. dirs. Wash. State Inst. for Pub. Policy, 1991-96, Wash. Tech. Ctr., 1992-96; trustee Wash. State U. Found., 1991-96; exec. com. Northwest Acad. Forum, 1992-96, chmn. 1994-95; rev. panel Grad. Rsch. Traineeships, NSF, 1992, rev. panel for sci. and tech. ctr. proposals, 1998, rev. panel for preproposals for sci. and tech. ctrs., 1998; mem. Project 435 Dist. Leadership Coun., Wis. Assn. Biomed. Rsch. and Edn./Rsch. Am., 1997; Comm. on the Future of Gettysburg Coll., 1997-98; bd. dirs. Portage County Bus. Coun., 1998-03, Stevens Point Area YMCA, 1998-03, v.p., 2002-03, United Way Portage County, Wis., 1997-2003, chmn. 1999 campaign, pres., 2002-04, Tech. Alliance State Wash., 1996, U. Wis., Stevens Point Found., 1996-03, Paper Sci. Found., 1996-03, St. Michael's Hosp., Stevens Point, 1999-03, Distributed Learning Workshop, Midwestern Higher Edn. Commn., 1999-03, Wis. Ctr. Acad. Talented Youth, 2001-03; Marathon County Ptnrs. in Edn., 2002, Civic Progress, 2003-, Ctr. for Emerging Tech., 2003-, Ctr. Rsch., Tech. and Entrepreneurial Expertise, 2003-, St. Louis Merc. Libr., 2003-, John W. Barringer III Nat. RR Libr., 2004, Christian Hosp., 2004-, United Way of Greater St. Louis, 2004-, Mo. Coun. Pub. Higher Edn., 2004-, bd. trustees, bd. dirs. Assoc. Western Univs., Atlanta, 1993-96; bd. dirs. alt. Joint Ctr. Higher Edn., Spokane, 1996; steering com. Ctr. for Advanced Tech. in Healthcare Instruments and Devices, 1988-90, Midwestern Higher Edn. Commn., 1999-03, 05-, chair policy rsch. adv. com.; exploring chair Mushkodany dist. Wis. Samoset coun. Boy Scouts Am., 1998, fin. chair, 1999, pres., 2002-03; bd. dirs. trustee WiSys Tech. Found., 2000-, Mo. Bot. Garden, 2003-; exec. bd. Greater St. Louis Area coun. Boy Scouts Am., 2004-, chmn. learning for life, 2006—; bd. commrs. Acad. Advanced Distributed Learning Lab. (UW-US Dept. Def.), 2001; adv. coun. Ednl. Directories Unltd., 2001-06; adv. bd. New Economy Workforce Coalition, Wausau, 2001, Mo. Coun. Pub. Higher Edn., 2003—; steering com. St. Louis Regional Competitiveness Coun. Initiative, 2004—; trustee St. Louis Sci. Ctr., 2005-; Met. bd. dirs. YMCA Greater St. Louis, 2005-; bd. dirs. coalition info. and comm. tech. St. Louis, 2006—; adv. bd. Halyard Edn. Partners, 2007-; Regional Chamber and Growth Assn., 2003-; chair. Plant and Life Sci. Network, 2007. Sloan fellow, 1976-80, postdoctoral fellow, 1990, Guggenheim fellow, 1983-84; recipient Disting. Alumni award Gettysburg Coll., 1987, Disting. Alumnus award Friends Ctr. Sch., 2003; Outstanding Cmty. Svc. award, NAACP St. Louis Branch, 2006. Fellow AAAS (chair St. Louis local com. 2006), Soc. Photo-Optical Instrumentation Engrs., Am. Phys. Soc., NY Acad. Scis., Inst. Superconductivity (steering com. 1987-91); mem. Am. Chem. Soc. (exec. com. phys. div. 1979-82, 85-89, 94-97, vice chmn. 1985-86, chmn.-elect 1986-87, chmn. 1987-88), Outstanding Contbns. to Chemistry award 2002, Am. Chem. Soc., Am. Assn. State Colls. and Univs. (acad. affairs subcom. on sci. edn. rsch. and tng., coun. state reps., mem. task force math. and sci. enrollments 2005), Wis. Assn. for Biomed. Rsch. and Edn., European Phys. Soc., Royal Soc. Chemistry (Marlow medal and prize 1979), Materials Rsch. Soc., Korean Acad. Sci. and Tech. (fgn.), Phi Beta Kappa, Sigma Xi (exec. com. U. Rochester 1984-85). Office: U Mo-St Louis Office of the Chancellor One Univ Blvd Saint Louis MO 63121 Office Phone: 314-516-5252. Business E-Mail: tfgeorge@umsl.edu.

GEORGE, TIMOTHY MERRILL, neurosurgeon, educator; b. Bklyn., Oct. 17, 1960; s. Carey and Gracie Mae (Gallman) G.; m. Rosalind Marie Jones; children: Kevin Randall James, Timothy Merrill George, Jr. BA, Columbia U., 1982; MD, N.Y. U., 1986. Diplomate Nat. Bd. Med. Examiners, Am. Bd. of Neurological Surgery, Am. Bd. of Pediatric Neurological Surgery. Asst. resident in surgery Yale U., New Haven, 1986-87, asst. resident in neurological surgery, 1987—93; trainee, pediatric neurosurgery Children's Mem. Hosp., 1993—95; assoc. prof. Duke U. Med. Ctr., Durham, 1995—. Rsch. assoc. Dept. Neuroanatomy Yale U., 1988—. Author: Symposium on Critical Care, 1989, Surgical Management of Supratentorial Gliomas: Contemporary Neurosurgery, 1989, Current Management of Aneurysmal Subasachnoid Hemorrhage, 1989, Lateral Ventricular Tumors: Complication Avoidance in Neurosurgery, 1990; designer (invention) Intracranial Localizer, 1988. Mem. NAACP, 1977-82. Recipient Merck Manual award Merck, Sharp & Dohme, 1986; named One of Outstanding Young Men in Am., 1990. Mem. AMA, Am. Assn. Neurol. Surgeons, Congress Neurol. Surgeons, Nat. Med. Assn. Avocations: disc jockey, basketball, music, jazz. Office: Pediat Neurosurgery 1601 Rio Grande Suite 340 Austin TX 78701-1149 E-mail: georg017@mc.duke.edu.

GEORGE, WALTER EUGENE, JR., architect; b. Wichita Falls, Tex., Oct. 28, 1922; s. Walter Eugene and Mamie Alta (Evans) G.; m. Mary Carolyn Hollers Jutson, May 20, 1980. BArch, U. Tex., 1949; MArch, Harvard U., 1950. Designer Wiltshire and Fisher (architects), Dallas, 1950-51; partner Pendley, George and Bowman (architects and engrs.), Austin, 1952-57; asst., then assoc. prof. architecture U. Tex., 1956-62; prof. architecture, chmn. dept. U. Kans., 1962-67; dean Coll. Architecture, U. Houston, 1967-69; practice of architecture Austin, 1969—71, 1974—; resident architect Colonial Williamsburg, Va., 1971-73; sr. lectr. engring. U. Tex., Austin, 1975-96, San Antonio Conservation Soc. prof. architecture San Antonio, 1997—2004. Served as pilot USAAF, 1943-46, ETO. Decorated Air medal with oak leaf cluster, Purple Heart; recipient 2d award 1st ann. Southwestern furniture competition, Dallas Mus. Fine Arts, Mont San Michele and Chartres award, 1949, D.B. Alexander Lifetime Achievement award, Heritage Soc. Austin, Tex., 2005. Fellow: AIA; mem.: Tex. Soc. Archs. (Edward J. Romieniec award for outstanding archtl. educator 2001), Soc. Archtl. Historians, Archaeol. Inst. Am., Tau Sigma Delta. Episcopalian. Office: PO Box 4426 Austin TX 78765-4426

GEORGE, WARREN S., labor union administrator; b. Pitts. m. Janice George; 3 children. Bus operator Critchlow Bus Lines, 1956—63; exec. bd. mem. operators, Local 85 Amalgamated Transit Union, 1963—76, exec. bd. mem. maintenance, Local 85, pres., fin. sec., treas., Local 85, 1970—75, del. Alleghany County Ctrl. Labor Coun., internat. v.p., 1975—93, spl. asst. to internat. pres., 1990, internat. exec., v.p., 1993—2002, internat. union pres., 2003—. Served with USN. Office: Amalgamated Transit Union International 2nd Floor 5025 Wisconsin Ave NW Washington DC 20016-4139 Office Phone: 202-537-1645. Office Fax: 202-244-7824.*

GEORGE, WILLIAM WALLACE, former manufacturing executive; b. Muskegon, Mich., Sept. 14, 1942; s. Wallace Edwin and Kathryn Jean (Dinkeloo) G.; m. Ann Tonnlier Pilgram, Sept. 6, 1969; children: Jeffrey, Jonathan. BS in Indsl. Engring. with honors, Ga. Inst. Tech., 1964; MBA with high distinction, Harvard U., 1966. Asst. to asst. sec. Dept. Def., Washington, 1966-68; spl. civilian asst. to sec. Navy, Washington, 1968-69; with Litton Industries, 1969-78, dir. long-range planning Cleve., 1969-70, v.p., 1976, Litton Microwave Cooking Products, Mpls., 1970-71, exec. v.p., 1971-73, pres., 1973-78; v.p. corp. devel. Honeywell, Mpls., 1978-80, exec. v.p., 1983-87; pres. Honeywell Europe (S.A.), 1980-82, Indsl. Automation, 1987, Space and Aviation Systems, Mpls., 1988-89; pres., chief oper. officer Medtronic Inc., Mpls., 1989-91, CEO, 1991—2002, chmn., 1996—2002. Bd. dirs. Dayton-Hudson, Imation., Goldman Sachs Group, Inc., Target Corp. and Novartis AG; sr. lecturer, Harvard Bus. Sch., prof. leadership and governance, Internat. Inst. Mgmt. Devel., 2002-2003, visiting prof. tech. mgmt., Ecole Polytechnique Federale de Lausanne, 2002-2003, exec.-in-residence, Yale Sch. Mgmt., 2003 Bd. dirs. Am. Red Cross, Minn. Symphony Orch., 1976-80, United Way, Minn. 1976-79, 96—, nat. chmn., Belgium, 1982-83, campaign chair, 1997; bd. dirs., pres., treas. Guthrie Theater, 1977-84; vice-chmn. United Theol. Sem., 1977-80, Abbott-Northwestern Hosp., 1984—, vice-chair, 1989-91, chair, 1991-93, Health Span, 1989-94; trustee Macalaster Coll., 1987-93, Allin Health Sys., 1994—, vice-chair, 1997—, Mlps. Inst. Arts, 1993—, chmn. Minn. Thunder Pro Soccer, 1994—. Recipient Meritorious Civilian Service Award Sec. Navy, 1969 Mem. Sigma Chi (Internat. Balfour award 1964, trustee 1971-77, Disting. Alumni award Harvard U., 1997). Clubs: Minneapolis, Minikahda. Episcopalian. Home: 2284 W Lake Of The Isles Pky Minneapolis MN 55405-2434 Office: George Family Found 1818 Oliver Ave S Minneapolis MN 55405

GEORGES, MARA STACY, lawyer; b. Sept. 2, 1963; married; 2 children. BA, U. Notre Dame, 1985; JD, Loyola U., 1988. Ptnr. Rock, Fusco, Reynolds, Crowe & Garvey, 1995-97; 1st asst. corporation counsel City of Chgo., 1997-99, corporation counsel, 1999—. Office: City Hall Law Dept 121 N Lasalle St Rm 600 Chicago IL 60602-1208 Office Phone: 312-744-0220. E-mail: mgeorges@cityofchicago.org.*

GEORGES, PETER JOHN, lawyer; b. Wilmington, Del., Sept. 8, 1940; s. John Peter and Olga Demetrius (Kazitoris) G. BS in Chemistry, U. Del., 1962; JD, John Marshall Law Sch., 1970; LLM in Patent and Trade Regulations, George Washington U., 1973. Bar: Ill. 1970, U.S. Ct. Appeals (fed. cir.) 1972, D.C. 1973, U.S. Supreme Ct. 1973, Del. 1977. Chemist engrng. labs Bell & Howell Co., Chgo., 1966; patent coordinator Armour & Co., Chgo., 1967; patent agt., atty. UOP Inc., Chgo., 1968-71, Washington counsel Arlington, Va., 1972-77; ptnr. Kile, Gholz, Bernstein & Georges, Arlington, 1977-78; assoc., then ptnr. Law Office Sidney W. Russell, Arlington, 1978-83; mng. officer Breneman & Georges (and predecessor law firms), Alexandria, 1983—; founding ptnr. Lenastri Properties and Joanastri Properties, Alexandria, Va. Served to 1st lt. USMC, 1963-65, Vietnam. Mem. Ill. Bar Assn., D.C. Bar Assn., Del. Bar Assn., Fed. Cir. Bar Assn., Assn. Am. Hellenic Lawyers Soc. Office: Breneman & Georges 3150 Commonwealth Ave Alexandria VA 22305-2712

GEORGES, RICHARD MARTIN, lawyer, educator, poet; b. St. Louis, Nov. 17, 1947; s. Martin Mahlon Georges and Josephine (Cipolla) Rice. AB cum laude, Loyola U., New Orleans, 1969; JD cum laude, Stetson Coll. Law, 1972. Bar: 1972, U.S. Dist. Ct. (mid. dist.) Fla. 1973, U.S. Ct.

Appeals (11th cir.) 1981, U.S. Supreme Ct. 1982. Ptnr. Kieffer & Georges, St. Petersburg, Fla., 1973-80, Kieffer, Georges & Ranter, St. Petersburg, Fla., 1980-85; pvt. practice St. Petersburg, Fla., 1985—. Adj. prof. Fla. Inst. Tech., Melbourne, 1977-86, Stetson Coll. Law, 1985-90, 2000-2002, Eckerd Coll., St. Petersburg, 1986-89; mem. Fla. Cts. Tech. Comm., 1998—. Author: Life is Simple Really, 2006; Contbg. author Florida Law of Trusts, 1983; contbr. Future Lawyer column on legal tech, poems. Arbitrator United Steelworkers Union, Continental Can Co., 1975-80; hearing examiner City of St. Petersburg, 1982—; me. citizen's adv. com. Pinellas County Met. Planning Orgn., 1986-87; exec. committeeman Pinellas County Rep. Party, Clearwater, Fla., 1981-82. 1st lt. U.S. Army, 1972. Recipient Rafael Steinhardt award Stetson Coll. Law, 1972, Clint Green award, 1972. Mem. ABA, Fla. Bar, St. Petersburg Bar Assn. (chmn. computer com.), Fla. Camera Club Coun. (pres. 1985), Suncoast Camera (Clearwater, v.p. 1982-84, pres. 1985), Phi Alpha Delta. Roman Catholic. Office: PO Box 14545 Saint Petersburg FL 33733 E-mail: futurelawyer@futurelawyer.com.

GEORGIADE, GREGORY STEPHEN, plastic surgeon, educator; b. Durham, NC, Nov. 16, 1947; BS, U. NC, Chapel Hill, 1970; MD, Duke U., Durham, 1973. Lic. NC, 1973, cert. Am. Bd. Gen. Surgery, 1979, Am. Bd. Plastic Surgery, 1981. Intern dept. surgery Duke U. Med. Ctr., 1973—74, asst. resident plastic surgery, 1974—78, instr. dept. surgery, 1977—78, resident, instr. plastic surgery, 1978—79, chief resident, instr. plastic surgery, 1979—80, asst. prof. surgery, 1980, asst. dir. trauma svc., unit physician Burn Unit, unit physician Surg. Intensive Care Unit, assoc. prof. dept. surgery and divsn. plastic, maxillofacial & reconstructive surgery, 1985—, interim life flight dir., 1994, dir. life flight/life care, 1994, vice chmn. dept. surgery, 1995, prof. surgery dept. surgery Divsns. Gen. Surgery and Plastic & Reconstructive Surgery, 1997, bd. dirs. Duke Ctr. Aesthetic Svcs., 1996, med. dir. Duke Ctr. Aesthetic Svcs., 1998, med. dir. 2B/2C clinic Duke Clinics, 2001, dir. peri-operative svcs., 2003; fellow hand surgery U. Louisville/Kleinert & Assocs., 1979; attending physician Durham VA Hosp., 1980; asst. prof. surgery and plastic surgery Duke U. Sch. Medicine, 1980; physician, med. control officer Duke Hosp. Helicopter Air Transport Svc.; attending physician dept. surgery and divsn. plastic surgery Durham Regional Hosp., 1991; clin. prof. divsn. plastic surgery U. NC, Chapel Hill, 1995, clin. prof. dept. surgery, 1996. Vice chmn. ACS NC Com. on Trauma, chmn., 1987—90; mem. med. policy com. Ctrl. Piedmont Profl. Stds. Rev. Orgn., Inc. Contbr. articles to med. jours., chapters to books. Fellow: ACS (v.p. NC chpt. 1995, pres. elect NC chpt. 1995—96, pres. NC chpt. 1996—97); mem.: AMA, Am. Soc. Plastic and Reconstructive Surgeons (mem. ethics com. 1997), So. Surgeons Club, Surg. Infection Soc., NC Soc. Plastic Maxillofacial and Reconstructive Surgeons, Southeastern Med.-Dental Soc., NC Indsl. Commn., NC Surg. Soc. (program chmn. 1988—89), Am. Burn Assn. (mem. burn prevention com.), Am. Assn. Plastic Surgeons (mem. constn. & by-laws com. 1995—96), Durham-Orange Med. Soc., NC Med. Soc., Am. Cleft Palate Assn. (assoc.). Office: Duke U Med Ctr Dept Surgery PO Box 3960 Durham NC 27710 Office Phone: 919-684-2854, 919-681-2670.

GEORGIADIS, MARGARET H. (MARGO), finance company executive; AB magna cum laude, Harvard Univ., MBA. Ptnr., head CRM practice McKinsey & Co., Chgo. & London; exec. v.p., chief mktg. officer Discover Fin. Services LLC div., Morgan Stanley, Riverwoods, Ill., 2004—. Baker Scholar. Mem.: Phi Beta Kappa. Office: Discover Fin Services LLC 2500 Lake Cook Rd Riverwoods IL 60015*

GEORGIOU, GEORGE, chemical engineer, educator; BSc, U. Manchester Inst. Sci. and Tech., 1981; MSChemE, Cornell U., 1983, PhD in Chem. Engring., 1987. Asst. prof. dept. chem. engring. U. Tex., Austin, 1986—91, assoc. prof., 1991—94, prof., 1994—, prof. biomedical engring., 1994—, Cullen Trust prof., 1997—98, Joan and Keys Curry/Cullen Trust endowed chair, 1998—2004, Joe C. Walter, Jr. endowed chair, 2004—. Mem. Inst. Molecular and Cellular Biology U. Tex., Austin, 1994—; R.B. Barton lectr. dept. chemistry & biochemistry U. Okla., 1997; B. Chance lectr. Inst. Medicine and Engring. U. Pa., 1998; Vaughan lectr. Calif. Inst. Tech., 1999; Bayer lectr. U. Calif., Berkeley, 2000; Caterpillar lectr. U. Iowa, 2001; Merck lectr. U. Va., 2003; Van Ness lectr. Rensselaer Poly. Inst., 2003; McCabe lectr. NC State U., 2005; Eastman Biotechnology lectr. Ga. Inst. Tech., 2005; Smith lectr. Cornell U., 2005. Contbr. articles to profl. jours. Recipient Presdl. Young Investigator award, NSF, 1987, E. Bergman award, US-Israel Sci. Found., 1995, Amgen Biochemical Engring. award, 2007. Fellow: AAAS, Am. Acad. Microbiol., Am. Inst. Med. and Biol. Engring.; mem.: NAE, AIChE (Profl. Progress award 2003, Food, Pharm. and Bioengineering award 2005), Protein Soc., Am. Soc. Engring. Edn., Am. Soc. Microbiol., Am. Chem. Soc. (Marvin J. Johnson award 2003). Achievements include patents in field. Office: Dept Chem Engring U Tex Austin 1 University Station C0400 Austin TX 78712-0231 Office Phone: 512-471-6975. Office Fax: 512-471-7963. E-mail: gg@che.utexas.edu.

GEORGOPOULOS, APOSTOLOS P., neuroscientist, neurologist, educator; b. Patras, Greece; MD, U. Athens, D of Physiology. Joined faculty Johns Hopkins U., 1976, prof., 1986; Am. Legion Brain Scis. chair, dir. Minneapolis Veteran Affairs Med. Ctr. U. Minn., 1991—; prof. neuroscience, neurology and psychiatry U. Minn. Med. Sch. Grantee McKnight Presdl. Endowed Chair, U. Minn., 2004. Mem.: Inst. Medicine, Nat. Acad. Scis. Office: U Minn Dept Neuroscience 6-145 JacH 1216 321 Church St S Minneapolis MN 55455 also: V A Med Ctr Brain Sci Ctr 11B 1 Veterans Dr Minneapolis MN 55417 Office Phone: 612-725-2282. E-mail: omega@umn.edu.

GEPFORD, BARBARA BEEBE, retired nutrition educator; b. Buffalo, Sept. 2, 1930; d. Kenneth Hildreth and Martha Bell (Griswold) Beebe; m. William George Gepford, Dec. 28, 1952; children: David, Scott, Joanna, Andrea. BS in Home Econs. Edn., Iowa State U., 1952. Nutrition instr. Sidon Girl's Sch., Lebanon, 1953-56; instr. textiles and clothing Beirut Univ. Coll., Lebanon, 1955-56, 62-63; nutrition cons. Hong Kong Coun. of Social Svcs., 1967-71; commd. fraternal worker Presbyn. U.S.A., Lebanon, Hong Kong, 1953-71; mgr. Lila's Fabric Store, Cambridge, Ohio, 1973-74. Overseas missionary advisor to Assembly Coun. of Presbyn. Ch., U.S.A., 1971-72. Elder Presbyn. Ch., New Concord, Ohio, 1974-79, mem. com. on Ministry, Detroit, 1987-94; pres. Presbyn. Women of Littlefield Ch., 1987-89, mem. session, 2006-; vice-moderator Presbyn. Women of Presbytery of Detroit, 1985-87, moderator, 1997-99; synod of covenant women's rep. Churchwide Coordinating Team of Presbyn. Women, 1999-2002; chair Presbyn. Women Triann. Global Exch. to Africa, 2002-03; elder, session mem. Littlefield Presbyn. Ch., Dearborn, Mich., 2006—; advisor YWCA Head Start Program, Dearborn, Mich., 1988-91; bd. dirs. YWCA, 1985-96, pres., 1993-95. Named Ohio Mother of the Yr., Am. Mothers Com., New Concord, 1978. Mem., AAUW (bd. dirs. 1987-89, internat. rels. area rep.). Democrat. Avocations: reading, gardening, sewing, knitting. Home: 9421 Westwind Dr Livonia MI 48150-4530 Personal E-mail: barbbgepford@msn.com, wiamfrd@msn.com.

GEPFORD, WILLIAM GEORGE, minister; b. Kansas City, Mo., Jan. 12, 1927; s. Herbert John and Anna Ruth (Minckemeyer) G.; m. Barbara Joan Beebe, Dec. 28, 1952; children: David Proctor, Scott Allen, Joanna Lynn, Andrea Laine. BS in Elec. Engring., Colo. State U., 1949; MDiv., McCormick Sem., 1953; MEd, U. Colo., 1957; DSc in Theology, San Francisco Sem., 1973. Ordained to ministry Presbyn. Ch. (U.S.A.), 1953. Edn. missionary Presbyn. Ch., Lebanon, 1953-63; dean students Am. U., Beirut, 1961-63; asst. min. First Presbyn. Ch., Boulder, Colo., 1963-65; missionary, student min. Presbyn. Ch., Hong Kong, 1965-71; chaplain, student life dir. Muskingum Coll., New Concord, Ohio, 1972-79; dir. Am./Arab Ministry Presbytery of Detroit, Mich., 1979—. Dean of students Am. U. Beirut, Lebanon, 1961-63; dir. student ctr. YMCA (Chinese), Hong Kong, 1965-71; acting assoc. dean of students, Muskingum Coll., New Concord, 1977-78; mem. gen. assembly, adv. study com. on Islam, N.Y., 1983-86; bd. dir. Interfaith Activities, Presbytery of Detroit; founder Muslim/Christian Dialogue Group, 1985; adv. bd. Arab Cmty. Ctr. of Econ. and Social Svcs., Dearborn, 1983-2003; mem. Am. Arab Anti-Discrimination com., adv. com., Detroit, 1984-2004, others; cons. Interfaith Ministries, Presbytery of Detroit, 1992—. Mem. adv. bd. ACCESS, Dearborn, Mich., 1985-2003; clergy participant Interfaith Round Table of Detroit, 1985—; bd. dir. Human Svcs., Inc., Dearborn; mem. citizens adv. bd. WTVS Ch. 56 PBS, Detroit, 1986-89; bd. dir. Freedom House, Detroit, McGehee Interfaith Loan Fund, 2001-2005, Mich. Interfaith Trust Fund, 2002-04; mem. Coalition Human Rights, 1999-2003, Met. Christian Coun., 1996—; mem. planning com. Detroit 300 Celebration. With USN, 1945-46. Recipient Steward Kerr Ecumenical award, Met. Christian Coun., 2007. Mem. McCormick Sem. Alumni Assn. (pres.-elect 1991-93), Kiwanis (pres. Dearborn 1986-87), Phi Delta Kappa. Democrat. Home: 9421 Westwind Dr Livonia MI 48150-4530 Personal E-mail: wiamfrd@msn.com.

GEPHARDT, DICK (RICHARD ANDREW GEPHARDT), consulting compay executive, lawyer, former congressman; b. St. Louis, Jan. 31, 1941; s. Louis Andrew and Loreen Estelle (Cassell) Gephardt; m. Jane Ann Byrnes, Aug. 13, 1966; children: Matthew, Christine, Katherine. BS, Northwestern U., 1962; JD, U. Mich., 1965. Bar: Mo. 1965. Ptnr. Thompson & Mitchell Law Firm, St. Louis, 1965-76; Dem. committeeman 14th ward, City of St. Louis, St. Louis, 1968—71, alderman 14th ward, 1971-76; mem. US Congress from 3d dist. Mo., 1977—2005, majority leader, 1989—94, minority leader, 1995—2002; founder, pres., CEO Gephardt Group LLC, Atlanta, 2005—; sr. counsel DLA Piper Rudnick Gray Cary US LLP, Washington, 2005—. Bd. dirs. Centene Corp., 2006—, Spirit Aerosystems Holdings, Inc., 2006—, Embarq Corp., 2007—, US Steel Corp. Co-author (with Michael Wessel): An Even Better Place: America in the 21st Century, 1999. Pres. Children's Hematology Rsch. Assn., St. Louis Children's Hosp., 1973-76. Served to capt. Air Nat. Guard, 1965—71. Mem.: US Assn. Former Members of Congress, Metro St. Louis Bar Assn., Mo. Bar Assn., Boy Scouts Am., Am. Legion, Mid-Town Club (St. Louis), Kiwanis. Democrat. candidate for Dem. presdl. nomination, 1987-88, 2003-04. Office: Gephardt Group LLC 2496 Jett Ferry Rd Ste 102 Atlanta GA 30338 also: DLA Piper Rudnick Gray Cary US LLP 1200 19th St NW Washington DC 20036*

GEPHARDT, DONALD LOUIS, music educator; b. St. Louis, Mar. 27, 1937; s. Louis Andrew and Loreen Estelle (Cassell) G.; m. Zenaida Otero Gephardt, June 10, 2000; children from previous marriage: Lisa Diane, Francis Joseph. B Music Edn., Drake U., 1959; BS, Juilliard Sch., 1961, MS, 1962; EdD, Washington U., St. Louis, 1978. Clarinet instr. Henry Street Settlement Music Sch., NYC, 1961-64; music tchr. Wantagh (N.Y.) Elem. Schs., 1962-67; music tchr., band and orch. dir. W.C. Mepham High Sch., Bellmore, N.Y., 1967-70; assoc. prof. music, band and jazz ensemble conductor Nassau C.C., Garden City, N.Y., 1970-83, chmn. music dept., 1977-83, dean instrn., 1984-90; dean Coll. Fine and Performing Arts, Rowan U., Glassboro, N.J., 1990—, acting exec. v.p., provost, 1994-95. Clarinetist Des Moines Symphony Orch., 1956-59, Aspen (Colo.) Festival Orchestra, 1959-60, Henry Schuman's Wind Ensemble Workshop, 1965-69, L.I. Symphony Orch., 1970-82; clarinetist Seuffert Band, 1962-90, Great Neck (N.Y.) Symphony, 1967-80; contbr. articles to profl. jours. Bd. dirs. L.I. Symphony, 1980-82; surrogate spkr. Richard Gephardt for Pres., 1987-88, 2004. Mem. Music Educators Nat. Conf. (chpt. advisor 1970-83, 2-yr. coll. chmn. Ea. divsn. 1982-83), N.Y. State Sch. Music Assn. (chmn. rsch. 1982-84), N.J. Music Educators Assn., Alliance for Arts Edn. N.J. (past pres.), Nassau Music Educators Assn. (rec. sec. 1968-69, 1st v.p. 1969-70, pres. 1970-71), Coll. Music Soc., Internat. Coun. of Fine Arts Deans (pres.-elect 2001-02, pres. 2003-05, past pres. 2005—), Arts Edn. Partnership (steering com.), Phila. Arts Edn. Partnership (bd. dirs. 2004—), Phi Mu Alpha Sinfonia. Democrat. Avocations: cooking, reading. Office: Rowan Univ Dept Music Glassboro NJ 08028-1701 Home Phone: 302-764-5755; Office Phone: 856-256-4551. Business E-Mail: gephardt@rowan.edu.

GERACHIS, GEORGE MATTHEW, lawyer; b. Washington, Dec. 7, 1957; BA with high distinction, U. Va., 1979, JD, 1983. Bar: Tex. 1983, US Dist. Ct., US Tax Ct. Ptnr., mem. firm mgmt. com., co-head Tax Sect., leader Fed. Tax Controversy and Litig. practice Vinson & Elkins LLP, Houston. Mem.: ABA, Internat. Fiscal Assn., Houston Bar Assn. Office: Vinson & Elkins LLP First City Tower 1001 Fannin St, Ste 2300 Houston TX 77002-6760 Office Fax: 713-758-1056. E-mail: ggerachis@velaw.com.

GERAGHTY, DIANE C., law educator; BA, U. California; MA, U. Chgo., 1967; JD, Northwestern U. Faculty mem. Loyola U. Chgo., 1977—, prof. law, dir. Civitas ChildLaw Ctr., acting dean, 2004—05. Author: Juvenile Law Bencbook, Vols. I and II, 2001; co-author: Training the Lawyer to Represent the Whole Child: In re Pena, 2003; mem. editl. bd. Ill. Child Welfare; contbr. articles to law jours. Named Juvenile Justice Pioneer, 2000; recipient Livingston Hall Juvenile Justice Award, ABA, 2001, Leonard Jay Schrager Award, Chgo. Bar Found., 2003. Mem.: Ill. State Ct. Improvement Project (co-chair), Ill. Juvenile Justice Initiative (hon. bd. mem.), Citizens Com. on Juvenile Ct. (chair), Chgo. Children's Advocacy Ctr. (bd. mem., co-chair Strategic Planning Com.), Am. Civil Liberties Union (mem. Nat. Bd. Dirs.). Office: Loyola U Chgo Sch Law 1 E Pearson St Rm 506 Chicago IL 60611 E-mail: dgeragh@luc.edu.

GERAGHTY, ELIZABETH, food products executive; b. 1966; MBA, Northwestern Univ. Kellogg Sch. Mgmt., Chgo., 2000. With Sara Lee Corp., Chgo., 1990—, food sci., 1990, v.p. coffee and tea brand mgmt., 2005—. Named one of 40 Under Forty, Crain's Bus. Chgo., 2005.*

GERAGHTY, JAMES D., health science association administrator; b. Bronx, July 8, 1971; s. James Joseph and Donna Elizabeth Geraghty. BA in Journalism, Temple U., Phila., 1994. Exec. asst. Walt Disney Co., NYC, 1994—96; sales assoc. Random Ho., Inc., NYC, 1996—97; mgr. subsidiary rights Penguin USA, NYC, 1997—2001, Random Ho., Inc., 2001—02; sr. mgr. subsidiary rights Harper Collins Pubs., NYC, 2003—06; devel. officer Alzheimer's Assn., Denville, NJ, 2006—. Mem.: Assn. Fundraising Profls.

GERAGHTY, PATRICK D., lawyer; b. Woodside, NY, Jan. 9, 1970; BA, SUNY, Stony Brook, 1992; JD, NY Law Sch., 1995. Bar: NJ 1995, NY 1996, US Dist. Ct. Dist. NJ 1996, US Dist. Ct. Ea. & So. Districts NY 1996. Ptnr. Wilson, Elser, Moskowitz, Edelman & Dicker LLP, NYC. Office: Wilson Elser Moskowitz Edelman & Dicker LLP 23rd Fl 150 E 42nd St New York NY 10017-5639 Office Phone: 212-490-3000 ext. 2524. Office Fax: 212-490-3038. Business E-Mail: geraghtyp@wemed.com.

GERAGHTY, PAUL D., bank executive; B, Villanova U., Pa., 1974; grad. student, Lehigh U., Bethlehem, Pa. With CoreStates; head Specialized Industries divsn. Nat. City Corp., 1999—2004, head Large Corp. and Treasury Mgmt. divsns., 2001—04, head Internat. divsn., 2002—04, sr. v.p., 2002, exec. v.p. comml. banking - regional. Office: Nat City Corp Nat City Ctr 1900 E Ninth St Cleveland OH 44114-3484 Office Phone: 216-222-2000.*

GERAGOS, MARK JOHN, lawyer; b. LA, Oct. 5, 1957; BA, Haverford Coll., 1979; JD, Loyola Marymount U., 1982. Pvt. practice, LA; with Calif. Legis. Assembly Resolution, 2003; mng. ptnr. Geragos & Geragos, P.C., LA. Legal cons. CNBC, MSNBC, Fox News Svc., CNN; spkr. in field. Guest, legal commentator Today Show, Good Morning America, Dateline NBC, Larry King Live, Greta Van Susteren's On the Record, 60 Minutes, 48 Hours. Named Trial Lawyer of Yr., LA Criminal Cts. Bar Assn., 2006; named one of 100 Most Influential Attys. in Calif., Calif. Bus. Law mag., LA's Superlawyers; recipient Jerry Giesler Meml. award, Criminal Cts. Bar Assn., 1999, Humanitarian of Yr. award, Mexican Am. Grocers Assn., 2001, Resolution award for pioneering work in internet TV, Calif. Legis. Assembly, 2003, Profl. of Yr. award, Am. Profl. Soc., 2004, Calif. Lawyer of Yr. award, Civil Litig., 2006. Mem.: LA County Bar Assn. (mem. jud. appointments com., mem. outstanding trial jurist award com. 1992—93, jud. com. 1994—), State Bar Calif. Office: Geragos & Geragos PC 644 S Figueroa St Los Angeles CA 90017 Office Phone: 213-625-3900. Office Fax: 213-625-1600. E-mail: geragos@geragos.com.*

GERAKITIS, RICHARD, lawyer; b. Atlanta, 1956; AB magna cum laude, Univ. Ga., 1978; JD, Mercer Univ., 1981. Bar: Ga. 1981. Assoc. Cashin, Morton & Mullins, 1981—85, ptnr., 1986—97; ptnr., practice group leader, labor and employment Troutman Sanders LLP, Atlanta, 1997—. Named a Super Lawyer, Atlanta Mag., 2004, Legal Elite in labor/employment, Ga. Trend Mag., 2004. Mem.: Atlanta Bar Assn., Nat. Coll. Trial Advocacy (instr. 1996—98), State Bar Ga., Old Warhorse Lawyers Club. Office: Troutman Sanders LLP One Logan Sq Ste 5200 600 Peachtree St NE Atlanta GA 30308-2216 Office Phone: 404-885-3328. Office Fax: 404-962-6568. Business E-Mail: richard.gerakitis@troutmansanders.com.

GERALD, BARRY, retired radiology educator, neuroscientist; b. Greenville, Miss., Feb. 10, 1934; s. Louis Elmo and Eula (Mitchell) G.; m. Marjorie Brown, Aug. 6, 1955; children: Lucy Gerald Cook, Lee, Paul. Student, U. Miss., Oxford, 1951-54; MD, U. Miss., Jackson, 1958. Diplomate Am. Bd. Radiology. Intern Hermann Hosp., Houston, 1958-59, resident in radiology, 1959-62; fellow in pediatric radiology Children's Hosp. Med. Ctr., Cin., 1962-64; mem. faculty dept. radiology U. Ark., Little Rock, 1964-65, 67-69; dir. radiology dept. Children's Hosp. Med. Ctr., Oakland, Calif., 1965-66; mem. faculty dept. radiology U. Tenn. Coll. Medicine, Memphis, 1969—2004, prof., chmn. dept., 1979-95; fellow in neuroradiology Tufts-New Eng. Med. Ctr., Boston, 1971-72, interim chair dept. radiology, 2004—. Dir. radiology dept. Le Bonheur Children's Hosp., Memphis, 1983-88, 1991-2002; acting dir. radiology dept. St. Jude Children's Rsch. Hosp., Memphis, 1985-87; trainee Nat. Cancer Inst., 1960-62. Contbr. articles to med. jours., chpts. to books. Fellow Am. Coll. Radiology; mem. Am. Soc. Neuroradiology, Soc. for Pediatric Radiology, Radiol. Soc. N.Am. (councillor 1980-85), Am. Roentgen Ray Soc., Southeastern Neuroradiologic Soc. (founder, pres. 1977-78), So. Radiologic Conf. (pres. 1975-76). Avocations: tennis, american history. Home: 694 Clanlo Dr Memphis TN 38104-5067 Office: U Tenn Dept Radiology 800 Madison Ave Memphis TN 38103-3400 E-mail: bgerald@utmem.edu.

GERALD, MICHAEL CHARLES, pharmacy educator; b. N.Y.C., Nov. 20, 1939; s. Tobias Gerson and Ruby Rose (Weinstock) G.; m. Gloria Elaine Gruber, Jan. 31, 1965; children— Marc Jonathan, Melissa Suzanne, B.S. in Pharmacy, Fordham U., 1961; Ph.D., Ind. U., 1968. Registered pharmacist, N.Y. Postdoctoral fellow USPHS, U. Chgo., 1968-69; asst. prof. Coll. Pharmacy Ohio State U., Columbus, 1969-74, assoc. prof., 1974-80, prof., 1980-93, prof. and assoc. dean., 1984-93; dean, prof. Sch. Pharmacy U. Conn., Storrs, 1993-02; prof., 2002—; cons. WHO, Geneva, 1983-84; mem. adv. panel U.S. Pharmacopeia Com. Revision, Washington, 1980-85; bd. dirs. Patient Access Network Found., 2006—. Author: Pharmacology: An Introduction to Drugs, 2d edit. 1981, Nursing Pharmacology and Therapeutics, 2d edit. 1988, The Poisonous Pen of Agatha Christie, 1993, Complete Idiot's Guide to Prescription Drugs, 2006; co-author: The Nurse's Guide to Drug Therapy: Drug Profiles for Patient Care, 1984; editor; Instruction in Pharmacology: New Approaches and New Faces, 1979. Mem. FDA Drug Abuse Adv. Com., 1993-96. Served to 1st lt. USAF, 1963-65. USPHS fellow Ind. U., 1965-68; Gustavus A. Pfeiffer Meml. rsch. fellow Am. Found. Pharm. Edn., 1983-84. Fellow Acad. Pharm. Scis. (sect. sec. 1975-77, sect. v.p. 1978-79). (sect. sec. 1975-77, sect. v.p. 1978-79); mem. Am. Assn. Colls. Pharmacy (bd. dirs. 1980-82), Am. Soc. Pharmacology and Exptl. Therapeutics. Avocations: photography, reading, music, walking. Home Phone: 860-487-4675; Office Phone: 860-486-5416. Business E-Mail: michael.gerald@uconn.edu.

GERALDSON, RAYMOND I., JR., lawyer; b. Racine, Wis., Oct. 19, 1940; s. Raymond I. Sr. and Evelyn (Thorpe) G.; m. Melinda Paine, June 13, 1964; children: Amy Geraldson-Bhote, Raymond I. III. BA, DePauw U., 1962; JD, Northwestern U., 1965. Bar: Ill. 1965, D.C. 1966, U.S. Dist. Ct. (no. dist.) Ill. 1967. Ptnr. Pattishall, McAuliffe, Newbury, Hilliard & Geraldson, Washington, 1965-67, Chgo., 1967—. Adj. prof. John Marshall Law Sch. 1978—; lectr. in field. Contbr. articles on trademark law to profl. jours. Trustee Kendall Coll., 1985—, chmn., 1990-2000. Mem. ABA, Ill. State Bar Assn. (coun. sect. intellectual property law 1978-82, chmn. 1980-81), Chgo. Bar Assn., 7th Cir., Intellectual Property Law Assn. Chgo. (bd. dirs. 1984-86, 92-93, pres. 1991-92), Internat. Trademark Assn. (bd. dirs. 1985-87), Am. Intellectual Property Law Assn., Lawyers for Creative Arts (hons. coun. 1994—, bd. dirs. 1974-94, pres. 1976-78), Lawyers Club Chgo., Econ. Club Chgo., Sunset Ridge Country Club, Union League Club of Chgo., Chi. Office: Pattishall McAuliffe Newbury Hilliard & Geraldson 311 S Wacker Dr Ste 5000 Chicago IL 60606-6631

GERARD, GARY, neurologist; b. NYC, Apr. 16, 1949; s. Victor and Sylvia G.; m. Pauline Judd; 1 child, Michael. BA, NYU, 1971; MD, Hahnemann U., 1975. Diplomate Am. Bd. Neurology and Psychiatry. Intern medicine Brookdale Med. Ctr., Bklyn., 1975-76; resident in diagnostic radiology Mt. Sinai Med. Ctr., NYC, 1976-78; resident in neurology L.I. Jewish Med. Ctr., New Hyde Park, NY, 1978-81; chief of neurology Winthrop U. Hosp., Mineola, NY, 1984-89; assoc. prof. neurology and radiology, dir. cerebrovascular lab. Med. Coll. Ohio, Toledo, 1990-94, vice chmn. neurology, 1991-94; med. dir. Neurology Ctr. Ohio, Toledo, 1994—, dir., 1994-96. Contbr. chpts. to books; guest editor jour. Seminars in Neurology, 1986. Bd. dirs. Ohio Rsch. Ctr., Toledo, 1994-97. Recipient Robert J. Tidrick award Med. Coll. Ohio, 1991. Mem. Am. Soc. Neuroimaging (bd. dirs. 1984-90).

GERARD, JAMES WILSON, publishing consultant; b. Chgo., May 16, 1935; s. Ralph Waldo and Margaret (Wilson) G. Student U. Vt., 1955, Roosevelt U., 1955-59. Ptnr. UNIPUB, NYC, 1962-77; pres. Brookfield (Vt.) Pub. Co., 1977—. Bd. dirs. Renouf Pub. Co., Ltd. Mem. Am. Assn. Scholarly Pub., Les Ambassadeurs Club. Democrat. Office: Brookfield Mktg Inc 1517 Sagebrush Rd Palm Springs CA 92264 Office Phone: 760-320-8663. Personal E-mail: jgerard@dc.rr.com.

GERARD, JULES BERNARD, law educator; b. St. Louis, May 20, 1929; s. John Baptist and Faith Vera (Clinton) G.; m. Camilla Roma Smith, Aug. 8, 1953; children: Lisa, Karen, Julia. Student, Iowa State Coll., 1947-49; AB, Washington U., St. Louis, 1957, JD, 1958. Bar: NY 1959, US Supreme Ct. 1979. Assoc. Donovan, Leisure, Newton & Irvine, NYC, 1958-60; asst. prof. law U. Mo., Columbia, 1960-62; asst. prof., assoc. prof. law Washington U., 1962-67, prof., 1967-99, prof. emeritus, 1999—. Author: Local Regulation of Adult Businesses, 1992, Proposed Washington DC Amendment, 1979, (with others) Sum and Substance Constitutional Law, 1976, (with others) Federal Land Use Law, 1986; editor: 100 Years of 14th Amendment, 1973; editor-in-chief Washington U. Law Quar., 1958; contbr. articles to profl. jours., chpts. to books. Mem. Mo. Adv. com. US Commn. on Civil Rights, 1987-92. Served to 1st lt. USAF, 1950-54 Mem. ABA. Republican. Avocations: collecting scrimshaw and antique photographica, photography. Home: 1564 Yarmouth Point Dr Chesterfield MO 63017-5639 Business E-Mail: gerard@law.wustl.edu.

GERARD, LEO W., labor union executive; b. Sudbury, Ont., 1947; m. Susan Gerard; children: Kari-Ann, Meaghan. LLD (hon.), Laurentian U., 1994; attended, Canadian Labour Congress Labour Coll., 1996—98. Staff rep. United Steelworkers Am. USWA, 1977, dir. Dist. 6 Ont., 1985—91, nat. dir. Can., 1991, internat. sec.-treas., 1993—2001, internat. pres., 2001—05, pres., 2005—; dir. Dist. 6 Ont., Canada, 1985—91; nat. dir. Can., 1991—93; chmn. Steelworkers Health and Welfare Fund, 1996—98; with Heartland Labor Capital Funds. Contbr. articles to profl. pubs. Office: United Steelworkers 5 Gateway Ctr Pittsburgh PA 15222

GERARD, ROY DUPUY, retired oil company executive; b. New Orleans, Sept. 14, 1931; s. Lester Charles and Helene (Dupuy) G.; m. Minnie Harper, May 17, 1958; children: Roy Dupuy Jr., Nannette Gerard Helmcamp, Carl, Denise Ingram. BSChemE, La. State U., 1953, MSChemE, 1958. Chemist, technologist various plants Shell Chem. Co., Houston, La., N.Y., Calif., 1958-69; dept. head Shell Devel. Co., Emeryville, Calif., 1969-71, dir. indsl. chems. and petrochems. Houston, 1973-75, mgr. chem. R & D, 1975-77, gen. mgr. Westhollow rsch., 1982-90; pres. Saudi Petrochem. Co., Al Jubail, Saudi Arabia, 1980-82; mgr. logistics econs., supply and econs. and mktg. Shell Oil Co., Houston, 1971-73, gen. mgr. engring. products, 1977-80, v.p. health, safety and environ., 1990-92, ret., 1992; pvt. investor, stocks, bonds, etc., 1992—. Vice chmn. coun. environ. affairs Conf. Bd., 1991—; chmn. chem. engring. vis. com. U. Tex., Austin, 1985-87; chem. engring. vis. com. La. State U., Baton Rouge, 1987-90, dean's adv. com., 1990-2001; chem. engring. vis. com. Tex. A&M U., College Station, 1989, U. Tenn., Knoxville, 1989 1st lt. C.E., U.S. Army, 1954-56. Named to Engring. Hall of Distinction, La. State U., 1996. Mem. AICE, Coun. for Chem. Rsch. (chmn. 1991—), Am. Indsl. Health Coun. (bd. dirs., exec. com. 1990—), Am. Petroleum Inst. (health and environ. gen. com. 1990—), Northgate Country Club, Raveneaux Country Club (Spring, Tex.). Republican. Roman Catholic. Avocations: fishing, golf, woodworking. Personal E-mail: rgerard914@aol.com.

GERARD, WHITNEY IAN, lawyer; b. NYC, Oct. 31, 1934; s. Harold Todd and Beatrice Roma (Meyer) G.; m. Marion Lehane, Apr. 1, 1966; children: Ian Alexandre, Stefan Meredith. AB, Princeton U., 1956; JD, Harvard U., 1963. Bar: N.Y. 1964. Wine exporter Alexis Lichine et Cie, Bordeaux, France, 1956-58; wine cons. S.S. Pierce Co., Boston, 1960-75; assoc., then ptnr. Alexander and Green, NYC, 1963-84; ptnr., chmn. internat. practice comm. Chadbourne and Parke LLP, NYC, 1984—. Bd. dirs. Dreyfus Liquid Assets, Inc., The Dreyfus Fund, Inc., Dreyfus Worldwide Dollar Money Market Fund, Inc., Dreyfus Lifetime Portfolios, Inc., Dreyfus Short Intermediate Mcpl. Bond Fund, Dreyfus Short Intermediate Govt. Fund. and other Dreyfus funds. 1st lt. USAF, 1958-60. Mem. ABA, N.Y. State Bar Assn., Internat. Bar Assn., Univ. Club, Ancient Order of Beefeaters (Chief Warder 1965-90). Democrat. Avocations: classical music, ballet, theater, mountain hiking, literature. Home: 940 Park Ave New York NY 10028-0311 also: 102 W Center Rd West Stockbridge MA 01266-9378 Office: Chadbourne & Parke LLP 30 Rockefeller Plz New York NY 10112-0129 Office Phone: 212-408-5265.

GERARD-SHARP, MONICA FLEUR, communications executive; b. London, Oct. 4, 1951; came to U.S., 1975; d. John Hugh Gerard-Sharp and Doreen May (Kearney) Dewhurst; m. Ali Edward Wambold, Nov. 21, 1981; children: Marina, Daniela, Dominica. BA in Philosophy and Lit. with honors, U. Warwick, Eng., 1973; MBA in Fin., Mktg. and Internat. Bus., Columbia U., 1980. Editor Inst. Chem. Engrs., London, 1973-74; sub-editor TV Times, London, 1974-75; press officer, editor UN, NYC, 1975-78; bus. mgr. Time-Life Video, NYC, 1980-81; mgr. fin. analysis Time-Life Films, NYC, 1981; v.p. T.V.I.S., NYC, 1982-83; dir. strategy and devel. HBO, ATC, NYC, 1984-85; asst. treas., officer Time Inc., NYC, 1985—87; pub. Travel Today and other mags. Fairchild Pubs. subs. Capital Cities/ABC, NYC, 1987-88; dir. video programming Fairchild Pubs., Capital Cities/ABC, NYC, 1988-89; pub. Entrée and Home Fashions Mags., NYC, 1988-90; pres. Monali Inc., NYC, 1991—. Cons. UN Bus. Council, N.Y.C., 1979; bd. rep. U.S.A. Network, N.Y.C., 1983-85. Editor: Everyone's United Nations, 1977; contbg. editor Asia Pacific Forum, 1976-77; contbr. articles to profl. jours. and mags., 1973-78. Treas. Help the Aged, Eng.; nat. devel. bd. Chances for Children, 1995-, pres. 2001-2003; adv. bd. Am. Mus. Natural History, 1998—; pres. bd. Am. Friends of Royal Ct. Theatre, 1998-2000, Historic Royal Palaces, 2005-, Nat. Theatre, 2006-. Bronfman fellow, 1979-80. Mem. Nat. Acad. Cable Programming, Am. Film Inst., Beta Gamma Sigma. Roman Catholic. Avocations: antiques, photography, wildlife. Home: Deer Park 128 Sunset Hill Rd Pleasant Valley NY 12569 Office: Monali Inc 26 E 80th St New York NY 10021-0110

GERATHY, E. CARROLL, retired insurance company executive, real estate developer; b. Long Island City, NY, June 25, 1915; s. Joseph Hewson and Emma E. (Donady) G.; m. Julia F. Gill, Sept. 7, 1942; children: Nancy, John; m. Joyce K. Baker, Dec. 31, 1972; children: Stephen Baker, Nancy Baker; m. Betty Ann Durkin, Jan. 27, 1984. MBA, U. Chgo., 1962. C.L.U. With McKesson & Robbins, Inc., 1933-48; with Prudential Ins. Co. Am., 1948-78, sr. v.p., 1964-78; project dir. Hilton Hawaiian Village, Hilton Hotels Corp., 1979-81, Third Newark Gateway Urban Renewal Assn., 1981-91. Mem. N.J. C. of C., Canoe Brook Country Club (N.J.). Home: 42 Knob Hill Dr Summit NJ 07901-3051 Personal E-mail: carbet@att.net.

GERATY, LAWRENCE THOMAS, academic administrator, archaeologist, educator; b. St. Helena, Calif., Apr. 21, 1940; s. Thomas Sinclair and Hazel Mae (McVicker) G.; m. Gillian Anne Keough, Aug. 5, 1962; children: Brent, Julie. BA, Pacific Union Coll., 1962; MA, Andrews U., 1963, BD, 1965; PhD, Harvard U., 1972. Pastor 7th Day Adventist Ch., Calif., 1962-66; instr. old testament Andrews U., Berrien Springs, Mich., 1966-72, asst. prof. archaeology and history, 1972-76, assoc. prof. archaeology and history, 1976-80, prof., 1980-85; curator S.H. Horn Archaeol. Mus., Berrien Springs, Mich., 1976-85; dir. Inst. Archaeology Andrews U., Berrien Springs, 1981-85; pres. Atlantic Union Coll., Lancaster, Mass., 1985-93, La Sierra U., Riverside, Calif., 1993—. Project dir. Excavation of Tell Hesban, Jordan, 1973-76, Madaba Plains Project, Jordan, 1984—; v.p. Am. Ctr. of Oriental Rsch., Amman, 1985-03; pres. Am. Schs. Oriental Rsch., Boston, 2003-07. Editor, contbr. articles to profl. jours. Bd. dirs. Thayer Symphony Orch., Lancaster, Mass., 1985-93; mem. Edn. Forum of Clinton, Mass., 1990-93. Fulbright fellow, 1970-71, Robert H. Pfeiffer fellow, 1970-71; grantee Ford Found., 1969-70, Ctr. Field Rsch., 1976, NEH, 1979. Mem. Soc. Bibl. Literature (pres. 1988-90), Archeol. Inst. Am., Am. Schs. Oriental Rsch., Clinton C. of C. (bd. dirs. 1985-92), Riverside C. of C. (bd. dirs. 1996—), Raincross Club, Employers Group (bd. dirs. 1996-, chair 2006-07), United Way (chair 2003-04), Monday Morning Group. Seventh-Day Adventist. Office: La Sierra U Office of Pres 4500 Riverwalk Pkwy Riverside CA 92515 Home Phone: 951-689-7562; Office Phone: 951-785-2020. Business E-Mail: lgeraty@lasierra.edu.

GERBA, CHARLES PETER, microbiologist, educator; b. Blue Island, Ill., Sept. 10, 1945; s. Peter and Virginia (Roulo) G.; m. Peggy Louise Scheitlin, June 6, 1970; children: Peter, Phillip. BS in Microbiology, Ariz. State U., 1969; PhD in Microbiology, U. Miami, 1973. Postdoctoral fellow Baylor Coll. Medicine, Houston, 1973-74, asst. prof. microbiology, 1974-81; assoc. prof. U. Ariz., Tucson, 1981-85, prof., 1985—. Cons. EPA, Tucson, 1980—, World Health Orgn., Pan Am. Health Orgn., 1989—; advisor CRC Press, Boca Raton, Fla., 1981—. Editor: Methods in Environmental Virology, 1982, Groundwater Pollution Microbiology, 1984, Phage Ecology, 1987, Pollution Sci., 1996; contbr. numerous articles to profl. and sci. jours. Mem. Pima County Bd. Health, 1986-92; mem. sci. adv. bd. EPA, 1987-95. Recipient McKee medal Water Environ. Fedn., 1996; named Outstanding Research Scientist U. Ariz., 1984, 92, Outstanding Rsch. Team, 1994. Fellow AAAS (environ. sci. and engring.), Am. Acad. Microbiology, Am. Soc. Microbiology (divsn. chmn. 1982-83, 87-88, pres. Ariz. chpt. 1984-85, councilor 1985-88); mem. Internat. Assn. Water Pollution Rsch. (sr. del. 1985-91), Am. Water Works Assn. (A.P. Black award 1997), Water Quality Assn. (Hom. Mem. award 1998). Achievements include research in environmental microbiology, colloid transport in ground water, wastewater reuse and risk assessment. Home: 1980 W Paseo Monserrat Tucson AZ 85704-1329 Office: U Ariz Dept Microbiol & Immunol Wat Tucson AZ 85721-0001 Office Phone: 520-621-6906. Business E-Mail: gerba@ag.arizona.edu.

GERBER, DANIEL J., lawyer; b. Greenville, SC, Jan. 14, 1963; BA in Polit. Sci., U. Fla., 1985, JD, 1988. Bar: Fla. 1988, cert.: US Ct. Appeals, 11th Cir. Ptnr. Rumberger, Kirk & Caldwell LLP. Gen. counsel Fla. Pest Mgmt. Assn. Author: Get an Annual Legal Audit, 2002; contbr. articles to profl. jours.; Lectr. in field. Named one of The Nation's Top Litigators, Nat. Law Jour., 2007; recipient Pres. award, Fla. Pest Mgmt. Assn., 2007. Mem.: Orange County Bar Assn., Def. Rsch. Inst., Fla. Pest Control Assn., Fla. Def. Lawyers Assn., ABA, Fedn. of Def. and Corp. Counsel. Office: Rumberger Kirk & Caldwell PA Lincoln Plz 300 S Orange Ave Ste 1400 Orlando FL 32801 Office Phone: 407-872-7300. Office Fax: 407-841-2133. E-mail: dgerber@rumberger.com.*

GERBER, DEAN N., lawyer; b. Chgo., Dec. 4, 1959; married. BS magna cum laude, U. of Delaware, 1982; JD cum laude, U. of Ill., 1985. CPA Ill., 1984; bar: Ill. 1985. Joined Chapman & Cutler; assoc. atty. Vedder, Price, Kaufman & Kammholz, 1991, shareholder, 1992—, chair equipment fin. practice group. Mem.: Omicron Sigma Delta, Phi Kappa Phi. Office: Vedder Price Kaufman & Kammholz 222 N LaSalle St Chicago IL 60601

GERBER, DOUGLAS EARL, classics educator; b. North Bay, Ont., Can., Sept. 14, 1933; s. Earl Jacob and Bertha (Cox) G.; m. Joan Isobel Warner, Nov. 22, 1986; 1 dau., Allison S. BA, U. Western Ont., London, 1955, MA, 1956; PhD, U. Toronto, 1959. Lectr. Greek U. Toronto, 1958-59; mem. faculty dept. classics U. Western Ont., London, 1959-99, assoc. prof., 1964-69, prof., 1969-99, chmn. dept., 1969-97, vice provost for acad. affairs, 1984-86, W.S. Fox chair of classics. Author: A Bibliography of Pindar, 1513-1966, 1969, Euterpe: An Anthology of Early Greek Lyric, Elegiac and Iambic Poetry, 1970, Emendations in Pindar, 1513-1972, 1976, Pindar's Olympian One: A Commentary, 1982, Lexicon in Bacchylidem, 1984, Greek Iambic Poetry, 1999, Greek Elegiac Poetry, 1999, A Commentary on Pindar Olympian Nine, 2002; editor Greek Poetry and Philosophy; Studies in Honor of Leonard Woodbury, 1984, A Companion to the Greek Lyric Poets, 1997. Mem. Classical Assn. Canada (treas. 1960-62, pres. 1988-90), Am. Philol. Assn. (editor trans. 1974-82), Classical Assn. Middle West and South, Classical Assn. (Gt. Britain). Home: 2 Grosvenor St London ON Canada N6A 1Y4 Office: U Western Ont Dept Classics London ON Canada N6A 3K7 E-mail: degerber@uwo.ca.

GERBER, JOEL, federal judge; b. Chgo., July 16, 1940; s. Peter H. and Marcia L. (Weber) G.; m. Judith R. Smilgoff, Aug. 18, 1963; children— Jay Lawrence, Jeffrey Mark, Jon Victor BSBA, Roosevelt U., Chgo., 1962; JD, DePaul U., Chgo., 1965; LLM, Boston U., 1968. Bar: Ill. 1965, Ga. 1974. Trial atty. IRS, Boston, 1965-72, staff asst. to regional counsel Atlanta, 1972-76, dist. counsel Nashville, 1976-80, dep. chief counsel Washington, 1980-83, acting chief counsel, 1983-84; judge US Tax Ct., Washington, 1984—99, 2000—06, sr. judge, 1999—2000, 2006—, chief judge Washington, 2004—06; gen. counsel ATF Credit Union, Boston, 1968-70; lectr. Vanderbilt U. Sch. Law, Nashville, 1976-80. Lectr. U. Miami Grad. Law Sch., 1986-90. Recipient awards US Treasury Dept., 1979, 81, 82; Presdl. Meritorious Exec. Rank award, 1983. Office: US Tax Ct 400 2nd St NW Rm 432 Washington DC 20217-0002*

GERBER, MELANIE K., lawyer; b. Jersey City, May 27, 1947; BA, Univ. Md., 1973; JD, Georgetown Univ., 1988. Bar: DC 1989, Pa. 1989, Supreme Ct. Pa., US Dist. Ct. (DC dist.), US Ct. Appeals (DC cir.), US Supreme Ct. Assoc. Morrison & Foerster, Washington; exec. dir. Legal Resource Ctr. for Housing & Cmty. Devel., Washington; pub. svc. counsel Patton Boggs LLP, Washington. Mem. oper. com. Whitman-Walker Legal Svc.; mem. adv. bd. DC Employment Justice Ctr.; mem. legal adv. bd. Capital Area Immigrants Rights Coalition; mem. editl. bd. Law Firm Pro Bono Project; vol. mentor Georgetown Univ. Law Ctr.; mem. regional leadership council Lawyers for Children Am.; mem. Legal Svc. Providers Consortium. Recipient Mayor's Arts award, DC Commn. on Arts & Humanities, 2003, Legal Assistance Disting. Svc. award, Sept. 11 Pro Bono Legal Relief Project, 2002, Servant of Justice award, Legal Aid Soc., 2001. Mem.: Washington Lawyers' Com. for Civil Rights (Vincent E. Reed award 2004, Outstanding Achievement award, Immigration & Refugee Rights 2003, Outstanding Achievement award, Equal Employment Opportunity 2000), Pa. Bar Assn., DC Bar (award for Pro Bono Work 2001). Office: Patton Boggs LLP 2550 M St NW Washington DC 20037-1350 Office Fax: 202-457-6315, 202-457-6312. Business E-Mail: mgerber@pattonboggs.com.

GERBER, MILO PHIL, urologist; b. Brainerd, Minn., May 11, 1940; s. Milo Phil and Edith (Heald) Gerber; m. Judith A. Gerber, Apr. 1978; children: Milo P. III, Nicole A., Kyra A. BS, Duke U., Durham, 1962; MD, U. Fla., Gainesville, 1966. Cert. Bd. Urology, 1973. Internship 1st surgery Western Reserve, Cleve., 1966—68; urology residency U. Ed., Denver, 1970—73; urologist St. Pete Med. Clinic, St Petersburg, Fla., 1973—77, Pueblo Urological, Colo., 1977—98; ret., 1998. Surgical chief St. Mary-Corwin Dept. Surgery, Pueblo, 1980. Capt. USAF, 1968—70, Vietnam. Recipient Eagle Scout, Boy Scouts of Am., 1950, Silver Explorer award, Explorers, 1950. Mem.: Am. Coll. Surgeons, Am. Urological Assn. Republican. Cath. Avocations: hunting, fishing, golf, skiing.

GERBER, MURRY S., gas, oil and utilities executive; b. 1953; BA with honors in Geology, Augustana Coll.; MS in Geology, U. Ill. Geologist Shell Oil, 1978, various mgmt. positions for exploration programs in the continental US, Alaska and the offshore Gulf of Mexico, gen. mgr. planning and finance Shell Exploration and Production, 1991—95, treasurer; CEO and co-creator of Shell affiliate formed from subs. of Shell Oil Co. and Tejas Gas Corp. Coral Energy, 1995—98; pres., CEO Equitable Resources, Inc., Pitts., 1998—, chmn., 2000—. Bd. mem., mem. exec. com. BlackRock, Inc., 2000—; bd. mem. Westport Resources Corp.; mem. Nat. Petroleum Coun. Bd. dirs. United Way of Allegheny County, 1999; chmn. bd. Education Policy and Issues Center, Pitts., 2001—; host com. chmn. Nat. Urban League Conference, Pitts., 2003. Recipient CEO Communicator of the Year Renaissance award, Pitts. Chap. Public Relations Society of Am., 2003, Frieda Shapira award, Heritage Health Found., 2003. Mem.: Pa. Roundtable (vol. chmn. early childhood initiative effort), Am. Gas Assn. (Com. on Security, Infrastructure Integrity and Reliability 2001—).

GERBER, ROBERT EVAN, judge; s. Milton M. and Miriam G. BS with high honors, Rutgers U., 1967; JD magna cum laude, Columbia U., 1970. Bar: N.Y. 1971, U.S. Dist. Ct. (so. and ea. dists.) N.Y. 1972, U.S. Ct. Appeals (2d cir.) 1973, U.S. Ct. Appeals (9th cir.) 1974, U.S. Ct. Appeals (10th cir.) 1975, U.S. Ct. Appeals (11th cir.) 1983, U.S. Supreme Ct. 1983, U.S. Ct. Appeals (5th cir.) 1987, U.S. Ct. Appeals (6th cir.) 1989, U.S. Ct. Appeals (3d cir.) 1997. Assoc. Fried, Frank, Harris, Shriver & Jacobson, NYC, 1970-71, 72-78, ptnr., 1978-2000; judge U.S. Bankruptcy Ct. (so. dist.) N.Y., NYC, 2000—. Served to 1st lt. USAF, 1971-72. James Kent scholar, 1970, Harlan Fiske Stone scholar, 1969. Fellow Am. Coll. Bankruptcy; mem. ABA, Assn. Bar City NY (sec. spl. com. on energy 1974-79), Fed. Bar Coun., Am. Bankruptcy Inst., Nat. Conf. Bankruptcy Judges, Tau Beta Pi. Office: US Bankruptcy Ct US Custom House One Bowling Green New York NY 10004 Office Phone: 212-668-5660.

GERBER, ROBERT SCOTT, lawyer; b. Lansing, Mich. s. Arnold William and Carol L. Gerber. BA with high honors, U. Mich., 1984, M of Pub. Policy, 1985; JD cum laude, Harvard U., 1988. Bar: Calif. 1988, US Dist. Ct. (so. dist.) Calif. 1989, US Dist. Ct. (ctrl. dist.) Calif. 1991, US Ct. Appeals (9th cir.) 1992, US Dist. Ct. Ariz. 1994, US Supreme Ct. 2000, US Dist. Ct. (ND, Calif.), 2001. Econ. devel. analyst Mich. Dept. Commerce, 1984-85, City of San Diego, 1985; summer assoc. Riker, Danzig, Scherer, Hyland & Perretti, Morristown, NJ, 1986, Lillick, McHose & Charles, San Diego, 1987, Debevoise & Plimpton, NYC, 1987; law clk. Hon. Rudi M. Brewster U.S. Dist. Ct. (so. dist.) Calif., San Diego, 1988-89; assoc. Sheppard, Mullin, Richter & Hampton LLP, San Diego, 1989-97, ptnr., 1997—. Contbr. articles to profl. jours. Active San Diego Vol. Lawyer Program, 1989—; judge pro tempore Small Claims Ct., Mspl. Ct. Calif., San Diego Jud. Dist., 1994—2001; mem. Calif. Jud. Nominees Evaluation Commn., 2004—06; bd. dirs. ch. coun. Christ Evang. Luth. Ch., Pacific Beach, Calif., 1991—94, 1995—96, long range planning com., 1994—95. Master: Am. Inns of Ct. (bd. trustees); mem.: ABA (asst. editor-in-chief profl. liability com. newsletter 1994—), San Diego Def. Lawyers, Assn. Bus. Trial Lawyers, State Bar Calif. (fed. rules subcom. 1991—92, ct. rules com. 1992—, exec. com. litig. sect. 1995—, treas. 1996—97, sec. 1997—, vice chair 1998—99, chair 1999—2000). Avocations: fine wines, collecting movies, golf. Office: Sheppard, Mullin, Richter & Hampton LLP Ste 200 12275 El Camino Real San Diego CA 92130 Office Phone: 858-720-8907. Office Fax: 858-509-3691. Business E-Mail: rgerber@sheppardmullin.com, rgerber@smrh.com.

GERBER, ROBIN, history and social sciences educator; b. Miles City, Mont. AA, Miles CC; BA in Anthropology and Hist., U. Mont., Missoula, MA in Hist. Mem. faculty to instr. hist. and social scis. Miles CC, Miles City, Mont., 1998—. Author: A Long Way From Anywhere - A History of Miles City, MT - For Kids, 2006. Recipient US Prof. of Yr. award, Carnegie Found. for Advancement of Tchg. and Coun. for Advancement and Support of Edn., 2006. Office: Hist and Social Scis Miles CC 2715 Dickinson Miles City MT 59301-4774 Office Phone: 406-874-6193. E-mail: gerberr@milescc.edu.*

GERBER, ROGER ALAN, lawyer, consultant; b. Bklyn., Jan. 27, 1939; s. Edward and Anne (Rothstein) G.; m. Jane E. Satlow, Sept. 20, 1964; children: Dina Huebner, Deborah Tor, Tamar Gerber. BA magna cum laude (Rufus Choate scholar), Dartmouth Coll., 1959; JD, Harvard U., 1962. Bar: N.Y. 1963. Real estate atty. ABC, Inc., 1965-68; assoc. Kaye, Scholer, Fierman, Hays & Handler, other law firms, 1968-75; v.p., gen. counsel ISS Internat. Service System, Inc., NYC, 1975-83; v.p., sec., gen. counsel Meyers Parking System, Inc., NYC, 1975-89, sr. exec. v.p., chief oper. officer, 1989-95, also bd. dirs., 1981-91; pres. Meyers Realty Co., NYC, 1982-95. Abritrator Am. Arbitration Assn., 1973—; bd. dirs. Nat. Parking Assn., 1991-92; mem. adv. bd. Mid. East Forum, 1995—; bd. dirs. Jewish Inst. for Nat. Security Affairs, 1995—. Treas. Scarsdale Democratic Com., NY, 1977-83; v.p., exec. com. Bd. Jewish Edn., Greater NY, 1977-2006; bd. trustees PEF-Israel Endowment Fund, 1997-2004; bd. dirs. Conf. Jewish Social Studies, 1975-93, Jewish Conciliation Bd., NY; class agt. Dartmouth Coll. Mem. N.Y. State Bar Assn., Phi Beta Kappa. Clubs: Harvard (N.Y.C.). Home: 26 Sage Ter Scarsdale NY 10583-2045 Office Phone: 212-983-4414. E-mail: RG26@aol.com.

GERBERDING, JULIE LOUISE, federal agency administrator; b. SD, 1956; m. David Rose; 1 child, Renada. BA in chemistry and biology, Case Western Reserve U., Cleve., 1971, MD, 1981; MPH, U. Calif., Berkeley, 1990. Intern and resident, internal medicine U. Calif., San Francisco, chief med. resident, fellow in clin. pharmacology and infectious diseases; clin. prof. medicine (infectious disease) Emory U.; assoc. prof. medicine, epidemiology and biostatistics U. Calif., San Francisco; founder, dir., Epidemiology Prevention and Interventions Ctr. San Francisco Gen. Hosp., 1987—98; dir., divsn. healthcare quality promotion CDC, Atlanta, 1998—2001, acting deputy dir. sci., 2001—02, dir., 2002—; adminstr. Agency for Toxic Substances and Disease Registry (ATSDR), 2002—. Dir., Prevention Epicenter U. Calif., San Francisco; mem., scientific program com. Nat. Conf. on Retroviruses CDC, mem., HIV adv. com., mem., scientific program com., Nat. Ctr. for Infectious Diseases; cons. NIH, AMA, Occupational Safety and Health Adminstrn., Nat. AIDS Commn., U.S. Congress, Congl. Office Tech. Assessment, and WHO.; invited spkr. in field. Edtl. bd. Annals Internal Medicine, assoc. editor Am. Jour. Medicine, peer-reveiwer for numerous types of jours. in the field, contbr. to profl. publs. and textbooks. Named one of 100 Most Powerful Women, Forbes mag., 2005—06; recipient Case Med. Alumni Assn. Disting. Alumnus/a award, Case Western Reserve U., 2003, President's award for Disting. Alumni, 2004. Fellow: Infectious Diseases Soc. Am. (chair and co-chair com. profl. devel. and diversity, mem. nominations com., co-chair. annual program com.); mem.: ACP, Nat. Acad. Pub. Adminstrn., Inst. Medicine, Am. Epidemiology Soc., Soc. for Healthcare Epidemiology Am. (mem. AIDS/Tuberculosis com., bd. acad. counselor), Am. Soc. Clin. Investigation, Alpha Omega Alpha, Phi Beta Kappa. Achievements include being the first female director for the CDC. Avocations: scuba diving, reading, gardening, beach, spending time with cats. Office: CDC 1600 Clifton Rd NE 214 Atlanta GA 30333*

GERBERDING, MILES CARSTON, lawyer; b. Decatur, Ind., Oct. 25, 1930; s. Arnold H. and Luella E. (Lapp) G.; m. Ruth H. Hostrup, Aug. 20, 1955 (dec. Mar. 1992); children: Karla M. Smith, Greta E. Cowart, Kent E., Brian K.; m. Joan W. Fackler, Jan. 2, 1993; stepchildren: Stephen W. Fackler, Deborah E. Holbrook. BS, Ind. U., 1954, JD, 1956. Bar: Ind. 1956, US Dist. Ct. (so. and no. dists.) Ind. 1956, Mich. 1984. Ptnr. Nieter & Smith, Ft. Wayne, Ind., 1956-58, Barrett, Barrett & McNagny, Ft. Wayne, 1958-85, Barnes & Thornburg, Ft. Wayne, 1985-97; pvt. practice Frankfort, Mich., 1998—. Lectr., writer Ind. Continuing Legal Edtl. Forum. Contbr. articles to profl. jours. Pres. Luth. Assn. Elem. Edn., 1968-69; vice chmn., mem. Ind. Supreme Ct. Commn. on Continuing Legal Edn., sec.; bd. dirs. Big Bros., Ft. Wayne, Jr. Achievement, Ft. Wayne, United Way Allen County; pres. Concordia Ednl. Found., Greater Ft. Wayne C. of C. Found.; chmn. bd. visitors Ind. U. Sch. Law, Bloomington, 1984-85, mem. 1979-94; vice chmn. United Way of Allen County Campaign, 1990-92, chmn., 1992-93, dir., 1992-98; trustee Boys and Girls Club Ft. Wayne; sec. Willoughby Rotary Found., 1999-2006. With USMC, 1950-52. Decorated UN medal, Korean Svc. medal with star; recipient Christus Magister award Luth. Edn. Assn., 1971, Disting Svc. award Ind. U. Sch. Law, 1999; named Grad. of Yr., Concordia Alumni Assn., 1993, named Citizen of Yr. Benzie County C. of C., 2003. Fellow: Mich. Bar Found., Ind. Bar Found. (dir.), Am. Coll. Trust and Estate Counsel, Am. Coll. Tax Counsel, Am. Bar Found.; mem.: VFW, ABA (rep. Nat. Conf. Lawyers and CPAs 1980—86, nominating com., ho. dels. credentials com., chmn. Ind. del. 1985—94, budget officer Sr. Lawyers divsn. 2005—07, ho. dels. mem. com., marital deduction com. taxation sect., com. on pub. understanding about law, standing com. on bar svc., coordinating com. on outreach, vice-chmn. com. on state and local bars-sr. lawyers divsn., med. profl. liability com.), Korean War Vets. Assn., Nat. Conf. Bar Pres. (exec. coun. 1983—86), Ind. CLE Forum (pres. 1978—79), Am. Judicature Soc., Allen County Bar Found. (former bd. dir., sec.), Lawyer-Pilot Bar Assn., Allen County Bar Assn. (dir.), Benzie County Bar Assn. (pres. 1999—2000), State Bar Mich.

(coun. 1998—, treas. 1999—2000, chmn.-elect 2000—01, chmn. sr. lawyers sect. 2001—02, Mich. del to ABA ho. of dels. 2004—06, com. on mandatory CLE, com. on quality profl. life), Ind. Bar Assn. (pres. 1979—80, del. ABA 1979—94), Endowment Com. (chair), Am. Legion, TerraLex (former co-vice chmn. N.Am., dir. 1993—96), Benzie Area Hist. Soc. (dir., chmn. endowment commn.), Frankfort Rotary Club, Arcadia Lions Club. Republican. Lutheran. Home: 17726 N Ridgewood PO Box 6 Arcadia MI 49613-0006 Office: PO Box 272 Frankfort MI 49635-0272 also: PO Box 118 Arcadia MI 49613-0118 Office Phone: 231-352-9526. Personal E-mail: mcgerb@bignetnorth.net.

GERBERDING, WILLIAM PASSAVANT, retired university president; b. Fargo, ND, Sept. 9, 1929; s. William Passavant and Esther Elizabeth Ann (Habighorst) G.; m. Ruth Alice Albrecht, Mar. 25, 1952; children: David Michael, Steven Henry, Elizabeth Ann, John Martin. BA, Macalester Coll., 1951; MA, U. Chgo., 1956, PhD, 1959. Congl. fellow Am. Polit. Sci. Assn., Washington, 1958-59; instr. Colgate U., Hamilton, N.Y., 1959-60; research asst. Senator E.J. McCarthy, Washington, 1960-61; staff Rep. Frank Thompson, Jr., Washington, 1961; faculty UCLA, 1961-72, prof., chmn. dept. polit. sci., 1970-72; dean faculty, v.p. for acad. affairs Occidental Coll., Los Angeles, 1972-75; exec. vice chancellor UCLA, 1975-77; chancellor U. Ill., Urbana-Champaign, 1978-79; pres. U. Wash., Seattle, 1979-95. Cons. Dept. Def., 1962, Calif. Assembly, 1965. Author: United States Foreign Policy: Perspectives and Analysis, 1966; co-editor, contbg. author: The Radical Left: The Abuse of Discontent, 1970. Trustee Macalester Coll., 1980—83, 1996—2001, Gates Cambridge Trust, U. Cambridge, England, 2000—. With USN, 1951—55. Recipient Distinguished Teaching award U. Calif., Los Angeles, 1966; Ford Found. grantee, 1967-68 Office: Univ Wash PO Box 352800 Seattle WA 98195-2800

GERBERDING COWART, GRETA ELAINE, lawyer; b. Ft. Wayne, Ind., Aug. 17, 1960; d.Ruth (Hostrup) G., stepmother Joanie Wyatt Gerberding; m. T. David Cowart, Aug. 12, 1995. BS with high distinction, Ind. U., Bloomington, 1982, JD cum laude, 1985. Bar: Ind. 1985, U.S. Dist. Ct. (so. dist.) Ind., CPA, Ind., CEBS. Sr. tax cons. Ernst & Whinney, Indpls., 1985-87; assoc. Klineman, Rose, Wolf and Wallack P.C., Indpls., 1987-89, Hall Render Killian Heath & Lyman P.C., Indpls., 1989-95; ptnr. Haynes and Boone, L.L.P., Dallas, 1996—. Presenter at seminars. Author: (with G.P. Gooch) Trust and Estate Income Tax Reporting and Planning, 1985; contbr. chpt. to books, articles to profl. jour. including Jour. Deferred Compensation, 403(b) Answer Book, Benefits Law Jour. Chmn. hospitality area Virginia Slims Tennis Tournament, Indpls., 1987-89; vol. Jello Tennis Classic Tennis Tournament, Indpls., 1990-91, Dallas Ramp Project, 2004; coord. Hospitality and Ball Kids, 1990, Jr. Jamboree GTE Tennis Tournament, Indpls., 1990; vol. Ctr. for Exploration The Children's Mus., Indpls., 1991-94; com. on funding Vision 2002 Luth. Camp Assn., Inc., 1993-94; bd. dir., 1997—, chmn., 2001; women's retreat com. King of Glory Luth. Ch., 1997—, fin. com., 2003—, adult edn. com., 2005—; bd. dirs. Brianwood Retreat Ctr., 1998-2001, Adult Edn. Com., 2004—; bd. dirs. Arcadia Found., 1997-2003, chmn., 2001-03. Glen Peters fellow, Ind. U., 1984. Fellow Ind. Bar Found., Am. Coll. Employee Benefits Counsel; mem. ABA (com. marital deduction legis. real property and probate sect. 1986-87, tax section, gen. income tax com. 1987-89, employee benefits com. 1988—, subcom. health plan design and state regulation 1993—, health care task force 1994—, chmn. COBRA subcom. 1997-2002, vice chair employee benefits com. 2002-2005, chair elect, 2005-2006, chair, 2006—), Ind. Bar Assn. (acct.-lawyers com. 1986-89, co-chmn. com. on legis. 1988-92, coun. tax sect. 1988-96, sec.-treas. 1991-92, vice-chmn. tax sect. 1992-93, chair elect 1993-94, chair 1994-95), Indpls. Bar Assn., Indpls. Jaycees (treas. 4th Festival 1987 monthly dinner meetings 1988), West Indy Racquet Club (USTA Volvo Tennis Team 1986-87, RCA tounament credentials com. 1993-94), Indpls. Racquet Club (USTA Volvo tennis team 1988-91, 96). Avocations: tennis, golf, skiing, swimming, artwork. Office: Haynes and Boone LLP 901 Main St Ste 3100 Dallas TX 75202-3789 Office Phone: 214-651-5000.

GERBERG, JUDITH LEVINE, career consultant; d. Murray Joseph and Pearl (Berens) Levine; m. Mort Gerberg; 1 child, Lilia Anya Berens. BS in Comparative Lit., Columbia U., 1963, postgrad. in organizational devel., 1989; MA in Psychology and Art, NYU. Registered art therapist; lic. clin. mental health counselor; cert. counselor, career mgmt. profl. Program dir. Women's Selling Game, NYC, 1979-84; mem. faculty Parsons Sch. Design, NYC, 1979-85; pres. gerberg & co., NYC, 1984—. Orgnl. devel. mgmt., leadership devel., valuing diversity, team bldg., comm. skills, stress mgmt.; founder Powerhouse, 1st outplacement for creative profls.; mem. N.Y. steering com. Women's Study in Religion Program Harvard Div. Sch.; pres. Career Counselors Consortium, 2000-03. Co-author: The New York Women's Directory, 1973; contbr. articles and book revs. to profl. jours. Chmn. pub. rels. Profl. Women's Caucus, 1972; facilitator NYC Contr.'s Women's Econ. Task Force, 1994-95; mem. Harvard Divinity Sch.: Women in Religion Leadership Conf. NY State scholar. Mem.: Career Counselors Consortium (pres. 2000—03), Internat. Assn. Career Mgmt. Profl. (co-chair future focus com.), Women's Venture Fund, Fin. Women's Assn. (bd. dirs. 2003—04), The Forum at Stephen Wise (co-chmn. 1986—87), N.Y. Art Therapy Assn., Am. Art Therapy Assn. (life; bd. dirs. 1980—84). Office: 250 W 57th St Ste 2315 New York NY 10107-2315 Home Phone: 212-873-6311; Office Phone: 212-315-2322. Business E-Mail: gerberg@gerberg.com.

GERBIE, ALBERT BERNARD, obstetrician, gynecologist, educator; b. Toledo, Nov. 20, 1927; s. Louis and Fay (Green) G.; m. Barbara Hirsch, June 29, 1952; children: Gail Diane, Stephen Ralph. MD, George Washington U., 1951. Intern Michael Reese Hosp., Chgo., 1951-52; preceptorship in ob-gyn. under Drs. R.A. Reis, J.L. Baer, E.J. DeCosta, Chgo., 1952-55; practice medicine specializing in ob-gyn. Chgo., 1955—; mem. faculty Northwestern U. Med. Sch., Chgo., 1952—, prof. ob-gyn., 1972—2007, prof. emeritus, 2007—, dir. continuing grad. edn., 1975—. Mem. staff Northwestern Meml. Hosp., 1955—; chief divsn. ob-gyn. Children's Meml. Hosp.; v.p., dir. Am. Bd. Ob-Gyn, 1976—, chmn. 1988—, pres. 1990, historian, 1998; chmn. liaison com. for ob-gyn., 1989; rep. Am. Bd. Med. Specialties; bd. dirs. Chgo. Maternity Ctr., Found. for Excellence in Women's Health Care. Author textbooks; assoc. editor Surgery, Gynecology, and Obstetrics, Am. Jour. Ob-Gyn.; editor ACOG Current Jour. Rev.; contbr. chpts. to books, articles to profl. jours. Served with U.S. Army, 1946-47. Mem. ACS (bd. govs.), ACOG (chmn. learning resources commn.), AMA, Am. Gynecol. Soc., Am. Assn. Obstetricians and Gynecologists, Am. Gynecol. and Obstet. Soc., Am. Bd. Med. Specialties, Am. Coll. Sports Medicine, Ctrl. Assn. Ob-Gyn, Soc. Human Genetics, Southwestern Ob-Gyn. Soc., Chgo. Gynecol. Assn. (pres. 1977-78), Skokie Valley Figure Skating Club, (pres. 2003). Office: Ste 900 251 E Huron St Chicago IL 60611-4814

GERDES, ANTHONY MARTIN, research scientist, health science association administrator; BS, Lamar U., 1974; PhD, U. Tex. Med. Br., Galveston, 1978. Asst. prof. U. South Fla., Tampa, 1982—88, assoc. prof.; prof., chmn. anatomy U. SD, Vermillion, 1993—98; dir. cardiovasc. rsch. inst. Sanford Rsch./U. SD, Sioux Falls, 1998—. Contbr. articles to scientific jours. Recipient Rsch. Excellence award, SD Bd. Regents, 2000. Fellow: Am. Heart Assn. (life). Achievements include discovery of Myocyte lengthening is largely responsible for chamber dilatation in heart failure; Low thyroid function alone can cause heart failure; Low thyroid function destroys coronary microcirculation. Avocations: scuba, sailing, canoeing, camping. Office: Sanford Rsch/U SD 1100 E 21st St Ste 700 Sioux Falls SD 57105 Home Phone: 605-339-7695; Office Phone: 605-328-1303. Office Fax: 605-328-1301. E-mail: mgerdes@usd.edu.

GERDES, DAVID ALAN, lawyer; b. Aberdeen, SD, Aug. 10, 1942; s. Cyril Fredrick and Lorraine Mary (Boyle) G.; m. Karen Ann Hassinger, Aug. 3, 1968; children: Amy Renee, James David. BS, No. State Coll., Aberdeen, 1965; JD cum laude, U. S.D., 1968. Bar: S.D. 1968, U.S. Dist. Ct. S.D., 1968, U.S. Ct. Appeals (8th cir.) 1973, U.S. Supreme Ct. 1973. Assoc. Martens, Goldsmith, May, Porter & Adam, Pierre, SD, 1968-73; ptnr. successor firm May, Adam, Gerdes & Thompson, Pierre, 1973—. Chmn. disciplinary bd. S.D. Bar, 1980-81, mem. fed. practice com. U.S. Dist. Ct., S.D., 1986-91, 1994-2000; mem. fed. adv. com. U.S. Ct. Appeals (8th cir.), 1989-93; bd. dirs. U.S.D. Law Sch. Found., 1973-84, pres., 1979-84. Mng. editor U. S.D. Law Rev., 1967—68; author: Physician's Guide to South Dakota Law, 1982. Chmn. Hughes County Rep. Ctrl. Com., 1979-81; del. Rep. State Conv., co-chair platform com., 1988, 90; state ctrl. committeeman, 1985-91. Served to lt. Signal Corps, AUS, 1965-68. Mem. ABA, Nat. Coun. Bar Pres., Internat. Assn. Def. Counsel, Am. Judicature Soc., Am. Bd. Trial Advocates, State Bar S.D. (chmn. professionalism com. 1989-90, pres. 1992-93), Pierre Area C. of C. (pres. 1980-81), S.D. C. of C. (bd. dirs. 1998-2004), Lawyer-Pilots Bar Assn., Def. Rsch. Inst., Am. Soc. Med. Assn. Counsel, Kiwanis, Elks. Republican. Methodist. Office: May Adam Gerdes & Thompson PO Box 160 503 S Pierre St Pierre SD 57501-0160 Office Phone: 605-224-8803.

GERDES, NEIL WAYNE, library director, educator; b. Moline, Ill., Oct. 19, 1943; s. John Edward and Della Marie (Ferguson) G. AB, U. Ill., 1965; BD, Harvard U., Cambridge, Mass., 1968; MA, Columbia U., NYC, 1971; MA in Libr. Sci., U. Chgo., 1975; DMin, U. St. Mary of the Lake, 1994. Ordained to ministry Unitarian Universalist Assn., 1975. Copy chief Little, Brown, 1968-69; instr. Tuskegee Inst., 1969-71; libr. asst. Augustana Coll., 1972-73; editl. asst. Library Quar., 1973-74; libr., prof. Meadville Theol. Sch., Chgo., 1973—; libr. program dir. Chgo. Cluster Theol. Schs., 1977-80; dir. Hammond Libr., 1980—; prof. Chgo. Theol Sem., 1980—. Affiliated minister 1st Unitarian Church, Chgo., 2002—. Mem. exec. bd. Sem. Coop. Bookstore, Chgo., 1982-2002, Ctr. for Religion and Psychotherapy, Chgo., 1984-97, Ind. Voters of Ill., 1986-89, Hyde Park-Kenwood Cmty. Orgn., Chgo., 1988-89; pres. Hyde Park-Kenwood Interfaith Coun., 1986-90, Inst. for Spiritual Leadership, 2000-07; chmn. libr. coun. Assn. Chgo. Theol. Sch., 1984-88, 96-98, pres.-elect, 2007—; chmn. adv. bd. LGBT Religious Archive Network, 2002—; trustee Civitas Dei Found., 1994—2006; mem. alumni coun. Harvard Div. Sch., 1999-2005, sec., 2001-05. Mem. ALA, Am. Theol. Library Assn., Chgo. Area Theol. Library Assn., Unitarian Universalist Mins. Assn. (sec., treas. nat. body 1990-94), Assn. Liberal Religious Scholars (sec., treas. 1975—), Phi Beta Kappa Office: Chgo Theol Sem Hammond Libr 5757 S University Ave Chicago IL 60637-1507 Office Phone: 773-752-5757. Business E-Mail: ngerdes@ctschicago.edu.

GERDES, RALPH DONALD, fire safety consultant; b. Cin., Aug. 11, 1951; s. Paul Donald and Jo Ann Dorothy (Meyer) G. BArch, Ill. Inst. Tech., 1975. Registered architect, Ill. Architect Schiller & Frank, Wheeling, Ill., 1976; sr. assoc. Rolf Jensen & Assocs., Inc., Chgo., 1976-84; pres. Ralph Gerdes & Assocs., Inc., Indpls., 1984-88, chmn., 1988—; gen. mgr. Ralph Gerdes Cons., LLC. Lectr. Purdue U., Ind. U., Ill. Inst. Tech., Butler U., Ball State U.; bd. dirs. Ind. Fire Svcs. Inst. Co-author: Planning and Designing the Office Environment, 1981. Recipient Joel Polsky prize Am. Soc. Interior Designers, 1983. Mem.: AIA (bldg. performance and regulations com., liaison to Nat. Fire Protection Agy.), ASHRAE, Archs. and Engrs. Bldg. Ofcls. (bd. dirs. 1994—, Ind. code devel. com.), Ind. Fire Safety Assn. (bd. dirs. 1986—92, pres. 1989—91, bd. dirs. 1994—95), Internat. Code Coun., Nat. Fire Protection Assn. (tech. coms., stds. council), Soc. Fire Protection Engring. (assoc.; exec. com. Ind. chpt. 1992—, pres. 1995—96), Indpls. Soc., Maple Creek Country Club. Roman Catholic. Home: 556 Lockerbie Cir N Indianapolis IN 46202-3600 Office: 5510 S East St Ste E Indianapolis IN 46227

GERDING, THOMAS GRAHAM, medical products executive; b. Evanston, Ill., Feb. 11, 1930; s. Louis Henry and Helen Frances (Graham) G.; m. Beverly Ann Starnes, June 18, 1955; children: Mark, David, Gail, Gene Ann. Student, U. Notre Dame, 1948-49; BS in Pharmacy, Purdue U., 1952, MS, 1954, PhD, 1960, D (hon.), 2002. From instr. to asst. prof. Purdue U., West Lafayette, Ind., 1956-61; dir. product devel. Pitman-Moore divsn. Dow Chem., Indpls., 1962-64; tech. dir. new products Glenbrook Labs., NYC, 1964-66; dir. product devel. Sterling-Winthrop Rsch. Inst., Rensselaer, NY, 1966-70; v.p. rsch. and devel. Calgon Consumer Products, Rahway, NJ, 1970-77; v.p., dir. rsch. and devel., quality assurance, consumer affairs, engring. Johnson & Johnson Products Inc., New Brunswick, NJ, 1977-88; pres. Thomas G. Gerding, Inc., Georgetown, Tex., 1988-96; dir. Drug Dynamics Inst. U. Tex., Austin, 1988-95; pres. Newform Devel. Labs., Inc., Georgetown, Tex., 1993—. Deans adv. coun. Purdue U. Sch. Pharmacy, 1996—2001, U. Tex. Coll. Pharmacy, 2002—07. Sgt. U.S. Army Med. Svc. Corp, 1954-56. Recipient Disting. Alumni award, Purdue U., 1984, Best Friend award, U. Tex., 2002. Mem.: Am. Assn. Pharm. Scientists, Am. Chem. Soc., Berry Creek Country Club, Union League Club (Chgo.). Republican. Achievements include research in pharmaceutics, wound care and unique drug delivery systems; patents in field. Home: 340 Shell Spur Georgetown TX 78628 Office: Newform Devel Labs Inc 340 Shell Spur Georgetown TX 78628

GERDNER, LINDA ANN, nursing researcher, educator; b. Burlington, Iowa, Sept. 17, 1955; d. Richard Paul and Edna Marie Gerdner. AA, Southeastern C.C., 1975, ADN, 1977; BSN, Iowa Wesleyan Coll., 1980; MA, U. Iowa, 1992, PhD, 1998. RN, Iowa, Ark., Minn. Staff devel. coord. Elm View Care Ctr., Burlington, Iowa, 1985—88, DON, 1988—89; tchg./rsch. asst. U. Iowa Coll. Nursing, Iowa City, 1989-92; nursing faculty Grand View Coll., Des Moines, 1992-93; project dir. Nat. Caregiver Tng. Project, U. Iowa Coll. Nursing, 1992-97, predoctoral fellow, 1996-98; postdoctoral fellow/faculty dept. psychiatry U. Ark. Med. Scis., VA Med. Ctr., Little Rock, 1998—2000; asst. prof. U. Minn. Sch. Nursing, 2001—06; asst. dir. Geriatric Edn. Ctr., Stanford U., Palo Alto, Calif., 2007—. Presenter in field; cons. Alverno Health Facility, Clinton, Iowa, 1997—2000. Mem. referee panel Clin. Nursing Rsch., 1997—, Western Jour. Nursing Rsch., 1998—, Jour. Gerontol. Nursing, 1999—, Internat. Jour. Geriatric Psychiatry, 2000—, Internat. Psychogeriatrics, 2002—, Alzheimer's Disease and Related Disorders, 2002—, Nursing Research, 2003—; contbr. chapters to books, articles to profl. jours. AARP Andrus Found. grad. fellow in gerontology Assn. Gerontology in Higher Edn., 1996-97, Rsch. award Am. Soc. Aging, 1999, mini-fellowship ethnogeriatrics, Stanford U., Palo Alto, Calif., 2004. Mem.: ANA, Coun. Nursing and Anthropology, Am. Assn. Geriatric Psychiatry, Midwest Nursing Rsch. Soc. (Outstanding Poster award 1993), Mid-Am. Contress on Aging (Best Grad. Paper award 1994), Am. Geriatric Soc., Internat. Psychogeriatric Assn. (task force on behavioral and psychol. symptoms of dementia 1999—, scientific advisory com. 2001, IPA/Bayer Rsch. award 1999), Sigma Theta Tau (Best of Image award 1997). Avocations: reading, travel, walking, music, photography. Home: care Richard Gerdner 1304 Lynnwood Dr Burlington IA 52601 Business E-Mail: gerdn001@umn.edu.

GERDTS, WILLIAM HENRY, art history educator; b. Jersey City, Jan. 18, 1929; s. William Henry and Suzanne (Zanowick) G.; m. Elaine Evans, Apr. 4, 1953 (div. 1962); 1 child, Jeffrey Evans Dee; m. Abigail Booth, July 23, 1976. BA, Amherst Coll., 1949; MA, Harvard U., 1950, PhD, 1966; LHD (hon.), Amherst Coll., 1992; DFA (hon.), Syracuse U., 1996. Resident dir. Hist. Myers House, curator Norfolk (Va.) Mus., 1953-54; curator paintings and sculpture Newark (N.J.) Mus., 1954-66; prof. art history U. Md., College Park, 1966-69; v.p. Coe Kerr Gallery, NYC, 1969-71; prof. art history CUNY, 1971-99, prof. emeritus, 1999—, exec. officer art history PhD program, 1977-79, exec. officer, 1979-85. Vis. lectr. Johns Hopkins U., Balt., 1969-71; adj. prof. Rutgers U., New Brunswick, N.J., 1975, Washington U., St. Louis, 1977; mem. adv. bd. Archives Am. Art, Smithsonian Instn., N.Y.C., 1981—. Author: American Still-Life Painting, 1971, American Neo-Classic Sculpture: The Marble Resurrection, 1973, The Great American Nude: A History in Art, 1974, A Man of Genius: The Art of Washington Allston, 1979, Masters of the Humble Truth: Masterpieces of American Still Life, 1801-1930, 1981, American Impressionism, 1984, rev., 2001, The Art of Henry Inman, 1987; (with James L. Yarnall) The National Museum of American Art's Index to American Art Exhibition Catalogues From the Beginning through the 1876 Centennial Year, 6 vols., 1986, Art Across America: Regional Painting in America through 1920, 3 vols., 1990, others. Summer Rsch. grantee U. Md., 1968, Mellon Found., 1974; Guggenheim Found. fellow, 1980, Am. Philos. Soc. fellow, 1980. Office: CUNY Grad Ctr 365 5th Ave New York NY 10016-4334

GERE, JAMES MONROE, civil engineering educator; b. Syracuse, NY, June 14, 1925; s. William S. and Carol (Hixson) G.; m. Janice M. Platt, June 1, 1946; children— Susan M., William P., David S. BS, Rensselaer Poly. Inst., 1949, MS, 1951; PhD, Stanford, 1954. Registered profl. engr., Calif., N.Y. Instr. Rensselaer Poly. Inst., 1949-51; faculty Stanford U., 1954—; prof. civil engring., 1962—; assoc. dean Sch. Engring., 1960-67, exec. head dept. civil engring., 1967-72. Cons., lectr. in field. Author 7 textbooks in field, also tech. papers. Served with USAAF, 1943-46, ETO. Fellow ASCE; mem. Am. Soc. Engring. Edn., Earthquake Engring. Resch. Inst., Sigma Xi, Tau Beta Pi.

GERE, RICHARD, actor; b. Phila., Aug. 31, 1949; s. Homer and Doris Gere; m. Cindy Crawford, Dec. 12, 1991 (div. 1995); m. Carey Lowell, Nov. 9, 2002; 1 child, Homer James Jigme. Attended, U. Mass. Played trumpet, piano, guitar and bass and composed music with various musical groups. acting appearances with Provincetown Playhouse in Great God Brown, Camino Real, Rosencrantz and Guildenstern are Dead; off-Broadway prodn. Killer's Head, Richard Farina: Long Time Coming and Long Time Gone, Back Bog Beast Bait; in Broadway prodn. Taming of the Shrew; London and Broadway prodns. Midsummer Night's Dream; Broadway prodns. Habeas Corpus, Bent; on Broadway Soon, Grease; appeared in and composed music for Volpone at Seattle Repertory Theatre; film debut in Report to the Commissioner, 1975; other films include Baby Blue Marine, 1976, Looking for Mr. Goodbar, 1977, Days of Heaven, 1978, Blood Brothers, 1978, Yanks, 1979, American Gigolo, 1980, An Officer and a Gentleman, 1982, Breathless, 1983, Beyond the Limit, 1983, The Cotton Club, 1984, King David, 1985, Power, 1986, No Mercy, 1986, Miles from Home, 1988, Internal Affairs, 1990, Pretty Woman, 1990, Rhapsody in August, 1991, Final Analysis, (also exec. prodr.) 1992, Sommersby, 1993, Mr. Jones, 1993, Intersection, 1994, First Knight, 1995, Primal Fear, 1996, Red Corner, 1997, The Jackal, 1997, An Alan Smithee Film: Burn Hollywood Burn, 1998, Runaway Bride, 1999, Autumn in New York, 2000, Dr. T and the Women, 2000, The Mothman Prophecies, 2002, Unfaithful, 2002, Chicago, 2002, Shall We Dance?, 2004, Bee Season, 2005, The Hoax, 2007; TV movie Strike Force, 1975, And the Band Played On, HBO, 1993 (Emmy nomination, Supporting Actor - Special, 1994), AFI's 100 Years.100 Movies, 1998; author: Pilgrim Photo Collection, 1998; exec. prodr. (films) Final Analysis, 1992, Mr. Jones, 1993, Sommersby, 1993; TV guest appearance Kojak, 1973. Alfred P. Sloan Found. fellow, 1941—43, Tax Found. fellow, 1943—44.*

GEREIGHTY, ANDREA SAUNDERS, diversified financial services company executive, poet; b. New Orleans, July 20, 1938; d. Andrew Jackson and Jeanne Teresa (Martin) Saunders; m. Dennis Anthony Gereighty Jr., May 19, 1959 (wid.); children: Deni Ann, David Dennis, Peggy T. Cert., Exeter Coll., Oxford, Eng., 1972; BA, U. New Orleans, 1974, MA in English with distinction, 1978. Cotton analyst Anderson-Clayton, Metairie, La., 1956; records retrieval profl. Shell Oil Co., New Orleans, 1956-60; census coord. St. Vincent De Paul Ch., New Orleans, 1960-65; bldg. funds dir. St. Francis Xavier Ch., Metairie, 1965-70; tchr. spl. edn. Deckbar Elem. Sch., Jefferson, La., 1966-70; tchr. English Chalmette (La.) H.S., 1971-73; assoc. prof. English dept. U. New Orleans, 1973-75; tchr. secondary edn. Berlin-Am. H.S., 1980-81; owner, founder, CEO New Orleans Field Svcs. Assocs., 1974—. Guest speaker Delgado Coll., New Orleans, 1989; guest presenter Rabouin Vo-Tech., New Orleans, 1980; lectr., guest presenter poetry at New Sarpy Sch., 1994-95; guest presenter St. Mark's Episcopal Ch., Latter Libr., N.O. Pub. Libr., others. Author: (public opinon polls book) Asking Q's, 1980; (poetry) Illusions and Other Realities, 1974, Restless for Cool Weather, 1990, Season of the Crane, 1994; publ., editor Desire Street, 1997—; author numerous poems. Recipient Coda award Poets and Writers, 1983, Poetry award of honor Nat. League Am. Pen Women, 1973, Deep South Writers, 1984, 88, 90, 92, 94, 95, 96, 97, 98, 99, 2d place award Nuyarikin Poet's Cafe, N.Y.C., Ellipsis Poetry prize, 1983, 85, 87, 90, other poetry awards. Mem. Am. Mktg. Assn., Mktg. Rsch. Assn., Nat. Geneal. Soc., Jefferson Geneal. Soc., Geneaol. Soc. of New Orleans, New Orleans Poetry Forum (dir. 1990—), New Orleans Track Club. Democrat. Roman Catholic. Avocations: poetry, jogging, genealogy, camping. Office: New Orleans Field Svcs 257 Bonnabel Blvd Rear Office Metairie LA 70005-3738

GEREN, BOB (ROBERT PETER GEREN), professional baseball manager; b. San Diego, Calif., Sept. 22, 1961; Catcher NY Yankees, 1988—91, San Diego Padres, 1993; mgr. Sacramento River Cats, 2000—02; bench coach Oakland Athletics, 2003—06, mgr., 2006—. Achievements include being bench coach Am. League All-Star Team, 2005. Office: Oakland Athletics 7000 Colliseum Way Oakland CA 94621*

GEREN, GERALD S., lawyer; b. Chgo., Nov. 10, 1939; s. Ben and Sara (Block) G.; m. Phyllis Freeman, Feb. 11, 1962; children: Suzanne, Gregory, Bradley. BSMetE, Ill. Inst. Tech., 1961; JD, DePaul U., 1966. Bar: Ill. Supreme Ct. 1966, U.S. Ct. Customs and Patent Appeals 1967, U.S. Patent and Trademark Office 1967, U.S. Dist Ct. (no. dist.) Ill. 1969, U.S. Supreme Ct. 1972, U.S. Ct. Appeals (7th cir.) 1972, U.S. Ct. Appeals (fed. cir.) 1982; cert. mediator. Engr. Internat. Harvester, Chgo., 1961-64; atty. Corning Glass Works, Corning, N.Y., 1966-69; assoc. Silverman & Cass, Chgo., 1969-70, Siegal & Geren, Chgo., 1970-71; ptnr. Epton, Mullin & Druth, Chgo., 1971-84, Hill, Steadman & Simpson, Chgo., 1984-94, Gerald S. Geren Ltd., Chgo., 1994-96, Lee, Mann, Smith, McWilliams, Sweeney & Ohlson, 1997—2002, Barnes & Thornburg, 2003, of counsel, 2004—. Contbr. articles to Indsl. Rsch. and Devel., Design News mags. Pres. Chgo. High Tech. Assn., 1981-86, v.p., 1986-87; mem. strategic planning com. Econ. Devel. Commn., Chgo., 1986-91; mem. Ill. Ctr. for Indsl. Tech., 1984-90, Ill. Mfg. Tech. Network, Chgo., 1986-91; mem. pres.' coun., rsch. coun., alumni bd. Ill. Inst. Tech., 1991—; Ill. chpt.b d. mem. The Leukemia Soc. Am., 1988-90; mem. pres. coun. Chgo. Mus. Sci. and Industry. Mem. ABA, Ill. Bar Assn., Chgo. Bar Assn., Patent Law Assn. Chgo., Am. Intellectual Property Law Assn., Execs. Club, Chgo. Econ. Club, Comml. Club Chgo. (small bus. com. 1985—). Office: Barnes & Thornburg 1 N Wacker Dr #4400 Chicago IL 60606-2807 Home Phone: 847-945-2624; Office Phone: 312-214-4803. Personal E-mail: ggeren@comcast.net. Business E-Mail: ggeren@btlaw.com.

GEREN, PETE (PRESTON M. GEREN III), civilian military employee, former congressman; b. Ft. Worth, Jan. 29, 1952; m. Beckie Ray; children: Tracy, Annie, Mary. Student, Ga. Inst. Tech., 1970—73; BA, U. Tex., 1974, JD, 1978. Atty. pvt. practice, 1978-83; exec. asst. to Senator Lloyd Bentsen US Senate, 1983-85; mem. US Congress from Tex. 12th dist., Washington, 1989—97; sr. v.p. Pub. Strategies, Inc., Ft. Worth, 1997-98, atty., 1997-99, Ft. Worth, 1999—2001; spl. asst. to the sec. US Dept. Def., Washington, 2001—05; acting sec. Dept. of Air Force, US Dept. Def., Washington, 2005; under sec. Dept. of Army, US Dept. Def.,

Washington, 2006—07, acting sec., 2007, sec., 2007—. Bd. dirs. Union Pacifi Resources Group , Inc., 1997—2000, Dallas/Ft. Worth Airport, 1999—2001, Anadarko Petroleum Corp., 2000—05, TNP Enterprises, Inc., 2000—04, Cullen/Frost Bankers, Inc., 2001—05. Office: US Army 101 Army Pentagon Rm 3E560 Washington DC 20310*

GEREN III, PRESTON M. See GEREN, PETE

GERETY, PETER LEO, archbishop; b. Shelton, Conn., July 19, 1912; s. Peter Leo and Charlotte (Daly) Gerety. Student, St. Thomas Sem., Bloomfield, Conn., 1934, Sem. St. Sulpice, Paris, 1939. Ordained priest Roman Catholic Ch., 1939. Asst. pastor, New Haven, 1939—42; dir. Blessed Martin de Porres Interracial Ctr., 1942—56; pastor New Haven, 1956—66; coadjutor bishop Portland, Maine, 1966—; apostolic adminstr., 1967—; bishop, 1969—74; archbishop of Newark, 1974—86; archbishop emeritus, 1986—. Roman Catholic. Address: St John Vianney Residence 60 Home Ave Rutherford NJ 07070-1760 Home Phone: 201-460-1369; Office Phone: 201-460-1369. Business E-Mail: abgerety@verizon.net.

GERETY, ROBERT JOHN, microbiologist, researcher, pediatrician, pharmaceutical executive; b. Jersey City, Oct. 16, 1939; s. James Leo and Helen (Beck) G.; m. Joan Imelda Grant, Feb. 3, 1967; children: Andrew, Kathleen, Nancy. BA with spl. honors, Rutgers U., 1962; MA, Stanford U., 1966, PhD, 1971; MD, George Washington U., 1970. Diplomate Nat. Bd. Med. Examiners. Rsch. assoc. dept. med. microbiology Stanford (Calif.) U. Med. Sch., 1969-70; intern in pediatrics Stanford U. Hosp., 1970-71, resident, 1974-75; staff assoc. Lab. Viral Immunology, NIH, Bethesda, Md., 1971-72; staff assoc. Bur. Biologics, FDA, Bethesda, 1972-73, dir. hepatitis br., 1973-84, assoc. dir. medicine and sci., chief infectious diseases br., 1984-85; exec. dir. virus & cell biology Merck Rsch. Labs., West Point, Pa., 1985-89, chief clin. evaluation of vaccines and antiviral drugs, 1985-89; v.p. devel. ops. Biogen, Inc., Cambridge, Mass., 1989-93; v.p. pharm. ops. Immulogic Pharm. Corp., Waltham, Mass., 1993-94, CEO, pres. and dir., 1994-96; v.p. devel. and regulatory affairs ORAVAX, Cambridge, Mass., 1997-99; exec. v.p. corp. devel. Cell Gate Inc., Sunnyvale, Calif., 1999-2000; v.p. regulatory affairs and clin. ops. Inhale Therapeutic Sys., San Carlos, Calif., 2000—02; v.p., head proprietary products, prin. devel. fellow Nektar Therapeutics, San Carlos, 2002—07. Mem. exec. com. Nektar Bus. Rev., chmn. product develop. team; adj. prof. medicine Jefferson Med. Sch., Phila., 1985; Plenary lectr. Internat. Symposium on Viral Hepatitis and Liver Disease, London, 1987; mem. U.S. Army Med. R&D Adv. Bd., 1987; mem. AIDS subcom. Nat. Inst. Allergy and Infectious Diseases, 1988; mem. Nat. Vaccine Adv. Com., 1990-92, sci. bd. Oravax, Cambridge, Mass., 1991-94, numerous others; participant confs., symposia and workshops. Editor: Non-A, Non-B Hepatitis, 1981, Hepatitis A, 1984, Hepatitis B, 1985; mem. editl. bd. Biols., 1990-94; contbr. over 200 articles to sci. jours. Med. dir. USPHS, 1970-85. Recipient commendation medal USPHS, 1975, Outstanding Svc. medal, 1982, Disting. Svc. medal, 1985; Patriotic Svc. award U.S. Dept. Treasury, 1983; Henry Rutgers fellow, 1961-62, fellow NIH, 1962-65, Calif. Tb and Health Assn., 1964-67, U.S. Health Professions scholar and microbiology fellow, 1966-70. Fellow Infectious Disease Soc. Am.; mem. AMA, Am. Soc. for Microbiology, Am. Acad. Pediatrics, Am. Assn. Immunologists, William Beaumont Soc., Henry Rutgers Soc., Internat. assn. for Biol. Standards, Internat. Soc. Interferon Rsch. Achievements include major contribution to development and/or approval of vaccine against Hepatitis A and Hepatitis B, pediatric vaccines including Hemophilus Influenza B and varicella, Biogen's beta interferon product to treat multiple sclerosis (Avonex) Medicines Company product (Angiomax) direct thrombin inhibitor); patents for Inactivation of Non-A, Non-B Hepatitis Agent; Hepatitis B Immune Globulin used to Inactivate Hepatitis B Virus in Injectable Biological Products; Detection of Non-A, Non-B Hepatitis Associated Antigen; Heat Treatment of a Non-A, Non-B Hepatitis Agent to Prepare a Vaccine; Hepatitis B Core Antigen Vaccine; Hepatitis B Core Antigen Vaccine Made by Recombinant DNA; Purified Antigen from Non-A, Non-B Hepatitis Causing Factor: Screening Test for Reverse Transcriptase Containing Viruses in human blood. Home: 103 Livingston Rd Wellesley MA 02482 E-mail: yteregb@yahoo.com.

GERETY, TOM R., former academic administrator, lawyer, educator, philosopher; b. NYC, July 22, 1946; m. Adelia Moore, Oct. 7, 1972; children: Finn, Carrick, Amias, Rowan. BA, Yale U., 1969, MPhil, 1974, JD, PhD, Yale U., 1976; MA, Amherst Coll., 1995; LLD (hon.), Williams Coll., 1995; LHD, Doshisha U., 1996; LLD (hon.), Wesleyan U., 2001. Tchr. Peru project Joint Ctr. Urban Studies Harvard-MIT, Lima, 1966—67; bilingual tchr. Boston Pub. Schs., 1970—71; assoc. lectr. philosophy, master's asst. Morse Coll. Yale U., New Haven, 1972—74; asst. prof., fellow Ctr. Profl. Ethics Chgo. Kent Coll. Law, Ill. Inst. Tech., 1976—78; prof. law U. Pitts., 1978—86; dean, Nippert prof. Coll. Law U. Cin., 1986—89; pres., prof. philosophy Trinity Coll., Hartford, Conn., 1989—94, Amherst Coll., 1994—2003; exec. dir., Brennan prof. Brennan Ctr. for Justice, NYC, 2003—05; sr. cons. Academic Search Consultation Svc., Washington. Vis. asst. prof. Ind. U. Sch. Law, Bloomington, 1977—78; vis. prof. constl. law and jurisprudence Stanford U. Sch. Law, 1983—84; occasional appellate litigation in constl. law ACLU, 1981—; chair New Engl. Small Coll. Athletic Conf., 1991—92, 2000—01; chair bd. dirs. Consortium on Financing Higher Edn., 1993—95; testimony before the Senate Judiciary Com., Subcom. on Constitution on various proposed amendments. Writer, cons., on-air corr., fundraiser Visions of the Constitution, Nat. Endowment for Humanities TV series in constl. law, 1985—88, commentaries in various media Washington Post, Boston Globe, Chgo. Tribune, Christian Sci. Monitor, L.A. Times, MacNeil Lehrer Report, Nat. Pub. Radio; contbr. articles to profl. jours. Bd. mem. Internat. Rescue Com., 1989—2003, Save the Children U.S., Conn. State Bd. Edn., 1992—94. Fellow Kent fellow, Danforth Found., 1972—76, Woodrow Wilson fellow, 1983. Office: Academic Search Consultation Svc Ste 705 1825 K St NW Washington DC 20006 E-mail: tom.gerety@academic-search.org.

GERGELY, TOMAS ESTEBAN, astronomer; b. Budapest, Hungary, Oct. 14, 1943; came to U.S., 1976, naturalized, 1982; s. Tibor and Magda (Szilasi) G.; m. Ana Lajmanovich, Mar. 6, 1970; children: Gabriela S., Esteban A., Daniel M. Licenciado in Physics, U. Buenos Aires, 1967; PhD in Astronomy, U. Md., 1974. Asst. prof. Nat. Tech. U., Buenos Aires, 1974, rschr., 1975; rsch. assoc. U. Md., College Park, 1976-81, sr. rsch. assoc., 1981-82, assoc. rsch. sci., 1982-85; astrophysicist NASA Hdqs., Washington, 1985-86; mgr. electromagnetic spectrum NSF, 1986—. Mem. U.S. del. to World Adminstrv. Radio Conf., 1987, 92, World Radio Comm. Conf., 1995, 97, 2000, 03. Editor: (with others) Radio Physics of the Sun; contbr. articles to profl. jours. Recipient Young Scientist award French Govt., 1976. Mem. Internat. Astron. Union, Am. Astron. Soc., Internat. Radio Physics Union. Office: NSF Divsn Astron Scis 4201 Wilson Blvd Arlington VA 22230-0001 Home: 5315 Sherier Pl NW Washington DC 20016 Office Phone: 703-292-4896. Business E-Mail: tgergely@nsf.gov.

GERGEN, DAVID RICHMOND, federal official, magazine editor; b. Durham, NC, May 9, 1942; s. John Gergen; m. Anne Gergen, 1967; children: Christopher, Katherine. BA, Yale U., 1963; LLB, Harvard U., 1967. Staff asst. Nixon Adminstrn., Washington, 1971-72, spl. asst. to Pres., chief White House writing/research team, 1973-74; spl. comm. counsel to Pres. Ford White House, Washington, 1975-77, dir. comm. staff, 1981, dir. comm. to Pres. Reagan, 1981-84, counselor to Pres. Clinton, 1993-94, spl. advisor to Pres. and Sec. of State, 1994-95; resident fellow Am. Enterprise Inst.; mng. editor Am. Enterprise Inst. Public Opinion mag., Washington, 1977-81; resident fellow Inst. Politics, John F. Kennedy Sch. Govt., Cambridge, Mass., 1983-85; dir., Ctr. for Pub. Leadership John F. Kennedy Sch. Govt., Cambridge, Mass., prof. pub. svc.; mng. editor U.S. News & World Report, Washington, 1985-86, from editor to editor-at-large, 1986-93, 96—; weekly polit. analyst MacNeil/Lehrer News Hour, 1987-93. Weekly contbr. Newshour with Jim Lehrer; vis. prof. Duke U. Mem.: Trilateral Commn., Coun. on Foreign Relations. Office: JFK Sch Govt Harvard U 79 JF Kennedy St Cambridge MA 02138

GERGES, RAFIK REFAAT WESSA, structural engineer; s. Refaat Wessa Gerges and Awatif Shafeek Rizkalla; m. Nivert Mansi, Feb. 24, 2003. BSc, El Minia U., Egypt, 1991; M of Applied Sci. in Structural Engring., U. Waterloo, Ont., 1997; PhD in Structural Engring., U. We. Ont., London, Ont., 2003. Registered profl engr., Egyptian Engring. Syndicate, 1991, Profl. Engineers Ont. (Can.), 1999, civil and structural engr., Calif. Bd. Profl. Engrs. and Land Surveyors, 2004. Structural design engr. SANES Cons. Engrs., Cairo, 1994—95; wind/structural engr. Rowan, Williams, Davis and Irwin Inc., Guelph, Ont., 1997; sr. project engr., sr. structural analyst Nabih Youssef & Assoc., LA, 2003—. Cons. engr. Boundary Layer Wind Tunnel Lab., London, 1998—2002; presenter in field. Contbr. scientific papers, articles to profl. jours. Scholar, U. Waterloo, 1996, Natural Sci. and Engring. Rsch. Coun. Can., 1998—99, Ministry of Edn., Ont., 2000—01. Mem.: ASCE, Structural Engring. Assn. Calif., Am. Concrete Inst., Earthquake Engring. Rsch. Inst., Coun. Tall Bldgs. and Urban Habitat, Am. Inst. Steel Constrn. Achievements include structural design of tall reinforced concrete and steel buildings in areas of high seismicity and strong wind; design of tuned mass dampers to control wind induced vibrations of structures; energy dissipation systems to reduce the level of damage of buildings due to earthquakes; development of design expression to predict web crippling resistance of cold-formed steel beams; mathematical model for the force-displacement relationship of coil springs; design of method for non-linear tuned mass dampers; development of large displacement finite element analysis of curved beams; research in structural reliability analysis. Avocations: swimming, table tennis, canoeing, bicycling. Office Phone: 213-362-0707. Personal E-mail: rafik_gerges@yahoo.ca.

GERHARD, H. JOHN, orthopaedic surgeon, military officer; b. Portsmouth, Va., Oct. 29, 1955; s. Harry E. and Barbara M. Gerhard; m. Dianne Heath, Aug. 17, 1990; children: Christopher Ansley, Katherine Leigh, J. Stephen, Ian Jonas. BS, US Naval Acad., 1977; MD, Harvard U., Boston, 1981; MS, Indsl. Coll. Armed Forces, 1998. Diplomate Am. Bd. Orthopaedic Surgery, cert. naval flight surgeon Naval Aerospace Med. Inst. Commd. Ens. USN, 1977, advanced through grades to capt.; intern Naval Regional Med. Ctr. San Diego, 1981—82; flight surgeon Carrier Air Wing Two, NAS Miramar, Calif., 1982—84; orthopaedic surgery resident Duke U. Med. Ctr., Durham, NC, 1984—89, fellow hand and upper extremity surgery, 1992—93; staff orthopaedic surgeon Naval Hosp., Camp Lejeune, NC, 1989—92, dir. clin. svcs.; chief orthopaedics, staff orthopaedic surgeon, 1993—96; staff orthopaedic surgeon Brigade Svc. Support Group 4, Ops. Desert Shield/Storm, Iraq, 1990—91, USNS Comfort, Operation Uphold Democracy, Haiti, 1994; physician adviser to pres. Nat. Def. U., Ft McNair, DC, 1996—97; force surgeon USMC Forces, Atlantic; USMC Forces, Europe; USMC Forces, South; Fleet Marine Forces, Atlantic; Fleet Marine Forces, Europe, Norfolk, Va., 1998—2001; staff orthopaedic hand surgeon Naval Med. Ctr., Portsmouth, Va., 2001—02; exec. officer/COO Naval Hosp., Beaufort, SC, 2002—05, commdg. officer/CEO NAS Lemoore, Calif., 2005—. Presenter in field. Decorated various campaign and svc. medals/ribbons Dept. Navy, Ground Combat Action ribbon Dept. Def., Navy And Marine Corps Commendation medal, Meritorious Svc. medal, Legion Of Merit,; recipient USN Surgeon Gen.'s award, Naval Aerospace Med. Inst., Pensacola, Fl, 1980; Trident scholar, US Naval Acad. Fellow: ACS, Am. Acad. Orthopaedic Surgeons; mem.: Piedmont Orthopaedic Soc., Soc. Med. Cons. to Armed Forces (assoc.), Am. Coll. Healthcare Execs. Office: Commdg Officer Naval Hosp 937 Franklin Ave Lemoore CA 93246 Personal E-mail: jdij1493@aol.com. Business E-Mail: hjgerhard@nhlem.med.navy.mil.

GERHARD, LEE CLARENCE, geologist, educator; b. Albion, NY, May 30, 1937; s. Carl Clarence and Helen Mary (Lahmer) G.; m. Darcy LaFollette, July 22, 1964; 1 dau., Tracy Leigh. BS, Syracuse U., 1958; MS, U. Kans., 1961, PhD, 1964. Exploration geologist, region stratigrapher Sinclair Oil & Gas Co., Midland, Tex. and Roswell, N.Mex., 1964-66; asst. prof. geology U. So. Colo., Pueblo, 1966-69, assoc. prof., 1969-72; assoc. prof., asst. dir. West Indies Lab. Fairleigh Dickinson U., Rutherford, NJ, 1972-75; asst. geologist State of N.D., Grand Forks, 1975-77, geologist, 1977-81; prof., chmn. dept. geology U. N.D., Grand Forks, 1977-81; mgr. Rocky Mountain div. Supron Energy Corp., Denver, 1981-82; owner, pres. Gerhard & Assocs., Englewood, Colo., 1982-87; prof. petroleum geology Colo. Sch. Mines, Denver, 1982—2004, Getty prof., 1984-87; state geologist, dir. geol. survey State of Kans., Lawrence, 1987-99, prin. geologist, 1999—2005; prin. Gerhard & Assocs., 2005—; founder, co-dir. Energy Rsch. Ctr., U. Kans., 1990-94. Presdl. appointee Nat. Adv. Com. on Oceans and Atmosphere, 1984-87. Contbr. articles to profl. jours. Served to 1st lt. U.S. Army, 1958-60. Danforth fellow, 1970-72; named to Kans. Oil and Gas Hall of Fame, 2002. Fellow Geol. Soc. Am.; mem. Am. Assn. Petroleum Geologists (hon., Disting. Svc. award 1989, Journalism award 1996, pres. divsn. environ. geosci. 1994-95, hon. divsn. environ. geoscis. 1998, v.p. divsn. profl. affairs 2003-04, Pub. Outreach award 1999, 2003, 07), Am. Inst. Profl. Geologists, Russian Acad. Natural Scis. (US Br.), Rocky Mountain Assn. Geologists, Colo. Sci. Soc., Kans. Geol. Soc. (hon.), Sigma Xi, Sigma Gamma Epsilon. Home: 1628 Alvamar Dr Lawrence KS 66047-1714 Personal E-mail: leeg@sunflower.com.

GERHARDT, CAROL, artist; b. Wabash, Ind., Aug. 10, 1946; d. Dale Martin Ashby and Helen Irene Harper; 2 children from previous marriage. BS, U. Houston, 1986, postgrad., 1994—96. Exec. dir. Penguin Photography Studio, Houston, 1986—87, photographer, 1987—90; photojournalism faculty North Harris County Coll., Houston, 1990—92; art faculty Houston Ind. Sch. Dist., 1992—2007. Exhibitions include UN/UNIFEM, Marias do Mundo, Brazil, 2001, Diverse Works Art Space, Houston, 1996, Cultural Arts Coun. Houston, 2005, 125 Gallery, 2005, Commerce St. Artsts, Houston, 2005, Poissant Gallery, 2006, 2007, Represented in permanent collections Lester Marks Collection. Personal E-mail: gerhardt1c@aol.com.

GERHARDT, E. ALVIN, JR., retired museum director; b. Lynchburg, Va., Oct. 15, 1930; s. Earl Alvin and Georgia Burton Gerhardt; m. Sally Tazewell Flournoy, Sept. 10, 1955; children: Beth, Fritz, Tom, Anna. BS in Bus., Davidson Coll., 1951; postgrad., Lebanon Valley Coll., 1952, Columbia U., 1955; MA in Mus. Studies, SUNY, 1974. Salesman Murphy, Brill & Sahner, Inc., NYC, 1954—56; sales mgr., treas. Lynchburg (Va.) Hosiery Mills, Inc., 1956—73; exec. dir. Rocky Mount Mus., Piney Flats, Tenn., 1974—92; mus. dir., tchr. Tusculum (Tenn.) Coll., 1992—2000. Pres., officer Lynchburg Hist. Soc., 1960—73, Tenn. Assn. Mus., Nashville, 1975—79, SE Mus. Conf., Atlanta, 1977—86; pres., founding dir. Va. Assn. Mus., Richmond, 1967—73; founding chmn. mus. assessment program Inst. Mus. Svcs. and Am. Assn. Mus., 1980—87; founding mem., bd. dirs. World's Fair Hospitality Assn., Knoxville, Tenn., 1979—83; chmn., officer Upper East Tenn.-SW Va. Tourism Coun., 1977—81; bd. dirs. Assn. Living History, Farms and Agrl. Mus., Ohio, 1990—93. 1st lt. inf. US Army, 1951—53. Decorated Combat Inf. badge; recipient James Short award, SE Mus. Conf., 1993, Millenium award, Tenn. Assn. Mus., 2000, Schlebecker award, Assn. Living History, Farms and Agrl. Mus., 2003. Mem.: Am. Assn. Mus. (coun. mem. 1979—89), Am. Assn. for State & Local History (treas., bd. exec. com. 1986—92). Presbyterian. Avocations: history, photography, genealogy. Home: 211 University Pkwy 4 Johnson City TN 37604 Home Phone: 423-926-2519. Personal E-mail: alvingerhardt@earthlink.net.

GERHARDT, EMERY WILLIAM, food products executive; b. Chgo., Aug. 3, 1940; s. William Harry and Lorraine F. Gerhardt; children: William A. Harris, Elizabeth M. Harris, Antoinette S. Biggs, Ana T. Degree in Pub. Adminstrn., San Diego State U., 1966. Sr. v.p. ops. Ne-Mo's Bakery Inc., Escondido, Calif., 1981—2006; v.p. ops. Horizon Food Group, Escondido, 2006—. Sr. warden Anglican Ch. of St. Timothy & Titus, San Diego, 2006—07. With US Army, 1963—65. Office: Horizon Food Group 416 N Hale Ave Escondido CA 92029 Office Phone: 760-300-3060.

GERHARDT, LESTER A., engineering educator, dean; b. Bronx, NY, Jan. 28, 1940; s. David and Mary G.; m. Karen Rita Zimmerman, Sept. 2, 1961; children: Brian, Douglas. BEE, CUNY, 1961; MSEE, SUNY, Buffalo, 1964, PhD, 1969; Doctorate (hon.), Danish Tech. U., 2000. Engr., asst. dir rsch. Bell Aerospace, Buffalo, 1961-70; assoc. prof. Rensselaer Polytechnic Inst., Troy, NY, 1970-74, prof., 1974—, chmn. elect., computer and systems engring. dept., 1975-86, dir. CIM Program, 1986-91, assoc. dean engring., 1991—, v.p. rsch. adminstrn. and fin., 2003—, acting dean engring., 2004—05, vice provost, dean grad. edn., 2005—, dir. internat. programs, 2007—. Acting dir. Ctr. for the Mfg. Productivity, 1991-92, founding dir., 1979-80, dir. Ctr. for indsl. Innovation, 1993—; nat. del. NATO, 1980—, chair Rsch. Collaborative Grants Programme; mem. AFSB com. on Robotics and Artificial Intelligence, 1986-89, mem. com. Tactical Communications Nat. Acad. Scis.; mem. adv. bd. N.Y. Gov. Carey's Panel on Telecommunications, NSF, chair. adv. bd.; active internat. cons. to industry, the gov't, and other Universities. Recipient Inventor of Yr. award NY State Intellectual Property Law Assn., 1997. Fellow: IEEE, ASEE (chmn. engring. rsch. coun. 1996—98, bd. dirs. 1996—98, Inaugural award Rsch. Adminstrn. Engring. Rsch. Coun. 2002). Avocations: sailing, photography, tennis. Office: Rensselaer Poly Inst Deans Office Sch Engring JEC 3002 Troy NY 12180 E-mail: gerhal@rpi.edu.

GERHART, EUGENE CLIFTON, lawyer; b. Bklyn., Apr. 7, 1912; s. Herman Eugene and Mary Elizabeth (Hamilton) G.; m. Mary Richardson Schreiber, Mar. 30, 1939; children: Catherine Gerhart Landon, Virginia Gerhart Mason. AB, Princeton U., 1934; LLB, Harvard U., 1937. Bar: N.J. 1938, N.Y. 1945. Practiced in, Newark, 1938-43, Binghamton, NY, 1946—; counsel firm Coughlin & Gerhart, Binghamton; sec. to Judge Manley O. Hudson, Secretariat/League of Nations, Geneva, 1934; lectr. bus. law U. Newark, 1942-43, Triple Cities Coll., 1946-48, Harpur Coll., Endicott, NY, 1953-55; lectr. indsl. and labor relations Cornell U., Ithaca, NY, 1946; dir., gen. counsel Columbian Mut. Life Ins. Co., 1949-83, acting pres., 1969-70, chmn. bd., 1970-82. Mem. coun. SUNY, Cortland, 1967-77, chmn., 1971-77; mem. Select Task Force on Ct. Reorgn. N.Y. State Senate; mem. jud. nominating com. 3d Jud. Dept., State of N.Y.; mem. N.Y. Unified Ct. Sys. Judicial Records Disposition and Archives Devel. Com. Author: American Liberty and Natural Law, America's Advocate: Robert H. Jackson, Robert H. Jackson: Lawyer's Judge, 2003, Arthur T. Vanderbilt: The Compleat Counsellor, Quote It!, Quote It II, The Lawyer's Treasury, Quote It Completely!, 1998, World Reference Guide to more than 5500 Memorable Quotations from Law and Literature, 1998; spl. contbg. author: Law Office Econs. and Mgmt, 1962—; mem. editl. bd. Quar. Report of Conf. on Personal Fin. Law, 1965; contbr. articles to legal, other publs. Chmn. Harpur Forum SUNY, Binghamton, 1983-84. Lt. USNR, 1943-46. Fellow Am. Bar Found., Am. Coll. Probate Counsel, N.Y. State Bar Found.; mem. ABA (editor Jour. 1946-67, Ross Essay award 1946), Internat. Assn. Ins. Counsel, Assn. Life Ins. Counsel, Am. Judicature Soc., Am. Law Inst., N.Y. State Bar Assn. (editor-in-chief jour. 1961-97, editor-in-chief emeritus 1997—, Disting. Svc. award 1998), Assn. Bar City N.Y., Broome County Bar Assn. (pres. 1961-62, Lifetime Achievement award 1995), Selden Soc., Broome County Princeton Alumni Assn., Harvard Law Sch. Assn. Upstate N.Y. (pres. 1955-57), Scribes (pres., dir. 1966-67), St. Andrew's Soc. Clubs: Rotary (pres. 1969-70), Cosmos, Oteyokwa Lake (pres. 1971-73), Nassau, Harvard of N.Y, Princeton of N.Y. Republican. Home: 34 W End Ave Binghamton NY 13905-4026 Office: 20 Hawley St Binghamton NY 13901-3216

GERHART, FREDERICK JOHN, lawyer; b. Osage, Iowa, Mar. 12, 1946; s. Grant George and Marjory Justine (Heckle) G.; m. Marcia Soast, Apr. 3, 1974 (div. May 1992); children: David, Ethan. BA, Drake U., 1968; JD, Harvard U., 1971. Bar: Iowa 1971, Minn. 1973, U.S. Tax Ct. 1973, Pa. 1977, U.S. Dist. Ct. (ea. dist.) Pa. 1978, U.S. Ct. Appeals (3d cir.) 1992. Atty., advisor U.S. Tax Ct., Washington, 1971-73; assoc. Gray, Plant, Mooty & Bennett, Mpls., 1973-77, Dechert, Price & Rhoads, Phila., 1977-80, ptnr., 1980, Dechert LLP, Phila. Taught Law Sch. Villanova U.; taught Temple U. Author: The Gift Tax, 1980, contbr. numerous articles to profl. jours. Mem. ABA (tax sect. com. on exempt orgns., health law sect.), Phila. Bar Assn. (tax sect.), Pa. Bar Assn., Phi Beta Kappa. Office: Dechert LLP Cira Ctr 2929 Arch St Philadelphia PA 19104-2808 Office Phone: 215-994-2838. Office Fax: 215-994-2222. E-mail: frederick.gerhart@dechert.com.

GERICKE, PAUL WILLIAM, minister, educator; b. St. Louis, Apr. 8, 1924; s. Orville Herman and Irma Rose (Reinhart) G.; m. Jean Fisher, Feb. 18, 1953; 1 child, Michael Paul. BSEE, Washington U., St. Louis, 1949; BD, So. Bapt. Theol. Sem., 1960; ThD, New Orleans Bapt. Theol. Sem., 1964; MA, U. New Orleans, 1972. Ordained to ministry So. Bapt. Conv., 1952. Instr. electronics USAF, 1949; calibration engr. Emerson Electric Co., St. Louis, 1950; asst. pastor Calvary Bapt. Ch., St. Louis, 1951-53, Forest Ave. Bapt. Ch., Kansas City, Mo., 1954; pastor First Bapt. Ch., Marceline, Mo., 1955-56, New Hope Bapt. Ch., St. Louis, 1957, Summit Park Bapt. Ch., Louisville, 1959-60, Logtown Bapt. Ch., Miss., 1960-64; asst. prof., dir. libr. svcs. New Orleans Bapt. Theol. Sem., 1965-73, assoc. prof., dir. libr., 1973-91, assoc. prof. comms., dir. Comm. Ctr., 1991-92, dir. rsch. and planning, 1992-93, prof. comms. N. Ga. Campus, 1993, acad. counselor, 1993, dir. of libr., 1993—99, prof. comms. emeritus, 1999—. Mgr. Sta. WSBN-FM, New Orleans, 1979-85, chmn., 1985-92; bd. dirs. religious access channel REACH, New Orleans, 1985-93. Author: The Preaching of Robert G. Lee, 1967, The Ministers Filing System, 1971, Sermon Building, 1973, Crucial Experiences in the Life of D.L. Moody, 1978, Pastor's Library, 1986, Great Preachers of the Church, 1996, Prince of Preachers: The Apostle Paul, 2005. Served with AC USNR, 1942-46. Mem. Am. Radio Relay League, Theta Xi. Republican. Avocation: amateur radio. Home: 482 Sletten Dr Lawrenceville GA 30045 *My life has been completely changed by a personal encounter with Jesus Christ in 1951. Through faith in Him as Savior and Lord, I received a new life, a new sense of values, a new purpose in life, and a new hope both for this life and the life to come. My purpose now is to seek first the kingdom of God and all the other things I need will be given unto me.*

GERJUOY, EDWARD, physicist; b. Bklyn., May 19, 1918; s. Abraham and Clara (Hirsch) G.; m. Clark Jacqueline Reid, Aug. 26, 1940; children: Neil, David Leif. BS cum laude, CCNY, 1937; MA, U. Calif., Berkeley, 1940, PhD, 1942; JD magna cum laude, U. Pitts., 1977. Bar: Calif. 1977, Pa. 1978. Assoc. dir. sonar analysis group Divsn. War Rsch., Columbia, 1942—46; mem. faculty U. So. Calif., LA, 1946—51; vis. assoc. prof. NYU, 1951—52; mem. faculty U. Pitts., 1952—58, 1964—82, prof. physics, 1964—82, prof. emeritus, 1982—; mem. Pa. Environ. Hearing Bd., 1982—86, cons. hearing examiner, 1987—89; of counsel Rose, Schmidt, Hasley & DiSalle, Pitts., 1987—2001. Mem. rsch. staff Gen. Atomic div. Gen. Dynamics Corp., San Diego, 1958-62; dir. plasma and space applied physics RCA Labs., Princeton, N.J., 1962-64; cons. Westinghouse Rsch. Labs., 1952-58; mem. adv. com. health physics divsn. Oak Ridge Nat. Labs., 1967-71, chmn. com., 1971-74; assoc. Tucker Arensberg Very & Ferguson, Pitts., 1978-80; vis. fellow Joint Inst. Lab. Physics, U. Colo., Boulder, 1970; vis. sci. USSR Acad. Sci. Lebedev Inst., Moscow, 1972; hearing examiner Pa. Environ. Hearing Bd., 1980-81; vis. scholar Stanford Math. Dept., 1987; cons. EPA, 1977-81,; cons. atty. Reed, Smith, Shaw & McClay, Pitts., 1993-2004; adj. prof. U. Pitts. Law Sch., 2000. Author: (with A. Yaspan) Reverberation, in series The Physics of Sound in the Sea, 1968; editor: Physics Text Series, 1960-62, Jour. Comments on Atomic and Molecular Physics, 1971-74, Jurimetrics Jour. of Law Sci. and Tech., 1980-87; contbr. chpts. and numerous articles to tech. and legal lit. Bd. dirs. Pitts. ACLU, 1975-80, 92-95, vice-chmn., chair-elect, chair Am. Phys. Soc. Forum on Physics and Soc., 1994-97; bd. dirs. Pitts. Group Against Smog and Pollution, 2002—04. Fellow AAAS, Am. Phys. Soc. (panel on pub. affairs 1976-79, 94-96, chmn. 1981, governing coun. 2000—03, audit com. 2002-04, chair com. on internat. freedom of scientists 2004, mem. Sakharov prize com. 2005-07), Inst. Physics, Phys. Soc. (Eng.); mem. ABA (chmn. phys. scis. com., sect. sci. and tech. 1976-77, coun. sci. and tech. 1977-80, 84, 87-91), Phi Beta Kappa, Sigma Xi, Order of Coif. Achievements include first predictions of interference in Zeeman Effect allowing magnetic dipole and electric quadrupole transitions, and (with others) of beats between photons of different frequencies; first derivation of transition rates in many-particle collisions from a purely time-independent formalism; first development (with others) of routine procedure for constructing variational estimates of very wide class of quantities. Home: 400 Richland Ln Pittsburgh PA 15208-2732 Office: Univ Pitts Dept Physics and Astronomy 100 Allen Hall Pittsburgh PA 15260 Office Phone: 412-624-2737. Business E-Mail: gerjuoy@pitt.edu. *I have tried to avoid overspecialization, while not letting myself descend into dilettantism. I believe I have succeeded in these endeavors. The last phase of my career, embarking on a law degree at age 56, earning the degree and passing the bar at 59, and then being employed full time as a judge in environmental disputes, probably is an extreme example of career restlessness. I am not sorry to have strayed from a straight line career path, and it has kept me feeling young in my so-called golden years. Nevertheless—and this is more a comment about the present world than about me— I do not believe I would advise young men today to be guided by me.*

GERJUOY, HERBERT GEORGE, information scientist, educator, psychologist, consultant, poet; b. Bklyn., Apr. 22, 1929; s. Abraham and Clara (Hirshkowitz) G.; m. Irma Lewis Rossman, May 6, 1952 (div. 1965); children: Judith Hope, Amy Beth; m. Carol Judith Arenberg, Dec. 30, 1966; children: Berenice Tamar, Ilana Martha. AB magna cum laude, U. So. Calif., 1949; MA, State U. Iowa, 1952, PhD, 1953. Cert. psychologist, Ohio. Rsch. assoc. in psychology State U. Iowa, Iowa City, 1953—54; instr. psychology Ind. U., Bloomington, 1954—57; assoc. prof. psychology U. Toledo, 1957—62; rsch. psychologist Ednl. Testing Svc., Princeton, NJ, 1962—67; sr. staff scientist HumRRO, Alexandria, Va., 1967—70; prof. pub. adminstrn. SUNY, Albany, NY, 1970—75; sr. staff scientist The Futures Group, Glastonbury, Conn., 1975—79; pres. Program Strategies, Inc., West Hartford, Conn., 1979—85; asst. prof. computer sci., soc. sci., psychology Three Rivers C.C., Norwich, Conn., 1987—99, coord. data processing, 1987—94; asst. prof. computer info. sys., adj. instr. psychology Tunxis C.C., Farmington, Conn., 1999—2001, coord. computer info. sys., 1999—2001, adj. instr. computer info. sys., 2001; adj. instr. pub. adminstrn Marist Coll., Poughkeepsie, NY, 1999—2002; adj. prof. econs. Tunxis C.C., Farmington, Conn., 2003. Pres. Bravo Corp., West Hartford, 1988-91; editor The Red Fox Rev., Norwich, 1992-99; sr. rsch. assoc. Ark. Inst., Little Rock, 1994; adj. lectr. math. & computer sci. Eastern Conn. State U., 1997-99; mem. prostate pathobiology peer rev. panel Dept. Def., US Army Med. Rsch. Unit, 2006. Editor: Rehabilitation: Pathways in a Changing World, 1962, Population, Education, and Social Welfare in Sub-Saharan Africa, 1995, (newsletter) Kol Kehilah (Voice of the Congregation), Hartford, 2002-05; co-author: Life-Extending Technologies, 1980, Youth Crime in Arkansas, 1994; co-editor: Prayer Book for Yom Kippur Evening, 2004. Chief observer Ground Observer Corps, so. Ind., 1956-57; cons. Schenectady Narcotics Info. Ctr., 1974-75; mem. edtl. bd. Future Rsch. Qtrly., 1984—. Recipient Outstanding Contbn. award Am. Acad. Rehab. Therapy, 1962. Mem.: AAAS, Assn. Humanistic Psychology, N.Y. Acad. Arts and Sci., Conn. Acad. Arts and Scis. (mem. steering com. Kehilat Chaverim 2002—06, mem. editl. bd. Kehilat Chaverim 2005—06), Network Spiritual Progressives, Stratford Writers Group, Sigma Xi. Democrat. Jewish. Avocations: foundations of mathematics, writing, music. Home: 8 Lexington Rd West Hartford CT 06119-1747 Personal E-mail: elementhg@yahoo.com.

GERKE, THOMAS A., telecommunications industry executive, lawyer; BBA, U. Mo., Columbia; MBA, Rockhurst Coll.; JD, U. Mo., Kansas City. Ptnr. Smith, Gill, Fisher & Butts, Kansas City; sr. atty. US Sprint, 1994—97, various mgmt. pos. in legal, including asst. v.p.-legal, corp. transactions, 1997—99, v.p.-legal gen. bus. and tech., 1999—2000; corp. sec., assoc. gen. counsel Sprint Corp., Overland Park, Kans., 2000—02, v.p.-bus. devel., strategic planning and alliances in the Global Markets Group, 2002—03, exec. v.p.-gen. counsel and external affairs, 2003—05; gen. counsel, external affairs Embarq Corp., Overland Park, Kans., 2005—. Office: Embarq Corp 5454 W 110 St Overland Park KS 66211*

GERKENS, HENRY H., trucking executive; m. Marcia Gerkens; 3 children. Degree, Adelphi U. CPA. Acct. Price Waterhouse, 1972; various positions Gen. Host Corp.; v.p. fin. admin. Chiquita Brands Inc.; v.p., CFO Landstar Sys., Inc., Jacksonville, Fla., 1989—94, exec. v.p., CFO, 1994—2001, pres., CFO, 2001, pres., COO, 2001—04, bd. dirs., pres., CEO, 2004—. Mem.: AICPA, N.Y. State Soc. CPAs. Office: Landstar Sys 13410 Sutton Park Dr S Jacksonville FL 32224*

GERKEY, STEPHEN J., management consultant, writer, speech educator; b. Eau Claire, Wis., Sept. 14, 1943; s. Joseph Thomas and Mary Jane (Lawrence) G. BA, U. Wis., Eau Claire, 1966; MA, Mich. State U., 1967; PhD, Ind. U., 1977. Cert. project mgr. IBM Corp., 1998, archives and records mgr. State Hist. Soc. of Wis., 1979. Instr. English U. Wis., Eau Claire, 1967-70, 76; assoc. instr., lectr. Ind. U., Bloomington, 1971—75; home sch.-coord. West Ctrl. Wis. Native Am. Comty., Inc., Eau Claire, 1977-78; archives asst. State Hist. Soc. of Wis., Eau Claire, 1978-79; chmn. dept. English, journalism, drama McDonell Ctrl. H.S., Chippewa Falls, Wis., 1981-82, dir. writing program, 1980-82; owner, prin. cons. NMB Assocs., Santa Fe, 1982—; sr. cons. BDM Internat., Albuquerque, 1995-96; project mgr. IBM Corp., Santa Fe, sys. change leader, 1997-98, edn. consulting practice leader, 1998-99; sr. business intelligence cons., 2000—02. Adj. asst. prof. English Iowa State U., Ames, Iowa, 1982-84; asst. prof. English Ea. N.Mex. U., Portales, 1984-88; asst. prof. bus. Ea. N.Mex. U., Portales, 1988-90, assoc. prof. bus., 1990-92; dir. N.Mex. Ctr. Tchg. Excellence, Ea. N.Mex. U., Portales, 1990-92; sr. rsch. and policy analyst, N.Mex. Legislature, Santa Fe, 1992-93; edn. summits steering com. Office N.Mex. Gov., Santa Fe, 1990-93; chair N.Mex.'s Gov., Edn. Renewal Task Force, Edn. Commn. States, Santa Fe, 1991-92; tchr. N.Mex. Author: Sources for the Study of Chippewa Valley History: A Preliminary Bibliography, 1977, A Manual for Full-Time Tutors, 1978, N.Mex. Gov.'s Edn. Summit Reports, 1991, 92, 93, The Navajo Code Talkers, 1996; assoc. editor rsch. and legis. ops. Capitol Govt. reports, Santa Fe, 1993-95; contbr. articles to profl. jours. including N.Mex. Jour. Reading, 1989. V.P. Roosevelt County Humane Soc., 1985-92; v.p., pres. faculty senate Ea. N.Mex. U., Portales, 1986-89. Hobbs Found. Doctoral fellow, 1969; Ind. U. scholar, Bloomington, 1971; Ea. New Mex. U. Faculty Devel. grantee. Mem.: Sigma Tau Delta (life; pres. 1964—65). Avocations: triathlons, road racing. Home and Office: 314 N 14th St Memphis TX 79245-2720 Home Phone: 806-259-9975. E-mail: sgerkey@valornet.com.

GERLACH, FRANKLIN THEODORE, lawyer; b. Portsmouth, Ohio, Apr. 11, 1935; s. Albert T. and Nora Alice (Hayes) G.; m. Cynthia Ann Koehler, Aug. 1, 1958; children: Valarie, Philipp. BBA, U. Cin., 1958; MPA, Syracuse U., NY, 1959; JD, U. Cin., 1961. Bar: Ohio 1961, US Dist. Ct. (so. dist.) Ohio 1969, US Supreme Ct. 1971. Dir. purchasing, planning and urban renewal City of Portsmouth, 1961-62, city mgr., 1962-66, mayor, 1990-97; asst. dir. Ohio U., Portsmouth, 1966-68; sole practitioner law Portsmouth, 1968—. Solicitor Village New Boston, Ohio, 1968-70; trustee Ohio Acad. Trial Lawyers, Columbus, 1984-85. Recipient Outstanding Young Man of Ohio award Portsmouth Jaycees, 1968, Ohio Jaycees, 1969. Mem. Scioto County Bar Assn. (pres. 1986). Democrat. Avocation: antiques. Home: 1221 20th St Portsmouth OH 45662-2924 Office: 814 7th St Portsmouth OH 45662-4128 Office Phone: 740-354-7755. E-mail: lawyergg@zoomnet.net.

GERLACH, JEANNE ELAINE, English language educator; b. Charleston, W.Va., Oct. 20, 1946; d. Lafayette and Edith Lorraine (Robinson) Marcum; m. Roger Thomas Gerlach Sr., Dec. 30, 1966; children: Roger Thomas Jr., Kristen Elaine. BS, W.Va. State Coll., Institute, 1974; MA, W.Va. State Coll., 1979; EdD, W.Va. U., 1985, U. North Tex., 1992. Lang. arts tchr. Ohio County Schs., Wheeling, W.Va., 1974-79; English instr. West Liberty (W.Va.) State Coll., 1979-82; continuing edn. instr. Seattle Pacific U., 1982-85; asst. prof. English W.Va. U., Morgantown, 1985-86, Tarrant County Jr. Coll., Ft. Worth, 1986-88; dir. Communications Unlimited, Dallas, Pitts., 1986—; assoc. prof. English edn. W.Va. U., Morgantown, 1989-97, spl. asst. to the provost, 1994-97, dir. ctr. women's studies, 1993-94; dean coll. edn. U. Tex., Arlington, 1997—, assoc. v.p. K-16 initiatives, 2003—. Cons. to bus. and corps., 1986—; co-dir. advanced writing project W.Va. U., Morgantown, 1989, lang. arts camps, 1988, 89, 90, young writers inst. Editor: English Internat.; contbr. articles to profl. jours. Mem. LWV, W.Va., DAR, Young Republicans, W.Va.; participant Leadership Tex., 2005. Recipient 1st place Creative Writing award, W.Va. Women's Clubs, 1976, Great Tex. Woman award, Ft. Worth Bus. Press, 2002; Faculty Devel. grantee, W.Va. U., 1989. Mem. AAUW, AAUP, Nat. Coun. Tchrs. English (chair women's com. 1986—, chair nominating com. 1988-89, Outstanding Tchr. in Coll. of Human Resources and Edn. award W.Va. U. 1992, Rewey Belle Inglis award 1992), Am. Ednl. Rsch. Assn., W.Va. U. Alumni Assn. (sec. 1990, pres.), Nat. Women's Studies Assn., Nat. Soc. Daus. Am. Revolution. Republican. Methodist. Avocations: tennis, golf, poetry, photography, doll collecting. Office Phone: 817-272-5476. Business E-Mail: gerlach@uta.edu.

GERLACH, JIM (JAMES WILLIAM GERLACH), congressman; b. Ellwood City, Pa., Feb. 25, 1955; s. Jack Allen and Helen (Fitzgerald) Gerlach; m. Karen Devanna, 1980; children: Katie, Jimmy, Robby. BA cum laude in Polit. Sci., Dickinson Coll., 1977; JD, Dickinson Coll. Sch. Law, 1980. Bar: Pa. Pvt. practice, Downingtown, Pa.; legis. aide Pa. Senate, Harrisburg, 1978-80; mem. Pa. State Ho. Reps. from Dist. 44, Harrisburg, Pa., 1991-94, Pa. State Senate from Dist. 44, Harrisburg, 1995—2002, US Congress from 6th Pa. dist., 2003—, mem. transp. and infrastructure com., mem. fin. svcs. com., founder, co-chmn. Land Trust Caucus. Bd. dirs. Brandywine Health & Wellness Found., Mission Educating Children with Autism. Named Guardian of Small Bus., Nat. Fedn. Ind. Bus., 1993, 1996; recipient Green Valleys Assn. Environ. award, 1995, Light of Long-Term Care award, Am. Health Care Assn., 2006, Legis. Leader award, Humane Soc., 2006, Disting. Cmty. Health Superhero award, Nat. Assn. Cmty. Health Ctrs., 2006. Mem.: Lions (bd. dirs. Downingtown), Pa. Bar Assn., Chester County Agr. Devel. Coun., Sigma Chi. Republican. Office: US House Reps 308 Cannon House Office Bldg Washington DC 20515 Office Phone: 202-225-4315. Office Fax: 202-225-8440.*

GERMAIN, CLAIRE MADELEINE, law librarian, educator; b. Chaumont, France, Sept. 22, 1951; d. Pierre and Jeanne (Despujols) G.; m. Stuart M. Basefsky, Aug. 16, 1976; 1 child, Nicolas. Licence-es. lettres, U. Paris, 1971, LLB, 1974; M in Comparative Law, La. State U., 1975; M in Law Librarianship, U. Denver, 1977. Reference librarian Duke U. Law Library, Durham, NC, 1977-80, head reference librarian, 1982-84, asst. librarian, sr. lectr. comparative law, 1984-89, assoc. dir., sr. lectr. comparative law, 1989-93; Edward Cornell law libr., prof. law Cornell U., Ithaca, NY, 1993—. Research fellow Max Planck Inst., Hamburg, Federal Republic of Germany, 1980. Author: Germain's Transnational Law Research: A Guide to Attorneys, 1991, (with Szladits) Guide to Foreign Legal Materials, French, 2d edit., 1985; contbr. and editor articles to profl. jours. Mem. ABA, Am. Assn. Law Librs. (chair fgn. law sect. 1985-86, v.p., pres.-elect 2004—, chair-elect sect. librs. 2003-), Am. Assn. Law Schs. (chmn. libr. and tech. com., chmn. elect libr. sect. 2003—). Roman Catholic. Office: Cornell Law Libr Myron Taylor Hall Ithaca NY 14853 Office Phone: 607-255-5857. E-mail: cmg13@cornell.edu.*

GERMAIN, PAMELA, health facility administrator, educator; b. Buffalo, Feb. 17, 1952; d. Philip William and Alma Thering Germain; children: Constantine Skagias, Amelia Katerina Skagias. BA in Econs., LeMoyne Coll., Syracuse, NY, 1973; MBA, Harvard U., Boston, 1985. Dist. mgr. comml. lines casualty property The Travelers, Worcester, Mass., 1981—83; assoc. dir. external rels. Harvard Bus. Sch., Boston, 1985—87; dir. corp. strategy and bus. diversification group The Travelers, Hartford, Conn., 1987—88; divsn. v.p. managed care and employee benefits ops. divsn. The Travelers Corp., Hartford, 1988—93; dir. network devel. and ops., COO MFHS Managed Care, Inc. Millard Fillmore Health Sys., Buffalo, 1995—97; v.p. managed care and outreach Roswell Pk. Cancer Inst., Buffalo, 1998—. Lectr. mgmt. devel. programs Harvard Bus. Sch. Club, Buffalo, 1995—; adj. faculty D'Youville Coll., Buffalo, 2004—05; products and svcs. com. mem. Nat. Comprehensive Cancer Network, Phila., 1997—; presenter in field. Bd. mem. Mid-Erie Treatment and Counseling Svcs., Buffalo, 1996—2007, pres., 2005—07. Roman Catholic. Avocations: travel, cultural arts, walking. Home: 59 Round Trail Rd West Seneca NY 14218-3723 Office: Roswell Park Cancer Institute Elm & Carlton Sts Buffalo NY 14263 Office Phone: 716-845-4552. Office Fax: 716-845-1610; Home Fax: 716-677-5515. Personal E-mail: pgermainsk@aol.com. Business E-Mail: pamela.germain@roswellpark.org.

GERMAN, DONALD FREDERICK, physician; b. San Francisco, Oct. 2, 1935; m. Marilyn Sue King; children: Susan, Charles, Donald. BS, U. San Francisco, 1956; MD, U. Calif., San Francisco, 1960. Diplomate Am. Bd. Pediats., Am. Bd. Allergy and Immunology. Intern Kaiser Found. Hosp., San Francisco, 1960-61, resident in pediats., 1963-65, resident, fellow in allergy, 1966-68; staff pediatrician Kaiser Med. Ctr., Santa Clara, Calif., 1965-66, staff allergist, 1968-69; chief dept. allergy Kaiser Permanente Med. Ctr., San Francisco, 1969-99, allergy staff physician, 1999—. Clin. prof. pediatrics U. Calif. Med. Sch., San Francisco, 1991—; bd. dirs. Asthma, Allergy and Immunology Found. No. Calif. Capt. USAF, 1961-63. Fellow Am. Acad. Pediats., Am. Coll. Allergy and Immunology, Am. Acad. Allergy and Immunology; mem. Calif. Soc. Allergy and Immunology (past pres.). Avocations: running, hiking, fly fishing, travel. Address: 1030 Sir Francis Drake Blvd Ste 110 Kentfield CA 94904 Office Phone: 415-460-6686. Personal E-mail: dfgerman2@yahoo.com. Business E-Mail: donald.german@kp.org.

GERMAN, JUNE RESNICK, lawyer; b. NYC, Feb. 24, 1946; d. Irving and Stella (Weintraub) Resnick; m. Harold Jacob German, May 31, 1974; children: Beth Melissa, Heather Alice, Bret. BA, U. Pa., 1965; JD, NYU, 1968. Bar: N.Y. 1968, U.S. Dist. Ct. (ea. and so. dists.) N.Y. 1974, U.S. Ct. Appeals (2d cir.) 1973, U.S. Supreme Ct. 1973. Atty., sr. atty., supervising atty. Mental Health Info. Svc., NYC, 1968-77; atty., advisor Course in Human Behavior Mems. of N.Y. State Judiciary, Nassau and Suffolk County, 1980; pvt. practice Huntington, NY, 1985—. Contbg. author: Bioethics and Human Rights, 1978, Mental Illness, Due Process and the Acquitted Defendant, 1979; contbr. chpts. to books, articles to profl. jours. Chmn. Citizen's Ad Hoc Com. Constrn. of the Dix Hills Water Adminstrn. Bldg., Huntington, N.Y., 1985-90; mem. Citizens Adv. Com. for Dix Hills Water Dist., Huntington, 1992—; dir. House Beautiful Assn. at Dix Hills, 1986—, Citizens for a Livable Environment and Recycling, Huntington, 1989-93; active Suffolk County (N.Y.) Dem. Com., 1986—, Deer Park Avenue Task Force, Town of Huntington, 1997-98, Dix Hills Revitalization Com., 1999-2000. Mem. Suffolk County Bar Assn. Jewish. Avocations: tennis, hiking, travel. Office: 150 Main St Huntington NY 11743-6908 Office Phone: 631-271-8711. Personal E-mail: junegerman@hotmail.com.

GERMAN, WILLIAM, newspaper editor; b. NYC, Jan. 4, 1919; s. Sam and Celia (Norack) G.; m. Gertrude Pasenkoff, Oct. 12, 1940 (dec. 1998); children: David, Ellen, Stephen. BA, Bklyn. Coll., 1939; MS, Columbia U., 1940; Nieman fellow, Harvard U., 1950. Mng. editor KQED, Newspaper of the Air, 1968; editor Chronicle Fgn. Service, 1960-77; reporter, asst. fgn., news, mng., exec. editor, editor San Francisco Chronicle, 1940-2000, editor emeritus, 2000—. Lectr. U. Calif., Berkeley, 1946-47, 68-70 Editor: San Francisco Chronicle Reader, 1962. Bd. trustees World Affairs Coun. Served with AUS, 1943-45. Mem. AP Mng. Editors Assn., Am. Soc. Newspaper Editors, Commonwealth Club of Calif. (pres. 1995). Office: San Francisco Chronicle 901 Mission St San Francisco CA 94103-2905 Home: 300 Deer Valley Rd #1B San Rafael CA 94903 Business E-Mail: wgerman@sfchronicle.com.

GERMANN, RICHARD P(AUL), pharmaceutical company chemist, chemicals executive; b. Ithaca, NY, Apr. 3, 1918; s. Frank E.E. and Martha Minna Marie (Knechtel) G.; m. Malinda Jane Plietz, Dec. 11, 1942 (dec. Dec. 2005); 1 child, Cheranne Lee (dec.). Student, U. N.Mex., 1938-39; BA, U. Colo., 1939, postgrad., 1940-41, Western Res. U., 1941-43, Brown U., 1954. Chief analytical chemist Taylor Refining Co., Corpus Christi, 1943-44; rsch. devel. chemist Calco Chem. divsn. Am. Cyanamid Co., 1944-52; devel. chemist charge pilot plant Alrose Chem. Co. divsn. Geigy Chem. Corp., 1952-55; new product devel. chemist, rsch. divsn. W.R. Grace & Co., Clarksville, Md., 1955-60; chief chemist soap-cosmetic divsn. G.H. Packwood Mfg. Co., St. Louis, 1960-61; coord., promoter chem. product devel. Abbott Labs., North Chicago, Ill., 1961-71; internat. chem. cons. to mgmt., 1971-73; pres. Germann Internat. Ltd., 1973-82, Ramtek Internat. Ltd., 1973-2000. Real estate broker, 1972-90; cons. major Japanese chem. cos., 1971-85; cons. dept. chemistry Bowling Green (Ohio) State U., 1988. Author: The Technical Man of the Sea of Change, 1965, Decontamination of Plant Wastes--An Overview, 1969, Science's Ultimate Challenge--The Re-evaluation of Ancient Occult Knowledge, 1978, Science and Innovation, 1993; patentee in U.S. and fgn. countries on sulfonamides, vitamins, detergent-softeners and biocides. Rep. Am. Inst. Chemists to Joint Com. on Employment Practices, 1969-72; vestryman St. Paul's Episc. Ch., Norwalk, Ohio, 1978-81, chmn. adminstrn. and long-range planning commn., 1980-81, The Ch. of Light; sec. Friends of the Norwalk Pub. Libr., 1996, pres., 1997-99, 2006—; trustee Svcs. for the Aging, Inc., 1982-94, treas., 1992-93, pres., 1994; mem. nutritional coun. Ohio Dist. Five Area Agy. on Aging, 1983-84; sr. adv. Ohio Assn. Ctrs. for Sr. Citizens, Inc., 1982-90; bd. dirs. Christie Lane Industries, 1981—2005, chmn., 1988-94; mem. com., sec. Huron County Disaster Svcs. Agy., 1987-89. Fellow AAAS, Am. Inst. Chemists (chmn. com. employment rels. 1969-72), Chem. Soc. (London); mem. Am. Chem. Soc. (councilor 1971-73, chmn. membership com. chem. mktg. and econs. divsn. 1966-68, chmn. program com. 1968-69, del. at large for local sects. 1970-71, chmn. 1972-73, chmn. Chgo. program com. 1966-67, chmn. Chgo. endowment com. 1967-68, dir. Chgo. sect. 1968-72, chmn. awards com. 1972-73, sec. chem. mktg. and econs. group Chgo. sect. 1964-66, chmn. 1967-68), Am. Numastic Soc., Internat. Sci. Found., Sci. Rsch. Soc. Am., Comml. Chem. Devel. Assn. (chmn. program com. Chgo. conv. 1966, mem. fin. com. 1966-67, ad hoc com. of Comml. Chem. Devel. Assn. and Chem. Market Rsch. Assn. 1968-69, co-chmn. pub. rels. Denver conv. 1968, chmn. membership com. 1969-70, mem. directory com. 1967-68, employment com. 1969-70), Nat. Security Indsl. Assn. (com. rep. ocean sci. tech. com., maintenance adv. com., tng. ad. com. 1962-70), Midwest Planning Assn., Am. Assn. Textile Chemists and Colorists, Am. Pharm. Assn., Midwest Chem. Mktg. Assn., Am. Mgmt. Assn., N.Y. Acad. Scis., Internat. Platform Assn., Am. Meteorol. Soc., Water Pollution Control Fedn., Lake County Bd. Realtors, World Future Soc., Midwest Planning Assn., Am. Fedn. Astrologers, Washington Astrological Assn. (v.p. 1959-60), Ancient Astronaut Soc., Am. Philatelic Soc., Am. Numismatic Assn., Am. Rose Soc., AARP (pres. Huron county Firelands chpt. #4110 1986-88, chmn. legis. com. 1988-90, active project vote, pres. 1997-98, bd. dirs. 1998—), Friends Norwalk Pub. Libr. (sec. 1997-98, pres. 1998-2000), Chemists Club (N.Y.C., Chgo.), Torch Club, Toastmasters, Lions (sec. Allview, Md. 1956-57), Kiwanis, Masons, (32nd degree, Knights Templar, Rotary, Gamma Delta (pres. Cleve. chpt. 1941-42), Sigma Xi, Alpha Chi Sigma (chmn. profl. activities com. 1968-70, pres. Chgo. chpt. 1968-70). Home and Office: 394 Cleveland Rd #11H Norwalk OH 44857-8500 Office Phone: 419-668-9640. *Total knowledge, whether it be in business, science, history, or religion, is a mirage. That which we believe to be true today will be subject to continuous modification throughout all eternity as understanding of the universe continues to expand. This belief has made my life an adventure in which I have attempted to find the many "reasons why" which determine the way we think and live. It is obvious that all the fields in question are interrelated in many ways. History shows that dogma in any discipline or a lack of knowledge of the past has always inhibited or prevented man's spiritual, scientific or material growth. The incorrect beliefs thus perpetuated become the cross we bear that prevents us in no small part from living our lives to the fullest during our short stay here on earth. Since I believe that there is a hidden reason for everything that happens during our lifetime, logic tells me that in the eons to come each soul will continue its adventures through many rebirths both here on this earth and on earths in many distant galaxies far out in the universe as God allows us to increase our knowledge of the real reason for our existence.*

GERMANO, THOMAS, art educator; s. Thomas J. and Rosalie M. Germano. AA, Nassau C.C., Garden City, NY, 1983; BFA, Cornell U., Ithaca, NY, 1985; MFA, Yale U., New Haven, Conn., 1989. Assoc. prof. SUNY, Farmingdale, NY, 1987—. Lectr. in field. Numerous exhibitions. Mem. Met. Mus. Art. Recipient Edwin Palmer award, Nat. Acad. Mus., NYC, 2004, award, Puffin Found., Teaneck, NJ, 2006. Mem.: Coll. Art Assn. Avocation: music. Studio: 45 Main St #519 Brooklyn NY 11201

GERMANO, WILLIAM PAUL, dean, former publishing executive; b. Yonkers, NY, Oct. 10, 1950; s. William Peter and Edna Mary (Gilmore) G.; m. Diane Grace Gibbons, July 21, 1973; 1 child, Christian. BA in English, Columbia U., 1972; PhD in English, Ind. U., 1981. Editor Columbia U. Press, NYC, 1980-83, editor in chief, 1983-85; v.p., editorial dir. Routledge, Chapman and Hall Inc., NYC, 1986-92, Routledge, Inc., NYC, 1992-96, v.p., dir. pub. humanities, 1996—2005; dean Faculty of Humanities and Social Scis., prof. English lit. The Cooper Union for Advancement of Sci. and Art, NYC, 2006—. Author: Getting It Published: A Guide for Scholars and Anyone Else Serious About Serious Books, 2001, From Dissertation to Book, 2005. Bd. suprs. The English Inst. Mem. MLA, PEN. Home: 33 Riverside Dr New York NY 10023-8020 Office Phone: 212-353-4273. Business E-Mail: germano@cooper.edu.

GERMOLUS, PENNY LYNN, music educator; b. Oxhard, Calif., Sept. 23, 1967; d. Carmen Lynn Bell and Karen Avon Gentry; m. Shaun Jeremy Germolus, Mar. 3, 2001; 1 child, Isabelle. BE, Moorehead State U., Minn., 1992. Cert. music & vocal K-12 tchr. Minn., 1992. Music tchr., 1992, Superior Mid. Sch., Wis., 2005—. Prodr.: (CD vocals) Wild Olive 3. Mem.: Phi Kappa Lambda. Luth.

GERN, RONALD L., lawyer, real estate company executive; m. Patti Gern; children: Andrew, Stephen, Alison. BA, BS, U. Pa, 1979; JD, U. Va., 1982. Bar: Ill. 1999. Assoc. Wolf, Block, Schorr & Solos-Cohen, 1982—85; counsel Kravco Co., 1985—90, v.p., gen. counsel, 1990—97; sr. v.p., gen. counsel, asst. sec. General Growth Properties, Inc., 1997—. Mem.: ABA, ICSC Law Conf. Prog. Com. (former chmn.), Am. Coll. Real Estate Lawyers. Office: General Growth Properties Inc 110 N Wacker Dr Chicago IL 60606 Office Phone: 312-960-5000. E-mail: rgern@generalgrowth.com.

GERNAND, BRADLEY ELTON, archivist, librarian; b. Hugo, Okla., Aug. 29, 1964; s. Charles D. Jr. and Mary Ellen (Akins) G. BA, U. Okla., 1985, MA, 1987, postgrad., 1987—. Archivist Western History Collections, Norman, Okla., 1982-89, Nat. Archives of U.S., Washington, 1989—91, Libr. of Congress, Washington, 1991—2001; libr. mgr. Inst. for Def. Analyses, Alexandria, Va., 2001—. Lachenmeyer Media fellow U. Okla., 1985-87. Independent. Baptist. Avocations: photography, reading, history. Office: Inst for Def Analyses 4850 Mark Center Dr Alexandria VA 22311-1882

GERNANDER, BARTON CARL, lawyer; b. Newport, RI, July 21, 1969; married. BA with honors in Philos., U. Pa., Phila., 1992; JD, U. Minn. Law Sch., 1996. Bar: Minn. 1996, US Dist. Ct. (dist. Minn.) 1998, US Ct. Appeals (8th cir.) 1999. Assoc. Hellmuth & Johnson, P.L.L.C., Eden Prairie, Minn. Bd. dirs. Bancroft Neighborhood Assn., Mpls. Named a Rising Star, Minn. Super Lawyers mag., 2006. Mem.: Fed. Bar Assn., Minn. State Bar Assn., Hennepin County Bar Assn. Office: Hellmuth & Johnson PLLC 10400 Viking Dr Ste 500 Eden Prairie MN 55344 Office Phone: 952-941-4005. E-mail: bgernander@hjlawfirm.com.

GERNER, EDWARD WILLIAM, medical educator; b. NYC, Nov. 8, 1940; s. David and Anne (Robbins) G.; m. Judith E. Delbaum, June 5, 1983; 1 child, Danielle. BA magna cum laude, Clark U., 1961; MD, NYU, 1965. Diplomate Am. Bd. Ophthalmology, Am. Bd. Neurology. Intern Presbyn. U. Pitts. Hosp., 1965-66; resident Hosp. U. Pa., Phila., 1967-69; instr. dept. neurology U. Pa. Sch. Medicine, Phila., 1967-69, instr. dept. ophthalmology, 1972-74; attending neurologist Tulane U. Sch. Medicine, New Orleans, 1969-71; asst. surgeon Wills Eye Hosp., Phila., 1981-88, assoc. surgeon, 1988—; asst. prof. dept. neurology T. Jefferson U. Sch. Medicine, Phila., 1978-88, asst. prof. dept. ophthalmology, 1982-88, assoc. prof., 1988—. Bd. dirs. Pa. Physicians Healthcare Plan, Harrisburg. Contbr. chpts. to books and articles to profl. jours. Lt. comdr. USPHS, 1969-72. N.Y. State Regent scholar N.Y. State Bd. Regents, 1957-61; Jones fellow Mayo Clinic, Rochester, Minn., 1965. Fellow Am. Acad. Ophthalmology, Am. Acad. Neurology; mem. Royal Soc. Medicine (affiliate), Phi Beta Kappa. Avocations: photography, gardening. Office: 1015 Chestnut St # 1125 Philadelphia PA 19107-5127 Office Phone: 215-928-1212.

GERNER, JOAN, foundation administrator; BArch, CCNY, BS in Arch.; MSc Hist. Preservation, Columbia U. Grad. Sch. of Arch.; grad., Exec. Edn. Program in Leadership Devel., Columbia U. Grad. Sch. of Bus. Bus. planning rschr. Lever Brothers Co.; constrn. engr./arch. Gen. Services Adminstrn.; joined Tishman Constrn. Corp., 1981, project mgr., v.p.; sr. v.p. Bovis Lend Lease, 1993—2007; exec. v.p. design constrn. & capital planning World Trade Ctr. Meml. Found., 2007—. Mem. bd. advisors Columbia U. Constrn., Engring, and Mgmt. Program, Columbia U. Sch. of Engring., NY Women Executives in Real Estate. Named one of 100 Women Real Estate Leaders for the 21st Century, Real Estate Weekly, 2000. Office: World Trade Ctr Meml Found One Liberty Plz 20th Fl New York NY 10006 Office Phone: 212-227-7722. Office Fax: 212-227-7931.*

GERO, ANTHONY GEORGE, securities and commodities trader; b. London, May 31, 1936; came to U.S., 1947; s. Stephen Gero and Ilona (Braun) Von Rieger; m. Joan Selinger, Nov. 20, 1969 (div. 1980); m. Gale Gendason, Feb. 14, 1989; 1 child, Danielle Joy. BS, NYU, 1959; cert., Investment Bankers Inst. U. Pa., 1965. Reporter USIS Chilean Eartquake Relief/Am. Embassy, 1959-60; ptnr. Goodbody & Co., 1960-64, Charles Plohn & Co., NYC, 1964-67; v.p., dir. Internat. First Hanover Corp., NYC, 1967-69; v.p. Drexel Burnham & Co., NYC, 1971-80; 1st v.p. Prudential Securities, NYC, 1981—2003; sr. v.p. Legg Mason Wood Walker Inc., NYC, 2003—06, RBC Capital Mkts., RBC Dain Rauscher, 2006—. Mem. U.S. Dept. Commerce, Nat. Def. Exec. Res., 1989—; bd. dirs. Commodity Clearing Corp.; arbitrator Nat. Assn. Securities Dealers, N.Y. Stock Exch., 1992—. Author: Precious Metals, 1985. Dir., treas. children's fund Commodities Exch. Ctr., N.Y.C., 1980—; chmn. NYMEX Charitable Trust, N.Y.C., 1990-95; dir. Futures Options for Kids, 1995—. Recipient Cert., Holocaust Meml., 1991. Mem. Internat. Precious Metals Inst. (dir. 2000—), N.Y. Produce Exch., N.Y. Merc. Exch. (bd. dirs., treas. N.Y.C. chpt. 1974—), Commodity Exch. (bd. dirs. 1995), N.Y. Coffee, Sugar and Cocoa Exch., N.Y. Cotton Exch. (bd. dirs. 1995), Commodity Floor Brokers and Traders Assn. (chmn. 1990—), Investment Brokers Assn., Ret. Westchester County Police Revolver League, Westchester County Sheriff's Assn., N.Y. Police Res. Assn., Securities Industry Assn. (swaps and derivatives commn.), Police Res. Assn. N.Y.C., N.Y. State Troopers Alumni Assn., Am. Radio Relay League. Republican. Avocations: photography, amateur radio, chess. Home: 180 East End Ave New York NY 10128-7763 Office: RBC Dain Rauscher 1211 Ave Of The Americas 33rd Fl New York NY 10036 Office Phone: 212-703-8230. Business E-Mail: george.gero@rbcdain.com.

GEROE, MICHAEL R., lawyer; JD, Columbia U., 1993. With Williams, Mullen, Dewey and Ballantine; gen. counsel Adknowledge, Inc., Kansas City, Mo., 2004—. Bd. dirs. Am. Hungarian Exec. Cir., Great Falls, Va. Trustee Bar Found. of the Bar Assn. of Dist. of Columbia, 2004—07. Office: Adknowledge Inc 4600 Madison 10th Fl Kansas City MO 64112 Office Phone: 816-931-1771.

GEROSA, PETER R., automotive executive; BA, U. Conn.; post grad., U. Ill., 1983, Harvard U., 1990. With GM Oldsmobile Div., 1964, asst. gen. sales. mgr., 1984; gen. sales svc. mgr. GM Cadillac Div., 1986; regional gen. mgr. GM N.E. Region Vehicle Sales Svc, Mktg., 1999, GM North Ctrl. Region, 2000; v.p. GM North Am., 2003—. Office: GM Corp 300 Renaissance Ctr PO Box 300 Detroit MI 48265-3000

GEROU, PHILLIP HOWARD, architect; b. Natick, Mass., July 20, 1951; s. James Francis and Enid (Meymaris) G.; m. Cheri Rodgers, Nov. 24, 1979; children: Gregory Bedford, Sara Christine. BArch, U. Nebr., 1974, MArch, 1975. Designer, owner Gerou & Assocs. Ltd., Evergreen, Colo., 1986—. Design cons. Kilimanjaro Children's Hosp., Tanzania, 1988-91, World Alpine Ski Championships, Vail, Colo., 1988. Pres. Colo. Soc. of Architects Ednl. Fund., Denver, 1986; del. State Rep. Assembly, Denver, 1986; trustee Rockland Community Ch., Denver, 1986-89. Recipient Citation award Nat. Assn. of Remodeling Industry, 1991, 96, Design Excellence Wood, Inc., 1990, Citation award, 1990. Fellow AIA (pres. Colo. chpt. 1986, bd. dirs. 1981-87, nat. dir. 1991-94, nat. v.p. 1995, dir. Nat. Ethics Coun. 1997—2002, chmn., 2001—02, conf. chair Western Mountain region design conf. 1990, Spl. Recognition award 1990), Nat. Coun. Archtl. Adminstrn. Bds. (examiner 1985). Republican. Mem. United Ch. of Christ. Avocations: skiing, travel, architectural design. Home Phone: 303-670-4587; Office Phone: 303-674-4177. E-mail: phil@gerou.net.

GERRARD, JOHN M., state supreme court justice; b. Schuyler, Nebr., Nov. 2, 1953; BS, Nebr. Wesleyan U., 1976; MPA, U. Ariz., 1977; JD, U. Pacific, 1981. Pvt. practice, Norfolk, 1981-95; city atty. City of Battle Creek, Nebr., 1982-95; justice Nebr. Supreme Ct., Lincoln, 1995—. Co-chair Minority and Justice Task Force; chair Nebr. Supreme Ct. Gender Fairness Implementation Com., Gender Fairness Implementation Com. Fellow: Nebr. Bar Found.; mem.: Nebr. State Bar Assn. (Nebr. State Bar Assn. Standing Com. on Professionalism). Office: Nebr Supreme Ct 2219 State Capitol Lincoln NE 68509-8000*

GERRARD, KEITH, lawyer; b. Malden, Mass., Feb. 8, 1935; s. William Francis and Mary Ethel (Compton) Gerrard; children: Jessica, Beth stepchildren: Elizabeth Perera, Jonathan Perera. AB, Harvard U., 1956; LLB, Harvard U. Law Sch., 1963. Bar: Wash. 1963. Assoc. Perkins Coie, Seattle, 1963—70, ptnr., 1970—. Trustee Mus. Flight. Trustee Mus. Flight, Seattle. Served to lt. USAF, 1956—59. Fellow: Am. Coll. Trial Lawyers; mem.: ABA, Seattle-King County Bar Assn., Wash. State Bar Assn., Rainier Club (Seattle). Office: Perkins Coie 1201 3rd Ave Fl 40 Seattle WA 98101-3029 Office Phone: 206-359-8462. Business E-Mail: kgerrard@perkinscoie.com.

GERRAS, STEPHEN JOSEPH, military officer, psychologist; b. Reading, Pa., June 23, 1960; s. Charles Stephen and Anne Christina Gerras; m. Ann Catherine Kelliher, Oct. 12, 1991; children: Joshua Stephen, Zachary Charles. PhD., Pa. State U., State Coll., Pa., 1992; BS, West Point Acad., West Point, NY, 1982; M Strategic Studies, U.S. Army War Coll., Carlisle Barracks, PA, 2002; MS, Pa. State U., State Coll., Pa., 1991. Bn. comdr. 24th Transp. Bn., Fort Eustis, Va., 1998—2001; liaison officer to Turkish mil. Office of Def. Cooperation, Ankara, Turkey, 2002—04; prof. US Army War Coll., 2004—. Mem., army chief of staff strategic leadership task force U. S. Army War Coll., Carlisle Barracks, Pa., 2001—02. Author article to profl. jours. Lt. col. US Army, 1982—2003. Recipient Douglas MacArthur Leadership Award, U.S. Army Command and Gen. Staff Coll., 1996. Mem.: Soc. of Indsl. and Orgnl. Psychologists. Avocations: travel, weight-lifting, reading. Home Phone: 717-241-4825; Office Phone: 717-245-3571. Personal E-mail: stevegerras@hotmail.com. Business E-Mail: stephen.gerras@us.army.mil.

GERRINGER, ELIZABETH (THE MARCHIONESS DE ROE DEVON, POET JULIE DE VONTINE), writer, lawyer; b. Edmund, Wis., Jan. 7, 1934; d. Clyde Elroy and Matilda Evangeline Knapp; m. Roe (Don Davis) Devon Gerringer-Busenbark, Sept. 30, 1968 (dec. Dec. 1972). Student, Madison Bus. Coll., 1952, San Francisco State Coll., 1953-54, Vivian Rich Sch. Fashion Design, 1955, Dale Carnegie Sch., 1956, Arthur Murray Dance Studio, 1956, Biscayne Acad. Music, 1957, L.A. City Coll., 1960-62, Santa Monica Jr. Coll., Calif., 1963; JD, U. Calif., San Francisco, 1973; postgrad., Wharton Sch., U. Pa., 1977, London Art Coll., 1979; PhD, U. Cambridge, 1979; student, Goethe Inst., 1985. Bar: Calif., 1965. Ordained to ministry, 1978. Atty. Dometrik's JIT-MAP, San Francisco, 1973—. Cons. in field; pres., tchr. Environ Improvement, Originals by Elizabeth. Actress Actors Workshop San Francisco, 1959, 65, Theater of Arts Beverly Hills, Calif., 1963, also radio; artist, poet, singer, songwriter, playwright, dress designer; author: The Cardinal, 1947, Explorations in Worship, 1965, The Magic of Scents, 1967, New Highways, 1967, The Grace of Romance, 1968, Happening-Impact-Mald, 1971, Seven Day Rainbow, 1972, The Day of the Lone Survivor, 1972, Zachary's Adversaries, 1974, Fifteen from Iowa, 1977, Bart's White Elephant, 1976, Skid Row Minister, 1978, Points in Time, 1979, Special Appointment-A Clown in Town, 1979, Happenings, 1980, Candles, 1980, The Stranger in the Train, 1983, Votes from the Closet, 1984, Wait for Me, 1984, The Stairway, 1984, The River is a Rock, 1985, Happenings Revisited, 1986, Comparative Religion in the United States, 1986, Lumber in the Skies, 1986, The Fifth Season, 1987, Summer Thoughts, 1987, Crimes of the Heart, 1987, Toast Thoughts, 1988, The Contrast of Russian Literature Through the Eyes of an American Artist, 1988, A Thousand Points of Light, 1989, The Face in The Mirror, 1989, Raining In My Heart, 1989, Sea Gulls, 1990, Voices on the Hill, 1991, It's Tough to Get a Matched Set, 1991, Equality, 1991, Miss Geranium, 1991, Forest Voices, 1991, Golden Threads, 1991, Castles in the Air, 1991, The Cave, 1991, Angels, 1991, Real, 1991, An Appeal to Reason, 1992, We Knew, 1992, Like It Is, 1992, Politicians Anonymous, 1993, Wheels Within Wheels, 1994, A Tree for All Seasons, 1995, The Visitor, 1995, The Stranger on the Train, 1995, Time Frames, 1996, Save the Dance, 1998, Flowers For My Grandfather, 1999, Last Day at Mission Rock, 1999, Waiting for the Train, 1999, The Influence of Rural Life Upon Culture, 1999, The Crowd, 2001, Without Saying Goodbye, 2002, The Moon's Agreement, 2003, The Avenues, 2003, Unplanned Schedule, 2004, The Possum, 2004, Picnic Table, 2004, The Owl, the Parrot and the Monkey, 2005, Julie Marie, 2005, The Radio, 2005, Interpretations, 2005, Social Commentaries, 2005, Heaven, 2005, Without Saying Goodbye, 2005, Tony and Randy, 2006, Message From the Tower, 2006, The Dream Heaven, 2006, Endings, 2006, Death Left a Box, 2006, The Dove Returns, 2006, While Good Men Sleep, 2006, The Dream, 2007, The Dance of Life, 2007. Steering com. Explorations in Worship. Home: 1017 10th St #275 Sacramento CA 95814 Personal E-mail: pagesuite171@yahoo.com.

GERRISH, BRIAN ALBERT, theologian, educator, retired minister; b. London, Aug. 14, 1931; s. Albert and Doris (King) G.; children from previous marriage: Carolyn, Paul; m. Dawn Ann De Vries, Aug. 3, 1990; 1 child, Heather. BA, Queens' Coll., Cambridge, Eng., 1952, MA, 1956; cert., Westminister Coll., Cambridge, 1955; S.T.M., Union Theol. Sem., NYC, 1956; PhD, Columbia U., 1958; D.D. (hon.), U. St. Andrews, Scotland, 1984. Ordained to ministry Presbyn. Ch., 1957. Asst. pastor West End Presbyn. Ch., NYC, 1956-58; tutor philosophy of religion Union Theol. Sem., NYC, 1957-58; instr. ch. history McCormick Theol. Sem., Chgo., 1958-59, asst. prof., 1959-63, assoc. prof., 1963-65; assoc. prof. hist. theology U. Chgo., 1965-68, prof., 1968-85, John Nuveen prof., 1985-96, John Nuveen prof. emeritus, 1996—. Disting. Svc. prof. theology Union Theol. Sem., Va., 1996—2002; Cunningham lectr. U. Edinburgh, 1990. Author: Grace and Reason: A Study in the Theology of Luther, 1962, 3d edit., 2005, Japanese transl. 1974, Tradition and the Modern World: Reformed Theology in the Nineteenth Century, 1978, 2d edit. 2007, The Old Protestantism and the New: Essays on the Reformation Heritage, 1982, 2d edit., 2004, A Prince of the Church: Schleiermacher and the Beginnings of Modern Theology, 1984, 2001, Korean transl., 1988, Grace and Gratitude: The Eucharistic Theology of John Calvin, 1993, 2002, Continuing the Reformation: Essays on Modern Religious Thought, 1993, Saving and Secular Faith: An Invitation to Systematic Theology, 1999, The Pilgrim Road: Sermons on Christian Life, 2000; editor: The Faith of Christendom: A Source Book of Creeds and Confessions, 1963, Reformers in Profile, 1967, 2d edit., 2004, Reformatio Perennis: Essays on Calvin and the Reformation in Honor of Ford Lewis Battles, 1981, Reformed Theology for the Third Christian Millennium: The 2001 Sprunt Lectures, 2003; co-editor: Jour. Religion, 1972-85; contbr. articles to profl. jours. Am. Assn. Theol. Schs. faculty fellow, 1961; Guggenheim fellow, 1970; Nat. Endowment Humanities fellow, 1980 Fellow Am. Acad. of Arts and Scis.; mem. Am. Soc. Church History (pres. 1979), Am. Theol. Soc. (Midwest divsn. pres. 1973-74). Home: 9142 Sycamore Hill Pl Mechanicsville VA 23116-5806

GERRITSEN, HENDRIK JURJEN, physics professor, researcher; b. The Hague, Netherlands, Jan. 19, 1927; came to U.S., 1957; s. Hendrik Pieter and Augusta (Koopmans) G.; m. Lida Buitelaar, June 13, 1955 (div. 1968); children: Robert (dec.), Steven, Albert (dec.), Leon, Jenine; m. Heide Robertson Hoppe, Dec. 28, 1978, (div. 2002); m. Maria Emilio, Jan. 17, 2003 (div. 2006). AB in Physics and Chemistry, U. Leiden, 1948; PhD in Physics, 1955. Scientist RCA Labs., Zurich, Switzerland, 1955-57, Princeton, NJ, 1957-67; lectr. electrophysics Chalmers U., Sweden, 1961-62; prof. physics Brown U., Providence, 1967-97, prof. emeritus, prof. rsch., 1997—; prof. physics U. Utrecht, Netherlands, 1974, U. Karlsruhe, W. Germany, 1981-82; cons. Polaroid Corp., Cambridge, Mass., 1968-70; prin. investigator U.S. Bur. Mines, Brewster, Pa., 1970-76, Honeywell, Mpls., 1980-87, NSF, Dept. Energy and AERG., 1968-98; cons. Krieger Corp., Providence, 1986-89. Dir. Ladd Observatory, Providence, 1985-89. Contbr. sci. articles to profl. jours., 1968—; patentee in field. Vis. IREX scholar, Baltic Republics. Fulbright grantee Rostock, Germany, 1995, 96. Mem. Fedn. Am. Scientists, Union of Concerned Scientists, Profl. Photographers Soc. Am. (hon.), Am. Optical Soc., Celestial Observers (hon.), Night Pilot (CEO R.I.), Sigma Xi. Achievements include patentee, co-founder Nightpilot a company devoted to producing universal devices for learning names of constellations and stars. Office: Brown U Physics Dept Hope/George St Providence RI 02912 Home Phone: 401-941-2510; Office Phone: 401-863-1488. Business E-Mail: gerritsen@physics.brown.edu.

GERRITSEN, MARY ELLEN, vascular and cell biologist; b. Calgary, Alta., Can., Sept. 20, 1953; arrived in US, 1978; d. Thomas Clayton and Alice Irene (Minton) Cooper; m. Paul William Gerritsen, May 24, 1975 (div. 1977); m. Thomas Patrick Parks, Oct. 11, 1980; children: Kristen, Madelene. BSc summa cum laude, U. Calgary, 1975, PhD, 1978. Postdoctoral fellow U. Calif., San Diego, 1978-80; asst. prof. N.Y. Med. Coll., Valhalla, 1981-86, assoc. prof., 1986-90; sr. staff scientist Pharm. divsn. Bayer Corp., West Haven, Conn., 1990-93, head inflammation exploratory rsch., 1990-96, prin. staff scientist, 1993-97; vis. scientist Harvard U., 1996; assoc. dir. cardiovasc. rsch. Genentech, South San Francisco, 1997—2001; sr. dir. Millennium Pharms., South San Francisco, 2003—04, Molecular and Cellular Pharm., Exelixis Inc., South San Francisco, 2004—. Cons. Insite Vision, Alameda, Calif., 1987-89, Boehringer Ingelheim Pharms., Ridgefield, Conn., 1985-88, Xoma, Berkeley, Calif, 2003-04, Frazier Health Care Ventures, Palo Alto, Calif, 2003—, Macusite, Union City, Calif., 2004—; adj. assoc. prof. N.Y. Med. Coll., 1990-99. Co-author: Masdevallias: Gems of the Orchid World, 2005, Calochortus, Mariposa Lilies and Their Relatives, 2007; editor: N.Am. Vascular Biology Orgn. Newsletter, —; mem. editl. bd. Microvascular Rsch., 1988—96, Am. Jour. Physiology, 1983—90, Am. Jour. Cardiovasc. Pathology, 1996—98, Circulation Rsch., 1997—99, Endothelium, 1999—, editor-in-chief Microcirculation, 1993—98, cons. editor, 1998—; contbr. articles to profl. jours. I. W. Killam Found. fellow, 1976, Med. Rsch. Coun. Can. fellow, 1978; Mary Weideman award, Sinsheimer Scholar. Mem. Am. Soc. for Pharmacology and Exptl. Therapeutics, Am. Physiol. Soc., Am. Soc. Investigational Pathology, Microcirculatory Soc. (mem. coun. 1989-92, chairperson publs. com. 1991-93, Mary Weideman award 1985, Young Investigator award 1984), N.Am. Vascular Biology Orgn. (mem. steering com. 1993, mem. coun. 1994-97, editor-in-chief newsletter 1994-97, sec.-treas. 1997-99, pres. 1999, chair devel. com., 2004-05), Peninsula Orchid Soc. (bd. dirs. 2001, v.p. 2005, 06), Am. Orchid Soc., Pleurothallid Alliance, Orchid Digest. Avocations: orchids, horticulture. E-mail: meg570@comcast.net.

GERRITSON, A. J., advertising executive; b. Weymouth, Mass., Oct. 19, 1976; s. Stephen L. Gerritson and Allcen J. McGowan. BA, U. Mass., Amherst, 1998. V.p. comm. Asiafoods.com, Woburn, Mass., 2000—02; v.p. mktg. ZEEO Interactive, Boston, 2002—04; prin. 451 Mktg., Watertown, Mass., 2004—. Bd. dirs. Christopher's Haven, Boston, 2007, Ireland C. of C. New Eng., 2007. Named Collegiate All-Am., USA Rugby, 1997, 1998. Mem.: Mass. Tech. Exch., Algonquin Club (mem. mktg. com. 2006—07), Ad Club New Eng. (trustee 2007). Avocations: rugby, sailing, golf. Office: 451 Mktg 203 Arlington St Watertown MA 02472

GERRY, DEBRA PRUE, psychotherapist, recording artist, writer; b. Oct. 9, 1951; d. C.O. and Sarah E. Rawl; m. Norman Bernard Gerry, Apr. 10, 1981 (div. 1998); 1 child, Gisele Psyche Victoria. BS, Ga. So. U., 1972; MEd, Armstrong State U., 1974; PhD, U. Ga., 1989. Cert. Ariz. Bd. Behavioral Health Examiners. Spl. edn. tchr. Chatham County Bd. Edn., Savannah, Ga., 1972-74; edn. and learning disabilities resource educator Duval County Bd. Edn., Jacksonville, Fla., 1974-77; ednl. resource counselor spl. programs adminstr. Broward County Bd. Edn., Ft. Lauderdale, Fla., 1977-81; pvt. practice Scottsdale, Ariz., 1990—. Contbr. author coll. textbooks; contbr. articles to profl. jours.; prodr. musical album Welcome to this World. Vol., fundraiser, psychol. cons., group leader Valley AIDS Orgns., Phoenix, 1990-96; fundraiser Hosp. Health Edn. Programs, Scottsdale, 1992-93; mem. com. for women's issues Plz. Club, Phoenix, 1992-93; pres. Laissez Les Bon Temps Rouler, Wrigley Club, Phoenix, 1993-96; mem. bd. Sojourner' Ctr., 1996, exec. bd., 1997-98, v.p., 1999; exec. bd. Breast Found., Inc., Phoenix, 1997-98; appointee Ariz. Supreme Ct., Foster Care Rev. Bd., Phoenix, 1996-2001. Recipient Rudy award Shanti Orgn., 1991. Mem. APA, NOW, ACA, Internat. Soc. Poets (disting., Poet of Merit award 1996), Nat. Assn. Women Bus. Owners, Assn. for Multicultural Coun., Assn. for Specialists in Group Work, Mensa, Phi Delta Kappa, Kappa Delta Epsilon, Sigma Omega Phi, Kappa Delta Pi. Avocations: ballroom dancing, playing musical instruments, singing, travel, air sports. E-mail: dgerryphd@aol.com.

GERSAPPE, SUNIL, marketing executive; b. Hyderabad, India, Mar. 30, 1951; arrived in U.K., 1971; s. Raghunandan and Radha Gersappe; m. Kalyani Ganguly, Jan. 24, 1975; children: Avynash, Arjun. B of Commerce, U. Calcutta, India, 1971. Chartered acct., London. Asst. mgr. Deloitte Haskins & Sells, London, 1975-79; mgr. Produce Brokers, London, 1979-82; v.p. Nascor, Fribourg, Switzerland, 1982-85; pres. Dash Internat., NYC, 1985—86, Indo-Med, NYC, 1986—97, mktg. mgr. London, 1995—; pres. Into-Med Commodities. Fellow Inst. Dirs., Assn. Business Leaders, Inst. Chartered Accts. in Eng. and Wales; mem. Rotary Club Huntington, N.Y.C., Rotary Club Ealing (treas.). Avocation: travel. Office: Indo-Med Commodities Ltd 67A Boston Manor Rd Brentford TW8 9JQ England Home: 1459 W Blackhawk St Apt 3R Chicago IL 60622-2313 Office Fax: 020 88472093; Home Fax: 020 8993 7131. E-mail: sunil@pabcor.co.uk.

GERSH, BERNARD J., cardiologist, researcher, educator; b. Johannesburg, Oct. 2, 1941; came to U.S., 1978; s. Maurice and Revee Gersh; m. Alison D. Brunette, 1967 (div. 1973); children: Brunette, Jonathan, Amanda; m. Ann Gersh, Oct. 28, 1977; children: Kate and Sarah (twins); 1 stepchild, Brione. MB ChB, U. Cape Town, South Africa, 1965; DPhil, Oxford U., Eng., 1970. Cons. Mayo Clinic, Rochester, Minn., 1978-93, 98—; prof. medicine Mayo Med. Sch., Rochester, 1985-93, 93-98, 98—; W. Proctor Harvey tchr. Georgetown U. Med. Ctr., Washington, 1993-98, chief divsn. cardiology, 1993-98, prof. medicine. Sr. specialist, sr. lectr. Groote Schuur Hosp. and U. Cape Town, 1973-78. Editor/author 9 books; contbr. 600 articles to profl. jours. Past chmn. coun. clin. cardiology Am. Heart Assn., 1995-98. Recipient Disting. Achievement award, Coun. Clin. Cardiology, Am. Heart Assn., 2004; Rhodes scholar, 1965. Fellow Royal Coll. Physicians, Am. Coll. Cardiology (trustee 1995-2000, Disting. Svc. award 2007); mem. Assn. Univ. Cardiologists, Am. Clin. and Climatol. Soc., Cosmos Club (Washington), Vincent's Club (Oxford U.), Western Province Cricket Club, Marylebone Cricket Club (London). Home: 2501 Institute Rd SW Rochester MN 55902-1156 Office: Mayo Clinic Cardiovasc Diseases 200 1st St SW Rochester MN 55905-0002 Home Phone: 507-529-8701; Office Phone: 507-284-4441. E-mail: gersh.bernard@mayo.edu.

GERSHAN, WILLIAM M., pediatrician, educator; b. Milw. BS, U. Wis., Milw., 1979; MD, Med. Coll. Wis., Milw., 1983. Instr. pediat. Wash. U. Sch. Medicine, St. Louis, 1989—90; asst. prof. pediat. Med. Coll. Wis., Milw., 1990—97, assoc. prof. pediat., 1997—, pediatric pulmonary fellowship dir., 1994—, dir. Cystic Fibrosis Ctr., 2003—; dir. pulmonary function lab. Children's Hosp. Wis. Cons. pediatric pulmonary Children's Hosp. Wis., Milw., 1990—. Contbr. articles to profl. jours., chapters to books. Mem. Milw. Childhood Asthma Project, 1998—2000. Fellow: Am. Acad. Pediat., Am. Coll. Chest Physicians; mem.: Pediatric Pulmonary Tng. Dirs. Assn., Am. Thoracic Soc. Avocations: athletics, travel, music. Office: Children's Hosp Wis 9000 W Wisconsin Ave Milwaukee WI 53226 Home Phone: 414-266-6731; Office Phone: 414-266-6731. Business E-Mail: wgershan@mcw.edu.

GERSHEL, ALAN M., prosecutor; b. Nov. 19, 1951; s. Marvin and Francine G.; m. Linda, Aug. 3, 1975; children: Jessica Sara, Bradley Ross. BS, Northeastern U., 1974; MS, Ind. State U., 1975; JD, U. Detroit, 1978. Bar: Mich. 1978, U.S. Ct. Appeals (6th cir.) Mich. 1980. Asst. atty., criminal chief ea. dist. U.S. Dept Justice, Detroit, 1993—; dep. asst. atty. gen. U.S. Dept. Justice, 2000; interim U.S. atty. U.S. Dept Justice, Detroit, 2000—01; adj. prof. U. Detroit Mercy Sch. Law, Mich. Office: Assist US Atty 211 W Fort St 2001 Detroit MI 48226-3211 Business E-Mail: alan.gershel@usdoj.gov.

GERSHENFELD, MATTI KIBRICK, psychologist; b. Phila. d. Hyman and Esther Kibrick; m. Marvin A. Gershenfeld, 1946 (dec. 1989); children: Robert, Howard, Richard, Kenneth. BA, U. Pa., 1947, M in Govt. Adminstrn., 1951; EdD, Temple U., 1967. Lic. psychologist, Pa.; cert. marriage and family therapist. Pres. MKG Assocs., Elkins Park, Pa., 1975—, Couples Learning Ctr., Jenkintown, Pa., 1975—. Mem. organizing com., co-chair 1st Internat. Interdisciplinary Conf. on Women, Haifa, Israel, 1982. Author: Groups: Theory and Experience, 1973, 7th edit., 2004, Making Groups Work, 1983, How to Find Love, Sex and Intimacy after 50: A Woman's Guide, 1991; contbr. chpts. to Contemporary Marriage, 1986, Adult Development, 1984, conservation of Marriage and the Family Studies, 1986. Chair bd. dirs. Gratz Coll., Elkins Park, 2001-04; pres. Hillel Greater Phila., 1996-99; mem. pres.' coun. Gwynedd (Pa.) Mercy Coll., 1981—; past pres. Am. Diabetes Assn., Phila., 1987-90, affiliate, past pres. Pa. affiliate, 1990-93. Fellow APA, Am. Assn. Marriage and Family Therapists; mem. Nat. Coun. on Family Rels., Pa. Coun. Family Rels. (past pres.), Assn. State Couns. Nat. Coun. Family Rels. (past pres.), Internat. Coun. Psychologists (past pres., sec.-gen.). Jewish. Avocations: travel, theater. Home: 8302 Old York Rd Philadelphia PA 19027-1522 E-mail: mattikg@comcast.net.

GERSHENGORN, MARVIN CARL, internist, researcher, educator; b. NYC; MD, NYU, 1971. Diplomate Am. Bd. Internal Medicine. Intern Strong Meml. Hosp., Rochester, NY, 1971-72, asst. resident in medicine, 1972-73; asst. prof. medicine NYU Sch. Med., 1976-80, assoc. prof., 1980-83; prof. medicine Cornell U. Med Coll., NYC, 1983-2001; Abby Rockefeller Mauze disting. prof. Weill Med. Coll. Cornell U.; sci. dir. divsn. Intramural Rsch. Nat. Inst. Diabetes & Digestive & Kidney Diseases, NIH, 2001—. Office: NIH Nat Inst Diabetes & Digestive & Kidney Diseases Bldg 10 Rm 9N222 Bethesda MD 20892-1818 Home Phone: 202-237-8228; Office Phone: 301-496-4128. Business E-Mail: marving@intra.niddk.nih.gov.

GERSHENHORN, ALAN, delivery service executive; B fin., Univ. Houston. Mgmt. positions UPS, Tex., 1979—93, mgmt. positions internat. mktg., 1993—2002; v.p. mktg. UPS Canada, v.p., ops. dist. mgr., pres., 2002; pres. supply chain solutions glob. transp. & shared services UPS, Atlanta, pres. UPS supply chain solutions ops. Europe, Asia, ME & Africa, 2004—07, pres. UPS Internat., mem. mgmt. com., 2007—. Office: UPS 55 Glendale Pky NE Atlanta GA 30328*

GERSHENSON, ALAN C., lawyer; b. Phila., June 15, 1947; BA, Pa. State U., 1967; JD, Harvard U., 1971. Bar: Pa. 1971, US Dist. Ct. (ea.dist.) Pa. 1972, US Ct. of Appeals (3rd cir.) 1973, US Supreme Ct. 1976, US Ct. of Appeals (2nd cir.) 1984, US Ct. of Appeals (6th cir.) 1987, US Dist. Ct. (mid.dist.) Pa. 2003. Mem. Blank, Rome, Comisky & McCauley, Phila.; councel Sirlin Gallogly & Lesser PC. Mem. ABA, Phi Beta Kappa, Phila. Bar Assn., Pa. Bar Assn. Office: Sirlin Gallogly & Lesser PC 1529 Walnut St Ste 600 Philadelphia PA 19102 Office Phone: 215-864-9700. Office Fax: 215-864-9669.

GERSHMAN, CARL SAMUEL, foundation administrator; b. NYC, July 20, 1943; s. Joseph Saul and Josephine (Cohen) G.; m. Laurie Pfeffer, Jan. 25, 1970; children: Sarah, Joseph, Jacob. BA, Yale U., 1965; MEd, Harvard U., 1968. Researcher Anti-Defamation League of B'nai B'rith, NYC, 1968; dir. rsch. A. Philip Randolph Inst., NYC, 1969-71; exec. dir. Youth Inst. for Peace in the Mid. East, NYC, 1971-74, Social Dems., U.S.A., NYC, 1974-80; sr. rsch. fellow Freeedom House, NYC, 1980-81; sr. counselor U.S. Mission to the U.N., NYC, 1981-84; pres. Nat. Endowment for Democracy, Washington, 1984—. Author: Foreign Policy of American Labor, 1975; editor: Israel, the Arabs and the Middle East, 1972; mem. editorial bd. Washington Quarterly, 1988—, Society Mag., 1989—; contbr. articles to popular mags. and jours. Avocations: reading, jogging, travel. Office: Nat Endowment for Democracy 1101 15th St NW Ste 700 Washington DC 20005-5013

GERSHON, NINA, federal judge; b. Chgo., Oct. 16, 1940; d. David and Marie Gershon; m. Bernard J. Fried, May 15, 1983. BA, Cornell U., 1962; LLB, Yale U., 1965; postgrad., London Sch. Econs., 1965-66. Staff atty. NY Supreme Ct. (Appellate div.), 1966—68; asst. corp. counsel, Appeals div. State of NY, 1968—69; lectr. law and political sci. U. of Calif. San Diego, 1969—70; chief fed. appeals State of NY, 1972—75, chief consumer protection div., 1975—76; magistrate judge U.S. Dist. Ct. (so. dist.) N.Y., NYC, 1976—96; U.S. dist. judge Eastern Dist. N.Y., Bklyn., 1996—. Adj. prof. law Cardozo Sch. Law, 1986—88. Fulbright scholar. Office: US Courthouse 225 Cadman Plz E Brooklyn NY 11201-1818 Office Phone: 718-613-2650.

GERSHTEYN, YEFIM, application developer, researcher; b. Borisov, Minsk Region, Belarus, Apr. 15, 1956; arrived in US, 1995; s. Feliks Gershteyn and Anna Royak; m. Marina Berkhman, Aug. 2, 1986; 1 child, Vadim. BSME, Belarus State Poly. U., Minsk, 1977; postgrad., Belarus State Econ. U., Minsk, 1982—86, DSc, 1993. Cert. sr. rsch. assoc. Highest Qualifying Com., Moscow. Exec. dir. market econ. rsch. divsn. Belarus Econ. Rsch. Inst., Minsk, 1990—94; database mktg. cons. Kestnbaum & Co., Chgo., 1995—97; mgr. stats. SCIREX, Bloomingdale, Ill., 1997—2000; dir. statis. programming, biometrics and data mgmt. Takeda Global R & D, Lincolnshire, Ill., 2001—. Author: Belarus Transition to Market Economy, 1991; contbr. articles to profl. jours. Office: Takeda Global R&D One Takeda Pkwy Deerfield IL 60015 Home Phone: 847-329-9560; Office Phone: 224-554-5350. Personal E-mail: fgershteyn@att.net. Business E-Mail: fgershteyn@tgrd.com.

GERSIE, MICHAEL H., insurance company executive; CLU, ChFC. Actuarial trainee Principal Fin. Group, Des Moines, 1970—74, actuarial assoc., 1974—75, asst. actuary, 1975—79, assoc. actuary, 1979—84, actuary, 1984—86, 2d v.p., 1986—90, v.p., 1990—94, sr. v.p., CIO, 1994—96, sr. v.p., CFO, 1996—2000, CFO, exec. v.p., 2000—. Office: Principal Fin Group 711 High St Des Moines IA 50392*

GERSON, DONALD FRANKLIN, pharmaceutical executive; b. Kansas City, Mo., Oct. 22, 1946; s. Nathaniel C. and Sareen R. (Epstein) Gerson; m. Mavis Gail Meadows, May 12, 1979; children: Benjamin Asa, Alexander Roald, Jonas Elliott. BSc, U. Western Ont., London, Can., 1968; PhD, McGill U., Montreal, Que., Can., 1972. Mem. Basel (Switzerland) Inst. for Immunology, 1979-82; mgr. process devel. Genex Corp., Gaithersburg, Md., 1982-83; head biotech. Alta. Rsch. Coun., Edmonton, Canada, 1983-87; asst. v.p. mfg. Connaught Labs., Toronto, 1987-92; v.p. R & D Apotex Fermentation, Inc., Winnipeg, Man., Canada, 1992-94; mng. dir. Wyeth-Lederle Vaccines, Pearl River, NY, 1994-2000; v.p. mfg. Acambis, Inc., Cambridge, Mass., 2000—03; pres. Axenic, Inc., 2003—05; COO, Celltrion, Inc., 2005—. Contbr. chapters to books, articles to profl. jours. Mem.: Cosmos Club (Washington). Achievements include patents for process for production of lovastatin using coniothyrium fuckelli; hydrocarbon extraction agents and microbiological processes for their production; microbiological production of novel biosurfactants; measuring degree of mixing in turbulent liquid; application for controlled dose dropper construction. Office: Celltrion Inc Incheon 406-130 Republic of Korea Business E-Mail: dg@celltrion.com.

GERSON, DONALD JEROME, computer scientist, consultant, photographer, small business owner; b. NYC, Apr. 26, 1934; s. Irwin I. Gerson and Helen Sacks; m. Barbara A. Jaques, Aug. 21, 1960 (dec. Oct. 1998); 1 child, Laura Melissa; m. Emma Sue Gaines, June 24, 2000. BA in Meteorology, N.Y.U., 1956; MS in Computer Sci., U. Md., 1975. Oceanographer Naval Oceanog. Office, Suitland, Md., 1956-78; phys. scientist Defense Mapping Agy., Bethesda, Md., 1978-83; imagery scientist CIA, Langley, Va., 1983-97; prin., owner Gerson Imaging Solutions, LLC, Silver Spring, Md., 1997—2006, Gerson Photography, 2006—. Instr. George Washington U., Washington, 1983-88; U.S. rep. working group on sea ice World Meteorological Org., Geneva, 1975-77. Co-author: Processes in Marine Remote Sensing, 1982, Radius, Image Understanding for Imagery Intelligence, 1997; contbr. articles to profl. jours. Recipient Goldsborough award for best tech. paper of yr., 1983, Intelligence Commendation medal CIA, 1997. Fellow: Royal Geog. Soc. (Eng.), Explorers Club (Wash. chpt. chmn. 1986—88); mem.: IEEE, Am. Soc. Media Photographers, Applied Imagery Pattern Recognition Com. (chmn. 1975—), Cosmos Club, Sigma Xi. Avocations: travel, photography, racewalking, hiking, book collecting. Home Phone: 240-293-6570. Personal E-mail: dgersonphoto@yahoo.com.

GERSON, ELLIOT FRANCIS, foundation administrator; b. New Haven, July 15, 1952; s. Louis Lieb and Elizabeth (Shanley) G; children: Emily, Hilary, Alexander, Marissa, Jillian; m. Amy Shapiro, May 23, 1993 (separated). AB summa cum laude, Harvard Coll., 1974; BA with first class honors, Oxford U., Eng., 1976, MA, 1981; JD, Yale U., 1979. Bar: Conn. 1981, D.C. 1982, U.S. Dist. Ct. Conn. 1982, U.S. Ct. Appeals (D.C. cir.) 1982, U.S. Supreme Ct. 1985. Law clk. to judge U.S. Ct. Appeals, Washington, 1979; staff asst. to sec. Dept. Def. The Pentagon, Washington, 1979-80; law clk. to Justice Stewart U.S. Supreme Ct., Washington, 1980-81; assoc. Verner, Liipfert, Bernhard & McPherson, Washington, Hartford, Conn., 1981-83; dep. atty. gen. State of Conn., Hartford, 1983-86; v.p. Travelers Corp., Hartford, 1986-90, sr. v.p., 1990-93; pres. Travelers Ins. Co., 1993-95; exec. v.p. MetraHealth Cos., Inc., 1995-96, United Healthcare, 1996; pres. ETC, Inc., 1996—97, CEO, 1997-99, Lifescape, LLC, 1999-2000; pres. FHC Health Sys., Inc., 2000—03, ValueOptions, Inc., 2001—03; policy dir., nat. fin. chair Joseph I. Lieberman for Pres., Inc., Vienna, Va., 2003—04; exec. v.p. The Aspen Inst., 2004—. Bd. dirs. Bazelon Ctr. Mental Health Law, Internat. Biomed. Rsch. Alliance. Editor: Conn. Law Tribune, 1986-88. Mem. Sec. State's Adv. Com. Internat. Law, Washington, 1984-86; mem. Gov.'s Commn. Design Environ. Policy for Conn., 1969; dir. Eastern Conn. Develop. Coun. Inc., 1981-86, Hartford State Co., 1985-95, pres., 1990-93, Hartford Ballet, 1986-88, Greater Hartford Arts Coun., 1986-90, 94-95; mem. Conn. Humanities Coun., 1987-90; dir. Conn. Civil Liberties Union, 1987-89, Conn. Women's Ednl. and Legal Fund, 1987-91; staff mem. commn. Critical Choices Ams., 1973-74; mem. Council Fgn. Rels. Inc., N.Y.C., 1981-86, 98—, Yale Law Sch. Com. Pub. Interest Law, New Haven, 1983-85; elector Wadsworth Atheneum, Hartford, 1983-93; sec. Conn. Rhodes Scholar Selection Com., 1982-94; asst. Am. sec. Rhodes Scholarship Trust, 1976-79, Am. sec., Eng., 1998—; treas. Am. South African Scholarship Assn., Inc., 1986-94; trustee Conn. Pub. Broadcasting, 1988-92, Conn. Histo. Soc., 1993-95, The Shakespeare Theatre, Washington, 1996—; founding trustee Mandela Rhodes Found. (USA), 2005—; bd. dirs. Internat. Biomed. Rsch. Alliance, 2005—; trustee Hartford Courant Found., 1988-95, pres., 1992-94. Rhodes scholar 1974; recipient Sec. Def. Meritorious Civilian Service medal, 1980. Mem.: Conn. Bar Assn. (long range planning com. 1984—87), Cosmos Club (Washington), Spee Club (Cambridge, Mass.) (pres. 1973—74), Phi Beta Kappa. Democrat.

GERSON, IRWIN CONRAD, advertising executive; b. NYC, Mar. 18, 1930; s. Leon and Charlotte (Steinhause) G.; m. Lenore Greenblatt, Nov. 29, 1953; children: Jill Beth, Matthew Ted. BS, Fordham U., 1953; MBA, NYU, 1959; DHL, Albany Coll. Pharmacy, 1992, L.I. U., 2001. Ter. mgr. Wyeth Labs. divsn. Am. Home Products, 1956-58; account exec., supr. William Douglas McAdams, Inc., NYC, 1958-66, v.p., 1966-68, sr. v.p., 1969-70, exec. v.p., 1971-74, pres., 1974-86, chmn. bd., 1987-96, Lowe McAdams Healthcare, NYC, 1996-98, chmn. emeritus, 1999-2000. Instr. sales mgmt. Columbia Coll. Pharm. Sci., 1967-77; bd. dirs. Enzo Biochem. Inc.; bd. advisors, v.p. Lifelong Learning Soc., Fla. Atlantic U., 2000-06, pres., 2006-. Mem. editl. adv. bd. US Jour. Drug and Alcohol Dependence, 1977-83. Trustee, bd. dirs. Chemotherapy Found., 1971-86; bd. dir. Nutritional Rsch. Found., 1977-85, Am. Found. for Pharm. Edn., 1996-2003, Conn. Grand Opera, 1983-93, Stamford Chamber Orch., 1985-93; mem. coun. overseers Arnold and Marie Schwartz Coll. Pharmacy and Health Sci., LI U., 1986-90, chmn., 1990-99; bd. trustees Bus. Publs. Audit of Circulation, 1988-95, vice chmn., 1992-93, chmn., 1993-94; bd. trustees LI U., 1989-99; trustee Albany Coll. Pharmacy, Union U., 1993-97. With AUS, 1954-56. Named to Med. Advt. Hall of Fame, 1999. Mem. Am. Assn. Advt. Agys. (bd. govs. NY coun. 1991-95, ea. region 1995-98), Pharm. Advt. Coun. (bd. dirs. 1974-84, treas. 1976-77, v.p. 1979-81), Alpha Zeta Omega. Home: 189 Spyglass Ln Jupiter FL 33477-4090 Office Phone: 561-307-8077.

GERSON, MICHAEL JOHN, journalist; b. May 15, 1964; s. Michael and Betty Gerson; m. Dawn Soon Gerson; 2 children. BA, Wheaton Coll., Il. Aide Indiana Senator Dan Coats; speechwriter Presidential campaign of Bob Dole, 1996; journalist U.S. News & World Report; sr. policy adv. The Heritage Found.; chief speechwriter and sr. policy advisor Bush Presidential Campaign, 1999—2000; dep. asst. to the pres., dir. presidential speechwriting Bush Adminstrn., 2001—02, asst. to the pres. for speechwriting and policy advisor, 2002—05, asst. to the pres. policy and strategic planning, 2005—06; sr. fellow Coun. Fgn. Relations, 2006—; op-ed. columnist Washington Post, 2007—. Named one of The 25 Most Influential Evangelicals In America, Time Magazine. Episcopalian. Office: Council on Fgn Relations 1779 Massachusetts Ave NW Washington DC 20036*

GERSON, RALPH JOSEPH, manufacturing executive; b. Detroit, Nov. 30, 1949; s. Byron Hayden and Dorothy Mary (Davidson) G.; m. Erica Ann Ward, May 20, 1979. BA, Yale U., New Haven, Conn., 1971; MSc, London Sch. Econs., 1972; JD, U. Mich., 1975. Bar: Mich. 1975, DC 1976, US Dist. Ct. DC 1976, US Ct. Appeals (DC cir.) 1976. Counsel Dem. Nat. Com., Washington, 1975-77; spl. asst. US Trade Rep., Washington, 1978-79; counselor to spl. Middle East negotiator Office of Pres., Washington, 1979-80; ptnr. Akin, Gump, Strauss, Hauer and Feld, 1981-83, 85-87; dir. Mich. Dept. Commerce, Lansing, 1983-84; exec. v.p. Guardian Industries Corp., Auburn Hills, Mich., 1988—, also bd. dirs., 1988—; pres., CEO Guardian Internat. Corp., 1993—. Bd. dirs. Pistons-Palace Found., US Spain Coun.; trustee Henry Ford Mus., Detroit Symphony Orch., Citizens Rsch. Coun. Mem. ABA, DC Bar Assn., Mich. Bar Assn., Coun. Fgn. Rels., World Pres. Orgn., Royal Automobile Club, Franklin Hills Country Club, Bloomfield Open Hunt Club, Yale Club (NYC). Office: Guardian Industries Corp 2300 Harmon Rd Auburn Hills MI 48326-1714

GERSON, STUART MICHAEL, lawyer; b. NYC, Jan. 16, 1944; s. James and Ethel (Cherney) G.; m. Pamela Somers, July 28, 1979; children: James Barker, Somers Elizabeth, Lindsey Dakota. BA in Polit. Sci., Pa. State U., 1964; JD, Georgetown U., 1967. Bar: DC 1968, NY 1999, US Ct. Appeals (DC cir.) 1972, US Ct. Appeals (5th cir.) 1972, 81, US Supreme Ct. 1974, US Ct. Appeals (9th cir.) 1978, US Ct. Appeals (2d cir.) 1979, US Ct. Appeals (11th cir.) 1981, US Ct. Appeals (6th cir.) 1982, US Ct. Appeals (4th cir.) 1984, US Ct. Appeals (3d cir.) 1985, US Ct. Appeals (8th cir.) 1986, US Ct. Appeals (1st, 7th, 10th, fed. cirs.) 1989. Asst. U.S. atty. City of Washington, 1972—75; assoc., then ptnr. Reed Smith Shaw & McClay, Washington, 1975—80; pvt. practice; ptnr. in charge litig. Epstein, Becker & Green, Washington, NYC, 1980—89; asst. atty. gen. in charge civil divsn. U.S. Dept. Justice, Washington, 1989—93; acting Atty. Gen. U.S., 1993; atty. and head of litig. Epstein, Becker & Green, P.C., Washington and NYC. Bd. dirs. Counsel for Ct. Excellence; mem. bd. legal advisors Heritage Found, Washington Legal Found., Nat. Legal Ctr. for the Pub. Interest; adj. prof. law Georgetown U., 1991. Contbr. articles to profl. jours. Gen. counsel Nat. Rep. Senatorial Com., Washington, 1985-86; sr. advisor presdl. campaign George Bush, 1988; leader transition team Office Pres. Elect, 1988; advisor Transition Office Pres. Elect, 2000; lay Eucharistic min.; vestryman All Saints Episcopal Ch. Capt. USAF, 1967-72. Decorated Meritorious Svc. medal. Fellow Am. Bar Found.; mem. ABA, D.C. Bar Assn. (steering com. litig. 1985-93), The Barristers (pres.), Am. Health Lawyers Assn., Am. Inns of Ct., Met. Club, Lawyers Club. Episcopalian. Avocations: competitive running, national track and field official, sailing, reading. Office: Epstein Becker & Green PC 1227 25th St NW Ste 700 Washington DC 20037-1175 also: 250 Park Ave New York NY 10177-0001 Home Phone: 301-657-8743; Office Phone: 202-861-4180. Personal E-mail: sgerson@ix.netcom.com. Business E-Mail: sgerson@ebglaw.com.

GERSONY, WELTON MARK, pediatrician, cardiologist, educator; b. Syracuse, NY, Nov. 19, 1931; s. Irving and Ann (Cohen) Gersony; m. Susan Gersony; children: Neal, Anne, Richard, Deborah. AB, Syracuse U., 1954; MD, SUNY, Syracuse, 1958. Diplomate Am. Bd. Pediatrics, Am. Bd. Pediatric Cardiology. Intern Cleve. Met. Gen. Hosp., 1958-59, resident in pediat., 1959-61; resident in pediatrics Babies and Childrens Hosp., Cleve., 1959-61; fellow in cardiology Harvard U., 1963-65; asst. prof. pediat. U. Tex., Dallas, 1965-68; from asst. prof. to assoc. prof. Columbia U., 1968—74, prof., 1974—, Alexander S. Nadas prof., 2000—. Dir. divsn. pediatric cardiology Columbia-Presbyn. Med. Ctr., 1974—2005, Columbia-Cornell Pediatric Cardiovasc. Ctr., 1999—2005, fellowship dir.; mem. Sub.-Bd. Pediatric Cardiology, 1976—83, chmn., 1981—83; vis. prof., named lectureships multiple US and Fgn. Med. Ctrs., 1982—2006; mem. com. ofcl. examiners, 1983—90; vis. dir. pediatric cardiology Gt. Ormond St. Hosp. Sick Children, London, 1984—85; organizer 2d World Congress Pediatric Cardiology, NYC, 1985; cons. Extramural Affairs divsn. Nat. Heart Lung and Blood Inst., 1988—; chmn. steering com. World Congress Pediatric Cardiology and Cardiac Surgery, 1989—97, plenary lectr., 2001, plenary chair, 05; pres. faculty practice orgn. Coll. Physicians and Surgeons Columbia U., 2003—05; mem. adv. bd. Congress Pediat. Cardiology Internat., 1998—; chmn. publ. com. Pediat. Heart Network; lectr. in field. Author: Nelson's Textbook of Pediatrics, 1983, 3d edit., 1991, Congenital Heart Disease in the Adult, 2002; assoc. editor: The American Heart Association Consultant, 2001, 2d edit., 2006; mem. editl. bd. Pediatric Cardiology, 1978—90, Jour. Pediat., 1986—93, Jour. Am. Coll. Cardiology, 1990—94, Cardiology in Young, 1990, Progress in Pediatric Cardiology, 1991—, Criculation, 1993—96; cons. editor: Circulation, 1996—2001; internat. adv. bd. Japanese Circulation Jour., 1996—2002, Cardiology, 2006—; contbr. revs. to profl. jours., chapters to books. Mem. internat. com., bd. dirs. Internat. Cardiology Found., 1993—; mem. program com. Internat. Kawasaki Disease Chmn. Cardiology Symposium, 1989, 1992, 1995, 1998, 2001, 2007. Capt. M.C. US Army, 1961—63. Recipient Disting. Practitioner award, Columbia U., 2005, Practitioner of Yr. award, NY Presbyn. Hosp., 2005; grantee, Pediat. Heart Network, 2002—, NH LBI, 2006—; NIH grantee, 1977, 1993, 1983, Falkner fellow, U. Sydney, 1983. Master: Am. Contract Bridge League (life); fellow: Am. Acad. Pediat., Am. Coll. Cardiology; mem.: AMA (cons. 1985—, accreditation coun. grad. med. edn. 1994—, cardiology sect. Founder's award 2007), Internat. Soc. Adult Congenital Heart Disease, Harvey Soc., Am. Fedn. Clin. Rsch., Assn. European Paediatric Cardiologists (corr.), Am. Heart Assn. (pres. coun. cardiovasc. disease in young 1989—90, T. Duckett Jones lectr. 1998, Disting. Achievement award 2003), Am. Pediatric Soc., Soc. Pediatric Rsch. Achievements include research in cardiovascular disease in infants, children and adults; natural history congenital heart disease in children; patents for ductus arteriosus in premature infants; persistence of the fetal circulation. Office: Columbia U 630 W 168th St New York NY 10032-3795

GERSPACH, THOMAS JOSEPH, lawyer; b. Mineola, NY, Dec. 16, 1960; s. John Charles and Claire Louise Gerspach; m. Eileen Elizabeth O'Reilly, Oct. 28, 1989; children: Ryan, Megan, Anne. BA, U. Notre Dame, 1983; JD, St. John's U. Sch. Law, 1987. Assoc. atty. Martin Clearwater & Bell, NYC, 1987—88; assoc., ptnr. Belair & Evans, NYC, 1988—99; founder, sr. ptnr. Garson, Gerspach, Decorato & Cohen, LLP, NYC, 1999—. Mem.: ATLA, NY Medical Defense Bar Assn., NY State Bar Assn. Avocations: skiing, coaching youth baseball, football, basketball and soccer. Office: Garson Gerspach Decorato & Cohen LLP 110 Wall St 10th FL New York NY 10005 Office Phone: 212-742-8700. Business E-Mail: gerspach@ggdc.com.

GERST, PAUL HOWARD, physician; b. Sept. 24, 1927; s. David and Hilde (Werbel) G.; m. Elizabeth Carlsen, Aug. 3, 1957; children— Steven R., Jeffrey C., Andrew L. AB, Columbia U., 1948, MD, 1952. Diplomate: Am. Bd. Surgery, Am. Bd. Thoracic Surgery. Intern Columbia Presbyn. Med. Center, NYC, 1952-53, resident, 1956-62, mem. staff, 1962—; instr. physiology U. Pa., 1955-56; practice medicine specializing in surgery NYC, 1962—; asst. clin. prof. surgery Columbia U., 1964-72; prof. surgery Albert Einstein Coll. Medicine, 1972—2003. Dir. surgery Bronx-Lebanon Hosp. Ctr., NYC, 1964—2003 Contbr. articles to profl. jours. Served to 1st lt. U.S. Army, 1953-55. USPHS postdoctoral fellow, 1955-56; recipient Rsch. Career Devel. award, 1964-65. Fellow ACS; mem. Am. Physiol. Soc., N.Y. Soc. for Thoracic Surgery, N.Y. Surg. Soc., N.Y. Soc. for Cardiovasc. Surgery, Am. Heart Assn. Home: 141 Tekening Dr Tenafly NJ 07670-1218 Fax: 201-569-5198. Personal E-mail: pgerst@msn.com.

GERSTEIN, DAVID BROWN, manufacturing and professional sports team executive; b. NYC, Jan. 30, 1936; s. Frank and May G.; m. Jane Ellen Bender, May 4, 1963; children: Mark, James. BS, Seton Hall U., 1959. With Thermwell Products Co., Paterson, NJ, 1958—, sales mgr., 1965-68, v.p., 1968-74, pres., 1974—. Prin. owner N. J. Nets NBA franchise, 1978—98; v.p. Lever Mfg. Co., Paterson; pres. Woodlowe Realty, Paterson, Wait Assocs., Paterson, Dim Assocs., Mahwah, N.J. Chmn. adv. council energy and conservation State of N.J.; co-chmn. athletic program Seton Hall U. Office: Thermwell Products Co Inc 420 Rte 17 S Mahwah NJ 07430 Mailing: 860 5th Ave New York NY 10021 Office Phone: 201-684-4440.

GERSTEIN, MORDICAI, illustrator, writer; b. LA, Nov. 24, 1935; s. Samuel and Fay Gerstein. Student, Chouinard Art Inst., 1953—56. Artist, designer United Prodrs. Am., LA, 1956—57; prin., owner Summer Star Prodns., NYC, 1969—79. Author and illustrator: Arnold of the Ducks, 1983, Tales of Pan, 1986, The Seal Mother, 1986, The Mountains of Tibet, 1987, Beauty and the Beast, 1988 (Golden Eagle award CINE, 1989), The Cataract of Lodore, 1990, The New Creatures, 1991, The Story of May, 1993, Jonah and theTwo Great Fish, 1997, Stop Those Pants!, 1998, The Wild Boy, 1998, Victor, 1998, Noah and the Great Flood, 1999, The Absolutely Awful Alphabet, 1999, Queen Esther, 2000, Fox Eyes, 2001, What Charlie Heard, 2002, Sparrow Jack, 2003, The Man Who Walked Between the Towers, 2003 (Caldecott award, 2004); author and illustrator The Old Country, 2005; illustrator: Dracula is a Pain in the Neck, 1983, FrankensteinMovedin on the Fourth Floor, 1987, Something Queer in the Wild West, 1997, A Hare Raising Tail, 2002, The Mixed-Up Mask Mystery, 2002, The Principal's on the Roof, 2003; author: (films) The Room, 1965, The Magic Ring, 1966 (Golden Eagle award CINE, 1967).

GERSTENMAIER, WILLIAM H., federal agency administrator, aerospace engineer; m. Marsha Ann Johnson; 2 children. B in Aero. Engring., Purdue U., Ind., 1977; M in Mech. Engring., U. Toledo, Ohio, 1981; doctoral student in Dynamics and Control, Purdue U., Ind., 1993. With Glenn Rsch. Ctr. NASA, Cleve., 1977—80, propulsion flight contr. Space Shuttle prog., 1980, head space shuttle/space sta. freedom assembly ops. office, 1990, mgr. orbital maneuvering vehicle project Johnson Space Ctr. Houston, 1992, space shuttle prog. integration mgr., 1998, dep. mgr. internat. space sta. prog., 2000, prog. mgr. internat. space sta. office Johnson Space Ctr. Houston, 2002—05, assoc. adminstr. space ops. Washington, 2005—. Fellow: AIAA. Office: Space Ops NASA Hdqs 300 E St SW Washington DC 20224-3210*

GERSTL, CYNTHIA KOREN, foreign and English language educator; b. Bklyn., May 18, 1942; d. Herman L. and Estelle Koren; m. Robert Gerstl, June 9, 1963; children: David, Sara, Noemi. BA, Bklyn. Coll., 1963; MAT, Trinity Coll., 1979; postgrad., U. Md., 1987—. Cert. tchr. French, spl. edn., reading, Md.; cert. tchr. fgn. lang., English, N.J. Tchr. N.Y.C. Pub. Schs., Bklyn., 1962-63, Woodbridge (N.J.) Pub. Sch., 1963-65, Metuchen (N.J.) Pub. Sch., 1965-67, Hebrew Acad., Washington, 1970-72, Bd. Jewish Edn., Rockville, Md., 1973-82, Prince George's County Pub. Sch., Md., 1986—. Co-author book chpt. in field, (curriculum) Flex Activities, 1990-92, Activities for Foreign Language Studies, 1986. Mem. Am. Assn. Tchrs. French, Am. Coun. Tchrs. Fgn. Langs., Coun. Exceptional Children, Tchrs. of English as Second Lang. Avocations: genealogy, miniatures. Home: 805 Hyde Rd Silver Spring MD 20902-3047 Office: Prince Georges Pub Sch 601 Suffolk Ave Capitol Heights MD 20743-3028

GERSTNER, JONATHAN NEIL, religious studies educator; b. Latrobe, Pa., Aug. 5, 1957; s. John H. and Edna Rachel Gerstner; m. Kathleen Jipping, June 20, 1987; children: Sarah Elizabeth, Jerusha Joy, Monica Kaye, Nathanael John, Micaia Eden. BA, Mich. State U., 1979; MA, U. Chgo., 1980, PhD, 1985. Ordained to ministry, Reformed Ch. in Am. Asst. prof. systematic and practical theology Payne Theol. Sem., Wilberforce, Ohio, 1986-89, acting acad. dean, 1988-89; exec. sec. Reformed Ch. in Can., Cambridge, Ont., 1989-94; prof. ch. history and apologetics Knox Theol. Sem., Ft. Lauderdale, Fla., 1994—98; prof. systematic theology and apologetics Knox Theol Sem., 1999; adj. prof. Ottawa Theol. Hall, Ottawa, Canada, 1997—2002, Sch. of Pastoral Studies, Rio de Janeiro, 1999—; dean and prof. of systematic theology and apologetics New Geneva Theol. Sem., Balt., 2001—02; corp. trainer MCI, Hunt Valley, Md., 2002—04, area mgr. Easton, Va., 2005; regional cons. in workforce devel. ACT Balt (Mid-Atlantic Region), 2004; adj. faculty, dept. religious studies Coll. Notre Dame, Balt., 2004—; chpt. support specialist ASTD, Alexandria, Va., 2005—. Mem. governing bd. Can. Coun. Ch., Toronto, Ont., Canada, 1989—94, Evang. Fellowship Can., Willowdale, Ont., Canada, 1989—94; bd. dir. Ligonier Ministries Can., Guelph, Ont., Canada, 1992—2002; radio program host, 1998—2002. Author: The Thousand Generation Covenant: Dutch Reformed Covenant Theology and Group Identity in Colonial South Africa, 1652-1814, 1991; (with others) Trust and Obey, 1996, Christianity in the History of South Africa, 1997, Onward Christian Soldiers, 1999. Grad. fellow Rotary Internat., 1983. Mem. ASTDm Am. Acad. Religion, Am. Soc. Ch. History, Am. Soc. Assn. Execs., Phi Beta Kappa, Phi Kappa Phi.

GERSTNER, LOUIS VINCENT, JR., investment company and retired information technology executive; b. Mineola, NY, Mar. 1, 1942; s. Louis Vincent and Marjorie (Rutan) Gerstner; m. Elizabeth Robins Link, Nov. 30, 1968; children: Louis, Elizabeth. BA in Engring., Dartmouth Coll., Hanover, NH, 1963; MBA with hon., Harvard U. Bus. Sch., Cambridge, Mass., 1965; DBA (hon.), Boston Coll., 1994; LLD (hon.), Wake Forest U., Winston-Salem, NC, 1997, Brown U., Providence, 1997, Notre Dame U., Ind., 2001; D of Engring. (hon.), Rensselaer Poly. Inst., Troy, NY, 1999. Dir. McKinsey & Co., NYC, 1965-78; exec. v.p. Am. Express Co., NYC, 1978-81, vice-chmn. bd., 1981-83, chmn. exec. com., 1983-85, pres., 1985-89, chmn., CEO travel related svcs., 1985-89; chmn., CEO RJR Nabisco Inc., NYC, 1989-93, IBM, Armonk, NY, 1993—2002; chmn. The Carlyle Group, Washington, 2003—. Mem. Pres.'s Nat. Security Telecom. Adv. Com., 1994-97, Adv. Com. for Trade Policy and Negotiations, 1995-2002; chmn. Computer Sys. Policy Project, 1999-2001; adv. bd. DaimlerChrysler, 2001-05, Sony Corp., 2002—. Author: Who Says Elephants Can't Dance: Inside IBM's Historic Turnaround, 2002; co-author: Reinventing Education: Entrepreneurship in America's Public School, 1994. Bd. dirs. Meml. Sloan Kettering Hosp., 1978-89, 98—, vice-chmn., 2000—, United Negro Coll. Fund, 1987-91, Lincoln Ctr. for Performing Arts, 1984-2002, NY Times Co., 1986-97, AT&T, 1987-93, Caterpillar, 1984-89, Jewel Co., Melville Corp, Coun. Fgn. Rels., 1995-2005; trustee Joint Coun. on Econ. Edn., 1975-87, chmn. 1983-85; active Bus. Roundtable, 1991-98, The Bus. Coun., 1992; vice-chmn., bd. dirs. New Am. Schs. Devel. Corp., 1991-98; trustee NY Pub. Libr., 1991-96; bd. regents Smithsonian Instn., 1996-99; co-chmn. Achieve, 1996-2002, chmn. emeritus, 2003-; chmn. The Teaching Commn., 2003-06; trustee Am. Mus. Natural History, 2004-. Recipient Cleveland E. Dodge Medal for disting. svc. to edn. Tchrs. Coll., Columbia U., Disting. Svc. to Sci. and Edn. award Am. Mus. Natural History, Award for Excellence in Bus., Engring. and Tech., John M. Olin Sch. of Washington U., 1999; named Knight of British Empire, 2001. Fellow Am. Acad. Arts and Scis., Am.-China Forum; mem. NAE Office: IBM Corp 20 Old Post Rd Armonk NY 10504-1709 Office Phone: 914-499-4900.

GERSTNER, MARY JANE, nurse; b. Rochester, NY, June 27, 1953; d. Thomas J. and Jane E. Gerstner. Diploma, St. Joseph's Hosp. Health Ctr. Sch. Nursing, 1974; BSN, Nazareth Coll., 1982. Cert. RN N.Y. Staff nurse oper. rm. U. Rochester Med. Ctr./Strong Meml. Hosp., 1974-79, staff nurse ob.-gyn. unit, 1981-83, 84-86; staff nurse oper. rm. St. Mary's Hosp., Rochester, 1983-84, Genesee Hosp., Rochester, 1985-95; nurse 1st asst. Genesee Valley Plastic Surgery, Canandaigua, NY, 1995; staff nurse oper. rm. U. of Rochester (N.Y.) Med. Ctr., 1996-00, nurse 1st asst., 2000—. Mem.: ARC, Genesee Valley Nurses Assn., Assn. Peri-Operative RNs, Sigma Theta Tau.

GERSTNER, ROBERT WILLIAM, structural engineering educator, consultant; b. Chgo., Nov. 10, 1934; s. Robert Berty and Martha (Tuchelt) G.; m. Elizabeth Willard, Feb. 8, 1958; children: Charles Willard, William Mark. BS, Northwestern U., 1956, MS, 1957, PhD, 1960. Registered structural and profl. engr., Ill. Instr. Northwestern U., Evanston, Ill., 1957-59, research fellow, 1959-60; asst. prof. U. Ill., Chgo., 1960-63, assoc. prof., 1963-69, prof. structural engring., architecture, 1969-92, prof. emeritus, 1992—. Structural engr. cons., 1959—; mem. State of Ill. Structural Engring. Bd., 1992-94. Contbr. articles to profl. jours. Pres. Riverside Improvement Assn., 1973-77, 79-82. Mem. AAUP, ACLU, ASCE, Am. Soc. Engring. Edn., Structural Engrs. Assn. Ill. (bd. dirs. 1986-89, 92-94, sec. 1989-91, pres. 1991-92). Home: 2628 W Agatite Ave Chicago IL 60625-3011 E-mail: robertwgerstner@aol.com.

GERSTUNG, ESTELLA ROSE, literature and language professor; b. Malta, Mont., Nov. 12, 1929; d. Ralph Sylvaneous and Rose (McLeod) Baker; m. Denman Wayne Gerstung, July 4, 1953; children: Stephen Denman, Roy Wayne, Monica Rose. BA, U. Mont., Missoula, 1951; MEd, Phillips U., Enid, Okla., 1968; MA, U. Okla., Norman, 1970; PhD, U. Ky., Lexington, 1976. Cert. tchr. Mont., Calif., Ohio, Ga., Minn., NY, SC. 6th gr. tchr. Charlo Sch. Dist., Mo., 1948—49; sec. grad. sch. dean U. Mont., Missoula, 1950—52; interviewer Cook County Sch. Nursing, Chgo., 1953—54; lang. arts tchr. Covina Unified Sch. Dist., Calif., 1955—56; English tchr. Northview HS, Covina, 1960—61, Southwest HS, Covina, 1964—66; Latin tchr. Whitewater Sch. Dist., Wis., 1966—67; English tchr. Cleveland Heights HS, Cleveland Heights, 1971—74; English tchr., dept. chair Macon Sch. Dist., Ga., 1974—76; substitute tchr. Winoma Sch. Dist., Minn., 1976—77; English tchr. Corning Sch. Dist., NY, 1977—80; assoc. prof., dept. chair Claflin Coll., Orangeburg, SC, 1980—85; English and Latin tchr. Orangeburg-Wilkinson HS, Orangeburg, 1985—91; reader State of Calif., San Diego, 1991—98, asst. to coord. bus. enterprise program, 1993—98; freelance editor Greenhaven Press, San Diego, 1999—2001; freelance proofreader and editor Paso Robles, Calif., 2002—05. Adj. faculty Corning C.C., Corning, 1977—80, Elmira Coll., NY, 1979—80; grammar tutor, Paso Robles, 2003—05. Mem. Am. Field Svc. Internat. Scholar Program, Covina, 1961—65, pres., 1962—64; mem. spkr. bur. League of Women Voters, Covina, 1962—65. Grantee, NEH, 1983, UNCF, 1984; Fulbright grant, U. Sheffield, Eng., 1952. Democrat. Anglican. Avocations: reading, travel, white-water rafting, Scrabble, walking. Home: 5145 White Tail Pl Paso Robles CA 93446

GERT, BERNARD, philosopher, educator; b. Cin., Oct. 16, 1934; s. Max and Celia (Yarnovsky) G.; m. Esther Libbye Rosenstein, Aug. 3, 1958; children: Heather Joy, Joshua Noah. BA, U. Cin., 1956; PhD, Cornell U., 1962; LHD (hon.), U. Cin., 2006. Instr. philosophy Dartmouth Coll., Hanover, NH, 1959-62, asst. prof. philosophy, 1962-66, assoc. prof., 1966-70, prof., 1970—, chmn. dept. philosophy, 1971—74, 1979—81, 1998—2001, Stone prof. intellectual and moral philosophy, 1981—92, 1998—, Eunice and Julian Cohen prof. ethics and human values, 1992-98. Vis. assoc. prof. philosophy Johns Hopkins U., Balt., 1967-68; vis. prof. philosophy Edinburgh U., fall 1974, Hebrew U. Jerusalem, 1985-86, Nacional U. de la Plata and U. Buenos Aires, Argentina, fall 1995, Ctr. Applied Philosophy Charles Sturt U., Canberra, Australia, 2004, 2007; adj. prof. psychiatry Dartmouth Med. Sch., 1976—; prin. investigator NIH, 1990-93; vis. rsch. prof. U. NC Med. Sch., Chapel Hill, 2007. Author: The Moral Rules: A New Rational Foundation for Morality, 1970, 1973, 1975, German edit. 1983, Morality: A New Justification of the Moral Rules, 1988, Morality: Its Nature and Justification, 1998, revised edit., 2005, Common Morality, 2004, paperback edit. 2007; co-author: Philosophy in Medicine: Conceptual and Ethical Issues in Medicine and Psychiatry, 1982, Japanese edit. 1984; first author: Morality and the New Genetics: A Guide for Students and Health Care Providers, 1996, Bioethics: A Return to Fundamentals, 1997, Bioethics: A Systematic Approach, 2006; editor: Hobbes' Man and Citizen, 1972, reprinted with revisions, 1991, Serbian edit., 2006, Rationality, Rules, and Ideals: Critical Essays on Bernard Gert's Moral Theory, 2002; contbr. chpts. to books, articles to profl. jours. Recipient NSF-NEH Sustained Devel. award, 1980—84, Fulbright lectureship, Israel, 1985—86, Argentina, 1995; fellow, NEH, 1969—70, Hastings Ctr., 1986—; prin. investigator grant, NIH, 1990—93. Fellow Nat. Humanities Ctr. 2001-2002; mem. Am. Philos. Assn., Am. Soc. Polit. and Legal Philosophy, Soc. Ethics Across the Curriculum, Assn. Practical and Profl. Ethics, Am. Soc. Bioethics and Humanities (Lifetime Achievement award, 2006). Avocation: poker. Home: 8 Bridgman Rd Hanover NH 03755-1302 Office: Dartmouth Coll Dept Philosophy Hanover NH 03755 Office Phone: 603-646-2022. Business E-Mail: bernard.gert@dartmouth.edu.

GERTEIS, CHRISTOPHER, history educator; b. Riverside, Calif., Sept. 15, 1968; s. George Vincent Byron and Joan Diane Gerteis, adopted s. Timothy C. and Briana Clifford; m. Jennifer Elizabeth Anderson. BA, U. Calif., Santa Cruz, 1992; MA, MA, U. Iowa, Iowa City, 1995, PhD, 2001. Vis. asst. prof. East Asian history U. Puget Sound, Tacoma, 2002—04; asst. prof. East Asian history Coastal Carolina U., Conway, SC, 2004—05; postdoctoral fellow, lectr. Yale U., New Haven, 2005—06; asst. prof. East Asian history Creighton U., Omaha, 2006—. Co-dir. Japan studies program Coastal Carolina U., 2004—05. Contbr. articles to profl. jours. Fellow Japan Studies Dissertation Workshop, Social Sci. Rsch. Coun., 2000; Postdoctoral Rsch. fellowship, 2001—02, Japan Soc. for the Promotion of Sci., 2001—02, Japan Studies Travel grant, NE Asia Coun., 2005, Postdoctoral fellowship, Yale U., 2005—. Mem.: Assn. Asian Studies, Am. Hist. Assn. D-Liberal. Avocations: sailing, snorkeling. Office: Creighton U Dept History 2500 California Plz Omaha NE 68178

GERTH, DONALD ROGERS, retired university president, educator; b. Chgo., Dec. 4, 1928; s. George C. and Madeleine (Canavan) G.; m. Beverly J. Hollman, Oct. 15, 1955; children: Annette, Deborah. BA, U. Chgo., 1947, AM, 1951, PhD, 1963. Field rep. S.E. Asia World Univ. Svc., 1950; asst. to pres. Shimer Coll., 1951; Admissions counselor U. Chgo., 1956-58; assoc. dean students, admissions and records, mem. dept. polit. sci. San Francisco St. U., San Francisco, 1958-63; assoc. dean instnl. relations and student affairs Calif. State U., 1963-64, chmn. commn. on extended edn., 1977-82, dean of students Chico, 1964-68, prof. polit. sci., 1964-76, assoc. v.p. acad. affairs, dir. internat. programs, 1969-70, v.p. acad. affairs, 1970-76, pres., prof. polit. sci. Dominguez Hills, 1976-84, pres., prof. pub. policy and adminstrn. Sacramento, 1984—2003, pres., prof. emeritus, 2003—; co-dir. Danforth Found. Research Project, 1968-69; coordinator Inst. Local Govt. and Public Service, 1968-70. Past chair Accrediting Commn. for Sr. Colls. and Univs. of Western Coll. Assn.; chmn. admissions coun. Calif. State U., 1974-03; bd. dirs. Ombudsman Found., L.A., 1968-71; lectr. U. Philippines, 1953-54, Claremont Grad. Sch. and Univ. Ctr., 1965-69; mem. World Trade Ctr. No. Calif., 1996, chair, 1996-03; chmn. Calif. State U. Inst., 1997-98; pres. Internat. Assn. Univ. Pres. 1996-99; mem. governing bd. UN Univ. Coun., 1998-2004, vice chair, 2002-04; mem. Am. Coun. for the UN Univ., 1998—, chair, 2004—. Co-author: The Learning Society, 1969; author, editor: An Invisible Giant, 1971; contbg. editor Education for the Public Service, 1970, Papers on the Ombudsman in Higher Education, 1979. Mem. pers. commn. Chico Unified Sch. Dist., 1969-76, chmn., 1971-74; adv. com. justice pgorams Butte Coll., 1970-76; mem. Varsity Scouting Coun., 1980-84; chmn. United Way campaign Calif. State Univs., LA County, 1981-82; bd. dirs. Sacramento Area United Way, campaign chmn., 1991-92, exec. com., 1991-96, vice chmn., 1992-94, chmn.-elect, 1994-95, chmn., 1995-96; bd. dirs. South Bay Hosp. Found., 1979-82; mem. Cultural Commn., LA, 1981-84; mem. com. govtl. rels. Am. Coun. Edn. Active USAF, 1952—56, released as capt. USAF, 1956. Mem. Internat. Assn. Univ. Pres. (pres. 1996-99), Am. Polit. Sci. Assn., Am. Soc. Pub. Adminstrn., Soc. Coll. and Univ. Planning, Western Govtl. Rsch. Assn., World Affairs Coun. No. Calif., Assn. Pub. Adminstrn. Edn. (chmn. 1973-74), Western Polit. Sci. Assn., Am. Assn. State Colls. and Univs. (bd. dirs.), Calif. State C. of C. (edn. com.), Calif. State U. Inst. (chmn. bd. dirs.), UN Ednl., Sci. and Cultural Orgn. (mem. adv. com.), UN U. Coun. (governing bd. 1998-04, vice chair 2001-04), Am. Coun. UN U. (chair 2004-). Democrat. Episcopalian. Avocations: tennis, skiing, reading. Mailing: 7132 Secret Garden Loop Roseville CA 95747-8339 Office: Calif State U Rm 3022 Libr 2000 State University Dr East Sacramento CA 95819-6039 Office Phone: 916-278-7400. Business E-Mail: dongerth@csus.edu.

GERTIS, NEILL ALLAN, writer; b. Buffalo, Mar. 24, 1943; s. Alfred Charles and Gertrude Charlotte (Hurst) Gertis; m. Gail C. Morgan, Oct. 3, 1966 (div. Aug. 1982); m. Alma Ann Sulivan, Sept. 15, 1984; children: Charlotte Ann, Joseph Alfred, Daniel Andrew, Martin Alexander. Community planner Alaska State Housing Authority, Anchorage, 1968-72, libr. dir., 1968-72; real estate appraiser Gertis Assocs., Buffalo, 1972-76; ops. mgr. Chem. Equipment Labs., Phila., 1979-83; tech. writer Gen. Dynamics, Groton, Conn., 1983-84; sr. tech. writer communication products MTS Sys. Corp., Mpls., 1984-94, mgr. tech. tng., 1994-97; supr. tech. publs. Rockwell Automation, Mpls., 1997—. Author: Student Housing Demand in Anchorage, 1972; editor: Storm Drainage for Chester Creek, Anchorage, 1969, Guide to Periodical Holdings in the Anchorage Area, 1970, Engring. Graphics, Anchorage, 1968—72. With US Army, 1965—69. Mem.: Alaska Libr. Assn. Republican. Avocations: computers, antiques, restoration, writing, reading. Home: 1157 Tyler St S Shakopee MN 55379-2070

GERTLER, FRED, librarian, dean; MLS, San Jose State U., 1978. With Rsch. Librs. Group; head customer svc. Santa Clara U. Libr., Calif., 1991—2006; asst. dean U. Pacific Libr., Stockton, Calif., 2006—07, interim dean, 2007—. V.p. north Calif. Academic & Rsch. Librs. Mem.: Spl. Librs. Assn. (mem. San Andreas Chap.). Office: U of Pacific 3601 Pacific Ave Stockton CA 95211 Office Phone: 209-946-2939. E-mail: fgertler@pacific.edu.*

GERTLER, JANOS JOHN, electrical engineer, educator; b. Vienna, Sept. 9, 1936; came to U.S., 1981; s. Mor and Marta (Ungar) Gertler; m. Judit Andai, July 29, 1965; 1 child, Nicholas Balazs; m. Eva Anna Vas, Dec. 30, 2000. Diploma in engring., Tech. U., Budapest, Hungary, 1959; candidate in sci., Hungarian Acad. Scis., Budapest, 1967, DSc, 1980. Rsch. assoc. Power Systems Rsch. Inst., Budapest, 1959-65; asst. prof. Tech. U., Budapest, 1965-67; postdoctoral fellow U. Toronto, Ont., Can., 1967-68; sr. rsch. assoc. Automation Rsch. Inst., Budapest, 1968-70, dep. dir., 1971-81; vis. prof., assoc. dean engring. Poly. Inst. N.Y., Bklyn., 1984-85; prof. George Mason U., Fairfax, Va., 1985—. Assoc. vis. prof. Case Western Res. U., Cleve., 1977, vis. prof., 1982-84; cons. Bailey Controls, Cleve., 1983-84, GM, Warren, Mich., 1989-96; plenary spkr. internat. confs., 1974, 86, 91, 92, 93, 94, 95, 00. Author: Fault Detection and Diagnosis, 1998; series editor Internat. Fedn. Automatic Control Procs., 1984-96; editor Ann. Revs. in Control, 1996—; contbr. articles to profl. jours. Fellow IEEE, Internat. Fedn. Automatic Control (chmn. publ. bd. 1993-96, 96-99, advisor for life, 1999—); mem. Hungarian Nat. Acad. Scis. (fgn. mem.). Achievements include rsch. in the theory and application of model-based diagnosis in engineering systems; development of generalized parity relation method; isolation-enhanced principal component analysis; application to car engines. Office: George Mason U Elec Engring Dept Fairfax VA 22030 Home Phone: 703-425-3419; Office Phone: 703-993-1604. Business E-Mail: jgertler@gmu.edu.

GERTLER, MENARD M., physician, educator; b. Saskatoon, Sask., Can., May 19, 1921; arrived in U.S., 1947, naturalized, 1953; s. Frank and Clara (Handelman) G.; m. Anna Paull, Sept. 4, 1943; children: Barbara Lynn, Stephanie Jocelyn, Jonathan Paull. BA, U. Sask., Saskatoon, 1940; MD, McGill U., Montreal, 1943, MS, 1946, DSc (hon.), 2003, U. Sask., 2006; DSc, NYU, 1960. Intern Royal Victoria Hosp., Montreal, Que., Canada, 1943—44; resident Mass. Gen. Hosp., Boston, 1947—50; rsch. fellow in medicine Mass. Gen. Hosp., Harvard Med. Sch., 1947—50; dir. cardiology Francis Delafield divsn. Columbia Presbyn. Med. Ctr., NYC, 1950—54; spl. rsch. fellow NIH, NYU Dept. Biochemistry, 1954—56; prof. Sch. Medicine, dir. cardiovascular rsch. Rusk Inst. NYU Med. Ctr., 1958—71; sr. med. examiner FAA, 1975; dir. Washington Fed. Savs. & Loan Assn., 1972—83; adj. prof. medicine McGill U., 1996—; clin. prof. medicine N.Y. Hosp.-Cornell Med. Ctr., attending physician. Prof. medicine Weill Med. Sch., Cornell U.; attending physician N.Y. Hosp./Presbyn. Hosp., 1998—; med. dir. Sinclair Oil Corp., 1958-68; internat. cons. cardiovascular diseases, social and rehab. svcs. HEW, Washington, 1968-92. Author: Coronary Heart Disease in Young Adults, 1954, Coronary Heart Disease, 1974; Contbr. articles to profl. jours. Pres. Friends of McGill U., 1983-2001; mem. dean's com. McGill U. Med. Sch. With M.C., Royal Can. Army, 1940-43. Recipient Founders Day award NYU, 1959, medal of honor McGill U., 1993, award of merit McGill U., 1993. Mem. Gallatin Assocs. NYU, Cosmos Club (Washington), Harvard Club (Boston), Univ. Club. Home and Office: 1000 Park Ave Apt 2C New York NY 10028-0934

GERTLER, MEYER H., lawyer; b. New Orleans, Oct. 28, 1945; s. David and Sadie (Redman) G.; m. Marcia Raye Goldstein, Aug. 23, 1967; children— Louis, Danielle, Joshua. B.A., Tulane U., 1967, J.D. 1969. Bar: La. 1970, U.S. Dist. Ct. (ea. and mid. dists.) 1970, U.S. Ct. Apppeals (5th cir.) 1970, U.S. Supreme Ct. 1970. Ptnr. Uddo & Gertler, New Orleans, 1970-76, Gertler & Gertler, New Orleans, 1977-86, Gertler, Gertler & Vincent, New Orleans, 1986-95, Gertler, Gertler, Vincent & Plotkin, 1996—. Mem. ABA, Am. Assn. for Justice, Asbestos Litigation Group., La. State Bar Assn., New Orleans Bar Assn. Democrat. Jewish. Office: Gertler Gertler Vincent & Plotkin 127 Carondelet New Orleans LA 70130 Business E-Mail: mhgertler@ggvplaw.com.

GERTRUDE, KATY See WILHELM, KATE

GERTZ, DAVID LEE, homebuilding company executive; b. Denver, July 30, 1950; s. Ben Harry and Clara (Cohen) G.; m. Bonnie Lee Schulein, June 2, 1973; children: Joshua, Eva. BS, U. Colo., 1972; MBA, U. Colo., Denver, 1993. Real estate broker Crown Realty, Denver, 1972-73; pres. Sunshine Plumbing Co., Lakewood, Colo., 1974-76, Sunshine Diversified, Inc., Lakewood, 1976—, Sunshine Master Builders, Ltd., Lakewood, 1990—. Sec.-treas. Wight Lateral Ditch Co., Lakewood, 1987-91. Builder Taylor Made semi-custom homes. Cub master Boy Scouts Am., Lakewood, 1989-91, asst. scout master, 1991-94; chmn. Parade of Homes com., 1999-2000, pres. Homebuilders Assn. of Metro Denver, 2004. Scholar, Evans Scholars, U. Colo., 1968-72. Mem.: Home Aid Denver (bd. dirs., pres.). Avocations: skiing, golf. Office: Sunshine Master Builders 7120 E Orchard Rd Englewood CO 80111 Office Phone: 303-932-9929. E-mail: dlgertz@sunshinemb.com.

GERTZ, THEODORE GERSON, lawyer; b. Chgo., Sept. 8, 1936; s. Elmer and Ceretta (Samuels) G.; m. Suzanne C., June 19, 1960; children: Craig M., Candace C., Scott W. BA, U. Chgo., 1958; JD, Northwestern U., 1962. Bar: Ill. 1962, U.S. Dist. Ct. (no. dist.) Ill. 1962. Assoc. Marks, Marks & Kaplan, Chgo., 1962-64, Lowitz, Vihons & Stone, Chgo., 1964-66, ptnr., 1966-71, Pretzel & Stouffer, Chgo., 1971-94, Shefsky, Froelich, Chgo., 1995—. Gen. counsel Hull House Assn., Chgo., 1977—, Blind Svc. Assn., Chgo., 1987—, Lawyers for the Creative Arts, Citizens Against Suburban Sprawl, Mettawa, Ill., 1995—. Author: A Guide to Estate Planning, Illinois Advance Estate Planning. Dir., treas. Mettawa Open Lands, 1987—; former trustee Village of Mettawa, 1994—, Pub. Interest Law Initiative, Chgo; bd. mem., Lawyers for the Creative Arts, 2002—. With U.S. Army, 1962-64. Fellow Ill. Bar Found., Ill. Bar Assn., Chgo. Bar Assn., Law Club. Democrat. Jewish. Avocations: reading, nature, working out, dance, travel. Office: Shefsky and Froelich 444 N Michigan Ave Ste 2600B Chicago IL 60611-3998

GERTZBEIN, STANLEY DAVID, orthopedic surgeon; b. Toronto, Can., Sept. 25, 1941; MD, U. Toronto, Can., 1966. Cert. Am. Bd. Orthop. Surgeons, Am. Bd. Spine Surgery. Fellow, orthop. surgery Royal Coll. Physicians and Surgeons (Can.), 1971; rsch. and clin. fellow Sunnybrook Med. Ctr., Toronto, 1972; spinal tng. London and Hong Kong, 1973; prof. U. Toronto, U. Tex. Med. Sch.; active staff mem. Christus St. Joseph Hosp., Houston; staff mem. Methodist Hosp., Houston; full prof., dept. orthop. surgery Baylor Coll. Medicine, Houston. Vis. prof. and guest lectr. at Colleges, Universities and symposia throughout the world; presenter in field. Adv. editor Spine, Spine Jour.; contbr. article to peer-reviewed jours., chapters to books; guest appearance Miracle Workers (ABC), 2006. Trustee AO Found.; chmn. AO Spine Courses. Mem.: Tex. Orthop. Assn., Tex. Med. Assn., Harris County Med. Soc., Canadian Orthop. Assn., AMA, Am. Acad. Orthop. Surgeons, Internat. Soc. for Study of the Lumbar Spine (exec. bd. dir., Volvo award for the best Basic Sci. Rsch. study 1984), N.Am. Spine Soc. (mem. exec. com.). Office: Baylor Coll Medicine Dept Orthopedic Surgery 6620 Main St 13th Fl Houston TX 77030 Address: Inst for Spinal Disorders 6560 Fannin St Houston TX 77030 also: Christus St Joseph Hosp 1401 St Joseph Pkwy Houston TX 77002 Office Phone: 713-986-5710. Office Fax: 713-986-5711. E-mail: bkdoctor@aol.com.*

GERUS, JOHN PATRICK, portfolio manager, retired educator; b. NYC, Mar. 17, 1935; s. Stephan and Vera (Spytkowski) G.; m. Elsa Ortiz, Feb. 22, 1979. Diploma, USN Fire Control Technician, 1954; diploma apprentice electrician program, Dept. Navy, 1961; diploma in indsl. tchr. edn., SUNY, 1968; BS in Edn., cum laude, CUNY, 1976; cert. completion, Queensborough C.C., 1982. Cert. completion in staff devel. N.Y.C. Bd. Edn., completion in elec. tech. Buck Engrng. Co., lic. tchr. secondary edn. Elec. technician Almar Electric Corp., Bklyn., 1956—57; electrician apprentice Dept. Navy, Bklyn., 1957—61, electrician, technician, 1961—65; tchr. vocat.-tech. edn. N.Y.C. Bd. Edn., Bklyn., 1965—91, examiner Bd. Examiners, 1972—88, mentor, 1988—91, 1993—95; financier portfolio mgmt., 1995—. Tutor, faculty advisor N.Y.C. Bd. Edn., 1985—91. With USN, 1953—56, With USNR, 1956—61. Recipient Letter of Commendation, Dept. Navy, 1965, N.Y.C. Bd. Edn., 1970, 1974—75, 1977—78, 1983—85, 1987, 1990, 1995. Mem.: Nat. Maritime Hist. Soc., USN Destroyer Escort Sailors Assn., Tin Can Sailors, Mensa. Avocations: antique cars, sailing, deep sea fishing, ballroom dancing. Office: PO Box 96 Bayside NY 11361-96 Home Phone: 718-631-2338.

GERVAIS, CHERIE NADINE, small business owner; b. Marysville, Calif. d. Victor H. and Gladys A. (Poissant) Fehr; 1 child, Dublin M. Ryan. Student, Yuba Coll., Coll. of Marin, 1977, Sonoma State Coll., 1994, student, 2002. Owner, operator Grandma's Trunk Doll Hosp., San Francisco, 1969-72, San Rafael, Calif., 1972-92, Cherie's Doll Hosp., Petaluma, Calif., 1992-93. Model various local fashion shows, San Francisco and Marin County, Calif., 1973-87; docent Petaluma Mus. Editor: U.F.D.C. Doll Convention Book; contbr. numerous poems to profl. publs., articles in mags. on doll history; paintings and scultpures exhibited at show in Petaluma Mus. Recipient many 1st, 2d and 3d place ribbons at doll shows, ribbons for quilts at fairs in Sonoma and Marin County, 1st place ribbons for paintings and sculptures Sonoma Fair, 1993, Best of Show Sonoma-Marin Fair, 2004, 1st and 2d ribbons, 2005; named Poet of Month, San Rafael (Calif.) Pointer News, 1975. Mem. Dolls from the Attic (pres. 1988-02, 06, v.p.), 101 Doll Club (pres. 1975-76), San Francisco Doll Club (pres. 1976-77), Women of the Moose. Episcopalian. Avocations: painting, sculpting, writing, sewing. Home and Office: Cherie's Doll Hosp 45 La Cresta Dr Petaluma CA 94952-2460

GERVAIS, SISTER GENEROSE, hospital consultant; b. Currie, Minn., Sept. 18, 1919; d. Philip Frederick and Elizabeth Eleanor (Sandgathe) Gervais. BS, Stout State U., Menomonie, Wis., 1945; M. Hosp. Adminstrn., U. Minn., 1954. Joined Sisters of St. Francis, Roman Catholic Ch., 1938; adminstrv. dietitian St. Marys Hosp., Rochester, Minn., 1948-50, adminstrv. asst., 1951-52, asst. adminstr., 1954-63, assoc. adminstr., 1963-71, hosp. adminstr., 1971-81, exec. dir., 1981-85, bd. trustees, 1968-86; hosp. cons., 1985-90. Cons. dietitian Mercy Hosp., Portsmouth, Ohio, 1950-51; v.p., sec. Family Health Ctr. LaCrosse, Inc., 1985-91, pres., 1991-93; residency adv. bd. St. Francis-Mayo Family Practice, 1993-95; v.p. Caledonia Health Care Ctr., 1986-90; treas. Franciscan Cmty. Programs 1985-94. Bd. dirs. United Way of Olmstead County, 1968-73, Sr. Citizens Svcs. Inc., Rochester, Minn., 1988-94, Diocese of Winona Found., 1991-2000; bd. dirs. Madonna Towers, Rochester, 1987—, chair, 1991-97, 2003-05; bd. dirs. Olmstead County Hist. Soc., 1994-97, Regina Med. Ctr., Hastings, Minn., 1996-02, Madonna Meadows, 2002—; pres. Poverello Found., Rochester, 1983—; bd. adv. Winona State U. Rochester Ctr., 1985-93; fin. coun. Diocese of Winona, 1986-91; mem. Franciscan Skemp Healthcare Cmty. Bd., LaCrosse, 1995—. Decorated Lady of Equestrian Order of Holy Sepulchre, 1989; recipient Alumni Disting. Service award U. Wis.-Stout, 1978, Teresa of Avila award Coll. of St. Teresa, 1980, Outstanding Achievement award Rochester chpt. U. Minn. Alumni Assn., 1981, Women of Achievement in Area of Bus. award YWCA, 1985, Pro Ecclesiae et Pontifice medal, 1985, Service to Mankind award Sertoma 700 Club, 1987, Mayor's Medal of Honor City of Rochester, 1990, The Athena award, 1994, Outstanding Alumni award Coll. Human Devel., U. Wis.-Stout, 2001; named Boss of Yr., Rochester Jaycees, 1980, named in her honor Sister Generose Gervais Bldg. St. Marys Hosp., 1991; Paul Harris fellow Nat. Rotary Club, 1998. Mem. Cath. Health Assn. U.S. (trustee 1979, vice chair 1981-82, chair 1982-83, speaker membership assembly 1983-84), Am. Coll. Hosp. Adminstrs., Am. Hosp. Assn., Minn. Hosp. Assn., Minn. Conf. Cath. Health Facilities (past dir.), Rochester Area C. of C. Republican. Address: 1216 2nd St SW Rochester MN 55902-1906 Office Phone: 507-255-5158. Business E-Mail: hanson.sandra@mayo.edu.

GERVAIS, MARK G., physical education educator; b. Oct. 10, 1954; s. Joseph F. and Dorothy F. Gervais. Bachelor's, NE Mo. State U., 1980; Master's, Ea. Ill. U., Charleston, 1985. Asst. instr. N.E. Mo. State U., Kirksville, Mo., 1978—81; asst. wrestling coach Ea. Ill. U., 1981—82, Marist H.S., Chgo., 1982—83, head wrestling coach, 1983—, tchr., 1983—, dept. chair health and phys. edn., 1995—. Named to Hall of Fame, Marist HS, 2003, East Suburban Cath. Conf., 2007; recipient Champnat Educator of Yr. award, Marist Bros., 2003, Heart of Sch. award, Marist HS, 2005. Mem.: ASCD, AAHPERD, Ill. Wrestling Coaches Ofcls. Assn. (Coach of Yr. 1987, named to Hall of Fame 1995). Office: Marist High Sch 4200 W 115th St Chicago IL 60655 Office Phone: 773-881-5300 Ext. 5360. Business E-Mail: gervais.mark@marist.net.

GERVAIS, PAUL NELSON, foundation administrator, psychotherapist, writer, public relations executive; b. Augusta, Maine, June 28, 1947; s. Adrien and Phyllis (Sullivan) G. B in Bible and Doctrine/Ministerial Studies, Berean Coll., 1975; M, U. Maine, 1987; M in Marriage and Family Therapy, Coll. Clin. Family Sci., 1988; cert. in Constl. Law, U. Maine, 1969; Dr., N.Am. Biblical Sem., Buffalo, 1987; M. in Marriage and Family, San Antonio Theol. Sem., 1988; PhD in Psychology, San Antonio Theol. Sem., St. Paul, 1989; PhD in Marriage and Family Therapy, Minn. Grad. Sch., 1990. Cert. behavioral analyst, clin. supr. Maine Criminal Justice Acad., Dept. Pub. Safety, registered clin. therapist, lic. marriage and family therapist, clin. profl. counselor, profl. counselor, pastoral counselor Maine. Reporter No. New Eng. divsn. News dept. NBC Radio divsn., NYC, 1966-70; dir. pub. rels. Kennebec Valley Med. Ctr., Augusta, 1970-73, Penobscot Bay Med. Ctr., Rockport, Maine, 1973-74; pres., chmn. bd. dirs. Ministry of Miracles Evangelistic Assn., Maine, 1975—; staff clinician Augusta Police Dept. News dir. Maine Broadcasting Sys., Augusta, 1966—70; advisor, assoc. dir. pub. rels. State VA Svcs., Maine, 1969—70; family counselor Gracelawn Meml. Park, Auburn, Maine, assoc. dir., 1987, COO; pres., CEO Motivational Resources; behavioral scientist Augusta Police Dept. Pioneered one of first radio and TV health edn. programs from which proceeded other nat. and internat. programs in field; mental health columnist Maine Sunday Paper; internat. network TV guest. Active Rep. Nat. Com., Washington, 1987, Dole for Pres. exploratory Com., 1987—, also adv. com., 1987, steering com. Campaign Am., 1987-88; mem. Presdl. Task Force, Washington, 1989, Rep. Senatorial Inner Circle, 1989—, U.S. Senatorial Club, Washington, 1989-90, Nat. Rep. Senatorial Com., Washington, 1990; CEO Gracelawn Meml. Park, Auburn, Maine, 1988—; spl. advisor, dep. Kennebec County Sheriff's Office, also dep. sheriff. Recipient vice-presdl. Citation Office of U.S. V.P. Hubert Humphrey, 1968, Malcolm T. MacEachern Citation Am. Health Congress, 1973; cert. in pub. rels. Chgo. chpt. Am. Hosp. Assn.; Presdl. Medal of Merit Pres. George Bush, 1989. Fellow Profl. Assn. Christian Counselors and Therapists; mem. AACD, Am. Acad. Family Therapists (exec. dir.), Acad. for Eating Disorders, Nat. Assn. Anorexia Nervosa and Associated Disorders, Publicity Club Boston (disting. bell ringer award 1974), Nat. Christian Counselors Assn. (mem. licensing bd., chmn. legal com.), Am. Mental Health Counselors Assn., Maine Network Associated Profl. Practitioners, Maine Assn. for Counseling and Devel., Mensa. Baptist. Home and Office: Am Acad Profl Family Therapists 16 Julianne Ln Augusta ME 04330-6251 Personal E-mail: pgerv14771@aol.com. Business E-Mail: clinicdrpng@aol.com.

GERVAIS, RICKY, actor, scriptwriter; b. Reading, Eng., June 25, 1961; BA in Philosophy, Univ. Coll., London. Disc jockey XFM Radio Sta., London. Actor: (films) Dog Eat Dog, 2001, For Your Consideration, 2006, (voice) Valiant, 2005; (TV films) Legend of the Lost Tribe, 2002,: (TV series) The 11 O'Clock Show, 1998, Meet Ricky Gervais, 2000, The Office, 2001—03, Extras, 2005—06; writer: TV series Bruiser, 2000, Meet Ricky Gervais, 2000, The Office, 2001—03, The Sketch Show, 2001; performer: (appeared in) Comic Relief, 2003, The Big Hair Do, 2003; author (illus. by Rob Steen): (children's books) Flanimals, 2005, More Flanimals, 2006; scriptwriter (TV series) Homer Simpson: This Is Your Wife, The Simpsons, Fox TV, 2006. Co-recipient Rave award for podcast, Wired mag., 2006; named No. 3 on the list Brit. ulture's Top 50 Movers and Shakers, BBC 3, 2004, London's Funniest Man, Time Out mag.; recipient O.K. Comedy award, 2003, Golden Globe best comedic actor (2), 2003, Aerial Gold award, 6 BAFTAs. Office: Plumplard Prodn 38 Pickwick House London SE16 4UT England*

GERVAIS-GRUEN, ELIZABETH, lawyer; b. Papa, Hungary, Feb. 04; arrived in U.S., 1921; d. Samuel Friedmann and Vilma Kohn; m. Ralph Gervais, Feb. 7, 1970; m. Rudolph Gruen, Aug. 2, 1934 (div.); children: Richard Gruen, Robert Gruen, S. Daniel Gruen, David Gruen. Student, St. John's U., 1929—31, LLB, 1934. Bar: N.Y. 1936, N.Y. Supreme Ct. 1936, U.S. Supreme Ct. 1969. Law clk. Law Office of Samuel Newfield, 1934—36; ptnr. Rudolf Gruen and Elizabeth Gruen, 1936—38; asst. to town atty. James Dowsey, Jr. Nassau County, NY, 1938—40, asst. to county atty. James Dowsey, 1940—43; pvt. practice, 1943—58; pvt. practice Immigration and Naturalization Law, 1958—. Pres. Nassau County Women's Assn., 1968—70; bd. trustees Blumenthal Jewish Home, 1989—93; pres. Durham-Chapel Hill Jewish Fedn., 1988—90; chair Am. Affairs com. Hadassah, 1960—64, 1972—74; founder, mem. Women's Ctr., Chapel Hill, NC; chair, advisor youth activity com. Temple Beth El, Great Neck, LI, NY, chair, advisor Temple Teens, chair, advisor Coll. Youth com., pres. Sisterhood; mem. long-term planning com. Temple Beth Zion, Buffalo; chair women's group Judea Reform Congregation, Durham, NC, 1976—78, mem. long-term planning com., hon. chmn. Capitol Campaign. Recipient Sara Mutt Evans award, Jewish Fedn. and Cmty. Svc., 1992. Mem.: Commn.-Status of Women Attys. (Status of Women Attys. in N.C. com. mem.), N.C. Bar Assn. (chair Immigration and Nationality com. 1981—99), Am. Immigration Lawyers Assn. (chair N.C. chpt. 1980—84, bd. govs., founder N.C. chpt., hon. fellow 2002, Sam Williamson Mentor award 2000, Carolinas chpt. Mentor award in honor Elizabeth Gervais-Gruen established 1999, Elizabeth F. Gervais-Gruen Mentor award 1999, Pres.'s Commendation 1992). Avocations: reading, analyzing law, collecting Judaic artifacts, collecting ancient glass, collecting minerals and fossils, stamp collecting/philately. Office: 914 Crestwood Ln Chapel Hill NC 27517 Office Phone: 919-933-6810.

GERWICK-BRODEUR, MADELINE CAROL, marketing and timing professional; b. Kearney, Nebr., Aug. 29, 1951; d. Vern Frank and Marian Leila (Bliss) Gerwick; m. David Louis Brodeur; 1 child, Aria Renée Brodeur. Student, U. Wis., 1970-72, U. Louisville, 1974-75; BA in Econs. magna cum laude, U. N.H., 1979; postgrad., Internat. Trade Inst., Seattle. Cert. profl. cycles cons., 1995; cert. bus. astrologer. Indsl. sales rep. United Radio Supply Inc., Seattle, 1980-81; mfrs. rep. Ray Over Sales Inc., Seattle, 1981-82; sales engr. Tektronix, Inc., Kent, Wash., 1982-83; mktg. mgr. Zepher Industries, Inc., Burien, Wash., 1983-85, Microscan Systems Inc., Tukwila, Wash., 1986; market devel. URS Electronics, Inc., Portland, 1986-88; sr. product specialist Fluke Corp., 1989-95; owner Astro Cycles Cons. L.L.C., Seattle, 1995—; co-founder Polaris Business Guides LLC. Co-found. Polaris Bus. Guides LLC, 2001; bd. dirs., sec. Starfish Enterprises Inc., Tacoma, 1984-87; com. chmn. Northcon, Seattle and Portland, 1984-86, 88, 90; speaker to Wash. Women's Employment and Edn., Tacoma, 1983—. Writer daily column for Zodiac Zone, 1995-96, Online Noetic Network; author, pub. The Good Timing Guide; co-author The Complete Idiot's Guide To Astrology, 1997, Pocket Idiot's Guide to Horoscopes, 1998-2000, (annual) Good Timing Guides, 1997—. Bd. dirs. Kepler Coll. of Astrol. Arts and Scis., 1998-2000. Recipient Jack E. Chase award for Outstanding Svc. and Contbr. Northcon Founder's Orgn., 1988. Mem. Electronic Mfrs. Assn. (sec. 1982, sec.-treas. 1988, v.p. 1989), Inst. Noetic Scis., Internat. Soc. for Astrol. Rsch., Wash. State Astrol. Assn. (bd. dirs. 1996-98), Columbia Tower Club, Phi Kappa Phi. Avocations: writing, healing arts, metaphysics. Home and Office: PO Box 160 Arlington WA 98223-0160 Office Phone: 877-524-8300. Business E-Mail: mgb@polarisbusinessguides.com.

GERWIN, LESLIE ELLEN, lawyer, consultant, public relations executive; b. LA, May 18, 1950; d. Nathan and Beverly Adele (Wilson) G.; m. Bruce Robert Leslie, July 3, 1978; 1 child, Jonathan Gerwin Leslie. BA, Prescott Coll., 1972; JD, Antioch Sch. Law, 1975; MPH, Tulane U., 1988; MPA, Harvard U., 2006. Bar: DC 1975, NY 1981, US Dist. Ct. DC 1977, US Dist. Ct. (so. dist.) NY 1980. Staff asst. U.S. Congress, Washington, 1970-72; cons. Congl. Subcom., Washington, 1972-73; instr. U. Miami Law Sch., Coral Gables, Fla., 1975-76; assoc. prof. law Yeshiva U., NYC, 1976-86; vis. assoc. prof. law Tulane Law Sch., New Orleans, 1983-84; pub. policy cons. New Orleans, 1987—; pres. Ariadne Cons., New Orleans, 1994—; dir. devel. and community rels. Planned Parenthood La., Inc., New Orleans, 1989-90; legal advisor La. Coalition for Reproductive Freedom, 1990-92; exec. v.p. Met. Area Com., New Orleans, 1992-94; exec. dir. Met. Area Com. Edn. Fund, New Orleans, 1992-94. Bd. dirs. Inst. for Phys. Fitness Rsch., NYC, 1982-86, Challenge/Discovery, Crested Butte, Colo., 1977-80; cons. FDA, Washington, 1977-78, U. Judaism, LA, 1974-75; mem. Met. Area Com. Leadership Forum, New Orleans, 1988; adj. asst. prof. La. State U. Sch. Medicine, 1996—, La. State U. Med. Sch., Dept. of Public Health and Preventive Medicine. Contbr. articles to profl. jours. Mem. Ind. Dem. Jud. Screening Panel, NYC, 1980; profl. adv. com. MAZON-A Jewish Response to Hunger, LA, 1986-89; bd. dirs. New Orleans Food Bank for Emergencies, 1987-89, Second Harvesters Food Bank Greater New Orleans, 1989-94, La. State LWV, 1990-91, Anti-Defamation League, New Orleans, 1989-95, Jewish Endowment Found., 1987-93, Contemporary Arts Ctr., 1993-97, Planned Parenthood La. and Miss. Delta, 2004—, Jewish Family Svc., 2004—; trustee Emergency Food and Shelter Program, SE La., 1988—, Jewish Fedn. Greater New Orleans, 1989-95, 97-99, exec. com., 1997-99; v.p. Tulane U. B'nai B'rith Hillel Found., 1987-90; steering com. Citizens for Pers. Freedom, 1989-91; steering com. Metro 2000, 1989-90; sec. New Orleans sect. Nat. Coun. Jewish Women, 1990-91, state pub. affairs chmn., 1992-96; chair, bd. advocates Planned Parenthood La., 1995—; v.p. Edn. Tikvat Shalom Conservative Congregation, 1995-97, chair New Orleans Israel Bonds, 1996-98; mem. Cmty. Rels. Com., 1986-99, vice chair, 1995-97, chair 1997-99; adminstr. Area Tng. Ctr., USTA, New Orleans, 1996-2001; v.p. ritual Shir Chadash Conservative Congregation, 2002— Fellow Inst. of Politics, 1990-91, Lucius N. Littauer Kennedy Sch. Govt., 2006; scholar Xerox Found., 1972-75; decorated Order of Barristers; named One of Ten Outstanding Young Women of Am., 1987; recipient Herbert J. Garon Young Leadership award Jewish Fedn. Greater New Orleans, 1990; named YWCA Role Model, 1992. Mem. ABA, NY Bar Assn., NY Acad. Scis., Am. Pub. Health Assn., DC Bar Assn., Nat. Moot Ct. Honor Soc., Pub. Health Honor Soc., Calif. State Dem. Club (Key Svc. award 1988), Delta Omega. Personal E-mail: lgerwin@aol.com.

GESCHKE, CHARLES M., computer company executive; b. Cleve., Sept. 11, 1939; married, 1964; 3 children. AB in Classics, Xavier U., 1962, MS in Math., 1963; PhD in Computer Sci., Carnegie-Mellon U., 1972. Instr. math. John Carroll U., 1963—68; rsch. scientist computer sci. LAB. Palo Alto Rsch. Ctr., Xerox Corp., 1972—80, mgr. Imaging Sci. Lab., 1980—87; co-founder Adobe Sys. Inc., Mountain View, Calif., 1982, pres., chmn. bd., 1987—2000, co-chmn. bd., 2000—. Bd. dirs. Rambus, Inc.; computer sci. adv. bd. Carnegie-Mellon U., Princeton U.; mem. Govt.-Univ. Industry Rsch. Roundtable NAS. Bd. govs. San Francisco Symphony; bd. trustees U. San Francisco. Named 7th most influential graphics person of last millennium, Graphic Exch. Mag., 2000; recipient award, Assn. Computing Machinery, Nat. Computer Graphics Assn., Rochester Inst. Tech., Fellow award, Computer History Mus., 2002. Mem.: NAE, IEEE (hon.), Math. Assn. Am., Assn. Computer Math. Achievements include research in programming languages; machine design for efficient emulation of higher level languages; computer imaging and graphics.

GESKE, JANINE PATRICIA, law educator; b. Port Washington, Wis., May 12, 1949; d. Richard Braem and Georgette (Paulissen) Geske; m. Michael Julian Hogan, Jan. 2, 1982; children: Mia Geske Berman, Sarah Geske Hogan, Kevin Geske Hogan. Student, U. Grenoble, U. Rennes; BA, MA in Tchg., Beloit Coll., 1971; JD, Marquette U., 1975, LLD, 1998, LLD (hon.), 1994; DHL (hon.), Mt. Mary Coll., 1999. Bar: Wis. 1975, U.S. Dist. Ct. (ea. & we. dists.) Wis. 1975, U.S. Supreme Ct. 1978. Tchr. elem. sch., Lake Zurich, Ill., 1970-72; staff atty., chief staff atty. Legal Aid Soc., Milw., 1975-78; asst. prof. law, clin. dir. Law Sch. Marquette U., Milw., 1978-81; hearing examiner Milw. County CETA, Milw., 1980-81; judge Milw. County Circuit Ct., Milw., 1981-93; justice Supreme Ct. Wis., 1993-98; disting. prof. law Marquette U. Law Sch., Milw., 1998—, interim Miles County exec., 2002, interim dean Sch. Law, 2002—03. Dean Wis. Jud. Coll.; mem. faculty Nat. Jud. Coll.; instr. various jud. tng. programs, continuing legal edn. Fellow ABA, mem. Am. Law Inst., Am. Arbitration Assn., Soc. Profls. in Dispute Resolution, Wis. Bar Assn., Wis. Assn. Mediators, Milw. Bar Assn., Nat. Women Judges Assn., 7th Cir. Bar Assn., Alpha Sigma Nu. Roman Catholic. Office: Marquette U Law Sch PO Box 1881 Milwaukee WI 53201-1881

GESKIN, LARISA, dermatologist, researcher; d. Rita Gurevich and Yuri Karpel; m. Gennady Geskin, Mar. 28, 1989; children: Albert Aron, Jacob Zalman, Sophie Ilana. MD, U. Pitts., 1998. Lic. Dermatology Bd. Internal Medicine, 2003. Dir. cutaneous oncology ctr. Dept. Dermatology, U. Pitts., 2001—; assoc. dir. dermatology residency program Dept. Dermatology, Pitts., 2006—. Dir. photopheresis unit U. Pitts. Med. Ctr., 2001. Adv. bd. Gen. Clinical Rsch. Ctr., Pitts., 2005—06. Recipient Physician Scientist Career Devel. award, Dermatology Found., 2004—06. Fellow: Am. Acad. Dermatology (assoc.). Achievements include development of cancer vaccine. Avocations: travel, skiing, theater. Office: U Pitts 190 Lothrop St Pittsburgh PA 15213 Office Phone: 412-648-3161.

GESLANI, GEMMA P., science educator, health researcher; b. San Jose, Negros Oriental, Philippines, Mar. 23, 1961; d. Justiniano P. Geslani and Paz Pareja. BS in Chemistry, Silliman U., Dumaguete City, Philippines, 1981; MS in Biochemistry, U. Philippines, Manila, 1988; MPH, U. SC, Columbia, 1998; PhD in Biochemistry, U. SC, 1996. Rsch. asst. U. of the Philippines, 1982—84, rsch. assoc., 1984—88; instr. RTR Sch. of Medicine, Tacloban City, Philippines, 1988—90; rsch. and tchg. asst. U. SC, 1990—98; health rschr. Survey Methods Group, San Francisco, 1999—99; asst. prof. Claflin U., Orangeburg, SC, 2000—05, assoc. prof., 2005—07, St. Louis Coll. Pharmacy, 2005—. Co-PI, co-dir. export grant Claflin U., 2005—, co-investigator, program coord. Kellogg grant, 2003—06, rsch. coord. Kellogg grant, 2005—. Co-author: Custom Made Laboratory Manual for Human Biology; contbr. articles to profl. jours. Active mem. Filipino-Am. Assn. of Greater Columbia, 1991—. Academic fellow, RTR Med. Sch., 1982—84, rsch. fellow, U. SC Sch. Pub. Health, 2006. Mem.: APHA, SC Pub. Health Assn. Roman Catholic. Avocations: reading, travel, gardening, cooking, dance. Home: Towne House Apt Apt 21-D 4400 Lindell Blvd Saint Louis MO 63108 Personal E-mail: gemma_11999@yahoo.com.

GESNER, LAWRENCE H., lawyer; b. NYC, 1958; BBA, George Washington U., 1980; JD cum laude, Georgetown U., 1983. Bar: DC 1983. Former ptnr. Arter & Hadden LLP, Washington; ptnr., real estate group Venable LLP, Washington, 2003—. Sr. lead articles editor Law and Policy in Internat. Bus., 1982—83. Mem.: ABA, DC Bar Assn. Office: Venable LLP 575 7th St NW Washington DC 20004 Office Phone: 202-344-4733. Office Fax: 202-344-8300. Business E-Mail: lhgesner@venable.com.

GESSAMAN, DONALD EUGENE, retired government executive; b. Dayton, Ohio, Nov. 11, 1939; s. Stanley Loran and Alma Elizabeth (Tevis) G.; m. Jane Alexander Giles, Oct. 16, 1965; 1 child, William Arthur. BS in Indsl. Mgmt., U. Cin., 1964; MS in Indsl. Engring., Stanford U., 1972. Exec. trainee Office of Sec. of Def., Washington, 1966; with nat security divsn., dep. divsn. chief Office Mgmt. and Budget, Exec. Office of Pres., Washington, 1967-90, dep. assoc. dir., 1990-95; cons. EOP Group, Inc., Washington, 1995—. Office: EOP Group Inc 819 7th St NW Washington DC 20001-3762 E-mail: gessaman@adelphia.net.

GESSAMAN, MARGARET PALMER, mathematician, educator, retired dean; b. Florence, Ariz., Oct. 7, 1934; d. William Lee Sr. and Lillian Maude (Henkle) Palmer; m. Paul Hayden Gessaman, June 11, 1965. BS, Mont. State Coll., 1956, MS, 1965, PhD, 1966. Statistician Fatstock Mktg. Corp., London, 1957-59; ops. researcher Richard, Thomas and Baldwin, Ebbw Vale, South Wales, 1959-60; market researcher Nestle Co., Inc., London, 1960-61; instr. Mont. State U., 1966-67; asst. prof. math. Ithaca Coll., 1967-70; asst. prof., assoc. prof., prof. math. U. Nebr., Omaha, 1970—, chmn. dept. math., computer sci., 1973—80, 1998—2000, dean grad. studies rsch., 1980-93. Cons. grad. and rsch. activities, Coll. Bd., Chgo., 1981-88, Ednl. Testing Svc., Princeton, N.J., 1976-80, various govt. units, univs.; panelist NSF, Washington. Contbr. articles to profl. jours. Program chair Nebr. Commn. United Ministries in Higher Edn., Lincoln, 1976-81, 88-90. Mem. Coun. Grad. Schs. (bd. dirs.), Inst. Math. Stats., Am. Statis. Assn., Grad. Women in Sci.(nat. treas. 1994-95), Fulbright Assn., Mid-Am. State Univs. Assn. (chair 1988-89), Midwestern Assn. Grad. Schs. (chair-elect, chair, past chair 1986-89). Methodist. Avocations: travel, Mayan history, cat lore.

GEST, HOWARD DAVID, lawyer; b. Bergenfield, NJ, Jan. 24, 1952; m. Lucy Acevedo; 1 child, Aaron. AB in Econs., U. Calif., Berkeley, 1974; JD, Hastings Coll., 1977. Bar: Calif. 1977. Staff atty. US Ct. Appeals (9th cir.), San Francisco, 1977-78; asst. U.S. atty. Cen. Dist. Calif., LA, 1978-83; assoc. Sidley & Austin, LA, 1983—86, ptnr., 1986—99, Burhenn & Gest, LA, 2000—. Office: Burhenn & Gest LLP Ste 2200 624 S Grand Ave Los Angeles CA 90017 Home Phone: 310-458-6258; Office Phone: 213-688-7715. Business E-Mail: hgest@burhenngest.com.

GEST, KATHRYN WATERS, public relations executive; b. Boston, Mar. 20, 1947; d. Mendal and Anna Waters; m. Theodore O. Gest, May 28, 1972; 1 child, David Mendal. BS, Northwestern U., 1969; MS, Columbia U., 1970. Reporter The Patriot-Ledger, Quincy, Mass., 1968; writer Europe desk Voice of Am., Washington, 1969; reporter St. Louis Globe-Democrat, 1970-77, Congl. Quar., Washington, 1977-78, news editor, 1978-80, asst. mng. editor, 1980-83, mng. editor, 1983-87; St. Louis corr. Time Mag., 1975-77, The Christian Sci. Monitor, 1976-77; press sec. to Sen. William S. Cohen, Washington, 1987-96; chmn., U.S. del. Internat. Labor Orgn. Tripartite Meeting on Conditions of Employment and Work of Journalists, Geneva, 1990; exec. v.p., dir. internat. issues Powell Tate/Weber Shandwick, 1996—. Election observer Nat. Dem. Inst., Albania, 1996, Azerbaijan, 2003, Ukraine, 04, Palestinian Terrs., 2006—. Recipient award for investigative reporting Inland Daily Press Assn., 1975 Bd. dirs. Nat. Press Found. Soc. Profl. Journalists, Women's Fgn. Policy Group, Internat. Women's Media Fund, Nat. Press Club. Office: Powell Tate/Weber Shandwick 700 13th St NW Washington DC 20005-6618 Business E-Mail: kgest@aol.com.

GESTON, MARK SYMINGTON, lawyer; b. Atlantic City, June 20, 1946; s. John Charles and Mary Tobiatha (Simmington) G.; m. Gayle Francis Howard, June 12, 1971 (div. Aug. 1972); m. Marijke Havinga, Aug. 14, 1976; children: Camille LaCroix, Robert L. LaCroix, Emily S. Geston. AB in History (with honors), Kenyon Coll., 1968; JD, NYU, 1971. Bar: Idaho, U.S. Ct. Appeals (9th cir.). With Eberle and Berlin, 1971—2003; atty. Stoel Rives LLP, Boise, Idaho, 2003—. Author: Lords of the Starship, 1967, Out of the Mouth of the Dragon, 1969, The Day Star, 1972, The Seige of Wonder, 1975, Mirror to the Sky, 1992, The Stronghold If, 1973; contbr. stories to Amazing Stories, Fantasy and Sci. Fiction. Recipient Kenyon Rev. prize for achievement in lit., Kenyon Coll., 1968; named Root-Tilden fellow NYU, 1968-71. Mem. Idaho State Bar Assn., Phi Beta Kappa. Avocation: writing. Office: Stoel Rives LLP 101 S Capitol Blvd Boise ID 83702 Home Phone: 208-343-0559; Office Phone: 208-387-4291. Business E-Mail: msgeston@stoel.com.

GESWEIN, GREGORY T., software company executive; m. Rose Geswein; 2 children. BBA, U. Cin., 1977, MBA in Fin., 1978. Joined Armco Inc., 1978; v.p., corp. contr., corp. treas. Mead Corp., Dayton, Ohio, 1985—89; sr. v.p., CFO Pioneer-Standard Electronics, Inc., Cleve., 1999, Diebold, Inc., North Canton, Ohio, 2000—04, Reynolds & Reynolds Co., 2005—. Office: Reynolds and Reynolds Co PO Box 1824 Dayton OH 45401-1824

GETCHELL, CHARLES WILLARD, JR., lawyer, publisher, foundation executive; b. LA, May 29, 1929; s. Charles Willard and Katharine (Fitch) G.; m. Angela Winthrop, Sept. 16, 1961; children: Katharine Chisholm, Emily Erskine, Sarah Fields. AB, Stanford U., 1951, JD, 1954. Bar: Calif. 1955, Mass. 1979, U.S. Dist. Ct. (no. dist.) Calif. 1960, Mass. 1983, U.S. Ct. Appeals, 9th cir. 1960, U.S. Supreme Ct. 1985. Atty. Air Materiel Force, Chateauroux, France, 1958-59; asst. U.S. atty. No. Dist. Calif., San Francisco, 1960-61; asst. mgr. Citibank, NYC, Brussels, 1961-68; v.p. Wood Struthers & Winthrop, NYC, Brussels, 1969-77; ptnr. Gray, Wendell, Chalmers & Dahlen, Boston, 1981-87; pub. The Ipswich (Mass.) Press, 1980—. Pres. Yorkham Timber Co., Inc., 1986-2000; chmn. Sabre Europe (Belgium); sec. Sabre Found., 1995—; sr. fellow Salzburg Seminar, 1997—. Translator: European Monetary Unity: For Whose Benefit? (Pascal Salin), 1980; contbr. articles and poetry to newspapers and mags. Mem. steering com. Bilderberg Meetings, The Hague, 1980—85; trustee Shore Country Day Sch., 1978—84; bd. dirs. Salzburg Seminar, 1985—89. Lt. j.g. USNR, 1955—58. Fellow: Mass. Hist. Soc., Tavern Club; mem.: Belgian Am. Ednl. Found. Office: Ipswich Press PO Box 291 Ipswich MA 01938-0291

GETCHELL, SYLVIA FITTS, librarian; b. Dover, NH, July 3, 1925; d. Perley Irving and Marguerite Elizabeth (Marden) F.; m. L. Forbes Getchell, July 17, 1948; children: Ann Marden, Faith Perley, Edward Fitts, William Forbes. BA in History magna cum laude, U. N.H., 1947; BS in Libr. Sci., Simmons Coll., 1948. Profl. cataloger Libr. Columbia U., NYC, 1948-51, U. N.H., Durham, 1951-52; sch. libr. Newmarket (N.H.) Pub. Schs., 1970-85; curator Stone Sch. Mus., Newmarket, 1966—. Author: Marden Family Genealogy, 1974, Tide Turns on the Lamprey: History of Newmarket, N.H., 1984, Fitts Families: A Genealogy, 1989, Getchell-Gatchell, a Family Genealogy of Maine Pioneers, 2005; co-editor: Piscataqua Pioneers, Selected Biographies of Early Settlers in Northern New England, 2000; editor: Living in the Lap of History: A Checklist of Historic Sites in New Hampshire, 2004. Libr. Am. Independence Mus., Exeter, N.H., 1990-2005, bd. govs., 1992-99; bd. dirs. Newmarket Hist. Soc., 1966-2005, past pres.; curator Stone Sch. Mus., 1966-; bd.dirs. Piscataqua Pioneers, Portsmouth, N.H., 1969—, past pres.; 18th century re-enactor 1st Newmarket Colonial Militia, 1973—; former chair ann. fund drive local chpt. ARC; past collector, Sun. sch. tchr. Newmarket Cmty. Ch.; former treas. Aux. of N.H. Dental Soc.; mem. N.H. Hist. Soc. Mem. DAR (mem. and past sec. N.H. attic commn. 1994-2000, N.H. state historian 2000-04), New Eng. Hist. Geneal. Soc., Newmarket Women's Club (past treas.), Huguenot Soc. N.H., Soc. Daus. Colonial Wars. Republican. Avocations: genealogy, painting, needlecrafts, travel. Home: 51 N Main St Newmarket NH 03857-1216

GETCHES, DAVID HARDING, lawyer, educator, dean; b. Abington, Pa., Aug. 17, 1942; s. George Winslow Getches and Ruth Erskine (Harding) Fossette; m. Ann Marks, June 26, 1964; children: Matthew, Catherine, Elizabeth. AB, Occidental Coll., 1964; JD, U. So. Calif., 1967. Bar: Calif. 1968, U.S. Supreme Ct. 1971, D.C. 1972, Colo. 1973. Assoc. Luce, Forward, Hamilton & Scripps, San Diego, 1967-69; directing atty. Calif. Indian Legal Services, Escondido, 1969-70; founding dir. Native Am. Rights Fund, Boulder, Colo., 1970-76; ptnr. Getches & Greene, Boulder, Colo., 1976-78; assoc. prof. U. Colo. Law Sch., Boulder, Colo., 1979—87, prof., 1987—94, Raphael J. Moses Prof. of Natural Resources Law, 1994—, interim dir. Natural Resources Law Ctr., 1995, dean, 2003—; exec. dir. Colo. Dept. Natural Resources, Denver, 1983-87; spl. consultant to sec. U.S. Dept. Interior, Washington, 1996. Ptnr. MB Land Co., Centro Bldg. Devel. Co. Author: Water Law in a Nutshell, 1997; co-author: Cases and Materials on Federal Indian Law, 2005, Water Resources Management, 5th edit., 2002; contbr. articles to profl. jours. Bd. trustees Rocky Mountain Mineral Law Fedn. Mem. Wilderness Soc. (governing coun.), Defenders of Wildlife (bd. dirs.). Democrat. Office: University Colorado School of Law Fleming Law Building 401 UCB Boulder CO 80309-0401 Home Phone: 303-449-4869; Office Phone: 303-492-3084. Business E-Mail: lawdean@colorado.edu.

GETER, RODNEY KEITH, plastic surgeon; b. Baton Rouge, La., Nov. 13, 1946; s. Argless William and Jewel Alma (Rudolph) G. BA in Chemistry with honors, U. Mo., 1975, MD, 1979. Resident in gen. surgery U. Mo., Columbia, 1979-83, fellow in microvascular surgery, 1983-84, resident in plastic surgery, 1984-86; pvt. practice Springfield (Mo.) Clinic, 1986—. Chmn. dept. surgery St. John's Regional Health Ctr., Springfield, 1992-94, chmn. two hosp. coms., 1994-97; v.p. med. staff St. John's Hosp., 1996-97, chmn. plastic surgery dept., 2000-02. Contbr. articles to profl. jours. Pres. Springfield Music Found., 1989—; leader troop 210 Boy Scouts Am., Springfield, 1995-98. Sgt. Spl. Forces, U.S. Army, 1968-71, Vietnam. Mem. Am. Soc. Plastic and Reconstructive Surgeons, Greene County Med. Soc., Mo. State Med. Assn., Phi Beta Kappa, Phi Lambda Upsilon. Avocations: playing keyboard in band, fishing, backpacking. Office: St Johns Clinic Plastic Surgery 1229 E Seminole Ste 340 Springfield MO 65804 Office Phone: 417-820-9330. E-mail: rkgeter@sprg.mercy.net.

GETIS, ARTHUR, geography educator; b. Phila., July 6, 1934; s. Samuel J. and Sophie Getis; m. Judith M. Marckwardt, July 23, 1961; children: Hilary Hope Tarazi, Victoria Lynn, Anne Patterson Tibbetts. BS, Pa. State U., University Park, 1956, MS, 1958; PhD, U. Wash., Seattle, 1961. Asst. instr. geography U. Wash., 1960-61; asst. prof. Mich. State U., 1961-63; faculty Rutgers U., New Brunswick, NJ, 1963-77, prof. geography, 1969-77, dir. grad. programs in geography, 1970-73, chmn. New Brunswick geography dept., 1971-73; prof. geography U. Ill., Urbana-Champaign, 1977-90, San Diego State U., 1990—, doctoral program coord., 1990-92, Stephen/Mary Birch Found. endowed chair geog. studies, 1992—2004, disting. prof. geography, 2004—, Albert W. Johnson univ. rsch. lectr., 1995; head dept. U. Ill., 1977-83, dir. Sch. Social Scis., 1983-84; centennial fellow Pa. State U., 1996; A. Robinson lectr. Ohio State U., 1999. Vis. lectr. Bristol U., Eng., 1966-67, UCLA, summers 1968, 74, U. BC, 1969; vis. prof. Princeton U., 1971-74; vis. disting. prof. San Diego State U., 1989; mem. Regional Sci. Rsch. Group, Harvard U., 1970; panelist NSF, 1981-83 Author: (with B. Boots) Models of Spatial Processes, 1978, Point Pattern Analysis, 1988, (with J. Getis and J.D. Fellmann) Geography, 1981, Human Geography, 8th edit., 2004, Introduction to Geography, 10th edit., 2006, (edited with J. Getis and J.D. Fallmann) The United States and Canada, 1995, 2d edit., 2001, The Tyranny of Data, 1996, (edited with M.M. Fischer) Recent Developments in Spatial Analysis, 1997, (with J. Mur and H. Zoller) Spatial Econometrics and Spatial Statistics, 2004; editor-in chief Jour. Geographical Systems, 1992—; contbg. editor, assoc. editor: Jour. Geography, 1972-74; mem. editl. bd. Nat. Geog. Rsch., 1984-90, Rsch. and Exploration, 1991-95, Geog. Analysis, 1991—, Papers in Regional Sci., 1999-02, Annals of Regional Sci., 1999—, Regional Rsch. Inst., 2003—; contbr. articles to profl. jours. Mem. Urbana Zoning Bd. Appeals, 1980-84; co-pres. Univ. High Sch. Parent-Faculty Orgn., 1982-83; bd. dirs. Univ. Consortium for Geog. Info. Scis., 1997-2004, pres.-elect, 2000-02, pres. 2002-03. Rutgers U. faculty fellow, 1970; East-West Center sr. fellow, 1974; NSF grantee, 1983-85, 1992-94, 99—, NIH grantee, 1999—; recipient Walter Isard award N.Am. Regional Sci. Coun., 1997. Fellow Western Regional Sci. Assn. (bd. dirs. 1992-97, pres. 1998-99), Regional Sci. Assn. Internat. (pres. N.E. sect. 1973-74, bd. dirs. 1998-2007); mem. Assn. Am. Geographers (grantee 1964-65, vis. scientist 1970-72, chair math. models and quantitative methods splty. group 1991-92, honors for disting. scholarship 2002), Internat. Inst. Brit. Geographers, Internat. Geog. Union (sec. commn. math. models 1988-96), Sigma Xi. Home: 5135 Jumilla St San Diego CA 92124-1503 Office: San Diego State U Dept Geography San Diego CA 92182 Business E-Mail: arthur.getis@sdsu.edu.

GETNICK, NEIL VICTOR, lawyer; b. Bklyn., Oct. 28, 1953; s. Irving Murray and Zita (Ellman) G.; m. Margaret Joan Finerty, May 21, 1978. BA in Govt. magna cum laude, Cornell U., 1975, JD, 1978. Bar: N.Y. 1979, U.S. Dist. Ct. (so. and ea. dists.) N.Y. 1983. Asst. dist. atty. trial divsn. N.Y. County, NYC, 1978-81, asst. dist. atty. frauds bur., 1981-82; ptnr. Getnick & Getnick, NY, 1983—. Mem. Criminal Justice Act panel U.S. Dist. Ct. for So. Dist. N.Y., N.Y.C., 1984-89. Editor-in-chief: Civil Prosecution News, 1994-96. Recipient Pub. Citizenship award N.Y. Pub. Interest Rsch. Group, 1977. Mem. ABA (litigation and criminal law sects.), N.Y. State Bar Assn. (exec. com. comml. and fed. litigation sect., chair com. on civil prosecution), Assn. of Bar of City of N.Y., N.Y. County Lawyers Assn., Internat. Assn. Ind. Pvt. Sector Inspectors Gen. (pres. 1994—), Internat. Assn. of Ind. Pvt. Sector Inspectors Gen. (pres. 1994—). Office: Getnick & Getnick Rockefeller Ctr 620 5th Ave 4th Flr New York NY 10020-2457

GETS, LISPBETH ELLA, retired educational administrator; b. Jhelum, Pakistan, Mar. 18, 1931; arrived in USA, 1952, naturalized, 1955; s. Henry Ellis and Constance Selina (Bodell) Glenn; m. Terence Mathew Gets, Jan. 19, 1952; children: Erik Charles, Alison Beth, Hugh Malcolm, Adrienne Lea. AA, Santa Fe Cmty. Coll., 1973—74; BA (hon.), U. Fla., 1976; postgrad, 1977—89, MS, 1989. Cert. ednl. specialist Fla., 1989. Cert. adminstr., supr., Fla. Editl. asst. John Trundell Pub., London, 1950—52; exec. secretarial positions, various co. Chgo., Ft. Smith, Ark. and Jamestown, NY, 1952—58; tchr. spl. edn. Buchholz HS, Gainesville, Fla., 1976—81; asst. prin. Sidney Lanier Sch., Gainesville, 1981—83, 1987—2003; prin. Monarch Ctr. for Exceptional Students, Gainesville, 1983—87; inclusion specialist Alachua County Pub. Schs., 2003—07; ret., 2007. Named Tchr. of Yr., Gatorland chpt. Coun. for Exceptional Children, 1981. Mem.: Fla. Assn. Exceptional Sch. Adminstrs. (state chmn. 1988—90), Coun. Exceptional Children (chpt. pres. 1983—), Phi Delta Kappa. Democrat. Episcopalian. Home: 4601 NW 13th Ave Gainesville FL 32605-4534 Personal E-mail: jblg31@aol.com.

GETTEL, JAMES JOSEPH, lawyer, consultant; b. Evanston, Ill., June 22, 1959; s. James Robert and Mary Ellen (Davis) G.; m. Jennifer Anne Vogel, Aug. 13, 1983; children: Katharine Elizabeth, Sarah Jane. BA in Philosophy, Northwestern U., 1980; MBA, JD, U. Ill., 1984. Bar: Wis. 1984, US Dist. Ct. Wis. 1984, US Ct. Appeals (7th cir.) 1984. Ptnr. Michael, Best & Friedrich, Milw., 1991-94; gen. counsel, exec. v.p. The Waterstone Group, Inc., Mequon, Wis., 1994—. Author: Fundamental Reform of Philosophy, 1987, God's Love, Human Freedom and Christian Faith, 2003. Bd. dirs. Our Next Generation, Milw., 1993-2002; congl. devel. officer Episcopal Diocese of Milw., 2000-01; cons. Middle Voice Cons., Grafton, Wis., 2005—. Mem. ABA, Nat. Assn. Corp. Dirs., Wis. Bar Assn., Soc. Human Resources Mgmt., Federalist Soc. Office: The Waterstone Group Inc 12075 North Corporate Pkwy Ste 100 Mequon WI 53092 Home: 390 Streamside Ct Grafton WI 53024-9420

GETTELFINGER, RON, labor union administrator; b. Aug. 1, 1944; m. Judy Gettelfinger; children: Dawn, Darin. B in Acctg., Ind. U., 1976. Local official, truck plant Ford Motor Co., Louisville, 1964—84; pres. Local 862 UAW, 1984—87, dir. Region 3, 1992—98, v.p., 1998—2002, pres., 2002—. Mem. UAW-Ford Motor Co. Bargaining Com., 1987—98; mem. supervisory bd. DaimlerChrysler AG, 2006—. Served in USMC, 1962—63. Office: UAW Solidarity House 8000 E Jefferson Detroit MI 48214 Office Phone: 313-926-5000.*

GETTIG, MARTIN WINTHROP, retired mechanical engineer; b. South Bend, Ind., Nov. 8, 1939; s. Joseph H. and Esther (Scheppele) G.; m. Nancy Caroline Buchannan, June 25, 1960 (dec. 1965). Student, Pa. State U., 1957-60, 89—. Process engr. Gettig Tech. Inc., Spring Mills, Pa., 1960-88. Inventor ultralight non-solid state miniature ignition systems for model aircraft employing small two cycle spark ignition engines. Staff sgt. Pa. N.G., 1961-67. Mem.: NRA, Acad. Model Awronautics, Soc. Antique Modelers and Model Airplanes, Model Engine Collectors Assn., Delta Phi. Republican. Lutheran. Home: PO Box 85 Boalsburg PA 16827-0085

GETTLEMAN, JEFFREY, journalist; BA in Phil., Cornell Univ, 1993; M in Social Anthrop., Oxford Univ. Reporter LA Times, New York Times. Author: (articles) For Iraqi's in Harm's Way, $5000 and I'm Sorry, Transfer of Power in Iraq Nearly Done, Officials Say, 2004, A Rough-and-Tumble Congressman Is Ready to Step Up, 2005. Finalist Livingston awards, 2004. Office: The New York Times Newark Bur 111 Mulberry St Newark NJ 07102 Office Phone: 973-623-3905. Office Fax: 973-802-1877.

GETTLEMAN, MARVIN E., retired history professor; b. NYC, Sept. 12, 1933; s. Arthur A. Gettleman and Pauline Antopol; m. Ellen Schrecker, Aug. 23, 1981; children: Michael Schrecker, Dan Schrecker; m. Susan Braiman, 1968; children: Dan, Todd, Eva Braiman, Rebecca. BA, CCNY, 1957; PhD, Johns Hopkins U., Balt., 1972. Lectr. CCNY, 1959—63; from instr. to prof. Poly. U., Bklyn., 1963—2005, emeritus prof. history, 2005—; exec. dir. Abraham Lincoln Brigade Archives, NYC, 1996—98. Vis. prof. Queens Coll., CUNY, 2000—05, NYU, 2005. Author: Vietnam: History, Documents and Opinions, 1965, 3d edit., 1970, The Dorr Rebellion: A Study in American Radicalism, 1933-49, 1973, An Elusive Presence: John Finley and His America, 1979, The Johns Hopkins Seminary of History and Politics, 1977-1912, 1988—90; co-editor: The Great Society: Failure of Liberalism, 1967, 1970, Vietnam and America, 1985, The Middle East and Islamic World Reader, 2003, 2005, others; contbr. numerous articles and revs. to profl. jours.; editor: The Volunteer, 1996—98; mem. editl. bd.: Science & Society, 1974—. Fellow, NEH, 1973—74, Woodrow Wilson Found., 1957—59. Mem.: Phi Beta Kappa. Avocations: swimming, painting.

GETTLER, BENJAMIN, lawyer, manufacturing company executive; b. Louisville, Sept. 16, 1925; s. Herbert and Gertrude (Cohen) G.; m. Deliaan Angel, Mar. 1972; children: Jorian, Thomas, Gail, John, Benjamin. BA in Econs. with high honors, U. Cin., 1945; JD (Frankfurter scholar), Harvard U., Cambridge, Mass., 1948. Bar: Ohio 1949, U.S. Supreme Ct. 1955. Ptnr. Brown & Gettler, Cin., 1951—73, Gettler, Katz & Buckley, Cin., 1973—87; chmn. bd. Am. Controlled Industries Inc., Cin., 1973—86; chmn. bd. dirs., pres. Colorpac Inc., Franklin, Ohio, 1973—86; chmn. exec. com. Valley Industries, Inc., Cin., 1973—86; chmn. bd., pres. Vulcan Internat. Corp., Wilmington, Del., 1988—, Vulcan Corp., Clarksville, Tenn., 1988—; vice chmn. bd. Cin. So. R.R., 1987—91; chmn. bd. Trusthouse, Inc., Cin., 1987—. Chmn. exec. com. Valley Industries, Inc., Cin., 1973-86; chmn. bd. dirs. ACI Internat., Inc., Cin., 1990—; spl. counsel U. Cin., 1975-77, trustee, 1994-2003, vice chmn. bd., 1999-2000, chmn., 2000-2002; bd. dirs. PNC Bank, Ohio, 1988-96. Chmn. bd. Jewish Inst. Nat. Security Affairs, 1994-98, chmn. policy com., 1998—; chmn. Cin. Bonds for Israel, 1969; chmn. Nat. Israel Commn., Nat. Jewish Cmty. Rels. Adv. Coun., 1981-82; mem. Ohio, Ky. and Ind. Mass Transit Policy Com., 1970-75; pres. Cin. Jewish Cmty. Rels. Coun., 1978-80; trustee Jewish Hosp. Cin., 1978-92, chmn., 1991-92; chmn. Midwest Hosp. Sys., Inc., 1987-90, 92-93; pres. Jewish Found. Cin., 1995-99, chmn., 1999-02; trustee Health Alliance Greater Cin., 1995-96, 2000-02; chmn. Cin. Coalition for Reagan, 1980; co-chmn. Hamilton County Reagan Bush Campaign Ohio, 1984; chmn. Rep. Fin. Com., Hamilton County, 1991-92; mem. Hamilton County Rep. Policy Com., 1990—; exec. dir. Rockwern Charitable Found., 1998—; trustee S.W. Ohio Regional Transit Authority, 2003-06, chmn., 2004-06. Capt. US Army, 1955—56. Mem. ABA, Cin. Bar Assn., Shoe Last Mfrs. Assn. (pres. 1984-85), Footwear Industries Am. (bd. dirs. 1989-2000), Phi Beta Kappa, Omicron Delta Kappa. Clubs: Coldstream Country, Harvard. Office: Vulcan Corp 30 Garfield Pl Ste 1040 Cincinnati OH 45202-4322 Office Phone: 513-621-2850.

GETTNER, ALAN FREDERICK, retired lawyer; b. NYC, Dec. 25, 1941; s. Victor Salomon and Henriette Seldner (Herrmann) G.; m. Monah Lawrence, Jan. 19, 1969. BA, Yale U., 1963; MA, U. Chgo., 1964; PhD, Columbia U., 1971, JD, 1979. Bar: N.Y. 1980. Assoc. Debevoise & Plimpton, NYC and Paris, 1979-84, Holtzmann, Wise & Shepard, NYC, 1984-85, ptnr., 1986-95, Patterson, Belknap, Webb & Tyler, LLP, NYC, 1995—2004, chmn. bus. devel. com., 2000—03, of counsel, 2005—06; mem. exec. com. Holtzmann, Wise & Shepard, 1992-94; ret., 2007. Bd. mem. Friends of the Neuberger Mus. Art; co-chmn. Finance Com., Hosp. Audiences Inc.; mem. profl. adv. com. Mus. Art and Design. Mem.: ABA (sect. on bus. law, mem. art and design profl. adv. com.), Profl. Advisory Com. Museum of Art and Design, Assn. Bar City N.Y., The Lotos Club. Office Phone: 212-877-2077. Business E-Mail: agettner@verizon.net.

GETTY, BALTHAZAR, actor; b. LA, Jan. 22, 1975; s. Paul and Gisela Getty; m. Rosetta Millington, May 3, 2000; 1 child. Former fashion model Calvin Klien, Tommy Hilfiger, Versace. Actor: (films) Lord of the Flies, 1990, Young Guns II, 1990, My Heroes Have Always Been Cowboys, 1991, The Pope Must Diet, 1991, Where the Day Takes You, 1992, Natural Born Killers, 1994, Judge Dredd, 1995, White Squall, 1996, Lost Highway, 1997, Habitat, 1997, Fait Accompli, 1998, Out in Fifty, 1999, Big City Blues, 1999, Shadow Hours, 2000, Four Dogs Playing Poker, 2000, Sol Goode, 2001, MacArthur Park, 2001, The Center of the World, 2001, Run for the Money, 2002, Deuces Wild, 2002, Ladder 49, 2004, Slingshot, 2005, Feast, 2005, (TV films) The Turn of the Screw, 1990, Corsairs, 2002, Dirtbags, 2006, (TV miniseries) Traffic, 2004, Into the West, 2005, (TV series) Charmed, 2003-04, Alias, 2005-06, Brothers & Sisters, 2006-.

GETTY, ESTELLE (ESTELLE SCHER), actress; b. NYC, July 25, 1923; m. Arthur Gettleman, Dec. 21, 1946 (dec. 2004); children: Barry, Carl. Student, New Sch. for Social Rsch., Herbert Berghof Studios; studied with Gerald Russak. Actress: numerous stage prodns. on and off Broadway including Death of a Salesman, The Glass Menagerie, All My Sons, 6 Rms Rv Vu, Blithe Spirit, Arsenic and Old Lace, I Don't Know Why I'm Screaming, Widows and Children, Torch Song Trilogy, 1981-83; (films) Team-Mates, 1978, Tootsie, 1982, Deadly Force, 1983, Mask, 1985, Mannequin, 1987, Stop! Or My Mom Will Shoot, 1992, Stuart Little, 1999, The Million Dollar Kid, 2000; (TV movies) No Man's Land, 1984, Victims for Victims: The Teresa Saldana Story, 1984, Copacabana, 1985, A Match Made in Heaven, 1997, The Sissy Duckling, 1999; (TV series) The Golden Girls, 1985-92, (Emmy award for outstanding supporting actress in a comedy series, 1988, Golden Globe award for best performance by an actress in a TV series - comedy/musical, 1986, Am. Comedy award for funniest supporting female performer in a TV series, 1991, 92), Golden Palace, 1992-93, Empty Nest, 1994-95; author: If I Knew Then What I Know Now.So What?, 1988. ret. 2000. Spokesperson Alternative Living for the Aging.

GETTYS, THOMAS WIGINGTON, medical researcher; BS in Biology, Lander Coll., 1978; PhD in Nutrition, Clemson U., 1984. Grad. rsch. asst. animal sci. dept. Coll. Agr. Clemson U., SC, 1979—84; rsch. assoc. Howard Hughes Med. Inst., Dept. Molecular Physiology and Biophysics Vanderbilt U. Sch. of Medicine, Nashville, 1985—87; rsch. assoc. divsn. gastroenterology, dept. medicine Duke U. Med. Ctr., Durham, NC, 1987—90, rsch. asst. prof. divsn. gastroenterology, dept. medicine, 1990—, rsch. asst. prof. dept. cell biology, 1992—93; assoc. prof. medicine Med. U. SC, Charleston, 1993—, assoc. prof. biochemistry and molecular biology, 1995—, prof. medicine, 2000—; prof., chief exptl. obesity divsn. Pennington Biomed. Rsch. Ctr., Baton Rouge. Contbr. articles to profl. jours., chapters to books. Fellow predoctoral rsch., Clemson U., 1981—82; grantee, NIH, 1990, 1994, 1996, 1998, 2003, 2005, 2006, 2007, USDA, 1997, 2000, Am. Diabetes Assn., 2006. Mem.: Am. Diabetes Assn. (grant review panel 2006, Rsch. award 1996, 2003—05), Am. Soc. Biochemistry and Molecular Biology, Sigma Xi. Office: Pennington Biomed Rsch Ctr 6400 Perkins Rd Baton Rouge LA 70808 Office Phone: 225-763-3165. Business E-Mail: gettystw@pbrc.edu.

GETZ, BERT ATWATER, investment company executive; b. Chgo., May 7, 1937; s. George Fulmer Jr. and Olive Cox (Atwater) G.; m. Sandra Maclean, July 17, 1958; children: Lynn Getz, George F., Bert A. Jr. BSBA, U. Mich., 1959. V.p. Globe Corp., Scottsdale, Ariz., 1960-74, pres., bd.

dirs., 1974—, CEO, 1992—. Bd. dirs. Bank of Am., Ill., Dean Foods Co., Franklin Park, Ill., Ameritas Life Ins. Corp., Lincoln, bd. trustees, Mayo Found., Rochester (chmn. 2002—), dir. and pres. Globe Found., Arthur R. Merch Found. Bd. dirs. Western Golf Assn., Golf, Ill., Ind. U. Found., Bloomington, Nat. Hist. Fire Found.; chmn. bd. govs. Merit Club, Libertyville, Ill.; trustee Lawrenceville (N.J.) Sch., 1972—, pres. bd. dirs. 1984-90, trustee emeritus, 1990; trustee Ariz. Cmty. Found., Phoenix, 1978—, chmn. bd. dirs., 1981-89, chmn. emeritus, 1989. Mem. Phoenix Thunderbirds, Paradise Valley Country Club, John Gardiners Tennis Ranch, Merit Club, Sigma Chi, Theta Theta. Republican. Episcopalian. Avocations: tennis, golf. Home: 6335 W Highway 120 Libertyville IL 60048-9788 Office: Globe Corp 6730 N Scottsdale Rd Ste 250 Scottsdale AZ 85253-4416

GETZ, LOWELL VERNON, financial advisor; b. Schenectady, NY, Feb. 28, 1932; s. Leon and Harriet Esther (Friedman) G.; m. Judith Ruth Schwartz, Oct. 14, 1956; children: Marshall, Andrew. BS in Econs., U. Pa., 1953; MBA, Harvard Univ., 1955. Treas. R. Dixon Speas Assocs., Inc., Manhasset, NY, 1969-72, Coverdale & Colpitts, Inc., NYC, 1972-74; fin. mgr. Bovay Engrs., Inc., Houston, 1974-79; sec., treas. Rice Center, Houston, 1979-82. Guest lectr. U. Houston, 1980-81, Harvard Grad. Sch. of Design, 1985—; Univ. of Wisconsin, Madison, 1998; overseas instr. Tongji U., Shanghai, People's Republic of China, 1990, Shanghai Mcpl. Constrn. Commn., 1992, Assn. Consulting Engrs., London, 1995 and 1998; condr. seminars in field. Author: Financial Management and Project Control for ConsultingEngineers, 1983; Financial Management for the Design Professional, 1984, Business Management in the Smaller Design Firm, 1986, Managing Ownership Transition in Design Firms, 1987, Mergers, Acquisitions, and Sales, 1987; co-author: Ownership Transition, Options and Strategies, 1996, 2d edit., 2003; contbg. editor: Valuation Survey of Design Firms, 1991-97, Insider's Guide to Cashing in on your Equity in an A/E/P or Environment Consulting Firm, 1993, Financial Management for Design Firms, 1997, (with others) Architect's Handbook of Professional Practice, 1993, (with others) Valuing Professional Practices and Licenses, 1998-2000, Financial Guidelines to Practice, 2004; contbr. articles to profl. publs. Served as lt. USNR, 1955-58. Mem. Profl Svcs. Mgmt. Assn. (pres. 1988, treas. 1981-82, bd. dirs. 1979-88, 86-88), Tex. Soc. CPAs (chmn. mgmt. adv. svcs. com. Houston chpt. 1982-83), Am. Inst. CPAs (mem. various mgmt. adv. svcs. subcoms. 1981-87, Cert. of Ednl. Achievement in Bus, Valuation, accredited in bus. valuations), Am. Soc. Appraisers (sr.), Inst. Mgmt. Cons. (cert.). Home: PO Box 19159 Houston TX 77224-9159 Office: 820 Gessner Rd Ste 265 Houston TX 77024-4258 E-mail: lgetz@swbell.net.

GETZENDANNER, SUSAN, lawyer; b. Chgo., July 24, 1939; d. William B. and Carole S. (Muehling) O'Meara; children— Alexandra, Paul. BBA, JD, Loyola U., 1966. Bar: Ill. bar 1966. Law clk. U.S. Dist. Ct., Chgo., 1966-68; assoc. Mayer, Brown & Platt, Chgo., 1968-74, ptnr., 1974-80; judge U.S. Dist. Ct., Chgo., 1980-87; ptnr. Skadden, Arps, Slate, Meagher & Flom, Chgo., 1987—2002. Recipient medal of excellence Loyola U. Law Alumni Assn., 1981 Mem. ABA, Chgo. Council Lawyers. Office Phone: 312-944-2629. E-mail: sgetzendanner@mindspring.com.

GETZLAF, RYAN, professional hockey player; b. Regina, Sask., Can., May 10, 1985; Center Anaheim Ducks (formerly Mighty Ducks of Anaheim), 2005—. Mem. Team Canada, World Junior Championships, Grand Forks, ND, 2005; player NHL YoungStars Game, 2007. Achievements include being a member of Gold Medal Team Canada, World Junior Championships, 2005; being a member of Stanley Cup Champion Anaheim Ducks, 2007. Office: Anaheim Ducks 2695 E Katella Ave Anaheim CA 92806*

GEURTS, TOM GEERD, real estate educator, consultant; m. Beate Klingenberg. B of Civil Engring., Higher Tech. Coll., Zwolle, Netherlands, 1987; M in Econs., U. Amsterdam, Netherlands, 1991, M in Polit. Sci., 1991; PhD, Pa. State U., State College, 1996. Asst. prof. fin. and real estate Calif. State U., San Bernardino, 1996—99; dir. econ. and market rsch. Newmark and Co, NYC, 1999—2000; assoc. prof. fin. Marist Coll., Poughkeepsie, NY, 2000—06; clin. assoc. prof. real estate NYU Real Estate Inst., NYC, 2006—. Prin. TGGC, Poughkeepsie, 2001—. Author: (book) Public-Private Partnerships: The Search for Equilibrium, 1991; contbr. articles to profl. jours. Mem. Hudson Valley Fed. Credit Union, Poughkeepsie, 2003—06. Philip H. Sieg fellow, Pa. State U., 1991. Office: NYU Real Estate Inst 11 West 42nd St Rm 509-A New York NY 10036-8083 Office Phone: 212-992-3241. Office Fax: 212-992-3686. Business E-Mail: tom.geurts@nyu.edu.

GEUSIC, JOSEPH EDWARD, physicist; b. Nesquehoning, Pa., Nov. 21, 1931; s. Joseph John and Mary Martha (Kosch) Geusic; m. Irene Jean Hosak, July 18, 1953; children: Patricia, Mark, Michael, Mary Ellen, Robert, Joseph. BS in Physics, Lehigh U., 1953; MS in Physics, Ohio State U., 1955, PhD in Physics, 1958. Rsch. assoc. physics dept. Ohio State U., Columbus, 1955-58; mem. tech. staff AT&T Bell Labs., Murray Hill, NJ, 1958-62, supr. solid state laser group, 1962-66, head solid state optical device dept., 1966-70, head magnetics dept., 1970-84, head semiconductor laser dept., 1984-94; pres. Geusic Info. Svcs., Inc., 1996—2005. Contbr. more than 63 to profl. publs. Recipient R. W. Wood prize, Optical Soc. Am., 1993, Clinton J. Davisson Patent award trophy, AT&T, 1993. Fellow: IEEE (Quantum Electronics award 1992); mem.: Am. Inst. Physics, Sigma Xi. Achievements include first to demonstrate Nd/YAG laser and first continuous operating optical parametric oscillator; development of semiconductor lasers for terrestrial and undersea lightwave communication systems, magnetic bubble materials and devices; 102 US patents in field. Home: 261 Lorraine Dr Berkeley Heights NJ 07922-2341 Personal E-mail: josephgeusic@comcast.net.

GEWARTOWSKI, JAMES WALTER, retired electrical engineer; b. Chgo., Nov. 10, 1930; s. Joseph Walter and Irene Dorothy (Dziekanowski) G.; m. Marion Ruth Wakeman, June 23, 1956; children: Marion, Diane, Patricia, John, Karen. BS in Elec. Engring., Ill. Inst. Tech., 1952; S.M., MIT, 1953; PhD, Stanford U., 1958. Research asst. Stanford Electronics Lab., Calif., 1954-57; supr. microwave sources AT&T Bell Labs., Inc, Murray Hill, NJ, 1957-71, supr. high bit rate optical data link group Allentown, Pa., 1971-88, supr. SL optical relay/receiver group Breinigsville, Pa., 1988-89, ret. Co-author: Principles of Electron Tubes, 1965, Fundamentals of Electron Tubes, 1969; contbg. author: Microwave Semiconductor Devices and Their Circuit Applications, 1969; contbr. articles to profl. jours. Fellow IEEE (Browder J. Thompson Meml. prize 1960); mem. Sigma Xi, Tau Beta Pi, Eta Kappa Nu, Serra Internat. Republican. Roman Catholic. Home: 2908 Edgemont Dr Allentown PA 18103-5410

GEWEKE, JOHN FREDERICK, economics professor; b. Washington, May 11, 1948; s. Robert William and Winnifred Lois (Quies) G.; m. Lynne Marie Osborn, Aug. 22, 1970; 1 child, Andrew Robert. BS, Mich. State U., 1970; PhD, U. Minn., 1975. Asst. prof. U. Wis., Madison, 1975-79, assoc. prof., 1979-82, prof., 1982-83, Duke U., Durham, NC, 1983-86, William R. Kenan Jr. prof., 1986-90, dir. Inst. Stats. and Decision Scis., 1987-90; prof. U. Minn., Mpls., 1990—99; McGregor Chair in econs. & stats. U. Iowa, 1999—. Editor Jour. Bus. and Econs. Stats., 1989-92; co-editor Jour. Applied Econometrics, 1993-2002, Jour. Econometrics, 2003-; assoc. editor Econometrica, 1984-88, 95-2002. Rsch. fellow Sloan Found., N.Y.C., 1982. Fellow Econometric Soc., Am. Statis. Assn.; mem. Am. Econ. Assn., Internat. Soc. for Bayesian Analysis (pres. 1999). Office: U of IA Dept Econs Iowa City IA 52242

GEWERTZ, BRUCE LABE, surgeon, educator; b. Phila., Aug. 27, 1949; s. Milton and Shirley (Charen) G.; children: Samantha, Barton, Alexis; m. Diane Weiss, Aug. 31, 1997. BS, Pa. State U., State Coll., 1968; MD, Jefferson Med. Coll., Phila., 1972. Diplomate Am. Bd. Surgery. Surg. resident U. Mich., Ann Arbor, 1972-77; asst. prof. U. Tex., Dallas, 1977-81; assoc. prof. U. Chgo., 1981-87, prof. surgery, 1988—, faculty dean med. edn., 1989-92, Dallas Phemister prof., chmn. dept. surgery, 1992—2006; chmn. dept. surgery, surgeon-in-chief, v.p. Cedars-Sinai Med. Ctr., LA, 2006—. Tchg. scholar Am. Heart Assn., Dallas, 1980-83; pres. Assn. Surg. Edn., 1983-84; dir. vascular surgery bd. Am. Bd. Surgery, 2001—. Author: Atlas of Vascular Surgery, 1989, 2005, Surgery of the Aorta and its Branches, 2000; editor Jour. Surg. Rsch., 1987-2002; patentee removable vascular filter. Recipient Jobst award Coller Surg. Soc., 1975, Coller award Mich. chpt. Am. Coll. Surgeons, 1975, Outstanding Sci. Alumnus award Pa. State U., 2003. Mem. Soc. Vascular Surgery, Midwestern Vascular Soc. (pres. 1993, 94-95), Soc. Clin. Surgery, Soc. Univ. Surgeons, Chgo. Surg. Soc. (treas. 1989-92, pres. 2005), Am. Surg. Assn. Office: Cedars-Sinai Med Ctr 8700 Beverly Blvd Los Angeles CA 90048 Office Phone: 310-423-5884. Business E-Mail: bruce.gewertz@cshs.org.

GEWIRTZ, ELLIOT, lawyer; b. NYC, Apr. 8, 1947; m. Barbara Gewirtz; children: Lisa D., Eric S. BA summa cum laude, Colgate U., 1969; JD cum laude, Harvard U., 1972; M in Pub. Adminstrn., Princeton U., 1973. Bar: N.Y. 1973. Assoc. Milbank, Tweed, Hadley & McCloy, NYC, 1973—78, assoc. to ptnr.-in-charge Tokyo, 1978—84, ptnr. global transp. fin. dept. NYC, 1984—. Mem.: ABA, N.Y. State Bar Assn., Assn. of the Bar of the City of N.Y. Home: 52 Greenacres Ave Scarsdale NY 10583-1436 Office: Milbank Tweed Hadley & McCloy 1 Chase Manhattan Plz Fl 47 New York NY 10005-1413 Office Phone: 212-530-5474. Office Fax: 212-530-5219. Business E-Mail: egewirtz@milbank.com.

GEWIRTZ, PAUL D., lawyer, educator; b. May 12, 1947; s. Herman and Matilda (Miller) Gewirtz; m. Zoë Baird, June 8, 1986; children: Julian, Alec. AB summa cum laude, Columbia U., 1967; JD, Yale U., 1970. Bar: D.C. 1973, U.S. Supreme Ct. 1976. Law clk. to Hon. Marvin E. Frankel US Dist. Ct (so. dist.) NY, 1970—71; law clk. to Justice Thurgood Marshal US Supreme Ct., Washington, 1971—72; assoc. Wilmer, Cutler & Pickering, Washington, 1972—73; atty. Ctr. Law and Social Policy, Washington, 1973—76; assoc. prof. then prof. Yale Law Sch., New Haven, 1976—, Potter Stewart prof. Law, 1992—, dir. The China Law Ctr., 1999—. Dir. Global Constitutionalism Project, 1996—; Spl. Rep. the Presdl. Rule of Law Initiative US Dept. of State, 1997—98; guest prof. Peking (China) U. Law Sch., 2003—; US rep. European Commn. on Democracy through Law, 1996—2000. Author: Law's Stories, 1996, The Case Law Sys. in Am., 1989; contbr. numerous articles to profl. jours. Mem.: Am. Law Inst., Coun. on Fgn. Rels. Office: Yale U Law Sch PO Box 208215 New Haven CT 06520-8215 Business E-Mail: paul.gewirtz@yale.edu.

GEWIRTZ-FRIEDMAN, GERRY, editor; b. NYC, Dec. 22, 1920; d. Max and Minnie (Weiss) G.; m. Eugene W. Friedman, Nov. 11, 1945; children: John Henry, Robert James. BA, Vassar Coll., 1941. Editor Package Store Mgmt., 1942-44, Jewelry Mag., 1945-53; freelance editor promotion dept. McCall's Mag., Esquire, 1953-56; free-lance fashion and gifts editor Jewelers Circular Keystone, NYC, 1955-71; editor, pub. The Fashionables, 1971-74, The Forecast, 1974—, Nat. Jeweler, Ann. Fashion Guide, 1976-80; editor, assoc. pub. Exec. Jeweler, 1980-83; editor The Fashion Source (formerly Internat. Fashion Index), NYC, 1984—; freelance editor and mktg. specialist, 1995—. Ptnr. Gary Gewirtz-Editl. and Mktg.; free-lance editl. wrtier, 1995—. Corr. Internat. Mktg. News. Mem. exec. com. Inner City Council of Cardinal Cooke, N.Y.; chairperson women's task force United Jewish Appeal Fedn.; former bd. govs. Israel Bonds; former trustee Israel Cancer Research Fund, Central Synagogue; bd. dirs. Double Image Theater; former pres. women's aux. Brandeis U. Honored guest Am. Jewish Com., 1978; Israel Cancer Research Fund, 1978-81; recipient Disting. Community Service award Brandeis U., 1987; named to Jewelry Hall Fame, 1988. Mem. N.Y. Fashion Group, Nat. Home Fashions League (former pres.), Women's Jewelry Assn. (pres. 1983-87, named editor who has contbd. most to jewelry industry 1984, free lance editor). Home: 45 Sutton Pl S New York NY 10022-2444

GEWIRTZMAN, GARRY BRUCE, dermatologist; b. Albany, N.Y., Mar. 26, 1947; s. Benjamin Joseph and Mary (Leibowitz) G.; m. Sheila Ellen Cuba, July 4, 1971; children: Beth Lauren, Aron Jeffrey. BA, Rutgers U., 1969; MD, Albany Med. Coll., 1973. Diplomate Am. Bd. Dermatology. Intern U. Miami (Fla.), 1973-74; resident in dermatology SUNY-Buffalo, 1974-77; practice medicine specializing in dermatology; attending staff Humana Hosp., Plantation (Fla.) Gen. Hosp.; pres. Arbet Enterprises Inc. Author: Smooth as a Baby's Bottom, Skin Care Tips and Skin Sense; contbr. articles to profl. jours. Fellow Am. Acad. Dermatology; mem. AMA, Fla. Med. Assn., Broward County Med. Assn., Fla. Soc. Dermatology, Soc. Dermatol. Genetics, Broward Bus. and Profl. Assn. (pres.), Broward County Dermatol. Soc. Office: Bennett Med Park 201 NW 82nd Ave Plantation FL 33324-7808

GEWITZ, MICHAEL HAROLD, pediatric cardiologist; b. Jan. 20, 1949; m. Judith Lipshutz, May 12, 1973; children: Emily, Andrew. BA, Yale U., 1970; MD, Hahnemann U., 1974. Intern Children's Hosp. Phila., Phila., 1974—75, resident, 1975—76, Hosp. Sick Children, London, 1976—77; fellow Yale New Haven Hosp., 1977—79; dir. noninvasive cardiology Children's Hosp. Phila., 1979—83; asst. prof. pediat. Sch. Medicine U. Pa., Phila., 1979—83; chief pediat. cardiology N.Y. Med. Coll. and Westchester Med. Ctr., 1983—; dir. pediat., chief pediat. cardiology Children's Hosp. Westchester, Valhalla, NY, 1991—; prof., vice chair dept. pediat. N.Y. Med. Coll., Valhalla, NY, 1992—; pres. med. staff Westch Med. Ctr., 1998—2002; chief pediat. cardiology Maria Fareri Children's Hosp., 1983—, physician in chief, 2004—, exec. dir., 2004—. Editor: (book) Primary Pediatric Cardiology, 1995; assoc. editor: (journal) Heart Diseases, 1999-2004; section editor (jour.) Cardiovasc Reviews, 2004—. Fellow Am. Acad. Pediat., Am. Coll. Cardiology, N.Y. Acad. Medicine, Am. Heart Assn. (exec. com. cardiovasc. disease in young 1999—, com. Rheumatic fever, endocarditis and Kawasaki disease 1995—, vice chmn. 2001-04, chmn. 2004—), Am. Coll. Physician Execs.; mem. Pediat. Acad. Soc. Office Phone: 914-493-6160.

GEWURZ, ANITA TARTELL, physician, medical educator; b. Buffalo, July 30, 1946; MD, Albany Med. Coll., 1970. Resident in pediat. U. Ill., Chgo., 1971—73; resident in allergy and immunology Rush-Presbyn.-St. Luke's Hosp., Chgo., 1974—76; fellow allergy and immunology Max Samter Inst., Grant Hosp., Chgo., 1976—77, Northwestern U. Med. Coll., Chgo., 1983—85; assoc. prof. immunology/microbiology, pediat. and internal med. Rush U. Med. Coll., Chgo., 1993—2003, prof. immunology/microbiology, pediat. and internal med., 2003—; physician Rush U. Med. Ctr., Chgo., 1974—. Chair, Tng. Program Dirs. Com. Am. Acad. Allergy, Asthma & Immunology, 2000—02; chair Am. Bd. Allergy and Immunology, 2004—05; initial cert. task force Am. Bd. Med. Specialties, 2004—, sub-com. chair, 2004—05; vol. physician pediats. St. Roger Hosp., Cook County, Ill., 1997—. Office: Rush Univ Med Ctr 1725 W Harrison St Ste 117 Chicago IL 60612 Office Phone: 312-942-6296. Business E-Mail: agewurz@rush.edu.

GEYER, GEORGIE ANNE, columnist, educator, commentator, writer; b. Chgo., Apr. 2, 1935; d. Robert George and Georgie Hazel (Gervens) G. BS, Northwestern U., 1956, LHD (hon.), 1993; postgrad., U. Vienna, Austria, 1956-57; LittD (hon.), Lake Forest Coll., 1980, Coll. Mt. St. Joseph, 1986, Notre Dame, 1986, Wilson Coll., 1987, Linfield Coll., 1987, St. Mary-of-the-Woods Coll., 1989, U. Indpls., 1991, Colby-Sawyer Coll., 1992, Franklin Coll., 1992, Cabrini Coll., 1994; LHD (hon.), Northwestern U., 1984, U. S.C., 1991, Rockhurst Coll., Kansas City, 1992, Spring Hill Coll., 1993, Lebanon Valley Coll., 1994, Hofstra U., 1995, Loyola U., Chgo., 1996, Westminster Coll., 1996, Govs. State U., 1997, Notre Dame Coll., 1999, Knox Coll., 1999. Reporter Southtown Economist, Chgo., 1958; soc. reporter Chgo. Daily News, 1959-60, gen. assignment reporter, 1960-64, corr. Lat. Am., Ctrl. Am., Soviet Union, Middle East, Europe, 1964-75, roving fgn. corr. and columnist, 1967-75; syndicated columnist Los Angeles Times Syndicate, 1975-80, Universal Press Syndicate, 1981—; Lyle M. Spencer prof. journalism Syracuse U., 1977. News commentator PBS' Washington Week in Review; questioner on Presdl. debate, Oct., 1984; steering com. Aspen Inst. Latin Am. Governance Project, 1981-82; commentator on the BBC; panelist Voice of America; sent by Internat. Communication Agy. on 3 worldwide speaking tours on Am. journalism: Nigeria, Zambia, Tanzania and Somalia, 1979, Philippines and Indonesia, 1981, Iceland, Norway, Belgium and Portugal, 1982; rep. Fulbright scholar program 40th anniversary, New Zealand, 1987; commencement speaker U. SC, Rockhurst Coll., St. Mary's Notre Dame; sr. fellow Annenburg Washington, 1992-93; columnist Chgo. Tribune, Wash. Times, Universal de Caracas, Dallas Morning News, Diario las Americas, Denver Post, others; speaker, lectr. in field. Author: The New Latins, 1970, The New 100 Years War, 1972, The Young Russians, 1976; (autobiography) Buying the Night Flight, (Weintal prize citation Sch. Fgn. Svc. Georgetown U. 1984, Chgo. Found. for Lit. award 1984), 1983, reissued, 1996, Guerilla Prince, The Untold Story of Fidel Castro, 1991, Waiting for Winter to End, An Extraordinary Journey Through Soviet Central Asia, 1994, Americans No More: The Death of Citizenship, 1996, Tunisia: A Journey Through the Country that Works, 2003, When Cats Reigned Like Kings: On the Trail of the Sacred Cats, 2004; subjects of interviews include Prince Sihanouk of Cambodia, Yassar Arafat, Anwar Sadat, King Hussein of Jordan, Pres. Khaddafy of Libya, the Ayatollah Khomeini, Sultan Qaboos of Oman, Pres. Juan Peron of Argentina, Pres. Siad Barre of Somalia, Prime Minister Mauno Koivisto of Finland, Anastasio Somoza, Jerzy Urban, Janusz Onyszkiewicz, Prime Minister Edward Seaga of Jamaica, Pres. Ronald Reagan, Pres. George W. Bush and Defense Secretary Donald Rumsfeld, others; discovered and had first interview with second most-wanted Nazi, Walter Rauff in Tierra del Fuego, Chile, 1966; found Dominican pres. Juan Bosch in hiding in P.R. during Dominican revolution, 1965; held by Palestinians as Israeli spy, 1973; imprisoned in Angola for writing about revolutionary government, 1976; contbr. chpts. to books, articles numerous pubs. Active Orgn. for S.W. Community Chgo., 1960-64; trustee Am. U., Washington, 1981-86; Coun. Fgn. Rels. Recipient 1st prize Am. Newspaper Guild, 1962; 2d prize Ill. Press Editors Assn., 1962; award for best writing on Latin Am. Overseas Press Club, 1967; Merit award Northwestern U., 1968; Nat. Headliner award Theta Sigma Phi, 1968; Maria Moors Cabot award Columbia U., 1971; Hannah Solomon award Nat. Council Jewish Women, 1973; Ill. Spl. Events Commn. Woman's award, 1975; Northwestern U. Alumni award, 1991; Fulbright scholar U. Vienna, 1956-57; Woodrow Wilson fellow Rollins Coll., Winter Park, Fla., 1982; Presdl. Citation award Am. Univ., 1985; Disting. fellow Mortar Bd. Nat. Sr. Honor Soc., Am. U., 1982, Sr. fellow Annenberg Washington Program, Washington, 1992-93; fellow Soc. Profl. Journalists, 1992; named Outstanding Illinoisian, Ill. State Assn., 2001; named to Hall of Fame of Soc. of Profl. Journalists, 2001, Stewart Alsop award Assn. Retired Intelligence Officers, 2001, Headliners Club Lifetime Achievement award, 2003, Woman Extraordinaire award Internat. Women Assn., 2004. Mem.: Coun. Fgn. Rels., Inst. Internat. Edn. (bd. dirs.), Soc. Profl. Journalists, Tavern Club (Chgo.), Cosmos Club (1st women mem.), Gridiron Club. Home and Office: The Plaza 800 25th St NW Washington DC 20037-2207 Personal E-mail: gigi_geyer@juno.com. *I have never compromised seriously on any ethical or moral principle, and I truly believe that the women of my generation can bring a new and cleansing element to American public life. Whatever I have accomplished I could not have done without profoundly analyzing myself: but I also find that in professional life the old injunction to "Know Thyself" reaches women more than men. It has been a constant struggle, often with little personal approval or backing, which I feel also adds to a woman's inner strength.*

GEYER, JAMES A, insurance company executive; BA in Math., U. Conn. V.p. and chief actuary Aetna Inc., 2000—; various positions with Aetna's Individual Life Divsn., Corp. Acutarial, Employee Benefits Divsn., 1980; head of planning and fin. reporting Employee Benefits Divsn. Fellow: Soc. of Actuaries; mem.: Am. Acad. of Acutaries. Office: Aetna Inc 151 Farmington Ave Hartford CT 06156 Home Phone: 860-647-1006; Office Phone: 860-273-6304. Business E-Mail: geyerja@aetna.com.

GEYER, MICHAEL, history professor; PhD, Albert Ludwigs U., Freiburg, Germany. Samuel N. Harper prof. history U. Chgo., 1986—. Trustee Am. Acad. in Berlin, 2007—. Guggenheim fellow, 2003. Office: U Chgo Dept History 1126 E 59th St Chicago IL 60637 Home Phone: 773-955-7204; Office Phone: 773-702-7934. E-mail: mgeyer@uchicago.edu.

GEYER, RICHARD DOUGLAS, librarian, editor, poet; b. Detroit, June 23, 1964; s. John Richard Geyer and Mary Jennie Winiarczyk. BA, U. Minn., 1989; MLS, U. Mich., 1990. Libr. Adrian Coll., Adrian, Mich., 1991—, head libr., 1996—2001. Pub. Yellow Bat Press, Adrian, 2003—06; editor Contemporary Rhyme, 2004—; dir. website Phantom-Wooer: Thomas Lovell, Adrian, 2004—; editor Contemporary Rhyme, 2004—. Author: The Phantasm of Despair, Sleepy Hollow, 1776, Old Tom's Skull, 2005, Gothic Extravaganza, 2006; contbr. poetry to jours. and mags. Mem.: ALA, Am. Soc. Info. Sci. and Tech., Thomas Lovell Beddoes Soc., Beta Phi Mu. Office: Adrian College 110 S Madison Adrian MI 49221 Office Phone: 517-265-5161. Business E-Mail: rgeyer@adrian.edu.

GEYER, THOMAS POWICK, newspaper publisher; b. Phila., Dec. 13, 1946; s. John Alvin and Jean (Powick) G. BA, St. John's Coll., 1969. Reporter The Mercury, Pottstown, Pa., 1969-73; editor Internat. Data Corp., Waltham, Mass., 1974, The Eagle-Times, Claremont, N.H., 1975; editor, pub. The Daily Freeman, Kingston, N.Y., 1976-81; pres. Ingersoll Pubs. Co., Princeton, N.J., 1982-86; pub. New Haven Register, 1986-91, The Daily Record, Parsippany, N.J., 1991-98. Bd. govs. St. John's Coll., Annapolis, Md., 1991—; chmn. First Night, Morristown, N.J., 1993. Fellow Berkeley Coll. Yale, 1988—. Address: Apt 15J 54 W 16th St New York NY 10011-6342

GEYMAN, JOHN PAYNE, physician, educator; b. Santa Barbara, Calif., Feb. 9, 1931; s. Milton John and Betsy (Payne) Geyman; m. Eugenia Clark Deichler, June 9, 1956; children: John Matthew, James Caleb, William Sabin. AB in Geology, Princeton U., 1952; MD, U. Calif., San Francisco, 1960. Diplomate Am. Bd. Family Practice. Intern L.A. County Gen. Hosp., 1960—61; resident in gen. practice Sonoma County Hosp., Santa Rosa, Calif., 1961—63; pvt. practice specializing in family practice Mt. Shasta, Calif., 1963—69; dir. family practice residency program Cmty. Hosp. Sonoma County, Santa Rosa, 1969—71; assoc. prof. family practice, chmn. divsn. family practice U. Utah, 1971—72; prof., vice chmn. dept. family practice U. Calif., Davis, 1972—77; prof., chmn. dept. family medicine U. Wash., 1977—90, prof. family medicine, 1990—93, prof. family medicine emeritus, 1993—. Author: The Modern Family Doctor and Changing Medical Practice, 1971, Family Practice: Foundation of Changing Health Care, 1980, 2d edit., 1985, Flight as a Lifetime Passion: Adventures, Misadventures and Lessons, 2000, Falling Through the Safety Net: Americans Without Health Insurance, 2005; editor: Content of Family Practice, 1976, Family Practice in the Medical School, 1977, Research in Family Practice, 1978, Preventive Medicine in Family Practice, 1979, Profile of the Residency Trained Family Physician in the U.S, 1970—79,

Funding of Patient Care, Education and Research in Family Practice, 1981, The Content of Family Practice: Current Status and Future Trends, 1982, Archives of Family Practice, 1980—82, Family Practice: An International Perspective in Developed Countries, 1983, Jour. Am. Bd. Family Practice, 1990—2003; founding editor Jour. Family Practice, 1973—90; co-editor: Behavioral Science in Family Practice, 1980, Evidence-Based Clinical Practice: Concepts and Approaches, 2000, Textbook of Rural Medicine, 2000, Health Care in America: Can Our Ailing System Be Healed?, 2002, The Corporate Transformation of Health Care: Can the Public Interest Still be Served?, 2004, Shredding of the Social Contract: The Privatization of Medicare, 2006, An Open Cockpit Biplane Dream: Honey Bee III, 2005. Pres. Physicians for Nat. Health Program, 2005—06. Served to lt. (j.g.) USN, 1952—55, PTO. Recipient Gold-Headed Cane award, U. Calif. Sch. Medicine, 1960, Alumnus of Yr. award, 1998. Mem.: Inst. Medicine NAS, Soc. Tchrs. Family Medicine, Am. Acad. Family Physicians. Unitarian Universalist. Home: 53 Avian Ridge Ln Friday Harbor WA 98250-8895 Business E-Mail: jgeyman@u.washington.edu.

GHADERI, BAHRAM, plastic surgeon; b. Tehran, Iran, Dec. 11, 1968; BA in Econs. cum laude, U. Calif., LA; MD, U. Mich., Ann Arbor, 1995. Diplomate Am. Bd. Plastic Surgery. Internship gen. surgery Loyola U. Med. Ctr., Maywood, Ill., 1995—96, resident plastic surgery, 1996—98, fellow, 1998—2001; surgeon St. Charles Plastic Surgery, Ill. Staff Delnor Cmty. Hosp., Provena Mercy Ctr., Suburban Surgery Ctr. DuPage, Dreyer Ambulatory Surgery Ctr., Valley Ambulatory Surgery Ctr.; chief plastic surgery sect. Ctrl. DuPage Hosp., 2007—. Contbr. articles to profl. jours. Fellow: ACS; mem.: Chgo. Soc. Plastic Surgeons, Am. Soc. Aesthetic Plastic Surgeons, Am. Soc. Plastic Surgeons, Phi Eta Sigma. Office: 2900 Foxfield Rd Ste 201 Saint Charles IL 60174 Office Phone: 630-762-9697. Office Fax: 630-762-9721.*

GHADERSOHI, ALI, veterinarian, researcher; arrived in U.S., 2000; DVM, Tehran U., 1986; PhD in Molecular Biology, Microbiology and Immunology, James Cook U., 1997. Dir. Vet. Orgn. and Microbiology Lab. Esfahan and Hamedan Provinces, Iran, 1985—92; ast. prof. Dept. Microbiology and Biotechnology Razi Vaccine and Serum Rsch. Inst., Iran, 1998—99; cons. microbiology James Cook U., North Queensland, Australia, 1999; rsch. affiliate Roswell Pk. Cancer Inst., Buffalo, 2000—07, rsch. scientist dept. pharmacology and therapeutics, 2007—. Contbr. articles to profl. jours. Mem.: AAAS, Am. Assn. Cancer Rsch. Achievements include patents in field. Home: 84A Grandview Dr Amherst NY 14228 Office: Roswell Park Cancer Inst Elm and Carlton St Buffalo NY 14263 Office Phone: 716-845-1565. Business E-Mail: ali.ghadersohi@roswellpark.org.

GHAFOURIFAR, PEDRAM, pharmacologist, director; b. Tehran, Iran, Dec. 23, 1965; s. Ahmad and Sorour (Ghashghai) G.; m. Zahra Ramezani, Feb. 17, 1987; children: Parnian, Parham. PharmD, U. Tehran, 1990, PhD, 1995. Postdoctoral fellow Swiss Fed. Inst. Tech., Zurich, 1996—2000; rsch. asst. prof. U. Mass. Med. Sch., Worcester, 2000—01; asst. prof. pharmacology La. State U., Shreveport, 2001—04; assoc. prof. pharmacology Marshall U., Huntington, W.Va., 2004—06; dir. basic sci. rsch. Dept. Surgery Ohio State U. Sch. Medicine, Columbus, 2006—. Hon. rsch. fellow Wolfson Inst. for Biomed. Rsch., U. Coll. London, 1999-2000; prin. rsch. fellow Univ. Coll. London, 1999-2000; invited vis. scientist Dana-Farber Cancer Inst., Harvard Med. Sch., Boston, 1999-2000. Author: Methods in Enzymology, 1998, 2002, 2005, Endocytobiology, 1999, Mitocondrial Ubiquinone, 2000, Nitric Oxide, Cell Signaling and Gene Expression, 2004; editor: Antioxidants and Redox Signaling, 2003; contbr. articles to profl. jours. Recipient The New Century award of the Europe 500, 2000. Mem.: AAAS, Mitochondrial Soc. (pres., chmn. bd. dirs. 2006—), Fedn. Am. Soc. for Exptl. Biology, Am. Soc. Pharmacology and Exptl. Therapy, Nat. Orgn. Outstanding Talents, The Cell Death Soc., Nitric Oxide Soc., Oxygen Soc., Iranian Pharm. Soc., Swiss Tissue Culture Soc., Soc. Physiology and Pharmacology, NY Acad. Scis. Office: Divsn Vascular Surgery Means Hall-N325 1654 Upham Dr Columbus OH 43210 also: 460 W 12th Ave Columbus OH 43210

GHALI, ANWAR YOUSSEF, psychiatrist, educator; b. Cairo, May 30, 1944; arrived in U.S.A., 1974, naturalized, 1980; s. Youssef and Insaf Wahba (Soliman) G.; m. Violette Fouad Saleh, May 23, 1968; 1 child, Susie MD, Cairo U., 1966, DPM, 1970, DM, 1971; MPA, NYU, 1999. Diplomate Am. Bd. Psychiatry and Neurology; cert. adminstrv. psychiatry. Registrar in psychiatry Woodilee Hosp., Glasgow, Scotland, 1973-74; resident in psychiatry N.J. Med. Sch., Newark, 1974-77, instr., 1977-78, clin. asst. prof., 1978-79, asst. prof., 1979-83, clin. assoc. prof., 1983—; chief Outpatient Dept.-Community Mental Health Ctr., N.J. Med. Sch., Newark, 1978-86; dir. Emergency Psychiat. Svcs. Univ. Hosp., U. Medicine and Dentistry of N.J., Newark, 1986-87; med. dir. Profl. Counsel Ctr., Westfield, NJ, 1984-87; med. chief ambulatory psychiat. svcs. Elizabeth (N.J.) Gen. Hosp., 1987-89; dir. psychiat. tng. VA Med. Ctr., East Orange, NJ, 1989—2001, asst. chief psychiatry, 1990—91, assoc. chief psychiatry, 1991—2001; chmn. psychiatry Trinitas Hosp., Elizabeth, NJ, 2001—. Contbr. articles to profl. jours. Recipient Exceptional Merit award Coll. Medicine & Dentistry, Newark, 1981 Mem. AMA, Christian Med. Soc., Am. Psychiat. Assn., N.J. Psychiat. Assn., N.Y. Acad. Scis. Republican. Presbyterian. Home: 22 Benvenue Ave West Orange NJ 07052-3202

GHANI, CYRUS, lawyer; b. Sabzevar, Khorasan, Iran, Nov. 8, 1929; came to U.S., 1980; s. Qasem and Maryam (Ghaffouri) G.; m. Caroline Bennett, May 19, 1956; children: Ali Ghani, Vida Ghani Touran. BA, Wagner Coll., Staten Island, NY, 1954; JD, NYU, 1958. Head contract dept. Plan Orgn., Tehran, Iran, 1958-59; dep. mgr. legal dept. Indsl. Mining Devel. Bank Iran, 1959-63, mgr. legal dept., 1963-70; sr. ptnr. Ghani & Tavakoli, Tehran, Iran, 1964-79; legal cons. NY and London, 1979-89. Mem. commn. drafting co. law, Iran, 1965-68; cons. and expert witness on Iranian law. Author: Iran and the West, 1987, Iran and The Rise of Reza Shah, 1998, My Favorite Films, 2004, A Man of Many Worlds, 2005; editor: 13 Vol. Memoirs of Ghassem Ghani, 1981-84. Mem.: Century Assn. NY. Home: 360 E 72nd St New York NY 10021-4753

GHARABAWI GARIBALDI, GEORGE MILAD, psychiatrist, neuroscientist; arrived in US, 1996; s. Milad Hanna Gharabawi and Ragaa Mitri Armand; m. Sonia Sami Boulos, Oct. 8, 1985; 1 child, Jesse Milad Gharabawi. MB, Cairo U., 1983; degree in Psychopharmacology, U. Pitie Salpetriere, Paris, 1991; D in Psychiatry, U. Rene Descartes, Paris, 1992. Cert. France, 1993. Primary care physician internship, residency Behman Hosp., Cairo, 1983—88; cons. child psychiatry Bobigny Med. Sch., France, 1989—93; med. expert Sandoz Pharmaceuticals, Basel, Switzerland, 1992—97; exec. dir. Novartis Pharmaceuticals, East Hanover, NJ, 1997—2001; lead therapeutic area Janssen Pharmaceuticals, Titusville, NJ, 2001—06; v.p. global clin. neurosciences Hoffman-La Roche, Nutley, NJ, 2006—. Contbr. chapters to books, articles to profl. jours. Master: Internat. Soc. Ctrl. Nervous Sys. Clin. Trial Methodology (pres. 2007—); mem.: Collegium Internationale Neuropsychopharmacologicum, Am. Acad. Child and Adolescent Psychiatry. Achievements include development of a treatment for the management of symptoms of Alzheimer's disease. Home Phone: 1 917 361 7947; Office Phone: 1 973 235 5516.

GHARIB, SUSIE, newscaster; b. NYC, Nov. 27, 1950; d. Ali and Homa (Razzaghmanesh) Gharib; m. Fereydoun Nazem, Jan. 20, 1973; children: Alexander Nazem, Taraneh Nazem. BA magna cum laude, Case Western Res. U., 1972; M in Internat. Affairs, Columbia U., 1974. Reporter Cleve. Plain Dealer, 1972-73; assoc. editor Fortune Mag., NYC, 1974-83; anchor, reporter Bus. Times/ESPN, NYC, 1983-85; bus. reporter ABC News, NYC, 1986-87; anchor Fin. News Network, NYC, 1989-90, CNBC Network, Ft. Lee, NJ, 1993-98, Nightly Bus. Report, NYC, 1998—. Moderator/host Xerox Corp., Stanford, Conn., 1989—95, KPMG Peat Marwick, NYC, 1992—95; cons. Adam Smith's Money World/PBS, NYC, 1987. Bd. dirs. First Fortis, Inc., 1991—2000, Ice Theatre N.Y., 1988—90; dir. SIPA adv. bd. Columbia U., 2006—; trustee Case Western Res. U., 2005—. Mem.: Econ. Club N.Y. (trustee 2003—), N.Y. Fin. Writers Assn., Fgn. Policy Assn., Phi Beta Kappa. Democrat. Avocations: ice skating, tennis, piano. Home: 44 E 73rd St New York NY 10021-4173 Office Phone: 212-560-8757.

GHASEMI, SEIFI, chemicals executive; MSME, Stanford Univ. Pres. BOC Gases Am. BOC Group Inc., chmn., CEO BOC Process Plants & Cryostar; chmn., CEO GKN Sinter Metals, GKN plc, 1997—2001, Hoeganes Corp., 1997—2001, Rockwood Holdings Inc., Princeton, NJ, 2001—, Rockwood Specialties Group Inc., 2001—. Office: Rockwood Holdings Inc 100 Overlook Ctr Princeton NJ 08540*

GHASEMI NEJHAD, MEHRDAD N., mechanical engineering educator; PhD, U. Del., 1992. Prof., mechanical engring. U. Hawaii at Manoa, dir., Composites, Smart Structures & Nanotechnology Labs. Founding dir. Advanced Materials Mfg. Lab., Intelligent and Composite Materials Lab., Hawaii Nanotechnology Lab.; spkr. in field. Contbr. articles to profl. jours.; assoc. editor Jour. Thermoplastic Composite Materials, reviewer for jours. in field. Named Advisor, Human Powered Vehicle (HPV) Nat. Champion, 1995, 1997; Block Fellowship, U. Del., 1990, DuPont Fellowship, E.I. DuPont de Nemours & Co., 1991, A.D. Welliver Faculty Fellow, Boeing Co., 1999, Scholars award, U. Del., Ctr. for Composite Materials, 1991. Mem.: ASME (co-chair, ASME/IMECE ASMS Symposium 2005, chair ASMS symposium and multifunctional nanocomposite internat. conf. 2006, faculty advisor, mem. technical com. Aerospace/Adaptive Structures & Material Systems, Region IX Outstanding Faculty Advisor 2001), Am. Soc. Composites, Soc. for the Advancement of Material and Process Engring. (faculty advisor). Received a Guinness Book of World Records Certificate in 2006 (with others) for creating the smallest nanotube brushes with bristles more than a thousand times finer than a human hair. Office: Dept Mechanical Engring U Hawaii at Manoa 2540 Dole St Holmes Hall 302 POST 207F Honolulu HI 96822 Office Phone: 808-956-7560. Office Fax: 808-956-2373. Business E-Mail: nejhad@hawaii.edu, nejhad@wiliki.eng.hawaii.edu.

GHASSOMIAN, KEVIN R., lawyer; b. Ashland, Ky., June 18, 1973; BA in Polit. Sci., U. Ky., 1995; JD, Vanderbilt U. Sch. of Law, 1998; LLM in Taxation, U. Miami Sch. of Law, 2001. Bar: Nev. 1999, Ky. 1999, Ohio 2002. Mem., Young Professionals Prog. World Affairs Coun., Cin., 2002—; supervising atty. Wills for Heroes Prog., 2004—; bd. trustees Corp. for Findlay Market, Cin., 2006—, devel. com. mem., 2006—; mem., C-Change Leadership Devel. Prog. Cin. USA Regional Chamber, 2006, mem., C-Change Steering Com., bd. dir., 2006—07. Mem. Cin. Downtown Resident's Coun., 2002—; trustee Children's Home Northern Ky., 2002—, mem., Exec. Com., 2003—, mem., Endowment Com., 2005—; mem., Prog. Com. LEGACY, Covington, Ky., 2002—03, mentor, 2003—; mem., Adv. Com. for Young Professionals Programming Cin. Art Mus., 2005—, shareholder, 2005—; trustee Invest in Neighborhoods, Inc., Cin., 2004—; mem. U. Club Cin., 2001—, mem., Membership Com., 2001—, mem., Bd. Governors, 2002—, chair, Membership Com., 2003—, chair, Law Com., 2004—; trustee Carnegie Visual & Performing Arts Ctr., Covington, Ky., 2004—, mem., Devel. Com., 2004—, chair, Devel. Com., 2005—06, v.p., 2006—; trustee Friends of U. Cin. Coll.-Conservatory of Music, 2005—, mem., Exec. Com., 2006—. Named Inspire Vol. of Yr., Inspire Cin. Mag., 2005; named one of 40 Under 40, Cin. Bus. Courier, 2004, Ohio's Rising Stars, Super Lawyers, 2005, 2006. Mem.: Bacchanalian Soc. (founding mem. 2002—), Cin. Paralegal Assn. (adv. counsel 2006—, Outstanding Svc. award 2005), Estate Planning Coun. Northern Ky., Ohio Bar Assn., Northern Ky. Bar Assn., Cin. Bar Assn. (Estate Planning and Probate Com. 2003—), Ky. Bar Assn., Nev. Bar Assn., ABA (Real Property, Probate and Trust Law Sect. 2001—), Phi Beta Kappa Soc. Office: Greenebaum Doll & McDonald PLLC 2800 Chemed Ctr 255 E 5th St Cincinnati OH 45202-4728 Office Phone: 513-455-7603. Office Fax: 513-762-7903.

GHAUSI, MOHAMMED SHUAIB, retired dean, electrical engineer, educator; b. Kabul, Afghanistan, Feb. 16, 1930; came to U.S., 1951, naturalized, 1963; s. Mohammed Omar; m. Marilyn Buchwold, June 12, 1961; children: Nadjya, Simine. BS summa cum laude, U. Calif., Berkeley, 1956, MS, 1957, PhD, 1960. Prof. elec. engring. NYU, 1960-72; head elec. scis. sect. NSF, Washington, 1972-74; prof., chmn. elec. engring. dept. Wayne State U., Detroit, 1974-77; John F. Dodge prof. Oakland U., Rochester, Mich., 1978-83, dean Sch. Engring. and Computer Sci., 1978-83; dean Coll. Engring., U. Calif., Davis, 1983-96, interim vice chancellor rsch., vice provost, dean grad., 1996-97; ret., 1997. Mem. adv. panel NSF, 1989. Author, co-author: Principles and Design of Linear Active Circuits, 1965, Introduction to Distributed-Parameter Networks, 1968, Electronic Circuits, 1971, Modern Filter Design: Active RC and Switched Capacitor, 1981, Electronic Devices and Circuits: Discrete and Integrated, 1985, Design of Analog Filters, 1990, Introduction to Electronic Circuit Design, 2003, also numerous articles.; cons. editor Van Nostrand Rinehold Pub. Co., 1968-71. Mem. disting. alumni rev. panel Elec. Engring. and Computer Sci. programs U. Calif., Berkeley, 1973; mem. external bd. visitors U. Pa., 1974. Recipient Outstanding Alumnus award in Elec. Engring. and Computer Sci., U. Calif., 1998. Fellow IEEE (chmn. edn. medal com. 1990-92, Centennial medal, Alexander von Humboldt prize 1983, circuits and systems soc. edn. award); mem. Circuits and System Soc. (v.p. 1970-72, pres. 1976), N.Y. Acad. Scis., Engring. Soc. Detroit, Sigma Xi, Phi Beta Kappa, Tau Beta Pi, Eta Kappa Nu. Business E-Mail: msghausi@comcast.net.

GHAVAMIAN, TAGHI, orthopedist, surgeon; arrived in US, 1956; s. Mohamad and Fatemah Ghavamian. MD, U. Tehran, 1953. Prof. orthopaedics, Tehran, Iran, 1956. Fellow: Am. Coll. Surgeons.

GHEBRHIWET, FREWEINY WENDY, real estate broker, consultant; d. Shashu Mana; children: Daniel Yafet Girmay, Abel Rafel Girmay. BBA, Coll. Alameda, Calif., 1990. Lic. real estate sales Calif., 1994. Sales/real estate broker Re/Max East Bay Hills, Oakland, Calif., 2000—02; assoc. sales Re/Max In Motion, Castro Valley, Calif., 2002—. Sales assoc. Better Homes, Oakland, Calif., 1998—2000; loan broker Am. Fin., Santa Rosa, Calif., 2006—. Mem. exec. bd. Morris Cerullo World Evangelism, San Diego, 1995—2004. Mem.: Nat. Assn. Realtors (licentiate). Office Phone: 510-536-0595.

GHERARDI, GHERARDO JOSEPH, pathologist; b. Lucca, Italy, July 1, 1921; came to U.S., 1933; s. Mario E. and Maria (Gilli) G.; m. Celeste Tranfaglia, Sept. 16, 1957; children: Roberta, Ronald, Mark, Peter. BA, Princeton U., 1942; MD, Columbia U., 1945. Diplomate Am. Bd. Pathology. Pathologist in charge, assoc. prof. pathology Tufts New Eng. Med. Ctr., Boston, 1954-70; assoc. prof. pathology Tufts Med. Sch., 1954-70; sr. pathologist Framingham (Mass.) Union Hosp., 1970-93; assoc. prof. pathology Boston U. Sch. Medicine, 1970—2003. Capt. AUS, 1945-48. Fellow Coll. Am. Pathologists; mem. N.E. Soc. Pathologists (past pres.).

GHERMAN, PAUL M., university librarian; BA, Wayne State U., Detroit, Mich.; MALS, U. Mich. Acting head humanities divsn. Wayne State U., 1971—72; pers. officer univ. libr. Pa. State U., 1972—74; asst. dir. adminstrv. svc. Iowa State U., 1977—85; univ. libr. Va. Poly. Inst. and State U., 1985—92; dir. libr. Kenyon Coll., Gambier, Ohio, 1992—96; univ. libr. Vanderbilt U., Nashville, 1996—. Mem.: ALA (Hugh C. Atkinson Meml. Award 2005). Office: Jean and Alexander Heard Libr Vanderbilt U 419 21st Ave S Nashville TN 37240-0007 Office Phone: 615-322-7120. Fax: 615-343-8279. E-mail: paul.m.gherman@vanderbilt.edu.*

GHESQUIÈRE, NICOLAS, apparel designer; Internship Agnès B., Paris, 1986; with Jean Paul Gaultier; freelance designer, 1992; designer Balenciaga, Paris, 1996—97, creative dir., 1997—. Named one of 100 Most Influential People, Time Mag., 2006.

GHETTI, BERNARDINO FRANCESCO, neuropathologist, educator; b. Pisa, Italy, Mar. 28, 1941; s. Getulio and Iris (Mugnetti) G.; m. Caterina Genovese, Oct. 8, 1966; children: Chiara, Simone. MD cum laude, U. Pisa, 1966, specialist in mental and nervous diseases, 1969; laureate (hon.), U. Siena, 2005. Lic. physician, Italy; cert. Edn. Coun. for Fgn. Med. Grads.; diplomate Am. Bd. Pathology. Postdoctoral fellow U. Pisa, 1966-70; rsch. fellow in neuropathology Albert Einstein Coll. Medicine, Bronx, NY, 1970-73, resident, clin. fellow in pathology, 1973-75, resident in neuropathology, 1975-76; asst. prof. pathology Ind. U., Indpls., 1976-77, asst. prof. pathology and psychiatry, 1977—78, assoc. prof. pathology and psychiatry, 1978—83, prof. pathology and psychiatry, 1983—91, assoc. dir. program in med. neurobiology, 1983—2000, assoc. dir. divsn. neuropathology, 1989-93, prof. pathology, psychiatry, med. and molecular genetics, 1991—97, dir. Alzheimer Disease Ctr., 1991—, dir. divsn. neuropathology, 1993—, Disting. prof. pathology and lab. medicine, psychiatry, med. and molecular genetics, neurology, 1997—, chancellor's prof., 2007—. Mem. Nat. Inst. Neurol. Disorders and Stroke rev. com. NIH, 1985-89; mem. NIH Reviewers Res., 1989-93. Contbr. articles to profl. jours. Alzheimer's disease rsch. sci. rev. com. Am. Health Assistance Found., 1998—2002. Recipient Potamkin prize, 1999. Mem. Internat. Soc. Neuropathology (v.p. 2000-03, pres.-elect 2005, pres. 2006—), Am. Acad. Neurology, Am. Neurol. Assn., Am. Assn. Neuropathologists (pres. 1996-97), Soc. Neurosci., Assn. Rsch. in Nervous and Mental Diseases, Internat. Brain Rsch. Orgn., Am. Soc. Cell Biology, Italian Soc. Psychiatry, Italian Soc. Neurology, Sigma Xi. Roman Catholic. Home: 1124 Frederick Dr S Indianapolis IN 46260-3421 Office: Ind U 635 Barnhill Dr Rm 138 Indianapolis IN 46202-5126 Office Phone: 317-274-7818. Business E-Mail: bghetti@iupui.edu.

GHEZ, ANDREA MIA, astronomy and physics educator; b. NYC, June 16, 1965; d. Gilbert and Susanne; m. Tom La Tourette, May 1, 1993; 1 child, Evan LaTourette-Ghez. BS, MIT, 1987; MS, Calif. Inst. Tech., 1989, PhD in Physics, 1992. Hubble postdoctoral fellow U. Ariz., Tucson, 1992-93; vis. rsch. scholar Inst. Astronomy, Cambridge, England, 1994; asst. prof. physics and astronomy UCLA, 1994-97, assoc. prof., 1997—2000, prof., 2000—. Contbr. articles to profl. jours. Recipient Amelia Earhart award, 1987, Young Investigator award, NSF, 1994, Fullam/Dudley award, 1995, Maria Goeppert-Mayer award, Am. Phys. Soc., 1999, Sackler prize, U. Tel Aviv, 2004; grantee Pacific Telesis fellowship, 1991, Alfred P. Sloan Rsch. fellowship, 1996, David and Lucile Packard fellowship, 1996. Fellow: Am. Acad. Arts & Scis.; mem.: AAUW, Am. Astron. Soc. (Annie Jump Cannon award 1994, Newton Lacy Pierce prize 1998), NAS, Phi Beta Kappa. Achievements include discovery of formation of young low mass stars in multiple star systems; production of the first diffraction-limited image with the keck 10-m telescope (the largest telescope in the world); measurement of stellar motions which indicate the presence of a supermassive black hole at the center of our own galaxy. Office: UCLA Divsn Astronomy and Astrophysics Physics and Astronomy Bldg 430 Portola Plz Box 951547 Los Angeles CA 90095-1547 E-mail: ghez@astro.ucla.edu.

GHIA, KIRTI N., fluid mechanics engineer, aerospace educator; b. Bombay; BS, Gujarat U., India, 1960; MS, Ill. Inst. Tech., 1965, PhD in Mechanical & Aerospace Engring., 1969. Rsch. engr. Premier Automobiles Ltd., India, 1960-61; rsch. asst. fluid dynamics Ill. Inst. Tech., 1961-62, instr., 1962, asst., 1962-69; from asst. prof. to assoc. prof. U. Cin., 1969—78, prof. fluid dynamics, 1978—. Dir. Inst. Computational Mechanics, 1986—; co-dir. Computational Fluid Dynamics Rsch. Lab., 1990—. Assoc. tech. editor Jour. Fluids Engring., 1981—90, Am. Inst. Aeronautics and Astronautics Jour., 2000—; co-editor: Internat. Computational Fluid Dynamics Jour., 1991—98; contbr. articles to profl. jours. Named Disting. Prof., U. Cin., 2005; recipient Dolly Cohen award, 2004. Fellow ASME (life, chair honors and awards com. fluids engring divsn. 1997-2000, Freeman scholar award 1995-96), AIAA (fluid mechanics tech. com. 1986—); mem. Am. Phys. Soc., Am. Soc. Engring. Edn., Sigma Xi, Sigma Gamma Tau, Tau Beta Pi. Hindu. Achievements include research in analysis and numerical solutions of three-dimensional viscous internal flow problems; use of numerical coordinate transformations and higher-order spline techniques and direct solvers in the solution of navier-stokes equations. Office: Univ Cin Aerospace/Engring Mech Rhodes 681 Cincinnati OH 45221-0070 Home Phone: 513-984-2252; Office Phone: 513-556-3243. Business E-Mail: kghia@cfdrl.uc.edu.

GHIARDI, JAMES DOMENIC, lawyer, educator; b. Gwinn, Mich., Nov. 10, 1918; s. John B. and Margaret M. (Trosello) G.; m. Phyllis A. Lindmeier, Sept. 5, 1945; children— Catherine, Jeanne, Mary. PhB, Marquette U., 1940, LLB, 1942, JD, 1968. Bar: Wis. bar 1942. Prof. law Marquette U. Law Sch., Milw., 1946-89, prof. law emeritus, 1990—; research dir. Def. Research Inst., Milw., 1962-72; of counsel firm Kluwin, Dunphy, Hankin & McNulty, Milw., 1972-87. Author: Personal Injury Damages, Wisconsin, 1964, Punitive Damages, Vol. I, 1981, Vol. II, 1985; contbr. articles to profl. jours. Served to capt. Med. Adminstrv. Br. U.S. Army, 1942-45. Recipient award for teaching excellence Marquette U. Faculty, 1971, Edward A. Uhrig Found., 1971, Alumni of Yr. award Marquette U. Law Sch., 1971, Charles L. Goldberg award for outstanding pub. svc. Wis. Law Found., 1986, Charles C. Pinckney award for legal scholarship and svc. to the legal profession N.Y. Def. Bar Assn., 1986. Fellow Am. Bar Found.; mem. ABA (mem. ho. of dels. 1967-80, Disting. Prof. Torts and Ins. Law award Torts and Ins. Practice sect. 1989), Milw. Bar Assn. (Lifetime Achievement award 1993), State Bar Wis. (gov., mem. exec. com. 1962-72, pres. 1970-71), Am. Law Ins., Wis. Bar Found., Am. Legion. Office: Sensenbrenner Hall Marquette U Law Sch PO Box 1881 Milwaukee WI 53201-1881 Office Phone: 414-288-5370.

GHIGLIONE, LOREN FRANK, journalism professor; b. NYC, Apr. 5, 1941; s. William John and Norma Rae (Whitney) G.; m. Nancy Ellen Geiger, Feb. 24, 1968; children: Jessica, Laura. BA, Haverford Coll., 1963; M of Urban Studies, Yale U., 1966, LLB, 1966; PhD in Am. Civilization, George Washington U., 1976. Asst. to dir. office of planning & analysis NEH, Washington, 1967-68; editor The News, Southbridge, Mass., 1969—95; pres. Worcester County Newspapers, Southbridge, Mass., 1969—95; former James M. Cox Chair in Journalism, dir. Journalism program Emory U., 1996—99; former dir. Sch. Journalism U. So. Calif., Annenberg Sch. Comm., 1999—2001; dean, prof. Medill Sch. Journalism, Northwestern U., 2001—06, Richard Schwarzlose prof. media ethics, 2007—. Author books and contbr. chpts. and essays to books and articles to profl. jours.; mem. editl. bd. Jour. Mass Media Ethics, 1990-. Congrl. fellow U.S. Congress, Washington, 1966-67, Freedom Forum Media Studies Ctr. fellow Columbia U., 1987-88, Joan Shorenstein Ctr. Harvard's John F. Kennedy Sch. Govt. fellow, 1988-89, Soc. Profl. Journalists fellow, 1990-91, Reuter fellow Oxford U., 1997. Fellow Am. Acad. Arts and Scis.; mem. Am. Soc. Newspaper Editors (pres. 1989-90), New Eng. Soc. Newspaper Editors (pres. 1978-79), New Eng. Press Assn. (pres. 1984), Internat. Press Inst. (dir. Am. com. 1989-94), Assn. Sch. Journalism and

Mass Comm.(pres., 2006-07), Coun. Fgn. Rels. Avocations: reading, wind surfing. Office: Medill School of Journalism Northwestern U 1870 Campus Dr Evanston IL 60208-2170 Office Phone: 847-491-4837. Business E-Mail: ghiglion@northwestern.edu.

GHISELLI, GARY, spine surgeon; BS (cum laude) in Biochemistry, UCLA; MD (summa cum laude), U. Tex., Southwestern Med. Sch., Dallas, Tex. Intern, gen. surgery UCLA, resident, chief resident; fellow, spine surgery U. Hosp. Cleve., Ohio; staff physician, Acute Spinal Cord Injury Ctr. Veterans Hosp. Cleve.; physician Denver Spine. Mem.: Am. Acad. Orthop. Surgeons, AMA, N.Am. Spine Soc. Office: Denver Spine 1601 E 19th Ave Ste 4000 Denver CO 80218 Office Phone: 303-860-1500. Office Fax: 303-860-0511.*

GHIU, SILVANA MELANIA STEFANIA, process and development engineer; b. Constanta, Romania, Dec. 27, 1971; d. Gheorghe and Camelia Ghiu. BSc, U. Bucharest, 1995, MSc, 1996, Ctrl. European U., Budapest, 1998; PhD, U. So. Fla., 2003. EIT 2000. Rsch. asst. Engring. and Environment Rsch. Inst., Bucharest, 1995—97; safeguards officer asst. Nat. Commn. of Nuc. Activities Control, Bucharest, 1996—97; rsch. asst. U. So. Fla., Tampa, 1999—2003; environ. engr. HSA, Tampa, 2004—06; sr. process and devel. engr. Doosan Hydro Tech., Tampa, 2006—. Contbr. articles to profl. jours. Fellow, U. So. Fla. Coll. Engring., 1998—2001, 2001; Govtl. fellow, U. Bucharest, 1995—96, George Soros Found. fellow, Ctrl. European U., 1997—98, Channabasappa Meml. scholar, IDA, 2001. Mem.: Internat. Desalination Assn., North Am. Membrane Soc., Am. Membrane Tech. Assn., Am. Water Works Assn. (v.p. Fla. sect. 2001—03), Nat. Soc. of Profl. Engr., Phi Kappa Phi. Achievements include patents pending for submersible pump; research in equations governing the process of direct osmosis. Office: Doosan Hydro Tech 912 Chad Ln Tampa FL 33619 Office Phone: 813-549-0182. Personal E-mail: silvanaghiu@yahoo.com. Business E-Mail: sghiu@doosanhydro.com.

GHOGAWALA, ZOHER, neurosurgeon; b. Dhaka, Bangladesh, Nov. 3, 1966; s. Honed and Nema (Mohammed) G.; m. Tasneem Haidermota, June 16, 1991; 3 children. AB, Harvard U., 1987; MD, Harvard Med. Sch., 1991. Diplomate Am. Bd. Neurol. Surgeons. Resident Mass. Gen. Hosp., Boston, 1991—99; clin. asst. prof. neurosurgery Yale U., New Haven, 2001—. Contbr. articles to profl. jours. Named one of, Best Drs. Am., 2006. Mem. Am. Assn. Neurol. Surgeons, Congress Neurol. Surgeons (prin. investigator study joint spine sect., clin. outcomes com.).

GHOSH, AJIT KUMAR, daycare administrator; b. Calcutta, India, May 20, 1922; arrived in U.S., 1987, naturalized, 1997; s. Rajendra Kumar and Uma Rani Ghosh; m. Sovana Sirkar, June 29, 1945; children: Baruna, Surajit. BSME, Bengal Engring. Coll., 1943. Asst. foreman Govt. Ctrl. Workshops, Kanpore, India, 1943; owner Gen. Engring. Co., Kanpore, 1943—46; lectr. applied mechanics Bengal Engring. Coll. U. Calcutta, Calcutta, India, 1946—48; with dept. prodn. and design office William Asquith, BSA Tools et al, Yorkshire, England, 1948—50; designer Newall Engring. Co. Ltd., Peterborough, England, 1950; chief process planning and rate fixing engr. Burn & Co., Howrah, India, 1951—54; mgr., machine shop Garden Reach Workshops Ltd., Calcutta, India, 1955; works mgr. Ctrl. Engring. Orgn., Howrah, 1956—59; gen. mgr. Heavy Machine Tools Plant, Heavy Engring. Corp., Ranchi, India, 1960—70; mng. dir. Rehab. Industries Corp., India, 1971—72; mem., CEO on-shore divsn. Oil & Natural Gas Commn., Dehradun, India, 1972—77; founder, mng. dir. Webel Toolsind Ltd. (a joint govt. & pvt. sector co.), Calcutta, 1977—87; co-prin., owner Incare Infant Care Day Nursery T/A Incare Inc., Parsippany, NJ, 1987—. Author: Practical Machine Design, 1969. Recipient Honor cert., Govt. India, 1963; scholar, U. Calcutta, 1940. Mem.: AARP, Instn. Engrs. India. Achievements include patents in field. Avocations: walking, cooking. Home: 25 Gilmar Rd Randolph NJ 07869 Office Phone: 973-887-2299.

GHOSH, AVIJIT, dean; m. Sara McLafferty; children: Smita, Priya. BS in chem. with honors, Calcutta U., 1970; postgrad. in mgmt., Xavier Inst., 1975; MA in geography, U. Iowa, 1977, PhD in geography, 1979. Asst. prof. mktg. Sch. Bus., U. Iowa, 1978—79; asst. to prof. mktg. Leonard N. Stern Sch. Bus., NYU, 1980—91, dir. Ctr. Entrepreneurial Studies, 1991—95, vice dean profl. programs, 1994—2001, dep. dean, 1998—2000; dean Coll. Bus., U. Ill., Urbana-Champaign, 2001—, assoc. editor: Jour. Retailing, 1983 (Best Article Yr., 1984); editor, 1985—91 (Best Article Yr., 1991); author: (books) Retail Management, 1990, 1994; co-author (with Sara McLafferty): Location Strategy for Retail and Service Firms, 1987; co-editor: Spatial Analysis and Location Allocation Models, 1987, Spatial Analysis in Marketing: Theory, Methods and Applications, 1991. Office: Coll Bus Univ Ill Urbana Champaign 1206 S Sixth St 260 Wohlers Hall Champaign IL 61820 Office Phone: 217-333-2747. Office Fax: 217-244-3113. Business E-Mail: ghosha@uiuc.edu.

GHOSH, BHASKAR KUMAR, statistics educator, researcher; b. Dibrugarh, India, Feb. 10, 1936; arrived in US, 1961; s. Saroj Kumar and Usha Rani (Bose) G.; m. Hedwig Graf, 1960; children: Monica, Anita, Rebecca. BSc, Calcutta U., 1955; PhD, London U., 1959. Statistician Atomic Power Constrn., London, 1959-60; asst. prof. U. London, 1960-61, Lehigh U., Bethlehem, Pa., 1961-63, assoc. prof., 1963-68, prof., 1968—. Vis. prof. MIT, Cambridge, Mass., 1968, Va. Tech., Blacksburg, 1978-80, U. Munster, Germany, 1986-87. Author: Sequential Tests of Statistical Hypotheses, 1970; editor: Handbook of Sequential Analysis, 1991; editor: Sequential Analysis, 1982-95. Recipient U.S. Sr. Rsch. Scientist award Alexander von Humboldt Found., 1986-87, 92. Fellow Royal Statis. Soc., Inst. Math. Statistics. Home: 1440 E University Ave Bethlehem PA 18015-4718 Office: Lehigh U Dept Math 14 E Packer Ave Bethlehem PA 18015-3175 Office Phone: 610-758-3722. Business E-Mail: bkg0@lehigh.edu.

GHOSH, SAMBHUNATH (SAM), environmental engineer, educator; BS, U. Calcutta, 1956; MS, U. Ill., 1963; PhD, Ga. Inst. Tech., Atlanta, 1970. Engr. Wiedeman & Singleton, Atlanta, 1963—65; mgr. bioengring. rsch. Gas Tech. Inst., Chgo., 1971—85; prof. civil engring. U. Utah, Salt Lake City, 1985—2000; prof. civil, agrl. and geol. engring. N.Mex State U., Las Cruces, 2000—01; pres. EnviroEnergetics, Salt Lake City, 1988—, EnviroEnergetics of Wis., Inc., 2005—. Recipient Ill. Energy award, 1985, Utah Gov.'s award for energy innovation, 1986, John Ericsson award and Gold medal in Renewable Energy, U.S. Dept. Energy, 1994, George Bradley Gascoigne medal, Water Environment Fedn., 1996, Thomas R. Camp medal, Water Environment Fedn., Alexandria, Va., 2001. Home: 1281 E Federal Heights Dr Salt Lake City UT 84103-4325 Office Phone: 801-355-1429. Personal E-mail: sambhughosh@aol.com.

GHOSSAINI, SOHA NADIM, medical educator; b. Beirut; d. Nadim and Noha Kaasamany Ghossaini. MD, Am. U., Lebanon, 1994, degree in otolaryngology head and neck surgery, 2000. Intern and resident Am. U. Beirut, 1994—2000; otology-neurotology fellow Columbia U., Coll. Physicians and Surgeons, NYC, 2000—02, cilincal instr., 2002—03, asst. prof., 2003—. Recipient Tchg. award, Columbia U., Coll. Physicians and Surgeons, 2005. Mem.: Am. Acad. Otolaryngology (mem. Head and Neck Surgery Found., grantee 2005, scholar 2004—05). Achievements include research in Baha; tinnitus; sudden hearing loss; cochlear implants; otosclerosis. Office: Columbia Univ Med Ctr 180 Fort Washington Ave HP706 New York NY 10032 Office Phone: 212-305-0029. Office Fax: 212-342-3050. Business E-Mail: sng27@columbia.edu.

GHOVANLOO, MAYSAM, engineer, educator; m. Azadeh N. Shahshahani, Sept. 8, 2001. BS, U. Tehran, Iran, 1990—94; MS, Amirkabir U. Tech., Tehran, Iran, 1994—97; PhD, U. Mich., Ann Arbor, 2000—04, MS, 2000—03. Sr. rsch. engr. IDEA Co. Ltd., Tehran, Iran, 1994—99; sr. engr. Ctr. for Repair and Reconstruction Med. Devices, Tehran, Iran, 1997—98; founder, CEO Sabz Nagar Rayaneh Co. Ltd., Tehran, Iran, 1998—99; rsch. asst. U. Mich., Ann Arbor, 2000—04; tech. intern Advanced Bionics Corp., Santa Clarita, Calif., 2002; asst. prof. N.C. State U., Raleigh, 2004—. Cons. Nitinol Devel. Corp., Fremont, Calif., 2004—. Contbr. articles to profl. jours. Grantee, N.C. State U., 2005. Mem.: IEEE, Tau Beta Pi. Achievements include patents pending for Frequency shift keying demodulation methods for wireless biomedical Implants; Three dimensional microassembly structures for micromachined planar microelectrode arrays; Shatter-proof microprobes; A compact large voltage compliance high output impedance programmable current source. Home Phone: 734-476-5738; Office Phone: 919-513-1923. Office Fax: 919-515-2285. Business E-Mail: mghovan@ncsu.edu.

GHRIST, CATHERINE ANN, religious organization administrator; b. St. Edward, Nebr., Nov. 27, 1946; d. William Roy and Catherine Theresa (King) Burney; m. David Henry Cates, Apr. 3, 1969 (div. Nov. 1973); 1 child, David Aaron; m. William John Ghrist, Mar. 5, 1975; children: Scott William, Catherine Ann. Postgraduate, Assumption U., Windsor, Ontario. Cert. youth min. level II Archdiocese of Detroit, 1991, youth min. level III Archdiocese of Detroit, 1996, youth min. level IV Archdiocese of Detroit, 2004, religious edn. dir. level III Archdiocese of Detroit, 2004, Nat. Ctr. Ctr. for Youth Min. Coord. youth ministry Sts. Kevin and Norbert/Holy Family Ch., Inkster, Mich., 1991-96, St. Albert the Great Ch., Dearborn Heights, Mich., 1993-98, St. Mary's Parish, Wayne, Mich., 1996—2002; DRE St. Sabina Parish, Dearborn Heights, 2002. Adj. staff mem. Cath. Youth Orgn., Detroit, 1991-98; mem. world youth day com. Archdiocese of Detroit, 1994—; mem. Youth Ministry Cert. Bd., 1998—. Mem. Detroit Soc. Profl. Catechetical Leaders. Democrat. Avocations: reading, camping, travel. Home: 33459 Somerset St Westland MI 48186-4847 Office: St Sabina Parish 8147 Arnold Dearborn Heights MI 48127 Office Phone: 313-274-5635. Personal E-mail: caghristdre@yahoo.com.

GHUZLAN, KHALID A., civil engineer; b. Huwwara, Irbid, Jordan, Feb. 2, 1970; s. Ahmad M. Ghuzlan and Tamam S. Shatnawi; m. Rana H. Athamneh, May 15, 2006; 1 child, Malaak K. BS in Civil Engring, Jordan U. Sci. and Tech., Irbid, 1993, MS in Civil Engring, 1996; PhD in Civil Engring, U. Ill., Urbana-Champaign, 2001. EIT Calif., 2002. Rsch. assoc. U. Ill., Urbana, 1996—2001; pavement rsch. specialist Calif. Dept. Transp., Sacramento, 2001—. Contbr. articles to profl. jours. Mem.: ASCE (assoc.), Profl. Engineers Calif. Govt. (assoc.), Engring. Assn. Jordan (assoc.), Assn. Asphalt Paving Technologists (assoc.). Achievements include development of energy fatigue model for asphalt concrete mixtures; research in pavement engineering. Office: Calif Dept Transp 5900 Folsom Blvd Sacramento CA 95819 Home Phone: 916-227-5848; Office Phone: 916-227-5848. Office Fax: 916-227-5856.

GIACCHI, RENATO, physician; b. Hoboken, NJ, Feb. 21, 1967; s. John and Valentina Giacchi; m. Anna Sasso; children: Nicola, Alexander. BA, Cornell U., Ithaca, NY, 1989; MD, NYU, 1993. Lic. Am. Bd. Otolaryngology, 2000. Otolaryngologist in head & neck surgery Otolaryngology, Morristown, NJ, 2000—. Office: Otolaryngology 95 Madison Ave Morristown NJ 07960

GIACCHINO, MICHAEL, composer; b. Riverside, NJ; Grad., Sch. Visual Arts, NYC; composition student, Juilliard Sch. With feature film publicity dept. Disney Studios, Burbank; asst. prodr. Disney Interactive. Composer: (films) Buffalo Soldiers, 1995, No Salida, 1998, Freight, 1998, My Brother the Pig, 1999, Los Gringos, 1999, The Trouble with Lou, 2001, Sin, 2003, The Incredibles, 2004 (ASCAP award, 2005, Annie award for Music in an Animated Feature Prodn., 2005, BMI Film Music award, 2005, World Soundtrack award, 2005), Sky High, 2005, The Family Stone, 2005, Looking for Comedy in the Muslim World, 2005, Tom & Jerry: The Karate Guard, 2005, One Man Band, 2005, M:i III, 2006, Lifted, 2006, Ratatouille, 2007, (TV films) Teen Angel, 1998, The Others, 1999, Semper Fi, 2001, Redemption of the Ghost, 2002, Phenomenon, 2004, The Muppets' Wizard of Oz, 2005, (TV series) Alias, 2001—06, Lost, 2004— (ASCAP award, 2005, 2006, BMI TV Music award, 2005, Emmy award for Outstanding Music Composition for a Series, 2005), What About Brian?, 2006, Six Degrees, 2006, (video games) The Lost World: Jurassic Park, 1998, The Lost World: Chaos Island, 1998, Squad Commander, 1998, Small Soldiers, 1998, T'Ai Fu, 1999, Warpath, 1999, Medal of Honor, 1999, Muppet Monster Adventure, 2000, Medal of Honor: Underground, 2000, Medal of Honor: Allied Assault, 2002, Medal of Honor: Frontline, 2002, Secret Weapons Over Normandy, 2003, Call of Duty, 2003, The Incredibles, 2004, Call of Duty: Finest Hour, 2004, Mercenaries: Playground of Destruction, 2004, Black, 2005, The Incredibles: Rise of the Underminer, 2005, (symphony) Camden 2000, 2000.*

GIACCIO, ANTHONY, lawyer; m. Jennifer Ellen Burns, Sept. 5, 1992; children: Anthony, John, Ashley. BS in Biology, SUNY Binghamton, 1988; JD, Albany Law Sch., NY, 1991; LLM in Trade Regulation, NYU Sch. Law, 1995. Bar: NY 1992, Ea. Dist. NY 1992, So. Dist. NY 1992, registered patent atty.: US Patent and Trademark Office 1996. Legis. atty. NYC Councilman John A. Fusco, 1992—94; patent atty. Brumbaugh Graves Donohue & Raymond, NYC, 1995—97, Baker Botts LLP, NYC, 1997—2003, Kenyon & Kenyon LLP, NYC, 2003—. Dir. Joint Patent Practice Continuing Legal Edn., Inc., NYC, 2001—. Founder, mng. editor lead articles: Albany Law Jour. Sci. and Tech., 1990—91. Pres. St. Bernardino Soc., SI, 1995—99; commr. NYC Redistricting Commn., 2002—03. Recipient Achievement award, St. Bernardino Soc., 1995, Mews Main St. Acknowledgement award, New Dorp Ctrl. Civic Assn., SI, 1998, Svc. award, Joint Patent Practice Continuing Legal Edn., Inc., 2005. Mem.: NY State Bar Assn., ABA, NY Intellectual Property Law Assn. (chair continuing legal edn. 1998—2003, bd. dir. 2003—05, 2d v.p. 2005—06, 1st v.p. 2006—07, pres.-elect 2007—), Am. Intellectual Property Law Assn., NY Acad. Scis., Am. Bar Found. (fellow). Business E-Mail: agiaccio@kenyon.com.

GIACCONI, RICCARDO, astrophysicist, educator; b. Genoa, Italy, Oct. 6, 1931; arrived in U.S., 1956, naturalized, 1967; s. Antonio and Elsa (Canni) Giacconi; m. Mirella Manaira, Feb. 15, 1957; children: Guia Giacconi Trutter, Anna Lee Bauze, Marc A. PhD, U. Milan, Italy, 1954; ScD (hon.), U. Chgo., 1983; laurea honoris causa in astronomy, U. Padua, 1984; ScD (hon.), Warsaw U., 1996; laurea honoris causa in physics, U. Rome, 1998; Dr Tech. and Sci. (hon.), U. Uppsala, 2000. Asst. prof. physics U. Milan, 1954—56; rsch. assoc. Ind. U., 1956—58, Princeton U., 1958—59; exec. v.p., dir. Am. Sci. & Engring. Co., Cambridge, Mass., 1959—73; prof. astronomy Harvard U.; also assoc. dir. high energy astrophysics divsn. Center Astrophysics, Smithsonian Astrophys. Obs./Harvard Coll. Obs., Cambridge, 1973—81; dir. Space Telescope Sci. Inst., Balt., 1981—92; prof. astrophysics Johns Hopkins U., 1981—99, U. Milan, Italy, 1991—97; dir.-gen. European So. Obs., Garching, Germany, 1993—99; pres. Assoc. Univs., Inc., Washington, 1999—2004; prof. Johns Hopkins U., 1999—. Richtmeyer meml. lectr. Am. Assn. Physics Tchrs., 1975; mem. space sci. adv. com. NASA, 1978—79, mem. adv. com. innovation study, 1979—; mem. NASA Astrophysics Coun., mem. adv. com. innovation study astronomy adv. com., 1979—; mem. high energy astronomy survey panel Nat. Acad. Scis., 1979—80, mem. Space Sci. Studies Bd., 1980—84, 1989—; mem. adv. com. Max-Planck Inst. für Physik und Astrophysik; chmn. bd. dirs. Instituto Guido Donegani, Gruppo Montedison, 1987—89; mem. vis. com. to divsn. of phys. scis. U. Chgo., U. Padua; chmn. ISC E-1 (galactic and extragalactic astrophysics) Com. on Space Rsch. (COSPAR), 1982—93; Russell lectr. Co-editor: X-ray Astronomy, 1974, The X-Ray Universe, 1985, author numerous articles and papers in field.; inventor x-ray telescope, discoverer of x-ray stars. Recipient Röntgen prize in astrophysics, Physikalish-Medizinische Gesellschaft, Wurzburg, Germany, 1971, Exceptional Sci. Achievement medal, NASA, 1971, 1980, Disting. Pub. Svc. award, 1972, 2003, Space Sci. award, AIAA, 1976, Elliot Cresson medal, Franklin Inst., 1980, Gold medal, Royal Astron. Soc., 1982, A. Cressy Morrison award, N.Y. Acad. Sci., 1982, Bruce medal, 1987, Heinneman award, 1987, Wolf Prize in Physics, 1987, Nobel prize in physics, 2002, Nat. medal of Sci., 2003; fellow, Fulbright, 1956—58. Mem.: Am. Philos. Soc., Royal Astron. Soc., Max-Planck Soc. (ext. mem.), Academia Nazionale dei Lincei (fgn.), Md. Acad. Sci. (sci. coun. 1982—), Internat. Astron. Union, Am. Acad. Arts and Scis., Italian Phys. Soc. (Como prize 1967), Am. Astron. Soc. (Henry Norris Russel lectr. 1981, Darwin lectr. Royal Soc. 1993, chmn. high energy astrophysics divsn., Helen B. Warner award 1966), NAS (rep. 1979—82), AAAS, Cosmos Club (Washington). Office: Johns Hopkins U Dept Physics & Astronomy 3400 N Charles St Baltimore MD 21218 Office Phone: 410-516-6021. Business E-Mail: rgiacconi@comsat.net.

GIACINO, JOSEPH T., psychologist, educator; BA in Psychology, Fairfield U., 1981; MA in Psychology, Hofstra U., 1982, PhD in Clin./Sch. Psychology, 1986. Lic. NJ. Assoc. dir. neuropsychology JFK Johnson Rehabilitation Inst. Ctr. for Head Injuries, NJ Neuroscience Inst., JFK Med. Ctr., Edison, NJ; clin. asst. prof. U. Medicine and Dentistry NJ Robert Wood Johnson Med. Sch., Piscataway, NJ; asst. prof., adjunct faculty mem. Seton Hall U. Sch. Grad. Med. Edn., Dept. Neuroscience, South Orange, NJ; contbg. faculty mem. Rutgers U., Grad. Sch. Applied and Profl. Psychology, Piscataway, NJ. Prin. investigator Investigation of the Utility of Functional MRI in Assessing Cognition, Predicting Outcome and Planning Treatment in Persons Diagnosed with Minimally Conscious State; invited lectr. in field. Contbr. articles to profl. jours.; mem. editl. bd. Jour. Head Trauma Rehabilitation, ad hoc reviewer Archives of Phys. Medicine, Rehabilitation, Brain, Nature Reviews-Neuroscience and Neuropsychological Rehabilitation. Fellow: Nat. Acad. Neuropsychology, Am. Congress Rehabilitation Medicine (program com. mem. 1999, program chair 2001—02, bd. governor 2002—05, brain injury inter-disciplinary spl. interest group, past chair 2003—04, brain injury inter-disciplinary spl. interest group, chair-elect 1999—2000, brain injury inter-disciplinary spl. interest group, chair 2001—02, Disting. Mem. award 2002); mem.: NJ Neuropsychology Soc., Brain Injury Assn. Am., Inc., APA. Achievements include the primary author of the JFK Coma Recovery Scale which is currently being used in brain injury facilities throughout the US and Europe. Office: NJ Neuroscience Inst JFK Med Ctr 65 James St Edison NJ 08818*

GIACINTI, LOUIS ANTHONY, science educator, writer; b. Racine, Wis., Sept. 16, 1948; s. Louis Anthony and Rosalie Giacinti; m. Christine Marie Isler, Apr. 9, 1989; 1 child, Christopher Peter. BA, U. Wis., Milw., 1971, BS, 1972, MS, 1974, PhD, 1989. Tchg. asst. U. Wis., Milw., 1972—74; prof. Milw. Area Tech. Coll., 1977—. Author: (computerized study guide) Anatomy and Physiology Study Guide, (study guide) Microbiology Study Guide and Student Manual, (teacher's manual for microbiology) Manual for Talaro Microbiology. Mem. Young Reps., Racine, Wis., 1966—68. Fellow, Med. Coll. Wis., 1974—75; scholar, U. Wis., Milw., 1970. Democrat. Roman Catholic. Avocations: guitar, writing. Office: Milw Area Tech Coll 700 W State St Milwaukee WI 53233 Home Phone: 414-297-7360; Office Phone: 414-297-7360.

GIAEVER, IVAR, physicist; b. Bergen, Norway, Apr. 5, 1929; arrived in Canada, 1954, arrived in U.S., 1957, naturalized, 1963; s. John A. and Gudrun (Skaarud) Giaever; m. Inger Skramstad, Nov. 8, 1952; children: John, Anne Kari, Guri, Trine. Siv. Ing., Norwegian Inst. Tech., Trondheim, 1952; PhD (hon.), Rensselaer Poly. Inst., 1964, Union College, 1974; PhD U. of Oslo (hon.), 1976; PhD (hon.), Michigan Tech. U., 1976, Worcester Polytechnic Inst., 1977, Norwegian Inst. of Tech., 1985, Clarkson U., 1985, SUNY, 1985. Patent examiner Norwegian Patent Office, Oslo, 1953—54; mech. engr. Can. Gen. Electric Co., Peterborough, Ont., Canada, 1954—56; applied mathematician Gen. Electric Co., Schenectady, 1956—58, physicist Research and Devel. Ctr., 1958—88; Inst. prof. Rensselaer Poly. Inst., Troy, NY, 1988—; and pres. Applied BioPhysics, Inc., Troy, NY. Prof.-at-large Univ. Oslo, Norway, 1988—. With Norwegian Army, 1952—53. Recipient Nobel prize for Physics, 1973; fellow Guggenheim, 1970. Fellow: Am. Phys. Soc. (Oliver E. Buckley prize 1965); mem.: NAS, IEEE, Korean Acad. of Sci., Swedish Acad. of Engring., Norwegian Acad. Tech., Norwegian Acad. Sci., Am. Acad. Arts and Scis., Nat. Acad. Engring. (V.K. Zworykin award 1974), Norwegian Profl. Engrs. Achievements include experimental discoveries regarding tunneling phenomena in semiconductors and superconductors. Office: Rensselaer Poly Ins Physics Dept 110 8th St Troy NY 12180-3590 E-mail: giaevi@rpi.edu.

GIAIMO, PAUL SEBASTIAN, English and philosophy educator; b. New Haven, May 8, 1962; s. Thomas John and Geraldine Carmel Giaimo; m. Sarah Therese Jeglosky, Oct. 1, 1988; children: Clare Rose, Michael Thomas. BA, Holy Cross Coll., 1984; MA, Clark U., 1988; PhD, Bowling Green State U., 1994. Instr. English Owens CC, Findlay and Toledo, Ohio, 1994—96; instr. English and philosophy Highland CC, Freeport, Ill., 1996—. Author: (workbook) Prentice Hall Philosophy Notes, 2005; contbr. articles to profl. jours., conf. procs. Roman Catholic. Avocations: swimming, running, yoga, guitar, singing. Home: 1540 West Logan Freeport IL 61032 Office: Highland CC 1540 West Logan Freeport IL Home Phone: 815-235-7075; Office Phone: 815-599-3431. Business E-Mail: paul.giaimo@highland.edu.

GIALANELLA, DONALD GEORGE, broadcast executive, sound recording engineer, sculptor; b. Plainfield, NJ, June 9, 1956; s. Angelo George and Helena Joan (Kreminski) G.; m. Phyllis Clare Orlowski, June 25, 1988; children: Max Philip, Julian Andrew. Student, Montclair State U., NJ, 1974-77; BFA cum laude, Cooper Union, 1979. Art dir. South Coast Publs., San Diego, 1981-83; artist, animator ABC News/Sports, NYC, 1983-84; assoc. network news graphics dir. ABC News, NYC, 1984-85; broadcast graphics artistic dir. ABC Sports/Entertainment, NYC, 1985—. Designer, producer (animation/graphics) Monday Night Football, 1990 (Emmy award 1990), (opening animation) Good Morning America, 1989. Recipient Elliot Lash Meml. prize Cooper Union, 1979, Page Design award Sigma Delta Chi, 1983, Gold Design award North County Press Club, 1984, Art Direction awards Art Direction mag., 1985; finalist Monitor Award Assn., 1986. Mem. Acad. TV, Arts and Scis. (Sports Emmy award 1990), Broadcast Designers Assn. Avocations: triathlons, biathlons. Home: 20 Sugar Ct Newtown CT 06470 Office: ABC Sports 47 W 66th St Fl 8 New York NY 10023-6201

GIALLOMBARDO, LESLIE, publishing executive; Adv. dir. The Desert Sun, Palm Springs, Calif., The Idaho Statesman, Boise; v.p. adv. The Tennessean, 1995, sr. v.p. mktg., 1999, pres., pub., 2002—05; v.p. advertising, newspaper div. Gannett Co., 2006—. Mgmt. positions Reno (NE) Gazette-Jour., Statesman Jour., Salem, Oreg. Named seven time winner Pres.'s Ring. Office: Gannett Co Inc 7950 Jones Branch Dr Mc Lean VA 22107 E-mail: lgiallom@tennessean.com.

GIALLORENZI, THOMAS GAETANO, optical engineer; b. NYC, Feb. 28, 1943; s. Amedeo and Eleanor (Spica) G.; m. Margaret Mary Marrin, Sept. 6, 1966; children: Thomas R., Kathy. BS in Engring. Physics, Cornell U., 1965, MS in Engring. Physics, 1966, PhD, 1969. Tech. staff Gen. Tel.

& Electronics Lab., Bayside, NY, 1969-70; sect. head, optical techniques br. Naval Rsch. Lab., Washington, 1970-76, head optical techniques br., 1976-79, supt. optical scis. divsn., 1979—. Lectr. in field and at profl. soc. confs. Editor Jour. Lightwave Tech., 1983-88; contbr. over 80 articles to profl. jours.; over 30 patents in field. Mem. adv. bd. U. Va., 1986-92. Recipient Applied Sci. award Rsch. Soc. Am., 1973, Meritorious Civilian Svc. award USN, 1978, Conrad award USN, 1985, Disting. Exec. Rank award Pres. of U.S., 1990, 98, Meritorious Exec. Rank award Pres. of U.S., 1984, 2004, Disting. Civilian Svc. award Dept. Def., 1987. Fellow IEEE (assoc. editor Procs. 1990-95, Lightwave Comms. 1989-92, Harry Diamond award 1986, John Tyndell award 1990), IEEE Laser and ElectroOptics Soc. (pres. 1996), Optical Soc. Am. (editor Jour. Lightwave Tech. 1983-89, assoc. editor Applied Optics 1991-94); mem. Nat. Acad. Engring., U.S. Naval League (Albert Michelson award 1995, USN Rodger Easton award Office of Naval Rsch. 1998). Home: 8704 Side Saddle Rd Springfield VA 22152-2731 Office: Naval Rsch Lab Optical Scis Divsn Washington DC 20375-0001 Business E-Mail: nrl5600@ccf.nrl.navy.mil.

GIAMBI, JASON GILBERT, professional baseball player; b. West Covina, Calif., Jan. 8, 1971; s. John and Jeanne Giambi; m. Dana Mandela, Nov. 9, 1996 (div.); m. Kristian Rice, Feb. 2002. Grad., Long Beach State U. 1st baseman U.S. Olympic Team, 1992; drafted Oakland A's, Calif., 1992, 1st baseman Calif., 1995—2001, N.Y. Yankees, 2002—. Named Am. League MVP, 2000; named to U.S. Olympic Baseball team, Barcelona, Spain, 1992, Am. League All-star team, 2000—04; recipient AL Comeback Player of the Yr., MLB, 2005. Avocations: off-roading, WWF. Office: NY Yankees Yankee Stadium 161st Street and River Avenue Bronx NY 10451

GIAMBRA, JOEL ANTHONY, municipal official; m. Michelle Giambra; children: Gabriella, Nicholas, Dominic, Joel Anthony. Student, Bryant & Stratton Bus. Inst., 1973; AAS in Bus. Adminstrn., Erie C.C., 1978. Legis. asst. Erie County Legis., Buffalo, 1975-76, cmty. aide, mem. citizens adv. com., 1976; sgt.-at-arms Buffalo Common Coun., 1976-77; dir. field ops. western N.Y. Carter/Mondale Re-Election Com., Buffalo, 1980; monitor/evaluator Divsn. Employment & Tng., Buffalo, 1982-90; comptroller City of Buffalo, 1990-2000; Erie County exec. Buffalo, 2000—. Bd. dirs. Buffalo Fine Arts Acad.; mem. Loaned Exec. Club, United Way Buffalo & Erie County. Recipient Bus. First 40 under 40 award, 1995, Erie C.C. Found. Disting. Alumni award, Be-A-Friend Big Brother/Big Sister Program Dir.'s award, Disting. Svc. to Preservation award Landmark Soc. Niagara Frontier, 1984, Appreciation award Preservation Coalition Erie County, 1984, Man of Yr. award YMCA, 1998, Donald A. Miller Cmty. Svc. award, 2000, Man of Yr. award Buffalo Renaissance Found., 2000, Italian-Am. Achievement award Good Govt. Club, 2000, Abraham Lincoln Leadership award, 2000, Paul Harris Fellow Rotary Found. Rotary Internat., 2001, Erie Cmty. Coll. Light of Leadership award, 2002, Frank E. Van Lare award, N.Y. Water Environ. Assn., 2002, Buffalo award, Buffalo Niagara Assn. of Realtors, 2002; named Buffalo News Outstanding Citizen, 2001. Mem. NCCJ, N.Y. State Fin. Officers Assn. (bd. govs. 1992), West Side Bus. & Taxpayers' Assn. (Man of Yr. 20024), Forest Dist. Civic Assn., Jr. C. of C., Kiwanis Club Buffalo, Leadership Buffalo (adv. bd.), Romulus Club. Office: Erie County 95 Franklin St Buffalo NY 14202-3925 Business E-Mail: giambraj@bflo.co.erie.ny.us.

GIAMPETRO, KATHLEEN A., school psychologist; b. Phila., Oct. 1943; d. Anthony N. and Theresa D. Giampetro. BA, Our Lady of Angels Coll., Ashton, Pa., 1973; MA, Immaculata Coll., Pa., 1989. Cert. sch. psychologist Rowan U., Glassboro, NJ, 1994, in supervision Rowan U., Glassboro, NJ, 1994, in social studies Rowan U., Glassboro, NJ, 1997, ednl. specialist Rowan U., Glassboro, NJ, 1999. Tchr. primary studies Sisters St. Francis, Phila. Found., Glen Riddle, Pa., 1964—70; interviewer, supr. Dept. Pub. Welfare, Phila., 1970—73; tchr. jr. HS Queen of Heaven Sch., Cherry Hill, NJ, 1974—86; prin. pre-kindergarten to grade 8 sch. Christ the King Sch., Haddonfield, NJ, 1986—92; sub. tchr. Audubon Jr.-Sr. HS, NJ, 1992—93; sch. psychologist Overbrook HS, Pine Hill, NJ, 1994—. Invited sch. psychologist Oxford Round Table Discussion, London, 2005. Mem.: NASP, Oxford Roundtable Sch. Psychologists (invited mem. 2005), NJ Edn. Assn., NJ Assn. Sch. Psychologists (co-chair com. children's svcs. 1994—97, newsletter editor 1995—97, editor newsletter 1995—97). Avocations: music, baking. Home: 6807 Normandy Dr Mount Laurel NJ 08054 Office Phone: 856-767-8000 ext. 3058. E-mail: k.giampetro@worldnet.att.net.

GIAMPIETRO, NICHOLAS L., lawyer; b. 1962; BBA, Univ. Notre Dame; JD, Northwestern Univ., 1987. Bar: Ill. 1987. Sr. v.p., gen. counsel, sec. Reyes Holdings LLC. Office: Reyes Holdings LLC Ste 700 9500 W Bryn Mawr Ave Des Plaines IL 60018

GIAMPIETRO, WAYNE BRUCE, lawyer; b. Chgo., Jan. 20, 1942; s. Joseph Anthony and Jeannette Marie (Zeller) G.; m. Mary E. Fordeck, June 15, 1963; children: Joseph, Anthony, Marcus. BA, Purdue U., 1963; JD, Northwestern U., 1966. Bar: Ill. 1966, U.S. Dist. Ct. (no. dist.) Ill. 1966, U.S. Ct. Appeals (7th cir.) 1967, U.S. Tax Ct. 1977, U.S. Supreme Ct. 1971. Assoc. Elmer Gertz, Chgo., 1966-73; mem. firm Gertz & Giampietro, Chgo., 1974-75; pvt. practice, 1975-76; ptnr. Poltrock & Giampietro, 1976-87, Witwer, Burlage, Poltrock & Giampietro, 1987-94, Witwer, Poltrock & Giampietro, Chgo., 1995—2002, Stitt, Klein, Daday, Aretos & Giampietro LLC, Arlington Heights, Ill., 2003—. Former cons. atty. Looking Glass divsn. Traveler's Aid Soc.; gen. counsel First Amendment Lawyers Assn., 2000—. Contbr. articles to profl. jours. Pres. Chgo. 47th Ward Young Republicans, 1968; bd. dirs. Ravenswood Conservation Commn. Lutheran. Avocation: stamp collecting/philately. Office Phone: 847-590-8700. Business E-Mail: wgiampietro@skdaglaw.com.

GIANCOLA, JAMES J., bank executive; Grad., Harvard U.; postgrad., Suffolk U., Boston; student, U. Colo. Pres. Gainer Bank, Ind.; exec. v.p. CNB Bancshares, Inc., 1992, pres., COO, 1994; CEO Midwest Banc, 2004—. Cmty. work U. So. Ind., U. Evansville, Evansville Dance Theatre, United Way, Leadership Evansville. Mem. Methodist Temple. Office: Midwest Banc 501 W North Ave Melrose Park IL 60160

GIANCOTTI, FILIPPO GIUSTO, molecular biologist, educator; b. Rome, Mar. 25, 1958; MD, U. Torino, Italy, 1981, PhD, 1987. Diplomate Italian Bd. Hematology/Oncology. Intern and resident dept. hematology U. Torino Sch. Medicine, 1979—83; sr. rsch. fellow La Jolla (Calif.) Cancer Rsch. Found., 1987—91; asst. prof. Sch. Medicine, NYU, 1991—96, assoc. prof., 1996; assoc. prof. Sch. Medicine Cornell U., NYC, 1996—2000, prof. Sch. Medicine, 2000—; assoc. prof. cell biology and genetics Weill-Cornell Grad. Sch. Biomed. Scis., 1996—2000, prof., 2000—. Cons. NIH, 1994—; assoc. mem. Sloan-Kettering Inst. Meml. Sloan-Kettering Cancer Ctr., 1996—2000, mem., 2000—. Contbr. articles to profl. jours. including, Cell, European Molecular Biology Orgn. Jour., Jour. of Cell Biology. Recipient Lucille P. Markey Charitable Trust award, 1992—96, Established Investigatorship award, Am. Heart Assn., 1996—; fellow Sr. postdoctoral fellow, European Molecular Biology Orgn., 1987—89, postdoctoral, European Orgn. for Rsch. and Treatment Cancer and Nat. Cancer Inst., 1987—89, Am. Cancer Soc., 1989—90, Arthritis Found., 1990—93, Whitehead Presdl., 1992—93. Mem.: ASCB, AAAS. Achievements include patent on novel fibronectin receptor. Office: Cell Biology Program Box 216/1275 York Ave Meml Sloan-Kettering Cancer New York NY 10021 Home: #9B 170 2nd Ave New York NY 10003-5754

GIANINNO, SUSAN MCMANAMA, advertising executive; b. Boston, Dec. 25, 1948; d. John Carroll and Barbara (Frances) Magner; m. Lawrence John Gianinno, June 7, 1970; 1 child, Alexandra Christin. BA in English Lit. and Psychology cum laude, Boston Coll., 1970; MA in Ednl. Psychology, Northwestern U., 1973; postgrad. in behavioral scis., U. Chgo., 1974-78. Psychiat. asst. Quinn Psychiat., Pavilion St Elizabeth's Hosp., Brighton, Mass., 1967-70; research assoc. com. human devel., dept behavioral scis. U. Chgo., 1973-79; resident adv. U. Chgo. Housing Systems, from 1979; research assoc., then research supr. Needham, Harper and Steers Advt. Inc., Chgo., 1979-80, dir. life style rsch., from 1981; v.p., dir. creative rsch. Young & Rubicam NY, then sr. and exec. v.p., dir. rsch. svcs., 1982-86, exec. v.p., dir. mktg., 1986-90, exec. v.p., worldwide group dir., 1990-92, exec. v.p. worldwide acct. mng. dir., 1992-94; exec. v.p., sr. dir. BBDO, NYC, 1994; chief branding officer D'Arcy; chairwoman, CEO Publicis USA, 2003—. Bd. dirs. United Way of NYC. Contbr. papers, reports to profl. jours. Trustee Boston Coll., 1991—. Univ. scholar U. Chgo., 1975-77 Office: Publicis USA 4 Herald Sq 950 Sixth Ave New York NY 10001 Office Phone: 212-279-5550. Office Fax: 212-279-5560.*

GIANITSOS, ANESTIS NICHOLAS, surgeon; b. Chios, Greece, Aug. 31, 1961; came to U.S., 1966; s. Dimitrios and Soultani (Zannikos) G.; m. Laurie S. Hallmark, children: Alexia Soultani, Dimitri Jacob. BA summa cum laude, Boston U., 1983, MD, 1987. Physician U. Wis. Hosp., Madison, 1987—92; pres. Tricorp Informational Svcs., Williams Bay, Wis., 1989—93; staff urologist Riverview Clinic, Janesville, Wis., 1992—98; pres. Geneva Mktg. Sys., Lake Geneva, Wis., 1996—; med. dir. Men's Health Ctr. Mercy Health Sys., So. Wis., No. Ill., 1998—; staff urologist Mercy Regional Urology Ctr., Janesville, 1998—, Mercy Walworth Hosp. and Med. Ctr., 1998—, Harvard Meml. Hosp., Ill., 2003—. Cons. Rural Wis. Hosp. Coop., Sauk City, 1989-93; staff urology Mercy Health Sys., Janesville, 1998—; med. dir. So. Wis. chpt. US TOO, 1993—. Mem. editl. bd. Men's Total Health Digest, 2001—; contbr. articles to profl. jours. Commonwealth scholar, Augustus Howe Buck scholar. Fellow Internat. Coll. Surgeons; mem. Am. Assn. Clin. Urologists, Am. Urologic Assn., Wis. Med. Soc., Pelvic Health Consortium, Inc. Republican. Greek Orthodox. Avocations: photography, travel, baseball, investing, rare wine. Home: 1237 Geneva National Ave W Lake Geneva WI 53147-5009 Office: Mercy Men's Health Ctr 1000 Mineral Point Ave Janesville WI 53545-2940 Home Phone: 262-245-1475; Office Phone: 800-662-6990. Personal E-mail: ngianitsos@wi.rr.com. Business E-Mail: ngianitsos@mhsjvl.org.

GIANLORENZI, NONA ELENA, art dealer, painter; b. Virginia, Minn., July 20, 1939; d. Teto Nicholas and Lena Dora (Zini) Gianlorenzi; m. George Michael Devlin, July 20, 1966 (dec. Feb. 1990); children: Gian Loren Kjellesvig Waering, Helena Nicole Devlin Seidel. BA, Bklyn. Coll./CUNY. Painter self employed, NYC, 1960—; asst. dir. Am. Art Gallery, NYC, 1961-67; owner, dir. Asage Art Gallery, NYC, 1977-88; pvt. art dealer Art Space Inc., Bklyn., 1989—. Tchr. art and aesthetics St. Francis Sch. Deaf, Bklyn., 1968-71, Mt. Carmel, Queens, N.Y., 1968-71, Charles Borromeo Sch., Bklyn., 1968-71. Ford fellow, 1992-94, Loy fellow, 1992-94; Art Studio scholar, 1961. Address: 415 Rugby Rd Brooklyn NY 11226-5611

GIANNAROS, DEMETRIOS SPIROS, economist, educator, state representative; b. Karlovasi, Samos, Greece, Oct. 4, 1949; came to U.S., 1964; s. Spiridon Demetrios and Irene (Kiriakou) G.; m. Elizabeth Sampson, June 5, 1977; children: Edward, Spiros Jason. BA in Econs., U. Mass., 1972; MA in Econ. Devel., Boston U., 1976, MAPE in Polit. Econ., 1977, PhD in Econs., 1981. Mgr. Samos Imex Corp., Boston, 1974—77; asst. prof. econs. Suffolk U., Boston, 1977—79; prof. U. Hartford, West Hartford, Conn., 1980—, dir. internat. programs, 1993—94, dir. exec. MPA program, 1986—88, assoc. to sr. v.p., dir. internat. studies, 1988—91; mem. Bd. Edn., Farmington, Conn., 1993—95; dir. U.S. Consortium for Mgmt. Edn. in Ctrl. and Ea. Europe, 1993—98; state rep. Conn. Legislature, 1995—, dep. majority leader, 2005—; vice chmn. fin. com. Conn. Gen. Assembly, 1995—98. Mem. Conn. Internat. Trade Coun., 1995-96; spl. asst. to pres. George Washington U., Washington, 1988-89; cons. to pub. and pvt. orgns., 1977—; bd. advisors Fatshoe.com, 2000-02; vice chmn. fin. com. Conn. Gen. Assembly, 1995-98, state rep., mem. fin. revenue and bonding coms., 1995—, chmn. energy and tech. com., 1999-2002, chmn. edn. com., 2003-05, commr. children's higher edn. and employment advancement com., 2002—. Bd. dirs. Coll. Southea. Europe, 1992-97, Nat. Dem. Ethnic Leadership Coun., 2005—, Conn. Invention Conv., 2005—; mem. Conn. Commn. on Children, 2003-05. NSF grantee, 1983-84, U. Hartford Coffin grantee, 1983-8, Mellon Found. grantee, 1991-92; Am. Coun. on Edn. fellow, 1988-89. Fellow Am. Coun. on Edn. (mem. exec. bd. coun.); mem. Am. Hellenic Ednl. and Progressive Assn., Am. Econ. Assn., Internat. Econ. Assn., N.E. Bus. and Econs. Assn. (pres. 1990-92, bd. dirs. 1989-95), Exchange Club, Helicon Soc. (pres., bd. dirs. 1975-78), Hellenic Soc. Paideia, World Affairs Coun., World Hellenic Interparliamentary Union (alt. pres. 1998-2002, pres. 2002—). Greek Orthodox. Avocations: travel, water sports, museums, political activities, nature. Home: 56 Basswood Rd Farmington CT 06032-1142 Office: U Hartford Econs Dept 200 Bloomfield Ave Hartford CT 06117-1545 Home Phone: 860-676-2850.

GIANNELLA, ANDREW R., lawyer; b. Apr. 1, 1970; BA, Colgate U., 1992; JD, U. Cin. Coll. Law, 1996. Bar: Ohio 1996, Ky. 2003. Of counsel Strauss & Troy, Cin. Named one of Ohio's Rising Stars, Super Lawyers, 2006; named to Best Lawyers in Am., Real Estate Law, 2006. Office: Strauss & Troy Fed Res Bldg 150 E Fourth St Cincinnati OH 45202-4018 Office Phone: 513-621-2120. Office Fax: 513-241-8259.

GIANNETTI, LOUIS DANIEL, film critic, educator; b. Natick, Mass., Apr. 1, 1937; s. John and Vincenza (Zappitelli) G.; m. Justine Ann Gallagher, Sept. 7, 1963 (div. 1980); children: Christina, Francesca. BA, Boston U., 1959; MA, U. Iowa, 1961, PhD, 1967. Asst. prof. English Emory U., Atlanta, 1966-70; prof. English and film Case Western Res. U., Cleve., 1970—2001, prof. emeritus English and film, 2002—. Author: Understanding Movies, 1972, rev. 11th edit., 2007, Godard and Others, 1975, Masters of the American Cinema, 1981, (with S. Eyman) Flashback, 1986, 5th rev. edit., 2005. Democrat. Office: Case Western Res U Dept English Euclid Ave Cleveland OH 44106-2706 E-mail: louisgiannetti@aol.com.

GIANNETTI, STEPHEN P., publishing executive; BA, Dickinson Coll., Carlisle, Pa. Ea. regional mgr. Reader's Digest; advt. dir. Prevention, 1993—96, assoc. pub., 1996—98, publisher Emmaus, Pa., 1998—2000; v.p., pub. Nat. Geog. Mag., NYC, 2000—; group pub. Nat. Geog. Mags., 2002—. Advisory bd. position Make-A-Wish Found. New York. Mem.: Am. Advt. Fedn., Consumer Healthcare Products Assn. Office: National Geographic 711 Fifth Ave New York NY 10022

GIANNETTI, THOMAS LEONARD, lawyer; b. Stamford, Conn., June 7, 1947; s. Thomas and Lucille Giannetti; m. Charlene Canape, Jan. 12, 1974; children: Joseph, Theresa. BS, Yale U., 1968; MSEE, Carnegie-Mellon U., 1970; JD, George Washington U., 1976. Bar: NY 1977, US Dist. Ct. (so. and ea. dists. NY) 1978, US Ct. Appeals (fed. cir.) 1984, US Dist. Ct. (no. dist.) Calif. 1993, US Supreme Ct. 1996, US Patent and Trademark Office 1975. Engr. Westinghouse Electric Corp., Pitts. and Phila., 1968-73; assoc. Fish & Neave, NYC, 1976-86, ptnr., 1986—2001, Jones Day, NYC, 2001—. Mem. ABA, Am. Intellectual Property Law Assn. NY Intellectual Property Law Assn., Assn. of Bar of City of NY, Fed. Cir. Bar Assn., Yale Club (NYC). Home: 1158 5th Ave New York NY 10029-6917 Office: Jones Day 222 E 41st St New York NY 10017-6702 Office Phone: 212-326-3917. Office Fax: 212-755-7306. Business E-Mail: tlgiannetti@jonesday.com.

GIANNINI, A. JAMES, psychiatrist, educator, researcher, author; b. Youngstown, Ohio, June 11, 1947; s. Matthew and Grace Carla (Nistri) G.; children: Juliette Nicole, Jocelyn Danielle. BS, Youngstown State U., Ohio, 1970; MD, U. Pitts., 1974; postgrad., Yale U., 1974-78, U. London, 1996-97. Diplomate Nat. Bd. Med. Examiners. Intern St. Elizabeth Med. Ctr., Youngstown, 1974, assoc. dir. family medicine, psychiatry, 1978-80; resident in psychiatry Yale U., New Haven, 1975-78, chief resident, 1977-78; assoc. psychiatrist Elmcrest Psychiat. Inst., Portland, Conn., 1976-78; acting ward chief Conn. Mental Health Ctr., New Haven, 1977; assoc. dir. family medicine, psychiatry St. Elizabeth Med. Ctr., Youngstown, 1978-80; from asst. prof. to assoc. prof. dept. psychiatry N.E. Ohio Med. Coll., 1978-84, program dir., 1980-88, prof., 1984-90, vice-chmn., 1985-89; assoc. clin. prof. dept psychiatry Ohio State U., 1983-89, clin. prof., 1989-96; chmn. depts. psychiatry and toxicology Western Res. Care System Hosp., 1985-87, med. dir. toxicology, 1987; acting dir. dual diagnosis unit Youngstown Osteo. Hosp., 1987—2000; pres., corp. med. dir. Chem. Abuse Ctrs., Inc., Ohio and Mich., 1987—2004; med. dir. substance abuse svcs. Cmty. Mental Health Ctr. of Mid. Ga., Dublin, 2004—; lt. col. M.C., U.S. Army, 2004—05. Dir. alumni schs. com. Yale U., New Haven, 1997-2005; vis. prof. Inst. for Scis. Comm. and Sci. Edn., Columbia Coll., Chgo., U. Naples, Italy, 1990, U. Zagreb, Croatia, 1990; examiner in psychology LaTrobe U., Bundoora, Australia, 1988-89; sr. mentor U. Pitts., 2001—05, U. Pitts. Alumni Recruitment Team, 2005-; sr. cons. Fair Oaks Hosp., Summit, N.J., 1979, Regent Hosp., N.Y.C., 1981-96, chmn. Nat. Adv. Council Prevention and Control of Rape, NIMH, Rockville, Md., 1983-86, spl. reviewer mood disorders com., 1995-97; mem. drug abuse clin., behavioral and rsch. rev. com. Nat. Inst. Drug Abuse, Rockville, Md., 1987-88; chief forensic psychiatrist Mahoning County Prosecutor, 1989-97; Am. Participant USIA Drug Abuse program to Cyprus, Italy, Can., Barbados, St. Lucia and Yugoslavia, 1990-94; panelist, moderator Renaissance Weekend, Hilton Head and Charleston, S.C., 1997—; cons. Smith-Kline Labs., McNeil Labs., Excerpta Medica Pubs., Amino Labs., Fund for Am. Renaissance; dir. clin. rsch. Princeton Diagnostic Labs., South Plainfield, N.J., 1987-89; med. dir. med. adv. bd. Neurodata Inc., 1987-89, pres., 1989-2004, med. dir. Chem. Abuse Ctrs. Inc., 1987, corp. med. dir., 1987-97; spl. reviewer initial review group, 1995-97, health, behavior and prevention review com. NIH, Rockville, Md.; ethics com. Mahoning County Mental Retardation Bd., Youngstown, Ohio, 1995-98, treas. 1996-97, vice-chmn., bd. treas., 1997-98; psychiatrist emeritus Stony Lodge Hosp., Briar Cliff Manor, NY; book reviewer Psychiat. Times, 2000—. Author: (with Henry Black) Psychiatric, Psychogenic, Somatopsychic Disorders, 1978; (with Robert Gilliland) Neurologic and Neuropsychiatric Disorders, 1983; (with Andrew Slaby) Overdose and Detoxification Emergencies, 1983; Biological Foundation of Clinical Psychiatry, 1988, (with Andrew Slaby) Drugs of Abuse, 1989, 2d edit., 1996, Comprehensive Laboratory Services in Psychiatry, 1986; (with Philip Jose Farmer) Red Orc's Rage, 1991; (with Andrew Slaby) The Eating Disorders, 1993, 2d edit., 1997, Drugs of Abuse, 2d edit., 1998, Drug Abuse: A Family Guide to Recognition and Treatment, 1999; contbr. numerous articles to profl. jours. Vice chmn. Mahoning County (Ohio) Mental Health Bd., 1982-84, chmn., 1984-86; councilor Nat. Italian Am. Found. Named Ky. Col., 2007; recipient Physician's Recognition award, 1978—, rsch. award Fair Oaks Hosp., 1979, bronze award Brit. Med. Assn., 1983, Outstanding Leadership award Mahoning County Mental Health Bd., 1986, Silver Rose award Assn. Italiano Donati d'Organo, Milan, 1990, Excellence award Yale U. Admissions Com., 2002, Rschr. of Yr. award Western Res. Behavioral Medicine Inst., 2006. Fellow: APA (disting. 2003—), Am. Coll. Clin. Pharmacology (sec.-treas. Ohio chpt. 1990—97, nat. govt. affairs com. 1990—2003, steering coun., exec. com. Ohio chpt. 1990—, pres. 1997—2004, nat. edn. com. 2003—04), Acad. Medicine, Royal Acad. Medicine (Eng.), N.J. Acad. Medicine; mem.: Royal Soc. Medicine (sub-dean 2005—), Ga. Psychiat. Assn., Acad. Clin. Psychiatry, N.Y. Acad. Scis., Royal Coll. Medicine, European Neurosci., Brit. Brain Soc., Soc. Neurosci., Am. Psychiat. Assn. (fellow 1989—2003, disting. fellow 2003—), Dublin C. of C., Youngstown C. of C. (vice-chmn. health com. 1986—89, chmn. 1989—96), Athletic Club (Atlanta), Domus (London), Youngstown Club, Yale Club (Cleve., Pitts., Atlanta), Atrium Club (Warren, Ohio), Morey's (New Haven), Dublin Country Club, Swim and Racquet Club (Poland, Ohio), Cercola di Corso (Florence, Italy), Sigma Xi. Republican. Roman Catholic. Office: 463 Deer Creek Trail Dublin GA 31021-3248 Office Phone: 478-272-1190.

GIANNINI, ANTOINETTE FRANCES, music educator, researcher; b. Worcester, Mass., Sept. 9, 1923; d. Domenic Giannini and Mary Margaret Amato-Giannini. MusB, Boston U., 1945, MA, 1948; postgrad., Juilliard Sch., NYC, Columbia U. Dir. music pub. schs., Spencer, Mass., 1948—51; tchr. Worcester Pub. H.S., 1958—91, instr. music history, 1962—91; ret., 1991. Concert pianist, New Eng., 1932—41, on tour, 1941—48, NYC, 1948—88. Mem.: Nat. Guild Piano Tchrs. (adjudicator 1965—94), Mu Phi Epsilon. Independent. Roman Catholic. Home: 196 Pakachoag St Auburn MA 01501

GIANNINI, FRIDA, apparel designer; b. Rome, 1972; Studied Fashion Design, Rome's Fashion Acad. Designer, ready to wear Fendi, 1997—98, designer, leathergoods, 1998—2002; design dir., handbags Gucci, 2002—04, creative dir., accessories, 2004—, creative dir., ready to wear women, 2005—06, creative dir., 2006—. Named one of 50 Women to Watch, Wall St. Jour., 2006. Avocations: horseback riding, collecting original vinyl records. Office: Gucci via Don Lorenzo Perosi 6 Casellina di Scandicci 50018 Florence Italy*

GIANNINI, GIANCARLO, actor, director, screenwriter; b. La Spezia, Italy, Aug. 1, 1942; m. Livia Giampalmo, 1967 (div. 1975); children: Lorenzo, Adriano. Student, Rome Acad. Drama, 1963. Ptnr. Liberty Films; translator Am. films. Actor: (theatre) A Midsummer Night's Dream, 1961, Romeo and Juliet, 1964, Two Plus Two No Longer Make Four, 1966; (films) Fango sulla metropoli, 1964, Rita the Mosquito, 1966, Don't Sting the Mosquito, 1967, Anzio, 1968, I'll Try Tonight, 1968, Arabella, 1969, Fraulein Doktor, 1969, Midnight Pleasures, 1975, The Innocent, 1979, Blood Feud, 1979, I Picari, 1987, New York Stories, 1989, The Fun of a Private Life, 1990, A Time to Kill, 1991, The Obscure Malady, 1992, Falcone, 1993, A Walk in the Clouds, 1995, Blood of a Poet, 1995, Like Two Crocodiles, 1995, The She-Wolf, 1995, Palermo Milan One Way, 1995, The Whole Shebang, 2000, Welcome Albania, 2000, Hannibal, 2001, Viper, 2001, CQ, 2001, The Whole Shebang, 2001, The Council of Egypt, 2002, Joshua, 2002, The Dark, 2002, The Heart is Elsewhere, 2003, The Water, 2003, Forever, 2003, Man on Fire, 2004, The Shadow Dancer, 2005, Casino Royale, 2006, numerous others; actor, prodr.: Seven Beauties, 1975 (Best actor Acad. award nomination 1976), Good News, 1979; actor, writer (with Lin Jannuzzi), dir.: Ternosecco, 1987; TV movies: Dune, 2000. Mem. Screen Actors Guild. Office: Julien and Assocs 1501 Broadway Ste 2600 New York NY 10036-5601

GIANNINI, VALERIO LOUIS, investment banker; b. NYC, Feb. 7, 1938; s. Gabriel M. and Luisa M. (Casazza) G.; m. Linda Martin, Oct. 6, 1979; children: Martin Louis, Alexander Elliot, Charles Gabriel. BSE, Princeton U., 1959. With Kidder Peabody & Co., NYC, 1961-64; sr. cons. IIT Rsch. Inst., Chgo., 1964-66; sec. Giannini-Voltex, LA, 1966-68; pres. V.L. Giannini & Co., LA, 1968-76; CEO Namco Chems., Inc., 1975; dir. White House ops., Washington, 1977-78; dep. spl. asst. to Pres. for adminstrn. White House, 1979-80; dep. asst. sec. Dept. Commerce, Washington, 1980-81; prin. Cumberland Investment Group, NYC, 1981-87; pres. Numex Corp., 1986-87; CEO, Geneva Bus. Network, Inc., Irvine, Calif., 1987-90. Adj. prof. Argyros Sch. Bus., Chapman U., 2001; founder Eurosearch Ptnr., Newport Beach, Calif., 1990; prin. Newcap Ptnr., 1995; bd. dir. Dudek & Assoc., Pro-Dex, Inc., Lynx Ednl. Found. Pres. Lido Jr.

Sailing Found., 2000-03. Lt. USNR, 1959-61 Mem. N.Y. Yacht Club, Newport Harbor Yacht Club. Office: 1122 Bristol St Costa Mesa CA 92626 Office Phone: 714-241-8686. Business E-Mail: vgiannini@att.net.

GIANNOPOULOS, ATHINA, physician, surgeon; b. Xanthi, Greece, May 12, 1962; arrived in US, 1990; d. Alexandros and Pipina (Papanikas) Giannopoulou; m. Nick Kanopoulos, Feb. 28, 1992; 1 child, Tasos Kanopoulos. MD with honors, U. Thessaloniki, Greece, 1987. Diplomate Am. Bd. Plastic and Reconstructive Surgery. Resident in gen. surgery Theagenio Med. Ctr., Thessaloniki, 1987-90; rsch. fellow Duke U. Hosp., Durham, N.C., 1991-92; resident in gen. surgery U. N.C. Hosps., Chapel Hill, 1992-96, resident in plastic surgery, 1996-98; fellow aesthetic and oculoplastic surgery Paces Plastic Surgery, Atlanta, 1998-99; pvt. practice Faces Plastic Surgery, Chapel Hill, N.C., 1999—. Contbr. articles to profl. jours. Avocations: skiing, swimming, gourmet cooking, fashion design. Home: 3723 Dairy Pond Pl Durham NC 27705 Office: 1515 W NC Hwy 54 Ste 130 Durham NC 27707 Office Phone: 919-419-8319. Personal E-mail: facesps@aol.com.

GIANNOULIAS, ALEXI, state official; b. 1976; BA, Boston Univ.; JD, Tulane Univ. V.p., sr. loan officer Broadway Bank, Chgo.; state treas. Ill., 2007—. Bd. dir. South Side/Wabash YMCA, Edgewater C. of C. Office: State Treas 219 Statehouse Capitol Bldg Springfield IL 62706 Office Phone: 217-782-2211. Office Fax: 217-785-2777.*

GIANNULLI, MOSSIMO, designer, apparel business executive; b. June 4, 1963; s. Gene and Nancy; m. Chris Clausen, 1988 (div. 1995); 1 child, Gianni; m. Lori Loughlin, 1997; children: Isabella Rose, Olivia Jade. Student, Orange Coast Cmty. Coll., U. So. Calif. Founder Mossimo Inc., Irvine, Calif., 1987, chmn. bd., 1988—, pres., 1988—98, 2000—02, CEO, 1995—96, 2000—; designer, exclusive clothing line Target, 2000—. Appeared in (music video) Janet Jackson's "You Want This?", 1994. Recipient Orange County Entrepreneur of Yr. award, 1992, Fashion Performance award, 1996. Office: Mossimo Inc 2016 Broadway Blvd Santa Monica CA 90404

GIANOPOULOS, JOHN GEORGE, obstetrician; b. 1952; MD, Loyola U., Stritch Sch. Medicine, Maywood, Ill., 1977. Cert. Am. Bd. Obstetrics and Gynecology, 1984, in Maternal and Fetal Medicine 1985. Resident, ob-gyn. Loyola U. Med. Ctr., Maywood, Ill., 1977—81, fellow, maternal fetal medicine, 1981—83; Mary Isabelle Caestecker prof., chmn. dept., ob-gyn. Loyola U., Stritch Sch. Medicine, Maywood, Ill., 1997—. Office: Loyola Univ Sch Medicine 2160 First Ave Maywood IL 60153 Business E-Mail: jgianop@lumc.edu.

GIANOPULOS, JIM, film company executive; b. Bklyn. m. Anne Gianopulos. JD, Fordham U. Bus. affairs RCA/Columbia Pictures Internat. Video, RCA Selectavision; sr. v.p. bus. affairs and internat. video divsn. Paramount Pictures, 1988—91; exec. v.p. internat. Carolco Pictures, 1991—92; pres. Twentieth Internat. TV, 1992—94, Twentieth Century Fox Internat. and Pay TV, 1994—2000; co-chmn., CEO Fox Filmed Enterainment, LA, 2000—. Named one of 50 Most Powerful People in Hollywood, Premiere mag., 2004—06. Office: Fox Filmed Entertainment 10201 W Pico Blvd Los Angeles CA 90035 Office Phone: 310-277-2211. Office Fax: 310-203-1558.

GIANOS, DIANE E., lawyer; BS, DePaul U., 1984; JD, Chgo.-Kent Coll. Law, 1989. Bar: Ill. 1989, US Dist. Ct. (no. and ctrl. dists. Ill.), US Ct. Appeals (5th & 6th cirs.) 1990. Ptnr., mem. labor & employment practice Foley & Lardner, Chgo. Office: Foley & Lardner Suite 2800 321 N Clark St Chicago IL 60610 Office Phone: 312-832-5158. Office Fax: 312-832-4700. E-mail: dgianos@foley.com.*

GIANOULAKIS, JOHN LOUIS, lawyer; b. St. Louis, Nov. 22, 1938; s. Louis John and Marie (Pappas) G.; m. Louise Marotta, Jan. 1961 (dec. 1970); children: Christopher Louis, Kia Louise, Candlin Hamilton Dobbs; m. Dora Rodliff Deady, Sept. 2, 1972. AB, Wash. U., 1960; JD, Harvard U., 1963. Bar: Mo. 1963, U.S. Dist. Ct. (ea. dist.) Mo. 1963, U.S. Ct. Appeals (8th cir.) 1974, U.S. Supreme Ct. 1975, U.S. Ct. Appeals (7th cir.) 1982, U.S. Ct. Appeals (6th cir.) 1987. From assoc. to ptnr. Thompson, Walther & Shewmaker, St. Louis, 1963-70; ptnr. Kohn, Shands & Gianoulakis, St. Louis, 1971-73, Kohn, Shands, Elbert, Gianoulakis & Giljum, LLP, St. Louis, 1973—. Pres. bd. dirs. Legal Svcs. of Ea. Mo., Inc., St. Louis, 1972-81; bar com. 22d Jud. Cir., St. Louis, 1977-85 V.p., pres. University City (Mo.) Sch. Bd., 1970-76; vice-chair Washington U. Alumni Bd. Govs., 2000-01, exec. vice-chair, 2001-2002, chair 2002-03. bd. trustees Washington U., 2001-03. Recipient Arts and Scis. Disting. Alumnus award Washington U., 2000, Founders Day Disting. Alumnus award Washington U., 2005; named Best Lawyer in Am., 2005, 06, Legal Malpractice Def. Chambers USA, 2005 Fellow: Am. Coll. Trial Lawyers; mem.: ABA, Bar Assn. Met. St. Louis, Mo. Bar Assn., Spanish Lake Cmty. Assn. (dir. 1999—), Mo. Bluffs Assn. (pres. 1999—2001), Noon Day Club, Norwood Hills Country Club. Democrat. Home: 44 Clearview Park Saint Louis MO 63138-3302 Office: Kohn Shands Elbert Gianoulakis & Giljum LLP One US Bank Plz 24th Fl Saint Louis MO 63101 Office Phone: 314-241-3963. Business E-Mail: jgianoulakis@ksegg.com.

GIANTURCO, DELIO EMANUELE, management consultant, educator, author; b. Washington, Sept. 28, 1940; s. Elio and Valentine (McGillycuddy) G.; m. Mary Elizabeth Jordan, Jan. 31, 1961; children: Lisa, Grace, Mark. BS in Fgn. Trade, Georgetown U., Washington, DC, 1963; MA, George Wash. U., Washington, DC, 1967. Staff asst. to Robert J. Corbett of Pa. US Ho. of Reps., Washington, 1960-62, legis. asst. to Robert L.F. Sikes of Fla., 1962-63; sr. v.p. guarantees, ins. and exporter credits, treas. , comptroller, exec. v.p., vice chmn., 1st v.p., dir. Export-Import Bank, Washington, 1963-77; pres. First Washington Assocs., 1978—2005. Dir. Fgn. Credit Ins. Assn., N.Y.C., 1971-76; adj. prof. George Mason U., 1995—.

GIARDINA, ELSA GRACE VONNA, cardiologist, educator; b. Newark, Aug. 1, 1941; d. John and Elsa (Freda) G.; m. Alan L. Saroff, June 1, 1974; 1 child, John Saroff. AB, Bryn Mawr Coll., 1961; MD, NY Med. Coll., 1965. Diplomate Am. Bd. Internal Medicine, Am. Bd. Cardiology; cert. internal medicine, cardiovascular disease. Resident Roosevelt Hosp., NYC, 1965-69; cardiology resident Columbia Presbyn. Med. Ctr., NYC, 1969-71, NIH cardiovascular pharmology fellow, 1971-72; asst. prof. medicine Columbia U., NYC, 1972-79, assoc. prof. medicne, 1980-87, prof. medicine, 1987—. Mem. cardiorenal adv. com. Food & Drug Adminstrn., Rockville, Md., 1984-88; mem. pharmacology study sect. NIH, Bethesda, Md., 1989-93; dir. Ctr. for Women's Health, Columbia-Presbyn. Med. Ctr., N.Y.C., 1994—. Contbr. articles to profl. jours. Sec., bd. dirs. Sarnoff Rsch. Found., 2004—; bd. dirs. Sarnoff Endowment for Cardiovascular Sci., 2000—. Fellow: ACP, Heart Rhythm Soc., Am. Heart Assn., Am. Coll. Cardiology. Office: Columbia U 630 W 168th St New York NY 10032-3795 Office Phone: 212-305-6154. Business E-Mail: evg1@columbia.edu.

GIBALA, RONALD, metallurgical engineering educator; b. New Castle, Pa., Oct. 3, 1938; s. Steve Anthony and June Rose (Frank) G.; m. Janice Claire Grichor; children: Maryellen, Janice, David, Kristine. BS, Carnegie Inst. Tech., 1960; MS, U. Ill., 1962, PhD, 1964. Engring. technician Crane Co., New Castle, Pa., 1956-59; engr. U.S. Steel Rsch. Labs., Monroeville, Pa., 1960; rsch. asst. U. Ill., Urbana, 1960-64; asst. prof. metallurgy Case Western Res. U., Cleve., 1964-69, assoc. prof., 1969-76, prof. metallurgy and materials sci. and macromolecular sci., 1976-84, co-dir. materials rsch. lab., 1981-84; dir. metallurgy program NSF, 1982-83; prof., chmn. dept. materials sci. and engring. U. Mich., Ann Arbor, 1984-94, L.H. and F.E. Van Vlack prof. materials sci. and engring., 1998—2004, L.H. and F.E. Van Vlack prof. emeritus, 2004—, interim dean Coll. Engring., 2005—06. Dir. electron microbeam analysis lab. U. Mich., Ann Arbor, 2002—04. Contbr. articles to profl. jours.; editor: Hydrogen Embrittlement and Stress Corrosion Cracking, 1984. Pres. Woodhaven Hills Homeowners Assn., 1989—91. Recipient Alfred Noble prize ASCE, 1969, NASA Materials Sci. Divsn. Paper award, 1992; Tech. Achievement award Cleve. Tech. Socs. Council, 1972; vis. research fellow C.E.N.G. Labs., Grenoble, 1973-74; Matthias fellow Los Alamos Nat. Lab., 1991-92, Disting. Merit award U. Ill., 1998; vis. scientist Sandia Nat. Labs., 1998-99. Fellow: TMS (bd. dirs. 1981—87), Am. Soc. Metals Internat. (life; chpt. chmn. 1975—76, Outstanding Young Mem. Cleve. chpt. 1971); mem.: AAAS, Materials Rsch. Soc. (councillor 1995—97, v.p. 1998, pres. 1999, exec. com. 1995—97), Suburban Ski (pres. 1981—82), Alpha Sigma Mu, Tau Beta Pi, Sigma Xi. Democrat. Home: 1543 Stonehaven St Ann Arbor MI 48104-4149 Office: U Mich Dept Materials Sci Engring Ann Arbor MI 48109-2136 Office Phone: 734-936-0178. Business E-Mail: rgibala@umich.edu.

GIBANS, JAMES DAVID, architect, consultant; b. Akron, Ohio, Feb. 10, 1930; s. Myer Jacob and Sylva (Hirsch) G.; m. Nina Freedlander, July 16, 1955; children: David Myer, Jonathan Samuel, Amy, Elisabeth. BA, Yale U., 1951, BArch, MArch, Yale U., 1954. Architect George K. Raad & Assocs. et al, San Francisco, 1958-63; project architect Ward and Schneider, Cleve., 1964-68; sr. assoc. William A. Gould and Assocs., Cleve., 1968-74, Don M. Hisaka and Assoc., Cleve., 1974-76; pvt. practice architecture Cleve., 1976-81; v.p. Teare Herman & Gibans, Inc., Cleve., 1981-89; v.p., treas. Herman Galvin Gibans, Inc., Cleve., 1989-91, HGG, Inc., Cleve., 1991-94, Herman Gibans Fodor, Inc., 1994—2000, v.p., 1994—2006; consulting arch., 2007—. Faculty Edn. for Aesthetic Awareness Cleve. State U., 1977—79. Mem. Cleve. Landmarks Commn., 1993—2006, chmn., 2004—06; trustee, mem. exec. com., 1st v.p. Cleve. Chamber Music Soc., 1970—78; mem. adv. bd. Environ. Resource Ctr. Cleve. Pub. Libr., 1973—76; mem. design rev. com. Shaker Sq. Hist. Dist., 1991—93; bd. dir. Cleve. Soc. Contemporary Art, 1985—86, Friends of Shaker Sq., 1994—96, Shaker Sq. Area Devel. Corp., 1996—, v.p., 1996—97, treas., 1997—2001, pres., 2001—03; trustee Cleve. Found. for Arch., 1999—2003, chair focus com., 1999—2001, pres., 2001—03; bd. dir. Bulldogs on the Cuyahoga, 2002—, treas., 2006—. With US Army, 1955—57. Fulbright grantee, 1954-55. Fellow AIA (sec. Cleve. chpt. 1972-74, bd. dirs. 1984-86, treas. 1989, v.p. 1990, pres. 1991); mem. Architects Soc. Ohio (trustee 1975-76, bd. dirs. 1985-88), Cleve. City Club, Fulbright Assn. (bd. dirs. N.E. Ohio chpt. 1995-99, treas. 1998-99), N.E. Ohio Jazz Soc. (bd. dirs. 1991-96, v.p. 1993-95, pres. 1995-96), Rowfant Club (chair bldgs. and furnishings com. 2002—, coun. of fellows, 2005—). Democrat. Jewish. Avocations: music, art, jogging, cross country skiing. Home and Office: 13800 Shaker Blvd 1108 Cleveland OH 44120-1585

GIBB, GINARI RENE, psychiatrist; d. Delores Morse and Rogelio Edwin Gibb; m. Michael Price, July 12, 1996; children: Evan Michael Price, Norman Louis Price, Corey Thomas Price. BS, Vanderbilt U., Nashville, 1995, Clark Atlanta U., Atlanta, 1996; MD, Meharry Med. Coll., Nashville, 2003. Diplomate Fedn. Of State Med. Boards, 2003. Office asst. Gibb Ins. Agy., Atlanta, 1988—93; dormitory asst. Vanderbilt U. Residential Affairs Dept, Nashville, 1992—95; adminstrv. asst. Mike's Electronics and More, 1997—2003; rschr. dept. psychiatry Meharry Med. Coll., 2002—03; resident physician dept. psychiatry Vanderbilt U. Med. Ctr., 2003—04, Morehouse Sch. Of Medicine, Atlanta, 2004—. Del. and rep. (Meharry chpt.) Am. Med. Student Assn., Nashville, 1999—2001; profl. in residence Hazelden Nat. Assn. Of Alcoholism And Drug Abuse Counselors, Center City, Minn., 2004; residency recruiting adv. com. dept. psychiatry Morehouse Sch. Of Medicine, Atlanta, 2004—; student advisor curriculum com. Meharry Med. Coll., Nashville, 2001—03. Mem. spl. events com. Apec Learning Ctr., Atlanta, 2004—; mem. steering com. and vol. tutor St. Vincent De Paul Cath. Sch., Nashville, 2001—03. Recipient Protection of Human Rights Cert., Nat. Inst. Mental Health, 2004; scholar, Clark Meml. Scholarship Fund, 2000—01; Meharry Assn. Office Personnel scholarship, Meharry Med. Coll., 2000—01. Mem.: AMA, Nat. Inst. Mental Health, Am. Psychiat. Assn. (Psychodynamic Psychotherapy Continuing Med. Edn. Cert. 2005), Ga. Psychiat. Physicians Assn. (Annual Meeting Resident Scholarship 2005), Delta Sigma Theta (chaplain, v.p. and treas. 1994—2000, Vol. of Yr. 1994—95). Achievements include research in forensic investigation and clinical consequences of violence and murder within families. Avocations: catering special events, gardening, roller skating, tutoring at local schools, national public radio.

GIBB, ROBERTA LOUISE, lawyer, artist; b. Cambridge, Mass., Nov. 2, 1942; d. Thomas Robinson Pieri and Jean Knox Gibb. BS, U. Calif., La Jolla, 1969; JD, New Eng. Sch. Law, 1982. Bar: Mass. 1978. Legal aide Mass. State Legis., 1973; practice law Mass., 1980—. Assoc. MIT, 1972—85. Author: To Boston With Love, 1980, The Art of Inflation, 1981, The Art of Economics, 1982; co-prodr.: (documentaries) Lovins on the Soft Path; Exhibited in group shows at Geraci Galleries, Rockport, Mass., 1996—2005, Rockport Art Assn. Gallery, Rockport, 1996—2005, Represented in permanent collections, Nat. Art Mus. Art, Indpls.; prodr.: (documentaries) Where the Spirit Leads, 2001—; Albert Einstein, Pres. Carter, Pres. Johnson, Pres. Reagan, Mother Theresa, Eleanor Roosevelt, The Marathon, Fire Dancers, Birth, Olympia, The Family, The Left Handed Squash Player, Basketball, Germain Gliddin, others. Bd. dir. Essex County Environ. and Conservation, Rockport, Mass., 1980-85; assoc. Mass. Gen. Hosp. Cecil B. Day Lab. Women winner Boston Marathon, 1966-68, 1st woman to run Boston Marathon, 1966; named to Road Runners of Am. Hall of Fame, 1982 Mem.: Inst. Study of Natural Sys. (founder, pres. 1976—), Rockport Art Assn., Mass. Bar, Nat. Sculpture Soc. (assoc.), Boston Athletic Assn.

GIBBES, WILLIAM HOLMAN, lawyer; b. Hartsville, SC, Feb. 25, 1930; s. Ernest Lawrence and Nancy (Watson) G.; m. Frances Hagood, May 1, 1954; children: Richard H., William H. Jr., Lynn. BS, U. S.C., Columbia, 1952, LLB, 1953. Bar: S.C. 1953, U.S. Ct. Mil. Appeals 1954, U.S. Dist. Ct. S.C. 1956, U.S. Supreme Ct. 1959, U.S. Ct. Appeals (4th cir.) 1965. Asst. atty. gen., Columbia, S.C., 1957-62; ptnr. Berry & Gibbes, Columbia, 1962-68, Berry, Lightsey, Gibbes, Columbia, 1968-72; mem. Gibbes Law Firm, P.A., Columbia, 1972—; house of dels. S.C. Bar, 1994-96, mem. exec. coun. sr. lawyers divsn., 2006. Chief judge U.S. Army Legal Svcs. Agy., 1980-83. Author: Control of Highway Access - Its Prospects and Problems, Legal Dimensions of Community Health Planning, 1969, Manual for Fee Appraisors, 1960; contbr. articles to S.C. Law Review, Law Rev. Digest, 1960. Chmn. bd. dirs. U. S.C. YMCA, 1956-60. Brig. gen. JAGC, USAR 1980-83. Recipient Legion of Merit, U.S. Army, 1983. Mem. ABA (mil. laws com. 1984-90, meml. com.), S.C. Bar Assn. (exec. com. 1961-62), Am. Bd. Trial Advocates (sec.-treas. 1994-95, pres.-elect 1995-96, pres. 1996-97), Judge Advs. Assn. (pres. 1982-83), Richland County Bar Assn., S.C. Credit Ins. Assn. (gen. counsel 1963-94), Tarantella Club, Caprician Club, Summit Club, Doonbeg (Ireland) Golf Club, Forest Lake Country Club, Kiawah Island Club, Kappa Sigma Kappa, Omicron Delta Kappa, founding mem. Doonberg Golf Club, Cnty. Clare Ireland, 2002. Episcopalian. Home: 35 Avian Tr Columbia SC 29206-4965 Personal E-mail: williamhgibbes@bellsouth.net.

GIBBON, MARY-LYNN, special education educator; b. La Jolla, Calif., Feb. 5, 1955; d. Leslie and Edith Gertrude Swaim; m. Mark Jeffrey Gibbon, Mar. 12, 1987; children: Shawna Odet Pedro, William Leslie Lower. BS, Excelsior Coll., 1995; MA in Edn., Chapman U., 1997; MA in Spl. Edn., Azusa Pacific U., 2004. Cert. mid. childhood generalist Nat. Bd. for Profl. Tchg. Standards, 2001. Substitute tchr. Dept. Def. Dependent Schs., Baumholder, Germany, 1993—94, Barstow Unified Sch. Dist., Calif., 1995—96; tchr. elem. Lenwood Sch., Barstow, 1996—97, Hinkley Sch., Barstow, 1997—2002, social studies tchr. mid. sch. spl. edn., 2002—04; tchr. sixth grade sci. and world history tchr. Barstow Intermediate Sch., 2004—. Bus. action plan com. mem. Barstow Unified Sch. Dist., Calif., 1996, report card revision adv. bd. mem., 1999—2000, schoolwide assessment rev. & revision adv. com. mem., 1999—2000, mem. sci., social studies standards adoption adv. com., 2000; tchr. participant Goldstone Apple Valley Radio Telescope, NASA, Barstow, Calif., 2002—04; mem. Excel tchr. tng. team Barstow Intermediate Sch., 2005—, provider Beginning Tchr. Support and Assessment, 2005—. Vol. Police Activities League, Barstow, Calif., 1997—2003; mem. delegation People to People, Beijing, 2005. Grantee, Barstow Rotary Club, 1996. Mem.: Delta Kappa Gamma (assoc.; chmn. spring fling fundraiser 2005—06, Continuing edn. grantee 2005), Pi Lambda Theta (hon.). Conservative. Roman Catholic. Avocations: reading, travel. Office: Barstow Unified Sch Dist 551 So Ave H Barstow CA 92311 Home Phone: 760-256-2630; Office Phone: 760-255-6304. Personal E-mail: mlg2555@cs.com.

GIBBONS, DONA ALDEN COE, electrical engineer, director; b. Springfield, Mass., Mar. 9, 1975; s. Arthur Coe and Virginia Elaine Fife Gibbons. BEE, Auburn U., 2000, B in Computer Engring., 2000, B in Software Engring., 2000; MS in Applied Computer Sci., Columbus State U., Ga., 2007. Cert. CompTIA Network profl. 03. Thinkpad product specialist, server qas analyst IBM Personal Sys. Group, Research Triangle Park, NC, 1996—98; govt. contractor US Army-Ft. Benning, Columbus, Ga., 1999—2002; network specialist instl. support eArmyU. Troy State U.-S.E. Regions, 2002—04, sys. integration and software devel. mgr., engr., 2004—06, edn. tech. coord., engr. ecampus, 2006—. Recipient Outstanding Achievement award, IBM, 1998. Mem.: Assn. Supervison and Curriculum, IEEE, Comptia Info. Tech. Profl., Math. Assn. Am., Assn. Computing Machinery, Auburn Alumni Assn., Phi Kappa Phi. Home: 8118 Alabama Hwy 169 Salem AL 36874-2562 Personal E-mail: gibbons.dona@gmail.com. Business E-Mail: gibbonsd@troy.edu.

GIBBONS, FRANKLIN (CHIP) ARTHUR, application developer, systems analyst, writer; b. Washington, Oct. 14, 1951; s. Franklin Arthur Gibbons Jr. and Ruth Cavanagh Gibbons. BS in Biology, Va. Commonwealth U., Richmond, 1977. Computer programmer, analyst Pacific Telesis, San Francisco, 1980—87; software engr. Charles Schwab and Co., Inc., San Francisco, 1988—90; computer programmer U. Calif., San Francisco, 1992—95. Cons. Charles Schwab, San Francisco, Bank Am., San Francisco. Author: Reality: The Taboo Against Truth. Vol. Shanti (AIDS) Project, San Francisco, 1994—96. Libertarian. Avocations: motorcycling, hiking, painting. Home: PO Box 10603 Bainbridge Island WA 98110

GIBBONS, JIM (JAMES ARTHUR GIBBONS), governor, former congressman; b. Sparks, Nev., Dec. 16, 1944; s. Leonard A. and Matilda (Hancock) Gibbons; m. T. Dawn Sanders-Snelling, June 21, 1986; children: Christopher, Jennifer, James A. Jr. BS in Geology, U. Nev., Reno, 1967, MS in Mining and Geology, 1973; JD, Southwestern U. Sch. Law, LA, 1979. Bar: Nev. 1982, admitted to practice: US Dist. Ct. Nev. 1982. Hydrologist Office of Fed. Watermaster, Reno, 1963-67; mining geologist Union Carbide Co., Reno, 1971—73; comml. pilot Western Airlines, LA, 1979—87; sr. land mgr., atty. Homestake Mining Co., Reno, 1980-82; lawyer Haase, Harris & Morrison, Reno, 1982—84; atty. pvt. practice, 1984—86; pilot Delta Airlines, Salt Lake City, 1987—97; mem. Nev. State Assembly, 1989—93, US Congress from 2nd Nev. dist., 1997—2006; gov. State of Nev., Carson City, 2007—. Mem. armed svcs. com. US Congress, mem. homeland security com., mem. resources com., chmn. subcommittee energy and mineral resources. Contbr. articles to profl. publs. Bd. dirs. Nev. Coun. Econ. Edn., 1984-1987. Col. USAF, 1967—71, col. Nev. Air Nat. Guard, 1975—96, vice comdr. Nev. Air Nat. Guard, 1990—96, col. USAF Res., 1996—98. Decorated Legion of Merit, DFC, Air Medal with Two Oak Leaf Clusters, Aerial Achievement medal, Air Force Commendation Medal with One Oak Leaf Cluster. Mem. Assn. Trial Lawyers of Am., Nev. Trial Lawyers Assn., Rocky Mt. Mineral Law Found., Comml. Law League Am., Am. Inst. Mining Engrs., Nev. Landman's Assn. (chmn. 1981-82, consulting atty. 1982-83). Republican. Avocation: flying. Office: Office of Gov Capitol Bldg 101 N Carson St Carson City NV 89701*

GIBBONS, JOE, filmmaker; Lectr., Visual Arts MIT. Exhibitions include AFI Video Festival, LA, 1989, Art of the Century, Whitney Mus., 1989—91, The Talking Cure, Artist's Space, NYC, 1990—91, Consumer Tools, Mus. Modern Art, 1991, The Kitchen, NYC, 1992, Whitney Biennial, 1993, 2000, 2002, 2006, Impakt Festival, Utrecht, The Netherlands, 1994—99, Black Maria Film and Video Festival, 1995—2000, NY Video Festival, Film Soc. Lincoln Ctr., 1995—2002, Internat. Film Festival, Rotterdam, 1995—2003, Viper Festival, Zurich, 1998, NY Film Expo, 1999, Pacific Film Archive, Calif., 2000. Recipient Best Experimental Film, New Eng. Film and Video Festival, 1986, 1992, award of Excellence, 27th Sinking Creek Film/Video Festival, 1994, Second prize, Black Maria Film and Video Festival, 1996, 1998—2001, 2004, First prize, Viper Video Festival, 1996; fellow Nat. Endowment for Arts, 1986, 1990, MacDowell, 1995, Guggenheim, 2001; grantee San Francisco Artspace, 1991. Office: MIT 265 Massachusetts Ave Cambridge MA 02139*

GIBBONS, JOHN HOWARD (JACK GIBBONS), federal official, physicist; b. Harrisonburg, Va., Jan. 15, 1929; s. Howard K. and Jessie Diana (Conrad) G.; m. Mary Ann Hobart, May 21, 1955; children: Virginia Neil, Diana Conrad, Mary Marshall. BS in Math. and Chemistry, Randolph-Macon Coll., 1949, ScD (hon.), 1977; PhD in Physics, Duke U., 1954, ScD (hon.), 1997; PhD in Humane Letters and Sci. (hon.), Ill. Inst. Tech., 1994; PhD in Sci. (hon.), Mt. Sinai Med. Sch., 1995; ScD (hon.), U. Delaware, 1996, U. Md., 1997. Physicist and group leader nuclear geophysics Oak Ridge Nat. Lab., 1954-69, dir. environ. program, 1969-73; dir. Energy Conservation Office, Fed. Energy Adminstrn., Washington, 1973-74; prof. physics, dir. Energy, Environ. and Resources Center, U. Tenn., Knoxville, 1974-79; dir. Office of Tech. Assessment, U.S. Congress, 1979-92; asst. to Pres. for sci. and tech. Exec. Office of the Pres., Washington, 1993-98; dir. of sci. and tech. policy Exec. Office of Pres., Washington, 1993-98; pres. Resource Strategies, 1998—; Karl T. Compton lectr. MIT, 1998-99; sr. fellow NAE, 1999-2000; sr. advisor U.S. Dept. State, 1999-2000. Adv. com. neutron cross sects. US Atomic Energy Commn., 1969—70; adv. com. nat. ctr. analysis energy sys. Brookhaven Nat. Lab., 1976—77; chmn. demand/conservation panel Com. Nuclear & Alternative Energy Sys., 1976—79; chmn. adv. com. energy and environ. sys. divsn. Argonne Nat. Lab., 1977—79; chmn. adv. com. nat. ctr. analysis energy sys. Brookhaven Nat. Lab., 1977; adv. bd. energy R&D US Dept. Energy, 1978—79; mem. Energy Resource Adv. Bd., 1978—79; mem. bd. sci. and tech. for internat. development Com. Nuclear & Alternative Energy Sys., 1979—87; energy and resources com. Aspen Inst., 1979—; sr. adv. panel Energy Modeling Forum Stanford U., 1980—92, mem. adv. com. Sch. Engring., 1984—87; bd. dirs. Resources in the Future, 1983—92; mem. steering com. Symposium Series Tech. & Soc., 1984—92; mem. adv. com. Electric Power Rsch. Inst., 1986—92; mem. exec. com. An Energy Agenda for 1990s, 1987—88; mem. Carnegie Corp. Sci., Tech. and Govt. Task Force on Long Term Goals and Priorities, 1990—92; bd. dirs. Dynamac Corp., 1998—; mem. coun. advisors Nat. Renewable Energy Lab., 1998—; mem. steering com. Nat. Climate Assessment, 1998—2001; bd. dirs. World Resource Inst., 1998—2003, chair program com., 1999—2000; bd. dirs. Interstate Waste Techs., LLP, 1999—, Black Rock Forest Consortium, 1999—, Action LLC; chair World Bank panel on millenium sci. initiatives, 2000—01, Com. Improving Effectiveness Environ. Non-Gov. Programs, Russia, 2000; mem. internat. adv. bd. com. on internat. programs Nat. Acads., 2001—06, divsn. advisor divsn. on phys. scis. and engring., 2001—; chief acad. advisor Shenglongda Co. Ltd., 2001—06; mem. strategic adv. com. Gas Tech. Inst., 2003—06; chmn. bd. Population Action Internat., 2003—06; mem. adv. bd. MIT Innovations Tech./Governance/Globalization Jour., 2005—; mem. Idaho Nat. Lab. Sci. and Tech. Com., 2005—; adv. bd. Airlie Found., 2006—; bd. dirs. Scientists and Engrs. Am., 2006—; sr. adviser Global Environment and Tech. Found., 2006; mem. adv. bd. Ctr. Am. Progress Jour. Sci. Tech. and Human Values, 2007—; bd. dirs. Transition Energy, 2007; cons. in field. Author: (with William U. Chandler) Energy: The Conservation Revolution, 1981, This Gifted Age: Science and Technology at the Millennium, 1997; contbr. articles to profl. jours. Trustee, Randolph-Macon Coll., Ashland, Va., 1977-79, chmn., bd. assocs. 1980-83; bd. dirs. World's Fair Enegy Expo, 1978-79, 1982, State Tenn. Energy Authority, 1977-1979; adv. com. Corp. Thomas Jefferson's Poplar Forest, 1983. Decorated comdr. Ordre des Palmes Academiques (France), 1994, officer's cross Order of Merit (Germany), 1991; recipient Disting. Svc. award Fed. Energy Adminstrn., 1974, Disting. Alumni award James Madison U., 1993, Life Achievement in Sci. award Commonwealth of Va., 1995, First Seymour Cray High Performance Computing Industry Recognition award, 1997, Disting. Svc. medal NASA, 1998, Alumni Excellence award Va. Found. for Ind. Colls., 2002, Disting. Career in Sci. and Engring. award Washington Acad. Scis., 2005, First George Brown award Coop. R&D Found., 2005. Fellow: AAAS (bd. dirs. 1988—90, Philip Hauge Abelson prize 1993), Am. Assn. Engring. Socs. (chmn.'s award 1998), Am. Phys. Soc. (Leo Szilard award for physics in pub. interest 1991), Am. Acad. Arts and Scis., Assn. for Women in Sci.; mem.: Am. Philos. Soc., N.Y. Acad. Scis. (bd. govs. 1998—2002), Coun. Fgn. Rels., Nat. Acad. Engring. (chmn. steering com. 2007, Arthur Bueche award 1998), Cosmos Club, Sigma Pi Sigma, Pi Mu Epsilon, Omicron Delta Kappa, Pi Gamma Mu, Phi Beta Kappa, Sigma Xi (nat. Sigma lectr. 1978—79, pres. 2000—01, John P. McGovern Sci. and Soc. award and medal 1997). Episcopalian. Avocations: hiking, farming. Home: PO Box 379 The Plains VA 20198 Home Phone: 540-253-5409; Office Phone: 540-253-9843. Personal E-mail: jackgibbons@hughes.net. *My formal training in physics, backed by a liberal arts education, enabled me to drink deeply from the sweet spring of basic research for many years. When I took leave from disciplinary research and became immersed in analysis of socio-technical issues, it was a most discomforting step. But having taken it, the new challenges were not only enlivening, but also surprisingly susceptible to the problem-solving approaches I had learned in science. The lessons: (1)Training in physics is an effective instrument to learn how to solve many kinds of problems; (2)A change in professional direction about every decade or so is a great tonic; (3)Attacking issues from fresh perspectives is a natural ingredient of creativity.*

GIBBONS, JOHN JOSEPH, lawyer, retired federal judge; b. Newark, Dec. 8, 1924; s. Daniel Lehane and Julia (Murray) G.; m. Mary Jeanne Boyle, Apr. 19, 1952; children: Daniel J., Mary E., Nora F., Richard G., Deirdre E., Maude A., David C. BS, Holy Cross Coll., 1947, LL.D., 1970; LLB cum laude, Harvard U., 1950; LLD, Seton Hall U., 1980, Suffolk U., 1982. Bar: N.J., 1950. Ptnr. Crummy, Gibbons & O'Neill, Newark, 1953-70; cir. judge U.S. Ct. of Appeals (3d cir.), 1970-90, ret. judge; spl. counsel Crummy, Del Deo, Dolan, Griffinger & Vecchione, Newark; dir. Gibbons, Del Deo, Dolan, Griffinger & Vecchione, Newark; chief judge U.S. Ct. Appeals (3d cir.), 1987-90. Richard J. Hughes prof. Constl. law Seton Hall U., 1989-97; adj. prof. Rutgers U., Suffolk U., Duke U.; mem. N.J. Bd. Bar Examiners, Trenton, 1959-64, chmn., 1963-64; mem. Gov.'s Select. Commn. on Civil Disorders, N.J. Coun. Against Crime; mem. vis. com. Law Sch., U. Chgo. Contbr. articles in field. Trustee Practicing Law Inst., 1973—99; trustee Holy Cross Coll., 1970—96. Served to lt. (j.g.) USNR, 1943-46. Named Lawyer of the Year, N.J. Law Jour., 2004; named one of 100 Most Influential Lawyers, Nat. Law Jour., 2006; recipient Lifetime Achievement award, Am. Law mag., 2005. Fellow Am. Bar Found.; mem. ABA (ho. of dels. 1968), N.J. Bar Assn. (pres. 1967-68), Essex County Bar Assn. (trustee 1961-64), Holy Cross Coll. Gen. Alumni Assn. (trustee, v.p. 1967-70) Office: Gibbons PC One Gateway Ctr Newark NJ 07102-5310 Home Phone: 973-376-2584; Office Phone: 973-596-4733. Business E-Mail: jgibbons@gibbonslaw.com.

GIBBONS, JOSEPH HARRISON, engineering educator, farmer; b. Turbeville, SC, Sept. 4, 1934; s. James Harry and Roxie Lanie Gibbons; m. Geneva F. Gibbons, June 10, 1956; children: Karen, Lisa. BS in Chem. Engring., U. S.C., 1956; MS in Chem. Engring., U. Pitts., 1958, PhD in Chem. Engring., 1961. Registered profl. engr., S.C. Chem. engr. Du Pont, Aiken, SC, 1955, Westinghouse, Pitts., 1956—63; assoc. prof. U. S.C., Columbia, 1963—74, prof., 1974—2005, Disting. prof., 2005, chair chem. engring. dept., 1977—93, assoc. dean, 1991—2001, dean, 1999—2000. Named Engr. of Yr., S.C. Soc. Prof. Engrs., Columbia, 1993, Disting. Alumnus, U. S.C., 1999; recipient Outstanding Svc. award, U. S.C. Ednl. Found., 2002, Order of Palmetto, Gov. S.C., 2005. Fellow: AIChE; mem.: NSPE, Am. Soc. for Engring. Edn., Am. Chem. Soc., Tau Beta Pi, Phi Beta Kappa. Baptist. Avocations: fishing, woodworking, classic cars. Home: 6300 Macon Rd Columbia SC 29209 Office: U SC Columbia SC 29208-0001 Office Phone: 803-777-8978.

GIBBONS, JUDITH A., librarian; b. Phila., Nov. 9, 1951; d. John J. and Margaret G. Gibbons; m. Harold M. Staton. BA, Pa. State U., State College, 1972; MS in Libr. Sci., U. Ky., Lexington, 1978; MPA, Ky. State U., Frankfort, 1994. Cert. libr. Ky. Ref. asst. Lexington Pub. Libr., 1977—78, asst. br. mgr., 1978—80, head children's dept., 1980—84; dir. Woodford County Libr., Versailles, Ky., 1984—98; dir. field svcs. divsn. Ky. Dept. Librs. and Archives, Frankfort, 1998—. Adj. faculty Sch. Libr. and Info. Sci. U. Ky., Lexington, 1993—98; mem. State Bd. for Cert. of Librs., Frankfort, 1994—98, State Archives and Records Commn., Frankfort, 1987. Contbr. articles to profl. jours. Pres. Woodford County Lit. Coun., Versailles, 1988; grants chair Ky. Book Fair, Frankfort, 2000—; adv. bd. Audio Studio for the Reading Impaired, Louisville, 2004—; bd. dirs. Woodford County C. of C., 1998, Woodford County Cmty. Edn. Adv. Coun., Versailles, 1989—93. Named Woman of Achievement, Versailles, 1994; recipient Outstanding Pub. Libr. Svc. award, Frankfort, 2006, Bus. Equity award, Versailles, 1997. Mem.: ALA (chair pub. awareness com. 2006—), Ky. Pub. Libr. Assn. (chair 1994—95), Ky. Libr. Assn. (sec. 1997—98), Southeastern Libr. Assn. (pres. 2004—06). Avocations: reading, hiking, bicycling, gardening. Office: Kentucky Dept for Libraries and Archives PO Box 537 300 Coffee Tree Rd Frankfort KY 40602

GIBBONS, JULIA SMITH, federal judge; d. John Floyd and Julia Jackson (Abernathy) Smith; m. William Lockhart Gibbons, Aug. 11, 1973; children: Rebecca Carey, William Lockhart Jr. BA, Vanderbilt U., 1972; JD, U. Va., 1975. Bar: Tenn. 1975. Law clk. to judge US Ct. Appeals, 1975-76; assoc. Farris, Hancock, Gilman, Branan, Lanier & Hellen, Memphis, 1976-79; legal advisor Gov. Lamar Alexander, Nashville, 1979-81; judge 15th Jud. Cir., Memphis, 1981-83, US Dist. Ct. (we. dist.) Tenn., Memphis, 1983—2002, chief judge, 1994-2000; judge US Ct. Appeals (6th cir.), Memphis, 2002—. Recipient Outstanding Judge of Yr. award, Memphis Lawyers, 1985, She Knows Where She's Going award, Girls, Inc., 1992. Master: Leo Bearman, Sr. Am. Inn of Ct.; fellow: Memphis and Shelby County Bar Found., Tenn. Bar Found., Am. Bar Found.; mem.: Ctrl. Gardens Assn., Tenn. Women's Forum, Assn. for Women Attorneys (pres. 1993, Marion Griffin-Frances Loring award 1992), Fed. Judges Assn., Memphis Bar Assn. (Heroine for Women in Law award 2000, Outstanding Judge of Yr. award 2001), Memphis Rotary Club (Treasurer 1991—92, v.p. 1992—93, Paul Harris Fellow, president 1994—95), Phi Beta Kappa, Order of Coif. Presbyterian. Office: US Ct Appeals 970 Federal Bldg 167 N Main St Memphis TN 38103-1816*

GIBBONS, LEEZA, television and radio talk show host, entertainment reporter; b. Hartsville, SC, Mar. 26, 1957; m. John Hicks, 1980 (div. 1982); m. Chris Quinten, 1988 (div. 1990); 1 child, Lexi; m. Stephen Meadows, 1991; children: Troy, Nathan. Student, U. S.C. CEO Leeza Gibbons Enterprises; former co-host Entertainment Tonight, Hollywood, Calif.; co-host John and Leeza, Hollywood, 1993; host, exec. prodr. Leeza, 1994—99; host Lezza Live Westwood One, host Hollywood Confidential. Host Miss Universe Pageant, The Hollywood Christmas Parade; host, co-prodr. (series) Growing Up Together; film appearances include Robocop, 1987, Robocop 2, 1990, Soapdish, 1991, The Player, 1992, Last Action Hero, 1993; performer Dancing with the Stars, 2007. Office: c/o KBIG #800 330 N Brand Blvd Glendale CA 91203*

GIBBONS, MARK, state supreme court justice; BA, U. Calif., Irvine, 1972; JD, Loyola U., LA, 1975. Assoc. atty. Woofter & Bilbray, 1975—86; partner Bilbray & Gibbons, 1976—85, Gibbons & Berman, 1985—90, Oshins & Gibbons, 1990—95; of counsel Streich Lang, 1995—96; judge Clark County Dist. Ct., Nev., 1996—98, presiding judge civil divsn. Nev., 1998—2001; chief judge 8th Jud. Dist. Ct., Nev., 2001—02; assoc. justice Nev. Supreme Ct., Carson City, 2003—. Advisory mem. Senior Citizens Law Project Las Vegas City Council, 1995, chair of advisory mem. Senior Citizens Law Project, 1998—2001. Mem.: Nev. Bar Assn., Clark County Bar Assn. Office: Nev Supreme Ct 201 Carson St Carson City NV 89701-4702 Office Phone: 775-684-1500.

GIBBONS, MILES JOSEPH, JR., foundation administrator; b. Scranton, Pa., June 25, 1935; s. Miles J. and Claire (Kennedy) Gibbons; m. Carole Forker; children: Miles D., Elisabeth D. BA, Dickinson Coll., Carlisle, Pa., 1957; JD, Georgetown U., 1964; postgraduate student, Harvard U., 1996. Cost acct. US Steel, Johnstown, Pa., 1957-60; atty. Keating, Waterval and Johnson, Falls Church, Va., 1964-65; staff atty. AMP Inc., Harrisburg, Pa., 1965-68; counsel to minority leader US Ho. of Reps. Commonwealth of Pa., Harrisburg, 1968—70; assoc. atty. Morgan, Lewis and Bockius, Harrisburg, 1968-71, ptnr., 1971-81, of counsel, 1981-84; exec. dir. The Franklin H. and Ruth L. Wells Found., Mechanicsburg, 1983—, The Helen F. Whitaker Fund, Mechanicsburg, Pa., 1984—; CEO, pres. The Whitaker Found., Rosslyn, Va. and Mechanicsburg, Pa., 1981-2000. Mem. sch. bd. No. York County Sch. Dist., Dillsburg, Pa., 1984-88; chair problem solving com. United Way of Capital Region, Harrisburg, 1990-91; bd. dirs. United Way of Pa., 1994-95; bd. dirs. Coun. for Pub. Edn., Harrisburg, 1989-92, Life Sci. Greenhouse, Harrisburg, 2002—, Whitaker Ctr. Sci. and the Arts, Harrisburg, 2001—, treas., 2007—; exec. dir. The Fredricksen Found., Mechanicsburg, Pa., 1990—; mem. adv. bd. Milton S. Hershey Med. Sch., 1992-98; vol. Big Bros./Big Sisters, Harrisburg, 1990-95; co-chair Found. Exec. Rountable, Harrisburg, 1989-99; bd. dirs. Capital Campaign Rev. Com., Harrisburg, 1989—, chair, 1992—. Recipient Pub. Svc. award Messiah Coll., 1997, Founder's Day award Lebanon Valley Coll., 1999. Mem. Rotary Club Harrisburg (pres. 1988-89, Cmty. Svc. award 1990). Office: FH and RL Wells Found 3607 Rosemont Ave ste 404 Camp Hill PA 17011 Home Phone: 717-691-7582; Office Phone: 717-763-1157. Personal E-mail: mgibbons989@earthlink.net.

GIBBONS, PATRICK CHANDLER, physicist, researcher; b. Washington, Dec. 18, 1943; s. Myles Francis and Margaret Mack (Chandler) G.; m. Jane Elizabeth Forsell, Aug. 17, 1968; children: Elizabeth Jane, Jonathan Myles, Jane Chandler, Katherine Forsell. BS, Georgetown U., 1965; PhD, Harvard U., 1971. Physics instr. Princeton (N.J.) U., 1971-73, asst. prof. physics, 1973-76, Washington U., St. Louis, 1976-79, assoc. prof. physics, 1979-89, prof. physics, 1989—. Contbr. articles to Philos. mag., Jour. Non-Crystal Solids. Trustee Univ. Hills Subdivsn., University City, Mo., 1984-87. Mem. Am. Phys. Soc., Univ. City Swim Club (pres. 1988-90, 94-95), Sigma Xi, Phi Beta Kappa. Office: Washington U PO Box 1105 Saint Louis MO 63188-1105 Office Phone: 314-935-6271.

GIBBONS, RAYMOND JOHN, cardiologist; b. NYC, Sept. 4, 1949; BSE in Aerospace and Mechanical Sciences, Princeton U.; MS, MSc in Math., U. Oxford, Eng.; MS, John Hopkins U.; MD, Harvard Med. Sch., 1976. Intern Mass. Gen. Hosp., Boston, 1976-77, resident, internal medicine, 1977-78; fellow, cardiovascular divsn., dept. medicine Duke U. Med. Ctr., Durham, 1978-81; prof. medicine Mayo Med. Sch., 1992—. Contbr. articles to profl. jours.; mem. editl. bd. Circulation, Jour. Am. Heart Assn., Jour. Am. Coll. of Cardiology, Annals of Internal Medicine and others. Fellow Am. Coll. Cardiology; Am. Heart Assn. (pres. 2006-). Office: Mayo Clinic 200 1st St SW Rochester MN 55905-0002*

GIBBONS, REX VINCENT, geologist; b. Lumsden, Nfld., Can., Feb. 12, 1946; s. Clayton Manuel and Nita Mildred (Vincent) G.; m. Marjorie Stagg, May 20, 1966; children: Kim, Emily, Vince. BA in Edn., BSc, Meml. U. of Nfld., 1967, MSc in Geology, 1969; PhD in Geology, Calif. Inst. Tech., Pasadena, 1974. Registered profl. geologist, Nfld. Rsch. scientist NASA/Johnson Space Ctr., Houston, 1974-76; sr. geologist Nfld. Dept. Mines & Energy, St. John's, 1976-89; mem. Ho. of Assembly, St. John's West, Nfld., 1989-97, minister of mines and energy, 1989-94, 96-97, minister of natural resources, 1994-96; exec. v.p., sr. geosci. cons. Jacques Whitford Environment Ltd., Nfld. Geoscis. Ltd., St. John's, Canada, 1997—2004; sr. v.p. Jacques Whitford Ltd., St. John's, 2004—07; ret., 2007. Contbr. articles to profl. jours.; assoc. editor Geosci. Canada, 1980-85. Mem. Avalon Consol. Sch. Bd., St. John's, 1982-89, chmn., 1986-89; bd. mgmt. St. James United Ch., 1983-87; bd. regents Meml. U. of Nfld., 1978-81; bd. dirs. Nfld. Lung Health Found., Nfld. Sci. Ctr., Nfld. Ocean Industries, 1998-2001, St. John's Bd. Trade, 1998-2000. Nat. Rsch. Coun. Can. grad. bursary, 1968-69; Nfld. Govt. grad. fellow, 1967-68; Centenary scholar, 1966-67. Mem.: Assn. Profl. Engrs. and Geoscientists of Nfld., Can. Inst. Mining, Metallurgy & Petroleum (councillor, nat. v.p. 1982—87, nat. pres. 2001—02). Liberal. Avocations: fly fishing, curling, canoeing, hunting, genealogy. Home: 34 Spratt Pl Saint John's NL Canada A1E 4M2 Office Phone: 709-685-4665. Personal E-mail: rex.gibbons@nf.sympatico.ca.

GIBBONS, ROBERT BUTLER, JR., retired military officer; b. Sumter, SC, Sept. 20, 1947; s. Robert Butler Gibbons Sr. and Dorothy Jean (Welsh) Gibbons; m. Patricia Theodora Atkins, July 7, 1970 (div. Aug. 1983); 1 adopted child, Carole Gibbons Taylor children: Robert Butler III, Hannah Gibbons Tremer; m. Jean Claire Kennedy Burttram, June 24, 1984; 1 stepchild, Paige Burttram Belt. AS in Bus. Admnstrn., Victor Valley Coll., Victorville, Calif., 1986; grad. Leadership course, Am. Legion Inst., New Orleans, 1998; grad., Nat. Am. Legion Coll., Indpls., 2000. Cert. instr. phase I security State Law Enforcement Divsn. Am. Legion, 1992, notary pub. Instrnl. sys. designer to devel. mgr. and instr. USAF, Southeast Asia, Europe and U.S., 1966—89, ret., 1989; security chief internat. cos., 1990—99. Instr. phase I security state law enforcement divsn. Am. Legion, 1992—2002, comdr. dist. 11 dept. S.C., 1998—2000, comdr. Black River post 149, 1998—, dept. S.C. 4th vice cmdr. and gen. chmn. dept. econ. com., 2000, dept. S.C. 3d vice comdr. and gen. chmn. dept. nat. security com., SD, 00, dept. S.C. 2d vice comdr. and gen. chmn. dept. Americanism com., SC, 01, facilitator nat. coll., 01, dept. S.C. 1st vice cmdr. and gen. chmn. dept. internal affairs com., SC, 02, comdr. state of S.C., 2003—04, Forty and Eight Grand Dir. Boys State S.C., 2003—, adjuntant Black River post 149, 2006—. Mem. edn. com. Clarendon C. of C., 1997—98; chmn. Clarendon County Planning Commn., Manning, SC, 1998, 1999, 2003—04, Clarendon County GOP, Manning, SC, 2002—, Clarendon County GOP Capital 1000 Club, 2003; candidate dist. 36 S.C. Senate, 1996, 2004; lay del. or alt. to ann. conf. United Meth. Ch. in S.C., 1994—2002; chmn. trustees New Zion Methodist Ch., 1991—94. Decorated Air Force Commendation medal, Air Force Achievement medal with Oak Leaf cluster, Disting. Presdl. Unit citation, Air Force Outstanding Unit award with 2 Oak leaf clusters, Nat. Def. Svc. medal, Vietnam Svc. medal with 3 Oak Leaf clusters, Republic of Vietnam Gallantry Cross with Device, Republic of Vietnam Campaign medal, Meritorious Svc. medal. Mem.: VFW (life), Am. Air Mus. Brit. (Forty and Eight Grand Dir. Boys State S.C. 2002—), Disabled Am. Vets. (life), Am. Legion (life; mem. nat. resolutions assignment com. 2002—04, mem. Americanism commn. 2004—, chmn. mem. and post-activities sub-com. 2002), Air Force Assn. (life), Nat. Assn. Uniformed Svcs., La Soc. Des Quarante Hommes Et Huit Chevaux, Sumter Voiture 1254 (Voiture of Yr. 2003, Grand Voiture of Yr. 2004), Army, Navy and Air Force Vets. in Can. (hon.; U.S. unit), Mason Fidelity Lodge. Republican. Methodist. Avocations: collecting models of presidents homes and European castles, gardening, birdwatching, travel. Home: PO Box 19 6877 Salem Rd New Zion SC 29111 Office Phone: 843-659-8793. E-mail: rbgibbonsjr@frc.net.

GIBBONS, ROBERT EBBERT, university official; b. Sharon, Pa., Nov. 15, 1940; s. Thomas Michael and Mary Jane (Ebbert) G.; m. Patricia Arlene Fox, Aug. 18, 1962; children: Patrick, Timothy, Roberta, Aaron. BS, John Carroll U., 1962; MA, Bowling Green State U., 1963, PhD, 1967. Pres. Viterbo Coll., La Crosse, Wis., 1980-91; asst. prof. English Our Lady of the Lake U., San Antonio, 1969-72, chmn. English dept., 1972-74, dir. humanities div., 1974-77, exec. asst. to pres., 1977-80, exec. v.p., 1991-99, prof. English, 1991—, pres., 2001—02. Bd. dirs. Wis. Found. of Ind. Colls., Milw., 1980-91, pres., 1987-88; mem. USCC Com. on Cert. and Accreditation, 1988-94, vice chair, 1991-93. Mem. Phi Kappa Phi. Roman Catholic. Home: 3518 Hunters Gate St San Antonio TX 78230-2820 Office: Our Lady of the Lake U 411 SW 24th St San Antonio TX 78207-4689

GIBBONS, ROBERT JOHN, lawyer; b. Bklyn., Dec. 3, 1944; s. David Thomas and Virginia Marie G.; m. Judith Ann Borst, Nov. 23, 1968; children: Robert, Sharon, Suzanne. BA, St. John's U., Jamaica, NY, 1966; JD, Fordham U., 1969. Bar: N.Y. 1970. Assoc. Mudge, Rose, Guthrie, Alexander & Ferdon, NYC, 1969-76; ptnr. Wood, Dawson et al, NYC, 1976-77, Debevoise & Plimpton LLP, NYC, 1977—, co-head Project Fin. Practice Group. Trustee New Canaan County Sch., Conn., 1983-91, pres. bd. trustees, 1988-91; bd. dirs. New Canaan Baseball Inc., 1982-88, Country Club of New Canaan; mem. Utilities Commn. Town of New Canaan, 1986-90. Mem. ABA, N.Y. State Bar Assn., Assn. of Bar of City of N.Y. Home: 221 Michigan Rd New Canaan CT 06840-2223 Office: Debevoise & Plimpton LLP 919 3rd Ave Fl 47 New York NY 10022-6225 Office Phone: 212-909-6303. Office Fax: 212-521-7303. E-mail: rjgibbons@debevoise.com.

GIBBONS, ROBERT PHILIP, management consultant, director; m. Mary Jane M. Jamieson, June 12, 1965; children: Laura Ann, Robert John. BSME, Stevens Inst. Tech., 1955; MS in Indsl. Mgmt., Purdue U., 1959. Ptnr. Touche Ross Co., NYC, 1959—74; v.p., gen. mgr. Carborundum Co., Niagara Falls, NY, 1975—78, Main Hurdman, NYC, 1978—84, Zolfo, Cooper & Co., NYC, 1984—86; ptnr. Gibbons, Quintero & Co., NYC, 1986—90, Gibbons & Co., Tenafly, NJ, 1990—. Apptd. trustee U.S. Trustee and U.S. Bankruptcy Ct. Contbr. Am. Mgmt. Assn. Mgmt. Handbook, 1970. Bd. dirs., chmn. audit com., compensation com. Weldotron Corp., 1974—91. With US Army, 1956—58. Mem.: Turnaround Mgmt. Assn., Am. Bankruptcy Inst., Inst. Mgmt. Cons. (cert.), Am. Prodn. and Inventory Control Soc. (cert.). Office: Gibbons and Co 118 Fisher Rd Mahwah NJ 07430 Office Phone: 201-760-0567.

GIBBONS, SAM MELVILLE, retired congressman, government agency administrator; b. Tampa, Fla., Jan. 20, 1920; s. Gunby and Jessie Kirk (Cralle) G.; m. Martha Hanley, Sept. 14, 1946; children: Clifford, Mark, Timothy. JD, U. Fla., 1947. Bar: Fla. 1947. Mem. Fla. Ho. of Reps., 1952-58, Fla. Senate, 1958-62, US Congresses from 7th Fla. dist., 1962—97; ranking minority mem. ways and means com.; chmn. ways and means com., 1994-95; mem. joint taxation com.; chmn. Gibbons & Co., Washington, 1996—. Founder, 1st pres. U.S. Fla. Found., 1958. Served to maj. AUS, 1941-45, ETO. Decorated Bronze Star; named Outstanding Young Man Tampa Jr. C. of C., 1954; recipient President's award Tampa C. of C., 1955; featured in Tom Brokaw book The Greatest Generation and Steve Ambrose's "D" Day. Mem. Tampa Bar Assn. (dir.), Hillsborough Bar Assn. (dir.), Greater Tampa C. of C. (dir.) Democrat. Presbyterian (deacon).

GIBBONS, WILLIAM JOHN, lawyer; b. Chgo., Jan. 22, 1947; s. Edward and Lottie (Gasiorek) G.; children: Maximilian Clay, Bartholomew David, Ariel Katherine. BA, Northwestern U., 1968, JD, 1972. Bar: Ill. 1972, U.S. Dist. Ct. (no. dist.) Ill. 1972, U.S. Ct. Appeals (9th cir.) 1980, U.S. Supreme Ct. 1982, U.S. Ct. Appeals (7th cir.) 1984, U.S. Ct. Appeals (3d cir.) 2002. Assoc. Kirkland and Ellis, Chgo., 1972-76; ptnr. Hedlund, Hunter and Lynch, Chgo., 1976-82, Latham and Watkins, Chgo., 1982—, mng. ptnr. Chgo. office, 1995-2000. Served with USAR, 1968-74. Mem.: ABA, Chgo. Coun. Lawyers, Seventh Cir. Bar Assn., Chgo. Bar Assn. (chair class action com. 1994—95), Riverpark Club (Chgo.). Home: 1515 S Prairie # 913 Chicago IL 60605-3024 Office: Latham & Watkins Sears Tower Ste 5800 Chicago IL 60606-6306 Home Phone: 312-588-0844; Office Phone: 312-876-7706. Business E-Mail: william.gibbons@lw.com.

GIBBONS, WILLIAM REGINALD, JR., poet, writer, translator, editor; b. Houston, Jan. 7, 1947; s. William Reginald and Elizabeth (Lubowski) G.; m. Virginia Margaret Harris, June 8, 1968 (div. July 1982); m. Cornelia Maude Spelman, Aug. 18, 1983. AB, Princeton U., 1969; MA, Stanford U., 1971, PhD, 1974. Instr. Spanish Rutgers U., Brunswick, NJ, 1975-76; lectr. creative writing Princeton U., 1976-80, Columbia U., NYC, 1980-81; prof. English Northwestern U., Evanston, Ill., 1981—, chair English, 2002—05, editor TriQuarterly mag., 1981-97; prof. MFA Program for Writers Warren Wilson Coll., 1989—. Author: Roofs Voices Roads, 1979 (Quar. Rev. prize), The Ruined Motel, 1981, Saints, 1986, Maybe It Was So, 1991, Five Pears or Peaches, 1991, William Goyen: A Study of the Short Fiction, 1991, Sweetbitter, 1994, Sparrow: New and Selected Poems, 1997, Homage to Longshot O'Leary, 1999, It's Time, 2002, In the Warhouse, 2004, Fern-Texts, 2005; translator: Selected Poems of Luis Cernuda, 1978, Guillén on Guillén, 1979, (with Charles Segal) Euripides' Bakkhai, 2001, (with Charles Segal) Sophokles' Antigone, 2003; editor: The Poet's Work, 1979; (with G. Graff) Criticism in the University, 1985, The Writer in Our World, 1986, Fiction of the Eighties, 1990, Thomas McGrath: Life and the Poem, 1991, New Writing from Mexico, 1992, Goyen: Autobiographical Essays, Notebooks, Evocations, Interviews, 2007. Woodrow Wilson fellow Stanford U., 1969-70; Fulbright fellow Spain, 1971-72; Guggenheim fellow, 1983-84; NEA fellow, 1984; Ill. Arts Coun. fellow, 1988; recipient Translation prize Denver Quar., 1977, Short Story award Tex. Inst. Letters, 1986, Carl Sandburg award, 1992, Anisfield-Wolf Book award, 1995, Jesse Jones award Tex. Inst. Letters, 1995, Ill. Arts Coun. Lit. awards, 1996, 97, Balcones Poetry prize, 1998, Best Book of Poetry award Tex. Inst. Letters, 2003, O.B. Hardison Jr. Poetry prize Folger Libr., 2004. Mem. PEN Am. Ctr., Poetry Soc. Am. (John Masefield Meml. award 1991), Associated Writing Programs (bd. dirs. 1984-87), The Guild Complex (bd. dirs. 1989—). Office: Northwestern U Dept English Univ Hall 215 Evanston IL 60208-0001 Office Phone: 847-491-7294. Business E-Mail: rgibbons@northwestern.edu.

GIBBS, ANTONY (TONY GIBBS), film editor; Editor: (films) The Loneliness of the Long Distance Runner, 1962, A Taste of Honey, 1962, Tom Jones, 1963, The Luck of Ginger Coffey, 1964, The Knack.And How to Get It, 1965, The Loved One, 1965, Petulia, 1968, Performance, 1970, Walkabout, 1971, (with Robert Lawrence) Fiddler on the Roof, 1971, Jesus Christ Superstar, 1973, Rollerball, 1975, The Sailor Who Fell from Grace with the Sea, 1976, A Bridge Too Far, 1977, (with Graeme Clifford)

F.I.S.T., 1978, Yesterday's Hero, 1979, (with George Trirogoff) Butch and Sundance: The Early Days, 1979, (with Anne V. Coates and Stanley Warnow) Ragtime, 1981, The Dogs of War, 1981, Bad Boys, 1983, Dune, 1984, Agnes of God, 1985, Tai-Pan, 1986, Russkies, 1987, Stealing Home, 1988, (with Lou Lombardo) In Country, 1989, The Runner, 1990, The Taking of Beverly Hills, 1992, The Man Without a Face, 1993, Don Juan DeMarco, 1995, Ronin, 1998, Reindeer Games, 2000, (TV movies) Devlin, 1992, A Case for Life, 1996, Crime of the Century, 1996, George Wallace, 1997, James Dean, 2001. Office: 15691 Royal Ridge Rd Sherman Oaks CA 91403-4208

GIBBS, DAVID RICHARD, musician, journalist, photographer, writer; b. Hammond, Ind. s. John and Grace Gibbs. BA, Ind. U., 1986; MA, Trinity Internat.U., 1998. Staff writer, photographer The Times, Bedford, Ind., 1986—87; photographer David Gibbs Photography, Seattle, 1988—92, The Times-Mail, Munster, Ind., 1992—93; market intelligence specialist Interactive Intelligence, Indpls., 1999—2002; adj. prof. Ind. Tech., 2004—06; pres. Folk Pop Music Inc., 2005—, Folk Pop Records, Inc., 2005—. Corp. rep. TechPoint, Indpls., 1999—2002; mem. dean's coun. Ind. U. Sch. Journalism; mem. Heartland Film Festival Jury, 2007. Singer, songwriter (CD) Welcome to Tomorrow, 2005. Vol. Habitat for Humanity, Zionsville, Ind., 2004, Cystic Fibrosis Found., Indpls., 2004; youth dir. Meadow Lane Bapt. Ch., Hammond, Ind., 1993; dir. Christian edn. Elim Bapt. Ch., Seattle, 1990—92. Scholar, Chgo. Press. Club, 1985. Mem.: Nat. Press Photographers Assn., Soc. Profl. Journalists, Am. Hist. Assn. E-mail: info@davidgibbs.com.

GIBBS, DENIS LAUREL, radiologist; b. Wayne, Mich., Mar. 6, 1945; s. Laurel Pierce and Alwyn Marie (Larson) G.; m. Paula Kay Lynn, Sept. 6, 1974 (div. Aug. 1988); children: Jeremy Paul, Matthew Ryan, Kevin Christopher, Denis Patrick; m. Kathleen Marie DeLaFuente, July 9, 1989; 1 child, Andrew Zachery. BS, Andrews U., Berrien Springs, Mich., 1967, postgrad., 1967-69; DO, Kansas City Coll. Osteopathic Medicine, 1974. Diplomate Am. Bd. Radiology. Intern, radiology resident Doctors' Hosps., Columbus, Ohio, 1974-78, staff radiologist, 1978; chmn. dept. radiology Rocky Mountain Hosp., Denver, 1978-88, vice chief of staff, 1982, chief of staff, 1983, 84; chmn. dept. radiology Colo. Plain Med. Ctr. Regional Trauma Ctr., Ft. Morgan, 1988—2002, vice chief of staff, 1992—93; staff radiologist, VICE CHMN. DEPT. Lakeland Med. Ctr., Niles, Mich., 2002—, radiologist, vice chair of dept., 2002—; ptnr., CFO Radiology Assn. Berrien County, Mich., 2005—; radiologist Lakeland Hosp. Systems, St. Joseph, Mich., 2005—; site chief Lakeland Hosp., Niles, 2005—. Med., legal cons., Colo., 1979—, Calif., 1979—, Fla., 1979—; consulting radiologist East Morgan Hosp., Luth. Health Sys., Brush, Colo., 1988—2002; CEO IRS Radiology Cons., P.C., Ft. Morgan, 1988—2002, Interstate Radiology Services, Henderson, Nev., 2002—; v.p. Niles Imaging Physicians, Mich., 2002—. Med. reviewer Post Grad. Medicine. Mem. Am. Osteopathic Assn., Am. Osteopathic Coll. Radiology, Am. Roentgen Ray Soc., Radiology Soc. N.Am., Soc. Nuc. Medicine, Mich. Radiologic Soc., Mich. Osteopathic Assn., Nat. Assn. Seventh-Day Adventist Osteopaths, Colo. Med. Soc., Soc. Nuclear Medicine Physicians. Republican. Avocations: snorkeling, skin diving, racquetball, sports car enthusiast and owner, travel. Office: PO Box 820 Niles MI 49120

GIBBS, FREDERICK WINFIELD, lawyer, communications executive; b. Buffalo, Mar. 22, 1932; s. Walter L. M. and Elizabeth Mari (Georgi) G.; m. Josephine Janice Jarvis, Dec. 20, 1954; children: Michael, Mathew, Robyn. BA cum laude, Alfred U., NY, 1954; JD with Tax honors, Rutgers U., Camden, 1989. Bar: Pa. 1989, N.J. 1989, U.S. Dist. Ct. N.J. 1989. With N.Y. Tel. Co., 1954-65, ITT, 1965-86; mng. dir. ITT Standard Electrica, S.A., 1971-75; CEO ITT Standard Electrica, Brazil, 1975-77; exec. dir. ops. ITT Communications Ops. Group ITT Comm. Ops. Group, 1977; corp. v.p. ITT, 1977-80; pres. U.S. Tel. and Tel. Corp., 1977-79, exec. dir., sr. group exec., 1980-86; dir. System 12, ITT, 1979-80; exec. v.p. ITT, 1980-86, ITT Telecom. Corp., 1983-86; pvt. practice law Pemberton, NJ, 1989-95; founding ptnr. Frederick W. Gibbs & Assocs. (formerly Gibbs, Gregory & Emmons Attys. at Law), Pemberton, 1995—. Cons. ITT, 1986-89, The World Bank/IFC, 1989—; pres. Mulberry Hill Enterprises, 1989—; bd. dirs. ACT Mfg., eOn Comm. Inc. Trustee Alfred U., 1981—; trustee Whitesbog Found., 1996—, pres. bd. trustees, 2000—; mem. planning bd. Barnegat Light, N.J., 1992-2002; elected Borough Coun., Barnegat Light, 1992, re-elected, 1995, 98; bd. dirs. Burlington County Red Cross, 1999—, Our Gang Players, Inc. Named Hon. Citizen of Rio de Janeiro, 1973; inducted to Alfred Univ. Athletic Hall of Fame, 1993. Mem. ABA, N.J. Bar Assn., Pa. Bar Assn., Burlington County Bar Assn., Barnegat Light Taxpayers Assn. (v.p. 1989-90, pres. 1990-92), Rotary Internat. (bd. dirs. Pemberton club 1996-97, v.p. 1997-98, pres. 1999-00, Pemberton Rotarian of Yr. 1996-97). Office Phone: 609-893-0900. E-mail: ggelaw@verizon.net.

GIBBS, JAMES ALANSON, geologist; b. Wichita Falls, Tex., June 18, 1935; s. James Ford and Clovis (Robinson) Gibbs; m. Judith Walker, June 18, 1966; children: Ford W., John A. BS, U. Okla., 1957, MS, 1962. Lic. geoscientist Tex. Geologist Calif. Co., New Orleans, 1961-63, Lafayette, La., 1963-64; cons. geologist, oil prodr. Dallas, 1964—. Chmn. Five States Energy Co., 1984—. Author: Finding Work as a Petroleum Geologist: Hints to the Jobseeker, 1984, Becoming an Independent Geologist: Thriving in Good Times and Bad, 1999. Trustee Inst. Study Earth and Man, So. Meth. U. Lt. USNR, 1957—59. Recipient Regents award, U. Okla., 1996. Mem.: AAAS, W. Tex. Geol. Soc., Houston Geol. Soc., Nat. Petroleum Coun., Ind. Petroleum Assn. Am., Am. Inst. Profl. Geologists, Geol. Soc. Am., Am. Geol. Inst. (trustee, William B. Heroy Disting. Svc. award 1994), Soc. Ind. Profl. Earth Scientists (hon.; past chmn. Dallas chpt.), Am. Assn. Petroleum Geologists (hon.; sec. 1983—85, pres. 1990—91, found. trustee 1998—, Disting. Svc. award 1987), Dallas Geol. Soc. (hon.; pres. 1975—76), Explorers Club, Dallas Petroleum Club, Dallas Country Club, Sigma Xi, Phi Delta Theta, Sigma Gamma Epsilon. Republican. Methodist. Home: 3514 Caruth Blvd Dallas TX 75225-5001 Office: 4925 Greenville Ave Ste 1220 Dallas TX 75206-4015 Office Phone: 214-363-3008. E-mail: jagibbs@fivestates.com.

GIBBS, JAMES HOWARD, broadcast executive; b. Dover, Ohio, Jan. 3, 1929; s. Howard James and Berniece Ruth (Spahr) Gibbs; m. Bettye Jean Porter, Nov. 10, 1956 (dec. June 7, 2003); children: Charles Kenneth(dec.) , Tammy Ann. Grad. H.S., Dover, 1947. Announcer KWED Radio, Sequin, Tex., 1947-48; owner KIVY Radio, Crockett, Tex., 1948—2003; news dir. Sta. WFAA-TV, Dallas, 1956-57. Home: 111 Valley Ln Crockett TX 75835-1325 Office: Kivy Radio 102 S 5th St Crockett TX 75835-2037 E-mail: jhgibbs@pcstx.net.

GIBBS, JAMES R., oil industry executive; BS, So. Methodist Univ., 1967, MA, 1969, PhD, 1972. Mgmt. positions through v.p. adminstrn. & fin. Frontier Oil Corp., Houston, 1982—87, bd. dir., 1985—, pres., COO, 1987—, CEO, 1992—, chmn., 1999—. Bd. dir. Smith Internat. Inc., Talon Internat., Veritas DGC Inc.; adv. dir. Frost Nat. Bank, Houston. Office: Frontier Oil Ste 600 10000 Memorial Dr Houston TX 77024-3411 Office Phone: 713-688-9600. Office Fax: 713-688-0616.*

GIBBS, JOE (JOSEPH JACKSON GIBBS), professional football coach; b. Mocksville, NC, Nov. 25, 1940; m. Pat Gibbs; children: Coy, J.D. BS, San Diego State U., 1964, MS, 1966. Asst. coach San Diego State U., 1964—66, Fla. State U., 1967-68, U. So. Calif., 1969-70, U. Ark., 1971-72, St. Louis Cardinals, 1973-77, Tampa Bay Buccaneers, 1978; offensive coord. San Diego Chargers, 1979-80; head coach Washington Redskins, 1981-93, 2004—. Founder, owner Joe Gibbs Racing, 1991—; sports commentator NBC, 1993—98. Co-author (with Ken Abraham): Racing to Win: Establish Your Game Plan For Success, 2002. Named NFL Coach of the Yr., AP, 1982, 1983; named to The Pro Football Hall of Fame, 1996. Achievements include leading the Washington Redskins to three Super Bowl titles, 1983, 1988, 1992; winning three NASCAR Championships. Office: c/o Washington Redskins 21300 Redskin Park Dr Ashburn VA 20147

GIBBS, JUNE NESBITT, state senator; b. Newton, Mass., June 13, 1922; d. Samuel Frederick and Lulu (Glazier) Nesbitt; m. Donald T. Gibbs, Dec. 8, 1945 (dec. 2001); 1 child, Elizabeth. BA in Math., Wellesley Coll., 1943; MA in Math., Boston U., 1947; postgrad. computer sci., U. R.I., 1981-84. Mem. from R.I. Rep. Nat. Com., 1969-80, sec., 1977-80; mem. R.I. Senate, Dist. 48, Providence, 1985—2003, R.I. Senate, Dist 12, Providence, 2003—, dep. minority leader. Mem. def. adv. com. Women in Svcs., 1970—72, vice chmn., 1972. Mem. Middletown (R.I.) Town Coun., 1974—80, 1982—84, pres., 1978—80. Lt. (j.g.) USNR, 1943—46. Avocation: windsurfing. Home: 163 Riverview Ave Middletown RI 02842-5324 Office: Senate Minority Office State House Providence RI 02903 Office Phone: 401-222-2708. Business E-Mail: sen-gibbs@rilin.state.ri.us. *To help restore faith in our government every elected official must constantly seek to do all he can for the people he serves and continually guard against doing anything which is self-serving or takes personal advantage of his office in any way.*

GIBBS, LAWRENCE BLAIR, lawyer; b. Hutchinson, Kans., Aug. 31, 1938; married; 2 children. BA, Yale U., 1960; JD, U. Tex., 1963. Assoc., then ptnr. Branscomb, Gary, Thomasson & Hall, Corpus Christi, Tex., 1963-72; dep. chief counsel IRS, Washington, 1972-73, acting chief counsel, 1973, asst. commr., 1973-75; ptnr. Johnson and Swanson, Dallas, 1976-86; commr. IRS, Washington, 1986-89; ptnr. Johnson & Gibbs, Washington and Dallas, 1989-94; mem. Miller & Chevalier, Washington, 1994—. Mem. bd. adv. com. Taxation Mergers & Acquisitions. Adv. trustee So. Fed. Tax Inst. Mem. ABA (vice chmn. adminstrn. sect. taxation 1991-92), FBA, State Bar Tex. (chmn. taxation sect. 1978-79), D.C. Bar Assn., Am. Law Inst., Communities Found. Tex. Adv. Bd., Am. Coll. Trust and Estate Counsel (bd. regents 1990-96). Office: Miller & Chevalier 655 15th St NW Ste 900 Washington DC 20005-5799 Office Phone: 202-626-6005. E-mail: lgibbs@milchev.com.

GIBBS, LEONARD (DOC GIBBS), musician; Studied, Pa. Acad. Fine Art. Music dir. Emeril Live Band, 1997—. Workshop leader Young Audiences Eastern Pa., Stings Sch. Orgns. Musician: (albums) Servin It Up! Hot!, 2002. Mem.: Nat. Assn. Rec. Artists and Scis. (bd. of directors). Achievements include touring and recording with many top artists in the music industry.

GIBBS, MARTIN, biologist, educator; b. Phila., Nov. 11, 1922; s. Samuel and Rose (Sugarman) G.; m. Svanhild Karen Kvale, Oct. 11, 1950; children: Janet Helene, Laura Jean, Steven Joseph, Michael Seland, Robert Kvale. BS, Phila. Coll. Pharmacy, 1943; PhD, U. Ill., 1947. Scientist Brookhaven Nat. Lab., 1947-56; prof. biochemistry Cornell U., 1957-64; Abraham S. and Gertrude Berg prof. biology, chmn. dept. Brandeis U., Waltham, Mass., 1965-93. Cons. NSF, 1961-64, 69-72, NIH, 1966-69, Cosmos Club, 1984; mem. corp. Marine Biol. Lab., Woods Hole, Mass., 1970, RESA lectr., 1969; NATO cons. fellowship bd., 1968-70; mem. Coun. Internat. Exch. of Scholars, 1976-82; chmn. adv. com. selection Fulbright Scholars for Eastern Europe; adj. prof. Bot. Inst., U. Munster, Fed. Republic of Germany, 1978, 80, 87; adj. prof. dept. botany U. Calif., Riverside, 1979-89. Author: Structure and Function of Chloroplasts, 1970, Crop Productivity-Research Imperatives, 1975, Crassulacean Acid Metabolism, 1982, Crassulacean Acid Biosynthesis and Function of Plant Lipids, 1983, Crop Productivity-Research Imperative, Revisited, 1985, Hungarian-USA Binational Symposium on Photosynthesis, 1986; editor-in-chief: Plant Physiology, 1963—92, assoc. editor: Physiologie Vegetale, 1966—76, Ann. Rev. Plant Physiology, 1966—71. Recipient Charles Reid Barnes award, 1984, Adolph E. Gude award, 1993, Martin Gibbs medal, 1993, U. Ill. Achievement award, 1996, Gold medal Bulgarian Acad. Scis.; Alexander von Humboldt fellow, 1987. Mem. NAS, AAUP, Am. Soc. Plant Physiologists (Barnes, Gude, Gibbs medal), Russian Soc. Plant Physiologists (hon. life mem.), Am. Acad. Arts and Scis., Am. Soc. Biochem. Molecular Biology, Can. Soc. Plant Physiologists (hon. life), Acad. Scis. France. Home: 32 Slocum Rd Lexington MA 02421-5622 Personal E-mail: mgibbs8912@aol.com.

GIBBS, MICHAEL G., not-for-profit fundraiser; BA in Polit. Sci., DePaul U., Chgo., 1995, MS in Pub. Svc. Mgmt., 1997, EdD, 2002. Asst. v.p. DePaul U., Chgo., 2001—04; v.p. devel. St. Mary's U. Minn., Winona, 2004—05; chief advancement officer Astron. Soc. of Pacific, San Francisco, 2005—. Dir. Nat. Hispanic Inst., Maxwell, Tex., 2000. Mem.: Assn. Fundraising Profls., Am. Edn. Rsch. Assn. Office: Astron Soc Pacific 390 Ashton Ave San Francisco CA 94112 Office Phone: 415-337-1100. Business E-Mail: mgibbs@astrosociety.org.

GIBBS, PATRICIA HELLMAN, physician; b. Boston, Oct. 22, 1958; d. Frederick Warren and Patricia Christina (Sander) H.; m. Richard D. Gibbs, Dec. 22, 1984; children: Ruth, Samuel, Matthew, Kate, Frank. BA summa cum laude, Williams Coll., 1982; MD, Yale U., 1987. Diplomate Am. Bd. Family Practice. Intern, resident in family practice U. Wash., Seattle, 1987-90; ptnr. Tricia Gibbs, MD and Richard Gibbs, MD, San Francisco, 1990-95; co-founder, med. dir. San Francisco Free Clinic, 1993—. Supervising physician San Francisco Ballet, 1990-95. Co-author: Medical and Orthopedic Issues of Active and Athletic Women-Skiing, 1993, Spine Care-Dance, 1993, Medical and Orthopedic Issues for Women, 1993; contbr. articles to profl. jours. Mem. US Alpine ski team, 1976-78; founder Sugar Bowl Acad., 1999. Women's scholar Williams Coll., 1982, Class of '25 Athlete scholar, 1982; named Family Physician of Yr., Calif. Acad. Family Physicians, 1998; recipient Pub. Health Heroes Institutional award Berkeley Sch. Pub. Health U. Calif., 2006, Positive Coaching Alliance Honoring the Game award, Sugar Bowl Ski Team Found., Williams Coll. Bicentennial award 2002. Mem. AMA, Am. Acad. Family Physicians, Am. Assn. Intercollegiate Athletics for Women (All-Am. Athlete 1979, 1981), Phi Beta Kappa, Sigma Xi. Jewish. Avocations: distance running, ski racing, computers. Office: San Francisco Free Clinic 4900 California St San Francisco CA 94118-1115 Office Phone: 415-750-9894. Business E-Mail: pgibbs@sffc.org.

GIBBY, DIANE LOUISE, physician, plastic surgeon; b. Miami, Feb. 5, 1957; d. John and Mabel (Kunce) G.; m. Rodney J. Rohrich, July 3, 1990; children: Taylor Rodney, Rachel Nicole. BS, Duke U., Durham, NC, 1975; MD, U. Miami, 1980. Diplomate Am. Bd. Gen. Surgery, Bd. Plastic and Reconstructive Surgery. Clin. asst. prof. U. Tex. Southwestern, Dallas, 1987—; pvt. practice plastic surgery Med. City Dallas, 1987—. Founder Women's Ctr. for Plastic and Reconstructive Surgery, 1992. Fellow Am. Coll. Surgeons; mem. Am. Soc. Plastic and Reconstructive Surgeons, Am. Med. Soc., Tex. Soc. Plastic Surgeons, Dallas Soc. Plastic Surgeons, Aesthetic Soc. Office: 7777 Forest Ln Ste C820 Dallas TX 75230-2552 Office Phone: 972-566-6323. Business E-Mail: dgmdpa@aol.com.

GIBBY-SMITH, BARBARA, psychologist, nurse; b. Woodburn, Oreg., Dec. 13, 1938; d. Chester Clifton and Marvel Elizabeth (Hill) Gibby; m. Roy Milton Smith, June 2, 1957 (div. June 1990); children: Thomas Clifton, Jeffery Shawn, Mark Anderson. ADN, Chemeketa C.C., Salem, Oreg., 1972; BS, SUNY, Albany, 1980; MS, Western Oreg. State Coll., 1982; D of Psychology, Pacific U., Forest Grove, Oreg., 1993. Diplomate Am. Bd. Profl. Disability Cons., Am. Bd. Specialist, Am. Bd. Forensics Medicine; cert. addiction examiner. Adminstr. Birch St. Manor, Dallas, Oreg., 1973—81; disability determination specialist State of Oreg. Workers' Compensation Dept., Salem, 1983—85; counselor Women's Crisis Ctr., Salem, 1986—88; rehab. counselor Employer Rehab. Svcs., Portland, Oreg., 1985—87; therapist, counselor Pacific U., Hillsboro, Oreg., 1988—89, Forest Grove, 1989—91; intern psychology Portland State U., 1991—92, Kaiser-Permanente, Salem, 1991—92; resident psychology Tillamook Counseling Ctr., Oreg., 1993—95; hosp. privileges psychology and medicine Quality Healthcare, Forest Grove, 1996—; pvt. practice clin. psychology Mountain View Counseling Ctr., Forest Grove, Oreg., 1993—. Group therapy counselor Women's Crisis Ctr., Dallas, 1982-83; eating disorders group therapy facilitator, Salem, 1986-88; nat. register Doctoral Addiction Examiner. Author: William G. Hill: Pioneer of Oregon, 2004. Active Women's Coalition Orgn., Salem, 1988—; active missionary work in schs. Bless the Children, Salem, Oreg., 2004—06, Gospel Messengers, 2004, 2005, 2006. Mem. APA, Am. Coll. Forensic Examiners (diplomate), Nat. Bd. Addiction Examiners (diplomate), Oreg. Psychol. Assn., Prescribing Psychologist Assn. (diplomate), Am. Mental Health Alliance (Oreg.). Democrat. Avocations: golf, bicycling, travel, genealogy, walking. Office: Mountain View Counseling Ctr 1911 Mountain View Ln Ste 500 Forest Grove OR 97116-2248 Office Phone: 503-357-0206. Personal E-mail: barbpg@juno.com.

GIBERSON, JOAN ALYNE, retired school nurse practitioner; b. Hammond, Ind., Jan. 10, 1947; d. John Harrison and Cleta Jean McFadden; m. Franklin Winston Giberson, Jan. 2, 1969; children: Patricia Melanie, Eric Louis. Diploma, James Ward Thorne Sch. Nursing, Northwestern U., Chgo., 1965—68. RN. Recovery rm. nurse Passayant Meml., Chgo., 1970—71; staff nurse Ingalls Meml., Harvey, Ill., 1972—74, Munster Cmty. Hosp., Ind., 1982—86; sch. nurse Hoover-Schrum Sch. Dist #157, Calumet City, 1986—2005; retired. Active South Side Christian Ch., choir mem., Sunday sch. tchr., past pres. Martha Group. Mem. Christian Ch. Avocations: music, drawing, sewing.

GIBLETT, ELOISE ROSALIE, retired hematologist; b. Tacoma, Jan. 17, 1921; d. William Richard and Rose (Godfrey) Giblett. BS, U. Wash., 1942, MS, 1947, MD with honors, 1951. Mem. faculty U. Wash. Sch. Medicine, 1957—, research prof., 1967—87, emeritus research prof., 1987—. Assoc. dir., head immunogenetics Puget Sound Blood Ctr., 1957—79, exec. dir., 1979—87, emeritus exec. dir., 1987—; former mem. several rsch. coms. NIH. Author: Genetic Markers in Human Blood, 1969; mem. editl. bd. numerous jours. including: Blood, Am. Jour. Human Genetics, Transfusion, Vox Sanguinis; contbr. over 200 articles to profl. jours. Recipient fellowships, grants Emily Cooley, Karl Landsteiner, Philip Levine and Alexander Wiener immunohematology awards, disting. alumna award, U. Wash. Sch. Medicine, 1987. Fellow: AAAS; mem.: NAS, Assn. Am. Physicians, Western Assn. Physicians, Am. Fedn. Clin. Rsch., Internat. Soc. Hematologists, Brit. Soc. Immunology, Am. Assn. Immunologists, Am. Soc. Hematology, Am. Soc. Human Genetics (pres. 1973), Alpha Omega Alpha, Sigma Xi. Home: 6533 53rd Ave NE Seattle WA 98115-7748 Office: Puget Sound Blood Ctr 921 Terry Ave Seattle WA 98104-1256

GIBLIN, JAMES CROSS, writer, publishing executive; b. Cleve., July 8, 1933; s. Edward Kelley and Anna Belle (Cross) G. BA, Case Western Res. U., 1954; MA, Columbia U., 1955. Asst. editor Criterion Books, NYC, 1959-62; editor Lothrop, Lee & Shepard Co., NYC, 1962-67; editor in chief Clarion Books, NYC, 1967-79, pub., 1979-89, contbg. editor, 1989—. Author: The Scarecrow Book, 1980, The Skyscraper Book, 1981, Chimney Sweeps: Yesterday and Today, 1982 (Am. Book award 1983, Golden Kite award 1983), Fireworks, Picnics and Flags: The Story of the Fourth of July Symbols, 1983, Walls: Defenses Throughout History, 1984 (Golden Kite award 1985), The Truth About Santa Claus, 1985 (Boston Globe-Horn Book Nonfiction Honor Book award 1986), Milk: The Fight for Purity, 1986, From Hand to Mouth, 1987, Let There Be Light: A Book About Windows, 1988 (Golden Kite award 1989), Writing Books for Young People, 1990, The Riddle of the Rosetta Stone: Key to Ancient Egypt, 1990, The Truth About Unicorns, 1991, Edith Wilson: The Woman Who Ran the United States, 1992, George Washington: A Picture Book Biography, 1992, Be Seated: A Book About Chairs, 1993, Thomas Jefferson: A Picture Book Biography, 1994, When Plague Strikes: The Black Death, Smallpox, AIDs, 1995, The Dwarf, the Giant and the Unicorn: A Tale of King Arthur, 1996, Charles A. Lindbergh: A Human Hero, 1997 (Orbis Pictus Honor Book award 1998), The Mystery of the Mammoth Bones, and How it Was Solved, 1999, The Amazing Life of Benjamin Franklin, 2000 (Orbis Pictus Honor Book award 2001), The Century That Was: Reflections on the Last One Hundred Years, 2000, Fireworks, Picnics and Flags: The Story of the Fourth of July Symbols, rev. edit., 2001, The Life and Death of Adolf Hitler, 2002 (Robert F. Sibert Informational Book award 2003), Secrets of the Sphinx, 2004 (Orbis Pictus Honor Book award 2005), Good Brother, Bad Brother: The Story of Edwin Booth and John Wilkes Booth, 2005 (Boston Globe-Horn Book Nonfiction Honor Book award 2005), The Giblin Guide to Writing Children's Books, 2005, The Boy Who Saved Cleveland, 2006, The Many Rides of Paul Revere, 2007; also numerous articles and short stories. Mem. Authors Guild, Soc. Children's Book Writers and Illustrators (bd. dirs.). Avocations: travel, museum exhibits, movies, plays, walking. Home: 200 E 24th St Apt 1606 New York NY 10010-3919 Office Phone: 212-679-7126. E-mail: jcgiblin@aol.com. *Having written books for both children and adults, I find the juvenile field more stimulating and exciting because of the responsibility the children's writer has to his or her impressionable young readers. If the writer gives them solid, truthful, imaginatively treated books, he or she is contributing in a very real sense to their education and development.*

GIBLIN, JENNIFER, chef; b. Houston; Degree in Psych., U. Ariz, 1994; attended, Le Cordon Bleu, Eng., 1997. Cook Tabla, pastry sous chef; cook Eleven Madison Park; pastry chef Blue Smoke Jazz Standard, NYC, 2002—. Named one of NYC's Rising Stars, StarChefs.com, 2006. Office: Blue Smoke Jazz Standard 116 E 27th St New York NY 10016 Office Phone: 212-447-7733.

GIBLIN, LOUIS, lawyer; b. Omaha, Nov. 1, 1944; s. Richard and Mary (Mahoney) G.; m. Janis Schoblocher, May 20, 1977; 1 child, Marijo. AB in Econs., Creighton U., 1966; MBA, U. Chgo., 1968; cert. in investment mgmt., Princeton U., 1986; MS, Northwestern U., 1998; JD, Chgo.-Kent Coll. Law, cert. in employment law, LLM, 2004. Asst. v.p. No. Trust. Co., Chgo., 1968-73; v.p. MGIC Investment Corp., Milw., 1973-85; 1st v.p. Smith Barney Co., 1985—93. Chmn. fin. analyst seminar Northwestern U., Evanston, Ill., 1990; adj. faculty U. Wis., Milw., 1985-2002; adviser Financiers U. Wis., Milw., 1986-2002; sr. exam. grader Inst. CFAs, 1986-2003; cons. Fin. Svcs. Vol. Corp., Skoda Koncern, Czech Republic, 1993-2001. Founder Joint Univ./Soc. Scholarship program, CFA exam, 1988; trustee St. Stephen's Ch., Milw., 1989-99; chmn. investment com., fin. com., ops. com. United Way, Milw., 1989-2002; Oak Creek (Wis.) Housing Authority, Creighton U. Alumni Senate, 1991-99; adv. com. Creighton U.; bd. dirs. Creighton U. Alumni, 1993. Nominee Pulitzer Prize, 1985. Mem. Internat. Soc. Fin. Analysts (charter), Internat. Inst. Forecasters, N.Y. Soc. Security Analysts, Nat. Assn. Bus. Economists, Nat. Options and Futures Soc. (bd. dirs. 1986-93), Deutsch-Amerikanischer Nat. Kongress, North Atlantic Cultural Exch. League, Internat. Inst. Am. Host, Milw. Investment Analysts Soc. (bd. dirs. 1988-99), CFA Inst. (bd. dirs.), Milw. Investment Analysts Soc. (pres. 1989-90), Mensa. Home: 7468 S Logan Ave Oak Creek WI 53154-2234 Personal E-mail: lgi319@aol.com.

GIBLIN, MICHAEL F., medical researcher, educator; b. LA; s. Francis J. and Alice C. Giblin; m. Tara L. Giblin. BA, UCLA, 1985; PhD, U. Mo., Columbia, 1997. Sr. rsch. chemist U. Mo., 2002—03, rsch. asst. prof.,

2003—. Rsch. grant, Dept. Def., 2004, Nat. Cancer Inst., 2005. Mem.: Soc. Radiopharmaceutical Scis., Soc. Molecular Imaging, Soc. Nuc. Medicine. Achievements include patents for melanotropin analogs for diagnosis and treatment of melanoma. Office: Univ Mo 330 Hadley Hall Columbia MO 65212 Business E-Mail: giblinm@health.missouri.edu.

GIBLIN, NAN J., psychologist, educator; b. Kankakee, Ill., Sept. 18, 1946; d. Kenneth Theodore Johnson and Rose Marie Pocock; m. Walter Patrick Giblin, Oct. 5, 1968; 1 child, Daniel. BS in English Lit., Loyola U. Chgo., 1968, PhD of Ednl. Counseling, 1984; MA in Ednl. counseling, Northeastern Ill. U. Chgo., 1978. Registered psychologist Ill. Tchr. Sacred Heart Acad., Chgo., 1968—70; asst. prof. Northeastern Ill. U., Chgo., 1985—90; pvt. practice psychology Park Ridge, Ill., 1986—95; assoc. prof., prof. Northeastern Ill. U., Chgo., 1990—. Chair counseling edn. Northeastern Ill. U., Chgo., 1987—92, 2005—, assoc. dean Coll. Edn., 1992—98, dean Coll. Edn., 1998—; mem. Ill. State Cert. Bd., Springfield, 2001—05. Co-author: Finding Help: A Resource Guide to Personal Concerns, Individual Counseling: Skills and Techniques; co-editor: Family Counseling in School Settings. Mem.: ACA, Am. Assn. Coll. Tchr. Educators. Office: Northeastern Ill Univ 5500 N Saint Louis Chicago IL 60025 Office Phone: 773-442-5552.

GIBLIN, PAMELA M., lawyer; b. NYC, June 7, 1946; BA, U. Tex., 1967, JD, 1970. Bar: Tex. 1970. Mem. Jones, Day, Reavis & Pogue, Austin; ptnr. environ. dept. Baker Botts LLP, Austin, Tex. Gen. counsel Tex. Air Control Bd., 1970-76; chmn. Commn. on Electric Rates, Austin, 1975-76. Named a Texas Super Lawyer, Texas Monthly mag. & Law & Politics mag., 2003—04; named one of Top 50 Female Super Lawyers, 2003—04, Top 50 Regional & West Texas Regular Super Lawyers, 2003—04; recipient Disting. Lawyer award, Travis County Bar Assn., 2003. Office: Baker & Botts LLP 98 San Jacinto Blvd Ste 1600 Austin TX 78701-4039 Office Phone: 512-322-2509. Office Fax: 512-322-8308. Business E-Mail: pam.giblin@bakerbotts.com.

GIBLIN, PATRICK DAVID, retired bank executive; b. St. Louis, July 24, 1932; s. Patrick Joseph and Ann Jane (Gill) G.; children: Mary Clare, Christopher, Gregory. BBA, Manhattan Coll., 1954; MBA, St. John's U., Jamaica, NY, 1965. Staff auditor KPMG Peat Marwick, NYC, 1956-59; chief plant acct. div. Am. Machine & Foundry, Bklyn., 1959-63; with CBS, NYC, 1963-73, controller electronic video rec. div., 1968-73, dir. corp. acctg., 1967-68; vice chmn., chief fin. officer CRESTAR Fin. Corp., Richmond, 1973-95; ret., 1995. Served with U.S. Army, 1954-56. Mem. Delta Mu Delta. Roman Catholic. Personal E-mail: pdg3silver@aol.com.

GIBLIN, VINCENT J., labor union administrator; married; 3 children. Grad. Trade Union Program, Harvard U. Bus. mgr. Local 68 Internat. Union of Operating Engrs., 1975—2004, internat. v.p., 1989—2002, sec.-treas., 2002—05, gen. pres. Washington, 2005—. Bd. dir. Blue Cross-Blue Shield of NJ, 1993—, chmn. bd., 1994—; with NJ Econ. Devel. Authority; with, Office of Boiler Pressure Vessel Compliance NJ Dept. Labor; with Atlantic City Gaming Commn.; bd. trustees Ctrl. Pension Fund. Office: Internat Union of Operating Engineers 1125 17th St NW Washington DC 20036-4707

GIBNEY, ALEX, producer, director, writer; Grad., Yale U. Pres. Jigsaw Productions Inc., NYC; dir. spl. projects Samuel Goldwyn Co.; sr. v.p. Offline Entertainment Group, 1998—2000. Dir., prodr. (films) The Ruling Classroom, 1980, Manufacturing Miracles, 1988, writer, dir. The Pacific Century, 1992, dir., prodr., writer (TV miniseries) The Fifties, 1997, AFI's 100 Years.100 Movies: Love Crazy, 1998, The Sexual Century: The Sexual Revolution, 1999, The Sexual Century: Sexual Explorers, 1999, (documentaries) Enron: The Smartest Guys in the Room, 2005 (Best Documentary, Independent Spirit award, 2006), (films) Behind Those Eyes, 2005, prodr., writer The Trials of Henry Kissinger, 2002; exec. prodr.: (TV films) The Huntress, 2000; (films) Brooklyn Babylon, 2001; sr. prodr. (films) Soldiers in the Army of God, 2000; prodr.: The Kennedy Ctr. Presents: Speak Truth to Power, 2000, The Soul of a Man, 2003, Lightening in a Bottle, 2004; series prodr. (TV miniseries) The Blues, 2003, cons. prodr. Who Killed the Electric Car?, 2006. Office: Jigsaw Productions Inc 601 W 26th Stt, 17th Fl New York NY 10001 Office Phone: 212-352-3010. Office Fax: 212-352-3015.

GIBNEY, JAMES S., editor; Grad., Middlebury Coll., 1982. Former fgn. svc. officer; exec. editor Foreign Policy Mag.; sr. editor Smithsonian Mag.; now dep. Op-Ed page editor NY Times. Office: Op-Ed Page NY Times 229 W 43rd St New York NY 10036 Office Phone: 212-556-7005. Office Fax: 212-556-4100, 212-556-3690.

GIBNEY, ROBERT L., JR., lawyer; b. Meriden, Conn., Mar. 9, 1947; BS psych., Yale U., 1969; MBA, JD with distinction, cum laude, Harvard U., 1973. Bar: Calif. 1973. Mem. Heller, Ehrman, White & McAuliffe, San Francisco; shareholder Heller Ehrman LLP, San Francisco. Mem. ABA, State Bar Calif., Bar Assn. San Francisco. Office: Heller Ehrman LLP 333 Bush St San Francisco CA 94104-2806 Office Phone: 415-772-6314. Office Fax: 415-772-6268. Business E-Mail: bob.gibney@hellerehrman.com.

GIBRALTER, JONATHAN C., academic administrator; BA, SUNY, Binghamton, 1978; MA, NYU, 1982; PhD, Syracuse U., 1996. Assoc. dean Sch. Liberal Arts SUNY, Morrisville, 1990—93; dean Rome Campus Mohawk Valley CC, 1993—98; dean academic affairs Corning CC, 1998—2000, interim pres., 2000—01; pres. SUNY, Farmingdale, 2001—06, Frostburg State U., Md., 2006—. Office: Frostburg State U Office of Pres 101 Braddock Rd Frostburg MD 21532 Office Phone: 301-687-4111. Office Fax: 301-687-7074. E-mail: jgibralter@frostburg.edu.

GIBRAN, KAHLIL, sculptor; b. Boston, Nov. 29, 1922; s. Nicholas and Rose (Gibran) G.; m. Jean English, July 1, 1957; children: Timothy; by previous marriage, Nicole. Student, Boston Mus. Sch., 1940-43. Exhibited widely as painter, 1949-52, life sized steel sculpture, 1953—, one person show bronzes, Cambridge Art Assn., 1977, Charlottesville, Va., 1993; exhbn.: Boston Arts Festival, 1985, Santa Fe, 1993, The Jean and Kahlil Gibran Collection, Danforth Mus. Art, Framingham, Mass., 2002-03; ann. exhbn. Bologna-Landi Gallery, East Hampton, L.I., N.Y., Denenberg Fine Arts, San Francisco, 1997, Contemporary Sculpture Chesterwood, 1997, St. Botolph Club, 1998, Art of the Spirit Forest Hills Cemetery, 1998, Copley Soc., 2001; included in Forum 49 Retrospective, Provincetown Art Assn., 1999; exhibited lifesize bronze Into the Millennium, Boston, 1999, commd. bronze plaque of Kahlil Gibran, Copley Sq., Boston, 1977, Judge Francis Ford, Fed. Ct. House, Boston, 1977, Judge Anthony Julian, Fed. Ct. House, Boston, Elliot Norton medal, Boston, 1983, bronze figure of Kahlil Gibran, Worcester State Coll., 1987, West Canton Street Child, Hayes Pk., Boston, 1992, Processional Cross All Soul's Episcopal Ch., San Diego, 1993, bronze plaque composer Amy Beach, 28 Commonwealth Ave., Boston; inventor Gibran Tripod, Mus. Modern Art collection; sculpture and painting show Copley Soc., 1994; represented in permanent collections Pa. Acad., Tenn. Fine Arts Ctr., Norfolk (Va.) Mus., Chrysler Mus., William Rockhill Gallery, Swope Gallery, Brockton Fine Arts Ctr.; author: Sculpture--Kahlil Gibran, 1970, (with wife Jean Gibran) Introduction to Lazarus and His Beloved, 1973, Kahlil Gibran, His Life and World, 1974, rev. edit., 1991; author: (monograph) Observations on the Reasons for the Cremona Tone, 1993. Pres. Kahlil Gibran Scholarship Fund, Boston, 1974. Recipient George Widener award Pa. Acad., 1958; Guggenheim fellow, 1959-61; award Nat. Inst. Arts and Letters, 1961; Grand prize Boston Arts Festival, 1964; John Gregory award sculpture, 1965; Gold medal Internat. Sacred Art Show, Trieste, Italy, 1966

GIBSON, ANN EDEN, art historian, educator; b. Hagerstown, Md., Apr. 30, 1944; d. James Orville and Mary Ellen (Ellis) G.; m. H. Thomas Simmons; 1 child, Jessica; m. Allan Federman, Jan. 10, 1982 (dec.); children: Elizabeth, Michele; m. Stephen Fogg, July 26, 2006. BS, Kent State U., 1965, MA, 1970, U. Pitts., 1978; PhD, U. Del., 1984. Tchr. art pub. schs., Hinckley and Wooster, Ohio, 1966-69; studio adj. Kent (Ohio) State U., 1969-72, Akron (Ohio) State U., 1970-72; art history adj. U. Pitts., 1979; instr. art Art Inst. Pitts., 1972-75, Point Park Coll., Pitts., 1975-79; assoc. prof. history art Yale U., New Haven, 1981-91; assoc. prof. art history SUNY, Stony Brook, 1992-98, acting chair dept. art, 1993-94; chair dept. art history U. Del., 1998—. Author: Issues in Abstract Expressionism, 1990, Abstract Expressionism: Other Politics, 1997, Judith Godwin, Style and Grace, 1997, Norman Lewis, Black Paintings, 1946-1977, 1998; guest editor (with Stephen Polcari), Art Journal; also articles. Andrew W. Mellon fellow Met. Mus. Art, 1981-83; Morse fellow Yale U., 1987-88, sr. fellow, 1990-91; Ailsa Mellon Bruce fellow Ctr. for Advanced Study in Visual Arts, Washington, 1990, postdoctoral fellow Smithsonian Instn., 1990-91, Getty Rsch. fellow, Guggenheim Meml. Found. fellow, 2005; recipient Disting. Alumna award, U. Pitts., 1995. Mem. Internat. Assn. Critics, Coll. Art Assn., Phi Kappa Phi. Office: U Del Dept Art History 206 Mechanical Hall Newark DE 19716 Business E-Mail: agibson@udel.edu.

GIBSON, ARLENE JOY, retired headmaster; BA, Bryn Mawr Coll., 1965; MA, Georgetown U., 1969. Dir. middle school Bryn Mawr Sch., Balt., 1981-84; dir. lower sch. Holton Arms Sch., Bethesda, Md., 1984-87; headmistress Kent Place Sch., Summit, N.J., 1987-96; head of sch. Spence Sch., NYC, 1998—2006. Office: Spence Sch 22 E 91st St New York NY 10128-0657 E-mail: agibson@spenceschool.org.*

GIBSON, BARRY JOSEPH, editor; b. Boston, Feb. 6, 1951; s. Joseph Wray and Marjorie Mitchell (Jacobs) Gibson; m. Jane Harley Reese, Oct. 11, 1980; 1 child, Michael Reese. BA, U. Miami, 1973. Assoc. editor Salt Water Sportsman, Boston, 1977-81, editor, 1981—2004, v.p., 1981-88; assoc. boating editor Outdoor Life, NYC, 1981-82; editor Directory Boats, Accessories and Fishing Tackle, Boston, 1981-83. Adviser Internat. Commn. Conservation Atlantic Tuna, Washington, 1986—89; mem. New Eng. Fishery Mgmt. Coun., 1987—96, chmn., 1992; mem. Nat. Marine Sanctary adv. coun. Stellwagen Bank, 2002—; New Eng. regional dir. Recreational Fishing Alliance, 2005—; cons. sports fishing industry. Contbr. articles to profl. jours. Charter boat capt., Boothbay Harbor, Maine, 1971—. Recipient Mako Outdoor Writer of the Yr., Mako Marine, Inc., 1982. Mem.: Atlantic Sportfishing Assn. (bd. dirs. Natick, Mass. 1988—90), N.E. Charterboat Capts. Assn. (founding mem. 1988—). Avocation: sport fishing. Home: 19 Royall Rd East Boothbay ME 04544 Personal E-mail: barry.gibson6@aol.com.

GIBSON, BEN S., art educator; s. Ben Grublauskas and Tophelia Trusis; m. Jane Gibson, June 15, 1995; children: Jeff, Dan, Jill; 1 child from previous marriage, Robyn. Cert. graduation, Kendall Coll. Art and Design, Grand Rapids, 1970; BA, Aquinas Coll., Grand Rapids, 1973; MFA, U. Nebr., Lincoln, 1976. Asst. prof. art Daemen Coll., Buffalo, 1973—76; prof. art Edinboro U. Pa., 1976—. Exhibitions include Marie Curie-Sklodowski U., Lublin, Poland, 2003, Kendall Coll. Art and Design, 2004. Recipient Best of Show Images award, Pa. State U., 2003.

GIBSON, BENJAMIN FRANKLIN, physicist; b. Madisonville, Tex., Sept. 3, 1938; s. Mitchell Osler and Christine (Bennett) G.; m. Margaret Alice Ferguson, July 20, 1968; children: James M., Michael W., Stuart W. BA, Rice U., Houston, 1961; PhD, Stanford U., Calif., 1966. Postdoctoral fellow Lawrence Livermore Nat. Lab., Calif., 1966-68; rsch. assoc. NAS, Nat. Bur. Stds., Gaithersburg, Md., 1968-70, CUNY, Bklyn., 1970-72; group leader, T-5 Los Alamos Nat. Lab., N.Mex., 1982-86, staff mem. N.Mex., 1972—; detailee Dept. of Energy Divsn. Nuclear Physics, 1980-81. Program adv. com. MIT Bates Electron Accelerator, Boston, 1985-89, 98-2003; mem. subatomic physics grant selection com. Can. Natural Scis. and Engring. Rsch. Coun., 1994-96, theory rev. panel NSF, 1997, 98, 2006. Co-editor: Three-body Force in the Three-Nucleon System, 1986, Procs. of LAMPF Workshop on pi K Physics, 1991, New Vistas in Physics with High-Energy Pion Beams, 1993, Properties and Interactions of Hyperons, 1994, Baryons '95, 1996, 20 Years of Meson Factory Physics: Accomplishments and Prospects, 1997; assoc. editor Phys. Review C, 1988-02, editor, 2002—, mem. editl. bd. 1978-79, 87-88; mem. editl. bd. FEW Body Sys., 1986—; contbr. articles to profl. jours. Recipient Sr. Scientist Rsch. award Alexander von Humboldt Found., 1992; Japan Soc. Promotion of Sci. rsch. fellow Tohoku U., 1984; vis. fellow U. Melbourne, Australia, 1986, Flinders U., Adelaide, Australia, 1987, Murdoch fellow Inst. for Nuclear Theory, U. Wash., Seattle, 1992. Fellow Am. Phys. Soc., Few-Body Sys. Topical Group (vice chmn. 1990-92, chmn. 1992-93, exec. com. 2004-06), Divsn. Nuc. Physics (sec.-treas. 1995—). Achievements include patents in field of epithermal-neutron well logging. Office: T-16 MS-B283 Los Alamos NM 87545-0001 Home Phone: 505-672-3609; Office Phone: 505-667-5059. Business E-Mail: bfgibson@lanl.gov.

GIBSON, CHARLES DEWOLF, newscaster; b. Evanston, Ill., Mar. 9, 1943; s. Burdett and Georgiana (Law) G.; m. Arlene Joy Gibson, July 20, 1968; children: Jessica Law, Katherine Burdett. AB, Princeton U., 1965. Washington prodr. RKO Network, Washington, 1966; news dir. Sta.-WLVA-TV, Lynchburg, Va., 1967-69; anchorman, reporter Sta.-WMAL-TV (now WJLA-TV), Washington, 1970-73; corr. TVN, Inc. (TV News, Inc.), Washington, 1974-75; joined ABC News, 1975, White House corr. Washington, 1976—77, corr., gen. assignment, 1977—81, Capitol Hill corr., 1981-87; co-host Good Morning America ABC TV, NYC, 1987—98, 1999—2006, anchor World News with Charles Gibson, 2006—. Bd. trustees Princeton U., 2006—; bd. dir. Knight-Wallace Fellows at Mich., 1988—. John Maclean Fellowship, Princeton U., 1992, Nat. Journalism Fellow NEH, U. Mich., 1973-74. Office: ABC World News Tonight 77 West 66th St New York NY 10023

GIBSON, DAVID MARK, biochemist, educator; b. Kokomo, Ind., Aug. 7, 1923; s. Carl Banta and Marie (Loop) Gibson; m. Margaret Lockhart, June 2, 1951 (dec. Apr. 1992); children: Carl L., John L., Shauna Gibson Ball, Heather Gibson Garrison, Mark C.; m. Wilda Lee Preston, July 7, 2001. AB, Wabash Coll., 1944; MD, Harvard U., 1948. Intern Northwestern U. Med. Sch., 1948—49; rsch. assoc. biochemistry U. Ill., Urbana, 1950—53; rsch. assoc., asst. prof. Inst. Enzyme Rsch. U. Wis., 1953—55, 1955—58; assoc. prof. biochemistry Ind. U. Sch. Medicine, Indpls., 1958—61, prof., 1961—, Grace M. Showalter prof., 1974—92, prof. emeritus, 1992—, chmn., 1967—88. Established investigator Am. Heart Assn., 1957—62; vis. prof. U. Padua, Italy, 1964—65, U. Utrecht, Netherlands, 1975. Author: (textbook) Metabolic Regulation in Mammals, 2002. Recipient Career Devel. award, NIH, 1962—67. Mem.: AAAS, Biochem. Soc. (Eng.), Am. Diabetes Assn., Am. Soc. Biol. Chemists, Am. Soc. Cell Biology, Sigma Xi. Achievements include research in biochemical mechanisms and control fatty acid synthesis and cholesterol synthesis. Home: 1745 Graham Rd Mansfield OH 44904-9744 E-mail: davegibson@core.com.

GIBSON, DAVID THOMAS, microbiology educator; b. Wakefield, Yorkshire, Eng., Feb. 16, 1938; U.S. citizen; married; two children. BSc in Biochemistry 1st class honors, U. Leeds, Eng., 1961, PhD in Biochemistry, 1964. Lectr. in biology Leeds Tech. Coll., 1962-63; rsch. assoc. U. Wis. Coll. Pharmacy, Madison, 1964-65; rsch. assoc. dept. microbiology U. Ill., Champaign-Urbana, 1965-67; asst. prof. microbiology dept. U. Tex., Austin, 1967-68, 69-71, assoc. prof. microbiology dept., 1971-75, prof. microbiology dept., 1975-88, dir. Ctr. for Applied Microbiology, 1981-88; Edwin B. Green prof. biocatalysis and microbiology Coll. Medicine, U. Iowa, Iowa City, 1988—2004; ret., 2004. Rsch. biochemist pharms. divsn. I.C.I. Ltd., Aderley Park, Cheshire, Eng., 1968-69; L.Am. vis. prof. Nat. Poly. Inst., Mexico City, 1976; mem. microbial chemistry study sect. NIH, 1977-80; mem. sci. adv. bd. AMGEN, 1981-88; mem. various univ. coms. Assoc. editor Devels. in Indsl. Microbiology, 1975-79; mem. editl. bd. Jour. Bacteriology, 1979-83, 88-91, 95-97, Jour. Biol. Chemistry, 1980-88, Biodegradation, 1989-96; contbr. numerous articles to profl. jours. Recipient Career Devel. award USPHS, 1972-77; grantee NIH, 1995—, USAF, 1996-99. Fellow AAAS; mem. Am. Soc. for Microbiology (Found. lectr. 1981-82, Procter and Gamble award in appled and environ. microbiology 1997), Am. Chem. Soc., Soc. for Indsl. Microbiology, Fedn. Am. Socs. for Exptl. Biology, Am. Acad. Microbiology (mem. nominating com. 1988-90), NAS, Sigma Xi, Phi Kappa Phi. Office: U Iowa Dept Microbiology 3733 Bowen Science Building Iowa City IA 52242-1109 E-mail: david.gibson@uiowa.edu.

GIBSON, EDGAR THOMAS, retired surgeon, educator; b. Phila., Mar. 23, 1915; s. Albert and Mabel (Cave) G.; m. Helen Tomlinson, Nov. 7, 1943; children: Ann Peluso, Barbara, Jeanne Rollins, Helen Tucker. BS, Villanova U., 1938; MD, Jefferson Med. Coll., 1942; postgrad., U. Pa., 1947-48. Resident surgery Cleve. Clinic, 1943-44, West Jersey Hosp., Camden, NJ, 1948-50; resident thoracic surgery Phila. Gen. Hosp., 1952-54; pres. staff Camden County Chest Hosp., 1950-88; chmn. dept. surgery West Jersey Hosp. Group, 1975-78; staff mem. Our Lady of Lourdes Hosp., Camden, NJ, 1950-88; instr. surgery Jefferson U., Phila., 1950-88. Pres. Camden County Heart Soc., 1960. Capt. U.S. Army, 1944-46, ETO. Fellow AMA, ACS, Am. Bd. Surgery, N.J. Soc. Surgeons; mem. Camden County Med. Soc. (pres.). Republican. Avocations: sailing, skiing, photography. Home: 8 Pond Head Rd Southport ME 04576-3343

GIBSON, EMMITT E., career officer; b. Feb. 7, 1944; Commd. officer U.S. Army, advanced through grades to maj. gen., commdg. gen. Aviation and Missile Redstone Arsenal, Ala., 1997-98, dep. dir. resources and requirements, 1998—. Office: FSRAD J-8 9000 Defense Pentagon Rm 1e962 Washington DC 20318-0001

GIBSON, ERNEST WILLARD, III, retired state supreme court justice; b. Brattleboro, Vt., Sept. 23, 1927; s. Ernest William and Dorothy Pearl (Switzer) G.; m. Charlotte Elaine Hungerford, Sept. 10, 1960; children: Margaret, Mary, John. BA, Yale U., 1951; LLB, Harvard U., 1956. Bar: Vt. State's atty. Windham County, Vt., 1957-61; mem. Vt. Ho. of Reps., 1961-63, chmn. judiciary com., 1963; chmn. Vt. Pub. Svc. Bd., 1963-72; judge Vt. Superior Ct., 1972-83; assoc. justice Vt. Supreme Ct., 1983-97, ret., 1997. Chancellor Episcopal Diocese Vt., 1977-98, trustee, 1972-99, pres. bd. trustees, 1991-99, dep. to gen. conv., 1976-94. Served in U.S. Army, 1945-46, 51-53, Major Army Nat. Guard, 1956-71. Mem. Vt. Bar Assn. Avocations: bridge, tennis. Home: 11 Baldwin St Montpelier VT 05602-2110

GIBSON, EVERETT KAY, JR., aerospace scientist, geochemist; b. Seagraves, Tex., May 13, 1940; s. Everett Kay and Lillie Gertrude (Ivey) G.; m. Mary Morgan Shott, Oct. 13, 1973; 1 son, Bradford Pierce Gibson. BS, Tex. Tech U., Lubbock, 1963, MS, 1965; PhD, Ariz. State U., 1969. Instr. Tex. Tech. U., 1963-65; postdoctoral research assoc. NASA Johnson Space Center, Houston, 1969-70, space scientist, geochemist, 1970-91; sr. scientist NASA-Johnson Space Ctr., 1991—; vis. program mgr. NSF, Washington, 1979; mission sci. advisor Apollo 14; test dir. Lunar Receiving Lab. NASA, 1971, prin. investigator Lunar Sample Analysis Program, 1971-90, mem. Lunar Sample Analysis Planning Team, 1974-77, prin. investigator Planetary Geology Program, 1978-86, prin. investigator Mars Data Analysis Program, 1979-84, prin. investigation Exobiology Program, 1983—. Mem. U.S. Antarctic Meteorite Search Team, 1979-80; adj. prof. geology U. Houston, 1975-90; sr. Leverhulme vis. fellow Open U., Milton Keynes, Eng., 1984-85; cons. The Economist (London), BBC, London; interdiscipline scientist Mars Express/Beagle 2 Mission to Mars, European Space Agy., 2001—. Assoc. editor 5th, 6th, 7th, 8th, 9th and 12th Proc. Lunar and Planetary Sci. Conf., 1974-81; assoc. editor: Chondrules and Their Origins, 1983; contbr. articles to sci. jours. Bd. dirs. Clear Creek Basin Authority, Harris County, Tex., 1974-75; col. Commemorative Air Force, 1983—, life mem., 1987, aircraft sponsor, 1988, exec. officer, 1990-2002; exec. bd. Wings Over Houston Air Show, 1990—. Recipient Laurel Space award Aviation Week and Space Tech., 1972, 97, award for lunar sci. team participation NASA Johnson Space Ctr., 1974, Disting. Achievement award Ariz. State U., 1980, Silver Magnolia award Commemorative Air Force, 1993, 99, Manned Flight Awareness award, 1993, Exceptional Sci. Achievement medal NASA, 1997, Ariz. State U. Hall of Fame award, 1998, Scientist of Yr. award Tex. Acad. of Sci., 2000; Papadopoulos fellow in biology Kinkaid Sch., 2006. Fellow Meteoritical Soc. (sec. 1974-80, councilor 1987-90); mem. Am. Chem. Soc., Internat. Soc. for Study of Origin of Life, AAAS, Am. Geophys. Union, Sigma Xi, Phi Lambda Upsilon. Baptist. Home: 1015 Trowbridge Dr Houston TX 77062-2726 Office: NOW KR Astromaterials Rsch Office NASA Johnson Space Ctr 2101 NASA Rd 1 Houston TX 77058 Personal E-mail: ekgmars@aol.com.

GIBSON, FLORENCE ANDERSON, talking book company executive, narrator; b. San Francisco, Feb. 7, 1924; m. V.H. Carlos Gibson, Aug. 30, 1947; children: Nancy Derwent, Christopher Carlos, Katherine Wayne Bolland, Diana Corona. Student, Finch Jr. Coll., NYC, 1941—42; BA in Dramatic Lit., U. Calif., Berkeley, 1944; student, Neighborhood Playhouse, NYC, 1944—45. Radio actress, San Francisco, 1944, 46, 47; chmn. Washington com. Am. Field Svc., 1958-60, 62-65, founder, chmn. Peruvian Com. Lima, 1960-62; treas., distbn. mgr. Living Garden and Concern 1975 calendars, 1971-75; sec. exec. com Fgn. Student Svc. Coun., 1973-76; narrator Talking Books Libr. of Congress div. for Blind and Physically Handicapped, 1975-96; narrator Recorded Books, Inc., 1979; founder, pres. Audio Book Contractors, Inc., 1982—. Actress Blithe Spirit, the USO Camp Show, 1944, Ah, Wilderness, 1946, Equity Libr. Theater, NYC, (TV series) Traffic Ct., others, narrator more than 1,025 unabridged classic books on cassette; author: (children's book) Three Tales in Verse, 2006. Bd. dirs. Fgn. Student Svc. Coun., Concern, Inc., Rec. for the Blind, Children's Theater of Washington; vol. in occupational therapy Children's Hosp., Washington, 1949-50; vol. lobbyist student exch. program Am. Field Svc. Recipient Parents' Choice awards, 1983, 84, 86, Audiophile Earphone award, 1999; named Best Female Narrator, Book World, 1989; selected as A Notable Children's Recording, ALA, 1983, 87, 88, 89. Home: 4626 Garfield St NW Washington DC 20007-1025 Office: Audio Book Contractors Inc PO Box 40115 Washington DC 20016-0115 Office Phone: 202-363-3429. Personal E-mail: flogibsonabc@aol.com. E-mail: flogibsonabc@verizon.com.

GIBSON, GORDON RONALD, chemist; b. Buffalo, Sept. 14, 1929; s. Sandy Wellington and Geneva Lucy (Hill) G.; m. Janet Long, Feb. 10, 1954 (dec. 1961); children: Andrew, Robert, Douglas; m. Marilyn Jean Kirkendoll, Oct. 20, 1966 (dec. 1997); children: Nicholas John, Holli Rae. BA in Chemistry, U. Buffalo, 1957. Process devel. chemist Dunlop Tire & Rubber Co., Buffalo, 1957—59; sr. process engr. Hercules Inc., Salt Lake City, 1961—68, Radford, Va., 1968—76; analytical chemist Biomed. Test Lab. U. Utah, Salt Lake City, 1976—77; analytical chemist OSHA U.S. Dept. Labor, Salt Lake City, 1977—81; chemistry specialist Aerojet Propulsion divsn. GenCorp, Sacramento, 1981—92. Active Reps., Sacramento. With

U.S. Army, 1951. Achievements include patent for Polyurethane Molding; development of solid propellant having highest delivered specific impulse in the world. Home: 6634 Quanah Way Orangevale CA 95662-3332

GIBSON, JAMES ELLIOTT, architect; b. McMinnville, Oreg., Aug. 14, 1922; s. James H. and Julia Etta (Cummins) G.; m. Clara June Bosson, Dec. 19, 1948 (dec. Sept. 1967); children: Graeme E.B., Randolph U., James B.P.; m. Suzan Bailliere Brand Brown, Jan. 1, 1980 (dec. June 1998); children: John W. Brown, Natalie T. Brown, Frank D. Brown, Susannah Brown Kavanaugh. BS in Music, U. Oreg., 1944; BArch, U. Mich., 1950. Registered arch., Mich., Fla., SC, Ohio, cert. NCARB. Arch. Harley, Ellington & Day, Inc., Detroit, 1950—69, James E. Gibson, Archs. & Assoc., Inc., Vero Beach, Fla., 1969—83, Gibson & Silkworth, Archs. & Assoc., Inc., Vero Beach, 1983—97, Gibson & Assoc., Archs., Inc., Vero Beach, 1997—. Pres. Vero Beach Concert Assn., 1971-79, 81-83, pres. Treas. Coast Opera Assn., Vero Beach, 1979-81; bd. dir. Atlantic Classical Orch., Vero Beach, 1992-03, pres. 1998-2003; bd. dir., mem. adv. bd. Riverside Theatre, Vero Beach; mem. adv. bd. Ctr. for the Arts, Vero Beach. Staff sgt. U.S. Army, 1942-46, ETO. Recipient Bus. in the Arts award, 1986, Aurora Grand award Assoc. Gen. Contractors, 1985. Mem. AIA, John's Island Club (Vero Beach), Carolina Yacht Club (Charleston, SC). Avocations: music, antiques, sculpting, historical preservation. Office: Gibson & Assocs Archs 606 Azalea Ln Vero Beach FL 32963-1832 Home Phone: 772-231-2318; Office Phone: 772-231-6008.

GIBSON, JERRY LEIGH, oil industry executive; b. El Dorado, Ark., Jan. 24, 1930; s. Oscar Edward and Ruth (Coleman) G.; m. Alma Gail Peoples, Apr. 11, 1953; children: Sallie Gail, Gregory Leigh. BBA with honors, U. North Tex., 1951; MBA, So. Meth. U., 1956. With Exxon Mobil, 1952-59, 60-66, asst. to asst. comptr.; mgmt. cons. KPMG CPAs LLP, 1959; v.p., sec., treas. Riviana Foods Inc., Houston, 1966-69; pres., treas., CEO Intermedco Inc., Houston, 1969-73; pres., CEO Automated Fin. Svcs., Houston, 1973-75; v.p. fin. A-Z Internat. Tool Co., Houston, 1975-80; pres., CEO, owner JHJ Drilling Co., Houston, 1980-85; pres., CEO Kellywood Corp., Houston, 1986—. Tchr. acctg. So. Meth. U., 1956-57. With USAF, 1950-52. Home and Office: 6801 Auckland Ct Austin TX 78749-4136 Home Phone: 512-301-2069; Office Phone: 512-289-0804. Personal E-mail: jgibson14@austin.rr.com.

GIBSON, JOHN, news anchor, correspondent; B film sch., UCLA. Reporter Hollywood Reporter, LA, 1969-72, various locations, Calif., 1974-77; bur. chief, anchor Weekend Mag., Sta. KCRA-TV, San Francisco, 1979-89; anchor, corr. In Am., 1989-92; corr. NBC News, Burbank, Calif., 1992-94; West Coast corr. NBC News Channel, 1994—2000; anchor News Chat and InterNight, Playback MSNBC, NYC; host, The Big Story with John Gibson Fox News, NYC, 2000—. Office: Fox News Channel 1211 Ave of the Americas New York NY 10036

GIBSON, JOHN ROBERT, federal judge; b. Springfield, Mo., Dec. 20, 1925; s. Harry B. and Edna (Kerr) G.; m. Mary Elizabeth Vaughn, Sept. 20, 1952 (dec. Aug. 1985); children: Jeanne, John Robert; m. Diane Allen Larrison, Oct. 1, 1986 (div. 2006); stepchildren: Holly, Catherine. AB, U. Mo., 1949, JD, 1952. Bar: Mo. 1952. Assoc. Morrison, Hecker, Curtis, Kuder & Parrish, Kansas City, Mo., 1952-58, ptnr., 1958-81; judge US Dist. Ct. (we. dist.) Mo., 1981-82, US Ct. Appeals (8th cir.), 1982-94, sr. judge, 1994—. Mem. Mo. Press-Bar Commn., 1979-81; mem. com. on adminstrn. of magistrate sys. Jud. Conf. U.S., 1987-91, mem. security and facilities com., 1995-2001. Vice chmn. Jackson County Charter Transition Com., 1971-72; mem. Jackson County Charter Commn., 1970; v.p. Police Commrs. Bd., Kansas City, 1973-77. With US Army, 1944—46. Recipient Citation of Merit award U. Mo. at Columbia Sch. of Law, 1994. Fellow Am. Bar Found.; mem. Mo. State Bar (gov. 1972-79, pres. 1977-78; Pres.' award 1974, Smithson award 1984), Kansas City Bar Assn. (pres. 1970-71), Lawyers Assn. Kansas City (Charles Evan Whittaker award 1980), Fed. Judges Assn. (bd. dirs. 1991-97), Phi Beta Kappa, Omicron Delta Kappa. Presbyterian. Office: US Ct Appeals 8th Cir 400 E 9th St Ste 1040 Kansas City MO 64106-2695*

GIBSON, JOHN ROBERT, software engineer; b. Murfreesboro, Tenn., Dec. 24, 1948; s. Donald Cotis Gibson and Sara Elizabeth Garner; m. Corinne de Marie Pallatto, Sept. 2, 1978 (div. July 1989). BSEE, U. Ala., 1973. Commd. 2d lt. USAF, 1973, advanced through grades to capt., 1977, resigned, 1983; computer programmer/analyst Computer Scis. Corp., Colorado Springs, Colo., Ridgecrest, Calif., 1984-90; sci. computer programmer Boeing Computer Support Svcs., Ridgecrest, 1990-91; computer engr. USAF, Edwards AFB, Calif., 1993-95; software tester EER Sys., Inc., Ridgecrest, 1996-97; software engr. EDO Tech. Svcs. Ops., Edwards AFB, 1997—2001; embedded programming AOA Inc., Westlake Village, Calif., 2002—04; software tester Boeing Svc. Co., Colorado Springs, Colo., 2005. Contbr. articles to profl. jours. Candidate for Calif. State Senate, Antelope Valley Libertarian Party, 2000, treas., 2000-02. Mem. Calif. Checker Assn. (pres. 1999-2005). Avocations: anime, checkers, coins, history, skiing. Home: 4040 Lacy Lane 15 Colorado Springs CO 80916-7316 Personal E-mail: jrgibson_7@hotmail.com.

GIBSON, JOHN THOMAS, academic administrator, consultant; b. Montgomery, Ala., Sept. 19, 1948; s. Herman Farris and Lillian Christine (Payload) G.; m. Mayme Voncile Pierce, Jan. 31, 1970; children: John Thomas II, Jerard Trenton, Justin Tarrance, Shayla Voncile. BS, Tuskegee U., Ala., 1970, EdM, 1971; EdS, U. Colo., 1972, PhD, 1973; cert. in mgmt., Harvard U., 1982. Dir. lab. experiences Ala. State U., Montgomery, 1973-75, coord. fed. rels., 1975-76, area head edn. adminstrn., 1976-83, exec. asst. to pres., 1983-86; v.p. bus. and fin. Ala. A&M U., Huntsville, 1986-90, assoc. v.p. adminstrn., 1990-97, pres., 1996—2005. Cons. Ala. Edn. Assn., Montgomery, 1975-76, Montgomery County Bd. of Edn., 1976, Gray, Seay & Langford, Montgomery, 1976, Thomas, Means & Gillis, Montgomery, 1990-91; bd. dirs. Am. Coun. Edn., Ala. Sci. & Math. Inst.; chmn. bd. dirs. Sci. & Engring. Alliance. Contbr. articles to profl. jours. Exec. com. Ala. Dem. Party, Montgomery, 1976-78. Capt. U.S. Army, 1970-73. Named one of Outstanding Young Men of Am., 1983. Mem. Masons (32d), Optimists, Kiwanis, Kappa Alpha Psi (Svc. award 1980-82), Phi Delta Kappa (chair fin. com. 1983), Kappa Delta Pi. A.M.E. Avocations: tennis, swimming. Home: 151 Heritage Ln Madison AL 35758-7975 E-mail: jgibson@aamu.edu.

GIBSON, JOHN W., gas industry executive; b. Kansas City, Kans. B in engring., Univ. Mo. Refinery engr. Exxon Co. USA; engring. mgmt. positions through exec. v.p. mktg. GPM Gas Corp. Phillips Petroleum Co., 1974—95; exec. v.p. Koch Energy Inc., 1995—2000; pres., COO ONEOK Partners, Tulsa, Okla., 2000—07, pres., CEO, 2007—; CEO ONEOK Inc., Tulsa, Okla., 2007—. Bd. mem. Assn. Tex. Intrastate Gas Pipelines, Gas Industry Standards Bd., Interstate Natural Gas Assn. Am. Office: ONEOK Inc 100 W Fifth St Tulsa OK 74103*

GIBSON, JUDITH W., psychotherapist; b. Syracuse, NY, Apr. 27, 1942; d. Nathan Whitney and Helen-Alycia (Fancher) Watson; m. Robert Glenn Gibson, Aug. 1964 (dec. Oct. 1966); children: Heidi, Mary Lou. BA in English, Syracuse U., 1978, MA in Religion, 1985, MSW, 1987. LCSW Acad. Cert. Social Workers. Bookkeeper Stickley Furniture, Fayetteville, N.Y., 1965-67; adminstrv. asst. Agway Inc., Dewitt, N.Y., 1967-82; asst. dir. housing Syracuse U., 1983-87; dir. preventive svcs. The Salvation Army, Syracuse, 1990—2002; clinician Psychol. Health Care PLLC, Syracuse, 2002—. Mem. NASW. Roman Catholic. Avocations: reading, arts, travel. Home: 9 Carriage House E # A Manlius NY 13104-2355 Home Phone: 315-682-8602; Office Phone: 315-422-0300.

GIBSON, KATHLEEN M., computer and electronics executive; b. Phila., Feb. 14, 1955; BA summa cum laude, Temple U.; JD cum laude, Harvard U. Bar: Pa. With Ballard, Spahr, Andrews and Ingersoll, 1984-87, Bell Atlantic Corp., 1987-97; v.p., corp. sec. Honeywell Inc., 1997-99, Honeywell Internat. Inc., 1999; v.p., sec., corp. governance officer Prudential Fin., Newark. Mem. ABA, Nat. Inst. Investor Rels., Am. Soc. Corp. Secs., former chmn.). Soc. Corp. Secretaries and Governance Profl., Phi Beta Kappa. Office: Prudential Fin Prudential Plz 751 Broad St Newark NJ 07102 Office Phone: 973-802-7770. Office Fax: 973-802-8287.

GIBSON, KEITH E., education educator; b. Columbia, Mo., Dec. 27, 1972; s. Kenneth E. and Carol Ann Gibson; m. Jocelin A. Anderson, June 14, 1996; children: Michal Anne, Samantha, Kenneth Eli. PhD in English, Pa. State U., University Park, 1999—2003. Asst. prof. Auburn U., Ala., 2003—. Office: Auburn Univ 9030 Haley Center Auburn University AL 36849 Home Phone: 334-821-8629. Business E-Mail: gibsoke@auburn.edu.

GIBSON, KEITH RUSSELL, lawyer, educator; b. Fulton, NY, Feb. 24, 1954; s. Keith Melvin and Retha (Thatcher) G.; m. Brandi Gibson; children: Emily Michelle, Robin Bethany, Kyle Russell. BA, Lycoming Coll., 1976; paralegal cert., Adelphi U., 1977; JD, Oklahoma City U., 1984. Bar: Okla. 1984, U.S. Dist. Ct. (no., we., ea. dists.) Okla. 1984. Paralegal Thatcher & Miller, Lewistown, Pa., 1978-81; law clk. Chief Justice Don Barnes Okla. Supreme Ct., Oklahoma City, 1983-84; assoc. Pate & Payne, Oklahoma City, 1984-91; sr. atty. Williams, Box, Forshee & Bullard, P.C., Oklahoma City, 1991—. Instr. Oklahoma City U. Legal Asst. Program, 1990-98, officer Sch. of Law Alumni Assn., 1994-96; lectr. Okla. Foreclosure and Repossession Nat. Bus. Inst.; paralegal issues instr. Inst. for Paralegal Edn.; legal advisor Okla. Just Compensation Act. Originator and participant Met. Ch. Legal Clearinghouse, Oklahoma City, 1995. Mem. Oklahoma City U. Law Alumni Assn. (officer 1994-96, participant fund-raising 1996), North Oklahoma City Rotary (bd. dirs. 1994-95, sec. 1995-96, Newcomer of Yr. 1991, Pres.'s award 1993-94, Benefactor award Rotary Found. 1993), Friends of the Oklahoma City Libr. Assn., Federalist Soc. (Okla. chpt.), Conf. Consumer Fin. Law. Republican. Home: 2713 NW 158th St Edmond OK 73013-8819 Office: Williams Box Forshee & Bullard PC 522 Colcord Dr Oklahoma City OK 73102-2202 Home Phone: 405-348-8071; Office Phone: 405-232-0080. Business E-Mail: kgibson@wbfblaw.com.

GIBSON, LISETTE L., elementary school and music educator; b. St. Louis, Dec. 14, 1945; d. Erwin L. and Anna Marie Lueker; children: Robert, Todd. BA, Concordia, River Forest, Ill., 1967; MA, U. Mich., 1989. Tchr. grades 3 and 4, music tchr. grades 5-8 St. Paul Luth. Ch. and Sch., Bay City, Mich., 1994—.

GIBSON, MCGUIRE, archaeologist, educator; b. Bushwood, Md., Nov. 6, 1938; s. Thomas Laurie and Essie Mae (Owens) Gibson. BA, Fordham U., 1959; MA, U. Chgo., 1964, PhD, 1968. Asst. prof. anthropology U. Ill., Chgo., 1968-71; asst. prof. U. Ariz., Tucson, 1971-72; from asst. prof. to assoc. prof. U. Chgo., 1972—81, prof., 1981—. Ann. prof. Am. Schs. Oriental Rsch., Baghdad, Iraq, 1969—70; dir. Nippur Expdn., Iraq, 1972—, Dhamar Expdn., Yemen, 1978—98, Hamoukar Expdn., Syria, 1999—; chmn. Coun. Am. Overseas Rsch. Ctrs., 1984—88, treas., 1988—92, mem. exec. com., 1995—2001; pres. Am. Acad. Rsch. Inst. in Iraq, 2003—. Author: (book) The City and Area of Kish, 1972; editor: Irrigation's Impact on Society, 1974, Seals and Sealing in the Ancient Near East, 1977, The Organization of Power: Aspects of Bureaucracy in the Ancient Near East, 1987, Uch Tepe II, 1990, Nippur III, 1993; author, editor: book Excavations in Nippur, 12th Season, 1978, Uch Tepe I, 1981. Mem. UNESCO Fact-Finding Mission to Iraq, 2003; mem. arts com. Union League Civic and Arts Found., Chgo., 1984—86; mem. adv. bd. Chgo. Humanities Festival, 2003—. Recipient Yemeni Arch. Svc. award, 1998; grantee, Am. Numismatic Soc., 1966, Am. Philos. Soc., 1969, Nat. Geog. Soc., 1978, 1989, NSF, 1994, 2000, NEH, 1995—98. Fellow: Deutsche Orient-Gesellchaft, Royal Anthrop. Inst., Brit. Sch. Archaeology Iraq; mem.: AAAS, Civil War Landscapes Assn., Am. Assn. Rsch. Baghdad, Mid. E. Studies Assn., Am. Inst. Yemeni Studies, Am. Anthrop. Assn., Archaeological Inst. Am., Quadrangle Club. Democrat. Avocations: architectural restoration, study of oriental rugs. Office: U Chgo Oriental Inst 1155 E 58th St Chicago IL 60637-1540 Home Phone: 773-862-7297; Office Phone: 773-702-9525. E-mail: m-gibson@uchicago.edu.

GIBSON, MEL, actor, film director and producer; b. Peekskill, NY, Jan. 3, 1956; emigrated to Australia, 1968; s. Hutton and Anne Gibson; m. Robyn Moore June 7, 1980; children: Hannah, Edward, Christian, Willie, Louis, Milo, Tommy. Grad., Nat. Inst. Dramatic Art, Sydney, Australia, 1977; LHD (hon.), Loyola Marymount U., 2003. Founder Icon Prodns. Works include: (films) Summer City, 1977, Mad Max, 1979, Tim, 1979, Attack Force Z, Gallipoli, 1981, The Road Warrior (Mad Max II), 1982, The Year of Living Dangerously, 1983, The Bounty, 1984, The River, 1984, Mrs. Soffel, 1984, Mad Max Beyond Thunderdome, 1985, Lethal Weapon, 1987, Tequila Sunrise, 1988, Lethal Weapon II, 1988, Bird on a Wire, 1989, Hamlet, 1990, Air America, 1990, Lethal Weapon III, 1992, Forever Young, 1992, Maverick, 1994, Pocahontas, 1995 (voice only), Ransom, 1996, Father's Day, 1997, Conspiracy Theory, 1997, Lethal Weapon 4, 1998, The Million Dollar Hotel, 1999, Payback, 1999, Chicken Run, 2000 (voice only), The Patriot, 2000, What Women Want, 2000, Signs, 2002, We Were Soldiers, 2003, The Singing Detective (also prodr.), 2003; actor, dir.: The Man Without a Face, 1993; actor, dir., prodr.: Braveheart, 1995 (Golden Globe award for best dir. of film 1996, Acad. award for best dir. 1996, Acad. award for best picture of yr. 1996, Outstanding Directorial Achievement in Motion Picture award nominee Dir. Guild Am. 1996, Oscar award for Best Dir.); dir., screenwriter, prodr.: The Passion of the Christ, 2004, Apocalypto, 2006; performed with Nimrod Theatre Co. in plays including Death of a Salesman, Romeo and Juliet, with South Australian Theatre Co., from 1978, appeared in plays including Oedipus, Henry IV, Cedoona; work in TV series includes The Sullivans, The Oracle (Australia); exec. prodr. (TV) The Three Stooges, 2000, Complete Savages, 2004-05, Clubhouse, 2004-05. Favorite Movie Actor, People's Choice award, 1997; named one of 50 Most Power People in Hollywood Premiere mag. 2003-06. Roman Catholic.

GIBSON, MELVIN ROY, retired pharmacology educator; b. St. Paul, Nebr., June 11, 1920; s. John and Jennie Irene (Harvey) G. BS, U. Nebr., Lincoln, 1942, MS, 1947, DSc (hon.), 1985; PhD, U. Ill., Chgo., 1949. Asst. prof. pharmacognosy Wash. State U., Pullman, 1949-52, assoc. prof., 1952-55, prof., 1955-85, prof. emeritus, 1985—, ret. Editor: Am. Jour. Pharm. Edn, 1956-61; mem. editl. bd., co-author: Remington's Pharm. Sci, 1970, 75, 80, 85; editor, co-author: Studies of a Pharm. Curriculum, 1967; author over 100 articles. Served as arty. officer AUS, 1942-46. Decorated Bronze Star, Purple Heart; sr. vis. fellow Orgn. for Econ. Cooperation and Devel., Royal Pharm. Inst. (now part of Uppsala U.), Stockholm, U. Leiden (Holland), 1962; recipient Rufus A. Lyman award, 1972, Wash. State U. Faculty Libr. award, 1984, Disting. Alumnus award U. Nebr., 1999; named Wash. State U. Faculty Mem. of Yr., 1985. Fellow AAAS, Am. Coll. Apothecaries (assoc.); mem. AAUP, VFW (life), NY Acad. Scis., Am. Pharm. Assn., Am. Soc. Pharmacognosy (pres. 1964-65), Am. Assn. Coll. Pharmacy (exec. com. 1961-63, bd. dirs. 1977-79, chmn. coun. faculties 1975-76, pres. 1979-80, Disting. Educator award 1984), U.S. Pharmacopeia (revision com. 1970-75), Am. Found. Pharm. Edn. (hon. life, bd. dirs. 1980-85, exec. com. 1981-85, vice chmn. 1982-85), Am. Inst. History of Pharmacy (sponsor), U. Nebr. Chancellor's Club, U. Nebr. Pres. Club, Sigma Xi, Phi Kappa Phi, Omicron Delta Kappa, Rho Chi, Spokane Club, Kappa Psi (Nat. Svc. citation 1961). Democrat. Presbyterian. Home: 707 W 6th Ave Apt 41 Spokane WA 99204-2813

GIBSON, MILTON EUGENE, cardiologist; b. Laporte, Ind., July 11, 1939; s. Maurice Wayne and Mary Leola Gibson; m. Gloria Jean Birky, Aug. 12, 1961; children: Kevin Scott, Bradley Mark. BA, Valparaiso U., 1961; MD, Ind. U., 1965. Diplomate Am. Bd. Internal Medicine, Am. Bd. Cardiovasc. Disease, Am. Bd. Interventional Cardiology. Rotating intern Meml. Hosp. of South Bend, 1965—66; resident in internal medicine Meth. Hosp. Grad. Med. Ctr., 1968—70, fellow in cardiology, 1970—72; cardiologist Cardiology Assocs., Inc., South Bend, Ind., 1972-88, pres., 1984-88; cardiologist, pres. Heart Group, South Bend, 1988—2004; cardiologist South Bend Clinic, 2004—05. Chmn. cardiac cath com. Meml. Hosp., South Bend, 1973-90, St. Joseph's Med. Ctr., South Bend, 1999-2001; chmn. dept. medicine Meml. Hosp., South Bend, 1976-79; asst. clin. prof. medicine Ind. U., Indpls., 1980—. Author: Heart Sounds and Murmurs, 1973; contbr. articles to profl. jours. Pres. Am. Heart Assn., Indpls., 1977, pres. St. Joseph County chpt., 1975; bd. dirs. Vis. Nurse Assn., South Bend, 1984; mem. adv. bd. South Bend Pops Orch., 1978. Capt. U.S. Army, 1966-68, Vietnam. Decorated Bronze Star; recipient Man of Yr. award St. Joseph County Heart Assn., 1976. Fellow Am. Coll. Cardiology, Am. Coll. Chest Physicians, Coun. Critical Cardiology, Am. Heart Assn., Soc. Cardiac Angiography and Interventions; mem. ACP. Personal E-mail: megibso@comcast.net.

GIBSON, PAMELA HEMENWAY, elementary school educator; b. Rocky Mount, NC, May 7, 1953; d. Robert Walter and Irene Hemenway; children: Deana G. Miller, Nikki G. Oates. BSEd, East Carolina U., 1976; postgrad., East Carolina Grad. Sch. Edn., 1982; MA in Reading Edn., N.C. State U., 1995—. Cert. reading, lang. arts, social studies tchr., elem. edn. Tchr. Tarboro (N.C.) City Schs., Wake County Pub. Schs., Raleigh, NC, Sampson County Schs., 1996, Durham Pub. Schs., NC, 2003—, literacy com. mem., 2004—05, site base decision making com. mem., 2005—; reading specialist Intercede to Succeed Chapel Hill (N.C.) Profl. Devel. Sch., 1996-98; exceptional children's tchr., I.E.P. chair Vance County Schs., 1998-2000; literacy and lang. arts specialist, grades 2-5 Wake County Pub. Schs., NC, 2000—01; with N.C. Dept. Corrections, 2001—03. Cons. N.C. Dept. Pub. Instrn., 1991, test reader, editor, 1991; adviser/advisee planning com. West Cary Middle Sch. Task Force; coord. KEYS mentoring/vol. program E.O. Young Elem; reading instr., Vance Granville C.C., 2001, Dept. Corrections Divsn. Criminal Investigations, 2003, Durham Pub. Schs., 2003— Recipient PTSA Svc. award, Cert. of Svc. Girl Scouts U.S.; N.C. Vets. scholar. Mem. NEA, NCAE (treas. local unit, Tarboro Pace rep., bldg. rep. Durham pub. schs.), N.C. English Tchrs. Assn., N.C. Social Studies Coun., Internat. Reading Assn., Bus. and Profl. Women's Club, Gamma Sigma Sigma. Republican. Baptist. Office Phone: 919-560-3963. Personal E-mail: pgibson50@aol.com.

GIBSON, PATRICK DANIEL, accountant, historian; b. Downey, Calif., May 4, 1973; s. Paul Bartholomew and Cynthia Jean Gibson. B in Bus. Adminstrn., Calif. State U., Fullerton, 1999, M in History, 2006. Staff acct. Lesley, Thomas, Schwarz, and Postma, Inc., Newport Beach, Calif., 1999—2003; sr. acct. Westcorp, Irvine, Calif., 2003—06; sr. tax acct. Mendoza, Berger & Co., LLP, Irvine, 2006—. Office: Mendoza Berger & Co LLP 9838 Research Dr Irvine CA 92618 Home: 240 E Taft St #3 Orange CA 92865 Office Phone: 949-387-9850. Office Fax: 949-387-9652. Personal E-mail: pgibson@mendozaberger.com.

GIBSON, RALPH H. (RALPH HOLMES GIBSON), photographer; b. Jan. 16, 1939; Student in photography, U.S. Navy, 1956-60, San Francisco Art Inst., 1960-61; DFA (hon.), U. Md., 1991, Ohio Wesleyan U., 1997. Lectr. at numerous schs., museums. Exhibited photography in one-man shows including Madison (Wis.) Arts Ctr., 1975, Hoesch Mus., Duren, W. Ger., 1975, Castelli Graphics, N.Y.C., 1976, 80, 82, 91, Balt. Mus. Art, 1976, Van Reekum Galerji Mus., Apeldoorn, Netherlands, 1977, Swedish Mus. Photography, 1977, Mus. Modern Art, Oxford, Eng., 1977, Photographers Gallery, Melbourne, Australia, 1977, Robert Self Gallery, London, 1978, Mus. Modern Art, Brisbane, Australia, 1978, I.C.A. Mus. Art, Richmond, Va., 1979, Canon Gallery, Geneva, 1979, Grapestake Gallery, San Francisco, 1979, Kunstmuseum, Dusseldorf, Fed. Republic Germany, 1980, Night Gallery, London, 1980, Mus. Folkwang, Essen, Fed. Republic Germany, 1981, Mattingly Baker Gallery, Dallas, 1981, Sprengel Mus., Hanover, W. Ger., 1981, Cantieri Navali, La Giudeca, Venice, Italy, 1981, F.I.A.C., Paris, 1982, Olympus Gallery, London, 1892, Centre Georges Pompidou, Paris, 1982, Shadai Gallery, Tokyo, 1982, Sun Valley Ctr. for the Arts, Idaho, 1983, Seattle Art Mus., 1983, Weston Gallery, Carmel, Calif., 1984, Consejo Argentino de Fotografia, Buenos Aires, Argentina, 1985, Bouwfonds Hovelaken, The Netherlands, 1985, Castelli Uptown, N.Y.C., 1985, Galerie Agathe Gaillard, Paris, 1985, Leo Castelli Gallery, N.Y.C., 1985, 87, Ministry of Culture Hall, Marrakech, Morocco, 1986, Nat. Exhibit Hall, Moabane, Swaziland, 1986, Musee Carnavalet, Paris, 1986, Hellenic Ctr. Photography, Athens, 1987, Mus. Fine Arts, Alexandria, Egypt, 1987, Museo Archivi Alinari, Florence, Italy, 1987, Circulo de Bellas Artes, Madrid, 1987, Internat. Ctr. Photography, N.Y.C., 1987, Villa Medici, Rome, 1987, Mpls. Inst. Arts, 1988, Bibliotheque Nationale, Paris, 1988, Moderna Museet, Fotografiska Museet, Stockholm, 1989, Arts Club Chgo., 1989, Albin O. Kuhn Libr. and Gallery, U. Md., Balt., 1990, Musee Nicephore Niepce, Chalon Sue Soane, France, 1990, Princessehof Mus., Leuwarden, Holland, 1991, Okla. City Art Mus., 1991, Espace Photo Paris Audiovisuel, 1991, Photography House, Prague, 1992, Kunstverein Emmerich, Haus imm Park, 1996—, High Museum of Art, Atlanta, GA., 1997, MMK, Frankfurt, Germany, 1998, Maison Européenne De La Photographie, Paris, 1999; Greenville Cnty. Museum of Art, Greenville, Whitney Museum of American Art- N.Y.C., Ger., 1992, Boca Mus. Art, Boca Raton, Fla., 1993, 94, Butler Mus. Am. Art, Ohio, 1994, Frankfurt Kunstverein, 1996, Internat. Ctr. Photography 5-yr. world wide travelling exhbn., Villa Medici, Rome, 1986—, Mus. Carnavalet, Paris, 1986—, Leo Castelli Gallery, N.Y., Galerie Eric Van de Weghe, Brussels, Expo 1991, ICAC/Weston Gallery, Tokyo, others; exhibited in numerous group shows, including, Mus. Modern Art, N.Y.C., 1978, Hayden Gallery, MIT, Cambridge, 1978, Bologna Art Fair, Italy, 1978, Walker Art Center, Liverpool, Eng., 1978, Cleve. Mus. Art, 1978, Musée Marseilles, 1980, Addison Gallery of Art, Phillips Acad., Andover, Mass., 1981, Mus. Folkwang, Essen, 1981, San Francisco Mus. of Modern Art, 1982, 84, 85, Met. Mus. Art, N.Y.C., 1982, Whitney Mus. Art, N.Y.C., 1983, Houston Ctr. for Photography, 1983, Mus. Art, Phila., 1983, Denver Art Mus., 1984, Nat. Mus. Art, Washington, 1984, Sesnon Gallery, U. Calif.-Santa Cruz, 1984, Mus. of Modern Art, Paris, 1984, Pace-McGill Gallery, N.Y.C., 1985, Barbican Art Gallery, London, 1985, Bronx Mus., N.Y.C., 1985, Kunsterin, Stuttgart, Fed. Republic Germany, 1985, Musee Cantonal, Lausanne, Switzerland, 1985, Lehigh U., Pa., 1985, Gallery Hirondelle, N.Y.C., 1986, Villa Medici, Rome, numerous others; represented in permanent collections, including Nat. Gallery Ottawa, Ont., Can., Whitney Mus. Am. Art, Bibliotheque National de France, Paris, Mus. Modern Art, N.Y.C., Internat. Mus. Photography, George Eastman House, Rochester, N.Y., Fogg Art Mus., Boston, Met. Mus. Art, N.Y.C., Australian Nat. Gallery, Canberra, Nat. Gallery Victoria, Australia, Art Gallery South Australia, Victoria and Albert Mus., London, Mus. Modern Art, Brisbane, Fotografiska Museet, Moderna Museet, Stockholm, Sweden, Musee Reattu, Arles, France, G. Ray Hawkins Gallery, Los Angeles, Mus. Fine Arts, Alexandria, Egypt, Mus. Art, Athens, Greece; author: Apropos de Mary Jane, 1990, Chiaroscuro, 1990; author, illustrator: The Strip, 1966, The Hawk, 1968, The American Civil Liberties Union Calendar, 1969, The Somnambulist, 1970, Deja-vu, 1973, Days at Sea, 1975, Syntax, 1983, Tropism, 1987, Archive-Early Work, 1988; navarin editor: In-Situ, 1988, Les Cahiers des La

Photographie, 1988, L'Histoire de France, 1991, Deux ex Machina, Taschen edits., 1999, Ex Libris Powerhouse edits., 2000, Light Strings, 2004, Refractions, 2005, Brazil, 2005, Piemonte, 2005. Decorated comdr. Ordre Arts et Lettres (France); recipient Leica medal of excellence award, 1988, grand medal City of Arles, France, 1994, Silver Plumb award Design Trust for Pub. Space, 2000; fellowship grantee Nat. Endowment for Arts, 1973, 75, 86-87, creative artists pub. svc. grantee N.Y. State. Coun. Arts, 1977, grantee Eastman Kodak Co., 1989, Murray and Isabella Rayburn Found., 1994; Guggenheim fellow, 1985-86. Address: 331 W Broadway New York NY 10013-2265 Office Phone: 212-334-1854. Business E-Mail: lustrum@pipeline.com. *Photography is a way for measuring my perception-I trust my photographs and study them intensely. After working over forty years, I realize that the years of struggle are over. Now begin the years of struggle.*

GIBSON, REGINALD WALKER, federal judge; b. Lynchburg, Va., July 31, 1927; s. McCoy and Julia Ann (Butler) G.; 1 child, Reginald S. BS, Va. Union U., 1952; postgraduate student, U. Pa. Wharton Grad. Sch. Bus. Adminstrn., 1952-53; LLB, Howard U., 1956. Bar: DC 1957, Ill. 1972. Agt. IRS, Washington, 1957-61; trial atty. tax divsn. US Dept. Justice, Washington, 1961-71; sr. tax atty. Internat. Harvester Co., Chgo., 1971-76, gen. tax atty., 1976-82; judge US Ct. Fed. Claims, Washington, 1982-95, sr. judge, 1995—. Mem. bus. adv. coun. Chgo. Urban League, 1974-82. Served with AUS, 1946-47. Recipient cert. award US Dept. Justice Atty. Gen., 1969, recipient spl. commendation US Dept. Justice Atty. Gen., 1970, Wall St. Jour. award, 1952, Am. Jurisprudence award, 1956; named Alumni of Yr. Howard U. Sch. Law, 1984. Mem. DC Bar Assn., Chgo. Bar Assn., Fed. Bar Assn., Nat. Bar Assn., Claims Ct. Bar Assn., J. Edgar Murdock Am. Inn of Ct. (taxation com.). Clubs: Nat. Lawyers (Washington). Baptist. Office: US Ct Fed Claims 717 Madison Pl NW Washington DC 20439-0002*

GIBSON, REX HILTON, lawyer; b. Galveston, Tex., May 17, 1963; BBA, So. Meth. U., 1985; JD, Southern Meth. U., 1988. Bar: Tex. 1988, U.S. Tax Ct. 1989, U.S. Ct. Claims 1992. Tax assoc. Exxon Co., U.S.A., Houston, 1988, tax atty., 1988-92, sr. tax atty., 1992, Exxon Co., Internat., Florham Park, NJ, 1992-95, Exxon Ventures (CIS) Inc., Houston, 1995-99; tax counsel ExxonMobil Internat. Ltd., London, 2000—01, ExxonMobil Devel. Co., Houston, 2001—03, ExxonMobil Exploration Co., Houston, 2003—07, ExxonMobil Gas & Power Mktg. Co., Houston, 2007—. Bd. dirs. Internat. Tax and Investment Ctr.; mem. tax com. Petroleum Adv. Forum, 2000—05; mem. US-Russia Bus. Coun., 2001—05; vice-chair Caspian Mineral Taxation Com., 2003—05. Mem. ABA (taxation sect., natural resources com. 1995—, environ. taxes com. 1990—), State Bar Tex. (taxation sect., oil, gas & minerals law sect. 1989—), Houston Bar Assn. (taxation sect. 1995—), Houston Livestock Show and Rodeo Assn., U.S. Ski Team Found., Beta Alpha Psi. Avocations: skiing, hiking, fishing, golf. Office: ExxonMobil Gas & Power Mktg Co EMB 3791N 800 Bell St Houston TX 77002 Office Phone: 716-656-4318. Business E-Mail: rex.h.gibson@exxonmobil.com.

GIBSON, RICK J., lawyer; b. Elmhurst, Ill., May 12, 1967; s. William George and Diane Gibson; m. Beth Ann Branscome, May 16, 1992; children: Keegan William, William Connor. BBA magna cum laude, Loyola U., Chgo., 1991, MBA, 1994; JD magna cum laude, U. Pitts., 1996. Bar: Ohio 96. Assoc. Jones Day, Columbus, Ohio, 1996—2005, ptnr., 2006—. Articles Editor Pitt. Law Rev. Office: Jones Day PO Box 165017 Columbus OH 43216-5017 Office Phone: 614-281-3654, 614-281-3654. Office Fax: 614-461-4198. Business E-Mail: rjgibson@jonesday.com.

GIBSON, ROBERT LEE, astronaut; b. Cooperstown, NY, Oct. 30, 1946; s. Paul A. Gibson; m. M. Rhea Seddon; 4 children. BS in Aero. Engring., Calif. Poly. State U., 1969. Commd. ensign USN, 1969, advanced through grades to capt., 1990; served in Vietnam; astronaut NASA, Houston, 1978—96; pilot Shuttle Mission 41-B, 1984; spacecraft comdr. Shuttle Mission 61-C, 1986, STS-27, 1988, STS-47, 1992, STS-71, 1995; chief astronaut office NASA, Houston, 1992—94; first officer to captain Southwest Airlines, 1996—2006; COO, chief test pilot Benson Space Co., Poway, Calif., 2006—. Decorated Defense Superior Service medal, Disting. Flying Cross, Navy Commendation medal with Combat "V", Navy Unit Commendation, Meritorious Unit Commendation, Armed Forces Expeditionary medal, Humanitarian Service medal, Vietnam Campaign medal; named to US Astronaut Hall of Fame, 2003; recipient Louis Bleriot medal, Federation Aeronautique Internationale, 1992, Freedom of Flight, Experimental Aircraft Assn., 1989. Achievements include participated in the investigation of the Space Challenger accident and contributed to the redesign of the solid fuel rocket boosters which caused the disaster; first astronaut to dock the American spacecraft with Russia's Mir space station, 1995.*

GIBSON, SIDNEY KAY, retired lawyer; b. Salina, Kans., Nov. 9, 1937; s. Melvin Merit and Katherine Pauline (Marlin) Gibson; m. Sandra Pauline Ogden, Dec. 21, 1959; children: Jeffery Merit, Russell Paul. Student, N.Mex. State U., 1955—58; BMus, U. Tex. El Paso, 1959, MEd, 1968; JD, St. Mary's U., San Antonio, 1971. Bar: Tex. 1971, U.S. Ct. Appeals (5th cir.) 1982. Tchr. El Paso Pub. Schs., Tex., 1959—68; assoc. H.T. Santiesteban and Assocs., El Paso, 1982—89; pvt. practice El Paso, 1989—2001; ret., 2001. Assoc. editor: St. Mary's Law Jour., 1970; contbr. articles to law jours. Recipient Outstanding Scholastic Achievement award, 1968, 1970, Liech-Semaan award, 1970, James R. Norvell Moot Ct. award, 1970, Achievement award, State Jr. Bar Tex., 1970, Internat. Trial Lawyers Outstanding Achievement award, Art and Sci. Adv., 1970. Mem.: El Paso Bar Assn., State Bar Tex. Presbyterian. Home: 437 Stonebluff Rd El Paso TX 79912-3310

GIBSON, TERRY GRANT, security firm executive; s. John and Lassie Gibson; m. Elizabeth Gibson; children: Jennifer, Amber. BS in Applied Scis., U. Ala. Dir. sales & mktg. Eastman Kodak, Motion Analysis Sys. Divsn., San Diego, 1996—2000; v.p. bus. devel. SAIC, Security & Transp. Tech. Bus. Unit, San Diego, 2000—07; v.p., gen. mgr. Integrated Security, Vienna, Va., 2007—. Sts 2 USN, 1973—77. Mem.: Nat. Def. Industry Assn. Home: 7140 Tatler Rd Carlsbad CA 92011 E-mail: terry_g_gibson@yahoo.com.

GIBSON, VIRGINIA LEE, lawyer; b. Independence, Mo., Mar. 5, 1946; BA, U. Calif., Berkeley, 1972; JD, U. Calif., San Francisco, 1977. Bar: Calif. 1981. Assoc. Pillsbury, Madison & Sutro, San Francisco, 1980-83; ptnr. Chickering & Gregory, San Francisco, 1983-85, Baker & McKenzie, San Francisco, 1985—2001, White & Case, LLP, Palo Alto and San Francisco, 2001—. Mem. ABA (internat. law and practice sect., labor and employment law sect.), Nat. Assn. Stock Plan Profls., Nat. Ctr. for Employee Ownership, Calif. Bar Assn. (exec. com. tax sect. 1985-88), San Francisco Bar Assn. (internat. taxation sect.), Western Pension and Benefits Conf. (pres. San Francisco chpt. 1989-91, program com. 1984-88). Office: White & Case LLP 5 Palo Alto Sq 3000 El Camino Real Palo Alto CA 94306 Business E-Mail: vgibson@whitecase.com.

GIBSON, WALKER, retired language educator, poet, writer; b. Jacksonville, Fla., Jan. 19, 1919; s. William Walker Sr. and Helen (Jones) G.; m. Nancy Close, 1942; children: David R., Susan M., William Walker. III, John S. BA, Yale U., 1940; MA, U. Iowa, 1946. Rsch. asst. writers workshop U. Iowa, 1945-46; instr. English Amherst (Mass.) Coll., 1946-48, asst. prof., 1948-54, assoc. prof., 1954-57; assoc. prof., dir. freshman English Washington Square Coll. NYU, NYC, 1957-61, prof., 1961-67; prof. English U. Mass., Amherst, 1967-87, dir. freshman English, 1967-70, dir. rhetoric program, 1970-72, dir. undergrad. studies in English, 1974-76, prof. emeritus, 1984. Lectr. Yale Summer Music Sch., 1948-56; dir. NYU Summer Inst. for Secondary Tchrs. English, 1962, NDEA Summer Inst. for Secondary Tchrs. English, NYU, 1965, Summer Seminars for Coll Tchrs, NEH, 1973-75; prof. summer intern teaching program Smith Coll., 1963-64, 66-67; vis. prof. Swarthmore Coll., 1965-66; prof. NDEA Summer Inst. at Mass., 1968, Bread Loaf Sch. English, Middlebury Coll., 1976, 77. Author: (verse) The Reckless Spenders, 1954 Come As You Are, 1957, (texts) Seeing and Writing: Fifteen Exercises in Composing Experience, 1959, Tough Sweet & Stuffy, 1966, Persona: A Style Study for Readers and Writers, 1969, (antholgy text) Poems in Progress, 1963; co-author: The Macmillan Handbook of English, 1960, 2nd edit, 1965; contbg. author: Traditions of Inquiry, 1985, The Legacy of Language, 1987, others; editor: Limits of Language, 1962, New Students in Two-Year Colleges, 1979; co-editor: The Play of Language, 1971; contbr. articles to profl. jours.; contbns. to TV and film include Sunrise Semester, CBS-TV, full-year course Modern Literature: British and American, 1962-63, semester course Studies in Style, 1966-67, film The Speaking Voice and the Teaching of Composition, 1963, videotapes on dramatic role-playing in student writing, 1971, 84; author numerous poems in publs. including The New Yorker, Harpers, Atlantic Poetry, others. 1st lt. U.S. Army Air Corps, 1941-45. Ford Found. fellow 1955-56; John Simon Guggenheim Found. fellow, 1963-64; grantee NEH, 1973-77. Mem. MLA (selection com. for scholar's libr. 1968-71, del. assembly 1976-77, exec. com. divsn. on tchg. of writing 1976-80, chmn. divsn. 1979), Nat. coun. Tchrs. English (commn. on curriculum 1962-65, chmn. coll. sect. 1969-71, pres. elect and pres. coun. 1971-73, com. pub. doublespeak 1972-90, chmn. emeritus assembly 1986-87, Disting. Lectr. award 1969, Disting. Svc. award 1988), CCCC (exec. com. 1966-69), 5 Coll. Learning in Retirement (pres. 1990-91). Avocations: reading, writing. Home: 331 Spencer Dr Amherst MA 01002

GIBSON, WILLIAM LEE, financial consultant; b. Newark, Dec. 1, 1949; S. Joseph Wilton Gibson and Margaret (Reynolds) Gibson Leavens; stepson William Barry Leavens, Jr.; m. Lorraine Wrightson Besch, July 10, 1982. BA in chemistry, Bucknell U., 1972; postgrad., Harvard Bus. Sch., 1977; MBA, NYU, 1987, Sch. of Advanced Fin. Mgmt., 1995. With Bur. Solid Waste Mgmt EPA, Cin., 1970-71; chemist Dow Chem. Co., Midland, Mich., 1972-75; mktg. cons. Westvaco, Charleston, SC, 1976; sales rep. Diamond Shamrock Co., Cleve., 19777-79; market devel. specialist strategic planing and ventures operation GE, Pittsfield, Mass., 1979-81; mktg. programs mgr. Allied-Signal Corp., Morristown, NJ, 1981-86, mgr. tech. and bus. devel., 1986-91, sr. sales mgr., 1991-93; v.p. Merrill Lynch, Short Hills, NJ, 1994—. Former pres., trustee Hartford Family Found; v.p. Leavens Found. Trustee N.J. Symphony Orch.; treas. Coun. N.J. Grantmakers. Mem. Harvard Bus. Sch. Club N.Y. Office: 51 John F Kennedy Pky Short Hills NJ 07078-2702

GIBSON, WILLIAM M., technology company executive; BA in Econs., Villanova U., 1966; grad. Exec. Edn. Program, Harvard U., 1979. With IBM, Applied Logic Corp., IIT Data Svcs., Chase Econometrics/Interactive Data Corp., Strategic Info. Inc.; with info. svcs. divsn. Ziff-Davis Corp.; COO Manugistics Group Inc., Rockville, Md., 1982, pres., 1982. Chmn. bd. dirs. Manugistics, 1986—. Recipient Entrepreneur of Yr. award Ernst & Young, 1997, High Tech Entrepreneur of Yr. award for Greater Washington region KPMG, 1997. Office: Manugistics Inc 9715 Key West Ave Rockville MD 20850-3915 Fax: 301-984-5370.

GIBSON, WILLIAM WILLARD, JR., law educator; b. Amarillo, Tex., Mar. 5, 1932; s. William Willard and Genelle (Works) G.; m. Beth Smyth, July 31, 1953; children— William Willard, Michael Murray, Timothy Thomas, Elizabeth Mills. BA, U. Tex., Austin, 1954, LLB, 1956. Assoc. Gibson, Ochsner, Harlin, Kinney & Morris, Amarillo, Tex., 1956-60, ptnr., 1960-65; assoc. prof. U. Tex.-Austin Sch. Law, 1965-69, prof., 1969-76, Albert Sydney Burleson prof. law, 1976-83, Sylvan Lang prof. law, 1983-98, Sylvan Lang prof. emeritus, 1998—, dir. continuing legal edn., 1981-85, assoc. dean, 1979-86; Austin. Provost jud. edn. Supreme Ct. Tex., 1992-93. Author: Teaching Materials on Wills and Estates, 1967; Selected Provisions from Texas Statutes Pertaining to Wills and Estates, 1973; also articles Vice chancellor Diocese of Tex., Protestant Episcopal Ch. Recipient Leon Green award Tex. Law Rev. Assn. of Ex-Editors, Austin, 1983. Mem. Am. Coll. Real Estate Lawyers. Democrat. Avocations: walking, fishing, hunting.

GIDDENS, DON PEYTON, engineering educator, researcher; b. Augusta, Ga., Oct. 24, 1940; m. Karin Baldzer; 1 child, Eric. BS in aerospace engring., Ga. Inst. Tech., 1963, MS in aerospace engring., 1965, PhD in aerothermodynamics, 1967. Assoc. aircraft engr. Lockheed-Ga. Co., Atlanta, 1963; mem. tech. staff Aerospace Corp., San Bernardino, Calif., 1966-67; asst. prof. Ga. Inst. Tech., Atlanta, 1968-70, assoc. prof., 1970-77, prof., 1977-82, regents prof., 1982-92, chair dept. aerospace engring., 1988-92, dean Coll. Engring., 2002—; eminent scholar Ga. Rsch. Alliance; co-dir. Biomedical Tech. Rsch. Ctr. Ga. Inst. Tech./Emory U., Atlanta, 1987—92, prof., chair Wallace H. Coulter Dept. Biomedical Engring., 1997—2002, now Lawrence L. Gellerstedt Jr. Chair in Bioengineering; dean Whiting Sch. Engring. Johns Hopkins U., Balt., 1992-97. Contbr. numerous articles to profl. jours. Fellow: Am. Heart Assn. Arteriosclerosis, Thrombosis and Vascular Biology Coun., Am. Inst. Med. and Biol. Engineers (founding fellow, pres. 2004—), ASME; mem.: NAE. Avocation: whitewater canoeing. Office: Ga Inst Tech Coll Engring Adminstrn Bldg 225 North Ave NW Atlanta GA 30332-0360

GIDDENS-JONES, EMILY JANE, architectural and interior designer, consultant; b. Jackson, Miss., Sept. 18, 1924; d. Jasper Franklin and Erma Jane (Simmons) Giddens; m. William Everard Jones, Nov. 10, 1947 (div. July 1967). BA with hons., Belhaven Coll., 1946; postgrad., Phila. Mus. Coll. Art, 1964. Dir. design Office Supply Co., Jackson, 1954-58; dir. design and prodn. Designers Fore Ltd., NYC, 1969-75, John F. Saladino, Inc., NYC, 1975-79; pres., CEO, owner Cross Quadrate Design, NYC, 1972—. Assoc. prof. interior design Post Coll., Waterbury, Conn., 1978-79; cons. Flexcon, Inc., Spencer, Mass., 1985-89; bd. dirs. Cornwall Assn., 2003— Contbr. articles to profl. jours. Sec. bd. dir. Cornwall Extras for Kids, Conn., 1993-2001. Scholar Belhaven Coll., 1942-46. Mem. Chi Delta. Presbyterian. Avocations: reading, writing, music, composing, painting. Home: 49 Popple Swamp Rd Cornwall Bridge CT 06754-1137 Office: Cross Quadrate Design 138 E 38th St New York NY 10016-2646

GIDDINGS, HELEN, state representative, personnel management director; b. Dallas, Apr. 21, 1942; d. Arthur and Catherine (Warren) Ferguson; m. Donald Giddings; children: Lizette, Lisa, Stanley. BA in Bus., U. Tex., 1968. Tng. dir. Sears, Roebuck, Dallas, 1975-77; personnel mgr. Sears, Roebuck & Co., Dallas, 1977-81, dir. community affairs for 11 states, 1979-81; pres. Select Personnel, Dallas, 1981-86; exec. dir. Leadership Dallas, 1985-86; state rep. dist. 109 State of Tex., 1982-86, 1992—. Trustee Dallas Alliance, 1981—, exec. dir., 1987. Gov. Dallas Symphony, 1980—; elected mem. Dallas Assembly, 1981—; mem. Dist. 6 State Bar Grievance Com.; bd. dirs. Dallas Theatre Ctr., 1984—; exec. dir. Leadership Dallas, 1984, state rep., 1992. Recipient Woman of Yr. award Committee of 100, Dallas, 1980, Achieving Against the Odds award East Oak Cliff-Dallas Ind. Sch. Dist., 1981. Mem. Dallas Black C. of C. (pres. 1981-82), Dallas Hist. Soc. (sec. 1983—, vice-chair), Zeta Phi Beta (Woman of Yr. award 1984), Alpha Phi Alpha (Community Service award 1987), Nat. Order Women Legislators (v.p. 1999, pres.-elect 2000). Democrat. Meth. Avocations: public speaking, the arts. Office: State Capital Rm CAP GN12 PO Box 2910 Austin TX 78768 Office Phone: 512-463-0953.

GIDDINGS, STEVEN B., physics professor; b. Murray, Utah, May 9, 1962; s. J. Calvin Giddings and Jennifer Sharp; m. Kristy Manning, July 23, 2005. BA in Math. and Physaics with honors, U. Utah, Salt Lake City, 1983; PhD, Princeton U., NJ, 1987. Jr. fellow Harvard Soc. Fellows, Cambridge, Mass., 1988—91; prof. physics U. Calif., Santa Barbara, 1990—. Recipient Par Excellence award, U. Utah, 1990, First Pl. Essay award, Gravitational Rsch. Found., 2002; grantee, Foundational Questions Inst., 2006; Outstanding Jr. Investigator grantee, Dept. Energy, 1990, Presdl. Young Investigator grantee, NSF, 1991. Mem.: Am. Phys. Soc. (life). Achievements include research in quantum gravity, string theory, black holes, cosmology. Avocations: alpinism, running, skiing, bicycling. Office: U Calif Dept Physics Santa Barbara CA 93106 Home Phone: 805-898-9026; Office Phone: 805-893-4750. Business E-Mail: giddings@physics.ucsb.edu.

GIDDON, DONALD B(ERNARD), psychologist, educator; b. Newark, May 1, 1930; s. William and Ruth (Franklin) G.; m. Phoebe L. Rothman, Aug. 28, 1955; children: David, Kenneth, Joanna, James. AB, Brown U., 1952; MA, Boston U., 1953; DMD, Harvard U., 1959; PhD in Psychology, Brandeis U., 1961. Lectr. psychology Brandeis U., 1954-71, 82-84, lectr. phys. edn., 1985-89; prof., chmn. dental ecology Harvard U., 1972-75, vis. prof., 1976-89, lectr., 1989-98, clin. prof. growth and devel., 1999—, lectr. health svcs. adminstrn. Sch. Pub. Health, 1972-75, asst. dean adminstrn. Sch. Dental Medicine, 1973-75; assoc. staff New Eng. Med. Center, 1964-73; assoc. prof., chmn. dept. social dentistry Tufts U., Boston, 1964-67, prof., chmn. dept. social dentistry, 1967-72, asst. dean, 1967-69, assoc. dean, 1969-71; dean NYU Dental Ctr., 1975-78, prof. epidemiology and health promotion, 1976—; prof. psychology Grad. Sch. Arts and Scis., prof. anesthesiology NYU Med. Center, 1976-80; prof. Faculty of Medicine, U. Groningen, The Netherlands, 1980-81. Cons. Astra Pharm. Products, Inc., 1960—, dept. medicine and surgery VA, 1966-69, med. rsch. cons., 1988-90, Peter Bent Brigham Hosp., 1975-76, Meml. Sloan-Kettering Cancer Ctr., 1976-78, psychologist dept. anesthesiology Brigham and Women's Hosp., 1979—; vis. prof. U. Gothenburg, Sweden, 1971, Royal Dental Coll., Aarhus, Denmark, 1972, U. Pa., 1972, medicine McGill Med. U., 1981-83, psychology Mass. Coll. Pharmacy and Allied Health Scis., 1984-89; mem. exec. com. Goldwater Meml. Hosp., 1976-78; vis. staff physician NYU Med. Ctr., 1976-2006; mem. med. staff Brookdale Hosp., 1977-2006; clin. prof. Brown U., 1989-2006, emeritus, 2006—; clin. prof. U. Ill., Chgo., 1994—, Health Scis. Ctr. Stony Brook U., 2004—; founding dir. Rsch. Inst., Royal Victoria Hosp., Montreal, 1981-82; mem. NIH study sect. 2000—. Contbr. articles to profl. jours. Bd. dirs. Mass. Health Coun., 1965-70, pres., 1968-69; pres. Hamilton sch. PTA, Newton Lower Falls, Mass., 1963-64; trustee Emerson Coll., 1991-2000, Berkshire Opera, 1996—; mem. Com. on Univ. Resources, bd. overseers Harvard U., 1991—, NIH study sect., 2000—. Named Fulbright scholar, 1971. Fellow AAAS, APA, Acad. Behavioral Med. Rsch., Am. Pub. Health Assn., Am. Coll. Dentists, Internat. Coll. Dentists, Internat. Coll. Psychosomatic Medicine, Royal Soc. Medicine; mem. AAUP, Am. Statis. Assn., Internat. Assn. Study Pain, Am. Psychosomatic Soc., Am. Coll. Sports Medicine, Am. Dental Soc. Anesthesiology (assoc. editor 1965-72, chmn. ethics com. 1979-81), Behavioral Sci. in Dental Rsch. (pres. 1976-77), Internat. Assn. Dental Rsch. (pres. Boston sect. 1965-66), Am. Pain Soc. (dir. 1977-79), Soc. Behavioral Med., Soc. Psychophys. Rsch., Soc. Clin. and Experimental Hypnosis, Sigma Xi. Office: 277 Linden St Wellesley MA 02482-5900 Business E-Mail: donald_giddon@hms.harvard.edu.

GIDEL, ROBERT HUGH, real estate investor; b. Ft. Dodge, Iowa, Sept. 19, 1951; s. Wayne D. and Mary A. (Ziegler) G.; m. Linda Carol Lombardo, Oct. 23, 1976; children: Jill, Allison, Robert. BSBA, U. Fla., 1973. Comml. loan officer Century Bank, St. Petersburg, Fla., 1975-77; asst. v.p. N.Y. Life, Washington, 1977-81; exec. v.p. Heller Real Estate Fin. Co., Chgo., 1981-86; pres., mng. dir., bd dirs. Alex Brown Realty Advisors, Balt., 1986-90; mng. dir., bd. dirs. Alex Brown Kleinwort Benson Realty Advisors, Balt., 1990-93; pres., bd. dirs. Brazos Ptnrs. L.P., Dallas, 1993-99; mng. ptnr. Liberty Ptnrs., Orlando, Fla., 1999—2005, also bd. dirs.; chmn. bd. LNR Property Holdings, 2005—; pres. Ginn Co. LLC, 2007—. Pres., COO, bd. dirs. ParagonGroup Inc., 1996-97; CEO, bd. dirs. Meridian Realty Trust VIII, 1997-98; bd. dirs. Fortress Registered Investment Trust, Developers Diversified Realty Corp., Lone Star Opportunity Fund I, II, III, IV, and V, Brazos Fund, 1996-05, Global Signal Inc., U.S. Restaurant Properties, 2001-05; exec. com. U. Fla. Ctr. Real Estate Studies. Contbr. articles to profl. publs. Bd. dirs. Gator Boosters, U. Fla. Found. Fellow Homer Hoyt Inst. Mem. Nat. Coun. Real Estate Investment Fiduciaries, Pension Real Estate Assn., Assn. Fgn. Investors in Real Estate, Nat. Assn. Real Estate Investment Trusts, Windermere Club, Golden Bear Club. Republican. Home: 6820 Valhalla Way Windermere FL 34786 Office: Liberty Ptnrs 7380 Sand Lake Rd Ste 500 Orlando FL 32819 Personal E-mail: RGidel@aol.com.

GIDEON, KENNETH WAYNE, lawyer; b. Lubbock, Tex., July 25, 1946; s. Melton Jean and Mary B. (Lanham) G.; m. Carol Almack, June 2, 1968; children: Christopher Lynn, Kevin Almack, Timothy Charles, Emily Susan BA, Harvard U., 1968; JD, Yale U., 1971. Bar: Tex. 1971, U.S. Tax Ct. 1971, U.S. Ct. Claims 1972, U.S. Supreme Ct. 1981, D.C. 1984. Assoc. Fulbright & Jaworski, Houston, 1971-78, ptnr., 1978-81, Washington, 1983-86; chief counsel IRS, Washington, 1981-83; ptnr. Fried, Frank, Harris, Shriver & Jacobson, Washington, 1986-89, 92-93; asst. sec. tax policy Dept. Treasury, Washington, 1989-92; ptnr. Wilmer, Cutler & Pickering, Washington, 1994-2000, Skadden, Arps, Slate, Meagher & Flom, 2000—. Mem. Spring Valley (Tex.) City Coun., 1978-79. Capt. U.S. Army, 1971-72. Fellow Am. Bar Found., Am. Coll. Tax Counsel (regent 1999-2004); mem. ABA (vice chair govt. rels. 1995-97, mem. coun. 1987-89, sect. taxation, chair, 2004-05), Am. Law Inst., Orgn. Econ. Cooperation and Devel. (Paris, vice chmn. com. on fiscal affairs 1990-92). Office: Skadden Arps Slate Meagher & Flom 1440 New York Ave NW Washington DC 20005-2111

GIEBEL, MIRIAM CATHERINE, librarian, genealogist; b. Williamsburg, Iowa, Oct. 10, 1934; d. John Timothy and Helen Gertrude (Wright) Donahoe; m. William Herbert Giebel, Sept. 30, 1967; 1 child, Sara Ann Giebel Ward. BS, Marquette U., 1956; MLS, Rosary Coll., 1960; cert. in paralegal, Roosevelt U.,., 1992; cert. in family history rsch., Brigham Young U., 1992. Asst. acquisitions dept. Marquette U. Libr., Milw., 1956—58; tech. svcs. libr. Chicago Heights Pub. Libr., Ill., 1959—63, ext., reference libr., 1974—99, vol. coord./webmaster, 1999—2000, webmaster, 2000—01, ind. geneal. rschr., 2002—; libr. Little Co. Mary Nursing, Evergreen Park, Ill., 1963—64; asst. libr. hdqrs. ALA, Chgo., 1964—67. Mem.: DAR (chpt. registrar 1994—2001), Fedn. Bus. Profl. Women (state libr. chair 1994—96), Nat. Soc. Sons and Daus. of Pilgrims, Daus. Union Vets. 1861-1865 (historian John Butler chpt. 2004—07), Daus. Colonial Wars, Dames Ct. Honor (historian Ill. soc. 2003—), Ill. Cameo Soc. of DAR (state v.p. 1996—99, state pres. 1999—2001), U.S. Daus. of 1812 (chpt. pres. 1991—97, Ill. state registrar 1994—97, Ill. state pres. 1997—99, nat. chair lineage and geneal. records 1997—2000, chpt. registrar 1997—, hon. state pres. life), Soc. Ind. Pioneers (life). Roman Catholic. Avocations: reading, personal genealogical research, Web surfing.

GIEDD, JAY NORMAN, psychiatrist; b. Bismarck, ND, July 11, 1960; MD, U. ND Sch. Medicine, 1986. Cert. Psychiatry (Gen., Child, Adolescent and Geriatric), Child and Adolescent Psychiatry. Intern, psychiatry Menninger Found., Topeka, 1986—87, resident, child and adolscent psychology, 1987—89; resident Duke U., Durham, NC, 1989—91; fellow NIMH, Rockville, Md., 1991, chief, Unit on Brain Imaging in Child Psychiatry Branch Bethesda, Md. Contbr. articles to profl. jours. Office: Nat Inst Mental Health (NIMH) 10 Center Dr Bethesda MD 20892-1381

GIEDT, BRUCE ALAN, paper company executive; b. Fargo, ND, May 7, 1937; s. Alexander and Alice Mildred (Rognaldson) G.; m. Suzanna Tae Abbott, Apr. 30, 1963; children: Alex, Jeffrey, Marybeth; m. 2d, Gail Ann Platt. BA, U. Wash., 1959; MBA, Harvard U., 1965. From regional sales mgr. to v.p. service products bus. units Crown Zellerbach Corp., San Francisco, 1965—; pres. Champion Paper Distbrs., Inc., Riverside, Calif., 1981-87, Pioneer Packaging, Phoenix, 1987—. Author: The Future of Commercial Arbitration, 1965. V.p. exec. com. Keep Riverside AHead, econ. devel. com., bd. dirs.; exec. com. mem. Riverside C. of C., devel. com. Served to Capt. USAF, 1959-63. Evans scholar Western Golf Assn., 1967. Mem. Am. Paper Inst. (past com. chmn.), Elks. Republican. Lutheran. Home: 704 Foothills East cir Payson AZ 85541 Office: 730 E University Dr Phoenix AZ 85034-6509 Personal E-mail: bgiedt@earthlink.net. Business E-Mail: bgiedt@pioneerpackaging.com.

GIEL, JAMES ARTHUR, JR., employee benefits management; b. Pitts., Aug. 29, 1952; s. James and Suan Helen (Barry) G.; m. Sharyl Dawn Unrath, Apr. 22, 1978; children: James Arthur III, Maggie Anne. BA, Westminster Coll., New Wilmington, Pa., 1974; MA in Pers. Administrn. and Indsl. Rels., St. Francis Coll., Loretto, Pa., 1987. Tchr. Shaler Area Schs., Glenshaw, Pa., 1974—77; group ins. underwriter Equitable Life Assurance Soc., NYC, 1977—79; pension clk. Allegheny Ludlum Industries, Inc., Pitts., 1979—80; benefits adminstr. Allegheny Internat., Pitts., 1980—86; mgr., asst. v.p. employee benefits Union Nat. Corp., Pitts., 1986—89; v.p., dir. employee benefits Integra Fin. Corp., Pitts., 1989—96; mgr. employee benefits Armco Inc., Pitts., 1996—99; mgr. employee benefits and relocation Heinz N.Am., Pitts., 1999—2001; cons. Todd Orgn. Pitts., 2001—02; mgr. employee benefits and HRIS, ANH Refractories Co., Pitts., 2002—05; mgr. benefits County Allegheny, Pitts., 2006—07; mgr. employee benefits Dollar Bank, Pitts., 2007—. Mem. Shaler Hist. Soc., 1972—, pres., 1982-86, v.p., 2007—; dir. Strawberry Way Child Ctr., Pitts., 1985-92; Rep. committeeman Allegheny County, Glenshaw, 1992-97; elder Elfinwild Presbyn. Ch., Glenshaw, 1986-2007, deacon, 1980-86, trustee, 2007—; bd dir. Shaler Twp.-Shaler Oaks, 1994-96; mem. strategic planning com. Shaler Area Sch. Dist., 1994-96, sch. bd. dir., 1997—, pres. 1999, 2000, 01, 06, 07, v.p., 2005, 06; dir. Bread of Life Food Pantry, 2003—, bd. sec., 2003—; mem. com. Allegheny Policy Coun., 1995-96; trustee ACSHIC, 2003—. Mem. Human Resource Info. Specialist Soc., Workers in Employee Benefits, Pitts. Human Resources Assn., Tristate Compensation Assn., Pitts. Bus. Group on Health (exec. com. 1997), Human Resources Sys. Profls., Travelers Aid Soc. Pitts. (bd. dir. 1994—, sec. bd. dir. 1998-2003, treas. bd. dirs. 2003-04), Westminster Coll. Alumni Assn. (alumni coord. 1988—), Towers Perrin Roundtable, Elfinwild Lions (pres. 1984), Shaler Soccer Club (treas. 1993-95, pres. 1995-97, bd. dirs. 1997-2002, Shaler Area Soccer Boosters 1997-2001, pres. 1998-2001), Rivers Club. Avocations: music, civic activities. Office: Dollar Bank Three Gateway Ctr Pittsburgh PA 15222 Personal E-mail: gielwest@verizon.net. Business E-Mail: jgiel224@dollarbank.com.

GIELOW, KATHLEEN LOUISE, career planning administrator, consultant, special education educator; b. Buffalo, July 8, 1951; d. James Elbert and Billie Elaine Robinson; m. Arthur William Gielow, Sept. 1, 1973; 1 child, James Arthur. BS in Edn., SUCNY, Buffalo, 1973, MS in Edn., 1979. Spl. edn. tchr. Buffalo Pub. Schools, 1974—98, career devel. coord., 1998—; ednl. founds. faculty SUCNY, Buffalo, 2001—04, prin. investigator, 2002; entrepreneurship coord. Buffalo Employment and Tng. Ctr., 2002—; owner Queen Creations, 2005—. Profl. devel. provider various ednl. and cmty. orgns., NY, 1997—; profl. conf. workshop presenter, NY, 1998—; conf. workshop presenter Coun. of Gt. City Schs., San Francisco, 1999; careerzone trainer N.Y. State Dept. of Labor, 2000—; cons. Syracuse U., NY, 2001—; career plan trainer N.Y. State Edn. Dept., 2001—; edn. adv. bd. mem. N.Y. State Electric and Gas, Lancaster, 2001—. Editor: (career development best practices collec) Best Practices in Career Development; contbr. nysbest practices in career development Career Development in the Automotive Industry. Vol. Aids Cmty. Svcs., Aids Family Svcs., Buffalo, 1998—; eucharistic min. St. Joseph U. Cath. Ch., Buffalo, 2002—. Recipient Partnership Svc. award, Sch. to Work Family Resource Ctr., 1998, Career and Tech. Educator award, Buffalo Career and Tech. Educators Guild, 2002, Vol. of Yr. award, AIDS Cmty. Svcs., 2003, Pathfinders award for forging partnerships between bus. and edn. in western NY, 2004, Entrepreneur award, Nat. Consortium for Enterpreneurship, 2004, Nat. Leavy Entrepreneurship award, Freedom Found., 2006; grantee School-To-Work (for Buffalo Pub. Schools), NY State Edn. Dept., 1997-1999; Urban/Rural Opportunity grantee, US Dept. Labor, 1998-2003, Youth Entrepreneurship grantee, Kidsway, Inc., 2000, Workforce Devel. Entrepreneurship grantee, Workforce Investment Bd. of Erie County, 2002, Tech Prep Planning grantee, NY State Edn. Dept., 2002-2003, Cornell Workforce Devel. grantee, Cornell U., 2004. Mem.: Assn. for Career and Tech. Educators Adminstrs. (licentiate), Nat. Educators Assn. (licentiate), Buffalo Tchrs. Fedn. (licentiate). Roman Catholic. Avocations: scrapbooking, travel, reading, musical theater. Home: 300 Hamilton Blvd Kenmore NY 14217-1811 Office: Buffalo Pub Schs 2201 City Hall 65 Niagara Sq Buffalo NY 14202 Office Phone: 716-816-3656. E-mail: klg7851@aol.com, kgielow@buffalo.k12.ny.us.

GIERAS, JACEK FRANCISZEK, engineering educator, research scientist; b. Maleniec, Voivodship Piotrkow Tryb, Poland, Apr. 2, 1947; s. Stanislaw Gieras and Zofia Rychlewska-Gieras; m. Janina Omilianczyk, Sept. 25, 1975; children: Izabella Anna, Karolina Maria, Michael Benjamin. MSEE, Tech. U., Lodz, 1971; PhD, Tech. U., Poznan, Poland, 1975, DSc, 1980. Project engr. Factory of Loudspeakers Tonsil, Wrzesnia, Poland, 1971; lectr. Tech. U. Poznan, 1971-73, sr. lectr., 1973-75, asst. prof., 1975-77, Acad. Technology and Agr., Bydgoszcz, Poland, 1977-81, assoc. prof., dean, 1981-83, assoc. prof., head of dept., 1985-87, prof., 1987—. Vis. assoc. prof. Queen's U., Kingston, Ont., Can., 1983-85; prof. U. Cape Town, 1989-98; vis. prof. endowed chair in transp. sys. engring. U. Tokyo, 1996; guest prof. Chungbuk Nat. U., Korea, 1996-97; scientist United Technologies Rsch. Ctr., East Hartford, Conn., 1998-2005; fellow Hamilton Sundstrand Aerospace, Rockford, Ill., 2005-. Author: Special Purpose Electric Machines, 1983, Linear Induction Motors, 1990, Linear Induction Drives, 1994; author: (with M. Dabrowski) Induction Machines with Solid Rotors, 1977; author: (W.H. Middendorf and R.H. Engelmann eds.) Handbook of Electric Motors, 1995, 2d edit., 2004; author: (with M. Wing) Permanent Magnet Motor Technology: Design and Applications, 1996, 2d edit., 2002; author: (with Z. Piech) Linear Synchronous Motor, 1999; author: (with R. Wang and M. Kamper) Axial Flux Permanent Magnet Machines, 2004; author: (with J. Lai and C. Wang) Noise of Polyphase Electric Motors, 2005; contbr. articles to profl. jours. Recipient Silver medal Polish Assn. of Elec. Engring., Poland, 1979; fellow Polish Ministry of Edn., 1976, 81, NSERC of Can., 1983, Italian Ministry of Sci. and Tech. Rsch., 1994, Merit awards U. Cape Town, 1995, 96, 97, 98. Fellow IEEE, Hamilton Sundstrand; mem. Internat. Acad. Electrotech. Scis. Roman Catholic. Avocations: railways, music, overseas travel, home improvement. Office: Hamilton Sundstrand PO Box 7002 Rockford IL 61125-7002 also: Univ Tech and Life Scis Al S Kaliskiego 7 85 796 Bydgoszcz Poland Office Phone: 815-226-6016. Business E-Mail: jgieras@ieee.org.

GIERER, VINCENT A., JR., tobacco and wine holding company executive; b. NYC, Oct. 21, 1947; s. Vincent A. Sr. and Isabel (McEwen) G.; m. Linda Bocek; children: Gregory, Vincent, Beth. BBA, Iona Coll., 1969. CPA, N.Y. Audit supr. Ernst & Ernst, White Plains, NY, 1971-77; dir. fin. reporting UST Inc., Greenwich, Conn., 1978-83, controller, 1983-86, sr. v.p., chief fin. officer, 1986-88, exec. v.p., chief fin. officer, 1988-90, pres., chief operating officer, 1990-93, chmn., pres., CEO, 1993—2005, chmn., CEO, 2005—07, non-exec. chmn., 2007—. With U.S. Army, 1969-71, Vietnam; trustee Fairfield Univ. Mem. N.Y. State Soc. CPAs, Fin. Executives Inst. Roman Catholic. Avocations: golf, gardening. Office: UST Inc 100 W Putnam Ave Greenwich CT 06830-5316*

GIESBRECHT, F. BRUCE, entertainment company executive; Founder, pres. RamSoft, Inc.; v.p. corp. info. systems, chief info. officer Hollywood Entertainment Corp., Wilsonville, Oreg., 1993—96, sr. v.p. product mgmt., 1996—98, sr. v.p. strategic planning, 1998—2000, exec. v.p. bus. devel., 2000—03, pres., chief operating officer, dir., 2004—, CEO, 2005—. Bd. dirs. Video Software Dealers Assn. Office: Hollywood Entertainment Corp 9275 W Peyton Ln Wilsonville OR 97070

GIESBRECHT, MARTIN GERHARD, retired economics professor, musician; b. Newark, Aug. 25, 1933; s. Theodore Gerhard and Martha Margarete (Thurm) G.; m. Patricia Maxine Berlin, July 4, 1957 (dec. Sept. 2000); children: Lisa, Martin F., Theodore K. BA, Rutgers U., 1955; Dr. Oec. Publ., U. Munich, 1958; diploma internat. bus., German-Am. C. of C., 1991. Asst. prof. econs. Wilmington (Ohio) Coll., 1958-63, assoc. prof. econs., 1963-75, prof. econs., 1975-87, No. Ky. U., Highland Heights, 1987—98, prof. emeritus, 1998—. Bd. dirs. Econs. Assocs., Villa Hills, Ky.; mem. spkrs. bur. WMKV-FM, Cin., 2002—; econ. commentator WNKU, Cin., 1989—2005, WMKV, Cin., 1997—, WVXU, Cin., 2006—, WOBO, Batavia, Ohio, 2007—; cons. No. Ky. U. Met. Edn. and Tng. Svcs., 2003—; columnist NKU Gold Times, Cin., 2006—. Author: The Evolution of Economic Society, 1972, Using Economics, 1976, Space Settlements, 1977, The Wealth of People, 1978, A Guide to Everyday Economic Statistics, 1990, 6th edit., 2003, A Guide to Everyday Economic Thinking, 1997, Markets, Money, Measures, 2005, revised edit., 2007. Chmn. Ohioans for the Merit Selection of Judges, Clinton County, 1979; mem. Cin. Silvers Jazz Quartet, 1995-, Over-the-Hill Gang, 1987-95, Bath House Five, 1958-89, The New Look Jazz Band, 1960-89, Riverboat Ramblers, 1970-74; guest artist Bone Voyage, 2006—. Fellow Ford Found., Ind. U., 1964, Gen. Electric Found., U. Chgo., 1966, NSF, Miami U., 1971, NASA-Am. Soc. Engring. Edn., Stanford U., 1975; Danforth Found. assoc. Wilmington Coll., 1969-82; recipient award Am. Heart Assn., Clinton County, 1977, Excellence award Soc. Profl. Journalists, 1993, award of distinction The Communicator, 2001. Mem. Cin. Musicians Assn., Ky. Econ. Assn. (trustee 1989-92, 96—), Ohio Assn. Economists (pres. 1977-78), Ohio Acad. Sci., Amyotrophic Lateral Sclerosis Assn. (bd. dirs. Ky. chpt. 2001-05), Am. Fedn. Musicians. Avocation: jazz clarinetist. Home: 2501 Kingston Ct Villa Hills KY 41017-3760

GIESE, WILLIAM HERBERT, tax accountant; b. Boston, Jan. 19, 1944; s. Robert Ewald and Harriet (Blaney) G.; m. Elaine Rabe, May 26, 1973; children: Amy Theiss, Katherine Clark, Lauren Stearns. BA, Amherst Coll., 1966; MBA, U. Pa., 1968. CPA. Staff acct. Price Waterhouse, Phila., 1968-70, sr. acct., 1970-73, mgr., 1973-79, ptnr., 1979-95; pres. William H. Giese, Ltd., Ardmore, Pa., 1995-97, Tax Counselors of Bryn Mawr, Inc., Pa., 1997-2000; ptnr. Tax Counsellors of Bryn Mawr, LLC, 2001—. Spkr. Wharton Tax Conf. Phila., 1988; bd. dirs. Verion, Inc., Exton, Pa. Treas. Dunwoody Home and Village, Newtown Square, Pa., 1988—2000; past pres. North Ardmore Civic Assn., Phila., Squash Racquets Assn., Bala Cynwyd; fin. chmn. U.S. Amateur Golf Tournament, 1989; past treas. U.S. Squash Racquets Assn., Bala Cynwyd; Bd. dirs. Dunwoody Home and Village, Newtown Square, Pa., 1998—2000; bd. dirs. Lankenau Found., Phila., 1990—2001. Mem. AICPA, Pa. Inst. CPA's, Merion Golf Club (Ardmore, Pa.), Merion Cricket Club (Haverford, Pa.), Phila. Racquet Club. Republican. Presbyterian. Avocations: squash, golf, tennis. Home: 133 Edgewood Rd Ardmore PA 19003-2507 Office: 101 S Bryn Mawr Ave Ste 360 Bryn Mawr PA 19010 Office Phone: 610-519-1721.

GIESECKE, JOAN RUTH, librarian, dean; MS in Mgmt., Ctrl. Mich. U.; MLS, U. Md.; D in Pub. Adminstrn., George Mason U. Dean librs. U. Nebr., Lincoln. Author: Scenario Planning for Libraries, Practical Help for New Supervisors, Practical Strategies for Library Managers; former editor Library Administration and Management. Office: University of Nebr - Lincoln Librs 318 Love Library Lincoln NE 68588-4100 Office Phone: 402-472-2526. E-mail: jgiesecke1@unl.edu.*

GIESEN, RICHARD ALLYN, manufacturing executive; b. Evanston, Ill., Oct. 7, 1929; s. Elmer J. and Ethyl (Lillig) G.; m. Jeannine St. Bernard, Jan. 31, 1953; children: Richard Allyn, Laurie J., Mark S. BS, Northwestern U., 1951. Research analyst new bus. and research depts. Glore, Forgan & Co., Chgo., 1951-57; asst. to pres. Gen. Dynamics Corp., NYC, 1957-60, asst. treas., 1960-61, asst. v.p. ops. and contracts, 1961-63; fin. cons. IBM Corp., 1963, exec. asst. to sr. v.p., 1964-65; treas. subs. Sci. Research Assocs., Inc., Chgo., 1965-66, v.p. fin. and adminstrn., 1966-67, exec. v.p., chief operating officer, 1967-68, pres., chief exec. officer, 1968-80; pres., chief exec. officer, chmn. exec. com., dir. Field Enterprises, Inc., Chgo., 1980-83; pres. RLM Investments, 1983-93; chmn., pres., CEO Am. Appraisal Assocs., Inc., 1984-93; chmn. Continental Pkg. Solutions, Chgo., 1988—; chmn., CEO Continere Corp., 1988—. Trustee Asia House Funds, 1994-98. Mem. bus. adv. coun. Chgo. Urban League, 1968-83; prin. Chgo. United, 1980-83; dir. GATX, Inc., 1982-2000, JWT Group, 1980-1985, Smurfit Stone Container, 1998-2001, Stone Container, 1973-98; mem. adv. coun. Technol. Inst., Northwestern U.; mem. pres.'s coun. Nat. Coll. Edn., Evanston, Ill., 1977-86; bd. dirs. Am. Cancer Soc.; mem. adv. coun. J.L. Kellogg Grad. Sch. Mgmt., Northwestern U.; dir. Jr. Achievement Chgo., 1993-2002; trustee Chgo. Edn. TV Assn., 1975-81, Inst. Internat. Edn., 1971-2003, chmn. midwest adv. bd., 1997-2003. Mem. Chief Execs. Orgn., Webhannet Golf Club, Chgo. Club, Shoreacres Club (Lake Bluff, Ill.), Alpha Tau Omega, Beta Gamma Sigma. Office: Continental Pkg Solutions Inc 230 W Monroe Chicago IL 60606 Fax: 312-666-7501. E-mail: rag@continentalpackagingsolutions.com.

GIESEY, RALPH EDWIN, retired historian; b. Detroit, Jan. 7, 1923; s. William Carl and Mary Thomas Giesey. AB, Wayne U., Detroit, 1943, MA, 1947; PhD, U. Calif., Berkeley, 1954. Asst. Inst. for Advanced Study, Princeton, NJ, 1953—55; instr. Vassar Coll., Poughkeepsie, NY, 1955—56, U. Wash., Seattle, 1956—59; assoc. prof. U. Minn., Mpls., 1959—66; prof. U. Iowa, Iowa City, 1966—88. Vis. prof. Folger Libr., Washington, 1972; dir. d'études Ecole des Hautes Etudes en Scis. Sociales, Paris, 1985. Author: The Royal Funeral Ceremony in Renaissance France, 1960, The Juristic Basis of Dynastic Right to the French Throne, 1961, If Not, Not, The Oath of the Aragonese and the Legendary Laws of Sobrarbe, 1968, Francogallia by François Hotman, 1972, Cérémonial et puissance souveraine: France, XVe-XVII siècles, 1987, Rulership in France, 15th-17th Centuries, 2004; editor: Selected Studies by Ernst H. Kantorowicz. Lt. j.g. USN, 1943—46, PTO. Fellow, Am. Coun. Learned Socs., 1952—53, Am. Numis. Soc., 1954, Inst. for Advanced Study, 1964—65, 1975—76, Guggenheim Found., 1970, NEH, 1974—75; grantee, Am. Coun. Learned Socs., 1960, Rockefeller Found., 1962, Am. Philos. Soc., 1966; Fulbright fellow, 1951—52. Democrat.

GIESZL, LOUIS ROGER, mathematician; b. Inglewood, Calif., Sept. 14, 1937; s. Clifford G. and Zelma R. (Thompson) G; m. Geraldine C. Cirigliano, Sept. 22, 1963; children: Louis G., Lisa M. BS in Math., U. Houston, 1958; MA in Math., Rice U., 1965; MS in Computer Sci., U. Md., 1976; MS in Tech. Mgmt., Johns Hopkins U., 1985. Designer large-scale simulations USN Ops. Analysis, 1967-80; cons. computer technology USAF, 1980-81; dir. info. sys. project Logistics Command/USAF, 1981-82; computer cons. Warfare Analysis Lab., Johns Hopkins U. Applied Physics Lab., Laurel, Md., 1982—, expert systems devel., 1983-87, test and evaluation mgmt., 1988-90, instr. software engring., 1988—. Referee, mem. editl. bd. and contbr. articles to profl. jours. and publs.; developer computer software/warfare simulation models. Capt. USAF, 1963-67. Mem. IEEE, Am. Legion. E-mail: L.R.Gieszl@ieee.org.

GIETSCHIER, STEVEN PHILIP, journalist, historian; b. NYC, July 21, 1948; s. Philip Herman Gietschier and Jacqueline Fern Noreyko; m. Donna Jean Peck, Aug. 30, 1975; children: Catherine Peck Meyers, Sarah Southard. BS in Fgn. Svc., Georgetown U., 1970; MA, Ohio State U., 1971, PhD, 1977. Archivist Ohio Hist. Soc., Columbus, 1975—78; supr. repository services divsn. SC. Dept. Archives and History, Columbia, 1978—86; dir. hist. records Sporting News, St. Louis, 1986—2000, sr. mng. editor rsch., 2000—. Exec. bd. Soc. for Am. Baseball Rsch., 1997—99; coun. mem. N.Am. Soc. for Sport History, 2001—03; treas. N.Am. Sport Libr. Network, 1992—. Editor: (reference work) Complete Baseball Record and Fact Book, 2004—. Mem. U. Kans. Parent Assn. Adv. Bd., Lawrence, 2006—07. Mem.: Spl. Librs. Assn., Midwest Archives Conf., Soc. Am. Archivists. Roman Catholic. Home: 3826 Secretariat Dr Florissant MO 63034 Office: Sporting News 14500 S Outer 40 Ste 300 Chesterfield MO 63017 Home Phone: 314-839-3839; Office Phone: 314-485-6387. Business E-Mail: sgietsch@sportingnews.com.

GIFFEN, DANIEL HARRIS, lawyer, educator; b. Zanesville, Ohio, Feb. 11, 1938; s. Harris MacArtor and Anne Louise (Crawford) G.; m. Jane Louise Cayford, Nov. 23, 1963 (div. 1970); children: Sarah Louise, Thomas Harris; m. Linda Eastin, Aug. 19, 1972. AB, Coll. of William and Mary, 1960; MA, U. Pa., 1962, MA, 1967; testamur, U. Exeter, Eng., 1971; JD, Case Western Res. U., 1973. Bar: Ohio 1973. Corp. asst. U. Pa. Lippincott Libr., Phila., 1961-63; assoc. curator La. State Mus., New Orleans, 1963-64; sec. N.H. Hist. Soc., Concord, 1964-69; asst. dir. Syracuse (N.Y.) U. Arents Rsch. Libr., 1969-70; pvt. practice Cleve., 1973-99; asst. prof. law Cleve. State U., 1976-79; asst. prof. Kent (Ohio) State U., 1980-98, prof. emeritus, 1998—. Editor Walter Drane Co., Cleve., 1974-76; lectr. Monadnock C.C., Peterborough, N.H., 1968-69; vis. scholar London Libr., 1991-92. Author: Adventures in Vermont, 1969, Adventures in Maine, 1969, New Hampshire Colony, 1970; contbr. articles to profl. jours. Hon. life mem. Pres.'s Coun., Coll. William and Mary, 1980. Recipient Kenyon English Prize scholarship, 1956; fellow Heritage Found., 1959-60, Nat. Trust, 1959-61, 67, 73. Fellow Saltire Soc. (Scotland); mem. ABA, Ohio Bar Assn., Am. Soc. Interior Design, Am. Assn. Mus., Am. Assn. State and Local Historians, Nat. Trust, Soc. Archtl. Historians, Masons, Shriners. Episcopalian. Home: 6058 Mad River Rd Centerville OH 45459-1508

GIFFEN, LOIS KEY, artist, psychotherapist; b. Hollis, Okla., Dec. 18, 1932; d. Andrew Finley and Audra Agnes (Griffith) Key; m. Robert Edward Giffen, June 26, 1954; children: John Andrew, Mark Alexander. BA, U. Chgo., 1951; diploma, Inst. Psychosynthesis, London, 1988. Artist, 1945—; social group worker Neighbourhood Clubs, Oklahoma City, Okla., 1956-59; tchr. Unity of the Keys, Key West, Fla., 1994—. Workshop facilitator Fla. Coalition Peace and Justice, 1990; organizer tchg. student mediators in elem. schs. Peace Edn. and Awareness Ctr., Santa Barbara, 1992-93; mentor Take Stock in Children Program; tchr. art program children Fla. Keys Land and Sea Trust. Editor: The London Bridge Mag., 1981—84, The CCL Cookbook, 1986; one-woman shows include Gippsland Regional Art Ctr., Sale, Victoria, Australia, 1973, Anjuian Angkatan Pelakis Semalaysia, Kuala Lumpur, 1976, Am. Consulate-USIS, Benghazi, Libya, 1962, exhibitions include Sculpture Key West, 2001—06, Ft. Zachary Taylor State Parks, Keys Women Arts, Key West Mus. Art and History, 2003—05, Gallery: Artists in Paradise, Big Pine Key, Fla. V.p., bd. dirs. Internat. Women's Club, Benghazi, Libya, 1960-65; mem. bd. dirs. Gippsland Regional Art Ctr., Sale, Victoria, Australia, 1971-73; com. chmn., mem. bd. dirs. Am. Women's Club, London, 1981-88; mem. bd. dir. Commonwealth Countries League, London, 1982-88, Welcome to London Internat. Club, London, 1983-88; mem. Univ. Women's Club, London, 1985-88; sec. bd. dirs. Fla. Keys Coun. of the Arts, Inc.; vol. Practical Acad. Cultural Edn. program teenage girls at risk, mem. Voices Fla. Keys Children. Mem. Assn. Transpersonal Psychology, Assn. for the Advancement of Psychosynthesis, Bus. and Profl. Women's Club, Fla. Keys Watercolor Soc., Lower Keys Artists Network, Marathon Sailing Club (rear commodore), Marathon Yacht Club. Democrat. Avocations: sailing, swimming, reading, astrology, gardening. Home: 2000 Manor Ln Marathon FL 33050

GIFFIN, GORDON D., former ambassador, lawyer; b. Springfield, Mass. m. Patti Alfred; 1 child, Kelley. BA, Duke U., 1971; JD, Emory U., 1974. Bar: Ga. 1974, DC 1979. Dir. legis. affairs, chief counsel to Senator Sam Nunn U.S. Senate, 1974-79; assoc. Hansell and Post, Atlanta, 1979-86; sr. ptnr. Long, Aldridge & Norman, Atlanta and Washington, until 1997; amb. to Can., Am. Embassy, Ottawa, Canada, 1997—2001; ptnr., co-chmn. pub. policy & regulatory affairs practice McKenna, Long & Aldridge LLP, Atlanta & Washington, 2001—. Former adj. prof. law Emory U. Sch. Law, Atlanta; bd. dirs. Overseas Pvt. Investment Corp., 1993-97; mem. bd. dirs. Can. Nat. Railway Co., Can. Imperial Bank of Commerce, Can. Natural Resources, Ltd., TransAlta Corp., Bowatee, Inc. and the Carter Presdl. Ctr. Treas. Senator Sam Nunn Campaign Com., 20 yrs.; with Senator Nunn and Gov. Clinton founder Dem. Leadership Coun., 1984, mem. bd., 1984-96; mem. com. to host Dem. Nat. Conv., Atlanta, 1988, chmn. site selection com., Chgo., 1996, gen. counsel, 1992, 96; presdl. elector, Ga., 1992, 96; chmn. Ga. Clinton primary campaign, 1992, Clinton-Gore Gen. Election Campaign, 1992; dep. dir. pers. White House Transition Team, 1992; sr. advisor on south, also chmn. Clinton-Gore effort in Ga., Clinton Reelection Campaign, 1996; active Atlanta Olympic Games Com., 1996; former mem. bd. dirs. Ga. C. of C., Trees Atlanta Found., Atlanta Hist. Soc., Atlanta Ballet. Named One of 100 Most Influential Georgians, Ga. Trend mag., 3 times. Democrat. Office: McKenna Long & Aldridge 1900 KSt NW Washington DC 20006-1108 Office Phone: 404-527-4020. E-mail: ggiffin@mckennaby.com.

GIFFIN, MARGARET ETHEL (PEGGY GIFFIN), management consultant; b. Cleve., Aug. 27, 1949; d. Arch Kenneth and Jeanne (Eggleton) G.; m. Robert Alan Wyman, Aug. 20, 1988; 1 child, Samantha Jean. BA in Psychology, U. Pacific, Stockton, Calif., 1971; MA in Psychology, Calif. State U., Long Beach, 1973; PhD in Quantitative Psychology, U. So. Calif., 1984. Psychometrician Auto Club So. Calif., LA, 1973-74; cons. Psychol. Svcs., Inc., Glendale, Calif., 1975-76, mgr., 1977-78, dir., 1979-94; rschr. Social Sci. Rsch. Inst., U. So. Calif., LA, 1981; dir. Giffin Consulting Svcs., LA, 1994—. Instr. Calif. State U., Long Beach, Long Beach, 1989—90; tech. adv. com. on testing Calif. Fair Employment and Housing Commn., 1974—80, steering com., 1978—80; pres. Pers. Testing Coun. So. Calif., 1980, exec. dir., 82, 88, bd. dirs., 1980—92. Mem. APA, Soc. Indsl. Organizational Psychology. Home and Office: 260 S Highland Ave Los Angeles CA 90036-3027 Office Phone: 323-939-0246. E-mail: peggygiffin@cs.com.

GIFFORD, CHARLES K., banker; b. Providence, Nov. 8, 1942; s. Clarence H. and Priscilla G.; m. Anne Gifford, Oct. 3, 1964; children: Ramsay, Charles, John, Jessica BA, Princeton U., 1964. Joined First Nat. Bank, Boston, 1966—67, loan officer, 1967—70, asst. v.p., 1970—73, v.p., 1973—78, first v.p., 1978, sr. v.p., 1979—81, exec. v.p., 1981—84, group exec. corp. banking group, 1984—87; vice chmn. Bank of Boston Corp. and First Nat. Bank of Boston (sub. of Bank of Boston), 1987—89, pres., 1989—95, chmn., CEO, 1995—99; pres., COO BankBoston and Fleet Fin. Group (merged), 1999—2001, CEO, 2001—02, chmn., 2002—04; chmn. emeritus Bank of Am., Boston, 2004—, bd. dirs., 2004—. Dir. NSTAR Corp.; bd. dir. CBS Corp., 2005—. Bd. mem. Northeastern U., Boston Symphony Orchestra, WGBH Pub. Broadcasting, Jr. Achievement, Dana Farber Cancer Inst., Dana Farber/Ptnrs. Cancer Care, Greater Boston C. of

C.; bd. dirs. Boston Pvt. Ind. Coun., Assn. Res. City Bankers; founding chmn. Success By 6, United Way, 1994-98; chmn. Boston Plan for Excellence in Pub. Schs. Mem. Greater Boston C. of C. (chmn.). Office: Bank of America 100 Federal St Boston MA 02110-2003

GIFFORD, DONALD GEORGE, dean, law educator, consultant; b. Medina, Ohio, July 26, 1952; s. George W. and Ruth Ann (Reed) G.; m. Nancy Ray Aten, Mar. 24, 1973; children: Rebecca Gifford Goldberg, Caroline. BA, Wooster Coll., 1973; JD, Harvard U., 1976. Bar: Ohio 1976, Fla. 1984. Assoc. Gallagher, Sharp, Fulton, Norman & Mollison, Cleve., 1976-77; ptnr. Noble & Gifford, Millersburg, Ohio, 1977-79; asst. prof. law U. Toledo, 1979-82, assoc. prof. law, 1982-84; prof. U. Fla., Gainsville, 1984-89; assoc. dir. academic task force for rev. ins. and tort systems Fla. Gov.'s Office, Gainsville, 1986-88; dean, prof. law W.Va. U., Morgantown, 1989-92; prof. law U. Md., Balt., 1992—, dean, 1992-99. Contbr. articles to profl. jours.; author 3 books. Chmn. Gov.'s Lead Paint Poisoning Commn., Md., 1992-94; vice chair Md. Alt. Dispute Resolution Task Force, 1997-2000. Mem. Ohio Bar Assn., The Fla. Bar, Am. Law Inst. Office: U Maryland Sch Law 500 W Baltimore St Baltimore MD 21201-1602 Office Phone: 410-706-1843. Business E-Mail: dgifford@law.umaryland.edu.

GIFFORD, GERALD FREDERIC, retired science educator; b. Chanute, Kans., Oct. 24, 1939; s. Gerald Leo and Marion Lou (Browne) Gifford; m. Cinda Jean Lowman, June 26, 1982. Student, Kans. U., 1957-60; BS in Range Mgmt., Utah State U., 1962, MS in Watershed Mgmt., 1964, PhD in Watershed Sci., 1968. Asst. prof. watershed sci. Utah State U., Logan, 1967-72, assoc. prof., 1972-80, prof., 1980-84, chmn. watershed sci. unit, 1967-84, dir. Inst. Land Reclamation, 1982-84; head range, wildlife and forestry U. Nev., Reno, 1984-92, chmn. environ. and resource sci. dept., 1992—94, prof. hydrology and natural resource mgmt., 1994—2000, ret., 2000. Exch. scientist NSF, Canberra, Australia, 1974; cons. in field. Author: (book) Rangeland Hydrology, 1981; assoc. editor: Jour. Range Mgmt., 1982—87, 1991—95, Arid Soil Rsch. and Rehab., 1985—90; contbr. scientific papers to profl. pubs. Mem.: Soil and Water Conservation Soc., Am. Water Resources Assn. Avocations: racquetball, antiques, garage sales. Home: 3880 Squaw Valley Cir Reno NV 89509-5663 Office Phone: 775-826-7932. Personal E-mail: fredandcinda@sbcglobal.net.

GIFFORD, JOHN F., retired electronics executive; b. 1941; Founder AMD, Sunnyvale, Calif., 1969, Maxim Integrated Products, Sunnyvale, Calif., 1983—2007, chmn., pres., CEO, 1992—2007, strategic adv., 2007—. Named one of Am.'s Most Powerful People, Forbes mag. Office: Maxim Integrated Products 120 San Gabriel Dr Sunnyvale CA 94086-5150*

GIFFORD, JOHN IRVING, retired agricultural equipment company executive; b. Lockport, NY, July 23, 1930; s. John Jacob and Carrie (McAdam) G.; m. Sara Jane Bauer, Jan. 28, 1955; children: John Hutchins, James Scott. BS, Purdue U., 1952, MS, 1956. Sales trainee Am. Nat. Foods, Inc., LA, 1956; economist Deere & Co., Moline, Ill., 1956-65, pers. adminstr., 1965-70, mgr. data svcs., 1970-96; stats. cons. to cos. and trade assns., 1996—. Bd. dirs., Rock Island (Ill.) sect. Easter Seal Found., 1981-87; v.p. coun., St. John Luth. Ch., Rock Island, 1981-82; pres., Rock Island Little League, 1981-82; v.p. Babe Ruth Baseball, Rock Island, 1983; mem. agrl. census adv. com. U.S. Dept. Commerce, 1997-98; mem. adv. com. stats. USDA, 1999-2004. 1st lt. U.S. Army, 1952-54, Korea. Recipient Leadership recognition Equipment Mfrs. Inst. Mem. Nat. Assn. Bus. Econs., Equipment Mfrs. Assn., Farm and Indsl. Equipment Inst., Constrn. Industry Mfrs. Assn., Outdoor Power Equipment Inst., Engine Mfrs. Assn., Internat. Farm Tractor Com., Internat. Harvesting Equipment Com. (chmn. statistics com. 1994-95), Rock Island (Ill.) Noon Kiwanis Club. Avocations: reading, golf. Office Phone: 309-788-5141. E-mail: gifford@revealed.net.

GIFFORD, JONATHAN LEWIS, transportation policy researcher, educator; b. Pitts., July 3, 1954; s. Richard Louis and Ardelle (S.) Gifford. BSCE, Carnegie Mellon U., 1976; MSCE, U. Calif., Berkeley, 1979, PhD in Civil. Engring., 1983. Jr. engr. Kaiser Engrs., Oakland, Calif., 1976-77; intern U.S. OMB, Washington, 1981, Congl. Budget Office, Washington, 1982; cons. Office Tech. Assessment, U.S. Congress, 1982, 83; asst. prof. pub. mgmt. and policy Sch. Urban and Pub. Affairs, Carnegie-Mellon U., Pitts., 1983-88; prof. pub. mgmt. and policy George Mason U., Fairfax, Va., 1988—, dir. Master's in Transp. Policy, Ops., Logistics, 2000—05. Cons. to industry and govt., 1985—; vis. assoc. prof. MIT, 1997; vis. fellow Transp. Rsch. Bd., 2005-06; chair com. for rev. of U.S. Dept. Transp. Intelligence Transp. Sys. standards program, NRC, 2002-03, 2006-07, co-chair com. workshop on developing a regional concept for mng. surface transp. ops., 2002-03. Author: Flexible Urban Transportation, 2003; mem. editl. adv. bd. Internat. Jour. Transport Mgmt., 2000-2003; co-editor, Infrastructure Planning and Management, 1993; script reviewer film Divided Highways, 1994-1997; assoc. editor Pub. Works Mgmt. and Policy; contbr. articles to profl. jours. Fenwick fellow, 1991-92, Carnegie Mellon U. Rsch. awardee, 1985, 84-86, grad. fellow Inst. Transp. Studies, U. Calif., Berkeley, 1981-83. Mem. ASCE, Soc. for History of Tech., Transp. Rsch. Bd. (chair com. on transp. and land devel.), Assn. for Pub. Policy and Mgmt., Intelligent Transp. Soc. Am., Cosmos Club. Office: George Mason Univ Sch Pub Policy MS 3B1 3401 Fairfax Dr Arlington VA 22201 Home Phone: 202-537-6722; Office Phone: 703-993-2275. Business E-Mail: jgifford@gmu.edu.

GIFFORD, KATHIE LEE, television personality, vocalist; b. Paris, Aug. 16, 1953; d. Aaron Leon and Joan Epstein; m. Paul Johnson, 1976 (div. 1983); m. Frank Gifford, Oct. 18, 1986; children: Cody Newton, Cassidy Erin. Student, Oral Roberts U., Tulsa. Gospel singer; singer $100,000 Name That Tune Quiz Show; co-host Morning Show, 1985-88, LIVE with Regis and Kathie Lee, 1988-2000, spl. corr. The Insider, 2005-; author: The Quiet Riot, 1976, I Can't Believe I Said That, 1992, (with Regis Philbin) Cooking With Regis and Kathie Lee, 1993, Entertaining With Regis and Kathie Lee, 1994, Christmas With Kathie Lee, 1997; marketer clothing collection Kathie Lee for Plaza South; singer (albums) Sentimental, 1993, It's Christmas Time, 1993, Born for You, 2000, A Gentle Grace, 2004; actress (plays) Annie, 2006; sang Nat. Anthem, Super Bowl, 1995; host, co-writer, co-producer, CBS television special, Kathie Lee.Looking for Christmas, 1994; co-writer (with David Pomeranz), Under the Bridge (play), 2004, Hurricane Amy, 2005 Office: The Insider Paramount Pictures 5555 Melrose Ave Los Angeles CA 90038 also: William Morris Agy 1325 Ave of Americas New York NY 10019*

GIFFORD, MARILYN JOYCE, emergency physician, consultant; b. Denver, Aug. 3, 1943; d. Leslie Arthur and Dorothy Marianne (Stevens) G.; m. Robert Bruce Caplan (div.); children: Eric Louis Caplan, Brian Matthew Caplan; m. Daniel Patrick McKenna, July 17, 1992. AA, Stephens Coll., Columbia, Mo., 1963; BS, Mich. State U., 1965; MD, Mt. Sinai Sch. Medicine, NYC, 1971. Diplomate Am. Bd. Emergency Medicine. Emergency physician Longmont (Colo.) United Hosp., 1974-80, Boulder (Colo.) Cmty. Hosp., 1976-78; dir. emergency svcs. Meml. Hosp., Colorado Springs, Colo., 1980—. Physician advisor Colorado Springs Fire Dept., 1980—; bd. dirs. Nat. Registry Emergency Med. Technicians, Columbus, Ohio, 1983—. Co-author: Protocols for Prehospital Emergency Medical Care, 1984, Prehospital Emergency Care, 1996. Advisor E-911 Authority Bd., Colorado Springs, 1996—. Lt. USNR, 1971-72. Recipient Kim Langstaff Meml. award for excellence Region IV EMs Coun., 1986, Val. Wolhauer award for physician excellence Emergency Med. Technician Assn. Colo., 1982, Pres.'s Leadership award Nat. Assn. Emergency Med. Technicians, 1983, ACEP contbn. in EMS, 2001. Fellow Am. Coll. Emergency Physicians (chair EMS com. 1979-81, Colo. coun. 1978-85); mem. El Paso County Med. Soc. (pres. 1993-94). Avocation: skiing. Office: Meml Hosp 1400 E Boulder St Colorado Springs CO 80909-5599 Home Phone: 719-576-8608; Office Phone: 719-365-2000. Personal E-mail: marilyngifford@hotmail.com.

GIFFORD, MARJORIE FITTING, mathematician, educator, consultant; m. Frederick N. Fitting, Feb. 25, 1972 (dec. 1985); m. Forrest W. Gifford, May 28, 1988 (div. 1992). BS in Math., Mich. State U., PhD in Math. Edn., 1968; AM in Math., U. Mich., 1966; postgrad., U. Nev., Las Vegas, 1995—97, U. Hawaii, Oahu, 2006—. Cert. tchr., Mich. Grad. asst. Mich. State U., East Lansing, 1966-68; prof. emeritus math. and computer sci. San Jose State U., Calif., 1968-92; CEO Metier Cons., Kauai, 2004—. V.p. fin. Metra Instruments, San Jose, 1972—82; pres. Metier, San Jose, 1982—98; cons. San Jose Unified Sch., 1969—71; instr. U. Nev., Las Vegas, 1993—94, U. Hawaii OutReach, 2006—. Author: (software) Math Test Generation, 1983; co-author: (book series) Computer Literacy Series, 1983-85, (book) Introduction to Geometry, 1996. Taxwise vol. AARP, 2006—; docent Na Aina Kai Bot. Gardens, 2006—; mem. Kani Lea Chorale, 2004—07. NSF fellow, 1965-66, Paul Harris fellow, Fulbright Sr. fellow, 1985-86. Mem. Am. Math. Soc., Calif. Math. Coun., Rotary Club Hanalei Bay, Zeta Tau Alpha. Roman Catholic. Avocations: gardening, bridge, photography, painting, singing.

GIFFORD, NELSON SAGE, finance company executive; b. Newton, Mass., May 3, 1930; s. Gordon Babcock and Hariette Rose (Dooley) G.; m. Elizabeth B. Brow, Nov. 12, 1955 (dec. Jan. 13, 2006); children: Susan Helen, Ian Christopher, Diane Brow. AB, Tufts Coll., 1952; HHD (hon.), U. Mass., 1989; PhD (hon.), Tufts U., 1996. With Dennison Mfg. Co., Framingham, Mass., 1954-90, mem. acctg. staff, 1954-63, controller, 1964-65, gen. mgr., 1965-67, v.p., 1967-72, pres., 1972-86, chmn., 1986-90; vice chmn. Avery Dennison Corp., Boston, 1990-91; prin. Fleetwing Capital, Boston, 1992—. Bd. dirs. Nypro Inc., Clinton, Mass., Doble Engring., Watertown, Mass. Past bd. dirs. New Eng. Colls. Fund, Reed and Barton, Taunton , Mass., John Hancock Fin. Svcs., Boston, J.M. Huber Corp., Edison, N.J., NSTAR, Boston, Avery Dennison, Pasadena, Calif.; corp. mem. Newton Wellesley Hosp., Mass. Gen. Hosp.; past chmn. Wellesley Pers. Bd.; past trustee Woods Hole Oceanographic Inst., Mass., 1984-90; chmn. bd. trustees Tufts U., 1986-95. Lt. comdr. USNR, 1952-60. Mem. Silvanus Packard Soc., Mass. Bus. Roundtable (bd. dirs., vice chmn. 1982-88), Assoc. Industries Mass. (bd. dirs. 1976-86), Kittansett Club, Brae Burn Country Club, Beverly Yacht Club, Soc. Tufts Followes. Office: Fleetwing Capital 75 Federal St Ste 1100 Boston MA 02110 Home: 224 Converse Rd Marion MA 02738 Office Phone: 617-357-9175. Personal E-mail: giffordn@msn.com.

GIFFORD, PROSSER, retired library administrator; b. NYC, May 16, 1929; s. John Archer and Barbara (Prosser) G.; m. Shirley Mireille O'Sullivan, June 26, 1954; children: Barbara, Paula, Heidi. BA, Yale U., 1951, PhD, 1964; BA, Oxford U., Eng., 1953, MA, 1958; LLB, Harvard U., 1956; MA, Amherst Coll., 1969, LHD, 1980; LLD, Doshisha U., Kyoto, Japan, 1979. Bar: DC 1956. Asst. to pres. Swarthmore Coll., 1956-58; asst. prof. history Yale, 1964-66; dir. 5 yr. B.A. program, 1965-66; dean faculty Amherst Coll., 1967-79, assoc. prof. history, 1967-69, prof. history, 1969-79; dep. dir. Woodrow Wilson Internat. Ctr. for Scholars, Washington, 1975-76, 80-87, acting dir., 1987-88; dir. scholarly programs Libr. Congress, 1990—2005. Chmn. Merton Coll. Charitable Corp., 1991-2006; Sir Thomas Bodley fellow Merton Coll., 2001. Co-editor, contbr.: Britian and Germany in Aftica, 1967, France and Britain in Africa, 1971, Transfer of Power in Africa, 1982, Decolonization and African Independence, 1988, Creating French Culture, 1995, Democracy and the Rule of Law, 2001. Trustee Hotchkiss Sch., 1971—81, Concord Acad., 1972—78; chmn. bd. trustees Woods Hole Marine Biol. Lab., 1978—90; bd. dirs. Woods Hole Pub. Libr. Rhodes scholar, 1951-53; Fgn. Area fellow No. Rhodesia, 1963-64 Mem. Assn. Yale Alumni (gov. 1972-77), Woods Hole Oceanographic Inst. (mem. corp.), Internat. House of Japan, India Internat. Ctr., Century Club, Cosmos Club, Elizabethan Club, Woods Hole Golf and Tennis Club, Quisset Yacht Club. Home: 59 Penzance Rd Woods Hole MA 02543-0005 Home Phone: 508-548-5727. Business E-Mail: pgifford@mbl.edu.

GIFFORD, THOMAS OWEN, physician; b. Scottsbluff, Nebr., May 9, 1978; s. Robert John and Rhonda Sue Gifford; m. Stephanie Berry, July 8, 2000; children: Brooklyn Lee, Ryan Thomas. BS in Biology, USAF Acad., Colo., 2000; MD, Loyola U. Chgo., Ill., 2004. Resident physician divsn. otolaryngology U. Utah, Salt Lake City, 2004—. Capt. USAF, 2004—07, Salt Lake City. Office: Univ Utah Divsn Otolaryngology 50 N Medical Dr Rm 3C120 Salt Lake City UT 84132 Office Phone: 801-581-2121.

GIFFORD, WILLIAM C., lawyer, educator; b. Aurora, Ill., Sept. 18, 1941; AB, Dartmouth Coll., 1963; LLB, Harvard U., 1966. Bar: Ill. 1966, D.C. 1968, N.Y. 1976, Paris 1994. Assoc., ptnr. Ivins, Phillips & Barker, Washington, 1967—74; assoc. prof. Cornell Law Sch., 1974—78; counsel, ptnr. Wilmer, Cutler & Pickering, 1978—83; ptnr. Davis Polk & Wardwell, NYC, 1983—98, sr. counsel, 1999—; prof. law Cornell U. Law Sch., 2001—03. Vis. lectr. Yale Law Sch., 2003, Columbia Law Sch., 2004—05. Author: International Tax Planning, 1974, 2d edit. (with W.P. Streng), 1979, (with E.A. Owens) International Aspects of U.S. Income Taxation, 1982. Office: Davis Polk & Wardwell 450 Lexington Ave New York NY 10017-3911 Home Phone: 917-865-6395; Office Phone: 212-450-4632. Business E-Mail: gifford@dpw.com.

GIFFORDS, GABRIELLE, congresswoman, former state senator; b. Tucson, June 8, 1970; m. Mark E. Kelly. BA in Sociology and Latin Am. History, Scripps Coll., 1993; M in Regional Planning, Cornell U., 1997. Rschr. Am. Friends Svc. Com., San Diego, 1995; planner bi-national bus. develop. San Diego Dialogue U. San Diego, 1995; assoc. regional econ. develop. Price Waterhouse LLP, NYC, 1996; pres. El Campo Tires Warehouses, Inc., Tucson, 1996—2000; mng. ptnr. Giffords Capital Mgmt, LLC, Tucson, 2000—07; mem. Ariz. Ho. of Reps from Dist. 13, 2001—03, Ariz. State Senate from Dist. 28, 2003—05, US Congress from 8th Ariz. dist., 2007—, mem. armed services com., fgn. affairs com., sci. & tech. com. Bd. adv. U. Ariz. Coll. Bus. and Pub. Adminstrn.; bd. dirs. Met. YMCA, Tucson, Ariz. Friends of Small Bus., 162nd Air Nat. Guard Minuteman Com., Ariz. Prevention Resource Ctr. Adv. Coun., Tohono Chul Pk., Anti-Defamation League, Ariz. Cultural Develop., Women's Campaign Sch. Yale, Tucson Regional Water Coun., Pres. Coun. Cornell Women, Breast Cancer Boot Camp, Friends Saguaro Nat. Pk., Arts Reach Inc. Named a Young Leader Worth Watching, Gannett News Svc., 2004; named Legis. of Yr., Ariz. Planning Assn., 2003, Ariz. Coalition to Prevent Homelessness, 2003, Mental Health Assn. Ariz., 2004, Most Valuable Player at Ariz. Legis., Sierra Club, 2005, Woman of Yr., Tucson Bus. Edge, 2005; named an Outstanding Legis., Ariz. Family Literacy, 2003, Outstanding Alumna, Scripps Coll., 2004; recipient Top 10 Tech award, Arizona Tech. Coun., 2003, 2004, Award of Distinction, League Ariz. Cities and Towns, 2005, 100% Rating, League Conservation Voters, 2005, Golden Eagle award, Independent Ins. Agents and Brokers Ariz., 2005, Eagle Enterprise award, Ariz. Small Bus. Assn., 2005, Women on the Move, YWCA Tucson, 2005; William J. Fulbright scholar, Chihualhua, Mexico, 1993—94, Fannie Mae fellow, Harvard U. Kennedy Sch. Exec. Mgmt., 2003, Eagleton Inst. Rutgers U. fellow, 2003. Mem.: Hadassah (life). Democrat. Jewish. Achievements include becoming youngest woman elected to Arizona State Senate. Avocation: reading. Office: 502 Cannon House Office Bldg Washington DC 20515 also: 1661 N Swam Ste 112 Tucson AZ 85712*

GIFT, JAMES JOSEPH, aquatic toxicologist; BA in Biology, Harvard U, 1964; MA in Environ. Sci., Rutgers U., 1968, PhD in Environ. Sci., 1970. Lab. rsch. dir. Ichthyological Assocs., Brigantine, NJ, 1970-75; sr. v.p., dir. sci. and tech. EA Engring., Sci. & Tech. Inc., Md., 1975-97; owner Quail's Roost Environ. Svcs., 1997—, Quail's Roost Photography, 1997—. Mem.: Am. Fisheries Soc. Achievements include direction of a multimedia assessment contrasting ocean disposal of sewage sludge with various land-based waste management options; direction of ocean site designation studies for New York City and other municipalities; preparation of the first Special Permit Application for ocean disposal of sewage sludge; direction of a wide variety of ecological and human health risk assessments; conducting of research on the physiological effects of thermal gradients of numerous marine, estuarine and freshwater fish species; award-winning nature photographer. Personal E-mail: jgift42@msn.com.

GIGANTELLI, JAMES WILLIAM, ophthalmic plastic surgeon; b. Dover, NJ, Sept. 3, 1959; BS, U. So. Calif., 1981; MD, Vanderbilt U., 1985. Diplomate Am. Bd. Ophthalmology. Resident Vanderbilt U., Nashville, 1985-86, Baylor Coll. Medicine, Houston, 1986-89; fellow Duke U., Durham, N.C., 1989-90; staff Alton Ochsner Med. Found., Baton Rouge, 1990-94; asst. prof. U. Mo., Columbia, 1994—. Fellow Am. Acad. Ophthalmology; mem. AMA, Assn. for Rsch. in Vision and Ophthalmology, Mo. State Med. Assn. Office: Dear A McGee Eye Inst U Okla 1000 N Limestone Ste 390 Oklahoma City OK 73104

GIGAS, GUNTER GEORGE, retired physicist, physician; b. Dürrenburg, Germany, Aug. 2, 1928; arrived in US, 1930; s. William Felix and Irmgard Erna (Behrend) Gigas; m. Joan E. Brinkman, Feb. 22, 1954 (dec.); children: Mark George, Marina Noelle. BSc with honors, U. Nev., Reno, 1950; MSc, U. So. Calif., LA, 1959, PhD, MD, 1962; PhD, Universidad de Autonoma, Juarez, Mex., MD, 1979. Lic. nuc. engr., Calif., 1976; diplomate Am. Bd. Forensic Medicine. Resident in internal medicine U. Health Sci. Chgo. Med. Sch., 1982; group leader High Altitude Lab. Air Rsch., LA, 1951—59; supr. radiation effects Rsch. Atomics Internat., Canoga Park, Calif., 1962—72; cons. space environ. effects JPL/CalTech, Pasadena, Calif., 1976—81; pvt. practice physician, surgeon LA, 1982—2005; ret., 2005. Lectr. Moorpark Coll., Calif., 1962—72. Contbr. articles to profl. jours. Mem. World Wildlife Fedn. Sta. chief USAF. Co-recipient Group Achievement award for Voyager Spacecraft Sys. Design and Devel., NASA, 1981; Rueben Thompson scholar, U. Nev., Phi Kappa Phi scholar, 1948, Major Max C. Fleischmann scholar, 1950. Mem.: Spanish Hills Country Club, Sigma Xi. Avocation: poetry. Home: 1300-1313 Ramona Dr Camarillo CA 93010

GIGER, MARYELLEN LISSAK, medical physicist, educator; d. Frank and Margaret Lissak; m. Charles Giger; children: Megan, Jennifer, Charlie, Eric. BS summa cum laude, Ill. Benedictine Coll., 1978; MSc, U. Exeter, Eng., 1979; PhD, U. Chgo., 1985. Asst. prof. U. Chgo., 1986—91, assoc. prof., 1991—2000, prof. radiology com. on med. physics and the coll., 2000—, vice-chair basic scientific rsch., radiology dept. Dir. advanced imaging program Cancer Rsch. Ctr. U. Chgo., 1994—, dir. grad. programs in med. physics, 1998—; presenter in field. Author: (manuscript in investigative radiology) Computerized Detection of Pulmonary Nodules in Computed Tomography Images (Stauffer Award, 1995), (manuscript in medical physics) Multifractal Radiographic Analysis of Osteoporosis (Sylvia Sorkin Greenfield Award, 1995); contbr. chapters to books, articles to profl. jours. Leader Girl Scouts, Elmhurst, Ill., 1994—2001. Recipient President's Scholarship award, Ill. Benedictine Coll., 1975, 1976, 1977, Rev. Shonka, O.S.B. Scholarship Award in Physics, 1977, First Pl. award Young Investigators' Symposium, Am. Assn. Physicists in Medicine, 1985, Jr. Faculty Rsch. award, Am. Cancer Soc., 1988, Faculty Rsch. award, 1991; grantee, Wendy Will Case Cancer Fund, 1989, NIH, Nat. Cancer Inst., 1989—95, 1999—2001, 2000—, 2001—, U.S. Army, DOD, 1993—96, 1996—2000, 1998—2001, 1999—2002; Rotary Internat. fellow, Rotary, 1978—79, Louis Block Rsch. grantee, U. Chgo., 1986, Am. Cancer Soc. Instl. grantee, 1986. Fellow: Am. Assn. Physicists in Medicine, Am. Inst. Med. Bioengring.; mem.: IEEE, Soc. for Computer Applications in Radiology, Assn. Univ. Radiologists, Internat. Soc. for Optical Engring. Achievements include first to in computer-aided diagnosis research; patents for computer-aided diagnosis for breast and lung cancer detection and diagnosis; assessment of breast cancer risk and assessment of osteoporosis. Office: U Chgo 5841 S Maryland Ave Chicago IL 60637 Business E-Mail: m-giger@uchicago.edu.

GIGLI, IRMA, dermatologist, educator, academic administrator; b. Cordoba, Argentina, Dec. 22, 1931; d. Irineo and Esperanza Francisca (Pons de Gigli) Gigli; m. Hans J. Muller-Eberhard, June 29, 1985. BA, Liceo Nacional Manuel Belgrano, Cordoba, 1950; MD, Universidad Nacional de Cordoba, 1957. Intern Cook County Hosp., Chgo., 1957—58, resident in dermatology, 1958—60; fellow in dermatology NYU, 1960—61; mem. faculty Harvard Med. Sch., 1967—75, asso. prof. dermatology, 1972—75; chief dermatology service Peter Bent Brigham Hosp., Robert B. Brigham Hosp., 1971—75; prof. dermatology and exptl. medicine N.Y. U. Med. Center, NYC, 1976—82, mem. Irvington Houst Inst., mem. faculty N.Y. Grad. Sch. Med. Scis., dir. Asthma and Allergic Disease Center for Immunodermatology Studies, 1980—91; prof. medicine, chief div. dermatology U. Calif.-San Diego, 1983—95; prof. medicine and dermatology, vice chair medicine for sci. U. Tex. Health Sci. Ctr., Houston, 1995—; assoc. dir. Inst. Molecular Medicine for Prevention Human Diseases U. Tex., Houston, 1998—2003, dep. dir., 2003—, Walter and Mary Mischer prof. molecular medicine Houston, 1998—; dir. Rsch. Ctr. Immunology and Autoimmune Diseases, 1995—. Mem. Nat. Inst. of Allergy and Infectious Diseases Coun., 1978—79, bd. sci. counselors, 1997—; chmn. study sect. Allergy and Immunology Inst., NIH, 1978—83; mem. Guggenheim Found. Western Hemisphere and Phillippines Com. of Selection; adv. bd. NIH Fogarty Internat. Ctr., 1984—97. Bd. dirs. U.S. Civilian R&D Found. for the Ind. States of the Former Soviet Union. Recipient Rsch. award, Am. Cancer Soc., 1970—72, NIH, 1972—76, Disting. Profl. Woman of Yr. award, U. Tex. Health Sci. Ctr. at Houston, 2003, David Martin Carter Mentor award, Am. Skin Assn., 2005; grantee, Guggenheim Found., 1974—75. Mem.: Acad. Medicine, Engring. & Sci. Tex. (bd. dirs.), Am. Acad. Arts and Scis., Henry Kunkel Soc. (councilor 1999—), PEW Latin Am. Fellows Program in Biomed. Scis. (nat. adv. com. 1998—2005), Inst. Medicine/NAS, Am. Dermatol. Assn., Assn. Am. Physicians, Am. Acad. Allergy, Am. Acad. Dermatology, Am. Assn. Immunologists, Am. Soc. Clin. Investigation, Soc. Investigative Dermatology (hon.; pres. 1990—91, Stephen Rothman Meml. award 1996). Office: U Tex Health Sci Ctr Inst Molecular Medicine 2121 W Holcombe Blvd Houston TX 77030-3303

GIGOT, PAUL ANTHONY, editor; b. San Antonio, 1955; AB in Govt., Dartmouth Coll., 1977. Editl. asst. Nat. Rev., 1978-79; reporter, editor Far Ea. Econ. Rev., 1979-80; reporter Wall St. Jour., 1980-82, Asia corr., 1982-84, editor editl. page Asian edit., 1984-86, columnist Potomac Watch, mem. editl. bd., 1987—2001, editl. page editor NYC, 2001—. Recipient Pulitzer prize, 2000; White House fellow, 1986—87. Office: The Wall St Jour 200 Liberty St New York NY 10281-1003

GIGUERE, FRANCOIS, professional sports team executive; b. June 24, 1963; m. Brigitte Giguere; children: Philippe, Frederique. Grad., Laval U., 1985. Controller fin. dept. Quebec Nordiques, 1990—93, adminstrv. asst., 1993—95; asst. gen. mgr. Colo. Avalanche, Denver, 1995—2000, v.p. hockey ops., 2000—01, gen. mgr., exec. v.p., 2006—; asst. gen. mgr. Dallas Stars, 2002—06. Office: Colo Avalanche Pepsi Ctr 100 Chopper Cir Denver CO 80204-1743

GIGUERE, JEAN-SEBASTIEN, professional hockey player; b. Montreal, Que., Can., May 16, 1977; m. Kristen Giguere; 1 child, Maxime Olivier. Goalie Hartford Whalers, 1996—97, Calgary Flames, 1998—2000, Anaheim Ducks (formerly Mighty Ducks of Anaheim), 2000—. Recipient Harry Holmes Meml. Trophy, Am. Hockey League, 1998, Conn Smythe Trophy, 2003. Achievements include being a member of Stanley Cup Champion Anaheim Ducks, 2007. Office: Anaheim Ducks 2695 E Katella Ave Anaheim CA 92806*

GIKAS, PAUL WILLIAM, medical educator; b. Lansing, Mich., July 23, 1928; s. John and Minnie (Neumann) G.; m. Lois Suzanne Haglund, Dec. 27, 1952; children— Sandra Jane, Sarah Elizabeth, Paula Suzanne. AB, U. Mich., 1950, MD, 1954. Diplomate: Am. Bd. Pathology. Chief lab. service VA Hosp., Ann Arbor, Mich., 1960-68; mem. faculty U. Mich. Med. Sch., Ann Arbor, 1959—, assoc. prof. pathology, 1966-69, prof., 1969-95, prof. emeritus, 1995—, faculty rep. to Big Ten Intercollegiate Conf., Nat. Collegiate Athletic Assn., 1982-88, asst. dean for admissions, 1990-97. Cons. Armed Forces Inst. Pathology, 1966-74 Author: The Accident Problem, 1976, Uropathology, 1976, Forensic Aspects of the Highway Crash, 1983; co-editor: The Prevention of Highway Injury, 1967. Mem. adv. com. traffic safety HEW, 1966-68; mem. Gov. Mich. Spl. Commn. Traffic Safety Mich., 1964; chmn. bd. dirs. Pub. Citizen, Inc., 1971-2002; co-trustee Center Study Responsive Law, Washington, 1969-71. Served to capt. M.C. AUS, 1956-58. Recipient Auto Safety award Med. Tribune, 1966-67, Distinguished Service award U. Mich., 1965, Disting. Svc. award U. Mich. Med. Ctr. Alumni Soc., 1998. Fellow Coll. Am. Pathologists, U.S. and Can. Acad. Pathology, Alpha Omega Alpha, Nu Sigma Nu. Lutheran. Achievements include research with preservation of blood for transfusion by freezing and rsch. in pathogenesis of injury in highway crashes. Home: 1900 Mershon Dr Ann Arbor MI 48103-5939

GIL, GUILLERMO, prosecutor; Acting U.S. atty. Dept. Justice, Hato Rey, PR, 1993—2002, asst. U.S. atty. PR, 2002—. Office: US Attys Office Fed Bldg 350Carlos E Chardon Ave Hato Rey San Juan PR 00918

GILBANE, THOMAS F., JR., construction executive; b. Providence, June 7, 1947; s. Thomas F. and Jean A. (Murphy) G.; m. Mary O'Donnell, June 9, 1973; children— Thomas F., Daniel, Martha, Michael. Student, Brown U., Providence; BSBA in Bus. Mgmt., Babson Coll., Mass., 1970; MS in Civil Engring. and Project Mgmt., MIT, Cambridge, 1975; postgraduate student in Advanced Mgmt., Harvard Bus. Sch., 1984. cert. in bldg. constrn., RI Sch. Design. Various positions Gilbane Bldg. Co., Providence, 1964-76, v.p., reg. mgr. Cleve., 1976-83, exec. v.p. Providence, 1983—2004, CEO, 2004—, chmn. Bd. dirs. Nynex, NY, New Eng. Tel., audit fin. com.; mem. Associated Gen. Contractors (AGC)of Am. Private Industry Adv. Coun., chmn. AGC Nat./Reg. Contractor's Com. Alumni dir., mem. corp. Babson Coll., Wellesley, Mass., 1974-76; bd. dirs. Boy Scouts Am., Cleve., 1981-83, Providence, 1985—; trustee Greater Cleve. Roundtable, 1983-85; RI Assn. for Blind, Providence, 1985—; bd. dirs. United Way-Southeastern New Eng., Providence, 1985-93, campaign chmn. 1986; bd. dirs. United Way Am., 1994—, fin. com., 1994—; trustee City of Hope, 1984—, Cath. Charities, US Lacrosse Found; Served to 2nd lt. RI N.G., 1970-76. Recipient Spirit of Life award City of Hope, 1984. Mem. Alexis de Tocqueville Soc. Am. (nat. chmn. 1994—), In-Sight Pro Am., New Albany Country Club, Sigma Chi, Phi Kappa Si, Sigma XI, Clubs: Union (Cleve.); Agawan Hunt (East Providence, RI), Point Judith Country (Narragansett, RI, Hope, US Golf Assn. Sectional Affairs Com., Lodges: Knights of Malta. Roman Catholic. Avocations: golf, skiing, fishing. Office: Gilbane Bldg Co 7 Jackson Walkway Providence RI 02903-3694 Office Phone: 401-456-5900. Office Fax: 401-456-5404.

GILBERG, KENNETH ROY, lawyer; b. Phila., Pa., Feb. 2, 1951; s. Leonard David and Roslyn (Tennis) G.; m. Nanci Jane Schwartz, Sept. 7, 1974. BA, Lebanon Valley Coll., 1973; JD, Widener U., 1976. Bar: Pa. 1976. Assoc. Pechner, Dorfman et. al., Phila., 1976-84, ptnr., 1984-87, Myerson & Kuhn, Phila., 1988-89; prin. Kenneth R. Gilberg and Assocs., Bala Cynwyd, Pa., 1989—99; ptnr. Mesirov Gelman Jaffe Cramer & Jamieson, LLP, Phila., 1990—2000, Schnader Harrison Segal & Lewis, LLP, Phila., 2000—02; shareholder Buchanan Ingersoll, Phila., 2002—06, Flaster/Greenberg PC, Phila., 2006—. Contbr. articles to profl. jours. Past pres. Golden Slipper Camp; past pres., past chmn. Golden Slipper Club and Charities. Recipient Meritorious Achievement award Pa. Sports Hall of Fame, 1974; named Most Valuable Player Mid-Atlantic Conf., 1973. Mem. Phi Alpha Delta (charter). Republican. Avocations: lacrosse, racquetball, photography, golf, tennis. Office: Flaster Greenberg PC Eight Penn Ctr 1628 John F Kennedy Bldg Fl 15 Philadelphia PA 19103 Office Phone: 215-279-9915. Business E-Mail: kenneth.gilberg@flastergreenberg.com.

GILBERT, ALAN T., conductor; b. NYC, Feb. 23, 1967; s. Michael Gilbert and Yoko Takabe; m. Kajsa William-Olsson; 2 children. Studies with Leon Kirchner, Peter Lieberson & Earl Kim, Harvard U.; studies with Masuko Ushioda, New England Conservatory of Music; studies with Otto-Werner Müller, Curtis Inst. of Music, Phila.; MusM, Juilliard Sch. Staff mem. The Cleveland Orch., 1994, asst. condr., 1995—97; music dir. Haddonfield Symphony, NJ, 1996—97; asst. concertmaster The Santa Fe Opera, Santa Fe, 1993—2001; chief condr. & artistic advisor Royal Stockholm Philharmonic Orch., 2000—; condr. & music dir. The Santa Fe Opera, Santa Fe, 2001—; principal guest condr. NDR Symphony Orch., Hamburg, 2004—. Guest condr. Orch. Philharmonique de la Radio, France, Tonhalle Orch., Orch. de la Suiss Romande, Bamberg Symphony, Phila. Orch., NY Philharmonic, Nat. Symphony Orch., Minnesota Orch., Atlanta Orch., Boston Orch., San Francisco Orch., Los Angeles Orch. Recipient Helen M. Thompson award, Am. Symphony Orch. League, 1994, First prize, Internat. Competition Mus. Performance, Geneva, 1994, Swiss prize, 1994, Bunkamura Orchard Hall award, 1994, Sir Georg Solti prize, 1994, Arts Conductors award, Seaver/Nat. Endowment for Arts, 1997. Office: Santa Fe Opera PO Box 2408 Santa Fe NM 87504-2408*

GILBERT, BLAINE LOUIS, lawyer; b. Phila., Aug. 26, 1940; s. Arthur I. and Marcia R. (Kaufman) G.; m. Sondra Gilbert; children: Beth M., Kimberly J. AA, Balt. Jr. Coll., 1961; postgrad., Am. U., 1962; JD, U. Balt., 1965. Bar: Md. 1966, U.S. Dist. Ct. Md. 1968, U.S. Supreme Ct. 1974. Exec. asst. ins. commr. State of Md., Balt., 1965-66; assoc. Polovoy & Polovoy, Balt., 1966-72; ptnr. Angeletti & Gilbert, Balt., 1972-79, Gilbert & Levin, Balt., 1979-92, Blaine L. Gilbert and Assocs. P.A., Balt., 1993—. Mem. ABA, Balt. Bar Assn., Am. Immigration Lawyers Assn., Am. Judicature Soc., Md. Trial Lawyers Assn. Avocations: music, screenwriting. Home: 2B Dorsett Hills Ct Owings Mills MD 21117-1131 Office: Blaine L Gilbert & Assocs PA Lower Level 200 E Lexington St Baltimore MD 21202-3530 Office Phone: 410-727-4970. Fax: 410-539-6440. E-mail: blglaw@aol.com.

GILBERT, BRADLEY, professional tennis coach, former professional tennis player, former Olympic athlete; b. Oakland, Calif., Aug. 9, 1961; m. Kim Gilbert; 3 children: Zachary, Julian Elizabeth, Zoe. Student, Foothills Jr. Coll., Pepperdine. Ranked 9th in U.S. Tennis Assn., 1993; played in over 35 USTA tour events; coach Andre Agassi, 1994—2002, Andy Roddick, 2003—04; commentator ESPN. Co-author: (books) Winning Ugly, 1994, I've Got Your Back, 2004. Recipient Bronze medal Olympics, Seoul, 1988. Achievements include winning 20 profl. singles titles. Office: USTA 70 W Red Oak Ln White Plains NY 10604-3602

GILBERT, BRUCE RITS, lawyer; b. Milw., Apr. 8, 1954; s. Eugene George and Inez Laurel (Rits) Gilbert; m. Andrea L. Fenton, Aug. 13, 1981; children: Molly, Emily, Casey. BBA, U. Wis., Madison, 1976; JD, Antioch Sch. Law, 1981. Bar: DC 1981, US Dist. Ct. DC 1982, US Ct. Appeals DC cir. 1982, Pa. 1985. Assoc. Weissburg and Aronson, Washington, 1981-84, Case & Cohen, Washington, 1984-85; named gen. counsel-health care, asst. sec. Universal Health Services, Inc., King of Prussia, Pa., 1985, gen. counsel, 1991—. Bd. dirs. Fedn. Am. Hospitals (formerly Fedn. Am. Health Systems), chmn., 1997, treas., 2003—. Mem. ABA, Nat. Assn. Health Lawyers. Jewish. Office: Universal Health Services Inc Universal Corp Ctr 367 S Gulph Rd King Of Prussia PA 19406-0958 Office Phone: 215-768-3300.*

GILBERT, CHARLES, performing arts educator, writer; b. West Chester, Pa., July 13, 1955; s. Charles Lewis Gilbert and Janet Earnshaw; m. D'Arcy Webb, July 19, 1980; children: Alex, Kerry. MFA in Directing, Carnegie-Mellon U., Pits., Pa., 1977. Asst. prof. drama U. Del., 1979—85; assoc. prof. drama Syracuse U., NY, 1985—86; prof. theater arts U. of the Arts, Phila., 1988—. Composer, lyricist: (musical) Gemini the Musical (nominee Barrymore award for excellence in theater, 2005); composer, lyricist, idea creator Assassins. Recipient Barrymore award for Excellence in Theater. Mem.: Musical Theater Educators Alliance Internat. (pres. 2006—). Liberal. Unitarian. Office: Univ of the Arts 320 S Broad St Philadelphia PA 19102 Home Phone: 302-383-4880; Office Phone: 215-717-6570. Business E-Mail: cgilbert@uarts.edu.

GILBERT, CHARLES D., neurobiologist; b. NYC, Jan. 15, 1949; s. Gustave M. and Matilda S. (Safran) G. BA in Biophysics, Amherst U., 1971; MD, Harvard U., 1977, PhD in Neurobiology, 1977. Tchg. fellow Harvard Med. Sch., Cambridge, Mass., 1977-79, prin. rsch. assoc., 1979-81, asst. prof., 1981-83, Rockefeller U., NYC, 1983-85, assoc. prof., 1985-91, prof. neurobiology, 1991—. Vice-chmn. Klingenstein Fund, N.Y.C., 1983—; adv. panel NSF, Washington, 1984-87. Contbr. articles to profl. jours. Exec. sec. Pew Charitable Trust Latin Am. Scholars, N.Y.C., 1989-91. Recipient Weill-Caulier award, 1984, Rita Allen Found. award, 1986, Presdl. Young Investigator award NSF, 1984, Devel. award McKnight Found., 1991, Cortical Discoverer award Cajal Club, 1993, W. Alden Spencer award Columbia U., 2002; fellow Danforth Found., 1971-75, Med. Found., 1978-80. Fellow AAAS (mem.-at-large neurosci. sect.), Am. Acad. Arts Scis.; mem. NAS, Assn. for Rsch. in Vision and Ophthalmology, Soc. for Neurosci.

GILBERT, CHARLES RICHARD ALSOP, obstetrician, gynecologist, surgeon, educator; b. Phila., May 26, 1916; s. Chauncey McLean and Frances Marguerite (Young) G.; m. Helene Scher, Dec. 24, 1973; children: Anita Ivonne, Charles Richard Alsop Jr. MD, U. Va., 1944. Diplomate Am. Bd. Abdominal Surgeons, Am. Bd. Ob-Gyn. Rotating intern N.Y.C. Hosp., 1944-45, asst. resident in internal medicine, 1945-46; resident in surgery Nix Hosp., San Antonio, 1946; resident in gen. surgery, chief female abdominal surgery Ryder Meml. Hosp., Hunacao, P.R., 1952-55; house staff gynecology Johns Hopkins Hosp., Balt., 1948-49; asst. resident in obstetrics U. Md., 1949, chief resident in obstetrics, 1949-50, asst. resident in gynecology, 1950-51, chief resident in gynecology, 1951-52, assoc. in gynecology, instr. gynecol. pathology, 1952; asst. clin. prof. obstetrics and gynecology U. P.R., 1952-55, George Washington U., 1972-74, assoc. clin. prof. obstetrics and gynecology, 1974-93, clin. prof. ob/gyn. Washington, 1994—; chief gynecology Doctors Hosp., 1973—; sr. attending in obstetrics and gynecology Washington Hosp. Center. Instr. internal medicine Randolph Sch. Aviation, San Antonio, 1946; cons. U.S. Air Force in obstetrics, gynecology, female urology, 1952-54 Author: Childbirth-The Modern Guide to Expectant Mothers, 1960, Better Health for Women, 1964, Abdominal Pelvic Surgery, 1969; co-editor, editor: Symposiumon Abdominal Pelvic Surgery, 1966; contbr. articles to profl. jours.; Mem. editorial staff: Jour. Abdominal Surgery, 1964-74. Served with M.C. USAF, as chief internal medicine, 1946-48, Selfridge AFB, Mt. Clemens, Mich. Fellow ACS (founding fellow), Am. Coll. Obstetrics and Gynecology, Am. Soc. Abdominal Surgeons (teaching faculty 1964-74, mem. exec. com. 1964-74, v.p. 1969-70, pres. 1971-72), Internat. Coll. Surgeons (U.S. sect., regent, exec. com. 1981—, chmn. bd. regents 1983-84, sec. 1982-83, membership chmn. 1983, 2d pres.-elect 1985, pres.-elect 1986, pres. 1987-88, coordinator diplomatic relations 1985—, spl. advisor to pres. 1989-90, mem. internat. bd. govs. 1990, sec. N.Am. fedn. 1991-92, Regent of Yr. award 1981, emeritus 1992, bd. trustees 1993, 96-98, hon. fellow 1995); mem. Pan Am. Med. Assn., Med. Soc. D.C., AMA, Med. and Surgery Soc. Johns Hopkins Hosp., Douglass Obstet. and Gynecol. Soc., Nat. Rifle Assn., African Safari Club Washington (v.p. 1974-77, pres. 1977), Am. Outdoors Council (dir.), Hunting Hall of Fame Found. (dir. 1978), Jefferson Soc. Club: Boone and Crockett. Clubs: Boone and Crockett. Achievements include developing first audiovisual med. corr. teaching courses for continuing med. edn., 1973. Home and Office: 705 E Franklin Ave Silver Spring MD 20901-4707 Home Phone: 301-565-8821.

GILBERT, CREIGHTON EDDY, art historian; b. Durham, NC, June 6, 1924; s. Allan H. and Katharine (Everett) G. BA, NYU, 1942, PhD, 1955; DHL (hon.), Adelphi U., 1990, U. Louisville, 1997. Assoc. prof. Brandeis U., 1961-65, Sidney and Ellen Wien prof. history of art, 1965-69; prof. Queens Coll. City U. N.Y., 1969-77; Jacob Gould Schurman prof. art history Cornell U., 1977-81; prof. Yale U., 1981-2000, prof. emeritus, 2000—. Fulbright sr. lectr. U. Rome, 1951-52; fellow Netherlands Inst. for Advanced Study, 1972-73; vis. prof. U. Leiden, 1974-75; Zacks Found. vis. prof. Hebrew U. Jerusalem, 1985. Author: Change in Piero della Francesca, 1968, History of Renaissance Art, 1972, The Works of Girolamo Savoldo, 1986, Poets Seeing Artists' Work: Instances from the Italian Renaissance, 1991, Michelangelo On and Off the Sistine Ceiling, 1994, Piero della Francesca et Giorgione: Problèmes d'Interpretation, 1994, Caravaggio and His Two Cardinals, 1995, The Saints' Three Reasons for Paintings in Churches, 2001, How Fra Angelico and Signorelli Saw the End of the World, 2002, Lex Amoris, 2005, Saint Bernardino, Preacher to the Eye, 2007; editor: Italian Art 1400-1500, Sources and Documents, 1979, enlarged Italian edit., 1988; editor-in-chief: The Art Bull, 1980-85; translator: Complete Poems and Selected Letters of Michelangelo, 1963, 3d edit., 1979. Recipient Mather award Coll. Art Assn., 1964 Fellow Am. Acad. Arts and Scis., Ateneo Veneto (fgn.). Office: Yale U Dept Art History Box 208272 New Haven CT 06520-8272

GILBERT, DANIEL, psychology professor; BA summa cum laude in Psych., U. Colo., Denver, 1981; PhD in Social Psych., Princeton U., NJ, 1985. Asst. prof. U. Tex., Austin, 1985—90, assoc. prof., 1990—95, prof., 1995—96, Harvard U., Cambridge, Mass., 1996—2005, Harvard Coll. prof., 2005—. Fellow Ctr. Advanced Study in Behavioral Scis., 1991—92; Ford vis. prof. behavioral sci. U. Chgo. Sch. Bus., 2003. Contbr. articles to profl. jours., to popular media; co-editor: Handbook of Social Psych., 4th edit., 1998; editor: Selected Works of Edward E. Jones, 2003; author: Stumbling on Happiness, 2006. Recipient Rsch. Scientist Devel. award, NIMH, 1991—96, James McKeen Cattell award, 1999; grantee John Simon Guggenheim Meml. Found. fellowship, 1999, Am. Philos. Soc. fellowship, 1999. Fellow: Soc. Exptl. Social Psych., APA (Disting. Sci. award, Early Career Contbn. to Psych. 1992), Soc. Personality and Social Psych. Office: Dept Psych Harvard U Cambridge MA 02138 E-mail: gilbert@wjh.harvard.edu.

GILBERT, DANIEL, professional sports team owner, mortgage company executive; married; 5 children. B, Mich. State U.; JD, Wayne State U. Bar: Mich. Founder, CEO, chmn. Rock Fin. Corp., 1985—99; founder, chmn. Quicken Loans, 2002—; ptnr. Camelot Ventures; majority owner NBA Cleve. Cavaliers, 2005—; operator Quicken Loans Arena, Cleve. Frequent guest on CNBC, including guest host on Morning Call; frequent guest ESPN, CNN, FOX, ABC and other networks. Past pres. Jewish Assn. Residential Care, Detroit; bd. dirs. Children's Tumor Found., NYC, Children's Hosp. Mich. Found. Named one of Forbes' Richest Ams., 2005, 2006; named to Jr. Achievement Hall of Fame; recipient Entrepreneur of Yr. award, Ernst and Young. Office: Quicken Loans 20555 Victor Pky Livonia MI 48152*

GILBERT, DAVID, chef; b. 1978; Grad., Johnson and Wales U., 1997. Cook Restaurant Vermeer, Amsterdam; chef Ritz-Carlton, Atlanta, head chef St. Thomas, 2000; exec. sous chef The Inn at Perry Cabin, Orient Express; chef de cuisine Eau Bistro, St. Louis; exec. chef Beverly Hilton; exec. chef, ptnr. Luqa, Dallas, 2006—. Featured in GQ mag., Gourmet Mag. Involved with North Tex. Food Bank. Named 2004 Best Chef in St. Louis, Riverfront Times; named one of Dallas' Rising Stars, StarChefs.com, 2007; recipient Bronze medal, Chaine des Rotisseurs jr. commis competition, 2000, silver medal, 2001. Office: Luqa Restaurant 1217 Main St Dallas TX 75202 Office Phone: 214-760-9000. Office Fax: 214-760-9321.*

GILBERT, DAVID A., lawyer; b. 1944; BA, Brown U., 1966; JD, U. Boston Coll., 1969. Bar: Mass. 1969, Colo. 1982, US Dist. Ct. (Dist. Mass.). Ptnr., dir., Real Estate Sect. Mintz, Levin, Cohn, Ferris, Glovsky & Popeo PC, Boston. Overseer Newton-Wellesley Hosp. Mem.: Internat. Assn. Corp. Real Estate Execs. (past pres. New Eng. Chpt.), Boston Bar Assn., Mass. Bar Assn., ABA. Office: Mintz Levin Cohn Ferris Glovsky & Popeo PC One Financial Ctr Boston MA 02111 Office Phone: 617-348-1645. Office Fax: 617-542-2241. Business E-Mail: dgilbert@mintz.com.

GILBERT, DAVID ERWIN, academic administrator, physicist; b. Fresno, Calif., June 23, 1939; s. Erwin Azel and Hester (Almond) G.; m. Carolyn Faye Parker, June 24, 1960; children: Ronald David, Joan Elaine. AB, U. Calif.-Berkeley, 1962; MA, U. Oreg., 1964, PhD, 1968. Prof. physics Eastern Oreg. U., La Grande, 1968-98, dean. acad. affairs, 1977-83, pres., 1983-98; pres. emeritus. Vis. rschr. Obs. Paris, 1975-82; commr. N.W. Assn. Schs. and Colls., 1982-88. Contbr. articles on physics to profl. jours. V.p. Ea. Oreg. Regional Arts Coun., 1979-80; vice chair, bd. dirs. Oreg. Ed-Net, 1989-97, Oreg. Pub. Broadcasting Found., 1991-93; mem. Oreg. Task Force Superconducting Super Collider, 1987, Oreg. Pub. Broadcasting Commn., 1991-01, Oreg. Bd. Forestry, 1991-2002, chair, 1996-2002; mem. Gov.'s Transition Team, 1990, Oreg. visibility adv. com. Dept. Environ. Quality, 1990-91; bd. dirs. Blue Mountains Natural Resources Inst., 1990-98, N.E. Oreg. Area Health Edn. Ctr., Gov.'s Telecomms. Forum Coun., 1996-97; bd. dirs. Oreg. Agr. Found., 1998—, Keep Oreg. Green Assn., 1999-2001, Tillamook Forest Heritage Trust, 1999-2002, North Ctrl. U., Ariz., 2002—04. Grantee NATO; grantee Research Corp. U.S.A., U.S. Govt., pvt. founds. Mem. Am. Assn. Colls. and Univs. (bd. dirs. 1995-97, chmn. com. econ. and cmty. devel. 1990-92), Am. Assn. Physics Tchrs. (pres. Oreg. chpt. 1973-74), Pacific N.W. Assn. Coll. Physics (bd. dirs. 1970-74), Sigma Xi, Sigma Pi Sigma, Phi Kappa Phi. Democrat. Home: PO Box 36 Joseph OR 97846-0036 Personal E-mail: deg@starband.net.

GILBERT, DONALD ROY, lawyer; b. Phila., June 6, 1946; BA, Stanford U., 1968; JD, U. Calif., 1971. Bar: Calif. 1972, Ariz. 1972. Ptnr., dir. Fennemore Craig, Phoenix, 1972—. Mem. ABA, State Bar Ariz., State Bar Calif., Maricopa County Bar Assn. Office: Fennemore Craig 3003 N Central Ste 2600 Phoenix AZ 85012-2913

GILBERT, DOUGLAS BRAINERD, telecommunications industry executive; b. Miami, Fla., July 4, 1957; s. Thomas Marshall Gilbert Jr. and Jeanne Brainerd; m. Susan M. Pace, Apr. 28, 2001; 1 child, Joshua Daniel. BA in Philosphy/Theology, Boston Coll., 1979; MDiv, Maryknoll Sch. of Theology, 1983; MA in Counseling, Duquesne U., 1995. Cert. sys. engr. Microsoft, project mgmt. profl. Microsoft, info. systems security profl. Microsoft, protection profl. Microsoft. Cons. Worklife Solutions, Old Greenwich, Conn., 1997; assignment dir. Deloitte & Touche, LLP, NYC, 1998-2000; sr. project mgr. Exodus Comms., Herndon, Va., 2000-01; svc. dir. Cable & Wireless, Sterling, Va., 2001—04; sr. mgr. Netsec, Herndon, Va., 2004—. Chmn. bd. SMA African Art Mus., 1997-98; exec. bd. Internat. Liaison of Lay Vols. in Mission, Washington, 1988-90. Mem.: Computer Security Inst., Internat. Info. Sys. Security Cert. Consortium, Project Mgmt. Inst. Republican. Roman Catholic. Avocations: travel, fishing, amateur radio. Office: Netsec 13525 Dulles Technology Drive Herndon VA 20171 Home Phone: 540-751-1544; Office Phone: 703-788-6391. E-mail: dbg1999@hotmail.com.

GILBERT, ELAYNE RHODA, writer; b. Bklyn., Oct. 22, 1940; d. Henry Albert and Sara Gilbert. *Ezra Pound reports in The Cantos that "Le prussien/C'est un chic homme." "A Prussian is a chic individual." Ms. Gilbert's paternal grandfather and his brother — both born in nineteenth century Germany — agree by posing in a photograph with trendy neckwear. Her grandpapa sports a necktie and her great-uncle wears a bow knot that depicts the alternative life choices for these bachelors. Their suit jackets display breast welt pockets with silk handkerchiefs spilling out in a style popular in the late nineteenth century (after 1850).* BA, U. Miami, 1964, MA, 1972; AA, Miami Dade C.C., 1997. With Dade County Cir. and County Cts., 1980—84; pollworker Dade County Election Days, 1988, 1990—2000, Broward County Election Days, 2002, 2004—06. Author: (books) Keepin' Up Kulcher: John Adams and Sidney Lanier Build Pound's Cantos, 1972, 4th edit, 2005, These Had Thrones: Edward Coke's Impact on 'The Cantos', 2001, 2nd edit., 2004, Ivory Dipping in Silver: Poetic Ideas Wrapped in Monographs and Murders, 2002, 3rd edit., 2006. Avocations: reading, theater, movies, music, book collecting.

GILBERT, ELMER GRANT, engineering educator, control theorist; b. Joliet, Ill., Mar. 29, 1930; s. Harry A. and Florence A. (Otterstrom) G.; m. Lois M. Verbrugge, Dec. 27, 1973. BSEE, U. Mich., 1952, MSEE, 1953, PhD in Instrumentation Engring., 1956. Instr. U. Mich., Ann Arbor, 1954-56, asst. prof., 1957-59, assoc. prof., 1959-63, prof. aerospace engring., 1963—94, prof. emeritus, 1994—. Founder, Applied Dynamics Inc., Ann Arbor. Patentee computer devices, 1968-74. Fellow IEEE (Control Engring. Field award 1994), AAAS; mem. Nat. Acad. Engring., Soc. Indsl. and Applied Math. Office: U Mich Dept Aerospace Engring Ann Arbor MI 48109-2140 Home Phone: 734-971-6753; Office Phone: 734-764-3355. Business E-Mail: elmerg@umich.edu.

GILBERT, FREDERICK E., development planner, Africanist, consultant; b. Mpls., May 28, 1939; s. Eugene Lester and Anne Cecelia (Omlie) G.; m. Jane Arey, June 30, 1962; children: Erik O., Christopher A., Peter A. BA, U. Minn., 1961; MALD, Tufts U., 1963, PhD, 1976. Desk officer for Niger, Upper Volta, Cote d'Ivoire, Dahomey and Togo U.S. AID, Washington, 1974-76, asst. dir. Yaounde, Cameroon, 1976-80, chief Africa econ. policy and analysis Washington, 1980-81, dir. Sahel and West Africa, 1981-83, prin. officer Dar es Salaam, Tanzania, 1983-86, dep. mission dir. Khartoum, Sudan, 1986-88, mission dir., 1988-90, regional dir. Abidjan, Cote d'Ivoire, 1990-93; ind. cons., 1994-97; dir. Famine Early Warning Sys., 1998-2000; ind. cons. Falls Church, Va., 2000—. Bd. dirs., treas. Am. Friends of Episcopal Ch. Sudan, 2005—. Mem. ACLU, Am. Fgn. Svc. Assn., Amnesty Internat., Sierra Club, World Resources Inst. (policy consultative group on natural resources mgmt. for Africa 1994-97). Episcopalian. Avocations: skiing, tennis, bicycling.

GILBERT, GLENN GORDON, retired linguistics educator; b. Montgomery, Ala., Sept. 17, 1936; s. William H. and Margaret (Christensen) G.; m. Erika Wrede, Aug. 8, 1964 (div. Nov. 1993); children: Alexander Martin, Christa Selene; m. Sharon Wright Pape, July 23, 1994. AB in German Lang. and Lit., U. Chgo., 1957; postgrad., U. Frankfurt, Fed.

Republic Germany, 1957—59; diplôme de la Langue Française with honors, Sorbonne, U. Paris, 1960; PhD in Linguistics, Harvard U., 1963. Instr. Germanic langs. and lits. U. Tex., Austin, 1963-66, asst. prof. Germanic langs., 1967-70; vis. asst. prof. linguistics Can. Summer Sch. Linguistics, U. Alta., Edmonton, summer 1966; Fulbright lectr. linguistics U. Marburg, Fed. Republic Germany, 1966-67; assoc. prof. So. Ill. U., Carbondale, 1970-74, prof., 1975—, chmn. dept. linguistics, 1987—89, 1999—2002; Fulbright lectr. linguistics U. Mainz, Fed. Republic Germany, 1973-74; Z.W.O. rsch. fellow in Creole langs. U. Nijmegen, Netherlands, 1984-85; ret., 2005. Active numerous univ. linguistics coms. and couns.; bd. dirs., mem. editl. bd., Ill. bus. rep. Papers in Linguistics, 1979-87; pres. Linguistic Rsch. Inc., 1983-87; lectr. in field. Founder, editor Jour. Pidgin and Creole Languages, 1985-2001; author: Linguistic Atlas of Texas German, 1972; editor: (books) Texas Studies in Bilingualism, 1970, The German Language in America, 1971, Pidgin and Creole Languages: Essays in Memory of John E. Reinecke, 1987, Pidgin and Creole Linguistics in the Twenty-First Century, 2002; co-editor (with Jacob Ornstein) Problems in Applied Educational Sociolinguistics, 1978; editor and translator: Pidgin and Creole Languages: Selected Essays by Hugo Schuchardt, 1980; editor: (book series) Studies in Ethnolinguistics, 1993-2003, Studies in Contact Linguistics: Essays in Honor of Glenn G. Gilbert, 2006; contbr. articles to profl. jours., chpts. to books; also revs. Translator, interpreter various cmty. orgns.; mem. Treasure Coast Unitarian Universalist Ch. NDEA fellow in Swedish, Harvard U., 1961-63; rsch. grantee U. Tex.-Austin, 1963-70, Nat. Carl Schurz Meml. Fund, 1968, So. Ill. U.-Carbondale, 1970-84, NEH, 1981, Am. Philos. Soc., 1982. Mem. Soc. Caribbean Linguistics, Soc. for Pidgin and Creole Linguistics, Harvard Club of the Palm Beaches. Home: 29 Fieldway Dr Stuart FL 34996 Personal E-mail: glenngilbert@comcast.net.

GILBERT, GORDON JOEL, neurologist, electroencelographer; b. NYC, Mar. 24, 1933; s. Benjamin Leon Henry and Lunny (Zalenko) Gilbert; m. Adele Schwartz, July 10, 1960; children: Benette Lisabeth Rosen, Stefanie Celeste, Benjamin Leon. AB, Harvard U., 1953; MD, NYU, 1957. Diplomate Am. Bd. Psychiatry and Neurology; diplomate Am. Electroencephalographic Soc. Intern Johns Hopkins Hosp., Balt., 1957-58; fellow in neurology Yale U. Sch. Medicine, New Haven, 1958-59, 60-61, Boston City Hosp., 1959-60; asst. prof. neurology Yale U. Sch. Medicine, New Haven, 1965; chief neurology St. Anthony's Hosp., Tampa, Fla., 1965-92; clin. prof. physiology and biophysics U. South Fla., Tampa, 1977—2006, clin. prof. molecular pharmacology and physiology, 1977—; chief of staff Humana Hosp., St. Petersburg, Fla., 1991-92, chmn. bd. trustees, 1996-97. Chmn. Med. Adv. Bd. MDA, St. Petersburg, 1966-81; expert witness Fla. Dept. Health, 2004-. Contbr. chpts. to books; Neurological Complications of Therapy, 1982, Spinocerebellar Degenerations, 1991; articles to jours: JAMA, New Eng. Jour. Medicine. Mem. collections com. Harvard Art Mus., 1996—;(paintings and sculpture subcom.); bd. govs. NYU Sch. Medicine, 1994—; trustee Mus. Fine Arts, St. Petersburg, 2000-06, 07-, chair accessions com., 2001-. Capt. USAF, 1961—63. Fellow Am. Acad. Neurology; mem. Pinellas County Med. Soc. (bd. govs. 1997-2004), Harvard Club (pres. Fla. west coast 1986-88), Harvard Alumni Assn. (bd. dir. 1991-94, regional dir. West Coast of Fla.), Phi Beta Kappa, Alpha Omega Alpha. Republican. Jewish. Achievements include discovery of effective treatment for spasmodic toricollis and for hemiballismus; description of spinocerebellar diseases, first descripton of turtle headache, quinidine dementia, pseudohemiparetic parkinsonism; first to describe the relationship of herpes zoster ophthalmicus to granulomatous angiitis of the central nervous system. Avocations: collection and study of 16th and 17 century Dutch and Flemish paintings. Office: Gordon J Gilbert MD PA 500 Pasadena Ave S Saint Petersburg FL 33707-2126 Office Phone: 727-345-7500. Business E-Mail: drgg22@tampabay.rr.com.

GILBERT, GREG, professional hockey coach, retired professional hockey player; b. Mississauga, Ont., Can., Feb. 22, 1962; Left wing NY Islanders, 1982—89, Chgo. Blackhawks, 1989—93, NY Rangers, 1993—94, St. Louis Blues, 1994—96; head coach Worcester IceCats, Mass., 1996—2000; asst. coach Calgary Flames, 2000, head coach, 2000—02, Mississauga Ice Dogs, 2003—06, Toronto Marlies, 2006—. Recipient AHL Coach of Yr., Louis A.R. Pieri Meml. award, Minor League Coach of Yr., The Sporting News. Achievements include being a member of Stanley Cup Champion, NY Islanders, 1982, 1983, NY Rangers, 1994. Office: Toronto Marlies Hockey Club Ricoh Coliseum at Exhibition Place 100 Princes' Blvd Toronto ON M6K 3C3 Canada

GILBERT, H. STEVEN, engineering and construction management company executive; B in Chem. Engring., Case Western Res. U., Cleve. With Fluor Corp., 1970—, various project mgmt. and gen. mgmt. positions including head telecom. bus. line and head fed. projects. bus. line, office mgr. Irvine, Calif., Houston, Calgary, Alta., Greenville, SC, Chgo., Phila., sr. v.p. bus. and work process integration, sr. v.p. human resources and adminstrn. Office: Fluor Corp 6700 Las Colinas Blvd Irving TX 75039 Office Phone: 469-398-7000. Office Fax: 469-398-7255.*

GILBERT, HARRIETTE GURLEY, retired music educator; b. Cherryville, NC, Apr. 7, 1950; d. Robert Clifton and Ruth McDowell Gurley; m. Richard Lee Gilbert, June 16, 1973; children: Lindsay McDowell, Kerstin Blair. AA, Peace Coll., 1970; MusB, Appalacian State U., 1973, MA cum laude, 1974; postgrad., Duke U., 1976—77. Cert. music edn., supervisn., cmty. & jr. coll. curriculum Appalacian State U., NC. Instrumental music specialist Gaston County Sch. Sys., Gastonia, NC, 1976—2006; ret., 2006. Condr. N.C. Assn. Educators convention music groups, educator confs. & county edn. functions, 1976—. Chmn. Am. Cancer Soc., Cherryville, 2000, Am. Heart Assn., Cherryville, 2003; vol. Leukemia & Lymphoma Soc., Gaston County, 2004; organist First United Meth. Ch., Cherryville, 1981—84, St. Luke's Episcopal Ch., Lincolnton, NC, 1985—. Mem.: NEA, NC Assn. Classroom Tchrs., NC Assn. Educators, Music Educators NC, Cherryville Music Club (program chmn. 1980—97). Democrat. Episcopalian. Avocations: historic home restoration, gardening, genealogy, landscaping.

GILBERT, HOWARD ALDEN, retired economics professor; b. Spokane, Wash., Feb. 1, 1935; s. Alden Phineas and Hester Anne (Warner) G.; m. Lucille Dorothy Weaver, June 28, 1957; children: Douglas Alden, Daniel William, Dawnna Faye Gilbert Berndt, Debra Anne Gilbert La Croix. BA, Cen. Bible Inst., Springfield, Mo., 1957; BS, Wash. State U., 1961, MA, 1962; PhD, Oreg. State U., 1967; postgrad., Vanderbilt U., 1971. Asst. prof. S.D. State U., Brookings, 1966-70, assoc. prof., 1970-76, prof., 1976—2001; ret., 2001. Expert witness retained by various attys. Mem. Mensa (pres. S.D. chpt. 1989-91, v.p. 1992-94, 96-97), Mortar Bd., Phi Kappa Phi (pres., v.p., sec., marshall), Pi Gamma Mu (sec., v.p., pres.), Gamma Sigma Delta (treas., pres.), Alpha Zeta, Omicron Delta Epsilon, Lambda Chi Alpha (head advisor 1967-97, ednl. advisor 1997—, order of merit, Alumni Hall of Fame). Democrat. Avocations: motorcycling, building restoration, running, piano, photography. Home: 708 8th St Apt 7 Brookings SD 57006-1559 Business E-Mail: purplesage@brookings.net.

GILBERT, HOWARD N(ORMAN), lawyer, director; b. Chgo., Aug. 19, 1928; s. Norman Aaron and Fannie (Cohn) G.; m. Jacqueline Glasser, Feb. 16, 1957; children: Norman Abraham, Harlan Wayne, Joel Kenneth, Sharon. PhB, U. Chgo., 1947; JD, Yale U., 1951. Bar: Ill 1951, U.S. Dist. Ct. (no. dist.) Ill. 1955, U.S. Ct. Appeals (7th cir.) 1956. Ptnr. Rusnak, Deutsch & Gilbert, Chgo., 1962-79, Aaron, Schimberg, Hess & Gilbert, Chgo., 1980-84, Holleb & Coff, Chgo., 1984-2000, Wildman, Harrold, Chgo., 2000—. Bd. dirs. Jewish Fedn. Met. Chgo., 1977-83; chmn. bd. dirs., pres. Mt. Sinai Hosp. Med. Ctr., Chgo., 1968-69; trustee Chgo. Hosp. Coun., 1979-84; mem. Bd. Jewish Edn., 1972-77; mem. vis. com. Coll. of U. Chgo., 1997-2003. Mem. ABA, Chgo. Bar Assn., Chgo. Coun. Lawyers, Ill. Soc. Health Lawyers, Standard Club, Bryn Mawr Country Club. Democrat. Jewish. Office: Wildman Harrold Allen & Dixon 225 W Wacker Dr Ste 3000 Chicago IL 60606-1224 Office Phone: 312-201-2722. Business E-Mail: gilbert@wildman.com.

GILBERT, J. PHIL, federal judge; b. 1949; BS, U. Ill., 1971; JD, Loyola U., Chgo., 1974. Ptnr. Gilbert & Gilbert, Carbondale, Ill., 1974-83, Gilbert, Kimmel, Huffman & Prosser, Carbondale, 1983-88; circuit judge First Jud. Circuit, Ill., 1988-92; fed. judge U.S. Dist. Ct. (so. dist.) Ill., Benton, 1992—, chief judge, 1993—2000. Spl. asst. atty. gen. Pub. Aid Enforcement Divsn., 1974-75; asst. city atty. City of Carbondale, 1975-78; active Nat. Coun. Govt. Ethics Laws, 1988—; mem. Ill. State Bd. Elections, 1982, vice chmn., chmn., 1983-85. Bd. dirs. Friends of Morris Libr., 1988—; active Edn. Coun. 100, 1989—, Boy Scouts Am. Mem. Ill. State Bar, Jackson County Bar Assn., Phi Alpha Delta. Office: US Dist Ct 301 W Main St Benton IL 62812-1362

GILBERT, JACK, poet; b. Pitts., 1925; Grace Hazard Conkling writer-in-residence Smith Coll., 1999—2000; vis. prof., writer-in-residence Univ. Tenn., 2004. Author: (poetry) Views of Jeopardy, 1962 (Yale Younger Poets Series award, 1962, Pulitzer Prize nominee), Monolithos (Stanley Kunitz Prize, Am. Poetry Rev. prize, Pulitzer Prize finalist), Kochan, The Great Fires: Poems 1982-1992, Refusing Heaven, 2005 (Nat. Book Critics Cir. award for poetry, 2005); contbr. poetry to Am. Poetry Rev., Quarterly, Poetry, Ironwood, Kenyon Rev., New Yorker, others. Recipient Guggenheim Fellowship, Nat. Endowment for Arts grant, Lannon Lit. award for poetry.

GILBERT, JAMES CAYCE, minister; b. Nashville, Feb. 26, 1925; s. Gettis and Delia Mae (Snyder) G.; m. Freda Mae Mitchell, Sept. 3, 1949; children— Elizabeth, Suzanne, Kathryn, Rosalie. BA, Bethel Coll., McKenzie, Tenn., 1945, DD (hon.), 1976; BD, Cumberland Presbyn. Theol. Sem., McKenzie, 1947; MA, Scarritt Coll., Nashville, 1948. Ordained to ministry Cumberland Presbyn. Ch., 1944; asso. pastor West Nashville Cumberland Presbyn. Ch., 1947-48; pastor River Oaks Cumberland Presbyn. Ch., Houston, 1948-55, Trinity Cumberland Presbyn. Ch., Ft. Worth, 1956-64; pastor emeritus Trinity Cumberland Presbyn. Ch, Ft. Worth; exec. dir. Cumberland Presbyn. Children's Home, Denton, Tex., 1964-90, dir. devel., 1991-94, exec. dir. emeritus; moderator gen. assembly Cumberland Presbyn. Ch., 1979-80. Stated clk., Red River Presbytery of the Cumberland Presbyn. Ch., 1993—. Mem. Nat. Assn. Homes Children, Southwestern Assn. Children's Home (past pres.), Tex. Assn. Execs. Homes Children (past pres.), Lions, Masons, K.T. Home: 3720 W Biddison St Fort Worth TX 76109-2705

GILBERT, JAMES EASTHAM, academic administrator; b. Bridgeport, Conn., July 1, 1929; s. Carl Ludwig and Anna Maude (Eastham) G.; m. Betty Lee Blankenship, Aug. 26, 1953; 1 child, Gregory Eastham. BS in Psychology, U. N.Mex., Albuquerque, 1952; MA in Psychology, Am. U., Washington, 1962, PhD in Psychology, 1969. Interviewer Va. State Employment Service, Alexandria, 1952-53; tng. officer Nat. Security Agy., Washington, 1953-55, rsch. psychologist Ft. Meade, Md., 1957-64, Hdqrs., Sec. to Air Staff, USAF, Washington, 1955-57; assoc. dean adminstrn. Northeastern U., Boston, 1964-71; assoc. vice-chancellor Ind. U.-Purdue U., Ft. Wayne, 1971-78; v.p. acad. affairs Pittsburg (Kans.) State U., 1978-86, interim pres., 1983; pres. East Stroudsburg (Pa.) U., 1986-96, pres. emeritus, 1996—; spl. asst. to provost Med. U. S.C., 1996—. Contbr. Vol. Office Academic Affairs Med. Univ. SC. Mem. USNR, 1948—60. NCES fellow, 1998, Robert Wood Johnson Exec. Nurse Fellow Mentor, 2003. Mem. Sigma Xi, Psi Chi, Phi Kappa Phi, Omicron Delta Kappa. Democrat. Presbyterian. Home: 1296 Waterfront Dr Mount Pleasant SC 29464-9493 Office Phone: 843-792-2010. Business E-Mail: gilbertj@musc.edu.

GILBERT, JAMES FREEMAN, geophysics educator; b. Vincennes, Ind., Aug. 9, 1931; s. James Freeman and Gladys (Paugh) G.; m. Sally Bonney, June 19, 1959; children: Cynthia, Sarah, James. BS, MIT, 1953, PhD, 1956; D honoris causa, Utrecht U., 1994; D in Engring. (hon.), Colo. Sch. Mines, 2004. Research assoc. MIT, Cambridge, 1956-57; asst. research geophysicist Inst. Geophysics and Planetary Physics at UCLA, 1957, asst. prof. geophysics, 1958-59; sr. research geophysicist Tex. Instruments, Dallas, 1960-61; prof. Inst. Geophysics and Planetary Physics, U. Calif. San Diego, La Jolla, 1961—2001, assoc. dir., 1976-88, prof. emeritus, 2001—; chmn. grad. dept. Scripps Inst. Oceanography, La Jolla, 1988-91. Chmn. steering com. San Diego Supercomputer, 1984-86. Contbr. numerous articles to profl. jours. Recipient Arthur L. Day medal Geol. Soc. Am., 1985, Internat. Balzan prize , 1990; Fairchild scholar Calif. Inst. Tech., Pasadena, 1987; fellow NSF, 1956, Guggenheim, 1964-65, 72-73, Overseas fellow Churchill Coll. U. Cambridge, Eng., 1972-73. Fellow AAAS, Am. Geophys. Union (William Bowie med. 1999); Nat. Acad. Scis., European Union Geoscis. (hon.); mem. Seismology Soc. Am. (medal 2004), Am. Math. Soc., Royal Astron. Soc. (recipient Gold medal 1981), Acad. Nat. dei Lincei (fgn.), Sigma Xi. Home: 780 Kalamath Dr Del Mar CA 92014-2630 Office: U Calif Inst Geophysics Planetary Physics 0225 La Jolla CA 92093-0225 Home Phone: 858-755-9287; Office Phone: 858-534-2470. Business E-Mail: fgilbert@ucsd.edu.

GILBERT, JAMES H., lawyer, former state supreme court justice; b. Minneapolis, Mar. 11, 1947; three children. BA, U. Minn., 1969, JD, 1972. Bar: Minn., 1972; Wis., 1984; U.S. Dist. Ct. Minn., 1974; U.S. Tax Ct., 1978; U.S. Ct. Appeals (8th cir.), 1989; U.S. Supreme Ct., 1988. Lawyer, v.p., mng. ptnr. Meshbesher, Singer, and Spence Ltd., Mpls., 1971—98; assoc. justice Minn. State Supreme Ct., Mpls., 1998—2004; atty. James H. Gilbert Law Group, Minnetonka, 2003—. Park Commr. City of Orono, Minn., 1988—92; bd. dir. Minn. Drug Abuse Resistance Edn. Inc.,(D.A.R.E.) Mem. Minn. Bar Assn. Avocations: skiing, hunting, golf, tennis, snowmobiling. Office: Gilbert Mediation Ctr Ltd 12700 Anderson Lakes Pkwy Eden Prairie MN 55344-7652

GILBERT, JAY, radio personality; FM rock DJ, 1969—; radio host WEBN-FM 102.7, Cin., 1974—. Composer, prodr.: numerous songs, jingles, & radio commercials. Recipient Marconi Radio award for Large Market Personality of Yr., Nat. Assn. Broadcasters, 2000. Office: WEBN-FM Ste 650 8044 Montgomery Rd Cincinnati OH 45236 Office Phone: 513-686-8300.

GILBERT, JILL BARSON, management consultant; b. Syracuse, NY, 1954; d. Zelmar and Thelma Simon Barson; m. Jeffrey S. Gilbert, 1986. MS in Environ. Mgmt., U. San Francisco, 1980; AB in Zoology, Miami U., Oxford, Ohio, 1976. Qualified environ. profl. Inst. Profl. Environ. Practice. Environ. specialist Diamond Shamrock Chem. Co., Pasadena, Tex., 1977—84; sr. advisor Pilko & Assoc., Inc., Houston, 1984—95; dir. product mgmt. Oracle Corp., 1996—98; dir., corp. strategy and comm. T3, Inc., 1998—2002; dir. InteGreyted Internat., 2002—03; pres., CEO Lexicon Systems, LLC, 2002—. Thought leader Environment, Health and Safety Mgmt. Info. Sys. Contbr. over 75 articles to profl. jours. Fellow: Air & Waste Mgmt. Assn. (chair gulf coast chpt. 1989—90, chair SW sect. 1994—95, bd. dirs. 1995—98, v.p. 1997—98, chair info. solutions com. 2000—04, charter mem. info. solutions com. 2000—, editl. adv. com. 2002—, vice chair editl. adv. com. 2007—); mem.: Women in Tech. Internat. Avocations: golf, gourmet cooking, travel. Office: Lexicon Systems LLC PO Box 890433 Houston TX 77289-0433 Office Phone: 281-280-8106. Business E-Mail: jbgilbert@lexicon-systems.com.

GILBERT, JOHN ALBERT, JR., lawyer; b. Boston, Sept. 30, 1957; s. John Albert Gilbert and Claire Ann Canavan; m. Claire Mary McGee, Aug. 8, 1987; children: Darcy, John III. BA, Westfield State U., Mass., 1979; JD, Cath. U., Washington, 1992. Bar: Va. 1992, DC 1995. Program assoc. Youthwork, Inc., Washington, 1978—80; cons. TATC, Washington, 1981—84, USA Today, Rosslyn, Va., 1985—86; dir. planning Corp. Open Sys., McLean, Va., 1986—89; law clk. Steptoe & Johnson, Washington, 1990—92; atty. US Dept. Justice, DEA, Washington, 1992—95; dir. Mymon, Phelps & McNamara, Washington, 1995—. Named to Atty. Gen. Honor Program, US Dept. Justice, 1992. Roman Catholic. Home: 2609 Woodlawn Tr Alexandria VA 22306 Office: Hyman Phelps & McNamara PC 700 13th St NW Washington DC 20005

GILBERT, JOHN F., retail executive; Sr. mktg. position PepsiCo, Inc., Gen. Cinema Corp., Carlson Restaurants Worldwide; chief mktg. officer KFC; v.p. mktg. Dunkin' Donuts, 2003—07; exec. v.p., chief mktg. officer TJX Cos., Inc., Framingham, Mass., 2007—. Office: TJX Cos Inc 770 Cochituate Rd Framingham MA 01701 Office Phone: 508-390-1000. Office Fax: 508-390-2091.*

GILBERT, JOHN JOUETT, aquatic ecologist, educator; b. Southampton, NY, July 18, 1937; s. Seymour Parker Gilbert and Louise Ross (Todd) Stanley; m. Caroline Spalding Colburn, June 16, 1959; children: John Spalding, Anne Gilbert Coleman. BA, Williams Coll., 1959; PhD, Yale U., 1963. Asst. prof. Princeton (N.J.) U., 1964-66; asst. prof. dept. biol. scis. Dartmouth Coll., Hanover, N.H., 1966-69, assoc. prof., 1969-74, prof., 1974—2004, prof. emeritus, 2004—. Contbr. numerous articles to profl. jours. Recipient Career Devel. award, 1973-78; NSF, NIH, EPA grantee, 1965—. Fellow AAAS; mem. Ecol. Soc. Am., Am. Soc. Limnology and Oceanography (Lifetime Achievement award 2003), Internat. Soc. Theoretical and Applied Limnology (nat. rep. 1971-83). Avocation: fly fishing. Office: Dartmouth Coll Dept Biol Scis Hanover NH 03755

GILBERT, JOHN RAY, geneticist, researcher; b. Erwin, NC, Dec. 7, 1947; s. William Henry and Grace Evelyn Gilbert; m. Colleen Justina Carman, June 14, 1975; children: Benjamin Kyle, Andrew Brenton. PhD, U. NC, Chapel Hill, 1982. Rsch. assoc. to rsch. assoc. prof. Duke U. Med. Ctr., Durham, NC, 1982—2003, assoc. dir. genomic genotyping and resource labs. Ctr. for Human Genetics, 1997—2004, rsch. prof. Ctr. Human Genetics, 2003—06; prof. Miami Inst. for Human Genomics U. Miami, Fla., 2007—, dir. Ctr. for Genome Tech., 2007—. Sci. adv. com. Muscular Dystrophy Assn., Tucson, 1999—2007. Contbr. articles to profl. jours. Fellow, U. NC, Chapel Hill, 1975—77; grantee, NIH, 1982—84; scholar, State of Va., 1974—75. Mem.: Soc. Movement Disorders, Am. Soc. Human Genetics. Independent. Methodist. Achievements include research in APOE in Alzheimers disease, Autism, Essential Tremor, Neural Tube Defects, Muscular dystrophies. Avocations: chess, history. Home: 7370 SW 156th Palmetto Bay FL 33158 Office: Univ Miami MIHG CRB Rm 814 M-860 Miami FL 33136 Office Phone: 305-243-2282. Business E-Mail: jgilbert@med.miami.edu.

GILBERT, KEITH THOMAS, lawyer, consultant; b. Harlingen, Tex., Jan. 29, 1959; BBA, Baylor U., 1982; JD, South Tex. Coll. Law, Tex. A & M U., 1989. Bar: Tex. 1990, U.S. Dist. Ct. (so. dist.) Tex. 1992. Ptnr. Gilbert & Mestemaker, Houston, 1991-96; pvt. practice Houston, 1996-2000, Gilbert & Maxwell, Houston, 2000—. Legal rep. Tex. Editor: World Trade Policy, 1979. Avocations: chess, muscle cars, stamp collecting/philately, wine. Office: PO Box 1984 Houston TX 77251-1984

GILBERT, LEONARD HAROLD, lawyer; b. Hutchinson, Minn., Apr. 3, 1936; s. Sidney and Clara (Franzblau) Gilbert; m. Jean Buchman, Apr. 21, 1963; children: Jonathan Stuart, Suzanne Elaine. BA, Emory U., 1958; LLB, Harvard U., 1961. Atty. Carlton Fields, Tampa, Fla., 1961—98, Holland & Knight LLP, Tampa, 1999—. Bd. dirs. Gasparilla Sidewalk Art Festival, Tampa, 1970—74, United Way; trustee Tampa Bay Performing Arts Ctr., Lowry Park Zool. Soc., Univ. Cmty. Hosp.; chmn. Art Coun. Tampa, 1973—74; mem. Hillsborough County Bicentennial Commn., Fla., 1973—76, Tampa Charter Revision Com., 1975; pres. Tampa Mus. Art, 1986—87; chmn. bd. fellows U. Tampa, 1986—87, trustee, 1987—2000. With USCGR, 1961—69. Fellow: Fla. Bar Found., Am. Bar Found. (chmn.); mem.: ABA (chmn. sect. gen. practice 1979—80, ho. dels. 1980—90, chmn. creditors' rights com. corps. sect., mem. coun. sect. bus. law 2000—04, standing com. on fed. judiciary 2006—, coun. sr. lawyer divsn.), Eleventh Cir. Hist. Soc. (trustee, v.p.), Am. Coll. Comml. Fin. Lawyers (pres. 1999—2000), NC Banking Inst., Internat. Insolvency Inst. (bd. dirs., sec. 2000—), Internat. Bar Assn., Am. Coll. Bankruptcy (bd. dirs. 1997—2003), Am. Law Inst., Am. Judicature Soc. (bd. dirs.), Bar Assn. Hillsborough County (pres. 1974—75), Fla. Bar (chmn. sect. corp. banking and bus. law 1970—71, chmn. sect. gen. practice 1972—73, bd. govs. 1975—79, pres. 1980—81), Tampa C. of C. (bd. dirs.), Harvard Law Sch. Assn. Fla. (pres. 1986), Univ. Club, Ye Mystic Krewe Gasparilla, Kiwanis (pres. 1972), Tampa Club (pres. 1986—87). Office: Holland & Knight LLP PO Box 1288 Tampa FL 33601-1288 Office Phone: 813-227-6481. Business E-Mail: leonard.gilbert@hklaw.com.

GILBERT, LUCIA ALBINO, psychology professor; d. William V. and Carmelina (Cutro) Albino; m. John Carl Gilbert, Dec. 18, 1965; 1 child, Melissa Carlotta. BA, Wells Coll., 1963; MS, Yale U., 1964; PhD, U. Tex., 1974. Lic. psychologist, Tex. Supr. research info. G.S. Gilmore Research Lab., New Haven, 1964-67; tchr. St. Stephen Sch., Austin, Tex., 1967-69; asst. prof. Iowa State U., Ames, 1974-76, U. Tex., Austin, 1976-81, assoc. prof., 1981-86, prof., 1986—, dir. women's studies, 1994—99, vice provost for undergrad. studies, 1999—2006; provost, prof. psychology Santa Clara U., 2006—. Author: Men in Dual Career Families, 1985, Sharing It All: The Rewards and Struggles of Two-Career Families, 1988, Two Careers/One Family: The Promise of Gender Equality, 1993, Gender and Sex in Counseling and Psychotherapy, 1999; editor spl. issue Parenting, Dual Career Families; assoc. editor Psychology of Women Quarterly, 1987—. Recipient Excellence in Teaching award U. Tex., 1981-86, Holland award, 1989, Carolyn Sherif award, 1998. Fellow AAUW, Am. Psychol. Soc., Am. Psychol. Assn. (rep. council 1980-83, 86-89, 93—96); mem. Assn. Women in Psychology. Avocations: swimming, progressive country music, ecology, theater. Office: Santa Clara U 204 Walsh Hall 500 El Camino Real Santa Clara CA 95053 Office Phone: 408-554-4533. Office Fax: 408-551-6075. E-mail: lgilbert@scu.edu.

GILBERT, MARGARET P., philosophy professor, researcher; b. England; d. Peter and Miriam Gilbert. DPhil, Oxford U. Prof. philosophy U. Conn., Storrs, 1983—2006; prof., Abraham Melden chair moral philosophy U. Calif., Irvine, 2006—. Vis. prof. Princeton U., NJ, King's Coll., London; vis. fellow Wolfson Coll., Oxford; vis. mem., Herodotus fellow Inst. for Advanced Study, Princeton; rsch. fellow St. Hilda's Coll., Oxford, St. Anne's Coll., Oxford, England; vis. fellow Swedish Collegium for Advanced Study in The Social Scis., Uppsala, Sweden, 2004. Author: On Social Facts, 1989, Living Together: Rationality, Sociality, and Obligation, 1996, Sociality and Responsibility: New Essays in Plural Subject Theory, 2000, Marcher Ensemble: Essais sur les Fondements des Phenomenes Collectifs, 2003, A Theory of Political Obligation: Membership, Commitment, and the Bonds of Society, 2006. Rsch. fellow, Am. Coun. Learned Socs., 1989—90, NEH fellow, 2003. Office: U Calif Irvine 201 Humanities Office Bldg 2 Irvine CA 92697 Office Phone: 949-842-8520. E-mail: margaret.gilbert@uci.edu.

GILBERT, MARIE ROGERS, poet; b. Florence, SC, Jan. 27, 1924; d. Frank Mandeville and Marie Barringer Rogers; m. Richard Austin Gilbert, Apr. 24, 1946; children: Richard Austin Jr., Laurie Gilbert Sanford. BA in Psychology and Theater Arts, Rollins Coll., 1945. Read poetry at Spoleto Festival, Charleston, S.C., 1999. Contbr. poetry to anthologies including Word and Witness: 100 Years of North Carolina Poetry, 1999; author: Freedom In the Twenty First Century, 2006, Brookgreen Oaks, 1999, Connexions, 1994, Myrtle Beach Back When, 1989, Forever New, 1987, The Song and the Seed, 1983, From Comfort, 1981. Driver ARC, Florence Army Air Base, 1943-44; trustee St. Andrews Presbyn. Coll., Laurinburg, NC, 2002 Recipient Poet Laureate Sam Ragan Fine Arts award St. Andrews Presbyn. Coll., 1994, Fortner award St. Andrews Presbyn. Coll., 2003. Mem. Poetry Soc. N.C. (v.p., 1988-89, pres. 1990-92), Poetry Soc. S.C. (1st pl. for lyric poetry 1987, 90), N.C. Writers Conf., N.C. Writers Network, Colonial Dames of Am. in state of N.C. (sec. 1990-91, v.p. 1992-93), Jr. League. Avocation: poetry readings and seminars. Home: 2200 Elm Ave # 1202 Laurinburg NC 28352

GILBERT, MELISSA, former actors guild executive, actress; b. LA, May 8, 1964; d. Paul and Barbara (Crane) G.; m. Bo Brinkman, 1988 (div. 1994); 1 son, Dakota; m. Bruce Boxleitner, Jan. 1, 1995; 1 son, Michael; stepchildren: Lee, Sam. Student, U. So. Calif. Actress: (TV movies) Little House on the Prairie, 1974, Christmas Miracle in Caulfield, U.S.A., 1977, The Miracle Worker, 1979, The Diary of Anne Frank, 1980, Splendor in the Grass, 1981, Little House: Look Back to Yesterday, 1983, Choices of the Heart, 1983, Little House: Bless All the Dear Children, 1984, Family Secrets, 1984, Little House: The Last Farewell, 1984, Choices, 1986, Penalty Phase, 1986, Family Secrets, Killer Instincts, Without Her Consent, Forbidden Nights, 1990, Blood Vows: The Story of a Mafia Wife, Joshua's Heart, 1990, Donor, The Lookalike, 1990, Conspiracy of Silence: The Shari Karney Story, 1992, With Hostile Intent, 1993, Shattered Trust, 1993, House of Secrets, 1993, Dying to Remember, 1993, Cries From the Heart, 1994, Against Her Will: The Carrie Buck Story, 1994, The Babymaker: The Dr. Cecil Jacobson Story, 1994, Danielle Steel's 'Zoya', 1995, Christmas in My Hometown, 1996, Seduction in a Small Town, 1996, Childhood Sweetheart, 1997, Her Own Rules, 1998, Murder at 75 Birch, 1999, Switched at Birth, 1999, A Vision of Murder: The Story of Donielle, 2000, Sanctuary, 2001, Then Came Jones, 2003; (TV series) Little House on the Prairie, 1974-82, Little House: A New Beginning, 1983, Stand By Your Man, 1992, Sweet Justice, 1994-95 (TV spls.) Battle of the Network Stars, 1978, 79, 81, 82, Celebrity Challenge of the Sexes, 1980, Circus Lions, Tigers and Melissa, Too, 1977, Dean Martin Celebrity Roast, 1984, (stage prodns.) Night of 100 Stars, 1982, The Glass Menagerie, 1985, A Shayna Maidel, 1987 (Outer Critics Circle Award), (feature films) Nutcracker Fantasy, 1979, Sylvester, 1985, Ice House, 1989. Mem.: SAG (pres. 2001—05).

GILBERT, NEIL ROBIN, social work educator, writer, consultant; b. NYC, Sept. 18, 1940; s. Alan and Ida (Bedzin) G.; children: Evan Mallory, Jesse Arthur; m. Rebecca A. Van Voorhis, 2002; children: George Nathaniel, Nicole. BA, Bklyn. Coll., 1963; MSW, U. Pitts., 1965, PhD, 1968. Caseworker Interdepartmental Service Ctr., NYC, 1963; dir. research Mayor's Com. on Human Resources, Pitts., 1967-69; prof. sch. social welfare U. Calif., Berkeley, 1969—, chmn. doctoral program, 1983—, acting dean sch. social welfare, 1986, 95-97, Milton and Gertrude Chernin prof. social welfare and social svcs., 1989—. Advisor Jour. Social Policy, 1982—. Author: Clients or Constituents, 1970, Capitalism and the Welfare State, 1983, (with others) Dimensions of Social Welfare Policy, 1974, 2d rev. edit., 1986, Dynamics of Community Planning, 1978, (with Barbara Gilbert) The Enabling State, 1989, Protecting Young Children from Sexual Abuse, 1989, Practical Program Evaluation, 1990, (with Jill Berrick) With the Best of Intentions, 1992, Welfare Justice, 1995, Transformation of the Welfare State, 2002; editor: (with Rebecca Van Voorhis) Activating the Unemployed; editor Social Welfare Series, 1977-83, Social Worker and Social Welfare Series, 1977—. Trustee Head Royce Sch., 1990-96; chair bd. dirs. Seneca Ctr. Fellow NIMH, 1966, U.N. Research Inst. for Social Devel., 1975; Fulbright scholar, U.S. Info. Agy, 1981; Fulbright Research fellow, London, 1981, Fulbright Western European scholar, 1987; recipient Medallion of Distinction U. Pitts., 1987. Mem. Nat. Assn. Social Workers, Assn. Pub. Policy Analysis and Mgmt. Avocations: skiing, mountain climbing. Office: U Calif Sch Social Welfare Haviland Hl Berkeley CA 94720-0001

GILBERT, PAUL H., engineering executive, consultant; b. Healdsburg, Calif., Apr. 23, 1936; s. Lindley D. and Beatrice Gilbert; m. Elizabeth A. Gilbert, July 13, 1963; children: Christopher, Gregory, Kevin. BSCE, U. Calif., Berkeley, 1959, MSCE, 1960. Registered profl. engr., in 17 states. Project mgr. Calif. State Water Project, Sacramento, 1959-68; officer U.S. Army Corp Engrs., Heidleberg, Germany, 1960-61, capt., 1961-68; project mgr. Parsons Brinckerhoff, NYC, 1969-73, regional mgr./ptnr. San Francisco, 1973-85, dir. NYC, 1973-98, sr. v.p., 1973—; vice chmn. Parsons Brinckerhoff Internat. Inc., 1973—99; chmn. bd. Parsons Brinckerhoff, Quade & Douglas, Inc., NYC, 1990-98; project dir. supercollider design and constrn. Parsons Brinckerhoff, Dallas, 1990-95. Prin.-in-charge award winning projects Glenwood Canyon I-70 tunnels, San Francisco Ocean Outfall, Seattle Bus. Tunnel, Hood Canal Floating Bridge and West Seattle High Level and Low Level Swing Bridges, others; reviewer Laser Interferometer Gravitational-Wave Obs. NSF, Washington, 1992—99; mem. faculties sub-com. for advising orgn. and mgmt. of major rsch. equipment & facilities contracting for NSF; program mgmt. advisor Railtrack West Coast Modernization Project, London, GM Design Ctr. Modernization, Warren, Mich.; mem. U. Calif. Pres.'s Coun.; chmn. project mgmt. panel U. Calif. Nat. Labs., 2000—07; chmn. oversight com. for nat. radio astronomy obs. Atacama Large Millimeter Array Radio Astronomy Obs., 2000—; mem. com. sci. and tech. countering terrorism NRC, 2001—07, spl. com. rev. and oversight project mgmt. program U.S. Dept. Energy, 1999—2002, mem. Grainger challenge com., 2004—07, chair bd. infrastructure and constructed environ., 2002—05, mem. organizing com. post-Katrina workshop, 2005; mem. Thirty Meter Optical Telescope External Adv. Panel, 2004—. Mem. external adv. panel Thirty Meter Telescape, 2006—; trustee Assoc. Univs., Inc., 1998—. Named Disting. Engring. Alumnus, U. Calif., Berkeley, 1998; recipient Lincoln Art Welding award, 1966. Fellow: ASCE (Rickey medal 1969, Constrn. Mgmt. award 1994); mem.: Nat. Acad. Engring., Moles, Project Mgmt. Inst. Republican. Roman Catholic. Office: Parsons Brinckerhoff 999 3rd Ave Ste 2200 Seattle WA 98104-4020 Office Phone: 206-382-6357. Business E-Mail: gilbert@pbworld.com.

GILBERT, RICHARD KEITH, biology professor, researcher; b. St. Louis, Apr. 23, 1958; s. William Ray and Janice Sylvia (Rephlo) Gilbert. BA, U. Calif., Santa Barbara, 1981, MA, 1990, postgrad., 1993; PhD, U. So. Calif., 1997. Cert. secondary tchr. Calif. Rschr. Marine Sci. Inst., Santa Barbara, 1979-82; rschr., coord. Catalina Isl. Marine Inst., Calif., 1983-85; tchr. sci. LA Unified Sch. Dist., 1985-87; sci. and calculus educator Am. Internat. Sch., Johannesburg, 1987-89; rschr. psychotherapy U. Calif., Santa Barbara, 1990-92; cons. advanced tech. divsn. spl. projects Gen. Rsch. Corp., Santa Barbara, 1992-94; instr., rschr. U. So. Calif., LA, 1993—; head dept. sci. Valley HS, 2002—. Rschr., cons. Human Scis. Rsch. Coun., Pretoria, South Africa, 1995; cons. spl. project divsn. binary sys. and geog. area specialist Akela Corp., 1994; team leader, cons. Tertiary Edn. Linkages Project USAID, Pretoria, 1996; profl. expert rsch. and evaluation dept. alternative edn. LA County Office Edn.; adj. prof., rschr. U. Southern Calif., 1993—; cons. tech. Capabilities, Assessment Geog. Info. Sys.; evaluator NSF, 1999—, evaluator MSP Projects, 2002—, evaluator TPC programs, 2003—; adj. prof. rsch. U. Phoenix; cons. UN Bangladesh Sci. Project, 2002, S.E. Asia Mins. Edn. Orgn., 2005—, Southern Africa Internat. Edn. Soc., 2006, Royal Acad. Cambodia Rsch. Devel., 2006—, Secondary Sci. and Math Edn., PDR Lao Ministry Edn., 2006—; chair sci. dept. Hacienda La Puente Sch. Dist., 2002—; facilitator organizational devel. tertiary edn. Republic Vietnam, South East Asia Ministries of Edn. Orgn., 2005; mem. edn. task force Hacienda La Puente, U. S.D.; cons., Cambodia rsch. devel. Royal Acad., 2006; Am. ambassador in residence Oxford U., 2006—; cons. Peoples Dem. Republic Lao Ministry Edn., Secondary Sci. and Math. Edn., 2006—, South African Educators Soc., 2006. Active re-election campaign Hon. Robert Lagomarsino, Santa Barbara, 1992. Named Outstanding Tchr. Advanced Biol. Sci., NSF, Calif. State U. Northridge, 1986—87; recipient Outstanding Mentor award, NSF Rsch. Dir. Fellow Program, 2002—; Calif. State U. fellow, U. So. Calif. fellow, 1993, Eisenhower fellow in marine rsch., NSF, 2002—, Calif. Sci. Project fellow, 2002—, NSF fellow, 2002, Robotics edn. grantee, NASA. Mem.: AAAS, Am. Ednl. Rsch. Assn., Comparative Internat. Edn. Soc., NY Acad. Sci., Order Internat. Ambs., Phoenix Soc. (Outstanding Achievement award 1987), US Naval Inst., Phi Beta Delta. Presbyterian. Avocations: scuba diving, photography, music, climbing, trekking. Home: 7931 Caldwell Ave Whittier CA 90602 Office: 6285 Avenida Ganso Goleta CA 93117-5485 Home Phone: 562-693-6260; Office Phone: 213-925-0082. Personal E-mail: richard.gilbert@mindspring.com.

GILBERT, RONALD RHEA, lawyer; b. Sandusky, Ohio, Dec. 29, 1942; s. Corvin and Mildred (Millikin) G.; children: Elizabeth, Lynne, Lisa; m. Wendy Wawrzyniak, Apr. 2, 2002; 1 stepchild, Joshua Sisco. BA, Wittenberg U., Springfield, Ohio, 1964; JD, U. Mich., 1967, postgrad., 1967-68, Wayne State U., Detroit, 1973-74. Bar: Mich. 1968, US Dist. Ct. (ea. and we. dists.) Mich. 1968, US Ct. Appeals (6th cir.) 1968, US Ct. Appeals (9th cir.) 1977, US Ct. Appeals (7th cir.) 1984, US Ct. Appeals (3d cir.) 1988, US Ct. Appeals (4th cir.) 1989, US Ct. Appeals (8th cir.) 1990, US Ct. Appeals (10th cir.) 1991, US Ct. Appeals (11th cir.) 1992, US Ct. Appeals (2nd cir.), 1992. Assoc. prosecutor Wayne County, Mich., 1969; assoc. Rouse, Selby, Dickinson, Shaw & Pike, Detroit, 1969-72; ptnr. Charfoos, Christensen, Gilbert & Archer, P.C., Detroit, 1972-84; pvt. practice, 1984—. Instr. Madonna Coll., Detroit, 1977-81; mem. faculty Inst. Continuing Legal Edn., 1977—; speaker symposium on social security law Detroit Coll. Law, 1984; state bar grievance investigator; vol. chmn. Aquatic Injury Safety Found; mgr. web sites Found. for Spinal Cord Injury Prevention, Care and Cure (fscip.org), Found. for Aquatic Injury Prevention (aquaticisf.org). Co-author: Social Security Disability Claims, 1983; contbr. articles to legal jours. Founder, chmn. Aquatic Injury Safety Group, 1982—89, Found. for Aquatic Injury Prevention, 1988, Found. for Spinal Cord Injury Prevention, 1988; chmn. aquatic safety com. Nat. Safety Coun., 1987; mem. data collection subcom. Nat. Swimming Safety Com. for Consumer Products Safety Commn.; patron Detroit Art Inst., Detroit Zool. Soc.; mem. Detroit Coun. World Affairs, 1968—73, Coun. for Nat. Coop. in Aquatics; mem. combined fed. campaign Nat. Health Agy. Mich.; founder adv. bd. spinal cord injury traumatic brain injury Mich. Pub. Health co-founder Safe Kids Coalition Southea. Mich.; mem. adv. bd. Nat. Drowning Prevention Alliance; bd. dirs. Nat. Coordinating Coun. on Spinal Cord Injuries, Drowning Prevention Found., Calif.; mem. Pres.'s Club U. Mich. Mem. ATLA, Mich. Trial Lawyers Assn., System Safety Soc., ABA, Mich Bar Assn., Detroit Bar Assn., Am. Arbitration Assn., Am. Judicature Soc., Nat. Spinal Cord Injury Assn. (sec. 1988, bd. dirs., exec. com., chmn. prevention com.), Nat. Head Injury Assn., Mich. Head Injury Assn., Am. Standards and Testing Materials (com. F-24 on water parks and playgrounds, mem. coms.), World Water Parks Assn., Nat. Environ. Health Assn., Nat. Pub. Health Assn., Nat. Safe Kids Coalition, Nat. Eagle Scout Assn. (alumni), Blue Key, Pi Kappa Alpha, Pi Sigma Alpha, Pi Delta Epsilon, Fenton Rotary, Fenton Village Theatre, U. Mich. Club, Spring Meadows Country Club. Office Phone: 800-342-0330. Personal E-mail: rrgjedi@aol.com.

GILBERT, ROSE BENNETT, journalist; b. High Point, NC, July 11, 1938; d. Ellis Howard and Sadie B. (Vernon) Bennett; children: Scott Randolph, Bennett J. BA, Mary Washington Coll., 1960; postgrad., George Washington U., 1964—65. Reporter Richmond (Va.) News-Leader, 1960—64; editor 1,001 Decorating Ideas Mag., NYC, 1973—75; columnist Chgo. Tribune-Daily News Syndicate, 1975—77; v.p., ptnr. Sweet & Co., NYC, 1978—80; pres. Gilbert/Green Comm., NYC, 1980—90, RBG Comm., NYC, 1990—. Assoc. editor Country Decorating Mag., NYC, 1982—2007; tchr. Maplewood/South Orange (NJ) Adult Sch., 1975—90; lectr. NY Sch. Interior Design, 1985—88; syndicated columnist Copley News Svc., San Diego, 1988—. Co-author: You-Do-It Book of Early American Decorating, 1978, Decorating Country-Style, 1980, Your Colors at Home, 1985, Manhattan-Style, 1990, Hampton Style, 1993; contbg. editor, columnist Cooking Light Mag., 2003—05. Fellow: Bd. Internat. Furnishings and Design Assn. (pres. N.Y. chpt. 2001); mem.: Mary Washington Coll. Alumni Assn. (v.p. 1966—67). Episcopalian. Home: 73 Jefferson Ave Maplewood NJ 07040-1228 Office: 101 W 23d St Ste 2396 New York NY 10011 Office Phone: 212-674-5108. E-mail: rose.gilbert@att.net.

GILBERT, SCOTT FREDERICK, biologist, educator, author; b. NYC, Apr. 13, 1949; s. Marvin Marshall and Elaine (Caplan) G.; m. Anne Marie Raunio, Dec. 30, 1971; children: Daniel, Sarah, David. BA, Wesleyan U., 1971; MA, PhD, Johns Hopkins U., 1976; PhD (hon.), U. Helsinki. Postdoctoral assoc. U. Wis., Madison, 1976-78, 1978-80; asst. prof. Swarthmore (Pa.) Coll., 1980-86, assoc. prof., 1986-92, prof., 1992—. Author: Developmental Biology, 1985, 88, 91, 94, 97, 2000, 03, 06, Embryology, 1997; zoology editor Jour. Irreproducible Results, 1979-93, Com. de Patronage, Annales Hist. Philosophie Sci.; mem. editl. bd. Embryo, Jour. Exptl. Zoology, Internat. Jour. Devel. Biol., Evolution and Devolution; contbr. articles to sci. jours. Recipient Dwight J. Ingle award Perspectives in Biology and Medicine, 1984, medal of Francois I, Coll. de France, 1996; Guggenheim fellow, 1999. Fellow AAAS; mem. Soc. Devel. Biology (Viktor Hamburger prize 2002), Soc. Integrative Comparative Biology, Internat. Soc. for Differentiation (exec. bd.), Soc. Human Genetics, Hist. Sci. Soc., St. Petersburg Soc. Naturalists (hon. fellow 2001, Kowalevsky prize 2004), Internat. Soc. Hist., Philos. Soc. Studies Biology, Phi Beta Kappa, Sigma Xi. Democrat. Jewish. Home: 224 Cornell Ave Swarthmore PA 19081-1932 Office: Swarthmore Coll Dept Biology 500 College Ave Swarthmore PA 19081-1306 Home Phone: 610-328-6086; Office Phone: 610-328-8047. Business E-Mail: sgilbe1@swarthmore.edu.

GILBERT, STANLEY DEAN, history educator; s. Ralph M. and Nellie L. Gilbert; m. Carolyn Gilbert, June 2, 1962; children: Angela, Julia, Christine, Geoff, Cara. MA, Huntington Coll., Ind., 1966. Tchr. Bluffton Harrison H.S., 1966—. Elder 1st Reformed Ch., Bluffton.

GILBERT, STEPHEN ALAN, lawyer, organization executive; b. NYC, Feb. 20, 1939; s. Ben Gilbert and Elsie (Alweiss) G. AB, Cornell U., 1960, JD, 1962. Bar: N.J. 1963, Fla. 1964, N.Y. 1984. From clk. to assoc. Carpenter, Bennett & Morrissey, Newark, 1961-63; assoc. Milton M. and Adrian M. Unger, 1963-67; vice chmn. bd. Preserver Group, Inc. (formerly Motor Club Am.), Paramus, 1967—, pres., 1988—2004, vice chmn. bd., 2004—. Pres. MCA Ins. Co., 1988-92, Property-Casualty Co. MCA, 1988-93, Motor Club Am. Ins. Co., 1989-2004, Preserver Ins. Co., 1992-2004, Am. Colonial Ins. Co., 1999—2003, Mountain Valley Ind. Co., 2000-2004; chmn. bd. N.E. Ins. Co., 1999-2004. Asst. editor Plain Language Law Dictionary, 1979, assoc. editor, 1995. Active Boys and Girls Clubs, Newark, 1970—, pres., 1977-80, 96-97, chmn. bd., 1980-81, 97-2003; active Newark Mus. Coun., 1975-87, chmn., 1981; active Natural Sci. Solar Ctr., Milford, Pa., 1981-87, v.p., 1982-84; trustee Natural Sci. for Youth Found., 1984-87. Recipient Man and Boy award Boys Clubs, Newark, 1980. Mem. Property Casualty Ins. Assn. Am. (bd. govs. 1989-2006). Jewish. Home: 8909 Francis Pl North Bergen NJ 07047-6001 Office: 95 Rte 17 S Paramus NJ 07653-0931 Office Phone: 201-291-2110. E-mail: sgilbert@preserver.com.

GILBERT, SUZANNE E., lawyer; b. Tampa, Fla., July 15, 1970; AB, Duke Univ., 1992; JD with honors, Univ. Fla., 1996. Bar: Fla. 1996, US Dist. Ct. (no., mid., so. dists.) Fla., US Ct. Appeals (11th cir.). Ptnr. Holland & Knight LLP, Orlando, Fla. Mem.: Orange County Bar Assn., ABA (bd. govs. 2005—), Duke Club Ctrl. Fla., Jr. League Greater Orlando. Office: Holland & Knight LLP 200 S Orange Ave PO Box 1526 Orlando FL 32802-1526 Office Phone: 407-425-8500. Office Fax: 407-244-5288. Business E-Mail: suzanne.gilbert@hklaw.com.

GILBERT, WALTER, molecular biologist, educator; b. Boston, Mar. 21, 1932; s. Richard V. and Emma (Cohen) G.; m. Celia Stone, Dec. 29, 1953; children: John Richard, Kate. AB, Harvard U., 1953, AM, 1954; PhD, Cambridge U., 1957; DSc (hon.), U. Chgo., 1978, Columbia U., 1978, U. Rochester, 1979, Yeshiva U., 1981. NSF postdoctoral fellow Harvard U., Cambridge, Mass., 1957-58, lectr. physics, 1958-59, asst. prof. physics, 1959-64, assoc. prof. biophysics, 1964-68, prof. biochemistry, 1968-72, Am. Cancer Soc. prof. molecular biology, 1972-81, prof. biology, 1985-86, H.H. Timken prof. sci., 1986-87, Carl M. Loeb Univ. prof., 1987—2005, chair dept. cellular and devel. biology, 1987-93; chmn. sci. bd. Biogen, 1978-83, co-chmn., supervisory bd., 1979—81, chmn. supervisory bd., chief exec. officer, 1981—84; vice chmn., bd. dirs. Myriad Genetics, Inc., 1992—; chmn. bd. dirs. Paratek Pharms., Inc., 1996—. V.D. Mattia lectr. Roche Inst. Molecular Biology, 1976; bd. sci. govs. Scripps Rsch. Inst., 1994—; bd. dirs. ActivBiotics, Inc., Memory Pharms., Inc., sci. adv. bd., 1998—, Trankaryotic Therapies, Inc., 2000—05; mng. ptnr. BioVentures Investors, 2001—. Recipient U.S. Steel Found. NAS, 1968, Ledlie prize Harvard U., 1969, Warren trienneal prize Mass. Gen. Hosp., 1977, Louis and Bert Freedman Found. N.Y. Acad. Scis., 1977, Prix Charles-Leopold Mayer Academie des Scis., Inst. de France, 1977, Nobel prize in chemistry, 1980, New Eng. Entrepreneur of Yr. award, 1991; co-winner Louisa Gross Horwitz prize Columbia U., 1979, Gairdner prize, 1979, Albert Lasker Basic Sci. award, 1979; Guggenheim fellow, 1968-69; hon. fellow Trinity Coll., Cambridge, U.K., 1991. Mem. Am. Phys. Soc., Nat. Acad. Scis., Am. Soc. Biol. Chemists, Am. Acad. Arts and Scis., Royal Soc. (fgn.), Harvard Soc. Fellows (chmn.). Office: BioVentures Investors 101 Main St Ste 17th Fl Cambridge MA 02142 Office Phone: 617-252-3443. Business E-Mail: wgilbert@bioventuresinvestors.com.

GILBERT-BARNESS, ENID F., pathologist, educator; b. Sydney, May 31, 1927; arrived in U.S., 1952, naturalized, 1975; d. Christian Henry and Mabel (Milne) Fischer; m. James Bryson Gilbert, Aug. 12, 1954; children: Mary M., Elizabeth A., James C. (dec.), Jennifer E., Rebecca D.; m. Lewis Barness, July 5, 1987. MBBS, U. Sydney, 1950, MD, 1983, MD (hon.), 1999; DSc (hon.), U. Wis., 1999; MD (hon.), U. Sydney, 2004. Diplomate Am. Bd. Pediat., Am. Bd. Clin. Pathology, Am. Bd. Anatomical Pathology, Am. Bd. Pediat. Pathology. Resident Children's Hosp., Boston, Phila., Washington, Brackenridge Hosp., Austin, Tex.; from asst. prof. to assoc. prof. U. W.Va., 1963-70; from assoc. prof. pathology and pediats. to prof. U. Wis., Madison, 1970-93, Disting. Med. Alumni prof., 1986-93, dir. pediat. pathology, 1970-93, prof. emeritus pathology and pediat., 1993—, Disting. Med. Alumni prof. emeritus, 1993—; prof. pathology, pediats. and ob-gyn. U. So. Fla., 1993—. Mem. editl. bds. Pediat. and Devel. Path. Med. jours., 1986—. Author: Introduction to Pathology, 1978, Genetic Aspects Developmental Pathology, 1987, Potters Pathology of the Fetus and Infant, 1997, Atlas Infant and Fetal Pathology, 1998, Metabolic Diseases, 2000, Atlas Embryo Fetal Pathology, 2004, Clinical Use of Pediatric Diagnostic Tests, 2003, Pediatric Autopsy Pathology, 2004; also numerous chpts., articles. Decorated Order of Australia; recipient Disting. Pathologist award, Royal Coll. Pathologists (Australia), 2002; grantee, NIH, 1972—92. Mem. Am. Soc. Clin. Pathology, Soc. Pediat. Pathology (pres. 1986-87), Internat. Acad. Pathology, Internat. Pediat. Pathology Assn. (pres. 1990-92), Teratology Soc., Cardiovasc. Soc. S.Am. (hon.), Am. Pediat. Soc., Am. Acad. Pediat., U.S. Can. Acad. Pathology, Arthur Purdy Stout Soc. Surg. Pathology, N.Y. Acad. Sci., Alpha Omega Alpha. Republican. Avocation: writing. Home: 3301 Bayshore Blvd #403 Tampa FL 33629 Office: Tampa Gen Hosp Dept Pathology Tampa FL 33601 Office Phone: 813-844-7565. Business E-Mail: egilbert@tgh.org.

GILBERTSON, DAVID, state supreme court justice; b. Milw., Oct. 29, 1949; BA, S.D. State U., 1972; JD, U. S.D. Sch. of Law, 1975. Atty. priv. practice, SD, 1975—86; dep. state atty. Roberts County; city atty. City of Sisseton; judge SC Cir. Ct. (5th jud. cir.), Pierre, 1986—95; assoc. justice SD Supreme Ct., Pierre, 1995—2001, chief justice, 2001—. Mem. Civil Pattern Jury Instruction Com., 1986—99, Tribal-State Judges Forum, 1992. Mem.: S.D. Bar Assn. (mem. Judicial-Bar Liaison Com.), Brown County Bar Assn., Glacial Lakes Bar Assn., S.D. Judges Assn. (past pres.). Office: 500 E Capitol Ave Pierre SD 57501-5070

GILBERTSON, ERIC RAYMOND, academic administrator, lawyer; b. Cleve., Mar. 5, 1945; s. Ewald R. and Esther V. (Johnson) G.; m. Cynthia F. Forrest, Jan. 25, 1974; children: Sara, Seth. BS, Bluffton Coll., 1966; MA in Econs., Ohio U., 1967; JD cum laude, Cleve. State U., 1970; DLitt (hon.), U. Mysore, Karnataka, India, 1993. Bar: Ohio 1970, Vt. 1984, U.S. Dist. Ct. (no. and so. dists.) Ohio 1971, U.S. Supreme Ct. 1981. Instr. econs. Kent State U., Ohio, 1969-70; law clk. Supreme Ct. of Ohio, Columbus, 1970-71; asst. atty. gen. State of Ohio, Columbus, 1971-73; exec. asst. to pres. Ohio State U., Columbus, 1973-79; assoc. Vorys, Sater, Seymore & Pease, Columbus, 1979-81; pres. Johnson State Coll., Vt., 1981-89, Saginaw Valley State U., University Center, Mich., 1989—. With Midland Tomorrow. Contbr. articles to profl. jours. Exec. com. Mich. Campus Compact; Pres. Coun. State Univs. Mich.; cmty. affairs com. Diocese Saginaw; active Bay County Bus. and Edn. Adv. Coun., Saginaw County Crime Prevention Coun., Vision Tri-County Steering Com.; trustee Citizens Rsch. Coun. Mich., 2003—. Mem. Am. Assn. State Colls. and Univs., Saginaw County C. of C., Torch Club, Saginaw Club, Bay City Country Club. Home: 7371 Glen Eagle Dr Bay City MI 48706-9316 Office: Saginaw Valley State U Office Of Pres University Center MI 48710-0001 E-mail: erg@svsu.edu.

GILBERTSON, JOEL WARREN, lawyer; b. Valley City, ND, Nov. 9, 1949; s. Roy W. and Gwen D. (Haugen) G.; m. Jan Erikson, June 11, 1972; children: David, Lisa. BA, Concordia Coll., Moorhead, Minn., 1972; JD, U. N.D., 1975. Bar: N.D. 1976, U.S. Dist. Ct. N.D. 1976. Ptnr. Binek & Gilbertson, Bowman, N.D., 1976; atty. N.D. Supreme Ct., Bismarck, 1976-78; exec. dir. N.D. Bar Assn., Bismarck, 1978-81; ptnr. Pearce & Durick, Bismarck, 1981-97; exec. v.p., gen. counsel Ind. Cmty. Banks of N.D., 1997—. Served with U.S. Army N.G., 1972-78. Mem. N.D. Bar Assn. (bd. govs. 1989-95, pres. 1992-93), N.D. Bar Found. (vice chmn. 1982-84, chmn. bd. dirs. 1986-89), South Cen. Dist. Bar Assn. (pres. 1987-89). Republican. Lutheran. Avocations: piano, softball. Home: 1025 Crescent Ln Bismarck ND 58501-2463 Office: Ind Comty Banks ND PO Box 6128 Bismarck ND 58506-6128

GILBERTSON, JOHN T., lawyer; b. Madison, Wis., Aug. 26, 1962; BA, Mich. State U., 1984; JD, Wake Forest U., 1991; LLM in taxation, Georgetown U., 1999. CPA Mich., 1986; bar: Calif. 1993. With Ernst & Young; ptnr. Sonnenschein Nath & Rosenthal LLP, LA, 2000—. Mem.: Am. Health Lawyers Assn., State Bar Calif. Office: Sonnenschein Nath & Rosenthal LLP 601 S Figueroa St, Ste 1500 Los Angeles CA 90017 Office Phone: 213-892-5077. Office Fax: 213-623-9924. Business E-Mail: jgilbertson@sonnenschein.com.

GILBERTSON, PHILIP, academic administrator; BA in Comparative Lit., Augustana Coll., SD, 1965; PhD in English, U. Ky., 1971. Prof. U. Idaho, 1969—73; tchg. and dept. chair positions Wartburg Coll., Iowa, 1973—79; chair humanities divsn. Tex. Luth. Coll., 1979—86; v.p. acad. affairs Doane Coll., Nebr., 1986—89, acad. dean Nebr., 1986—89, prof. Nebr., 1986—89; dean Coll. Arts and Scis. Valparaiso U., Ind., 1989—96, prof. Ind., 1989—96; provost U. of the Pacific, Stockton, Calif., 1996—. Office: Office of the Provost Anderson Hall 2nd Fl Univ of the Pacific Stockton CA 95211*

GILBERT-TIEGS, MARION ANN, gifted and talented educator, consultant; b. Donora, Pa., Jan. 24, 1927; d. Walter C. and Madelyn Elaine Grantham; m. Albert D. Gilbert (div.); children: Eric Gilbert, Richard Gilbert; m. Frank Tiegs, May 5, 1996 (dec.). BS in Psychology, U. Pitts., 1950; MS in Edn., Ill. State U., Normal, 1970; EdD, Ill. State. U., Normal, 1980. Tchr. We. Sch. Dist., Buda, Ill., 1968—78; adminstr. Ill. State Bd. Edn., Springfield, Ill., 1988—91, ret., 1991. Cons. Gifted Area Svc. Ctr., Bloomington, Ill.; gifted edn. del. to China Person to Person, gifted edn. del. to Russia, 2006. Gifted edn. del. Person to Person, China, 2005, Russia, 2006; mem. LWV. Mem.: Gifted Assn. for Gifted Children, Nat. Assn. Gifted Children. Independent. Protestant. Avocations: reading, travel, skiing. Home: 7367 Country Club Dr Pinetop AZ 85935

GILBRIDE, KEVIN, professional football coach; b. New Haven, Aug. 27, 1951; m. Deborah DiNuzzo, Jan. 4, 1975; children: Kelly, Kristen, Kevin. Degree in phys. edn., So. Conn. State U.; M in Sports Adminstrn., Idaho State U. Coach Idaho State U., 1974-75; linebacker coach Tufts U., Medford, Mass., 1976-77; defensive coord. Am. Internat., Springfield, Mass., 1978-79; passing game coord. East Carolina U., 1987, offensive coord., 1988; head coach So. Conn. State U., 1980-84; quarterbacks/receivers coach Ottawa Rough Riders, Can. Football League, 1985, offensive coord., 1986; quarterbacks coach Houston Oilers, 1989, offensive coord., 1990-93, asst. head coach, 1994; offensive coord. Jacksonville Jaguars, 1995-96; head coach San Diego Chargers, 1997—98; offensive coord. Pitts. Steelers, 1999—2000; analyst ESPN, 2000—02; offensive coord. Buffalo Bills, 2002—03; quarterbacks coach NY Giants, 2004—07, offensive coord., 2007—. Office: c/o NY Giants Giants Stadium East Rutherford NJ 07073

GILBURNE, MILES R., venture capitalist; b. NYC, Apr. 2, 1951; AB summa cum laude, Princeton U., 1972; JD cum laude, Harvard U., 1975. Bar: Calif. 1975. Founding ptnr. tech. & media law firms, The Cole Gilburne Fund; ptnr. Weil, Gotshal & Manges, Menlo Park, Calif., sr. v.p. corp. devel. for AOL, 1998-2000; mng. mem. ZG Ventures, 2000—. Bd. Pharmacyclics Inc. & Revolution Health Grp., mem. bd. dirs. Found. Nat. Insts. of Health. Editor in chief Computer Lawyer, 1983-91; co-editor Computer Law Annual, 1985; contbr. articles to profl. jours. Bd. trustees Am. Cancer Soc. Found., Nat. Archives Found., Wash. Shakespeare Theatre; vice chmn. In2Books. Mem. Am. Arbitration Assn. (panel arbitrators), State Bar Calif., Computer Law Assn. (bd. dirs. 1984-87). Office: ZG Ventures LLC 1250 Connecticut Ave NW Ste 200 Washington DC 20036 Office Phone: 202-663-9536.*

GILCHREST, THORNTON CHARLES, retired association executive; b. Chgo., Sept. 1, 1931; s. Charles Jewett Gilchrest and Patricia (Thornton) Thornton; m. Barbara Dibbern, June 8, 1952; children: Margaret Mary, James Thornton. BS in Journalism, U. Ill., 1953. Cert. tchr. Ill. Tchr. pub. high sch., West Chicago, Ill., 1957; exec. dir. Plumbing-Heating-Cooling Info. Bur., Chgo., 1958-64; asst. to pres. A.Y. McDonald Mfg. Co., Dubuque, Iowa, 1964-68; exec. dir. Am. Supply Assn., Chgo., 1968-77, exec. v.p., 1977-82, Nat. Safety Coun., Chgo., 1982-83, pres., 1983-95; chmn. Internat. Safety Coun., Chgo., 1992-95. Pres. Nat. Safety Coun. Found. for Safety and Health, 1986-95. Bd. dirs. Prevent Blindness Am., 1993. With USN, 1953-55. Mem. Am. Soc. Assn. Execs., Chgo. Soc. Assn. Execs. Methodist.

GILCHREST, WAYNE THOMAS, congressman, secondary school educator; b. Rahway, NJ, Apr. 15, 1946; s. Arthur and Elizabeth Gilchrest; m. Barbara Rawley; children: Kevin, Joel, Katie. AA in Liberal Arts, Wesley Coll., 1971; BA in History, Del. State Coll., 1973; postgrad., Loyola Coll., Balt., 1984—. Tchr. social studies Warren Hills Jr. H.S., Washington, N.J., 1973-76; tchr. history St. Alban's City (Vt.) Elem. Sch., 1976-79, Kent County H.S., Worton, Md., 1979-90; mem. U.S. Congress from 1st Md. dist., 1991—; mem. resources com., transp. and infrastructure com., sci. com. Vol. Nat. Forest Svc., Bitterroot Nat. Forest, Idaho, 1986-87. Sgt. USMC, 1964-68, Vietnam. Decorated Purple Heart, Bronze Star. Mem. Kent Country Tchrs. Assn., VFW, Am. Legion, Mil. Order Purple Heart. Republican. Methodist. Office: US Ho Reps 2245 Rayburn Ho Office Bldg Washington DC 20515-2001*

GILCHRIST, ANN ROUNDEY, medical/surgical nurse; b. Utica, NY, Dec. 21, 1948; d. William Gilchrist and Adele (Cobb) Roundey; married; children: Kristie Ann Hughes, Megean Elizabeth Hughes Holden. Student, Cazenovia Coll., 1967-68; LPN, Utica Sch. Practical Nursing, 1972; postgrad., Mohawk Valley C.C., 1972-75; ADN, SUNY, Morrisville, 1976; Forensic Nursing Specialist, Kaplan U., 2006. RN, Nev.; CNOR. Obstetrics and med., surg. staff nurse St. Elizabeth Hosp., Utica, 1972-76; asst. charge nurse CCU and ICU Mohawk Valley Gen. Hosp., Ilion, N.Y., 1976-78; staff nurse operating room Tucson Med. Ctr., 1978-80, El Dorado Hosp., Tucson, 1978-80; staff nurse oper. room and post anesthesia care unit Tucson Gen. Hosp., 1980-85; charge nurse oper. room Desert Springs Hosp., Las Vegas, Nev., 1985-87, staff nurse GI Lab., 1988-90; charge nurse GI Lab, staff nurse operating room Lake Mead Hosp., Las Vegas, 1991-93; supr. operating room Red Rock Surg. Ctr., Las Vegas, 1993-95; staff nurse Endoscopy Lab., Sunrise Flamingo Surg. Ctr., Las Vegas, 1995-97; RN case mgr. Home Side, at Odyssey Hospice, Las Vegas, 1998—. Mem.: Assn. Hospice and Palliative Care Nurses. Avocations: professional doll artist, learther artist, ceramicist, equestrian. Home: 4552 Scott Ave Las Vegas NV 89102-8107 Office: 4011 Mcleod Dr Las Vegas NV 89121-4305 Office Phone: 702-301-9540. E-mail: annzart@msn.com.

GILCHRIST, DEBRA L., college librarian; BS, Calif. State U., Northridge, 1977; MLS, U. Denver, 1983; MS, SD State U., 1987; PhD candidate, Oreg. State U. Asst. reference libr. & asst. prof. SD State U., 1984—87; asst. prof. & instr. libr. Pacific Lutheran U., Tacoma, 1987—91; dean libr. & media svcs. Pierce Coll. Dist., Lakewood & Puyallup, Wash., 1991—. Mem.: ALA (councilor-at-large 1995—2001), Assn. Coll. & Rsch. Librs. (faculty mem. Inst. Info. Literacy Immersion 1998—, chair Appts. com. 2001—02, ACRL Task Force on the Future 2001—02, dean faculty Inst. Info. Literacy Immersion 2001—, co-chair Virtual Conf. com. 2005—, Miriam Dudley Instruction Libr. award 2007). Office: Pierce Coll Libr Fort Steilacoom Cascade 400F 9401 Farwest Dr SW Lakewood WA 98498 also: Pierce Coll Libr Puyallup 1601 39th Ave SE Puyallup WA 98374 Office Phone: 253-964-6553. E-mail: dgilchrist@pierce.ctc.edu.

GILCHRIST, GERALD SEYMOUR, pediatric hematologist, oncologist, educator; b. Springs, Transvaal, South Africa, May 25, 1935; arrived in U.S.A., 1962; s. David and Anne (Lipschitz) G.; m. Antoinette E. Besset, May 7, 1967; children: Daniel J., Michael A., Lauren D. MB BCh, U. Witwatersrand Med. Sch., Johannesburg, South Africa, 1957; Diploma in Child Health, Royal Coll. Physicians and Surgeons, London, 1961. Diplomate Am. Bd. Pediat. Intern Johannesburg Gen. Hosp., 1958-59; resident Transvaal Meml. Hosp. for Children and Baragwanath Hosp., Johannesburg, 1959-60; resident in pediatrics Hosp. for Sick Children, London, 1961; resident in pediat. Children's Hosp., Cin., 1962-63; fellow pediat., hematology/oncology Children's Hosp. of L.A., 1963-65, cons. hematology and blood banking, 1965-71, attending physician, 1968-71; asst. prof. pediat. U. So. Calif., LA, 1966-71; assoc. prof. pediat. Mayo Med. Sch., Rochester, Minn., 1972-78, chmn. dept. pediat., 1984-96; cons. pediatric hematology/oncology Mayo Clinic and Found., Rochester, 1971-2000; prof. pediat. Mayo Med. Sch., Mayo Clinic and Found., Rochester, 1978-2000; Helen C. Levitt prof. Mayo Clinic and Found., Rochester, 1987-2000; prof. emeritus Mayo Found. and Med. Sch., 2000—. Mem. Commn. on Cancer ACS, 1982—85; bd. dirs. Hemophilia Ctr., Dept. Maternal and Child Health, Rockville, Md., 1978—2000; prin. investigator Children's Cancer Study Group Nat. Cancer Inst., Bethesda, 1981—99; mem. Accreditation Coun. Grad. Med. Edn. Residency Rev. Com. Pediat., 1997—2002. Co-author: You and Leukemia, 1976; contbr. chpts. to books, numerous articles to profl. jours. Med. advisor Northland Childrens Oncology Svcs., Rochester, Minn., 1978-80; bd. dirs. Minn. chpt. Nat. Hemophilia Found. Found., Mpls., 1981-84; chpt sec. Physicians for Social Responsibility, Rochester, 1982-85; bd. dirs. Nat. Childhood Cancer Found., 1990-97; chair med. and sci. adv. bd. Nat. Children's Cancer Found., 1995-97; mem. adv. com. Reach Out and Read MN, 2005—. Named to Children's Med. Ctr. Hall of Honor, Cin., 1994; recipient Joseph D. Early award, Nat. Hemophilia Found., 1997, Lifetime Achievement award, Minn., Dakotas Chpt. Nat. Hemophilia Found., 2000, Abraham Jacobi Meml. award, Am. Acad. Pediat., AMA, 2001. Fellow: Am. Acad. Pediat. (chmn. sect. on pediat. hematology-oncology 1988—90, chair coun. on sects. 1999—2002, com. on pediat. edn. 1999—2005, com. on pediat. workforce 2003—05); mem.: European and Am. Osteosarcoma Study Group (ind. data monitoring com. 2005—), Children's Oncology Group (data monitoring and safety comm. 2000—), Am. Soc. Pediat. Hematology/Oncology (trustee 1996—98), Soc. Pediat. Rsch. Accrediation Coun. Grad. Med. Edn. (residency rev. com. pediat. 1997—2002), Am. Bd. Pediat. (chmn. sub-bd. pediat. hematology-oncology 1989—91, bd. dirs. 1990—91), Am. Pediat. Soc., Am. Soc. Hematology, Am. Soc. Clin. Oncology, Reach Out and Read (mem. adv. com. 2005—). Democrat. Jewish. Avocations: sailing, bicycling, kayaking, scuba diving.

GILCHRIST, HENRY, lawyer; b. Austin, Tex., Nov. 6, 1924; s. Gibb and Vesta (Weaver) G.; m. Patricia Ann Lynch, Nov. 24, 1951; children: Thomas Gibb, Terri Lynn. BS in Civil Engring., Tex. A&M U., 1948; LLB with honors, U. Tex., 1950. Bar: Tex. 1950, US Supreme Ct. 1971. Assoc. Douglass & McGuire, Pampa, Tex., 1951-52; co-founder Jenkens & Gilchrist, P.C., Dallas, 1952—, now of counsel, corp. & securities practice group. Mem. Rsch. Fellows Southwestern Legal Found., 1976—. Contbr. articles to profl. jours. Bd. dirs. Dallas County Heritage Soc., 1984-87, chmn. bd. trustees, 1978-81, Ctrl. Dallas Assn., exec. com., chmn., 1984-85, Dallas World Salute 1985—, chmn. pres., 1988-90, Theatre Three, 1986-87, Tex. A&M U. Pvt. Enterprise Rsch. Ctr., 1987—, Dallas Bus. Com. for Arts, exec. com. 1988—; adv. coun. Communities Found. Tex., Inc., Dallas Citizens Coun., mem. cultural arts task force; mem. planning and zoning commn. Town of Highland Park, Tex., 1976-84; mem. exec. com. Dallas Mus. Art Trustee and Audit Com., 1988—, chmn. 1988-91, TACA Inc., v.p. 1986-89; mem. devel. coun. Tex. A&M U. Coll. Liberal Arts; mem. Tex. A&M U. Commn. Visual Arts, 1982—, chmn. 1982-88; mem. exec. bd. So. Meth. U. Sch. Theology, 1992—; founder Park Cities Hist. Soc. Served US Army, 1943—46. Mem.: ABA, Ctr. for Am. and Internat. Law, Dallas Bar Assn., Tex. State Bar Assn., Tex. Bar Found. (life), Greater Dallas C. of C. Methodist. Avocations: reading, walking, gardening. Office: Jenkens & Gilchrist PC 1445 Ross Ave Ste 3700 Dallas TX 75202-2799 Office Phone: 214-855-4301. Office Fax: 214-855-4300. Business E-Mail: hgilchrist@jenkens.com.

GILCHRIST, WILLIAM AARON, architect; b. NYC, Jan. 31, 1956; s. Johnie Aaron and Juanita Marcella (Hunt) G. BS, MIT, 1977, MArch, MS, MIT, 1982; postgrad., Harvard U., 1996. Registered arch., Ga., Ala., Nat. Coun. Archtl. Registration Bds. Project engr. H.J. Russell & Co., Atla., 1982-84, project mgr., 1987-88, project dir. Birmingham, Ala., 1988-90; br. mgr. H.J. Russel & Co., Birmingham, Ala., 1990-93; dir. planning and engrng. City of Birmingham, 1993-97, dir. planning, engrng. and permits, 1997—; architect intern Cherry Roberts Sullivan, Atla., 1984-87. Project dir. Birmingham Civil Rights Inst., 1988-91; mem. vis. com. dept. architecture MIT, Cambridge, 1997—; mem. adv. com. on cmty. devel. Auburn U., Ala., 1994—; mem. internat. adv. bd. remaking cities institute Carnegie Mellon U., 2006-. Contbg. editor articles to Birmingham News, 1997—. Bd. dirs. Discovery 2000 Sci. Mus., Birmingham, 1991-93, Birmingham Festival of Arts, 1993—, Ala. Symphony Found., Birmingham, 1997-99. Recipient James C. Howland award Nat. League of Cities, 1995, Karl Taylor Compton prize, 1979, Chandler prize MIT, 1982; Aga Khan fellow MIT-Harvard U., 1981. Fellow AIA (Ala. state coun., chmn. com. on design asst. team, urban design com. 1999-); mem. Am. Planning Assn. (del. 1996), Constrn. Specifications Inst., Urban Land Inst. (trustee, vice chair pub./pvt. partnership coun.), Kiwanis. Roman Catholic. Avocations: linguistics, photography, graphic arts, Aikido. Office: City of Birmingham 710 20th St N Birmingham AL 35203-2216

GILDAN, PHILLIP CLARKE, lawyer; b. West Palm Beach, Fla., July 17, 1959; AB magna cum laude, Dartmouth Coll., 1981; JD cum laude, Harvard U., 1984. Bar: Fla. 1984, U.S. Ct. Appeals (11th cir.) 1986, U.S. Supreme Ct. 1989. Prin. shareholder, Greenberg Traurig PA, West Palm Beach, 1997—. Mem. Fla. Bar Assn., Palm Beach County Bar Assn., Phi Beta Kappa. Office: Greenberg Traurig PA 777 S Flagler Dr Ste 300 West Palm Beach FL 33401-6161 Business E-Mail: gildanp@gtlaw.com.

GILDEA, BRIAN MICHAEL, lawyer; b. New Haven, Nov. 1, 1939; s. Thomas Michael and Lillian Frances (Reilly) G.; children: Larysa Albina, Stefan Bohdan. AS, New Haven U., 1964; BA, Providence Coll., 1967; JD, Suffolk U., 1970. Bar: Conn. 1970, U.S. Dist. Ct. Conn. 1971, U.S. Ct. Appeals (2d cir.) 1975, U.S. Ct. Appeals (3d cir.) 1979, U.S. Ct. Appeals (5th cir.) 1984, U.S. Supreme Ct. 1975. Legal adviser City of Boston, 1969-70; assoc. Celentano, Ivey & Gery, New Haven, 1970-73; ptnr. Celentano & Gildea, New Haven, 1973-74; pvt. practice New Haven, 1974—. Bd. dirs. St. Mary's High Sch., New Haven, 1975-77; mem. Bethany (Conn.) Town Charter Commn., 1976; del. U.S./Japan Bilateral Session, 1988, U.S./China Joint Session on Trade and Econ. Law, 1987. With USAF, 1958-62. Recipient Svc. award Providence Coll., New Haven, 1979, Friar award St. Mary's Alumni Assn., 1980. Mem. ABA, Def. Rsch. Inst., Conn. Bar Assn., New Haven County Bar Assn., Am. Lawyers Assn. Democrat. Roman Catholic. Avocations: bicycling, tennis, skiing, photography. Office: 512 Blake St New Haven CT 06515-1287 Home Phone: 860-945-9898; Office Phone: 203-387-7493. Business E-Mail: b.m.gildea@att.net.

GILDEA, LORIE SKJERVEN, state supreme court justice; BA, U. Minn. Morris, 1983; JD magna cum laude, order of the coif, Georgetown U. Law Ctr., 1986. Pvt. litig. practice Arent Fox LLP, Washington, 1986—93; assoc. gen. coun. U. Minn., 1993—2004; prosecutor Hennepin County Atty.'s Office, Minn., 2004—05; judge 4th Jud. Dist., Minn., 2005—06; assoc. justice Minn. Supreme Ct., 2006—, chair, gender fairness implementation com., liason, legal cert. bd. & adv. com. on juvenile protection rules. Mem. adv. com. on rules of civil procedure Minn. Supreme Ct., 2004—06. Adv. bd. MINNCORR Industries, 2000—02; bd. dirs. YWCA, Mpls., 2000—03. Mem.: Hennepin County Bar Assn. (co-chair Hennepin lawyer com. 2001—02, chair fin. & planning com. 2002—03), Minn. State Bar Assn. (bd. dirs. 2000—04, governing coun., civil litig. sect. 2000—06, assembly 2000—, coun. 2003—). Office: Minn Supreme Ct 25 Rev Dr Martin Luther King Jr Blvd Saint Paul MN 55155 Office Phone: 651-296-2581.*

GILDEA, THOMAS ROBERT, pulmonologist; b. Wilkes-Barre, Pa., Mar. 10, 1970; s. Susan Davis Hankey; m. Reena Mehra, Aug. 13, 2005; 1 child, Rohan Robert. BS, U. Scranton, Pa., 1992; MD, Hahnemann U., Phila., 1996. Diplomate Am. Bd. Internal Medicine, 1999, cert. pulmonary disease Am. Bd. Internal Medicine, 2002, critical care medicine Am. Bd. Internal Medicine, 2003. Resident, intern Yale U., New Haven, 1996—99, cheif resident, 1999—2000, clin. instr., 1999—2000; mem. staff Cleve. Clinic, 2000—, pulmonary, critical care fellow, 2000—03, med. dir. Ctr. Maj. Airway Diseases, 2004—07. Vol. pulmonologist Free Med. Clinic of Greater Cleve., 2005—07. Recipient Innovator award, Cleve. Clinic, 2006; grantee, AlphaOne Found., 2007—. Fellow: Am. Coll. Chest Physicians (Sixth Leadership Devel. Program for Academic Physicians 2005). Episcopalian. Office: The Cleve Clinic 9500 Euclid Ave Cleveland OH 44195 Home Phone: 216-444-6490; Office Phone: 216-444-6490. Business E-Mail: gildeat@ccf.org.

GILDENHORN, JOSEPH BERNARD, lawyer, real estate company executive, retired diplomat; b. Washington, Sept. 17, 1929; s. Oscar and Celia (Koval) G.; m. Alma Lee Gross, June 28, 1953; children: Carol Winer, Michael Saul. BS, U. Md., 1951; LLB, JD, Yale U., 1954. Bar: DC 1954, US Ct. Appeals (DC cir.) 1954, US Supreme Ct. 1954. Ptnr. Brown, Gildenhorn & Jacobs, 1955—; vice chmn. DC Nat. Sovran Bank, Washington, 1979—89; amb. to Switzerland Dept. State, Bern, 1989—93; ptnr. The JBG Cos., 1960—. Adj. prof. George Washington U.; pres. JBG Properties, Inc., 1956—88; vice chmn. adv. bd. DC metro region BB&T Bank, 1985—2003. Mem. editl. bd. Yale Law Jour., 1954. Past pres., bd. dirs. Hebrew Home Greater Washington, 1975—77; treas. Coun. Am. Ambs., 2000; pres. bd. dirs. Jewish Fedn. Greater Washington, 1988—89; vice chmn. DC Sports and Entertainment Commn., 1996—2003; chmn. bd. trustees Woodrow Wilson Internat. Ctr. for Scholars, 2002—; trustee, chmn. exec. com. U. Md. College Park Found., Inc.; DC campaign chmn. Bush-Quayle, 1988; DC chmn. George W. Bush for Pres., 2000; DC del. Rep. Conv., NYC, 2004; participant Nat. Prayer Breakfast, 2000; bd. dirs. Washington Jewish Cmty. Found., Inst. for Study of Diplomacy, Georgetown U., Ctr. for Strategic and Internat. Studies, UN Watch, Geneva, Internat. Inst. Strategic Studies, Am. Joint Distbn. Com., 1999—2006. With AUS, 1954—56. Named Washingtonian of Yr., Washingtonian mag., 1996, Philanthropist of the Yr., Nat. Soc. of Fundraising Execs., 2000; recipient David Ben Gurion award, State of Israel, 1977, B'nai B'rith Disting. Alumnus award, 1983, Hyman Goldman Humanitarian award, 1984, B'nai B'rith Humanitarian award, 1985, Ourisman Cmty. Svc. award, 1987, Ottenstein Cmty. Svc. award, 1991, Jewish Inst. for Nat. Security Affairs Leadership award, 1993, U. Md. Disting. Alumnus award, 1996, Leadership award, Washington Inst., 1999, Corp. Citizenship award, Woodrow Wilson Internat. Ctr. for Scholars, 2000. Mem. Order of Coif, Team 100, Presdl. Trust. Republican. Home: 2030 24th St NW Washington DC 20008-1608 Office: 4445 Willard Ave Ste 400 Chevy Chase MD 20815 Office Phone: 240-333-3702. Business E-Mail: jgildenhorn@jbg.com.

GILDERHUS, MARK THEODORE, historian, educator; b. Rochester, Minn., Nov. 15, 1941; s. M.R. and Thea L. (Enderson) Gilderhus; m. Nancy Loutzenheiser, June 24, 1967; children: Kirsten, Lesley. AB, Gustavus Adolphus Coll., 1963; MA (NDEA Title IV fellow), U. Nebr., 1965, PhD, 1968. Asst. prof. Colo. State U., Fort Collins, 1968-72, assoc. prof., 1972-77, prof. history, 1977—, chmn. dept., 1980-93, John N. Stern disting. prof., 1996—97; Lyndon B. Johnson prof. history Tex. Christian U., 1997—. Editorial cons. jours. and pubs. Author: Diplomacy and Revolution: U.S.-Mexican Relations Under Wilson and Carranza, 1977, Pan American Visions: Woodrow Wilson in the Western Hemisphere, 1986, History and Historians, A Historiographical Introduction, 1987, 5th edit., 2000, The Second Century: U.S.-Latin American Relations Since 1889, 2000. Nat. Endowment for Humanities grantee, 1972 Mem. Orgn. Am. Historians, Am. Hist. Assn. (pres. 1996), Soc. Historians Am. Fgn. Rels., Conf. on Latin Am. History. Democrat. Unitarian Universalist. Home: 5112 Blue Sage Rd Fort Worth TX 76132-2009 Office: History Dept Tex Christian Univ Fort Worth TX 76129 Home Phone: 817-263-2972; Office Phone: 817-257-6299. Business E-Mail: m.gilderhus@tcu.edu.

GILE, CAROLE S., retired education educator; d. Everett Howard and Violet June Rouse; m. Richard L. Gile, July 14, 1961; children: Sherrie Sue, David Charles. BS in Edn., Truman State U., Kirksville, Mo., 1978, MEd, 1982; PhD in Curriculum and Instrn., Reading Edn., U. Mo., Columbia, 1988. Cert. tchr. Iowa, 1978, Mo., 1978, Ind., 1990. Asst. prof. Ea. Ill. State U., Charleston, Ill., 1988—89, Purdue U. Calumet, Hammond, Ind., 1989—91, NW Mo. State U., Maryville, 1993—95; assoc. prof. St. Mary of Woods Coll., Terre Haute, Ind., 1991—92, William Penn U., Oskaloosa, Iowa, 2003—05; vis. prof. Ind. U., Bloomington, 1995—96; classroom tchr. St. Mary Sch., Paris, Ill.; ret. Recipient Superior Grad. Achievement award, U. Mo., Columbia, 1987; Transfer Hon. scholar, Truman State U., 1976—78, Ruth A. Norris scholar, U. Mo., Columbia, 1985, Robert M. Frank fellow, 1986. Home Phone: 641-673-4064.

GILES, ALLEN, pianist, composer, music educator; b. Cambridge, Mass., Dec. 26, 1924; s. Allen Lester and Clara Lillian (Collins) G.; m. Marilla Jane Roberts, May 26, 1950 (div. 1970); children: Marilyn, Andrea, Cynthia; m. Anne Watson Diener, Sept. 26, 1970 (div. 1996); 1 child, Katherine Anne. MusB in Piano, Boston U., 1946, MA in Music, 1949; EdD in Music Edn., Columbia U., NYC, 1981. performing pianist, soloist and chamber musician, U.S., Europe, Japan, 1945—; adjudicator for competitions nationwide, 1956—. Pvt. piano tchr., Mass., NY, Calif., 1944—; head piano dept., assoc. dir. music dept. SUNY, Buffalo, 1952-64; chair, music dept., dir. Inst. of Music Villa Maria Coll., Buffalo, 1964-68; prof. music, chair performing arts Golden West Coll., Huntington Beach, Calif., 1972-93, prof. emeritus, 1993-2000; exec. dir. South Bay Conservatory, Torrance, Calif., 1997-98; owner, pres. GME Piano Video, 1984—; artistic dir. Learning Ctr. for Arts Excellence, Torrance, Calif., 1999-2000; DVD annotator Media Hyperium/Pioneer Classics, 2000—; piano and musicianship tchr. Rivers Music Sch., Weston, Mass., 2001—05. Author: (books) Beginning Piano-An Adult Approach Vol. 1, 1978, Vol. 2, 1988, Beginning Piano Telecourse Student Study Guide, 1979; Learning To Play The Piano By Television, 1982; course designer, tchr. on camera (video series) Beginning Piano-An Adult Approach, 1978—; contbr. articles to profl. jours. Recipient Annual Piano Tchr. award SUNY, Fredonia, 1968; Radio and TV award for Noteworthy Achievement in Serious Music, Sigma Alpha Iota, 1980; named Master Tchr., Univ. Tex., Austin, 1986, Master Tchr. (piano), Music Tchrs. Nat. Assn., 1989. Mem. Music Tchrs. Nat. Assn., New Eng. Piano Tchrs. Assn. Office: GME Piano Video PO Box 6035 Lincoln MA 01773-4912 Home: 6 Appletree Ln Wayland MA 01778 Personal E-mail: gmegiles@comcast.net.

GILES, BRIAN STEPHEN, professional baseball player; b. El Cajon, Calif., Jan. 20, 1971; m. Doddie Giles; children: Alexis, Avery. Grad., Granite Hills HS, 1989. Profl. baseball player Cleve. Indians, 1995—98, Pitts. Pirates, 1998—2003, San Diego Padres, 2003—. Named 2 time Nat. League All-Star, 2000, 2001, 4 Time Nat. League Player of Week, 1999, 2000, 3 time Triple-A All-Star, 1994—96; recipient Robert Clemente award, BBWAA Pitts. chpt., 1999, 2000. Office: San Diego Padres Petco Park 100 Park Blvd San Diego CA 92101 Business E-Mail: pirates@mlb.com.

GILES, BRIAN T., lawyer; b. Louisville, Dec. 30, 1974; BA, Miami U., 1996; JD, U. Ky., 2000. Bar: Ohio 2000. Named one of Ohio's Rising Stars, Super Lawyers, 2006. Office: Statman Harris Siegel & Eyrich LLC 441 Vine St Ste 3700 Cincinnati OH 45202-3009 Office Phone: 513-621-2666. Office Fax: 513-587-4477.

GILES, CONRAD LESLIE, ophthalmic surgeon; b. NYC, July 14, 1934; s. Irving Samuel Giles and Victoria Ampole; m. Marilyn Toby Schwartz, June 20, 1955 (div. 1978); children: Keith Martin, Suzanne Speer, Kevin William, Brian Alan; m. Lynda Fern Schenk, Nov. 26, 1978; stepchildren: Jared Schenk, Jamie Schenk. MD, U. Mich., 1957, MS, 1961. Diplomate Am. Bd. Ophthalmology. Clin. assoc. NIH, Bethesda, Md., 1961-63; clin. asst. prof. Wayne State U. Sch. Medicine, Detroit, 1965-72, clin. assoc. prof. ophthalmology, 1973-89, clin. prof. ophthalmology, 1989—; chief ophthalmologist Children's Hosp. Mich., 1985-99, emeritus chief, 1999—, chief emeritus, 2000—. Contbr. articles to profl. jours. Active Jewish Welfare Fedn., Detroit, 1981-86, pres., 1986-89; bd. govs. Jewish Agy. for Israel, 1995-2000; vice-chair United Jewish Communities, 2000-2002; vice chair Jewish Coun. Pub. Affairs, 2005— Fellow: Am. Acad. Ophthalmology; mem.: AMA, Mich. State Ophthalmol. Soc., Jewish Coun. Pub. Affairs (vice chair 2005—), United Jewish Cmtys. (vice chair 2000—02), Mich. Jewish Conf. (pres. 1992—95), United Jewish Appeal Fedns. N.Am. (co-pres. 1997—99), Coun. Jewish Fedns. (v.p. 1992—95, treas. 1995—96, pres. 1996—99). Avocation: golf. Home: 6300 Westmoor Rd Bloomfield Hills MI 48301-1359 Office: 31500 Telegraph Rd Bingham Farms MI 48025 Office Phone: 248-594-6702. Personal E-mail: clgiles@sbcglobal.net.

GILES, EUGENE, anthropology educator; b. Salt Lake City, June 30, 1933; s. George Eugene and Eleanor (Clark) G.; m. Inga Valborg Wikman, Sept. 9, 1964; children: Eric George, Edward Eugene. AB, Harvard U., 1955, AM, 1960, PhD, 1966; MA, U. Calif., Berkeley, 1956. Diplomate Am. Bd. Forensic Anthropology (bd. dirs. 1996-2002). Instr. in anthropology U. Ill., Urbana, 1964-66, assoc. prof., 1970-73, prof., 1973-99, head dept. anthropology, 1975-80; asst. prof. Harvard U., Cambridge, Mass., 1966-70; assoc. dean Grad. Coll. U. Ill., 1986-89, assoc. dean Liberal Arts and Scis. Coll., 1995-99, prof. emeritus, 1999—. Editor: (with J.S. Friedlaender, jr. editor) The Measures of Man: Methodologies in Biological Anthropology, 1976. Served with U.S. Army, 1956-58. NSF postdoctoral fellow, 1967-68; NSF grantee, 1970-72, NIH grantee, 1965-68 Fellow Am. Anthropol. Assn., AAAS, Am. Acad. Forensic Scis. (T. Dale Stewart award 2004); mem. Am. Assn. Phys. Anthropologists (exec. com. 1973-76, v.p. 1979-80, pres. 1981-83, Charles R. Darwin Lifetime Achievement award 2005), Human Biology Assn. (exec. com. 1974-77), Phi Beta Kappa, Sigma Xi. Home: 1001 Ross Dr Champaign IL 61821-6631 Office: U Ill Dept Anthropology 607 S Mathews Ave Urbana IL 61801-3635 Home Phone: 217-359-5925; Office Phone: 217-333-0801. E-mail: e-giles1@uiuc.edu.

GILES, JOE W., music educator; b. Clarksville, Tenn., Mar. 29, 1940; s. Emmett J. and Rubye Elizabeth Waters Giles. BS in Music Edn., Austin Peay State U., 1961, M (hon.) in Music Edn., 1972. Tchr. choral and gen. music Met. Nashville Pub. Sch., 1961—84; music cons. Tenn. Dept. Edn., Nashville, 1984—85, dir. arts edn., 1985—99; arts edn. cons. Ctr. Creative Arts, Clarksville, Tenn., 1999—2001; adj. faculty McLean Sch. Music, Mid. Tenn. State U., Murfreesboro, 2003—. Presenter in field; conductor DeGraffenried Chorale, 2001—. Vol. Nashville Pub. Libr., 1999—2001; mem. FIND-18, Nashville, 2003—05; lay reader Christ Ch. Cathedral, Nashville, 1992—97; founding bd. dirs. Tenn. Arts Acad., 1986—. Recipient Gov.'s award, State of Tenn., 1988, Friends award, Tenn Art Edn. Assn., 1988. Mem.: Tenn. Music Educators (pres. 1980—82), Music Educators Nat. Conf. (divsn. pres. 1996—98, past nat. exec. bd. dirs.), Nat. Coun. State Supr. Music (pres. 1992—94), Kappa Delta Pi, Phi Beta Mu. Democrat. Episcopalian. Avocations: genealogy, travel, reading. Home: 4487 Post Pl Nashville TN 37205

GILES, KATHLEEN C., headmaster; m. Ralph Giles; children: Kait, Daniel, Eileen. AB in English and Am. Lit. magna cum laude, Radcliffe Coll.; JD cum laude, Harvard Law Sch. Teaching intern Groton Sch., coach; assoc. Gaston Snow, Boston; law clerk to Chief Justice Vincent McKusick Supreme Judicial Ct., Maine; coll. advisor Groton Sch., 1985—96, asst. dean of academic affairs, 1996—2002, dean of academic affairs, 2002—03; head of sch. Middlesex Sch., Concord, Mass., 2003—. Mem.: Phi Beta Kappa. Office: Middlesex Sch 1400 Lowell Rd Concord MA 01742-9122 Office Phone: 978-371-6537.*

GILES, ROBERT EDWARD, JR., lawyer; b. Bremerton, Wash., Dec. 17, 1949; s. Robert Edward Sr. and Alice Louise (Morton) G.; m. Barbara Susan Miller, Aug. 21, 1971; children: Steven, William, Thomas, James. BA in Fin., summa cum laude, U. Washington, 1971, JD, 1974. Bar: Wash. 1974, US Tax Ct. 1974. From assoc. to fin. ptnr. Perkins Coie, Seattle, 1974-86, mng. ptnr., 1986—, chmn. mgmt. com. Bd. dirs. Jr. Achievement, Seattle, 1984—; bd. dirs., sec. Wash. Coun. Econ. Edn., 1981—91; v.p., chief Seattle coun. Boy Scouts Am., 1996—2002; pres. Seattle Sports Commn., 2005—06. Capt. US Army, 1974. Mem.: ABA, Seattle C. of C. (trustee 1994—97, 2000—02), Wash. State Bar Assn. Avocations: hiking, climbing. Office: Perkins Coie 1201 3rd Ave 48th Fl Seattle WA 98101-3029 Office Phone: 206-359-8536. Office Fax: 206-359-9536. Business E-Mail: rgiles@perkinscoie.com.

GILES, ROBERT HARTMANN, journalist, educator; b. Cleve., June 6, 1933; s. Robert Hamilton and Grace (Hartmann) G.; m. Nancy May Morgan, Feb. 6, 1960; children: David Morgan, Megan Elisabeth, Robert Hamilton II. BA, DePauw U., 1955; MS, Columbia U., 1956; D of Journalism (hon.), DePauw U., 1996. Reporter Newport News Daily Press, 1957-58; reporter Akron (Ohio) Beacon Jour., 1958-63, editorial writer, 1963-65, city editor, 1966-68, met. editor, 1968-69, mng. editor, 1969-73, exec. editor, 1973-76; spl. lectr. Sch. Journalism, U. Kans., 1976-77; exec. editor Gannett Rochester (N.Y.) Newspapers, 1977-81, editor, 1981-86; v.p., exec. editor Detroit News, 1986-89, editor, pub., 1989-97; sr. v.p. The Freedom Forum, 1997-2000; exec. dir. Media Studies Ctr., 1997-2000; curator Nieman Found. Harvard U., Cambridge, Mass., 2000—. Pres. Media Mgmt. Books Inc. Author: Newsroom Management: A Guide to Theory and Practice. Trustee William Allen White Found., U. Kans., 1978—. With AUS, 1956-58. Nieman fellow Harvard, 1965-66; co-recipient Pulitzer prize for local reporting, 1971, Scripps-Howard 1st Amendment award, 1978 Mem. AP Mng. Editors Assn. (pres. 1988), Am. Soc. Newspaper Editors (bd. dirs., treas. 1994, v.p. 1995, pres. 1996), Soc. Profl. Journalists, Found. Am. Comm. (chmn. 1993-97), Accrediting Coun. for Edn. in Journalism and Mass Comm. (pres. 1992-98), Alpha Tau Omega. Office: Harvard U One Francis Ave Cambridge MA 02138 Office Phone: 617-496-5827. Business E-Mail: bob_giles@harvard.edu.

GILES, SCOTT MARCUS ANTHONY, composer, artist; b. Monroe, Mich., May 16, 1965; s. James Thomas and Veronica Thornhill (Franks) Giles; m. Candice Gabriella Elizabeth Wilken-Ranellone; children: Cecilia Susan, Marcus Aurelius, Roman Augustus; m. Cynthia Louise White, Apr. 17, 1993 (div. 2007). BA in Comm., Calif. State U., Sacramento, PhD in Music & History; PhD in Music with honors, U. Kuwait. Condr., artistic dir. Aug. Ensemble, Carmichael, Calif., 1995—2001. Composer over 100 symphonies in field; over 500 painings & graphics; writer (over 500 poems & essays);, musician performances; conductor Melodia & Hermatage. Vol. Roman Cath. Chs., Calif., 1978. Mem.: ASCAP, Am. Composers Assn., Am. Fedn. Musicans. Roman Cath. Achievements include development of sonata form and augmentation of general compositional practices. Avocations: chess, history. Home: 2008 N St #3 Sacramento CA 95814 Home Phone: 916-224-0908. Personal E-mail: scottgilesmusic@yahoo.com.

GILES, THOMAS DAVIS, cardiologist, internist, educator; b. Greenwood, Miss., Feb. 24, 1938; s. John Thomas and Aliece (Davis) G.; children: Helene, Denise, Lizette. AA, East Ctrl. Jr. Coll., Decatur, Miss., 1957; student, Millsaps Coll., Jackson, Miss., 1957-58; MD, Tulane U., 1962. Diplomate Am. Bd. Internal Medicine, Am. Bd. Cardiovasc. Diseases. Med. intern Charity Hosp. New Orleans, 1962-63, resident in internal medicine, 1963-65, chief resident, 1965-66; cardiology fellow Tulane U. Sch. Medicine, New Orleans, 1966, 68-70; chief of cardiology U.S.A. HSTC, Ft. Gordon, Ga., 1968; instr. medicine Tulane U. Sch. Medicine, 1964-70, asst. prof. medicine, 1970-73, assoc. prof. medicine, 1973-74, 76-77, clin. assoc. prof. medicine, 1974-76, prof. medicine, 1977-92, La. State U. Med. Sch., New Orleans, 1992—, dir. cardiovasc. rsch., 1992—, dir. program in hypertension and heart failure, 1992—. Adj. prof. physiology, Tulane U. Sch. Medicine, 1989-92, dir. cardiovasc. rsch. lab., 1989-92; chief med. svc. VA Med. Ctr., New Orleans, 1976-92; dir. quality assurance program, Charity Hosp. of La., 1974-76; dir. quality assurance program Tulane Med. Ctr. Hosp. and Clinic, 1976-92, mem. program, 1992—; mem. Coun. on Geriatric Cardiology, 1996; med. cons. Hospital Centro Medico, Guatamala, 1988; chmn. cardiovasc. task force Joint Commn. on Accreditation of Health Care Orgns., 1988—; bd. dirs. New Orleans Area/Bayou River Health Systems Agy., Inc., 1977-82, project rev. com., 1977-80, vice chmn. 1979-80, pres.-elect, 1980-81, pres., 1981-82. Asst. editor Am. Heart Jour., 1973-78; editor Am. Jour. Hypertension, 1987—; editl. bd. Residents' Forum in Internal Medicine, 1988—, Critical Reading in Cardiology, 1991—; editl. bd. Am. Jour. Geriatric Cardiology, 1992—, Hypertension: Index & Revs., 1993—. Capt. U.S. Army Med. Corps, 1966-68. Gillentine fellow, Tulane U., 1969, named one of Top Doctors La., La. Life mag., 2007. Fellow Am. Coll. Angiology (v.p. sci. affairs 1980—, program chmn. nat. mtg. 1981, gov.-elect 1990, gov. 1991—, com. on econs. of health care delivery 1994—, com. on chpt. rels.; pres. local chpt. 1991—), Am. Coll. Chest Physicians, Am. Coll. Physicians; Am. Heart Assn. (coun. on circulation, coun. on basic sci., coun. for high blood pressure rsch.; mem. affiliate rsch. peer rev. com.); mem. Am. Coll. Clin. Pharmacology, Am. Fedn. Clin. Rsch., Am. Soc. Clin. Pharmacology and Therapeutics, Am. Soc. Hypertension (organizing com., co-chair publs. com., nom. com. 1986-90, exec. coun. 1990-93, continuing edn. com. 1994—, membership com. 1994—, exec. com. 2000—, pres. 2006-07), Am. Soc. Pharmacology and Exptl. Therapeutics, Musser-Burch Soc. (sec.-treas. 1964-79, v.p. 1979-80, 87-88, pres.-elect 1980-81, 1988-89, pres. 1981-82, 1989-90), New Orleans Acad. Internal Medicine (pres. 1988), Southern Soc. Clin. Investigation, Phi Theta Kappa, Alpha Epsilon Delta, Alpha Omega Alpha. Office: LSU Sch Medicine Sect Cardiology 1430 Tulane Ave SL 48 New Orleans LA 70112-2825 Office Phone: 504-220-6275.*

GILES, WILLIAM ELMER, editor; b. Somerville, NJ, July 5, 1927; s. Elmer and Mary Jane (Reed) G.; m. Gloria Mastrangelo, June 4, 1949; children: William J., Michael E., Richard H. and Paul L. (twins), Joseph R. AB in Government, Columbia U., 1950, MS in Journalism, 1951. Reporter Plainfield Courier-News, NJ, 1946-47; copyreader, reporter Wall Street Jour., 1951- 58, mng. editor S.W. edit. Dallas, 1958-61, news editor Washington bur., 1961; an organizer nat. weekly newspaper Nat. Observer, 1961, editor, 1962-71; asst. gen. mgr. Dow Jones & Co., Inc.; pub. Dow Jones & Co., Inc. (Wall Street Jour. and Nat. Observer), 1971-76; dir. mgmt. programs, mem. Dow Jones mgmt. com., 1972-76; disting. editor in residence Baylor U., 1976; exec. editor Detroit News, 1976-77, editor, v.p., 1977-83; editor-in-residence, lectr. Mich. State U., East Lansing, 1983—; Sunday editor Singapore Monitor, 1984-85; v.p. Sandy Corp., Troy, Mich., 1985-87; prof. journalism La. State U., Baton Rouge, 1987-91, dir. Manship Sch. Journalism, 1988-91; prof. So. U., Baton Rouge, 1992-97; mng. editor The Washington Times, 1997—2002; ret., 2002. Mem. Assn. Educators in Journalism and Mass Comm., Soc. Profl. Journalists, Nat. Press Club. Personal E-mail: billgiles75@hotmail.com.

GILES, WILLIAM (BILL) T., retail executive; BA in Acct. and Mgmt., Alfred Univ. CPA. With PriceWaterhouse LLP, 1981—90; dir. fin. reporting Melville Corp., 1990—91; asst. contr. Linens 'n Things Inc., Clifton, NJ, 1991—97, CFO, 1997—2000, sr. v.p., CFO, 2000—03, exec. v.p., CFO, 2000—06; exec. v.p. fin., IT & store develop., CFO AutoZone Inc., 2006—. Office: AutoZone Inc 123 S Front St Memphis TN 38103*

GILFORD, STEVEN ROSS, lawyer; b. Chgo., Dec. 2, 1952; s. Ronald M. and Adele (Miller) Gilford; m. Anne Chrstine Johnson, Jan. 2, 1974; children: Sarah Julia, Zachary Michael, Eliza Rebecca. BA, Dartmouth Coll., 1974; JD, Duke U., 1978, M of Pub. Policy Scis., 1978. Bar: Ill. 1978, U.S. Dist. Ct. (no. dist.) Ill. 1978, U.S. Ct. Appeals (7th cir.) 1981, U.S. Ct. Appeals (DC cir.) 1984, U.S. Ct. Appeals (5th cir.) 1988, U.S. Dist. Ct. (ea. dist.) Mich. 1995. Assoc. Isham, Lincoln & Beale, Chgo., 1978—85, ptnr., 1985—87, Mayer, Brown, Rowe & Maw, Chgo., 1987—. Adminstrv. law editor: Duke Law Jour., 1976—77. Participating atty. ACLU, 1983—2000; bd. dirs. Evanston (Ill.) YMCA, 1982—92, 2005—, sec., 1985, vice chmn., 1986—92; bd. dirs. ACLU, Ill., 1991—96, v.p. Ill., 1995—96; elected mem. bd. edn. dist. 202 Evanston Twp. HS, 1993—2005, v.p., 1995—96, 2003—04, pres., 1996—98, 2004—05, mem. joint task force on safety, 1995—96, chmn. fin. com., 2001—04; mem. Legal Aid Soc., 2001—, chmn., 2005—; mem. Met. Family Svcs., Evanston Skokie Valley Cmty. Adv. Bd., 1997; mem., bd. dirs. Met. Family Svcs., 1998—; mem. exec. com. ED-RED, 2002—05; bd. dirs. Dem. Party Evanston, Ill., 2004—05, Roger Baldwin Found., 1993—96. Mem.: ABA, Chgo. Bar Assn., Ill. Bar Assn. Home: 2728 Harrison St Evanston IL 60201-1216 Office: Mayer Brown Rowe & Maw 190 S La Salle St Ste 3100 Chicago IL 60603-3441 Office Phone: 312-701-7909.

GILFOYLE, NATHALIE FLOYD PRESTON, lawyer; b. Lynchburg, Va., May 4, 1949; d. Robert Edmund and Dorothea Henry (Ward) Gilfoyle; m. Christopher Y.W. Ma, Sept. 9, 1978; children: Olivia Otey, Rohan James. BA, Hollins Coll., 1971; JD, U. Va., 1974. Bar: Mass. 1974, D.C. 1977. Staff counsel Rate Setting Commn., Boston, 1974-76; ptnr. Peabody, Lambert & Meyers, Washington, 1976-84, McDermott, Will and Emery, 1984-96; gen. counsel Am. Psychol. Assn., 1996—. Bd. dirs. ACLU Nat. Capital Area, Washington, 1980-83, St. Columbia's Nursery Sch., 1992-99, D.C. Bar Atty. Client Arbitration bd., chmn., 1994-95. Mem.: ABA, Mass. Bar Assn., Women's Bar Assn., DC Bar Assn. (legal ethics com. 1999—2001, gen. counsel 2002—04, bd. govs. 2004—). Office: Am Psychol Assn 750 1st St NE Washington DC 20002-4241 Office Phone: 202-336-6186. Business E-Mail: ngilfoyle@apa.org.

GILHAM, HANNA KALTENBRUNNER, writer; b. Linz, Austria, July 1, 1943; arrived in U.S., 1977; d. Werner and Marianne Kaltenbrunner; m. Royce Edward Gilham, Sept. 13, 1971. BA, East Carolina U., Greenville, 1994. Office worker Teekanne, Salzburg, Austria, 1959—64; ground hostess Lufthansa, Frankfurt, Germany, 1965—66; distbr. Oefag Car Dealership, Salzburg, 1966—67; receptionist Europea Hotel Mirabell, Salzburg, 1968—71. Author: Sechsundsechzig Seiten, 1996, The Secret Rock, 1997, The King, Short Stories, 1998, Poetry, 1999, Elite, 2000, CET, Color Equals Time, 2000, Gravity, 2001, VS-VE=EA, 2002, Five Pieces, Five Narrative Renderings on Cloning, 2002, MS to VS-VE=EA, Mathematical Solution to Volume Sun Minus Volume Earth Equals Earth's Age, 2005, Die Fruehen, 2005, The Minstrel, 2006. Roman Catholic. Avocation: painting. Home: 401 Summit St Greenville NC 27858 Office Phone: 252-758-7322.

GILHOOLY, DAVID JAMES, III, artist; b. Auburn, Calif., Apr. 15, 1943; s. David James and Gladys Catherine (Schulte) G.; m. Camille Margot Chang, Aug. 23, 1983; children: David James, Andrea Elizabeth, Abigail Margaret, Peter Rodney, Hakan Yuatutsu, Kiril Shintora, Sorqan Subetei. BA, U. Calif., Davis, 1965, MA, 1967. Tchr. San Jose (Calif.) State Coll., 1967-69, U. Sask. (Can.), Regina, 1969-71, York U., Toronto, Ont., Can., 1971-75, 76-77, U. Calif.-Davis, summer 1971, 75-76, Calif. State U.-Sacramento, summers 1978-79; lectr. in field. One-man shows include San Francisco Museum Art, 1967, M. H. deYoung Meml. Mus., San Francisco, 1968, Matrix Gallery, Wadsworth Athenuem, Hartford, Conn., 1976, Mus. Contemporary Art, Chgo., 1976, Vancouver (B.C., Can.), Art Gallery, 1976, ARCO Ctr. for Visual Arts, L.A., 1977, Mus. Contemporary Craft, N.Y.C., 1977, E.B. Crocker Art Mus., Sacramento, 1980, St. Louis Mus. Art, 1981, Smith-Anderson Gallery, Palo Alto, 1985, San Jose Mus. Art, 1992, De Saisset Mus., Santa Clara U., 1999, Hallie Ford Mus. Art, Salem, Oreg., 2000, Micaela Art Gallery, San Francisco, 2006; group shows include U. Calif.-Berkeley Art Mus., 1967, Inst. Contemporary Art, Boston, 1967, Whitney Mus. Am. Art, N.Y.C., 1970, 74, 81, Musee d'art de la Ville Paris, 1973, Chgo. Art Inst., 1975, San Francisco Mus. Art and Nat. Collection Fine Art, Washington, 1976-77, Stedelijk Mus., Amsterdam, Netherlands, 1979, Everson Mus. Art, Syracuse, N.Y., 1979, Whitney Mus. Am. Art, N.Y.C., 1981, Palm Springs Desert Art Mus., 1984, Oakland Mus., 1985, Stanford Mus. Art, 1987, Inst. Contemporary Art, Boston, 1994, Mus. Glass, Tacoma, 2005, Pence Art Mus., Davis, Calif., 2005; represented in permanent collections S. Bronfman Collection Can. Art, Montreal, Que., San Francisco Mus. Art, Phila. Mus. Art, Vancouver Art Gallery, Art Gallery Greater Victoria (B.C.), Albright-Knox Art Gallery, Buffalo, San Antonio Mus. Art, Oakland (Calif.) Mus. Art, Stedelijk Mus., Stanford U., Palo Alto, Calif., Australian Nat. Gallery, Canberra, Govt. Can., Calgary, Alta., Whitney Mus. Am. Art, Eugene (Oreg.) Ctr. Performing Arts. Can. Coun. grantee, 1975, 78. Mem. Royal Can. Acad. Republican. Mem. Ch. of Scientology. Office: 4385 Yaquina Bay Rd Newport OR 97365-9618 Personal E-mail: dgilhooly@earthlink.net.

GILHOUSEN, BRENT, lawyer; b. Anacortes, Wash., Sept. 24, 1946; BA, Wash. State U., 1968; JD, U. Oreg., 1973. Bar: Wash. 1973, Mo. 1981. U.S. Dist. Ct. (we. dist.) Wash. 1973, U.S. Ct. Appeals (9th cir.) 1973, U.S. Supreme Ct. 1980, U.S. Ct. Appeals (4th cir.) 1986. From atty.-advisor to sr. atty. U.S. EPA, Seattle, 1973-80; from environ. atty. to asst. gen. counsel-environ. Monsanto Co., St. Louis, 1980-97; asst. gen. counsel-environ. Solutia Inc., St. Louis, 1997—2003; of counsel Husch & Eppenberger, LLC, 2004—; exec. in residence U. Calif.-Riverside at Palm Desert, 2007. Mem. Superfund Settlements Project, Washington, 1988-95, 01-03; legal com. Chem. Industry Inst. Toxicology, Rsch. Triangle Park, N.C., 1986-99; mem. environ. law adv. com. Nat. Chamber Litigation Ctr., Washington, 1992-97. Mem. editl. bd. Hazardous Waste Strategies Update, 1994-01, RCRA and Superfund Quar., Environ. Hazards. With USAR, 1968-74. Recipient Bronze medal, EPA, 1978. Mem. ABA (sect. environ., energy and resources, chair corp. counsel com. 1994-96, vice-chair hazardous waste com. 1991-99, adv. panel 2006—), The Mo. Bar, Wash. State Bar Assn., Environ. Law Inst., Am. Chem. Coun. (gen. counsel's group, enforcement subgroup 1995-2003), Def. Rsch. Inst., Indian Wells Country Club. Avocations: golf, boating. Office: Husch Eppenberger LLC Ste 600 190 Carondelet Plz Saint Louis MO 63105 Home: 1911 24th St Anacortes WA 98221 Office Phone: 314-480-1500. Business E-Mail: brent.gilhousen@husch.com.

GILIBERTI, ORAZIO LUCIA, ophthalmologist; BA, Rutgers U., Newark, 1977; MD, St. George's U., Grenada, WI, 1982. Cert. VISX physician. Fellow Pa. Hosp., Phila., 1983—84; dir. Giliberti Eye and Laser Ctr., Totowa, NJ, 1985—, Vision Sculpting Ctr., Totowa, 1995—; head divsn. ophthalmology St. George's Hosp. U. Sch. Medicine, Greneda, 1995—, assoc. clin. dean, 1997—; chmn. dept. ophthalmology Seton Hall U. Sch. Grad. Med. Edn., South Orange, NJ, 2000—. Cons. US Dept. HHS, NY, 1991—, HCFA-Empire BC&BS, NJ and NY, 1999—; profl. ophthalmic cons. Med. Inter Ins. Exch., NJ, 1993—; ophthalmic cons. Alcon Pharm. Spkr. Bur.; mem. physician asst. program in ophthalmology Seton Hall U. Author: Chlamydial Conjunctivitis and Chlamydial, 1986; co-author: Pneumonitis, A Review of Three Pediatric Cases. Mem. Eye Care Am., San Francisco, 1990—; dir. med. edn., vis. cons. Grenada Eye Care Project, 1990—; mem. Unico, Passic, Unico Cedar Grove, 2000—04. Named Top Dr. NY Metro Area, Castle Connolly Med. TTD, 1999—2006; recipient Physician Recognition award, AMA, 2003—, 20 Yr. Achievement award, St. George's U. Sch. Medicine, 2002; fellow, St. Georges U. Sch. Medicine, Windret Rsch. Found. Fellow: ACS; mem.: Am. Soc. Cataract and Refractive Surgeons, Am. Acad. Ophthalmology. Home: 415 Totowa Rd Totowa NJ 07512 Office: Giliberti Eye and Laser Ctr 415 Totowa Rd Totowa NJ 07512

GILKES, CHERYL LOUISE TOWNSEND, sociologist, educator, minister; b. Boston, Nov. 2, 1947; d. Murray Luke Jr. and Evelyn Annette (Reid) Townsend. BA, MA, PhD, Northeastern U.; postgrad., Boston U., 1988; DD (hon.), Ursinus Coll., Collegeville, Pa., 2006. Lectr. Univ. Coll. Northeastern U., Boston, 1973-78; instr. sociology Boston State Coll., 1974-78, U. Mass., 1976; asst. prof. sociology Boston U., 1978-87; MacArthur assoc. prof. African-Am. studies and sociology Colby Coll., Waterville, Maine, 1989-2000, MacArthur asst. prof., 1987-89, MacArthur prof. African Am. studies and sociology, 2000—. Vis. lectr. Tufts U., 1974, Ashland Theol. Sem., McCreary Inst., 2006; rsch. assoc., vis. lectr. sociology of religion Harvard U. Div. Sch., 1981-82, vis. lectr. African-Am. religious studies, 1992-93; vis. lectr. Afro-Am. studies Simmons Coll., Chgo. Theol. Sem., 1989, Iliff Sch. Theology, 1989, Temple U., 1989; faculty fellow Bunting Inst., Radcliff Coll., 1982-84; vis. scholar Episcopal Div. Sch., 1992-93; fellow W.E.B. DuBois Inst. for Afro-Am. Rsch., Harvard U., Inst. Advanced Study Religion, Yale U., 1999-2000; host gospel music radio sta. WMHB Waterville, 2002—. Author: If It Wasn't for the Women.: Black Women's Experience and Womanist Culture in Church and Community, 2000; contbr. articles and revs. to profl. jours., chpts. to books. Sec. Cambridge Civic Unity Com., 1978-87; mem. adv. com. Schlessinger Libr., Radcliffe Coll., 1984-86; pres. Cambridge Black Cultural and Hist. Assn., 1978-87; parliamentarian, asst. dean congress Christian Edn. United Bapt. Conv., Mass., R.I. and N.H., 1986—; assoc. min. Union Bapt. Ch., Cambridge, Mass., 1982-97, asst. pastor, 1998—. Nat. Fellowships fund dissertation fellow, 1977-78, Socialization Tng. fellow Northeastern U., 1970-73. Fellow: Inst. Advanced Study Religion; mem.: NAACP, Nat. Coun. Negro Women, Urban League Ea. Mass., Assn. for Sociology of Religion, Soc. Study Black Religion, Soc. Sci. Study of Religion (exec. coun. 1995—97), Sociologists Women in Soc. (lectr. 2002—), Assn. Black Sociologists, Soc. Study of Sybolic Interaction, Am. Acad. Religion, Assn. Humanist Sociology, Soc. Study of Social Problems (v.p. 1990—91), Mass. Sociol. Assn., Ea. Sociol. Soc. (v.p. 1995—96, Robin M. Williams lectr. 1998—99), Am. Sociol. Assn. (Spivak dissertation fellow 1977—78, mem. coun. 1995—98), Delta Sigma Theta, Phi Kappa Phi. Office: Colby Coll Dept Sociology Waterville ME 04901

GILL, ANGELA SUE, clinical psychologist; b. Springfield, Mo., Mar. 8, 1972; d. Ronald Eugene and Connie Sue Gill. BS in Polit. Sci., S.W. Mo. State U., 1994, BS in Psychology, 1994; MA in Clin. Psychology, SW Mo. State U., 1999; PsyD in Psychology, Forest Inst. Profl. Psychology, 2002. Lic. clin. psychologist Mo., cert. pain mgmt. Intern Family Svc. and Guidance Ctr., Topeka, 2001—02, postdoctoral trainee, 2002—03, coord. ADHD program, 2002—04, supr., 2002—04; clin. psychologist St. John's Hosp., Springfield, Mo., 2004—. Mem.: APA. Office: St Johns Springfield MO 65804 Business E-Mail: agill@sprg.mercy.net.

GILL, BECKY LORETTE, retired psychiatrist; b. Phoenix, Mar. 16, 1947; d. David Franklin and Lorette (Cooper) Brinegar; m. Jim Shack Gill, Jr., Aug. 5, 1978. BA in Biology, Stanford U., 1968; MD, U. Ariz., 1973. Diplomate Am. Bd. Psychiatry and Neurology, cert. addiction counselor, substance abuse residential facility dir., addictions specialist, clin. supr. Clerk typist Ariz. Med. Ctr. Med. Libr., Tucson, 1970, asst. ref. libr., 1971; surg. extern Tucson Med. Ctr., summer 1970; med. extern Fed. Reformatory for Women, Alderson, W.Va., 1972-73; commd. lt. USN, 1974, advanced through grades to capt., 1992; intern in medicine USPHS Hosp., Balt., 1973-74; resident in psychiatry Nat. Naval Med. Ctr., Bethesda, Md., 1974-77; head alcohol rehab. svc./substance abuse dept., staff psychiatrist Naval Hosp., Camp Lejeune, N.C., 1977-85, head alcohol rehab. svc./substance abuse dept., head psych. Millington, Tenn., 1985-88, head alcohol rehab. dept. Long Beach, Calif., 1988-94; head Navy Addictions Rehab. and Edn. Dept., Camp Pendleton, Calif., 1994-2001; ret., 2001; owner, mgr. Curves of Chiefland, Fla., 2001—. Mem. tumor bd. Naval Hosp., Camp Lejeune, 1977—85, watch officer Acute Care Clinic, Millington, 1985—86; cons. Tri-Command Consol. Drug and Alcohol Adv. Coun., 1977—85, phys. fitness program com., 1980—85, med. liaison substance abuse, 1982—85, drug/alcohol program advisor, cons., 1983—85; cons. Counseling and Assistance Ctr., 1985—88, mem. bioethics com., chmn. med. records utilization rev. com., 1985—88, mem. exec. com. med. staff, chmn., 1986—87; psychiat. cons. NAS Brig, 1986—88, mem. quality assurance com., mem. pharmacy and therapeutics com., dir. surg. svcs., 1986, mem. credentials com., commd. duty watch officer, 1986—87, dir. med. svcs., 1986—88, watch officer Acute Care Clinic, 1987—88; mem., preceptor to social worker Navy Drug and Alcohol Adv. Coun., 1987—88, mem. pos. mgmt. com., mem. commd. retention coun., 1988; owner Curves, Chiefland, Fla., 2006—. Capt. USN. Decorated Legion of Merit. Mem.: Levy County Fla. Humane Soc., Nat. Assn. Alcoholism and Drug Abuse Counselors, Addiction Profls. N.C. (chmn. pub. info. com. 1979—80, eastern regional v.p. 1981—82, chmn. fall meeting planning com. 1983, sec. 1984—85), Am. Soc. Addiction Medicine, Am. Acad. Psychiatrists Alcoholism and Addictions (founding mem.), U.S. Lawn Tennis Assn. (life), U. Ariz. Alumni Assn., Stanford Alumni Assn., VFW Aux., Stanford Cardinal Club, Am. Legion, Stanford Cap and Gown. Democrat. Avocations: tennis, swimming, jogging. Home: PMB 8187 PO Box 2428 Pensacola FL 32513-2428 Office Phone: 352-490-6289. Personal E-mail: beckyjgill@bellsouth.net.

GILL, DAVID BRIAN, electrical engineer, educator; b. Columbus, Ohio, Oct. 23, 1957; s. Emery Jr. and Norma Jean Gill; m. Karen Marie Schaar, June 25, 1988. BSEE with highest distinction, Purdue U., 1978, MSEE, 1979, MBA, 1981. Registered profl. engr., Tex. Systems design engr. Owens-Ill., Toledo, 1976-80; engr. Tex. Instruments Def. Group, Dallas, 1981-84, lead engr., 1984-86, mem. group tech. staff, 1986-88, br. mgr., 1988-95, sr. mem. tech. staff, 1995—2001; sr. fellow Raytheon, 2001—. Instr. Purdue U., West Lafayette, Ind., 1978-80, Richland Coll. Engring. Lab., Dallas, 1982-96. Editor lab. manual Control Systems Workbook, 1979. Krannert scholar, 1981. Mem. Purdue Alumni Assn. (life), IEEE, Assn. Old Crows, Phi Eta Sigma, Tau Beta Pi, Eta Kappa Nu, Beta Gamma Sigma, Phi Kappa Phi. Avocations: golf, skeet shooting, hunting. Office: Raytheon 2501 W University Dr Mc Kinney TX 75071-2813

GILL, E. ANN, lawyer; b. Elyria, Ohio, Aug. 31, 1951; d. Richard Henry and Laura (Beeler) G.; m. Robert William Hempel, Aug. 4, 1973; children: Richard, Peter, Mary. AB, Barnard Coll., NYC, 1972; JD, Columbia U., NYC, 1976. Bar: NY 1977, US Supreme Ct. 1982. Assoc. Mudge, Rose, Guthrie & Alexander, NYC, 1976-77, Dewey Ballantine LLP, NYC, 1977-84, ptnr., 1985—2004, Thelen Reid Brown Raysman & Steiner LLP, NYC, 2004—. Mem. ABA. Home: 255 W 90th St New York NY 10024-1109 Office: Thelen Reid Brown Raysman & Steiner LLP 875 Third Ave New York NY 10022 Office Phone: 212-603-2412. Business E-Mail: agill@thelenreid.com.

GILL, GEORGE NORMAN, newspaper publishing company executive; b. Indpls., Aug. 11, 1934; s. George E. and Urith (Dailey) G.; m. Kay Baldwin, Dec. 28, 1957; children— Norman A., George B. AB, Ind. U., 1957. Reporter Richmond (Va.) News Leader, 1957-60; copy editor, reporter, acting Sunday editor, city editor, mng. editor Courier-Jour., Louisville, 1960-74; v.p., gen. mgr. Courier-Jour. and Louisville Times Co., 1974-79, sr. v.p. corp. affairs, 1979-80, pres., chief exec. officer, 1981-86. Chief exec. officer affiliates Standard Gravure Corp., WHAS, Inc., 1981-86; pres., pub. Courier-Jour. and Louisville Times Co., 1986-93. Served with USNR, 1954-56. Recipient Picture Editors award Nat. Press Photographers Assn., 1965 Mem. Am. Soc. Newspaper Editors, Asso. Press Mng. Editors, Alpha Tau Omega, Sigma Delta Chi. Home: PO Box 108 Pewee Valley KY 40056-0108 E-mail: gillg@BellSouth.net.

GILL, GEORGE WILHELM, retired anthropologist; b. Sterling, Kans., June 28, 1941; s. George Laurance and Florence Louise (Jones) Gill; m. Carol Anne Livesay, Aug. 11, 1962 (div. 1974); children: George Scott, John Ashton; m. Pamela Jo Mills, July 26, 1975 (div. 1988); children: Bryce Thomas, Jennifer Florence; m. Denise Ann Royer, Oct. 30, 2001. BA in Zoology with honors (NSF grantee), U. Kans., 1963, MPhil Anthropology (NDEA fellow, NSF grantee), 1970, PhD in Anthropology, 1971. Diplomate Am. Bd. Forensic Anthropology, 1978. Mem. faculty U. Wyo., Laramie, 1971—, dir. Anthropology Mus., 1979—87, prof. anthropology, 1985—2006, chmn. dept. anthropology, 1993—96, prof. emeritus anthropology, 2006—. Forensic anthropologist law enforcement agys., 1972—; sci. leader Easter Island Anthrop. Expdn., 1981; chmn. Rapa Nui Rendezvous: Internat. Conf. Easter Island Rsch., U. Wyo., 1993. Author: articles, monographs; editor: (with S. Rhine) Skeletal Attribution of Race, 1990. Capt. US Army, 1963—67. Recipient J.P. Ellbogen meritorious classroom tchg. award, 1983; rsch. grantee U. Wyo., 1972, 78, 82, Nat. Geog. Soc., 1980, Ctr. for Field Rsch. 1980, Kon-Tiki Mus., Oslo, 1987, 89, 94, 96, World Monuments Fund, 1989, Mus. Inventory and Curation co-grantee BLM, Bur. Reclamation, Wyo. DOT, Fish and Wildlife Svc., 1994-99, Disting. Emeritus Prof., Coll. Arts & Sci., 2007. Fellow: Am. Acad. Forensic Scis. (sec. phys. anthropology sect. 1985—87, chmn. 1987—88); mem.: Wyo. Archaeol. Soc., Plains Anthrop. Soc., Am. Assn. Phys. Anthropologists. Republican. Unitarian. Office: U Wyo Dept Anthropology Laramie WY 82071 Office Phone: 307-766-5136. Business E-Mail: ggill@uwyo.edu.

GILL, GERALD LAWSON, librarian; b. Montgomery, Ala., Nov. 13, 1947; s. George Ernest and Marjorie (Hackett) G.; m. Nancy Argroves, Mar. 5, 1977 (div. 1982). AB in History, Philosophy Religion, U. Ga., Athens, 1971; MA in Libr. Sci., U. Wis., Madison, 1973; postgrad. in Bus. Adminstrn., James Madison U., Harrisonburg, Va., 1978—79. Cert. profl. libr., Va. Cataloger James Madison U., Harrisonburg, Va., 1974-76, reference libr., 1976-87, bus. reference libr., 1987-99, govt. documents libr., 1998—2003, head of reference and govt. documents, 2003—, instr., 1974-80, asst. prof., 1980-90, assoc. prof., 1990—2002, prof., 2002—. Lectr., spkr. nat. and regional groups; cons. in field; mem. faculty senate James Madison U., 1975-79, 96-98, sec. curriculum and instrn. com., 1976-78, chair, 1978-79, univ. coun., 1996-98. Mem. editl. bd. James Madison Jour., 1977-80; reviewer Am. Reference Books Ann.; contbr. articles to profl. jours. Mem. libr. adv. com. State Coun. for Higher Edn. in Va., 1986-87; virtual Va. Coord. Mgmt. Bus. com.; pres. Minor Hill Manorhomes Home Owners Assn., 2004-05, bd. mem., 2006-08. Mem. ALA (chmn. bus. reference svcs. com. 1984-86, sec. law and polit. sci. sect. 1982-85, chmn. bus. reference svcs. discussion group 1986-87, chmn. bus. reference in acad. librs. com. 1988-91, Gale Rsch. award 1991, Bus. Librarianship Excellence award, 1991), AAAS, Am. Soc. for Info. Sci., Va. Libr. Assn. (coun. 1986-87, parliamentarian 1979, 81), Spl. Librs. Assn. (treas. Va. chpt. 1983-85, pres. 1986-87), World Future Soc., Harrisonburg C. of C., Sierra Club. Democrat. Roman Catholic. Avocations: art collecting, writing. Home: 326 Westfield Rd Charlottesville VA 22901-1660 Office: James Madison Univ Carrier Library Mail Stop Code 1704 Harrisonburg VA 22807-0001 Business E-Mail: gillgl@jmu.edu.

GILL, GORDON N., medical educator; b. Dec. 19, 1937; BA in Chemistry and Lit., Vanderbilt U., 1960, MD, 1963. Diplomate Am. Bd. Internal Medicine with subspecialty in endocrinology and metabolism. Internal medicine intern Vanderbilt U. Hosp., Nashville, 1963-64; resident Yale-New Haven Hosp., 1964-66; fellow postdoctoral fellow metabolism/endocrinology NIH/Yale U., 1966-68; spl. postdoctoral rsch. fellow NIH/U. Calif., San Diego, 1968-69; asst. prof. medicine U. Calif., San Diego, 1969-73, assoc. prof., 1973-78, prof. medicine, 1978—, prof. cellular and molecular medicine, 2000—, chief divsn. endocrinology dept. medicine, 1971-83, chief divsn. endocrinology/metabolism, 1983-95, assoc. chair sci. affairs, 1992-95, chmn. faculty basic biomed. scis., 1995—2002, dean sci. affairs, 2001—03, interim dir. Moores/UCSD Cancer Ctr., 2003, dean translational medicine, dir. Coll. Integrated Life Scis., 2006—. Chmn. endocrinology study sect. NIH, 1979-80, chmn. task force on endocrinology, 1978, dir. tng. grant on exptl. endocrinology and metabolism, 1978-; prin. investigator interdisciplinary program to study macromolecules regulating growth and oncogenesis U. Calif., San Diego, 1988-95; chmn. Gordon Conf. on Hormone Action, 1979, Gordon Conf. on Peptide Growth Factors, 1990; mem. sci. adv. bd. BioCryst, 1990-; sci. and med. adv. bd. chair Whittier Inst., 1991-95; sci. adv. bd. Liver Ctr., U. Calif., San Francisco, 1991-95, Charles E. Culpepper Found., 1992—2001, Coun. for Tobacco Rsch. USA, 1991-97, ICN Pharms., 1992-; internat. adv. bd. dept. molecular and structural biology U. Grenoble, France, 1993-98; S. Richardson Hill vis. prof. U. Ala., Birmingham, 1991; Berlin lectr. Northwestern U. Sch. Medicine, 1994, sci. adv. bd. Chau, Kirsch Found., 2001-04. Mem. editl. bd. Jour. Cyclic Nucleotide and Protein Phosphorylation Rsch., 1974-84, Endocrinology, 1978-82, Am. Jour. Physiology, Cell Physiology, 1981-87, Jour. Biol. Chemistry, 1983-88, Jour. Cellular Biochemistry, 1984-89, Ann. Rev. Medicine, 1986-91, Analytical Biochemistry, 1980-92; editor Molecular and Cellular Endocrinology, 1974-92; cons. editor Jour. Clin. Investigation, 1992-97; sect. editor: Endocrinology, Best and Taylor Physiological Basis of Medical Practice, 11th-12th edits., Endocrinology and Metabolism, Cecil's Textbook of Medicine, 20th-22nd edit. Bd. dirs. Med. Rsch. and Edn. Found., The Agouron Inst., 1985—; mem. biochemistry and endocrinology sci. adv. com. Am. Cancer Soc., 1989-91; adv. com. Markey Charitable Trust, 1990-97; peer rev. com. Am. Heart Assn., 1991-96. Helen Hay Whitney Found. fellow, 1969-73; NIH Rsch. Career Devel. awardee, 1969-73, Merit award. Fellow ACP, Am. Acad. Arts and Scis.; mem. AAAS, Assn. Am. Physicians, Am. Fedn. Clin. Rsch., Am. Soc. Clin. Investigation, Am. Soc. Biol. Chemistry and Molecular Biology, Endocrine Soc., Western Assn. Physicians, Western Soc. for Clin. Investigation, Am. Soc. for Cell Biology, Phi Beta Kappa, Alpha Omega Alpha. Office: Univ Calif 9500 Gilman Dr La Jolla CA 92093-0650 Office Phone: 858-534-4310.

GILL, GURDEV S., orthopaedic surgeon; b. India; m. Savita Gill; children: Anju, Rajeev. MD, Punjab U., 1966. Cert. Am. Bd. Orthopaedic Surgery. Intern, med. officer, registrar, Kenya, 1967—71; resident orthopaedic surgery Harlem Hosp., Columbia U., 1972—75; pvt. practice in orthopaedic surgery Lubbock, Tex.; prof. clin. orthopaedic surgery Tex. Tech. U. Sch. Medicine, Lubbock. Presenter in field. Contbr. articles to profl. jours. Named to Am.'s Top Physicians, Consumers' Rsch. Coun. Am., 2004—05, Orthopedic Surgery and Am.'s Top Surgeons, 2006. Mem.: World Med. Assn., West Tex. Orthopedic Surg. Soc. (founding mem.), Internat. Coll. Surgeons, Lubbock Surg. Soc., Lubbock-Crosby-Garza Med. Soc., Tex. Med. Assn., So. Orthopedic Assn., Tex. Orthopedic Assn., Western Orthopedic Assn., Am. Acad. Orthopedic Surgeons, Assn. for Arthritic Hip and Knee Soc. (charter mem.), Am. Bd. Orthopedic Surgery (diplomate). Office: 3601 22d Pl Lubbock TX 79410

GILL, HARDAYAL SINGH, electrical engineer; b. Amritsar, Punjab, India, Aug. 18, 1952; came to U.S., 1974; BSc with honors, Punjabi U., Patiala, 1971, MSc, 1973; PhD, U. Minn., Mpls., 1978. Sr. engr. Nat. Semiconductor, Santa Clara, Calif., 1978-81; mem. tech. staff Hewlett-Packard, Palo Alto, Calif., 1981-83, project leader, 1983-85, project mgr., 1985-90; sr. engr. IBM, San Jose, Calif., 1990-94, sr. tech. staff, 1994-97; IBM Disting. engr., 1997—. Contbr. over 100 articles to profl. jours. Fellow IEEE (chmn. Magnetics Soc. 1987-88, chmn. Santa Clara sect. 1992-93, adminstrv. com. Magnetics Soc. 1992-94); mem. Am. Phys. Soc. Achievements include more than 200 U.S. patents on data storage devices. Avocations: tennis, bike riding. Office: IBM Corp MS N17/142 5600 Cottle Rd San Jose CA 95123-3696 Office Phone: 408-717-5568. Personal E-mail: hsgill@aol.com.

GILL, HENRY HERR, photojournalist; b. Detroit, July 21, 1930; s. Henry Herr and Esther (King) G.; m. Mary Jane Brown, Aug. 26, 1957. Student, Vincennes U., 1948, Northwestern U., 1949, Ind. U., 1951, McNeese State U., La., 1952, U. Miami, 1962. Mem. publ. staff U. Miami, 1960; fgn. service photographer, then dir. photography Chgo. Daily News, 1976; dir. photography Chgo. Sun-Times, 1978-83; pres., exec. editor Globalfoto/Roma, 1983-87; pres., film dir. Fotostar Prodns., 1987—. Lectr. in field, exhibitor of photographs, 1964- Co-author: Mississippi Notebook, 1964; photographer: film A War of Many Faces, 1965, The Cocaine Express, 1982. Recipient photo reporting award on Vietnam Nat. Headliners Club, 1967, Overseas Press Club award, 1967, 81, Emmy award for documentary Nat. Acad. TV Arts and Scis., 1965, Best News Picture of Yr. award Inland Press Assn., 1968, 69, Faculty citation Vincennes U., 1979, Baker Meml. Journalism award, 1980; named to Journalism Hall of Fame, 1994, Ind. Journalism Hall of Fame, 2004. Mem. Internat. Press Club (Chgo.), Headliner Club (Chgo.), Sigma Delta Chi (Disting. Journalism award 1965). Personal E-mail: gattolv@earthlink.net.

GILL, JANE ROBERTS, retired psychotherapist, clinical social worker; b. Boston, Dec. 6, 1923; d. Penfield Hitchcock and Cecilia (Washburn) Roberts. Student, Wellesley Coll., 1941-43; BA, Boston U., 1954, MSW, 1956; m. Peter Lawrence Gill, Dec. 24, 1943 (div. 1973); children: Jonathan Penfield, Dorcas Pearson, Nicholas Brinton, Timothy Roberts. Diplomate Clin. Social Work. Social worker Beth Israel Hosp., Boston, 1956-57, S. End Family Program, Boston, 1957-58, Margaret Gifford Sch., Cambridge, Mass., 1963-65; Adams House Psychiat. Clinic, Boston, 1967-76; supr. sr. clin. social work, coord. outpatient clinic, Faulkner Hosp., Boston, 1975-87, instr. family program NAMI, Springfield, Vt., 2000, staff mem. The Headache Rsch. Found., 1976-94; pvt. practice psychotherapy, Brookline, 1970-95; ret., 1995; With John R. Graham Headache Ctr., 1970-94; rsch. interviewer Stone Ctr. for Women's Studies, Wellesley Coll., 1989-90; clin. instr. Smith Coll. Sch. of Social Work, 1971-79, Simmons Sch. Social Work; Contbr. chpt. to book, papers to profl. meetings; Mem. social svc. com. Am. Heart Assn., 1979-83; program chmn. Mass. Mental Health Ctr. Aux. Bd., 1969-71; bd. dirs. Rutland Corner House, 1982-96, Town of Putney Libr., 1996-2006; cons. to bd. dirs. Putney Cares, 1998-2006, invited spkr. Brazilian Headach Soc., 1996, poster Internat. Headache Soc., London, 1994, 2002, 04; mem. Dem. Town Com., Newton-Wellesley, 1959-64. Mem. NASW, Acad. Psychosomatic Medicine, Internat. Headache Soc., Internat. Stress and Tension Control Soc., Peacham (Vt.) Hist. Assn., Putney Sch. Alumni Assn. Home: 30 W Hill Rd Putney VT 05346 Personal E-mail: jrgill@sover.net.

GILL, LINDA A., advertising executive; b. Buffalo, May 8, 1942; d. Elvin R. Albee and Marian Elizabeth Beardsley; m. W. Richard Davy, Apr. 4, 1964 (div. Oct. 1973); children: Ashley, Jennifer, Kit; m. Edward W. Fallon, June 14, 1992. AS, Endicott Coll., 1962; student, Rutgers U., 1984—85. Sales rep., account mgr. Ciba-Geigy Pharm., Summit, NJ, 1980—87; account supr., v.p. Bozell, NYC, 1987—90; sr. v.p., mgmt. supr. FCB, NYC, 1990—94; exec. v.p., mng. dir. Healthworld, NYC, 1994—. Tchr. music/piano, 1979—87. Recipient Clio award, 1986. Mem.: Healthcare Mktg. and Comm. Coun., Healthcare Bus. Woman's Assn., Jr. League. Avocations: piano, golf, reading, horseback riding. Office: Healthworld 100 6th Ave New York NY 10013 Business E-Mail: fallonle@yahoo.com.

GILL, MADELINE KAY, school and youth counselor; d. Joseph Paul and Earline Hart LeBlanc; m. H. Glenn Gill, Mar. 8, 1974; 1 child, Jason Glenn. Secretarial degree, Massey Bus. Coll., Nacogdoches, Tex., 1970; BEd, Stephen F. Austin U., Nacogdoches, 1979, MEd, 1982. Lic. profl. counselor Tex.; cert. mid-mgmt. Tex. Edn. Agy. Sec. Tom Senff, Atty., Nacogdoches, 1970—74; elem. tchr. Joaquin Ind. Sch. Dist., Tex., 1979—92; sch. counselor Garrison Ind. Sch. Dist., Tex., 1992—2004; youth counselor Joaquin Meth. Ch., 2002—; tutor for youth, dir. MK Leadership & Guidance, Joaquin, 2004—. Mem. Tex. Sch. Initiative, Austin, 2002—03; sec. Garrison Ind. Sch. Dist. Site Base Team, Garrison, 2003—04; cons. MK Leadership & Guidance, Joaquin, 2004—. Author: (guidelines) Seniors to College Freshman. Office mgr. vol. Shelby County Sheriff Office, Joaquin, 2005—; program dir. Meth. Ch. Youth Program, Joaquin; vol. Tex. Counselor Assn. Growth Conf., El Paso, 2004—05. Named Counselor of Yr., Piney Woods Counseling Assn., 2002. Mem.: ACA (assoc.), Piney Woods Counseling Assn. (sen. 2001—), Tex. Assn. Adult Devel. and Aging (assoc.; sec.), Tex. Counseling Assn. (assoc. Award of Merit 2001—04), Delta Kappa Gamma, Chi Sigma Iota. Democrat. Methodist. Avocations: reading, dance, jet ski, church activities, scrapbooks. Home: 12113 FM 699 Joaquin TX 75954 Office: MK Leadership & Guidance 12113 FM 699 Joaquin TX 75954 Home Phone: 936-248-5307; Office Phone: 936-248-5307.

GILL, MARGARET GASKINS, lawyer; b. St. Louis, Mar. 2, 1940; d. Richard Williams and Margaret (Cambage) Gaskins; m. Stephen Paschall Gill, Dec. 21, 1961; children: Elizabeth, Richard. BA, Wellesley Coll., 1962; JD, U. Calif., Berkeley, 1965. Bar: Calif. 1966. Assoc. Pillsbury, Madison & Sutro, San Francisco, 1966-72, ptnr., 1973-94, mem. mgmt. com., 1973-94, head corp. securities group, mem. assoc., rev. com., 1981-91, chair asoc., rev. com., 1988-91; sr. v.p. legal, external affairs & sec. AirTouch Communications, San Francisco, 1994—. Referee Calif. State Bar Ct., 1979-82; bd. dirs. Consolidated Freightways. Mem. steering com. Trinity Episcopal Ch., Menlo Park, Calif., 1980-82, com. to revise constitution, Diocese Calif., 1981-82; trustee St. Luke's Hosp. Found., San Francisco, 1983-93; mem. adv. coun. Ch. div. Sch. of the Pacific, 1986; bd. dirs. Episcopal Diocese Calif., 1989—; trustee San Francisco Ballet, 1991—; bd. dirs., gen. counsel United Way Bay Area, San Francisco, 1993-94. Fellow Am. Bar Found.; mem. ABA (spl. com. on internat. practice 1979-82, spl. com. negotiated acquisition 1988-90), Calif. Bar Assn. (corp. com. 1982-85, chairperson 1985, exec. com. 1985-88, vice chairperson 1987-88, chair nominating com. bus. law sect. 1988), San Francisco Bar Assn. Republican. Episcopalian. Office: Airtouch Communications 2999 Oak Rd #5 Walnut Creek CA 94597-2066

GILL, MICHELE GREGOIRE, education educator; b. Bronx, NY, June 15, 1967; d. Salvatore and Dolores Gregoire; m. Tracy R. Gill, Aug. 9, 1997; 1 child, Aaron. BA in Humanities, New Coll. Fla., 1988; postgrad., U. N.Mex., 1991—92; MA in Ednl. Psychology, U. Fla., 1999; PhD, U. Fla., Gainesville, 2002. Cert. tchr. Colo. Dept. Edn., 1992. Tchr. Carbondale Mid. Sch., Colo., 1992—96; asst. prof. U. Ctrl. Fla., Orlando, Fla., 2003—. Lector coord. St. Peter and St. Paul's Cath. Ch., Winter Park, Fla., 2005—. Acad. Faculty fellow, UCF Tchg. Acad., 2005—06. Mem.: APA, Am. Ednl. Rsch. Assn. Avocations: cooking, reading, gardening, bicycling. Office: U Ctrl Fla PO Box 161250 Orlando FL 32816-1250 Business E-Mail: mgill@mail.ucf.edu.

GILL, MILVI KOSENKRANIUS, artist, photographer; b. Geislingen, Germany, Sept. 25, 1948; d. Hans Edgar Kosenkranius and Georgine Marie Tomberg; m. Robert Earl Gill, Mar. 14, 1986; m. Robert Bruce Graham, Mar. 23, 1974 (div. Dec. 2, 1985); children: Dean James Graham, Alan Robert Graham. BA in Art History magna cum laude, U. Md. European Divsn., Brussels, 1992; cert. in Iconography, St. John of Damascus Sacred Art Acad., Ligonier, Pa., 1999. Cert. sys. adminstr. WANG Labs., Arlington, Va., 1987. Various office positions U.S. Army, Navy, Smithsonian Instn., NIH, Washington, 1973—83; office adminstrn. Smithsonian Instn., Washington, 1982—83, Office Sec. of Def., Arlington, 1983—84, Office Joint Chiefs of Staff, Arlington, 1984—88, NATO, Brussels, 1988—89; artist Old Towne Art Gallery, Fredericksburg, Va., 1993—98, Brush Strokes Gallery, Fredericksburg, 2004—, Edgy Studios, Fredericksburg, 2005—. Photographer (exhibitions) Corner Window, Fredericksburg (1st Pl., Bldg. and Arch. Category, 2005), Below Deck (Hon. Mention, Enhanced Photography, 2005), Old Vine (3d Pl., Buildings and Arch., 1995), Belmont Garden, Fredericksburg Ctr. for Creative Arts, 2007 (1st pl. pastel, 2007); exhibitions include Joy, Spotsylvania Co. Mus. (award of excellence, 2007), Madonna and Child, The Plains, Va. (1st Pl., Mixed Media, 1994), Hanover Street Balcony, Fredericksburg (Hon. Mention, 2004), Bills (Hon. Mention, Drawing Category, 1994), Byzantine Angel (Hon. Mention, Mixed Media, 1995), Mary and Child, Old Towne Art Gallery (1st Pl., 1997), Father's Day (2nd Pl., 1997). Treas. Banner Plantation Homeowners Assn., Fredericksburg, 1998—2004; team leader Therapy Dogs Internat., Inc., Fredericksburg, 1996—2004; sponsor Christian Children's Fund, Richmond, Va., 1980—2006; treas. ASPCA, Fredericksburg, 1997—98, team leader, vis. pet program, 1994—98. Recipient Neighbors in Action - Adult Vol. of Yr., Rappahannock United Way, 1998, Best Essay, U. Md. European Divsn., 1991. Mem.: AAUW (assoc.), Nat. Mus. for Women in the Arts (assoc.), Fredericksburg Ctr. for Creative Arts (assoc.; ednl. com. 2005—06). Lutheran. Avocations: art workshops, computer graphics, travel, gardening. Home: 12720 Isle of Pines Blvd Fredericksburg VA 22407 Office: Brush Strokes Gallery 810 Caroline St Fredericksburg VA 22401 Studio: Liberty Town Arts Workshops 916 Liberty St Fredericksburg VA 22401 Home Phone: 540-786-6566; Office Phone: 540-368-0560. Personal E-mail: milvig@msn.com.

GILL, PHUPINDER, mercantile exchange executive; b. 1960; m. Margaret Mary Burns. BA, Wash. State U., 1985, MBA, 1987. Joined Chgo. Merc. Exch. Inc. (CME), 1988, v.p. Clearing House Divsn., 1994—97, sr. v.p., 1997—98, pres., 1998—2000, mng. dir. Clearing House Divsn. and GFX Corp., 2000—04, pres., COO, 2004—07, Chgo. Merc. Exch. Holdings Inc., 2004—07, CME Group Inc. (formerly Chgo. Merc. Exch. Holdings Inc.), 2007—. Former bd. mem. Youth Svcs. of Glenview / Northbrook. Office: CME Group Inc 20 S Wacker Dr Chicago IL 60606*

GILL, RICHARD LAWRENCE, lawyer; b. Chgo., Jan. 8, 1946; s. Joseph Richard and Dolores Ann (Powers) Gill; m. Mary Helen Walker, July 14, 1990; children: Kyla Marie, Matthew Joseph. BA, Coll. of St. Thomas, St. Paul, 1968; JD, U. Minn., 1971. Bar: Minn. 1971, U.S. Dist. Ct. Minn. 1971, U.S. Supreme Ct. 1979, U.S. Ct. Appeals (8th cir.) 1983, U.S. Ct. Appeals (4th cir.) 1990, Ill. 1992. Spl. asst. atty. gen. State of Minn., St. Paul, 1971-73; assoc. Maun, Hazel, Green, Hayes, Simon & Aretz, St. Paul, 1974-77; ptnr. Gill & Brinkman, St. Paul, 1978-84, Robins, Kaplan, Miller & Ciresi, Mpls., 1984—2002, of counsel, 2002—. Vol. Courage Ctr., Golden Valley, Minn., 1981—; youth football coach Maplewood (Minn.) Athletic Assn., 1978-80; youth basketball coach Orono (Minn.) Athletic Assn., 1999—; mem. athletics adv. bd. U. St. Thomas, 2002—. Mem. ABA, Minn. Bar Assn., Hennepin County Bar Assn., Ramsey County Bar Assn., Assn. Trial Lawyers Am., Minn. Trial Lawyers Assn., Town and Country Club, Windsong Farm Golf Club. Avocations: skiing, tennis, golf. Office: Robins Kaplan Miller & Ciresi 800 Lasalle Ave Ste 2800 Minneapolis MN 55402-2015 Office Phone: 612-349-8430. Business E-Mail: rlgill@rkmc.com.

GILL, ROBERT TUCKER, lawyer; BA, Union U., 1969; JD, MA, Boston Coll., 1973. Bar: Ga. 1973, Mass. 1973, U.S. Ct. Appeals (1st and 5th cirs.) 1973, U.S. Supreme Ct. 1993. Staff atty. Ga. Indigents Legal Svcs., Savannah, Ga., 1973-74; assoc. Sherwin & Gottlieb, Fall River, Mass., 1974-75; ptnr. Parker, Coulter, Daley & White, Boston, 1975-95, Peabody and Arnold, Boston, 1995—. Chmn. Weston (Mass.) Transp. Commn., 1984—89; mem., chmn. Weston (Mass.) Cable TV Com., 1987-88. Mem. ABA, Am. Arbitration Assn. (panel of arbitrators), Mass. Bar Assn., Boston Bar Assn., State Bar of Ga., Mass. Trial Lawyers Assn., Wianno Yacht Club. Avocations: sailing, skiing. Office: Peabody & Arnold 30 Rowes Wharf Fl 6 Boston MA 02110-3339 Office Phone: 617-951-4706.

GILL, STEPHEN PASCHALL, retired physicist, mathematician; b. Balt., Nov. 13, 1938; s. Robert Lee and Charlotte (Olmsted) G.; m. Margaret Ann Gaskins, Dec. 21, 1961; children: Elizabeth Olmsted, Richard Paschall. BS, MIT, 1960; MA, Harvard U., 1961, PhD, 1964. Cons. hypersonic aerodynamics Raytheon Corp., Bedford, Mass., 1963-64; research physicist Stanford Research Inst., Menlo Park, Calif., 1964-65, head high energy gasdynamics, 1965-68, Physics Internat. Co., San Leandro, Calif., 1968-70, mgr. shock dynamics dept., 1970-72; founder, pres. Artec Assocs., Inc., Hayward, Calif., 1972-77, chief scientist, 1977-91; founder, pres. Votan Corp., Hayward, Calif., 1979-91, chief scientist, chmn. bd., 1981-85; ret., 1999. Founder, chief scientist Magnetic Pulse Inc., 1985-99. Mem. San Francisco Symphony Assn.; mem. San Francisco Mus. Art. Mem. IEEE, Am. Phys. Soc., Am. Math. Soc., MIT Alumni Assn., Sigma Xi, Delta Kappa Epsilon. Clubs: MIT. Republican. Episcopalian. Home: 32 Flood Cir Atherton CA 94027-2151 Personal E-mail: stephen@gillfamily.name.

GILL, THOMAS EDWARD, science educator; b. Walnut Creek, Calif., Aug. 13, 1961; s. Bruce Arthur and Virginia Phyllis Gill. BS, U. Calif., Davis, 1984, PhD, 1995. Cert. geologist Tex. Rschr. U. Calif., Davis, 1984—95; phys. scientist USDA Agrl. Rsch. Svc., Lubbock, Tex., 1995—98; rsch. assoc. Tex. Tech. U., Lubbock, 1998—2000, rsch. asst. prof., 2000—04; assoc. prof. U. Tex., El Paso, 2004—. Presenter in field. Contbr. articles to profl. jours. Co-founder Ecotema, Calif., 1995; country specialist Amnesty Internat. USA, Washington, 1988—. Envi. Sci. fellow, Switzer Found., 1992, numerous rsch. grants, 1985—. Mem.: Am. Geophys. Union, Am. Meteorol. Soc., Geol. Soc. Am. Avocations: photography, writing. Office: Univ Tex Dept Geol Sci 500 W University Ave El Paso TX 79968 Home: 5525 N Stanton St El Paso TX 79912

GILL, THOMAS JAMES, III, pathologist, educator; b. Malden, Mass., July 2, 1932; s. Thomas James and Marguerite (Capobianco) G.; m. Faith Libbie Etoll, July 8, 1961; children: Elizabeth Ruth, Thomas James IV, Christopher Gregory. AB summa cum laude, Harvard U., 1953, AM in Chemistry, 1957, MD, 1957. Diplomate Am. Bd. Pathology. Asst. in pathology Peter Bent Brigham Hosp., Boston, 1957-58; intern N.Y. Hosp.-Cornell Med. Center, 1958-59; jr. fellow Soc. Fellows Harvard U., 1959-62; mem. faculty Harvard U. Med Sch., 1962-71, asso. prof. pathology, 1970-71; prof. pathology, chmn. dept. U. Pitts. Med. Sch., 1971-90; pathologist-in-chief Univ. Health Ctr. Pitts., 1971-90, Maud L. Menten prof. exptl. pathology, 1988—98, prof. human genetics, 1988-98, prof. emeritus human genetics and exptl. pathology, 1999—; prof. clin. immunology for postgrad. studies U. Rijeka, Croatia, 1996—; fellow U. Pitts. Ctr. for Philosophy Sci., 1996—98, assoc., 1999—2001; vis. scholar in biology Harvard U., 1998-2001. Affiliate of Eliot House, Harvard Coll., 1998—; cons. to govt. and industry; mem. sci. adv. bd. St. Jude Children's Rsch. Hosp., Memphis, 1969—77, chmn., 1974-76; mem. allergy and immunology rsch. com. Nat. Inst. Allergy and Infectious Diseases, 1973-76; mem. med. rsch. svc. merit rev. bd. in immunology VA, 1976-79, chmn., 1977-79; mem. sci. adv. com. Damon Runyon-Walter Winchell Cancer Fund, 1978-81; mem. com. on animal models and genetic stocks NRC, 1978-86, chmn. com., 1983-86, mem. com. on rabbit genetic resources, 1979-80, mem. coun. Inst. Lab. Animal Resources, 1986-92, mem. com. on preservation of lab. animal resources, 1985-90, com. on transgenic animals, 1991-92; mem. surgery, anesthesiology and trauma study sect. NIH, 1983-84; sci. adv. com. on immunology and immunotherapy Am. Cancer Soc., 1986-88; mem. Armed Forces Epidemiol. Bd., 1966-72; adj. prof. U. Milan, 1990-92; nutrition found. Italy lectr. U. Milan, 1986-97; trustee Am. Bd. Pathology, 1981-92, life trustee, 1992—, pres., 1992; mem. Maternal and Child Health com. Nat. Inst. Child Health and Human Devel., 1992-96; chmn., 1995-96; mem. immunology task force Nat. Inst. Allergy and Infectious Diseases, 1996-98; mem. adv. com. for the Rat Genome Project and Rat EST Project, Nat. Heart, Lung, and Blood Inst., 1998; rsch. scientist, dir. rsch. in sports medicine Mass. Gen. Hosp., 2004—; instr. orthopaedic surgery Harvard Med. Sch., 2004—. Mem. editl. bd. several sci. and med. jours.; contbr. articles to profl. jours. Bd. dirs. Easter Seal Soc., Allegheny County, 1972-77, Univs. Assn. for Rsch. and Edn. in Pathology, 1979-90. Recipient Lederle med. faculty award, 1962-65, rsch. career devel. award NIH, 1965-71, MERIT award NIH, 1992-2002, cert. of appreciation for patriotic civilian svc. Dept. Army, 1973, Spl. Qualification in Pathology: Immunopathology, 1983, Disting. Scientist award in genetics S.W. Found. for Biomed. Rsch., 1986, Charter with medal U. Rijeka, 1990, medal U. Pitts., 1990; named George H. Fetterman lectr. U. Pitts., 1981, George Hoyt Whipple lectr. U. Rochester, N.Y., 1984, Aron E. Szulman lectr. U. Pitts., 1993, Raymond O. Berry Meml. lectr. Tex. A&M U., 1995, Mühlblock lectr. Internat. Coun. for Lab. Scis., 1995, Spiridion Brusina award Croatian Soc. Natural Scis., 1997. Fellow Assn. Pathology Chairmen (pres. 1978); mem. AMA, Am. Assn. Immunologists, Am. Assn. Pathologists, Am. Soc. Molecular Biology and Biochemistry, Am. Soc. Human Genetics, Transplantation Soc. (v.p. 1982-84), Am. Soc. for Immunology of Reprodn. (v.p. 1988-89, Disting. Investigator award 1991, pres. 1995-96), Genetics Soc. Am., Internat. Acad. Pathology, Internat. Soc. Immunology of Reprodn. (pres. 1992-95, hon. pres. 1995—), Alps Adria Soc. for Immunology of Reprodn. (hon. pres. 1994—), Mass. Med. Soc., Harvard Club (Boston), Harvard Varsity Club. Business E-Mail: gilliii@massmed.org.

GILL, WILLIAM NELSON, chemical engineering professor; b. NYC, Sept. 13, 1928; s. William Nelson and Frances (Murphy) G.; m. Chandlee Stevens, Aug. 13, 1982; children: Alison Louise, Christine Marie, Douglas Max, Max William. BSChemE, Syracuse U., 1951, MA, 1955, PhD, 1960. Field engr. Am. Blower Corp., 1951-55; mem. faculty Syracuse U., 1957-65, assoc. prof., 1963-65; prof. chem. engring., chmn. dept. Clarkson U., 1965-71; provost engring. and applied sci. SUNY, Buffalo, 1971-78, prof. chem. engring., 1982-87; Glenn Murphy Disting. prof. engring. Iowa State U., Ames, 1980-82; Russell Sage disting. prof. chem. engring. Rensselaer Poly. Inst., Troy, NY, 1987—. Cons. in field. Editor: Chem. Engring. Communications, 1979—; mem. editorial adv. bd. Fuel, Processing Tech.; mem. bd. cons. editors Elsevier Texts in Engring.; editor Chem. Engring. series Elsevier Sci. Pub. Co.; author numerous articles in field. Named Alumnus of Yr., Bklyn. Tech. H.S., 1977; recipient William H. Wiley Disting. Faculty award in recognition of outstanding tchg. and scholarship Rensselaer Poly. Inst., 1994; Fulbright-Hays sr. rsch. scholar Univ. Coll., London, 1977-78, U. Queensland, Australia, 1986-87, Best Paper award Interconnect Scis. & Tech., Techcon 96 Semiconductor Rsch. Corp., 1996, Lecturship award Chem. Eng. Divsn. ASEE, 1992, Best Paper award Interconnect Modeling and Simulation, Techcon 98, Semiconductor Rsch. Corp., 1998. Fellow AIChE, AAAS; mem. AAAS, AAUP, Am. Chem. Soc., Am. Soc. Engring. Edn. (lectureship award chem. engring. divsn. for fundamental contbns. to chem. engring. theory and practice 1992), N.Y. Acad. Scis., Sigma Xi. Office: Rensselaer Poly Inst Chem Engring Ricketts Troy NY 12180 Home Phone: 518-274-0748; Office Phone: 518-276-6929. Personal E-mail: wngill@aol.com. Business E-Mail: gillw@rpi.edu.

GILLAN, KAYLA J., lawyer; b. 1958; Grad., Calif. St. U.; JD, U. Calif., Davis, 1984. Gen. counsel Calif. Pub. Employees Ret. Sys., Sacramento, 1996—2002; v.p. Ind. Fiduciary Services, 2002—; mem. Pub. Co. Acctg. Oversight Bd., Washington, 2002—. Named one of Top 50 Women Lawyers Nat. Law Jour., 1998. Office: Pub Co Acctg Oversight Bd 1666 K St NW Washington DC 20006

GILLANI, NOOR VELSHI, atmospheric scientist, researcher, educator; b. Arusha, Tanzania, Mar. 8, 1944; came to the U.S., 1963, naturalized, 1976; s. Noormohamed Velshi and Sherbanu (Kassam) G.; children: Michael, Michelle, Nicole. Cert. Edn., U. Cambridge, 1960; advanced level, U. London, 1963; AB cum laude, Harvard U., 1967; MSME, Washington U., St. Louis, 1969, DSc, 1974. Rsch. assoc. Washington U., St. Louis, 1975—76, rsch. scientist, 1976—77, asst. prof., 1977—80, assoc. prof., 1981—84, prof. mech. engring., 1984—91, faculty assoc. Ctr. Air Pollution Impact and Trend Analysis, 1979—91, dir. air quality spl. studies data ctr., 1981—88, dir., mech. engring. rsch. computing facility, 1988—90; pres. N.V. Gillani & Assocs., Inc., 1991—; prin. rsch. scientist Nat. Space Sci. & Tech. Ctr. NASA, Ala., 1995—; adj. prof. atmospheric sci. U. Ala., Huntsville, 1995—. Vis. scientist Stockholm U., 1977, Brookhaven Nat. Lab., 1990—91, EPA/RTP, 1992—93, TVA Environ. Rsch. Ctr., 1994—95; organizer NATO CCMS 15th internat. tech. meeting on air pollution modeling and its applications, St. Louis, 1985; mem. Sci. Bd. NATO/Commn. for the Challenges of Modern Soc. Air Pollution Pilot Study, 1984—92; mem. tech. adv. bds. U.S. EPA, DOE and others, 1980—; hon. mem. Aga Khan Edn. Bd. for U.S.A. (AKEB/USA), 1987—90; vis. prof. NC State U., NC, 1993—94. Author: (with others) Critical Assessment Document on Acidic Depositions, 1984, EPA Criteria Document for Particulate Matter, 1994-95; editor: Air Pollution Modeling and Its Applications V, vol. 10, 1986; contbr. chpts. to book and articles to profl. jours. Dir., founder AKEB/USA Program (PIAR)for Parental Involvement in Children's Edn., 1987-97; pres. Pyar Found. for Humanitarian Assistance, 2000—. Scholar, Harvard Coll., 1963—67; Aga Khan travel grantee, 1961—63, grad. fellow, Washington U., 1967—74, rsch. grantee, EPA, DOE, Elec. Power Rsch. Inst., NASA, NOAA, NSF, TVA, Tex. Commn. Environ. Quality, 1978—. Mem. Am. Meteorol. Soc., Am. Chem. Soc., Am. Geophys. Union, Nat. Assn. for Edn. Young Children, N.Y. Acad. Scis. Achievements include research on superconductivity, bioengring., atmospheric scis., air pollution and Islamic humanism. Office: NASA-UAH Nat Space Sci and Tech Ctr 320 Sparkman Dr Huntsville AL 35805 Office Phone: 256-961-7942. E-mail: gillani@nsstc.uah.edu.

GILLARD, MONTGOMERY, dermatologist; b. Des Moines, Iowa, Feb. 3, 1967; m. Gabrielle Allegra Tuchow, June 15, 1996; children: Isabelle Rose children: Benjamin Joel. MD, U. Mich. Diplomate Am. Bd. Dermatology. Lectr. U. Mich. Med. Ctr., Ann Arbor, 2002—04; dir. Ctr. for Skin Cancer Surgery, Clinton Township, Mich., 2004—07; co-dir. The Boyd Gillard Inst. Aesthetic and Dermatol. Surgery, Ypsilanti, Mich., 2007—. Contbr. articles to profl. jours. Mem.: AMA, Am. Soc. Dermatol. Surgery, Am. Coll. Mohs Micrographic Surgery and Cutaneous Oncology, Am. Acad. Dermatology. Office: Boyd Gillard Inst Aesthetic and Dermatol Surgery 4990 W Lark Rd Bldg A Ste 200 Ypsilanti MI 48197 Home: 1101 Martin Pl Ann Arbor MI 48104-3512 Office Phone: 734-572-7500. Office Fax: 734-572-7777. Personal E-mail: montgomery_gillard@ihacares.com.

GILLECE, JAMES PATRICK, JR., lawyer; b. Annapolis, Md., May 26, 1944; s. James Patrick and Erna Virginia (Barling) G.; m. Jane C. Szczepaniak, Apr. 24, 1971 (div. 1998); children: Jessica K., Jocelyn J., Jillian N., James P. III, Juliette A., John M. Szczepaniak -Gillece; m. Rosa Beza, Feb. 12, 1999. BA, LaSalle U., 1966; JD, U. Notre Dame, 1969. Bar: Md. 1969, U.S. Dist. Ct. Md. 1969, U.S. Ct. Appeals (4th cir.) 1972, U.S. Supreme Ct. 1974, U.S. Ct. Appeals (7th cir.) 1992, U.S. Ct. Appeals (8th and 11th cir.) 1995, U.S. Ct. Appeals (D.C. cir.) 2000. Assoc. Piper & Marbury, Balt., 1969-77, ptnr., 1977-92, dir. poverty law program, 1971-72; ptnr. Miles & Stockbridge, Balt., 1992-93; prin. Miles and Stockbridge, Balt., 1994-98; ptnr. McGuire, Woods, Battle & Boothe, Balt., 1998—2005, Whiteford, Taylor & Preston LLP, 2005—. Cons. Mercy Hosp. Dietitians Program, Balt., 1986-95. Mem. law adv. coun. U. Notre Dame, 1983—95; mem. Com. to Keep Supreme Bench Judges; trustee Everyman Theatre, 1996—; mem. com. for Mayor Kurt Schmoke, 1987; mem. Lawyers' Com. for Jerry Brown, 1976; mem. fin. com. Mayor Martin O'Malley, 2000—; bd. dirs. Balt. City Fair, 1984—88, Legal Aid Soc, Balt., Family Crisis Ctr., Balt. County, Inc., 1992—97, Everyman Theatre, 1995—, Justice for Children, 2004—. Mem. ABA, FBA, Am. Judicature Soc. (bd. dirs. 1988-90), Md. State Bar Assn. (Disting. Svc. award), Balt. Bar Assn., Notre Dame Law Assn. (pres. 1983-99, bd. dirs. 1977—, exec. coun., life mem.), U. Notre Dame Law Assocs., Internat. Childbirth Edn. Assn. (cons. 1987-97). Democrat. Roman Catholic. Home: 3809 Greenway Baltimore MD 21218-1826 Office: Whiteford Taylor & Preston LLP 1 St Paul St Ste 1300 Baltimore MD 21202-1626 Home Phone: 410-261-5520; Office Phone: 410-659-4421, 410-347-9470. Fax: 410-659-4455. E-mail: jgillece@Mcguire.woods.com.

GILLELAND, JOHN ROGERS, technology company executive; b. Gadsden, Ala., Jan. 12, 1941; s. Earl Rogers and Margaret Eta Gilleland; m. Kim Denise Turos, Aug. 23, 1987. BS in Physics, Yale U., 1963; MS in Physics, U. Mich., 1964, PhD in Physics, 1969. Scientist Gulf Gen. Atomics, La Jolla, Calif., 1970-72, dir. Doublet III program, 1972-78, sr. v.p. fusion energy program, 1985-87; program dir. U.S.-Japan Fusion rsch. Collaboration, La Jolla, 1978-85; mng. dir. Internat. Thermonuclear Exptl. Reactor Project, Garching, Germany, 1987-91; v.p., chief scientist Bechtel Corp., San Francisco, 1991-98; pres., CEO Archimedes Tech. Group, San Diego, 1998—, chmn. bd., 2006—; dir. Archis, LLC, 2005—. Advisor space def. initiative Dept. Def., Washington, 1985-86; advisor Nat. Acad. Scis., Washington, 1984-87; chmn. bd. dirs. Archis, LLC; program dir. Intellectual Ventures, Bellevue, Wash. Named Young Engr. of the Yr. Am. Nuc. Soc., 1980; recipient Achievement award Am. Nuc. Soc., 1992. Avocations: cello, squash, art installation, philosophy, carpentry. Home: 13226 67th Ave NE Kirkland WA 98034

GILLEN, JAMES ROBERT, lawyer, insurance company executive; b. NYC, Nov. 14, 1937; s. James Matthew and Katharine Isabel (Fritz) G.; m. Rita Marie Wahleithner, June 15, 1963 (div. 1992); children: Jennifer Elaine, Nancy Louise, Paula Anne; m. Edda Lya Pacheco, Dec. 10, 1994 AB magna cum laude, Harvard U., 1959, LLB cum laude, 1965. Bar: N.Y. 1966, N.J. 1975. Assoc. White & Case, NYC, 1965—72; v.p., assoc. gen. counsel Prudential Ins. Co. Am., Newark, 1972—77, sr. v.p., assoc. gen. counsel, 1977—80, sr. v.p. pub. affairs, 1980—84, sr. v.p., gen. counsel, 1984—98. Mem. bd. trustees Columbia Inst. Investor Project, 1981—97; legal adv. com. N.Y. Stock Exch., 1986—89; mem. adv. bd. Ascertain Solutions, Inc., 2001—02. Trustee United Way Essex and West Hudson Counties, 1981-90, pres., 1986-88; mem. Mendham Twp. Bd. Edn., 1981-82, NJ; trustee NJ Shakespeare Festival, 1991-99, Mendham Twp. Libr., 1979-82; dir., chmn. Neurol. Inst. NJ, 1998, 2005; bd. dirs. New Philharm. Orch. NJ, 2005—. Lt. (j.g.) USN, 1959-62 Mem. ABA, N.J. Bar Assn., Assn. Life Ins. Counsel, Harvard Club N.Y.C., Morris Country Golf Club Avocations: opera, theater, concerts, reading. Home and Office: 72 Washington Valley Rd Morristown NJ 07960-3332 Personal E-mail: jrgillen1@verizon.net.

GILLER, EDWARD BONFOY, retired government official, military officer; b. Jacksonville, Ill., July 8, 1918; s. Edward Bonfoy and Ruth (Davis) G.; m. Mildred Florana Schmidt, July 2, 1943; children— Susan Ann, Carol Elaine, Bruce Carleton, Penny Marie, Paul Benjamin. BS in Chem. Engring, U. Ill., 1940, MS, 1948, PhD, 1950. Chem. engr. Sinclair Oil Refining Co., 1940-41; commd. 2d lt. USAAF, 1942; advanced through grades to maj. gen. USAF, 1968; pilot, 1941-46; chief radiation br. (Armed Forces Spl. Weapons Project), Washington, 1950-54; dir. research directorate Air Force Spl. Weapons Center, Albuquerque, 1954-59; spl. asst. to comdr. (Office Aerospace Rsch.), Washington, 1959-64; dir. sci. and tech. Hdqrs. USAF, 1964-67; asst. gen. mgr. for mil. application U.S. AEC, 1967-72; ret. USAF, 1972; asst. gen. mgr. for nat. security AEC, 1972-75; dep. asst. adminstr. for nat. security U.S. ERDA, 1975-77; rep. of Joint Chiefs of Staff to Comprehensive Test Ban Negotiations, Geneva, 1977-84; sr. scientist Pacific-Sierra Rsch. Corp., Arlington, Va, 1984-92; v.p. Trans Mar Inc., Spokane, Wash., 1992-96; cons. Sandia Nat. Labs., Albuquerque, 1990—2004, ret., 2004. Cons. in the field. Decorated Silver Star, D.S.M., Legion of Merit with oak leaf cluster, D.F.C., Air medal with 17 oak leaf clusters, Purple Heart; Croix de Guerre France). Fellow Am. Inst. Chemists; mem. Am. Inst. Chem. Engrs., Sigma Xi, Alpha Tau Omega. Episcopalian. Home: 14415 Soula Dr NE Albuquerque NM 87123-1941

GILLERS, STEPHEN, law educator; b. Nov. 3, 1943; BA, Bklyn Coll., 1964; JD cum laude, NYU, 1968. Bar: NY 1968. Law clk. to Hon. Gus J. Solomon US Dist. Ct. Oreg., Portland, 1968-69; assoc. Paul, Wiess, Rifkind, Wharton & Garrison, NY, 1969-71; exec. dir. Com. for Pub. Justice, 1971—73; ptnr. Warner & Gillers, P.C., NYC, 1975—78; assoc. prof. law NYU Law Sch., NYC, 1978—81, prof. law, 1981—99, vice dean, 1999—2004, Emily Kempin prof. law, 2003—. Mem. com. on profl. & jud. ethics Assn. Bar City of NY, 1979—82, mem. criminal law com., 1992—95; mem. Departmental Disciplinary Com., First Jud. Dept., 1980—83; mem. exec. com. profl. responsibility section Assn. Am. Law Schools, 1985—91; counsel NY State Blue Ribbon Commn. to Review Legis. Practice in Relation to Polit. Campaign Activities of Legis. Employees, 1987—88; chair American Bar Assn. (ABA) Joint Com. on Lawyer Regulation, 1989—90; adj. ass. prof. law Bklyn. Law Sch., 1976—78; vis. prof. law Harvard U., 1988, Yeshiva U., 1986—88. Author: Getting Justice: The Rights of People, 1971, I'd Rather Do It Myself: How to Set Up Your Own Law Firm, 1977, The Rights of Lawyers and Clients, 1979; co-editor: None of Your Business: Government Secrecy in America, 1975, Looking at Law School: A Student Guide From the Society of American Law Teachers, 1977, Regulation of Lawyers: Statutes and Standards, 1989, Regulation of Lawyers: Problems of Law and Ethics, 2005. Exec. dir. Soc. Am. Law Teachers, Inc., 1975-78, 78-80 Recipient Order of Coif, 1968. Mem.: ABA (chair policy implementation com. 2005—). Office: NYU Sch Law 40 Washington Sq S New York NY 10012-1099 Office Phone: 212-998-6264. Business E-Mail: stephen.gillers@nyu.edu.

GILLESPIE, CHARLES KEVIN, priest, educator; b. Phila., Jan. 25, 1951; s. Francis John and Sara Ann Gillespie. BS in Psychology, St. Joseph's Coll., Phila., 1972; MA in Psychology, Duquesne U., Pitts., 1974; MDiv, Jesuit Sch. Theology, Berkeley, Calif., 1986, MST, 1989; PhD, Boston U., 1997. Cert. profl. counselor Md. Danielsen clin. fellow Boston U., 1991—94; assoc. prof. Loyola Coll., Balt., 1996—, dir. MA in spiritual and pastoral care, 1996—, assoc. chmn. internat. studies, 2001—, chair dept. pastoral counseling, 2007—. Bd. dirs. Pastoral Counseling Services of Md., Balt., 1999—, Transplant Resource Ctr. Md., Balt., 1997—2002, Transplant Resource Centers Md., Balt.; dir. Loyola Overseas Gifts of Solidarity, Balt., 1998—2004; fellow Inst. Ecumenical and Cultural Rsch., Collegeville, Minn., 2001; spiritual dir. SJ Spiritual Ctr., Wernersville, Pa.; presenter in field. Author: Psychology and American Catholicism: From Confession to Therapy?; contbr. articles to profl. publs. Bd. mem. St. Joseph's U., 2006—. Grantee, Raskob Found., 2000—01, Mercy Sisters of Balt., 2003—04. Fellow: Am. Assn. Pastoral Counselors (mem. exec. com. 2004—06); mem.: Coll. Theology Soc., Spiritual Dirs. Internat. Democrat. Roman Catholic. Avocations: travel, athlectics, gardening, photography. Office: Loyola Coll Md 8890 McGaw Rd Columbia MD 21045 Office Phone: 410-617-7651. Business E-Mail: kgillespie@loyola.edu.

GILLESPIE, DANNY, JR., management consultant, music foundation administrator; m. Surrenden Gillespie. BA, U. Tex., Austin; MBA, Baylor U. Dir. bus. solutions programs RLX Technologies; with MHM, Inc., Perryman Consultants, Andersen Consulting (name changed to Accenture), Cold Spring Consulting; prin. & co-founder IdealFlow, Austin. Pres. Austin Music Found.; ptnr. Tex. Music Roundup, Austin; co-chair KLRU Assoc. Prodr.'s Cir., Austin. Recipient Austin Under 40 award for Arts/Entertainment, 2006. Office: Austin Music Found PO Box 4309 Austin TX 78765 Office Phone: 512-323-0787. E-mail: info@austinmusicfoundation.org.

GILLESPIE, ED (EDWARD WALTER GILLESPIE), federal official, former political organization administrator; b. Browns Mills, NJ, 1962; m. Catherine Hay; children: John Patrick, Carrie, Mollie Brigid. BA in Polit. Sci., Cath. U., 1983. Asst. to Rep. Andy Ireland US Congress, Fla., 1983—84, press spokesman to Rep. Dick Armey Tex., 1985—95; dir. comm. & cong. affairs Rep. Nat. Com., 1996; pres., CEO Policy Impact Communications, 1997—99; founder, prin. Quinn Gillespie & Assocs., Washington, 2000—; chmn. Rep. Nat. Com., Washington, 2003—05, Va. Rep. Party, 2006—07; counselor to Pres. The White House, Washington, 2007—. Adv. to Hon. Samuel J. Alito during his Supreme Ct. confirmation hearings, 2006. Editor: Contract with America, 1995 (NY Times bestseller list, 1995). Comm. dir. Pres. George W. Bush Inauguration, 2001; mgr. Phila. conv. Rep. Nat. Com., 2000; sr. comm. adv. George W. Bush Presdl. Campaign, Austin, 2000, spokesman for Fla. election recount, 2001; gen. strategist Elizabeth Dole Senate Campaign, NC, 2002. Republican. Office: The White House 1600 Pennsylvania Ave Washington DC 20001*

GILLESPIE, EDWARD MALCOLM, hospital administrator; b. Mpls., Oct. 19, 1935; s. Harold Livingston and Alice May (Thompson) G.; children: Karin, Timothy, Kenneth. BS, U. Minn., 1957, MPA, 1959, MHA, 1962. Engaged in refugee adminstrn., Linz, Austria, 1958-60; asst. adminstr. Luth. Med. Ctr., Denver, 1962-66; asst. gen. sec. Meth. Bd. Health and Welfare Ministries, Evanston, Ill., 1966-69; adminstr. Meth. Hosp., Rochester, Minn., 1969-74, Univ. Hosp., Augusta, Ga., 1974-91, pres. Health Advance, 1991-92. Bd. dirs. Augusta Area Mental Health, Augusta Speech and Hearing Ctr., St. John's Towers, CSRA Blood Assurance; chmn. hosp. divsn. certification coun. Meth. Health and Welfare. Bd. dirs. local United Way, Boy Scouts Am., Blue Cross Ga., Bankers First; chmn. Augusta Resource Ctr. on Aging, Brandon Wilde. Fellow ACHA; mem. Am. Hosp. Assn., Ga. Hosp. Assn. (chmn.), Rotary Internat. (bd. dirs. Augusta chpt.). Methodist. Home and Office: Health Advance 12 Shadow Brook Cir Augusta GA 30909-3749

GILLESPIE, GARY DON, physician; b. Jackson, Mich., Apr. 23, 1943; s. Harold Don and Marion Estella (Diemer) G.; m. Nancy Bliven Hinkle, June 29, 1969 (div. July 1980; children: Brian James, Julie Elizabeth; m. Elaine Marie Beard, July 25, 1984. BS, U. Mich., 1966, D of Medicine, 1971. Diplomate Am. Bd. Family Practice. Intern Edward W. Sparrow Hosp., Lansing, Mich., 1971-72, resident in family practice, 1971-74; physician Dept. Family Practice, USN Med. Corps., Orlando, Fla., 1974-76; pvt. practice Okemos, Mich., 1976—2001; ret., 2001. Chmn. continuing edn., dept. family practice Edward W. Sparrow Hosp., 1976-91; asst. clin. prof. dept. family practice Mich. State U. Coll. Medicine, East

Lansing, 1981-2001. Lt. comdr. USN, 1974-76. Mem. AMA, Am. Acad. Family Physicians, Am. Bd. Family Practice, Mich. Acad. Family Physicians (treas. Capitol chpt. 1982-92). Republican. Avocations: reading, music, photography, travel, golf.

GILLESPIE, GEORGE JOSEPH, III, lawyer; b. NYC, May 18, 1930; s. George Joseph Jr. and Dorothy Elizabeth (McKenna) Gillespie; m. Eileen Tracy Dealy, July 27, 1955; children: Gail Gillespie Garcia, John D., Myles D., Eileen G. Fahey. AB magna cum laude, Georgetown U., 1952; LLB magna cum laude, Harvard U., 1955. Bar: N.Y. 1957. Assoc. Cravath, Swaine & Moore, LLP, NYC, 1956-62, ptnr., trusts, estates, 1963—2005, spl. counsel, 2006—. Bd. dirs. White Mountains Holdings, Inc. Trustee, pres. John M. Olin Found., 1976—; pres. Pinkerton Found., 1971—, Arthur Ross Found., 1986—, William S. Paley Found., 1984—, Edward E. Ford Found., Edmond J. Safra Philanthropic Found.; trustee, sec. Mus. TV and Radio, 1997—; vice-chmn. exec. com. Madison Sq. Boys and Girls Club; chmn. emeritus, hon. life dir. Nat. Multiple Sclerosis Soc.; mem. corp. Jackson Lab., Bar Harbor, Maine. Frederick Sheldon Travel fellow, Harvard U., 1955—56. Mem.: Century Assn., Blind Brook Golf Club, Portland Country Club, Am. Yacht Club, Double Eagle Club, Prouts Neck Country Club, Winged Foot Golf Club. Republican. Roman Catholic. Office: Cravath Swaine & Moore Worldwide Pla 825 8th Ave Fl 43 New York NY 10019-7475 Office Phone: 212-474-1700. Office Fax: 212-474-3700. Business E-Mail: ggillesp@cravath.com.

GILLESPIE, GERALD ERNEST PAUL, comparative literature educator, writer; b. Cleve., July 12, 1933; s. Francis and Nora Veronica (Quinn) G.; m. Adrienne Amalia Galante, Sept. 5, 1959. AB, Harvard U., 1956; postgrad., U. Tübingen, Germany, 1956—57; MA, Ohio State U., 1958, PhD, 1961; postgrad., U. Munich, 1960—61. Asst. prof. U. So. Calif., LA, 1961-65; from assoc. prof. to prof. SUNY, Binghamton, 1965-74; prof. Stanford (Calif.) U., 1974—. Vis. prof. U. Pa., Phila, 1969, NYU, 1970, U. Minn., Mpls., 1978, Peking U., Beijing, 1985, U. East Anglia, Norwich, Eng., 1988, U. Munich, 1993, U. Hagen, Germany, 2002; hon. prof., Liaoning U., China. Author: Lohenstein's Historical Tragedies, 1965, German Baroque Poetry, 1972, Evolution of the European Novel, 1987, Garden and Labyrinth of Time, 1988, Proust, Mann, Joyce in the Modernist Context, 2003, By Way of Comparison, 2004, Echoland: Readings from Humanism to Postmodernism, 2006; author, editor: Herkommen und Erneuerung, 1976, Studien zum Werk D.C. von Lohenstein, 1983, German Theater Before 1750, 1992, Romantic Drama, 1994, Narrative Ironies, 1997, Mallarmé in the Twentieth Century, 1998, Romantic Nonfictional Prose, 2004; translator, editor: Night Watches, 1972, Puss-in-Boots, 1974, Bohemian Lights, 1976; editor: Littérature Comparée, Littérature Mondiale, 1991, Visions in History, 1995, Powers of Narration, 1995; mem. editl. bd.: Comparative Lit., 1977—, Internationales Archiv, 1975—, Utrecht Studies in Comparative Lit., 1987-2004, Recherche Littéraire, 1991—, Literary Imagination, 1998-2004; co-editor: German Life and Letters, 1987-2004, advisor, 2005—. Andrew Mellon Found. fellow, 1966—67, John S. Guggenheim Found. fellow, 1967—68, NEH sr. fellow, 1973—74, vis. fellow Clare Hall, Cambridge U., Eng., 1979. Mem.: MLA (exec. com. comparative studies in romanticism and the 19th century 1982—87, mem. nat. program com. 1985—88, mem. exec. com. classical studies and modern lit. 1986—91), Calif. Assn. Scholars (bd. dirs. 1992—), Assn. Lit. Scholars and Critics (coun. 1998—2001), Renaissance Soc. Am., Brit. Comparative Lit. Assn., Am. Comparative Lit. Assn., Internat. Comparative Lit. Assn. (sec. 1979—85, mem. editl. bd. bull. 1979—85, v.p. 1985—88, pres. 1994—97), Berliner Wissenschaftliche Gesellschaft (corr.). Office Phone: 650-723-3266.

GILLESPIE, J. MARTIN, sales and distribution company executive; b. Detroit, Sept. 27, 1949; s. John Martin and Shirley Ann (Rees) G.; children: Heather, Tara. BBA, Xavier U., 1971; MBA, U. Mich., 1973. Account exec. Foote Cone & Belding, Chgo., 1973-76, account supr., 1976-77; mktg. mgr. Hansen Corp., Walled Lake, Mich., 1977-80, gen. mgr., 1980-82; chmn., CEO Hansen Mktg. Svcs., Inc., Walled Lake, 1982—. Founder Hickory Stick Invitational Charity Tournament; bd. dirs. Xavier U. Alumni Assn., 2001—. Recipient Merit award Nat. Alliance Businessmen, 1973. Mem. Assn. MBA Execs., Am. Mgmt. Assn., Nat. Acad. TV Arts and Scis., Nat. Assn. Credit Mgmt., Nat. Bldg. Materials Distbn. Assn., Alpha Kappa Psi. Office: Hansen Mktg Svcs Inc PO Box 640 1000 Decker Rd Walled Lake MI 48390-0640 Office Phone: 248-669-2323.

GILLESPIE, JOHN DAVID, political science educator, former academic administrator; b. Oxford, NC, Sept. 22, 1944; s. Arthur S. and Pauline M. (Pittard) G.; m. Judi K. Flowers, June 11, 1966. BA, Wake Forest U., 1966, MA, 1967; PhD, Kent State U., 1973. Instr., history and polit. sci. Davidson C.C., Lexington, NC, 1967-70; asst. prof. Samford U., Birmingham, Ala., 1973-79; from assoc. prof. to prof. to Charles A. Dana prof. polit. sci. Presbyterian Coll., Clinton, SC, 1979—2006, v.p. academic affairs, dean of faculty, 1997-2005, former chmn. dept. polit. sci.; pres. SC Ind. Colls. Deans' Coun., 1999-2000; part-time prof. polit. sci. Coll. of Charleston, 2007—; spkr. at colloquia, profl. confs. in field; interviewee ABC-TV, BBC-Radio, CNN-TV, PBS-TV, NPR, and others; testimony expert in fed. and state ballot access cases. Author: Politics at the Periphery: Third Parties in Two-Party America, 1993. Contbr. chpts. to anthologies, articles to profl. jours.; former chmn. Laurens County Dem. Party, mem. SC Dem. Exec. Com., v.p. Ala. Polit. Sci. Assn., 1978-79, pres. SC Polit. Sci. Assn., 1985-86; NDEA Title IV fellow, 1970-73; grantee NEH 1978, Fulbright group project, China, 1988; Fulbright scholar, Tartu U., Estonia, 1997; named SC Prof. of Yr., 1993-94; Designated Exemplary Tchr., US Dept. Edn., 1996. Mem. Am. Polit. Sci. Assn., Internat. Soc. for Sci. Study Subjectivity. Presbyterian. Home: 6023 Grand Council St Daniel Island SC 29492-8035 E-mail: jdavidgi@gmail.com.

GILLESPIE, JOHN THOMAS, retired university administrator; b. Thunder Bay, Ont., Can., Sept. 25, 1928; came to U.S., 1954, naturalized, 1961; s. William and Jeannie (Barr) G. BA, U. B.C., 1948; MA, Columbia U., 1957; PhD, NYU, 1969. High sch. tchr., Powell River, B.C., Canada, 1949-53; libr. Roslyn (N.Y.) Pub. Sch. Dist., 1955-63; mem. faculty Palmer Grad. Library Sch., C.W. Post Center, LIU, NY, 1963—, prof., 1975-80, dean, 1981-83; acad. v.p. C.W. Post Ctr., LIU, 1983-85; ret., 1985. Vis. prof. Syracuse (N.Y.) U., SUNY, Albany; cons. in field. Author: Juniorplots, 1966, Introducing Books, 1970, Young Phenomenon, 1971, Creating the School Media Program, 1973, A Model School Media Program, 1973, Paperback Books for Young People, 3d edit., 1987, More Juniorplots, 1977, Best Books for Children, Administering the School Library Media Center, 1983, Elementary School Paperback Collection, 1985, Senior High School Paperback Collection, 1986, Juniorplots 3, 1987, Seniorplots, 1989, Best Books for Junior High Readers, 1991, Best Books for Senior High Readers, 1991, Juniorplots 4, 1993, Middleplots 4, 1994, Best Books for Children, 5th edit., 8th edit., 2006, 1994, Guides to Library Collection Development, 1994, The Newbery Companion, 1996, 2d edit. 2000, Characters in Young Adult Literature, 1997, Guides to Library Collection Development for Children and Young Adults, 1997, Best Books for Young Teen Readers, 1999, Teenplots, 2003, Best Books for Middle and Jr. High School Readers, 2004, supplement, 2006, Best Books for High School Readers, 2004, supplement, 2006, The Children's and Young Adult Literature Handbook, 2005, The Newbery/Printz Companion, 2006, Classic Teenplots, 2006. Mem. ALA, N.Y. Libr. Assn., Phi Delta Kappa, Kappa Delta Pi. Home: 360 E 72nd St New York NY 10021-4753 Home Phone: 212-861-9294. Personal E-mail: bestgill@aol.com.

GILLESPIE, MICHAEL J., lawyer; b. Feb. 21, 1960; AB summa cum laude, Amherst Coll., 1982; JD, Harvard U., 1986. Bar: NY 1987. Assoc. Debevoise & Plimpton LLP, NYC, 1986—95, mem., 1995—, ptnr., co-chair Media and Tech. Group. Mem.: ABA, Assn City Bar NY. Office: Debevoise & Plimpton LLP 919 Third Ave New York NY 10022 E-mail: mjgillespie@debevoise.com.

GILLESPIE, ROBERT WAYNE, banker; b. Cleve., Mar. 26, 1944; s. Robert Walton and Eleanore (Parsons) G.; m. Ann. L. Wible, June 17, 1967; children: Laura, Gwen. BA, Ohio Wesleyan U., 1966; MBA, Case Western Res. U., 1968; postgrad., Harvard U., 1979. Credit analyst Soc. Nat. Bank, Cleve., 1968-70, v.p., 1970-76, sr. v.p., 1976-79; exec. v.p. Soc. Nat Bank, Cleve., 1979-81; vice-chmn., chief operating officer Soc. Nat. Bank, Cleve., 1981-83, pres., chief operating officer, 1983-85, CEO, 1985—, pres., 1987-94; pres., CEO, Key Corp., Cleve., 1995—, chmn., 1996—, CEO, 1996—. Trustee Case Western Res. U., Ohio Wesleyan U., Cleve. Mus. Art, Cleve. Initiative for Edn. and Musical Arts, Greater Cleve. Roundtable, Cleve. Tomorrow and North Coast Harbor; bd. dirs. Greater Cleve. Growth Assn. Office: Key Corp 127 Public Sq Cleveland OH 44114-1306

GILLESPIE, RONALD JAMES, chemistry professor, researcher, writer; b. London, Aug. 21, 1924; arrived in Can., 1958; s. James Andrew and Miriam (Kirk) G.; m. Madge Garner, July 5, 1950; children: Ann, Lynn. BSc, London U., 1945, PhD, 1949, DSc, 1957; LLD (hon.), Concordia U., Montreal, Can., 1988, Dalhousie U., Halifax, Can., 1988; D Honoris causa, U. des Scis. et Techniques du Languedoc, 1991; DSc (hon.), McMaster U., 1993; DSc (hon.), U. Lethbridge, 2007. Asst. lectr. dept. chemistry U. Coll., U. London, 1948-50, lectr., 1950-58; assoc. prof. dept. chemistry McMaster U., Hamilton, Ont., Canada, 1958-60, prof., 1960-87, prof. emeritus, 1988—, chmn. dept., 1962-65. Vis. prof. U. Manchester (Eng.), 1965-66, U. des Scis. et Techniques du Languedoc, Montpellier, France, 1972-73, U. Geneva, 1976, U. Göttingen, Fed. Republic Germany, 1978, Australian Nat. U., Canberra, 1979, U. Melbourne, Australia, U. Auckland, New Zealand, 1980, Panjab U., Chandigarh, India, 1983; Nyholm lectr. Chem. Soc., London, 1978; Gillespie lectr. U. Coll., London, 1990; Muetterties vis. scholar U. Calif., Berkeley, 1990. Author: Molecular Geometry, 1972, (with others) Chemistry, 1986, 2d edit., 1989, (with I. Hargittai) The VSEPR Model of Molecular Geometry, 1991, (with others) Atoms, Molecules and Reactions: An Introduction to Chemistry, 1994, (with P. Popelier) Chemical Bonding and Molecular Geometry: From Lewis to Election Densities, 2001; contbr. over 380 articles to profl. jours. Recipient Can. Centennial medal, 1967, Coll. Chemistry Tchr. award Mfg. Chemists Assn., 1972, Silver Jubilee award, 1977, Excellence in Teaching award McMaster u. Students Union, 1983, Izaak Walter Killam Meml. Prize of Can. Coun. for Pure Sci., 1987; Commonwealth Fund fellow Brown U., 1953-54. Fellow Royal Soc. London, Royal Soc. Can. (Henry Marshall Tory medal 1983), Royal Soc. Chemistry (Harrison Meml. medal 1953), Royal Inst. Chemistry, Chem. Inst. Can. (Noranda award 1966, Union Carbide award 1976, medal 1977); mem. Am. Chem. Soc. (N.E. Region award 1971, Tour Speaker of Yr. award 1971, Disting. Svc. award 1973, fluorine chemistry award 1981). Avocations: sailing, skiing, travel. Office: McMaster U Dept Chemistry Hamilton ON Canada L8S 4M1 Home Phone: 905-628-1502; Office Phone: 905-628-1502. Business E-Mail: ronald.gillespie@sympatico.ca.

GILLESPIE, THOMAS STUART, investment company executive; b. Montreal, July 18, 1938; s. Alexander Robert and Lois Tully (O'Brien) G.; m. Caroline Pierce Doyle, June 28, 1963; children: Caroline Alexandra, Alexandra Olivia, Vanessa Margaret, Joshua William. BA, McGill U., 1959, BCL, 1963. Assoc., Ogilvy, Renault, Montreal, 1964-72, ptnr., 1972-89, sr. ptnr., 1989-2001; pres. Tyringham Investments Ltd., 2001—07. Pres., bd. dirs. Bouverie Investments Ltd.; chmn., bd. dirs. Imperial Tobacco Can. Ltd.; bd. dirs. Daily Mail and Gen. Trust plc, Biomosaics Inc., Nuera Internat. Inc., Tyringhaus Instruments Ltd. Bd. dirs. Carnegie Instn. Can. Mem. Que. Bar Assn., Mt. Bruno Country Club, Orleans Fish and GameClub, Univ. Club, Tarratine Club Dark Harbor, Toronto Golf Club. Roman Catholic. Home: 48 Aberdeen Ave Westmount PQ Canada H3Y 3A4 Office: 1800 McGill College Ave Ste 2430 Montreal PQ Canada H3A 3J6 Business E-Mail: tgillespie@tyringham.ca.

GILLET, PAMELA KIPPING, special education educator; EdB in Elem. Edn., Chgo. Tchrs. Coll., 1963; MA in Mental Retardation, Northeastern Ill. U., 1966; PhD in Gen. Spl. Edn./Adminstrn., Walden U., 1976. Cert. elem. edn., early childhood edn., learning disabled, mental retardation, behavior disorders, supt., supr. and dir. spl. edn. 4th grade tchr. Dist. # 83 Mannheim, Franklin Park, Ill., 1963—64; h.s. spl. edn. tchr. Dist. # 207 Maine Twp., Park Ridge, Ill., 1964—67, prevocational coord., 1967—69, dept. chmn. spl. edn. dept., 1969—70; dir. EPDA tchr. tng. program Chgo. Consortium Colls. and Univs., Northewst Ednl. Coop., Palatine, Ill., 1970—71; prin. West Suburban Spl. Edn. Ctr., Cicero, Ill., 1971—73; supr. West Suburban Assn. Spl. Edn., Cicero, 1973—75; asst. dir. Northwest Suburban Spl. Edn. Orgn., Palatine, 1975—78, supt. Mt. Prospect, Ill., 1978—96; spl. edn. cons., 1996—. Adj. instr. Northeastern Ill. U., Chgo. State U., Corcordia Coll., Barat Coll., Nat. Coll. Edn., Roosevelt U.; mem. task forces ISBE, 1975—2007, cons. career edn. project, 1977—78, spl. edn. demandate study group, 1983—85; cons. Ednl. Testing Svc.; tchr. edn. coun. Northeastern Ill. U., 1981—97, dean's grant program, 1982—97; workshop leader, 1974—; lectr., cons. in field. Author: Auditory Processes, 1974, rev., 1992, Career Education for Children, 1978, Of Work and Worth: Career Education Programming for Exceptional Children and Youths, 1981; contbr. articles to profl. jours., chapters to books. Bd. dirs. Found. Exceptional Children, 1996—, pres., 1999—2004. Recipient Cmty. Svc. award, Am. Legion, 1976, 1980, Alumnus of Yr. award, Northeastern Ill. U., 1984, Learning Disabilities of Am. Contributors award, Coun. Understanding Learning Disabilities, 1992, Those Who Excel award of excellence, Ill. State Bd. of Edn., 1994, Outstanding Svc. award, Divsn. Mental Retardation and Devel. Disabilities, 1994, Sleznick award, Coun. of Admin. of Spl. Edn., 1996, Outstanding Contbr. award, Coun. Exceptional Children, 1996, Burton Blatt award, Divsn. on Mental Retardation and Devel. Disabilities, 1997, Spl. Edn. Leadership award, Ill. Adminstrs. of Spl. Edn., 1995, Outstanding Spl. Edn. Adminstr. of Yr. award, 1997. Mem.: Found. for Exceptional Children (pres. 2000—04, v.p. CEC Pioneers divsn. 2006—), Ill. Adminstrs. Spl. Edn. (pres. 1994—95), Coun. Exceptional Children (pres. Ill. chpt. 1975—77, bd. govs. 1977—80, pres. mental retardation divsn. 1983—85, bd. govs. 1986, exec. com. 1989—92, v.p. internat. 1992—93, pres.-elect 1993—94, pres. 1994—95, bd. govs. 1996—2000, bd. dirs. 2000—04, pres. Pioneers divsn. 2007, pres.-elect. 2005—06, Meritorious Svc. award Ill. 1983), Am. Assn. Sch. Adminstrs. Home and Office: 413 Courtlea Oaks Blvd Winter Garden FL 34787

GILLETT, GEORGE NIELD, JR., professional sports team executive, communications executive; b. Racine, Wis., Oct. 22, 1938; s. George Nield and Alyce (Herbert) G.; m. Rose Foster, Aug. 5, 1967; children: George Nield III, Alexander, Andrew, Foster. Student, Amherst Coll.; BA, Dominican Coll., Racine, 1961. With McKinsey and Co., Inc., 1964-67; bus. mgr. Miami Dolphins, 1966-67; pres. Harlem Globetrotters, Inc., 1967-70, Globetrotter Comms., Inc., Chgo., 1970-76; vice-chmn. Globe Broadcasting Co., 1976-78; chmn. Wausau Fin. Corp., Wis., 1969, Lease Mgmt. Corp., Chgo., 1973; pres. Juneau Supply Co., Inc., 1977, Wausau Energy Corp., 1977; chmn. Gillett Holdings, Inc., 1978, Gillett Comms. Co., 1978, Packerland Packing Co., Inc., 1978-94; owner, chmn. Vail Assocs., Inc., Colo., 1985; chmn. Citizens Bank & Trust, Wausau, Wis., 1986; chmn, CEO Gillett Holdings Inc., Vail, Colo.; chmn. Booth Creek Mgmt. Corp.; owner Montreal Canadiens, 2000—. Chmn. The Norris Farm, Inc., 1988—; dir. Endata, Inc., Third Nat. Bank, Nashville. Mem. Young Presidents Orgn.; mem. exec. com. Middle Tenn. council Boy Scouts Am.; bd. dirs. United Way; trustee U.S. Ski Edns. Found.; mem. Vail Valley Found. Named to Colo. Ski and Snowboard Hall of Fame, 2005. Mem. Am. Meat Assn., Alexis de Tocqueville Soc., Nat. Ski Areas Assn. Clubs: Racquet (Chgo.); Belle Meade Country, Onwentsia, Oneida; Colo. Ski (bd. dirs.), Cascade (Vail, Colo.); Beaver Creek, Buck Point, Honors Course, Richland, Country of the Rockies. Roman Catholic. Office: c/o Montreal Canadiens 1275 St Antoine St W Montreal PQ Canada H3C 5L2

GILLETT, GROVER, author; b. Whitewright, Tex., June 22, 1927; s. Grover Cleveland and Gertrude (Holland) G.; m. Mary Margaret Landress, Aug. 16, 1963. BBA, Tex. Tech. U., 1949; MBA, U. Tex., 1951; postgrad., Columbia U., NYC, 1953. CPA, Tex. Auditor Lumberman's Mutual Casualty Co., Dallas, 1954-56; operational auditor Dept. of Def., Dallas, 1956-58; self-employed CPA Dallas, 1958-64; asst. prof. McMurry Coll., Abilene, Tex., 1964-66; sr. internal auditor Ling-Temco-Vought Aerospace Corp., Dallas, 1966-67; instr. El Centro Coll., Dallas, 1967-96. Author: Personnel Policies of Public Accounting Firms in Texas, 1951, (booklet) 1002 Trends and Forecasts, 2005, 124 other books and booklets. Bd. dirs. Twenty-One Turtle Creek Homeowners Assn., Dallas, 1996-98; mem. World Affairs Coun. With USN, 1945-46, Korea, lt. (j.g.) USNR ret. Mem. AICPA, Tex. Soc. CPAs, World Future Soc., Dallas UN Assn., S.W. Social Sci. Assn., Lions. Democrat. Unitarian Universalist. Avocations: reading, collecting antiques. Home and Office: Apt 1103 3883 Turtle Creek Blvd Dallas TX 75219-4426 Personal E-mail: gmgillett@sbcglobal.net.

GILLETT, JAMES WARREN, retired ecotoxicology educator; b. Sept. 18, 1933; s. Ira Elijah and Atha Arthela (Morlan) Gillett; m. Mary Francis Hebert, Aug. 7, 1970; children: Grant Jameson, Iain Michael; m. Mary Alexia Stuart, June 26, 1958 (div. Apr. 1970); children: John Stuart, Peter Warren. BS, U. Kans., 1955; PhD, U. Calif., Berkeley, 1962. Postdoctoral rsch. chemist U. Calif., Berkeley, 1962-64; asst. prof. agrl. chemistry Oreg. State U., Corvallis, 1964-69, assoc. prof., 1969-74; rsch. ecologist EPA/Environ. Rsch. Lab., Corvallis, 1974-81, rsch. environ. scientist, 1981-83; prof. ecotoxicology dept. natural resources Cornell U., Ithaca, NY, 1983—2006, dir. superfund basic rsch. program, 1992—2001; prof. emeritus, 2006—. Dir. Inst. for Comparative and Environ. Toxicology, 1986-92, Risk Analysis Studies minor field of grad study. Editor, pub.: Biological Impact of Pesticides in the Environment, 1971; editor: Terrestrial Microcosms, 1979; editor: (jour.) Hazard Assessment, Environ. Toxicology & Chemistry, 1988-93; contbr. articles to profl. jours. Chmn. bd. Oreg. Mus. Sci. and Industry, 1969-71, Cmty. Action Program, 1970-72; sec. Willamette Soccer League, 1970-74; coach Corvallis Womens Soccer Team, 1979-81; pres., founder Esophagal Cancer Awareness Assn., 2002-06. Summerfield scholar, 1951-54. Mem.: Soc. Risk Analysis, Soc. Environ. Toxicology and Chemistry (bd. dirs. 1984—88), Toastmasters (pres. 1974), Alpha Kappa Lambda. Home Phone: 607-257-2447. Personal E-mail: jwg3@cornell.edu.

GILLETT, MARY CAPERTON, military historian; b. Richmond, Va., Apr. 28, 1929; d. Lewis Hopkins and Mary Caperton (Horsley) Renshaw; m. Richard Clark Gillett, June 7, 1949; children: Richard Clark Jr., Glenn Douglas, Mary Caperton, Priscilla Elizabeth, Blakeney Diana. Student, Wellesley Coll., 1946-49; BA, Am. U., 1966, MA, 1971, PhD, 1978. Historian U.S. Navy Dept., Washington, 1966-69, U.S. Dept. Army, Washington, 1972-96. Author: The Army Medical Department, 1775-1818, 1981, The Army Medical Department, 1818-1865, 1988, The Army Medical Department, 1865-1917, 1995; contbr. articles to profl. jours. Mem. Am. Assn. for History of Medicine, Nat. Wildlife Fedn., We. Hist. Assn., The Nature Conservancy, The Wilderness Soc., The Sierra Club, Nat. Audubon Soc., Audubon Naturalist Soc. Avocations: backpacking, gardening. E-mail: mcgillett@mindspring.com.

GILLETTE, DALE ALAN, retired research scientist; b. Lincoln, Nebr., Mar. 24, 1943; s. Francis Joseph and Julia Philomena Gillette; m. Jane Ashbel Edson, Dec. 15, 1979; children: Kimberly Jane Irlbeck, Robin Christopher Doner, Franklin Emerson, Jonathan Blake. BS, U. Mich., Ann Arbor, 1965, MS, 1967, PhD, 1970. Scientist Nat. Ctr. Atmospheric Rsch., Boulder, Colo., 1970—79, U. Colo., Boulder, 1979—81; phys. scientist Nat. Oceanic & Atmospheric Adminstrn., Research Triangle Park, NC, 1991—2007; ret., 2007. Contbr. over 125 articles to sci. jours. Mem. Unitarian Universalist Ch. Achievements include research in emissions of dust and sand transport. Avocations: philosophy, travel. Home: 3619 Lion Ridge Ct Raleigh NC 27612 Home Phone: 919-541-1883.

GILLETTE, FRANK C., JR., retired mechanical engineer; m. Jane Gillette; 3 children. BS in Mech. Engring., U. Fla. Mech. designer Pratt & Whitney, 1962-77, chief of structures, 1977-80, engring. mgr. YF119 program, dir. engring. programs F119 engine projects for Govt. Engines and Space Propulsion, 1980-95, dir. advanced mil. programs, 1995-97, dir.-chief engr. F119/JSF engine programs, 1997-98, ret., 1998. Mem. adv. bd. U. Fla. Coll. Engring.; cons. in field. Recipient Disting. Alumnus Disting. Svc. award U. Fla. Coll. Engring., Laurels award Aviation Week, 1991. Fellow ASME, AIAA (assoc.; Nat. Engr. of Yr. award 1991); mem. Soc. Automotive Engrs. (Cliff Garrett Turbomachinery Engring. award 1994). Achievements include design of the RL10 rocket chamber, the turbine section of the J58, F119 engine; management of the overall structural engineering effort of the J52, TF30, F100 rockets and preliminary design Nat. Acads., Air Force & Dept. Def. Aerospace Propulsion Commn.; patents in field. Home: 8325 Nashua Dr Palm Beach Gardens FL 33418 E-mail: fcgillette@yahoo.com.

GILLETTE, FRANKIE JACOBS, retired savings and loan association executive, federal agency administrator, social worker; b. Norfolk, Va., Apr. 1, 1925; d. Frank Walter and Natalie (Taylor) Jacobs; m. Maxwell Claude Gillette, June 19, 1976. BS, Hampton U., 1946; MSW, Howard U., 1948. Lic. clin. social worker; cert. jr. coll. tchr., life. Youth dir. YWCA, Passaic, N.J., 1948-50; dir. program Ada S. McKinley Community Ctr., Chgo., 1950-53; program dir. Sophie Wright Settlement, Detroit, 1953-64; dir. Concerted Services Project, Pittsburg, Calif., 1964-66, Job Corps Staff Devel., U. Calif., Berkeley, 1966-69; spl. program coordinator U.S. Community Services Adminstrn., San Francisco, 1969-83; pres. G & G Enterprises, San Francisco, 1985—. Chmn. bd. dirs. Time Savs. and Loan Assn., San Francisco, 1986-87. Commr. San Francisco Human Rights Commn., 1988-93; bd. dirs. Urban Econ. Devel. Corp., 1980-93, San Francisco Conv. and Visitors Bur.; trustee Fine Arts Mus. of San Francisco, 1993—; chmn. San Francisco-Abidjan Sister City Com., 1990—; founding bd. dirs. Mus. African Diaspora, 2002—. Mem. Nat. Assn. Negro Bus. and Profl. Women's Clubs (pres. 1983-87), The Links, Inc., Delta Sigma Theta, Inc. Office: G & G Enterprises 85 Cleary Ct Apt 4 San Francisco CA 94109-6518

GILLETTE, MURIEL DELPHINE, nurse; b. Pasadena, Calif., Nov. 10, 1945; d. Edwin and Jean Helen (Fremont) Gillette; m. Larry Houston Potter, Dec. 31, 1971 (dec. 1979); children: Melissa Darlene Genevieve Potter Stephens, Bryan Scott; m. Robert George Baumann Jr., Aug. 18, 1980 (annulled 2000); children: Robert George III; m. Michael Ray Alexander, Sept. 9, 2001. Student, Western Coll. for Women, Oxford, Ohio, 1963-65; BSN, UCLA, 1968; M of Nursing, Oreg. Health Scis. U., 1991. Sch. nurse, health tchr. Hawthorne Intermediate Sch., Calif., 1969-70; nurse St. John's Hosp., Santa Monica, Calif., 1969-71; camp nurse L.A. Girl Scout Coun., 1969-71; nurse UCLA Med. Ctr., 1967-70; ICU/CCU/pediatrics nurse Mercy Med. Ctr., Roseburg, Oreg., 1971-79; nurse Umpqua Valley Community Hosp., Myrtle Creek, Oreg., 1981-91; camp nurse, health coord. Western Rivers Girl Scout Coun., Roseburg, 1984-90; health edn. dir. City of Myrtle Creek, 1986-91; nurse practitioner

Umpgua Nat. Forest, Roseburg and Glide, Oreg., 1991-93; camp nurse, health coord. Oreg. Trail Boy Scout Coun., Roseburg, 1981-91, Western Rivers Girl Scout Coun., Roseburg, 1984-90; cmty. health cons. Roseburg, 1984-98; home health nurse, 1995-98; pub. health nurse State of Alaska Epidemiology, Anchorage, 1998—, Dept. Corrections, Alaska Psychiat. Hosp. Musician quartet, orch., soloist; artist in oils; poet. Bd. dirs. River 'N Dell Day Care Ctr., Myrtle Creek, 1983-85; trustee Augusta Bixler Farms, Inc., Stockton, Calif., 1976—; mem. Douglas County Cancer Screening Com.; vol. ARC, 1982-. Capt. USAF, 1970-89. Umpqua Valley Hosp. Aux. scholar, 1989; L.A. Watercolor Soc. traveling art collection award, 1963. Mem. DAR, UCLA Alumni Assn., Umpqua Valley Hosp. Aux., Oreg. Health Sci. U. Alumni Assn., OES, Delta Zeta. Republican. Presbyterian. Avocations: painting, tennis, music, skiing, raising arabian horses. Home: PO Box 521171 Big Lake AK 99652-1171 Personal E-mail: alex7@mtaonline.net.

GILLETTE, P. ROGER, physicist, systems engineer; b. Mt. Vernon, Iowa, May 12, 1917; s. Clinton Edgar and Celia (Rogers) G.; m. Bettelaine Dunbar, Apr. 26, 1947 (dec. Mar. 1986); children: Kenneth Lee, Sandra Jo. BA in Physics, Cornell Coll., 1937; BS in Engring. Physics, U. Ill., 1938, MS in Physics, 1939, PhD in Physics, 1942. Staff mem. Radiation Lab, MIT, Cambridge, Mass., 1942-45; rsch. engr. Sperry Gyroscope Co., Great Neck, NY, 1945-48; physicist Hanford Works Gen. Electric Co., Richland, Wash., 1948-50; sr. rsch. physicist SRI Internat., Menlo Park, Calif., 1950-92, ret. Co-author: Pulse Generators, 1948. Bd. dir. West Bay Opera Assn., Palo Alto, Calif., 1959—64, 1977—79, Inst. Continued Learning Willamette U., Salem, Oreg., 1996—98, 2004—05. Mem. AAAS, IEEE (sr. life), Am. Phys. Soc. (life), Am. Acad. Religion, Inst. on Religion in an Age of Sci., Sigma Xi, Phi Beta Kappa, Tau Beta Pi, Phi Kappa Phi. Achievements include development of pulse transformer theory, system design concepts for command, control, communications and intelligence systems, electronic combat systems, and air combat training systems and of theology, religion and ethics for a scientific age. Home: 2385 Crestview Dr S, Salem OR 97302-5373

GILLETTE, PATRICIA K., lawyer; b. LA, Aug. 7, 1951; AB, Occidental Coll., 1973; JD cum laude, U. San Francisco, 1976. Bar: Calif., Am. Bar Assoc. In-house counsel Bank of Am.; atty. private practice; ptnr. Heller Ehrman LLP, San Francisco, 1990—. Co-chmn. labor and employment practice group Heller Ehman LLP, co-chmn. gender diversity com., 2006—. Office: Heller Ehrman LLP 333 Bush St San Francisco CA 94104-2806 Office Phone: 415-772-6456. Business E-Mail: pgillette@hewm.com.

GILLETTE, PAUL CRAWFORD, pediatric cardiologist; b. Winston-Salem, NC, Dec. 1, 1942; s. Crawford Paul and Eileen Marie (O'Rourke) G.; m. Vicki Lynn Zeigler, 1992; 2 children. BA in Chemistry, U.N.C., 1965; MD, Med. Coll. S.C., 1969. Intern, then resident in pediatrics Baylor U. Coll. Medicine, Houston, 1969-71, fellow in pediatric cardiology and cell biophysics, 1971-74, mem. faculty, 1974-84, assoc. prof. exptl. medicine, 1977-84, prof. pediatrics, 1980-84, Med. U. S.C., Charleston, 1984-96, chmn. promotions com., dept. pediatrics, 1989-96; dir. S.C. Children's Heart Ctr., Charleston, 1984-96; med. dir. Cook Children's Cardiology, 1996—, Cook Childrens Cardiac Ctr., Fort Worth, Tex., 1996—. Dir. electrophysiology and electrocardiography Tex. Children's Hosp.; co-dir. Palmetto Heart Inst., 1988-96; mem. tng. grant manpower rev. com. Nat. Heart, Lung and Blood Inst., 1989-93, chmn., 1992-93. Co-author: A Guide to Pediatric Cardiac Dysrhythmias, 1980, Pediatric Cardiac Dysrhythmias, 1981, A Practical Guide to Cardiac Pacing, 1986, Pediatric Electrophysiology, Arrythmia and Pacing, 1990, Pediatric Cardiac Pacing, 1995, Clinical Pediatric Arrythmias, 1999, Cardiac Arrhythmias after Surgery for Congential Heart Disease, 2001; editl. bd. Circulation, Am. Heart Jour., Pediatric Cardiology, Jour. Am. Coll. Cardiology; contbr. articles to profl. jours. Mem. sports com., treas. St. Thomas More Sch., Houston; bd. dirs. Toler's Cove Homeowners Assn. Charleston, 1989-94, Ronald McDonald House of Ft. Worth, 2001—. Nat. Heart, Lung and Blood Inst. grantee; named Disting. Alumni, Medical Univ. S.C., 1991; recipient Rsch. award So. Med. Assn., 1994. Fellow Am. Acad. Pediatrics (exec. com. cardiology sect. 1979, ednl. grantee 1970, Young Investigator award 1975, trustee 1987—, chmn. rsch. rev. com. 1987-88 S.C. chpt.), Am. Coll. Cardiology (trustee 1984-90, learning ctr. com. 1984-88, strategic planning com. 1986-90, long range planning com. 1987-88, chmn. pacemaker com. 1990-95, mem. rsch. com. 1990—); mem. Soc. Pediatric Rsch., So. Soc. Pediatric Rsch., Southeastern Pediatric Cardiology Soc. (pres. 1987), N.Am. Soc. Pacing and Electrophysiology (pres. 1986-87, trustee 1987-90, program com. 1987, Pioneer in Cardiac Pacing and Electrophysiology award 1998, Healthcare Hero 2004, Tex. Super Doc 2004), Am. Heart Assn. (chmn. rsch. peer rev. com. S.C. chpt. 1989, chmn. rsch. com. 1990, pres.-elect Ft. Worth chpt. 1998-98, pres. 1998-99), Tex. Pediatric Soc., Harris County Med. Soc., Houston Cardiology Soc., North Tex. Electrophynology Soc., Houston Pediatric Soc., S.C. Med. Soc., Charleston County Med. Soc., Tarrant County Med. Soc. (bd. dirs. 2001—), S.C. Heart Assn. (rschr. of the yr. 1991), Alpha Omega Alpha, Phi Chi. Republican. Roman Catholic. Office: Cook Childrens Cardiac Ctr 901 7th Ave Ste 301 Fort Worth TX 76104-2724 Office Phone: 682-885-7940. E-mail: pgillette@cookchildrens.org.

GILLETTE, ROBERT J., aerospace transportation executive; BS in Fin., Ind. U. With GE Plastics; v.p., gen. mgr. AlliedSignal Engring. Plastics; v.p. strategic growth, v.p., gen. mgr. Asia Worldwide aftermarket Garrett Engine Boosting Sys., pres., 2000—01; pres., CEO Honeywell Transp. Systems Honeywell Internat. Inc., Torrance, Calif., 2001—04, pres., CEO, Honeywell Aerospace Phoenix, 2005—. Office: Honeywell Aerospace 1944 E Sky Harbor Cir N Phoenix AZ 85034*

GILLETTE, W. MICHAEL, state supreme court justice; b. Seattle, Dec. 29, 1941; s. Elton George and Hazel Irene (Hand) G.; children: Kevin, Saima. AB cum laude in German, Polit. Sci., Whitman Coll., 1963; LLB, Harvard U., 1966. Bar: Oreg. 1966, U.S. Dist. Ct. Oreg. 1966, U.S. Ct. Appeals (9th cir.) 1966, Samoa 1969, U.S. Supreme Ct. 1970, U.S. Dist. Ct. Vt. 1973. Assoc. Rives & Rogers, Portland, Oreg., 1966-67; dep. dist. atty. Multnomah County, Portland, 1967-69; asst. atty. gen. Govt. of Am. Samoa, 1969-71, State of Oreg., Salem, 1971-77; judge Oreg. Ct. Appeals, Salem, 1977-86; justice Oreg. Supreme Ct., Salem, 1986—. Instructor constitutional and criminal law Portland State U., 1971—74; mem. bd. Oreg. Law-Related Education Project, 1980—88; mem. advisory com. Scholars for Constitution Project, 1984; prof. administrative, constitutional, and consumer law Nat. Jud. Coll. Bd. trustees Oreg. Museum of Science and Industry, 1977—80. Avocation: basketball. Office: Oreg Supreme Ct Supreme Ct Bldg 1163 State St Salem OR 97310-1331 Office Phone: 503-986-5705.*

GILLETTE, WILLIAM, historian, educator; b. Bridgeport, Conn., Mar. 2, 1933; s. Samuel William and Lillian (Abeson) G.; m. Elisabeth L. Janes, May 23, 1971; children: Scott Douglas, Wendy Elisabeth. BS, Georgetown U., 1955; MA, Columbia U., 1956, postgrad., 1958-59; PhD, Princeton U., 1963. Instr. Ohio State U., 1962-64; acting asst. prof. U. Conn., Storrs, 1965-66; asst. prof. Bklyn. Coll. CUNY, 1966-67; asso. prof. Rutgers U., 1967-81, prof., 1981—. Fulbright prof. U. Salzburg (Austria), 1982-83, Japan Women's U. and Tsuda Coll., 1997-98, Lomonosov Moscow State U., 1998. Author: The Right to Vote: Politics and the Passage of the Fifteenth Amendment, 1969, Retreat From Reconstruction, 1869-1879, 1979, Jersey Blue: Civil War Politics in New Jersey, 1995. With AUS, 1956—58. Social Sci. Rsch. Coun. faculty fellow, 1970; recipient Landry award La. State U. Press, 1979, Chastain award So. Polit. Sci. Assn., 1980, award of merit Am. Assn. for State and Local History, 1996, McCormick award N.J. Hist. Commn., 1997; grantee Am. Philos. Soc., N.J. Hist. Commn. Mem. AAUP, N.J. Hist. Soc., Advs. for N.J. History. Democrat. Unitarian Universalist. Home: 43 South Dr East Brunswick NJ 08816-1134 Office: Rutgers U Dept History New Brunswick NJ 08901-1108 Office Phone: 732-932-6779.

GILLEY, JENNIFER R., librarian; BA, Hiram Coll., Ohio, 1994; MA, Ohio State U., 1995; MSLIS, U. Ill., Urbana-Champaign, 1998. Asst. libr. Penn State New Kensington U. Librs., 1998—. Recipient New Libr. Honors award, Pa. Libr. Assn., 2000. Mem.: ALA, Assn. Coll. & Rsch. Librs. (Women's Studies sect., Women's Studies rsch. com., WSS Significant Achievement award 2007). Office: Penn State New Kensington 3550 7th St Rd 0001 Faculty & Admin Bldg New Kensington PA 15068 Office Phone: 724-334-6076. E-mail: jrg15@psu.edu.

GILLEY, MICKEY LEROY, musician; b. Natchez, Miss., Mar. 9, 1936; s. Arthur Philmore and Irene Frances (Lewis) G.; m. Vivian McDonald, Dec. 27, 1962; 1 son, Gregory Brent. Prtnr. Gilley's Club, Pasadena, Tex., 1971-89; owner Gilley's Theatre, Branson, Mo., 1990—; pres., owner Gilley's Tex. Cafe, 1992—, owner Myrtle Beach, SC, 1995—2000, Gilley's Rest., Pasadena, Tex., 2002—05. Appeared in night clubs in, Houston, New Orleans, Biloxi, Miss., Mobile, Ala., Lake Charles, La., 1957-59; appeared at, Nesadel Club, Houston, 1960-70. Named Most Promising Male Artist, Acad. Country Music 1974, Most Promising Male Artist, Record World 1974, Top New Country Singles Artist, Billboard 1974, Top New Male Vocalist in Album Category, Record World 1975, Most Promising Male Artist, Music City News 1976, Best Male Vocalist, Entertainer of Year, Acad. Country Music 1976; recipient Star in Walk of Fame on Hollywood Blvd., 1984, over 17 #1 records, Grammy award for Orange Blossom Special Nat. Acad. Rec. Arts and Scis., 1981. Mem. Country Music Assn., Acad. Country Music, AFTRA, Musicians Local 65. Clubs: Moose. Office: 3737 Lily St Pasadena TX 77505-2927 E-mail: mickey@gilleys.com.

GILLHAM, JOHN KINSEY, chemical engineering professor; b. London, Aug. 7, 1930; came to U.S., 1959, naturalized, 1968; s. Gerald Albert and Doris (Kinsey) G.; m. Helen Alyce Currier, Sept. 18, 1961; children: Matthew, Jane, Martha. BA, Cambridge U., 1953, MA, 1957; PhD in Chemistry, McGill U., Montreal, 1959. Research chemist Am. Cynamid Co., Stamford, Conn., 1958-65; vis. rsch. chemist Princeton (NJ) U., 1964-65, mem. faculty, 1965—, prof. chem. engring., 1975-98, prof. emeritus, 1998—. Cons. to chem. and polymer industries; vis. fellow Japan Soc. Promotion Sci., 1983; vis. scholar Chinese Acad. Scis., 1984; sci. exch. visitor USSR Acad. Scis./NAS, 1986. Author papers in field. Recipient 1st prize for best tech. paper Roon Found. Awards Competition of Fedn. Socs. for Coatings Techs., 1983, 89, Outstanding Rev. Paper award Electronics Components Conf. of IEEE, 1985. Fellow Soc. Plastics Engrs. (Internat. Rsch. award 1988, Best Paper award 1991, Founders award Polymer Analysis Divsn., 2005); mem. Am. Chem. Soc. (Borden award 1978, Doolittle award 1980, Roy W. Tess award 1996, fellow divsn. Polymeric Materials: Sci. and Engring. 2000), N.Am. Thermal Analysis Soc. (Mettler award 1978, Spl. Recognition award 2005). Home: 11 Vernon Cir Princeton NJ 08540-5415 Office: Princeton U Dept Chem Engring Princeton NJ 08544-0001 Office Phone: 609-258-1830. Personal E-mail: jkgillham@yahoo.com.

GILLHAM, NICHOLAS WRIGHT, geneticist, educator; b. NYC, May 14, 1932; s. Robert Marty and Elizabeth (Enright) G.; m. Carol Lenore Collins, June 2, 1956. BA, Harvard, 1954, MA, 1955, PhD (USPHS fellow), 1962. From instr. to asst. prof. Harvard U., 1963-68; assoc. prof. zoology Duke U., 1968-72, prof., 1973-82, James B. Duke prof. biology, 1982—2002, chmn. dept. zoology, 1986—89, profl. emeritus, 2002—. Mem. biochemistry, molecular genetics and cell biology interdisciplinary cluster Pres.'s Biomed. Rsch. Panel, 1975; mem. study sect. in genetics NIH, 1976-80; mem. N.C. Gov.'s Bd. Sci. and Tech., N.C. Gov.'s Task Force on Sci. and Tech., chmn., bd. dirs. Am. Type Culture Collection, 1993-96. Author: (with R. Krueger and J. Coggin) Introduction to Microbiology, 1973, Organelle Heredity, 1978, Organelle Genes and Genomes, 1994, A Life Sir Francis Galton: From African Exploration to the Birth of Eugenics, 2001; mem. editl. bd. Genetics, 1975-78, Jour. Cell Biology, 1977-79, Intl. Review of Cytology, 1987-97; sr. editor Plasmid, 1977-86. Served to 1st lt. Med. Service Corps USAF, 1955-58. Postdoctoral fellow USPHS, 1962-63 Spl. fellow, 1967-68; Rsch. Career Devel. grant USPHS, 1972-77; Guggenheim fellow, 1984-85. Mem. Genetics Soc. Am., Sigma Xi. Office: Duke Univ Dept Biology PO Box 90338 Durham NC 27708-1000 Business E-Mail: gillham@duke.edu.

GILLIAM, SAM, artist; b. Tupelo, Miss., Nov. 30, 1933; s. Sam and Estery C. (Cousins) G.; children: Stephanie, Melissa, Leah. BA, U. Louisville, 1955, MA, 1961, LHD (hon.), 1980; ArtsD (hon.), Northwestern U., 1990; numerous DFA (hon.). Instr. art Pub. Sch. Sys., Washington, 1958—67; instr. painting Corcoran Sch. Art, Washington, 1964—67, Md. Inst. Art, Baltimore, 1967—82; prof. painting U. Md., 1982—85, Carnegie Mellon U., Pitts., 1985—89. Exhibitions include "Arts on Line: Art Pub. Transit Spaces" Hayden Gallery, MIT, Cambridge, Mass., 1980, "Am. Abstraction Now" Va. Mus. Fine Arts, 1982, "Painting in South" Va. Mus. Fine Art, 1984, "Experienced Eye" Owensboro Mus. Fine Art, Ky. 1988, African Am. Art from Collection, Phila. Mus. Art, 1990, "Golden Windows Inside Gold" an installation Whitney Mus. Am. Art, Phillip Morris, N.Y.C., 1993-1995, Baumgartner Galleries, Washington, 1994, 44th Biennian Exhbn. Contemporary Am. Painting, Corcoran Gallery Art, Washington, 1995; numerous one-man shows of paintings, include Univ. Gallery, U. Mass., Amherst, 1978, Dart Gallery, Chgo., 1979, Florence Dugl Gallery, N.Y.C., 1979, Nina Freudenheim Gallery, Buffalo, 1979, Hamilton Gallery of Contemporary Art, N.Y.C., 1979, U. Wis., Stevens Point, 1980, Hamilton Gallery Contemporary Art, 1981, Galerie Darthea Speyer, Paris, France, 1983, Alice Simsar Gallery, Ann Arbor, Mich., 1986, Davis/McClain Gallery, Houston, 1986, G H Dalsheimer Gallery, Baltimore, 1986, Robert Kidd Gallery, Birmingham, Mich., 1987, Carl Solway Gallery, Cin., 1987, Klein Gallery, Chgo., 1987, 88, Iannetti-Lanzone Gallery, San Francisco, 1988, Middendorf Gallery, Washington, 1989, Frederick Gallery, N.Y.C., 1991, Gallery Simmone Stern, New Orleans, 1991, Smith Andersen Gallery, Palo Alto, Calif., 1992, Whitney Mus., N.Y.C., 1993—; numerous group shows including Galerie Darthea Speyer, Paris, 1978, Dade County Library, Miami, Fla., 1978, Grey Gallery, N.Y.C., 1979, Hamilton Gallery of Contemporary Art, N.Y.C., 1979, Alternative Mus., Washington, 1980, SUNY, 1980, N.J. State Mus., Trenton, 1980, "Afro-Am. Abstraction" L.A. Municipal Art Gallery, 1982, "10+10+10" Corcoran Gallery Art, Washington, 1982, "Abstraction/Abstraction" Carnegie Mellon U. Art Gallery, Pitts., 1986, "Contemporary Visual Expressions" Anacostia Mus. Smithsonian Inst., Washington, 1987, "Looking South: Different Dixie" Birmingham Mus. Art, Ala., 1988; represented in numerous permanent collections including, Nat. Gallery Art, Washington, Mus. Modern Art, N.Y.C., Rockefeller Collection, N.Y.C., Corcoran Gallery Art, Washington, Howard U., Washington, Phillips Collection, Washington, Gallery Modern Art, Washington, Mus. African Art, Washington, IBM Co., Washington, Carnegie Inst., Pitts., Balt. Mus. Art, Art Inst., Chgo., Hirschhorn Mus. and Sculpture Gardern, Smithsonian Inst., Met. Mus. Art, Walker Art Ctr., Tate Gallery, London, Musée d'art Moderne de la Ville de Paris, France, Beymans Mus., Rotterdam, Holland, and others; commissions include "Circles, Circuits, Boxes" Fed. Sys. Commn., Chantilly, Va. 1990, "Windows Go Orange" (ee cummings), Am. Craft Mus., 1991, "Washington Coulours" Kaempfer Corp., Washington, 1991, "Riders Blue" Archer St. Sta., Met. Transit Authority, Jamica, N.Y.C., 1991, Norfolk, USAA Ins. Co., MARO Bldg. Norfolk, Va., 1992; pub. works include Phillips Collection, Nat. Collection Fine Arts, Howard U., Mus. Modern Art, Met. Mus. Art, Princeton U., Rutgers U., Madison Art Ctr. Bd. dir. Washington Project Arts, 1980—85; art com., bd. dir. Coll. Art Assn., 1985—88; pub. art work com., adv. bd. Anacostia Cmty. Orgn., 1987—88. Recipient Norman W. Harris Prize Award, Art Inst. Chgo., 1969, Disting. Alumnus Award, U. Louisville, 1975, Pres. Award, Md. Coll. Art & Design, 1987, Order Merit Award, U. Louisville Alumni Assn., 1987; grantee, Nat. Endowment Arts, 1967, 1989. Fellow: Washington Gallery Modern Art, 1968, Guggenheim, 1971. Office: c/o Workshop Inc 3145 Newark St NW Washington DC 20008

GILLIAM, TERRY VANCE, film director, actor, writer, illustrator; b. Mpls., Nov. 22, 1940; s. James Hall and Beatrice (Vance) G.; m. Margaret Weston, 1973; children: Amy Rainbow, Holly du Bois, Harry Thunder. BA, Occidental Coll., 1962, DFA (hon.), 1988; doctorate (hon.), Royal Coll. Art, London, 1987; DFA (hon.), Occidental Coll., 2004; D (hon.), Wimbledon Sch. of Art. Assoc. editor HELP! mag., 1962-64; free-lance illustrator, 1964-65; advt. copywriter, art dir., 1966-67; TV resident cartoonist We Have Ways of Making You Laugh, 1968; animator Do Not Adjust Your Set, 1968-69, The Marty Feldman Comedy Machine, 1971-72; with Monty Python's Flying Circus, 1969-76. Animator (film) And Now For Something Completely Different; illustrator (book) The Cocktail People, 1966; co-dir., actor (film) Monty Python and the Holy Grail, 1974, The Do It Yourself Animation Film, 1974, The Miracle of Flight, 1974; dir. (film) Jabberwocky, 1976; designer, actor, animator (film) Monty Python's Life of Brian, 1978; co-writer, producer, dir. (film) Time Bandits, 1980; actor, dir. (film) Monty Python Live at the Hollywood Bowl, 1982; dir., actor, animator, co-writer (film) Monty Python's Meaning of Life, 1983; dir., writer (film) Brazil, 1985; dir., co-writer (film) The Adventures of Baron Munchausen, 1988; dir. (film) The Fisher King, 1991, Twelve Monkeys, 1995; co-writer, dir. Fear and Loathing in Las Vegas, 1998, Lost in La Mancha, 2002, The Brothers Grimm, 2005, Tideland, 2005; author: Gilliam on Gilliam, 1999, Dark Knights and Holy Fools, 19989 co-author: The Brand New Monty Python Book, 1973, Monty Python and the Holy Grail, 1977, Monty Python Life of Brian, 1979 Monty Python's Big Red Book, Monty Python's Papperbok, 1977, Monty Python's Scrapbook, 1979, Animations of Mortality, 1979, Time Bandits, 1981, Monty Python's The Meaning of Life, 1983, The Adventures of Baron Munchausen, 1989, Not the Screenplay of Fear and Loathing in Las Vegas, 1998; presenter TV series The Last Machine, 1995; exec. prodr. (CD ROM) Monty Python's Complete Waste of Time, 1995.

GILLIAND, TOM, chef, Restaurant Owner; Grad., U. Nebr., U. Tex., Austin; studied, Universidad Nat. Autónoma de Mex., Mex. City, Am. Inst. Fgn. Trade, Glendale, Ariz. Co-founder San Angel Inn, Houston, Fonda San Miguel, Austin, 1975—. Co-author: Fonda San Miguel: Thirty Years of Food and Art, 2006 (Cookbook award for Design, Internat. Assn. Culinary Professionals, 2006). Mem.: Internat. Assn. Culinary Professionals. Office: Fonda San Miguel Restaurant 2330 W N Loop Blvd Austin TX 78756 Office Phone: 512-459-4121.*

GILLIAR, BEATE C., educator; b. Karlsruhe, Germany, Oct. 17, 1959; arrived in US, 1981; d. Arno and Erna Gilliar. BA in English, U. Ariz., Tucson, 1984, MA in English, 1986, MA in German, 1988, PhD in English, 1993. Rsch. asst. U. Ariz., 1984—90, tchg. asst., 1991—92. Mem.: Nat. Coun. Tchrs. English, Nat. Assn. Poetry Therapy. Avocations: travel, knitting, writing, dance.

GILLIBRAND, KIRSTEN RUTNICK, congresswoman, lawyer; b. Albany, NY, Dec. 9, 1966; m. Jonathan Gillibrand; 1 child, Theodore. AB magna cum laude, Dartmouth Coll., 1988; JD, UCLA, 1991. Bar: NY 1992, DC 1993, US Dist. Ct. So. & Ea. Dist. NY. Law clk. to Hon. Roger J. Miner US Ct. Appeals (2nd Cir.), 1992—93; sr. assoc. Davis, Polk & Wardwell; spl. counsel to sec. US Dept. Housing & Urban Devel., Washington, 2000—01; ptnr., comml. litigation practice Boies, Schiller & Flexner LLP, Albany, NY, 2001—07; mem. US Congress from 20th NY Dist., 2007—, mem. agr. com., armed services com., 2007—. Mem. adv. bd. Brennan Ctr. for Justice; chmn. Women's Leadership Forum Network; bd. mem. Eleanor Roosevelt Legacy Com., Commn. Greenway Heritage Conservancy for Hudson River Valley. Recipient Am. Jurisprudence Book award. Mem.: ABA, Assn. Bar City of NY (chmn. com. on govt. ethics 1998—99, 2000—), Women's Bar Assn., Blue Dog Coalition. Democrat. Roman Catholic. Office: US House Reps 120 Cannon House Office Bldg Washington DC 20515 also: 333 Glen St Ste 302 Glens Falls NY 12801 Office Phone: 202-225-5614, 518-743-0964. Office Fax: 202-225-1168, 518-743-1391.*

GILLICE, SONDRA JUPIN, sales and marketing executive; b. Urbana, Ill. d. Earl Cranston and Laura Lorraine (Rose) Jupin; m. Gardner Russell Brown, Jan. 12, 1980; 1 child, Thomas Alan Gillice. BS, Lindenwood Coll., 1968; MBA, Loyola Coll., 1983. Pers. officer N.Y. Citibank, 1968-70, 1st Nat. Bank Chgo., 1970-72; mgr. human resources Potomac Electric Power Co., Washington, 1973-81; dir. pers. U.S. Synthetic Fuels Corp., Washington, 1981-86; v.p. human resources Guest Svcs., Inc., 1987-90, v.p. sales and mktg., 1990-93; sr. v.p. govt. rels. Drake Beam Morin, Inc., 1994-98; pres. RusSon, Inc., 1998—. Bd. govs. Nat. Coal Coun., exec. com. Bd. dirs. Nat. Womens Econ. Alliance, Life With Cancer; dir. Black Bear Energy Corp., Capital Speakers Club; treas. Arts for the Aging. Mem. AAUW (pres. Falls Church br.), Edison Electric Inst. (chair tng. and mgmt. devel. com.), Soroptimists (pres. Washington chpt. 1979-80), DAR, Army Navy Country Club, Army Navy Club, Soc. Magna Charta Dames, Edgartown Yacht Club, Georgetown Club.

GILLICK, PATRICK, b. Chico, Calif., Aug. 22, 1937; s. Larry G.; m. Doris Sander, Nov. 1968; 1 child, Kimberly BS, U. So. Calif., 1958. Minor league baseball player, 1958-63; asst. farm dir., regional scout Houston Astros, coordinator, dir. scouting, 1963-73; coordinator player devel. and scouting N.Y. Yankees, 1974-76; v.p. player personnel Toronto Blue Jays, 1976-77, v.p. baseball ops., 1977-84, exec. v.p. baseball, 1984-95; gen. mgr. Baltimore Orioles, 1995—98, Seattle Mariners, 2000—03, Philadelphia Phillies, 2005—. Consul. Seattle Mariners, 2003—05. Named Baseball Exec. of Yr., UPI, 1985; Gen. Mgr. World Series Champions, 1992, 1993. Office: Philadelphia Phillies Citizens Bank Park One Citizens Bank Way Philadelphia PA 19148-5249

GILLIES, DONALD RICHARD, marketing and advertising consultant, educator; b. Sioux Falls, SD, Jan. 14, 1939; s. Donald Franklin and Gladys O. (Gullickson) G.; m. Twyla Elaine Bloomquist, Apr. 7, 1962; children: Dawn, Trent, Tara. BA in Journalism/Advt., U. Minn., 1961. Writer, producer Sta. WCCO-TV, Mpls., 1954-60; mgmt. supr., sr. v.p., bd. dirs. Campbell-Mithun Advt., Mpls., 1960-86; pres., chief oper. officer Colle & McVoy Inc., Mpls., 1987-89; prin. Gillies group inc. (Gg), Minnetonka, Minn., 1989—. Adj. prof. U. St. Thomas, 1990-97, asst. prof., 2001—07. Bd. dirs. Guthrie Theater, Mpls., 1979-84; ch. coun. Mt. Olivet Ch., Mpls., 1988-94; Midwest adv. rev. bd. BBB, 1996—. Mem. Am. Assn. Advt. Agencies (regional gov.), Minn. Advt. Fedn. (bd. dirs. 1973-76). Lutheran. Home and Office: Gillies group inc (Gg) 5942 Fairwood Ln Minnetonka MN 55345-6533 Personal E-mail: dongillies@prodigy.net.

GILLIG, PAULETTE MARIE, psychiatry educator, researcher; b. Boston, Mar. 24, 1949; d. Franklin Joseph and Marie Robichaud (Collins) G.; m. Douglas K. Fairobent, June 13, 1981. BA cum laude hons. psychology, SUNY, Buffalo; MA, PhD, Ohio State U., Columbus, 1973; MD, Med. Coll. Ohio, 1977. Diplomate Am. Bd. Psychiatry and Neurology, Am. Bd. Geriat. Psychiatry. Resident in neurology Med. Coll. Ohio, 1978-79, U. Mich., Ann Arbor, 1979-81; resident in psychiatry Ohio State U., Columbus, 1981-83; med. dir. North Ctrl. Mental Health Ctr., Columbus, 1985; clin. asst. prof. Ohio State U., Columbus, 1983-85; asst. prof. U. Cin., 1985-90; assoc. prof. Wright State U., Dayton, 1990-2000, prof. psychiatry, 2000—; chief clin. officer Mental Health Drug and Alcohol Svcs. Bd., Champaign and Logan Cos., 1995—2005. Prof. rural psychiatry Ohio Dept. Mental Health, 1997—; mem. strategic planning coun. Wright State U., Dayton, 1998-2001. Sect. editor Psychiatry, 2004—07; editor: Clinical Guide to the Treatment of the Homeless Mentally Ill Person, 2006; contbr. chapters to books, articles to profl. jours. Founding Bd. Domestic Abuse and Violence Inst. of Dayton, 2000—; patron Cin. Ballet Co., Xavier U., Humane Soc. U.S., Dayton Opera Co., Cin. Symphony Orch., Sorg Opera Co., Middletown, Ohio,Lebanon Police Children's Fund, Balletech Ohio, Warren County Animal Shelter, Nat. Wildlife Fedn.; chair Domestic Violence Rsch. Group, 1999-2002. Named one of Top Psychiatrists, Consumers Rsch., 2007; recipient Clin. Neuroscis. award, Med. Coll. Ohio, Best Dr. in Am., Bestdoctors.com, 2005—06; grantee Pruitt Found., 1992, Ohio Dept. Mental Health, 1995—. Fellow Am. Psychiat. Assn. (disting.; com. on poverty, homelessness, and psychiatric disorders 1999-2006, Nancy Roeske Med. Student Tchg. award 2007); mem. Am. Assn. Women Psychiatrists, Am. Assn. Cmty. Psychiatrists (Midwestern rep. 2002—, chair tng. com., Moffic award 1999), Ohio Psychiat. Assn. (chmn. com. on minorities 1999-2002, Pres.'s award 2001), WHO (dir. internat. classification diseases), Nat. Wildlife Fedn. (cert.), Univ. Club, Nat. Bd. Psychiatry and Neurology (bd. examiner 2005—), Alpha Omega Alpha. Avocations: classical piano, opera, companion animals, ballet, horticulture. Office: Wright State U Dept Psychiatry PO Box 927 Dayton OH 45401-0927 E-mail: paulette.gillig@wright.edu.

GILLIGAN, CAROL, psychologist, writer; b. NYC, Nov. 28, 1936; d. William Edward and Mabel (Caminez) Friedman; m. James Frederick Gilligan, June 12, 1960; children: Jonathan Mark, Timothy David, Christopher James. AB, Swarthmore Coll., 1958, degree (hon.), 1985; AM, Radcliffe Coll., 1961; PhD, Harvard U., 1964; degree (hon.), Regis Coll., 1983, Haverford Coll., 1987, Fitchburg State Coll., 1989, Wesleyan U., 1992, Smith Coll., 1999, John Jay Coll., 2006, U. Haifa, 2006. Instr. U. Chgo., 1965—66; lectr. Harvard U., Cambridge, Mass., 1967-69, rsch. asst., 1969-70, asst. prof., 1970-78, assoc. prof., 1978-86, prof., 1986—97, Patricia Alberg Graham prof. gender studies, 1997—2001; Laurie chair in Women's Studies Rutgers U., New Brunswick, NJ, 1986-87; univ. prof. NYU, NYC, 2001—. Founding mem. Harvard Project on Women's Psychology and the Devel. of Girls, 1987—2001; co-dir., The Company of Women and Girls, 1991—96; mem. coun. scholars Erikson Inst. Austen Riggs Ctr.; Pitt prof. U. Cambridge, 1992—93, vis. prof., 1993—94, fellow commoner Jesus Coll., 2004—. Author: In a Different Voice, 1982; author: (with Lyn M. Brown) Meeting at the Crossroads: Women's Psychology and Girls Development, 1992; author: (with J. Taylor and A. Sullivan) Between Voice and Silence: Women and Girls, Race and Relationship, 1995; author: The Birth of Pleasure: a new map of love, 2002; editor (with J. Ward and J. Taylor): Mapping the Moral Domain: A Contribution of Women's Thinking to Psychological Theory and Education, 1988; composer (with N. Lyons and T. Hanmer): Making Connections: Relational Worlds of Adolescent Girls at Emma Willard School, 1990; editor (with A. Rogers and D. Tolman): Women, Girls, and Psychotherapy: Reframing Resistance, 1991, 2d edit., 2001. Bd. dir. Facing History and Ourselves. Sr. rsch. fellow Spencer Found., 1984—2001; Mellon Faculty fellow Bunting Inst.-Radcliffe Coll., 1982-83; recipient Grawemayer award U. Louisville, 1992, Heinz award, 1997, Medallion of the Univ., SUNY, Albany, 2006. Fellow: Brit. Acad. Vis. Profs.; mem.: APA, Assn. Women in Psychology, Nat. Acad. Edn. Democrat. Jewish. Avocations: music, piano, modern dance, theater. Office: NYU Sch Law 511 Vanderbilt Hall New York NY 10012 Office Phone: 212-998-6048. Business E-Mail: carol.gilligan@nyu.edu.

GILLIGAN, EDWARD P., diversified financial services company executive; Pres. corp. services American Express Co., NYC, 1996—2000, group pres., global corp. services, 2000—07, vice-chmn., 2007—. Mem. Am. Express Global Leadership Team, Am. Express Planning and Policy Com.; bd. dirs. Ketera Tech. Office: Am Express Co World Fin Ctr 200 Vesey St New York NY 10285*

GILLIGAN, SANDRA KAYE, private school director; b. Ft. Lewis, Wash., Mar. 22, 1946; d. Jack G. and O. Ruth (Mitchell) Wagoner; m. James J. Gilligan, June 3, 1972 (div. June 1998); 1 child, J. Shawn Gilligan. BS in Edn., Emporia State U., 1968, MS in Psychology, 1971; postgrad., Drake U., 1976, U. Mo., St. Louis, 1977-79. Tchr. Parklane Elem. Sch., Aurora, Colo., 1968-69, Bonner Springs (Kans.) Elem., 1970; stewardess Frontier Airlines, Denver, 1969; grad. teaching asst. Emporia (Kans.) State U., 1970-71; lead tchr. Western Valley Youth Ranch, Buckeye, Ariz., 1971-74; staff mem. program devel., lead tchr. The New Found., Phoenix, 1974; ednl. therapist Orchard Pl., Des Moines, 1974-76; ednl. cons. Spl. Sch. Dist. of St. Louis County, 1976-79; founding dir. The Churchill Ctr. and Sch. Learning Disabilities, St. Louis, 1978—. Instr. Webster Coll., Webster Groves, Mo., 1978-80; adj. prof. Maryville Coll., St. Louis, 1985; keynote spkr. Miss. Learning Disabilities Assn. Conv., 1991; site visitor blue ribbon schs. program U.S. Dept. Edn., 1992; bd. dirs. Ind. Schs. St. Louis; evaluation rev. com. ISACS, 1996—; presenter in field. Recipient Spirit Care & Counseling award, 2004, Deans Excellence in Ednl. Leadership award, U. Mo., 2006—07. Mem. Learning Disabilities Assn., Internat. Dyslexia Assn. (chpt. bd. dirs.), St. Louis Jr. League. Avocations: gardening, painting. Office: The Churchill Ctr and Sch Learning Disabilities 1035 Price School Ln Saint Louis MO 63124-1596 Office Phone: 314-997-4343. Business E-Mail: sgill@churchillstl.org.

GILLIGAN, THOMAS W., dean, finance educator; b. San Diego, Calif., Aug. 21, 1954; s. Thomas F. and Neva S. Gilligan; m. Christie L. Skinner; children: Leah S., Laura S., Patrick J. BA in econ., U. of Okla., 1979; PhD in Economics, Wash. U., St. Louis, 1984. Vice dean Marshall Sch. of Bus., U. of So. Calif., LA, 2004—06, dean, 2006—. Chair, dept. fin. and bus. econs. Marshall Sch. of Bus., U. of So. Calif., LA, 2000—03, prof. fin. and bus. econs.; asst. prof. econs. Divsn. of Humanities and Social Sciences, Calif. Inst. of Tech., Pasadena. Elder La Can. (Calif.) Presbyn. Ch., 2002—06. Sgt. USAF, 1972—76. Decorated Air medal (with cluster) USAF; fellow Nat. Fellow, Hoover Instn. on War and Peace, Stanford U., 1992. Mem.: Am. Econ. Assn. (assoc.). Avocation: golf. Home: 4355 Oakwood Ave La Canada CA 91011 Office: Marshall Sch of Bus Univ of Southern Calif Los Angeles CA 90089 Home Phone: 818-790-7850; Office Phone: 213-740-6422. Business E-Mail: gilligan@marshall.usc.edu.

GILLILAND, JOHN CAMPBELL, II, lawyer; b. Bellefonte, Pa., June 4, 1945; s. John Campbell and Miriam Ruth (Forsythe) G.; m. Karen Gardner, Nov. 2, 1997; children: Jennifer, John, David. BA. Pa. State U., 1967; JD, Georgetown U., Washington, DC, 1971. Bar: Pa. 1971, Ind. 1979, Ky. 1991, Ohio 1992. Ptnr. McQuaide, Blasko & Brown, Inc., State College, Pa., 1974-79, DeFur, Voran, Hanley, Radcliff & Reed, Muncie, Ind., 1979-90; prin. Gilliland & Assocs., Covington, Ky., 1991-2000; sr. counsel Locke Reynolds LLP, Indpls., 2000—01; prin. Gilliland Law Office, Indpls., 2001—02; ptnr. Gilliland Markette & Milligan LLP, Indpls., 2002—. Lectr. econs. dept. Ball State U., Muncie. Bd. dirs. United Way Delaware County, v.p., 1983—85; bd. dirs. Vis. Nurses Assn.; v.p. Muncie chpt. ARC, 1983—85; bd. govs. Friends of Bracken Libr.; bd. dirs. USO Ind., 2007—, pres., 2007—. Capt. US Army, 1971—72. Fellow, Rotary Found., Queens Coll., Belfast, Ireland, 1968—69. Mem. ABA, Ind. Bar Assn., Ky. Bar Assn., Ohio Bar Assn., Am. Health Lawyers Assn., Ind. Soc. Hosp. Attys. (chmn. 1989), Pa. Soc. Hosp. Attys. (pres. 1978-79), East Ctrl. Ind. Pers. Assn. (bd. dirs.). Republican. Unitarian. Home: 3446 Kenilworth Dr Indianapolis IN 46228 Office: 3905 Vincennes Rd Indianapolis IN 46268 Office Phone: 317-704-2400. Business E-Mail: jcg@gilliland.com.

GILLILAND, MICHAEL S. (SAM GILLILAND), travel company executive; m. Shannon Gilliland; 2 children. BS in Elec. Engring., U. Kans., 1985; MBA, U. Tex., Dallas. With Lockheed Missiles and Space, Austin, Tex.; sr. v.p., gen. mgr., Sabre Bus. Travel Solutions Sabre Holdings, Southlake, Tex., exec. v.p., chief mktg. officer, 2000—02, group pres., Airlines Solutions bus., 2001—02, sr. v.p., gen. mgr., product mktg., pres., CEO, Travelocity, 2002—03, bd. dirs., pres., CEO, 2003—, chmn., 2004—. Office: Sabre Holdings 3150 Sabre Dr Southlake TX 76092*

GILLILAND, RICHARD, actor; b. Ft. Worth, Tex., Jan. 23, 1950; m. Jean Smart, June 7, 1987; 1 child, Connor. Actor: (films) Bug, 1975, Stay Hungry, 1976, The White Buffalo, 1977, Airplane II, 1982, Happy Hour, 1987, Escape, 1990, Playing Dangerous 2, 1996, Dog Watch, 1996, Star Kid, 1997, Home Room, 2002, Vampire Clan, 2002, The Powder Puff Principle, 2006; (TV films) Operation Petticoat, 1977, Little Women, 1978, A Wedding on Walton's Mountain, 1982, Mother's Day on Walton's Mountain, 1982, A Day for Thanks on Walton's Mountain, 1982, The Night the Bridge Fell Down, 1983, Challenge of a Lifetime, 1985, Embassy, 1985, Acceptable Risks, 1986, Police Story: Monster Manor, 1988, A Killing in a Small Town, 1990, Bad Attitudes, 1991, Just My Imagination, 1992, Not in My Family, 1993, Take Me Home Again, 1994, The Man Next Door, 1996, Two Voices, 1997, Audrey's Rain, 2003, Kim Possible, 2003; (TV series) McMillan & Wife, 1976—77, Operation Petticoat, 1977, Little Women, 1979, Just Our Luck, 1983, Heartland, 1989, (appeared on) The Love Boat, 1978—85, Thirtysomething, 1989—90, Designing Women, 1986—91, Murder, She Wrote, 1991—93, Matlock, 1991—95, Party of Five, 1997—98, Judging Amy, 2000, Joan of Arcadia, 2003; (plays) It Had to Be You, Beyond Therapy, Cops, When in Rome, House of Blue Leaves, Balancing Act, 2007.*

GILLINGHAM, BRYAN REGINALD, music educator; b. Vancouver, BC, Can., Apr. 12, 1944; s. Reginald Pearce and Ethel Gladys (Collier) G.; m. Helen Campbell, Aug. 11, 1970 (div. 1980); children: Gregory, Sara; m. Susanna Catharine Burton, Oct. 29, 1984; children: Gwendolyn, Miranda, Jeremy. BA, U. B.C., 1966, MusB, 1968; MusM, U. London, 1972; PhD, U. Wash., 1976. Lectr. Mt. Allison U., Sackville, N.B., Canada, 1972-73, U. Alta., Edmonton, Canada, 1975-76; prof., chmn. Carleton U., Ottawa, Ont., Canada, 1976-83. Dir. Inst. Medieval Music, Ottawa, 1985—. Author: The Polyphonic Sequences in Codex Wolfenbüttel 677, 1982, Saint-Martial Mehrstimmigkeit, 1984, Medieval Polyphonic Sequences, 1985, Modal Rhythm, 1986, Secular Medieval Latin Song, 1993, A Critical Study of Secular Medieval Latin Song, 1995, The Social Background to Secular Medieval Latin Song, 1998, Chant and Its Peripheries, 1998, Music in the Cluniac Ecclesia, 2006; editor (with Donald Beecher) Dovehouse early music edits.; contbr. articles and book revs. to profl. jours. Avocations: winemaking, squash, cross country skiing. Office: Carleton U Dept Music Colonel By Dr Ottawa ON Canada K1S 5B6 Office Phone: 613-520-3791.

GILLINGHAM, ROBERT FENTON, economist, consultant; b. Newark, Nov. 13, 1944; s. Evan Stevenson and Eleanor (Fenton) G.; m. Deborah Lynn Wickham, 1989; children: James Stevenson, Sarah Eleanor. BA, Haverford Coll., 1965; PhD, U. Pa., 1973. Economist Bur. Labor Stats., Washington, 1968-73, chief price rsch. div., 1973-82, dep. assoc. commr., 1982-85; dir. office econ. analysis Dept. Treasury, Washington, 1985-88, dep. asst. sec. for econ. policy, 1988-98; cons. Internat. Monetary Fund, Washington, 1998—. Assoc. editor Jour. Bus. and Econ. Stats., 1982-93; contbr. articles to profl. jours. Mem. Am. Econ. Assn., Am. Statis. Assn., Econometric Soc., Western Econ. Assn. (bd. dirs. 1995-98), Conf. on Income and Wealth, Nat. Acad. Social Ins. Home: 20448 Tappahannock Pl Sterling VA 20165-4786 Office: Internat Monetary Fund 700 19th St NW Washington DC 20431-0001

GILLINGHAM, STEPHEN THOMAS, financial planner; b. St. Paul, May 30, 1944; s. Thomas Elmwood and Barbara Alice (Sickles) G.; m. Carolyn Jean Alvey, June 5, 1976; children: Kenneth, Brett. BA, Juniata Coll., 1966; JD, The George Washington U., 1969. Bar: Va. 1971; CFP; ChFC. Tax specialist Price Waterhouse, Washington, 1969-71; tax law specialist IRS, Washington, 1971-77; sr. tax lawyer Internat. Paper Co., NYC, 1977-83; dir. tax rsch. and planning The Singer Co., Stanford, Conn., 1983-88; tax counsel Am. Cyanamid Co., Wayne, N.J., 1988-95; fin. planner The Thompson Group, Inc., White Plains, NY, 1995—2004, Fin. Planning Assocs., White Plains, 2004—. Lectr. World Trade Inst., 1980-90. Contbg. editor Tax Lawyer, 1984-88. With US Army, 1970—75. Named one of Outstanding Young Men in Am., Jaycees, 1979, one of Am.'s Top Fin. Planners Consumer Rsch. Coun. Am., 2006-07. Mem. Va. Bar Assn., N.J. Tax Group (chmn. 1991-95), Tax Execs. Inst., Fin.Planning Assn. Avocations: golf, swimming, hiking. Home: 4 Northway Hartsdale NY 10530-2109 Office: Financial Planning Assocs 244 Westchester Ave White Plains NY 10604-2907 Office Phone: 914-997-9229. E-mail: stgill@cyburban.com.

GILLINGS, DENNIS B., medical products executive; Prof. biostats. U.N.C., Chapel Hill; cons. various pharm. cos.; founder, chmn., CEO Quintiles Transnat. Corp., Durham, N.C., 1982—. Named One of 15 Top Biotechnology Execs., Genetic Engring. News, 1994. Office: Quintiles Transnat Corp 4709 Creekstone Dr Ste 200 Durham NC 27703

GILLINSON, SIR CLIVE DANIEL, music executive, former musician; b. Bangalore, India, Mar. 7, 1946; arrived in Eng., 1948; s. Stanley and Regina Rebecca (Schein) G.; m. Susan Sheppard, 1980 (div. 1986); m. Penelope Sara Morsley, June 1, 1989; children: Sarah Helen, Miriam Catherine, David Michael. Student, Queen Mary Coll., London, 1963-64; diploma, recital, Royal Acad. Music, 1968; diploma in music (hon.), Guildhall Sch., London, 1992, City U., 1994; doctorate, City of London U., 1995. Cellist London Symphony Orch., 1970-84, mng. dir., 1984—2005; ptnr. Clive Daniel Antiques, London, 1980-86; exec. and artistic dir. Carnegie Hall, 2005—. Named Freeman of the City of London, Corp. of London, 1984, Comdr. British Empire, 1998; knighted, 2005 Fellow Royal Acad. Music; mem. Assn. Brit. Orchs. (chmn. 1982-85), Nat. Youth Orch. Avocations: theater, reading, skiing, tennis, concerts. Office: Carnegie Hall 881 7th Ave New York NY 10019-3210 Office Phone: 212-903-9820. Business E-Mail: cgillinson@carnegiehall.org.

GILLIOM, JUDITH CARR, federal official; b. Indpls., May 19, 1943; d. Elbert Raymond and Marjorie Lucille (Carr) G. BA, Northwestern U., 1964; MA, U. Pa., 1966. Feature writer, asst. women's editor Indpls. News, summers 1961-63; rsch. asst. cultural anthropology Northwestern U., 1963-64, asst. instr. freshman English, 1964; editorial asst. to dir. div. cardiology Phila. Gen. Hosp., 1965-67; asst. to ophthalmologist-in-chief Wills Eye Hosp., Phila., 1967-69; editor, writer Nat. Assn. Hearing and Speech Agencies, Washington, 1969-70; free-lance speech writer White House Conf. Children and Youth, 1969-70; free-lance editor, writer, abstractor, 1971-78; free-lance speechwriter President's Com. Mental Retardation, 1971-78; from dir. publs. to dir. comm. Nat. Assn. Hearing and Speech Action, Silver Spring, Md., 1972-77; editor Hearing & Speech Action mag., 1969-70, 72-77; program mgr. Interagy. Com. on Handicapped Employees, 1978, dep. exec. sec., 1979-83; mgr. disability program Dept. Def., 1983—. Cons. U.S. Archtl. and Transp. Barriers Compliance Bd., 1976-77, Office Ind. Living for Disabled, HUD, 1977-78, Office for Handicapped Individuals, HEW, 1978, Women's com. Pres.'s Com. Employment Handicapped, 1985-86. Mem. Nat. Spinal Cord Injury Assn., 1970-90, editor, pub. conv. jour., 1974-82, bd. dirs. D.C. chpt., 1975-81, 89-90, nat. trustee, 1975-81, nat. bd. dirs., 1978-79; bd. dirs. Nat. Ctr. for a Barrier-Free Environment, 1979-84, v.p., 1980-81, pres., 1981-82; nat. bd. dirs., treas. League Disabled Voters, 1980-85; local bd. dirs. Easter Seal Soc. Disabled Children and Adults, 1985-90; active Montgomery County Commn. on People with Disabilities, 1989-95; mem. Taxicab Svcs. Adv. Com., 1995-99. Recipient Smittkamp award Nat. Paraplegia Found., 1976, Outstanding Svc. award Fed. Asian Pacific Am. Coun., 1990, Geico Pub. Svc. award, 1996, Civilian Career Svc. award Office of Sec. of Def., 1997, Outstanding Leadership award Fed. Asian Pacific Am. Coun., 2002; Woodrow Wilson fellow, 1965. Mem. Phi Beta Kappa, Delta Delta Delta. Home: 901 Arcola Ave Silver Spring MD 20902-3401 Office: Dept Def The Pentagon Rm 5D641 Washington DC 20301-4000 Office Phone: 703-571-9330. Business E-Mail: judy.gilliom@osd.mil.

GILLIOM, MORRIS EUGENE, social studies and global educator; b. Bluffton, Ind., Feb. 10, 1932; s. William Orel and Zella Leota (Gallimore) G.; m. Bonnie Lee Cherp, Dec. 29, 1956; children: Gregor William, Julia Lee. BA, Heidelberg Coll., 1954; MA, Ohio State U., 1958, PhD, 1962. Cert. tchr., Ohio. Tchr. social studies Cleve. Pub. Schs., 1956-59; instr. Ohio State U., Columbus, 1959-62; asst. prof. San Francisco State Coll., 1962-65, U. Chgo., 1965-66; from assoc. prof. to prof. social studies, global edn. Ohio State U., Columbus, 1966-95, prof. emeritus, 1995—, dir. social studies edn. program abroad, 1969-95. Cons. TraveLearn, Lakeville, Pa., group leader programs worldwide; group leader Smithsonian Instn. Programs to China. Author, sr. editor: Practical Methods for the Social Studies, 1977; author, co-editor: Perspectives of Global Education, 1981; contbr. chpts. to books, articles to profl. publs. Mem. Heidelberg Coll. Fellows, Heidelberg Coll. Global Edn. Adv. Coun. With US Army, 1954—56. Recipient Disting. Tchg. award Ohio State U., 1985, Outstanding Alumni award, Heidelberg Coll., 2005; Malone fellow. Mem. Nat. Coun. Social Studies (coll. and univ. faculty assembly), Ohio Soc. Sci. Edn. Consortium (bd. dirs. 1986-90), Ohio Coun. Social Studies, Torch Club. Democrat. Avocations: photography, travel, skiing, reading. Home: 2495 Haverford Rd Columbus OH 43220-4203 Office: Ohio State U 1945 N High St Columbus OH 43210-1120 Fax: 614-451-1763. E-mail: genegilliom@mac.com.

GILLIS, CHRISTINE DIEST-LORGION, financial planner, stockbroker; b. San Francisco, Apr. 26, 1923; d. Evert Jan and Christine Helen (Radcliffe) Diest-Lorgion; children: Barbara Gillis Pieper and Suzanne Gillis Seymour (twins). BS, U. Calif., Berkeley, 1944; MS, U. So. Calif., 1968. Cert. fin. planner, 1978. Account exec. Winslow, Cohu & Stetson, NYC, 1962-63, Paine Webber, NYC, 1964-65; sr. investment exec. Shearson Hammill, Beverly Hills, Calif., 1966-72; fin. planner, asst. v.p. E.F. Hutton, LA, 1972-87; 2d v.p. Shearson Lehman Hutton, Glendale, Calif., 1988; v.p. investments Dean Witter Reynolds, Glendale, Calif., 1988-90. Mem. AAUW (life; trustee ednl. found.), Town Hall. of Calif. (life; corp. sec. 1974-75, dir., gov. 1976-80), Women Stockbrokers Assn. (founding pres. N.Y.C. 1963), Women of Wall Street West (founder, pres. 1979-84), Navy League (life), U. Calif. Berkeley Alumni Assn. (life), U. So. Calif. Alumni Assn. (life), Town and Gown (life). Episcopalian. Home: 1099 Pine Oak Ln Pasadena CA 91105

GILLIS, EDWIN, information technology executive; BA in Govt., Clark U.; MA in Internat. Rels., U. So. Calif.; MBA, Harvard Bus. Sch. CPA, gen. practice ptnr. Coopers & Lybrand, 1976—91; CFO Lotus Devel. Corp., 1991—95; exec. v.p., CFO Parametric Tech. Corp., 1995—2002, VERITAS Software Corp., Mountain View, Calif., 2002—. Office: VERITAS Software Corp 350 Ellis St Mountain View CA 94043

GILLIS, JAMES R., consumer products company executive; Exec. v.p. Globe Comm. Corp.; mng. ptnr. Aders, Wilcox, Gillis; pres., CEO Brand Mfg. Corp.; pres. Source Interlink Cos., 1998—2006, COO, 2000—06, bd. dirs., 2000—, interim co-CEO, 2006—. Office: Source Interlink Cos 27500 Riverview Center Blvd Bonita Springs FL 34134 Office Phone: 239-949-4450.*

GILLIS, JOHN LAMB, JR., lawyer; b. St. Louis, June 13, 1939; 5. John L. and Carol (Randolph) G.; m. Nichola Mitchell, Aug. 1965; children: John Mitchell, Suzanne Lamb. Student, Brown U.; AB, Washington U., 1965; LLB, Stanford U., 1968. Bar: Mo. 1968. Sr. counsel Armstrong Teasdale LLP, St. Louis. Address: Armstrong Teasdale LLP 1 Metropolitan Sq Saint Louis MO 63102-2733 E-mail: jgillis@armstrongteasdale.com.

GILLIS, JOHN SIMON, retired psychologist, educator; b. Washington, Mar. 21, 1937; s. Simon John and Rita Veronica (Moran) G.; m. Mary Ann Wesolowski, Aug. 29, 1959; children: Holly Ann, Mark, Scott. BA, Stanford U., 1959; MS (fellow), Cornell U., 1961; PhD (NIMH fellow), U. Colo., 1965. Lectr. dept. psychology Australian Nat. U., Canberra, 1968-70; sr. psychologist Mendocino (Calif.) State Hosp., 1971-72; asso. prof. dept. psychology Tex. Tech U., Lubbock, 1972-76; prof. psychology Oreg. State U., Corvallis, 1976—2004, chmn. dept. psychology, 1976—84, 1997—2004; ret., 2004. Cons. VA, Ciba-Geigy Pharms., USIA, UN High Commn. for Refugees; commentator Oreg. Ednl. and Pub. Broadcasting System, 1978-79; Fulbright lectr., India, 1982-83, Greece, 1992, Kyrgyzstan, 2001; vis. prof. U. Karachi, 1984, 86, U. Punjab, Pakistan, 1985, Am. U., Cairo, 1984-86. Contbr. articles to profl. jours. Served with USAF, 1968-72. Ciba-Geigy Pharms. grantee, 1971-82 Roman Catholic. Home: 7520 NW Mountain View Dr Corvallis OR 97330-9106 Office: Oreg State U Dept Psychology Corvallis OR 97331 Business E-Mail: jgillis@orst.edu.

GILLIS, JOHN W., federal agency administrator; Grad., Calif. State U., LA, U. So. Calif. Lt., asst. comdg. officer L.A. Police Dept., 1962—88; ret., 1988; dir. victims of crime U.S. Dept. Justice, Washington, 2001—. Commr. Calif. Bd. Prison Terms, chmn., 1991—93; mem. crime victims and corrections com. Calif. State Bar Assn.; mem. victim com. Am. Legis. Exch. Coun. Founding mem. Justice for Homicide Victims; founder Coalition of Victims Equal Rights, Victims and Friends United; active Memory of Victims Everywhere, Parents of Murdered Children. Named to Am. Plice Hall of Fame; recipient Nat. Crime Victim Svc. award, 1991, Spl. Commendation award, 1993. Achievements include being one of six Black students to integrate the University of Kentucky in 1954. Office: US Dept Justice Victims of Crime 810 7th St NW Washington DC 20531 Office Phone: 202-307-5983, 202-305-2984. Personal E-mail: jwgillis@aol.com.

GILLIS, MARVIN BOB, retired chemical executive, consultant; b. Treutlen County, Ga., Apr. 5, 1920; s. Bob Lee and Pearl (Gillis) G.; m. Helen Reed, Dec. 23, 1946; children: Margaret Susan, Marvin Reed, Kenneth Robert. BSA., U. Ga., 1940; PhD, Cornell U., 1947. Rsch. assoc. Cornell U., 1947-51; sr. rsch. chemist Internat. Minerals and Chem. Corp., from 1947, asst. dir. rsch., 1956-57, dir. rsch., 1957-64, dir. animal health and nutrition, 1964-66, div. v.p., 1966-70, corp. v.p., 1970-72, sr. v.p., 1972-82; pres., dir. IMC Chem. Group, Inc., 1976-78; pres. Animal Products Group, 1978-82, cons. to exec. office, 1982-86. Sec. Agrl. Rsch. Inst., 1958-59, v.p., 1960-62, 66-67, pres., 1962-63, 68-69; mem NRC Agrl. Bd., 1962-67; bd. dirs. Animal Health Inst., 1966-69 Author numerous papers in field; patentee in field Served to 1st lt. USAAF, 1942—45. Decorated DFC with oak leaf cluster, Air medal with 3 oak leaf clusters. Mem. North Shore Country Club (Glenview, Ill.), Blue Key, Sigma Xi, Gamma Alpha, Alpha Zeta, Phi Kappa Phi. Baptist. Home: 2500 Indigo Ln 409 Glenview IL 60026

GILLIS, RUTH ANN M., utilities executive; married; 2 children. BS magna cum laude in Econs., Smith Coll., Northampton, Mass., 1977; MBA in Fin., U. Chgo., 1980. Various lending and staff positions First Chgo. Corp. (now JPMorgan Chase & Co.), 1977—95; CFO, treas., v.p. U. Chgo. Hosps. and Health Sys.; v.p., treas. Unicom Corp., 1997, sr. v.p. competitive ops., CFO; CFO Exelon Corp., 2000—02, exec. v.p. ComEd, sr. v.p., pres. Exelon Bus. Svcs. Co., mem. ops. coun. and corp. risk mgmt. com. Bd. dirs. Potlatch Corp.; trustee Archstone-Smith Trust. Pres. bd. trustees U. Chgo. Cancer Rsch. Found.; trustee Goodman Theatre Bd.; mem. U. Chgo. Cancer Rsch. Found. Women's Bd., 1986—. Mem.: Chgo. Network, Econ. Club Chgo., Phi Beta Kappa. Office: Exelon Corp 37th Fl 10 S Dearborn St Chicago IL 60603*

GILLISPIE, BILLY CLYDE, men's college basketball coach; b. Abilene, Tex., Nov. 7, 1959; Student, Sam Houston State U.; BA in Edn., S.W. Tex. State U., 1983. Grad. asst. Tex. State U., 1982—85; asst. coach Killeen HS, Tex., 1985—87, U. Tulsa, 1997—2000; head coach Copperas Cove HS, Tex., 1987—88, New Braunfels Canyon HS, Tex., 1988—90, Killeen Ellison HS, Tex., 1990—93, U. Tex., El Paso, 2002—04, Tex. A&M U., 2004—07, U. Ky., 2007—; asst. coach, recruiting coord. South Plains Jr. Coll., 1993—94, Baylor U., 1994—97, U. Ill., 2000—02. Named Big 12 Coach Yr., 2005, 2007. Mem.: Tex. HS Coaches Assn., Tex. Assn. Basketball Coaches, Nat. Assn. Basketball Coaches, Fellowship of Christian Athletes. Office: U Ky Mens Basketball Athletics Dept Rupp Arena Lexington KY 40506*

GILLISPIE, HAROLD LEON, minister; b. Levant, Kans., May 11, 1933; s. Harold Leon and Agnes Anne (Dryden) G. BA in Bus. Adminstrn., Kans. Wesleyan U., 1955. Youth dir. Cen. YMCA, Des Moines, 1957-61; exec. dir. West Des Moines br. YMCA, 1961-65; exec. dir. Aurora Br. YMCA, Denver, 1965-69, YMCA, McCook, Nebr., 1969-75, Junction City, Kans., 1975-79; owner H & R Block Franchise, Manhattan, Kans., 1979-91; lay pastor Presbyn. Ch., Oak Hill, Kans., 1996—; vice moderator Presbytery of No. Kans., 1999-00, moderator, 2000-01. Proofreader text H & R Block, Kansas City, Mo., 1986-92. Bd. dirs. Flint Hills Breadbasket, Manhattan, Kans., 1982-89, treas., 1987; bd. dirs. Big Bros. Big Sisters, Manhattan, 1981-85, pres., 1983-85; pres. Downtown Manhattan, Inc., 1986; bd. dirs. Manhattan Main Street, 1986-89; bd. dirs. Ecumenical Campus Ministry, Kans. State U., 1995-99, 2002-2005, chmn., 1996-98 Republican. Presbyterian. Avocations: theology, tennis, baking, working with youth. Home: 710 Bertrand St Manhattan KS 66502-5156 E-mail: pastogil@flinthills.com.

GILLISPIE, ROBERT J., lawyer; b. Washington, Aug. 25, 1943; s. Eugene Render and Gertrude (Pensock) G.; m. Susan Scott (div. Jan. 1977); children: Robert, Megan; m. Barbara Farrell, Oct. 23, 1982; children: Bradley, Todd John. BEE, Catholic U., 1965, JD magna cum laude, 1968. Bar: NY 1969, DC 1977, US Supreme Ct. 1977. Assoc. Mudge, Rose, Guthrie, Alexander & Ferdon, NYC, ptnr., 1977—95; ptnr., corp. dept., leasing & tax dept. Cahdbourne & Parke LLP, NYC, 1995—. Adj. prof. Rutgers U., 1972—76. Contbr.; lectr. in field, editor-in-chief Catholic U. Law Rev., 1967—68. Mem.: DC Bar, ABA, NY Bar Assn. Roman Catholic. Avocation: golf. Office: Chadbourne & Parke LLP 30 Rockefeller Plz New York NY 10112 Office Phone: 212-408-1154. Office Fax: 212-541-5369. Business E-Mail: rgillispie@chadbourne.com.

GILLISPIE, STEVEN BRIAN, systems analyst, researcher; b. Seattle, Oct. 19, 1955; s. Edwin B. and Claudia Mae (Cooper) G. BS in Physics with distinction, U. Wash., 1979, BS in Math., 1979, BS in Psychology, 1983, BA in Gen. Studies, 1983, MS in Math., 1998. Software specialist Fla. Computer Graphics, Seattle, 1983-84; data analyst coronary artery surgery study U. Wash., Seattle, 1985-87, sci. programmer dept. radiology, 1987-88, systems analyst dept. radiology, 1988—. Dir. devel. med. imaging software Viewbox, 1992; contbr. articles to profl. jours. Mem. Woodland Park Zool. Soc., Seattle, 1986—; contbg. mem. Nordic Heritage Mus., Seattle, 1991—; patron The High Desert Mus., Bend, Oreg., 1991—. Mem. Soc. for Indsl. and Applied Math., U. Wash. Alumni Assn. (life), So. Oreg. Hist. Soc. Office: U Wash Dept Radiology Box 357987 Seattle WA 98195-7987 Business E-Mail: gillisp@u.washington.edu.

GILLISS, CATHERINE LYNCH, vice chancellor, dean, nursing educator; b. New Britain, Conn., Apr. 18, 1949; d. James A. and Lorraine Lynch; m. Thomas P. Gilliss, June 6, 1970. BS in Nursing, Duke U., 1971; MS in Nursing, Cath. U. Am., Washington, 1974; D of Nursing Sci., U. Calif., San Francisco, 1983; cert. adult nurse practitioner, U. Rochester, 1979; D (hon.), U. Portland, Oreg., 2007. Staff and charge nurse Duke U. Med. Ctr., Durham, NC, 1971, VA Hosp., Washington, 1971-72; asst. prof. U. Md., Balt., 1974-76, The Cath. U. Am., 1976-79, U. Portland, Oreg., 1979—83, assoc. prof., 1983—84; lectr. in nursing Sonoma State U., Rohnert Park, Calif., 1983-84; prof., chmn. dept. family health care U. Calif., San Francisco, 1984-98, prof. emeritus, 1999—; prof. Sch. Nursing, Yale U., New Haven, 1998—2004, dean Sch. Nursing, 1998—2004; dean Sch. Nursing Duke U., 2004—; vice chancellor nursing affairs, 2004—. Chair NIH, Nat. Inst. Nursing Rsch. Study Sect., 1997-2000. Co-author: Toward a Science of Family Nursing, 1989, The Nursing of Families, 1993; mem. editl. bd. Families, Systems and Health, Jour. Family Nursing, Jour. Nat. Assn. Hispanic Nurses, Jour. Nat. Black Nurses Assn., Nursing Outlook; contbr. articles to profl. jours. Bd. dirs. Nat. Coun. Family Relations, 1986-88, Am. Acad. Nursing, 2000-04, Soc. Primary Care Policy Fellows, 1996-99, Nat. Orgn. Nurse Practitioner Faculties, 1994-97. Recipient Disting. Alumna award Duke U. Sch. Nursing, 1991; Pres.'s Fellowship award U. Calif., 1983; Sr. fellow Ctr. for Health Professions, 1996-99, Primary Health Care Policy fellow USPHS, 1993; Regent U. Portland, Oreg., 1994-2000; named to Wall of 100 Disting. Alumni, U. Calif. San Francisco Sch. Nursing, 2007. Fellow Am. Acad. Nursing; mem. ANA, Nat. Coun. on Family Rels., Nat. Orgn. Nurse Practitioner Faculties (pres. 1995-96), Soc. Primary Care Policy Fellows (pres. 1997-98), Am. Assn. Colls. Nursing (fin. com., 2006—). Office: Duke Univ Sch of Nursing DUMC 3322 Durham NC 27710

GILLISS, EDWARD JOHNSON, lawyer; b. Balt., Oct. 23, 1955; s. Rollie Downing and Ethel May (Rankin) G.; m. Barbara Stultz, Sept. 25, 1982; children, Ned, Tim, Tom. BA, Coll. of Wooster, 1977; JD, U. Md., 1980. Bar: Md. 1980, U.S. Dist. Ct. Md. 1980, U.S. Supreme Ct. 1986. With gen. counsel's office U.S. Dept. HHS, Balt., Washington, 1980-82; assoc. Lord, Whip, Coughlan & Green, Balt., 1982-86; ptnr. Royston, Mueller, McLean & Reid L.L.P., Towson, Md., 1986—; county atty. Baltimore County, 2001—04. Pres. The Towson Partnership, 1995-97. Bd. dirs. Rodgers Forge Cmty. Assn., Balt., 1986-91, pres., 1988-90; bd. dirs. Catonsville C.C. Found., 1993-95, St. Joseph's Hosp.; deacon 2d Presbyn. Ch., Balt., 1987-93, moderator, 1992-93, trustee, 1993—; trustee Md. Inst. for Continuing Profl. Edn. of Lawyers, 1988-91, 94-. Fellow Md. Bar Found.; mem. ABA, Md. State Bar Assn. (bd. govs. 1989-91, 96-98, budget and fin. com. 1989, exec. com. young lawyers sect., pres. 2006-07), Maritime Law Assn., Balt. County Bar Assn. (chair constitution and bylaws com. 1991-92, bench-bar com. 1993-97, chmn. 1996-97), Md. Assn. Def. Trial Counsel. Office: Royston Mueller McLean & Reid LLP 102 W Pennsylvania Ave Ste 600 Towson MD 21204-4510

GILLMAN, DEREK A., museum director, academic administrator; m. Yael Gillman; 3 children. MA, Oxford U., England; LLM, U. East Anglia, England. Curator British Mus.; keeper (dir.) Sainsbury Centre Visual Arts, U. East Anglia, Norwich, England; dep. dir. Nat. Gallery Victoria, Melbourne, Australia; exec. dir. & provost Pa. Acad. Fine Arts, Phila., 1999—2001, pres. & CEO, 2001—06, pres., CEO, Edna S Tuttleman dir.; dir. Barnes Found., Pa., 2006—. Mem. Getty Trust Mus. Mgmt. Inst., 1991. Author: The Idea of Cultural Heritage, 2006. Mem.: Assn. Art Mus. Dirs., Norfolk Inst. Art & Design (gov. 1990—95). Office: Barnes Foundation 300 N Latch's Lane Merion Station PA 19066-1729 Office Phone: 610-667-0290. Office Fax: 610-664-4026.

GILLMAN, LEONARD, mathematician, educator; b. Cleve., Jan. 8, 1917; s. Joseph Moses and Etta Judith (Cohen) G.; m. Reba Parks Marcus, Dec. 24, 1938; children: Jonathan Webb, Michal Judith. Diploma (fellow in piano 1933-38), Juilliard Grad. Sch. Music, 1938; BS, Columbia U., 1941, MA (Carnegie fellow math. statistics 1942-43), 1945, PhD, 1953. Asst. in math. dept. Columbia U., 1941-42, lectr., 1942-43; ops. analyst Tufts Coll., MIT, 1943-51; from instr. to assoc. prof. math. Purdue U., 1952-60; prof. math., chmn. dept. U. Rochester, 1960-69; prof. math. U. Tex., Austin, 1969-87, prof. emeritus, 1987, chmn. dept., 1969-73. Mem. Inst. Advanced Study, Princeton, 1958-60; cons. editor W.W. Norton Co., Inc., 1967-80. Author: (with Meyer Jerison) Rings of Continuous Functions, 1960, 76, You'll Need Math, 1967, (with Robert H. McDowell) Calculus, 1973, 78, Writing Mathematics Well, 1987; mem. editorial bd. Topology and Its Applications, 1971-94. Guggenheim fellow, 1958-59; NSF sr. post-doctoral fellow, 1959-60. Mem. Am. Math. Soc. (assoc. sec. 1969-71, mem. com. to monitor problems in commn. 1972-77), Nat. Coun. Tchrs. Math., Math. Assn. Am. (bd. govs. 1973-95, treas. 1973-86, pres.-elect 1986-87, pres. 1987-89, past pres. 1989-90, Lester R. Ford award for expository writing 1994, 2003, Yueh-Gin Gung and Dr. Charles Y. Hu award for disting. svc. to math. 1999). Home and Office: 1606 The High Rd Austin TX 78746-2236 Personal E-mail: lgillman@austin.rr.com.

GILLMOR, CHARLES STEWART, historian, researcher, educator; b. Kansas City, Mo., Nov. 6, 1938; s. Charles Stewart and Evelyn (Noland) G.; m. Rogene Marie Godding, Nov. 28, 1964; children: Charles Stewart III, Alison Bogue. BSEE, Stanford U., 1962; MA, Princeton U., 1966, PhD, 1968; postgrad., U. Colo., 1963. Ionospheric physicist Bur. Standards, Antarctica and Boulder, Colo., 1960-62; instr. history Wesleyan U., Middletown, Conn., 1967-68, asst. prof., 1968-72, assoc. prof., 1973-79, prof. history and sci., 1979—, chmn. dept. history, 1986-88, 91-94; cons. Office Sci. Edn., AAAS, 1973-75. Adv. com. Coun. Internat. Exch. Scholars, 1978—82; cons. NSF, 1983; Hennebach vis. prof. Colo. Sch. Mines, 1996—97; vis. prof. elec. engring. Stanford u., 1998—2001. Author: Coulomb and the Evolution of Physics and Engineering in 18th Century France, 1971, Fred Terman at Stanford, 2004; editor: The History of Geophysics, Vol. 1, 1984, Vol. 2, 1986, Vol. 4, 1990, Vol. 7, 1997; jour. editor: Transactions Am. Geophys. Union, 1983-86; mus. dir. Nutmeg Foxtrot-Jazz Orch., 1990-96; contbr. articles to profl. jours.; recording artist with Leo Records, 1998. Deacon Higganum Congl. Ch., Conn., 1978-96. Mt. Gillmor in Antarctica named in his honor, 1963; Social Sci. Rsch. Coun. grantee, 1971; NSF rsch. grantee, 1972-74, 75-77, 76-79; sr. Fulbright rsch. scholar Cambridge U., Eng., 1976; NASA History scholar, 1980-81; U.S.-France NSF research fellow, Paris, 1984-85; Joseph J. Malone fellow to Tunisia Nat. Coun. U.S.-Arab Rels., 1989; Smithsonian Instn. Lemelson fellow, 2005. Fellow Am. Phys. Soc. (sec.-treas. history of physics divsn. 1988-94, exec. com. 1996-98, chair 1997-98); mem. AAAS, IEEE, History of Sci. Soc., Soc. History of Tech. (adv. coun. 1978-82). Home: 29 Spencer Rd Higganum CT 06441-4034 Office: Wesleyan Univ Dept History Middletown CT 06459-0002 Office Phone: 860-685-2378. E-mail: sgillmor@wesleyan.edu.

GILLMOR, HELEN, federal judge; BA, Queen's Coll. of CUNY, 1965; LLB magna cum laude, Boston U., 1968. With Ropes & Gray, Boston, 1968-69, Law Offices of Alexander R. Gillmor, Camden, Maine, 1970, Torkildson, Katz, Jossem, Fonseca, Jaffe, Moore & Hetherington, Honolulu, 1971-72; law clk. to Chief Justice William S. Richardson Hawaii State Supreme Ct., 1972; dep. pub. defender Office of Pub. Defender, Honolulu, 1972-74; dist. ct. judge per diem Family Ct. (1st cir.) Hawaii, 1977-83; per diem judge Dist. Ct., 1st circuit, 1983-85; pvt. practice Honolulu, 1985-94; district judge U.S. Dist. Ct. Hawaii, 9th circuit, 1994—2005, chief dist. judge, 2005—. Counsel El Paso Real Estate Investment Trust, 1969; lectr. U.S. Agy. Internat. Devel., Seoul, South Korea, 1969-70, Univ. Hawaii, 1975. Office: Prince J K Kuhio Fed Bldg 300 Ala Moana Blvd Rm C-400 Honolulu HI 96850-0400

GILLMOR, JOHN EDWARD, lawyer; b. Phila., Oct. 26, 1937; s. John Edward and Louise Ann (Porter) G.; m. Allis Dale Brannon, Aug. 17, 1968; children: Sarah, Abigail, Susan, Eleanor, John, Matthew. BA, Swarthmore Coll., 1959; LL.B., U. Pa., 1962. Bar: DC 1962, NY 1963, Tenn. 1972, Pa. 1980. Assoc. Dewey Ballantine Bushby Palmer & Wood, 1962-63, 66-71; v.p., corp. counsel Hosp. Affiliates Internat., Nashville, 1971-78, sr. v.p., gen. counsel, 1978-79; staff v.p., asst. gen. counsel INA Corp., Phila., 1980; sr. v.p., gen. counsel INA Health Care Group, 1981; partner Gillmor, Mills & Gillmor, 1981-83; dir., exec. v.p. Health Am. Corp., 1983-86; ptnr. Gillmor, Anderson & Gillmor, 1986-89, Dearborn & Ewing, 1989-92, Boult, Cummings, Conners & Berry, Nashville, 1992—. Trustee U. Sch. Nashville, 1990-02; bd. dirs. Nashville Opera Assn., 1996-2007; bd. dirs. Hoosier Care, Inc., 1988-, Am. Eagle Life Care Corp., 2004-, Edn. Networks Am., 2003-. With USMC, 1963-66. Mem.: ABA, Nashville Bar Assn., Nashville Bar Found., Tenn. Bar Assn. Republican. Home: 1700 Graybar Ln Nashville TN 37215-2106 Office: Boult Cummings Conners & Berry 1600 Division St Ste 700 Nashville TN 37203 Home Phone: 615-297-3149; Office Phone: 615-252-2305. Business E-Mail: jgillmor@bccb.com.

GILLMOR, KAREN LAKO, state agency administrator; b. Cleve., Jan. 29, 1948; d. William M. and Charlotte (Sheldon) Lako; m. Paul E. Gillmor, Dec. 10, 1983; children: Linda D., Julie E., Paul Michael, Connor W., Adam S. BA cum laude, Mich. State U., 1969; MA, Ohio State U., 1970, PhD, 1981. Asst. to v.p. Ohio State U., Columbus, 1972-77, spl. asst. dean law, 1979-81, assoc. dir. Ctr. Healthcare Policy and Rsch., 1991-92; asst. to pres. Ind. Cen. U., Indpls., 1977-78; rsch. asst. Burke Mktg. Rsch., Indpls., 1978-79; v.p. pub. affairs Huntington Nat. Bank, Columbus, 1981-82; fin. cons. Ohio Rep. Fin. Com., Columbus, 1982-83; chief mgmt. planning and rsch. Indsl. Commn. Ohio, Columbus, 1983-86; mgr. physician rels. Ohio State U. Med. Ctr., Columbus, 1987-91; cons. U.S. Sec. Labor, Washington, 1990-91; mem. Regional Bd. Rev./Indls. Commn., Ohio, 1991-92; state senator Ohio Gen. Assembly, 1993-97; vice-chair State Employment Rels. Bd., 1997—. Legis. liaison Huntington Bancshares, Ohio, Ohio State U., Columbus; trustee Heidelberg Coll., 1999—, Rutherford B. Hayes Presd. Ctr., 2002—. Mem. adv. coun. The Childhood League Ctr., 2003—06; nat. bd. dirs. Nat. First Ladies' Libr., 2004—; bd. dirs. Congl. Childcare Ctr., 2003—. Named Outstanding Freshman Ohio Legislator, 1994, Outstanding Nat. Freshman Legislator of the Yr., 1995, Watchdog of the Treasury, 1994, 1996, Hon. Alumna, Heidelberg Coll., 2006; named to Rocky River H.S. Hall of Fame, 1998; recipient Pres. award, Ohio State Chiropractic Assn., 1994, Pub. Svc. award, Am. Heart Assn., 1995, Ctr. Advancement and Study of Ethics award, Capital U. and Trinity Luth. Sem., 1996, cert. of Achievement, U.S. Dept. of Army, 1997, Friend of Medicine award, Ohio State Med. Assn., 1997, Legis. Achievement award, Ohio chpt. Am. Acad. Pediat., 1997, Spirit of Women award, 1999, Civic Leadership award, Ohio Assn. for Gifted Children, 2006; grantee, Andrew W. Mellon Found., 1978, Carnegie Corp., 1978. Mem.: DAR, Coun. Advancement and Support Edn., Am. Assn. Higher Edn., Ohio Fedn. Rep. Women, Women's Roundtable, Women in Mainstream, Phi Delta Kappa. Methodist. Office: 65 E State St Ste 1200 Columbus OH 43215-4209

GILLMOR, PAUL EUGENE, congressman, lawyer; b. Tiffin, Ohio, Feb. 1, 1939; s. Paul Marshall and Lucy Jeannette (Fry) Gillmor; m. Karen Lee Lako, Dec. 10, 1983; children: Linda Dianne, Julie Ellen, Paul Michael, Connor Sheldon, Adam William BA, Ohio Wesleyan U., Delaware, 1961; JD, U. Mich. Law Sch., 1964; LLD (hon.), Tiffin U., Ohio, 1985; degree (hon.), Defiance Coll., Ohio U., Rio Grande Coll. Bar: Ohio 1965. Mem. Ohio State Senate, 1967-89, minority leader, 1978—81, 1983—85, pres., 1981—83, 1985—88; mem. US Congress from 5th Ohio dist., 1989—, mem. fin. svcs. com., ranking mem. subcommittee on fin. instns. and consumer credit, dep. minority whip. Assoc. firm Tomb and Hering, Tiffin, 1967-88; bd. dirs. Old Fort Banking Co., Ohio; chmn. econ. and security com. NATO Parliamentary Assembly. Pres. Ohio Electoral Coll., Columbus, 1984. Served to capt. USAF, 1965—66. Recipient Gov.'s award, Ohio, 1980, Phillips medal of Pub. Svc. Ohio U. Coll. Osteopathy, 1981, Exec. Order, Ohio Commodores Assn., 1981, Disting. Citizen award Med. Coll. Ohio, 1982, FT Stone Lab. Partnership award, Ohio State U., 1995, Ground Water Protector award, Nat. Ground Water Assn., 2004; named Legislator of Yr., Ohio VFW, 1994. Mem. ABA, Ohio State Bar Assn., Nat. Rep. Legislators Assn. (named Outstanding Legislator of Yr. 1983). Republican. Methodist. Office: US House Reps 1203 Longworth House Office Bldg Washington DC 20515-3505 Office Phone: 202-225-6405.*

GILLON, PETER M., lawyer; b. Phila., Mar. 9, 1957; AB magna cum laude, Duke Univ., 1979; JD, Georgetown Univ., 1983. Bar: Fla. 1983, DC 1984. Shareholder, chair nat. insurance coverage and adv. practice, co-chair nat. environ. practice Greenberg Traurig LLP, Washington. Assoc. editor Tax Lawyer; contbr. articles to profl. journals. Mem.: ABA (chmn., subcom. bankruptcy and litig., litig. sect. com.). Office: Greenberg Traurig LLP Ste 500 800 Connecticut Ave NW Washington DC 20006 Office Phone: 202-331-3100. Office Fax: 202-331-3101. Business E-Mail: gillonp@gtlaw.com.

GILLOOLY, EDNA RAE See BURSTYN, ELLEN

GILLUM, RODERICK D., automotive executive; b. Detroit; BA, Mich. State U., 1972; JCD, Northeastern U. Sch. Law, 1975; MS in Mgmt., Mass. Inst. Tech., 1985. Atty. Nat. Labor Rels. Bd., Detroit; with GM Corp., mgr. strategic planning, 1985—86, v.p., gen. coun., sec., 1988—93; sec. GM Bd. Dirs., 1986—88; chief pers. labor atty. GM Corp., 1988—97, v.p. corp. respsibility, diversity, 1997—. Admin. asst. Mich. Senator Arthur Cartwright. Mem.: ABA Coll. Labor Employment (fellow), New Detrot (bd.mem.), Mich. Colls. Found. (bd.mem.), Detroit Econ. Corp. (bd. mem.), Martin Luther King Jr. Nat. Meml. Project Found. (bd.mem.), Charles H. Wright Mus. African Am. His (bd.mem.), Harvard U. Kennedy Sch. Govt. (bd. mem.), Hispanic Assn. Corp. Responsibility (bd. mem.), Nat. Coun. LaRaza (bd. mem.), Congl. Black Caucus Found. (bd. mem.), Nat. Urban League (bd. mem.), Holcim Inc. (chair, audit com.). Office: GM Corp 300 Renaissance Ctr Detroit MI 48265-3000

GILMAN, ALAN B., restaurant company executive; b. South Bend, Ind., Sept. 24, 1930; s. Sol M. and Lee R. (Rintzler) G.; m. Phyllis Schrager, Feb. 16, 1951; children: Bruce, Jeffrey, Lynn. AB with highest honors, Ind. U., 1952, MBA, 1954. With Lazarus Co. div. Federated Dept. Stores, Inc., Columbus, Ohio, 1954-64, div. mdse. mgr., 1961-64; with Sanger Harris div. Federated Dept. Stores, 1965-74, chmn. bd., chief exec. officer, 1970-74; corp. v.p. Federated Dept. Stores, 1974-80; with Abraham & Straus div. Federated Dept. Stores, 1975-80, chmn. bd., chief exec. officer, 1978-80; pres. Murjani Internat. Ltd., NYC, 1980-85; pvt. investor, 1985-87; chmn. At Ease of Newport Beach (Calif.) Inc., 1988-91; pres., CEO Consol. Products Inc., 1992—2002; chmn. Steak 'n Shake Co., Indpls., 2002—. Vice-chmn. bd. dirs. Ind. U. Found., 2000-03, nat. chmn. ann. giving, 1983, presdl. search com., 1987-88; chmn. dean's adv. coun. Ind. U. Grad. Sch. Bus., 1976-86; dean's adv. coun. Coll. Arts and Scis., Ind. U., 1989—, pres.'s cabinet, 1995=2003; bd. dirs., pres., exec. com. Greater N.Y. Fund-United Way, 1984-87; bd. dirs., exec. com., chmn. strategic planning com. United Way of N.Y.C., 1982-88; dir. Corp. Comty. Coun., Indpls., 1992-2001, Greater Indpls. Progress Com., Kelley Restaurants, Inc.; trustee Com. for Econ. Devel. Recipient Humanitarian of Yr. award Juvenile Diabetes Found., 1979, Disting. Alumni Svc. award Ind. U., 1996. Mem. Young Pres. Orgn. 49'er, Ind. U. Acad. Alumni Fellows, World Pres.'s Orgn., Phi Beta Kappa Fellows, Phi Alpha Theta, Beta Gamma Sigma (charter mem. dirs. table). Office: The Steak and Shake Co 500 Century Bldg 36 S Penn Ave Indianapolis IN 46204 Office Phone: 317-633-4100. *Value intellectual curiosity, an open mind, the greater import of tomorrow over yesterday, and recognize rapid change as the definition of opportunity while maintaining a sense of humor and honest humility.*

GILMAN, ALFRED GOODMAN, pharmacologist, educator; b. New Haven, July 1, 1941; s. Alfred and Mabel (Schmidt) Gilman; m. Kathryn Hedlund, Sept. 21, 1963; children: Amy, Anne, Edward. BS, Yale U., 1962, DMS (hon.), 1997; MD, PhD, Case Western Res. U., 1969, DSc (hon.), 1995, U. Chgo., 1991, U. Miami, 1999. Pharmacology rsch. assoc. NIH, Bethesda, Md., 1969—71; from asst. prof. to assoc. prof. pharmacology U. Va., Charlottesville, 1971—77, prof., 1977—81, dir. med. sci. tng. program, 1979—81; prof. pharmacology, chmn. dept. U. Tex. Southwestern Med. Ctr., Dallas, 1981—, Raymond and Ellen Willie disting. chmn. molecular neuropharmacology, 1987—, regental prof., 1994—, acting dean, 2004—, dir. Cecil H. and Ida Green Comprehensive Ctr. for Molecular Computational and Sys. Biol., 2004—, interim dean Southwestern Med. Sch., 2004—05, dean Southwestern Med. Sch., 2005—. Mem. pharmacology study sect. NIH, 1977—81, mem. nat. adv. gen. med. scis. coun., 1992—95; bd. sci. counselors Nat. Heart, Lung and Blood Inst. NIH, 1982—86; sci. adv. com. Am. Cancer Soc., NYC, 1982—86; adv. com. Lucille P. Markey Charitable Trust, Miami, 1984—96; sci. rev. bd. Howard Hughes Med. Inst., Bethesda, 1986—93; dir. Regeneron Pharmaceutics, 1989—, Eli Lilly and Co., Inc., 1995—; mem. vis. com. Sch. Medicine Case Western Reserve U., 1995—99; mem. sci. adv. bd. Huntsman Cancer Inst., U. Utah, 1995—2000, Ernest Gallo Clinic and Rsch. Ctr., U. Calif., San Francisco, 1996—2001; chmn. steering com. The Alliance for Cellular Signaling, 2000—. Editor The Pharmacological Basis of Therapeutics, 1975, 1980, 1985, 1990, cons. editor, 1996, 2001, contbr. over 240 articles to profl. jours. Recipient Poul Edvard Poulsson award, Norwegian Pharmacology Soc., 1982, Gairdner Found. Internat. Award, Can., 1984, Albert Lasker Basic Med. Rsch. award, 1989, Passano Sr. award, Passano Found., 1990, Waterford Biomed. Sci. award, Scripps Clinic and Rsch. Found., 1990, Basic Sci. Rsch. prize, Am. Heart Assn., 1990, City of Medicine award, Durham, N.C., 1991, Ciba-Geigy Drew award, 1991, Nobel prize in Physiology or Medicine, 1994, ACP award, 1995, Disting. Alumnus award, Case Western Reserve U., 1995, Am. Acad. Achievement award, 1995, Med. Honor Basic Rsch. award, Am. Cancer Soc., 1995. Mem.: NAS (Richard Lounsbery award 1987), Am. Acad. Arts and Scis., Inst. Medicine NAS, Am. Soc. Biol. Chemistry, Am. Soc. Pharmacology and Exptl. Therapeutics (John J. Abel award in pharmacology 1975, Louis S. Goodman and Alfred Gilman award 1990, Torald Sollman award 1997). Office: U Tex Southwestern Med Ctr Office of the Dean 5323 Harry Hines Blvd Dallas TX 75390-9003 Office Phone: 214-645-6128. E-mail: alfred.gilman@utsouthwestern.edu.

GILMAN, BENJAMIN ARTHUR, former congressman, lawyer; b. Poughkeepsie, NY, Dec. 6, 1922; s. Harry and Esther (Gold) G.; m. Jane Prizant, Oct. 19, 1952 (div. 1978); children: Jonathan, Harrison, Susan, David (dec.), Ellen (dec.); m. Rita Gail Kelhoffer, Nov. 9, 1984 (div. 1996); m. Georgia Nickles Tingus, Jan. 12, 1997; children: Nicole, Peter. BS, U. Pa., Phila., 1946; LLB, NY Law Sch., 1950; degree (hon.), St. Thomas Aquinas Coll., Sparkill, NY, 1977, Mercy Coll., Dobbs Ferry, NY, 1984, Yeshiva U., NYC, 1995, Dominican Coll., Orangeburg, NY, 2003, U. Bridgeport, Conn., 2003, Inje U., South Korea, 2004. Bar: NY 1952. Dep. asst. atty. gen. NY State Dept. Law, 1952-54, asst. atty. gen., 1954-55; ptnr. Gilman & Gilman, Middletown, NY, 1955-72; counsel NY Assembly's Com. on Local Fin., 1956-64; mem. NY State Assembly, 1967-72; congressman 93d-97th Congresses from 26th NY dist., 1972-82, 20th dist. NY, 1983—2002; sr. counsel Finkelstein & Ptnrs., New Windsor, NY, 2003—04. Mem. Rep. Congl. Policy Com., 1997-2002; mem. Presdl. Commn. on World Hunger, 1978-80, co-chair Ad Hoc Com. on Irish

Affairs, Rep. Task Force on Handicapped and Task Force on Econ. Policy; mem. U.S.-Mex. Consultative Mechanism Subcom. on Narcotics Trafficing, Govt. Reform Com., House Public Office and Civil Svcs. Com., co-founder House Select Com. on Narcotics; U.S. Congl. rep. to 36th session UN Gen. Assembly; pub. del. U.S. UN Mission 58th Gen. Assembly, 2003; mem. Spkr.'s Task Force on Narcotics; chmn. House Task Force on Prisoners of War and Missing in Action, 1983-85, Human Rights Caucus; mem. World Hunger Yr. Bd.; mem. adv. com. NY State Divsn. Youth's Start Ctr., 1962-67; mem. NY State Southeastern Water Study Com., 1971-73, Lawyers' Com. for Civil Rights Under Law, 1963-75; mem. adv. com. Otisville Fed. Correctional Instn.; v.p., bd. dirs. Orange County Health Assn.; adv. coun. Lamont-Doherty Geol. Obs., Columbia U., 1979-82; chmn. House Internat. Com. on Fgn. Affairs, 1995-2001; bd. dirs. Co-Operation Ireland, US, 2004-, Am. Internat. Learning Corp., 2003. Bd. dirs. Bnai Zion, 2003-, Humpty Dumpty Inst., Nat. Legis. Office Jewish War Vets., 2000—, Columbia U. Gilman Fellows, 2002, Am. Friends of Shakespeare Birthplace Trust, 2004-; mem. chmn.'s adv. bd. US Inst. for Peace; advisor Internat. Med. Relief Found., 2004-; mem. adv. coun. US Global Leadership Campaign, 2005-; mem. adv. com. on Public Policy for Population Inst., World Hunger Yearmem. Com. on Present Danger, 2005—, Haiti Internat. Assessment Com., Internat. Rep. Inst., 2005—; chmn. bd. dirs. Middletown Little League; trustee Am. U. Antigua, 2005—; bd. visitors U.S. Mil. Acad., 1973-83; mem. Asia-Pacific CEO Assn., US World Holocaust Mem. Coun., 1993-2002. Lt. col. USAAF, 1943-45, Japan, C.A.P., staff sgt.; col. NY N.G. Decorated D.F.C., Air medals, VFW Medal of Merit, 1972; recipient Peace Thru Strength award, Am. Security Coun., Disting. Svcs. award HHS Adminstrn. Law Judges, 1980, Silver Beaver award Boy Scouts Am., 1994, Am. Hellenic Pericles award, 1996, Theodore Herzel award, 1997, Distinguished Svc. medal, NY Grand Lodge of Masons, 1998, NY Law Sch. Judge Chas W. Froessel award, 1999, Stephen Duggan award for Internat. Understanding, Inst. of Internat. Edn., 2000, FBI and DEA Jt. award for promoting internat. fight vs. drugs and crime, 2000, Padma Vibhuswan, India, 2001, Assn. Interat. Microenterprise award, 2002, Disting. Svc. award U.S. Dept. State, 2002, award Anti Defamation League, 2004; named to St. Thomas Aquinas Hall of Fame, 2004; established Grad. Sch. scholarships U. Belfast, No. Ireland, U. Limerick, Ireland; Benjamin A. Gilman Internat. Congl. Ann. Internat. Scholarship named in his honor, 2000. Mem. ABA, D.C. Bar Assn., NY State Bar Assn., Assn. of Bar of City of NY, Middletown Bar Assn., Orange County Bar Assn., Assn. Trial Lawyers Am., VFW (past county comdr.), Am. Legion, Masonic War Vets. (lt. comdr.), Jewish War Vets., Forty and Eight, Air Force Assn., Internat. Narcotics Enforcement Officers, NY Law Sch. Alumni (advisor), NY Soc. in Washington (pres.), Grange, La Société des 40 Hommes et 8 Chevaux, Masons (33 deg.), Shriners (Capitol Hill pres.), Elks, DAV (hon.), Vietnam Vets. (hon.), Nat. Sojourners. Republican. Jewish. Achievements include the creation of the Gilman International Library at SUNY Orange County Community College named in his honor. Office: The Gilman Group 1625 K St Ste 1070 Washington DC 20006 Home Phone: 845-341-0098; Office Phone: 202-659-3333. Personal E-mail: gntgilman@optonline.net.

GILMAN, DAVID ALAN, education educator; b. Terre Haute, Ind., Sept. 26, 1933; s. Albert Maynard and Ruth Edna (Parsons) G.; m. Elizabeth Ann Barlow, Oct. 7, 1956; children— Ruth Ann, Thomas Alan, William Michael. BS, Ind. State Tchrs. Coll., Terre Haute, 1955; MA, Mich. State U., East Lansing, 1962; PhD (NSF fellow), Pa. State U., 1967. Tchr. Flint Pub. Schs., Mich., 1955-56; tchr. Utica Pub. Schs., Mich., 1957-62; prof. Shippensburg State Coll., Pa., 1963-65; prof. edn. Ind. State U., Terre Haute, from 1967, Holmstedt disting. prof. edn., 1994-95, Coffman dist. prof. edn., from 2004, Lotus Delta Coffman disting. prof. edn., from 2004. Author: A Course-writer Guide for Teacher-Authors of Materials for Computer-Assisted Instruction, 1967, Alternatives to Tests, Marks and Class Ranks, 1974, Portfolios: They're Not Just Work Folders Anymore, 1996; editor Contemporary Edn., 1990-98; contbr. articles to profl. jours. Served with CIC AUS, 1956-58. Recipient Caleb Mills Disting. Tchg. award Ind. State U., 1973, Theodore Dreiser Disting. Contbn. to Rsch. and Creativity award, 2003. Mem. Blue Key, Kappa Delta Pi, Phi Delta Kappa. Home: Terre Haute, Ind. Died June 13, 2007.

GILMAN, JOHN JOSEPH, research scientist; b. St. Paul, Dec. 22, 1925; s. Alexander Falk and Florence Grace (Colby) G.; m. Pauline Marie Harms, June 17, 1950 (div. Dec. 1968); children: Pamela Ann, Gregory George, Cheryl Elizabeth; m. Gretchen Marie Sutter, June 12, 1976; 1 son, Brian Alexander. BS, Ill. Inst. Tech., 1946, MS, 1948; PhD, Columbia, 1952. Research metallurgist Gen. Electric Co., Schenectady, 1952-60; prof. engring. Brown U., Providence, 1960-63; prof. physics and metallurgy U. Ill., Urbana, 1963-68; dir. Materials Research Center Allied Chem. Corp., Morristown, N.J., 1968-78; dir. Corp. Devel. Center, 1978-80; mgr. corp. research Amoco Co. (Ind.), Naperville, Ill., 1980-85; assoc. dir. Lawrence Berkeley Lab./U. Calif., Calif., 1985-87; sr. scientist Lawrence Berkeley Lab., Calif., 1987-93; adj. prof. UCLA, 1993—. Author: Micromechanics of Flow in Solids, 1969, Inventivity-The Art and Science of Research Management, 1992, Electronic Basis of the Strength of Materials, 2003; editor: The Art and Science of Growing Crystals, 1963, Fracture of Solids (with D.C. Drucker), 1963, Atomic and Electronic Structures of Metals, 1967, Metallic Glasses, 1973, Energetic Materials, 1993; editl. bd. Jour. Applied Physics, 1969-72; contbg. editor Materials Tech., 1994-99; contbr. over 325 papers, articles to tech. jours. Served as Ensign USNR, 1943-46. Recipient Mathewson gold medal Am. Inst. Metal Engrs., 1959, Disting. Service award Alumni Assn. Ill. Inst. Tech., 1962, Application to Practice award, 1985. Fellow AAAS, Am. Phys. Soc., The Materials Soc., Am. Soc. for Metals (Campbell lectr. 1966); mem. Nat. Acad. Engring., Phi Kappa Phi, Tau Beta Pi. Home: 2852 Forrester Dr Los Angeles CA 90064-4662 Office: UCLA 6532 Boelter Hl Los Angeles CA 90095-0001 Business E-Mail: gilman@seas.ucla.edu.

GILMAN, RICHARD CARLETON, retired academic administrator; b. Cambridge, Mass., July 28, 1923; s. George Phillips Brooks and Karen Elise (Theller) G.; m. Lucille Young, Aug. 28, 1948 (dec. 1978); children: Marsha, Bradley Morris, Brian Potter, Blair Tucker; m. Sarah Gale, Dec. 28, 1984 (dec. 1986). BA, Dartmouth Coll., 1944; student, New Coll., U. London, Eng., 1947-48; PhD (Borden Parker Bowne fellow), Boston U., 1952, LHD, 1969; LLD, Pomona Coll., 1966, U. So. Calif., 1968, Coll. Idaho, 1968; LHD, Chapman Coll., 1984, Occidental Coll., 1988. Teaching fellow religion Dartmouth, 1948; mem. faculty Colby Coll., 1950-56, assoc. prof. philosophy, 1955-56; exec. dir. Nat. Council Religion Higher Edn., New Haven, 1956-60; dean coll., prof. philosophy Carleton Coll., 1960-65; pres. Occidental Coll., LA, 1965-88, pres. emeritus, 1988—. Past mem. bd. dirs. Am. Coun. on Edn., Assn. Am. Colls., Assn. Ind. Calif. Colls. and Univs., Coun. for Fin. Aid to Edn., Coun. on Postsecondary Accreditation, Nat. Coun. Ind. Colls. and Univs., Ind. Coll. Funds Am.; mem. Intergovtl. Adv. Coun. on Edn., 1980-84; mem. pres.'s commn. NCAA, 1984-86; exec. asst., counselor to sec. of edn., 1979-80; mem. Calif. Student Aid Commn., 1988-92; mng. trustee S.W. Mus., LA, 1994-95. Bbd. dirs. Wellness Cmty.-Foothills, pres., 1996-98; past bd. dirs. Calif. Mus. Found., Cape of Good Hope Found., Exec. Svc. Corp. Calif., S.W. Mus., LA World Affairs Coun., Calif. C. of C. Fellow Soc. for Values in Higher Edn.; mem. Calif. Club LA, Twilight Club (Pasadena), Phi Beta Kappa. Home: 131 Annandale Rd Pasadena CA 91105-1405 Personal E-mail: rcgilman@earthlink.net.

GILMAN, RONALD LEE, federal judge; b. Memphis, Oct. 16, 1942; s. Seymour and Rosalind (Kuzin) Gilman; m. Betsy Dunn, June 11, 1966; children: Laura M., Sherry I. BS, MIT, 1964; JD cum laude, Harvard U., 1967. Bar: Tenn. 1967, US Supreme Ct. 1971. Mem. Farris, Mathews, Gilman, Branan & Hellen, Memphis, 1967—97; judge US Ct. Appeals (6th cir.), 1997—. Judge Tenn. Ct. Judiciary, 1979—87; lectr. trial advocacy U. Memphis Law Sch., 1980—97; arbitrator, mediator Am. Arbitration Assoc., 1988—97; arbitrator NASD, 1993—97; referee Pvt. Adjudication Ctr., 1994—97. Contbr. articles to profl. jours. Regional chmn. ednl. coun. MIT, 1968—88; active Chickasaw coun. Boy Scouts Am., 1993—2000; mem. Leadership Memphis; bd. dirs Memphis Jewish Home, 1984—87. Recipient Sam A. Myar Jr. Meml. award for outstanding svc. to legal profession and cmty., 1981. Mem.: ABA (ho. of dels. 1990—97, chmn. appellate judges conf. jud. divsn.), Am. Arbitration Assn. (mem. large, complex case panel 1993—97), Tenn. Bar Assn. (spkr. ho. of dels. 1985—87, pres. 1990—91), Memphis Bar Assn. (pres. 1987), Am. Coll. Trust and Estate Counsel, Am. Judicature Soc., Am. Law Inst., 6th Cir. Jud. Conf. (life). Democrat. Jewish. Office: Fed Bldg 167 N Main St Ste 1176 Memphis TN 38103-1824*

GILMAN, SHELDON GLENN, lawyer; b. Cleve., July 20, 1943; BBA, Ohio U., 1965; JD, Case Western Res. U., 1967. Bar: Ohio 1967, Ky. 1971, Ind. 1982, Fla. 1984, DC 1985, Tenn. 1985, U.S. Supreme Ct. 1987. From assoc. to ptnr. law firms, Louisville, 1972—; ptnr. Lynch, Cox, Gilman & Mahan, P.S.C., Louisville, 1987—. Gen. counsel Louisville Assn. Life Underwriters, 1977, 78, 90; adj. prof. law U. Louisville Sch. Law; spkr. in field. Author: Kentucky Estate Planning, 2d edit., 2003; contbr. chapters to books, articles to profl. jours. Bd. dirs., chmn. Louisville Minority Bus. Resource Ctr., 1975—80; bd. dirs., v.p., sec. Louisville Orch., 1982—85; bd. dirs. City of Devondale, Ky., 1976; pres. Congregation Adath Jeshurun, 1986—88; bd. dirs. United Synagogue Cons. Judaism, NY, pres. Ohio Valley region. With JAGC US Army, 1968—71. Named one of Best Lawyers in Am. Employee Benefits Law, Trusts, Estates, 2007. Fellow: Am. Bar Found., Am. Coll. Trust and Estate Counsel; mem.: ACLU (bd. dirs. 1998—2002), Louisville Employee Benefit Coun. (pres. 1980), Ky. Bar Assn. (mem. ethics com. 1982—, mem. ethics hotline com. 1990). Office: Lynch Cox Gilman & Mahan 500 W Jefferson St Ste 2100 Louisville KY 40202 Office Phone: 502-589-4215. Business E-Mail: sgilman@lcgandm.com.

GILMAN, SID, neurologist; b. LA, Oct. 19, 1932; s. Morris and Sarah Rose (Cooper) G.; m. Carol G. Barbour. BA, UCLA, 1954; MD, 1957, FRCP, 2001. Intern UCLA Hosp., 1957-58; resident in neurology Boston City Hosp., 1960-63; from instr. to assoc. in neurology Harvard Med. Sch., 1965-68; from asst. prof. to prof. neurology Columbia U., NYC, 1968-76, H. Houston Merritt prof. neurology, 1976-77; prof., chair dept. neurology U. Mich., Ann Arbor, 1977—2004, William J. Herdman prof. neurology, 1997—2005, William J. Herdman disting. univ. prof. neurology, 2005—. Cons. VA Hosp., Ann Arbor, 1977—; mem. peripheral and ctrl. nervous sys. drugs adv. com. FDA, 1983-85, 86-87, 90-94, chmn., 1996-2000, cons., 2000—; adj. attending neurologist Henry Ford Hosp., Detroit; mem. chronic disease adv. com. Mich. Dept. Pub. Health, 1988-94; mem. neurol. sci. rsch. and tng. com. NIH, 1971-73, mem. neurol. disorders program project B com., 1976-80, mem. sci. programs adv. com. Nat. Inst. Neurol. Diseases, Communicative Disorders and Stroke, 1982-84, mem. nat. adv. neurol. disorders and stroke coun., 1994-97; mem. clin. trials subcom. Nat. Adv. Neurol. Disorders and Stroke Coun., 2001-04; dir. Mich. Alzheimer's Disease Rsch. Ctr., 1991—; mem. rsch. adv. coun. United Cerebral Palsy Found.; mem. sci. adv. coun. Nat. Ataxia Found., Nat. Amyotrophic Lateral Sclerosis Found., Inc.; mem. profl. adv. bd. Epilepsy Found. Am.; mem. rsch. adv. com. Nat. Multiple Sclerosis Soc., 1986-90; mem. exec. bd. Nat. Coalition for Rsch., 1989-95, Nat. Found. for Brain Rsch., 1989-95; mem. rsch. adv. com. Dana Alliance; mem. sci. adv. bd. Merck, Inc., 2000-04, PPD Devel., 1999—, INC Rsch., 2000—; Henry Russel lectr. U. Mich., 2001. Author: (with J.R. Bloedel and R. Lechtenberg) Disorders of the Cerebellum, 1981, (with S.W. Newman) Manter and Gatz's Essentials of Clinical Neuroanatomy and Neurophysiology, 10th edit., 2003, (with J.C. Mazziotta) Clinical Brain Imaging: Principles and Applications, 1992, Clinical Examination of the Nervous System, 2000; editor: Neurobiology of Disease, 2007; sect. editor editl. bd. Exptl. Neurology, Current Opinion in Neurology and Neurosurgery, Neurology, Annals Neurology, Jour. Neuropathology and Exptl. Neurology, Neurobase Arbor Pub. Co.; editor-in-chief MedLink Neurology, 1992—, Contemporary Neurology Series, 1995—, Neurology Network Commentary, 1996-2000, Lancet Neurology Network, 2000-02, Exptl. Neurology, 2003—, Neurolobiology of Disease, 2005-; contbr. articles to profl. jours. Dir. Mich. Dem. Program, 1994-2000. With USPHS, 1958-60. Recipient Lucy G. Moses prize Columbia U., 1973, Weinstein Goldenson award United Cerebral Palsy Assn., 1981, UCLA Alumni Profl. Achievement award, 1992, UCLA Med. Alumni Profl. Achievement award, 1992. Fellow AAAS, Royal Soc. of Medicine, Royal Coll. Physicians, Am. Acad. Arts and Scis.; mem. Am. Neurol. Assn. (hon.; 1st v.p. 1985-86, pres.-elect 1987-88, pres. 1988-89), Mich. Neurol. Assn. (pres. 1987-88), Soc. Clin. Investigation, Am. Physiol. Soc., Am. Assn. Neuropathologists, Soc. Neurosci., Am. Acad. Neurology (vice chmn. geriatric neurology subcom. 1992-94, chmn. 1994-96, chmn. Decade of Brain com. 1990-95, AB Baker award 2004), Am. Epilepsy Soc., Assn. Rsch. in Nervous and Mental Disease, Assn. Am. Physicians, Inst. Medicine, Nat. Acad. Scis., The Nat. Acads. (nat. assoc.), Phi Beta Kappa, Alpha Omega Alpha. Home: 3411 Geddes Rd Ann Arbor MI 48105-2518 Office: U Mich Dept Neurology 300 N Ingalls 3D15 Ann Arbor MI 48109 Office Phone: 734-936-1808. Business E-Mail: sgilman@umich.edu.

GILMAN-ANDERSON, SUSAN ELLEN, real estate company executive, consultant; b. Brockton, Mass., June 18, 1962; d. Alden Reed and Phoebe Ames Gilman. BA, Green Mountain Coll., 1985. Dir. relocation Relocation Resources Internat. Inc, Norwell, Mass., 1995—2002; dir. relocation and corp. svcs. ERA Stirling Properties, Covington, La., 2003—. Cons. relocation Rockport Co., Marlboro, Mass., 1995. Mem. Relocation Dirs. Coun. Mem.: Relocation Dirs. Coun., Profl. Employee Relocation Coun. (assoc. cert. relocation profl. 1998, PERC 2003), St. Tammany C. of C. Conservative-R. Protestant. Avocations: travel, swimming, camping, hiking. Office: ERA Stirling Properties 109 Northpark Blvd Ste 300 Covington LA 70433 Home Phone: 985-875-9757; Office Phone: 985-246-3400. Office Fax: 504-523-8577, 985-246-3420; Home Fax: 504-523-8577, 985-246-3420. Business E-Mail: sanderson@stirlingprop.com, sanderson@erastirling.com.

GILMARTIN, GEOFFREY SCOTT, physician, researcher; m. Jessica Kiernan Gilmartin. MD, Brown U., Providence, 1997. Physician Beth Israel Deaconess Med. Ctr., Boston, 2004—.

GILMARTIN, MARYANNE, real estate company executive; b. May 28, 1964; married; 3 children. Asst. v.p. comml. devel. NYC Econ. Devel. Corp.; mng. dir. consulting svcs. Grubb & Ellis Cos.; positions up to exec. v.p., dir. comml. and residential devel. & Atlantic Yards Forest City Ratner Cos., Bklyn., 1994—. Mem. adv. com. NYC Ballet. Named one of 40 Under 40, Crain's NY Bus., 2003. Mem.: NY Women Execs. in Real Estate, CoreNet Global, Assn. Real Estate Women (named a Rising Star in NY Real Estate 2004). Office: Forest City Ratner Cos 1 MetroTech Ctr N Brooklyn NY 11201 Office Phone: 718-923-8420. Office Fax: 718-923-8720. E-mail: mgilmartin@fcrc.com.*

GILMARTIN, RAYMOND V., pharmaceutical company executive; b. Washington, Mar. 6, 1941; m. Gladys Higham; 3 children. BS in Elect. Engring., Union Coll., 1963; MBA, Harvard U., 1968. Sr. cons. Arthur D. Little Inc., 1968-76; v.p. corp. planning Becton Dickinson & Co., Paramus, NJ, 1976-79, pres. Becton Dickinson divsn., 1979-87, group pres., 1982-83, sr. v.p., 1983-86, exec. v.p., 1986-87, pres. Franklin Lakes, NJ, 1987-94, CEO, 1989-94; chmn., pres., CEO Merck & Co. Inc., Whitehouse Station, NJ, 1994—2005, spl. adviser to the bd. exec. com. Whitehouse, NJ, 2005—. Bd. dirs. Merck & Co. Inc., 1994-2005, Microsoft Corp., 2001-, Gen. Mills, Inc.; chmn. Inter-faculty initative in Health Policy. Trustee Healthcare Leadership Coun., Healthcare Inst. NJ; bd. dirs. Alliance for Healthcare Reform, Am. Enterprise Inst.; Pharm. Rsch. and Mfrs. Am.; chmn. United Negro Coll. Fund; active Bus. Coun., Bus. Roundtable, Pres. Export Coun.; mem. exec. com. Coun. on Competitiveness. Mem.: Internat. Fed. Pharm. Mfrs. Assn. (chmn.). Office: Merck & Co Inc 1 Merck Dr Whitehouse Station NJ 08889-0100

GILMER, PENNY JANE, biochemist, educator; b. Hackensack, NJ, Aug. 19, 1943; d. Peter E. and Barbara D. (Joynt) Gilmer; m. Sanford A. Safron, Sept. 9, 1980; children: Helena M., Nathaniel S. BA in Chemistry, Douglass Coll., 1965; MA in Organic Chemistry, Bryn Mawr Coll., 1967; PhD in Biochemistry, U. Calif.-Berkeley, 1972; DSc in Sci. Edn., Curtin U. Tech., 2004. Bank Am.-Giannini postdoctoral fellow Stanford U. (Calif.), 1973—75, USPHS and NIH postdoctoral fellow, 1975—77, acting asst. prof. human biology, 1976—77; asst. prof. chemistry Fla. State U., Tallahassee, 1977—84, assoc. prof., 1984—96, interim assoc. dean coll. arts and scis., 1990—91, assoc. chair chemistry, 1991—93, prof., 1996—. Lectr. in field. Contbr. articles to profl. jour. Recipient Faculty Rsch. award, Fla. State U., 1978, 1984, 1986, 1990, Tchg. Incentive award, 1993—94, Outstanding Cmty. Women award, Am. Assn. U. Women, Tallahassee br., 2006, GK-12 Dissemination award, Nat. Sci. Found., 2006; grantee NIH, 1979—81, Rsch. Corp., 1979—86, 1990—96, Am. Cancer Soc., 1981—83, Jessie Ball duPont Fund, 1987—89, NSF, 1990—2007. Mem.: AAAS, Assn. Sci. Tchr. Edn. (Outstanding Sci. Tchr. Educator 2006), Nat. Assn. Rsch. Sci. Tchg. (bd. 2003—, pres.-elect 2006—07, pres. 2007—), Assn. Women in Sci., Southeastern Immunology Conf. (dir. 1979—84, pres. 1982), Audubon Soc., Am. Chem. Soc., Fedn. Biol. Chemists, Zonta Internat. (pres. Tallahassee Club 1992—93, area 4 dir. dist. 11 2006—), Sierra Club, Sigma Xi. Democrat. Office: Fla State U Dept Chemistry and Biochemistry Tallahassee FL 32306-4390 Home Phone: 850-385-5762; Office Phone: 850-644-4026. Business E-Mail: gilmer@chem.fsu.edu.

GILMER, ROBERT, mathematics professor; b. Pontotoc, Miss., July 3, 1938; s. Robert William and Lucy Marie (Jernigan) G.; m. Rachel Grace Colson, Aug. 24, 1963; children: David Patrick, Stephen Douglas. Student, Itawamba Jr. Coll., 1955-56; BS, Miss. State U., 1958; MS, La. State U., 1960, PhD, 1961. Instr., Miss. State U., Starkville, 1959, vis. prof., 1962; research instr. La. State U., Baton Rouge, 1961-62; vis. lectr. U. Wis., Madison, 1962-63; mem. faculty Fla. State U., Tallahassee, 1963—2003, prof. math., 1968—2003, Robert O. Lawton Disting. prof., 1981—2003, prof. emeritus, 2003—. Vis. prof. Latrobe U., Bundoora, Victoria, Australia, 1974, U. Tex., Austin, 1976-77; vis. rsch. prof. U. Conn., Storrs, 1982; visitor Inst. for Advanced Study, 1990; vis. scholar U. N.C., Chapel Hill, 1997. Author: Multiplicative Ideal Theory, 1967, 72, 92, Commutative Semigroup Rings, 1984; also articles; assoc. editor Am. Math. Mo., 1971-73; mem. editl. bd. Jour. Communications in Algebra, 1974-85. Named Barrett Meml. Lectr., U. Tenn., Knoxville, 1994; Office Naval Rsch. fellow, 1962-63; Alfred P. Sloan Found. fellow, 1965-67; NSF grantee, 1965-89; Fulbright sr. scholar to Australia, 1974. Mem. Am. Math. Soc., Math. Assn. Am. (gov. Fla. sect. 1986-89, cert. meritorious svc. 1992). Baptist. Home: 2414 Perez Ave Tallahassee FL 32304-1329 Office Phone: 850-644-8705. Business E-Mail: gilmer@math.fsu.edu.

GILMER-HILL, HOLLY, medical educator; d. Anderson Gilmer and Bennie Glenn; m. Carl Hill; children: Christopher, Susan. Degree in pediatric neurosurgery, Wayne State U., Detroit, 2000. Diplomate Am. Bd. Neurological Surgery, Calif., 2003, Am. Bd. Neurological Surgery, La., 2003, Am. Bd. Neurological Surgery, Mich., 2003. Attending Children's Hosp. Mich., Detroit, 2000; asst. prof., dept. neurol. surgery Wayne State U., Detroit, 2001—. Rsch. Wayne State Univ., 2000—. Mem.: Confress Neurol. Surgeons (assoc.; edn. com. 2005). Office: Pediatric Neurosurgery Grp PC 3901 Beaubien Carl's Bldg 2d Fl Detroit MI 48201 Office Fax: 313-993-8744.

GILMORE, BRENDA RENÉ, literature and language educator, theater director; BA in English, Northern Ill. U., Dekalb, 1990; MA in speech, Northern Ill. U., Chgo., 2002. Theatre dir. Camp Kamaji, Benidji, Minn., 1990; speech coach Wanbondie Valley HS, Aurora, Ill., 1991—95; English tchr. Wanbondia Valley HS, Aurora, Ill., 1991—99, theatre dir., 1993—99, Neugua Valley HS, Naperville, Ill., 1999—2001, English and theatre tchr., 1999—; speech coach Nequa Valley HS, Naperville, Ill., 1999—2000; theatre dir. Summer Place Theatre, Naperville, Ill., 2001, 2002. Prodr.: Boy the Musical, 2004; (plays) She Loves Me, 2005. Bd. mem. Summer Place Theatre, 2003—, sec., 2004—. Avocations: tennis, music, theater. Office: Neuqua HS 2360 95th St Naperville IL 60564

GILMORE, CLARE MAE, writer; d. Clarence Mansel and Ida Jane Smith; m. Calvin Hobert Gilmore, Dec. 24, 1935 (dec.); 1 child. Student, New Concord, Ohio, 1934—35. Mem.: Christian Writer's Fellowship Internat. Home: 7915 Blackrun Rd Nashport OH 43830

GILMORE, CLARENCE PERCY, editor-in-chief, writer; b. Baton Rouge, Feb. 8, 1926; s. Clarence Percy and Clara (Cobb) G.; m. V. Elaine Oliver, 1985; children: Robert Dillard, Patricia Anne. Student, La. State U., 1942-44, 46-48. Reporter various radio, TV stas., 1948-56; free-lance mag. writer, 1956—; sci. editor Metromedia TV, 1967-84; exec. editor Popular Sci. Mag., 1971-80, editor-in-chief, 1980-89; dep. editorial dir. Times Mirror Mags., NYC, 1989-92, ret., 1992. Cons. in field. With USNR, 1944-46. Recipient Claude Bernard sci. journalism award Nat. Soc. Med. Rsch., 1969, Albert and Mary Lasker Found. award, 1969, Howard W. Blakeslee award Am. Heart Assn., 1969, Spl. Commendation for med. journalism AMA, 1969, 70, Sci. Writing award for physics and astronomy Am. Inst. Physics, 1970, Sci. Writing award AAAS, 1980. Home: 1629 Boston Post Rd Westbrook CT 06498 Home Phone: 860-339-5280. Personal E-mail: kengilmore@comcast.net.

GILMORE, DENNIS J., insurance company executive; BBA, San Diego State U.; MBA, Loyola Marymount U. With TRTS Data Svcs. (acquired by First Am. Corp. in 1991), 1988—91; v.p., area mgr. First Am. Corp., 1991—93, regional v.p., 1993—96, regional v.p., nat. dir., 1996—98, pres. First Am. Real Estate Solutions LLC, 1998, COO. Office: First Am Corp 1 First American Way Santa Ana CA 92707 Office Phone: 714-250-3000.*

GILMORE, GUY L., publishing executive; m. Donna Gilmore; 3 children. BA magna cum laude, U. Calif., Riverside. Regional gen. mgr. USA Today, Kansas City, Mo., Cin./Indpls.; v.p. circulation Little Rock Gazette; circulation dir. Reno (Nev.) Gazette-Jour., Fla. Today, Brevard, Fla., Nashville Tennessean & Banner, Portland Oregonian; v.p. circulation & prodn. Balt. Sun; pres. & pub. Allentown (Pa.) Morning Call, 2000—05; v.p. circulation St. Paul Pioneer Press, 2005—07, pub., 2007—. Mem.: Phi Beta Kappa. Office: Pioneer Press 345 Cedar St Saint Paul MN 55101 Office Phone: 651-222-1111.*

GILMORE, H. JAMES, film producer, educator; b. Park Forest, Ill., Mar. 25, 1961; s. Harold James Gilmore, Jr. and Mary Emily Curtis; m. Sheryl Ann Christy, June 22, 1991; children: Grace, Griffin, Ronan. BA, Kalamazoo Coll., 1983; MA, U. Iowa, 1984. Writer/prodr. WSBT-TV, South Bend, Ind., 1985—86; field prodr. The Christian Sci. Monitor, Boston, 1986—88; coordinating prodr./dir. N.H. Pub. TV, Durham, 1989—95; exec. prodr. Acadia Pictures, St. Augustine, Fla., 1995—. Assoc. dir. Acadia Inst. Oceanography, Seal Harbor, Maine, 1992—; asst. prof. St. Joseph's Coll., Standish, Maine, 1999—2000, Flagler Coll., St. Augustine, 2000—06, assoc. prof., 2006—. Prodr.: (documentaries) Great Lakes/Toxic Lakes, 1987, Zimbabwe: A Racial Revolution, 1988 (Gold Plaque, Chgo. Intnl.

Film Festival, 1988), The Rhino War, 1988, Dare Not Walk Alone, 2005; prodr., dir. (documentaries) Happy Talk, 2007; dir.: (documentary film) The Shipyard Dance, 1999, (editor) Alone Together, 1990 (AFI Robert M. Bennett Award, 1990), (writer, editor) Soul of a Woman: The Life & Times of Mary Baker Eddy, 1994 (Wilbur, Telly, 1994), Chronicle of an American Suburb, 2002, (film) Pale in Your Shadow, 1997 (Gold Aurora, 1998). Mem.: Internat. Documentary Assn., Univ. Film and Video Assn. (Award of Merit in Documentary Film 2002). Avocations: theater, piano, photography, travel. Office: Acadia Pictures Inc PO Box 1860 Saint Augustine FL 32085 Business E-Mail: hjames@acadiapictures.com.

GILMORE, JAMES STUART, III, lawyer, former governor; b. Richmond, Va., Oct. 6, 1949; s. James Stuart, Jr. and Margaret Kandle G.; m. Roxane Gilmore; children: Jay, Ashton BA, U. Va., 1971, JD, 1977. Atty. Harris, Tuck, Freasier & Johnson, 1977-80, Benedetti, Gilmore, Warthen & Dalton, 1984-87; commonwealth's atty. Henrico County, Va., 1987-93; atty. gen. Commonwealth of Va., 1993-97; ptnr. LeClair Ryan, Richmond, Va., 1997; gov. Commonwealth of Va., 1998—2002; ptnr. Kelley Drye & Warren LLP, Washington, 2002—. Alt. del. Rep. Nat. Conv., 1976; chmn. Henrico County Rep. Com., 1982-85. With U.S. Army, 1971-74. Mem. Nat. Dist. Atty. Assn., Va. Bar Assn., Va. Trial Lawyers Assn., Va. Commonwealt Attys. Assn. Methodist. Office: Kelley Drye & Warren LLP Washington Harbour Ste 400 3050 K St Washington DC 20007 Business E-Mail: jgilmore@kelleydrye.com.*

GILMORE, JENNIFER A.W., computer specialist, educator; b. San Fernando, Trinidad, Jan. 12, 1954; arrived in US, 1972, naturalized, 1993; d. Fitzroy Grant and Zelma (Williams) Oudkerk; m. Frederick R. Gilmore, June 17, 1983. BA, MA, Bklyn. Coll., NY, 1984; BBA, MS, Baruch Coll., NYC, 1993; MBA, LI U., NY, 1994; PhD, Kennedy-Western U., Cheyenne, Wyo., 2001, Walden U., Mpls., 2001. Cert. Microsoft Office Specialist (MOS) 2002, Internet Computing Core (IC3) Certiport, 2003, IC3 Instr. Certiport, 2003, Online Tchr. U. Md. Univ. Coll., 2003; coll. tchg. Kaplan U., 2005, blackboard tchg. Baker Coll., 2006. COBOL programmer MetLife, NYC, 1972-86; project mgr., human resources adminstrn. mgmt. info. sys. City of N.Y., 1990—. Adj. prof. NYC Coll. Tech., 1997, Kingsborough C.C., 1998, St. Francis Coll., Bklyn., 1998, Medgar Evers Coll., 1998, Borough of Manhattan C.C., 1998, Touro Coll., 1999—, Baruch Coll., 1999—2000, Monroe Coll., 1999—, U. Md., 2003—, Kaplan U., 2005—, Baker Coll. Online, 2006—. Author: (books) A Case Study of Two System Development Projects and their Implementation, 2003, An Analysis of Computer and Telephone Usage in the New York City Metropolitan Area, 2003. Democrat. Adventist. Home: 47 Mckeever Pl Apt 16J Brooklyn NY 11225-2537 Office: NYC-HRA-MIS 15 Metrotech Brooklyn NY 11201 Personal E-mail: jgilmore102716560@yahoo.com.

GILMORE, JUDITH MARIE, physician; b. Houston, Dec. 28, 1942; d. Howard Ray and Mary Gardner (Currier) G.; m. Richard E. Kelley, July 21, 1974 (div. 1981); 1 child, Lisa Kelley. BA, U. Maine, 1965; MA, NYU, 1968; MD, Woman's Med. Coll., 1972. Diplomate Am. Bd. Internal Medicine, Am. Bd. Endocrinology. Resident St. Vincent's Hosp., NYC, 1972-74; fellow in endocrinology St. Raphael's Hosp., New Haven, 1974-75, West Haven VA-Yale Hosp., New Haven, 1975-76; pvt. practice Bridgeport, Conn., 1976-80, Cranston, R.I., 1986—; mem. staff St. Joseph's Hosp., Providence, 1986—; mem. cons. staff Newport (R.I.) Hosp., 1986—; mem. courtesy staff Roger Williams Hosp., Providence, 1994—, R.I. Hosp., Providence, 1995, Kent County Hosp., Pawtucket Meml. Hosp. Lt. comdr. USNR, 1980-86. Mem. ACP, AMA, Am. Assn. Endocrine, Am. Diabetes Assn., R.I. Endocrine Assn. Avocations: hiking, music, art. Office: 725 Reservoir Ave Ste 2 Providence RI 02910-4450 Office Phone: 401-943-5120. E-mail: JP1994@msn.com.

GILMORE, KATHI, former state treasurer; b. Dec. 23, 1944; m. Richard Gilmore; children: Suzi, Barb, Jeff, Amy. Mem. N.D. Ho. of Reps. from Dist. 6, 1989-92; treas. State of N.D., 1993—2004. Mem. Bd. Tax Equalization, State Hist. Bd., State Investment Bd., Tchrs. Fund for Retirement Bd., State Canvassing Bd., Bd. of Univ. and Sch. Lands Mem.: Assn. Securities Profls. (hon. co-chair pension fund conf. 1994, Task Forces Orgnl. Planning and Coordinating Com. 1993), Retirement and Investment Office Internal Audit Com., Nat. Assn. State Treas. (pension com.). Democrat. Presbyterian.

GILMORE, MARSHALL, bishop; b. Hoffman, NC, Jan. 4, 1931; m. Yvonne Dukes; children: John Marshall, Joan Michele. BA, Paine Coll., 1957, LLD (hon.); MDiv, Drew U., 1960; D of Ministry, United Theol. Seminary, 1974; DD, Texas Coll., Interdenominational Theol. Ctr. Ordained Deacon 1955. Bishop Christian Meth. Episcopal Ch., Ga., Ill., Mich., Phillips Temple Christian Meth. Episcopal Ch., Dayton, Ohio; presiding sr. bishop 8th Episcopal Dist., Dallas, 1994—. Past chair Dept. of Evangelism; chair Dept. of Personnel Svcs.; rep. Christian Meth. Episcopal Ch. on Consultation on Ch. Union. Chair bd. trustees Tex. Coll.; mem. bd. trustees Paine Coll. Mem. USAF, 1950—54. Named one of 100 Most Influential Black Americans, Ebony mag., 2006.

GILMORE, MAURICE EUGENE, mathematics professor; b. NYC, Jan. 2, 1938; s. Maurice Eugene and Mary Wells (Barnes) G.; m. Julie Anne Rogers, June 20, 1964 (div. 1989); children: Peter Barnes, Christopher Alan, Jessica Lynn; m. Cathi Leslie Sonneborn, Sept. 1, 1991. BA, Georgetown U., 1959; MS, Syracuse U., 1961; PhD, U. Calif., Berkeley, 1967. Instr. Northeastern U., Boston, 1966-68, asst. prof., 1968-72, assoc. prof., 1972-78, prof., 1978—, chmn. math. dept., 1975-88. Vis. prof. U. Tecnica Del Estado, Santiago, Chile, 1968, U. of Sussex, Falmer, U.K., 1989. Grantee, NSF, 1979, 1992, 1999, CNSF, 1999, Nellie Mae, 2001. Mem.: Assn. Tchrs. Math. Mass., Nat. Coun. Tchrs. Math., Am. Math. Soc., Math. Assn. Am. Office: Northeastern U 360 Huntington Ave Boston MA 02115-5000 Office Phone: 617-373-5675. Business E-Mail: gilmore@neu.edu.

GILMORE, W. FRANKLIN (FRANK), academic administrator; BS, Va. Mil. Inst.; PhD in organic chemistry, MIT; postdoctoral study, Inst. Molecular Biophysics, Fla. State U. Prof., dept. chmn., rsch. prof. med. chemistry dept. U. Miss.; exec. v.p. W.Va. U. Inst. Tech.; chancellor Mont. Tech, U. Mont., Butte. Bd. dir. Butte-Silver Bow United Way, Butte Family YMCA; mem. Goldwater Scholarship Selection Com.; mem. NAPLEX steering com. Nat. Assn. Boards of Pharmacy. With USMCR, 1952—55, capt. USAR, 1957—65. Mem.: Sigma Xi (past pres.). Office: Montana Tech Office of the Chancellor 1300 W Park St Butte MT 59701-8997 Home Phone: 406-782-6994; Office Phone: 406-496-4129. Business E-Mail: fgilmore@mtech.edu.

GILMOUR, D(AVID) JAMES, financial and systems analyst; b. Phila., July 10, 1947; s. James William and Florence Elizabeth (Weisbrod) Gilmour; m. Deborah Anne Kaufold, July 2, 1977. BS, Muhlenberg Coll., 1969; MS in Adminstrn., George Washington U., 1974; MBA, Temple U., 1981, MEd, 2005; MS, U. Pa., 1995, MPhil, 1998. Analyst Nat. Security Agy., Ft. Meade, Md., 1970-74; programmer, analyst Rohm & Haas Co., Phila., 1974-77; staff economist Sun Oil Co., Radnor, Pa., 1977-85; project leader Arco Chem. Corp., Phila., 1985-87; asst. v.p. Corestates Fin. Corp., Phila., 1987-98, cons., 1998—. Hon. amb. Ctr. Orgnl. Dynamics U. Pa., Phila.; MEd, PhD student asst., grad. rsch. asst. Temple U. Author: (book) An Economic Model of Core States Financial Corporation, 1994, How to Write Term Papers Real Good, 1996, The Corestates/University of Pennsylvania Strategic Planning Model, 1997, The Philadelphia Ethos, 1998, 1776 and All That: A Memorable History of Philadelphia, 2002. With USN, 1970—74. Mem.: NEA, NRA, NJ Edn. Assn., Pa. Edn. Assn., Clan Morrison Soc., Mensa, Beta Gamma Sigma, Alpha Tau Omega (exchequer 1965—69, Thomas Arcle Clark award 1969). Republican. Anglican. Achievements include co-inventor semi-automatic pistol. Home and Office: 15 Keats Rd Yardley PA 19067-3219 Office Phone: 215-204-6107. Business E-Mail: jgilmour@grad.upenn.edu.

GILMOUR, JOSEPH A., insurance company executive; m. Cathy Gilmour; 3 children. Grad., U. Toronto, Ont. Various positions in group life ins. and pension, strategic planning, mergers and acquisitions and product devel. Canada Life, sr. v.p. Internat. and Reinsurance Divsn.; exec. v.p., CFO NY Life Internat. NY Life Ins. Co., 2003—05, pres., CEO NY Life Internat., exec. v.p., 2005—, chmn. NY Life Internat., 2006—. Fellow: Soc. Actuaries. Office: NY Life Ins Co 51 Madison Ave Ste 3200 New York NY 10010 Office Phone: 212-576-7000.*

GIL ORRIOS, ANGEL, theater director, lighting designer, translator; b. Cariñena, Zaragoza, Spain, Oct. 7, 1956; s. Angel Gil Sebastian and Cristina Orrios Ruiz; m. Soledad Lopez, Feb. 22, 1980; children: Sebastian Orrios, Mariana Orrios. MFA in Directing, Sch. Dramatic Arts, Zaragoza, Spain, 1974. Artistic dir. Royal Theatre Of Spain, NYC, 1980—85, Internat. Art Theatre Inst., NYC, 1995—99; artistic, exec. dir. Thalia Spanish Theatre, Sunnyside, NY, 2000—. Cultural corr. El Pais, NY, 1988—92; cons., lectr. in field. Dir.(prodr., set & lighting designer): (musical) Pablo Picasso's the Four Little Girls, Picasso's Guernica (Best Dir. and Best Prodn. award Assn. Critics of Entertainment, 2000); (plays) Ramos Perea's We Women Do It Better, Jardiel Poncela's Brake Four Hearts (Best Dir. award Assn. Critics of Entertainment, 2001), (writer, prodr., set & lighting designer): (musical) Maestro Jaurena's I Love Tango, Tangomania, Life's Tango, All That Tango (Best Musical Prodn. award Assn. Critics of Entertainment, 2001), (translator, prodr., set & light designer): (plays) Carlos Fuentes' The One-eyed Man Is King (Best Dir. and Best Prodn. award Hispanic Orgn. Latin Actors, 2003, Best Set Designer award Assn. Critics of Entertainment, 2003), Jaime Salom's Almost a Goddess, Calderon De La Barca's The Great Theatre of the World (Hola award for best dir. and best prodn., 2000). Recipient Prince Ferdinand award, Radio Juventud De Zaragoza, Spain, 1975, Silver medal, French Acad. Arts, Sci. and Letters, Paris, 1987, Best Short Film award, XVIII San Francisco Poetry Film Festival, 1993. Mem.: Spanish Soc. Authors, Composers & Publ., Dramatists Guild, Soc. Stage Dir. & Choreographers. Office: Thalia Spanish Theatre 41-17 Greenpoint Ave Sunnyside NY 11104 Home Phone: 718-786-5632; Office Phone: 718-729-3880. E-mail: angel@thaliatheatre.org.

GILPATRICK, RUSSELL O., dean, dental educator; married; 1 child, Nicholas. Degree, Chico State U.; DDS, U. Pacific Sch. Dentistry. Pvt. practice; mem. faculty U. Conn. Sch. Dentistry; joined faculty, Health Sci. Ctr. Sch. Dentistry, U. Tenn., 1988; prof. gen. dentistry Health Sci. Ctr. Sch. Dentistry, U. Tenn., 1993, chmn. gen. dentistry dept., exec. assoc. dean academic affairs, dean, 2003—. Recipient Outstanding Tchr. award, U. Tenn. Alumni Assn., 1992, Fellowship award, Tenn. Dental Assn., 2003. Office: U Tenn Health Sci Ctr 875 Union Ave Memphis TN 38163 Home Phone: 901-748-9006; Office Phone: 901-448-6202. Office Fax: 901-448-7104. Business E-Mail: rgilpatrick@utmem.edu.

GILPIN, PERI, actress; b. Waco, Tex., May 27, 1961; m. Christian Vincent, 1999; children: Ava Vincent, Stella Vincent. Former student, Dallas Theatre Ctr., U. Tex., Brit.-Am. Acad., London. Owner prod. co. (with Jane Leeves) Bristol Cities. Actress (TV series) Frasier, 1993-2004 (SAG award outstanding performance ensemble, 2000), The Lionhearts (voice), 1998; (TV guest appearances) 21 Jump Street, 1988, Matlock, 1990, Wings, 1992, Designing Women, 1993, Cheers, 1993, Pride & Joy, 1995, The Outer Limits, 1996, Early Edition, 1996, Superman, 1998, Hercules (voice), 1998, Baby Blues, 2000, The Chris Isaak Show, 2001, King of the Hill (voice), 2003, Justice League (voice), 2003, I'm With Her, 2003; (TV movies) Fight for Justice: The Nancy Conn Story, 1995, The Secret She Carried, 1996, Laughter on the 23rd Floor, 2001, (films) Spring Forward, 1999, How to Kill Your Neighbor's Dog, 2000, Finaly Fantasty: The Spirits Within (voice), 2001; guest appearance Later with Greg Kinnear, 1994, Early Edition, 1996, The Outer Limits, 1995, Superman, 1996, Pride & Joy, 1995, Talk Soup, 1991, Matlock, 1986, 21 Jump Street, 1987. Office: William Morris Agy One William Morris Place Beverly Hills CA 90212-2775

GILPIN, ROBERT GEORGE, JR., political science professor; b. Burlington, Vt., July 2, 1930; s. Robert George and Beatrice (Sandspra) G.; m. Jean Millis, Aug. 13, 1955; children— Linda, Elizabeth, Robert. BA, U. Vt., 1952; MS, Cornell U., 1954; PhD, U. Calif., Berkeley, 1960. Fellow Harvard U., 1960-61; lectr. Columbia U., 1961-62; faculty Princeton U., 1962—68, prof. polit. sci., 1970-98, Eisenhower prof. internat. affairs, 1975-98, prof. emeritus, 1998—. Mem. Pres.'s Advisory Group Tech. and the Economy, 1975-76. Author: American Scientists and Nuclear Weapons Policy, 1962, France in the Age of the Scientific State, 1968, U.S. Power and the Multinational Corporation, 1975, War and Change in World Politics, 1981, The Political Economy of International Relations, 1987, The Challenge of Global Capitalism: The World Economy of the 21st Century, 2000, Global Political Economy: Understanding the International Economic Order, 2001; co-author (co-editor): Scientists and National Policy Making, 1964. Served with USNR, 1954-57. Congl. fellow, 1959-60, Guggenheim fellow, 1969, Rockefeller fellow, 1967-68, 76-77 Fellow AAAS; mem. Am. Polit. Sci. Assn. (v.p. 1984-85). Home: PO Box 105 Greensboro VT 05841 Business E-Mail: rggilpin@princeton.edu.

GILROY, FRANK DANIEL, playwright; b. NYC, Oct. 13, 1925; s. Frank B. and Bettina (Vasti) Gilroy; m. Ruth Dorothy Gaydos, Feb. 13, 1954; children: Anthony, John, Daniel. BA magna cum laude, Dartmouth Coll., 1950; postgrad., Yale Sch. Drama. Author became TV writer, (TV series) (originated) Burkes Law, (TV writer, scripts prod. on programs) Playhouse 90, U.S. Steel Hour, Omnibus, Kraft Theatre, Lux Video Theatre, Studio One; dir.(writer): 40 Gibbsville, 1975, The Doorbell Rang, 1977, Money Plays, 1997; author: (plays) Who'll Save the Plowboy? (presented off-Broadway, 1962), 1957, (completed) The Subject Was Roses, 1962, (presented on Broadway, 1964), 1962; presented (Broadway plays) That Summer-That Fall, 1967, The Only Game in Town, 1968, Last Licks, 1979, Any Given Day, 1993, (off Broadway plays) Contact With the Enemy, 1999, one-act (produced off-Broadway plays) The Next Contestant, 1978, Real to Reel, 1987, Match Point, 1990, A Way With Word, 1991, Give the Bishop My Faint Regards, 1992, Contact with the Enemy, 2000, Inspector Ohms, 2001; prodr.(writer, dir.): (films) Desperate Characters, 1970 (best screenplay award Berlin Film Festival), From Noon Till Three, 1977, The Gig, 1985, Once in Paris (original screenplay), 1978; writer, dir. (films) The Luckiest Man in the World, 1989; author: Present Tense, prod. off-Broadway, 1972, (novels) Private, 1970, (with Ruth Gilroy) Little Ego, 1970, From Noon till Three, 1973, (non-fiction) I Wake Up Screening-Everything You Need to Know About Making Independent Films Including A Thousand Reasons Not To, 1993, Writing for Love and/or Money: Outtakes From a Life on Spec-The Early Years, 2007, (screenplays) (with Russell Rouse) The Fastest Gun Alive, 1956, (with Beirne Lay Jr.) Gallant Hours, 1960, Desperate Characters, 1971, The Subject was Roses, The Only Game in Town, From Noon till Three, Once in Paris. With US Army, 1943—46, ETO. Nominee Best Play N.Y. Drama Desk, 1999—2000; recipient Obie award for best Am. play, 1962, Outer Circle award, 1964, Drama Critics Circle award, 1964, N.Y. Theatre Club award, 1964—65, Antoinette Perry award, 1965, Pulitzer prize for drama, 1965. Mem.: Writers Guild Am., Dirs. Guild Am., Dramatists Guild (pres. 1969—71).

GILROY, KEVIN, electronics executive; BS in Fin., LI U. Various positions up to sr. v.p., gen. mgr. worldwide small and medium businesses (SMB) ops. segment HP; CEO OnForce, Inc.; sr. v.p., pres. Enterprise Computing Solutions Arrow Electronics, Inc., Melville, NY, 2007—. Bd. dirs. Computing Tech. Industry Assn. Named Channel Exec. of Yr., VARBusiness, 2003. Office: Arrow Electronics Inc 50 Marcus Dr Melville NY 11747-4210 Office Phone: 631-847-2000.*

GILROY, SUE ANNE, hospital administrator, former state official; b. Ind., 1948; m. Dick Gilroy; children: Emily (dec. 1989), Grant. Grad. cum laude, DePauw U.; MA, Ind. U. Ordained elder Presbyn. Ch. Profl. assoc. Office of Mayor Lugar; dir. Parks and Recreation; asst. to pres. Ind. Ctrl. U. (now U. Indpls.); chair Mayor Steve Goldsmith's Transition Team, 1991-92; state dir. for Senator Richard Lugar US Senate, Ind., 1990-93; sec. state State of Ind., Indpls., 1994—2003; dir. advancement Univ. H.S., Carmel, Ind., 2003—05; v.p. for devel. St. Vincent Hospital, Indpls., 2005—; exec. dir. St. Vincent Hosp. Found., Indpls., 2005—. Cons. in fundraising and bus. adminstrn. Tabernacle Presbyn. Ch.; bd. dirs. St. Vincent Hosp Found., Cathedral H.S., U. Indpls.; mem. adv. bd. Salvation Army. Mem. Indpls. Rotary Club. Republican. Office: St Vincent Hosp 2001 W 86th St Indianapolis IN 46260*

GILSON, JEROME, lawyer, writer; b. Chgo., Jan. 12, 1931; s. William George and Clara Margaret (Loewe) G.; m. Jamie Marie Chisam, June 19, 1955; children: Thomas, Matthew, Anne. AB, U. Mo., 1952; JD, Northwestern U., 1958. Bar: Ill. 1958, U.S. Dist. Ct. (no. dist.) Ill. 1958, U.S. Ct. Appeals (7th cir.) 1962, U.S. Supreme Ct. 1966, U.S. Ct. Appeals (3d cir.) 1967, U.S. Ct. Appeals (5th cir.) 1968, U.S. Ct. Appeals (fed. cir.) 1982, U.S. Ct. Appeals (11th cir.) 1985, U.S. Ct. Appeals (4th cir.) 1988, U.S. Ct. Appeals (8th cir.) 1994. Assoc. Rooks, Pitts, Fullagar & Poust, Chgo., 1958-63; ptnr. Brinks Hofer Gilson & Lione, Chgo., 1963—. Faculty John Marshall Law Sch., Chgo., 1961-63; advisor Am. Law Inst.-Unfair Competition Law Restatement, Phila., 1986-91. Author: Gilson on Trademarks 1974, also supplements 1977-2006; contbr. articles to profl. jours. Served as sgt. U.S. Army Security Agy., 1952-55. Named as top trademark law practitioner in world Managing Intellectual Property, 1998; recipient Burton award for legal achievement The Burton Found., 2003, 05-06. Mem. ABA, Internat. Trademark Assn. (reporter trademark rev. com. 1985-88, counsel 1991-94), Intellectual Property Law Assn. Chgo., Union League, Mich. Shores Club Avocations: tennis, piano. Office: Brinks Hofer Gilson & Lione 445 N Cityfront Plaza Dr Chicago IL 60611-4316 Home Phone: 847-256-6230; Office Phone: 312-321-4205. Business E-Mail: jg@brinkshofer.com.

GILTNER, PHIL (F. PHILLIPS GILTNER III), food distributing executive; BSBA, U. Nebr.; MS in Acctg., U. Pa., Phila. CPA Ariz. Various auditing positions Deloitte, Price Waterhouse; v.p., CFO Wells Fargo Credit Corp.; v.p., asst. to chmn. Inertia Dynamics Corp.; CFO, sr. v.p. Shamrock Foods, Phoenix. Bd. dirs., mem. audit com. Poore Bros., Inc., 2003—. Mem. Ariz. Bus. Leadership Assn. (founding pres., spkr.). Office: Shamrock Foods 2540 N 29th Ave Phoenix AZ 85009 Office Phone: 602-233-6400.*

GIMBEL, HERVEY WILLIS, public health physician, medical administrator; b. Calgary, Alta., Can., Nov. 25, 1926; s. Jacob Allen Gimbel and Ruth Helen Johnson; m. Ann Matterand Gimbel, Dec. 23, 1951; children: Shirley Tetz, Denise Job, Kenneth, Marlin, Beverly Kramer. BA, Walla Walla Coll., 1950; MD, Loma Linda U., 1955, MPH, 1978. Diplomate Nat. Bd. Medicine; cert. Am. Bd. Preventive Medicine. Med. dir. North Hill Med. Clinic, Calgary, 1957-82; assoc. prof. Loma Linda U., Calif., 1982-84; area med. dir. Calif. Indsl. Med. Clinics, Irvine, Calif.; med. dir. Parkview Ctr. for Occupl. Medicine, Riverside, Calif., 1985-91, Rancho Canyon Occupl. Medicine, Temecula, Calif., 1991-2001, Steck Meml. Medica Ctr., Centralia, Wash., 2002—06. Founder, dir. Health Edn. Ctr., Calgary, 1969-82; dir. China-USA Health Project, Loma Linda, Calif., 1991—; cons. China Nat. Health Edn. Inst., Beijing, 1992—; guest prof. Huazhong U., Wuhan, China, 2002-04. Contbr. articles to profl. jours. Flight lt. Royal Can. Air Force Res., 1958—60. Named an Honored Alumus, Loma Linda U., 2005, Canadian U. Coll., 2006; named one of Am.'s Top Physicians, Consumers' Rsch. Coun. Am., 2004; recipient China Tobacco Control award Chinese Assn. Smoking and Health, 2000. Fellow Am. Coll. Preventive Medicine; mem. Am. Coll. Environ. and Occupl. Medicine, Med. Coll. Can. (licentiate), Delta Omega. Avocations: travel, photography, history. Home: 911 Landing Way Centralia WA 98531 Office Phone: 951-316-4945. Personal E-mail: gimbelhw@compprime.com.

GIMBRONE, MICHAEL ANTHONY, JR., research scientist, pathologist, educator; b. Buffalo, Nov. 16, 1943; married, 1971; 3 children. AB, Cornell U., 1965; MD, Harvard U., 1970. Intern, resident fellow Mass. Gen. Hosp., Boston, 1970-72; staff assoc. Nat. Cancer Inst., Bethesda, Md., 1972-74; resch. assoc. Harvard Med. Sch., Boston, 1974-76, from asst. prof. to assoc. prof., 1979-85, Elsie T. Friedman prof. pathology, 1985—; chmn. dept. pathology Brigham and Women's Hosp., Boston, 2001—. Cons. Nat. Heart, Lung and Blood Inst., NIH, 1976—; established investigator Am. Heart Assn., 1977-82; head Vascular Pathophysiol. Rsch. Lab., 1977-85; dir. vascular rsch. div. Brigham and Women's Hosp., 1985—, dir. Ctr. for Excellence in Vascular Biology. Recipient Achievement award in cardiovascular scis. Bristol-Myers Squibb, 2001, King Faisal prize (medicine), King Faisal Found., 2006. Fellow NIH, AAAS, Nat. Acad. of Scis., Am. Acad. Arts and Scis.; mem. Inst. of Medicine, Am. Heart Assn. (Basic Rsch. prize 1993), Am. Soc. Cell Biologists, Tissue Culture Assn., Am. Soc. Hematology, Am. Assn. Pathologists (v.p. 1991-92), Am. Soc. Invest. Pathology (pres. 1992-93), Am. Assn. Physicians, Fedn. Am. Socs. for Exptl. Biology (Exptl. Pathologist award 1982, bd. dirs. 1990-94), N.Am. Vascular Biology Orgn. (founding pres. 1994—, J. Allyn Taylor Internat. prize in medicine). Achievements include research in cardiovascular pathophysiology, especially atherosclerosis, thrombosis and inflammation, vascular cell biology. Office: Brigham and Womens Hosp Dept Pathology 75 Francis St Boston MA 02115 E-mail: mgimbrone@rics.bwh.harvard.edu.

GIMENES, SONIA REGINA ROSENDO, family therapist, psychologist; b. São Paulo, Brazil, Jan. 25, 1953; arrived in U.S., 1996; d. Joao and Luzia (Pragelis) Rosendo; m. Airton Jose Gimenes, May 7, 1976; children: Erika, Rodrigo. BS in Psychology, U. Mogi Cruzes, São Paulo, 1980; M in Sci. Psychology with honors, U. Americas, Mexico City, 1988; postgrad. in psychology; cert. in clin. psychology, U. Paulista, São Paulo, 1994. Registered family therapist intern Fla., lic. clin. psychologist Brazil. Family therapist intern Clinica Oira, Mexico City, 1987—88; psychologist intern Clinica Psicologia Objetivo, São Paulo, Brazil, 1994, Pontificia U. Cath., São Paulo, 1995; clin. psychologist Human Inst., São Paulo, 1995—96; family therapist Counseling and Hypnosis Inc., Miami, Fla., 1999—. Author: Domestic Violence, 2001; contbr. monography project Child Abuse, 1988, articles to profl. jours. Established Internat. C. of C. Nonprofit Bus. Network. Mem.: ACA, Assn. Bi-Nat. C. of C. Fla., Am. Bd. Hypnotherapy, Am. Coll. Forensic Examiners, Am. Psychotherapy Assn., Rotary Internat. (Paul Harris medal of honor 1976). Avocations: music, dance, piano, arts and crafts.

GIMENEZ, LUIS FERNANDO, physician, educator; b. Antofagasta, Chile, Mar. 3, 1952; came to U.S., 1979; s. Luis Sr. and Nelly (Basulto) G.; m. Diane Marie Salazar, Sept. 20, 1957; children: Luis Andres, Pilar Elizabeth, Nicholas Miguel, Catherine Anne. MD, U. Chile, Valparaiso, 1976. Diplomate Am. Bd. Internal Medicine, Am. Bd. Nephrology. Intern U. Chile Sch. Medicine, Valparaiso, 1975-76; resident U. Concepcion Sch.

Medicine, Chile, 1976-77, U. Chile Sch. Medicine, Valparaiso, 1977-79; research fellow in nephrology Johns Hopkins U. Sch. Medicine, Balt., 1979-81; intern Johns Hopkins Hosp., Balt., 1981-82, resident, 1982-84, clin. fellow nephrology div., 1984-85; instr. Johns Hopkins U. Sch. Medicine, Balt., 1985-86, asst. prof. medicine, 1986—. Dir. dialysis unit The Good Samaritan Hosp., Balt., 1985—, chief renal div., 1990; med. cons. to Social Security Administrn., 1985-93; mem. med. adv. bd. Am. Kidney Found., Balt., 1987-95. Contbr. articles to profl. jours. Recipient Outstanding Civic Svc. award Chilean Med. Assn., Valparaiso, 1974. Mem. Am. Fedn. for Clin. Research., Am. Soc. Nephrology, Am. Coll. Physicians, Internat. Soc. Nephrology, Internat. Soc. Peritoneal Dialysis, Md. Kidney Comn. Avocation: philatelist. Office: Johns Hopkins Hosp Renal Divsn 1830 Bldg Baltimore MD 21205-2109 Home: 5601 Loch Raven Blvd Ste 3N Baltimore MD 21239 Office Phone: 410-532-3775. Personal E-mail: lgimene@yahoo.com.

GINEPRI, ROBBY (ROBERT LOUIS GINEPRI), professional tennis player; b. Ft. Lauderdale, FL, Oct. 7, 1982; s. Rene and Nancy Ginepri. Profl. tennis player ATP Tour, 2001—. Achievements include winner, Newport, RI, 2003, Indpls., 2005. Office: c/o ATP Tour 201 ATP Boulevard Ponte Vedra Beach FL 32082

GINER, A. SILVANA, lawyer; b. 1959; BA cum laude, Univ. Mass., Amherst, 1982; JD, Stanford Univ., 1985. Bar: Mass. 1985. Assoc. to ptnr. Wilmer Cutler Pickering Hale & Dorr, Boston, 1985—, vice chmn. Private Client dept. Contbr. chapters to books. Trustee Boston Social Law Libr., Brain Sci. Found., Medfield, Mass.; mem. adv. bd. Commonwealth Coll., Univ. Mass. Amherst; overseer Opera Boston. Fellow: Am. Coll. Trust & Estate Counsel; mem.: Boston Estate Planning Council, Phi Beta Kappa. Office: Wilmer Cutler Pickering Hale & Dorr 60 State St Boston MA 02109 Office Phone: 617-526-6327. Office Fax: 617-526-5000. Business E-Mail: nan.giner@wilmerhale.com.

GINGER, ANN FAGAN, lawyer; b. Nov. 25, 1925; Exec. dir. Meiklejohn Civil Liberties Inst., Berkeley. Vis. prof. law Univ. Calif. Hastings Coll., Univ. San Francisco, Univ. Santa Clara, New Coll. Calif., Univ. Puget Sound. Author: Calif. Criminal Law Practice (vol. I & II), The National Law Guide, Jury Selection in Civil & Criminal Trials, & other books and articles on civil liberties law. Office: Meiklejohn Civil Liberties Institute PO Box 673 Berkeley CA 94701-0673

GINGERICH, OWEN JAY, astronomer, educator; b. Washington, Iowa, Mar. 24, 1930; 3 children. BA, Goshen Coll., Ind., 1951; MA, Harvard U., Cambridge, Mass., 1953, PhD in Astronomy, 1962. Dir. obs. Am. U., Beirut, 1955-58, from instr. to asst. prof., 1955-58; lectr. astronomy Wellesley Coll., 1958-59; astrophysicist Smithsonian Astrophys. Obs., 1961-87, sr. astronomer, 1987-2000; from lectr. to assoc. prof. astronomy and history of sci. Harvard U., 1960-69, prof., 1969-2000, chmn. history of sci. dept., 1992-93, emeritus prof., 2000—. Astronomy cons. Harvard Project Physics, 1964-69; dir. ctrl. telegram bur. Internat. Astronomical Union, 1965-67, pres. commn. history astronomy, 1970-76, chmn. U.S. nat. com., 1982-84; Sigma Xi nat. lectr., 1971; George Darwin lectr. Royal Astron. Soc., 1971; adv. com. Ctr. Theol. Inquiry, Princeton, 1988-97; adv. bd. John Templeton Found., 1994-99, 2001-2003, trustee, 2003—. Assoc. editor: Jour. History Astronomy, 1975-; mem. editorial bd. Am. Scholar, 1975-80; dir. Harvard mag., 1978-85, incorporator, 1986—; contrb. over 500 publications to profl. jours. on model stellar atmospheres and history of astronomy. Overseer Boston Mus. Sci., 1979-96, 1998—2004. Decorated Order of Merit comdr. class People's Republic of Poland, 1981; recipient prix Janssen French Astron. Soc., 2006. Fellow AAAS (chmn. sect. L 1974, sect D 1981); mem. Academie Internationale d'Histoire des Sciences, Am. Acad. Arts and Scis., Am. Philos. Soc. (v.p. 1982-85, John F. Lewis prize 1976, councilor 1994-2000), Am. Astron. Soc. (chmn. hist. astronomy div. 1983-85, Doggett prize 2000, Edn. prize 2004), Royal Astron. Soc. Can. (hon.), Examiner Club, Phi Beta Kappa. Achievements include research on model stellar atmospheres (to 1971) and in history of astronomy. Office: Harvard-Smithsonian Ctr for Astrophysics Cambridge MA 02138 Office Phone: 617-495-7216. Business E-Mail: ginger@cfa.harvard.edu. *Our most earnest ambitions are in effect unspoken prayers-they define our deepest views on the meaning of life far more precisely than any outward profession of religion or ethics.*

GINGOLD, GEORGE NORMAN, insurance company executive, lawyer; b. NYC, Aug. 2, 1939; s. Josef and Gladys (Anderson) G.; m. Anne Brenda Davis, July 7, 1963; children— Rachel June, David Bruce AB magna cum laude, Harvard U., 1960, JD, 1963. Bar: Ariz. 1964, Conn. 1968, Mass. 1989. Pvt. practice law, Phoenix, 1964-65; atty. SEC, Washington, 1965-67; counsel AEtna Life & Casualty, Hartford, Conn., 1967-94; counsel, corp. sec. AEtna Life Ins. and Annuity Co., Hartford, 1981-94; pvt. practice ins. securities law, 1994—. Mem. com. on securities regulation Am. Council of Life Ins., Washington, 1978-94, chmn., 1986-88; instr. Hartford Coll. for Women, 1983-95. Author articles in field Vice pres., bd. dirs. United Cerebral Palsy Assn., Hartford, 1980-87; vice chmn. West Hartford Human Rights Commn., Conn., 1975-79; pres. West Hartford PTA, 1976-78 Mem. ABA (mem. fed. regulation of securities com. 1978—), Am. Soc. Corp. Secs., Fed. Bar Assn. (pres. Hartford County chpt. 1974-76) Lodges: B'nai B'rith Unity (pres. 1971-72). Avocations: classical music, theater, chess. Office: PO Box 155 West Hyannisport MA 02672-0155 Personal E-mail: gingoldga@comcast.net.

GINGREY, PHIL (JOHN PHILLIP GINGREY), congressman; b. Augusta, Ga., July 10, 1942; m. Billie Ayers; children: Billy, Gannon, Phyllis, Laura Neill. BS in Chemistry, Ga. Inst. Tech., 1965; MD, Med. Coll. Ga., 1969. Intern Grady Meml. Hosp., Atlanta; ob-gyn. resident Med. Coll. Ga., Augusta; physician Ga. Ob-Gyn. Affiliates, Marietta, Ga.; mem. Ga. State Senate, Atlanta, 1999—2002, mem. banking and fin. instns. com., edn. com., retirement com., transp. com.; mem. US Congress from 11th Ga. dist., 2003—. Mem. St. Joseph's Cath. Ch., Marietta; mem. Marietta Sch. Bd., 1993-97, also chmn.; bd. dirs. North Cobb divsn. Am. Cancer Soc. Mem.: Ga. Ob-Gyn. Soc., Med. Assn. of Ga., Cobb County Med. Soc., AMA. Republican. Roman Catholic. Office: US Ho Reps 119 Cannon Ho Office Bldg Washington DC 20515-1011 also: Marietta Dist Office 219 Roswell St Marietta GA 30060 Office Phone: 202-225-2931. Office Fax: 202-225-2944. E-mail: gingrey.ga@mail.house.gov.*

GINGRICH, NEWT (NEWTON LEROY GINGRICH), former congressman; b. Harrisburg, Pa., June 17, 1943; s. Robert Bruce and Kathleen (Daugherty) G.; children: Linda Kathleen, Jacqueline Sue.; m. Jackie Battley, June 19, 1962 (div. Feb. 1981), m. Marianne Ginther, Aug. 8, 1981 (div. 2000), children: Linda Kathleen, Jacqueline Sue; m. Callista Bissek, Aug. 18, 2000. BA, Emory U., 1965; MA, Tulane U., 1968, PhD in European History, 1971. Asst. prof. history W. Ga. Coll., Carrollton, 1970—78; mem. Congress from 6th Ga. dist. Washington, 1979-99; spkr. of the House, 1995-99; founder The Com. for New Am. Leadership, Washington, Ctr. for Health Transformation; chmn. The Gingrich Group, 1999—; polit. analyst Fox News Network; sr. fellow Am. Enterprise Inst.; Disting. vis. fellow Hoover Instn. Speaker, chmn. emeritus GOPAC; co-founder Conservative Opportunity Soc., congl. mil. caucus, space caucus; mem. joint com. on printing, house adminstrn. com.; co-chmn. Leader's Task Force on Health, US Commn. on Nat. Security/21st Century, 1999-, co-chair Task Force on the UN, 2005-, co-chair Nat. Commn. for Quality Long-term Care, 2005-; adj. prof. Reinhardt Coll., Waleska, Ga., 1994-95. Author: (non-fiction) To Renew America, 1995, Lessons Learned the Hard Way: A Personal Report, 1998, Winning The Future: A 21st Century Contract With America, 2005, Rediscovering God in America: Reflections on the Role of Faith in Our Nation's History and Future, 2006; co-author:(with Marianne Gingrich) Window of Opportunity: A Blueprint for the Future, 1984, Renewing American Civilization, 1995; co-author: (novels) (with William R. Forstchen) Nineteen Forty-Five, 1995, Gettysburg: A Novel of the Civil War, 2003, Grant Comes East: A Novel of the Civil War, 2003, Never Call Retreat: Lee and Grant: The Final Victory, 2005, Pearl Harbor: A Novel of December 8th, 2007 Named Man of Yr. TIME mag., 1995, Ga. Citizen of the Year, March of Dimes, 1995, Legislative Conservationist of the Year, Ga. Wildlife Found., 1998, Sci. Pioneer award, Sci. Coalition, 2001, Health Quality award, Nat. Com. for Quality Assurance, 2005, Nat. Minority Health Month Found. award, 2005. Mem. AAAS, Ga. Conservancy. Lodges: Kiwanis, Moose. Republican. Baptist. Office: Ctr for Health Transformation 1425 K St NW Ste 750 Washington DC 20005*

GINIGER, KENNETH SEEMAN, publisher; b. NYC, Feb. 18, 1919; s. Maurice Aaron and Pearl (Triester) G.; m. Carol Virginia Wilkins, Sept. 27, 1952 (dec. Aug. 1985); m. Bernice Dees Ellinger Cullinan, Apr. 13, 2002. Student, U. Va., 1935-39, N.Y. Law Sch., 1940-41. Ptnr. Signet Press, 1939-40; assoc. editor Arts and Decoration and The Spur, 1940-41; dir. pub. relations Prentice-Hall, Inc., 1946-49, editor-in-chief trade book div., 1949-52; v.p., gen. mgr. Hawthorn Books div., 1952-61; pres. Hawthorn Books, Inc., NYC, 1961-65, K.S. Giniger Co., Inc., NYC, 1965—, Consol. Book Pubs. div. Processing & Books, Inc., Chgo., 1969-74, Tradewinds Group div. IPC Ltd., Sydney, Australia, 1974-76. Lectr. New Sch. Social Rsch., 1948—49, NYU, 1979—81, adj. asst. prof., 1981—83, adj. assoc. prof., 1983—85; asst. to dir. CIA, 1951—52. Author: The Compact Treasury of Inspiration, 1955 (NCCJ Brotherhood Week citation), America, America, America, 1957, A Treasury of Golden Memories, 1958, A Little Treasury of Hope, 1968, A Little Treasury of Comfort, 1966, A Little Treasury of Christmas, 1968, The Sayings of Jesus, 1968, The Family Advent Book, 1979, Pope John Paul II: Pilgrim of Faith, 1987; author: (with Walter Russell Bowie) What is Protestantism?, 1965; author: (with Will Yolen) Heroes for Our Times, 1969; author: (with Sir John Templeton) Spiritual Evolution, 1998; editor: Internat. Pub. News, 1983—91, European Bookseller Pub. World/Update Newsletter, 1991—92; mem. editl. bd. RAM Reports, 1977—83, Communications and the Law, 1978—94. Sec. Com. Collective Security, 1952—65; nat. adv. bd. Found. Religious Action, 1956—94; dir. Layman's Nat. Bible Com., 1957—2006, pres., 1963—71, chmn., 1987—94, chmn. emeritus, 1994—; mem. adv. bd. Templeton Found., 1992—2000, 2004—06, Am. Theater Wing, 1999, Blanton-Peale Inst., 2002—06. From pvt. to capt. AUS, 1941—45. Decorated French Legion of Honor; recipient Norman Vincent Peale award for Positive Thinking, Elanton-Peale Inst., 2006. Mem.: PEN, Church Club (NYC), Dutch Treat Club, Players Club, Arts Club (London), Garrick Club (London), Authors Club (London), Army and Navy Club (Washington), Yale Club, Phi Delta Phi. Republican. Episcopalian. Home: 1045 Park Ave New York NY 10028-1030 Office: 250 W 57th St New York NY 10107 Office Phone: 212-570-7499.

GINLEY, THOMAS H., JR., urologist; b. Pa., June 30, 1924; s. Thomas H. Ginley Sr. and Helen Meisinkel; m. Emma Catherine Ginley, June 12, 1954; children: Deborah Fabian Ginley Lewis, Vanessa Noel. MD, Georgetown U. Sch. Medicine, Washington, 1948; postgrad. in Urology, U. Pa. Sch. Medicine, Phila., 1950—50. Diplomate Am. Bd. Urology, 1960. Intern Guthrie Clinic and Robert Packer Hosp., Mpls., 1948—49; resident U. Minn. N.W. Hosp., Mpls., 1949—50; resident in urology Hahnemann U., Phila., 1950—51, assoc. prof. urology; staff urologist Our Lady Lourdes, 1955—, Hahemann U., Phila., 1958—, West Park Hosp., 1963—. Cons. urologist Nantucket Cottage Hosp., 1976—82. Founder, dir. West Park Hosp.; dir. sec. Entercom Corp.; pres. Gem Treasury Mgmt. Inc.; dir. Devon Horse Show, 1977—84, African Safari Club, Phila., 1980—86. Surg. staff US Naval Hosp. USN, 1952—53, Yohoska, Japan. Recipient Legion Honor award. Fellow: Coll. Physicians Phila., Internat. Coll. Surgeons, Am. Coll. Surgeons; mem.: Quaker City Farmers (1st v.p.), Phila. Soc. Promoting Agr. (1st v.p.), Urol. Soc. Urodynamics, Phila. Urol. Sco., Mid Atlantic Urol. Soc., Am. Urol. Soc., Pa. Med. Soc., Sankaty Head Golf Club, Phila. Penn Club, Radnor Hunt Club, Rittenhouse Club.

GINN, JOHN ARTHUR, JR., financial consultant; b. Palatka, Fla., June 2, 1918; s. John Arthur and Violet Maude (Merwin) g.; m. Lou Eliska Cone, Feb. 4, 1945; children: Judith Ann, John Arthur III. BS, Fla. So. Coll., 1940. CLU; chartered fin. cons. Agt. N.Y. Life, Palatka, Fla., 1938—; v.p. Ginn Fin. Group, 1938—. Chmn. N.Y. Life Chmn. Coun., 1981; mem. N.Y. Life Adv. Bd. Dirs., 1981-95. Mem. Fla. Assn. Life Underwriters (pres. 1969), Nat. Assn. Life Underwriters. Republican. Methodist. Office: Ginn Fin Group Inc 421 Saint Johns Ave Ste 3 Palatka FL 32177-4700 Office Phone: 386-325-4501. Business E-Mail: ginnfingrp@funport.net.

GINN, RICHARD VAN NESS, retired military officer, healthcare executive; b. Miami, Fla., Mar. 23, 1943; s. Philander Jerome and Alida Loring (Van Ness) G.; m. Angelica Suarez, June 29, 1968; children: Angie Ann, Richard Van Ness. BA, Stetson U., 1965; MHA, Baylor U., 1978; MA, Duke U., 1980; grad. with honors, Army Command/Gen. Staff Coll., 1981, Army War Coll., 1990. Commd. 2d lt. U.S. Army, 1965, advanced through grades to col.; chief force devel. USAMRDC; exec. officer US Army 173rd Airborne Birgade, Vietnam, 1970—71; exec. sec. US Army Med. R&D Adv. Panel, Washington, 1972—76; resident Office Asst. SEc. Def., Health Affairs, Pentagon, Washington, 1977—78; profl. svcs. adminstr. BAMC, Ft. Sam Houston, 1978—80; pers. policy officer Office of Army Surgeon Gen., Washington, 1981-83; spl. asst. to chief Med. Svc. Corps, U.S. Army, Washington, 1983-86; dep. comdr. for adminstrn. SHAPE (Belgium) Med. Ctr., 1986-89; insp. gen. 7th Med. Command, Heidelberg, Germany, 1989-91; chief of staff USAMRDC, Ft. Detrick, Md., 1991-92; chief edn. and tng. Office of Army Surgeon Gen., Va., 1992-93; chief Health Svcs. divsn. Officer Pers. Mgmt., PERSCOM, Alexandria, Va., 1993-95; ret. U.S. Army, 1995; sr. v.p. Capital Health Svcs., Inc., 1996-97, pres., CEO, 1998—2000; historian Office of Army Surgeon Gen., Va., 2001—. Author: The History of the U.S. Army Medical Service Corps, 1997; contbr. numerous articles to profl. jours. Bd. dirs., sec., v.p. Daventry Cmty. Assn., pres., 2005—. Recipient Sir Henry Wellcome medal and prize, 1977, George Washington Honor medal Freedoms Found., 1978, Pres.'s award Daventry Cmty. Assn., 2005; named Young Fed. Health Care Adminstr., Assn. Mil. Surgeons U.S., 1982, Disting. Honor Grad., U.S. Army-Baylor U. Program in Health Care Adminstrn., 1977, Disting. Mem. U.S. Army Med. Dept. Rgt., 1998. Fellow Am. Coll. Healthcare Execs.; mem. Nat. Capital Healthcare Execs. (prizes scholarly competition 1982, 84), Fed. Health Care Execs. Inst. Alumni Assn., Soc. History of Fed. Govt., Soc. 173d Airborne Brigade, Order Mil. Med. Merit, U.S. Army War Coll. Alumni Assn., SHAPE Officers Assn., Omicron Delta Kappa (chpt. pres. 1964-65), Sigma Tau Delta, Pi Kappa Phi, Kappa Kappa Psi. Home: 6825 Spring Beauty Ct Springfield VA 22152-3111 Office Phone: 703-912-4326. E-mail: dickginn@aol.com.

GINN, RONN, architect, urban planner, general contractor; b. Jacksonville, Fla., Apr. 17, 1933; s. Angus Theodore and Joan Adelaide (Bailey) Ginn; children: Sharon Lee, John Norman, Pat C. AA, U. Fla., 1957, B.Arch., 1960, B.Landscape Architecture, 1961. Lic. Lic. bldg. ofcl. Fla. Urban design specialist Model Cities Adminstrn., HUD, Washington, 1967-68; pvt. practice landscape architecture, constrn., urban planning St. Petersburg, Fla., 1968—; pres. ARG Constrn. Corp., 1975-76, ARG Corp., 1977—, Ginn Corp., 1967-70, Atrium Corp., 1965-72. Urban design lectr. U. N.Mex., 1967; planning cons. State Dept., 1967-68; design cons. Am. Revolution Bicentennial Commn., 1967-69; vis. design critic Rice U., 1974; mem. Pinellas County (Fla.) Bd. Adjustments and Appeals, 1981-88; mem. Albuquerque Fine Arts Commn., 1965-67, St. Petersburg Design Goals Com., 1971-73; moderator radio program Design in Our Community WPKM, Tampa, Fla., 1971-72; founder, bd. dirs. Pinellas County Red Flag Charrette, 1972-76, Catalyst, St. Petersburg; bd. dirs. Fla. Council Clean Air, Fla. Red Flag Charrette; mem. Pinellas County Planning Council, 1972-73 Supervising architect, urban designer: Roswell (N.Mex.) Ctrl. bus. dist. redesign, 1964, Tucumcari (N.Mex.) ctrl. bus. dist. redesign, 1967, Treasure Island (Fla.) civic ctr. design, 1971; architect, urban designer, prin. Atrium One, Albuquerque, 1965-67; contbg. editor Urban Affairs Symposia, 1965-73; guest columnist St. Petersburg Evening Ind., 1974; important works include Albuquerque ctrl. bus. dist. redesign (nat. AIA award 1966), new town Fla. Ctr. (nat. Am. Soc. Landscape Architects award 1970), Brown residence (AIA merit award 1975), Penguin Restaurant, Treasure Island, Fla., 1973, Cross residence, 1974, Sheridan Gallery, 1974, Madeira Beach C. of C., 1975, Greenpepper Restaurant, 1975, Mixon Bldg., Ruskin, Fla., 1976, Congregation Beth Chai Synagogue, Seminole, Fla., 1979, Villa Dos Santos Master Plan, St. Petersburg Beach, Fla., 1979, Congregation Kol Ami Synagogue, Tampa, 1981, Markham residence, St. Petersburg, 1981, The Moorings, Tierra Verde, Fla., 1981, Ginn Residence, St. Petersburg, 1981, Congregation B'nai Israel Synagogue, Clearwater, Fla., 1981, Suncoast Seabird Sanctuary, St. Petersburg, 1982, Lilly Residence, Treasure Island, Fla., 1983, Anchor Bank Office Bldg., St. Petersburg, 1984, 1600 Pasadena Office Bldg., 1984 (nat. design patent), Lighthouse Harbor Marina, 1984, Tugaloo Environ. Edn. Ctr., 1989, Latorre Chiropractic Clinic, 1990, Johnnie Ruth Clarke Health Ctr., 1986, 92. Mayoral candidate City of Treasure Island, Fla., 1973; bldg. dir. City of Seminole, 1975-78; mem. Leadership St. Petersburg, 1978-79; mem. permitting task force City of St. Petersburg, 1999-2001. Named Spiffs Person of Courage, 1984; recipient numerous archtl., landscape architecture, urban design awards, Addy awards, 1981, 1982. Mem. AIA (nat. com. on regional devel. 1969-76, vice chmn., commr. pub. affairs Fla. chpt.), Am. Inst. Planners, Constrn. Specifications Inst., Am. Inst. Landscape Architects, So. Bldg. Code Congress, Fla. Planning and Zoning Assn., Nat. Eagle Scout Assn. (chpt. chmn.). Democrat. Presbyterian. Office: Ginn Arch PO Box 1541 Robbinsville NC 28771-1541 Home Phone: 727-302-0080; Office Phone: 828-479-2188. Personal E-mail: ronnginn@aol.com.

GINN, SAM L., telephone company executive; b. Saint Clair, Ala., Apr. 3, 1937; s. James Harold and Myra Ruby (Smith) G.; m. Meriann Lanford Vance, Feb. 2, 1963; children: Matthew, Michael, Samantha. BS, Auburn U., 1959; postgrad., Stanford U. Grad. Sch. Bus., 1968. Various positions AT&T, 1960-78; with Pacific Tel. & Tel. Co., 1978—, exec. v.p. network San Francisco, 1979-81, exec. v.p. services, 1981-82, exec. v.p. network services, 1982, exec. v.p., strategic planning and adminstrn., 1983, vice chmn. bd., strategic planning and adminstrn., 1983-84; vice chmn. bd., group v.p. PacTel Cos. Pacific Telesis Group, San Francisco, 1984-86; pres. Air Touch Commn., San Francisco, 1984-87; vice chmn. bd., pres., chief exec. officer PacTel Corp. Pacific Telesis Group, San Francisco, 1986; pres., chief operating officer Pacific Telesis Group, San Francisco, 1987-88, former chmn., pres., chief exec. officer; chmn. Air Touch Commn., San Francisco, 1993—, now chmn. bd., CEO. Mem. adv. bd. Sloan program Stanford U. Grad. Sch. Bus., 1978-85, mem. internat. adv. council Inst. Internat. Studies; bd. dir. 1st Interstate Bank, Chevron Corp., Safeway, Inc. Trustee Mills Coll., 1982—. Served to capt. U.S. Army, 1959-60. Sloan fellow, 1968 Mem.: Blackhawk Country (Danville, Calif.); World Trade, Pacific-Union; Rams Hill Country (Borrego Springs, Calif.), Bankers. Republican. Office: Ste 1400 400 S El Camino Real San Mateo CA 94402-1740

GINOBILI, MANU, professional basketball player; b. Argentina, June 28, 1977; Player Andino, La Rioja, Argentina, 1995—96, Olimpo de Bahía Blanca, Argentina, 1996—97, Basket Viola Reggio Calabria, Italy, 1998—2000, Kinder Bologna, Italy, 2001—02, San Antonio Spurs, 2002—. Player Argentina Nat. Olympic Team, Athens, Greece, 2002. Named Euroleague Finals MVP, 2001, Italian League MVP, 2000—01, 2001—02; named to NBA All-Star game, 2005. Achievements include being a member of Argentina Olympic Gold Medal Men's Basketball team, 2002; being a member of NBA Champion San Antonio Spurs, 2003, 2005; being the only player in NBA history to win Olympic Gold medal, NBA Championshiop, and Euroleague Championship. Office: c/o San Antonio Spurs 1 SBC Center San Antonio TX 78219

GINSBERG, BARRY GAVRILLE, psychologist, marriage and family therapist; b. Bklyn., July 25, 1936; s. Elias Ginsberg and Leah Schwartz Ginsberg Epstein; m. Mindi Silverberg, Feb. 22, 1962; children: Joshua, Neil Daniel, Jeremy Marc. BS in Pharmacy, columbia U., 1958; MS in Edn./Clin. Sch. Psychology, CCNY, 1969; PhD in Human Devel. and Family Studies, Pa. State U., 1971. Diplomate Am. Bd. Profl. Psychology, Am. Family Therapy Acad.; lic. pharmacist, NY, NJ, Calif., Fla.; cert. tchr., NY; lic. psychologist, Pa., Mass.; cert. play therapist/supr., cert. marriage and family therapist; nat. cert. sch. psychologist. Pharmacist, mgr. Ginsberg Pharmacy, Bronx, N.Y., 1958-63; tchr. jr. and sr. h.s. N.Y.C. Bd. Edn., 1963-69; psychologist Bucks County Psychiat. Ctr., Chalfont, Pa., 1971-73; dir. child and family unit Lenape Valley Found., Chalfont, 1973-75, dir. cmty. svcs., 1975-78; psychologist dir. Ginsberg Assocs., Doylestown, Pa., 1978—; cons. and trainer, dir. Ctr. Relationship Enhancement, Doylestown, 1981—. Adj. assoc. prof. Temple U., 1975-85; cons. Bucks County Area Coun. Aging, 1988—, Bucks County Children and Youth, Doylestown, 1989—, Bucks County Head Start, Bucks County Assn. Retarded Citizens, Doylestown, 1982—; adj. prof. psychology Phila. Coll. Osteo. Medicine, 1997; adj. prof. clin. psychology Chestnut Hill Coll., 2000. Author: Relationship Enhancement Family Therapy, 1997, 50 Wonderful Ways to Be a Single Parent Family, 2002; columnist Parenting, 1988-89; co-host (cable TV) Parenting, 1994—; host (cable TV) Parent Connection. Bd. dirs. Big Bros./Big Sisters of Bucks County, 1972—, Bucks County Drug and Alcohol Commn., 1981-87, Network of Victims Asistance, 1990-95. Recipient Sterling Vol. award Ctrl. Bucks C. of C., 1996, Meritorious award Am. Bd. Profl. Psychology, 1992, Meritorious award Bucks County Drug and Alcohol Commn., 1987. Fellow APA (bd. dirs. divsn. family psychology, Meritorious awards divsn. family psychology 1986, 87, 88, 89), Pa. Psychol. Assn. (bd. dirs., pres. cmty. divsn.), Am. Assn. Marriage and Family Therapists (clin. mem., approved supr.), Ctrl. Bucks C. of C. (v.p., bd. dirs. 1975-89, chmn. parenting and family com. 1990—). Avocations: racquetball, folk dancing, ballet. Office: Ctr Relationship Enhancement 70 W Oakland St Ste 313 Doylestown PA 18901 Home Phone: 215-345-7543; Office Phone: 215-348-2424. Personal E-mail: enhancerelations@aol.com. Business E-Mail: barry@relationshipenhancement.com.

GINSBERG, BARRY HOWARD, endocrinologist, educator; b. Bklyn., May 9, 1945; s. Emanuel and Ruth (Friedman) G.; m. Marjorie Ellen Kanef, Aug. 20, 1967; children: Susan, David. BA, SUNY, Binghamton, 1965; PhD, Yeshiva U., NYC, 1971, MD, 1972. Intern Beth Israel Hosp., Boston, 1972-73, resident in internal medicine, 1973-74; fellow in endocrinology NIH, 1974-77; asst. prof. U. Iowa, Iowa City, 1977-82, assoc. prof. medicine and biochemistry, 1982—87, prof., 1988-90, assoc. dir. Diabetes-Endocrinology Rsch. Ctr., 1982-84, dir., 1984-86, co-dir. diabetes control and complications trial, 1984—86, dir., 1986-90; med. dir. worldwide diabetes healthcare Becton Dickenson and Co., Franklin Lakes, NJ, 1990—98; v.p. med. affairs BD Consumer Healthcare, 1999—2007; pres. Diabetes Tech. Cons., Wyckoff, NJ, 2007—. Adj. prof. medicine Robert Wood Johnson Coll. Medicine, 1990-2005 Contbr. chpts. to med. books. Comdr. USPHS, 1974-77. Mem. Am. Fedn. Clin. Rsch., Endocrine Soc., Ctrl. Soc. Clin. Rsch., Am. Diabetes Assn. (pres. Iowa chpt. 1982-84, bd. dirs. 1982-85, bd. dirs. N.E. chpt. 1989—). Avocation: computer programming. Office: PO Box 462 Wyckoff NJ 07481-1712 Office Phone: 201-665-9152. Personal E-mail: diabetes.consultants@yahoo.com.

GINSBERG, DAVID BARON, retired management consultant; b. Detroit, May 29, 1946; s. Bernard and Rebecca Ginsberg; m. Leslie Ann Wiggins, Jan. 2, 1982; children: Roman Wiggins, Rex Wiggins. B, Ctrl. Mich. U., Mt. Pleasant, 1964—68, M, 1968—74. Cert. secondary schs. adminstr. Mich., 1996, contract seminar leader Fred Pryor Seminars/Career Track, 2005. Tchr., basketball coach Leslie Pub. Schs., Mich., 1968—69, Battle Creek Pub. Schs., Mich., 1969—72, Grand Rapids Pub. Schs., Mich., 1972—75; basketball coach Ctrl. Mich. U., 1975—91; retail jewelry mgr. Osterman Jewelers, Traverse City, Mich., 1991—93; tchr., basketball coach, prin. Flint Cmty. Schs., Mich., 1993—2005; ind. contractor, trainer Mgmt. & Motivational Strategies, LLC, Traverse City, 2005—06; ret., 2006. Facilitator, activist Cmty. Flint, 1993—2005. Recipient Coach of Yr. award, Big-9 Athletic Conf., 1995. Mem.: Mich. Assn. Secondary Sch. Prins. (assoc.), Nat. Assn. Basketball Coaches (life), Basketball Coaches Assn. Mich. (life), Mich. Sports Sages (life). Office: Mgmt & Motivational Strategies LLC 1192 Piccadilly Rd Traverse City MI 49684 Home Phone: 231-943-3509. Personal E-mail: hoopster33@hotmail.com.

GINSBERG, DAVID LAWRENCE, architect; b. NYC, Sept. 21, 1932; s. Harry Seaman and Zena (Sagal)S.; m. Emily (Boor), Dec. 29, 1969; children: Stuart Samuel, Daniel Paul, Laura Ruth. BArch, Cornell U., Ithaca, NY, 1955. Ptnr. charge N.Y. offices Perkins and Will, NYC, 1957-78; exec. v.p. Perkins and Will, Chgo., 1978-79; exec. v.p. and chief planning officer Columbia-Presbyn. Health Svc., Inc., NYC, 1979-92; v.p. Columbia-Presbyn. Health Sys., Inc.; dep. to pres. Presbyn. Hosp., 1993—95; ptnr. Larsen, Shein, Ginsberg, and Snyder LLP, 1995—2005; v.p. and prin. Perkins Eastman Archs., 2006—. Mem. adv. group, asst. clin. prof. pub. health Columbia U., N.Y.C., 1979-97, adj. prof. pub. health, 2005—; sr. cons. U.S. Global Health Svc., 1992-94; mem. Nat. Healthcare Guidelines Com. Mem. parents coun. Washington U., St. Louis, 1988-91; mem. Scarsdale Planning Bd., 1980-90; sec. bd. trustees N.Y. Presbyn. Hosp. Infant and Child Care Ctr.; v.p., bd. dirs. Stephen Wise Free Synagogue. Recipient medal N.Y. Soc. Architects, 1955, award N.Y. Soc. for Health Planning, 1993, Modern Healthcare Design award. Fellow A1A (nat. guidlines revision com.); mem. APHA, Acad. Architecture for Health, Forum for Healthcare Planning, Am. Hosp. Assn., Assn. Am. Med. Colls., Soc. Hosp. Planning, Regional Planning Assn., Gargoyle Soc. Office: Perkins Eastman Architects 115 Fifth Ave New York NY 10003 Home Phone: 212-799-8275; Office Phone: 212-353-7200. Business E-Mail: d.ginsberg@perkinseastman.com.

GINSBERG, ERNEST, lawyer, banker; s. Morris Henry and Mildred Florence (Slive) G.; m. Harriet Gay Scharf, Dec. 20, 1959; children: Alan Justin, Robert Daniel. BA, Syracuse U., 1953, JD, 1955; LLM, Georgetown U., 1963. Bar: N.Y. 1955, U.S. Supreme Ct. 1964. Pvt. practice law, Syracuse, 1957-61; mem. staff, office chief counsel IRS, Washington, 1961-63; tax counsel Comptr. of Currency, Washington, 1964-65, assoc. chief counsel, 1965-68; v.p. legal affairs, sec. Republic Nat. Bank N.Y., NYC, 1968-74; sr. v.p. legal affairs, sec. Republic Nat. Bank, NYC, 1975-86, exec. v.p., gen. counsel, sec., 1984-86, vice chmn. bd., gen. counsel, 1986-94, vice chmn. bd., 1990-99. Sr. v.p., sec. legal affairs Republic N.Y. Corp., N.Y.C., 1974-84, exec. v.p., gen. counsel, sec., 1984-86, vice chmn. bd., gen. counsel, sec., 1986-94, vice chmn. bd., 1986-99, also bd. dirs.; bd. visitors Syracuse U. Coll. Law, 1980-2005. Chmn. emeritus Roundabout Theatre Co., N.Y.C. With U.S. Army, 1955-57. Mem. Am. Bankers Assn. (bd. dirs. 1995-97), Am. Bankers Coun. (co-chmn. 1992-94), N.Y. State Bankers Assn. (pres. 1993-94), Bankers Roundtable (bd. dirs. 1995-97), Phi Sigma Delta, Phi Delta Phi.

GINSBERG, HENRY, medical educator, researcher; b. NYC, July 13, 1945; s. Stanley and Irene Ginsberg; m. Barbara Goldberg, Jan. 2, 1946; children: David, Michael. MD, SUNY Downstate Med. Ctr., Bklyn., 1970. Lic. physician NY, 1970. Assoc. prof. of medicine Mt Sinai Sch. of Medicine, NYC, 1978—85; Irving prof. of medicine Columbia U. P&S, NYC, 1985—. Dir. Irving Ctr. for Clin. Rsch. Lt comdr. USN, 1974—76, San Diego. Achievements include research in lipid disorders and diabetes mellitus. Office: Columbia University College of P&S 630 West 168th Street New York NY 19932 Office Phone: 212-395-9562. Office Fax: 212-305-3213. E-mail: hng1@columbia.edu.

GINSBERG, HERSH MEIER, rabbi, religious organization administrator; b. Vienna, July 8, 1928; s. Lazar Yonah Ginsberg and Perl Roth; m. Fradel Levy; children: Lazar Yonah, Meshulim, Chana. Dir. Union Orthodox Rabbis of U.S. and Can.; rabbinical ct. judge; dean Rabbi Jacob-Joseph Sch., NYC, 1955-73. Founder Kolel Ohel Elemelech Rabbinical Coll., Jerusalem. Jewish. Office: Union Orthodox Rabbis US & Can 235 E Broadway New York NY 10002-5600

GINSBERG, MARC CHARLES, former diplomat, investment company executive; b. NYC, Oct. 18, 1950; m. Janet Louise Ginsberg; two children. BA, MBA, Am. U.; JD, Georgetown U., 1978. Legis. asst. to Sen. Edward Kennedy, 1973-76; spl. asst. to under sec. of mgmt. Dept. State, 1977-80; dep. sr. adviser to Pres. for Middle East affairs, 1980-81; atty. Surrey & Morse, D.C., 1981-87, Galland, Kharasch, Morse & Garfinkle, D.C., 1987-93; U.S. amb. to Morocco, 1993-98; pres. Georgetown Global Investments Corp., Washington, 1998-2000; CEO, mng. dir. Northstar Equity Group Inc, Washington, 2000—. Contbr. FOX News Channel. Mem. ABA, D.C. Bar Assn. Office: Northstar Equity 700 12th St NW Ste 800 Washington DC 20005-3949

GINSBERG, MYRON, computer scientist; b. Brockton, Mass., May 3, 1943; s. Frank and Evelyn Hazel (Spekin) Ginsberg; m. Judith Beverly Rosenbaum, Nov. 19, 1989; 1 child, Ellen Joy Hochberg. BA in Math., Boston U., 1965; MA in Math., Clark U., 1967; PhD in Computer Sci., U. Iowa, 1972. Instr. dept. computer sci. U. Iowa, Iowa City, 1969-72; from asst. prof. to assoc. prof. computer sci. So. Meth. U., Dallas, 1972-77, 77-79; NASA/ASEE rsch. fellow NASA Langley Rsch. Ctr, Hampton, Va., summer 1979, summer 2000; assoc. sr. rsch. scientist GM Rsch. Labs., Warren, Mich., 1979-81, sr. rsch. scientist, 1981-82, staff rsch. scientist, 1982-92; cons. sys. engr. EDS Advanced Computing Ctr., GM NAO R & D Ctr., Warren, 1992-96, EDS High Performance Computing Group, Troy, Mich., 1996-97; ind. cons. HPC Rsch. and Edn., Farmington Hills, Mich., 1997—. Mathematician U.S. Army Ballistics Rsch. Lab., Aberdeen Proving Ground, Md., 1964—67; data sys. analyst NASA Electronics Rsch. Ctr., Cambridge, Mass., 1968—69; adj. assoc. prof. U. Mich., Ann Arbor, 1990; mem. adv. bd. Cray Rsch. Fortran, 1991—92; grant rev. panelist NSF, 1992—93, 1996—97; GM/EDS rep. Supercomputing Automotive Applications Partnership, 1992—94; founder, first chmn. AUTOBENCH Project U.S. Coun. Automotive Rsch., 1995—96; mem. couns. advisors HPC area Gerson Lehrman Group, NYC, 2002—. Editor: Supercomputers in the Auto Industry, 1985, Automotive Applications of Supercomputers, 1988, High-Speed and Large-Scale Computing: A Panoramic View, 1988, Automotive Applications of Vector/Parallel Computers: State-of-the-Art, 1992; contbr. articles to profl. jours.; mem. editl. bd. Computing Sys. Engring., 1988—93. Grantee, Mobil Oil Found., 1975, Alfred P. Sloan Found., 1975—78, U.S. Army C.E., 1977—78, NSF, 1977—79, 1983—84. Fellow: Assn. Computing Machinery (lectr., bd. dirs. SIGNUM, editor-in-chief SIGNUM newsletter 1976—80); mem.: ASME (lectr.), IEEE (sr.; program evaluator 2003—), Soc. Automotive Engr. (founder, 1st chmn. com. high performance computing stds. for automotive mfg. 1996—97, lectr., award for excellence in oral presentation 1985—87, Disting. Spkr. plaque 1988, Forest R. McFarland award 1994), Soc. Indsl. and Applied Math. (lectr. spl. group supercomputing), Computer Soc. of IEEE (lectr.), Sigma Xi (lectr.). Avocations: playing alto sax, tenor sax, soprano sax, clarinet and flute, jazz. Office: HPC Rsch & Education 35764 Congress Rd Ste 100 Farmington MI 48335-1222 E-mail: m.ginsberg@ieee.org.

GINSBERG, MYRON DAVID, neurologist; b. Denver, Aug. 26, 1939; s. Morris Seymour and Evelyn (Fishman) G.; children: Deborah Mara, Emily Michelle. BA, Wesleyan U., 1961; MD, Harvard U., 1966. Intern, resident Harvard Med. Svc., Boston City Hosp., 1966-68; neurology resident, fellow Mass. Gen. Hosp., Boston, 1968-70, 72-73; staff assoc. Lab. Perinatal Physiology, NIH, Bethesda, Md., 1970-72; asst. prof., assoc. prof. dept. neurology U. Pa., Phila., 1973-79; assoc. prof. neurology U. Miami Sch. Medicine, 1979—81, prof. neurology, 1981—, dir. cerebral vascular disease rsch. ctr., 1981—2006, dir. neurotrauma clin. rsch. ctr., 1991—95, Peritz Scheinberg endowed chair of neurology, 1992—. Mem. study sect. NIH, Bethesda, 1982-86; nat. rsch. com. Am. Heart Assn., Dallas, 1986-91. Editor: Cerebrovascular Diseases, 16th Princeton Conf., 1989; editor Jour. Blood Flow and Metabolism, 1992-97; contbr. over 300 articles to profl. jours. Lt. comdr. USPHS, 1970-72. Fulbright scholar U.S. Govt., 1961-62; recipient Jacob Javits Neuroscience Investigator award NIH, 1985-92, Willis Lectr. award, Am. Stroke Assn., 2002, Disting. Scientist award Am. Heart Assn., 2003, Disting. Faculty Scholar award U. Miami, 2004. Fellow Am. Acad. Neurology; mem. Am. Neurol. Assn. (membership com. 1990-91), Am. Physiol. Soc., Internat. Soc. Cerebral Blood Flow & Metabolism (dir. 1985-89), Phi Beta Kappa, Alpha Omega Alpha. Office: U Miami Sch Medicine Dept Neurology D4-5 PO Box 016960 Miami FL 33101-6960 Office Phone: 305-243-6103.

GINSBURG, ALLEN J., lawyer; b. July 5, 1944; BS, Northwestern U., 1965, JD cum laude, 1968. Bar: Ill. 1969, U.S. Tax Ct. 1973; CPA, Ill. Ptnr.-in-charge Chgo. office DLA Piper US LLP, Chgo. Address: DLA Piper US LLP Ste 1900 203 N La Salle St Chicago IL 60601-1210 Office Phone: 312-368-4025. Office Fax: 312-630-5357. Business E-Mail: allen.ginsburg@dlapiper.com.

GINSBURG, CHARLES DAVID, lawyer; b. NYC, Apr. 20, 1912; s. Nathan and Rae (Lewis) G.; m. Marianne Laïs; children by previous marriage: Jonathan, Susan, Mark. AB, W.Va. U., 1932; LLB, Harvard U., 1935. Bar: W. Va. 1935, U.S. Supreme Ct. 1940, D.C. 1946, U.S. Ct. Appeals (2d, 3rd, 4th, 7th, and Fed. cirs.) 1946, U.S. Claims Ct. 1960, U.S. Tax Ct. 1961. Atty. for public utilities div. and office of gen. counsel SEC, 1935-39; law sec. to Justice William O. Douglas, 1939; asst. to commr. SEC, 1939-40; legal adviser Price Stblzn. Div., Nat. Def. Adv. Com., 1940-41; gen. counsel Office Price Adminstrn. and Civilian Supply, 1941-42, OPA, 1942-43; pvt. practice law Ginsburg, Feldman and Bress, Washington, 1946-98; founding ptnr. Ginsburg, Feldman & Bress, 1946-98; sr. counsel firm Powell, Goldstein, LLP, 1998; adminstrv. asst. to Senator M.M. Neely, W.Va., 1950; adj. prof. internat. law Georgetown U. (Grad. Sch. Law), 1959-67. Dep. commr. U.S. del. Austrian Treaty Commn., Vienna, 1947; adviser U.S. del. Council Fgn. Ministers, London, 1947; Mem. Presdl. Emergency Bd. 166 (Airlines), 1966; mem. Pres.'s Commn. on Postal Orgn., 1967; chmn. Presdl. Emergency Bd. 169 (Railroads), 1969; exec. dir. Nat. Adv. Commn. Civil Disorders, 1967 Author: The Future of German Reparations; Contbr. to legal jours. Bd. mem., chmn. exec. com. Nat. Symphony Orch. Assn., 1960-69; bd. govs. Weizmann Inst., 1965 (hon. fellow 1972); mem. vis. com. Harvard-Mass. Inst. Tech. Joint Ctr. on Urban Studies, 1969; trustee St. John's Coll., 1969-76, chmn. bd., 1974-76; overseers com. Kennedy Sch. Govt. Harvard, 1971—; mem. coun. Nat. Harvard Law Sch. Assn., 1972—, gen. counsel Dem. Nat. Com., 1968-70. Served from pvt. to capt. AUS, 1942-46; dep. dir. econs. div. Office Mil. Govt., 1945-46, Germany. Decorated Bronze Star, Legion of Merit; recipient Presdl. Cert. of Merit. Mem. ABA, Fed. Bar Assn, Am. Law Inst., Coun. on Fgn. Rels., Met. Club, Army and Navy Club, Phi Beta Kappa. Democrat. Home: The Alexandra House 400 Madison St Apt 1303 Alexandria VA 22314-1723 Personal E-mail: davginsburg@comcast.net.

GINSBURG, DAVID, genetics educator, researcher; b. Newburgh, NY, Aug. 11, 1952; s. Leonard and Ruth Helena Henrietta (Falkson) G.; m. Maureen Rose Kushinsky, June 7, 1981; children: Daniel William, Leah Beth. BA (magna cum laude) in Molecular Biophysics and Biochemistry, Yale U., 1974; MD, Duke U. Sch. Medicine, 1977. Diplomate Am. Bd. Internal Medicine, subspecialties in med. oncology and hematology; diplomate Am. Bd. Med. Genetics. Resident in pathology Presbyn. Hosp., San Francisco, 1977-78; intern, resident in internal medicine Peter Bent Brigham Hosp., Boston, 1978-81; fellow tng. program in hematology and med. oncology Brigham and Women's Hosp., Harvard Med. Sch., Boston, 1981-84; instr. medicine Harvard Med. Sch., Boston, 1984-85; asst. prof. dept. medicine U. Mich., Ann Arbor, 1985-89, assoc. prof. with tenure, 1989-93, assoc. prof. human genetics, 1989-93, dir. divsn. med. genetics, dept. medicine, 1993—2002, prof. internal medicine and human genetics, 1993—2004, James V. Neel Disting. U. prof. internal medicine and human genetics, 2004—, Warner-Lambert/Parke Davis prof. medicine, 2005—, mem., Life Sci. Inst., 2003—; asst. investigator Howard Hughes Med. Inst. Howard Hughes Med. Inst., Ann Arbor, 1985-89, assoc. investigator, 1989-93, investigator, 1993—. Contbr. numerous articles to profl. jours. Recipient Cotlove award, Acad. Clin. Lab. Physicians and Scientists, 2006. Fellow AAAS; mem. ACP, Am. Soc. Human Genetics, Am. Soc. Hematology (E. Donnall Thomas lectr. and prize 2000), Am. Heart Assn. (Sol Sherry lectr., 2002, Basic Rsch. prize 2003), Assn. Am. Physicians, Am. Soc. for Clin. Investigation (pres., 2002, ASCI award, 2004), Inst. Medicine, Am. Acad. Arts and Scis., NAS, Alpha Omega Alpha. Jewish. Office: Life Scis Inst Rm 5028 210 Washtenaw Ave Ann Arbor MI 48109 Business E-Mail: ginsburg@umich.edu.*

GINSBURG, DOUGLAS HOWARD, federal judge; b. Chgo., May 25, 1946; Diploma, Latin Sch. Chgo., 1963; BS, Cornell U., 1970; JD, U. Chgo., 1973. Bar: Ill. 1973, Mass. 1982, US Supreme Ct. 1984, US Ct. Appeals (9th cir.) 1986. Assoc. Covington & Burling, Washington, 1972; law clk. to Hon. Carl McGowan US Ct. Appeals, Washington, 1973—74; law clk. to Justice Thurgood Marshall US Supreme Ct., Washington, 1974—75; prof. Harvard U., 1975—83; dep. asst. atty. gen. for antitrust divsn US Dept. Justice, Washington, 1983—84; adminstr. for info. and regulatory affairs Exec. Office Pres., Office Mgmt. and Budget, Washington, 1984—85; asst. atty. gen. antitrust divsn. US Dept. Justice, Washington, 1985—86; judge US Ct. Appeals (DC cir.), 1986—2001, chief judge, 2001—. Vis. prof. law Columbia U., NYC, 1987—88; lectr. law Harvard U., Cambridge, Mass., 1988—89; disting. prof. law George Mason U., Arlington, Va., 1988—; Charles J. Merriam vis. scholar, sr. lectr. U. Chgo., 1990—. Author: Regulation of Broadcasting: Law and Policy Towards Radio, Television and Cable Communications, 1979, Antitrust, Uncertainty, and Technological Innovation, 1980; co-author: Regulation of the Electronic Mass Media, 1991; editor (with W. Abernathy): Government, Technology and the Future of the Automobile, 1980; contbr. articles to profl. jours. Recipient Casper Platt award, U. Chgo. Law Sch., 1973; Mecham scholar, 1970—73. Mem.: ABA (jud. rep. antitrust sect. coun. 2000—03), Ill. State Bar Assn., Mont Pelerin Soc., Am. Law and Econs. Assn., Am. Econ. Assn., Phi Kappa Phi, Order of Coif. Avocations: historic preservation, land conservation. Office: US Ct Appeals 333 Constitution Ave NW Washington DC 20001-2866

GINSBURG, GERALD J., lawyer, management consultant; b. Poughkeepsie, NY, Aug. 29, 1930; s. Abraham and Anna (Murkoff) G.; children: Jason Andrew, Stephanie Carla. BS, Syracuse U., 1952; JD, Bklyn. Law Sch., 1958. Bar: N.Y. 1959. Pub. acct., 1954-59; v.p. fin. and ops., dir. Sheffield Watch Corp., NYC, 1959-70, dir., 1967-70; exec. v.p., dir. Kurt Orban Co., Wayne, NJ, 1971-83; pres., dir. Pacific Marine Holdings Corp., 1983-87; pres. J&S Cons., Walnut Creek, Calif. Dir. Ramapo Fin. Corp., Pilgrim State Bank Served with USNR, 1952-53. Mem. ABA, N.Y. Bar Assn. Office: PO Box 5314 Walnut Creek CA 94596-1314

GINSBURG, LYNN, writer; b. Detroit, July 16, 1965; d. Werner (Stepfather) and Suzanne Heim; m. Josef J. Pusedu, June 26, 1990. BFA (hons.), NYU, 1988. Sr. account exec. Creamer Dickson Basford, NYC, 1993—95; freelance author self employed, Boulder, Colo., 1995—. Author: (nonfiction book) What Are You Hungry For? Women, Food and Spirituality, (musical) Lonely on the Bayou, (play) Going to Pay, (freelance articles) O, The Oprah Mag., Wired, Travel and Leisure, N.Y. Daily News, LA Times, Alternative Medicine, Yoga Jour.; assoc. editor PC Sources Mag., N.Y.C., 1993—95. Nat. Merit Scholar, Nat. Merit Scholarship Orgn., 1983. Home Phone: 303-473-9493.

GINSBURG, MARTIN DAVID, lawyer, educator; b. NYC, June 10, 1932; s. Morris and Evelyn (Bayer) Ginsburg; m. Ruth Bader, June 23, 1954; children: Jane, James. AB, Cornell U., 1953; JD, Harvard U., 1958; LLD (hon.), Lewis and Clark Coll., 1992, Wheaton Coll., 1997. Bar: N.Y. 1959, D.C. 1980. Practiced in N.Y.C., 1959-79; mem. firm Weil, Gotshal & Manges, NYC, 1963-79; of counsel firm Fried, Frank, Harris, Shriver and Jacobson, Washington, 1980—; Charles Keller Beekman prof. law Columbia U. Law Sch., NYC, 1979-80; prof. law Georgetown U. Law Center, Washington, 1980—; lectr. U. Leiden, The Netherlands, 1982; lectr. Salzburg Seminar Austria, 1984; mem. tax divsn adv. group Dept. Justice, 1980-81; mem. adv. group to Commr. Internal Revenue, 1978-80; mem. adv. bd. U. Calif. Securities Regulation Inst., 1973-91. Adj. prof. law NYU, 1967—79; vis. prof. law Stanford U., Calif., 1978, Harvard U., Cambridge, Mass., 1986, U. Chgo., 1990, NYU, 1993; cons. joint com. on taxation U.S. Congress, 1979—80, acad. advisor, 2000—01; chmn. tax adv. bd. Commerce Clearing House, 1982—94; mem. bd. advisors NYU/IRS Continuing Profl. Edn. Program, 1983—88, co-chmn., 1986—88; sub coun. on capital allocation, co-chmn. taxation expert group Competitiveness Policy Coun., 1993—95; chmn. tax adv. bd. Little, Brown, 1994—96; bd. dirs. Millennium Chems., Inc., 1996—2003, Chgo. Classical Rec. Found.; lectr. various tax insts.; Mandella Inst. Disting. Vis. lectr. U. Witwatersrand, South Africa, 2006. Co-author, editor Tax Consequences of Investments, 1969; spl. editor: Structuring Venture Capital, Private Equity, and Entrepreneurial Transactions, 2007; co-author: Mergers, Acquisitions, and Buyouts, 2007; contbr. articles to legal jours. Mem. vis. com. Harvard Law Sch., 1994—98. 1st lt. arty. US Army, 1954—56. Recipient Chair named in his honor, Georgetown U. Law Ctr., 1986, Marshall-Wythe Medallion, Coll. of William and Mary Sch. Law, 1996, Outstanding Achievement award, Tax Soc. NYU, 1993, Viccenial medal, Georgetown U., 2000, Disting. Svc. award, ABA section of Taxation, 2006. Fellow: Am. Bar Found. (bd. dirs. 2000—03), Am. Coll. Tax Counsel; mem.: ABA (mem. com. corp. taxation, tax sect. 1973—, chmn. com. simplification 1979—81, mem. tax sect. coun. 1984—87, tax systems task force 1995—97), Assn. Bar City N.Y. (chmn. com. taxation 1977—79, mem. audit com. 1980—81), N.Y. State Bar Assn. (mem. tax sect. exec. com. 1969—, chmn. tax sect. 1975, ho. of dels. 1976—77), Am. Law Inst. (cons. Fed. Income Tax Project 1974—93). Office: 600 New Jersey Ave NW Washington DC 20001-2022 Home Phone: 202-298-3202; Office Phone: 202-639-7030. Business E-Mail: ginsbma@ffhsj.com.

GINSBURG, NORTON SYDNEY, retired geographer; b. Chgo., Aug. 24, 1921; s. Morris and Sarah (Ginsberg) G.; m. Diana Roselle Peterson, Aug. 12, 1973; children: Jeremy, Alexander. BA, U. Chgo., 1941, MA, 1947, PhD, 1949. Geographer U.S. Army Map Service, 1941-42; prof. geography U. Chgo., 1947-86, assoc. dean Coll., 1963-66, assoc. dean social scis., 1967-69; dean academic program, sr. fellow Center for Study Democratic Instns., Santa Barbara, 1971-74; chmn. dept. U. Chgo., 1978-85; retired, 1986; dir. Environment and Policy Inst. East-West Ctr., Honolulu, 1986-91. Cons. Social Sci. Research Council, Ency. Brit., Ford Found. East-West Center, Nat. Acad. Sci., NRC, SCOPE, UN, UNESCO Author: Atlas of Economic Development, 1961, The Urban Transition: American and Asian Experiences, 1990; co-author, editor: Pattern of Asia, 1958, Malaya, 1958, Essays on Geography and Economic Development, 1960, China: Urbanization and National Development, 1980, China: The 80s Era, 1984, Geographic Perspectives on the Wealth of Nations, 1986; co-author, editor: The Extended Metropolis in Asia, 1991; co-editor: The Ocean Yearbooks, 1978-96. Served to lt. USNR, 1942-46. Guggenheim fellow, 1983 Mem. Assn. Am. Geographers (pres. 1970-71), Phi Beta Kappa, Sigma Xi.

GINSBURG, PAUL B., health facility administrator; Degree, Binghamton U.; PhD in Econs., Harvard U. Dep. asst. dir. Congl. Budget Office, Washington, 1978—84; sr. economist RAND, 1984—86; founding exec. dir. Physician Payment Rev. Commn., 1986—95; pres. Ctr. for Studying Health Sys. Change, Washington, 1995—. Mem. adv. bd. Nat. Inst. for Health Care Mgmt. Rsch. and Ednl. Found., Washington, 2003—. Office: Ctr for Studying Health Sys Change 600 Maryland Ave SW Ste 550 Washington DC 20024 Business E-Mail: pginsburg@hschange.org.

GINSBURG, RUTH, state representative; b. Bklyn., July 18, 1931; m. George S.; two children. Grad., Bklyn. Coll., 1954. Mem. Mayor's Adv. Com. for Social Svc. Funding; mem. dist. 26 N.H. Ho. of Reps., 1996—. Mem. sci., tech. and energy com., children and family law com. N.H. Ho. Reps. Former mem. Nashua Sch. Bd.; bd. dirs. Nashua Children's Assn.; mem. Nashua Ethnic Awareness Com. Jewish. Office: NH State Legis State House Concord NH 03301

GINSBURG, (JOAN) RUTH BADER, United States supreme court justice; b. Bklyn., June 23, 1933; d. Nathan and Celia (Amster) Bader; m. Martin David Ginsburg, June 23, 1954; children: Jane Carol, James Steven. AB, Cornell U., 1954; postgrad., Harvard Law Sch., 1956—58; LLB Kent scholar, Columbia Law Sch., 1959; LLD (hon.), Lund U., Sweden, 1969, Am. U., 1981, Vt. Law Sch., 1984, Georgetown U., 1985, DePaul U., 1985, Bklyn. Law Sch., 1987, Amherst Coll., 1991, Rutgers U., 1991, Lewis and Clark Coll., 1992, Radcliffe Coll., 1994, NYU, 1994, Columbia U., 1994, Smith Coll., 1994, L.I. U., 1994, U. Ill., 1995, Brandeis U., 1996, Wheaton Coll., 1997, Jewish Theol. Sem. of Am., 1997, George Washington U. Law Sch., 1997, U. Pa., 2007; DHL (hon.), Hebrew Union Coll., 1988. Bar: N.Y. 1959, D.C. 1975, U.S. Supreme Ct. 1967. Law sec. to Hon. Edmund L. Palmieri U.S. Dist. Ct. (so. dist.) N.Y., 1959—61; rsch. assoc. Columbia Law Sch., NYC, 1961—62, assoc. dir. project internat. procedure, 1962—63; asst. prof. Rutgers U. Sch. Law, Newark, 1963—66, assoc. prof., 1966—69, prof., 1969—72, Columbia U. Sch. Law, NYC, 1972—80; judge U.S. Ct. Appeals, (DC cir.), Washington, 1980—93; assoc. justice U.S. Supreme Ct., Washington, 1993—. Phi Beta Kappa vis. scholar, 1973—74; fellow Ctr. for Advanced Study in Behavioral Scis., Stanford, Calif., 1977—78; lectr. Aspen (Colo.) Inst., 1990, Salzburg (Austria) Seminar, 1984; gen. counsel ACLU, 1973—80, bd. dirs., 1974—80. Author (with Anders Bruzelius): Civil Procedure in Sweden, 1965, Swedish Code of Judicial Procedure, 1968; author: (with H.H. Kay & K. M. Davidson) Text, Cases and Materials on Sex-Based Discrimination, 1974; contbr. numerous articles to books and jours. Named one of World's 100 Most Powerful Women, Forbes mag., 2004, Most Powerful Women, 2005. Fellow: Am. Bar Found.; mem.: AAAS, Coun. Fgn. Rels., Am. Law Inst. (coun. mem. 1978—93). Office: US Supreme Ct One First St NE Washington DC 20543*

GINSBURG, SIGMUND G., management and executive search consultant; b. NYC, Oct. 12, 1937; s. Saul and Rose (Rich) Ginsburg; m. Judith Ann Jacobson, July 4, 1965; children: Beth Alison, David Grant. BA magna cum laude, Dartmouth Coll., 1959; postgrad., London Sch. Econs., 1959-60; MPA, Harvard U., 1961. Mgmt. intern Office of Sec. of Def., Washington, 1961-62; asst. to pres. Hudson Inst., 1964; asst. mgr. pers. adminstrv. svcs., mgmt. analyst Port Authority of N.Y. and N.J., 1964-66; sr. mgmt. cons. and spl. asst. to dep. mayor Office of the Mayor, City of N.Y., 1966-67, asst. city adminstr., 1967-72; v.p. for adminstrn. and planning, treas. Adelphi U., Garden City, NY, 1972-78; v.p. for fin., treas. U. Cin., 1978-84, adj. prof. higher edn. adminstrn., bus. adminstrn., 1980-84; v.p. fin. and adminstrn. Barnard Coll., NYC, 1984-94; v.p. bus. devel. Am. Mus. Natural History, NYC, 1994, sr. v.p. fin. and bus. devel., 1995—2002; project. exec. Rose Ctr. Earth and Space, 1995—2000; exec. v.p., dir. nonprofit practice DHR Internat., NYC, 2003—; pres. Sigmund G. Ginsburg Cons., 2003—. Adj. asst. prof., lectr. CUNY, 1966—72; founder, dir. N.Y.C. Urban Fellows Program, 1969—72; adj. assoc. prof. Adelphi U., 1972—78; mem. City Mgrs. Working Rev. Com. Cin. 2000 Plan, 1979—82; mgmt. commentator Sta. WGUC, Cin., 1980; instr. Fordham U., 1985—95, New Sch. U., 1986, 91; adv. coun. Tchrs. Ins. and Annuity Assn.-Coll. Retirement Equities Fund, 1993—96, chmn., 1994—95; lectr. profl. meetings; cons. in field. Co-author: Managing the Higher Education Enterprise, 1980; author: Management: An Executive Perspective, 1982, Ropes for Management Success: Climb Higher, Faster, 1984, Managing with Passion: Making the Most of Your Job and Your Life, 1996; editor: Paving the Way for the 21st Century: The Human Factor in Higher Education Financial Management, 1993; contbr. chapters to books, articles to profl. jours. Mem. citizens adv. com. Wyo. Bd. Edn., 1980; bd. dirs. Greenwich House, 1994—97, chmn., 1994—95. Lt. US Army, 1962—64. Decorated Army Commendation medal; recipient Merit award, City. of N.Y., 1969, Neil O. Hines Publ. award, Nat. Assn. Coll. and Univ. Bus. Officers, 1992, Disting. Svc. award, N.Y.C. Urban Fellows Program, 1994; Littauer fellow, Harvard U., 1961. Mem.: Phi Beta Kappa. Office: DHR Internat 280 Park Ave 43d Fl West New York NY 10017 Home Phone: 212-585-4474.

GINSPARG, PAUL, physicist; married; 2 children. AB in Physics, Harvard U., 1977; PhD in Physics, Cornell U., 1981. Asst. prof. physics Harvard U., 1984—86, assoc. prof. physics, 1986—90; mem. tech. staff Los Alamos Nat. Lab., 1990—2001; prof. physics, computer sci. Cornell U., 2001—. Vis. prof. CEN, Saclay, France, Princeton U.; vis. scientist Stanford Linear Accelerator Ctr.; vis. prof. U. Calif., Santa Barbara, vis. scientist, Berkeley; vis. prof. Hebrew U., Jerusalem. Contbr. articles to profl. jours. Named Outstanding Jr. Investigator, Dept. Energy, 1986—91; recipient Physics, Astronomy and Math award, Spl. Libr. Assn., 1998; fellow A.P. Sloane fellow, 1986—90; grantee MacArthur Found., 2002. Fellow: Am. Phys. Soc. Achievements include development of website www.arXiv.org. Office: Cornell U 325 Clark Hall Ithaca NY 14853

GINTAUTAS, JONAS, physician, scientist, administrator; b. Justinava, Lithuania, Oct. 3, 1938; came to U.S., 1967; s. Jonas and Elena (Zavadzkyte) Sinsinas; m. Kristina Zebrauskaite, June 13, 1970 (div. June 1992); children: Stasys, Pasaka, Vadas; m. Lilija Isodaite, July 13, 2002; 1 child, Justinas. PhD, Northwestern U., 1976; MD, U. Juarez, Mex., 1984; MBA, Century U., 1996. Assoc. prof. Tex. Tech. U., Lubbock, 1975-77; assoc. prof. and dir. rsch. Tex. Tech. U. Health Scis. Ctr., Lubbock, 1979-82; dir. basic and clin. rsch., prof. neurology The Brookdlae U. Hosp. Med. Ctr., NYC, 1985—2002; dir. clin. rsch., prof. neurology MediaSys Corp., 2002—. Cons. Amtorg Corp., N.Y.C., 1987-94, Ralex Internat. Co., Boston, 1988-91, Arrow Biomed Inc., Metuchen, N.J., 1988—. Editorial cons. Jour. Aphasia Agnosia Apraxia, 1979—; contbr. articles on pharmacology, anesthesia and surgery to profl. jours. Charter mem. Rep. Presdl. Task Force, Washington, 1982—, Platinum mem., 2002—; mem. Nat. Rep. Senatorial Com., Washington, 1984—, U.S. Senatorial Club, Washington, 1984—; nat. campaign advisor Nat. Rep. Senatorial Com., Washington, 1995-96. Recipient medal of honor Rep. Presdl. Task Force, 1982; rsch. grantee various pvt. and govtl. agys. Fellow Internat. Coll. Physicians and Surgeons (hon.); mem. U.S. Senatorial Club (preferred). Avocations: woodworking, camping, scuba diving, fishing, reading. Home: 84-19 107th St Richmond Hill NY 11418-1140 Home Phone: 718-850-0505; Office Phone: 718-206-5800. E-mail: jgintautas@jhmc.org.

GINTER, CAROLYN AUGUSTA ROMTVEDT, retired underwriter; b. Toledo, Oreg., May 24, 1926; d. Fred and Mary Elizabeth (Whitney) Romtvedt; m. Paul Peter Ginter, June 2, 1951 (dec. Dec. 1995); children: Joan Paula, Teresa Ginter Ward, Philip M., Jeffrey G. Student, U. Oreg., 1945—46. Clk. office and dispatch Oregonian Newspaper, Portland, 1943—45; clk. typist USN Supt. of Ships, Portland, 1945; clk. gen. ins. Fidelity & Deposit Co., Portland, 1946—48; bond clk. Aetna Casualty & Surety Fireman's Fund, Transamerica, Portland, 1956—65; surety bond underwriter Cole, Clark & Cunningham/Rollins, Burdick Hunter, Portland, 1965—79; freelance publicity specialist Waldport, Oreg., 1986—. Pub., coord. family history Fred Romtvedt, His Life and Loves, 1980. Lay min. Sacred Heart Cath. Ch., Newport, 1990—; vol. blood drive ARC, Newport, 2000-2005; mem. Oreg. Hist. Soc.; vol. Rep. Ctrl. com. Mem. Bayshore Women's Club (sec. 1984-94, 96, 98), Waldport C. of C. (vol. visitors ctr. 1995—), Lincoln County Hist. Soc. (assisting oral histories Toledo Centennial 2005), Alsi Hist. Soc., Bayshore Beach Club (bd. dirs. publicity), Lincoln County Geneal. Soc. (v.p. 2003), Daus. Union Vets. Civil War (chaplain Oreg. dept. 2005, instr. patriotism 2006, charter mem., v.p. Mary Walker M.D. Tent #28 Waldport, Oreg.) Republican. Avocations: water exercise, travel, gardening. Home: 1802 NW Canal St Waldport OR 97394-9424 Personal E-mail: caginter@peak.org.

GINTER, VALERIAN ALEXIUS, urban historian, educator; b. Chgo., Nov. 4, 1939; s. Valerian Adalbert and Bernice (Podraza) G.; m. Linda Garner Tadlock, Feb. 24, 1968 (div. 1973). BS in Speech, Northwestern U., Evanston, Ill., 1962; postgrad., LI U., 1979—81; MA in Liberal Studies, SUNY, 2006. Investigator Acme Secret Svc. Ltd., Chgo., 1960-62; prodr., dir. Sta. WAAY-TV, Huntsville, Ala., 1965-68; comml. coord. CBS TV, NYC, 1968-70; buyer SSC&B Lintas Worldwide, Furman-Roth Inc., SFM Media Corp., NYC, 1970-79; prin. Ginter-Gotham Urban History, NYC, 1981—. Adj. lectr. Kingsborough CC, NY, 1990—98; adj. lectr. LaGuardia CC, NY, 1998-2006, lectr., 2007—. Author: Manhattan Trivia: The Ultimate Challenge, 1985; contbr. articles to profl. jours., The Ency. NYC, 1995. Cons., lectr. Mcpl. Art Soc., NY, 1975—2000, dir. video tng., St. Bartholomew's Cmty. House, NYC, 1974-77. With U.S. Army, 1962-68. Mem. Theatre Hist. Soc., Victorian Soc. Am., Nat. Trust Hist. Preservation, Soc. Archtl. Historians. Roman Catholic. Avocation: jazz accordionist. Home and Office: 50 W 72nd St Ste 312 New York NY 10023 Home Phone: 212-496-6859. Personal E-mail: gintgotham@aol.com.

GINTY, KAREN, elementary school educator; married. BS in Elem. Edn., Lynchburg Coll., 1972; MS in Early Childhood Edn., Kean Coll., NJ, 1978. Tchr. Monmouth Beach Elem. Sch., 1973—. Former mem. planning bd. Monmouth County Assn. Kindergarten Educators. Named NJ Tchr. of Yr., 2007. Office: Monmouth Beach Elem Sch 7 Hastings Pl Monmouth Beach NJ 07750 Business E-Mail: ginty@mbschool.org.*

GINZEL, ANDREW H., artist; b. Chgo., July 14, 1954; s. Roland F. and Ellen (Laynon) Ginzel; m. Kristin A. Jones, June 14, 1986. Student, SUNY, 1978-81, Bennington Coll., 1972-74. Sculpture faculty Sch. of Visual Arts, NYC, 1986—. Artistic cons. Hudson River Park Conservancy, NYC, 1997. Solo shows include: Polarities Kansas City Internat. Airport, 2004, Metronome Union Square South Project, NYC, 1999, TZ'Art, NYC, 1996, Acqario Romano, Rome, 1995, Madison Art Ctr., Wis., 1992-93, Three Rivers Arts Festival, Pitts., 1991, Mpls. Coll. Art and Design, 1991, Damon Brandt Gallery, NYC, 1990, Kunsthalle, Basel, 1989, others; commns. include: Panopia, Chgo., 2005, Spiraculum, Tampa Internat. Airport, 2005, Oculus, MTA, NYC, 1999, Olympic Arts Festival, Atlanta, 1996, Battery Park City, NYC, 1992, Pa. Conv. Ctr., 1994, Oreg. Conv. Ctr., Portland, 1990, Kunsthalle, Basel, Switzerland, 1989; group shows include Contemporary Artists and the Am. Acad. in Rome, 1995, 96, Equitable Gallery, NYC, 1996, Paine Webber Gallery, NYC, 1994, The Drawing Ctr., NYC, 1993-94, 181st Ann.: An Invitational Contemporary Art, Nat. Acad. Mus., NYC, 2006, numerous others; selected collections include: Bklyn. Mus., Beckton Dickinson and Co., Franklin Lakes, NJ, Bklyn. Mus., Centro per L'Arte Contemporanea Luigi Pecci, Prato, Italy, Hoffmann-La Roche, Inc., Pacific Enterprises, LA, Progressive Corpn., Cleve., Prudential Life Ins. Co., others. Recipient Visual Arts fellowship Nat. Endowment for the Arts, 1986, 94, awards Pollack-Krasner Found., 1994, Louis Comfort Tiffany Found., 1991, fellowship for Indo-Am. Coun. for Internat. Exch. of Scholars, 1990, numerous others in field. Fellow Am. Acad. in Rome (Rome prize 1994-95). Home: 289 Bleecker St New York NY 10014-4106 Office Phone: 212-691-9549.

GIOBBI, EDWARD GIACCHINO, artist; b. Waterbury, Conn., July 18, 1926; s. Achille and Teresa (Gasparetti) G.; m. Elinor E. Turner, Feb. 14, 1959; children: Eugenia, Elizabeth, Chambless Martino. Student, Whitney Sch. Art, New Haven, 1946-47, Vesper George Sch. Art, Boston, 1947-50, Cape Sch. Art, Provincetown, Mass., summer, 1949-50, Art Students League, NYC, 1950-51, 55-56, Acad. Fine Arts, Florence, Italy, 1951-54. One man shows include Ward Eggleston Gallery, N.Y.C., 1951, Mattatuck Mus., Waterbury, Conn., 1955, 78, Artists Gallery, N.Y.C., 1956, Contempories Gallery, N.Y.C., 1956, 60-61, 63, Heller Gallery, N.Y.C., 1957, 58, Brooks Meml. Art Gallery, Memphis, 1961, 72, 80, New Arts Ctr., London, 1964. 67, Bear Lane Gallery, Oxford, Eng., 1964, Queen Sq. Gallery, Leeds Gallery, 1964, Tirca Karlis Gallery, Provincetown, 1964-66, 67, Michelson Gallery, Washington, 1966, Alan Gallery, N.Y.C., 1966, Ark. Art Centre, Little Rock, 1966, Waddell Gallery, N.Y.C., 1967, Obelisk Gallery, Boston, 1968, Gertrude Kasle Gallery, Detroit, 1968, Hopkins Ctr., Dartmouth, 1972, Galleria del Obelisco, Rome, 1974, Crane Kalman Gallery, London, 1975, Neuberger Mus., Purchase, N.Y., 1977, 92, Gruenbaum Gallery, N.Y.C., 1977, (sculpture), 1979, Katonah (N.Y.) Gallery, 1978, Irving Gallery, Palm Beach, 1978, Norton Gallery, Palm Beach, 1988, Long Point Gallery, Provincetown, 1987, 93, Sta. Gallery, Katonah, 1989, Armstrong Gallery, N.Y.C., 1987, Alice Ringham Gallery, Memphis, 1980, Hudson River Mus., 1995; two-man shows include Galeries an der Reuss, Lucerne, Switzerland, 1953, Nexus Gallery, Boston, 1956, Hudson River Mus., 1995; group exhbns include Recent Drawings U.S.A. Mus. Modern Art, 1956, Am. Fed. Arts Travelling Show, 1956, 58, 61, 63, Whitney Mus. Ann., 1957-61, 66, Corcoran Gallery, 1958, Pa. Acad. Fine Arts, 1961, Young Am., Whitney Mus., 1961, 40 Painters Under 40, Whitney Mus., 1962, Figure USA, Mus. Modern Art, 1962, Art in Progress, Finch Coll., N.Y.C., 1967. Mem. adv. bd. Westchester Coun. Arts, Katonah Gallery. Served with inf. AUS, 1944-46, ETO. Recipient Emily Lowe award, 1951-52; Guggenheim fellow, 1972; decorated Combat Inf. Badge. Mem. NAD, Coll. NAD., Century Assn. (mem. adv. bd.): Address: 161 Croton Lake Rd Katonah NY 10536-1201

GIOCOMO, LISA, research scientist; b. Glenwood Springs, Colo., July 4, 1981; d. David and Helen Giocomo. BA, Baylor U., Waco, Tex., 2003; MA, Boston U., 2004. Rsch. asst. Boston U., 2003—. Contbr. articles to profl. jours. Mem.: Psi Chi, Sigma Nu Honor Soc., Golden Key Honor Soc. Home Phone: 617-530-0477.

GIOCONDA, THOMAS F., program manager, retired military flag officer; BA in History, St. Joseph's U., 1970; grad., Squadron Officer Sch., 1974; MBA, U. Mont., 1975; grad., Air Command and Staff Coll., 1976; M in Ednl. Adminstrn., Seton Hall U., 1979; grad., Air War Coll., 1986. Commd. 2d lt. USAF, 1970, advanced through grades to brig. gen., 2001; stationed at Malmstrom AFB, Mont., 1970-75; asst. prof. aerospace studies AFROTC detachment 750 St. Joseph's U., Phila., 1975-76, prof., 1976-77, detachment comdr., detachment closure officer, 1976-77; adminstrn. officer, asst. prof. aerospace studies N.J. Inst. Tech., Newark, 1977-79; missile launch instr./evaluator Vandenberg AFB, Calif., 1979-83; mission analyst strategic programs Hdqs. SAC, Offutt AFB, Nebr., 1983, congl. liaison br. chief, action officer, 1983-85; congl. affairs and resources planner, dep. chief of staff plans and ops. Hdqs. USAF, Washington, 1985-89; comdr. ICBM Squadron, Whiteman AFB, Mo., 1989-91; dep. legis. asst. to chmn. joint chiefs of staff USAF, Washington, 1991-93; legis. asst. to chmn. joint chiefs of staff Washington, 1993-97; prin. dep. asst. sec. mil. application Dept. Energy, Washington, 1997-99, acting asst. sec. energy for defense programs, 1999—2001; ret., 2001; v.p. govt. programs Bechtel Nat. Inc., 2001—. Mem.: KC, Air Force Assn. (life), Mil. Officers Assn. Am. (life), Am. Legion (life), Soc. SAC (life), Kappa Delta Phi. Home: 4818 Hercules Ct Annandale VA 22003-4243 Home Phone: 703-425-5878; Office Phone: 202-828-7375. Business E-Mail: tfgiocon@bechtel.com.

GIOFFRE, BRUNO JOSEPH, lawyer; b. June 27, 1934; s. Anthony B. and Louise (Giorno) G.; m. Kathleen M. Bartlik, Nov. 14, 1959; children: Kathleen, Lisa, Michael, Christopher, B. Scott, David, Kerry. BA, Cornell U., 1956, JD, 1958. Bar: N.Y. 1958, U.S. Dist. Ct. (so. dist.) N.Y. 1973. Prin. atty. Gioffre & Gioffre, P.C., Purchase, NY, 1958—99, of counsel, 2000—. Justice Town of Rye, N.Y., 1965-99. Past vice-chmn. bd. trustees United Hosp.; counsel Port Chester Pub. Libr.; trustee, Greenwich Conn. Hosp; chmn. bd. dirs. Sound Fed. Savs. Bank and Charitable Found., 1998-2006; mem. bd. dir. Hudson Valley Holding Corp. and Hudson Valley Bank, 2006-. Mem. ABA, N.Y. Bar Assn., N.Y. Magistrate's Assn., Westchester County Magistrate's Assn., Westchester Bar Assn., Port Chester-Rye Bar Assn., Elks, KC. Home and Office: 2900 Westchester Ave Purchase NY 10577-2552 Office Phone: 914-696-3800. Business E-Mail: bgioffre@gioffrelaw.com.

GIOIA, DANA (MICHAEL DANA GIOIA), poet, critic, cultural organization administrator; b. LA, Dec. 24, 1950; s. Michael and Dorothy (Ortiz) G.; m. Mary Hiecke, 1980; children: Michael (dec.), Theodore, Michael Frederick. BA, Stanford U., 1973, MBA, 1977; MA, Harvard U., 1975; PhD in Lit. (hon.), St. Andrews Coll., 2003; LittD (hon.), St. Andrew Presbyterian Coll., 2003; LHD (hon.), Lehigh U., 2003; LittD, West Chester U., 2003, Chapman U., 2005, U. Pacific, 2005; LittD (hon.), Seton Hall U., 2005. V.p. mktg. General Foods Corp., White Plains, NY, 1977-92; pres., bd. dirs. Story Line Press, 1992-2001; chmn. Nat. Endowment Arts, Nat. Found. Arts & Humanities, 2003—. Editor Sequoia mag., 1971-73, poetry editor, 1975-77; literary editor Inquiry mag., 1977-79, poetry editor, 1979-83; mem. bd. dirs. Wesleyan U. Writers Conf., 1985-99; commentator BBC Radio, 1992-2003; founder & co-dir. West Chester Writers Conf., 1995-2002; music critic San Francisco mag., 1997-2003; librettist for opera Nosferatu, 2001; founder & dir. Tchg. Poetry Conf., 2001-02; vis. writer John Hopkins U., Sarah Lawrence Coll., Colo. Coll., Wesleyan U. Author: (poetry) Daily Horoscope, 1986, The Gods of Winter, 1991, Interrogations at Noon, 2001 (Am. Book award, 2002); (criticism) Can Poetry Matter? Essays on Poetry an American Culture, 1992, 2d edit., 2002; editor: The Ceremony and Other Stories, 1984, Poems from Italy, 1985, New Italian Poets, 1991; co-editor: Literature: An Introduction to Fiction, Poetry and Drama, 2001, Longman Anthology of Short Fiction, 2001, Selected Short Stories of Weldon Kees, 2002, Twentieth-Century American Poetry, 2003, Disappearing Ink, 2004; translator: Eugenio Montale's Mottetti: Poems of Love, 1990; contbr. to periodicals including New Yorker, Atlantic, Washington Post, Hudson Rev., Poetry. Recipient Frederick Bock prize for poetry, 1986. Mem.: Nat. Fed. Coun. on Arts and Humanities, Poetry Soc. Am. (v.p. 1992—2003). Office: Nat Endowment for Arts 1100 Pennsylvania Ave NW Washington DC 20506 Office Fax: 212-682-5611.

GIONFRIDDO, MAURICE PAUL, aeronautical engineer, research and development company executive; b. Medford, Mass., Feb. 19, 1931; s. Santo and Germaine Camille (Gaillard) G.; m. Joan Marie Powers, Apr. 21, 1956; children: Marianne E., Linda. BS in Aero. Engring., MIT, 1953, MS in Aero. Engring., 1969. Rsch. asst. Aeroelastic and Structures Rsch. Lab., MIT, Cambridge, Mass., 1953-54; aero. rsch. engr. Air Force Cambridge Rsch. Ctr., Bedford, Mass., 1956-57; aero. engr. Army Natick (Mass.) Rsch., Devel. and Engring. Ctr., 1957-94; cons. MPG Cons., Westborough, Mass., 1994—. Mem. Nat. Parachute Tech. Coun., 1991—. Class agt. MIT Class of 1953, 1968-78. 1st lt. USAF, 1954-56. Fellow AIAA (assoc., charter, aerodyn. decelerator tech. com. 1964-67, Aerodyn. Decelerator award 1990), Parachute Industry Assn. (v.p. 2006—, Mem. of Yr. 2002). Roman Catholic. Home and Office: MPG Cons 20 Westminster Way Westborough MA 01581-3410 Home Phone: 508-366-4079; Office Phone: 508-366-1042. E-mail: mgion@charter.net.

GIONTA, BRIAN, professional hockey player; b. Rochester, NY, Jan. 18, 1979; s. Sam and Penny Gionta; m. Harvest Gionta; 1 child, Adam Joseph. BA, Boston Coll., 2001. Right wing Albany River Rats (AHL), 2001—02, 2005, NJ Devils, 2001—. Mem. USA Olympic Hockey Team, Torino, Italy, 2006. Recipient Walter Brown Award, 2001. Achievements include being a member of NCAA National Championship Team, Boston College, 2001; being a member of Stanley Cup Champion NJ Devils, 2003; set the NJ Devils franchise record for goals in a season, 2006. Office: c/o NJ Devils Nat Newark Bldg 744 Broad St, 33rd Fl Newark NJ 07102

GIORDANO, ANDREW ANTHONY, retired naval officer; b. Passaic, NJ, May 17, 1932; s. Samuel and Sarah (Pollara) G.; m. Felice Rochman, Mar. 3, 1957; children: Andrew Anthony, II, Dean James, Catherine Lisa. BBA cum laude, CCNY, 1953; MBA with distinction, Harvard U., 1962; student, Naval War Coll., 1965; L.H.D. (hon.), Nat. U., San Diego, 1982. Commd. ensign U.S. Navy, 1953, advanced through grades to rear adm., 1978; supply officer U.S.S. Kitty Hawk, Vietnam, 1968-70; ops. officer Aviation Supply Office, Phila., 1970-72; dir. material div. Office of Chief of Naval Ops., Washington, 1977-81; comdr. Naval Supply Systems Command, Chief Supply Corps, 1981-84; sr. v.p. control and ops. Donaldson's of Mpls. unit Allied Stores, 1984-87; exec. v.p., CFO Lamonts Corp., 1987-93; assoc. prof. acctg. George Washington U., 1966-67, Nat. U., 1970-72; prin. The Giordano Group, Ltd., Arlington, Va., 1993—. Bd. dirs. Dale Carnegie Assocs.; chmn., interim CEO, Jos. A. Bank, Inc. Treas., trustee Navy Marine Coast Guard Residence Found., 1993-98; pres., COO Graham Field, 1998. Decorated Legion of Merit, DSM; recipient Navy Civilian Svc. award, Disting. Grad. award Navy SC Found., 2004. Mem. NAS (Naval studies bd. 1996), Army-Navy Country Club (chmn. bd. govs. 1993-96). Roman Catholic. Address: PO Box 31059 Palm Beach Gardens FL 33420-1059 Office Phone: 561-776-6298. Personal E-mail: tggltd@aol.com.

GIORDANO, BILL A., psychotherapist; b. Newark, June 15, 1957; s. John and Marie Giordano. BA in Polit. Sci. cum laude, Fairleigh Dickinson U., Rutherford, NJ, 1979; postgrad. cert. in clin. social wk., NYU, 1982, MSW, 1992, postgrad., 2003—. LCSW N.Y. Case worker Cath. Charities, NYC, 1982; social worker Bklyn. Bur. C.C., 1986—89; primary therapist South Beach Psychiat. Ctr., SI, 1989—93; sr. therapist day tx. coord. H.S.S. Cmty. Cons. Ctr., NYC, 1993—. Cons., Think Tank mem. On Step Inst., NYC, 1998—; presenter in field. Mem. Dem. Nat. Com., 1976—; bd. trustees On Step Inst. Mental Health Rsch. Mem.: NASW, Phi Omega Epsilon. Achievements include research in paternal instinct; symptoms of parental alienation and its implications for clinicians and patients; coordination of multicultural day treatment program; depression in men. Home: 98 Ann St Newark NJ 07105-3110 Office: On Step Inst 169 E 74th St New York NY 10021 E-mail: bgeo15@aol.com.

GIORDANO, LAWRENCE FRANCIS, lawyer; b. Buffalo, Feb. 17, 1953; s. Anthony Jerome and Martha Ann (Taylor) G.; m. Elaine Kristie Thomas, May 29, 1976; children: Bradley Thomas, Evan Taylor. BS with highest honors in Psychology, Denison U., 1975; JD, Georgetown U., 1978. Bar: Tenn. 1978, U.S. Dist. Ct. (ea. dist.) Tenn. 1979, U.S. Ct. Appeals (6th cir.) 1980, U.S. Supreme Ct. 1983. Assoc. Stone & Hinds, P.C., Knoxville, Tenn., 1978-81, ptnr., 1981-88, Thomforde & Giordano, P.C., Knoxville, 1988-90, McCampbell & Young, P.C., Knoxville, 1990-91, London, Amburn & Giordano, Knoxville, 1991-92, Susano, Sheppeard & Giordano, Knoxville, 1993-94; spl. counsel Lewis, King, Krieg & Waldrop, P.C., Knoxville, 1994-97, shareholder, 1997—. Spl. judge Knox County Gen. Sessions Ct., 1988—; adminstrv. law judge State of Tenn. Dept. Edn., 1994-96; adj. prof. U. Tenn. Coll. Law, 1993—; instr. Knoxville Police Acad., 1989. Mem. exec. bd. Knoxville Metro Soccer League, 1980-85; mem. community network Knox County Youth Alcohol Hwy. Safety Project, Knoxville, 1987-90. Nat. Merit scholar, 1971-75, Kenneth I. Brown scholar, 1974. Mem. ABA, Tenn. Bar Assn. (Law Through Liberty award, 2000), Knoxville Bar Assn. (bd. govs. 1986-92, treas. 1986-90, sec. 1991-92), Def. Rsch. Inst., Am. Inns of Ct. (master of the bench 1991—, pres. 1994-95), Sertoma (v.p. chpt. 1987-89, pres. 1989-90), Phi Beta Kappa, Omicron Delta Kappa. Democrat. Roman Catholic. Avocations: soccer, gardening, reading, theater. Home: 1822 Nantasket Rd Knoxville TN 37922-5769 Office: Lewis King Krieg & Waldrop 620 Market St Fl 5 Knoxville TN 37902-2231 Office Phone: 865-541-5229. E-mail: giordano@lewisking.com.

GIORDANO, MARY ANN, editor; Reporter The Daily News; met. polit. editor NY Times, dep. met. editor, regional coverage, dep. editor Thursday Styles, 2006—. Office: NY Times 229 West 43rd St New York NY 10036 Business E-Mail: magior@nytimes.com.

GIORDANO, NICHOLAS ANTHONY, brokerage house executive; b. Phila., Mar. 7, 1943; s. Nicola and Aida (Gioioso) G.; m. Joanne M. Pizzuto, Oct. 21, 1967; children: Jeannine, Colette and Nicholas (triplets). BS, LaSalle Coll., 1965. CPA Pa. Mem. staff Price Waterhouse & Co., Phila., 1965-68; with various brokerage cos. Phila., 1968-71; controller stock exchange and stock clearing corp PBW (later Phila.) Stock Exch., Inc., 1971-72, v.p. ops., 1972-75, sr. v.p., 1975-76, exec. v.p., 1976-81, pres., CEO, 1981-97, bd. dirs.; pres. La Salle U., 1998—99. Cons. in field. Former vice-chmn. LaSalle U., bd. trustees; former chmn. bd. dirs. Mt. St. Joseph Acad.; trustee Am. U. Rome; trustee, bd. dirs. Kalmar Investments, Inc.; bd. dirs. Intricon Corp. (formerly Selas Corp.), Ind. Blue Cross; chmn. bd. trustees WT Mut. Fund. Office: PO Box 984 Blue Bell PA 19422-0984 Personal E-mail: nagiordano@yahoo.com.

GIORDMAINE, JOSEPH ANTHONY, physicist; b. Toronto, Can., Apr. 10, 1933; came to U.S., 1955; s. John Nichol and Anna Katherine (Cain) G.; m. Mary Auxilda Mills, Sept. 13, 1958; children: Paul, Anne, Claire. BA in Physics and Chemistry, U. Toronto, 1955; MA in Physics, Columbia U., 1957, PhD in Physics, 1960. vis. prof. Tech. U., Munich, 1966. Instr. Columbia U., NYC, 1959-61; mem. tech. staff AT&T Bell Labs., Murray Hill, N.J., 1961-88, rsch. dept. head, 1967-71, rsch. lab. dir., 1971-81, devel. lab. dir., 1981-87; v.p. to sr. v.p. NEC Rsch. Inst., Princeton, N.J., 1988-98, exec. advisor, 1998, sr. v.p. emeritus, 1998—. Bd. dirs. NEC Rsch. Inst., 1992-98; adv. coun. Princeton U., Materials Inst., 1993-98; mem. adv. com. Lehigh U., Fairchild Ctr., Allentown, Pa., 1994-98; vis. lectr., fellow, sr. rsch. scientist Princeton U., 1998-2005; rsch. scientist Tex. A&M U., Coll. Sta., Tex., 2004-05; mem. indsl. adv. bd. CUNY Ctr. Advanced Tech. in Ultrafast Photonics, 2004—. Assoc. editor Optics Letters, 1977-79, Annual Review of Material Sci., 1983-98. Fellow AAAS, IEEE (nat. lectr. 1983, Dist. Lectr. award 1983), Optical Soc. Am. (bd. dirs. 1991-94, R.W. Wood prize 1986), Am. Phys. Soc. (mem. nominating com. 1973), N.Y. Acad. Scis. Roman Catholic. Achievements include advances in tunable light sources; optical frequency conversion; nonlinear optics; detection of ultrashort light pulses; compression of light pulses; low-noise amplifiers for radio astronomy; analysis of gas flow in tubes. Office: NEC Labs America 4 Independence Way Princeton NJ 08540-6634 Home Phone: 609-921-7458; Office Phone: 609-951-2605. Business E-Mail: jag@nec-labs.com.

GIORGADZE, TAMAR ALFRED, pathologist, physician; b. Tbilisi, Georgia, Apr. 6, 1960; d. Alfred G. Giorgadze and Venera O. Iosava; m. Archil G. Tsuladze, May 26, 1991. MD, Tbilisi State Med. Inst., 1982, PhD, 1987. Diplomate Am. Bd. of Pathology, 2002, in cytopathology Am. Bd. of Pathology, 2004, lic. physician Mich., 2002, Tenn., 2005. Resident in oncology Tbilisi State Med. Inst., Chair of Oncology, Tbilisi, Georgia, sr. lab. asst., 1985—94; staff oncologist Rep. Cancer Ctr., Dept. of Pediatric Oncology, Tbilisi, Georgia, 1984—85; rsch. fellow Patho Lab Ltd, Sci. Pk., Kiryat-Weizmann, Rechovot, Israel, 1995—96; pathology resident East Tenn. State U., Dept. Pathology, James H. Quillen Coll. Med., Johnson City, Tenn., 1998—2001, chief resident, 2001—02, asst. prof., 2004—; surg. pathology fellow Dept. Pathology and Lab. Medicine Hosp. U. Pa., Phila., 2002—03, cytopathology fellow Dept. Pathology and Lab. Medicine Hosp., 2003—04. Sr. lab. asst. editl. bd. chair of oncology Tbilisi State Med. Inst., Tbilisi, Georgia, 1987—89; manuscript reviewer Hosp. U. Pa., Phila., 2003—04, East Tenn. State U., 2006—. Contbr. chapters to books, articles to profl. jours. Grantee, East Tenn. State U., 2005. Fellow: Coll. Am. Pathologists; mem.: Internat. Acad. Cytology, Internat. Acad. Pathology, Am. Soc. Cytopathology, US and Can. Acad. Pathology. Orthodox Christian. Achievements include patents for Method of forming of the high oncoproctological risk groups; first to Innovative methodologies in cytopathology and endocrine pathology. Avocations: opera, art, reading, swimming, tennis. Office: East Tenn State Univ Dept Pathology PO Box 70568 Johnson City TN 37614 Home Phone: 423-926-5616; Office Phone: 423-439-6328. Business E-Mail: giorgadz@etsu.edu.

GIOSEFFI, DANIELA (DOROTHY DANIELA GIOSEFFI), poet, writer, playwright, critic; b. Orange, NJ, Feb. 12, 1941; d. Daniel Donato Gioseffi and Josephine Buzevska; m. Richard J. Kearney, Sept. 7, 1965 (div.); 1 child, Thea D. Kearney; m. Lionel B. Luttinger, June 6, 1986. BA, Montclair State U., 1963; MFA, Cath. U. Am., 1966. Cons., poet, tchr. Poets-in-the-Schs., Inc., NYC, 1972-85. Freelance writer, lectr. at numerous univs. throughout U.S. and Europe; appeared on Nat. Pub. Radio, CBC, BBC; spkr. in field. Author: The Great American Belly, 1977, The Great American Belly, 4th edit., 1979; author: (collections of poems) Eggs in the Lake, 1979, Word Wounds and Water Flowers, 1995, Going On, 2000; author: Earth Dancing: Mother Nature's Oldest Rite, 1981, Women on War: International Voices for the Nuclear Age, 1988 (Am. Book award, 1990), rev. edit., 2003, On Prejudice: A Global Perspective, 1993—, Dust Disappears: Translations of Carilda Oliver Labra of Latin America, 1995—, (poems) In Bed With the Exotic Enemy, 1997—, (stories and novella) The Psychic Touch, 1996—; author: (play) The Golden Daffodil Dwarf, 1988—, Care of the Body, 1988—, The Sea Hag in the Cave of Sleep, 1988—; author: (radio play) Fathers and Children, 1988—, 1998—; author: Symbiosis, 2002, Symbiosis: Poems, 2003, Women on War: International Writings From Antiquity to the Present, 2003, Blood Autumn: New & Selected Poems, 2006, performer (stage presentations throughout U.S. and Europe), composer (and lyricist), singer (many concert series); editor-in-chief Wise Women's Web: Internet Mag. of Lit. and Art, 2001— (Best of Web award, 1998), creator The First Bklyn. Bridge Poetry Walk, 1972; verses etched in marble: Penn Sta., 2002; mem. editl. bd. Voices in Italian Americana -Grad. Ctr. CUNY, 1990—; contbr. numerous periodicals and anthologies. Pres. Bklyn. Citizens for Sane Nuclear Policy, 1987—89; mem. exec. bd., chmn. media watch com. Writers and Pubs. Alliance for Nuclear Disarmament, 1978—91. Named Featured poet, The Peoples' Poetry Gathering: The Great Hall, Cooper Union, 2003; recipient World Peace award, Ploughshares Fund, 1989, 1999, John Ciardi Lifetime Achievement award - Poetry, 2007; grantee poetry and fiction, Creative Artists' Pub. Svc. Program - N.Y. State Coun. on Arts, 1971—77, Thanks Be to Grandmother Winifred Found., 1996. Mem.: Poet's House, Nat. Book Critics Cir., Actors Equity Assn., Acad. Am. Poets, PEN Am. Ctr. Office: Box 8G 57 Montague St Brooklyn NY 11201-3356 Office Phone: 718-643-3837. Personal E-mail: daniela@garden.net.

GIOVANIELLI, DAMON VINCENT, physicist, consultant; b. Teaneck, NJ, May 8, 1943; s. Dominick John and Marie Concetta (Conti) G.; m. Eleanor Ruth Rand, Aug. 18, 1968; children: Kira, Tina. AB, Princeton U., 1965; PhD in Physics, Dartmouth Coll., 1970. Instr. dept. engring. and applied sci. Yale U., New Haven, 1970-72; with Los Alamos (N.Mex.) Nat. Lab., 1972-93, leader physics divsn., 1987—93; ret., 1993; pres. Sumner Assocs., Sante Fe, 1993—; chmn. bd. dirs. La Mancha Co., 1997—. With J. Robert Oppenheimer Meml. Com. Contbr. articles to profl. jours. Mem. alumni schs. com. Princeton U.; trustee Coll. Santa Fe. Fellow AAAS; mem. Am. Phys. Soc., Fusion Power Assocs., Sigma Xi. Episcopalian. Home: 12 Loma Del Escolar Los Alamos NM 87544-2524 Office: Sumner Assocs 100 Cienega St Ste D Santa Fe NM 87501-2003

GIOVANNOLI, JOSEPH LOUIS, entrepreneur, lawyer; B of Engring., Stevens Inst. Tech., 1962; JD, Fordham U., 1967. Bar: N.Y. 1967, N.J. 1971, Fed. Dist. Ct. 1967. Mgmt. sci. engr. corp. acctg. Am. Can Co., NYC, 1962-64; atty. dept. law Union Carbide Corp., NYC, 1967-71; ptnr. Weir & Giovannoli, South Orange, N.J., 1971-74; of counsel Fischer, Kagan, Ascione and Zaretsky, Clifton, N.J., 1974-84; pres., co-founder Capital Resources Corp., Clifton, 1971-80; entrepreneur Saddle River, N.J., 1980-87; chmn., founder U.S. Technologies, Inc., Fair Lawn, NJ, 1987—98; mng. mem. SST, LLC, Upper Saddle River, NJ, 2005—. Author: The Biology of Belief, 2001. Achievements include patents for computerized quotation system and method; field of electric distance measurement. Home: 280 Hampshire Ridge Park Ridge NJ 07656

GIOVINAZZO, VIVIAN CURRY, writer; b. Gstaad, Switzerland, Dec. 7, 1945; arrived in U.S., 1949, naturalized, 1959; d. Hugo Alexander and Beatrice Ferdinand (Wärtli) Curry; m. George Potts, Dec. 30, 1965 (dec.); m. Anthony Gioviazzo, Sept. 10, 1995 (dec. 2002). Grad., Edgewater HS, Orlando, Fla. Author children's books; athletic (Tennis) Champion, Fla. and NY, 1950—59; author: (children's stories) Those Scary Dust Bunnies, 2001—02, Daddy, I Don't Want To Go To School, 2001—02, New Puppy on the Block, 2001—02, Bubbles for My Birthday, 2001—02, (novel) Twisted Love.net, 2007. Named N.Y. State Tennis Champion, FIA. Avocation: stamp collecting/philately. Personal E-mail: whocares12745@wmconnect.com.

GIOVINCO, JOSEPH, non profit agency administrator, writer; b. San Francisco, Oct. 12, 1942; s. Joseph Bivona and Jean Andrews Giovinco; m. Sally Garey, Aug. 31, 1970 (div. Mar. 1982); 1 child, Gina Lorraine. BA, U. Oreg., 1964; MA in History, San Francisco State U., 1968; PhD in History, U. Calif., Berkeley, 1973. Asst. prof. history SUNY, Albany, 1974-76; instr. multicultural studies Sonoma State U., Cotati, Calif., 1976-79; exec. dir. Hist. Mus. Found., Sonoma County, Santa Rosa, Calif., 1977-80; exec. dir. no. Calif. affiliate Am. Diabetes Assn., San Francisco, 1980-81; exec. dir. San Francisco Sch. Vols., 1981-85, Calif. Hist. Soc., San Francisco, 1985-87; dir. Ctr. Advancement & Renewal of Educators, San Francisco, 1988—. Contbr. articles to profl. pubs. Named Alumnus of the Yr., San Francisco State U., 1987; recipient Covello prize, Italian Am. Hist. Assn., 1976; fellow, NEH, Harvard U., 1973; scholar, U. Minn. Ctr. Immigration History, 1975; Rockefeller Found. grantee, 1977. Roman Catholic. Avocations: rose gardening, classical music. Office: Ctr Advancement & Renewal Educators 25550 25th Ave San Francisco CA 94116

GIPPLE, ELLEN A., elementary school educator; b. Apr. 21, 1950; BS, Ctrl. Mich. U., Mt. Pleasant, 1972; MA in Edn., Olivet Nazarene U., Bourbonnais, Ill., 2000. Tchr. Lapeer Pub. Schs., Mich., 1972—73, Bourbonnais Elem. Schs. Dist. # 53, 1994—. Mem.: Ill. Reading Coun., Internat. Reading Assn., Nat. Coun. Tchrs. English, Kappa Delta Pi. Home: 197 Nottingham Ln Bourbonnais IL 60914

GIPSON, ILENE KAY, ophthalmologist, educator; b. Hoberg, Mo., Oct. 13, 1944; d. Ferdinand Robert and Margaret Marie (Fritz) Quade; m. Philip Gipson, June 1967 (div. 1974); m. Henry T. Keutmann, June 23, 1984. BA in Biology, Drury Coll., Springfield, Mo., 1966; MS in Zoology, U. Ark., Fayetteville, 1968, PhD in Zoology, 1973; MA (hon.), Harvard Med. Sch., Boston, 1997; DSc (hon.), Drury U., Springfield, Mo., 1999. Rsch. assoc. dept. plant pathology U. Ark., Fayetteville, 1973-74; rsch. assoc., instr. dept. ophthalmology U. Oreg. Health Scis. Ctr., Portland, 1974-76, asst. prof., 1976-79; asst. prof. ophthalmology Harvard Med. Sch., Boston, 1979-85, assoc. prof., 1985—97, prof., 1997—; assoc. scientist Schepens Eye Rsch. Inst., Boston, 1979-83, sr. scientist, 1983—, ocular surface scholar, 1997—. Head morphology unit Schepens Eye Rsch. Inst., 1980—91, head cornea unit, 1985—94; mem. study sect. divsn. rsch. resources NIH, Bethesday, Md., 1983, 84, 88; mem. cornea diseases panel Nat. Eye Inst., 1990; Leverhulme vis. prof. dept. anatomy U. Bristol, England, 1997. Contbr. articles to profl. jours.; mem. editl. bd.: Ocular Surface, exec. editor cornea and ocular surface sect.: Exptl. Eye Rsch., 2001—, guest editor: Investigative Ophthalmology & Visual Sci. Bd. trustees Drury U., 1999—2003, 2004—. Recipient Rsch. Career Devel. award, Nat. Eye Inst., 1978—83, MERIT award, 1990—2000, Alcon Rsch. award, 1984, Rsch. to Prevent Blindness Sr. Sci. Investigator award, 2001. Mem.: Internat. Soc. Eye Rsch., Assn. Rsch. in Vision and Ophthalmology (2007 Friedenwald award), Am. Soc. Cell Biologists. Democrat. Achievements include patents in field. Avocations: birding, gardening, cooking, travel. Office: Schepens Eye Rsch Inst 20 Staniford St Boston MA 02114-2508 E-mail: gipson@vision.eri.harvard.edu.

GIPSON, STEPHEN RICHARD, journalist, construction executive; b. Tacoma, Apr. 29, 1945; s. William Richard and Justina Pauline Gipson; m. Helen Therese Cory (div. Feb. 1981); 1 child, Mark Tyler. Diploma in acctg., Western Bus. Coll., 1974; degree in bus. law, Mt. Hood CC, Gresham, Oreg., 1975; studies in bus. admin., U. Md., 1966. Exec. v.p. Pioneer Optics, Beaverton, Oreg., 1974—76; founder, pres. Group Optical, Portland, Oreg., 1976—78; founder, CEO Gipson Optical & Safety, Portland, 1978—81; founder, publ. Comon Cents Newspaper, Cour d'Alene, Idaho, 1981—85; founder, pres. Gipson Bus. Cons., Portland, 1985—93, House Calls Contractors, Portland, 1993—2001; writer, pres. Gipson Lit. Svcs., Milton-Freewater, Oreg., 2001—; pres. Western Dolphin Pub., 2000—; CEO River Ratz News N.W. Regional Recreation Paper, 2004. Prin., owner Western Dolphin Gems, 2002—, Western Dolphin Wholesalers Jewelers, 2002—. V.p. Mid Atlantic Pistol & Rifle Club, 1965—66. With USAF, 1962—66. Decorated Def. medal USAF. Mem.: River Ratz Yacht Club (founder 2005), Eagles, Am. Legion. Democrat. Methodist. Avocations: flying, skydiving. Home and Office: Gipson Lit Svcs PO Box 417 Milton Freewater OR 97862

GIPSTEIN, MILTON FIVENSON, lawyer, psychiatrist, health facility administrator; b. Schenectady, NY, Aug. 31, 1951; s. Milton and Evelyn G.; m. Carol Grace Gipstein, July 21, 1974; children: Steven Mark, Richard Seth. BA, Columbia U., 1972; MD, SUNY, Syracuse, 1976; JD, U. N.C., 1981. Bar: Mass., 1982; Diplomate Am. Bd. Psychiatry and Neurology. Resident psychiat. U. N.C., Chapel Hill, 1976-79; pvt. practice of psychiat. Dept. Corrections N.C., Raleigh, 1979-81; med. dir. Brockton (Mass.) Dist. Ct. Clinic, 1981-86, Bridgewater (Mass.) St. Hosp., 1986-87, Charter Hosp. of Aurora, Colo., 1988—91; med. dir. of forensic svcs. Columbine Psychiatric Hosp., Littleton, Colo., 1991—96; med. dir. outpatient forensic svcs. Jefferson Ctr. Mental Health, Littleton, Colo., 1996—98; med. dir. forensic psychiatry divsn. Marvin Foote Youth Detention Facility, Englewood, Colo., 1997—2001; med. dir. ctrl. region Dept. Corrections, Raleigh, NC, 2001; med. dir. diagnostic and sexual offender units Kids Peace Nat. Ctrs. N.Y., Romulus, NY, 2003—04; med. dir. Advanced Health Resources, 2004—. Cons. med.-legal N.C. Legal Aid Soc., Raleigh, 1976-81, forensic Mass. Treatment Ctr. Sexually Dangerous, Bridgewater, 1981-88, psychiat. La. Gov.'s Task Force Mental Health, Baton Rouge, 1982, Jefferson Ctr. Mental Health, 1996-98; med.-legal cons. Med. Evaluators, Inc., Denver, 1991-2001; legal counsel indigent clients mental health Com. Pub. Counsel Svcs., Boston, 1982-88; lectr. mental health legal advisors com. Law and Mental Health for Mass. Supreme Ct., Boston, 1982-88. Cons. Pub. Health Adv. Com. Town of Sharon, Mass., 1983-88, Mental Health Legal Advisors Com. Mass. Supreme Ct., Boston, 1985-88; v.p. cmty. affairs Heights Elem. Sch. PTA, Sharon, 1983-88; adv. com. gifted and talented Cherry Creek H.S., 1992-97, Campus Middle Sch., 1993-96. Mem. ABA, Mass. Bar Assn., Am. Profl. Practice Assn. Avocations: boating, swimming, antiques.

GIRAGOSIAN, C. CHRISTOPHER, lawyer; b. Richmond, Va., Oct. 15, 1951; BA in Math., magna cum laude, Washington & Lee Univ., 1973; JD, Univ. Richmond, 1976. Corp. counsel Bank of Va. (now Signet Bank), 1976—84; ptnr., capital fin. , real estate Hunton & Williams LLP, McLean, Va. Mem.: ABA, Fairfax Bar Assn., Va. State Bar. Office: Hunton & Williams Ste 1700 1751 Pinnacle Dr Mc Lean VA 22102 Office Phone: 703-714-7426. Office Fax: 703-714-7410. Business E-Mail: cgiragosian@hunton.com.

GIRALDI, ROBERT NICHOLAS, film director; b. Paterson, NJ, Jan. 17, 1939; B.F.A., Pratt Inst., 1960. Assoc. creative dir. Young & Rubicam, NYC, 1960-71; v.p., head creative dept. Della Femina, NYC, 1971-73; ptnr. Ampersand Prodns., NYC, 1973-74, dir.; pres. Giraldi, NYC, 1974—. Head advt. and design, asst. dir. Sch. Visual Arts, N.Y.C., 1969-73, instr. 2002—; owner N.Y.C. restaurants, Vong, Lipstick Cafe, Patria, Gigino, Jean-Georges, Prime Las Vegas, The Mercer Kitchen, Bread Tribeca, Diablo Royale, European Union. Dir.: (play) Laughing on the Outside, 1982, (music videos) Say Say Say, 1983, Love Is a Battlefield, 1984, Hello, 1984, Don't Drive Drunk, 1984, Beat It. (Michael Jackson), 1983, World Series (Baseball Hall Fame), (TV special) A Christmas to Remember with Dolly Parton and Kenny Rogers, 1985, (feature film) Hiding Out, 1987, (feature film) Dinner Rush with Danny Aiello, 2000, (short films) The Routine, 2002 (Best Drama award L.A. Internat. Short Film Festival), The Dream Begins for N.Y.C. 2012 Olympic Bid, 2002, Honey Trap, 2005; art represented in permanent collection Mus. Modern Art, N.Y.C. Bd. dirs. Hamptons Internat. Film Festival, 2004-; appears in numerous ads against AIDS. Recipient numerous gold awards Art Dirs. Club N.Y., N.Y.C., numerous Andy awards Advt. Club N.Y., N.Y.C., numerous Clio awards, numerous One Show awards Copy Club N.Y., N.Y.C., numerous N.Y. Festival awards, numerous Mobius awards, Gold award Cannes Film Festival, 1974, 76, 79, 81, 88, 96, AICP MOMA gold award, 1992, 94, London Internat. Film Festival gold award, 1992, Italian Key awards, 1990, numerous other awards for excellence in advt., 1993-96, MTV Best Male Video award Will Smith's Just The Two of Us; Herschel Levit Scholarship award Pratt Inst., 1994; named to N.Y. Dir.'s Hall of Fame, 1991. Mem. Dirs. Guild Am. Roman Catholic. Office: Giraldi 149 Wooster St 2d Fl New York NY 10012-3327 *If you do quality you will always do quantity, but it never works the other way around.*

GIRARD, C. JACK, artist, educator; b. Ft. Knox, Ky., May 15, 1951; s. Charles Jack and Joan Elizabeth Girard; m. Shannon Easley Girard, June 24, 1994; children: Ethan, Clare, Kate. BFA, East Carolina U., 1970, MFA, 1973. Gallery dir. G.W. Gallery, Columbia, SC, 1976—78; vis. artist Carterat Tech. Coll., Morehead City, NC, 1978—79; instr. Berea (Ky.) Coll., 1979—80; asst. prof. Ctr. Coll., Danville, Ky., 1980—81; prof. Transylvania U., Lexington, Ky., 1981—. Instr. Govs. Sch. for Arts, Louisville, 1989—91; prof. KIIS, Murray, Ky., 1992. One-man shows include The Carnegie, 2003, Vanderbilt U., 2004, Ill. Ctrl. Coll., 2005, Wofford Coll., 2007, exhibited in group shows at Northampton Art Ctr., 2003, Ea. Ky. U., 2004, 2005, Chapman Friedman Gallery, 2004, Wingspan Gallery, 2004, TW Wood Gallery, 2005, East Carolina U., 2006. Recipient Bingham award for excellence in tchg., Transylvania U., 1993. Mem.: Coll. Art Assn. Office: Transylvania Univ 300 N Broadway Lexington KY 40508

GIRARD, FRANCOIS, film director; b. Lac St-Jean, Que., Can. Founder, prin. Zone Prodns., 1988-92, Velvet Camera, 1988-92. Writer, dir. feature films including Cargo, 1990, Thirty Two Short Films About Glenn Gould, 1993 (Best Film prix Genie award, 1993, Best Dir. prix Genie award, 1993, Best photography prix Genie award, 1993, Best Editing prix Genie award, 1993, mention Festival of Festival Toronto, 1993, mention Festival du Film de Vancouver, 1993, Prize Figueira Da Foz Festival de Lisbonne, 1994, Badeira Paulista award Mostra de Sao Paulo, 1994), Peter Gabriel's Secret World, 1994 (Prix du Pub. Festival Internat. du Nouveau Cinéma Mtl., 1994, silver rose for best concert film Montreux Film Festival, 1995, Internat. Grammy award for Music Video long version, 1996); dir. medium-length films including Le Dortoir, 1991 (Internat. Emmy award, Gold FIPA, Gemeau award), Le Jardin des Ombres, 1993, After Othello, 1994, Souvenirs d'Othello, 1994; dir. short films including Das Brunch, 1983, Human Scope, 1984, Le Train, 1985, Monsieur Léon, 1986, Tango Tango, 1986, Montréal Danse, 1988, Mourir, 1988, Supect No 1, 1989, CCA, 1989, Vie Et Mort De L'Architecte, 1989; co-dir. short films including Distance, 1984; co-writer: Thirty Two Short Films About Glenn Gould; dir. various commls.; dir.: The Red Violin, 1998 (8 Genie awards including best film and best dir., Oscar for best original soundtrack). Office: c/o Chantal Neveu 1435 St Alexandre Ste 500 Montreal PQ Canada H3A 2G4 Office Phone: 514-937-3198. E-mail: chantal.neveu@videotron.ca.

GIRARD, JAMES EMERY, chemistry professor; b. Joliet, Ill., July 1, 1945; s. George I. and Mary C. (Jones) G.; children: Krista, Jon, Mark, Steven, Lauren, Alexis. BA, Lewis Coll., Lockport, Ill., 1967; PhD, Pa. State U., University Park, 1971. Research fellow Pa. State U., Univ. Park, 1967-71, postdoctoral fellow, 1971-72; NIH postdoctoral fellow U. Calif., San Diego, 1972-73, vis. prof., summer 1974; asst. prof. Coll. the Holy Cross, Worcester, Mass., 1973-77; staff scientist Gen. Elec. Co. Corp. Research and Devel. Ctr., Schenectady, NY, 1977-79; assoc. prof. The Am. U., Washington, 1979-84, prof., 1984—, chmn. dept. chemistry, 1984—91, 2003—06. Cons., expert witness in field. Author: (textbooks) Chemistry: An Environmental Perspective, 1994, Chemistry Fundamentals: An Environmental Perspective, 1994, 2d edit., 2003, Principles of Environmental Chemistry, 2005, Criminalistics: Forensic Science and Crime, 2007; contbr. articles to profl. jours. Recipient Sr. Scholar award The Am. U., 1986-87, Leo Schubert award for outstanding teaching of sci. in coll. Washington Acad. Scis., 1995. Mem.: Am. Chem. Soc. Home: 6328 Karmich St Fairfax Station VA 22039-1621 Office: Am U Dept Chemistry 4400 Massachusetts Ave NW Dept Washington DC 20016-8003

GIRARD, JONATHAN RICHARD, conductor; b. Fall River, Mass., Apr. 25, 1978; s. Richard Joseph and Janet Theresa Girard. MusB in Saxophone Performance Summa Cum Laude, Hartt Sch. Music, 2000. Music dir., organist St. Robert Bellarmine Ch., Windsor Locks, Conn., 1996—2000; asst. condr. Portland Opera Repertory Theatre, Portland, Maine, 1996—2000; assoc. condr. Brockton Symphony Orch., Mass., 1998—2006; orch. condr. Wellesley H.S., 2000—; music dir., organist Ch. of St. George, Framingham, 2000—02; music dir. Waltham Philharm., 2002—; music dir., organist St. Mary of the Assumption Ch., Boston, 2002—, Dedham, 2002—; assoc. condr. Mass. Philharmonic Orch., 2006—. Named one of Top 50 Orch. Condrs. U.S., Sch. Band and Orch. Mag., 2001; Conducting fellow, Pierre Monteux Sch., 2001—02. Mem.: Am. Guild Organists, Phi Kappa Lambda (hon.). Achievements include Premiered the work Tribute to Kerouac by composer David Alpher - Hartford, 2000; premiered the work Sonata by Saxaphone by composer Gunther Schuller. Avocations: flying, skiing, golf. Home: 108 Farquhar St 3 Roslindale MA 02131 Home Phone: 617-876-8171. Personal E-mail: jg@jonathangirard.com.

GIRARD, LOUIS JOSEPH, retired ophthalmologist, educator; b. Spokane, Wash., Mar. 29, 1919; s. Harry and Agnes (Cain) G.; m. Bonita Crossnay, Mar. 31, 1945; children: Hilaire Michelle Bryan, Suzanne Christina Ann, Michael Sanford (dec.), Hugh Ashley, Gabrielle Inez; m. Loraine McMurrey, June 30, 1967; 1 son, Louis McMurrey; m. Louise Bell, June 14, 1975. BA, Rice U., 1941; MD, U. Tex., 1944; postgrad., NYU, Med. Sch., 1947-48. Diplomate: Am. Bd. Ophthalmology. Intern Jersey City Med. Ctr., 1944-45; assoc. Dr. Conrad Berens, NYC, 1947—49; asst. attending St. Clare's Hosp., 1948—53; resident ophthalmology NY Eye and Ear Infirmary, 1949-51; asst. attending Willard Parker Hosp., 1949-53; dir. chronic infection project, 1949-52; asst. attending N. Country Community Hosp., 1951-53; assoc. Dr. Conrad Berens, 1951—53; asst. attending Nassau Hosp., 1951-53, asst. surgeon, 1951-53; assoc. dir. dept. rsch. NY Eye and Ear Infirmary, 1953—57, founder dept. rsch., 1956; cons. ophthalmologist Southside Hosp., 1951-53; attending ophthalmologist Jefferson Davis Hosp., 1953-59, VA Hosp., Houston, 1954—98, Tex. Children's Hosp., 1954—98, St. Luke's Episcopal Hosp., 1954—98, Meth. Hosp., 1955—98; cons. Montgomery County Hosp., 1955—98, Tex. Children's Hosp., 1953—57; assoc. prof., assoc. chmn. dept. ophthalmology Baylor Coll. Medicine, Houston, 1957—70, prof., chmn. dept., 1953—70; cons. VA Hosp., Houston, 1958—98; sr. attending Ben Taub Gen. Hosp., 1959—98, Meth. Hosp., 1959—98; cons. St. Luke's Episcopal Hosp., 1961—98, St. Joseph's Hosp., 1965—98; chief ophthalmology, co-chief surgery Ctr. Pavilion Hosp., 1970-76; clin. prof. Baylor Coll. Medicine, Houston, 1971—. Coord. grad. course ophthalmology NYU Postgrad. Med. Sch., 1948-49, instr., 1951-53; clin. asst. prof. U. Tex. Postgrad. Sch. Medicine, 1953-57, lectr., 1946; assoc. mng. dir. Ophthal. Found., N.Y., 1951-55, cons., 1957; founder Tex. Med. Ctr.-Lions Eye Bank, 1953; exec. dir. Girard Ophthal. Found., 1971—; cons. Meth. Hosp., St. Luke's Hosp.; founder, exec. dir. Inst. Ophthalmology, Tex. Med. Ctr., 1958—70; founder ophthal. tissue culture lab. Baylor U., 1954; mem. Am. Orthoptic Coun., 1962-72; pres. Internat. Eye Film Library, 1967-71; med. adv. bd. Internat. Eye Bank, 1965-70; Pres. IX Pan Am. Congress Ophthalmology, 1972; presenter in field. Author: Advanced Techniques in Ophthalmic Microsurgery, Vol. I: Ultrasonic Fragmentation for Intraocular Surgery, 1979, Vol. II: Corneal Surgery, 1981; author, editor 11 books; prodr. 70 films.; editor: Corneal Contact Lenses, 1964, 2d edit., 1971, Corneal Scleral Contact Lenses, 1967, Procs. of XI Pan Am Congress of Ophthalmology, 1974; mem. editl. bd. Ophthalmologia, 1965-72, Annals of Ophthalmology, 1968-74; contbr. articles to profl. jours.; cons. Highlights Ophthalmology, 1972; founded the Lions Ey Bank; founded the first Tissue laboratory devoted to ophthalmology in the world, 1959; established the first inst. of ophthalmology in southwestern USA at Baylor Coll. Medicine, 1961. Recipient Alfred H. Bond award for rsch. in ophthalmology, 1950, Prof. Ignacio Barraquer Meml. award Inst. Barraquer, 1965, 2d prize Internat. Eye Film Festival, 1966, 1st prize, 1970, 1st prize, 1972, Golden Eagle award Internat. Film Festival Nantes, France, 1970, 71, Alumnus award Baylor U., 1984, First Disting. Alumnus award NY Eye and Ear Infirmary, 1984, Disting. Alumnus award Rice U., 1985, Disting. Alumnus award U. Tex. Med. Br. at Galveston, 1991; named to Hall of Fame, Alcon Labs., 1990. Fellow ACS (bd. gov. 1966-72); mem. Am. Acad. Ophthalmology (2d pl. award sci. exhibits 1960, Honor award, Sr. Honor award), Pan Am. Assn. Ophthalmology (1st pl. award sci. exhibits 1960, 62, vis. prof. 1967, v.p. 1972), Assn. Research Ophthalmology, N.Y. Acad. Medicine, NY Acad. Sci., Nassau, Houston ophthal. socs., French Soc. Ophthalmology, Houston Neurol. Soc., Jules Gonin Club, Tex. Opthal. Assn., Alumni Assn. NY Eye and Ear Infirmary, AMA (certificate of merit sci. exhibit 1961), So. Med. Assn., Nat. Med. Found. Eye Care, Assn. Am. Physicians and Surgeons, Am. Assn. Ophthalomologists, Nat. Med. Found. Eye Care, Tex. Rehab. Assn., Harris County Med. Soc., Am. U. Prof. Ophthalmologists (founder, chmn. com. on ophthalmic asst.), Med. Rsch.

Found. Tex., Contact Lens Soc. Ophthalmologists (Exceptional Merit award 1968), Inst. Horacio Ferrer (corr., lectr. 1959), Am. Eye Study Club (pres.) Achievements include inventing several instruments; originator numerous surg. techniques. Home: 20126 Indigo Lake Dr Magnolia TX 77355-3163 Personal E-mail: louisgirardmd@sbcglobal.net.

GIRARD, NETTABELL, lawyer; b. Pocatello, Idaho, Feb. 24, 1938; d. George and Arranetta (Bell) Girard. Student, Idaho State U., 1957—58; BS, U. Wyo., 1959, JD, 1961. Bar: Wyo. 1961, D.C. 1969, U.S. Supreme Ct. 1969. Practiced in, Riverton, Wyo., 1963-69; atty.-adviser on gen. counsel's staff HUD; assigned Office Interstate Land Sales Registration, Washington, 1969-70; sect. chief interstate land sales Office Gen. Counsel, 1970-73; ptnr. Larson & Larson, Riverton, 1973-85; pvt. practice Riverton, 1985—. Condr. course on women and law; lectr. in field. Editor Wyoming Clubwoman, 1966-68; bd. editors Wyo. Law Jour., 1959-61; writer Obiter Dictum column Women Lawyers Jour., Dear Legal Advisor column Solutions for Seniors, 1988-94; featured in Riverton Ranger, 1994; also articles in legal jours. Chmn. fund dr. Wind River chpt., ARC, 1965; chmn. Citizens Com. for Better Hosp. Improvement, 1965; chmn. subcom. on polit. legal rights and responsibilities Gov.'s Commn. on Status Women, 1965—69, mem. adv. com., 1973—93; local chmn. Law Day, 1966, 1967, county chmn., 1994—97; mem. state bd. Wyo Girl Scouts USA, sec., 1974—89, bd. dirs., 2001—04; state vol. adv. Nat. Found. March of Dimes, 1967—69; legal counsel Wyo. Women's Conf., 1977; gov. apptd. State Wyo. Indsl. Siting Coun., 1995—2001; rep. Nat. Conf. Govs. Commn., Washington, 1966. Recipient Spl. Achievement award HUD, 1972, Disting. Leadership award Girl Scouts USA, 1973, Franklin D. Roosevelt award Wyo. chpt. March of Dimes, 1985, Thanks Badge award Girl Scout Coun., 1987, Women Helping Women award Riverton Club Soroptimist Internat., 1990, Spl. award 27 yrs. svc. Wyo. Commn. for Women, 1964-92, Appreciation award Wyo. Sr. Citizens and Solutions for Srs., 1994, Arts in Action Pierrot award for outstanding musician, 1998, Disting. Svc. award Wyo. Music Edn. Assn., 2003, Leadership award 9th Jud. Dist., Wyo. Bar Assn., 2005. Mem. AAUW (br. pres., condr. seminar on law for layman Riverton br. 1965), Wyo. Bar Assn., Fremont County Bar Assn. (Spl. Recognition cert. 1997), DC Bar Assn., Women's Bar Assn. DC, Wyo. Trial Lawyers Assn., Nat. Assn. Women Lawyers (del. Wyo., nat. sec. 1969-70, v.p. 1970-71, pres. 1972-73), Wyo. Fedn. Women's Clubs (state editor, pres.-elect 1968-69, treas. 1974-76), Prog. Women's Club (pres.-elect. 1994-95), Riverton Chautauqua Club (pres. 1965-67, 2000-01), Riverton Civic League (pres. 1987-89), Kappa Delta, Delta Kappa Gamma (state chpt. hon.). Home: PO Box 687 Riverton WY 82501-0687 Office: 513 E Main St Riverton WY 82501-4440 Home Phone: 307-856-5048; Office Phone: 307-856-9339. Business E-Mail: ngirard@tcinc.net. *I believe first and foremost in the freedom of the individual: the right of the individual to be different, to be unique, and to pursue his or her particular heart's desire so long as that pursuit does not endanger the life or freedom of another. Perhaps because as a woman lawyer in predominately a man's profession, I have experienced the bitterness and dissolutionment of discrimination, I have actively worked through the equal rights movement toward the realization of individual freedom for all people. I support equality, not in the sense of "sameness," but in the realization of greater opportunities for individual development and differentiation.*

GIRARD, ROBERT DAVID, lawyer; b. Pitts., Aug. 2, 1946; s. Oscar L. and Ruth (Alpern) G. AB, UCLA, 1967; LLB, Yale U., 1970. Bar: Calif. 1971, U.S. Dist. Ct. (ctrl. dist.) Calif. 1971. Ptnr. Musick, Peeler & Garrett, LA, 1970-85, Girard, Ellingsen, Christensen & West, LA, 1985-88, Jones, Day, Reavis & Pogue, LA, 1988-92, Musick Peeler & Garrett, LA, 1992—97; with Sonnenschein Nath & Rosenthal LLP, LA, 1997—. Bd. dirs. Eisner Pediatric and Family Med. Ctr., L.A., 1980—, chmn., 1998-2002. Mem. ABA, L.A. County Bar Assn., Am. Health Lawyers Assn., Calif. Health Care Lawyers Assn. (bd. dirs. 1982-85), Phi Beta Kappa. Office: Sonnenschein Nath & Rosenthal LLP 601 S Figueroa St Ste 1500 Los Angeles CA 90017-5720 Office Phone: 213-892-5074. Business E-Mail: rgirard@sonnenschein.com.

GIRARD-DICARLO, DAVID FRANKLIN, lawyer; b. Bryn Mawr, Pa., Jan. 20, 1943; m. Constance Jean Bricker, Apr. 5, 1973. BS, St. Joseph's U., 1970; JD, Villanova U., 1973. Bar: DC 2002, NY 2006, US Dist. Ct. (ea. dist.) Pa. 1973, US Ct. Appeals (3d cir.) 1973, US Supreme Ct. 1978, US Ct. Appeals DC 2002. Assoc. Wolf, Block, Schorr & Solis-Cohen, Phila., 1973—74, Dilworth, Paxson, Kalish, Levy & Kauffman, Phila., 1974—78, ptnr., 1979, Fell, Spalding, Goff & Rubin, Phila., 1979—82, Blank, Rome, Comisky & McCauley, Phila., 1982—, chmn., labor and employment law section, 1982—86, mng. ptnr. & CEO, 1987—99; co-chair, CEO & mng. ptnr. Blank Rome LLP (formerly Blank, Rome, Comisky & McCauley), Phila., 2000—03, chmn., 2003—, Blank Rome Govt. Rels. LLC, Washington, 2003—. Mem. hearing com. Disciplinary Bd. of Supreme Ct. of Pa., Phila., 1981-84, chmn. hearing com., 1984-87; faculty mem. Workshop on Urban Mass Transp., Practicing Law Inst., San Francisco and Washington, 1978; corp. mem. bd. Continental Bank, Midatlantic Corp., PNC Bank, 1987-01; trustee Phila. Belt Line R.R. Co., 1992; Editor-in-chief Villanova Law Rev., 1972, Transit Law Rev., 1977-81; mem. Phila. Cmty. Leadership Seminar Program, 1978-79; chmn. bd. Southeastern Pa. Transp. Authority, 1979-82; mem. transp. taxation task force Tax Commn. of Commonwealth of Pa., 1981-82; chmn. N.E. Corridor Commuter Rail Authorities Com., 1981-83; mem. Pa. Rep. State Fin. Com., 1982—. Trustee Ariz. Heart Found., 2006—, Phila. Acad. of Music, Phila. Orch., 1988—95, mem. exec. com., 1988—95, vice chmn., 1991—94, St. Joseph's U., 1994, Drexel U., 1988—92, Harcum Jr. Coll., 1987—92, Pennoni Assocs. Inc., Phila. Belt Line RR Co., Phila. Found., Walnut St. Theatre, 1986—93; treas. Ridge for Gov. Commn., 1994; co-chmn., Host Com. Repub. Nat. Convention, 2000; chair Sen. RickSantorum's Fed. Judicial Nominating Comm., chmn., 2005; Pa. state fin. chair Bush-Cheney campaign, 2000, 2004; co-chair Bush-Cheney 04 campaign; fin. com. John McCain 2008; bd. mem. Gettysburg Found., 2003—, John F. Kennedy Ctr. Performing Arts, 2001—, mem. exec. com., 2002—; mem. Wilson Coun. Woodrow Wilson Internat. Ctr. for Scholars, 2002—; former bd. chair, former chair exec. com. Greater Phila. C. of C.; mem. bd. consultors Villanova U. Sch. Law, 1992; bd. dir. SEPTA, 1979—82; chair Am. Public Transit Assn., 1981; bd. mem. Amtrak, 1990—93. Recipient Edwin Forrest award, Walnut St. Theater, Judge Learned Hand Human Relations award, Am. Jewish Comm., 1996, Gerald Abraham award for Disting. Svc., Villanova U. Law, 1999, Pontifical Honor of Knight of the Order of St. Gregory the Great, Pope John Paul II, 2003, Americanism award, Anti-Defamation League, 2005. Mem. ABA, Pa. Bar Assn., Phila. Bar Assn., Am. Pub. Transit Assn. (bd. dirs. 1979-82, chmn. bd. dirs. 1982, chmn. legis. com. 1980-81, mem. exec. com. 1980-82, v.p. govt. affairs 1981-82, mem. various coms.), Greater Phila. C. of C. (bd. dirs., sec., mem. exec. com. 1990). Office: Blank Rome LLP One Logan Sq Philadelphia PA 19103-6998 Office Phone: 215-569-5500. Office Fax: 215-569-5555. Business E-Mail: girarddicarlo@BlankRome.com.

GIRARDEAU, MARVIN DENHAM, physics professor; b. Lakewood, Ohio, Oct. 3, 1930; s. Marvin Denham and Maude Irene (Miller) G.; m. Susan Jessica Brown, June 30, 1956; children: Ellen, Catherine, Laura. BS, Case Inst. Tech., 1952; MS, U. Ill., 1954; PhD, Syracuse U., 1958. NSF postdoctoral fellow Inst. Advanced Study, Princeton, NJ, 1958—59; rsch. assoc. Brandeis U., 1959—60; staff mem. Boeing Sci. Rsch. Labs., 1960—61; rsch. assoc. Enrico Fermi Inst. Nuc. Studies, U. Chgo., 1961—63; assoc. prof. physics, rsch. assoc. Inst. Theoretical Sci., U. Oreg., Eugene, 1963—67, prof. physics, rsch. assoc., 1967—95, dir., 1967—69, chmn. dept. physics, 1974—76, prof. emeritus, 1995—; rsch. prof. optical scis. U. Ariz., 2000—. Contbr. articles to profl. jours. Recipient Humboldt Sr. U.S. Scientist award, 1984-85. NSF rsch. grantee, 1965-79; ONR rsch. grantee, 1981-87, 99—. Fellow Am. Phys. Soc.; mem. AAUP. Achievements include research on quantum-mech. many-body problems, statis. mechanics, atomic, molecular and chem. physics; Bose-Einstein condensation of atomic vapors, coherent control of quantum systems. Home: 288 N Bent Ridge Dr Green Valley AZ 85614-5949 Office: Optical Scis Ctr Univ Arizona Tucson AZ 85721-0001 E-mail: girardeau@optics.arizona.edu.

GIRARDI, JOE (JOSEPH ELLIOT GIRARDI), sports announcer, former professional baseball manager, former professional baseball player; b. Peoria, Ill., Oct. 14, 1964; m. Kimberly Girardi; 3 children. BS in Indsl. Engring., Northwestern U., 1986. Catcher Chgo. Cubs, 1989—92, 2000—02, Colo. Rockies, 1993—95, NY Yankees, 1995-2000, St. Louis Cardinals, 2003; bench coach NY Yankees, 2004—05; mgr. Fla. Marlins, Carol City, 2005—06. Baseball announcer YES Network, 2004, 2007—. Named to Nat. League All-Star Team, 2000; recipient Nat. League Mgr. Yr., Major League Baseball Writers Assn., 2006. Achievements include being a member of 3 NY Yankees World Series Championship Teams, 1996, 1998-99. Office: YES Network LLC Chrysler Bldg 405 Lexington Ave 36th Fl New York NY 10174*

GIRARDI, THOMAS VINCENT, lawyer; b. Denver, June 3, 1939; s. Albert Girardi; married, Sept. 11, 1993; children: Jacqueline, Matthew, Jennifer. BS, Loyola U., LA, 1961, LLB, 1964; LLM, NYU, 1965. Bar: Calif. 1964. Sr. ptnr. Girardi & Keese, LA, 1965—. Assoc. prof. law Loyola U., L.A., 1976—; apptd. mem. Jud. Coun. Calif., 2005. Contbr. over 50 articles to profl. jours. Fellow Internat. Acad. Trial Lawyers (pres. 2005-06); mem. The Am. Bd. Trial Advocates (nat. pres. 1999), The Inner Circle of Advocates, The Am. Bd. Profl. Liability Lawyers, The Internat. Soc. Barristers, The Consumer Attys. Assn. L.A., The L.A. Trial Lawyers (Trial Lawyer of Yr. 1995-96). Democrat. Roman Catholic. Avocations: golf, aviation. Home: 100 Los Altos Dr Pasadena CA 91105-1240 Office: Girardi & Keese 1126 Wilshire Blvd Los Angeles CA 90017-1904

GIRARDS, JAMES EDWARD, lawyer; b. Manhasset, NY, Aug. 16, 1963; s. H.V. and Barbara (Davis) G.; m. Julie Ann Calame, June 27, 1987; children: Jessica Lauren, James Edward. BS, Baylor U., Waco, Tex., 1986; JD, St. Mary's Law Sch., 1989. Bar: Tex. 1989, US Dist. Ct. (no., so. and ea. dists.) Tex. 1991, US Ct. Appeals (5th cir.) 2000. Assoc. Law Offices Windle Turley, PC, Dallas, 1989-94; prin. Tracy & Girards, Dallas, 1994-97, The Girards Law Firm, Dallas, 1997—. Contbr. articles to profl. jours. Recipient Am. Jurisprudence Contracts award AmJur Pub. Co., 1986. Mem. ATLA (pres.'s club 1999-, state del. 2003—), Tex. Trial Lawyers Assn. (dir. 1999—), Dallas Trial Lawyers Assn. (dir. 1998-2004, v.p. 2005, pres.-elect 2006, pres. 2007), Dallas Bar Assn., Dallas Assn. Young Lawyers, State Bar Tex., Tarrant County Trial Lawyer Assn., Coll. of State Bar Tex., Am. Mensa, Ltd., Million Dollar Advocates Forum. Office: 10000 N Central Expy Ste 750 Dallas TX 75231 Office Phone: 214-346-9529. Business E-Mail: info@girardlaw.com.

GIRDLER, SUSAN SCOTT, psychologist, educator, researcher; b. Rockledge, Fla., Mar. 18, 1960; d. Harry Bell and Nancy Jackson Girdler; m. Charles Edward Pettee, Aug. 6, 1957; children: Jackson Charles Pettee, Noah Scott Pettee. BS in Psychology, U. Fla., 1982; MS in Counseling Psychology, Nova Southeastern U., Fla., 1986; PhD, U. N.C., 1991. Asst. clin. prof. U. Calif., Fresno, 1992—93; prof. U. NC, Chapel Hill, 1993—. Cons. NIH, Bethesda, Md., 2001—06. Assoc. editor: Biol. Psychology, 2000—05, guest editor:, 2005, assoc. editor: Psychophysiology, 2006—. Sunday Sch. tchr. U. Bapt. Ch., Chapel Hill, 2002—, tchr. Vacation Bible Sch., 2002—. Grantee, NIMH, 1995—, Nat. Heart, Lung and Blood Inst., 1997—2002, Nat. Inst. Drug Abuse, 2001—. Mem.: Soc. for Psychophysiological Rsch., Internat. Orgn. Psychophysiology, Soc. Behavioral Medicine (Young Investigator award 1996), Am. Psychosomatic Soc. (Early Career Contributions to Psychosomatic Rsch. award 2001). Democrat. Baptist. Avocations: swimming, hiking, backpacking. Office: U NC CB7175 Dept Psychiatry Chapel Hill NC 27599 Home Phone: 919-967-1381. Personal E-mail: sgirdler@med.unc.edu.

GIRGIS, MICHAEL M., physician; b. Spring, Tex., Feb. 10, 1976; s. George and Nora Girgis. BS, Tex. A&M U., Coll. Sta., 1998; MD, St. George's U., Grenada, 2003. Diplomate Am. Bd. Family Medicine, 2006. Family practice residency Charlton Meth. Med. Ctr., Dallas, 2003—05, chief resident, 2005—. Ring side physician Golden Gloves Boxing, Dallas, 2006. Recipient Disting. Biomedical Sci. award, Tex. A&M U., 1998, Outstanding Academic Achievement award, 1998, Prof. of Aerospace Studies award, 1998, Mr. Humanitarian Class award, St. George's U., 2000; Lawrence Sullivan Ross scholar, Tex. A&M U., 1994—98, Gunther Meml. scholar, St. George's U., 1999—2003. Mem.: AMA, Dallas County Med. Soc., Tex. Acad. Family Physicians, Am. Soc. Bariatric Physicians, Am. Acad. Family Physicians. Home Phone: 214-953-0125; Office Phone: 972-664-0404. Office Fax: 972-664-9797; Home Fax: 214-953-0125. Personal E-mail: girgismichael@yahoo.com.

GIRGIS-HANNA, MARY FAHIM, music educator; b. Assiut, Egypt, Mar. 6, 1935; arrived in U.S., 1989; d. Fahim Girgis and Emily Matta Boctor; m. Fadel M. Hanna, Nov. 25, 1954; children: Baher, Farid, Wagih. BA in Edn., Am. U., Cairo, 1958, MA in Sociology, 1978; ATCL in Piano Tchg., Trinity Coll., London, 1972; PhD in Spl. Edn., U. Toledo, 1997. Tchr. Manor House H.S., Cairo, 1967—69; pvt. piano tchr. Cairo, 1972—88; tchr. family sociology Prebyn. Sem., Cairo, 1984—88; cons. gerontology Egyptian Ministry of Health, Cairo, 1980—83; instr. sociology U. Toledo, 1989—2000; dir., founder Rhapsody Sch. Music, Toledo, 1994—. Founder, bd. dirs. Ctr. for Geriatric Svcs., Cairo, 1976—88. Author: The Gerontologist, 1983. Bd. dirs. Lucas County Bd. Mental Retardation, Toledo, 1998—2000; Ohio rep. Trinity Coll. London, 1995—; chmn. internat. com. World Day of Prayer, 1978—82; active Christian Med. Commn., World Coun. Chs., Geneva, 1980—83; organist Judson Bapt. Ch., Toledo, 1992—2006, deacon of missions, 1997—2002. Named Model Mother, Presbyn. Women's Assn., 1980. Mem.: Toledo Piano Tchr. Assn. (pres. 2001—03), Nat. Piano Tchr. Assn. Avocations: piano, organ, accordion, singing, reading. Home: 3006 E Lincolnshire Blvd Toledo OH 43606 Office Phone: 419-866-4640.

GIRGUIS, PETER RIAD, microbiologist, entrepreneur, educator; s. Mounir R. and Farida A. Girguis; m. Christen M. Herren. BSc, UCLA, 1994; PhD, U. Calif., Santa Barbara, 2000. Postdoctoral fellow Monterey Bay Aquarium Rsch. Inst., Moss Landing, Calif., 2000—02, rsch. scientist, adj. engring. assoc. Grantee Innovative Rsch. award, Merck Inc, 2006, Sci. and Innovation award, Lindbergh Found., 2007; UC Regents fellow, U. Calif. Santa Barbara, 2000, Biotechnology fellow, Dept. Energy, 2002. Fellow: NSF RIDGE Program (steering com. 2004—); mem.: Am. Geophys. Union, Am. Soc. Limnology and Oceanography, Am. Soc. Microbiology. Achievements include patents pending for microbial fuel cells; alternative energy systems; patents in field of bioreactors. Office: Harvard University 16 Divinity Ave Rm 3085 Cambridge MA 02138 Home Phone: 7818749137. Office Fax: 617 4958848. Business E-Mail: pgirguis@fas.harvard.edu.

GIRGUS, JOAN STERN, psychologist, educator, director; b. Albany, NY, Mar. 21, 1942; d. William Barnet and Louise (Mayer) Stern; m. Alan Chimacoff, Jan. 2, 1981; 1 child, Katherine Louise Stern. BA, Sarah Lawrence Coll., 1963; MA, The Grad. Faculty New Sch. for Social Research, 1965, PhD, 1969. Asst. prof. dept. psychology CCNY, NYC, 1969-72, assoc. prof., 1972-77, assoc. dean div. social sci., 1972-75, dean, 1975-77; prof. psychology Princeton U., 1977—, dir. Pew Sci. Program Undergrad. Edn., 1987—2002, chair dept. psychology, 1996—2002, spl. asst. to dean of faculty, 2003—. Contbr. articles and chpts. to profl. jours. and books. NSF fellow, NIH fellow; Research grantee CUNY, 1971-74; Nat. Inst. Child Health and Human Devel. research grantee, 1972-74; NSF grantee, 1975-79; NIMH grantee, 1985-91. Fellow APA, Am. Psychol. Soc.; mem. Eastern Psychol. Assn., Soc. Rsch. in Child Devel. Home: 306 Ridgeview Rd Princeton NJ 08540 Office: Princeton U Green Hall Princeton NJ 08544

GIRGUS, SAM B., English literature educator; b. Dec. 30, 1941; m. Judith Scot-Smith; children: Katya Roberts, Meighan St. John, Jennifer Scot-Smith. BA in American Studies, Syracuse U., NYC, 1962; MA in English, State U. Iowa, Ames, 1963; PhD in American Studies, U. N.Mex., Albuquerque, 1972. Reporter, critic Providence Jour., RI, 1967-69; asst. prof. in Am. studies and English U. Ala., 1972-75, dir., 1973-75; assoc. prof., chmn. dept. Am. studies U. N.Mex., 1975-84, prof. English and Am. studies, 1980-87; prof. English, dir. Am. studies U. Oreg., Eugene, 1987-90; prof. English Vanderbilt U., Nashville, 1990—, dir. Am. studies, 1990-92, chair, dir., film studies, 2003—04. Chmn. disciplinary adv. com. Fulbright Scholars Awards in Am. Culture, 1989-93; cons. USIA visit at Sofia U., Bulgaria, 1985, Los Andes U., Bogota, Columbia, 1992, Hankuk U., Seoul, Korea, 1993, Aarhus U., Odense U., Denmark, 1995; Uppsala chair in Am. studies Uppsala U., Sweden, 1996; acting dir. film studies Vanderbilt U., 2003-04; mem. tchg. com. Soc. for Cinema and Media Studies, 2006, Cinema of Redemption, Levinas and Cinema, King's Coll., London, 2006; lectr. in field. Author: The Law of the Heart: Individualism and the Modern Self in American Literature, 1979, The New Covenant: Jewish Writers and the American Idea, 1984, Desire and the Political Unconscious in American Literature, 1990, The Films of Woody Allen, 1993, 2d edit., 2002, Hollywood Renaissance: The Cinema of Democracy in the Era of Ford, Capra and Kazan, 1998, America on Film: Modernism, Documentary, and a Changing America, 2002; editor: The American Self: Myth, Ideology and Popular Culture, 1981, The New Eden: Consensus and Regeneration in America, 1988, The Outsider: Dissent and Alienation in America, 1988; guest editor: Am. Literary Realism 1870-1910, 1977; prodr., writer: (film) In Loco Amicis: The New Vanderbilt Story, 2001, Beyond Ontology, 2006, Divine comedy in Woody Allen, Capra and Levinas, 1938 in Am. Cinemas; contbr. articles to profl. jours. With USN, 1963-67. Rockefeller Humanities fellow, 1980-81; Sr. Fulbright lectr. U. Heidelberg, Germany, 1984; named Prof. of the Semester Vanderbilt U., 2006. Fellow Vanderbilt Ctr. Nashville Studies, Ctr for Religion and Cultures; mem. MLA, Cinema Studies Assn., Am. Studies Assn., Modernist Studies Assn. Home: 402 Lynwood Blvd Nashville TN 37205-3435 Office: Vanderbilt U Dept English PO Box 1654 Sta B 318 Benson Hall Nashville TN 37235 Office Phone: 615-322-2271. Business E-Mail: sam.b.girgus@vanderbilt.edu.

GIRI, CHANDRA PRASAD, research scientist; b. Chimchima, Khotang, Nepal, May 13, 1961; s. Kul Prasad and Rupa Giri; m. Tejaswi Giri, Dec. 15, 1989; children: Medhawi, Ashwat Chandra. PhD, Asian Inst. Tech., Bangkok, 1998. Sr. staff assoc. Columbia U., NYC, 2000—02; prin. scientist SAIC/USGS/EROS, Sioux Falls, SD, 2002—. Cons. UN Environment Programme, Nairobi, Kenya, 2004—06. Recipient Mahendra Vidya Bhushan, King of Nepal, 2000; Austrian scholar, Austrian Govt., 1992—93, Environ. Assessment grantee, Asian Devel. Bank, 1999, Venture Capital Fund grantee, US Geol. Survey, 2006, Mangrove Study of Asia grantee, NSF, 2007. Mem.: IEEE (sr.). Achievements include research in the application of remote sensing and GIS technology. Home: 5312 S Ash Grove Ave Sioux Falls SD 57108 Office: SAIC/USGS/EROS 47914 252 St Sioux Falls SD 57198 Business E-Mail: cgiri@usgs.gov.

GIRMAN, DEE-MARIE, retired artist, singer; b. Duquesne, Pa., Apr. 10, 1919; d. Michael Girman and Marie Schuster. Student, Pitts. Musical Inst., Fillion Ballet Sch.; studied dress design with Louise Salinger; student, Barry U. Singer, Pitts.; iconographer, artist Barry U., Miami Shores, Fla.; ret. Author: Sandtrap, The Mathematical Genius Dog, 2003; one-woman shows include Chase Showing, 1974, Barrry U., 1983, Miami Art Ctr. Entertainer specialist Spl. Svc., USAAC, 1942—45. Named to Hall of Fame, Barry U., 1995, Meml. Hist. Roll of Honor, Am. Meml. Found., 1997. Republican. Roman Catholic. Avocation: golf. Home: Sunset Lake Village 1121 Jacaranda Blvd Rm 309 Venice FL 34292 Personal E-mail: sansydee@msn.com.

GIROLO, NELLA SUE, retired voice educator; b. Newton, Iowa, Aug. 21, 1938; d. Dorman Daane and Clara Winifred (Bond) Hundling; m. Patrick C. Murphy, Jan. 2, 1990; children: Janella Wilimek Ingle, James Powell Wilimek II. MusB, Drake U., 1960, M, 1964; student, Music Acad. of the West, 1973, U. Calif., Irvine, 1976. Cert. Elem. and Secondary Sch. Educator. Music instr. Johnston HS, 1960—63; asst. voice prof. Iowa State U., 1966—70; voice, theater instr. Cuesta Coll., San Luis Obispo, Calif., 1972—2003, drama, music coord., 1993—96, chmn. performing arts., 1996—2003; ret., 2003. Adv. bd. Pacific Repertory Opera, San Luis Obispo, Calif., 1986—89; pres. Ctrl. Coast Music Teachers, San Luis Obispo, 1975—76; alumni adv. bd. Cuesta Coll., 1986—. Performer: Concerts, Operas and Musicals, 1960—86; author: (historical book) Uncommon Letters from a Common Man, 1993, (cookbook) Grandma's Recipe Album, 1995, Plain and Fancy, 1999. Bd. mem. Cuesta Coll. Found., 1990—, Project Theatre Found., Paso Robles, 2003—06; spl. events coord. Cuesta Coll. Found., 1998—; grant reviewer Women's Legacy Fund, 2005, co-chair grant revs., 2007. Named Layperson of Yr., Phi Delta Kappa, 2006; recipient Outstanding Kappa of Yr., Drake U., 1959—60, Outstanding Acad. Employee, Cuesta Coll., 1997, Outstanding Vol., Bd. Mem. of Yr., Equal Opportunity Commn., 2003. Mem.: AAUW, Woman's Legacy Fund (bd. mem. 2006—), Nat. Assn. Teachers of Singing, Women's Power Lunch, Kappa Kappa Gamma. Avocations: gourmet cooking, writing, swimming. Home: 1374 Shane Lane Templeton CA 93465

GIRONDA, RONALD JAMES, psychologist; b. Charlotte, NC, Feb. 26, 1967; PhD, Kent State U., Ohio, 1998. Lic. psychologist Fla. Bd. Health, 1999. Staff psychologist James A. Haley Veterans Hosp., Tampa, Fla., 2005—. Pain investigator VA Rehab. R&D Svc., Tampa, 2003—06. Contbr. articles to profl. jours. Recipient VA Olin Teague award, Dept. Vets Affairs, 2004, Scholar award, Eastern Paralyzed Veterans Assn., 2002. Mem.: Am. Pain Soc. (web editor 2007—). Achievements include research in pain treatment outcomes assessment. Office: James A Haley Veterans Hospital 13000 Bruce B Downs Blvd Tampa FL 33612 Home Phone: 813-632-4840; Office Phone: 813-972-2000 4363. Office Fax: 813-903-4847. Business E-Mail: ronald.gironda@va.gov.

GIROUARD, MARVIN J., retired retail executive; b. 1939; B in Mktg., Tex. A&M U., 1961. Various mktg. positions Pier 1 Imports Inc., Ft. Worth, 1975—85, sr. v.p. merchandising, 1985—88, pres., COO, 1988—98, pres., CEO, 1998—99, chmn., CEO, 1999—2007. Bd. dirs. Brinker Internat., Tandy Brands Accessories, Inc. Mem. exec. com. U.S. Com. for UNICEF; mem. devel. coun. Coll. Bus. Adminstrn. Tex. A&M U.; bd. visitors M.J. Neeley Sch. Bus. Tex. Christian U. Commd. ensign USNR, 1963, advanced though grades to comdr. USNR, 1983, ret. USNR, 1983. Recipient Hugh Downs award, U.S. Com. for UNICEF, 1994, Outstanding Alumni award, Coll. Bus. Adminstrn. and Grad Sch., Tex. A&M U., 1995.*

GIROUARD, PEGGY JO FULCHER, ballet educator; b. Corpus Christi, Tex., Oct. 25, 1933; d. J.B. and Zora Alice (Jackson) Fulcher; m. Richard Ernest Girouard, Apr. 16, 1954 (div. Mar. 1963); children: Jo Linne, Richard Ernest; m. James C. Boles, May 4, 1996. BS in Elem. Edn., U. Houston, 1970. Ballet instr. Emmamae Horn Studio, Houston, 1951-81;

owner, dir. Allegro Acad. Dance, Houston, 1981—. Artistic dir. Allegro Ballet Houston, 1976—; asst. mgr. Sugar Creek Homes Assn., Sugar Land, Tex., 1979-90; coord. 1st Regional Dance Am. Nat. Festival, Houston, 1997. Choreographer (with Glenda W. Brown) Masquerade Suite, 1983, Sebelius Suite, 1983, Shannan, 1984, Papa Shamus, 1986, Silhouettes, 1987, Aspirations, 1989, Here Come the Clowns, 1990. Mem. Cultural Arts Coun. Houston; founding officer Regional Dance Am., 1988, bd. dirs., 1988—, sec., 1996-2001. Mem. Dance Masters Am. (dir. 1977-80), S.W. Regional Ballet Assn. (chmn. craft of choreography 1983-85, coord. to nat. assn. 1983-2003, Stream award 1986). Democrat. Home: 9945 Warwana Rd Houston TX 77080-7609 Office Phone: 281-496-4670. Personal E-mail: pgirouard77080@yahoo.com.

GIRTH, MARJORIE LOUISA, lawyer, educator; b. Trenton, NJ, Apr. 21, 1939; d. Harold Brookman and Marjorie Mathilda (Simonson) G. AB, Mt. Holyoke Coll., 1959; LLB, Harvard U., 1962. Bar: NJ 1963, US Supreme Ct. 1969, NY 1976. Pvt. practice, Trenton, 1963-65; rsch. assoc. Brookings Instn., 1965-70; assoc. prof. law SUNY Law Sch., Buffalo, 1971-79, prof., 1979-91, assoc. dean, 1986-87; dean Ga. State U. Coll. Law, Atlanta, 1992-96, prof., 1992—. Vis. prof. U. Va. Law Sch., 1979-80, Southeastern Bankruptcy Law Inst., Emory Law Sch., spring 1991, vis. scholar, spring 1996; vis. prof. Warsaw, Poland, 2003, Law Sch. Vytautus Magnus U., Lithuania, 2006; vis. legal educator W.Va. U. Coll. Law Vis. Com., 1994-95; chancellor's search adv. com. Bd. of Regents, 1993-94; mem. com. on standards of the profession State Bar Ga., 1996-; mem. commn. on racial and ethnic bias in ct. sys. Ga. Supreme Ct, 1993-95, mem. commn. on equality, 1995-2004, sec., 1998-2000, mem. commn. on access and fairness in the cts., 2004-06; mem. Atlanta Foreclosure Prevention Task Force, Fed. Reserved Bd., 2004-. Author: Poor People's Lawyers, 1976, Bankruptcy Options for the Consumer Debtor, 1981, (co-author) Bankruptcy: Problem, Process, Reform, 1971. Bd. dirs. Buffalo and Erie County YWCA, 1972-76, Buffalo Unitarian-Universalist Ch., 1981-84, Feminist Women's Health Ctr., 1993-94, ACLU, Ga., 1995-2001, Unitarian-Universalist Congregation of Atlanta, 1999—2003; mem. commn. on peace, justice and human rights Internat. Assn. Religious Freedom, 1976-79; mem Ga. Ct. appeals Centennial Celebration, 2005-06; chmn. Erie County Task Force on Status of Women, 1985-87 Recipient Centennial award for profl. achievement, Alumnae Assn. of Mt. Holyoke Coll., 1972, award for pioneering achievements NY State 8th Jud. Dist. Splty. Bar Assn. and Com. on Women in the Cts., 2000. Fellow Lawyers Found. Ga.; mem. ABA (mem. coun. bus. law sect. 1985-89, chmn. consumer bankruptcy com. 1983-86), Am. Arbitration Assn. (nat. comml. arbitration panel 1997—), Assn. Am. Law Schs. (profl. devel. com. 2002-06, nominations com. 1996), Am. Law Inst., Law Sch. Admission Coun. (audit com. chair 2007—, fin. and legal affairs com.), N.Y. State Bar Assn. (mem. exec. com. bus. law sect. 1980-91, chmn. bankruptcy law com. 1980-82, chmn. banking corp. bus. law sect. 1986-87, mem. ho. of dels. 1990-91), Ga. Assn. Women Lawyers, Law Sch. Admissions Coun. (audit com. 1995-97, 1999—, chair, 2007-, fin. and legal affairs com., 1997-99). Unitarian Universalist. Office: Ga State U Coll Law PO Box 4037 Atlanta GA 30302-4037 Office Phone: 404-413-9196. Business E-Mail: mgirth@gsu.edu.

GIRVIGIAN, RAYMOND, architect; b. Detroit, Nov. 27, 1926; s. Manoug and Margaret G.; m. Beverly Rae Bennett, Sept. 23, 1967; 1 son, Michael Raymond. AA, UCLA, 1947; BA with honors, U. Calif., Berkeley, 1950; MA in Architecture, U. Calif.-Berkeley, 1951. With Hutchason Architects, LA, 1952-57; owner, prin. Raymond Girvigian, LA, 1957-68, South Pasadena, Calif., 1968—. Co-founder, advisor LA Cultural Heritage Bd., 1961—; vice chmn. Hist. Am. Bldgs. Survey, Nat. Park Svc., Washington, 1967-71; co-founder Calif. Hist. Resources Commn., 1970-78; co-founder, chmn. governing bd. Calif. Hist. Bldgs. Code, 1976-91, chmn. adminstrv. law, 1992—, chmn. emeritus, 1993—; co-founder, chmn. Calif. State Capitol Commn., 1985-98, chmn. emeritus, 1998—. Co-editor, producer: film Architecture of Southern California for Los Angeles City Sch., 1965; hist. monographs of HABS Landmarks, Los Angeles, 1958-80; historical monographs of Calif. State Capitol, 1974, Pan Pacific Auditorium, 1980, LA Meml. Coliseum, 1984, Powell Meml. Libr., UCLA, 1989; designed: city halls for Pico Rivera, 1963, LaPuente, 1966, Rosemead, 1968, Lawndale, 1970 (all Calif.); hist. architect for restoration of Calif. State Capitol, 1975-82, Workman/Temple Hist. Complex, City of Industry, Calif., 1974-81, Robinson Gardens Landmarks, Beverly Hills, Calif., 1983-92, Pasadena (Calif.) Ctrl. Libr., 1982-92, 95—, Mt. Pleasant House Mus., Heritage Sq., LA, 1972-95. Mem. St. James' Episcopal Ch., S. Pasadena, Calif. With US Army, 1944—46. Recipient Outstanding Achievement in Architecture award City of Pico Rivera, Calif., 1968, Preservationist of Yr. award Calif. Preservation Found., 1987, LA Mayor's award for archtl. preservation, 1987, Gold Crown award Pasadena Arts Coun., 1990, Golden Palm award Hollywood Heritage, 1990, Design award for Oaklawn Bridge Rehab., Merit award Heritage Coalition of So. Calif., 2003, Cert. Spl. Congl. Recognition award, Cert. Spl. Recognition award Calif. State Assembly, 2006, Proclamation Commendation award City of South Pasadena, Calif., 2006; named Hist. Architect Emeritus Calif. State Capitol, Calif. Legislature, 1998, Commendation award Calif. Legislature, 1998; co-recipient honor award rehab. Los Altos Apts., Calif. Preservation Found., 1999, Lifetime Achievement award Calif. Preservation Found., 2007. Mem. AIA (mem. Coll. Fellows 1972, Calif. state preservation chmn. 1970-75, state preservation coord. 1970-89, co-recipient Nat. Honor award for Restoration Calif. State Capitol 1983, co-recipient Honor award for Restoration Pasadena Cen. Libr., Pasadena chpt. 1988, Regional and Urban Design award Pasadena and Foothill chpts., 2005); mem. Soc. Archtl. Historians, Nat. Trust for Historic Preservation, Calif. Preservation Found., Calif. Hist. Soc. (Neasham award 1982), Xi Alpha Kappa. Office: PO Box 220 South Pasadena CA 91031-0220 *I believe that we must all serve society in whatever way that we are best able; and if a worthy cause I have undertaken appears to have failed, I should ignore that possibility and press on with even greater determination and vigor to succeed. I would hope by that example to encourage others to join the cause and thereby futher the likelihood of a successful effort for the good of all.*

GIRVIN, STEVEN MARK, physicist, researcher; b. Austin, Tex., Apr. 5, 1950; s. Allen Fitzhugh and Margaret (Trowbridge) Girvin; m. Diane Desjardins, Jan. 1, 1972; children: Andrew T., Joshua M. BS magna cum laude, Bates Coll., 1971; MS, U. Maine, 1973, Princeton U., 1974, PhD, 1977. Postdoctoral rsch. assoc. Ind. U., Bloomington, 1977-79; staff scientist Nat. Inst. Stds. and Tech., Gaithersburg, Md., 1979-87; prof. Ind. U., Bloomington, 1987-92, disting. prof., 1992—2001; prof. physics Yale U., 2001—. Mem. Aspen Ctr. Physics, Colo., 1990-94, NRC Panel on Condensed Matter and Materials Physics, Washington, 1996—; pres. adv. bd. Inst. Theoretical Physics, Santa Barbara, Calif., 1997-98. Contbr. articles to sci. jours.; editor: The Quantum Hall Effect, 1990. Fellow Am. Phys. Soc. (Oliver E. Buckley prize, 2007), Am. Acad. Arts & Sci.; mem. NAS, Royal Swedish Acad. Sci. (fgn. mem.). Avocation: amateur astronomy. Office: Yale U Dept Physics PO Box 208120 New Haven CT 06520-8120 Office Phone: 203-432-5082. Business E-Mail: steven.girvin@yale.edu.

GISO, FRANK, III, lawyer; b. Haverhill, Mass., Feb. 14, 1949; s. Frank and Clementina Paula (Foresta) G; m. Deborah Jean Kracht, May 5, 1979; children: Christopher Anderson, Benjamin Hilding. BA Econs. magna cum laude, Brown U., 1971; JD magna cum laude, Cornell U., 1975. Bar: Mass. 1975, U.S. Dist. Ct. Mass. 1976, U.S. Ct. Appeals (1st cir.) 1976. Law clerk Mass. Superior Ct., Boston, 1975—76; assoc. Peabody & Brown, Boston, 1976—83, ptnr., 1983—88, Choate, Hall & Stewart, Boston, 1988—, chmn. real estate dept., 1988—98. Bd. dirs. Melrose (Mass.) Coop. Bank; pres. Melrose (Mass.) Affordable Housing Corp., 2003—. Vice chmn. Melrose Housing Authority, 1986-98, chmn. 1998—. Mem. ABA, Mass. Bar Assn., Boston Bar Assn., Phi Beta Kappa, Order of Coif. Avocations: tennis, golf. Office: Two International Pl Boston MA 02110 Home Phone: 781-665-9589; Office Phone: 617-248-5117. Business E-Mail: fgiso@choate.com.

GISOLFI, DIANA (PECHUKAS), art history educator; b. NYC, Sept. 12, 1940; d. Anthony M. and Eleanor (Hayes) Gisolfi; m. Philip Pechukas, June 15, 1963 (div. Sept. 1991); children: Rolf, Maria, Sarah, Fiona (dec.), Amy. Student, Manhattanville Coll., Purchase, NY, 1958-60; BA magna cum laude, Radcliffe Coll., Cambridge, Mass., 1962; postgrad., Yale U., New Haven, Conn., 1962-63; MA, U. Chgo., 1964, PhD, 1976. Instr. CUNY, 1967-68, Marymount Manhattan Coll., NYC, 1977-79; asst. prof. art history Pratt Inst., Bklyn., 1979-84, assoc. prof., 1984-90, prof., 1990—, chmn. dept., 1981—99. Vis. asst. prof. Pratt Inst., 1976-79; dir. Pratt in Venice, Italy, 1984—; spkr. Conv. on Veronese, Venice, 1988, Conv. on Tintoretto, Venice, 1994, Symposium on Italian Art in Am., Fordham U., 1993, Mass. Coll. Art, 1998, AM Berger lecture, Manhattanville Coll., 2001; invited participant Veronese Reconsidered, CASVA, Washington, 1988; invited spkr. Coll. Art. Assn. 1990, 93, 95, 2002, 07, discussant session Benedictine patronage, Medieval Conf., Kalamazoo, Mich., 2003; invited spkr. Medievel Conf. Kalamazoo, Mich., 2004; chmn. two Renaissance Art sessions, Renaissance Soc. Meeting, NYC, 2004; chair session Alterations in Italian Art, Italian Art Soc., Coll. Art Assn., 2006; invited spkr. on antiquity Renaissance Soc. Meeting, Miami, 2007, session chair Life of St. Benedict. Illustrator: On Classic Ground, 1982; designer: Caudine Country, 1987; author: (with S. Sinding-Larsen) The Rule, the Bible, and the Council: The Library of the Benedictine Abbey at Praglia, 1998; contbr. articles to profl. jours. including Art Bull., Arte Veneta, Artibus et Historiae, Burlington Grove Dictionary of Art. Am. Philos. Soc. grantee, 1989, Delmas Found. grantee, 1995-96. Mem. Italian Art Soc., Renaissance Soc., Coll. Art Assn., Phi Beta Kappa. Democrat. Roman Catholic. Home: 843 President St Brooklyn NY 11215-1405 Office: Pratt Inst Dept Art History East 250 Brooklyn NY 11205 Office Phone: 718-636-3598. Personal E-mail: dianagisolfi@aol.com. Business E-Mail: dgisolfi@pratt.edu.

GISSLER, SIGVARD GUNNAR, JR., journalist, educator, retired editor; b. Chgo., July 2, 1935; s. Sigvard Gunnar Sr. and Louisa (Anderson) Gissler; m. Mary Catherine Engman, Oct. 23, 1954; children: Gary, Glenn, Gregory. BA in Am. Civilization, Lake Forest Coll., 1956, LLD (hon.), 1991; student, Northwestern U., 1958-61. News editor Ind. Register, Libertyville, Ill., 1958-59; exec. editor News-Sun, Waukegan, Ill., 1963-67; editl. writer Milw. Jour., 1967-77, editl. page editor, 1977-84, assoc. editor, 1984-85, editor, 1985-93; v.p. Jour. Comm., Milw., 1987-93, also bd. dirs.; sr. v.p. Jour./Sentinel Inc., Milw., 1987-93, also bd. dirs.; assoc. prof. grad. sch. journalism Columbia U., NYC, 1994—2003, acting assoc. dean, 1997, founder, dir. workshops on journalism, race and ethnicity, 1998-2000, sr. adviser, 2000—, adminstr. Pulitzer Prizes, 2002—, spl. faculty mem., 2003—. Vis. prof. dept. comm. Stanford U., 1993; mem. jury Pulitzer Prize. Recipient Disting. Svc. citation, Lake Forest Coll., 1977, Pub. of the Yr. award, Wis. Newspaper Assn., 1987, 1991, 1992; Journalism fellow, Stanford U., 1976, Sr. fellow, Freedom Forum Media Studies Ctr. Columbia U., 1993—94. Mem.: Soc. Profl. Journalists (Tchr. of the Yr. award 1998), Internat. Press Inst., Am. Soc. Newspaper Editors, Phi Beta Kappa. Home: 101 W 79th St Apt 6D New York NY 10024-6475 Home Phone: 212-595-2938; Office Phone: 212-854-7327. E-mail: sg138@columbia.edu.

GIST, HOWARD BATTLE, JR., lawyer; b. Alexandria, La., Sept. 17, 1919; s. Howard Battle and Marcie (Luckett) G.; m. Rosemary Flynn, Sept. 30, 1950; children: Howard Battle III, Marcie, Stephanie, Robert C., Ellen K., William M. Student, Washington and Lee U., 1936—38; BA, Tulane U., 1941, JD, 1943. Bar: La. 1943. Of counsel Gist Firm, Alexandria, La. Bd. dirs. Security First Nat. Bank, Alexandria, chmn. bd., 1983-93, dir. emeritus, 1993. Named 2000 Disting. Atty., La. Bar Found., 2000. Fellow Am. Coll. Trial Lawyers; mem. La. State Bar Assn. (pres. 1977-78), Alexandria Bar Assn. (pres. 1967), La. Def. Attys. Assn. (past pres.), La. Def. Attys. (pres. 1972-73), La. State Law Inst. (mem. coun. 1964—, past v.p.). Office: The gist Firm 4119 Parliament Dr Ste 101 Alexandria LA 71303-1871 also: PO Box 13705 Alexandria LA 71315 Home Phone: 318-442-5708; Office Phone: 318-448-1632.

GIST, JOHN MONTFORT, publishing executive, educator; b. Denver, Oct. 26, 1963; s. Christopher Gist and Phyllis Ann (Angevine) Jozwik. BA, U. Wyo., 1992; MFA, U. Alaska, 1996. Editor, pub. Exegesis Writing Svcs., Laramie, Wyo., 1992-96; tchr. English U. Alaska, Fairbanks, 1994-96; owner Gist Ink. Writing Cons., 2000—; prof. creative non-fiction Western Carolina U., 2001—; owner, editor-in-chief High Sierra Books, 2003—06. Adj. prof. English Western N.Mex. U. Author: Crow Heart, 1999, Lizards Dreaming of Birds, 2004; co-author: Angst & Evolution, 2007; editor: Plants for Profit, 1998, Perennial Plants for Profit, 1998, Angst and Evolution, 2007; editor: The Greenhouse & Nursery Handbook, 1999, Illustrated Handbook of Landscape Plants, 2000, Make Money Growing Trees, 2000, Creation Through Evolution, 2000, The Voice of Creation, 2000, The Dawn of Satisfaction, 2001, The Liberty of Man & Eternity of Mind, 2002, Beyond Charles Darwin, 2003, Environmental Vitalism, 2004. Tchr. Acad. Decathlon, Fairbanks, 1994-96, Upward Bound, Laramie, 1998—. Mem. Am. Philos. Assn., Nat. Assn. Scholars, Poets and Writers, U. Alaska Alumni Assn., U. Wyo. Alumni Assn. Avocations: hunting, fishing, reading, quantum theory. Personal E-mail: gist@cybermesa.com.

GIST, WILLIAM CLAUDE, JR., retired dentist; b. Chattanooga, May 14, 1935; s. William Claude and Dorothy Virginia (Gibbs) Gist; m. Barbara Roppel Babcock, May 9, 2003. BSc, U. Tenn., Knoxville, 1958; DMD, U. Louisville, 1967. Diplomate Am. Bd. Forensic Dentistry, Am. Bd. Forensic Medicine, Am. Bd. Forensic Examiners. Pvt. practice, Louisville, 1967-2001. Chmn. celebrations Bicentennial of Pres. Zachary Taylor's Birth, Louisville, 1984; pres. Louisville Civil War Roundtable, 1990-91. Recipient Presdl. commendation Pres. Ronald Reagan, 1985, DAR medal of honor, 1996, DAR history award, 1985. Mem.: ADA (life), Gen. Soc. War 1812 (Ky. pres. 1986—88, v.p. gen. 1990—93, 2001—), Hereditary Order Descs. Loyalists-Patriots, Gen. Soc. Sons Revolution, Nat. Soc. Sons and Daus. of Pilgrims (Ky. gov. 1990—93), Colonial Order of Acorn, Gen. Soc. Colonial Wars, Jamestowne Soc., Order Ams. Armorial Ancestry, Magna Charta Barons (Somerset chpt.), Nat. Gavel Soc., Nat. Order of the Blue and Gray (comdg. gen. 1996—98), Continental Soc. Sons of Indian Wars (nat. gov. 1990—92), Nat. Soc. SAR (Ky. pres. 1985—86, nat. chmn. centennial observances com. 1985—90, nat. trustee 1986—87, v.p. gen. Ctrl. dist. 1989—90, nat. chmn. hdqrs. com. 1989—94, historian gen. 1991—93, registrar gen. 1993—94, sec. gen. 1994—95, pres. gen. 1995—96, nat. chmn. nominating com. 1996—97, dir. mus. 1998—, nat. chmn. ethics com. 1999—2003, Gold Good Citizenship award 1996, Minuteman award 1990, Disting. Svc. medal 1999), St. Matthews Hist. Soc. (life), Ky. Hist. Soc. (life), Louisville Dental Soc. (life), Ky. Dental Assn. (life), Aztec Club, Filson Club (life), Buechel Rotary Club (pres. 1979—80), Honorable Order of Ky. Cols., Order Stars-Bars (Ky. comdr. 1988—90), Kappa Sigma (asst. dist. grand master 1999—). Republican. Roman Catholic. Avocations: history, genealogy, historic preservation.

GITELSON, SUSAN AURELIA, corporate executive, philanthropist; b. NYC; d. Moses Leo and Miriam Evelyn (Silverman) G. BA, Barnard Coll.; MIA, Columbia Sch. Internat. Affairs; PhD, Columbia U.; postgrad., Univ. Calif., Berkeley; degree (hon.), Hebrew U., 2004. Trainee Rockefeller Found.; asst. prof. internat. rels. Hebrew U., Jerusalem; rsch. assoc. Columbia U., NYC; dir. internat. affairs and third world World Jewish Congress, NYC; pres. Internat. Cons., Inc., NYC, Magic Touch Icewares Internat. Corp., NYC. Author: Multilateral Aid for National Development and Self-Reliance; editor, author: Israel in the Third World; contbr. articles to profl. jours.; mem. editl. com. Jerusalem Papers on Peace Problems. Mem. nat. adv. coun., sponsor Gitelson Essay awards Ctr. for Study of Presidency, Washington; co-chair dean's coun. Columbia Sch. Internat. and Pub. Affairs, sponsor Dr. Susan Aurelia Gitelson Fund for Innovative Programs; pres. Dr. Susan Aurelia Gitelson Found. Inc.; sponsor Gitelson Lecture on Human Rights and U.S. Fgn. Policy Columbia U.; sponsor Gitelson award for human values in internat. affairs Columbia Sch. Internat. and Pub. Affairs; sponsor Gitelson-Meyerowitz Human Rights essay award Columbia Ctr. for Study of Human Rights; sponsor Gitelson Peace prize Truman Inst.; sponsor Gitelson Peace Papers and Publs.; mem. bd. overseers Truman Inst. Hebrew U., Jerusalem; v.p. bd. dirs. Am. Friends of Hebrew U.; mem. Columbia U. seminars; trustee Nat. Com. Am. Fgn. Policy; sponsor Dr. Susan Aurelia Gitelson Fund for Innovative Programs Columbia U. Faculty Arts and Scis.; sponsor Gitelson Policy Forum Columbia Sch. Internat. and Pub. Affairs; trustee Sutton Pl. Synagogue, sponsor Gitelson-Meyerowitz Disting. Svc. award; mem. internat. bd. govs. Hebrew Univ. Jerusalem; mem. bd. overseers Mus. Jewish Heritage-A Living Meml. to the Holocaust. Recipient Outstanding Service award, Columbia Sch. Internat. and Public Affairs, Alumni medal for conspicuous svc., Columbia U. Mem. Nat. Inst. Social Scis., Columbia Sch. Internat. and Pub. Affairs Alumni Assn. (pres. 1980-84), Columbia U. Alumni Fedn. (mem. exec. com.), Nat. Com. on Am. Fgn. Policy (mem. bd. trustees), Carnegie Coun. on Ethics and Fgn. Affairs, Am. Jewish Com., Women's Fgn. Policy Group. Office Phone: 212-679-5260. Personal E-mail: susangitel@aol.com.

GITENSTEIN, DONNA M., academic administrator; b. Florala, Fla. m. Donald Hart; children: Pauline, Samuel. BA in English, Duke U.; PhD in English and Am. Lit., U. N.C., Chapel Hill. Asst. prof. English Ctrl. Mo. State U.; prof. English SUNY, Oswego, chair English dept., assoc. provost; provost Drake U., 1992—98, exec. v.p., 1997—98; pres. Coll. of N.J., Ewing, 1998—. Commr. Mid. States Commn. on Higher Edn. Author: (book) Apocalyptic Messianism and Contemporary Jewish-Am. Poetry; contbr. articles and reviews on Jewish and Am. Lit. Named Salute to Policy Makers, Exec. Women of N.J., 2002, Tribute to Women, YWCA of Princeton, N.J., 2003; recipient Woman of Distinction award, Girl Scouts of Del.-Raritan Coun., 2002. Mem.: Am. Coun. on Edn. (mem. commn. on minorities in higher edn., pres. sponsor (N.J. chapt.) network of women leaders in higher edn.). Office: Office of the Pres Coll of NJ PO Box 7718 Ewing NJ 08628

GITLER, BERNARD, cardiologist, critical care specialist; b. Munich, Aug. 14, 1950; arrived in U.S., 1953, naturalized, 1957; s. Abe and Lola (Greenberg) G.; m. Ellen Spielman, Aug. 4, 1974; children: Stefanie, Cynthia, Bryan. BS in Chemistry, MIT, 1972, BS in Life Scis., 1972; MD, Cornell U., 1976. Diplomate Nat. Bd. Med. Examiners; diplomate in internal medicine, cardiovasc. diseases, critical care medicine Am. Bd. Internal Medicine; cert. Nat. Bd. Echocardiography; cert. Bd. Nuclear Cardiology. Resident in internal medicine Bronx Mcpl. Hosp. Ctr., Albert Einstein Coll. Medicine, Bronx, NY, 1976—79; cardiology fellow Montefiore Med. Ctr., Albert Einstein Coll. Medicine, 1979—81, chief fellow, 1980—81; clin. instr. Albert Einstein Coll. Medicine, 1981—84, asst. clin. prof. medicine, 1984—92, assoc. clin. prof. medicine, 1992—; attending cardiologist Sound Shore Med Ctr. Westchester, New Rochelle, 1981—; chief divsn. cardiology Sound Shore Med. Ctr. Westchester, 2002—, dir. Chest Pain Ctr., 2005—, dir. cardiology fellowship program, 2005—; assoc. attending cardiologist Montefiore Med. Ctr., Bronx, 1981—; pvt. practice cardiology Westchester Heart Specialists, New Rochelle, 1981—; asst. attending cardiologist Columbia-New York. Presbyn. Med. Ctr., NYC, 1992—; asst. prof. clin. medicine Columbia U., 1992—; attending cardiologist Westchester Med. Ctr., 2002—. Adj. assoc. prof. medicine N.Y. Med. Coll., 2006—; physician cons. Island Peer Rev. Orgn., N.Y., 1985-88; faculty senator Albert Einstein Coll. Medicine, 1987-89, co-dir. cardiology curriculum New Rochelle Hosp. Med. Housestaff, 1985-92; attending cardiologist dept. electrocardiography Montefiore Med. Ctr., Bronx, 1983—; pres. med. staff Sound Shore Med. Ctr. Westchester, 1996-99, bd. govs., 1993-99, clin. cardiology rschr., 1985—. Referee Am. Heart Jour., 1983-95, Jour. Am. Coll. Cardiology, 1987-89, N.Y. State Jour. of Medicine, 1990-91, Chest, 1998—; contbr. articles to profl. jours. Recipient Attending of the Yr. award Montefiore Hosp. Med. House Staff, 1985, Tchr. of the Yr. award New Rochelle Hosp. and Med. Ctr., 1986, William C. Schraft Jr. Meml. Tchg. award New Rochelle Hosp., 1996, Robert D. Brandstetter Meml. Tchg. award Sound Shore Med. Ctr. Westchester, 2006. Fellow: ACP (Outstanding Tchg. Preceptorship award 1996, Cmty. Based Excellence in Tchg. award 2004), NY Cardiol. Soc., Am. Soc. Nuc. Cardiology, Am. Heart Assn., Am. Coll. Cardiology, Am. Soc. Echocardiography, Am. Coll. Chest Physicians; mem.: AMA, NY Acad. Scis., Am. Coll. Sports Medicine, NY State Med. Soc., Soc. Chest Pain Ctrs., Am. Assn. Med. Rsch., Am. Med. Athletic Assn., Soc. Critical Care Medicine, Nat. Strength and Conditioning Assn., Mensa, Phi Beta Kappa, Phi Lamba Upsilon. Democrat. Jewish. Achievements include completion of ten marathons. Avocations: Okinowan Goju-ryu karate (black belt), marathon running. Office: Westchester Heart Specialists 150 Lockwood Ave New Rochelle NY 10801-4916 Personal E-mail: bgmd@aol.com.

GITLIN, RICHARD D., telecommunications technology executive; BS with honors, CCNY; MS, Columbia U., PhD in Elec. Engring. Sr. v.p. comms. and network rsch. Bell Labs.; CTO Lucent's Data Networking Bus. Unit; v.p. tech., chief tech. officer NEC Labs Am.; chief tech. officer Hammerhead Sys. Inc., 2006—. Prof. elec. engring. Columbia U.; adv. com. mem. Computer Sci. and Engring. NSF. Contbr. articles to profl. jours.; edtl. bd. Jour. Comms. Networks; co-author: Data Comms. Principles, 1992. Co-recipient Thomas Alva Edison Patent Award, 2005; vis. scholar Bell Labs. fellow. Fellow: IEEE; mem.: NAE. Office: Hammerhead Sys, Inc 640 Clyde Ct Mountain View CA 94043 Office Phone: 650-210-3318. E-mail: richgitlin@ieee.org.

GITLOW, ABRAHAM LEO, retired dean; b. NYC, Oct. 10, 1918; s. Samuel and Esther (Boolhack) G.; m. Beatrice Alpert, Dec. 12, 1940; children: Allan Michael, Howard Seth. BA, U. Pa., 1939; MA, Columbia U., 1940, PhD, 1947. Substitute instr. Bklyn. Coll., 1946-47; instr. NYU, NYC, 1947-50, asst. prof., 1950-54, assoc. prof., 1954-59, prof. econs., 1959-89, prof. emeritus, 1989—; acting dean NYU Coll. Bus. and Pub. Adminstrn., 1965-66, dean, 1966-85, dean emeritus, 1989—. Hon. dir. Bank Leumi USA; pres. bd. edn. Ramapo (N.Y.) Ctrl. Sch. Dist. 2, 1963-66; pres., sec. Samuel and Esther Gitlow Found., Miami Beach, Fla. Author: Economics of the Mt. Hagen Tribes, New Guinea, 1947, Economics, 1962, Labor and Manpower Economics, 1971, Being the Boss: The Importance of Leadership and Power, 1992, NYU's Stern School: A Centennial Retrospective, 1995, Reflections on Higher Education: A Dean's View, 1995, Corruption in Corporate America, 2005, 2007; co-editor: General Economics: A Book of Readings, 1963; contbr. articles to profl. jours. Served to 1st lt. USAAF, 1943-46, PTO. Recipient Univ. medal Luigi Bocconi U., 1983. Mem. Am. Econ. Assn. Home and Office: 9 Island Ave Apt T3 Miami Beach FL 33139-1349

GITNER, GERALD L., air transportation executive, investment banker; b. Boston, Apr. 10, 1945; s. Samuel and Sylvia (Berkovitz) Gitner; m. Deanne Gebell, June 24, 1968; children: Daniel Mark, Seth Michael. BA cum laude, Boston U., 1966. Staff v.p. TransWorld Airlines, NYC, 1972-74; sr. v.p. mktg. and planning Tex. Internat. Airlines, Houston,

1974-80; pres., founder People Express Airlines, Newark, 1980-82; chmn. Pan Am. World Svcs. Inc., NYC, 1982-85, exec. v.p., chief fin. officer, 1983-85; vice chmn. Pan Am. World Airways, NYC, 1982-85, Pan Am Corp., 1984-85; pres. Tex. Air Corp., Houston, 1985-86; CEO, pres. ATASCO USA, Inc., aircraft trading firm, NYC, 1986-89; chmn. D. G. Assocs. Inc., 1986—, Avalon Group, Ltd., NYC, 1990-98; co-chmn. Global Aircraft Leasing Ltd., 1991-98; dir. TWA, Inc., 1993—2002, CEO, 1996-99, chmn., 1997—2002; chmn. bd. Kitty Hawk, Inc., 2002—07; dir. Tricom, S.A., 2004—. Bd. advisers econs. dept. Boston U.; mem. chancellors coun. U. Mo., St. Louis, 1997—2000. Trustee, mem. exec. com. Boston U., 1984—96; trustee Rochester (N.Y.) Inst. Tech., 1999—2004. Recipient Disting. Alumni award, Boston U., 1982, 1984. Mem.: Cornell Club N.Y., Phi Alpha Theta.

GITTER, ALLAN REINHOLD, lawyer; b. Yonkers, NY, Aug. 26, 1936; s. George Reinhold and Katherine (Allan) G.; divorced; children: Alison, Ryne, Kent; m. Sandra Case Gitter, Apr. 2, 1988. BA, Washington & Lee U., 1958; LLB, U. Mich., 1961. Bar: NC 1963, US Dist. Ct. (mid., ea. and we. dists.) NC 1964, US Ct. Appeals (4th cir.) 1964, US Dist. Ct. (mid. dist.) Pa. 1998, US Dist. Ct. (ea. dist.) Pa. 2006. From assoc. to ptnr. Womble, Carlyle, Sandridge & Rice, Winston-Salem, NC, 1969—. Fellow: Am. Coll. Trial Lawyers; mem.: Am. Bd. Trial Advs. Home: 1077 E Kent Rd Winston Salem NC 27104-1113 Office: Womble Carlyle Sandridge & Rice One W 4th St Winston Salem NC 27101 Office Phone: 336-721-3615. Personal E-mail: agitter@wcsr.com.

GITTER, MAX, lawyer; b. Samarkand, Uzbekistan, Nov. 17, 1943; came to U.S., 1950; s. Wolf and Paula (Nissenbaum) G.; m. Elisabeth Karla Gesmer, June 22, 1969; children: Emily F., Michael A. AB, Harvard U., 1965; LLB, Yale U., 1968. Bar: N.Y., D.C., U.S. Dist. Ct. (so. and ea. dists.) N.Y., U.S. Ct. Appeals (2d, D.C., 4th and 9th cirs.), U.S. Supreme Ct. Instr. U. Chgo. Law Sch., 1968-69; assoc. Paul, Weiss, Rifkind, Wharton & Garrison, NYC, 1969-76, ptnr., 1976-99, Cleary, Gottlieb, Steen & Hamilton, NYC, 1999—. Vis. lectr. law Yale U., 1986-88; mem. Internat. Steering Com. on Free Trade with Israel; vice-chmn., Yivo Inst. for Jewish Rsch. Spl. counsel Mayor of N.Y.C. to Investigate Office of Chief Medical Examiner, 1985. Mem. Fed. Bar Coun., Assn. Bar City of N.Y. (vice chmn. com. on profl. and jud. ethics 1985-86), Am. Law Inst. (spkr., panelist 1985-89), Practicing Law Inst. (spkr., panelist 1983-92), N.Y. State Bar Assn. (exec. com. sect. on comml. and fed. litigation 1994-99), Internat. Arbitration Inst. Office: Cleary Gottlieb Steen & Hamilton Rm 200 One Liberty Plz Ste 4300 New York NY 10006-1470 Office Phone: 212-225-2610. Business E-Mail: mgitter@cgsh.com.

GITTERMAN, ALEX, social work educator; b. Kolomea, Poland; came to U.S., 1948; s. Paul and Fay (Hirsch) G.; m. Naomi Janet Pines, Sept. 1963; children: Daniel Paul, Sharon Lynn. BA, Rutgers U., 1960; MSW, Hunter Coll., 1962; EdD, Columbia U., 1972. Div. dir. Bronx River Settlement, 1962-65; dir. East Side House Millbrook Ctr., Bronx, 1965-66; mem. faculty Columbia U., NYC, 1966—, prof., 1972—, assoc. dean, 1981-85; mem. faculty U. Conn. Sch. Social Work, 2000—. Cons. Manhattan VA, N.Y.C., 1974-80, Family Service of Westchester (White Plains), N.Y., 1978-80, Bur. Child Welfare, 1977-80, Drug Abuse Prevention Program, Archdiocese of N.Y., 1985—, Keio Acad.; vis. prof. U. Conn. Sch. Social Work, 2000--. Author: (with C.B. Germain) The Life Model of Social Work Practice, 1980, (with L. Shulman) Mutual Aid Groups and The Life Cycle, 1986, Handbook of Social Work Practice with Vulnerable Populations, 1991, Mutual Aid Groups, Vulnerable Populations and the Life Cycle, 1994, (with C.B. Germain) The Life Model of Social Work Practice: Advances in Theory and Practice, 1996, Handbook of Social Work Practice with Vulnerable and Resilient Populations, 2001, Mutual Aid Groups, Vulnerable and Resilient Populations and the Life Cycle, 2005; contbr. articles to profl. jours. Recipient Hexter award Hunter Coll., 1981 Mem. Con. on Social Work Edn., Nat. Assn. Social Workers Democrat. Jewish. Office: U Conn Sch Social Work 1798 Asylum Ave West Hartford CT 06117-2001 Office Phone: 860-570-9016. Business E-Mail: Alex.Gitterman@uconn.edu.

GITTES, FRANKLIN M., lawyer; b. Newark, 1947; BSChE, Lehigh U., 1969; JD, Georgetown U., 1973. Bar: DC 1973, NY 1975. Law clk. to Hon. John Biggs, Jr. US Ct. Appeals (3d cir.), 1973-74; ptnr., corp. mergers and acquisitions Skadden, Arps, Slate Meagher & Flom, NYC. Editor: Georgetown Law Jour., 1972-73; contbr. articles to jours. Office: Skadden Arps Slate Meagher & Flom 4 Times Sq New York NY 10036 Office Phone: 212-735-3760. Office Fax: 917-777-3760. Business E-Mail: fgittes@skadden.com.

GITTINGER, D. WAYNE, lawyer; b. Kellogg, Idaho, Jan. 22, 1933; s. Daniel Reese and Evelyn Caroline (Knudson) G.; 1 child, Marni; m. Anne Elizabeth Nordstrom, Dec. 17, 1984; stepchildren: John Hopen, Susan Dunn. BA, U. Wash., 1955, JD, 1957. Bar: Wash. 1957, U.S. Ct. Appeals (9th cir.) 1957, Tax Ct. of U.S., U.S. Supreme Ct. Teaching assoc. Northwestern U. Law Sch., Chgo., 1957-58; ptnr. Lane Powell PC, Seattle, 1959—. Active U. Wash. Alumni Assn., 1965—. Lt. USCGR, 1958-67. Mem. Vintage Club, Seattle Golf Club, Seattle Yacht Club, 101 Club, Overlake Golf and Country Club (past pres. 1978-79). Republican. Avocations: golf, yachting. Office: Lane Powell PC 1420 5th Ave Ste 4100 Seattle WA 98101-2338 Office Phone: 206-223-7053. E-mail: gittingerw@lanepowell.com.

GITTINGER, LAURIE ELLEN, music educator, elementary school educator; b. Berea, Ohio, May 17, 1964; d. William Alfred and Patricia Ann Gittinger. MusB in Instrumental Music Edn., Bowling Green State U., 1986; MA in Adminstrn., Furman U., 1997. Cert. Music Education K-12 SC. State Dept. Edn., 1987, Educational Leadership K-8 SC. State Dept. Edn., 1997. Asst. dir. bands, instr. strings Bowling Green City Schs., Ohio, 1986—87; dir. bands D.W. Daniel HS, Clemson, 1987—89; dir. strings program Travelers Rest High/Blue Ridge Mid./NW Mid./Gateway Elem., Greer, 1989—97; supervising coop. tchr. Furman U. and Bob Jones U., Greenville, 1991—97; lead tchr. strings Sch. Dist. Greenville County, 1992—97; state pres., pres.-elect, and festival chmn. SC Music Educators Assn., 1993—2001; program coord., adminstrv. asst. Beck Acad. Mid. Sch., 1997—2002; program dir. The 21st Century Cmty. Learning Ctr. After Sch. Program, 1999—2002; program coord. Bob Jones U., 1999—2002; dir. bands, program coord., adminstrv. asst. J.L. Mann HS, 2002—03; dir. bands LaGrange HS and Gardner Newman Mid. Sch., 2003—05, Westside Fine Arts Magnet Sch., La Grange, Ga., 2005—. Percussion instr. Travelers Rest HS, Travelers Rest, 1990—98; strings coach Carolina Youth Symphony Repertory Orch., Greenville, 1997—2000; guest condr. full orch. Florence City Sch. Dist., 1999—2000; accompanist St. Giles Presbyn. Ch., Greenville, 2001—02; program dir. Mathematica Policy Rsch. Program, Washington, 2000—02; accompanist St. Giles Presbyterian Ch., Greenville; rep. Greenville County Schools Tchr. Yr. Luncheon, 2000—01; coord. United Way Beck Mid. Sch., 1999—2000; mentor Greenville Sch. Dist. ADEPT Program, 1997—98; participant Ohio State U. Midwest Summer String Conf., 1997—98; sponsor Mid. Sch. Beta Club, 2000—02; participant Master Scheduling Com. Greenville Schs., 2001—02; guest condr. Florence City Sch. Dist., 2000—00; guest spkr. Anderson County Sch. Dist. Adminstrn. Students, 1996—99; adjudicator SC Music Educators Assn., Greenville, 1997—2000; mem. sch. dist. fine arts adv. coun. Troup County Schs., 2003—. Musician (performer): (orchestra performance in carniege hall) Lexington County School District (Invitation/Cert., 1992); percussion director (south carolina upper state marching fest) Performance (Third in Upper State of SC., 1993). Ch. accompanist adult/elem. chior program St. Giles Presbyn. Ch., Greenville, 2001—02. Named one of Superior Drumline/Marching Percussion Travelers, Rest HS; named to Nat. Residence Hall Honorary, Bowling Green State U.; recipient SC Outstanding Performance award for Bands, Daniel HS, Keith Montgomery Outstanding Music Performance award, Port Clinton HS, Nat. Hon. Roll Outstanding Educators, 2005—06. Fellow: Ga. Music Educators Assn., Nat. Residence Hall Hon. (life Outstanding Performance in Residence Hall); mem.: Assn. Supervision and Curriculum Devel., Music Educators Nat. Conf. Achievements include winning the Bowling Green State Univ. Music Dept. organ competition; receiving an invitation/performance to Washington DC for Band Program of Daniel HS, Clemson, SC; invitation to Blue Ridge HS Orch. to Univ. of Mississippi's Tenth Annual Am. Honor Orchestra Conf; invitation from LaGrange High Marching Band to perform for 65th Celebration of Pearl Harbor Honorary Parade, Hawaii. Office: Westside Fine Arts Magnet Middle Sch 301 Forrest Ave Lagrange GA 30240 Home Phone: 706-837-0556; Office Phone: 706-883-1550. Home Fax: 706-812-7976. Personal E-mail: gittingerle@troup.org.

GITTINS, TIMOTHY, military officer; b. IA, 1976; Instructor Captains Career Course, 2007—. Capt. 101st Airborne US Army, Co. C, 1st Sqdn., 61st Cav. Regt. Decorated Purple Heart, Bronze Star, General Douglas MacArthur Leadership Award; named one of The World's Most Influential People, TIME Mag., 2007. Southern Baptist. Office: Captains Career Course Fort Benning GA 31905*

GITTLEMAN, RICHARD M., lawyer; b. Providence; BA, Brown Univ., 1977; JD cum laude, Am. Univ., Washington, 1982. Bar: DC 1983. Ptnr., head project devel. and fin. practice group and chair info. tech. com. Akin Gump Strauss Hauer & Feld LLP, Washington. Scholar T. Morton McDonald Scholarship and Dean's Fellow, Am. Univ. Fluent in French. Office: Akin Gump Strauss Hauer & Feld LLP Robert S Strauss Bldg 1333 New Hampshire Ave NW Washington DC 20036-1564 Office Phone: 202-887-4444. Office Fax: 202-887-4288. E-mail: rgittleman@akingump.com.

GITTLER, JOSEPHINE, law educator; b. Richmond, Va., May 13, 1943; d. Joseph and Lamie Gittler. BA, Barnard Coll.; JD, Northwestern Coll., 1968. Bar: Conn. 1969. Law clk. US Dist. Ct., New Haven, 1969-70, Conn. Supreme Ct., Hartford, 1970-71, US Dist. Ct. Conn., 1971-72; assoc. prof. Coll. Law to prof. Coll. Pub. Health U. Iowa, Iowa City, 1973—2002, prof. Coll. Law, 2002—. Chief counsel subcommittee to investigate juvenile deliquency jud. com. US Senate, Washington, 1977-78; coord. US Surgeon Gen.'s Conf., Washington, 1988; mem. exec. com. Consortium Ctrs. on Children Families & Law, 1989-2000; legis. cons. Nat. Assn. State and Territorial Maternal and Child Health and Crippled Children's Progs., 1982-86, recipient Pub. Svc. award 1982, 84; counsel interim study com. juvenile justice Iowa Gen. Assembly, Des Moines, 1975-77; vis. scholar Justice Ctr. of Atlanta, 1999; cons. in field. Contbr. articles to profl. jours., chpts. to books. Chair Iowa Maternal and Child Health Adv. Coun., Des Moines, 1983-88; mem. Iowa Juvenile Justice Adv. Com., Des Moines, 1975—83, Iowa Crime Commn., Des Moines, 1974-75, interim com. Penal Reform and Correction, Des Moines, 1973-74. Office: Coll Law U Iowa 290 Boyd Law Bldg Iowa City IA 52242-1113 E-mail: josephine-gittler@uiowa.edu.

GITTLER, MICHELLE S., physiatrist; B, U. Mich., 1984; MD, U. Ill., Chgo. Diplomate Am. Bd. Phys. Medicine and Rehab. Residency Northwestern U. Med. Sch., Rehab. Inst. Chgo.; physiatrist, residency program dir. Schwab Rehab. Hosp., Chgo.; physiatrist Mount Sinai Hosp., Chgo., Weiss Meml. Hosp., Chgo., Cook County Hosp.; physiatrist, assoc. prof. surgery U. Chgo. Med. dir. spinal cord injury program. Mem.: Am. Acad. Phys. Medicine and Rehab., Assn. Acad. Physiatrists. Office: Schwab Rehab Hosp 1401 S California Blvd Chicago IL 60608

GIUFFRÉ, JOHN JOSEPH, lawyer; b. Bklyn., Nov. 30, 1963; s. John B. and Marilyn N. G.; m. Lauren P. Dippel, Sept. 1, 1990; children: John Paul, Danielle Emily. BA, Columbia Coll., 1984; JD cum laude, U. Pa., 1987. Bar: N.J. 1987, N.Y. 1988, Conn. 1988, Pa. 1988, U.S. Dist. Ct. (so. and ea. dists.) N.Y. 1989. Assoc. labor and employment law sect. Morgan, Lewis & Bockius, NYC, 1987-88; assoc. McLaughlin & McLaughlin, Bklyn., 1988-93; founding ptnr. Giuffré & Kaplan, PC, Hicksville, NY, 1994—2007, Giuffré Law Offices, PC, Floral Park, NY, 2007—. Editor: U. Pa. Jour. Comparative Bus. and Capital Market Law, 1985-86; sr. editor: U. Pa. Jour. Internat. Bus. Law, 1986-87. Vol. lawyer Bklyn. Bar Assn. Vol. Lawyer Project, 1992-93; trustee 1st Presbyn. Ch., Flushing, N.Y., 1991-92, pres. bd. trustees, 1993, elder, 1996—, Sunday Sch. tchr., 1989—; trustee Flushing Christian Sch., 1994-2002, pres. bd. trustees 2004—; mem. Nassau County Rep. Com., 2002—. Mem. Nassau County Bar Assn., Phi Beta Kappa. Office: Giuffré Law PC 99 Tulip Ave Ste 307 Floral Park NY 11001-1974 Office Phone: 516-358-5300.

GIUFFRIDA, THEODORE JOHN, dermatologist; BS, U. Fla., Gainesville, 1994; MD, Emory U., Atlanta, 1998. Intern Emory U.; resident dermatology U. Miami, 1999—2002; pvt. practice dermatology Miami, Fla., 2002—; mohs surgery fellow Dermatology and Skin Cancer Ctr., Leawood, Kans., 2003—04. Vol. faculty U. Miami, 2002—. Contbr. articles to profl. jours. Recipient Outstanding Surg. Resident award, U. Miami, 2002, Cancer Rsch. award, 2002, Resident Rsch. award, Sylvester Cancer Ctr., 2002; fellow, Am. Coll. Mohs Micrographic Surgery, 2003—04; Fla. Academic scholar, 1990—94. Mem.: Mohs Coll. (assoc.), Am. Acad. Dermatology (assoc.). Office: Dermatology and Skin Cancer Center 3275 Ponce de Leon Blvd Coral Gables FL 33134 Office Phone: 305-461-2000.

GIUFFRIDA, TOM A., publisher; b. Glendale, Calif., Feb. 24, 1946; s. Alfred and Anna (LiPera) G.; m. Judith Lynn Price, Aug. 22, 1970; children: Jeffrey, Gregory, Christopher. BA in Journalism, Calif. State U., Northridge, 1967. Copy editor Santa Barbara (Calif.) News-Press, 1967, 69-70; copywriter to asst. dir., promotion and pub. relations L.A. Times (Times Mirror), 1971-79; from promotion dir. to v.p. and gen. mgr. Atlanta Jour. & Constitution (Cox Enterprises), 1979-85; publisher Palm Beach (Fla.) Post, 1985—. Bd. dirs. Palm Beach County Cmty. Found. Lt. (j.g.) USNR, 1967-69. Mem. Am. Newspaper Pubs. Assn., Fla. Press Assn. (pres. 1995-96), Soc. Profl. Journalists, Palm Beach Yacht Club. Home: 6325 S Flagler Dr West Palm Beach FL 33405 Office Phone: 561-820-4124. E-mail: tgiuffrida@pbpost.com.

GIULIANI, JUDITH ANN, not-for-profit executive; b. Hazelton, Pa.; d. Donald and Joan Stish; m. Jeffrey Scott Ross, Dec. 8, 1974 (div. 1979); m. Bruce Nathan, 1979 (div. 1992); 1 child, Whitney; m. Rudy Giuliani, May 24, 2003. From 2000-06, Mrs. Giuliani was a Managing Director of Changing Our World, Inc., a national fundraising and philanthropic services company headquartered in New York. She is a registered nurse with an extensive medical and scientific background. She worked with U.S. Surgical Corporation and Bristol-Myers Squibb. Mrs. Giuliani coordinated the efforts at the Family Assistance Center on Pier 94 in the aftermath of the September 11, 2001 terrorist attacks. In 2001, she became a founding member of the Board of Trustees of the Twin Towers Fund, which raised and distributed all of the $216 million to over 600 families/individuals. Contributions to the fund helped to create the TTF Scholarship Fund, and America's Camp for victims' children. Mrs. Giuliani currently serves as the Executive Director of the Campaign for Saint Vincent Catholic Medical Centers in New York. This campaign includes the construction of a state-of-the-art Level 1 Trauma Center. As the only Level 1 Trauma Center below 14th Street, Saint Vincent's plays a key role in protecting the lives of hundreds of thousands of New Yorkers and visitors to New York City. The Trauma Center will also include a comprehensive educational and instructional component focusing on bio-terrorism. Mrs. Giuliani is the recipient of numerous awards, including the New York Junior League's "Community Award" for her commitment, support and love for New York City and its people. In November, 2005, she received the "Spirit of Cabrini Service Award" from the Cabrini Mission Foundation for her work with Cabrini High School for Girls in the Bronx. This award is presented to those who represent the finest in the tradition of public service to the community and who are involved in the facets of charity and philanthropy which are the hallmarks of the Cabrini Mission Foundation: healing, teaching and caring. In 2006, Mrs. Giuliani was awarded New York University's College of Nursing's "Humanitarian Award" in recognition of using her nursing identity for humanitarian work and charitable endeavors as well as for being a powerful voice that enhances the visibility of nursing and elevates the profession. Also in 2006, Mrs. Giuliani received the "St. Francis Xavier Cabrini Service Award" from Mother Cabrini High School an award honoring her commitment to young women and their education. She was further honored by the McCarton Foundation, who presented Mrs. Giuliani with their "Leadership Award" at the foundation's "Celebration of Learning 2006." The McCarton School is a full-time school in New York City dedicated to the treatment of children with autistic spectrum disorders. Mrs. Giuliani is a frequent speaker on medically related philanthropic issues. *

GIULIANI, RUDY (RUDOLPH WILLIAM LOUIS GIULIANI III), consultant, lawyer, former mayor; b. Bklyn., May 28, 1944; s. Harold A. and Helen (D'Avanzo) Giuliani; m. Regina Peruggi, Oct. 26, 1968 (annulled 1982); m. Donna Hanover, Apr. 15, 1984 (div. July 10, 2002); children: Andrew, Caroline; m. Judith Nathan, May 24, 2003. AB, Manhattan Coll., 1965; JD magna cum laude, NYU, 1968. Law clk. to Hon. Lloyd F. McMahon US Dist. Ct. (So. dist.) NY, NYC, 1968-70; asst. U.S. atty. (So. dist.) N.Y. US Dept. Justice, 1970-73, exec. asst. U.S. atty., chief narcotics sect., and chief spl. prosecutions sect., 1973-75, assoc. dep. atty. gen., 1975-77, assoc. atty. gen., 1981-83, U.S. atty. (So. dist.) N.Y., 1983-89; atty. Patterson, Belknap, Webb and Tyler, NYC, 1977-81, White & Case, NYC, 1989-90, Anderson Kill Olick & Oshinsky PC, NYC, 1990-93; mayor N.Y.C., 1994—2001; chmn., CEO Giuliani Partners LLC, NYC, 2002—; ptnr. Bracewell & Giuliani, NYC, 2005—. Rep. candidate for mayor N.Y.C., 1989, 93; spkr. Rep. Nat. Convention, NYC, 2004; mem. Iraq Study Group, 2006. Author (with Ken Kurson): Leadership, 2002. Decorated Knight Commander of the British Empire; named Person of the Year, Time Mag., 2001, Consultant of the Year, Consultant mag., 2002. Republican. Office: Giuliani Partners 5 Times Sq New York NY 10036*

GIULIANO, LOUIS J., former industrial manufacturing company executive; BS in Chemistry, Syracuse U., 1968, MBA in Mktg., 1969. Various mgmt. positions Bendix, v.p., gen. mgr. Gen. Aviation Avionics divsn., v.p., group exec. Avionics Sys. Group Arlington, Va.; pres. Avionics Sys. Group Allied-Signal Aerospace Co.; v.p. def. ops. ITT Def., 1988; v.p. ITT Corp., 1988; sr. v.p. ITT Industries, Inc., pres., chief exec. def. and electronics White Plains, NY, 1991-98, pres., COO, 1998—2001, chmn., 2001—04, pres., CEO, 2001—04, non-exec. chmn., 2004. Mem. bd. govs. US Postal Service, Washington, 2005—. Mem. Nat. Def. Indsl. Assn. (vice chmn., bd. dirs.), Aerospace Industries Assn. (bd. govs.). Office: US Postal Svc 475 L Enfant Plz SW Rm 10300 Washington DC 20260

GIULIANO, NEIL GERARD, civil rights organization executive, former mayor; b. Bloomfield, NJ, Oct. 26, 1956; s. Jacqueline Ann (Enright) G. BA, Ariz. State U., 1979, MEd, 1983. Pres. Circle K. Internat., Chgo., 1977-78, conv. cons., 1983-91; counselor disabled students Ariz. State U., Tempe, 1980-81, pres. associated students, 1982-83, coord. leadership devel., 1983-87, constituent dir., 1988-91, dir. fed. and community rels., 1991; pres. Valley Achievement, Tempe, 1987—; mem. Tempe City Coun., 1990—94; vice mayor City of Tempe, 1992—94, mayor, 1994—2004; pres. Gay & Lesbian Alliance Against Defamation, 2005—. Speaker, trainer in field. Bd. dirs. Tempe Community Coun., 1990—2003, Valley Big Bros.-Big Sisters, Tempe, 1987—; pres. Tempe Leadership, Inc., 1990-91; mem. gov.'s task force on drug abuse, 1990—. Recipient Selected Participant award Ctr. for the Study of the Presidency Symposium, Washington, 1983. Mem. Tempe C. of C., Kiwanis (pres. 1986-87), Sigma Nu (conv. cons. 1988), Key Club Internat. (conv. cons. 1983-87). Republican. Roman Catholic. Avocations: reading, rock climbing, tennis.

GIULIANO, ROBERT PAUL, pharmacist; b. NYC, Mar. 7, 1943; s. Salvatore Anthony and Marie Rita (LoScalzo) G.; m. Maja Hreljanovic, July 2, 1966; children: Christopher Robert, Kenneth Paul. BS in Pharmacy, Fordham U., 1965; MS in Hosp. Pharmacy Adminstrn., L.I. U., 1970. Diplomate Am. Bd. Pharmacy, Nat. Registy Emergency Med. Technicians. Clin. pharmacist Columbia-Presbyn. Med. Ctr., NYC, 1965—70; dir. pharmacy dept. St. Barnabas Hosp., NYC, 1970—71; dir. dept. pharm. scis. Misericordia Hosp. Med. Ctr., NYC, 1971—78, adminstrv. dir. material mgmt., 1978—79, asst. adminstrv. dir., 1979—81; pres. Apotheke Assos. Ltd., NYC, 1980—81; pres., dir., CEO U.S. Home Health Care Corp. and Steri-Pharm subs., 1981—91; also chmn. bd.; mem. Tech. Adv. Svc. for Attys., 1988—. Pres. RPG Assoc., 1991—, pres. dir.; chmn. bd. Bryce Rx Labs Inc., 1995—; pres., dir. Red Rock Labs, Inc., 1997-99; v.p. Red Rock Rsch., 2001-06, Scarguard Labs, LLC, 2006—; affil. clin. instr. St. John's U., 1971-81; cons. Weleda Internat., 1991-92, Healix Health Care, 1992-96, Rye Beach Pharmacy, 1992-96, Champlain Valley Physicians Hosp., 1993-94, Columbia Presbyn. Med. Ctr., 1984-97, Transworld Home Health Corp., 1991-93, NY Med. Coll., 1992-95, ROR Group, 1992-93, Geneva Gen. Regional Hosp., 1994-95; home health care cons. Alternative Care Svcs., Inc., 1988-90, Robert Wood Johnson Found., 1985; clin. pharmacy adv. bd., 1971-81; exec. com. Bronx Emergency Med. Svcs. Coun., 1975-80; sr. emergency med. technician instr./coord. NY State Dept. Health, Bur. Emergency Med. Svcs., 1975-81; spkr.'s bur., CPR instr. AHA, 1975-81; CPR instr. Westchester Heart Assn., 1977-80; mem. spkrs. bur. Misericordia Hosp. Med. Ctr., Westchester County Soc. Hosp. Pharmacists; cons., surveyor Pharmacy Compunding Accreditation Bd., 2006—. Author: (with others) RX Technician Manual, 1994; editor: Misericordia Hosp. Pharmacy Newsletter, 1971-78. Asst. cubmaster Boy Scouts Am., Eastchester, NY, 1976-78; coach youth baseball T.Y.A., Eastchester, 1975-83. Mem. Am. Pharm. Assn., Italian Pharm Assn., Am. Soc. Cons. Pharmacists, Am. Soc. Healthcare Pharmacists, N.Y. State Coun. Hosp. Pharmacists, Nat. Assn. Sr. Emergency Med. Technician Instrs., Nat. Assn. Emergency Technicians (founding), Am. Soc. Parenteral-Enteral Nutrition, League IV Therapists, Nat. IV Therapy Assn., Nat. Assn. Retail Druggists, Pharmacy Compounding Ctrs. Am., Internat. Acad. Compounding Pharmacists, Fordham U. Pharmacy Alumni Assn. (dir. 1982-98, 1st v.p. 1990-91, pres. 1992-95), N.Y. Athletic Club. Republican. Roman Catholic. Home: 157 Oakland Ave Eastchester NY 10709-5403 Office: PO Box 1 Eastchester NY 10709-1403 Office Phone: 800-798-7279. Personal E-mail: bobgrx@optonline.net, brycerx@hotmail.com. Business E-Mail: rx@brycerx.com.

GIULIANO, ROSEMARY E., lawyer; b. Waterbury, Conn. BA, Smith Coll.; JD, Univ. Conn. Bar: Conn. 1979, US Dist. Ct. Conn. 1979. Ptnr. Giuliano & Richardson LLC, Woodbury, Conn. Mem.: Waterbury Bar Assn. (dir.), New Eng. Bar Assn. (pres. 2003, vp, dir.), Conn. Bar Assn. (pres. 1994—95, John Eldred Shields Meml. Disting. Prof. Svc. award 1999), ABA (bd. govs. 2005—). Office: Giuliano & Richardson LLC 39 Sherman Hill Rd Woodbury CT 06798-3650

GIULIANTI, MARA SELENA, mayor; b. NYC, June 3, 1944; d. Leon and Bertha (Jablonky) Berman; m. Donald Giulianti, May 29, 1966; children: Stacey Alexander, Michael Alan. BA, Tulane U., 1966. Social worker L.A. County Social Svcs., 1966-68; adminstrv. asst. neurosurg. cons. D. Giulianti, MD, Hollywood, Fla., 1980-83; campaign mgr. City Commr. Suzanne Gunzburger, Hollywood, 1982; mayor City of Hollywood, 1986-90, 92—. Vice chmn. Broward Employment and Tng. Adminstrn., 1987-89, 92-94, 96-00, 01-02, chmn., 1989-90, 94-96, 00-01, Work Force One chmn., 2002-04, 06-, chmn. pro tem, 2004-05, vice chair 2005-06; exec. bd. Fla. League Cities, Tallahassee, 1986-90, 92—), bd. dirs.; econ. devel. pol. com. Nat. League Cities, Washington, 1987-90, human devel. policy com., 1992-94, fin., adminstrn. and intergovtl. rels. steering com., 1994-02; active Broward County Met. Planning Orgn., 1986-90. Columnist The Digest, Hallandale, Fla., 2001-02, South Fla. Sun-Times, 2002—, Beach Digest, 2002-03; contbr. articles to local newspapers. Pres. Women in Distress, Broward County, 1982-83, bd. dirs., 1983-90, 2006—, trustee, 1994-97, 05-; exec. bd. Nat. Jewish Cmty. Rels. Adv. Coun., 1985-87; v.p. CHARLEE Family Care Homes, Broward County, 1986-88, bd. dirs., 1988-92; mem. Broward County Commn. on Status Women, 1984-86, Fla. Commn. on Drug and Alcohol Concerns, Tallahassee, 1984-85, Broward County Dem. Exec. Com., 1984-88; pres. Hills Dem. Club, 1991-94; trustee Graves Mus. of Archeol. and Nat. History, Dania, Fla., 1993-97; bd. dirs. Hollywood Econ. Growth Corp., 1994-95, 98-99; chmn. Hollywood Comty. Redevel. Agy., 1992—; v.p. South Broward unit Am. Cancer Soc., 1992-93, bd. dirs., 1993-99. Recipient Hannah G. Solomon award, 1983, Giraffe Stick Your Neck Out award Women's Advocacy--the Majority/Minority, 1986, Leadership award Leadership Hollywood Alumni, 1987, City of Peace award Israel Bonds, Broward County, 1987, Menorah award Histadrut, 1990, Juliette Gordon Low award Girl Scouts Broward County, 1997, Govt. Leadership award, ArtServe, 2002, Gracias award Hispanic Unity, 2000, Cmty. Covenant award, Broward Outreach Ctr., 2001, Breaking the Glass Ceiling award, Ziff Jewish Mus. of Fla., 2002, Spirit of Excellence award Am Bus. Women's Assn., 2003, Woman of Valor award Broward County Jewish Cmty. Ctr., 2003, Founders award Chaminade-Madonna Coll. Prep., 2004; named Broward County Woman of Yr., Am. Jewish Congress, 1988, Woman of Yr. Women in Comms., Inc., 1990, Crystal Vision award Hollywood Art and Culture Ctr., 2000; Honoree Boys & Girls Clubs of Broward, 2001, honoree Holocaust Documentation and Edn. Ctr., 2005; inducted Broward County Women's Hall of Fame, 1996. Mem. Nat. Coun. Jewish Women (nat. bd. dir. 1985-89), Jewish Fedn. So. Broward (chair community rels. com. 1981-82, bd. dir. 1982-90), Broward County Med. Aux. (br. pres. 1977-78), Rotary. Democrat. Avocations: writing, volunteer work, travel. Office: PO Box 229045 Hollywood FL 33022-9045 Home Phone: 954-961-5959; Office Phone: 954-921-3321. Business E-Mail: mgiulianti@hollywoodfl.org.

GIUSTI, JOSEPH PAUL, retired academic administrator, consultant; b. Harrisburg, Pa., Mar. 4, 1935; s. Joseph and Ellen C. (Carletti) G.; m. Marie D. Mazza, Jan. 30, 1960; children: Jeannine Carolyn, Lynn Christine, Susan Marie. BA in English Lit., Villanova U., 1957; MSBA, Pa. State U., 1959, PhD in Higher Edn. Adminstrn., 1962; LHD (hon.), St. Vincent Coll., 1976. Instr. dept. commerce and fin. Pa. State U., 1958-60, grad. asst., 1961-62, asst. to v.p., 1963-65, mem. grad. faculty, 1963-79, assoc. prof. higher edn., 1965-79; campus dir., chief exec. officer Beaver campus, 1965-79; chancellor univ., prof. higher edn. Ind. U.-Purdue U., Fort Wayne, 1979-85; prof. edn. Ind. U., 1985-87; dir. global human resource devel. edn. programs/scholarships AMP, Inc., 1987-98; ret., 1998; cons. AMP, Inc., 1998-99. Cons. hemolytic disease study group divsn. blood diseases and resources Nat. Heart, Lung and Blood Inst., NIH, 1975-79; mem. adv. com. Edn. Mgmt. Info. Sys., Commonwealth of Pa., 1971-79; mem. joint adv. coun. Ft. Wayne Med. Edn. Program, 1979-85; mem. exec. com. Ft. Wayne Future, Inc., 1979-85, Ft. Wayne Ednl. Found., 1979-85, Allen County (Ind.) United Way, 1979-80; sec. Beaver Campus Adv. Bd., 1966-79, dir. emeritus, 1979—; mem. Corp. Coun., Ft. Wayne, 1981-85, also bd. dirs. Contbr. articles on fin. mgmt. and ednl. adminstrn. to profl. publs.; contbr. chpts. to books on fin. mgmt. and edn. Bd. dirs. Med. Ctr. Beaver County, Pa., 1966-79, chmn. bd. dirs., 1972-75, dir. emeritus, 1979—; bd. dirs. Parkview Meml. Hosp., 1982-85. Recipient Beaver Campus Disting. Service award, 1974; Trustee award Community Coll. of Beaver County, 1972; Civic Improvement League award, 1972; Benjamin Rush award Med. Soc. of Beaver County, 1976; resolutions in his honor for contbrs. to edn. and health care delivery in state Pa. State Senate and Ho. Reps., 1979; Beaver Campus Community Cultural Ctr.'s 1000 seat amphitheater named in his honor, 1980; lit. collection named in his honor Beaver Campus Library, 1980 Mem. Greater Fort Wayne C. of C. (dir. 1981-85), Ind. U. Ft. Wayne Alumni Assn. (life dir. 1982—), Purdue U. Ft. Wayne Alumni Assn. (life dir. 1982—). Roman Catholic.

GIUSTI, WILLIAM ROGER, lawyer; b. NYC, Oct. 27, 1947; s. John Eletto and Rita Marie (Lucarini) G. AB, Columbia Coll., 1969; postgrad., Oxford U., 1969-71; JD, Yale U., 1974. Bar: N.Y. 1975. Law clk. to judge U.S. Ct. Appeals (2d cir.), NYC, 1974-75; assoc. Cravath, Swaine & Moore LLP, NYC, 1975—80, Shearman & Sterling LLP, NYC, 1980—82, ptnr., 1983—2006, Baker Botts LLP, NYC, 2006—. Mem.: Yale (N.Y.C.). Roman Catholic. Office: Baker Botts LLP 30 Rockefeller Plaza New York NY 10112-4498 Business E-Mail: william.giusti@bakerbotts.com.

GIVEN, KENNA SIDNEY, surgeon, educator; b. Charleston, W.Va., Nov. 22, 1938; s. Virgil and Chessie Given; m. Charlene K. Given; children: Kari, Patrick, Amy. BA, W.Va. U., 1960; MD, Duke U., 1964. Diplomate Am. Bd. Surgery, Am. Bd. Plastic Surgery (chairperson-elect 1996-97, bd. dirs. 1992—). Intern Ind. U. Med. Ctr., Indpls., 1964-65; resident, then chief resident gen. surgery Grady Meml. Hosp./Emory U. Hosp., Atlanta, 1965-69; asst. resident, then chief resident plastic surgery Duke U. Med. Ctr., Durham, NC, 1975-77; clin. instr. surgery Emory U., Atlanta, 1972-74; chief surgery Lanier Meml. Hosp., Langdale, Ala., 1974; prof., chief divsn. plastic surgery Med. Coll. Ga., Augusta, 1977—2001, med. dir. oper. rm., 1989-90. Assoc. dir. burn unit Med. Coll. Ga. Hosp.; cons. Augusta Correctional and Med. Instrn.; plastic surgery dir. Children's Med. Svc., 1981—; mem. Residency Rev. Commn. for Plastic Surgery, 1991-2001, chmn., 1994-96; chair Am. Bd. Plastic Surgery, Inc., 1997-99; chmn. residency rev. com. Accreditation Coun. for Grad. Med. Edn., 1994-96; lectr. in field. Contbr. articles to profl. jours. Pres. Med. Rsch. Found. Ga., 1985-88; trustee Plastic Surgery Edn. Found., 1994-97, pres.-elect, 1997; bd. dirs. Augusta Country Day Sch.; bd. dirs. Augusta Prep. Day Sch., 1988, trustee, 1989-90. Fellow ACS; mem. AMA, Am. Assn. Plastic Surgeons (trustee 1994-97), Assn. Acad. Chmn. in Plastic Surgery (pres. 1996-97, bd. dirs. 1985-88, 93—), Southeastern Plastic and Reconstructive Surgery (chmn. continuing med. edn. com. 1987, bd. dirs. 1992-95), Am. Soc. Plastic and Reconstructive Surgery (bd. dirs. 1988), Am. Assn. Hand Surgery, Am. Cleft Palate Assn., Am. Soc. Aesthetic Plastic Surgeons, Internat. Soc. Clin. Plastic Surgeons, Ga. Plastic Surgery Soc. (pres. 1985), Med. Assn. Ga., Richmond County Med. Soc., Southeastern Surg. Congress., So. Med. Assn., Southeastern Soc. Plastic and Reconstructive Surgeons (pres. 1997), So. Surg. Soc. Baptist. Home: 748 Tripps Ct Augusta GA 30909 Office: Med Coll Ga Divsn Plastic Surgery HB-5049 Augusta GA 30912-4080 Office Phone: 706-721-6945. Business E-Mail: kgiven@mcg.edu.

GIVEN, MARK, religious studies educator; b. Gassaway, W.Va., Oct. 14, 1961; s. James Bruce and Lola Faye Given; m. Janet Sue Griffin, June 6, 1982. BA, Alderson-Broaddus Coll., Philippi, W.Va.; MDiv, So. Bapt. Theol. Seminary, 1989; PhD in Religious Studies, U. NC, Chapel Hill, 1998. Asst. prof. Mo. State U., Springfield, 1998—2003, assoc. prof. religious studies, 2003—07. Author: (book) Paul's True Rhetoric: Ambiguity, Cunning, and Deception in Greece and Rome, 2001; contbr. articles to profl. jours. Recipient Soc. Bibl. Lit. Regional Scholar award, Southeastern Region Soc. Bibl. Lit., 1996, Coll. award for excellence in rsch., Mo. State U., 2002, U. Award in tchg., 2003. Mem.: Am. Guild Organists, Am. Acad. Religion, Soc. Bibl. Lit. Office: Mo State Univ 901 S National Ave Springfield MO 65897 Business E-Mail: markgiven@missouristate.edu.

GIVENCHY, HUBERT JAMES MARCEL TAFFIN DE, fashion designer; b. Beauvais, France, Feb. 20, 1927; s. Lucien and Béatrice (Badin) Taffin de G. Student, École nationale supérieure des beaux-arts. Faculty of Law U. Paris; Apprenticeship fashion houses of Lelong, 1945-46; apprentice fashion houses of Piquet, 1946-48; Apprenticeship fashion houses of Fath, 1948-49, Schiaparelli, 1949-51; opened his own fashion house, Paris, 1952—88; pres., dir. gen. Givenchy-Couture, 1954—; pres. Christie's France, 1997—. Pres. Cristobal Balenciaga Found., Spain, 2003. Designer costumes for films Breakfast at Tiffany's, 1961, Charade, 1963, Paris When It Sizzles, 1964, How To Steal a Million, 1966 Decorated chevalier Legion of Honor; recipient award for design excellence Chgo. Hist. Soc., 1995. Avocations: tennis; swimming; skiing; horseback riding.

GIVENS, JACK RODMAN, lawyer; b. Wichita, Kans., Oct. 28, 1928; s. Clarence William and Marie Irene (Smith) G.; m. Phyllis Jean Starner, May 22, 1955; children: Rene, Blake. BS in Mech. Engring., Okla. State U., 1955; LLB, U. Okla., 1958. Bar: Okla. 1958, U.S. Supreme Ct. 1971, U.S. Dist. Ct. (no. dist.) Okla. 1958, U.S. Dist. Ct. (we. dist.) Okla. 1959, U.S. Ct. Appeals (5th cir.) 1970, U.S. Ct Appeals (10th cir.) 1967, U.S. Tax Ct. 1976; U.S. Dist. Ct. (ea. dist.) Okla. 1989. Assoc. Spillers & Spillers, Tulsa, 1958-64; ptnr., dir. Jones, Givens, Gotcher & Bogan, Tulsa, 1964—2004; ptnr. Givens & Givens, PLLC, Tulsa, 2006—. Guest lectr. U. Okla., Norman, 1969, Tulsa U., 1992-93; faculty Okla. Bar Rev., 1970; adj. settlement judge U.S. Dist. Ct. (no. dist.) Okla., 1988—98; judge Okla. Temporary Ct. Appeals, 1982. Chmn. Citizens Bond Adv. Authority, Tulsa, 1976; mem., chmn. Okla. Jud. Nominating Commn., 1969-75; founding dir. Okla. Inst. for Justice, 1965. 1st lt. USAF, 1952-54. Fellow Am. Coll. Trial Lawyers, Am. Coll. Real Estate Lawyers, Am. Bar Found., Okla. Bar Found.; mem. Am. Judicature Soc. (dir. 1972), Am. Inns. of Ct. (master 1988, Outstanding Mem. award 1989, 91, Leadership award 1993), Okla. Bar Assn. (chmn. young lawyers conf. 1963, v.p. 1964, Lifetime Profl. award 2005), Tulsa County Bar Assn. (pres. 1967, Outstanding Atty. 1974, Golden Rule award, 1991), Order of Coif, Sigma Phi Epsilon, Sigma Tau, Phi Eta Sigma. Democrat. Methodist. Avocations: tennis, boating, fishing, history. Home: 10137 S 77th East Pl Tulsa OK 74133-6814 Office: Givens & Givens PLLC 1010 Williams Ctr Tower 1 Tulsa OK 74103 Business E-Mail: jgivens@givensgivens.com.

GIVENS, JANET EATON, writer; b. NYC, July 5, 1932; d. Irving Daniel and Matilda (Schmelzle) E.; m. Richard Ayres Givens, Aug. 24, 1957; children: Susan Ruth, Jane Lucile. BA, Queens Coll., 1953; MA, Columbia U., 1955. Lic. tchr. NY. Tchr. pub. elem. schs., Silver Spring, Md., 1953—55, Mamaroneck, NY, 1955—59; supr. prospective tchrs., part-time ledctr. Queens Coll., NYC, 1959—68. Author: The Migrating Birds, 1964, Something Wonderful Happened, 1982, Just Two Wings, 1984; contbg. author: Tensions Our Children Live With, 1959. V.p. PTA, Pub. Sch. 219, Queens, NY, 1972—73, del. to United Parents Assn., 1971—72, editor PS 219 News, 1971—73. Home: 600 E Cathedral Rd Ste D208 Philadelphia PA 19128-1928 E-mail: janet.givens@Owanputall.net.

GIVENS, JOHN KENNETH, automotive executive; b. Highland Park, Mich., Aug. 21, 1940; s. John Hamilton and Marion Florence G.; children: Kevin John, Kirk David; m. Patricia Ann Bowlby, May 23, 1980. BA, Mich. State U., 1963. With Lincoln-Mercury divsn. Ford Motor Co., Cleve., 1963-71, sales promotion mgr. Lincoln-Mercury divsn. Dearborn, Mich., 1971-73; dir. sales and mktg. Ford South Africa, 1973-75; car advt. mgr. Ford Divsn., 1975-77; sr. v.p. Wells. Rich, Greene Advt., LA, 1977-79; v.p. mktg. Chrysler Corp., Highland Park, 1979-82; pres. Seal-Dry USA, Inc., Little Rock, 1982-92; chmn. Eastar, Inc. Holding Co., 1982-98, Spash Superpools, LLC, 1988—2005, SanduskyAthol Internat., 1992—, Deckrite, LLC, 1997—2005, Aqua Ventures, LLC, 2002—05. also: Eastar Inc 15 Hickory Hills Cir Little Rock AR 72212 Personal E-mail: jg82140@aol.com.

GIVENS, ROBIN, actress; b. NYC, Nov. 27, 1964; d. Reuben Givens and Ruth Roper; m. Mike Tyson, Feb. 7, 1988 (div. Feb. 14, 1989); m. Svetozar Marinkovic, Aug. 22, 1997 (separated); children: Michael, William. Grad., Sarah Lawrence Coll.; postgrad., Harvard U.; student in Dramatic Arts, Am. Acad., NYC. Founder, dir. Never Blue Prodns., 1990—. Worked as model Ford Agy., N.Y.C. Appeared in (daytime TV series) The Guiding Light, Loving; (films) Fort Apache: The Bronx, The Wiz, A Rage in Harlem, 1991, Boomerang, 1992, The Foreign Student, 1994, Blankman, 1994, Dangerous Intentions, 1995, Everything's Jake, 2000, The Elite, 2001, Book of Love, 2002, Head of State, 2003, A Good Night to Die, 2003, Love Chronicles, 2003, Flip the Script, 2005, Restraining Order, 2006, 4-Bidden, 2007; (TV series) The Cosby Show, Head of the Class, 1986-91, Angel Street, 1992, Courthouse, 1995, Sparks, 1996, Forgive of Forget, 2000—; (TV films) Beverly Hills Madam, 1986, The Women of Brewster Place, 1989, The Penthouse, 1989, A Face to Die for, 1996, The Expendables, 2000, Spinning Out of Control, 2001, Hollywood Wives: The New Generation, 2003, Captive Hearts, 2005; (cable TV series) Philip Marlow: Private Eye. Avocations: swimming, working out, viewing movies.*

GIVHAN, ROBERT MARCUS, lawyer; b. Mineral Wells, Tex., May 10, 1959; s. Walter Houston Givhan and Marion Blackwell Callen Stothart; m. Janet Lee Dothard, May 6, 1989; children: Vivian Lee, Charlotte Ann, Virginia Mae. BA, U. Ala., Tuscaloosa, 1981; JD, Cumberland Sch. Law, Birmingham, 1986. Bar: Ala. 1987, DC 1989, US Supreme Ct. 1989, US Ct. Appeals (DC and 11th cirs.), US Dist. Ct. (so., mid. and no. dists.) Ala. 1987. Assoc. Perry and Russell, Montgomery, Ala., 1987-88; dep. dist. atty. 15th Jud. Cir. Ala., Montgomery, 1988-91; dep. atty. gen. Office Atty. Gen. of Ala., Montgomery, 1991-95; ptnr. Johnston Barton Proctor & Rose LLP, Birmingham, 1995—. Contbr. articles. Fellow: Am. Coll. Pros. Attys.; mem.: Am. Health Lawyers Assn., Birmingham Bar Assn. (co-chmn. econs. law practice com. 1998, chmn. 1999, co-chmn. jud. and legal reform com. 2002, chmn. 2003, chmn. cts. and legis. com. 2004), Ala. State Bar Assn., ABA (vice chmn. antitrust competition and trade regulation com. adminstrv. 1994—2000). Episcopalian. Avocations: whitewater rafting, hiking, music collecting, book collecting. Home: 1601 Shades Park Cove Birmingham AL 35209 Office: Colonial Brookwood Ctr 569 Brookwood Village Ste 901 Birmingham AL 35209 Home Phone: 205-423-9313; Office Phone: 205-458-9444. Business E-Mail: rmg@jbpp.com.

GIVHAN, ROBIN DENEEN, journalist; b. Detroit, Sept. 11, 1964; d. Robert Earl and Stella Mae (Thompson) G. BA in English, Princeton U., 1986; MA in Journalism, U. Mich., 1988. Staff writer Detroit Free Press, 1988-92, San Francisco Chronicle, 1992-93; fashion editor Detroit Free Press, 1993-95, Washington Post, 1995—; assoc. editor Vogue, NYC, 2000. Recipient Outstanding Achievement in Media award Nat. Coalition of 100 Black Women, 1992, Pulitzer Prize for criticism, 2006, Eugenia Sheppard award for Fashion Journalism, Coun. Fashion Designers Am., 2007. Methodist. Avocations: bicycling, aerobics, reading, photography. Office: Washington Post Style News Desk 1150 15th St NW Washington DC 20006 Office Phone: 212-445-4900. Office Fax: 202-334-5587. E-mail: givhanr@washpost.com.*

GIVONE, DONNA MARIE, pharmacologist; d. Donald Daniel and Louise Maria Givone. BS in Pharmacy, SUNY, Buffalo, 1998; PharmD, Med. U. SC, Charleston, 2000. Cert. Bd. Pharm. Specialties, 2003. Clin. pharmacy specialist in psychiatry Jesse Brown VA Med. Ctr., Chgo., 2002—. Mem.: Am. Coll. Clin. Pharmacy, Coll. Psychiat. and Neurologic Pharmacists. Office: Jesse Brown VA Med Ctr 820 S Damen Ave Chicago IL 60612 Office Phone: 312-569-7936.

GIZA, DAVID ALAN, lawyer; b. Chgo., May 16, 1958; s. Bruno Frank and Marianne Theresa (Mozdren) G.; m. Karen Ann Van Maldegiam, Nov. 5, 1988. BS, DePaul U., 1981; JD, John Marshall U., 1984. Bar: Ill. 1985, U.S. Dist. Ct. (no. dist.) Ill. 1985, Wis., 2005. Atty. pvt. practice, Chgo., 1985-86; assoc. Larry Karchmar, Ltd., Chgo., 1986-87, Kovitz, Shifrin & Waitzman, Chgo., 1987; atty. W.W. Grainger, Inc., Skokie, Ill., 1987-91, Lincolnshire, Ill., 1991—, divsn. atty., 1993-96, sr. atty., 1996-98, asst. gen. counsel, 1998—2002; pvt. practice Corp. Law Assocs., Northfield, Ill., 2002—03; corp. atty. Snap-On Inc., Kenosha, Wis., 2003—07; ethics and compliance atty. Hewlett-Packard Co., Palo Alto, Calif., 2007—, dir. compliance. Trustee Village of Libertyville, Ill., 1995—07; chmn. Camp Lake/Ctr. Lake Rehab. Dist., Wis., 1990-06. Mem. Am. Corp. Counsel Assn., Ill. State Bar Assn., Chgo. Bar Assn., Wis. State Bar Assn. Roman Catholic. Avocations: politics, water sports, reading, travel, cooking. Office: Hewlett-Packard Co 3000 Hanover St Mail Stop 1050 Palo Alto CA 94304-1112 Home Phone: 847-816-1602; Office Phone: 650-857-5905.

GIZZI, MARTIN SHERMAN, neurologist, neurophysiologist; b. Yonkers, NY, Jan. 1, 1957; s. Vincent George and Laura (Cronkhite) G.; m. Barbara Buono, Mar. 15, 2002; children Sarah, Allegra, Lance, Tessa, Ariella, Sofia. PhD, NYU, 1983; MD, U. Miami, Fla., 1985. Diplomate Am. Bd. Psychiatry and Neurology. Med. intern New Rochelle Hosp., NY, 1985-86; resident in neurology Mt. Sinai Hosp., NYC, 1986-89; asst. prof. neurology Mt. Sinai Sch. Medicine, NYC, 1989-92; assoc. prof. neurosci. Seton Hall U. Sch. Grad. Med. Edn., 1992-96, prof., assoc. chair, 1996—2002, chair, 2002—, assoc. dean, 2005—. Mem. editl. bd. Vision Rsch.; bd. examiner Am. Bd. Psychiatry Neurology; sci. cons., co-investigator Microgravity Vestibular Investigations Group, NASA, Johnson Space Ctr., 1990—99; program dir. neurology residency Seton Hall U., JFK Med. Ctr., 1995—99. Pres. med. adv. bd. Music for all Seasons, NJ; grants officer JFK Med. Ctr., 2004—; bd. dirs. DeVry U. Named Best Dr. in NY, NY mag., 1990, 2002—07, Best Dr. in NY Met., Castle-Connoly Med. Ltd., 1994—2007; named to Best Drs. in NJ, NJ Monthly, Life, 2001—06, Am. Top Drs., Castle-Connoly Med., 2002—07; recipient Physician Scientist award, Nat. Eye Inst., 1989, Best Dr. in NY, NY mag., 2006, Joint Legis. Resolution award, NJ Senate and Gen. Assembly, 2004. Fellow Am. Acad. Neurology, N.Am. Neuro-Ophthalmol. Soc., Barany Soc., Am. Neurotology Soc. Democrat. Achievements include research in The Analysis of Moving Visual Patterns, Reprinted in SM Kosslyn and RA Andersen (Eds) Frontiers in Cognitive Neuroscience, 1995 MIT Press, Cambridge, MA; The familial incidence of benign paroxysmal positional vertigo. Acta Otolaryngologica (Stockh) 118:774-777,1998; Vestibular dysfunction does not directly cause cognitive or psychological symptoms. Journal of Head Trauma Rehabilitation, 18:398-407, 2003. Avocations: music, exercise. Office: JFK Med Ctr PO Box 3059 Edison NJ 08818-3059 Office Phone: 732-632-1624. Business E-Mail: mgizzi@solarishs.org.

GJERDE, ROSALIE CAROLYN, music educator, conductor; b. Fort Bragg, Calif., May 23, 1941; d. Julius Nathaniel and Lucille Agnes Prince; children: Carolyn Anne Gjerde-Tu, Daniel William, Thomas Edward. BA, Humboldt State Coll., 1963. Cert. tchr Calif., 1963, nat. cert. music Music Tchrs. Nat. Assn., 1981. Tchr. Coll. of Redwoods, 1971—78; choral dir. Mendocino Presbyn. Ch., Calif., 1986—93; owner, head tchr. Gjerde Music Studio, Fort Bragg, 1979—. Composer of various choral works. Arts activist Arts for All, Fort Bragg, 2000—; aids activist, 1992—. Mem.: Nat. Guild Piano Tchrs. (Hall of Fame award 1982), Calif. Assn. Profl. Music Tchrs. (dist. coord., various com. chairs, workshop leader 1981—), Music Tchrs. Nat. Assn. Avocations: photography, travel. Home and Office: Gjerde Music Studio 315 Park St Fort Bragg CA 95437 Home Phone: 707-964-4338; Office Phone: 707-964-4338. Personal E-mail: mwgjerde@adelphia.net.

GJERTSEN, O. GERARD, lawyer; b. Bklyn., June 24, 1932; s. Ole Gerhard and Hilma (Jorgensen) G.; m. Carol Ann Jurkops, June 2, 1962; children: Gerard, Gary, Krista, Karen. BA, Columbia Coll., 1954; JD, NYU, 1958. Bar: N.Y. 1958, U.S. Dist. Ct. (so. dist.) N.Y. 1960. Ptnr., counsel Thacher Proffitt & Wood, NYC, 1964—. Vice chmn. Tuckahoe (N.Y.) Urban Renewal Agy. With U.S. Army, 1954-55. Mem. ABA, N.Y. State Bar Assn., Assn. of Bar of City of N.Y., Westchester County Bar Assn., White Plains Bar Assn., Scarsdale Golf Club. Avocations: music, sports. Home: 262 Dante Ave Tuckahoe NY 10707-3015 Office: Thacher Proffitt & Wood 50 Main St White Plains NY 10606-1934

GJERTSON, STEPHEN ARTHUR, artist, writer; b. Mpls., Minn., May 21, 1949; s. Arthur Clarence and Betty Lou Gjertson; m. Patricia Teresa Campion, Nov. 1, 1975; children: Stephanie Patricia, Philip Allen, Andrew Christopher, Elizabeth Mary. Artist Stephen Gjertson Studios, Mpls., 1975—. Creative cons. Atelier LeSueur, Excelsior, Minn., 1985—94; instr. Atelier Lack, Mpls., 1973—88. Exhibition, Classical Realism: The Other Twentieth Century, Beauty: A Rebirth of Relevance, For Glory and For Beauty, Triad: Three American Painters; author: (biography) Richard F. Lack: An American Master, (book) For Glory and For Beauty; editl. adviser: essays and revs. Classical Realism Quarterly, essays Classical Realism Journal, editor, author: Classical Realism Newsletter. Ch. drummer, Mpls., 1986—2004. Grantee, Elizabeth T. Greenshields Meml. Found., 1973—75. Mem.: TRIAD: Three Am. Painters, Am. Soc. Classical Realism (guild dir. 1988—2005, v.p. 1994—2003, pres. 2003—05). Republican. Home: 3855 Colfax Ave N Minneapolis MN 55412-2029 Home Phone: 612-522-1557.

GJESSING, DAG TRYGVESON, physicist; b. Talvik, Norway, Feb. 24, 1930; s. Trygve Ragnvaldson Gjessing and Ruth Lofting-Hansen; m. Toril Johansen, Sept. 15, 1958; children: Trygve, Randi. BSEE, London U., 1954; PhD in Geophysics, Oslo U., 1964. Staff mem. Norwegian Def. Rsch. Establishment, Kjeller, Norway, 1954—76, chief scientist, 1969—76; chief tech. program remote sensing Norwegian Rsch. Coun., Oslo, 1977—97; mng. dir. TRIAD AS, Lillestrøm, Norway, 1997—. Rsch. assoc. Stanford U., Calif., 1960—61; mem. tchg. staff Inst. Theoretical Physics, Trieste, Italy, 1981—83; adj. prof. physics U. Tromsø, 1982—97; cons. scientist remote sensing com. Swedish Space Ctr., Stockholm, 1985—90; vis. scientist Johns Hopkins Applied Physics Lab., Balt., 1986—95. Author: Remote Surveillance by Electromagnetic Waves for Air-Water-Land, 1978, Adaptive Radar in Remote Sensing, 1981, Target Adaptive Matched Illumination RADAR: Principles and Applications, 1986; contbr. articles to profl. jours. Recipient prize for paper, IEE, London, 1963. Mem.: IEEE (sr.), Electromagnetics Acad., Norwegian Geophys. Soc., Norwegian Acad. Tech. Scis. Home: Skogfaret 54 N-2020 Skedsmokorset Norway Office: Triad AS Storgaten 6 N-2000 Lillestrøm Norway Business E-Mail: dag.gjessing@triad.no.

GJØNNES, JON KJELL, physics professor; b. Brevik, Norway, Jan. 26, 1931; s. Knut and Ulrikka (Bjørnstad) G.; m. Joy Suzanne Angell-Baustad, Dec. 31, 1955 (dec. Dec., 2004); children: Kjersti, Liv. BS, U. Oslo, 1955, MS, 1957, PhD, 1967. Rsch. assoc. Ctr. for Indsl. Rsch., Oslo, 1957-59; rsch. fellow Chem. Rsch. Labs. Commonwealth Sci. and Indsl. Rsch. Orgn., Melbourne, Australia, 1960-61; rsch. fellow U. Oslo, 1961-63, sr. lectr., 1965-81, prof. physics, 1981—99, head physics dept., 1970-72; sr. rsch. fellow Melbourne U., 1964. Vis. prof. Tohoku U., Sendai, Japan, 1974, 94, Ariz. State U., Tempe, 1986. Contbr. articles to profl. jours. Mem. coun. County of Baerum, 1972-83, chmn. planning com., 1972-79; polit.

advisor Ministry of Local Govt. and Labour, 1980-81; mem. Royal Norwegian Coun. Sci. and Indsl. Rsch., 1975-81; chmn. Norwegian Coun. Info. Tech. Policies, 1987-90. Mem. Royal Norwegian Acad. Sci., Norwegian Adv. Coun. Physics (chmn. 1973-75), Commn. Electron Diffraction. Home: Maridalsveien 238 N-0467 Oslo Norway Personal E-mail: jongjn@bbse.no.

GJOVIG, BRUCE QUENTIN, entrepreneur, consultant; b. Crosby, ND, Mar. 24, 1951; s. Ronald Daniel and Agnes (Smedberg) G.; children: Mike Mohn, Todd Chaffee. BA, BS, U. N.D., 1974. Rsch. chemist Man-in-the-Sea Project, Grand Forks, ND, 1975-76; campaign advisor Elkin for Gov. Com., Bismarck, ND, 1976; exec. officer Grand Forks Bd. Realtors, 1977-81; devel. officer U. N.D. Found., 1981-84; founder, dir. Ctr. for Innovation, Grand Forks, 1984—. Bd. dirs. Valley Angel Investment Fund, Grand Forks, 2006-, SBIR Project West, Phoenix; founder, chmn. N.D. Entrepreneur Hall of Fame, 1985—, innovate website; founder Skalicky Tech. Incubator, 1994—, N.D. Angel Capital Network, 1998—, Ina Mae Rude Entrepreneur Ctr., 2005—. Editor: The Business Plan: Step-by-Step, 1988, The Marketing Plan: Step-by-Step, 1990; author, editor: Boxcar of Peaches: Nash Finch Co., 1990, Pardon Me, Your Manners are Showing!, 1992; contbr. articles to profl. jours. Founder, sponsor 67th Patent & Trademark Depository Libr., 1991-2003; chair N.D. Mus. Art; chair U. N.D. Nordic Initiative, 1997—. Recipient Outstanding Svc. award U. N.D. Alumni Assn., 1984, Western U.S. SBIR Support Person award, 1997, Tibbetts award SBA, 1998, Kauffman Leadership award 1998, SBA Nat. Vision 2000 award, 1999, Rsch. Advocate of Yr., 2003, Entrepreneur Spirit award Greater ND Assn., 2004, Hon. Innovator, Sarpsborg, Norway, 2004, Soft Landings Internat. Incubator, NBIA, others; named Friend of Small Bus., Fargo C. of C. 1988, U. ND Outstanding Greek Alumnus, 1990, ANSA Norseman of Yr., 2001, Rsch. Adv. of Yr. for N.D. and Six States in Region VIII, SBA, 2003, #8 Top Entrepreneur Program Princeton Rev.& Entrepreneur mag., 2006; named to ND Entrepreneur Hall of Fame, 2001. Mem. Assn. Univ. Tech. Mgrs., Assn. Univ. Related Rsch. Pks., Univ. Small Bus. Tech. Consortium (state dir. 1986-90), Alumni Inter-Fraternity Coun. (chmn. 1982-86, 90-95, Outstanding Alumnus 1990), Midwest Assn. Seed and Venture Funds, Rotary, Delta Tau Delta. Republican. Episcopalian. Avocations: reading, politics, art collector, fund raising, entrepreneur history collector. Office: Ctr for Innovation PO Box 8372 Ina Mae Rude Entrepreneur Ctr Grand Forks ND 58202-8372 Home: Condo #2013 111 N 3d St Grand Forks ND 58203 Home Phone: 701-775-3484; Office Phone: 701-777-3134. Business E-Mail: bruce@innovators.net.

GLAAB, CHARLES NELSON, historian, educator; b. Williston, ND, Dec. 19, 1927; s. Reuben and Betty (Nelson) G.; m. Mary Ellen Anderson, Nov. 5, 1949; children— Martha Ann, John Reuben. BPh, U. N.D., 1951, MA, 1952; PhD, U. Mo., 1958. Rsch. assoc. history Kansas City project U. Chgo., 1956-58; from instr. to asst. prof. history Kans. State U., 1958-60; from assoc. prof. to prof. history U. Wis., Milw., 1960-68; dir. urban history sect. Wis. Hist. Soc., 1960-63; prof. history U. Toledo, 1968—. Dir. Fox Valley research project Wis. Hist. Soc., 1963-64; mem. Milw. Landmarks Commn., 1965-68, Toledo Landmark Com., 1968-70, Ohio Hist. Site Preservation Bd., 1979-81 Author: Kansas City and the Railroads, 1962, The American City: A Documentary History, 1963, (with A.T. Brown) A History of Urban America, 1967, (with L.H. Larsen) Factories in the Valley, 1969, (with Morgan A. Barclay) Toledo: Gateway to the Great Lakes, 1983; editor: Urban History Group Newsletter, 1962-68; co-editor, 1968-70, N.W. Ohio Quar., 1994-99; mem bd. editors Urban Affairs Quar. 1966-74, Soc. Press Wis, 1966-7 Jour. Urban History, 1973-88, Urban Affairs Ann. Rev, 1978-82, Frederick Law Olmsted Papers, 1985-90, Hayes Hist. Jour., 1987-91. Served with AUS, 1946-48. Mem. Orgn. Am. Historians, Am. Hist. Assn., Urban History Assn., VFW, Am. Legion, Phi Beta Kappa. Home: 2662 Densmore Dr Toledo OH 43606 Office Phone: 419-530-2296. E-mail: cglaab@accesstoledo.com.

GLACEL, BARBARA PATE, management consultant; b. Balt., Sept. 15, 1948; d. Jason Thomas Pate and Sarah Virginia (Forwood Pate) Wetter; m. Robert Allan Glacel, Dec. 21, 1969; children: Jennifer Warren, Sarah Allane, Ashley Virginia. AB, Coll. William and Mary, 1970; MA, U. Okla., 1973, PhD, 1978. Tchr. Harford County Schs., Md., 1970—71, Dept. Def. Schs., Germany, 1971—73; ednl. counselor U.S. Army, Germany, 1973—74; mgmt. cons. Barbara Glacel & Assocs., Anchorage, 1980—86, Washington, 1986—88; ptnr. Pracel Prints, Williamsburg, Va., 1981—85; sr. mgmt. tng. specialist Arco Alaska, Inc., 1984—85; gen. mgr. mgmt. programs Hay Sys., Inc., Washington, 1986—88; CEO VIMA Internat., Burke, Va., 1988—99, chmn. emeritus, 2000; 2d v.p., bd. dirs. Chesapeake Broadcasting Corp. Md.; prin. The Glacel Group, 2000—. Adj. prof. U. Md., 1973—74, Suffolk U., Boston, 1975—77, C.W. Post Ctr., L.I. U., John Jay Coll. Criminal Justice, NYC, 1979—80, St. Thomas Aquinas Coll., NYC, 1981, St. Mary's Coll., Leavenworth, Kans., 1981, Anchorage C.C., 1982; acad. adviser Ctrl. Mich. U., 1981—82; asst. prof. U. Alaska, Anchorage, 1983—85; mem. adj. faculty Ctr. for Creative Leadership, 1986—; guest lectr. U.S. Mil. Acad.; mem. U.S. Army Sci. Bd., 1986—90, U.S. Dept. Def. Sci. Bd. Quality of Life Panel, 1994—95, Def. Adv. Com. on Women in the Svcs., 2000—02, Consumer Rev. Bd. DOD Breast Cancer Rsch. Program, 2001—02; mem. adv. coun. Reves Ctr. for Internat. Studies Coll. William and Mary, 2001—; bd. dirs. Fund for William and Mary, 2001—07. Author: Regional Transit Authorities, 1983; (with others) 1000 Army Families, 1983, The Army Community and Their Families, 1989, Light Bulbs for Leaders, 1994, Hitting the Wall: Memoir of a Cancer Journey, 2001. Chmn. 172d Inf. Brigade Family Coun. Recipient Comdr.'s award for pub. svc. U.S. Dept. Army, 1984, U.S. Army Patriotic Civilian Svc. award 1991, U.S. Army Forscom Svc. award 1993, Dept. of Army Outstanding Civilian Svc. medal, 1999, Yellow Rose of Tex. award, 1999, Helping Hand Cmty. Svc. award, 1999, Coll. William & Mary Alumna medallion, 2001; AAUW grantee, 1977-78. Mem. ASTD (bd. dirs. Anchorage chpt.), APA, Soc. for Indsl. and Orgnl. Psychology, Instrnl. Sys. Assn. (v.p. 1993-96), Soc. Alumni Coll. William and Mary (bd. dirs. 1992-98, v.p., 1997-98). Personal E-mail: bpglacel@aol.com.

GLACEL, ROBERT ALLAN, retired military career officer; b. Frankfurt, Germany, Oct. 31, 1947; (parents Am. citizens); m. Barbara Pate; children: Jennifer, Sarah, Ashley. Grad., U.S. Mil. Acad., 1969; M in Civil and Mech. Engring., MIT, 1977; MBA, Boston U., 1977; grad., Command and Gen. Staff Coll., 1982, Indsl. Coll. Armed Forces, 1990. Commd. 2d lt. U.S. Army, 1969, advanced through grades to brig. gen., 1995, FO, fire dir. officer 3d bn., 319th field arty. Vietnam, 1970-71, comdr. B battery, 1st Bn., 10th Field Arty., 3rd Inf. Divsn. Germany, 1971-72, S-2 (Intelligence) Divsn. Arty., 1972-74, asst. prof. engring. U.S. Mil. Acad. W. Point, NY, 1977-81, ops. officer, exec. officer 1st Bn., 37th Field Arty. Ft. Richardson, Alaska, 1982-85, with office Dep. Chief of Staff Pers. Hdqrs., Pentagon Washintgon, 1985-87, comdr. 1st Bn., 4th Field Arty., 2d Inf. Divsn. Republic of Korea, 1987-89, polit. mil. planner J-5 (Plans), the Joint Staff, Pentagon Washington, 1990-92, divsn. arty. comdr. 7th Inf. Divsn. (Light) Ft. Ord, Calif., 1992-93, exec. officer to the Under Sec. of the Army, Pentagon Washington, 1993-95; chief requirements and programs br. Office of Asst. Chief of Staff for Policy in SHAPE, Belgium, 1995-97; comdr. U.S. Army Test and Experimentation Command, Ft. Hood, Tex., 1997-99; ret. from active duty, 1999; v.p. America Online, Inc., Herndon, VA, 1999—. Decorated Legion of Merit, Bronz Star, Def. Meritorious Svc. medal, Meritorious Svc. medal, Disting. Svc. medal, Def. Superior Svc. medal. Office: America Online Inc 22020 Broderick Dr Dulles VA 20166-9323

GLAD, BETTY, political scientist, educator; b. Salt Lake City, Sept. 27, 1927; d. Harluf Anderson and Edna Janette (Geertsen) G.; m. Irving T. Diamond, Sept., 1954 (div. Jan. 1957). BS magna cum laude, U. Utah, 1949; PhD, U. Chgo., 1962. Instr. Mt. Holyoke Coll., 1958-59; lectr., instr. Bklyn. Coll., 1960-64; from asst. prof. to assoc. prof. U. Ill., Urbana, 1964-72, prof., 1973-89, dept. head, 1972-73; prof. U. S.C., Columbia, 1989-93, Caroline disting. prof., 1993-95, Olin D. Johnston prof., 1995—. Mem. hist. adv. com. U.S. Dept. State, Washington, 1990; rev. panelist NEH, Washington, 1980-83; chair Midwest Univs. Seminar in U.S. Fgn. Policy, 1972. Author: Charles Evans Hughes and the Illusion of Innocence, 1966, Jimmy Carter: In Search of the Great White House, 1980, Key Pittman: Tragedy of a Senate Insider, 1985; editor, contrbr. Psychological Dimension of War, 1990, The Russian Transformation, 1999, Striking First, 2004; mem. numerous editl. bds., 1968-73; contbr. articles to profl. jours.; appeared on numerous TV and radio shows. Nat. Pub. Svc. fellow, 1952, Kappa Kappa Gamma nat. fellow, 1952, Disting. Alumnus award Coll. of Behavioral and Social Scis., U. Utah, 2007. Mem. Internat. Soc. for Polit. Psychology (pres. 1993-94, Harold Lasswell award 1997), Am. Polit. Sci. Assn. (treas. 1978-79, v.p. 1994-95, pres. Presidency Rsch. Group 1989-90, women's caucus, Mentor of Distinction award 1989, Women's Caucus Frank Goodnow award 2000), U. Utah Beehive Soc., Mortar Bd., Phi Beta Kappa. Democrat. Unitarian Universalist. Avocations: jazz, piano, dance, theater, travel. Home: 1317 Belmont Dr Columbia SC 29205-1507 Office: U SC Dept Polit Sci Columbia SC 29208-0001 Business E-Mail: glad@gwm.sc.edu.

GLADDEN, DEAN ROBERT, arts administrator, educator, consultant; b. Columbus, Ohio, Dec. 27, 1953; s. Cyril Robert and Eileen (Faulkner) G.; m. Jane Frances Tellers, Aug. 27, 1953; children: John Dean, Catherine Eileen. B in Music Edn., Miami U., Oxford, Ohio, 1976; MS in Urban Arts Mgmt., Drexel U., 1978; postgrad., Harvard U., 1998. Exec. dir. Council for Arts of Greater Lima, Ohio, 1977-80, Arts Comm. Greater Toledo, 1980-82; dir. devel. and adminstrn. Great Lakes Theater Festival, Cleve., 1982-86; assoc. mng. dir. The Cleve. Play House, 1986, mng. dir., 1987—2006, Alley Theatre, Houston, 2006—. Cons. Ohio Arts Coun., Cleve., 1977—, chmn. sponsor/touring panel, 1981-83; adj. assoc. prof. U. Akron, Ohio, 1984-87; mem. adv. com. Mandel Sch. of Non-Profit Mgmt., Case Western Res. U., Cleve. Author booklets on the econs. of arts in Ohio, 1981, 83, 85, 87, 89, 91, 93. Mem. League Resident Theatres (exec. com.), Ohio Citizens for Arts (v.p.), Rotary (pres.). Episcopalian. Avocations: piano, drums. Home: 4022 Lanark Ln Houston TX 77025 Office: Alley Theatre 615 Texas Ave Houston TX 77002 Office Phone: 716-315-3372.

GLADDEN, GARNETT LEE, psychologist, educator; b. May 8, 1922; s. Martin L. and Beatrice G. (Palmer) Gladden; m. Vivianne C. Gladden, 1958; children: Mark L., Jeanne Sue. AB, U. Calif., Berkeley, 1943; MA, Claremont Coll., Calif., 1948; PhD, Honolulu U., 1989. Prof. Riverside C.C., Calif., 1946—77, prof. emeritus, 1976—; v.p. Golden State U., LA, 1978—82; dean Grad. Studies and provost Honolulu U., 1982—98; scientific cons. Japan Life Ltd., LA & Tokyo, 1986—98. Adj. prof. San Bernardino Valley Coll., 2002; faculty Osher Lifelong Learning Inst. U. Calif., Riverside, 2003—06; adj. prof. Riverside C.C., 2006. Author (with Vivianne Cervantes Gladden): How to Win the Aging Game, 1958. Fellow, Internat. Acad. Edn., 1983. Home: 6148 Turnberry Dr Banning CA 92220 Personal E-mail: gordont24@adelphia.net.

GLADDEN, JAMES WALTER, JR., lawyer; b. Pitts., Feb. 23, 1940; s. James Walter and Cynthia Unice (Hales) G.; m. Patricia T. Kuehn, Aug. 21, 1993; children: James, Thomas, Robert. AB, DePauw U., 1961; JD, Harvard U., 1964. Bar: Ill. 1964, U.S. Sup. Ct. 1978. Ptnr. Mayer, Brown, Rowe & Maw, Chgo., 1964—2005, sr. counsel, 2005—. Mem. ABA. Home: 1426 Chicago Ave Apt 5N Evanston IL 60201 Office: Mayer Brown Rowe & Maw 71 S Wacker Chicago IL 60603-3441 Home Phone: 847-475-4230; Office Phone: 312-701-7253. E-mail: jgladden@mayerbrownrowe.com.

GLADDEN, JOSEPH RHEA, JR., lawyer; b. Atlanta, Oct. 5, 1942; s. Joseph Rhea I and Frances (Baker) G.; m. Sarah Elizabeth (Bynum), Aug. 21, 1965; children: Joseph III, Elizabeth. BA, Emory U., 1964; LLB, U. Va., 1967. Bar: Ga., 1968; U.S. Dist. Ct. (no. dist.) Ga., 1968; U.S. Ct. Appeals (5th cir.), 1968; U.S. Ct. Appeals (11th cir.), 1985. Assoc. King and Spalding, Atlanta, 1967-73, ptnr., 1973-85; v.p., sr. staff counsel The Coca Cola Co., Atlanta, 1985-87, v.p., dep. gen. counsel, 1987-90, v.p., gen. counsel, 1990-91, sr. v.p., gen. counsel, 1991—99, exec. v.p., gen. counsel, 1999—2000; ret. Atlanta, 2001. Bd. dirs. Coca Cola Enterprises, Emory Healthcare; chmn. bd. dir. Wesley Woods Inc., Coca Cola Amatil. Chmn. bd. trustees Agnes Scott Coll.; bd. dir. Atlanta Ballet; trustee Lovett Sch.; Acad. Search Cons. Svc. Mem. ABA (com. corp. law, gen. counsel), Am. Corp. Counsel Assn., Ga. Bar Assn., State Bar Ga., Assn. Gen. Counsel; Atlanta Bar Assn., Health Svcs. Found. (bd. mem.), Commerce Club, Piedmont Driving Club. Home Phone: 540-456-8353, 540-456-8353. Personal E-mail: sjgladden@mindspring.com.

GLADDEN, ROBERT WILEY, healthcare executive; b. Barnesville, Ohio, Dec. 17, 1958; s. William R. Gladden and Clara M. (Sidebottom) Dimitro; m. Jorja Abernethy, Nov. 6, 1959; children: Teri Marie, Scott Robert, Corey William, Sara Sylvia, Bridget Kay. BS, West Liberty State Coll., 1981; MA, Bowling Green State U., Ohio, 1983. Actuarial rsch. analyst Blue Cross of N.W. Ohio, Toledo, 1983-85; dir., actuarial svcs. Co-Med Inc., Dublin, Ohio, 1985-87; sr. v.p., rsch. and analysis McNerney Heintz, Inc., Barrington, Ill., 1987-93; exec. dir. managed care numerics Luth. Gen. Health System, Park Ridge, Ill., 1993-96; exec. Ernst & Young, LLP, Chgo., 1996-99; asst. v.p. Evanston Northwestern Healthcare, 1999—2004; v.p. decision support/informatics CareSource, Dayton, Ohio, 2004—. Advancement chair, Cub Scout den leader, cubmaster, com. mem. Boy Scouts Am.; treas., dir., soccer coach Palatine Celtic Soccer; svc. unit cookie coord. Girl Scouts Am.; student fund acct. Palatine H.S. Music Dept.; team bus. mgr. N.W. Travelers Baseball; Steven min., worship com. mem. Westminster Presbyn. Ch.; fin. chmn., treas., fin. com. chair First United Meth. Ch., Palatine, Ill.; mem. worship com. Presbyn. Ch., Dayton, Ohio, 2007—. Avocations: reading, wine. Office: 1 S Main St Dayton OH 45402 Personal E-mail: bobgladden@yahoo.com.

GLADDEN, VIVIANNE CERVANTES, healthcare consultant, writer; b. Brookhaven, Miss., Oct. 8, 1927; d. Thomas James Guillory and Edna Beatrice Torry; m. Garnett Lee Gladden; children: Mark Lee, Jeanne Sue Wood. Grad., Edwin Lester Sch. Musical Theater, 1976; LittD (hon.), Union U., 1979; BA, Golden State U., 1980, PhD, DHL, Honolulu U., 1993. Ordained to ministry Cmty. Ch. of the Bay, 1985. Stage, film and TV actress, NYC, Hollywood, 1950—64; model Harry Conover, NYC, 1951; mannequin Jacques Heim, Paris, 1951; featured singer La Vien Rose, NYC, 1951—52, Copa City, Fla., 1951—52; nutritional cons. Ctr. Holistic Health Cedars-Sinai Hosp., LA, 1975—77; health and lifestyle counselor Beverly Hills and Newport, Calif., 1977—; lectr., cons. health sci. and products All Natural Products, Honolulu, Japan Life Inc., Tokyo. Radio ministry Sta. KIEV, Glendale, Calif., 1985—86; mem. adv. bd. Nat. Acad. Sports Medicine, Chgo., 1993—2002. Author (with Lee Gladden): (book) Heirs of the Gods, 1978 (Bronze Halo award So. Calif. Motion Picture Coun., 1982); author: (with Lee Gladden and Gary Couture) How to Win the Aging Game, 1979; author: Archeolinguistics, 1984. Chmn. Eco World, Hollywood, Calif., 1971; master of ceremonies Opening Ahmanson Theatre, LA, 1976. Named to Hall of Fame, Oakwood Coll., Huntsville, Ala., 1956; recipient Gold award of merit, Martin Luther King Jr. Campaign Ctr., Port Arthur, Tex., 1988. Avocations: singing, piano, yoga, running. Personal E-mail: gordont24@adelphia.net.

GLADE, WILLIAM PATTON, JR., economics professor; b. Wichita Falls, Tex., July 29, 1929; s. William Patton and Billie (Hatcher) G.; m. Marlene Louise Joseph, July 10, 1954; children: Anita, Genie, Patton, John. BBA, U. Tex., 1950, MA, 1951, PhD, 1955. Instr., asst. prof. econs. U. Md., 1957-60; asst., assoc. prof. U. Wis., Madison, 1960-65, prof. Sch. Bus. and dept. econs., 1966-71; prof. econs. U. Tex., Austin, 1970—2007, prof. emeritus, 2007—, dir. Inst. L.Am. Studies, 1971-86, dir. Mex. Ctr., 1997-2001; sr. program assoc. Smithsonian Instn. Wilson Ctr., 1987-88, acting sec. L.Am. program, 1989, sr. scholar, 1990-2000; assoc. dir. USIA, 1989-92; mem. rsch. adv. coun. Ctr. for Arts and Culture, 1998—2005. Mem. Mex.-U.S. Commn. Ednl. and Cultural Exch./Fulbright Commn., 2002—07, Am. co-pres., 2002—04. Author: Las empresas gubernamentales descentralizadas, 1959, The Political Economy of Mexico, 1963, The Latin American Economies, 1969, Marketing in a Developing Economy - The Case of Peru, 1970; co-editor (with Charles A. Reilly) Inquiry at the Grassroots, 1993; contbr., editor Privatization of Public Enterprises in Latin America, 1991; author, editor: Bigger Economies, Smaller Governments: The Role of Privatization in Latin America, 1996. Mem. Latin Am. Studies Assn. (v.p. 1978, pres. 1979), S.W. Coun. Latin Am. Studies Assn. (v.p. 1995, pres. 1996), Assn. Cultural Econs., Cosmos Club. Office: U Tex Dept Econs Austin TX 78712

GLADFELTER, WILBERT EUGENE, physiology educator; b. York, Pa., Apr. 29, 1928; s. Paul John and Marea Bernadette (Miller) G.; m. Ruth Isabelle Ballantyne, Jan. 26, 1952; children: James W., Charles D., Mary A. AB magna cum laude, Gettysburg Coll., Pa., 1952; PhD, U. Pa., 1960. NSF fellow U. Pa., Phila., 1956-58, NIH fellow, 1958-59, asst. instr., 1954-56; instr. physiology W.Va. U., Morgantown, 1959-61, asst. prof., 1961-69, assoc. prof., 1969-96, prof. emeritus, 1996—. Contbr. articles to profl. jours. Treas., Monongalia County chpt. W. Va. Heart Assn., 1976-95. With USN, 1946-48. Fellow, NSF, 1956—58. Mem. Am. Physiol. Soc., Soc. Neurosci., Soc. for Integrative and Comparative Biology, Sigma Xi, Phi Beta Kappa, Beta Beta Beta. Lutheran. Home: 70 Pine Tree Ln Morgantown WV 26508-2929 Office: WVa U Health Sci Ctr Dept Physiology Morgantown WV 26506

GLADISH, DAVID STEPHEN, lawyer; b. Cedar Rapids, Iowa, Apr. 20, 1969; s. Allen and Michelle Gladish. BA in Criminal Justice cum laude, Calumet Coll. of St. Joseph, Hammond, Ind., 1991; JD, Valparaiso U., 1995. Bar: Ind. 1995, Ill. 1995, U.S. Dist. Ct. (no. and so. dists.) Ind. 1998, U.S. Dist. Ct. (no. dist.) Ill. 1998, U.S. Ct. Appeals (7th cir.) 1998, bd. cert. civil trial specialist, Nat. Bd Trial Advocacy, 2002. Probation officer Hammond City Ct., 1992-96; ptnr. Smith & DeBonis, Highland, Ind., 1995—; pvt. law practice Highland, 2006—. Office: Law Office of David Gladish 8320 Kennedy Ave Highland IN 46322 Office Phone: 219-838-1900.

GLADSTEIN, MIMI REISEL, theater and literature educator; d. Emil and Regina Rosen Reisel; m. Jay Stephen Gladstein, Aug. 18, 1956; children: Clifford Eric, Denise Robin Halikman-Gladstein, Alfred Martin. BA in Speech and Drama, Tex. Western Coll., 1959; PhD, U. N.Mex, Albuquerque, 1973. Prof. English and Theatre U. Tex., El Paso, Tex., 1968—. Dir. Women's Studies Program U. Tex., 1981—83, chmn. Depts. English and Philosophy, 1985—88, chmn. Dept. English, 1985—88, exec. dir. Diamond Jubilee, 1988—90, dir. We. Cultural Heritage Program, 1995—97, assoc. dean, 1997—2002, chmn. Dept. Theatre, Dance, and Film, 2002—06. Author: 5 books; contbr. articles to profl. jours. Mem. edn. and content com. El Paso Holocaust Mus. and Study Ctr., Tex., 1995—2006. Named Woman of Yr., El Paso Women's Polit. Caucus, 1975; recipient Burlington No. award, 1988, Angeline Pruis award, 1987, Burkhardt award, 1996, Mentor Appreciation award, Ariz. State U., 2002, Disting. Achievement Svc. to Students award, UTEP, 2006, Sterling Membership award, Rocky Mountain Modern Lang. Assn., 2006; grantee, Fulbright Found., 1995, Outstanding Achievement award, Coll. Liberal Arts, 2003. Home: 5464 Cactus Hill Drive El Paso TX 79912 Office: University of Texas at El Paso El Paso TX 79968 Office Phone: 915-747-6259.

GLADSTONE, ARTHUR M., artist, writer, aerospace engineer; b. NYC, Sept. 22, 1921; m. Margaret SeBastian, July 14, 1948 (dec. Mar. 1972); m. Helen Worth, Feb. 3, 1980 (dec. Aug. 2002); m. June Doris Bailey, Mar. 11, 2004. BA cum laude, NYU, 1942, MS in Chemistry, 1947. Cert. propulsion engr., U.S. Civil Svc. Rsch. chemist Am. Cyanamid, Bridgeville, Pa., 1947-48; rsch. supr. Pitts. Coke and Chem., 1978-53; product mgr. Nopco Chem., Harrison, NJ, 1953-59; v.p. Anchor Serum, St. Joseph, Mo., 1959-61; engr. advanced propulsion Hercules Powder, Rocket City, W.Va., 1961-68. Author (under pseudonym Margaret SeBastian): (novels) Miss Letty, My Lord, Rakehell, The Courtship of Colonel Crown, The Fortunate Belle, A Lesson in Love, Dilemma in Duet, A Keeper for Lord Linford; author: (as Maggie Gladstone) The Love Tangle, The Reluctant Debutante, The Impudent Widow, A Lesson in Love, others; author: (as Cilla Whitmore) His Lordship's Landlady; Represented in permanent collections Fed. Res., Richmond, Va. 1st lt. USAF, 1944—46, maj. USAF, ret. Decorated Meritorious Svc. medal USAF. Mem.: Authors Guild. Avocations: theatre organ, cooking, cosmology, literature. Home: 323 Logtrac Rd Stanardsville VA 22973 Office Phone: 434-985-6211. Personal E-mail: amgladstone@hotmail.com.

GLADSTONE, BERNARD, columnist; b. NYC; m. Sandra Gladstone. Contbr. expert Motor Boating mag.; Home Improvement editor NY Times, 1956—86, Leisure editor, 1972—83, syndicated columnist. Author: (books include) Hints & Tips for the Handyman, 1960, NY Times Complete Manual of Home Repair, 1966; co-author: Boatkeeper: The Boatowner's Guide to Maintenance, Repair & Improvement, 1984. Recipient Lawrence Tiefer award. Office: NY Times Syndication Sales Corp 14th Fl 122 E 42nd St New York NY 10168 also: Motor Boating Ste 114 18 Marshall St Norwalk CT 06854 Office Phone: 941-371-7822, 203-299-5950. Office Fax: 212-499-3382, 212-299-5951.

GLADSTONE, HERBERT JACK, manufacturing executive; b. NYC, May 12, 1924; s. Joseph D. and Ella (Shabman) G.; m. Sylvia Rosenberg, Dec. 28, 1946; children: Alan, Linda, Karen. Student, Hamilton Coll., 1944, Harvard U., 1945; BBA, CCNY, 1947. Mem. staff Gershon & Strell, CPAs, NYC, 1947-51; budget dir. F.M.C., NYC, 1951-55; v.p., treas. Condec Corp., Old Greenwich, Conn., 1955-85; treas., chief fin. officer Cober, 1985-92; ret., 1992. Prof. acctg. Sacred Heart U.; lectr. MBA program U. Conn.; bd. dirs. Consol. Controls Corp., Hammond Valve Corp. Pres. PTA, 1956-57; asst. scoutmaster Toquam coun. Boy Scouts Am., 1960-63. With US Army, 1943—46. Mem. AICPA, Fin. Execs. Inst. (dir.), N.Y. State Soc. CPAs. Clubs: Roxbury Country (dir.), Roxbury Tennis and Swim (trustee). Home: 284 W Hill Rd Stamford CT 06902-1713 E-mail: shglad284@aol.com.

GLADSTONE, RICK, editor; Dep. Sunday bus. editor New York Times, assignment editor, fgn. desk. Office: New York Times 229 W 43d St New York NY 10036 Office Phone: 212-556-7415. Office Fax: 212-556-7278. Business E-Mail: rickg@nytimes.com.

GLADSTONE, WILLIAM LOUIS, accountant; b. Bklyn., May 23, 1931; s. Archie C. and Bernice T. (Turk) G.; m. Mildred G. Rosenberg, June 21, 1953; children: Susan, Douglas. BS, Lehigh U., 1951; LLB, Bklyn. Law Sch., 1955; grad., Harvard U. Advanced Mgmt. Program, 1970; LLD (hon.), Lehigh U., 1992. CPA, N.Y. Staff acct. Arthur Young & Co., NYC, from 1951, ptnr., 1963, mng. ptnr., 1981-88, chmn., 1985-89; co-chief exec. Ernst & Young, NYC, 1989-91; pres. Tri-City ValleyCats, Inc. Baseball Club, 1992—. Lectr. acctg. Columbia U., N.Y.C., 1962-64; ptnr. N.Y.C. Partnership, 1989-91; bd. dirs. Nat. Baseball Hall of Fame and Mus., Inc., 1991—. Contbr. articles to profl. jours. Mem. Corp. Congress

N.Y. Pub. Libr., 1987-91, mem. conf. bd., 1987-93, trustee com. for econ. devel., 1988-94; bd. dirs. N.Y.-Pa. Baseball League, 1992—; trustee Nat. Asn. Profl. Baseball Leagues, 2000--. Lt. USAF, 1952-53. Mem. AICPA, N.Y. State Soc. CPAs, Lehigh Alumni Assn. (award 1976), Bklyn. Law Sch. Alumni Assn., Fin. Acctg. Found. (trustee 1988-91). Home: 30 Clubhouse Ln Scarsdale NY 10583-3146

GLADWELL, GRAHAM MAURICE LESLIE, mathematician, civil engineering educator; b. Otford, Kent, Eng., Feb. 21, 1934; emigrated to Can., 1969; s. Basil Maurice Edwin and Doris Alexandra (New) G.; m. Joyce Eugenie Nation, Mar. 29, 1958; children: Graham Hugh, Geoffrey Norman, Malcolm Timothy. B.Sc., U. London, 1954, PhD, 1957, D.Sc., 1969. Lectr. U. London, 1956-60, U. West Indies, Jamaica, 1960-62; sr. lectr. U. Southampton, Eng., 1962-69; prof. dept. civil engring. U. Waterloo, Ontario, Canada, 1969-99, prof. dept. applied math., 1979-99, Disting. prof. emeritus, 2001—. Author: Matrix Analysis of Vibration, 1965, Contact Problems in the Classical Theory of Elasticity, 1980, Inverse Problems in Vibration, 1986, 2d edit., 2004, Inverse Problems in Scattering, 1993, Functional Analysis: Applications to Mechanics and Inverse Problems, 1996; editor: Computer Aided Engineering, 1971, Contact Mechanics and Wear of Rail/Wheel Systems, 1983; series editor Solid mechanics and its Applications, 1989—. Fellow Am. Acad. Mechanics (dir. 1979-82), Inst. Math. and Its Applications, Royal Soc. Arts, Royal Soc. Can. Presbyterian. Office: Dept Civil Engring Univ Waterloo Waterloo ON Canada N2L 3G1 Business E-Mail: graham@gladwell.com.

GLADWELL, MALCOLM, writer; b. Fareham, Eng., Sept. 3, 1963; s. Graham and Joyce Gladwell. BA in history, U. Toronto, 1984. Intern The Am. Spectator, Bloomington, Ind., 1984; freelance writer Washington, 1985—87; reporter The Washington Post, 1987—96, bus. reporter, sci. writer, NYC bureau chief, 1993—96; staff writer The New Yorker, 1996—. Author: The Tipping Point: How Little Things Can Make a Big Difference, 2000 (NY Times bestseller), Blink: The Power of Thinking Without Thinking, 2005 (#1 NY Times bestseller). Named one of 100 Most Influential People of 2005, Time mag. Office: The New Yorker 4 Times Sq New York NY 10036*

GLAESER, EDWARD LUDWIG, research economist, educator; b. NYC, May 1, 1967; s. Ludwig and Elizabeth Abigail (Bayne) Glaeser; m. Nancy Schwartz, Oct. 2003. AB, Princeton U., 1988; PhD, U. Chgo., 1992. Asst. prof. Harvard U., Cambridge, Mass., 1992-96, prof. polit. econ., Paul Sack assoc., 1996-98, prof. econ., 1998—, Fred and Eleanor Glimp prof. econs., 2005—, prof. econs., 2005—. Dir. Taubman Ctr., Kennedy Sch. Govt., Harvard U., Rappaport Inst. for Greater Boston Office: Harvard U 315 Littauer Ctr Cambridge MA 02138 Office Phone: 617-495-5140. Business E-Mail: glaeser@fas.harvard.edu.

GLANCY, DAVID LUCAS, internist; b. Cin., 1934; MD, Johns Hopkins U., 1961. Diplomate Am. Bd. Internal Medicine. Intern Johns Hopkins Hosp., Balt., 1961-62, resident in internal medicine, 1962-63, Grady Meml. Hosp., Atlanta, 1963-65; fellow cardiology Nat. Heart Inst., Bethesda, Md., 1966-69; physician Univ. Hosp., New Orleans, 1972—, med. dir. cardiology, 1974—93; mem. faculty La. State U., 1972—, prof. medicine, (now emeritus) chief cardiology sect., 1993—; med. dir. cardiology Med. Ctr. La., New Orleans, 1993—. Named one of Top Doctors in La., La. Life mag., 2007. Fellow ACP, Am. Coll. Cardiology (La. chpt.). Office: 3535 Bienville St Ste W420 New Orleans LA 70119-5260 also: La State U Med Ctr 1542 Tulane Ave New Orleans LA 70112-2825 Office: University Hospital 1541 Tulane Ave New Orleans LA 70112-2821 also: Sect Cardiology Earl K Long Med Ctr 5825 Airline Hwy Baton Rouge LA 70805 Office Phone: 225-358-3918. Business E-Mail: dglanc@lsuhsc.edu.*

GLANCY, DOROTHY JEAN, lawyer, educator; b. Glendale, Calif., Sept. 24, 1944; d. Walter Perry and Elva T. (Douglass) G.; m. Jon Tobias Anderson, June 8, 1979. BA, Wellesley Coll., 1967; JD, Harvard Law Sch., 1970. Bar: D.C. 1971, Calif. 1976, U.S. Dist. Ct. D.C. 1971, U.S. Ct. Appeals (D.C. cir.) 1972. Assoc. Hogan & Hartson, Wash., 1971-73; counsel U.S. Senate Judiciary Subcomm. on Constitutional Rights, Wash., 1973-74; fellow in Law & Humanities Harvard U., Cambridge, Mass., 1974-75; asst. to assoc. prof. law Santa Clara U., Calif., 1975-82, prof. law Calif., 1984—; vis. prof. law U. Arizona, Tucson, 1979; asst. gen. counsel U.S. Dept. of Agr., 1982-83. Cons. Commn. Fed. Paperwork, Wash., 1976; dir. summer Law Study Program in Hong Kong, 1985-90; advisor Restatement, Third Property: Servitudes, 1986-97; mem. ct. tech. adv. com. Calif. Jud. Coun. Dir. legal rsch. project regarding privacy and intelligent trnsp. systems Fed. Hwy. Adminstrn., 1993-95; bd. dirs. Presidio Hts. Assn. Neighbors, 1990—. Fellow Wellesley Coll., Harvard U. Mem. ABA (chair ethics com. of sect. on natural resources, energy and environ. law, 1993-95, coun. mem. 1995-98), State Bar Calif. (mem. environ. law sect., adv. exec. com. 1993-96, advisor 1996—), Am. Assn. Law Schs. (chair environ. law sect. 1992-93, chair property sect. 1996-97, chair defamation and privacy sec., 1997-98), Am. Law Inst., Calif. Women Lawers, Soc. Am. Law Tchrs., Phi Beta Kappa. Democrat. Avocations: gardening, travel. Office: Santa Clara U Sch Law Santa Clara CA 95053-0001 Home Phone: 415-922-4495. Business E-Mail: dglancy@scu.edu.

GLANCY, WALTER JOHN, lawyer; b. LA, Mar. 8, 1942; s. Walter Perry and Elva Thomasin (Douglass) Glancy; children: Jill Marie, Gregory Owens. AB, Princeton U., 1964; BA, Oxford U., Eng., 1966; LLB, Yale U., 1969. Bar: Tex. 1971. Law clk. to assoc. justice Byron R. White U.S. Supreme Ct., 1969-70; staff asst. NSC, 1970-71; staff asst. to Peter M. Flanigan, The White House, 1971; assoc. then ptnr. Jackson, Walker, Winstead, Cantwell & Miller, Dallas, 1972-76; ptnr. Hughes & Luce and predecessor, Dallas, 1976-85, Baker & Botts, Dallas, 1985-88, Hughes & Luce, Dallas, 1988-90; pvt. practice Dallas, 1991-95, 97-99; cons. Meyer, Hendricks, Victor, Osborn & Maledon, Phoenix, 1991-95; ptnr. Weil, Gotshal & Manges LLP, Dallas, 1995-96; sr. v.p., gen. counsel, dir Holly Corp., 1999—. Adj. lectr. corp. taxation So. Meth. U. Sch. Law, 1988. Note and comment editor Yale Law Jour., 1968-69. Bd. mgmt. Dallas YMCA Urban Svcs., 1975—84; bd. dirs. Dallas Family Guidance Ctr., 1982—96, pres. bd. dirs., 1985—86; bd. dirs. Child & Family Guidance Ctrs., Dallas, 1996—2003, pres. bd. dirs., 2001—02; bd. dirs. Dallas Opera, 1984—88, 1996—97; bd. trustees Hockaday Sch., Dallas, 1989—95; mem. adminstrv. bd. Lovers Ln. United Meth. Ch., Dallas, 1984—86, 1988—89; deacon Park Cities Bapt. Ch., Dallas, 1996—. Nat. Merit scholar, 1960-64, Marshall scholar, 1964-66. Mem.: ABA, State Bar Tex. (profl. ethics com. 1982—, chmn. tax sect. 1985—86, chmn. profl. ethics com. 1999—), Am. Law Inst., Dallas Bar Assn. (chmn. legal ethics com. 1980—81), Order of Coif, Park Cities Rotary Club (pres. 2003—04), Phi Beta Kappa. Republican. Office: 100 Crescent Ct Ste 1600 Dallas TX 75201-6915

GLANCZ, RONALD ROBERT, lawyer; b. Bay City, Mich., Jan. 29, 1943; s. Alexander and Ella (Josehart) Glancz; m. Margie Joan Pensler, Dec. 28, 1969. BA in Pre-Legal Studies, U. Mich., 1964, JD cum laude, 1968. Bar: Mich. 1968, U.S. Ct. of Appeals (D.C. cir.) 1969, U.S. Supreme Ct. 1972, D.C. 1974. Atty. civil divsn. Appellate Sec. U.S. Dept. Justice, Washington, 1968-75, asst. dir. civil divsn., 1975-79; dir. litigation divsn. Office of the Comptr. of the Currency, Washington, 1979—84; asst. gen. counsel Fed. Deposit Ins. Corp., Washington, 1984—88; ptnr. Venable LLP, Washington, 1991—. Contbr. Named one of Am.'s Leading Lawyers for Bus., Chambers U.S.A., 2006; recipient, 2007. Mem.: ABA (past vice-chmn. banking law com.), Jewish Found. for Group Homes (bd. dirs., past pres., chancellor), Exchequer Club (Washington), Order of Coif. Office: Venable LLP 575 7th St NW Washington DC 20004-1601 Office Phone: 202-344-4947. Business E-Mail: rglancz@venable.com.

GLANDT, EDUARDO DANIEL, chemical engineering educator; b. Buenos Aires, Mar. 4, 1945; arrived in US, 1973; s. Jacob and Matilde (Reidich) G. BS in chem. engring., U. Buenos Aires, 1968; M in chem. engring., U. Pa., 1975, PhD in chem. engring., 1977. Researcher Nat. Inst. Indsl. Technology, Buenos Aires, 1968-73; asst. prof. U. Pa., Phila., 1977-81, assoc. prof., 1981-85, prof., 1985—, chair dept. chem engring., 1990—94, Carl V.S. Patterson Prof., 1990—95, Russell P. and Elizabeth C. Heuer Prof., 1995—98, interim dean Sch. Engring. & Applied Sci., 1998—99, dean Sch. Engring & Applied Sci., 1999—, Robert D. Bent Prof. Chem. and Biomolecular Engring. Contbr. articles to profl. jours. Recipient S. Reid Warren Award for Disting. Tchg., Sch. Engring. and Applied Sci., U. Pa., 1977, Christian R. and Mary F. Lindback Award for Disting. Tchg., U. Pa., 1980. Mem. NAE, AAAS, AIChE, Am. Chem. Soc. (Viktor K. LaMer Award, Surface and Colloid Sci. Divsn., 1979), Am. Phys. Soc. Office: Dept of Chem Engring U Pa 220 S 33rd St, 311A Towne Bldg Philadelphia PA 19104-6393

GLANTZ, LAWRENCE G., special education and social studies educator; b. Irvington, NJ, Sept. 15, 1965; s. Ernest and Judith Glantz. BA in Polit. Sci. and Spl. Edn., Kean U., Union, NJ, 1996; MEd, Seton Hall U., South Orange, NJ, 1991. Asst. mgr. sales Macys, Shorthills, NJ, 1995—2003; tchr. spl. edn., social studies Montclair Bd. Edn., NJ, 2003—04; tchr. spl. edn. Passaic Bd. Edn., NJ, 2005—. Mem.: Nat. Coun. Social Studies, Kappa Delta Pi. Avocations: travel, exercise, history, museums. Personal E-mail: lhist123@mac.com.

GLANTZ, STANTON A., medical researcher; BS, U. of Cincinnati, 1969; MS, Stanford U., 1970, PhD, 1973. Student trainee NASA Manned Spacecraft Ctr., Houston, 1965—68, aerospace engr., 1969; post-doctoral trainee Stanford U., 1973—75, U. Calif. San Francisco, 1975—77, asst. prof. medicine in residence, 1977—80, assoc. prof. medicine in residence, 1981—82, assoc. prof. medicine, 1983—87, prof. medicine, 1987—; dir. UCSF Ctr. Tobacco Control Rsch. & Ed., 2002—. Contbr. scientific papers; assoc. editor: Jour. Am. Coll. Cardiology, 1992—97. Recipient NIH Rsch. Career Devel. award, 1977—82, James Madison Freedom of Information award, Soc. Profl. Journalists, 1996, Alton Ochsner award, 1996, UCSF Chancellor's award for Pub. Svc., 1997, Am Soc. Addiction Medicine Annual award, 1998, Gleitsman Found. Citizen Activist award, 1998, Taking the Heat award, U. Calif. Tobacco Related Diseases Rsch. Program, 1999, Common Cause Pub. Svc. Achievement award, 2000, Cahan Disting. Prof. award, Flight Attendant Med. Rsch. Inst. (FAMRI), 2002; fellow Am. Coll. Cardiology, 1992. Mem.: Inst. Medicine. Office: UCSF Box 1390 513 Parnassus Ave San Francisco CA 94143-1390 Office Phone: 415-476-3893. Office Fax: 415-514-9345. E-mail: glantz@medicine.ucsf.edu.

GLANVILLE, JERRY, college football coach, former professional football coach; b. Detroit, Oct. 14, 1941; m. Brenda Glanville; 1 child, Justin. Student, Mont. State U.; BS, No. Mich. U., 1964; MS, Western Ky. U. Defensive coord. We. Ky. U. Hilltoppers, 1967; defensive ends & outside linebackers coach Ga. Tech. U. Yellow Jackets, Atlanta, 1968-74; spl. teams coach, defensive asst. Detroit Lions, 1974-77; defensive backs coach Atlanta Falcons, 1977—78, defensive coord., 1979—82; defensive backfield coach Buffalo Bills, 1983; defensive coord. Houston Oilers, 1984-85, head coach, 1986-90, Atlanta Falcons, 1990-94; defensive coord. U. Hawaii Warriors, Honolulu, 2005—07; head coach Portland State U. Vikings, Oreg., 2007—; sports analyst NFL Today, CBS, Inside the NFL, Home Box Office, 1994—2005. Co-author (with J. David Miler): Elvis Don't like Football: The Life and Times of the NFL's Most Outspoken Coach, 1990. Named to The No. Mich. U. Hall of Fame, 1992; recipient Disting. Alumnus award, No. Mich. U. Office: Portland State U PO Box 751 Portland OR 97207

GLANVILLE, ROBERT EDWARD, lawyer; b. Binghamton, NY, Aug. 1, 1950; s. Robert S. and Betty J. (Garlick) G.; m. Susan Anne Kime, Sept. 3, 1970. BA magna cum laude, SUNY, Binghamton, 1972; JD magna cum laude, Cornell U., 1976. Bar: N.Y. 1977, U.S. Dist. Ct. (we. dist.) N.Y. 1978, U.S. Supreme Ct. 1981, U.S. Ct. Appeals (2d cir.) 1985, U.S. Ct. Appeals (D.C. cir.) 1991. Law clk. Appellate Divsn., 4th Dept., Rochester, 1976-78; from assoc. to ptnr. Phillips, Lytle, Hitchcock, et. al., Buffalo, 1978-85, 88—; ptnr. Prahl & Glanville, Buffalo, 1986-88. Mem. ABA, N.Y. State Bar Assn., Erie County Bar Assn., Am. Gas Assn. Avocations: whitewater kayaking, sailing, mountain climbing, flying. Home: 9385 S Hill Rd Boston NY 14025-9667 Office: Phillips Lytle Hitchcock 3400 HSBC Ctr Buffalo NY 14203-2887 Office Phone: 716-847-7019. Business E-Mail: rglanville@phillipslytle.com.

GLANZE, WALTER D., editor, writer, lexicographer, publishing consultant; b. Leipzig, Germany, July 9, 1928; arrived in US, 1959, naturalized, 1965; s. Walther and Erna (Spangenberg) Glanze; m. Gertraude Marie Felsmann, 1953; 1 child, Yvonne Manuela; m. Rita Maria Obrecht, 1956; m. Vion Vivian Starks, 1962; m. Agnes Thornton Rios, 1979; 1 child, Kim Jennifer. Multilingual interpreter, orgn. and methods examiner, adminstr. US Army and Air Force in Europe, 1948—59; export order mgr. Bell & Howell, Chgo., 1959—60, efficiency analyst, 1960—62; sr. editor Scott Foresman, Chgo., 1962—67, Bantam Books, NYC, 1967—79; mem. editl. bd. Am. Rev., 1973—77; lit. agt., 1985—. Cons. to pubs., 2000—; originator The Glanze Intersound Sys. (GIS). Author, compiler, primary editor over 70 books, including Guinness Book of World Records, ann. US edits., 1968—82, series editor Bantam Coll. Dictionaries (French, German, Hebrew, Italian, Latin, Spanish), 1967—82; editor (with J.J. Mulligan): Gestern, heute und morgen: Prose of Our Century, 1968; editor: (with R.W. Marks) Simplifying Computer Math, 1968, The New Dictionary and Handbook of Aerospace, 1969; editor: (with R. Buckminster Fuller) Utopia or Oblivion: The Prospects for Humanity, 1969; editor: (with N. McWhirter) Dunlap Illustrated Encyclopedia of Facts, 1969; editor: (with J. Pittaro) Spanish Panorama, 1973; editor: (with H. Osmond) Understanding Understanding: The New Guide to Getting Along with Others, 1974; editor: (with Carl Sagan) Other Worlds, 1975; editor: (with N. McWhirter) Guinness en Español e Inglés, 1981; editor: (with J. Agel) Test Your Word Power, 1984; editor: (with R.J. Steiner and G.J. MacDonald) Langenscheidt's Pocket Spanish Dictionary, 1985; editor: (with R. Goldenson) The Language of Sex from A to Z, 1986, also Chinese, Japanese, Brazilian and UK edits., Sex A-Z, 1987; editor: (with J.R. Childs) Casanova: A New Perspective (A Revisionist Biography), 1987, The Condom Book: A Survey of 100 Brands, 1987; editor: (with J. Agel) Pearls of Wisdom, 1987, expanded 2-vol. edit. in Mandarin, 1992; editor: (with C.F. von Weizsäcker) The Ambivalence of Progress: Essays on Historical Anthropology, 1988; editor: (with R.J. Steiner and G.J. MacDonald) Langenscheidt's New Standard Spanish Dictionary, 1988; editor: (with J.L. Ferrier) Art of Our Century: The Chronicle of Western Art, 1900 to the Present, 1989; editor: (with J. Agel) Cleopatra's Nose, the Twinkie Defense, & 1500 Other Shortcuts in Popular Parlance, 1990, 2d edit., 1993; editor: (with J.E. Kahn) The Reader's Digest Illustrated Reverse Dictionary, 1990, also later edits.; editor: (with S. Serafin) Encyclopedia of World Literature in the 20th Century, vol. 5, 1993; contbr.; editor Langenscheidt's European Phrasebook in 7 Languages, 2001, mng. editor The Scribner-Bantam English Dictionary, 1977, also later edits., Methodological Problems in Monolingual and Bilingual Lexicography, 1978, The Bantam Crossword Dictionary, 1979, Isaac Asimov's Book of Facts, 1979, A Word Finder Thesaurus of Selected Words (in The World Book Complete Word Power Libr.), 1981, Longman Dictionary of Psychology and Psychiatry, 1984, Mosby's Medical, Nursing and Allied Health Dictionary, 1984—2001, Longman Dictionary and Handbook of Poetry, 1985, The Mosby Medical Encyclopedia, 1985, The Signet/Mosby Medical Encyclopedia, 1987. Co-chmn., strategist Dick Gregory campaign for US Pres. Freedom and Peace Party, 1967—68. Named hon. citizen, Nashville, 1977. Mem.: AAUP, MLA (chmn. lexicography session 1978, 1982), Am. Philos. Assn., Am. Math. Soc., Internat. Linguistic Assn., PEN Am. Ctr., Dictionary Soc. N.Am. (founding mem.). Avocations: swimming, sailing, chess. Home and Office: 280 Riverside Dr New York NY 10025 Office Phone: 212-666-6993. E-mail: wdglanze@aol.com.

GLASBERG, H(ERBERT) MARK, psychiatrist, educator; b. NYC, Oct. 11, 1939; s. Joesph and Elsa (Haber) G.; m. Paula Drillman, June 19, 1960; children: Scot Bradley, Hilary Jennifer. BA, Yeshiva U., 1953; MS, Columbia U., 1954; MD, SUNY, 1958. Diplomate Am. Bd. Psychiatry and Neurology. Intern Maimonides Hosp., NYC, 1958-59; resident in psychiatry Kings County Hosp., NYC, 1959-60; resident in internal medicine Kingbridge VA Hosp. of Columbia U. Coll. Med. Program, NYC, 1960-61; resident Payne Whitney Psychiat. Clin., N.Y. Hosp., 1963-65; psychiatrist pvt. practice, NYC, 1968—; attending physician dept. psychiatry Columbia U. Coll. Physicians & Surgeons; instr. Cornell U. Med. Sch., 1966-68; assoc. prof. psychiatry Mt. Sinai Sch. Medicine, 1968-80; dir. psychiat. outpatient svcs. Beth Israel Hosp., NYC, 1968-74, assoc. attending physician, 1968-74, chief psychiat. emergency & cons. svcs., 1974-75; attending psychiatrist & clin. prof. psychiatry Coll. Physicians & Surgeons, Columbia U., 1986—; neurosurgery Coll. Physicians & Surgeons, N.Y. Presbyn. Med. Ctr., 1982, clin. prof. neurosurgery, 1995; clin. prof. neurosurgery, attending neurosurgeon N.Y. Presbyn. Med. Ctr., 1995. Examiner Am. Bd. Psychiatry & Neurology, 1988—; cons. mem. panel of ind. psychiatrists N.Y.C. Mental Health Info. Svc., 1968—. Mem. Manhattan physicians com. United Jewish Appeal, 1970—; mem. com. admission sel. Cornell U. Med. Coll., Ctr. Alumni Assn. N.Y. Hosp. Col. M.C. AUS, 1961-63. Fellow N.Y. Hosp., 1965-66, spl. rsch. fellow Nat. Inst. Mental Health, 1966-68, Cornell U. Med. Sch. Fellow ACP, Am. Soc. Neurosurgeons, Am. Psychiat. Assn. (internat. platform com. 1980—); mem. APA, AAAS, Am. Psychosomatic Soc., N.Y. Acad. Scis., N.Y. Acad. Medicine, Soc. Adolescent Psychiatry, Internat. Platform Assn. Office: 14 E 73rd St New York NY 10021-4128 Office Phone: 212-744-6600.

GLASBERG, LAURENCE BRIAN, investment company executive; b. NYC, Apr. 28, 1943; s. William and Tillie (Liebowitz) G.; m. Lana Lucille Pollack, Aug. 10, 1963; children: Jeffrey Scott, Glenn David. BBA, CUNY, 1964, MBA, 1968. Mgr. bus. affairs Sta. WCBS-TV, NYC, 1970-72, dir. planning and adminstrn., 1972-74; gen. auditor Ea. ops. CBS Inc., NYC, 1975-76; v.p. fin. and adminstrn. CBS Publs., 1976-82, v.p., gen. auditor, 1982-88; sr. v.p. fin. and adminstrn. N.Am. ops. AEG Corp., 1988-89; pres. Nat. Mgmt. Resources Group Inc., 1990—. Mng. dir. Future Resource Sys., Inc., 1994-96, exec. v.p. Future Bus. Ctr., Inc., 1995-96; sr. v.p., CFO MacDonald Comms. Corp., 1996-98; bus. and fin. mgr. Mus. Mags., 1998-2000; co-chmn. Media Resources Group, LLC, 2001-02. Fin. and tax com. Princeton Twp., NJ, 1991, elected committeeman, 1992, elected mayor, 1993; bd. dirs. AMAS Mus. Theatre, Inc., 1998-99. 1st lt. inf. U.S. Army, 1964-65. Mem. Fin. Execs. Inst. (nat. com. on govt. liaison, local bd. dirs. 1987-88, chpt. sec. 1989-92), Econ. Club (N.Y.C.). Avocations: physical fitness, outdoor and environmental activities, reading. E-mail: lglas2@yahoo.com.

GLASBERG, SCOT BRADLEY, plastic surgeon; b. NYC, June 30, 1964; s. H. Mark and Paula (Drillman) G.; m. Alisa Goldman, Oct. 17, 1999; children: Alexander Zachary, Evan Blake. BA cum laude, Columbia U., 1986; MD with honors, NYU, 1990. Diplomate Am. Bd. Plastic Surgery, Am. Bd. Surgery, Nat. Bd. Med. Examiners. Resident in surgery U. Conn./Hartford Hosp., 1990-95, chief resident, 1995-96; craniofacial rsch. fellow Inst. Reconstructive Plastic Surgery, NYU Med. Ctr., NYC, 1992-93; fellow SUNY Health Sci. Ctr., Bklyn., 1996-98, program dir., dir. plastic surgery edn., 1998—2000. Contbr. articles to profl. jours.; featured on shows such as Today show (NBC), Good Morning America (ABC), the Paula Zahn show (CNN) and the Morning show (WB)., guest appearances on nat. and local networks of NBC, CBS, ABC, WB and CNN. Mem. Plastic Surgery Ednl. Found. NY State Regents scholar, 1982-86; recipient first prize for presentation at the annual meeting, Soc. of Former Residents and Associates of Plastic Surgery, 1998. Fellow ACS; mem. AMA (del. resident physician sect. 1990-93, 96—98, plastic surgery caucus 1996-97, 99—, del. young physicians sect. 1999-2004, young physicians sect. governing coun. 2002-2004), Am. Soc. Plastic Surgeons (vice chmn. govt. rels. com., chmn. govt. rels. com. 2005—, plastypac bd. govs. 2001—, Maliniac cir., parliamentarian bd. dirs. 2005-06), Am. Soc. Aesthetic Plastic Surgery (legis. com. 2000-02), Northeastern Soc. Plastic Surgery (Resident/Fellows award 1997), Med. Soc. State NY (del. AMA resident physician sect. 1996-98, young physician sect. 1999-2006, mem. med. liability task force, legis./advocacy steering com., Outstanding Svc. award 1990), NY County Med. Soc.(litigation com., managed care task force), NY Regional Soc. Plastic Surgeons (exec. bd. 2006-, winner clin. paper competition 1997). Avocations: tennis, golf, swimming, card collecting. Office: Cosmetic & Reconstructive Plastic Surg 42A E 74th St New York NY 10021-2735 Address: 900 Park Ave Apt 19AB New York NY 10021 Office Phone: 212-717-8550. Business E-Mail: info@DrGlasberg.com. E-mail: scotbg@juno.com.

GLASBRENNER, KARL CHRISTIAN, federal agency administrator; s. Heinz Wilhelm Glasbrenner and Mariann Theresa Byrne; m. Brenda W. Wilkinson, Apr. 8, 1989; m. Irma Julia Monclova, Sept. 11, 1976 (div. Dec. 13, 1984); children: Jeromy Alan, Justin Tyler. BS, Pa. State U., 1976; MA, Pepperdine U., 1980. Cert. clin. hypnotist (Ericksonian hypnotherapy) Am. Hypnosis Tng. Acad., Inc., 2003; neurolinguistic programming practitioner Am. Neuro-Linguistic Programming Assn., 2000, pistol instr. NRA, 2002. Police officer Selfridge Air N.G. Base, Mt. Clemens, Mich., 1976—76; supervisory supply technician U.S. Army Garrison, Arlington Hall Station, Va., 1981—82; spl. agt. investigations br. Def. Intelligence Agy., Washington, 1982—86, spl. agt. overseas security ops., 1986—91, chief investigations br., 1991—96, chief force protection and tech. security br., 1996—2000, acting chief security ops. divsn., 1998, chief pers. security divsn., 2000—. Charter mem. East Coast chpt. Assn. of Threat Assessment Profls., Washington, 1995—; fellow Excellence in Govt. fellows program Coun. for Excellence in Govt., Washington, 1995—96, co-coach Excellence in Govt. fellows program, 1997—2000, vice chair sr. fellows bd. leaders, 1997—2001; mem. def. and intelligence coun. Am. Soc. for Indsl. Security, Alexandria, Va., 2003—. Singer: Alexandria Harmonizers (Internat. Chorus Champion, 1986); contr.: book The Colors of Poetry, 2003 (Best 100 Poets, 2003). Capt. US Army, 1976—81. Recipient Res. Officer Tng. Corps scholarship, U.S. Army, 1974-1976, Achievement award, Coun. for Excellence In Govt., 2000, Def. Intelligence Dir.'s award, Def. Intelligence Agency, 2002. Master: Masons (25 Yr. Pin 2001); mem.: Fed. Exec. Inst. Alumni Assn., Am. Soc. for Indsl. Security (def. and intelligence coun. 2003). Avocations: singing, writing, swimming, traveling, genealogy. Office: Def Intelligence Agy Bldg 6000 Bolling AFB CLAR DAC-3 Washington DC 20340-5300 Home Phone: 703-494-5949; Office Phone: 703-907-1309. Business E-Mail: karl.glasbrenner@dia.mil.

GLASER, ARTHUR HENRY, lawyer, mediator; b. Jersey City, May 1, 1947; s. Ned C. and Lorraine I. (Neil) G.; m. Waynelia Potter, Mar. 19, 1994; children: Kimberly N., Kevin M., Daniel J. BS, Hampden-Sydney Coll., 1968; JD, U. Va., 1973. Bar: Ga. 1973, U.S. Dist. Ct. (no. and mid. dists.) Ga., U.S. Ct. Appeals (11th cir.). Assoc. Swift, Currie, McGhee & Hiers, Atlanta, 1973-78, ptnr., 1978-83, Drew, Eckl & Farnham, Atlanta, 1983-98, Self, Glaser & Davis, LLP, Atlanta, 1999—2004, Glaser, Currie, Bullman, Atlanta, 2004—; with Henning Mediation, 1999—. Mem. ABA, Ga. Bar Assn., Atlanta Bar Assn. Presbyterian. Home: 1540 Burnt Hickory Rd NW Marietta GA 30064-1308 Office: Glaser Currie Bullman LLP 1455 Lincoln Pkwy Ste 300 Atlanta GA 30346 Home Phone: 770-424-7634; Office Phone: 770-563-9305. Business E-Mail: ahg@gcblaw.net.

GLASER, DAVID, painter, sculptor; b. Bklyn., Sept. 29, 1919; s. Samuel and Jennie (Oiffer) Glaser; m. Millie Sappol, Feb. 19, 1944; children: Susan, Sherry. Student, NY Sch. Indsl. Art, 1937, NY Sch. Contemporary Art, 1947-48, Bklyn. Mus. Art Sch., 1948-50. Illustrator, cartoonist comic books Popular Mechanics, Electronics Illustrated, Popular Sci., NYC, 1939—42, 1946—50; pres., designer, inventor Mosamics Co., Bklyn., 1948—50; art dir., advt. mgr. Univ. Loudspeakers, White Plains, NY, 1951—60; owner, mgr., graphic designer Studio Concepts, Wantagh, NY, 1957—. Artist Civilian Conservation Corps, Adirondacks, 1936; tchr. art Ctr. Island Jewish Sch., Freeport, NY, 1959; newspaper artist Bering Breeze, Aleutian Islands, 1945-46; co-founder Northwest Pacific chpt. AVC Adak, 1945; worked with North Am. Philips, Amperex, Gen. Instruments, Gen. Signal, Cardion, Schweber Electronics, Singer-Telesignal; Veeco/Lambda Electronics, Plessey Inc.; Polytech. R&D, Univ. Loudspeakers, Harmon Kardon, Brit. Industries, Hohner Harmonicas; lectr. career guidance Mid. Sch. East students; presenter in field Author: (poetry) My Mother Died Dancing, 1960; designer, creator illuminated slide series LI Comty. chorus; contbr. poetry to anthologies; three-man show Heckscher Mus., Huntington, NY, 1964; exhibited in group shows Mcpl. Gallery, Jackson, Miss., 1943, Allied Artists of Am., 1957-85, Nat. Art Club, NYC, 1959, Art Directions, 1959, ACA Galleries, 1960, Hofstra U., Adelphi U., Nassau CC, 1980, LI Art Dirs. Exhbn. Firehouse Gallery, 1980, Nassau County Art Mus., 1980, Hempstead Harbor Art Assn., Glen Cove, LI, 1982, Knickerbocker Artists, Islip Mus., 1983, Wantagh Libr., 1975, Levittown Libr., 1986, Freeport Libr., 1987, Plainview Libr., 2002, Brandeis U. Men's Club lecture series, 2002; illustrator: Planets (Willie Ley); author, creator: American Indian, Crime and Punishment, Superstition and Parapsychology, 1947-50; prodr. bicentennial pictorial chronological map of Entire Am. Revolution, Spirit of '76, 1975; inventor process for mass prodn. ceramic and transparent mosaics, silk screen sys. for printing inside compound curves; creator innovative 2 color graphics method; new age art: developer combining chemically colored copper (sculpture) plastic, resins and reflective integral elements with electronics, 1973—; prodr. crossover filming of painting, sculpture and poetry recitation as ongoing creative product of Bridges of Mind, 1993—, Career Forum, 1999—. Designer war posters visual aids for U.S. Army, 1942-44; creator comic character Giggy F. Useless, used in basic tng. and theatre dramatizations and for Army newspaper, 1943-46. Sgt. AUS, 1942-46. Art Student's League scholar, 1936-37; recipient grand prize for redesign Levitt Home, 1967, Printing Industries, NY, 1973, numerous graphics awards, 1973-84, graphic excellence award Monadnock Mills, 1975, Desi grand award, 1980-82, poetry award Nassau County Fine Arts Mus., 1981, award of excellence IEEE, World Trade Ctr., NYC, 1984, Vets. Soc. Am. Artists, 1984, award of excellence Long Beach Art League, 1989 Mem. Internat. Soc. Poets, Freeport Arts Coun., Allied Artists Am. (pres. 1985-86), Huntington Twp. Art League, DAV, Comic Artist Guild (treas.), Nature Conservancy, various environ. groups. Achievements include development of process for mass-producing mosaics, both traditional and current for architecture as well as home decor; transparent (per-stained glass) and opaque. Home and Office: 33 Downhill Ln Wantagh NY 11793-1817 Office Phone: 516-785-5440.

GLASER, DONALD ARTHUR, physicist; b. Cleve., Sept. 21, 1926; s. William Joseph Glaser; m. Lynn Bercouitz, 1975. BS, Case Inst. Tech., 1946, ScD (hon.), 1959; PhD, Calif. Inst. Tech., 1949; ScD (hon.), U. Mich., 2002. Prof. physics U. Mich., 1949—59; prof. physics U. Calif., Berkeley, 1959—, prof. grad. sch., divsn. neurobiology, 1964—. Recipient Henry Russel award, U. Mich., 1955, Charles V. Boys prize, Phys. Soc., London, 1958, Nobel prize in Physics, 1960, Gold medal, Case Inst. Tech., 1967, Golden Plate award, Am. Acad. of Achievement, 1989; fellow NSF, 1961, Guggenheim, 1961—62, Smith-Kettlewell Inst. for Vision Rsch., 1983—84. Fellow: AAAS, Am. Physics Soc. (prize 1959), Neuroscis. Inst., Royal Swedish Acad. Sci., Royal Soc. Sci., Assn. Rsch. Vision and Ophthalmology, The Exploratorium (bd. dirs.), Fedn. Am. Scientists; mem.: NAS, Am. Philos. Soc., Internat. Acad. Sci., N.Y. Acad. Scis., Am. Assn. Artificial Intelligence, Sigma Xi, Theta Tau, Tau Kappa Alpha. Achievements include invention of the Bubble Chamber. Office: U Calif 221 Donner Lab Dept Physics and Neurobio 237 Hildebrand Hall #3206 Berkeley CA 94720-3206 Business E-Mail: glaser@berkeley.edu.

GLASER, GERARD R., science administrator; Acting exec. officer Nat. Sci. Bd., Arlington, Va., 2002—03, dir. divsn. grants and agreements, 2003—. Office: Nat Sci Found 4201 Wilson Blvd Arlington VA 22230

GLASER, GILBERT HERBERT, retired neuroscientist, educator; b. NYC, Nov. 10, 1920; s. Burnard Richard and Sidelle (Rogers) G.; m. Morfydd Mai Pugh, Mar. 17, 1946; children: Gareth Evan, Sara Elizabeth. AB, Columbia, 1940, MD, 1943, Med. Sc.D., 1951; MA (hon.), Yale, 1963. Diplomate: Am. Bd. Psychiatry and Neurology. Intern Mt. Sinai Hosp., NYC, 1943-44; resident neurology N.Y. Neurol. Inst., 1944-46; research asst. to assoc. neurology Columbia Coll. Physicians and Surgeons, 1948-52; research scientist N.Y. Psychiat. Inst., 1948-50; head. sect. neurology Sch. Medicine Yale U., 1952-71, chmn. dept. neurology Sch. Medicine, 1971-86, asst. prof. neurology Sch. Medicine, 1952-55, assoc. prof. Sch. Medicine, 1955-63, prof. neurology Sch. Medicine, 1963-91, prof. neurology emeritus, 1991—. Commonwealth Fund vis. prof. neurology U. London, Eng., 1965-66; cons. West Haven (Conn.) VA Hosp., 1955-91; vis. prof. neurology Nat. Hosp., London, 1972, Park Hosp., Oxford, Eng., 1973-86, Hunan Med. Coll., Peoples Republic of China, 1986, U. Niigata, Kyoto, Japan, 1989; Fulbright Disting. prof. neurology Zagreb U., Yugoslavia, 1981; vis. scholar Green Coll. Oxford U., Eng., 1987-88; mem. neurology research adv. com. USPHS, 1956-60, 68-72, spl. cons., 1973, epilepsy adv. com., 1974-77, chmn. basic sci. subcom., 1977-80; mem. neurobiology rev. com. VA, 1975-78, chmn., 1977-78. Author: EEG and Behavior, 1963; Editor: Epilepsia, 1958-76; adv. editor, 1976-86; editor: Recent Advances in Clinical Neurology, 1978, 81, 84, Antiepileptic Drugs: Mechanisms of Action, 1980; mem. editorial bd.: Jour. Nervous and Mental Diseases, Annats of Neurology, Jour. of Neurological Sci.; Contbr. articles to profl. jours. Capt. M.C. AUS, 1946-48. Recipient Janeway prize Columbia U., 1943, Bicentennial medal award, 1968, Book award Commonwealth Fund, 1975. Fellow Royal Soc. Medicine, ACP; mem. Am. Neurol. Assn. (hon., 1st v.p. 1977-78), Am. Acad. Neurology (pres. 1973-75 hon. mem. 1998), Am. Epilepsy Soc. (pres. 1963, Lennox lectr. 1985), Am. Electroencephalographic Soc. (council 1958-61, bd. qualifications), Eastern Assn. Electroencephalographers (pres. 1958), EEG Soc. (Gt. Britain), Assn. Brit. Neurologists, Soc. for Neurosci. (hon.), Epilepsy Found. Am. (med. adv. bd.), Myasthenia Gravis Foundation (med. adv. bd. chmn. 1964-65), Multiple Sclerosis Soc. (chmn. research programs com. 1973-74, med. adv. bd.). Clubs: Athenaeum (London). Home: 205 Millbrook Rd North Haven CT 06473-4334

GLASER, LUIS, biochemistry educator; b. Vienna, Mar. 30, 1932; came to U.S., 1953, naturalized, 1961; s. Hermann and Gisela (Kohn) G.; m. Ruth Walliser, May 18, 1961; children: Miriam, Nicole. BA, U. Toronto, Ont., Can., 1953; PhD, Washington U., St. Louis, 1956. Asst. prof. biol. chemistry Washington U., 1959-62, asso. prof., 1962-67, prof., 1967-75, chmn. dept. biol. chemistry, 1975-86; dir. Div. Biology and Biomed. Scis., 1980-86; exec. v.p., provost U. Miami, 1986—2005, prof. Biology and spl. asst. to the pres., 2005—. Contbr. numerous articles on bacterial and mammalian metabolism to profl. jours.; editor Jour. Biol. Chemistry, 1969-74, 81-86, Jour. Supramolecular Structures, 1979-86, Jour. Cell Biology, 1981-92. Helen Hay Whitney fellow, 1956-59; NIH grantee; NSF grantee. Mem. Am. Soc. Biol. Chemists, Am. Chem. Soc., Am. Soc. Microbiology, Am. Soc. Neurochemists, AAAS. Jewish. Office: PO Box 248033 Coral Gables FL 33124-8033 Office Phone: 305-284-3356. E-mail: lglaser@umiami.edu.

GLASER, MILTON, graphics designer, illustrator; b. NYC, June 26, 1929; s. Eugene and Eleanor (Bergman) G.; m. Shirley Girton, Aug. 13, 1957. Student, Cooper Union Art Sch., 1948-51; DFA (hon.), Mpls. Inst. Arts, 1971; postgrad., Moore Coll., Phila., 1975, Phila. Mus. Sch. Visual Arts, 1979, SUNY, Buffalo, 1987; degree (hon.), Queen's Coll., CUNY, 1990; doctorate (hon.), Royal Coll. Art, London, 1995. Co-founder, pres. Push Pin Studios, NYC, 1954-74; co-founder, pres., chmn. bd., design dir. N.Y. mag., 1968-77; v.p., design dir. Village Voice, NYC, 1975-77; pres. Milton Glaser, Inc., NYC, 1974—. Designer Grand Union Supermarkets, 1978-97; art dir. graphics, chmn. art selection com. for restoration Rainbow Room at Rockefeller Ctr., 1987-88, pres., 1990—; bd. dirs. Internat. Design Conf., Aspen, Colo., 1972—, co-chmn., 1973, pres., 1990; mem. total identity program mktg. & advt. Queens Coll. Author: If Apples Had Teeth, 1960, Milton Glaser: Graphic Design, 1973, The Underground Gourmet, 1974, The Milton Glaser Poster Book, 1977, Milton Glaser Barcelona, 1989, Giorgio Morandi Milton Glaser, I Manifesti Di, Art Is Work, 2000; Co-author:(with Shirley Glaser) The Alphazeds, 2003, (with Mirko Ilic & Tony Kushner) The Design of Dissent: Socially and Poltically Driven Graphics, 2005; illustrator numerous books; designed observation deck and restaurant graphics for World Trade Ctr. Twin Towers, N.Y.C., 1975; graphic and interior designer Sesame Pl., Bucks County, Pa., 1980; designer restaurants Aurora, N.Y.C., Tratorria dell'Arte, N.Y.C., La Hosteria; graphics and signage Rainbow Room, Rockefeller Ctr., N.Y.C.; designer N.Y. Unearthed Mus., N.Y.C., 1990; logo for Tony Kushner's Tony-award-winning play Angels in America, 1993; designer new Windows on the World Bar and Restaurant at the World Trade Ctr., N.Y.C., 1996, Land's End Direct Merchants; design cons. Stony Brook U., others; exhbns. include Mus. Modern Art, N.Y., 1975, Centre Georges Pompidou, Paris, 1977, Lincoln Ctr. Gallery, N.Y., 1981, Houghton Gallery, Cooper Union, N.Y., 1984, Vicenza Mus., Italy, 1989, Galleria Communale d'Arte Moderna, Bologna, 1989, Nuages Gallery, Milan, 1988, Am. Inst. Graphic Arts, N.Y.C., 2000, Phila. Mus. Art, 2000; retrospective at 2000 Carnevale, Venice; represented in permanent collections Mus. Modern Art, N.Y., Israel Mus., Jerusalem, Nat. Archive, Smithsonian Inst., Washington, Cooper Hewitt Nat. Design Mus., N.Y. Trustee Cooper Union Art Sch., Maine Sch. Visual Arts; bd. dirs. Sch Visual Arts, N.Y., 1961—. Recipient St. Gauden's medal Cooper Union, 1972, gold medal Soc. Illustrators, 1979, Soc. Indsl. Artists and Designers medal 1985, honors award AIA, 1992, Fulbright award for individual achievement Metro Internat., 1992, Lifetime Achievement honor, Smithsonian Cooper-Hewitt Nat. Design Museum, 2004; Fulbright scholar Acad. Fine Arts, Bologna, Italy, 1952-53; hon. fellow Royal Soc. Arts, 1979. Mem. Am. Inst. Graphic Arts (co-chair nat. conf. 1989, Gold medal 1972), Art Dirs. Club (Hall of Fame 1979), Alliance Graphique Internat. (Prix Savignac 1996). Jewish. Office: Milton Glaser Inc 207 E 32nd St New York NY 10016-6305

GLASER, PATRICIA L., lawyer; b. Charleston, W.Va., Sept. 15, 1947; d. Richard Stanley and Tilda Jane (Rosen) G.; m. Samuel Hunter Mudie, May 19, 1978; stepchildren: Heather and Jason Mudie. BA, Am. U., 1969; JD, Rutgers U., 1973. Bar: Calif. 1973, U.S. Dist. Ct. (no. and cen. dists.) Calif. 1973, U.S. Dist. Ct. (so. dist.) 1976, U.S. Ct. Appeals (9th cir.), U.S. Supreme Ct. Law clk. to presiding justice U.S. Dist. Ct.; from assoc. to ptnr. Wyman, Bautzer, Rothman, Kuchel & Silbert, Los Angeles, 1973—. Judge pro tem West br. Los Angeles Mcpl. Ct., panelist legal continuing edn. programs. Mem. fund-raising com. Deukmejian for Gov. of Calif.; participant Parole-Aide program. Mem. Los Angeles County Bar Assn. (fed. cts. and practices com.). Avocations: travel, skiing, tennis, reading.

GLASER, PETER EDWARD, retired mechanical engineer, consultant, educator; b. Zatec, Bohemia, Czechoslovakia, Sept. 5, 1923; came to U.S., 1948, naturalized July, 1954; s. Hugo and Helen (Weiss) G.; m. Eva F. Graf, Oct. 16, 1955; children: David, Steven, Susan. Diploma, Leeds Coll. Tech., Eng., 1943; 1st state exam, Czech Tech U., Prague, Czechoslovakia, 1948; MS, Columbia U., NYC, 1951, PhD, 1955. Head design dept. Werner Mgmt. Co., NYC, 1948-53; from mem. profl. staff to cons. Arthur D. Little, Inc., Cambridge, Mass., 1955—94, v.p., 1985, cons., 1994—99; pres. Power from Space Cons., Inc., Lexington, Mass., 1995—2005; ret., 2005. Cons. NASA, Washington, 1963-67, mem. adv. coun., 1986; mem. case study task force Lunar Energy Enterpise, 1988-89; mgmt. adv. bd. Ctr. for Space Power, Tex. A&M U. System, 1990-94; sr. adv. bd. mem. Space Studies Inst., 1990—; mem. bd. assessment NIST program NRC, 1993-96; cons. NRC, Washington, 1960-62, panel mem., 1994-95, Heritage Found., Washington, 1982-83; adv. panelist Office Tech. Assessment, Washington, 1980-81; mem. Awards Adv. Coun. of Space Found., 1988-96. Editor: The Lunar Surface Layer, 1964, Thermal Imaging Techniques, 1964, Solar Power Satellites-The Emerging Energy Option, 1993, Solar Power Satellites-A Space Energy System for Earth, 2d edit., 1998, Solar Power Systems in Space; contbr. Standard Handbook of Powerplant Engineering, 1998; assoc. editor Space Power Jour., 1980-86; editor-in-chief Jour. Solar Energy, 1972-85, mem. editl. bd., 1985-93; mem. editl. bd. Space Policy, Space Power, Jour. Practical Applications in Space, Solar Energy; patentee solar power satellite, 1973; guest editor spl. issue of "Space Policy" on Space Solar Power, 1999-2000. Mem. bd. overseers Combined Jewish Philanthropies, Boston, 1984-88; voting mem. engrng. coun. Columbia U., N.Y.C., 1984; advisor Space Solar Power Rsch. Soc., Japan, 1998—. Recipient Carl F. Kayan medal Columbia U., 1974, Farrington Daniels award Internat. Solar Energy Soc., Australia, 1983; named to U.S. Space Found. Space Tech. Hall of Fame, 1996. Fellow AAAS, AIAA; mem. ASME, Internat. Astron. Fedn. (chmn. space power com. 1984-89), Internat. Acad. Astronautics, Internat. Solar Energy Soc. (pres. 1967-72), Am. Astron. Soc. (bd. dirs. 1977-84), Sunsat Energy Coun. (pres. 1978-94, chmn. 1994—2000), Nat. Space Soc. (bd. advisors 1990-94, dir. 1994-97, bd. govs. 1997—), United Socs. in Space (regent 1997—), Am. Soc. for Macro-Engrng. Avocation: archaeology.

GLASER, ROBERT, communications executive; BA in Econ., MA in Econ., Yale U., BS in Computer Sci. CEO and chmn. Progressive Networks, Seattle; various pos. Microsoft Corp., 1983—93; founder, CEO, chmn. RealNetworks, Seattle, 1995—. Adv. com. on pub. interest Pres. Clinton; spkr. in field. Editor: Yale Daily News. Office: Real Networks 2601 Elliott Ave Ste 1000 Seattle WA 98121

GLASER, ROBERT EDWARD, lawyer; b. Cin., Jan. 12, 1935; s. Delbert Henry and Rita Elizabeth (Arlinghaus) G.; m. Kathleen Eileen Grannen, June 17, 1961; children— Petra M., Timothy X., Mark G., Bridget M., Christopher D., Jenny M., Michael F. BS in Bus. Adminstrn. cum laude, Xavier U., Cin., 1955; LLB, U. Cin., 1960; LLM, U. Chgo., 1962; postgrad., U. Tuebingen, Fed. Republic of Germany, 1961. Bar: Ohio 1960, U.S. Dist. Ct. (no. dist.) Ohio 1963, (so. dist.) Ohio 1964, U.S. Ct. Appeals (6th cir.) 1964, U.S. Tax Ct. 1970, U.S. Ct. Internat. Trade 1971, U.S. Ct. Fed. Claims 1992, U.S. Ct. Appeals (fed. cir.) 2000. Assoc. Arter & Hadden, Cleve., 1963-69, ptnr., 1970-2001, chmn., 1983-92; owner Law Office of Robert E. Glaser, 2001—. Arbitrator Cuyahoga County Ct. Common Pleas, Ohio, 1972—, Med. Malpractice Panel, 1985—, Mediator Settlement Week, 1990; lectr. Cleve. Tax Inst., 1966—2000, mem. exec. com., 1980—84, chmn., 1982; lectr. Can.-U.S. Law Inst., 1980, Res. Officers Assn., 1970—, Ret. Officers Assn., 1985—; mem. qualified list of neutrals IRS Rev. Proc., 2003—. Contbr. articles to legal jours. Sec. Bay View Hosp., 1972-81; trustee Mental Health Rehab. and Rsch., Inc., 1975-86, mem. exec. com., 1977-81, pres., 1979-81; trustee Cmty. Legal Svcs. Cleve., Inc., 2004—06, legal counsel, 2004—06, v.p. 2006; mem. men's com. Cleve. Play House, 1965-2003; mem. joint mental health and corrections com. Fedn. Cmty. Planning, 1978-81; mem. Cleve. Coun. on Fgn. Affairs, 1987-2002; mem. vis. com. Coll. Law Cleve. State U., 1987-97; mem. Soc. of Benchers, Case Western Res. Univ. Coll. Law, 1988—; trustee Univ. Circle, Inc., 1989-99, mem. exec. com., 1989-99. Col. U.S. Army, ret. Ford Found. grantee, 1960. Fellow Am. Bar Found. (life); mem. Ohio Bar Assn. (gen. tax com. 1998—, lawyer assistance com. 1999—), Nat. Bar Assn., Cleve. Bar Assn. (trustee 1983-87, chmn. bd. of com. grievance and discipline trial com. 1993, gen. tax com. 1983-2004, lawyer assistance com. 1999-2004), Legal Aid Soc. Cleve., Am. Judicature Soc., 8th Jud. Conf. (life), Am. Arbitration Assn. (nat. and internat. panel arbitrators 1969—), Citizens League Greater Cleve., Cleve. Cath. Lawyer Guild (pres. 1969-70, St. Thomas More award 2006), Tax Club Cleve., Order of Coif, Union Club, Pentagon Officers Athletic Club, Serra Internat., Cleve. Club (exec. com. 1987-88, 90-91, 93-98, 2000-04, pres. 1994-96, 2002-04), KC. Roman Catholic. Office: Law Office of Robert E Glaser Ste 1150 925 Euclid Ave Cleveland OH 44115-1475 Home: 33750 Lorain Rd North Ridgeville OH 44039 Office Phone: 216-696-2938. Business E-Mail: robert.glaser@tuckerellis.com.

GLASER, ROBERT JOY, retired internist, foundation administrator; b. St. Louis, Sept. 11, 1918; s. Joseph and Regina Glaser; m. Helen Louise Hofsommer, Apr. 1, 1949 (dec. Oct. 1999); children: Sally Louise, Joseph II, Robert Joy. SB, Harvard U., 1940, MD magna cum laude, 1943; DS (hon.), U. Health Scis.-Chgo. Med. Sch., 1972; DS (hon.), Temple U., 1973; DS (hon.), U. N.H., 1979, U. Colo., 1979; LHD, Rush Med. Coll., 1973; DS, Mt. Sinai Med. Sch., 1984; DS (hon.), Washington U., 1988, Thomas Jefferson U., 1991; DHL, Johns Hopkins U., 2000; DS (hon.), Watson Sch. of Biol. Scis., 2001. Diplomate Am. Bd. Internal Medicine. Med. intern Barnes Hosp., St. Louis, 1944, asst. resident physician, 1945—46, resident physician, 1946—47, asst. physician, 1949—57; asst. resident physician Peter Bent Brigham Hosp., Boston, 1944—45; NRC fellow med. scis. Wash. U. Med. Sch., 1947—49, instr. medicine, 1949—50, asst. prof., 1950—56, assoc. dean., 1947, asst. dean, 1953—55, assoc. prof., 1956—57, assoc. dean, 1955—57; dean, prof. medicine Med. Sch. U. Colo., 1957—63, v.p. for med. affairs, 1959—63; vis. physician Washington U. Med. Service, St. Louis City Hosp., 1950; chief svc. Washington U. Med. Svc. St. Louis City Hosp., 1950—53; cons. Washington U. Med. Service, St. Louis City Hosp., 1953—57; attending physician Colo. Gen. Hosp., Denver, 1957—63; prof. social medicine Harvard U., Boston, 1963—65; pres. Affiliated Hosps. Ctr., Inc., 1963—65; v.p. med. affairs, dean Sch. Medicine, prof. medicine Stanford U., 1965—70, acting pres., 1968, cons. prof., 1972—97, prof. emeritus, 1997—; bd. dirs. Henry J. Kaiser Family Found., 1970—83, pres., chief exec. officer, 1972—83; attending physician Columbia-Presbyn. Med. Ctr., NYC, 1971—72, clin. prof. medicine, 1971—72; dir. for med. sci. Lucille P. Markey Charitable Trust, 1984—97, trustee, 1989—97. Bd. dirs. Maxygen; cons. medicine VA Hosp., Denver, 1957—63, Fitzsimons Army Hosp., Aurora, Colo., 1957—63, Lowry AFB, Denver, 1957—63; mem. nat. adv. coun. NIMH, 1970—72, Harvard Fund Coun., 1953—56, Harvard Med. Alumni Coun., 1956—59, 1991—94, pres., 1993—94; assoc. mem. streptococal commn. Armed Forces Epidemiologic Bd., 1958—61; chmn. com. study nat. needs biomed. and behavioral rsch. pers. NAS-NRC, 1974—77; mem. vis. com. Med. Sch. Harvard U., 1968—74, Sch. Pub. Health, 1971—77; bd. visitors Charles Drew Postgrad. Med. Sch., 1972—79; mem. com. on med. affairs Yale U., 1969—82, adv. bd. Sch. Orgn. and Mgmt., 1976—84; vis. com. Tufts Med. Sch., 1974—84. Editor: Pharos, 1962—97; editor emeritus:, 1997—; contbr. articles to sci. jours., chapters to books. Bd. regents Georgetown U., 1976—78; trustee Commonwealth Fund, 1969—88, v.p., 1970—72; trustee David and Lucile Packard Found., 1984—96, trustee emeritus, 1996—; trustee Pacific Sch. Religion, 1972—77, Washington U., St. Louis, 1979—87, 1988—, trustee emeritus, 1996—; trustee Albert and Mary Lasker Found., 1998—2003, Palo Alto Med. Found., 1974—, vice chmn., 1991—2000, trustee emeritus, 2000—; mem. Sloan Commn. on Govt. in Higher Edn., 1977—79; bd. dirs. Kaiser Found. Hosps., Kaiser Found. Health Plan, 1969—79, Coun. on Founds., 1974—79, Packard Humanities Inst., 1987—. Recipient William Greenleaf Eliot Soc. Search award, 1998, Hubert H. Humphrey Cancer Rsch. Ctr. award, Disting. Citizen award for outstanding leadership of med. edn. and rsch., Harvard Club of San Francisco, Harvard medal, 2003. Master: ACP; fellow: AAAS, Royal Coll. Physicians London, Am. Philos. Soc., Am. Acad. Arts and Scis. (exec. bd., v.p. 1972—76); mem.: N.Y. Acad. Medicine (John Stearns award for lifetime achievement in medicine 2000), Inst. Medicine NAS (acting pres. 1970—71, chmn. membership com. 1970—72, mem. exec. com. 1971—73), Nat. Inst. Allergy and Infectious Disease (tng. grant com. 1957—60), Am. Soc. Exptl. Pathology, Western Assn. Physicians (councillor 1960—63), Assn. Am. Physicians, Assn. Am. Med. Colls. (asst. sec. 1956—60, chmn. com. edn. and rsch. 1958—63, mem. exec. coun. 1959—63, v.p. 1963—64, chmn.exec. coun. and assembly 1968—69, mem. exec. coun. 1976—79, Abraham Flexner award, Disting. Svc. award), Am. Soc. Clin. Investigation, Ctrl. Soc. Clin. Rsch. (councillor 1955—58), Am. Fedn. Clin. Rsch. (chmn. midwestern sect. 1954—55), Am. Clin. and Climatological Assn. (pres. 1982—83), Century Club, Harvard Club (N.Y.C.), Alpha Omega Alpha (bd. dirs. 1963—77), Sigma Xi. Personal E-mail: robert.glaser@stanford.edu.

GLASER, RONALD, microbiologist, educator; b. NYC, Feb. 27, 1939; s. Irving and Pauline G.; m. Janice Kiecolt, Jan. 17, 1980; children: Andrew, Erik. BA, U. Bridgeport, 1962; MS, U. R.I., 1964; PhD, U. Conn., 1968; postgrad., Baylor Coll. Medicine, 1968-69. Asst. prof. microbiology Pa. State U., Hershey, 1970-73, assoc. prof., 1973-77, prof., 1977-78; prof. chmn. dept. med. microbiology and immunology Coll. Medicine Ohio State U., Columbus, 1978—92; reviewer NIH and NASA study sects.; assoc. dean for rsch. and grad. edn. Med. Ctr. Ohio State U., Columbus, 1992-94, assoc. v.p. health sci. rsch. Med. Ctr., 1994-2001, assoc. v.p. rsch., 2001—03. Editor: (with T. Gottleib-Stematsky) Human Herpes Virus Infections: Clinical Aspects, 1982; (with others) Epstein-Barr Virus and Human Disease, 1987; (with J. Jones) Human Herpes Virus Infections, 1994; (with J. Kiecolt-Glaser) Handbook of Human Stress, 1994. NIH postdoc. fellow, 1968-69; Franco-Am. Exch. Program; Fogarty Internat. Ctr.; NIH and INSRM fellow, 1975, 77; Leukemia Soc. Am. scholar, 1974-79. Fellow: AAAS, Acad. Behavioral Medicine Rsch. (pres. psychoneuroimmunology rsch. soc. 2003, pres. behavioral med. rsch. 2007—); mem.: Am. Soc. Microbiology. Office: Ohio State U 2175 Graves Hall 333 W 10th Ave Columbus OH 43210-1239 Home Phone: 614-771-9119; Office Phone: 614-292-5526. E-mail: ronald.glaser@osumc.edu.

GLASER, THOMAS WILLIAM, educational administrator; b. Chgo., May 2, 1952; s. Thomas Harry and Cecelia Martha (Hirsch) G.; m. Nancy Lee Poole, Mar. 16, 1983. B.A., Tex. Christian U., 1974; m. Internat. Mgmt., Am. Grad. Sch. Internat. Mgmt., 1975; postgrad. Tex. State U., 1980. Gun dept. mgr. Zales Corp., Cullum & Boren Sporting Goods, Ft. Worth, 1971-75; family security analyst Met. Life Ins. Co., Arlington, Tex., 1975-76; telephone sales coordinator Stocksill Shooters Supply, Grapevine, Tex., 1976-79; coordinator customer service/cost control Greif Bros. Co., Ft. Worth, 1979-82; v.p. mktg. Holloway Arms Co., Ft. Worth, 1982-84; asst. curator exhibits DeGolver Library So. Meth. U., Dallas, 1984-85; dean of students, tchr. The Oakridge Sch., Arlington, Tex., 1985-86; dir. edn. Mansfield Bus. Sch., Dallas, 1986—. Served as maj. Tex. State Guard Mem. Nat. Rifle Assn. (life), Internat. Mil. Arms Soc., Nat. Guard Assn. Tex. (life), Tex. State Rifle Assn. (life.), Civil War Round Table Tex. (treas. 1979-81), Am. Def. Preparedness Assn. (life), Tex. State Guard Assn. (life), Dallas Arms Collectors Assn. (life), So. Hist. Assn., Soc. Historians of Early Am. Republic, Orgn. Am. Historians, Res. Officers Assn., Assn. U.S. Army, Am. Mgmt. Assn., Mensa (nat. coordinator Civil War spl. interest group 1976-80, sec. Ft. Worth 1976-80), Am. Hist. Assn., U.S. Naval Inst., Société Internationale des Officers, Alpha Phi Omega, Phi Alpha Theta (pres. Alpha Lambda chpt. 1983-84). Office: Sch for Avanced Studies N 1380 NW 27th Ave Ste 1111 Miami FL 33125-2510

GLASER, VERA ROMANS, journalist; b. St. Louis, Apr. 21, 1916; d. Aaron L. and Mollie (Romans); m. Herbert R. Glaser, Apr. 16, 1939; 1 dau., Carol Jane Barriger. Student, Washington U., St. Louis, George Washington U., Am. U., 1937-40. Reporter-writer Nat. Aero. mag., 1943-44; reporter Washington Times Herald, 1944-46; pub. relations specialist Great Lakes-St. Lawrence Assn., 1950-51; promotion specialist, writer Congl. Quar. News Features, 1951-54; writer-commentator radio sta. WGMS, Washington, 1954-55; mem. Washington bur. N.Y. Herald Tribune, 1955-56; press officer U.S. Senator Charles E. Potter, 1956-59; dir. pub. relations, women's div. Rep. Nat. Com., 1959-62; press officer U.S. Senator Kenneth B. Keating, 1962-63; Washington corr. N.Am. Newspaper Alliance, 1963-69, bur. chief, 1965-69; columnist, nat. corr. Knight-Ridder Newspapers, Inc., 1969-81; assoc. editor Washingtonian Mag., 1981-88, contbg. editor, 1988—; columnist Maturity News Svc., 1988-94. Mem. Pres.'s Commn. on White House Fellows, 1969, Pres.'s Task Force on Women's Rights and Responsibilities, 1970; judge 1981 Robert Kennedy Journalism Awards. Free-lance writer nat publs., radio and TV appearances Stas. WTOP-TV, ABC, PBS, C-SPAN. Mem. nat. bd. Med. Coll. Pa., 1977-88; bd. dirs. Washington Press Club Found., 1986-88; bd. dirs. Internat. Women's Media Found., 1990-98. Mem. White House Corrs. Assn., Nat. Press Club (bd. govs. 1988, 89), Washington Press Club (pres. 1971-72), Cosmos Club. Unitarian Universalist. Home and Office: 5555 Friendship Blvd Apt 724 Chevy Chase MD 20815-7243

GLASGOW, NORMAN MILTON, lawyer; b. Washington, Aug. 14, 1922; children: Norman M., Heather Glasgow Harris, Glenn. BS, U. Md., 1943; LLB, JD, BA, George Washington U., 1949. Bar: D.C. 1949, U.S. Supreme Ct. 1956, Md. 1960. Assoc. Wilkes, McGarraghy & Artis, Washington, 1949-55; ptnr. Wilkes & Artis, Washington, 1955-82; pres. Wilkes, Artis, Hedrick & Lane, Washington, 1982-86, sr. prin., 1988-2000; ptnr. Holland & Knight, LLP, Washington, 2001—. Bd. dirs., gen. counsel Greater Washington Bd. Trade, 1966, 87, 88; mem., chmn. Md. PAC, 1981-93; bd. govs. Washington Bldg. Congress; mem. Citizens Tech. Adv. Com. for Drafting Bldg. Code and Zoning Regulations, Washington, Commrs. Citizens Adv. Com. on Zoning, Washington, Balt. conv. Ctr. Authority Transp. Revenue Com., Gov.'s Salary Commn., Gov.'s Spl. Com. Vehicle Emissions Inspection Program, Gov.'s Adv. Redistricting Com.; chmn. Gov.'s Task Force Statewide Bldg. Performance Stds., Md. Stadium Authority, 1993-97, Md. Econ. Growth, Resource Protection and Planning Commn., co-chair subcom. for updating state planning and zoning laws, 1993-97; chmn. Md. Econ. Growth Task Force; mem. Gov.'s Western Md. Econ. Devel. Strategies Task Force, 1998—, co-chair Updating Md. Zoning and Planning Regulations (Article 66B). 1st lt. U.S. Army, 1942-46, ETO. Recipient Outstanding Alumni award George Washington U., 1985, Outstanding Svc. award D.C. Real Estate, Greater Washington Bd. Trade, 1978. Mem. Supreme Ct. Bar Assn., D.C. Bar Assn., Md. Bar Assn., Urban Land Inst., Am. Soc. Planning Ofcls., Washington Bldg. Congress, Nat. Assn. Bus. Economists, Nat. Conf. States in Bldg. Codes and Stds., Lambda Alpha. Avocation: gardening. Office: Holland & Knight 2099 Penn Ave NW Washington DC 20006-2803

GLASGOW, WILLIAM JACOB, lawyer, venture capitalist, business executive; b. Portland, Oreg., Sept. 29, 1946; s. Joseph Glasgow and Lena (Friedman) Schiff; m. Renée Vonfeld, Aug. 30, 1969; children: Joshua, Andrew. BS in econ. magna cum laude, U. Pa., 1968; JD magna cum laude, Harvard U., 1972. Bar: Oreg. 1972, U.S. Dist. Ct. Oreg. 1972, U.S. Ct. Appeals (9th cir.) 1978. Assoc. Rives, Bonyhadi & Drummond, Portland, 1972-76, ptnr., 1976-79; mng. ptnr. Perkins Coie, Portland, 1983-88; sr. v.p., gen. counsel PacifiCorp Fin. Svcs. Inc., Portland, 1988-89, chmn., CEO, 1989-95; sr. v.p. PacifiCorp, Portland, 1992-93, sr. v.p., CFO, 1993-95; pres. PacifiCorp Holdings Inc., Portland, 1992-95; pres., dir. NERCO, Inc., Portland, 1992-93; dir. Pacific-Telecom, Inc., 1992-93; ret. PacifiCorp, Portland, 1996; co-chmn. Shaw, Glasgow & Co. LLC, 1995-96; pres., CEO BCN Data Sys. (a Bechtel/CellNet Data Sys. joint venture), Portland, 1996-2000, Madrona Venture Group LLP, Portland, 2000—03; coo Fish & Neave LLP/Ropes & Gray LLP, NYC, 2003—05; ptnr. Perkins Coie LLP, Portland, Oreg., 2005—. Pres. bd. trustees Oreg. Mus. Sci. and Industry, Portland, 1976-82; mem. exec. com. bd. Portland C. of C. 1982-1983; pres. N.W. Fin. Symposium, Portland, 1985; trustee Oreg. Art Inst., 1990-92, 94-, Oreg. Grad. Inst. Sci. and Tech., 1991-97, Discovery Inst., 1992-; pres. Portland Met. Sports Authority, 1992-; trustee Portland Art Mus. 1992-1997; v.p. NIKE World Masters Games, 1994-; bd. dirs. Internat. World Masters Games, 1994-, pres., bd, trustees, chmn. emertius Oreg. Sports Authority 1992-1998. Mem. Oreg. Bar Assn., Portland C. of C. (bd. dirs. 1983), Harvard Law Sch. Alumni Assn. (pres. Oreg. chpt. 1981). Democrat. Office: Perkins Coie LLP 1120 NW Couch St 10th Fl Portland OR 97209-4128 Office Phone: 503-727-2118. Office Fax: 503-346-2118. Business E-Mail: wglasgow@perkinscoie.com.*

GLASHAUSSER, CHARLES MICHAEL, physicist, researcher; b. Newark, Dec. 7, 1939; s. Charles Michael and Ruth Mary (Dietz) G.; m. Suellen O'Brien, Sept. 7, 1965; children: Alexander, Allegra. BS, Boston Coll., 1961; PhD, Princeton U., 1966. Physicist Ctr. d'Etude Nucléaires, France, 1965-67; rsch. assoc. Lawrence Berkeley Lab., Calif., 1967-69; from asst. prof. to prof. Rutgers U., New Brunswick, NJ, 1969—, also chmn., Dept. Physics. Chmn. Los Alamos (N.Mex.) Users Group, Inc.; mem. Nuclear Sci. Adv. Com., Washington, 1987-91; mem. program adv. com. Brookhaven, U. Ind., Triumf; guest prof. Univ. Munich, 1975-1976; exchange prof. Univ. Paris, 1991. Contbr. articles to profl. jours. NSF grantee, 1969—. Fellow Am. Phys. Soc. Office: Rutgers U Dept Physics 136 Frelinghuysen Rd Piscataway NJ 08854-8019 Office Phone: 735-445-2501. Business E-Mail: chair@physics.rutgers.edu.

GLASHOW, SHELDON LEE, physicist, researcher; b. NYC, Dec. 5, 1932; s. Lewis and Bella (Rubin) Glashow; m. Joan Glashow; children: Jason David, Jordan, Brian Lewis, Rebecca Lee. AB, Cornell U., 1954; AM, Harvard U., 1955, PhD, 1959; DSc (hon.), Yeshiva U., 1978, U. Marseille, 1982, Adelphi U., 1989, Bar Ilan U., 1989, Gustave Adolphus Coll., 1989, Case Western Res. U., 2001. NSF fellow U. Copenhagen, Denmark, 1958—60; rsch. fellow Calif. Inst. Tech., 1960—61; asst. prof. Stanford U., 1961—62; asst. prof., assoc. prof. U. Calif., Berkeley, 1962—66; prof. physics Harvard U., 1967—84, Higgins prof. physics, 1979—2000; disting. sci. Boston U., 1984—2000; Mellon prof. scis. Harvard U., 1988—93, Higgins prof. of physics emeritus, 2000—; Arthur G.B. Metcalf prof. sci. Boston U., 2000—. Cons. Brookhaven Nat. Lab., 1964, 1966—73; vis. prof. U. Marseille, 1970, MIT, 1974; cons. Brookhaven Nat. Lab., 1975; mem. sci. policy com. CERN, 1979—84; vis. prof. MIT, 1980, Boston U., 1983; affiliated sr. scientist U. Houston, 1983—; univ. scholar Tex. A&M U., 1983—86; hon. prof. U. Nanjing, 1998—. Author (with Ben Bova): Interactions, 1988; author: Charm of Physics, 1990, From Alchemy to Quarks, 1994; contbr. articles to profl. jours. and popular mags.; founding editor Quantum mag., 1989—2000. Pres. Andrei Sakharov Inst., 1980—85, Nat. Com. for Excellence in Edn., 1985—88. Recipient J.R. Oppenheimer Meml. prize, 1977, George Ledlie prize, 1978, Nobel prize in Physics, 1979, Castiglione di Sicilia prize, 1983, Erice Sci. for Peace prize, 1991; fellow NSF, 1955—60, Sloan, 1962—66, CERN vis., 1968. Fellow: AAAS, Am. Phys. Soc.; mem.: NAS, Am. Philosophical Soc., Costa Rica Acad. Sci. (fgn.), Korean Acad. Sci. (fgn.), Russian Acad. Sci. (fgn.), Am. Acad. Arts and Scis., Sigma Xi, Phi Beta Kappa. Achievements include contbns. to theory of unified weak and electromagnetic interactions between elementary particles, including alia the prediction of the weak neutral current. E-mail: slg@bu.edu.

GLASKY, ALVIN JERALD, retired medical research scientist; b. Chgo., June 16, 1933; s. Oscar and Bessie (Akwa) G.; m. Rosalie Anne Hanfling, Aug. 25, 1957; children: Michelle S., Karen R., Mark J., Ira D. BS in Pharmacy, U. Ill., Chgo., 1954, PhD in Biochemistry, 1958. Dir. biochem. research Michael Reese Hosp., Chgo., 1959-61; research pharmacologist Abbott Labs., North Chicago, Ill., 1961-66; v.p. research ICN, Burbank, Calif., 1966-68; pres., CEO Newport Pharms., Inc., Newport Beach, Calif., 1968—86, Neo Therapeutics, Inc., Irvine, Calif., 1987—2002; regents prof. U. Calif., Irvine, 1998—2000. Contbr. articles to profl. jours. Mem. AAAS, Am. Pharm. Assn., Calif. Pharm. Assn., Am. Soc. Microbiology, Am. Chem. Soc., Rho Chi. Jewish. Avocations: tennis, swimming, theater, wine. Home: 28872 Alanya Mission Viejo CA 92692-4965

GLASOFER, ERIC DAVID, allergist, immunologist, pediatrician, educator; b. Bklyn., May 23, 1950; BS, Lehigh U., 1971; PhD in Pharmacology, Thomas Jefferson U., 1975; MD, Jefferson Med. Coll., 1978. Resident pediat. Thomas Jefferson U. Hosp., Phila., 1978-81, fellow allergy and immunology, 1981-83; attending physician Our Lady of Lourdes Med. Ctr., Camden, NJ, West Jersey/Virtua Health Sys. Clin. asst. prof. pediat. Jefferson Med. Coll. Mem. AMA, Am. Acad. Allergy, Asthma and Immunology, Am. Coll. Allergy, Asthma and Immunology Office: 1000 White Horse Rd Ste 904 Voorhees NJ 08043-4415 Office Phone: 856-772-1200.

GLASS, ANDREW JAMES, newspaper editor; b. Warsaw, Nov. 30, 1935; came to U.S., 1941, naturalized, 1948; s. Martin Allan and Wanda (Mosewicka) G.; m. Eleanor Attianese Sorrentino, June 3, 1962; 1 child, Samuel Sorrentino. BA, Yale U., 1957. Fin. reporter N.Y. Herald Tribune, 1959-62, chief congl. corr., 1963-66; mem. nat. staff Washington Post, 1966-68; exec. asst. to Senator Charles Percy, U.S. Senate, Washington, 1968-70; sr. editor Nat. Jour., Washington, 1970-74; Washington corr. Cox Newspapers, 1974-77, chief Washington Bur., 1977-97, sr. corr., 1997—2001; mng. editor The Hill Newspaper, Washington, 2002—04, columnist, 2003—06; sr. editor The Politico, Arlington, Va., 2006—. Syndicated columnist N.Y. Times News Svc., 1980-2001; adj. prof. Philip Merrill Sch. Journalism, U. Md., 2005—. Chmn. Corr. Com. for Refugee Relief, 1975—78. With US Army, 1958, mem. USAR, 1958—64. Fellow Shorenstein, J.F. Kennedy Sch. Govt., Harvard U., 2001. Mem.: Am. Soc. Newspaper Editors, Cosmos Club, Gridiron Club (chmn. Gridiron Found. 2005—), Met. Club Washington. Office: 1100 Wilson Blvd Arlington VA 22209-3921 Home Phone: 202-363-2389; Office Phone: 703-647-7681. E-mail: aglass@politico.com.

GLASS, BRIAN JAY, aerospace scientist; b. Atlanta, July 22, 1960; s. Jack and Gail Hawver Glass; m. Patricia Greene, July 2, 1983; children: James, David, Kevin. BSc in Aeronautics and Astronautics, MIT, Cambridge, 1982; MS in Aerospace Engring., Ga. Inst. Tech., Atlanta, 1984, PhD in Robotics, 1987; MS in Geophysics, Stanford U., Palo Alto, Calif., 1992. Scientist NASA Ames Rsch. Ctr., Moffett Field, Calif., 1987—. Contbr. articles to profl. jours. Recipient Grp. Achievement award, NASA, 1990, 1997, 1999, 2001, 2006, Space Act award, 1990, 2000. Fellow: AIAA (assoc.); mem.: Soc. Petroleum Engrs., Am. Geophys. Union, Alpha Phi Omega (life). Achievements include patents for air traffic management algorithms. Avocation: flying. Office: NASA Ames Rsch Ctr Mail Stop 269-4 Moffett Field CA 94035 Office Fax: 650-604-4036. Business E-Mail: brian.glass@nasa.gov.

GLASS, DAVID CARTER, psychologist, educator; b. NYC, Sept. 17, 1930; s. Samuel and Dorothy (Braunstein) Glass; m. Kathleen Kehoe, May 15, 1982. AB, NYU, 1952, MA, 1954, PhD, 1959, postdoctoral fellow, 1959—62. Mem. staff social psychologist Russell Sage Found., NYC, 1963—71; assoc. prof. psychology Rockefeller U., NYC, 1966—68; prof. psychology NYU, NYC, 1968—72; chmn., prof. dept. psychology U. Tex., Austin, Tex., 1972—75; vis. scholar Russell Sage Found., 1975—76; prof. psychology, dir. Lab. Biobehavior CUNY Grad. Ctr., NYC, 1976—82; prof. psychology and psychiatry SUNY, Stony Brook, 1982—94, vice provost for rsch. and grad. studies, 1982—86, spl. advisor to provost, 1987—89, v.p. for rsch., 1990—93, prof. emeritus psychology, 1994—. Vis. prof. psychology Inst. Health Rutgers U., New Brunswick, NJ, 1994—96; interim dir. rsch. Kessler Inst., West Orange, NJ, 1997—98; cons. in field. Author: Behavior Patterns, Stress and Coronary Disease, 1977; co-author (with J.E. Singer): Urban Stress: Experiments in Noise and Social Stressors, 1972 (AAAS prize, 71); contbr. articles to profl. jours. Fellow: AAAS, APA; mem.: Acad. Behavioral Medicine Rsch. (pres. 1981—82), Soc. Expl. Social Psychology, Soc. Psychophysiol. Rsch., Am. Psychosomatic Soc., Phi Kappa Phi, Sigma Xi. Home: 330 E 33rd St Apt 11J New York NY 10016-9437

GLASS, DAVID D., retail and professional sports team executive; b. Liberty, Mo., 1935; m. Ruth Glass; 3 children. Gen. mgr. Crank Drug Co., 1957-67; v.p. Consumers Markets Inc., 1967-76; exec. v.p. fin. Wal-Mart Stores Inc., Bentonville, Ark., to 1976, vice chmn., CFO, 1976-84, bd. dir., 1977—, pres., 1984-2000, COO, 1984-88, CEO, 1988-2000, chmn. exec. com., 2000—; CEO, chmn. bd. dirs. Kansas City Royals, 1993—. Bd. dir. Nat. Baseball Hall of Fame, Cooperstown. Office: Wal-Mart Stores Inc 702 SW 8th St Bentonville AR 72716-6299 also: Kansas City Royals PO Box 419969 Kansas City MO 64141-6969*

GLASS, DAVID J., lawyer; b. Union, NJ; BA, U. Pa., 1990; JD, Villanova U., 1996; PhD in Clin. Psychology, Drexel U., 1997. Bar: Pa. 1996, NJ 1996, Calif. 2003. Internship in clinical psychology Albert Einstein Coll. Medicine, Bronx, NY; atty. Schnader Harrison Segal & Lewis, Pa., Kolodny & Anteau, Beverly Hills, Calif., Law Offices of Alexandra Leichter, Beverly Hills, Calif.; prin., family law practice Glass Family Law, Beverly Hills, Calif. Co-editor: Ziskin's Coping with Psychiatric and Psychological Testimony, 2000 Supplement; co-author: Family Law chapter in Practicing Therapeutic Jurisprudence: The Law as a Helping Profession; editor (mng.): Villanova Law Rev. Named a Rising Star, So. Calif. Super Lawyers, 2005—06. Mem.: Am. Psychological Assn., LA Psychological Assn., Beverly Hills Bar Assn., LA County Bar Assn. Office: Glass Family Law 3d Fl 499 N Canon Dr Beverly Hills CA 90210 Office Phone: 310-777-5206. Office Fax: 310-777-5266. Business E-Mail: info@glassfamilylaw.com.

GLASS, DENNIS ROBERT, insurance company executive; b. Milw., Oct. 4, 1949; s. Robert Joseph and Carmella (Bellart) Glass; m. Deborah Glass, 1984; 2 children. BBA, U. Wis.-Milw., 1971, MBA, 1973. Investment analyst Northwestern Mut. Life Ins. Co., Milw., 1973-77, v.p., treas., 1977-82, mgr. treasury ops., 1983; dir. fin., treas. Portman Cos., Atlanta, 1983, sr. v.p., chief fin. officer, 1983-91; exec. v.p., CFO Protective Life Corp., 1991-93; sr. v.p., CFO Jefferson-Pilot Corp., 1993, exec. v.p., CFO, pres. fin. operations, CFO, 1999—2001, pres., COO, 2001—04, pres., CEO, 2004—06; pres., COO Lincoln Fin. Group, Phila., 2006—07, pres., CEO, 2007—. Mem. academic staff U. Wis., Mliw., 1973-83; mem. adv. bd. Wachovia. Organizer United Way, Milw.; mem. Leadership Atlanta, 1985—86, Greensboro Partnership; bd. mem. Am. Coun. Life Insurers, Ins. Marketplace Stds. Assn., Life Office Mgmt. Assn., Wachovia Bank NC, Greensboro. Office: Lincoln Fin Group Ctr Sq W Tower Ste 3900 1500 Market St Philadelphia PA 19102-2112*

GLASS, DONALD DAVID, anesthesiologist; b. Johnston, Pa., May 1, 1942; s. Donald S. and Meriel L. Glass; m. Bonnell W. Glass, Sept. 5, 1965 (div. Nov. 1992); children: David J., Jennifer J.; m. Alice M. Goldwine, June 27, 1998. Student, U. Pitts., 1960-62; MD, W.Va. U., 1966. Diplomate Am. Bd. Anesthesiology (chmn. CCM examination com. 1988—, asst. sec.-treas. 1991-94, chair com. on Americans and Disabilities Act 1991, chair credentials com. 1992, sec.-treas. 1994-96, pres. 1996-97); cert. spl. qualifications in critical care medicine, cert. continued demonstration of qualifications; lic. anethesiologist Miss., N.H. Rsch. assoc. dept. surgery W.Va. U., 1965-66; intern in surgery U. Pitts., 1966-67, resident in surgery, 1969-70; asst. resident in anesthesia Mass. Gen. Hosp., Boston, 1970-71, chief resident in anesthesiology, 1971-72; clin. fellow Harvard U., 1972; dir. edn. dept. anesthesiology, dir. cardiovascu. anesthesia U. Miss. Med. Ctr., Jackson, 1972-77, asst. dir. inhalation therapy, 1972-77, asst. prof. anesthesia, 1972-76, med. dir. ICU, 1975-77, assoc. prof. anesthesiology and surgery, 1976-77; assoc. prof. surgery and medicine Med. Sch., Dartmouth Coll., Hanover, NH, 1977-84, prof. surgery and medicine, 1984-88, prof. anesthesiology and medicine, 1988—; med. dir. adult unit ICU Dartmouth-Hitchcock Med. Ctr., Hanover, 1977-87, chief sect. anesthesiology, 1983-89, chmn. dept. anesthesiology, 1989. Mem nat. com. Accreditation Coun. for Grad. Med. edn., 1997—. Co-editor: (with M.P. Yeager) Anesthetic Management of the Vascular Surgical Patient, 1990; contbr. chpts. to books including Rhoads Textbook of Surgery, 1976, Intensive Care Therapeutics, 1980, Cardiac Anesthesia, 1987, Anesthesia in Vascular Surgery, 1989; contbr. numerous articles to med. jours. Elected rep. to ACGME Coun. Am. Bd. Med. Specialists. Recipient Lange Med. Publs. award, 1966. Fellow Am. Coll. Anesthesiology, Am. Coll. Chest Physicians, Faculty of Anesthesiologists of Royal Australian Coll. Surgeons; mem. Am. Soc. Anesthesiologists (U. Miss. preceptorship com. liaison 1974, coord. ICU workshop 1976, chmn. com. on sci. papers 1986, vice chmn. ann. meeting 1987, chmn. ann. meeting 1988, chair ABA-ASA joint select com. on recertification 1988), Internat. Anesthesia Rsch. Soc., Soc. Critical Care Medicine, Assn. Cardiac Anesthesiologists (elected), Assn. Univ. Anesthesiologists, Assn. Critical Care Anesthesiologists, N.H./Vt. Soc. Anesthsiologists, Soc. Acad. Anesthesia Chairmen, Alpha Omega Alpha. Home: 261 River Rd Lyme NH 03768-3008 Office: Dartmouth Hitchcock Med Ctr Dept Anesthesiology Medical Center Dr Lebanon NH 03756

GLASS, DOROTHEA DANIELS, physiatrist, educator; b. NYC; d. Maurice B. and Anna S. (Kleegman) Daniels; m. Robert E. Glass, June 23, 1940; children: Anne Glass Roth, Deborah, Catherine Glass Barrett, Eugene. BA, Cornell U., 1940; MD, Woman's Med. Coll. Pa., 1954; postgrad., U. Pa., 1960—61; DMS (hon.), Med. Coll. Pa., 1987. Diplomate Am. Bd. Phys. Medicine and Rehab. (guest bd. examiner 1978, 89). Intern Albert Einstein Med. Ctr., Phila., 1954-55, clin. asst. dept. medicine, 1956-59, attending phys. medicine and rehab., 1968-70, chmn. dept. phys. medicine and rehab., sr. attending, 1971-85; chief rehab. medicine VA Med. Ctr., Miami, Fla., 1985-95; clin. prof. dept. orthop. and rehab. U. Miami Sch. Medicine, 1985—. Lois Mattox Miller fellow preventive medicine Woman's Med. Coll. Pa., 1955-56, instr. preventive medicine, 1956-59, instr. medicine, 1960-62; resident phys. medicine and rehab. VA Hosp., Phila., 1959-62, chief phys. medicine and rehab., 1966-68, cons., 1968-82; asst. clin. dir. Jefferson Med. Coll. Hosp., Phila., 1963-66, Camden County Stroke Program, Cooper Hosp., Camden, N.J., 1963-66; gen. practice medicine, Phila., 1956-59; asst. med. dir., chief phys. medicine and rehab. Moss Rehab. Hosp., Phila., 1968-70, med. dir., 1971-82, sr. cons., 1982-; mem. active staff Temple U., Phila., 1968-, asso. prof. rehab. medicine, 1968-73, prof., 1973-, dir. residency tng. rehab. medicine, 1968-82; program dir. Rehab. Rsch. and Tng. Ctr., 1977-80, chmn. dept. rehab. medicine, 1977-82; staff physician Hosp. Med. Coll. Pa., Phila., 1955-59, vis. assoc. prof. neurology, 1973-79, clin. prof., 1977-82, vis. prof., 1982-96; mem. cons. staff Frankford Hosp., Phila., 1968-82, Phila. Geriatric Center, 1975-82; mem. active staff Willowcrest-Bamberger Hosp., Phila., 1980-82; asso. phys. medicine and rehab. U. Pa. Sch. Medicine, Phila., 1962-66; asst. prof. clin. phys. medicine and rehab., 1966-68; asst. clin. dir. dept. phys. medicine and rehab. Jefferson Med. Coll., Phila., 1963-66; cons. Vols. in Medicine Clinic, Stuart, Fla., 1996—. Contbr. articles to profl. jours. Mem. profl. adv. com. Easter Seal Soc. Crippled Children and Adults Pa., 1975-82; active Goodwill Industries Phila., 1973-82, Cmty. Home Health Svcs. Phila., 1974-82, Ea. Pa. chpt. Arthritis Found., 1968-82. Recipient Humanitarian Svc. cert. Gov.'s Com. on Employment Handicapped, 1974, Outstanding Alumnae award Commonwealth of Pa. Bd., Hosp. Med. Coll. Pa., 1975, Humanitarian award Pa. Easter Seal Soc., 1981, John Eiselie Davis award Am. Kinesiotherapy Assn., 1988, Carl Haven Young Svc. award, 1994, Disting. Career award Moss Rehab. Hosp., 1997, Outstanding Svc. and Accomplishments award Fla. Soc. Phys. Medicine and Rehab., 2001, Susan B. Anthony award LWV of Martin County, 2002. Fellow Am. Congress Rehab. Medicine; mem. AMA, Am. Acad. Med. Dirs., Am. Acad. Phys. Medicine and Rehab. (Disting. Clinician award 1995, Krusen award 2000), Am. Assn. Electromyography and Electrodiagnosis (assoc.), Am. Assn. Sex Educators, Counselors and Therapists, Am. Burn Assn., Am. Coll. Angiology, Am. Coll. Utilization Rev., Am. Congress Rehab. Medicine (bd. govs. 1979-85, pres. 1986-87, gold Key award 1989), Am. Heart Assn. (coun. on cerebrovascular disease), Am. Lung Assn. Phila. and Montgomery County (bd. dirs. 1977-79), Am. Med. Women's Assn., Assn. Acad. Physiatrists, Assn. Med. Rehab. Dirs. and Coords., Coll. Physicians Phila., Emergency Care Rsch. Inst., Gerontol. Soc., Internat. Assn. Rehab. Facilities, Internat. Rehab. Medicine Assn., Pan Am. Med. Assn., Fla. Med. Assn., Fla. Soc. Phys. Medicine and Rehab. (pres. 1975-77, Award for Outstanding Svc. in Rehab. Medicine 2001), Pa. Med. Soc. (phys. medicine and rehab. adv. com. 1975-82), Pa. Thoracic Soc., Delaware Valley Hosp. Coun. Forum, Phila. Med. Soc., Phila. PSRO (bd. dirs. 1975-82), Phila. Soc. Phys. Medicine and Rehab. (pres. 1968-69), Laennec Soc. Phila., Royal Soc. Health, Alpha Omega Alpha. E-mail: glassrd@earthlink.net.

GLASS, FRED STEPHEN, lawyer; b. Asheboro, NC, Oct. 17, 1940; s. Emmett Frederick and Colene F. (Foust) G.; m. Gloria A. Grant, June 12, 1964; 1 child, Elizabeth Foust; m. Martha G. Daughtry, June 9, 1982. BA, Wake Forest U., 1963, JD, 1966. Bar: N.C. 1966, U.S. Dist. Ct. (ea. dist.) N.C. 1966, (mid. dist.) N.C., (we. dist.) N.C.; U.S. Ct. Appeals (4th cir.), U.S. Supreme Ct. Rsch. asst. presiding justice N.C. Supreme Ct., 1966-67; ptnr. Miller, Beck, O'Briant and Glass, Asheboro, N.C., 1971-77; exec. dir. and legal counsel N.C. Democratic Party, 1977-78; dep. commr. N.C. Indsl. Commn., 1978; spl. Congl. asst. 4th Congl. Dist., N.C., 1979; ptnr. Harris, Cheshire, Leager and Southern, Raleigh, N.C., 1979-86, Poyner and Spruill, Raleigh, 1987-94, Brooks, Stevens & Pope, P.A., Cary, 1994-98; mng. ptnr. Glass & Vining, LLC, Cary, 1998-2000, Johnson, Hearn, Vinegar, Gee & Glass, PLLC, 2001—. Prof. law and govt. Asheboro Jr. Coll. Bus., 1973-76; bd. dirs. Capital Bank; mem. Gov.'s commn. mil. affairs, N.C., commn. Battleship N.C. Author: The Legal Handboook for North Carolina Businesses, 2003, Your Estate Planning Handbook, Business Considerations for North Carolina Healthcare Providers; contbg. editor: N.C. Will Drafting and Probate Practice Handbook, 1983; contbr. articles to profl. jours. Pub. chmn., United Appeal; bd. dirs., Randolph County Emergency Med. Technician Bd., Capital Bank; chmn.-elect Cary C. of C., bd. dirs., vice-chair govt. relations com.; mem. adv. bd. Naval War Coll. ops. law; active Dem. campaigns, Boy Scouts Am., council commr. for Roundtables, 1980-89, asst. dist. commr. 1979-84, asst. scoutmaster; mem. nat. com. Boy Scouts of Am., council ex. bd., council commr., chancellor, council commrs. coll., 1980-83, Boy Scouts Am. Nat. Com., 1987-90, coun. pres. 1994-96; force judge adv. COMRNCF, 1985-89; v.p. Healthcare Bus. Mgmt., LLC. Rear adm. JAGC, USNR. Disting. Svc. Medal award, 1996. Meritorious Svc. medal with gold star, Meritorious Unit Commendation, Nat. Meritorious Svc. award USNR, 1995, Navy Commendation medal with Gold Star, Nat. Defense Svc. medal with Bronze Star, Seabee Combat Warfare Specialist Cert.; recipient numerous Scouters Tng. award Boy Scouts Am., Disting. Eagle Scout award, 1991, Young Man of Yr. award City Asheboro. Mem.: ABA (standing com. on armed forces law), N.C. Bar Found., N.C. Coun. Entrepreneurial Devel., N.C. Def. Lawyers Assn. (computers in litigation support 1989), N.C. Bar Assn. (chmn. young lawyer sect. Randolph County, computers in law office 1995), 19th Jud. Dist. Bar Assn. (pres. 1974—75), Randolph County Bar

Assn. (pres. 1971—74), Cary C. of C. (bd. dirs., chmn. elect), Club, Sovereign Mil. Order Temple Jerusalem, Naval Order U.S. Democrat. Methodist. Home: 108 Forest Hills Ct Cary NC 27511 Office: PO Box 1776 Raleigh NC 27602 Home Phone: 919-467-5809; Office Phone: 919-743-2200. Office Fax: 919-743-2201. Business E-Mail: sglass@jhvgglaw.com.

GLASS, IRA, radio producer, radio personality; b. Balt., Mar. 3, 1959; s. Barry and Shirley Glass; m. Anaheed Alani, Aug. 2005. BA, Brown U., 1982. From intern to reporter, editor, & prodr. NPR, Washington, 1978—94; prodr., radio show host Chgo. Pub. Radio WBEZ 91.5 FM, 1994—. Host, reporter (radio series) Morning Edition, All Things Considered, co-host The Wild Room, host, prodr. This American Life, 1995—; exec. prodr.: (films) Unaccompanied Minors, 2006; writer, host (TV series) This American Life, 2007—. Co-recipient Thomas Lowell award, Overseas Press Club, 2006; named a Young Journalist of Yr., Livingston Found., 1988.

GLASS, JOANNE WISSMAN, lawyer; b. Covington, Ky., Nov. 6, 1969; BA, Xavier U., 1991; JD, Salmon P. Chase Coll. Law, 1994. Bar: Ohio 1994, Ky. 1995, US Dist. Ct. Eastern Dist. Ky. 1995, US Dist. Ct. Western Dist. Ky. 1995, US Dist. Ct. Southern Dist. Ohio. Ptnr. Frost Brown Todd LLC, Cin., chairperson, Cmty. Opportunity Com. Vol., firm coordinator St. Francis Soup Kitchen; bd. mem., sec. Queen City Found.; bd. mem. Transitions, Inc., 1996—; vol. Ky. Lawyers Assistance Prog. Nominee 40 Under 40 awards, Cin. Bus. Courier, 2005, 2006; named one of Ohio's Rising Stars, Super Lawyers, 2005, 2006. Mem.: ABA, Ohio State Bar Assn. (mem., Workers' Compensation Com.), Northern Ky. Bar Assn. (mem., Young Lawyers Sect., mem., Workers' Compensation Com.,), Ky. Bar Assn., Cin. Bar Assn. (sec., Workers' Compensation Com., Young Lawyers Sect., chairperson, Bridge the Gap Com.). Office: Frost Brown Todd LLC 2200 PNC Ctr 201 E Fifth St Cincinnati OH 45202-4182 Office Phone: 513-651-6132. Office Fax: 513-651-6981.

GLASS, JOHN DEREK See HOOPER, IAN

GLASS, JULIA, writer; b. NY; d. John and Kerry G.; life ptnr. Dennis Cowley; children: Alec, Oliver. BA in Art summa cum laude, Yale Univ., 1978. Figurative painter; copy editor Cosmopolitan mag.; freelance editor JP MorganChase. Author: (novels) Three Junes, 2002 (Nat. Book award for fiction, 2002), The Whole World Over, 2006, (novella) Collies, 1999 (Faulkner Soc. medal for best novella, 1999). Recipient Nelson Algren award for a short story, Chgo. Tribune, 1993, two other Nelson Algren awards, Tobias Wolff award, Ames Meml. Essay award for nonfiction; grantee Nat. Endowment for the Arts fellowship, NY Found. for Arts fellowship, Radcliffe Inst. Fellow, 2004—05. Mailing: Author Mail - Pantheon Books Random House 1745 Broadway New York NY 10019

GLASS, KENNETH EDWARD, management consultant; b. Fort Thomas, Ky., Sept. 28, 1940; s. Clarence E. and Lucille (Garrison) Glass; m. Nancy Romanek, May 9, 1964; children: Ryan, Lara. ME, U. Cin., 1963, MS, 1965, grad. student, 1967. Registered profl. engr., Ohio; lic. Airline Transport Pilot. With Allis Chalmers Mfg. Co., Cin. and Eng., 1963—73; v.p. mfg. Fiat Allis Contrn. Machinery, Inc., Chgo., 1973—75; pres. Perkins Diesel Corp., Canton, Ohio, 1975—77; pres., CEO Massey-Ferguson, Inc., Des Moines, 1978; v.p., gen. mgr. N.Am. ops. Massey Ferguson Ltd., Des Moines, 1978; chmn., pres., CEO Union Metal Mfg. Co., Canton, Ohio, 1979—85; pres. Glass & Assocs. Inc. Glass & Assocs. Inc., 1985—2004, chmn., 1996—2005; pres. Stony Point Group, Inc., 1996—, also bd. dirs., chmn., 2005—. Chmn. Utica Corp., 2001—, UCA Holdings, 2001—, TECT Corp. Trustee U. Cin. Found.; dir. N.C. Outward Bound Sch., bd. dirs. Mem.: Young Presidents Orgn., Turnaround Mgmt. Assn. (bd. dirs.), Assn. Cert. Turnaround Profls. (bd. dirs., v.p. 1993—94, pres. 1995—96), Am. Bankrupcy Inst., Pi Tau Sigma. Achievements include patentee in field. Office Phone: 828-210-8120. Personal E-mail: keglass@attglobal.net.

GLASS, LAWRENCE, research scientist; Sr. v.p., dir. devel. SRA Technologies, Inc., Falls Church, Va.; pres., CEO SRA Life Sci., 1998—2000; exec. v.p. Corp. Develop. Virco Lab, Inc.; chief strategy officer, sr. cons. Panacea Pharmaceuticals, Inc., Gaithersburg, Md. Office: Panacea Pharms, Inc 207 Perry Pkw, Ste 2 Gaithersburg MD 20877 Office Phone: 240-243-8000. Office Fax: 240-465-0450. E-mail: LGlass@PanaceaPharma.com.

GLASS, LINDA L., elementary school educator; b. Hamilton, Ohio, June 1, 1959; d. Chester L. and June E. Morgan; m. Robert E. Glass, June 6, 1981; 1 child, Bethany L. BS in Edn., Miami U., Oxford, Ohio, 1993; MAT, Marygrove Coll., Detroit, 2005. Tchr. grade 1 St. Joseph Consol. Schs., Hamilton, Ohio, 1995—99, Fairfield West Elem. Sch., Ohio, 1999—. Mentor Fairfield City Schs., Fairfield, Ohio, 2004—06. Mem.: Kappa Delta Pi. Mailing: 4700 River Rd Fairfield OH 45014-1606 Home: 6209 Morris Rd Fairfield OH 45011

GLASS, MARY JEAN, management executive; b. Urbana, Ill., Nov. 27, 1964; d. Sandra Kay and Bobby Dee Egner; 1 child, Jacob Steven. BS in Orgnl. Leadership, Mid-Continent U., 2001. Cert. quality auditor Am. Soc. Quality, 1995. Staff sgt. USAF, 1985, med. svc. specialist Belleville, Ill., 1985—89, med. svc. technician RAF Greenham Common, 1989—91; quality assurance technician North Star Steel Ky., Calvert City, Ky., 1991—99; quality assurance supr. Dura Automotive Sys., Inc., Fulton, Ky., 1999—2002; ISO coord. Jakel, Inc., Murray, Ky., 2002—04; with Newcomb Oil, Benton, Ky., 2004—. Internat. peace amb. Am. Biog. Soc.; capt. Dem. Nat. Party, Benton, Ky., 2003. Decorated Outstanding Unit with one oak leaf cluster USAF, Nat. Def. Svc. medal; named Woman of Yr., Am. Biog. Inst., 2002. Mem.: Am. Soc. Quality (publicity officer 1987—89). Democrat. Pentecostal. Avocations: reading, writing, internet. Home: 279 US Hwy 68E Benton KY 42025 Office: Newcomb Oil LLC 406 Main St Benton KY 42025 Office Phone: 270-527-3004. Personal E-mail: glaspane@bellsouth.net.

GLASS, NOAH N., entrepreneur; b. 1981; BA with honors, Yale U., 2003. Product mgr. Shutterfly.com, 2000; online ordering strategist Braun Consulting, Boston, 2003; global expansion mgr. Endeavor Global, South Africa, 2004; founder & CEO Mobo Systems Inc., NYC, 2005—. Guest lectr. Harvard Bus. Sch., Kellogg Sch. Mgmt., World Bank. Named one of Best Entrepreneurs Under 25, Bus. Week, 2006. Achievements include development of Shutterfly Express application materials. Avocation: lacrosse. Office Phone: 888-411-MOBO. E-mail: info@gomobo.com.

GLASS, PHILIP, composer, musician; b. Balt., Jan. 31, 1937; s. Benjamin C. and Ida (Gouline) Glass; m. JoAnne Akalaitas (div.); children: Juliet, Zachary; m. Luba Burtyk, 1980 (div.); m. Candy Jernigan (dec. 1991); m. Holly Critchlow, 2001; 1 child, Cameron. AB, U. Chgo., Ill., 1956; MS in Composition, Julliard Sch. Music, 1964; composition studies with, Vincent Persichetti, 1962, William Bergsma, Nadia Boulanger, Paris, 1964—66, Steve Reich, Darius Milhaud; studied flute, Peabody Conservatory. Began creating music for theatre while studying in Paris; composer in residence Pitts. Pub. Sch., 1962—64; worked and studied with Ravi Shankar, 1965—66; founder, dir. Philip Glass Ensemble, 1967—; owner Dunvagen Music Pubs.; founder Chatham Sq. Prodns., NYC, 1972. Composer of incidental music, film scores, chamber music, choral works and songs; various European concert tours, 1968—, US tours, 1972—; composer: Strung Out, 1967, In Again Out Again, 1967, Pieces in the Shape of a Square, 1968, How Now, 1968, Red Horse Animation, 1968, Two Pages, 1968, Music in Similar Motion, 1969, Music in Contrary Motion, 1969, Music in Eight Parts, 1969, Music in Fifths, 1969, Gradus, 1969, Music with Changing Parts, 1971, Music in Twelve Parts, 1971—74, Music for Voices, 1972, Another Look at Harmony, 1975, The Lost Ones, 1975, The St. and the Football Player, 1975, Einstein On The Beach, 1976, Modern Love Waltz, 1977, Dressed Like an Egg, 1977, Fourth Series Part I, 1978, Music for a Performance/Reading by C. DeJong: Fourth Series Part II, 1978, Cascando, 1979, Geometry of a Cir., 1979, Mercier and Camier, 1979, Dance No. 2, 1979, Dance No. 4, 1979, Mad Rush: Fourth Series Part III, 1979, Madrigal Opera: The Panther, 1980, Satyagraha, 1980, Facades, 1981, Vessels, 1981, Habeve Song, 1982, The Photographer, 1982, Hymn to the Sun, 1982, The Photographer, 1983, Akhnaten, 1983, The Civil Wars: A Tree is Best Measured When It Is Down, 1983, Pages from Cold Harbor, 1983, Floe, 1983, String Quartet No. 2: Co., 1983, Endgame, 1984, Glassworks, 1984, Dance from Akhnaten, 1984, String Quartet No. 3: Mishima, 1985, The Juniper Tree, 1985, Songs from Liquid Days, 1986, Three Songs, 1986, In the Upper Room, 1986, Dialogue, 1986, A Descent Into the Maelstrom, 1986, The Light for Orchestra, 1987, Itaipu, 1988, The Fall of the House of Usher, 1988, 1000 Airplanes on the Roof, 1988, The Making of the Representative for Planet 8, 1988, The Canyon, 1988, String Quartet No. 4: Boczak, 1989, Hydrogen Jukebox, 1989, The White Raven, 1991, The Voyage, 1992, Orphée, chamber opera after Cocteau, 1993, Low Symphony, 1993, La Belle et la Bête, 1994, Symphony No. 2, 1994, The Marriages Between Zones Three, Four and Five, 1997, Aguas de Amazonia, 1999, Passage, 2001, The Man in the Bath, 2001, Dancissimo, 2001, Notes, 2001, Diaspora, 2001, Voices for Organ, Didgeridoo and Narrator, 2001, Philip on Film, 2001, The Elephant Man, 2002, Symphony No. 6 Plutonian Ode, 2002, Glasswork, 2003, Taoist Sacred Dance, 2003, Orion, 2004, A Musical Portrait of Chuck Close, 2005, Chaotic Harmony, 2006, Life: A Journey Through Time, 2006, Passion of Ramakrishna, 2006, (films) North Star: Mark Di Suvero, 1977, Koyaanisqatsi, 1983, Mishima, 1984, Dead End Kids, 1986, Hamburger Hill, 1987, Powaqqatsi, 1987, The Thin Blue Line, 1988, Mindwalk, 1990, A Brief History of Time, 1992, Candyman, 1992, Anima Mundi, 1992, Compassion in Exile, 1992, Candyman II: Farewell to the Flesh, 1995, Jenipapo, 1995, The Secret Agent, 1996, Bent, 1997, Kundun, 1997, Dracula, 1999, The Hours, 2002 (The Anthony Asquith Award for Achievement in Film Music, British Acad. Film Award (BAFTA), 2003), Nagoygatsi, 2002, The Fog of War, 2003, Secret Window, 2004, Taking Lives, 2004, Undertow, 2004, Declaring Genius, 2004, La Moustache, 2005, Faith's Corner, 2005, Neverwas, 2005, The Giant Buddhas, 2005, Roving Mars, 2006, Nasiona, 2006, Notes on a Scandal, 2006, The Illusionist, 2006 (Best Composer, 2006 Critics Choice award, Broadcast Film Critics Assn., 2007); composer, keyboard artist (films) The Truman Show, 1998 (Golden Globe award, ASCAP Film & TV award, 1999); composer: (ballets) Witches of Venice, 1995, (dance opera) Les enfants terrible, 1996, (theatre) In the Penal Colony, 2000, (Operas) Monsters of Grace, 1999, Galileo Galilei, 2002, Waiting for the Barbarians, 2005; composer: (with Henry Hwang) The Sound of Voice, 2003; composer: (spl. events) Ceremonial Music at 1984 Olympics, original music for Atlanta Olympic Games, 1996, (benefit compact disc for Gehlek Rimpoche and Jewel Heart Orgn.) Dreaming Awake, Concerto for violin and orch., 1987, Concerto Fantasy for Two Timpanists and Orchestra, 2000, Tirol Concerto, piano and orchestra, 2000, Concerto for Cello and Orchestra, 2001, Concerto for Harpsichord and Orchestra, 2002, (Pandemic) Facing AIDS (documentary), 2002, (chamber and instrumental music) String Quartet, 1966, (vocal and choral music) Knee Play No. 3, 1976; Collaboration with David Bowie on Heros Symphony, 1997; author (with C. DeJong): Satyagraha: M.K. Gandhi in South Africa 1893-1914, 1980; author: Music by Philip Glass, 1987, Writings on Glass: Essays, Interviews, Criticism, 1997. Named composition grantee, Fulbright, 1966—67, Found. for Contemporary Performance Arts, 1970—71, Changes, Inc., 1971—72, Nat. Endowment for the Arts, 1974—75, Menil Found., 1974, Musician of Yr., Musical Am. mag., 1985; recipient Broadcast Music Industry award, 1960, Lado prize, 1961—67, Benjamin award, 1961—62, Art of Freedom award, Om Sarwasvati Hring Soha Tibet House, 2000, George Peabody medal, Peabody Cons. Music, 2000, Contemporary Music award, Classical Brit Awards, 2004, Frederick Loewe award for Film Composing, Palm Springs Internat. Film Soc., Palm Springs Internat. Film Festival, 2007, Young Composer's award, Ford Found., 1964—66. Mem.: PRS, ASCAP. Office: Dunvagen Music 632 Broadway Ste 902 New York NY 10012 Address: Orange Mountain Music 632 Broadway Rm 902 New York NY 10012-2614 also: Nonesuch Records 75 Rockefeller Plz 8th Fl New York NY 10019 Office Phone: 212-979-2080. Fax: 212-353-2007, 212-315-1124; Office Fax: 212-473-2842. E-mail: info@dunvagen.com.

GLASS, RENÉE, educational health foundation executive; b. Elizabeth, NJ, Jan. 27, 1928; d. Samuel and Helen Peritz m. Milton L. Glass, Feb. 5, 1950; children: Jill S., Mikel L. Student, Tufts U., 1952, Northeastern U., 1954, U. Mass., 1984-85. Bd. dirs. Inst. of Contemporary Art, Boston, 1979-83; pres. Connoisier Network, Boston, 1981; founder, pres. Jaw Joints Found., Boston, 1982—. Dir. Goldberg Ctr., Northeastern U., Boston, 1993—, exec.-in-residence, 1994—, mem. wellness com., 1994—, dir. Ctr. Health in Soc., 1999; participant, lectr. health forums, NIH, 1982—; bd. dirs. Health Practice and Policy Inst. Author numerous booklets and pamphlets on temporomandibular joint disorders, 1982—; mem. editl. bd. Bus. Ethics Resource. Mem. examining com. Boston Pub. Libr., 1983-84; bd. dirs. Boch Ctr. for the Performing Arts, Cape Cod. Mem. Internat. Catacomb Soc. (bd. dirs. 1987-97). Office: Jaw Joints/Musculo-Skeletal Disorders Found Forsyth Inst 140 Fenway Boston MA 02115-3782 Office Phone: 617-266-2550.

GLASS, ROGER I., virologist; b. Somerville, NJ, Jan. 10, 1946; MD, Harvard U., 1972. Intern Cambridge City Hosp., Mass., 1972—73; resident Mt. Sinai Hosp., NYC, 1974—76; resident in microbiology U. Goteborg, 1984; chief viral gastroenteritis sect. Nat. Ctr. Infectious Diseases, Ctrs. Disease Control and Prevention, Atlanta, 1986—; staff Grady Meml. Hosp., Atlanta, 1990—. Co-recipient Pasteur award, Children's Vaccine Initiative, 1998. Mem.: Inst. Medicine (life). Office: Nat Ctr for Infectious Diseases Ctrs for Disease Control/Prevention 1600 Clifton Rd NE Atlanta GA 30333 Office Phone: 404-639-3577. Business E-Mail: rglass@cdc.gov.

GLASS, RONALD BERNHARD JACOB, radiologist; b. Salisbury, Rhodesia, Dec. 20, 1952; arrived in U.S., 1984; s. Joseph and Inge Selma Glass. MB BCh, U. Witwatersrand, 1976. Diplomate Am. Bd. Radiology. Fellow pediat. radiology Northwestern U., Chgo., 1984—86; radiologist U. Chgo., 1986—87, Loyola U., Maywood, Ill., 1987—88, Children's Nat. Med. Ctr., Washington, 1988—92, R.I. Hosp., Providence, 1992—93, U. Tex., Houston, 1993—95, Mt. Sinai Hosp. Med. Ctr., NYC, 1995—2005, Beth Israel Med. Ctr., NYC, 2005—06, Children's Meml. Hosp., Chgo., 2006—. Reviewer Am. Jour. of Roentgenology, Radiology, Radiographics. Contbr. numerous articles to profl. jours.; editor (assoc. editor): Radiology, Examiner Am. Bd. of Radiology. Jewish. Office: Children's Meml Hosp Dept Radiology 2300 Childrens Plz Chicago IL 60614 Office Phone: 773-880-3520. Personal E-mail: salisb1@yahoo.com. Business E-Mail: rglass@childrensmemorial.org.

GLASS, ROY LEONARD, lawyer; b. Littleton, NH, Jan. 27, 1947; s. Jack Irving and Noreen (Leiuthwait) Kline; children: Shannon Renee, Ashley Leigh; m. Lauren Rachel Adams, Aug. 8, 1998; 1 stepchild, Ariel Adams. AA with honors, St. Petersburg Jr. Coll., Fla., 1971; BA, U. South Fla., 1972; JD, Fla. State U., 1975. Bar: Fla. 1976, U.S. Dist. Ct. (mid. dist.) Fla. 1977, U.S. Dist. Ct. (no. dist.) Fla. 1978, U.S. Supreme Ct. 1979, U.S. Ct. Appeals (11th cir.) 1983; cert. state and fed. mediator, 2005. Assoc. Meyers, Mooney & Adler, Orlando, Fla., 1976-78, Barrett, Boyd & Bajoczky, Tallahassee, 1978-79; sole practice Tallahassee, 1979-81; ptnr. Deserio & Glass, St. Petersburg, Fla., 1981-82; assoc. Battaglia, Ross, Hastings, Dicus & Andrews, St. Petersburg, 1982-85; sole practice St. Petersburg, 1985—. Lectr. Floridians Against Constl. Tampering, Fla., 1984. Past mem. Roscoe Pound Inst., Capt. U.S. Army, 1966-70, Vietnam. Mem. ABA, ATLA (sustaining mem.), Am. Arbitration Assn., Fla. Acad. Trial Lawyers (mem. spkrs. bur.), Fla. Bar Assn. (health law com. 1984-85, chmn. health care profls. subcom. 1984-85, mem. exec. coun. health care sect. 1986-94, mem. spkrs. bur., chair client security fund com. 2003-04, Meritorious Svc. award health law sect. 1994, client security fund com. award for outstanding leadership 2004), St. Petersburg Bar Assn. (legis. com. 1983-85, liaison med. soc., med. rels. com. 1985—, trial lawyers 1987—, mem. spkrs. bur.), Pinellas County Trial Lawyers Assn., St. Petersburg C. of C. (urban solutions task force 1983-84), Phi Delta Phi, Phi Kappa Phi, Beta Gamma Sigma. Clubs: Suncoast Tiger Bay (St. Petersburg, Fang & Claw award 1983), Breakfast Sertoma (Cert. of Appreciation 1984), Westgate High Twelve (Cert. of Appreciation 1987), Am. Coll. Barristers (sr. counsel). Office: 5501 Central Ave Saint Petersburg FL 33710-8050 Office Phone: 727-384-8888. Personal E-mail: lroyglas@tampbay.rr.com.

GLASS, WILLIAM ROBERT, history professor; b. Ft. Lauderdale, Fla., Sept. 24, 1952; arrived in Poland, 2003; s. Theodore Rufus and Lois Glass. BA, Centre Coll., Danville, Ky., 1974; PhD, Emory U., Atlanta, Ga., 1991. Prof. history Miss. U. Women, Columbus, 1994—2005; lectr. Am. studies ctr. Warsaw U., 2003—04, prof. social history Am. studies ctr., 2005—. Author: (book) Strangers in Zion: Fundamentalist in the South, 1900-1950; contbr. articles to profl. jours.

GLASSCOCK, LARRY CLABORN, health insurance company executive; b. Cullman, Ala., Apr. 4, 1948; s. Oscar Claborn and Betty Lou (Norman) Glasscock; m. Lee Ann Roden, Sept. 13, 1969; children: Michael, Carrie BBA, Cleve. State U., 1970; postgraduate student, Columbia U. Am. Inst. Banking. V.p. pers. and orgn. AmeriTrust Co., Cleve., 1974-75, v.p. nat. divsn., 1976-78, v.p., mgr. credit card ctr., 1978-79, sr. v.p. consumer fin., 1980-81, sr. v.p. nat. divsn., 1981-83, exec. v.p. corp. banking adminstr., 1983-87; group exec. v.p. AmeriTrust Corp. and AmeriTrust Co., Cleve., 1987-92; pres., CEO Essex Holdings, Inc.; pres., COO First Am. Bank, N.A.; pres., CEO Blue Cross and Blue Shield of the Nat. Capital Area; COO CareFirst, Inc.; senior exec. v.p., COO Anthem Ins., Indpls., 1998—99, pres., CEO, 1999—2004, chmn., 2003—04; pres., CEO WellPoint, Inc. (formerly Anthem Ins.), Indpls., 2004—07, chmn., 2005—. Chmn. Coun. Affordable Quality Healthcare, Washington, 2002-03; bd. dirs. Nat. Inst. Healthcare Mgmt., Zimmer Inc., 2001-, AT Fin. Corpn., AT Capital Corpn., AmeriTrust Internat. Banking, AmeriTrust Devel. Bank, CT Leasing Corpn., Sprint Nextel Corp. Trustee Cleve. State U. Devel. Found.; campaign chmn. Geauga County United Way, 1989; mem. adv. bd. N.E. Ohio Employee Ownership Ctr. Kent State U., 1987—. Served in USMC, 1970—76. Co-recipient Ind. Entrepreneur of Yr. award, Ernst & Young, 2003. Mem. Am. Inst. Banking, Am. Bankers Assn., Assn. Res. City Bankers, Greater Cleve. Growth Assn., Cleve. State U. Alumni Assn. (pres. 1987). Clubs: Union (Cleve.); Hillbrook (Chagrin Falls, Ohio); The Country (Pepper Pike, Ohio). Office: WellPoint Inc 120 Monument Cir Indianapolis IN 46204-4906*

GLASSE, JOHN HOWELL, retired philosophy and theology educator; b. Buffalo, June 1, 1922; s. John Alfred and Jessie Elizabeth (Howell) G.; m. Wanda Lou Howard, June 16, 1950; children: Jeffrey Howell, Paulding Howard. BA, Williamette U., 1945; B.D., Yale U., 1948, PhD, 1961. Ordained to ministry Presbyn. Ch., 1948. Dir. field work Christian Activities Council, Hartford, Conn., 1948-50, exec. dir., 1950-52; dir. Danish program Scandinavian Seminar, Inc., 1952-53; mem. faculty Vassar Coll., Poughkeepsie, N.Y., 1956—, prof. religion, 1969-90, prof. emeritus, 1990—, Frederick Weyerhaeuser chair, 1971-90, chmn. dept. religion, 1965-67, 77-83, 87-90. Vis. prof. Harvard Div. Sch., 1970, vis. scholar, 1962, 69; vis. scholar Columbia U., Union Theol. Sem., 1980-81. Contbr. articles to profl. jours. Trustee Scandinavian Seminar, 1950—. Hon. fellow Am. Scandinavian Found., 1952; grantee Am. Philos. Soc., 1964; grantee Am. Council Learned Socs., 1965, 67 Mem. Am. Acad. Religion, Am. Philos. Assn., Metaphys. Soc. Am., Soc. Values in Higher Edn., AAUP. Address: Box 347 Vassar Coll 124 Raymond Ave Poughkeepsie NY 12604-0347

GLASSELL, ALFRED CURRY, JR., investor; b. Cuba Plantation, La., Mar. 31, 1913; s. Alfred Curry and Frances (Lane) G.; m. Clare Attwell; children: Jean Curry, Alfred Curry III. BA, La. State U., 1934. Investor, 1936—; cons. Glassell Producing Co., 1938—. Past bd. dirs. Transco Cos., El Paso Nat. Gas, First City Bancorp. Trustee Houston Mus. Natural Sci., Internat. Oceanographic Found.; truste, chmn. emeritus Houston Mus. Fine Arts; former trustee Kinkaid Sch., Tex. Children's Hosp., Smithsonian Nat. Bd. Recipient Marine Sci. ann. award Internat. Oceanographic Found., 1971, Soc. Grand Founders medallion U. Miami, 1984, James Smithson award, 1991. Mem. Am. Geog. Soc., Am. Mus. Natural History, Tex. Angus Assn., Can. Chianini Assn., Houston Horse Show Assn., Tex. Cattle Breeders Assn., Am. Nat. Cattlemen's Assn., Tex. and Southwestern Cattle Raisers Assn., Mil. and Hospitaller Order St. Lazarus of Jerusalem. Clubs: Atlantic Tuna (Providence), Boston (New Orleans), Cabo Blanco Fishing (Peru), Tex. Game Fishing (Dallas), Tex. Corinthian Yacht (Kemah), Bay of Islands Swordfish and Mako Shark (New Zealand), Anglers of N.Y., Houston, Petroleum, Ramada, Bayou, Houston Country, River Oaks Country. Achievements include being a holder of the record of world's largest fish, former holder of numerous world record salt water game fish. Office: 1021 Main St Ste 2300 Houston TX 77002-6606

GLASSER, IRA SAUL, former civil liberties organization administrator; b. Bklyn., Apr. 18, 1938; s. Sidney and Anne (Goldstein) Glasser; m. Trude Maria Robinson, June 28, 1959; children: David, Andrew, Peter, Sally. BS in Math., Queens Coll., 1959; MA in Math., Ohio State U., 1960; LLD (hon.), N.Y. Law Sch., 2001. Instr. math. Queens Coll., NYC, 1960—63; lectr. math. Sarah Lawrence Coll., Bronxville, NY, 1962—65; assoc. editor Current Mag., NYC, 1962—64, editor, 1964—67; assoc. dir. N.Y. Civil Liberties Union, NYC, 1967—70, exec. dir., 1970—78, ACLU, 1978—2001. Cons. U. Ill.-Champaign-Urbana, 1964—65; dir. Asian Am. Legal Def. and Edn. Fund, NYC, 1974—2004; pres., bd. dirs. Drug Policy Alliance NY, 1991—; cons. Legal Svcs. of NY, 2006—. Author: Visions of Liberty: The Bill of Rights for All Americans, 1991; co-author: Doing Good: The Limits of Benevolence, 1978; contbr. articles to profl. jours. Chmn. St. Vincents Hosp., NYC, Cmty. Adv. Bd., NYC, 1970—72. Recipient Martin Luther King, Jr. award, N.Y. Assn. Black Sch. Suprs., 1971, Gavel award, ABA, 1972, Allard K. Lowenstein award, Park River Ind. Dem., 1981, Malcolm, Martin, Mandela award, Greater Bapt. Trinity Ch., 1993, Justice in Action award, Asian Am. Legal Def. and Edn. Fund, 1999, Lifetime Achievement in Advocacy award, Correctional Assn. N.Y., 2005. Avocation: sports.

GLASSER, ISRAEL LEO, federal judge; b. NYC, Apr. 6, 1924; s. David and Sadie (Krupp) G.; m. Grace Gribetz, Aug. 24, 1952; children—Dorothy, David, James, Marjorie. LL.B., Bklyn. Law Sch., 1948; BA, CUNY, 1976. Bar: N.Y. 1948. Fellow Bklyn. Law Sch., 1948-49, instr., 1950-52, asst. prof. law, 1952-53, asso. prof., 1953-55, prof., 1955-69, adj. prof., 1969-77, dean, 1977-81; judge U.S. Dist. Ct. N.Y., 1981—99, sr. judge, 1993—. Judge N.Y. State Family Ct., N.Y.C., 1969-77 Mem. ABA, Assn. of Bar of City of N.Y. Office: US Dist Ct 225 Cadman Plz E Brooklyn NY 11201-1818 Office Phone: 718-613-2440. Business E-Mail: leo_glasser@nyed.uscourts.gov.

GLASSER, JOSEPH, management consultant, educator; b. Phila., May 17, 1925; BS in Econs., U. Pa., Phila., 1947, MBA, 1948, postgrad.,

1948—51. With NLRB, 1948-51; internal mgmt. cons., 1954-55; mem. faculty Sch. Bus. Adminstrn., U. Conn., 1955-81, prof. emeritus, 1981—; pres. Eljen Corp., 1971—. Arbitrator Fed. Mediation and Conciliation Service, VA, Nat. Mediation Bd., Soc. Security Adminstrn., Am. Arbitration Assn.; fact finder Mass. Bd. Mediation and Arbitration, Ct. Bd. Mediation and Arbitration, N.H. Pub. Employee Labor Relations Bd.; mediator Conn. Bd. Edn.; rev. officer FAA; mem. Nat. Def. Exec. Res.-Fed. Emergency Mgmt. Agy.; speaker seminars, also mgmt. groups in Eng., Austria and Hungary, Am. Mgmt. Assn. Author: Fundamentals of Applied Industrial Management; contbr. articles to profl. jours. Served to lt. col. USAF, ETO. Decorated Air medal with four oak leaf clusters, Air Force commendation medal. Mem. Soc. Profls. in Dispute Resolution, Indsl. Rels. Rsch. Assn., Nat. Assns. Mgmt. Educators (Innovative Mgmt. Edn. award 1976), Nat. Assn. Suggestion Systems (winner internat. papers competition 1975), Res. Officers Assn., Air Force Assn. Office: Eljen Corp 10 N Main St #216-217 West Hartford CT 06107-1968 Business E-Mail: eljencorporation@aol.com.

GLASSER, LYNN SCHREIBER, publisher; b. Chgo., Sept. 19, 1943; d. Alexander Paul and Beatrice (Bollard) Schreiber; m. Stephen A. Glasser, Dec. 30, 1965; children: Susan, Laura, Jeffrey, Jennifer. BA, Chatham Coll., 1965. Publs. editor Inst. CLE U. Mich. Law Sch., Ann Arbor, 1966-68; asst. to dir. Practising Law Inst., NYC, 1968-71; v.p., COO Law Jour. Press and Law Jour. Seminars, NYC, 1971-78; exec. v.p., pub. Law & Bus./Harcourt Jovanovich, Inc., NYC, 1978-86; co-pres. Prentice Hall Law & Bus., Englewood Cliffs, NJ, 1986-94; cons. Simon and Schuster, NYC, 1994-95; pres. Glasser Publ. Inc., Little Falls, NJ, 1995—; co-pres. Glasser Legal Works, a Thomson Bus., 2003—04; pres. Sandpiper Ptnrs., LLC, Bloomfield, NJ, 2005—. Organizer, originator over 1000 CLE seminars, 1986—; organizer Woman Advt. Conf., N.Y.C., Chgo. and San Francisco, 1993-94; chmn. Woman Bus. Lawyer Conf., N.Y.C. and San Francisco, 1994; adj. assoc. prof. Stony Brook U., 2004-. Trustee N.J. Chamber Music Soc., Montclair, 1989—, Montclair Art Mus., 1998—; Cmty. Found. of N.J., Morristown, 1995—; co-donor Lynn & Stephen Glasser Scholarship Fund, Colgate U., 1988—, Bloomfield Coll., 1993—. Office: 1515 Broad St Bldg B Bloomfield NJ 07003

GLASSER, PAMELA JEAN, musician, educator; b. Livonia, Mich., June 26, 1953; d. Walter and Margaret Julia (Geersens) Glasser; m. Richard Barth Turner, Sept. 7, 1996 (div. Mar. 2006). BEd in Music, Wayne State U., 1976; M of Music, Rice U., 1982. Prin. hornist Wyo. Symphony Orch., Casper, 1994—, Jackson Hole Symphony, 1999—2002; adj. prof. horn Casper Coll., 1998—2001; artistic dir. Casper Chamber Music Soc., 2001—; dir. music Fremont Sch. Dist. # 2, Dubois, Wyo., 2001—. Hornist music edn. programs Wyo. Arts Coun., 1993; hornist, solo performer Llangollen Eisteddfod North Wales, 1978. Mem.: VFW Aux., SPLC, NEA, ACLU, Casper Chamber Music Soc. (ednl. liaison 1997—2001), Wyo. Edn. Assn., Am. Fedn. Musicians. Democrat. Episcopalian. Avocations: field and space science, organic gardening, cross country skiing, science fiction, crystal and mineral collecting, world music, religion. Home: PO Box 1357 Dubois WY 82513-1357 E-mail: pjglasser@yahoo.com.

GLASSER, PAUL HAROLD, sociologist, educator, social worker, university administrator; b. NYC, Aug. 21, 1929; s. David and Rae (Startz) G.; m. Lois Hannah Naefach, Nov. 25, 1954 (div. June 1993); children: Heather Denys, Frederick Naefach. BS, CCNY, 1949; MS, Columbia U., 1951; PhD, U. N.C., 1961. Chief psychiat. social work sect. Mental Hygiene Clinic, Camp Chaffee Army Hosp., Ark., 1952-53; asst. dir. residence Child Guidance Home, Inc., 1953-55; instr. psychiat. group work, dept. psychiatry Med. Sch. U. Cin., 1953-55; asst. prof. U. Mich., Ann Arbor, 1958-63, assoc. prof., 1963-65, prof. Sch. Social Work, 1965-78; dean Grad. Sch. Social Work U. Tex., Arlington, 1978-88; dean Sch. Social Work Rutgers U., State U. of N.J., New Brunswick, 1988-92, prof. II, 1988—. Vis. prof. Paul Baerwald Sch. Social Work, Hebrew U., Jerusalem, spring 1987, City U. Hong Kong, fall 1993, Bar-Ilan Sch. Social Work, spring 1997, Tel Aviv U., 2002-03. Author: Small Groups in Hospital Community, 1967, Families in Crisis, 1970, Social Work Education for Family and Population Planning, 1973, Individual Change Through Small Groups, 1974, 2d edit., 1985, Social Work Roles and Functions in Family and Population Planning, 1974, Child Abuse and Neglect: A Challenge to the Caring Community, 1977, Group Workers at Work: Theory and Practice in the 80's, 1986, The First Helping Interview: Engaging the Client and Building Trust, 1996, in Russian, 2003, Il Primo Colloquio: Coinvolgiemento e Relazione Nelle Professioni D'aruto, 1999; sr. editor: Ency. Social Work, 1971, LaRicerca Valutative, 1972; editor Jour. Health and Social Behavior, 1970-73, Jour. Social Work, 1965-69, Jour. Marriage and Family Counseling, 1974-82, Social Work with Groups, Hong Kong Jour. Social Work, 1998—, Jour. Social Work and Social Policy in Israel, 1988—. Bd. dirs. Washtenau County Family Svc., 1964-66, 69-70. Served to 1st lt. AUS, 1952-53. Fulbright Hays lectr. Italy, 1971; Fulbright Hays lectr. U. Philippines, 1966-67; Fulbright Hays lectr. Australia, 1973-74. Mem. NASW (chpt. chmn. 1962-63), Am. Sociol. Soc. Office: State U of NJ Rutgers Sch Social Work 536 George St New Brunswick NJ 08901-1167 Business E-Mail: pglasser@rci.rutgers.edu. *The generation and the dispersal of knowledge are the two primary ways in which the academician contributes to the society. He is an agent of change as he studies what is, in order to suggest what might be, and communicates this to his students. My career has been devoted to these principles and to stimulating others to follow them.*

GLASSER, STEPHEN ANDREW, publishing executive, lawyer; b. Memphis, July 27, 1943; s. Melvin A. and Esther (Kron) G.; m. Lynn Schreiber, Dec. 30, 1965; children: Susan, Laura, Jeffrey, Jennifer. BA cum laude, Colgate U., 1965; JD, U. Mich., 1968. Bar: D.C., 1968. Asst. dir. Practising Law Inst., NYC, 1968-71; exec. v.p., exec. editor N.Y. Law Pub. Co., NYC, 1971-77; pres. Law & Bus. Inc. div. Harcourt Brace Jovanovich, NYC, 1977-86, Prentice Hall Law & Bus. div. Simon & Schuster Profl Info Group, Englewood Cliffs, NJ, 1986-94; chmn. Glasser Publs. Inc., Little Falls, NJ, 1995—2003; co-pres. Glasser Legal Works, a Thomson Bus., 2004; chmn. Sandpiper Ptnrs., LLC, Bloomfield, NJ, 2005—. Adj. assoc. prof. SUNY Coll. Bus., Stony Brook, NY, 2004—. Co-founder, editor, publisher Legal Times of Washington, 1978-86. Former trustee Mental Health Assn. of Essex County; trustee Bloomfield Coll., chmn. bd., 1999—2000, former chmn. fin. and property com., 2000—01, 1st vice chair, 2001—; former trustee The Hospice Inc.; adv. bd. SUNY (Stony Brook) Coll. Bus. Mem. ABA, D.C. Bar Assn., Assn. Bar City N.Y., Phi Beta Kappa, Montclair Golf Club. Home: 86 Highland Ave Montclair NJ 07042-1910 Office: Sandpiper Partners LLC 1515 Broad St Bldg B Bloomfield NJ 07003 Business E-Mail: steveglasser@sandpiperpartners.com.

GLASSER, STEPHEN C., lawyer; b. Bklyn., Jan. 11, 1951; BS, Bklyn. Coll.; JD, Bklyn Law Sch., 1976. Bar: NY 1977, Calif. 1983, US Dist. Ct. (so., ea. dist. NY) 1977, US Ct. Appeals (2d cir.) 1982. Law asst. Justices of NY State Supreme Ct. Appellate Div. 2d Compartment, 1976—80; of counsel Sullivan Papain Block McGrath & Cannavo PC, NYC, 1984—97, chief appellate counsel, 1997—. Mem.: Assn. Trial Lawyers Am., NY State Bar Assn., NY State Trial Lawyers Assn., NY County Trial Lawyers Assn. Office: Sullivan Papain Block McGrath & Cannavo PC 120 Broadway New York NY 10271 Office Phone: 212-732-9000. Office Fax: 212-266-4141.

GLASSER, WOLFGANG GERHARD, science researcher, educator; b. Oct. 9, 1941; came to U.S., 1969, naturalized, 2001; s. Joachim and Charlotte (Syjatz) G.; m. Heidemarie Reinecke, Mar. 18, 1969; children: Christine Glasser Sutherland, Stephan A Degree wood tech., U. Hamburg, 1966, PhD Wood Chemistry, 1969. Rsch. assoc. U. Wash., Seattle, 1969—70, rsch. asst. prof., 1970—71; asst. prof. Va. Poly. Inst. and State U., Blacksburg, 1972—75, assoc. prof., 1975—80, prof. wood chemistry, 1980—2002, assoc. dean rsch. and grad. studies Coll. Forestry and Wildlife Resources, 1993—98, prof. emeritus wood sci. and forest products, 2002—. Adj. prof. Inst. Paper Sci. and Tech., Atlanta, 1999-2003; dir. Pulp and Paper Rsch. Inst., Sao Paulo, Brazil, 1976, Biobased Materials Ctr., 1988-91; vis. prof. U. Grenoble (France), Centre de Recherche sur Macromolecules Vegetales, Grenoble, 1985, Nat. U. Singapore, 1993, Kyoto (Japan) U., 1998, U. Toulouse, France, 2000, 03, Chalmers U. Tech., Gothenborg, Sweden, 2001-02, U. de Guadalajara, Jalisco, Mex., 2005, U. Henri Poincaré, Nancy, France, 2006; vis. scientist Weyerhaeuser Corp., 2004; chmn. panel NAS, 1974-76; cons. to industry and govt. Mem. editl. adv. group Holzforschung, Braunschweig, Germany, 1985—, Cellulose Chem. Tech., Romania, 1987—, Cellulose, 1994-99, editor-in-chief, 2000—; mem. editl. adv. group Jour. Wood Sci. (Japan), 1998—, Jour. Applied Polymer Sci., 1989—; patentee in field; contbr. articles to profl. jours.; book editor Co-recipient George Olmsted award Am. Paper Inst., 1974; recipient Sci. Achievement award Internat. Union Forest Rsch. Orgns., 1986, Anselme Payen award Cellulose, Paper and Textile divsn. Am Chem. Soc., 2000 Fellow Internat. Acad. Wood Sci. Tech.; mem. Am. Chem. Soc. (fellow Cellulose and Renewable Materials divsn., 2003, alt. councilor 1983-85, pub. chmn. 1985-88, chmn. 1990, councilor 1991-2000, program chmn. 1993-96, nominations chair 2002—), Soc. Wood Sci. Tech., Sigma Xi, Phi Beta Delta. Lutheran. Office: Va Tech 230 Julian Cheatham Hall Wood Sci Forest Products Blacksburg VA 24061 Office Phone: 540-231-4403. Business E-Mail: wglasser@vt.edu.

GLASSHEIM, ELIOT ALAN, editor, state legislator; b. NYC, Feb. 10, 1938; s. Raymond S. and Edith (Ruthizer) G.; m. Patricia Sanborn, July 20, 1969 (div. Feb. 1979); children: Eagle, Don; m. Dyan Rey, Feb. 14, 1996. BA, Wesleyan U., 1960; MA, U. N.Mex., 1966, PhD, 1972. Copy boy, book reviewer Wash. Post, 1960-61; editl. proofreader Wall St. Jour., NYC, 1962-64; mgmt. trainee Accessory Fashions, NYC, 1964-66; asst. prof. English, Augusta (Ga.) Coll., 1968-70; fellow U. N.D., Grand Forks, 1971-73; mem. N.D. Ho. of Reps., Grand Forks, 1975-76, 93—, house appropriations com., 2001—, asst. Dem. leader, 2003—04; grant writer, dir. oral history project of 97 flood N.D. Mus. Art, Grand Forks, 1993-99; owner used bookstore and Internet sales Dr. Eliot's Twice Sold Tales, Grand Forks, 1992—; policy analyst No. Great Plains, Inc., Fargo, ND, 1999—. Dir. Population/Food Fund, Grand Forks, 1977-79; housing coord., grantswriter N.D. Migrant Coun., Grand Forks, 1979-81. Editor: Population and Food Issues, 1977, 1978, Voices from the Flood, 1999, Behind the Scenes, 2002, Renewing the Countryside--North Dakota, 2004, Toward New Horizons: Moving the Northern Great Plains Region to a Stronger Economic Future, 2002, Traceability in Agriculture, 2003; author: The New Marketplace in European Agriculture: Environmental and Social Values Within the Ford Chain, 2005; author: (poems) The Restless Giant, 1968. Exec. dir. Quad County Cmty. Action Agy., Grand Forks, 1981—87; field rep., office mgr. U.S. Senator Quentin Burdick, Grand Forks, 1987—92; mem. Grand Forks City Coun., 1982—, Grand Forks Planning and Zoning Com., 1984—96, mem. flood response com., 1997—2000, chmn. population task force, 2001; chmn. interim legis. Commerce Commn., 1999—2000; founder, dir. Red River Valley Habitat for Humanity, Grand Forks, 1988—99; chmn. Dist. 17/18 Dems., Grand Forks, 1980—81; bd. dirs. Prairie Pub. TV, 1997—2000. Home: 619 N 3rd St Grand Forks ND 58203-3203 E-mail: eglass@infionline.net.

GLASSHEIM, JEFFREY WAYNE, allergist, immunologist, pediatrician; b. Far Rockaway, NY, Sept. 16, 1958; s. Ronald Alan and Glenda (Deitch) G.; m. Paulette Renée, Apr. 16, 1989; children: Elyssa Gwen, Brenna Chase. BA cum laude, Temple U., 1980; DO in Osteo. Medicine (hon.), U. New. Eng., 1984. Diplomate Am. Bd. Pediatrics, 1989, Am. Bd. Allergy and Clin. Immunology, 1995. Commd. 2d lt. U.S. Army, 1980, advanced through grades to maj., 1989; intern pediat. Winthrop-Univ. Hosp., Mineola, NY, 1984-85; resident pediat. Madigan Army Med. Ctr., Tacoma, 1985-87; fellow allergy/immunology Fitzsimons Army Med. Ctr. and Nat. Jewish Med. Ctr., Denver, 1990—92, chief fellow allergy-clin. immunology, 1990—92; chief allergy-clin. immunology and immunizations svcs. Silas B. Hays Army Community Hosp., Fort Ord, Calif., 1992—93; resigned commn. USAR, 1993; dir. allergy-immunology Pediatric Med. Group of Fresno, Calif., 1994-95, Northwest Med. Group, Fresno, 1995-97; pvt. practice allergy and immunology Fresno, Calif., 1997—2005, Oshkosh, Wis., 2005—06; dir. allergy, asthma and immunology Theda Care Physicians, Inc., Oshkosh, 2006—. Cons. numerous pharm. companies. Contbr. articles to profl. jours.; mem. editl. adv. bd. Unique Opportunites, 1998—, contbg. editor, 2004—. Bd. dirs. Am. Lung Assn. Ctrl. Calif., 1999—2002. Fellow Am. Acad. Allergy Asthma and Immunology, Am. Coll. Allergy, Asthma and Immunology; mem. AMA, Am. Osteo. Assn., Am. Physicians Fellowship for Medicine in Israel, Wis. Med. Soc., Winnebago County Med. Soc., Wis. Asthma Coalition, Wis. Assn. for Osteopathic Physicians and Surgeons. Republican. Jewish. Avocations: meteorology, sports, reading, gardening, walking. Home Phone: 920-385-0028; Office Phone: 920-738-6444. Personal E-mail: glasjw@juno.com.

GLASSICK, CHARLES ETZWEILER, foundation administrator; b. Wrightsville, Pa., Apr. 6, 1931; s. Gordon J. and Melva G. (Etzweiler) Glassick; m. Mary Williams, Feb. 27, 1952; children: Bruce, Judith, Jeffrey, Robert, Jonathan. BS with honors, Franklin and Marshall Coll., 1953; MA, PhD, Princeton U., 1957; D.Sc. (hon.), U. Richmond, 1977; L.L.D. (hon.), Dickinson Sch. Law, 1986; LLD, Pepperdine U., 1996, Adrian Coll., 1997; LHD (hon.), Franklin & Marshall Coll., 1997. Rsch. chemist Rohm & Haas Co., Phila., 1957-62; instr. gen. chemistry Temple U., Phila., 1957-62; prof. chemistry Adrian Coll., Mich., 1962-68; v.p. Great Lakes Colls. Assn., Ann Arbor, Mich., 1968-69; assoc. dean acad. affairs Albion Coll., Mich., 1969-71, v.p. acad. affairs, 1971-72; pres. Va. Inst. Scientific Research, Richmond, 1972-77; provost, v.p. acad. affairs U. Richmond, Va., 1972-77; pres. Gettysburg Coll., Pa., 1977-89, Woodruff Arts Ctr., Atlanta, 1990-96; sr. scholar Carnegie Found. Advancement Tchg., Stanford, Calif., 1989-90, acting pres. Menlo Park, Calif., 1995, interim pres., 1996-97, sr. assoc., 1997-2001, sr. assoc. emeritus, 2001—; interim pres. NC Wesleyan Coll., 2000-01, Reinhardt Coll., 2001—02, Thomas U., 2005—06. Cons. NSF, 1963—67, NEH, 1971—72, Va. Coun. High Edn., 1972—76; mem. exec. com. Luth. Ednl. Conf. N.Am., 1983—86; mem. Pres.'s Commn. Nat. Collegiate Athletic Assn., 1988—89; interim pres. Converse Coll., 1998—99; interim dir. Scholars Press, 1999—2000; vis. fellow Cambridge U., 2002. Mem. editl. bd. Liberal Education, 1978—82, Educational Record, 1985—97; co-author: Scholarship Assessed-Evaluations of the Professoriate, 1995. Mem. Mental Health and Mental Retardation Task Force Manpower Devel., Richmond, 1975—77, ACE Commn. Minorities; bd. dirs. Hist. Gettysburg/Adams County, 1979—89, Meth. Conf. Homes Aging, 1985—89, Atlanta Cultural Olympiad, 1991—96, Midtown Alliance, 1991—97; bd. dirs., exec. com. Spartanburg Habitat for Humanity, 2002—; bd. dirs. Cmty. Campus Partnership Health, 2003—; trustee, vice-chmn. Eisenhower Soc., 1985—95, Carnegie Found. Advancement in Tchg., 1991—97, Ga. Found. Ind. Colls., 1992—, Literacy Action, Inc., 1994—97, Found. Hosp. Art, 1994—; bd. trustees Ga. Found. Ind. Colls., 1996—, Thomas U., 2006—; bd. curators Ga. Hist. Soc., 1997—99; bd. regents Am. Arch. Fedn., 1998—2007; Fulbright sr. scholar specialist, 2002—. Mem.: AAUP, AAAS, Danforth Assocs., NY Acad. Scis., Am. Chem. Soc., Phi Beta Kappa (hon.), Alpha Chi Omega, Omicron Delta Kappa, Beta Gamma Sigma. Methodist. Personal E-mail: CEGlassick@aol.com.

GLASSMAN, ALEXANDER HOWARD, psychiatrist, researcher; b. Chgo., Feb. 4, 1934; s. Morris and Mindelle (Sosna) G.; m. B. Judith Cohen, Mar. 28, 1958; children: Steven, Laura Glassman Hercher. BS, U. Ill., Chgo., 1956, MD, 1958. Diplomate Am. Bd. Neurology and Psychiatry. Resident in psychiatry Albert Einstein Med. Coll. Medicine, Yeshiva U., NYC, 1954-62; USPH fellow, 1963-64; asst. prof. psychiatry Albert Einstein Coll. Medicine, Bronx, NY, 1964-65, cons. psychopharmacologist, 1972-78; dir. residency tng. Letterman Gen. Hosp., San Francisco, 1967-68, chief psychiatry svc., 1968-69; dir. affective diseases N.Y. State Psychiat. Inst., NYC, 1973-78, chief clin. psychopharmacology, 1978—; prof. clin. psychiatry Coll. Physicians and Surgeons, Columbia U., NYC, 1980—. Mem. merit rev. bd. VA, Washington, 1987-90. Editor: Treatment Strategies in Refractory Depression, 1990, also 5 other books; contbr. articles to jours. in field; patentee in field. Lt. col. U.S. Army, 1967-69. Recipient Established Investigator award Nat. Assn. for Rsch. Affective Diseases and Schizophrenia, 1990, also Disting. Investigator award, 2005, N.Y. State Psychiat. Rsch. award, 1994; invited spkr. Nobel Com. Conf. of Depression, Stockholm, 1983; Plenery spkr. German Psychiat. Assn., Fed. Republic Germany, 1990, Plenery spkr. Japanese Neurosci. Soc., Nagoya, 1994. Fellow Am. Coll. Neuropsychopharmacology, Am. Psychiat. Assn. (Lifetime achievement prize 1989); mem. AAAS, Am. Psychopath. Assn. (trustee), N.Y. Acad. Sci. Achievements include patent for clonidine in smoking cessation; first to recognize unique treatment response of delusionally depressed patients, to demonstrate relationship between antidepressant drug treatment outcome and individual differences in drug metabolism, to describe the cardiac antiarrhythmic effects of antidepressant drugs, to describe relationship between depression and cigarette smoking. Office: Columbia U Dept Psychiatry 1051 Riverside Dr New York NY 10032-2695 Business E-Mail: ahg1@columbia.edu.

GLASSMAN, ARMAND BARRY, physician, educator, scientist, administrator, pathologist; b. Paterson, NJ, Sept. 9, 1938; s. Paul and Rosa (Ackerman) G.; m. Alberta C. Macri, Aug. 30, 1958; children: Armand P., Steven B., Brian A. BA, Rutgers U., 1960; MD magna cum laude, Georgetown U., DC, 1964. Diplomate in anatomic, clinical pathology & tranfusion medicine Am. Bd. Pathology, Am. Bd. Nuc. Medicine. Intern Georgetown U. Hosp., Washington, 1964-65; resident Yale-New Haven Hosp., West Haven VA Hosp., 1965-69; asst. prof. pathology, Coll. Medicine U. Fla.; chief radioimmunoassary lab. Gainesville VA Hosp., Fla.; practice lab. and nuc. medicine, 1969-71; dir. clin. labs., assoc. prof., prof. pathology, cellular, molecular biology Med. Coll. Ga., Augusta, 1971-76; cons. physician in nuc. medicine Univ. Hosp., Augusta, 1973-76; med. dir. clin. labs. Med. U. SC Hosp., Charleston, 1976-87; attending physician in lab. and nuc. medicine Med. U. SC, 1976-87, assoc. med. dir. Med. U. Hosp. and Clinics, 1982-86, prof., chmn. dept. lab. medicine, 1976-87, med. dir. MT and MLT programs, 1976-87, clin. prof. pathology, lab. medicine, and radiology, 1987—, acting chmn. dept. immunology and microbiology, 1985-87, assoc. dean Coll. Medicine, 1979-85, asst. and assoc. dean Coll. Allied Health Sci., 1984-87, chmn. hosp. exec. com., 1985-86, acting med. dir. Univ. Hosp. and Clinics, 1985-86; med. dir. clin. labs. Charleston Meml. Hosp., 1976-87; cons. VA Hosp., Charleston, 1976-87; sr. v.p. med. affairs, prof. lab. medicine and nuc. medicine Montefiore Med. Ctr. and Albert Einstein Coll. Medicine, Bronx, NY, 1987-89; v.p., lab. dir. Nat. Reference Lab., Nashville, 1989-92; from clin. prof. to prof. dept. pathology Vanderbilt U., Nashville, 1990-94; dir. Vanderbilt Pathology Lab. Svcs., 1992-94; dir. clin. labs. Vanderbilt U. Med. Ctr., 1993-94, O. Stribling chair, prof., 1994—2006; head and chair divsn./dept. lab. medicine, med. dir. med. tech. and cytogenetic tech. programs U. Tex., M.D. Anderson Cancer Ctr., Houston, 1994—96, med. dir. Med. Tech. & Cytogenetic Tech. programs, 1994—96, 2001—06, dir. sect. cytogenetics, 1994—2006, chair ops. and improvement mgmt. com. dept. hematopathology, 1998—2002; prof. Grad. Sch. Biol. Scis. U. Tex., 1994—2006; prof. emeritus Med. U. SC, 2006—. Adj. prof. Grad. Sch. Biol. Scis. and U. Tex. Health Scis. Med. Sch., 1994-2007; adv. coun. Trident Tech. Coll., 1976-87; bd. dirs. Fetter Family Health Ctr.; mem. steering com. pathology and lab medicine U. Tex. M.D. Anderson Cancer Ctr., 1998-2000, mem. radiation safety com., 1998-, pharmacy and therapeutics com., 2000-06, vice chmn., 2004—06, credentials com., 2002—06, radiation drug rsch. com., 2003—06, chmn. task force on antiemetic drugs, 2003—06, chmn. medication process com., 2004—06, faculty senate rep., 2004—06; founding dir. Sealite, Inc., 1987-99, chmn. bd. dirs., 1995-99; founding dir., bd. dirs. SynthRx, Inc., 2003-07; med. adv. com. Nashville Red Cross Blood Ctr., 1991-94, acting med. dir., 1991-92; v.p., bd. sci. advisors Nat. Health Labs./Nat. Reference Lab., 1992-94; trustee, bd. dirs. Gulf Coast Cmty. Blood Ctr., 1994—2006; cons. in field. Editor, co-editor 4 books; bd. editors Annals of Clin. and Lab. Scis., 1981—, book editor, 2005—; contbr. articles to profl. jours., chpts. to books. Trustee Coll. Prep. Sch., 1979-84, chmn. bd., 1983-84; trustee, bd. dirs., v.p. Mason Prep. Sch., 1984-87; bd. dirs. United Way, 1983-87, Am. Cancer Soc., 1984-87; co-founder, bd. dirs. Glassman Family Fund, 1998—; bd. mem., sec. Kiawah Island Cmty. Assn., 2007-; mem. comm. com. Town of Kiawah Island, SC, 2007-; donor M.D. Anderson Cancer Ctr., U. Tex., 1994-, Charleston Breast Cancer, 2006-; founder, chmn. Glassman Family Fund/Fidelity Charitable Gift Fund, 1996-. With USMCR, 1956—64. Johnson and Avalon Found. scholar Georgetown U., 1961-64, State scholar Rutgers U., 1956-60; Recipient Jacobi award in pediatrics, Washington, 1964; named Young Investigator of Yr. Soc. Nuclear Medicine 1971, Outstanding Tchr. Med. Coll. Ga., 1974, Olla Stribling Disting. Chair Cancer Rsch. U. Tex., M.D. Anderson Cancer Ctr., 1994-2006. Fellow ACP, Coll. Am. Pathologists (numerous coms. 1971-), Assn. Clin. Scientists (Diploma of Honor 1987, pres. 1990-91, exec. com. 1990-95, Clin. Scientist of Yr. 1993, C.P. Brown lectr. 1995, numerous coms. 1969-), Am. Soc. Clin. Pathology (coun. immunohematology and blood banking 1983-89, coun. grad. med. edn. and rsch. 1998—2004, Commr.'s award for Continuing Edn. 1989, nat. contbg. editor to Resident In-Svc. Exam. 2000-04), Coll. Nuc. Medicine, NY Acad. Medicine; mem. Am. Bd. Pathology (transfusion medicine/blood bank test com. 1984-88), Internat. Acad. Pathology, Am. Assn. Pathologists, Soc. Nuc. Medicine (chmn. edn. com. 1973-77, acad. coun. 1979-92), AMA (Physician's Recognition award, instnl. rep. to sect. on med. schs., 1987-94, 2003—), So. Med. Assn., Am. Geriat. Soc. (founding fellow So. divsn.), Am. Soc. Microbiology, Am. Assn. Blood Banks (chmn. cryobiology com. 1974-83, edn. com. 1978-85, sci. program com. 1981-84, autologous transfusion com. 1979-83, bd. dirs. 1984-87, transfusion practices com. 1992-96), Assn. Schs. Allied Health Professions (bd. editors jour. 1979-83), Soc. Cryobiology (treas., bd. dirs. 1978-80), AAAS, NY Acad. Scis., Acad. Clin. Lab. Physicians and Scientists (exec. coun. 1978-85, pres. 1982-83), S.E. Area Blood Bankers (pres. 1979-81, exec. coun. 1980-85), Tenn. Assn. Blood Banks (treas. 1993-94), Am. Coll. Physician Execs., Kiawah Island Cmty. Assn. (bd. sec., mem. various coms. 2007—), Sigma Xi, Alpha Eta, Alpha Omega Alpha. Avocations: tennis, community service. Office: Med U SC Dept Microbiology Immunology BSB201 173 Ashley Ave Charleston SC 29425 Personal E-mail: abglassmn@yahoo.com. Business E-Mail: glassma@musc.edu.

GLASSMAN, CAROLINE DUBY, state supreme court justice; b. Baker, Oreg., Sept. 13, 1922; d. Charles Ferdinand and Caroline Marie (Colton) Duby; m. Harry Paul Glassman, May 21, 1953; 1 son, Max Avon. LLB summa cum laude, Williamette U., 1944. Bar: Oreg. 1944, Calif. 1952, Maine 1969. Atty. Title Ins. & Trust Co., Salem, Oreg., 1944-46; assoc. Belli, Ashe, Pinney & Melvin Belli, San Francisco, 1952-58; ptnr. Glassman & Potter, Portland, Maine, 1973-78, Glassman, Beagle & Ridge, Portland, 1978-83; justice Maine Supreme Judicial Ct., Portland, 1983-97. Lectr. Sch. Law, U. Maine, 1967-68, 80 Author: Legal Status of Homemakers in State of Maine, 1977. Mem.: ATLA, Russian Am. Rule of Law Consortium, Maine Trial Law Assn., Maine Bar Assn., Calif. Bar Assn., Oreg. Bar Assn., Am. Law Inst., Supreme Ct. Hist. Soc. Roman Catholic. Home: 56 Thomas St Portland ME 04102-3639

GLASSMAN, CYNTHIA AARON, federal agency administrator, former commissioner; m. Len Glassman. BA, Wellesley Coll., 1967; MA in Econs., PhD in Econs., U. Pa., 1975. With Fed. Res. Bank, Phila, 1971—74; econ. supr. U. Cambridge, 1974—77; economist fin. structure sect., spl. asst. to Henry C. Wallich, economist capital markets sect., then chief fin. reports sect. Fed. Res. Sys., Washington, 1977—86; sr. economist Economists Inc., 1986—88; dir. rsch. then mng. dir. fin. services regulatory & pub. policy practices Furash & Co., 1988—97; dir. comml. bank risk mgmt. Ernst & Young, 1997—99, prin. nat. tax dept. quantitative economics & statistics divsn., 1999—2001; commr. SEC, NYC, 2002—06, acting chmn., 2005; under sec. for econ. affairs & statistics adminstrn. US Dept. Commerce, Washington, 2006—. Prof. econs. U. Cambridge, England, 1977—86; sr. mem. Lucy Cavendish Coll., England. Mem.: Commn on Savings and Investment in Am., Women in Housing and Finance, Fed. Res. Bd Credit Union, Nat Economists Club. Office: US Dept Commerce 1401 Constitution Ave NW Washington DC 20230*

GLASSMAN, DEBRA, dentist; m. Steven Glassman; 3 children. BA in dental hygiene, Columbia U.; DDS, NYU Col. Dentistry. Dentist Glassman Dental Care, NYC. Office: NYC Cosmetic Dentists Glassman Dental Care 160 West End Ave New York NY 10023 Office Phone: 212-787-4860. Office Fax: 212-787-9238.

GLASSMAN, EDWARD, public relations executive, educator, journalist; b. NYC, Mar. 18, 1929; s. Jacob S. and Riesa (Bronfman) F.; children: Lyn Judith, Susan Fiona, Ellen Ruth, Marjorie Riesa. AB, NYU, 1949, MS, 1951; PhD, Johns Hopkins U., 1955. Mem. staff City of Hope Med. Ctr., Duarte, Calif., 1959-60; prof., faculty biochemistry dept. med. sch. U. N.C., Chapel Hill, 1960-90, head program for team effectiveness and creativity, 1981-90; prof. emeritus, 1990—; pres. Leadership Cons. Svcs., Inc., Creativity Coll., Chapel Hill, 1990—. Mem. grants and rev. study sect. NIMH, 1966-69, U. Calif., Irvine, 1978; vis. fellow Ctr. Creative Leadership, Greensboro, N.C., 1983; vis. scientist Stanford Rsch. Inst., Menlo Park, Calif., 1986; pres. Creativity Coll. divsn. Leadership Consulting Svcs., Inc., Chapel Hill. Author: Molecular Approaches to Neurobiology, 1967, For Presidents Only: Unlocking the Creative Potential of Your Management Team, 1990, Creativity Handbook, 1991, The Creativity Factor: Unlocking the Potential of Your Team, 1991; columnist Creativity at Work, Chapel Hill Newspaper, 1991-92, Triangle Bus. Jour., 1992-95, Chapel Hill Herald, 1992-94, Moore County Citizens News Record, 1994-96; mem. editl. adv. bd. Behavioral Biology, 1971-78, Pharmacology, Biochemistry and Behavior, 1973-88; mem. bd. advisors Neurochem. Rsch., 1975-78; contbr. 95 articles to profl. jours. Pub. rels. specialist Lions Club, 1995—. Adam T. Bruce fellow, 1954-55; Am. Cancer Soc. fellow, 1955-57; NIH fellow, 1958-59; NIH Career Devel. award, 1961-71; Guggenheim fellow, 1968-69 Fellow AAAS, Royal Soc. Edinburgh; mem. Soc. Neurosci. (pres. N.C. chpt. 1974-75), Elisha Mitchell Sci. Soc. (v.p. 1965-66) Home and Office: 679 Cedar Pt Vass NC 28394-8686

GLASSMAN, GERALD SEYMOUR, metal products executive; b. Hartford, Conn., July 6, 1932; s. Abram and Lena (Rulnick) Glassman; BS, U. Vt., 1954. Exec. Bland Co., Hartford, Conn., 1954-63, Coleco Industries, Hartford, 1963-75; pres. Stanley Plating Co., Forestville, Conn., 1977-82; chmn. CBR Industries, Plainville, Conn., 1977-82; pres. Plainville Plating Co., 1975-97, chmn., 1998—; pres. Internat. Metal Finishing, Inc., 1986—90; mem. regional adv. bd. Bank of Boston Ct., Plainville, 1979-89; mem. adv. bd. 1st Nat. Bank of New Eng., 1991—99. Pres. Tunxis CC Found., 1978-88; trustee Wheeler Clinic, 1979-89, Plainville YMCA, 1980-84; mem. Assocs. U. Hartford. Mem. Nat. Assn. Metal Finishers, Conn. Assn. Metal Finishers (v.p.), Metal Finishers Assn. Conn. (pres.), NAM, Am. Electroplaters Soc., Plainville C. of C., Masons. Jewish. Home: 2 Abbottsford Avon CT 06001 Office: 21 Forestville Ave Plainville CT 06062-2159 E-mail: gsglassman@comcast.net.

GLASSMAN, HILARY E., lawyer, communications executive; BS with honors, NYU, JD. Bar: NY. Assoc. Weil, Gotshal & Manges, 1987—93; v.p., corp. counsel Reliance Group Holdings, Inc., 1987—93; v.p., gen. counsel NewView Technologies, Inc., 2000—03; dep. gen. counsel, mng. dir. Sandler O'Neill & Partners, LP, 2003—05; sr. v.p., gen. counsel, sec. Citizens Communications Co., Stamford, Conn., 2005—. Office: 3 High Ridge Park Stamford CT 06905

GLASSMAN, JAMES KENNETH, editor, writer, publishing executive; b. Washington, Jan. 1, 1947; s. Stanley G. and Elaine Ruth (Schiff) Garfield; children: Zoe Ann, Kate Julia. BA, Harvard, 1969. Editor, pub. Provincetown (Mass.) Advocate, 1971-72; editor-in-chief, exec. pub. Figaro, New Orleans, 1972-78; exec. editor Washingtonian Mag., 1979-81; pub. New Republic mag., Washington, 1981-84; pres. Atlantic mag., Washington, 1984-86; exec. v.p. U.S. News & World Report, Washington, 1984-86; editor-in-chief Roll Call, Washington, 1987-93; fin. and polit. columnist Washington Post, 1993—; resident fellow Am. Enterprise Inst., Washington, 1996—. Host Capital Gang Sunday, CNN-TV, 1995-98, Techno Politics, PBS-TV, 1995-99. Co-author: Dow 36,000, 1999; host www.TechCentralStation.com, 2000—; author: The Secret Code of the Superior Investor, 2002; columnist: Scripps Howard News Svc., 2004—. Office: Am Enterprise Inst 1150 17th St NW Washington DC 20036-4603 Home: 15 Battle Hill Rd Falls Village CT 06031

GLASSMAN, JON DAVID, aerospace executive; b. NYC, Jan. 8, 1944; s. J. and Dorothy (Witkin) G.; m. Ann Tracy Holtz, Nov. 12, 2003; 1 child, Amanda Louise. B in Fgn. Svc., U. So. Calif., 1965; MA, Columbia U., 1968, cert. Russian Inst., 1968, PhD, 1976. Joined Fgn. Svc. Dept. State, 1968; officer Am. Embassy, Madrid, 1968-70, Moscow, 1971-73, Havana, Cuba, 1977-79, Mexico City, 1979-81, Dept. State, Washington, 1974-77, 81-87; charge d'affaires Am. Embassy, Kabul, Afghanistan, 1987-89; dep. asst. for nat. security affairs to V.p. The White House, 1989-90, asst. to V.p. of U.S., 1990-91; amb. to Paraguay Asuncion, 1991-94; dept. state chair Indsl. Coll. of the Armed Forces, Washington, 1994-96; dep. for Balkan mil. stabilization Dept. State, Washington, 1996-97; v.p. internat. bus. devel. electronic sys. sector Northrop Grumman Corp., Balt., 1998—2006, dir. govt. policy, electronics sys. setor, 2006—. Mem. bd. Bus. Coun. for Internat. Understanding, 1999—. Author: Arms for the Arabs, 1976. Bd. dirs. Bus. Coun. for Internat. Understanding. Recipient Presdl. Meritorious Svc. award, 1991. Office: Northrop Grumman Corp Elec Sys Sector PO Box 451 MS A275 Baltimore MD 21203 Office Phone: 410-765-9353. Business E-Mail: jon.glassman@ngc.com.

GLASSMAN, M. MELISSA, lawyer; b. Ft. Rucker, Ala., 1955; BS summa cum laude, U. Tex., Austin, 1976; JD magna cum laude, George Mason U., Arlington, Va., 1987. Bar: Va. 1987, DC 1988, Md. 1995. Assoc. McGuireWoods LLP, Tysons Corner, Va., 1987—96, ptnr., comml. litig. dept., 1996—, mng. ptnr. Tysons Corner office, 2004—. Mem.: Va. Bar Assn. (bd. mem. comml. litig. sect., chmn. constrn. & pub. contracts sect.). Office: McGuireWoods LLP Ste 1800 1750 Tysons Blvd Mc Lean VA 22102-4215 Office Phone: 703-712-5351. Office Fax: 703-712-5228. Business E-Mail: mglassman@mcguirewoods.com.

GLASSMAN, PAUL, library administrator, architecture educator; b. Providence, Dec. 19, 1952; s. Samuel H. and Stella Simons Glassman; life ptnr. Ernest H. Rubinstein. BA, Bowdoin Coll., 1974; MArch, U. Colo., 1979; MS in Libr. Sci., Simmons Coll., 1984. Asst. dir. Frank Lloyd Wright Preservation Trust, Oak Park, Ill., 1992—93; dir. Morris-Jumel Mansion, NYC, 1993—95; art and arch. libr. and asst. prof. Pratt Inst., Bklyn., 1995—97; exec. dir. Old Ch. Cultural Ctr., Demarest, NJ, 1997—98; instr. arch. Yeshiva U., NYC, 1994—; libr. dir. N.Y. Sch. Interior Design, NYC, 1998—2003; asst. dean for reference services and collection devel. Hofstra U., Hempstead, NY, 2003—06; dir. pub. svcs. Pratt Inst., Bklyn., 2006—. Co-author: The Library and the Accreditation Process in Design Disciplines, 2003; contbr. articles to publs. Treas. Hebrew Tabernacle Congregation, 2006—. Mem.: Art Librs. Soc. N.Am, Soc. Architectural Historians (treas. N.Y. Metro. chpt. 2005—), Am. Assn. Museums, Art Librs. Soc. N.Am. (editor 1999—2005, moderator art and design sch. libr. divsn. 2000—01, chair-elect NY met. chpt. 2007). Home: 200 Cabrini Blvd New York NY 10033 Office: Pratt Inst Librs 200 Willoughby Ave Brooklyn NY 11205

GLASSMAN, STEVEN, dentist; m. Debra Glassman; 3 children. BA cum laude, Brandeis U.; DDS, Columbia Col. Dentistry. Pvt. practice, NYC. Office: 160 West End Ave New York NY 10023 Office Phone: 212-787-4860. Office Fax: 212-787-9238.

GLASSMAN, STEVEN J., lawyer; b. NYC, 1944; BS, MIT, 1964; JD, Georgetown U., 1968. Bar: NY 1970, US Supreme Ct., US Cts. of Appeal (Fed. and 2nd Cirs.), US Dist. Cts. (So. and Ea. Dists. NY). Patent examiner U.S. Patent Office, 1964-65; asst. sect. chief, counsel tech. utilization Nat. Aeronautics and Space Adminstrn., 1966-71; asst. U.S. Atty. so. dist. N.Y. U.S. Atty's. Office, 1971-76, chief civil rights sect. so. dist. N.Y., 1974-75, chief civil appellate atty. so. dist. N.Y., 1975-76; ptnr. Kaye Scholer LLP, NYC, 1979—. Editor: Georgetown Law Jour., 1967—68; contbr. articles to law jours. Mem. ABA, Assn. Bar City N.Y., Fed. Bar Coun., Phi Delta Phi. Office: Kaye Scholer LLP 425 Park Ave New York NY 10022-2598 Office Phone: 212-836-8651. E-mail: sglassman@kayescholer.com.

GLASSMEYER, JAMES MILTON, aerospace, computer, and electronics engineer; b. Cin., Mar. 31, 1928; s. Howard Jerome and Ethel Marie (Nieman) G.; m. Anita Mary Tschida, Apr. 21, 1979 Student, U. Cin., 1947-49; BSEE with spl. honors, U. Colo., Boulder, 1958; MS in Aeronautics and Astronautics, MIT, 1960. Commd. 2d lt. USAF, 1950, advanced through grades to lt. col., 1971, astron. engr. Air Force Space Systems Div. Hdqrs. LA, 1960-64, astronautical engr. and astronautics intelligence analyst Air Force Rocket Propulsion Lab Edwards AFB, Calif., 1967-73, ret., 1973; aerospace, computer, and electronics rsch. and analysis and analysis, 1973—. Contbr. articles to jours. in field. Recipient Air Force Inst. Tech. scholarship, U. Colo., 1956-58, MIT, 1958-60, Am. Rocket Soc. Grad. Student Nat. 1st Pl. award, MIT, 1960, USAF Master Missileman badge, Air Force Rocket Propulsion Lab., 1970. Mem. AIAA, IEEE, Air Force Assn., Planetary Soc., Ret. Officers Assn., Tau Beta Pi (1st grand prize Greater Interest in Govt. Nat. Essay Contest 1957), Eta Kappa Nu, Sigma Tau, Sigma Gamma Tau, Sigma Xi. Roman Catholic. Home: 61 Brookhill Woods Ln Tipp City OH 45371-1951 Office: 4017 Tipp Elizabeth Rd Tipp City OH 45371-9443

GLASSON, LLOYD, sculptor, educator; b. Chgo. s. Albert and Fay G.; m. Cathleen Naso, 1968. BFA, Sch. Art Inst. Chgo., 1957; MFA, Tulane U., 1959. Mannequin sculptor, 1959-60; exhibits designer Newark Mus., 1961-62; prof. emeritus U. Hartford, (Conn.), 1964—. Co-founder Artists Tenants Assn., 1961— One-man shows Dorsky Gallery, N.Y.C., 1966, 74, Trinity Coll., Hartford, 1977, SaltBox Gallery, West Hartford, 1985, The Greene Art Gallery, Guilford, Conn., 1997, Sculpture Showcase, Ltd., New Hope, Pa., 1997; represented in permanent collections Wadsworth Atheneum, Hartford, Bushnell Auditorium, Hartford, Ch. of St. Helena, West Hartford, U. N.H., Karen Horney Inst., N.Y.C., Yale U., New Haven, Hartford Hosp., Samuel Dorsky Mus., SUNY, Purchase, Wichita Mus. Art, Kans., Forma Viva, Kostanjevica, Slovenia, ACMAT Corp., New Britain, Conn., Wichita Art Mus., Kans., New Britain Mus. Am. Art, Conn.; recreated the 2 bronze angels atop Soldiers and Sailors Meml. Arch, Hartford; designer, Albert Schweitzer Humanitarian award. With US Army, 1952—54, Korea. Recipient Gold medal 52d ann. exhbn. Nat. Sculpture Soc., 1985, James E. and Frances W. Bent award for Creativity, 1989. Fellow Nat. Sculpture Soc.; mem. NAD (Thomas Proctor prize 1985, Gold medal 1986), Sculptors Guild. Home Phone: 860-342-3469; Office Phone: 212-431-3313.

GLASSROTH, JEFFREY, internist, educator; b. NYC, Oct. 28, 1948; s. Murray and Marie (Cheynoweth) G.; m. Carol Holton, July 22, 1972; children: Marley, Drew. AB, Columbia U., 1969; MD, U. Cin., 1973. Diplomate Am. Bd. Internal Medicine, Subspecialty Bd. Pulmonary Medicine. Intern U. Cin. Med. Ctr., 1973-74, intern, resident, 1973-75, 77-78, resident, 1974-75, 77-78; fellow in pulmonary and critical care medicine Boston U., 1978-81, instr. medicine, 1979-81; from asst. to assoc. prof. medicine Northwestern U., Evanston, Ill., 1981-90, prof. medicine, 1990—95; prof. medicine, chair dept. Allegheny U. Health Scis., Phila., 1995—98; pres. Am. Thoracic Soc., NYC, 1999—2000; chmn., dept. of med. Univ. Wisconsin, 1998—2005; vice dean, prof. medicine Tufts U. Sch. Medicine, 2005—. Cons. Astra N.Am., Westboro, Mass., 1993-99, Genentech/Novartis, San Francisco, 2000-02; mem. adv. coun. for elimination of Tb, CDC, Atlanta, 1993-97; mem. ad hoc study sect. NIH, Bethesda, Md., 1993, 97, 2005. Editor: Scientific Basis Respiratory Infection, 1993; co-editor: Baum's Textbook of Pulmonary Diseases, 7th edit., 2003; assoc. editor Am. Jour. Respiratory Critical Care Medicine, 1994-99; mem. editl. bd. Chest, 1988-93. Surgeon, USPHS, 1975-77, Atlanta. Rsch. grantee NIH, 1987-97, recipient Pulmonary Acad. awards, 1983-89. Master ACP; fellow Am. Coll. Chest Physicians; mem. AAAS, Am. Thoracic Soc. (sec. 1996-97, v.p. 1997-98, pres.-elect 1998, pres. 1999-2000), Ctrl. Soc. for Clin. Rsch. (pres. 2002-03), European Respiratory Soc., Internat. Union Against TB and Lung Disease, Assn. Profs. Medicine (pres.-elect 2003, pres. 2004-05). Avocations: skiing, distance running. Office: Tufts Univ Sch Med 136 Harrison Ave Boston MA 02111 Home Phone: 617-850-5755; Office Phone: 617-636-2727. Business E-Mail: jeff.glassroth@tufts.edu.

GLASSROTH, STEPHEN R., lawyer; Prin. Glassroth Law Firm, P.C. and predecessors, Montgomery, Ala., 1986. Mem. Ala. Sentencing Commn. Contbr. articles to profl. publs. Mem.: Ala. Criminal Def. Lawyers Assn. (pres. 1995—96), Nat. Assn. Criminal Def. Lawyers (2nd v.p. 2006—07). Office: Glassroth Law Firm PC 615 S McDonough St Montgomery AL 36104-5811 Office Phone: 334-263-9900. Office Fax: 334-263-9940. E-mail: srg@glassrothlaw.com.*

GLAT, PAUL MITCHELL, plastic surgeon; b. NYC, Aug. 4, 1962; married; 2 children. Cert. in French Language and Civilization, Sorbonne; BA in Molecular Biology, Princeton U., 1984; MD, NY Med. Coll., 1988. Diplomate Nat. Bd. Med. Examiners, Am. Bd. Surgery, Am. Bd. Plastic Surgery, lic. Pa., NJ, NY. Resident, gen. surgery, dept. surgery NYU Med. Ctr., NYC, 1988—89, rsch. fellow, craniofacial surgery, Inst. Reconstructive Plastic Surgery, 1991—92, chief resident, gen. surgery, 1993—94, resident, plastic surgery, 1994—96; fellow, craniofacial surgery Children's Hosp. Phila. & U. Pa., Phila., 1996—97; asst. prof., surgery MCP-Hahneman (merged in 2002 into Drexel U. Sch. Medicine), 1997—; chief, divsn. plastic surgery St. Christopher's Hosp. for Children, 1997—, dir., cleft palate and craniofacial programs, dir., burn unit; attending physician Hahnemann U. Hosp., Lankenau Hosp., Bryn Mawr Hosp., Elkins Park Hosp.; private practice Pa. Mem. craniomaxillofacial subcommittee Nat. Bd. Med. Examiners, 1998—; treas. Pa. Fedn. Cleft Palate Clinics, 1999—2002; presenter in the field. Contbr. articles to profl. jours., chapters to books; interviewed on the subject of plastic surgery on ABC and NBC News, interviewed by Main Line Today Mag., 2001. Named one of Top Plastic Surgeon, Phila. Mag., 2001, 2002, 2003, 2004, 2007, Best Plastic Surgeons, Main Line Mag. Fellow: ACS; mem.: Am. Burn Assn., Robert H. Ivy Soc. Plastic and Reconstructive Surgeons, Am. Cleft Palate-Craniofacial Assn., Northeastern Soc. Plastic and Reconstructive Surgeons, Am. Soc. Plastic and Reconstructive Surgeons, Am. Soc. Aesthetic Plastic Surgery. Achievements include being recognized for innovations and expertise in the cosmetic surgery of the face. Office: 555 City Line Ave Ste 1170 Bala Cynwyd PA 19004 Office Fax: 866-472-6009.*

GLATER, JONATHAN D., reporter; b. Sept. 1971; Grad., Swarthmore Coll., 1993; JD, Yale Univ., 1998. Reporter Washington Post; lawyer Buenos Aires, 1998—99, NYC, 1999—2000; acctg., consulting firms reporter NY Times, NYC, 2000—. Avocation: running. Office: Bus Day Desk NY Times 229 W 43rd St New York NY 10036 Office Phone: 212-556-1474. Office Fax: 212-556-1448.

GLATT, MITCHELL STEVEN, consumer products company executive; b. NYC, Sept. 2, 1957; s. Herbert and Gloria (Comita) G.; m. Randy Ginsburg, Oct., 1987. BA, NYU, 1978, MBA, 1980. Agt. trainee Internat. Creative Mgmt., NYC, 1980-81; exec. asst. to chmn. bd. Bozell, Jacobs, Kenyon & Eckhardt, Inc., NYC, 1981-87; chmn. of bd. Magla Products Inc., Chatham, 1987—. Pres. GiGi Products, Inc., pres. Am. Med. Acceptance Corp., 1998—. Cons. Statue of Liberty Ellis-Island Found., N.Y.C., 1983-87, Juvenile Diabetes Found., N.Y.C., 1987; adv. bd. NYU Sch. of the Arts; mem. Playwrights Theater N.J. Recipient Commendation Advt. Women of N.Y., N.Y.C., 1986. Mem. Am. Mgmt. Assn., Young Pres. Orgn. Office: Am Med Acceptance Corp 11 West 42nd St New York NY 10036-4011

GLATTER, REBECCA JAN, secondary school educator; BA in religion cum laude, U. Rochester, NY, 2000; MS, Syracuse U., NY, 2002. Cert. tchr. secondary edn. N.Y., 2003. Tchr. Am. history and govt. C. W. Baker H.S., Baldwinsville, NY, 2003—. Tchg. fellow C-SPAN, 2007. Recipient Bryan Swayze Meml. award, NY State Coun. Social Studies, 2005; grantee, Fulbright-Hays, 2004, Freeman Found. Grant, 2004, Japan Fulbright Meml. Fund, 2005, Cornell U., 2005, Inst. African Devel. Cornell U., 2005, Inst. European Studies, 2006, Goethe Inst., 2006, Ctrl. NY Tchg. Ctr., 2006. Mem.: Nat. Coun. Social Studies, N.Y. State Coun. Social Studies, Ctrl. N.Y. Coun. Social Studies (chmn. profl. devel. 2004—). Office Phone: 315-638-6001. Personal E-mail: rjglatter@yahoo.com. Business E-Mail: rglatter@bville.org.

GLAUBER, ROBERT R., former financial regulatory service executive; b. NYC, Mar. 22, 1939; married; 2 children. BA in Econ., Harvard Coll., 1961; Ph.D in Fin., Harvard Bus. Sch., 1965. Instr. Harvard Bus. Sch., 1964—65, asst. prof. fin., 1965—68, assoc. prof. fin., 1968—72, prof. fin., 1972—2000; under sec. for fin. US Dept. Treasury, 1989—92; lectr. Ctr. Bus. and Govt., John F. Kennedy Sch. Govt., Harvard U., 1992—2000; pres. Nat. Assn. Securities Dealers, Washington, 2000—01, CEO, 2000—06, chmn., 2001—06; sr. adv. Peter J. Solomon Co., NYC, 2006—. Exec. dir. Pres. Ronald Reagan's Task Force on Market Mechanisms (Brady Commn.), 1987—88; bd. govs. Nat. Assn. Securities Dealers, 1996—2006; vis. prof. Harvard Law Sch., 2006—; dir. Moody's Corp., Bermuda, Freddie Mac, Quadra REIT, XL Capital Ltd.; mem. internat. adv. bd. Korean Fin. Supervisory Svc. Mem.: Boston Com. Fgn. Rels., Coun. Fgn. Rels. Office: Peter J Solomon Co 520 Madison Ave New York NY 10022

GLAUBER, ROY JAY, physics professor; b. NYC, Sept. 1, 1925; s. Emanuel B. and Felicia (Fox) G.; m. Cynthia Marshall Rich, July 26, 1960 (div. June 1976); children: Jeffrey M., Valerie M. BS in Physics summa cum laude, Harvard U., 1946, MA, 1947, PhD in Physics, 1949; D in Naturwissenschaften (hon.), U. Essen, Germany, 1997; D in rer. nat. ehrenhaber (hon.), Friedrich-Alexander U., Erlangen-Nürnberg, Germany, 2006; DSc, U. Ariz., Tucson, 2006. Staff mem. theoretical physics div. Los Alamos (N.Mex.) Lab., 1944-46; mem. Inst. for Advanced Study, Princeton, NJ, 1949-51; research fellow Swiss Fed. Polytech. Inst., Zürich, 1950; lectr. Calif. Inst. Tech., Pasadena, 1951-52, Harvard U., Cambridge, Mass., 1952-53, asst. prof., 1953-56, assoc. prof., 1956-62, prof., 1962-76, Mallinckrodt Prof. of Physics, 1976—. Vis. lectr. Ecole d'Été de Phys., Théorique, Les Houches, France, 1954, 64, U. Calif., Berkeley, 1955, 57, 63, U. Colo., Boulder, 1958, 61, U. Wash., Seattle, 1960, Brandeis U., Waltham, Mass., 1961, U. Leningrad, USSR, 1964, CUNY, 1970; adj. prof. physics U. Ariz., Tucson, 1988—; dir. Enrico Fermi Internat. Sch. Physics, Varenna, Italy, 1967; guest prof. CERN, Geneva, 1972-73, vis. staff, 1983; vis. prof. NORDITA, Copenhagen, 1974; Lorentz prof. U. Leiden, The Netherlands, 1974; vis. prof. Coll. France, Paris, 1983; Freese lectr. Rensselaer Poly. Inst., 1986; Racah lectr. Hebrew U., Jerusalem, 1988; Touschek lectr. Frascati Lab., Italy, 1988; adv. bd. Program for Sci. and Tech. for Internat. Security, MIT, 1983—; trustee Ivy Fund, 1961-92, 95-2004; dir. Mackenzie Funds, Inc., 1993-2004; cons. Clinton Anderson Lab., Los Alamos Nat. Lab., N.Mex.; bd. dirs. Ctr. Arms Control and Non Proliferation, 2006-; hon. prof. Zhejiang U., Hangzhou, China, 2007, Xian Jiaotong U., China, 2007, Tongji U., Shanghai, 2007. Author: Quantum Theory of Optical Coherence, 2007; editor Quantum Optics, 1989-95; mem. editl. bd. Jour. Math. Physics, 1961-63, Nuc. Physics B., 1972-93; contbr. articles to profl. jours. Named Fulbright Lectr., 1954 hon. prof. Zhejiang U., Hangzhou, China, 2007, Xian Jiaotong U., Xian, 2007, Tongji U., Shanghai, 2007; recipient A.A. Michelson Medal Franklin Inst., 1985, A. von Humbolt Rsch. award, 1989, Dannie Heineman prize, 1996, Willis E. Lamb prize, 2006; co-recipient Nobel Prize in Physics, 2005; fellow NRC, 1946-49, AEC, 1949-50, Frank B. Jewett Bell Labs., 1950-51, Guggenheim, 1966-67, 72-73. Fellow Am. Acad. Arts and Scis., Am. Phys. Soc. (Dannie N. Heineman Prize in Mathematical Physics 1996), Am. Optical Soc. (Max Born award 1985), Royal Soc. New Zealand (hon.); mem. NAS, Royal Soc. London (fgn.), Nat. Ctr. Arms Control Non-Proliferation (mem. adv. bd.), Phi Beta Kappa, Sigma Xi. Office: Harvard U Lyman Lab Physics Lyman 331 17 Oxford St Cambridge MA 02138

GLAUBINGER, LAWRENCE DAVID, retired manufacturing company executive; b. Newark, Nov. 26, 1925; s. Samuel I. and Pauline (Sandler) G.; m. Lucienne Lefebvre, Nov. 11, 1967. BS with honors, Ind. U., 1949; MBA, Columbia U., 1977; LLD (hon.), Ind. U., 1993. Adminstrv. asst. to pres. Ronson, Inc., Newark, 1949-51; mdse. mgr. United Mchts., NYC, 1951-65; v.p. Marietta Silk Mills, Pa., 1965-66; pres., CEO Channel Textile Co. Inc., Bradford, Vt., 1966-75; chmn. bd., CEO Stern & Stern Industries, Inc., NYC, 1977-2000; ret., 2000. Pres. Lawrence Econ. Cons. Inc., Melbourne Beach, Fla., 1977—; mgr. Beegee Trading Co. LLC, 2000—; bd. dir. Leucadia Nat. Corp. Bd. overseers Columbia U. Sch. Bus., chmn. ann. funds campaigns, 1980-82; bd. dirs. Ind. U. Found.; mem. Ind. U. Bus. Sch. Acad. Alumni Fellows; bd. dirs. Ind. U. Varsity Club. Served with USCGR, 1943-46. Recipient Disting. Alumni Svc. award, Ind. U. Mem. Hoosier Hundred, Ind. U. Dean's Assocs., Columbia U. Bus. Assocs., Campaign for Columbia (co-chmn. bus. sch.), Am. Arbitration Assn., Princeton Club (N.Y.), Green Brook Country Club, Beta Gamma Sigma. Republican. Jewish. Home: Sterling House # 253 6307 S Hwy AIA Melbourne Beach FL 32951

GLAUS, TROY, professional baseball player; b. Newport Beach, Calif., Aug. 3, 1976; Attended, UCLA. Player Anaheim (Calif.) Angels, 1998—2004, Arizona Diamondbacks, 2004—05, Toronto Blue Jays, 2005—. Named World Series MVP, 2002; named to, Am. League All Star Team, 2000—03. Achievements include led American League in Home Runs (47), 2000; member of World Series Champion Anaheim Angeles, 2002. Office: Toronto Blue Jays Rogers Centre One Blue Jays Way Toronto ON Canada M5V 1J3

GLAUTHIER, T. J., management consultant; b. Durham, NC, Jan. 3, 1944; s. Theodore and Martha May (Myers) G.; m. Carrie L. Bostrom, June 11, 1966 (div. 1973); children: Jeff, Paul, Tad; m. M. Brigid O'Farrell, July 9, 1977; 1 child, Patrick O. AB, Claremont Coll., Calif., 1965; MBA, Harvard Bus. Sch., 1967. Cons. Peat, Marwick, Livingston, LA, 1967-68; with Applied Computer Tech., LA, 1968-70; cons. Applied Decision Systems, Cambridge, Mass., 1970-74; v.p. Temple, Barker & Sloane, Inc., Lexington, Mass., 1974-90; head Pub. Policy Practice, 1980-90; head Washington office, 1986-90; dir. energy and climate change World Wildlife Fund, Washington, 1990-93; assoc. dir. nat. resources, energy and sci. U.S. Office Mgmt. and Budget, Exec. Office of Pres., Washington, 1993-98; dep. sec., COO U.S. Dept. Energy, 1999-2001; pres., CEO Electricity Innovation Inst., Palo Alto, Calif., 2001—04; pres. TJG Energy Assocs., LLC, Moss Beach, 2005—. Bd. dirs. Union Drilling, Inc., 2006—, San Mateo County Resource Conservation Dist., 2006—. Pres. Lake Barcroft Assn., 1989—94; assoc. Lake Barcroft Watershed Improvement Dist., 1989—2001; del. Va. State Dem. Conv., 1993, 1997. Democrat. Unitarian. Home: 1001 Ocean Blvd Moss Beach CA 94038 Office Phone: 650-353-6061. Personal E-mail: tjglauthier@aol.com.

GLAVIN, A. RITA CHANDELLIER (MRS. JAMES HENRY GLAVIN III), lawyer; b. Schenectady, NY, May 11, 1937; d. Pierre Charles and Helen C. (Fox) Chandellier; m. James H. Glavin, III, June 1, 1963; children: Helene, James, Rita, Henry. AB cum laude, Middlebury Coll., Vt., 1958; JD, Union U. Albany Law Sch., 1961. Bar: N.Y. 1961, U.S. Dist. Ct. (no. dist.) N.Y. 1961, U.S. Tax Ct. 1965, U.S. Supreme Ct. 1978. Assoc. Eugene Steiner, Albany, N.Y., 1961-64, Helen Fox Chandellier, Schenectady, 1965-76; mem. Glavin and Glavin, Waterford, Schenectady, 1965-86, 87—, Albany, 1965-86, 87—. Del. 4th Jud. Dist. Nominating Conv., 1966—67; confidential law clk. justices N.Y. State Ct. Claims, 1968—71; surrogate judge Saratoga County, 1986; dir. assn. coun. mems. and coll. trustees SUNY, 1991—2002, sec., 1996—2002. Mem. editl. bd. Albany Law Rev., 1960-61. Sec. Bellevue Women's Med. Ctr., 2001—02; bd. dirs., chmn. fin. com. Schenectady YWCA, 1979—81; bd. dirs. Schenectady Jr. League, 1974, 1976; del. pub. affairs com. N.Y. State Jr. League, 1976; sec. Bellevue Maternity Hosp., Inc., 1966—2001, bd. dirs., 1966—83, bd. advisors, 1984—2001; bd. dirs. Bellevue Women's Med. Ctr., 2001—02; trustee Middlebury Coll., 1978—88, chmn. law com., 1982—88, vice chmn. bd. dirs., 1986—87; trustee Waterford Hist. Mus. and Cultural Ctr., Inc., 2000—06, sec., 2002—06; mem. univ. coun. SUNY, Albany, 1985—2002; tech. advisor HSA Northeastern N.Y. Maternity and Pediat. Com., 1976. Mem. N.Y. State Bar Assn. (mem. ho. of dels. 1987-88, nominating com. 1988-90), Saratoga County Bar Assn. (exec. com. 1981—, v.p. 1985, pres. 1986), Schenectady County Bar Assn., Phi Beta Kappa, Kappa Kappa Gamma. Office: Glavin & Glavin PO Box 40 69 2nd St Waterford NY 12188-0040 Personal E-mail: gglaw@mindspring.com.

GLAVIN, EDWARD P., television producer; b. Phila., Sept. 8, 1963; s. Maurice Denis and Maureen Elizabeth Glavin; m. Deborah Harwick, Aug. 22, 1992; 1 child, Emily Maureen. Degree, Glassboro Coll., NJ, 1985. Mem. staff KYW-TV, 1985-88, CNBC, Ft. Lee, NJ, 1988-92, Donahue Shoe, NYC, 1990-92; exec. prodr. Jenny Jones Show, Warner Bros., LA, 1992, Caroline Rhea Show, 2002, Change of Heart, 2003, The Ellen Degeneres Show, 2004—. Recipient Best Television Series or Special (Variety), The Producers Guild Am., 2006. Mem. NATAS. Office: The Ellen Degeneres Show Warner Bros Studio 4000 Warner Blvd Burbank CA 91522

GLAVIN, JAMES EDWARD, landscape architect; b. Syracuse, NY, Aug. 18, 1923; s. James Edward and Florence Ellen (Nelson) G.; m. Helen Catherine Hartnett, Aug. 24, 1946; children— Kathleen Glavin Kopitsky, Timothy, David, Matthew, Martin, Maureen. BS in Landscape Architecture, SUNY Coll. Environ. Sci. and Forestry, Syracuse, 1948. City planner Syracuse Planning Commn., 1948-49; chief land planning dept. Sargent Webster Crenshaw & Folley, Syracuse, 1951-56; partner Hueber Hares Glavin (architects, landscape architects, and engr., and predecessor), Syracuse, 1956-88, James E. Glavin & Assos. (landscape architects), Syracuse, 1956-88, Syracuse Scale Models, 1968-88, Glavin & Van Iderstine Landscape Architects, 1980-88; pvt. cons., 1988—. Vis. juror, lectr. State U. Coll. Environ. Sci. and Forestry, 1959, 65, 69, State U. Coll. Agr., Cornell U., 1970—; mem. faculty adv. coun. Sch. Landscape Architecture, NY State U. Coll. Environ. Sci. and Forestry, 1990—; cons. NY State Council Arts, 1971; mem. NY State Bd. Landscape Architects, 1987-91. Contbr. articles to profl. publs.; contbg.; editor: Empire State Architect, 1957-60. Mem. Citizens Found., Syracuse, 1957-77, St. Thomas More Found, 1965-88; bd. dirs. Hiawatha coun. Boy Scouts Am., 1980-88, adv. bd., 1988-2003; bd. dirs. Adirondack Archtl. Heritage, 1993-2000, Clifton-Fine Hosp., 1998-2000; trustee Clifton Cmty. Libr., 1994-2000. Recipient Design award Am. Assn. Nurserymen, 1969, 71; named Outstanding Alumni, SUNY Coll. Environ. Sci. and Forestry Alumni Assn., 1994. Fellow Am. Soc. Landscape Architects (past co-chmn. pvt. practice com., Design award 1968, 71); mem. ASCE (past v.p. Syracuse chpt.), Sigma Lambda Alpha. Home and Office: PO Box 491 Cranberry Lake NY 12927-0491

GLAVIN, WILLIAM FRANCIS, JR., insurance company executive; BA, Coll. Holy Cross, Worcester, Mass. Various sr. mgmt. positions in sales and mktg. Procter & Gamble, State St. Bank and Trust Co., Boston Co., Dreyfus Corp.; pres. Scudder Funds; with Babson Capital Mgmt. LLC (subs. of MassMutual Fin. Group), 2003—06, pres., CEO, 2005—06; exec. v.p. US Ins. Group MassMutual Fin. Group, 2006—, co-COO, 2007—. Office: MassMutual Fin Group 1295 State St Springfield MA 01111-0001 Office Phone: 800-767-1000.*

GLAVINE, TOM (THOMAS MICHAEL GLAVINE), professional baseball player; b. Concord, Mass., May 25, 1966; s. Fred and Millie Glavine; m. Carri Dobbins, Nov. 7, 1992 (div.); 1 child, Amber; m. Christine Glavine; children: Peyton, Mason 1 stepchild, Jonathan. Grad., Billerica Meml. HS, Mass., 1984. Pitcher Atlanta Braves, 1987—2002, NY Mets, 2002—. Vol. Nat. Sports Com., Leukemia Soc. Am.; hon. chmn. Ga. Coun. on Child Abuse; host Ga. Transplant Found. Ann. Spring Tng. Named Nat. League Pitcher Yr., Sporting News, 1991, World Series Most Valuable Player, 1995, 2005 Mets honoree of the Roberto Clemente award for civic involvement, cmty. endeavors, and general caring about his fellow man.; recipient Nat. League Cy Young award, Baseball Writers Assn. Am., 1991, 1998, Babe Ruth award, 1995, Good Guy award, NJ Sportswriters, 2004, NY Chpt. Baseball Writers Assn. Am., 2007, Joan Payson award for humanitarian svc., NY Chpt. Baseball Writers of Am., Bart Giamatti award for cmty. svc., Baseball Assistance Team, 2006. Achievements include the only pitcher to throw two shutouts at Coors field, with Atlanta Braves; 4-time Silver Slugger winner, 1991, 1995-96, 1998; 5-time National League leader in wins, 1991-1993, 1998, 2000; 10-time National League All-Star, 1991-93, 1996-98, 2000, 2002, 2004, 2006; tied as leader of the National League pitching victories, 1991-92; starting National League pitcher Major League Baseball All-Star Game, 2006; being one of only 23 pitchers in MLB history to earn 300 career wins, August 5, 2007. Office: NY Mets Shea Stadium 123 01 Roosevelt Ave Flushing NY 11368-1699*

GLAZE, LYNN FERGUSON, pre-school administrator; b. Oakland, Calif., May 24, 1933; d. Kenneth Loveland and Constance May (Pedder) Ferguson; m. Harry Smith Glaze, Jr., July 3, 1957; children: Catherine, Charles Richard. BA, Stanford U., 1955, MA, 1966. Devel. dir. Greenwich Acad., Conn., 1982-84, Am. Lung Assn. of Del., 1988—89; devel. cons. St. Michael's Sch. and Nursery, Brandywine Mus., Opera Del., others, 1990—99. Author: Seasons of the Trail, 2000. Pres. Darien-Norwalk YWCA, Conn., 1973-76; sec. Darien Republican Town com., 1974-76; dist. chmn. Darien Rep. Meeting, 1974-76, mem. Rep. Nat. Conv. Platform Com., 1988; vestry St. Luke's Ch., Darien, 1979-82; justice of the peace, Darien, 1981-84; bd. dirs. Ingleside Homes, Inc., 1986-92, Henrietta Johnson Med. Ctr., 1994-97; pres. Del. ProChoice Med. Fund, 1997-99; mem. Gov.'s Small Bus. Coun., 1987, EEOC, New Castle County, 1991-94, Del. Common Cause, 1999—. Coro Found. fellow.

GLAZE, THOMAS A., state supreme court justice; b. Jan. 14, 1938; s. Phyllis; children: Steve, Mike, Julie, Amy, Ashley. BSBA, U. Ark., 1960, JD, 1964. Exec. dir. Election Research Council Inc., 1964-65; legal advisor Winthrop Rockefeller, 1965-66; staff atty. Pulaski County Legal Aid, 1966-67, asst. then dep. atty. gen., 1967-70; pvt. practice law, 1970-79; chancellor Ark. Chancery Ct., 6th Jud. Cir., 1979-80; judge Ark. Ct. Appeals, 1981-86; assoc. justice Ark. Supreme Ct., 1987—. Lecturer U. Ark., Little Rock, 1971, 72, 79, 80; lecturer U. Ark. Sch. Law, 1981, 82, 85, 87; chmn. Election Laws Inst., 1970-78. Past bd. dirs. Vis. Nurses Corp., Youth Home Inc. Office: Ark Supreme Ct Justice Bldg 625 Marshall St Justice Bldg Little Rock AR 72201-1054 Home Phone: 501-223-4880; Office Phone: 501-682-6870.

GLAZER, BARRY DAVID, lawyer; b. Cleve., Oct. 10, 1948; s. Jacob J. and Constance (Schwartz) Glazer; m. Deborah Werbner, Sept. 28, 1984. AB, Miami U., Oxford, Ohio, 1970; JD, Mich. Law Sch., 1973. Bar: Minn. 1973, U.S. Dist. Ct. Minn. 1973, France Conseil Juridique 1981. Assoc. Dorsey & Whitney, Mpls., 1973—78, ptnr., 1979—80, resident ptnr. Paris, 1980—86, London, 1986—91, mng. ptnr. Brussels, 1991—2000, resident ptnr. London, 2001—. Mem.: ABA, Internat. Bar Assn. Office: Dorsey & Whitney LLP 21 Wilson St London EC2 England Office Phone: 44-207-588-0800. Business E-Mail: glazer.barry@dorsey.com.

GLAZER, CHARLES LOUIS, ambassador; b. Greenwich, Conn., June 21, 1943; s. Charles Sidney and Jeaney Meyer (Mellitz) Glazer; m. Janet H. Glazer; children: Lindsay Hollis, Charles Louis Jr., Alexander Herbert. BS in Fin., U. Va. Sr. v.p., dir. Jefferies & Co., NYC; sr. v.p. Blyth Eastman Dillon & Co., Inc., NYC; pres., CEO C.L. Glazer Co., Greenwich, 1981—2007; US amb. to El Salvador US Dept. State, San Salvador, 2007—. Officer 502nd Mil. Intelligence Bn. US Army, 1965—67, Seoul, Korea. Republican. Mailing: DOS Amb 3450 San Salvador Pl Washington DC 20521-3450*

GLAZER, DONALD WAYNE, lawyer, corporate financial executive, educator; b. Cleve., July 26, 1944; s. Julius and Ethel (Goldstein) G.; children: Elizabeth M., Mollie S. AB summa cum laude, Dartmouth Coll., 1966; JD magna cum laude, Harvard U., 1969; LLM, U. Pa., 1970. Bar: Mass. 1970. Assoc. Ropes & Gray, Boston, 1970-78, ptnr., 1978-92, counsel, 1992-96; ptnr. Am. Bus. Ptnrs. LLC, Boston, 1996-98; pres. Mugar/Glazer Holdings, Inc., Boston, 1992-95; vice chmn. fin. New Eng. TV Corp. and WHDH-TV, Inc., Boston, 1992-93; adv. counsel Goodwin Procter LLC, Boston, 1997—; co-founder, corp. sec. Provant, Inc., Boston, 1998—, vice-chmn., 2002. Instr. corp. fin. Boston U. Law Sch., 1975; lectr. law Harvard U., Cambridge, Mass., 1978-91; trustee GMO Trust, Boston, 2000—, lead trustee, 2004, chmn. bd., 2005. Co-author: Massachusetts Corporation Law and Practice, 1991, Glazer and FitzGibbon on Legal Opinions, 1992, 2d edit., 2001; co-editor First Ann. Inst. on Securities Regulation, 1970; contbr. articles to legal jours. Past chmn., trustee Cowen Slavin Found.; past trustee Santa Fe Neuroscis. Inst.; past dir. Newton Girls Soccer League, past co-chmn. intramural com.; past trustee, past treas. Hillel Founds. of Greater Boston Inc.; past trustee Program for Young Negotiators. Fellow Salzburg Seminar in Am. Studies, 1975. Mem.: ABA (coun. Bus. Law Sect., past chmn. legal opinions com., co-reporter Legal Opinions Prins., past chmn. subcom. on employee benefits and exec. compensation, fed. securities law com., past co-chmn. task force on sect. 16 devels.), TriBar Legal Opinions Com. (co-chmn., editor-in-chief The Remedies Opinion, co-reporter Third-party Closing Opinions, co-reporter Opinions on Limited Liability Cos.), Am. Law Inst. (Members Consultative Group Restatement Law Governing Lawyers), Boston Bar Assn. (past chmn., corp. sec., past co-chmn. legal opinions com., past chmn. securities law com.). Jewish. Home: 225 Kenrick St Newton MA 02458-2731

GLAZER, GILDA F., musician, educator; b. NYC, June 9, 1944; d. Naphtali Zvi and Lena Esther Frishberg; m. Robert B. Glazer, June 8, 1968. BA in Music, Queens Coll., 1966; MA in Music, Columbia U., 1968; postgrad., Wake Forest U., 1980. Mem. piano faculty Roosevelt U., Chgo., 1971—81; ofcl. pianist Chgo. Symphony Orch., 1971—81; touring concert pianist Prestige Concerts, 1980—; ofcl. pianist St. Louis (Mo.) Symphony, 1981—86; prof. piano Wake Forest U., Winston-Salem, NC, 1986—89; mem. piano faculty Hartt Coll. Music, Hartford, Conn., 1989—98; pianist Glazer Duo, NYC and Hartford, 1986—, N.Y. Piano Quartet, NYC, 1995—. Condr. master classes U. Conn., U. Mo., others, 1971—; leader chamber music workshop and inst. faculty Columbia U., NYC; jury mem. Bergen Festival Competition, Bergen County, NJ, 1995—, dir.; mem. jury Heida Hermanns Internat. Piano Competition, St. Louis Symphony Young Artist Awards. Editor: (piano book) Album for Two, 1989; musician: (CD) The Glazer Duo, 2005, CD solo and duo compositions, CD solo and chamber compositions; author: Training the Pianist as An Ensemble Player, 2004. Recipient piano fellowship, Tanglewood Music Ctr., 1st prize in piano, Nat. Fedn. Music Clubs, Nat. Guild Piano Awards. Mem.: Chamber Music Am., Coll. Music Soc., Chgo. Symphony Alumni, Bohemian Club of N.Y., Phi Beta Kappa. Office: Prestige Concerts PO Box 342 Bergenfield NJ 07621

GLAZER, GUILFORD, real estate developer; b. Knoxville, Tenn., July 17, 1921; s. Aaron Usher and Ida (Bressoff) G.; children: Emerson, Erika; m. Diane Pregerson, Jan. 29, 1967. Mech. Engr., George Wash. U., 1939; Metallurgy, U. Louisville, 1943. Bd. dirs. The Torrance (Calif.) Co., 1990, Del Amo Fashion Ctr., Torrance, Calif., 1990; partial owner Allegheny Ctr., Pitts. Bd. dirs. Rand Corp. Ctr. for Middle East Pub. Policy. Developer various shopping ctrs. and office bldgs. in U.S. Pres. Reagan Libr. Found., Nixon Libr. Foun.; trustee L.A. Holocaust Meml., Stop Cancer, Bell Shelter for Homeless, Tel Aviv U.; founder Ford's Theatre, Washington, Am. Friends of the Israel Def. Force, Sino Judaic Inst., Nanjing, China, Moshe Dayan Ctr., Tel Aviv U. for Ea. and African Studies, U. Tenn. Judaic Studies Dept.; mem. Wilshire Blvd. Temple, L.A.County Mus. Art, Unified Fund Music Ctr. With USN, 1942-45, WWII. Recipient Hon. Fellow U. Tel Aviv. Mem. World Affairs Coun., Hillcrest Country Club, Monterey Country Club. Jewish. Avocation: golf. Office: Ste 610 9440 Santa Monica Blvd Beverly Hills CA 90210

GLAZER, JACK HENRY, lawyer; b. Paterson, NJ, Jan. 14, 1928; s. Samuel and Martha (Merkin) G.; m. Zelda d'Angleterre, 1979. BA, Duke U., 1950; JD, Georgetown U., 1956; postgrad., U. Frankfurt, Germany, 1956-57; SJD, U. Calif., Berkeley, 1977. Bar: D.C. 1957, Calif. 1968. Atty. GAO and NASA, 1958-60; mem. maritime divsn. UN Internat. Labour Office, Geneva, Switzerland, 1960, spl. legal adv., 1960-62; atty. NASA, Washington, 1963-66; chief counsel NASA-Ames Rsch. Ctr., Moffett Field, Calif., 1966-88; gov. Calif. Maritime Acad., 1975-78; asst. prof. Hastings Coll. Law, 1985-87; prof., assoc. dean bus. sch. San Francisco State U., 1988-92; dir. San Francisco Palace Fine Arts, 1995. Contbr. articles to profl. jours. Comdr. Calif. Naval Militia, ret. Capt. JAGC, USNR, ret. Mem. Calif. Bar Assn., D.C. Bar Assn., White's Inn (reader). Office: White's Inn 37 White St San Francisco CA 94109-2609 Home Phone: 415-776-1629; Office Phone: 415-441-0236. Personal E-mail: whitesinn@comcast.net.

GLAZER, MALCOLM, professional sports team executive; b. Rochester, NY, Aug. 25, 1928; m. Linda; children: Avram, Kevin, Bryan, Joel, Ed, Darcie. Owner, pres. Tampa Bay Buccaneers, Fla., 1995—; shareholder Manchester United, 2003—, owner, 2005—. Pres., CEO First Allied Corp.; chmn. of bd. Zapata Corp., Houston, 1994-2002; bd. dirs. Splty. Equipment Cos. Active Am. Cancer Soc., Sloan-Kettering Cancer Ctr., United Jewish Appeal, Jewish Guild for the Blind. Named one of 400 Richest Ams., Forbes mag., 2006. Office: Tampa Bay Buccaneers One Buccaneer Pl Tampa FL 33607

GLAZER, MARTIN A., lawyer; b. Brookline, Mass., May 19, 1946; AB magna cum laude, Bowdoin Coll., 1968; JD, Harvard U., 1971. Bar: Mass. 1971. Ptnr. Goulston & Storrs, P.C., Boston, dir. Trustee, v.p. & treas. Temple Shalom Newton; trustee Jewish Vocat. Svc. Named Mass. Super Lawyer, 2006. Mem.: Internat. Coun. of Shopping Ctrs. Office: Goulston & Storrs PC 400 Atlantic Ave Boston MA 02110-3333 Office Phone: 617-574-6439. Office Fax: 617-574-7582. E-mail: mglazer@goulstonstorrs.com.

GLAZER, MICHAEL, lawyer; b. LA, Oct. 10, 1940; BS, Stanford U., 1962; MBA, Harvard U., 1964; JD, U. Calif., LA, 1967. Bar: Calif. 1967. Law clk. to Hon. Roger J. Traynor Calif. Supreme Ct., 1967-68; commr. L.A. Dept. of Water & Power, 1973-76; chmn. Calif. Water Commn., 1976-78; asst. adminstr. nat. oceanic and atmospheric adminstrn. U.S. Dept. of Commerce, 1978-80; dir. Met. Water Dist. of So. Calif., 1984-91; ptnr. Paul, Hastings, Janofsky & Walker LLP, LA. Articles editor U. Calif. at L.A. Law Rev., 1966-67. Mem. State Bar Calif. (com. on corps. 1986-87), L.A. County Bar Assn. (chair fed. securities regulation com. 1988-90, chair exec. com. bus. and corp. law sect. 1995-96), Order of the Coif, Phi Beta Kappa. Office: Paul Hastings Janofsky & Walker LLP 515 S Flower St Los Angeles CA 90071-2300

GLAZER, REA HELENE See KIRK, REA

GLAZER, ROBERT BOYD, musician, educator; b. Anderson, Ind., Aug. 24, 1939; s. Samuel and Dorothy Siegel Glazer; m. Gilda F. Frishberg, June 8, 1968. MusB, Roosevelt U., Chgo., 1960, MusM, 1962; postgrad., Columbia U., NYC, 1986. Mem. Pitts. Symphony, 1963—71, Chgo. Symphony, 1971—81; co-prin. violist St. Louis Symphony, 1981—86; prof. viola and conducting U. NC, Charlotte, 1986—94; violist NY Piano Quartet, NYC, 1995—. Touring soloist Prestige Concerts, NYC, 1980—; violist Glazer Duo, NYC, 1986—; dir. chamber music workshop and instrumental faculty Columbia U., NYC, 1987—; conductor NY String Symphony, 1987—, NC All-State Orch., Charlotte, 1989; prof. viola Hartt Coll. Music, Hartford, Conn., 1994—99; prin. violist Hartford Symphony, Conn., 1994—99; jury mem. Washington U. Internat. String Competitions, St. Louis, 1995—, St. Louis Symphony Internat. String Competitions, 1995—. Musician (soloist): (CD) Viola Concerto by Morton Gould, 1995; musician: The Glazer Duo Plays American Music, 2005; contbr. articles to profl. jours. Recipient Tanglewood award, Tanglewood Music Ctr., Boston; fellow, Aspen Music Festival, Colo.; scholar, Roosevelt U., Chgo. Mem.: Chamber Music Am., Coll. Music Soc., Chgo. Symphony Alumni, Bohemian Club NY. Avocations: photography, art, exercise, reading.

GLAZER, SIDNEY, physician, director; b. Decatur, Ill., Mar. 16, 1948; s. Benjamin and Lucille Glazer; m. Janice Lysiak, July 2, 1977. BA, U. Calif., Berkeley, 1966—70; MD, Loyola U. Stritch Sch. Medicine, Maywood, Ill., 1970—74. Diplomate Med. Bd. Calif., 1975, cert. General surgery Am. Bd. Surgery, 1981. Ptnr. physician in vascular surgery Kaiser Permanente, Anaheim, 1982—, lead physician hemodialysis access cqi com. Pasadena, 1997—. Pres. Orange County Surg. Soc., Anaheim, 2001—02; clin. assoc. prof. surgery U. Calif., Irvine, 2006—. Contbr. articles to profl. jours. and pubs. Recipient Physicians' Exceptional Contbn. award, Kaiser Permanente , So. Calif. Permanente Med. Group, 1997, Physician of Excellence, Orange County Med. Assn., 2005. Fellow: ACS; mem.: Soc. Clin. Vascular Surgery, So. Calif. Vascular Surg. Soc., Vascular Access Soc. of Americas, Soc. Vascular Surgery, Alpha Omega Alpha. Avocation: travel. Office: Kaiser-Permanente 411 Lakeview Ave Anaheim CA 92807 Home Phone: 714-639-4526; Office Phone: 714-279-4013. Office Fax: 714-279-4029. Business E-Mail: simglazer@scal.kp.org.

GLAZER, WILLIAM H., real estate developer; b. Pa. BA, UPenn. Lic. Pa. Real Estate Broker. Founder & pres. Keystone Property Group, Conshohocken, Pa., 1991—. With Nat. Assn. Indsl. & Office Properties, Wharton Sch. Zell/Lurie Real Estate Ctr., Tristate Comml. Alliance, Urban Land Inst. Recipient 40 Under 40 award, Phila. Bus. Jour., 2006. Office: Keystone Property Group Ste 400 1 W First Ave Conshohocken PA 19428 Office Phone: 610-825-2060. Office Fax: 610-825-2009.

GLAZIER, KENNETH M., lawyer; b. May 17, 1948; BA magna cum laude, Harvard Coll., 1969; JD, Yale U., 1973. Bar: Calif. 1973. Assoc. O'Melveny & Myers, LA, 1973—78; trial atty. U.S. Dept. of Justice, Wash., 1979—80; mem. Morrison & Foerster, LA, 1980—93; ptnr. Ross, Sacks & Glazier, 1993—2001, Sacks, Glazier, Franklin & Lodise, LA, 2001—. Lectr. Practicing Law Inst., 1986—, panelist Calif. Continuing Edn. Bar. Editor Yale Law Jour., 1972. Mem. LA County Bar Assn., 1986-88, Jud. Evaluation Com. Office: Sacks Glazier Franklin & Lodise 350 S Grand Ave Ste 3500 Los Angeles CA 90071 Office Phone: 213-617-7455. Office Fax: 213-617-9350.

GLAZIER, PENNY PORT, property and event manager; m. Peter Glazier. Principal Glazier Group (properties incude Monkey Bar, Michael Jordan's Steak House, NYC Strip House, NJ Strip House); pres. Seaport Merchants Assn., 1995—95; former columnist TV Guide's Celebrity Dish. Bd. mem. Children's Hearing Inst.; mem. Joseph Papp Theatre Bd. Named one of 50 Taste Makers, Nation's Restaurant News, Movers and Shakers, Hamptons Mag.; recipient Judy Silberstein Volunteerism award, Children's Hearing Inst., 2001. Office: Glazier Group 535 Fifth Ave New York NY 10017*

GLAZIER, ROBERT CARL, publishing executive; b. Brandsville, Mo., Mar. 26, 1927; s. Vernie A. and Mildred F. (Beu) G.; m. Harriette Hubbard, June 5, 1949; children: Gregory Kent, Jeffrey Robert. Student, Drury Coll., 1944-46; BA, U. Wichita, 1949. Reporter Springfield (Mo.) Daily News, 1944-46; asst. city editor Wichita Eagle, 1946-49; journalism instr. U. Wichita, 1949-53; dir. pub. relations Springfield (Mo.) Pub. Schs., 1953-59; asso. dir. dept. radio and TV The Methodist Ch., Nashville, 1959-61; gen. mgr. WDCN-TV (Channel 2), Nashville, 1961-65, KETC (Channel 9), St. Louis, 1965-76; also exec. dir. St. Louis Ednl. TV Commn.; pres. So. Ednl. Communications Assn., 1976-80; chmn. bd. Springfield Communications, Inc., Mo., 1980—. Bd. dir. Systematic Savs. & Loan Assn., Cox Health Sys.; pres. Lester E. Cox Med. Ctrs., 1999-2000 Bd. dir. Adult Edn. Council Greater St. Louis, 1965-76, United Meth. Communications, 1980-86, Springfield Area Council of Chs., 1980-86. Served with AUS, 1945-46. Named to, Writers Hall of Fame of Am., 2003; recipient Ozarks Heritage award, Mus. of the Ozarks, 1990, Silver Beaver award, Boy Scouts Am., 2003. Mem. Nat. Sch. Public Relations Assn. (past regional dir.), Nat. Acad. TV Arts and Scis. (gov.), Mo. Instructional TV Council, Ill. Instructional TV Commn., Nat. Assn. Ednl. Broadcasters. Clubs: Rotary Internat. Methodist. Home: 2305 E Meadow Dr Springfield MO 65804-4536 Office: 520 S Union Ave Springfield MO 65802-2660 Office Phone: 417-831-1600 417. E-mail: pub@sgfmag.com.

GLEASON, ABBOTT, history professor; b. Cambridge, Mass., July 21, 1938; s. Sarell Everett and Mary Eleanor (Abbott) G.; m. Sarah Caperton Fischer, June 11, 1966; children: Nicholas Abbott, Margaret Holliday BA, Harvard U., 1961, PhD, 1969. Asst. prof. history Brown U., Providence, 1969-73, assoc. prof. history, 1973-78, prof. history, 1978—; sec. Kennan Inst. for Advanced Russian Studies, Woodrow Wilson Ctr., Washington, 1980-82, chmn. history, 1989-92; dir. Watson Inst., 1999-2000, dir. univ. rels., 2000—03; Keeney prof. history Brown U., 1993—2005, prof. emeritus, 2005—. Mem. overseers com. to visit Davis Ctr. for Russian Studies, Harvard U., Cambridge, 1981-85, 91-97; bd. dirs. Fabergé Arts Found. Author: European and Muscovite, 1972, Young Russia, 1980, Totalitarianism, 1995 (with William Taubman and Sergei Khrushchev), Nikita Khrushchev, 2000; co-editor: Bolshevik Culture, 1985, Shared Destiny, 1985, Nineteen Eighty-Four: George Orwell and our Future, 2005. Fellow, Howard Found., 1973—74; Rockefeller fellow, Aspen Inst., 1977, Mellon fellow, Harvard U., 1985. Mem. Am. Hist. Assn., Am. Assn. Advancement Slavic Studies (del. to Am. Coun. Learned Socs. 1984-87, bd. dirs. 1991-97, exec. com. 1994-97, pres. 1995). Democrat. Home: 30 John St Providence RI 02906-1043 Office: Brown U PO Box 1970 Providence RI 02912 also: Watson Inst for Internat Studies 111 Thayer St Providence RI 02912 E-mail: abbott_gleason@brown.edu.

GLEASON, BARBARA JO, literature and language professor; b. San Diego, Aug. 10, 1952; d. George Donald and Virginia Lee Gleason; m. Edward Gerard Quinn, Mar. 17, 2001. BS, U. Mo., Columbia, 1974; MA, Okla. State U., Stillwater, 1984; PhD, U. So. Calif., LA, 1989. Vol. Peace Corps, Abong Mbang, Eastern Province, Cameroon, 1978—81; assoc. prof. english City Coll. NY, 1990—, dir. composition, 1992—94, writing cons. supr. Ctr. Worker Edn., 1997—2006, dir. MA in lang. and literacy, 2005—. Exec. bd. mem. Conf. Basic Writing, NY, 2005—. Co-editor: Composition in Four Keys; contbr. chapters to books. Grantee, Fund for Improvement in Post-Secondary Edn., 1993—96. Mem.: Internat. Writing Ctr. Assn., Writing Program Adminstrn. Coun., Coll. Composition and Communication Conf., Nat. Coun. Tchrs. English. Office: City Coll NY 138th St at Convent Ave New York NY 10031 Office Phone: 212-650-6329. Business E-Mail: bgleason@ccny.cuny.edu.

GLEASON, DANIEL J., lawyer; b. New Haven, Sept. 22, 1944; BA magna cum laude, Harvard Coll., 1967; JD cum laude, Harvard U., 1970. Bar: Mass. 1971, N.H. 1992. Ptnr., co-chmn. intellectual property litig. group Nutter, McClennen & Fish, Boston. Arbitrator. Mem. exec. com. Mass. Appleseed Ctr. for Law and Justice. Named Mass. Super Lawyer, Boston mag., 2004. Fellow: Am. Coll. Trial Lawyers; mem.: ABA (chmn., subcom. on intellectual property litigation), Boston Bar Assn. (bd. dris., lawyers com. for civil rights under law), Mass. Bar Assn., Phi Beta Kappa. Office: Nutter McClennen & Fish World Trade Ctr West 155 Seaport Blvd Boston MA 02210-2604 Office Phone: 617-439-2233. Office Fax: 617-310-9233. Business E-Mail: dgleason@nutter.com.

GLEASON, JAMES MULLANEY, lawyer, insurance company executive; b. Sept. 27, 1948; s. Harry H. and Dorothy (Mullaney) Gleason; m. Margaret McGuire; children: Matthew, Katherine. BA, Briar Cliff Coll., 1973; JD, Creighton U., 1976. Bar: (Iowa) 1976, Nebr. 1976. From asst. counsel to asst. v.p. Woodmen of the World, Omaha, 1976—93, asst. v.p., 1993—2004, v.p., 2004—, v.p. gen. coun., 2005—. With US Army, 1968—69. Fellow: Life Mgmt. Inst. (master), Life Office Mgmt. Assn.; mem.: Assn. Life and Health Claims, Nebr. Fraternal Congress (pres. 1993—94), Internat. Claim Assn. (pres. 2002—03, exec. com.), Assn. Fraternal Benefit Counsel. Democrat. Roman Catholic. Office: Woodmen of World Life Ins Soc 1700 Farnam St Ste 2200 Omaha NE 68102-2007 E-mail: jgleason2@cox.net.

GLEASON, JEAN BERKO, psychology professor; b. Cleve., Dec. 19, 1931; d. Arthur E. and Alice (Gelberger) Berko; m. Andrew Mattei Gleason, Jan. 26, 1959; children: Katherine, Pamela, Cynthia. AB, Radcliffe Coll., 1953, AM, 1955, PhD, 1958. USPHS fellow MIT, 1958—59; research assoc. VA Med. Ctr., Boston, 1961—2000; from vis. asst. prof. psychology to prof. emerita Boston (Mass.) U., 1972—2005, prof. emerita, 2005—, chairperson dept. psychology, 1985—89, acting chair dept. psychology, 1997, dir. grad program devel. psychology, 1975—78, 1982—85, dir. grad. program human devel., 1997—2002; research assoc. edn. Harvard U., Cambridge, Mass., 1968—70, prin. research assoc. psychiatry, 1970—72. Rsch. scholar in residence Inst. Linguistics, Hungarian Acad. Sci., 1981, 83; mem. mental retardation rsch. com. Nat. Inst. Child Health and Human Devel., 1981-85; trustee Ctr. for Applied Linguistics, Washington, 1989-94. Author: The Development of Language, 1983, 6th edit., 2005, You Can Take It with You, 1989, Psycholinguistics, 1993, 2nd edit., 1998; mem. editl. bd. Child Development, 1971—77, Discourse Processes, 1982—2002, assoc. editor Language, 1997—2000; contbr. articles. Recipient Editors award Jour. Speech and Hearing Research, 1970. Fellow: APA, AAAS (coun. del. 2002—05); mem.: ACLU, Internat. Assn. for Study of Child Lang. (pres. 1990—93), Soc. for Rsch. Child Devel., Linguistic Soc. Am. (chmn. program com. 1980—81, resolutions com. 2004), Radcliffe Alumni Assn. (bd. dirs. 1969—72), Radcliffe Grad. Soc. (past pres.), Gypsy Lore Soc. (exec. bd. 1983—87, 1992—2002, pres. 1996—99, exec. bd. 2003—06), Acad. Aphasia, Phi Beta Kappa (pres. Radcliffe chpt. 1965—68). Home: 110 Larchwood Dr Cambridge MA 02138-4639 Office: Boston U Dept Psychology 64 Cummington St Boston MA 02215-2407 Business E-Mail: gleason@bu.edu.

GLEASON, JOHN PATRICK, JR., trade association executive; b. NYC, Nov. 11, 1941; s. John Patrick Sr. and Ruth T. (Madigan) G.; m. Judith Peper (dec. 1980); children: John P. III, Megan K.; m. Susan Leigh Collier, Mar. 31, 1984; children: Kevin M., Colin P. BS in Fgn. Service, Georgetown U., 1963; PMD, Harvard Bus. Sch., 1972. Gen. mgr. Pappagallo, Inc., Washington, 1964-67; export project mgr. U.S. Dept. Commerce, Washington, 1967-68; investment banker Blyth, Eastman Dillon, Inc., Washington, 1968-70; with U.S. Dept. Commerce, Washington, 1970-77, chief staff domestic and internat. bus. adminstrn., 1970-77, dep. asst. sec. commerce, 1970-77; pres. Brick Inst. Am., Reston, Va., 1977-86, Portland Cement Assn., Skokie, Ill., 1986—. Bd. dirs., chmn. Coun. Masonry Rsch., Reston, 1985—, Masonry Industry Com., Washington, 1984—. Recipient Silver medal U.S. Dept. Commerce, Washington, 1978. Mem. Am. Soc. Assn. Execs., Chgo. Soc. Assn. Execs., River Bend Country Club (Great Falls, Va.), Carlton Club (Washington), Skokie Country Club (Glencoe, Ill.). Republican. Office: Portland Cement Assn 5420 Old Orchard Rd Skokie IL 60077-1053

GLEASON, ROBERT LYLE, financial analyst, realtor; b. Fullerton, Nebr., Aug. 21, 1932; s. Charles Streeter Gleason and Pearl Allington; m. Betty Ann Rolf, Dec. 28, 1958; children: Robert Scott, Brett Christopher. BSBA, U. Nebr., Lincoln, 1959; degree in banking, Rutgers U., New Brunswick, NJ, 1969. Asst. bank examiner Fed. Deposit Ins. Corp., Columbus, Nebr., 1960—61, Denver, 1961—65, bank examiner Oklahoma City, 1965—68, Cedar Rapids, Iowa, 1968—70, field office supr. North Platte, Nebr., 1970—79, sr. bank examiner Des Moines, 1979—86, fin. analyst Chgo., 1986—87; realtor Coldwell Banker & Iowa Realty, West Des Moines, Iowa, 1992—2000; ret. Coach Little League Baseball, North Platte, Nebr., 1975—77, West Des Moines, 1984—85, 1988—89; rep. Rep. Conv., West Des Moines. Sgt. USMC, 1953—56. Recipient Spl. Achievement award, Fed. Deposit Ins. Corp., Wash., DC, 1982. Mem.: Am. Assn. Rep. Persons, Am. Legion. Republican. Avocations: baseball, bowling, politics. Home: 407 38th St West Des Moines IA 50265-3925

GLEAVES, LEON ROGERS, marketing and sales executive; b. Louisville, May 4, 1939; s. Leon Rogers and Fain Mae (King) G.; m. Hallie Virginia Dumke, Apr. 9, 1966 (dec. Dec. 20, 1990); 1 child, Keith Browning; m. Elizabeth Ann Smith, June 25, 2000 BS, U. Louisville, 1961, MBA, 1966. Sales mgmt. trainee GM, Louisville, 1965-67; advt. rep. The Christian Sci. Monitor, NYC, 1967-72; mktg. and sales coord. White Lily Foods Co., Knoxville, Tenn., 1972-75; v.p. mktg. and sales Wilkins-Rogers, Inc., Ellicott City, Md., 1975—2002; pres., CEO, LRG, Ltd., 2002—. Spkr. in field. Bd. dirs. Bucknell U. Parents Assn., Lewisburg, Pa., 1992-95; adv. com. Md. Agrl. Edn. Found., Balt., 1993-96, Md. Food Bank, Inc., Balt.; home econ. adv. bd. Howard County Schs., Columbia, Md., 1993-2003, Balt. City Schs., 1994-97; mem. fin. com. So. Assn. State Depts. Agr., 1997, Md. Agrl. Commn., 2002-03; Md. Agrl. Commn., 2002-2003; spkr. Future Bus. Leaders Am., 1997-99. Mem. Balt./Washington Grocery Mfr. Rep., Md. Food Exporters Assn., Am. Mktg. Assn., Home Baking Assn. (dir. 1990-92), So. Assn. State Dept. Agr. (fin. com. 1997), Md. Agriculture Commn., 2002-2003. Avocations: tennis, classical and vintage jazz music, English mystery books and movies.

GLEESON, THOMAS ALEXANDER, retired meteorologist; b. NYC, Aug. 11, 1920; s. John and Bertha Alexander Gleeson; m. Jeanette Lucas, Nov. 21, 1942; children: Vicki, Keith Thomas. BS, Harvard U., 1946; MS, NYU, 1947, PhD, 1950. Professional Member Am. Meteorol. Soc., Mass., 1945. Asst. prof. Fla. State U., Tallahassee, 1949—54, assoc. prof., 1954—59, full prof., 1959—94. Cons. USN, Norfolk, Va., 1962—67, NASA, Huntsville, Ala., 1964—73; state climatologist U.S. Weather Svc., Tallahassee, 1984—94. Contbr. articles to profl. jours. First lt. US Army, 1942—45, U.S. and Middle East. Fellow: Am. Meteorol. Soc. (hon.; com. chmn. 1974—75); mem.: Sigma Xi (corr.). Home: 2106 Old Bainbridge Rd Tallahassee FL 32303 Office: Univ Dept Meteorology Fla State Tallahassee FL 32306

GLEICH, CAROL S., health professions education executive; b. Kewanee, Ill., Jan. 18, 1935; d. Carl and Edna (Krause) Gleich. BA, U. Iowa, 1958, MS, 1967, PhD in Health Sci. Edn., 1972. Cert. clin. chemistry technologist, Nat. Registry Clin. Chemistry. From instr. to asst. prof. pathology U. Iowa Sch. Medicine, Iowa City, 1972-77, edn. specialist divsn. allied health, 1977-88, chief resource devel. sec., 1988-90, health manpower edn. officer, physician manpower and credentialing, chief spl. projects and data analysis br. divsn. medicine, 1991-95, exec. sec. coun. grad. med. edn., 1996-99; dir. area health edn. ctr. nat. program Bur. Health Professions, Health Resources & Svcs. Adminstrn., Rockville, Md., 1977—. Allied health cons. to Egypt; gov. cons. in internat. health profl. ed., Russia, 1993-99; dir. Geriatric Edn. Ctrs. PHS; adj. assoc. prof. U. Md. Sch. Medicine; meme. Iowa Health Manpower Com., 1972—; cons. U. Wis. System Acad. Affairs, 1974; panelist and participant workshops; presenter and U.S. chief del. internat. congress. Assoc. editor Am. Jour. Med. Tech., 1974-83, Jour. Allied Health, 1982-85; contbr. articles to profl. jours. Mem. Am. Soc. Clin. Pathologists (assoc., cert. med. technologist, sec. ASCP Bd. Registry 1975-77), Am. Soc. Clin. Lab. Sci., D.C. Soc. Med. Tech. (Outstanding Med. Technologist of Yr. 1975), Beta Beta Beta (Pub. Health Svc. award 1995), Alpha Mu Tau. Home: 7340 35th Avenue Ct Moline IL 61265-8067 E-mail: carolgleich@mindspring.com.

GLEICH, GERALD JOSEPH, immunologist, researcher, educator; b. Escanaba, Mich., May 14, 1931; s. Gordon Joseph and Agnes (Ederer) G.; m. Elizabeth Louise Hearn, Aug. 16, 1955 (div. 1976); children: Elizabeth Genevieve, Martin Christopher (dec.), Julia Katherine; m. Kristin Marie Leiferman, Sept. 25, 1976; children: Stephen Joseph, David Francis, Caroline Louise, William Gerald. BA, U. Mich., 1953, MD, 1956. Diplomate Am. Bd. Internal Medicine, Am. Bd. Allergy and Immunology. Intern Phila. Gen. Hosp., 1956-57; resident Jackson Meml. Hosp., Miami, Fla., 1959-61; instr. in medicine and microbiology U. Rochester, NY, 1961—65; cons. in medicine, prof. immunology and medicine Mayo Clinic-Med. Sch., Rochester, Minn., 1965—2001; chmn. dept. immunology Mayo Clinic, Rochester, Minn., 1982-90, George M. Eisenberg prof., 1995—2001; disting. investigator Mayo Found., Rochester, 1988—2001; prof. medicine & dermatology U. Utah, Salt Lake City, 2001—. Mem. bd. sci. counselors Nat. Inst. Allergy and Infectious Disease, 1981-83; chmn. subcom. on standardization allergens WHO, Geneva, 1974-75; lectr. Am. Acad. Allergy, 1976, 82; mem., chmn. immunological scis. study sect. NIH, 1984-87; John M. Sheldon Meml. lectr., 1976, 82, 88; Steve Lang Meml. Lectureship, 1980, Stoll-Stunkard lectr. Am. Soc. Parasitologists, 1986, David Talmage Meml. lectureship, 1987, Disting. lectr. Med. Scis. Mayo Clinic, 1988; original mem. Highly Cited Rschrs. Database, 2002. Contbr. articles on eosinophilic leukocyte to profl. jours. Served to capt. USAF, 1957-59. Recipient Landmark in Allergy award, 1990; grantee Nat. Inst. Allergy and Infectious Disease, 1970—; AAAS fellow for studies of structure, biol. properties and role in pathogenesis of disease of basic proteins present in cytoplasmic granules of eosinophilic leukocytes, 1993. Fellow ACP, Am. Acad. Allergy and Immunology (hon. fellow award 1992), AAAS; mem. Am. Soc. Clin. Investigation, Am. Assn. Immunologists, Assn. Am. Physicians, Phi Beta Kappa, Phi Kappa Phi, Alpha Omega Alpha. Roman Catholic. Office: Univ Utah 4B454 Sch Medicine 30 North 1900 East Salt Lake City UT 84132-2409 Home Phone: 801-949-0324; Office Phone: 801-581-6465. Business E-Mail: gerald.gleich@hsc.utah.edu.

GLEICHMAN, JOHN ALAN, protective services official; b. Anthony, Kans., Feb. 11, 1944; s. Charles William and Caroline Elizabeth (Emch) G.; m. Martha Jean Cannon, July 1, 1966; 1 son, John Alan Jr. BS in Bus. Mgmt., Kans. State Tchrs. Coll., 1966. Cert. hazard control mgr.; cert. safety profl. with a speciality in constrn. safety; cert. safety exec. Office mgr. to asst. supt. Barton-Malow Co., Detroit, 1967—72, coord. safety, 1972—76, corp. mgr. safety and security, 1976—89, dir. corp. safety and loss control, 1989—2006; safety officer Walbridge Barton Malow Jt. Venture, North Terminal Redevel. Project, Wayne County Airport Authority, Romulus, Mich., 2006—07. Instr. U. Mich., Wayne State U., 1977-81, Lawrence Tech. U., 1994-96; constrn. safety stds. commn. adv. com. for concrete constrn. and steel erection Bur. Safety and Regulations, Mich. Dept. Labor, 1977-2007; rep. constrn. stds. com. Am. Nat. Stds. Inst., 1984-2007. Author: (with others) You, The National Safety Council, and Voluntary Standards, 1981, Construction Accident Analysis: The Inductive Learning Approach, 1991; mem. editl. bd. Safety and Health: Internat. Safety, Health and Environ. Mag., 1989—; contbr. chpts. to books. Instr. multimedia first aid ARC, 1976-89; past trustee Apostolic Christian Ch., Livonia, Mich. Recipient Safety Achievement awards Mich. Mut. Ins. Co., 1979-83; Cameron award Constrn. sect. Indsl. divsn. Nat. Safety Coun., 1982, 87. Mem. Mich. Safety Conf. (pres. 1984-85), Am. Soc. Safety Engrs. (pres. Detroit chpt. 1982, nat. adminstr. constrn. divsn. 1988-89, bd. dirs. 1988-90, Safety Profl. of Yr. 1984), Nat. Safety Coun. (chmn. tech. rev. constrn. sect. indsl. divsn. 1980-84, chmn. stds. com. indsl. divsn. 1983-85, chmn. assn. com. indsl. divsn. 1986-87, dir. sects. group indsl. divsn. 1987-89, chmn. elect indsl. divsn. 1989-90, chmn. 1990-91, bd. dirs. 1987-92, Disting. Svcs. to Safety award 1993), Am. Arbitration Assn. (panel arbitrators 1985). Office: Barton Malow Co 26500 American Dr Southfield MI 48034 Office Phone: 248-436-5402.

GLEICK, PETER H., conservationist; BS cum laude with distinction, Yale U., 1978; MS, U. of Calif., Berkeley, 1980; PhD, U. of Calif., 1986. Ecology rsch. grp. asst. Lawrence Berkeley Nat. Lab. Energy and Environment Divsn., Calif., 1978—80; dep. asst. for energy and environment Office Gov. of Calif., 1980—82; rsch. and tchg. assoc. U. Calif. Energy and Resources Grp., Berkeley, 1980—81, rsch. assoc., 1983—86, postdoctoral rschr., 1986—88; co-founder, pres. Pacific Inst. for Studies in Devel., Environment, and Security, Oakland, Calif., 1987—. Mem. climate and water panel AAAS, 1986—90, sci. and internat. security com., 1993—95; rsch. and writing fellow MacArthur Found., 1988—90; bd. dirs. Pacific Inst. for Studies in Devel., Environment, and Security, 1988—; co-chair working grp. 2, adv. grp. on greenhouse gases World Meteorol. Orgn. and UN Environment Prog., 1989—91; mem. water task grp. Second World Climate Conf., Geneva, 1990; bd. dirs. Environ. Sci. and Policy Inst., 1991—97; mem. surface water com. Am. Geophys. Union, 1992—93, mem. global environ. change com., 1993—98; mem. adv. com. Climate Inst. Environ. Refugee Prog., 1993—95; mem. public adv. forum Am. Water Works Assn., 1993—98; mem. sci. rev. grp. President's Coun. on Sustainable Devel., 1994—96; interim bd. dirs. Middle East Water Info. Network, 1994—96; adv. comprehensive freshwater assessment Stockholm Environment Inst., 1996—97; bd. dirs. Internat. Water Resources Assn., 1997—2000; co-chair water sector Nat. Assessment of Potential Impacts of Climatic Variability and Change on the US, 1998—2000; mem. project steering com. on water demand mgmt. in so. Africa World Conservation Union (IUCN), 2000—03; mem. Calif. Water Plan 2003 public adv. com. Dept. Water Resources, Calif., 2001—; adv. coun. Internat. Water Acad., Oslo, 2003—05. Contbr. articles profl. jours., chapters to books; editl. bd.: Climatic Change, 1990, Environment and Security, 1993—2001, Ency. Global Change, 1996—2000, Ency. Life Support Systems, 1997—2002, Water Policy, 1997, Global Change and Human Health, 1999—2003, Annual Revs. of Energy and Environment, 2001—; sci. adv. IMAX Film The Water Planet, 2003—; editor: Water in Crisis: A Guide to the World's Fresh Water Resources, 1993; adv. bd.: (documentaries) Cadillac Desert, 1995—97; author: (book) The World's Water: The Biennial Report on Freshwater Resources, 2002. Named a visionary on the environment, BBC Essential Guide to 21st Century; named academician, Internat. Water Acad., Oslo, Norway, 1999; named one of 90 People to Watch in the '90s, San Francisco Chronicle; fellow MacArthur Found., 2003. Mem.: NAS (water sci. and tech. bd. 2001—), Phi Beta Delta. Office: Pacific Inst 654 13th St Preservation Pk Oakland CA 94612

GLEIJESES, MARIO, holding company executive; b. Italy, Feb. 27, 1955; came to US, 1985; s. Luigi Gleijeses and Rosalba Catanoso; m. Betsy L. Miller, Mar. 14, 1992; children: Rosalba, Caterina. Student, U. Naples, 1973-77. Chartering mgr. Itex subs. Italgrani, Zurich, 1977-82; asst. to pres. Italgrani Spa, Naples, Italy, 1982-85; exec. v.p., bd. dirs. Italgrani USA Inc. and Italgrani Elevator Co., St. Louis, 1985-89; v.p., bd. dirs. New Eng. Milling Co., Ayer, Mass., 1987-89; bd. dirs. Green Bay Elevator Co., Burlington, Iowa; v.p., bd. dirs. Mayco Export, Inc., Mpls., 1988-89; pres., bd. dirs. McLean Elevator Co., Benedict, ND, 1989; founder, pres., bd. dirs. Agricorp Holding Inc., 1989-92; pres., bd. dirs. Granicorp Inc., 1989-92, Granicorp Export, Inc., Uganda, 1989-92; chmn., CEO, bd. dirs. Granicorp France, S.A., Paris, 1991-92; founder, pres., bd. dirs. Gleijeses, Inc., 1993—; founder, chmn. bd. dirs. LithoFlex Corp., St. Louis, 1994—; pres. Hoky-Contico, LLC, 1995-96.

GLEIN, RICHARD JERIEL, SR., lawyer; b. LA, Aug. 20, 1929; s. Henry Carl Glein and Elsie B. (Drummond) Glein Schurman; m. Rosalind Bell; children: Valerie, Kimberly, Richard Jr., Stacy (dec.); 1 stepchild, Steven Anders Bell. Student, U. Wash., 1953-58. Bar: Wash. 1963, US Dist. Ct. (ea. and we. dists.) Wash. 1963, US Ct. Appeals (9th cir.) 1963; registered law clerk, 1958-63. Police officer, Seattle, 1952-63; dep. pros. atty. King County, Wash., 1963-65; from assoc. to ptnr. Clinton, Fleck & Glein, Seattle, 1965-92; pvt. practice Seattle, 1992—; pro-tem judge, arbitrator Superior Ct.; owner Legal Alternatives, LLC, Anacortes, Wash. Sgt. 1st class USAF, 1946-49, US Army, 1950-51. Mem. FBA, Wash. State Bar Assn., Snohomish County Bar Assn., Skagit County Bar Assn., Internat. Footprint Assn. (pres. Seattle chpt. 1969-70, grand pres. 1982-83), Masons (master 1973). Republican. Home and Office: 5301 Sterling Dr Anacortes WA 98221-3037 Office Phone: 360-293-2930. Personal E-mail: RG1fun@aol.com, rnrlegalt@aol.com.

GLEKEL, JEFFREY IVES, lawyer; b. NYC, Apr. 8, 1947; s. Newton and Gertrude (Burr) G.; m. Cynthia R. Leder, June 18, 1988; 1 child, David L. AB magna cum laude, Columbia U., 1969; JD, Yale U., 1972. Bar: NY 1973, US Supreme Ct. 1981, US Ct. Appeals (2d cir.) 1974, US Dist. Ct. (so. Dist.) NY 1974. Law clk. to Hon. Edward Weinfeld US Dist. Ct. (So. Dist.) NY, 1972-73; asst. US atty. So. Dist. NY, 1973-77; law clk. to Hon. Byron R. White US Supreme Ct., Washington, 1977-78; ptnr., criminal and constitutional law and bus. fraud matters Skadden, Arps, Slate, Meagher & Flom, LLP, NYC, 1980—. Co-chmn., Civil Litigation Seminar, NY Law Jour., 1982—90; spkr. 2nd Cir. Jud. Conf., 1983. Editor, contbr., Civil Litigation Practice, 1990; Business Crimes: A Guide for Corporate and Defense Counsel, 1982; note and comment editor Yale Law Jour., 1971-72; contbr. articles to law jours. Mem. Assn. Bar City of NY (chmn. com. fed. legislation 1984-87), ABA. Office: Skadden Arps Slate Meagher & Flom 4 Times Sq New York NY 10036 Office Phone: 212-735-3460. Office Fax: 917-777-3460. Business E-Mail: jglekel@skadden.com.

GLEKLEN, JONATHAN IAN, lawyer; b. NY, Aug. 28, 1966; s. Donald Morse and Carol Platzker Gleklen; m. Amy Jaller, May 28, 1989; children: Brandon Leo, Ryan Jaller, Jamie Elizabeth, Mia Danielle. BA, Yale U., 1988; JD, U. Chgo., 1993. Bar: Md. 1993, D.C. 1994. Cons. Strategic Planning Assocs., Washington, 1988—90; assoc. Arnold & Porter LLP, Washington, 1993—2001, ptnr., 2001—. Editor: Ann. Review Antitrust Law Devels., 2003, 6th edit., 2007, Antitrust Law Jour., 2001—. Mem.: ABA, Anti-Defamation League (bd. dirs.Wash. Regional Office 1998—, chmn. civil rights com. Wash. Regional Office 1998—). Home: 14 Greentree Court Bethesda MD 20817 Office: Arnold & Porter LLP 555 12th Street NW Washington DC 20004 Office Phone: 202-942-5454. Business E-Mail: jonathan.gleklen@aporter.com.

GLEN, NIKI, artist, sculptor; b. Milw., Nov. 14, 1950; d. Alan and Janet (Marx) G.; children: Dana Alan Knops, Laramie Ann Glen. BS in Art Edn., U. Wis., 1973. Cert. in art edn. K-12. Pub. artist, muralist numerous orgns., various locations, 1973—; co-founder Madison (Wis.) Graphics, 1973-76; art educator various schs. various locations, 1973—; dir. S.W. Pub. Art Group, Phoenix, Ariz., 1996—. Exhibited in group shows Corcoran Gallery, Washington, 1986, Williams Ratliff Gallery, Sedona, Ariz., 1988, Veneble Neslage Galleries, Washington, 1989-92, Spirit of N.Mex. Art Exhbn., Washington, 1990, Marin-Price Galleries, Bethesda/Chevy Chase, Md., 1992, Am. Bank Gallery, Chevy Chase, 1994, Artisimo Gallery, Scottsdale, Ariz., 1995, Nat. Soc. Mural Painters Centennial Exhibit, N.Y.C., 1996, Exit Gallery, NYC, 1996, 2002, 1st Internat. Pub. Art and Mural Congress, Mexico City, 1998, Sietz Gallery, Harrisburg, Pa., 2003 (art installation) Phoenix Coll., Ariz. Ctr. Blind and Visually Impaired, Phoenix Childrens Hosp.; featured in publs. including Community Murals, 1984, Street Murals: The Most Exciting Cities of America, Britain and Western Europe, 1982, The Art of Handmade Tile, also numerous covers and illustrations for textbooks and periodicals; works featured in Mosaic: Techniques and Traditions. Pres. Arts and Creativity in Early Childhood, 1993-96; bd. dirs. Gaynor Mus. and Found., 1993-95, Cmty. Built Assn., 2000-; mem. Ariz. Alliance for Art Edn., 1990-95. Recipient Orchid award City of Madison, 1975, Tempe Diablo award of excellence in edn., 1996, 97, Livable Cities award, 2001, Beautification award Art in Pvt. Devel.; Ariz. Artist Project grantee Ariz. Commn. on Arts, 1994, Phoenix Children's Hosp.; grantee numerous orgns. including Atlantic Richfield, City of Whitewater, The Mills Corp., Phoenix Arts Commn., Medtronics Inc., Phoenix (Ariz.) Coll., NEA, YMCA, City of Tempe, IKEA Corp., Desert Bot. Garden, Phoenix Coll. Mem. Nat. Soc. Mural Painters. Avocations: swimming, reading, sailing, dance. Office Phone: 602-690-9399. Personal E-mail: publicartdesign@aol.com.

GLEN, ROBERT ALEXANDER, state agency administrator; b. Phila., July 13, 1957; s. John Alexander and Natalie (Musser) G.; m. Lee Taylor Glen, Oct. 20, 1984; children: Elizabeth Anne, Catherine Lee. BA in Econs., Williams Coll., Williamstown, Mass., 1979; MS in Acctg., NYU, 1981; JD, U. Pa., 1986. Acct. Ernst & Whinney, NYC, 1979—80; vol. Peace Corps, Fiji, 1981—82; atty. Skadden, Arps, Slate, Meagher & Flom, Washington, 1986—94; dep. atty. gen. State of Del., Wilmington, 1994, dep. bank commr. Dover, 1994—98, bank commr., 1999—. Mem.: Conf. State Bank Suprs. (chmn. dist. 1). Office: Office of the State Bank Commr 555 E Loockerman St Ste 210 Dover DE 19901 Office Phone: 302-739-4235. Office Fax: 302-739-3609.

GLENDENING, EVERETT AUSTIN, architect; b. White Plains, NY, May 20, 1929; s. Gilbert Leslie and Elsie Jane (Fanjoy) G.; m. Wilhelmina Louise Hanley, Nov. 26, 1949; children: Nancy, James, Thomas, Terry, Susan. B.Arch., U. Cin., 1953; M.Arch., M.I.T., 1954. With Duffy Constrn. Co., Cleve., 1951-55, SIS Architects, Cin., 1956-58, T.J. Moore (architect), Denver, 1959; prof. architecture U. Cin., 1960-67; pvt. practice architecture Cin., 1959—. Prin. works include Queen's Towers, Cin., 1964, Summit Chase, Columbus, Ohio, 1966, Norwood High Sch., Cin., 1972, W.Va. State Mus., 1978, Douglass Montessori Sch., Cin., 1979, Christie Lane Workshop, Norwalk, Ohio, 1980, Coll. Law U. Cin., 1981, Elks Lodge, Columbus, Ind., 1981, Geology/Physics Sci. Ctr. U. Cin., 1983, U. Rio Grande Dormitory, 1989, U. Rio Grande Student Ctr., 1994, U. Rio Grande Math-Sci.-Nursing Bldg., 1995, Planetarium, Shawnee State U., 1998, Sch. for Creative and Performing Arts Auditorium, Cin. Pub. Schs., 1997, U. Rio Grande Student Conf. Ctr. Served as 1st lt. USAF, 1954-56. Fellow AIA (honor awards Ohio chpt. 1966-70, 74, 82, 90, 91, Cin. chpt. 1966-68, 70, 76, Bronze medal 1969, Apple award for arch. 1995, mem. U.S. delegation of architects to People's Republic China and Hong Kong 1990); mem. Architect's Soc. Ohio, Scarab. Methodist. Office: 8050 Montgomery Rd Cincinnati OH 45236-2950 Fax: (513) 791-2794. *A consistently positive point of view has perhaps been the single, most important factor in making possible what has been accomplished in my lifetime. I have always felt that anything was possible as long as I was willing to make the effort and, in fact, I can recall telling myself as a new college freshman that "while I may not be the most intelligent man in the class, there was no reason why I should not be the hardest working member of that class.".*

GLENDENING, PARRIS NELSON, former governor, political science educator; b. Bronx, NY, June 11, 1942; m. Jennifer Elizabeth Crawford; children: Raymond Hughes, Gabriella Mona. AA, Broward County Jr. Coll., Ft. Lauderdale, Fla., 1962; BA, Fla. State U., Tallahassee, 1964, MA, 1965, PhD, 1967; LLD (hon.), Bowie State U., Md., 1995, U. Balt., 1996, U. Md., Balt., 1998; Dr. Pub. Svc. (hon.), Wash. Coll., Chestertown, Md., 1995, Carroll C.C., 1997, U. Md., 2000, Bridgewater State Coll., Mass., 2003; LHD (hon.), Towson U., Md., 2000. Asst. prof. U. Md., College Park, 1967-72, assoc. prof., 1972-94; coun. mem. Hyattsville City Coun., Md., 1973-74, Prince George's County Coun., Upper Marlboro, Md., 1974-82, coun. chmn., 1980, 81, county exec., 1982—94; gov. State of Md., 1995—2003; pres. Smart Growth Leadership Inst., Washington, 2003—. Vice chair state of Md.'s Chesapeake Bay Critical Area Commn., 1984-94; vice chair bd. dirs. World Trade Ctr., 1990-97; mem. bd. visitors U. Md. Sch. Pub. Affairs, 1990-97; trustee Ptnrs. for Livable Places, 1990— Author: (with Mavis Mann Reeves) Controversies of State and Local Political Systems, 1972, Pragmatic Federalism, 1977, 2nd edit., 1984; contbr. numerous articles to profl. jours. Del. to Dem. Nat. Conv., San Francisco, 1984, Atlanta, 1988, NYC, 1992; bd. govs., steering com. Am.'s Clean Water Found.; co-chair (with Gov. Christine Todd Whitman) Smart Growth Coun., 2004-; sec., treas. State Capitol Media Project, 2004-; bd. mem. Land Trust Alliance, 2003-05, Ptnrs. for Livable Communities, 1990-, mem. exec. com., Smart Growth Am., 2003-; chmn. bd. dirs. Smart Growth Investments, 2003-; mem. Nat. Govs. Assn., 1995-2003, chair, 2000-01, vice chair, 1999-2000, mem. exec. com., 1999-2002, co-chair growth and quality of life task force, 2000-01, mem. econ. devel. and commerce com., 1995-97, mem. fin. com., 1999-2001, chair fin. com., 1999-2000, mem. human resources com., 1997-98, mem. natural resources com., 1998, 2001-02, chair, 1998-99, mem. transp. task force, 1996-97, co-lead gov. tech., 1996-97, mem. children's task force, 1997-98, mem. task force on Ideas That Work-Tax Reform, 1995, lead gov. federalism, 1995, mem. state mgmt. task force, 1995; mem. Dem. Govs. Assn., 1995-03, chair, 2002, mem. exec. com., 1998-2002, Coun. State Govts., 1995-03, v.p., 2000, pres., 2002, So. Govs. Assn., 1995-2003, mem. exec. com., 1996, 2001, Am. Legacy Found., bd. dirs., 2001-03, Chesapeake Exec. Coun., 1995-2003, chair, 1997-2000, So. Regional Edn. Bd., 1995-97, chair, 1995-96, Md. Mcpl. Assn., Nat. Forum for Black Pub. Adminstrs.; pres. Nat. Coun. Elected County Execs., 1992-93; bd. dirs. Md. Assn. Counties, 1978-87, treas., 1984-85, sec., 1985-86, 1st v.p./pres., 1986-87, pres., 1987-88; mem. Chesapeake Bay Critical Area Commn., 1984-94; mem. task force on indsl. revenue bonds Nat. Assn. Counties, 1982, mem. taxation and fin. steering com., 1984-87, vice chair intergovernmental rels. policy steering com., 1987-88, adv. commn. on fed.-state-local rels., 1987-94; mem. bd. govs. Md. World Trade Inst., 1992-2002; chair regional environ. policy com. Met. Wash. Coun. Govts., 1992; mem. State Trade Policy Coun., 1985-94; bd. visitors U. Md. Sch. Pub. Affairs, 1988-94; mem. profl. ethics com. Am. Soc. Pub. Adminstrs., 1989-90. Recipient numerous awards, including City and State mag., Prince George's County, Prince George's High Sch. Prins. Assn., State Assn. Retarded Citizens, Nat. Bus. League So. Md., Spanish Speaking Communities Md., Inc., Elizabeth and David Scull award for disting. leadership to Washington met. region Coun. Govts., 1995, Dr. Nathan Davis award The Am. Med. Assn., 1991; Disting. Alumni award Fla. State U. Coll. Social Svcs., 1993, Outstanding Alumni The Am. Assn. of Com. Coll., 1997, Friend of Edn. award Md. State Tchrs. Assn., 1997, Nat. Leadership award Outside the Field Nat. Coun. for Continuing Edn. and Tng., 1998, Pres.'s Medal Johns Hopkins U., 2001, Heart of the Cmty. award Cmty. Tchrs. Inst., 2004, numerous other environ., health and safety, human rights and advocacy and profl. awards. Mem. AAUP, AAAS (profl. ethics group 1990-94), Am. Polit. Sci. Assn., ASPA (profl. ethics com. mem. 1989—, chmn. 1991-92, SIAM mem. 1991—). Democrat. Office: Smart Growth America Ste 1050 1707 L St NW Washington DC 20036 Office Fax: 410-974-3275. Business E-Mail: pglendening@sgli.org.

GLENDENING, TERRY SKY, psychologist; b. Cin., Apr. 19, 1961; BA, Cornell U., 1983; MA, U. Cin., 1986, PhD, 1995. Lic. psychologist Ohio, Ky., cert. corrective thinking practitioner 1999. Dir. recreation Indian Hill Cmty. Edn., Cin., 1986—92; pvt. practice in clin. psychologist, psychotherapist, 1982—. Tchg. asst. Cornell U., Ithaca, NY, 1982—83; cons. IHHS Peer Counseling Program, Indian Hill, Ohio, 1987—96; lectr. in field. Author: (book) Thought Patterns in Depression and Somatization, 1986, Cognitive Specificity in Non-Clinical Depressive Manifestations of Distress, 1995, Timeless Parenting Techniques: Fair, Firm and Functional, 2002, (workshop series) Beating Anxiety: A Structured Approach for Children, 2006, Coping Skills for a New Millenium, 2000. Vol. recreation for disabled Camp Stepping Stones, Cin., 1997—98; vol. Spl. Olympics, Cin., 1997—98. Named Outstanding Young Woman of Am., 1986, Diplomate, Nat. Inst. Sports, 2004—; recipient Sons and Daughters Am. Revolution award, 1974. Mem.: APA, Nat. Inst. Sports (diplomate 2004), Ohio Psychol. Assn., Psi Chi. Avocations: hiking, camping, art, sports, rock collecting. Office Phone: 513-688-7555.

GLENDENNING, DON MARK, lawyer; b. Dallas, Dec. 24, 1953; s. Don Thomas and Nancy (Malloy) G.; m. Carol Peterson, Dec. 30, 1979. BA, Rice U., 1976; JD, Stanford U., 1979. Bar: Tex. 1979. Assoc. Rain Harrell Emery Young & Doke, Dallas, 1979-85; ptnr. Rain, Harrell, Emery, Young & Doke, Dallas, 1985-87; shareholder Locke Purnell Rain Harrell, P.C., Dallas, 1987-98; ptnr. Locke Liddell & Sapp LLP, Dallas, 1999—. Past pres. Human Rights Initiative North Tex., Tex.; pres. Scenic Dallas, Scenic Tex.; chair Dallas Zool. Soc.; bd. dirs. Nat. Tree Trust, Tex. Trees Found.; chmn. Thanks-Giving Found. Republican. Presbyterian. Office: Locke Liddell & Sapp LLP 2200 Ross Ave Ste 2200 Dallas TX 75201-6776 Office Phone: 214-740-8623. E-mail: dglendenning@lockeliddel.com.

GLENDON, MARY ANN, law educator; b. Pittsfield, Mass., Oct. 7, 1938; m. Edward R. Lev; 3 children. BA, U. Chgo., 1959, JD, 1961, M of Comparative Law, 1963, LLD (hon.), 1992; DHL (hon.), Brigham Young U., 1990. Bar: Ill. 1964, Mass. 1980. Legal intern EEC, Brussels, 1963; assoc. Mayer, Brown & Platt, Chgo., 1963-68; asst. prof. Boston Coll. Law Sch., 1968—71, assoc. prof., 1971—73, prof., 1973—86; prof. law Harvard Law Sch., Cambridge, Mass., 1986—, Learned Hand prof. law, 1993—. Vis. prof. Harvard Law Sch., 1974, U. Chgo. Law Sch., 1983, 84, 86, Gregorian U., Rome. Author: Abortion and Divorce in Western Law, 1987 (Scribes Book Award, Am. Soc. Writers on Legal Subjects, 1988), The Transformation of Family Law, 1989 (Order of the Coif Triennial Book Award, 1993), Rights Talk: The Impoverishment of Political Discourse, 1991, A Nation Under Lawyers, 1994, A World Made New: Eleanor Roosevelt and the Universal Declaration of Human Rights, 2001, Traditions in Turmoil, 2006; co-author: Comparative Legal Traditions, 2d edit., 2007; co-editor: Seedbeds of Virtue: Sources of Competence, Character, and Citizenship in Am. Soc., 1995; editor: Intergenerational Solidarity, Welfare, and Human Ecology, 2004. Recipient Nat. Humanities medal, 2005; fellow, Radcliffe Inst., 1975—76; Fgn. Law fellow, U. Libre de Bruxelles, 1962—63, Ford Found. fellow, 1975—76. Mem.: Pontificial Acad. Social Sci. (pres. 2002—), Am. Acad. Arts and Scis. Office: Harvard Law Sch 1563 Massachusetts Ave Cambridge MA 02138 Office Phone: 617-495-4769. Office Fax: 617-496-4913.

GLENISTER, BRIAN FREDERICK, geologist, educator; b. Albany, Western Australia, Sept. 28, 1928; came to U.S., 1959, naturalized, 1967; s. Frederick and Mabel (Frusher) G.; m. Anne Marie Treloar, Feb. 16, 1956; children: Alan Edward, Linda Marie, Kathryn Grace. BSc, U. Western Australia, Perth, 1949; MSc, U. Melbourne, Australia, 1953; PhD, U. Iowa, 1956. Lectr., then sr. lectr. geology U. Western Australia, 1956-59; asst. prof. U. Iowa, Iowa City, 1959-62, assoc. prof., 1962-66, prof., 1966-74, chmn. geology dept., 1968-74, A.K. Miller prof. geology, 1974-97, A.K. Miller prof. geology emeritus, 1997—. Mem. AAAS, Paleontol. Soc. (pres. 1988-89), Geol. Soc. Am., Geol. Soc. Iowa (pres. 1991), Paleontol. Rsch. Inst. Office Phone: 319-335-1828. Business E-Mail: brian-glenister@uiowa.edu.

GLENN, CHANCE MICHAEL, engineering educator, researcher, singer, writer; s. Wallace Edward and Shirley Janice Glenn; m. Marsha Ilean Hamilton, July 14, 1990; children: Michael Jonathan, Chance Markiss, Rebecca Melissa, Abigayle Morgen. A in Elec. Engring. Tech., Alabma A&M U., Huntsville, 1987; BS in Elec. Engring., U. Md., College Park, 1991; M in Elec. Engring., Johns Hopkins U., Balt., 1992, PhD in Elec. Engring., 2003. Dir. Lab. Advanced Comm. Tech., Rochester, NY, 2004; assoc. prof. Rochester Inst. Tech., 2003—; founder Morningbird Music, Fairport, NY, 1999—. Cons. Glenn Tech., Fairport, 2006—. Composer: (gospel, pop, jazz, r&b music) The Morningbird Music Collection - Catalogs (Nomination 43rd Grammy award, 2001); editor-in-chief Jour. Applied Sci. and Engring. Tech., 2005—. Pres. bd. advisors Davis Coll., Binghamton, NY, 2004—07. Grantee, Office Naval Rsch., 1998, 1999, 2000, 2001. Mem.: IEEE (assoc.), AAUP (assoc.), Am. Soc. Engring. Edn. (assoc.), Rochester High Tech Bus. Coun. (assoc.), Internat. Assn. Devel. Advances Tech. (assoc.), Nat. Ctr. Telecom. Tech. (assoc.), Internat. Telecom. Edn. and Rsch. Assn. (assoc.), Soc. Cable Telecom. Engrs. (assoc.), Nat. Soc. Black Engrs. (assoc.). Independent. Achievements include patents pending for quasi-active delay line limiter/filter; linear amplification by synchronized chaotic oscillation; methods for data compression based on nonlinear dynamical systems and systems thereof; patents for non-reflective limiter (limiting attenuator); exponentially amplified sampling and reconstruction of weak signals using controlled chaotic orbits; microwave field-emitter array limiter; discovery of D-transform, DYNAMAC compression algorithm; research in biomedical data analysis utilizing nonlinear systems theory; advanced communications development using nonlinear and chaotic systems theory. Office Phone: 585-475-4261.

GLENN, CHRISTOPHER MARK, music educator; b. Booneville, Miss., Sept. 2, 1972; s. Alvin E. and Sue Carol Glenn. BS, Lipscomb U., Nashville, 1994; MEd, Tenn. State U., Nashville, 2006. Lic. profl. tchr. Tenn., Miss. Band dir. Itawamba County Schs., Fulton, Miss., 1995—97; music tchr. Metro Nashville Pub. Schs., 1997—. Dist. dir. Metro Nashville Edn. Assn., 1999. Mem.: NEA (licentiate), Am. Mensa, Music Educators Nat. Conf. (licentiate), Phi Mu Alpha. Republican. Church Of Christ. Avocation: travel. Home: 3224 Penn Meade Way Nashville TN 37214 Office: Park Ave Elem Sch 3703 Park Ave Nashville TN 37209 Home Phone: 615-886-7177; Office Phone: 615-298-8412.

GLENN, CONSTANCE WHITE, art museum director, educator, consultant; b. Topeka, Oct. 4, 1933; d. Henry A. and Madeline (Stewart) White; m. Jack W. Glenn, June 19, 1955; children: Laurie Glenn Buckle, Caroline Glenn Galey, John Christopher. BFA, U. Kans., 1955; grad., U. Mo., 1969; MA, Calif. State U., 1974. Dir. U. Art Mus. & Mus. Studies program, from lectr. to prof. Calif. State U., Long Beach, 1973—2004, prof. and dir. emeritus, U. Art Mus. and Mus. Studies program, 2004—. Art cons. Archtl. Digest, L.A., 1980-89. Author: Jim Dine Drawings, 1984, Roy Lichtenstein: Landscape Sketches, 1986, Wayne Thiebaud: Private Drawings, 1988, Robert Motherwell: The Dedalus Sketches, 1988, James Rosenquist: Time Dust: The Complete Graphics 1962-92, 1993, The Great American Pop Art Store: Multiples of the Sixties, 1997, The Artist Observed: Photographs by Sidney B. Felsen, 2003, Candida Höfer: Architecture of Absence, 2004; contbg. author: Encyclopedia Americana, 1995-, The Grove Dictionary of Art, 1989-, Carrie Mae Weems: The Hampton Project, 2000, Double Vision: Photographs from the Strauss Collection, 2001, Tom Wesselmann, 2005. Vice-chair Adv. Com. for Pub. Art, Long Beach, 1990-95; chair So. Calif. adv. bd. Archives Am. Art, LA, 1980-90; mem. adv. bd. ART/LA, 1986-94, chair, 1992. Recipient Outstanding Contbn. to Profession award Calif. Mus. Photography, 1986, Women of Distinction award Soroptimist Internat., 1999. Mem. Am. Assn. Mus., Assn. Art Mus. Dirs. (trustee 2000-02, emeritus 2004—), Coll. Art Assn., Art Table, Long Beach Pub. Corp. for the Arts (Arts Adminstr. of Yr. 1989), Kappa Alpha Theta. Home Phone: 949-715-0933; Office Phone: 949-715-0933. Business E-Mail: cglenn@csulb.edu. E-mail: connieglenn@hotmail.com.

GLENN, EDWARD VERNON FERRELL, lawyer, consultant; b. Winston-Salem, NC, Jan. 10, 1950; s. Douglas (Stepfather) and Rosena Ferrell Dillard, Joseph Henry Glenn; m. Andrea Leigh Hilsman, Apr. 8, 1985; children: Catherine Courtney Hilsman, Douglas Tyree Tinsley, Rosena Ferrell. BA in Polit. sci., U. N.C., Chapel Hill, 1972; JD, Wake Forest Sch. of Law, Winston-Salem, NC, 1975. Cert.: Nat. Bd. of Trial Advs. (civil trial lawyer) 1994, advocate: Nat. Trial Coll. - Harvard Law 1998, cert.: S.C. Bd. of Arbitrators (cir. ct. mediator) 2004, bar: N.C. 1976, S.C. 1985, (U.S. Ct. Appeals (4th dist.)), (U.S. Supreme Ct.). Trial atty. Glenn & Crumpler, Winston-Salem, NC, 1977—84, Few & Glenn, Greenville, SC, 1984—87, McCoy , Taylor & Glenn, Charleston, SC, 1987—98, Law Office of E.Vernon F. Glenn, Mount Pleasant, SC, 1998—2006; of counsel Allman, Spry, Leggett & Crumpler PA, Winston Salem, NC, 2006—. Author: (articles) The Charlotte Observer, The Post & Courier, SCTLA Bulletin, ABA The Jour., S.C. Trial Lawyers Jour. Bd. dirs. U. N.C. Ednl. Found., 1977—99, Life Mgmt. Ctrs., Charleston, SC, 1999—2002, Carolina Low Country Girl Scout Coun., Charleston, SC, 1990—93, USO Coun., Charleston, SC; exec. com. U. North Carolina Parents Coun., 2006—; bd. trustees Charleston Day Sch., SC, 1999—2002. Fellow: Delta Kappa Epsilon (life; pres. collegiate chpt. 1971—72); mem.: ATLA (assoc.), ABA (assoc.), Am. Bd. of Trial Advs., N.C. Acad. of Trial Lawyers (assoc.), SC Trial Lawyers Assn. (assoc.; chair ethics com. 1990—92), NC Bar Assn. (assoc.), SC Bar Assn. (assoc.; medico-legal affairs 1985—86, secty. trial & appellate sect. 2006—), So. Trial Lawyers Assn. (assoc.). Independent. Methodist. Achievements include Testified before Senate special committes on legal issues; Lobbyist - Republican Caucus of ATLA. Avocations: college athletics, travel, radio sports commentary, sports handicapper, hiking and biking. Office: Law Offices of Vernon Glenn 211 Scott St Mount Pleasant SC 29464 Home Phone: 843-971-1515; Office Phone: 866-252-3834. Office Fax: 843-971-0194; Home Fax: 843-971-0194. Personal E-mail: evfg@lowcountrylawyer.com, evfg@comcast.net.

GLENN, GERALD MARVIN, marketing, engineering and construction executive; b. Greenville, SC, Aug. 20, 1942; s. Oscar Marvin and Lorene (Ashmore) G.; m. Candice Wilson, Oct. 24, 1986; children: Regina Lynn, Gerald Marvin II, Charles Wilson. BSCE, Clemson U., SC, 1964; Exec. Program Bus. Adminstrn., Columbia U., Harriman, NY, 1980. With Daniel Constrn. Co., Greenville, SC, 1964-77, Fluor Corp., Santa Ana, Calif., 1977-94, sr. v.p. mktg., 1982-85, pres. U.S. ops., 1985-86, exec. v.p., 1986, group pres., dir. Irvine, Calif., 1986-94; owner, prin. The Glenn Group LLC, Cimarron, Colo., 1994—, Eagle Glen Ranch LLC, Cimarron, Colo., 1994—; chmn., pres., CEO, mng. dir. Chgo. Bridge & Iron Co. NV, The Woodlands, Tex., 1996—2006. Bd. dir. Woodforest Fin. Group, The Woodlands, Tex., Gas Tech. Inst. Chmn. bd. dirs. Chgo. chpt. Am. Heart Assn., 1999—2001; vice chmn. bd. dir. John Cooper Sch., The Woodlands, Tex.; bd. dir. Jr. Achievement Southeast Tex. Mem.: ASCE, AIChE, Am. Petroleum Inst., Chgo. Soc., Econ. Club Chgo., Grand Pines Golf Club, Bentwater Yacht and Country Club, 25 Yr. Club Petroleum Industry, Club at Carlton Woods, Woodlands Country Club, Execs. Club Chgo., Fairway Pines Golf Club. Republican. Methodist. Home: 3 Grand Regency Cir The Woodlands TX 77382 Office: 3 Grand Regency Cir The Woodlands TX 77382 Office Phone: 281-681-2261.

GLENN, GUY CHARLES, pathologist; b. Parma, Ohio, May 13, 1930; s. Joseph Frank and Helen (Rupple) G.; m. Lucia Ann Howarth, June 13, 1953; children: Kathryn Holly, Carolyn Helen, Cynthia Marie. BS, Denison U., 1953; MD, U. Cin., 1957. Diplomate Am. Bd. Pathology, Am. Bd. Radioisotopic Pathology. Intern Walter Reed Army Med. Ctr., Washington, 1957-58; resident in pathology Fitzsimons Army Med. Ctr., Denver, 1959-63; commd. 2d lt. U.S. Army, 1956; advanced through grades to col., 1972; demonstrator pathology Royal Army Med. Coll., London, 1970-72; chief dept. pathology Fitzsimons Army Med. Ctr., Denver, 1972-77. Past pres. med. staff St. Vincent Hosp., Billings, Mont.; past mem. governing bd. Mont. Health Sys. Agy. Contbr. articles to profl. jours. Fellow: Coll. Am. Pathologists (chmn. chemistry resources com., chmn. commn. sci. resources, mem. budget com., coun. on quality assurance, chmn. practice guidelines com., bd. govs., chmn. nominating com.); mem.: Midland Empire Health Assn. (past pres.), Soc. Med. Cons. to Armed Forces, Am. Registry Pathology (bd. dirs., exec. com., search com., planning com.), Am. Soc. Clin. Pathology, Rotary (bd. dirs. emeritus local chpt.). Home: 3225 Jack Burke Ln Billings MT 59106-1113 Personal E-mail: guyglenn@bresnan.net.

GLENN, JAMES FRANCIS, urologist, educator; b. Lexington, Ky., May 10, 1928; s. Cambridge Francis and Martha (Morrow) G.; children: Cambridge Francis II, Sara Brooke, Nancy Carrick, James Morrison Woodworth; m. Gay Elste Darsie, Jan. 11, 2002. Student (Yale Regional scholar), Univ. Sch., Lexington, 1946; BA in Gen. Sci. (Bausch and Lomb Nat. Sci. scholar), U. Rochester, 1949; MD, Duke U., 1952; DSc, U. Ky., 1998, Transylvania U., 2004. Diplomate Am. Bd. Urology (mem.), Nat. Bd. Med. Examiners. Intern Peter Bent Brigham Hosp., Boston, 1952-54; asst. resident urology Duke U. Med. Ctr., 1956-58, resident, 1958-59; instr. urology Duke U., 1958-59, prof., chief div. urology, 1963-80; asst. prof. Yale U., 1959-61; assoc. prof. Bowman Gray Sch. Medicine, Wake Forest Coll., 1961-63; practice medicine specializing in urology New Haven, 1959-61, Winston-Salem, N.C., 1961-63, Durham, N.C., 1963-80; prof. surgery, dean Med. Sch., Emory U., 1980-83; pres. Mt. Sinai Med. Ctr., 1983-87; prof. surgery U. Ky. Coll. Medicine, Lexington, 1987—; CEO Markey Cancer Ctr., 1989-93; chief staff Univ. Hosp., Lexington, 1993-95, chmn. dept. surgery, 1996-97. Sci. dir. Coun. for Tobacco Rsch. U.S.A., 1987-91, chmn. bd., 1991—. Contbg. author: Renal Neoplasia, 1967, Urodynamics, 1971, Textbook of Surgery, 1972, Plastic and Reconstructive Surgery of The Genital Area, 1973, Current Operative Urology, 1975, Campbell's Urology, 1977; author, editor: Diagnostic Urology, 1964, Ureteral Reflux in Children, 1966, Urologic Surgery, 1969, rev. edit., 1975, 84, 90; contbr. numerous articles to profl. jours. Capt. M.C., USAF, 1954-56. Mem. Am. Assn. Genitourinary Surgeons (pres. 1992-93, hon. 1998), Am. Surg. Assn., ACS, AMA (sec. sect. urology 1972-73, chmn. 1975-77), Assn. Am. Med. Colls., Internat. Urol Soc. (v.p. 1985-91, pres. 1991-94), Clin. Soc. Genito-Urinary Surgeons (pres. 1990-91), N.Y. Acad. Medicine, Soc. Pediatric Urology (pres. 1972-73), Soc. Pelvic Surgeons (pres. 1980-81), Soc. Univ. Surgeons, Soc. Univ. Urologists (pres. 1971-72), Royal Coll. Surgeons (hon. fellow 1987), German Urol. Assn. (hon.), Australasian Urologic Soc. (hon.), Brit. Assn. Urologic Surgeons (hon.)

GLENN, JERRY HOSMER, JR., retired language educator; b. Little Rock, Sept. 5, 1938; s. Jerry Hosmer and Anne (Matthews) G.; m. Renate Drexl, July 29, 1978 BA, Yale U., 1960; MA, U. Tex., 1962; postgrad., Free U. Berlin, 1962—63; PhD, U. Tex., 1964. Asst. prof. German U. Wis., Milw., 1964—67; asst. prof. German U. Cin., 1967—69, assoc. prof., 1969—72, prof., 1972—2003, prof. emeritus, 2003—. Dir. honors program U. Cin., 1977—79, head dept., 1980—83. Author: Deutsches Schrifttum der Gegenwart (ab 1945), 1971, Paul Celan, 1973, Paul Celan: Eine Bibliographie, 1989, Paul Celan: A Bibliography of English Lang. Secondary Lit. 1955-1996, 1996; (with Jeffrey Todd) Paul Celan: Die zweite Bibliographie, 1998; mng. editor: Lessing Yearbook, 1969-74; editor: (with Uwe Faulhaber and others) Exile and Enlightenment, 1987; (with Joachim Herrmann and Rebecca Rodgers) Alfred Gong, Early Poems, 1987, Max Kade Occasional Papers, 2001—, (with J. Clausen and others) Iceland's Foggy Nights, 2005; transl. (with Jennifer Kelley) On the Wrong Track, 1993, International Zone, 1999, Too-Late, Too-Early, 2000, (with Clarise Samuels) Landing Attempts, 2000, (with Aine Zimmerman) StadtFluchten/City Escapes, 2004, (with Andrea Engels) Iceland's Foggy Nights, 2005 Mem. Lessing Soc. (sec-treas. 1968-74), Mideast Honors Assn. (exec. sec. 1977-78, pres. 1979-80), Am. Assn. Tchr. German, Soc. German-Am. Studies (v.p. 1987-89) Republican. Home: 54 Fairway Dr Southgate KY 41071-3025 Personal E-mail: jerry.glenn@uc.edu.

GLENN, JOHN HERSCHEL, JR., former senator, astronaut; b. Cambridge, Ohio, July 18, 1921; s. John Herschel and Clara (Sproat) G.; m. Anna Margaret Castor, Apr. 1943; children: Carolyn Ann, John David. Student, Muskingum Coll., 1939-42, B.Sc., 1962; naval aviation cadet, U. Iowa, 1942; grad. flight sch., Naval Air Tng. Center, Corpus Christi, Tex., 1943, Navy Test Pilot Tng. Sch., Patuxent River, Md., 1954. Commd. 2d lt. USMC, 1943, assigned 4th Marine Aircraft Wing, Marshall Islands campaign, 1944, assigned 9th Marine Aircraft Wing, 1945-46; with 1st Marine Aircraft Wing, North China Patrol, also Guam, 1947-48; flight instr. advanced flight tng. Corpus Christi, 1949-51; asst. G-2/G-3 Amphibious Warfare Sch., Quantico, Va., 1951; with Marine Fighter Squadron 311, exchange pilot 25th Fighter Interceptor Squadron USAF, Korea, 1953; project officer fighter design br. Navy Bur. Aero. Washington, 1956-58;

astronaut Project Mercury, Manned Spacecraft Center NASA, 1959-65; pilot Mercury-Atlas 6, 1st orbital space flight launched from Cape Canaveral, Fla., Feb. 1962; ret. as col., 1965; v.p. corp. devel. and dir. Royal Crown Cola Co., 1966-74; pres. Royal Crown Internat.; U.S. senator from Ohio, 1975-99; mem.-at-large Ohio State Dem. Com., 1999—. Mem. Spl. Com. on Aging, Armed Svcs. Com., Senate Dem. Tech. and Comm. Com., Intelligence Com.; ranking minority mem. Govtl. Affairs Com.; vice-chmn. Senate Dem. Policy Com. Co-author: We Seven, 1962; author: P.S., I Listened to Your Heart Beat. Made first supersonic transcontinental flight, July 16, 1957; trustee Muskingum Coll. Decorated D.F.C. (six), Air medal (18); recipient Astronaut medal USMC, Navy unit commendation, Korean Presdl. unit citation, Disting. Merit award Muskingum Coll., Medal of Honor N.Y.C., Congl. Space Medal of Honor, 1978, Centennial awd., Nat. Geographic Soc., 1988, other decorations, awards and hon. degrees. Mem. Soc. Exptl. Test Pilots, Internat. Acad. of Astronautics (hon.) Democrat. Presbyterian. Office: Ohio State U John Glenn Inst 100 Bricker Hall 190 N Oval Mall Columbus OH 43210-1321

GLENN, MARSHALL ANDREW, psychologist; b. Wynnewood, Okla., Feb. 12, 1952; s. Marshall Neal Glenn and Reba Pauline Flippen; 1 stepchild, Jason Travis Seay. BSE, East Ctrl. State U., 1974; MEd, U. Okla., 1975, PhD, 1995; post grad. program, Fielding Inst., 2002. Recreational aide Pauls Valley State Sch. for the Mentally Retarded, 1972—74; grad. rsch. asst./test libr. U. Okla., 1974—76; sch. psychologist Okla. State Dept. Edn., Okla. City, 1976—88, Western Heights Sch., 1988—93, Norman Schools, 1993—2004, Frisco Ind. Sch. Dist., 2004—. Delegate for Okla. Nat. Assn. of Sch. Psychologist, Bethesda, Md., 2001—05; exec. bd. Okla. Sch. Psychol. Assn., 1991—2004, vol., 1991—96. Psychologist Okla. Cmty. Children and Youth, 1999; bd. dirs. Okla. Inst. for Child Advocacy, 1998. Mem.: Tex. Assn. of Sch. Psychology, Nat. Assn. of Sch. Psychologists, Okla. Sch. Psychol. Assn., Phi Kappa Phi. Avocation: fly fishing. Home: 8513 Forest Highlands Dr Plano TX 75024 Office Phone: 469-633-6916.

GLENN, MICHAEL B., forest products executive; Joined Universal Forest Products, Grand Rapids, Mich., 1974, sr. v.p., Southwest ops., 1989—97, pres., Western divsn., 1997—2000, pres., COO, 2000—06, bd. dir., CEO, 2006—. Bd. dirs. Outdoor Advantage, Inc., 2000—. Office: Universal Forest Products 2801 E Beltline NE Grand Rapids MI 49525 Office Phone: 616-364-6161.*

GLENN, MORTON BERNARD, retired internist; b. NYC, Mar. 21, 1922; s. Harold and Mimi (Steinberg) Glenn; m. Justine Manheim, July 21, 1963 (dec. Dec. 29, 2004); stepchildren: Adrienne Harkauy, Marcia Stamberg;children from previous marriage: Wendy, Valerie Jorgensen, John. AB, U. Pa., Phila., 1942; MD, NYU Sch. Medicine, NYC, 1946. Intern Bellevue Hosp., NYC, 1946, resident, 1949—52, chief obesity clinic, Knickerbocker Hosp., NYC; asst. attending physican U. Hosp., NYC; pvt. practice specializing nutrition and internal medicine; physician-in-charge Kips Bay and Morrishnia Obesity Clincs. Med. cons. UN, 1954—56; asst. clin. prof. medicine NYU Sch. Medicine, Bronx, NY; pres. Food and Nutrition Coun. Greater NY, 1962—64; cons. NYC Dept. Health Bur. Nutrition; asst. vis. physician Bellevue Hosp., chief obesity clinic. Lt. USNR, 1943—45, lt. USNR, 1947—49. Fellow: NY Acad. Medicine, Am. Coll. Nutrition; mem.: AMA, NYC and NY State Med. Soc., Am. Inst. Nutrition (Travel award 1962), Bellevue Alumni Soc. (pres.), N.Am. Assn. Study Obesity, Food and Nutrition Coun. Greater NY.

GLENN, NORVAL DWIGHT, sociologist, educator; b. Roswell, N.Mex., Aug. 13, 1933; s. William N. and Mary E. (Cochrain) Glenn. BA, N.Mex. State U., 1954; PhD, U. Tex., 1962. Instr. Miami U., Oxford, Ohio, 1960—61, U. Ill., 1961—63, asst. prof., 1963—64; asst. prof. to assoc. prof. sociology U. Tex., Austin, 1964—70, prof., 1970—84, Ashbel Smith prof. sociology, 1984—, Raymond Dickson, Alton C. Allen and Dillon Anderson centennial prof., 1990—91, Stiles prof. Am. studies, 1991—. Author (with Leonard Broom): Tranformation of the Negro American, 1965, Cohort Analysis, 1977, 2004; author: (with Elizabeth Marguardt) Hooking Up, Hanging Out, and Looking for Mr. Right, 2001; author: With This Ring, 2005; editor (with Charles Bonjean): Blacks in the United States, 1969; editor: (with Marion Coleman) Family Relations, 1989; editor: Contemporary Sociology, 1977—80, Jour. Family Issues, 1984—89; compiler (with John Alston and David Weiner) Social Stratification: A Research Bibliography, 1969; contbr. articles to profl. jours. Mem. coun. Inter-Univ. Consortium Polit. and Social Rsch., 1980—84, assoc. dir., 1984—2000. Served to 1st lt. US Army, 1954—56. Mem.: Population Assn. Am., Nat. Coun. Family Rels., Am. Assn. Pub. Opinion Rsch., Am. Sociol. Assn. Office Phone: 512-232-6320. Business E-Mail: ndglenn@mail.la.utexas.edu.

GLENN, ROBERT EASTWOOD, lawyer; b. Catlettsburg, Ky., Dec. 24, 1929; s. Albert Sidney and Pauline Elizabeth (Eastwood) Glenn; m. Clydenne Reinhard, Mar. 16, 1956 (dec. Apr. 2007); children: Pauline Glenn O'Brien, Robert Eastwood Jr. BS cum laude, Washington and Lee U., 1951, JD cum laude, 1953. Bar: Va. 1952, US Dist. Ct. (we. dist.) Va. 1958, US Ct. Appeals (4th cir.) 1974, US Supreme Ct. 1975, US Tax Ct. 1994. Assoc. Eggleston & Holton, Roanoke, Va., 1957-60; ptnr. Glenn, Feldmann, Darby & Goodlatte, Roanoke, 1960—2003, of counsel, 2003—. Mem. Va. Bd. Bar Examiners, Richmond, 1982—, pres., 1993—. Mem. State Coun. for Higher Edn. for Va., 1980-84; rector Radford U., Va., 1975-79, bd. visitors, 1972-79; chmn. Roanoke City Rep. Com., 1968-70, Roanoke Valley ARC, 1974-76; mem. Va. Found. for Humanities, 1995-01. Lt. col. (ret.) USAF. Fellow: Va. Bar Found., ABA Found.; mem.: ABA, Roanoke Bar Assn. (pres. 1980—81), Va. Bar Assn., Roanoke Regional C. of C. (pres. 1988), Shenandoah Club (pres. 2001—03), Roanoke Country Club, Order of Coif, Beta Gamma Sigma. Roman Catholic. Home: 3101 Allendale St SW Roanoke VA 24014-3118 Office: Glenn Feldmann Darby & Goodlatte 210 1st St SW Ste 200 Roanoke VA 24011-1607 E-mail: rglenn@gfdg.com.

GLENN, ROLAND DOUGLAS, chemical engineer; b. Somerville, Mass., Mar. 22, 1912; s. Charles Rathford and Anna Amanda (Card) G.; m. Eleanor Norwood Greene, June 19, 1939; children: Meg Mary Eleanor Glenn-Albiez, Nancy Anne Hansen, Sara Elisabeth Baker, Rolene Douglas Ramsey. BSChemE, MIT, 1933, MSChemE, 1934, postgrad. Registered profl. engr., N.Y., Conn., Va. Prodn. supr. Union Carbide Corp., South Charleston, W.Va., devel. group leader, plant mgr., 1934-56, div. v.p. NYC, 1957-68; v.p. Pope, Evans & Robbins, NYC, Alexandria, Va., 1969-71; pres. Combustion Processes, Inc., NYC, 1972-90, Darien, Conn., 1991-93. Editor: (directory) Consulting Services, 1978-88; contbr. numerous reports and papers to profl. jours. Sloan fellow MIT, 1939. Mem. Am. Inst. Chem. Engrs., Am. Chem. Soc., Assn. Cons. Chemists & Chem. Engrs. (dir. 1974-92).

GLENN, (THEODORE) SCOTT, actor; b. Pitts., Jan. 26, 1941; s. Theodore Glenn; m. Carol Schwartz, Sept. 10, 1967; 2 daughters, Dakota, Rio. BA, Coll. William and Mary; student, Actors Studio, NYC, from 1968. Made Broadway debut in The Impossible Years, 1965; other theater performances include Zoo Story, Long Day's Journey Into Night, Actors Studio, 1968, Collision Course, Angelo's Wedding, Circle Repertory Theater, 1985, Burn This, 1988; motion pictures include The Baby Maker, 1970, Angels Hard As They Come, 1971, Hex, 1973, Nashville, 1975, Fighting Mad, 1976, Apocalypse Now, 1979, More American Graffiti, 1979, Urban Cowboy, 1980, Cattle Annie and Little Britches, 1981, The Challenge, 1982, Personal Best, 1982, The Keep, 1983, The Right Stuff, 1983, The River, 1984, The Wild Geese II, 1985, Silverado, 1985, Man on Fire, 1987, Off Limits, 1988, Verne Miller, 1988, Miss Firecracker, 1989, The Hunt for Red October, 1990, Silence of the Lambs, 1991, My Heroes Have Always Been Cowboys, 1991, Backdraft, 1991, The Player, 1992, The Flight of the Dove, 1994, The Spy Within, 1995, Tall Tale, 1995, Reckless, 1995, Edie and Pen, 1996, Courage Under Fire, 1996, Carla's Song, 1996, Absolute Power, 1997, Lesser Prophetes, 1997, Larga Distance, 1998, Firestorm, 1998, The Last Marshall, 1999, The Virgin Suicides, 1999, Vertical Limit, 2000, Training Day, 2001, Buffalo Soldiers, 2001, The Shipping News, 2001, Puerto Vallarta Squeeze, 2004, Journey to the End of the Night, 2006, Freedom Writers, 2007, The Bourne Ultimatum, 2007; appeared in TV films Gargoyles, 1972, As Summers Die, 1986, Intrigue, 1988, The Outside Woman, 1989, Women & Men 2: In Love There Are no Rules, 1991 (HBO), Shadow Hunter, 1993, Extreme Justice, 1993, Slaughter of The Innocents, 1993, Past Tense, 1994, Night of The Running Man, 1994, Naked City: Justice with a Bullet, 1998, Naked City: A Killer Christmas, 1998, The Seventh Stream, 2001, A Painted House, 2003, Gone But Not Forgotten, 2004, Homeland Security, 2004, Faith of My Fathers, 2005, Code Breakers, 2005. Served M.C. Office: William Morris Agy c/o Lee Stallman 151 S El Camino Dr Beverly Hills CA 90212-2775*

GLENN, T. MICHAEL, delivery/messenger service executive; b. Memphis; Bachelor's, U. Miss.; MBA, U. Memphis. With sales div. Dover Elevator Co.; with dept. corp. sales Fed. Express Corp. (now FedEx Corp.), 1981-83, mgr., 1983-84, mng. dir. dept. mktg., 1984-85, v.p. mktg. N.Am., 1985-92, sr. v.p. Catalog and Remail Svcs. div., 1992-93, sr. v.p. worldwide mktg., customer svc., corp. comm., 1993-98; exec. v.p. market devel. and corp. comm. FedEx Corp., Memphis, 1993—, overseer FedEx Custom Critical, 1993—. Bd. dirs. Make-A-Wish Found., United Way. Office: Fed Ex Corp 942 S Shady Grove Rd Memphis TN 38120-4117

GLENN, TERRY, professional football player; b. Columbus, Ohio, July 23, 1974; Student, Ohio St. Univ., 1994. Wide receiver New Eng. Patriots, 1996—2001, Green Bay Packers, 2002, Dallas Cowboys, 2003—. Office: Dallas Cowboys One Cowboys Pkwy Irving TX 75063-4999

GLENNEN, ROBERT EUGENE, JR., retired academic administrator; b. Omaha, Mar. 31, 1933; s. Robert E. and La Verda (Elledge) G.; m. Mary C. O'Brien, Apr. 17, 1958; children: Maureen, Bobby, Colleen, Billy, Barry, Katie, Molly, Kerry AB, U. Portland, 1955, M.Ed., 1957; PhD, U. Notre Dame, 1962. Asst. prof. U. Portland, 1956-60; asst. prof., assoc. prof. Eastern Mont. Coll., Billings, 1962-65; assoc. dean U. Notre Dame, South Bend, Ind., 1965-72; dean, v.p. U. Nev.-Las Vegas, 1972-80; pres. Western N.Mex. U., Silver City, 1980-84, Emporia (Kans.) State U., 1984-97; acting vice-chancellor U. Ark., Montecello, 1999; interim provost U. So. Colo., 1999-2000, interim pres., 2001—02. Bd. dirs. Emporia Enterprises; cons. HEW, Washington, 1964-84 Author: Guidance: An Orientation, 1966. Contbr. articles to profl. jours. Pres. PTA, South Bend, Ind., 1970-71; bd. trustees Am. Coll. Testing Corp., Iowa City, 1977-80; chmn. Kans. Regents Coun. of Pres., 1986-87, 92-93, 95-96. Recipient award of excellence Nat. Acad. Advising Assn., Disting. Alumnus award U. Portland, 1993, Kans. Master Tchr. award, 1994; named Coach of Yr., Coach and Athletic mag., 1958, Pub. Adminstr. of Yr., 1994, Athletic Hall of Fame, Portland, 1995; Rotary Paul Harris fellow, 1995, Ford Found. fellow, 1961-62. Mem. Kans. C. of C. (bd. dirs.), Emporia C. of C. Regional Devel. Assn. (bd. dirs., Bank IV), Am. Personnel and Guidance Assn., Am. Assn. State Colls. and Univs. (chair pres's. commn. on tchr. edn.), Am. Assn. Higher Edn., Nev. Personnel and Guidance Assn., Assn. Counselor Educators and Suprs., Am. Assn. Counseling and Devel., Nat. Assn. Student Personnel Adminstrs. Republican. Roman Catholic. Avocations: walking, reading. Home: 1591 Meadow Hills Dr Richland WA 99352

GLENNER, RICHARD ALLEN, dentist, dental historian; b. Chgo., Apr. 14, 1934; s. Robert Joseph and Vivian (Prosk) G.; m. Dorothy Chapman, July 13, 1957; children: Mark Steven, Alison, Scott Jay. BS, Roosevelt U., 1955; BS in Dentistry, U. Ill., 1958, DDS, 1959; student, Army Med. Svc. Sch., 1960. Pvt. practice, Chgo., 1962—. Cons. on dental history to Smithsonian Instn., ADA, various corps., librs., univs., museums, dental jours, Dr. Samuel D. Harris Nat. Mus. Dentistry; dental and anthropol. rschr. Nat. Park Svc., Nat. Mus. Health and Medicine, 1993—; lectr. to various orgns. Author: The Dental Office: A Pictorial History, 1984, How it Evolved: Dentistry's Pursuit for Excellence, 1997; co-author: The American Dentist, 1990, A Visit to the Dentist: Then & Now, 1996; appeared in PBS video Sci. Am. Frontiers: The Wild West, 1995; cons. editor A Bicentennial Salute to Am. Dentistry, 1976; contbr. articles to profl. and popular jours.; film maker The Dental Office, 1994; reviewer Jour. ADA, 1999—. Served to capt. AUS, 1960—68. Mem. ADA (life), Ill. Dental Assn., Chgo. Dental Soc., Acad. Gen. Dentistry, Assn. Mil. Surgeons U.S., Am. Acad. History of Dentistry (historian 1984, chmn. smithsonian Instn. adv. group 1987, Hayden-Harris award 1983, columnist Jour. History of Dentistry 1989—, mem. editl. bd. 1993—, hist. display com. 1993—, pub. com. 1993—, Hayden-Harris award com. 1995-99), Fedn. Dentaire Internat., Lindsay Soc. G.B., Ill. Dental Soc. (history com.), Pierre Fauchard Acad. (life), Am. Med. Writers Assn., Sci. Instrument Soc., Jewish War Vets. U.S., Westerners, Titanic Hist. Soc., Titanic Internat. Soc. (rschr.), Alpha Omega. Home: 6715 N Lawndale Ave Lincolnwood IL 60712-3711 Office: 3414 W Peterson Ave Chicago IL 60659-3447

GLENNON, CHARLES EDWARD, retired judge, lawyer; b. Monticello, Ill., Apr. 5, 1942; s. William Edward and Beatrice Jane (Pierson) G.; m. Sylvia Ann McClintock, Aug. 24, 1965 (div. Aug. 1972); children: David, Caroline; m. Victoria Louise Pearre, Oct. 26, 1974 (div. May 2001); 1 child, Andrew; m. Bonnie Jane Krueger, July 5, 2003. BA, U. Ill., 1964, JD, 1966. Bar: Ill. 1966, U.S. Supreme Ct. 1974. Assoc. Fellheimer & Fellheimer, Pontiac, Ill., 1968-73; ptnr. Gomien & Glennon Ltd., Dwight, Ill., 1973-75; cir. judge State of Ill., Pontiac, 1976-98; temporarily recalled to bench, 1999, 2003; chief judge 11th cir., 1991-95. Lectr., author criminal law Ill. Village atty., Dwight, 1973-75; chmn. Salvation Army Adv. Bd., Pontiac, 1976; chmn. criminal law com. Ill. Jud. Conf., 1989-99, del., mem. exec. com., 1993-98; former mem. Regional Youth Planning Commn., Livingston County Commn. on Children and Youth; mng. dir. Nat. Arts Found., 1998—; pres. Alta Vista Assn., 2005—; With U.S. Army, 1966-68. Fellow Ill. Bar Found.; mem. Livingston County Bar Assn. (pres. 1991-93), Ill. Bar Assn., Ill. Judges Assn., Am. Assn. Juvenile and Family Ct. Judges, Lions, Rotary, Elks. Republican. Episcopalian. Personal E-mail: chasness@aol.com.

GLESBY, MARSHALL JAY, physician, educator; b. Winnipeg, Manitoba, Canada, Sept. 27, 1963; U.S., 1985; MD, Johns Hopkins U., 1989, PhD, 1997; BSc, McGill U., 1985. Diplomate Am. Bd. Internal Medicine, Am. Bd. Infectious Diseases. Intern, resident Johns Hopkins Hosp., 1989—92, post-doctoral fellow divsn. infectious diseases, 1992—96; med. dir. Cmty. Rsch. Initiative on AIDS, NYC, 1996—99; asst. prof. medicine Weill Med. Coll. Cornell U., 1999—2005; assoc. prof. medicine and pub. health Weill Med. Coll. Cornell U., NYC, 2005—. Office: Weill Medical College of Cornell Univ 525 E 68th St Box 566 New York NY 10025 Office Phone: 212-746-4177.

GLESMANN, SYLVIA-MARIA, artist; b. Spardorf, Erlangen, Germany, June 8, 1923; arrived in the US, 1925; d. Rolf-Joseph and Auguste (Schultheiss) Hoffmann; m. John Brainerd Glesmann, Apr. 30, 1948; children: Glenn M., Eric B., Jonathan M. Degree, Acad. Fine Arts, Nurnberg, Germany, 1940, Acad. Fine Arts, Munich, 1944. Instr. Somerville Adult Edn. Exhibited in group shows at Carrier Clinic, 1993, Bergen Mus., 1993, Morris Mus., 1993, Nabisco Brands, 1993, Cultural and Heritage Gallery, Somerville, N.J., 1993-95, Salmagundi Club, 1994, Garden State Water Color Assn., Princeton, N.J., 1994, Barrons Art Ctr., 1993, Art on the Ave. Group Show of Flowers, 1991, Nat. Assn. Women Artists, N.Y.C., 1991, 94, SoHo, 1994, Bridgewater N.J. County Libr., 1996, 2001-02, Nat. Assn. Women Artists New World Art Ctr., Soho, N.Y., 1999, Children's Specialized Hosp., Westfield, N.J., 2002, Barrons Art Ctr, Woodbridge, 2002, Creative Arts Com. Show, Bridgewater, N.J., 2006, Trinity United Ch. Art Show, Warren, N.J., 2006; one-woman shows include N.U.I. Corp., Bridgewater, 1987, Salmagundi Club, N.Y.C., 1995, 2000, Am. Artists Profl. League, 1995-97, Somerset County Libr., Bridgewater, 1996, 2001-02, Barrons Art Ctr., Woodbridge, 1997, Barrons Art Ctr., Bridgewater Mcpl. Bldg, 1999-2001, Nat. Assn. Women Artists, Balt. Conv. Ctr., 2000, Bridgewater Libr., 2001, Nat. Assn. Women Artists, UN Visitors Lobby, 2002, Georgio Zikos Gallery, New Hope, Pa., 2002-03, over 25 one woman shows; author numerous poems. Recipient over 50 awards in water color, Editor's Choice award, 1998, Poetry Editors Choice award, 2002, Poetry award, Intenat. Libr. Poetry, 2003. Mem. Am. Artists Profl. League (pres. N.J. chpt. 1988-91, 2001, 06-07, Bridgewater NJ Artists shows, 2002-2003), Nat. Assn. Woman Artists, Raritan Valley Arts Assn. (pres. 1976-78), Somerset Art Assn. (chairwoman 10th outdoor art show, participant shows 2004, 05, 06), Salmagundi Club, Nat. Mus. for Women in Arts (charter). Lutheran. Avocations: sports, music, reading, poetry, traveling and sketching. Home and Office: 36 Twin Oaks Rd Bridgewater NJ 08807-2343 *To be of cultural stamina in the arts - to help and influence the American public. To see the world through art-music poetry painting also Philosophy. To make people see and feel. And to look at nature as a miracle.*

GLETHEROW, JAMIE, computer scientist; b. London, Dec. 17, 1968; Grad. in media studies with honors, U. Westminster, London, 1998. Tech. dir. Atticmedia, London, 2003—06.

GLIATTA, STEPHEN, lawyer; BS, Fordham U., 1980; JD, NYU, 1983. Bar: NY 1984. Ptnr., co-chair Real Estate Dept., mem. exec. com. Kaye Scholer LLP, NYC. Mem.: Nat. Assn. Real Estate Investment Trusts. Office: Kaye Scholer LLP 425 Park Ave New York NY 10022 Office Phone: 212-836-8618. E-mail: sgliatta@kayescholer.com.

GLICK, ANNA MARGARET, real estate broker, consultant; d. John Dale and Lena Iris Thomas; m. Alfred Dean Glick, June 1, 1986; m. Lealon Maynard Stoy, Oct. 16, 1966 (div. July 8, 1983); children: Lee Matthew Stoy, John Dale Stoy. Student, Indiana-Purdue U., 1979—82, Okla. City C.C., 1985—86; cert., Coldwell Banker U., 1992, cert., 1999. Real estate broker State of Ind. Lic. Bd., 1989. Mathematician to sec. Lincoln Nat. Life Ins. Co., Fort Wayne, Ind., 1965—69; exec. sec. Magnavox Corp., Fort Wayne, 1969—71; tri-state dir. Tammey Jewels, Inc., Indpls., 1970—73; owner, operator LeAn's Family Footwear, Hamilton, Ind., 1973—78; dep. auditor DeKalb County Ct. Ho., Auburn, Ind., 1974—83; fin. contr. Price Comm., Inc, Oklahoma City, 1983—86; auditing State of Ind., State Bd. of Accounts, Idpls., 1987—90; trust, ira adminstr. Ft. Wayne Nat. Bank, Fort Wayne, 1987—90; real estate broker, realtor RE/MAX Results, Fort Wayne, 1989—. Presenter A & A Unlimited Budget Workshops, Fort Wayne, 2004—. Bd. dirs. Nat. Kidney Found. of Ind., Fort Wayne, 1986—95. Recipient Gift of Life award, Nat. Kidney Found. of Ind., 1987, President's Cir. award, Coldwell Banker, 1996, 1998, 2000—03, Diamond Cir. award, 1997, Multi-Million Dollar Club award, 1990—94, President's Elite Distinction, 1995, 100% Club, RE/MAX, 2004, 2005. Mem.: Ft. Wayne Area Assn. Realtors (forms and govtl. affairs com. mem. 2001—), Providence Seminars, Inc. (club net leader 2004—05). R-Consevative. Protestant. Avocations: genealogy, decorating, piano, computers, reading. Home: 11626 Sycamore Hills Dr Fort Wayne IN 46814 Office: RE/MAX Results 7806-A W Jefferson Fort Wayne IN 46804 Home Phone: 260-625-5357; Office Phone: 260-436-6363. Office Fax: 260-436-6364. E-mail: anna@annaglick.com.

GLICK, CHARLES L., lawyer, insurance company executive; b. Cleve., Ohio, Sept. 8, 1954; BA magna cum laude, Ind. Univ., Bloomington, Ind., 1976; JD, Yale Univ., New Haven, Conn., 1982. Bar: Ill. 1982, NY 1991, Tenn. 2006. Founding ptnr. Hedlund Hanley & John, Chgo., 1991—99; dep. gen. counsel Bank One Corp., Chgo., 2001—03; prin. Orchard Equity, Inc., 2003—05; exec. v.p., gen. counsel Unum Group, Chattanooga, 2005—. Editor (sr.): Yale Law Rev., 1981—82. Mem.: ABA, Assn. Corp. Counsel, Phi Beta Kappa. Office: Unum Group One Fountain Sq Chattanooga TN 37402 Office Phone: 423-294-3118. Business E-Mail: cglick@unum.com.

GLICK, EARL A., lawyer; b. Chgo., Feb. 20, 1930; s. Simon and Eva (Cohen) G.; m. Janet Esther Klein, Aug. 22, 1953; children: Michael J., Daniel H., Linda J. Richardson, Steven B. BS, U. Ill., 1951; JD, Northwestern U., 1953. Bar: Ill. 1953, Calif. 1962. Asst. atty. gen. State of Ill., Chgo., 1953-57; ptnr. Gerwin & Glick, Chgo., 1957-61; gen. counsel S & S Corp., Beverly Hills, Calif., 1961-62; ptnr. Gendel, Raskoff, Shapiro & Quittner, LA, 1962-90, Orrick, Herrington & Sutcliffe, LA, 1990-2000; of counsel Murphy & Assocs. Capital, LLC, Westlake Village, Calif., 2000—04, 2004—. Bd. govs. Fin. Lawyers Conf., LA, 1965—2000. Fellow Am. Coll. Comml. Fin. Lawyers; mem. ABA (chair program com. fin. svcs. subcom., 1993-96). Republican. Jewish. Avocations: travel, walking, reading. Home: 5560 Ostin Ave Woodland Hills CA 91367-3976 Personal E-mail: eglick@socal.rr.com.

GLICK, GARLAND WAYNE, retired theological seminary president; b. Bridgewater, Va., Jan. 27, 1921; s. John T. and Effie (Evers) G.; m. Barbara Roller Zigler, Jan. 1, 1943; children— Martha (Mrs. Carl Barlett), Ted, Mary. B.D., Bethany Bibl. Sem., Chgo., 1946; MA in N.T, U. Chgo., 1949, PhD in Ch. History, 1957; LL.D., Bridgewater Coll., 1969. Ordained to ministry Ch. of Brethren, 1942, United Ch. Christ, 1978. Pastor, Lombard, Ill., 1945-48; instr., then asst. prof. Bibl. studies Juniata Coll., Huntingdon, Pa., 1948-53; mem. faculty Franklin and Marshall Coll., 1955-65, assoc. prof. religion, 1958-65, prof., 1965, v.p., 1962-65, acting pres., 1962-63, dir. rsch. and long-range planning, 1960, asst. to dean, 1960-61, dean coll., 1961-65; pres. Keuka Coll., Keuka Park, NY, 1966-74; dir. Moton Center Ind. Studies, Gloucester, Va., 1975-78; pres. Bangor (Maine) Theol. Sem., 1978-86. Vis. prof. Lancaster (Pa.) Theol. Sem., 1958-60, 64; coord. cons. Knox Seminars Ednl. Mgmt., 1963-65; seminar dir. Nat. Cath. Assn. Long-Range Planning Seminars, 1968; bd. dirs. Empire State Found. Ind. Liberal Arts Colls., Fund for Theol. Edn. (pres. 1988-92), Lancaster Guidance Ctr. Author: Maker of Modern Theology: Adolf von Harnack, 1967, Songs for my God, 1998; contbr. to Ency. Brit. Mem. Nat. Assn. Bibl. Instrs., Am. Soc. Ch. History, Lancaster Cliosophic Soc. (pres. 1995-97), Am. Conf. Acad. Deans (treas. 1965-66), Societas Orphea, Pi Gamma Mu, Tau Kappa Alpha. Mem. United Ch. Of Christ. Home: 1834 Ridgeview Ave Lancaster PA 17603-4316 *Clearly, a revolution has taken place in the last generation. The meaning of that revolution is not yet clear. I believe the name of the revolution is "longing" and Augustine's "God and the soul I want to know, nothing more," demarks its direction.*

GLICK, GINA PHILLIPS MORAN, retired physician; b. Chgo., Dec. 6, 1931; d. Edward Langan Moran and Virginia Louise Phillips; m. L. Michael Glick, Feb. 9, 1957; children: Mark Michael, Celeste Michele, Felicia Michele, Matthew Michael. Student, Mundelein Coll., Chgo., 1949-52; MD, Loyola U., Chgo., 1956. Diplomate Am. Bd. Anesthesiology. Intern Mercy Hosp., Chgo., 1956-57; resident in anesthesia Chgo. Wesley Mem. Hosp., 1957-59; pvt. practice anesthesia Cumberland, Md., 1959-83; clin. instr. anesthesia U. Md., Balt.; chmn. dept. anesthesia Sacred Heart Hosp., Cumberland, 1967-83; asst. prof. anesthesia U. Tex. S.W. Med. Ctr., 1985—99; ret., 1999. Dir. Jenkins Anesthesiology Libr. Recipient gold, silver and bronze medals Md. chpt. Am. Heart Assn., Community Achievement award Sta. WCBC, 1981, St. Benedict medal St. Scholastica

High Sch., Chgo., 1978. Mem. Am. Soc. Anesthesiologists, Tex. Soc. Anesthesiologists, Dallas County Soc. Anesthesiologists, Dallas County Med. Soc. Roman Catholic. Office: U Tex Sci Med Ctr Dept Anesthesiology 5323 Harry Hines Blvd Dallas TX 75390-7208

GLICK, J. LESLIE, entrepreneur; b. NYC, Mar. 2, 1940; s. Arthur Harvey and Hilda Lillian (Lichtenfeld) G.; m. Judith Sumiye Mihara; children: Geoffrey Michael, Jessica Michele. AB, Columbia U., 1961, PhD, 1964. Nat. Cancer Inst. postdoctoral fellow Princeton U., 1964-65; sr., then asso. cancer research scientist Roswell Park Meml. Inst., Buffalo, 1965-69; assoc. rsch. prof. physiology, physiology chmn. Roswell Park div. SUNY, Buffalo, 1968-70; from exec. v.p. to chmn. bd. Asso. Biomedic Systems, Inc., Buffalo, 1969-77; pres. Inst. Sci. and Social Accountability, Washington, 1975-79; pres., chief exec. officer Genex Corp., Gaithersburg, Md., 1977-87; chmn., CEO Bionix Corp., Potomac, Md., 1987-93. Chmn. HTI Corp., Buffalo, 1972-75; dir. Nat. Assn. Life Sci. Industries, 1975-77; rsch. prof. biology Niagara U., N.Y., Canisius Coll., Buffalo, 1968-70; mem. exec. com. SUNY Grad. Sch., Buffalo, 1968-70; vis. lectr. NATO Adv. Study Inst., Brussels, 1970; mem. biotech. tech. adv. com. U.S. Dept. Commerce, 1985-87; adj. prof. tech. mgmt. Grad. Sch., U. Md. Univ. Coll., 1988-2004, mem. adv. panel, 1988-2000, mem. grad. coun., 1992-94, mem. dr. mgmt. adv. bd., 2006-; professorial cons. NTU Satellite Network, Nat. Tech. U., 1989-90; vis. lectr. tech. mgmt. Johns Hopkins U., 1993-97; external examiner doctoral program Sch. Mgmt. Asian Inst. Tech., 1998-99, Sch. Mgmt. U. Western Sydney, 2006; mng. dir. Cooper Alport Prodns., 1998—; chmn. bd. Marco Polo Techs., Inc., 1998-2003; bd. dirs. Advanced Processing and Imaging, Inc., vice chmn. bd., 1999—; vice chmn. bd. Advanced Tracking Svcs., Inc., 2000-01, chmn. bd., 2001-03. Author: Fundamentals of Human Lymphoid Cell Culture, 1980; also articles; patentee in field; mem. editorial advisors bd. Strategic Direction, 1984-87; mem. adv. coun. High Tech. Mktg. Rev., 1986-87; mem. indsl. adv. bd. Biotech. Process Engrng. Ctr., MIT, 1986-87; mem. editorial bd. Accountability in Rsch.: Policies and Quality Assurance, 1989—; editor-in-chief Tech. Mgmt., 1992-2001. Bd. overseers Simon's Rock of Bard Coll., 1984-85; trustee Nat. Faculty Humanities, Arts and Scis., 1985-87. Mem. Internat. Assn. for Mgmt. Tech., Am. Physiol. Soc., Indsl. Biotech. Assn. (pres. 1981-83, bd. dirs.1981-84), N.Y. Acad. Scis., Sigma Xi. E-mail: jlglick@ix.netcom.com.

GLICK, JANE MILLS, biomedical researcher, educator; b. Memphis, Nov. 26, 1943; d. Albert Axtell Jr. and Mary Louise (Baynes) Mills; m. John Harrison Glick, May 25, 1968; children: Katherine Anne, Sarah Stewart. AB, Randolph-Macon Woman's Coll., 1965; PhD, Columbia U., 1971. Postdoctoral trainee NIH, Bethesda, Md., 1971-73; postdoctoral fellow Sch. of Medicine Stanford (Calif.) U., 1973-74; rsch. asst. prof. biochemistry Sch. Dental Medicine U. Pa., Phila., 1974-77; asst. prof. biochemistry Med. Coll. Pa., Phila., 1977-82, assoc. prof. biochemistry, 1982-90, prof. biochemistry, 1990-94; sr. rsch. investigator Inst. Human Gene Therapy Sch. Medicine U. Pa., 1994—2002, faculty adminstr. cell and molecular biology group. Mem. metabolism study sect. NIH, 1993—97; adj. assoc. prof. Sch. Medicine U. Pa., 1996—. Assoc. editor: Jour. Lipid Rsch., 1985-86, mem. editorial bd., 1987-99; contbr. articles to profl. jours. Trustee Episcopal Acad., Merion, Pa., 1989-95, Swarthmore Presbyn. Ch., 1995-97, pres. 1997. Recipient Rsch. Svc. award NIH, 1975-77, Young Investigator award, 1980-83, Teaching award Lindback Found., 1985. Mem. AAAS, AAUP (sec. 1990-92), Arteriosclerosis Coun. Am. Heart Assn. (program com. 1990-93), Am. Soc. for Biochemistry and Molecular Biology, Am. Soc. for Human Genetics, Phi Beta Kappa, Sigma Xi. Presbyterian. Office: U Pa Sch Medicine 652 BRB II/III 421 Curie Blvd Philadelphia PA 19104 Home Phone: 610-328-1795. Business E-Mail: glickj@mail.med.upenn.edu.

GLICK, JOHN H., oncologist, medical educator; b. NYC, May 9, 1943; s. Arthur W. and Sybil (Goldman) Glick; m. Jane Mills, May 25, 1968; children: Katherine, Sarah. AB magna cum laude, Princeton U., 1965; MD, Columbia U., 1969. Diplomate Am. Bd. Med. Oncology, (sec. subsplty. com. med. oncology 1976-83, mem. subsplty. bd. med. oncology 1983-87, chmn. 1987-89, cert. exam. com. 1986-88, mem. bd. govs. 1987-89) Am. Bd. Internal Medicine. Intern in medicine Presbyn. Hosp., NYC, 1969-70, asst. resident in medicine, 1970-71; commd. surgeon, clin. assoc. medicine br. Nat. Cancer Inst., USPHS, Bethesda, Md., 1971-73; postdoctoral fellow in med. oncology Stanford (Calif.) U., 1973-74; asst. prof. medicine U. Pa., Phila., 1974-79, Ann B. Young asst. prof. cancer rsch., 1974, assoc. prof., 1979-83, prof., 1983—, Madlyn and Leonard Abramson prof. clin. oncology, 1988—; dir. clin. trials U. Pa. Cancer Ctr., Phila., 1977-79, assoc. dir. for clin. rsch., 1980-85, dir. Cancer Ctr., 1985—2006, mem. numerous acad. coms., dept. medicine coms., hosp. coms., 1974—; pres. Abramson Family Cancer Rsch. Inst., Phila., 1998—; v.p. U. Pa. Health Sys., 2006—; assoc. dean U. Pa. Sch. Medicine, 2006—. Attending physician Hosp. U. Pa., 1974—, dir. Hematology-Oncology Clinic, 1974—76; cons. Phila. VA Hosp., 1974—; mem. clin. trials rev. com. NIH, Bethesda, Md., 1980—83, mem. radiosensitizer /radioprotector working group, radiotheraphy devel. br., 1980—85, chmn. consensus devel. panel conf. adjuvant therapy for breast cancer, 1985; mem. com. accreditation med. oncology tng. programs Accreditation Coun. Grad. Med. Edn., Phila., 1983—, mem. appeals panel, 1984—94; prin. investigator Ea. Coop. Oncology Group U. Pa.; pres., dir. Abramson Family Cancer Rsch. Inst. U. Pa., Phila., 1987—; dir. Pa. Cancer Ctr. U. Pa., Phila., 1985—. Mem. editl. bd.: Am. Jour. Clin. Oncology, 1983—89, Blood, 1983—86, Jour. Clin. Oncology, 1987—93, Internat. Jour. Radiation Oncology, Biology and Physics; editor (assoc. editor): Cancer Rsch., 1984—88; contbr. articles to profl. jours. Recipient Faculty Rsch. award, Am. Cancer Soc., 1982—86; Rsch. grantee, Nat. Cancer Inst., Ea. Coop. Oncology Group, Am. Cancer Soc., others. Master: ACP (mem. various splty. coms. 1983—84); fellow: Coll. Physicians and Surgeons; mem.: John Morgan Soc. U. Pa., Am. Fedn. Clin. Rsch., Am. Soc. Hematology, Am. Radium Soc. (mem. exec. com. 1986—87), Am. Assn. Cancer Rsch., Am. Assn. Cancer Edn., Am. Soc. Clin. Oncology (chmn. program com. 1983—84, nominating com. 1983—84, mem. pub. issue com. 1984—85, bd. dirs., pres. 1995—96), Alpha Omega Alpha, Phi Beta Kappa. Office: Abramson Cancer Ctr of Univ Pa 3400 Spruce St Philadelphia PA 19104-4283 Office Phone: 215-662-6065. Business E-Mail: glickjh@mail.med.upenn.edu.

GLICK, LESLIE ALAN, lawyer; b. NYC, May 22, 1946; s. Leo S. and Sylvia (Hall) G. BS, Cornell U., 1967, JD, 1970. Bar: N.Y. 1971, D.C. 1971, Md. 1974, U.S. Ct. Internat. Trade 1971, U.S. Supreme Ct. 1974. Ptnr. Porter Wright Morris & Arthur, Washington, 1987—. Author: Multilateral Trade Negotiations, 1984, Trading with Saudi Arabia, 1980, Guide to U.S. Customs and Trade Laws, 1991, 2d edit., 1996, Understanding the North American Free Trade Agreement, 1993, 2d edit., 1995; author, co-editor, contbr. Manual for the Practice of U.S. International Trade Law, 2001. Active Dem. State Cen. com., Md., 1982-84; chmn. adv. com. on Consumer Affairs, Montgomery County, Md., 1982-84. Mem. ABA (intrnat. trade and customs law com., chmn. sec. adminstrv. law and regulatory practice 2004—), FBA (chmn. internat. law sect. 1986-88). Office: Porter Wright Morris & Arthur 1919 Pennsylvania Ave NW Washington DC 20006 Office Phone: 202-778-3022. Business E-Mail: lglick@porterwright.com.

GLICK, MILTON DON, academic administrator, chemist; b. Memphis, July 30, 1937; s. Lewis S. and Sylvia (Kleinman) G.; m. Peggy M., June 22, 1965; children: David, Sander. AB cum laude, Augustana Coll., 1959; PhD, U. Wis., 1965. Asst. prof. chemistry Wayne State U., Detroit, 1966-70, assoc. prof., 1970-74, prof., 1974-83, chmn. dept., 1978-83; dean arts & scis. U. Mo., Columbia, 1983-88; provost Iowa State U., Ames, 1988-91, interim pres., 1990-91; sr. v.p., provost Ariz. State U., Tempe, 1991—2002, exec. v.p., provost, 2002—06; pres. U. Nev., Reno, 2006—. Contbr. articles to profl. jours. Fellow dept. chemistry Cornell U., Ithaca, N.Y., 1964-66. Office: Office of President Univ Nev Reno/001 Reno NV 89557-0154 Office Phone: 775-784-4805. Office Fax: 775-784-6429. Business E-Mail: glick@unr.edu.

GLICK, RICHARD STEPHEN, internist, rheumatologist; b. Pitts., May 18, 1947; s. William and Ruthe (Scher) Glick; m. Joan Marie Skaf, Nov. 2, 1986; children: William Spencer, Michael Andrew. BA cum laude, U. Pa., 1969, MD, 1973. Diplomate Am. Bd. Internal Medicine (also subsplty. bd. rheumatology). Intern U. Mich. Hosp., Ann Arbor, 1973-74, resident, 1974-77; fellow in rheumatology U. Pa., 1977-78, Albany Med. Coll. Hosp., 1978-79; practice medicine specializing in rheumatology and internal medicine Ft. Lauderdale, Fla., 1979—. Contbr. articles to profl. jours. Mem. Am. Coll. Rheumatology, So. Med. Assn., Fla. Soc. Rheumatology. Office: 6405 N Federal Hwy Ste 105 Fort Lauderdale FL 33308-1414

GLICK, RUTH BURTNICK, literature educator, writer; b. Lexington, Ky., Apr. 27, 1942; d. Lester Leon and Beverly (Miller) Burtnick; m. Norman Stanley Glick, June 30, 1963; children: Elissa, Ethan. BA, George Washington U., 1964; MA, U. Md., 1967. Lectr. S.W. Writers Conf., Houston, 1984, Nebr. Writers' Guild, Omaha, 1985, Bouchercon, Balt., 1986, Triangle Romance and Fiction Writers' Conf., Raleigh, 1988, Romantic Times Booklovers Conf., San Antonio, 1990, Orlando, 2001, Kansas City, 2003, St. Louis, 2005, Malice Domestic, Bethesda, 1993, Howard C.C., 1995—, World Fantasy Conv., 2003, Desert Dreams Conf., Phoenix, 2004, Writers Weekend, Seattle, 2004. Author: (with Nancy Baggett) Dollhouse Furniture You Can Make, 1977, Dollhouse Lamps and Chandeliers, 1979, Soup's On, 1985, Oat Bran Baking, 1989, Skinny Soups, 1992, 100 Percent Pleasure, 1994 (US Today list of 12 best cookbooks of 1994), Skinny Italian, 1996, One-Pot Meals for People with Diabetes, 2002; (with Eileen Buckholtz, Carolyn Males and Louise Titchener) Love Is Elected, 1982 (named one of best romances 1982), Southern Persuasion, 1983, (with Titchener) In the Arms of Love, 1983 (Romance best seller list), Brian's Captive, 1983 (Romance best seller list), Reluctant Merger, 1983 (Romance best seller list), Summer Wine, 1984, Beginner's Luck, 1984, Mistaken Image, 1985, Hopelessly Devoted, 1985, Summer Stars, 1985, Stolen Passion, 1986, Indiscreet, 1988, (with Baggett and Gloria Kaufer Greene) Don't Tell 'Em It's Good for 'Em, 1984, Eat Your Vegetables!, 1985, (with Buckholtz) End of Illusion, 1984, Space Attack, 1984, Mission of the Secret Spy Squad, 1984, Mindbenders, 1984, Doom Stalker, 1985, Captain Kid and the Pirates, 1985, The Cats of Castle Mountain, 1985, Logical Choice, 1986, Great Expectations, 1987, A Place in Your Heart, 1988, Saber Dance, 1988, Postmark, 1988, Roller Coaster, 1989 (Young Adult Best Seller List), Silver Creek Challenge, 1989, Needlepoint, 1989, Life Line, 1990, Shattered Vows, 1991, Whispers in the Night, 1991, Only Skin Deep, 1992, Trial By Fire, 1992, Hopscotch, 1993, Cradle and All, 1993, What Child is This, 1993, Midnight Kiss, 1994, Tangled Vows, 1994, Till Death Us Do Part, 1995, Prince of Time, 1995, Face to Face, 1996, For Your Eyes Only, 1997, Father and Child, 1997 (Peregrine Connection series) Talons of the Falcon, 1986, Flight of the Raven, 1986, In Search of the Dove, 1986 (Lifetime Achievement award for romantic suspense series 1987), (with Kathryn Jensen) The Big Score, 1989 (Young Adult Best Seller List), Night Stalker, 1989 (Young Adult Best Seller List), (sole author) Dollhouse Kitchen and Dining Room Accessories, 1979, Invasion of the Blue Lights, 1982, More Than Promises, 1985, The Closer We Get, 1989, Make Me a Miracle, 1992, Bayou Moon, 1992, Skinny One Pot Meals, 1994, The Diabetes Snack, Munch, Nibble, Nosh Book, 1998, Simply Italian, 1998, Nowhere Man, 1998, Shattered Lullaby, 1999, Midnight Caller, 1999, Never Too Late, 2000, Amanda's Child, 2000, Fabulous Lo-Carb Cuisine, 2001, The Man from Texas, 2001, Never Alone, 2001, Lassiter's Law, 2001, Body Contact, 2002 (Waldenbooks Series Best Seller List), From the Shadows, 2002, Phantom Lover, 2003, Killing Moon, 2003 (Berkley Sensation Launch Book), Intimate Strangers, 2003, Edge of the Moon, 2003, Witching Moon, 2003, Bedroom Therapy, 2004, Out of Nowhere, 2004, Undercover Encounter, 2004, Crimson Moon, 2005, Spellbound, 2005, Beyond Control, 2005, Riley's Retribution, 2005, others; contbr. articles to profl. jours. U. Md. Am. studies fellow, 1964-65; recipient Career Achievement award for series Romantic Mystery, 1994, Romantic Times Career Achievement award for series Romantic Suspense, 2000, Golden Leaf award for Best Long Contemporary novel and Best Novella, N.J. Romance Writers, 2001, Golden Leaf award for Best Paranormal novel N.J. Romance Writers, 2003, 04, Best Selling Author, NY Times, USA Today, 2003, Barclay Gold award for Best Futuristic, Fantasy and Paranormal novel Lake Country Romance Writers, 2004; nominee Best Series Romance Book of the Yr. 1993-94 Romantic Times, 1995, 99, 2001, nominee Series Storyteller of Yr., 1996, nominee Best Harlequin Intrigue of Yr., 1998, nominee Best Series Romantic Suspense Writer of Yr., 2000. Mem. Author's Guild, Romance Writers Am. (lectr. Detroit, 1984, Atlanta 1985, Dallas 1987, 96, 2004, Boston 1989, San Francisco 1990, New Orleans 1991, 2001, Denver 2002, N.Y.C. 2003, Reno, 2005), Washington Romance Writers (bd. dirs.), Sisters in Crime, Novelists Inc., Md. Romance Writers, Internat. Thriller Writers. E-mail: rglick@capaccess.org.

GLICK, WILLIAM H., dean; AB in Psychology, U. Mich., 1975; PhD in Bus. Adminstrn., U. Calif., Berkeley, 1981. Mem. faculty U. Tex., Austin, 1981—95, dir. bus. honors program; mem. faculty Ariz. State U. W.P. Carey Sch. Bus., Tempe, 1995—2005, chair dept. mgmt.; dean Rice U. Jesse H. Jones Grad. Sch. Mgmt., Houston, 2005—, H. Joe Nelson III prof. mgmt., 2005—. Vis. prof. INSEAD, 2002. Co-editor (with G.P. Huber): (books) Organizational Change and Redesign: Ideas and Insights for Improving Performance, 1993. Office: Rice U Jesse H Jones Grad Sch Mgmt PO Box 2932 Houston TX 77252-2932 Office Phone: 713-348-5928. E-mail: bill.glick@rice.edu.

GLICKENHAUS, SARAH BRODY, speech therapist; b. Mpls., Mar. 8, 1919; d. Morris and Ethel (Silin) Brody; BS, U. Minn., 1940, MS, 1945; m. Seth Morton Glickenhaus, Oct. 23, 1944; children: James Morris, Nancy Pier. Speech therapist Davison Sch. Speech Correction, Atlanta, 1940-42; speech pathologist U. Minn., Mpls., 1945-46; speech therapist Queens Coll., N.Y.C., 1946-48; speech therapist VA, N.Y.C., 1949-50; pvt. practice, New Rochelle, N.Y., 1950-71; speech therapist Abbott Sch. United Free Sch. Dist. 13, Irvington, N.Y., 1971-79; pvt. practice, Scarsdale, N.Y., 1979—; tutor learning disabled children New Rochelle Public Schs., 1968-71. Mem. AAAS, Am. Speech Hearing & Lang. Assn., N.Y. State Speech &Hearing Assn., Westchester Speech & Hearing Assn. Club: Harvard (N.Y.C.). Jewish. Home and Office: 100 Dorchester Rd Scarsdale NY 10583-6051

GLICKMAN, CARL DAVID, banker; b. Cleve., July 29, 1926; s. Jack I. and Dora R. (Rubinowitz) G.; m. Barbara H. Schulman, Oct. 16, 1960; children: Lindsay Dale, David Craig, Robert Todd. Student, U. Minn., 1944, Inst. Fin. Mgmt., Harvard U., 1970. Pres. Glickman Orgn., Cleve., 1953—; chmn. bd., chief exec. officer Computer Research, Inc., Pitts., 1964-67, Am. Steel & Pump Corp., NYC, 1968-71, Shelter Resources Corp., Cleve., 1971-75; pres. Leader Bldg., Inc., Cleve., 1959—2004, Capital Bancorp., Cleve., 1971-75, Real Property Corp., Cleve., 1975—; spl. ltd. ptnr. Bear Stearns & Co., 1978-85, dir., 1985—. Chmn. exec. com. Franklin Corp., N.Y.C., 1986-98, Cook United Inc., Cleve., 1986-87, Capital Nat. Bank Cleve., 1970-75; chmn. bd. dirs. Univ. Nat. Bank, Chgo., 1968-70; ltd. ptnr. S.B. Lewis & Co., N.Y.C., 1980-89; gen. ptnr. Millbrook Assocs., Chester Union Assocs.; founding gen. ptnr. Park Ctrl. Assocs.; pres. LGT Industries, Durham, N.C., 1987-95; bd. dirs. Royal Petroleum Properties Corp., Jerusalem Econ. Corp., Israel, Custodial Trust Co., Alliance Tyre and Rubber Co., Tel Aviv,Tnuport Ltd., Tel Aviv, Indsl. Structures, Inc., Tel Aviv, Office Max, Inc., InfoTech, Englewood Cliff, NJ, Lexington Corp. Properties, NYC, presiding trustee, chmn. exec. com. Active Mayor's Com. Urban Renewal, 1965-67, Mayors Task Force on Higher Edn., 1967-69; trustee Cleve. Growth Assn., 1972-75; co-chmn. Herzog Loan Fund Cleve. State U., 1970-76; chmn. Med. Arts Hosp., Houston, 1976-86; bd. visitors Case Western Res. Sch. Law; trustee Montefiore Home Aged, Mt. Sinai Hosp., Cath. Diocese Found., Cleve.; grievance com. Cleve. Bar Assn., 1982-85; foreman Cuyahoga County Grand Jury, Cleve., 1984-85; trustee Cleve. State U., 2000—, Cleve. Cath. Diocese Found.; disting. fellow, hon. trustee Cleve. Clinic; nat. co-chmn. Glickman Urol. Inst. Cleve. Clinic; trustee Cleve. Jewish Fedn., 2006—. With USAAF, 1944-46. Mem. Am. Bankers Assn., Am. Arbitration Assn. (arbitrator), Beechmont Country Club, Shaker Heights Country Club, Union Club, Standard Club, Harmonie Club, Town Club, Friars Club, Palm Beach Club, Yacht Club, High Ridge Country Club, John Carroll Univ. Club (trustee), Masons, Phi Sigma Delta, Phi Eta Sigma. Office: 1140 Leader Bldg Cleveland OH 44114 also: 383 Madison Ave New York NY 10167-0002 also: 1 N Breakers Row Palm Beach FL 33480-4021 Office Phone: 216-696-2650. E-mail: carldglickman@hotmail.com.

GLICKMAN, DANIEL ROBERT, motion picture association executive, former congressman; b. Wichita, Kans., Nov. 24, 1944; s. Milton and Gladys Anne (Kopelman) G.; m. Rhoda Joyce Yura, Aug. 21, 1966; children: Jonathan, Amy. BA, U. Mich., Ann Arbor, 1966; JD, George Washington U., Washington, 1969. Bar: Kans. 1969, Mich. 1970. Trial atty. SEC, 1969-70; assoc. Sargent, Klenda & Glickman, Wichita, 1971—73, ptnr., 1973—76; mem. 95th-103rd Congresses from 4th Kans. Dist., 1977-95, mem. agrl. com., mem. judiciary, sci., space and tech. coms.; chmn. permanent select com. on intelligence 103d Congress; sec. USDA, Washington, 1995-2001; sr. advisor pub. law and policy group Akin Gump Strauss Hauer & Feld LLP, Washington, 2001—04; dir. Inst. Politics, John F. Kennedy Sch. Govt. Harvard U., 2002—04; pres. Motion Picture Assoc. Am., Encino, Calif., 2004—. Mem. Wichita Bd. Edn., 1973-76, pres., 1975-76. Mem. Order of Coif, Phi Delta Phi, Sigma Alpha Mu. Democrat. Jewish. Office: Motion Picture Assn Amer 15503 Ventura Blvd Encino CA 91436

GLICKMAN, FRANKLIN SHELDON, dermatologist, educator; b. Bklyn., Dec. 14, 1929; s. Arthur Zachary and Hilda (Kurtz) G.; m. Leatrice Sallie Alter, Mar. 29, 1953; children: Todd Scott, Jeff Bret. BA cum laude, Hofstra Coll., 1950; MD, SUNY-Bklyn., 1954; MS in Health Care Mgmt., NYU, 1990. Diplomate: Am. Bd. Dermatology. Intern Flushing (N.Y.) Hosp., 1954-55; resident in dermatology Kings County Hosp., Bklyn., 1957-58, Bronx VA Hosp., 1958-60; practice medicine specializing in dermatology Bklyn., 1960-94; mem. faculty dermatology dept. SUNY-Bklyn., 1960—82, clin. prof., 1982-93, adj. clin. prof., 1993—96; dir. med. edn. Wyckoff Heights Med. Ctr., Bklyn., 1990-96, chmn. dept. grad. med. edn., 1992-96. Author: General Dermatology, 1978, Fundamentals of Dermatology: A Study Guide, 1990; contbr. articles to profl. jours. Served to capt. M.C. USAF, 1955-57. Fellow N.Y. Acad. Medicine, ACP; mem. Am. Acad. Dermatology, Bklyn. Dermatol. Soc. (pres. 1970-72), N.Y. State Med. Soc., Kings County Med. Soc., AMA, N.Y. State Soc. Dermatology (pres. 1983-85), Phi Beta Kappa. Home: 6841 Treves Way Boynton Beach FL 33437-6485

GLICKMAN, MARLENE, non-profit organization administrator; b. Evansville, Ind., May 13, 1936; d. Morris Jack and Sarah (Krawll) Foreman; m. Marshall Levi Glickman, Jan. 9, 1956 (dec. 2002); children: Cynthia Anne, Joseph Leonard. Student, Ohio State U., 1954-56. Area dir. Am. Jewish Com., Buffalo, 1981-2000; v.p. adminstrn. and fin. Network of Religious Cmtys., 2000—05, co-pres., 2006—. Pres. Meals on Wheels of Buffalo and Erie County, 1981—83, N.E. Lakes Coun. and UAHC, Coun. Congl. Pres. Erie County, 1979—81; vice chair gen. campaign United Jewish Appeal, 1980, chair woman's divsn., 1979; pres. N.E. Lakes coun. Union Am. Hebrew Congregations, 1982—86; pres. Temple Beth Am, 1978—80, 2002—03, chair 50th anniversary, 2005; pres. Sisterhood Temple Beth Am, 1969—71, 1976—77; agy. allocations com. United Way, chair Towns and Villages divsn., 1981; pres. Human Rights Adv. Coun. Western N.Y., 1988—96; bd. dirs. YWCA, Buffalo and Erie County, 1990—96, Buffalo Fedn. Neighborhood Ctrs., Inc., 1994—98; exec. com., sec. Sheehan Meml. Hosp., Inc., 1994—98; pres., bd. dirs. Western N.Y. Martin Luther King Jr. Commn., 1991—97; active Western N.Y. Vision for Tomorrow 2000 C. of C./Buffalo Partnership. Recipient Abraham Pugash Cmty. Rels. award for establishing Kosher Meals on Wheels, Jewish Family Svc., Buffalo and Erie County, N.Y., 1975, NAACP Human Rels. award, 1997, Cmty. Rels. award Am. Jewish Com. Western N.Y., 2001; Marlene Glickman H.S. Human Rels. Award of Western N.Y. named in her honor for Am. Jewish Com., 2004; Am.-Pol Eagle Citizen of Yr., 1995. Mem. NAACP (life), Union Am. Hebrew Congregations (exec., bd. dirs. 1982-99, exec. com.), Commn. on Synagogue Music, Joint Cantorial Placement Commn., FRJ Admin. (budget and finance), New Congregations, Maintenance of Union Membership, Hadassah (life), Assn. Reform Zionists Am. (del. to Israel 1987), Brandeis Women's Com. (life), Nat. Coun. Jewish Women (life, Hannah G. Solomon award 1985), Assn. Jewish Comty. Rels. Workers, Jewish Communal Svc. Assn., Arza/World Union (bd. dirs. 1992-2000). Avocation: singing. Office: PMB 361 425 Carr 693 Dorado PR 00646 Home: 63 Hidden Creek Ct Buffalo NY 14221 Personal E-mail: mglickman5@cs.com.

GLICKMAN, MICHAEL RICHARD, social studies educator; b. NYC, Nov. 15, 1946; s. George Osiris Glickman and Hilda Ann Milmed; m. Irma S. Glickman, June 10, 1990; stepchildren: Scott D., Shari E. BA, Franklin Coll., Ind., 1969; MS, Coll. of S.I., 1997. Cert. tchr. social studies, N.Y. Paraprofl. N.Y.C. Bd. Edn., Bklyn., 1974—82, tchr. social studies, 1992—. Adj. prof. sociology Kings Borough Coll., Bklyn., 1998—; lectr. Housatonic C.C., Bridgeport, Conn., 2004—; tutor Williamsburg Settlement House, Bklyn., 1966-67, computer svcs. for children John Jay H.S., 1990-91. Head Young Dems., Dem. Party, Franklin Coll., Ind., 1968; vol. VISTA, 1969-70; tchr. Literacy Program John Jay H.S. Mem. United Fedn. of Tchrs., Am. Fedn. of Tchrs. Republican. Jewish. Avocations: reading, astronomy, computers, painting, music. Home: 22 Lincoln Pl Apt H North Brunswick NJ 08902 Office: Murray Bergtraum HS 411 Pearl St New York NY 10002 E-mail: glickmoid@optonline.net.

GLICKMAN, NORMAN JAY, economist, urban policy analyst; b. Bklyn., July 27, 1942; s. Harry and Beatrice (Frankel) G.; m. Elyse M. Pivnick, May 8, 1983; children: Katy Rose, Madeline Claire. BA, U. Pa., 1963, MA, 1967, PhD, 1969. Prof. urban and regional planning U. Pa., Phila., 1980-82; Hogg prof. urban policy U. Tex., Austin, 1983-89; State of N.J. prof. urban planning Rutgers U., New Brunswick, 1989, dir. Ctr. for Urban Policy Rsch. State of N.J., 1989—, Disting. Univ. prof., 2000—. Vis. scholar U.S. HUD, Washington, 1978-79; fellow Netherland Inst. Advanced Studies, Wassenaar, 1981-82; sr. rsch. scholar Internat. Inst. Applied Systems Analysis, Laxenburg, Austria, 1977; appointee N.J. Coun. on Job Opportunities, N.J., 1992—. Co-author: The New Competitors, 1989 (Top 10 Bus. Week 1989). Chmn. Econ. Devel. Commn., Austin, 1985-89. Recipient Lindback award U. Pa., 1976, named Disting. Fulbright Prof., Monterrey (Mex.) Inst. of Tech., 1985; fellow Japan Found., 1976. Mem. EEFMS (charter), Regional Sci. Assn. (v.p. 1988-89), Am. Econ. Assn. Office: Rutgers U Ctr Urban Pol Rsch 33 Livingston Ave Ste 400 New Brunswick NJ 08901-1982 Office Phone: 732-932-3133 570.

GLICKMAN, ROBERT JEFFREY, bank executive; b. Mpls., Feb. 10, 1947; s. Joseph Charles and Beverly (Willis) G.; m. Hardye Simons Moel (div. 1983); children: Kate, Adam; m. Caryn Chernick, June 26, 1988. BA,

Cornell U., 1969. Pres. River Forest Bancorp, Inc., Chgo., 1969—2004; CEO Corus Bankshares, Chgo., 2004—. Mem. Young Presidents Orgn. Jewish. Office: Corus Bancshares Inc 3959 N Lincoln Ave Chicago IL 60613-2431*

GLICKMAN, ROBERT MORRIS, health facility administrator, dean; b. Bklyn., June 23, 1939; s. David B. and Sally G.; m. Mary Holahan, June 20, 1961; children: Jonathan, Michael. BA magna cum laude, Amherst Coll., 1960; MD cum laude, Harvard U., 1964. Diplomate Am. Bd. Internal Medicine. Resident in medicine Harvard U. Med. Services, Boston City Hosp., 1965-66; research fellow in medicine Med. Sch., Harvard U., Boston, 1966-68; from instr. medicine to assoc. prof. Harvard U. Med. Sch., Boston, 1970-77; clin. and rsch. fellow in medicine Mass. Gen. Hosp., Boston, 1966-68, asst. in medicine, 1970-74, asst. physician, 1974-75; intern Harvard U. Med. Services, Boston City Hosp., 1964-65; chief divsn. gastroenterology, asst. physician Beth Israel Hosp., Boston, 1975-77, physician-in-chief, 1990—96; from assoc. prof. to prof. Coll. Physicians and Surgeons, Columbia U., NYC, 1977-82, Samuel Bard prof. medicine, chmn. dept. medicine, 1982-90, chief divsn. gastroenterology, 1977-84, chmn. gastrointestinal sect. abnormal biology, 1978-84; attending physician Presbyn. Hosp., NYC, 1981—90, dir. med. svc., 1982—90; Herrman L. Blumgart prof. medicine Harvard Med. Sch., Boston, 1990—98, chmn. exec. com. dept. medicine, 1996—98; physician-in-chief Beth Israel Deaconess Med. Ctr., 1996—98, sr. v.p. acad. and clin. strategies, 1996; dean NYU Sch. Medicine, NYC, 1998—2007; CEO NYU Hosps. Ctr., NYC, 1998—2007, prof. medicine and gastroenterology, 2007—. Mem. Nat. Digestive Diseases Adv. Bd., 1985—. Mem. editorial bd. Jour. Lipid Research, 1978-79, Jour. Clin. Investigation, 1979-84, Am. Jour. Medicine, 1981—; contbr. articles to med. jours. Maj. M.C. U.S. Army, 1968-70. Fellow ACP; mem. AMA (pres. 1997-98), Am. Fedn. Clin. Rsch. (councillor Eastern sect. 1975-79, sec.-treas. 1976-79), Am. Gastroent. Assn. (v.p. 1985-87, pres. elect 1987, pres. 1988), Nat. Acad. Medicine, Inst. Medicine NAS, Harvey Soc., Interurban Clin. Club, Assn. Am. Physicians (v.p. 1997, pres.), Nat. Found. Ileitis and Colitis (mem. sci. adv. bd. 1978), Am. Soc. Clin. Investigation (councillor 1981-84, pres. elect 1983, pres. 1984-85), Assn. Profs. Medicine (councillor 1989-94, pres. 1992-93), Am. Bd. Internal Medicine (sub-splty. bd. on gastroenterology 1988-93), Harvard Soc., Phi Beta Kappa, Sigma Xi, Alpha Omega Alpha. Office: NYU Sch Med 550 First Ave New York NY 10016 Business E-Mail: glickr04@med.nyu.edu.

GLICKMAN, SALLIE A., professional society administrator; BA, Temple U., 1988, EdM, 1991. With Crime Prevention Assn., Phila., 1989—94; sr. assoc. DTI Assocs., Arlington, Va., 1995—96; dir. membership svcs. Nat. Assn. Pvt. Industry Couns. (name changed to Nat. Assn. Workforce Bds.), Washington, 1996—98; v.p. instl. advancement Pvt. Industry Coun. Phila., 1998—99; founding exec. dir. & CEO Phila. Workforce Investment Bd., Inc., 1999—. Trustee US Conf. Mayors Workforce Devel. Coun., 2002—, pres., 2006—; co-founder, bd. mem. Life Sci. Career Alliance, 2003—; mem. Nat. Re-Entry Policy Coun., 2003—. Mem. econ. devel. cabinet City of Phila.; mem. Jewish Ednl. & Vocat. Svc. Coun., 2004—; co-founder, co-chair Graduate! Phila., 2005—; vol. United Way S.E. Pa., 2002—. Recipient 40 Under 40 award, Phila. Bus. Jour., 2006. Office: Philadelphia Workforce Investment Bd Ste 1500 1601 Market St Philadelphia PA 19103 Office Phone: 215-717-2010. Office Fax: 215-717-2020. E-mail: sglickman@pwib.org.

GLICKMAN, STEPHEN H., judge; b. Bklyn. AB, Cornell U., 1969; JD, Yale U., 1973. Former law clerk Supreme Ct. of Conn.; ptnr. Zuckerman Spaeder LLP, 1980-99, mng. ptnr., 1991—98; assoc. judge DC Ct. Appeals, 1999—. Seminar instructor Yale U.; atty. Federal Trade Commn., Bureau of Competition, DC Public Defender Svc. Office: DC Ct Appeals 500 Indiana Ave NW 6th Fl Washington DC 20001-2131

GLICKSMAN, ARVIN S(IGMUND), radiation oncologist; b. Bklyn., Mar. 14, 1924; s. Charles and Myrtle (Fetner) G.; m. Bernice R. Grobstein, Jan. 30, 1956; children: Jonathan, Jane Ellen, Merrylee, Caroline, Jeanette. MB, MD, Chgo. Med. Sch., 1949. Intern Kings County Hosp., Bklyn., 1948-50; AEC postdoctoral research fellow Duke U., 1950-51; postgrad. rsch. fellow Brookhaven Nat. Labs., Upton, NY, 1951-52; resident in medicine Meml. Hosp., NYC, 1952-54, clin. asst. physician in medicine, 1955-64, asst. attending radiation therapist, 1964-65; rsch. fellow Sloan-Kettering Inst., NYC, 1954-60, assoc., 1960-65; mem. med. rsch. inst. Michael Reese Hosp., Chgo., 1964-65, assoc. chmn. dept. radiation therapy, 1965-67; dep. dir. radiotherapy Mount Sinai Hosp., NYC, 1967-73; prof. radiotherapy Mount Sinai Sch. Medicine, 1971-73; dir. radiation oncology R.I. Hosp., Providence, 1973-84, chmn. dept. radiol. medicine and biol. rsch., 1984-89; prof. med. scis., founding chair dept. radiation medicine Brown U., 1973-95, prof. emeritus, 1995—; chmn. dept. radiation oncology Roger Williams Med. Ctr., 1989-95; practice medicine specializing in radiation oncology. Hon. med. cons. NIH, Royal Marsden Hosp.; mem. cancer clinic, investigation rev. com. Nat. Cancer Inst., 1975-79, mem. radiation oncology com., 1976-86, mem. cancer intervention study sect., 1991-94. Editor: (with others) Computers in Radiotherapy, 1970, 73; contbr.: numerous articles to profl. jours. Mem. exec. com. Am. Cancer Soc., R.I., 1987-96, pres., 1987-89, nat. bd. dirs., 1980-93; chmn. radiotherapy com. Cancer and Leukemia Group B.; dir. Quality Assurance Rev. Ctr., R.I. Cancer Control Bd., 1980-98, chmn. task force info. sys., mem. exec. com.; co-chmn. exec. com. ASSIST Program Nat. Cancer Inst./Am. Cancer Soc., 1991-98; exec. dir. R.I. Cancer Coun., 1999—. Dillon fellow Royal Marsden Hosp., Surrey, Eng., 1961-62; Rsch. Career Devel. awardee NIH, 1962-64; Fulbright sr. scholar, 1986-87; recipient St. George medal Am. Cancer Soc., 1991, Disting. Svc. award Am. Cancer Soc., 2003, Excellence in Cancer Awareness award Congl. Families Action for Cancer, 2006. Fellow Am. Coll. Radiology; mem. New England Soc. Radiation Oncologists (pres. 1975-76), N.Y. Roentgen Ray Soc. (chmn. sect. therapeutic radiology 1972-73), Am. Soc. Clin. Oncology, Am. Assn. Cancer Edn., Am. Assn. Cancer Rsch., Am. Radium Soc., Am. Soc. Therapeutic Radiologists, Brit. Inst. Radiology. Home: 15 Brown Ter Uxbridge MA 01569 Office: RI Cancer Coun Inc 249 Roosevelt Ave Ste 201 Pawtucket RI 02860-2134 Office Phone: 401-728-4800. Office Fax: 401-728-4816. Business E-Mail: glicksman@ricancercouncil.org.

GLICKSMAN, MARTIN EDEN, materials engineering educator; b. NYC, Apr. 4, 1937; s. Nathan Henry and Ruth Elaine (Rosensaft) G.; m. Lucinda Jeanette Mulder, May 7, 1967 B in Metall. Engring., Rensselaer Poly. Inst., 1957, PhD, 1961. Metall. engr. Procter & Gamble Co., Cin., 1957-58; research metallurgist Naval Research Lab., Washington, 1961-75, assoc. supt. materials sci. divsn., 1974-75; chmn. materials engr. dept. Rensselaer Poly. Inst., Troy, N.Y., 1975-86, prof., 1986—; prof. materials engring., chmn. dept. materials engring. Rensselaer Poly. Inst., Troy, N.Y., 1975-86, John Tod Horton prof. materials engring., 1986—. Van Horn lectr. Case Western Res. U., 1984; cons. in field. Author: Diffusion in Solids, 2000; contbr. in articles to profl. jours. Recipient Pure Sci. Rsch. award Rsch. Soc. of Am., 1968, Arthur Flemming award Washington Jr. C. of C., Space Processing medal AIAA, 1998; Minerals Metals and Materials Soc. fellow AIME, 1994. Fellow AAAS, ASM (M.E. Grossman award 1971), AIAA; mem. AIME (Bruce Chalmers award 1992), Am. Soc. Metals Internat. (Gold medal 2003), Univ. Space Rsch. Assn. (chmn. bd. trustees 1986, dir. microgravity divsn. 1986—), Nat. Acad. Engring. (Alexander von Humboldt Rsch. prize, 2001). Office: Rensselaer Poly Inst CII-9111 Troy NY 12180-3590 Home Phone: 518-436-7878. Business E-Mail: glickm@rpi.edu.

GLICKSMAN, MAURICE, engineering educator, retired dean, provost; b. Toronto, Oct. 16, 1928; came to U.S., 1949, naturalized, 1961; s. Robert Maxwell and Fanny Bella (Lachowitz) G.; m. Yetta Leich, Dec. 18, 1949; children: Howard David, Roslynn Sue, Marcie Ann. Student, Queen's U., 1946—49; MSc, U. Chgo., 1952, PhD, 1954; ScD (hon.), Brown U., 1997. Rsch. assoc. Inst. Nuc. Studies, U. Chgo., 1954; mem. tech. staff RCA Labs., Princeton, NJ, 1954-61, head Plasma Physics Group, 1961-63; dir. rsch. RCA Rsch. Labs., Tokyo, 1963-67; head Gen. Rsch. Group, Princeton, 1967-69; Univ. prof., prof. engring. Brown U., 1969-94, dean Grad. Sch., 1974-76, dean faculty and acad. affairs, 1976-78, provost, dean faculty, 1978-86, provost, 1986-90, prof. physics, 1990-94, prof. engring. rsch., 1994—2002, provost emeritus, 1990—, univ. prof. emeritus, 1994—, prof. engring. and physics emeritus, 1994—. Cons. RCA Corp., 1969-77; vis. scientist MIT, 1983-84; chmn. com. materials for radiation detection devices NAS, 1971-74; chmn. vis. com. U. Pa., 1977-83, Vanderbilt U., 1977-81; mem. vis. com. Emory U., 1981, U. Miami, 1990, Northwestern U., 1991, U. N.C., Greensboro, 1992; bd. dirs. Ctr. Rsch. Librs., 1981-87, chmn., 1983-84; mem. bd. overseers Fermilab, 1983-99, chmn., 1989-94; trustee OCLC, Dublin, Ohio, 1993-2004, vice chmn., 2002-04; dir. Manisses Comm. Group, Providence, 1993-2004. dir. Lifespan Corp., Providence, 1994-2000, NELINET, Southbridge, Mass., 2005-. Contbr. rsch. articles to profl. jours.; patentee frequency multipliers, hall-effect devices, semiconductor devices and circuits. Pres. Jewish Ctr., Princeton, 1962-63; v.p. cultural and ednl. affairs Jewish Cmty. Ctr., Tokyo, 1965-67; mem. Bur. Jewish Edn., R.I., 1974—, v.p., 1975-80; v.p. Jewish Fedn. R.I., 1980-83; trustee Miriam Hosp., 1979-85, 87-2003, chmn., 1993-97; v.p. Jewish Srs. Agy. R.I., 1998-2000, pres., 2000-03; chmn. World Affairs Coun. R.I., 1999—; pres. Tamarisk, Inc., 2003-05. Recipient Outstanding Achievement award RCA, 1956, 62. Fellow IEEE, Am. Phys. Soc.; mem. AAAS, Am. Soc. Engring. Edn., N.Y. Acad. Scis., Phi Beta Kappa (pres. R.I. Alpha chpt. 1993-96), Sigma Xi. Home: 10 Westwood Ln Barrington RI 02806-2614 Office: Brown U Box D 79 Waterman St Providence RI 02912-9079 Personal E-mail: maurice_glicksman@brown.edu.

GLICKSTEIN, STEVEN, lawyer; b. Bklyn., Jan. 3, 1952; s. Alexander and Esther (Camhi) G. BA, Lehigh U., 1973; JD, Columbia U., 1976. Assoc. Kaye Scholer, LLP, NYC, 1976-84, ptnr., 1985—, co-chair Product Liability Dept. Mem. ABA, DC Bar Assn., Fla. Bar Assn., NY State Bar Assn. Home: 144 Walnut St Englewood NJ 07631 Office: Kaye Scholer LLP 425 Park Ave New York NY 10022-3506

GLICK-WEIL, KATHY, library director; b. Milw., Jan. 11, 1950; d. Irving Robert and Janice Esther (Rosner) Glick; m. Gordon Weil, June 20, 1971; children: Jeffrey, Aaron. BA, Tulane U., 1971; MLS, U. Calif., Berkeley, 1972. Children's libr. Thayer Pub. Libr., Braintree, Mass., 1972-73; reference libr. Stoughton (Mass.) Pub. Libr., 1973-77; br. libr. Brockton (Mass.) Pub. Libr., 1977-78; asst. dir. Medford (Mass.) Pub. Libr., 1978-84; dir. Lincoln (Mass.) Pub. Libr., 1984-93, Newton (Mass.) Free Libr., 1993—. Trustee Beaver Country Day Sch.; mem. assocs. bd. dirs. Tulane U. Mem. ALA, Mass. Libr. Assn. (pres. 2006-07). Home: 46 Acacia Ave Chestnut Hill MA 02467-1351 Office: Newton Free Library 330 Homer St Newton MA 02459-1429 Office Phone: 617-796-1400. Business E-Mail: kglickweil@mlnlib.net.

GLIDDEN, JOHN REDMOND, lawyer; b. Sanford, Maine, July 24, 1936; s. Kenneth Eugene and Kathryn (Gilpatrick) G.; m. Jacqueline R. Scales, Aug. 6, 1964; children— Ian, Claire, Jason Student, U. Wis., 1954-55; BS, Coe Coll., 1958; LL.B., U. Iowa, 1961. Bar: Iowa 1961, Ill. 1965. Assoc. firm Williams & Hartzell, Carthage, Ill., 1965-67; ptnr. Hartzell, Glidden, Tucker & Hartzell and predecessor firms, Carthage, 1969—. City atty. City of Carthage, 1969—. Capt., judge advocate USAF, 1961-65. Mem. ABA, VFW, Ill. Bar Assn., Iowa Bar Assn., Hancock County Bar Assn., Am. Trial Lawyers Assn., Ill. Trial Lawyers Assn. (governing bd. 1973-80), Am. Legion, Carthage Golf Club (bd. dirs. 1967—2005), Phi Delta Phi, Sigma Nu. Home: PO Box 70 Carthage IL 62321-3435 Home Phone: 217-357-2334; Office Phone: 217-357-3121. Personal E-mail: jrglaw@frontiernet.net.

GLIDDEN, ROBERT BURR, academic administrator, consultant, music educator; b. Rippey, Iowa, Nov. 29, 1936; s. Burr Harold and Lora Elsie (Groves) Glidden; m. Rene Colete Siefken, Apr. 26, 1964; children: Melissa, Michele, Briana. BA, U. Iowa, 1958, MA, 1960, PhD, 1966; D of higher edn. adminstrn. (hon.), Bowling Green State U., 2004. Tchr. instrumental music Morrison Community High Sch., Ill., 1958-63, Univ. Schs., Iowa City, 1963-66; asst. prof. music Wright State U., Dayton, Ohio, 1966-67, Ind. U., Bloomington, 1967-69; assoc. prof. music U. Okla., Norman, dir. grad. studies in music, 1969—72; exec. dir. Nat. Assn. Schs. Music, 1972—75, treas., 1977-82, v.p., 1982-85, pres., 1985-88; dean Coll. Musical Arts, Bowling Green State U., Ohio, 1975-79; dean Sch. Music Fla. State U., Tallahassee, 1979-91, provost, v.p. for acad. affairs, 1991-94; pres. Ohio U., Athens, 1994—2004, pres. emeritus, 2004—. Cons., higher edn., condr.; chmn. Coun. Specialized Accrediting Agys., 1976—77; chair Am. Coun. Edn. Commn. Leadership and Instnl. Effectiveness, 1998—2000; chair coun. pres. Mid-Am. Conf., 1997—99. Bd. dirs. Coun. on Postsecondary Accreditation, 1977—84, exec. com., 1979—84, chmn., 1981—83; bd. dirs. Arts, Edn. and Ams., Inc., 1978—81; chmn. advanced placement music com. Coll. Bd., 1977—79; mem. Coun. on Arts Task Force on Edn. Tng. and Devel. Profl. Artists and Art Educators, 1977—78; adv. coun. on accreditation Nat. League for Nursing, 1977—81; edn. adv. com. Nat. Endowment for Arts, 1987, adv. com. for arts in edn., 1989—90; bd. dirs. Coun. for Higher Edn. Accreditation, 1996—2004, chmn., 1996—98. Recipient Disting. Alumni award, U. Iowa, 1997. Mem.: Ohio Inter-Univ. Coun. (chair 2001—02), Ohio Aerospace Inst. (exec. com. 1995—2004, chair 1998—2000), Ohio Supercomputer Ctr. (governing bd. 1996—2004), Ohio Sci. and Tech. Coun. (biotech. com. 1996—2004), So. Assn. Colls. and Schs. (commn. on coll. 1993—94), Assn. Specialized and Profl. Accreditors (bd. dirs. 1994—96), Coll. Music Soc. (chmn. govt. rels. com. 1976—78, task force on edn. coll. music tchrs. 1987), Mortar Bd., Pi Kappa Lambda (nat. v.p. 1979—81, pres. 1981—85), Omicron Delta Kappa, Phi Kappa Phi, Phi Beta Kappa. Episcopalian. Home: PO Box 88 140 Gibraltar Forge Dr Rockbridge Baths VA 24473 Office Phone: 540-348-6360. Business E-Mail: gliddenr@ohio.edu.

GLIEBERMAN, HERBERT ALLEN, lawyer; b. Chgo., Dec. 6, 1930; s. Elmer and Jean (Gerber) G.; m. Evelyn Eraci; children— Ronald, Gale, Joel Student, U. Ill., 1947, Roosevelt U., 1948-50; JD, Chgo. Kent Coll. Law, 1953. Bar: Ill. 1954, D.C. 1987. Pvt. practice, Chgo., 1954—; lectr. Chgo. Kent. Coll. Law, Ill. Inst. Continuing Legal Edn. Lectr. in field numerous instns. including ABA, ATLA, Am. Acad Matrimonial Lawyers, Inst. Law Inst., others. Author: Some Syndromes of Love, 1965, Know Your Legal Rights, 1974, Confessions of A Divorce Lawyer, 1975, Closed Marriage, 1978, Four Weekends to an Ideal Marriage, 1981; former host 2 radio shows for NBC Sta. WMAQ: Ask the Lawyer, Law and Controversy; contbr. articles to profl. jours. Former trustee Chgo. Kent. Coll. Law; former bd. dirs. Chgo. Coun. on Alcoholism. Mem. Am. Acad. Matrimonial Lawyers (cert. of appreciation 1967), Decologue Soc. Lawyers (cert. of appreciation 1965, 66, 68), Assn. Trial Lawyers Am. (cert. of appreciation 1973), Ill. Trial Lawyers Assn. (cert. of appreciation 1974), ABA, Ill. State Bar Assn., Chgo. Bar Assn., N.C. Bar Assn., Idaho Bar Assn., Internat. Law Inst., Wash., D.C. Jewish (bd. dirs., pres. Temple) Office: 19 S La Salle St Chicago IL 60603-1401 Office Phone: 312-236-2879. Office Fax: 312-236-3417. Personal E-mail: hglieber@aol.com.

GLIEDMAN, MICHAEL SETH, sports association executive; s. Monroe M. Gliedman; m. Jennifer Bersch; children: Daniel, Jacob. BA in Computer Sci., Brandeis U.; MBA in Mktg., Columbia Bus. Sch. Prin. Booz Allen & Hamilton; sr. v.p. application devel. infoworks Viacom; v.p. info. tech. to sr. v.p., chief info. officer, head info. tech. NBA, NYC, 1999—. Office: NBA Olympic Tower 645 5th Ave Fl 10 New York NY 10022-5986 E-mail: mgliedman@nba.com.*

GLIKLICH, JERRY, physician, educator; b. Jelenia Góra, Poland, May 6, 1948; came to U.S., 1958; s. Henry and Henia (Gotajner) G.; m. Jane Salmon, Sept. 12, 1976; children: David, Benjamin. AB, Columbia U., 1969, MD, 1975. Intern N.Y. Hosp., NYC, 1975-76, resident, 1977-78; fellow in cardiology Presbyn. Hosp., NYC, 1978-81, attending physician, 1981—; asst. prof. medicine Columbia U., NYC, 1981-91; assoc. clin. prof. Presbyn. Hosp., NYC, 1991-97, clin. prof., 1997—2001, David A. Gardner prof. medicine, 2001—. Cons. in field. Contbr. articles to profl. jours. Mem. ACP, Am. Coll. Cardiology, Phi Beta Kappa. Office: NY Presbyn Hosp 161 Fort Washington Ave New York NY 10032-3713

GLIMCHER, ARNOLD B., art gallery executive; b. Duluth, Minn., Mar. 12, 1938; s. Paul and Eva (Fishman) G.; m. Mildred Louise Cooper, Dec. 20, 1959; children: Paul William, Marc Cooper. BA, Mass. Coll. Art., 1969; postgrad., NYU Sch. Psychology, Boston U. Founder, owner Pace Gallery, Boston, 1961-63; founder, chmn. Pace Wildenstein , NYC, 1963—; founder Pace Editions, 1968—. Author: Louise Nevelson, 1972, paperback edit., 1976; (with Paul Vitz) Modern Art and Modern Science: The Parallel Analysis of Vision; contbr. articles to art jours.; prodr.: (films) Gorillas in the Mist, The Good Mother; prodr., dir.: (film) The Mambo Kings, Just Cause; editor, cataloger, text writer for various art vols. selector, installer various mus. exhibits and retrospectives. Named Chevalier de la Légion d'honneur. Fellow Israel Mus. (chmn. devel. com. 1976-77); mem. Am. Acad. Arts and Letters, Officier des Arts and Lettres, Art Dealers Assn. Am. (bd. dirs.). Office: Pace Wildenstein 32 E 57th St New York NY 10022-2513 Office Phone: 212-421-3292.

GLIMCHER, MELVIN JACOB, orthopedic surgeon; b. Brookline, Mass., June 2, 1925; s. Aaron and Clara (Fink) Glimcher; m. Karin Wetmore, Mar. 8, 2000; children from previous marriage: Susan Deborah, Laurie Hollis, Nancy Blair. Student, Duke U., 1943-44; BS in Mech. Engring. with highest distinction; BS in Physics with highest distinction, Purdue U., 1946; MD magna cum laude, Harvard, 1950; postgrad., Mass. Inst. Tech., 1956-59; PhD in Engring. (hon.), Purdue U., 2004. Intern surgery Strong Meml. Hosp., Rochester, NY, 1950-51; 3d asst. resident surgery Mass. Gen. Hosp., Boston, 1951-52, 2d asst. resident, 1952-53, asst. resident orthopedic surgery, 1954-55, chief resident, 1956, chief orthopedic service, 1965-71, chmn. dept. orthopedic surgery, 1968-71; asst. resident orthopedic surgery Children's Med. Center, Boston, 1953-54, jr. resident, 1955-56; mem. faculty Harvard Med. Sch., 1956—, Edith M. Ashley prof. orphopedic surgery, 1965-71, Harriet M. Peabody prof., 1971—; also chmn. dept.; orthopedic surgeon-in-chief Children's Hosp. Med. Center, Boston, 1971-81, dir. Lab. for Study of Skeletal Disorders and Rehab., 1980—. Trustee Forsyth Dental Infirmary, New England Sinai Hosp. With USMCR, World War II. Recipient Soma Weiss award Harvard Med. Sch., 1950, Borden Research award, 1950; Kappa Delta award, 1959; Internat. Assn. Dental Research award, 1964; Ralph Pemberton award Am. Rheumatism Soc., 1969; Bristol-Meyers/Zimmer inst. grant for excellence; Disting. Achievement in Orthopaedic Research award Orthopaedic Research Edn. Found.; William Neuman award Am. Soc. Bone and Mineral Rsch., 1996; Physician Achievement award Arthritis Found., 1996. Fellow Am. Acad. Arts and Scis., Am. Acad. Orthopaedic Surgeons (Silver anniversary Kappa Delta prize 1974, Alfred Shands award jointly awarded with Orthop. Rsch. Soc 1997), Am. Orthopedic Assn.; mem. Orthopedic Research Soc. (past pres.), Assn. Bone and Joint Surgeons (Nicholas Andry award 1978), Internat. Soc. for Study Lumbar Spine (Volvo award 1983), Societe Internationale de Chirurgie Orthopedique et de Traumatologie. Office: 300 Longwood Ave Boston MA 02115-5724

GLIMM, JAMES GILBERT, mathematician, educator; b. Peoria, Ill., Mar. 24, 1934; s. William Frederick and Barbara Gilbert (Hooper) G.; m. Adele Strauss, June 30, 1957; 1 dau., Alison. AB in engring. (hon.), Columbia U., 1956, AM (hon.) in math., 1956, PhD (hon.) in math., 1959. From asst. prof. to prof. math. MIT, 1960-69; prof. Courant Inst., NYU, 1969-74; prof. math. Rockefeller U., NYC, 1974-82; prof. Courant Inst., NYU, NYC, 1982-89; disting. prof., chair dept. applied math. and statis. SUNY, Stony Brook, 1989—; dir. Ctr. for Data Intensive Computing Brookhaven Nat. Labs., 1999—2004. Co-author: Quantum Physics, 1981; Collected Papers, Vols. I and II, 1985; mem. editorial bds. profl. jours.; contbr. articles to sci. publs. Guggenheim fellow, 1963, 65; recipient Dannie Heineman prize in math. physics, 1980, Nat. Medal Sci. award, 2002. Mem. NAS, Internat. Assn. Math. Physicists, Am. Phys. Soc., Am. Math. Soc. (pres. elect 2006, Leroy P. Steele prize 1992), Soc. Indsl. and Applied Math., Math. Assn. Am., Am. Acad. Arts and Scis., Soc. Petroleum Engrs., NY Acad. Scis. (award in phys. and math. scis. 1979) Office: Stony Brook U Dept Applied Math and Stats Math Bldg Rm P-138A Stony Brook NY 11794-3600 Office Phone: 631-632-8355. Business E-Mail: glimm@ams.sunysb.edu.

GLINDEMAN, HENRY PETER, JR., real estate developer; b. Coeur d'Alene, Idaho, Sept. 26, 1924; s. Henry Peter and Laura Mae (Buchanan) Glindeman; children: Pamela, Henry Peter III, John. BS, U.S. Naval Acad., 1945; postgrad., U.S. Naval War Coll., 1959-60. Commd. ensign U.S. Navy, 1945, advanced through grades to rear adm., 1973; exec. officer, comdg. officer Fighter Squadron 154, 1962-63; comdr. Attack Carrier Air Wing 15 Attack Carrier Air Wing 15, 1964-65; tng. officer attack carrier air wing, staff, comdr. U.S. Naval Air Forces, U.S. Pacific Fleet, 1965-66; readiness officer, staff comdr. U.S. First Fleet, 1966-68; comdg. officer U.S.S. Passumpsic, 1968-69; head Attack Carrier Weapons Requirements br. Office Chief Naval Ops., 1970-71; comdg. officer U.S.S. Ranger, 1971-73; chief Fleet Coordinating Group Nakhon Phanom, Thailand, 1973-74; dir. Office Program Appraisal, Office Sec. Navy, 1974-75; comdr. Carrier Group 7, 1975-76; comdr. Carrier Group 3, 1976; comdr. Carrier Group 5, Carrier Strike Force, 7th Fleet, 1976-77; comdr. Naval Safety Center, 1977-78; pres. Mr. Quick Lube Inc., Clearwater, Fla., 1978-81; v.p. Fla. Light and Save Inc., 1981-83; real estate developer, 1983-85; pres. GBS Devel. Inc., Redwood City, Calif., 1985-87; chmn., CEO Stormy Weather Guard, Inc., Clearwater, Fla., 1988-94. Bd. dirs., sec.-treas. Guardian Marine Corp., 1990—91; pres. Fiber Am. Inc., Clearwater, 1991—96. V.p. Edgar Allan Poe Jr. HS PTA, Annandale, Va., 1960—61, Annandale Am. Little League, 1961—62; sec. exec. com. Troop 674 Boy Scouts Am., Annandale, 1961—62; chmn. bd. dirs. USS Ranger Mus. Found., 2001—05. Decorated Legion of Merit with 4 gold stars, DFC, Air medal with gold star. Mem.: Tailhook Assn., Mil. Officer Assn. Am., Assn. Naval Aviation, Mil. Order World Wars, U.S. Naval Acad. Alumni Assn., Navy League, Breakfast Club (San Francisco), Golden Gate Club. Episcopalian. Personal E-mail: radmu@earthlink.net.

GLINES, CARROLL VANE, JR., magazine editor; b. Balt., Dec. 2, 1920; s. Carroll Vane and Elizabeth Marion (Cross) G.; m. Mary Ellen Edwards, Oct. 1, 1943; children: Karen Ann, David Edwards, Valerie Jean Student, Drexel Inst. Tech., 1938-40, Canal Zone Jr. Coll., 1946-48, U. Munich, 1948; BBA, U. Okla., 1952, MBA, 1954; MA, Am. U., 1969. Commd. 2d lt. USAF, 1942, advanced through grades to col., 1965; military service, 1941-68; mgr. publs. Nat. Bus. Aircraft Assn., Washington, 1968; assoc. editor Armed Forces Mgmt. mag., Washington, 1969-70; editor Air Cargo mag., Washington, 1970-71, Air Line Pilot mag., Washington, 1971-85, cons. editor, 1985-86, contbg. editor, 1989—; sr. editor Aviation Space mag., 1982-85; editor Profl. Pilot Mag., Alexandria, Va., 1986-88, sr. contbg. editor, 1988—, Aviation History mag. (formerly Aviation Heritage mag.), Leesburg, Va., 1990—. Mgr. publs. Air Line

Pilots Assn., 1971-85, dir. comms., 1983-85; lectr. U. Dayton, U. Alaska, Am. U Author 36 books; contbr. articles to mags.; gen. editor MacMillan, Air Force Acad. series, 1970-74; editl. cons. Van Nostrand Reinhold, 1980-85; contbg. editor Nation's Bus., 1981-86; mem. adv. bd. Hist. of Aviation Collection, U. Tex., Dallas, 1981-90, 95—, Alaska Aviation Heritage Mus., Anchorage, 1993-99; curator Doolittle Libr., U. Tex., Dallas, 1995— Asst. to v.p. for spl. projects Evergreen Internat. Aviation, 1988-93; active Frontiers of Flight Mus., Dallas Recipient numerous awards from press assns. Freedoms Found., Pres. award Air Force Pub. Affairs Alumni Assn., 2003; inducted into Interboro Hall of Fame, 2003, Glen-Nor Wall of Fame, 2005. Mem. Aviation-Space Writers Assn. (Lauren D. Lyman award), Air Force Assn., Air Force Hist. Found., Soc. Aerospace Communicators, Quiet Birdmen, Soc. Profl. Journalists, Order of Daedalians Home: 1531 San Rafael Dr Dallas TX 75218-4444 Personal E-mail: ceevee1531@sbcglobal.net.

GLINSEK, GERALD JOHN, lawyer; b. Akron, Ohio, Jan. 16, 1939; s. Rudolph Paul and Angela Louise (Stanger) G.; m. Karen Rosemary Mehen, Oct. 17, 1968 (div. Aug. 1990); children: Kelli, Daniel; m. Maureen Louise Nuosce, May 7, 1994 (dec. Aug. 1998); 1 child from previous marriage, Rebecca Ann; m. Debra K. Gable, Oct. 22, 2002. BA, U. Akron, 1963, JD, 1967. Bar: Ohio 1967, U.S. Dist. Ct. (no. dist.) Ohio 1969, U.S. Ct. Appeals (6th cir. 1986), U.S. Supreme Ct. 1986. Asst. pros. atty. Summit County Prosecutors Office, Akron, 1967-71; pvt. practice Akron, 1971—. With U.S. Army, 1957. Mem. ABA, Ohio Bar Assn., Akron Bar Assn. (treas. 1981, trustee 2005—), Akron Coun. on World Affairs (trustee 2005—), Summit County Legal Aid Soc. (pres. 1978-82), Phi Kappa Tau (advisor 1982-2006). Democrat. Roman Catholic. Avocations: travel, skiing. Home: 1861 Wiltshire Rd Akron OH 44313-6101 Office: 88 S Portage Path Akron OH 44303-1023 Home Phone: 330-864-4901; Office Phone: 330-867-6600. Personal E-mail: glinseklaw@sbcglobal.net.

GLISMANN, CLEMENTINE, retired elementary school educator; b. Oakland, Nebr., Aug. 4, 1917; d. Louis Martin Larson, Edvinna Josephine Young; m. Leonard William Glismann, Feb. 24, 1940 (dec. Feb. 1997). BA, Midland Luth. Coll., Fremont, Nebr., 1939; postgrad., U. Nebr., 1942—43, Weber Coll., Ogden, Utah, 1945—47, U. Utah, 1963—78. Tchr. 1st grade Bd. Edn., Norfolk, Nebr., 1939—40, secondary tchr. Madrid, Nebr., 1941—42, 3d grade tchr. Ogden, Utah, 1945—56, 4th grade tchr., 1957—63, Salt Lake City, 1964—79; ret., 1979. Traveling dealer Lenswood, 1977—91. Author, prodr. (TV program) Wheels, KSL-TV Salt Lake City, Utah, 1951, Paper, 1952, Rubber, 1953, Clothes, 1954, Historical Masquerade (Great Americans), 1955, Mother Earth's Rock Family, Ogden City Schs. TV, 1962—63, There's More to Say to Your Story. State chmn. Luth. Ch. Women, Utah, 1963. Mem.: Golden Spike Gem and Mineral Soc., Delta Kappa Gamma. Republican. Lutheran. Achievements include having a 50-year collection of fossils, petrified wood, minerals and butterflies on permanent display at Midland Lutheran College in Fremont, Nebraska. Avocations: faceting gemstones, poetry. Office Phone: 801-359-1508.

GLOCER, THOMAS HENRY, publishing executive; b. NYC, Oct. 8, 1959; s. Walter W. and Ursula (Goodman) G.; m. Maarit Hanelle Leso, Aug. 5, 1988. BA, Columbia Coll., 1981; JD, Yale U., 1984. Atty. Davis, Polk & Warswell, NYC, 1985-93; corp. counsel Reuters Am. Inc., NYC, 1993-94; exec. v.p., gen. counsel Reuters Am. Holdings Inc., NYC, 1995-98; CEO Reuters L. Am., 1996—98; pres. Reuters Am., NYC, 1998—2001; CEO Reuters Info., 2000—01, Reuters Group PLC, 2001—. Dir. TVT Records, N.Y.C., 1985-93. Author compter software. Mem. Coney Island Assn. (founder, ptnr.); bd. dirs., Reuters, 2000-. Avocations: windsurfing, skiing, running. Office: Reuters Group PLC, Corporate Headquarters 85 Fleet Street London EC4P 4AJ England*

GLOCK, CHARLES YOUNG, sociologist, writer; b. NYC, Oct. 17, 1919; s. Charles and Philippine (Young) G.; m. Margaret Schleef, Sept. 12, 1950; children: Susan Young, James William. BS, N.Y. U., 1940; MBA, Boston U., 1941; PhD, Columbia U., 1952. Research asst. Bur. Applied Social Research, Columbia U., 1946-51, dir., 1951-58, lectr., then prof. sociology, 1956-58; prof. sociology U. Calif. at Berkeley, 1958-79, prof. emeritus, 1979—, chmn., 1967-68, 69-71; dir. Survey Research Center, 1958-67; adj. prof. Grad. Theol. Union, 1971-79; Luther Weigle vis. lectr. Yale U., 1968. Co-author: American Piety, 1968, Wayward Shepherds, 1971, Anti-Semitism in America, 1979, The Anatomy of Racial Attitudes, 1983; author (sr.): Religion and Society in Tension, 1965, Christian Beliefs and Anti-Semitism, 1966, To Comfort and To Challenge, 1967, Adolescent Prejudice, 1968, The Apathetic Majority, 1975; contbg. editor: Rev. Religious Rsch. Sociol. Analysis; editor: Survey Research in the Social Sciences, 1967, Prejudice U.S.A., 1969, Beyond the Classics, 1973, Religion in Sociological Perspective, 1973, The New Religious Consciousness, 1975, Unison-Newsletter of One Voice, 1990—96; contbr. numerous articles on social scis. Active parish edn. Luth. Ch. Am., 1970-72; mem. mgmt. com. Office Rsch. and Planning, 1973-80; bd. dirs. Pacific Luth. Theol. Sem., 1962-74, 80-86, Inst. Rsch. in Social Behavior, 1962-90, Interplayers, 1990-92, Sandpoint Christian Connection, 1995-97; pres. Cornerhouse Fund, 1982-92, One Voice, 1994-95, bd. dirs., 1995-97; mem. adv. com. Office Rsch. and Evaluation Evang. Luth. Ch. Am., 1988-94; mem. history com. Soc. Study of Religion, 1993-94; v.p. Sandpoint chpt. Idaho Writers' League, 2003—. Capt. USAAF, 1942-46. Decorated Bronze Star, Legion of Merit; recipient Roots of Freedom award Pacific bd. Anti-Defamation League, 1977, Garman-Hidy award for Disting. Contbn. to Life of Luth. Ch. in the West, 1999; Berkeley citation U. Calif., Berkeley, 1979; Rockefeller fellow, 1941-42; fellow Center Advanced Study Behavioral Scis., 1957-58; fellow Soc. for Religion in Higher Edn., 1968-69 Fellow Soc. Sci. Study Religion (Western rep., pres. 1968-69); mem. Am. Assn. Pub. Opinion Research (v.p., pres. 1962-64, pres. Pacific chpt. 1959-60), Am. Sociol. Assn. (v.p. 1978-79), Religious Research Assn., Sociol. Research Assn. Home: 319 S 4th Ave Sandpoint ID 83864-1219 Personal E-mail: chyogl@yahoo.com.

GLOCKNER, PETER G., civil and mechanical engineering educator; b. Moragy, Hungary, Jan. 26, 1929; emigrated to Can., 1949; BSc in Civil Engring., McGill U., Montreal, Que., Can., 1955; MSc in Civil Engring., MIT, 1956; PhD in Civil Engring., U. Mich., 1964. Asst. prof. applied mechanics U. Alta., Canada, 1958-60; from asst. prof. to prof. emeritus U. Calgary, Alta., Canada, 1960-94, prof. emeritus Alta., 1994—, chmn. dept. mech. engring. Alta., 1976-87. Author: A Place of Ingenuity, 1994, more than 300 articles on shell theory, stability and non-linear behavior of thin-walled structures, dielectrics and non-linear constitutive theory. Whitney fellow, 1955-56, Ford Found. fellow, 1962-64; recipient CANCAM medal, 1993. Fellow ASCE (Moisseiff award and medal 1983), Can. Soc. Mech. Engring., Engring. Inst. Can. (Gzowski Gold medal 1971), Am. Acad. Mechanics (pres. 1995-96); mem. Can. Soc. Civil Engring., Assn. Profl. Engrs., Geologists and Geophysicists Alta., Order of U. Calgary. Home: 2536 Charlebois Dr Calgary AB Canada T2L OT6 E-mail: glockner@ucalgary.ca.

GLOGAU, RICHARD G., dermatologist; b. Camden, NJ, Dec. 28, 1947; m. Pamela Ann Baj, June 11, 1977; 1 child, Gordon. AB, Dartmouth Coll., Hanover, NH, 1969; BMS, Dartmouth Med. Sch., Hanover, NH, 1971; MD, Harvard U., 1973. Diplomate Am. Bd. Dermatology, cert. in Dermatopathology, Am. Bds. Dermatology & Pathology. Intern, medicine Pa. Hosp., Phila., 1973-74; resident, dermatology U. Calif., San Francisco, 1974-77, chief resident, dept. dermatology, 1977-78, fellow, dermatologic surgery, 1978-79; active med. staff U. Calif. Hosps., 1979—2006; pvt. practice, 1979—. Departmental clin. adv. bd. mem., dept. dermatology, U. Calif., San Francisco, 1980-1998, mem. utilization review com., 1982-2000, mem. alternate dept. rep. clin. faculty assn., 1984-98, co-dir., dermatologic surgery fellowship, 1988-, Chancellor's Assocs., 1990-2006, clin. assoc. prof. dermatology, attending physician, 1988-94, clin. prof. dermatology, 1994-; cons. for Allergan Corp., Revance Therapeutics, Bioformis-Genzyme, Fibrogen, Inammed Corp., Medicis Corp., Neutrogena Corp., Liposonix, Inc.; commr., bd. examiner, Calif. State Bd. Med. Quality Assurance, 1989-95; lectr. in field. Co-author: Basics of Dermatologic Surgery, 1982, Flaps and Grafts, 1988, Cosmetic Dermatologic Surgery, 2d edit., 1989; co-editor: Dermatologic Surgery Year Book, 1991, 92, 93, 94; sect. editor Cosmetic Surgery, 1997-2004; mem. editl. bd. Archives of Dermatology, 1999-; contbg. editor Dermatologic Surgery, 2004-; featured on ABC's 20/20; contbr. chpts. to books and articles to profl. jours.; featured in several mag. articles. Pub. svc. U. Calif., San Francisco Med. Ctr. Glogau Teddy Bear Rescue Fund for Pediatrics, 2000—. Named one of "Top Docs", San Francisco Mag., 2001, 2003, 2004, 2005. Fellow Am. Acad. Dermatology (founder & chmn., DermPAC-Dermatology Polit. Action Com., 1994-2000, mem sect. on health policy, practice & rsch., 1996-2002, chmn., 1998-2002, bd. dir. SkinPAC-Dermatology Polit. Action Com., 2000-03), Am. Dermatol. Assn., Am. Acad. Facial Plastic and Reconstructive Surgery, Am. Coll. Mohs' Micrographic Surgery and Cutaneous Oncology (bd. dirs. 1989-92, chmn. bylaws com., 1989-92, mem. task force on CPT Coding, 1991-92), Am. Soc. for Dermatol. Surgery (chmn., practice support & liability com., 1985-87, chmn. task force on surgery & AIDS, 1989-93, mem. quality assurance com., 1994-97, dermatologic surgery fellowship task force, 1994-96, bd. dir. 1991-94, prog. dir. annual mtg. Rancho Mirage, Calif., 1986, Scottsdale, Ariz., 1992), Am. Soc. for Dermatopathology, Am. Acad. Cosmetic Surgery (bd. dir. 1993-98, chmn. exhibitos com., 1993-95), Am. Soc. Liposuction Surgery (charter fellow), N.Am. Soc. Phlebology (charter fellow); mem. Dermatology Found. Leaders Soc. (Calif. State chmn. (North), 1990-95, bd. trustee 1993-98), Calif. Dermatology Soc.(At-Large mem., bd. dir., 1993-2002, mem. legis. task force on AB 595 and AB1841, 1993-94, legis. task force on cosmetic surgery, 1997-98), San Francisco Dermatol. Soc., San Francisco Med. Soc., San Mateo County Med. Soc. Office: Dermatology 350 Parnassus Ave Ste 400 San Francisco CA 94117-3608 Office Phone: 415-564-1261.*

GLOGOWER, MICHAEL HOWARD, real estate company executive, consultant; b. Louisville, Jan. 6, 1944; s. Louis R. and Elaine R. (Switow) G. Student, Louisville Country Day Sch., 1958—61; BA in Polit. Sci., Kenyon Coll., 1965. Cert. lic. real estate broker Ky., Fla. Asst. gen. mgr. Mail Photo Svc. Inc., Louisville, 1966-69; pres. Mi-Glo Corp., Louisville, 1969-70; v.p. ops. Cherokee Coal Co. Inc., Louisville, 1970-71; area mgr. Owens/Corning Fiberglas Corp., Toledo, 1971-73; gen. mgr. Redd's Auto Parts Inc., Louisville, 1973-74; dist. mgr. Hackney Corp., Birmingham, Ala., 1974-75; area sales rep. J&W Fence Supply Co. Inc., Indpls., 1975-76; broker, salesman comml./investment divsn. Bass & Weisberg Realtors, Louisville, 1976-79; owner Michael H. Glogower Investment Realtor & Bus. Consulting, 1979—; housing programs specialist office pub. and Indian housing HUD, Washington, 1991-96, sr. functional specialist Honolulu, 1996-98, Miami, Fla., 1998—2005, sr. pub. housing specialist Louisville, 2005—. Former mem. edn. com. Bd. Realtors, Louisville; former subs. instr. Jefferson C.C., Louisville; former moderator, ace designee, counselor Acad. Network II-Nat. Real Estate Exch. Former pres. bd. dirs. Waterford House Condo Assn., Arlington, Va., 1993—96; bd. dirs. Palace Condominium Assn., Miami, 1999—2002; pres. Am. Fedn. Govt. Employees HUD Union Local 1516, 1999—2001; pres. bd. dirs. Costa Brava Condo. Assn., Miami Beach, Fla., 2003—04, v.p., bd. dirs., 2004—05. Avocations: photography, antiques, art. Office: US Dept HUD Ste 110 601 W Broadway Louisville KY 40202 Home: 5100 US Highway 42 Apt 632 Louisville KY 40241-6050 Office Phone: 502-582-6163 ext. 379. E-mail: michael_h._glogower@hud.gov. *Living different places, doing different things, I have never ceased to be impressed by the resiliance and humanity of my fellow human beings. We should never sell our fellow man short.*

GLOSBAND, DANIEL MARTIN, lawyer; b. Salem, Mass., July 3, 1944; s. Leon Glosband and Ruth Pauline (Wentworth) Glosband School; m. Merrily Cotton, Dec. 23, 1967; children: Alexander, Gabriel, Oliver. BA, U. Mass., 1966; JD, Cornell U., 1969. Bar: Mass. 1969, NY 2005, US Dist. Ct. Mass. 1970, US Dist. Ct. Conn. 1971, US Dist. Ct. Vt. 1974, U.S. Dist. Ct. (so. dist.) N.Y. 2006, US Ct. Appeals (1st cir.) 1971, US Supreme Ct. 1982. From assoc. to ptnr. firm Widett & Widett, Boston, 1969—75; ptnr. Goldstein & Manello, Boston, 1976—87, Goodwin, Procter LLP, Boston, 1988—. Advisor Am. Law Inst. Transnat. Insolvency Project, 1994—2000. Contbr. articles to profl. jours. Fellow: Mass. Bar Found., Am. Bar Found., Am. Coll. Bankruptcy (sec. 2001—05, v.p. 2005—); mem.: ABA (sect. on corps., chmn. internat. bankruptcy com. 1990—95), Conf., Nat. Bankruptcy Conf., Boston Bar Assn. (chmn. bankruptcy com. 1977—80), Mass. Bar Assn. (chmn. bankruptcy com. 1980—83), Internat. Bar Assn. (sect. bus. law, vice chmn. insolvency and creditors rights com. 1997—2000, del. UN Commn. Internat. Trade Law 1995—2004). Democrat. Jewish. Home: 34 Atlantic Ave Swampscott MA 01907-2404 Office: Goodwin Procter LLP Exchange Pl Boston MA 02109-2803 Office Phone: 617-570-1930. Business E-mail: dglosband@goodwinprocter.com.

GLOSS, LAWRENCE ROBERT, fundraising executive; b. Colorado Springs, Oct. 31, 1948; s. Kenneth Edwin and Clara U. Gloss; children: Alexander Edwin, Carolyn Claire. BA, U. Denver, 1970. Vol. Peace Corps, Colombia and Peru, 1970—75; dir. natl. congress on volunteerism and citizenship NCVA, Washington, 1975—76; dir. devel. Vis. Nurses Assn., Washington, 1976—77; devel. cons. Am. Lung Assn., Washington and NYC, 1977—78; exec. dir. Colo. Conservation Fund, Denver, 1978—79; dir. devel. Rose Med. Ctr., Denver, 1985—86; exec. dir. Rose Found., Denver, 1979—86; sr. campaign dir. J. Panas, Young and Ptnrs., San Francisco, 1986—88; pres. Gloss and Co., Denver, 1988—. Adv. coun. non-profit mgmt. Metro State Coll., Denver, 1994; cons. Native Am. Rights Fund, Boulder, Colo., Arts at the Sta., Denver, 1994, Up With People, 1995-96, Emily Griffith Ctr. Found., 1995-96, Colo. CASA, 1998-99, Women of the West Mus., 1998, 2000, Sister Cities-Denver and Kumming, China, 1999, sec. bd. Ctr. for Tax Policy. Guest spkr. Tech. Assistance Ctr., Denver, 1992—94; bd. dirs. Alzheimer's and Related Disorders Assn., Denver, 1985—86, Woman's Sch. Network, Denver, 1984—85, Colo. PTA, Englewood, 1991—92; active Emily Griffith Ctr. Found., 1997, U. Denver; active Episc. Ministries U. Colo., Boulder, 1996—2001; active Ctr. for Tax Policy, 1998—, Columbine H.S. Permanent Meml., Srs. Resource Ctr., 1998—99, Am. Humane Assn., 1998—99, Colo. Mil. History Mus., 2001—, Noah's Ark Pk., 2001—, Humane Soc. Pagosa Springs, 2001—02; mem. Prairie Wind Aninal Refuge, 2004; active Colorado Springs Soc. CPA Ednl. Found., 2004—05, Boulder Cmty. Hosp. Found.; mem. BMH-BJ Congregation, 1999—2003, sec., 2001. Mem.: Boulder Cmty. Hosp. Found. (active KUVO Radio Jazz 89), Colo. Soc. CPAs (mem. ednl. found. 2004—), Acad. Charter Schs., Assn. Profl. Rschrs. Advancement, Assn. Healthcare Philanthropy (region XII 1993—94), Am. Prospect Rsch. Assn., Nat. Com. on Planned Giving, Assn. Fund-Raising Profls., Assn. Profl. Fundraisers (Colo. chpt. 1992—94, bd. dirs.), Am. Lung Assn. of Colo., Nat. Assn. Mus. Exhibitors, Women of the West Mus., Arapahoe Ho., Englewood Hist. Soc., Colo. Planned Giving Roundtable, Soccer Ofcls. Assn. Colo., Colo. State Youth Soccer Assn., U.S. Soccer Assn., Rotary Club of Denver. Lutheran. Avocations: dressage, art, soccer. Office: Morris Animal Found 45 Inverness Dr E Englewood CO 80112-5488

GLOSSER, JEFFREY MARK, lawyer; b. 1936; married; 1 child. BS in Econs. with distinction, U. Pa., 1958; LLB, Harvard U., 1961. Bar: D.C. 1962. Law clk. U.S. Ct. Claims, 1963-64; assoc. Emery & Wood, Washington, 1965-69; ptnr. Jeffrey M. Glosser, P.C., Washington, 1969-86, Whiteford, Taylor & Preston, Washington, 1987-95. Instr. CLE courses sponsored by D.C. Bar, 1976-95. Mem. ABA (adminstrv. law sect., various coms.), D.C. Bar Assn. (numerous coms.), Fed. Bar Assn. (U.S. Claims Ct. com.), Fed. Cir. Bar Assn. (rules com. 1985-95). Personal E-mail: glosser@mac.com.

GLOTFELTY, CHERYLL, literature and language professor; m. Steve Glotfelty; 1 child, Rosa Ramona. BA, U. Calif., Davis; MA, PhD, Cornell U., Ithaca, NY. Assoc. prof. lit. and the environment U. Nev., Reno, Sanford Disting. prof. humanities, 2000—02. Contbr. articles to profl. jours., chapters to books; co-editor: The Ecocriticism Reader: Landmarks in Literary Ecology, 1996. Recipient US Prof. of Yr. award, Carnegie Found. for Advancement of Tchg. and Coun. for Advancement and Support of Edn., 2006. Mem.: Assn. for Study of Lit. and Environment (founder). Avocations: reading, rock climbing, hiking, basket weaving. Office: English Dept 098 U Nev Reno Reno NV 89557 Office Phone: 775-682-6395. Office Fax: 775-784-6266. E-mail: glotfelt@unr.edu.*

GLOTTA, RONALD DELON, lawyer; b. Lajunta, Colo., Mar. 18, 1941; s. John Wallace and Marian (Kisner) G.; m. Sharon S. Glotta, Aug. 27, 1961 (div. Mar. 1986); children: Holly Ann, Jeffrey Delon; m. Marietta Lynn Baba, June 23, 1990 (div. Oct. 1998). BA with honors, U. Kans., 1963; JD, U. Mich., 1966. Bar: Mich. 1966. Atty. Marcus, McCroskey, Libner, Reamon, Williams & Dilley, Muskegon, Mich., 1966-68; ptnr. Philo, Maki, Moore, Pitts, Ravitz, Glotta, Cockrel & Robb, Detroit, 1968-70; prin. Glotta & Adelman, Detroit, 1970-85, Glotta, Rawlings & Skutt, Detroit, 1985-96, Glotta, Skutt & Assts., Detroit, 1996—2004, Glotta & Assts., Detroit, 2004—. Author: The Road to Hell is not Paved with Good Intentions. Mem. Phi Beta Kappa. Home: 2065 Hyde Park Rd Detroit MI 48207-3885 Office Phone: 313-963-1320. E-mail: rglotta@glottaassociates.com.

GLOTZBACH, PHILIP A., academic administrator, philosopher, educator; m. Marie B Glotzbach; children: Jason, Elizabeth. BA summa cum laude, U. Notre Dame, 1972; PhD, Yale U., 1979. Assoc. prof. to chair of Philosophy dept. to chair of the faculty sen. Denison U., Granville, Ohio, 1977—92; dean of coll. of arts and scis., v.p. for academic affairs U. of Redlands, 1992—2003; pres. Skidmore Coll., 2003—. Mem.: Phi Beta Kappa. Office: Skidmore Coll 815 N Broadway Saratoga Springs NY 12866 Office Phone: 518-580-5700. Office Fax: 518-580-5699. E-mail: pglotzba@skidmore.edu.*

GLOTZER, LIZ, film company executive; BA, Bennington Coll., 1983; MFA, U. So. Calif., 1985. Dir. devel. Samuel Goldwyn Co., 1984-97; v.p. prodn. Castle Rock Pictures, Beverly Hills, Calif., 1987-94, pres. prodn., 1994—. Prodr. (film) Sibling Rivalry, 1990; exec. prodr. (film) The Shawshank Redemption, 1994, Chaos Theory, 2007, Fracture, 2007. Office: Castle Rock Pictures 335 N Maple Dr Ste 135 Beverly Hills CA 90210-3879*

GLOVER, CLIFFORD CLARKE, retired construction company executive; b. Newnan, Ga., May 15, 1913; s. Howard Clarke and Fannie Virginia (Jones) G.; m. Louise Liles, Jan. 16, 1937; children: Edmund Cook, Nancy Liles Glover Kennedy, Virginia Johnston Glover Lee, Laura Clarke Glover Thatcher. BCE, U. N.C., 1934. With Batson-Cook Co., West Point, Ga., 1934-94; ret., 1994. Mem. West Point Sch. Bd., 1951-69, chmn., 1964-68; chmn. West Point Planning Bd., 1964-2007; trustee LaGrange Coll.; pres. George H. Lanier council Boy Scouts Am., 1977-78, dir. Southeast regional bd., 1987, recipient Silver Antelope award, 1992; bd. dirs. Joint Tech. Ga. Devel. Fund, 1987. Served with USNR, 1944—45. Recipient Silver Beaver award Boy Scouts Am., Silver Antelope award Boy Scouts Am.; Presdl. award George H. Lanier Coun. Boy Scouts Am., Disting. Citizen's award, 1988; Award of Merit Greater Valley C. of C., 1984; Golden Hammer award Profl. Constrn. Estimators Assn. Am., 1988; fellow La Grange Coll. Mem. Assoc. Gen. Contractors (past pres. Ga. br., Skill, Integrity and Responsibility award 1991) Methodist (ofcl. bd.). Clubs: Rotary (Paul Harris fellow); Capital City (Atlanta); Riverside (West Point). Office: Batson-Cook Co PO Box 151 West Point GA 31833-0151 Business E-Mail: cglover@batson-cook-wp.com.

GLOVER, CRISPIN HELLION, actor; b. NYC, Apr. 20, 1964; s. Bruce Herbert and Betty Lillian Marie (Koerber) G. Stage debut The Sound of Music, L.A., 1977; appeared in My Tutor, 1982, Racing With the Moon, 1983, The Orkly Kid, 1983, Friday 13th-The Final Chapter, 1983, Teachers, 1984, Back To The Future, 1984, At Close Range, 1984, Rivers Edge, 1985, Twister, 1987, Where the Heart Is, 1989, Wild At Heart, 1989, The Doors, 1991, Ferdydurke, 1991, Little Noises, 1992, Rubin and Ed, 1992, Crime and Punishment, 1994, What's Eating Gilbert Grape, 1993, Chasers, 1994, Even Cowgirls Get the Blues, 1994, Dead Man, 1995, The People Vs. Larry Flynt, 1996, Nurse Betty, 1999, Charlie's Angels, 2000, Bartleby, 2000, Crime and Punishment, 2002, Like Mike, 2002, Willard, 2003, Charlie's Angels Full Throttle, 2003, What is it?, 2005 (also dir.), Drop Dead Sexy, 2005, It Is Fine. Everything is Fine!, 2007 (also dir.), Epic Movie, 2007; (TV film) High School U.S.A., 1983; author, pub.: (books) Rat Catching, 1987, Oak Mot, 1990, Concrete Inspection, 1992, What It Is and How It Is Done, 1995; dir., screenwriter, actor, prodr. What is It?, 1997, 98, 99.*

GLOVER, DANNY, actor; b. San Francisco, July 22, 1947; s. Carrie Hunley Glover; m. Asake Bomani, 1975; 1 child, Mandisa. Degree in Econs., San Francisco State Univ.; DFA (hon.), San Francisco State U., 1997. Rschr. Mayor's Office, San Francisco, 1971-75. Apptd. goodwill amb. for UN Devel. Program, 1998; mem. Am. Conservatory Theatre's Black Actor Workshop. Actor: (Broadway debut) Master Harold.and the Boys, Lyceum Theatre, 1982 (Theatre World award 1982), (stage prodns.) The Blood Knot, 1982, The Island, Sizwe Banzi is Dead, Macbeth, Suicide in B Flat, Nevis Mountain Dew, Jukebox; (feature films) Escape from Alcatraz, 1979, Chu Chu and the Philly Flash, 1981, Out, 1982, The Stand-In, 1984, Iceman, 1984, Places in the Heart, 1984, Birdy, 1984, Silverado, 1985, Witness, 1985, The Color Purple, 1985, Lethal Weapon, 1987, Bat 21, 1988, Lethal Weapon II, 1989, To Sleep with Anger (also exec. prodr.), 1990, Predator 2, 1990, Flight of the Intruder, 1991, A Rage in Harlem, 1991, Pure Luck, 1991, Grand Canyon, 1992, Lethal Weapon III, 1992, The Saint of Fort Washington (also co-prodr.) 1993, Bopha!, 1993, Maverick, 1994, Angels in the Outfield, 1994, Operation Dumbo Drop, 1995, America's Dream, 1996, The Rainmaker, 1997, Wings Against the Wind, 1998, Beloved, 1998, Lethal Weapon 4, 1998, (voice) Prince of Egypt, 1998, (voice) Antz, 1998, The Monster, 1999, Boesman and Lena, 2000, Wings Against the Wind, 1999, The Royal Tenenbaums, 2001, The Cookout, 2004, Saw, 2004, Manderlay, 2005, Missing in America, 2005, The Shaggy Dog, 2006, Bamako (also exec. prodr.), 2006, (voice) Barnyard: The Original Party Animals, 2006, Dreamgirls, 2006, Shooter, 2007; (TV films) The Face of Rage, 1983, Mandela, 1987, Dead Man Out, 1989, America's Dream (also exec. prodr.), 1996, Freedom Song, 2000, Good Fences (also prodr.), 2003, Legend of Earthsea, 2004, The Exonerated, 2005; (TV mini-series) Chiefs, 1983, Lonesome Dove, 1989, Queen, 1993; (TV episodes) Hill Street Blues, Lou Grant, Many Mansions, others; host: Civil War Jour., 1993. Address: Cary Prodns Inc PMB 352 6114 LaSalle Ave Oakland CA 94611*

GLOVER, DAVID LLOYD, artist; b. Victoria, BC, Canada, Oct. 25, 1949; s. David Edward and Iris Diane Glover; m. Judith Rose, Dec. 3, 2000; children: Guy Patrick, Darren Randall. Polit. cartoonist, op ed illustrator Victoria Times Newspaper, 1967—72; prin. Truman/Glover

Advt., Ltd., Victoria, 1973—77; v.p., account supr. W. Can Comm., Calgary, Alberta, Canada, 1980—82; exec. v.p. Freeman Yipp Advt., Ltd, Calgary, 1982—84; fine artist Vancouver, 1986—88; internat. fine artist Masterworks Fine Art, Inc., LA, 1986—, Tokyo. Internat. cir. diplomat LA World Affairs Coun., 1999—2004. One-man shows include fine art oil & watercolor paintings, book, White Bears & Other Curiosies, by Peter Corly-Smith. Bd. trustees, chmn. bd. Hugh O'Brian Youth Leadership, LA, 2000—05. Recipient Best in Show award, Premio Nacional de Artes Graficas, Mex. City, 1990. Achievements include development of a marketing strategy for winning 1988 Calgary winter olympic bid. Home Phone: 323-822-1056.

GLOVER, DOUGLAS DENNIS, obstetrics, gynecology and pharmacology educator; b. Rowlesburg, W.Va., Feb. 7, 1929; s. Douglas and Iva (Hughes) G.; m. Barbara Anne Brady, Sept. 6, 1958; children: Joseph, William, Donald, Geoffrey, Robert. BS in Pharmacy, W.Va. U., Morgantown, 1951, BS in Medicine, 1959; MD, Emory U., Atlanta, 1961. Diplomate Am. Bd. Ob-gyn. Intern Grady Meml. Hosp., Atlanta, 1961-62, resident, 1962-65; pvt. practice, Marietta, 1965-82; prof. ob/gyn. Marshall U. Sch. Medicine, Huntington, W.Va., 1982-87, W.Va. U., Morgantown, 1987—2004, prof. Sch. Pharmacy, 1987—2004, prof. emeritus, 2004—. Vis. prof. Zhejiang Med. U., Hangzhou, People's Republic of China, 1993; past operator of 4 rural outreach clinics for disadvantaged pregnant women. Editor: Current Therapy in Obstetrics, 1988; contbr. articles to profl. jours. Mem. U.S. Pharmacopeial Conv., Inc., 1990—, gen. com. of revision, 1990-2000, chmn. ob-gyn adv. panel, 1990-2000, expert com. on nomenclature and labeling, 1990-2005. Served to 1st lt. AUS, 1952-53, Korea Decorated Bronze Star, Purple Heart; recipient Outstanding Svc. award W.Va. U., 1972, 87, Outstanding Alumnus award W.Va. U. Sch. Pharmacy, 1982, Disting. Alumnus award, 1999, Dr. James H. Beal award W.Va. Pharmacists Assn., 1989, Sch. Medicine Faculty Recognition award, 1997, 2002, 2005, W.Va.Gov.'s Meritorious Svc. award, 2004, W.Va. U. Most Loyal Mountaineer, 2004, W.Va. U. Sch. Medicine award Excellence Svc. to Sch., 2005, Fellow Am. Coll. Ob-Gyn., Am. Soc. Reproductive Medicine (co-chair sessions mgmt. com. 1990—, chair registrations com. 1992-98), Internat. Infectious Diseases Soc. for Ob-Gyn. (mem. nat. steering com.), Masons (32d deg.), Sigma Xi, Phi Delta Theta (chpt. advisor 1988-2000), Phi Chi, Phi Lambda Sigma. Republican. Presbyterian. Achievements include patents in field; research in placental metabolism and pharmacokinetics of drugs during pregnancy. Avocation: military history. Home: 5 Maple Ave Morgantown WV 26501-6542 Office: Dept Ob/Gyn WVa U Morgantown WV 26506 Office Phone: 304-293-4198. Business E-Mail: dglover@hsc.wvu.edu.

GLOVER, FRED WILLIAM, information scientist, director, educator; b. Kansas City, Mo., Mar. 8, 1937; s. William Cain and Mary Ruth (Baxter) G.; m. Diane Tatham, June 4, 1988; 1 child, Lauren Glover; children from previous marriage: Dana Reynolds, Paul Glover. BBA, U. Mo., 1960; PhD, Carnegie-Mellon U., 1965; DSc (hon.), Nat. Acad. Sci., Ukraine, 2006. Asst. prof. U. Calif., Berkeley, 1965-66; assoc. prof. U. Tex., Austin, 1966-69; prof. U. Minn., Mpls., 1969-70, U. Colo., Boulder, 1970—, Media One chair in sys. sci., 1998—; rsch. dir. Artificial Intelligence Ctr., Boulder, 1984-90; disting. prof. U. Colo. Sys., 2006—. Bd. dirs. Heuristec, Boulder, OptTek, Boulder, Decision Analysis, Rsch. & Computation, Austin. Author: Netform Decision Models, 1983 (DIS award 1984), Tabu Search I, 1989, Tabu Search II, 1990, Tabu Search (book and special vols.) 1993, 97, 98, 2003, Ghost Image Processes for Neural Networks, 1993, Linkages with Artificial Intelligence, 1990, Network Models in Optimization and Their Application in Practice, 1992, Handbook of Metaheuristics, 2003, others; contbr. over 350 articles on math. optimization and artificial intelligence to profl. jours. Recipient Internat. Achievement award Inst. Mgmt. Scis., 1982, Energy Rsch. award Energy Rsch. Inst., 1983, Univ. Disting. Rsch. Lectr. award U. Colo., 1988, Rsch. Excellence prize Ops. Rsch. Soc., 1989, Nat. Best Theoretical/Empirical Rsch. Paper award Decision Scis. Inst., 1993, Computer Sci. Rsch. Excellence award Ops. Rsch. Soc. Am., 1994, Nat. Rsch. Excellence award Comp. Sci. Ops. Rsch. Soc., 1994, John Von Neumann Theory award Inst. Ops. Rsch. Mgmt. Sci., 1998, Spl. Recognition award Inst. Ops. Rsch. and Mgmt. Scis., 2004; named first U.S. West Disting. fellow, 1987. Fellow: AAAS, ICC Inst., Am. Assn. Collegiate Schs. Bus., Am. Inst. Decision Scis. (lectr. 1984, Outstanding Achievement award 1984); mem.: NAE, Alpha Iota Delta. Achievements include invention of tabu search methodology for optimization, design of software systems used throughout the U.S. and abroad. Office: U Colo Coll Bus Box 419 Boulder CO 80309-0419 Home Phone: 303-442-3559; Office Phone: 303-492-8589. Business E-Mail: fred.glover@colorado.edu.

GLOVER, GARY H., radiologist, educator; b. Mpls., Aug. 8, 1942; s. Harold E Glover, Margaret Glover; m. Anne-Marie Sawyer; children: Peter, Julie, Susan, Nickolas. PhD, U. Minn., 1969. Physicist GE Corp. Rsch. & Devel. Ctr., Schenectady , NY; sr. physicist GE Med. Systems, Milw., 1977—89; prof. radiology dept. Stanford U. Sch. Medicine, Calif., 1990—. Recipient Outstanding Rschr. award, Radiol. Soc. N.Am., 2002, Gold Medal award, Internat. Soc. Magnetic Resonance in Medicine, 2000; fellow, 2000, Am. Inst. Med. & Biomed. Engring., 1997. Fellow: AIMBE, ISMRM (numerous coms. 1985—, pres., v.p., bd. trustees); mem.: NAE, AAPM. Office: Stanford U Lucas Ctr P-262 1201 Welch Rd Stanford CA 94305-5488 Office Phone: 650-723-7577. Office Fax: 650-723-5795. Business E-Mail: gary@s-word.stanford.edu.

GLOVER, JAMES TODD, manufacturing executive; b. Aberdeen, SD, Apr. 30, 1939; s. Fay and Vi (Bruns) G.; m. Joann Elizabeth House; children: Jason, Jeffrey, Jamie. Student, S.D. State U.; BS in Math., No. State Coll., Aberdeen, 1961. Inside sales engr. Aberdeen Ops. Safeguard, 1961-64, asst. sales engr., 1965-67, mktg. mgr., 1968-72, gen. mgr., 1973-77; v.p. ops. Safeguard PowerTech Systems, Aberdeen, 1978-83, exec. v.p., 1984-85, pres., 1986-89; pres., chief exec. officer, chief ops. officer, dir. Hub City, Inc., Aberdeen, 1989—. Officer Safeguard Sci. Co., Inc.; v.p. corp. devel. Regal-Beloit (Wis.) Corp., 1990-93; v.p. HQ Cos., Mpls., 1993-98, gen. mgr. Pixall Ltd. Partnership, Clear Lake, Wis., 1993-98; pres. JTG Solutions, Inc., Peoria, Ariz., 1998-. Bd. mem. S.D. Swimming Assn.; S.D. Dist. Export Council. Export Devel. Authority; bd. dirs. No. State Found., James River Water Devel.; bd. mem., chmn. James River Water Devel. Dist. Recipient Ernie Gunderson award S.D. Swimming Assn. Mem. Power Transmission Distbrs. Assn. (past bd. dirs., past chmn. allied adv. bd.), Power Transmission Rep. Assn. (past bd. dirs., past chmn. allied adv. bd.), Aberdeen C. of C., S.D. Mfrs. Assn. (past dir.). Republican. Roman Catholic. Avocations: hunting, fishing, music.

GLOVER, JOHN, actor; b. Salisbury, Md., Aug. 7, 1944; s. John S. and Cade (Mullins) G. Student, Towson State Coll. Appeared in plays Look Homeward Angel, 1963, A Scent of Flowers, 1969, Subject to Fit, 1971, House of Blue Leaves, 1971, The Great God Brown, 1972, Don Juan, 1972, The Selling of the President, 1972, The Visit, 1973, Chemin de Fer, 1973, Holiday, 1973, Rebel Women, 1976, The Importance of Being Earnest, 1977, Treats, 1977, A Man for All Seasons, 1979, Frankenstein, 1981, Hedda Gabler, 1981, Booth, 1982, The Doctor's Delemma, 1982, A Doll's House, 1982, Whodonnit, 1982-83, Criminal Minds, 1984, Design for Living, 1984, Linda Her and the Fairy Garden, 1984, Digby, 1985, Henceforward, 1991, Love! Valour! Compassion!, 1994 (Tony award Featured Actor in a Play, 1995), The Paris Letter, 2005, The Drowsy Chaperone, 2007; films include Shamus, 1972, Annie Hall, 1977, Julia, 1977, Somebody Killed Her Husband, 1978, The Last Embrace, 1979, American Success Company, 1979, Mountain Men, 1980, Melvin and Howard, 1980, Brubaker, 1980, The Incredible Shrinking Woman, 1981, A Little Sex, 1982, The Evil That Men Do, 1984, A Flash of Green, 1985, White Nights, 1985, Willy/Milly, 1985, My Sister's Keeper, 1986, 52 Pick-up, 1986, Masquerade, 1988, A Killing Affair, 1988, Rocket Gibraltar, 1988, The Chocolate War, 1988, Scrooged, 1988, Meet the Hollowheads, 1989, Gremlins 2: The New Batch, 1990, Robocop 2, 1990, Dora Was Dysfunctional, 1993, Ed and His Dead Mother, 1993; TV movies include The Face of Rage, 1983, Ernie Kovacs: Between the Laughter, 1984, An Early Frost, 1985, Moving Target, 1988, Hot Paint, 1988, David, 1988, The Traveling Man, 1989, Twist of Fate, 1989, Breaking Point, 1989, El Diablo, 1990, What Ever Happened to Baby Jane?, 1991, Dead on the Money, 1991, Drug Wars: The Cocaine Cartel, 1992, Majority Rule, 1992, Assault at West Point, 1994, Night of The Running Man, 1995, In the Mouth of Madness, 1995, Schemes, 1995, Batman & Robin, 1997, Love! Valour! Compassion!, 1997, The Broken Giant, 1998, Dead Broke, 1999, Payback, 1999; mini-series include Kennedy, 1983, Rage of Angels, 1983, George Washington, 1984, Nutcracker: Money, Madness and Murder, 1987, Grass Roots, 1992; TV series appearances include (voice) The Adventures of Batman and Robin, 1992, South Beach, 1993, (voice) Batman: Gotham Knights, 1997, Dead Man's Gun, 1997, The Tempest, 1998, Brimstone, 1998, Macbeth in Manhattan, 1999, Dead Broke, 1999, On Edge, 2001, Sex & Violence, 2002, Mid-Century, 2002, Sweet Union, 2003, Tricks, 2003; (TV series) Smallville, 2001. Office: The Gersh Agy care Ken Kaplan 232 N Canon Dr Beverly Hills CA 90210-5302*

GLOVER, KAREN ELAINE, lawyer; b. Nampa, Idaho, Apr. 14, 1950; d. Gordon Ellsworth and Cora (Frazier) G.; m. Thaddas L. Alston, Aug. 17, 1979; children: Samantha Glover Alston, Evan Glover Alston. AB magna cum laude, Whitman Coll., 1972; JD cum laude, Harvard U., 1975. Bar: Wash. 1975, U.S. Dist. Ct. (we. dist.) Wash. 1975. Assoc. Preston, Thorgrimson Ellis & Holman, Seattle, 1975-80; ptnr. Preston Gates & Ellis LLP, Seattle, 1981—2006, mng. ptnr., 2005—06; global integration ptnr. K&L Gates, Seattle, 2007—. Bd. dirs. Adaptis, Inc. Chmn. bd. dirs. United Way King County, Seattle, 1993-94; chmn. trustees Whitman Coll., Walla Walla, Wash., 2004-06; bd. trustees King County Libr. Sys., Seattle, 1992-01. Mem. Wash. State Bar Assn. (corp. and health sects.), Columbia Tower Club, Rainier Club. Episcopalian. Office: K&L Gates 925 4th Ave Ste 2900 Seattle WA 98104-1158 Office Phone: 206-370-7624. Business E-Mail: kari.glover@klgates.com.

GLOVER, MELVIN (MELLE MEL, GRANDMASTER MELLE MEL), rap artist; b. NYC, May 15, 1962; Lead lyricist, rapper Three MC's, 1978, Grandmaster Flash & the Furious Five, 1979—83, Grandmaster Melle Mel & the Furious Five. Musician: (albums) The Message, 1982, Work Party, 1984, Stepping Off, 1985, Sun City: Artists United Against Apartheid, 1985, Adventures of Grandmaster Flash, Melle Mel & the Furious Five, 1996, Grandmaster Flash vs. the Sugarhill Gang, 1997, Right Now, 1997, Adventures on the Wheels of Steel, 1999, Muscles, 2007, (with Chaka Khan) I Feel for You, 1984, (with Quincy Jones) Back on the Block, 1989 (Grammy award, Best Group Rap Performance, 1990), Q's Jook Joint, 1994; actor: (films) Beat Street, 1984, Police Academy 6, 1989, Who's the Man?, 1993; author: The Portal in the Park, 2006. Named to Rock & Roll Hall of Fame, with Grandmaster Flash & the Furious Five, 2007.*

GLOVER, SAVION, actor, dancer; b. Newark, Nov. 19, 1973; Head dance co. TiDii; founder NYOTs (Not Your Ordinary Tappers), 1997; choreographer Washington Soc. for Performing Arts. Performer: (Broadway plays) The Tap Dance Kid, 1985, Black and Blue (Tony award nomination), Jelly's Last Jam (Jefferson award for supporting role in nat. tour); choreographer, co-creator (Broadway plays) Bring In the Noise, Bring in Da Funk, 1995 (Tony award, best choreography, 1996, Drama Desk award, Outer Critics Cir. award, Obie award (2), Fred Astaire award (2), 1996); performer: (films) Tap, 1989, Bamboozled, 2000; choreographer & exec. prodr. (films) Savion Glover's Nu York; performer: (TV Spl.) Dance in America: Tap!, Black Filmmaker's Hall of Fame, Sesame Street Jam: A Musical Celebration, 1994, (TV series) Sesame Street, 1990—95, (nat. tour) Footnotes: The Concert, (TV films) The Wall, 1998, Bojangles, 2001; choreographer (TV films) The Rat Pack, 1998, Nike Free Style commls., Improvography, 2004, Improvography II, 2005; performer (with Reg e gaines & Matana Roberts): If Trane Wuz Here, 2004; performer: (with The Otherz) Classic Savion, 2005. Recipient Choreographer of Yr. award, Dance mag., 1996, Martin Luther King Jr. Outstanding Youth award, 1991, Capezio Dance award, 2004; Endowment Grant for Choreography, NEA. Office: William Morris Agy 151 El Camino Dr Beverly Hills CA 90212 Mailing: c/o Nederlander Worldwide Entertainment 1450 Broadway 20th Floor New York NY 10018

GLOVSKY, MYRON MICHAEL, medical educator; b. Boston, Aug. 15, 1936; divorced; five children. BS magna cum laude, Tufts U., 1957, MD, 1962. Bd. cert. Nat. Bd. Med. Examiners, Am. Bd. Allergy & Immunology, Am. Bd. Diagnostic Lab. Immunology. Intern Balt. (Md.) City Hosp., 1962-63; resident New Eng. Med. Ctr., Boston, 1965-66; spl. NIH fellow allergy and immunology Walter Reed Army Inst. Rsch., Washington, 1966-68; fellow hematology and immunology U. Calif., San Francisco, 1968-69; staff physician dept. internal medicine So. Calif. Permanente Med. Group, LA, 1969-72, dir. allergy & immunology lab., 1970-84, chief dept. allergy and clin. immunology, co-dir. residency program in allergy & clin. immunology, 1974-84, dir. pheresis unit, 1978-80; dir. L.A. County Gen. Hosp./U. So. Calif. Asthma Clinic; prof. medicine, head allergy and immunology labs. pulmonary divsn., head allergy and clin. immunology divsn. pulmonary medicine. U. So. Calif., Sch. Medicine, 1984-89, prof. pathology, 1986-89; clin. prof. medicine, clin. prof. pathology U. So. Calif., 1989—2003; dir. asthma and allergy referral ctr. Huntington Meml. Hosp., Pasadena, 1989—2003. Head fellowship and career devel. program Nat. Heart Inst., NIH, Bethesda, Md., 1963-65, fellowship bd. mem., 1964-65; vis. assoc. in chemistry Calif. Inst. Tech., Pasadena, 1977—; acad. assoc. complement and allergy Nichols Inst., San Juan Capistrano, Calif., 1980-2003, med. dir. immunology, 1980-89, 2003-06; clin. prof. medicine UCLA, 1983-84; vis. prof. clin. scholars program Eli Lilly & Co., Indpls., 1988; mem. steering com. Aspen Allergy Conf., 1988—. With USPHS, 1963-65. Fellow Am. Acad. Allergy; mem. AAAS, Am. Assn. Immunologists, Am. Thoracic Soc., Am. Fedn. for Clin. Rsch., Am. Coll. Allergy, L.A. Soc. Allergy and Clin. Immunology (pres. 1979-80), Collegium Internat. Allergolicum. Home: 287 Grace Dr South Pasadena CA 91030 Office: Huntington Asthma & Allergy Ctr 960 E Green St Pasadena CA 91106 Home Phone: 626-755-7783; Office Phone: 626-793-6680. Business E-Mail: yksvolg@caltech.edu.

GLOVSKY, SUSAN G.L., lawyer; b. Boston, Apr. 16, 1955; d. Leonard B. and Marilyn S. (Shapiro) Loitherstein; m. Steven M. Glovsky, May 25, 1980; 1 child, Lowell Eliott. BS in Chemistry, U. Vt., 1977; JD, Boston U., 1980. Bar: Mass. 1980, Mich. 1980, U.S. Dist. Ct. (ea. dist.) Mich. 1980, U.S. Patent Office 1981, N.Y. 1982, U.S. Dist. Ct. Mass. 1982, U.S. Ct. Appeals (1st cir.) 1982, U.S. Ct. Appeals (fed. cir.) 1991, U.S. Supreme Ct. 1995. Assoc. Levin, Levin, Garvett & Dill, Southfield, Mich., 1980-81, Ladas & Parry, NYC, 1981-82, Dahlen & Gatewood, Boston, 1982-83; ptnr. Dahlen & Glovsky, Boston, 1983-85; pvt. practice Boston and Salem, Mass., 1985-93; of counsel Hamilton, Brook, Smith & Reynolds, Mass., 1993-97, prin. Concord, 1998—. Mem.: ABA, Am. Arbitration Assn. (nat. roster neutrals), Boston Patent Law Assn. (past pres., founder, chmn. litig. com. 1989—2001, co-founder, chmn. contested matters com.), Boston Bar Assn., Mass. Bar Assn. Jewish. Avocations: swimming, skiing. Home: 36 Shaw Dr Wayland MA 01778-3214 Office: Hamilton Brook Smith & Reynolds 530 Virginia Rd PO Box 9133 Concord MA 01742 Home Phone: 508-358-3540; Office Phone: 978-341-0036. Business E-Mail: susan.glovsky@hbsr.com.

GLOWCZEWSKA, KLARA, editor-in-chief, translator; b. Warsaw; BA magna cum laude, Yale U. Editor Condé Nast Traveler, 1987—92, exec. editor, 1992—2005, editor-in-chief, 2005—. Staff mem. Random House, The New York Review of Books; contbg. editor Vanity Fair, The New Yorker. Translator: Beautiful Mrs. Seidenman, 1989, Shadow of the Sun, 2001. Office: Conde Nast Traveler 360 Madison Ave New York NY 10017*

GLOWINSKI, ROLAND, mathematics professor; b. Paris, Mar. 9, 1937; s. Nathan and Anna (Cukiernik) G.; m. Angela Rimok, Nov. 3, 1963; children: Anne, Tania. B, Ecole Polytechnique, Paris, 1960; M, Ecole Nationale Supérieure des Télécommunications, Paris, 1963; PhD, U. Paris, 1971; D (hon.), U. Jyvaskyla, Finland, 2004. Registered profl. engineer; cert. prof. math. Rsch. engr. Office de Radio et Télévision Françaises, Paris, 1963-68, Institut National de Recherches en Informatique et Automatique, Paris, 1968-70; prof. U. Paris VI, 1970—98, chmn. math dept., 1981-85; Disting. prof. U. Houston, 1985—. Adj. prof. Rice U., Houston, 1986—; Sherman Fairchild Disting. visitor Calif. Inst. Tech., 1988-89; cons. CNET, Paris, 1968-85, Sci. Rsch. Coun., London, 1978-81; bd. dirs. Electricite de France, Paris, 1990-96, U. Leonardo da Vinci, Paris; dir. Centre Européen de Recherches et de Formation Avancée en Calcul Scientifique, Toulouse, France, 1992-94; docent prof. U. Jyvaskyla, Finland, 2001—; sci. bd. French Petroleum Inst., 2005— Lt. France Signal Corps, 1958-61. Decorated officer Nat. Merit, knight Order of Acad. Palms, knight Order Legion of Honor, France; recipient Cray prize Selected Jury, Paris, 1988, Marcel Dassault prize French Nat. Acad. Scis., 1996, Zienkiewicz Disting. lectureship, 1999, IMA, 1999, others. Mem. Soc. for Indsl. and Applied Math. (Theodore von Kármán Prize, 2004, selected jury), Am. Math. Soc., Academia Europea (London), French Nat. Acad. Tech., French Nat. Acad. Scis. Office: U Houston Dept Math 651 Philip G Hoffman Hall Houston TX 77204-3008 Home Phone: 713-523-5270; Office Phone: 713-743-3473. Personal E-mail: angelarim@aol.com. Business E-Mail: roland@math.uh.edu.

GLOYD, RITA A., retired social worker; b. Gaithersburg, Md., Sept. 10, 1918; d. Henry Dorsey Gloyd and Margaret Lavenia Arnold. RN, Georgetown U., 1939; BA in Art, Notre Dame Md., 1960; MSW, U. Md., 1970. Cert. Acad. Cert. Social Workers. Delivery rm. nurse Georgetown U. Hosp., Washington, 1939; obstet. nurse Washington, 1939; stewardess Am. Airline, Flushing, NY, 1940—43; from novice to superior Good Sherperd, Balt., 1943—68; social worker stroke unit Johns Hopkins Hosp., Balt., 1970—71; social worker Montgomery County Pub. Schs.-Mark Twain Spl. Sch., Rockville, Md., 1971—73; social worker, adminstr. Diagnosis and Profl. Support Team, Rockville, 1975—84; ret., 1984. Democrat. Roman Catholic. Home: Apt 315 403 Russell Ave Gaithersburg MD 20877 Personal E-mail: rgloydrag@aol.com.

GLUBE, CONSTANCE RACHELLE, retired judge; b. Ottawa, Ont., Can., Nov. 23, 1931; d. Samuel and Pearl (Slonemsky) Lepofsky; m. Richard Hillard Glube, July 6, 1952 (dec.); children: John B., Erica D. Glube Kolatch, Harry S., B. Joseph. BA, McGill U., Montreal, Can., 1952; LLB, Dalhousie U., Halifax, Can., 1955, LLD (hon.), 1982, Mount St. Vincent U., 1998, St. Mary's U., 2000. Bar: N.S. 1956, created queen's counsel, 1974. Assoc. Kitz, Matheson, Halifax, 1964-66; ptnr. Fitzgerald & Glube, Halifax, 1966-68; sr. solicitor City of Halifax, 1969-74, city mgr., 1974-77; puisne judge Supreme Ct. of N.S., Halifax, 1977-82, chief justice, 1982-98, N.S. Ct. Appeals, 1998—2004; ret., 2004. Vice chair Can. Judges Conf.; bd. dirs. Can. Inst. Adminstrs. Justice. Contbr. articles to profl. jours. Co-chair Can. Coun. Christians and Jews; bd. dirs. Halifax Heritage Found., 1984—95, Internat. Commn. Jurists, Can. br., 2003—, Queen Elizabeth II Found., 2005—, vice chmn., 2006; bd. dirs. Can. Civil Liberties Assn., 2005—, chmn., 2007; bd. dirs. Halifax Cmty. Learning Network, 2005; chmn. bd. N.S. Archives, 1998—2004; chmn. Lt. Govs. Arts Award Found., 2005—; chair (hon.) N.S. divsn. Can. Mental Health Assn., 1984—98; mem. adv. coun. Order N.S., 2001—04. Recipient award of merit City of Halifax, 1977, Frances Fish award, 1997, N.S. Women Lawyers Achievement award, Confedn. Can. medal (1867-1992), 1992, Commemorative medal Golden Jubilee of Her Majesty Queen Elizabeth II, 2002, Justice award Can. Inst. Adminstrn. Justice, 2003. Fellow: Law of the Future (hon.); mem.: Order of Can. (apptd. officer 2006), Order of N.S., Nat. Jud. Inst. (bd. dirs. 1998—2004), Can. Jud. Coun. (chmn. edn. com. 1986—88; adminstrn. of justice com. 1992—94, equality com. 1994—99, jud. benefits com. 1994—99, fin. com. 1999—2002, chmn. edn. com. 2000—04, exec. com. 2001—04, vice chair jud. conduct com. 2001—04), Assn. Women Judges (hon.), Internat. Assn. Women Judges (hon.), Can. Bar Assn. (hon.; fellow Law of the Future Fund), Golden Key Internat. Honor Soc. (hon.). Jewish. Avocations: swimming, gardening, bridge. Home: 5920 Inglewood Dr Halifax NS Canada B3H 1B1 Personal E-mail: cglube@judicom.ca.

GLUCH, STEFFEN, company executive; b. Dresden, Saxony, Germany, Aug. 17, 1954; D of Engring., Tech. U., Dresden, 1984. Cert. in engring. Asst. Tech. U. Dresden, 1979—84, asst. lectr., 1988—92; project leader PLANETA Printing Machines , Radebeul, 1984—87; freelance engr., 1992—; exec. Inst. for Prodn. and Environ. Engring., Dresden, 1993—2001; CEO GMT Precision Mfg. GmbH, Glashutte, Germany, 1994—. Lay judge Comml. Ct. of Dresden, 2000; mem. facultas Tech. U. Dresden, 1991. Inventor in field. Mem.: Soc. for Ops. Rsch. Office: GMT Precision Mfg GmbH Bertolt-Brecht-Allee 24 D-01309 Dresden Germany E-mail: ipudresden@t-online.de.

GLUCK, CAROL, history professor; b. Newark, Nov. 12, 1941; d. David E. and Doris S. Newman; m. Peter L. Gluck, May 1, 1966; children: Thomas Edward, William Francis. Student, U. Munich, 1960-61, U. Tokyo, 1972-74; BA, Wellesley Coll., 1962; MA, Columbia U., 1970, PhD, 1977. Asst. prof. Columbia U., NYC, 1975-83, assoc. prof., 1983-86, prof., 1986-88, George Sansom prof. history, 1988—. Vis. rsch. assoc. faculty law Tokyo U., 1978-79, 85-86, 92; vis. prof. Harvard U., Cambridge, Mass., 1991, Inst. Social Sci. Tokyo U., 1993, Ecole des Hautes Etudes en Scis. Sociales, Paris, 1995, 98; fellow Inst. for Advanced Studies in the Behavioral Scis., 1999-2000; mem. Inst. for Advanced Study, Princeton, 2005-06; publs. bd. Columbia U. Press, N.Y.C., 1991-96; co-dir. project on Asia in the core Curriuculm NEH, N.Y.C., 1987—; Am. adv. com. Japan Found., 1986-96, chair, 1991-96; disting. lectr. N.E. Area Coun., 1988, Japan Soc. for Promotion of Sci., 1989. Author: Japan's Modern Myths, 1985 (Fairbank prize 1986, Trilling award 1987); co-editor: Showa: The Japan of Hirohito, 1992, Asia in Western and World History, 1997, Thinking with the Past, 2006; contbr. numerous articles to profl. publs. Mem. Coun. on Fgn. Rels., U.S.-Japan Friendship Commn., 1994—2001; mem. com. on rsch. librs. N.Y. Pub. Libr., 1987—, mem. humanities adv. coun., 1996—. Recipient Fulbright 50th Anniversary Disting. Fellow award, 2002, Order of Rising Sun, Japanese Govt., 2006; fellow, Woodrow Wilson Found.; grantee, Japan Found.; Fulbright grantee, 1985—86, Fgn. Area fellow. Fellow: Am. Acad. Arts and Scis.; mem.: Am. Philos. Soc., Asia Soc. (trustee 1992—98, 2002—), Japan Soc. (bd. dirs. 1990—), Assn. Asian Studies (coun. 1981—84, nominating com. 1985—86, pres. 1996—97, bd. dirs. 1995—99), Am. Hist. Assn. (coun. 1987—90), Phi Beta Kappa. Home: 440 Riverside Dr New York NY 10027-6828 Office: Columbia U East Asian Inst 420 W 118th St New York NY 10027-7213

GLÜCK, LOUISE ELISABETH, poet, educator; b. NYC, Apr. 22, 1943; d. Daniel and Beatrice (Grosby) G.; m. Charles Hertz (div.); 1 child, Noah Benjamin; m. John Dranow, 1977 (div.). Student, Sarah Lawrence Coll., 1962, Columbia U., 1963-65; LLD, Williams Coll., 1993, Skidmore Coll., 1995, Middlebury, 1996. Vis. poet Goddard Coll., U. N.C., U. Va., U. Iowa; Elliston prof. U. Cin., 1978; vis. faculty Columbia U., 1979; faculty M.F.A. program Goddard Coll., also Warren Wilson Coll., Swannanoa, NC;

Holloway lectr. U. Calif., Berkeley, 1982; vis. prof. U. Calif.-Davis, 1983; Scott prof. poetry Williams Coll., 1983; Regents prof. poetry UCLA, 1985-88; faculty Williams Coll., 1984—, Preston Parrish 3d century prof., 1997—2003, Margaret Scott Bundy lectr., 2003—04; Rosenkranz writer-in-residence Yale U., New Haven, 2004—. Vis. prof. Harvard U., 1995; Hurst prof. poetry Brandeis U., 1996; delivered Phi Beta Kappa poem Harvard U. commencement, 1990; baccalaureate spkr. Williams Coll.; Hopwood lectr. U. Mich.; spl. cons. Libr. of Congress, 2000; judge younger poets competition Yale U. Press, 2003—. Author: Firstborn, 1968, The House on Marshland, 1975, Descending Figure, 1980, The Triumph of Achilles, 1985, Ararat, 1990, The Wild Iris, 1992 (Pulitzer Prize for poetry 1993), Proofs and Theories (collected essays), 1994, Meadowlands, 1996, Vita Nova, 1999, The Seven Ages, 2001, October (chapbook), 2004, Averno, 2006. Grantee Rockefeller Found., Nat. Endowment for Arts, 1969-70, 79-80, 88-89, Guggenheim Found., 1975-76, 87-88, NEA, 1988-89; recipient lit. award Am. Acad. and Inst. Arts and Letters, 1981, award in poetry Nat. Book Critics Cir., 1985, Melville Cane award Poetry Soc. Am., 1986, Sara Teasdale Meml. prize Wellesley Coll., 1986, Bobbitt Natil prize Libr. Congress, 1992, Pulitzer prize, 1993, William Carlos Williams award, 1993, PEN/Martha Albrand award Non-Fiction, 1995, Lannan Found. award in poetry, 1999, New Yorker mag. award, 1999, Ambs. award English Spkg. Union, 1999, 2006, 50th Anniversary medal MIT, 2000, Bollingen prize, 2001, Medal for lifetime distinction Barnard Coll., 2004; named Poet Laureate of Vt., 1994, U.S. Poet Laureate, 2003. Fellow Am. Acad. Arts and Scis.; mem. Am. Acad. Arts & Letters, Am. Acad. Poets (chancellor 1999-2006), Phi Beta Kappa (hon.).

GLUCK, MATTHEW, lawyer; b. NYC, Oct. 16, 1942; BA, Cornell U., 1963; LLB, Harvard U., 1966. Bar: N.Y. 1967. Ptnr. Fried, Frank, Harris, Shriver & Jacobson, NYC, 1973—2006; sr. ptnr. Milberg Weiss Bershad & Schulman LLP, 2006—. Office: Milberg Weiss Bershad & Schulman LLP 49th Fl One Pennsylvania Plaza New York NY 10119*

GLUCK, MICHELLE H., lawyer; b. Apr. 1959; m. Robert J. Gluck. BA, JD, U. Mich. Bar: Va. 1983. Assoc. Hunton & Williams, 1983—89; legal cons. Am. Household Inc., 1996—99, Office Depot, 1996—99; v.p., assoc. gen. counsel, asst. sec. The Sports Authority Inc., Ft. Lauderdale, Fla., 1999—2001, Kmart Corp., Troy, Mich., 2001—03; exec. v.p., chief legal officer, corp. sec. LandAmerica Fin. Group Inc., Richmond, Va., 2004—. Mem.: Am. Corp. Counsel Assn. (sec., bd. mem. South Fla. Chpt. 2001). Office: LandAmerica Fin Group Inc PO Box 27567 Richmond VA 23261-7567 Office Phone: 804-267-8383. Business E-Mail: mgluck@landam.com.*

GLUCK, PETER L., architect; BA, Yale U., New Haven; MArch, Yale Sch. Art and Architecture, New Haven. Owner Peter L. Gluck & Ptnrs., Archs., NYC, 1972—. Tchr. design studios Yale U., Columbia U., NYC, CCNY. Prin. works include Little Sisters of the Assumption Family Health Service, East Harlem, NY (Design award, AIA NY chpt., 2004), Affordable Housing, Aspen, Colo. (Architecture Merit award, AIA NY chpt., 2007). Office: Peter L Gluck & Ptnrs Archs 646 W 131st St New York NY 10027 Office Phone: 212-690-4950. Office Fax: 212-690-4961.*

GLÜCK, SEBASTIAN M., pipe organ builder; b. Sept. 26, 1960; BA in Architecture, Columbia U., NYC, 1982, MS in Historic Preservation, 1987. Colleague's cert. Am. Inst. Organ Builders. Pres. Glück Orgelbau, Inc., NYC, 1985—. Builder Laurance Spellman Rockefeller Organ, Union Ch. of Pocantico Hills, Tarrytown, NY, 2006, Sanctuary Organ, Beth-El Chapel Organ, Congregation Emanu-El of City of NY, Rees Jones Meml. Pipe Organ, Alexander Chapel, 1st Presbyn. Ch. in City of NY, organ Ch. of Jesus Christ of LDS, NY Stake Ctr.; contbr. articles to profl. jours.; editor Jour. Am. Organbuilding, 2001—05. Mem.: Am. Inst. Organbuilders, Am. Guild Organists, Internat. Soc. Organbuilders, Organ Hist. Soc. (nat. councillor for rsch. and publs. 2005, mem. restoration guidelines bd.), NY Landmarks Conservancy. Office: 170 Park Row Ste 20A New York NY 10038 Office Phone: 212-608-5651.

GLUCKMAN, PETER, endocrinologist, fetal physiologist; b. New Zealand; s. Laurie and Ann Gluckman. With U. Auckland, New Zealand, 1974—, prof. pediat. & perinatal biology, dean, faculty med. & health scis., 1992—2001, founding dir. Liggin's Inst., 2001—; chief scientific officer Neuren Pharmaceuticals; founding dir. Nat. Rsch. Ctr. Growth & Development, New Zealand. Chmn. pregnancy nutrition com. WHO, NIH. Named New Zealander of Yr., NZ Herald, 2004, U. Disting. Prof., U. Auckland, 2001; recipient Rutherford medal for sci. & tech., New Zealand Royal Soc., 2001, World Class New Zealand award, 2006, Companion of New Zealand Order of Merit, 1997. Fellow: London Royal Soc.; mem.: Inst. Medicine (fgn. assoc.). Office: The Liggins Inst U Auckland Private Bag 92010 Auckland New Zealand also: Neuren Pharmaceuticals Ltd Level 3 2-6 Park Ave Grafton Auckland New Zealand Office Phone: 64 9 373 7599 ext. 86476. Office Fax: 64 9 373 7497. E-mail: director@liggins.auckland.ac.nz.

GLUCKSTEIN, FRITZ PAUL, veterinarian, biomedical information specialist; b. Berlin, Jan. 24, 1927; came to U.S., 1948; s. Georg Jakob and Hedwig Emilie (Heinrich) G.; m. Ethel Gold, July 31, 1955 (dec. Nov. 1993); 1 child, Ruth; m. Maran Ostchega, Nov. 29, 1996. BS, U. Minn., 1953, DVM, 1955; MLS, U. Md., 1984. Diplomate Am. Coll. Vet. Preventive Medicine. Vet. meat insp. U.S. Dept. Agr., South St. Paul, Minn., 1955-56, asst. vet. pathologist Ames, Iowa, 1958-59, vet. analyst Washington, 1959-63; chief microbiology br. Sci. Info. Exchange Smithsonian Instn., Washington, 1963-66; coordinator for vet. affairs Nat. Library of Medicine, Bethesda, Md., 1966-93; biomed. info. cons., 1993—. Mem. coordinating com. for research animal resources NIH, 1982-93; adv. sci. bd. Gorgas Meml. Inst. Tropical Preventive Medicine, Washington, 1967-70; chmn. continuing edn. com. 1989-90. Author: (annotated bibliography) Laboratory Animal Welfare, 1984-93; contbr. chpts. to books. Served to 1st lt. U.S. Army, 1956-58; commd. officer USPHS, 1966-93. Recipient cert. merit U.S. Dept. Agr., 1962 Fellow Royal Soc. Health (London); mem. AVMA, APHA, Assn. Mil. Surgeons of U.S., Am. Assn. Lab. Animal Sci., Am. Soc. Lab. Animal Practitioners, Med. Libr. Assn., Beta Phi Mu. Avocation: music. Home: 11801 Rockville Pike Apt 812 Rockville MD 20852-2723 Personal E-mail: opera.buff@verizon.net.

GLUCKSTERN, ROBERT LEONARD, physics professor; b. Atlantic City, July 31, 1924; BEE, CCNY, 1944; PhD, MIT, 1948. Asst. prof. physics Yale U., New Haven, 1950-57, assoc. prof., 1957-64; prof. physics U. Mass., Amherst, 1964-75, head dept., 1964-69, assoc. provost, 1969-70, provost, vice chancellor for acad. affairs, 1970-75; prof. physics U. Md., College Park, 1975-97, chancellor, 1975-82, sr. rsch. scientist, 1997—2005; ret., 2005. Vis. prof. U. Tokyo, Japan, 1969; cons. on theory of high energy particle accelerators Brookhaven Nat. Lab., Fermi Nat. Accelerator Lab., Lawrence Berkeley Nat. Lab., Los Alamos Nat. Lab., Stanford Linear Accelerator Ctr. With USNR, 1944-46. AEC fellow U. Calif., Berkeley, 1948-49, Cornell U., Ithaca, N.Y., 1949-50, Yale fellow, 1961-62. Fellow AAAS, Am. Phys. Soc.; mem. SSC (bd. overseers 1990-93), SURA (trustee 1982-98, chmn. bd. trustees 1994-96, high energy physics adv. panel 1990-93), Fedn. Am. Scientists, Am. Assn. Physics Tchrs. Business E-Mail: RLG@physics.umd.edu.

GLUECK, JEFFREY, travel company executive; b. Newport Beach, CA; BA social studies, Harvard U.; MA internat. rels., Oxford U. Strategy cons. Monitor Co.; chief strategic officer, v.p. bus. and product devel. Site59.com; head product team, TotalTrip Travelocity, 2002—04, chief mtkg. officer, 2004—. White house fellow Export-Import Bank of the US, 1998—99. Named one of 40 under 40, Advt. Age, 2007. Office: Travelocity 3150 Sabre Dr Southlake TX 76092*

GLUECKMAN, ALAN JAY, writer, producer, director; b. Detroit, Oct. 24, 1944; s. Saul Hyman and Lillian Rose (Stern) G. BA in Econs., U. Mich., 1966; MBA in Mktg., Columbia U., 1968. Creative dir. Ted Bates Hellas, Athens, Greece, 1974-76, Ted Bates, NYC, 1977; writer, dir. Am. Internat. Pictures, 1979; screenwriter Melvin Simon Prodns., 1980, 82, Universal Pictures, Universal City, Calif., 1980, Walt Disney Prodns., LA, 1981, Ray Stark Prodns., LA, 1983-84, Paramount Pictures, LA, 1984, 86; pres. Glueckman Entertainment, LA, 1984—92; screenwriter Columbia Pictures, LA, 1985; chmn. & pres. eJamming AUDiiO, 2002—. Screenwriter: Night Warning, 1982 (Best Horror Film award 1982), Russkies, 1987, Gross Anatomy, 1989; writer, dir. (film) Pickup starring Glenn Close, 1977; writer: Crash Course (NBC), 1988, Jamboree (NBC), 1989, The Face of Fear (CBS), 1990; writer, producer: It Almost Wasn't Christmas (LBS), 1989, Have You Seen Me?, 1991; writer, exec. producer The Fear Inside, 1991; prodr. Ravager, 1997; exec. prodr. (TV series) Scoring, 2002; writer & lyricist (stage musicals) Starr Struck: A Musical Investigation, Stalag 17: The Musical, Friday Saturday Sunday; writer & designer: Mission Impossible: The Web Adventure, You're Gotta Believe Me, Disco-Rama. Mem. Writers Guild Am. West. Office: 77 Federal St 2nd Fl San Francisco CA 94107-1414 Office Phone: 408-832-7627. E-mail: info@ejamming.com.*

GLUSBAND, STEVEN JOSEPH, lawyer; b. Berlin, Jan. 15, 1947; came to U.S., 1949; s. Morris and Docia (Waitman) G.; m. Roberta Gail Jacobs, Nov. 22, 1981; children: Ilana, Jonathan. BBA, CCNY, 1969; JD, Fordham U., 1973; LLM, NYU, 1978. Bar: N.Y. 1974, U.S. Dist. Ct. (so. dist.) N.Y. 1974, U.S. Ct. Appeals (2nd cir.) 1974. Trial atty. SEC, NYC, 1974-75, spl. trial counsel, 1976-77; assoc. Sage Gray Todd & Sims, NYC, 1977-80, ptnr., 1981-87; mem. exec. com. Carter, Ledyard & Milburn, NYC, 1987—. Dir. MER Telemanagement Solutions Ltd. Mem. ABA (com. fed. regulation of securities, securities litigation), Assn. of Bar of N.Y.C. (com. on futures regulation 1986-88). Home: 343 E 30th St New York NY 10016-6417 Office: Carter Ledyard & Milburn 2 Wall St Fl 13 New York NY 10005-2072

GLUSKER, JENNY PICKWORTH, chemist; b. Birmingham, Eng., June 28, 1931; came to U.S., 1955, naturalized, 1977; d. Frederick Alfred and Jane Wylie (Stocks) P.; m. Donald Leonard Glusker, Dec. 18, 1955; children: Ann, Mark John, Katharine. BA in Chemistry, Oxford U., Eng., 1953, MA, DPhil, Oxford U., Eng., 1957; DSc (hon.), Coll. of Wooster, Ohio, 1985. Postdoctoral rsch. fellow Calif. Inst. Tech., Pasadena, 1955-56; rsch. fellow Inst. Cancer Rsch., Phila., 1956, rsch. assoc., 1957-67, asst. mem., 1967, assoc. mem., 1967-79, sr. mem., 1979—. Adj. prof. U. Pa., 1969—; vis. prof. Nat. Inst. Health, 1972—76, Internat. Union Crystallography, Egypt, 1997, Turkey, 2006, chmn. tchg. commn., 1987—93; chmn. selection com. Rhodes Scholarship, Pa., 1984—89; mem. US Nat. Com. for Crystallography, 1974—90, sec.-treas., 1977—79, chmn., 1982—84; mem. biotech. resources rev. com. NIH, 1977—80, chmn. biotech. resources rev. com., 1979—80, mem. adv. com. divsn. rsch. grants; dir.-at-large, mem. gov. bd. Am. Inst. Physics, 1980—83, exec. com., 1981—82, mem. adv. com. Ctr. History of Physics, 2003—05; mem. Metallo Biochem. Study Sect., 1983—87, Divsn. Rsch. Grants Adv. Com., 1989—92, computer graphics lab. adv. com., U. Calif., San Francisco, 1985—, chmn., 1988—; mem. gov. bd. Cambridge Structural Database Ctr., England, 1988—2001, vice chmn., 1998—2001; vis. fellow Oriel Coll., Oxford, England, 1994—95; mem. exec. com. Los Alamos Neutron Sci. Ctr. user group Los Alamos Nat. Lab., 2007—; cons., lectr. in field. Co-author (with K.N. Trueblood): (book) Crystal Structure Analysis: A Primer, 1972, Crystal Structure Analysis: A Primer, 2d edit., 1985; co-author: (with Dodson, Ramaseshan and Venkatesan) The Collected Works of Dorothy Crowfoot Hodgkin; editor: Structural Crystallography in Chemistry and Biology, Structures of Molecules of Biological Interest, 1981; co-editor (with McLachlan): Crystallography in North America, 1982; co-editor: (with S. Parthasarathy) Aspects of Crystallography in Molecular Biology, 1997; editor: Acta Crystallographica sect. D. Biological Crystallography; co-editor (with M. Lewis, M. Rossi): Crystal Structure Analysis for Chemists and Biologists, 1994; co-editor: (with Patterson and Rossi) Patterson and Pattersons, 1987; mem. adv. bd. Molecular Structures in Biology, 1991, mem. editl. bd. Biophys. Jour., 1981—86; contbr. articles to profl. jours. Hon. fellow Somerville Coll., Oxford U. (Eng.), 2001. Fellow AAAS; mem. Am. Assn. Cancer Rsch., The Chem. Soc., Am. Soc. Biol. Chemists, Biophys. Soc., Am. Crystallog. Assn. (pres. 1979, Pub. Svc. award 1991, Fankuchen Meml. award 1995), Am. Chem. Soc. (Phila. sect. award 1978, Garvan medal 1979), Am. Phys. Soc., Sigma Xi. Office: Inst Cancer Rsch Fox Chase Cancer Ctr 333 Cottman Ave Philadelphia PA 19111-2497 Home Phone: 215-379-3449; Office Phone: 215-728-2220. Business E-Mail: jenny.glusker@fccc.edu.

GLUSS, BRIAN, mathematician, statistician, engineer, systems expert; s. Joseph and Otilie (Tenenhaus) Gluss; m. Joan Marie Chodorow (div.); 1 stepchild, Lori Kim Smallwood. BA in Math., Cambridge U., Eng., 1952, MA, 1957; diploma in Stats, Cambridge U., 1953; PhD in Electrical Engring., U. Calif., Berkeley, 1965. Rsch. asst. London Sch. Econs., 1953—54; actuarial clk. Prudential Assurance Co., London, 1954—55; statistician Jury Project U. Chgo., 1955—56; asst. to sr. rschr. bur. of stats. Canadian Govt., Ottawa, 1956—58; staff mem. Ill. Inst. Tech. Rsch Inst., Chgo., 1958—62; mathematician Rand Corp., Santa Monica, Calif., 1964—66; rsch. staff GE-TEMPO, Santa Barbara, 1966—68; prof. U. Ill., Chgo., 1968—83, emeritus prof., 1983—. Cons. Ill. Inst. Tech. Rsch. Inst., Chgo., 1962—64; reviewer Math. Rev., 1966—74. *Gluss is an expert on victims of violent death in war and peace, on healing their families-termed "survivors" by pioneer William Niederland, and on the condition of "survivor guilt." Inspired by Niederland, he uses his own family experiences (bombing, London, 9/24/1940; murder, Santa Barbara, 5/31/1980) in his one-on-one work with other survivors. During wartime, Gluss keeps track of the numbers and conditions of civilian casualties. He researches and works politically on gun issues in America and their relation to murder, suicide, and fatal accidents. He has worked with victims of brain damage and disease to help ease their final years.* Author: (Book) Introduction to Dynamic Programming, 1972; contbr. articles to profl. jours. and newspapers. Vol. performer for retirement homes etc., Berkeley, Calif., 2000—; vol. grief mentor; polit. and human rights activism. With RAF, 1949, England. State scholar, Brit. Govt., 1948, Found. scholar, Pembroke Coll., Cambridge, 1952. Fellow: Royal Stats Soc. (London). Democrat. Avocations: acting, singing, dance, volunteering. Home: 3242 Idaho St Berkeley CA 94702 Office Phone: 510-428-2708.

GLUYS, CHARLES BYRON, retired marketing management consultant; b. Richmond, Ind., Apr. 16, 1928; s. J. Howard and Reba Anna (Macy) G.; children: Gary William, Robert Lee, Marcia Kay, James Duke. BS in Indsl. Econs., Purdue U., 1955. Sales mgr. Carlyle Constrn., Columbus, Ohio, 1958; asst. product mgr. Palmer-Donavin Mfg., Columbus, 1958-61; new product mgr. KCL Corp., Shelbyville, Ind., 1963-64; prin. Gluys & Assocs., Greenfield, Ind., 1964—. Asst. scoutmaster Boy Scouts Am., Greenfield, 1953-54, Columbus, 1958-60, chmn. orgn. and extension com., Columbus, 1960-61; vol. counselor Small Bus. Adminstrn., 1976-. Mem. Am. Mktg. Assn. (bd. dirs. 1970-73), Inventors Assn. Ind. (1st v.p. 1986), Assn. Indsl. Advertisers (treas. 1971-72), Masons.

GLYMPH, DIANNE TYLER, librarian; b. Burlington, NC, Sept. 10, 1958; d. Earle Goodson and Mayme Alcora (Ellis) Tyler; m. Michael Joe Glymph, Sept. 26, 1981. BA cum laude, Presbyn. Coll., 1980; MLS, Univ. S.C., 1981. Head libr. Christ Ch. Episc. Sch., Greenville, S.C., 1981-83; reference libr. Greenville County Libr., 1983-90, br. mgr., 1990; reference libr. Midlands Tech. Coll., Columbia, S.C., 1991-94. Reference libr./webmaster Trident Tech. Coll., Charleston, SC, 1996—99; libr. Drug Free Am. Found., St. Petersburg, Fla., 2001—. Mng. editor: Jour. Global Drug Policy and Practice; contbr. articles to profl. jours. Singer Greenville Chorale, 1982-90; bd. dirs. Walter Johnson Club of Presbyn. Coll., 1987-89, Pebble Ridge Homeowners Assn., 1989-90; libr., editor Drug Free Am. Found. Mem. S.C. Libr. Assn. (sec. archives and spl. collections 1987-88), Piedmont Libr. Assn., Staff Assn. Greenville County Libr. (pres. 1987-88), Alumni Assn. Presbyn. Coll. (bd. dirs. 1999-2004) Avocations: music, calligraphy. Home: 2212 Riverside Dr N Clearwater FL 33764-6722 Business E-Mail: dglymph@dfaf.org.

GLYNN, CARLIN (CARLIN MASTERSON), actress; b. Cleve., Feb. 19, 1940; d. Guilford Cresse and Lois Carlin (Wilks) G.; m. Peter Masterson, Dec. 29, 1960; children: Carlin Alexandra, Mary Stuart, Peter C.B. Student, Sophie Newcomb Coll., 1957-58. Prof. Columbia U. Grad. Film Sch., NYC; prof. MFA program Actors Studio at Pace U. Creative advisor Sundance Inst. Film Lab. Appeared in N.Y. as Miss Mona in: The Best Little Whorehouse in Tex., 1978-80; in London, 1981; starred in Pal Joey, Goodman Theatre, Chgo., 1988 (Joseph Jefferson award 1988), Cover of Life, Am. Place Theatre, N.Y., 1994, The Young Man from Atlanta, Signature Theatre Co., 1995 (Pulitzer prize for drama 1995), Amazing Grace, 1998, The Chemistry of Change, 1999, Frame 312, 2002, Safe, 2003, Spring Storm, 2004, The Oldest Profession, 2004, A Lovely Sunday for Creve Coeur, Hartford Stage, Conn., 2006; films include Three Days of the Condor, 1974, Resurrection, 1978, Continental Divide, 1981, Sixteen Candles, 1984, The Trip to Bountiful, 1985, Blood Red, Night Game, Convicts, 1989, Blessing, 1992, Judy Berlin, 1997, West of Here, 2001, Lost Junction, 2001, Whiskey School, 2004; TV series Mr. President, 1987; dir. short film Love Divided By, 1993; dir. contemporary opera Cheri at Actors Studio, 2005. Recipient Theatre World award, 1978, Antoinette Perry award, 1979, best actress award in musical Soc. West End Theatres, Lawrence Olivier award, London, 1981 Mem. SAG, AFTRA, Actor's Studio (bd. dirs., co-artistic dir.), Actors' Equity Assn. Episcopalian.

GLYNN, EDWARD, retired academic administrator; b. Clarks Summit, Pa., Oct. 6, 1935; s. John J. G. AB, Fordham U., 1960, PhL, 1961, MAT, 1962; STB, Woodstock Coll., 1967; STM, Yale Divinity Sch., 1968; ThD, Grad. Theol. Union, 1971; LLD (hon.), Monmouth Coll., 1984, U. Scranton, 1990; LHD (hon.), Seton Hall U., 1989, St. Peter's Coll., 1990, Loyola Coll., 1993. Entered Soc. Jesus 1955; ordained 1967. Instr. Gonzaga H.S., 1961—64; asst. prof. Georgetown U., 1971-77; acad. v.p. Gonzaga U., Spokane, 1977-78, pres., 1996—97, St. Peter's Coll., Jersey City, 1978-90; provincial Md. Province Soc. of Jesus, Balt., 1990-96; interim provost U. Mass., Boston, 1997—98; pres. John Carroll U., Cleve., 1998—2005. Acting dir., mem., bd. dir. Churches' Ctr. for Theology and Pub. Policy, 1976-77; exec. dir. Woodstock Theol. Ctr., Washington, 1974-76, bd. dirs., 1974-76. Contbr. articles to profl. jours. Bd. dirs. U. Scranton, 1973-78, Fordham U., 1981-87, Canisius Coll., 1982-88, 2001—, LeMoyne Coll., 1983-89, 2000—04, St. Louis U., 1986-91, John Carroll U., 1987-90, 1998—2005, Seton Hall U., 1990-96, St. Mary's Sem. and U., 1991-96, Weston Sch. Theology, 1990-96, NCAA's Pres. Commn., 1984-88, Commn. on Higher Edn., Mid. States Assn., 1988-90, Fairfield U., 1997-, Marquette U., 1998-, U. Detroit Mercy, 1999-, Wheeling Jesuit U., 2004-, Am. Coun. of Edn., 2001-2004, U.S. Dept. of Edn. (nat. adv. bd. 1999-2001), Fund for Improvement of Post Secondary Edn. Mem.: FIPSE. Home Phone: 202-625-2589; Office Phone: 216-397-4209, 202-625-2589. Personal E-mail: lgly@aol.com.

GLYNN, EDWARD F., JR., lawyer; b. Boston, May 5, 1947; BA, McGill U., 1968; JD, Cornell U., 1971. Bar: NY 1972, DC 1975, Md. 1981, US Ct. of Appeals (2d, 4th, 9th and D.C. cirs.), US Dist. Ct. (no., so. and ea. dists.) NY, US Dist. Ct., Md., US Dist. Ct., DC. Various positions including trial atty. and asst. dir., internat. antitrust FTC, 1976—89, assoc. dir., bur. of competition, 1989—90; of counsel, ptnr., antitrust, consumer protection and trade regulation Venable LLP, Washington, 1991—. Mem.: ABA (former chmn. consumer protection com., antitrust sect., mem. coun.), DC Bar Assn., Md. Bar Assn., NYC Bar Assn. Office: Venable LLP 575 7th St NW Washington DC 20004 Office Phone: 202-344-4805. Office Fax: 202-344-8300. Business E-Mail: efglynn@venable.com.

GLYNN, JAMES A., sociology educator, writer; b. Bklyn., Sept. 10, 1941; s. James A. and Muriel M. (Lewis) G.; m. Marie J. Gates, Dec. 17, 1966 (div. Apr. 1995); 1 child, David S. AA, Foothill Coll., 1961; BA in Sociology, San Jose State U., Calif., 1964, MA in Sociology, 1966; PhD, U. Calif. at Riverside, 1972. Instr. in sociology Bakersfield Coll., Calif., 1966-98, prof. sociology, 1972—98; prof. sociology State Ctr. Cmty. Coll. Dist. Clovis Ctr. and Madera Ctr., 1998—2002, prof. emeritus State Ctr. Cmty. Coll. Dist., 2003. Adj. prof. Fresno (Calif.) State U., 1971-72, Chapman Coll., Orange, Calif., 1972, Calif. State U., Bakersfield, 1989-98, Chapman U., Visalia, Calif., 1997-98; del. acad. senate Calif. C.C., Sacramento, 1980-89; mem. coun. Faculty Assn. Calif. C.Cs., 1981—; columnist Madera Tribune, 1999-2001, 2004—. Author: Studying Sociology, 1979, Writing Across the Curriculum Using Sociological Concepts, 1983, Hands On: User's Manual for Data Processing, 1986; (with Elbert W. Stewart) Introduction to Sociology, 1972, 4th edit., 1985; (with Crystal Dea Moore) Guide to Social Psychology, 1992, Understanding Racial and Ethnic Groups, 1992, 98, 2001, Guide to Human Services, 1994, Focus on Sociology, 1994, 98; (with Charles F. Hohm and Elbert W. Stewart) Global Social Problems, 1996; contbg. editor Introduction to Sociology, 1996; contbg. author: California's Social Problems, 1997; editor, contbg. author (with Charles F. Hohm) California's Social Problems, 2d edit., 2001 Mem. Madera County Arts Coun., 2000—, co-chair fin. com., 2001—02, pub. rels. chmn., exec. bd., 2001—, v.p., 2002—03, pres., 2003—04, 2006—; mem. citizens adv. com. of govt. ctrs. and hall of justice Madera County Bd. Suprs., 2000—01; chairperson pub. rels. com. City of Madera; bd. dirs. San Joaquin Paleontology Found., 2004—06; chair pub. rels. com. Implementation Com. for City of Madera Vision Project, 2007—. Recipient Innovator Yr. award League Innovations C.C., 1989, Innovator Yr. award Kern C.C. Dist., 1992. Mem. Calif. Sociol. Assn. (founder, treas. 1990-92, editor newsletter 1991-92, pres. 1992-93, exec. dir. 1993-2001), Commn. on Tchg., Pacific Sociol. Assn. (mem. editl. bd. Sociol. Perspectives 1996-99, awards com. 2000-03, Disting. Prof. award for Contbn. to Edn. 1997,), Population Reference Bur., World Watch Inst., World Future Soc., Kiwanis (editor newsletter 2001—, pres. 2001-02, bd. dirs. 2004—). Democrat. Home: 135 N Park Dr Madera CA 93637-3041 Office Phone: 559-674-4490. Personal E-mail: j_glynn@sbcglobal.net.

GLYNN, KEVIN PELTIER, pulmonologist; b. Chgo., Ill., July 17, 1936; s. Edward Kevin and Marguerite (Peltier) Glynn; m. Patricia Harrington Glynn, Sept. 1, 1962; children: Kevin H., MaryEllen, Kathleen, Patrick, Terrence. BA, Northwestern U., Evanston, Ill., 1957, MD, 1961. Intern Chgo. Wesley Meml. Hosp., 1961—62; resident U. Mich., 1962—63, 1965—67; pvt. practice San Diego, 1967—2003; med. cons. Healthways, Inc., San Diego, 2002—, Scripps Health, San Diego, 2003—. Med. dir. Scripps Mercy Hosp., San Diego, 1981—2003, respiratory care chief staff, 1999—2000. Author: (book) Beyond Training, 2000. Capt. USAF, 1963—65, Altus, Okla. Fellow, Milw. County Gen. Hosp., 1967—69. Mem.: Rotary Internat. Roman Catholic. Avocation: golf.

GLYSCH, RANDALL LEE, research scientist; s. Alvin Joseph and Marlene Lou Glysch; life ptnr. William Roy Kunzelman. BS in Psychology and Human Devel. cum laude, U. Wis., Green Bay, 1988; MS in Ednl. Psychology, U. Wis., Madison, 2000. Rsch. scientist Wis. Dept. Health and Family Svcs., Madison, 1998—. Author, pub.: Injury Prevention, Human

Development, Maternal and Child Health, Tobacco Prevention & Control. V.p. to pres. Carpenter-Ridgeway Neighborhood Assn., Madison, 1996—2007, founder, neighborhood planning coun., 2000; founder East Isthmus Neighborhoods Planning Coun., 2000; bd. mem. Transit and Parking Commn., 1998—2000, Motor Vehicle and Pedestrian Commn., 1999—2001, Madison Pks. Commn., 2001—05, Madison Pool Com., 2005—06; sec. Madison Pks. Found., 2004—06, Friends of Starkweather Creek, Madison, 2004—06; active Madison Citizen Police Acad., 2007, mem., 2007—. Yeoman 1st class USN, 1976—84. Decorated Navy Achievement medal USN, Sailor of Yr. (2 commands); nominee Sailor of Yr., Pacific Fleet; Injury Prevention grantee, Ctr. for Disease Control and Prevention, 2002, 2005, 2006—07. Mem.: APHA (assoc.), Profl. Employees in Rsch. and Statis. Analysis (assoc.; sec. 2000—03). Progressive. Avocations: walking, gardening, stain glass windows. Home Phone: 608-244-0054; Office Phone: 608-266-9708. Personal E-mail: rgbk@sbcglobal.net.

GMACHL, CLAIRE, electrical engineer, educator; MS in Physics, U. Innsbruck, 1991; PhD in Electrical Engring., Tech. U., Vienna, 1995. Mem. tech. staff, Walter Schottky Inst. Tech. U., Munich, 1992—94, mem. tech. staff, Ctr. Microstructures Vienna, 1993—94, asst. prof., Dept. Solid State Electronics, 1995—96; post-doctoral mem. tech. staff Lucent Technologies-Bell Laboratories, NJ, 1996—98, mem. tech. staff NJ, 1998—2002, disting. mem. tech. staff NJ, 2002—03; assoc. prof. Dept. Electrical Engring. Princeton U., 2003—. Contbr. articles to profl. jour. Named a MacArthur Fellow, John D. and Catherine T. MacArthur Found., 2005; recipient Group Achievement award, NASA, 2000, Outstanding Performer award, US Dept. Def. (Def. Advanced Rsch. Projects Agy.), 2001, Commendation for Excellence in Tech. Comm., Laser Focus World mag., 2001, The Snell Premium award, IEE UK, 2003. Mem.: Laser and Electro-Optics Soc., Austrian Physical Soc. (Solid State Physics award 1996), AAAS, Optical Soc. Am., Am. Physical Soc., NY Acad. Sci., Internat. Soc. Optical Engring., Materials Rsch. Soc., IEEE (sr.). Achievements include granted 15 patents. Office: Princeton Univ Engineering Quadrangle B 326 Olden St Princeton NJ 08544 Office Phone: 609-258-4641. Office Fax: 609-258-3745. E-mail: cgmachl@princeton.edu.

GMEINER, TIMOTHY J., music librarian, music director; b. Neenah, Wis., June 15, 1949; s. Russell Elwood and Elvera L. (Fink) Gmeiner; life ptnr. Dale Manning, 1976. BA in Creative Comm., U. Wis., Green Bay, 1971; MusM in Piano Performance, Vanderbilt U., Nashville, 1975, MLS, 1978. Organist, asst. dir. music Hillsboro Presbyn. Ch., Nashville, 1976—; music libr. Belmont U., Nashville, 1979—. Adjudicator Nat. Guild Piano Tchrs., 1978. Mem.: Music Libr. Assn. (Southeastern Chpt.), Am. Guild Organists. Home: 3024 Brightwood Ave Nashville TN 37212 Office: Belmont U 1900 Belmont Blvd Nashville TN 37212 Home Phone: 615-297-7958; Office Phone: 615-460-5495. Office Fax: 615-460-6095. Business E-Mail: gmeinert@mail.belmont.edu.

GNANARAJ, JOSEPH SATHIYA, scientist; b. Kovilpatti, Tamil Nadu, India, Mar. 10, 1963; arrived in US, 2003, permanent resident, 2005; s. Joseph Vedgnanamuth and Paranjothi Vedanayagam; m. Jeyarani Paulinal, Aug. 27, 1993; 1 child, Lincy. MSc, Bharathidasan U., India, 1989, MPhil, 1990; PhD, U. Pune, India, 1998. Postdoctoral rschr. Bar-Ilan U., Ramat-Gan, Israel, 1999—2001, sr. rschr., 2001—03; scientist Worcester Poly. Inst., Mass., 2003—06, Yardley/Lithion Inc., 2006—. Dir. Bible Study Groups, Sunday Sch. New Eng. Tamil Ch., Wakefield, Mass., 2004; mng. trustee Follow Jesus Ministries, India. Grantee, Dept. Energy, 2005—06, Dept. Defense, 2006—07, NASA, 2007—, OSD, 2007—. Mem.: Electrochem. Soc. Achievements include research in lithium ion batteries. Office: Yardney Technical Products 82 Mechanic St Pawcatuck CT 06379 Home: 104 Litton Ct Groton CT 06340 Office Phone: 860-599-1100 ext. 480. Personal E-mail: js_gnanaraj@yahoo.com. Business E-Mail: joeg@lithion.com.

GNAT, RAYMOND EARL, librarian; b. Milw., Jan. 15, 1932; s. John and Emily (Syperek) Gnat; m. Jean Helen Monday, June 19, 1954; children: Barbara, Richard, Cynthia. BBA, U. Wis., 1954, postgrad., 1959; MS, U. Ill., 1958; MPA, Ind. U., Indpls., 1981. Page Milw. Pub. Libr., 1950-53, jr. libr., 1954, librarian, 1958-63; circulation asst. U. Ill., 1956-57, serials cataloger, 1957-58; asst. dir. Indpls.-Marion County Pub. Libr., 1963-71, dir., 1972-94. Exec. dir. Ind. Nat. Libr. Week, 1965. With AUS, 1954—56. Mem.: ALA, Bibliog. Soc. Am., Ind. Libr. Assn. (pres. 1980), Portfolio Club, Lit. Club. Home: 8246 Shadow Cir Indianapolis IN 46260-2761

GNEHM, EDWARD W., JR., ambassador; b. Nov. 10, 1944; s. Edward, Sr. and Beverly (Thomasson) Gnehm; m. Margaret Scott, June 13, 1970; children: Cheryl Lynn, Edward William III. BA, George Washington U., 1966, MA, 1968; postgrad., Am. U., Cairo, 1966—67; LLD, Thiel Coll., 2000. Head U.S. liaison office Dept. of State, Riyadh, Saudi Arabia, 1976-78, dep. chief of mission Am. Embassy Sanaa, Yemen, 1978-81, dir. jr. officer divsn. pers. Washington, 1982-83, dir. secretariat staff, 1983-84, dep. chief mission Am. Embassy Amman, Jordan, 1984-87; dep. asst. sec. def. for Near East and South Asia Dept. of Def., 1987-89, dep. asst. sec. state Bur. Near East and South Asian Affairs, 1989-90, U.S. amb. to Kuwait, 1990-94, dep. U.S. Permanent Rep. to UN, 1994-97; dir.-gen. of fgn. svc., dir. pers. U.S. Dept. of State, Washington; US amb. to Australia, 2000-2001; US amb. to Jordan, 2001—04; Kuwait prof. internat. affairs Elliot Sch. Internat. Affairs George Washington U., 2004—. Shapiro vis. prof. Elliott Sch. Internat. Affairs George Washington U., vice chmn. bd. Bd. dirs. Am. Near East Refugee Aid, Am.-Kuwait Alliance; mem. exec. bd. Nat. U.S.-Arab C. of C. Recipient Presdl. Disting. Honor award, 2000. Mem.: Am. Acad. Diplomacy, Am. Fgn. Svc. Assn., Mid. East Inst., Am. Philatelic Soc., Sigma Chi, Omicron Delta Kappa. Presbyterian. Avocations: history, bicycling, stamp collecting/philately, hiking. Office: George Washington U Elliott Sch Internat Affairs 1957 E St NW Ste 501 Washington DC 20052 Office Phone: 202-994-0155. Business E-Mail: ambgnehm@gwu.edu.

GNICHTEL, WILLIAM VAN ORDEN, lawyer; b. Summit, NJ, Jan. 11, 1934; s. William Stone and Edith Parrot (Van Orden) G.; m. Emily Hopkins Martenet, July 11, 1959 (dec.); children: William Van Orden Jr., Edwin Martenet; m. Mary B. Gayley, June 7, 1996. BA, Trinity Coll., 1956; LLB, Columbia U., 1959. Bar: N.Y. 1961, Mass. 1997. Ptnr. Whitman & Ransom, NYC, 1968-88, Chadbourne & Parke, NYC, 1988-92; spl. counsel Law Firm of Salah Al-Hejailan, Riyadh, Saudi Arabia, 1986-95. Lectr. in field. Contbr. articles to profl. jours. Mem. Assn. Bar City N.Y. (mem. com. internat. security affairs 2001-04, mem. com. fgn. and comparative law 2006—), Boston Bar Assn. (chmn. pub. policy com. bus. steering com. 1999-2004), Union Club, Knickerbocker Club (N.Y.C.), Onteora Club (Tannersville, N.Y.; exec. vp. 1974-75, pres. 1976-77, bd. dirs. 1970-77), Masons, Phi Delta Phi. Episcopalian. Address: PO Box 431 Lincoln MA 01773-0431 Personal E-mail: WVOGLAW@mindspring.com.

GNIEWEK, DEBRA LYMAN, school librarian, consultant; b. Philadelphia, Pa., Apr. 6, 1951; d. Bernard and Lois Lyman; m. Edwin Joseph Gniewek, Jan. 15, 1983; 1 child, Andrew Lyman. BA, Temple U., 1972; MEd, Arcadia U., 1989; MIS, Drexel U., 1991. Cert. ednl. adminstrn. Temple U., 1999, sch. libr. Drexel U., 1991, secondary English tchr. Gwynned-Mercy Coll., 1977. Sch. libr. Sch. Dist. Phila., 1991—96, mgr. libr. programs and svcs., 1996—2001; sch. libr. Coun. Rock Sch. Dist., Holland, Pa., 2001—. Exec. bd. mem. Assn. Phila. Sch. Librs., 1994—2000; dir. and sec. Pa. Sch. Librs. Assn., 2000—04; mem. adv. bd. The Multicultural Resource Ctr., Phila., 1998—; tchr. adv. com. Am. Immigration Law Found., Washington, 2005—. Author: (articles) American Librs., (article) Sch. Libr. Jour.; conf. presenter From Aesop to e-book. Recipient Libr. Advocacy award, Assn. Phila. Sch. Librs., 2001, Commendation, Pa. Sch. Librs. Assn., 2000, 2004; scholar Governor's Inst. for Literacy and Info. Literacy, Pa. Dept. Edn., 2005. Master: Bucks County Librs. Assn. (corr.; steering com. 2005—06). Avocations: reading, travel, theater. Office: Council Rock HS South 2002 Rock Way Southampton PA 18966 Home Phone: 215-673-5352; Office Phone: 215-944-1175. Business E-Mail: dgniewek@crsd.org.

GOACH, KENNETH EDMUND, professional counselor; b. Hazle Brook, Pa., July 26, 1929; s. John and Elizabeth Goach; m. Ruth Helen O'Quinn, Mar. 13, 1953; 1 child, Kenneth Edmund Jr. BA, S.E. State U., Durant, Okla., 1956, M of Tchg., 1960; grad., Northwestern U. Marching Band Sch., Evanston, Ill., 1964. Cert. counselor, prin. West Tex. State U., 1966. Band and orch. dir. Nixon Jr. High, Amarillo, Tex., 1956—58, Fannin Jr. High, Amarillo, 1958—67, counselor, 1967—81, Sam Houston Jr. High, Amarillo, 1981—91; lic. prof. counselor Amarillo Ind. Sch. Dist., 1984—91; ret. Dir. Khiva Shrine Band, Amarillo. Fundraiser Khiva Shrine, Amarillo, 1980—, arranger music, 1980—. With USAF, 1950—53, Alaska, Tex. Mem.: NEA (life), Tex. State Tchrs. Assn., Masonic Lodge, Kappa Delta Phi. Avocations: dance, writing, walking, movies.

GOATS, DEBBIE, elementary school educator; b. Panorama City, Calif., July 11, 1964; d. Mandel and Joan Buchbinder; m. Michael Goats, May 26, 1991; children: Sarah, Mandy. EdB in Elem. Edn. summa cum laude, Temple U., Phila., 1990. Cert. elem. edn. Okla., sci. endorsement mid. sch./jr. HS Okla. 4th and 5th grade sci. tchr. Crutcho Pub. Schs., Oklahoma City, 1990—95, mid. sch. sci. tchr., 1995—2002; jr. high sci. tchr. Advanced Sci. and Tech. Edn. Ctr., Oklahoma City, 2003—05, sci. dept. chair, student health advisor, 2003—05; 6th grade tchr. McLoud (Okla.) Pub. Sch., 2005—. After sch. tutor Crutcho Pub. Schs., Oklahoma City, 1990—94, sci. club and field rsch. sponsor, 1996—97, sci. coord. lab. sci., sci. fair dir. local level, 1996—2002, asst. dir. bird and butterfly cmty. courtyard, 2002—03; sq. foot gardens facilitator, sci. fair dir. local level Advanced Sci. and Tech. Edn. Ctr., Oklahoma City, 2003—05. Recipient Dean Willard Zahn Tribute award, Temple U., 1990; Pres.'s scholar, 1990. Office: McLoud Schs 529 W Park Mcloud OK 74851 Home Phone: 405-769-2727; Office Phone: 405-964-3306.

GOBAR, ALFRED JULIAN, retired economic consultant, educator, investor; b. Lucerne Valley, Calif., July 12, 1932; s. Julian Smith and Hilda (Millbank) G.; m. Sally Ann Randall, June 17, 1957, (dec. 2005); children: Wendy Lee, Curtis Julian, Joseph Julian; m. Cathleen Jane Anderson, Feb. 26, 2006. BA in Econs., Whittier Coll., 1953, MA in History, 1955; postgrad., Claremont Grad. Sch., 1953-54; PhD in Econs., U. So. Calif., 1963; DHL (hon.), Whitter Coll., 2005. Asst. pres. Microdot Inc., Pasadena, Calif., 1953—57; regional sales mgr. Sutorbilt Corp., LA, 1957—59; mktg. rsch. assoc. Beckman Instrument Inc., Fullerton, Calif., 1959—64; sr. mktg. cons. We. Mgmt. Consultants Inc., San Diego, 1964—66; ptnr., prin., chmn. bd. Darley/Gobar Assocs., Inc., San Diego, 1966—73; pres., chmn. bd. Alfred Gobar Assocs., Inc., Anaheim, 1973—. Asst. prof. finance U. So. Calif., LA, 1963-64; assoc. prof. bus. Calif. State U., LA, 1963-68, 70-79, assoc. prof. Calif. State U.-Fullerton, 1968-69; mktg., fin. adviser 1957—; pub. spkr. seminars and convs. Contbr. articles to profl. publs. Trustee Whittier Coll., 1992—. Office: 300 S Harbor Blvd Ste 900 Anaheim CA 92805-3721 Home: 1215 Margarita Dr Fullerton CA 92833 Office Phone: 714-772-8900 ext. 309. Business E-Mail: al@gobar.com. *I try not to be too quick to cast aside the social protocol that has taken centuries to evolve and test in order to define effective behavior.*

GOBEL, JOHN HENRY, lawyer; b. Oak Park, Ill., Oct. 21, 1926; s. Henry Andrew and Mary Ann (Coughlan) G.; m. Carol Zvara, Mar. 8, 1969; children: Kristina, Gregory. BA cum laude, DePaul U., 1950, JD cum laude, 1952. Bar: Ill. 1951, Md. 1975, Ohio 1976. Various positions law dept. Chgo. and North Western R.R. Co., Chgo., 1952-60, Balt. and Ohio R.R. Co., Balt., 1960-75; asst. gen. counsel Chesapeake and Ohio Ry. Co., Cleve., 1975-77, gen. solicitor, 1977-80, gen. counsel, 1980-82; v.p. govt. relations CSX Corp., Cleve., 1982-86; v.p., regional trial counsel CSX Transp., 1987. Served with U.S. Army, 1945-46. Fellow Internat. Soc. Barristers; mem. ABA (spl. com. on rules 1967-71), Ill. Bar Assn. (chmn. profl. ethics com., mem. assembly 1973-74), Nat. Assn. R.R. Trial Counsel (nat. sec. 1971-75), Soc. Trial Lawyers Ill. (dir. 1968-70), Ohio C. of C. (bd. dirs.), Ohio Pub. Expenditures Council (v.p. 1979-88), Ohio R.R. Assn. (chmn. 1979-87), W.Va. R.R. Assn. (chmn. 1975-87). Clubs: Union League (Chgo.), Law (Chgo.). E-mail: gobel-john@webtv.net.

GOBLE, DAVID S., library director; BA, The Citadel; MA, U. SC; MLS, U. NC-Chapel Hill. V.p. NationsBank, Charlotte, NC; asst. v.p. SC Nat. Bank, Columbia; with U. NC-Chapel Hill Sch. Info. & Libr. Sci., NC State U. Librs., Charlotte-Mecklenburg Pub. Libr., NC; dean of librs. Ctrl. Piedmont Cmty. Coll., Charlotte, NC; state libr. SC State Libr., Columbia, 2007—. Capt. USMC. Recipient Outstanding Svc. to the Sch. award, U. NC Sch. Info. & Libr. Sci., 1993. Mem.: ALA, U. NC Sch. Info. & Libr. Sci. Alumni Assn. (pres. 2001—02), Metrolina Libr. Assn. (immediate past pres.), NC Coun. Cmty. Coll. Libr. Adminstrs., NC Libr. Assn. Office: SC State Libr PO Box 11469 Columbia SC 29211 Office Phone: 803-834-8656. Office Fax: 803-734-8676. E-mail: dgoble@statelibrary.sc.gov.*

GOBLE, PAUL, writer, illustrator, artist; b. Haslemere, Eng., Sept. 27, 1933; s. Robert John and Elizabeth Marian (Brown) G.; m. Janet A. Tiller, June 2, 1978; 1 son, Robert George; children by previous marriage: Richard, Julia. Nat. Diploma in Design with distinction, Central Sch. Art and Design, London, 1959; LHD (hon.), S.D. State U. Vis. lectr. indsl. design Central Sch. Art and Design, London, 1960-68; sr. lectr. indsl. design Ravensbourne Coll. Art and Design, London, 1968-77. Author, illustrator numerous children's books including: Custer's Last Battle, 1969, The Fetterman Fight, 1972, Lone Bull's Horse Raid, 1973, The Friendly Wolf, 1974, The Girl Who Loved Wild Horses, 1978 (Caldecott medal), The Gift of the Sacred Dog, 1980, Star Boy, 1983, Buffalo Woman, 1984, The Great Race, 1985, Death of the Iron Horse, 1987, Her Seven Brothers, 1988, Iktomi and the Boulder, 1988, Beyond the Ridge, 1989, Iktomi and the Berries, 1989, Dream Wolf, 1990, Iktomi and the Ducks, 1990, Iktomi and the Buffalo Skull, 1991, I Sing for the Animals, 1991, Crow Chief, 1992, Love Flute, 1992, The Lost Children, 1993, Iktomi and the Buzzard, 1994, Adopted by the Eagles, 1994, Hau Kola—Hello Friend, 1994, The Return of the Buffaloes, 1996, Remaking the Earth, 1996, The Legend of the White Buffalo Woman, 1998, Iktomi and the Coyote, 1998, Iktomi Loses His Eyes, Paul Goble Gallery: Three Native American Stories, 1999, Storm Makers Tipi, 2001, Mystic Horse, 2003, A Song of Creation, 2004, All Our Relatives, 2005, Tipi: Home of the Nomadic Buffalo Hunters, 2007. Recipient Regina medal, Cath. Libr. Assn., 2006. Fellow Royal Soc. Arts, Soc. Indsl. Artists and Designers, Grey Owl Soc. (hon.), Eagle Cir. Soc. (hon.). *I have felt the pull of the Native American tradition as long as I can remember, probably since the time my mother read to me stories of Grey Owl and Ernest Thompson Seton. As I grew up in England, I read everything I could lay my hands on about Indians. It was the books concerning the wisdom of Black Elk which finally determined my life's orientation.*

GOCHBERG, THOMAS, real estate investor, investment banker; b. Boston, Jan. 18, 1939; s. Hyman and Lee (Goredetsky) G.; m. Leatrice Eckber, Mar. 28, 1965; children: John, Sarah. AB, Columbia U., 1961. Pres., CEO Smith Barney Real Estate Corp., NYC, 1969-84; dir. Smith Barney, Inc., NYC, 1980-84; pres., CEO Security Capital Corp., NYC, 1978—90, dir., 1978—2000. Chmn. Benjamin Franklin Savs. Assn. 1985-89, dir. 1981-89; chmn. Foster Mortgage Co., 1985-89, dir. 1981-89; pres., sole shareholder TJG Holdings Inc., 1991—; ptnr. TGM Assocs. L.P., 1991—; pres., dir. TGM Realty Corp. I, II, III, IV, V, VI, VII, X, XX, XXX, XL, 1993—. V.p. Rep. County Com. of NY, 1985—95, 2001—; trustee Birch Wathan Sch., NYC, 1980—88; trustee, treas. Nat. Maritime Hist. Soc., 1990—92; trustee South Street Seaport Mus., NYC, 1992—2005, 2006—, co-chair waterfront com., 1995—98, co-chair devel. com., treas. exec. com., treas., 2006—; bd. dirs. Am. Sail Tng. Assn., 1994—2003, exec. com., chmn. devel. com., 1996—98, vice chair, 1999—2003; bd. assocs. The Whitehead Inst. Biomed. Rsch., 1995—; co-chair pres.'s coun. NY Hist. Soc., 2006—. With US Army, 1960—63. Mem.: Pension Real Estate Assn. (pres. 1982—84, chmn. 1984—85), Ocean Cruising Club, Cruising Club of Am. (treas. NY sta. 1996—2000, rear commodore NY sta. 2000—02), Royal Western Yacht Club Eng., Univ. Club (N.Y.C.), NY Yacht Club (seamanship com. 1995—, membership com. 1998—2001). Jewish. Office: TGM Assocs 650 5th Ave Fl 28 New York NY 10019-6108 Business E-Mail: tgochberg@tgmassociates.com.

GOCHNAUER, RICHARD WALLIS, wholesale distribution executive; b. Kansas City, Mo., Dec. 3, 1949; s. Harry Wallis and Janet Elizabeth (Huff) G.; m. Beth Andrea Splinter, Dec. 18, 1971; children: Grant D., Mary E. BS in Indsl. Engring., Northwestern U., 1972; MBA, Harvard U., 1974. From shift supr. to pres. Schreiber Internat., Schreiber Foods, Green Bay, Wis., 1974-82; exec. v.p., gen. mgr. Dial Corp., Phoenix, 1989—93; pres. cheese div. Universal Foods, Milw., 1982-89; pres. Golden State Foods, 1993—2002; COO United Stationers Inc., Des Plaines, Ill., 2002, pres., CEO, 2002—. V.p. Nat. Cheese Inst., Washington, 1988-89. Chmn. bd. dirs. YMCA, Green Bay, 1981, Milw., 1988; mem. met. bd. dirs. YMCA, Phoenix, 1990. Mem. Soap and Detergent Assn. Office: United Stationers Inc 2200 E Golf Rd Des Plaines IL 60016*

GOCKEL, JOHN RAYMOND, construction executive; b. Ft. Madison, Iowa, June 12, 1947; s. Carl R. and Virginia Jeanne (Schultz) Gockel; m. Joleen E. Gunst, Sept. 9, 1989; children: Rose Marie Kuehni, Christina Ann Rathman. BSCE, Iowa State U., 1970. Registered profl. engr., Mich., Minn., Wis. Cost estimator Barton Malow Co., Detroit, 1975-76, project mgr., 1976-82, project adminstr., 1982-83; project exec. Gilbane Bldg. Co., Maplewood, Minn., 1983-84; constrn. mgr., dir. phys. plant Minn. Racetrack, Inc., Shakopee, 1984-85; v.p. Scottland, Inc., Shakopee, 1985-86, Knutson Constr. Co., Mpls., 1987-88, Encompass Inc., Bloomington, Minn., 1988-89; ind. constrn. cons. Bloomington, 1989—; pres. John R. Gockel & Assocs., Inc., 1990—. Project mgr. Mpls. Metrodome; constrn. mgr. Canterbury Downs, Mpls.; owner's rep. Minn. Twins Ballpark, 2007—; cons., lectr. in field. Minn. arbitrator Am. Arbitration Assn., 1982. Recipient Honor award, Cons. Engrs. Coun., Minn., 1985. Mem.: Minn. Consulting Engrs. Coun., Minn. Soc. Profl. Engrs. (bd. dirs. 1985—86, Seven Wonders of Engring. award 1982, 1985), Profl. Engrs. Contrn. (v.p. 1983, pres. 1984, bd. dirs. 1984—93), Internat. Congress Bldg. Ofcls., Am. Acad. Forensic Examiners, Iowa State U. Alumni Assn., Tau Beta Pi. Republican. Roman Catholic. Avocations: history, woodworking, boating, fishing. Home and Office: 11120 Stanley Cir S Minneapolis MN 55437-3315 Home Phone: 952-888-5362; Office Phone: 952-888-5362. Personal E-mail: jrgockel@aol.com.

GOCKLEY, (RICHARD) DAVID, opera company director; b. Phila., July 13, 1943; s. Warren and Elizabeth S. Gockley; children: Meredith, Lauren, Adam. BA, Brown U., 1965; MBA, Columbia U., 1970; DHL (hon.), U. Houston, 1992; DFA (hon.), Brown U., 1993. Dir. music Newark Acad., 1965-67; dir. drama Buckley Sch., NYC, 1967-69; mgr. box office Santa Fe Opera, 1969-70; bus. mgr. Houston Grand Opera, 1970-71, assoc. dir., 1971-72, gen. dir., 1972—2005, San Francisco Opera, 2006—. Co-founder Houston Opera Studio, 1977. Prodr. (operas): Nixon in China (Emmy award 1988), Harvey Milk, Florencia en el Amazonas, Porgy and Bess (Tony award, Grammy award 1977), Treemonisha, A Quiet Place, Willie Stark, Resurrection, Carmen. Bd. dirs. Tex. Inst. Arts in Edn.; past pres. OPERA Am.; past chmn. Houston Theater Dist. Recipient Tony award League of N.Y Theaters and Producers, 1977, Dean's award Columbia Bus. Sch., 1982, Music Theater award Nat. Inst. Music Theater, 1985, William Rogers award, Brown U., 1995; named one of Outstanding Men Am., Nat. Jr. C. of C., 1976. Mem. OPERA Am. Avocation: tennis. Office: San Francisco Opera 301 Van Ness Ave San Francisco CA 94102 Office Phone: 415-551-6271. Business E-Mail: dgockley@sfopera.com.*

GODAGER, JANE ANN, retired social worker; b. Blue River, Wis., Nov. 29, 1943; d. Roy and Elmyra Marie G. BA, U. Wis., 1965; MSW, Fla. State U., 1969. LCSW, diplomate Acad. Cert. Social Workers. Social worker III State of Wis. Dept Corrections, Wales, 1965—71; supervising psychiat. social worker I State of Calif., San Bernardino, 1972—75, La Mesa, 1975—77, psychiat. social worker San Bernardino, 1978—85; supr. mental health svcs. Riverside County Dept. Mental Health, Calif., 1985—86; mental health counselor Superior Ct. San Bernardino County, 1986—2001; staff asst. to dist. dir. Calif. State Assembly, 2002, ret., 2002. Former mem. adv. bd. Grad. Sch. Social Work Calif. State U., San Bernardino, Mental Health Assn.; mem. County Hosp. Re-Use Com. Mem. commn. sr. affairs City of San Bernardino, Calif.; mem. County Mental Health Commn.; sr. assemblyperson Calif. Sr. Legislature; legis. com. Mayor's Blue Ribbon Com. Mem.: NASW, Acad. Cert. Social Workers, Kappa Kappa Gamma Alumnae Assn. Avocations: travel, reading, music.

GODBEY, ROBERT CARSON, lawyer; b. Houston, June 7, 1953; s. Charles Perry and Bobbye Lee Godbey; m. Ellen Carson, June 2, 1979. BS, BSEE magna cum laude, So. Meth. U., 1975; JD cum laude, Harvard U., 1980. Bar: U.S. Patent Office, 1981, Hawaii 1988. Telecom. engr. Southwestern Bell, Dallas, 1975—76, Tex. Instruments, Dallas, 1976—77; assoc. Peabody, Lambert & Meyers, Washington, 1980—84; asst. U.S. atty. U.S. Dept. Justice, Washington, 1984—87, Honolulu, 1987—91; ptnr. Godbey Griffiths Reiss LLLP, 1991—. Mem. ABA, IEEE, Hawaii State Bar Assn. (past chmn. intellectual property sect. 1994-96, past chmn. tech. com., 1995-97), Phi Beta Kappa, Tau Beta Pi. Office: 2300 Pauahi Tower 1001 Bishop St Honolulu HI 96813-3429 Office Phone: 808-523-8894.

GODBOLD, FRANCIS STANLEY, investment banker, security firm executive; b. Charleston, SC, Mar. 4, 1943; s. Francis Stanley and Ula Leigh (Waddey) G.; m. Lelia Elizabeth Harman, Sept. 24, 1966; children: John A., Laura H. Blair. BS in Indsl. Engring. with honors, Ga. Inst. Tech., 1965; MBA, Harvard U., 1969. V.p. Raymond, James & Assocs., Inc., St. Petersburg, Fla., 1969-74, sr. v.p., 1974-78, exec. v.p., 1978—; pres. Raymond James Fin., Inc., 1987—2002, vice chmn., 2002—. Regional firms adv. com. NY Stock Exch., 1990-93; bd. dirs. Raymond James Bank, Raymond James Fin. Pres. Baypoint Mid. Sch. Parent Action Com., 1982-83, Bay Vista Parent Action Com., 1979-80; mem. Leadership St. Petersburg, 1974—; mem. Lakewood H.S. Parent Action Com., 1984-90, pres., 1987-88, trustee Ga. Tech. Found., Inc., 2003-; dir. Ga. Tech. Indsl. and Sys. Engring. Alumni award, 1997, mem. Tampa Bay area regional devel. coun., 1995; bd. dirs. Acad. Prep., 1999-, Elk River Properties Owners Assn., chmn. fin. com., 2003-04, pres., 2004-2006; bd. dirs. Banner Elk Heritage Found. Capt. AUS US Army, 1965—67. Mem. Securities Industry Assn. (vice chmn. so. dist. 1980, chmn. 1987, treas. 1986, exec. com. 1988-96, nat. dir. 1995-97, regional firms com. 1995-99, chmn. regional firms com. 1998, tax policy com. 1995-97, nominating com. 1997), Ga. Tech. Alumni Assn. (trustee 2002-05), Harvard Club of West Coast Fla. (sec.-treas 1971-72, v.p. 1972-73, pres. 1973-74), Harvard Bus. Sch. Club (treas. 1984), St. Petersburg Country Club, Elk River Club, Diamond Creek Golf Club, Tau Beta Pi, Phi Kappa Phi, Alpha Pi Mu, Phi Delta Theta. Republican. Office: Raymond James Fin Inc 880 Carillon Pkwy Saint Petersburg FL 33716-1100 Home Phone: 727-867-1962; Office Phone: 727-567-5003.

GODBOLD, JOHN COOPER, federal judge; b. Coy, Ala., Mar. 24, 1920; s. Edwin Condie and Elsie (Williamson) Godbold; m. Elizabeth Showalter, July 18, 1942; children: Susan, Richard, John C., Cornelia. BS, Auburn U., 1940; JD, Harvard U., 1948; LLD (hon.), Samford U., 1981, Auburn U., 1988, Stetson U., 1994. Bar: Ala. 1948. With firm Richard T. Rives, Montgomery, Ala., 1948-49; ptnr. Rives & Godbold, 1949-51, Godbold & Hobbs and successor firms, 1951-66; cir. judge US Ct. Appeals (5th cir.), 1966-81, chief judge, 1981, US Ct. Appeals (11th cir.), 1981-86, sr. judge, 1987—; dir. Fed. Jud. Ctr., Washington, 1987-90. Mem. Fed. Jud. Ctr. Bd., 1976—81. With field arty. US Army, 1941—46. Mem.: FBA, ABA, Montgomery County Bar Assn., Ala. Bar Assn., Phi Kappa Phi, Omicron Delta Kappa, Alpha Tau Omega. Episcopalian. Office: US Ct Appeals 11th Circuit One Church Street Montgomery AL 36104 Office Phone: 334-954-3920.*

GODBOUT, ARTHUR RICHARD, JR., lawyer; b. Hartford, Conn., Oct. 7, 1957; s. Arthur Richard and Elizabeth Anne (Desmond); m. Elizabeth G. Godbout. BSBA, Georgetown U., 1979, JD, 1986. Bar: Conn. 1987. Pres. A.R. Godbout & Co., Avon, Conn., 1987—. Home: 8 Cheltenham Way Avon CT 06001-2444 Office: PO Box 1175 Avon CT 06001-1175

GODDARD, BRYAN LANCE, physician, director; b. July 13, 1954; s. Charles William and Alice Lance Goddard; m. Nancy Baumback, June 24, 1978; children: David, Jonathan. MD, NY Med. Coll., 1980. Diplomate Am. Bd. of Family Practice, 1983. Pvt. practice Self-employed, Gloversville, NY, 1983—87; residency faculty Wilson Family Practice Residency, Johnson City, NY, 1987—; med. dir. Johnson City Family Care Ctr., NY, 1983—91; med. dir. info. technologies United Health Services, Johnson City, NY, 1998—. Domestic cons. Lockheed-Martin Healthcare Systems, Owego, NY, 1999—2000; chmn., aids policy group NY Penn Health Systems Agy., Binghamton, 1988—89; med. cons. Broome County Child Protective Services, Binghamton, 1989—98; bd. mem. Rural Health Network of South Ctrl. NY, Whitney Point, NY, 2001—. Contbr. articles to profl. jours. Recipient Recognition for Outstanding Svc., Broome County Child Abuse Coun., 1989—97. Fellow: Am. Acad. of Family Physicians; mem.: Am. Med. Informatics Assn., Soc. of Teachers of Family Medicine. Christian, United Methodist. Office: United Health Services 40 Arch St Johnson City NY 13790

GODDARD, CLAUDE PHILIP, JR., lawyer; b. Long Beach, Calif., Oct. 31, 1952; s. Claude Philip and Doris Marian (Dow) G.; m. Ellen Kohn, May 23, 1981; children: Marian Laura, Nora Margaret. BS with distinction, US Naval Acad., 1974; JD cum laude, U. Pa., 1979. Bar: N.H. 1979, D.C. 1985, Va. 1999, U.S. Dist. Ct. D.C. 1989, U.S. Ct. Appeals (9th cir.) 1985, U.S. Ct. Appeals (fed. cir.) 1991. Ensign USN, 1974, advanced through grades to lt. comdr., 1987, atty., 1979—87, resigned, 1987; assoc. Keck, Mahin & Cate, Washington, 1987—89, ptnr., 1990, Jenner & Block, Washington, 1990—95; shareholder Kilcullen, Wilson and Kilcullen, Chartered, Washington, 1995—99, Wickwire Gavin, P.C., Vienna, Va., 1999—2006, Akerman Senterfitt Wickwire Gavin, Tysons Corner, Va., 2006—. Office Phone: 703-790-8750. Business E-Mail: claude.goddard@akerman.com.

GODDARD, DONALD LETCHER, writer, editor; b. Cortland, NY, Apr. 16, 1934; s. Donald Gay and Adele Fournier (Letcher) G.; m. Connie Heaton (div. 1977); m. Hannah Wilke (dec. 1993); m. Helen Oppenheimer, 2000; children: Kathlyn Adele, Cornelia Marion. AB, Princeton U., 1956; postgrad., Columbia U., 1958-60, NYU, 1966-68. Admitting clk. St. Vincent's Hosp., NYC, 1956-58, St. Luke's Hosp., NYC, 1958-59; with picture rsch. dept. Reader's Digest, NYC, 1959-60; editor Am. Archives World Art, NYC, 1960-65, McGraw-Hill Book Co., NYC, 1966-68; dir. Editorial Photocolor Archives, NYC, 1968-74; mng. editor Art News, NYC, 1974-78, contr., editor, 1978—90; editor Harry N. Abrams, Inc., 1979—82; sr. editor Wildlife Conservation Soc., Bronx, 1981-96; art reviewer newyorkartworld.com, 2000—. Mem. adv. bd. art gallery Lehman Coll., Bronx, 1985-96. Author: Mark di Suvero: An Epic Reach, 1976, Harry Jackson, 1981, The Fashion Photographer, 1981, Sound/Art, 1983, American Painting, 1990, Saving Wildlife, 1995. Mem.: Internat. Assn. Art Critics. Office: 463 West St New York NY 10014-2010 Business E-Mail: hgoddard3@rr.nyc.com.

GODDARD, PETER, academic administrator, mathematical physicist; b. Woking, Surrey, UK, Sept. 3, 1945; s. Herbert Charles and Rosina Sarah (Waite) G.; m. Helen Barbara Ross, Aug. 24, 1968; children: Linda Jane, Michael Alan Edward. BA, U. Cambridge, 1966, PhD, 1970, Sc.D, 1996. Rsch. fellow Trinity Coll., Cambridge U., 1969-73; vis. scientist CERN, Geneva, 1970-72; lectr. applied math. U. Durham, U.K., 1972-74; univ. asst. lectr. in math. U. Cambridge, 1975-76; tutor St. John's Coll., U. Cambridge, 1980-87, sr. tutor, 1983-87; univ. lectr. math. U. Cambridge, 1976-89, reader in math. physics, 1989—92, prof. theoretical physics, 1992—2004; dep. dir. Isaac Newton Inst. for Mathematical Sciences, Cambridge, England, 1991—94; master St. John's Coll., U. Cambridge, 1994—2004; chmn. local exam. syndicate U. Cambridge, 1998—2003; dir. Inst. of Advanced Study, Princeton, NJ, 2004—. Fellow St. John's Coll., U. Cambridge, 1975-1994, 2004-; vis. prof. U. Va., Charlottesville, 1983; mem. Inst. Advanced Study, Princeton, NJ, 1974, 88, Inst. Theoretical Physics, U. Calif., Santa Barbara, 1986, 90. Contbr. articles to profl. jours. Decorated comdr. Order Brit. Empire; recipient Dirac prize and medal, Internat. Ctr. for Theoretical Physics, Trieste, 1997. Fellow: Inst. Physics, Royal Soc., Trinity Coll. Dublin (hon.); mem.: London Math. Soc. (pres. 2002—03). Office: Inst for Advanced Study Einstein Dr Princeton NJ 08540 Office Phone: 609-734-8200. Business E-Mail: pgoddard@ias.edu.

GODDARD, TERRY, state attorney general; BA, Harvard U., 1969; JD, Ariz. State U., 1976. Bar: Ariz. 1976, U.S. Ct. Appeals (9th cir.) 1980, U.S. Supreme Ct. 2003. Mayor City of Phoenix, 1983-90; of counsel Bryan Cave, Phoenix, 1990-94; atty. gen. State of Ariz., 2003—. Bd. dirs. Ariz Theatre Co.; former pres. Nat. League of Cities, 1989; former chmn. Ariz Mcpl. Water Users Assn., Maricopa Assn. Govts., Regional Pub. Transp. Authority, Rebuild Am. Coalition; adv. bd. State and Local Legal Ctr. With USNR, 1970—98. Mem.: ABA, Maricopa County Bar Assn., Ariz. State Bar Assn. Democrat. Office: Office of Atty General 1275 W Washington St Phoenix AZ 85007 Office Phone: 602-542-4266. E-mail: ag.inquiries@azag.gov.*

GODDE, JAMES SCOTT, molecular biologist; b. Aurora, Ill., Feb. 20, 1967; s. James Carl Godde and Ruth Gundlach; m. Trudy Lynn Tolliver, Oct. 4, 1986; children: Justin Quade, Brennan Scott. PhD, U. Ill., Urbana-Champaign, 1993. Postdoctoral fellow NIH, Bethesda, Md., 1993—97; asst. prof. Bklyn Coll., CUNY, 1997—2001; assoc. prof., chmn. biology Monmouth Coll., Ill., 2001—. Avocation: acting. Office: Monmouth Coll 700 East Broadway Monmouth IL 61462 Office Phone: 309-457-2350. Office Fax: 309-457-2226. Business E-Mail: jgodde@monm.edu.

GODDESS, LYNN BARBARA, real estate investor; b. NYC, Mar. 3, 1942; d. Eugene Daniel and Hazel Cecile (Kinzler) Goddess. BS, Columbia U., 1963, postgrad., 1964—66. Coord. John M. Burns Assembly Campaign, NYC, 1963; dir. spl. events, projects Kenneth B. Keating Senatorial Campaign, NYC, 1964; dist. dir. fund raising Muscular Dystrophy Assn. Am. Inc., NYC, 1965-66; exec. acct. fund raising, pub. relations Victor Weingarten Co., NYC, 1966-67, Oram Group (formerly Harold L. Oram Inc.), NYC, 1967-70; dir. devel. City Ctr. Music Drama Inc., NYC, 1970; sales person Whitbread-Nolan, NYC, 1971-73; from asst. v.p. to sr. v.p. Cross and Brown Co., NYC, 1973-1985; sr. dir., comml. real estate Cushman & Wakefield, Inc., NYC, 1985—2004; chmn./CEO LYNN LLC, 2004—. Trustee Young Adult Inst.; founder, chmn. The Hazel K. Goddess Fund for Stroke Rsch. in Women., 2000—; mem. external adv. bd. Ga. Brain and Spinal Injury Rsch. Ctr., 2004—. Mem. Nat. Soc. Fund Raisers, Assn. Fund Dirs., Real Estate Bd. NY (named Most Ingenious Broker Yr. 1975), Women's Forum (bd. dirs.). Home Phone: 212-288-4287. Personal E-mail: lbg22@earthlink.net.

GODDU, KEVIN ALBERT, secondary school educator; b. Lowell, Mass., Mar. 13, 1962; s. Albert Peter and Rita Theresa Goddu; m. Lorraine Ann Dolat, Oct. 4, 1997; children: Matthew Thomas, Alan Kevin. BA, U. of Lowell, Mass., 1989; MEd, U. of Mass., 1993; MA, Salem State Coll., Mass., 1999. Long-term substitute tchr. Nashua Sr. H.S., Nashua, NH, 1993—94, spl. edn. tchr. asst., 1994—95; social studies tchr. Timberlane Regional H.S., Plaistow, NH, 1995—. Author: (book) Monday's Mourning: A Retrospective of the 1915 Strike at the Nashua Manufacturing Company; contbr. articles to profl. jours. Bd. dirs. Nashua Hist. Soc., NH, 1991—92, 2d v.p., 1992—95; town meeting rep. Chelmsford, Mass., 2005—; mem. Chelmsford Hist. Commn., 2005—. Mem.: Am. Polit. Sci. Assn., The Omohondro Inst. of Early Am. History and Culture, The Soc. for Historians of the Early Am. Republic, New Eng. Hist. Assn., Am. Hist. Assn., Phi Theta Kappa, Pi Lambda Theta. Avocations: golf, travel. Home: 402 Wellman Ave North Chelmsford MA 01863-1364 Office: Timberlane Regional High School 36 Greenough Rd Plaistow NH 03865 Office Phone: 603-382-6541 482. Personal E-mail: kagoddu@comcast.net. Business E-Mail: kgoddu@timberlanehs.com.

GODENNE, GHISLAINE DUDLEY, physician, psychotherapist, educator; b. Brussels; came to U.S., 1951; d. Pierre and Olive Dudley (Short) G. BS, Universite Catholique de Louvain, Belgium, 1948, MD, 1952. Intern Providence Hosp., Washington, 1951-52; resident in pediatrics, 1952-54; fellow in pediatrics Mayo Clinic, Rochester, Minn., 1954-57; fellow in pediatric research Johns Hopkins U., 1957-58, assoc. prof. mental hygiene, 1966-82, assoc. prof. psychiatry and pediatrics, 1966-82, psychoanalyst, 1972—, prof. psychology, 1973-90, prof. psychiatry, pediatrics, and mental hygiene, 1982—; resident in psychiatry Johns Hopkins Hosp., Balt., 1958-62, chief adolescent psychiat. service, 1964-73, dir. counseling and psychiat. services, 1973-90, dir. health svcs., 1978-88, dir. emeritus, 1990—; mem. staff various hosps. Balt., 1978-88; clin. prof. psychiatry U. Md., Balt., 1986—. Cons. psychiatrist Cylburn Children's Home, Balt., 1960-81, Catonsville (Md.) C.C., 1968-75, Good Shepherd Ctr., Balt., 1970-74, Assoc. Cath. Charity, Balt., 1970-77, Jewish Family of Children's Svcs., Balt., 1972-77, Mt. Washington Pediat. Hosp., Balt., 1974-81, Sheppard and Enoch Pratt Hosp., Balt., 1973-80, Loyola Coll., Balt., 1990-92. Mem. editorial bd.: Adolescent Psychiatry, 1978-83, Clinical Update Adolescent Psychiatry, 1982-85; contbr. articles to profl. jours. Bd. dirs. Balt. Girl Scouts Assn., 1958-60, 81-82, Met. Balt. Assn. Mental Health, 1965-69, Florence Crittendon Home, 1966-68; trustee McDonough Sch., 1975-83; pres. bd. Trustees Richmond Fellowship Md., 1975-77. Decorated Knight and Officer Order of Leopold (Belgium); recipient Christophe Plantin prize, Belgium, 1989; awarded Nobility Concession with the title of Baroness (Belgium) 1991; recipient Career Teaching award NIMH, 1963-65, Schonfeld award Am. Soc. Adolescent Psychiatry, 1995; grantee Fulbright Found., 1951-52, Parke Davis Co., 1957-58, NIMH, 1961-63. Fellow ACP, Am. Psychiat. Assn. (life), APHA (life), Am. Orthopsychiat. Assn. (life), Am. Soc. Adolescent Psychiatry (life, pres. 1981-82); mem. AAUP, Am. Psychoanalytic Soc., Md. Soc. Adolescent Psychiatry (pres. 1968-69), Md. Psychiat. Soc. (past chmn. program com., co-chmn. women's com. 1991-96), Md. State Conf. Social Welfare (past mem. child welfare com.), Am. Soc. Adolescent Medicine (charter), Am. U. and Coll. Counseling Ctr. Dirs., Internat. Soc. Adolescent Psychiatry (v.p. 1989-92, sec.-gen. 1992-95, v.p. 1995-99, co-editor monograph 2000-05), Women's Club of Johns Hopkins U. (pres. 1999-2000). Home: 15 Edgevale Rd Baltimore MD 21210-2215 Business E-Mail: gigodenn@jhmi.edu.

GODFREY, CULLEN MICHAEL, lawyer, academic administrator; b. Ft. Worth, Apr. 8, 1945; s. Cullen Aubrey and Agnes (Eiland) Godfrey; m. Melinda McDonald, Aug. 29, 1970. BA, U. Tex., 1968, JD, 1970. Bar: Tex. 1969, U.S. Dist. Ct. (we. dist.) Tex. 1971, U.S. Ct. Appeals (5th cir.) 1979, U.S. Supreme Ct. 2004. Ptnr. Sloan, Muller & Godfrey, Austin, Tex., 1969—72; staff atty. Hunt Oil Co., Dallas, 1972—74, Tesoro Petroleum Corp., San Antonio, 1974—75, sr. atty., 1975—78, asst. gen. counsel, 1978—82, FINA, Inc., Dallas, 1982—88, gen. counsel, 1988—90, v.p., sec., gen. counsel, 1990—95, sr. v.p., sec., gen. counsel, 1995—2000; vice chancellor, gen. counsel U. Tex. Sys., Austin, 2000—04; ptnr. Jackson Walker LLP, Austin, 2004—06; gen. counsel Tex. A&M U. Sys., 2006—. Author: Legal Aspects of the Purchase and Sale of Oil and Gas Properties, 1992; contbr. articles to profl. jours. Trustee Dallas Mus. Art, 1993—95, 1998—2000; gen. campaign chmn. United Way Met. Dallas, Inc., 1999; bd. dirs. Greater Dallas Crime Commn., 1991—2000, chmn. bd. dirs., 1997—99; bd. dirs. Dallas County Heritage Soc., 1998—2000, United Way Met. Dallas, Inc., 1999—2000, United Way Capital Area, 2005—06; bd. dirs. Cir. 10 Boy Scouts Am., 1999—2000; bd. dirs. Greater Austin Crime Commn., 2003—06, v.p., 2004—06. Recipient Excellence in Corp. Practice award, Am. Corp. Counsel Assn., 1998, Jurisprudence award, Anti-Defamation League, 1999. Fellow: Austin Bar Found. (founder), Dallas Bar Found. (sustaining life fellow), Tex. Bar Found. (sustaining life fellow); mem.: ABA (chmn. subcom. on fgn. investment reporting, internat. law sect. 1984—87), Nat. Conf. Commr. on Uniform State Laws, Am. Law Inst., Ctr. Am. and Internat. Law (rsch. fellow), Tex. Bus. Law Found. (chmn. bd. dirs. 1995—98, bd. dirs.), Tex. Bd. Legal Specialization (bd. cert. oil, gas and mineral law), State Bar Tex. (coll. mem. 1989—, coun. oil, gas and mineral law sect. 1992—95, coun. bus. law sect. 1998—2004, chmn. bus. law sect. 2002—03, Cert. Merit 1999, 2003, Friends of CLE award 2004). Office: Tex A&M U Sys 200 Tech Way Ste 2079 College Station TX 77845 Home Phone: 979-690-0987. Business E-Mail: mgodfrey@tamu.edu.

GODFREY, JOHN CARL, medicinal chemist; b. Cornelius, Oreg., Mar. 11, 1929; s. Carl H. and Ruth Emma (James) G.; m. Nancy Jane Williams, June 12, 1954; children: Laura Alexis, Helen Rebecca, Sabrina Lee. BA in Chemistry, Pomona Coll., Claremont, Calif., 1951; PhD in Organic Chemistry, U. Rochester, 1954. Rsch. chemist Shell Devel. Co., Emeryville, Calif., 1954-55; instr. chemistry Rutgers U., New Brunswick, NJ, 1955-59; asst. dir. clin. rsch. Bristol Labs., Syracuse, NY, 1959-79, Revlon Health Care, Tuckahoe, NY, 1979-86; assoc. dir. clin. rsch. Rorer Pharm. Corp., Horsham, Pa., 1986-90; pres. Godfrey Sci. & Design, Inc., Huntingdon Valley, Pa., 1979—, cons., 1990—. Mem. sci. adv. bd. Quigley Corp., Doylestown, Pa., 1992—. Contbr. more than 60 articles to profl. jours. NSF fellow, 1951; DuPont fellow, 1952-53. Fellow Am. Inst. Chemists; mem. AAAS, Am. Soc. Microbiology, Am. Chem. Soc. Achievements include patents for formulation to deliver active zinc in treatment of common cold (U.S., U.K., Can., Europe), 57 total in U.S.; elucidation of mechanism of action of zinc against common cold in humans; invention of original and enhanced formulations of major common cold intervention lozenges; Godfrey Stereomodels which uniquely demonstrate mechanisms of formation, properties and reactions. Office: Godfrey Sci & Design 1649 Old Welsh Rd Huntingdon Valley PA 19006-5835 Office Phone: 215-947-1861. Personal E-mail: jcandnj@aol.com.

GODFREY, JOHN MUNRO, economic consultant; b. San Antonio, Mar. 20, 1941; s. George Phillips and Frieda (Allen) G.; m. Nancy Porter, June 4, 1966 (div. 1976); 1 son, John Munro, Jr.; m. Flavel Mcmichael, July 30, 1994. AA, Armstrong State Coll., 1964; BBA, U. Ga., 1964, PhD, 1976. Rsch. officer, sr. fin. economist Fed. Res. Bank, Atlanta, 1969-81; sr. v.p., chief economist Barnett Banks Inc., Jacksonville, 1981-95; prin. Fla. Econ. Assocs., Jacksonville. Adj. prof. econs. and fin. Davis Coll. Bus., Jacksonville (Fla.) U., 1995-97; mem. Gov.'s Econ. Adv. Com.; mem. econ. adv. com. Am. Bankers Assn. Author: Monetary Expansion in the Confederacy, 1977. Mem. econ. adv. com. U.S. C. of C.; bd. dirs. Fla. Ballet at Jacksonville, Jacksonville Symphony Orch., Cummer Mus. of Art and Gardens; chmn. St. Vincent's (Hosp.) Found.; trustee St. Johns Country Day Sch.; vestryman St. Marks Episcopal Ch., Jacksonville; trustee, treas. St. Marks Episcopal Ch. Found. Recipient Disting. Alumnus award Terry Coll. of Bus., U. Ga., 1994. Mem. Econ. Roundtable of Jacksonville (pres. 1982-89), Nat. Assn. Bus. Economists (dir.), Am. Econ. Assn., So. Econ. Assn., U. Ga. Coll. Bus. Alumni Assn. (bd. dirs., pres.), Ponte Vedra Club, Fla. Yacht Club (bd. dirs.), Meninak Club (bd. dirs. Jacksonville chpt.), Timuquana Country Club, Epping Forest Yacht Club. Episcopalian. Office: Fla Econ Assocs 4168 Oxford Ave Jacksonville FL 32210-4464 Home: 4849 Ortega Blvd Jacksonville FL 32210-7637 E-mail: godfreyjon@aol.com.

GODFREY, NORMAN V., plastic surgeon; BS, Yale U., 1979; MD, Harvard U., 1973. Lic. physician N.Y., diplomate Am. Bd. Plastic Surgery. Resident in gen. surgery NYU-Bellevue Hosp. Med. Ctr., 1973—78, resident in plastic surgery, 1978—80; fellow in microvascular surgery Bellevue Hosp., 1978—80; pvt. practice plastic surgery NYC, 1980—. Chief divsn. plastic surgery N.Y. VA Hosp., 1980—81; clin. instr. plastic surgery NYU-Bellevue Med. Ctr., 1980—; attending surgeon N.Y. Hosp. Med. Ctr. of Queens, 1982—, St. Vincent's Hosp. Med. Ctr., 1982—, Manhattan Eye, Ear and Throat Hosp., 1982—, N.Y. Flushing Hosp., 1997—; asst. clin. prof. surgery N.Y. Med. Coll., 1995—98, Cornell U. Weill Med. Coll., 1998—; co-dir. divsn. plastic surgery N.Y. Hosp. Med. Ctr. of Queens, 1982—. Contbr. articles to profl. jours. Mem.: AMA, Am. Soc. Plastic and Reconstructive Surgeons, N.Y. State Med. Soc.

GODFREY, PHILIP M., plastic surgeon; BS, Yale U., 1974; MD, Med. Coll. Pa., 1981; DDS, U. Pa., 1981. Lic. physician N.Y., diplomate Am. Bd. Plastic Surgery. Resident in surgery Hartford Hosp., Conn.; resident in plastic surgery NY Hosp./Cornell Med. Ctr.; fellow in plastic surgery of the breast Meml. Sloan-Kettering Cancer Ctr.; pvt. practice plastic surgery Fresh Meadows, NY. Co-dir. divsn. plastic surgery N.Y. Hosp. Med. Ctr. of Queens, 1982—, attending surgeon, 1986—, St. Vincent's Hosp. and Med. Ctr., 1987—, Manhattan Eye, Ear and Throat Hosp., 1994—, N.Y. Flushing Hosp., 1997—; asst. clin. prof. surgery N.Y. Med. Coll., 1995—98, Cornell U. Med. Coll., 1998—; contbr. Found. Reconstructive Plastic Surgery; spkr. in field. Contbr. articles to profl. jours. Named to Castle-Connolly Guide to Best Drs. in area. Mem.: AMA, Am. Soc. Plastic and Reconstructive Surgeons, N.Y. State Med. Soc. Office: 16303 Horace Harding Hwy Fresh Meadows NY 11365

GODFREY, RICHARD CARTIER, lawyer; b. Harvey, Ill., Sept. 25, 1954; s. Richard L. and Rosemary (Cartier) G.; m. Alice Bacon Woolsey, Aug. 27, 1983; children: John Cartier, Polly Woolsey. BA magna cum laude, Augustana Coll., 1976; JD magna cum laude, Boston U., 1979. Bar: Ill. 1979, US Dist.Ct. (no. dist.) Ill. 1979, US Dist. Ct. (ctrl. dist.) Ill. 1988, US Dist. Ct. (we. dist.) Mich. 1990, US Dist. Ct. (no. dist.) Ind. 1999, US Dist. Ct. Colo. 2002, US Dist. Ct. (ea. dist.) Mich. 2005, US Ct. Appeals (7th cir.) 1983, US Ct. Appeals (6th cir.) 1988, US Ct. Appeals (8th cir.) 1994, US Ct. Appeals (10th cir.) 1996, US Ct. Appeals (11th cir.) 1997, US Ct. Appeals (5th and 9th cirs.) 1999, US Ct. Appeals (2d. cir.) 2002, US Ct. Appeals (1st cir.) 2003, US Ct. Appeals (3d cir.) 2003, US Ct. Appeals (4th cir.) 2005, US Claims Ct. 1990, US Supreme Ct. 2000, US Tax Ct. 2006. Assoc. Kirkland & Ellis LLP, Chgo., 1979-85, ptnr., 1985—. Named one of Am. Leading. Bus. Lawyers Litig./Gen. Comml., Chambers USA, 2004—05. Mem. ABA, Ill. Bar Assn., Chgo. Bar Assn., Bd. Visitors Boston U. Sch. Law, Bd. Trustees Augustana Coll., Lawyers' Com. Nat. Ctr. State Cts., Office: Kirkland & Ellis LLP Ste 6048 200 E Randolph Dr Chicago IL 60601 Office Phone: 312-861-2391. Office Fax: 312-861-2200. Business E-Mail: rgodfrey@kirkland.com.

GODFREY, ROBERT DOUGLAS, lawyer; b. Danbury, Conn., Sept. 11, 1948; s. Douglas and Rita (Cardinale) G. BA, Fordham U., 1970; JD, U. Conn., 1985. Bar: Conn. 1985. Com. clk. Conn. Gen. Assembly, Hartford, 1977-78; v.p. pub. affairs Greater Danbury C. of C., 1978-82; law clk. to presiding judge Probate Ct., City of Danbury, 1983; atty. Conn. Bank & Trust Co., Hartford, 1986-90; justice of the peace State of Conn., 1977—. Mem. Common Coun. of Danbury, 1985-89; mem. Charter Rev. Commn., Danbury, 1988; with Conn. Ho. of Reps., 1989—, dep. maj. leader, 1995-2005, dep. spkr., 2005—; mem. exec. com. Coun. State Govts., 1997-99, 2005—; mem. exec. com. Ea. Regional Coun., Coun. State Govts., 2000—, vice chair, 2004, chair, 2005; bd. dirs. AIDS Project Greater Danbury, 2003—. With USNR, 1970-77. Recipient reproductive rights award Conn. Coalition for Choice, 1990, environ. energy award Peoples Action for Clean Energy, 1992, legis. leadership award Housing Authority Danbury, 1995, legis. svc. award Conn. Med. Assn., 1996, cmty. svc. award Midwestern Conn. Coun. on Alcoholism, 1998, Outstanding State Legislator award AFL-CIO, 2000, Apple Pie award Million Mom March, 2001, leadership award Conn. After Sch. Svc., 2003, disting. svc. award Conn., Freedom of Info. Commn., 2003, Disting. Svc. award Conn. Found. for Environmentally Safe Schs, 2004, legislative award Am. Legion of Conn., 2005, legis. award Uniformed Profl. Fire Fighters Assn. of Conn., 2005, cmty. leadership award Head Start No. Faifield County, 2005; recognized Conn. Coalition Against Gun Violence, 1993, spl. recognition award Danbury Dept. Elderly Svcs., 1995, sponsor youth and govt. Conn. YMCA; named Champion for Children Conn. Coalition for Children, 1990, Legislator of Yr. Conn. Police Chiefs Assn., 1993, Legislator of Yr. Conn. Assn. Bd. Edn., 2006. Mem. Cath. War Vets. (judge advocate 1978—) Home: 13 Stillman Ave Danbury CT 06810-8007 Office: Conn Ho of Reps Legis Office Bldg Rm 4107 Hartford CT 06106 Home Phone: 203-778-5127; Office Phone: 860-240-8500. E-mail: bob.godfrey@cga.ct.gov, robert.godfrey@snet.net.

GODHARDT, KAREN, information technology executive; b. NYC, Oct. 25, 1957; d. James Bertrand and Beatrice (Kaufman) B.; m. Kenneth Mark Curry, Nov. 24, 1979 (div. Dec. 1991); m. Thomas J. Godhardt, Dec. 25, 2004. BS, Fordham U., 1979; MBA, Calif. State Poly. U., 1982; postgrad., George Mason U., 1994-98; PhD, Kennedy Western U., 2000. Software engr. Hughes Aircraft Co., Fullerton, Calif., 1979-81; microprocessor engr. Beckman Instruments Co., Fullerton, 1981-82, Singer Co., Glendale, Calif., 1982-83; sr. software engr. Sanders Assocs., Nashua, NH, 1983-85; software project mgr. GTE Corp., Billerica, Mass., 1985-86; sr. software engr. Wang Labs., Lowell, Mass., 1986-87; project task leader Vanguard Rsch., Lexington, Mass., 1987-88; program mgr. Applied Rsch. & Engring., Bedford, Mass., 1989-91, Sparta, McLean, Va., 1992-93; prin. software engr. Sci. Applications Internat., Arlington, Va., 1993-94; tech. mgr. CACI, Arlington, 1994, Booz-Allen & Hamilton, Vienna, Va., 1995, MRJ Tech. Solutions, Inc., Fairfax, Va., 1996-97, Softek Systems, Inc., Fairfax, 1998—2001; pres. QSCI, Ashburn, Va., 2001—. 1st lt. U.S. Army, 1979-88. Scholar Gov. N.Y. Scholarship Com., 1975-79, Beta Gamma Sigma, 1978—. Mem. IEEE, AAUW, Am. Women in Sci., Am. Brokers Network, Assn. Computing Machinery, Soc. Women Engrs., Wash. Soc. of Engrs. Office Phone: 703-328-9661. Personal E-mail: karens_mail2007@yahoo.com.

GODIN, SETH WARREN, video production executive, writer, entrepreneur, blog website writer; b. Mt. Vernon, NY, July 10, 1960; s. William Neal and Lenore Diane (Leinwand) G.; m. Helene S. Aronson, June 22, 1986. BS, Tufts U., 1982; MBA, Stanford U., 1984. Founder, gen. mgr. TSR, Medford, Mass., 1980-82; brand mgr. Spinnaker Software, Cambridge, Mass., 1983-86; founder, mgr. The Skeibo Press, Inc., Mt. Vernon, 1986-89; pres. Seth Godin Prodns., Inc., Mt. Vernon, 1989—; founder, CEO Yoyodyne (acquired by Yahoo!), 1995—98; v.p., permission mktg. Yahoo!, 1998—99; founder Squidoo, LLC, 1996—. Copy writer Javelin, BMW, Kodak, Ricoh, Lotus Software, others, 1987-, Gridworks/Sci. Methods, Inc., Austin, Tex., 1988; cons., Media Syndicate, Boulder, Colo., 1987-, Internat. Ctr. Creative Thinking, Mamaroneck, N.Y., 1989-; invited spkr. in field Author: Business Rules of Thumb, 1987, Purple Cow: Transform Your Business by Being Remarkable (on NY Times and Wall Street Journal bestseller lists), All Marketers Are Liars: The Power of Telling Authentic Stories in a Low-Trust World (named to Amazon.com Top 100 List, own blog: allmarketersareliars.com), The Big Moo: Stop Trying to Be Perfect and Start Being Remarkable, Permission Marketing: Turning Strangers Into Friends and Friends Into Customers (named Top 100 Bestseller for the Yr., Amazon.com, Fortune Mag. Best Bus. Book, on Business Week bestseller list for four months, appeared on NY Time bestseller list), Free Prize Inside: The Next Big Marketing Idea, Survival Is Not Enough: Why Smart Companies Abandon Worry and Embrace Change (bestsellers lists in Germany, UK and US), The Big Red Fez: How To Make Any Website Better (#1 ebook worldwide Amazon.com, until published in paperback in 2002, Miami Herald named it one of the best bus. books of the yr.), Free Prize Inside/Purple Cow, Small Is the New Big: and 183 Other Riffs, Rants, and Remarkable Business Ideas, 2006 (Amazon Top 50 Bestsellers list, NY Times Bus. Bestseller), The Dip: A Little Book That Teaches You When to Quit (and When to Stick)(NY Times Bestseller), Survival Is Not Enough: Why Smart Companies Abandon Worry and Embrace Change; co-author (ebook)Unleashing the Ideavirus (on Amazon-.com best seller list-Japan and U.S.A.), The Guerrilla Marketing Handbook; producer: Robots, 1988, Score More Points, 1989; columnist: MacGuide mag., 1989, Fast Company; writer, exec. producer, producer, dir. home videos; creator software; maintains blog sethgodin.typepad.com (named best bus. blog by several publications). Named Ultimate Entrepreneur for the Information Age, Business Week, No. 5 of 25 Top Web Celebs, Forbes mag., 2007. E-mail: sethgodin@yahoo.com.*

GODINE, DAVID RICHARD, publishing executive; b. Cambridge, Mass., Sept. 4, 1944; s. Morton Robert and Bernice (Beckwith) G.; m. Sara Eisenman, 1987; children: Addison Reuben, Madeline Sangree. BA (Sr. fellow), Dartmouth Coll., Hanover, NH, 1966; Ed.M., Harvard U., Cambridge, Mass., 1968. Founder David R. Godine, Pub., Inc., Boston, 1969, pres., 1969—, pub., editor, 1969—. Author: Renaissance Books of Science, 1970, Five Decades of the Burin, 2004. Trustee Mass. Hort. Soc., Mass. Ctr. for the Book. Served with AUS, 1967. Fellow Pierpont Morgan Libr.; mem. Mass. Hist. Soc., Am. Antiquarian Soc., Soc. Printers, St. Botolph Club (Boston), Grolier Club (NYC). Office: David R Godine Pub Inc 9 Hamilton Pl Boston MA 02108-4715 Home Phone: 617-698-7417; Office Phone: 617-451-9600 x22. Business E-Mail: drg@godine.com.

GODINER, DONALD LEONARD, lawyer; b. Bronx, NY, Feb. 21, 1933; s. Israel and Edith (Rubenstein) G.; m. Caryl Mignon Nussbaum, Sept. 7, 1958; children: Clifford, Kenneth. AB, NYU, 1953; JD, Columbia U., 1956. Bar: N.Y. 1956, Mo. 1972. Gen. counsel Stromberg-Carlson, Rochester, NY, 1965-71; assoc. gen. counsel Gen. Dynamics Corp., St. Louis, 1971-73; v.p., gen. counsel Permaneer Corp., St. Louis, 1973-75; ptnr. Gallop, Johnson, Godiner, Morganstern & Crebs, St. Louis, 1975-80; sr. v.p., gen. counsel, sec. Laclede Gas Co., St. Louis, 1980-98; of counsel Stone, Leyton and Gershman, P.C., St. Louis, 1999—. Editor Columbia U. Law Rev., 1955-56. Served with U.S. Army, 1956-58. Mem.: ABA, Bar Assn. of Metropolitan St. Louis. Office: Stone Leyton & Gershman PC 7733 Forsyth Blvd Ste 500 Saint Louis MO 63105-2122 Office Phone: 314-721-7011.

GODINEZ, JOSHUA RAY, social sciences educator; b. Palm Springs, Calif., June 18, 1979; s. Richard and Debra Susan Godinez. BA, U. Calif., Riverside, 2001; MA, Claremont Grad. U., Calif., 2002. Clear credential in single subject social sci. Calif. Outreach specialist Comty. Settlement, Riverside, Calif., 1997—2001; mktg. specialist Desert Sun Pub. Co., Palm Springs, Calif., 2000—01; tchr. social sci. AB Miller HS, Fontana, Calif., 2001—06, Summit HS, Fontana, 2006—. Instr. Calif. std. ednl. testing Claremont Grad. U., 2002—; mem. adv. bd. Claremont Grad. Sch., 2002—. Exec. bd. dir. Cmty. Settlement Assn. Named Highest Caliber Achievement Tchr. of Yr., Vista Metals, 2007; recipient Tchr. Recognition award, U. Calif., San Diego. Mem.: Civil Rights Ctr., Social Studies Educators, Pi Lambda Theta. Avocation: theater. Office Phone: 909-357-5950 ext. 4032. Personal E-mail: godijr@fusd.net.

GODINEZ, MARYE H., anesthesiologist; b. Louisville, Aug. 19, 1945; d. Jerome and Hilda Marie Durbin; m. Rodolfo I. Godinez, June 28, 1969; children: Lucas, Peter, Paul, Adela, Sarah, Ruth. BS, Gonzaga U., Spokane, Wash., 1967; MD, St. Louis U. Sch. Medicine, 1971. Diplomate Am. Coll. Anesthesiologists, 1974. Dir. ENT, neuro and opthalmology anesthesia Barnes Hosp., St. Louis, 1974—77; dir. obstet. anesthesia Temple U. Hosp., Phila., 1978—79; rsch. assoc. Dept. Anesthesiology and Critical Care Children's Hosp., Phila., 1985—. Contbr. articles to sci. jours. Home: 1036 Sproul Rd Bryn Mawr PA 19010

GODINEZ FLORES, RAMON, bishop; b. Jamay, Jalisco, Mexico, Apr. 18, 1936; s. Ortega J. Cleofas G. and Maria del Refugio (Flores). Lic. in Philosophy, Sem. Guadalajara, (Jalisco, Mexico); theology degree, U. Gregoriana, Rome, postgrad. in canon law. Ordained priest Roman Catholic Ch., 1959. Prof., superior Diocesan Sem., Guadalajara; chaplain religious communities, Templo de San Jorge, Vallarta-San Jorge, Guadalajara; pastor Parroco de Nuestra Senora de la Luz, Guadalajara; sec. Archdiocese of Guadalajara, 1972—80, aux. bishop, 1980—. Sec. gen. Conferencia del Episcopado Mexicano, 1991—98; bishop of Aguascalientes, Mex., 1998. Contbr. articles to religious jours. Home and Office: Galeana 105 Norte Apartado Postal 167 CP 20000 Aguascalientes Mexico Home Phone: 01-449-9146716; Office Phone: 01-449-9153261.

GODLASKY, THOMAS C., insurance company executive; BS, Indiana Univ., Pa.; MA, Univ. Pitts. Mgmt. positions Mellon Bank, Federated Investors Inc.; mgr. fixed income & derivatives Providian Corp., 1988—95; exec. v.p., chief investment officer AmerUs Group Co., Des Moines, 1995—2003; pres. AmerUs Capital Mgmt., Des Moines, 1998—2003; bd. dir. AmerUs Group Co., Des Moines, 2003—, pres., COO, 2003—05, chmn., pres., CEO, 2005—06; pres., CEO Aviva USA, Des Moines, 2006—. Office: Aviva USA 699 Walnut Des Moines IA 50309 Mailing: Aviva USA PO Box 1555 Des Moines IA 50306*

GODLEY, JOANNE, city health department administrator; 2 children. BA in Human Biology, Stanford U., 1973; MPH, Yale U. Sch. Pub. Hlth., 1977; MD, Yale U. Sch. Medicine, 1977. Area med. officer Abidjan, Ivory Coast and Pretoria, South Africa Peace Corps; med. dir. Phila. Divsn. Social Services, Phila. Dept. Public Health, acting commr., 2005—. Mem.: Am. Bd. Quality Assurance and Utilization Review (diplomat), Am. Bd. Gastroenterology (diplomat), Am. Bd. Internal Medicine (diplomat). Office: Phila Dept Public Health 1101 Market St Ste 840 Philadelphia PA 19107 Office Phone: 215-685-5683. Office Fax: 215-685-5398.

GODOFSKY, STANLEY, lawyer; b. NYC, May 24, 1928; s. Eli and Lily (Deutsch) G.; m. Elaine Gloria Weiss, Dec. 15, 1951 (dec. Feb. 1994); m. Phyllis A. Schaevitz, Jan. 16, 2000. AB, Columbia U., 1949, JD, 1951. Bar: N.Y. 1951, U.S. Supreme Ct. 1961. Assoc. Rogers & Wells, and predecessors, NYC, 1951-64, ptnr., 1965-89. Co-adj. lectr. Rutgers Law Sch., 1990-91, adj. prof., 1992-93; adj. prof. Nova U. Law Sch., 1991-93; spl. asst. counsel N.Y. State Crime Commn., 1952. Bd. editors Columbia Law Rev., 1950, bd. revising editors, 1951. Trustee Jewish Cmty. Ctr. White Plains, N.Y., 1983-89; commn. on law and social action Am. Jewish Congress, 1986-98; mem. bd. advisors Lifelong Learning Soc. Fla. Atlantic U., 2004—. Mem. ABA, Am. Law Inst., N.Y. State Bar Assn., Assn. Bar City N.Y., Internat. Assn. Jewish Lawyers and Jurists (bd. govs. Am. sect. 1990-98, exec. com. and coun. 1999—), World Jurist Assn., Am. Assn. Jewish Lawyers and Jurists (bd. govs. 2006—). Home: 17858 Deauville Ln Boca Raton FL 33496-2457 Personal E-mail: jenice45@bellsouth.net.

GODRIDGE, LESLIE V., bank executive; married; 2 children. AB in History, Smith Coll., 1978; MBA, NYU, 1981. Head asset mgmt. and pvt. bank, head consumer bank and regional comml. lending Bank of NY, NYC, 1981—, sr. exec. v.p., 2004—. Trustee Mus. City of NY; financial leadership forum NY Public Libr.; adv. coun. NY Botanical Gardens; bd. mem. Jr. Achievement of NY. Named one of 25 Women to Watch, US Banker Mag., 2003. Office: The Bank of NY One Wall Street New York NY 10286

GODSCHALK, DAVID ROBINSON, architect, urban development planner, educator; b. Enid, Okla., May 14, 1931; s. Harold J. and Helen Faye (Robinson) G.; m. Lallie Moore Kain, June 27, 1959; 1 child, David Kennedy. BA, Dartmouth Coll., 1953; B.Arch., U. Fla., 1959; M.Regional Planning, U. N.C., 1964, PhD, 1971. Vice pres. Milo Smith Assos., Tampa, Fla., 1959-61; planning dir. City of Gainesville, Fla., 1964-65; asst. prof. Fla. State U., Tallahassee, 1965-67; editor AIP Jour., Chapel Hill, NC, 1968-71; assoc. prof. U. N.C., Chapel Hill, 1972-77, prof., 1977-94, Stephen Baxter prof. planning, 1994—2004, chmn. dept. city and regional planning, 1978-83. Adj. prof. Kenan Flagler Bus. Sch., U. NC, Chapel Hill, 2005-07; cons. and expert witness in field. Author: (with others) Constitutional Issues of Growth Management, 1979, Land Supply Monitoring, 1986, Planning in America: Learning from Turbulence, 1974, Catastrophic Coastal Storms: Hazard Mitigation and Development Management, 1989, Urban Land Use Planning, 5th edit., 2006, Pulling Together: A Planning and Development Consensus Building Manual, 1994, Cooperating with Nature: Confronting Natural Hazards with Land Use for Planning Sustainable Communities, 1998. Natural Hazard Mitigation: Recasting Disaster Policy and Planning, 1999, Monitoring Land Supply with Georgaphic Information Systems, 2000; editor: (with others) Understanding Growth Management, 1989, The Planner as Dispute Resolver, 1989; editor Am. Inst. Planners Jour., 1968-71; mem. editl. bd. Jour. Planning Edn. and Rsch., 1983-89, 93-97, Jour. Am. Planning Assn., 1983-96, Jour. Archtl. Planning Rsch., 1991—, Australian Planner, 1997- Mem. Town Coun., Chapel Hill, 1985-89, NC Legis. Rsch. Commn. on Statewide Comprehensive Planning, 1991-93, NC Legis. Commn. on Smart Growth, 1999-2001; bd. dirs. Carol Woods Continuing Care Cmty., 2004—. With USNR, 1953-56, 61-62; comdr. Res.; ret., 1980. Recipient Disting. Alumnus award Dept. City and Regional Planning, U. N.C., 1996; Disting. Grad. Tchg. awd., U.N.C., 1999. Fellow AICP; mem. Am. Planning Assn. (bd. govs. 1978-79, Profl. Achievement award 1983, Elected Ofcl. award N.C. chpt. 1990), Am. Soc. Planning Ofcls. (bd. dir. 1974-77), Am. Inst. Cert. Planners (Svc. medal 1971), Assn. Collegiate Schs. Planning (Disting. Educator award 2002), NC Botanical Garden Found. (bd. dirs. 2003—). Office: Univ NC Dept City & Regional Planning Chapel Hill NC 27599-3140 Business E-Mail: dgod@email.unc.edu.

GODSELL, RICHARD VERNON, elementary school educator, researcher; b. Detroit, June 18, 1949; s. Roy John and Bernadene Rosella Godsell; m. Marion Jures-Godsell, June 4, 1999. BS, U. Ctrl. Fla., 1997, MEd, 2004, PhD in Edn., 2005. Plumber Plumbers Union Local #98, Detroit, 1968—78; master plumber Wayne County Plumber Union Local #98, 1978—92; tchr. Orange County Pub. Schs., Ocoee, Fla., 1997—. With USN, 1966—67. Decorated Purple Heart Silver Star USN. Mem.: ASCD, Orange County Classroom Tchrs. Assn., Nat. Coun. Tchrs. Math. Democrat. Avocations: reading, swimming, walking. Office: Ocoee Elem Sch 400 S Lakewood Ave Ocoee FL 34761 Business E-Mail: m.jures@sympatico.ca.

GODSEY, JOHN DREW, retired minister, theology educator emeritus; b. Bristol, Tenn., Oct. 10, 1922; s. William Clinton and Mary Lynn (Coma) Godsey; m. Emalee Caldwell, June 26, 1943 (dec. Oct. 1993); children: Emalee Lynn Godsey Murphy, John Drew Jr., Suzanne Godsey Douglas, Gretchen Godsey Brownley; m. Cozette Hapney Barker, Sept. 23, 1995. BS, Va. Poly. Inst. and State U., 1947; BD, Drew U., 1953; D.Theol., U. Basel, Switzerland, 1960. Ordained to ministry United Meth. Ch., 1952. Instr. systematic theology, asst. dean Drew U., Madison, N.J., 1956-59, asst. prof., 1959-64, assoc. prof., 1964-66, prof., 1966-68; prof., assoc. dean Wesley Theol. Sem., Washington, 1968-71, prof. systematic theology, 1971-88, emeritus prof., 1988—. Author: The Theology of dietrich Bonhoeffer, 1960, Karl Barth's Table Talk, 1963, Preface to Bonhoeffer, 1965, Introduction and Epilogue to Karl Barth's How I Changed My Mind, 1966, The Promise of H. Richard Niebuhr, 1970; co-editor: Ethical Responsibility: Bonhoeffer's Legacy to the Churches, 1981, Dietrich Bonhoeffer, Discipleship, 2000. Mem. Montgomery County Fair Housing Assn., Md. With US Army, 1943—46. Recipient Disting. Svc. Alumni award, Drew U. Theol. Alumni Assn., 1995; Faculty fellow, Am. Assn. Theol. Schs., 1964—65, Fulbright scholar, U. Goettingen, Germany, 1964—65. Mem.: Am.'s Registry Outstanding Profls., New Haven Theol. Discussion Group, Karl Barth Soc. N.Am., Internat. Bonhoeffer Soc. (editor newsletter 1989—92), Bibl. Theologians, Am. Theol. Soc. (pres. 1985—86), Am. Acad. Religion, Common Cause, Alpha Zeta, Phi Kappa Phi, Omicron Delta Kappa. Democrat. Home: 8306 Bryant Dr Bethesda MD 20817-3137 Office: Wesley Theol Sem 4500 Massachusetts Ave NW Washington DC 20016-5690 *My goal has been to serve others with integrity, to do every job to the best of my ability, and to respect and further the rights and welfare of my fellow creatures on planet earth. Thus should my life be a testimony to my faith.*

GODSOE, PETER COWPERTHWAITE, retired banker; b. Toronto, Can., May 2, 1938; s. J. Gerald and Margaret (Cowperthwaite) G.; m. Shelagh Cathleen Reburn, Nov. 30, 1963; children: Craig, Cynthia, Eden. BSc in Math. and Physics, U. Toronto, 1961; MBA, Harvard U., 1966. Chartered acct., Can. Joined The Bank of N.S., various locations, 1966-71, various positions with internat., corp. banking divsn., 1971-82, vice chmn. bd., bd. dirs., 1982-92, pres., COO, vice chmn. bd., 1992—93, pres., CEO, 1993—2003, dep. chmn. bd., 1993—95, chmn. bd., 1995—2004. Chmn. Sobeys Inc.; bd. dirs. Lonmin Plc, Ingersoll-Rand Co., Barrick Gold Corp., Rogers Comms. Inc., Templeton Emerging Markets Investment Trust, Onex Corp. Bd. dirs. Can. Coun. Christians and Jews, Toronto, 1972—, Mt. Sinai Hosp., 1986; pres. Bd. Trade, Toronto, 1984-85; mem. adv. com. Western Bus. Sch., Richard Ivey Sch. Bus.; assoc. mem. bd. govs. Dalhousie U.; mem. chancellor's coun. Victoria U.; hon. dir. Sheena's Pl. Fellow Inst. Chartered Accts.; mem. Can. Bankers Assn. (past chmn.), Jr. Achievement of Met. Toronto and York Region (bd. govs.), Can. Club (past pres. 1982-83). Office: Scotia Plz 40 King St W Toronto ON Canada M5H 1H1

GODSON, GODFREY NIGEL, molecular geneticist, educator; b. London, June 20, 1936; s. Godfrey Edward and Elsie Louise (Harrington) G.; m. Barbara Cohen, Aug. 9, 1969; children: Rebecca Charlotte, Vanessa Alexandra. BS, London U., 1957, PhD, 1961, D.Sc. (hon.), 1984. Research fellow Calif. Inst. Tech., 1964-67; staff scientist Nat. Insts. Med. Research, Med. Research Council, Mill Hill, London, 1968-69; asst. prof., assoc. prof. radiobiology Yale Med. Sch., New Haven, 1969-74, 1974-80; prof. dept. biochemistry NYU Med. Sch., NYC, 1980—2006, chmn. dept. biochemistry, 1980—2006, prof. emeritus biochemistry, 2006—. Mem. biochemistry sect. Nat. Bd. Med. Examiners, 1985-89; mem. tropical medicine and parasitology study sect. NIAID, 1985-90. Editor: Gene jour., 1984-96, Jour. Cell and Molecular Biology, 1984-86; contbr. chpts. to books, articles to profl. jours. Mem. Am. Soc. for Biochemistry and Molecular Biology, N.Y. Acad. Scis. Office: NYU Med Sch 550 1st Ave New York NY 10016-6402

GODWIN, DONALD EVERETT, lawyer; b. Dunn, NC, Oct. 14, 1947; s. Lewis E. and Lois G.; m. Carmen Q.; children: Eric, Natalie. BS, U. N.C., Wilmington, 1969; MS in Acctg., Memphis State U., 1970; JD, So. Meth. U., 1973. Bar: U.S. Dist. Ct. (we. dist.) Okla., U.S. Ct. Appeals (5th cir.) 1982, U.S. Supreme Ct. 1979. Mng. dir. Godwin & Carlton, P.C., Dallas, 1980—2006; chmn., CEO Godwin Pappas Langley Ronquillo , LLP (formerly Godwin Gruber, LLP), Dallas, 2006—. Bd. dirs. Haggard Clothing Co., 2003—. Bd. dirs. Dallas Opera, 1990—; advisor Tex. Tycoon Gala, Dallas, 1990—; mem. Dallas Citizens Coun., 1993—, Dallas Crime Commn., 1993—; exec. bd. mem., So. Methodist U. Dedman Sch. Law, 2002-; outside counsel, Episcpal Sch. Dallas, 2002-, Dallas Symphony Assn., 2002- Recipient Disting. Alumni award for Pvt. Practice, So. Methodist U. Sch. Law, 2003. Fellow Tex. Bar Assn.; mem. ABA, Dallas Bar Assn. (coun. mem., bus. litigation sect. 1990), S.W. Legal Found. (rsch. fellow, com. anti-trust sec. 1978-79), Dallas C. of C. (chmn. minority affairs com. 1990—), City Club (bd. dirs. 1990—). Office: Godwin Pappas Langley Ronquillo LLP Renaissance Tower 1201 Elm St Ste 1700 Dallas TX 75270 E-mail: dgodwin@godwinpappas.com.

GODWIN, GAIL KATHLEEN, writer; b. Birmingham, Ala., June 18, 1937; d. Mose Winston and Kathleen (Krahenbuhl) G.; m. Douglas Kennedy, 1960 (div. 1961), m. Ian Marshall, 1965 (div. 1966). Student, Peace Jr. Coll., Raleigh, NC, 1955-57; BA in Journalism, U. NC, 1959, PhD (hon.), 1987; MA in English, U. Iowa, 1968, PhD, 1971; PhD (hon.), U. So.-Sewanee, 1994, SUNY, 1996. News reporter Miami Herald, 1959-60; rep., cons. US Travel Svc., London, 1961-65; editorial asst. Saturday Evening Post, 1966; instr. Univ. Iowa, Iowa City, 1967-71; lectr. Iowa Writer's Workshop, 1972-73, Vassar Coll., 1977, Columbia U. Writing Program, 1978, 81. Author: (novels) The Perfectionists, 1970, Glass People, 1972, The Odd Woman, 1974 (Nat. Book award nomination 1974), Violet Clay, 1978 (Am. Book award nomination 1980), A Mother and Two Daughters, 1982 (Nat. Book award nomination 1982), The Finishing School, 1985, A Southern Family, 1987, Father Melancholy's Daughter, 1991, The Good Husband, 1994, Evensong, 1999, Evenings at Five, 2003; (short stories) Dream Children, 1976, Mr. Bedford and The Muses, 1983; editor: (with Shannon Ravenel) The Best American Short Stories 1985, 1985, Evensong, 1999, Heart: A Personal Journey Through Its Myths & Meanings, 2001, Evenings at Five, 2003, Queen of the Underworld, 2006, The Making of a Writer: Journals, 1961-1963, 2006; librettist: (with Robert Starer) The Last Lover, 1975, Journals of a Songmaker, 1976, Apollonia, 1979, Anna Margarita's Will, 1981, Remembering Felix, 1987, Gregory The Great, 1996, The Other Voice: A Portrait of Hilda of Whitby in Words and Music, 1998, Magdalene At The Tomb, 1999, Abraham Remembers, 2000. Recipient Thomas Wolfe Meml. award Lipinsky Endowment of Western NC Hist. Assn., 1988, Janet Heidinger Kafka award U. Rochester, 1988; fellow Center for Advanced Study, U. Ill., Urbana, 1971-72; Am. specialist USIS, 1976; Nat. Endowment Arts grantee, 1974-75; Guggenheim fellow, 1975-76; recipient award in lit. Am. Acad. and Inst. of Arts and Letters, 1981 Mem. ASCAP, Authors Guild, Authors League. Mailing: PO Box 946 Woodstock NY 12498-0946

GODWIN, HAROLD NORMAN, pharmacist, educator; b. Ransom, Kans., Oct. 9, 1941; s. Harold Joseph and Nora Elva (Welsh) G.; m. Judy Rae Ricketts, June 9, 1963; children: Paula Lynn, Jennifer Joy. BS in Pharmacy, U. Kans., 1964; MS in Hosp. Pharmacy, Ohio State U., 1966. Lic. pharmacist, Kans., Ohio. Instr. Ohio State U. Coll. Pharmacy, Columbus, 1966-69; asst. dir. pharmacy Ohio State U., Columbus, 1966-69; dir. pharmacy U. Kans. Med. Ctr., Kansas City, 1969—2004; asst. prof. U. Kans. Sch. Pharmacy, Kansas City, 1969-74, assoc. prof., 1974-80, prof. pharmacy, 1980—, asst. dean pharmacy, 1975-89, assoc. dean pharmacy, 1989—, chmn. pharmacy practice, 1984—2006. John W. Webb lectr., vis. prof. Northeastern U., 1999; chmn. pharmacy exec. com. U. HealthSys. Consortium, 2001-04, exec. com., 2004-07; mem. exec. com. Novation Pharmacy, 2003-05. Author: Implementation Guide to IV Admixtures, 1977; (with others) Remington's Pharmaceutical Sciences, 1980, 85, 90, 95, 2000; contbr. over 100 articles to profl. jours. Recipient Clifton J. Latiolais award Ohio State U. Residents Alumni, 1986, Disting. Alumni award Ohio State U. Coll. Pharmacy, 1995; named Tchr. of the Yr., U. Kans. Sch. Pharmacy, 2001, Harold N. Godwin Leadership Legacy award U. Kans. Med. Ctr., 2004. Fellow: Am. Soc. Health System Pharmacists (bd. dir. 1978—81, pres. 1982—83, bd. dir. rsch. and edn. found. 2002—06, Harvey A.K. Whitney award 1991); mem.: Kans. Pharmacy Found. (v.p. 2004—), Am. Coun. Pharm. Edn. (bd. dir. 1988—2000, pres. 1992—96), Greater Kansas City Soc. Hosp. Pharmacists (pres. 1972), Kans. Soc. Hosp. Pharmacists (Kans. Hosp. Pharmacist of Yr. 1982, Harold N. Godwin award 1984), Kans. Pharmacists Assn. (pres 1977, Kans. Pharmacist of Yr. 1982), Am. Pharm. Assn. (bd. trustees 2006—, Disting. Achievement award 2000). Republican. Methodist. Avocations: tennis, bicycling, cooking, wine tasting. Home: 10112 W 98th St Shawnee Mission KS 66212-5238 Office: U Kans Med Ctr MS4047 Rainbow Blvd At 39th St Kansas City KS 66106-7231 Office Phone: 913-588-2399. Business E-Mail: HGodwin@kumc.edu.

GODWIN, HILARY A., chemistry professor, research scientist; BS in chemistry with honors, Univ. Chgo., 1989; PhD in phys. chemistry, Stanford Univ., 1994; NIH post doctoral fellow, Johns Hopkins Univ. Sch. Medicine, 1994—96. Preceptor Interdepartmental Biol. Sci. Program Northwestern Univ., 1996—, asst. prof. Dept. Chemistry and Dept. Biochemistry, Molecular Biology & Cell Biology, 1996—2001, assoc. prof., 2001—. Mem. Lurie Cancer Ctr. Northwestern Univ., 1997—, Dow Chem. Co. Rsch. Prof. in Chemistry, 2002—; prof. Howard Hughes Med. Inst., 2002—. Recipient Stanford Centennial Tchg. Asst. Award, Stanford Univ., 1992, Toxicology New Investigator Award, Burroughs Wellcome Fund, 1998, CAREER Award, Nat. Sci. Found., 1999, Camille Dreyfus Tchr.-Scholar Award, 2000, Paul Saltman Award, 2001; grantee Grad. Rsch. Fellowship, Nat. Sci. Found., 1989—92, Postdoctoral Rsch. Fellowship, Nat. Inst. Health, 1994—96. Mem.: Am. Assoc. Women in Sci., Am. Assoc. for Advancement of Sci., Biophysical Soc., Soc. for Neuroscience, Am. Chem. Soc., Iota Sigma Pi, Phi Beta Kappa. Office: Dept Chemistry Northwestern Univ 2145 Sheridan Rd Evanston IL 60208-3113 Office Phone: 847-467-3543. Office Fax: 847-491-5937. E-mail: h-godwin@northwestern.edu.

GODWIN, JOHN E., hematologist; b. Mobile, Ala., Dec. 28, 1951; married; 3 children. BS summa cum laude, U. Montevallo, Ala., 1970—74; MD, U. Ala. Sch. Medicine, Birmingham, 1974—78; MS in Epidemiology, U. Tex. Sch. Pub. Health, Houston, 1981—83. Cert. Nat. Bd. Med. Examiners, 1979, Am. Bd. Internal Medicine, 1981, in Hematology 1986. Intern, internal medicine Baylor Coll. Medicine, Houston, 1978—79, resident, internal medicine, 1979—81, fellow, internal medicine, 1981—82, fellow, hematology and oncology, 1982—83; instr., dept. medicine Ben Taub Hosp., Houston, 1981—83; fellow, hematology and oncology U. N.C., Chapel Hill, 1983—85; instr., dept. medicine N.C. Meml. Hosp., Chapel Hill, 1983—85; cons. Hines Veterans Hosp., Ill., 1985—96; attending physician Foster G. McGaw Hosp., Maywood, 1985—2006, assoc. dir., spl. hematology clin. coagulation lab., dept. pathology, 1996—2006; asst. prof., dept. medicine and pathology Loyola U., Maywood, 1985—96, assoc. prof., dept. medicine and pathology, 1996—2006, prof., dept. medicine and pathology, 2002—06; prof. dept.

medicine So. Ill. U. Sch. Medicine, Springfield, 2006—, chief divsn. hematology/oncology, 2006—. Chmn., blood utilization com. Loyola U. Med. Ctr., Maywood, 1990—2006, dir., dept. medicine, bone marrow lab., 1993—2006, asst. dir., hematology and oncology fellowship program, 1995—98, mem., pharmacy and therapeutics com., 2001—06; mem. Ctr. for Excellence in Molecular Hematology; assoc. dir. clin. svcs. Simmons Cooper Cancer Inst., Springfield, 2006—. Reviewer for various jours. Fellow, Coun. on Arteriosclerosis, Thrombosis and Vascular Biology, 1997. Fellow: Am. Heart Assn.; mem.: AAAS, Am. Soc. Hematology. Achievements include research in leukemia, its biology and treatment, and in clinical thrombosis. Office: Div Hematology/Oncology Southern Ill U Sch Medicine PO Box 19678 Springfield IL 62794-9678 Office Phone: 217-545-8124. Office Fax: 217-545-7021.

GODWIN, KIMBERLY ANN, federal agency administrator, lawyer; b. Fargo, ND, July 18, 1960; d. Robert Chandler and Kathryn Marie (Haney) G. BA in Polit. Sci., U. N.H., 1980; MS in Mass Comm., Boston U., 1984, JD, 1984. Bar: D.C. 1984, U.S. Supreme Ct. 1990. Legal intern Army Corps of Engrs., Waltham, Mass., 1983-84; assoc. Booz, Allen & Hamilton, Inc., Bethesda, Md., 1986-88; cons. Dept. State, Washington, 1984-86, asst. dir. comm. internat. affairs, 1988-92, chief of policy diplomatic telecom. svc., 1992-96, dir. external affairs, 1997—. Cons. Elton Assocs., Inc., Arlington, Va., 1984—. Mem. ABA (vice chmn. internat. comm. com. 1989—), Phi Beta Kappa, Pi Sigma Alpha. Avocations: flying, tennis, skiing. Home: 6215 Walhonding Rd Bethesda MD 20816-2138 Office: Dept State IRM/EA Rm 4428 2201 C St NW Washington DC 20520-0001 Office Phone: 202-647-1438. Business E-Mail: godwinka@state.gov.

GODWIN, PAMELA JUNE, financial services executive; b. Council Bluffs, Iowa, Mar. 29, 1949; BA in French, Pa. State U., 1970; postgrad., West Chester U., Pa., 1971-74. Tchr. various schs., Phila., 1971-74; various underwriting/tng. positions Colonial Penn Ins. Co., Phila., 1974-77, mgr., 1977-81, dir., 1981-84, v.p., 1984-86, Colonial Penn Group, Inc., Phila., 1986-87, sr. v.p., 1987-88; sr. v.p. customer mgmt. Nat. Liberty Corp., Valley Forge, Pa., 1988-93; pres., COO, Acad. Ins. Group, Frazer, Pa., 1993-95, Nat. Home Life Assurance Co., Frazer, Pa., 1993-95; pres. Change Ptnrs., Inc., Havertown, Pa., 1995—96, 2002—; acting pres. Womens Way, Phila., 1998-99; pres., COO agy. divsn. GMAC Ins. Personal Lines (formerly Integon Corp.), Winston-Salem, NC, 1999—2001; pres. Change Ptnrs., Inc., Havertown, 2001—. Bd. dirs. Wheels, Inc., J.F. Kennedy Vocat. Tech. Sch., Phila., 1987-88; bd. dirs. Gt. Valley Cmty. Edn. Found., 1991-95, past pres.; mem. Westgate Hills Civic Assn., Havertown, 1974-; mem. Wharton Exec. Edn. adv. bd.; chmn. adv. bd. Pa. State Great Valley, 1996-2000, 2002-; bd. dirs. Winston-Salem C. of C., 1996-2001, Phila. Found., 2003-; mem. Com. of 200, 2000-. Named to Pa. Honor Roll of Women, 1996. Mem. Phila. Forum of Exec. Women (pres. 1998-99), Soc. Property and Casualty Underwriters (past pres. Phila. chpt. 1987-88), Phi Beta Kappa, Phi Sigma Iota. Democrat. Lutheran. Avocations: skiing, walking, reading. E-mail: changepartners@comcast.net.

GODWIN, RALPH LEE, JR., real estate executive; b. Raleigh, NC, July 20, 1954; s. Ralph Lee Sr. and Hilda Faye (Sellars) G. BS in Commerce, U. Va., 1976; MBA, Dartmouth Coll., 1982. Fgn. exchange trader N.C. Nat. Bank, Charlotte, 1976-78; mgr. N.Y. office 1st Nat. Bank Atlanta, NYC, 1979-80; assoc. corp. fin. Goldman Sachs & Co., NYC, 1982-84; assoc. Eastdil Realty, Inc., NYC, 1984-88; dir. Jones Lang Wootton, U.S.A., NYC, 1988-92; mng. dir., head real estate group Gruntal & Co., Inc., NYC, 1993-98; sr. mng. dir., head equity capital markets Landauer Assocs., Inc., NYC, 1998-99; gen. ptnr. Centurion Realty Ptnrs., L.P., Charlotte, 1999—2005; pres. RCG Longview Realty Svcs., LLC, New Orleans, 2006—. Recipient Devel. cert. DARE Inc., Wilmington, 1984, 88. Mem. NAREIT, Real Estate Bd., N.Y., Urban Land Inst., N.C. Soc. N.Y., U. Va. Alumni Assn., Dartmouth Coll. Alumni Assn., N.Y. Athletic Club, Omicron Delta Kappa. Republican. Episcopalian. Avocations: fishing, bridge, golf, tennis. Office Phone: 504-799-3281. Personal E-mail: rlgodwinjr@hotmail.com.

GODWIN, ROBERT ANTHONY, lawyer; b. Phila., Apr. 24, 1938; s. Robert Anthony and Mary (MacElderry) G.; m. Isabel A. Tumelty; children: Cara G., Marisa A., Elise D. BS, Villanova U., 1960, JD, 1963. Bar: Pa. 1964, U.S. Dist. Ct. (ea. dist.) Pa. 1964, U.S. Ct. Appeals (3d cir.) 1964, U.S. Supreme Ct. 1980. Vol. defender, Phila., 1964; assoc. Eastburn & Gray, Doylestown, Pa., 1968-70; asst. pub. defender Bucks County, Pa., 1969-71; sole practice Newtown, Pa., 1971—73; ptnr. Timby and Godwin, 1973—75; atty. Robert A. Godwin & Assocs., 1975—. Served with JAG, USMC, 1964-68, JAG, USMCR, 1968-92, col. USMCR, ret. Mem. Pa. Bar Assn., Pa. Trial Lawyers Assn., Bucks County Bar Assn., Rotary. Office: Box 450 110 S State St Newtown PA 18940-3508 Office Phone: 215-968-6763. Personal E-mail: ragodwinlaw@aol.com.

GODWIN, SARA, writer; b. St. Louis, Feb. 18, 1944; d. Robert Franklin, Jr. and Annabelle Godwin; m. Charles D. James, May 1, 1990; children: Jane, Josh. BA, Calif. State U., 1967; postgrad., UCLA, 1968-70, U. Calif., Berkeley, 1970-71, W.I. Inst. Fairleigh Dickinson U., St. Croix, V.I., 1971-72; MA, Dominican Coll., 1974. Writer, editor Ortho Books, Std. Oil Calif., San Francisco, 1975-77; writer, editor Gannett Corp., San Rafael, Calif., 1977-79; sr. writer Shaklee Corp., San Francisco, 1979-88; freelance writer Marin County, Calif., 1988—. Featured spkr. Ask the Gardener Sta. KSFO, San Francisco, 1980—81; contbr., prodr. Raw Radio Travel, 1998—. Author: (book) Seals, 1990, Gorillas, 1990, The Angler's Companion, 1992, Hummingbirds, 1991, The Gardener's Companion, 1992 (N.Y. Times Rev., Garden Book Club selection), Landscaping Decks and Patios, 1994, Scott's See and Do: Lawns and Groundcovers, 1995; contbr. book Last Puff, 1990 (Lit. Guild selection), book The Sea, 1993; author (with others): (book) Smith and Hawken Book of Outdoor Gardening, 1996 (Book-of-the-Month club selection Rodale Books, selection Country Homes and Gardens Club, selection Newbridge Garden Book Club); author: (screenplays) Discover Canada, Discovering The USA; manuscript editor: All About Perennials, 1992, prin. lexicographer: Nat. Gardening Assn. Dictionary of Horticulture, 1994; scriptwriter, prodr.: China: The Middle Kingdom; contbr. CD ROM Microsoft Complete Gardening, 1996, CD ROM Frommer's Boston, 1996, articles to numerous U.S. and fgn. mags. Recipient 1st prize for personal column, Calif. Press Women, 1984. Mem.: PEN, Garden Writers Assn., Am. Soc. Journalists and Authors, Authors Guild. Avocations: reading, travel, gardening, fly fishing. Home: PO Box 1503 Ross CA 94957-1503

GODZAK, ROMAN PAUL, archivist; b. Syracuse, NY, Nov. 6, 1954; s. Walter and Stephanie Godzak. BA, Wayne State U., 1980, MA, 1988. Tech. Archives of Labor and Urban Affairs, Wayne State U., Detroit, 1983—85; archives asst. Archdiocese Detroit, 1985—87, archivist, records mgr., 1987—. Author: Make Straight The Path, 2000 (Cath. Comm. Campaign award, 2001), Archdiocese of Detroit, 2000, Catholic Churches of Detroit, 2004. Adv. bd. Mich. Hist. Records, 1992—94; speaker various area hist. and genealogical soc. mtgs.; host Historical Minutes. Mem.: Assn. Cath. Diocese Archivists, Soc. Am. Archivists, Midwest Archives Conf. (program com. mem. 1994), Mich. Archival Assn. (exec. bd., nominating com. 1980—93). Democrat. Roman Cath. Avocations: creative writing, swimming, bicycling, pop culture. Office: Roman Cath Archdiocese Detroit 1234 Wash Blvd Detroit MI 48226 Office Phone: 313-237-5846.

GODZALA, JESSE THOMAS, history educator; b. Grand Forks, ND, Nov. 20, 1976; s. Thomas and Bridget Godzala. MA, St. Cloud State U., Minn., 2006; BA, U. St. Thomas, St. Paul. Tchr. history Foley H.S., Minn., 1999—2006. Cons. in field. Named Minn. State History Tchr. Yr., 2005. Mem.: Nat. Coun. History Edn., Minn. Coun. History Edn. (founder), Minn. Coun. for the Social Studies (mem./presenter 1999—2006, Presenter at ann. Conf. 1999). Home and Office: 210 4th Ave S Saint Cloud MN 56301 Office Phone: 320-309-7335. Office Fax: 320-968-8456. E-mail: jgodzala@foley.k12.mn.us.

GOEBEL, JENS, physician; b. Hannover, Germany, Aug. 19, 1961; MD, U. Heidelberg, 1989. Diplomate Am. Bd. Pediat., 1994, cert. pediatric nephrology Am. Bd. Pediat., 1999. Asst. prof. pediat. U. Ky., Lexington, 1998—2002; assoc. prof. pediat. Children's Hosp., Cin., 2003—. Med. dir. kidney transplantation Children's Hosp., Cin., 2003—. Named one of Best Doctors in Am., Best Doctors, 2003—. Office: Nephrology 7022 Children's Hospital 3333 Burnet Ave Cincinnati OH 45229-3039 Office Phone: 513-636-4531. Office Fax: 513-636-7407. Business E-Mail: jens.goebel@cchmc.org.

GOEBEL, JOHN J., lawyer; b. St. Charles, Mo., Feb. 3, 1930; s. Francis Joseph and Elizabeth (Lawler) G.; m. Margaret Mary Rooney, May 10, 1958; children— Laura, Margaret, John, Matthew BS, LL.B., St. Louis U., 1953. Bar: Mo. 1953, U.S. Dist. Ct. (ea. dist.) Mo. 1957. Jr. exec. Constrn. Escrow Service Inc., St. Louis, 1955-56; jr. ptnr. Bryan Cave LLP, St. Louis, 1956-66, ptnr., 1966-98, sr. counsel, 1998—. Served to 1st lt. USAF, 1953—55. Mem.: ABA, Mo. Bar Assn., St. Louis Bar Assn., Port Royal Club, St. Louis Club, Bellerive Country Club. Roman Catholic. Home: 245 Little Harbour Ln Naples FL 34102-7606 Office: Bryan Cave 1 Metropolitan Sq Ste 3600 Saint Louis MO 63102-2750 Business E-Mail: jjgoebel@comcast.net.

GOEBEL, WILLIAM HORN, lawyer; b. NYC, Dec. 7, 1941; s. Harry H. and Maxine (Hamburger) G.; m. Barbara Golden, July 30, 1966; children: Jason, Pamela. AB, Columbia U., 1963; JD, NYU, 1966. Bar: NY 1966. Assoc. Bernard Trencher, NYC, 1966-69; real estate atty. J.C. Penney Co., Inc., NYC, 1969-71; assoc. gen. counsel N.K. Winston Corp., NYC, 1971-72; Teachers Ins. and Annuity Assn. Am./Coll. Retirement Equities Fund, NYC, 1972-2000; bus. devel. and legal cons. Stewart Title Ins. Co., NYC, 2000—04. Lectr. NYU Sch. Continuing Edn., 1985-88; mem. adv. bd. Commonwealth Land Title/Transamerica Title Ins. Co., 1992-2000; v.p. M.O.A. Enterprises, Inc./M.O.A Holdings, Inc., 1992-2000. Mem. Town of Oyster Bay Arts Coun., 2002—; sustaining mem. Rep. Nat. Com., 2004—; pres. Oyster Bay Jewish Ctr., 1976—78. Mem. Assn. Bar City of NY (legal history com. and real property com. 2005—), NY State Bar Assn. (fin. subcom. of real estate sect. 1998—, subcom. on zoning and land use planning), Barnard-Columbia Hillel Soc. (pres.'s coun. 2002-05), Woodbury Jewish Ctr. Men's Club (treas. 2003—). Office Phone: 516-921-3425. E-mail: bgoebel@optonline.net.

GOEDDE, ALAN GEORGE, financial company executive; b. Irvington, NJ, Feb. 27, 1948; s. Albert and Herta (Konrad) G.; m. Julie S. Withers, June 30, 1981. BS in Engring., Duke U., 1970, PhD in Econs., 1978. Economist U.S. Treasury, Washington, 1976-79, Export-Import Bank, Washington, 1979-81; mgr. Arthur Andersen & Co., Chgo., 1981-84; v.p. bus. planning 1st Nat. Bank Chgo., 1984-86; dir. strategic planning The NutraSweet Co., Chgo., 1986-87; pres., CEO Mentor Internat., Northbrook, Ill., 1987-88; cons. Coopers & Lybrand, Chgo., 1988-90, Freeman & Mills, LA, 1990-94, Putnam, Hayes and Bartlett, LA, 1994-2000, Freeman & Mills, LA, 2000—. Office: Freeman & Mills Inc 350 S Figueroa St Ste 900 Los Angeles CA 90071 Office Phone: 213-620-9535.

GOEDE, MICHAEL JON, secondary school educator; b. Milwaukee, Wis., Sept. 26, 1979; s. Ned Harold and Marguerite Elizabeth Goede. BA, Valparaiso U., Ind., 2003, MusB in Edn., 2003. Dir. choral programs, English instr., coach Kettle Moraine Luth. HS, Jackson, Wis., 2003—. Mem.: ACDA (assoc.). Home: 8031 W Locust St Milwaukee WI 53222 Office: Kettle Moraine Luth HS 3399 Division Rd Jackson WI 53051 Home Phone: 414-526-7964; Office Phone: 262-677-4051. Business E-Mail: mgoede@kmlhs.org.

GOEHRING, KENNETH, artist; b. Evansville, Wis., Jan. 8, 1919; s. Walter A. and Ruth I. (Rossman) G.; m. Margretta M. MacNicol, Dec. 1, 1945. Student, Cass Tech. Inst., 1933-35, Meinzinger Sch. Applied Art, 1945-46, Colorado Springs Fine Arts Ctr., 1947-50. Works have appeared in over 100 exhibitions in 17 states and 20 museums; 17 one-man shows; Terry Inst., Miami, Symphony Hall, Boston, de Cordova Mus., Fitchburg Mus., Mass., Farnsworth Mus., Maine, Corcoran, Washington, Joslyn Meml. Mus., Nebr., Detroit Inst. Arts, Nebr. Galleries, Stanford U. Galleries, Calif, De Young Mus., San Francisco, Denver Art Mus., Okla. Art Ctr., La Jolla Art Ctr., Calif., Colorado Springs Fine Arts Ctr., 1998, 99, Boulder Mus. Avant Garde Art, 1999, others; represented in permanent collections, Sheldon Art Ctr., Lincoln, Nebr., Colorado Springs Fine Arts Ctr., Foothills Gallery, Golden Colo., Canon City Fine Arts Ctr., Colo., Washburn U. Gallery, Wichita, Kans., Swedish Consulate, Washington, El Pomar Found., Colo. Springs, in many pvt. collections Purchase awards include Colorado Springs Fine Arts Ctr., 1958; Washburn U., 1957; Am. Acad. Design, 1977. Address: 2017 W Platte Ave Colorado Springs CO 80904-3429

GOEI, BERNARD THWAN-POO (BERT GOEI), retired architectural and engineering firm executive; b. Semarang, Indonesia, Jan. 27, 1938; came to US, 1969; naturalized, 1976; s. Ignatius Ing-Khien Goei and Nicolette Giok-Nio Tjioe; m. Sioe-Tien Liem, May 26, 1966; children: Kimberley Hendrika, Gregory Fitzgerald. BA in Fine Arts, Bandung Inst. Tech. State U. Indonesia, 1961, MA in Archtl. Space Planning, 1964; postgrad., U. Heidelberg, Germany, 1967—68. Co-owner, chief designer Pondok Mungil Interiors Inc., Bandung, 1962-64; dept. mgr., fin. advisor Gumarna Architects, Engrs. and Planners, Inc., Bandung, Jakarta, Indonesia, 1964-67; shop supr., model maker Davan Scale Models, Toronto, Ont., Can., 1968-69; chief archtl. designer George T. Nowak Architects and Assocs., Westchester, Calif., 1969-72; sr. archtl. designer Krisel & Shapiro Architects and Assocs., LA, 1972-74; sr. supervising archtl. designer The Ralph M. Parsons A/E Co. (now Parsons Infrastructure and Tech. Group Inc.), Pasadena, Calif., 1974—2006; ret., 2007. V.p. United Gruno U.S.A. Corp. Import/Export, Monterey Park, Calif., 1980-89. Mem. Rep. Presdl. Task Force, Washington, 1982—, Nat. Rep. Senatorial Com., Washington, 1983—, Nat. Rep. Congrl. Com., Washington, 1981—, Rep. Nat. Com., Washington, 1982—; active Am. Indonesian Cath. Soc. Recipient Excellent Design Achievement commendation Magneto-Hydro-Dynamics Program, 1976, Strategic Def. Initiative "Star Wars" Program, 1988, USAF Space Shuttle Program, West Coast Space-Port, 1984; scholar U. Heidelberg, 1967-68. Mem. NRA, Am. Air Gunner Assn., Tech. Comm. Soc., Indonesian Am. Soc., Dutch Am. Soc., Second Amendment Found., The Right to Keep and Bear Arms Com. Republican. Roman Catholic. Avocations: antique weapons, photography, hi-tech electronics, stamp collecting/philately, travel. Home: 154 Ladera St Monterey Park CA 91754-2125

GOEKE, JOSEPH ROBERT, federal judge, lawyer; b. Covington, Ky., June 22, 1950; BS cum laude, Xavier U., 1972; JD, U. Ky., 1975. Bar: Ky. 1975, US Tax Ct. 1975, Ill. 1988-. Trial atty. Office Chief Counsel IRS, Cin., 1975—80, sr. trial atty., 1980—85, internat. trial atty., 1985—88; ptnr. Mayer, Brown & Platt, Chgo., 1988—2003; judge US Tax Ct., Washington, 2003—. Mem. ABA, Ky. Bar Assn., Order of Coif. Office: US Tax Ct 400 2nd St NW Washington DC 20217*

GOEL, KARAN, entrepreneur; b. New Delhi, 1983; BA, U. Chgo., 2004; MBA, U. Chgo. Grad. Sch. Bus., 2006. Metcalf fellow fin. & equity rsch. Pritzker Orgn.; intern Boston Consulting Group; co-founder & CEO PrepMe.com, Chgo., 2005—. Former chmn. Internat. Leadership Coun. Co-recipient New Venture Challenge award, U. Chgo. Grad. Sch. Bus., 2005, 1st place, Fortune Small Bus. Student Startup Competition, 2006; named Young Entrepreneur of Yr., US SBA, 2004; named one of Best Entrepreneurs Under 25, Bus. Week, 2006. Avocation: bhangra.

GOEL, STEVE, treasurer; b. Elk Grove Village, Ill., July 18, 1968; m. Julie Magary, July 2, 2000; 1 child, Flynn. BS in Acctg. and Fin., U. Ill., Champaign, 1991; MBA, U. Chgo., 2000. CPA Ill., 1993; cert. CFA Inst., 2003. Various treasury positions to asst. treas. AutoNation, Fort Lauderdale, Fla., 2000—06; asst. treas. Ryder, Miami, Fla., 2006—. Home: 1370 S Ocean Blvd # 2406 Pompano Beach FL 33062 Office: Ryder 11690 NW 105th St Miami FL 33178 Home Phone: 954-785-9154; Office Phone: 954-785-9154. Personal E-mail: stevegoel@bellsouth.net.

GOELET, ROBERT G., investment company executive; b. Sandricourt, France, Sept. 28, 1923; s. Robert Walton and Anne Marie (Guestier) G.; m. Alexandra Gardiner Creel, Sept. 9, 1976. AB, Harvard U., 1945. Trustee Am. Mus. Natural History, 1958—, pres., 1975-88, chmn., 1988-89; trustee Boscobel Restoration Inc., 1976—, French Inst.-Alliance Francaise N.Y., 1951—, pres., 1967-93; trustee N.Y. Zool. Soc., 1951—, pres., 1971-75; trustee Carnegie Instn. of Washington, 1980—, Mus. Comparative Zoology, 1980—, N.Y. Geneal. & Biographical Soc., 1998—. Office: 540 Madison Ave Ste 21A New York NY 10022-3244

GOELL, JAMES EMANUEL, electronics executive; b. NYC, Oct. 13, 1939; s. Milton Jacob and Amy (Jacob) G.; m. Tamara Greenberg, Sept. 11, 1960; children: Lisa Sue, Fredric Scott. BEE, Cornell U., 1962, MS, 1963, PhD, 1965. Tech. staff Bell Labs., Holmdel, NJ, 1965—74; v.p., dir. engring., dir. fiber optics lab. Electro-Optical Products div. ITT, Roanoke, Va., 1974-81; pres. Lightwave Technologies, Inc., Van Nuys, Calif., 1981-85; v.p. mktg. PCO, Chatsworth, Calif., 1985-91; program mgr. HBT Ericsson Components, LA, 1991-92; dir. engring. end-user bus. AMP, Harrisburg, Pa., 1992-97; dir. Netconnect Engring. Amp, Harrisburg, Pa., 1997-2000; mng. dir. program mgmt. TyCom, Eatontown, NJ, 2000—02; v.p. engring. Omni Guide, Cambridge, Mass., 2002—05, product devel. cons. Lexington, Mass., 2005—. V.p. Middletown Twp. (N.J.) Bd. Edn. Fellow IEEE; mem. Optical Soc. Am., Am. Phys. Soc., Sigma Xi, Eta Kappa Nu, Tau Beta Pi, Phi Kappa Phi. Home: 6 Boxwood Ln Lexington MA 02420 Office Phone: 781-274-8151. E-mail: jim.goell@ieee.org.

GOELTZ, RICHARD KARL, finance company executive; b. Chgo., Sept. 11, 1942; s. Karl George and Adeline Caroline Goeltz. AB, Brown U., 1964; MBA, Columbia U., 1966; student, London Sch. Econs., 1962-63. Fin. analyst, Office Treas. Exxon Corp., NYC, 1966—70; asst. treas. Joseph E. Seagram & Sons, Inc., NYC, 1970—73, treas., 1973—76, v.p., fin., 1976—86, exec. v.p. fin., 1986—92; bd. dirs., CFO Nat. Westminster Bank, London, 1992—96; vice chmn., CFO Am. Express Co., NYC, 1996—2000; ret., 2000. Bd. dirs. The New Germany Fund, Warnaco Group, Fed. Home Loan Mortgage Corp. (Freddie Mac), Aviva plc; trustee 59 Wall Street Fund, NYC, 1984—92; bd. overseers Columbia Bus. Sch.; mem. ct. of govs. London Sch. Econs., dep. chmn., fin. and gen. purposes com. Bd. dirs., past pres. Opera Orch. of N.Y., 1980—. With USAR, 1966-72. Mem. Beta Gamma Sigma. Republican. Episcopalian.

GOELZER, DANIEL LEE, lawyer; b. Milw., Feb. 14, 1947; s. Gerald Howard and Roberta (Hart) G.; m. Angela C. Carcone, Jan. 9, 1988; children: Christina H., Mary E., Michael W. BBA, U. Wis., 1969, JD, 1973; LLM, George Washington U., 1979. Bar: Wis. 1973, DC 1979, US Dist. Ct. (ea. dist.) Wis. 1973, US Ct. Appeals (7th cir.) 1974, US Ct. Appeals (2d, 9th and DC cirs.) 1975, US Supreme Ct. 1976. Auditor Touche, Ross & Co., Milw., 1969-70; law clk. U.S. Ct. Appeals, Chgo., 1973-74; atty. SEC, Washington, 1974-78, exec. asst. to chmn., 1978-83, gen. counsel, 1983-90; ptnr. Baker and McKenzie, Washington, 1990—2002; mem. Pub. Co. Acctg. Oversight Bd., Washington, 2003—. Adj. prof. Georgetown U. Law Ctr., Washington, 1986-92. Contbr. articles to profl. jours. With USAR, 1969-75. Mem. ABA, AICPA, Fed. Bar Assn. Republican. Congregationalist. Avocation: amateur radio. Home: 5941 Searl Ter Bethesda MD 20816-2022 Office: Pub Co Acctg Oversight Bd 1666 K St NW Washington DC 20006 Office Phone: 202-207-9070. Personal E-mail: dgoelzer@aol.com.

GOEN, BOB, television show host; b. Long Beach, Calif., Dec. 1, 1954; Grad., San Diego State U., 1976. DJ Stint Sta. KPRO-FM, Riverside, Calif., 1977-81; anchor, reporter, prodr., writer, editor Sta. KESQ-TV, Palm Springs, Calif., 1981—86; game show host Perfect Match, 1986, The Home Shopping Game, Blackout; daytime host Wheel of Fortune, 1989-92; game show host The Hollywood Game, 1992; corr., weekend anchor Entertainment Tonight, 1993—96, co-host, 1996—2004. Host Miss Universe, Miss USA, Miss Teen USA, 1993-96. Named to, Long Beach City Coll. Hall of Fame.

GOERGEN, ROBERT B., consumer products company executive; BA in Physics cum laude, Univ. Rochester, NY, 1960; MBA in Fin., Univ. Pa., 1962. With Procter & Gamble, Donaldson, Lufkin & Jenrette, McCann-Erickson; ptnr. McKinsey & Co.; founder, chmn. Blythe Inc., Greenwich, Conn., 1977—, CEO, 1978—. Chmn. Ropart Group, private equity investments, 1979—, XTRA Corp. trailer leasing, 1990—; bd. dir. Bionutrics Inc., 1999—, Protein Sciences Corp. Bd. trustees Univ. Rochester, 1982—; bd. overseers Wharton Sch., Univ. Pa., 1997—. Office: Blythe Inc 1 E Weaver St Greenwich CT 06831 Office Phone: 203-661-1926.

GOERING, JACOB D., retired psychoanalyst; b. Galva, Kans., Jan. 12, 1918; s. Christian B. and Adina Goering; m. Beth Eldridge Goering, Aug. 23, 1941; children: J. Daniel, Kathleen, Barbara. AB, Bethel Coll., North Newton, Kans., 1941; BD, Bethany Sem., Chgo., 1949; PhD, U. Md., College Park, 1959. Mgr. coll. book store Bethel Coll., North Newton, 1941—42; asst. dir., dir. Civilian Pub. Svc. Camps, Oreg., Calif., 1943—45; asst. dir. relief Mennonite Ctrl. Comm., Akron, Pa., 1945—47; psychologist Brook Lane Hosp., Hagerstown, Md., 1950—57; instr., prof. U. Md., College Park, 1957—83, prof. emeritus, 1983; pvt. practice psychoanalyst Silver Spring, 1983—96; ret., 1996. Cons. in field. Contbr. chapters to books. Mem. Newton-North Newton Hist. Preservation Commn., 1998—2003; chmn. Sand Creek Trial com., North Newton, Kans., 1998—2006. Recipient Disting. Achievement award, Bethel Coll. Alumni, 2000; vis. scholar Fulbright, Fulbright Found., Berlin Germany, 1964; Grant Found. fellowship, W.T. Grant Found., Univ. Md., 1956—57. Fellow: Md. Psychol. Assn.; mem.: Nat. Assn. Advancement Psychoanalysis. Democrat. Mennonite. Achievements include proclamation and plaque by city North Newton honoring creation of Sand Creek Trial, 2001. Avocations: music, reading, hiking, gardening. Home: 3043 Ivy Ct North Newton KS 67117 Personal E-mail: jdgoering@sbcglobal.net.

GOERZ, MARY ELIZABETH LARSEN, civic worker; b. Mpls., Apr. 1, 1935; d. David Paul and Myrtle Mary (Grunnet) Larsen; m. David J. Goerz, Jr., Jan. 26, 1962; children: David J. III, Karen Goerz Preston, Julie Goerz Mulvaney. BA, Stanford U., 1957. Mem. pers. staff Hewlett-Packard Corp., Palo Alto, Calif., 1960—62. Founder Roth Aux., 1989; pres. Assn. of Auxs., 1986—89; pres. PTA, La Entrada Sch., Menlo Park, 1976—77; sec. Mid-Peninsula Access Corp., 1986—87; pres. of corp. Menlo Park Presbyn. Ch., 1989—91, moderator women's ministries, 1989—91, elder, 1983—; bd. dirs. Packard Children's Hosp., Stanford, Calif., 1985—96, chair art and display com., 1989—2007; bd. dirs. Ch. of the Pioneers Found., Menlo Park, 1991—, pres., 1999—2003; bd. dirs. Lucile Packard Found. for Children's Health, Stanford, 1996—2001. Mem. Stanford Alumni Assn., Stanford Club of Palo Alto (dir. 1971-73). Personal E-mail: margrz@aol.com.

GOESSL, CELINE, head of religious order; d. Irving Charles Goessl and Theresa Marie Decker. BS Edn., Alverno Coll., Milw., 1971; ThM, St. John U., Collegeville, Minn., 1973; D Ministry, St. Mary U. & Sem., Balt., 1988, Myers-Briggs Personality Profile MBTI, 1982, Enneagram Aspell Assocs., 1992. Dir. religious edn., musician Diocese of Superior Wis., Mercer, 1954—57; tchr., prin. St. Joseph Sch., Rhinelander, Wis., 1957—71; pastoral assoc. Diocese of Green Bay Wis, Appleton/Omro, 1976—85; pastoral adminstr. Diocese of Gaylord Mich., Bellaire, 1987—2004; provincial leader Holy Cross Sisters, Merrill, Wis., 2006—. Spiritual dir. Holy Cross Sisters, Merrill, 1990—. Dir.: (human development workshops) Titles are on web site www.crossbeams.org. Mem. Big Bros.-Big Sisters, Appleton, Wis., 1980—85, Bus. & Profl. Women, Mancelona, Mich., 1987—90, Midwest Pastoral Adminstrs., Racine, Wis., 1990—2005; treas. Women's Ordination Conf., Washington, 2004—06; bd. mem. Habitat for Humanity, Mancelona, 1988—91. Mem.: Leadership Conf. Women Religious (assoc.). Roman Catholic. Home: 700 East Riverside Avenue Merrill WI 54452 Office: Holy Cross Sisters 1400 O'Day Street Merrill WI 54452 Home Phone: 715-536-1896.

GOESTENKORS, GAIL ANN, women's college basketball coach; b. Waterford, Mich., Feb. 26, 1963; d. John and Martha Goestenkors; m. Mark Simons. BA, Saginaw Valley State U., 1985. Grad. asst. Iowa State U., 1985-86; asst. coach Purdue U., West Lafayette, Ind., 1986-92; head coach Duke U., Durham, NC, 1992—2007, U. Tex., 2007—. Head coach Festival Trials, 1991, 95, Atlantic Coast Conf. All-Star Team, 1994, US Jones Cup Team, 1997, U.S.A. Under 19 World Championship Team, 2005; asst. coach U.S.A. World Championship Team, 2002, 06, Olympic Team, 2004. Named Atlantic Coast Conf. Coach of Yr., 1996, 98, 99, 2002, 03, 04, Basketball Times Nat. Coach of Yr., 2000, Dist. II Coach of Yr., Women's Basketball Coaches Assn., 2001, Coach of Yr., 2002, GBallmag.com Coach of Yr., Russell Athletic/Women's Basketball Coaches Assn., 2007, Women's Basketball Coach of Yr., AP, 2007; recipient Victor award, 1999, 2003, Carol Eckman award, Women's Basketball Coaches Assn., 2006, Naismith Women's Coll. Basketball Coach of Yr. award, 2007. Office: U Tex Womens Basketball Athletics Dept PO Box 7399 Austin TX 78713*

GOETSCHEL, ROY HARTZELL, JR., mathematician, researcher; b. Oak Park, Ill., Apr. 19, 1930; s. Roy Hartzell and Elizabeth Wilhelmina Johanna (Gaude) G.; m. Jane Peterson, June 6, 1971. BS, Northwestern U., 1954; MS, DePaul U., 1958; PhD, U. Wis., 1966. Asst. prof. math. Sonoma State U. of Calif., Rohnert Park, Calif., 1966-69; prof. math. U. Idaho, Moscow, Idaho, 1969-97, prof. emeritus math., 1997—. Author: Advanced Calculus, 1981; contbr. articles to Fuzzy Sets and Systems. Mem. N.Y. Acad. Scis. Achievements include introduction and development of concept of fuzzy darts and fuzzy dart representations of fuzzy numbers; introduction of the topic of fuzzy hypergraphs including methodology and applications (especially Hebbian structures) to the literature through papers published in Fuzzy Sets and Systems; conceptualization and development of the basis of a fuzzy matroid theory. Home: 1721 Atsirk St Moscow ID 83843-9302 Office Phone: 208-882-1030.

GOETSCHIUS, JAMES BRIAN, military officer, urban planner; b. Bremerton, Wash., Feb. 22, 1972; s. Garrett Abram and Holly Jane Goetschius; m. Nicole Marie Santillie, Oct. 8, 2004. BA in Psychology, Norwich U., 1995, BS in Arch., 1995; M in City Planning, U. Pa., Phila., 2003. Level II cert. facilities engring. Def. Acquisition U., 2005. Med. platoon leader 1st Bn., 503d Inf. Rgt., Tongduchon, Korea (South), 1995—96; constrn. project officer Health Facility Project Office - NE, Forest Glen, Md., 1996—97; command facility planner US Army Med. Rsch. and Materiel Command, Fort Detrick, Md., 1997—99; officer-in-charge, ops. US Army Health Facility Planning Agy., Falls Church, Va., 1999—2001; officer-in-charge, constrn. Office of the Command Surgeon, US Army Europe, Camp Bondsteel, Serbia-Monteneg (Yugoslavia), 2001—01; chief, health facility project office - korea 121st Gen. Hosp., Seoul, Korea (South), 2003—04; detachment comdr. 6th Med. Logistics Mgmt. Ctr., Fort Detrick, Md., 2004—06; chief health facilities planning Multi-Nat. Force, Iraq, 2006—07; program mgr. med. edn. and tng. campus Army Med. Dept. Ctr. and Sch., 2007—. Decorated Korea Def. Svc. medal US Army, Meritorious Svc. medal with 3 oak leaf clusters, Kosovo Campaign medal, Def. Meritorious Svc. medal, Iraq Campaign medal; named Disting. Mil. Grad., Norwich U. Res. Officer Tng. Corps, 1995; recipient Comdrs. award for Merit in Health Facility Planning, Health Facility Planning Agy., 1997, Erwin Gutkind Travel award, U. Pa., 2002, medal, NATO, 2001; Res. Officer Tng. Corps scholar, US Army, 1991—95, Gen. I. D. White scholar, Norwich U., 1991—95, Dept. City Planning Chair's Merit scholar, U. Pa., 2001—03, Outstanding Planning Student scholar, Pa. Planning Assn., 2003, Long Term Health Edn. and Tng. fellow, US Army, 2001—03, Robert Scott Brown fellow, U. Pa., 2001—03. Mem.: VFW (life), Assn. Mil. Surgeons of the US, Am. Inst. Cert. Planners (cert. profl. planner), Soc. Am. Mil. Engrs. (treas. 2005—06), Nat. Soc. of the SAR, Appalachian Trail Conservancy (life), Upper Saddle River Hist. Soc. (life; trustee 2002—07). Presbyterian. Avocations: photography, travel, running. Office: Brac Program 2250 Stanley Rd Ste 270 Fort Sam Houston TX 78234

GOETZ, CHARLES JOHN, law and economics educator; b. NYC, 1939; AB, Providence Coll., 1961; PhD, U. Va., 1965. Asst. prof. U. Ill., 1965-67; assoc. prof. Va. Poly. Inst. & State U., 1967-72, prof. economics, dir. grad. program economics, 1972-75; vis. prof. U. Va. Sch. Law, Charlottesville, 1975-76, prof., 1976-83, Joseph M. Hartfield prof. law, 1983—. Co-author: Social Security Hearings and Appeals: A Study of the Social Security Administration Hearing System, 1978, Using Experts: Pretrial Preparation, Trial Testimony and Settling Cases, 1985, Antitrust Law: Interpretation and Implementation, 1998, 2002; author: Cases and Materials on Law and Economics, 1984, Uncommon Common-Sense vs. Conventional Wisdom: The Virginia School of Economics, 1991. NATO postdoctoral fellow, 1964-65. Mem. Phi Beta Kappa. Office: U Va Sch Law 580 Massie Rd Charlottesville VA 22903-1789 Office Phone: 434-924-3456. E-mail: cjg4t@virginia.edu.

GOETZ, DOUGLAS NEIL, contract management educator; b. Forest Hills, NY, Aug. 3, 1953; s. Ambrose J. and Frances G.; m. Kathryn Deike, Jan. 22, 1978; 1 child, Michael. BA, Hunter Coll., 1975, MA, 1977; PhD, The Ohio State U., 1989. Park ranger Nat. Park Svc., NYC, 1977-78; dir. edn. Bklyn. Archdiocese, NYC, 1978-80; property adminstrn. Def. Logistics Agy., NYC, 1980-84; prof. contract mgmt. edn. Air Force Inst. Tech., Dayton, 1984—2000; prof. Def. Acquisition U., 2000—. V.p., prof. devel. Nat. Property Mgmt. Assn., Dunedin, Fla., 1987-90, liaison Nat. Contract Mgmt. Assn., Vienna, 1987—. Editor: Property Administration, 1986, 12th edit., 1993, The Property Professional, 1990—; contbr. more than 100 articles to profl. jours. Mem. ASTD, Nat. Property Mgmt. Assn., Nat. Contract Mgmt. Assn. (liaison 1987-90), Am. Soc. Composers Authors and Pub. Democrat. Lutheran. Home: 233 N Maple Ave Fairborn OH 45324-5103 Office Phone: 937-781-1077. E-mail: douglas.goetz@au.mil.

GOETZ, KENNETH LEE, cardiovascular physiologist, research consultant, writer; b. Java, SD, Jan. 7, 1932; m. Shirley Anne Caldwell, July 14, 1962 (div. 2003); children: Gregory Earl, Anne Katherine. PhD, U. Wis., 1963; MD, U. Kans., 1967. Instr., asst. prof. dept. physiology U. Kans. Med. Ctr., Kansas City, 1963-69; med. intern St. Luke's Hosp., Kansas City, 1969, head, div. of exptl. medicine, 1970-91, dir. rsch., 1980-91. Adj. prof. dept. physiology U. Kans. Med. Ctr., 1976-92; vis. prof. U. Kuopio, Finland, 1985, 91, U. Munich, 1992; vis. scientist German Inst. Aerospace Medicine, Cologne, 1993-94. Author (memoir): Bending the Twig, 2002. Recipient Alexander von Humboldt award, 1992. Fellow Am. Phys. Soc. (circulation sect.); mem. Am. Physiol. Soc., Alexander von Humboldt Assn. of Am. Achievements include research in Neurohumoral control of body fluid balance; influence of vasoactive peptides on hemodynamics; Vasopressin, atriopeptin, renal natriuretic peptide, endothelin; reflex control of the circulation. Home: 9535 Ash St # 211 Overland Park KS 66207 Personal E-mail: klg101@sbcglobal.net.

GOETZ, KENNETH M., bank executive; BBA in Fin., Bowling Green State U., Ohio. With Nat. City Corp., Cleve., 1980—, various positions in retail, comml. lending and nat. lending, pres., sr. mng. dir. comml. real estate - nat. markets, exec. v.p. Office: Nat City Corp Nat City Ctr 1900 E Ninth St Cleveland OH 44114-3484 Office Phone: 248-729-8477. E-mail: Kenneth.Goetz@NationalCity.com.*

GOETZ, MAURICE HAROLD, lawyer; b. NYC, Mar. 29, 1924; s. Morton M. and Elsie (Klein) G.; m. Pearl Goldberg, Sept. 12, 1948; children: Susan Goetz Zwirn, Janet L., Jill K. B Social Scis. in Econs. and History, CCNY, 1947; JD, Harvard U., 1950. Bar: N.Y. 1951. Assoc. Bandler Haas & Kass, NYC, 1951-57; ptnr. Bandler Kass & Goetz, NYC, 1957-66, Friedlander, Gaines, Ruttenberg & Goetz, NYC, 1966-74, Rosenman & Colin, NYC, 1974-92; of counsel KMZ Rosenman, NYC, 1993—. Lectr. on labor law Contbr. articles to Nat. Law Jour., Fed. Publs., Inc., others. Office: KMZ Rosenman 575 Madison Ave New York NY 10022-2585

GOETZ, RICHARD J., communications executive; BSME, Ga. Inst. Tech., Atlanta, 1994. Cert. energy mgr. Assn. Energy Engrs. Dir. Linc Network, Alpharetta, Ga., 1996—. Home: 165 Chaseland Rd NE Atlanta GA 30328 Office: Linc Network 1005 Windward Ridge Pkwy Alpharetta GA 30005 Personal E-mail: rickyg623@comcast.net.

GOETZ, ROGER MELVIN, minister; b. Chgo., May 17, 1940; s. Charles Albert and Sidonia Helene (Heck) G.; m. Betty Jean Bokelheide, Nov. 22, 1969; 1 child, Anne Katharine. BS in Chemistry, Iowa State U., Ames, 1962, BS in Math., 1967; MDiv, Concordia Theol. Sem., 1967; STM, Luth. Theol. Sem., 1972. Ordained minister Luth. Ch., 1968. Asst. pastor, dir. music Gethsemane Luth. Ch., St. Paul, 1968-80; assoc. pastor, kantor St. John's Luth. Ch., Topeka, 1980—; instr. Walther Luth. Jr. HS, St. Paul, 1968-80; archivist Kans. Dist. Luth. Ch.-Mo. Synod, Topeka, 1985-89, chmn. worship com., 1985-94, chair floor com. edn., 2000; instr. organ Luth. Ch. - Mo. Synod, 2000—02. Organ recitalist various Luth. chs., 1970—. Author: The Descendants of Johann Georg Götz, 1976, Double Cousins by the Dozens, 1982; editor: A Century of Grace: Centennial History of the Kansas District, 1888-1988, 1988; contbr. articles to profl. jours. including Luth. Witness and Concordia Hist. Inst. Quarterly; composer work for double mixed chorus. Bd. edn. Topeka Luth. Sch., 1996-2004; Rep. precinct committeeman Ward 11/Precinct 3, Topeka, 1996-98, 2002—. Mem.: Am. Guild Organists (chpt. pres. 1983—84, chpt. chaplain 1994—2001, v.p. 2001—02, chpt. pres. 2004—07), Cosmopolitan Internat. (chpt. pres. 2005—06, chpt. chmn. bd. 2006—07), Alpha Chi Sigma, Phi Mu Alpha. Office: St Johns Luth Ch 901 SW Fillmore St Topeka KS 66606-1445 *In my life I have found that the less I try to control things and people and rather leave things in the hands of my loving God, the more God brings gifts and joy into my life.*

GOETZMAN, BRUCE EDGAR, architecture educator; b. Rochester, June 6, 1931; s. Benjamin Byron and Ila Flowers G.; m. Jane Grady McRae,June 25, 1955; children: Adam Brit, Ben Evan. BArch, Carnegie Mellon U., 1954; MS in Architecture, Columbia U., 1956; M in Cmty. Planning, U. Cin., 1965; postgrad., U. London, 1968. Asst. prof. Univ. Cin., 1956-66; prin. Bruce Goetzman & Assocs., Cin., 1965-77; acting chmn. grad. div. Univ. Cin., 1966-67, assoc. prof., 1967-99; prof. emeritus, 1999; ptnr. Goetzman & Follmer Architects, Cin., 1977-85; prin. Bruce Goetzman, Restoration Architect, 1985--. Trustee Miami Purchase Assn. Hist. Preservation, Cin., 1972-91, Ohio Hist. Sites Preservation Adv. Bd., 1980-92; pres. Better Housing League of Cin., 1979-81; trustee Ohio Hist. Soc., 1986-96, pres., 1995-96; pres. Ohio Preservation Alliance, 1986-88; trustee Cin. Preservation Assn., 1993-2000. Mem.: AIA, Assn. Preservation Tech., Architects Soc. Ohio, Cincinnatus Assn. Democrat. Home: 187 Greendale Ave Cincinnati OH 45220-1223 Home Phone: 513-751-3332; Office Phone: 513-281-7244. Business E-Mail: bg@pastarc.com.

GOEWEY, DAVID W., lawyer; b. Andrews AFB, Md., Aug. 22, 1962; BA in Economics & Am. Govt., U. Va., 1984; JD, Coll. William & Mary, 1987. Bar: Va. 1987, DC 1988, Md. 2000, US Ct. of Appeals, Federal, DC & Fourth Circuit. Ptnr., civil litigation Venable LLP, Washington, 1987—. Prof., intensive trial advocacy program & deposition skills program Nat. Inst. for Trial Advocacy, Georgetown U. Office: Venable LLP 575 7th St NW Washington DC 20004 Office Phone: 202-344-4853. Office Fax: 202-344-8300. Business E-Mail: dwgoewey@venable.com.

GOFF, BARBARA ANN, obstetrician, gynecologist, gynecologic oncology; b. Seattle, Aug. 22, 1960; married; 2 children. Cert. med. mgmt., U. Wash., 1999; MD, U. Pa., 1986. Diplomate Am. Bd. Ob-Gyn; Lic. Wash. 1992. Intern Brigham & Women's Hosp., Boston, 1986-87, resident in ob-gyn., 1987-90, mem. staff ob-gyn., 1990-93; resident in ob-gyn. Mass. Gen. Hosp., Boston, 1987-90, fellow in gynecol. oncology, 1990-93, mem. staff ob-gyn., 1990-93, U. Wash., Seattle, 1993—, prof., dir. gynecology oncology. Asst. prof. Harvard Med. Sch., 1992-93; asst. prof. U. Wash., Seattle, 1993-97, assoc. prof., 1997-, adj. prof., dept. medicine, divsn surgery; mem. Gynecologic Oncology Group, Puget Sound Oncology Consortium. Contbr. articles to profl. jours. Named one of Best Doctors in Am. award, 1999, 2000; recipient Good Housekeeping award: Best Doctors for Women, Gynecologic Oncologists, 1997, Seattle Mag. Best Doctor award, 1998. Mem. ACOG, Am. Soc. Clin. Oncology, Soc. Gynecol. Oncologists, Assn. Profs. Gynecology and Obstetrics (Abbott Med. Edn. award, 1997), Western Assn. Gynecologic Oncologists. Office: U Wash Dept Ob-Gyn PO Box 356460 Seattle WA 98195-6460 Office Phone: 206-543-3669. Office Fax: 206-288-6200.*

GOFF, JAMES FRANKLIN, physicist, consultant; b. Louisville, Aug. 1, 1928; s. James Robert and Mary Louise (Kubaugh) Goff; m. Barbara Louise Kral, June 20, 1959; children: Sidra Denise, Alexandra Kral. BS in Physics, MIT, 1950; PhD in Physics, Purdue U., 1962. Rsch. physicist Naval Ordnance Lab., Silver Spring, Md., 1961—80; dir. materials applications office Naval Surface Weapons Ctr., Silver Spring, 1980—90. U.S. nat. leader (Army, Navy, Air Force) Dept. Def. Program in Non-Destructive Evaluation for Coordination with Australia, Can., and Gt. Britain, 1981. Editor: Gaelic Jour. of An Comunn Gaidhealach Am., 1993—2000; contbr. articles to profl. jours. With US Army, 1953—55. Hon. fellow, Internat. Thermal Conductivity Conf. Com., 2003. Fellow: Washington Acad. Scis. (pres. 1982); mem.: Nat. Insts. Sci. and Tech. Alumni Assn. (invited mem.), Philos. Soc. Washington (pres. 1980), Cosmos Club (program chmn. 1986—90). Achievements include research in reformulation of thermoelectric figure-of-merit so that it could be computed from realtistic band structure and scattering; electron-phonon interactions in Ge at low temperatures, contributions of real density states to anomalous electronic transport properties of transition metals and alloys. Home: 3405 34th Pl NW Washington DC 20016-3135

GOFF, RENEE ROSENSTOCK, gifted and talented educator; b. Chgo., May 15, 1956; d. Alfred and Alice (Bronstein) Rosenstock; m. Gerald M. Goff; children: Gregory Scott, Carly Michelle. BA, Northeastern Ill. U., 1978; MEd, Nat. Louis U., 2001. Tchr. 5th and 6th grades Talala Elem. Sch., Park Forest, Ill., 1978—88; tchr. lang. arts and social studies West Oak Mid. Sch., Diamond Lake, Ill., 1989—2003; tchr. gifted grades 2-5 Mount Prospect Sch. Dist. 57, Ill., 2003—. Leader 4-H Clubs, Park Forest and Diamond Lake, 1978—; Washington trip sponsor/assembly chairperson. Nominee Disney Am. Tchr. award, 2001, 2005; recipient Golden Apple nominee, 2003. Mem. Nat. Mid. Sch. Assn., Nat. Assn. Gifted Children, Ill. Assn. Gifted Children Personal E-mail: reneegoff@hotmail.com.

GOFF, ROBERT BURNSIDE, retired food company executive; b. Arcadia, La., Aug. 8, 1924; s. Carl and Ruth (Capers) G.; m. Mary Jane Ellis, June 14, 1947; children— Gayle M., Robert B. BS, Rice U., 1947. Engr. Tex. Pipe Line Co., Tulsa, 1947-48; v.p., dir. Comet Rice Mills, Inc., Houston, 1948-58; sr. v.p., dir. Riviana Foods, Inc., Houston, 1958-75; pres., dir. Food Corp. Internat., Houston, 1975-86. Trustee Found. for Retarded, 1982-90. Served to lt. (j.g.) USNR, 1942-46. Mem. Rice U. Alumni Assn. (exec. bd. 1985-88), River Oaks Country Club. Presbyterian. Home: 2710 Essex Ter Houston TX 77027-5212

GOFF, STEPHEN PAYNE, molecular biologist, educator; b. Providence, Oct. 22, 1951; s. Godfrey and Virginia (Ross) G.; m. Marian B. Carlson, Oct. 15, 1977; children: Sarah Carlson Goff, Thomas Carlson Goff. AB, Amherst Coll., 1973; PhD, Stanford U., 1978; DSc (hon.), Amhert Coll., 1996. Postdoctoral fellow MIT, Cambridge, 1978-81; asst. prof. biochemistry Columbia U., NYC, 1981-85, assoc. prof., 1985-86, prof., 1986—90, Higgins prof. biochemistry and molecular biophysics, 1990—; investigator Howard Hughes Med. Inst., 1993—. Mem. NIH study sect., 1984-88, virology sci. adv. bd. Progenics Pharms., 1988-, chmn. 1991-. Mem. edit. bd. Jour. Virology, Molecular Cell Biology; editor Jour. Virology; contbr. articles to profl. jours. Recipient Irma T. Hirschl Career Devel. award Hirschl Found., 1982-1986, Searle Scholarship award G.D. Searl, Chgo., 1982-1985, Merit award NIH, 1990, 2004, Retrovirology prize 2005. Fellow Am. Acad. Arts Scis., Am. Acad. Microbiol.; mem. NAS. Office: Columbia U Coll of Physicians and Surgeons 701 W 168th St HHSC 1310 New York NY 10032

GOFF, WILLIAM M., JR., art director, graphics designer, animator, artist; b. Tampa, Fla., June 21, 1959; s. Willam M. and Flora G. Goff. Degree in gen. aviation, Ala. Aviation Tech. Coll., 1983; BA, Spring Hill Coll., 1990; cert. in advanced graphic design, Chyron Corp., Melville, NY, 1993; cert. in animation design, Alias/Wavefront Animation, Santa Barbara, Calif., 1995. Cert. in advanced graphic design Chyron Corp. Disk jockey, mem. prodn. staff Sta. WABB-FM Radio, Mobile, Ala., 1975-78; photographer Palmer Photography, Mobile, Ala., 1978-79; mem. gen. maintenance staff Mobile Air Ctr., 1980-83; courier, mem. office svcs. staff Delchamps, Inc., Mobile, 1983-87; art dir., animator Sta. WKRG-TV 5, Inc., Mobile, 1988-98, dir. art internships, 1995-98; digital graphic cons., tech. dir., freelance animator/artist, 1998—. Art dir. (TV spl.) Someone You Know-AIDS, 1992 (AP award 1993); graphic design (documentary) Indian Blood, 1993 (award 1994). Troop leader Boy Scouts Am., Eagle Scouts, Mobile, 1977-79; past pres. Explorers Am., Mobile, 1977-78; prodr. dir. Jr. Achievement, Mobile, 1975-78. Recipient Excellence in Broadcasting award CBS, 1993, Best Sports Event award AP/Afa., 1995, 96, Best Scheduled Live Event award, 1995. Avocations: music, art, outdoor activities, writing, movies. Office: Global Village PO Box 91594 Mobile AL 36691-1594

GOFFARD, LUCIEN H., language educator; b. Paris, May 24, 1938; arrived in US, 1984; s. Julien and Lucienne (Wargny) Goffard; m. Susan Lee Robbin, Aug. 5, 1968; children: Eliane, Sandrine. B, Ecole Normale Instituteurs, Evreux, France, 1957; cert. aptitude pédagogigue, Ecole Normale, Rouen, France, 1958; BA, U. South Fla., Tampa, 1986, MA, 1988. Tchr., counselor French Ministry Edn., 1960—86; adj. instr. U. South Fla., 1986—88; French tchr. Pres Prep. Sch., Sarasota, Fla., 1988—90; French and Spanish tchr. Bloomingdale HS, Bloomingdale, Fla., 1990—92; Latin and Spanish tchr. Pine View Sch., Osprey, Fla., 1992—. Office: Pine View Sch 7 Python Path Osprey FL 34229 Office Phone: 941-486-2001.

GOFFART, WALTER ANDRÉ, history professor; b. Berlin, Feb. 22, 1934; emigrated to U.S., 1943, naturalized, 1959; s. Francis Leo and Andrée Juliette (Steinberg) G.; m. Ellen Horvath, May 19, 1961; children: Vivian, Andrea Judith; m. Roberta Frank, Dec. 31, 1977. AB, Harvard U., Cambridge, Mass., 1955, AM, 1956, PhD, 1961; postgrad., École pratique des Hautes-Études, Paris, France, 1957-58. Lectr. history U. Toronto, Ont., Canada, 1960—63, asst. prof., 1963-66, assoc. prof., 1966-71, prof., 1971-99, acting dir. Ctr. for Medieval Studies, 1971-72, prof. emeritus, 1999; sr. rsch. scholar and lectr. history Yale U., 2000—. Vis. asst. prof. U. Calif. at Berkeley, 1965—66; vis. fellow Inst. Advanced Study, Princeton, NJ, 1967—68, Dumbarton Oaks Ctr. Byzantine Studies, Washington, 1973—74; residency Rockefeller Found. Study and Conf. Ctr., Bellagio, Italy, 2001. Author: The Le Mans Forgeries, 1966, Caput and Colonate, 1974, Barbarians and Romans, A.D. 418-584, 1981; The Narrators of Barbarian History: Jordanes, Gregory of Tours, Bede, and Paul the Deacon, 1988, 2d edit., 2005, Rome's Fall and After, 1989, Historical Atlases: The First Three Hundred Years, 1570-1870, 2003, Barbarian Tides: The Migration Age and the Later Roman Empire, 2006; translator: The Origin of the Idea of Crusade (C. Erdmann), 1978. Fellow Berkeley Coll. (Yale). Recipient Haskins medal Medieval Acad. Am., 1991; Can. Coun. fellow, 1967-68; Am. Coun. Learned Socs. fellow, 1973-74; Guggenheim fellow, 1979-80; Connaught sr. fellow in humanities U. Toronto, 1983-84; Newberry Libr. fellow, 1989. Fellow Medieval Acad. Am. (councillor 1977-80), Royal Hist. Soc., Royal Soc. Can.; mem. Internat. Soc. Anglo-Saxonists, Phi Beta Kappa. Office: Yale U Dept History PO Box 208324 New Haven CT 06520-8324 Business E-Mail: walter.goffart@yale.edu.

GOFFIGAN, CHRISTOPHER WAYNE, research associate; b. Norfolk, Va., June 10, 1960; s. James Edward and Lillie Pearl (Jones) G. AAS in Mgmt., Tidewater C.C., 1982, AAS in Merchandising, 1982; diploma Internet specialist, Stratford Career Inst., 2006. Cert. in profl. comm. Christopher Newport Coll.; cert. profl. cons. Libr. aide Tidewater C.C., Virginia Beach, Va., 1980-82; inventory taker Miller Rhodes, Virginia Beach, Va., 1984, 88; telephone sales rep. Energy Savs. Exterior Inc., Virginia Beach, Va., 1985, Sears Svc. Ctr., Virginia Beach, Va., 1985-86; credit clerical Sears Credit Ctrl., Virginia Beach, Va., 1986-87; telephone interviewer Issues Answers, Norfolk, Va., 1988; rsch. assoc. Leading Nat. Advertisers/Competitive Media Reporting/TNS Media Intelligence, Virginia Beach, 1990—. New mem. adv. panel Am. Mktg. Assn., Chgo., 1992-93. Vol. City of Virginia Beach, 1989. Recipient Cert. of Appreciation, Mil. Mail Call, 1984, Editors Choice award Nat. Libr. Poetry, 1996, 97; named Knight Chevalier Venerable Order of the Knights of Michael the Archangel, 1992, Hon. Sgt. At Arms, Nat. Assn. Chiefs of Police, 1993, named to Internat. Poetry Hall of Fame, 1997. Mem. Am. Fedn. Police and Concerned Citizens, Am. Police Hall of Fame & Mus., U.S. Marshals and Peace Officers Assn. Am., Nat. Assn. Chiefs of Police (hon. chief 1995, Good Samaritan award 1995, Gold Seal award 1995), Internat. Soc. Poets (Internat. Poet of Merit award 1996), Soc. for Human Resource Mgmt., Internat. Guild Profl. Cons. (cert.), Nat. Geographic Soc., Am. Biog. Inst. Rsch. Assn., Va. Employment Law Inst., Va. Crime Prevention Assn., Air Force Assn., History Channel Club, Nat. WWII Mus. (charter). Avocations: bowling, pool, travel, reading, shopping. Home: 740 Cason Ln Virginia Beach VA 23462-1197

GOFFMAN, THOMAS EDWARD, radiation oncologist; b. Chgo., Apr. 16, 1953; s. E. and A. (Choate) G.; divorced; 1 child, James Edward. BA, Yale U., 1975; MD, Hahnemann U., 1979. Diplomate Am. Bd. Radiology, Am. Bd. Internal Medicine, Am. Coll. Radiation Oncology. Intern, resident Georgetown U. Hosp., Washington, 1979-82; med. staff fellow, epidemiology tng. program Nat. Cancer Inst., NIH, Bethesda, Md., 1982-83; resident in radiotherapy, Joint Ctr. for Radiation Therapy Harvard U. Med. Sch., Boston, 1983-86; instr. in radiation oncology Columbia U., NYC, 1986-87, asst. prof. of radiation oncology, 1987; attending in radiation oncology Washington Hosp. Ctr., 1987-89, vice chmn. dept. radiation oncology, 1988-89; asst. dir. radiation oncology Sibley Meml. Hosp., 1989; asst. clin. prof. radiation medicine Georgetown U., 1989—; assoc. prof. dept. radiation oncology/biophysics, med. dir. Sentora Norfolk (Va.) Gen. Hosp., 1997—, chief radiation oncology, 1997—99. Head clin. therapy sect., radiation oncology br. Nat. Cancer Inst., Bethesda, 1989—; asst. prof. radiology USUHS, Bethesda, 1989-91, dir. radiation oncology tng., 1989-92, assoc. prof. radiology, 1991-92; dir. radiation oncology tng. Nat. Cancer Inst. USUHS, Bethesda, 1990-92; dir. radiation oncology St. Agnes Hosp., Balt., 1992-93; rschr. internat. epidemiology nat. radiation NIH, 1983-84; med. dir. radiol. oncology Sentara Norfolk Gen. Hosp., 1999-2000; adj. prof. microbiology and molecular cell biology, Eastern Va. Med. Sch.; dir. Cancer Intelligence and Rsch., PC, 2005—; pres. Premier Avian Bird Flu Newsletter. Contbr. articles to numerous profl. jours. Bd. dirs. Lee's Friends, 2000—. Recipient Excellence in Medicine award, 1979, Blue Ribbon award, 1979; Mosby scholar, 1979, Nat. Rsch. Svc. award, 1983, Epidemiology Tng. fellow Nat. Cancer Inst.-NIH, 1983; named one of Top Physicians in Am., 2003; Internat. Healthcare Profl. of Yr. (Gt. Britain), 2006. Fellow ACP; mem. AAAS, ACS (oncology com. 2001—, bd. dirs.), Am. Soc. Clin. Oncology, Am. Soc. Therapeutic Radiology and Oncology (CMS com. 2003—), N.Y. Acad. Scis., Com. on Physicians Assn., D.C. Med. Soc. (legis. com.), Nat. Cancer Inst. (internal rev. bd. 1989-90, biol. operating com. 1991-), Va. Med. Soc. (dir. cancer intelligence and rsch. com. 2005-, grant reviewer several jours.). Office Phone: 757-363-9885. Personal E-mail: tomeg2@juno.com.

GOFFMAN, WILLIAM, mathematician, educator; b. Cleve., Jan. 28, 1924; s. Sam and Mollie (Stein) G.; m. Patricia McLoughlin, Feb. 7, 1964. BS, U. Mich., 1950, PhD, 1954. Math. cons., 1954-59; research asso. prof. Case Western Res. U., Cleve., 1959-71; dean Case Western Res. U. (Sch. Library Sci.), 1971-77; dir. Case Western Res. U. (Complex Systems Inst.), 1972-75. Contbr. numerous publs. to sci. jours. Served with USAAF, 1943-46. Recipient research grants NSF, research grants NIH, research grants USAF, research grants others. Fellow AAAS Home: Apt 1304 1 Bratenahl Pl Bratenahl OH 44108-1183 Office: Case Western Res Univ Cleveland OH 44106

GOFORTH, DEBORAH S., school librarian, educator; BS in Early Edn., Mid. Edn., Libr. Sci., Tenn. Tech. Univ.; MA, So. Bapt. Theol. Sem. Elem., mid. sch. tchr. Tenn., SC, NC, 1977—89; sch. libr., 1989—; libr. Courtland Elem. Sch., Spotsylvania, Va. Finalist GEICO Excellence in Edn. award, 1998; named Tenn. Region III Tchr. of Yr., 2005, Va. Tchr. of Yr., 2006. Mem.: Va. Ednl. Media Assn. Office: Courtland Elem Sch 6601 Smith Station Rd Spotsylvania VA 22553 Business E-Mail: dgoforth@es.spotsylvania.k12.va.us.*

GOFORTH, JILL HASTINGS, principal; b. Gainesville, Ga., Feb. 19, 1952; d. John Clifton and Enid McKinley Hastings; m. Charles Butler Goforth, July 9, 1977; children: Elizabeth Key, Charles Preston. AA, Gainesville Jr. Coll., Ga., 1972; BS in edn., U. Ga., Athens, 1974, MEd, 1978; EdS, Brenau U., Gainesville, Ga., 2001. Tchr. Oakwood Elem., Oakwood, Ga., 1975—82; dir. First Bapt. Preschool, Gainesville, Ga., 1985—87; tchr. Enota and Centennial Elem. Sch., Gainesville, Ga., 1987—2001; lit. coach Enota Elem., Gainesville, Ga., 2001—03; asst. prin. New Holland Core Knowledge Acad., Gainesville, Ga., 2003—06, prin., 2006—. Cons. Core Knowledge Found., Charlottsville, 2005—. Mem. Gainesville Hall County Jr. League, 1994—2000. Recipient Tchr. of the Yr., Enota Elem., 1997—98, Gainesville City Schools, 1997—98. Mem.: ASCD, Internat. Reading Assn., Profl. Assn. Ga. Educators, Kappa Delta Pi Internat. Honor Sci. Baptist.

GOGAN, PETER JOHN PATRICK, biologist, researcher; s. Patrick John and Winiifred Joan Gogan; m. Dana Lee Waring, Dec. 20, 1975; children: Sloane Waring, Devlynn Ross. AB in Zoology, U. Calif., Berkeley, 1968, PhD, 1986; MS in Wildlife Sci., Tex. A&M U., College Station, 1973. Cert. wildlife biologist Wildlife Soc., 1978. Rsch. wildlife biologist Voyageurs Nat. Pk., International Falls, Minn., 1987—92, US Geol. Survey No. Rocky Mountain Sci. Ctr., Bozeman, Mont., 1992—. Soccer coach Am. Youth Soccer Orgn., Bozeman. Fellow, Welder Wildlife Found., 1979—81. Office: USGS No Rocky Mountain Science Cen Forestry Sci Lab Montana State U Bozeman MT 59717 Home Phone: 406-585-7181. Business E-Mail: peter_gogan@usgs.gov.

GOGBASHIAN, ANDREW, surgeon, researcher; b. Welwyn Garden City, Eng., Oct. 31, 1977; s. Charles Andrew and Hilda Gogbashian; m. Lisa Suzanne Rogers, Dec. 23, 2000; 1 child, Luke Andrew. MD, Imperial Coll., London, 2001. Hon. rsch. fellow Royal Coll. Surgeons Eng., London, 2003—04; rsch. fellow Brigham & Women's Hosp., Boston, 2004—05, Beth Israel Deaconess Med. Ctr., Boston, 2004—05, Harvard Med. Sch., Boston, 2004—05; resident in surgery Hammersmith Hosp., London, 2005—06, resident in radiology, 2006—. Coord. endovascular aneurysm rsch. trial Charing Cross Hosp., London, 2001—02; anatomy instr. Imperial Coll. Sch. Medicine, London, 2002—03; spkr. in field. Contbr. articles to profl. jours. Recipient Burns prize, Imperial Coll. Sch. Medicine, 1996, Cert. of Merit in anatomy, 1995, Cert. of Merit in biochemistry, 1997, Rheumatology prize, Arthritis Rsch. Coun. United Kingdom, 2001; Rsch. fellow, Brigham & Women's Hosp., 2004. Mem.: Royal Coll. Surgeons Edinburgh, Royal Coll. Surgeons Eng. (George Quist Anatomy prize 1996). Evangelical. Achievements include development of novel device for treatment of aortic regurgitation secondary to aortic root dilatation; risk stratification scoring system to predict risk of atrial fibrillation in cardiac surgery utilizing nationwide US data; first to create meta-analysis of a risk scoring system within cardiac surgery. Avocations: computers, tennis. Home Phone: +44 208 998 1816. Personal E-mail: andrew@cardiacforum.com.

GOGEL, RAYMOND E., energy executive; B in philosophy, Upsala Coll.; M in philosophy, Drew U., Madison, NJ, PhD; doctoral rsch, U. Freiburg, Germany. Various positions Pub. Svc. Electric & Gas Co. of NJ; with bus. process mgmt. group IBM Corp., sr. project exec., 1999—2001, v.p. client services, 2001—02; v.p. & chief info. officer Xcel Energy Inc., Mpls., 2002—, v.p. customer & enterprise solutions group, chief human resource officer, chief adminstrv. officer, 2005—. Bd. dirs. Seren Innovations (subs. Xcel Energy); bd. advisors IBM. Author: (books) Quest for Measure. Bd. dirs. MedicAlert Found.; bd. trustees Denver Chpt. Mile High United Way. Named one of Premier 100 IT Leaders, Computerworld, 2005. Office: Xcel Energy Inc 800 Nicollet Mall Minneapolis MN 55402

GOGGINS, COLLEEN A., health products executive; B in Mktg., U. of Wis.; grad., Northwestern U. Kellogg Sch. Mgmt., 1979. With Johnson & Johnson, New Brunswick, NJ, 1981—, dir. mktg. GmbH Germany, 1990—92, pres. Can., 1992—94, pres. consumer products, 1995—98, co. grp. chmn., 1998—2001, worldwide chmn. consumer and personal care grp., mem. exec. com. New Brunswick, NJ, 2001—. Exec. advisory bd. U. of Wis Madison Sch. of Bus. Named one of 50 Most Powerful Women in Business, Fortune mag., 2006. Office: Johnson & Johnson 1 Johnson & Johnson Plz New Brunswick NJ 08933

GOGLIA, CHARLES A., JR., lawyer; b. Phila., Aug. 26, 1931; s. Charles and Marie A. (Beckman) G.; m. Patricia A. Morrissey, July 26, 1958; children: Philip L., Catherine A. BS, St. Joseph's U., Phila., 1953; LLB, Boston Coll., 1958. Bar: Mass. 1958, U.S. Dist. Ct. Mass. 1959, U.S. Ct. Appeals (1st cir.) 1964, U.S. Tax Ct. 1977, U.S. Supreme Ct. 1993. Atty. Sheff & Gens, Boston, 1958-61, Foley, Hoag & Eliot, Boston, 1961-68, ptnr., 1968-74; pvt. practice Wellesley, Mass., 1974—2003. Corporator, trustee, mem. bd. investment, exec. com. Bank Five for Savs., Burlington, Mass., 1974-92; mem. hearing com. Bd. Bar Overseers, Boston, 1984-86; arbitrator Nat. Assn. Dispute Resolution, Inc., 2002—. Counsel Town of Nantucket, Mass., 1970-82, spl. counsel, 1982-85, Town of Weston, Mass., 1974-85, town counsel, 1986-92, spl. counsel, 1992—, mem. zoning bd. appeals, 1964-66, 74-85, mem. planning bd., 1973-74; spl. counsel Mass. Cable TV Commn., Boston, 1973-74. With USNAR, 1951-59. Mem. Wellesley Country Club (past pres.). Avocations: golf, travel. Home and Office: 43 Kendall Ave G-07 Sherborn MA 01770 Office Phone: 508-655-6292.

GOGOTSI, YURY, materials scientist, educator; b. Kiev, Ukraine, Dec. 16, 1961; s. George A. and Svetlana (Potarykina) G.; m. Larissa Ganzha, Mar. 18, 1989; children: Pavel, Natalie. MS with honors in Metallurgy, Kiev Poly. Inst., Ukraine, 1984, PhD in Phys. Chemistry, 1986; DSc in Materials Engring., Nat. Acad. Scis., Ukraine, Kiev, 1995. Rsch. assoc. Inst. Materials Sci. Nat. Acad. Scis., Kiev, Ukraine, 1986-90; Alexander von Humboldt fellow U. Karlsruhe, Germany, 1990-92; Japan Soc. for Promotion of Sci. fellow Tokyo Inst. Tech., 1992-93; NATO/Norwegian Rsch. Coun. fellow U. Oslo Ctr. Materials Rsch., 1993-95; rsch. scientist U. Tübingen, Germany, 1995-96; asst. prof. mech. engring. U. Ill., Chgo., 1996-99, assoc. prof., asst. dir. Rsch. Resources Ctr., 1999-2000; prof. materials sci. and engring. Drexel U., Phila., 2000—, prof. chemistry, 2000—02, prof. mech. engring. and mechanics, 2001—06. Adj. prof. mech. engring. U. Ill., Chgo., 2001—; assoc. dean Coll. Engring. Drexel U., 2002—, dir. A.J. Drexel Nanotechnology Inst., 2003—; cons. NanoBlox Inc., Foster-Miller, Kurth, Ylitalo and Couden, Asea Brown Boveri, Heidelberg, Germany, Microsin, Kiev, Ukraine. Contbr. articles to sci. jours., chapters to books; co-author: Corrosion of Structural Ceramics, 1989, Corrosion of High-Performance Ceramics, 1992; mem. internat. editl. bd.: Advanced Ceramics and Glass, 1992—93, Jour. Materials Processing and Mfg. Sci., 1997—2002, Advances in Tech. of Materials and Materials Processing Jour., 1998—2004, Revs. in Advanced Materials Sci., 1999—, Materials Physics and Mechanics, 2000—, British Ceramic Transactions, 2004—05, Advances in Applied Ceramics, 2005—, Applied Ceramic Tech., 2005—, AZojomo, 2005—, Sci. Nanoscale Materials, 2005—; co-editor: Materials Sci. of Carbides, Nitrides and Borides, 1999, High Pressure Surface Sci. and Engring., 2003, Nanostructured Materials and Coatings for Biomedical and Sensor Applications, 2003; editor: Nanomaterials Handbook, 2006, Nanotubes and Nanofibers, 2006, Carbon Nanomaterials, 2006, Carbon, 2007—; assoc. editor: Internat. Jour. Applied Ceramic Tech., 2003—, Sci. Sintering, 2005—. Recipient I.N. Frantsevich prize, Ukrainian Acad. Scis., 1993, Career award, NSF, 1998, S. Somiya award, Internat. Union Materials Rsch. Societies, 2002, R&D 100 award, R&D Mag., 2003; grantee, Dept. Energy, NSF, 1999. Fellow: World Innovation Found., Am. Ceramic Soc. (Roland Snow award 2003, 2005); mem.: Am. Chem. Soc., Internat. Inst. Sci. Sintering (G.C. Kuczynski prize 2002), World Acad. Ceramics (academician 2004), Electrochemical Soc., Materials Rsch. Soc., AAAS. Achievements include patents in field. Avocations: travel, reading. Office: Dept Materials Engring Drexel U 3141 Chestnut St Philadelphia PA 19104 Business E-Mail: gogotsi@drexel.edu.

GOGUE, JAY (G. JAY GOGUE), academic administrator; b. Waycross, Ga., Sept. 21, 1947; m. Susie Gogue; 3 children. BS, MS, Auburn U.; PhD in Horticulture, Mich. State U. Rsch. scientist Ecological Svc. Div. Nat. Park Svc., 1973—77, chief scientist, 1977—79, chief scientist Div. Interpretation, Park Protection, and Natural Resources Mgmt., 1979—86; prof. Coll. Forest and Recreation Resources Clemson U., 1986—95, assoc. dir. Office Univ. Rsch., 1986—88, v.p. rsch., 1988—95, interim dean Grad. Sch., 1991—92, acting dean Coll. Forest and Recreation Resources, 1994—95, v.p./vice provost agr. and natural resources, 1994—95; provost Utah State U., 1995—2000, prof. Coll. Natural Resources, 1995—2000; pres. N.Mex. State U., 2000—03; chancellor U. Houston Sys., 2003—07; pres. U. Houston, 2003—07, Auburn U., Ala., 2007—. Mem. Tex. Internat. Edn. Consortium; bd. dirs. Greater Houston Partnership, Conference—USA, BioHouston, Inc.; bd. govs. Houston Forum. Mem.: Nat. Assn. State Univs. and Land Grant Colls. (bd. mem. Nat. Resources Ecology Sect.), Sigma Chi, Phi Kappa Phi. Office: Auburn U Office of Pres 107 Samford Hall Auburn University AL 36849 Office Phone: 713-743-8820.*

GOH, CHAN HON, ballerina; b. Beijing, Feb. 1, 1969; arrived in Can, 1977; d. Choo Chiat and Lin Yee Goh. Attended Goh Ballet Academy, Vancouver. Corp de ballet dancer Nat. Ballet of Can., Toronto, 1988-90, second soloist, 1990-92, first soloist, 1992-93, prin. dancer, 1994—, The Suzanne Farrell Ballet, 1999—. Guest artist various ballet companies in Europe, Australia, N. Am., Asia; entrepreneur, owner Principal by Chan Hon Goh Inc., TM Dance Supplies and Dance Shoes, 1996—. Dancer (prin. roles) The Sleeping Beauty, La Fille Mal Gardée, Don Quixote, Romeo & Juliet, Tristan and Isolde, The Nutcracker, Taming of the Shrew, Swan Lake, Giselle, Cinderella, La Boutique Fantasque, La Sylphide, The Dream, Paquita, La Ronde, Desir, Mozartiana, La Bayadere, Apollo, Jewels, Afternoon of a Faun, Forgotten Land, Polyphonia, others; author: Beyond the Dance: A Ballerina's Life, 2002; prodr., star and lead: The Stars of N.Am. Ballet, 2002; Dance at the Main Stage, 2003; An Evening with Dancers of the Nat. Ballet of Can, 2003; Chan Hon Goh and Friends, 2007. Recipient Prix de Lausanne, 1986, Solo Seal award, Royal Acad Dance, 1987, Silver Medal, Adelene Genee Internat. Competition, London, 1988, New Pioneers Arts award, 2005, ACCE Entrepreneurial award for the innovation of prin. shoes, 2005; Can. Coun. grantee, 1987. Office: Nat Ballet of Canada 470 Queens Quay W Toronto ON Canada M5E 3K4 Office Phone: 416-345-9686.

GOHEEN, JANET MOORE, counseling administrator, sales executive; b. Everett, Mass., Sept. 29, 1945; d. Franklin Pierce and Virginia Louise (Murphy) Moore; m. Peter Arthur Goheen, Apr. 2, 1967; children: Kevin Murphy Moore, Andrew Hudson Moore. BA, Ohio Wesleyan U., 1967; MS, U. Bridgeport, 1979. Cert. profl. sch. counselor Ohio. Tchr. English Nordinia Hills HS, Macedonia, Ohio, 1967-69, White Plains (N.Y.) HS, 1969-71, Hudson (Ohio) HS, 1982-83; tchr. emotionally disturbed Palisades Learning Ctr., Paramus, NJ, 1986-87; sales cons. Longaberger Co., Dresden, Ohio, 1983-84, br. advisor, 1984-90, regional advisor, 1990—2004, nat. sales leader, 2004—; counselor Hudson Mid. Sch., 1988—. Tchr. ESL Hitchcock Presbyn. Ch., Scarsdale, NY, 1976—79, Aurora (Ohio) City Schs., 1979—81, Hudson Local Schs., 1980—82. Mem. Jr. League Scarsdale, 1976—79, Jr. League Akron, 1979—82, Jr. League No. N.J., Ridgewood, 1983—85; trustee Am. Found. Suicide Prevention N.E. Ohio, 1997—2005; founder Anna Lee chpt. Questers, Hudson, 1981, Hudson Presbyn. Ch., 1980; mem. alumni bd. dirs. Ohio Wesleyan U., Delaware, 1990—93. Mem.: Ohio Sch. Counselors Assn., Am. Sch. Counselors Assn., Kappa Delta Pi, Kappa Kappa Gamma. Home: 97 Manor Dr Hudson OH 44236-3406 Office: Hudson Middle Sch 77 N Oviatt St Hudson OH 44236-3043 Office Phone: 330-653-1320.

GOHEEN, ROBERT FRANCIS, classicist, educator, former ambassador; b. Vengurla, India, Aug. 15, 1919; s. Robert H.H. and Anne (Ewing) G.; m. Margaret M. Skelly, June 21, 1941; children: Anne Goheen Crane, Gertrude Goheen Swain, Stephen, Margaret Goheen Lower, Elizabeth, Charles. BA, Princeton U., 1940, MA, 1947, PhD, 1948; degree (hon.). Instr. classics Princeton U., 1948-50, asst. prof., 1950-57, prof., 1957, pres., 1957-72, emeritus, 1972—; chmn. Coun. on Founds., 1972-77; pres. Edna McConnell Clark Found., 1977; amb. to India, 1977-80; sr. fellow Woodrow Wilson Sch., 1981—. Dir. Mellon Fellowships in the Humanities, 1981-92; mem. adv. com. Nat. Fgn. Lang. Ctr., Ctr. for Advanced Study of India. Author: The Imagery of Sophocles' Antigone, 1951, The Human Nature of a University, 1969. Trustee emeritus Bharatiya Vidya Bhavan (USA), Nat. Humanities Ctr., Village Charter Sch., Trenton, N.J., Woodrow Wilson Nat. Fellowship Found. Decorated Legion of Merit, Bronze Star. Mem. Am. Philos. Soc., Coun. Fgn. Rels., Am. Acad. Arts and Scis., Am. Acad. Diplomacy, Phi Beta Kappa, Princeton Club (N.Y.C.), Century Assn. (N.Y.C.), Cosmos Club (Washington), Nassau Club (Princeton), Springdale Club (Princeton), Eastward Ho Club (Mass.), Gymkhana and Delhi Golf Club (India). Address: 1 Orchard Cir Princeton NJ 08540-3025 E-mail: rfgoheen@princeton.edu.

GOHH, REGINALD YUCHENGCO, nephrologist; s. Kiatsu and Aurora Yuchengco Go; m. Victoria Miranda, June 20, 1993; children: Miranda Elizabeth, Benjamin Andrew. MD, Meharry Med. Coll., Nashville, 2000. Diplomate Am. Bd. Nephrology, 2000. Med. dir., divsn. organ transplantation RI Hosp., Providence, 1997—; assoc. prof. medicine Brown U. Sch. Medicine, Providence, 2005—. Bd. dirs. RI Organ Donor Awareness Com., Providence. Mem.: Am. Soc. Transplantation, Internal Soc. Nephrology. Achievements include research in clinical transplantation. Office: RI Hosp 593 Eddy St APC-921 Providence RI 02903 Home Phone: 401-481-2967; Office Phone: 401-444-8345. Office Fax: 401-444-3283; Home Fax: 401-444-3283. Business E-Mail: rgohh@lifespan.org.

GOHMERT, LOUIS BULLER, JR., (LOUIE GOHMERT), congressman, former judge, lawyer; b. Pittsburg, Tex., Aug. 18, 1953; s. Louis B. and E. Sue (Brooks) Gohmert; m. Kathryn Ann Bledsoe, June 24, 1978; children: Kathryn Blair, Caroline Sue, Sarah Louise. Student, Sch. Internat. Tng., Putney, Vt., 1973; BA, Tex. A&M U., 1975; JD, Baylor U. Sch. Law, 1977; postgraduate student, U.S. Army Judge Adv. Gen. Sch., 1978. Bar: Tex. 1978, US Dist. Ct. (ea. and so. dists.) Tex. 1978, US Ct. Appeals (5th cir.) 1986, US Supreme Ct. 1986. Asst. dist. atty. 76th Judicial Dist., Mt. Pleasant, Tex., 1978; assoc. Potter Guinn Law Firm, Tyler, Tex., 1982-86; ptnr. Freeman, Smithson & Gohmert, Tyler, 1986; pvt. practice law Tyler, 1986—92; judge Smith County Dist. Ct., Tex., 1992—2002, 12th Cir. Appeals Ct. Tex., 2002—03; mem. US Congress from 1st Tex. dist., 2005—, mem. judiciary com., mem. resources com., mem. small bus. com. Deacon, Green Acres Bapt. Ch., Tyler; mem. E. Tex. Coun. World Affairs, Tyler. Capt. JAGC US Army, 1978—82. Mem. Smith County Bar Assn. (treas. 1989), State Bar Tex. (litigation sect.), Tex. A&M Alumni Assn. (pres. Smith County chpt. 1988), Rotary (pres. local chpt. 1990-91). Republican. Baptist. Avocations: sports, creative writing. Office: US Ho Reps 508 Cannon Ho Office Bldg Washington DC 20515-4301 Office Phone: 202-225-3035.*

GOIN, MARCIA KRAFT, physician; b. Portsmouth, NH, June 27, 1932; d. Wendell Everett and Dorothy (Spurr) Kraft; m. John Morehead Goin, Mar. 5, 1960 (dec. May 1995); children: Suzanne J., Jessica M. BA, Middlebury Coll., 1954; MD, Yale U., 1958; PhD, So. Calif. Psycho-Analytic Inst., 1972; DSc (hon.), Middlebury Coll., 2004. Intern in medicine U. Calif., San Francisco, 1958-59; resident in psychiatry U. So. Calif. Med. Sch., LA, 1959-62; pvt. practice psychiatry and psychoanalysis LA, 1962—; dir. residency edn. psychiat. outpatient dept. L.A. County/U. So. Calif. Med. Ctr., 1980—; clin. prof. psychiatry and behavioral scis. U. So. Calif. Sch. Medicine, 1980—. Co-author: Changing the Body: Psychological Effects of Plastic Surgery, 1981; author (med. jour. column) Practical Psychiatry and Behavioral Health, 1998—; contbr. articles to profl. jours. Mem. L.A. Coun. World Affairs. Recipient Humanitarian Svc. award AMA, 1964, Cert. of Merit, Am. Soc. Plastic Surgeons, 1985, Exemplary Psychiatrist award Nat. Alliance Mentally, Ill. chpt., 2005, Exceptional Mentoring award U. So. Calif., 2005. Fellow Am. Psychiat. Assn. (cons. commn. on psychotherapy 1993—, cons. steering com. practice guidelines 1993—, com. on grad. edn. 1997-99, elected trustee-at-large bd. trustees 1997-2000, v.p. 2000-2002, pres.-elect 2002-2003, pres. 2003-2004), Am. Coll. Psychiatrists; mem. Am. Soc. Aesthetic Surgery (assoc.), So. Calif. Psychoanalytic Inst. (faculty), So. Calif. Psychiat. Soc. (Disting. Svc. award 1991, 2005). Episcopalian. Avocations: tennis, travel, international politics. Office: 1127 Wilshire Blvd Ste 1115 Los Angeles CA 90017-4002 Home Phone: 323-469-5267; Office Phone: 213-977-1129. Business E-Mail: mgoin@usc.edu.

GOIN, PETER JACKSON, art educator; b. Madison, Wis., Nov. 26, 1951; children: Kari, Dana. BA, Hamline U., 1973; MA, U. Iowa, 1975, MFA, 1976. Found. prof. art U. Nev., Reno, 1984—. Author: Tracing the Line: A Photographic Survey of the Mexican-American Border, 1987, Nuclear Landscapes, 1991, Arid Waters: Photographs from the Water in the West Project, 1992, Stopping Time: A Rephotographic Survey of Lake Tahoe, 1992, Humanature, 1996, Atlas of the New West, 1997, A Doubtful River, 2000, Changing Mines in America, 2004, Lake Tahoe, 2005, Black Rock, 2005; one-man shows include Duke U. Mus. Art, Durham, N.C., 1992, Phoenix Mus. Art, 1992, Indpls. Mus. Art, 1992, Savannah (Ga.) Coll. Art and Design, 1992, Nev. Humanities Com. Traveling Exhibit, 1992, NICA, Las Vegas, Nev., 1997, Mus. for Photographie, Braunschweig, Germany, 1997, U. Oreg. Mus. of Art, Eugene, 1997, Nev. Mus. Art, Reno, 1996, 99, 2005-06, Princeton (N.J.) U. Art Mus., 1996, Whitney Mus. Am. Art, N.Y.C., 1996, Museet for Fotographie, Denmark, 1999. Recipient Millennium award for Excellence in Arts, Nev., 1999; named Outstanding Rschr. of Yr., U. Nev., Reno, 2007; grantee NEA, 1982, 90. Office: Univ Nev Dept Art Reno NV 89557-0007 Office Phone: 775-784-4994. Business E-Mail: pgoin@unr.edu.

GOINES, LEONARD, music educator, consultant; b. Jacksonville, Fla., Apr. 22, 1934; s. Buford and Willie Mae (Lamar) G.; m. Margaretta Bobo (div.); 1 child, Lisan Lynette. BMus, Manhattan Sch. Music, 1955, MMus, 1956; Cert., Fontainebleau Sch. Music, France, 1959; MA, Columbia U., 1960, profl. diploma, 1961, EdD, 1963; BA, New Sch. Social Rsch., 1980; MA, NYU, 1980; cert. in clin. counseling, Postgrad. Ctr. for Mental Health, NYC, 1983; CAS, Harvard U., 1984. Lectr. music Queens Coll. CUNY, 1969, York Coll. CUNY, 1969, NYU, 1970—93; trumpeter Symphony New World, NYC, 1965-76; assoc. prof. music Morgan State Coll., Balt., 1966-68, Howard U., Washington, 1970-72; prof. Manhattan C.C. CUNY, NYC, 1970—92; freelance musician Broadway shows, theatre, orchestras, recording ensembles, jazz groups, 1959—. Vis. prof. Williams Coll., Williamstown, Mass., 1984, Vassar Coll., Poughkeepsie, N.Y., 1985; co-exec. prodr., 651 at the Bklyn. Acad. Music Majestic Theatre, 1988-96; dist. vis. prof. Lafayette Coll., Easton, Pa., 1986; postdoctoral fellow Harvard U., Cambridge, Mass., 1982-85; ptnr. Shepard & Goines Orgnl. and Ednl Art. cons., Jazz rsch. cons. Nat. Endowment Arts, 1983; appointee U.S. Dept. Interior, Smithsonian Inst.; mem. Preservation Jazz Adv. Commn., 1992-93; cons. in field. Contbr. articles to profl. jours. Folklore cons., field rschr., African Diaspora, Smithsonian Instn., 1972-76; trustee Nat. Assn. Community Schs. of Arts, N.Y.C., 1982-85; chmn. spl. arts section panel N.Y. State Council on Arts, N.Y.C., 1982-85; music panelist Arts Connection, N.Y.C., 1985. Recipient Pub. Svc. award U.S. Dept. Labor, 1980, Scholar Incentive award CUNY, 1983-84; named Hon. Citizen City of Winnipeg, Can., 1958; Coll. Tchrs. fell NEH, 1982-83; Faculty Rsch. grantee Howard U., CUNY, NYU, 1971-73. Mem. Local 802 of Am. Fedn. Musicians, AAUP, Nat. Acad. Rec. Arts and Scis., Phi Delta Kappa, Phi Mu Alpha. Democrat. Episcopalian. Avocations: running, photography, travel.

GOINGS, EVERETT VERNON (RICK), consumer products company executive; b. Chgo., Oct. 13, 1945; s. Louise Goings; m. Carol Panella; children: Rett, Todd. AB, Guilford Coll., 1969. Dist. sales mgr., regional v.p. Renn Enterprises, 1969-70; pres. Dynamics Inc. (name changed to Dynamark Sec. Ctrs.), 1970-78, Fortcorp, 1979-85; with Avon Products Inc., 1986—, exec. v.p. N.Am. ops. NYC, 1989, exec. v.p., 1989—; pres. (world-wide) Tupperware (formerly Avon U.S.), NYC, 1989—97; chmn., CEO Tupperware Brands, 1997—. Bd. dirs. Boys & Girls Clubs of Am., N.Y., 1989—. Mem. Direct Selling Assn. (bd. dirs. Washington chpt. 1989—), CTFA, Farmington Country Club. Home: 5163 Fairway Oaks Dr Windermere FL 34786-8934 Office: Tupperware 14901 S Orange Blossom Trl Orlando FL 32837-6600*

GOINS, FRANCES FLORIANO, lawyer; b. Buffalo, Jan. 30, 1950; d. William and Anita (Graziano) Floriano; m. Gary Mitchell Goins; children: Matthew W., Mark W. MusB, Cleve. Inst. Music, 1971; MusM, Case Western Res. U., 1973, JD, 1977. Bar: Ohio 1977, U.S. Dist. Ct. Ohio 1978, U.S. Ct. Appeals (6th cir.) 1979, N.Y. 1984, U.S. Dist. Ct. NY 1984, U.S. Supreme Ct. 2002. Law clk to Hon. Frank J. Battisti U.S. Dist. Ct. (no. dist.) Ohio, Cleve., 1977-78; ptnr. Squire, Sanders & Dempsey, Cleve., 1986—2003, Ulmer & Berne LLP, Cleve., 2004—. Mem. vis. com. bd. overseers Case Western Res. U., Cleve., 1984-2000; faculty Nat. Inst. Trial Advocacy, Cleve.; faculty, lectr. trial advocacy seminar Cleve. State U. Sch. Law, 1989-90. Editor-in-chief law rev. Case Western Res. Sch. Law, 1976-77. Trustee, chairperson devel. com. Lyric Opera Cleve., 1985-92, 2003—; founding trustee Shoreby Club Cleve.; v.p. bd. trustees Bay Village Montessori Sch., 1994-96; chmn. bd. trustees No. Ohio Breast Cancer Coalition, 2003—. Mem. ABA (bus. law sect., bus. lit. com., governance com. 1995—, fed. regulation of securities com., subcom. on civil litigation and SEC enforcement 1992—), Ohio Women's Bar Assn. (founding mem.), Ohio State Bar Assn. (ad hoc com. on bus. cts. 1994-99), Cleve. Bar Assn. (com. on women and the law 1987-2000, ethics com. 1988-90, securities law inst., jud. selection com. 1996-2001). Democrat. Roman Catholic. Office: Squire Sanders & Dempsey 4900 Key Tower 127 Public Sq Ste 4900 Cleveland OH 44114-1304

GOINS, MICHAEL ROY, otolaryngologist; b. Charleston, W.Va., Jan. 10, 1974; s. Curtis Lee and Connie Sue Goins. BA, W.Va. U., Morgantown, 1996; MD, W. Va. U., Morgantown, 2000. Cert. Am. Acad. Otolaryngology. Intern in gen. surgery Mercy Hosp. Pitts., 2000—01; resident in otolaryngology Wake Forest U., Winston-Salem, NC, 2004—08; with EN&T Assoc. of Charleston, W.Va., 2005—. Asst. clin. prof. W.Va. U., Charleston, 2005—. Office: EN&T Assoc Charleston 500 Donnally St Charleston WV 25326

GOINS, RICHARD ANTHONY, lawyer, educator; b. New Orleans, Mar. 1, 1950; s. James Milton and Vivian (Wiltz) G.; m. Jane Parker, Aug. 18, 1973 (div. Sept. 1987); m. Nannette Smith, Mar. 3, 1990. BA in History cum laude, Yale U., 1968—72; JD, Stanford U., 1972—75. Bar: La. 1975, Calif. 1977. Dep. dir. New Orleans Legal Asst. Corp., 1977-78, exec. dir., 1978-81; law clk. to Hon. A. Duplantier U.S. Fed. Dist. Ct., New Orleans, 1982; asst. prof. Loyola U. Law Sch., New Orleans, 1981-84; ptnr. Adams and Reese, New Orleans, 1987-96, The Goins Law Firm, New Orleans, 1997-99; shareholder Goins Aaron, PLC, 2000—. Asst. bar examiner torts La. Bar Exam., 1991-96, bar examiner civil procedure, 1996-2004; sec., dir. character and fitness La. Com. on Bar Admissions, 2004—; mem. merit selection panel for selection and appt. of U.S. Magistrate for Ea. Dist. La., 1992-95, 2000; mem. host com. jud. conf. Fed. 5th Cir. Ct. Appeals, 1995; mem. civic justice reform act adv. com. Ea. Dist. La., 2000-; adj. prof. Loyola U. Law Sch., New Orleans, 1984-92, 2003—. Co-author: Practical Issues in Class Action Litigation, 1995. Mem. Mayor of New Orleans Overall Econ. Devel. Plan Com., 1991, Orleans Intercmty. Coun., 1992; mem. spl. gifts. com. Yale Alumni Fund, 1991-92; bd. dirs. New Orleans Home Mortgage Authority, 1991-94, City Trust, New Orleans, 1983-94, State Mental Health Advocacy Sys., New Orleans, 1983-84, New Orleans Legal Assistance Corp., 1982-83, Milne Asylum for Destitute Orphan Boys, Inc., 1994-97. Fellow: La. Bar Found; mem.: ABA (conf. minority ptnrs. 1990—96), Calif. State Bar Assn., 5th Cir. Bar Assn., Fed. Bar Assn. (bd. dir. New Orleans chpt. 1992—99), Nat. Bar Assn. (comml. law sect. 1989—), La. State Bar Assn. (legal aid com. 1978—81, uniform fed. rules com. 1991—92, fed. ct. bench-bar liason com. 1993—99), Master Thomas Moore Inn of Ct. Democrat. Roman Catholic. Avocations: reading, computers. Home: 860 S Clearview Pkwy Apt 121 New Orleans LA 70123-6315 Office Phone: 504-569-1800. Business E-Mail: rgoins@goinsaaron.com.

GOIZUETA, ROBERTO SEGUNDO, theology studies educator; b. Havana, Cuba, Dec. 8, 1954; s. Roberto Crispulo and Olga Casteleiro de Goizueta; m. Elizabeth Thompson; children: Cristina Marie, Roberto Carlos, Gabriela Isabel. BA, Yale U., 1972—76; MA, Marquette U., 1979—82, PhD, 1982—84; DHL (hon.), U. San Francisco, 1998, Elms Coll., 1998. Asst. prof. of theology Loyola U., New Orleans, 1983—; program dir. Aquinas Ctr. of Theology at Emory U., Atlanta, 1986—92; assoc. prof. of theology Loyola U., Chgo., 1992—99; prof. of theology Boston Coll., Chestnut Hill, Mass., 1999—. Pres. Cath. Theol. Soc. of Am., 2004—, Acad. of Cath. Hispanic Theologians of the US, 1990—91. Author: (book) Caminemos con Jesus: Toward a Hispanic/Latino Theology of Accompaniment (Cath. Press Assn. Book Award, Theology Category, Hon. Mention, 1996). Mem. Stonehill Coll., Easton, Mass., 1993—99, The Louisville Inst., 2002—04, The Goizueta Found., Atlanta, 1998—2004, Cristo Rey SJ H.S., Chgo., 1996—99. Named one of Ten Most influential Hispanic Am. educators, pastors, and theologians, Nat. Cath. Reporter, 1992; recipient Virgilio Elizondo award, Acad. Cath. Hispanic Theologians of US, 1996, Awarded key to City, Miami/Dade County, Fla., 1998. Roman Catholic. Office: Boston Coll Theology Dept 21 Campanella Way Chestnut Hill MA 02467 Office Phone: 617-552-1226. Office Fax: 617-552-0794. E-mail: goizueta@bc.edu.

GOKEL, GEORGE WILLIAM, organic chemist, educator; b. June 27, 1946; s. George William and Ruth Mildred G.; m. Kathryn Smiegocki, June 2, 1978; children: Michael Robert, Matthew George, Mark Arlington. BS in Chemistry, Tulane U., 1968; PhD in Organic Chemistry, U. So. Calif., 1971. Postdoctoral fellow UCLA, 1972-74; chemist cen. rsch. dept. E.I. Du Pont de Nemours & Co., Wilmington, Del., summer 1974; asst. prof. chemistry Pa. State U., University, 1974-78; assoc. prof. chemistry U. Md., College Park, 1978-82, prof. chemistry, 1982-85, U. Miami, Coral Gables, Fla., 1985-93, prof. dept. molecular biology and pharmacology Sch. Medicine, 1993—2006; dir. bioorganic chemistry program Washington U., 1993—; Disting. prof. sci. dept. chemistry and biochemistry U. Mo., St. Louis, 2006—; assoc. dir. Ctr. Nanosci., St. Louis, 2006—. Cons. W.R. Grace Co., 1977-86, Lion Detergent Co., Tokyo, 1985—, Seal Sands Chem. Co., Stockton-on-Tees, Eng., 1983-88, Monsanto Co., St. Louis, 1989-91, A.H. Marks, Eng., 1990-99; dean's adv. com. Tulane U., 1997—; lectr. in field. Editor Supramolecular Chemistry jour., 1992-2000, Advances in Supramolecular Chemistry, 1990—, Jour. Supramolecular Chemistry, 2001—; mem. editl. adv. bd. Chemical Communications, 1998—; mem. editl. bd. New Jour. Chemistry, 2001—; author: Phase Transfer. Recipient Allan C. Davis medal Md. Acad. Sci., 1979; Leo Schubert award Washington Acad. Scis., 1980, Macrocycle Chemistry award Izatt-Christensen, 1996, Tomen Agro award excellence, 2000; Petroleum Rsch. Fund grantee, 1976-78; grantee NIH, 1979—, NSF, 1998—. Fellow AAAS; mem. Biophys. Soc., Protein Soc., Am. Chem. Soc., Chem. Soc. (London), Sigma Xi, Alpha Chi Sigma. Republican. Methodist. Home: 1817 Stenton Path Chesterfield MO 63005-4733 Office: Washington U Sch Medicine Dept Molecular Biology & Pharmacology Saint Louis MO 63110

GOKSEL, TAMER, oral surgeon, director; b. Istanbul, Turkey, Aug. 6, 1960; s. Ruhan Etem and Sevgi Ayse Goksel; m. Denise Ladd; children: Will, Kate. BA, U. Va., Charlottesville, 1987; DDS, U. Tenn., Memphis, 1992; MD, U. Tex., San Antonio, 1999. Lic. Oral and Maxillofacial Surgery San Antonio Uniformed Svcs. Health Edn. Consortium, Tex., 2002, Gen. Cosmetic Surgery Am. Acad. Cosmetic Surgery, Ill., 2003, diplomate Am. Bd. Oral and Maxillofacial Surgery, Ill., 2004. Fellow gen. cosmetic surgery Am. Acad. Cosmetic Surgery, Little Rock, 2002—03; chief oral and maxillofacial surgery 31st Combat Support Hosp., Baghdad, 2004; asst. program dir. Oral and Maxillofacial Surgery Residency, Brooke Army Med. Ctr., Ft. Sam Houston, Tex., 2004—05, chief, program dir., 2006—. Lt. col. US Army, 1995. Decorated Meritorious Svc. medal Pres. US, Bronze Star medal, Combat Action Badge US Army. Fellow: Am. Assn. Oral and Maxillofacial Surgeons, ACS; mem.: AMA. Conservative. Home: 5146 Dagger Flats San Antonio TX 78244 Office: Brooke Army Med Ctr 3851 Roger Brooke Dr San Antonio TX 78234 Home Phone: 210-381-1504; Office Phone: 210-916-1701. Home Fax: 210-916-4453.

GOKTEPE, JANET ROSE, retired financial analyst; b. Anniston, Ala., Nov. 27, 1950; d. Clifton Frank and Bertha Ezel (Yates) Yeager; children: Katherine Emel, Joy Saadet. BS in Bus. & Mgmt. magna cum laude, U. Md., 1976, MBA with honors, 1979, PhD in Bus. & Mgmt. with honors, 1986. Sec. dept. of justice FBI, Washington, 1969-72, Dept. of Treasury, Washington, 1972-75; rsch. analyst Comptroller of Currency, Washington, 1975-77, fin. analyst, 1977, Interstate Commerce Commn., Washington, 1978-86, Farm Credit Adminstrn., McLean, Va., 1986—2005; ret., 2005. Lectr. bus. Montgomery Coll., Rockville, Md., 1979-80, U. Md., College Park, 1980-82, U. Md. Grad. Sch., College Park, 1988-89. Author: (with others) Small Groups and Social Interaction, 1983; contbr. articles to profl. jours. Co-chair fed. women's program Interstate Commerce Commn., Washington, 1980-81; vol. Seven Locks Elem. Sch., Bethesda, Md., 1986-94; chair child care task force Farm Credit Adminstrn., McLean, 1989-90. Recipient Outstanding Vol. Svc. certs. Seven Locks Elem. Sch., 1987, 91, 94, Commendation letter Pres. Gerald Ford, 1974. Mem. Nat. Assn. Female Execs., Nat. Capitol Women's Network, Exec. Women in Govt., Assn. Investment Mgmt. and Rsch., Wash. Assn. Money Mgrs., Beta Gamma Sigma, Phi Kappa Phi. Avocations: biking, walking, listening to music. Home: 1439 Mclean Mews Ct Mc Lean VA 22101-3800 Personal E-mail: janetgoktepe@yahoo.com.

GOLAN, DAVID ERIC, biophysicist, pharmacologist, hematologist, medical educator; b. Boston, Mar. 10, 1953; s. Harold Philip and Irene Judith (Soble) G.; m. Laura Carolyn Green, Nov. 29, 1981; children: Liza Green-Golan, Sarah Green-Golan. AB, Harvard Coll., Cambridge, Mass., 1975; MD, Yale U., New Haven, Conn., 1979, PhD, 1982. Diplomate Am. Bd. Internal Medicine, Am. Bd. Hematology. Clin. and rsch. fellow Harvard Med. Sch., Brigham and Women's Hosp., Boston, 1979-83; intern Brigham & Woman's Hosp., Boston, 1979-80, resident in internal medicine, 1980-83, fellow in hematology/oncology, 1983-85; instr. Harvard Med. Sch., Brigham and Women's Hosp., Boston, 1983-87, asst. prof., 1987-94, assoc. prof., 1994-2001, prof., 2001—; assoc. physician Brigham and Women's Hosp., Boston, 1985-92, physician, 1992—. Co-dir. MD-PhD program Harvard-MIT, 2000-03; reviewer study sect. NIH, 1997—; med.-sci. adv. bd. Alza Corp., 1994-2000; Applied Pharm. Task Force and Test Material Devel. com. Nat. Bd. Med. Examiners, 1996-98, Pharm. Test Com. and Test Material Devel. Com. 1998-2001, Interdisciplinary Test Com., 1999-2000; founding mem. Harvard Med. Sch. Acad. Author: (software) Pharm Aid, 1991, (textbook) Principles of Pharmacology: The Pathophysiologic Basis of Drug Therapy, 2004, 2d edit., 2007; contbr. 90 articles to profl. jours. Recipient Faculty prize for excellence in tchg., 1996, Merit award, NIH, 1997—, Student awards for excellence in tchg., Harvard Med. Sch., 1998—2004, AOA Robert J. Glaser Disting. Tchr. award, Assn. Am. Med. Colls., 2005; rsch. fellow, Med. Found., 1985—87. Fellow Molecular Med. Soc.; mem. ACP, Acad. at Harvard Med. Sch. (founder), Biophys. Soc., Am. Soc. for Cell Biology, Am. Chem. Soc., Am. Soc. Hematology, Am. Soc. for Clin. Investigation (elected). Achievements include demonstration of control of transmembrane protein diffusion by membrane skeletal proteins in human red blood cells, development of novel system for visualization of contact area between cell membrane and target membrane, and elucidation of molecular mechanisms by which cells respond to ac electric fields. Office: Harvard Med Sch 250 Longwood Ave Boston MA 02115-5731 Business E-Mail: dgolan@hms.harvard.edu.

GOLAN, KIM MARIE, facility interior designer; b. Pekin, Ill., May 29, 1959; d. Kenneth Frank and Kathleen Marie Golan; 1 child, Julianne Elizabeth. BS in Interior Design and Consumer Comm., Ill. State U., Normal, 1981. Cert. interior designer Nat. Coun. for Interior Design Qualification, 1990, registered Ill., 2001. Jr. interior designer Lincoln Office, Ill., 1981—83, facility asset mgr. Morton, Ill., 1996—2000; sr. interior designer Loth, Inc., Cin., 1983—87; asst. interior design mgr. Miami Bus. Interiors, Dayton, Ohio, 1987—89; interior designer, CAD specialist PEDCO Engring. and Archtl. Svcs., Inc., Cin., 1989—96; registered interior designer Ethan Allen, Peoria, Ill., 2000—02; facility interior designer, office planner Citizens Equity Fed. Credit Union, Peoria, 2002—. Author: Workplace Safety, 2006. Mem.: Internat. Facility Mgmt. Assn. (assoc.). Methodist. Avocations: knitting, board games, fishing, bicycling. Office: CEFCU PO Box 1715 Peoria IL 61656-1715 Home: 404 Fairlane Ave Pekin IL 61554 Business E-Mail: kmgolan@cefcu.com.

GOLAN, STEPHEN LEONARD, lawyer; b. Chgo., Oct. 22, 1951; s. Leonard Walter and Carol (Pepper) G.; m. Sharon D. Robson, Aug. 16, 1980; children: Brianna, Jenna, Melissa. BA, Claremont Coll., Calif., 1974; MBA, JD, Northwestern U., 1978. Bar: Ill. 1978, U.S. Dist. Ct. (no. dist.) Ill. 1978, U.S. Ct. Appeals (7th cir.) 1993. Ptnr. Seyfarth, Shaw, Fairweather & Geraldson, Chgo., 1978—93; founding ptnr. Golan & Christie LLP, Chgo., 1993—. Fellow ABA; mem. AICPA, Nat. Assn. JD-MBA Profls. (bd. dirs. 1984-86), Ill. Bar Assn., Chgo. Bar Assn., Leading Lawyers Network, Leading Lawyers Adv. Bd., Ill. Superlawyers, Tavern Club (mem. jr. com. 1984-86), Exmoor Country Club (Highland Park, Ill.), Lake Forest Caucus. Republican. Episcopalian. Office: Golan & Christie LLP 70 W Madison St 15th Fl Chicago IL 60602 E-mail: slgolan@golanchristie.com.

GOLANSKI, ALANI, lawyer; b. Hartford, Conn., May 29, 1954; s. Solomon and Etta Golanski; m. Gina Gabriella Schmeling, Oct. 30, 1999; children: Cy Sherman Schmeling children: Creeley Leon Schmeling. BA in Philosophy, Trinity Coll., Hartford, Conn., 1983; JD, U. Conn., Hartford, 1986; LLM, Columbia U., 2003; MA in Philosophy, CUNY, 2004. Bar: Conn. 1986, NY 1988, NJ 1990, US Dist. Ct. (ea. and so. dists.) NY 1990, US Dist. Ct. NJ 1990, US Ct. Appeals (2d cir.) 1990, US Ct. Appeals (5th cir.) 1993, US Ct. Appeals (8th and 10th cirs.) 1996, US Ct. Appeals (1st and 6th cirs.) 2004, US Ct. Appeals (fed. cir.) 2005, US Ct. Appeals (3rd cir.) 2007, US Supreme Ct. 1999. Law clk. Conn. Supreme Ct., Hartford, 1986—87; appellate counsel Criminal Appeals Bur., Legal Aid Soc., NYC, 1987—90, Levy Phillips & Konigsberg, NYC, 1990—2003; founder, chmn., pres. ALGOLAW, LLC, Bklyn., 2003—. Articles editor Conn. Law Rev., 1985-86; contbr. articles to profl. jours. James Kent scholar, Columbia U. Sch. of Law, 2003. Mem. Assn. Bar City NY, Phi Beta Kappa. Avocations: philosophy of science, jazz history, Afro-Cuban drumming, swimming, poetry. Office: Ste 547 25 Washington St Brooklyn NY 11201 Home Phone: 718-260-0827; Office Phone: 718-406-4488. Office Fax: 718-852-3465. Personal E-mail: alanigolanski@gmail.com.

GOLD, ALAN H., plastic surgeon; b. Bronx, NY, 1946; MD, SUNY-Downstate Med. Ctr., 1971. Diplomate Am. Bd. Plastic Surgery. Intern North Shore U. Hosp., Manhasset, NY, 1971—72, resident in gen. surgery, 1972—75; resident in plastic surgery Kings County-SUNY Med. Ctr., Bklyn., 1976—78; fellow in hand surgery Nassau County Med. Ctr., East Meadow, NY, 1975—76; pvt. practice plastic surgery Great Neck, NY, 1979—. Attending plastic surgeon North Shore U. Hosp., Manhassett; clin. assoc. prof. surgery Weill Med. Coll. of Cornell U. Mem.: Am. Soc. Plastic Surgeons, Am. Soc. for Aesthetic Plastic Surgery. Office: 833 Northern Blvd Ste 240 Great Neck NY 11021-5308 Home Phone: 516-496-9229; Office Phone: 516-498-2800.

GOLD, ALLAN HAROLD, architect, structural engineer, educator; b. Chgo., Jan. 12, 1942; s. Melvin King and Estelle M. (Zucker) G.; m. Barbara Gail Edelstein, June 20, 1967 (div. Feb. 1989); children: Grant, Ross, Susan; m. Susan Carlucci, Dec. 30, 1989. BArch, U. Ill., Urbana, 1966, MS, 1967. Registered architect, Conn., Colo., Ill., Ind., La., Okla., Wis.; registered structural engr., Ill; registered profl. engr., Ind., La., Okla., Wis., Tex., Mich.; cert. Nat. Coun. Archtl. Registration Bds. (juror registration exam. 1985); Nat. Coun. Examiners Engring. and Surveying Cert., Structural Engrs. Cert. Bd. Architect, project engr. various archtl., engring. cos., Chgo. area, 1963—68; project structural engr. Perkins & Will Archs., Chgo., 1968—70; structural engr. Chgo. Dept. Bldgs., 1970—73; owner, operator Allan H. Gold Arch./Structural Engr., Hazel Crest, Ill., 1973—81; project mgr., sr. structural engr. HKS/Structures, Dallas, 1981—84; dir. architecture and structural engring. URS Engrs., Dallas, 1984; owner, operator Allan H. Gold, Architect/Structural Engr., Dallas, 1985—88; project mgr. Hoffmann Architects, North Haven, Conn., 1988—90; prin. Allan H. Gold, Archt. & Structural Engr., Chgo., 1990—93; v.p. Salse Engrs., Northbrook, Ill., 1993—96; assoc. Thornton-Tomasetti Engrs./LZA Tech., Chgo., 1996—2001; prin. AHG Structural Engring. PC, Chgo., 2001—; asst. prof. archtl. tech. dept. constrn. tech. Purdue U., Hammond, Ind., 1976—80; assoc. prof. architecture U. Okla., Norman, 1980—81. Adj. assoc. prof. architecture U. Tex., Arlington, 1983-85; guest lectr. U. Wis. Ext., 1981; mem. credentialing com. Structural Engrs. Cert. Bd., 2005—. Structural engr. Century Shopping Ctr., Chgo., 1973, Phoenix Tower, Houston, 1983, Xerox II, Irving, Tex., 1984. Mem. Village of Hazel Crest Plan Commn., 1979-81. Fellow: ASCE (tall bldgs. com. 1983—86, std. com. design loads on structure during constrn. 1989—, std. com. design engineered wood constrn. 1989—, editl. bd. Jour. Archtl. Engring. 1995—); mem.: AIA, Am. Inst. Steel Constrn., Am. Arbitration Assn., Structural Engrs. Assn. Ill. (chmn. structural engrs. polit. action com. 2004—06), Am. Concrete Inst., Shriners, Scottish Rite, Masons. Jewish. Home: 360 E Randolph St # 4204 Chicago IL 60601-7341 Office: AHG Structural Engring PC 120 W Madison St Ste 702 Chicago IL 60602 Office Phone: 312-782-2600. Business E-Mail: ahgold@ahgse.com.

GOLD, ANNE MARIE, library director; b. NYC, Feb. 24, 1949; d. James Raymond and Marion Rita (Magner) Scully; m. Steven Louis Gold, Aug. 9, 1974; 1 child, Lauren Z. BA in English, St. Lawrence U., Canton, NY, 1971; MS in Libr. Svc., Columbia U., NYC, 1972. Libr. NY Pub. Libr., NYC, 1972—74, Oakland Pub. Libr., Calif., 1975—80; dir. libr. svcs. Solano County Libr., Fairfield, Calif., 1980—90; county libr. Contra Costa County Libr., Pleasant Hill, Calif., 1990—98; interim mgr. Libr. Calif., Calif. State Libr., Sacramento, 1999; exec. dir. Stanford-Calif. State Libr. Inst. 21st Century Librarianship, Calif., 1999—2001; dir. Sacramento Pub. Libr. Authority, 2002—. Guest lectr. U. Calif., Berkeley Grad. Sch. Libr. Sci., 1975—85, San Jose State U. Sch. Libr. and Info. Sci., 1994—; chair bd. dirs. Califa, 2004—07; mem. coun. Online Computer Libr. Ctr., 2006—. Contbr. articles to profl. jours. Bd. trustees Lafayette Sch., 1993-97; mem. adv. com. San Jose State U. Sch. Libr. and Info. Sci., 2002-07. Recipient Award for Excellence, Contra Costa County Bd. Suprs., 1997. Mem. ALA, Pub. Libr. Assn. (bd. dirs. 1992-93, 2004-07, met. librs. sect., pres. 1992-93), Libr. Adminstrn. and Mgmt. Assn. (various coms.), Calif. Libr. Assn. (coun. mem. 1985-87, 90-92, exec. bd. 1991-92, co-chair legis. com. 1992-94, pres. 1998, Mem. of Yr. award, 1994), Calif. Inst. Librs. (v.p. 1990-91), Restructuring Calif. Pub. Librs. Task Force (1994-95), Calif. County Librs. Assn. (pres. 1996), Urban Librs. Coun. Office: Sacramento Pub Libr 828 I St Sacramento CA 95814 Office Phone: 916-264-2830. Office Fax: 916-264-2755. E-mail: amgold@saclibrary.org.

GOLD, ARNOLD HENRY, judge; b. Santa Monica, Calif., Apr. 12, 1932; s. Louis and Rose (Shalat) G.; m. Gloria Victor; children: Jeffrey Alan, Kenneth Clarke, Susan Elizabeth. AB with distinction, Stanford U., 1953, JD, 1955. Bar: Calif. 1955, U.S. Dist. Ct. (so., ctrl. and no. dists.) Calif. 1955, U.S. Ct. Appeals (9th cir.) 1955, U.S. Supreme Ct. 1955. Law clk. to Hon. John W. Shenk Supreme Ct. of Calif., San Francisco, 1955-56; assoc. atty. Loeb & Loeb, LA, 1956-61; pvt. practice Beverly Hills, Calif., 1961-70; ptnr. Pachter, Gold & Schaffer, and predecessors, LA, 1970-88; judge Calif. Superior Ct. for County of L.A., 1988-2001, supervising judge probate dept., 1993-94. Mem. Calif. Atty. Gen.'s Com. on Charitable Reporting Stds., 1970—71; mem. exec. com. Stanford Law Soc. So. Calif., 1973—77; mem. Calif. Atty. Gen.'s Task Force on Charitable Solicitation Legis., 1975—78; chmn. probate and mental health com. Calif. Judges Assn., 1995—96; pres. bd. trustees Los Angeles County Law Libr., 1998—2000; Calif. rep. Nat. Coll. Probate Judges, 2003—; bd. dirs. Dispute Resolution Svcs., 2003—04; mem. adv. com., advisor Calif. Jud. Coun. Probate and Mental Health, 1997—2004, 2005—; lectr. in field. Co-author: Probate Module, California Civil Practice, 1993-; contbg. author: California Family Law Handbook, California Nonprofit Corporations Handbooks; mng. editor, bd. editors Stanford Law Rev., 1954-55. Mem. ABA, State Bar Calif. (vice chmn. conf. dels. 1986-87), L.A. County Bar Assn. (trustee 1981-83), Los Angeles County Bar Found. (bd. dirs. 1985-91), Mulholland Tennis Club, Phi Beta Kappa, Alpha Epsilon Pi, Phi Alpha Delta, Delta Sigma Rho. Office: 10842 Alta View Dr Studio City CA 91604-3901 Office Phone: 310-312-6002. Personal E-mail: judgeagold@aol.com.

GOLD, ARNOLD P., neurologist; b. NYC, Aug. 8, 1925; s. Michael and Rebecca (Perlman) Gold; m. Sandra Orenberg, Nov. 17, 1969; children: Jeffrey, Stephen, Jennifer, Amelia, Margaret. BA, U. Tex., 1947; MS, U. Fla., 1949; MD, U. Lausanne, 1954; D (hon.), U. Medicine & Dentistry N.J., 2001; DSc (hon.), Sacred Heart U., 2003. Diplomate Am. Bd. Pediatrics, in child neurology Am. Bd. Psychiatry and Neurology. Intern Charity Hosp of La., New Orleans, 1954—55; resident, chief resident in pediat. Children's Hosp., Cin., 1955—58; NIH fellow in pediatric neurology Columbia Presbyn. Med. Ctr., NYC, 1958—; prof. clin. neurology Columbia U., NYC, 1976—, prof. clin. pediat., 1976—, attending neurologist, 1958—, attending pediatrician, 1958—; advisory bd. Winston Sch., Short Hills, NJ, 2004—. Cons. Cmty. Sch., Teaneck, NJ, 1975—; mem. interdisciplinary coun. Devel. and Learning Disabilities, Bethesda, Md., 1997—; attending neurologist and pediatrician N.Y. Presbyn. Hosp., 1999—; attending pediatrician Stanley Morgan Children's Hosp., NYC, 1999. Editor, author: Neurology of Infancy and Childhood, 1974, Pediatric Therapy, 1963—80, Pediatrics, 1968, 1996; author: Merritt's Textbook of Neurology, 1984—2005. Chmn. bd. emeritus Arnold P. Gold Found., 2005—06; bd. dirs. Homes for Developmentally Disabled, NJ, 1984—; pres. Myoclonus Rsch. Found., 1992—2004; trustee, sec. AMA Found., 1999—2004; adv. coun. Naomi Berrie Diabetes Ctr., NYC, 1997—; adv. bd. Winston Sch., Short Hills, NJ; pres. Arnold P. Gold Found., Engelwood Cliffs, NJ, 1989—2005, pres. bd. dirs., 1999—2005, chmn. bd. dirs., 2005—; admissions com. Ben Guron U., Beer-Sheeva, Israel, 1997—98; trustee, bd. advisors N.J. Med. Sch., 2001—. Named Best Dr. in Am., Am. Health Mar. issue, 1996, Best Dr. in N.Y., 1997, 1998, 1999, 2000, 2001; recipient Brennerman award in pediat., 1968, Man of Yr. award, Assn. Brain Injured Children, 1968, Disting. Svc. award, Speech-Lang.-Hearing Assn., 1993, Miracle Maker of N.Y., Children's Miracle Network, 1994, Practitioner of Yr. award, Columbia Presbn. Med. Ctr., 1992, Disting. Svc. award, Columbia U., 1999, Lifetime Cmty. Svc. award, Autism Soc. Am.,

2000, Humanitarian award, Sinai Inst., 2002, Humanitarian award multiple sclerosis rsch., U. Medicine and Dentistry N.J., 2003, Humanitarian award, N.J. Coun. for the Humanities, 2004, Disting. Citizen award, NJ Med. Sch., 2005, Pres.'s award, AMA Found., 2006, Edward J. Ill Excellence in Medicine award, 2007. Fellow: Internat. Child Neurology Soc., Child Neurology Soc. (Lifetime Achievement award 2005), Am. Acad. Neurology, Am. Pediatric Soc., Am. Acad. Pediat. Avocations: gardening, stamp collecting/philately, travel, reading. Office: Neurol Inst NY 710 W 168th St New York NY 10032-2603 Office Phone: 212-305-5483. Business E-Mail: apg1@columbia.edu.

GOLD, BELA, economist, educator; b. Kolozsvar, Hungary, Jan. 30, 1915; came to U.S., 1920, naturalized, 1927; s. Leo and Esther (Ludwig) G.; m. Sonia Steinman, July 5, 1938; 1 son, Robert. BS in Mech. Engring, NYU, 1934; PhD (Univ. fellow 1936-37), Columbia U., 1948. Research cons. Life Ins. Sales Research Bur., Hartford, Conn., 1938-39; asst. head div. program surveys Bur. Agr. Econs., 1939-42; econ. cons. subcom. war mblzn. U.S. Senate, 1943-44; econ. adviser FEA and Dept. Commerce, 1944-46; prof. indsl. econs. U. Pitts. Grad. Sch. Bus., 1947-66; Timken prof. and William E. Umstattd prof. indsl. econs., dir. research program indsl. econs. Case Western Res. U., 1966-83, chmn. dept. econs., 1967-73; Fletcher Jones prof. tech. and mgmt. Claremont Grad. Sch. (Calif.), 1983-2000; pres. Indsl. Econs. and Mgmt. Assocs., 1980-2000. Vis. professorial fellow Nuffield Coll., Oxford (Eng.) U., 1964; vis. prof. Imperial Coll. Scis. and Tech., London, 1967, 73; Disting. Internat. Sr. Rsch. fellow Centre Internat. Rsch. on Computer and Info. Tech., Melbourne, Australia, 1989, Adminstrv. Staff. Coll. India, Hyderabad, 1992, Rand Afrikaans U., South Africa, 1995; cons. to industry and ednl. instns., 1950—; mem. com. on steel industry Nat. Acad. Scis.-Nat. Materials Adv. Bd., 1977-78; mem. assembly of engring. com. on computer-aided mfg. NRC, 1978-82, mem. mfg. studies bd., 1982-86, mem. com. on machine tool industry, 1982-84; mem. Interdepartmental Adv. Com. on Fed. Policy on Indsl. Innovation, 1978-79; mem. ferrous metals panel Nat. Acad. Engring., 1980-84, panel on improving the competitiveness of U.S. Industries, 1985. Author: Wartime Economic Planning in Agriculture, 2d edit., 1969, How is Higher Education Financed, 1959, Foundations of Productivity Analysis, 1955, Explorations in Managerial Economics, 1971, Japanese edit., 1977, Technological Change: Economics Management and Environment, 1975, 80, Applied Productivity Analysis for Industry, U.K. edit., 1976, Russian edit., 1981, Chinese edit., 1982, Research, Technological Change and Economic Analysis, 1977, Productivity, Technology and Capital, 1979, 2d edit., 1982, Evaluating the Effects of Technological Innovations, 1980, Appraising and Stimulating Technological Advances in Industry, 1980, Improving Managerial Evaluations of Computer-Aided Manufacturing, 1981, Technological Progress and Industrial Leadership, 1984, 85, On the Increasing Role of Technology in Corporate Policy, 1991, Strengthening Corporate and National Competitiveness Through Technology, 1992, New Technological Foundations of Strategic Management: Some International Perspectives, 1993, Needed Technological Responses to International Competition, 1994, Emerging Technological Frontiers in International Competition, 1995, Changing the Technological Determinants of International Competitiveness, 1996, Advancing the International Competitiveness of U.S. Manufacturing, 1999; mem. editl. bd. Acad. Mgmt. Jour., 1962-73, Omega: Internat. Jour. Mgmt. Scis., 1972-99, Jour. Product Innovation Mgmt., 1983-99, Internat. Jour. Tech. Mgmt., 1989-99; corr. mem. editl. bd. Revue d'Économie Industrielle, 1978-90; mem. adv. editl. bd. Jour. Computer Integrated Mfg., 1985—,Transactions in Engring. Mgmt., 1986—, Jour. Engring. and Tech. Mgmt., 1988—, Mfg. Rev., 1989—, Prodn. and Ops. Mgmt., 1991—, Mng. Tech. Today, 1992—; contbr. numerous articles to profl. jours., chpts. in books. Social Sci. Research Council fellow, 1937-38, 77, 83; Ford Found. fellow, 1961-62, 66-67, 72 Mem. Am. Econ. Assn., Inst. Mgmt. Scis. (chmn. Coll. on Mgmt. of Technol. Change 1970-85), Nat. Assn. Accts. (subcom. on productivity measurement 1977-79), AAUP. Home: 130 Wellington G West Palm Beach FL 33417-2562

GOLD, CAROL SAPIN, international management consultant, speaker, writer; b. NYC; d. Cerf Saul and Muriel Louise (Fudin) Rosenberg; children: Kevin Bart Sapin, Craig Paul Sapin, Courtney Byrens Sapin. BA, U. Calif., Berkeley, 1955. Asst. credit mgr. Union Oil Co., 1956; with U.S. Dept. State, 1964—66; mem. dept. pub. rels. Braun & Co., LA, 1964—66; corp. dir. pers. tng. Gt. We. Fin. Corp., LA, 1967—71; pres. Carol Sapin Gold & Assocs., LA, 1971—. Bd. dirs. Marathon Nat. Bank, L.A.; host radio program The Competitive Edge; mem. expdn. to Syria and Jordan, 1994, to Morocco, 1995; mem. WORID Bus. Acad.; instr. Learning Annex; instr. Asian program U. So. Calif., 1998; presenter, cons., spkr. in field. Author: Solid Gold Customer Relations and Success Secrets, Travel for Scholars, Paris, 1999; featured in tng. films Power of Words; author: Cassette Libraries, How to Present Seminars, Sound Selling. Bd. dirs. Ctr. Theatre Group, Town Hall, Music Ctr., Odyssey Theater; asst. dir. Burnhill Prodns., 1992—, asst. dir. Cabaret, Palisades Theatre; dir. Improv Corp.; vol. Exec. Svc. Corp., 1996—, CEO Leadership Forum, Lacma Coun. Mem. ASTD, Am. Film Inst. Assn., Sales and Mktg. Execs., Nat. Spkrs. Assn., Nat. Platform Assn., Women in Bus., KCET Women's Coun., Exec. Svc. Corps, World Affairs Coun., Blue Ribbon, Women in Arts, Women in Film, Manuscript Soc. Forum Scotland, Plato Soc., Brandeis U. Women, Sierra Club (Toure de Mt. Blanc), Supreme Ct. Hist. Soc., Dispute Resolution Svcs., Faces of History, Women of LA, Marina Del Rey C. of C., Internat. CEO Exec. Forum, Manuscript Soc., Brandeis Film Group. Avocations: collecting famous manuscripts, music, theater, writing. Office: PO Box 11447 Marina Del Rey CA 90295 Office Phone: 310-823-0202. Personal E-mail: cconsult@aol.com.

GOLD, CHRISTINA A., data processing company executive; b. Can., 1947; d. Peter. BA, Carleton U., Ottawa, 1969; degree (hon.), U. Montreal, 1991. With human resources, sales, mktg., fin. and mgmt. depts. Avon Can., 1970-89, pres., CEO, 1989-93, head oper. bus. unit, 1993; sr. v.p., pres. Avon North Am., NYC, 1993-98; exec. v.p. Global Direct Selling Devel., NYC, 1997-98; co-CEO Teleglobe, Inc.; CEO Beaconsfield Group, 1998—99; chmn., pres., CEO Excel Comm., Inc., Dallas, 1999—2002; sr. exec. v.p. First Data Corp., 2002—06; pres. The Western Union Co. (divsn. First Data Corp.), Greenwood Village, Colo., 2002—06; pres., CEO The Western Union Co., Greenwood Village, Colo., 2006—. Bd. dirs. Meredith Corp., 1999—2001, The Torstar Corp., The Conf. Bd., ITT Industries, NY Life Investment Mgmt. LLC, Western Union Co., 2006—. Named one of 50 Most Powerful Women in Business, Fortune mag., 2006, 50 Women to Watch, Wall St. Jour., 2006. Mem.: Direct Selling Assn. (bd. dirs.), Conf. Bd. NY and Can. (bd. dirs). Office: Western Union Co PO Box 6992 Greenwood Village CO 80155*

GOLD, DEIDRA D., lawyer; b. Jan. 1955; m. Stephen A. Gold. BA, Wellesley Coll.; JD, Columbia U., 1979. Assoc. Jones Day Reavis & Pogue, Cleve., 1983—88, ptnr., 1988—91; v.p., gen. counsel Premier Industrial Corp., Cleve., 1991—97; ptnr. Goldberg Kohn Bell Black Rosenbloom & Mortiz, Chgo., 1998; counsel, corp. sec. Ameritech Corp., 1998—99; v.p., gen. counsel eLoyalty Corp., 2000—01; sr. v.p., gen. counsel, sec. United Stationers Inc., Des Plaines, Ill., 2001—06; exec. v.p., gen. counsel N.Am. Wolters Kluwer, Riverwoods, Ill., 2006—. Office: Wolters Kluwer US 2700 Lake Cook Rd Riverwoods IL 60015*

GOLD, EDWARD DAVID, lawyer; b. Detroit, Jan. 17, 1941; s. Morris and Hilda (Robinson) Gold; m. Francine Sheila Kamin, Jan. 8, 1967; children: Lorne Brian, Karen Beth. Student, Wayne State U., 1958-61; JD, Detroit Coll. Law, 1964. Bar: Mich. 1965, U.S. Dist. Ct. (ea. dist.) Mich. 1965, U.S. Ct. Appeals (6th cir.) 1965, D.C. 1966. Atty. gen. counsel FCC, Washington, 1965-66; ptnr. Conn, Conn & Gold, Detroit, 1966-67, May, Conn, Conn & Gold, Livonia, Mich., 1967-69, Oakland County Legal Aid Soc., 1969—71, Hyman, Gurwin, Nachman, Gold & Alterman, Southfield, Mich., 1971-88, Butzel Long, Bloomfield Hills, Mich., 1988—. Mem. Oakland County Criminal Justice Coordinating Coun., 1976—77; chmn. Friend of the Ct. Adv. Com., Lansing, Mich., 1982—88; contbr. lectr. Inst. Continuing Legal Edn., Ann Arbor, Mich., 1981—, Mich. Trial Lawyers Assn.; adj. prof. U. Detroit Mercy Sch. Law, 2001—05. Author: (book) Michigan Family Law, 1988; contbr. articles to legal jours. Mem. Southfield Transp. Commn., 1975—77; chairperson atty. disp. bd. Tri-County Hearin Panel 71, 1994—2004; chmn. attys.' divsn. Jewish Welfare Fedn., Detroit; mem. nat. young leadership cabinet United Jewish Appeal, NYC, 1978—80; pres. Jewish Family Svc., Detroit, 1988—90; bd. dirs. Oakland County Legal Aid Soc., 1979—84. Scholar Tau Epsilon Rho, 1963. Fellow: Am. Acad. Matrimonial Lawyers (bd. dirs. 1988—93, nat. bd. govs. 1988—2001, pres. Mich. chpt. 1992—93, nat. v.p. 2001—05), Am. Coll. Family Trial Lawyers; mem.: Am. Arbitration Assn., Bar Assn. D.C., Southfield Bar Assn. (pres. 1975—76), Oakland County Bar Assn. (bd. dirs. 1984—93, pres. 1992—93), Mich. Bar Assn. (coun. real property law sect. 1973—81, coun. family law sect. 1974—75, 1977—82, rep. assembly 1978—82, chmn. family law sect. 1981—82, Lifetime Achievement award 2001), Alpha Epsilon Pi (nat. pres. 1976—77, Order of Lion award 1986). Avocation: golf. Office: Butzel Long Ste 200 100 Bloomfield Hills Pkwy Bloomfield Hills MI 48304 Office Phone: 248-258-1416. Business E-Mail: Gold@Butzel.com.

GOLD, GEORGE MYRON, lawyer, editor, writer, consultant; b. Bklyn., June 28, 1935; s. Harry and Rose Miriam (Meyerson) G.; m. Bunny Winters, Dec. 24, 1960; 1 child, Seth Harris AB, U. Rochester, 1956; JD, NYU, 1959. Bar: NY 1960. Practice, NYC, 1960-64, 67-78; legal editor Prentice-Hall, Inc., Englewood Cliffs, NJ, 1960-62; assoc. Speiser, Shumate, Geoghan & Law, NYC, 1962-64; assoc. editor Rsch. and Rev. Svc. Am., Inc., Indpls., 1964-67; dir. publs., mng. editor Estate Planners Quar., Farnsworth Pub. Co., Inc., Rockville Centre, NY, 1967-69; editor-in-chief Trusts & Estates Mag., NYC, 1969-76; mng. editor Trust News, NYC, 1976-78; dir. news publs. and info., editor ABA, Chgo., 1978-83; sr. assoc. editor and dir. book divsn. ABA Jour., Chgo., 1984-87; dir. publs. and editor Trial Mag. Assn. Trial Lawyers Am., 1988-89; exec. sr. law editor Lexis/Nexis, Dayton, 1990-93; exec. editor Stevens Pub., Washington, 1993-94, corp. editl. dir., 1994-95, v.p. editl., 1995; sr. acq. editor Harcourt Profl. Pub., Alexandria, Va., 1998—2000; sr. writer, editor Arnold & Porter, 2003—04. Cons., Ashburn, Va., 1995—. Author: The Propriety, Procedure and Evidentiary Effect of a Jury View, 1959, Investments by Trustees, Executors and Administrators, 1961, What You Should Know About Intestacy, 1962, What You Should Know About the Common Disaster, 1962, The Powers of Your Trustee, 1962, What You Should Know About the Antenuptial Agreement, 1963, Who May Be the Beneficiary of Your Will, 1963, What You Should Know About The Spendthrift Trust, 1963, Comprehensive Estate Analysis, 1966, You're Worth More Than You Think, 1966, Medicare Handbook, 1966, The ABCs of Administering Your Estate, 1966, The Will: An Instrument for Service and Sales, 1966, A Tax-Sheltered Pension Plan for the Close-Corporation Stockholder, 1968, Social Security Law in Nutshell, 1968, What You Should Know About Custodial Gifts to Minors, 1968, The Short-Term Trust and Estate Planning, 1976, The Importance of a Will, 1976, The Need for an Experienced Executor, 1976, Tax Tips-99 Ways to Reduce the Bite, 1976, Investment Management: No Job for the Amateur, 1971, Who Manages Your Securities?, 1972, A Woman's Need for Financial Planning, 1972, The Lawyer's Role in the Search for Peace, 1982, True Counselors: Helping Clients Deal with Loss, 1983, Evaluating and Settling Personal Injury Claims, 1991, Cite Checking: A Guide to Validating Legal Research, 1992, The Compliance Pak for HR Managers-Book I (Hiring, Evaluation & Separation), Book II (Severance), 1993, Selling Life Insurance: Overcoming Objections, 1996; editor: Fundamentals of Federal Income Estate and Gift Taxes, 1965-67 (ann.), The R & R Tax Handbook, 1965-67 (ann.), Tax-Free Reorganizations, 1968, Guide to Pension and Profit Sharing Plans, 1968, A Life Underwriter's Guide to Equity Investments, 1968, The Tired Tirade, 1968, A Handbook of Personal Insurance Terminology, 1968, The 15th Anniversary Edition of Estate Planners Quar., 1968, You, Your Heirs and Your Estate, 1968, The Farnsworth Letter for Estate Planners, 1968-69, How to Use Life Insurance in Business and Estate Planning, 1969, Human Drama in Death and Taxes, 1970, Don't Bank on It, 1970, The Feldman Method, 1970, Directory of Trust Instns., 1969-75 (ann.), LawTalk, 1986-87, The Supreme Court and Its Justices, 1987, Aaron J. Broder on Trial: Reflections of a Famous Litigator, 1994, Examining the Science Behind Nutraceuticals, 2001. Mem. Soc. Law Writers (dir. 1972-75), ABA, Am. Law Inst., NY State Bar Assn., Assn. Bar City NY, Estate Planning Council NYC, Nat. Press Club, Soc. Bus. Press Editors, Soc. Scholarly Publ., Soc. Human Resources Mgmt., Am. Soc. Assn. Execs., Newsletter and Electronic Publishers Assn., Washington Independent Writers, Loudoun County Cable TV Commn., Kappa Nu, Pi Alpha Lambda. Clubs: KP. Office: 43325 Dovetail Pl Ashburn VA 20147 Office Phone: 703-729-7315. Personal E-mail: gmgold@erols.com.

GOLD, GERALD SEYMOUR, lawyer; b. Cleve., Feb. 2, 1931; s. David N. and Geraldine (Bloch) G.; 1 child, Anne; m. Rosemary Grdina, 1994. AB, Case-Western Res. U., 1951, LLB, 1954. Bar: Ohio 1954, US Supreme Ct. 1961. Practiced in, Cleve., 1954-60; chief asst. legal aid defender Cuyahoga County, Cleve., 1960-61, chief legal aid defender, 1961-65; assoc. Ulmer, Byrne, Laronge, Glickman & Curtis, Cleve., 1965-66; ptnr. Gold, Rotatori, Schwartz & Gibbons, Cleve., 1966—. Instr. in law Case-Western Res. U., 1965-66, Cleve. State Law Sch., 1968-69, Case-Western Res. Law-Medicine Center, 1961-77; lectr. to bar assns. commr. Cuyahoga County Pub. Defender, 1977-81. Contbg. author: American Jurisprudence Trials, 1966; Contbr. articles to profl. jours. Fellow Am. Coll. Trial Lawyers, Am. Bd. Criminal Lawyers, Ohio State Bar Found., Internat. Soc. Barristers; mem. ABA (criminal justice coun.), Cuyahoga County Criminal Ct. Bar Assn. (chmn., Lifetime Achievement award 1995), Ohio Bar Assn. (chmn. criminal law sect. 1974-78, ho. of dels. 1986—), Greater Cleve. Bar Assn. (Merit award 1974, trustee 1978—, pres. 1982-83), Nat. Assn. Criminal Def. Lawyers (pres. 1977, Merit award 1975), Ohio Acad. Trial Lawyers (chmn. criminal law sect. 1970-75), Ohio Assn. Criminal Def. Lawyers (bd. dirs. 1990), Case-Western Res. U. Law Alumni Assn. (pres. 1974-75, Outstanding Alumnus award 1991), Soc. Benchers, Court of Nisi Prius Club, Cleve. Skating Club. Home: 33000 Pinetree Rd Pepper Pike OH 44124-5514 Office: 526 Superior Ave E Ste 1140 Cleveland OH 44114-1497 Office Phone: 216-696-6122. Personal E-mail: goldjero@aol.com.

GOLD, HAROLD ARTHUR, lawyer; b. Pitts., Jan. 13, 1929; m. Anita Hubert, Aug. 18, 1937; children: Howard, Bradley. BBA, U. Pitts., 1952; JD, Georgetown U., 1956. Bar: Pa. 1956, D.C. 1956. Sole practice law, Pitts., 1956-64; atty. City of Pitts., 1960-69; ptnr. Baskin and Sears, Pitts., 1965-84, Reed, Smith, Shaw & McClay, Pitts., 1985-93; pres., chief exec. officer Coventry Care, Inc., Monongahela, Pa., 1970-86, chmn. bd., chief exec. officer, 1986-87. Adj. prof. law Duquesne U. Pres. Young Dem. Club of Pitts., 1960-66; presdl. elector Pa., 1960; chmn. bd. Mayview State Hosp., Pitts., 1971-75. Served to lt. U.S. Army, 1948-49, 52-53. Mem. ABA, Pa. Bar Assn., Allegheny County Bar Assn. (real property council 1983-86).

GOLD, I. RANDALL, lawyer; b. Chgo., Nov. 2, 1951; Albert Samuel and Lois (Rodrick) G.; m. Marcey Dale Miller, Nov. 18, 1978; children: Eric Matthew, Brian David. BS with high honors, U. Ill., 1973, JD, 1976. Bar: Ill. 1976, U.S. Dist. Ct. (no. dist.) Ill. 1976, Fla. 1979, U.S. Dist. Ct. (so. dist.) Fla. 1979, U.S. Ct. Appeals (5th and 7th cirs.) 1979, U.S. Tax Ct. 1979, U.S. Ct. Appeals (11th cir.) 1981, U.S. Supreme Ct. 1982, U.S. Dist. Ct. (mid. dist.) Fla. 1987; CPA, Ill., Fla. Tax staff Ernst & Ernst, Chgo., 1976-77; asst. state atty. Cook County, Ill., 1977-78, Dade County, Miami, Fla., 1978-82; spl. atty. Miami Strike Force U.S. Dept. Justice, Fla., 1982-87; pvt. practice Miami, 1987-92; asst. U.S. atty. U.S. Dist. Ct. (mid. dist.) Fla., 1992—, dep. chief Orlando div., 2002—. Lectr. Roosevelt U., Chgo., 1976-77; vice-chmn. fed. practice com. on criminal sect. Fla. Bar, 1986-88, profl. ethics com., 1992-2001; instr. Rollins Coll. paralegal program, 1992-97; adj. prof. criminal justice program U. Ctrl. Fla., 1994—; adj. prof. law U. Orlando, 1998-99; adj. prof. law Barry U., 2007; online faculty U. Phoenix, 2003. Former co-author: Supplement to Vol. 2 of Tax Fraud and Evasion, 6th edit. Co-chmn. Greater Oviedo Cmty. Devel. Program, 1992-93; adviser Jr. Achievement, Chgo., 1976-78, Miami, 1982-84; coach, judge Nat. Trial Competition, U. Miami Law Sch., 1983-86, 88, 90; mentor Seminole County Sch., 1994—, coach mock trial program legal project, 2003—; coach, mock trial program legal project Dade County Pub. Schs., 1985-89, 91-92, ptnr. program, 1989-92. Mem.: FBA, ATLA, AICPA, ABA (govt. litigation counsel, complex crimes com.litigation sect.), Am. Assn. Atty. CPAs, Seminole County Bar Assn., Orange County Bar Assn. (bankruptcy com.), Fla. Inst. CPAs (com. on rels. with Fla. Bar 1985—86, bd. dirs. South Dade chpt. 1987—92), Ill. Soc. CPAs, Ill. Bar Assn., Fla. Bar, U. Ill. Alumni Club (v.p.), Delta Sigma Pi. Jewish. Office: 501 W Church St Ste 300 Orlando FL 32805 Home Phone: 407-366-9662; Office Phone: 407-648-7506. Personal E-mail: eyerandall@aol.com.

GOLD, JAMES PAUL, museum director; b. Seattle, Sept. 26, 1944; s. William J. and Madlyn (Hunsberger) G.; m. Cheryl Magruder, Apr. 6, 1968. BA, Hiram Coll., 1966; MA, Cooperstown Sch. SUNY, 1967. Tchr., curator Elwood Mus., Amsterdam, NY, 1968-71; dir. New Eng. Fire and History Mus., Brewster, Mass., 1972-74; site mgr. Senate House, N.Y. State Parks Recreation and Hist. Preservation, Kingston, 1974-77; regional historic sites supr. Bear Mountain, 1977-79; dir. N.Y. State Bur. Historic Sites and Resource Ctr., Waterford, 1979—. Chair Design Rev. commn. Saratoga springs, 1992-2002; mem. N.Y. State Document Conservation Adv. Coun., 1984-87; mem. Saratoga Springs Open Space Com., 2003—, Saratoga Springs Comprehensive Plan Com., 2006—. Recipient Lifetime Achievement award, Saratoga Springs Preservation Found., 2003. Mem. Cooperstown Grad. Assn. (bd. dirs. 1983-93), N.Y. State Assn. Museums (bd. dirs. 1985-92), Am. Assn. Museums (bd. dirs. 1988-93), Am. Assn. State and Local History, Assn. Preservation Tech., Mid-Atlantic Assn. Mus. (bd. dirs. 1988-93, 94-98, pres. 1994-97, Katherine Coffey award for disting. svc. to mus. profession 2003). Democrat. Avocations: architecture, gardening. Home: 199 Woodlawn Ave Saratoga Springs NY 12866-1507 Office: NY State Parks Recreation and Historic Preservation Peebles Island Waterford NY 12188

GOLD, JANET NOWAKOWSKI, Spanish language educator; b. Torrington, Conn., Oct. 24, 1948; d. Peter S. and Virginia (Eseppi) Nowakowski; m. Hector Zamora, Dec. 1974 (div. Sept. 1978); m. Stephen Gold, June 28, 1981. BA, Albertus Magnus Coll., 1971; MEd, Worcester State Coll., 1981; PhD, U. Mass., 1990. Elem. sch. tchr., Tegucigalpa, Honduras, 1971-72; instr. English Centro Internat. de Idiomas, Cuernavaca, Mexico, instr. ESL, 1973; tchr. Spanish-English bilingual program Worcester (Mass.) Elem. Sch., 1974-82; tchg. asst. U. Mass., Amherst, 1984-88; instr. Spanish lang. and lit. Bates Coll., Lewiston, Mass., 1989-91; asst. prof. Spanish La. State U., Baton Rouge, 1991-95; assoc. prof. Spanish U. N.H., Durham, 1995—. Author: Clementina Suarez: Her Life and Poetry, 1995; contbr. books Reinterpreting the Spanish American Essay: Studies in Nineteenth and Twentieth Century Women's Essays, 1994, A Dream of Light and Shadow: Portraits of Latin American Women Writers, 1995; contbr. articles and revs. to Hispanic studies jours. Fulbright grantee, Honduras, 1988-89. Mem. MLA, Am. Assn. Tchrs. Spanish and Portuguese,Latin Am. Studies Assn., Millay Soc., Asociacion de Literatura Femenina Hispanica, Maine Writers and Publ. Alliance. Home: PO Box 357 Eliot ME 03903-0357 Office: U NH Dept Spanish Murkland 209 Durham NH 03824

GOLD, JEFFREY MARK, investment banker; b. Bronx, NY, Jan. 7, 1945; s. Samuel L. and Sylvia E. Gold; m. Lenore N. Gold, May 29, 1966; children: Brian, Steven, Samuel. BBA in Acctg, Pace U., 1967. Sr. acct. KPMG Peat, Marwick, NYC, 1967—71; v.p., corp. contr. Nat. Patent Devel. Corp., NYC, 1971—78; exec. v.p. fin. and adminstrn., CFO Esquire, Inc., NYC, 1978—84; exec. v.p. strategic planning and corp. devel. Simon & Schuster divsn. of Paramount Comm., NYC, 1984; pres. Goldmark Advisers, Inc., NYC, 1985—; chmn. Quarto Holdings, Inc., 1994—; dir. Vision Fund Am., 2002—. Home: 351 E 84th St New York NY 10028 Office: Goldmark Advisers Inc 276 5th Ave Rm 205 New York NY 10001-4509 Office Phone: 212-779-6059. Personal E-mail: gold1745@aol.com.

GOLD, JONATHAN, restaurant critic, columnist; Restaurant critic California, LA Times, Los Angeles mag., Gourmet, LA Weekly, 1984—. Author: Counter Intelligence: Where to Eat in the Real LA, 2000, (columns) Counter Intelligence, 1986—. Recipient James Beard Found. Journalism award, 1999, 2001, 2005, 2006, Pulitzer Prize for Criticism, 2007. Office: LA Weekly 6715 Sunset Blvd Los Angeles CA 90028 Office Phone: 323-465-9909.*

GOLD, JOSEPH, medical researcher; b. Binghamton, NY, Jan. 17, 1930; s. Leon and Gertrude J. G.; m. Judith Barbara Taylor, June 12, 1955; children: Shannon Gabriel, Skye Raphael. AB, Cornell U., 1952; MD, Upstate Med. Univ., Syracuse, 1956. Diplomate Nat. Bd. Med. Examiners. USPHS postdoctoral rsch. fellow U. Calif. Sch. Medicine, 1956—58; fellow dept. pharmacology Upstate Med. Univ., Syracuse, 1961—62, rsch. asst. prof., 1962—64, asst. prof. pathology, 1964—65; dir. Syracuse Cancer Rsch. Inst., 1965—, trustee, 1965—. Editor: Monsters and Madonnas, The Roots of Christian Antisemitism, 1999; contbr. numerous articles on cancer research and therapy; contbr. chpts. to books. Served with USAF, 1958-61. Recipient Presdl. citation for work in Mercury Astronaut Selection Program, 1960; named Disting. Grad. Binghamton Sch. Dist., 1994. Mem. Am. Assn. Cancer Rsch., Am. Assn. for Lab. Animal Sci., N.Y. Acad. Scis., Onondaga County Med. Soc., Med. Soc. State N.Y. Achievements include pioneering work in proposing gluconeogenesis as a biochemical mechanism of cancer cachexia, 1968; development of hydrazine sulfate, 1st specific anti-cachexia drug to be used in human cancer; invention of process for the synthesis and prodn. of DL-Glyceraldehyde-3-phosphate in a pure and stable form; patentee in field. Home: 127 Edgemont Dr Syracuse NY 13214-2010 Office: 600 E Genesee St Syracuse NY 13202-3111 Office Phone: 315-472-6616.

GOLD, JUDITH HAMMERLING, psychiatrist; b. NYC, June 24, 1941; d. James S. and Anne (Linder) Hammerling; m. Edgar Gold, June 27, 1965. MD, Dalhousie U., 1965; DHumL (hon.), Mt. St. Vincent U., 2002. Intern Victoria Gen. Hosp., Halifax, N.S., Canada, 1964-65; resident Dalhousie U., Halifax, 1967-71; practice medicine specializing in psychiatry Halifax, 1971—2002; staff psychiatrist Dalhousie U. Student Health Clinic, 1971-73; vis. colleague U. Wales Med. Sch., 1973-75; asst. prof. dept. psychiatry Dalhousie U., Halifax, 1975-78, assoc. prof., 1978-80, part-time, 1980-87; pvt. practice Brisbane, 1998—. Vis. prof., reader in psychotherapy studies dept. psychiatry U. Queensland, Brisbane, 1998-99. Editor: Clinical Practice Series, 1987-2001, 6 books; contbr. articles to profl. jours. Bd. govs. Mt. St. Vincent U., 1981-87, chmn., 1986-87. Med. Research Council Can. fellow, 1973-75; Health and Welfare Bd. Can. grantee, 1976-78 Fellow Am. Psychiat. Assn., Am. Coll. Psychiatrists (1st v.p. 1990-91, pres.-elect 1991-92, pres. 1992-93); mem. Can. Psychiat. Assn. (pres.

1981-82), Royal Coll. Phys. Surgeons Can. (exec. mem. 1992-94, coun. 1991-98), Order Can., Alpha Omega Alpha. Home Phone: 61-7-3831-5034; Office Phone: 61-7-3839-4788.

GOLD, LEONARD SINGER, librarian, translator, curator; b. Bklyn., July 3, 1934; s. Hyman B. and Gertrude (Singer) G.; m. Stella Schmidt, June 5, 1960; children: Yael, Dalia. BA, McGill U., 1956; MS in Libr. Service, Columbia U., 1966; MA, NYU, 1967, PhD, 1975; student, C. Redmond Art Students League, 1998—2001. Cert. profl. librarian, N.Y. Tchr. high sch., Kiryat Hayim, Israel, 1960-61; tchr. Hugim High Sch., Haifa, Israel, 1961-63; tech. asst. N.Y. Pub. Libr., NYC, 1963-66, chief Jewish div., 1971-98, Dorot chief libr. Jewish div., bibliographer Jewish studies, 1987-98, asst. dir. Jewish, Oriental and Slavonic studies, 1980-88. Chmn. Jewish and Middle East studies program com. Rsch. Librs. Group, Inc., 1989-91; curator hist. exhbns. A Sign and A Witness: 2000 Years of Hebrew Books and Illuminated Manuscripts, N.Y. Pub. Libr., 1988-89, The Dead Sea Scrolls: Ancient Civilization, Modern Scholarship, N.Y. Pub. Libr., 1993-94. Translator (Nathan Shaham): The Other Side of the Wall, 3 novellas, 1983; editor: A Sign and A Witness: 2000 Years of Hebrew Books and Illuminated Manuscripts, 1988; exhibitions include Bob Laurie Gallery, N.Y.C., 2000, Broome St. Gallery, 2001, 2002, 1st Presbyn. Ch., 2007; assoc. editor: Jewish Book Annual, 1979—94; contbr. to bibliog publs. Astor fellow, 1986-87. Mem. Assn. Jewish Librs. (pres. 1974-76, lifetime mem. award 1998), Coun. Archives and Rsch. Librs. in Jewish Studies (pres. 1978-80, disting. svc. award 1998), Jewish Book Coun. (v.p. 1980-90, pres. 1990-94), Assn. Jewish Studies, Rsch. Librs. Group (chmn. Jewish and Mid. East studies program com. 1989-91, mem. programs adv. group 1991-92), Jewish Publ. Soc. (editl. com. 1986-2002, nat. coun. 2002—). Personal E-mail: leonardgold@rcn.com.

GOLD, LORNE W., Canadian government official; b. Saskatoon, Sask., Can., June 7, 1928; s. Alexander Stewart and Grace Dora (Davis) G.; m. Elizabeth Joan L'Ami, Sept. 8, 1951; children: Catherine Anne, Patricia Ellen, Judith Sharon, Kenneth Robert. BSc, U. Sask., 1950; MSc in Physics, McGill U., 1952, PhD, 1970. Research officer div. bldg. research Nat. Research Coucil Can., Ottawa, Ont., 1950-52, head snow and ice sect., 1953-69, head geotech. sect., 1969-74, asst. dir. div., 1974-79, assoc. dir. div., 1979-86, chmn., assoc. com. geotech. research, 1976-83, guest worker inst. research on constrn., 1987; rschr. emeritus Nat. Rsch. Coun. of Can., Ottawa, Ont., 1988—. Canadian del. to Intern. Union of Testing and Research Labs. for Materials and Structures, 1982-87, bd. dirs. Coun. Internat. du Batiment, 1983-86; sr. visiting scientist Ctr. for Cold Oceans Resources Engring., Meml. U. of Newfoundland, 1987-88; vis. rschr. Inst. for Marine dynamics, NRC of Can., 1990-91. Author: The Canadian Habbakuk Project, 1993. Chair coun. Rideau Park United Ch., Ottawa, 2003—05. Fellow Royal Soc. Can. (sec. Acad. Sci. 1997-01), Can. Acad. Engring., Engring. Inst. Can. (hon. treas. 1991-96), Can. Soc. Civil Engrs. (Horst Leipholz medal 1991), Soc. Sr. Engrs; mem. Internat. Glaciol. Soc. (pres. 1978-81), Assn. Profl. Engrs. Ont., Engring. Inst. Can. (hon. treas. 1991-96), Can. Geotech. Soc. (Roger Brown Meml. award 2003). Mem. United Ch. Of Canada. Home: 1903 Illinois Ave Ottawa ON Canada K1H 6W5 Office: Nat Rsch Coun Can Inst for Research in Constrn Ottawa ON Canada K1A 0R6

GOLD, MARC J., secondary school educator, supervisor; b. Bklyn., Aug. 7, 1959; s. Morton and Shirley Gold; m. Alison R. Paul; children: Benjamin Paul, Melanie Paul. MA, Columbia U., NYC, 1987. Cert. Tchr. NJ, 1984. Vice prin. Tenafly HS, NJ, 2000—01, tchr., dept. supr., 2001—. Tchr. EvenStart, Tarrytown, NY, 2004—06. Grantee Summer Inst., Nat. Endowment for the Humanities, 1987, 1990. Mem.: NJ Social Studies Supervisors Assn. (assoc.). Liberal. Avocations: reading, travel, basketball, crossword puzzles. Office: Tenafly HS 19 Comubus Dr Tenafly NJ 07670 Office Phone: 201-816-6654. Business E-Mail: mgold@tenafly.k12.nj.us.

GOLD, MARI S., public relations executive; b. NYC, June 17, 1940; d. George B. and Natalie (Machol) Sour; m. Joel S. Ullman, May 27, 1983. BA, Vassar Coll., 1962. Coord. Family Book Svc., Meredith Pub. Co., NYC, 1962-64; assoc. producer Tanglewood Theatre, Lords Valley, Pa., 1966-68; producer CasperCitron Program, NYC, 1968-70; free-lance publicist NYC, 1970-74; with Lobsenz-Stevens Inc., NYC, 1974—, exec. v.p., 1981—, assoc. gen. mgr., 1985-92; dep. press sec. N.Y.C. Health & Hosps. Corp., 1992-93, dr. mktg. and comm., 1993-95; dir. comm. MetroPlus Health Plan, NYC, 1995—. Office: MetroPlus Health Plan 160 Water St New York NY 10038 E-mail: goldm@nychhc.org.

GOLD, MARTIN ELLIOT, lawyer, educator; b. NYC, Jan. 6, 1946; s. Herman and Rose (Zippin) G.; m. Mary Byrne. BA, Cornell U., 1967; JD, Harvard U., 1970, MPA, 1971. Bar: NY 1972, US Dist. Ct. (so. and ea. dists.) NY 1974, US Ct. Appeals (2d cir.) 1974. With Operation Crossroads Africa, The Gambia, 1965; cons. US Dept. Justice, 1968; assoc. Freshfields, London, 1969; rsch. fellow Ctr. Law and Devel. Sri Lanka, Cambridge, Mass., 1971—73; assoc. Debevoise & Plimpton, NYC, 1973—78; chief econ. devel. divsn. NYC Law Dept., 1978—85, NYC dir. corp. law, 1980—85; ptnr. Sidley Austin LLP, NYC, 1985—. Adj. prof. Columbia U., 1987—; guest lectr. Fordham U., Yale U., Cornell U., US Conf. Mayors, US Justice Dept., Nat. Conf. State Legislatures, others. Author: Law and Social Change: A Study of Land Reform in Sri Lanka, 1977; contbr. articles to numerous profl. jours. Mem. Legal Aid Soc., 1975-81, Cornell Real Estate Coun., 1988—; bd. dirs. Environ. Action Coalition, 1988-2002, INFORM, J.F. Kennedy Sch., Tri State Coun., 1991-97; chmn. Ridgefield Coun. Lake Assns. Recipient awards, Rockefeller Bros. Fund, 1979, 1980, Fund for City N.Y., 1981, Leadership award, J.F. Kennedy Sch. Mem. ABA (NY Super Lawyer award), Internat. Assn. Attys. and Execs. in Corp. Real Estate, Nat. Coun. for Pub. and Pvt. Partnerships, Natural Resources Def. Coun., Assn. Bar City NY (environ., mcpl., energy and real property and housing law coms.), Urban Land Inst., Common Cause, Cornell Club. Avocations: tennis, gardening, travel. Home: 140 Riverside Dr Apt 12H New York NY 10024 Home Phone: 212-496-8235; Office Phone: 212-839-5481. Business E-Mail: megold@sidley.com.

GOLD, MICHAEL EVAN, law educator; b. Oakland, Calif., Apr. 14, 1943; s. Ellis and Ruth Lorraine Gold; m. Sarah Dogbe, Apr. 20, 1971; children: Elijah Laoba, Kebbeh Calypso. BA, U. Calif., Berkeley, 1965; LLB, Stanford U., 1967. Bar: Calif. 72, NY 78, U.S. Supreme Ct. 78. Vol. Peace Corps, Liberia, 1968—70; atty. Schwartz, Steinsapir & Dohrmann, LA, 1972—75; assoc. prof. San Fernando Valley Coll. Law, LA, 1975—77, Cornell U., Ithaca, NY, 1977—. Author: A Dialogue on Comparable Worth, 1983; contbr. articles to profl. jours. Home: 102 Oxford Pl Ithaca NY 14850-4720 Office: Cornell U Ives Hall Ithaca NY 14853-3901 Business E-Mail: meg3@cornell.edu.

GOLD, MONIQUEKA E., education educator; d. John Wesley and Julia H. Gold. EdD, Vanderbilt U., Nashville, 1998. Cert. tchr. Tenn. Vision specialist Dept. Def. Schs., Ft. Campbell, Ky., 1992—99; assoc. prof. edn. Austin Peay State U., Clarksville, Tenn., 1999—. 2nd grade tchr., 4th and 5th grade resource tchr., vision specialist Clarksville Montgomery County Schs., 1985—92. Contbr. articles to profl. jours. (Who's Who Among Teachers, 2005), chapters to books. Active mem. Boiling Spring Missionary Bapt. Ch., Clarksville, 1969—. Mem.: Societas Docta. Baptist. Office: Austin Peay State Univ 601 College St Clarksville TN 37044 Home Phone: 931-645-6373; Office Phone: 931-221-7518. Office Fax: 931-221-1292. Business E-Mail: goldm@apsu.edu.

GOLD, NEIL D., lawyer; b. NYC, Jan. 28, 1948; s. Henry and Rose (Siegel) G.; m. Ellen Toff, Aug. 24, 1969; children: Jeffrey, Jason. BA honors, in polit. sci., U. Rochester, 1969; JD honors, Harvard U., 1972. Bar: NY 1973. Assoc. Rosenman, Colin, Freund, Lewis & Cohen, NYC, 1972-81, ptnr., 1981-86, Gelberg & Abrams, NYC, 1986-87, Reavis & McGrath, NYC, Fulbright & Jaworski, NYC, 1987—. Contbr. articles to profl. journs. Recipient Who's Who in Am. Law. Mem. ABA, Assn. Bar NYC, Atrium Club. Avocations: golf, travel. Office: Fulbright & Jaworski 666 5th Ave Fl 30 New York NY 10103-3198 Office Phone: 212-318-3000, 212-318-3022. Office Fax: 212-318-3400. Business E-Mail: ngold@fulbright.com.

GOLD, PAUL ERNEST, psychology and behavioral neuroscience educator; b. Detroit, Jan. 7, 1945; s. Hyman and Sylvia Gold; children: Scott David Gold, Zachary Alexander Korol-Gold. BA, U. Mich., 1966; MS, U. N.C., 1968; PhD, 1971. NIH postdoctoral fellow, lectr. psychobiology U. Calif., Irvine, 1972-76; asst. prof. U. Va., Charlottesville, 1976-78, assoc. prof., 1978-81, prof., 1981-97, Commonwealth prof., 1997—99, dir. neurosci. grad. program, 1991-95; prof. Binghamton (N.Y.) U., 1999-2000, U. Ill., Urbana-Champaign, 2000—. Dir. Med. Scholars Program U. Ill. Coll. Medicine, Urbana-Champaign, 2000—02, exec. com. Inst. Aging, 2001—, interim dir. neurosci. program, 2004—05. Editor Psychobiology, 1990-97, Neurobiology of Learning and Memory, 1998—; contbr. numerous articles to sci. publs. Mem. Commonwealth of Va. Alzheimer's and Related Disorders Commn., 1998-99. Recipient James McKeen Cattell award, 1983, Sesquicentennial Assn. award, U. Va., 1983, 90-93, Disting. Alumni award U. N.C., Chapel Hill, 2000; named APA Master Lectr., 2000; NIH fellow, 1967. Fellow APA (com. animal rsch. and ethics), AAAS, Am. Psychol. Soc. (mem. com. 1990-91, program com. 1991); mem. Soc. for Neurosci. (com. on animals in rsch. 1993-98, com. on women in neurosci. 2005—), NSF Adv. Panel for Behavioral and Computational Neurosci., 1993-96. Office: U Ill at Urbana-Champaign Dept Psychology Champaign IL 61820 Business E-Mail: pgold@uiuc.edu.

GOLD, PETER FREDERICK, lawyer; b. NYC, Nov. 10, 1945; s. John and Dolores (Soyer) G.; m. Jill Finder; children: Joshua, Katharine. BA, Cornell U., 1967; MSc, London Sch. Econs., 1968; JD, NYU, 1971. Bar: D.C. 1988, N.Y. 1972, U.S. Dist. Ct. (so. dist.) N.Y. 1972, U.S. Dist. Ct. (ea. dist.) N.Y. 1972. Assoc. atty. Paul, Weiss, Rifkind, Wharton & Garrison, NYC, 1971-75; legis. dir. Senator Gary Hart, Washington, 1975-81; ptnr. Wellford, Wegman, Krulwich, Gold & Hoff, Washington, 1981-84, Winthrop, Stimson, Putnam & Roberts, Washington, 1984-94; pres. The Gold Group, Chartered, Washington, 1994—, C.G. Sloan & Co., Inc., 1995-97. Editor in chief Review of Law and Social Change, 1970. Nat. policy dir. Hart for Pres. Campaign, Washington, 1984; chmn., founder First Book, Washington, 1992—; dir. Share Our Strength, Washington, 1990—; mem. Clinton-Gore Transition Team, Washington, 1992. Recipient Disting. Visitor Program European Econ. Community, Brussels, Belgium, 1982. Mem. D.C. Bar Assn., Fed. Bar Assn., N.Y.C. Bar Assn., Kenwood Golf & Country Club, Four Streams Golf Club (dir.). Democrat. Jewish. Avocations: tennis, golf. Home: 13640 Glenhurst Rd North Potomac MD 20878-3921 Office: The Gold Group Chartered 1319 F St NW Ste 1000 Washington DC 20004-1106 Home Phone: 301-963-2239; Office Phone: 202-347-5542. Personal E-mail: pfg2000@aol.com.

GOLD, PHIL, immunologist, educator, researcher; b. Montreal, Sept. 17, 1936; m. Evelyn Katz; 3 children. BSc in Physiology with honors, McGill U., Montreal, 1957, MSc, MD, 1961, PhD in Physiology, 1965; DSc (hon.), McMaster U., 1986. Licentiate Med. Coun. Can. Jr. rotating intern Montreal Gen. Hosp., 1961—62, jr. asst. resident in medicine, 1962—63, sr. resident in medicine, 1965—66, jr. asst. physician, asst. and assoc. physician, 1967—73, sr. physician, 1973—2003, physician-in-chief, 1980-95, dir. divsn. clin. immunology and allergy, 1977—80, dir. McGill U. Med. Clinic, 1980—95, also sr. investigator Research Inst.; faculty dept. physiology McGill U., 1964—, mem. faculty of medicine, 1965—, prof. medicine and clin. medicine, 1973—, chmn. dept. medicine and clin. medicine, 1985—90, prof. physiology, 1974—, prof. oncology, 1989—, mem. faculty of medicine exec. com. representing clin. depts., 1985—, D. G. Cameron prof. medicine (inaugural), 1987—; exec. dir. Clin. Rsch. Ctr. Mont. Gen. Hosp. and McGill U. Hosp. Ctr., 1995—. Vis. scientist Pub. Health Research Inst. N.Y.C., 1967-68; Chester M. Jones Meml. lectr. Mass. Gen. Hosp., 1974; vis. prof. U. Caracas, Venezuela, 1974; Squires Club vis. prof. Wellesley Hosp., Toronto, 1983; Cecil H. and Ida Green vis. prof., 1984 autumn lectures U. Brit. Columbia; cons. in allergy and immunology Mt. Sinai Hosp., St. Agathe des Monts, Quebec, 1975—; hon. cons. dept. medicine Royal Victoria Hosp., Montreal; cons. dept. internal medicine Douglas Hosp. Ctr., Montreal; vice chmn. med. adv. com. Council of Physicians, Dentists and Pharmacists, 1985-90; mem. Conseil d'Adminstrn., Found. Quebecoise du Cancer, 1986-88, adv. com. Burroughs Wellcome fellowship fund, 1998—; health com. mem. Centre d'Entreprises et d'Innovation de Montreal, 1996—; Sir Arthur Sims travelling prof., 1998; inaugurator Phil Gold chair medicine cGill U. Health Ctr, 2006. Mem. editorial bd. Clin. Immunology and Immunopathology, 1977—, Immunopharmacology, 1978—, Diagnostic Gynecology and Obstetrics, 1978-83, Oncodevelopmental Biology and Medicine, 1979—, Modern Medicine of Can., 1984-90, Jour. Internal Medicine, 1988—, Canadians for Health Rsch., 1989—, Current Therapeutic Rsch., 1992—, Nutrition Quar., 1992—; editorial cons. Jour. Chronic Diseases, 1981-84; mem. editorial adv. bd. Cancer Research, 1971-73, assoc. editor 1973-80; contbg. editor Practical Allergy and Immunology, 1991—; editl. bd. Can. Jour. Allergy & Clin. Immunology, 1996—; contbr. over 140 articles to med. jours. External referee Can. Red Cross Soc. Decorated companion Order of Can., officer L'ordre nat. du Quebec, Great Montrealer, knight comdr. Sovereign Order St. John Jerusalem, Knights of Malta; named Most Outstanding Can. Med. Personality of the past 25 years, MacLean's Mag., 1986, establishment of Phil Gold Chair Medicine, McGill U., 2006; recipient Hiram Mills Gold medal, Mosby Scholarship Book award, Wood Gold medal, E.W.R. Steacie prize, Nat. Rsch. Coun. Can., 1973, Can. Silver Jubilee medal, 1977, Johann-Georg-Zemmerman prize for cancer rsch., Medizinische Hochschule, Hannover, Germany, 1978, Gold medal award of merit, Internat. award, Gardner Found., Ernest C. Manning prize, F.N.G. Starr award Izzak Walton Killam prize, Can. Coun., 1985, Tower of Hope award, Israel Cancer Rsch. Fund, 1985, Sci. Achievement medal, Govt. of Italy, 1990, Agora trophy, Ambassador's Club, 1991, Internat. Soc. Oncodevel. Biol. Medicine Internat. Abbott award, 1992, Commemorative medal 125th Anniversary of Can. Confedn., Govt. of Can., 1992, Carl Goresky Meml. award, 1999, Christie award, Can. Assn. of Profs. of Medicine, 1999, 20th Anniversary of L'Actualité Medicale award for outstanding contbns. to medicine, 2000, Queen Elizabeth II Golden Jubilee medal, 2002, Edwin F. Ullman award, Am. Assn. for Clin. Chemistry, 2004, Alpha Omega Achievement medal, 2005; MacDonald scholar, J. Francis Williams scholar, Univ. scholar. Fellow: AAAS; mem.: Internat. Assn. Health Profls. (chmn. 1998). Achievements include discovery of carcinoembryonic antigen. Office: Clin Rsch Ctr Montreal Gen Hosp 1650 Cedar Ave Montreal PQ Canada H3G 1A4 Office Phone: 514-934-1934 x430. E-mail: phil.gold@mcgill.ca.

GOLD, PHRADIE KLING See KLING, PHRADIE

GOLD, RICHARD L., lawyer; b. NYC, Feb. 23, 1950; s. Murray and Ruth Lillian (Nesselson) G.; m. Mary Laroe, Mar. 15, 1975; 1 child, Scott. BA, SUNY, Binghamton, 1972; student, Columbia U., 1972-73; JD, NYU, 1976. Bar: N.Y. 1976. From assoc. to ptnr. Bandler & Kass, NYC, 1976-85; ptnr. Sylvor, Schneer, Gold & Morelli, NYC, 1985—, Morelli & Gold, LLP, NYC, 1996—. Contbr: You and the Law, 1984. Coach baseball Stamford (Conn.) Am. Little League, 1994-97, Stamford Babe Ruth, 1998. Mem. ABA, N.Y. State Bar Assn., Bar Assn. City of N.Y., Phi Beta Kappa. Avocation: sports. Office: 605 Third Ave New York NY 10158 Office Phone: 212-972-1100 237. E-mail: rlgold1977@aol.com.

GOLD, RICHARD N., management consultant; b. Chgo., May 27, 1945; s. Irving Louis and Victoria (Saltzman) G.; m. Renee Bonnie Rein, Nov. 3, 1968; children: Jedd Steven, Amanda Caryn. BSI, U. Wis., Madison, 1967; MBA with honors, Columbia U., NYC, 1971; MA with honors, NYU, 1971. Tchr., supr. Ocean-Hill Brownsville, NYC Pub. Schs., 1968—71; brand mgr. packaged soap and detergent divsn. Procter & Gamble Co., Cin., 1971—76; exec. v.p. Glendinning Assocs., Westport, Conn., 1976—81; pres. R.N. Gold & Co., 1981—; prodr., ptnr. Enterplan, NYC, 1983—85; dir. mktg. Downtown Coun., Cin., 1975—77. Bd. dirs. Hampton Products Internat. Corp., SoftLock.com Inc., Luminary Graphics Inc., Rally Ptnrs. Inc., Autolink.com Data Nat. Corp.; bd. advs. LA Brewing Co., Designer Fragrances Internat., Seattle Med., Evolve Products Inc., Cursor-Mate.com. Mem.: Am. Mgmt. Assn., Pres. Assn. Avocations: sports, theater, collecting antique electronic musical devices. Office: RN Gold & Co 19 Rowayton Ave Norwalk CT 06853-1627 Office Phone: 203-831-0001. Business E-Mail: rngoldco@aol.com.

GOLD, SHARON CECILE, artist, educator; b. NYC, Feb. 28, 1949; d. Henry Joseph and Betty (Kopan) G.; m. William McKay Watson III, July 12, 1992; 1 child, Miranda Cecile. Student, CUNY, 1967-68, Columbia U., 1968-70; BFA, Pratt Inst., 1976. Adj. prof. Art NYU, 1983; vis. artist SUNY, Purchase, 1985; assoc. prof. painting and critical theory Syracuse (N.Y.) U., 1986—; vis. artist The Art Inst. Chgo., Chgo., 1990. Lectr. in field; guest critic Sch. Visual Arts, N.Y.C., 1987, N.Y. Studio Sch., 1988. Solo exhibits include Stephen Rosenberg Gallery, N.Y.C., 1987, 89, 91, 55 Mercer St., N.Y.C., 1986, John Davis Gallery, Akron, Ohio, 1986, Pam Adler Gallery, N.Y.C., 1986; group exhibits include IRIS House, N.Y.C., 1992, Everson Mus. of Art, Syracuse, 1991, ARTSTAR, L.A., 1991, Stephen Rosenberg Gallery, N.Y., 1991, Rose Art Mus. Brandeis U., 1990, Robert Pardo Gallery, N.Y.C., 2001; performance/video works include A Video Tape 1990-1991 Stephen Rosenberg Gallery, 1991, North South Consonance St. Stephen's Ch., N.Y.C., 1984. Pratt Inst. Acad. fellow, 1974-76, NEA grantee, 1981, Penny McCall Found. grantee, 1988. Home: 10 Leonard St New York NY 10013-2929 Office Phone: 212-925-6885. Business E-Mail: sharon@watsongold.com.

GOLD, SIMEON, lawyer; b. Hartford, Conn., Jan. 3, 1949; s. Charles and Claire (Goldschein) G.; m. Heide Aline Turkel, Aug. 30, 1970; children: Jana, Craig. BS, Cornell U., 1970; JD, Harvard U., 1973. Bar: N.Y., U.S. Dist. Ct. (so. dist.) N.Y., U.S. Ct. Appeals (2d cir.). Assoc. Weil, Gotshal & Manges LLP, NYC, 1973-81, ptnr., 1981—. Bd. dirs. Lawyers Alliance for N.Y. Contbr. articles to profl. jours. Mem. Coun. of Bus. Exec. Assn. for Help of Retarded Children, N.Y.C., Legal Aid Soc., N.Y.C.; bd. trustees Dalton Sch., 1997-2000. Mem. ABA, N.Y. State Bar Assn. (chair bus. law sect. 2000-01, chair corp. law com. 1993-97), Assn. of Bar of City of N.Y., N.Y. County Lawyers Assn., Harmonie Club, Old Oaks Country Club. Avocations: skiing, tennis, golf, travel. Office: Weil Gotshal & Manges LLP 767 5th Ave Fl Concl New York NY 10153-0119 Office Phone: 212-310-8226. Business E-Mail: simeon.gold@weil.com.

GOLD, STEVEN MICHAEL, lawyer; b. Bklyn., Sept. 19, 1953; s. Joseph and Gladys (Guss) G.; m. Susan Schwartz, Jan. 9, 1977; children: Rachel, David, Hannah. BA, Hobart Coll., 1975; JD, Cornell U., 1978. Bar: Conn. 1979, N.Y. 1979, U.S. Dist. Ct. Conn. 1979, U.S. Dist. Ct. (no. dist.) N.Y. 1979. Confidential law asst. 3d dept. appellate div. N.Y. Supreme Ct., Albany, 1978-79; assoc. Schatz & Schatz, Ribicoff & Kotkin, Hartford & Stamford, Conn., 1979-86, ptnr. Stamford, 1987-96, Shipman & Goodwin, LLP, Stamford, 1996—. Treas. Cmty. Coun. Westport/Weston, Conn., 1985, 1st v.p., 1987, bd. dirs., 1985-87; bd. dirs., counsel Urban League Greater Bridgeport, 1987-92; bd. dirs., v.p. Stamford Symphony Soc., 1990-95, counsel, 1994-95; bd. dirs. Nursing and Home Care, 1996-97, Women's Bus. Devel. Ctr., 2001-, Housatonic Cmty. Coll. Found., 2005-. Mem. ABA, N.Y. State Bar Assn., Conn. Bar Assn., Fairfield County Bar Assn. (dir. 2002-06), Assn. Comml. Fin. Attys., Assn. Corporate Growth, Nat. Assn. Transp. Practitioners (treas. Conn. chpt. 1983-85), Entrepreneurship Inst. (adv. bd. 1989-91), Phi Delta Phi, Pi Gamma Mu. Democrat. Jewish. Office: Shipman & Goodwin LLP 300 Atlantic St Stamford CT 06902-3522 Office Phone: 203-324-8102. Business E-Mail: sgold@goodwin.com.

GOLD, STUART WALTER, lawyer; b. NYC, Mar. 3, 1949; s. Morris I. and Barbara (Walters) G.; m. Michele M. Cardella, June 26, 1983. BA in Polit. Sci., Bklyn. Coll., 1969; JD, NYU, 1972. Bar: N.Y. 1973, U.S. Supreme Ct. 1983, U.S. Ct. Appeals (2d, 3d, 7th, 8th, 9th and D.C. cirs.). Law clk. to judge U.S. Dist. Ct. (so. dist.) N.Y., 1972-73; assoc. Cravath, Swaine & Moore LLP, NYC, 1973-80, ptnr., 1980—. Mem. ABA, N.Y. State Bar Assn., Assn. of Bar City of N.Y. Democrat. Avocations: scuba diving, travel. Office: Cravath Swaine & Moore LLP 825 8th Ave Fl 40 New York NY 10019-7475 Office Phone: 212-474-1394. Office Fax: 212-474-3700. E-mail: sgold@cravath.com.

GOLD, WILLIAM ELLIOTT, health care management consultant, educator; b. Bklyn., Oct. 21, 1948; s. Theodore David and Debra (Fridovich) Gold; m. Nili Rachel Scharf, June 1, 1972; children: Avitai, Doria, Michelle. BA, SUNY, Stony Brook, 1970; MSS, Hebrew U. Jerusalem, Israel, 1972; PhD, U. Minn., 1982. Rsch. asst. Hebrew U. Jerusalem, 1971—72; rschr. Mt. Sinai Hosp., Mpls., 1973—74; instr. hosp. adminstrn. U. Minn., Mpls., 1974—75; coord., dir. Blue Cross/Blue Shield Greater N.Y. HMO, NYC, 1975—85; v.p. Rush-Presbyn. St. Luke's Med. Ctr., Chgo., 1985—88; pres. Gold Health Strategies Inc., NYC, 1988—. Cons. Dept. Health, Mpls., 1973—74; pres. ANCHOR, Chgo.; bd. dirs. NY Bus. Group Health, chmn. managed care task force, 1989—; vice chmn. The HMO Group, 1987—88; mem. steering com. U. Mo-Kansas City Nat. Ctr. Managed Care Adminstrn., 1986—98; asst. adj. prof. Columbia U., NYC, 1989—99, clin. prof., 1999—. Founding editor: Managing Employee Health Benefits. Mem. task force pub. health and managed care PEW Charitable Trust, 1995—96; mem. task force improving cardiovasc. health Am. Heart Assn., NYC, 1995—96. Fellow, Caldwell B. Esselstyn Found., 1991—92. Avocations: clarinet, music, sports, photography. Home: 322 W 72nd St # 14B New York NY 10023-2676 Office: Gold Health Strategies Inc 250 Park Ave Ste 2020 New York NY 10177-0001 Home Phone: 212-724-1148; Office Phone: 212-953-1504. Business E-Mail: bgold@goldhealthstrategies.com.

GOLDBARD, LAURA E., lawyer; b. NYC, June 14, 1956; BA, Emory Univ., Atlanta, 1978; JD, Univ. Miami, 1981. Bar: NY 1983. Adminstrv. ptnr., intellectual property practice area Stroock & Stroock & Lavan LLP, NYC. Contbr. articles to profl. journals. Mem.: ABA, Copyright Soc. USA, Internat. Trademark Assn. Office: Stroock & Stroock & Lavan LLP 180 Maiden Ln New York NY 10038-4982 Office Phone: 212-806-6675. Office Fax: 212-806-6006. Business E-Mail: lgoldbard@stroock.com.

GOLDBERG, ADELE J., computer scientist; b. July 1945; BS in Math., U. Mich.; MS in Info. Sci., U. Chgo., PhD in Info. Sci., 1973; PhD (hon.), Open U., 1998. Researcher, lab. mgr. Xerox Palo Alto Rsch. Ctr.; founder, chmn., CEO ParcPlace-Digitalk, Inc.; founder Neometron, Inc., Redwood City, Calif., 1996—; chief tech. officer AgileMind, Inc., San Francisco. Lectr. in field; cons. in field. Co-author, co-developer (books) Smalltalk-80 programming system; author: numerous papers on project mgmt., programming and analysis methodology using object-oriented tech., & on-line project communities; edited The History of Personal Workstations, 1988, co-editor Visual Object-Oriented Programming. Bd. dir. The San Francisco Exploratorium, chair, adv. coun.; bd. dir., trustee Internat. Computer Sci. Inst., Berkeley, Calif.; mem. vis. com., divsn. physical sciences U. Chgo. Recipient Lifetime Achievement award, PC Mag., 1990, Howard Vollum award, Reed Coll., 1995, Dr. Dobbs Mag. Excellence in Programming award, 2000. Fellow: Assn. Computing Machinery (pres. 1984—86, former nat. sect. and editor-in-chief, Computing Surveys, Software Systems award 1987). Office: AgileMind Inc 582 Market St Ste 1215 San Francisco CA 94104 E-mail: adele@neometron.com.

GOLDBERG, ALAN JOEL, lawyer; b. Bklyn., Jan. 22, 1943; s. Ralph and Dorothy (Rolnick) G.; 1 child, Cary Adam. BA, U. Miami, 1965, JD, 1968. Bar: Fla. 1968, U.S. Supreme Ct., U.S. Ct. Appeals (4th cir.). Ptnr. Goldberg, Young, Goldberg & Borkson, P.A., Ft. Lauderdale, Fla., 1968-82; atty. City of Margate, Fla., 1969-70, City of Tamarac, Fla., 1970-71; pvt. practice Ft. Lauderdale, 1982—. Pres. Diversified Realty Devel., Co., 1996—. Mem. Citizen's Task Force on Transp., State of Fla.; mem. Broward County Planning Coun., 1984-92, chmn., 1988, 91; bd. dirs. Boys and Girls Clubs of Broward County, Inc., 1995—, pres., 1999-2000, chmn. bd. dirs., 2000-01 Mem. ABA, Fla. Bar Assn. Republican. Office: 2700 West Cypress Creek Rd Ste C105 Fort Lauderdale FL 33309 Office Phone: 954-935-0820.

GOLDBERG, ALAN MARVIN, toxicologist, educator; b. Bklyn., Nov. 20, 1939; s. William and Celia Ida (Rudman) G.; m. Helene Schoenbach, Aug. 14, 1960; children: Michael David, Naomi Jill BS, Bklyn. Coll. Pharmacy, 1961; PhD in Pharmacology, U. Minn., 1966; DSc (hon.), L.I. U, 1995. Rsch. asst. U. Wis., 1961-62, U. Minn., 1962-66; rsch. assoc. Inst. Psychiat. Rsch. Ind. U., 1966-67, asst. prof. dept. pharmacology, 1967-69; asst. prof. environ. medicine Johns Hopkins U., Balt., 1969-71, assoc. prof., 1971-78, prof. dept. environ. health scis., 1978—, assoc. chmn. dept., 1978-80, acting dir. div. toxicology, 1979-80, dir. div. toxicology, 1980-82, dir., chmn. bd. Ctr. Alternatives to Animal Testing, 1981—, assoc. dean rsch., 1984-94; assoc. dean corp. affairs Sch. Pub. Health, Balt., 1994-99; adminstrv. head health edn. program Johns Hopkins U./Nat. Basketball Player Assn., 1990-95; cons. OECD, Paris, 1998—; commr. Pew Trust Nat. Comm. on Indsl. Animal Production, 2006—; participant Woodrow Wilson Program Nanotechnology, 2006—. Prin. rsch. scientist Chesapeake Bay Inst., 1979-84; mem. health hazard evaluation team of chem. waste dumps State of Tenn., 1980; mem. rev. panel EPA, 1980-82; mem. working group on harmonization of in vitro methods Orgn. Econ. and Cmty. Devel., 1995—; organizer 1st World Congress on Alternative and Animal Use in Life Scis., 1993; sci. adv. bd. subcom. on toxicology U.S. FDA, 1996-2001; mem. interagy. coord. com. for validation of alternative method HHS, 1998-2002; bd. sci. advisors Xenogen, Inc.; mem. sci. adv. com. Alternative Tchg. Methods, NIEHS, 2002— vis. prof. U. Utrecht Ctr. Animals and Society, 2002, chmn. bd. Ctr. Alternatives to Animal Testing, John Hopkins U., 2005-. Mem. editorial bd. Jour. Am. Coll. Toxicology, assoc. editor In Vitro Toxicology; contbr. articles to profl. jours. Trustee Hildergard Doerenkamp-Gerhard Zbinden Found., 1985-2001, hon. mem., 2002—; mem. Pew Trust Commn. on Farm Animal Welfare and Indsl. Animal Prodn., 2006—; mem. Woodrow Wilson Panel on Nanotechs., 2006—; chmn. external adv. bd. dept. cell biology and anatomy Med. U. SC., 2006—; mem. chem. prioritization com. FDA, 2006—. Recipient award Ind. Neurol. Soc., 1967, Russell and Burch award Human Soc. of U.S., 1991; named Disting. Alumnus, L.I. U., 1992. Mem. AAAS, Am. Soc. Pharmacology and Exptl. Therapeutics, Soc. Neurosci. (pres. Balt. chpt. 1971-73), Am. Soc. Neurochemistry, Am. Epilepsy Soc., Assn. Univ. Tech. Mgrs., Internat. Soc. Neurochemistry, Soc. Toxicology (Ambassador Mid-Atlantic sect. 1998), Soc. Toxicology (Enhancement of Animal Welfare award 2001, Hildergard Doerenkamp-Gerhard Zbinden award 2001), Internat. Study Group on Memory Disorders, Internat. Union Pharmacology, Office of Tech. Assessment Panel on Alternatives to Animal Use in Rsch. Testing and Edn. and Frontiers in Neuroscience, Nat. Acad. Sci., Inst. for Lab. Animal Resources. Office: 111 Market Pl Ste 840 Baltimore MD 21202-7113 Office Phone: 410-223-1692. Business E-Mail: goldberg@jhsph.edu.

GOLDBERG, ANNE CAROL, physician, educator; b. Balt., June 12, 1951; d. Stanley Barry and Selma Ray G.; m. Ronald M. Levin, July 29, 1989. AB, Harvard U., 1973; MD, U. Md., 1977. Diplomate Am. Bd. Internal Medicine, Am. Bd. Endocrinolgy and Metabolism. Intern in medicine Michael Reese Hosp., Chgo., 1977-78, resident in medicine, 1978-80; fellow in endocrinology Washington U., St. Louis, 1980-83, instr. medicine, 1983-85, asst. prof. medicine, 1985-94, assoc. prof. medicine, 1994—. Fellow ACP, Am. Heart Assn.; mem. AMA, Am. Diabetes Assn., Am. Med. Women's Assn., Endocrine Soc., Nat. Lipid Assn., Alpha Omega Alpha. Democrat. Jewish. Office: Washington U Med Sch Box 8127 660 S Euclid Ave Saint Louis MO 63110-1010

GOLDBERG, ARNOLD IRVING, psychoanalyst, educator; b. Chgo., May 21, 1929; s. Morris Henry and Rose (Auerbach) Goldberg; m. Constance Obenhaus; children: Andrew, Sarah. BS, U. Ill., Chgo., 1949, MD, 1953. Diplomate Am. Bd. Psychiatry and Neurology, cert. psychoanalyst. Intern Cin. Gen. Hosp., 1954-55; psychiat. resident Michael Reese Hosp., Chgo., 1957-59; tng. and supervising analyst Chgo. Inst. for Psychoanalysis, 1970—, dir., 1990-92; assoc. psychiatrist Rush Presbyn. St. Luke's Hosp., Chgo., 1982—; prof. psychiatry Rush Med. Coll., Chgo., 1982-97, Cynthia Oudejans Harris MD prof. psychiatry, 1997—. Author: (book) Models of the Mind, 1973, A Fresh Look at Psychoanalysis, 1988, The Prisonhouse of Psychoanalysis, 1990, The Problem of Perversion, 1995, Being of Two Minds, 1999, Misunderstanding Freud, 2004, Moral Stealth, 2006; editor: Future of Psychoanalysis: Progress in Self Psychology, Vols. 1-16, 1976—99, Errant Selves, 2000; contbr. articles to profl. jours. Capt. US Army, 1955—57. Fellow: Am. Psychiat. Assn. (life); mem.: Am. Psychoanalytic Assn. Home: 844 W Chalmers Pl Chicago IL 60614-3223 Office: Inst for Psychoanalysis Chgo 122 S Michigan Ave Ste 1305 Chicago IL 60603-6107 Home Phone: 773-348-0771; Office Phone: 312-922-6797. Personal E-mail: docaig@aol.com.

GOLDBERG, ARTHUR, merchant banker, financial consultant, educator; b. Jersey City, Nov. 25, 1940; s. Jack Geddy and Ida (Steinberg) G.; m. Jane Elizabeth Gottlieb, Aug. 10, 1968; children: Ari Matthew, Shoshana Eve, Benjamin Saul, Talia Akiva. AB with honors, Am. U., 1962; JD, Cornell U., 1965; PhD (hon.), HHD (hon.), Natchez Coll., 1992. Intern, staff mem. to senator, 1962; law clk. DeSevo & Cerutti, Jersey City, 1964; pvt. practice Jersey City, 1965-89; asst. prof. law U. Conn. Sch. Law., 1965-67; cooperating atty. NAACP Legal Def. Fund, 1965-72; adminstrv. asst. to congressman Ohio, 1966-67; dep. atty. gen. N.J., counsel Dept. Community Affairs and Housing Finance Agy., 1967-70; exec. v.p., dir., mgr. mcpl. fin. dept. Matthews & Wright, Inc., NYC, 1970-88; exec. v.p., dir. Landamatic Systems Corp., NYC, 1982-85; vice chmn. Matthews & Wright Realty, NYC, 1986-88, Matthews & Wright Pacific, NYC, 1986-88; pres. New Am. Fed. Credit Union, 1981-87; dir., treas. Fedn. Community Devel. Credit Unions, 1985-88; v.p. Alfus Corp., 1958-85, Basow Corp., 1965-86; ptnr. Shayna Enterprises, York Builders, Hudson Mgmt. Svcs., 1978-87; dir. investment strategies FAB Capital Corp., 1998-99; spl. asst. to pres. TCI Coll., 2005—. Mng. ptnr. Bank Bldg. Assocs., 1974—86, Inst. Profl. and Exec. Devel.; vis. lectr. Rutgers U., 1971—80, Practising Law Inst., 1969—76; mem. exec. com. NJ Commn. Discrimination in Housing, 1975—80; mem. urban adv. coun. Anti-Defamation League, 1965—72; spl. cons. Exclusionary Zoning Nat. Com. Discrimination in Housing, 1965—70; cons. scholarship edn. Def. Fund for Racial Equality, 1965—72; gen. counsel NJ chpt. Mcpl. Fin. Officers Assn., NJ chpt. Nat. Assn. Housing and Redevel. Ofcls., 1966—74; chmn. Com. for Absorption of Soviet Emigrees (CASE), 1973—; pres. CASE-UNA Cmty. Devel. Corp., 1976; co-dir. Jews Offering New Alternatives to Homosexuality (JONAH), 1999—; bd. mem. Ophthalmic Mission Trust, India, 1988—91, 2003—; fin. advisor Nat. Found. Manufactured Home Owners, 1994—, EVCI Career Colls., 1997—; adv. bd. Parents and Friends of Ex-gays and Gays, 2001—, Internat. Healing Found., 2000—; mem. adv. bd. Inst. for Youth and Soc., Germany, 2005—; chmn. monitoring of rsch. com. Nat. Assn. Rsch. Therapy Homosexuality, 2001—02, exec. sec., 2003—; pres. Positive Alternative to Homosexuality, 2003; facilitator People Can Change and Internat. Healing Found., 2003—; v.p. Cong. Mt. Sinai, Jersey City, 2004—05, pres., 2005—06. Author: Financing Housing and Urban Development, 1975, Zoning and Land Use, 1972; adv. bd. Housing and Devel. Reporter, 1975-89; contbr. articles to law revs. Co-pres. New Synagogue, Jersey City, 1974-80; bd. dirs. Jersey City Hebrew Free Loan Assn., 1976-77; pres. Met. N.Y. Coord. Com. for Resettlement of Soviet Jewry, 1978-80; treas. Hebrew Free Loan N.J., 1977-90, pres., 1995—; bd. dirs. Hillel Acad., 1985-87; dir. Bayonne Jewish Cmty. Ctr., 1987-88, Jersey City United Jewish Appeal, 1984—, chmn. allocation com., 1994, chmn. nominating com., 1996; bd. dirs. South Bronx Cmty. Housing, Inc., 1977-81; chmn. Novy Americanitz, 1980-84; bd. dirs. Citizens Housing and Planning Coun., 1980-84, Boys Club of Jersey City, 1975-92; pres. CASE Mus. Contemporary Russian Art, 1980—; pres. Freedom Synagogue, 1982—85; v.p. Congregation Mt. Sinai, 2004-05, pres., 2005—; mem. Settlement House Fund; treas. Coun. Jewish Orgns., Jersey City, 1977; mem. bd. edn. Yeshiva of Hudson County, 1977-85; pres. Hudson Yeshiva Parents Orgn., 1980-88. Mem. Conn. Assn. Mcpl. Attys. (exec. com., editor newsletter 1965-68), Nat. Housing Conf., Am. Polit. Sci. Assn., Nat. Acad. Polit. and Social Sci., Nat. Leased Housing Assn. (nat. pres. 1972-74, chmn. emeritus 1975—), Public Securities Assn. (legis. com. 1978), Nat. Housing Rehab. Assn. (dir. 1982-89, v.p. 1985), Omicron Delta Kappa, Pi Gamma Mu, Pi Sigma Alpha, Pi Delta Epsilon, Phi Alpha Delta. Home: 83 Montgomery St Jersey City NJ 07302-3723 Office: 80 Grand St Jersey City NJ 07302-4522 Office Phone: 917-929-0087. Personal E-mail: jonahhelp@aol.com. Business E-Mail: agoldberg@tcicollege.edu.

GOLDBERG, CATHERINE T., lawyer; b. Devils Lake, ND, June 28, 1950; AB summa cum laude, U. ND, 1971; JD magna cum laude, U. N. Mex., 1975. Bar: N. Mex. 1975. Law clk. to Hon. Howard C. Bratton U.S. Dist. Ct., Dist. N. Mex., 1975—76; dir. Rodey, Dickason, Sloan, Akin & Robb PA, Albuquerque. Named to Best Lawyers in Am. in real estate and banking, 1995—, Chamber's America's Leading Lawyers for Bus., 2004, 2005. Mem.: Albuquerque Mus. Art, History & Sci. (found. bd. 1987—93, 1994—2000, art adv. com. 1996—, bd. trustees 2000—), Albuquerque Econ. Devel. Forum, Albuquerque Bar Assn. (former pres.), ABA (real property probate & trust law sect., bus. law sect.), Am. Coll. Mortgage Attys. (trustee, opinions com.), Am. Coll. Real Estate Lawyers (new mem.'s com.), Phi Beta Kappa, Order Coif. Office: Rodey Dickason Sloan Akin & Robb PA 201 Third St NW Ste 2200 PO Box 1888 Albuquerque NM 87103 Office Phone: 505-768-7318. Business E-Mail: ctgoldberg@rodey.com.

GOLDBERG, DANNY, recording industry executive; b. NYC, July 4, 1950; s. Victor and Mimi (Paul) G.; m. Rosemary Carroll, Feb. 25, 1988; children: Kathryn G., Max. Diploma, Fieldston Sch., 1967. Freelance journalist, reviewed Woodstock Billboard Mag., 1969; freelance journalist, editor NYC, 1969-72; dir. pub. rels. rock music div. Solters & Roskin, NYC, 1973-74; v.p. Swan Song Records, U.S.A., LA, 1974-76; pres. Danny Goldberg, Inc., NYC, 1978-79; co-founder Modern Records, LA, 1979-83; music cons. 20th Century Fox, LA, 1983-84; pres. Gold Mountain Entertainment, LA, 1984-92; sr. v.p. Atlantic Records, LA, 1992-94, pres., 1994; chmn., CEO Warner Bros. Records, Inc., Burbank, Calif., 1995; co-publisher (with father Victor Goldberg) Tikkun mag., 1997—2001; founder, CEO Artemis Records, 1999—2005; CEO Air America Radio Network, 2005—06, vice chmn., 2006; founder, pres. Gold Village Entertainment, 2006—. Author: Dispatches From the Culture War - How the Left Lost Teen Spirit. Bd. dirs. Children Now, 1990, Show Coalition, 1990, New York Civil Liberties Union; pres. ACLU Found. Southern Calif. Recipient 1st Amendment award in Arts and Entertainment. Mem. ACLU (chair so. Calif. found. 1988-90). Democrat. Jewish. Office: Gold Village Entertainment 37 W 17th St Ste 7W New York NY 10011

GOLDBERG, DAVID, lawyer, retail executive; Chief legal counsel RadioShack Corp., Fort Worth, Tex., sr. v.p., gen. counsel, corp. sec., 2006—. Office: RadioShack Corp 300 RadioShack Cir Fort Worth TX 76102-1964 Office Phone: 817-415-3700, 817-415-3011.

GOLDBERG, DAVID ALAN, investment banker, lawyer; b. NYC, Oct. 31, 1933; s. Joseph R. and Rose (Trutt) G.; m. Victoria Liebson, July 7, 1957 (div. Mar. 1976); children: Eric S., Jeremy P. AB magna cum laude, Harvard U., 1954, JD, 1957, postgrad. in bus. adminstrn, 1956-57. Bar: N.Y. 1958. Counsel firm R.W. Pressprich & Co., Inc., NYC, 1958-64, gen. partner, 1965-68, exec. v.p., 1968-78, also chmn. exec. com. Bd. dirs. Gen. Atomics, Gen. Atomics Techs. Corp. Trustee Beth Israel Med. Center, N.Y.C., Continuum Health Ptnrs. Inc., St. Luke's and Roosevelt Hosp. Ctr.; trustee, bd. regents The L.I. Coll. Hosp. Served with AUS, 1957-58. Mem. Harvard Club (N.Y.C.), Phi Beta Kappa. Office Phone: 212-765-1164.

GOLDBERG, DAVID MEYER, retired biochemist; b. Glasgow, Scotland, Aug. 30, 1933; arrived in Can., 1975; s. Samuel Simon and Ethel (Elyan) G.; m. Pearl Gertrude Goldberg; children: Susan Simone, Tanya Marion. BSc with honors in Biochemistry, U. Glasgow, 1959, MB, ChB, 1959, PhD, 1966, MD, 1974. Intern Stobhill Hosp., Glasgow, 1960, So. Gen. Hosp., Glasgow, 1961; resident We. Infirmary, Glasgow, 1962—66; prof. dept. clin. biochemistry U. Toronto, Canada, 1975—2002, chmn., 1977—88, prof. emeritus, 2002—; biochemist-in-chief dept. biochemistry Hosp. for Sick Children, Toronto, 1975—88. Cons. chem. pathology and hon. lectr. United Sheffield Hosp., U. Sheffield, Eng., 1967-75 Joint editor-in-chief Clin. Biochemistry, 1982-94, Critical Revs. Clin. Lab. Scis., 1992—; mem. editl. bd. Enzyme, 1978-89, Clin. Chimica Acta, 1981-2004, Clin. Biochem. Physiology, 1982-96, Clin. Chemistry, 1986-88, Jour. Clin. Lab. Analysis, 1987—, European Jour. Lab. Medicine, 1993-2001, Am. Jour. Enology Viticulture, 1995-2001, Jour. Agrl. Food Chemistry, 1999-2004. Recipient Van Slyke award Am. Assn. Clin. Chemistry, 1982, Roman award Australian Assn. Clin. Chemists, 1983, Nova Idea prize Italian Soc. Clin. Pathologists, 1985, Norman Kubasick award Am. Assn. Clin. Chemistry, 1996. Mem. Can. Soc. Clin. Chemists (Ames award 1990, Beckman award 1999), Can. Assn. Med. Biochemists, Can. Soc. Clin. Investigation, Internat. Soc. Clin. Enzymology (pres. 1995-2000), Can. Atherosclerosis Soc. (chmn. edn. com. 1994-97). Jewish. Home: 9 Harrison Rd Willowdale ON Canada M2L 1V3 Personal E-mail: david.goldberg@utoronto.ca.

GOLDBERG, EDWIN, rehabilitation specialist, interfaith clergyman; b. Jan. 12, 1937; D in Chiropractic magna cum laude, Columbia Inst. Chiropractic, 1960; grad. in edn. of blind, Columbia U. Tchrs. Coll., NYC, 1967—68; postgrad., C.G. Jung Found., NYC, 1972—73; postgrad. in edn. of blind, NYU, NYC, 1973—74, postgrad. in tng. and devel., 1972; postgrad., Am. Inst. Psychoanalysis, Moreno Inst. Psychodrama, Karen Horney Clinic; postgrad. in spl. edn., Fordham U., NYC, 1971; cert. of study, Alfred Adler Inst., 1970; MA in Edn., Hebrew Union Coll., 1971; cert. rehab. mgmt., Cornell U., 1973; grad., All Faiths Sem., 1999—2000; student, Camden County Coll., 1994; studied under, Kurt Adler, MD and Helene Papanak, MD, Dr. Joseph Gelberman, Prof. Robert Bowers, Harold Richtirman. Cert. med. rehab. coord., rehab. therapist in mobility tng. of the blind Am. Assn. Med. Rehab. Therapists and Specialsts, rehab. counselor, master therapeutic recreation specialist, Nat. Bd. Cert. Counselor' registered recreation adminstr., NJ; cert. mobility instr., rehab. tchr., NY; nat. cert. profl. rehab. tchr. the blind AER.; cert. rehab. dir. OVR accredited facilities, lic. rehab. counselor State of NJ; profl. cert. in crisis mgmt. Cornell U., 1972, rehab. mgmt., 1973; cert. assessment in aging U. Pa., 1987; cert. in microcounseling U. Buffalo, 1999; cert. in cane mobility tng. blind Joseph Kohn Rehab. Ctr., 1992; cert. in low vision, 1995; cert. in drug and alcohol counseling, Mercer Coun. Coll., NJ, 1997; profl. disability examiner; ordained clergy All Faiths Sem., 2001; qualified mental retardation profl., NJ; lic. in human and group rels. workshop, NYC, 1973, health edn. tchr. NJ Dept. Edn. State Bd. Examiners, cert. group psychotherapist, Am. Assn. Group Psychotherapy, 2005, drug and alcoholism treatment Resource CASAC Group, 2005-07. Mem. Dr. Samuel Losner staff coagulation lab. Isaac Albert Rsch. Inst., Bklyn., 1957-60; tech. eye bank and clin. lab. Bklyn. Eye & Ear Hosp., 1958-59; exec. Greater NY couns. Boy Scouts Am., 1961—63; supr. blood products divsn. Knickerbocker Biologicals, Charles Pfizer & Co., NYC, 1963-64; assoc. dir. Western Mediterranean ops. St. Jean Cap Ferrat A.M. USO, Nice, France, Naples, Italy, 1964-65; coord. rehab. skills Jewish Guild Blind, NYC, 1965-68, asst. dir., 1968-77; grad. thesis adviser on edn. and creative arts with the blind Columbia U., NYC, 1975—76; sect. chief Trenton Psychiat. Hosp., 1977-78; mobility cons. Elm & Maple Halls, Ancora Hosp., 1977-82; dir. Work Adjustment Ctr. Jewish Employment and Vocat. Svc., Phila., 1979-80; dir. Mary Campbell Ellis Vocat. Rehab. Ctr. S.I. (N.Y.) Aid for Retarded Children, 1980-86; sr. rehab. counselor/acting dir. Vocat. Rehab. dept. Ancora Hosp., Hammonton, NJ, 1982-87; rehab. cons. Dominican Coll. of Blauvet; tchr. blind military personnel Ministry Health, State Israel, 1969—71; program chmn. NY Fed. of Workers for the Blind, 1972; rehab. cons. Shield Inst., Flushing and Manhattan, NY, 2003—04, FEGS, NYC, 2003—04; dir. Seamark Ctr. Goodwill Industries NY and No. NJ, Bklyn., 2003—04; rehab. counselor Inter-Care Substance Abuse Treatment Ctr., NYC, 2004—06; counselor for blind children early intervention and transition program NY State Commn. for Blind, Exchange Place, 2006. Habilitation plan coord. State of NJ Div. Devel. Disabilities, Hammonton, 1988-91, New Lisbon Devel. Ctr., 1991-93; sr. rehab. counselor NJ State Commn. for the Blind, 1992-2002; rehab. cons. Beth Israel Hosp., NYC, Goldwater Meml. Hosp., NYC, Montefirore Med. Ctr., Bronx, NY, Harlem Med. Ctr., Bklyn., Jewish Home and Hosp. for Aged, NYC, Inst. Rehab. Medicine, NYU, Hillside Med. Ctr., Bklyn. Devel. Ctr., Manhattan Psychiat. Hosp., Keener Unit of Gov. Hosp., Albert Einstein Coll. Medicine, Bronx, Downstate Med. Ctr., Bklyn., Manhattanville Coll., Westchester, NY, LI U., Bklyn., Yonkers Home for the Aged Blind, Trenton State Coll., Bank Street Coll. of Edn., Staten Island CC, Kingsbrook CC, Exxon Homes, Morris Hall Rehab. Ctr., Jewish Geriatric Ctr., Phila., Nat. Rehab. Assocs.; mobility specialist for severely disabled blind State of NY, 1968-2003; coord. corrective therapy, internship program rehab dept. Manhattan Vets. Hosp., 1970-77; rehab. tng. specialist multiple disabled blind in NY area, 1970-77; instr. group rels. ongoing workshops; sr. vocat. counselor, summer camp. coord. for blind adolescents program Joseph Kohn Rehab. Ctr., New Brunswick, NJ, 2000-04; vocat. sr. counselor Bus. Enterprise Program State of NJ, Trenton, 1998-2002, sr. counselor coll. edn. unit NJ Commn. for Blind and Visually Impaired, Newark, 2002—2003; cons. rehab. Shield Inst., NY, 2002-03; adj. asst. prof. health and phys. edn. and adapted phys. edn. Hunter Coll., NYC, 1971-76; adj. field supr. art psychotherapy Trenton State Coll.in conjuction with C.G. Jung Inst., NYC and Trenton Psychiat. Hosp., 1977-78; lectr. N.Am. Indian myth and medicine Found. Faith Sem., NYC, 1976-77; lectr. in field, 1970—, Zeman Ctr. Instrn., NYC, 1965-78; mobility cons. Yonkers Home for Aged Blind, 1968-71; contbr. to developing tchr. tng. on phys. edn. of physically disabled Chung Yuan U., Republic of China, 1973-77; cons. devel. disabled Keener Unit Goodwater Meml. Hosp. NYC, 1968-1970, Blind Vocational Rehab. Inst. Rehab. Medicine, 1966-1969; cons. on brain damage and visual loss JFK Rehab. Ctr., Edison, NJ, 1996-2000; presenter in field. Author: Mobilitiy Training Manual for Teachers of Visually Impaired Children, 1969, Isolation From the Human Scene: The Meaning and Direction of Loneness, 1972, Adapted and Corrective Physical Education Curriculum Handicapped, 1972, Rehabilitation Assessment in Psychiatric Facilities, 1984, Overcoming Feelings of Inferiority: The Role of Mobility Training for the Blind An Adlerian Viewpoint, 1986; TV appearances include Am. Speaks, 1960-62. Legis rep. NY State Fedn. Workers Blind, 1973-76, program chmn., 1974; cons. legis. US Senate and Congl. Subcoms., 1972-77; lectr. mobility tng. the blind, Rusk Inst., 1965—1969, rehab. skills tng. vision impaired Geriatrics Ctr. Instrn., 1968-77; mem. Nat. Eagle Scout Assn. Boy Scouts Am.; program chmn. NY Fedn. Blind, 1976; chaplain Warner Brothers TV, 2005-06. Recipient Silver award Nat. Coun. Boy Scouts Am., 1958, Recognition citation Rotary Club NYC, 1959, Dr. Frank E. Dean Meml. award for outstanding contbns. to sci. edn., 1976, Thomas E. Watson Silver citation Citizenship in Action medal SAR, Lydia Hayes Disting. Svc. award NJ Commn. for Blind and Visually Impaired, 2000. Fellow: NY Hist. Soc., World Med. Assn., Am. Inst. Sci., World Assn. Social Psychiatry, N.Y. Acad. Scis., Royal Soc. Promotion Health; mem.: APA, Am. Assn. Workers for the Blind, Am. Orthopsychia. Assn., Am. Social Hygiene Assn., Am. Public Health Assn., Royal Inst. Pub. Health and Hygiene London, Assn. Med. Rehab. Dirs. Coords., Am. Assn. Rehab. Therapy, Royal Inst. Pub. Health and Hygiene, Royal Soc. Health, Am. Congress Rehab. Medicine, Assn. Edn. and Visually Handicapped and Blind, Royal Soc. Medicine (London), Am. Assn. Med. Rehab. Specialists and Therapists, Nat. Therapeutic Recreation Assn., Am. Orthopsychiat. Assn. for Applied Psychoanalysis, N.Y. Counseling Assn., N.Am. Soc. Adlerian Psychology, Am. Rehab. Counseling Assn., John Burroughs Meml. Assn. (life). Personal E-mail: dredgoldberg@yahoo.com.

GOLDBERG, EVGUENI, computer scientist; b. Minsk, Russia, July 8, 1960; s. Isaac Lvovich and Klara Khaimovna Goldberg. MS, Belorussian State U., Minsk, Russia, 1982; PhD, Belorussian Acad. Scis., Minsk, Russia. Rschr. Inst. of Engring. Cybernetics, Belorussian Acad. of Scis., Minsk, Belarus, 1983—96; vis. rschr. U. Calif., Berkeley, 1996—97; rsch. scientist Cadence Design Systems, Berkeley Labs., Calif., 1997—. Recipient Best paper award, DATE conf., 2002. Mem.: IEEE. Achievements include development of theory of testing satisfiability by building a stable set of points; a method of logic synthesis and equivalence checking of circuits with a common specification; a method of extracting tests from proofs; co-authored development of the SAT-solver , BerkMin that was a winner of SAT-2002 and SAT-2003 international competitions; patents pending for on checking satisfiability, equivalence checking and logic synthesis, test generation. Office: Cadence Design Systems 1995 University Ave Ste 460 Berkeley CA 94704 Home Phone: 510-528-3577; Office Phone: 510-647-2825. Business E-Mail: egold@cadence.com.

GOLDBERG, FRED T., JR., lawyer; b. St. Louis, Oct. 15, 1947; m. Wendy Meyer; 5 children. BA in Econs., Yale U., 1969, JD, 1973. Instr. polit. sci. and econs., Yale Coll., asst. dean Calhoun Coll. Yale U., New Haven, 1971-73; assoc. then ptnr. Latham, Watkins & Hills, Washington, 1973-81; asst. to commr. IRS, Washington, 1981-82, chief counsel, prin. legal advisor to commr., 1984-86, commr., 1989-92; asst. sec. for tax policy US Dept. of Treas., Washington, 1992; ptnr. Skadden, Arps, Slate, Meagher & Flom, LLP, Washington, 1986—89, ptnr., tax, 1993—. Mem. Nat. Commn. on Restructuring the IRS, Ctr. for Strategic and Internat. Studies Nat. Commn. on Retirement Policy; exec. dir. Bi-Partisan Congressional Commn. on Entitlement and Tax Reform. Editorial bd. Yale Law Jour.; Author, "Filling the Void: Can the IRS Restructuring Bring Purpose and Meaning to the Random World of Tax Litigation?," TAXES Mag. 1999; Co-Author (with Michael Graetz) "Reforming Social Security: A Practical and Workable System of Personal Retirement Accounts," Administrative Aspects of Investment-Based Social Security Reform, 2000. Office: Skadden Arps Slate Meagher & Flom LLP 1440 New York Ave NW Ste 600 Washington DC 20005 Office Phone: 202-371-7110. Office Fax: 202-661-8216. Business E-Mail: fgolder@skadden.com.

GOLDBERG, HARRY FINCK, lawyer, business consultant; b. Boston, May 5, 1936; s. Benjamin and Helen Sonia (Finck) G.; m. Vicki Lou Katz, Oct. 9, 1971 (div. Aprl. 1985); children: Andrew Seth, Ross Charles. BA magna cum laude, Yale U., 1958; JD cum laude, Harvard U., 1961. Bar: Mass. 1961, N.Y. 1966, Pa. 1973. Assoc. Cowan, Liebowitz & Latman, N.Y.C., 1965-68, Powers and McNiff, N.Y.C., 1969-70, Austrian, Lance & Stuart, N.Y.C., 1970-71; assoc. Blank, Rome, Comisky & McCauley, Phila., 1971-76, ptnr. 1976-84; ptnr. Wiener, Zuckerbrot & Weiss, N.Y.C., 1984-89; mem. firm Sills Cummis Zuckerman Radin Tischman Epstein & Gross, P.A., Newark, 1989-94; of counsel Law Office of Robert M. Becker, Newark, 1995-96; lectr. Pa. Bar Inst., 1981, 82, 83, N.Y. State Bar Assn., 1983, 84, 86. Bd. dirs. Soc. Hill Civic Assn., Phila., 1977-80, pres., 1978-79. Capt. U.S. Army, 1962-65. Mem. Fort Lee Hist. Soc. Co-author: Real Estate Limited Partnerships, 3d edit., 1991. Home and Office: 4 Horizon Rd Fort Lee NJ 07024-6743 E-mail: hfgoldberg@hotmail.com.

GOLDBERG, HARVEY, corporate financial executive; b. Bklyn., Jan. 30, 1940; s. Joseph and Regina (Goldkrantz) Goldberg; m. Joyce Baron, Nov. 22, 1962; children: Keith, Jodi. BS in Acctg., Bklyn. Coll., 1962; postgrad., CCNY, 1963. CPA NY. Sr. acct. Schwartz, Zelin & Weiss CPA's, NYC, 1962-66; mgr. fin. analysis Columbia Records div. CBS, Inc., NYC, 1966-70; asst. contr. Revlon, Inc., NYC, 1970-71; treas. Ctrl. Textile, Inc., Jersey City, 1971-74; contr. Marcade Group, Inc., Jersey City, 1974-81, v.p., contr., 1981-86; v.p., CFO Paul Marshall Products, Inc., subs. Marcade Group, Long Beach, Calif., 1982-86, Player's Internat., Inc., Calabasas, Calif., 1988-93, sr. v.p., CFO, 1988-93; exec. v.p., CFO Adesso, Inc., Culver City, Calif., 1994-98; CFO, dir. Hollywood Beauty Corp., Encino, Calif., 1997-99; CFO YellowOnline.Com, Inc., LA, 1999; fin. cons., 1999—. Bd. dirs. Tarzana Improvement Assn., Calif., 2000—; treas., bd. govs. Tarzana Neighborhood Coun., 2003, bd. govs., treas., 2003—; chmn. adv. bd. High Point Ctr., Marlboro, NJ, 1978—82; active Marlboro Twp. Bd. Edn., 1980—82, v.p., 1981—82; bd. dirs. Family Consultation Ctr., Freehold, NJ, 1982—83; county committeeman Monmouth County Dem. Com., NJ, 1979—80. Mem.: AICPA, NY State Soc. CPAs. Home and Office: 19798 Greenbriar Dr Tarzana CA 91356-5442 E-mail: harveygoldberg98@yahoo.com.

GOLDBERG, HERB, psychologist, educator; b. Berlin, July 14, 1937; arrived in US, 1941; s. Jacob and Ella (Nagler) Goldberg; 1 child, Amy Elisabeth. BA cum laude, CUNY, 1958; PhD, Adelphi U., Garden City, NY, 1963. Lic. psychologist Calif. Pvt. practice, LA, 1965—. Prof. psychology Calif. State U., LA. Author: Creative Aggression, 1972, The Hazards of Being Male, 1976, Money Madness, 1978, The New Male, 1979, The Inner Male, 1986, The New Male/Female Relationship, 1982, What Men Really Want, 1991, What Men Still Don't Know About Women, Relationships and Love, 2007. Mem.: APA, Phi Beta Kappa. Office: 3739 Mayfair Dr Los Angeles CA 90065-3208 Office Phone: 323-225-4649, 323-225-7770. Personal E-mail: drherbgoldberg@aol.com.

GOLDBERG, HOMER BERYL, language educator; b. Chgo., Feb. 4, 1924; married, 1956; 2 children. AB, U. Chgo., 1947, AM, 1948, PhD in English, 1961. Instr. English U. Chgo., 1950-54, asst. prof., 1954-60, Haverford (Pa.) Coll., 1960-61; assoc. prof. SUNY, Stony Brook, 1961-70, prof. English, 1970-88, Disting. teaching prof., 1988—, emeritus, 1991—. Fulbright lectr., Italy, 1956-57; dir. NDEA English Inst., 1965-66; editl. cons. L.I. Rsch. Inst., 1992-97. Author: The Art of Joseph Andrews, 1969; editor: Norton Critical Edition of Joseph Andrews and Shamela, 1987; contbr. articles to profl. jours. Mem. Suffolk County Campaign Fin. Bd., 1999—2005. Recipient Chancellor's award for Excellence in Teaching SUNY, 1973, Pres.'s award for Excellence in Teaching SUNY, 1987, others; faculty rsch. fellow SUNY, 1962, 67, 69. Mem. MLA. Office: SUNY Dept English Stony Brook NY 11794-5350

GOLDBERG, IRVING HYMAN, molecular pharmacology and biochemistry educator; b. Hartford, Conn., Sept. 2, 1926; s. Morris Wolfe and Rose (Krechevsky) Goldberg; m. Margaret Field Ziskin, Apr. 15, 1956; children: Daniel Eliot, Nancy Elizabeth. BS, Trinity Coll., 1949; MD, Yale U., 1953; PhD, Rockefeller U., 1960; AM (hon.), Harvard U., 1964. Intern Columbia-Presbyn. Med. Ctr., NYC, 1953—54; asst. resident, chief resident, instr. medicine Columbia-Presbyn. Med. Ctr. (Coll. Phys. and Surgs.), 1954—57; asst. prof. medicine, biochemistry U. Chgo., 1960—64, assoc. prof., 1964; assoc. prof. medicine Med. Sch. Harvard, 1964—68; prof. medicine Med. Sch. Harvard U., 1968—, chmn. divsn. med. scis. Faculty Arts and Scis., 1968—70, Gustavus Adolphus Pfeiffer prof. pharmacology, 1972—83, chmn. dept. pharm., 1972—86, Otto Krayer prof. pharmacology, 1983—86, Otto Krayer prof. biol. chemistry and molecular pharmacology, 1986—; chief endocrinology-metabolism unit Beth Israel Hosp., 1964—68, physician, 1964—72, mem. bd. consultation in medicine, 1972—; cons. in pharmacology Dana-Farber Cancer Inst., Boston, 1980—87. Mem. rev. panel internat. program Howard Hughes Med. Inst., 1994; cons. in clin. pharmacology Children's Hosp. Med. Ctr., Boston, 1972—91; mem. rsch. com. Med. Found., Boston, 1968—77; mem. exptl. therapeutics study sect. NIH, 1974—77; mem. com. proposed legis. to restructure FDA Assembly Life Scis. NAS-NRC, Inst. Medicine, 1976; mem. sci. adv. com. Rite Allen Found., 1976—2006, Damon Runyon-Walter Winchell Cancer Fund, 1982—86; mem. life scis. panel NRC, 1992—93. Mem. editl. bd. Endocrinology, 1964—68, Antimicrobial Agents and Chemotherapy, 1974—88, Jour. Biochem. Pharmacology, 1973—84, Biochemistry, 1986—97. Rev. panel Internat. Program Howard Hughes Med. Inst., 1994; sci. adv. com. Rita Allen Found., 1976—2006. With USNR, 1945—46. Recipient Faculty Rsch. award, Am. Cancer Soc., 1960—71; fellow Guggenheim, dept. genetics, Oxford (Eng.) U., 1970—71, sr., Trinity Coll., 1974—76. Mem.: Brit. Pharm. Soc., Am. Soc. Microbiology, Am. Soc. Pharmacology and Therapeutics (Otto Krayer award 1994), Am. Chem. Soc., Assn. Am. Physicians, Am. Acad. Arts and Scis., Am. Soc. Clin. Investigation, Am. Soc. Biochemistry and Molecular Biology, Inst. Medicine NAS, Alpha Omega Alpha, Sigma Xi, Phi Beta Kappa. Home: 987 Memorial Dr Apt 472 Cambridge MA 02138-5737 Office: Harvard U Med Sch 45 Shattuck St Boston MA 02115-6091 Home Phone: 617-864-3111; Office Phone: 617-432-1787. Business E-Mail: irving_goldberg@hms.harvard.edu.

GOLDBERG, JACK, hematologist; b. Ulm, Germany, Feb. 7, 1948; came to U.S., 1952; s. Isaac and Mary (Selitska) G.; m. Doreen, July 28, 1970; children: Joshua, Alexis. BA, Boston U., 1969; MD, SUNY, 1973. From asst. prof. medicine to assoc. prof. medicine SUNY Health Sci. Ctr., Syracuse, 1977-89; prof. medicine Robert Wood Johnson Med. Sch., Camden, NJ, 1989—2003, Am. Cancer Soc. prof. clin. oncology, 1992—2002; head divsn. hematology-oncology U. Pa. Presbyn. Med. Ctr., 2003—; vice chmn. Abramson Cancer Ctr. U. Pa. Network. Prof. medicine Coriell Inst. for Med. Rsch., Camden, 1990-2002; med. dir. blood bank Cooper Hosp., Camden, 1990-2002, head divsn. hematology/oncology, 1989-2002; med. dir. CorCell, 1996—; head Cooper Cancer Inst., 1998-2002. Bd. mem. N.J. divsn. Am. Cancer Soc., 1989-99; vol. Leukemia, Lymphoma Soc., Camden, 1990—. Fellow Am. Coll. Medicine. Jewish. Avocations: exercise, travel. Office: Penn Medicine at Cherry Hill 409 Rte 70 East Cherry Hill NJ 08034 Office Phone: 856-429-1519. Business E-Mail: jack.goldberg@uphs.upenn.edu.

GOLDBERG, JAY, lawyer; b. NYC, Jan. 2, 1933; s. Joseph and Lillian (Adler) G.; m. Rema, Dec. 27, 1959; children: Justin, Julie. BA, Bklyn. Coll., 1954; JD, Harvard U., 1957. Bar: N.Y. 1957, U.S. Ct. Appeals (2d, 4th and 9th cirs.) 1971, U.S. Supreme Ct. 1961. Asst. dist. atty. N.Y. County Dist. Atty. Office, NYC, 1957-61; spl. asst. to atty. gen. Washington, 1961-63; spl. asst. to U.S. Atty. NJ Hammond, Ind., 1961-67; lawyer, sole practice NYC, 1963—. Lectr. trial practice Harvard Law Sch., 1976-88; com. on grievances U.S. Dist. Ct. (so. dist.) N.Y., 1989—. Editorial mgr. White Collar Crime Law Reporter, 1989—; contbr. articles to profl. jours. Recipient Merit award for Advocacy of Individual Rights for Persons Advised, N.Y. Criminal Bar Assn., 1989. Mem. Friars Club (gov. 1988-92). Home: 200 E 65th St New York NY 10021-4451 Office: 250 Park Ave New York NY 10177-0001

GOLDBERG, JEROLD S., academic administrator; b. NJ, 1945; m. Michele Goldberg; children: Megan, Abby. BS, Case Western Res. U., 1968, DDS, 1970. Mem. faculty Sch. Dentistry, Case Western Res. U., 1974, chmn. oral and maxillofacial surgery dept., 1985—96, dean, 1997—; interim dean Sch. Medicine, Case Western Res. U., 2002—03; interim provost Case Western Reserve U., 2007—. Rschr. in field; co-founder Partnership in Hope Case Western Res. U. and City Hosp. of Klapeda, Lithuania, 1995—; Chair-elect of Coun. of Deans Am. Dental Edn. Assn., 2005—. Bd. mem. Ohio Dental Assn. Found. Recipient Cross of the Knight of the Order of the Lithuanian Grand Duke Gediminas, Govt. Lithuania, 2002. Mem.: Ohio Dental Assn. (mem. Ohio Dental Assn. Coun. on Dental Edn. and Licensure, del. and alt., House of Dels.). Office: Case Western Res U 10900 Euclid Ave Cleveland OH 44106-4920 Home Phone: 216-292-2744; Office Phone: 216-368-3266. Office Fax: 216-368-3204. Business E-Mail: jsg@case.edu.

GOLDBERG, JOLANDE ELISABETH, law librarian; b. Pforzheim, Germany, Aug. 11, 1931; came to U.S., 1967; d. Eugen and Luise Rosa (Thorwarth) Haas; m. Lawrence Spencer Goldberg, Sept. 7, 1969; children: Daniel Scott, Elisa Miriam, Clarissa Anna. Referendar, U. Heidelberg, 1957, PhD, 1963; postdoctoral, U. London, 1976-77. Bar: Germany 1961. Mem. rsch. staff Acad. Scis. and Humanities, Heidelberg, 1961-67; rsch. assoc. U. Heidelberg, 1964-67; cataloger, law specialist Libr. of Congress, Washington, 1967-72, asst. law classification specialist, 1972-80, law classification specialist, 1980—97, sr. cataloging policy specialist, 1997—. Sculptor, potter Torpedo Factory Art Ctr., Alexandria, Va., 1974—; lectr. Smithsonian Inst., Washington, 1988-90. Author: Probschlag & Meistersignatur, 1963, Library of Congress Law Library: An Illustrated Guide, 2005; contbr. articles to profl. jours. Exec. bd. dirs. Friends Torpedo Factory Art Ctr., Alexandria, 1987—2003. Volkswagenwerk Found. Rsch. fellow, Fed. Republic of Germany, 1964-65, German Rsch. Assn. fellow, 1966, German Libr. Inst. grantee, 1981, Robbins Collection Sr. Rsch. fellow U. Calif. Berkeley, 1995; Hon. Mention award Best of Va. Artists and Artisans, 2005. Mem. ABA, ALA (Marta Lange award for disting. librarianship in law and polit. sci. 1999, Assn. Coll. and Rsch. Librs. divsn. Marta Lange Congl. Quarterly award 1999), Am. Soc. Internat. Law, Indigenous Rights Group (exec. bd. dir., 2005—), Am. Assn. Law Librs. (Tech. Svcs. Spl. Interest sect. exec. bd. dirs. 1987-91, 2003-05, ednl. com., 2006-, citation for exceptional contbn. 1992, Reneé Chapman Meml. award 1999, Joseph L. Andrews Bibliographie award 2002), Torpedo Factory Artist Assn., The Art League. Democrat. Jewish. Office: Libr Of Congress Washington DC 20540 Office Phone: 202-707-4386. Office Fax: 202-707-6629. Business E-Mail: jgol@loc.gov.

GOLDBERG, JONAH JACOB, political columnist; b. NYC, Mar. 21, 1969; s. Sid and Lucianne (Steinberger) Goldberg; m. Jessica Gavora; 1 child. BA, Goucher Coll., 1991. V.p. Lucianne Goldberg Lit. Agy., NYC, 1991—; tchr. Prague, Czech Republic, 1991-92; rschr. Am. Enterprise Inst., Washington, 1993-94; prodr. New River Media, Washington, 1994; contributing ed. Nat. Review Online, Washington, 1998—, columnist Goldberg File, 1998—, editor. Prodr. Think Tank with Ben Wattenberg, Washington, 1996; writer, prodr. (documentary) Gargoyles: Guardians of the Gate, 1995, Notre Dame: Witness to History, 1996; contbr. articles to mags. and jours. Trustee Goucher Coll., Balt., 1992-95. Conservative. Jewish. Avocations: reading, international intrigue. Office: National Review 221 Pennsylvania Ave SE Washington DC 20003 Office Phone: 202-543-9226.

GOLDBERG, JOSEPH, lawyer; b. Washington, Aug. 21, 1950; s. Morris and Rose (Levin) G.; m. Christine Marie Riggott, Mar. 29, 1980; children: Benjamin R., Louis E. BS, Ohio U., 1972; JD, U. Pa., 1975. Bar: Pa. 1975, N.J. 1981, D.C. 1980, U.S. Ct. Appeals (3d cir.) 1980, U.S. Dist. Ct. (mid. dist.) Pa. 1987, U.S. Supreme Ct. 1989. Assoc. Margolis, Edelstein & Scherlis, Phila., 1975—81; ptnr. Margolis Edelstein, Phila., 1982—2005, Weber Gallagher Simpson Stapleton Fires and Newby LLP, Phila., 2005—. Author: State and Local Government Immunity to Tort Claims, 1992, 2d edit., 1997. Mem. ABA, Pa. Def. Rsch. Inst., Pa. Jud. Rules Com., Phila. Assn. Def. Counsel, Phila. Bar Assn. Avocation: scuba diving. Office: Weber Gallagher Simpson Stapleton Fires and Newby LLP 2000 Market St 13th Flr Philadelphia PA 19103 Home Phone: 610-649-7184; Office Phone: 215-825-7225. Business E-Mail: jgoldberg@wglaw.com.

GOLDBERG, KENNETH YIGAEL, computer engineering educator, artist; b. Ibadan, Nigeria, Oct. 6, 1961; came to U.S., 1962; s. Melvin Morris and Ann Natalie G.; m. Tiffany Shlain; 1 dau., Odessa. BSEE, U. Pa., 1984, BS in Econs., 1984; MS in Computer Sci., Carnegie Mellon U., 1988, PhD in Computer Sci., 1990. Asst. prof. computer sci. U. So. Calif., 1991—95, assoc. dir. Inst. Robotics and Intelligent Systems, 1991—95; asst. prof. U. Calif. Berkeley, 1995—97, asst. prof. indsl. engring. and ops. rsch. (IEOR) dept., 1995—97, assoc. prof. indsl. engring. and ops. rsch. (IEOR) dept., 1997—2002, prof. robotics indsl. engring. and ops. rsch. (IEOR) dept. secondary appt. elect. engring. and computer sci. (EECS), artist, 2002—. Vis. prof. San Francisco Art Inst., MIT Media Lab, Pasadena Art Ctr., Calif. Editor: Robot in the Garden: Telerobotics and Telepistemology in the Age of the Internet, 2000; exhbns. include Siggraph Art Show, 1991, 92, 93, 95, 96, Ars Electronica, Austria, Dutch Electronic Art Festival, 1996, ZKM, Karlsruhe, ICC Biennale, Tokyo, Kwangju Biennale, Seoul, Artists Space, The Kitchen, NY, Whitney Biennial, Venice Biennial, Pompidou Ctr., Paris, Walker Art Ctr., Ars Electronica, Linz, Australia; contbr. over 100 rsch. papers to profl. pubs.; inventor low friction gripper. Co-founder Melvin M. Goldberg fellowship U. Pa.; founding dir. Art, Tech., and Culture Colloquium, U. Calif. Berkeley. Recipient Kobe prize 1995, Young Investigator award NSF, 1994, Joseph Engelberger Robotics award, 2000; finalist Nat. Info. Infrastructure awards 1995, 96; Rsch. grantee NSF 1992, 93, 95, 96, 97; named Nat. Young Investigator 1994, Presdl. Faculty fellow NSF 1995. Fellow: IEEE (Major Ednl. Innovation award 2001), World Technol. Network. Office: U Calif Berkeley 4189 Etcheverry Hall Berkeley CA 94720-1777

GOLDBERG, LAURENCE, investment banker; BS, U. Pa. Mng. dir., tech. group Credit Suisse First Boston, NYC; head, global tech. investment banking group Lehman Brothers, NYC, 2005—. Named a Top Rainmaker, Dealmaker mag., 2006. Office: Global Tech Lehman Brothers 745 Seventh Ave New York NY 10019*

GOLDBERG, LEE DRESDEN, endocrinologist, educator; b. Point Pleasant, NJ, July 29, 1937; s. Milton J. and Maude (Dresden) G.; m. Lana Ditchek, July 23, 1967 (dec. 1991); children: Marissa Julie, Sara Amy, Rachel Sherry; m. Rhoda Kuperman, Mar. 10, 1994. BS summa cum laude, Yale U., 1959, MD, 1963. Diplomate Am. Bd. Internal Medicine, Am. Bd. Endocrinology, Nat. Bd. Med. Examiners. Rotating intern Mt. Sinai Hosp., NYC, 1963—64; resident in internal medicine Montefiore Hosp., Bronx, NY, 1964, 1966—68; clin. rsch. fellow in endocrinology Albert Einstein Coll. Medicine, Bronx, 1968—69; fellow in endocrinology Bellevue Hosp.-NYU Med. Ctr., NYC, 1969—70; pvt. practice Miami, Fla., 1970—. Co-chief endocrinology Mt. Sinai Hosp., Miami Beach, Fla., 1974-91, chief endocrinology, 1991—; tchg. asst. NYU Sch. Medicine, 1969-70; clin. instr. medicine U. Miami Sch. Medicine, 1970-71, clin. asst. prof., 1971-80, clin. assoc. prof., 1980-99, vol. prof. medicine, 1999—; chief internal medicine South Shore Hosp., Miami Beach, 1975-79; assoc. chmn. med. svcs. St. Francis Hosp., Miami Beach, 1977-78. Author: (with Goldberg) The Jewish Student's Guide to American Colleges, 1989; contbr. articles on endocrinology to med. jours. Bd. dirs. Hebrew Acad. Greater Miami, 1975-79. Lt. M.C., USNR, 1964-66. Fellow ACP, Am. Coll. Endocrinology; mem. Endocrine Soc., Am. Diabetes Assn. (past dir. Miami chpt.), Am. Assn. Clin. Endocrinologists, Yale Club, B'nai B'rith, Phi Beta Kappa, Sigma Xi. Office Phone: 305-672-2244.

GOLDBERG, LEE WINICKI, furniture company executive; b. Laredo, Tex., Nov. 20, 1932; d. Frank and Goldie (Ostrowiak) Winicki; m. Frank M. Goldberg, Aug. 17, 1952; children: Susan, Arlene, Edward Lewis, Anne Carri. Student, San Diego State U., 1951—52. With United Furniture Co., Inc., San Diego, 1953—83, corp. sec., dir., 1963—83, dir. environ. interiors, 1970—83; founder Drexel-Heritage store Edwards Interiors subs. United Furniture, 1975; founding ptnr., v.p. FLJB Corp., 1976—86; 1980founding ptnr., sec., treas. Sea Fin., Inc., 1980; founding ptnr. First Nat. Bank San Diego, 1982. Den mother Boy Scouts Am., San Diego, 1965; vol. Am. Cancer Soc., San Diego, 1964-69; chmn. jr. matrons United Jewish Fedn., San Diego, 1958; del. So. Pacific Coast region Hadassah Conv., 1960, pres. Galilee group San Diego chpt., 1960-61; supporter Marc Chagall Nat. Mus., Nice France, U. Calif. at San Diego Cancer Ctr. Foun., Smithsonian Instn., L.A. (Calif.) County Mus., San Diego (Calif.) Mus. Contemporary Art, San Diego (Calif.) Mus. Art; pres. San Diego (Calif.) Opera, 1992-94; bd. dirs. The Old Globe, 2002-05 Recipient Hadassah Svc. award San Diego chpt., 1958-59; named Woman of Dedication by Salvation Army Women's Aux., 1992, Patron of Arts by Rancho Santa Fe Country Friends, 1993. Republican. Jewish.

GOLDBERG, LENA G., lawyer, investment company executive; b. 1949; BA, Chatham Coll.; JD, Harvard Univ., 1978. Bar: Mass. 1978. Sr. v.p., gen. counsel FMR Corp. (Fidelity Investments), Boston. Dir. New Eng. Legal Found.; mem. exec. com. Boston Lawyers Group; mem. bd. overseers Mass. Supreme Judicial Ct. Hist. Soc. Mem.: Boston Bar Found. (pres. bd. trustees 2003—04), Boston Bar Assn. Office: FMR Corp 82 Devonshire St Boston MA 02109

GOLDBERG, LOIS D., health facility administrator, disability analyst; b. Mar. 30, 1940; m. Gerald Allen Goldberg, Dec. 18, 1960; children: Sheri Goldberg Smith, Nancy Cozart, Karen Galinkin. BS in Elem. Edn., U. Wis., Milw., 1961, MS in Spl. Edn., 1977. Cert. Am. Inst. Hypnotherapy and Psychotherapy, 1986, disability analyst 2000; in reading & learning disabilities 1980, mental health counselor Dept. Health and Social Svcs. Wis., 1985, Wis. Alcohol and Drug Abuse Cert. Bd., 1985, nat. acupuncture detoxification specialist NY, 1992. Tchr. elem. edn. Fox Point Sch., 1961—63; tchr. spl. edn. Juneau Acad., 1977—79; edn. dir. Commando Acad., 1979—81; with Counseling Ctr. Milw., 1984—85, St. Charles Boys Home, 1981—87; health svcs. adminstr. Eastside Clinic, Milw., 1985—; acupuncture detox specialist, 1992-98. Pres. Eastside Youth and Family Clinic, 1981—87; weight therapist, 1984—85. Pres. Fox Point PTA, Milw., 1980; bd. dirs. Close Encounters Chamber Music. Recipient Fighting Back Initiative Cert. Recognition award, Milw. County for Reduction of Substance Abuse and Improvement of Life of Milw. County Residents, 2000. Mem.: Pi Lambda Theta (assoc. v.p. 1982). Avocations: music, swimming, tennis. Personal E-mail: ldgl@bellsouth.net.

GOLDBERG, LUCIANNE, literary agent; b. Apr. 1935; m. Sidney Goldberg. Gen. clerk promotion dept. Washington Post, 1957—65; press aide Lyndon Johnson's presdl. campaign; lit. agent, publicist Washington, DC, NYC, 1963—; columnist Lucianne.com. Author: Madame Cleo's Girls, 1992. E-mail: Lucianneg@aol.com.

GOLDBERG, LUELLA GROSS, diversified financial services company executive; b. Mpls., Feb. 26, 1937; d. Louis and Beatrice (Rosenthal) Gross; m. Stanley M. Goldberg, June 23, 1958; children: Ellen Goldberg Luger, Fredric, Martha Goldberg Aronson. BA, Wellesley Coll., 1958; postgrad. in philosophy, U. Minn., 1958-59. Dir. Reliastar Fin. Corp., 1976—2000, NRG Energy, Inc., Mpls., 2001—04. Bd. dirs. ReliaStar, Mpls. TCF Fin. Corp., Mpls., Hormel Foods Corp., Austin, Minn., Personnel Decisions Internat., 1997-2004, dir. Comm. Sys., Inc., 1997—, ING Group, Amsterdam, 2001—. Pres. Minn. Orch. Women's Assn., Mpls., 1972-74; bd. dirs. Minn. Orch. Assn., 1972—, chmn., 1980-83, Mpls. chpt. United Way, 1978-88, Ind. Sector, Washington, 1984-90; regent St. John's U., Collegeville, Minn., 1974-83; trustee U. Minn. Found., Mpls., 1978—, chmn. bd. trustees, 1996-98; bd. overseers Sch. Mgmt., U. Minn., Mpls., 1980—; chmn. bd. trustees Wellesley (Mass.) Coll., 1985-93, acting pres., 1993; trustee Wellesley Coll., 1978-96, emerita, 1996—, Northwest Area Found., 1994-2000. Recipient Disting. Svc. award, Minn. Orch. Assn., 1983, Community Svc. Leadership award, Mpls. YWCA, 1986, Disting. Svc. to Higher Edn. award, Minn. Pvt. Coll. Coun., 1992, Humanitarian award, NCCJ, 1992, Regents award, U. Minn., 2000, Alumnae Achievement award, Wellesley Coll., 2002, Disting. Women's award, Northwoods U., 2001, Lifetime Achievement award as Outstanding Dir., Twin Cities Bus. Monthly, 2001, Minn. Bus. Hall Fame, Jr. Achievement Upper Midwest, 2005. Mem. Minn. Women's Econ. Round Table, Mpls. Club, Phi Beta Kappa. Avocations: water-skiing, wind surfing, travel. Home: 7019 Tupa Dr Minneapolis MN 55439-1643

GOLDBERG, MARC EVAN, healthcare venture capitalist; b. Boston, Mar. 14, 1957; s. Ray Allan and Thelma (Englander) G.; children: Frederick Warren, Alyssa Rachel, Meredith Hayley AB, Harvard U., 1979, MBA, JD, 1983. Bar: Mass. 1985. Mgr. bus. devel. Genetics Inst., Inc., Cambridge, Mass., 1983—87; v.p. fin. and corp. devel., CFO, treas. Safer, Inc., Newton, Mass., 1987—91; pres., CEO Mass. Biotech. Rsch. Inst., Worcester, 1991—97; mng. dir. BioVentures Investors, Cambridge, 1997—. Bd. dirs. Enanta Pharms., Applied Spine Technologies, Verax Biomed., Spirus Med., Gulfstream Bioinformatics, Claros Diagnostics; founder Mass. Biotech. Coun., pres., 1985-87, 90-92. Mem., prin. author Gov.'s Task Force on Biotech., 1991—98; trustee Worcester State Coll., 1991—2002, vice chmn., 1993—95, chmn., 1995—97; trustee Harvard Yearbook Pubs., 1981—; exec. adv. bd. Harvard Varsity Club, 1982—, bd. dirs., treas., 2004—07, pres., 2007—; adv. com. Town of Wellesley, 1992—94, mem. town meeting, 1993—95; trustee Mass. Taxpayers Found., 1993—99; bd. dirs. rsch. adv. com. Beth Israel Deaconess Med. Ctr. Mem. Mass Bar Assn., New Eng./Israel C. of C. (trustee 1993-2000), Harvard Bus. Sch. Assn. Boston (bd. govs. 1993-96) Office: BioVentures Investors 101 Main St Ste 1750 Cambridge MA 02142

GOLDBERG, MARK ARTHUR, neurologist; b. NYC, Sept. 4, 1934; s. Jacob and Bertha (Grushlawska) G.; 1 child, Jonathan. BS, Columbia U., 1955; PhD, U. Chgo., 1959, MD, 1962. Resident neurology NY Neurol. Inst., NYC, 1963-66; asst. prof. neurology Columbia U. Coll. Phys. and Surgs., NYC, 1968-71; assoc. prof. neurology and pharmacology UCLA, 1971-77, prof. neurology and pharmacology, 1977—; chair dept. neurology Harbor UCLA Med. Ctr., Torrance, 1977—2005. Contbr. articles to profl. jours., chpts. to books. Capt. US Army, 1966-68. Fellow Am. Neurol. Assn., Am. Acad. Neurology; mem. L.A. Neurol. Soc., Palos Verdes Land Conservancy. Avocation: oriental cusine. E-mail: mrkgldbrg@yahoo.com, mgoldberg@labiomed.org.

GOLDBERG, MARK JOEL, lawyer; b. Pitts., June 2, 1941; s. Charles J. and Eleanore (Letwin) Goldberg; 1 child, Wendy. BA, Washington and Jefferson Coll., 1963; JD, Case Western Res. U., 1966. Bar: Pa. 1966, Ohio 1966, U.S. Tax Ct. 1969, U.S. Supreme Ct. 1972. Assoc. Jerome Silver, Cleve., 1966-67; pvt. practice, Pitts., 1967-69; ptnr. Goldberg & Wedner, Pitts., 1969-80; ptnr., shareholder Gillotti Goldberg & Capristo, Pitts., 1981-91, Goldberg Gentile & Voelker, Pitts., 1991-92, Goldberg, Gruener, Gentile, Horoho & Avalli, P.C., Pitts., 1992—. Mem. drafting com. Pa. Divorce Code, 1978—80, 1988; lectr. Pa. Bar Inst., Pa. Trial Lawyers Assn. Contbr. articles to profl. jours. Pres. bd. dirs. Parent and Child Guidance Ctr., Pitts., 1984—86; committeeman Dem. Party, Pitts., 1970. Fellow: Am. Acad. Matrimonial Lawyers (lectr., pres. Pa. chpt. 1988—90, nat. bd. govs. 1991—95); mem.: Pa. Bar Assn. (family law sect. chmn. 1986—88), Allegheny County Bar Assn. (coun. mem. family law sect. 1972—, chmn. 1982—84), Am. Coll. Family Trial Lawyers (diplomate, officer), Rivers Club, Westmoreland Country Club. Jewish. Avocations: golf, travel. Office: Goldberg Gruener Gentile Horoho & Avalli PC 230 Grant Bldg Pittsburgh PA 15219-2200 Home: 128 N Craig St Apt 316 Pittsburgh PA 15213 Office Phone: 412-261-9900. Business E-Mail: mgoldberg@ggpha.com.

GOLDBERG, MARTIN, internist, educator; b. Phila., Sept. 15, 1930; s. Samuel and Esther (Shreibman) Goldberg; m. Lynn Taksey, June 17, 1951 (dec. Aug. 31, 1976); children: Meryl I, Karen L, Dara S; m. Marion Lindblad, May 26, 1978; 1 child, David S. BA, Temple U., 1951, MD, 1955; MA (hon.), U. Pa., 1971. Diplomate Am. Bd. Internal Medicine, Nat. Bd. Med. Examiners. Intern Phila. Gen. Hosp., 1955-56, resident, 1957-59, sr. attending physician, 1970-76; resident Cleve. Clinic, 1956-57; fellow nephrology Hosp. U. Pa., Phila., 1959-61, sr. attending physician, 1962-79; mem. faculty U. Pa. Sch. Medicine, 1960-79, prof. medicine, 1970-79, chief renal electrolyte sect., 1966-79, acting chmn. dept. medicine, 1975-76; sr. attending physician Phila. VA Hosp., 1968-79; Gordon and Helen Hughes Taylor prof. medicine U. Cin., 1979-86; chmn. internal medicine U. Cin. Coll. Med. and Hosp., 1979-86; prof. medicine Temple U. Sch. Medicine, Phila., 1986-96, dean, vice pres., 1986-89, prof. emeritus, 1997—, asst. to dean for computer assisted instrn., 1997-2000; chmn. sci. adv. com. Gen. Clin. Rsch. Ctr. Temple U. Hosp., 1993—. Bd. mgrs. St. Christopher's Hosp. for Children, 1986—89; chmn. nephrology com. Am. Bd. Internal Medicine, 1976—79, bd. govs., 1976—79. Mem. editl. bd.: Jour Clin Investigation, 1969—70, Kidney Internat., 1972—74, Jour. Mineral and Electrolyte Metabolism, 1977—91, Am. Jour. Hypertension, 1990—97, First Consult, 2000—, mem. editl. adv. bd.: others. Recipient Alumni prize, Temple U. Sch. Medicine, 1955, Rsch. Career Devel. award, NIH, 1963—70, Lindback award for disting. tchg., U. Pa., 1972, Disting. Med Scientist of Yr. award, Med. Alumni Temple U. Sch. Medicine, 1985, Honoree of the Yr. award, Greater Delaware Valley Kidney Found., 1997, A.N. Richards award, U. Pa., 1998, Centennial award, Assn. Chmn. Depts. Physiology, 1989; rsch. grantee, NIH, 1962—89, John Hartford Found., 1970—73. Master: ACP (nat. sci. program com. 1976—81); fellow: Royal Soc. Medicine, Am. Coll. Clin. Pharmacology; mem.: Physicians for Social Responsibility (adv. bd. Phila. chpt. 1988—98), Coll. Physicians Phila., Am. Med. Informatics Assn., Internat. Soc. Nephrology (coun. 1975—84), Am. Soc. Nephrology (sec.-treas. 1975—78), Am. Fedn. Clin. Rsch. (chmn. eastern sect. 1967), Am. Physiol. Soc., Am. Soc. Clin. Investigation, Assn. Am. Physicians, Assn. Am. Med. Colls. (coun. deans 1986—89), Interurban Clin. Club, Alpha Omega Alpha. Achievements include research in renal physiology and disease; electrolyte and acid-base metabolism, computer assisted instruction and diagnosis. Business E-Mail: marting@temple.edu.

GOLDBERG, MARVIN ALLEN, lawyer, consultant; b. Phila., Jan. 9, 1943; s. Daniel and Elizabeth (Katz) G.; m. Kathryn Elizabeth Balotsky, Apr. 27, 1974; children: Robert Andrew, MaryBeth Anne. BS, Temple U., 1964, JD, 1967. Bar: Pa. 1968, U.S. Dist. Ct. (ea. dist.) Pa. 1980, U.S. Supreme Ct. 1976. Estate tax atty. IRS, Phila., 1967—68; staff atty. Legal Aid Soc. Northampton County, Easton, Pa., 1969-70, Northampton County Pub. Defender, Easton, Pa., 1969-70; pvt. practice law Phila., 1970-76; tchr. Inst. for Paralegal Tng., Phila., 1973; staff atty. Legal Aid Soc. Phila., 1974-76; CEO Goldberg & Assocs., P.C., Phila., 1976—. Cons. Butcher Trade Exchange, Ft. Washington, Pa., 1982-92. Mem. Chestnut St. Assn., Phila; dir. Sr. Citizen Judicare Project, Phila., 1977. With USAF, 1967-73. Fellow Roscoe Pound Inst.; mem. ABA, Phila. Bar Assn., Phila. Trial Lawyers Assn., Assn. Trial Lawyers Am., Pa. Trial Lawyers Assn., Attys. Across Am. (founding mem.), Jewish War Vets, Beta Gamma Sigma, Phi Alpha Delta. Avocations: running, flying, sailing, chess, 19th century physics. Office: Goldberg & Assocs PC 1334 Walnut St Fl 5 Philadelphia PA 19107-5311

GOLDBERG, MAUREEN MCKENNA, state supreme court justice; b. Pawtucket, RI, Feb. 11, 1951; m. Robert D. Goldberg. Grad., St. Mary's Acad., 1969; AB cum laude, Providence Coll., 1973; JD cum laude, Suffolk U., 1978, LLD (hon.), 1999. Bar: R.I. 1978, Mass. 1978, U.S. Ct. of Appeals (1st cir.) 1979. Asst. atty. gen. Adminstr. of the Criminal Divsn., 1978-84; town solicitor South Kingstown, 1985-87, Town of Westerly, 1987-90, acting town mgr., 1990; spl. legal counsel RI State Police; apptd. assoc. justice Superior Ct., 1990-96; assoc. justice RI Supreme Ct., 1997—. Mem. Com. to Study Proposed Amendments to R.I. Rules of Evidence, 1998—99; co-chair R.I. Supreme Ct. Law Day Com., 2001—, Advisory Com. on Code of Jud. Conduct, 2002; chair Indigent Defense Task Force, 2003, Jud. Performance Evaluation Com., 2003. Mem. ABA, R.I. Bar Assn., R.I. Trial Judges Assn., Pawtucket Bar Assn., R.I. Bar Found., Nat. Assn. of Women Judges, Mass. Bar Assn. Office: Rhode Island Supreme Ct 250 Benefit St 7th Fl Providence RI 02903-2719*

GOLDBERG, MELVIN ARTHUR, communications executive; b. NYC, Feb. 5, 1923; s. Louis and Anna (Bergman) G.; m. Norma N. Nertz, Oct. 18, 1956; children: Ronald, Richard, Joan Sandra. BS, CCNY, 1942; AM, Columbia U., 1950. Mem. staff Bur. Applied Social Rsch., Columbia, 1946-47; news editor, rsch. dir. TV mag., 1947-49; dir. sales planning and rsch. DuMont TV Network, 1949-52; dep. dir. Office Rsch. and Evaluation, U.S. Info. Agy., 1952-53; exec. sec. Ultra-High Frequency TV Assn., 1953-54; cons., chief of rsch. M-G Rsch., 1954-56; dir. rsch. Westinghouse Broadcasting Co., 1956-62; v.p., dir. rsch. Nat. Assn. Broadcasters, 1962-64; v.p. planning and rsch. John Blair & Co., 1964-69; pres. Melvin A. Goldberg Inc., NYC, 1969-77; v.p. primary and social rsch. ABC-TV, 1977-80, v.p. news, social and tech. rsch., 1980-85; v.p. market planning, tech. and social rsch. ABC Inc.; exec. dir. Electronic Media Rating Coun., 1985-93; pres. Melvin A. Goldberg Inc., NYC, 1993—. Former mem. ABA Commn. on Pub. Understanding About the Law. Mem. editorial bd. TV Quar.; Contbr. articles to profl. publs. Mem. Great Neck/North Shore Cable Commn., chmn. long range planning com. Decorated D.F.C., Air medal with clusters. Mem. Am. Assn. Pub. Opinion Rsch., Radio-TV Rsch. Coun., Nat. Acad. TV Arts and Scis. Home: 17 North Dr Great Neck NY 11021-1337 Office: Melvin A Goldberg Inc Comm 17 North Dr Great Neck NY 11021-1337

GOLDBERG, MICHAEL ELLIS, neurologist, neuroscientist; b. New York, NY, Aug. 10, 1941; s. Samuel Goldberg; m. Deborah Baron Goldberg, July 31, 1966; children: Joshua, Jonathan. AB, Harvard Coll., 1963; MD, Harvard Med. Sch., 1968. Asst. prof. to prof. neurology NIH Georgetown U. Sch. Medicine, Washington, 1978—2001; med. rsch. officer Lab. Sensorimotor Rsch. Nat. Eye Inst., Bethesda, Md., 1978—2001; David Mahoney prof. brain and behavior, dept. neurology, psychiatry, and the Center for Neurobiology and Behavior Columbia U. Coll. Physicians and Surgeons, NYC, 2001—. Guest investigator Lab. Sensorimotor Rsch. Nat. Eye Inst., 2001—02; James M. Sprague lectr. U. Pa., 2000. Author: (Journal Articles) Science, Nature, Journal of Neurophysiology, Journal of Neuroscience, Experimental Brain Research, Vision Research, 2001; contbr. articles to profl. jours. Grantee, McDonnell Found., 2003—, Nat. Eye Inst., 2004—. Fellow: Am. Acad. Arts & Sciences; mem.: Internat. Neuropsychol. Symposium (pres. 1990—94), Soc. Neurosci. (treas. 2005, Spl. Achievement award 2000), Am. Neurol. Assn. Home Phone: 212-678-9035. Business E-Mail: meg2008@columbia.edu.

GOLDBERG, MICHAEL IRA, obstetrician, gynecologist; b. Bklyn., June 8, 1944; MD, U. Rome, 1970. Diplomate Am. Bd. Ob-Gyn., Am. Bd. Gynecol. Oncology. Intern Maimonedes Med. Ctr., Bklyn., 1971, resident in ob-gyn., 1972-75; fellow in gynecol. oncology Miami (Fla.)-Jackson Meml. Hosp., 1975-77; pvt. practice New Brunswick, NJ. Mem. staff RW Johnson U. Hosp., New Brunswick; clin. prof. ob-gyn. U. Medicine and Dentistry of N.J., RW Johnson Med. Sch.; chief gynecol. oncology St. Peter's U. Hosp., New Brunswick. Fellow ACS, ACOG; mem. Soc. Gynecol. Oncology. Office: 78 Easton Ave New Brunswick NJ 08901-1865 Office Phone: 732-828-3300. Fax: 723-937-5739.

GOLDBERG, MORTON EDWARD, pharmacologist; b. Phila., July 11, 1932; s. Herman and Ethel (Shill) G.; m. Janet Louise Werlin, Aug. 15, 1954; children— Shellie, Ellen, David. BS, Phila. Coll. Pharmacy and Sci., 1954, MS in Pharmacology, 1955, DSc in Pharmacology, 1958. Sr. pharmacologist Abbott Labs., North Chgo., 1958-60; asst. dir. pharmacology Union Carbide Corp., Tuxedo, NY, 1960-69; dir. pharmacodynamics Warner Lambert Research Inst., Morris Plains, NJ, 1969-73; dir. pharmacology Squibb Inst. Med. Research, Princeton, NJ, 1973-77; v.p. biomed. research Stuart Pharms. div. ICI Americas, Wilmington, Del., 1977-84; v.p. rsch., devel., and regulatory affairs ICI Pharm. Group divsn. ICI Ams. (now Astra Zeneca Pharm.), Wilmington, 1984-92; clin. prof. pharmacology and exptl. therapeutics Dept. Pharmacology U. Pa. Sch. Medicine, Phila., 1992-96; advisor, cons. several pharm. cos., 1996—. Vis. prof. toxicology Phila. Coll. Pharmacy and Sci.; vis. prof. pharmacology, Allegheny U. Med. Sch., Phila., 1978-2001, U. Pa. Sch. Med., Phila., 1996-2001; cons. to pharm. industry in drug discovery and devel., 1992—; mem. extramural sci. adv. bd. NIDA, 1993-95, mem. nat. adv. bd. 1996-2000. Editor-in-chief: series Pharmacological and Biochemical Properties of Drug Substances; contbr. articles to profl. jours. Asst. scoutmaster Boy Scouts Am., Glen Rock, N.J., 1968-72. NIH grantee, 1961-64 Fellow Acad. Pharm. Sci., AAAS, N.Y. Acad. Sci.; mem. Am. Soc. Pharmacology and Exptl. Therapeutics, Behavioral Pharmacology Soc., Internat. Soc. Biochem. Pharmacology, Soc. Toxicology (charter), Sigma Xi, Rho Chi. Home: 715 Severn Rd Wilmington DE 19803-1725 Personal E-mail: mortjan@comcast.net.

GOLDBERG, MORTON FALK, ophthalmologist, educator; b. Lawrence, Mass., June 8, 1937; s. Maurice and Helen Janet (Falk) G.; m. Myrna Davidov, Apr. 6, 1968; children— Matthew Falk, Michael Falk AB magna cum laude, Harvard U., 1958, MD cum laude, 1962; Doctoris honoris causa, U. Coimbra, Portugal, 1995. Diplomate Am. Bd. Ophthalmology. Intern Peter Bent Brigham Hosp., Boston, 1962-63; resident Wilmer Inst. Johns Hopkins Hosp., Balt., 1963—67, head dept., dir. Wilmer Inst., 1989—2003; prof. and head ophthalmology Eye and Ear Infirmary U. Ill. Hosp., Chgo., 1970-89; Joseph Green prof. ophthalmology Johns Hopkins Med. Sch., 2003—. Author: (with D. Paton) Injuries of the Eye, the Lids and the Orbit: Diagnosis and Management, 1968, Management of Ocular Injuries, 1976; editor: Genetic and Metabolic Eye Disease, 1974, (with G.A. Peyman and D.R. Sanders) Principles and Practice of Ophthalmology (3 vols.), 1980; editor-in-chief Archives of Ophthalmology, Chgo., 1984-94; contbr. articles to profl. jours. Lt. comdr. USPHS, 1967-69 Recipient award for outstanding contbns. in the field of vision rsch. Alcon Research Inst., 1987, Univ. Scholar award U. Ill.-Chgo., 1986, Michaelson medal Israel Acad. Scis. and Humanities, 2000, Greatest Living Ophthalmologists award Ophthalmology Times, 1999, Mildred Weisenfeld Lifetime Achievement award Fight for Sight, Inc., 2001, Pryor award Am. Soc. Retinal Specialists, 2004, Heritage award Johns Hopkins U., 2007. Fellow: Am. Acad. Ophthalmology (Inaugural Helen Keller lectr. 2007, sr. honor award 1985), Royal Australian Coll. Ophthalmologists (hon.); mem.: Internat. Academia Ophthalmologia, Academia Ophthalmologica Internationalis, Macula Soc. (pres. 1980—82, Patz medal 1999, David Paton medal 2002), Assn. Univ. Profs. Ophthalmology (trustee 1985—91, pres. 1990—91), Assn. Rsch. in Vision and Ophthalmology (trustee 1985—90, pres. 1989—90, Weisenfeld award 2000), Chgo. Ophthal. Soc. (pres. 1985—86), Am. Ophthal. Soc., Inst. Medicine-NAS. Avocation: snorkelling. Office: Johns Hopkins Med Insts Wilmer Eye Inst 600 N Wolfe St Baltimore MD 21287-0005 E-mail: mgoldberg@jhmi.edu.

GOLDBERG, NEIL ALAN, lawyer; b. NYC, Dec. 24, 1947; s. Bernard G. Goldberg and Hortense (Goldman); children: Jane Hana, Robert Saul. BA cum laude, SUNY, Stony Brook, 1969; JD cum laude, SUNY, Buffalo, 1973. Bar: N.Y. 1974, U.S. Dist. Ct. (we. dist.) N.Y. 1974. Sr. ptnr. Saperston & Day P.C., Buffalo, 1974—2001; founding ptnr. Goldberg Segalla LLP, Buffalo, 2001—. Editor, contbg. author: Products Liability in New York Strategy and Practice, 1997; co-editor in chief: Preparing for and Trying the Civil Lawsuit, 2d edit., 2004; editor-in-chief: Daubert Compendium, Def. Rsch. Inst.; editor-in-chief, contbg. author: 7 books def. complex personal injury cases, Def. Rsch. Inst. Mem.: ABA, Trial Lawyers Am., Internat. Assn. Insurance Law, Fedn. Def. Corp. Counsel, Lawyers for Civil Justice (pres. 2004—05, bd. chmn.), Erie County Bar Assn., NY State Bar Assn. (past chmn. torts ins. and compensation law sect. product liability com, past chmn. product liability com. torts, Disting. Svc. award), Am. Arbitration Assn. (product liability adv. coun. bd. mem.), Def. Rsch. Inst. (pres. 2000—01, fmr. chair products liability com.), Internat. Assn. Def. Counsel. Office: Goldberg Segalla LLP Ste 400 665 Main St Buffalo NY 14203 Home Phone: 716-992-1224; Office Phone: 716-566-5475. Business E-Mail: ngoldberg@goldbergsegalla.com.

GOLDBERG, NIECA, cardiologist, educator; b. Bkyln., Oct. 21, 1957; BA, Barnard Coll., 1979; MD, SUNY, Bklyn., 1984. Diplomate Am. Bd. Internal Medicine. Resident in internal medicine St. Lukes-Roosevelt Hosp., NYC, 1985-87; fellow in cardiology SUNY Health Sci. Ctr., Bklyn.; chief women's cardiac care Lenox Hill Hosp., NYC; asst. clin. prof. of medicine NYU Sch. Medicine, NYC; and co-med. dir. 92nd St. YMCA Cardiac Rehabilitation Ctr., NYC. Nat. spokesperson Am. Heart Assn. Go Red campaign; adv. bd. Woman's Day mag. Author: Women Are Not Small Men: Life-Saving Strategies for Preventing and Healing Heart Disease in Women, 2003, The Women's Health Heart Program: Life-saving Strategies for Preventing and Healing Heart Disease in Women, 2006. Named to New York mag. Best Doctors issue, 1999, 2000, 2001, 2004, 2005; recipient Dr. with Heart award, Am. Heart Assn., Red Dress award, Woman's Day mag., Women to Watch award, Jewish Women Internat. Mem. ACP, Am. Coll. Cardiology, Am. Heart. Assn., Am. Soc. Echocardiography, Am. Coll. Physicians. Office: Total Heart Care PC 177 E 87th St #503 New York NY 10128 Office Phone: 212-289-2045. Office Fax: 212-289-2473. Business E-Mail: Echodocs2@cs.com.*

GOLDBERG, PAMELA WINER, entrepreneur, educator; b. Boston, Oct. 14, 1955; d. Arthur Leonard and Marilyn (Miller) Winer; children from previous marriage: Frederick Warren, Alyssa Rachel, Meredith Hayley. BA, Tufts U., 1977; MBA, Stanford U., 1981. Day care dir. Cmty. Action Inc., Haverhill, Mass., 1977-79; lending assoc. Bankers Trust Co., NYC, 1980-81; mgr., bank officer, corp. fin. dept. Citicorp, NYC, 1981-82; assoc. dir., mergers and acquisitions group State St. Bank, Boston, 1983-85; ind. strategic cons. Wellesley, Mass., 1986-97; dir. bus. rels. Babson Coll., Wellesley, 1998—2002; prof., dir. Ctr. for Entrepreneurial Leadership Tufts U., 2002—. Exec. bd. friends Beth Israel Hosp., Boston, 1987—96; trustee Recuperative Ctr., Boston, 1988—95; exec. bd. trustees Temple Beth Elohim, Wellesley, 1992—2000, treas., 1997—2000, Synagogue 2000 nat. com., 2000—04; bd. dirs. Hunnewell Sch. PTO, 1991—96, Wellesley LWV, 1995—98. Mem.: US Assn. Small Bus. and Entrepreneurship, The Commonwealth Inst., The Boston Club. Avocations: swimming, tennis, singing. Home: 34 Ivy Rd Wellesley MA 02482-4554 Office: Tufts University 4 Colby St Medford MA 02155 Office Phone: 617-627-2153. Personal E-mail: pwg14@aol.com. Business E-Mail: pamela.goldberg@tufts.edu.

GOLDBERG, PAUL BERNARD, gastroenterologist, clinical researcher; b. Bklyn., Apr. 11, 1950; s. Samuel and Eva (Turkenitz) G.; m. Harriet Ruth Ferrer, July 8, 1973 (div. 1987); children: Deborah Lynn, Susan Michelle; m. Mary Alice Denaro, June 23, 1990; 1 child, Laura Alicia. BA in Chemistry summa cum laude, Cornell U., 1967-71, MD, 1971-75. Diplomate Am. Bd. Internal Medicine, Am. Bd. Gastroenterology. Intern in medicine Hosp. of U. of Pa., Phila., 1975-76, resident in medicine, 1976-78, fellow in gastroenterology, 1978-80, fellow in nutritional support svc., 1979-80; med. coord. and founder nutritional support svc. Lakeland (Fla.) Gen. Hosp., 1980-81; attending physician Halifax Med. Ctr., 1980—, Ormond Meml. Hosp., 1980—, Atlantic Med. Ctr., 1980-2000, Fish Meml. Hosp., New Smyrna Beach, Fla., 1989-99, Peninsula Med. Ctr., 1989-94. Pres. Sunshine Health Care Plan, Inc., 1983-86, v.p., 1986-87; chief staff Humana Hosp., Daytona Beach, 1986-88, trustee, 1986-89, mem. exec. com., 1984-91; mem. rev. bd. Coastal Instnl. Rev., 1990-93, chmn. rev. bd., 1993-96; expert reviewer Fla. Dept. Profl. Regulation, 1990—; pres. med. staff Halifax Hosp., 1996-97; clin. asst. prof. medicine dept. family medicine U. South Fla., 1987-2007. Rschr. and author in field. Physician adv. Daytona chpt. Crohn's and Colitis Found., 1991-95. Recipient Nat. award Ford Future Scientists of Am., 1967, Westinghouse Sci. Talent Search finalist, 1967. Fellow ACP, Am. Coll. Gastroenterology, Am. Gastroent. Soc.; mem. Am. Soc. Gastrointestinal Endoscopy, Am. Soc. for Parenteral and Enteral Nutrition (pres. Fla. chpt. 1991-92), Volusia County Med. Soc. (exec. com. 1991-94, co-chmn. mini internship program 1992-94, 2000-01), Fla. Gastrointestinal Soc., Fla. Med. Assn. (alt. del. to ho. of dels. 1990-95), Fla. Assn. Nutritional Support (1st pres.), Rotary, Phi Beta Kappa, Alpha Omega Alpha. Office: 1070 N Stone St Ste D Deland FL 32720 Office Phone: 386-822-9410. Personal E-mail: pbgoldberg@aol.com.

GOLDBERG, RAY ALLAN, agriculturist, educator; b. Fargo, ND, Oct. 19, 1926; s. Max and Anne G.; m. Thelma R. Englander, May 20, 1956; children: Marc E., Jennifer E., Jeffrey L. AB, Harvard U., 1948, MBA, 1950; PhD, U. Minn., 1952; D Polit. Sci. (hon.), U. Buenos Aires, Argentina, 2000. Officer, dir. Moorhead Seed & Grain Co., Minn., 1952—62; dir. Experience, Inc., Mpls., 1963—78, Arbor Acres Farm, Inc., NYC, H.K. Webster Co.; mem. faculty Harvard U. Grad. Bus. Sch., 1955—, Moffett prof. agr. and bus., 1970—97, Moffett prof. agr. and bus. emeritus, 1997—, dir. continuing edn. programs, participant seminars. Bd. dirs. Daymon Assn., Smithfield Foods; hon. prof. Royal Agrl. Coll., Cirencester, Eng., 1996; vis. prof. U. Minn. Grad. Sch., 1960; adv. coun. Foods Multinat., Inc., 1972-77; agrl. investment com. John Hancock Ins. Co., 1971-95; cons. in field; adviser Instituto Centroamericano de Administracion de Empresa, Managua, Nicaragua, 1973—, Inst. Panamericano de Alta Direccion de Empressa, Mexico City, 1973—, U.S. Comptr. Currency, 1975—, Food and Agr. Policy Project, Ctr. Nat. Policy, 1984—; study team, subgroup chmn. world food and nutrition study NRC, 1975—; com. tech. factor contbg. to nation's fgn. trade positions Nat. Acad. Engring., 1976—; chmn. agribus. adv. com. on Caribbean Basin USDA, 1982—; com. on indsl. policy for developing countries Commn. on Engring. and Tech. Systems, NRC, 1982—; task force on agr. Fowler-McCracken Commn., 1984—; adv. bd. The First Mercantile Currency Fund Inc., 1985—; internat. adv. bd. Atlantic Exch. Program, 1987—; mem. V.I. Lenin All-Union Acad. Agrl. Scis., 1988—; mem. U.S. Presdl. Econ. Del. to Poland, Nov., 1989; sci. adv. bd. Sepragen Corp., 1993—, Inst. Food Technologists, 1999—; chmn. joint bus. sci. pub. policy consumer policy tech. com. U.S. Food Sys. and Seminar, 1994—; internat. bd. vis. Zamorano, 1995—; adv. com. Foodfit.com., 1999—, sci. adv. bd., IFT/FDA Rsch. Contract, 1999, chmn. adv. panel for World Bank Guide to Developing Agrl. Markets and Agro-Enterprises, 1999, chmn. subcom. on Econ. and Social Devel. in Global Context, Nat. Rsch. Coun., 2002; chmn. Task Force to utilize Tobacco Funds for Econ. Devel., Ky., Long Term Plan for Agrl. and Rural Devel. for state of Ky., 2001; chmn. sub. com. on Econ. and Social Devel. in a Global Context for com. on opportunities in Agr.-NRC Bd. on Agr. and Natural Resources, 2001; co-chmn. European Food and Agribus, Seminar, Rome, 2005. Author: (with Hohn H. Davis) A Concept of Agribusiness, 1957, Agribusiness Coordination, 1968, Agribusiness Management for Developing Countries-Latin America, 1974, (with Lee F. Schrader) Farmers' Cooperative and Federal Income Taxes, 1974, (with John T. Dunlop et al) The Lessons of Wage and Price Controls-The Food Sector, 1977, (with Richard C. McGinity et al), Agribusiness Management for Devloping Countries-Southeast Asia Corn Study, 1979; editor: Research in Domestic and International Agribusiness Management, Vol. 1, 1980, Vol. 2, 1981, Vol. 3, 1982, Vol. 4, 1983, Vol. 5, 1984, Vol. 6, 1986, Vol. 7, 1987, Vol. 8, 1988, Vol. 9, 1989, Vol. 10, 1981, Vol. 11, 1995, Vol. 12, 1996; co-editor; (with Gerald E. Gaul) New Technologies and the Future of Food and Nutrition, 1991, The Emerging Global Food System: Public and Private Sector Issues, 1993; contbr. numerous articles to profl. jours.; chmn. editl. adv. bd. Agribus.: An Internat. Jour., 1983—. Bd. govs. Internat. Devel. Rsch. Ctr., Govt. Can., 1978—; trustee Roxbury Latin Sch., Boston, 1973-76, Beth Israel Hosp., Boston, 1978—, mem. com. on patents and tech. transfer, 1982—, chmn. gerontology com., 1991—; mem. adv. com. to prep. sch. New Eng. Conservatory Music, 1974—, assoc. trustee, 1978—; vice chmn. bd. Spoleto Festival U.S.A., 1993; adv. mem. Polish Investment Fund, 1994—; chmn. adv. com. Sonoma Internat. Capital Assocs., 1994—; trustee Global Conservation Trust, Rome, 2002 Recipient Outstanding Alumni award, Dept. Agrl. Econs. U. Minn., 1992, 2d pl. McKinsey award, Harvard Bus. Rev., 2000, Disting. Svc. award, Harvard Grad. Sch. Bus. Adminstrn., 2001. Fellow Internat. Agribus. Mgmt. Assn. (pres. 1990-92, bd. dirs., chmn. Russian food mgmt. program sponsored rsch. project 1994—, coord. non-partisan ednl., govt., pvt., sci., med. and consumer group for food, safety, nutrition and environ. 1994—, chmn. subcom. econ. and social devel.), Agribus. Inst. Cambridge (chmn. bd., treas. 1991-93), Am. Agrl. Econ. Assn. (editl. coun. 1974-78, nat. agribus. edn. commn. 1988—), Am. Econ. Assn.; mem. Royal Agrl. Coll. Eng. (hon. prof. 1996—), V.I. Lenin All-Union Acad. Agrl. Scis. (fgn.), Am. Mktg. Assn., Am. Dairy Sci. Assn., Food Distbn. Rsch. Soc., Harvard Club (Boston and NYC), Bus. Coun. for Sustainable Devel. (adv. group for sustainable paper cycle project 1994—) Address: 975 Memorial Dr Apt 701 Cambridge MA 02138-5803 Office Phone: 617-495-6496. Business E-Mail: rgoldberg@hbs.edu.

GOLDBERG, RICHARD ROBERT, lawyer; b. NYC, Apr. 27, 1941; s. Joseph and Anne (Blumfield) G.; m. Rita Ann Zieve, June 30, 1963; 1 child, Andrew Louis. BA, Pa. State U., 1961; LLB, U. Md., 1964. Bar: Md. 1964, U.S. Ct. Appeals (4th cir.) 1970, U.S. Supreme Ct. 1974, U.S. Ct. Appeals (5th cir.) 1978, U.S. Ct. Appeals (D.C. cir.) 1992, Pa. 1994, N.J. 1994. Asst. city solicitor to Mayor and City Coun. City of Balt., 1965-70; atty. The Rouse Co., Columbia, Md., 1970-78, v.p., assoc. gen. counsel, 1978-94; ptnr. Ballard, Spahr, Andrews & Ingersoll, Phila., 1994—. Author: Real Estate Development of Downtown Projects, 1981; author and editor: (handbooks) Commercial Real Estate Leasing, Commercial Real Estate Financing; contbr. numerous articles to profl. publs. Chmn. Jewish Coun. of Howard County, Md., 1975-77, chmn. ann. campaign, 1978, 80, 87; pres. Temple Isaiah, Columbia, 1978-79; bd. trustees Jewish Fedn. Howard County, 1993-94. Mem. ABA (sec. real property, probate and trust law, chmn. prohibited transactions com. 1983-85, chmn. mgmt. property com. 1985-87, chmn. nat. insts. and satellite programs 1987-89, advisor UCC drafting com. article 1, article 3, article 9), Md. State Bar Assn., Pa. Bar Assn., Phila. Bar Assn., Am. Law Inst. (advisor restatement law of mortgages), Anglo-Am. Real Property Inst. (sec. 1990-92, chair-elect 1994, chair 1995), Am. Coll. Real Estate Lawyers (v.p. 1989-90, pres.-elect 1990-91, pres. 1991-92), Am. Coll. Mortgage Attys., Internat. Coun. Shopping Ctrs. (past chmn. law conf. com., mem. govtl. affairs com., econ. affairs subcom.). Office: Ballard Spahr Andrews & Ingersoll 1735 Market St Ste 5100 Philadelphia PA 19103-7599 Home: 319 Vine St Apt 301 Philadelphia PA 19106 Office Phone: 215-864-8730. Business E-Mail: goldbergr@ballardspahr.com.

GOLDBERG, RICHARD W., federal judge; b. Fargo, ND, Sept. 23, 1927; s. Jacob H. and Frances (Gilles) G.; m. Mary Borland, Apr. 26, 1964; children: Julie, John. BBA, U. Miami, Fla., 1950, JD, 1952. Bar: Fla. 1952, N.D. 1952, DC 1957. Pres., chief exec. officer Goldberg Feed & Grain Co.; acting and dep. under sec. of internat. affairs & commodity program USDA, Washington, 1983-89; pvt. practice Anderson Hibey and Blair, 1990—91; judge US Ct. Internat. Trade, NYC, 1991—2001, sr. judge, 2001—. Served to capt. USAF, 1953-56. Office: US Ct Internat Trade 1 Federal Plz New York NY 10278-0001

GOLDBERG, RITA MARIA, foreign language educator; b. NYC, Oct. 1, 1933; d. Abraham Morris and Hilda (Weinman) G. BA, Queens Coll., 1954; MA, Middlebury Coll., 1955; PhD, Brown U., 1968. Mem. faculty Queens Coll., NYC, 1956, Oberlin (Ohio) Coll., 1957; mem. faculty St. Lawrence U., Canton, NY, 1957—2001, Dana prof. modern langs., 1975—2000, emerita, 2001—, chmn. dept., 1972—75, 1983—91, 2000—01. Chmn. Regional Conf. Am. Programs in Spain, 1979-81; mem. Nat. Fulbright Selection Com., 1990-92; mem. advanced placement devel. com. for Spanish, Ednl. Testing Svc., 1993-2000, chair, 1996-99, chief reader AP Spanish 2000-04. Spanish Ministry of Fgn. Affairs scholar, 1954-56; Danforth grantee, 1960-62, 63-64; N.Y. State Regents scholar, 1950-54, Brown U. scholar, 1960-62. Mem. Am. Assn. Tchrs. Spanish and Portuguese, AAUP, MLA, Am. Council Teaching of Fgn. Langs., N.Y. State Assn. Fgn. Lang. Tchrs., Phi Beta Kappa, Sigma Delta Pi. Roman Catholic. Office: St Lawrence U Dept Modern Langs Lits Canton NY 13617 Business E-Mail: ritagoldberg@stlawu.edu.

GOLDBERG, ROBERT B., molecular biologist, educator; b. Cleve., May 28, 1944; BS in botany, Ohio Univ., Athens, OH, 1966; MS in genetics, Univ. Ariz., Tucson, 1969, PhD in genetics, 1971. Asst. prof. Wayne State U., Detroit, 1973—76, UCLA, 1976—78, assoc. prof., 1978—83, prof., 1983—96, Disting. Prof. Molecular, Cell, and Devel. Biology, 1996—. Program dir. Genetic Mechanisms for Crop Improvement USDA, 1983, program dir. Plant Genetics and Molecular Biology, 84; chmn. Divsn. Cell, Molecular and Plant Biology UCLA, 1983, dir. Plant Molecular Biology Program, 1991—96, dir. Multicampus Seed Inst., 1986—; chair Edn. Found. Am. Soc. Plant Biologists, 1998—2002; co-founder and dir. Ceres Inc., Malibu, Calif., 1996—. Edtl. bd. (jour.) Developmental Genetics, 1981—84, Plant Molecular Biology, 1982—87, Molecular and General Genetics, 1982—87, Science, 1986—89, Sexual Plant Reproduction, 1998—, founding editor and editor-in-chief The Plant Cell, 1988—93. Named to NAS, 2001; recipient Recognition Disting. Tchg. and Rsch., Ohio House Rep., 1991, Disting. Svc. Award, Am. Soc. Plant Physiologists, 1993, Nat. Order Sci. Merit, Pres. of Brazil, 1998, Gold Shield Award, UCLA, 1998; grantee Professorship, Howard Hughes Med. Inst., 2002—. Office: UCLA Life Sciences Building 2835 Los Angeles CA 90095 Office Phone: 310-825-9093, 310-825-3270. E-mail: bobg@ucla.edu.

GOLDBERG, SAMUEL, retired mathematician, foundation administrator; b. NYC, Mar. 14, 1925; s. Gedalia and Fannie (Lieberman) G.; m. Marcia Chinitz, June 21, 1953; 1 son, David. BS, CCNY, 1944; PhD, Cornell U., 1950. Instr., then asst. prof. math. Lehigh U., Bethlehem, Pa., 1950-53; mem. faculty Oberlin (Ohio) Coll., 1953—, prof. math., 1961-85, emeritus prof., 1985—; program officer Alfred P. Sloan Found., NYC, 1985-90, cons., 1990—. Vis. assoc. prof. Harvard U. Grad. Sch. Bus. Adminstrn., 1959-60; vis. prof. U. W.Australia, 1976; mem. com. math. in social scis. Social Sci. Research Council, 1979; participant African Math. Project, Mombasa, Kenya, 1965, 68 Author: Probability: An Introduction, 1960 (translated into Greek, German and Spanish, paperback edit.), Introduction to Difference Equations, 1958 (translated into Spanish, German and Japanese, also paperback edit.), Some Illustrative Examples of the Use of Undergraduate Mathematics in the Social Sciences, 1977, Probability in Social Science, 1983. Bd. dirs. Allen Meml. Hosp., Oberlin, 1980-85, 92-2000. Served with AUS, 1944-46. NSF sci. faculty fellow, 1960-61, 67-68. Mem. Math. Assn. Am., Am. Math. Soc., Phi Beta Kappa, Sigma Xi.

GOLDBERG, SETH A., lawyer; b. NYC, Aug. 20, 1953; s. Seymour I. and Florence (Rovensky) Goldberg; m. Joan E. Shapiro, July 29, 1978; children: David, Emily. BA in History, SUNY, Binghamton, 1975; JD, Stanford U., 1978. Bar: D.C. 1978, Calif. 1991. Assoc. Steptoe & Johnson, Washington, 1978-86, ptnr., 1986—. Mem.: ABA, Am. Inn Ct. Found. (pres. 2005—06, trustee 2006—). Home: 8303 Whittier Blvd Bethesda MD 20817-3124 Office: 1330 Connecticut Ave NW Washington DC 20036-1704 Home Phone: 301-469-7823; Office Phone: 202-429-6213. Business E-Mail: sgoldberg@steptoe.com.

GOLDBERG, STANLEY IRWIN, real estate company executive; b. Newport News, Va., May 13, 1934; s. David and Sara (Levy) G.; m. Marilyn Levin, Nov. 22, 1963 (dec. Oct. 1970); 1 child, Andrew Garfield. Student, Coll. William and Mary, 1952—54, U. Va., 1954—55. Lic. real estate broker, Va. V.p. Bedding Supply Co., Inc., Newport News, 1956-59, exec. v.p., 1960-61, pres., 1962-70; mng. ptnr. Goldkress Investment Co., Newport News, 1970—, also bd. dirs.; pres. Mut. Realty Corp., Newport News, 1973—. Trustee Temple Sinai, Newport News. Served with USAF, 1957-58. Mem. Nat. Assn. Realtors, Va. Assn. Realtors, Va. Peninsula Assn. Realtors, Elks. Home: 19 Hopemont Dr Newport News VA 23606-2146 Office: 11116 Jefferson Ave Newport News VA 23601-2551 Office Phone: 757-595-9529. Personal E-mail: asc67@aol.com.

GOLDBERG, STANLEY JOSHUA, federal judge; b. Balt., Feb. 16, 1939; s. Isidore and Lillian Frances (Kravatz) G.; m. Susan Jane Coplin, July 1, 1962; Rachel Hilary, David Mark. BS, U. Md., 1960, LLB, 1964; postgraduate student, NYU, 1966-69. Bar: Md. 1964, US Dist. Ct. Md. 1964, NJ 1967, US Dist. Ct. NJ 1967, US Tax Ct. 1968. Tax trial atty. Office of Chief Counsel IRS, NYC, 1965-69, 1971-76; assoc. Buckmaster, White, Mindel & Clarke, Balt., 1970; spl. trial atty. IRS, NYC, 1976-84, asst. dist. counsel, 1984-85; spl. trial judge US Tax Ct., Washington, 1985—. Mem.: DC Bar Assn. (hon.), Am. Coll. Tax Counsel (hon.). Office: US Tax Ct 400 2nd St NW Washington DC 20217-0002

GOLDBERG, STANLEY MORTON, surgeon, educator; b. Mpls., May 20, 1932; s. Isadore Meyer and Blanche Halpern Goldberg; m. Luella Gross, June 23, 1958; children: Ellen Goldberg Lugar, Frederic Gross, Martha Goldberg Aronson. BA cum laude, U. Minn., Mpls., 1953, BS, 1954, MD, 1956; Doctors Honoris Causa (hon.), U. Lleida, 2005. Diplomate Am. Bd. Colon and Rectal Surgery. Intern Mpls. Gen. Hosp., Hennepin County Med. Ctr., 1956—57; resident in gen. surgery Vets. Hosp., Mpls., 1957—60; resident in colon and rectal surgery U. Minn., Mpls., 1960—62, sr. resident in gen. surgery, 1962—63; Am. Cancer Soc. fellow St. Mark's Hosp., London, 1962; cons. colon and rectal surgery dept. surgery VA Med. Ctr., Mpls., 1964, head divsn. colon and rectal surgery, 1969—92; dir. residency program divsn. colon and rectal surgery U. Minn. Med. Sch., Mpls., 1972—92, clin. prof. surgery, 1972—; med. dir. enterstomal therapy edn. program Abbott Northwestern Hosp., Mpls., 1979—95. Bd. advisors Cine'-Med Inc., 1985—; mem. staff Fairview Southdale Hosp., 1965—, Hennepin County Med. Ctr., 1963—2001, U. Minn. Hosps., 1972—; lectr, spkr. in field; vis. prof. numerous univs. Mem. editl. bd.: Internat. Jour. Colorectal Disease, others; contbr. articles to profl. jours., chapters to books. Named Surg. Alumnus of Yr., U. Minn., 2006; recipient Diehl award, Minn. Med. Found., 1996; Stanley M. Goldberg chair named in his honor, U. Minn. Med. Sch., 2000. Fellow: ACS (mem. grad. edn. com. 1977—81), Am. Soc. Colon and Rectal Surgeons, Assn. Coloproctology Gt. Britain and Ireland (hon.), Philippine Coll. Surgeons (hon.), Royal Soc. Medicine (hon.), French Assn. Surgeons (hon.), Royal Can. Soc. Colon and Rectal Surgeons (hon.), Royal Australasian Coll. Surgeons (hon.), Assn. Surgeons Gt. Britain and Ireland (hon.), Royal Coll. Physicians and Surgeons Glasgow (hon.), Philippine Soc. Colon and Rectal Surgeons (hon.), Filipino Soc. Colon and Rectal Surgeons (hon.); mem.: AMA, numerous others, Western Surg. Assn., Pan Pacific Surg. Assn. (v.p. 2002), Nat. Found. Ileitis and Colitis, Milligan Surg. Soc. Perth, Mpls. Acad. Medicine (v.p. 2002, pres. 2003), Mpls. Surg. Soc. (pres. 1977—78), Midwest Soc. Colon and Rectal Surgeons (sec. 1970—82), Lillehei Surg. Soc., Collegium Internat. Chirurgie, Crohn's Colitis Found. Am., European Assn. Coloproctology, Assn. Coloproctology Gt. Britain and Ireland, Am. Surg. Assn., Am. Gastroenterol. Assn., Am. Cancer Soc. (mem. nat. adv. com. on colorectal cancer 1983—86), Am. Bd. Colon and Rectal Surgery (v.p. 1979—80, pres. 1980—81, mem. adv. coun. 1985—88), Royal Soc. Medicine (hon.), Sydney Colo-Rectal Surg. Soc. (hon.), Mex. Assn. Gen. Surgeons (hon.), Chilean Surg. Soc. (hon.), Royal Coll. Surgeons Eng. (hon.), Uruguayan Surg. Soc. (hon.), Hitchcock Surg. Soc. (hon.), Bolivian Soc. Coloproctology (hon.), Spanish Assn. Surgeons (hon.), European Soc. Coloproctology, Am. Soc. Colon and Rectal Surgeons (mem. coun. 1978—79, v.p. 1978—79, mem. coun. 1982—85, pres. 1983—84, Mentor's award 1993), St. Mark's Assn., Phi Rho Sigma. Office: Colon and Rectal Surgery Assoc Ltd 6363 France Ave S Ste 212 Minneapolis MN 55435 Home: 7019 Tupa Dr Minneapolis MN 55439 Office Phone: 651-312-1700.

GOLDBERG, STEVEN MURRAY, lawyer; b. San Francisco, Feb. 25, 1957; s. Daniel T. and Tanette Goldberg; m. Renée Miguel, Aug. 25, 1984; children: Rachel, Sarah. BA in Journalism, San Jose State U., 1979; JD, U. Calif., Berkeley, 1984. Bar: Calif. 1984, US Dist. Ct. (no. dist. Calif.) 1984. Assoc. Schwab & Hibser, San Francisco, 1985-89, Goldberg & Brauer, San Francisco, 1989-92, Ropers, Majeski, Kohn & Bentley, Santa Rosa, Calif., 1992-96, Lanahan & Reilly, Santa Rosa, Calif., 1997; ptnr. Friedemann Goldberg, Santa Rosa, Calif. Mem. Redwood Empire estate planning coun., Santa Rosa, 1993—. Contbr. articles to profl. publs. Pres. bd. dirs. Village in the Park Homeowners Assn., Daly City, Calif., 1991-92; mem. estate planning subcommittee Marin and Sonoma Jewish Cmty. Fedn., San Rafael, Calif., 1992—. Named a Super Lawyer, No. Calif. Super Lawyers, 2006; named one of Top 100 Attys., Worth mag., 2005, 2006. Mem. State Bar of Calif. (estate planning and taxation sects. 1989—), Sonoma Bar Assn. Avocations: fiction writing, science, astronomy, sports. Office: Friedemann Goldberg LLP Ste 201 420 Aviation Blvd Santa Rosa CA 95403 Office Phone: 707-543-4900. Office Fax: 707-543-4910. E-mail: sgoldberg@frigolaw.com.

GOLDBERG, SUSAN, editor; b. 1959; m. Gary Blonston (dec. Apr. 1999). Reporter Seattle Post-Intelligencer; asst. city editor Detroit Free Press, San Jose Mercury News, 1987—89, acting city editor, mng. editor, 1999—2003, v.p., 2001—07, exec. editor, 2003—07; dep. mng. editor USA Today, 1989—99; editor Cleve. Plain Dealer, 2007—. Chair mng. editors leadership and mgmt. com. AP. Mem. bd. visitors Northwestern U. Medill Sch. Journalism; bd. mem. Silicon Valley chpt. Am. Cancer Soc., 2003—. Mem.: Am. Soc. Newspaper Editors (bd. dirs.), Downtown San Jose Rotary Club. Office: Cleve Plain Dealer 1801 Superior Ave NE Cleveland OH 44114-2198 Office Phone: 216-999-4800. Office Fax: 216-999-6354.*

GOLDBERG, VICTOR JOEL, retired data processing company executive; b. Chgo., Oct. 19, 1933; s. Albert J. and Ruth R. (Rosenberg) Goldbert; m. Harriet A. David, June 1, 1958 (dec. Apr. 1998); children: Susan A., Alan J.; m. Patricia A. Waldeck, Aug. 11, 2001. BS, Northwestern U., 1955, MBA, 1956. With IBM Corp., Armonk, NY, 1959-93, corp. dir. bus. plans, 1977-78, v.p. communications, 1979-81, corp. v.p., pres. communication products div., 1981-83, pres. nat. distbn. div., 1983-86, v.p. asst. group exec. marketing, 1986-88, v.p. mgmt. systems, 1988-93; dir. Edn. Through Music, 1998—. Mem. Forum for World Affairs, 1988-97; mem. planning bd. Village of Scarsdale, 1999—, chmn., 2002-05; bd. govs. Am. Jewish Com., 1998-06; trustee Inst. Internat. Edn., 1978—, mem. exec. com., 1984—, vice chmn., 1988-2004; trustee Mental Health Assn., Westchester, 1984-99, exec. v.p., 1997-99; trustee Westchester Reform Temple, 1995-98, Scarsdale Found., 1998—, v.p. 1999-2004; dir. Actors Shakespeare Co., 1995-98; chmn. adv. com. Long Term Care Ombudsmen Program, Westchester County, 1995-98; trustee New Alternatives for Children, 1997-2001, treas., 1998-2001; v.p. Thanks to Scandavia, Inc., 2001—; trustee Ford Found. Internat. Fellowships program, 2001—. With US Army, 1956—59. Mem.: Beta Gamma Sigma.

GOLDBERG, VICTOR PAUL, law educator; b. 1941; BA, Oberlin Coll., Ohio, 1963, MA, 1964; PhD, Yale U., 1970. From asst. to full prof. U. Calif., Davis, 1967-83; prof. Northwestern U., Evanston, Ill., 1983-88; prof., co-dir. Ctr. Law and Econ. Studies Columbia U., NYC, 1988—, Thomas Macioce prof. law. Assoc. prof. U. Calif., Berkeley, 1977; prof. U. Va., Charlottesville, 1981; mem. Inst. for Advanced Study, Princeton, N.J., 1978-79. Fellow Ctr. for Study of Pub. Choice, Blacksburg, Va., 1975-76. Office: Columbia U Sch Law JG810 435 W 116th St New York NY 10027-7297 Office Phone: 212-854-8380. E-mail: vpgol@yahoo.com, vpg@law.columbia.edu.

GOLDBERG, WHOOPI (CARYN ELAINE JOHNSON), actress, comedienne; b. NYC, Nov. 13, 1955; d. Robert and Emma (Harris) Johnson; m. Alvin Martin, 1973 (div. 1979); 1 child, Alexandrea Martin; m. David Claessen, 1986 (div. 1988); m. Lyle Trachtenberg, 1994 (div. 1995). Mem. San Diego Repertory Theatre, 1975—80, Blake St. Hawkeyes, Berkeley, Calif., 1980—84. Actor: (plays) Living on the Edge of Chaos, 1988 (Calif. theatre award outstanding achievement, 1988); prodr.: (Broadway plays) Thoroughly Modern Millie (Tony award for best musical, 2002); actor: A Funny Thing Happened on the Way to the Forum, 1996—98, Funny Girl, 2002; actor, prodr. (Broadway plays) Ma Rainey's Black Bottom, 2003, actor, writer (one-person show Broadway plays) Whoopi Goldberg on Broadway, 1984—85; actor: (films) Citizen, 1982, The Color Purple, 1985 (Golden Globe for best actress motion picture drama, 1986), Jumpin' Jack Flash, 1986, Burglar, 1986, Fatal Beauty, 1987, The Telephone, 1987, Clara's Heart, 1988, Homer and Eddie, 1989, Beverly Hills Brats, 1989, Comicitis, 1989, The Long Walk Home, 1990, Ghost, 1990 (Acad. award for best supporting actress, 1991, Golden Globe for best supporting actress motion picture, 1991), Soapdish, 1991, Blackbird Fly, 1991, The Player, 1992, Sister Act, 1992, House Party 2, 1992, Sarafina!, 1992, Made in America, 1993, National Lampoon's Loaded Weapon 1, 1993, Sister Act 2: Back in the Habit, 1993, Naked in New York, 1993, (voice) The Lion King, 1994, Naked in New York, 1994, The Little Rascals, 1994, Corrina, Corrina, 1994, Star Trek: Generations, 1994, (voice) The Pagemaster, 1994, Boys on the Side, 1995, Moonlight and Valentino, 1995, Theodore Rex, 1995, Bogus, 1996, The Ghost of Mississippi, 1996, Eddie, 1996, Tales from the Crypt Presents: Bordello of Blood, 1996, The Associate, 1996, (voice) A Christmas Carol, 1997, How Stella Got Her Groove Back, 1998, (voice) The Rugrats Movie, 1998, Alegria, 1998, Deep End of the Ocean, 1999, Jackie's Back!, 1999, Girl, Interrupted, 1999, (narrator) A Second Chance at Life, 2000, More Dogs Than Bones, 2000, Kingdom Come, 2001, Monkeybone, 2001, Rat Race, 2001, (narrator) Golden Dreams, 2001, Star Trek: Nemesis, 2002, Blizzard, 2003, Jiminy Glick in La La Wood, 2004, (voice) Pinocchio 3000, 2004, (voice) Racing Stripes, 2005, (voice) Doogal, 2006, (voice) Everyone's Hero, 2006; (TV films) My Past Is My Own, 1989, Kiss Shot, 1989, Defenders of Dynatron City, 1992, (voice) Yuletide in the 'hood, 1993, In the Gloaming, 1997, (voice) Mother Goose: A Rappin' and Rhymin' Special, 1997, Cinderella, 1997, A Knight in Camelot, 1998, Jackie's Back!, 1999, The Magical Land of the Leprechauns, 1999, Alice in Wonderland, 1999, (voice) Madeline: My Fair Madeline, 2002, It's a Very Muppet Christmas Movie, 2002; actor, exec. prodr. (TV films) Call Me Claus, 2001, What Makes a Family, 2001, actor, prodr. Good Fences, 2003; actor: (TV series) Star Trek: The Next Generation, 1988—94, (voice) Captain Planet and the Planeteers, 1990, Baghdad Cafe, 1990, (voice) Happily Ever After: Fairy Tales for Every Child, 1997, (voice) Foxbusters, 1999, (voice) Liberty's Kids, 2002, Littleburg, 2004; host: (TV series, talk show) The Whoopie Goldberg Show, 1992—93; actor, exec. prodr. (TV series) Whoopi, 2003; actor: (TV specials) Circus of the Stars #15, 1990, Tales from the Whoop: Hot Rod Brown, Class Clown, 1990; dir., writer, performer (TV specials) Comic Relief, 1986; co-prodr.: (films) The Mao Game, 1999; exec. prodr.: (TV films) Ruby's Bucket of Blood, 2001; prodr.: (TV series) Hollywood Squares, 1998—2002; exec. prodr.: Strong Medicine, 2000; prodr.: (TV miniseries) Oh What A Time It Was, 1999; author: Alice, 1992, Whoopi Goldberg Book, 1997, Whoopi's Big Book of Manners, 2006; disc jockey Wake-up with Whoopi, 103.5 KTU, NYC, 2006—, co-host The View, 2007—. Named Entertainer of the Yr., NAACP, 1990; recipient Grammy award for album of Broadway show, 1985, Hans Christian Andersen award for outstanding achievement by a dyslexic, 1987, Humanitarian of Yr. award, Starlight Found., 1989, Star on Hollywood Walk of Fame, 2001, Mark Twain Prize for Am. Humor, Kennedy Center, 2001.*

GOLDBERGER, ALAN STEVEN, lawyer; b. Newark, Jan. 31, 1949; s. Milton Howard and Miriam (Kaplan) G.; m. Carole Selikowitz, Oct. 13, 1985. AB, Franklin and Marshall Coll., 1971; JD, Rutgers U., 1974. Bar: N.J. 1975, N.Y. 1985, Md. 1999, U.S. Dist. Ct. N.J. 1975, U.S. Dist. Ct. (so. dist.) N.Y. 1992, U.S. Dist. Ct. Md. 1999. Ptnr. Goldberger & Goldberger, Clifton, N.J., 1975—. Author: Sports Officiating: A Legal Guide, 1984, 2d edit., 2007; co-author: Sport, Physical Activity, and the Law, 1993, 3d edit., 2007. Mem.: ABA (bus. law sect., co-chmn. nonprofit athletic orgn. sub-com., chmn. trade assns. com.), Nat. Assn. Girls and Women in Sport (chmn. com. legal issues), Internat. Assn. Approved Basketball Ofcls. Jewish. Avocations: officiating basketball, baseball and football. Office: Goldberger & Goldberger 1373 Broad St PO Box 447 Clifton NJ 07015-0447 Office Phone: 973-471-9200. E-mail: alan@reflaw.com.

GOLDBERGER, ARTHUR EARL, JR., information technology executive; BS in Systems Engring., U. Ariz., 1974, BS in Indsl. Engring., 1975; MS in Indsl. Engring., Tex. A&M U., 1977; MBA, U. Denver, 2005. Cert. Novell engr.; cert. Microsoft sys. engr.; registered profl. engr., Ky., Tex., Mo., Ariz., Fla. Gen. engr. DARCOM/RRAD, Texarkana, Tex., 1975-77; mgr. DARCOM/AVSCOM, St. Louis, 1977-81; div. dir. prodn. improvement McDonnell Douglas, St. Louis, 1981-90; pres. Spectrum Techs., Inc., St. Louis, 1990—2001; founder, pres. Salientinfo Inc., Littleton, Colo., 2001—, Salient Global Resources, Inc., 2006—. Chmn. CAD/Expert System Tool Design, Seattle, 1991; cons. in field. Author: Real Leadership, 1993, Radical Leadership, 1997; contbr. articles to profl. jours. Bd. dirs. Engrs. Club St. Louis, 1978, Nat. Com. on U.S. Competitiveness, Washington, 1989—; judge, coach Scientific Olympiad, Mo., 1989. Recipient Quality Leadership award McDonnell Douglas Corp., 1988; named expert in inventory and prodn. mgmt. Am. Prodn. and Inventory Control Soc. Mem. IEEE (chmn. 1987-88, vice chmn. vehicle tech. soc. conf. 1991, bd. dirs. nat. com. on U.S. competitiveness, Leadership award 1988), Inst. Indsl. Engrs., Soc. Mfrg. Engrs., Data Mgmt. Assn. (bd. dirs. 1999—), Alpha Pi Mu, Tau Beta Pi Achievements include rsch. in strategic marketing, global business strategy, radio frequency identification, information systems, and supply chain execution, mfg. technology, process engring., healthcare operations and mgmt., RF and Network Comm., info. sys., ops. analysis, integration, and six sigma quality/process improvement.

GOLDBERGER, ARTHUR STANLEY, economics professor; b. NYC, Nov. 20, 1930; s. David M. and Martha (Greenwald) G.; m. Iefke Engelsman, Aug. 19, 1957; children: Nina Judith, Nicholas Bernard. BS, N.Y.U., 1951; MA, U. Mich., 1952, PhD, 1958. Acting asst. prof. econs. Stanford U., 1956-59; assoc. prof. econs. U. Wis., 1960- 63, prof., 1963-70, H.M. Groves prof., 1970-79, Vilas research prof., 1979-98, prof. emeritus, 1998—. Vis. prof. Center Planning and Econ. Rsch., Athens, Greece, 1964-65, U. Hawaii, 1969, 71, Stanford U., 1990, 96, 2000; Keynes vis. prof. U. Essex, 1968-69. Author: (with L.R. Klein) An Econometric Model of the United States, 1929-52, 1955, Impact Multipliers and Dynamic Properties, 1959, Econometric Theory, 1964, Topics in Regression Analysis, 1968, Functional Form and Utility, 1987, A Course in Econometrics, 1991, Introductory Econometrics, 1998; editor: (with O.D. Duncan) Structural Equation Models in the Social Sciences, 1973, (with D.J. Aigner) Latent Variables in Socioeconomic Models, 1976; Assoc. editor: Jour. Econometrics, 1973-77; bd. editors: Am. Econ. Rev, 1964-66, Jour. Econ. Lit, 1975-77. Fulbright fellow Netherlands Sch. Econs., 1955-56, 59-60; fellow Ctr. for Advanced Study in Behavioral Scis., Stanford, 1976-77, 80-81; Guggenheim fellow Stanford U., 1972-73, 85. Fellow Am. Statis. Assn., Econometric Soc. (council 1975-80, 82-87), Am. Acad. Arts and Scis., AAAS; mem. Am. Econ. Assn. (Disting. fellow 1988), Nat. Acad. Scis., Royal Netherlands Acad. Scis. Home: 2828 Sylvan Ave Madison WI 53705-5228 Office: U Wis Dept Econs 1180 Observatory Dr Madison WI 53706-1320 Business E-Mail: asgoldbe@wisc.edu.

GOLDBERGER, GEORGE STEFAN, finance company executive; b. Oradea, Romania, July 3, 1947; arrived in U.S., 1962; s. Ladislau and Margareta (Schwartz) Goldberger; 1 child, David Michael. BS in Systems Engring., Bklyn. Poly. U., 1969; MBA in Fin., U. Pa., 1975. Sys. analyst Grumman Corp., Bethpage, NY, 1969-73; ops. analyst Internat. Paper Co., NYC, 1973—74; mgmt. cons. Booz, Allen & Hamilton, 1975; asst. to chmn. W.R. Grace & Co., 1977—85; pres. Citizens Against Govt. Waste, Washington, 1986-89; COO Pres.'s Pvt. Sector Survey on Cost Control (Grace Commn.), 1986—89; dir. mergers and acquisitions Figgie Internat., Inc., Willoughby, Ohio, 1989-90; pres. Goldberger & Assoc., Inc., NYC, 1991—98; chief bus. officer, CFO Progenitor Cell Therapy, LLC, Hackensack, NJ, 1999—. Contbr. articles to publs. Avocation: skiing. Personal E-mail: georgegoldberger@aol.com.

GOLDBERGER, MELVIN TOBIAS, bank executive; b. Knoxville, Tenn., June 6, 1919; s. Harry and Grace (Reich) G.; m. Betty Knox, June 4, 1944; children: Diane, Susan, Margy. BSBA, Ohio State U., 1940; postgrad., U. Tenn., 1940—41. Pres. Sq. Supply Co., Knoxville, 1946-64; chmn. Vector Co., 1965-72; pres. Seventh Investment Bancing Corp., Boca Raton, Fla., 1973—, Regency Highland Corp., Boca Raton, 1973—81. Treas. Fla. Philharm. Orch., Ft. Lauderdale, Fla., 1985-94, life bd. dirs., hon. life treas. emeritus, 1992-. Shrine mem. Kerbela Temple, 1947—; vice chmn. bd. dirs. Mae Volen Sr. Ctr., Boca Raton, 1989-2000, chmn. bd. dirs., 2001-02. Capt. Med. Adminstrn. Corps, U.S. Army, 1943-46. Mem. Elks Club. Avocations: golf, tennis, sports. Office: Seventh Investment Bancing Corps 1599 NW 9th Ave Boca Raton FL 33486 Office Phone: 561-417-4100. Personal E-mail: bocagrove6@woh.rr.com.

GOLDBERGER, PAUL JESSE, dean, architecture critic, writer; b. Passaic, NJ, Dec. 4, 1950; s. Morris and Edna (Kronman) G.; m. Susan Lynn Solomon, Feb. 17, 1980; children: Adam Hirsh, Benjamin James Solomon, Alexander David Solomon. BA, Yale U., 1972; LHD (hon.), Pratt Inst., 1992; LHD (hon.), Ctr. Creative Studies; doctoral degree (hon.), NY Sch. Interior Design; LHD (hon.), U. Miami, 2004, Kenyon Coll., 2005. Staff editor The New York Times Mag., NYC, 1972-73; architecture critic The New York Times, NYC, 1973—90, editor cultural news, 1990-94, chief cultural corr., 1994—97, freelance contbr., 1995; architecture critic-Sky Line Column The New Yorker, NYC, 1997—; dean The New Sch. Parsons Sch. Design, NYC, 2004—06; Joseph Urban prof. design and arch. The New Sch., 2006—. Vis. lectr. architecture Yale U., 1984— Author: The City Observed: New York, An Architectural Guide to Manhattan, 1978, The Skyscraper, 1981, On the Rise: Architecture and Design in a Post-Modern Age, 1983, Houses of the Hamptons, 1986, Above New York, 1988, The World Trade Ctr. Remembered, 2001, Up From Ground Zero, 2004; contbr. articles and essays to profl. publs. Bd. trustees Nat. Trust Historic Preservation, 2005—; mem. bd. overseers Parsons Sch. Design, 1986—90, 1994—2004; bd. dirs. Jewish Found. for Christian Rescuers, 1994—2004, Guild Hall, East Hampton, NY, 1986—90; bd. trustees Kenyon Coll., 2003—; bd. trustees ethical culture Fieldston Sch., 2004—. Recipient Pres. medal Mcpl. Art Soc., NYC, 1984, Pulitzer prize for Disting. Criticism, 1984, Roger Starr Journalism award Citizens Housing and Planning Coun., 1987, medal of honor NY Landmarks Preservation Found., 1991, Lit. Lion award NY Pub. Libr., 1993, Preservation Achievement Award, NYC Landmarks Preservation Commn, 1996. Mem. AIA (hon., medal 1981), Soc. Archtl. Historians (bd. dirs. 1977-79), Century Assn. Office: The New Sch 72 Fifth Ave New York NY 10011 Home Phone: 212-874-0505; Office Phone: 212-229-1112. Business E-Mail: pjg@newschool.edu.

GOLDBERG-SCHAIBLE, JOCELYN HOPE SCHNIER, market research professional; b. NYC, Mar. 29, 1953; d. Alex and Eileen Rosalie (Firstenberg) Schnier. AB, Princeton U., 1974; MBA, Harvard U., 1977. Statis. technician John Hancock Inc., Boston, 1974-75; product mgr. Gen. Foods Corp., White Plains, N.Y., 1977-78; strategic and tactical bus. planning analyst Bausch & Lomb Corp., Rochester, N.Y., 1979-81; mgmt. assoc. Gordon S. Black Corp. Harris Interactive, Rochester, 1981-84; pres. Rochester Rsch. Group, 1985—. Dirs. adv. coun. M&T Bank. Bd. dirs. U. Rochester Med. Ctr., 1991-98; life mem. JCC Greater Rochester, 1998-2004; trustee Geva Theater, 1992-99; v.p. class of '74, Princeton U., 1999—. Recipient achievement award Wall Street Jour., 1977. Mem. Profl. Ski Instrs. Am. (cert.), Harvard U. Bus. Sch. Club (bd. dirs.), Princeton Club Rocheater (pres. 2007—), Princeton Alumni Coun. (mem. exec. com. 2006—). Home: 1666 Strong Rd Victor NY 14564-9133 Office: PO Box 22954 Rochester NY 14692-2954 Home Phone: 585-924-3942; Office Phone: 585-924-3620. Business E-Mail: Jocelyn@RochesterResearchGroup.com.

GOLD-BIKIN, LYNNE Z., lawyer; b. NYC, Apr. 23, 1938; d. Herbert Benjamin Zapoleon and Muriel Claire (Wimpfheimer) Sarnoff; m. Roy E. Gold, Aug. 20, 1956 (div. July 1976); children: Russell, Sheryl, Lisa, Michael; m. Stephen L. Fine, Dec. 17, 2006. BA summa cum laude, Albright Coll., 1973; JD, Villanova Law Sch., 1976; degree (hon.), 1996. Bar: Pa. 1976, U.S. Dist. Ct. (ea. dist.) Pa. 1976, U.S. Supreme Ct. 1979. Assoc. Pechner, Dorfman, Wolffe, Rounick & Cabot, Norristown, Pa., 1976-81; ptnr. Olin, Neil, Frock & Gold-Bikin, Norristown, 1981-82; pres. Gold-Bikin, Welsh & Assocs., Norristown, 1982-96, Wolf, Block, Schorr & Solis-Cohen, Norristown, 1996—. Course planner for 12 manuals on continuing legal edn., 1978—; pres. coun. Albright Coll., Reading, Pa., 1982-87. Author: Pennsylvania Marital Agreements, 1984, Divorce Practice Handbook, 1994, The Divorce Trial Manual, 2003; contbg. editor, Fairshare Mag., 1987—. Bd. trustees Albright Coll., 2000—. Named Pa. Honor Roll of Women, 1996, Pa. Super Lawyers, 2004. Fellow Am. Acad. Matrimonial Lawyers, Internat. Acad. Matrimonial Lawyers, Am. Coll. Matrimonial Trial Lawyers, Am. Bar Found., Am. Law Inst., Pa. Bar Found.; mem. ABA (family law sect. chair 1994-95, ho. of dels. 1995-2001, 2002—, bd. govs. 1998-2001), Pa. Bar Assn. (family law sect. coun. mem. 1980-89), Montgomery County Bar Assn. (chmn. family law com. 1984-86), Pa. Trial Lawyers Assn. (chmn. family law sect. 1988-90). Office: Wolf Block Schorr & Solis-Cohen One West Main St Norristown PA 19401-0869 Office Phone: 610-278-1511. Business E-Mail: lgold-bikin@wolfblock.com.

GOLDBLATT, BARRY LANCE, manufacturing executive; b. Palo Alto, Calif., July 29, 1945; s. Samuel and Joan Charlotte (Morton) Goldblatt. BS, U. So. Calif., 1967, MBA, 1968. Supr. market rsch. for brands Procter & Gamble Co., Cin., 1968-71; mgr. market rsch. Personal Products Co. subs. Johnson & Johnson, 1971-74; assoc. dir. consumer rsch. Johnson & Johnson Baby Products Co., Skillman, NJ, 1974-87; dir. market rsch. Johnson & Johnson Dental Care Co., New Brunswick, NJ, 1987-89, Johnson & Johnson Consumer Products Inc., Skillman, 1989-93; exec. dir. mktg. rsch. Johnson & Johnson Consumer Products Worldwide, 1994—2002; dir. market rsch. Church & Dwight Co., Inc., Princeton, NJ, 2002—. Bd. dirs. New Brunswick Hot Line, 1973; vol. Urban Cons. Group, 1977—. Recipient Cert. of Recognition Nat. Symposium Hispanic Bus. and Economy, Chgo., 1981, Cert. of Appreciation U. So. Calif., 1981. Mem. Am. Assn. Pub. Opinion Rschrs., U. So. Calif. MBAs, U. So. Calif. Commerce Assocs., Advt. Rsch. Found., Am. Mktg. Assn., Assn. MBA Execs., Mktg. Rsch. Coun.-The Conf. Bd., Am. Philat. Soc., U. So. Calif. Assocs., U. So. Calif. Alumni Club, Skull and Dagger, U. So. Calif. Alumni of N.J. (pres.), Zeta Beta Tau (asst. chpt. advisor Princeton U.). Republican. Home: 20 Andrews Ln Princeton NJ 08540-7633 Office: Church & Dwight Co Inc 469 N Harrison St Princeton NJ 08543 Office Phone: 609-279-7679. Business E-Mail: barry.goldblatt@churchdwight.com.

GOLDBLATT, HAL MICHAEL, photographer; b. Long Beach, Calif., Feb. 6, 1952; s. Arnold Phillip and Molly (Stearns) Goldblatt; m. Shawn Naomi Doherty, Aug. 27, 1974; children: Eliyahu Yonah, Tova Devorah, Raizel, Shoshana, Reuven Lev, Eliezer Noach, Esther Bayla, Rochel Leah, Zalman Ber, Perle Sara. BA in Math., Calif. State U., Long Beach, 1975; MBA, Trinity U., 2003. Owner Star Publs., Las Vegas, 1975—; treas. Goldblatt, Inc., Las Vegas, 1980—; pres. SDG Computer Svc., Las Vegas, 1985—; CFO Martin & Mills Ltd., Las Vegas, 1992-93; contr. Amland Devel., Las Vegas, 1993-95; CFO Stewart Constrn., Las Vegas, 1995-96; CEO Goldblatt, Inc., Las Vegas, 1996-97; cost acct. Ameristar Casinos, Inc., Las Vegas, 1997-99; dir. spl. projects Chabad So. Nev., Las Vegas, 1999-2000; dir. photography Lightons Creations, Las Vegas, 2000—; contr. Nev. Hand, Las Vegas, 2001—04; exec. MBA Trinity So. Univ., 2003; budget mgr. Rhodes Homes, 2004—06; mgr. Fountainbleau Resorts, 2006—; dec ch. mgr. Turnberry West Constrn., 2007—. Photographer Mikveh Yisorel, 1978, Chassidic Fabrangen, 1979, A Day at Disneyland, 1985, Shavous Trek, 1997, Garth Brooks World Tour, 1998, Care for Kids Telethon, 1998, 1999, Chanukah - Festival of Lights 1998-2004, 2006, prodr., engr. (audio cassettes) From the Heart of My Dreams, 1980, Middle Class Dreams, 1981, Uforatzta Trio, 1982. Fundraising chmn. Friends of Lubavitch, Long Beach, 1977; treas. Actor's Repertory Theatre, 1995—98, adv. bd., 1998—2003; founder, pres. Jews for Judaism, Long Beach, 1975—82, v.p., 1983—; bd. dirs. Congregation Lubavitch, Long Beach, 1987, 1991—92. Recipient Gold Press Card award, Forty Niner Newspaper, 1973, 1974, Floyd Durham Meml. award for outstanding cmty. svc., 1973, Georgie award, Actor's Repertory Theatre, 1995, ART Disting. Svc. award, 1996. Office: Turnberry West Constrn 2755 Las Vegas Blvd S Las Vegas NV 89109 Office Phone: 702-495-7367, 702-349-4538. Personal E-mail: halgoldblatt@cox.net.

GOLDBLATT, LAWRENCE I., dean, educator, researcher; Undergrad., Georgetown U., DDS cum laude, 1968; grad. oral pathology residency program, Ind. U., 1971, MSD, 1973. Diplomate Am. Bd. Oral and Maxillofacial Pathology. Rotating dental intern U.S. Naval Hosp., St. Albans, NY; lt. to comdr. U.S. Naval Res. U.S. Navy Dental Corps., 1971—89, ret., 1989; asst. prof. oral pathology Ind. U. Sch. Dentistry, 1973—77, assoc. prof. oral pathology, 1977—82, prof. oral pathology, 1982—93, 1997—, named assoc. dean grad. and postgrad. edn., 1988, named assoc. dean acad. affairs, 1990, dean, 1997—; prof. oral pathology, dean Case Western Res. U. Sch. Dentistry, 1994—96. Tchr., rschr. in field; past. commr. and chmn. ADA Joint Commn. on Nat. Dental Exams.; commr. ADA Commn. Dental Accreditation, 1998—2002. Contbr. scientific papers, articles to peer-reviewed jours. Fellow: Internat. Coll. Dentists, Am. Coll. Dentists; mem.: Internat. Assn. Dental Rsch., ADA, Am. Dental Edn. Assn. (v.p. deans), Am. Assn. Dental Rsch., Am. Acad. Oral and Maxillofacial Pathology, Ind. U. Sch. Dentistry Alumni Assn. (ad hoc mem. assn.'s bd. dirs.), Omicron Kappa Upsilon (past pres. Supreme chpt.). Office: 1121 West Michigan St Indianapolis IN 46202 Office Phone: 317-274-7461. Office Fax: 317-274-7188. Business E-Mail: lgoldbla@iupui.edu.

GOLDBLATT, SAMUEL, lawyer; b. NYC, 1953; BS, SUNY, Brockport, 1974; JD, SUNY, Buffalo, 1977. Bar: N.Y. 1978, U.S. Dist. Ct. (we. and so. dist. N.Y.) 1978, U.S. Dist Ct. (no. dist. Ill.) 1979. Ptnr., practice group leader Products Liability, Toxic and Complex Tort Nixon Peabody LLP, Buffalo, 1978—. Mem.: ABA, Defense Rsch. Inst. (mem. Drug & Medical Device Steering Com.), Product Liability Adv. Coun. Office: Nixon Peabody LLP 40 Fountain Plz Buffalo NY 14202-3716 Address: 437 Madison Ave New York NY 10022 Office Phone: 716-853-8121. E-mail: sgoldblatt@nixonpeabody.com.

GOLDBLATT, STANFORD JAY, lawyer; b. Chgo., Feb. 25, 1939; s. Maurice and Bernice (Mendelson) G.; m. Ann Dudley Cronkhite, June 17, 1968; children: Alexandra, Nathaniel, Jeremy. BA magna cum laude, Harvard U., 1960, LLB magna cum laude, 1963. Bar: Ill. 1963. Law clk. U.S. Ct. Appeals, 5th Jud. Circuit, New Orleans, 1963-64; mem. firm Winston & Strawn, Chgo., 1964-67; v.p. Goldblatt Bros., Inc., Chgo., 1967-76, pres., chief exec. officer, 1976-77, chmn. exec. com., 1977-78; ptnr. Hopkins & Sutter, 1978-97, Winston & Strawn, Chgo., 1997—. Bd. dirs. MacLean-Fogg Co., Divergence, Inc. Trustee U. Chgo., Cancer Rsch. Found., U. Chgo. Hosps. Mem. Econ. Club, Racquet Club, Comml. Club. Office: Winston & Strawn 35 W Wacker Dr Ste 4200 Chicago IL 60601-9703

GOLDBLATT, STEVEN HARRIS, law educator; b. Bklyn., Apr. 30, 1947; s. J. Irving and Ethel (Epstein) G.; m. Irene P. Burns, June 12, 1981; children: Sarah P., Elizabeth G.B. BA, Franklin & Marshall Coll., 1967; JD, Georgetown U., 1970. Bar: Pa. 1970, D.C. 1981. With Phila. Dist. Atty.'s Office, 1970-81; dir. Appellate Litigation Program Georgetown U. Law Ctr., Washington, 1981-83, prof. law, dir. Appellate Litigation Progam, 1983—. Chair rules adv. com. U.S. Ct. Appeals for Armed Forces, 1998—; dir. Supreme Ct. Inst., 2005—. Co-author: Analysis and Commentary to the Pennsylvania Crime Code, 1973, Three Prosecutors Look at the Crimes Code, 1974, Ineffective Assistance of Counsel: Attempts to Establish Minimum Standards for Criminal Cases, 1983; reporter Criminal Justice in Crisis, 1988, Achieving Justice in a Diverse America, 1992, An Agenda for Justice: ABA Perspectives on Criminal and Civil Justice Issues, 1996. Mem. ABA (criminal justice sect. chmn. amicus curiae briefs com. 1981-99, crisis in criminal justice com. 1990-91, criminal justice standards com. 2002-04) Office: Georgetown U Law Ctr 600 New Jersey Ave NW Washington DC 20001-2075 E-mail: goldblat@law.georgetown.edu.

GOLDBLOOM, VICTOR CHARLES, pediatrician; b. Montreal, Que., Can., July 31, 1923; s. Alton and Annie (Ballon) G.; m. Sheila Barshay, June 15, 1948; children: Susan, Michael, Jonathan. *Father Dr. Alton Goldbloom (1890-1968) was a pioneer of Canadian pediatrics. Wife Sheila is a retired professor of Social Work at McGill University and maintains varied comunity involvement. Daughter Susan Restler is founding partner in Knowledge in the Public Interest (kpublic.com) in New York which serves non-profit organizations. Son-in-law Peter Restler heads CAI (Canadian American Investments) in New York and Montreal. Son Michael, married to Fiona Macleod, vice-principal for Governmental and Inter-Institutional Relations of McGill University. Son Jonathan, married to Alice Switocz, heads his own communications firm in Montreal.* MD, McGill U., Montreal, 1945; LLD (hon.), U. Toronto, Ont., Can., 1980, Concordia U., Montreal, 1993, St. Anne's U., NS, Can., 1996; LittD, McGill U., Montreal, 1992; Dr. of Univ., U. Ottawa, Ont., 1994. Intern Montreal Children's Hosp., 1945-47, 1949-50; resident Babies Hosp., NYC, 1947-48; pvt. practice, 1950-80; min. environment and mcpl. affairs Govt. of Province Que., Quebec, 1970-76; pres., CEO Can. Coun. Christians and Jews, Toronto, 1979-87; pres. Internat. Coun. Christians and Jews, 1982-90, Environ. Pub. Hearings Bd., Quebec, 1987-90; exec. dir. Fonds de la recherche en santé du Qué., Montreal, 1990-91; commr. Official Langs. of Can., 1991—99. Can. del. UN Environment Conf., Stockholm, 1972, UN Habitat, Vancouver, B.C., 1976; tchr. McGill U., 1950—66; chair Montreal Regional Health and Social Svc. Bd., 2002—. Pres. (hon.) Jules and Paul-Emile Léger Found., Montreal; pres. Temple Emanu-El-Beth Sholom, Montreal, 2000—04, Jewish Immigrant Aid Svcs. of Montreal, 2005—. Decorated Companion Order of Can., officier Ordre Nat. du Que.; recipient Govt. of Can. award, 1990, James H. Graham award, Royal Coll. Physicians and Surgeons of Can., 1996, Centennial medal, Assn. médecins langue française du Can. Mem.: Can. Jewish Congress (chair Quebec region 2007—, Samuel Bronfman medal 2004), Allied Jewish Cmty. Svcs. Montreal (Samuel Bronfman medal 1989), Alliance Israelite Universelle (Rene Cassin medal 1987). Avocations: opera, singing. Home: 1455 Sherbrooke St W #701 Montreal PQ Canada H3G 1L2 Office Phone: 514-949-5043. E-mail: sgoldbloom@sympatico.ca.

GOLDBLUM, JEFF, actor; b. Pitts., Oct. 22, 1952; m. Patricia Gaul, 1980 (div 1986.), m. Geena Davis, Nov. 1, 1987, (div. Oct. 17, 1990). Studied at, Neighborhood Playhouse, NYC. Broadway theater debut in Two Gentlemen of Verona, 1971, also appeared in The Mooney Shapiro Songbook, 1981; off-Broadway appearances in Our Late Night, El Grande de Coca-Cola, City Sugar, 1978, The Pillowman, 2005 (Outer Critics Cir. award, outstanding featured actor in a play, 2005); films include California Split, 1974, Death Wish, 1974, Nashville, 1975, Next Stop Greenwich Village, 1976, Annie Hall, Between the Lines, 1977, Invasion of the Body Snatchers, 1978, Remember My Name, 1978, Thank God It's Friday, 1978, The Big Chill, 1983, The Right Stuff, 1983, Threshold, 1983, The Adventures of Buckaroo Banzai, 1984, Silverado, 1985, Into the Night, 1985, Transylvania 6-5000, 1985, The Fly, 1986 (Saturn award), Beyond Therapy, 1987, Vibes, 1988, Earth Girls Are Easy, 1989, The Tall Guy, 1990, The Bad Monkey, 1990, Mr. Frost, 1990, Deep Cover, 1992, The Favor, the Watch and the Very Big Fish, 1992, Fathers and Sons, 1992, Jurassic Park, 1993, Hideaway, 1995, Nine Months, 1995, Mad Dog Time, 1996, Independence Day, 1996, The Great White Hype, 1996, Lost World: The Jurassic Park, 1997, Hideaway, 1995, Nine Months, 1995, Mad Dog Time, 1996, The Great White Hype, 1996, Independence Day, 1996, Welcome to Hollywood, 1998, The Prince of Egypt (voice), 1998, Holy Man, 1998, Popcorn, 1999, Chain of Fools, 2000, Auggie Rose, 2000, One of the Hollywood Ten, 2000, Perfume, 2001, Cats & Dogs, 2001, Igby Goes Down, 2002, Dallas 362, 2003, Spinning Boris, 2003, Supermarket, 2004; TV movies include The Legend of Sleepy Hollow, 1980, Rehearsal for Murder, 1982, Ernie Kovacs: Between the Laughter, 1984, Lush Life, 1994, One of the Hollywood Ten, 2000, Legend of the Lost Tribe (voice), 2002, War Stories, 2003, The Life Aquatic with Steve Zissou, 2004, Mini's First Time, 2006, Fay Grim, 2006, Man of the Year, 2006; TV series Tenspeed and Brownshoe, 1980, Future Quest, 1994, Crank Yankers (voice), 2002; prodr. short action film: Little Surprises, 1995 (Acad. award nominee for best live short action film 1996); TV guest appearences Will & Grace, 2005.*

GOLDEN, ARTHUR, writer; b. Chattanooga, Tenn., 1956; m. Trudy Legee, 1982; 2 children. B in Art History, Harvard Coll.; MA in Japanese History, Columbia Univ., 1980; student, Beijing Univ.; MA in English, Boston Univ. Writer-in-residence Northwestern Univ., 2006. Author: (novels) Memoirs of a Geisha, 1997 (NY Times bestseller list, nominee, Am. Book award, 1999, made into feature film, 2005). Home: Brookline MA Mailing: care Lynn Pleshette Lit Agy 2700 N Beachwood Dr Los Angeles CA 90068-1922 Address: care Leigh Feldman Darhansoff Verrill & Feldman Lit Agy 236 W 26th St ste 802 New York NY 10001

GOLDEN, ARTHUR F., lawyer; b. Bklyn., Apr. 14, 1946; s. Isadore and Dorothy (Schisel) G.; m. Elisabeth Lee Smith, Aug. 28, 1971; children: Frederick Tucker, James Alexander, Eliza Emerson. BS, Rensselaer Poly. Inst., 1966; JD, NYU, 1969. Bar: NY 1970, US Ct. Appeals (2d cir.) 1970, US Dist. Ct. (so. dist.) NY 1972, US Supreme Ct. 1975, US Ct. Appeals (DC cir.) 1979, DC 1980, US Dist. Ct. DC 1980, US Dist. Ct. (ea. dist.) NY 1972, US Dist. Ct. (no. dist.) Ohio 1985, US Ct. Appeals (6th cir.) 1985, US Ct. Appeals (7th cir.) 1996. With Davis Polk & Wardwell, NYC, 1969—, ptnr., 1978—, co-founder Washington office, 1980—82, mem. mgmt. com., 1996—2005. Bd. dirs. Emerson Electric Co., 2000-; mem. fin. and governance com., ESCO Electronics Corp.; mem. exec. com., chmn. compensation com., 1990-96, Burns Internat. Svcs. Corp.; mem. exec. and audit and fin. coms., 1996-2000, Allegiance Corp., mem. audit and pub. policy com., 1996-99. Trustee Rensselaer Poly. Inst., 2005—. With USAR, 1968—74. Mem. ABA, Assn. of Bar of City of NY, NY State Bar Assn., NY State Cmtys. Aid Assn. (bd. mgrs. 1986-89), New Canaan Winter Club (pres. 1988-91, bd. govs. 1987-93), Country Club New Canaan, River Club NYC. Office: Davis Polk & Wardwell 450 Lexington Ave Fl 29 New York NY 10017-3911 Home Phone: 203-966-5484; Office Phone: 212-450-4388. Office Fax: 212-450-3388. Business E-Mail: arthur.golden@dpw.com.

GOLDEN, BRYAN, management consultant, writer; s. Samuel and Rachelle Golden; life ptnr. Sally Delmerico. BA with honors, SUNY, Purchase, 1978. Syndicated columnist various newspapers, Hopewell Junction, NY; mgmt. cons., owner Power Point Group, 1983—. Curriculum adv. com. mem. Dutchess C.C., Poughkeepsie, NY, 1984—; lead cons. N.Y. State Dept. Econ. Devel., Marist Coll., 1989—90; adj. prof. Marist Coll., 1983—98, Dutchess C.C., 1983—, Culinary Inst. Am., Hyde Park, NY, 1999. Author: Dare to Live Without Limits; editor: (newspaper) Common Sense Monthly; contbr. columns in newspapers. Founder People Beekman, NY, 1986—89. Regents scholar, N.Y. State, 1974. Mem.: Nat. Soc. Newspaper Columnists. Office Phone: 845-223-7223. E-mail: bryan@columnist.com.

GOLDEN, CHARLES EDWARD, retired pharmaceutical company executive; b. Ft. Wayne, Ind., 1946; BA in Econ., Lafayette Coll., 1968; MBA, Lehigh U., 1970. From treas. to corp. v.p. GM, United Kingdom, 1970—96; exec. v.p., CFO Eli Lilly and Co., Indpls., 1996—2006.

GOLDEN, DANIEL, journalist; b. Toledo, Ohio; BA magna cum laude, Harvard U. Staff reporter Springfield Daily News, Mass., 1978—81; regional corr. Boston Globe, 1981, gen. assignment reporter and investigative reporter, 1982—86, Sunday "Focus" section and magazine writer, 1986—93, med. investigative reporter, 1993—94, projects reporter, 1994—98; reporter Wall St. Jour., 1999—2000, sr. special writer, 2000—, dep. bur. chief Boston. Author: The Price of Admission: How America's Ruling Class Buys Its Way into Elite Colleges-and Who Gets Left Outside the Gates, 2006. Recipient George Polk award for bus. reporting, 1985, George Polk award for edn. reporting, 2004, Nat. Headliner award, feature writing category, 1989, Nat. Headliner award, beat reporting category, 1999, First Place award for mag. reporting, Sigma Delta Chi, 1989, First Place award for investigative reporting, Sunday Mag. Editors, 1990, award for mag. reporting, Soc. Profl. Journalism, 1990, First Place award for investigative reporting, AP Sports Edit., 1993, Edn. Writers Assn., 1995, Nat. award for edn. reporting, 2002, 2004, Nat. award for edn. reporting special citation award, 1999, 2000, Pulitzer Prize for beat reporting, 2004; John S. Knight fellowship, Stanford U., 1998—99. Office: Wall Street Jour 10 Post Office Square Boston MA 02108

GOLDEN, DANIEL H., lawyer; b. NYC; BA, Univ. Wis., Madison, 1974; JD, SUNY, Buffalo, 1977. Bar: NY 1978, US Dist. Ct. (so., ea. dist.) NY. Sr. ptnr. Akin Gump Strauss Hauer & Feld LLP, NYC, ptnr., head financial restructuring practice group and mem. mgmt. com. Mem. SUNY Buffalo Law Rev. Mem.: ABA. Office: Akin Gump Strauss Hauer & Feld LLP 590 Madison Ave New York NY 10022-2524 Office Phone: 212-872-8010. Office Fax: 212-872-1002. Business E-Mail: dgolden@akingump.com.

GOLDEN, DAVID EDWARD, physicist; b. NYC, May 27, 1932; s. Barnet Dade and Rose (Rosenbaum) G.; m. Paula Englander, July 18, 1962; children: Richard, Jeffrey Bertram, Leila Justine. AB, NYU, 1954, PhD in Physics, 1960. Asst. prof. NYU, 1960-61, Adelphi U., Garden City, NY, 1961-62; engring. specialist GTE Lab., Palo Alto, Calif., 1962-63; staff scientist Lockheed Lab., Palo Alto, 1963-68; vis. prof. U. Bari, Italy, 1968-69; sr. scientist Sylvania Electric Products, Danvers, Mass., 1969-70; prof. U. Nebr., Lincoln, 1970-75; George Lynn Gross rsch. prof., chmn. U. Okla., Norman, 1975-85; provost, v.p. acad. affairs, prof. physics U. North Tex., Denton, 1985-89, prof., dir. ctr. for materials characterization, 1989-94, regents prof., 1993—2004; pres. Say It Straight Found., Carlsbad, Calif., 2004—. Cons. autometric divsn. Paramount Pictures, N.Y.C., 1961-62, Tracor, Austin, Tex., 1969-74, Lawrence Radiation Lab., Livermore, Calif., 1975-78, Minn. Mining and Mftg., Mpls., 1984-86, Motorola, 1997-2000, Charles Evans & Assocs., 1998—; hon. lectr. Mid-Am. State U. Assn., 1982-83; chmn. Tex. Higher Edn. Coordinating Bd. Com. on Satellite Ednl. Delivery Systems, 1986; lectr. in field. Contbr. articles to profl. jours., chpts. to books. Sr. cons. Say It Straight Found. Grantee various orgns.; fellow Centennial Edn. Program U. Nebr., 1974-75. Fellow Am. Phys. Soc. (com. mem.); mem. AAAS, Materials Rsch. Soc., Sigma Xi. Lodges: Kiwanis. Avocations: jogging, tennis. Home Phone: 760-431-1147; Office Phone: 760-586-6301. E-mail: goldene@unt.edu.

GOLDEN, E(DWARD) SCOTT, lawyer; b. Miami, Fla., Sept. 25, 1955; s. Alvan Leonard and Fay Betty (Gray) G.; m. Jane Eileen DeKlavon, June 9, 1979; children: Daniel Bryan, Kimberly Michelle. Student, So. Fla. Christian Coll., 1975-76; BS, MIT, 1978; JD, Harvard U., 1981. Bar: Fla. 1981, U.S. Dist. Ct. (so. dist.) Fla. 1982, U.S. Tax Ct. 1982, U.S. Supreme Ct. 1991, U.S. Dist. Ct. (mid. dist.) Fla. 1993, U.S. Ct. Appeals (11th cir.) 2003, U.S. Ct. Fed. Claims 2005. Assoc. Roberts and Holland, Miami, 1981-82, Valdes-Fauli, Richardson, Cobb & Petrey, P.A., Miami, 1982-83; v.p. Buck and Golden, P.A., Ft. Lauderdale, Fla., 1983-88; prin. E. Scott Golden, Ft. Lauderdale, 1988—2004, E. Scott Golden & Assocs., Ft. Lauderdale, 2004—06, Golden & LaNeve, Ft. Lauderdale, 2007—. Judge negotiations competition Nova Southeastern U. Editor-in-chief Harvard Jour. of Law and Pub. Policy, 1980-81; contbr. articles to profl. jours. Mem. West Lauderdale Bapt. Ch., Broward County, Fla., 1982-98, chmn. deacons, 1984-86, 87-88, elder, 1994-98; mem. MIT Ednl. Coun., 1995—; del. Fla. Rep. Conv., 1987, 90; mem. Rep. Exec. Com., Broward County, 1984-94. Named one of Outstanding Young Men of Am., 1986; Western

Electric grantee, 1972-74. Mem. Broward County Bar Assn. (mem. bench bar com. 2004-), Christian Legal Soc., Broward County Christian Legal Soc. (pres. 1985-86, 94-95, 2000), Optimists, Zeta Beta Tau. Avocations: sports, politics, bible study. Home: 5410 Buchanan St Hollywood FL 33021-5708 Office: Golden & La Neve 644 SE 4th Ave Fort Lauderdale FL 33301-3102 Home Phone: 954-983-4464; Office Phone: 954-764-6766. Personal E-mail: esglaw@bellsouth.net.

GOLDEN, ELLIOTT, judge; b. Bklyn., June 28, 1926; s. Barnet David and Rose (Fistel) G.; m. Ana Valbuena, July 8, 1990; children: Jeffrey Stephen, Marjorie Ruth, Peter Michael (dec.); stepchildren: Robert, Elizabeth, William, John. Student, Maritime Acad., 1944-46, NYU, 1947-48; LLB, Bklyn. Law Sch., 1951. Bar: N.Y. 1952, U.S. Dist. Ct. (ea. dist.) N.Y. 1953, U.S. Tax Ct., U.S. Dist. Ct. (so. dist.) N.Y. 1953, U.S. Supreme Ct. 1961. Assoc. Golden & Golden, 1952-64; asst. dist. atty. Kings County, 1956-64, chief asst. dist. atty., 1964-76, acting dist. atty., 1968; judge Civil Ct. of City of N.Y., 1977-78; justice Supreme Ct. State of N.Y., 1979-98, jud. hearing officer, 1998-2000. Adj. assoc. prof. N.Y.C. Tech. Coll., 1987-93; arbitrator, mediator Nat. Arbitration & Mediation, 1998—; cons. in field. Contbr. articles to profl. jours. Bd. trustees Greater N.Y. coun. Boy Scouts Am.; hon. vice chmn. March of Dimes; bd. dirs. Bklyn. Philharmonia; mem. adv. bd. Bklyn. PAL; chmn. Bklyn. Lawyers div. Fedn. Jewish Philanthropies; co-chmn. Bklyn. Lawyers div. State of Israel Bonds; assoc. trustee Temple Beth Emeth of Flatbush; mem. exec. com. Lawyers div. United Jewish Appeal; past pres. counsel Hosp. Relief Assn.; bd. dirs. Kings Bay YM-YMHA of Bklyn.; bd. dirs. Bklyn. ARC, Archway Sch. for Spl. Children, Bklyn. Sch. for Spl. Children. Recipient Cert. of Merit, Hosp. Relief Assn., numerous plaques, awards and certs. of appreciation various civic orgns. Mem. Nat. Dist. Attys. Assn. (dir. 1976-77, Disting. Svc. award), Combined Coun. Law Enforcement Ofcls. State N.Y., N.Y. State Dist. Attys. Assn. (sec. 1965-77), K.P. (supreme coun.). Avocations: golf, fishing, computers. Home and Office: 49 E Glenwild Dr PO Box 762 Smallwood NY 12778-0762 Personal E-mail: egolden@hvc.rr.com.

GOLDEN, GAIL (GAIL GOLDEN ICAHN), travel company executive; m. Carl Icahn, 1999. Office mgr. Icahn & Co.; founder, former CEO Gutsy Women Travel; vice chmn., CEO Maupintour LLC, Las Vegas. V.p. Carl C. Icahn Charter Sch., Bronx. Founder Found. for a Greater Opportunity. Office: Carl C Icahn Charter Sch 1525 Brook Ave Bronx NY 10457 also: Maupintour LLC 2688 S Rainbow Blvd, Ste D Las Vegas NV 89146-5196 Office Phone: 718-716-8105.*

GOLDEN, GERALD SAMUEL, retired national medical board executive; b. Newark, June 8, 1935; s. Clement Harold and Jeanette (Bellat) G.; m. Deborah Ann Berlatsky, March 22, 1959 (dec. 1984); children: Leah Rachel, Ruth Naomi; m. Constance Reisa Abramson, Jan. 26, 1985. AB, Princeton U., 1957; MD, Columbia U., 1961. Diplomate Am. Bd. Pediat., Am. Bd. Psychiatry and Neurology. Asst. prof. of neurology and pediatrics Albert Einstein Coll. of Medicine, Bronx, NY, 1967-73, assoc. prof., 1973-77; prof. pediatrics and neurology U. Tex., Galveston, 1977-84; prof. pediatrics and neurology, dir. ctr. for devel. disabl. U. Tenn., Memphis, 1984-92; v.p. Nat. Bd. Med. Examiners, Phila., 1993—2002, con., 2002—. Adj. prof. neurology U. Pa., 1993—98. Author: Textbook of Pediatric Neurology; assoc. editor: Pediatric Neurology Jour., 1987-92, Jour. of Devel. and Behavioral Pediatrics, 1987-2000, Jour. Epilepsy, 1987-92; contbr. numerous articles to profl. jours. Bd. dirs. Harwood Day Tng. Ctr., Memphis, 1987-92 Memphis-Shelby County Assn. for Retarded Citizens, 1987-92, Memphis Oral Sch. for Deaf, 1987-92, Temple Israel Memphis, 1989-92. Recipient fed. grant Adminstrn. on Devel. Disabilities, 1990, Dept. of Human Svcs., 1990. Fellow Am. Acad. Pediat. (neurology sect. head 1981-83), Am. Assn. Mental Deficiency (v.p. for medicine, 1984-86); mem. Am. Assn. U. Affiliated Programs (bd. dirs. 1987-92, pres. elect 1988-89, pres. 1989-90). Democrat. Jewish. Avocations: amateur radio, travel, bird watching. Personal E-mail: docsg@verizon.net.

GOLDEN, HAL, artist, consultant; b. Bklyn., Dec. 10, 1925; s. Benjamin and Dora Golden; m. Kitty Hanson, Apr. 27, 1957; children: Cynthia, Deborah. Student, Art Students League, NYC, 1945—46, CUNY, 1946. Dir. advt. and promotion Swivelier Lighting Corp., NYC, 1951—53; dir. nat. advt. pub. rels. Fred Astaire Corp., NYC, 1953—55; dir. pub. rels. Gimbel's, NYC, 1956—57; v.p. and dir. pub. rels. United Fund N.Y., NYC, 1957—76; exec. v.p. United Way of Tri-State, NYC, 1976—79; faculty New Sch. U., NYC, 1970; exec. v.p., COO United Way Tri-State, NYC, 1979—80; pres. Hal Golden Assocs. Pub. Rels. Cons. and Svcs., NYC, 1981—83, Huntington's Disease Found. Am., NYC, 1983—85; artist, conservator Hal Golden Studios, Patterson, NY, 1985—92, NYC, 1992—99, Providence, 2000—. Cons. in field. Author: How to Plan, Produce and Publicize Special Events, 1960, Working with the Working Press, 1962, The Grant Seekers, 1972; creator: mag. Telefare Weekly, 1946; two-person show, Providence Art Club, 2000, 2005, exhibitions include Gracie Square Art Show, NYC, 1997, Stamford Art Assn., Conn., 1999, Am. Artists Profl. League 74th Grand Nat. Exhbn., NYC, 2002, Oil Painters Am. S.E. Regional Exhbn., Richmond, Va., 2002, Salmagundi Club, NYC, 2003, 2004, Attleboro Mus. Ctr. for the Arts, Mass., 2003, Cmty. Arts Assn., Ridgewood, NJ, 2003, 2005. Pvt. USMC, 1943—44. Recipient Silver Anvil award, Pub. Rels. Soc. Am., 1976, Cert. of Excellence internat. poster contest, Latham Found., 1951, Louis Kuriansky Found. award, 1999. Mem.: Am. Inst. for Conservation Historic and Artistic Work, Oil Painters Am. (exhibiting mem.), Am. Artists Profl. League, Providence Art Club. Office Phone: 401-421-0164. Personal E-mail: hgolden4@cox.net.

GOLDEN, JOHN DENNIS, lawyer; b. Providence, May 18, 1954; s. Edward J. and Ann V. (Cahill) G.; m. Olga Iglesias, Aug. 2, 1980; children: Jennifer, Jackelyn, John. BA, Providence Coll., 1976; JD, Thomas M. Cooley, 1980. Bar: Mich. 1980, Fla. 1981. Assoc. Harvey Kruse & Weston, Detroit, 1980-82, Blackwell & Walker, Miami, Fla., 1982-83; ptnr. Rumburger Kirk et al, Miami, 1983-89; mng. ptnr. Roth, Edwards & Smith, Miami, 1989-91; shareholder, dir. Popham, Haik, Schnobrich & Kaufman, Ltd., Miami, 1991-95; shareholder Carlton, Fields, Ward, Emmanuel, Smith & Cutler, Miami, 1996; assoc. Golden & Grimes, LLC, Miami. Sustaining mem. Product Liability Adv. Coun. Mem. ABA (sustaining, mem. products liability adv. coun.), Mich. Bar Assn., Fla. Bar Assn., Dade County Bar Assn, Am. Bd. Trial Advocates, Fla. Republican. Roman Catholic. Avocations: golf, skiing. Office: Golden & Grimes LLC Ste 1550 9350 S Dixie Hwy Miami FL 33156 Office Phone: 305-670-4421. Office Fax: 305-670-4353.

GOLDEN, JOHN JOSEPH, JR., information technology executive; b. New Milford, Conn., Jan. 13, 1943; s. John Joseph and Anne Munroe (Hope) Golden; m. Carolyn Joan Pachesa, May 29, 1965 (div. July 1984); children: Elizabeth Susan, Jennifer Leigh, John Joseph III, Matthew Benjamin; m. Ethel M. Piercy, July 8, 1991; 1 stepchild, Michael Joseph O'Neill. BS, MIT, Cambridge, 1966. V.p. systems devel. Quantum Computing Corp., Newton, Mass., 1968-70; mgr. computer ops. Polaroid Corp., Cambridge, Mass., 1970-75; dir. info. processing Schering-Plough Corp., Kenilworth, NJ, 1975-78; dir. info. systems Compugraphic Corp., Wilmington, Mass., 1978-80; dir. info. systems electro-optics div. Honeywell, Lexington, Mass., 1981-83, dir. adminstrn. electro-optics div. Wilmington, Mass., 1983-87, dir. materials electro-optics div. Marlboro, Mass., 1987-90; dir. ops. Micracor, Acton, Mass., 1990-96; dir. info. sys. Fresenius Med. Care, Lexington, Mass., 1996-97; mgr. computing and telecom. U.S. Postal Svc., Washington, 1997-2000; sr. v.p. ops. Ethentica., Lake Forest, Calif., 2000—01; dir. bus. devel. Legato, Inc., Mountain View, Calif., 2001—03, Nakuurug Solutions, Fairfax, Va., 2003—. With USAR, 1964—70. Mem.: IEEE, Assn. Computing Machinery, MIT Alumni Orgn., Sigma Alpha Epsilon, Mass. Iota Tau Assn. (treas. 1970—). Roman Catholic. Home: 5013 Ox Rd Fairfax VA 22030-4561 Office: Nakuurug Solutions Herndon VA 22030 Office Phone: 571-323-5975. Personal E-mail: jjgmit@prodigy.net.

GOLDEN, JOSEPH AARON, lawyer; b. Detroit, Oct. 27, 1940; s. Milton and Sally (Schweitzer) G.; m. Frances Miriam Rubenstein, Aug. 16, 1965 (div. Apr. 1973); children: Manine Rosa, Jay Dylan, Nicholas Michael Estuardo, Samuel Marcos, Jennifer Rose Cetnar, Natalie Elizabeth Mead; m. Cynthia Sisson Mead, June 24, 1979. BBA, Wayne State U., 1962; JD, U. Detroit, 1967. Bar: Mich. 1968, U.S. Ct. Appeals (6th cir.) 1974, U.S. Ct. Appeals (3d cir.) 1995, U.S. Supreme Ct. 2004. Supervising atty. Wayne County Neighborhood Legal Services, Ecorse, Mich., 1968-70; ptnr. Craig, Fieger & Golden, Southfield, Mich., 1970-73, Fieger, Golden & Cousens, Southfield, 1973-78; pvt. practice, Southfield, 1978-85; prin. Sommers, Schwartz, Silver & Schwartz, P.C., Southfield, 1985—2007, Pitt Mcgehee Palmer Rivers & Golden PC, 2007—. Adj. prof. labor law U. Detroit, 1987—. Co-author: Wrongful Termination Litigation in Mich., 1986; contbrg. author: Employee Dismissal Law: Forms and Procedures, 1986. Founder, pres. Coalition for Fairness in Workplace, 1993. Fellow Coll of Labor and Employment Lawyers; mem. ABA (pub. co-chmn. employee rights and responsibilities com. labor and employment law sect., sect. coun. 1988-92), ATLA, Mich. Trial Lawyers Assn., Nat. Employment Lawyers Assn. (nat. exec. bd. 1984-95, pres. 1991-93), Mich. Employment Lawyers Assn. (founder, v.p.). Office Phone: 248-398-9800. Business E-Mail: jgolden@pittlawpc.com.

GOLDEN, JOSEPH DAVID, music educator; b. McKinney, Tex., Aug. 26, 1951; s. Joseph Tyler and Jo W. Golden. B in music, U. No. Tex., 1976, M in music, 1980. Assoc. organist, choirmaster Ch. of St. John the Divine, Houston, 1979—83; organist, choirmaster Hist. Trinity Espis. Ch., Columbus, Ga., 1983—95; prof. of music Schwab Sch. of Music, Columbus State U., Columbus, Ga., 1989—. Adv. Metropolitan Opera, NYC, 2000—; coun. on creating original opera Lincoln Ctr., NYC. Editor: RILM Jour., 1986—89. Mem.: Nat. Convention Steering Com., Music Tchr's Nat. Assn., Nat. Assn. Tchrs. of Singing, Am. Guild of Organists. Episcopalian. Achievements include development of James H. Thompson Scholarships @ U. of No. Tex; The Jordan Internat. Organ Competition at River Ctr. for the Performing Arts. Avocation: gourmet cooking. Office: Schwab Sch of Music Columbus State U 4225 U Ave Columbus GA 31907 Office Phone: 706-649-7246. E-mail: golden_joseph@colstate.edu.

GOLDEN, JUDITH GREENE, artist, educator; b. Chgo., Nov. 29, 1934; d. Walter Cornell and Dorothie (Cissell) Greene; m. David T. Golden, Oct. 10, 1955 (div.); children: David T. Golden III, Lucinda Golden Rizzo. BFA, Art Inst. Chgo., 1973; MFA, U. Calif., Davis, 1975; PhD Art (hon.), Moore Coll. Art, Phila., 1990. Assoc. prof. art U. Ariz., Tucson, 1981-88, prof. art, 1989-96, prof. emerita, 1996—. NEA forum pub. grants panelist, 1987; project dir. U. Calif. L.A. NEA Lecture series, 1979, 84; archives founder Ctr. Creative Photography, Tucson, 1996. One woman shows include Women's Bldg., LA, 1977, G. Ray Hawkins Gallery, LA, 1977, Quay Gallery, San Francisco, 1979, 81, A. Nagel Galerie, Berlin, 1981, Ctr. Creative Photography, U. Ariz., 1983, Colburg Gallery, Vancouver, Can., 1985, Etherton Gallery, Tucson, 1985, 89, 91, 95, Mus. Photog. Arts, San Diego, 1986, Friends of Photography, Carmel, Calif., 1987, Tucson Mus. Art, 1987, Mus. Contemporary Photography, Chgo., 1988, Visual Arts Ctr., Anchorage, Alaska, 1990, Temple Music and Art, Tucson, 1992, 97, 05, Scottsdale (Ariz.) Ctr. Arts, 1993, Arte de Oaxaca, Mex., 1995, Etherton Gallery, Tucson, 1995, Columbia Art Ctr., Dallas, 1997, U. Arts, Phila., 2002, Temple Music & Art, Tucson, 2005; exhibited in group shows at Centre Georges Pompidou, Paris, 1981, Security Pacific Bank, LA, 1985, Phoenix Mus. Art, 1985, LA County Mus. Art, 1987, 03, Tokyo Met. Mus. Photography, 1991, Laguna Art Mus., 1992, U. N.Mex. Mus. Art, Albuquerque, 1993, LA County Mus., 1994, Hara Contemporary Mus., Tokyo, 1995, Mus. Women in Arts, Washington, 1997, Santa Barbara Mus. Art, Calif., 1997, 05, Mus. Cont. Photography, 1998, Tucson Mus. Art, 1999, Calif. Mus. Photography, 1999, Ctr. for Creative Photography, 1999, 04, Santa Barbara Mus. Art, 1999, 05, Mus. Fine Arts, Santa Fe, N.Mex., 2002, U. Ariz. Mus. Art, 2003, Akron (Ohio) Mus. Art, Mus. Photog. Art, San Diego, 2006, Albuquerque Mus. Art, 2007, others; represented in permanent collections at Art Inst. Chgo., Calif. Mus. Photography, Ctr. Creative Photography U. Ariz., Denver Art Mus., Fed. Res. Bank San Francisco, Fogg Mus. Art, Grunwald Ctr. Graphic Arts, UCLA Mus. Contemporary Art, Mus. Contemporary Photography, Chgo., Internat. Mus. Photography George Eastman House, LA County Mus. Art, Mpls. Inst. Arts, Mus. Photog. Arts, San Diego, Calif., Mus. Fine Arts, Santa Fe, N.Mex., Newport Harbor Mus. Art, Oakland Mus. Art, Photography Mus. Osaka, Polaroid Corp., San Francisco Mus. Modern Art, Security Pacific Bank, Tokyo Met. Mus. Photography, Tucson Mus. Art, Weisman Found., LA, Mus. Cont. Photography, Chgo., Seattle Art Mus., Wash., Akron (Ohio) Art Mus., Avon Collection, N.Y.C.; resident Harvard Mus. Art, Taos, N.Mex., 2006. Individual artist grantee Tucson Pima Arts Coun., 1987; faculty rsch. grantee U. Ariz., 1986-87, 93-94; Ariz. Found. grantee U. Ariz., 1984; fellow Ariz. Commn. Arts, 1984; individual photography fellow NEA, 1979; Regent's faculty fellow Creative Rsch. U.Calif. L.A., 1977. Personal E-mail: judithgolden@earthlink.net.

GOLDEN, KIMBERLY KAY, critical care nurse; b. Munich, July 31, 1961; arrived in US, 1961; d. Henry Davis and Mary Walker G. AA, Hinds Jr. Coll., Raymond, Miss., 1980, ASN, 1984; BSN, U. Miss., Jackson, 1987, AS in EMT-Paramedic, 1990; postgrad., U. Health Scis., Antigua, W.I., 1997—. Cert. ACLS, PALS provider and instr.; emergency nurse, crit. care RN; cert. paramedic, Miss., Tenn. Staff nurse neuro ICU U. Miss. Med. Ctr., 1984-85, staff nurse surg. ICU, 1985-87; staff nurse emergency rm. Rankin Gen. Hosp., Brandon, Miss., 1987-88; flight nurse Lifestar Helicopter Flight Svc., 1988-91; staff nurse emergency rm., ICU Nightingale Nursing, Jackson, 1988-91, Riveroaks Hosp., Jackson, 1990-91; staff RN emergency rm., Aerovesta flight Midland Meml. Hosp., Tex., 1991-93; flight nurse Hosp. Wing BTLS, Memphis, 1993-99, U. Health Sci. Med. Sch., Antigua, West Indies, 1997—; nurse Univ. Health Scis./Antigua Sch. Medicine, 1997—; emergency rm. staff nurse U. Nebr. Health Systems, 2001—. Examiner Nat. Registry EMT-P; advanced trauma life support station instr.; affiliate faculty paramedic program U. Miss. Faculty scholar Hinds Jr. Coll., 1983. Mem. AACN, Nat. Flight Assn., Emergency Nurses Assn. Baptist. Avocations: Karate, skiing, horse back riding, camping. Office: PO Box 140466 Austin TX 78714-0466 Home: 1211 Brentwood Dr Pine Bluff AR 71601-5414

GOLDEN, LEON, classicist, educator; b. Jersey City, Dec. 25, 1930; s. Nathan and Regina (Okun) G. BA, U. Chgo., 1950, MA, 1953, PhD, 1958. Instr. ancient langs. Coll. William and Mary, 1958-60, asst. prof. ancient langs., 1960-65; assoc. prof. classical langs. Fla. State U., Tallahassee, 1965-68, prof., 1968—, dir. program in humanities, 1976—, chmn. dept. classics, 1986-95. Bd. dirs. Fla. Endowment for Humanities, 1983-87. Author: In Praise of Prometheus: Humanism and Rationalism in Aeschylean Thought, 1966, (with O.B. Hardison Jr.) Aristotle's Poetics, 1968, Aristotle: On Tragic and Comic Mimesis, 1992, Horace for Students of Literature, 1995, Understanding the Iliad, 2004. With AUS, 1953-55. Fellow coop. program humanities U.N.C. and Duke, 1964-65; fellow coop. program humanities Soc. for Religion in Higher Edn., 1971-72 Mem. Am. Philol. Assn., Archeol. Inst. Am., Classical Assn. Mid. West and South (pres. So. sect. 1972-74), Phi Beta Kappa. Address: 1526 Parchment Cove Tallahassee FL 32308 E-mail: lgolden352@msn.com.

GOLDEN, LOUIS JOSEPH, retired editor, publishing executive; b. Hartford, Conn., Oct. 19, 1952; s. Merrill S. and Marjorie (Louis) G.; m. Christine Palm, June 27, 1981 (div. Dec. 1988); children: James Joseph, Daniel Louis. BA, U. Conn., 1975. Copy editor Hartford Courant, 1974-77, night city editor, 1977-79, editor Bus. Weekly, 1987-89, bus. editor, 1989-94, v.p. mktg. and bus. developer, 1994-98; v.p. external rels., dep. publ., 1998—; asst. editor Weekly World News, Lantana, Fla., 1979-80, editor, 1980-81; v.p. Greater Hartford C. of C., 1981-85, Decker Guertin Cheyne, Hartford, 1985-87.

GOLDEN, MARITA, literature educator, writer, foundation administrator; b. Washington, Apr. 28, 1950; d. Francis Sherman and Beatrice Lee Golden; m. Joseph Butlar Murray, Aug. 23, 1991; 1 child, Akintunde Michael Kayode. BA, Am. U., 1972; MSc, Columbia U., 1973; LittD (hon.), U. Richmond, 1998. Lectr. U. Lagos, Nigeria, 1975-79; asst. prof. Roxbury C.C., Boston, 1979-81, Emerson Coll., Boston, 1981-83; assoc. prof. George Mason U., Fairfax, Va., 1989-94; prof. English Va. Commonwealth U., Richmond, 1994—2001; writer-in-residence U. DC, 2005—. Author: Migrations of the Heart, 1983, A Woman's Place, 1986, Long Distance Life, 1989, And Do Remember Me, 1992, Wild Women Don't Wear No Blues, 1993, Saving Our Sons, 1995, Skin Deep, 1997, The Edge of Heaven, 1998, A Miracle Everyday, 1999, Gumbo, An Anthology of African American Writing, 2003, Don't Play in the Sun: One Woman's Journey Through the Color Complex, 2004. Pres. Hurston Wright Found., Hyattsville, Md., 1990—. Recipient Disting. Alumni award Am. U., 1994, Woman of Yr. award Zeta Phi Beta, 1997, Writers for Writers award Poets and Writers mag., 2001, Authors Guild Disting. Svc. award, 2002; named to Literary Hall of Fame, Chgo. State U., 2000. Mem. African Am. Writers Guild (pres. Washington 1986-90). Office: Hurston Wright Found Ste 531 6525 Belcrest Rd Hyattsville MD 20782

GOLDEN, MICHAEL, publishing executive; BA, Lehigh U., Pa., 1971, M Ed, 1974; MA, U. Mo., 1977; MBA, Emory U., 1984. English tchr. Inst. Franco-Am., Rennes, France, 1974-76; various editorial, mgmt. positions The Chattanooga (Tenn.) Times, 1976-84; prodn. mgr. Family Circle The N.Y. Times Co., Mag. Group, 1984—86; sr. v.p. retail mag. mktg. co. NY Times Co., 1986—88, gen. mgr. Child mag., 1988—90, pub. McCall's mag., 1990—91, exec. v.p., gen. mgr. Women's Pub. Div., 1991—94, exec. v.p., pub. Tennis mag., 1994—96, v.p. operations devel., 1996—97, vice chmn., 1997—; publ. Internat. Herald Tribune, 2003—. Office: The New York Times Co 229 W 43rd St New York NY 10036-3959

GOLDEN, OLIVIA ANN, state official, human services administrator; b. NYC, May 23, 1955; BA in Philosophy and Govt., Harvard U., MPP, PhD. Budget dir. office human svcs. State of Mass., 1983-85; lectr. in pub. policy J.F. Kennedy Sch. Govt. Harvard U., Cambridge, Mass., 1987-91; dir. programs and policy Children's Def. Fund, Washington, 1991-93; commr. on children, youth & families US Dept. Health & Human Services, Washington, 1993-97, prin. dep. asst. sec. for children & families, 1997, asst. sec. for children and families, 1997—2001; dir. D.C. Child and Family Svcs. Agy., 2001—04; sr. fellow Urban Inst., Washington, 2004—07; dir. state ops. State of NY, 2007—. Mem. adv. com. children and youth City of Cambridge. Author: Poor Children and Welfare Reform, 1992. Candidate for state senator, Mass. Business E-Mail: ogolden@ui.urban.org.*

GOLDEN, REYNOLD STEPHEN, geriatrician, educator; b. Herkimer, NY, Jan. 11, 1937; s. Harold Theodore and Ethel Anne (Myers) G.; m. Gale Holtz, Nov. 26, 1959 (div. May 1978); children: Nathan Myers, Jennifer Lynn (dec.), Laura Beth (Lieba); m. Ellen Jeanne Moore, Sept. 9, 1978; children: Melissa Nan, Benjamin Harold. AB cum laude, Harvard Coll., 1958; MD, SUNY, Syracuse, 1962. Diplomate Am. Bd. Family Practice, Am. Bd. Internal Medicine; cert. added qualifications in geriatrics. Intern Lankenau Hosp., Phila., 1962-63; resident in internal medicine SUNY, Syracuse, 1963-66; pvt. practice Utica, NY, 1966-78; dir. family practice residency St. Elizabeth Hosp., Utica, 1978-92, St. Francis Hosp., Poughkeepsie, NY, 1992-95; clin. assoc. prof. dept. family medicine SUNY, Syracuse, 1991-96; chief of geriatrics Unity Med. Group (formerly Rochester Park Med. Group), 1995—; med. dir. continuing care svcs. Park Ridge Health Sys. (now Unity Health Sys.), Rochester, 1995—; clin. asst. prof. dept. internal medicine U. Rochester, 1999—. Cons. residency assistance program, Kansas City, Mo., 1988-96; pres. med. staff St. Elizabeth Hosp., Utica, N.Y., 1978-80, Pk. Ridge Hosp., Rochester, N.Y., 2004; charter mem. N.Y. State Coun. on Grad. Med. Edn., N.Y.C., 1987-89. Editor: N.Y. Family Physician, 1987—92. Recipient Vincentian Award, Unity Health Sys., 2000. Jewish. Avocations: travel, computers, music, theater, wine. Office: Ste 216 1561 Long Pond Rd Rochester NY 14626 Personal E-mail: GoldenREN@aol.com.

GOLDEN, RICHARD M., history professor; b. NYC, June 14, 1947; s. Herbert and Sylvia Mintz Golden; m. Hilda Schlanger, June 8, 1969; children: Davina Golden Weinstein, Irene Golden Meehan, Jeremy Herbert. BA, Vanderbilt U., Nashville, 1969; MA, Johns Hopkins U., Balt., 1972, PhD, 1975. From asst. prof. to prof. dept. of history Clemson U., SC, 1974—94; prof., chair dept. history U. North Tex., Denton, 1994—2001, dir. Jewish studies program, 2001—. Editor: Encyclopedia of Witchcraft: The Western Tradition, 4 vols.; author: (book) The Godly Rebellion: Parisian Curés and the Religious Fronde, 1652-1662; editor: The Social Dimension of Western Civilization, 5 edits., The Edict of Nantes, Its Revocation, and Early French Migration to South Carolina, Church, State, and Society under the Bourbon Kings of France; coeditor (book) Western Societies: Primary Sources in Social History. Recipient Regents' Faculty Lectr., U. North Tex. Bd. of Regents, 1997, Jewish Profl. of Yr. in Dallas and Ft. Worth, Regional Hillel of North Tex., 2006. Mem.: Assn. for Israel Studies, Assn. for Jewish Studies, Soc. for French Hist. Studies, Hist. Soc., Am. Hist. Assn. (life). Home: 2285 Strathmore Dr Highland Village TX 75077 Office: Univ North Texas Box 310650 Dept History Denton TX 76203-0650 Office Fax: 940-369-8838. E-mail: rmg@unt.edu.

GOLDEN, ROBERT CHARLES, finance company executive; b. Bklyn., July 12, 1946; s. Charles Joseph and Audrey (Griffin) Golden. BS in Acctg., Fordham U., Bronx, NY, 1968, MBA in Fin., 1978. V.p. internal audit Walston & Co., Inc., NYC, 1969-73; v.p.-fin. Acan X-Ray Co., Inc., Detroit, 1973-76; exec. v.p. Prudential Securities Inc., NYC, 1976-97, Prudential Fin., Roseland, NJ, 1997—. Bd. dirs. HeartShare Human Svcs. NY, 1985—; trustee Xaverian HS, Bklyn., 1987—93; v.p. Ireland-US Coun. on Commerce and Industry. Named Educator of Yr., Assn. of Tchrs. of NY, 1986, Cath. Guardian Soc. Humanitarian of Yr., 1985, Chief Brehon of the Great Irish Fair, 1992, Knight of the Sovereign Mil. Order of Malta, 1995, Man of Yr., Cath. Big Bros. and Big Sisters, 2002; named to Diocesan Ct. of Honor, Diocese of Bklyn., Assembly of Stewarts, Diocese of NY, 1995, Knights of the Equestrian Order of the Holy Sepulchre, 1998; recipient citation, Coun. of the City of NY, Franciscan Heritage award, Franciscan Sisters of the Poor at Pla. Hotel, 1987, Apple award, Prudential Pacesetters, 1989, St. Francis Xavier Soc. award, Xaverian Bros., 1990, Thomas J. Cuite award, Irish Am. Heritage Wk. Com. of NYC Hall, 1991, Crystal Shield award, Salvation Army, 1992, Disting. Alumni award, Xaverian HS, 1993, Constance O. Garreson award, Minority Interchange, Inc., 1999, Ellis Island medal of honor, 2000, Bishop's Humanitarian award, Cath. Charities Diocese, Bklyn., 2001, Bus. 100 award, Irish Am. Mag., 2001—06, Disting. Leadership award, NY Aquarium, 2001, Caritas award, Catholic Tchr. Assn, Diocese of Bklyn., 2003, Outstanding Vol. award, OPUS, 2005, Cmty. Svc. award, Bay Ridge Ctr. Older Adults, 2005, Disting. Irish American commendation, NYC Comptroller William Thompson, 2006, Person of Yr. award, SI Ctr. for Ind. Living, 2007. Mem.: Ft. Hamilton Hist. Soc., Securities Industry Assn., Friendly Sons St. Patrick

City of NY, Acad. Magical Arts, St. Patrick Soc. Bklyn., Emerald Assn. LI (past pres.), Bishop's Coat of Arms Club, Fordham U. Pres. Club, Bay Ridge Men's Club, Cathedral Club Bklyn. (past pres., Man of Yr. 1994), Mcpl. Club Bklyn., Bayfort Benevolent Assocs. (past pres.), KC, Ancient Order Hiberians (divsn. 22). Roman Catholic. Home: 33 Columbia Ave Staten Island NY 10305-3739 Office: Prudential Fin Inc 80 Livingston Ave Roseland NJ 07068-1798

GOLDEN, ROLLAND HARVE, artist; b. New Orleans, Nov. 8, 1931; s. John Ferdinand and Ione (Rolland) G.; m. Stella Anne Doussan, Aug. 31, 1957; children: Carrie Marie Lambert, Mark Damian, Lucille Marie. Grad., John McCrady Art Sch., 1955-57. Author: Vieux Carre Courier-Golden Show Tours USSR, 1976-77; one man shows include Moscow, Leningrad, Kiev, Odessa, 1976-77, touring show France, 1993-94; exhibited in group shows at Mo. Bicentennial, 1976, Musee Marzelles, Bon Encontre Cultural Ctr., Galleries in Marseille, Toulouse, Agen. Bd. dirs. Vieux Carre Property Owners, New Orleans, 1970-81, Folsom, La., 1982-90. Served with USN, 1951-55. Mem. Nat. Watercolor Soc., Watercolor U.S.A. (v.p. 1992-96), Midwest Watercolor Soc., Nat. Soc. Painters in Casein and Acrylic, Nat. Arts Club, Rocky Mountain Nat. Watermedia, Allied Artists Am., Artists Fellowship (N.Y.). Republican. Roman Catholic. Home: 215 St Charles Ave Natchez MS 39120 Home Phone: 601-443-9852. Personal E-mail: rollandgolden@aol.com.

GOLDEN, SHEILA S., retired special education educator; d. Harley Wade and Ruby Richards Golden. Student, Salem Coll., 1966—68; BS in Speech Pathology and Audiology, W.Va. U., 1970. Advanced Profl. Cert.in Spl. Edn.Grades K-12 Md. State Dept. Edn., 1980. Speech, lang. pathologist Bd. of Edn. of Mineral County, Keyser, W.Va., 1971—74; spl. edn. inclusion support tchr. Bd. of Edn. of Allegany County, Cumberland, Md., 1974—2004. Speech, lang. pathologist for summer head start program Bd. of Edn. of Mineral County, Keyser, 1971; ednl. coord. for summer programs for disabled students Clary St. Learning Ctr., Keyser, 1972—77. Contbr. articles to profl. jours. Vol. crisis counselor Family Crisis Ctr., Inc., Keyser, 1982—87, bd. dirs., 1982—87, sec., 1982—87, pres., 1982—87; vol. during 1985 flood disaster ARC; vol. Fire Escape Youth Ctr., Keyser, W.Va., 2005—; mem. Keyser-Mineral County C. of C., 1984—86, Mineral County Hist. Soc., Keyser, 2003—, Keyser Mineral County Friends of Libr. Assn., 2003—, vol., 2005—; mem. relay for life team Am. Cancer Soc., 2003—04; sec. exec. com. McNeill's Rangers Apple Alley Players, Inc., 1983—87, mem. funding com., 1983—87, chairperson box office, 1983—87, pub. rels. and media coord., 1983—87; bd. dirs. Potomac Kinship, 1983—86, pres., 1983—86, mem. spl. events com., 1983—86, chairperson, 1983—86, chairperson pub. rels. com., 1983—86; steering com. mem. Mineral County Substance Abuse Task Force, 1984—87, chairperson intervention com., 1984—87; bd. dirs. Mineral County Chpt., Am. Cancer Soc., 1984—87, fundraising chairperson, 1984—87, media chairperson, 1984—87; mem. programming com. Highland Arts Unlimited, Inc., 1982—89, 2003—05, mem. publicity com., 2003—, mem. accountability com., 2003—; mem. AAUW, 1985—87; life mem. Westernport Elem. Sch. PTA, Md., 2005—, Md. PTA, 2005—; vol. fundraiser Warm the Children Project, 2005—, shopper, 2005—; vol. Keyser After-Sch. Program, 2005—; mem. RCIA program Ch. of the Assumption, 1990—98; nursing home vol. Heartland of Keyser, 1999—, Clarksburg Continuous Care Ctr., Clarksburg, W.Va., 1987—, Moran Manor Care & Rehab. Ctr., Westernport, Md., 2000—. Named Vol. of Yr., Mineral County Mental Health Assn., 1985, Clarksburg Continuous Care Ctr., 2000; recipient Cert. of Appreciation for Outstanding Svc. to Cmty. and to Victims of Domestic Violence, Family Crisis Ctr., Inc., 1987, Plaque of Appreciation, Recognition as Exec. Com. Sec. and Publicity Coord., McNeill's Rangers, Apple Alley Players, Inc., 1987, Rose Dunlap award for Outstanding Vol., Heartland of Keyser, 2004, Cert. of Recognition for Vol. Svcs., 2005, Cert. of Recognition for Vol. Svc., Clarkesburg Continuous Care Ctr., W.Va., 2005, Heartland of Keyser Nursing Ctr., W.Va., 2005; scholar, scholar, 1968. Mem.: NEA (life), Nat. Ret. Tchrs. Assn. (life), Allegany County Tchrs. Assn. (life), Md. State Tchrs. Assn. (life). Roman Catholic. Achievements include research in Co-authored a research study on receptive language assessment scales; 1973-74. Avocations: volunteering-particularly with the geriatric population, attending concerts and stage shows, walking, crafts, reading. Home Phone: 304-788-0184. Personal E-mail: sgolden@pennswoods.net.

GOLDEN, STEPHEN L., lawyer; b. San Antonio, Tex. BA, Tulane U., 1975; JD, St. Mary's U., 1978. Bar: Tex. 1978. Various exec. positions in real estate sales and devel. and utilities, 1984—90; ptnr., head San Antonio office real estate sect. Akin, Gump, Straus, Hauer & Feld, LLP, 1990—2005; ptnr., co-founder Drenner & Golden, Stuart, Wolff LLP, San Antonio, 2005—, mem. exec. com. head San Antonio office, 2005—. Assoc. editor St. Mary's Law Jour., 1977—78. Mem.: ABA, San Antonio Bar Assn., State Bar Tex. (real estate and probate and trust sects.), Phi Delta Phi. Office: Drenner & Golden Stuart Wolff LLP Ste 2600 300 Convent St San Antonio TX 78205-3732 Office Phone: 210-745-3777. Office Fax: 210-745-3737. Business E-Mail: sgolden@drennergolden.com.

GOLDEN, T. MICHAEL, state supreme court justice; b. 1942; BA in History, U. Wyo., 1964, JD, 1967; LLM, U. Va., 1992. Bar: Wyo. 1967, U.S. Dist. Ct. 1967, U.S. Ct. Appeals (10th cir.) 1967, U.S. Supreme Ct. 1970. Mem. firm Brimmer, MacPherson & Golden, Rawlins, Wyo., 1971-83, Williams, Porter, Day & Neville, Casper, Wyo., 1983-88; chief justice Wyo. Supreme Ct., Cheyenne, 1994—96, justice, 1988—. Mem. Wyo. State Bd. Law Examiners, 1977-82, 86-88. Capt. US Army, 1967—71. Mem.: Wyo. State Bar Assn. Office: Wyo Supreme Ct Bldg 2301 Capitol Ave Cheyenne WY 82001*

GOLDEN, THELMA, curator; BA in Art History & African Am. Studies, Smith College. Visual arts dir. Jamaica Arts Ctr., Jamaica, NY, 1989—91; dir., exhbn. coord. Whitney Mus. Am. Art at Philip Morris, 1991—93; assoc. curator, dir. br. museums Whitney Mus. Am. Art, 1993—96, curator, 1996—98; spl. projects curator Peter Norton Family Found., 1998—99; dep. dir. exhbns. and programs Studio Mus., Harlem, NY, 2000—05, chief curator, 2000—, exec. dir., 2005—. Lectr. in field. Curator (exhibitions) Black Male: Representations of Masculinity in Contemporary American Art, 1994, Bob Thompson: A Retrospective, 1998, Isaac Julien: Vagabondia, 2000, Martin Puryear: The Cane Project, 2000, Freestyle, 2001, Black and Green, 2001, Yinka Shonibare, 2002, Black Romantic: The Figurative Impulse in Contemporary American Art, 2002, Aaron Siskind: Harlem Document, 2003, Harlemworld: Metropolis as Metaphor, 2004, others. Office: The Studio Mus in Harlem 144 W 125th St New York NY 10027 Office Phone: 212-864-4500. Office Fax: 212-864-4800.

GOLDEN, THOMAS M., federal judge; b. Pottsville, Pa., Nov. 1, 1947; BA, Pa. State U., 1969; JD, Dickinson Sch. Law, 1972. Mng. ptnr. Golden Masano Bradley, 1972—2006; judge US Dist. Ct. (Ea. dist.) Pa., Phila., 2006—. Mem. adv. bd. Nat. Penn Bank. Mem. adv. bd. Jesuit Ctr. for Spirtual Growth. Fellow: Pa. Bar Found.; mem.: Pa. Bar Assn. (pres.-elect, pres. 2003—04, Ho. of Dels., zone 2 gov., vice chair editl. com., chair client and cmty. rels. com., task force for quality of life/balance, task force on entities and ops., Spl. Achievement award 2000), Berks County Bar Assn. (dir. 1990—93, pres. 1992), Berks County Golf Assn. (past pres.). Office: US Courthouse Rm 3041 601 Market St Philadelphia PA 19106 also: Madison Bldg Rm 401 400 Washington St Reading PA 19601-3956 also: Pa Bar Assn PO Box 186 100 South St Harrisburg PA 17108-0186*

GOLDEN, WILLIAM THEODORE, trustee, corporate director; b. NYC, Oct. 25, 1909; s. S. Herbert and Rebecca (Harris) Golden; m. Sibyl Levy, May 2, 1938 (dec. 1983); children: Sibyl Rebecca, Pamela Prudence; m. Jean E. Taylor, July 8, 2001 (div. Aug. 3, 2005); m. Catherine Morrison, Feb. 3, 2007. AB, U. Pa., 1930, LLD (hon.), 1979; postgrad. bus. adminstrn., Harvard U., 1930-31; DSc (hon.), Poly. Inst. N.Y., 1975, Bard Coll., 1988; MA, Columbia U., 1979, LLD (hon.), 1986, Hamilton Coll., 1987; DHL (hon.), CUNY, 1997, Mt. Sinai Sch. Medicine, NYU, 2000. Lic. amateur radio operator, 1922—, station 2AEN. Asst. to pres. Cornell, Linder & Co., NYC, 1931-34; with Carl M. Loeb & Co., Carl M. Loeb, Rhoades & Co., 1934-41; dir. Woodward Iron Co., 1940-68; asst. to commr. AEC, Washington, 1946-50, cons., 1950-58; chmn. bd. Nat. U.S. Radiator Co. (and successor cos.), 1952-74; dir. Pitts. Railways Co., 1952-63, United Carbon Co., 1957-63, Crowell-Collier and Macmillan, Inc., 1964-71, Paribas Corp., 1965-69; trustee Mitre Corp., 1958-72, 76-85, System Devel. Corp., 1957-66, chmn. bd. trustees, 1961-66. Spl. cons. on rev. govt. sci. activities Pres. Truman, Washington, 1950-51; advisor on NSF to dir. Bur. Budget, 1950-51; mem. mil. procurement task force Commn. on Orgn. Exec. Br. Govt., Hoover Commn., 1954-55; adv. com. on pvt. enterprise in fgn. aid U.S. State Dept., 1964-65; pub. mem. Hudson Inst., 1964-94; mem. commn. on delivery personal health svcs. Mayor's Piel Commn., 1966-68; adv. coun. Sch. Gen. Studies, Columbia U., NYC, 1966-2001, emeritus, 2001; vis. com. on astronomy Princeton U., NJ, 1969—, chmn., 1976-89; vis. com. on engring. and applied physics and on medicine and dental medicine Harvard U., Cambridge, Mass., 1969-77, vis. com. on astronomy, 1976-90; vis. com. Assn. Univs. for Research in Astronomy, 1973-76, dir. at large, 1988-91, Disting. advisor, 1991—; mem. vis. com. Space Telescope Sci. Inst., 1982-87; adv. panel on space transp. ops. NASA, 1976-77; adv. panel U.S. Postal Svc., 1981-83; vice chmn. Mayor's Commn. on Sci. and Tech., 1983-91, hon. chair, 1992—, Commn. Coll. Retirement, 1984-88, Scientists Inst. Pub. Info., 1985-94; co-chmn. Carnegie Commn. on Sci., Tech. and Govt., 1988-96; bd. dirs. Verde Exploration, Ltd., Inc., Block Drug Co., Inc.; founder Carnegie Group of Ministers of Sci. and Sci. Advisors to Heads of G8 countries, Russia and European Union, 1991- Editor, co-author: Science Advice to the President, 1980, 2d rev. edit., 1993, Science and Technology Advice to the President, Congress and Judiciary, 1988, 2d rev. edit., 1993, Worldwide Science and Technology Advice to the Highest Levels of Governments, 1991; contbr. articles to profl. jours. Trustee Hebrew Free Loan Soc., 1935—, treas., 1985—2000, United Neighborhood Hos., 1952—61, Associated Hosp. Svc. NY, 1959—74, Univ. Corp. for Atmospheric Rsch., 1965—74, Riverside Rsch. Inst., 1967—76, NYC-Rand Inst., 1969—75, Ctr. for Advanced Study Behavioral Scis., 1970—76, Bennington Coll., 1971—76, Haskins Labs., 1971—92, SIAM Inst. Math. and Soc., 1973—91, Columbia U. Press, 1974—77, John Simon Guggenheim Meml. Found., 1978—81, Nat. Humanities Ctr., 1978—90, emeritus, 1990—; trustee Population Coun., 1979—89, Catskill Ctr. for Conservation and Devel., 1981—, U. Pa. Press, 1985—; mem. Marine Biology Lab., Woods Hole, Mass., 1968—, trustee, 1968—87, trustee emeritus, 1987; trustee Mt. Sinai Hosp., NYC, 1955—, vice chmn., 1977—; governing coun. Courant Inst. Math. Scis., NYU, 1962—91, vice chmn., 1962—86, chmn., 1986—91; trustee Mt. Sinai Med. Sch., 1963—, vice chmn., 1977—; trustee NY Found., 1963—84, treas., 1974—78; chmn. bd. trustees City Univ. Constrn. Fund, 1967—71; exec. com. Health Rsch. Coun., NYC, 1968—75; trustee Am. Mus. Natural History, 1968—, v.p., 1971—88, vice chmn., 1988—89, chmn., 1989—94, chmn. emeritus, 1994—; trustee Carnegie Instn. Washington, 1969—, sec., 1971—99, sr. trustee, 2000—; trustee Barnard Coll., 1973—, vice chmn., 1975—79, 1986—92, treas., 1980—83, hon. vice chmn., 1992—98, emeritus, 1998—; trustee NY Coun. for Humanities, 1975—78, chmn., 1976—78; bd. overseers Sch. Arts and Scis., U. Pa., Phila., 1976—97, emeritus, 1997—; coun. mem. Rockefeller U., 1978—; bd. visitors Grad. Sch. and Univ Ctr., CUNY, 1979—96, bd. dirs. Grad. Ctr. Found., 1996—; trustee Am. Trust for Brit. Libr., 1980—92, 1998—, vice chmn., 1985—92, co-chmn., treas., 1998—; trustee Neurosci. Rsch. Found., 1981—99, chmn., 1981—87, Black Rock Forest Consortium, 1988—; adv. bd. Johns Hopkins Sch. Hygiene and Pub. Health, 1995—98; trustee After Sch. Corp., 1999—2007; bd. dirs. Grad Sch. Arts and Sci. Alumni Assn., Columbia U., 1984—93, vice chmn., 1984—91; bd. dirs. Internat. Univ. Exch., Inc., 1996—2007. Lt. comdr. USNR, 1941—45. Recipient Letters of Commendation with ribbon Sec. of Navy and chief Bur. Ordnance for invention of naval gunfire device used in WWII, Pub. Svc. award Mus. City of N.Y., 1981, Disting. Pub. Svc. award NSF, 1982, Tribute of Appreciation, Nat. Sci. Bd., 1991, Pub. Welfare medal NAS, 1996, medal of distinction Barnard Coll., Columbia U., 1999, Dean's award for disting. achievement Grad. Sch. A&S, Conservation Citizen award Ctr. Environ. Rsch. and Conservation, 2003. Fellow AAAS (treas., bd. dirs. 1969-2000, treas. emeritus 2000, Lifetime Achievement award 2001), N.Y. Acad. Scis. (hon. life; mem. bd. govs. 1977—, pres. 1988, chmn. 1989, life gov. 1991), Am. Acad. Arts and Scis. (Scholar-Patriot award 2001), Assn. Women in Sci., N.Y. Acad. Medicine; mem. Nat. Acad. Pub. Adminstrn., Am. Philos. Soc. (mem. coun. 1985-91, v.p. 1992—, Benjamin Franklin award for disting. pub. svc. 1995), History of Sci. Soc., Coun. Fgn. Rels., Army and Navy Club, Cosmos Club (Washington), Century Assn. Office: 500 Fifth Ave 50th Fl New York NY 10110-5099

GOLDEN, WILSON, lawyer; b. Holly Springs, Miss., Feb. 15, 1948; s. Woodrow Wilson and Constance Annette (Harris) G.; m. Krista Nix, July 10, 1999; children from previous marriage: Wilson Harris, Lewis Hamilton, Pamela Camille. BPA, U. Miss., 1970, JD, 1977. Bar: Miss. 1977, U.S. Dist. Ct. (no. and so. dists.) Miss. 1977, U.S. Ct. Appeals (5th cir.) 1977. Pub. affairs journalist PBS/Miss. Authority for Ednl. TV, Jackson, 1970-72; asst. sec. Miss. State Senate, Jackson, 1972-76; ptnr. Lane & Henderson, Greenville, Miss., 1977-80, Watkins Ludlam & Stennis, Jackson, 1980-89; pvt. practice Jackson, Washington, 1990-96; v.p. govt. rels. ICF Kaiser Internat., Inc., Fairfax, Va., 1996—99; sr. congl. liaison US Dept. Transp., Washington, 1999-2001; v.p., of counsel Jefferson Govt. Rels., Washington, 2001—. Prin. Golden & Assocs., Falls Church, Va., 2005—. Mem. Dem. State Exec. Com., 1976-84, 88-96; mem. Miss. Gov.'s Constl. Study Commn., 1986; mem. Dem. Nat. Com., 1990-92; charter mem. Dem. Leadership Coun. NETWORK, 1988; USDOT rep. Miss. Spl. Task Force for Econ. Devel. Planning, 2000—. Major USAR, 1970-90. Recipient Disting. Reporting award Am. Polit. Sci. Assn. 1971, U.S. Law Week award Bur. Nat. Affairs, Inc., Washington, 1978. Mem.: Miss. Bar Assn. Democrat. Presbyterian. Home: 7037 E Haycock Rd Falls Church VA 22043-2319 Home Phone: 703-531-0144. Personal E-mail: wilsongolden@aol.com.

GOLDENBERG, CHARLES LAWRENCE, real estate company executive; b. NYC, Sept. 4, 1933; BS, NYU, 1955, JD, 1958. Associated with Brown, Harris, Stevens, Inc., 1955-75, officer, 1960-75, sr. v.p., dir. fin. dist. office; pres., CEO Sylan Lawrence Co., Inc., NYC, 1975—. Former adj. prof. real estate NYU; cons., lectr. in field. Contbr. articles to N.Y. Times, Real Estate Weekly, and other profl. jours. Mem. Nat. Assn. Real Estate Bds., Internat. Real Estate Fedn., Real Estate Bd. N.Y. Inc. (gov.). Address: 980 Fifth Ave New York NY 10021-0126 Office Phone: 212-344-0044 x300. E-mail: clg_ny@yahoo.com.

GOLDENBERG, DAVID MILTON, experimental pathologist, oncologist; b. NYC, Aug. 2, 1938; s. Leo and Lillie (Spivak) G.; m. Hildegard Gruenbaum, Apr. 28, 1961 (div. 1996); children: Eva, Deborah, Marc, Denis, Neil, Lee; m. Cynthia Sullivan, Aug. 13, 1997. Student, Shimer Coll., 1954-56; BS, U. Chgo., 1958; ScD, U. Erlangen-Nuremberg, Fed. Republic of Germany, 1965; MD, U. Heidelberg, Fed. Republic of Germany, 1966. Assoc. rsch. prof. pathology U. Pitts. Med. Sch., 1968-70; assoc. prof. pathology Temple U. Med. Sch., Phila., 1970-72, U. Ky. Med. Ctr., Lexington, 1972-73; prof., dir. div. exptl. pathology U. Ky., Lexington, 1973-83; pres. Ctr. for Molecular Medicine and Immunology, Belleville, NJ, 1983—; founder, pres. Garden State Cancer Ctr., Belleville, NJ, 1992—; adj. prof. surgery N.J. Med. Sch., U. of Medicine and Dentistry of N.J., Newark, 1983—93. Adj. prof. microbiology immunology N.Y. Med. Coll., Valhalla, 1993-2000; mem. VA Merit Rev. Bd. for Oncology, Washington, 1974-77; exec. dir. Ephraim McDowell Cmty. Cancer Network, Lexington, 1975-80; pres. Ephraim McDowell Cancer Rsch. Foun., 1978-80; sec., treas. Ky. Cancer Commn., Frankfort, 1978-80; mem. sci. adv. bd. German Fund for Cancer Rsch., Bonn, 1980-90; mem. exptl. immunology study sect. NIH, Bethesda, Md., 1980-83; chmn bd. Immunomedics inc., Morris Plains, NJ, 1983-; bd. trustees, Ctr. Molecular Medicine and immunology, Belleville, NJ, 1983-. Author more than 1500 articles, book chpts., abstracts, 1962—; mem. editl. bd. Tumor Biology, Antibody, Immunoconjugates and Radiopharms., Jour. Nuclear Medicine, Qtly. Jour. Nuclear Medicine, Tumor Targeting. Outstanding Investigator grantee Nat. Cancer Inst., 1985, 92; recipient Rsch. Found. award U. Ky., 1978, N.J. Pride award in sci. and tech. N.J. Monthly, 1986, Excellence in Cancer Rsch. award N.J. Legis., 1986, Herz Meml. lectureship Tel Aviv U., 1991, 3M/Mayneord Meml. lectureship Brit. Inst. Radiology, 1991, Abbott prize Internat. Soc. Oncodevelopmental Biol. Medicine, 1994, Vikram Sarabhai Meml. Oration award, Soc. Nuclear Medicine, India, 1994, Ted Bloch Meml. lectr. Southwestern chpt. Soc. Nuc. Medicine, 1999, Elis Bervin lecture and medal, Swedish Oncology Soc., 2002, Garden State Cancer Ctr. Special Sci. award, 2003, Dist. Scientist award, Clinical Ligand Assay Soc., 2004, Paul Aebersold award, Soc. Nuclear Medicine, 2005; named Inventor of Yr., N.J. Rsch. Devel. Coun., 2005. Hon. mem. Argentine Cancer Assn. Jewish. Achievements include several U.S. and fgn. patents in field; Pioneered the development of radiolabeled antibodies for various applications in the detection, diagnosis and therapy of cancer. Under his leadership, the scientists and clinicians at the Garden State Cancer Center have developed antibodies for the diagnosis, detection and treatment of solid tumors such as colorectal, pancreatic, lung, breast and ovarian cancers, as well as certain hematologic cancers such as lymphoma and multiple myeloma. He has overseen the in-house clinic as well as clinical outreach at affiliated institutions in the United States and Europe for treatment of cancer patients with radiolabeled antibodies. He also helped develop two diagnostic radiopharmaceuticals marketed by Immunomedics Inc., which he established in 1982. Office: Immunomedics Inc 300 American Rd Morris Plains NJ 07950 also: CMMI 520 Belleville Ave Belleville NJ 07109 Personal E-mail: dmg.gscancer@att.net.*

GOLDENBERG, FELIX, retired electrical engineer, researcher; b. Yalta, Ukraine, Apr. 24, 1939; arrived in US, 1993; s. Moisey Goldenberg and Ida Koretskaya; m. Leeza Kaschuk, Jan. 12, 1961; children: Michael, Irina. MS in Electro-Mech. Engring., Russian So. State Poly. U., 1961; PhD, Russian State Supreme Air Force Engring. Acad., Moscow, Russia, 1977. Head sci. rsch. lab. Ramenskoye Design Co., Ramenskoye, Moscow Region, Russia, 1961—91; rsch. engr. Watson Industries, Inc., Eau Claire, Wis., 1995—98; v.p. engring. Humprey, Inc., San Diego, 1998—2001; engring. fellow advanced sensors tech. ctr. Goodrich Corp., Burnsville, Minn., 2001—. Contbr. articles to profl. jours. Mem.: IEEE, Inst. Nav. (Walter R. Fried Best Paper award 2006). Achievements include patents for method of adjusting a fluxgate magnetometer apparatus; patents pending for force balanced impeller flow meter for mass flow rate control; high performance MEMS gyroscope. Home: 12653 NW 13 Ct Sunrise FL 33323 Personal E-mail: fgoldenberg@usfamily.net.

GOLDENBERG, GEORGE, retired pharmaceutical executive; b. NYC, Mar. 12, 1929; s. Gersh and Rose (Kolpacci) G.; m. Arlene Sandra Yudell, May 22, 1955; children: Steven Alan, Heidi Michele Goldenberg Handelsman, Jeffrey Evan. Student, Bklyn. Coll., 1946-47; BS, Bklyn. Coll. Pharmacy L.I. U., 1951. Pharmacist Dolcorts Pharmacy, NYC, 1951-56; export mgr. Chem. Specialties Co., Inc., NYC, 1956-58; sales mgr. Syntex Chem. Co., Inc., NYC, 1958-60; asst. to pres. Syntex Labs., Inc., NYC, 1960-61; gen. sales mgr. Panray-Parlam Corp., Englewood, NJ, 1961-63; v.p. Ormont Drug & Chem. Co., Inc., Englewood, 1963-64, exec. v.p., dir., 1964-66, pres., dir., 1966-81; sec., dir. Goldleaf Pharmacal Co., Inc., Englewood, 1966-81; pres., dir. Moleculon, Inc., 1982-88; pres., CEO, dir. Argus Pharms. Inc., The Woodlands, Tex., 1988-92. Bd. dirs. Fed. Pharmacal Co., Ft. Lauderdale, Fla., Bedford Acme Surg. Co., Inc., Bklyn., Lawton Labs., Inc., Englewood, Ormont Diagnostics Ltd., London. Trustee L.I. U., Bklyn. Coll. Pharmacy. Mem. Bklyn. Coll. Pharmacy Alumni Assn. (pres.), Fedn. Alumni Assns. L.I. U. (pres.), Am. Pharm. Assn., Englewood Jr. C. of C., Young Pres. Orgn., Am. Mgmt. Assn., Drug and Allied Trades Assn., Delta Sigma Theta. Clubs: B'nai B'rith, The Polo Club of Boca Raton (past pres. bd. govs.), Jewish Fedn. of S. Palm Beach County (chmn.). Home: 16730 Colchester Ct Delray Beach FL 33484-6946 E-mail: aggpolo@aol.com.

GOLDENBERG, KIM, retired academic administrator, internist, consultant; BS, SUNY, Stonybrook, 1968; MS, Polytech. Inst. N.Y., 1972; MD, Albany Med. Coll., NYC, 1979. Test engr. lunar lander and naval jets, Grumman, NY, 1968—75; resident internal medicine Western Res. Care Sys., Youngstown, Ohio, 1979—82; dir. gen. internal medicine Sch. Medicine Wright State U. Sch. Medicine, Dayton, Ohio, 1983—89, vice chair medicine, 1988—89, assoc. dean for students and curriculum, 1989—90, dean, 1990—98; pres. Wright State U., Dayton, Ohio, 1998—2007.

GOLDENBERG, WILLIAM BRUCE, musician, educator; b. Cleve., Nov. 1, 1950; s. David and Helen Goldenberg. BA, Oberlin Coll., 1972; MusM, SUNY, Stony Brook, 1974, Juilliard Sch., 1976; MusD, Ind. U., 1991. Head tchg. asst. SUNY, Stony Brook, 1972—74; piano tchg. fellow and accompanist Juilliard Sch., NYC, 1974—76; personal asst. to Menahem Pressler Ind. U. Sch. of Music, Bloomington, 1976—80; disting. prof. piano and chamber music No. Ill. U., DeKalb, 1980—; chair dept. piano and collaborative piano No. Ill. U. Sch. Music, DeKalb, 1996—. Concert pianist Idyllwild (Calif.) Arts Music Festival, 1995—, Grand Teton Music Festival, Jackson Hole, Wyo., 1983—84; guest prof. Ind. U., 1995; adjudicator Joanna Hodges Piano Competition, Palm Springs, Calif., 1983, Grace Welsh Internat. Piano Competition, Chgo., 2002, Music Tchrs. Nat. Assn., Decatur, Ill., 2003, St. Charles (Ill.) Internat. Art and Music Festival Piano Competition, 1987—88; masterclass tchr. Shanghai Conservatory of Music, 2001; masterclasses tchr. Liszt Acad., Budapest, 2003. Musician: (CDs) Violin Sonatas with Vermeer Quartet Violinist Pierre Menard, Contemporary Chamber Music, Door County Suite, Petite Suite for my Grandchildren, (concert tours) Asia, 2001, 2004, Europe, 2003—, 2004, Scandanavia, 2005, Can., 2006, Australia and New Zealand, 2007; contbr. articles to profl. publs. Named winner Concerto Competition, Oberlin Coll., 1971, Ind. U., 1978; Piano fellow, Tanglewood Music Festival, 1975. Mem.: East Meets West Music Arts- Chgo. (adv. bd. 1993—), Pi Kappa Lambda, Phi Beta Kappa. Achievements include grants for research in non-traditional repertoire from diverse cultures (Asian, Hispanic, Black) and contemporary music. Home: PO Box 165 Dekalb IL 60115 Office: No Ill U Dekalb IL 60115 Business E-Mail: goldenberg@niu.edu.

GOLDENKRANZ, ANDREW, principal, educator; married; 2 children. BS, Stanford U. With Linus Pauling Inst. for Sci. and Medicine; asst. prin., tchr. Aptos HS, Calif.; prin. Pacific Collegiate Sch., Santa Cruz, Calif., 2005—. Dir. summer residential biology inst. Woodrow Wilson Found., 1998—2002; spkr. in field. Office: Pacific Collegiate Sch Office of Prin/Supt PO Box 1701 Santa Cruz CA 95061-1701 Office Phone: 831-479-7785. Office Fax: 831-427-5254. E-mail: Andrew.goldenkranz@pcsed.org.*

GOLDER, HERBERT ALAN, classics educator; b. Oct. 29, 1952; BA, Boston U., 1975; MA, Yale U., 1977, MPhil, 1979, PhD, 1984; postgrad., Oxford U., 1982. Tchg. fellow, instr. in classics Yale U., New Haven,

1977-80; asst. prof. of classics Syracuse (N.Y.) U., 1982-85, Emory U., Atlanta, 1985-87, Boston U., 1988-93, assoc. prof. classics, 1993—2004, prof. classics, 2004—. Vis. asst. prof. classics Emory U., Atlanta, 1984-85. Archival rschr. The White Diamond, 2004 (Best Non-Fiction Film award N.Y. Film Critics Circle, 2005), The Wild Blue Yonder, 2005 (Internat. Critics prize The Internat. Fedn. Film Critics, 2005), Rescue Dawn, 2007; asst. dir.: (documentary) Little Dieter Needs to Fly, 1997 (Emmy nomination 1999, Disting. Achievement award Internat. Documentary Assn. 1998, Spl. Jury prize Amsterdam Internat. Documentary Film Festival 1997), Wings of Hope, 1999, My Best Fiend, 1999, The Lord and the Laden, 2000; asst. dir., co-writer, actor (film) Invincible, 2002; gen. editor: (with William Arrowsmith) The Greek Tragedy in New Translations, 1985-96, editor-in-chief: Arion, A Jour. Humanities and the Classics, 1990— (CELJ Phoenix award for significant editl. achievement 1992, APA Inaugural Scholarly Outreach award 2004); author: Sophocles' Aias, 1999, Euripides' Bacchae, 2001. Office: 621 Commonwealth Ave Boston MA 02215 Home Phone: 617-424-1130; Office Phone: 617-353-6480. Business E-Mail: redlog@bu.edu.

GOLDFARB, ALVIN, academic administrator; b. NYC, Apr. 1, 1951; s. Martin and Shirley Goldfarb; m. Elaine Carol Johanson, Apr. 3, 1973; children: Deborah Anne, Jason Benjamin. BA, CUNY, Queens, NY, 1972; MA, CUNY, NYC, 1974, PhD, 1978. Asst. prof. theatre Ill. State U., Normal, 1977—81, chair theatre dept., mng. dir. Ill. shakespeare festival, 1981—88, dean fine arts, 1988—98, provost, acad. v.p., 1998—2002; pres. We. Ill. U., Macomb, 2002—. Co-author: (textbook) Living Theatre, Theater: The Lively Art; co-editor: Anthology of Living Theater, (anthology) Theatrical Performance during the Holocaust (Finalist Nat. Jewish Book awards). Mem. Ill. Arts Coun., 1996—2000; chair Am. Coll. Theatre Festival-Region III, 1985—88; pres. Ill. Alliance for Arts Edn., 1997—99. Recipient Kennedy Ctr. medallion, Am. Coll. Theatre Festival, Region III, 1989, Outstanding Contbn. award, Ill. Theatre Assn., 1991, Svc. award, Ill. Alliance for Arts Edn., 1993, Alumni Achievement award, CUNY Grad. Ctr., 2001, Hunter Coll., CUNY, 2003. Mem.: Phi Beta Kappa. Avocation: travel. Home: 2001 N Wigwam Hollow Rd Macomb IL 61455 Office: Western Ill Univ 1 University Cir Macomb IL 61455 Home Phone: 309-837-5700; Office Phone: 309-298-1824. Business E-Mail: a-goldfarb@wiu.edu.

GOLDFARB, BERNARD SANFORD, lawyer; b. Cleve., Apr. 15, 1917; s. Harry and Esther (Lenson) Goldfarb; m. Barbara Brofman Goldfarb, Jan. 4, 1966; children: Meredith Stacy, Lauren Beth. AB, Case Western Res. U., 1938, JD, 1940. Bar: Ohio 1940. Since practiced in, Cleve.; sr. ptnr. firm Goldfarb & Reznick, 1967-95; pvt. practice Cleve., 1997—. Spl. counsel to atty. gen. Ohio, 1950, 1971—74; mem. Ohio Commn. Uniform Traffic Rules, 1973—80. Contbr. articles to profl. jours. With USAAF, 1942—45. Mem.: ABA, Cuyahoga County Bar Assn., Greater Cleve. Bar Assn., Ohio Bar Assn. Home: 39 Pepper Creek Dr Pepper Pike OH 44124-5279 Office: 55 Public Sq Ste 1500 Cleveland OH 44113-1998 Office Phone: 216-696-0606 ext. 250. Personal E-mail: bunnysgoldfarb@aol.com.

GOLDFARB, C. RICHARD, radiologist, educator; b. NYC, Feb. 22, 1946; s. Harold and Lenore (Goldenheim) G.; m. Linda Markovitz; children: Adina R., Akiva M., Aviva S., Aliza L., Atara C. AB, Columbia U., 1966; MD, N.Y. Med. Coll., 1970. Diplomate Am. Bd. Radiology, Am. Bd. Nuclear Medicine. Intern Met. Hosp. Ctr., NYC, 1970-71; resident in diagnostic radiology St. Luke's Med. Ctr., NYC, 1971-74, fellow in nuclear medicine and ultrasound, 1974-75; dir. nuclear medicine Nassau County Med. Ctr., East Meadow, NY, 1976-79; chief nuclear medicine Beth Israel Med. Ctr., NYC, 1979—; assoc. prof. radiology Albert Einstein Coll. Medicine, NYC, 1988—. Editor Practical Reviews in Nuclear Medicine, 1992—; author: 2 books; contbr. articles to profl. jours. Maj. U.S. Army, 1971-84. Named Tchr. of the Yr. Radiology Dept., Nassau County Med. Ctr., 1979, Beth Israel Med. Ctr., 2004. Mem. N.Y. Acad. Sci., Radiol. Soc. N.Am., Soc. Nuclear Medicine, Am. Coll. Radiology. Jewish. Home: 490 W End Ave New York NY 10024-4329 Office: Beth Israel Med Ctr 1st Ave and 16th St New York NY 10003 Home Phone: 212-874-2915; Office Phone: 212-420-2339. Business E-Mail: rgoldfar@chpnet.org.

GOLDFARB, DAVID, investment banking executive; Grad., Robert H. Smith Sch. Bus., U. of Md., 1979. Various positions to sr. ptnr. Ernst & Young, 1979—93; joined Lehman Bros. Inc., 1993, controller, 1995—2000, CFO, 1998—; exec. v.p., CFO Lehman Bros. Holdings Inc., 2000—04, chief adminstrv. officer, 2004—06, global head strategic partnerships, 2006—. Mem. Lehman Bros. Operating com. Recipient Disting. Alumnus award, Robert H. Smith Sch. Bus., U. Md., 2004. Mem.: SIA Fin. Mgmt. and Internal Audit divisions, AICPA Stock Brokerage Com. Office: Lehman Bros Holdings Inc 745 7th Ave 31st Fl New York NY 10019-6801*

GOLDFARB, DONALD, industrial engineering educator; b. NYC, Aug. 14, 1941; s. Leon and Hannah (Marcus) G.; m. Ranny Lichtman, June 29, 1968; children: Benjamin, Cora. B.Chem. Engring., Cornell U., 1963; MA, Princeton U., 1965, PhD, 1966. Asst. research scientist Courant Inst. Math. Sci., NYC, 1966-68; mem. faculty CCNY, 1968-83, prof. computer sci., 1977-83; prof. indsl. engring. and ops. research Columbia U., NYC, 1982—, chmn. dept. indsl. engring. and ops. research, 1984, 1995—2002, acting dean Sch. Engring. and Applied Sci., 1994-95, Alexander and Hermine Avanessians prof. indsl. engring. and ops. rsch., 2002—. Mem. com. recommendations U.S. Army Basic Sci. Rsch. of NRC; rsch. faculty mem. T.J. Watson Rsch. Lab., IBM, Yorktown Heights, N.Y., summers 1972, 76, 91; rsch. assoc. Atomic Energy Rsch. Establishment, Harwell, Eng., 1974-75; vis. prof. Cornell U., Ithaca, N.Y., 1979-80; mem. adv. coun. dept. civil engring. and ops. rsch. Princeton (N.J.) U.; cons. in field. Editor SIAM Jour. Numerical Analysis, 1982-84, SIAM Jour. on Optimization, 1989-95; editor-in-chief Math. Programming, Series A, 1994-99; assoc. editor Math. of Computation, 1969-90, mem. editl. com., 1982-85; assoc. editor Ops. Rsch., 1983-95, Math. Programming, 1983-95, 99—. NSF fellow, 1963-66; grantee NSF, 1973-75, 80—, ARO, 1977-80, 82-85, ONR, 1987-1990, 2003—, DOE, 1992—. Mem. Inst. for Ops. Rsch. and Mgmt. Scis. (prize for rsch. excellence in the interface between ops. rsch. and computer sci. 1995), Am. Math. Soc. (mem. coun. 1985-87), Soc. Indsl. and Applied Math., Math. Programming Soc. (mem. coun. 1982-85, Hon. Mention prize SIAG/OPT 1996). Home: 6 Peter Cooper Rd Apt 8C New York NY 10010-6709 Office: Columbia U Dept Indsl Engring Ops Rsch 316 SW Mudd Bldg New York NY 10027 E-mail: goldfarb@columbia.edu.

GOLDFARB, ERIC DANIEL, information technology executive; b. Kalamazoo, Mich., Apr. 29, 1964; s. Russell Marshall and Clare Sara (Rosett) Goldfarb; m. Gwen Julia Oberman, Aug. 20, 1989; children: Adam, David. Bachelors, U. Mich., 1986. Project leader Domino's Pizza, Inc., Ann Arbor, Mich., 1986—90; mgr. info. sys. Interpublic Group (Lintas), Warren, Mich., 1990-91; mgr. bus. sys. The Limited Inc. (Express), Columbus, Ohio, 1991-94; CIO Elder-Beerman Stores Corp., Dayton, Ohio, 1994—96; CIO and CTO Pearson plc (Viacom-Macmillan), Indpls., 1996—2001; CIO Global Knowledge Inc., Cary, NC, 2001—02; CIO and exec. v.p. PRG-Schultz Internat., Inc., Atlanta, 2002—06, BearingPoint, Inc., McLean, Va., 2006—. Spkr. in field. Author: Ways to Reduce IT Spending, 2004, Staying Ahead of the Technology Curve, 2005, Strategies Today for Preventing Tomorrow's Technology Nightmares, 2005, Developing a Technology Strategy for Your Company, 2006, The CTO Best Practices Collection, 2006; contbr. articles to profl jours., chapters to books. Named Premier 100 IT Leader, IDG ComputerWorld, 2003; recipient nat. Arthur D. Little Best of the Best award. Republican. Achievements include patents in field. Avocations: painting, sailing, golf. Office: 115 Perimeter Pl Atlanta GA 30346

GOLDFARB, IRENE DALE, retired financial planner; b. Newark, Jan. 13, 1929; d. Philip and Lucie (Mintz) Dale; m. Samuel Goldfarb, Jan. 28, 1951; children: Ruth Goldfarb Koizim, David Alan, Sally Fay, Judith Valerie. BS in Chemistry, Rutgers U., 1950; MBA, U. Pa., 1979. CFP. Asst. to assoc. provost Princeton (N.J.) U., 1968-70, asst. to provost, 1970-72, tech. staff, 1972-74, mgr. pers. svcs., 1974-75, asst. dir. pers. svcs., 1975-84; fin. planner, mgr. A.L. Herst Assocs., Inc., Princeton, 1984-86; pvt. practice Princeton, 1986-90; v.p. A.L. Herst Assocs., Inc., Princeton, 1990-92; fin. planner Glenmede Trust Co. N.J., Princeton, 1992—2001; ret., 2002. Cons. in field. Mem. Fin. Planning Assn. (founding officer Princeton-Western N.J. chpt. 1986-98, pres. 1988-89, chmn. 1989-90), Assoc. Alumnae Douglass Coll. (chmn. ann. fund 1982-84, v.p. adminstrn. 1988-94), Phi Beta Kappa. Avocations: music, gardening, travel. Home and Office: 69 Balsam Ln Princeton NJ 08540-5326

GOLDFARB, JOEL PETER, internist, gastroenterologist; b. Fitchburg, Mass., Jan. 17, 1949; s. Abraham and Eunice (Caplan) G.; m. Elizabeth Weinshel, Dec. 5, 1954. BA, Yale U., 1971; MD, NYU, 1975. Diplomate Am. Bd. Internal Medicine, Am. Bd. Gastroenterology. Resident NYU Bellevue, NYC, 1975-78; fellow (liver) Yale, New Haven, 1978-79; fellow (G.I.) Columbia, NYC, 1979-81; asst. prof. medicine Yeshiva U., Bronx, NY, 1981-84; ptnr. D. Penn MD, J. Patrowitz MD, J. Goldfarb MD, PA., Fort Lee, NJ, 1984—. Asst. clin. prof. medicine Mt. Sinai. Named one of Best Doctors of N.J., N.J. Monthly Mag., 1996, 2001, N.Y. Mag., 2001, 2002, N.J. Life Mag., 2005. Fellow Am. Coll. Physicians, Am. Coll. Gastroenterology. Avocations: cross country skiing, swimming, hiking, scuba diving, opera. Home: 2621 Palisade Ave Apt 5B Bronx NY 10463-6108 Office: 1600 Parker Ave Fort Lee NJ 07024-7050 E-mail: jpgoldfarb@cs.com.

GOLDFARB, MURIEL BERNICE, marketing and advertising consultant; b. Bklyn., Mar. 29, 1920; d. Barnett and May (Steinberg) Goldfarb. BA, U. Miami, Coral Gables, Fla., 1942; postgrad., CCNY, 1950. Pub. info. asst. UNESCO, Paris, 1946—47; advt. mgr. Majestic Specialties Co., NYC, 1947—50; retail promotion mgr. Glamour Mag., 1955—61; advt. dir. Country Tweeds Co., NYC, 1961—65, S. Augstein & Co., NYC, 1966—72, Feature Ring Co., Inc., Gotham Ring Co., Inc., Fidco Inc., NYC, 1972—77; dir. advt. promotion Wasko Gold Products Corp., NYC, 1977—81; advt. mktg. cons. specializing promotions sale vintage jewelry Bric-a-Brac, 1982—. Lt. WAVES, 1943—46. Mem.: Women's Jewelry Assn. (corr. sec. 1983—85). Jewish.

GOLDFARB, ROBERT PAUL, neurological surgeon; b. St. Paul, July 17, 1936; s. Jack and Frances S. (Singer) G.; m. Lesley G. Zatz, Aug. 11, 1963; children: Jill, Pam. BA with distinction, U. Ariz., 1958; MD, Tulane U., 1962. Diplomate Am. Bd. Neurol. Surgery. Intern Michael Reese Hosp., Chgo., 1962-63; resident gen. surgery Presbyn. St. Luke's Hosp., Chgo., 1963-64; resident neurol. surgery U. Ill. Rsch. Hosp., Chgo., 1963-67; pres. med. staff Crippled Children's Svc. So. Ariz., Tucson, 1973-75; chief staff Tucson Med. Ctr., 1978-80; neurol. surgeon Western Neurosurgery, Ltd., Tucson, 1980—. Bd. disr. S.W. Physician Network; neurosurg. cons. U. Ariz. athletic teams, Tucson, 1980—; trustee El Dorado Hosp., 1999—2005; mem. Ariz. Bd. Med. Examiners, 2002—, bd. sec., 2003-04, chmn. bd., 2006. Maj. USAFR, 1962-70. Baird scholar U. Ariz., 1958. Fellow ACS; mem. Am. Assn. Neurol. Surgeons, Congress Neurol. Surgeons, Am. Coll. Physician Exec., Rocky Mountain Neurosurg. Soc. (v.p. 1979). Office: Western Neurosurgery Ltd 4753 E Camp Lowell Dr Tucson AZ 85712

GOLDFARB, RONALD LAWRENCE, lawyer, writer, literary agent; b. Jersey City, Oct. 16, 1933; s. Robert S. and Aida J. (Weintraub) G.; m. Joanne Jacob, June 9, 1957; children: Jody, Nicholas, Maximilian Goldfarb. AB, Syracuse U., 1954, LLB, 1956; LLM, Yale, 1960, JSD, 1962. Bar: N.Y. 1956, Calif. 1959, D.C. 1962, U.S. Supreme Ct. 1965. Spl. asst. to U.S. atty. gen. (organized crime sect.), 1961-64; ptnr. Goldfarb and Assocs. and predecessor law firms, 1966—. Dir. Brookings Instn. program on cts. and adminstrn. Justice, 1966-67; mem. staff counsel com. on law and social action Am. Jewish Congress, 1960-61; cons. Pres.'s Poverty Program, 1964, Riots Commn., 1967-68 Author: The Contempt Power, 1963, Ransom: A Critique of the American Bail System, 1965, (with Alfred Friendly) Crime and Publicity, 1967, (with Linda Singer) After Conviction--A Review of the American Correction System, 1973, Jails: The Ultimate Ghetto, 1975, Migrant Farm Workers: A Caste of Despair, 1981, (with James Raymond) Clear Understandings: A Guide to Legal Writing, 1983, (with Gail Ross) The Writer's Lawyer: Essential Legal Advice for Writers and Editors in All Media, 1989, Perfect Villains, Imperfect Heroes: Robert F. Kennedy's War Against Organized Crime, 1995, TV or Not TV: Television, Justice and Courts, 1998, In Confidence, 2007. Bd. dir. Va. Ctr. for the Creative Arts, The Alliance for Justice. Capt. JAG Corp. USAF, 1957—60. Arthur Garfield Hays fellow N.Y.U., 1960-61; Woodrow Wilson fellow. Mem. ACLU, D.C. Bar Assn., N.Y. Bar Assn., Calif. Bar Assn., Cosmos Club, Sigma Alpha Mu, Phi Delta Phi. Office: 721 Gibbon St Alexandria VA 22314 Office Phone: 202-466-3030. Personal E-mail: rglawlit@aol.com.

GOLDFARB, RUTH, poet, educator; b. Bklyn., Aug. 13, 1936; d. Nathan Alter and Florence Goldfarb. BA in Psychology, L.I. Univ., 1980; MA in Edn., NYU, 1984. Tchr. kindergarten N.Y.C. Bd. Edn., 1963-64, early childhood tchr., 1993-94, NYC, Bklyn., 1970-84; tchr. common br. Bklyn. Bd. Edn., 1986-93; clk. Primary Health Care Ctr. North Broward Med. Ctr., Pompano Beach, Fla., 1998—. Author (poetry) Whispers and Chants, 1997, Poems That Elevate the Soul, 2006; CD recs. include Christmas Memories, 1999, The Miracle of Christmas, 2000, Songs of Praise, 2000. Mem.: AARP, Gold Coast Poetry Group, Acad. Am. Poets, Internat. Soc. Poets. Avocations: poetry, music, sculpture, writing stories.

GOLDFARB, STANLEY, internist, educator; b. NYC, Dec. 18, 1943; s. Robert Melvin and Mary Ann (Siegel) G.; m. Rayna Lynne Block, Aug. 30, 1970; children: Rachael, Michael. AB, Princeton U., 1965; MD, U. Rochester, 1969; MS, U. Pa., 1986. Intern Hosp. U. Pa., Phila., 1969-70, resident, 1970-73; asst. prof. U. Pa., Phila., 1974-84, assoc. prof., 1984-88, prof. medicine, 1988—. Mem. nephrology bd. Am. Bd. Internal Medicine, Phila., 1988—. Editor: Hormones, Autocoids and Kidney, 1991. Bd. dirs, bd. regents ACP; bd. dirs. Nat. Kidney Found. Pa., Phila, 1988-90. NIH grantee, Washington, 1984-88; recipient Vol. award Nat. Kidney Found., N.Y.C., 1990. Mem. Am. Soc. Clin. Investigation. Avocation: golf. Home: 801 Muirfield Rd Bryn Mawr PA 19010-1940 Office: Hosp of the U of Pa 3400 Spruce St Philadelphia PA 19104-4206

GOLDFARB, WILL, chef; Attended, Duke U. Apprentice, commis El Bulli, 1999—2000; pastry chef Ryland Inn, Whitehouse, NJ, 1999—2001; garde mgr. Atlas, NYC, 2001; pastry chef Papillon, NYC, 2001—02, Castine Inn, Maine, Morimoto, Phila., 2002—04, Cru, NYC, 2004—05; owner, chef Room 4 Dessert, NYC, 2006—. Founder AKWA. Named one of NYC's Rising Stars, StarChefs.com, 2006. Office: Room 4 Dessert 17 Cleveland Pl New York NY 10012 Office Phone: 212-941-5405.

GOLDFARB, WILLIAM D., underwriter, investor; b. El Paso, Tex., Sept. 16, 1921; s. Sol and Leona Goldfarb; m. Miriam Kahn Goldfarb, Aug. 22, 1951; children: Allan, Pamela, Cathy, Thomas. BBA, U. Tex., Austin, 1942. CLU, ChFC. Life underwriter Southwestern Life, El Paso, 1946—96; investor El Paso, 1956—. Chmn. Pres.'s Coun., Southwestern Life, Dallas, 1980—82. Pres. BBB, El Paso, 1970, El Paso Jewish Fedn. and Ctr., 1967—69; dir. Tex. Leaders Round Table, 1970—80. Lt. USN, 1942—46, PTO. Mem.: Nat. Assn. Ins. and Fin. Advisors (Life Underwriter Man of Yr. 1966), Assn. Advanced Life Underwriters, Soc. Fin. Svc. Profls. (founding), Estate Planning Coun. El Paso (founding). Office: David Dick and Assocs Inc 501 Executive Ctr # 100 El Paso TX 79902 Office Phone: 915-533-9901. Fax: 915-533-2205. Business E-Mail: bill.goldfarb@dwdassoc.com.

GOLDFEIN, SHEPARD, lawyer; b. Englewood, NJ, 1948; AB, Rutgers U., 1970, JD, 1975; MA, U. Chgo., 1977. Bar: NY 1976, NJ 1977. Practice leader for antitrust Skadden, Arps, Slate, Meagher & Flom LLP, NYC, 1975—. Editor: Rutgers Law Rev., 1974-75; contbr. articles to profl. jours.; co-author, monthly trade regulation column, NY Law Jour., 1983-. Mem.: Assn. Bar City of NY (chmn., sports law com. 1996—99), NY State Bar Assn. (chmn., civil practice and procedure com., antitrust sect. 1982—84), Phi Beta Kappa, Pi Sigma Alpha. Office: Skadden Arps Slate Meagher & Flom LLP 4 Times Sq 34th Fl New York NY 10036-6595 Home Phone: 201-568-0610; Office Phone: 212-735-3610. Business E-Mail: sgoldfei@skadden.com.

GOLDFIELD, EMILY DAWSON, finance company executive, artist; b. Bklyn., May 31, 1947; d. Martin and Renee (Solow) Dawson; m. Stephen Gary Goldfield, June 17, 1973; children: Stacy Rose, Daniel James. BS, U. Mich., 1969; MEd, Pa. State U., 1971; PhD, U. So. Calif., 1977. Chmn. bd. Union Home Loan, Inc. Author: The Value of Creative Dance, 1971; Development of Creative Dance, 1977. U. Mich. scholar, 1969; Pa. State U. fellow, 1970, U. So. Calif. fellow, 1972. Mem.: Pastel Soc. San Diego, Allied Artists of the Santa Monica Mountains, Pastel Soc. of the West Coast, Calif. Art Club, Calif. Mortgage Assn. Office: 23586 Calabasas Rd Ste 201 Calabasas CA 91302-1322

GOLDFRANK, LEWIS ROBERT, physician; b. NYC, Sept. 8, 1941; s. Herbert John and Helen (Colodny) G.; m. Susan M. Harrington, Aug. 29, 1964; children: Michelle, Andrew, Jennifer, Rebecca. BA, Clark U., 1963; MD, U. Brussels, Belgium, 1970. Diplomate Am. Bd. Med. Toxicology (dir., chmn. 1985-90), Am. Bd. Internal Medicine, 1973, Am. Bd. Emergency Medicine, 1979. Resident Montefiore Hosp., Bronx, NY, 1971-73; dir. emergency medicine Morrisania Hosp., Bronx, 1973-76, North Cen. Bronx Hosp., 1976-79, Montefiore Hosp., 1976-79, Bellevue Hosp., NYC, 1979—, NYU Med. Ctr., NYC, 1979—; dir. N.Y.C. Poison Ctr., 1979—; prof. and chmn. dept. emergency medicine Sch. Medicine NYU, NYC, 2003—. Author, editor: Goldfrank's Toxicologic Emergencies, 1978, 8th edit., 2006, Emergency Doctor, 1987, Diagnostic Testing in the Emergency Department, 1984, 2d edit., 1995; editor: Preparing for Terrorism, 2002, Preparing for Psychological Consequences of Terrorisn, 2003. Recipient hon. mention Am. Med. Writers Assn., 1988, Disting. Tchr. award NYU, 2003; faculty scholar NYU, 1999. Fellow: ACP, Am. Acad. Clin. Toxicology, Am. Coll. Emergency Physician; mem.: NAS (Inst. Medicine), Soc. for Acad. Emergency Medicine (Hal Jayne Acad. Excellence award 1990, Leadership award 1999). Avocation: gardening. Home: 55 Grace Ln Ossining NY 10562-2129 Office: Bellevue Hosp Ctr 1st Ave and 27th St New York NY 10016 Office Phone: 212-562-3346. Fax: 212-562-3001. Business E-Mail: goldfl03@med.nyu.edu.

GOLDGAR, BERTRAND ALVIN, historian, educator; b. Macon, Ga., Nov. 17, 1927; s. Benjamin Meyer and Annie (Shapiro) G.; m. Corinne Cohn Hartman, Apr. 6, 1950; children: Arnold Benjamin, Anne Hartman. BA, Vanderbilt U., 1948, MA, 1949, Princeton U., 1957, PhD, 1958. Instr. in English Clemson (S.C.) U., 1948-50, asst. prof., 1951-52; instr. English Lawrence U., Appleton, Wis., 1957-61, asst. prof., 1961-65, assoc. prof., 1965-71, prof. English, 1971—, John N. Bergstrom prof. humanities, 1980—. Mem. fellowship panel NEH, 1979 Author: The Curse of Party: Swift's Relations with Addison and Steele, 1961, Walpole and the Wits: The Relation of Politics to Literature, 1722-1742, 1976; editor: The Literary Criticism of Alexander Pope, 1965, Henry Fielding's The Covent-Garden Jour., 1988, Henry Fielding's Miscellanies, Vol. 2, 1993, Jonathan Wild, 1997, The Grub Street Jour. 1730-1733, 2002; adv. editor: 18th Century Studies, 1977-82; contbr. essays to books. With AUS, 1952-54. Fellow, Am. Coun. Learned Socs, 1973-74, NEH, 1980-81. Mem. Am. Soc. 18th Century Studies, Johnson Soc. Cen. Region. Home: 914 E Eldorado St Appleton WI 54911-5536 Office: Lawrence U Dept English Appleton WI 54912 Home Phone: 920-734-8676; Office Phone: 920-832-6694. Business E-Mail: bertrand.a.goldgar@lawrence.edu.

GOLDHABER, GERSON, astrophysicist, researcher; b. Chemnitz, Germany, Feb. 20, 1924; came to US, 1948, naturalized, 1953; s. Charles and Ethel (Frisch) G.; m. Judith Margoshes, May 30, 1969; children: Amos Nathaniel, Michaela Shally, Shaya Alexandra M.Sc., Hebrew U., Jerusalem, 1947; PhD, U. Wis., 1950; PhD honoris causus, U. Stockholm, 1986. Instr. Columbia U., NYC, 1950-53; acting asst. prof. physics U. Calif., Berkeley, 1953-54, asst. prof., 1954-58, assoc. prof., 1958-63, prof. physics, 1963-92, prof. physics emeritus, 1992—; Miller research prof. Miller Inst. Basic Sci. U. Calif.-Berkeley, 1958-59, 75-76, 84-85, prof. Grad. Sch., 1994—; Morris Loeb lectr. in physics Harvard U., 1976-77. Named Calif. Scientist of Yr., 1977, Sci. Assoc., CERN, 1986; Ford Found. fellow CERN, 1960-61; Guggenheim fellow CERN, 1972-73 Fellow Am. Phys. Soc. (Panofsky prize 1991, co-recipient Gruber prize 2007), Sigma Xi; mem. Am. Astron. Soc., Royal Swedish Acad. Sci. (fgn.), Nat. Acad. Sci. Office: Lawrence Berkeley Nat Lab Physics Ms 50 R5008 Berkeley CA 94720-0001 Office Phone: 510-486-6210. Business E-Mail: gerson@lbl.gov.

GOLDHABER, MAURICE, physicist, researcher; b. Lemberg, Austria, Apr. 18, 1911; arrived in U.S., 1938, naturalized, 1944; s. Charles and Ethel (Frisch) Goldhaber; m. Gertrude Scharff, May 24, 1939; children: Alfred S., Michael H. PhD, Cambridge U., Eng., 1936; PhD (hon.), Tel Aviv U., 1974; D (hon.), U. Louvain-La-Neuve, Belgium, 1982; DSc (hon.), SUNY, Stony Brook, 1983, U. Notre Dame, 1992. Bye fellow Magdalene Coll., Cambridge, 1936—38; asst. prof. physics U. Ill., 1938—43, assoc. prof., 1943—45, prof., 1945—50; sr. scientist Brookhaven Nat. Lab., 1950—60, chmn. dept. physics, 1960—61, dir., 1961—73, disting. scientist emeritus, 1973—. Cons. labs. AEC; Morris Loeb lectr. Harvard U., 1955, 93, Rabi Scholar lectr., 55; adj. prof. physics SUNY, Stony Brook, 1965—; Royal Soc. Rutherford Meml. lectr., Canada, 1987; nuc. sci. com. NRC. Assoc. editor Phys. Rev., 1951—53; contbr. articles on nuc. physics and elem. particles to sci. jours. Bd. govs. Weizmann Inst. Sci., Rehovoth, Israel, Tel Aviv U.; trustee Univs. Rsch. Assn. Co-recipient Rossi prize, Am. Astron. Soc., hign energy physics divsn., 1989; recipient citation for meritorious contbns., U.S. AEC, 1973, J. Robert Oppenheimer Meml. prize, 1982, Nat. medal of Sci., 1983, Am. Acad. Achievement award, 1985, Wolf prize in physics, Wolf Found., Israel, 1991, Enrico Fermi award in physics, 1998. Fellow: AAAS, Am. Acad. Arts and Scis., Am. Phys. Soc. (pres. 1982); mem.: NAS, Am. Philos. Soc. (Lanutti Meml. lectr. 2003, Tom W. Bonner prize in nuc. physics 1971). Office: Brookhaven Nat Lab Bldg 510 Upton NY 11973

GOLDHAGEN, JEFFREY LEE, city health department administrator; m. Diana Goldhagen; children: Mia, Alanna, Tess, Eva, Julian. MD, U. Pitts.; MPH, U. Minn. Dir., med. programs for surg. aid Children of the World; co-dir., med. anthropology program Case Western Reserve U., Cleve.; med. dir. Cleve. Pub. Health Dept.; assoc. prof., pediat. U. Fla.; dir. Duval Co. Health Dept., Jacksonville, Fla., 1993—. Fellow: Am. Acad. Pediat. Office: Duval County Pub Health 515 W Sixth St MC #24 Jacksonville FL 32206

GOLDIE, SUE J., health service researcher; b. Washington, Dec. 14, 1961; m. Aaron Bradley Waxman, Apr. 17. 1986; children: Jacob Benjamin Waxman, Matthew Ariel Waxman. BS, Union Coll., 1984; MD, Albany Med. Coll., 1988; MPH, Harvard U., 1997. Bd. cert. Nat. Bd. Med. Examiners; diplomate, bd. cert. Am. Bd. Internal Medicine; lic. physician, Conn., Mass. Intern in internal medicine Yale New Haven Hosp., Yale U. Sch. Medicine, 1988-89, resident in internal medicine, 1989-91; fellow AHCPR policy award Harvard Sch. Pub. Health, Boston, 1996-98; attending physician Yale New Haven Hosp., 1990, Brigham and Women's Hosp., 1998; clin. asst. prof. medicine Yale U. Sch. Medicine, 1994-98; instr. medicine Harvard Med. Sch., Boston, 1998; asst. prof. health policy and health decision sci. Harvard Sch. Pub. Health, Boston, 1998, 1998—. Presenter in field. Contbr. articles to med. jour. Dana scholar Charles A. Dana Found., 1981, Dana fellow, 1982-84; Charles P. Drumm and Harold C. Wiggers merit scholar, 1984-88; MacArthur Fellow, John T. and Catherine MacArthur Found., 2005. Mem.: Soc. Med. Decision Making (editl. bd.), Am. Program Dirs. Internal Medicine (Original Investigation Competition award for innovative programs in med. edn. 1995), Soc. Gen. Internal Medicine (Larry Lynn award 1998), ACP, Alpha Omega Alpha. Office: Harvard Sch Pub Health 718 Huntington Ave Fl 2D Boston MA 02115-5924 Office Phone: 617-432-2010. Office Fax: 617-432-0190. E-mail: sgoldie@hsph.harvard.edu.

GOLDIN, CLAUDIA DALE, economics professor; b. NYC, May 14, 1946; d. Leon and Lucille (Rosansky) G. BA magna cum laude with distinction, Cornell U., 1967; MA, U. Chgo., 1969, PhD, 1972; MA (hon.), U. Pa., 1985, Harvard U., 1990; DHL (hon.), U. Nebr., Lincoln, 1994. Asst. prof. econs. U. Wis., Madison, 1971-73; asst. prof. Princeton U., NJ, 1973-79, vis. fellow indsl. relations sec., 1987-88; assoc. prof. U. Pa., Phila., 1979-85, prof., 1985-90; vis. lectr. econs. Harvard U., Cambridge, Mass., 1975-76, Henry Lee prof., 1990—; dir. Develop. of the Am. Econ. Program, rsch. assoc. Nat. Bur. Econ. Rsch., Cambridge, Mass. Mem. Inst. Advanced Study, Princeton, 1982-83; dir. grad. studies U. Pa., 1983-1984; vis. fellow Brookings Instn., 1993-1994; vis. scholar Russell Sage Found., 1997-98; Bogen vis. prof. econs., Hebrew U. of Jerusalem, 1999; Katherine Hampson Bessell fellow Racliffe Inst. for Advanced Study, 2005-2006. Author: Urban Slavery in the Am. South, 1976, Understanding the Gender Gap (Allan Sharlin Book award, Richard Lester Book award), 1990; editor: Strategic Factors in 19th Century Am. Econ. Hist., 1992, The Regulated Economy, 1994, The Defining Moment: The Great Depression and the Am. Economy in the 20th Century, 1998; editor: Jour. Econ. Hist., 1984-88, NBER Series on Long-Term Factors in Econ. Devel., 1990-; co-editor: Corruption and Reform: Lessons from America's Hist., 2005; mem. editl. bd. Hist. Methods, 1978-1983, Jour. Econ. Hist., 1978-1984, Explorations in Econ. Hist., 1978-1985, 1991-1998, Am. Econ. Rev., 1985-91, Quar. Jour. Econs., 1991—, Rev. Econs. and Stats., 1992-, Jour. Interdisciplinary Hist., 1998; mem. adv. bd. Jour. Econ. Perspectives, 2001-2003; contbr. articles to profl. publs., chapters to books. Recipient NSF award, 1975-77, 79-81, 81-82, 84-86, 87-89, 92-93, 96-99, Spencer Found. rsch. award, 1996, 2001—; Guggenheim fellow, 1987-88. Fellow Econometric Soc., Am. Acad. Arts and Scis.; mem. Am. Econ. Assn. (v.p. 1990-1991), Econ. History Assn. (pres. 1999-2000, trustee 1984-1988, v.p. 1988-1989), NAS. Avocations: aerobics, hiking, bird watching. Office: Harvard U Dept Econs Littauer Building 217 1805 Cambridge St Cambridge MA 02138 E-mail: cgoldin@harvard.edu.

GOLDIN, LEON, artist; b. Chgo., Jan. 16, 1923; s. Joseph P. and Bertha (Metz) G.; m. Meta Solotaroff, July 30, 1949; children: Joshua, Daniel. BFA, Art Inst. Chgo., 1948; MFA, U. Iowa, 1950. From instr. to assoc. prof. Columbia U., NYC, 1964-82, prof., 1982-92, prof. emeritus, 1992—. Former tchr. Calif. Coll. Arts and Crafts, Phila. Coll. Art, Queen's Coll., Cooper Union; vis. prof. painting Stanford, summer 1973 One-man shows Oakland Art Mus., 1955, Felix Landau Gallery, LA, 1956, 57, 59, Galleria L'Attico, Rome, 1958, Kraushaar Galleries, NYC, 1960, 64, 68, 72, 84, 88, 90, 93, 96, 98, 2001, 04 U. Houston, 1981, Binghamton U. Art Mus., 2000, Ctr. for Maine Contemporary Art, 2000; represented in permanent collections Bklyn. Mus., City Mus. St. Louis, Worcester Mus., Addison Gallery Am. Art, Pa. Acad. Fine Arts, LA County Mus., Santa Barbara Mus., Oakland Art Mus., Munson Proctor Inst., Va. Mus. Fine Arts, Portland Mus., Maine, Everson Mus., U. Ark., Okla. Art Ctr., Cleve. Mus. Fine Art. Served with AUS, 1943-46, ETO. Fulbright scholar to France, 1952, Prix de Rome Am. Acad. Rome, 1955-58, Jennie Sesnan Gold medal Pa. Acad. Fine Arts, 1966; Tiffany grantee, 1951; Guggenheim fellow, 1959, Nat. Endowment for Arts grantee, 1967, 80; Nat. Inst. Arts and Letters grantee, 1968, NY Caps grantee, 1981, Ranger Fund Purchase award, 2005. Mem. NAD (Benjamin Altman Landscape prize 1993, 1999, Adolph and Clara Obrig prize, 2003). Office Phone: 212-666-5559.

GOLDING, BRAGE, university president; b. Chgo., Apr. 28, 1920; s. Leon M. and Viola B. (Brage) G.; m. Hinda F. Wolf, Dec. 21, 1941; children: Brage, Susan, Julie. BS, Purdue U., 1941, PhD, 1948; LLD, Wright State U., 1975. Assoc. dir. research Lilly Varnish Co., Indpls.; also research assoc. Purdue U., 1948-57; vis. prof. engring. Purdue U., dir. research Lilly Varnish Co., 1957-59; head Sch. Chem. Engring. Purdue U., 1959-66; v.p. Ohio State U. and; Miami U., 1966-67; pres. Wright State U., Dayton, Ohio, 1967-72, San Diego State U., 1972-77, Kent State U., 1977-82, Met. State Coll., Denver, 1984-85; acting pres. Western State Coll., Gunnison, Colo., 1985, ret. Cons. Dept. Higher Edn., Pa. and N.J. Author: Polymers and Resins, 1959; Contbr. articles to profl. jours. Fellow AAAS; mem. Am. Chem. Soc., Phi Beta Kappa (hon.) Address: 3990 Foothill Ave Carlsbad CA 92010-7053 Personal E-mail: bgolding@mail.sdsu.edu.

GOLDING, CAROLYN MAY, former government senior executive, consultant; b. Essex County, NJ, July 1, 1941; d. Wesley Irwin and Florence Grace (Smith) G.; m. Gary Anthony Derosa, Oct. 18, 1975 (div. Sept. 1982). BA, Duke U., 1963, postgrad., 1965—66. English tchr. Parkersburg (W.Va.) H.S., 1963; asst. to registrar Duke U., Durham, NC, 1963-65; mgmt. intern Dept. Labor, Washington, 1966-67, various other positions, 1967-72; dep. assoc. regional adminstr. Employment and Tng. Adminstrn., San Francisco, 1972-77, comptroller Washington, 1977-78, regional adminstr. San Francisco, 1979-82, dir. Unemployment Ins. Svc. Washington, 1982-87, adminstr. employment security, 1987-88, dep. asst. sec. employment and tng., 1988-96. Cons. on mgmt., labor force, long-range planning, workforce edn. issues and exec. coaching, 1996—; judge Arthur S. Flemming Award for Excellence in Fed. Svc. Recipient Disting. Career Svc. award Dept. Labor, 1979, Fed. Women's Career award Sec. Labor, 1983, Presdl. Meritorious rank, 1987, 95, Philip Arnow award Dept. Labor, 1988. Mem. Internat. Women's Forum, Women's Forum of Washington, Coun. for Excellence in Govt. (prin.), Women Mean Business (co-chair, Judge Arthur S. Flemming award Excellence Pub. Svc.) Episcopalian.

GOLDING, SUSAN G., former mayor; b. Muskogee, Okla., Aug. 18, 1945; d. Brage and Hinda Fay (Wolf) G.; children: Samuel, Vanessa. Cert. Pratique de Langue Francaise, U. Paris, 1965; BA in Govt. and Internat. Rels., Carleton Coll., 1966; MA in Romance Philology, Columbia U., 1974. Assoc. editor Columbia U. Jour. of Internat. Affairs, NYC, 1968-69; teaching fellow Emory U., Atlanta, 1973-74; instr. San Diego Community Coll. Dist., 1978; assoc. pub., gen. mgr. The News Press Group, San Diego, 1978-80; city council mem. City of San Diego, 1981-83; dep. sec. bus., transp., housing State of Calif., Sacramento, 1983-84; county supr. dist. 3 County of San Diego, 1984-92; mayor City of San Diego, 1992—2000; pres. & CEO The Golding Group, Inc., San Diego, 2000—; head Homeland Security Office, Titan Corp., San Diego, 2000—. Chmn. San Diego Drug Strike Force, 1987-88, Calif. Housing Fin. Agy., Calif. Coastal Commn.; bd. dirs. San Diego County Water Authority; trustee So. Calif. Water Com., Inc.; founder Mid City Comml. Revitalization Task Force, Strategic Trade Alliance, 1993, Calif. Big 10 City Mayors, 1993; mem. Gov. Calif. Mil. Base Reuse Task Force, 1994; established San Diego World Trade Ctr., 1993, San Diego City/State/County Regional Permit Assistance Ctr., 1994; mem. adv. bd. U.S. Conf. of Mayors, 1994; chair Gov. Wilson's Commn. on Local Governance for 21st Century. Bd. dirs. Child Abuse Prevention Found., San Diego Conv. and Vis. Bur., Crime Victims Fund, United Cerebral Palsy, San Diego Air Quality Bd., San Diego March of Dimes, Rep. Assocs.; adv. bd. Girl Scouts U.S.; trustee So. Calif. Water Comm.; mem. Rep. State Cen. Com.; co-chair com. Presidency George Bush Media Fund, Calif.; chair San Diego County Regional Criminal Justice Coun., race rels. com. Citizens Adv. Com. on Racial Intergration, San Diego Unified Sch. Dist.; hon. chair Am. Cancer Soc's. Residential Crusade, 1988. Recipient Alice Paul award Nat. Women's Polit. Caucus, 1987, Calif. Women in Govt. Achievement award, 1988, Willie Velasquez Polit. award Mex. Am. Bus. and Profl. Assn., 1988, Catalyst of Chance award Greater San Diego C. of C., 1994, Woman Who Means Bus. award San Diego Bus. Jour., 1994, Internat. Citizen award World Affairs Coun., 1994; named One of San Diego's Ten Outstanding Young Citizens, 1981, One of Ten Outstanding Rep. County Ofcls. in U.S.A., Rep. Nat. Com., 1987, San Diego Woman of Achievement Soroptimists Internat., 1988. Mem. Nat. Assn. of Counties (chair Op. Fair Share, mem. taxation and fin. com.), Nat. Women's Forum. Republican. Jewish. Office: The Golding Group Inc 9276 Scranton Rd Ste 600 San Diego CA 92121 E-mail: commerce@golding.org.

GOLDMAN, ALAN IRA, brokerage house executive; b. NYC, July 29, 1937; s. Julius and Florence (Blum) G.; m. Joanne T. Marren. AB, Cornell U., 1958; MBA, NYU, 1962; grad., Stonier Grad. Sch. Banking, 1967. Methods analyst, personnel-researcher Fed. Res. Bank of N.Y., NYC, 1958-62; platform asst. Bankers Trust Co., NYC, 1962-63, asst. mgr., 1963-64, mgr., 1964-65, asst. treas., 1965-66, asst. v.p., 1967-69; assoc. investment banking dept. Lehman Bros., NYC, 1969-70; v.p. fin., chief fin. officer, treas. Interway Corp., NYC, 1970-74; mgmt. cons. Montclair, NJ, 1974-75; v.p. fin. Mgmt. Assistance Inc., NYC, 1975-80, sr. v.p. fin., 1980-85; ind. investment banker, bus. cons., 1985—; pres. Goldmark Capital, 1987-88. Lectr., adv., examiner Stonier Grad. Sch. Banking, 1968-71; lectr. Am. Inst. Banking, 1968-69; chair SGA Interactive Corp.; chair SGA Interactive, Inc. Co-chmn. Montclair chpt. campaign ARC, 1970-73; chmn. Cornell Funds' N.Y. Area Phonathons, 1972-74, UN Week, Montclair, 1973; trustee, treas., co-chair Cocteau Repertory Theatre, 1985-2000; chair bd. dirs. Planned Parenthood Fedn. Am., 1986-88; bd. dirs., treas. Planned Parenthood Met. N.J.; bd. dirs., former chair, treas. Montclair ARC; vice chair adv. bd. Columbia U. Mailman Sch. Pub. Health; co-chair Class of 1958 reunion com. Cornell U. Mem. Orange Lawn Tennis Club, Univ. Club (N.Y.C.), Aspatuck Tennis Club, Surf Club of Quogue, Phi Beta Kappa, Phi Kappa Phi, Zeta Beta Tau. E-mail: alangoldman@comcast.net.

GOLDMAN, ALLAN BAILEY, lawyer; b. Auburn, NY, Jan. 1, 1937; s. Charles and Rose Hortense (Abrahams) G.; m. Eleanor Ruth Levy, May 26, 1963; children; Jennifer Brooke Horwitz, Andrea Allison Gellert. AB magna cum laude, Harvard U., 1958, JD, 1963; LHD (hon.), Hebrew Union Coll.-Jewish Inst. Religion, 1992. Bar: Calif. 1964, D.C. 1977, U.S. Supreme Ct. 1977. Assoc. Wyman, Bautzer, Kuchel & Silbert, Beverly Hills, Calif., 1963-67, ptnr. LA, 1967-91, Katten Muchin Rosenman, LLP, LA, 1991—. Judge pro-tem Calif. Mcpl. and Small Claims Cts.; arbitrator Calif. Superior Ct. Contbr. articles to profl. jours. Chmn. Attys. for Brown for Gov., officer Brown for Pres., 1976; founder LA Com. for Civil Rights Under Law, Mus. Contemporary Art., LA, Fraternity of Friends of LA Music Ctr.; trustee Calif. Mus. Sci. and Industry, 1981-89, St. John's Hosp. and Health Ctr. Found., 1978—, exec. com., 1979-89, 2006-, bd. dirs., 1989-95, 2006—, treas., 1990-94, chmn., 1994-95; chmn. nat. bd. trustees Union of Am. Hebrew Congregations, 1987-91, trustee, 1977-, officer, 1985-; bd. govs. Hebrew Union Coll.-Jewish Inst. Religion, 1988—, bd. overseers LA campus, 1981-85, 1988-, vice chair, 1997-; trustee HUC Skirball Cultural Ctr., 1997—; pres. Leo Baeck Temple, LA, 1975-77; mem. Conf. Pres.'s Major Jewish Orgns., 1987-91; mem. synagogue funding com. Jewish Fedn. Coun. of Greater LA, 1979, chmn., 1985-88; Calif. Commn. Jud. Nominees Evaluation, 1999-2002. Lt. USN, 1958—60. Named Humanitarian of Yr., NCCJ, 1995. Mem. Calif. Bar Assn., D.C. Bar Assn. Democrat. Jewish. Avocations: trekking, running, tennis. Home: 347 Conway Ave Los Angeles CA 90024-2603 Office: Katten Muchin Rosenman LLP 2029 Century Park E Ste 2600 Los Angeles CA 90067 Home Phone: 310-475-5621; Office Phone: 310-788-4520. Business E-Mail: allan.goldman@kattenlaw.com.

GOLDMAN, ALLEN MARSHALL, physics professor; b. NYC, Oct. 18, 1937; s. Louis and Mildred (Kohn) Goldman; m. Katherine Virginia Darnell, July 31, 1960; children: Matthew, Rachel, Benjamin. AB in Chemistry and Physics, Harvard U., Cambridge, Mass., 1958; PhD in Physics, Stanford U., Calif., 1965. Rsch. asst. Stanford U., Calif., 1960-65, rsch. assoc., 1965; asst. prof. physics U. Minn., Mpls., 1965-67, assoc. prof., 1967-73, prof., 1974—, dir. Ctr. Sci. and Application of Superconductivity, 1989—, inst. tech. prof., 1992—, head Sch. Physics and Astronomy, 1996—. Co-chmn. Gordon Conf. quantum Liquids and Solids, 1981; dir. NATO Advanced Study Inst., 1983; mem. materials rsch. adv. com. NSF, 1985—88; mem. vis. com. Francis Butter Nat. Magnet Lab., 1986—89, chmn., 1987—89; mem. vis. com. Nat. Nanofabrication Facility Cornell, 1988—90, mem. user com., 1997—99; mem. vis. com. U. Chgo. Materials Program Argonne Nat. Lab., 1992—98, chmn., 1995; mem. Buckley prize com., 1994—95, London prize com., 1994—98; mem. Helium res. com. NAS/NRC, 1998—99. Assoc. editor: Revs. Modern Physics, 1999—2005; contbr. articles to profl. jours. Vis. divsn. materials rsch. grantee, NSF, 1999, Alfred P. Sloan Found. fellow, 1966—70. Fellow: AAAS, Am. Phys. Soc. (councilor divsn. condensed matter physics 1994—96, mem. publs. oversight com. 1996—99, chair 1997, councilor divsn. condensed matter physics 1999—2003, mem. exec. com. 2001—03, vice chair divsn. condensed matter physics 2006, chair elect 2007, Fritz London Meml. prize 2002); mem.: NAS, Am. Inst. Physics (pub. policy com. 1999—). Jewish. Home: 1015 James Ct Mendota Heights MN 55118-3640 Office: U Minn Sch Physics and Astronomy 116 Church St SE Minneapolis MN 55455-0149 Office Phone: 612-624-6062. Business E-Mail: goldman@physics.umn.edu.

GOLDMAN, ALVIN IRA, philosopher, educator; b. Bklyn., Oct. 1, 1938; s. Nathan and Frances (Krugman) G.; m. Holly Martin Smith, June 15, 1969; children: Raphael, Sidra. BA, Columbia U., 1960; MA, Princeton U., 1962, PhD, 1965. From asst. prof. to prof. U. Mich., Ann Arbor, 1963-80; prof. U. Ill., Chgo., 1980-83, U. Ariz., Tucson, 1983-94, Regents' prof. philosophy, 1994—2002; Bd. Govs. Prof. Philosophy Rutgers U., New Brunswick, NJ, 2002—. Author: A Theory of Human Action, 1970, Epistemology and Cognition, 1986, Liaisons: Philosophy Meets., 1992, Philosophical Applications of Cognitive Science, 1993, Knowledge in a Social World, 1999, Pathways to Knowledge, 2002. Guggenheim fellow, 1975-76, Ctr. for Advanced Study in Behavioral Scis. fellow, 1975-76, Nat. Humanities Ctr. fellow, 1981-82. Fellow: Am. Acad. Arts and Scis.; mem.: Soc. for Philosophy and Psychology (pres. 1987—88), Am. Philos. Assn. (Pacific divsn. pres. 1991—92). Avocations: music, athletics.

GOLDMAN, ALVIN LEE, lawyer, educator, arbitrator; b. NYC, Feb. 27, 1938; s. Joseph I. and Emma (Berger) G.; m. Elisabeth C. Paris, Nov. 23, 1956; children— Paula, Douglas AB, Columbia U., 1959; LL.B., NYU, 1962. Bar: Ky. 1969. Assoc. Parker, Chapin & Flattau, NYC, 1962-65; mem. faculty U. Ky., Lexington, 1965—, prof. law, 1972—. Prof. in residence NLRB Zagoria staff, 1967-68; vis. scholar Inst. for Labor Law, U. Lueven, 1973; vis. prof. U. Calif., Davis, 1976-77. Author: Processes for Conflict Resolution, 1972, The Supreme Court and Labor-Management Relations Law, 1975, Labor Law and Industrial Relations in the USA, 2d edit., 1983, (with R. Covington) Legislation Protecting the Individual Employee, 1982, (with M. Finkin, C. Summers and K. Dau-Schmidt) Legal Protection for the Individual Employee, 1989, 2d edit., 1995, 3d edit., 2002, Settling for More: Mastering Negotiating Strategies and Techniques, 1991, Labor and Employment Law in the United States, 1996, (with J. Rojot) Negotiation: Theory and Practice, 2003. Bd. dirs. Central Ky. Jewish Assn., 1978-80, 81-84. Fellow Coll. Labor and Employment Lawyers; mem. ABA, Ky. Bar Assn., Nat. Acad. Arbitrators (bd. govs. 1994-97), Labor Law Group Trust (chmn. 1988-94), Internat. Soc. Labor Law (internat. v.p. 2000-03, exec. bd. U.S. br. 1982-85, 88—, vice-chair 1995-2001, chair 2001-06, sec.-treas. 2006-), Internat. Indsl. Rels. Assn. Democrat. Office: U Ky Coll of Law Lexington KY 40506-0048 Office Phone: 859-257-3325. E-mail: agold00@email.uky.edu.

GOLDMAN, BENJAMIN EDWARD, lawyer; b. NYC, Feb. 25, 1940; s. William Wolfe and Blanche (Kallenburg) G.; m. Lynda Ann Schwartz, July 27, 1950; children: Brian Edward, Victoria Beth, Adam Edward BS, NYU, 1965; JD, Fordham U., 1968; LLM, Georgetown U., 1970. Bar: N.Y. 1968, D.C. 1972, U.S. Dist. D.C., U.S. Ct. Appeals (D.C., 4th, 5th and 9th cirs.), Calif. 1986, U.S. Dist. Ct. (cen. dist.) Calif. 1986. Atty., advisor to chmn. NLRB, Washington, 1968-72; assoc. Arent, Fox, Kitner, Plotkin, Kahn, Washington, 1972-75; ptnr. Feldman, Krieger, Goldman, Tisch, Washington, 1976-83, Memel, Jacobs, Pierno, Gersh & Ellsworth, LA, 1984-87, Graham and James, LA, 1987-2001, Squire, Sanders & Dempsey LLP, LA, 2001—07, Squire Sanders, LA, 2007—. Mem. com. on devel. law under NLRB Act, 1968—; speaker Healthcare Fin. Mgmt. Assn., Calif., 1987, Nat. Health Edn. Conf. on AIDS, 1987, Inst. Corp. Counsel, 1986, Hosp. Coun. N. Calif., 1985, others. Contbr. articles to profl. jours. Mem. ABA (forum com. on health law 1983, mem. labor and employment law sect. 1968—), Nat. Health Lawyers Assn. (speaker ann. healthlaw update 1985), Calif. Bar Assn., N.Y. Bar Assn., D.C. Bar Assn., Am. Acad. Hosp. Attys. Office: Squire Sanders Ste 3100 555 S Flower St Los Angeles CA 90071-2300 Home Phone: 310-375-4521; Office Phone: 213-624-2500. Office Fax: 213-623-4581. E-mail: bgoldman@ssd.com.

GOLDMAN, BERT ARTHUR, psychologist, educator; b. NYC, Apr. 4, 1929; children: Lisa, Linda. BA, U. Md., 1951; M.Ed., U. N.C., 1956; Ed.D., U. Va., 1960. Mem. faculty U. N.C., Greensboro, 1965—, prof. ednl. psychology, 1971-85, dean acad. advising, 1970-85, prof. higher ednl. adminstrn., 1985—86, acting chair dept. ednl. adminstrn., higher edn. and ednl. rsch., 1987-88, dept. coord. of higher edn., 1991—. Served with U.S. Army, 1951-53. Mem. APA. Office: U NC at Greensboro Dept Curriculum and Instrn PO Box 26170 Greensboro NC 27402-6170

GOLDMAN, BRIAN ARTHUR, lawyer, accountant; b. Balt., June 30, 1946; s. Marvin L. and Edythe R. Goldman; m. Eileen G. Safro, Aug. 22, 1970; children: Jonathan S., Evan M. BS in Real Estate Planning, Am.U., 1968; JD, U. Md., 1971. Bar: Md. 1972, U.S. Dist. Ct. Md. 1972, U.S. Tax Ct. 1977, U.S. Supreme Ct. 1977. Acct., Balt., 1974—; mem. Burke, Gerber & Wilen, 1972-77, Sapero & Sapero, 1977-78; pvt. practice, 1978-83; ptnr. Goldman and Fedder, P.A., Balt., 1983—85, Fedder & Garten, P.A., Balt., 1986—88, Goldman & Vetter, P.A., Balt., 1989—2004, Goldman & Goldman, PA, Balt., 2004—. Asst. prof. income taxation U. Balt., 1974-75. Mem. ABA, Md. Bar Assn., Balt. City Bar Assn., Md. Assn. CPAs, Ctr. Club, Woodholme. Office: Goldman & Goldman PA 36 S Charles St Ste 2401 Baltimore MD 21201-3108 Business E-Mail: bgoldman@goldmangoldman.com.

GOLDMAN, CHARLES A., science administrator; SB, MIT, 1986; PhD, Stanford U., 1993. Assoc. dir. edn. RAND Corp., Santa Monica, Calif., 2004—, sr. economist, 1993—. Prof. econs. Pardee RAND Grad. Sch., Santa Monica, 1996—. Author: (books) Paying for University Research Facilities and Administration, 2000, PhD Factory, 2001, In Pursuit of Prestige, 2002, Education for a New Era, 2007. Office: RAND Corp 1776 Main St Santa Monica CA 90401 Office Phone: 310-393-0411.

GOLDMAN, CHARLES NORTON, retired corporate lawyer; b. NYC, Feb. 15, 1932; s. Morris and Mary Celia (Tames) G.; m. Jane Barbara Webbink, July 21, 1968; children: Alexander Daniel, Jeffrey David. AB with honors, Columbia U., 1953, LLB, 1955. Bar: N.Y. 1956. Practiced in, NYC, 1955-60; atty.-advisor AID, Washington, 1960-62; regional legal advisor for India, Nepal and Ceylon AID mission to India, New Delhi, 1962-64; asst. gen. counsel for Latin Am. AID, 1965-68, dep. gen. counsel, 1968-69; staff counsel for Latin Am. ITT, NYC, 1969-72, sr. counsel, asst. to gen. counsel, 1972-74, sr. counsel for Latin Am., 1974-75; v.p., gen. counsel ITT Europe Inc., Brussels, 1975-81; v.p. ITT, 1976-95, assoc. gen. counsel, 1981-95. Mem. Overseas Devel. Coun., 1988-95, Bretton Woods Com., 1992-95. Dir. Jewish Repertory Theater Inc., 1999—2001; bd. dirs. The Internat. Shakespeare Globe Ctr. Ltd., 2003—05, Alliance of Resident Theatres, NYC, 1996—98, The Shakespeare Globe Ctr. (USA) Inc., 1996—, pres., 2001—04. Mem. Coun. on Fgn. Rels., Mid-Atlantic Club N.Y. Inc. (pres. 1996-2001), Phi Beta Kappa. Home: 139 E 94th St New York NY 10128-1761

GOLDMAN, DONALD AARON, lawyer; b. NYC, Sept. 11, 1947; BA, UCLA, 1969, JD, 1972. Bar: Calif. 1972. Dep. atty. gen. Calif. Dept. Justice, LA, 1972-79; ptnr. Memel, Jacobs & Ellsworth, LA, 1979-87; ptnr., mem. firm exec. mgmt. com., chmn. firm compensation com. McDermott, Will & Emery LLP, LA, 1987—. Mem. Nat. Health Lawyers. Avocations: golf, music. Office: McDermott Will & Emery LLP 2049 Century Park E Los Angeles CA 90067-3101 Office Phone: 310-551-9319. Office Fax: 310-277-4730. Business E-Mail: dogoldman@mwe.com.

GOLDMAN, DUFF (JEFFREY ADAM GOLDMAN), chef; b. Dec. 17, 1974; Grad., Corcoran Sch. of Art, Washington, DC; BA in Hist., U. Md., Balt., 1997; grad., Culinary Inst. Am., Napa Valley, 1998. Stagiere French Laundry; exec. pastry chef Vail Cascade Hotel, Colo.; sous chef Olives, Washington; founder, exec. pastry chef Charm City Cakes, Balt., 2000—. Bass player, band mem. So I had to. Chef, host (TV series) Ace of Cakes, Food Network, 2006—. Home: 2936 Remington Ave Baltimore MD 21211-2830 Office Phone: 410-235-9229. Business E-Mail: duff@charmcitycakes.com.*

GOLDMAN, ERIC SCOT, lawyer; b. Quincy, Mass., Mar. 5, 1957; s. Terry and Harriet (Goldstein) G.; m. Lora Anderson, June 18, 1983; children: William, Daniel, Leigh. BA, Boston Coll., 1979; MS in Criminal Justice, Northeastern U., 1980; JD, Suffolk U., 1987. Bar: Mass. 1987, U.S. Dist. Ct. Mass. 1987, U.S. Mil. Ct. Appeals. Adminstr. McLean Hosp., Belmont, Mass.; caseworker Norfolk County Dist. Atty.'s Office, Dedham, Mass.; atty. McDermott & Padis, Milton, Mass., 1983-93; assoc. Lynch & Lynch, South Easton, Mass., 1993-98, Lang & Morgera, Boston, 1998-99; ptnr. Finneran, Byrne & Drechsler, LLP, Boston, 1999—. Mediator Norfolk-Plymouth County; bd. dirs. Criminal Justice Scis. Inst., Washington. Recipient Cert. of Recognition, Norfolk County Dist. Atty., Commonwealth of Mass. Dist. Ct. Mem. Mass Acad. Trial Attys., Norfolk, Plymouth and Bristol County Bar Assn., Braintree Rifle and Pistol Club (pres. 1988—). Avocations: scuba diving, Karate, music, firearms training. Home: 36 Forge Way Duxbury MA 02332-4743 Office: Finneran Byrne & Drechsler Eastern Harbor Office Pk 50 Redfield St Boston MA 02122-3630 Office Phone: 617-265-3900. Business E-Mail: esgoldman@fbdlegal.com.

GOLDMAN, GARY CRAIG, lawyer; b. Dec. 28, 1951; s. Ronald Walter and Connie Sylvia (Stein) G.; m. Diane Rose Lane, Oct. 1, 1977; children: Justin Edward, Gregory David. BA magna cum laude, Temple U., 1973; JD, Villanova U., 1976. Bar: Pa. 1976, U.S. Dist. Ct. (ea. dist.) Pa. 1981. Jud. law clk. Common Pleas Ct., Northampton County, Pa., 1976-77; asst. atty. gen. office of legal counsel Pa. Dept. Pub. Welfare, Phila., 1977-81, asst. counsel, 1981-84; staff counsel CDI Corp., Phila., 1984-86, v.p., assoc. gen. counsel, 1986—. Mem. faculty, planning chmn. Nationwide Comml. Real Estate Leasing Programs. Author: Drafting a Fair Office Lease, 1989, 2d edit., 2000; contbg. author: The Commercial Real Estate Tenant's Handbook, 1987, The Practical Real Estate Lawyer's Manual, 1987, Commercial Tenants' Leasing Transactions Guide, 1991, Office Planning and Design Desk Reference, 1992, Negotiating and Drafting Office Leases, 1995; assoc. editor: Villanova Law Rev., 1974-76; contbr. articles to legal jours. Mem. ABA, Am. Corp. Counsel Assn., Phila. Bar Assn. Republican. Jewish. Avocations: golf, running. Home: 210 Fox Hollow Dr Langhorne PA 19053-2477 Office: CDI Corp 1717 Arch St Fl 35 Philadelphia PA 19103-2713 Home Phone: 215-322-0065; Office Phone: 215-636-1114. Business E-Mail: gary.goldman@cdicorp.com.

GOLDMAN, GARY STEVEN, computer scientist, consultant; b. LA, Apr. 7, 1954; s. Fred and Claire Goldman; m. Rusty Lynn Goldman, May 7, 1983; children: Stephanie Lynn, Casondra Claire, Dora Nicole. BS in Computer Sci., Calif. State U., 1976, BS in Engring., 1976; PhD in Computer Sci., Pacific Western U., 1982. Lic. gen. contractor Calif. State Lic. Bd., 1989. Rsch. analyst L.A. Dept. Health Svcs., Lancaster, Calif., 1995—2002; dir. Pearblossom Pvt. Sch., Inc., Pearblossom, 1988—. V.p. systems devel. Cascade Graphics Devel., Irvine, Calif., 1980—84; founder, pres. Med. Veritas Internat. Inc., 2005—07. Author: INJECTION!, The Chickenpox Vaccine: A New Epidemic of Disease and Corruption; editor-in-chief: Medical Veritas: Journal of Medical Truth; author: numerous med. jour. publs. concerning MMR vaccination and autism, varicella vaccination, and impact on herpes-zoster epidemiology and capture-recapture methodology. Dir. Pearblossom Pvt. Sch. Inc., 1988—2004. Mem.: Phi Kappa Phi. Achievements include invention of first microcomputer-based computer aided drafting (CAD) system; patents for power wheel-efficient microprogrammed electric motor for vehicular transportation. Home: PO Box 847 Pearblossom CA 93553 Office: Pearblossom Pvt Sch Inc PO Box 847 Pearblossom CA 93553 Home Phone: 661-944-5661; Office Phone: 800-309-3569. Office Fax: 661-944-4483; Home Fax: 661-944-4483. Personal E-mail: pearblossominc@aol.com.

GOLDMAN, GEORGE DAVID, psychologist; b. NYC, Jan. 8, 1923; s. Irving Israel and Hattie Anna (Bennett) G.; m. Belle Hans, Sept. 11, 1948; children: Ira Stephen, Carol Marcia Goldman Reife, Deborah Sue Goldman Cohen. BS in Social Sci., CCNY, NYC, 1943; MA, NYU, NYC, 1946, PhD, 1950; cert. in psychoanalysis, William A. White Inst., NYC, 1958. Diplomate Am. Bd. Profl. Psychology, Am. Bd. Psychoanalysis in Psychology. Fellow CCNY, 1946-47, instr. psychology, 1947-53, NYU, 1948-51; pvt. practice psychology NYC, 1952—; pvt. practice Jericho, NY, 1956-95; clin. psychologist Bronx VA Hosp., Montrose VA Hosp., 1947-52; staff psychotherapist Low Cost Psychoanalytic Svc. William Alanson White Inst., NYC, 1952-58; clin. prof., supr., dir. clin. svcs. Postdoctoral Psychotherapy Ctr., Derner Inst., Adelphi U., Garden City, NY, 1958-94; supr. psychotherapy grad. div. Ferkauf Sch., Yeshiva U., Bronx, 1976-80. Cons. to supt. Manhasset Pub. Schs., NY, 1956-61; cons. psychotherapy VA, NY area, 1959-79; mem. arbitration panel on marital conflicts Am. Arbitration Assn., 1968—94; bd. dirs. Am. Bd. Psychoanalysis in Psychology, 1983—; trustee Am. Bd. Profl. Psychology, 2000—. Co-editor: (with D.S. Milman) Modern Woman: Her Psychology and Sexuality, 1969, Psychoanalytic Contributions to Community Psychology, 1970, Innovations in Psychotherapy, 1971, The Neurosis of Our Time: Acting Out, 1973, Group Process Today, 1974, Man and Woman in Transition, 1978, Psychoanalytic Perspectives on Aggression, 1978, Modern Man: The Psychology and Sexuality of the Contemporary Male, 1979, Parameters in Psychoanalytic Psychotherapy, 1979, Therapists at Work: A Demonstration of Theory and Technique, 1979, Addiction—Theory and Treatment, 1980, Techniques of Working with Resistance, 1987; (with G. Stricker) Practical Problems of a Private Psychotherapy Practice, 1972, 2d edit., 1981; (with L. Saretsky) Integrating Ego Psychology and Object Relations Theory: Psychoanalytic Perspectives on Psychopathology, 1979; contbr. articles to profl. jours. Mem. profl. adv. bd. Nassau County chpt. Parents Without Ptnrs., 1970-95; pres. psychology divsn., bd. dirs. Am. Friends of Hebrew U. of Jerusalem, NYC, 1975-2002. With US Army, 1943-45. Decorated Bronze Star, Purple Heart with oak leaf cluster; named Disting. Practitioner in Psychology, Nat. Acads. of Practice, 1983; recipient Outstanding Contbn. to Psychology award CCNY, 1989, Disting. Svc. to Profession of Psychology award Am. Bd. Profl. Psychology, Inc., 1999. Fellow APA (pres. divsn. psychologists in ind. practice 1987, psychotherapy, clinic psych., pres. divsn. psychoanalysis, 1982, Disting. Contbn. award 1988, Disting. Psychologist award divsn. 42 1989, divsn. 39 award 1990, Disting. Lifetime Svc. award divsn. 39 2000), NY State Psychol. Assn. (past bd. dirs. clin. div.), Nassau County Psychol. Assn. (past bd. dirs.), NY Soc. Clin. Psychologists (pres. 1979), Am. Acad. Psychotherapists (past bd. dirs. and sec.), Am. Bd. Psychoanalysis in Psychology (bd. dirs. 1983—), Am. Bd. Profl. Psychology (trustee). Democrat. Jewish. Avocations: swimming, travel. Office: 305 E 86th St Apt 22aw New York NY 10028-4751 Office Phone: 212-722-6515. Personal E-mail: drgdgoldman@aol.com.

GOLDMAN, GLENN, architect, educator; b. NYC, Apr. 7, 1952; s. Herbert and Tamara G.; m. Elizabeth Anne Strub, May 31, 1982; children: Aaron, Nathan, Jacob. BA, Columbia U., 1974; M in Architecture, Harvard U., 1978. Registered arch. and planner. Instr. career discovery program Harvard U., Cambridge, Mass., 1978; asst. prof. architecture Iowa State U., Ames, 1978-80; design critic Boston Architectural Ctr., 1981; prof., dir. imaging lab. NJ Inst. Tech., Newark, 1982—. Graphic designer Skidmore, Owings and Merrill, Boston, 1975; designer Moshe Safdie Archs., Ltd., Jerusalem, 1976; arch. Jung/Brannen Assocs., Boston, 1980-82, J.F. Caulfield Assocs., Hoboken, NJ, 1983-86, Glenn Goldman, Arch., Tenafly, NJ, 1984—. Author: Architectural Graphics: Traditional and Digital Communication, 1997; co-author, photographer: (video) Iowa: Downtowns in Transition, 1980; co-editor: Reality and Virtual Reality, 1991; contbr. articles to profl. jours. Mem. adv. bd. Tech. Sch., Morris County, NJ, 2000—, Sussex County, 2000—. Named Innovator for Advancement in Tech. and Edn., Campus Tech. mag., 2005; recipient Applied Rsch. citation, Progressive Architecture Awards Program, 1991; Tech. Engring. Pre-Visualization Archl. Design grantee, NJ Dept. Higher Edn., 1985, 1989, Imaging Lab grantee, numerous corp. sponsors, 1990—2006. Fellow: AIA (honorable mention edn. honors program 1989, 2004); mem.: Assn. Computer Aided Design in Architecture (pres. 1996—97), NJ Soc. Archs. (edit. bd. Architecture N.J. 1983—93), Assn. Computing Machinery Spl. Interest Group in Graphics, Tenafly United Soccer Club (youth soccer coach 1999—2005, v.p.), Tenafly Swim Club (trustee 1999—2004, pres. 2001—04). Home: 11 Ravine Rd Tenafly NJ 07670-2124 Office: NJ Inst Tech Sch of Architecture Newark NJ 07102 Office Phone: 973-596-3012. Personal E-mail: glenn_goldman@hotmail.com.

GOLDMAN, GLORIA A., lawyer; b. Bamberg, Germany, Oct. 7, 1948; d. Esther and Harry Praw (Stepfather); m. Michael V. Goldman, Dec. 11, 1945; children: Maurice H., Larissa A. BS, Wayne State U., 1970; JD, U. Ariz., 1990. Bar: Ariz. 1991, D.C. 2001. Pvt. practice, Tucson. Named one of Top 50 Pro Bono Attys. in Ariz., Ariz. Bar Found., 2002, Best Lawyers in Am., 2001—. Mem.: U. Ariz. Law Coll. Assn. (bd. mem. 1991—), Am. Immigration Lawyers Assn. (Ariz. state chairperson 1997—98, enforcement com. liaison 2001—, bd. govs. 2002—05, Pro Bono award 1996). Avocation: travel. Home: 6919 Gleneagles Tucson AZ 85718 Office: Gloria A Goldman PC 1575 W Ina Rd Tucson AZ 85704 Office Phone: 520-797-9229. Business E-Mail: gloria@ggoldmanlaw.com.

GOLDMAN, IRA STEVEN, gastroenterologist; b. Bronx, NY, May 19, 1951; s. George David and Belle (Hans) G.; children: Zachary, Joshua. BA, U. Rochester, 1973; student, Oxford U., 1972; MD, Columbia U., 1977. Diplomate Am. Bd. Internal Medicine, Am. Bd. Gastroenterology. Intern Columbia Presbyn. Med. Ctr., NYC, 1977-78, resident in internal medicine, 1978-80; fellow in gastroenterology and liver diseases U. Calif. Sch. Medicine, San Francisco, 1980-83; instr. in anatomy Columbia U., NYC, 1978; asst. prof. medicine U. Calif., San Francisco, 1983-85, Cornell U. Med. Coll., NYC, 1985-91, assoc. prof. clin. medicine, 1991-96; attending physician North Shore Univ. Hosp., Manhasset, N.Y., 1985—; assoc. prof. clin. medicine NYU Sch. Medicine, 1996—. Attending physician St. Francis Hosp., Roslyn, N.Y.; physicians adv. bd. Am. Liver Found., Greater N.Y. chpt., 1985—; sci. adv. commn. L.I. chpt. Nat. Found. for Ileitis and Colitis, 1985-91; vice chair clin. practice sec. Am. Gastroent. Assn., 1995-97, chmn., 1997-2000. Reviewer jours. Gastroenterology; contbr. articles to profl. jours., chpts. to books. Rsch. fellow Am. Liver Found., 1982, Clin. Investigator award NIH, 1983. Fellow ACP, Am. Coll. Gastroenterology, Am. Gastroenterol. Assn.; mem. Am. Assn. for Study of Liver Diseases, Med. Soc. State of N.Y., Nassau County Med. Soc., Nassau County. Acad. Medicine, N.Y. Soc. for Gastrointestinal Endoscopy (pres. 1996-97), Alpha Omega Alpha. Avocations: sailing, tennis. Office: 310 E Shore Rd Great Neck NY 11023-2432 Home Phone: 516-482-7650; Office Phone: 516-487-7677. Personal E-mail: isgoldman@aol.com.

GOLDMAN, JAY, industrial engineer, educator, dean emeritus; b. Norfolk, Va., Apr. 15, 1930; s. Louis H. and Rose O. Goldman; m. Renitta Librach, Dec. 20, 1959 BSME, Duke U., 1950; MSME, Mich. State U., 1951; DSc in Indsl. Engring., Washington U., St. Louis, 1955. Registered profl. engr., Mo. Lectr. indsl. engring. Washington U., 1952-56, asst. prof., 1956-64, acting chmn. human and orgn. factors, 1963-64; dir. dept. indsl. engring. Jewish Hosp., St. Louis, 1960-64; research assoc. dept. hosp. adminstr. U. N.C., Chapel Hill, 1964-68; prof., grad. adminstr. dept. indsl. engring. N.C. State U., Raleigh, 1964-68; prof., chmn. dept. indsl. engring. U. Mo., Columbia, 1968-84, prof. bioengring., 1969-75, prof. bioengring. and advanced automation, 1975-84; Disting. Svc. prof. and dean emeritus U. Ala., Birmingham, 1984—, dean, 1984-96. Cons. to fed., state agys., pvt. industry Contbr. to textbooks, profl. jours.; producer 6 tech. motion pictures; patentee in field V.p. Boone County Cmty. Svcs. Coun., 1973-76; v.p., exec. com., treas. Cmty. Rels. Coun.; bd. dirs. Birmingham Jewish Fedn.; vice-chmn., bd. dirs. Sloss Furnaces Nat. Hist. Landmark, bd. dirs., treas. Jewish Family Svcs. Named Ala. Engr. of Yr., ASPE; recipient Editl. award, Hosp. Mgmt. mag., 1969, U. Mo. Faculty Alumni award, 1981, Outstanding Engr. Educator in State award, ASPE. Fellow Inst. Indsl. Engrs. (trustee, exec. v.p., regional v.p., chpt. pres., v.p. edn. and profl. devel., editl. bd. Trans., Health Svcs. Devel. award 1981, Fred C. Crane award 1999, Medallion award, 2004), Accreditation Bd. Engring. and Tech. (dir., treas., fellow); mem. NSPE, Soc. Health Sys. (bd. dirs., pres.), Nat. Coun. Indsl. Engrs. Acad. Dept. Heads (chmn.), Ala. Soc. Profl. Engrs., Am. Soc. Engring. Edn., Sigma Xi, Alpha Pi Mu, Tau Beta Pi, Phi Kappa Phi, Omicron Delta Kappa. Home: 6068 Brookhill Cir Birmingham AL 35242 Office: U Ala-Birmingham Sch Engring 1075 13th St S Ste 310 Birmingham AL 35205-3430 Home Phone: 205-980-5822. Business E-Mail: jgoldman@uab.edu.

GOLDMAN, JEFFREY ADAM See GOLDMAN, DUFF

GOLDMAN, JERRY S., lawyer; b. Bklyn., Sept. 7, 1951; s. Bernard I. and Charlotte (Emerling) G.; children by previous marriage: Rachel Dawn, Samantha Blair. BA with honors, NYU, 1973; JD, Boston U., 1976; LLM in Taxation, Temple U., 1983. Bar: Mass. 1977, N.Y. 1977, U.S. Dist. Ct. (ea. and so. dists.) N.Y. 1980, U.S. Supreme Ct. 1981, Pa. 1982, U.S. Tax Ct. 1983, U.S. Dist. Ct. (ea. dist.) Pa. 1983, U.S. Ct. Appeals (3d cir.) 1983, U.S. Dist. Ct. Mass. 1997, U.S. Ct. Appeals (2nd cir.) 1996, U.S. Ct. Appeals (1st cir.) 1997. Sr. asst. dist. atty. Kings County Dist. Atty.'s Office, Bklyn., 1976-82; pvt. practice NYC, Phila., 1982—; mng. ptnr. Law Offices of Jerry S. Goldman and Assocs., P.C. Dir., pres. Huntingdon Brook Cmty. Assn., Bucks Co, Pa., 1985-89. Chmn. Upper Southampton Planning Commn., 1984—90; counsel Citizens Crime Commn., Phila., 1983—95, bd. dirs., 1983—, NYU Alumni Assn., 1998—; pres. NYU, Coll. Arts and Scis. Alumni Assn., 2004—; mem. Phila. Estate Planning Coun., N.Y. Estate Planning Coun.; atty. Phila. Vol. Lawyers for the Arts, 1983—. Mem. ABA, N.Y. State Bar Assn., Pa. Bar Assn., Phila. Bar Assn., Fed. Bar Assn. Avocations: cross country skiing, music. also: 13th Fl 111 Broadway New York NY 10006 Office: Two Penn Center Plaza 1500 JFK Boulevard Ste 1411 Philadelphia PA 19102 Office Phone: 215-569-4500, 212-242-2232.

GOLDMAN, JOEL A., lawyer; b. NYC, May 27, 1942; s. Solomon and Lee Goldman; m. Shirley Ann Curnow, Jan. 15, 1967; children: David Abraham, Nanette Francis, Jonathan Michael. BA, Grinnell Coll., Iowa, 1964; JD, U. So. Calif., LA, 1967. Bar: Calif. Assoc. Getz, Akins & Manning, LA, 1967—71; ptnr. Buchalter, Nemer, Fields, LA, 1971—94, Heenan Blaikie, Beverly Hills, Calif., 1994—95, Stephens Berg & Lasater McKenna & Cuneo, LA, 1995—2002, Russ, August & Kabat, LA, 2002—03, Lewis Brisbois Bisgaard & Smith LLP, LA, 2004—. Mem. grants com. Robert Russell Found., Miami, Fla., 1984—; v.p. Bell Canyon Assn., 1999—2002; bd. dirs. Encino Property Owners' Assn., Calif., 1978—94, Bell Canyon Assn., Calif., 1999—2002. Younker Acad. scholar, Grinnell Coll., 1960—64. Mem.: Comm. Law League Am., Assn. Bus. Trial Lawyers, LA Complex Litigation Inn of Ct., LA County Bar Assn. (comm. law and bankruptcy sect.), Calif. Bar Assn. (com. adminstrn. justice, litigation sect.). Jewish. Avocations: fishing, sports. Office: Lewis Brisbois Bisgaard & Smith LLP 221 N Figueroa St Ste 1200 Los Angeles CA 90012

GOLDMAN, JOEL J., retired lawyer; b. NYC, Sept. 7, 1940; s. Myron and Pearl (Jacobs) G.; m. Jane I. Stalker, July 23, 1973; children: Elizabeth Ann, Rebecca Lynn. BS, U. Va., 1962; JD, Syracuse U., 1965. Bar: N.Y. 1966, U.S. Dist. Ct. (we. dist.) N.Y. 1966. Law clk. Myron Goldman, NYC, 1965; staff atty., chief trial counsel Legal Aid Soc., Rochester, NY, 1966-73; ptnr. Kaman, Berlove, Marafioti, Jacobstein & Goldman, Rochester, 1973-97; ret., 1997. Lectr. family law; spl. investigator N.Y. State Spl. Commn. on Attica, 1972; mem. panel arbitrators Am. Arbitration Assn.; mem. faculty Nat. Bus. Inst., 1985-97. Author continuing edn. materials; contbg. editor Bender's Forms for Civil Practice, 1986, Medina's Bostwick, 1986. Referee Ea. Assn. Inter-Collegiate Football Ofcsls., 1974-95, v.p. Empire chpt., 1988, pres., 1989, Observer, Ea. Coll. Athletic Conf., 1996—. Inductee Jewish Athletes Sports Hall of Fame, 1996. Fellow Am. Acad. Matrimonial Lawyers (ret.); mem. ABA, N.Y. State Bar Assn. (exec. com. family law sect. 1982, mem. exec. com. 1981-97), Monroe County Bar Assn. (chmn. family law sect. 1982, exec. com. 1981-86), Assn. Trial Lawyers Am. Jewish. also: 21 Bluebill Ave Apt 1005B Naples FL 34108-1765 Personal E-mail: jjgesq@att.net.

GOLDMAN, JOHN ABNER, rheumatologist, immunologist, educator; b. June 9, 1940; s. Leon and Belle (Hurwitz) G.; children from previous marriage: Joey, Beth; m. Deborah J. Staples, Aug. 1, 1993; children: Shelley, Michael. BS, U. Wis., 1962; MD, U. Cin., 1966. Diplomate Am. Bd. Internal Medicine, subsplty. in rheumatology, allergy-immunology, advanced achievement in internal medicine, 1987. Intern U. Oreg. Med. Sch., Portland, 1966-67; resident U. Cin. Med. Ctr., 1967-69, postdoctoral fellow in rheumatology and immunology, 1969-71; clin. prof. medicine Emory U. Sch. Medicine, Atlanta, 1973—. Contbr. numerous articles to sci. jours. Bd. dirs. Atlanta Arthritis Found.; med. adv. com. Lupus Erythematosus Found., Inc. Maj. U.S. Army, 1971-73. Fellow ACP, Am. Soc. Lasers in Medicine and Surgery, Am. Coll. Rheumatology (chair CORC SE network); mem. Ga. Soc. Rheumatology (pres. 1974-75), Med. Assn. Atlanta, Med. Assn. Ga. (chmn. 3d party payers com. 2004-05), Met. Atlanta Rheumatology Soc. (co-pres.), Am. Soc. Clin. Densitometry (cert.), Ga. Medicare Carrier Adv. Com. (rheumatology rep.), Lupus Rsch. Inst. (adv. physician adv. coun.), Atlanta Bone Club (co-pres.). Office: Med Quarters Ste 293 5555 Peachtree Dunwoody Rd NE 293 Atlanta GA 30342-1711 Office Phone: 404-252-0230.

GOLDMAN, JUDITH, writer, editor, curator, consultant, publisher; b. Chgo. d. Emmanuel M. and Irene (Mirotsnic) G. BA, Bard Coll., 1964; postgrad., Ill. Inst. Tech., 1965. Editor Print Collector's Newsletter, NYC, 1970-73; mng. editor Artnews, NYC, 1973-75; curator prints Whitney Mus. of Am. Art, NYC, 1978-91; contbg. editor Artnews, NYC, 1975—. Cons. to bd. The Andy Warhol Authentication Bd., 1999—, mem., 2005—. Author: Windows at Tiffany: The Art of Gene Mone, 1980, American Prints: Process & Proofs, 1981, Jasper Johns Prints: 1977-81, 1981, Jasper Johns: 17 Monotypes, 1982, Frank Stella, Fourteen Prints with Drawings, Collages and Working Proofs, 1983, James Rosenquist, 1985, James Rosenquist, The Early Pictures, 1992, The Pop Image, Prints and Multiples, 1994, Frank Stella: Painting Retrospective, 1995, Frankenthaler: The Woodcuts, 2002, The Painted Sculpture of Betty Parsons, 2005. McDowell Colony fellow, 1976; NEA grantee, 1978. Personal E-mail: judithdg@earthlink.net.

GOLDMAN, LAWRENCE SAUL, lawyer; b. Phila., Mar. 25, 1942; s. Ephraim and Belle G.; m. Kathi Sue Schleifer, June 20, 1965; children: Carolyn, Jonathan. BA, Brandeis U., 1963; JD, Harvard U., 1966. Bar: N.Y. 1966. Asst. dist. atty. New York County, NYC, 1966-71; asst. gen. counsel N.Y. State Commn. To Investigate N.Y.C., 1971-72; pvt. practice NYC, 1972—; principal Law Offices of Lawrence S. Goldman, 2001—. Cons. N.Y.C. Commn. on Police Corruption, 1972. Contbg. author: Criminal Trial Advocacy. Trustee Congregation Rodeph Sholom, N.Y.C., 1984-92; bd. dirs. William F. Ryan Comty. Health Ctr., N.Y.C., 1987-90, Bronx Defenders, 1997-2004; mem. N.Y. State Commn. on Jud. Conduct, 1990-2006, chmn., 2004-06, mem. adv. com. on the criminal law, 1992—, mem. N.Y. State Commn. on Future of Indigent Def. Svcs., 2003—. Recipient Man of Yr. award Hogan Assocs., 1984. Fellow Am. Bd. Criminal Lawyers; mem. NACDL (chmn. ethics adv. com. 1988-92, white collar com. 1992-97, 2004—, Robert C. Heeney award 1998, pres. 2002-03), N.Y. State Assn. Criminal Def. Lawyers (pres. 1987-89, Thurgood Marshall award 1999), N.Y. Criminal Bar Assn. (pres. 1982-85, Outstanding Practitioner award 1994), N.Y. State Bar Assn. (mem. exec. com. criminal justice sect. 1987—, Outstanding Practitioner award criminal justice sect. 1996), Harvard Club. Democrat. Office: 500 Fifth Ave 29th Flr New York NY 10110-0002 Home Phone: 212-362-8042; Office Phone: 212-997-7499. E-mail: LSG@lsgoldmanlaw.com.

GOLDMAN, LOUIS B., lawyer; b. Chgo., Apr. 11, 1948; s. Jack Sidney and Lorraine Goldman; m. Barbara Marcia Berg, Oct. 2, 1983; children: Jacqueline Ilyse, Annie Dara, Michael Louis. BA magna cum laude, U. Calif., Berkeley, 1970; JD cum laude, U. Chgo., 1974. Bar: Calif. 1975, US Dist. Ct. (no. dist.) Calif. 1975, US Ct. Appeals (9th cir.) 1975, NY 1976, US Dist. Ct. (so. and ea. dists.) NY 1976, US Ct. Appeals (2nd cir.) 1976, Ill. 1991, Czech Republic, 1997; registered fgn. lawyer, Eng. 1999, Wales 1999. Law clk. US Dist. Ct., San Francisco, 1974-75; assoc. Cleary, Gottlieb, Steen & Hamilton, NYC and Paris, 1975-81, Edwards & Angell, NYC, 1981-83, ptnr., 1986-88, Wald, Harkrader & Ross, NYC, 1983-86, Altheimer & Gray, Chgo., 1989—2003, co-chmn., 1999—2003; ptnr., mem. global bd. Salans, NYC, 2003—. Mng. dir. Abacus & Assocs. Inc., NYC; supervisory bd. Pudliszki S.A. Mem. U. Chgo. Law Rev.; contbr. articles to profl. jours. Mem. Chgo.-Prague Sister Cities Com., Chgo.-China Sister Cities Com.; bd. dirs. Lyric Opera Ctr. for Am. Artists, New Trier Swim Club; sec. class of 1970, U. Calif., Berkeley; bd. trustees The Ravinia Festival. Mem. ABA, Calif. Bar Assn., Assn. of the Bar of City of NY, Chgo. Bar Assn., Ill. State Bar Assn., Internat. Bar Assn., Order of Coif, Northwestern Assocs., Chgo. China Sister Cities Comm., Old Willow Club, The Law Club, Phi Beta Kappa. Home: 465 Grove St Glencoe IL 60022-1844 Office: Salans 620 Fifth Ave New York NY 10020 Office Phone: 312-622-8448. Business E-Mail: goldmanlb@yahoo.com.

GOLDMAN, LYNN ROSE, medical educator; b. Galveston, Tex., Apr. 24, 1951; d. Armond Samuel and Barbara Jean (Bangert) G.; m. Douglas George Hayward. BS, U. Calif., 1976; MPH, Johns Hopkins U., 1981; MS, U. Calif., Berkeley, 1979; MD, U. Calif., San Francisco, 1981. Diplomate Am. Bd. Pediatrics; lic. physician, Calif. Resident in pediatrics Children's Hosp. Med. Ctr., Oakland, Calif., 1985; resident in preventive medicine U. Calif., Berkeley, 1985; pub. health med. officer Calif. Dept. Health Svcs., Berkeley, 1985-91, pub. health med. adminstr., 1991-93; asst. adminstr. Office of Prevention, Pesticides and Toxic Substances, EPA, Washington, 1993-98; prof. Sch. Hygiene and Pub. Health, Johns Hopkins U., Balt., 1999, prof. Environ. Health Sci., Occupational and Environ. Health, chair Interdepartmental Prog. in Applied Pub. Health. Named Alumna of Yr., U. Calif. Berkeley Sch. Pub. Health, 2002; recipient Woodrow Wilson award disting. govt. svc., John Hopkins U. Alumni Assn., 1999. Democrat. Office: Johns Hopkins U Bloomberg Sch Pub Health 615 N Wolfe St Rm E6636 Baltimore MD 21205-1900 Office Fax: 443-287-7375. E-mail: lgoldman@jhsph.edu.*

GOLDMAN, MARK S., alcohol/drug abuse services professional, educator, reseracher; b. Bklyn., Dec. 1, 1946; s. Paul and Vera Goldman; m. Elana Solome, Mar. 23, 1974; children: David, Gregory, Lisa. BS in Psychology, Bklyn. Coll., 1967; MS in Clin. Psychology, Rutgers U., NJ, 1971, PhD in Clin. Psychology, 1972. Staff psychologist Beth Israel Med. Ctr. Gouver Hosp., NYC, 1972—73; adj. asst. prof. clin. psychology Rutgers U., New Brunswick, NJ, 1972—73; prof. Wayne State U., Detroit, 1973—85; dir. Wayne State Ctr. Alcohol Studies, Detroit, 1978—85; prof. psychology U. South Fla., Tampa, 1985—94, dir. alcohol & substance use rsch. inst., 1993—, disting. rsch. prof., 1994—; assoc. dir. Nat. Inst. Alcohol Abuse & Alcoholism, Bethesda, Md., 2003—06. Cons. addiction studies doctoral program U. Iowa, Iowa City, 2001; cons. PIPSA project U. Fla., 2001—. Contbr. articles to profl. jours. Recipient Merit Award, Nat. Inst. Alcohol Abuse & Alcoholism, 1991—2001, Outstanding Faculty Rschr. award, Sigma Xi, Tampa Bay Chpt., 2004; numerous rsch. grants, 1976—. Fellow: APA (Disting. Sci. Contributions to Pub. Interest award 2004); mem.: AAAS, Rsch. Soc. Alcoholism, Assn. Psychol. Sci. Office: Univ S Fla 4202 E Fowler Ave PCD 4118G Tampa FL 33620 Home Phone: 813-963-5331. Office Fax: 813-974-3409; Home Fax: 813-974-3409. Business E-Mail: goldman@cas.usf.edu.

GOLDMAN, MEIR, lawyer; b. South Amboy, NJ, Feb. 19, 1957; s. Harry Goldman and Hannah Roll; children: Joseph, Aryeh, Yaakov Zelig. B in Talmudic Law, Ner Israel Rabbinical Coll., Balt., 1979; MEd, Loyola Coll., Balt., 1980; JD, U. Balt., 1989. Self inspector OSHA, CPR/multimedia first aid instr. ARC, asbestos inspector Aerosol Monitoring Assocs., lead inspector Md. Dept. of Environment. Emergency shelter coord. City of Balt. Social Svcs., 1980; safety enforcement officer Divsn. of Occupl. Safety, Balt., 1981—90; OSHA atty. Divsn. Occupl. Safety, Balt., 1990—. Prof. CC Balt., 1982—85; CPR/multimedia first aid instr. ARC, Balt., 1981—86; patrolman NW Citizens Patrol, Balt., 1980—90; editor advt. Agudah of Balt., 1986—87. Coach Little League, Balt., 1987—97; svc. coord. Ahavas Yisroel Tzemach Tzedeck, Balt., 1985—90. Mem.: ABA (licentiate), Md. Bar Assn. (licentiate), U. Balt. Alumni Assn. (life), Mensa.

Democrat. Jewish. Avocations: travel, games, computers, electronics, gambling. Home: 3609 Labyrinth Rd Apt 2C Baltimore MD 21215 Office: OSHA Divsn Occupl Safety Ste 700 401 E Fayette St Baltimore MD 21202 Home Phone: 410-764-6948; Office Phone: 410-396-3738. Office Fax: 410-396-7278; Home Fax: 410-396-7278. Personal E-mail: meirgoldman@hotmail.com. Business E-Mail: meir.goldman@baltimorecity.gov.

GOLDMAN, MICHAEL S., lawyer; b. NYC, Nov. 4, 1962; BA cum laude, Univ. Pa., 1984; JD cum laude, Fordham Univ., 1987. Bar: NY 1988. Assoc. Cravath Swaine & Moore LLP, NYC, 1987—95, ptnr., corp., 1995—. Mem.: ABA, Assn. of Bar of City of NY, NY State Bar Assn. Office: Cravath Swaine & Moore LLP Worldwide Plz 825 Eighth Ave New York NY 10019-7475 Office Phone: 212-474-1929. Office Fax: 212-474-3700. Business E-Mail: mgoldman@cravath.com.

GOLDMAN, MITCHEL PAUL, dermatologist; b. Miami Beach, Fla., Apr. 5, 1955; s. Arnold Leonard and Betty (Freedman) G.; children: Risa D., Melissa D; m. Dianne York-Goldman. BA in Biology summa cum laude, Boston U., 1977; MD, Stanford U. Sch. Medicine, 1982. Diplomate Am. Bd. Dermatology. Intern, internal medicine U. Calif., San Diego, 1982-83; resident, dermatology UCLA, 1983-86; with Dermatology Assocs., La Jolla, Calif., 1996—; assoc. clin. prof. dermatology, medicine Univ. Calif., San Diego; founder, med. dir. La Jolla Spa MD. Mem. staff U. Calif. VA Med. Ctr., La Jolla, San Diego Med. Ctr., Scripps Meml. Hosps., Encinitas and La Jolla, Children's Hosp., 1987—; adv. bd. 3-M Pharma. Johnson and Johnson, Allergen, Lumenis Laser Corp., DUSA Pharm., Galderma, COOLTOUCH Laser Corp., Cynosure Laser Corp., Medicis, Cosmetic Surgery Expos, Consumer Guide to Plastic Surgery; presenter in field. Author of several med. textbooks; contbr. several articles to profl. jours.; assoc. editor Dermatologic Surgery, Jour. Cosmetic Dermatology; editl. reviewer Jour. Am. Acad. Dermatology; quoted in Bus. 2.0 mag, Oprah mag., San Diego mag., More mag. Bd. dirs. San Diego chpt., Am. Cancer Soc. Fellow Am. Soc. for Dermatologic Surgery (bd. dirs. 1995—), Am. Acad. Dermatology, Am. Acad. Cosmetic Surgery, Am. Soc. for Laser Medicine and Surgery; mem. Am. Coll. Phlebology (founding mem., past pres.), Am. Venous Forum (bd. dirs. 1993-95), San Diego County Dermatol. Soc. (past pres.), Sonoran Dermatology Soc. (past pres.), Calif. Med. Assn., AMA, San Diego Med. Soc., Am. Acad. Cosmetic Surgery, Space Dermatol. Found. (founding mem.), Pacific Dermatol. Assn., Am. Acad. Aesthetic & Reconstrucive Surgery, Am. So. Liposuction, Am. Med. Soc., Calif. Med. Soc., Phi Beta Kappa. renowned for pioneering research and development of multiple laser techniques, and for advancing the technique widely used for liposuction and leg vein treatment. Office: La Jolla Spa MD 7630 Fay Ave La Jolla CA 92037-4841 Office Phone: 858-459-6868. Office Fax: 858-459-4894.*

GOLDMAN, NATHAN CARLINER, lawyer, educator; b. Charleston, SC, Mar. 19, 1950; s. Reuben and Hilda Alta (Carliner) G.; m. Judith Tova Feigon, Oct. 28, 1984; children: Michael Reuben, Miriam Esther. BA, U. S.C., 1972; JD, Duke U., 1975; MA, Johns Hopkins U., 1978, PhD, 1980. Bar: N.C. 1975, Tex. 1985, U.S. Dist. Ct. (mid. dist.) N.C. 1975. Paralegal City Atty.'s Office, Durham, NC, 1975-76; asst. prof. govt. dept. U. Tex., Austin, 1980-85; pvt. practice Houston, 1985-86; assoc. Liddell, Sapp, Zivley, Hill & LaBoon, Houston, 1986-88; pvt. practice Houston, 1988-2000; atty. Amdur Law Office, 2000—. Adj. prof. space law U. Houston, 1985-88; rsch. assoc. Rice U. Inst. Policy Analysis, 1986—; lectr. bus. law, 1988-95; mem. coordinating bd. Space Architecture, U. Houston, 1985—; v.p. Internat. Design in Extreme Environments Assn., U. Houston, 1991—; vis. asst. prof. U. Houston-Clear Lake, 1989-91, 99—; adj. prof. South Tex. Coll. Law, 1994-95; gen. counsel Internat. Space Enterprises, 1993—, Globus Ltd. Co., 1994—; info. officer Israel Consulate, 1996-97, atty. Judith G. Cooper, P.C. Author: Space Commerce, 1985, American Space Law, 1988, 2d edit., 1996, Space Policy: A Primer, 1992; editor: Space and Society, 1984; assoc. editor Jour. Space Commerce, 1990-91; exec. editor Space Governance, 1996-99; more than 40 articles, 100 poems published. Mem. com. on governance of space U.S. Bicentennial Commn., 1986-88, Clear Lake (Tex.) Area Econ. Devel. Found., 1987, Space Collegium, Houston Area Rsch. Ctr., 1987; pres. Windermere Civic Assn., 1990-92; bd. dirs. Hebrew Acad., 1994-96, Men's Club United Orthodox Synagogues, 1994-98, pres., 1999-2002. U.S. Dept. Justice grantee, 1979-80, U. Tex. Inst. for Constructive Capitalism U. grantee, 1983; E.D. Walker Centennial fellow, 1984; NASA Summer fellow U. Calif., 1984. Fellow Internat. Inst. Space Law; mem. ABA, Tex. Bar Assn., Nat. Space Soc. (v.p. 1989-91), Inst. for Social Sci. Study Space (mem. adv. bd. 1990, editor Space Humanization Jour. 1993-2000), Am. Astronautical Soc. (history com. 2005—), Inst. for Design in Extreme Environment Assn. (v.p. 1991-96), Space Bus. Roundtable. Avocations: poetry, reading, hiking, baseball, softball. Home: 9406 Cliffwood Dr Houston TX 77096

GOLDMAN, NEAL, entrepreneur, information technology executive; b. 1971; MBA, Columbia Bus. Sch. With Lehman Bros.; founder & chief exec. Capital IQ, NYC, 1998—2004, Inform Technologies LLC, NYC, 2004—. Named one of 40 Under 40, Crain's NY Bus., 2007. Office: Inform Technologies LLC 6th Fl 145 E 57th St New York NY 10022*

GOLDMAN, NORMAN LEWIS, chemistry professor; b. Bklyn., Aug. 11, 1933; s. Sam and Rose (Schrager) G. BS in Chemistry, CCNY, 1954; AM in Chemistry, Harvard U., Cambridge, Mass., 1956; PhD in Chemistry, Columbia U., NYC, 1959. Postdoctoral NSF fellow Imperial Coll., U. London, 1959—60; NIH postdoctoral fellow Columbia U., NYC; mem. faculty Queens Coll., CUNY, 1961—, prof. chemistry and biochemistry, 1976-98; prof. chemistry emeritus Queens Coll., 1998—; chmn. dept. Queens Coll., CUNY, 1972-77, acting assoc. dean faculty, 1977-78, acting dean faculty, div. math. and natural scis., 1978-79, dean faculty, div. math. and natural scis., 1979-98. Contbr. articles to profl. jours. Mem. Am. Chem. Soc., NY Acad. Sci. (vice chair chem. sci. sect. 1998-99, chair 1999-2000), Sigma Xi, Phi Beta Kappa. Home: 75-10 Grand Central Pky Forest Hills NY 11375-5562 Office: CUNY Queens Coll 120 Remsen Hall Flushing NY 11367-1597 Office Phone: 718-997-4196. Business E-Mail: norman.goldman@qc.cuny.edu.

GOLDMAN, PETER LOUIS, writer; b. Phila., Feb. 8, 1933; s. Walter and Dorothy (Semple) G.; m. Helen Dudar, July 16, 1961. BA, Williams Coll., 1954; MS, Columbia U., 1955. Staff writer St. Louis Globe Democrat, 1955-62; assoc. editor Newsweek, NYC, 1962-64, gen. editor, 1965-68, sr. editor, 1968-88, contbg. editor, 1988—. Field dir. Spl. Election Unit, 1984—. Author: Civil Rights: The Challenge of the Fourteenth Amendment, 1965, Report from Black America, 1970, The Death and Life of Malcolm X, 1973, rev. 2d edit., 1979; co-author: Charlie Company: What Vietnam Did to Us, 1983, The Quest for the Presidency 1984, 1985, The Quest for the Presidency 1988, 1989, Quest for the Presidency 1992, 1994, The End of the World That Was, 1986, Brothers, 1988; editor: The Attentive Eye: Selected Journalism by Helen Dudar, 2002. Nieman fellow, Harvard U., 1961; recipient Sigma Delta Chi award 1962, Robert F. Kennedy Journalism award 1972, ABA Silver Gavel award 1972, Page One awards N.Y. Newspaper Guild, 1967, 72, 86, 88, 89, Nat. Mag. award, 1982, 92, Freedom Found. award, 1982, Am. Legion Fourth Estate award 1982, N.Y. Bar Media award, 1984. Home: 36 Gramercy Park E New York NY 10003-1741 Office: Newsweek 251 W 57th St New York NY 10019 E-mail: petergoldman@msn.com.

GOLDMAN, PHYLLIS E., psychology educator; BA, Rutgers U., 1966; MA, Seton Hall U., 1969; MS, Stevens Inst. Tech., 1978; EdD, Seton Hall U., 1983. Rsch. asst. Rutgers Univ., Newark, 1965-66; counselor N.J. Dept. of Labor and Industry, Newark, 1967-69; prof., psychology County Coll. of Morris, Randolph, N.J., 1969—; pvt. practice cons., 1978—. Author: Academic Self-Concept, 1992; editor: Dimensions of Work and Human Behavior, 1980, 85, (jour.) Morris Manager, 1988, 89, 90; contbr. articles to profl. jours. Speakers bur. County Coll. Morris, Randolph, 1976—2005; bd. adv. Cath. Cmty. Svcs., Newark, 1978—80; adv. coun. US Postal Svc., 2003—04. Mem. Am. Psychological Assn., Psi Chi, Kappa Delta Pi, Phi Delta Kappa. Avocation: reading. Office: County Coll of Morris Rt 10 & Center Grove Rd Randolph NJ 07869 Office Phone: 973-328-5622.

GOLDMAN, RALPH FREDERICK, research physiologist, educator; b. Boston, Mar. 3, 1928; s. Harry and May (Field) G.; m. Joan R. Krinsky, May 27, 1956; children: Harry, Ellen. BS in Chemistry, U. Denver, 1949; MA in Physiology, Boston U., 1951, PhD in Physiology, 1954; MS in Engring., Northeastern U., Boston, 1962. Rsch. physiologist Natick Labs. U.S. Army, Mass., 1955—61; dir. div. environ. medicine U.S. Army Rsch. Inst., Natick, 1961—82; prin. cons. Dept. of Army for Environ. Physiology, Natick, 1971—82; chief scientist Multi-Tech Corp., Natick, 1982—88; chief scientist, R&D, clothing and human comfort Comfort Tech., Inc., Framingham, Mass., 1989—; sr. cons. tech. and product devel. Arthur D. Little, Inc., Cambridge, Mass., 1993—97. Adj. prof. Boston U., 1970—2005, N.C. State U., 1989—2005; lectr. MIT, Cambridge, 1974-94; vis. scientist Peoples Rep. of China, 1981—2005; vis. scholar lectr. Springfield (Mass.) Coll., 1977, Ohio State U., 1977, 88; chmn. rsch. group biomed. effects of clothing, NATO, 1981-86. Author: 2 books; contbr. 26 chpts. to books, over 500 articles, abstracts and tech. reports to profl. jours. Scoutmaster Boy Scouts Am., Framingham, Mass., 1956-90, exec. bd., 1991-2002; mem. town meeting Town of Framingham, 1983-88. Recipient Meritorious Civilian Svc. award U.S. Army R&D Command, 1963, Exceptional Civilian Svc. award Sec. of Army, 1976, Sr. Exec. Svc. award U.S. Civil Svc., 1979, Silver Beaver award Boy Scouts Am., 1981. Fellow: ASHRAE (life; bd. dirs. 1982—85, assoc. editor HVAC&R Rsch. 1995—2001, Disting. Fellow award 1992), Am. Coll. Sports Medicine (editl. bd. 1979—85), Ergonomics Soc. (hon.); mem.: ASTM, IEEE (life; AEMB Coun. 1978—84), Assn. Mil. Surgeons U.S., Am. Physiol. Soc. (editl. bd. 1972—78), Framingham Amateur Radio Assn. (treas. 1970—84), Tarpon Cove Yacht and Racquet Club, Naples, Fla. Jewish. Avocations: piano, gardening, duplicate bridge, tennis. Office: Comfort Tech 7 W Trevor Hill Plymouth MA 02360 Home Phone: 239-597-1973; Office Phone: 508-397-3886. Personal E-mail: ralphgoldman@cs.com. Business E-Mail: comfortcorp@cs.com.

GOLDMAN, RICHARD HARRIS, lawyer, director; b. Boston, June 17, 1936; s. Charles M. and Irene M. (Marks) Goldman; m. Patricia Grollman, June 21, 1959; children: Elaine, Stephen. BA, Wesleyan U., 1958; LLB, NYU, 1961. Bar: Mass. 1961, U.S. Dist. Ct. Mass. 1961. Mem. Slater & Goldman, Boston, 1961—76, Widett, Slater & Goldman, PC, Boston, 1976—93, Sullivan & Worcester LLP, Boston, 1993—. Past trustee, chmn. audit com. and clk. Grove Bank. Co-author: The Ritual Dance Between Lessee and Lender; contbr. articles to profl. jours. Former chmn. Newton (Mass.) Human Rights Commn.; hon. trustee, former v.p. Temple Israel. Recipient Cmty. Svc. award, Am. Jewish Cmty., 2003, Mass. Super Lawyers, 2005. Mem.: ABA, Mass. Conveyancers Assn., Boston Bar Assn. (chmn. leasing com. 1996—97, lectr., chmn. seminar comml. real estate fin. 1997, real estate steering com. 1997—2004, co-chair real estate sect. 1999—2002, co-chair sr. lawyer sect. 2003—04), Mass. Bar Assn., Belmont Country Club (v.p., sec., bd. govs.). Home: 47 Vaughn Ave Newton MA 02461-1038 Office: Sullivan & Worcester LLP 1 Post Office Sq Ste 2300 Boston MA 02109-2129 Office Phone: 617-338-2942. Business E-Mail: rgoldman@sandw.com.

GOLDMAN, RICHARD N., foundation administrator; b. San Francisco, Apr. 16, 1920; s. Richard and Alice Goldman; m. Rhoda Haas (dec.); children: Richard (dec.), John, Douglas, Susan. BA, U. Calif., Berkeley, 1941, postgrad. Chmn. Goldman Ins. Svcs.; pres. Richard and Rhoda Goldman Fund. Former mem. port commn., pub. utilities commn., chief of protocol City and County of San Francisco. Trustee World Fine Arts Mus. San Francisco, Nat. Symphony, U. Calif.-Berkeley Berkeley Found., Washington Inst. for Near East Policy, World Affairs Coun. No. Calif.; bd. dirs. Am. Jewish History Soc., Internat. House, Berkeley, Jerusalem Found., League to Save Lake Tahoe, San Francisco Ballet; mem. coun. Yosemite Fund; mem. exec. com. Bay Area Internat. Forum; mem. dv. com. Bus. Execs. for Nat. Security; bd. visitors Inst. for Internat. Studies, Stanford U.; bd. dirs., former pres. Jewish Cmty. Fedn., San Francisco; mem. adv. coun. Pacific Grad. Sch. Psychology; mem. governing coun. Save-the-Redwoods League; mem. pres.' adv. coun. San Francisco State U. With U.S. Army, 1942-46. Recipient The Chairman's Medal, Heinz Awards, 2005. Mem. San Francisco Planning and Urban Renewal Assn. (mem. adv. coun.), Concordia-Argonaut Club, The Family, Villa Taverna, Calif. Tennis Club. Office: Richard Rhoda Goldman Fund PO Box 29924 San Francisco CA 94129-0924

GOLDMAN, STANFORD MILTON, medical educator; b. Salt Lake City, Nov. 28, 1940; s. Osher and Miriam (Solomon) G.; m. Harriet Kaplow, Apr. 2, 1965; children: Etan, Nava. BA, BRE, Yeshiva U., 1961; MD, Einstein Coll. Medicine, 1965. Intern Jefferson U. Sch. Medicine, Phila., 1965-66; resident Einstein Coll. Medicine, Bronx, 1966-69; chmn. dept. radiology USPHS Phoenix Indian Med. Ctr., 1969-71; asst. prof. radiology Einstein Coll. Medicine, Bronx, 1971-72; from instr. to asst. prof. radiology Johns Hopkins U. Sch. Medicine, Balt., 1972-79; from asst. prof. to assoc. prof. U. Md., Balt., 1975-81; assoc. prof. Johns Hopkins U., 1979-86; clin. prof. Uniformed Svcs. U., Bethesda, Md., 1981-94; prof. radiology Johns Hopkins U., 1986-94, prof. urology, 1988-93; prof., chmn. radiology U. Tex. Med. Sch., Houston, 1993—2000, prof. urology, 1995—, prof. radiology, 1993—. Adj. prof. radiology and urology Baylor Coll. Medicine, Houston, 1994—; med. dir. radiol. sch. tech. Houston C.C., 1994, ultrasound sch. tech., 1999-2001; prof. radiology M.D. Anderson Cancer Ctr., Houston, 1995-2003, adj. prof., 2007—. Editor: Computed Tomography of Kidneys & Adrenals, 1983, CT & MRI of the Genitourinary Tract, 1990, Tc E Rm Del Trattos Genito-Urinario, 1994; assoc. editor: Urologic Radiology, 1982-85, Radiology, 1986-94, European Urology, 1993-2004; cons. editor Urology, 1998—. Chair bd. edn. Beren Acad. Houston, 2005—; mem. Radiation Control Adv. Bd., Md., 1989—93. Lt. comdr. USPHS, 1969—71. Recipient Albert Einstein Disting. Alumni award, 1996; grantee, Royal Coll. Physicians, 2006—. Fellow: Royal Coll. Physicians, Soc. Uroradiology (bd. dirs. 1992—98, med. equipment com. 2000—01, ethics com. 2003), Am. Soc. Emergency Radiology (bd. dirs. 1994—, indsl. com. 1994—, abstract com. 1995—97, chmn. audit com. 1995—99, chmn. sci. program com. 1996—97, vice chair program com. 1996—97, fin. com. 1996—98, site com. 1996—98, sec.-treas. 1998—2000, exec. com. 1998—, 1998—, sec.-treas. 2001, pres. 2002—04, chair site selection com. 2002—04, nominating com. 2002—04, chmn. bylaws com. 2004—06, alt. counselor to ACR 2007—, 2-H counselor 2007—, Gold medal 2006), Radiol. Soc. N.Am. (chmn. sci. exhibits awards com. 1988—90, chmn. program coms. subcom. on gu radiology 1996—99), Am. Coll. Radiology (counselor from Tex. 1996—2002, mem. com. on coding and nomenclature of commn. on econs. 1996—2002, nominating com. 1999, co-chmn. nominating comm. 2000—01, alt. counselor 2002—, liason to com. on trauma ACS 2004—, subcom. on radiation in pregnancy com. on safety 2007—, liaison to publ. subcom., liaison to performance improvement and patient safety subcom.); mem.: ACS, AMA, Johns Hopkins Med. and Surg. Assn., Assn. Univ. Radiologists (ethics com. 1997, nominating com. 1997—98), European Soc. Urogenital Radiology, Houston Radiol. Soc. (treas. 2000—, pres. 2002), Houston Med. Soc., Tex. Radiol. Soc. (program com. 1994—96, chmn. long range planning com. 1996—97, bd. dirs. 1996—, fellowship nominating com. 1998—2000, 2d v.p. 2001, 1st v.p. 2002, chmn. program com. 2002—03, exec. com. 2002—, chmn. legis. com. 2003—04, pres. 2004—05, chair orgnl. structure coun. 2005—06, bd. govs. 2005—06, chair jud. affairs com. 2005—06, chair nominating soc. 2005—06, chmn. bylaws com. 2005—06, trustee 2005—06, chair bd. trustees 2005—06), Tex. Med. Soc., Am. Urol. Assn. (hematuria guidelines panel 1998—99), Am. Roentgen Ray Soc., U.S.-Israel Bi-Nat. Sci. Found., Albert Einstein Alumni Assn. (bd. dirs. 1991—2002, 2003—, Disting. Alumni award 1996), U. Md. Alumni Assn. (assoc.). Jewish. Avocations: swimming, music. Office: U Tex Med Sch Dept Radiology 6431 Fannin St Ste 2100 Houston TX 77030-1501 Business E-Mail: stanford.m.goldman@uth.tmc.edu.

GOLDMAN, STEVEN ANDREW, plastic surgeon, educator; s. John and Margaret Goldman; m. Jodie Lynn Goldman, June 11, 1995; children: Max, Mollie, Eli, Jacob. BA in Chemistry with honors, Dartmouth Coll., 1989; MD, U. Pitts., 1993. Cert. Am. Bd. Plastic Surgery. Intern in surgery U. Pitts. Sch. Medicine, 1993—94; resident in otolaryngology U. Pitts. Med. Ctr., 1994—98; resident in plastic surgery U. Hosps. Cleve., 1998—2000; asst. prof. plastic surgery Case Western Res. U. Sch Medicine, U. Hosps. Cleve., 2000—. Contbr. articles to profl. jours., chapters to books. Named Top Doc in Reconstructive Surgery, No. Ohio Live Mag., 2005; named to Who's Who in Execs. and Profls., Nat. Register, 2004. Fellow: ACS, Am. Acad. Facial Plastic and Reconstructive Surgery; mem.: Am. Acad. Otolaryngology/Head and Neck Surgery (cert.), Am. Rhinologic Soc., Am. Soc. Plastic Surgeons, Alpha Omega Alpha. Home: 2490 Blossom Ln Beachwood OH 44122 Office: Case Sch Medicine 11100 Euclid Ave Cleveland OH 44106 Office Phone: 216-514-8899. Office Fax: 216-884-8667. E-mail: into@drgoldman.com.

GOLDMAN, STEVEN M., state agency administrator; married; 3 children. AB cum laude in Polit. Sci., Boston U., 1973; JD with honors, George Washington U., 1976; LLM in Taxation, NYU, 1980. Bar: NJ 1976, Fla. 1978, NY 1988. Sr. mem. Sills, Cummis, Epstein & Gross, P.C.; commr. NJ Dept. Banking and Ins., 2006—. Mem.: Phi Beta Kappa. Office: NJ Dept Banking and Ins PO Box 325 20 W State St Trenton NJ 08625 Office Phone: 609-633-7667. Office Fax: 609-984-5273. E-mail: commissioner@dobi.state.nj.us.

GOLDMAN, STEVEN MARK, lawyer; s. Alan Ben and Joan Phyllis Goldman; m. Constance Helen Cantrell, May 16, 1992; children: Charlotte, David, Grace. BA in Historycum laude, U. Vt., 1982; JD cum laude, U. Ga., 1985. Intern Judge Hugh Gibson U.S. Dist. Ct., So. Dist. Tex., Galveston, 1985—87; intern Judge Will Garwood U.S. Ct. Appeals, 5th Cir., Austin, 1987—88; assoc. Kilpatrick & Cody, Atlanta, 1988—89, Asbill & Brennan, Atlanta, 1990—91; sr. counsel Holiday Inn Worldwide, Atlanta, 1991—95; gen. counsel Franchise divsn. ITT Sheraton Corp., Atlanta, 1995—96, gen. counsel, v.p. franchise adminstrn., 1996—97; v.p., asst. gen. counsel Marriott Internat., Inc., Bethesda, Md., 1997—2002, sr. v.p., assoc. gen. counsel, 2002—, corp. officer, 2004—. Lectr. in field. Editl. bd. LJN's Franchising Bus. Alert, 1998—; contbr. articles to profl. jours. Mem.: ABA (co-chair S.E. regional workshops sect. of litigation, com. on corp. co 1995—97), Nat. Franchise Coun. (bd. dirs. 1998—2003, corp. governance/mission task force 1999), Atlanta Bar Assn. (bd. dirs. corp. counsel sect. 1996—98). Avocations: travel, road biking, golf, mountaineering. Office: Marriott International Inc One Marriott Dr Washington DC 20058

GOLDMAN, STUART MILES, podiatrist; b. Phila., Pa., May 26, 1955; s. Albert and Minnie Goldman; m. Debbie Schlecker, Sept. 4, 1988; children: Nechama, Aryeh, Goldie, Shoshana, Avraham. BA, Dickenson Coll., 1976; Doctorate in podiatric medicine, PA Coll. of Podiatric Medicine, 1980. Cert. Foot and Ankle Surgery Am. Bd. of Podiatric Surgery, 1984. Author: Neurogenic Positional Pedal Neuritis: Pedal Manifestations of Spinal Stenosis, Value of a Grocery Cart and Wheeled Walker in Identification and Management of Symptomatic Spinal Stenosis in Patients presenting with Neuropathy or Claudication., Diabetic Peripheral Neuropathy or Spinal Stenosis: Prevalence of Overlap or Misdiagnosis, Spinal Stenosis: Positional History, Positional Testing, Positional Therapy Facilitate Identification and Management of Lower Extremity Symptoms, Nocturnal Neuropathic Pain in Diabetics: It may be Caused by Spinal Stenosis; contbr. articles various profl. jours. Mohel, Fla. Fellow: Am. Coll. of Foot and Ankle Surgeons. Jewish. Achievements include research in spinal stenosis: A common cause of podiatric symptoms; diabetic peripheral neuropathy or spinal stenosis: Prevelance of overlap of misdiagnosis. Avocations: story teller, teacher, guitar. Office: 4419 Paris Rd Baltimore MD 21211 Personal E-mail: podmohel@aol.com, podmohel@yahoo.com.

GOLDMAN, WILLIAM, writer, scriptwriter; b. Chgo., Aug. 12, 1931; s. M. Clarence and Marion (Well) Goldman; m. Ilene Jones, Apr. 15, 1961; children: Jenny, Susanna. BA, Oberlin Coll., 1952; MA, Columbia U., 1956. Author: (novels) The Temple of Gold, 1957, Your Turn to Curtsy, My Turn to Bow, 1958, Soldier in the Rain, 1960, Boys and Girls Together, 1964, No Way to Treat a Lady, 1964, The Thing of It Is, 1967, Father's Day, 1971, The Princess Bride, 1973, Marathon Man, 1974, Wigger, 1974, Magic, 1976, Tinsel, 1979, Control, 1982, The Silent Gondoliers, 1983, The Color of Light, 1984, Heat, 1985, Brothers, 1987, (non-fiction) The Season: A Candid Look at Broadway, 1969, Adventures in the Screen Trade, 1983; author: (with Mike Lupica) Wait Until Next year, 1988, Hype and Glory, 1990, Four Screenplays, 1995, Five Screenplays, 1997, Which Lie Did I Tell, 2000; author: (essays) The Big Picture, 1999; author: (with James Goldman) (plays) Blood Sweat and Stanley Poole, 1961; author: (with James Goldman and John Kander) (musical) A Family Affair, 1962; author: (films) Masquerade, 1965, Harper, 1966, Butch Cassidy and the Sundance Kid, 1969 (Acad. award Best Original Screenplay, 1970), The Hot Rock, 1972, The Stepford Wives, 1974, The Great Waldo Pepper, 1975, Marathon Man, 1976, All the President's Men, 1976 (Acad. award Best Screenplay Adaptation, 1977), A Bridge Too Far, 1977, Magic, 1978, The Princess Bride, 1987, Heat, 1987, Misery, 1990, The Year of the Comet, 1992, Memoirs of an Invisible Man, 1992, Chaplin, 1992, Maverick, 1994, Ghost and the Darkness, 1996, Absolute Power, 1997, Hearts in Atlantis, 2001, Dreamcatcher, 2003. Recipient Laurel award for Lifetime Achievement in Screenwriting, 1983. Personal E-mail: longbaugh@aol.com.

GOLDMANN, JAMES ALLEN, healthcare consultant; b. Milw., Feb. 26, 1952; s. Allen Abraham and Ruth Lois (Kolbur) G.; m. Pamela Anne McCole, June 6, 1980; children: Michael, Elissa, Kerry. AB, Harvard Coll., 1974; MHA, Washington U., St. Louis, 1979. V.p. Riverside Meth. Hosp., Columbus, Ohio, 1980—85; COO Children's Med. Ctr., Dallas, 1986—92; cons. APM, Inc., NYC, 1993—96; ptnr. Arthur Andersen, Dallas, 1996—2000, IBM, Dallas, 2001—03, JHD Group, Dallas, 2004—. Bd. dirs. Hope Cottage, Dallas, 1989-93; scout leader Boy Scouts Am., Columbus and Grapevine, Tex., 1980-84, 92, 93. Fellow Am. Coll. Healthcare Execs. Office: JHD Group 5055 Keller Springs Addison TX Business E-Mail: jgoldmann@jhdgroup.com.

GOLDMANN, MORTON AARON, cardiologist, educator; b. Chgo., July 11, 1924; s. Harry Ascher and Frieda (Cohon) G.; m. Doris-Jane Tumpeer, July 18, 1951; children: Deborah, Jory, Erica, Leslie BS, U. Ill., 1943, MD, 1946. Diplomate Am. Bd. Internal Medicine. Intern Cook County Hosp., Chgo., 1946-47, resident physician, 1949-52, practice medicine specializing in internal medicine and cardiology Skokie, Ill., 1952—2003, trustee emeritus, 2003—; chief of medicine Rush North Shore Med. Ctr. (formerly Skokie Valley Hosp.), 1964-65, also trustee, 1968—2002, trustee emeritus, 2002—, pres. med. staff, 1968-69, attending physician, med. dir. heart sta. and cardiac rehab. unit, 1973-96, bd. dirs., 1970—; former attending physician Ill. Rsch. Hosp.; former assoc. prof.

Abraham Lincoln Sch. Medicine, U. Ill., Chgo.; prof. Cook County Grad. Sch. Medicine. Pres. Heart Assn. North Cook County, 1978-81, North Suburban Assn. Health Resources, 1974-77 Contbr. numerous articles to profl. jours. Capt. M.C., AUS, 1947-49, PTO Fellow ACP, Inst. Medicine Chgo., Am. Coll. Cardiology; mem. AMA, Am. Soc. Internal Medicine, Am. Heart Assn., Ill. Med. Soc., Chgo. Med. Soc., Chgo. Heart Assn. (bd. govs., bd. dirs. 1978-87, bd. trustees 1979-83).

GOLDMARK, PETER FRANCIS, banker; b. Budapest, Hungary, Nov. 27, 1946; came to U.S., 1964; s. Francis Martin Goldmark and Eva Magdolna (Balla) Sander; m. Cassandra K. Masson; children: Alexander, Nicolas. BS, Fairleigh Dickinson U., 1968; MBA, Columbia U., 1970. Asst. treas. Am. Express Bank, NYC, 1970-74; dir. Coun. of the Ams., NYC, 1974-76; group mgr. N.Y. Times, NYC, 1976-82; v.p. Chase Manhattan Bank, NYC, 1982-91; rep. Union Bancaire Privee, NYC, 1991—; exec. v.p. Inter-Nation Capital Mgmt. Corp., NYC, 1997—; pres. Rockport Capital Group, NYC, 1995—. Chmn., pres. The Ams. Found., N.Y.C., 1993—. Mem. Ams. Soc., Columbia U. Bus. Sch. Counseling Bd., Colombian-Am. Assn., N.Am. Chilean C. of C., Argentine-Am. Assn., European-Am. Assn., Venezuelan-Am. Assn. (dir., asst. treas. 1991—), Bolivarian Soc. U.S. (dir. 1992—). Democrat. Avocations: skiing, tennis, scuba diving. Office: 230 Park Ave Rm 1536 New York NY 10169-9415 Office Phone: 212-687-5245. Business E-Mail: pfgoldmark@usa.net.

GOLDNER, SHELDON HERBERT, retired import/export company executive; b. Bklyn., Aug. 3, 1928; s. David and Esther (Maskowsky) G.; m. Lila Diane Silber, Aug. 14, 1954; children: Jonathan Shepard, Jeffrey Scott, Barbara Jill. BS in acctg., L.I. U., 1950. C.P.A., N.Y. Acct. S.H. Goldner & Co., NYC, 1950-59; v.p. fin. Connell Rice & Sugar Co., Inc., Westfield, NJ, 1959-89, ret., 1989. Pres., trustee Temple Israel, Union, N.J. Served with U.S. Army Signal Corps, 1946-47, PTO. Mem. AICPA, N.Y. State Soc. CPAs, Halloween Yacht Club (Stamford, Conn.), Royal Veere (Netherlands) Yacht Club, Dartmouth Yacht Club (Devon, Eng.), Miles River Yacht Club (St. Michaels, Md.).

GOLDREICH, PETER MARTIN, astrophysics and planetary physics educator; b. NYC, July 14, 1939; s. Paul and Edith (Rosenfield) Goldreich; m. Susan Kroll, June 14, 1960; children: Eric, Daniel. BS in Engring. Physics, Cornell U., Ithaca, NY, 1960, PhD in Physics, 1963. Part-time instr. Cornell U., 1961—63; postdoctoral fellow Cambridge U., 1963—64; asst. prof. astronomy and geophysics UCLA, 1964—66; assoc. prof. planetary sci. and astronomy Calif. Inst. Tech., Pasadena, 1966—69, prof., 1969—81, Lee A. DuBridge prof. astrophysics and planetary physics, 1981—, emeritus prof., 2003—; prof. sch. natural scis. Inst. Advanced Study, Princeton, NJ, 2003—. Named Calif. Scientist of Yr., 1981; recipient Chapman medal, Royal Astron. Soc., 1985, Gold medal, 1990, Nat. Medal of Sci., 1995, Antoinette de Vaucouleurs medal, U. Tex., 1999, Grande médaille, French Acad. Scis., 2006, Shaw prize, Astronomy, Shaw Prize Found., Hong Kong, 2007; fellow NSF, 1961—63, Sloan Found., 1968—70; grantee Woodrow Wilson Hon. fellowship, 1960—61. Fellow: NAS, Am. Acad. Arts and Scis.; mem.: Royal Soc. (foreign mem. 2003—), Am. Astron. Soc. (Henry Norris Russell lectr., Dick Brouwer award 1986, George P. Kuiper prize divsn. planetary sci. 1992). Office: Calif Inst Tech Msc 150-21 1200 E California Blvd Pasadena CA 91125-0001 also: Sch Natural Scis Inst Advanced Study Einstein Dr Princeton NJ 08540 Office Phone: 626-395-6193, 609-734-8016. Office Fax: 609-951-4402. E-mail: pmg@ias.edu.*

GOLDRICH, MICHAEL SETH, otolaryngologist; s. David and Agnes Goldrich; m. Judith Ilana Goldberg, July 6, 1986; children: Eliana, David, Gavriella. BA, Johns Hopkins U., Balt., 1984; MD, George Washington U., Washington, 1989. Diplomate Am. Bd. Otolaryngology-Head and Neck Surgery, 1998. Intern, resident in surgery George Washington U. Med. Ctr., Washington, 1989—91; rsch. fellow Nat. Inst. Allergy and Immunology, Bethesda, Md., 1991—92; resident in otolaryngology Manhattan Eye Ear and Throat Hosp., NYC, 1992—96; fellow on laryngology Vanderbilt U. Med. Ctr., Nashville, Tex., 1996—97; mem. staff Univ. Otolaryngology Assocs., New Brunswick, NJ, 1997—. Clin. assoc. prof. U. Medicine and Dentistry NJ, New Brunswick, 1998—, clin. asst. environ. and occupl. medicine, 2004—, chief divsn. otolaryngology, 2007—, Robeet Wood Johnson U. Hosp., New Brunswick, 2007—; presenter in field. Contbr. articles, sci. papers to profl. jours. Trustee Ray Kushner Yeshiva HS, Livingston, NJ, 2006—; pres. Rabbi Pesach Rayman Yeshiva, Edison, NJ, 2002—04. Recipient Vol. Faculty award, U. Medicine and Dentistry NJ, 2002. Fellow: ACS, Am. Acad. Otolaryngology-Head and Neck Surgery (del., chmn. com. residents and fellows in tng. 1994—95); mem.: AMA (trustee 1993—97, mem. exec. com. Physician Health Found. 1994—95, v.p. Edn. and Rsch. Found. 1994—97, chmn. coun. ethical and jud. affairs 2002—04, trustee fin. com. 1996—97, sec.-treas. Edn. and Rsch. Found. 1993—94), Am. Laryngological, Rhinological and Otological Soc., Middlesex County Med. Soc., Med. Soc. NJ (trustee found. 1998—). Office: Univ Otolaryngology Assocs 181 Somerset St New Brunswick NJ 08901

GOLDRING, NORMAN MAX, marketing professional; b. Chgo., June 22, 1937; s. Jack and Carolyn (Wolf) G.; m. Cynthia Lois Garland, Dec. 20, 1959; children: Jay Marshall, Diane. BS in Bus., Miami U., Ohio, 1959; MBA, U. Chgo., 1963. Advt. account mgr. Edward H. Weiss & Co., Chgo., 1959-61; sr. v.p., dir. mktg. svcs. Stern, Walters & Simmons, Inc., Chgo., 1961-68; chmn. Goldring & Co., Inc., Chgo., 1968-89; pres., CEO CPM, Inc., 1969-93, chmn., 1994-99; pres. CPO Inc., 1994—. Dir. Creative Works, Inc., 1994-97, MediaSmith, Inc., 2004—; instr. mktg. and advt. mgmt. Roosevelt U., 1965-68. Mem. editl. bd. Jour. Media Planning; mem. editl. bd. advisors Response Mag., 2001—. Commr. Ridgeville Park Dist., Evanston, Ill., 1971-75, pres. 1974-75; bd. dirs., v.p. Mus. Broadcast Comm., 1983-92; bd. dirs. Chgo. Chamber Musicians 1988—, Chgo. Metro History Fair, 1990; bd. dirs. Lake Forest Grad. Sch. Mgmt., 2000—, mem. exec. com., 2002—, chmn. mktg. com., 2005—; trustee Chgo. Assn. Dirs. Mktg. Ednl. Found., 2001-05. Mem. Am. Mktg. Assn. (speaker), Advt. Coun. Inc. (Midwest adv. bd. 1983-90), Am. Mgmt. Assn., Direct Mktg. Assn. (mem. chmn., broadcast coun.), Chgo. Assn. Dirs. Mktg., Elec. Ret. Assn. Home: 855 Beverly Pl Lake Forest IL 60045-3901 Office: CPO Inc 736 N Western Ave # 147 Chicago IL 60045 Home Phone: 847-735-8055; Office Phone: 847-735-7365. Business E-Mail: ngoldring@cpodirect.com.

GOLDSBOROUGH, ROBERT GERALD, publishing executive, author; b. Chgo., Oct. 3, 1937; s. Robert Vincent and Wilma (Janak) G.; m. Janet Elizabeth Moore, Jan. 15, 1966; children: Suzanne Joy, Robert Michael, Colleen Marie, Bonnie Laura. BS, Northwestern U., 1959, MS with honors, 1960. Reporter A.P., 1959, City News Bur., Chgo., 1959; with Chgo. Tribune, 1960-82, reporter neighborhood news sect., asst. editor Sunday mag. and TV sect., 1963-66, editor TV Week mag., 1966-67, asst. to features editor, 1967-71, asst. to editor, 1971-72, Sunday editor, 1972-75, editor Sunday mag., 1975-82; exec. editor Advt. Age Mag., Chgo., 1982-88, spl. projects dir., 1988-91; corp. projects editor Crain Comm., Chgo., 1991-96, spl. projects dir., 1997—2004, spl. projects cons., 2005—. Author: Great Railroad Paintings, 1976, Nero Wolfe Mysteries: Murder in E-Minor, 1986, Death on Deadline, 1987, The Bloodied Ivy, 1988, The Last Coincidence, 1989, Fade to Black, 1990, The Crain Adventure, 1992, Silver Spire, 1994, The Missing Chapter, 1994, The Year Diz Came to Town, 2003, Three Strikes You're Dead, 2005, Shadow of the Bomb, 2006, A Death in Pilsen, 2007. Served with AUS, 1961. Recipient Svc. award, Northwestern U. Alumni, 2001. Mem. Arts Club. Presbyterian. Personal E-mail: goldsborough@sbcglobal.net.

GOLDSCHEIDER, FRANCES K., sociologist, educator; b. Balt., June 12, 1942; d. George Hyde and Ida Thomas (Sledge) Engeman; m. David R. Kobrin, Sept. 23, 1961 (div. 1978); children: Sarah, Janet; m. Calvin Goldscheider, Aug. 18, 1983. BA, U. Pa., Phila., 1965, MA, 1967, PhD, 1971. Asst. prof. sociology Skidmore Coll., 1969-74, Brown U., Providence, 1974-86, prof., 1986—2006, prof. emeritus, 2006—, chair dept. sociology, 1984-87, dir. Social Sci. Data Ctr., 1984-85, dir. Population Studies and Tng. Ctr., 1989-92, 94-95, 2003—04; rsch. assoc. RAND Corp., 1980—, Inst. Social Rsch., U. Mich., Ann Arbor, 1989—; College Park prof. family studies U. Md., College Park. Vis. assoc. prof. demography The Hebrew U., 1983—84; vis. prof. sociology Stockholm U. Author: (with C. Goldscheider) The Ethnic Factor in Family Structure and Mobility, 1978, Ethnicity and the New Family Economy, 1989, (with Linda Waite) New Families, No Families: The Transformation of the American Home, 1991, (with C. Goldscheider) Leaving Home Before Marriage, 1993, (with C. Goldscheider) The Changing Transition to Adulthood: Leaving and Returning Home, 1999; editor: Demography, 1994-95; assoc. editor: Jours. of Gerontology, 1992-94, Am. Sociol. Rev., 1990-92, 2005—, Jour. Marriage and Family, 1987-2006, Demographic Research, 2002-, (with others) Immigration, Gender, and Family Transitions to Adulthood in Sweden, 2007; contbr. articles to profl. jours. NEH grantee, 1973-74; Fulbright fellow, 1983-84, 2001-02. Mem. Am. Sociol. Assn. (chair population sect. 1988-89), Internat. Union for Sci. Study of Population, Population Assn. Am. (bd. dirs. 1987-90, 2nd v.p. 1991-92, chair Dorothy Swaine Thomas Award com. 1985-86, chmn. pubs. com. 2002-03). Home: 2737 Devonshire Pl NW Apt 423 Washington DC 20008 Business E-Mail: frances_goldscheider@brown.edu.

GOLDSCHMID, HARVEY JEROME, law educator, commissioner; b. NYC, May 6, 1940; s. Bernard and Rose G.; m. Mary Tait Seibert, Dec. 22, 1973; children: Charles Maxwell, Paul MacNeil, Joseph Tait. AB, Columbia U., 1962, JD, 1965. Bar: N.Y. 1965, U.S. Supreme Ct. 1970. Law clk. to judge 2d Circuit Ct. Appeals, NYC, 1965-66; assoc. firm Debevoise & Plimpton, NYC, 1966-70; asst. prof. law Columbia U., 1970-71, assoc. prof., 1971-73, prof., 1973-84, Dwight prof. law, 1984—, founding dir. Ctr. for Law and Econ. Studies, 1975-78; gen. counsel SEC, 1998-99, adv. to chmn. Washington, 2000, commr., 2002—05; sr. counsel Weil, Gotshal & Manges, NYC, 2000—02, 2005—. Mem. Pub. Govt. Fin. Industry Regulatory Authority, 2007—; mem. legal adv. com. N.Y.S.E., 1997-98, chmn. subcom. on corp. governance; adv. bd. Millstein Ctr. Corp. Governance and Performance, Yale U., 2005—; cons. in field. Author: (with others) Cases and Materials on Trade Regulation, 1975, 5th edit., 2003; editor: (with others) Industrial Concentration: The New Learning, 1974, Business Disclosure: Government's Need to Know, 1979, The Impact of the Modern Corporation, 1984. Chmn. bd. advisors program on philanthropy and the law NYU Sch. Law, 1992-94; bd. dir. Nat. Ctr. on Philanthropy and the Law, 1996—; nat. coun. Washington U. Sch. of Law, 1999-2006; bd. dir. Greenwall Found., 1996—, vice chair, 1999-2002, chair, 2006— Fellow Am. Bar Found. (life); mem. ABA (task force on lawyers polit. contbns. 1997-98), Am. Law Inst. (reporter part IV, duty of care and the bus. judgment rule, corp. governance project 1980-93), N.Y. State Bar Assn., Assn. Bar City N.Y. (v.p. 1985-86, chmn. exec. com. 1984-85, chmn. com. on antitrust and trade regulation 1971-74, com. on the 2d century, chmn. com. on securities regulation 1992-95, chmn. audit com. 1988-96, chmn. com. on corp. takeover legislation 1985-86, 88-92, treas., mem. exec. com. 1996-98, chmn. nominating com. 2000-01), Assn. Am. Law Schs. (chmn. sect. antitrust and econ. regulation 1976-78), Am. Assn. Internat. Commn. Jurists (sec.-treas., bd. dir. 1969-2002, 05—), Transparency Internat. USA (bd. dir. 2001-02, 05—), Century Assn., Riverdale Yacht Club (bd. dir. 1987-90), Phi Beta Kappa. Office: Columbia Univ Sch Law 435 W 116th St New York NY 10027 Home Phone: 212-933-0988; Office Phone: 212-854-2654. Business E-Mail: goldschm@law.columbia.edu.

GOLDSCHMIDT, ARTHUR EDUARD, JR., historian, educator, writer; b. Washington, Mar. 17, 1938; s. Arthur Eduard and Elizabeth (Wickenden) G.; m. Louise Robb, June 17, 1961; children: Stephen Robb, Paul William. AB, Colby Coll., Waterville, Maine, 1959; AM, Harvard U., 1961, PhD, 1968. Asst. prof. history Pa. State U., University Park, 1965-73, assoc. prof., 1974-89, prof. Mid. East History, 1989-2000, prof. emeritus, 2000—. Vis. assoc. prof. mid. east history Haifa U., Israel, 1973-74; vis. prof. Semester at Sea, 1987, 2001, vis. rsch. fellow Durham U., 1989, 90; acad. dean N.J. Scholars, Lawrenceville, 1985. Author: Concise History of the Middle East, 1979, 8th edit., 2006, Modern Egypt, 1988, 2d edit., 2004, The Memoirs and Diaries of Muhammad Farid: An Egyptian Nationalist Leader (1868-1919), 1992, Historical Dictionary of Egypt, 3d edit., 2003, Biographical Dictionary of Modern Egypt, 2000, Brief History of Egypt, 2007; contbr. AHA Guide to Historical Literature, 3d edit., 1995, American National Biography, 1999, Understanding the Contemporary Middle East, 2000, 2d edit., 2003, Literature of Exploration and Travel, Encyclopedia of African History, History in Dispute: The Middle East; cons., contbr. The Encyclopedia of the Modern Middle East, 1996, 2d edit., 2004, Encarta On-Line Encyclopedia, 2000, 2d edit., 2005, Encyc. Britannica, 2000, 07; editor: Articles on the Middle East, 1947-71, 1980; editor, contbr.: Re-Envisioning Egypt, 1919-1952, 2005; cons. contbr., editor: Contemporary Middle East, 2005. Trustee Unitarian-Universalist Fellowship, State College, Pa., 1977-80, 85-87, 2000-04. Recipient AMOCO Tchg. award Pa. State U., 1981, Mentoring award Mid. East Studies Assn., 2000; Fulbright rsch. fellow, 1981-82; faculty fellow Am. Rsch. Ctr. Egypt, 1998. Mem. Mid. East Studies Assn., Am. Rsch. Ctr. Egypt (bd. govs. 1989-92), Am. Hist. Assn., Ctrl. Pa. Torch Club (pres. 1993), Voices Ctrl. Pa. (founding pres. 1993-97, v.p. 2002-04, pres. 2004—). Democrat. Avocations: cooking, reading. Home: 1173 Oneida St State College PA 16801-5938 Business E-Mail: axg2@psu.edu.

GOLDSCHMIDT, CHARLES, advertising agency executive; b. NYC, June 15, 1921; s. Harry and Adele (Safir) G.; m. Patricia Nevins, Jan. 17, 1951; children: Richard Walter, Jane, Peter. BA, NYU, 1941. Advt. copywriter Warner Bros. Pictures Co., 1946-48, Buchanan & Co., NYC, 1948-49, Ray Austrian Assocs., NYC, 1949-52; founder, ptnr. Daniel & Charles Inc., NYC, 1952; chmn. bd. dirs. LCF&L, Inc., 1980—. Author fiction, play, articles. Served to lt. USNR, 1941-46. Mem. Beach Point Club, Phoenix Country Club. Democrat. Home: 710 The Crescent Mamaroneck NY 10543-4531 Office: LCF&L Inc 260 Madison Ave New York NY 10016-2401

GOLDSCHMIDT, LYNN HARVEY, lawyer; b. Chgo., June 14, 1951; d. Arthur and Ida (Shirman) H.; m. Robert Allen Goldschmidt, Aug. 27, 1972; children: Elizabeth Anne, Carolyn Helene. BS with honors, U. Ill., 1973; JD magna cum laude, Northwestern U., 1976. Bar: Ill. 1976. Ptnr. Hopkins & Sutter, Chgo., 1976-2001, Foley & Lardner, Chgo., 2001—02; prin. D and G Cons. Group, 2002—. Articles editor Northwestern U. Law Rev. Mem. Airport Coun. Internat., N. Am., Order of Coif. Personal E-mail: lhg@dg-cg.com.

GOLDSCHMIDT, ROBERT ALPHONSE, financial executive; b. Cin., July 3, 1937; s. Alphonse Francis and Lillian Mary (Ashbrock) G.; m. Karen Ann Koehnemann, June 10, 1961; children: Diane, Kristine, Linda, Mark, Erik. BA, U. Notre Dame, 1959, BSME, 1960; MS in Indsl. Mgmt., Purdue U., 1961. CPA; registered profl indsl. engr. Mgmt. cons. Touche Ross & Co., NYC, 1961-66; mgr. planning and control Litton Med. Group, Des Plaines, Ill., 1966-68; v.p. fin. Bell TV, NYC, 1968-70; pres., chief exec. officer Living Industries, Farmingdale, N.Y., 1971-72; asst. to pres. Gen. Instrument Corp., NYC, 1972-73; v.p. ops. Jackson Communications, Dayton, Ohio, 1973-74; v.p., chief fin. officer Esterline Corp., Darien, Conn., 1974-87; v.p. fin. controls The Dyson-Kissner-Moran Corp., NYC, 1987-93; CFO The Archdiocese of New York, 1994—2002. Treas. YMCA, Tarrytown, N.Y., 1980-82. Mem.: Sleepy Hollow Country (Scarborough, N.Y.) (treas. 1982-84). Republican. Roman Catholic. Home: 226 River Rd Briarcliff Manor NY 10510-2414 Office Phone: 914-923-9220. E-mail: rgoldschmidt@earthlink.net.

GOLDSCHMIDT, WALTER ROCHS, anthropologist; b. San Antonio, Feb. 24, 1913; s. Hermann and Gretchen (Rochs) G.; m. Beatrice Lucia Gale, May 27, 1937 (dec.); children: Karl Gale (dec.), Mark Stefan. BA, U. Tex., 1933, MA, 1935; PhD, U. Calif., Berkeley, 1942. Social scientist Bur. Agrl. Econs., 1940-46; mem. faculty UCLA, 1946—, prof. anthropology, 1956—, chmn. dept., 1964-69, prof. anthropology and psychiatry, 1970-83, prof. emeritus, 1983—. Vis. lectr. Stanford, 1945, U. Calif., Berkeley, 1949, Harvard, 1950 Dir. radio program: Ways of Mankind, 1951- 53, Culture and Ecology in E. Africa, 1960-68. Spl. editor: World of Man Series, Aldine Pub. Co., 1966-75. Author: Small Business and the Community, 1946, As You Sow, 1947, 2nd edit., 1978, Nomlaki Ethnography, 1951, Ways to Justice, 1953, Man's Way, 1959, Exploring the Ways of Mankind, 1960, 3rd edit., 1977, Comparative Functionalism, 1966, Sebei Law, 1967, Kambuya's Cattle, The Legacy of an African Herdsman, 1968, On Being an Anthropologist, 1970, Culture and Behavior of the Sebei, 1976, The Sebei: A Study in Cultural Adaptation, 1986; The Human Career: The Self in The Symbolic World, 1990, The Bridge to Humanity: How Affect Hunger Trumps the Selfish Gene, 2006; co-author: Haa Aaní, Our Land: Tlingit and Haida Land Rights and Use, 1998; editor: The U.S. and Africa, rev, 1963, French edit., 1965, The Anthropology of Franz Boas, 1959, (with H. Hoijer) The Social Anthropology of Latin America, 1970, The Uses of Anthropology, 1979, Anthropology and Public Policy: A Dialogue, 1986, Am. Anthropologist, 1956-59; founding editor: Ethos, 1972-79. Fulbright scholar U.K., 1953; grantee Social Sci. Rsch. Coun., 1953, Wenner-Gren. Found., 1953; NSF postdoctoral fellow, 1964-65, fellow Center Advanced Study Behavioral Scis., 1964-65, sr. sci. fellow NIMH, 1970-75; disting. lectr. U. Indonesia, 1993. Fellow Am. Anthrop. Assn. (pres. 1975-76, Dist. Svc. award 1994), African Studies Assn. (founding, bd. dirs. 1957-60); mem. Southwestern Anthrop. Assn. (pres. 1950-51), Am. Ethnol. Soc. (pres. 1969-70), Phi Beta Kappa, Sigma Xi. Home: 842 E Villa St #146 Pasadena CA 91101 Business E-Mail: walterg@ucla.edu.

GOLDSEN, BRUCE I., radio executive; b. Norwalk, Conn., Aug. 5, 1959; s. Leonard and Esther (Rosenfeld) G.; m. Susan Eva Szanti, Sept. 15, 1984; 1 child, David Tyler. BA, Western Conn. State U., 1981. Music dir. Sta. WRKI, Danbury, Conn., 1981-83; program dir. Sta. WINE, Danbury, 1983-85, Sta. WTFM, Kingsport, Johnson City, Tenn., 1986-87, Sta. WIVY-FM, Jacksonville, Fla., 1987-90; v.p., gen. mgr. Sta. WABJ/WQTE, Adrian, Mich., 1990—95; v.p. Sta. WMXE, Hudson and Hillsdale, Mich., 1995—97; pres. & gen. mgr. Jackson Radio Works, Inc./WKHM-AM/FM, Jackson, Mich., 1997—. Mem. Dem. Town Com., Weston, Conn., 1982-83; bd. dirs. Lewanee United Way and Vol. Ctr., 1992—, ann. campaign co-chair, 1992-94, pres. 1995-96; bd. dirs. Croswell Opera House, 1995—. Mem. Mich. Assn. of Broadcasters (bd. dirs. 1993-, pres. 1998-2001, chmn. elect. 2007-), Nat. Assn. Broadcasters (bd. dirs.), Adrian Rotary Club (bd. dirs. 1996-, pres. 2005-06, Internat. Ave. Svc. award, 2006). Avocations: racquetball, music, finance, computers. Office: Jackson Radio Works 1700 Glenshire Dr Jackson MI 49201 Office Phone: 517-787-9546. Office Fax: 517-787-7517.*

GOLDSMAN, MELVIN SAUL, lawyer; b. LA, Mar. 25, 1947; BA, UCLA, 1969; JD, Southwestern U., 1975. Bar: Calif. 1975, cert.: Family Law (specialist). Editl. asst. LA County Bar Assn. Family Law Symposium, 1976—77; ptnr. Freid & Goldsman, L.A. Editl. asst. LA County Bar Assn. Family Law Symposium, 1976—77. Co-author: (law text) Selection, Preparation of, Preparation by and Protection of Expert Witnesses; editor: Tax Aspects of Dissolution, the Apportionment of Property on Dissolution and Avoiding Malpractice. Recipient Super Lawyer in family law, So. Calif., 2004, 2005, 2006. Fellow: Am. Acad. of Matrimonial Lawyers; mem.: ABA. Office: Freid & Goldsman 2029 Century Pk E Ste 860 Los Angeles CA 90067 Office Phone: 310-552-2700. Office Fax: 310-552-2770.*

GOLDSMITH, BARRY RICHARD, lawyer, former federal agency administrator; b. NYC, Dec. 28, 1949; s. Milton Theodore and Sylvia Goldsmith; m. Beverly Jane Bernstein, June 18, 1978; children: Adam Avery, Jacob Bradley. BS, U. Pa., 1972; JD, Georgetown U., 1975. Bar: Ill. 1976, U.S. Dist. Ct. (no. dist.) Ill. 1976, D.C. 1977, U.S. Dist. Ct. D.C. 1977. Law clk. to Hon. Thomas R. McMillen US Dist. Ct. (no. dist.) Ill., Chgo., 1975-76; assoc. Bergson, Borkland, Margolis & Adler, Washington, 1976-83, ptnr., 1983-86; asst. chief litigation counsel SEC, Washington, 1986-88, dep. chief litigation counsel, 1988-90, sr. dep. chief litigation counsel, 1990-93, chief litigation counsel, 1993—96; exec. v.p. enforcement NASD, Washington, 1996—2006; ptnr. Gibson, Dunn & Crutcher LLP, Washington, 2006—. Editor: Antitrust Law Developments, 2d edit., 1986. Mem. ABA, Beta Gamma Sigma. Avocation: running. Office: Gibson Dunn & Crutcher LLP 1050 Connecticut Ave NW Washington DC 20036 Office Phone: 202-955-8580. E-mail: BGoldsmith@gibsondunn.com.

GOLDSMITH, BILLY JOE, real estate broker, rancher; b. Blum, Tex., Nov. 6, 1933; s. John T. and Gladys Aileen (Curlee) G.; m. Jean Elizabeth Wendel, Oct. 20, 1962; 1 child, Anne. BS, Tex. A&M U., 1955. Asst., county agrl. agt. Harris County Tex. Extension Svc., Houston, 1957-64; mgr. Rice Coun., Houston, 1964-75, exec. v.p., 1975-95, ret., 1995; owner, broker real estate co. Houston, 1995—; owner Goldsmith Realty, Houston, Bill Goldsmith Agrl. Consulting. Arena dir. Houston Livestock Show and Rodeo, 1966-73; bd. dirs. Tex. Soc. to Prevent Blindness. With U.S. Army, 1955-57. Internat. Rice Festival honoree, 1992, Paul Harris fellow, Rotary. Mem. Tex. Cattle Raisers Assn., Southwestern Cattle Raisers Assn., Nat. Cattlemen's Assn., Houston Livestock Show and Rodeo Rancher, Res. Officer Assn., Harris County Ext. Bd. Advisors. Home: 5826 Cheena Dr Houston TX 77096-5928

GOLDSMITH, BRAM, banker; b. Chgo., Feb. 22, 1923; s. Max L. and Bertha (Gittelsohn) G.; m. Elaine Maltz; children: Bruce, Russell. Student, Herzl Jr. Coll., 1940, U. Ill., 1941—42. Asst. v.p. Pioneer-Atlas Liquor Co., Chgo., 1945-47; pres. Winston Lumber and Supply Co., East Chicago, Ind., 1947-50; v.p. Medal Distilled Products, Inc., Beverly Hills, Calif., 1950-75; pres. Buckeye Realty and Mgmt. Corp., Beverly Hills, 1952-75; exec. v.p. Buckeye Constrn. Co., Inc., Beverly Hills, 1952-75; chmn. bd., CEO City Nat. Corp., Beverly Hills, 1975-95; CEO City Nat. Bank, 1975-96, chmn., 1975-95, City Nat. Corp., 1995—. Mem., bd. dirs. L.A. Philharm. Assn.; bd. dirs. Cedars/Sinai Med. Ctr.; pres. Jewish Fedn. Coun. Greater L.A., 1969-70; nat. chmn. United Jewish Appeal, 1970-74; regional chmn. United Crusade, 1976; co-chmn. bd. dirs. NCCJ; chmn. Am. com. Weizman Inst. Sci. With signal corps U.S. Army, 1942-45. Mem. Masons, Hillcrest Country Club, Balboa Bay Club. Office: City Nat Corp 400 N Roxbury Dr Beverly Hills CA 90210 Home Phone: 310-271-1309; Office Phone: 310-888-6711. Business E-Mail: bram.goldmith@cnb.com.

GOLDSMITH, CLIFFORD HENRY, retired consumer products company executive; b. Leipzig, Germany, Sept. 6, 1919; came to U.S., 1940, naturalized, 1943; s. Conrad and Elise (Stahl) G.; m. Katherine W. Kaynis; children: Corinne Elizabeth Goldsmith Dickinson (dec.), Audrey Jane Goldsmith Kubie, Alexandra Eve Goldsmith Fallon. Grad., Bradford U., Eng., 1939. Technologist, Glenside Mills Corp., Skaneateles, NY, 1940-41; supt. Falls Yarn Mills, Woonsocket, RI, 1941-42, Aldon Spinning Mills, Talcotville, Conn., 1942-43; with Benson & Hedges Co., 1945-53, plant mgr., 1945-53; with Philip Morris, Inc., 1954-84, pres., 1978-83, vice chmn., 1983-84; chmn. Prendel Co., LLC, 2005—. Chmn. emeritus Nat.

Multiple Sclerosis Soc., FOJP Svc. Corp.; trustee Mr. Sinai Sch. Medicine, Mt. Sinai Hosp. and Med. Ctr. With inf. US Army, 1943—45. Mem. Textile Inst. (Manchester, Eng., assoc.), Commonwealth Club (Richmond), Univ. Club (N.Y.), Century Club (N.Y. Office: 900 Park Ave New York NY 10075

GOLDSMITH, DONNA, sports association executive; b. Long Island; Degree in comm., SUNY, Oswego. Worked at Swatch Watch USA, Revlon Inc.; v.p. licensing NBA; sr. v.p. consumer products World Wrestling Fedn. Entertainment Inc., Stamford, Conn., 2000—. Mem.: NY Women in Comm. Office: World Wrestling Fedn Entertainment Inc 1241 E Main St Stamford CT 06902 Home Phone: 917-841-3871; Office Phone: 203-328-2561. E-mail: donna.goldsmith@wwecorp.com.

GOLDSMITH, ELEANOR JEAN, retired hospital administrator; b. Mount Vernon, NY, Aug. 16, 1929; d. Elias Benjamin Jacobson and Rose Millicent Liebowitz; m. Myles Robert Goldsmith, Mar. 8, 1981 (dec.); m. Marshall H. Numark (div.); children: Deborah Lynn Numark, Laura Ellen Madere, Neil Joseph Numark. BS in commerce, Coll. of New Rochelle, NYC, 1949; MA in Edn., NYU, 1950, EdD, 1979. Cert. tchr. NY, 1950, lic. nursing home adminstr. Tex., 1983. Tchr. Mount Vernon Sch. Bus., Mount Vernon, 1949—50, Northport HS, NY, 1950—51; supr. recreation Greystone Park Psychiatric Hosp., Morris Plains, NY, 1969—80; dir. activities therapy Bellevue Psychiatric Hosp., NYC, 1980—82; adminstr. Mesquite Tree Nursing Home, Tex., 1983—84; edn. coord. dept. ophthalmology U. Tex. Southwestern Med. Ctr., Dallas, 1984—92; ret., 1992. Author several mag. articles. Elected mem. Bd. Edn., Fair Lawn, NJ, 1957—59. Mem.: Women's Am. Orgn. for Rehab. and Tng., Bridgeport Upper Merion Lions Club (pres.). Avocations: travel, reading, bridge, skiing, ice skating. Home: 3000 W Valley Forge Cir #941 King Of Prussia PA 19406 Personal E-mail: elgoldsmith@comcast.net.

GOLDSMITH, GARY NORMAN, psychiatrist, psychoanalyst; b. NYC, Oct. 30, 1948; s. Walter J. and Mildred (Cohen) G. BA, Brandeis U., Waltham, Mass., 1969; MD, Georgetown U., 1973. Intern Evanston Hosp., Ill., 1973-74; clin. fellow in psychiatry Med. Sch. Harvard U., Boston, 1974-77; resident in psychiatry Mass. Mental Health Ctr., Boston, 1974-77; pvt. practice psychiatry Brookline, Mass., 1977—; faculty Psychoanalytic Inst. New Eng., Needham, Mass., 1988—; mem. faculty, supervising analyst Mass. Inst. for Psychoanalysis, 1994—96. Cons. in psychiatr. R.I. Inst. Mental Health, Cranston, 1977-78; staff psychiatrist VA Med. Ctr., Brockton, mass., 1978-82; med. dir. Brockton Area Multi-Svcs., Inc., 1982-84; staff psychiatrist Tufts-New Eng. Med. Ctr., 1984-86; assoc. in psychiatry Beth Israel Hosp., Boston, dir. Russian lang. psychiat. svcs., 1994—; clin. instr. psychiatry Harvard U., 1977-82, 89—; faculty mem., Psychoanalytic Inst. of Eastern Europe, 2002-. Mem. Am. Psychiat. Assn., Am. Psychoanalytic Assn. (chair com. on Russian ednl. exch. 2000—). Office: 1419 Beacon St Brookline MA 02446-4808 Office Phone: 617-731-6888. Personal E-mail: G6676@aol.com.

GOLDSMITH, HARRY LOUIS, lawyer; b. Memphis, Sept. 4, 1951; s. Robert Tobias and Elvis (Ginsberg) G. Student, Washington and Lee U., 1969-71; BBS, U. Tex., 1973; JD, Memphis State U., 1977. Bar: Tenn. 1977. With Goodman, Glazer, Greener, Schneider & McQuiston, Memphis, 1977-82, Brown, Reese & Goldsmith, Memphis, 1984-89, Fed. Express Corp., Memphis, 1982-84; v.p., gen. counsel, sec. AutoZone, Inc., Memphis, 1993—96, sr. v.p., gen. counsel, sec., 1996—2005, exec. v.p., gen. counsel, sec., 2005—. Trustee Goldsmith Found. Mem. Beta Alpha Psi, Beta Gamma Sigma. Office: Autozone Inc 123 S Front St Memphis TN 38103-3607 Office Phone: 901-495-6500. Office Fax: 901-495-8300.*

GOLDSMITH, HARRY SAWYER, surgeon, educator; b. Newton, Mass., Sept. 30, 1929; s. Leo and Dorothy Amy (Appleton) G.; m. Linda Perry, Dec. 8, 1961; children: John, Robert, Lynne. AB, Dartmouth, 1952; MD, Boston U., 1956; degree in medicine (hon.), Shanghai Second Med. U., 1988, Xuzhou Med. Coll., China, 1995. Intern Boston (Mass.) City Hosp., 1956-57, resident surgery, 1957-61, Meml. Sloan Kettering Inst., NYC, 1963-65, chief gastric, mixed tumor svc., 1965-70; Samuel D. Gross prof. surgery, chmn. dept. Jefferson Med. Coll., Phila., 1970-77, disting. prof. surgery, 1977; surgeon in chief Jefferson U. Hosp., Phila., 1970-77; prof. surgery Dartmouth Coll. Med. Sch., Hanover, NH, 1977-83; prof. surgery, adj. prof. neurosurgery Boston (Mass.) U. Sch. Medicine, 1983-95; clin. prof. surgery U. Nev., Reno, 1996—2005, cons. surgery, 2006—. Author: A Conspiracy of Silence: The Health and Death of Franklin D. Roosevelt, 2007; editor-in-chief: Goldsmith's Practice of Surgery, 1976-89; editor: The Omentum: Research and Clinical Applications, 1990, The Omentum: Application to Brain and Spinal Cord, 2000; contbr. articles to profl. jours. Capt. U.S. Army, 1961-63. Mem. ACS, Soc. Vascular Surgery, Brit. Assn. Surg. Oncology, Soc. for Surgery Alimentary Tract, Internat. Surg. Soc., Ctrl. Surg. Assn., New England Surg. Soc. Address: PO Box 493 Glenbrook NV 89413-0493 Office Phone: 775-749-5801. Office Fax: 775-749-5861. Personal E-mail: hlgldsmith@aol.com.

GOLDSMITH, HOWARD, writer, consultant; b. NYC, Aug. 24, 1945; s. Philip and Sophie (Feldman) G. BA with honors, CUNY, 1965; MA with honors, U. Mich., Ann Arbor, 1966. Research psychologist Mental Hygiene Clinic, Detroit, 1966-70; freelance writer Ency. Britannica Ednl. Corp., Chgo., 1970; writer, pvt. practice editorial cons. Flushing, NY, 1970—. Editorial cons. Mountain View Ctr. for Environ. Edn., U. Colo., Boulder, 1970-85. Author poetry, videos, plays, numerous short stories, books, novels including: The Whispering Sea, 1976, What Makes a Grumble Smile?, 1977, The Shadow and Other Strange Tales, 1977, Terror by Night, 1977, Spine-Chillers, 1978, Sooner Round the Corner, 1979, Invasion: 2200 A.D., 1979, The Ivy Plot, 1981, Three-Ring Inferno, 1982, Plaf Le Paresseux, 1982, Ninon, Miss Vison, 1982, Toufou Le Hibou, 1982, Fourtou Le Kangourou, 1982, The Tooth chicken, 1982, Mireille l'Abeille, 1982, Little Dog Lost, 1983, Stormy Day Together, 1983, The Sinister Circle, 1983, Shadow of Fear, 1983, Treasure Hunt, 1983, The Square, 1983, The Circle, 1983, The Contest, 1983, Welcome, Makoto!, 1983, Helpful Julio, 1984, The Secret of Success, 1984, Pedro's Puzzling Birthday, 1984, Rosa's Prank, 1984, A Day of Fun, 1984, The Rectangle, 1984, Kirby the Kangaroo, 1985, Ollie the Owl, 1985, The Twiddle Twins' Haunted House, 1985, Young Ghosts, 1985, Von Geistern Besessen, 1987, The Further Adventures of Batman, 1989, Visions of Fantasy, 1989, The Pig and the Witch, 1990, The Mind-Stalkers, 1990, Spooky Stories, 1990, Little Quack and Baby Duckling, 1991, The Proust Syndrome, 1992, The President's Train, 1993, Thomas Edison Had A Bright Idea, 1993, The Day My Dad and I Got Mugged, 1993, Evil Tales of Evil Things, 1993, The Christmas Star, 1994, The Curiosity Kid, 1994, Tales of the Batman, 1995, Dream Weavers, 1996, The Gooey Chewy Contest, 1997, The Twiddle Twins' Music Box Mystery, 1997, The Twiddle Twins' Amusement Park Mystery, 1998, Science Through Stories (series), 1998-99, The Twiddle Twins' Single Footprint Mystery, 1999, The Tooth Fairy Mystery, 1999, Roundabout the Rain, 2000, Three Bags of Chips, 2000, See It Fly!, 2000, Strike up the Band, 2000, Danger Zone, 2000, Thomas Edison to the Rescue!, 2003, Mark Twain at Work, 2003, John F. Kennedy and the Stormy Sea, 2005, Thomas Jefferson and the Ghost Riders, 2007. Fellow U.S. Pub. Health Svc., 1965; Rackham predoctoral fellow U. Mich., 1966; recipient Phi Sigma Sci. award, 1966. Mem. Poets and Writers, Sci. Fiction Writers of Am., Soc. Children's Book Writers and Illustrators, Phi Beta Kappa, Psi Chi, Sigma Xi, Phi Kappa Phi. Avocations: classical music, book collecting, chess, old movies. Home: 41-07 Bowne St Apt 6B Flushing NY 11355-5629

GOLDSMITH, JACK LANDMAN, III, law educator, former federal agency administrator; b. Sept. 26, 1962; married; 2 children. BA summa cum laude, Washington & Lee U., 1984; BA, Oxford U., Eng., 1986, MA with hons., 1991; JD, Yale U., 1989; diploma in Pvt. Internat. Law, Hague Acad. Internat. Law, 1992. Bar: D.C. Law clk. to hon. J. Harvie Wilkinson U.S. Ct. Appeals (4th cir.), 1989—90; law clk. to Hon. Anthony M. Kennedy U.S. Supreme Ct., 1990—91; legal asst. to Hon. George Aldrich Iran-U.S. Claims Tribunal, Netherlands, 1991—92; assoc. Covington & Burling, Washington, 1992—94; assoc. prof. law U. Va., 1994—97, prof. law, 2003—04, U. Chgo., 1997—2003; spl. counsel to gen. counsel US Dept. Def., Washington, 2003; asst. atty. gen. Office Legal Counsel US Dept. Justice, 2003—04; prof. law Harvard U., Cambridge, 2004—. Visiting scholar Am. Enterprise Inst., 2004—. Editor: (novels) Internat. Dispute Resolution: The Regulation of Forum Selection, 1997; co-author Fgn. Rels. Law: Cases and Materials, 2002, Conflicts of Laws: Cases and Materials, 2003, The Limits of Internat. Law, 2005, On "Nineteen Eighty-Four": Orwell and Our Future, 2005, Who Controls the Internet? Illusions of a Borderless World, 2006; contbr. articles to profl. jours. Mem.: ABA, Am. Soc. Internat. Law. Office: Harvard Law Sch Griswold 304 1563 Massachusetts Ave Cambridge MA 02138 E-mail: jgoldsmith@law.harvard.edu.*

GOLDSMITH, JEFF CHARLES, management consultant; b. Portland, Oreg., Oct. 31, 1948; children: Jason, Trevor, Amelia. BA, Reed Coll., 1970; PhD, U. Chgo., 1973. Dir. health planning, regulatory affairs U. Chgo. Med. Ctr., 1975-82; nat. advisor Ernst & Young, 1982-94; pres. Health Futures, Inc., 1982—; dir. Cerner Corp., 1999—2005, Essent Healthcare, 2000—; assoc. prof. med. edn. Sch. Medicine U. Va., 1997—. Lectr. U. Chgo. Grad. Sch. Bus., 1979—90, Wharton Sch., U. Pa., 1994—; adv. Burrill Biotech. Capital Fund. Author: Can Hospitals Survive?, 1981, Digital Medicine, 2003; mem. editl. bd. Health Affairs, 1990--; contbr. articles to profl. jours. including Harvard Bus. Rev., Jour. AMA, Health Affairs. Recipient Woodrow Wilson Nat. Fellowship, 1971. Avocations: skiing, audiophile, native american art, whitewater. E-mail: hfutures@healthfutures.net.

GOLDSMITH, JOHN ANTON, linguist, educator; b. NYC, Nov. 7, 1951; s. Simon Albert and Thelma Margaret (Ettesvold) G.; m. Jessie Elizabeth Pinkham, Nov. 20, 1982; children: Elizabeth, Paul, Julia. BA, Swarthmore Coll., 1972; PhD, MIT, 1976. Asst., assoc. then prof. Ind. U., Bloomington, 1976-84; prof. U. Chgo., 1984—, Edward Carson Waller Disting. Svc. prof., 1997—. Bd. dirs. U. Chgo. Press, 1990-94. Author: Autosegmental and Metrical Phonology, 1990, (with G. Huck) Ideology and Linguistic Theory, 1995, (with J. Komlos and P. Gold) The Chicago Guide to Your Academic Career; editor, translator Syntax and Human Experience, 1991; editor: The Last Phonological Rule, 1993, Handbook of Phonological Theory, 1995, Phonological Theory: The Essential Readings, 1999. Fellow Am. Acad. Arts & Scis.; Mem. Linguistics Soc. Am. (mem. exec. com. 1988-91). Office: U Chgo Dept Linguistics 1010 E 59th St Chicago IL 60637-1512*

GOLDSMITH, LEE SELIG, lawyer, physician; b. NYC, Nov. 18, 1939; s. Isidore L. and Elsie (Friedman) G.; m. Arlene F. Applebaum, June 10, 1962; children: Ian Lance, Helena Ayn, Jordan Seth. BS with honors, N.Y. U., 1960, MD, 1964, LL.B., 1967. Bar: N.Y. 1968, N.J. 1974; cert. civil trial atty. 2000. Assoc. clk. Speiser, Shumate, Geoghan Krause & Rheingold, 1965-70; individual practice law, 1970-72; mem. firm Lea, Goldberg, Goldsmith & Spellen, NYC, 1972-74; of counsel Newark, 1974-77; mem. firm Goldsmith, Cohen & Simon, 1976-77, Goldsmith & Cohen, 1977-80, Greenstone, Greenstone, Naishuler & Goldsmith, Newark, 1981, Goldsmith & Richman, P.C., NYC, 1981-2000, Goldsmith & Richman, P.A., Englewood, NJ, 1981-2000. Adj. prof. law Fordham U., 1976-88; spl. counsel N.Y. State Senate health com., 1971; lectr. Practicing Law Inst.; chmn. Am. Bd. Law in Medicine, 1984-85. Author: Malpractice Made Easy, 1976, Hospital Liability Law, 1972, 2d edit. 1979; editor: Jour. Legal Medicine, 1978-81, Legal Aspects of Med. Practice, 1981—, Medical Malpractice, Guide to Medical Issues, 7 vols., 1986; contbr. articles to various publs. Fellow: NY Acad. Medicine, Am. Coll. Legal Medicine (bd. govs. 1982, pres.-elect 1986—87, pres. 1987—88, chmn. com. legis. rev.); mem.: ATLA (sec. NJ chpt. 1988—89, treas. 1989—89, 2d v.p. 1990—91, 1st v.p. 1991—92, pres. 1993—94, PAC bd. govs. 1996—2000, treas. NJ PAC 1996—97, bd. govs. 2000—), AMA, NY Trial Lawyers Assn., Assn. Bar City NY (sec. sci. and law com. 1985—87), NY County Med. Soc., NY Med. Soc. Home: 1 Kelwynne Rd Scarsdale NY 10583-4507 Office: Goldsmith Richman & Harz LLP 747 3rd Ave New York NY 10017-2803 also: 140 Sylvan Ave Englewood Cliffs NJ 07632-2502 Office Phone: 201-363-1122. Business E-Mail: lee@goldrich.com.

GOLDSMITH, LOWELL ALAN, medical educator; b. Bklyn., Mar. 29, 1938; s. Isidore Alexander and Ida (Kaplan) G.; m. Carol Amreich, June 11, 1960; children: Meredith, Eileen. AB, Columbia Coll., 1959; MD, SUNY, Bklyn., 1963; MPH, U. Rochester Sch. Medicine & Dentistry, 2002. Diplomate Am. Bd. Dermatology. Intern, then resident in medicine UCLA Med. Ctr., 1963-65; resident in dermatology Harvard U. Med. Sch., Boston, 1967-69, asst. prof. dermatology, 1970-73; asst. in dermatology Mass. Gen. Hosp., Boston, 1970-71, asst. dermatologist, 1971-73; assoc. prof. medicine Duke U. Med. Ctr., Durham, NC, 1973-78, prof., 1978-81; James H. Sterner prof. dermatology Sch. Medicine and Dentistry, U. Rochester (NY), 1981-96, chief dermatology unit, 1981-87, acting chmn. dept. medicine, 1985-87, chmn. dept. dermatology, 1987-96; dean Sch. Medicine and Dentistry U. Rochester, 1996-2000, dean emeritus, 2000—; prof. dermatology U. NC, Chapel Hill, 2002—, clin. prof. epidemiology Sch. Pub. Health, 2002—. Mem. dermatology adv. com. FDA, 1983-87; chmn. Gordon Rsch. Cong. on Epithelial Differentiation and Keratiniazation, 1987, AAD-CDC Conf. on skin cancer prevention and edn., Washington, 1995; mem. gen. medicine A study sect. USPHS, NIH, 1988-92, chmn., 1990-92; mem. coun. NIAMS, NIH, 1996-99; chmn. med. adv. bd. Nat. Alopecia Areata Found., 1981-87, 90-2002, bd. dirs.; bd. dirs. Monroe Cmty. Hosp., Rochester, Ctr. for Alternatives in Animal Testing, Balt.; chmn. NIH Consensus Conf. on Diagnosis and Treatment of Early Melanoma, Bethesda, Md., 1992. Author, editor: Biochemistry and Physiology of the Skin, 1983, 2d edit., 1991, Physiology, Biochemistry and Molecular Biology of the Skin, 1991, Differential Diagnosis of Skin Disease, 2d edit., 1996; mem. editl. bd. Archives Dermatology, 1981-92, Clinics in Dermatology, 1982-96, Seminars in Dermatology, 1991-96, Jour. Dermatological Sci., 1994-2002; mem. editl. bd. Jour. Investigative Dermatology, 1987-95, editor, 2002-07; editor in chief Journal Watch Dermatology 2006—, also numerous articles. With USPHS, 1965-67. Recipient Rsch. Career Devel. award USPHS, 1975-80; Macy Found. fellow, 1978-79. Mem. Assn. Am. Physicians, Am. Soc. Clin. Investigation, Am. Acad. Dermatology (bd. dirs., Presdl. citation 2003), Soc. Investigative Dermatology (bd. dirs., pres. 1994-95, Rothman Gold medal), Nat. Ichthyosis Found. (chmn. adv. bd. 1981-85), Assn. Profs. Dermatology (bd. dirs. 1984-87, pres. 1992-94), Am. Bd. Dermatology (bd. dirs. 1993-96), NY State Soc. Dermatology (pres. 1985-89), Am. Dermatol. Assn. (bd. dirs. 1996-2001, pres. 2002—03, Buffalo-Rochester Dermatology Soc. (pres. 1987), Rochester Dermatology Soc., Rochester Acad. Medicine, Polish Dermatol. Assn. (hon.), Brit. Dermatology Assn. (hon.), Japanese Dermatology Assn. (hon., DOHI lectr. 2003), Am. Skin Assn. (Martin Carter Mentorship award 2006), Berlin Dermatology Soc. (hon.), Deutsche Dermatologische Gesellschaft (hon.), Alpha Omega Alpha. Office: U NC Dept Dermatology 3100 Thurston-Bowles Bldg CB #7287 Chapel Hill NC 27599 Home Phone: 919-942-9263; Office Phone: 919-843-3097. Business E-Mail: Lowell_Goldsmith@med.unc.edu.

GOLDSMITH, MERWIN, actor, theater director; b. Detroit, Aug. 7, 1937; s. Max Harold and Alice Flora (Singer) Goldsmith; m. Susan Leigh Benson, Mar. 1966 (div. 1969); m. Barbara Parry, July 1996. BA in Theater, UCLA, 1960; student, Bristol Old Vic Theatre Sch., Bristol. Actor: (plays) Aunti Mame, 1958, License to Murder, 1964, The Tempest, Trap for a Lonely Man, Phaedra, Gentlemen Prefer Blondes, 1965, Billy Budd, 1967, Fiddler on the Roof, 1968—69, Minnie's Boys, 1970, Much Ado About Nothing, Pal Joey, 1973, Last of the Red Hot Lovers, 1974, Hedda Gabler, 1975, Dirty Linen, 1977, Oklahoma!, 1978, Death of a Salesman, The Importance of Being Ernest, 1982, Hello Dolly!, 1983, La Boheme, 1984, The Taming of the Shrew, 1985, Hamlet, 1986, Me & My Girl, 1988, 1989, Grand Hotel, The Musical, 1991, Merry Widow, 1991, Learned Ladies, 1991, Ain't Broadway Grand, 1993, The Little Prince, 1993, An Imaginary Life, 1993, Beau Jest, 1994, After-Play, 1995, By Jeeves, 1996, Loot, 2000, The Investigation, 2001, Bloomer Girl, 2001, The Pajama Game, 2001, Franklin of Philadelphia, 2002, 70 Girls 70, 2002; (films) Shamus, 1972, Boardwalk, 1979, So Fine, 1981, Blue Heaven, 1984, Making Mr. Right, 1986, Cadillac Man, 1991, It Could Happen to You, 1993, Quiz Show, 1993, Rounders, 1998, The Hurricane, 1998, Company Man, 1999, Joe Gould's Secret, 1999, Au Plus Pres du Paradis, 2001, Unholy, 2005; (TV series) All My Children, Ryan's Hope, The Guiding Light, Search for Tomorrow, As the World Turns, Another World, Wide World of Mystery, The Connection, Law & Order; dir.: (theater) Vanities, 1980. With USAFR. Nominee Best Actor in a Musical, Variety Critics Poll, 1972, Best Supporting Actor in a Musical, 1973, Best Actor in a Musical, Joseph Jefferson Awards, 1972. Mem.: NARAS (Grammy awards voter), SAG, AFTRA, Actors Equity Assn., The Century Assn., The Players. Avocations: photography, studying French and Hebrew. Office: Leading Artists Inc 145 W 45th St New York NY 10036-4008 Office Phone: 212-391-4545. Personal E-mail: merwinsg@yahoo.com.

GOLDSMITH, MICHAEL ALLEN, oncologist, educator; b. Bronx, NY, Jan. 28, 1946; s. Walter and Bertha (Tannenberg) G.; m. Judith Harriet Plaut, June 6, 1971; children: Sharon, Esther, Eva, Steven. BA, Yeshiva U., 1967; MD, Albert Einstein Coll. Medicine, 1971. Diplomate Am. Bd. Internal Medicine. Intern Bronx Mcpl. Hosp. Ctr., 1971-72; staff assoc. Nat. Cancer Inst., Bethesda, Md., 1972-74; resident in medicine Mt. Sinai Hosp., NYC, 1974-75, fellow in neoplastic diseases, 1975-77, asst. clin. prof. medicine and neoplastic diseases, 1977—; attending physician Oncology Consultants, P.C., NYC, 1977—. Assoc. editor Cancer Investigation, 2001—07, reviewer Jour. AMA, 1988—90, New Eng. Jour. Medicine, 1995—; contbr. articles to med. jours. Vice-pres. Congregation Orach Chaim, N.Y.C., 1978-83. Lt. comdr. USPHS, 1972-74. Fellow ACP; mem. Am. Soc. Clin. Oncology, Am. Assn. Cancer Rsch. Achievements include research in new anticancer drugs. Office: Oncology Cons PC 1045 5th Ave New York NY 10028-0138 Office Phone: 212-628-6800.

GOLDSMITH, PAUL FELIX, astronomy and physics professor; b. Washington, Nov. 5, 1948; s. Raymond William and Selma Evelyn (Fine) G.; m. Sheryl E. Reiss, June 5, 1988. AB, U. Calif., Berkeley, 1969, PhD., 1975. Mem. tech. staff AT&T Bell Labs., Holmdel, NJ, 1975-77; asst. prof. U. Mass., Amherst, 1977-82, assoc. prof., 1982-85, prof. physics and astronomy, 1985-92; prof. astronomy, dir. Nat. Astronomy and Ionosphere Ctr. Cornell U., Ithaca, NY, 1993—2002, James A. Weeks prof. phys. sci., 1999—. Cons. MIT Lincoln Lab., Lexington, Mass., 1977-80; v.p. R & D Millitech Corp., South Deerfield, Mass., 1983-92. Author: Quasioptical Systems, 1998; editor: Instrumentation and Techniques for Radio Astronomy, 1988; contbr. articles on radio astronomy and millimeter and submillimeter wavelength tech. to profl. jours. Fellow IEEE; mem. Microwave Theory Tech. Soc. of IEEE (mem. spkr.'s bur. 1989-90, Disting. lectr. 1992-93), Am. Astron. Soc. Office: Dept Astronomy Cornell University Space Sciences Building Ithaca NY 14853 Office Phone: 607-255-0606. Business E-Mail: pfg@astro.cornell.edu.

GOLDSMITH, STANLEY JOSEPH, nuclear medicine physician, educator; b. Bklyn., Aug. 17, 1937; s. Jack and Mae (Greenzweig) G.; m. Miriam Schulman, June 6, 1959; children: Ira, Arthur, Beth, Mark. BA, Columbia U., 1958; MD, SUNY, Bklyn., 1962. Diplomate Am. Bd. Internal Medicine, Am. Bd. Nuclear Medicine (bd. dirs. 1990-96, treas. 1995-96). Intern SUNY-Kings County Med. Ctr., Bklyn., 1962-63, resident, 1965-66, chief resident, 1966-67; fellow in endocrinology Mt. Sinai Hosp., NYC, 1967-68, dir. physics nuclear medicine, 1973-92; clin. dir. nuclear medicine Meml. Sloan-Kettering Cancer Ctr., NYC, 1992-95; dir. nuclear medicine N.Y. Hosp.-Cornell Med. Ctr., NYC, 1995—. Rsch. assoc. radioisotope svc. Bronx (NY) VA Hosp., 1968-69; dir. nuclear medicine, asst. dir. endocrine dept. Nassau County Med. Ctr., East Meadow, NY, 1969-73; asst. prof. medicine radiology SUNY-Stony Brook Health Sci. Ctr., 1971-73; asst. prof. medicine Mt. Sinai Sch. Medicine, 1973-76, assoc. prof., 1976-84, prof. clin. medicine, 1985-91, prof. radiology and medicine, 1991-92, Cornell U. Med. Coll., 1993—, prof. radiology, medicine; bd. dirs. Capintec, Inc., Ramsey, NJ; rsch. collaborator Brookhaven Nat. Labs., Upton, NY, 1971-75; cons. nuclear medicine; cons. dept. health State of N.Y., 1973-77, Health Svcs. Adminstrn., NYC, 1976; radiopharm. adv. com. FDA, 1987-90, low level radioactive waste disposal site commn., N.Y., 1987-95. Assoc. editor Newline, 1984-93, Jour. Nuclear Medicine, editor-in-chief, 1993-98; mem. editl. bd. Am. Jour. Cardiology, 1978-82, European Jour. Nuclear Medicine, 1993-98, Cancer Biotherapy and Radiopharm., 1998—, Jour. Nuc. Medicine, 1999—; reviewer Israeli Jour. Med. Scis., 1979, JAMA, 1983-92, Jour. Am. Coll. Cardiology, 1984-94, Jour. Nuclear Medicine, 1989-93, 99—, Cancer, 2003—, Jour. Clin. Oncology, 2002—, Kidney Internat., 2004—. Capt. U.S. Army, 1963-65. Recipient Harry Z. Mellino Master Tchr. in Radiology award, SUNY Downstate Alumni, 2000, Frank A. Babbott award, 2007, DeWitt Clinton award for cmty. svc., NY State Masons, 2006. Fellow ACP, Am. Coll. Cardiology, Am. Coll. Nuclear Physicians (chmn. nuclear med. tech. affairs, chmn. Washington oversight com.), N.Y. Acad. Sci.; mem. AAAS, Am. Fedn. Clin. Rsch., Am. Coll. Radiology, Endocrine Soc., N.Y. Acad. Medicine (pres sect. on nuclear medicine 2004-2006), Radiol. Soc. N.Am. (program com. 2002-06), Soc. Nuclear Medicine (trustee 1982-84, pres.-elect 1984-85, prse. 1985-86, chmn. govt. rels. com. 1991-93, sec. Greater N.Y. chpt. 1975-78, pres. 1979-80, pres. therapy coun. 2001-2003). Office: NY Presbyn Hosp Weill Cornell Med Ctr 525 E 68th St New York NY 10065-4885 Home Phone: 212-421-3467; Office Phone: 212-746-4588. Business E-Mail: sjg2002@med.cornell.edu.

GOLDSMITH, STEPHEN, investment company executive, former mayor; b. Indpls., Dec. 12, 1946; s. Joseph F. and Marjorie (Holmes) G.; m. Margaret McDaniel, June 15, 1988; children: Reid, Elizabeth, Devereaux, Olivia. AB, Wabash Coll., 1968; JD (hon.), U. Mich., 1971; LLD (hon.), Wabash Coll., 1993. Pvt. practice atty., 1972-78, 91; dep. corp. counsel City of Indpls., 1974-75, chief trial dep., 1976-78, mayor, 1992—99; pros. atty. Marion County, Ind., 1979-90; chief domestic policy adv. to George W. Bush Bush-Cheney Campaign, 2000; chmn. Corp. for Nat. & Community Svc., Washington, 2001—; spl. adv. to Pres. on Faith Based and Not-for-Profit Initiatives The White House, Washington, 2000—01; dir. infrastructure fin. & investment group CapitalSource Fin. LLC, Chevy Chase, Md., 2007—. Chmn. Ctr. Civic Innovation, Manhattan Inst.; adv. bd. Bur. Justice and Stats.; chmn. Indpls. & Ctrl. Ind. Tech. Partnership; co-chmn. domestic strategy group, Aspen Inst.; hon. co-chmn. Nat. Coun. Pub.-Pvt. Partnerships; mem. def. reform group, US Dept. Def.; various adv. and peer rev. bds., Nat. Inst. Justice; adv. bd. Office Juvenile Justice and Delinquency; adv. bd. Pres.'s Commn. on Missing and Exploited Children; vice chmn. Pres.'s Commn. on Model State Drug Laws; Dan Paul prof. govt., John F. Kennedy Sch. Govt., Harvard U.; asst., adj. prof. I.U.; adj. fellow The Manhattan Inst.; adj. faculty, Columbia U. Author: The Twenty-first Century City; editor (Jour.) Prosecutor's Perspective; contbr. Jerusalem Post, Harvard Bus. Rev., Wall St. Jour., others.

USAR, 1968-74. Office: CapitalSource Fin LLC 4445 Willard Ave 12th Fl Chevy Chase MD 20815 also: John F Kennedy Sch Govt Harvard U Mailbox 101 79 JFK St Cambridge MA 02138 E-mail: steve_goldsmith@ksg.harvard.edu.*

GOLDSMITH, WILLIS JAY, lawyer; b. Paris, Feb. 21, 1947; arrived in U.S., 1949; s. Irving and Alice (Rosenfeld) Goldsmith; m. Marilynn Jacobson, Aug. 12, 1973; children: Andrew Edward, Helene Sara. AB, Brown U., 1969; JD, NYU, 1972. Bar: N.Y. 1973, U.S. Ct. Appeals (2d cir.) 1975, D.C. 1978, U.S. Ct. Appeals (4th cir.) 1979, U.S. Ct. Appeals (D.C. cir.) 1979, U.S. Supreme Ct. 1980, U.S. Ct. Appeals (6th cir.) 1985, U.S. Ct. Appeals (7th cir.) 1989, U.S. Ct. Appeals (3d cir.) 1991, U.S. Ct. Appeals (5th cir.) 1998. Atty. Dept. Labor, Washington, 1972-74; assoc. Guggenheimer & Untermyer, NYC, 1974-77, Seyfarth, Shaw, Fairweather & Geraldson, Washington, 1977-79, ptnr., 1979-83, Jones Day, Washington, 1983—2006, chmn. labor and employment law practice, 1991—2006, with NYC, 2006—. Adj. prof. law Georgetown U., 1988—91; mem. Nat. Adv. Com. on Ergonomics; adv. Am. Law Inst., 2004—. Editor (contbg.): Employee Rels. Law Jour., 1983—91; editor: (assoc.) Occupl. Safety and Health Law; mem. editl. adv. bd. Benefits Law Jour., 1991—2002. Fellow, Coll. Labor and Employment Law, 1997—. Mem.: ABA (sec. labor and employment law com. on employee benefits, com. on occupl. safety and health), D.C. Bar Assn., Apple Seed Found. (bd. mem.), NYU Ctr. for Labor and Employment Law (bd. dirs.), Kenwood Golf and Country Club Bethesda, Met. Club Washington. Democrat. Jewish. Business E-Mail: wgoldsmith@jonesday.com.

GOLDSPIEL, ARNOLD NELSON, real estate executive; b. NYC, Aug. 4, 1949; s. Julius and Minna (Nelson) G. BA in Econ., Rutgers U., 1971. Elec. data processing auditor Chubb and Son, Inc., Short Hills, N.J., 1972-74; audit coord., tech. support Merrill Lynch and Co., NYC, 1974-76; sr. EDP auditor Hoffman-LaRoche, Inc., Nutley, N.J., 1976-78; sr. EDP auditor then EDP audit assoc. Mut. Benefit Life Ins. Co., Newark, 1978-82, asst. comptr. corp. data security, 1982-85; sr. EDP auditor Bristol-Myers Co., NYC, 1985-88; sales rep. Century 21 Valerius Realty, Belleville, N.J., 1989-90, Century 21 Stanford Agy., Nutley, N.J., 1990—; sr. EDP auditor Securitas Security Svcs. USA, Inc. (formerly Pinkerton), 1994—2001, mgr. quality assurance and change mgmt., 2002—04; info. tech. auditor Valley Nat. Bank, Wayne, 2005—06, asst. cashier, sr. info. tech. auditor, 2006—. Mem. Info. Mgmt. System com. IBM Share-Audit Project, 1980-81. Citizens planning adv. com. Nutley Sch. Bd., 1978. Staff sgt. N.J. Air N.G., 1968-74. Mem. Info. Sys. Audit and Control Assn. (cert.), Inst. Internal Auditors, Nat. Assn. Realtors, United Assn. Realtors.

GOLDSTEIN, ADAM M., cruise line executive; m. Cheryl Goldstein; children: David, Julie. Grad. with honors, Princeton U.; JD, Harvard U.; MBA, INSEAD. Sr. v.p. Total Guest Satisfaction, sr. v.p. mktg. Royal Caribbean Internat., Miami, 1988—2002, exec. v.p. brand ops., 2002—05, pres., 2005—. Bd. mem. Trust of Our Kids, Inc. Mem.: Travel Industry Assn. Am. (nat. chair 2001). Office: Royal Caribbean Internat 1050 Caribbean Way Miami FL 33132 Office Phone: 305-539-6082. Business E-Mail: agoldstein@rccl.com.

GOLDSTEIN, ALFRED GEORGE, consumer products company executive; b. NYC, Sept. 22, 1932; s. Milton and Pauline M. G.; m. Hope D. Perry, July 5, 1959; children: Mark, Robert. AB, CCNY, 1953; MS, Columbia U., 1954. With Sears, Roebuck & Co., Chgo., 1957—79, v.p. mdse, group nat. mdse. mgr., 1976-79; sr. v.p. consumer bus. Am. Can Co., Greenwich, Conn., 1979-81, sr. v.p. waste recovery bus., 1981-82, exec. v.p. plastics packaging bus., 1982-83, pres. splty. retailing sector, 1983-87; pres. splty. merchandising and direct mktg. group, Sears Can., Sears Logistics Svc. Sears, Roebuck & Co., Chgo., 1987-93; pres., CEO AG Assocs., Chgo., 1993 —; bd. dirs. Sears Mdse. Group, Sears Can., Ltd. Former vice chmn., CEO, bd. dirs. Fingerhut Corp.; chmn. bd. dirs. Pickwick Internat.; chmn., CEO, Musicland Group; bd. dirs. Gander Mountain Corp., 1994; adv. bd. in bus. ethics Kellogg Grad. Sch. Bus. Northwestern U., 1995-2004 Exec. editor: Internat. Jour. Addictions, 1975-80. Trustee Archaeus Found., 1978—90; bd. dirs. United Negro Coll. Fund, 1991—, mem. exec. com., 1996, vice chmn., 2001—, trustee com. econ. devel., 1999—; mem. mktg. com. bd. trustees Art Inst. Chgo., 1988—2002; mem. adv. bd. Goizueta Bus. Sch. Ctr. Leadership and Career Studies, Emory U., 1990—97; mem. exec. com. Columbia U. Grad. Sch. Bus. Alumni Assn., 1980—86, Am. Can Co. Found.; bd. dirs. Art Americana, 1996; mem. adv. bd. chief exec. leadership inst. Yale U., 2000—. With US Army, 1954—57. Mem. Am. Arbitration Assn. (arbitrator), Bus. Execs. Nat. Security.

GOLDSTEIN, ALLAN LEONARD, biochemist, educator; b. Bronx, NY, Nov. 8, 1937; s. Morris and Miriam (Siegel) G.; m. Linda Jo Tish, Dec. 23, 1975; children: Jennifer Joy, Dawn Eden, Adam Lee. BS, Wagner Coll., 1959, DSc (hon.), 1997; MS, Rutgers U., 1961, PhD, 1964. Tchg. asst. Rutgers U., New Brunswick, NJ, 1959-61, asst. instr. biology, 1961-63, instr. physiology, 1963-64; rsch. fellow Albert Einstein Coll. Medicine, 1964-66, instr. biochemistry, 1966-67, asst. prof., 1967-71, asso. prof., 1971-72; prof., dir. divsn. biochemistry U. Tex. Med. Br., Galveston, 1972-78, acting dir. multidisciplinary rsch. program in mental health, 1973-78; prof., chmn. dept. biochemistry and molecular biology George Washington U. Sch. Medicine, Washington, 1978—, pres., sci. dir. Inst. for Advanced Studies in Immunology and Aging, 1985-95; chmn. bd. Alpha 1 Biomeds., 1982-2000, RegeneRX Biopharms., Inc., 2000—. Cons. Syntex Rsch., 1972-74, Hoffmann-LaRoche, 1974-82; spl. cons. bd. sci. counselors Nat. Inst. Allergy and Infectious Diseases, 1975; mem. med. rsch. svc. rev. bd. in oncology VA, 1977-80; cons. decisive network com. Biol. Response Modifiers program Divsn. Cancer Treatment, Nat. Cancer Inst., 1982-84; sci. adv. com. to pres. Papanicolaou Cancer Rsch. Inst. Miami, Inc., 1981-84; mem. AIDS task force adv. com. Nat. Cancer Inst., 1983-84; sci. bd. Alliance for Aging Rsch., 1986—; trustee Albert Sabin Vaccine Inst., 2000—. Discoverer (with Abraham White) Thymosins, hormones of thymus gland and HGP-30 a "core" based p17 AIDS Vaccine. Decorated chevalier des Palmes Academiques (France), comdr. Order Vasco Nuñez de Balboa; recipient Career Scientist award NYC Health Rsch. Coun., 1967, Alumni Achievement award Wagner Coll., 1974, Gordon Wilson medal Am. Clin. and Climatol Soc., 1976, Disting. Faculty Rsch. award U. Tex. Sch. Biomed. Scis., 1976, Van Dyke award in pharmacology Columbia Coll. Physicians and Surgeons, 1984, award Burroughs Wellcome Found., FASEB, 1986, Fernandez-Cruz award, 1989, Martin Rubin award Am. Coll. Advancement in Medicine, 1990, Michele Fodera Internat. prize for Biomed. Rsch., Italy, 1990, Disting. Rsch. award George Washington U. Med. Sch., 2003, Catherine Birch McCormick medal George Washington U. Med. Sch., 2005. Mem. AAAS, Endocrine Soc., Am. Soc. Biol. Chemists and Molecular Biologists, Am. Assn. Immunologists, Internat. Soc. Immunopharmacology (coun. mem. 1985-94), Assn. Med. Sch. Chm. of Depts. Biochemistry, AAUP, Acad. Medicine of Washington, Toastmasters Internat. (pres. NY chpt. 1971), Sigma Xi. Home: 800 25th St NW Apt 1005 Washington DC 20037-2207 Office: George Washington U Med Ctr Dept Biochemistry/Molecular Biology 2300 I St NW Washington DC 20037-2336 Business E-Mail: bcmalg@gwumc.edu.

GOLDSTEIN, ALVIN, lawyer; b. NYC, Nov. 21, 1929; s. Abraham and Florence (Bruckner) G.; m. Eleanor Kronish, Dec. 27, 1959; children—Eric, Michael, Eileen. BSS., Coll. City N.Y., 1950; LL.B., Bklyn. Law Sch., 1953, SJD magna cum laude, 1960. Bar: N.Y. State 1953, U.S. Supreme Ct. Asso. firm Levine & Berman, NYC, 1955-59, partner, 1963; practiced in NYC, 1960-62; partner firm Berman, Paley, Goldstein, Kanry, NYC, 1964—. Contbr. articles to profl. pubs. Served with AUS, 1953-55. Mem.: ABA, Assn. Bar City of N.Y., N.Y. State Bar Assn. Home: 1 Chester Ter Hastings On Hudson NY 10706-3907 Office: Berman Paley Goldstein & Kannry 500 5th Ave Fl 43 New York NY 10110-0375 Office Phone: 212-354-9600. Business E-Mail: agoldstein@bpgk-law.com.

GOLDSTEIN, ARTHUR LOUIS, retired utilities executive; s. David and Henrietta (Frankfort) Goldstein; m. Vida F. Fishbach; children: Jonathan M., Susanne B., James A. BSChemE, Rensselaer Poly. Inst., 1957; MSChemE, U. Del., 1959; MBA, Harvard U., 1960. Pres., CEO Ionics, Inc., Watertown, Mass., 1971—2003, chmn., 1991—2004; ret., 2004. Bd. dirs. State St. Corp., State St. Bank and Trust Co., Cabot Corp., Ptnrs. Healthcare Sys. Inc., trustee, treas., chmn. Fin. Com. Trustee Calif. Inst. Tech., Mass. Gen. Physicians Orgn., Inc.; exec. com. CEOs for Fundamental Change in Edn., Inner-City Scholarship Fund; chmn. Mass. High Tech. Coun., 1985—87, bd. dirs., mem. exec. com.; past pres. Rensselaer Coun.; former bd. dirs. Jobs for Mass., Inc.; former mem. vis. com. Harvard Bus. Sch., Harvard Sch. Pub. Health; cardiovasc. adv. coun. Harvard Environ. Health Coun. Mem.: Nat. Acad. Engring. (industry adv. bd). Achievements include patents for purification and processing of liquids. Office: 24 Hubbard Rd Weston MA 02493 Personal E-mail: arthurlgoldstein@yahoo.com.

GOLDSTEIN, AVRAM, pharmacology educator; b. NYC, July 3, 1919; s. Israel and Bertha (Markowitz) Goldstein; m. Dora Benedict, Aug. 29, 1947; children: Margaret, Daniel, Joshua, Michael. AB, Harvard, 1940, MD, 1943. Intern Mt. Sinai Hosp., NYC, 1944; successively instr., assoc., asst. prof. pharmacology Harvard U., 1947—55; prof. dept. pharmacology Stanford U., Palo Alto, Calif., 1955—89, exec. head dept., 1955—70, prof. emeritus, 1989—. Dir. Addiction Rsch. Found., Palo Alto, Calif., 1973—87. Author: Biostatistics, Principles of Drug Action, 1965, ADDICTION: From Biology to Drug Policy, 2001. Served from 1st lt. to capt., Med. Corps US Army, 1944—46. Mem.: AAAS, Am. Soc. Biol. Chemists, Am. Soc. Pharmacology and Exptl. Therapeutics, Am. Acad. Arts and Scis., Inst. Medicine NAS.

GOLDSTEIN, BENJAMIN, lawyer, educator; b. Phila., Dec. 2, 1949; s. Harry and Bella (Hochman) G. BS in Education, Temple U., 1971; JD, John Marshall U., Chgo., 1975. Bar: Ill. 1975, N.J. 1976, U.S. Ct. Appeals (7th cir.) 1975, (3rd cir.) 1978; U.S. Supreme Ct. 1978. Law clerk Cir. Ct. Cook County, Chgo., 1973-75; pvt. practice Chgo., 1975-76, Voorhees, NJ, 1976-80; atty., shareholder Maressa, Goldstein, Patterson & Drinkwater, Berlin, NJ, 1980—2006; solicitor Zoning Bd., Waterford, NJ, 1987-90, Township Com., Winslow, NJ, 1987-90; solicitor for mayor and coun. City of Lavallette, NJ, 1995—98. Adj. prof. law Camden County Coll., Blackwood, N.J., 1984-2000; arbitrator Superior Ct. N.J., Camden, 1990—; cons. Camden County Dem. Com., Runnemede, N.J., 1988-89; solicitor Kennedy Hosp. Sys., Stratford, N.J., 1994—. Author: (chpt.) Opening Statements, 1995, 2001; spkr. in field. Mem. ATLA, N.J. Trial Lawyers Assn., ABA, N.J. State Bar Assn. (mock trial judge 1994—). Avocations: flying, scuba diving, boating, horseback riding, piano. Office: Drinkwater & Goldstein LLP 277 White Horse Pike Atco NJ 08004 Office Phone: 856-753-5131. Personal E-mail: goldsteinlaw@comcast.net.

GOLDSTEIN, BERNARD, transportation and hotel executive; b. Rock Island, Ill., Feb. 5, 1929; s. Morris and Fannie (Borenstein) G.; m. Irene Alter, Dec. 18, 1949; children: Jeffrey, Robert, Kathy, Richard. BA, U. Ill., 1949, LLB, 1951. Bar: Iowa 1951. With Alter Co., Bettendorf, Iowa, 1951—, chmn. bd., 1979—, Isle of Capri Casinos, Inc., St. Louis, 1992—, chmn., CEO, 1997—. Bd. vis. U. Ill. Coll. Law, 2005—. Pres. Quad City Jewish Fedn., 1975; mem. U. Ill. Coll. Law Bd. Visitors. Named Top Performing Gaming CEO of the Yr., Am. Gaming Assn., 2001; recipient Ernst and Young Entrepreneur of the Yr. award, 1999, Rivers Hall of Fame Achievement award, 1999, Simon Wiesenthal Disting. Cmty. award, Compass award, Passenger Vessel Assn., Outstanding Bus. Leader award, Jewish Fedn. South Palm Beach County, Jerusalem medal, State of Israel Bonds, Disting. Alumnus award, U. Ill. Coll. Law Bd. Visitors. Jewish.

GOLDSTEIN, BERNARD DAVID, public health service officer, educator; b. Bronx, NY, Feb. 28, 1939; m. Russellyn Carruth, May 6, 1995; children: Lara, Ross, Casey. BS, U. Wis., 1958; MD, NYU, 1962. Diplomate Am. Bd. Toxicology, Am. Bd. Internal Medicine, Am. Bd. Hematology. Faculty depts. environ. medicine and medicine NYU Med. Ctr., NYC, 1968—80; prof., chmn. dept. environ. and cmty. medicine U. Medicine and Dentistry, NJ-Robert Wood Johnson Med. Sch., Piscataway, 1980—2001, dir. grad. program in pub. health, 1982—89, dir. environ. and occupl. health scis. inst., 1985—2000; asst. adminstr. for R & D EPA, Washington, 1983—85; acting dean Sch. Pub. Health NJ, Piscataway, 1998—99; dir. Nat. Inst. Environ. Health Scis. Ctr. Excellence, 1988—94; prof. environ. and occupl. health sch. Pub. Health, U. Pitts., 2001—, dean, 2001—05. Chmn. clean air sci. adv. com. EPA, 1982—83; toxicology study sect. NIH, 1980—84, chmn., 1982—84; bd. sci. dirs. Risk Sci. Inst., 1986—2005, nat. adv. environ. health effects coun., 1987—91; chmn. ad hoc com. on dioxin EPA, 1988—89, vice-chmn., chmn. sci. group on methodology for sci. evaluation chems., 1989—, chmn. working group on Air Quality Guidelines for Major Urban Air Pollutants, 1985; health rev. com., chmn. health rsch. com. Health Effects Inst., 1987—2000; bd. dirs. Internat. Life Sci. Inst., Roy F. Weston, Inc.; pres. Soc. Risk Analysis, 2002; chair Nat. Bd. Pub. Health Examiners, 2006—. Recipient Solomon Berson Med. Alumni Achievement award, NYU, 1989, Kehoe award, Am. Coll. Occupl. Environ. Medicine, 1993, Sturgis award, Am. Coll. Preventive Medicine, 1995, Sullivan award, N.J. Pub. Health Assn., 1998, Disting. Achievement award, Soc. for Risk Analysis, 1999, Sen. Frank Lautenberg award, UMDNV Sch. Pub. Health, 2005, Disting. Svc. award, Am. Coll. Toxicology, 2005. Mem.: Am. Soc. Clin. Investigation, Inst. Medicine NAS. Achievements include research in in concept of biological markers in the field of risk assessment. Office: Deans Office U Pitts Grad Sch Pub Health 130 Desoto St Rm A710 Pittsburgh PA 15261 Business E-Mail: bdgold@pitt.edu.

GOLDSTEIN, BRUCE I., lawyer; b. Newark, Nov. 4, 1942; s. Samuel C. and Gertrude A. Goldstein; m. Marjorie R. Goldstein, Aug. 21, 1969; children: Jed, Geoffrey. JD, Cornell U., 1967. Exec. asst., U.S. atty., chief spl. prosecutions U.S. Atty.'s Office Dist. N.J., Newark, 1971-77; mng. ptnr., trial lawyer Saiber Schelsinger Satz & Goldstein LLC, Newark, 1977—. Adj. prof. Rutgers U. Law Sch., N.J., 1975-78; mediator U.S. Dist. Ct. N.J., 1989—, mem. lawyer's adv. com., 1993; chmn. fee arbitration com. N.J. Supreme Ct., 1989—; pres. comml. subtrack adv. com. Supreme Ct. Complex. Fellow Am. Bar Found., Am. Coll. Trail Lawyers; mem. Assn. Fed. Bar State N.J. (pres. 1988-89, mem. adv. bd.). Home: 15 Deerwood Trail Warren NJ 07059 Office: Saiber Schlesinger Satz and Goldstein 1 Gateway Ctr Newark NJ 07102-5311 E-mail: big@saiber.com.

GOLDSTEIN, BURTON JACK, psychiatrist; b. Balt., Sept. 23, 1930; s. Hyman and Roz (Levin) C.; m. Linda Feuer, June 16, 1989; children: Howard, Herbert, Brian, Esther, Leonard, Mark. BS in Pharmacy, U. Md., 1953, MD, 1960. Diplomate Am. Bd. Psychiatry and Neurology (bd. examiner). Intern Jackson Meml. Hosp., Miami, Fla., 1960-61, NIMH fellow in psychiatry, 1961-63, chief resident, 1963; dir. div. clin. psychopharmacology, dept. psychiatry U. Miami, 1964-92, chief div. research, 1964-71, prof. pharmacology, 1973—, prof. psychiatry, 1973—, acting chmn. dept. psychiatry, 1983-85, prof. epidemiology, pub. health Sch. Medicine, 1999; sr. cons. in psychopharmacology Mt. Sinai Med. Ctr., Miami Beach, 1993—; dir. psychiat. consultation liaison svc. Mt. Sinai Hosp., Miami Beach, 1993—; med. dir., behavioral health U. Miami, Miller Sch. Medicine, 2005—. Mem. bd. advisors Fla. Mental Health Inst., U. South Fla.; cons. in psychiat. rsch. South Fla. State Hosp., West Hollywood; cons. indsl. security program Dept. Def.; cons. VA Psychiatry Svc., Miami; chmn. panel on neuropharmacologic drugs U.S. Pharmacopeial Conv., Inc., mem. exec. com.; mem. faculty Health Svcs. Ctr., U. Miami, 1996; med. rev. officer dept. athletics U. Miami, 1996—. Mem. editorial bd. Miami Medicine, Clin. Advancement in Treatment of Depression; contbr. chpts. to books, articles to profl. publs. Served to maj. AUS, 1953-62. Fellow Am. Psychiat. Assn. (life), Am. Coll. Psychiatrists, Am. Coll. Clin. Pharmacology, Am. Coll. Neuropsychopharmacology (life); mem. Royal Soc. Health, Am. Assn. Clin. Pharmacology and Chemotherapy, Am. Soc. Addiction Medicine, Collegium Internationale Neuropsychopharmacologium. Personal E-mail: bhls@earthlink.net. Business E-Mail: bgoldste@med.miami.edu.

GOLDSTEIN, CHARLES ARTHUR, lawyer; b. NYC, Nov. 20, 1936; s. Murray and Evelyn V. Goldstein; m. Judith Stein, Sept. 29, 1962 (div. 1982); 1 child, Deborah Ruth; m. Carol Sager, Nov. 10, 1990 (div. 1995). AB, Columbia U., 1958; JD cum laude, Harvard U., 1961. Bar: N.Y. 1962. Law clk. U.S. Ct. Appeals (2d cir.), 1961-62; assoc. Fried, Frank, Harris, Shriver & Jacobson, NYC, 1962-69; ptnr. Schulte Roth & Zabel, NYC, 1969-79, Weil, Gotshal & Manges, NYC, 1979-83, counsel, 1983-85; ptnr. Shea & Gould, NYC, 1985-94, Sutherland, Asbill & Brennan, NYC, 1994-95; counsel Squire, Sanders & Dempsey, NYC, 1996-01; counsel to amb. Ronald S. Lauder, 2001—06; counsel Herrick Feinstein, NYC, 2001—. Lectr. Columbia U. Law Sch. Gen. counsel to Citizens Budget Commn., 1980-87; mem. Temp. Commn. on City Fins., 1975-77; mem. Gov.'s Task Force on World Trade Ctr. Mem. Am. Coll. Real Estate Lawyers. Republican. Home: 220 E 65th St New York NY 10021-6620 Office: Herrick Feinstein LLP 2 Park Ave New York NY 10016 Home Phone: 212-207-8565; Office Phone: 212-592-1523. Business E-Mail: cgoldstein@herrick.com.

GOLDSTEIN, CHARLES HENRY, architect, consultant; b. Winthrop, Mass., Mar. 23, 1938; s. Daniel and Rose (Shulman) G.; children: Brent R., Scott H., Nathan H., Lindsay H., Vanessa H. Cert., Boston Archtl. Ctr., 1965. Registered architect, Mass., N.H., Conn. Chief designer Milo Hart Assocs., Lynnfield, Mass., 1970-72; prin. C.H. Goldstein Assocs., Methuen, Mass., 1972-73; ptnr. Sarver & Goldstein, Saugus, Mass., 1973-75; chief architect A.D. Maclaren Assocs., Andover, Mass., 1975-80, Allen & Demurjian, Boston, 1980-83; prin. Archtl. Energies, North Hampton, NH, 1983—, North Andover, Mass., 1983—. Guest lectr. Wentworth Inst., Boston, 1982—, Merrimack Coll., North Andover, Mass.1978—, U. Debrecen, Hungary, 1992. Mem. bd. selectmen, bd. of health Town of Tewksbury (Mass.), 1969-72; mem. sch. coms., Merrimac and West Newbury, Mass., 1977-87. Recipient Honorable Mention award Interval Internat., 1982, N.H. Sam awards (5) for design, 1989-91; Boston Soc. Architects scholar, 1960; John Worthington Ames scholar, 1964; Rotch scholar finalist, 1964. Mem. Nat. Council Archtl. Registration Bds., Boston Soc. Office: Archtl Energies 200 Sutton St North Andover MA 01845-1656 E-mail: aearchitect@verizon.net.

GOLDSTEIN, DANIEL ROBERT, cardiologist; b. London, Apr. 22, 1968; MD, St. George's Hosp. Med. Sch., London, 1992. Bd. cert. Cardiology, Internal Medicine. Intern Johns Hopkins Hosp., Balt., 1993—94, resident, internal medicine, 1994—96; fellow U. Alabama, Birmingham, 1996; asst. prof., internal medicine, cardiology Yale Sch. Med. Recipient Wyeth Basic Sci. Career Devel. award (Asst. Prof. Level), Am. Soc. Transplantation, 2007. Office: Yale Congestive Heart Failure Program Ste 301 135 College St New Haven CT 06510 Office Phone: 203-785-3271. Office Fax: 203-785-2917. Business E-Mail: daniel.goldstein@yale.edu.*

GOLDSTEIN, DAVID ARTHUR, biophysicist, educator; b. Rochester, NY, Nov. 8, 1934; s. Jacob David and Elizabeth Maude (Brown) G.; m. Marie Elaine Nardone, May 25, 1969; 1 child, David James. AB in Physics, Harvard U., 1956, MD, 1960. Rsch. fellow biophys. lab Harvard Med. Sch., Cambridge, Mass., 1960-62, rsch. assoc. biophys. lab., 1964-65; asst. prof. radiation biology and biophysics Rochester Sch. Med. and Dentistry, 1965-68, assoc. prof. biophysics, 1968—, assoc. prof. biomath., 1969-74, assoc. prof. med. informatics, 1988—98, prof. emeritus med. informatics, 1999—. Dir. Med. Ctr. Computing, U. Rochester Med. Sch., 1975-77, assoc. chmn. dept. radiation biology and biophysics, 1980-85, dir. divsn. med. informatics, 1988-98; cons. mathematician NIMH, Bethesda, Md., 1963-64. Contbr. articles to profl. jours. Treas. Stormers Soccer Club, Rochester, 1983-93; bd. dirs. Monroe County Girls Soccer League, Rochester, 1988-93. Surgeon, USPHS, 1963-64. Grantee AEC, NIH, NSF, ERDA, DOE, 1965-96. Mem. Biophys. Soc., N.Y. Acad. Scis. Home: 75 Deer Creek Rd Pittsford NY 14534-4147 E-mail: dgoldst2@frontiernet.net.

GOLDSTEIN, DAVID BAIRD, energy executive, physicist; b. Cleve., June 29, 1951; s. Laurence and Gloria Reta (Baumgarten) G.; m. Julia Beth Vetromile, May 17, 1980; children: Elianna Louise, Abraham Micah. AB in Physics, U. Calif., Berkeley, 1973; PhD in Physics, U. Calif., 1978. Rsch. asst. Lawrence Berkeley (Calif.) Lab., 1975-78, staff scientist, 1978-80; sr. scientist, dir. energy program Natural Resources Def. Coun., San Francisco, 1980—. Sub-com. chair standing standards project com. 90.1 ASHRAE, Atlanta, 1983-96; vice-chmn. bd. Consortium for Energy Efficiency, Inc., Sacramento, 1991-93, 99-02, 06-, bd. dirs., 2002—, advisor, 1993-96; initiator and advisor Super Efficient Refrigerator Program, Inc., 1991-96. Author: Saving Energy, Growing Jobs, 2007; contbr. articles to profl. jours. Recipient Champion of Energy Efficiency award Am. Coun. for an Energy Efficient Economy, 1988, 94, Excellence in Achievement award Calif. Alumni Assn., 2003; MacArthur Found. fellow, 2002. Fellow: Am. Phys. Soc. (Leo Szilard award 1998); mem.: Sigma Xi, Phi Beta Kappa. Jewish. Avocations: travel, hiking, music, photography. Home: 1240 Washington St San Francisco CA 94108-1041 Office: Natural Resources Def Coun 111 Sutter 20th Fl San Francisco CA 94104 Home Phone: 415-771-7959; Office Phone: 415-875-6100. Business E-Mail: dgoldstein@nrdc.org.

GOLDSTEIN, DEBRA HOLLY, judge; b. Newark, Mar. 11, 1953; d. Aaron and Erica (Schreier) Green; m. Joel Ray Goldstein, Aug. 14, 1983; children: Stephen Michael, Jennifer Ann. BA, U. Mich., 1973; JD, Emory U., Atlanta, 1977. Bar: Ga. 1977, Mich. 1978, DC 1978, Ala. 1984. Tax analyst atty. Gen. Motors Corp., Detroit, 1977-78; trial atty. US Dept. Labor, Birmingham, Ala., 1978-90; US adminstrv. law judge Social Security Adminstrn., Birmingham, 1990—. Mem. Gov.'s Commn. Quality Tchg., 2006—. Troop leader Girl Scouts, 1992—2004, bd. dirs. Cahaba coun., 1996—2002; chmn. Success By 6 Blue Ribbon adv. com., 2003—05; bd. dirs. Temple Emanu-El, 2000—03, Leadership Birmingham Mems. Assn., 2004—, United Way, Birmingham, 2004—, exec. com., 2005—; bd. dirs. YWCA, 2002—, treas., 2007—; bd. dirs. Pathways, 2007—; exec. bd. Women's Network, 2007—. Mem. ABA, Ga. Bar Assn., DC Bar Assn., Birmingham Bar Assn. (bd. dir. women's sect. 1999-2003, 2006—), Ala. Bar Assn. Forum (pres. 2004-06), Leadership Ala., Leadership Birmingham, Momentum, Zonta, Hadassah, Leadershp Shelby County. Jewish. Office Phone: 800-940-0923. Business E-Mail: debra.goldstein@ssa.gov.

GOLDSTEIN, DONALD MAURICE, historian, educator; b. Dec. 15, 1932; s. Max A. and Jean M. Goldstein; m. Mariann Norma Zinck, Aug. 5, 1961; children: Tammie, Timmie, Tommie, Teri. BA, U. Md., 1954, MA, 1962; MS, Georgetown U., 1963; MPA, George Washington U., 1965; PhD, U. Denver, 1970; grad., War Coll., 1973, Air Command and Staff Coll., 1965. Commd. 2d. lt. USAF, 1955, advanced through grades to lt. col., 1972, comdr. missile site Taiwan, 1958-59; staff officer US Strike Command, 1961-64; rsch. assoc. Airstaff Pentagon; assoc. prof. history

USAF Acad., 1965-71, asst. track coach, 1965-71; ret., 1977; assoc. prof. history Troy State U., Ala., 1971-74; prof. aerospace studies U. Pitts., 1975-77, assoc. prof. pub. and internat. affairs, 1975-92, prof., 1993, dir. placement and alumni, 1977-85, assoc. dean, 1985-88. Author: Ennis C. Whitehead Aerospace Commander, 1970, Adolph Hitler in the Perspective of the Am. Press, 1961, Adolph Hitler Administr. of a Society, 1965, (with others) Miracle at Midway, 1982, 2001, 3d edit., 2002, Target Tokyo: The Story of the Surge Spy Ring in Japan, 1984, 3d edit., 2001; collaborator: At Dawn We Slept: The Untold Story of Pearl Harbor, 1981, 3d edit., 2001, Pearl Harbor: The Verdict of History, 1985, 3d edit., 2001, December 7, 1941: The Day the Japanese Attacked Pearl Harbor, 1990, Fading Victory: The Diary of Matome Ugaki, 1991, The Way It Was: A Pictorial Hist.of Pearl Harbor, 1991, The Williwar War: The Arkansas Nat. Guard in World War II, 1992, The Pearl Harbor Paper, 1993, Classics in Internat. Affairs with Others, 1993, 3d edit., 2005, D Day: A Pictorial Hist., 1994, Nuts: The Battle of the Bulge, 1994, Security in Korea: War, Stalemate and Negotiation, 1994, Rain of Ruin: A Photographic Hist. of Hiroshima and Nagasaki, 1995, Amelia Earhart: A Biography, 1997, Vietnam: A Pictorial History, 1997, The Spanish American War: A Centennial Hist., 1998, The Korean War: The Story and Photographs, 2000, World War I: The Story and Photographs, 2002, God's Samurai: Lead Pilot at Pearl Harbor, 2003, The Pacific War Paper, 2004, Classics in International Affairs, 3d edit., 2005; asst. editor papers on fgn. policy for House Com. on Internat. Affairs, 1947-54; contbr. articles on def. policy and nat. security affairs to profl. jour. Decorated Soldiers medal, Meritorious Svc. medal with 2 oak leaf clusters, Joint Svc. Commendation medal, Air Force Commendation medal with oak leaf cluster; recipient Peabody award, 1991, U. Pitts. Tchr. of Yr., 2003, Chancellor Disting. Tchr. award, U. Pitts., 2003. Mem. Nat. Assn. Soc. Pub. Adminstrs. (Tchr. of Yr. award 2001), Am. Hist. Assn., Internat. Studies Assn., Am. Soc. Pub. Adminstr., Am. Polit. Sci. Assn., Air Force Assn., Toastmasters, Omicron Delta Kappa, Phi Kappa Phi, Phi Alpha Theta, Sigma Nu. Roman Catholic. Home: 2146 Meadowmont Dr Upper St Clair Pittsburgh PA 15241 Office: U Pitts Grad Sch Pub Intl Affairs Rm# 3617 Posvar Hall Pittsburgh PA 15260 Home Phone: 412-221-5241; Office Phone: 412-648-1026. Business E-Mail: goldy@pitt.edu, dmgh@aol.com.

GOLDSTEIN, DORA BENEDICT, pharmacologist, educator; b. Milton, Mass., Apr. 25, 1922; d. George Wheeler and Marjory (Pierce) Benedict; m. Avram Goldstein, Aug. 29, 1947; children: Margaret E. Wallace, Daniel P., Joshua S., Michael B. Student, Bryn Mawr Coll., 1940-42, Stanford U., 1945. Rsch. assoc. Stanford U., 1955-70, sr. rsch. assoc., 1970-74, adj. prof., 1974-78, prof. pharmacology, 1978-92, prof. pharmacology emerita, 1992—, co-dir. faculty mentoring program sch. medicine, 1994—2001. Author: Pharmacology of Alcohol, 1983; contbr. articles to sci. jours. Bd. dirs. Parents, Families and Friends of Lesbians and Gays, 2000-06. Mem.: Intersex Soc. N.Am. (med. adv. bd. 2003—05). E-mail: dody@stanford.edu.

GOLDSTEIN, EDWARD DAVID, lawyer, former glass company executive; b. NYC, July 12, 1927; s. Michael and Leah (Kirsh) G.; m. Rhoda Gordon, Apr. 18, 1950; children: Linda, Ellen, Ruth, Michael. BA, U. Mich., 1950, JD with distinction, 1952. Bar: Calif. 1952. Assoc. Orrick, Dahlquist, Herrington & Sutcliffe, San Francisco, 1952-54, Johnston & Johnston, San Francisco, 1954-56; with legal dept. Ohio Match Co., Hunt Foods & Industries, 1956-58; asst. gen. mgr., sales mgr. Glass Containers Corp., Fullerton, Calif., 1958-62, v.p., gen. mgr., 1962-68, pres., CEO, 1968-83. Chmn. bd. Knox Glass Co., Fairmount Glass Co., 1967-68; gen. counsel FHP, Internat., FHP, Inc., 1985-87. Chmn. bd. trustees St. Jude Hosp., Fullerton, 1984-88. Served with USNR, 1945-46. Mem. ABA, State Bar Calif., Orange County Bar Assn., Nat. Health Lawyers Assn., Am. Arbitration Assn., Calif. Soc. Healthcare Attys. Home: 2230 Yucca Ave Fullerton CA 92835-3320 Office: 110 E Wilshire Ave STe 305 Fullerton CA 92832-1900 Office Phone: 714-525-5055. Personal E-mail: edgatty@aol.com.

GOLDSTEIN, ELLIOTT, lawyer, director; b. Atlanta, Oct. 23, 1915; s. Max Fullmore and Sarah Ray (London) G.; m. Harriet Weinberg, Oct. 24, 1942 (dec. Dec. 2004); children: Lillian, Ellen. Student, Ga. Sch. Tech., 1932—33; BS, U. Ga., 1936; LLB, Yale U., 1939. Bar: Ga. 1938, D.C. 1977. Asso. firm Little, Powell, Reid & Goldstein, Atlanta, 1939-40; partner firm Powell, Goldstein, Frazer & Murphy, Atlanta, 1946-77, 80—, Washington, 1977-80. Spl. counsel com. on standards ofcl. conduct U.S. Ho. of Reps., 1978; mem. legal adv. com. N.Y. Stock Exchange, 1982-85. Author: Counselling the Board of Directors in its Structure, Functions and Compensation, 1985, Georgia Corporation Law and Practice, 1989; contbr. articles to profl. jours. Hon. v.p. Am. Jewish Com.; chmn. Atlanta Hist. Soc., 1990-94. Lt. col. F.A., U.S. Army, 1941-46, ETO. Decorated Bronze Star with V. Fellow ABA Found.; mem. ABA (chmn. com. corp. laws 1979-84, chmn. ad hoc com. ALI Corp. governance project 1982-86, mem. coun. sect. corp. banking and bus. law 1983-86, sr. del. ho. of dels. 1986-94), Am. Law Inst., Ga. Bar Assn., Atlanta Bar Assn., Lawyers Club Atlanta, Commerce Club, Standard Club. Democrat. Home: 2660 Peachtree Rd NW Atlanta GA 30305-3673 Office: Powell Goldstein LLP One Atlantic Center 1201 West Peachtree St NW 14th Fl Atlanta GA 30305 Office Phone: 404-572-6605. Business E-Mail: egoldste@pogolaw.com.

GOLDSTEIN, ERIC L., historian, educator; b. Annapolis, Md. s. Lawrence B. and Betty S. Goldstein; m. Cheryl L. Haas-Goldstein; 2 children. BA, Emory U., Atlanta, 1992, MA, U. Mich., Ann Arbor, 1994, PhD, 2000. Asst. prof. history and Jewish studies Mich. State U., East Lansing, 2000, Emory U., Atlanta, 2000—06, assoc. prof. history and Jewish studies, 2006—. Author: (book) The Price of Whiteness: Jews, Race and American Identity; editor: (quar. jour.) Am. Jewish History, 2006—. Office: Dept History Emory University 561 S Kilgo Cir Atlanta GA 30322

GOLDSTEIN, FRANK ROBERT, lawyer; b. July 31, 1943; s. Morris Herman and Maxine (Herzfeld) G.; m. Phyllis Ellen Levy, Jan. 26, 1967; children: Matthew Alexander, Andrew Stephen. AB, Duke U., 1964; LLB, U. Md., 1967. Bar: Md. 1967, D.C. 1981, Mass. 1985. Clk. to chief justice U.S. Dist. Ct. Md., Balt., 1967—68; assoc. Piper & Marbury, Balt. and Washington, 1968—74, ptnr. Washington, 1974—88, Morgan, Lewis & Bockius LLP, Washington, 1989—96, Sidley Austin LLP, Washington, 1997—2007; ret., 2007. Bd. govs. Reconstructionist Rabbincal Coll., Wyncote, Pa. 1992-94; bd. dirs. Washington-Balt. Regional Assn., 1984-93, Al Marah Neighborhood Assn., Bethesda, Md., 1982-85, Paine Webber Mortgage Fin. Inc., Columbia, Md., 1987-93 Author: Mournful Numbers, 1995; co-author: District of Columbia Limited Liability Company Forms and Practice Manual, 1995. Pres. Meadowbrook Neighborhood Assn., Potomac, Md., 1990—93, Tidesfall Neighborhood Assn., Columbia, Md., 1972; bd. visitors U. Md. Sch. Law, Balt., 1992—2001; pres. Adat Shalom Reconstructionist Congregation, Bethesda, Md., 1992—95. Fellow Am. Bar Found.; mem. ABA, D.C. Bar Assn. (chmn. ptnr. com. 1985-86, treas. 1988-89), Mass. Bar Assn., Md. State Bar Assn. (chmn. ptnr. com. 1980-82, chmn. sect. legal edn. and admission to bar com. 1975, chmn. D.C. corp. code rev. project 1989-93), Order of Coif. Jewish. Home: 4301 Military Rd NW #310 Washington DC 20015 E-mail: frgold@aol.com.

GOLDSTEIN, GARY SANFORD, executive recruiter; b. Rochester, NY, Nov. 29, 1954; s. Perry Leon and Joyce Lorraine (Hoffman) G.; m. Lisa Ann Bernstein, Sept. 24, 1977 (div. 1980); m. Alicia de la Caridad Lazaro, Jan. 3, 1983 (div. 1992); children: Jessica Leigh, Vanessa Kyle; m. Jill Allyson Brooke, June 11, 1995; 1 child, Parker Leon. BS in Acctg., Canisius Coll., 1976; OPM, Harvard U. Acct. Arthur Andersen & Co., NYC, 1976-79; mng. dir. A-L Assocs., NYC, 1979-84; chmn., pres. The Whitney Group, NYC, 1984—; chmn., CEO Headway Corp. Resources, 1992—2003; CEO Whitney Group LLC, NYC, 2003—. Coun. mem. The Brookings Instn., Washington, 1990—; mem. bd. dirs. Rippowam Cisqa Sch., 1992—2000. Mem. Young Pres. Orgn. Avocations: horseback riding, tennis, collecting photorealistic art, basketball. Home: 161 Buxton Rd Bedford Hills NY 10507-2310 Office: Whitney Group LLC 850 3rd Ave New York NY 10022-6222 E-mail: ggoldstein@whitneygroup.com.

GOLDSTEIN, GEORGE A., school system administrator; b. Bklyn., Sept. 28, 1942; s. Alex and Mary (Zeluck) G. AAS, N.Y.C. Community Coll., 1962; BS, L.I. U., 1965, MS, 1969; EdD, Nova U., 1975. Cert. sch. dist. adminstr., fin. planner. Tchr. Sewanhaka Cen. High Sch. Dist., Elmont, N.Y., 1965-71, chair dept., 1971-77, asst. supt., 1978-84, dep. supt., 1984-86; asst. prof. CUNY, Bklyn., 1971-78, Staten Island, 1980-86; supt. schs. Sewanhaka Cen. High Sch. Dist., Elmont, N.Y., 1986—. Area leader State Edn. Dept., Albany, N.Y., 1974-77, chair bd. trustees, 1975-78; pvt. mgmt. cons., 1980—; disting. fellow Harvard U. Supts. Symposium, 1989; examiner N.Y. State Excelsior Awards Program. Contbr. articles to profl. jours. Bd. dirs. Patchogue Homes Corp., Howard Beach, N.Y., 1984, S.E. Sr. Citizens, Howard Beach, 1985, Elmont Youth Outreach, 1987. NSF computer/data processing fellow, Stanford, Calif., 1969, IDEA fellow Kettering Found., San Diego, 1984, IBM Corp. exec. leadership fellow, San Jose, Calif., 1987; recipient AASA award, 1994. Mem. Am. Assn. Sch. Adminstrs. (apptd. mem. Nat. Supts. Acad. 1985), Nat. Assn. Secondary Prins., Soc. Profl. Mgmt. Cons. (v.p. 1984-87), Am. Mgmt. Assn., Am. Bd. Masters Edn., Internat. Assn. Planning Cons., Assn. Cert. Fin. Planners (bd. dirs. 1986—), Phi Delta Kappa (Educator of Yr. 1990). Lodges: Lions (v.p. Elmont chpt. 1985). Jewish. Avocations: travel, theater. Home: PO Box 81 Elmont NY 11003-0081 Office: Sewanhaka Central High School District 77 Landau Ave Floral Park NY 11001-3603

GOLDSTEIN, GERALD H., lawyer; b. Santa Monica, Calif., Jan. 29, 1944; BBA, Tulane U., 1965; LLB, U. Tex., 1968. Bar: Tex. 1968, Colo. 1970, U.S. Dist. Ct. (We. Dist. Tex.) 1970, U.S. Ct. Appeals (5th cir.) 1970, U.S. Supreme Ct. 1975, U.S. Ct. Appeals (9th cir.) 1979, U.S. Ct. Appeals (11th cir.) 1981, U.S. Ct. Appeals (4th cir.) 1982, U.S. Ct. Appeals (8th and 10th cir.) 1983, bd. cert. criminal law: Tex. Bd. Legal Specialization. Ptnr. Goldstein, Goldstein & Hilley, San Antonio. Mem. dean's roundtable sch. law U. Tex., 1989—93; lectr. Fed. and State Criminal Law Institutes, 1974—; adj. prof. U. Tex., Austin, 1982—93, St. Mary's U., 1998—; faculty mem. Nat. Criminal Def. Coll., 1975—; gen. counsel Tex. Civil Liberties Union, 1979—; chmn. legal com. Nat. Orgn. Reform Marijuana Law, 1979—; bd. dirs. Tex. Death Penalty Resource Ctr. Fellow: State Bar Found.; mem.: ABA, Tex. Criminal Def. Lawyers Hall of Fame, Tex. Trial Lawyers Assn., Tex. Criminal Def. Lawyers Assn. (past pres. 1992—93), Nat. Assn. Criminal Def. Lawyers (past pres. 1994—95, Robert C. Heeney Meml. award 1991), Internat. Acad. Trial Lawyers, Am. Bd. Criminal Lawyers, Am. Coll. Trial Lawyers, State Bar Tex. (Outstanding Criminal Def. Atty. 1991), San Antonio Bar Assn. Office: 29th Fl Tower Life Bldg 310 S St Marys St San Antonio TX 78205 Office Phone: 210-226-1463. Office Fax: 210-226-8367. Personal E-mail: ggandh@aol.com.

GOLDSTEIN, HOWARD BERNARD, investment banker; b. Bronx, NY, Dec. 4, 1943; s. Maurice and Matilda Goldstein; m. Susan Nadine Goldberg, June 25, 1967; children: Jill Alecya, Brett Adam. Student, Bernard Baruch/CCNY, 1962-63; BFA, Pratt Inst., 1970. Lic. ins. agt., N.Y., spl. tng. radiation detection, chemical, electrical and fire disaster, damage assessment specialist; lic. health and life ins. agt.; cert. for 1st responder hazardous materials ops., N.J. State Police/Bergen County Law and Pub. Safety Inst., trained spotter, Nat. Weather Svc., 2006; registered security broker; spl. training, Ft. Lee Police Dept. SWAT Team, 2005, WMD response, U.S. Dept. Homeland Sec., 2005, FEMA nat. incident mgmt. tng. sys., 2005; cmty. emergency response team tng., Bergen County Law and Pub. Safety Inst. Police Acad., 2006. Art dir. Fairfax Advt. divsn. Ogilvy & Mather, Inc., NYC, 1968—72; creative dir. Hoffman Advt., NYC, 1972—80, Miller, Addison, Steele, Inc., NYC, 1980—82; pres. Gould Advt., Cliffside Park, NJ, 1969—; br. officer, tax shelter coord. E.F. Hutton & Co., Inc., NYC, 1983—85; security broker, sr. v.p., mem. chmn.'s coun., dir.'s coun. Lehman Bros., 1985—94, mem. guided portfolio mgmt. program, 1985—94; securities broker, sr. v.p. Gruntal & Co., NYC, 1994—2002; securities broker, sr. v.p., health and life ins. agt. Ryan Beck & Co., Ft. Lee, NJ, 2003—07, Stifel Nicolaus & Co. Inc., 2007—. V.p. bd. dirs. Winston Tower 200, Condominium Assn.; mem. Internat. Assn. Fin. Planning, Inst. Cert. Fin. Planners, Coll. Cert. Fin. Planners, Denver Grad. Police & Fire Acad. of Bergen County, N.J., 1986; capt., team leader Dept. Justice Emergency Response to Terrorism, 2000; trainee Nat. Fire Acad., Fed. Emergency Mgmt. Agy.; spl. trainee radiation detection, chm., elec. and fire disaster; damage assessment specialist ARC, Bergen Crossroads chpt., 1998; terrorism cons. Ft. Lee Office of Emergency Mgmt., 2002—; mem. Bergen County Weapons of Mass Destruction, Terrorism Task Force, 2003--. Designed Seal for art svcs. for ARC, 1961; exhibited photo show Bronx Hist. Soc., N.Y.C., 1970, paintings Soc. of Illustrators show, 1971-72, numerous other shows; represented in permanent collection Smithsonian Inst. Fin. officer N.J. State Police Office of Emergency Mgmt., Cliffside Park, 1986; spl. police officer Cliffside Park Police Dept., N.J. State Police Benevolent Assn., 1986—, Montclair State Coll. World of Computers, 1981; mem. steering com. Coalition Bus., Labor and Cmty. Orgns. N.Y., 1992, mem. exec. com., chmn. fin., 1992—; bd. advisor to UN Nat. Com. for Habitat, 1993—; first Am. investment banker to coord. pvt. bus. coun. meeting N.Y.C. with His Excellency Saparmurad A. Niyazov (1st elected pres. The Rep. of Turkismanistan, previously part of USSR) and cabinet of ministers, 1993; mem. Rep. Senatorial Inner Circle, 1992; mem. Graphic Artists Guild, 1976-80, Bronx County Hist. Soc., 1968-71, Cliffside Park Baseball Assn., 1979—, coach, 1981, 83; sponsor Project High Frontier, U.S. Govt., 1986, sustaining mem. Rep. Nat. Com., 1981—; preferred mem. U.S. Senatorial Club, 1984—; majority mem. Nat. Rep. Senatorial Com., 1984—; mem. Heritage Found., 1990—, Nat. Rep. Congrl. Com., 1984—, N.J. Rep. State Com., 1994—; capt., team leader emergency response to terrorism Dept. Justice, 2000; terrorism cons. Ft. Lee Office of Emergency Mgmt., 2002—, emergency man. first response team task forse exercise, Fort Lee , Bergen County 2003. Sachs Art scholar, 1955; recipient medal for art svc. Youth Friends Assn., 1961, Ga. Pacific award, 1978, Scholastic Mixed media award Scholastic Mag., 1961. Mem. Citizens Against Govt. Waste, The City Club N.Y. (govt. ops. com.), Tenafly Rifle and Pistol Club Inc., Nat. Rifle Assn. Clubs: Fort Lee Racquetball. Lodges: Bnai Brith. Jewish. Achievements include being first responder to World Trade Center Disaster, Sept. 11, 2001. Address: 200 Winston Dr Cliffside Park NJ 07010-3235 Office Phone: 201-585-6183. Business E-Mail: howard.goldstein@stifel.com.

GOLDSTEIN, HOWARD SHELDON, lawyer; b. Apr. 22, 1952; s. Jerome Harold and Goldie Goldstein; m. Amy Ruth, 1980. BA, CUNY, 1974; JD, Bklyn. Law Sch., 1977. Bar: N.Y. 1978, U.S. Dist. Ct. (so. and ea. dists.) N.Y. 1978. Assoc. Loew & Cohen, Esquires, NYC, 1976-82, ptnr., 1982-87, Cohen & Goldstein Esquires, LLP, NYC, 1988—. Contbr. articles to profl. jours. Mem.: N.Y.C. Bar Assn. (legal referral svcs.), Nassau County Bar Assn., N.Y. County Lawyers Assn., N.Y. State Bar Assn. (mem. family law com., mem. legis. com.). Republican. Jewish. Office: Cohen & Goldstein Esqs LLP 32 Broadway Rm 1700 New York NY 10004-1670 Office Phone: 212-797-5400. Business E-Mail: goldstein@cohengoldstein.com.

GOLDSTEIN, HOWARD WARREN, lawyer; b. NYC, Mar. 29, 1949; s. Murray and Claire (Millrod) G.; m. Wendy Jo Zacharius, Sept. 9, 1973; children: Lindsay Rebecca, Amanda Mikael, Justin Zacharius. BA, Northwestern U., 1970; JD, NYU, 1973. Bar: N.Y. 1974, U.S. Dist. Ct. (so. and ea. dists.) N.Y. 1974, U.S. Ct. Appeals (2d cir.) 1975, U.S. Ct. Appeals (10th cir.) 1984, U.S. Ct. Appeals (6th cir.) 1985, U.S. Ct. Appeals (3d cir.) 1997, U.S. Supreme Ct. 1984, U.S. Claims Ct. 1988. Law clk. to judge U.S. Dist. Ct. (ea. dist.) N.Y., 1973-74; assoc. Cravath, Swaine & Moore, NYC, 1974-76; asst. U.S. atty. Office of U.S. Atty. (so. dist.) N.Y., NYC, 1976-80; assoc. Mudge, Rose, Guthrie, Alexander & Ferdon, NYC, 1980-81, ptnr., 1982-90, Fried, Frank, Harris, Shriver & Jacobson, NYC, 1990—. Author: Grand Jury Practice, 1998; co-author: The Rights of Crime Victims, 1985, RICO: Civil and Criminal, Law and Strategy, 1989, Corporate Sentencing Guidelines, 1993. Mem. Fed. Bar Coun., Assn. of Bar of City of N.Y., Nat. Assn. Criminal Def. Lawyers, N.Y. Coun. Def. Lawyers, Order of Coif, Phi Beta Kappa. Jewish. Office: Fried Frank Harris Shriver & Jacobson One New York Plz New York NY 10004

GOLDSTEIN, IRA MORRIS, neurosurgeon; s. Michael and Diane Goldstein; m. Sophia Goldstein, July 2, 2006. BS, Cornell U., Ithaca, NY, 1993; MD, U. Chgo., 1997. Resident neurol. surgery Albert Einstein Coll. Medicine, 2003; asst. prof. neurol. surgery NJ med. sch. UMDNJ, Newark, 2004—; attending surgeon, neurosurgery and spine surgery U. Hosp., Newark, 2004—, Jersey City Med. Ctr., 2004—, Overlook Hosp., Summit, NJ, 2006—. Clin. instr. sch. medicine Presbyn. Hosp. U. Pitts., 2003—04; cons. in field. Contbr. articles to profl. jours. Recipient Elsberg Award, NY Neurosurgical Soc., 2001; fellow, NIH, 1994, Am. Heart Assn., 1996—97, U. Pitts. Med. Ctr., 2004; scholar, Bausch & Lomb, 1988, NY Bd. Edn., 1989—93; Calvin Fentress Rsch. fellow, U. Chgo., 1996—97. Mem.: NJ Spine Soc., N.Am. Spine Soc., NJ Med. Soc., Congress Neurol. Surgeons, Am. Assn. Neurol. Surgeons (assoc.), Phi Kappa Phi, Golden Key. Achievements include research in VEGF gene transduction to improve survival of transplanted embryonic mouse mesencephalon. Avocations: fishing, kayaking, mountain biking, photography. Office: NJ Med Sch UMDNJ 90 Bergen St Ste 8100 Newark NJ 07103 Office Phone: 973-972-8211. Office Fax: 973-972-2333.

GOLDSTEIN, IRVIN L., elementary school educator; b. Louisville, Aug. 12, 1929; s. Henry S. and Dorothy (Zillman) G.; m. Daisy Baker, Aug. 21, 1955; children: Steven, Alan, Sara, Lynne. BA in Edn., U. Ky., 1951; MEd in Supervision and Adminstrn., U. Louisville, 1961. Camp dir. Jewish Community Ctr., Louisville; elem. tchr. Louisville Pub. Schs.; elem. tchr., coord. camping New Albany (Ind.) Floyd County Schs. Speaker profl. confs.; prin. religious sch. The Temple, Louisville, 1957-98, life mem. bd. trustees, 1998; exch. tchr., Vancouver, B.C., Can., 1955-56; mem. leadership edn. adv. bd. Bellarmine Coll., 1987-96. Contbr. articles to profl. mags; author Teacher's Handbook for Creative Learning, 2004 Mem. Floyd County Comprehensive Health Planning Coun., South Ind. Comprehensive Health Plan; active numerous community orgns. Named Valley Forge Classroom Tchr. of Yr., 1963, Floyd County Conservation Classroom Tchr. of Yr., 1973, 88, Reform Jewish Educator, 1986; recipient Tchr. of Yr. award Floyd County Schs., 1990; finalist Ind. Tchr. Yr., 1990; Ind. Coun. on Econ. Edn. grantee, 1989, 90, 91, 92, 93, Olin Davis award, Tchr. Creativity award Lilly Found., 1992. Mem. NEA, Nat. Assn. Temple Educators (nat. bd. dirs. 1994-98), Ind. Tchrs. Assn., Environ. Edn. Assn. Ind., NAFCEA (pres. 1968-69), Leadership Edn. Alumni Assn. (pres. 1990-91), Phi Delta Kappa. Home: 3430 Bryan Way Louisville KY 40220-1930

GOLDSTEIN, IRVING SOLOMON, chemistry professor, consultant; b. Bronx, NY, Aug. 20, 1921; s. Jacob and Jennie (Rathsprecher) G.; m. Helen Haft, Dec. 16, 1945; children: Ardath Ann, Darra Jane, Jared. BS in Chemistry, Rensselaer Poly. Inst., 1941; MS in Chemistry, Ill. Inst. Tech., 1944; PhD in Organic Chemistry, Harvard U., 1948. Teaching asst. Ill. Inst. Tech., Chgo., 1941-42; teaching fellow Harvard U., Cambridge, Mass., 1946-48; rsch. chemist N.Am. Rayon Corp., Elizabethton, Tenn., 1948-51; mgr. wood chemistry rsch. Koppers Co., Inc., Pitts., 1951-63; sr. rsch. scientist Nalco Chem. Co., Chgo., 1963-66; mgr. paper rsch. Continental Can Co., Chgo., 1966-68; prof. forest sci. Texas A&M U., College Station, 1968-71; prof., head wood and paper sci. dept. N.C. State U., Raleigh, 1971-78, prof. wood chemistry, 1978-92; prof. emeritus, 1992—. Editor: Wood Technology: Chemical Aspects, 1977, Organic Chemicals From Biomass, 1981, Composition and Structure of Wood, 1991; contbr. articles to profl. jours.; 15 inventions in field. Lt. USNR, 1942—46, ATO, PTO. Fellow Internat. Acad. Wood Sci.; mem. AAAS, Am. Chem. Soc. (chmn. cellulose div. 1982), Tech. Assn. Pulp and Paper Industry, Forest Products Rsch. Soc., Soc. Wood Sci. and Tech. E-mail: isgold@unity.ncsu.edu.

GOLDSTEIN, JACK, biopharmaceutical executive, microbiologist; b. NYC, June 7, 1947; s. Arnold L. and Rachel (Vogel) G.; m. Laurie Ann Sacks, Aug. 28, 1969; 1 child, Justin T. BA, Rider U., Trenton, NJ, 1969; MS, St. John's U., Jamaica, NY, 1974, PhD, 1976. Diplomate Am. Bd. Med. Microbiology. Asst. dir. microbiology Queens Hosp. Ctr., Jamaica, 1976-81; dir. diagnostic labs. API div. Sherwood Med. Co., Plainview, NY, 1981-83; v.p. research and devel. MicroScan div. Baxter, Sacramento, 1983-86; group v.p. Ortho Diagnostic Systems Inc. div. Johnson & Johnson Co., Raritan, NJ, 1986-88; group v.p., gen. mgr. infectious disease bus. Ortho Diagnostic Systems, Inc. div. Johnson & Johnson Co., Raritan, NJ, 1988-92; exec. v.p. worldwide Ortho Diagnostic Sys. Inc. divsn. Johnson & Johnson Co., Raritan, NJ, 1992-93, pres. Ortho Diagnostic Sys. Inc. divsn., 1993-97; pres., CEO Applied Imaging Corp., Santa Clara, Calif., 1997-2001, chmn. bd., 2001—02; gen. ptnr. Windamere Venture Ptnrs., San Diego, 2001—02; pres. blood testing divsn. Chiron Corp., Emeryville, Calif., 2002—04, interim COO, 2004—05, pres., COO, 2005—. Mem. exam. com. Am. Bd. Med. Microbiology, Washington, 1984-91. Mem. editl. bd. Jour. Clin. Microbiology, Wasington, 1983-91; contbr. articles to profl. jours. Mem. Am. Soc. Microbiology, Am. Soc. Clin. Chemistry, Beta Beta Beta. Avocations: reading, skiing. Office: Chiron Corp 4560 Horton St Emeryville CA 94608-2916 Office Phone: 510-923-3850. E-mail: jack_goldstein@chiron.com.

GOLDSTEIN, JANE D., lawyer; b. Oct. 21, 1960; BA magna cum laude, Boston Univ., 1982, JD magna cum laude, 1989. Bar: Mass. 1989. Assoc. Ropes & Gray, Boston, 1989—98, ptnr. corp. dept., 1998—, head, retail & consumer branded products practice group. Mem.: Mad River Ski Club (bd. dir.). Office: Ropes & Gray 1 International Pl Boston MA 02110-2624 Office Phone: 617-951-7431. Office Fax: 617-951-7050. Business E-Mail: jane.goldstein@ropesgray.com.

GOLDSTEIN, JEFFREY ALAN, corporate financial executive; b. Dec. 2, 1955; m. Nancy Coles Goldstein; 3 children. Student, London Sch. Econs., 1976; BA in Econs. with honors, Vassar Coll., 1977; MA in Econs., MPhil in Econs., Yale U., 1980, PhD in Econs., 1983. Rsch. asst. Brookings Instn., Washington, 1977—78; instr. econs. Princeton U., NJ, 1982—83; ptnr. BT Wolfensohn, NYC, 1984—99, co-chmn., 1996—99; mng. dir., CFO World Bank, Washington, 1999—2004; mng. dir. Hellman & Friedman, NYC, 2004—. Guest lectr. fin. Grad. Sch. Orgn. and Mgmt. Yale U., 1982; bd. dirs. Internat. Ctr. Rsch. Women; cons. in field. Contbr. chapters to books. Bd. trustees, chmn. investments com. Vassar Coll.; bd. trustees German Marshall Fund US; former pres., bd. trustees Big Brothers/Big Sisters NYC, 1997—99; fin. com. Rockefeller Family Fund, 1997—99; photography coun. Mus. Modern Art. Fellow, Yale U. Grad. Sch.; Wells fellow for grad. study in econ., Vassar Coll. Mem.: Coun. Fgn. Rels., Social Sci. Rsch. Coun. (mem. investment com. 1989—98), Fgn. Policy Assn., Omicron Delta Epsilon, Phi Beta Kappa. Office: Hellman & Friedman 375 Park Ave 20th Fl New York NY 10152 Office Phone: 212-871-6680. Business E-Mail: jgoldstein@hf.com.

GOLDSTEIN, JEROME ARTHUR, mathematics professor; b. Pitts., Aug. 5, 1941; s. Morris and Henrietta (Vogel) G.; children: Maurice Roland, David Jonathan, Devra. BS, Carnegie-Mellon U., 1963, MS, 1964, PhD, 1967; S.MD (hon.), Internat. Boswell Inst., Loyola U., New Orleans,

1973. Mem. Inst. Advanced Study, Princeton, NJ, 1967-68; asst. prof. math. Tulane U., New Orleans, 1968-71, assoc. prof., 1971-75, prof., 1975-91; prof. Math. Sci. Rsch. Inst. U. Calif., Berkeley, 1990-91; prof. math. La. State U., Baton Rouge, 1992-96, U. Memphis, 1996—. Author: Semigroups of Linear Operators and Applications, 1985; editor: P.D.E. and Related Topics, 1975, Mathematics Applied to Science, 1988, Differential Equations in Biology, Physics and Engineering, 1991, Semigroups of Operators and Applications, 1993, Stochastic Processes and Functional Analysis, 1997, Applied Analysis, 1999, Semigroup Forum, 1982—, Applied and Computational Mathematics, 1983—, Differential and Integral Equations, 1988—, Electronic Jour. Differential Equations, 1992—, Advances in Differential Equations, 1995—, Communications in Applied Analysis, 1995—, Positivity, 1996—, Jour. Math. Analysis and Applications, 1998—, Jour. of Computational Analysis and Applications, 1998—, Internat. Jour. Differential Equations and Applications, 1999—, Jour. Evolution Equations, 2000—, Electronic Jour. Math. Phys. Sci., 2002-, others; contbr. articles to profl. jours. Recipient Faculty Excellence in Research award Coll. Arts and Scis., Tulane U., 1985; NSF grantee, 1968-96. Mem. Am. Math. Soc., Math. Assn. Am., Soc. Indsl. Applied Math., London Math. Soc. Soc. Math. Brazil, Edinburgh Math. Soc., Assn. Women in Math., Sigma Xi (Rsch. award 1972, Alumni Assn. Rsch. award 2002, Eminent Faculty award 2006). Jewish.

GOLDSTEIN, JEROME CHARLES, retired professional society administrator, otolaryngologist, surgeon; b. Glens Falls, NY, Nov. 4, 1935; s. Morris and Estelle (Ginsburg) G.; m. Rochelle Jacobs; children: Harry Glenn, Bradley John, Brian Louis. AB, U. Rochester, 1957; MD, SUNY, Syracuse, 1963. Diplomate Am. Bd. Otolaryngology (bd. dirs. 1982-2000). Intern Phila. Gen. Hosp., 1963-64; resident in gen. surgery Bronx Mcpl. Hosp. Ctr., NYC, 1964-65; resident in otolaryngology SUNY, Syracuse, 1965-68; asst. prof. Northwestern U. Med. Sch., Chgo., 1968-71; pvt. practice Glens Falls, NY, 1971-74; prof. surgery, head divsn. otolaryngology Albany (N.Y.) Med. Coll., 1974-83; exec. v.p. Am. Acad. Otolaryngology-Head and Neck Surgery, Washington, 1984-94, sr. exec. v.p., 1995-96, exec. v.p. emeritus, 1997-99. Otolaryngologist-in-chief Albany Med. Ctr. Hosp., 1974-83; prof. dept. otolaryngology, head and neck surgery Johns Hopkins Med. Sch., 1986—, Georgetown Med. Sch., 1990; chair sec. com. Combined Otolaryngology Spring Meeting., 1985—; pres. Centurions of Deafness Rsch. Found., N.Y.C., 1987-88. With USAFR, 1965-70. Fellow ACS, Royal Coll. Surgeons Edinburgh, Am. Acad. Facial, Plastic and Reconstructive Surgery, Triologic Soc., Am. Laryngol. Assn., Am. Soc. for Head and Neck Surgery (pres. 1982-83), Soc. Head and Neck Surgeons, Am. Neurotol. Soc. (hon.), Am. Bronchoesoph. Soc., Am. Head and Neck Soc., Nat. Assn. Physicians for the Environment (founding pres. 1993-95, pres. 1999-2000); mem. AMA, Am. Otol. Soc. (hon.), Internat. Fedn. Otorhino-Laryngol. Socs. (regional sec. for N.Am. 1985-2000), Coun. of Med. Splty. Socs. (pres. 1996), Pan Pacific Surg. Assn. (pres. 2004—06), Am. Soc. Geriatric Otolaryngology (founding pres. 2007—). Home and Office: 4119 Manchester Lake Dr Lake Worth FL 33467-8175 Office Phone: 561-432-7220. Office Fax: 561-649-9412. Personal E-mail: JCGMD@aol.com.

GOLDSTEIN, JERRY, physicist, educator; BS in Physics, Bklyn. Coll.; PhD in Physics, Dartmouth Coll., Hanover, NH. Prin. scientist space sci. and engring. divsn. S.W. Rsch. Inst., San Antonio, 2003—; adjoint asst. prof. physics and astronomy U. Tex., San Antonio. Contbr. articles to sci. jours. Named one of Brilliant 10, Popular Sci. mag., 2006, Forty Under Forty, San Antonio Bus. Jour.; recipient Macelwane medal, Am. Geophys. Union, 2006. Office: Space Sci and Engring Divsn SW Rsch Inst PO Drawer 28510 San Antonio TX 78228-0510 Office Phone: 210-522-5633.

GOLDSTEIN, JON, investment advisor; m. Joanne Goldstein; 3 children. BS, Univ. Calif., Berkeley; MBA, Wharton Sch. Bus. Univ. Pa. CPA Deloitte & Touche, San Francisco; mng. dir. wealth mgmt., sr. advisor Citigroup family office, leader Peninsula group Citi Smith Barney, Menlo Park, Calif. Named one of Top 15 Fin. Advisors, Registered Rep & Research mag., 2002—03, Top 100 Fin. Advisors, Barron's Mag., 2004—07. Office: Citi Smith Barney Bldg 3 Ste 230 3000 Sand Hill Rd Menlo Park CA 94025*

GOLDSTEIN, JONATHAN, lawyer; b. NYC, Nov. 20, 1943; BA, Yale U., 1965; LLB, Harvard U., 1968. Bar: NY, 1969. Assoc. to mng. ptnr. Winston & Strawn LLP, NYC, 1968—. Mem.: NY State Bar Assn., Phi Beta Kappa. Office: Winston & Strawn 200 Park Ave Rm 4100 New York NY 10166-0005

GOLDSTEIN, JOSEPH IRWIN, materials scientist, educator; b. Syracuse, NY, Jan. 6, 1939; s. Louis and Sylvia (Scharfeld) G.; m. Barbara Hammond, June 30, 1963; children: Steven (dec.), Anne. BS in Metallurgy, MIT, 1960, MS, 1962, ScD in Metallurgy, 1964. Instr. metallurgy dept. MIT, 1960-63; phys. metallurgist Smithsonian Astron. Obs., Cambridge, Mass., 1963-64; aerospace technologist NASA-Goddard Space Ctr., Greenbelt, Md., 1964—68; lectr. chem. engring. U. Md., 1966-68; asst. prof. metall. and materials sci. Lehigh U., Bethlehem, Pa., 1968-70, assoc. prof., 1970-75, prof., 1975-93, T.L. Diamond Disting. prof., 1976—83, v.p. rsch., 1979-83, 1983-90, R.D. Stout prof. materials sci. and engring., 1990-93; dean engring. U. Mass., Amherst, 1993—2004, disting. prof., 2003—. Author, editor 8 books; contbr. more than 200 articles to profl. jours. Recipient Nat. Environ. Rsch. Coun. award, Britain, 1974, Leonard medal, 2005. Fellow Am. Soc. Metals; mem. Microbeam Analysis Soc. (pres. 1977-78, Sci. award 1991, Svc. award 1984), Meteoritical Soc. (mem. coun. 1979-81, treas. 1995-99, v.p. 2005-06, pres. 2007—). Democrat. Jewish. Home: 49 Sheerman Ln Amherst MA 01002-1584 Office: U Mass Mech and Indsl Engring Amherst MA 01003 Business E-Mail: JIG0@ecs.umass.edu.

GOLDSTEIN, JOSEPH LEONARD, molecular biologist, educator; b. Sumter, SC, Apr. 18, 1940; s. Isadore E. and Fannie A. Goldstein. BS, Washington and Lee U., 1962, DSc, 1986; MD, U. Tex., Dallas, 1966; DSc (hon.), U. Chgo., 1982, Rensselaer Poly. Inst., 1982, U. Paris, 1988, U. Buenos Aires, 1990; DSc (hon.), So. Meth. U., 1993, U. Miami, 1996; DSc (hon.), Rockefeller U., 2001. Intern, then resident in medicine Mass. Gen. Hosp., Boston, 1966—68; clin. assoc. NIH, 1968—70; fellow U. Wash., Seattle, 1970—72; faculty U. Tex. Southwestern Med. Ctr., Dallas, 1972—77, Paul J. Thomas prof. medicine, chmn. dept. molecular genetics, 1977—85, regental prof., 1985—. Harvey Soc. lectr., 1977; mem. sci. rev. bd. Howard Hughes Med. Inst., 1978—84, med. adv. bd., 1985—90, chmn. med. adv. bd., 1995—2002, trustee, 2002—; non-resident fellow Salk Inst., 1983—94; chmn. award jury Albert Lasker Med. Rsch., 1996—; mem. bd. sci. govs. Scripps Rsch. Inst., 1996—. Co-author: The Metabolic Basis of Inherited Disease, 5th edit., 1983; mem. editl. bd. Jour. Biol. Chemistry, 1981—95, Cell, 1983—, Jour. Clin. Investigation, 1977—82, Ann. Rev. Genetics, 1980—85, Arteriosclerosis, 1981—87, Sci., 1985—98. Trustee Rockefeller U., 1994—; mem. sci. adv. bd. Welch Found., 1986—; bd. dirs. Passano Found., 1985—. Recipient Heinrich-Wieland prize, 1974, Pfizer award in enzyme chemistry, ACS, 1976, Passano award, Johns Hopkins U., 1978, Gairdner Found. award, 1981, award in biol. and med. scis., NY Acad. Sci., 1981, Lita Annenberg Hazen award, 1982, Rsch. Achievement award, Am. Heart Assn., 1984, Louisa Gross Horwitz award, 1984, 3M Life Sci. award, 1984, Albert Lasker award in basic med. rsch., 1985, Nobel Prize in physiology or medicine, 1985, Trustees's medal, Mass. Gen. Hosp., 1986, US Nat. medal of sci., 1988, prize, Warren Alpert Found., 2000, prize in Medicine and Biomed. Rsch., Albany Med. Ctr., 2003, Builders Sci. award, Rsch. Am., 2007, Woodrow Wilson award for pub. svc., 2005, Builder of Sci. award, Research!America, 2007. Mem.: Tex. Philos. Soc., Royal Soc. London (fgn. mem.), Inst. Medicine, Am. Philos. Soc., Am. Fedn. Clin. Rsch., Am. Soc. Biol. Chemists, Am. Acad. Arts and Scis., Am. Soc. Human Genetics (William Allan award 1985), Am. Soc. Clin. Investigation (pres. 1985—86), Assn. Am. Physicians, ACP (award 1986), NAS (coun. 1991—94, Lounsbery award 1979), Alpha Omega Alpha, Phi Beta Kappa. Home: 3831 Turtle Creek Blvd Apt 22B Dallas TX 75219-4538 Office: U Tex Southwestern Med Ctr 5323 Harry Hines Blvd Dallas TX 75390-9046 E-mail: jgolds@mednet.swmed.edu.

GOLDSTEIN, JULIA SONIA, librarian; b. Balt., Mar. 20, 1923; d. Fred Soloman and Etta (Marburg) Deutsch; m. Harold Goldstein, Nov. 4, 1943 (dec.); children: William M., Richard H. BS, U. Ill., 1963, MLS, 1968. Tchr. Thomas Paine Sch., Urbana, Ill., 1963-65; libr. Flossie Wiley Sch., Urbana, 1965-67; interlibr. loan libr. State Libr. Fla., Tallahassee, 1968-71; interlibrary libr. State Library of Fla., 1972—76; libr. Fla. Dept. Commerce, Tallahassee, 1976-78, Fla. Dept. Labor, Tallahassee, 1978-80, labor and employment and tng. specialist, 1980-85; ret., 1985; labor, employment and tng. rep. Fla. Dept. Labor, 1989. Mem. Fla. State U. Oxford (Eng.) U., 1988, 90, libr. Florence, Italy, 1992; mem. U. Okla. libr. seminar Oxford U., 1992. Bd. dirs. Tallahassee Opera Guild, 1988—94, Tallahassee Theatre Guild, 1997—99, pres., 1987—; founder Living Learning Libr., Frostproof, Fla., 1971; mem. exec. com. Music Assocs., Sch. Music Fla. State U., 1993—2000. Mem. Internat. Torch Club (pres. Tallahassee chpt. 1988-89), Univ. Club Fla. State U. (pres. 1989-90), Assn. Ret. Faculty (bd. dirs. 1994—, pres. 1998-99), Toastmasters Internat. (pres. Fla. Dept. Transp. chpt. 1983). Home: 1911 Angel Hollow Rd Tallahassee FL 32308-6189 E-mail: carnabubbl@aol.com.

GOLDSTEIN, JULIUS LESTER, biomedical engineer, consultant; b. Bklyn., July 9, 1935; s. Benjamin and Dorothy (Steinberg) G.; m. Batya Abramson, June 17, 1962; children: Hillel N., Miriam D., Naama L., Avi D. BEE, Cooper Union, 1957; MEE, Poly. Inst. Bklyn., 1960; PhD, U. Rochester, 1965. Postdoctoral fellow Inst. for Perception Rsch., Eindhoven, Netherlands, 1965-66; rsch. assoc., Lab. Psychophysics Harvard U., Cambridge, Mass., 1966-68; asst. prof. elec. engring. MIT, Cambridge, Mass., 1968-71, assoc. prof. elec. engring., 1971-73; dir. biomed. engring. Tel Aviv U., Israel, 1973-76, chmn. dept. electronics, 1976-78, assoc. prof., 1973-82, prof. elec. engring., 1982-90; vis. prof. Johns Hopkins U., Balt., 1986-88; rsch. prof. Ctrl. Inst. for the Deaf, St. Louis, 1988-96; adj. prof. elec. engring. Washington U., St. Louis, 1996—, adj. prof. biomed. engring., 2001—. Pres. Israel Soc. for Med. and Biomed. Engrs., Tel Aviv, 1975-77; dir. biomed. engring. program Tel Aviv U., 1973-76; cons. Digital Speech Systems, Tel Aviv, 1984-86, Models of Human Hearing, AT&T Bell Labs., Murray Hill, NJ, 1991-96; co-founder, pres. Hearing Emulations, LLC, 2000. Contrb. articles profl. jour. Achievements include the discovery and formulation of math models of basic principles of auditory signal processing, including nonlinear cochlear sound analysis, detection of signal peaks and intervals, central processing in pitch perception, hearing aids based on auditory models. Bd. dir. Epstein Hebrew Acad., Block Yeshiva HS, St. Louis, 1991-94, 98-2003; organizer, symposium chmn. Assn. for Rsch. in Otolaryngology 17th Midwinter meeting, 1994. NIH grantee MIT, 1972, Johns Hopkins U., 1986-88, U.S./Israel Binational Fund grantee, 1977-80, NIH-NIDCD grantee Ctrl. Inst. for the Deaf, 1990-95, NSF-IBN grantee Washington U., 1998-00, NIH-NIDCD SBIR grantee BECS Tech., 1999-2004. Fellow Acoustical Soc. Am., Collegium Oto-Rhino-Laryngologicum Amicitae Sacrum, 1980; mem. IEEE (life). Achievements include invention of hearing aids with instantaneous gain compression and adaptive nonlinear waveform compression. Office: Hearing Emulations LLC 9479 Dielman Rock Island Dr Saint Louis MO 63132 Personal E-mail: julius@hearem.com.

GOLDSTEIN, KENNETH B., lawyer; b. Bklyn., Sept. 16, 1949; s. Nathan and Isabella (Solow) G. BA, Tulane U., 1973, JD, 1974; postdoctoral, Fordham U., 1979. Bar: N.Y. 1977, U.S. Dist. Ct. (so. and ea. dist.) N.Y. 1980, U.S. Ct. Appeals (D.C. cir.) 1981. Gen. mgr., v.p. Middletown (N.Y.) Window Cleaning Co., Inc., 1974; tchr. various schs., Middletown and Chester, N.Y., 1975-77; asst. sr. v.p., dir. mktg. Saks Fifth Ave, NYC, 1977-79; sr. asst. dist. atty. Orange County, Goshen, N.Y., 1979-81; assoc. Zola & Zola, NYC, 1981-83, Freedman, Weisbein & Samuelson P.C., Garden City, N.Y., 1983-85, Jaffe & Asher, NYC, 1985-91, Raoul Lionel Felder P.C., NYC, 1991—. Bd. dirs. Middletown Window Cleaning Co., Inc. Bd. dirs. New Orleans Jazz and Heritage Found., 1972-74, Jewish Family Svcs. Orange County, 2000—. Named one of Outstanding Young Men in Am., 1980. Mem. ABA, N.Y. State Bar Assn., Middletown Bar Assn., Orange County Bar Assn., Order of DeMolay. Republican. Jewish. Avocations: swimming, art, dance, opera. Home: 145 E 35th St Apt 2me New York NY 10016-4121 also: PO Box 3 Middletown NY 10940-0003 Office: Raoul Lionel Felder PC 437 Madison Ave New York NY 10022-7001 Home Phone: 212-689-3842; Office Phone: 212-832-3939.

GOLDSTEIN, KENNETH F., entertainment and publishing company executive; b. Detroit, Mar. 10, 1962; s. Earl Goldstein and Sarita (Bow) Snow; m. Shelley Wood, 2007. BA in Philosophy and Theater, Yale U., 1984. Freelance writer, TV and film producer, LA, 1984-89; writer, producer Cinemaware Corp., Westlake Village, Calif., 1989-91; designer, producer Philips Interactive Media, LA, 1991-92; exec. publisher Carmen Sandiego series Broderbund Software, Inc., Novato, Calif., 1992-96, v.p. entertainment, gen. mgr. divsn. Red Orb Entertainment Myst, Riven Series, 1996-98, Journeyman Project series, Warlords series, 1996-98; sr. v.p., gen. mgr. Disney Online, 1998-2000; exec. v.p., mng. dir. Walt Disney Internet Group, 2000—06; chmn., CEO shop.com, 2006—. Author: (screenplays) 8; designer (software programs) Carmen Sandiego: Jr. Detective Edition, 1994 (Software Publs. Assn. award 1995), Reading Galaxy, 1994 (Family PC, Mac World awards 1996), In the 1st Degree, 1995 (Software Publs. Assn. award 1996); pub. Blast, 1998-06, FamilyFun Online, 1999-06, Disney's Toontown Online, 2002-06, Playhouse Disney Preschool Time Online, 2005-06, Movies.com website, 2002-06, Pirates of the Caribbean Online, 2006. Vol. Olive Crest Treatment Ctr., 1986, Free Arts Abused Children, 1988; sec. bd. trustees Full Circle Programs, Marin County, Calif., 1992-98; vice chmn. bd. trustees Hathaway Children and Family Svcs, 2002-05; bd. trustees Hathaway-Sycamores Child and Family Svcs., 2005—; bd. advs. Mediascope, 2002-04; bd. dirs. LA Make-A-Wish Found., 2005—; chair exec. com. Berit Mexia Peace Inst., 2006—. Recipient Pub. Svc. awards, Olive Crest Treatment Ctrs., 1986, Free Arts for Abused Children, 1988; named one of Top 100 Multimedia Producers, Multimedia Producer Mag., 1995, Best of What's New in Computers, Electronics, Popular Sci. Mag., 1995, Upside Mag. Elite 100, Digital Entertainment, 1998, Best of Festival award Internat. Web Awards, 2000, Web Mktg. Assn. Web Awards Best Game, Family, Movie, Entertainment Sites award 2001, Modalis Rsch. Excellence award, 2001, Outstanding Achievement award Web Mktg. Assn., 2002, 03, Web Internet Visionary award, Best of the Web, 2001, All Star Software award Software Rev., 2003, People's Voice award kids' category Webby Awards, 2003, Internet Safety award WiredKids website, 2005. Mem. Writers Guild of Am. West, Acad. Interactive Arts and Scis (founding mem., bd. govs. L.A.), Yale Univ. Alumni (schs. com. 1988—), Internat. Game Developers Assn. Office: shop.com Bldg 1 Ste 210 1 Lower Ragsdale Dr Monterey CA 93940

GOLDSTEIN, LEONARD BARRY, dentist; b. Seaford, NY, Feb. 6, 1944; s. Jacob Martin and Adele (Pelzner) G.; m. Phyllis Lynn Kerwin, June 25, 1967; children: Marcie Ilene, Sherri Elysse. Student, Ind. U., 1961-63; DDS, Case Western Reserve U., 1967; Cert. in Orthodontics, Dewey Sch. Orthodontics, NYC, 1969; PhD in Electro-Medicine, City U., LA, 1988. Diplomate Am. Acad. of Pain Mgmt., Am. Bd. Forensic Medicine, Am. Bd. Forensic Dentistry. Gen. practice dentistry, Smithtown, 1969—; attending orthodontist Abe Stark Philanthropies Dental Clinic, Bklyn., 1970-77; med. dir. TMJ Facial Pain Ctr. Southside Hosp., Bay Shore. Guest prof. dept. phys. edn. Queens Coll., N.Y., 1979—; guest lectr. dept. phys. edn. Queensboro (N.Y.) C.C., 1980—; dir. dental svcs. Good Samaritan Profl. Svcs., St. James, N.Y., 1979—, v.p. med. bd., 1979—; attending dental staff St. John's Episc. Hosp., 1980—, Cmty. Hosp. Western Suffolk, 1980—; bd. dirs. L.I. Ctr. for Cranio-Facial Pain, Smithtown; med. dir. TMJ/Facial Pain Ctr., Southside Hosp.; dir. grad. program in forensic exam. Touro Coll. Sch. Health Scis., Bay Shore; chmn. Instnl. Rev. Bd., Touro Coll.; vice chmn. com. on scholarly rsch., Touro Coll. Sch. Health Scis., asst. dean grad. program devel.; assoc. dir. program devel. NY Coll. Osteo. Medicine, assoc. prof. Dept. Family Medicine. Contbr. articles to profl. jours. Served to capt. Dental Corps, U.S. Army, 1967-69. Fellowship in removeable prosthetics, U.S. Army Dental Corps, 1967. Fellow Acad. Stress and Chronic Disease, Acad. Gen. Dentistry, Am. Endodontic Soc., Internat. Coll. Dentists; mem. Am. Equilibration Soc., Am. Coll. Sports Medicine, Internat. Acad. Preventive Medicine, Cranial Acad. of Am. Osteopathic Soc., Am. Orthodontic Soc., Internat. Soc. Orthodontists, Am. Dental Soc., N.Y. Coll. Osteo. Medicine (assoc. dir. program devel.), Cronio-Mandibular Study Club of N.Y., L.I. Gnathological Study Club, Northeastern Gnathological Soc. Office Phone: 516-686-1408. Personal E-mail: ddsphd@aol.com.

GOLDSTEIN, MANFRED, retired management consultant; b. Vienna, Jan. 30, 1927; arrived in US, 1939, naturalized, 1945; s. Isidore and Anna (Hahn) G.; m. Shirley Marie Lavine, Aug. 27, 1950 (dec. Feb. 2001); children: Cindy Marie, Lynn Alyse; m. Rhonda J. Demarsh, Mar. 23, 2005 Student, Manhattan Trade Ctr., 1947; E.E., Capitol Radio Engring. Inst., 1963; student, L.I. U., 1961, Indsl. Coll. Armed Forces, 1967-68; postgrad., SUNY at Delhi, 2003. Sr. technician Bklyn. Radio, 1953-55, Budd Stanley, Inc., Long Island City, N.Y., 1955; lead engr. telephone equipment Precision Indsl. Design Newark, 1955-57; project engr., contract adminstr., sales mgr. Leico, Inc., Syossett, N.Y., 1957-65, v.p., 1964-65; mgmt. and engring. cons., 1965-91; ret. Pres. Positive Cons. Inc., Bellmore, N.Y., 1967-86, Lake Luzerne, N.Y., 1986-91, 95—; owner Lake Luzerne Seaplane Base, 1969-2005; tchr. intermediate computer courses Hadley-Luzerne Pub. Libr., Lake Luzerne, 2003—. Mem. small bus. adv. com. to Congressman Thomas J. Downey, 1977-91; mem. small bus. adv. council L.I. Assn. Commerce; founder NCMA L.I. Scholarship Fund; pilot Civil Air Patrol, 1968-74; mem. Town of Lake Luzerne Zoning Bd. of Appeals, 2002-07. Served with AUS. Fellow Nat. Contract Mgmt. Assn. (bd. dirs. L.I. chpt., v.p. 1983-85); mem. IEEE (sr.), Soc. Plastics Engrs., Am. Indsl. Preparedness Assn. (exec. bd. mgmt. div.), ABA (assoc.), Air Force Assn., Capitol Radio Engring. Inst. Alumni (sr.), Nat. Pilots Assn., Aircraft Owners and Pilots Assn., Internat. Platform Assn., Am. Legion, VFW. Inventor torpedo fire control cable and connector for Polaris, high pressure seals for Polaris submarine antennae. Home: 18 Bay Rd PO Box 11 Lake Luzerne NY 12846-0011

GOLDSTEIN, MARC, surgeon, urologist, educator, health facility administrator; b. NYC, Mar. 22, 1948; BS cum laude, CUNY, Bklyn., 1968; MD summa cum laude, SUNY, Bklyn., 1972. Diplomate Nat. Bd. Med. Examiners, Am. Bd. Urology. Surgical intern Columbia-Presbyn. Med. Ctr., NYC, 1972-73, surgical resident, 1973-74; asst. instr., resident, chief resident dept. urology Downstate Med. Ctr. SUNY, Bklyn., 1977-80, asst. prof. urology dept. urology Downstate Med. Ctr., 1980-82; asst. attending surgeon U. Hosp., SUNY Downstate Med. Ctr., and Kings County Hosp. Ctr., Bklyn., 1980-82; fellow-in-residence Population Coun. Rockefeller U., NYC, 1980-82, rsch. assoc., 1980-83; assoc. physician Rockefeller U. Hosp., NYC, 1980-86, vis. assoc. physician, 1986-87; asst. attending surgeon urology NY Hosp., NYC, 1982-88; asst. prof. surgery Cornell U. Med. Ctr., NYC, 1982-88; staff scientist Population Coun. Ctr. Biomed. Rsch., NYC, 1982—2002, sr. scientist, 2002—; dir. divsn. male reproductive medicine and microsurgery, dept. urology NY Hops.-Cornell Med. Ctr., NYC, 1982—; assoc. attending surgeon NY Hosp., NYC, 1988-94; assoc. prof. surgery Cornell U. Med. Coll., NYC, 1988-94; attending surgeon NY Hosp., 1994—; prof. urology Cornell U. Med. Coll., NYC, 1994—, prof. urology and reproductive medicine, 1999—, dir. ctr. for male reproductive medicine and microsurgery, 1982—, co-exec. dir. Cornell Inst. Reproductive Medicine, 1999—; surgeon-in-chief Inst. Reproductive Medicine Cornell Ctr., 2001—. Mem. adv. com. Assn. Voluntary Surg. Contraception, 1984—; participant concept clearance meeting NIH, 1989; mem. editl. bd. Microsugery, 1983—, Jour. Andrology, 1991-93, Andrology Report, 1992—. Author: (with M. Feldberg) The Vasectomy Book: A Complete Guide to Decision Making, 1982, 2nd edit., 1985, (with G. Berger, M. Fuerst) The Couples Guide to Fertility, 1989, 2nd edit., 1995, 3rd edit., 2001, (with Doubleday Co.) Surgery of Male Infertility, 1995, Atlas of the Urology Clinics: Surgery for Male Infertility, 1999; contbr. chpts. to books, articles to profl. jours.; patentee in field. Maj. USAF, 1974—77, maj. USAFR, 1977—90. Honor scholar Downstate Med. Ctr., 1969; Summer Rsch. fellow Downstate Med. Ctr., 1969-70, Ferdinand C. Valentine fellow NY Acad. Medicine, 1980-82; recipient Ferdinand C. Valentine Urology prize NY Acad. Medicine and NY sect. Am. Urological Assn., 1981, Best Movie award Am. Fertility Soc. and Can. Fertility and Andrology Soc., 1986, 96, Excellence in Video Prodn. award Video Urology, 1987, 90, SUNY Coll. Medicine, Downstate Med. Ctr. Master Urology Tchr. award, 1997, Outstanding Dedication and Commitment to Family Bldg. award, 1997, RESOLVE, The Nat. Fertility Assn. and Am. Infertility Assn.; commd. Ky. Col., Commonwealth of Ky., 1988. Fellow ACS; mem. AMA, Am. Soc. Andrology (mem. various coms.), Am. Fertility Soc., Am. Urological Assn. (scholar 1980-82, mem. various coms., Best Movie award vasectomy reversal 2004), NY County Med. Soc., Internat. Microsurgical Soc., Soc. Study Reproduction, Soc. Reproductive Surgeons (fellowship com. 1989—), Soc. for Male Reproduction and Urology (pres. 1996), Alpha Omega Alpha, NY Rd. Runners Club (completed 20 NYC marathons), Brit. Mountaineering Coun. Office: Ctr Male Reproductive Medicine and Microsurgery 525 E 68th St Box 580 New York NY 10021-4885 Home Phone: 212-308-3992; Office Phone: 212-746-5470. Business E-Mail: mgoldst@med.cornell.edu.

GOLDSTEIN, MARCIA LANDWEBER, lawyer; b. Bklyn., Aug. 7, 1952; d. Jacob and Sarah Ann (Danovitz) Landweber; m. Mark Lewis Goldstein, June 3, 1973. AB magna cum laude, Cornell U., 1973, JD cum laude, 1975. Bar: NY 1976, US Dist. Ct. (So. and Ea. dists.) NY, US Ct. Appeals (2nd, 3rd, 5th, 7th and 9th cirs.); cert. mediator, So. Dist. NY. Assoc. Weil, Gotshal & Manges LLP, NYC, 1975-83, ptnr. to mng. ptnr., 1983—, co-chair, bus. fin. & restructuring devel. Adv. bd. Colliers on Bankruptcy, 15th edit., editor (15th edit. revised); vis. lectr. Yale Law Sch., 1986-88; lectr. Columbia Law Sch., Practicing Law Inst. ALI-ABA, Southeastern Bankruptcy Law Inst., NYU bankruptcy workshop; served as mediator for several Chapter 11 cases; trustee Chapter 11; serves on the Law Sch. Adv. Coun.; mem. Cornell Law Sch. Dean's Spl. Leadership Com. Articles editor Cornell Law Review, 1974—75. Named one of The 50 Most Influential Women Lawyers in Am., Nat. Law Jour., 2007. Mem. ABA (com. on creditors' rights, corp. counse. com.), Assn. of Bar of City of NY (chair bankruptcy and reorgn. com.), Nat. Bankruptcy Conf. (chair misc. com.), Am. Coll. Bankruptcy, Internat. Insolvency Inst. Office: Weil Gotshal & Manges LLP 767 5th Ave New York NY 10153 Office Phone: 212-310-8214. Office Fax: 212-310-8007. Business E-Mail: marcia.goldstein@weil.com.*

GOLDSTEIN, MARK KINGSTON LEVIN, information technology executive, researcher; b. Burlington, Vt., Aug. 22, 1941; s. Harold Meyer Levin and Roberta (Butterfield) Goldstein; m. Kyoko Matsubara, Mar. 8, 1984; 1 child, Amanda Kellie. BS in Chemistry, U. Vt., 1964; PhD, U. Miami, Coral Gables, 1971. Pres. IBR, Inc., Coral Gables, Fla., 1970-74; group leader Brookhaven Nat. Lab., Upton, NY, 1974-77; sr. rschr. East-West Ctr., Honolulu, 1977-79; sr. tech. advisor JGC Corp., Tokyo,

1979-81; pres., chmn. bd. Quantum Group, Inc., La Jolla, Calif., 1981—; exec. dir. Magnatek, Inc., Brotas, Brazil, 1982—. Project leader proliferation and waste mgmt. policy study for Pres. Ford's sci. advisor. Fellow NSF, 1964, 1965. Mem.: AAAS, Am. Chem. Soc., Hawaii Yacht Club (Honolulu). Achievements include patents for biomimetic carbon monoxide sensors, carbon monoxide catalyst, fuel cell reform catalyst and sensors; thaser co-generators; supermitters; thermphotovolaics self powered gas appliance; photon control systems; gas safety valve; eyesafe laser radar; photon wedding; fuel cell reformer catalyst; superemissive light pipe. Home: 2248 Del Mar Heights Rd Del Mar CA 92014-3022 Office: Quantum Group Inc 7737 Kenamar Ct San Diego CA 92121-2425 E-mail: mklgoldstein@aol.com.

GOLDSTEIN, MARTIN S., obstetrician, gynecologist, educator; b. NYC, Aug. 21, 1940; MD, SUNY Syracuse, 1966. Diplomate Am. Bd. Ob-Gyn. Intern Bronx Mcpl. Hosp. Ctr., NYC, 1966-67; resident Mt. Sinai Hosp., NYC, 1967-71; ob-gyn NYC, 1971—. Assoc. clin. prof. ob-gyn Mt. Sinai Sch. Medicine, N.Y.C. Fellow Am. Coll. Ob-Gyn; mem. N.Y. Ob-Gyn Soc. Office: 40 E 84th St New York NY 10028-1115 Office Phone: 212-472-6500.

GOLDSTEIN, MARVIN EMANUEL, aerospace scientist; b. Cambridge, Mass., Oct. 11, 1938; s. David and Evelyn (Wilner) G.; m. Priscilla Ann Beresh, July 5, 1965; children: Deborah, Judy. BS in Mech. Engring., Northeastern U., 1961; MS in Mech. Engring., MIT, 1962; PhD in Mech. Engring., U. Mich., 1965. Engr. Arthur D. Little, Inc., Cambridge, 1958-61; rsch. asst. MIT, Cambridge, 1961-63, rsch. assoc., 1965-67; aerospace engr. Lewis Rsch. Ctr., NASA, Cleve., 1967-79, chief scientist, 1980—2004. Adj. prof. math dept. Case Western Res. U., 1998—. Author: Aeroacoustics, 1976; contbr. articles to profl. jours. Recipient Outstanding Alumni award, Northeastern U., 2002, Fluids Engring. award, ASME, 2003. Fellow AIAA (assoc. editor jour. 1977-79, chmn. aeroacoustics tech. com., 1979-81, mem. publs. com. 1980-83, Aeroacoustics award 1983, Pendray award 1983), Am. Phys. Soc. (exec. com. div. fluid dynamics 1991-93, Otto Laporte award in fluid mechanics 1997); mem. Nat. Acad. Engring. (elected). Jewish. Avocations: auto racing, auto restoration. Office: NASA Lewis Rsch Ctr MS 54-3 21000 Brookpark Rd Cleveland OH 44135-3191 Home Phone: 440-365-6745; Office Phone: 216-433-5825. Business E-Mail: marvin.e.goldstein@nasa.gov.

GOLDSTEIN, MARVIN MARK, lawyer; b. Bklyn., Jan. 24, 1944; s. Abraham and Regina (Winkler) G.; m. Linda Ann Sinkoff, Aug. 4, 1969; 1 child, Randal Ian. BS, Cornell U., 1966; JD, Boston U., 1969. Bar: NY 1969, NJ 1972. Corp. labor counsel Gen. Cable Corp., NYC, 1970-72; assoc. Grotta, Oberwager & Glassman, Newark, 1972-76; ptnr. Grotta, Glassman & Hoffman P.A., Roseland, NJ, 1976-99; resident, ptnr. Proskauer Rose LLP, Newark, 1999—. Asst. sec. Hackensack U. Med. Ctr., NJ, 1987-93, mem. exec. com., 1987-96; bd. trustees United Jewish Community Bergen County, NJ, 1984-90; bd. visitors Sch. Law Boston U., 1998-2006. Office: Proskauer Rose LLP 1 Newark Ctr Fl 18 Newark NJ 07102-5211 Home Phone: 201-261-6951; Office Phone: 973-274-3200. E-mail: mmgoldstein@proskauer.com.

GOLDSTEIN, MATTHEW, academic administrator; BA in Stats. and Math., City Coll. CUNY, 1963; PhD, U. Conn., 1970. Asst. prof. math. Polytech. Inst. N.Y., 1971-75; assoc. prof., assoc. provost CUNY, 1976-78, prof. stats., mem. doctoral faculty, 1978-98, pres. Rsch. Found., 1982-90, acting vice chancellor acad. affairs, 1990-91, pres. Bernard M. Baruch Coll., 1991-98, chancellor, 1999—; pres. Adelphi U., 1998-99; mem. commn. leadership devel. Am. Coun. Edn., 1996—; mem. bd. overseers Albert Einstein Sch. Medicine, 1998—; mem. bd. dirs. Lincoln Ctr. Inst. Arts in Edn., 1999—, New Plan Excel Realty Trust, Inc., 2000—07; mem. Jewish Cmty. Relations Coun. of NY, 2000—, United Way of NY, 2002—. Mem. Nasulgc's Commn. of Sci. and Math. Tchr Imperative. Co-author: Discrete Discriminant Analysis, 1978, Intermediate Statistical Methods and Applications, 1983, Multivariate Analysis, 1984; contbr. articles for leading scholarly publs. in math. and stats. Recipient Jewish Nat. Fund Tree Life award, Townsend Harris medal, Liberty award for Disting. Accomplishments in Field Edn., Lower East Side Multicultural Fest., 2001, Leadership in Edn. and Pub. Svc. award Italo-Am. Assn., 2002, Ellis Island medal of honor, 2002, Max Rowe Ednl. Leadership award Am. Friends Open U. Israel, 2003, Pres.'s award NY Found. Arch., 2004, John H. Finley award, 2005, Australian Cross of Honor for Science and Art, 2005, Carnegie Corp. NY Acad. Leadership award, 2007 Fellow NY Acad. Scis., Am. Acad. Arts & Sciences; mem. Golden Key (hon.), Beta Gamma Sigma. Achievements include being the first graduate of City College to lead the nation's most prominent urban public university in 1963. Office: CUNY 535 E 80th St New York NY 10021-0795

GOLDSTEIN, MICHAEL B., lawyer; b. NYC, Sept. 29, 1943; s. Isaac and Betty (Friedman) G.; m. Jinny M. Loewenthal, Dec. 18, 1966; 1 child, Eric Loren. BA in Govt., Cornell U., 1964; JD, NYU, 1967. Bar: N.Y. 1967, Ill. 1974, D.C 1978. Spl. asst. to the dep. mayor Office of Mayor, NYC, 1965-66, asst. city adminstr., dir. univ. rels., 1969-72; dir. N.Y.C. Urban Corps, 1966-69; assoc. vice chancellor for urban and govtl. affairs, assoc. prof. urban sci. U. Ill., Chgo., 1972-78; mem. Dow Lohnes PLLC, Washington, 1978—. Practice leader Higher Edn.; chmn. task force on pub. policy Commn.on Higher Edn. and Adult Learner Am. Coun. on Edn. Contbr. articles to profl. texts and jours. Pres. Nat. Ctr. Pub. Svc. Internship Programs, 1975-77; bd. dirs. Washington Ctr. Internships and Acad. Seminars, 1977—; bd. dirs. and gen. counsel Washington Ballet, 1978—; bd. dirs. Greater Washington Rsch. Ctr., 1982-96, Chgo. Urban Corps, 1972-75, Am. Assoc. Higher Edn., 1998-05; trustee, chmn. acad. affairs com. Fielding Grad. U., 1989-94, 98—; trustee, chmn. fin. com. Mt. Vernon Coll., 1991-96; dir. Am.-Russian Cultural Cooperation Found., 1995—; bd. visitors Mt. Vernon Coll., 1996-98; bd. dirs. Sta. WETA, 1997-99; mem., pres. Friendship Fire Assocs., DC Fire Dept., 1985-, pres., 2004-. Wall St. Jour. Newspaper Fund fellow, 1963, Loeb fellow Harvard U., 1972. Mem. ABA (chmn. edn. law com. 1991-92), D.C. Bar Assn. (vice chair edn. task force 1999—2003), FBA (co-chmn. edn. grants com. 1985-86, 91-92), Nat. Assn. Coll. and Univ. Attys. (mem. ctrl. office com. 1986-88, vice chmn. pvt. bar com. 1989-90, chair continuing legal edn. com. 2001-2004, mem. fin. com. 2004—), Nat. Soc. Internships and Exptl. Edn. (pres. 1972), Am. Assn. Higher Edn. (bd. dirs. 1997—). Democrat. Jewish. Office: Dow Lohnes PLLC 1200 New Hampshire Ave NW Washington DC 20036-6802 Office Phone: 202-776-2569.

GOLDSTEIN, MICHAEL GERALD, lawyer, director; b. St. Louis, Sept. 21, 1946; s. Joseph and Sara G. (Finkelstein) G.; m. Ilene Marcia Ballin, July 19, 1970; children: Stephen Eric, Rebecca Leigh. BA, Tulane U., 1968; JD, U. Mo., 1971; LLM in Taxation, Washington U., 1972. Bar: Mo. 1971, U.S. Dist. Ct. (ea. dist.) Mo. 1972, U.S. Tax Ct. 1972, U.S. Ct. Appeals (8th cir.) 1974, U.S. Supreme Ct. 1976. Atty. Morris A. Shenker, St. Louis, 1972—78; ptnr. Lashly, Caruthers, Baer & Hamel and predecessor, St. Louis, 1978—84, Suelthaus & Kaplan, P.C. and predecessors, St. Louis, 1974—91; ptnr., chmn. dept. tax & estate planning Husch & Eppenberger, 1991—99; pres., CEO 1st Fin. Resources, 1999—2001; sr. v.p. EPS Fin. Solutions Corp., 1999—2000; sr. v.p., gen. counsel The Benefits Group, Inc., 2001—03; pres., COO Benefits Group Worldwide, 2003—05; sr. v.p. and counsel The Newport Group, 2005—. Adj. prof. tax law Washington U. Sch. Law, 1986-97; planning com. Mid-Am. Tax Confs., chmn. ALI/ABA Tax Seminar; lectr. in field. Author: BNA Tax Mgmt. Portfolios, ABA The Insurance Counselor Books; contbr. articles to profl. jours. Bd. dirs. Jewish Family and Children's Svc. St. Louis, 1980—, pres., 1986-88; bd. dirs. Jewish Fedn. of St. Louis; trustee United Hebrew Temple, 1986-88; grad. Jewish Fedn. St. Louis Leadership Devel. Coun.; co-chmn. lawyers divsn. Jewish Fedn. St. Louis Campaign, 1981-82, Leadership St. Louis, 1988-89. Capt. USAR, 1970-78. Capt. USAR, 1970—78. Recipient Kenneth Black Jr. Jour. Author award, Jour. Fin. Svc. Profl., 2001. Fellow Am. Bar Found., Am. Coll. Tax Counsel, Am. Coll. Trust and Estate Counsel; mem. ABA (chmn. tax seminar, group editor newsletter taxation sect. 1989-97, books editor real property, probate and trust sects. 1998—), Am. Law Inst., Mo. Bar Assn., Bar Assn. Met. St. Louis, St. Louis County Bar Assn. Office: 2011 Yacht Mischief Newport Beach CA 92660-6713 Office Phone: 949-760-9098. Business E-Mail: mgoldstein@newportgroup.com.

GOLDSTEIN, MICHAEL I., ecologist; children: Jacob, Ella, Benjamin. BS, Colo. State U., Fort Collins, 1989; MS, Clemson U., SC, 1997; PhD, Tex. A&M U., College Station, 2000. Cert. mediation USDA Forest Svc. and State of Ga., 2004. Wildlife progam mgr. Mendocino Redwood Co., Fort Bragg, Calif., 2000—02; wildlife ecologist Chugach Nat. Forest, Anchorage, 2002—04; regional wildlife ecologist USDA Forest Svc., Juneau, Alaska, 2004—. Contbr. chapters to books, articles to profl. jours. Mem. steering com. Project Playground, Juneau, 2005—07, chair materials com., build site coord.; bd. mem., v.p. Juneau Montessori Sch., 2004—; bd. mem., web chair Congregation Sukkat Shalom, Juneau, 2005—. Mem.: The Wildlife Soc. (pres. NW sect. 2004—07), Raptor Rsch. Found. (assoc. editor 2003—).

GOLDSTEIN, MORRIS, retired consumer products company executive; b. Pitts., Feb. 2, 1945; s. Irving and Clara (Caplan) G.; m. Diane Donna Davis, Aug. 21, 1966 (div. Nov. 1985); children: Jonathan, Julie; m. Kathy Evelyn Niemeier, July 7, 1990. BS, Carnegie Inst. Tech., 1967; MBA, U. Pa., 1979. Sales rep. computer divsn. RCA, Cherry Hill, NJ, 1968-70; sales mgr. Sedgwick Printout Sys., Princeton, NJ, 1970-76, pres., 1976-80; v.p. Courier-Jour. Louisville Times, 1980-81; mgr. bus. devel. Ziff-Davis Pub., NYC, 1982-2000; pres. Information Access Corp. divsn., Foster City, Calif., 1982-2000; pres., COO Imagination Network Inc., Oakhurst, Calif., 1994; sr. v.p. Ziff-Davis Pub., Foster City, Calif., 1994; CEO Info. Access Co., A Thomson Corp. Co., Foster City, Calif., 1995-96, Thomson Tech. Ventures, San Mateo, Calif., 1997; pres., CEO Alliance Gaming Inc, Las Vegas, Nev., 1997-99; pres. entertainment bus. divsn. InnoVentry LLC, Las Vegas, 1999-2000; ret., 2000; exec. v.p. Global Cash Access, Las Vegas, 2001—03; prin., owner Nev. Slots and Supplies. Founder Nev. Slots and Supplies, Las Vegas, 2002. Dep mayor Mt. Laurel Twp., N.J., 1974-78. Home: 3581 E Maule Ave Las Vegas NV 89120-2918 Office: Nevada Slots and Supplies 2245 N Green Valley Pkwy Ste 283 Henderson NV 89120 Office Phone: 702-596-8609.

GOLDSTEIN, MURRAY, medical epidemiologist and research administrator; b. NYC, Oct. 13, 1925; s. Israel and Yetta (Zeigen) G.; m. Sue Mary Michael, June 13, 1957; children: Patricia Sue Robertson, Barbara Jean Warner. BA, NYU, 1947; DO, Des Moines U., 1950; MPH, U. Calif., 1959; DSc (hon.), Kirksville Coll. Osteo. Medicine, 1970, U. New Eng., 1984, Ohio U., 1986, U. Osteo. Medicine and Health Scis., 1990, Mich. State U., 2000; LLD (hon.), NY Inst. Tech., 1982; Dr. honoris causa, Med. Univ. Pecs, Hungary, 1985; LHD (hon.), Coll. Osteo. Medicine Pacific, 1988; Dr. honoris causa, Med. Sch. U. Lund, Sweden, 1994. Diplomate Am. Osteo. Bd. Preventive Medicine (sec.-treas. 1987-88, vice chmn. 1988-92). Rotating intern Still Coll. Osteo. Hosp., Des Moines, 1950-51, resident internal medicine, 1951-53; commd. corps USPHS, 1953, advanced through grades to asst. surgeon gen., 1980, ret., 1993; asst. to chief, then asst. chief, grants and tng. br., Nat. Heart Inst. NIH, Bethesda, Md., 1953-58, dir. epidemiology and biometry tng. grant program, divsn. rsch. grants, 1956-58, asst. chief rsch. grants rev. br., divsn. rsch. grants, 1959-60; exec. sec. joint coun. subcom. cerebrovascular disease Nat. Inst. Neurol. Diseases and Stroke and Nat. Heart and Lung Inst., NIH, Bethesda, Md., 1961-67, 69-75; dir. extramural programs Nat. Inst. Neurol. and Communicative Disorders and Stroke, NIH, Bethesda, Md., 1961-76, dir. stroke and trauma program, 1976-78, dep. dir., 1978-81, acting dir., 1981-82, dir., 1982-93; pub. health trainee epidemiology Calif. State Dept. Pub. Health, Berkeley, 1958, acting chief sect. virus diseases ctrl. nervous system, Bur. Acute Communicable Disease, 1958; bd. dirs. United Cerebral Palsy Rsch. and Edn. Found., Washington, 1972-93, 2005—, med. dir., COO, 1993—2005, chmn. sci. adv. coun., 2005—; clin. prof. neurol. medicine NY Coll. Osteo. Medicine, 1977—; sr. lectr. dept. neurology Uniformed Svcs. U. Health Scis., 1986—; osteo. pioneer Des Moines U., 2000; chair Middle East Rsch. Cerebral Palsy Collaborative Project State Dept., 2005—. Bd. dirs. Nat. Stroke Assn., Burke Rsch. Inst., Robarts Rsch. Inst., Soc. Supranuclear Palsy; adj. prof. pub. health Nova-Southeastern U., 1995—; chmn. Commd. Corps Adv. Com. to NIH dir., 1990-93, WHO Task Force on stroke and other vascular cerebral disorders, 1986-89; dir. WHO Neurosci. Collaborating Ctr., Bethesda, 1981-93; liaison, mem. sci. adv. bd. Kent Waldrep Nat. Paralysis Found., 1989-94; vis. prof. med. rsch. Semmelweis Med. U., Budapest, Hungary, 1975; vis. sci. sect. neurology Mayo Clinic and grad. sch., Rochester, Minn., 1967-68; vis. scholar Henry Ford Hosp., 1979-80; v.p. Eisenhower Inst. Stroke Rsch., 1975-88; cons. bur. rsch. Am. Osteo. Assn., 1990-99; mem. nat. adv. coun. Nat. Ctr. Complimentary and Alternative Medicine/NIH, 2000-06; pres. Acad. Medicine, Washington, DC, 2004-06; mem. nat. adv. bd. rehab. rsch. NICHD/NIH, 2004—; chmn. UCP Sci. Adv. Coun., 2005—; chmn. MERC Sci. Adv. Coun. on CP, 2006—; lectr., cons. in field. Assoc. editor Stroke: A Journal of Cerebral Circulation, 1976-91, consulting editor, 1992—; mem. editl. bd. Osteo. Annals, 1973-85, 87-88, Internat. Jour. Neurology, 1980-04, Jour. Neuroepidemiology, 1981-90, Hosp. and Community Psychiatry, 1980—, Alzheimer Disease: An Internat. Jour., 1985-93, Cerebralvascular and Brain Metabolism Revs., 1985-93; contbr. articles to profl. jours. Bd. dirs. Bapt. Home for Children and Adults, 1999-2001. With U.S. Army, 1943-45. Decorated DSM, Silver Star, Purple Heart; recipient USPHS Disting. Svc. medal with oak leaf cluster, Surgeon Gen.'s Exemplary Svc. medal, Surgeon Gen.'s medallion, Founders Day medal U. Osteo. Medicine and Health Scis., 1983, Patenge Pub. Svc. medal Mich. State U., 1987, Marjorie Guthrie award The Huntington's Disease Soc. Am., 1988, Burke award Buke Found., 1988, Spl. Leadership award United Cerebral Palsy Rsch. & Ednl. Found., 1989, Phillips Pubs. Svc. medal Ohio U., 1990, others; named Pioneer in Osteo. Medicine, Des Moines U., 2000. Fellow: Am. Acad. Neurology (mem. long range planning com. 1972—75, mem. manpower com. 1979—85, mem. neurology in govtl. svcs. and insts. com. 1979—85, chmn. 1981—83, 1981—83, mem. internat. affairs com. 1981—90, mem. com. govt. rels. 1983—85, ANA-AAN del. to World Fedn. Neurology 1983—85, mem. AAN com. on pub. comm. and legislation 1983—85, mem. ad hoc com. for soc. neurology liaison 1987—89, sr. advisor uniformed svcs. orgn. neurologists com. 1987—93, chmn. 1993—95, bd. dirs. 1993—95); mem.: Soc. Supranuclear Palsy (bd. dirs. 2006—), Acad. of Medicine of Washington (pres. 2004—06), NIH Alumni Assn. (v.p. bd. dirs. 1999—2004), Am. Acad. Cerebral Palsy and Devel. Medicine (liaison mem., bd. dirs. 1993—2005), United Cerebral Palsy Assn. (interim dir. 1998). Avocations: gardening, golf, swimming. Home: 6210 Swords Way Bethesda MD 20817-3349 Personal E-mail: goldstein5@verizon.net. Business E-Mail: mgoldstein@ucp.org.

GOLDSTEIN, NATHAN, artist, writer; b. Chgo., Mar. 26, 1927; s. Joseph and Sarah (Kommisarov) G.; m. divorced; 1 child, Sarah; m. Harriet Joan Fishman; 1 child, Jessica. MFA, Sch. of Art Inst. Chgo., 1952. Instr. in drawing and painting New Eng. Sch. Art, Boston, 1957-61; inst. De Cordova Mus. Sch., Lincoln, Mass., 1959-63; asst. prof. Sch. Visual Arts Boston U., 1962-63, assoc. prof., 1973-77; instr. Northeastern U., Boston, 1973-75; assoc. prof. Mount Ida Coll., Newton, Mass., 1966-71; prof., chmn. Found. Program Art Inst. Boston, Lesley U., 1972—2001. Author: The Art of Responsive Drawing, 6th edit., 2005, Figure Drawing: The Structure, Anatomy, and Expressive Design of Human Form, 6th edit., 2005, A Drawing Handbook: Themes, Tools, and Techniques, 1986, Painting: Visual and Technical Fundamentals, 1979, 100 American and European Drawings: A Portfolio, 1982, Design and Composition, 1989; co-author: (with Harriet Fishman) Drawing To See, 2004. With USNR, 1945-47. Inducted into Nat. Acad. Design, 1996. Office: Art Inst Boston 700 Beacon St Boston MA 02215-2598 Personal E-mail: ngstein222@comcast.net.

GOLDSTEIN, SIR NORMAN, dermatologist; b. Bklyn., July 14, 1934; s. Joseph H. and Bertha (Docteroff) Goldstein; m. Ramsay Goldstein, Feb. 14, 1980; children: Richard, Heidi. BA, Columbia Coll., 1955; MD, SUNY, 1959. Intern Maimonides Hosp., NYC, 1959—60; resident Skin and Cancer Hosp., 1960—61, Bellevue Hosp., 1961—62, N.Y.U. Postgrad. Ctr., 1962—63; ptnr. Honolulu Med. Group, 1967—72; pvt. practice dermatology Honolulu, 1972—; clin. prof. dermatology U. Hawaii Sch. Medicine, 1973—. Bd. dir. Pacific Laser, Skin Cancer Found.; trustee Dermatol. Found., 1979—82; pres. Hawaii Med. Libr., 1987. Editor (emeritus): Hawaii Med. Jour.; contbr. articles to profl. jours. Pres. Hawaii Theater Ctr., 1985—89; mem. Oahu Heritage Council, 1986—94, Hawaii Govs. Blue Ribbon Panel on Living and Dying with Dignity. With US Army, 1960—67. Named Physician of Yr., Hawaii Med. Assn., 1993, 2003, Physcians Adv. Coun., 2003, Businessman of Yr., Bus. Adv. Coun., 2003; recipient Henry Silver award, Dermatol. Soc. Greater N.Y., 1963, Husik award, NYU, 1963, Spl. award, Acad. Dermatologia Hawaiiana, 1971, Outstanding Scientific Exhibit award, Calif. Med. Assn., 1979, Spl. Exhibit award, Am. Urologic Assn., 1980, Svc. to Hawaii's Youth award, Adult Friends for Youth, 1991, Nat. Cosmetic Tattoo Assn. award, 1993, Cmty. Svc. award, Am. Acad. Dermatology, 1993, Nat. Leadership award and hon., Physians Adv. Bd., Washington, 2003. Fellow: ACP (Laureate award 2005, Laureate award 2005), Royal Soc. Medicine, Am. Soc. Lasers Medicine & Surgery, Am. Acad. Dermatology (Silver award 1972); mem.: AAAS, Internat. Soc. Dermatology (bd. dirs.), Hawaii Public Health Assn., Hawaii Dermatol. Soc. (sec.-pres.), Am. Coll. Sports Medicine, Honolulu County Med. Soc. (gov.), Pacific Health Research Inst., Pacific Dermatol. Assn., Hawaii State Med. Assn. (mem. public affairs com.), Am. Soc. Preventive Oncology, Internat. Soc. Dermatol. Surgery, Am. Coll. Cryosurgery, Physicians Exchange of Hawaii (bd. dir.), Am. Med. Writers Assn., Am. Soc. Micropigmentation Surgery, Internat. Soc. Cryosurgery, Am. Soc. Photobiology, Soc. Investigative Dermatologists, Internat. Soc. Tropical Dermatologists (Hist. and Culture award), C. of C., Pacific Telecom Council, Soc. for Computer Medicine, Pacific and Asian Affairs Council, Health Sci. Communication Assn., Am. Assn. for Med. Systems and Info., Biol. Photog. Assn., Assn. Hawaii Artists, Chancellor's Club, Plaza Club, Outrigger Canoe Club (pres. bd. dir. 1990—92), Ancient Gaelic Nobility Soc. (named Knight of the Niadh Nask 1995), Hemlock Soc. USA (mem. bd.), Rotary, Preservation Action, Nat. Wildlife Fedn., Japan Am. Soc. Hawaii (bd. dir.), Navy League. Office: Tan Sing Bldg 1128 Smith St Honolulu HI 96817-5197 also: Puuone Plz 1063 E Main St C-225 Wailuku HI 96793 Office Phone: 808-538-7044. Personal E-mail: skinyouluv@aol.com.

GOLDSTEIN, NORMAN RAY, international trading company executive, consultant; b. Chgo., Nov. 20, 1944; s. Max and Rose (Weiner) G.; m. Bonnie A. Brod, Aug. 31, 1969; children: Russell, Matthew, Jamie. AA, Wright Jr. Coll., 1965; BS in Fin., No. Ill. U., DeKalb, 1967; MS in Acctg. cum laude, Roosevelt U., 1986. Cert. treasury profl., Assn. Fin. Profls. Gen. bus. mgr. Greenstreet Corp., Whiting, Ind., 1967; wholesale credit mgr. Atlantic Richfield Co., Chgo., 1968-74; v.p. fin., treas. Barton Inc. (Barton Brands, Ltd.), Chgo., 1974-96; chmn., CEO Gold Internat., 1996—. Spl. master U.S. Dist. Ct., 1998; chmn. ABC Fin. Comm. Forum, Chgo., 1987-88; v.p. Consort Corp., Chgo., 1971-80; spl. master U.S. Dist. Ct., 1998; adj. prof. fin. No. Ill. U., 2000-, mem. adv. bd. dept. fin., 2003-; instr. Ctr. Profl. Edn., 1997-2007; bd. mgrs. No. Ill. Angels LLC, 2004-07; spkr. in field. Contbg. author: Handbook of Cash Flow and Treasury Management, 1987; contbr. articles to profl. publs. Bd. dirs. Maine Twp. Jewish Congregation Shaare Emet, Des Plaines, 1986—, pres. 1989-91. Named Outstanding Credit Exec. of Yr., Nat. Assn. Credit Mgmt., 1987, Disting. Alumnus Coll. Bus. No. Ill. U., 1998, Outstanding Alumnus Dept. Fin., No. Ill. U., 2001. Fellow Nat. Inst. Credit; mem. Fin. Mgrs. Assn. Chgo. (treas. 1991-92), Treasury Mgmt. Assn. Chgo. (chmn. ednl. scholarship com. 1995-99, chmn. Windy City Summit Treasury Conf. 1999-2000, 2003-04, 2007—, bd. dirs. 2003—), Distillers Imports and Vintners (chmn. 1980-82), N.Y. Credit and Fin. Mgmt. Assn., Chgo. Midwest Credit Mgmt. Assn. (bd. dirs. 1984-87), Dept. Fin. Advisors Bd. No. Ill. U 2003-, No. Ill. U. Exec. Club (bd. dirs., v.p. 2003—).

GOLDSTEIN, PAUL, lawyer, educator; b. Mount Vernon, NY, Jan. 14, 1943; s. Martin and Nan Goldstein; m. Jan Thompson, Aug. 28, 1977. BA, Brandeis U., 1964; LLB Columbia U., 1967. Bar: NY 1968, Calif. 1978. Asst. prof. law SUNY-Buffalo, 1967-69, assoc. prof., 1969-71, prof., 1972-75; vis. assoc. prof. Stanford U., Calif., 1972-73, prof. law Calif., 1975—, Stella W. and Ira S. Lillick prof. law Calif., 1985—; of counsel Morrison and Foerster, San Francisco, 1988—. Author: Changing the American Schoolbook--Law, Politics and Technology, 1978, Real Estate Transactions--Cases and Materials on Land Transfer, Development and Finance, 1980, 3d edit. (with G. Korngold), 1993, Real Property, 1984, Copyright, 4 vols., 3d edit., 2005, Copyright, Patent, Trademark and Related State Doctrines--Cases and Materials on the Law of Intellectual Property, revised 5th edit., 2002, Copyright's Highway: From Gutenberg to the Celestial Jukebox, 1995, revised edit., 2003, International Copyright Law, 2001, International Intellectual Property Law, 2001, Errors and Omissions, 2006. Mem. Assn. Litteraire et Artistique Internationale, Copyright Soc. U.S.A. Office: Stanford U Law Sch Nathan Abbott Way Stanford CA 94305 Office Phone: 650-723-0313. E-mail: paulgold@stanford.edu.

GOLDSTEIN, PETER DOBKIN, lawyer; b. Bklyn., Apr. 12, 1953; s. Louis B. and Martha (Dobkin) G.; m. Marge W. Lilienthal, Aug. 28, 1982; children: Jenna Lilienthal, Daniel Reid. BA cum laude, Brandeis U., 1974; MS, Harvard U., 1977; JD magna cum laude, Boston Coll., 1980. Bar: Conn. 1980, N.Y. 1981, U.S. Dist. Ct. Conn. 1981, U.S. Dist. Ct. (so. and ea. dists.) N.Y. 1983, U.S. Ct. Appeals (2d cir.) 1982, U.S. Ct. Appeals (3d cir.) 1990, U.S. Supreme Ct. 1990. Assoc. Cummings & Lockwood, Stamford, Conn., 1980-82, Bond and Camhi, NYC, 1982-84; ptnr. Dorsey & Whitney, NYC, 1988-92; br. chief divsn. enforcement SEC, NYC, 1992-97; dep. gen. counsel Gabelli Asset Mgmt. Inc., Rye, 1997-2000; v.p. Goldman Sachs Asset Mgmt., NYC, 2000—04; dir. regulatory affairs Gabelli Asset Mgmt. Inc., 2004—. Editor Am. Jour. Law and Medicine, 1979-80. Office: One Corp Ctr Rye NY 10580 Office Phone: 941-921-7732. E-mail: pgoldstein@gabelli.com.

GOLDSTEIN, ROBERT DAVID, law educator; b. 1947; BA, Harvard U., 1969, MEd, 1976, JD, 1977. Bar: Mass. 1977, D.C. 1979. Law clk. to Hon. Raymond Pettine U.D. Dist. Ct. Providence, R.I., 1977-78; assoc. Foley, Hoag & Eliot, Boston and D.C., 1978-83; acting prof. UCLA, 1983-89, prof. law, 1989—, assoc. dean LA, 1998—2002, spl. asst. to vice chancellor. Author: Mother-Love and Abortion: A Legal Interpretation 1988, Child Abuse and Neglect: Cases and Materials 1999. Office: UCLA Sch Law Box 951476 Los Angeles CA 90095-1476 Office Phone: 310-825-4841. Business E-Mail: goldstei@law.ucla.edu.

GOLDSTEIN, SANDRA CARA, lawyer; b. Bklyn., May 12, 1964; BA, Barnard Coll., 1984; JD, NYU, 1987. Bar: N.Y. 1988. Assoc. Cravath Swaine and Moore LLP, NYC, 1987—94, ptnr., 1994—, mng. ptnr. litig.,

2005—. Office: Cravath Swaine & Moore LLP Worldwide Plz 825 8th Ave Fl 38 New York NY 10019-7475 Office Phone: 212-474-1000. Office Fax: 212-474-3700. Business E-Mail: sgoldstein@cravath.com.

GOLDSTEIN, SIDNEY, sociologist, educator, demographer; b. New London, Conn., Aug. 4, 1927; s. Max and Bella (Hoffman) G.; m. Alice Dreifuss, June 21, 1953; children: Beth Leah, David Louis, Brenda Ruth. BA, U. Conn., 1949, MA, 1951; PhD, U. Pa., 1953. Instr. sociology U. Pa., 1953-55; mem. faculty Brown U., Providence, 1955—, prof. sociology, 1960—, George Hazard Crooker Univ. prof., 1977—, prof. emeritus, 1993—, rsch. prof. population studies, 1997—, chmn. dept. sociology and anthropology, 1963-70, dir. Population Studies & Tng. Ctr., 1965-89. Demographic advisor Chulalongkorn U., Bangkok, 1968-69; cons. UN Econ. and Social Commn. for Asia and Pacific, 1971-72, 77-82, Nat. Ctr. Health Stats., 1970-77, Internat. Program Population Analysis, Smithsonian Instn., 1971-76; mem. U.S. Bur. Census Adv. Com., 1965-71, Rand Corp., 1975-83; nat. com. rsch. 1980 census Social Sci. Rsch. Coun., 1981-88; mem. governing bur. Com. Internat. Cooperation in Nat. Rsch. Demography, 1981-98, treas., 1994-98; com. on population Nat. Rsch. Coun., Nat. Acad. Scis., 1983-87; chmn. nat. tech. adv. com. Jewish population studies Coun. Jewish Fedns., 1984-95; co-chmn. internat. sci. com. 1990 census surveys world Jewry, Jerusalem, 1988-92 Author: Patterns of Mobility, 1910-1950, 1958, Consumption Patterns of the Aged, 1960, The Norristown Study: An Experiment in Interdisciplinary Research Training, 1961, (with K.B. Mayer) The First Two Years: Problems of Small Business Growth and Survival, 1961, Migration and Economic Development in Rhode Island, 1958, (with Calvin Goldscheider) Jewish Americans, 1968, Urbanization in Thailand, 1947-1960, 1970, The Demography of Bangkok, 1972, (with V. Prachuabmoh and A. Goldstein) Urban-Rural Migration Differentials in Thailand, 1974, (with A. Speare and W. Frey) Residential Mobility, Migration and Metropolitan Change, 1975, Circulation in the Context of Total Mobility in Southeast Asia, 1978; editor: (with D.F. Sly) Basic Data Needed for the Study of Urbanization, 1975, The Measurement of Urbanization and the Projection of Urban Population, 1975, Patterns of Urbanization: Comparative Country Studies, 1977, (with wife) A Test of the Potential Use of Mulltiplicity in Research on Population Movement, 1979, Population Mobility in the People's Republic of China, 1985, Surveys of Migration in Developing Countries: A Methodological Review, 1981, Migration and Fertility in Peninsular Malaysia, 1983, Urbanization in China, 1985, (with wife) Migration in Thailand: A Twenty-Five Year Review, 1986, (with C. Goldscheider) The Jewish Community of Rhode Island: A Social and Demographic Survey, 1988, Comparative Migration Patterns to Shanghai and Bangkok, 1989, Urbanization in China, 1982-1987, The Role of Migration and Reclassification, 1990, (with wife and Zai Liang) Migration, Gender, and Labor Force in Hubei Province, 1985-90, (with wife) Permanent and Temporary Migration Differentials in China, 1991, Demographic Issues and Data Needs for Mega-City Research, 1994, The Impact of Temporary Migration on Urban Places, 1993, (with R. Neupert) Urbanization and Population Redistribution in Mongolia, 1994, (with wife) Jews on the Move, 1996, (with Gang Liu) Migrant-Non Migrant Fertility in Anhui China, 1996, (with Dang Anh) Internal Migration and Development in Vietnam, 1997, (with wife and Michael White) Migration Fertility and State Policy in Hubei Province, China, 1997, (with wife) Lithuanian Jewry, 1993: A Demographic and Sociocultural Profile, 1997, (with wife) Conservative Jewry in the United States: A Sociodemographic Profile, 1998,(with wife and Yanyi Djamba) Permanent and Temporary Migration During Periods of Economic Change: Vietnam and China Compared, 1999, (with Uzi Rebhun) Changes in the Geographic Dispersion and Mobility of American Jews 1990-2001, 2006. Bd. dirs. Jewish Fedn. R.I., 1964-68, 78-82, 85—, area v.p., 1997-2000; bd. dirs. Bur. Jewish Edn., Providence, 1959-82, 94—, bd. dirs.; bd. dirs. Coun. Jewish Fedns., 1987-94 Recipient Disting. Svc. medal Chilalongkorn U., 1969, Disting. Svc. medal Mahidol U., 1992, Disting. Leadership award Coun. Jewish. Fedns., 1992, Tribute award, 1998, Lifetime Achievement award Assn. Social Sci. Study of Jewry, 1992, sr. rsch. award CSC-PRC , NAS, 1983, Jewish Cultural Achievement award Nat. Found. Jewish Culture, 2002, Laureate award Internat. Union for Sci. Study of Population, 2005, Tribute award Builders Jewish Edn., Bur. Jewish Edn., RI, 2007; Harrison fellow, 1953, Social Sci. Rsch. Coun. fellow, 1961-62, Guggenheom fellow, 1961-63, Rsch. fellow Inst. Contemporary Jewry, Hebrew U. Jerusalem, 1969—, sr. fellow East-West Population Inst., Honolulu, 1976, 82, 90, fellow Inst. Advanced Study Ind. U., 1995, vis. fellow Australian Nat. U., Canberra, 1977; scholar-in-residence Rockefeller Study Ctr., Bellagio, 1990, sr. vis. scholar Hebrew U., 1990. Mem. Am. Sociol. Assn., Population Assn. Am. (pres. 1975-76), Assn. Jewish Demography and Stats. (dir.), Internat. Union Sci. Study Population (chair com. urbanization and population distbn. 1971-76), Assn. Sociol. Study Jewry, Phi Beta Kappa. Home: 95 Kiwanee Rd Warwick RI 02888-4040 Office: Brown U Sociology Dept Box 1916 Providence RI 02912-9079 Business E-Mail: sidney_goldstein@brown.edu.

GOLDSTEIN, SIDNEY, pharmacist; b. Phila., Mar. 27, 1932; s. Israel and Gertrude (Stein) G.; m. Janice Levy, June 19, 1955; children: Rhonda, David, Nina. BSc in Pharmacy, Phila. Coll. Pharmacy & Sci., 1954, MSc in Pharmacy, 1955, DSc in Pharmacy, 1958. Cardiovascular unit head Eaton Labs, Norwich, NY, 1958—59; anti-inflammatory unit head Lederle Labs, Pearl River, NY, 1959-61; with Merrell Dow Rsch. Inst., Cin., 1961-93; v.p. global pharm. and analytical scis. Marion Merrell Dow Inc., Kansas City, Mo., 1991-93; v.p. sci. and tech. Duramed Pharm., Inc., Cin., 1994-98, v.p. bus. devel., sci. and tech., 1998—2002; chief sci. officer Prasco, Cin., 2002—. Adj. assoc. prof. U. Cin. Coll. Pharmacy, 1984-98, dean's adv. coun., 1998—; lectr. pharmacology Phila. Coll. Pharmacy, 1967-70, chair PQRI-drug product tech. com., 1997-2004, mem. steering com., 2003-05; mem. So. Ohio Life Sci. Task Force, 1999-2001, GPhA sci. com., 2001—; mem. tech. validation adv. bd. Cinn. Children's Hosp., 2003—. Contbr. articles to profl. jours. Bd. trustees Glen Manor Home for Aged, Cin., 1983-89. Recipient Award for Nicoderm, R&D Mag., 1992. Mem. Am. Assn. Pharm. Scientists, Am. Soc. Clin. Pharmacology and Therapeutics, Soc. Exptl. Biology and Medicine, Am. Soc. Pharmacology and Exptl. Therapeutics, B'nai B'rith (chpt. v.p. 1978). Home: 1125 Fort View Pl Cincinnati OH 45202-1713 Office: Prasco 7155 Kemper Rd Cincinnati OH 45249 Home Phone: 513-651-5575; Office Phone: 513-618-3333. E-mail: s.goldstein@prasco.com.

GOLDSTEIN, STANLEY PHILIP, engineering educator; b. Bklyn., Feb. 3, 1923; s. Max and Rose (Ahrenstein) G.; m. Wanda Rouse, June 6, 1949; children— Bruce, Richard. BS, U. Okla., 1949; MS, NYU, 1956; PhD in Astronautics, Poly. Inst. Bklyn., 1969. Engr. Vapor Recovery Systems Corp., Compton, Calif., 1950-52; project engr. Alderson Research Labs., NYC, 1952-54; mem. faculty Hofstra U., Hempstead, NY, 1954—, prof. engring., 1957-84, prof. emeritus, 1984—, chmn. engring. sci. dept., 1956-68, 70-72, 80-83, dir. acad. computer center, 1970-72; assoc. dean Hofstra U. (Coll. Arts and Scis.), 1973-74, 77, assoc. provost for planning, budgeting and instl. research, 1974-76. Pres. Techmark Enterprises, Inc.; Alcorn Combustion Co., N.Y.C. Transit Authority, Hofstra Internat. Trade & Devel. Corp.; dir. Collegiate Sci. and Tech. Entry Program Hofstra U., 1987-89 Served to 1st lt. USAAF, 1942-45, ETO. Decorated DFC, Air medal with four oak leaf clusters, French Normandy medal. Mem. Sigma Xi. Home: 18 Millers Ln Kingston NY 12401-4426 Office: Hofstra U Engring Dept Hempstead NY 11550 Personal E-mail: stanwand@aol.com.

GOLDSTEIN, STEVEN, lawyer; b. St. Louis, Sept. 8, 1950; s. Alexander Julius and Dorothy Lea (Matier) G.; m. Laura Lou Staley, July 20, 1980. BS in Speech, Northwestern U., Evanston, Ill., 1972; JD, U. Mich., 1975. Bar: Mo. 1975. Prin. Goldstein & Pressman, P.C., St. Louis, 1993—. Mem. ABA, Mo. Bar Assn. (chmn. bankruptcy com. 1983-85), Bar Assn. of Met. St. Louis. Home: 712 Swarthmore Ln Saint Louis MO 63130-3618 Office: Goldstein & Pressman PC 121 Hunter Ave Ste 101 Saint Louis MO 63124-2082 Office Phone: 314-727-1717. Business E-Mail: stg@goldsteinpressman.com.

GOLDSTEIN, STEVEN ALAN, medical and engineering educator; b. Reading, Pa., Sept. 15, 1954; m. Nancy Ellen Gehr, Aug. 22, 1976; children: Aaron Michael, Jonathan David. BS in Mech. Engring., Tufts U., 1976; MS in Bioengring., U. Mich., 1977, PhD in Bioengring, 1981. Rsch. investigator dept. surgery U. Mich., Ann Arbor, 1981-83, asst. prof. surgery, 1983-88, assoc. prof. surgery, 1988-92, prof. surgery, 1992—, prof. mech. engring., applied mechanics and biomedical engring., assoc. dean rsch. and grad. studies, Med. Sch., Henry Ruppenthal Family prof. orthopaedic surgery and bioengineering, dir. Ctr. for Biomedical Engring. Rsch., dir. Orthopaedic Rsch. Labs. Co-dir. orthopaedic biomechanics lab. U. Mich., 1981-82, dir. orthopaedic rsch. labs. U. Mich., 1982—; prof. mech. engring. and applied mechanics, 1992—, mem. faculty bioengring. program, 1982-96, prof. biomed. engring., 1996—, interim chmn., 1985-89, rsch. scientist Inst. Gerontology, 1993—, asst. dean rsch. & grad. studies U. Mich. Med. Sch., 1993-98, assoc. dean, 1999—; rsch. asst. bioengring. ctr. Tufts New England Med. Ctr., 1974-76; mem. calcium homeostasis adv. group NASA, 1987-89; cons. Libbey-Owens Ill., Gen. Tire & Rubber, Upjohn, Ethyl Corp., Norwich Eaton, KMS Fusion, Whitby Pharmaceuticals, Norian Corp., Genetics Inst., Therics Inc., Osteo Biologics Inc., Matrigin Inc.; chair NIH study sect. on orthopaedics and musculoskeletal diseases, 1993-95. Author: Advances in Engineering, 1991; author (with others) Biomechanics of Diathrodial Joints, 1990, Molecular Biology of the Cardiovascular System, 1991, Surgery: Scientific Principles and Practice, 1993, Limb Development and Regeneration, 1993, Accidental Injury: Biomechanics and Prevention, 1993; reviewer Math. Bioscis., 1982—, Annals of Biomed. Engring., 1983—, Clin. Orthopaedics and Related Rsch., 1983—, Jour. Rehab. Rsch. and Devel., 1987—; reviewer Jour. Biomechanics, 1982—, editorial cons., 1992—; reviewer Jour. Biomech. Engring., 1982—, assoc. editor, 1991-97; reviewer Jour. Orthopaedic Rsch., 1984—, mem. bd. assoc. editors , 1992—; reviewer Jour. Bone and Joint Surgery, 1987—, mem. bd. assoc. editors for rsch., 1989—; reviewer, mem. study section NIH, NSF, NASA, Nat. Inst. Occupational Health & Safety, 1983—; contbr. more than 100 articles to profl. jours. Recipient Young Rsch. Investigator award 3M Corp., 1984, Nicolas Andre award Assn. Bone & Joint Surgeons, 1987-88. Mem. NAE, ASME (chair program com. 1989-92, sec.-elect 1993, exec. com. bioengring. divsn. 1989—, chair bioengring. divsn. 1995-96, Y.C. Fung Young Investigator award 1987), Am. Soc. Biomechanics (exec. bd. 1984-85), Am. Acad. Orthopaedic Surgeons (com. biomed. engring. 1991—, Kappa Delta award 1989-90), Orthopaedic Rsch. Soc. (adj. program com. 1990-91, program com. 1992, sec. 1997—), Biomed. Engring. Soc., Engring. Soc. Detroit (Young Engr. of Yr. award 1987), The Knee Soc. Achievements include patents (with other) for Intracone Reamer, Instacone Prosthetic Surface, Flexible Connecting Shaft for Intramedullary Reamer, Tissue Pressure Measurement Transducer System, Continuous Flow Tissue Pressure Measurement Transducer System, Prosthesis Interface Surface and Method of Implanting, Direct Gene Transfer in Wounds. Office: U Mich Orthopaedic Rsch Labs 400 N Ingalls St Rm G161 Ann Arbor MI 48109-2003 Office Phone: 734-936-7417. Office Fax: 734-647-0003. E-mail: stevegld@umich.edu.

GOLDSTEIN, STUART N., lawyer; b. Rochester, NY, May 26, 1967; BS, Cornell Univ., 1989; JD, Boalt Hall Sch. Law, Univ. Calif., 1992. Bar: Calif. 1992, NY 1996. Ptnr. Cadwalader Wickersham & Taft LLP, Charlotte, NC. With CDO group, Cadwalader, CMBS group, Cadwalader. Mem. ABA, NY State Bar Assn. Office: Cadwalader, Wickersham & Taft LLP Ste 2400 227 W Trade St Charlotte NC 28202 Office Phone: 704-348-5100, 704-348-5258. Fax: 704-348-5200. Business E-Mail: stuart.goldstein@cwt.com.*

GOLDSTEIN, STUART WOLF, lawyer; b. Buffalo, Sept. 9, 1931; s. Joseph and Esther (Wolf) G.; m. Myra Saft Stuart, June 1960 (dec. Aug. 1981); children: Jeffrey, Jonathan, Meryl; m. Nancy Baynes Lux, 1993. Student, U. Buffalo, 1949-52, JD, 1955; postgrad., U. Va., 1956. Bar: NY 1956, Fla. 1974, Ariz. 1977, US Supreme Ct. 1960, US Dist. Ct. (we. dist.) NY 1956, US Ct. Mil. Appeals 1957, US Ct. Appeals (2d cir.) NY, 1978, US Dist. Ct. Ariz. 1981. Sole practice, Buffalo, 1960-79, 82-85, Phoenix, 1980-82, 85—. Pres., founder Cystic Fibrosis Found., Buffalo, 1960; fund-raiser United Fund, United Jewish Appeal; pres. Boys League; active Erie County Spl. Task Force on Energy, Buffalo, 1978. 1st lt. JAG, US Army, 1956-60. Fellow Ariz. Bar Found.; mem. Am. Assn. Justice, Ariz. State Bar Assn., NY Trial Lawyers Assn., NY State Bar Assn., Fla. Bar Assn., Maricopa County Bar Assn. Avocations: astronomy, breeding boston terriers. Office: 2700 N 3rd St Ste 2010 Phoenix AZ 85004-4602 Office Phone: 602-279-1666. Personal E-mail: stugoldstn@aol.com. Business E-Mail: stuart@stuartgoldsteinlaw.com.

GOLDSTEIN, SYDNEY RACHEL, photographer, writer, radio producer; b. San Francisco, Oct. 13, 1944; d. Edward William and Dorian Claire G.; m. Charles R. Breyer, Jan. 18, 1976; children: Katherine, Joseph. Grad. h.s., San Francisco. Photographer, writer, 1970—; prodr., founding exec. dir. City Arts & Lectures, Inc., San Francisco, 1981—; exec. prodr. City Arts & Lecturs, Radio Broadcasts, 1997—. Author: Earned Income, 2001. Adv. bd. Grants for the Arts, San Francisco Hotel Tax Fund, 1979-82. Recipient Koret Israel prize Koret Found., 1990. Democrat. Office: City Arts & Lectures Inc 1955 Sutter St San Francisco CA 94115

GOLDSTEIN, TAMARA BETH, musician; b. Tenafly, NJ, Dec. 20, 1961; d. Nathan and Beatrice Goldstein. MusB, Ind. U, Bloomington, 1984; MusM, Juilliard Sch., NYC, 1987; Mus D, U Colo., Boulder, 1996. Accompanist faculty Aspen Music Festival, Colo.; asst. prof., artist-in-residence Metro State Coll. Denver, 2002—. Founder, dir. www.pianocelebration.com. Mem.: Coll. Music Soc. (bd. dirs.), Colo. State Music Tchrs. Assn. (bd. dirs.), Suzuki Assn. Am., Denver Musicians Assn./Am. Fedn. Musicians, Music Tchr. Nat. Assn., Pi Kappa Lambda. Office Phone: 303-556-3391. Business E-Mail: goldstet@mscd.edu.

GOLDSTEIN, THOMAS C., lawyer; b. 1970; m. Amy Howe. BA, U. NC, Chapel Hill, 1992; JD summa cum laude, Am. U. Washington Coll. Law, 1995. Law clk. to Hon. Patricia M. Wald US Ct. Appeals (DC cir.), 1995—96; assoc. Jones, Day, Reavis & Pogue, 1996—97, Boies & Schiller, LLP, 1997—99; founding ptnr. Goldstein & Howe, P.C., 1999—2006; ptnr. Akin, Gump, Strauss, Hauer & Feld, LLP, Washington, 2006—. Lectr. Supreme Ct. litig. Stanford Law Sch.; lectr. Harvard Law Sch. Named one of Top 45 Lawyers in Country Under Age of 45, Am. Lawyer Mag., 2003, Top 40 Lawyers Under 40, Nat. Law Jour., 2005, 100 Most Influential Lawyers, 2006. Office: Akin Gump Strauss Hauer & Feld LLP 1333 New Hampshire Ave NW Washington DC 20036-1564

GOLDSTEIN, WALTER ELLIOTT, biotechnology executive; m. Paula G. Copen. BS in Chem. Engring., Ill. Inst. Tech., 1961; MBA, Mich. State U., 1968; MSChemE, U. Notre Dame, 1971, PhDChemE, 1973. Registered profl. engr., Ind. Process devel. engr. Linde div. Union Carbide, Tonawanda, NY, 1961-64; assoc. project engr. Miles Labs., Elkhart, Ind., 1964-67, assoc. rsch. scientist, 1967-72, rsch. scientist, 1972-73, rsch. supr., 1973-76; mgr. chem. engring. rsch. & pilot svcs. Chem. Engring. Rsch. & Pilot Svcs., Elkhart, Ind., 1976-78, dir., 1978-82; chem. engring. rsch. v.p. Biotech. Group, Elkhart, 1982-87; v.p. R&D ESCAgenetics Corp., San Carlos, Calif., 1987-94; pres. Goldstein Cons. Co., Foster City, Calif., 1994—; co-founder Transcyte Corp., Inc., 1996—, Phytonic Corp., 2001—; coord. Biotech. Ctr., Shadowlane Campus, U. Nev., Las Vegas, 2003—. Adj. prof. chem. engring. U. Notre Dame, 1974-75, San Jose State U., 1995—; cons. Bernard Wolnak, Chgo., 1987 Contbr. chpts. to books; inventions and publs. in chem. engring., pharm., food, diagnostics and biotech. field. Vice-pres. B'nai B'rith, South Bend., Ind., 1978-89. Mem. AAAS, Am. Chem. Soc., Am. Soc. Pharmacognosy, Soc. for Competitive Intelligence Profls., Am. Inst. Chem. Engrs., N.Y. Acad. Scis., Inst. Food Technologists, Sigma Xi. Avocations: reading, computers, sports, charitable causes. Office Phone: 702-774-2325, 702-804-5952. E-mail: goldconsul@aol.com, walter.goldstein@ccmail.nevada.edu.

GOLDSTEIN, WILLIAM A., investment counsel; b. Chgo., June 24, 1939; s. Jacob E. and Marion B. G.; m. Anne B. Goldstein, Aug. 19, 1962; chidlren: Deborah, Catherine. BS, Purdue U., West Lafayette, Ind., 1962. Registered rep. Hornblower & Weeks-Hemphill Noyes, Chgo., 1962-70; exec. v.p. Burton J. Vincent-Chesley & Co., Chgo., 1970-83; chmn. Prescott Asset Mgmt., Prescott, Ball & Turben, Chgo., 1983-89; pres. Lodestar Investment Counsel LLC, Chgo., 1989—; dir. The Pvt. Bank, Chgo. Trustee Chgo. Symphony Orch., chmn. governing mems., 1997-99, vice chmn., treas.; bd. dirs. Grant Park Concert Soc., Chgo., 1995-97. Mem. Standard Club, Chgo. Yacht Club. Avocations: sailing, bicycling, golf, reading. Office: Lodestar Investment Counsel LLC 208 S Lasalle St Chicago IL 60604-1000 Home Phone: 847-491-1352; Office Phone: 312-630-9666.

GOLDSTEIN, WILLIAM MARKS, lawyer; b. Phila., Aug. 28, 1935; s. David and Estelle (Marks) Goldstein; m. Lillia E. Demchuck; 1 child, Laura;children from previous marriage: Adam, Benjamin, Daniel. AB, Princeton U., 1957; JD magna cum laude, Harvard U., 1960. Bar: Pa. 1961, DC 1977. Law clk. to judge U.S. Ct. Appeals, Phila., 1960-61; assoc. firm Morgan Lewis & Bockius, Phila., 1961-66, ptnr., 1967-75, 77-82, Drinker, Biddle & Reath LLP, Phila., 1982—; dep. asst. sec. tax policy Dept. Treasury, Washington, 1975-76. Contbr. articles to profl. jours. Mem. Lower Merion (Pa.) Dem. Com., 1965—68; candidate Sch. Bd. Lower Merion, 1965, state legis., 1966. Mem.: ABA, Am. Coll. Tax Counsel, Am. Law Inst., DC Bar Assn., Phila. Bar Assn., Pa. Bar Assn. Jewish. Home: 787 Trephanny Ln Wayne PA 19087-1931 Office: Drinker Biddle & Reath LLP 1 Logan Sq 18th & Cherry St Philadelphia PA 19103-6996 Office Phone: 215-988-2982. Business E-Mail: Goldstwm@dbr.com.

GOLDSTICK, THOMAS KARL, biomedical engineering educator; b. Toronto, Ont., Can., Aug. 21, 1934; came to U.S., 1955, naturalized. s. David and Iva Sarah (Kaplan) G.; m. Marcia Adrienne Jenkins, July 4, 1982. BS, MIT, 1957, MS, 1959; PhD, U. Calif., Berkeley, 1966, U. Calif., San Francisco, 1966-67. Asst. prof. Northwestern U., Evanston, Ill., 1967-71, assoc. prof. chem. engring. and biol. sci., 1971-81, prof. chem. engring., neurobiology and physiology, 1981-85, prof. chem. engring., biomed. engring., neurobiology and physiology, 1985-99, prof. emeritus, 1999—. Adj. prof. ophthalmology U. Ill., Chgo., 1981-91. Editor: Oxygen Transport to Tissue V, 1983, VII, 1985, X, 1988, XI, 1989, XII, 1990, XIII, 1992. Rsch. grantee NIH, 1968—; Spl. Rsch. fellow U. Calif., San Diego, LaJolla, 1971-73. Mem. Internat. Soc. Oxygen Transport to Tissue (sec. 1980-86, exec. com. 1986-93), Biomed. Engring. Soc. (bd. dirs. 1983-86, chmn. publs. bd. 1985-86). Home: 2025 Sherman Ave Apt 504 Evanston IL 60201-3269 Office: Biomed Engring Dept Northwestern U Evanston IL 60208-3107 Home Phone: 847-328-2624; Office Phone: 847-491-5518. Business E-Mail: t-goldstick@northwestern.edu.

GOLDSTINE, STEPHEN JOSEPH, art educator; b. San Francisco, Nov. 16, 1937; s. Edgar Nathan and Regina Thelma (Benno) G.; m. Emily Raechel Miller Keeler, Apr. 12, 1981; children: Rachel, Bettina, Simone Massimiliana Student, Calif. Sch. Fine Arts, 1951-58; BA, U. Calif., Berkeley, 1961, postgrad. in philosophy, 1962-67. Teaching asst. rhetoric dept. U. Calif., Berkeley, 1963-66; asst. prof. St. Mary's Coll., Moraga, Calif., 1964-70, chmn. art dept., 1969-70; cons. Freeman & Gossage, San Francisco, 1967-69; dir. neighborhood arts program Art Commn. City and County San Francisco, 1970-77; exec. sec. Mayor's Interagency Com. for Arts, San Francisco, 1971-75; founding dir. Performing Arts for the Third Age, San Francisco, 1973; co-dir. Rockefeller Tng. Fellowships in Mus. Edn., San Francisco, 1975; pres. San Francisco Art Inst., 1977-86; dir. grad. programs Calif. Coll. Arts and Crafts, 1983—2003, Dennis Leon prof. grad. studies, 2002—; vis. faculty San Francisco State U. Sr. cons. Daniel Solomon Architects and Planners, 1988; mem. chancellor's adv. bd. Univ. Art Mus., U. Calif., Berkeley, 1979—; exec. com., trustee San Francisco Arts Edn. Found., 1985—; mem. Oakland Cultural Affairs Commn., 2002—; mem. prominent orgns. panel Calif. Arts Coun., 1981, vice chmn., 1983, chmn., 1985-87; chmn. invited session Am. Philos. Assn. (Pacific divsn.), 1986, lectr. UCLA, 1976, Stanford U., 1966, Harvard U., 1976, 71; docent Lycee Internat. Franco-Am., 1993—. Editor: Western Round Table on Modern Art, 1993; co-prodr., co-dir. (film) Walz um die Wände hoch zu gehen, 1999. Condr. The Art Orch., Calif. Palace of the Legion of Honor, 1997. Democrat. Jewish. Home: 1331 Green St San Francisco CA 94109-1926 Office: Calif Coll Arts Crafts 1111 Eighth St San Francisco CA 94107-2206 Home Phone: 415-474-0838; Office Phone: 415-551-9212. E-mail: mrgoldstine@earthlink.net.

GOLDSTON, JAMES, television producer; Grad., Oxford U. Sr. prodr.: (current affairs news series) Tonight with Trevor McDonald, ITV1 network, England, 1999—2001 (Nominee BAFTA TV award for Best News and Current Affairs Journalism, 2000); exec. prodr.: Tonight with Trevor McDonald, 2002—04 (Three-time award winner of Royal TV Soc. Program of Yr. award), ABC News Nightline, Washington and NYC, 2004—. Office: ABC 77 W 66th St New York NY 10023

GOLDSTON, ROBERT J., research scientist; BS magna cum laude, Harvard U., 1972; PhD in Astrophysical Sci., Princeton U., 1977. Rsch. asst. Princeton Plasma Physics Lab. Princeton U., NJ, 1972—77, assoc. dir. rsch. NJ, 1995—97, dir. NJ, 1997—, head Tokamak Fusion Test Reactor physics program divsn. NJ. Prof. astrophysical sci. Princeton U., 1992—. Co-author: (textbook) Introduction to Plasma Physics. Achievements include research in high temperature plasmas required for thermonuclear fusion leading to the National Spherical Torus Experiment (NSTX), an experimental nuclear reactor promoting plasma efficiency. Office: Princeton Plasma Physics Lab PO Box 451 Princeton NJ 08543-0451 Office Phone: 609-243-3553. Office Fax: 609-243-2749. E-mail: rjg@princeton.edu.

GOLDSTON, STEPHEN EUGENE, community psychologist, educator, consultant; b. NYC, Apr. 19, 1931; s. Michael Louis and Molly Ruth (Rothenberg) G.; children: Beth Karen, Lisa Robin BA, NYU, 1952; MSPH, Columbia U., 1953, MA, 1957, EdD, 1958. Lectr., instr. Columbia U., NYC, 1956-58; asst. to dir. Westchester County Cmty. Mental Health Bd., White Plains, NY, 1958-60; chief mental health edn. unit, dir. mental health consultation program N.Y.C. Cmty. Mental Health Bd., 1960-62; staff asst. to assoc. dir. extramural programs NIMH, Rockville, Md., 1962-63, tng. specialist pilot and spl. grants sect. Tng. and Manpower Resources br., 1963-65, tng. specialist exptl. and spl. tng. br., 1966-67, chief pub. health sect. exptl. and spl. tng. br., 1967-69, spl. asst. to dir. for preventive programs, 1967-71, coord. primary prevention program, 1972-80, chief primary prevention service programs, Div. Mental Health Service Program, 1980-81, dir. office of prevention, 1981-85; cons. in preventive psychiatry Neuropsychiat. Inst., UCLA, 1985-87; assoc. dir. UCLA Preventive Psychiatry Ctr., 1987-89, chair ann. nat. conf., 1987, 88; staff dir. Mayor's Citizen's Task Force on Cen. City East, Los Angeles, 1986-88; pres. Goldston & Assocs., Chgo., 1986—. Chmn. nat. conf. UCLA Preventive Psychiatry Ctr., 1987-88; coord. nat. conf. Mental Health in Pub. Health Tng., 1967-68; lectr. Bar-Ilan U. Sch. Social Work, Ramat

Gan, Israel, 1996-98, 2000—03, The Hebrew U. Sch. Social Work, Jerusalem, Israel, 1997-2000, 03; sr. editor NIMH Prevention Publ. Series, 1976-85; assoc. editor coun. Am. Assn. Applied and Preventive Psychology, 1991—. Mem. editl. bd. Jour. Preventive Psychiatry, Jour. Primary Prevention; contbr. articles to profl. jours. With U.S. Army, 1953-55, USPHS, 1957-85. Recipient Sustained High Quality Peformance award HEW, 1968, 72, 76; Superior Work Performance award HEW, 1970; Outstanding Contbn. to Prevention in Mental Health award Nat. Council Community Mental Health Ctrs., Washington, 1985 Fellow Am. Psychol. Assn. (Disting. Profl. Contbns. award 1984), Am. Pub. Health Assn. (chmn. com. on prevention, mental health sect. 1974-77). Personal E-mail: goldston@netvision.net.il.

GOLDSTONE, JEFFREY, physicist, educator; b. Manchester, Eng., Sept. 3, 1933; arrived in U.S., 1977; m. Roberta Gordon; 1 child, Andrew. BA, Cambridge U., Eng., 1954, PhD, 1958. Fellow Trinity Coll., Cambridge, 1956-60, 62-82, hon. fellow, 2000; lectr., reader U. Cambridge, England, 1961-76, MIT, Cambridge, Mass., 1977—2004, Cecil and Ida Green prof. physics, 1983—2004, prof. emeritus, 2004. Recipient Dannie Heineman prize, Am. Phys. Soc., 1981, Guthrie medal, Inst. Physics, 1983, Dirac prize, Internat. Ctr. Theoretical Physics, 1991. Mem.: Am. Acad. Arts and Scis., Royal Soc. Office: MIT 77 Massachusetts Ave 6-407 Cambridge MA 02139-4307 Business E-Mail: goldston@mit.edu.

GOLDSTONE, ROBERT ALLEN, orthopaedic surgeon; b. NYC, Sept. 28, 1935; married; 3 children. BS (with honors) in Psychology, U. Wis., Madison, 1955; MD, Harvard Med. Sch., 1959. Diplomate Am. Bd. Orthop. Surgery, lic. NJ. Intern, gen. surgery St. Vincent's Hosp., NYC, 1959—60, resident, gen. surgery, 1962—64; resident, orthop. surgery The Hosp. for Spl. Surgery, NYC, 1964—68, hand fellow, 1967; attending orthop. surgeon St. Joseph's Hosp. and Med. Ctr., NJ, 1968—88, Valley Hosp., Ridgewood, NJ, 1987—; clin. asst. prof., orthop. Cornell Med. Sch., NYC, 1968—77; clin. asst. prof., orthop., dept. surgery NJ Coll. Medicine and Dentistry, 1969—86; private practice Glen Rock, NJ. Dir., hand svc. St. Joseph's Hosp. and Med. Ctr., Paterson, NJ, 1970—87, courtesy staff orthop., 1988—97, mem. med. bd., 1971—74, Paterson, 1976—83, v.p., med. staff, NY, 1976—78, pres., med. staff, NJ, 1979—80, chmn. operating room com., 1976—78, chmn., staff develop. com., 1980—82, planning com. mem.; courtesy staff orthop. Barnert Meml. Hosp., Paterson, NJ, 1988—97, Fair Lawn Meml. Hosp., NJ, Preakness Hosp., Wayne, NJ, Daughters Miriam Ctr. for the Aged, Clifton, NJ; surgeon, out-patient dept. Hosp. for Spl. Surgery, NYC, 1968—77, NY Hosp., 1968—77; testimony before US Senate Subcommittee, Lawn Mower Injuries, 1978; med. advisor, compensation claims Liberty Mutual Ins. Comp., Saddle Brook, NJ, 1979—94; med. cons., Consumer's Union Com. on Lawn Mower Safety US Consumer Product Safety Commn.; bd. dir. Action for Child Product Safety, Nat. Consumers League, 1982—86; adv. bd. mem. Berdan Inst., Totowa, NJ, Quackwatch; mem. med. expert adv. panel Dept. Law & Pub. Safety, NJ Bd. Med. Examiners, 2002—; spkr. in field. Contbr. articles to profl. jours.; manuscript review bd. mem. Journal of the Med. Soc. NJ (Orthop. Surgery). Battalion Surgeon (Capt. Med. Corp.), 8th Cavalry (Germany) US Army, 1960—62. Fellow: NJ Acad. Medicine (sec. orthop. sect. 1979—80); mem.: Eastern Orthop. Assn., NJ Orthop. Soc. (mem. exec. com. 1976—82, symposium chmn. 1981, mem. com. on insurance and liasion for physician/carrier relationships 1981—82, mem. ann. orthop. symposium com. 1981—82, awards com. mem. 1981—82, chmn. manpower com. 1978—82), NJ Med. Soc. (del., Passaic County 1972—82), ACS (assoc.; chmn., NJ Com. on Trauma, Acad. Medicine NJ (Orthop. Sect.) 1980—81), Bergen County Med. Soc., Passaic County Med. Soc., Am. Acad. Orthop. Surgeons (mem. regional admissions com. 1975—81, chmn. regional admissions com. 1978—80, mem. com. injuries 1978—81, mem. manpower com. 1981—84, emeritus fellow). Avocations: photography, computers, skiing, sailing, tennis, magic, chess, flying, golf. Office: 1000 Maple Ave Glen Rock NJ 07452 Office Phone: 201-444-1166. Office Fax: 201-445-8282. Business E-Mail: goldstone@compuserve.com.*

GOLDSTONE, SANFORD, psychologist, educator; b. NYC, July 17, 1926; s. Albert and Anna (Steckel) G.; children: Susan Beth, Arthur Craig, Nancy Lynn; stepchildren: Peter B., Anthony A., Jane P., Elisabeth W.; m. Lois Adams. BS, CCNY, 1947; PhD, Duke U., 1953. Intern Duke Sch. Medicine, 1949-51; chief clin. psychologist Duke Sch. Medicine (Psychiat. Out-Patient Clinic), 1951-54, lectr. psychology, 1953-54, asso. dept. psychiatry, 1953-54; asst. prof. to prof. psychiatry, chief psychologist, program dir. Baylor U. Coll. Medicine, 1955-67; prof., head div. psychology dept. psychiatry Cornell U. Med. Coll., 1967-79; prof. psychology field neurobiology Cornell U. Med. Coll. (Grad. Sch. Med. Scis.), 1969-79; prof., dir. clin. tng., dept. psychology U. Maine, Orono, 1979-86, prof. psychology emeritus, 1986—. Cons. VA Hosps., Durham, NC, 1953-54, Houston, 1959-67, Temple, Tex., 1964-67, Montrose, N.Y., 1968-79, Togus, Maine, 1979-88; profl. staff Eastern Maine Med. Center and; Bangor Mental Health Inst., 1980-86; trustee Miles Meml. Hosp., Damariscotta, Maine, 1990-99; cons. criminal law sect. Am. Bar Assn., 1967-69, Westchester County Probation Dept., 1968-71, Community Service Bur., NY State Tng. Schs., 1969-75; head divsn. psychology Houston State Psychiat. Inst., 1958-67, acting bus. mgr., 1959-60, head divsn. crime and delinquency, 1966-67; clin. assoc. prof. to clin. prof. U. Houston, 1958-67; dir. mental health svcs. Harris County Probation Dept., Houston, 1963-67; cons. Silver Hill Found., 1974-81; psychologist-in-chief Payne Whitney Psychiat. Clinic, 1967-74, Westchester divsn. N.Y. Hosp., 1967-74; attending psychologist NY Hosp., 1967-79; head, community cons. svcs. outpatient dept. Payne Whitney Psychiat. Clinic, 1970-73; head cmty. cons. services Westchester divsn. NY Hosp.-Cornell Med. Center, 1973-75 Contbr. numerous articles to profl. jours. Served with USAAF, 1945. USPHS grantee, 1955-65, 79-86. Fellow APA (life); mem. Am. Psychopath. Assn. (life). Home: PO Box 282 East Boothbay ME 04544-0282 Office: U Maine Psychology Little Hall Orono ME 04469 Personal E-mail: sanfordg@adelphia.net. Business E-Mail: sanfordg@maine.edu.

GOLDSTONE, STEVEN F., former consumer products company executive; b. NYC, Jan. 30, 1946; s. Milton Harold and Beatrice (Chase) G.; m. Elizabeth Caravella; children: Elissa Eve, Margaret Chase, Douglas. BA, U. Pa., 1967; JD, NYU, 1970. Bar: N.Y. 1971, U.S. Dist. Ct. (so. dist.) N.Y. 1972, U.S. Ct. Appeals (2d cir.) 1971). Assoc. Davis, Polk & Wardwell, NYC, 1970-78, ptnr., 1978-95; gen. counsel RJR Nabisco, Inc., 1995; chmn., CEO, bd. dirs. RJR Nabisco Inc., 1995-2000; also bd. dirs. Nabisco Holdings, Inc., 1997-2000; pvt. exec. Silver Spring Group, NYC, 2000—. Bd. dirs. ConAgra Foods, Inc., Am. Standard Cos., Greenhill & Co. Chmn. Ridgefield Sr. Ctr. Found., Roundabout Theatre Co., NY. Office: Silver Spring Group 570 Lexington Ave Fl 37 New York NY 10022-6837

GOLDTHWAIT, CHRISTOPHER E., ambassador; b. Atlanta; s. John and Betty Goldthwait. BA, Am. U.; MPA, Harvard U. Joined U.S. Fgn. Agrl. Svc., agrl. attaché Germany, 1978-82, agrl. counselor Lagos, Nigeria, 1982-86, various positions, then Gen. Sales Mgr., 1993-99; U.S. ambassador to Republic of Chad, 1999—. Author: (books) Salvation is a Homecoming, 2001. Achievements include first Fgn. Agrl. administr. to become a chief of mission. E-mail: goldthwaitce@state.gov.

GOLDWASSER, SHAFRIRA, computer scientist; b. NYC, 1958; BS in math., Carnegie Mellon U., 1979; MS in computer sci., PhD in computer sci., U. Calif., Berkeley. RSA prof. elec. engring. and computer sci.; co-leader cryptology and info. security group Lab. Computer Sci. Prof. math. scis. Weitzmann Inst. Sci., Israel. Recipient Göbel prize, Theoretical Computer Sci., 1993, 2001, ACM Gracy Murray Hopper award, 1996, RSA award in math., 1998. Mem.: NAE, Am. Acad. Arts and Scis., NAS. Office: MIT Dept Elec Engring and Computer Sci 77 Massachusetts Ave Cambridge MA 02139 Business E-Mail: shafi@csail.mit.edu.

GOLDWATER, MARILYN R(UBIN), medical/surgical nurse, state legislator; b. Boston, Jan. 29, 1927; d. Frederick and Rebecca (Geller) Rubin; m. William H. Goldwater, Aug. 8, 1948; children: Charles Alan, Diane Louise. Diploma, Mt. Sinai Hosp. Sch. Nursing, NYC, 1948. RN, Md. Legislator State of Md., Annapolis, 1975-86; dir. Office Fed. Rels. Md. Dept. Health and Mental Hygiene, 1987-90; exec. asst. for health issue Gov.' Office, 1990—; mem. Md. Ho. of Dels., 1995—. Speaker on econs. and politics of health care; faculty assoc. U. Md., George Mason U. and Johns Hopkins U. schs. nursing. Author: (with Mary Jane Lloyd Zusy) Prescription for Nurses: Effective Political Action, 1990; mem. editl. adv. bd. Policy, Politics, and Nursing Practice, 2000; contbr. articles to profl. jours. Recipient Ann London Scott Legis. Excellence award, 1979, Legislator of Yr. award Md. Pub. Health Assn., 1982, Legis. Contbns. to Home Health Care award Upjohn Co., 1982, Disting. Alumna award Mt. Sinai Hosp. Sch. of Nursing, 1993; honored MedStar Health Vis. Nurse Assn., 2000. Fellow: Am. Acad. Nursing (hon.); mem.: ANA (bd. dirs. Hon. Recognition award 1980), Nat. Assn. Jewish Legislators, Order Women Legislators, Sigma Theta Tau. Office: Md Gen Assembly Lowe House Office Bldg Rm 221 Annapolis MD 21401-1691 Home: Apt 1927 5801 Nicholson Ln Rockville MD 20852-5738

GOLDWAY, RUTH Y., postal regulatory commissioner; d. David and Mathilda G.; children: Casey, Anthony, Julie. BA, U. Mich., 1965; MA, Wayne State U., 1968; postgrad., UCLA, 1970-71. Asst. dir. Dept. Consumer Affairs, LA, 1975-78; mayor City Santa Monica, Calif., 1979-83; dir. pub. affairs Calif. State U., LA, 1984-91; mgr. pub. affairs Getty Trust, LA, 1991-94; commr. US Postal Regulatory Comm., Washington, 1998—. Chair and founder Santa Monica Pier Restoration Corp., 1981-94; founding mem. Consumer Adv. Panel, GTE, San Francisco, 1974-76. Author: Letters From Finland, A Memoir, 1998; contbr. articles to mags., profl. jours., and newspapers, 1994-2006; actress in film Dave, 1992. Bd. dirs. New Visions Found., Ctr. for Sustainable Cities, USC, Tree People, 2002-, So. Calif. Consumer Affairs Profls., 1986-92. Recipient Best Diplomatic Role Model, Helsinik City Mag., 1996. Democrat. Avocations: biking, cooking, travel. Office: Postal Regulatory Commn 901 New York Ave NW Ste 200 Washington DC 20001 Office Phone: 202-789-6810. Business E-Mail: ruth.goldway@prc.gov.

GOLDWEBER, ROBERT, emergency physician; BA, UCLA, 1974, MD, 1978. Emergency physician Huntington Meml. Hosp., Pasadena, Calif., 1978—, residency dir., 1987—, asst. dir. emergency dept., 1989—. Assoc. prof. emergency dept. LA County, U. So. Calif., 1985—; expert reviewer Med. Bd. Calif., 1995—, LUmetra, 2005—. Office: Huntington Meml Hosp 100 W California Blvd Pasadena CA 91105

GOLDWEIT, RICHARD SCOTT, cardiologist; b. NYC, 1956; MD, Cornell U., 1982. Diplomate Am. Bd. Internal Medicine. Asst. attending physician N.Y. Hosp., 1987—; intern NYU-Bellevue Med. Ctr., NYC, 1982—83; resident in internal medicine N.Y. Hosp., NYC, 1983—85, fellow in cardiology, 1985; attending physician Englewood (N.J.) Hosp., 1988—, Hackensack (N.J.) Med. Ctr., 1988—, Holy Name Hosp., Teaneck, NJ, 1988—. Named one of Top Drs. in N.Y. Metro Area, Castle Connolly, Top Drs., NJ Monthly Mag., 2003, 2006. Office: Cardiology Consultants 200 Grand Ave Ste 202 Englewood NJ 07631-4363 Office Fax: 201-569-6111.*

GOLEMAN, DANIEL JAY, psychologist, journalist; b. Stockton, Calif., Mar. 7, 1946; s. Irving and Fay Goleman; m. Tara Bennett-Goleman, July 27, 1982; children: Gov, Hanuman. PhD, Harvard U., Cambridge, Mass., 1973; Doctorate (hon.), U. Mass., Boston, 2000, Univ. of Pacific, 2002. Sci. writer NY Times, NYC, 1984—96; co-dir. Consortium for Rsch. on Emotional Intelligence in Organizations, Rutgers U., New Brunswick, NJ, 1996—. Co-founder Collaborative for Acad., Social, and Emotional Learning, U. Ill., Chgo., 1993—. Author: (non-fiction book) Emotional Intelligence, 1995 (Best-seller, 1995). Post-Doctoral fellowship, Social Sci. Rsch. Coun., 1973. Fellow: AAAS. Office Phone: 413-268-3590.

GOLEMBESKI, JEROME JOHN, manufacturing executive; b. Nanticoke, Pa., Mar. 16, 1931; s. Edward and Mary Ellen (Grozio) G.; m. June Beverly Chadwick, Aug. 9, 1958; children— Dale, Gary, Gregg, Cheryl, Kim. BS, U. Conn., 1957. Auditor Price Waterhouse & Co., Hartford, Conn., 1957-59; mem. controller's staff Insilco Corp., Meriden, Conn., 1959-86; Times Fiber Comm. Inc. Times Wire & Cable Co., Wallingford, Conn., 1959-86; contr., treas. Uniset Inc., Wallingford, 1986—. Served with USNR, 1949-53. Mem. Nat. Assn. Accountants (Cost Accounting award Hartford chpt.) Office: Uniset Inc 258 Legend Hill Rd Madison CT 06443-1879

GOLEMON, RONALD KINNAN, lawyer; b. Atlanta, Tex., Nov. 22, 1938; s. William Layton and Avis (Bogle) G.; m. Jacqueline Alice Burst, Sept. 2, 1966; children: Donald Brent, Jennifer Alice. BS in Indsl. Mgmt. Engring., U. Okla., 1961; LLB, U. Tex., 1967. Bar: Tex. 1967, U.S. Ct. Appeals (5th cir.) 1970, U.S. Dist. Ct. (so. dist.) Tex. 1968, U.S. Dist. Ct. (we. dist.) Tex. 1981, U.S. Dist. Ct. (no. dist.) 1986. Engr. asst. Tex. Water Pollution Control Bd., Austin, 1964-67; assoc. Keys, Russell, Watson & Seaman, Corpus Christi, Tex., 1967-71, ptnr., 1971-73, Brown McCarroll, LLP (formerly Brown McCarroll & Oaks Hartline), Austin, 1973—; mng. ptnr. Brown McCarroll & Oaks Hartline, 1989-94. Contbg. author The Southwestern Legal Foundation, 40th Annual Institute on Oil and Gas Law and Taxation, 1989, The Southwestern Legal Foundation, 43rd Annual Institute on Oil and Gas Law and Taxation, 1992; contbr articles to profl. jours. Alt. mem. RCRA permit adv. com. U.S. EPA, 1983; mem. Gov.'s Hazardous Waste Task Force, 1984-85; v.p. St. Stephen's Sch. PTA, 1985-86, pres., 1986-87; mem. cmty. adv. bd. Ronald McDonald House, Austin, 1990—. Fellow Am. Bar Found.; mem. ABA (mem. ho. dels. 2000—, standing com. on membership, 1997-2000, constnl. and by-laws 2000-03, environl. law 2004—, chmn. standing com. environ. law 2004—, constnl. and by-laws, 2001-03, market rsch. task force 1995-96, chmn. sect. natural resources, energy and environ. law 1994-95, chmn.-elect 1993-94, vice-chmn. 1992-93, coun. liaison environ. group 1989-91, chmn. air quality com. 1986-89, vice-chmn. 1982-86), State Bar Tex. (chmn. environ. law sect. 1971-72), Tex. Mining and Reclamation Assn. (dir. 1988-00), Travis County Bar Assn., U. Tex. Law Alumni Assn. (pres. 1984-85, exec. bd. 1984-86), N.Am. Corriente Assn (bd. dirs. 2004—, pres. 2005—), Tex. Corriente Cattle Assn. (bd. dirs. 2002-05). Avocations: ranching, hunting, skiing, golf. Office: Brown McCarroll LLP 111 Congress Ave Ste 1400 Austin TX 78701-4043 Home Phone: 512-327-0721; Office Phone: 512-479-9707. Personal E-mail: kgolemon@mailbmc.com.

GOLER, MICHAEL DAVID, lawyer; b. Cleve., June 29, 1952; s. George and Harriet G.; children: Jonathan A. Jennifer S. BA with honors in Classics (Greek), Union Coll., 1974; JD, Case Western Res. U., 1977. Bar: Ohio 1977, US Dist. Ct. Ohio 1977, US Ct. Appeals (6th cir.) 1982. Assoc. Persky, Marken, Konigsberg & Shapiro, Cleve., 1977-81; assoc. counsel Cardinal Fed. Savings Bank, Cleve., 1981-84; assoc. Arter & Hadden, Cleve., 1984-86, Kohrman, Jackson & Krantz, Cleve., 1986—94, ptnr., 1988-94, Goodman Weiss Miller LLP, Cleve., 1994—. Panelist Nat. Arbitration Forum, 2005—. Bd. dirs. Jewish Cmty. Ctr. Cleve., 1998—2005, The Cleve. Hearing and Speech Ctr., 1998—, pres.-elect, 2005—06, pres., 2006—. Fellow Am. Coll. Mortgage Attys., Cleve. Bar Assn. (founder, chmn. environ. law sect. 1991-95, chmn. real estate sect. 1989-90, real estate inst. com. 1989—); mem. ABA (sect. real property probate and trust law, chmn. com. enforcement of creditors rights and bankruptcy, 1991-95, vice chair, 1995-97, chair, 1997-2001, com. on econs., tech. and practice methods, mng. editor EDirt electronic newsletter 1999—2006, editor EReport electronic newsletter 2006-07, mem. coun. 2001-07, mem. tech standing com. 1999-, vice chmn. 2005-07, chair 2007—, mem. planning com., liaison to ABA sect. law practice mgmt. sect. 1999—, CLE com. 1999-2006, liaison to ABA soc. tech. com. 2003—; mem. law practice mgmt. sect., co-chair membership and mktg., 2004—, mem. soc. joint membership com., mem. nominating com. 2005-07, named Ohio Super Lawyer 2004, 05, 06, 07). Avocations: music, golf, bicycling, skiing, travel. Office: Miller Goler Faeges LLP 100 Erieview Plz Fl 27 Cleveland OH 44114-1824 Home: 12931 Shaker Blvd #301 Cleveland OH 44120 Office Phone: 216-696-3366. E-mail: goler@millergolerfaeges.com.

GOLICI, NICOLAE, sculptor; MFA in Sculpture, Inst. Fine Arts, Bucharest, Romania. Exhibited in group shows at Place as Act and Metaphor, Village Mus., Bucharest, Romania, 1983, Contemporary Images, Mus. Art, Craiova, Romania, 1984, Arts of Today, Internat. Exhbn., Budapest, Hungary, 1986, Cultural Anthropology: Altars and Symbols, 14 Sculptors Gallery, NYC, 1990, Columns, Lehigh U. Art Gallery, 1991, Challenging Utopia, 14 Sculptors Gallery, NYC, 1992, Springworks, NY Hall of Sci., 1992, Sculptor's Drawing, 14 Sculptors Gallery, NYC, 1993, Fulton Ferry Outdoor Sculpture Show, NYC, 1993, Material Presence, 14 Sculptors Gallery, NYC, 1994, The Raw and the Cooked, 1995, Drawn to the Third Dimension, 1996, Cmty. Warehouse, Interchurch Ctr., NYC, 1998, Urban Air Forms, NJ City U., 1999, 181st Ann.: An Invitational Exhbn. Contemporary Art, Nat. Acad. Mus., NYC, 2006, one-man shows include Amfora Gallery, Bacau, Romania, 1984, Atelier 35 Gallery, Bucharest, Romania, 1985, 14 Sculptors Gallery, NYC, 1989, 1991, Mills Pond House, Smithtown Arts Coun. St. James, NY, 1993, Hurlbutt Gallery, Greenwich, Conn., 1996, Firehouse Art Gallery, Garden City, NY, 1998. Recipient Frederich Storck Studio Space award, City of Bucharest, Romania, 1980—82. Mailing: 225 Guy Lombardo Ave Freeport NY 11520-4456

GOLICK, TOBY, law educator, legal services administrator; b. Boston, Apr. 9, 1945; d. Albert David and Sara (Sharaf) G.; children: Benjamin Taylor, Samuel Taylor. BA, Columbia U., 1966, JD, 1969. Bar: NY 1969. Mng. atty. Queens Legal Svcs., NY, 1969-70; atty. Columbia Ctr. on Social Welfare Policy, NYC, 1970-71; sr. atty. Legal Svcs. for Elderly, NYC, 1972-74, 76-85; clin. prof. Yeshiva U. Cardozo Law Sch., NYC, 1985—; dir. Cardozo Bet Tzedek Legal Svcs., NYC, 1985—, Southside Guitars. Recipient Eleanor Roosevelt award State of NY, 1986, Disting. Svc. award Brookdale Ctr. on Aging, NYC, 1998. Mem. NY State Bar Assn., Assn. Bar City NY Home: 54 Morningside Dr New York NY 10025-1740 Office: Yeshiva U Cardozo Law Sch 55 5th Ave New York NY 10003-4301 Office Phone: 212-790-0240. Business E-Mail: tgolick@yu.edu.

GOLIGHTLY, DOUGLAS RAYMOND, artist; b. Milw., Feb. 13, 1931; s. William Bruce and Dorothy Agnes (Klein) G.; m. Patricia Anne Jelinek, June 20, 1959; children: Christine Marie Golightly Richter, William James. BS in Art, U. Wis., 1957, MS in Art, 1959, MFA, 1960. Instr. Layton Sch. Art, Milw., 1964-65. One-man shows Bradley Galleries, Milw., 1962, 66, 69, Wustum Mus. Art, Racine, Wis., 1968, Madison Art Ctr, Wis., 1968, Rahr Civic Ctr. and Pub. Mus., 1968, Manitowoc, Wis., Kenosha (Wis.) Pub. Mus., 1968, Hardy Gallery, Door County, Wis., 1969, Santa Cruz (Calif.) Art League, 1986-87, Sunset Cultural Ctr., Carmel, Calif., 1989, C.L. Clark Gallery, Bakersfield, Calif., 1993, Kings Art Ctr., Hanford, Calif., 1994, Merced Coll. Art Gallery, Calif., 2004, Bakersfield Mus. Art, Calif., 2006; 2-person shows include Layton Sch. Art, Milw., 1965, Sanchez Art Ctr., 2002; 3-person shows Sun Gallery, Hayward, Calif., 1985, San Luis Obispo art Ctr., Calif., 2006; exhibited in group shows Milw. Art Inst., 1950, 55, U. Wis. Meml. Libr., Madison, 1960, Milw. Art Ctr., 1960, 61, 66, 67, 68, Capitol Ct., Milw., 1961, 62, C.W. Post Coll., L.I., N.Y., 1962 (hon. mention), Nat. Arts Club, N.Y.C., 1962, Long Beach (N.Y.) Art Assn., 1962, Madison Gallery, N.Y.C., 1962, Lynn Kottler Galleries, N.Y.C., 1964, Marquette U., Milw., Wis., 1966, Wis. State Fair, Milw., 1967, Mus. Fine Art, Springfield, Mass., 1968, Las Vegas (Nev.) Art Roundup, 1968, Butler Inst. Am. Art, Youngstown, Ohio, 1972, Janacek Atelier, Madison, 1978, Milw. Symphony Showcase, 1980, Santa Cruz Art League, 1987-88, 00-01, Gallery Imago, San Francisco, 1987, Tulare County Fair, Tulare, Calif., 1989-94 (3d prize for oil 1989, 1st and 2d prizes for oils 1990, 92, Best in Show award 1991, 1st prize for oil 1993, 94), Visions Gallery, Reedley, Calif., 1989, 93 (hon. mention 1993) Fanny Garver Gallery, Madison, Wis., 1989, 90, 91, C.L. Clark Galleries, 1990, 91, 92, Mus. Fine Arts, Mus. N.Mex., Santa Fe, 1991, La. State U., Baton Rouge, 1992, Northlight Gallery, West Los Angeles, Calif., 1994, Kings Art Ctr., Hanford, Calif., 1995-03, Gallery 198, Three Rivers, Calif., 1999-00, San Luis Obispo Art Ctr., Calif., 2000-05, Carnegie Art Mus., Oxnard, Calif., 2000, 02, 03, 04, Pacific Grove Art Ctr., Calif., 2000, 02, 03 Second City Coun., Long Beach, Calif., 2000-02, 05, 40-Year Retrospective Exhibit, Wylie & May Louise Jones Gallery, Bakersfield Coll., Calif., 2000, Berkeley Art Ctr., 2001-05, San Francisco State U., 2001, Porterville Art Assn., Calif, 2001-06, Sanchez Art Ctr., Pacifica, Calif., 2001-02 (Grand Prize co-winner 2001), Sun Gallery, Hayward, Calif., 2001, 2002, Orange County Ctr. Contemporary Art, Santa Ana, Calif., 2001, Bedford Gallery at the Dean Lesher Regional Ctr. for Arts, Walnut Creek, Calif., 2001, 03, San Jose Art League, 2002, Sebastopol (Calif.) Ctr. for the Arts, 2002, 04, Nicolet Coll. Rhinelander, Wis., 2002, 2004, Armory Art Ctr., West Palm Beach, Fla., 2002, 2004, Artisans Gallery, Mill Valley, Calif., 2002, Palos Verdes (Calif.) Art Ctr., Rancho Palos Verdes, Calif., 2003, Chris Vanderlei Gallery, Bakersfield, Calif., 2003-06, City of Brea (Calif.) Gallery, 2004, Olive Hyde Gallery, Calif., 2004-06, Absolute Art Gallery, Calif., 2004-06, Long Beach Art Gallery, Calif., 2004-06, Millard Sheets Gallery, Calif., 2004-06, Carl Cherry Ctr. Art, Calif., 2004-06, others; represented in permanent collections Milw. Jour., Wis., Milw. Pub. Libr., Chazen Mus. Art, U. Wis., Madison; represented in pvt. collections C.L. Clark, Bakersfield, Calif., Ms. Jane Doud, Elm Grove, Wis., many others. With U.S. Army, 1953-55, Korea. Recipient purchase award Milw. Pub. Libr., 1961, Best in Show Award, Second City Coun., Long Beach, Calif., 2000, Third Place prize, Second City Coun., 2002. Mem. Berkeley Art Ctr., Elvehjem Mus. Art (Madison, Wis.), San Luis Obispo Art Ctr. Avocations: philosophy, theology, ethics, Hebrew, Greek and Arabic linguistics. Home: 1901 Dayton Rd 167 Chico CA 95928-6956 Office Phone: 530-894-1756.

GOLIN, MARK, editor; b. 1962; Dep. editor Cosmopolitan; editor Maxim, NYC, 1998—99, Details, NYC, 1999—2000; sr. v.p. Moviefone.com, NYC, 2000; v.p. & creative dir. Am. Online (AOL), NYC, 2000; creative dir. Time Inc. Interactive, NYC; editor-at-large Time Inc., NYC; editor Office Pirates, NYC, 2006, People.com, NYC, 2006—. Office: People Online Rockefeller Ctr New York NY 10020-1939

GOLINKIN, WEBSTER FOWLER, healthcare executive, media consultant; b. NYC, Aug. 3, 1951; s. Joseph Webster and Ruth Forman (Fowler) G.; m. Allison Ann Willeford, Apr. 19, 1985; children: Joseph Webster, George Willeford. BA, Harvard U., 1973. Comms. project adminstr. IBM Corp., Armonk, N.Y., 1974-76; v.p. Geer, DuBois Advtg., NYC, 1976-79, Reeves Comm. Corp., 1979-88; sr. v.p. Reeves Entertainment Group, 1986-88; pres. Reeves Corp. Svcs., NYC, 1979-88; co-chmn., CEO, Am. Med. Comms., Inc., Houston, 1988-93; chmn., CEO, America's Health Network, Inc., Orlando, Fla., 1993-99; vice chmn., chief mktg. and sales officer Norwood Promotional Products Inc., Austin, Tex., 1999—2001; pres., CEO Rediclinic LLC, Houston, 2001—. Mem. World

Presidents' Orgn. Home: 806 Briar Ridge Dr Houston TX 77057-1116 Office: Nine Greenway Plz Houston TX 77046 Office Phone: 713-935-0333. E-mail: w.golinkin@worldnet.att.net.

GOLINSKI, JOSEPH ANTONI, mechanical engineer; b. Krakow, Poland, Mar. 11, 1916; s. Walenty and Maria (Surowka) G.; m. Zofia Maria Wimmer, Apr. 10, 1944; children: Peter, Matthew. MSME, Tech. U. of Silesia, Gliwice, Poland, 1946; M in Applied Sci., U. Toronto, Can., 1950; D in Engring., Tech. U. of Krakow, Poland, 1960, DSc, 1963. Machine designer L. Zieleniewski-Fitzner Gam., Krakow, Poland, 1937-45, Casting Coop., Krakow, Poland, 1946-47; sr. asst. Mining Acad., Krakow, Poland, 1947-49; cons., owner Machine Shop Design, Krakow, Poland, 1947-48; demonstrator mech. dept. U. Toronto, Can., 1950-51; group leader design office Can. Vicers Co., Montreal, 1951-52; sessional lectr. mech. dept. McGill U., Montreal, 1952-56; design engr. Inst. Fluid-Flow Mach., Gdansk, Poland, 1956-58; assoc. prof., full prof. Tech. U., Wroclaw, Poland, 1959-77, 81-86; head dept. environ. engring., 1968-72; prof. emeritus Tech. U., Wroclaw, Poland, 1986—; sr. lectr. mech. dept. Auchi (Nigeria) Poly., 1977-81; dep. dir. Inst. Chem. Engring., 1881-86. Presenter 7 papers on gas turbine systems to ASME, 1990-98. Author: Vibration Isolation of Rotary Machinery, 1964, Vibration Isolation of Machines and Mechanical Systems, 1979; co-author: Jet Pumps, 1st edit., 1968, 2d edit., 1979, Binary Steam/Air Turbine Plants (Selected Thermodynamic/Design Problems), 2006. Recipient Individual awards Ministry Higher Edn., 1964, 86, Collective awards, 1969, 80. Mem. ASME. Home: Ul Olszewskiego 23C/19 51-642 Wroclaw Poland

GOLIS, PAUL ROBERT, lawyer; b. San Francisco, Sept. 25, 1954; BA with high distinction, Calif. State U., Long Beach, 1977; JD, Syracuse U., 1981. Bar: Fla. 1984, U.S. Dist. Ct. (so. dist.) Fla. 1985, U.S. Ct. Appeals (11th cir.) 2000. Assoc. Russell L. Forkey, P.A., Ft. Lauderdale, Fla., 1984-85, Josias & Goren, P.A., Ft. Lauderdale, 1985-88; sr. trial atty. State of Fla. Dept. Transp., Ft. Lauderdale, 1988-90; asst. county atty. Palm Beach County, West Palm Beach, Fla., 1990-91; assoc. Scott, Royce, Harris, Bryan & Hyland, Palm Beach Gardens, Fla., 1991-93, Watterson, Hyland & Klett, Palm Beach Gardens, 1993-98; pvt. practice Boca Raton, Fla., 1998—. Featured spkr. on eminent domain issues Palm Beach County Bar Assn., West Palm Beach, 1993, West Palm Beach, 96, West Palm Beach, 99, West Palm Beach, 2001; on legal ethics Nat. Bus. Inst., West Palm Beach, 1999, West Palm Beach, 2001, on land use, 00; on eminent domain issues Fla. Bar, 2002; spl. magistrate code enforcement issues Town of Hypoluxo, 2002—; spl. magistrate tax assessment issues Palm Beach County Value Adjustment Bd., 2002—. Bd. dirs. Aid to Victims of Domestic Abuse, Inc., 1990-99, v.p., 1993-97, pres. 1997-99, mem. adv. bd., 1999-2001, aux. bd., 2002—; bd. dirs. Boca Raton Soc. for Disabled, Inc., 1999-2002, treas. 2001-02. Mem. Fla. Bar Assn. (eminent domain com. 1989—, vice chair 2002-03, chair 2003-04), Palm Beach County Bar Assn. (vice chmn. environ., land use and eminent domain CLE com. 1993-95, chmn. 1995-99, mem. 2000—, jud. rels. com. 1996-99, professionalism com. 2001—, co-chair 2005-06, chair 2006—). Office: 2000 Glades Rd Ste 306 Boca Raton FL 33431-8504 Personal E-mail: paulgolis@yahoo.com.

GOLISANO, B. THOMAS, financial services company and professional sports team executive; b. Irondequoit, NY, 1941; BS, SUNY, Alfred, 1961. Founder, chmn., CEO Paychex, Inc., Rochester, NY, 1971—2004, founder, chmn., 2004—. Owner Buffalo Sabres hockey club, 2003—. Mem. exec. com. Prevention Ptnrs; founder B. Thomas Golisano Found; chmn. capital campaign for Sch. of the Holy Childhood; trustee Rochester Inst. Tech., past mem. bd. dirs. Rochester Gen. Hosp. and St. John Fisher Coll.; founding mem. Independence Party. Named to INC mag.'s Dream Team of the Eighties list, Entrepreneur of the Decade, Rochester Bus.; Paychex listed with 200 Best Growth Cos. by Fin. World, among the 1000 Most Valuable in Am. by Forbes, Forbes' Richest Americans, 2006; recipient Herbert W. VanderBrul Entreprenurial award, 1987, Humanitarian of Yr. award, Boy's Town of Italy, 1993, Commerce and Industry award, Rochester C. of C., 1993, Shumway Disting. Svc. award, 1995. Office: Paychex Inc 911 Panorama Trl S Rochester NY 14625-2396*

GOLITZ, LOREN EUGENE, dermatologist, pathologist, medical association administrator; b. Apr. 7, 1941; s. Ross Winston and Helen Francis (Schupp) G.; m. Deborah Burd Frazier, June 18, 1966; children: Carrie Campbell, Matthew Ross. MD, U. Mo., 1966. Diplomate Am. Bd. Dermatology, Nat. Bd. Med. Examiners. Intern USPHS Hosp., San Francisco, 1966—67, med. resident, 1967—69, resident in dermatology SI, 1969—71, dep. chief dermatology, 1972—73; vis. fellow dermatology Columbia-Presbyn. Med. Ctr., NYC, 1971—72; asst. in dermatology Coll. Physicians Surgeons, Columbia, 1972—73; vice-chmn. Residency Rev. Com. for Dermatology, 1983—85; assoc. prof. dermatology, pathology Med. Sch. U. Colo., Denver, 1974—88, prof., 1988—97, clin. prof. pathology, dermatology, 1997—. Chief dermatology Denver Gen. Hosp., 1974-97; med. dir. Ambulatory Care Ctr., Denver Gen. Hosp., 1991-97. Mem. editl. bd. Jour. Cutaneous Pathology, Jour. Am. Acad. Dermatology, Advances in Dermatology (editl. bd. Current Opinion in Dermatology); contbr. articles to med. jours. Fellow Royal Soc. Medicine; mem. AMA (residency rev. com. for dermatology 1982-89, dermatopathology test com. 1979-85), AAAS, Am. Soc. Dermatopathology (sec., treas. 1985-89, pres.-elect 1989, pres. 1990), Am. Acad. Dermatology (chmn. coun. on clin. and lab. svcs., coun. sci. assembly 1987-91, bd. dirs. 1987-91, chmn. joint dermatopathology com.), Soc. Pediat. Dermatology (pres. 1981), Soc. Investigative Dermatology, Pacific Dermatol. Assn. (exec. com. 1979-89, sec.-treas. 1984-87, pres. 1988), Noah Worcester Dermatol. Soc. (publs. com. 1980, membership com. 1989-90), Colo. Dermatol. Soc. (pres. 1978), Am. Bd. Dermatology Inc. (chmn. part II test com. 1989—, exec. com. 1993—, v.p. 1994, pres.-elect 1995, pres. 1996, dir. Emeritus, cons. to bd. 1997—), Colo. Med. Soc., Denver Med. Soc., Denver Soc. Dermatopathology, Am. Dermatol. Assn., Women's Dermatologic Soc., So. Med. Assn., Internat. Soc. Pediat. Dermatology, Am. Contact Dermatitis Soc., Am. Soc. Dermatologic Surgery, Physicians Who Care, Am. Bd. Med. Specialties (del.), N.Y. Acad. Scis., Brit. Assn. Dermatologists (hon.), Brazilian Soc. Dermatology (hon.), U. Mo. Med. Alumni Orgn. (bd. govs. 1993—). Office: Dermatopathology Svc PO Box 6218 Denver CO 80206-0218

GOLKIEWICZ, GARY J., federal official; b. Corning, NY, June 15, 1955; m. Cindy Golkiewicz; children: Keli Lynn, Kate Marie. BS in Acctg., Canisius Coll., 1977; JD, Cath. U., 1980. Law clk. SEC, 1980; staff atty. Grant Appeals Bd. US Dept. Health & Human Svcs., Washington, 1980—84; sr. atty. US Ct. Fed. Claims, 1984—87, chief of staff to Chief Judge Loren A. Smith, 1987—88, chief spl. master, 1988—. Mem.: DC Bar, Ct. Fed. Claims Bar Assn., Fed. Bar Assn., DC Bar Assn. Office: US Ct Fed Claims Office of Spl Masters 717 Madison Pl NW Washington DC 20005 Office Phone: 202-219-9657.*

GOLL, GEOFFREY STEVEN, lawyer; b. Columbus, Ohio, Feb. 2, 1944; s. Carl F. and Dru R. Goll; m. Kim Shauck; children: Megan E., Yvonne M. B.A., Denison U., 1966; J.D., Ohio State U., 1973. Bar: Ohio 1973, U.S. Dist. Ct. (no. dist.) Ohio 1974, U.S. Supreme Ct. 1980. Ptnr. Law Offices of Geoffrey S. Goll L.P.A., Salem, Ohio, 1982—. Mem. exec. bd. Columbiana coun. Boy Scouts Am., 1978, mem. nat. coun., 1981-92, pres., 1984-85; mem. exec. bd. Mobile Meals of Salem, Inc., 1976—; mem. adv. bd. Salem Salvation Army, 1979-81, chmn., 1981; mem. exec. bd. Salem Area Indsl. Devel. Corp., 1980— , Columbiana County Port Authority, 1981-96, Columbiana Bd. Elections, 1984-91; vice chmn. Columbiana County Republican Central Com., 1977-84; elder Presbyn. Ch.; trustee Salem Cmty. Found., 1995—2005, Salem Rotary Club Found., 1995—, Saxon Scholarship Found., 1988—; mem. Salem Ohio Utilities Com., 1993—, chair, 1995—. Served to lt. col. USAFR, 1966-93. Recipient District Merit award Boy Scouts Am., 1980, Silver Beaver award, 1984. Mem. ABA, Columbiana County Bar Assn. (sec.-treas. 1979—2004), Ohio State Bar Assn. (local com. 1980—), Columbiana County Mental Health Assn., Ohio State U. Alumni Assn. (trustee Columbiana County 1979-81, pres. 1984-86, 86-2000), Salem C. of C. (bd. dirs. 1979, 81-85, pres. 1984-85). Clubs: Saxon. Lodges: Elks, Rotary (pres. 1985, dist. gov. 2006—). Avocations: golf; travel. Home: 1989 Quaker Ln Salem OH 44460-1875 Office: PO Box 92 Salem OH 44460-0092 Office Phone: 330-337-9529. E-mail: ggull1@aol.com.

GOLL, PAULETTE SUSAN, education educator; b. Cleve., June 5, 1947; d. Ferdinand Paul and Lillian Clarice (Mehalko) Goll. BA in English, Cleve. State U., 1969, MEd, 1974; MA in English, U. Bridgeport, Conn., 1979; PhD in English, Case Western Res. U., Cleve., 1987. Cert. secondary tchr. Ohio, English tchr. Ohio, asst. supr. Ohio, secondary prin. Ohio. Part-time instr. U. Bridgeport, 1978-79, Case Western Res. U., Cleve., 1985-87, lectr., 2002—; tchr. English, Cleve. Pub. Schs., 1969—99, chmn. dept., coord. Ohio Proficiency Test, 1991—96; regional dir. Summer Inst. Gifted Midwest Region, Granville, Ohio, 2000—02. Advisor Students Against Drunk Drivers, 1985—86; coord. project success Lincoln West HS, Cleve., 1987—90; ACT vis. tchr., 1999; adj. instr. English Case Western Res. U., Cleve. State U., 1999—2000; vis. assoc. prof. edn. Dickinson Coll., Carlisle, Pa., 2000; external reviewer Bedford/St. Martins, Reading Critically, Writing Well, 2003, Wadsworth, the Informal Reader, 2004; presenter in field. Co-author: Shakespearean Comedies, 1985; textbook cons. McDougal Littel, 1999—2000. Mem. com. human rels. Cleve. Partnerships, 1989—92; co-chmn. High Schs. for Future, 1985—86; liaison Metrohealth/Lincoln-West Partnership, 1989—92. Named Master Tchr., Martha Holden Jennings Found., 1988; recipient Congl. Commendation Mary Rose Oaker, 1988, award of Excellence, Rotary, 1989, Tchr. of the Yr., Brit. Petroleum, 1997; fellow, NEH, 1985, 1993, Baker-Nord Seminarion, 2007; Jennings scholar, 1985, 1988. Mem.: ASCD (presenter), Case Showcase (presenter 2006, 2007), North Ctrl. Assn. (chair vis. team 1991, 1993), Nat. Assn. Gifted (presenter 2001), Phi Delta Kappa (v.p. programs 1993). Republican. Roman Catholic. Avocations: travel, music, needlepoint, writing, camping. Home: 11366 Clarke Rd Columbia Station OH 44028-9626 Personal E-mail: gollp@earthlink.net. Business E-Mail: psg3@case.edu.

GOLLAHALLI, SUBRAMANYAM RAMAPPA, engineering educator; b. Sadali, Karnataka, India, Nov. 26, 1942; came to U.S., 1976; s. Bagepalli Rampappa and Nagalakshamma Rao Ramappa; m. Rangamani Nadig Gollahalli, Dec. 25, 1967; children: Suma, Anil. BE Mech. Engring., U. Mysore, Karnataka, India, 1963; ME Mech. Engring., Indian Inst. Sci., Bangalore, 1985; MSc Mech. Engring., U. Waterloo, Ont., Can., 1970; PhD Mech. Engring., U. Waterloo, 1973. Registered profl. engr., Okla. Lectr. Indian Inst. Sci., Bangalore, 1965—68; asst. prof. U. Waterloo, 1973—76; from asst. prof. to full prof. U. Okla., Norman, 1976—92, Lesch Centennial prof., 1992—. Lesch Centennial chair U. Okla., Norman, 1998—, dir. Aerospace and Mech. Engring. Rsch. Ctr., 2001—; cons. in field Editor: ASME Conf. Proc., 1990, 91, 92; assoc. editor Jour. Energy Resources Tech., 1994-2000, Jour. Equipment Gas Turbines and Power, 1999-2005. Advance com. chair Boy Scouts Am., Norman, 1988-90 Recipient Ralph Angus medal Inst. Engrs. Can., 1978, Ralph Teetor award Soc. Automotive Engrs., 1978 Fellow ASME (Ralph James award 1993, chair emerging energy tech. com. 1990-93, George Westinghouse gold medal 2005), AIAA (assoc., tech. com., Energy Sys.award 2001, Sustained Svc. award 2006); mem. Pi Tau Sigma Achievements include research in spray combustion, particularly for delineating the structure of droplet wake flames, and turbulent flames in cross-flows. Office: Univ of Oklahoma 865 Asp Ave Norman OK 73019-1050 Office Phone: 405-325-1728. Business E-Mail: gollahal@ou.edu.

GOLLANCE, ROBERT BARNETT, ophthalmologist; b. NYC, Oct. 25, 1937; s. Harvey and Sarah (Chinitz) G.; m. Carmen Côté Gollance, Nov. 8, 1969; 1 child, Stephen Andrew. BA cum laude, Harvard Coll., 1958; MD, Columbia Coll., 1962. Diplomate Am. Bd. Ophthalmology, Nat. Bd. Med. Examiners. Intern in medicine NYU-Bellevue, 1962-63, resident and chief resident in ophthalmology, 1963-66; fellowship NIH, 1964-69; sec.-treas. Ophthalmology Assocs., Wayne, NJ, 1970-93; pres. Eye Assocs. of Wayne, 1993—; lectr. in ophthalmology Columbia U., NYC, 1998-2001; adv. bd. for devel. UMDNJ, 2002—. Chmn. ophthalmology Chilton Meml. Hosp., Pompton Plains, NJ, 1987-89, pres. med. staff, 1991; great hands adv. com. Becton Dickinson Corp., Franklin Lakes, NJ, 1990—; adv. com. Bausch & Lomb Corp., Rochester, NY, 1980-83; found. bd. Eye Inst. NJ Med.-Dental Sch., faculty cataract surgery and lens implantation; cons. Pharmacia Corp. Clin. Rsch. Glaucoma Medications, 2002—. Contbr. articles to profl. jours. Chmn. parents fund raising Loomis Chaffee Sch., Windsor, Conn., 1989-90. Capt. U.S. Army, 1966-68. Recipient Letter of Appreciation Korean Opthalomology Soc., 1967, Cath. Med. Ctr., 1967. Fellow ACS, Am. Soc. Cataract and Refractive Surgery, Am. Acad. Ophthalmology, European Soc. Cataract and Refractice Surgery. Office: Eye Assocs of Wayne 968 Hamburg Tpke Wayne NJ 07470-3225 Home Phone: 973-872-1710; Office Phone: 973-696-0300. E-mail: rbgollance@yahoo.com, rbgollance@njeyeinstitute.com.

GOLLATA, JAMES ANTHONY, library director, educator; b. Manitowoc, Wis., Aug. 18, 1945; s. Anthony Francis and Evelyn Marion (Terens) G.; children: Davis, Adrian. BS, U. Wis., 1969, MA, 1973. Libr. dir. Mt. Senario Coll., Ladysmith, Wis., 1974-87, U. Wis., Richland Center, 1987—. Pres. Wis. Ctr. for the Book, Madison, 1997-98, bd. dirs. Author numerous poems; appeared (several films and videos), hosted (jazz radio program); contbr. articles pub. to profl. jours. Mem. Wis. Libr. Assn. (newsletter editor 1986—, Literary award 1984-87, 96-99), Wis. Acad. Scis., Arts and Letters (chmn. Gordon MacQuarrie com. 1997). Avocations: music, art, book collecting, theater, acting. Home: 489 S Ira St Richland Center WI 53581-2617 Office: Univ Wis 1200 US Hwy 14 W Richland Center WI 53581-1316 Office Phone: 608-647-6186 ext. 220. Business E-Mail: jgollata@uwc.edu.

GOLLIN, MICHAEL A., lawyer; b. Rochester, NY, July 3, 1957; AB, Princeton U., 1978; MS, U. Zurich, 1981; JD, Boston U., 1984. Bar: NY 1985, Mass. 1985, DC 1991, Md. 1991, US Patent and Trademark Office. Ptnr., intellectual property, patent law, environmental law Venable LLP, Washington. Adjunct prof. McDonough Sch. of Bus., Georgetown U., 2001—. Founder Public Interest Intellectual Property Advisors, chair; trustee Rene Dubos Ctr. for Human Environments, Inc., 1994—2004. Recipient Young Lawyer's Chair award, 1994, Benjamin R. Civiletti Pro Bono Lawyer of the Yr. award, 2004. Mem.: ABA (vice chair, emerging tech. com., nat. resources & environ. law section 1992—2000). Office: Venable LLP 575 7th St NW Washington DC 20004 Office Phone: 202-344-4072. Office Fax: 202-344-8300. Business E-Mail: magollin@venable.com.

GOLLIN, STUART ALLEN, accountant; b. Bronx, NY, Aug. 7, 1941; s. Samuel and Suggie (Schreiber) G.; m. Harriet Joy Friedlander, Aug. 16, 1964; children: Deborah Lynn, Mark David, Adam Douglas, Seth Craig. BBA, CCNY, 1963. CPA, N.Y., N.J. Ptnr., nat. dir. retailing Touche Ross & Co., Newark, 1963-80; ptnr., nat. dir. retailing, nat. dir. bankruptcy and insolvency, dir. litigation and ins. cons. svcs. Laventhol & Horwath, NYC, 1980-90; ptnr. in charge bankrupty litig. support and ins. cons. David Berdon & Co., NYC, 1990-92; v.p. insolvency Buccino & Assocs., NYC, 1993-94; dir. litig. and appraisal svcs. J.H. Cohn & Co., NYC, 1994-96; mng. dir. corp. transactions KPMG Peat Marwick, NYC, 1996-97, Morrison & Gollin LLP, NYC, 1998—. Bd. dirs. Dad's Club of Hartsdale, Mid-Westchester YM/YMHA; treas. Am. Liver Found.; bd. dirs. The Transplant Living Ctr.; pres. Scarsdale Sports Assn. Mem. AICPA, N.Y. State Soc. CPAs, Am. Bankruptcy Inst., Nat. Cert. Insolvency & Reorgn. Acct., N.J. Soc. CPAs (acctg. and auditing stds., rels. with bankers, rels. with fin. writers coms., rels. with credit unions, chmn. bankruptcy and involvency com., litig. support com.), Nat. Assn. Accts. (dir. Westchester chpt.), Turnaround Mgmt. Assocs., Nat. Retail Mchts. Assn., Nat. Mass Retailers Inst., N.J. Retail Mchts. Assn., Met. Retail Fin. Execs. Assn., White Plains Jaycees, Bergen County C. of C., Ardsley Swim Club (dir.), Ridgeway Country Club, Beta Alpha Psi. Home: 34 Benedict Rd Scarsdale NY 10583-7340

GOLLIN, SUSANNE MERLE, cell biologist, researcher; b. Chgo., Sept. 22, 1953; d. Harvey A. and Pearl (Reiffel) G.; m. Lazar M. Palnick; 1 child, Jacob Hillel. BA in Biology, Northwestern U., 1974, MS, 1975, PhD, 1980. Diplomate Am. Bd. Med. Genetics with cert. in clin. cytogenetics; cert. food protection specialist. Postdoctoral fellow U. Rochester (N.Y.) Med. Ctr., 1979-81; rsch. assoc. in cell biology Baylor Coll. Medicine, Houston, 1981-83, rsch. assoc. in genetics, 1983-84; asst. prof. dept. pathology and pediat. U. Ark. for Med. Sci., Little Rock, 1984-87; dir. cytogenetics lab. Ark. Children's Hosp., Little Rock, 1984-87; assoc. mem. Pitts. Cancer Inst., 1987-95, mem., 1995—; dir. U. Pitts. Cancer Inst. Cytogenetics Facility, 1989—; asst. prof. human genetics U. Pitts., Grad. Sch. Pub. Health, 1987-95, dir. clin. cytogenetics lab., 1988-99, assoc. prof., 1995—2003, prof., 2003—, prof. human genetics, otolaryngology, pathology, 2003—; dir. rsch., clin. cons. Pitts. Cytogenetics Lab., 1999—. Pediat. oncology group, exec. com. Ark. Genetics Program, 1984-87; organizing com. Am. Cytogenetics Conf., 1990-2002; mem. Allegheny County Bd. Health, 1992-2004, vice chmn., 1997, 2000-04; bd. dirs. Tobacco-Free Allegheny; clin. lab. improvement adv. com. Ctrs. Disease Control and Prevention, HHS, 1994-2000, mem. genetic testing subcom., 1997-2000; founding fellow, Internat. Acad. Oral Oncology, 2005-; vis. sci. German Cancer Rsch. Ctr., Heidelberg, 1995; cons. med. devices adv. com. FDA, 1996—; mem. oral biol. med. I study sect. NIH, 1997; master gardener, 2000; spl. emphasis panel Nat. Cancer Inst., 2000; genetics spl. emphasis panel ZRG1-GEN-01S, NIH Ctr. for Sci. Rev., 2000, spl. emphasis panel Nat. Cancer Inst., Minority Instn./Cancer Ctr. Partnerships, 2000, 05, mammalian genetics study sect., 2002; lectr. U.S.-Japanese Cancer Rsch. Collaborative Conf., Tokyo, 2001; lectr. 1st Dhirubhai Ambani Life Scis. Symposium, Mumbai, 2006; immunol. devices panel FDA, 2004—; lectr. in field. Contbr. articles to profl. jours., chpts. to books; mem. editl. bd. Cytogenetics and Genome Rsch., 2005—, Genes, Chromosomes, & Cancer, 2007—. Mem. deans' adv. com. Pa. Sch. Excellence for Healthcare Profls., 1991-95; v.p. faculty senate U. Pitts. Grad. Sch. Pub. Health, 1994-95, senate anti-discriminatory policies com., 1999-2002, faculty senate athletics com., 2004—, search com. dean Grad. Sch. Pub. Health and chair human genetics, 2004-06., faculty adv. promotion tenure com., 2005—; mem. U. Pitts. Grad. Sch. Pub. Health Task Force on Smoking, 2007—; vol. Lighthouse for Blind, Houston, 1983; vol. hort. dept. Pitts. Zoo, 2000-01; chmn. med. ethics and civil liberties com. ACLU, Pitts., 1989-91; alt. del. Dem. Nat. Conv., 1992, 96, 2000, mem. rules com., 2004. Fellow Am. Coll. Med. Genetics (founder); mem AAAS, Internat. Acad. Oral Oncology, Am. Assn. Cancer Rsch., Am. Soc. Human Genetics (info. and edn. com. 2004-2005, mem. program com. 2005—), Am. Soc. Cell Biology, Soc. Analytical Cytology, Pitts. Cancer Inst., Pitts. Cytogenetics Club (founder, coord. 1989-95), Phipps/Pitts. Garden Place, Western Pa. Conservancy, Rivers Club, Carnegie Museums, Pitts. Zoo, Orchid Soc. Western Pa., Sigma Xi. Avocations: mountain dulcimer, gardening, photography, pulled thread embroidery. Office: U Pitts Dept Human Genetics Grad Sch Pub Health 130 Desoto St Pittsburgh PA 15213-2535 Home Phone: 412-661-3633; Office Phone: 412-624-5390. Business E-Mail: sgollin@hgen.pitt.edu.

GÖLLNER, MARIE LOUISE, musicologist, retired educator; b. Ft. Collins, Colo., June 27, 1932; d. Francis Gilbert and Gertrude Valentine (Steele) Martinez; m. Theodor W. Göllner, Sept. 30, 1959; children: Katharina, Philipp. BA, Vassar Coll., 1953; postgrad., Eastman Sch. Music, 1953-54, U. Heidelberg, Germany, 1954-56; PhD summa cum laude, U. Munich, 1962, Dr. phil. habil., 1975. Research asst. Bavarian State Library, Munich, 1964-67; lectr. Coll. Creative Studies, U. Calif., Santa Barbara, 1968; asst. prof. UCLA, 1970-74, assoc. prof., 1974-78, prof. musicology, 1978-2000, chmn. dept. music, 1976-80, chmn. dept. musicology, 1985-89; ret., 2000. Author: Die Musik des frühen Trecento, 1963, Katalog der Musikhandschriften der Bayerischen Staatsbibliothek München, vol. 2, 1979, vol. 1, 1989, Joseph Haydn, Symphonie 94, 1979, Orlando di Lasso: Sämtliche Werke, Neue Reihe, Das Hymnarium, (1580-82), 1980, Eine neue Quelle zur italienischen Orgelmusik des Cinquecento, 1982, The Manuscript Cod. lat. 5539 of the Bavarian State Library (Musicological Studies & Documents 43), 1993, Essays on Music and Poetry in the Late Middle Ages, 2003, The Early Symphony: 18th-Century Views on Composition and Analysis, 2004, The Echo of Music: Essays in Honor of Marie Louise Göllner, 2004; contbr. articles to profl. jours. NEH grantee, 1983, Fulbright grantee, 1954-56; Gordon Anderson Meml. lectr. U. New Eng., Armidale, Australia, 1984. Mem. Internat. Assn. Music Libraries, Am. Musicol. Soc., Internat. Musicol. Soc., Medieval Acad. Am. Episcopalian. Home: 817 Knapp Dr Santa Barbara CA 93108-1941 Business E-Mail: gollner@ucla.edu.

GOLLOB, HERMAN COHEN, retired publishing executive; b. Waco, Tex., July 7, 1930; s. Abe and Ruybe (Cohen) G.; m. Barbara Kowal, Apr. 9, 1961; children: Emily, Jared. BA, Tex. A & M U., 1951. Lit. agt. MCA, Beverly Hills, Calif., 1956-58, William Morris, NYC, 1958-59; editor Little, Brown & Co., Boston, 1959-64, Atheneum Pubs., NYC, 1964-68, v.p., editor-in-chief, 1971—; editor-in-chief Harper's Mag. Press, NYC, 1968-71; v.p., editorial dir. The Literary Guild, NYC, 1979-81; v.p., sr. editor Simon & Schuster, NYC, 1981-86; sr. v.p., editor-in-chief Doubleday Pub. Co., 1986-90, editor-at-large, 1990-95; ret., 1995. Author: Me and Shakespeare, 2002. Served to lt. USAF, 1951-53. Home: 40 Frederick St Montclair NJ 07042-4106

GOLLOBIN, LEONARD PAUL, chemical engineer; b. NYC, July 2, 1928; s. Morris and Jennie (Levine) G.; m. Charlotte Weissman, Jan. 21, 1951; children: Michael L., Susan D. Brown. BSChemE, CUNY, 1951; MS, Kans. State U., 1952; grad. mgmt. program, Harvard U., 1975. Design engr. Foster Wheeler Corp., NYC, 1952-55; mfg. engr. Gen. Electric Co., Waterford, NY, 1955-58; program dir. ORI, Inc., Silver Spring, Md., 1958-63; chmn., chief exec. Presearch, Inc., Fairfax, Va., 1963—2004; dir., mgr. Level II Sys., Longboat Key, Fla., 2004—; chief scientist, engr. Hicks and Assocs., Sci. Applications Internat. Corp., McLean, Va., 2004—. U.S. del. NATO Indsl. Avd. Group, 1989, chmn., 1992-93, chmn. emeritus, 1994-95; bd. visitors Nat. Def. U., Washington, 1989-98. Bd. dirs. Cultural Alliance Greater Washington, 1980-88, northern Va. bd. Va. Opera, 2000-01; trustee Washington Opera, 1988-90. Recipient NSIA Adm. Charles Weakley award, 1986, Meritorious Pub. Svc. award U.S. Dept. Navy, 1987, U.S. Marine Corps, 1989. Mem. Nat. Security Indsl. Assn. (exec. com. 1986—, chmn. antisubmarine warfare com. 1981-84, chmn. amphibious warfare com. 1986-89, chmn. environ. com. 1990-92, chmn. internat. com. 1991-93, vice chmn. exec. com. 1993, chmn. 1994, chmn. bd. trustees 1994-95), Nat. Def. Indsl. Assn. (chmn. fin. com. 1998—, mem. exec. com., chmn. energy security com. 2006-), Am. Chem. Soc., Naval Undersea Warfare Found. Mus., Loudon Golf and Country Club (Purcellville, Va.), Lougboat Key Club. Home: 3010 Grand Bay Blvd 425 Longboat Key FL 34228

GOLLUB, JERRY PAUL, physics professor; b. Mont. BA, Oberlin Coll., 1966, AM, 1967; PhD in Exptl. Condensed Matter Physics, Harvard U., 1971. Prof. physics Haverford Coll., Pa., 1979—, provost, prof. Pa., 1988—90, John and Barbara Bush prof. in natural scis. Pa., 1996—. Adj. prof. physics dept. U. Pa.; Sigma Xi lectr., 1983—85; mem. grad. group in mech. engring. and applied mechanics, 1985—99; vis. prof. Paris VII, 1985, Ecole Normale, 1991; project dir. Mid-Atlantic Pew Sci. Program in Undergraduate Edn., 1987—90; provost, prof. Haverford Coll., 1988—90, John and Barbara Bush prof. natural scis., Pa., 1996—; Morris Loeb lectr. in Physics Harvard U., 1990; Belkin prof. Weizmann Inst. Sci., 1997—98; mem. comm. on phys. scis., math., and applications NRC, 1998—2000, co-chair com. programs for advanced high sch. sci. and maths. edn., 2000—02, mem. governing bd., 2007—, mem. steering com. math/sci. partnership project. Co-author: Chaotic Dynamics: An Introduction; divisional assoc. editor Physical Review Letters, editl. bd. Physics of Fluids, invited columnist Physics Today, bd. editor American Journal of Physics, 1985—88, Physical Review, 1986—89, Nonlinearity: Journal of Nonlinear Science, 1990—93; contbr. articles tp profl. jours. Vis. scholar Danforth Fellowship; Guggenheim Fellow, 1984—85, Woodrow Wilson Fellowship. Fellow: Am. Physical Soc. (mem. exec. bd. and coun. 2001—02, chair-elect, divsn. fluid dynamics, chair, program com., sec.-treas., divsn. fluid dynamics 1985—88, APS award for Rsch. in an undergraduate institution 1985), Am. Acad. of Arts and Scis.; mem.: NAS (mem. 1993—, adv. bd., Nat. Sci. Resource Ctr. 1995—2000, mem. gov. coun. 2005—). Office: Haverford Coll 370 Lancaster Ave Haverford PA 19041-1392 Office Phone: 610-896-1196. Office Fax: 610-896-4904. Business E-Mail: jgollub@haverford.edu.

GOLOBY, GEORGE WILLIAM, JR., environmental scientist, editor, ornithologist; b. Franklin, Ky., Mar. 21, 1949; s. George William Sr. and Katherine Jacqueline (Panchot) G.; m. Diane Grayson, Dec. 29, 1974; children: Amy Vanessa, George William III. BS in Wildlife Sci., Tex. A&M U., 1971. Zookeeper of birds Houston Zool. Gardens, 1971—72; warehouseman, driver Houston Ind. Sch. Dist., 1972—76; lab. mgr. Empak Inc., Houston, 1976—80; asst. sect. chief City of Houston Dept. Pub. Works, 1980—90; environ. quality specialist III City of Houston Dept. Pub. Works & Engring., 1990—2007; project mgr. City of Houston, 2007—. Founder, owner Penfeathers Tours, Houston, 1984—; instr. Houston Arboretum and Nature Ctr., 1999; instr. Tex. birding cert. Armand Bayou Nature Ctr., U. Houston, 1999-2003. Editor (newsletters) Water Environment Assn. Tex. Pipeline 1984-2001, Tex. Ornithol. Soc. Newsletter, 1989-99, Penfeathers Newsletter, 1986—, Panchot Paper, 1989-93, Houston Audubon Soc., 1977-80, The Naturalist, 1986-89; asst. editor (books) Houston, 1978, Encyclopedia of American Cities, 1979; advt. mgr. Tex. WET Mag., 2002—. Mem. Houston Proud, 1986, Cy-Fair Houston C. of C., 1986, Greater Houston Conv. and Vis. Bur., 1986-88. Mem. Water Environ. Assn. Tex. (com. chmn. 1984—2006), Tex. Water Utilites Assn., Houston Audubon Soc. (v.p. adminstrv. affairs 1986-89), Am. Birding Assn., Outdoor Nature Club, Parrot People Club (v.p. Houston chpt. 1985-86), Purple Martin Conservation Assn., Whooping Crane Conservation Assn., Tex. Nature Conservancy. Office: City Houston 4545 Groveway Dr Houston TX 77087-1122 Office Phone: 713-641-9169. E-mail: pfcompany@aol.com.

GOLODNER, JACK, labor association official; b. NYC, Nov. 2, 1931; s. Maurice S. and Regina (Gaber) G.; m. Linda Louise Fowler, June 14, 1964; children: Dean Dovid, Daniel Dimmick, Jonathan Wilmot. BS, Cornell U., 1953; JD, Yale U., 1958. Labor arbitrator, Washington, 1958-60; exec. asst. to U.S. Congressman Giaimo, 1960-62; cons. pub. affairs, 1962-80; exec. sec. Coun. AFL-CIO Unions for Profl. Employees, 1967-77; dir. dept. for profl. employees AFL-CIO, 1977-89, pres., 1989—2001. V.p. bd. trustees Ford's Theater, Washington, 1973-79, Actors Studio, NY, 1982-87; bd. dir. Nat. Theatre, 1978—; mem. gen. bd. Am. Coun. for the Arts, 1981-96; presdl. appointee Nat. Info. Infrastructure adv. coun., 1994-96; mem. adv. coun. nat. orgns. Corp. Pub. Broadcasting, 1973-79; mem. Labor Adv. Com. for Multilateral Trade Negotiations of Dept. of Labor, 1975-2002; mem. arts and humanities com. Pres.'s Commn. on Internat. Women's Year, 1975-76; mem. US del. UNESCO govtl. experts meeting, Paris, 1980; US del. to adv. com. on salaried and profl. workers Internat. Labor Orgn., 1981, 85, 94, US labor del. Plenary Internat. Labor Orgn. Conf., 1981, 82; chmn. labor del. tripartit meeting on salaried authors and inventors, 1987, Internat. Labor Orgn.; mem. coun. Cornell U., 1987-93; chmn., mem. adv. coun. Cornell Sch. of Indsl. and Labor Rels., 1980-88, 90-94, mem. outside rev. com., 1986-87; mem. US govt. del. Diplomatic Conf. on Certain Copyright and Neighboring Rights Questions, World Intellectual Property Orgn., Geneva, 1996. Capt. USAF, 1953-55. Recipient William B. Groat award Cornell U., 1979 Mem. Indsl. Rels. Rsch. Assn. (exec. bd. 1993-96), Internat. Secretariat Arts, Mass Media and Entertainment Trade Unions (world v.p. 1987-93), Media and Entertainment Internat. (1st v.p. 1993-97), Nat. Policy Assn. (exec. com. New Am. Realities Program 1987-2003, co-chair nat. digital econ. opportunity com. 2000-2002), Phi Kappa Phi. Home: 1739 Q St NW Washington DC 20009-2407 Office: 1140 Conn Ave NW Washington DC 20036

GOLOMB, FREDERICK MARTIN, surgeon, educator; b. NYC, Dec. 18, 1924; s. Jacob J. and Hannah (Loewy) G.; m. Joan E. Schneider, Nov. 28, 1954; children: James Bradley, Susan Lynn. BS, Yale U., 1945; MD, U. Rochester, 1949. Diplomate: Am. Bd. Surgery. Intern Johns Hopkins Hosp., 1949-50; resident NYU Hosp., 1950-56; mem. staff NYU Med. Ctr., 1950—, dir. chemoimmunotherapy divsn. tumor svc. dept. surgery, 1967-96; attending surgeon Tisch Hosp.; mem. faculty NYU Sch. Medicine, 1956—, prof., clin. surgery, 1977—. Mem. clin. trials rev. com. Nat. Cancer Inst., 1976-79; chmn. melanoma com. Eastern Coop. Oncology Group, 1978-80; prin. investigator Central Oncology Group, 1969-77, exec. com., 1976-77; co-prin. investigator Ea. Coop. Oncology Group NYU, 1978-95. Contbr. articles to profl. jours. Served with M.C. AUS, 1953-54, Korea. Recipient John E. Sullivan award Beth Israel Med. Ctr., 1993. Fellow ACS; mem. AMA, Am. Assn. Cancer Rsch., Am. Soc. Clin. Oncology, N.Y. Cancer Soc. (pres. 1974-75), N.Y. Surg. Soc., N.Y. State Med. Soc., N.Y. County Med. Soc., Soc. Surg. Oncology, George Hoyt Whipple Soc., Brit. Assn. Surg. Oncology (editl. adv. panel 1980-85), Am. Alpine Club, Explorers Club, Sigma Xi. Office: Frederick M Golomb MD 59 Churchill Rd Tenafly NJ 07670-3123 Home Phone: 201-567-3680. Business E-Mail: frederick.golomb@med.nyu.edu.

GOLOMB, HARVEY MORRIS, hematologist, oncologist, educator; b. Pitts., Feb. 13, 1943; s. Russell Austin and Dorothy (Simon) G.; m. Lynne Rooth, Dec. 28, 1965; children: Adam, Sara. BA, U. Chgo., 1964; MD, U. Pitts., 1968. Diplomate Am. Bd. Internal Medicine, Am. Bd. Med. Oncology. Intern Boston City Hosp., 1968-69; resident Johns Hopkins U., Balt., 1971-72, fellow, 1972-73, U. Chgo., 1973-75, asst. prof. dept. medicine, 1975-79, assoc. prof., 1979-83, prof., 1983—, chief sect. hematology/oncology, 1981-98, chmn. dept. medicine, 1998—2005, dean clin. affairs divsn. biol. scis., 2005—. Chmn. subspecialty bd. med. oncology Am. Bd. Internal Medicine, 1991-95. Contbr. over 300 articles, papers to profl. publs.; co-editor: Lung Cancer, 1988, Oncologic Therapies, 1999, 2003. Capt. U.S. Army, 1971-73. Mem. Am. Soc. Hematology (bd. dirs. 1987-91), Am. Soc. Oncology (pres. elect 1989-90, pres. 1990-91). Office: U Chgo MC 1000 5841 S Maryland Ave Chicago IL 60637-1463 Business E-Mail: hgolomb@medicine.bsd.uchicago.edu.

GOLOMB, SOLOMON WOLF, mathematician, electrical engineer, director, educator; b. Balt., May 31, 1932; s. Elhanan Hirsh and Minna (Nadel) G. AB, Johns Hopkins U., 1951; MA, Harvard U., 1953, PhD, 1957; postgrad., U. Oslo, 1955—56; DSc (hon.), Dubna Internat. U., Russia, 1995; DHL (hon.), Hebrew Union Coll., LA, 1996. Mem. faculty Boston U., 1954-55, Harvard U., 1954-55, UCLA, 1957-61, Calif. Inst. Tech., 1960-62; sr. rsch. engr. Jet Propulsion Lab., Pasadena, Calif., 1956-58, rsch. group supr., 1958-60, asst. chief telecom. rsch. sect., 1960-63; assoc. prof. U. So. Calif., LA, 1963-64, prof. elec. engring. and math., 1964—, vice provost for rsch., 1986-89, univ. prof., 1993—, dir. tech. Annenberg Ctr. for Comm., 1995-98, Viterbi prof. comm., 1997—. Cons. to govt. and industry. Author: Digital Communications with Space Applications, 1964, 81, Polyominoes, 1965, rev. edit., 1994, Shift Register Sequences, 1967, 82, Basic Concepts in Information Theory and Coding, 1994, Signal Design for Good Correlation, 2005; contbr. articles to profl. jours. Recipient Lomonosov medal Russian Acad. Sci., 1994, Disting. Alumnus award Johns Hopkins U., 2002. Fellow IEEE (Shannon award Info. Theory Soc. 1995, Hamming medal 2000), AAAS, Am. Acad. Arts and Scis.; mem. NAS, NAE, Internat. Sci. Radio Union, Russian Acad. Natural Scis. (fgn., Kapistsa medal 1995), Am. Math. Soc., Math. Assn. Am., Soc. Indsl. and Applied Math., Golden Key, Phi Beta Kappa, Sigma Xi, Pi Delta Epsilon, Eta Kappa Nu, Phi Kappa Phi. Office: U So Calif Univ Park Dept Elec Engring Eeb 504A Los Angeles CA 90089-2565 Home Phone: 818-790-1745. E-mail: milly@usc.edu.

GOLOMB, SUSAN L., literary agent; b. NYC, Feb. 17, 1960; d. Frederick Martin and Joan Ellen Golomb; m. Gregory Thomas Martin, July 17, 1999; 1 child, Jacob Gabriel Golomb Martin. BA, U. Pa., 1982. Prodn. coord. WNET-TV Great Performances, NYC, 1982; asst. agt. Harold Ober Assocs., NYC, 1982—83; reader Samuel Goldwyn Prodns., NYC, 1984; agt. Rosenstone/Wender, NYC, 1984—88; story editor Mirage Prodns., NYC, 1988—89, Hearst Entertainment, NYC, 1989—91; owner Susan Golomb Lit. Agy., NYC, 1991—. Mem.: Women's Media Group. Avocations: rock climbing, hiking, theater. Office: The Susan Golomb Literary Agy 875 6th Ave #2302 New York NY 10001 Home Phone: 212-533-0876. E-mail: susan@sgolombagency.com.

GOLOMBEK, MATTHEW PHILIP, research scientist, planetary geologist; b. New Haven, Sept. 20, 1954; s. Martin I. and Sonia G.; m. Connie M. Morgan, Apr. 26, 1980; children: Sydney, Benjamin. AB in Geology with honors, Rutgers U., 1976; MS in Geology, U. Mass., 1978, PhD in Geology, 1981. Rsch. asst. in sedimentology Rutgers U., New Brunswick, NJ, 1976; tchg. asst. U. Mass., 1979, rsch. asst. in structural and planetary geology, 1976-81; vis. postdoctoral fellow Lunar and Planetary Inst., Houston, 1981-82, vis. scientist, 1982-83; rsch. scientist Jet Propulsion Lab. Calif. Inst. Tech., Pasadena, 1983—2000, Mars Pathfinder project scientist Jet Propulsion Lab., 1994-98, sr. rsch. scientist Jet Propulsion Lab., prin. scientist, 2000—. Lectr. U. Houston, Clear Lake City, 1983, Calif. State Poly. U., Pomona, 1986; Viking guest investigator Jet Propulsion Lab., 1977, US Geol. Survey, Astrogeology Br., Flagstaff, Ariz., 1978; mem. Mars Sci. Working Group, 1989-96, Mars Exploration Edn. Outreach Adv. Bd., 1994-98; chmn. Mars Pathfinder Project Sci. Group, 1994-98; mem. Am. Geophys. Union, Planetology Exec. Com., 1994-97; mem. assessment group Mars Exploration Program, 1999—, landing site scientist, 2000—, Mars Exploration Rover sci. ops. working group chair, 2002—; vis. scientist U. Colo., Boulder, 2000; vis. full prof. Inst. de Physique du Globe de Paris, 2001; spkr., lectr. in field. Planetology editor EOS, Transactions Am. Geophy. Union; assoc. editor Tectonophysics, 1986; contbr. articles to profl. jour. Recipient Vinton Gwinn Meml. prize, Rutgers U., 1976, Laurels award for outstanding achievement in space, Aviation Week and Space Tech., 1997, award for excellence, Jet Propulsion Lab./Project Scientist for Mars Pathfinder Mission, 1998, Disting. Alumni award for Profl. Svc., U. Mass., 1998, Hall of Disting. Alumni award, Rutgers U. Alumni Fedn., 1998, Exceptional Sci. Achievement medal, NASA, 1998, others, Dr. Matt Golombek Day named in his honor, City of Hackensack, NJ, 1998, asteroid named Golombek in his honor, 1992, Schlumberger scholar, Rutgers U., 1975—76, numerous grants, 1983—. Fellow Geol. Soc. Am.; mem. Am. Geophy. Union. Office: Jet Propulsion Lab MS 183-501 4800 Oak Grove Dr Pasadena CA 91109-8001 Business E-Mail: mgolombek@jpl.nasa.gov.

GOLOMSKI, WILLIAM ARTHUR JOSEPH, consulting company executive; b. Custer, Wis. s. John Frank and Margaret Sophie (Glisczinski) G.; m. Joan Ellen Hagen; children: Gretchen E., William A. Jr. MS, Marquette U.; MBA, U. Chgo; MS in Engring. Mgmt., Milw. Sch. Engring; MA, Roosevelt U. Registered profl. engr., Calif. Prin. W.A. Golomski & Assocs., Algoma, Wis., 1949—, pres., 1971—. Judge Malcolm Baldridge Nat. Quality award, 1988; sr. lectr. Grad. Sch. Bus., U. Chgo., 1990-95. Author chpts. in books; co-editor A Quality Revolution in Manufacturing, 1989; founding editor Quality Mgmt. Jour., 1993. Mem. Avoca Sch. Bd., Wilmette, Ill.; adv. bd. Milw. Sch. Engring., 1967-72, 83-87, indsl. engring. com. Hon. mem. Philippine Soc. Quality Control, 1992. Fellow AAAS, Am. Soc. Quality Control (Eugene L. Grant award 1991, Edwards medal, William A. Golomski rsch. award named in his honor 1986, Am. Deming medal met. sect., hon. mem. 1993), N.Y. Acad. Scis., Royal Soc. Health, Am. Statis. Assn., Inst. Indsl. Engrs. (Frank and Lillian Gilbreth Indsl. Engring. award 1999), World Assn Productivity Sciences; mem. NAE. Achievements include devel. of world class orgns.; first jour. for quality mgmt. and quality in higher edn. Office: N9690 County Road U Algoma WI 54201-9528

GOLOVKIN, IGOR, physicist; b. Moscow, May 27, 1968; s. Evgeny Golovkin and Alexandra Golovkina; m. Victoria Bagdanskite, Aug. 30, 1970; 1 child, Maria Golovkina. MS, Moscow State U., 1993; PhD, U. Nev., Reno, 2000. Rschr. U. Wis., Madison, 2001—02; scientist Prism Computational Scis., Inc., Madison, 2002—. Office: Prism Computational Scis Inc 455 Science Dr Ste 140 Madison WI 53711 Home Phone: 608-833-8721; Office Phone: 608-268-0465.

GOLSHANI, S. DANIEL, plastic surgeon; BS in Biology magna cum laude, UCLA, 1987; MD, U. Calif. Irvine Sch. Medicine, 1991. Diplomate Am. Bd. Plastic Surgery, Am. Bd. Surgery. Gen. surgery resident U. So. Calif., 1991—97, rsch. fellow, plastic surgery, 1993—94; plastic & reconstructive surgery resident U. Calif., San Francisco, 1997—99; clin. fellow in microsurgery and hand surgery U. So. Calif., So. Calif. Orthopedic Inst., 1999—2000; clin. instr., plastic surgery LA County-U. So. Calif. Med. Ctr., 1999—2000, clin. instr., hand surgery/replantation, 1999—2000; emergency room surgical attending physician Kaiser Permanente Hosp., 1999—2000; staff plastic surgeon, hand surgeon West Hills Hosp., 1999—, Tarzana/Encino Hosp., 1999—; plastic & reconstructive surgery, hand surgery Comprehensive Outpatient Surgery Ctr., 2001—; private practice Beverly Hills Advanced Surgical Inst., 2001—, West Hills Surgery Ctr., 2001—. Conducted rsch. projects; spkr. in field. Contbr. articles to profl. jours. Regent's Scholar, U. Calif., 1987—91, Nat. Cancer Inst. Student Fellowship, 1990. Fellow: Am. Coll. Surgeons; mem.: LA Surgical Soc., Am. Assn. for Surgery of the Hand, LA County/U. So. Calif. Soc. Grad. Surgeons, AMA, Am. Soc. Plastic Surgeons, Phi Eta Sigma, Phi Beta Kappa. Office: 9301 Wilshire Blvd Ste 401 Beverly Hills CA 90210-6133 Address: 7301 Medical Ctr Dr Ste 304 West Hills CA 91307 Office Phone: 310-274-3481, 818-887-9974. Office Fax: 310-274-3482. E-mail: doctorgolshani@yahoo.com.*

GOLSTON, ALLAN C., foundation administrator; BS in acctg., U. Colo.; MBA, Seattle U. Mem. audit practice KPMG Peat Marwick; dir. fin. Swedish Health Services; chief fin. and adminstrv. officer Bill & Melinda Gates Found., Seattle, 2000—. Bd. dirs. Pub. Libr. of Sci.; treas. Philanthropy N.W.

GOLTZ, JAY, small business owner; BA acctg., Northern Ill Univ, 1978. Founder and pres. Artists' Frame Services, Chgo., 1978—, Chgo. Art Source, Chgo., 1991—, Jayson Home and Garden, Chgo., 1997—, Bella Mouldings, Chgo.; CEO, founder The Goltz Group, Chgo. Minority advocate of the yr. US Small Bus. Adminstrn., 1989; Inc. Mag. Conf. spkr. for Customer Svc. Strategies; Nat. speaking tour on "How to Make Money" The Fletcher-Terry Co., 1999; keynote spkr. Chgo. Area Entrepreneurship Hall of Fame, 2000; cons. Nielsen-Bainbridge, 2004—05, Cresent Cardboard Co., 2004—06; nationwide ins., regional conf. spkr. and workshop leader, 2005; chmn. bd. Local Econ. and Employment Develop, 2006; bus. cons. Second City Comm., 2006; bus. mentor William J. Clinton Foundation's Urban Initiative, 2006; spkr. Inc. 500 Conf., 2006. Author: The Street-Smart Entrepreneur, 1997; bus. editor, monthly columnist Goltz on Business, Picture Framing Mag., 1996—. Bd. dir. Am. Cancer Soc., 1999—2002; co-founder Business Wise, 1998—2001. Finalist Mag. Entrepreneur of Yr., Ernst & Young Inc., 1990, 1993; named one of Top 100 Young Entrepreneurs, Assn. Collegiate Entrepreneurs, 1988, 40 under 40, Crain's Chgo. Bus., 1990, 1999; named to Arthur Anderson Entrepeneurship Hall of Fame, U. Ill. Chgo., 1992; recipient Biz Kid, Forbes, 1987. Office: The Goltz Group 1871 N Clybourn Ave Chicago IL 60614 Office Phone: 773-755-8301. Office Fax: 773-880-8801.

GOLTZ, PAT, artist, web site designer; m. John Goltz; children: Tom, Marti Robbins, Allen, Kenneth, Heidi Short, Philip, Victor. BA, Ohio Dominican U., 1975. Web designer Extraplicity, 2002—. Exhibitions include LA Ctr. Digital Art, 2005, Energy Gallery Toronto, 2006, Upstream People Gallery, Omaha. Co-founder Feminists for Life, Columbus, Ohio, 1972—77, pres., 1972—77. Lutheran. Avocations: piano, organ, singing, languages, Tae Kwon Do. Home: Box 36508 Tucson AZ 85740 Personal E-mail: pgoltz@extraplicity.com.

GOLTZ, ROBERT WILLIAM, dermatologist, educator; b. St. Paul, Sept. 21, 1923; s. Edward Victor and Clare (O'Neill) G.; m. Patricia Ann Sweeney, Sept. 27, 1945; children: Leni, Paul Robert. BS, U. Minn., 1943, MD, 1945. Diplomate: Am. Bd. Dermatology (pres. 1975-76). Intern Ancker Hosp., St. Paul, 1944-45; resident in dermatology Mpls. Gen. Hosp., 1945-46, 48-49, U. Minn. Hosp., 1949-50; practice medicine specializing in dermatology Mpls., 1950-65; clin. instr. U. Minn. Grad. Sch., 1950-58, clin. asst. prof., 1958-60, clin. assoc. prof., 1960-65, prof., head dept. dermatology, 1971-85; prof. medicine and dermatology U. Calif., San Diego, 1985—2004, emeritus prof., 2004—, acting chair divsn. dermatology, 1995-97; prof. dermatology, head div. dermatology U. Colo. Med. Sch., Denver, 1965-71. Former mem. editl. bd. Archives of Dermatology; editor Dermatology Digest. Served from 1st lt. to capt., M.C. U.S. Army, 1946-48. Mem. Assn. Am. Physicians, Am. Dermatol. Assn. (dir. 1976-79, pres. 1985-86), Am. Soc. Dermatopathology (pres. 1981), Am. Dermatologic Soc. Allergy and Immunology (pres. 1981), AMA (chmn. sect. on dermatology 1973-75), Dermatology Found. (past dir.), Minn. Dermatol. Soc., Soc. Investigative Dermatology (pres. 1972-73, hon. 1988), Histochem. Soc., Am. Acad. Dermatology (pres. 1978-79, past dir.) (hon.), Brit. Assn. Dermatology (hon.), Chilean Dermatology Soc. (hon.), Colombian Dermatol. Soc. (corr. mem.), Can. Dermatol. Soc. (hon. mem.), German Dermatol. Soc. (hon.), Pacific Dermatol. Soc. (hon.-mem.), S. African Dermatol. Soc. (hon. mem.), N.Am. Clin. Dermatol. Soc., Assn. Profs. Dermatology (sec.-treas. 1970-72, pres. 1973-74), West Assn. Physicians. Home: 6097 Avenida Chamnez La Jolla CA 92037-7404 Office: U Calif San Diego Med Ctr Divsn Dermatology H-8420 200 W Arbor Dr San Diego CA 92103-1911 Personal E-mail: rwgoltz@san.rr.com.

GOLTZMAN, DAVID, endocrinologist, educator, researcher; s. Jack and Lily (Roth) G.; m. Naomi Lyon, Dec. 29, 1968; children: Jonathan, Rebecca, Daniel. BSc, McGill U., 1966, MD, 1968. Diplomate Am. Bd. Internal Medicine, Am. Bd. Endocrinology and Metabolism. Med. intern Royal Victoria Hosp., Montreal, 1968-69; med. resident Columbia U. Coll. Physicians and Surgeons, NYC, 1969-71; clin. and rsch. fellow in endocrinology Mass. Gen. Hosp., Boston, 1971-75; instr. medicine Harvard Med. Sch., Boston, 1974-75; asst. prof. medicine McGill U., Montreal, 1976-78, assoc. prof., 1978-83, prof., 1983—, chmn. physiology, 1988-93, dir. calcium rsch. lab., 1981—, hosmer prof. physiology, 1992-93, Massabki prof. medicine, 1994—, chmn. medicine, 1994—2004; dir. Ctr. Bone and Periodontal Rsch., 2002—. Sr. physician dept. medicine Royal Victoria Hosp., 1987—, physician-in-chief, 1994-98; physician-in chief, McGill U. Hlth. Ctr., 1998-2004; chmn. exptl. medicine com. Med. Rsch. Coun. Can., Ottawa, Ont., 1984-88; mem. gen. medicine B study sect., NIH, Bethesda, Md., 1987-91; active Exec. Med. Rsch. Coun. Can., 1993-99; hon. prof. Nanjing Med. U., China, 2006—. Author: (with others) Principles of Bone Biology, 2001, Primer of Metabolic Bone Disease and Disorders of Mineral Metabolism, 1996, 1989, Primer of Osteoporosis, 2000, Principles and Practice of Endocrinology and Metabolism, 2001; editl. bd. Endocrinology Jour., 1985-90, Jour. Bone Mineral rsch., 1985-90, Bone and Mineral, 1991-94, Osteoporosis Internat., 1991-94, Assoc. Edn. Bone, 1989-94; assoc. editor: Jur. Bone Mineral research, 1995-2002; contbr. numerous articles to profl. jours. Recipient Chercheur Boursier award Que. Med. Rsch. Coun., 1980-83, Scientist award Med. Rsch. Coun. Can., 1983-88, Andre Lichtwitz prize Nat. Inst. for Med. Rsch., France, 1987; named officer Order of Can., 2000—, John G. Haddad Meml. Lectr. Penn. U, 2004 Fellow Royal Coll. Physicians and Surgeons, Royal Soc. Can., Can. Acad. Health Scis.; mem. Can. Soc. Endocrinology and Metabolism (pres. 1990-92), Am. Soc. for Bone and Mineral Rsch. (chmn. program com. 1989-90, pres. 1999-00), Am. Assn. Physicians, Endocrine Soc. (program com. 1989-91), Can. Soc. Clin. Investigation (councillor 1986-89, pres. 1998-99) Am. Soc. Clin. Investigation, Can. Assn. Profs. of Medicine (pres. 1998-99). Avocations: classical music, gardening, tennis. Office: Royal Victoria Hosp 687 Pine Ave W Montreal PQ Canada H3A 1A1 Business E-Mail: david.goltzman@mcgill.ca.

GOLUB, HARVEY, food products and former financial services company executive; b. NYC, Apr. 16, 1939; Student, Cornell U., 1956-58; BS, NYU, 1961. Jr. ptnr. McKinsey & Co. Inc., NYC, 1967-74, sr. ptnr., 1977-83; pres. Shulman Air Freight, NYC, 1974-77; pres., CEO IDS Fin. Svc., Mpls., 1984-90; chmn., CEO IDS Fin. Svcs. (name changed to Am. Express Fin. Advisors), Mpls., 1990—2001; vice chmn., dir. Am. Express Co., NYC, 1990-91, pres., 1991-93, chmn., CEO, 1993-2001, Am. Express Travel Related Svcs. Co. Inc., NYC, 1991; chmn. AirClic, Blue Bell, Pa., 2001—04, Campbell Soup Co., Camden, NJ, 2004—. Bd. dir. Campbell Soup Co., 1996—, Dow Jones & Co. Inc. Bd. dirs. Am. Enterprise Inst., Columbia Presbyn. Hosp., Carnegie Hall, N.Y.C. Partnership, N.Y. C. of C. and Industry, United Way of N.Y.C.; mem. Bus. Roundtable, Bretton Woods Com.; apptd. mem. Pres.'s Com. for Arts and Humanities, Pres.'s Adv. Trade and Policy Negotiations. Mem. World Travel and Tourism Coun. (exec. com., chmn.-elect). Office: Campbell Soup Co 1 Campbell Pl Camden NJ 08103*

GOLUB, HOWARD VICTOR, lawyer; b. NYC, Jan. 20, 1945; s. Irving W. and Mary Golub. AB cum laude, Hunter Coll., 1965; JD, Harvard U., 1968. Bar: N.Y. 1968, Mass. 1970, Calif. 1973, U.S. Dist. Ct. (no. dist.) 1972, U.S. Ct. Appeals, D. C. 1973, U.S. Ct. Appeals. (9th cir.) 1973, U.S. Supreme Ct. 1973. Asst. dist. atty. N.Y. Dist. Atty.'s Office, NYC, 1968-69; US military judge Judge Adv. General's Corps of US Navy, 1969—73; atty. Pacific Gas and Electric Co., San Francisco, 1973-86, v.p., gen. counsel, 1986—94; ptnr. McKenna & Cuneo, San Francisco, 1995, Nixon Peabody LLP. Contbr. articles to profl. jours. Bd. dirs. Legal Aid Soc. of San Francisco, Renew Am. Capt. JAGC, USNR. Recipient Northern Calif. Super Lawyer, by Law & Politics, 2004, nation's highest environmental medal, by pres. of US. Mem. ABA, Am. Law Inst., Phi Beta Kappa, fellow Am. Bar Found. Office: Nixon Peabody LLP 2 Embarcadero ctr San Francisco CA 94111 Office Phone: 415-984-8200. Office Fax: 415-984-8300. Business E-Mail: hgolub@nixonpeabody.com.

GOLUB, LEWIS, supermarket company executive; b. 1931; BS, Mich. State U., 1953; LHD (hon.), SUNY--Empire State Coll., 1998. With Golub Corp., 1953—, v.p., 1963-71, exec. v.p., 1971-72, pres., treas., 1972-82, chmn. bd., 1982—, also chief exec. officer, dir. Schenectady. Bd. dirs. Taylor Made Co., Racemark Internat., Dot Foods Inc., Paradigm Value Fund, CIES; mem. regional adv. bd. Chase Bank. Advisor MBA program Russell Sage Coll.; mem. adv. coun. grad. mgmt. inst. Union Coll.; bd. dirs. Empire State Coll. Found., Saratoga Performing Arts Ctr., Proctor's Theatre, Food Mktg. Inst., N.Y. State Bus. Coun.; active Found. SUNY. Served with U.S. Army. Recipient Marketer Exec.-Citizen award Sales and Mktg. Execs. Ea. N.Y., 1988, Disting. Citizen award SUNY, 1989, Dr. Norman D. Kathan Cmty. Svc. award YMCA, 1990, Tree of Life award Jewish Nat. Fund, 1992, Disting. Cmty. Svc. award Chinese Cmty., 1993, Cmty. Svc. award Inter-Faith Cmty. of Schenectady, 1993, Cmty. Svc. accolate Northeastern N.Y. chpt. Arthritis Found., 1993, Achievement award Am. Diabetes Assn., 1994, Disting. Citizen Laureate award U. Albany Found., 1994, John J. O'Connor Excellence in Leadership award United Way, 1995, Disting. Citizen award Boy Scouts Am., 1995, N.Y. State Chiefs of Police, 1995, Cmty. Svc. awar Office of Aging, 1996, Legends of the Industry award N.Y. State Food Mchts. Assn., 1996, Corning award N.Y. State Bus. Coun., 2003; named Man of Yr., Am. Jewish Com., 1981, Exec. of Yr., The Capital Dist. Bus. Rev., 1989, Humanitarian of Yr., Ctr. for Disabled, 1999; named to Hall of Fame, Capital Region Bus., 1997, Jr. Achievement, 1997; Paul Harris hon. fellow Rotary Internat., 1992. Office: Golub Corp 501 Duanesburg Rd Schenectady NY 12306-1092

GOLUB, MIKE, professional sports team executive; m. Sam Golub. BA, Dartmouth Coll., 1983; MBA, Stanford U., 1988. Dir. mktg. Oakland-Alameda County Coliseum, 1988—91; mng. dir. events and attractions NBA, 1991—97; founding mem. Nike Sports Entertainment, 1996—99; v.p. mktg. Trakus Inc., Boston; exec. v.p. NBA Memphis Grizzlies, 2000—05; sr. v.p. mktg. and bus. ops. NHL NY Rangers, 2005—06; exec. v.p. bus. ops. NBA Portland Trail Blazers, 2006—07, COO, 2007—. Office: Portland Trail Blazers Rose Garden One Center Ct Portland OR 97227*

GOLUB, NEIL M., supermarket chain executive; b. 1937; married. BA, Mich. State U., 1959; MS, Cornell U., 1961. With Golub Corp., Schenectady, NY, 1962—, asst. sec., 1967-72, v.p., 1972-77, exec. v.p., 1977-82, pres., 1982—, COO, 1982—2000, CEO Schenectady, NY, 2000—. With US Army. Office: Golub Corp 501 Duanesburg Rd Schenectady NY 12306-1092

GOLUB, SHARON BRAMSON, retired psychologist, educator; b. NYC, Mar. 25, 1937; m. Leon M. Golub, June 1, 1958; children: Lawrence E., David B. Diploma, Mt. Sinai Hosp. Sch. Nursing, 1957; BS, Columbia U., 1959, MA, 1966; PhD, Fordham U., 1974. Head nurse Mt. Sinai Hosp., NYC, 1957—59; contbg. editor RN Mag., Oradell, NJ, 1967—74; asst. prof. psychology Coll. New Rochelle, NY, 1974—79, assoc. prof., 1979—86, prof., 1986—98, prof. emeritus, 1998—; ret. Pvt. practice individual and group psychotherapy, 1976—2005; dir. women's studies Coll. New Rochelle, 1978—79, chmn. dept. psychology, 1979—82; adj. prof. psychiatry N.Y. Med. Coll., Valhalla, 1980—94. Editor: Menarche, 1983 (Assn. Women in Psychology Disting. Pub. award 1984, Book of Yr. award Am. Jour. Nursing 1984), Lifting the Curse of Menstruation, 1983, Health Care of the Female Adolescent, 1984, Health Needs of Women as They Age, 1984, PERIODS from Menarche to Menopause, 1992; (with Rita Jackaway Freedman) Psychology of Women: Resources for a Core Curriculum, 1987; editor Women and Health, 1982-86, mem. editorial bd., 1986—; mem. editorial bd. Psychology of Women Quar., 1989-2000. Grantee Nat. Libr. Medicine, 1983-84; NIH rsch. fellow, 1971-74. Fellow Am. Psychol. Assn. (chmn. task force on teaching psychology of women 1980-83), Am. Psychol. Soc.; mem. Soc. for Menstrual Cycle Rsch. (pres. 1981-83, bd. dirs. 1981-93), Assn. Women in Psychology, Westchester County Psychol. Assn. (pres. acad. divsn., Disting. Svc. award 2003), Phi Beta Kappa, Sigma Xi, Psi Chi. Home Phone: 212-879-0560. Personal E-mail: sgolubny@aol.com.

GOLUB, STEVEN J., investment company executive; b. Feb. 19, 1946; Dep. chief acct., chief acct. office SEC, 1979—80; ptnr. Deloitte Haskins & Sells, 1980—84; sr. v.p. Lazard Group, NYC, 1984—86, mng. dir., 1986—97, CFO, 1997—2001, vice chmn., 2004—, chmn., fin. adv. group, 2005—. Bd. dirs. Minerals Technologies Inc., 1993—. Office: Lazard Group 30 Rockefeller Ctr New York NY 10020 Office Phone: 212-632-2000.*

GOLUBITSKY, MARTIN AARON, mathematician, educator; b. Phila., Apr. 5, 1945; s. Isaac and Rose (Sarvetnick) G.; m. Barbara Lee Keyfitz, May 30, 1976; children: Elizabeth Ann, Alexander. AB, AM, U. Pa., 1966; PhD, MIT, 1970. Vis. lectr. UCLA, 1970-71; lectr. MIT, Cambridge, 1971-73; from asst. prof. to assoc. prof. Queens Coll., CUNY, NYC, 1973-79; prof. math. Ariz. State U., Tempe, 1979-83, U. Houston, 1983—. Co-author: Stable Mappings and Their Singularities, 1978, Singularities and Groups in Bifurcation, vols. I and II, 1985, 88, Fearful Symmetry, 1992, Symmetry in Chaos, 1992, Linear Algebra and Differential Equations Using MATLAB, 1999, The Symmetry Perspective, 2002; editor-in-chief SIAM Jour. Applied Dynamic Systems, 2001-05; mem. editl. bd. Jour. Nonlinear Sci., 1990-. Cullen prof. U. Houston, 1989. Fellow AAAS, Am. Acad. Arts and Sciences; mem. Am. Math Soc., Soc. Indsl. and Applied Math. (past pres.). Office: Univ Houston Dept Math 4800 Calhoun Rd Houston TX 77204-3008 Home: 4899 Montrose Blvd Houston TX 77006 E-mail: mg@uh.edu.

GOLUSIN, MILLARD R., obstetrician, gynecologist; b. Detroit, Feb. 14, 1947; s. Raddie and Joan (Lalich) Golusin; m. Yvonne Marie Cronovich, Sept. 29, 1974 (dec.); m. Cvetana Cindy Pavlovich, June 4, 2005. BS with honors, Wayne State U., 1968, MS, 1970, MD, 1975. Diplomate Am. Bd. Ob-Gyn. Intern, then resident William Beaumont Hosp., Royal Oak, Mich., 1975-78; practice medicine specializing in obstetrics and gynecology Village Gynecologic and Obstetric Assocs., P.C., Southfield and Troy, Mich., 1978-92; pvt. practice specializing in obstetrics and gynecology Troy, Mich., 1992-98; assoc. Wilshire Obstetrics-Gynecol. Assocs. PC, Troy, 1998—. Mem. quality assurance com. William Beaumont Hosp., Royal Oak, Mich., 1979—, mem. gynecol. quality assurance com., 1993—; charter mem., pres. Preferred Ob-Gyn. Mgmt. Group, LLC; bd. dirs., ptnr. Unasource Health, Troy, 2000—; trustee, mem. credentials com. Preferred Provider Network, 2000; trustee United Beaumont Physicians Group, 1993—. With US Army, 1969—71. Fellow: ACOG; mem.: Am. Inst. Ultrasound Medicine, Mich. State Med. Soc., Am. Soc. Reproductive Medicine, Serbian Singing Soc., Ravanica (musical dir. 1967—, pres. 1981—82). Republican. Serbian Eastern Orthodox. Avocations: music, golf. Office: Wilshire Obstetrics-Gynecol Assocs PC 4550 Investment Dr Ste 200 Troy MI 48098-6369 Office Phone: 248-267-5040.

GOMBOCZ, ERICH ALFRED, biochemist; b. Vienna, Aug. 29, 1951; came to U.S., 1990; s. Erich and Maria (Mayer) G.; m. Gisela M. Dorner, June 12, 1973 (div. Apr. 1992); 1 child, Manfred Alexander (dec.). Cert., T.U., Vienna, 1970-75. With Fed. Inst. for Food Analysis and Rsch., Vienna, 1975-90, head of sect. dept. biochem. analysis, 1980-90, contbr. Cen. Lab. Info. Mgmt. System, 1987-90; chmn. scientific adv. bd. LabIntelligence, Inc., Menlo Park, Calif., 1989-99, COO, v.p. R & D, 1989-99; chief sci. officer NucleoTech Corp., San Mateo, Calif., 1999-2000; chief sci. officer, chief tech. officer Biosentients, Inc., Emeryville, Calif., 2000—03; v.p., chief sci. officer IO Informatics, Inc., Emeryville, 2003—. Speaker and lectr. in field. Editor: Computers in Electrophoresis, Jour. Proteome Rsch.; contbr. articles to profl. jours.; patentee in field. Postdoctoral Rsch. award NIH, Bethesda, Md., 1985-86, 88. Mem. Internat. Assn. for Cereal Chemistry, Internat. Electrophoresis Soc., Am. Electrophoresis Soc., Am. Chem. Soc., N.Y. Acad. Scis., Microsoft Developers Network, Silicon Valley Computer Soc., Human Proteome Orgn. Roman Catholic. Avocation: photography. Office: IO Informatics Inc 2000 Powell St Ste 520 Emeryville CA 94608 Home Phone: 415-665-7289; Office Phone: 510-420-8400. E-mail: egombocz@ix.netcom.com.

GOMELSKY, BORIS, geneticist, educator; s. Iliya and Elizabeth Gomelsky; m. Natalie Gomelsky; 1 child, Vladimir Boris. MS, U. Fisheries, Kaliningrad, Russia, 1977; PhD, Inst. Devel. Biology Russian Acad. Scis., Moscow, 1985. Rsch. scientist Rsch. Inst. Freshwater Aquaculture, Rybnoe, Russia, 1977—91, Aquaculture Rsch. Sta., Dor, Israel, 1992—97; assoc. prof. Ky. State U., Frankfort, Ky., 1997—. Office: Aquaculture D Ky State Univ 103 Athletic Dr Frankfort KY 40601 Office Phone: 502-597-8114. E-mail: boris.gomelsky@kysu.edu.

GOMER, ROBERT, chemistry professor; b. Vienna, Mar. 24, 1924; m. Anne Olah, 1955; children: Richard, Maria. BA, Pomona Coll., 1944; PhD in Chemistry, U. Rochester, 1949; AEC fellow chemistry, Harvard, 1949-50. Instr. dept. chemistry James Franck Inst. U. Chgo., 1950-51, asst. prof., 1951-54, assoc. prof., 1954-58, prof., 1958-96, Carl William Eisendrath Disting. Service prof., 1984-96, prof. emeritus, 1996—. Dir. James Franck Inst. U. Chgo., 1977-83 Bd. dirs. Bull. Atomic Scientists, 1960-84. Served with AUS, 1944-46. Recipient Kendall award in surface chemistry Am. Chem. Soc., 1975, Davisson Germer prize Am. Phys. Soc., 1981, Medard W. Welch award Am. Vacuum Soc., 1989, Arthur W. Adamson award Am. Chem. Soc., 1996; Sloan fellow, 1958-62, Guggenheinm fellow, 1969-70; Bourke lectr. Eng., 1959. Mem. Leopoldina Acad. Scis., Nat. Acad. Scis., Am. Acad. Arts and Sci. Home: 4824 S Kimbark Ave Chicago IL 60615-1916 Office: 5640 S Ellis Ave Chicago IL 60637-1433 Office Phone: 773-702-7191. Business E-Mail: r-gomer@uchicago.edu.

GOMERY, DOUGLAS, communications educator, writer; b. NYC, Apr. 5, 1945; s. John Edgar and Julia G.; m. Marilyn L. Moon, Jan. 13, 1973. BS, Lehigh U., 1967; MA, U. Wis., 1970, PhD, 1975; DHL (hon.), Marrietta Coll., 2007. Asst. prof. mass communication U. Wis., Milw., 1974-79, assoc. prof., 1980, U. Md., College Park, 1981-87, prof., 1987—2006, prof. emeritus, 2006—. Sr. rschr. media studies project Woodrow Wilson Ctr. for Internat. Scholarship, Washington, 1988-92; vis. prof. Northwestern U., Evanston, Ill., 1980, U. Iowa, Iowa City, 1982, U. Utrecht, The Netherlands, 1990, 92; cons. Am. Film Inst., Washington, 1982-90; resident scholar Libr. Am. Broadcasting, 2004-. Author: High Sierra, 1979, The Hollywood Studio System, 1986, Movie History: A Survey, 1991, Shared Pleasures, 1992 (Am. Theater Libr. Assn. Book award, 1992), The FCC's Newspaper-Broadcast Cross-Ownership Rule: An Analysis, 2002, The Coming of Sound, 2005—, The Hollywood Studio System: A History, 2005, A History of Broadcasting in the United States, 2007; co-author (with Robert C. Allen): Film History: Theory and Practice, 1985; co-author: (with Phil Cook and L.W. Lichty) American Media, 1988; co-author: (with Annette Michelson) The Art of Moving Shadows, 1989; co-author: (with Ben Compaine) Who Owns the Media, 2000 (Picard prize award Assn. for Edn. in Journalism and Mass Comm., 2001); co-author: The Television Industries, 2006; editor: The Will Hays Papers, 1987, Marquee, 1991, The Future of News, 1992;: Media in America, 1998;; mem. editl. bd.: Cinema Jour., 1983—92, Jour. Film and Video, 1983—, Jour. Media Econs., 1989—, contbg. editor: Iris, 1983—89, Screen, 1984—89, Jour. of Comm., 1995—, columnist: Am. Journalism Rev., 1995—; contbr. articles to profl. jours. Cons. Joint Com. on Landmarks Washington, 1983, 85, 86, 90, NEH, 1980—. Nat. Endowment Arts, 1980—, Md. State Hist. Preservation Office, 1988, Voice of Am., Nat. Gallery Art., Wis. Dept. Revenue, 1978; trustee Am. Film Inst., 1986-89. Mem. Theatre Hist. Soc. (chmn. Weiss award com. 1984-87, bd. dirs. 1987-89, Weiss prize 1988), Soc. Cinema Studies, Univ. Film and Video Assn. (editorial bd. jours. 1983-92), Broadcast Edn. Assn. (Disting. Scholar award 2007), Assn. for Edn. in Journalism and Mass Comm., Internat. Comm. Assn. Avocation: economics. Home: 4817 Drummond Ave Chevy Chase MD 20815-5428 Office: U Md Coll Journalism College Park MD 20742-0001 Home Phone: 301-951-4385; Office Phone: 301-405-9160. Business E-Mail: dgomery@umd.edu.

GOMES, IVAN JOAQUIM, computer network designer; b. Malacca, Malaysia, Jan. 5, 1967; arrived in Australia, 1978; s. Benny Thomas and Judith (Athaide) G.; m. Shelomi Belinda Gordon, Oct. 14, 1995. BEng with honors, U. NSW, Sydney, Australia, 1988. Rsch. asst. BHP Australia, Newcastle, 1987-88; computer engr. Oasys Computers, Sydney, Australia, 1989-93; computer cons. MicroHelp Computer, Sydney, 1993-94; computer designer, cons. Res. Bank Australia, Sydney, 1994—. Mem. IEEE. Avocations: 32 bit operating systems, chess, real estate markets. Office: Res Bank Australia 65 Martin Pl Sydney NSW 2000 Australia

GOMES, NEIL DOMNIC, director; b. Margao, Goa, India, 1976; s. Januario Bricio and Maria Nivea Gomes; m. Cacilda Barros. BS, Goa U., India, 1996, Ms of Mgmt. Studie, 1999; MEd Instrnl. Design, U. South Fla., Tampa, 2004, postgrad., 2004—. Sales exec. Premier Sci. Instruments Co., Margao, Goa, India, 1996—97; mgmt. trainee Global Tele-Systems Ltd., Mumbai, Maharashtra, India, 1998; asst. mgr. mktg. Hello Info. Services Pvt. Ltd., Porvorim, Goa, 1999; mgr. instrnl. design, content devel. Tata Interactive Systems, Mumbai, 2000—01; mgmt. trainee Progen ERP Systems Pvt. Ltd., Ponda, Goa, 1999—2000; grad. asst. U. South Fla., Tampa, 2002—03, project mgr., instrnl. designer, aux. bus. growth cons., 2003—. Contbr. chapters to books; singer: (tenor in polyphonic choir) Juventus. Student mem. Nat. Social Svcs., Margao, Goa, 1993—96; contbr. Cath. Student Ctr., Tampa, 2002. Mem.: ASTD, Assn. Ednl. Comm. and Tech., Nat. Geog. Soc., Mensa, Phi Kappa Phi. Roman Catholic. Achievements include research in the effects of time-compressed audio on learner performance and satisfaction; the facilitation of faculty development through mentorship; game-based learning in higher education; development of web tutorial on plagiarism in higher education used by several universities worldwide; instructional materials used in several workshops at the University of South Florida; design of several instructional tutorials for multi-national firms and Fortune 500 companies; delivery and administration process for the synchronous virtual classroom tool Elluminate at the University of South Florida. Avocations: singing, guitar, piano, coin collecting/numismatics, stamp collecting/philately. Office: University of South Florida 4202 E Fowler Avenue SVC1072 Tampa FL 33620 Home Phone: 813-598-8131; Office Phone: 813-974-1839. Personal E-mail: neilgomes@yahoo.com. E-mail: ngomes@cte.usf.edu.

GOMES, PETER JOHN, clergyman, educator; b. Boston, May 22, 1942; s. Peter L. and Orissa Josephine (White) G. AB, Bates Coll., Lewiston, Maine, 1965; STB (Rockefeller fellow 1967-68), Harvard U., 1968; DD (hon.), New Eng. Coll., 1974; LHD (hon.), Waynesburg Coll., 1978; HumD (hon.), Gordon Coll., 1985; LittD (hon.), Knox Coll., 1987; DD (hon.), U. South, 1989, Bates U., 1997; LHD (hon.), Duke U., 1997, U. Nebr., 1997, Wooster Coll., Trinity Coll., Bowdoin Coll., Colby Coll., Olivet Coll., Mount Holyoke Coll., Furman U., Baker U., Mount Ida Coll., Willamette U., SUNY at Geneseo, Ursinus Coll., Wagner Coll., Lesley U., Williams Coll., Morris Coll., Ursinus Coll., U. NC, Chapel Hill, Hamilton Coll., Hebrew Union Coll. Ordained to ministry Am. Bapt. Ch., Mass., 1968. Instr. history, dir. freshmen exptl. program Tuskegee (Ala.) Inst., 1968-70; asst. minister, then acting minister Meml. Ch. Harvard U., 1970-74, Pusey minister Meml. Ch., 1974—, Plummer prof. Christian morals, 1974—. Nat. chaplain Am. Guild Organists, 1978-82; hon. fellow Emmanuel Coll., U. Cambridge, Eng.; vis. prof. Duke U., Durham, N.C., 1993-94; presenter numerous sermons, addresses and lectures throughout the US and British Isles. Author: Proclamation Series Commentaries, Lent, 1985, Proclamation Series Lent, 1995, History of Harvard Divinity School, 1992, The Good Book: Reading the Bible With Mind and Heart, 1996, Sermons: Biblical Wisdom for Daily Living, 1998, Sundays at Harvard, 1995, 96, 97, 98, The Good Life: Truths That Last in Times of Need, 2002, Strength for the Journey: Biblical Wisdom for Daily Living, 2003, The Backward Glance, 2005, Forward Look, 2005; co-author: Books of the Pilgrims; editor: Parnassus, 1970, History of the Pilgrim Society, 1970; editor: Harvard Divinity School History, 1992; contbr. articles and papers to profl. jours.; mem. edtl. bd. Pulpit Digest; mem. adv. bd. The Living Pulpit; profiled in The New Yorker, 60 Minutes, Talk mag. article Best Talkers in Am.: Fifty Big Mouths We Hope Will Never Shut Up, 1999. Trustee Bates Coll., 1973-78, 80-94, Pilgrim Soc., 1970—, pres. 1989, 93, Charity of Edward Hopkins, 1974—, Donation to Liberia, 1973—, Plimoth Plantation, 1977—, Roxbury Latin Sch., 1982—, Wellesley Coll., 1985—, Boston Found., 1985—, Plymouth Pub. Libr., 1985—, Harvard U. trustee Mus. Fine Arts; acting dir. W.E.B. DuBois Inst. for Afro-Am. History Harvard U., 1990—. Named Clergy of Yr., Religion in Am. Life, 1998; recipient Phi Beta Kappa tchg. award, Harvard U., 2001. Fellow Royal Soc. Arts; mem. Royal Soc. Ch. Music, Colonial Soc. Mass., Mass. Hist. Soc., Handel and Hayden Soc. (trustee), New Eng. Conservatory (trustee), Signet Soc. (former pres.), Country Day Sch. Headmasters Assn. (hon.), Phi Beta Kappa. Clubs: Tavern. Office: Harvard U Meml Ch Cambridge MA 02138 E-mail: jan_randolph@harvard.edu.

GOMES, RYAN, professional basketball player; b. Sept. 1, 1982; Attended, Providence Coll. Basketball player Boston Celtics, 2005—. Named to All-Big East Team, 2003—04. Office: The Boston Celtics 100 Legends Way Boston MA 02114

GOMES, WAYNE REGINALD, academic administrator; b. Modesto, Calif., Nov. 15, 1938; s. Frank C. and Mary (Rogers) G.; m. Carol L. Gerlach, Sept. 2, 1964 (deceased); children: John Charles, Regina Carol; m. Anne Freitas, Nov. 27, 2004. BS, Calif. Poly. State U., 1960; MS, Wash. State U., 1962; PhD, Purdue U., 1965. Asst. prof. dairy sci. Ohio State U., Columbus, 1965-69, assoc. prof. dairy sci., 1969-72, prof. dairy sci., 1972-81; prof., head dept. dairy sci. U. Ill., Urbana, 1981-85, prof., head dept. animal scis., 1985-89, acting dean Coll. Agr., 1988-89, dean, 1989-95; v.p. agr. and natural resources U. Calif. System, Oakland, 1995—2007. Fulbright prof. Zagreb U., Yugoslavia, 1974; vis. scholar Kyoto U., Japan, 1980; mem. bd. on agr. and natural resources NRC. Editor: The Testis, Vols. 1-4, 1970—77; contbr. over 100 articles to jours., chapters to books. Mem. Coun. for Agrl. Sci. and Tech., Am. Soc. of Animal Sci., Am. Dairy Sci. Assn., Soc. for Study of Reprodn., Endocrine Soc., others. Lodges: Rotary. Office: U Calif 1111 Franklin St Oakland CA 94607-5201 Home Phone: 510-841-3581; Office Phone: 510-986-0060. Business E-Mail: regmail@ucop.edu.

GOMEZ, CURTIS V., judge; b. St. Croix, VI, Mar. 26, 1962; Transfer, Dickinson Coll., 1981—84; BA, George Washington U., 1983—84; JD, Harvard U. Law Sch., 1986—89. Bar: V.I. 1989, DC 1990. Assoc. Patton, Boggs & Blow, 1989—93; atty. US Attorney's Office, 1997—2001, asst. US Atty., Ea. Dist. Va., 2001—02, asst. US Atty., Dist. V.I., 2002—05; US dist. judge US Dist., V.I., 2005—. Office: US Dist Judge US Courthouse and Federal Bldg 5500 Veterans Dr Rm 310 St Thomas VI 00802 Office Phone: 340-774-1800. Office Fax: 340-777-8532.*

GOMEZ, DAVID FREDERICK, lawyer; b. LA, Nov. 19, 1940; s. Fred and Jennie (Fujier) G.; m. Kathleen Holt, Oct. 18, 1977. BA in Philosophy, St. Paul's Coll., Washington, 1965, MA in Theology, 1968; JD, U. So. Calif., 1974. Bar: Calif. 1975, US Dist. Ct. (cen. dist.) Calif. 1975, US Dist. Ct. (ea. dist.) Calif. 1977, Ariz. 1981, US Dist. Ct. Ariz. 1981, US Ct. Claims 1981, US Ct. Appeals (9th cir.) 1981, US Supreme Ct. 1981; ordained priest Roman Cath. Ch., 1969; law clk. Law clk./field atty. Nat. Labor Rels. Bd., LA, 1974-75; ptnr. Gomez, Paz, Rodriguez & Sanora, LA, 1975-77, Garrett, Bourdette & Williams, San Francisco, 1977-80, Van O'Steen & Partners, Phoenix, 1981-85; pres. Gomez & Petitti, PC, Phoenix, 1985—. Faculty Practicing Law Inst., 1989; instr. contracts law Nat. Lawyers Guild, Peoples Coll. Law, 1975-76; mem. Missionary Soc. St. Paul the Apostle (Paulist Fathers), 1963-75; jud. oversight coun. ltd. jurisdiction Cts. Maricopa County, 2002—. Author: Somos Chicanos: Strangers in Our Own Land, 1973; contbg. author: Advanced Strategies in Employment Law, 1988, Arizona Employment Law Handbook, Vol. 2, 1995, 2000, 07. Fellow: Ariz. Bar Found.; mem.: ABA, Ariz. State Bar Assn. (com. on rules of profl. conduct 1991—97, civil jury instrns. com. 1992—94, peer rev. com. 1992—2000, task force on future of the legal profession 1998—2001), Ariz. Employment Lawyers Assn. (bd. dirs. 1996—), Calif. State Bar Assn., Nat. Employment Lawyer's Assn., Los Abogados Hispanic Bar Assn., Maricopa County Bar Assn. Democrat. Office: 2525 E Camelback Rd Ste 860 Phoenix AZ 85016-4279 Office Phone: 602-957-8686. Business E-Mail: dfg@gomezlaw.net.

GÓMEZ, EDWIN, social sciences educator; b. Southbridge, Mass., Mar. 24, 1968; s. Natividad and Julia Gomez. BS in Geography, Salem State Coll., Mass., 1993; MS in Hospitality and Tourism Mgmt., Rochester Inst. Tech., NY, 1994; PhD in Pk., Recreation, Tourism and Urban Studies, Mich. State U., East Lansing, 1999. Coord. acad. and counseling svc. McNair program Salem State Coll., 1999—2000; assoc. prof. Old Dominion U., Norfolk, Va., 2000—. Bd. dirs. Norfolk Conv. and Visitors Bur., Va., 2005—07. Decorated Army Achievement medal US Army. Office: Old Dominion Univ 115 Spong Hall Norfolk VA 23529 Office Phone: 757-683-6309. Business E-Mail: egomez@odu.edu.

GOMEZ, JAIME LUIS (TABOO), rap artist; b. July 14, 1975; 1 child, Joshua Parish. Band mem. Black Eyed Peas, 1995—. Actor: (films) Dirty, 2005; singer: (albums) Behind the Front, 1998, Bridging the Gap, 2000, Elephunk, 2003, Monkey Business, 2005 (Favorite Rap/Hip-Hop Album, Am. Music Awards, 2006), (songs) Joints & Jams, 1998, Fallin' Up, 1998, Where is the Love? (feat. Justin Timberlake), 2003, Shut Up, 2003, Hey Mama, 2004 (MTV Music Video award), Let's Get It Started, 2004 (Grammy award, Best Rap Performance, 2005), Don't Phunk with My Heart, 2005 (Grammy award, Best Rap Group Performance, 2006), Don't Lie, 2005, My Humps, 2005 (MTV Video Music award for Best Hip-Hop Video, 2006, Grammy award for Best Group Pop Vocal Performance, 2007, 2007). Recipient MTV Europe award, Best Pop Act (with Black Eyed Peas), 2004, 2005, Favorite Pop Group & Rap Group, Am. Music Awards, 2005, Favorite Soul/Rhythm & Blues Grp., 2006, Favorite Rap/Hip-Hop Grp., 2006.*

GOMEZ, JOSÉ H., archbishop; b. Monterrey, Mex., Dec. 26, 1951; arrived in US, 1987, naturalized, 1995; s. Jose H and Esperanza (Velasco) Gomez. Degrees in acctg. and philosophy, Nat. U., Mex., 1975; BA in theology, U. Navarre, Rome, 1978; PhD in theology, U. Navarre, Pamplona, Spain, 1980. Ordained as priest, Prelature of Opus Dei by Cardinal Franz Konig, Shrine of Torreciudad, Spain, 1978; in residence Our Lady of Grace, San Antonio, 1987—99; ministered St. Bartholomew Parish, Katy, Tex.; vicar Del. of Tex. Prelature of Opus Dei, 1999—2001; auxiliary bishop, vicar gen. Archdiocese of Denver, 2001—05, moderator of the curia, 2003—05; pastor Cathedral of the Immaculate Conception, Denver, 2001—03, Mother of God Ch., Denver, 2004—05; archbishop Archdiocese of San Antonio, 2005—. Mem. at large bd. dirs. Nat. Cath. Coun. Hispanic Ministry, 1997—98, treas., 1999; steering com. Encuentro 2000, LA, 1998—2000. Named one of 25 Most Influential Hispanics, Time Mag., 2005. Mem.: US Conf. Cath. Bishops (Com. on Doctrine 2003—, Com. on Priestly Formation 2003—06, Com. on Hispanic Affairs 2002—, Com. for

Priestly Life & Ministry 2003—06, Ad Hoc Com. on the Span. Lang. Bible for the Ch. in Am. 2003—), Nat. Assn. Hispanic Priests (regional rep. 1991, pres. 1995, exec. dir. 1999—2001, El Buen Pastor Award 2003). Office: Archdiocese of San Antonio 2718 W Woodlawn San Antonio TX 78228-5195 Business E-Mail: archbishop.gomez@archdiosa.org.

GOMEZ, LARRY, prosecutor; US atty. US Dept. Justice, Albuquerque, 1993—, asst. US atty. N.Mex., acting US atty. N.Mex., 2007—. Office: Federal Bldg US Attys Office PO Box 607 Ofc Albuquerque NM 87103-0607*

GOMEZ, LUIS OSCAR, Asian and religious studies educator, clinical psychology educator; b. Guayanilla, PR, Apr. 7, 1943; s. Manuel Gomez and Lucila Rodriguez; m. Ruth Cedenia Maldonado, Dec. 24, 1963; children: Luis Oscar, Jr., Miran Ruth. BA, U. P.R., 1963; PhD Asian Langs. and Lit., Yale U., 1967; MA in Clin. Psychology, U. Mich., 1991, PhD, 1998. Lic. clin. psychologist. Vis. asst. prof. U. P.R., Rio Piedras, 1967, lectr., 1969-70, assoc. prof., 1970-73; assoc. prof. dept. Asian langs. and cultures U. Mich., Ann Arbor, 1973-80, prof. Buddhist studies, prof. religious studies dept. Asian langs. and cultures, 1980—, chmn. dept., 1981-89, 2002—, prof. psychology dept. psychology, 1999—. Vis. asst. prof. U. Wash., Seattle, 1967-68; Evans-Wentz Disting. lectr. Stanford (Calif.) U., 1983, vis. prof., 1985; vis. prof. Otani U. Kyoto, Japan, 1991-94. Author: The Land of Bliss, 1996; co-editor: Barabudur, Problemas de Filosofia, Studies in the Literature of the Great Vehicle, 1989. Mem. Am. Psychol. Assn., Soc. for Sci. Study Religion, Am. Acad. Religion, Internat. Assn. Buddhist Studies (gen. sec. 1986-89), Assn. Asian Studies. Home: 3204 Lockridge Dr Ann Arbor MI 48108-1722 Office: U Mich Dept Asian Langs & Cultures 105 S State St Ann Arbor MI 48109-1285

GÓMEZ, MARTÍN, library association executive; BA in English, UCLA; MA Library Sci., U. Ariz., Tucson. Dir. Oakland City Pub. Libr., Calif., 1990—95; exec. dir. Bklyn. Pub. Libr., 1995—2002, Friends & Family Found., San Francisco Pub. Libr., 2002—04. Bd. mem. Online Computer Libr. Ctr., Dublin, Sesame Workshop, NYC, Friends of Libraries USA, Phila. Mem.: Urban Libraries Coun. (pres. 2004—). Office: Urban Libraries Council 125 S Wacker Dr Ste 1050 Chicago IL 60606 Office Phone: 312-676-0999. Office Fax: 312-676-0950.*

GOMEZ, MELISSA MORDELL, trial consultant; b. Phila., Oct. 28, 1973; d. Leonard E. and Virginia M. Mordell; m. Nicolas Luis Gomez, May 4, 2002. Vis. student, Cath. U., Leuven, Belgium, 1993—94; BA, Loyola Coll., Balt., 1995; MS in Edn., U. Pa., Phila., 1997, PhD, 2001. Cert. sch. psychologist Pa. Sr. assoc. cons. Hay Group, Jersey City, 2000—02; trial cons. TrialGraphix, Inc., NYC, 2003—05, Phila., 2005—. Child and family therapist Cmty. Counsel Phila., 1999—2001, clin. supr., 1999—2001; cons. Kenwood Psychol. Assocs., NYC, 2000—01; group therapist for sexually abused children and their non-offending parents U. of Medicine and Dentistry N.J., Stratford, 1998—99; prof. psychology of personality U. Pa., 1999—2000, seminar leader grad. student practicum in psychol. svcs., 1998—2000; presenter in field. Illustration for coll. publ., The Forum; contbr. articles to profl. jours. Recipient dissertation rsch. grant, Applied Psychol. Measurement Inc., 2000. Mem.: APA, Am. Soc. of Trial Consultants (mem. rsch. and membership com. 2004—05), Psi Chi. Achievements include research in Parent Ratings of Behavior: Contextually Based Assessment for Children and Adolescents. Independently developed behavior-rating scale, designed research methodology, collected and analyzed data. Avocations: travel, running, studio arts, writing. Office Phone: 215-988-8200. Business E-Mail: mgomez@trialgraphix.com.

GOMEZ, SCOTT, professional hockey player; b. Anchorage, Dec. 23, 1979; Center NJ Devils, 1999—2007, NY Rangers, 2007—. Mem. USA Olympic Hockey Team, Torino, Italy, 2006; player NHL All-Star Game, 2000. Named to All-Rookie Team, NHL, 2000; recipient Calder Meml. Trophy, 2000. Achievements include being a member of Stanley Cup Champion NJ Devils, 2000, 2003. Office: NY Rangers 2 Pennsylvania Plaza New York NY 10121

GOMEZ, TERRINE, school director; b. Trivandrum, India, Jan. 29, 1928; came to U.S., 1977; Tchr. Tng. Degree, Trinity Coll. Music, London, 1949; BA in History of Music, U. Ill., 1982. Licentiate in violin; assoc. in voice; Rolland specialist. Head dept. music Internat. Sch., India, 1959-72; head string dept. Am. Internat. Sch., India, 1972-77; asst. to artistic dir. Nat. Acad. of Arts and Conservatory of Champaign, Ill., 1983-89; major instr. violin CCI assisting Ian Hobson, 1983-89; dir. Young Artists' Studio, Champaign, 1989—. Condr. nat. and internat. workshops in preparation for Rolland Specialist category, Cambridge, Eng., 1976, Chichester, Eng. and Lausanne, Switzerland, 1977, Laval U., Que., 1981. Author: The Young Violinist (in 3 parts), 1985. Mem. European String Tchrs. Assn., Am. String Tchrs. Assn., Soc. Am. Musicians, Chamber Music Am. (Heidi Castleman award 1994). Roman Catholic. Avocations: languages, history, art, literature, shih-tzu dogs. Office: Young Artists Studio 1305 Mayfair Rd Champaign IL 61821-5023

GOMEZ, WILLIAM, orthopedist; b. NYC, Apr. 29, 1955; Degree, NYU, 1976; MD, Columbia U., NYC, 1982. Diplomate Am. Bd. Orthop. Surgeons. Intern in gen. surgery St. Vincent's Hosp., NYC, 1982—84; resident in orthop. Columbia-Presbyn. Med. Ctr., NYC, 1984—87; fellow in sports medicine U. Pitts., 1987—88; pvt. practice Trenton, NJ. Orthop. team physician Trenton Titans, Trenton Thunder; affiliated physician St. Francis Med. Ctr., Trenton, Robert Wood Johnson Univ. Hosp., Hamilton, NJ, Capital Health Sys., Trenton. Named one of Top Drs. NY Metro Area, Castle Connolly, 2001—06, Top Drs. 2003, NJ Monthly Mag. Fellow: Am. Acad. Orthop. Surgeons; mem.: NJ Orthop. Soc., Mercer County Med. Soc., NJ Med. Soc., Am. Orthop. Soc. Sports Medicine. Office: Orthop Surgery Bldg D Ste 220 1225 Whitehorse Mercerville Rd Trenton NJ 08619-3882 Office Phone: 609-581-2200.

GOMEZ-CAMBRONERO, JULIAN, cell biologist, biochemist, educator; arrived in U.S., 1986; s. Juan Jose and Maria Gomez-Cambronero; m. Teresa Madrid; children: David, Julia. PhD, Complutense U., Madrid, 1986. Instr. U. Conn. Health Ctr, Farmington, 1990—91, rsch. asst. prof., 1992—95; asst. prof. Wright State U. Sch Medicine, Dayton, Ohio, 1995—2000, assoc. prof., 2000—04, prof., 2004—, dir. blood/hematology course, 2004—. Office: Wright State U Sch Medicine 3640 Colonel Glenn Hwy Dayton OH 45435 Office Phone: (937)775-3601.

GÓMEZ-JIMÉNEZ, CARLOS, science educator, microbiologist, geneticist; s. Carlos Gómez-Vázquez, Sr. and Emma Jiménez-Gómez BS in Biology with honors, U. PR, 1986, MS in Microbiology and Genetics, 1992; postgrad., Alliance Theol. Sem. Tchr. asst. U. PR, Mayagüez, 1986-88, 91, biochemistry lab. technician, 1988, full prof. Aguadilla, 1992—; quality assurance analyst Microbiology and Cell Culture Lab. Ortho Biologics, Inc., Manatí, PR, 1989-90; prof. Inter Am. U., Aguadilla, PR, 1991-92, San Germán, 1992—; MCAT, PCAT, and DAT invited prof. Kaplan PR Ctr., 1997—; prof. Pontifica Cath. U. PR, 2000—. Acad. counselor sci. rsch. acad. tchrs. and gifted students Am. U., San Germán, PR, 1992-; sci. advisor Young Scholars Program-NSF-Inter Am. U., San Germán, 1992-; cons. drugs, alcohol, violence and HIV/AIDS Prevention programs U. PR, Aguadilla, 1992-; curriculum and course dir., U. PR-Aguadilla, 1992-; mem. over 40 coms. U. PR pres. office & U. PR-Aguadilla, 1992-; dir. honor program, 1996-98, mem. exec. com. Superior Edn. Coun., 1996, 2001; mem. Nat. Collegiate Honors Coun., 1996-; bd. dirs. Assn. Hon. Programs; mentor prof. NSF and U. PR Program, 2001-. Editor (newsletters) The Probe-Caribbean Soc. Biotech., Inc., 1994-, Biosfera-U. PR-Aguadilla, 1994-; contbr. articles to profl. jours.; author acad. manuals and modules in Microbiology, Genetics, Human Genetic, and General Biology Co-founder Leguísamo First Baptist Ch., Mayagüez, 1977-; first tenor Mayagüez Municipal Choir, 1994-, ROMANTIEZER Interdenominational Singing Ministry, 1996-; judge,advisor HS and Undergrad. Sci. Competitions, 1987-; liaison U. PR-Aguadilla & Am. Red Cross Assn. Communitarian Svc., 1994-. Mem.: AAAS, Assn. U. Honor Programs (bd. dirs. 1997—), Biostudy I (counselor, bd. dirs. 1997—), Assn. Food Sci, Tech., P.R. Sci. Tchr. Assn., Soc. Mycology (bd. dirs. 2002, pres. 2003—04, bd. dirs. 1995—97), Caribbean Soc. Biotech. (bd. dirs. 1995—2005), Am. Soc. Microbiology, Bapt. Student Union, Beta Beta Beta. Baptist. Avocations: singing, book collecting, French cooking. Office: U PR Aguadilla Dept Nat Scis PO Box 250160 Aguadilla PR 00604-0160 Office Phone: 787-890-2681 ext. 230, 226. E-mail: cgj_upra@yahoo.com.

GÓMEZ MARTINEZ, JUAN CARLOS, advertising executive; b. Caracas, Venezuela, Sept. 20, 1965; arrived in U.S., 1997; s. Nicolas Gomez Dosantos and Elsa Martinez Rosales; m. Pauline Gaspard Morell, Nov. 30, 1996; 1 child, Nicolas Antonio Gomez Gaspard. BA in Pub. Acctg., Universidad Catolica Andres Bello, Caracas, Venezuela, 1990; MBA with Specialization in Internat. Bus., U. Miami, Miami, Fla., 2000. Auditor i Price Waterhouse, Caracas, Venezuela, 1988—91; contr. Reckitt & Colman de Venezuela, Caracas, 1991—94; Andean region corp. contr. Motorola de los Andes y el Caribe, Caracas, 1994—97; sr. ops. contr. L.Am. north, south & Mex. Motorola Inc., Ft. Lauderdale, Fla., 1997—2000, dir. fin. Ams. supply chain orgn. Harvard, Ill., 2001—02, dir. fin. L.Am. Ft. Lauderdale, 2003—03; sr. divsn. contr., mfg. ops. Motorola Do Brasil, Campinas, Brazil, 2000—01; sr. v.p., CFO Foote Cone and Belding L.Am., Miami, 2003—. Mem.: Weston Rotary Club, Fla. (dir. 2007—), Beta Gamma Sigma. Roman Catholic. Office: Foot Cone and Belding LAm 1401 Brickell Ave Miami FL 33131 Home Phone: 954-349-3954; Office Phone: 305-372-8235. Personal E-mail: juancarlosgomez@bellsouth.net. Business E-Mail: juan-carlos.gomez@draftfcb.com.

GOMORY, RALPH EDWARD, foundation administrator, mathematician; b. NYC, May 7, 1929; s. Andrew L. and Marian (Schellenberg) Gomory; m. Laura Dumper, 1954 (div. 1968); children: Andrew C., Susan S., Stephen H. BA, Williams Coll., 1950, ScD (hon.), 1973; postgrad., Kings Coll., 1950—51, Cambridge U., Eng., 1950—51; PhD in Math., Princeton U., 1954; LHD (hon.), Pace U., 1986; DSc (hon.), Poly. U., 1987, Syracuse U., 1989, Worcester Poly. U., 1989, Carnegie-Mellon U., 1989. Rsch. assoc. Princeton U., 1951—54, asst. prof. math., Higgins lectr., 1957—59; with IBM, Yorktown Heights, NY, 1959—86, dir. math. scis., rsch. div., 1965—67, dir. rsch., 1970—86, v.p., 1973—84, sr. v.p., 1985—89, sr. v.p. for sci. and tech., 1986—89, mem. corp. mgmt. bd., 1983—89, dir. Asia Pacific Group, 1982—88; pres. Alfred P. Sloan Found., NYC, 1989—. Served President's Coun. Advisors on Sci. and Tech., 1984—92; mem. President's Coun. Advisors on Sci. and Tech. and Committee on Science, Engineering, and Pubic Policy. Co-author (with William J. Baumol): MIT Press book. Mem. governing bd. NRC, 1980—83, 1980—, chmn. com. on mandatory retirement in higher edn., 1989—91; trustee Hampshire Coll., 1977—86, Alfred P. Sloan Found., 1988—, Princeton U., 1985—89; bd. dir. Washington Post Co., Lexmark Internat. Inc. With USN, 1954—57. Recipient Lanchester prize, Ops. Rsch. Soc. Am., 1963, Harry Goode Meml. award, Am. Fedn. Info. Processing Socs., 1984, John Von Neumann Theory prize, Ops. Rschl. Soc. Am. and Inst. Mgmt. Scis., 1984, IRI medal, Indsl. Rsch. Inst., 1985, Engring. Leadership Recognition award, IEEE, 1988, Arthur M. Bueche award, NAE, 1993, Heinz award for Tech., the Economy and Employment, 1998; fellow IBM, 1964; Sheffield Fellowship award, Yale U. Faculty Engring., 2000. Fellow: NAS (coun. 1977—78, 1980—83, 1997—, com. sci. engring. and pub. policy 1985—), Am. Acad. Arts and Scis., Econometric Soc.; mem.: IEEE (hon.), Am. Philos. Soc. (coun. 1986—92), Nat. Acad. Engring. (coun. 1986—92). Home: 260 Douglas Rd Chappaqua NY 10514-3100 Office: Alfred P Sloan Found 630 5th Ave Ste 2550 New York NY 10111-0100*

GONÇALVES, C. LOURENÇO, metal products executive; B, Mil. Inst. Engring., Rio de Janeiro; M in Metall. Engring., Fed. U. Minas Gerais. Various positions up to mng. dir. Companhia Siderurgica Nacional, Brazil, 1981—98; pres., CEO Calif. Steel Industries, Inc., 1998—2003; pres., CEO, bd. dirs. Metals USA, 2003—, chmn., 2006—. Office: Metals USA One Riverway Ste 1100 Houston TX 77056 Office Phone: 713-965-0990. Office Fax: 713-965-0067.*

GONCHAROV, VIKTOR, biochemist, researcher; b. Znamenka, Ukraine, June 5, 1949; US, 1989; s. Michal Goncharov and Elena Goncharova; m. Marina Gankina, Jan. 7, 1984 (div. 1991); 1 child, Vladislav. MS in Biology, U. Grozny, Russia, 1986, PhD, 1987. Med. cons., Bklyn., 1992—2007. Med. dir. Inst. Accelerated Rejuvenation, 1992—2007. Achievements include research in bio-oxydative therapy of endocrinology disorders and orgins of malignancies; claimed largest drop in cholesterol to Guinness Book of World Records 1999.

GONDER, DARYL WILLIAM, art and literature educator; b. Chambersburg, Pa., Aug. 7, 1956; s. Jacob William and Nancy Marie Gonder; m. Kathleen Siobhan Wright, May 20, 1989; children: Maeve Elizabeth, Gillian Grace. BA in Lit. in English, Shippensburg State Coll., Pa., 1982; MA in Film Theory and Criticism, Ohio U., Athens, 1983; MA in Lit. in English, Pa. State U., University Park, 1989; PhD in English, U. Md., College Park, 2001. Assoc. prof. visual arts and english Anne Arundel C.C., Arnold, Md., 1991—. Pres. faculty orgn. Anne Arundel C.C., 2005—, chmn. faculty senate, 2005—. Democrat. Home Phone: 410-777-2551; Office Phone: 410-777-2551.

GONDOLESI, GABRIEL EDUARDO, transplant surgeon; b. Tandil, Buenos Aires, Argentina, Nov. 6, 1968; s. Carlos Eduardo Gondolesi and Marta Esther Bahi; m. Carolina Rumbo, May 15, 1998; children: Manuel, Florencia children: Ignacio. MD, U. Nat. Plata, La Plata, Buenos Aires, 1987—92. Diplomate Buenos Aires, 1993. Chief resident on gen. surgery Surgery Svc., pavilion Finochietto of the Hosp. Interzonal de Agudos, La Plata, Buenos Aires, Argentina, 1993—97; fellow hepatobiliary surgery and liver transplantation. Liver and Liver Transplant Unit at Fundación Favaloro, Buenos Aires, 1997—99; fellow multi-organ transplantation Recanati/Miller Transplantation Inst., NYC, 1999—2001, asst. prof. pediatric and adult liver transplant, surgical dir. intestinal transplant, 2002—06; assoc. dir. of liver transplant program, dir. intestinal and pancreas transplant Found. Favaloro, Buenos Aires, 2003—. Contbr. chapters to books, scientific papers, articles to profl. jours. including Jour. Gastrointestinal Surgery, Annals Surgery. Recipient Gold Medal, Best med. student (9, 9/10 pints average qualifications at the end of the 6 years of med. sch.). Facultad de Ciencias Medicas, UNLP., 1986-1992, Rotary Club prize for performance in the med. field, La Plata's Rotary Club, Argentina, 1996, 2004, award, Olivieri's Found., 2006. Fellow: Am. Coll. Surgeons; mem.: Soc. Surgery of Alimentary Track, Miembro de la Asociacion Argentina de Cirugia (assoc.), Internat. Hepato-Bilio-Pancreatic Assn. (assoc.), Am. Assn. of Transplant Surgeons (assoc.), Transplantation Soc. Office: Av Belgrano 1782 1st Fl C1093AAS Buenos Aires Argentina Office Phone: 54 11 4378 1366/3180. Personal E-mail: gegondolesi@yahoo.com. Business E-Mail: ggondolesi@ffavaloro.org.

GONDRY, MICHEL, film director; b. Versailles, France, May 8, 1963; Dir.: (films) Vingt p'tites tours, 1989, Human Nature, 2001, Block Party, 2005; writer, dir., actor (films) The Letter, 1998, writer, dir. One Day, 2001, Pecan Pie, 2003, Eternal Sunshine of Spotless Mind, 2004 (Best Dir., Washington, DC Film Critic award, 2004, Academy award for best original screenplay, 2005), The Science of Sleep, 2006; dir.: (music video for Björk: Volumen) (Human Behavior, Army of Me, Isobel, Hyperballad, Jóga, Bachelorette), 1998, (music videofor Clip Cult Vol. 1: Exploding Cinema) Sugar Water, 1999, (video) Massive Attack: Eleven Promos, 2001, The Chemical Brothers: Singles 93-03, 2003, The Work of Directo Michel Gondry, 2003, I've Been Twelve Forever, 2003, (commercials) for Gap, Smirnoff, Air France, Nike, Coca Cola, Adidas, Polaroid, & Levi. Address: Commerical/Music Video Partizan Entertainment 7083 Hollywood Blvd Ste 401 Los Angeles CA 90028 Office Phone: 323-468-0123.*

GONG, EDMOND JOSEPH, lawyer; b. Miami, Fla., Oct. 7, 1930; s. Joe Fred and Fayline G.; m. Sophie Vlachos, July 25, 1957 (dec.); children: Frances Fayline, Peter Joseph (dec.), Madeleine, Joseph Fred, II, Edmond Joseph; m. Dana Leigh Clay, Dec. 7, 1988. AB cum laude, Harvard U., 1952, postgrad. in law, 1954-55; JD, U. Miami, 1960. Bar: Fla. 1960. Spl. writer Hong Kong Tiger Standard, 1955-56; staff writer Miami Herald, 1958-59; assoc. firm Helliwell, Melrose and DeWolf, 1960-61; asst. U.S. atty. So. Dist. Fla., 1961-62; mem. Fla. Ho. of Reps., 1963-66, Fla. Senate, 1966-72; trustee Fla. Gulf Realty Trust, 1974-80; pres. Inflahedge Resources Fund, 1969—, Pub. Policy Cons. Inc., 1988—. Sr. pub. policy analyst and legal counsel Everett Clay Assocs., Inc., 1988—; chmn. Fla. Land Sales Advisory Council, 1974-76; vice chmn. Bd. Bus. Regulation, State of Fla., 1976-77; fellow Inst. Politics John Fitzgerald Kennedy Sch. Govt., Harvard U., 1969-70, assoc. dir., 1971-72 Mem. Harvard 350th Commn., 1984-86; mem. com. on univ. resources, bd. overseers and pres. and fellows Harvard Coll., 1984-86; mem. North Key Largo Habitat Conservation Planning Study Com., 1984-88; regional chmn. Selection Com. for Anglo-Am. Conf., Johns Hopkins Sch. Advanced Internat. Studies, 1985; mem. Fairbanks Ctr. Com., Fairbank Ctr. for East Asian Research, Harvard U., 1987-90. Mem. ABA, Fla. Bar, Harvard U. Alumni Assn. (dir.-at-large), Fla. Audubon Soc. (bd. dirs. 1990-93), Coral Reef Yacht Club. Episcopalian. Office: Pub Policy Cons 6161 Blue Lagoon Dr #270 Miami FL 33126

GONG, GLORIA MARGARET, lawyer, pharmacist; b. Yreka, Calif., Oct. 12, 1953; d. Kenneth Wayne and Patricia Ann (Farley) McCain; m. Peter-Poon Ming Gong, Apr. 3, 1976; children: George-Wayne, Cynthia-May, Miranda-Lin. Pharmacist Degree, U. of the Pacific, Stockton, Calif., 1976; JD, Calif. Pacific Law Sch., Bakersfield, 1992. BAr: Calif. 1992, U.S. Dist. Ct. (ea., ctr. and so. dists.) Calif. 1992. Pharmacist Gong's Pharmacy, Tehachapi, Calif., 1978-93; atty. Gong & Hirsch, Bakersfield, 1994-97; pvt. practice, 1997—. Mem.: ATLA, ABA, Kern County Bar Assn., L.A. County Bar Assn., Lambda Kappa Sigma. Office: 6840 District Blvd Bakersfield CA 93313 E-mail: ggong@legalemail.com.

GONGAWARE, ACEY M., music educator; m. Robert A. Gongaware; children: Katherine H., Sarah J., Molly A. MusB in Edn., Grove City Coll., Pa., 1982. Dir. christian edn. Presbyn. Ch., Pa., 1982—94; tchr. music St. Bernard's Sch., Ind., Pa., 1994—99; tchr. choral United Jr. Sr. H.S., Armagh, Pa., 1999—. Mem.: Music Educators Nat. Conf. Republican. Presbyn. Avocations: reading, piano. Office: United Jr Sr High School 10780 Route 56 Hwy E Armagh PA 15920-9038 Office Phone: 814-446-5615. Business E-Mail: agongaware@unitedsd.net.

GONICK, HARVEY CRAIG, nephrologist, educator; b. Winnipeg, Man., Can., Apr. 10, 1930; s. Joseph Wolfe and Rose (Chernick) G.; m. Gloria Granz, Dec. 16, 1967; children: Stefan, Teri, Julie, Suzanne. BS in Chemistry, UCLA, 1951; MD, U. Calif., San Francisco, 1955. Diplomate Am. Bd. Internal Medicine, Am. Bd. Nephrology. Intern Peter Bent Brigham Hosp., 1955-56; fellow in nephrology Mass. Meml. Hosp., 1956-57; fellow in nephrology, resident in internal medicine Wadsworth VA Hosp., Los Angeles, 1959-61, clin. investigator, 1961-64, chief metabolic balance unit, 1964-67, rsch. assoc. LA, 2002—; instr. medicine Sch. Medicine, UCLA, 1961-64, asst. prof., 1964-69, assoc. prof., 1969-72, adj. assoc. prof., 1972-76, adj. prof., 1976—2003, clin. prof., 2003—, assoc. chief div. nephrology, 1965-72, co-dir. Bone and Stone Clinic, 1972-76, coordinator postgrad. nephrology edn., 1975-78; mem. staff St. John's Hosp., Santa Monica, Calif., Century City Hosp., LA, med. dir. dialysis unit, 1972-79, chief medicine, 1978-79; mem. staff Cedars-Sinai Med. Ctr., LA, dir. trace element lab., 1979-96, clin. chief nephrology, 1983-85, coord. renal tng., dir. hypertension rsch., 1996—2003; practice medicine specializing in nephrology Los Angeles, 1972-94. Co-founder, med. dir. Berkeley East Dialysis Unit, Santa Monica, 1971-75; co-founder, cons. Kidney Dialysis Care Units Inc., Lynwood, Calif., 1971-78; co-dir. Osteoporosis Prevention and Treatment Ctr., Santa Monica, 1987-93; mem. numerous adv. coms. to state and fed. agys., 1969-83. Contbr. articles to profl. jours.; editor: Current Nephrology, 1977-96. Served to capt. M.C., USAF, 1957-59. Fellow Charles Nelson Fund, Kaiser Found., NIH; recipient Oliver P. Douglas Meml. award Los Angeles County Heart Assn., 1959, Vis. Scientist award Deutscher Academischer Austauschendienst, 1978. Fellow ACP; mem. AMA, AAAS, Internat. Soc. Nephrology (organizing com. internat. cong. 1984), Am. Soc. Nephrology, European Dialysis and Transplant Assn., Soc. Exptl. Biology and Medicine, Calif. Med. Assn., Los Angeles County Med. Assn., Nat. Kidney Found. (active ann. conf. 1963-65, sec. nat. med. adv. coun. 1969-70, regional rep. and legis. com. nat. med. adv. coun. 1970-73, grantee 1963), So. Calif. Kidney Found. (chmn. sci. adv. coun. 1968-70, co-chmn. legis. com. 1970-73, bd. dirs. 1974-83, honoree 1979), Am. Soc. Bone and Mineral Rsch., Am. Coll. Toxicology, Soc. Toxicology, Am. Heart Assn. (renal sect. of coun. on circulation), Am. Fedn. Clin. Rsch., Western Soc. Clin. Rsch., Western Assn. Physicians, Phi Beta Kappa, Sigma Xi, Alpha Omega Alpha, Phi Eta Sigma, Alpha Mu Gamma, Phi Lambda Upsilon. Avocation: tennis. Office: West LA VA Hosp Rsch Svc 11301 Wilshire Blvd Los Angeles CA 90073 Business E-Mail: hgonick@ucla.edu.

GONNELLI, PATRICK M., finance company executive; BS in Econs., U. Pa. CPA, Pa. Various exec. positions KPMG Peat Marwick, Revlon Corp.; CFO, Simon & Schuster, Towers Perrin, Phila., 1991-2000. Office: Towers Perrin 1 Stanford Plaza 263 Tresser Blvd Stamford CT 06901-3226

GONNERING, RUSSELL STEPHEN, ophthalmic plastic surgeon; b. Milw., Nov. 21, 1949; s. Russell Richard and Virginia Mary (Minar) G.; m. Sandra Lynne Brubaker, Aug. 6, 1971; children: Julie Kathleen, Stephen Russell, Scott Duncan. Student, U. Vienna, Austria, 1969—70; AB in History cum laude, Boston Coll., 1971; MD, Med. Coll. Wis., 1975; M of Med. Mgmt., U. So. Calif., LA, 2007. Diplomate Am. Bd. Ophthalmology; lic. physician, Wis.; cert. profl. in healthcare quality. Intern St. Luke's Hosp., Milw., 1975-76; resident in ophthalmology Med. Coll. Wis., Milw., 1977-80, asst. clin. prof. dept. ophthalmology, 1985-2000, prof. ophthalmology, 2000—05, clin. prof. ophthalmology, 2006—; fellow in ophthalmic plastic and reconstructive surgery U. Wis., Madison, 1980-81, asst. clin. prof. dept. ophthalmology, 1981-92, assoc. clin. prof. dept. ophthalmology, 1992-96, clin. prof. dept. ophthalmology, 1996—, Kambara lectr., 1997; ophthalmologist Children's Hosp. Wis., Milw., St. Luke's Hosp., Milw., chief ophthalmologist, 1983-94, 97-99, vice chief staff, 2000; pvt. practice Ophthalmic Plastic and Reconstructive Surgery, 1981-2000, 2006—. Full-time acad. practice, 2000-05; rsch. assoc. in corneal physiology Med. Coll. Wis., 1976-77; rsch. advisor to fellowship in ophthalmic plastic and reconstructive surgery U. Wis., Madison, 1983-2002; presenter in field. Author: (with others) Infections of the Eye and Ocular Adnexa, 1986, Oculoplastic, Orbital and Reconstructive Surgery, 1988, Oculoplastic and Orbital Emergencies, 1990, Ophthalmic Plastic, reconstructive and Orbital Surgery, 1997, Ophthalmic Surgery: Principles and Techniques, 1999; sect. editor: Principles and Practice of Ophthalmic Plastic and Reconstructive Surgery, 1995; contbr. numerous articles to profl. jours. Recipient Wisdom Soc. Honor award, 1999. Fellow: ACS (coun. Wis. chpt.

1996—2000), Am. Soc. Ophthalmic Plastic and Reconstructive Surgery (editl. bd. 1987—99, edn. com. 1988—99, vice chmn. edn. com. 1995—97, chmn. edn. com. 1997—99, Marvin H. Quickert award 1982, Rsch. award 1982, Reeh Pathology award 1999), Am. Acad. Ophthalmology (basic and clin. sci. course com. 1986—92, chmn. 1988—92, Honor award 1990, Ruedemann lectr. 1994, Sr. Achievement award 2001); mem.: Am. Coll. Physician Execs., Nat. Assn. for Healthcare Quality (cert. profl.), Project Mgmt. Inst., Christian Med. and Dental Assn., Am. Soc. Quality, Milw. Surg. Soc., Nat. Soc. to Prevent Blindness (mem. adv. bd. Wis. chpt. 1987—88), Am. Soc. Ocularists (med. adv. bd. 1987—2001), Milw. Ophthalmol. Soc. (treas. 1989—90, sec. 1990—91, v.p. 1991—92, pres. 1992—93), Milw. Acad. Surgery, Milw. Acad. Medicine, Milwaukee County Med. Soc. (del. to state med. soc. 1987—90, bd. dirs. 1989—94, Dirs. citation 1994), Med. Soc. Wis., Assn. for Rsch. in Vision and Ophthalmology, Internat. Dacryology Soc., European Soc. Ophthalmic Plastic and Reconstructive Surgery, Internat. Soc. Orbital Disorders, Black Belt Six Sigma (Villanova Univ.), Mensa. Avocations: sailing, skiing, tai kwon do, bicycling. Office Phone: 262-754-9921. Personal E-mail: rsgonnering@hotmail.com. Business E-Mail: info@rsgonnering.com.

GONNERMAN, JENNIFER, writer, journalist; b. Jan. 24, 1971; Attended, Cambridge U.; BA, Columbia U., 1994. Staff writer The Village Voice, 1997—2006. Author: Life on the Outside: The Prison Odyssey of Elaine Bartlett, 2004 (Nat. Book Award finalist, 2004). Finalist Nat. Mag. Award; recipient Livingston award, Gold Typewriter Award, N.Y. Press Club, Meyer Berger Award, Columbia U. Sch. Journalism, Front Page Award, Newswomen's Club N.Y. Office: Village Voice 36 Cooper Square New York NY 10003

GONSALVES, PATRICIA E., surgical nurse; b. NYC, Oct. 28, 1943; d. John A. Gonsalves and Julia Rivera Brosa. Diploma in practical nursing, Caledonian Hosp., Bklyn., 1963; student, Cornell Med. Ctr., 1965-66, L.I. U., 1971, SUNY, LI, 1988. Lic. practical nurse; cert. surg. technologist, preceptor, oper. rm., med. photographer. Lic. practical nurse Luth. Med. Ctr., Bklyn.; assoc. primary nurse, lic. practical nurse Maimonides Med. Ctr., Bklyn., LPN, surg. technologist, oper. rm. vascular surg. specialist, sr. tech. and neuro., 1980—. Contbr. articles to profl. jours. Guild del. Local 1199, Freedom of Health Choice; polit. Dem. endorser; lay min. Bay Ridge Christian Ctr., Bklyn. Mem.: NAACOG (Outstanding Leadership Recognition award), Found. for Advancement of Innovative Medicine, Nat. Ctr. Homeopathy, Assn. Surg. Technologists (pres. chpt. Metro 47 1994—96, nat. bd. dirs. 1993—94, apptd. mem. exam. rev. com. various awards 1992), Soc. Peripheral Vascular Nursing, Nat. Surg. Asst. Assn., Nat. Assn. Practical Nurse Edn. and Svc. Home: 814 57th St Apt 2A Brooklyn NY 11220-3631

GONSALVES, PHILIP, music educator; s. William Costa and Jocelyne Camille Gonsalves. BS in Math., Calif. State U., Hayward, 1986, MS in Edn. and Curriculum, 2004. Cert. tchr. single subject Calif., 1986. Contbr. articles to profl. jours. Named Tchr. of Yr., Calif. State U., Hayward, 2005. Office Phone: 510-670-4214.

GONSHAK, ISABELLE LEE, nurse, volunteer; b. Newark, Apr. 4, 1932; d. Robert John and Clara Kate (Cooperman) McClelland; m. David M. Gonshak, Aug. 8, 1953; children: Evan J., Brett A., Kathryn Susan. RN, N.J., Fla. Nurse Newark City Hosp., 1953; tchr. Ideal Sch. for Nurse's Aides, Miami, Fla., 1972-74. Vocal soloist numerous TV and social affairs; photographer multiple media, multi-faceted subjects. Bd. dirs. Miami Beach Symphony, 1971—, pres., 1978-79; bd. dirs. South Fla. Symphony; life mem. Opera Guild Soc. Ft. Lauderdale; active Statue of Liberty Refinishing Com. Mem. Greater Miami Opera Assn., Hadassah (life). Jewish. Home: 1700 SW 72d Ave Plantation FL 33317-5037

GONSON, S. DONALD, lawyer; b. Buffalo, June 13, 1936; s. Samuel and Laura Rose (Greenspan) G.; m. Dorothy Rose, Aug. 28, 1960; children: Julia, Claudia AB, Columbia U., 1958; JD, Harvard U., 1961; postgrad., U. Bombay, India, 1961-62; cert., London Sch. Econs., Eng., 1957. Bar: Mass. 1962, N.Y. 1983. With Hale and Dorr, Boston, 1962—, sr. ptnr., 1972-2000; of counsel Wilmer, Cutler, Pickering, Hale and Dorr LLP, Boston, 2000—. Co-chmn. Speech-Tech., NYC, 1987; instr. in law Boston U., 1963-65, bd. trustees Boston Five Cents Savs. Bank, 1978-83, bd. advisors, 1983-88; adj. prof. internat. law Tufts U. Fletcher Sch. Law and Diplomacy, 1999—; lectr. Fin. Times (UK), instnl. investor, New Eng. Law Inst., Mass. Soc. CPAs; vis. scholar Green Coll., Oxford U., 2004-05. Chmn. Mass. Comty. Devel. Fin. Corp., 1976-82; pres. Cambridge Ctr. for Adult Edn., 1985-88; bd. dirs. Boston Psychoanalytic Soc. and Inst., 1994—. Fulbright scholar, 1961-62. Fellow Am. Bar Found.; mem. ABA, Internat. Bar Assn., Mass. Bar Assn., Boston Bar Assn. (chmn. internat. law sect. 1998-2001), Harvard Faculty Club, Mount Auburn Club. Home: 32 Hubbard Park Rd Cambridge MA 02138-4731 Office: Wilmer Cutler Pickering Hale & Dorr LLP 60 State St Boston MA 02109-1816 Office Phone: 617-526-6735. Business E-Mail: donald.gonson@wilmerhale.com.

GONTHIER, CHARLES DOHERTY, retired judge; b. Montreal, Que., Can., Aug. 1, 1928; m. Mariette Morin; children: Georges, François, Pierre, Jean-Charles, Yves. BA, Paris Coll. Stanislas, Montreal, 1947; BCL, McGill U., Montreal, 1951, LLD (hon.), 1990; DHC (hon.), U. Montreal, 2002; DU (hon.), U. Ottawa, 2003. Queen's counsel, 1971. Atty. Hackett, Mulvena and Laverty, Montreal, 1952-57, Laing, Weldon, Courtois, Clarkson, Parsons, Gonthier & Tetrault (now McCarthy & Tetrault), Montreal, 1957-74; judge Superior Ct. Que., Montreal, 1974-88, Que. Ct. Appeal, Montreal, 1988-89, Supreme Ct. Can., Ottawa, 1989—2003; ret., 2003; of counsel McCarthy Tetrault LLP, 2004. Sec. Montreal br. Can. Inst. Internat. Affairs, 1957-58; pres. Jr. Bar Montreal, 1960-61; mem. Com. on Bldg. Contracts Que. Civil Code Rev., 1969-72; com. on discipline Bar Que., 1973-74; chmn. Commn. for Nat. Judges, 1st World Conf. on Independence of Justice, Montreal, 1983; pres. Can. Judges Conf., 1988-89; commr. Comm. Security Establishment, Ottawa, 2006. Chmn. Assn. Anciens Coll. Stanislas, Montreal, 1954-55; hon. sec. Montreal Mus. Fine Arts, 1961-76; bd. dirs. McCord Mus. Can. History, Montreal, 1976-89; chmn. bd. Coll. Stanislas, Montreal, 1984-90; mem. Internat. Commn. Jurists; chmn. bd. govs. Ctr. for Internat. Sustainable Devel. Law. Decorated knight L'Ordre des Palmes Académiques (France); Wainwright Sr. Rsch. fellow McGill U. Law Faculty, 2004. Fellow Am. Coll. Trial Lawyers (hon.); mem. Univ. Club (Montreal), Can. Bar Assn. (hon., pres. jr. bar sect. 1961-62, sec. Que. divsn. 1963-64), Can. Inst. Adminstrn. Justice (pres. 1986-87), Assn. Henri Capitant, Que. Assn. Comparative Law, Internat Acad. Comparative Law. Roman Catholic. Office: McCarthy Tetrault LLP 1000 De La Gauchetiere W Ste M2 400 Montreal PQ Canada H3B OA2 Office Phone: 514-397-4165. Business E-Mail: cdgonthier@mccarthy.com.

GONTIER, JEAN ROGER, medicine and physiology educator; b. Lens, France, Mar. 8, 1927; s. Paul Maurice and Marie Jeanne (Tricoche) G.; m. Sylviane Prevost, Dec. 8, 1968; children: Sylviane, Yannick, Jean-Yves, Yann. BA magna cum laude, Arras Coll., France, 1944; BS summa cum laude, Etampes Coll., Paris, 1946; MS magna cum laude, Coll. Scis., Paris, 1948; MD summa cum laude, Sch. Medicine, Paris, 1965. Prof., chair dept. physiology UGSEL, Paris, 1957-62; instr. in medicine Sch. Medicine, Paris, 1960-65; resident Hop Cochin, Paris, 1964; assoc. prof. medicine Hop Bicetre, Paris, 1966; dir. physiology Sch. Medicine, Reims, 1966-68; prof. physiology U. Montreal, 1970-78; cons. in internal medicine Paris, 1979—. Prof. physiology Bicetre U. Hosp., Paris, 1967-68; cons. editor various pubs., N.Y.C., 1975-78, Paris, 1969-73, Montreal, 1986-89; rsch. in diving physiology in man. Author: (textbooks) Hormones, Nervous System and Digestion, 1968, Respiration, 1977, Digestion, 1969, Textbook of Medical Physiology, 1980, Human Physiology, 1989, Biochemistry For Medical Students, 2000, Physiology for Medical Students, 2001, Human Genetics, 2001, Biochemistry, 2004, Organic Chemistry, 2004. Recipient Silver medal Sch. Medicine, Paris, 1965. Mem. AAAS, Am. Physiol. Soc. (tchr. physiology, respiration, cardiovasc. and history sects.), Can. Physiol. Soc., N.Y. Acad. Scis., French Physiol. Soc., Cercle de l'Etrier Club, La Baule Country Club. Roman Catholic. Achievements include research in diving physiology in man. Avocation: sailing. Home and Office: 133 Rue Michel Ange F75016 Paris France Home Phone: 0146512505; Office Phone: 0146512505. Personal E-mail: jean.gontier@wanadoo.fr.

GONTRUM, BARBARA, law librarian, educator; BA, Purdue U., 1972; MS, U. Ill., 1973; JD, Duke U., 1978. Law libr. Taft, Stettinius & Hollister, Cin.; assoc. law libr., reference/documents libr. Duke U. Law Libr.; dir. Thurgood Marshall Law Libr. U. Md., Sch. Law, Balt., 1979—, asst. dean libr. tech, prof. law. Chair Coun. Libr. Dirs. U. Md. and Affiliated Insts. Librs. Consortium. Mem.: ABA, Assn. Am. Law Schs. (chair, Sect. Law Librs.), Am. Assn. Law Librs. (chair, Spl. Interest Sect.). Office: U Md Sch Law 500 W Baltimore St Baltimore MD 21201-1786 Office Phone: 410-706-7270. E-mail: bgontrum@law.umaryland.edu.*

GONYA, JEFFREY KEENAN, lawyer; b. Manchester, NH, Mar. 15, 1961; m. Ann Martin; 1 child, Caroline P. BA with high honors, U. Va., 1983, JD, 1986. Bar: Ga. 1986, Md. 1988. Assoc. O'Callaghan, Saunders and Stumm, Atlanta, 1986-87; assoc. then ptnr., taxation, trusts & estates Venable LLP (formerly Venable, Baetjer and Howard), Balt., 1987—. Trustee Balt. Bar Found., 1993—. Trustee Mpala Wildlife Found., Inc., Balt., 1992—, mem. Reading, Runs & Ripken Com., Balt. Reads, Inc., Fund Mgmt. Com., Ctr. Health & Population Rsch. Mem. ABA (mem. tax section com. on estate & gift taxes), Md. Bar Assn., Bar Assn. Balt. City (sec.-treas. young lawyers sect. 1991-92, chmn.-elect 1992-93, chmn. 1993-94). Office: Venable LLP 1800 Two Hopkins Plz Baltimore MD 21201-2930 Office Phone: 410-244-7507. Office Fax: 410-821-0147. Business E-Mail: jkgonya@venable.com.

GONYNOR, FRANCIS JAMES, lawyer; b. Cambridge, Mass., Nov. 6, 1959; s. James Francis and Beverly Joan (Lintz) G.; m. Deborah Lynn Snyder, July 25, 1981; children: Brian Christopher, Caroline Jane, Madeline Marie. AA, U. Fla., 1978, BA, 1980; JD, U. Houston, 1983, postgrad., 2003. Bar: Tex. 1983, U.S. Dist. Ct. (so. dist.) Tex. 1983, U.S. Ct. Appeals (5th cir.) 1983. Assoc. Eastham Watson Dale & Forney, Houston, 1983-88, ptnr., 1988—. Mediator Am. Arbitration Assn., 1992; adj. prof. U. Houston Law Ctr., 2006—. Contbr. articles to profl. jours. Mem. Maritime Law Assn., Houston Bar Assn., Coll. of the State Bar of Tex. Home: 3327 Spring Trail Dr Sugar Land TX 77479-3050 Office: Eastham Watson Dale Forney 808 Travis St Fl 20 Houston TX 77002-5706 Office Phone: 713-225-0905. Business E-Mail: gonynor@easthamlaw.com.

GONZALES, ALBERTO R., former United States attorney general, former state supreme court justice; b. San Antonio, Tex., Aug. 4, 1955; s. Pablo and Maria Gonzales; m. Rebecca Turner; 3 children. Student, U.S. Air Force Acad., 1975-77; BA, Rice U., 1979; JD, Harvard U., 1982. Bar: Tex. Ptnr. Vinson & Elkins, LLP, Houston, 1982-95; gen. counsel Gov. George W. Bush, 1995-97; sec. state State of Tex., 1997—99; justice Supreme Ct of Texas, Austin, Tex., 1999—2000; asst. to Pres. & gen. counsel The White House, Washington, 2001—05; atty. gen. US Dept. Justice, Washington, 2005—07. Adj. prof. U. Houston Law Ctr. Trustee Tex. Bar Found., 1996-99; mem. Tex. Jud. Dists. Bd., 1996-97; bd. dirs. United Way of Tex. Gulf Coast, 1993-94; pres. Leadership Houston, 1993-94; chair Commn. for Dist. Decentralization of Houston Ind. Sch. Dist., 1994; mem. com. on undergrad. admissions Rice U., 1994; chair Rep. Nat. Hispanic Assembly of Houston, 1992-94; pres. Houston Hispanic Forum, 1990-92; chair adv. com. Tex. Real Estate Ctr., 1989-90; bd. dirs. Big Bros. and Sisters, Houston, 1985-91, Cath. Charities, Houston, 1989-93, others. With USAF, 1973—75. Recipient Commitment to Leadership award United Way, 1993, Hispanic Salute award Houston Metro Ford Dealers, 1989, Presdntl. Citiation, State Bar of Tex., 1997, Latino Lawyer of the Year, Hispanics Nat. Bar Assn, 1999, Harvard Law Sch. Assn. award, 2002, Good Neighbor award, US-Mex. C.of C., 2003, Presl. award, US Hispanic CofC and League of United Latin Am. Citizens, Golden Plate award, Acad. Achievement, 2005; named one of Five Outstanding Young Texans, Tex. Jaycess, 1994, Outstanding Young Lawyer of Tex., Tex. Young Lawyers Assn., 1992; inducted into the Hispanics Scholarship Fund Alumni Hall of Fame, 2003; named Disting. Alumnus of Rice U., Assn. of Rice Alumni; named one of 25 Most Influential Hispanics, Time Mag., 2005. Mem. Houston Bar Assn., Houston Hispanic Bar Assn. (pres., 1990-91), State Bar Tex. (bd. dirs. 1991-94), Am. Law Inst. Republican.*

GONZALES, DANIEL S., lawyer; b. San Antonio, Nov. 10, 1959; s. Sam and Mary Louise (Stewart) G.; m. Mary David McCauley, May 16, 1980 (div. 1983); m. Devon Elaine Cattell, Jan. 1, 1988 (div. 2001). BA, U. Notre Dame, 1981; JD, Stanford U., 1984. Bar: Calif. 1986, U.S. Dist. Ct. (no. dist.) Calif. 1986, U.S. Tax Ct. 1987, U.S. Ct. Appeals (9th cir.) 1988, U.S. Dist. Ct. (ea. dist.) Calif. 1990. Trivia game writer Axlon Games, Sunnyvale, Calif., 1984; legal writer Matthew Bender & Co., San Francisco, 1984—86; assoc. Carey & Carey, Palo Alto, Calif., 1986—96, Ferrari, Olsen, Ottoboni & Bebb, San Jose, Calif., 1996—97, Bryant, Clohan, Eller, Maines & Baruh, San Jose, 1997—2001, Eller & Assocs., San Jose, 2002—. Mng. editor Stanford Jour. Internat. Law, 1983-84. Candidate Menlo Park City Coun., Calif., 1988; bd. dirs. Page Mill YMCA, Palo Alto, 1993-99, YMCA Midpeninsula, 1999—, Sr. Housing Solutions, San Jose, 1997-2006, pres., 1998-99, 2002-03; pres. Menlo Park Dispute Resolution Svc., 1994-95; backup guitarist, keyboardist Beau Brummels 35th Anniversary Summer of Love Concert, San Francisco, 2002. U. Notre Dame scholar, 1977, Nat. Merit scholar, 1977, scholar Nat. Hispanic Scholarship Bd., 1980. Mem. ABA, San Mateo County La Raza Lawyers (pres. 1994), Santa Clara County Bar Assn. (chmn. minority access com. 1994, chmn. judiciary com. 1995), San Mateo County Bar Assn., Palo Alto Area Bar Assn. Democrat. Avocations: guitar, college football. Office: Eller & Assocs 60 S Market St Ste 1201 San Jose CA 95113 Office Phone: 408-299-0180. Personal E-mail: dsgonzale6@yahoo.com.

GONZALES, ERNESTO LUIS B., bank executive; b. May 16, 1958; MA in Internat. Econs., NYU, 1983, MBA, 1985. Treasury officer Asian Devel. Bank, Manila, 1985-91; fin. cons. European Bank, London, 1991-92; financing specialist PDVSA B.V., The Hague, The Netherlands, 1992-94; dep. gen. mgr. Nomura Bank Netherland, N.V., Amsterdam, The Netherlands, 1994-98; 1st v.p., head risk mgmt. and compliance Nomura Bank Ltd., Zurich, Switzerland, 1998—2003; sr. global compliance officer SVB Fin. Group, Santa Clara, Calif., 2005—06; dir. risk and compliance State St. Corp., Irvine, Calif., 2006—. Mem. Inst. Chartered Fin. Analysts, NYU Exec. Forum. Avocations: swimming, sailing, classical guitar, theater, opera. Office Phone: 949-932-1957. Personal E-mail: elgonzales@aol.com. Business E-Mail: ernesto.gonzales@sscims.com.

GONZALES, GREG, state agency administrator; B cum laude in Hist., Tenn. Technol. U., Cookeville, 1980; law degree, U. Tenn. Rsch. asst. to Sir Patrick Cormack Brit. Parliament, 1980; spl. asst. to Senator Albert Gore Jr., 1985—86; positions including gen. counsel, dir. budget, dir. human resources and dir. legis. efforts Tenn. Dept. Fin. Instns., Nashville, 1986—, acting commr., 2005—07, commr., 2007—. Bd. dirs. Money Transmitter Regulators Assn. Office: Tenn Dept Fin Instns 511 Union St Ste 400 Nashville TN 37219 Office Phone: 615-741-5603. Office Fax: 615-253-6306. E-mail: Greg.Gonzales@state.tn.us.

GONZALES, LOUISE MICHAUX, lawyer; b. Balt., Dec. 28, 1949; BA, Univ. Md., 1971, JD, 1976. Bar: Md. 1976. Atty. Blades & Rosenfield, Baltimore, Md., 1976—80; ptnr. Hylton & Gonzales, Baltimore, Md., 1980—. Bd. dir. Legal Mutual Insurance. Bd. regents Univ. Sys. Md., 1997—2002; bd. visitors Univ. Md. Law Sch., 2003. Recipient Md. Leadership in Law, 2001. Fellow: Md. Bar Found.; mem.: Am. Bar Found., Bar Assn. Balt. City, Md. State Bar Assn. (pres. 1991—92), ABA (bd. gov. 2004—). Office: Hylton & Gonzales Suite 2200 201 N Charles St Baltimore MD 21201 Office Phone: 410-547-0900. Office Fax: 410-625-1516.

GONZALES, RICHARD ROBERT, counselor; b. Palo Alto, Calif., Jan. 12, 1945; s. Pedro and Virginia (Ramos) G.; m. Jennifer Ayres; children: Lisa Dianne, Jeffrey Ayres. AA, Foothill Coll., 1966; BA, San Jose State U., Calif., 1969; MA, Calif. Poly. State U., San Luis Obispo, 1971; grad., Def. Info. Sch., Def. Equal Opportunity Mgmt. Inst. Lic. marriage family child counselor, Calif.; cert. counselor Nat. Bd. Cert. Counselors. Counselor student activities Calif. Poly. State U., San Luis Obispo, 1969-71, instr. ethnic studies, 1970-71; counselor Ohlone Coll., Fremont, Calif., 1971-72, coord. coll. readiness, 1971; counselor De Anza Coll., Cupertino, Calif., 1972-78, mem. cmty. spkrs. bur., 1975-78; counselor Foothill Coll., Los Altos Hills, Calif., 1978—, mem. cmty. spkrs. bur., 1978—. Instr. Def. Equal Opportunity Mgmt. Inst., 1984-96; mem. U. Calif. C.C. Counselor Adv. Com., 1998—. Mem. master plan com. Los Altos (Calif.) Sch. Dist., 1975-76; vol. worker, Latino/Chicano cmtys., Calif.; active mem. Woodside (Calif.) Recreation Commn. Commd. officer Calif. Army N.G., now ret. Adj. Gen. Corps, USAR. Masters and Johnson fellow. Mem. ACA, Am. Coll. Counseling Assn., Calif. Assn. Marriage and Family Therapists, Calif. C.C. Counselor Assn. (former pres.), Calif. Assn. Counseling and Devel. (former pres. Hispanic Caucus, former pres.), Calif. Assn. for Humanistic Edn. and Devel. (former pres.), Calif. Assn. for Multi-Cultural Counseling, Res. Officers Assn., La Raza Faculty Assn. Calif. C.C., Nat. Career Devel. Assn., Phi Delta Kappa, Chi Sigma Iota. Republican. E-mail: rrgincal@hotmail.com.

GONZALES, RON, mayor, former county supervisor; b. San Francisco, 1951; m. Alvina Gonzales; 3 children: Miranda, Rachel, Alejandra. BA in Community Studies, U. Calif., Santa Cruz. Formerly with Sunnyvale (Calif.) Sch. Dist., City of Santa Clara, Calif.; then human resource mgr. Hewlett-Packard Co.; market program mgmt. cons. state and local govts.; mem. city coun. City of Sunnyvale, 1979-87, mayor, 1982, 87; mem. bd. suprs. Santa Clara County, 1989-96; edn. program mgr. Hewlett Packard Co., 1996-98; mayor City of San Jose, Calif., 1999—2006. Bd. chair, 1993; bd. transit suprs. Santa Clara County, 1989—; bd. dirs. Joint Venture: Silicon Valley, The Role Model Program, Bay Area Biosci. Ctr., Am. Leadership Forum, Santa Clara County.

GONZALES, SARAH, women's organization director; b. 1976; Dir., Racial Justice Prog. YWCA. Mem. Ariz. Collegiate Leadership Conf. Mem. Jewish Cmty. Rels. Coun., Tunnel of Oppression, U. Ariz., Tucson Save Darfur Coalition. Named one of 40 Under 40, Tucson Bus. Edge, 2006. Office: YWCA 738 N 5th Ave Tucson AZ 85705 Office Phone: 520-884-7810. Office Fax: 520-884-5205.

GONZALEZ, ANTONIO, academic administrator, educator, title company executive; b. Edinburg, Tex., Mar. 14, 1943; s. Manuel Gonzalez and Natalia Torres; m. Elma De Luna, Oct. 10, 1975; 1 child, Julissa Priscilla. BA, U. Md., Balt., 1971; MA, U. Tenn., 1973; JD, Miles Coll., 1979. Law clk. Crain Caton James & Oberwetter, Houston, 1979-81; instr. U. Houston, 1981-83, asst. dir., 1983-86; instr. Houston C.C., 1982—85, 1995, 2001—02; assoc. dir. No. Ill. U., Dekalb, 1986-88; adminstr. Prairie View (Tex.) A&M U., 1988—96; instr. Houston Internat. U., 1988-89, pres., CEO, 1989-90, Am. Fidelity Mortgage & Title Co., Houston, 1992-95; instr. North Harris Coll., Houston, 1994-95, Wharton County Jr. Coll., 1996—2002, Tomball Coll., 2001—02, Montgomery Coll., 2002—03, Tex. So. U., 2003. Mem. adv. com. Houston C.C., 1994-95. Editor: Mexican-American Musicians, 1987; mem. editl. bd. Jour. Minority Issues, 1993-94. Chair tng. and devel. LULAC Dist. 18, Houston, 1994-96; dir. Inst. Chicano Culture, Houston, 1995; mem. SER Jobs for Progress, Houston, 1994-96; Dem. candidate Tex. Ho. Reps. Dist. 130, 1994; mem. Tejano Ctr. for Cmty. Concerns. With USAF, 1966-70, Vietnam. Named Man of Yr. LULAC, Ill., 1987. Mem.: VFW, AAUP, Tex. Assn. Coll. and Univ. Student Pers. Adminstrs., Nat. Bar Assn., Tex. Fgn. Lang. Assn., Tex. Assn. Mortgage Brokers, Tex. C.C. Tchrs. Assn., Tex. Assn. Coll. Admissions Counselors, Tex. Assn. Chicanos in Higher Edn., Am. Hist. Assn., Am. GI Forum (comdr. 2006—), Air Force Assn., Vietnam Vets. Assn., Am. Legion, Delta Theta Phi, Phi Delta Kappa. Roman Catholic. Avocations: writing, research. Home: 16614 Dounreay Dr Houston TX 77084-3410 Office: 3100 Cleburne St Houston TX 77004 Office Phone: 713-313-1335. Business E-Mail: amerfideli@aol.com, gonzaleza@tsu.edu.

GONZALEZ, ARTHUR PADILLA, artist, educator; b. Sacramento, July 22, 1954; s. John and Rita (Padilla) G.; m. Christine Carol Ciavarella, Feb. 11, 1988; stepchild, Nick Port. BA, Calif. State U., Sacramento, 1977, MA, 1979; MFA, U. Calif., Davis, 1981. Vis. artist La. State U., Baton Rouge, 1982-83, U. Ga., Athens, summer 1984, R.I. Sch. Design, Providence, 1985; asst. prof. U. Calif., Davis, 1985-86, Berkeley, 1987-88; vis. artist, instr. San Francisco Art Inst., 1990-91; assoc. prof. art Calif. Coll. Arts, Oakland, 1991—. Juror Sacramento Met. Arts Commn., 1994-95. One-person shows include Sharpe Gallery, N.Y.C., 1984, 85, 86, 88, Phyllis Kind Gallery, N.Y.C., 1995, John Elder Gallery, N.Y.C., 1999, 2002. Recipient awards Nat. Endowment for Arts, 1982, 84, 86, 90, Virginia Groot award, 1997. Democrat. Avocation: polynesian dance. Home: 1713 Versailles Ave Alameda CA 94501-1650 Office: Calif Coll Arts & Crafts 5212 Broadway Oakland CA 94618-1426 Office Phone: 510-594-3617. Business E-Mail: art@arthurgonzalez.com. E-mail: windeater@alamedanet.net.

GONZALEZ, CALEB, ophthalmologist, educator; b. Humacao, P.R., May 1, 1929; s. Carlos Pilar and Julia (Mercado) Gonzalez; m. Flora Caroline Harrison, June 29, 1956; children: Lisa Gay, Patricia Jo, Sandra Pilar, Erica Irene, Kristie Juliana. BA, Inter Am. U., San German, PR, 1949; MD, U. P.R., 1954; MA, Yale U., 1981. Intern Wayne County Gen. Hosp., Eloise, Mich., 1954—55; resident in ophthalmology Kings County Hosp., Bklyn., 1959—62; fellow pediat. ophthalmology Bellevue Hosp., NYC, 1962—64; assoc. prof. ophthalmology U. P.R., San Juan, 1971—76; chmn. dept. ophthalmology, chief ophthalmology Yale U., New Haven, 1977—96, prof. ophthalmology, 1981—. Mem. editl. bd.: Jour. Pediat. Opthalmology, 1977—85; author: Strabismus and Ocular Motility, 1983. Pres. local chpt. Exch. Club, San Juan, 1974; active Congregational Ch., Woodsridge, Conn., 1976—. Lt. comdr. USNR. Recipient Disting. Alumnus award, Inter Am. U., 1983. Fellow: Am. Bd. Ophthalmologists, Am. Assn. Pediat. Ophthalmology (Honor award 1997), Am. Acad. Ophthalmology (Honor award 1992); mem.: Alpha Omega Alpha. Republican. Avocation: tennis. Office: Yale Sch Medicine 330 Cedar St New Haven CT 06520

GONZALEZ, CECILIA H., lawyer; b. 1956; BA, McGill U., 1976; JD, Georgetown U., 1979. Bar: DC 1980. Ptnr. Howrey LLP, Washington, 1986, co-chair intellectual property practice grp., mem. exec. bd., mem. intellectual property grp. mgmt. team, co-chair bus. affairs com., mng. ptnr. practice devel. Named one of 15 of DC Area's Top IP Attorneys, Legal Times, 2003, The 50 Most Influential Women Lawyers in Am., Nat. Law Jour., 2007. Mem.: US Internat. Trade Commn. Trial Lawyers Assn., Minority Corp. Counsel Assn., Hispanic Bar Assn., Am. Intellectual Property Law Assn., ABA, DC Bar Assn. Office: Howrey LLP 1299

Pennsylvania Ave NW Washington DC 20004 Office Phone: 202-383-6595. Office Fax: 202-383-6610. Business E-Mail: gonzalezC@howrey.com.*

GONZALEZ, CHARLES A., congressman; b. San Antonio, May 5, 1945; s. Henry B. and Bertha Gonzalez; m. Becky Whetstone (div.); 1 child: Leo Gonzalez. BA in Govt., U. Tex., Austin, 1969; JD, St. Mary's Sch. Law, San Antonio, 1972. 5th grade tchr. Kindred Elem. Sch. Soth San Antonio Ind. Sch. Dist.; lawyer pvt. practice, San Antonio, 1972-82; mcpl. ct. judge San Antonio; judge Bexar County Ct. at Law Number 2, 1983-87; dist. ct. judge Bexar County, Tex., 1989-97; mem. US Congress from 20th Tex. dist., 1999—, mem. energy and commerce com. Appointed regional whip for the Dem. Caucus; elected v.p. freshman class for 106th Congress; mem. of Congl. Hispanic Caucus, named chair of Census Task Force; co-chair Census Task Force for Dem. Caucus Bd. dirs. Arthritis Found., Literacy Coun., YMCA Metroboard, Camp Fire Girls, March of Dimes, Easter Seals. Democrat. Roman Catholic. Achievements include being recognized as one of the highest rated trial judges; responsible for introducing the latest in technology into the courtroom and streamlining the dockets; earned reputation as ardent mediator. Office: US Ho Reps 327 Cannon Ho Office Bldg Washington DC 20515-4320 Office Phone: 202-225-3236.*

GONZALEZ, EDDIE, advertising executive; With Young & Rubicam Puerto Rico, 1982, mng. dir., 1983; pres., CEO Young & Rubicam Spain, Madrid; chmn., CEO L.Am. Young & Rubicam Brands, Miami, 2003—, chmn., CEO Bravo Grp., 2006—. Named to 100 Influentials List, Hispanic Bus. Mag., 2006. Office: Young & Rubicam Latin Am Courvoisier Ctr 11 601 Brickell Key Dr Ste 1100 Miami FL 33131 Office Phone: 305-347-1950.*

GONZALEZ, EMILIO BUSTAMANTE, rheumatologist, educator; b. Asuncion, Paraguay, Jan. 9, 1949; came to U.S., 1974; s. Emilio Gonzalez-Jovellanos and Clara (Bustamante) Gonzalez; m. Elizabeth Ferreira, Jan. 4, 1973; 1 child, Daniel BS Scis. and Humanities, C.A.L. Coll., Asuncion, 1972; MD summa cum laude, Nat. U., Asuncion, 1972. Diplomate Am. Bd. Internal Medicine, Am. Bd. Rheumatology, Am. Bd. Allergy and Immunology. Intern U. Hosp., Asuncion, 1973—74; resident Danbury Hosp., Conn., 1975—78; tchg. fellow allergy and clin. immunology U. Pitts. Sch. Medicine and VA Med. Ctr., 1978—79; mem. staff allergy and clin. immunology Nat. Jewish Hosp. and U. Colo. Affiliated Hosps., Denver, 1979—80; mem. staff clin. immunology and rheumatology U. Tex. Med. Br., Galveston, 1980—81, clin. instr. dept. medicine, 1981—82, asst. prof. medicine, 1982—89, assoc. prof. medicine, 1989—, dir. rheumatology, 2004—, prof. medicine, 2004—; chief rheumatology svc. Grady Meml. Hosp. and Emory U. Sch. Medicine, Atlanta, 1989—; attending physician rheumatology sect. med. svc. VA Med. Svc., Emory U., Decatur, Ga., 1989—; attending physician divsn. rheumatology Emory U. Hosp., Atlanta, 1989—; cons., part-time mem. divsn. rheumatology Emory Clinic and Emory U., Atlanta, 1989—; dir. rheumatology Atlanta Med. Ctr., 1998—2004. Bd. dirs. Arthritis Found., Ga., sci. com.; presenter in field Contbr. articles to profl. jours.; reviewer in field:. Fellow ACP, Am. Coll. Rheumatology; mem. AMA, Am. Acad. Allergy and Immunology, Ga. Rheumatism Soc. (program chmn. 1993-94), Ga. Soc. Rheumatology (pres. 1995-96), Sigma Xi Office: Univ Tex Med Branch Dir Rheumatology 301 University Blvd Galveston TX 77555-1165 Office Phone: 409-772-2863. Office Fax: 409-772-7355. Business E-Mail: ebgonzal@utmb.edu.

GONZALEZ, EMILIO T., federal agency administrator; BA in Internat. Studies, So. Fla.; MA in Latin Am. Studies, Tulane U.; Ph.D in Internat. Rels., U. Miami; Grad., Naval War Coll. Dir. office spl. assistants U.S. So. Command U.S. Army; instr. U.S. Military Acad., West Point, NY; dir. we. hemisphere affairs NSC, Washington; sr. mng. dir. global and govt. affairs Tew Cardenas, LLP, Miami; dir. U.S. Citizenship and Immigration Services, US Dept. Homeland Security, Washington, 2006—. Named a Knight of Malta; recipient Grad. Sch. award for Acad. Achievement, U. Miami. Office: US Citizenship and Immigration Svcs US Dept Homeland Security 20 Massachusetts Ave Washington DC 20524 Office Phone: 202-272-1000. Office Fax: 202-272-1134.

GONZALEZ, EUGENE ROBERT, investment banker; s. Eugenio Tomas and Alice Marie (Macdonald) Gonzalez-Mandiola. BA in Internat. Rels., Yale U., 1952; postgrad., Georgetown U., 1954; postgrad. sem. in advanced mgmt., Internat. Mgmt. Devel. Inst., Lausanne, Switzerland, 1967. Econ. officer Dept. Defense, Washington, 1954-57; project fin. officer Devel. Loan Fund (now AID), Washington, 1957-58; fin. mgr. RCA Internat., NYC, 1958-61; fin. instns. specialist Interam. Devel. Bank, Washington, 1961-62, fin. officer, 1962-63, dep. regional rep. for Europe Paris, 1964; exec. v.p. Adela Investment Co., Luxembourg, 1964-74; pres., chief exec. officer Adelatec Mgmt. Cons. Co., 1969-72; mng. dir. Adela Investment Co., 1974-75, pres., chief exec. officer, 1975-76; adviser, regional coordinator Ibero Am. Morgan Stanley Internat., NYC, 1977-89; sr. v.p., head internat. pvt. banking Barclays Bank, NYC, 1989-91; mng. dir. Kidder, Peabody & Co., NYC, 1992-94; pres. Quasar Capital Corp., S.A., 1995—. Author: International Sources of Financing, 1961. Served with U.S. Army, 1952-54. Mem. Nat. Com. on Am. Fgn. Policy, Internat. Assn. Fin. Planners, Am. Soc. Profl. Cons., Presidents Assn., Americas Soc., Spanish Inst., Met. Club (Washington), City Tavern Club (Washington), Brook Club (N.Y.C.), Racquet and Tennis Club (N.Y.C.), Yale Club (N.Y.C.), Pacific Union Club (San Francisco), Zeta Psi Soc. N.Am. Home: 165 E 66th St # 9K New York NY 10021-6132 Personal E-mail: egonz88888@aol.com.

GONZALEZ, FREDI, professional baseball manager; b. Cuba, 1964; m. Pamela Gonzalez; 1 child, Gabrielle; 1 child, Alex Christopher. Mgr. Triple-A Richmond Affiliate Atlanta Braves, 2002; third base coach Atlanta Braves, 2003—06; minor league coach Fla. Marlins, 1992—99, third base coach, 2000—01, mgr., 2006—. Achievements include being first minor league mgr. hired in history Fla. Marlins franchise, 1991.*

GONZALEZ, GABRIELA, history professor; d. Jorge German and Maria Bernardina Gonzalez. BS, U. Tex., Austin, 1988—91; MA in History, U. Tex., San Antonio, 1992—95, Stanford U., Calif., 1996—2001, PhD in History, 1996—2004. Rsch. asst. Inst. Texan Cultures, San Antonio, 1994; grad. asst. Coll. Social & Behavioral Scis. U. Tex., San Antonio, 1994, grad. asst. Ctr. for Study of Women & Gender, 1994—96, asst. prof. history, 1995—, tchg. assoc., 1996; rsch. asst. Stanford U., 1996—2001, tchg. asst., 1998—99, instr., 2000. Author: (book reviews) Reinventing the Melting Pot: The New Immigrants and What It Means to Be American, Lulac: Mexican Americans and National Policy; contbr. articles to profl. jours. & encyclopedias. Mem. Orgn. Am. Historians, 2005, Berkshire Conf. Women's Historians, 2006. Mem.: Tex. State Hist. Assn., We. Hist. Assn., Pacific Coast Branch-Am. Hist. Assn., Orgn. Am. Historians, Am. Hist. Assn. Avocations: reading, writing, music, exercise.

GONZALEZ, GABRIELA INES, physics professor; b. Cordoba, Argentina, Feb. 24, 1965; d. Pedro Arnaldo Gonzalez Bofill and Dora Luisa Trembinsky de Gonzalez; m. Jorge Alfredo Pullin, Oct. 7, 1988. Lic. in Physics, Cordoba U., Argentina, 1988; MSc in Physics, Syracuse U., 1993, PhD in Physics, 1995. Asst. tchr. Manuel Belgrano HS, Cordoba, 1983-85; tchg. asst. physics dept. Cordoba Nat. U., 1988—89; tchg. asst. Syracuse U., NY, 1990—91, rsch. asst., 1990—94, univ. fellow physics dept., 1994—95; rsch. scientist Ctr. Space Rsch. MIT, Cambridge, 1995-97; asst. prof. physics Pa. State U., University Park, 1997—2001, La. State U., Baton Rouge, 2001, assoc. prof. Mem. coun. Laser Interferometric Gravitational Wave Obs. project Laser Interferometric Gravitational Wave Obs. Sci. Collaboration, Pasadena, Calif., 1997—. Grantee NSF, 1998—. Mem. AAAS, Am. Phys. Soc. (exec. com. topical group on gravitation, Edward A. Bouchet award, 2007), ACLU, Nat. Geog. Soc. Achievements include research in gravitational wave detection, associated with the Laser-Interferometer Gravitational-wave Observatory project. E-mail: gonzalez@lsu.edu.*

GONZALEZ, HECTOR HUGO, nursing educator; b. Roma, Tex., Mar. 9, 1937; s. Amadeo Lorenzo and Carlotta (Trevino) G. BSN, Incarnate Word Coll., 1963; MSN, Cath. U. Am., 1966; PhD in Edn., U. Tex., 1974. RN, Tex. Staff nurse Santa Rosa Med. Ctr., San Antonio, 1962-65; asst. dir. nursing divsn. Incarnate Word Coll., San Antonio, 1968-72; prof., chmn. dept. nursing San Antonio Coll., 1972-92, dir. Ctr. for Assoc. Degree Edn. Rsch. and Svc., 1987-92, prof. and chmn. emeritus, 1993—. Cons. NIMH, 1973, FDA, 1989-93, mem. anesthesiology and respiratory devices panel, mem. dispute resolution panel, 2000—01; numerous ednl. instns. and hosps. in U.S., Mex., P.R., Kuwait; mem. Nat. Adv. Coun. on Alcohol Abuse and Alcoholism, 1976-80; mem. nat. adv. coun. nurses edn. and practice, 1992-96; mem. panel on nursing practice U.S. Pharmacopeia, 1985-2000. Contbr. articles to profl. jours.; peer reviewer Nursing Outlook, 1983, Advancing Clinical Care. Mem. legis. affairs adv. com. State Senator Glen Kothman, San Antonio, 1983; bd. dirs. Family Svcs. Assn. San Antonio; mem. multidisciplinary academic external com. U. Autonoma de Nuevo Leon, Mex., 1986-88. Capt. nurse corps U.S. Army, 1966-68. Recipient cert. of appreciation Citizens of Bexar County, San Antonio, 1970, Nat. Student Nurses Assn., 1977. Mem. ANA (mem. adv. bd. minority fellowship program 1976-80, Trail Blazer award Minority Fellowship Program 2004), Nat. Assn. Hispanic Nurses (pres. 1982-84, bd. dirs. 1995-97, CEO San Antonio chpt. 1998—, project dir. breast cancer tng. grant Am. Cancer Soc. and Nat. Assn. Hispanic Nurses 1992-96, historian 2000—), Nat. League for Nursing (bd. dirs. 1973-81). Democrat. Roman Catholic. Home: 114 Magnolia Dr San Antonio TX 78212-3115 Office Phone: 210-733-7460. Personal E-mail: hhgzz@sbcglobal.net.

GONZALEZ, IRMA ELSA, federal judge; b. Palo Alto, Calif., 1948; BA, Stanford U., 1970; JD, U. Ariz., 1973. Law clk. to Hon. William C. Frey US Dist. Ct. (Ariz. dist.), 1973-75; asst. U.S. atty. US Attys. Office Ariz., 1975-79, US Attys. Office (ctrl. dist.) Calif., 1979-81; trial atty. antitrust divsn. US Dept. Justice, 1979; assoc. Seltzer Caplan Wilkins & McMahon, San Diego, 1981-84; judge US Magistrate Ct. (so. dist.) Calif., 1984-91; ct. judge San Diego County Superior Ct., 1991-92; judge US Dist. Ct. (so. dist.) Calif., San Diego, 1992—, chief judge, 2005—. Adj. prof. U. San Diego, 1992; trustee Calif. Western Sch. Law; bd. visitors Sch. Law U. Ariz. Mem. Girl Scout Women's Adv. Cabinet. Mem. Lawyers' Club San Diego, Inns of Ct. Office: Edward J Schwartz US Courthouse 940 Front St Ste 5135 San Diego CA 92101-8911

GONZALEZ, JOE FRED, JR., mathematical statistician, educator; b. San Antonio, Tex., Jan. 16, 1947; s. Joe Fred Gonzalez, Sr. and Gloria Rodriquez Gonzalez; m. Patricia Vaive Gonzalez, July 15, 1987; children: Joe Fred III, Jennifer Melanie Wasko, Michele Yvette Frates, Francesca Joelle. BS in Math., St. Mary's U., 1965—70; MS in Stats., The George Wash. U., 1979—81. Math. statistician Office of Rsch. and Methodology, Nat. Ctr. for Health Stats., Hyattsville, Md., 1972—. Adj. asst. prof. Montgomery Coll., Rockville, Md., 1985—99; adj. assoc. prof. U. of Md. U. Coll., Coll. Pk., Md., 1990—; lead organizer, chair Discrete Math. and Theoretical Computer Sci. Working Group Rutgers U.; presenter in field. Co-author (with Lester R. Curtin): (math. computer graph) The Bivariate Normal Distbn. (Rho=0.8) (Most Creative Use of Software, First Place-monochrome, 1986); co-author: (online modules) Modules for UMUC Online BMGT 230 Bus. Stats. Class; contbr. articles to profl. jours., papers to conf. procs. Pres. Richard Montgomery H.S. Band Parents Orgn., Rockville, Md., 1984—85; swim team rep. Hungerford Stoneridge Swim Club, Rockville, pres., 1984—86. Recipient Cited with biosketch and photo in a textbook Advanced Math., Precalculus with Discrete Math. and Data Analysis, Houghton Mifflin Co., 1992, U. Md. Univ. Coll. Tchg. Recognition award, 2005; scholar LULAC Scholarship Award, League of United Latin Am. Citizens, 1965. Mem.: Internat. Statis. Inst., Wash. Statis. Soc. (assoc.), Am. Statis. Assn. (assoc.; chair, com. on minorities in stats. 1992—95), Math. Assn. of Am. (assoc.), Am. Statis. Assn. (assoc.; mem. asa adv. com. on continuing edn. 1999—2002). Office: Nat Ctr for Health Statistics 3311 Toledo Rd Rm 3121 Hyattsville MD 20782 Office Phone: 301-458-4239. Personal E-mail: joefredg2@aol.com. E-mail: jgonzalez@cdc.gov.

GONZALEZ, JOE MANUEL, lawyer; b. NYC, Aug. 18, 1950; s. Reinaldo Fabregas and Mary Louise (Cermeno) G.; m. Ruia Jane Whiteside, Dec. 30, 1977; children: Matthew Ray, Jane Marie, Jeffrey Joseph, Joseph Manuel. BA, U. South Fla., 1972; JD, Gonzaga U., 1980; LLM in Taxation, Georgetown U., 1981. Bar: Fla. 1981, U.S. Tax Ct. 1983, U.S. Dist. Ct. (mid. dist.) Fla. 1984, U.S. Ct. Appeals (11th cir.) 1984, U.S. Supreme Ct. 1985. Atty. Gonzaga U. Legal Services, Spokane, Wash., 1980; mng. ptnr. Cotterill, Gonzalez, Hayes & Grantham, Fla., 1981-88, Cotterill & Grantham, Pa., 1982-92, Cotterill, Gonzalez & Grantham, Pa., Pa., 1992-93; prin. Joe M. Gonzalez, P.A., 1993—; atty. Hispanic Def. League, Tampa, Fla., 1982-90. Assoc. editor Gonzaga Law Rev. Spl. Report: Pub. Sector Labor Law, 1980. Mem. Sheriff's Hispanic Adv. Coun., Hillsborough County, Fla., 1982-93, City of Tampa Hispanic Adv. Coun., 1983-2006, chmn. 1993-95, U. So. Fla. Hispanic Adv. Bd., 1999-2001; chmn. citizens adv. com. Hillsborough County Planning Commn., 1988-90; pres. Tampa Hispanic Heritage, Inc., 1985-87; co-founder Carnavale En Tampa, Inc., 1986-90; master of ceremonies Gasparilla Sidewalk Art Festival, 1988; mem. police chief's adv. com., 1988-93; sec. Hispanic Bus. Inst. Fla., Inc., 1988-93; dir. Housing and Edn. Alliance, 2001—. Mem. ABA, Fla. Bar Assn. (jud. nominating prodedures com. 1988-89), Hillsborough County Bar Assn., Assn. Trial Lawyers Am., Nat. Inst. for Trial Advocacy, Complete Census Count Com., Ybor City Rotary Club (Paul Harris fellow 2006), Ybor City Rotary Found. (co-founder, charter mem.), Phi Delta Phi. Democrat. Presbyterian. Home: 5801 Mariner St Tampa FL 33609-3411 Office: 304 S Willow Ave Tampa FL 33606-2147 Home Phone: 813-639-0680; Office Phone: 813-254-0797. E-mail: joegonzalez@aol.com.

GONZALEZ, JOSE ALEJANDRO, JR., federal judge; b. Tampa, Fla., Nov. 26, 1931; s. Jose A. and Luisa Secundina (Collia) G.; m. Frances Frierson, Aug. 22, 1956 (dec. Aug. 1981); children— Margaret Ann, Mary Frances; m. Mary Sue Copeland, Sept. 24, 1983 BA, U. Fla., 1952, JD, 1957; LLD, Nova Southeastern U., 1998. Bar: Fla. 1958, U.S. Dist. Ct. (so. dist.) Fla. 1959, U.S. Ct. Appeals 1959, U.S. Supreme Ct. 1963. Practice in, Ft. Lauderdale, 1958-64; claim rep. State Farm Mut., Lakeland, Fla., 1957-58; assoc. firm Watson, Hubert and Sousley, 1958-61, ptnr., 1961-64; asst. state atty. 15th Cir. Fla., 1961-64; cir. judge 17th Cir. Ft. Lauderdale, 1964-78, chief judge, 1969-70; assoc. judge 4th Dist. Ct. Appeals, West Palm Beach; U.S. dist. judge So. Dist. Fla., 1978—, sr. judge, 1996—. Bd. dirs. Arthritis Found., 1962-72; bd. dirs. Henderson Clinic Broward County, 1964-68, v.p., 1967-68. Served to 1st lt. AUS, 1952-54. Recipient Kupferman award Laymen's Nat. Bible Assn., 1991; named Broward County Outstanding Young Man, 1967, one of Fla.'s Five Outstanding Young Men, Fla. Jaycees, 1967, Broward Legal Exec. of Yr., 1978. Mem.: ABA, Broward County Bar, Fla. Bar Assn., Fed. Bar Assn., Am. Judicature Soc., Pittsfield Country Club, Fla. Blue Key, Kiwanian Club (pres. 1971—72), Lauderdale Yacht Club, Ft. Lauderdale Jaycees (dir. 1960—61), Phi Alpha Delta, Sigma Chi (Significant Sig). Democrat. Office: US Dist Ct 205 US Courthouse 299 E Broward Blvd Fort Lauderdale FL 33301-1944

GONZALEZ, JUAN (ALBERTO VAZQUEZ), professional baseball player; b. Vega Baja, Puerto Rico, Oct. 16, 1969; Outfielder Tex. Rangers, 1989—99, 2002—03; designated hitter Detroit Tigers, 2000; outfielder Cleve. Indians, 2001, Kansas City Royals, 2004, Cleve. Indians, 2005—06, Boston Red Sox, 2006—. Named Most Valuable Player, Am. Assn., 1990, Am. League Most Valuable Player, Baseball Writers' Assn. of Am., 1996, 1998; named to Am. League Silver Slugger Team, 1992—93, Am. League All-Star Team, 1993, 1998, 2001. Achievements include leading Am. League in home runs, 1992-93. Office: Boston Red Sox 4 Yawkey Way Boston MA 02215

GONZALEZ, KAREN EILEEN, middle school educator; b. Cin., Jan. 30, 1960; d. Charles Franklin and Doris Jean (Smith) Surber; children: Rachel Elizabeth, Mark Joseph. BA, Harding U., 1983. Elem. educator Wood County Pub. Schs., Parkersburg, W.Va., 1983—85; learning disabilities educator Upper Arlington City Schs., Columbus, Ohio, 1985—86, Columbus Pub. Schs., 1986—2005, Metro Nashville Public Schs., 2005—. Women's min. leader Indian Springs Ch. of Christ, 1987-91; vol. Spl. Olympics, 1981-85, Easter Seals of W.Va., Parkersburg, 1984-85, Elizabeth Blackwell at Riverside Meth. Hosp., Columbis, 1988—, Race for the Cure, Festival Latino, Bishop Watterson Mothers Club, Columbus Children's Theater, Ballet Met Columbus; mem. Children's Hosp. Aux. Twig, 1992—; troop leader Girl Scouts Am., 1992—; kids' voting coord. Power of the Pen sponsor; youth to youth advisor Project Tolerance; active Woodmont Hills Ch. of Christ, Nashville. Named Tchr. of Yr., Papa John's, 2005, Columbus Pub. Sch. Tchr. Vol. of Yr., 2002; fellow, COSI; Martha Holdings Jennings scholar, 2004—05, HistoryWorks fellow, Ohio State U., Growing to Green grantee, Scotts Found. Mem. NEA, Tenn. Educators Assn., Tenn. Social Studies Educators Assn., Coun. for Exceptional Children, Columbus Educators Assn., Phi Delta (pres., v.p. 1980-82). Avocations: reading, travel, scrapbooks, genealogy. Personal E-mail: kgonzalezfam@aol.com.

GONZALEZ, MARIO M., librarian; BA, City Coll. NY; MLS, Pratt Inst. Dir. Greenwich Libr., Conn., 1999—. Named to Advocacy Honor Roll, Assn. Libr. Trustees and Advocates, 2005. Mem.: Reference and User Services Assn. (mem. exec. bd.), Nat. Assn. to Promote Libr. and Info. Svcs. to Latinos and the Spanish-Speaking (pres. 1991—92, treas. north-east chpt. 2002, Libr. of Yr. 1994), ALA (councilor at large 1995—, mem. exec. com. 2006—, mem. Spectrum Scholarship Jury, chmn. Ethnic and Multicultural Info. Exchange Roundtable, mem. com. on committees). Office: Greenwich Library 101 W Putnam Ave Greenwich CT 06830 Office Phone: 203-622-7961. Office Fax: 203-625-6555. E-mail: mgonzalez@greenwichlibrary.org.

GONZALEZ, PEDRO BLAS, philosopher, educator; b. Ciego de Avila, Camaguey, Cuba, July 8, 1964; arrived in US, 1970; m. Anne Chung. BA, U. Ala., Tuscaloosa, 1988; MA, Depaul U., Chgo., 1989; PhD, DePaul U., Chgo., 1991. Assoc. prof. philosophy Barry U., Miami Shores, Fla., 1998—. Author: (books) Human Existence as Radical Reality: Ortega's Philosophy of Subjectivity / Fragments: Essays in Subjectivity, Individuality and Autonomy, Orteg's The Reuch Of The Masses And The Triumph Of The New Man, 2007, Unamuno: A Lyrical Essay, 2007. Office: Barry Univ 11300 NE Second Ave Miami Shores FL 33161-6695 Home Phone: 305-441-6453. Business E-Mail: pgonzalez@mail.barry.edu.

GONZALEZ, RICARDO, surgeon, educator; b. Buenos Aires, June 26, 1943; s. Salvador Maria and Clyde Alcira (Prevettoni) G.; children: Diego Andres, Carlos Ricardo. BA, Coll. Nat. San Isidro, 1959; MD, U. Buenos Aires, 1965. Diplomate Am. Bd. Urology. Resident in surgery Hosp. Mil. Ctr., Buenos Aires, 1966—68; intern in surgery U. Minn., Mpls., 1969—70, resident, med. fellow in urologic surgery, 1970—74, from instr. to prof. urology, 1974—85, prof. urology, 1985—94, prof. pediat., 1993—94; chief, pediat. urology Children's Hosp. of Mich., Detroit, 1994; prof. urology Wayne State U., Detroit, 1995—99; prof. urology and pediat., chief pediat. urology divsn. U. Miami /Jackson Meml. Hosp., Fla., 1999—2002; dir. pediat. urology fellowship A.I. du Pont Hosp. for Children, Wilmington, Del., 2002—; prof. urology Thomas Jefferson U., Phila., 2002—, pres., 2002. Pres. Pediat. Urology P.C., Detroit, 1995-00; vis. prof. Harvard U., Cambridge, Mass., 1994, John Hopkins U., Balt., 1995, U. Washington, Seattle, 1995, U. Calif., San Francisco, 1996, Cornell U., NY, 1998, U. Montreal, 2000, McGill U., 2000, U. Vienna, Austria, 2003, Chinese U. Hong Kong, 2003, SUNY Upstate Med. Coll., Syracuse, 2003, U. Zurich, Switzerland, 2005, 06, U. Belgrade, 2005; vis. prof., acting chief pediatric urology Kinderspital U. Zurich, Switzerland, 2006, 07; cons. pediat. urologist Italian Hosp., Buenos Aires; presenter in field. Contbr. over 340 articles to profl. jours., over 50 chpts. to books; editor 2 books. Am. Acad. Pediat. fellow, 1981, Nat. Kidney Found. rsch. fellow 1974-76; co-prin. investigator USPHS cancer grant 1976-78. Fellow Am. Acad. Pediat. (exec. sect. on urology com. 1995-98); mem. Am. Urol. Assn., Mex. Coll. Urology (hon.), Venezuelan Soc. Spina Bifida, Argentine Confedn. Urology, Societé Internat. d'Urologie, Ibero-Am. Soc. Pediat. Urology (pres. 1995-98, Medal of Merit 2000), Soc. Pediat. Urol. Surgeons (by invitation), European Soc. Paediat. Urology (hon.), Swiss Assn. Pediatric Surgeons. Avocations: opera, music, language, reading, writing. Office: AI duPont Hosp for Children Dept Urology 1600 Rockland Rd Wilmington DE 19899 Office Phone: 302-651-5701. Personal E-mail: ricardo_gonzalez33154@yahoo.com. Business E-Mail: rgonzale@nemours.org.

GONZALEZ, RICHARD, maritime safety officer; b. 1966; BA in Spanish with honors, U. Minn., 1991; BA in Polit. Sci., 1991; MPA, Fla. Atlantic U., 1998; JD, U. Miami, 2002. Regulatory project officer, analyst USCG Hdqtrs., Washington, 1992-93; divsn. head, supply dept., deck watch officer CGC Courageous, Panama City, Fla., 1993-95; chief, uninspected vessel safety sect. (7th Dist.) USCG, Miami, 1995-98, quality performance cons., 1998—2001, maritime safety officer, 2002—. With USCG, 1987. Decorated Nat. Def. Svc. medal, numerous commendation medals USCG, others. Mem. Phi Gamma Delta, Alpha Phi Omega, Alpha Mu Gamma, Pi Alpha Alpha, Pi Gamma Mu, Phi Alpha Delta.

GONZALEZ, RICHARD A., pharmaceutical executive; b. Jan. 21, 1954; B in BioChemistry, U. Houston; M in BioChemistry, U. Miami. Rsch. biochemist U. Miami Sch. Medicine; numerous positions in divsn. diagnostics Abbott Labs., Abbott Park, Ill., 1977—92, divisional v.p., gen. mgr., 1992—95, v.p. HealthSystems divsn., 1995—98, sr. v.p. hosp. products, 1998—2001, pres., COO med. products, 2001—06, pres., COO, 2006—. Mem. bd. dirs. Abbott Labs. Mem. bd. dirs. Lyric Opera Chgo., Shed Aquarium. Named one of 50 Most Important Hispanics in Tech. & Bus., Hispanic Engr. & Info. Tech. mag., 2005. Office: Abbott Labs 100 Abbott Park Rd Abbott Park IL 60064-6400*

GONZALEZ, RICHARD THEODORE, photographer; b. Trona, Calif., Nov. 9, 1939; s. Alfonso Contreras and Mary (Duarte) G.; m. Gerry Price, Oct. 30, 1958 (div. 1972); children: Richard K., Debra G., Maria E., Felicia F.; m. Yolanda Quijano, Apr. 18, 1991; 1 child, Andrea. Degree in profl. still photography, N.Y. Inst. Photography, 1962. Photographer Kerr McGee Chem. Corp., Trona, 1962-86, San Bernadino, Calif., 1987-89; founder Gonzalez's Modeling Agy., Midwest City, Okla., 1996—. Newspaper photographer Trona Argonaut, 1962-86; freelance photographer, Trona, 1962-86. Democrat. Roman Catholic. Home: 769 NW 1st St Moore OK 73160-2329 Office: 700 S Air Depot Blvd Ste D-366 Midwest City OK 73110-4833

GONZALEZ, ROLANDO NOEL, secondary school educator, theology studies educator, photographer; b. Rio Grande City, Tex., Sept. 10, 1947; s. Ubaldo and Beulah (Gutierrez) G. BA, U. Tex., 1968; MA, Tex. A&I U., 1972. Cert. tchr. all scis., guidance and counseling. Tchr., head sci. dept. Roma H.S., Tex., 1968-71; migrant/Title I counselor Roma Elem. and Roma Jr. H.S., 1972-76; head sci. dept. Rio Grande H.S., Rio Grande City, Tex., 1976-78; tchr., head sci. dept. Ringgold Jr. H.S., Rio Grande City, 1982-83, Pharr-San Juan-Alamo H.S., Pharr, Tex., 1986—, 1983—90, 1990—2004; seminarian Diocese of Brownsville, San Antonio, 1979-82; pastoral asst. Our Lady, Queen of Angels Ch., La Joya, Tex., 1982-83; coord., lay ministries Brownsville Diocese, McAllen, Tex., 1983-85; lectr., tchr. on scripture Perpetual Help Ch., McAllen, 1986-88, Holy Spirit Ch., McAllen, 1989—; tchr. psychology South Tex. C.C., 2003—; tchr., head sci. dept. St. Philip Neri Athenaeum High Sch., 2004—05; tchr. chemistry and biology I.D.E.A. Coll. Prep., Donna, Tex., 2005—07, St. Joseph Cath. Sch., Edinburg, Tex., 2007—. Instr. history of chemistry U. Tex.-Pan Am., Edinburg, 1990; wedding and portrait photographer, 1973—; psychology tchr., South Tex. C.C., 2003—. Contbr. articles to profl. jours. Tchr. scripture, lectr. Sts. Mary and Margaret Ch., Pharr, Tex., 1988, Sacred Heart Ch., Mercedes, Tex., 1990; tchr. scripture Holy Spirit Parish, McAllen, Tex., 1992—. Recipient Appreciation award Sacred Heart Ch., 1990, Tchr. of Yr. award Rio Grande Valley Sci. Assn., 1996-97, Holy Spirit Parish Vol. award, 2000. Home: 2800 W Iris Ave Mcallen TX 78501-6200 *Humans are so resilient and basically optimistic. I marvel at how humans reach for the stars even though they see around them a planet full of woes.*

GONZALEZ, ROSE MARIE JUAREZ, retired education educator; d. Charles Rosales and Rosie Solis Juarez; m. Mauro Rolando Gonzalez, Oct. 4, 1958; children: Roland Charles, Armand Michael, Rose Marie. BA in Human Devel., BA in Early Childhood Edn., Pacific Oaks Coll., 1974; tchg. credential, UCLA, 2005. Cert. elem. tchr. Calif., tchr. early childhood pre-K-1st grades Calif., bilingual, bicultural, Spanish Calif. Bilingual tchr. L.A. Unified Sch. Dist. 1974—2001, instr. pre-intern tchg. prog., 1999—2003, consulting tchr. peer assistance and rev. program, 2003—; supr./support provider UCLA, 2001—06; organizing coord. east area United Tchrs. L.A., 2005—. Cons./instrnl. transformation team LAUSD, 1993—99, cons./budget steering comm., 1993—99; lang. curriculum and instrn. committe L.A. Unified Sch. Dist. 1994—96. Contbr. biography. Mem. Polit. Action Program/UTLA, LA, 1989—. Save Our Cmty., Rosemead, Calif., 2004—06, Calif. Assn. Bilingual Edn., Covina, Calif., 1974—. Recipient Chpt. Chair of Month, UTLA, 1996, Unsung Hero award, 2000, We Honor Ours, 2003. Mem.: Calif. Tchr. Assn., NEA (del. 1990—2005, rep. assembly 1999—, Ho. of Reps. 1990—), Delta Kappa Gamma Soc. (scholarship chair person 2002—03, 2d v.p. 2004—05). Democrat. Roman Catholic. Achievements include del. NEA Internat; presenter L.A. County Office Edn. Avocations: travel, painting, gardening, dance, arts and crafts. Home Phone: 626-280-0301; Office Phone: 213-385-5398. Personal E-mail: rmgonz2@charter.net.

GONZALEZ, RUBEN RENE, biochemist, researcher, educator; s. Rafael Angel Gonzalez-Carabia and Maria del Rosario Perez-Rivera; m. Margarita Perla Ramos-Garcia, Dec. 2, 1996; children: Ruben Gonzalez-Ramos, Rene Gonzalez-Ramos, Frank Angel Gonzalez-Ramos, Roni-Shanon Gonzalez-Ramos. Biochemist, U. Havana, 1974, PhD, 1985. Scientist Nat. Inst. Endocrinology, Havana, Cuba, 1987—96; vis. scientist Boston Biomed. Rsch. Inst., Watertown, Mass., 2000—02, instr., 2002—; assoc. scientist Vincent Ctr. for Reproductive Biology Mass. Gen. Hosp., Boston, 2003—; rsch. asst. prof. Morehouse Sch. Medicine, Atlanta, 2006—. Rschr. fellow in enzymology-microbiology Moscow Rsch. Inst. Food Sci., 1978—79; rsch. fellow enzymology-microbiology INSA, Toulouse, 1983—84; rsch. fellow immunoassay-reproductive hormones Karolinska Inst., Stockholm, 1989, U. Oulu, Finland, 1989—90; fellow in vitro fertilization technologies IVI-Madrid, 1999; rsch. fellow embryo implantation Inst. of Mother and Child Rsch. U. Chile, Santiago, 1996—2000; rsch. fellow embryo implantation U. Geneva, 1998—99; rsch. fellow embryo implantation IVI-Valencia U. Valencia, Spain, 1998—99; adj. scientist Boston Biomed. Rsch. Inst., 2006; spkr. in field. Contbr. articles to profl. jours. Sci. adviser, rev. com. WHO-Rockefeller Found. Initiative on Embryo Implantation Rsch., 2000—04; sci. reviewer CONRAD Twinning Program, 2003. Grantee, Susan G. Komen Found., 2005—, Cancer Rsch. and Prevention Found., 2005—; CONRAD Grant, Leptin Peptide Antagonists, 2002—07. Mem.: Am. Assn. for Cancer Rsch., Am. Soc. Biochemistry and Molecular Biology, Spanish Soc. Fertility (assoc. Serono Sci. prize XIII Nat. Congress 2000), Am. Soc. Reproductive Medicine (assoc.). Achievements include development of novel inhibitors of leptin function; discovery of expression of leptin and leptin receptor by human and rabbit endometrium; patents in field; research in leptin role in embryo implantation; blockade of leptin signaling for cancer prevention and treatment. Office: Morehouse Sch Medicine Dept Microbiology Immunology and Biochem 720 Westview Dr SW Atlanta GA 30310 Office Fax: 404-752-1179. Personal E-mail: rrglez@yahoo.com. Business E-Mail: rgonzalez@msm.edu.

GONZALEZ, TONY, professional football player; b. Huntington Beach, California, Feb. 27, 1976; Attended, Univ. Calif. Tight end Kans. City Chiefs, 1997—. Spokesperson Midwest Donor Organ Bank, U.S. Dept. Transp. Safety Campaign, Sch. Safety Hotline, Kans. Cons. (movie) Any Given Sunday, appeared (HBO episode) Arliss, 2000, host (TV series) KCTV-5, appeared Buckle Up: Football is a Game, Your Life is Not. Founder Tony Gonzalez Found.; contbr. Shadow Buddies Program, Boys & Girls Clubs; donator Kans. City Boys & Girls Club, 1999. Named to AFC Pro Bowl team, 1999—2005; recipient Mack Lee Hill award. Office: 1 Arrowhead Dr Kansas City MO 64129

GONZALEZ-DEL-VALLE, LUIS TOMAS, Spanish language educator; b. Nov. 19, 1946; BA in Spanish cum laude, Wilmington Coll.-U. N.C., Wilmington, 1968; MA in Spanish and Spanish-Am. Lits., U. Mass., 1972; Phd in Spanish and Spanish-Am. Lits. five coll. coop. program, Amherst Coll., Hampshire Coll., Mt. Holyoke Coll., Smith Coll., U. Mass., 1972. Asst. prof. modern langs. Kans. State U., 1972-75, assoc. prof. modern langs., 1975-77; assoc. prof. modern langs. and lits. U. Nebr., Lincoln, 1977-79, prof. modern langs. and lits., 1979-86; prof. Spanish and Portuguese U. Colo., Boulder, 1986—, chmn. dept. Spanish and Portuguese, 1986-98, assoc. chair undergrad. studies, 2001—02, assoc. chair for grad. studies, 2003—04; prof. Spanish Temple U., Phila., 2007—, chmn. dept. Spanish and Portuguese, 2007—. Reading cons. South-Western Pub. Co., Inc., 1974, Eliseo Torres & Sons, 1974; dir. Ibero-Latin Am. Studies Ctr., 1987—; lectr. in field. Author: La nueva ficcion hispanoamericana a traves de M.A. Asturias y G. Garcia Marquez, 1972, La ficcion breve de Valle Inclán, 1990, El Canon: Reflexiones Sobre la Recepcion Literaria-Teatral, 1993, La canonización del Diablo: Baudelaire y la estética moderna en España, 2002, Quiroga's Viages, 2005, J. Benavente's Obras, 2007; co-author: Luis Romero, 1979; gen. editor Anales de la literatura española contemporánea, 1975—, Siglo XX/20th Century, 1985—; editor: Jour. Spanish Studies: 20th Century, 1972—80, Studies in 20th Century Lit., 1975—79, Annual Bibliography of Post-Civil War Spanish Fiction, 1977—82, Ecos de Cuba, 1997; co-editor: La generacion de 1898 ante España, 1997; contbr. articles to profl. jours. Recipient Postdoctoral Rsch. award Coun. for Internat. Exch. Scholars, 1984, 500th Rsch. award Spanish Fgn. Ministry, 1992, Silver Medal of Honor Galician Govt., 2000; grantee Coun. on Rsch. and Creative Work, U. Colo., 1986-87, Com. for Edtl. & Cultural Affairs, U. Nebr.-Lincoln, Chancellor's Rsch. Initiation Fund, U. Nebr.-Lincoln, 1980-81, Rsch. Coun., U. Nebr.-Lincoln, 1978-79; Sr. Faculty Summer Rsch. fellow Rsch. Coun., U. Nebr.-Lincoln, 1978, Woodrow Wilson Dissertation fellow, 1971-72, Univ. fellow U. Mass., 1968-72, Grad. fellow, 1969-70. Mem.: MLA, Nebr. Fgn. Lang. Assn., Cervantes Soc. Am., Cir. de Cultura Panamericano (exec. coun. 1972), 20th Century Spanish Assn. (exec. sec. 1982—), Soc. Spanish and Spanish-Am. Studies (bd. dirs. 1975—), Am. Assn. Tchrs. Spanish and Portuguese (Excellence in Tchg. award Colo. chpt. 1996), Assn. Europea de Profesores de Espanol, Fgn. Lang. Adminstrs. of Colo., Assn. de Escritores y Artistas Espanoles (U.S. rep.), Assn. Colegial de Escritores (spl. rep. to U.S., v.p.), Spain's Pen Club (founding 1984), Conf. Editors of Learned Jours. (bd. dirs. 1987—), N.Am. Acad. Spanish Lang. (corr.), Castilian Assn. Writers (hon.), others, Phi Kappa Phi.

GONZALEZ-FALLA, SONDRA GILMAN, art collector; Trustee Whitney Mus. Am. Art, NYC; chmn. bd. Am. Theatre Wing. Avocation: collector of Am. photography. Mailing: c/o Whitney Mus Am Art 945 Madison Ave New York NY 10021 also: c/o American Theatre Wing 570 Seventh Ave Ste 501 New York NY 10018

GONZALEZ-GERTH, MIGUEL, literature and language educator, writer; b. Mexico City, Aug. 15, 1926; arrived in U.S., 1957; s. Miguel S. Gonzalez and Claire E. Gerth; m. Tita Valencia, Oct. 9, 1994; m. Betty Brumbalow (dec.). BA, U. Tex., 1950, MA, 1955, Princeton U., 1960, PhD, 1970. Master of Spanish, French, The Lawrenceville Sch., NJ, 1956—58; instr. romance langs. Bryn Mawr Coll., Pa., 1960—65; asst. prof. Spanish, U. Tex., Austin, 1965—72, assoc. prof. Spanish, 1973—87, prof. Spanish, 1987—95, prof. Spanish and comparative lit., 1995—2001, prof. emeritus, 2001—. Cons. Coll. Bd., NYC, 1960—70, Ednl. Testing Svc., Princeton, NJ, 1960—75, Ransom Ctr., U. Tex., Austin, 1972—. Author: Labyrinth of Imagery: Ramón Gómez de la Serna's Novelas de la Nebulosa, 1986, The Musicians and Other Poems, 1991, T.E. Lawrence, Richard Aldington, and the Death of Heroes, 1994, En Busca de las Calmas Ecuatoriales, 1996, The Branadywine in Winter, 2004, Nueve Musas Eróticas, 2005; editor: (jour.) Tex. Quar., 1972—78. Bd. dirs. Humanities Tex., 2007—. Recipient Pro Bene Meritus award, Coll. Liberal Arts, U. Tex., 2006. Achievements include special consultant Harry Ransom Humanities Research Center, Austin, Tex; founding member faculty seminar of British studies U. Tex. Avocations: antique and art collecting, book collecting, nature watching. Home: 4109 Avenue G Austin TX 78751 Office: Harry Ransom Ctr 3.202 Guadalupe St Austin TX 78712 Business E-Mail: gonzalez-gerth@mail.utexas.edu.

GONZALEZ-LICEA, AUGUSTIN, pathologist, public health service officer; b. Mexico City, Sept. 27, 1936; arrived in U.S., 1981; s. Benjamin and Guadalupe (Licea) Gonzalez; m. Virginia Marcela Hernandez, Jan. 5, 1970; children: Monica Rosanne, Karla Gabriella. BS, Ctr. U. Mex., Mexico City, 1953; MD, Nat. Autonomous U. Mex. (UNAM), Mexico City, 1960. Diplomate Mex. Bd. Pathology. Intern in pathology UNAM Gen. Hosp., Mexico City, 1960-61, resident in pathology, 1961-64; fellow in pathology Johns Hopkins U., Balt., 1964-67; rschr., dept. scientific investigation Nat. Med. Ctr., Mexico City, 1969-80, head evaluation and control, Rsch. Programs Office, 1974-77, dir. Biomed. Rsch. Unit, 1978-80; med. dir., blood chemistry Miles Labs., Inc., Elkhart, Ind., 1981-89; dir. med. affairs Technicon Instruments, Inc., Tarrytown, N.Y., 1990-92; med. officer FDA, Rockville, Md., 1992—. Republican. Roman Catholic. Avocation: tennis. Office: FDA/ODE OIVD HFZ-440 2098 Gaither Rd Rockville MD 20850-4009 Business E-Mail: alg@cdrh.fda.gov.

GONZALEZ-MARRERO, VIRNALISIS M., dermatologist; d. Juan Gonzalez and Josefina Marrero; m. William Ramirez, 1993. MD, U. PR, San Juan, 1990—94. Diplomate Am. Acad. Dermatology, 1998. Dermatologist Hosp. Ryder Meml., Humacao, 1998—2006; solo practitioner Humacao; dermatologist Dermatology Assocs. San Antonio. Recipient Achievement award, Janet M. Glasgow. Fellow: Am. Acad. Dermatology; mem.: Tex. Dermatol. Assn. (assoc.), Tex. Med. Soc. (assoc.), PR Dermatol. Soc. (assoc.), Alpha Omega Alpha (assoc.). Office: Dermatology Assocs San Antonio 12602 Toepperwein Rd Ste 114 San Antonio TX 78233 Office Fax: 210-657-9478.

GONZÁLEZ NIEVES, ROBERTO OCTAVIO, archbishop; b. Elizabeth, NJ, June 2, 1950; Student, St. Joseph Seraphic Sem., Sienna Coll., Washington Theol. Union, Fordham U. Joined Franciscan Order, 1976, ordained priest Roman Cath. Ch., 1977. Titular bishop Ursona and aux. bishop, Boston, 1988-95; coadjutor bishop Diocese of Corpus Christi, 1995-97, bishop, 1997-2000; archbishop Archdiocese of San Juan, 1999—. Roman Catholic. Office: PO Box 9021967 San Juan PR 00902-1967

GONZALEZ-PITA, J. ALBERTO, lawyer, food products executive; b. Havana, Cuba, Aug. 20, 1954; came to U.S., 1960; s. Benigno Jesus and Maria Modesta (Diaz) G.P.; m. Suzanne J. Martin, Apr. 7, 1984; children: Roberto Martin, Antonio Martin. AA, Miami-Dade Community Coll., 1973; BA, U. Miami, 1974; JD, Boston U., 1977. Bar: Fla. 1977, U.S. Dist. Ct. (so. dist.) Fla. 1977, U.S. Ct. Appeals (5th cir.) 1977, U.S. Ct. Appeals (11th cir.) 1981. Assoc. Walton, Lantaff, Schroeder & Carson, Miami, Fla., 1977-80, Patton & Kanner, Miami, 1980-82, ptnr., 1982-86, mng. ptnr., 1986-89; ptnr. McDermott, Will & Emery, Miami, 1989-91, White & Case, Miami, 1991-99; v.p. group counsel, International BellSouth Corp, 1999—2001; v.p. International Legal, Regulatory and External Affairs BellSouth Corp., 2001—04; exec. v.p., gen. counsel Tyson Foods, Inc., Springdale, Ark., 2004—. Chair Worldwide Privatization Practice Group; co-chair Latin Am. Practice Group. Mem. Acad. for Community Edn., Miami, 1980-90; bd. dirs. Inst. Innovative Intervention, Miami, 1980-90; trustee St. Thomas U., Miami, 1991-96. Mem. ABA, Internat. Bar Assn. (co-chair corp. coun. com. 2002-2004), Inter-Am. Bar Assn., Cuban-Am. Bar Assn., Maritime Law Assn. U.S. Roman Catholic. Office: Tyson Foods Inc 2310 West Oakburn Springdale AR 72762-6999 Office Phone: 479-290-7100.*

GONZALEZ-SCARANO, FRANCISCO ANTONIO, neurologist, virologist; b. Ponce, PR, Mar. 23, 1950; s. Francisco and Genoveva (Scarano) Gonzalez-Hernandez; m. Barbara Jean Turner, June 23, 1979; children: Genevieve Carre, Stephanie Katharine, Lisa Frances. BA, Yale U., 1971; MD, Northwestern U., Chgo., 1975; MA (hon.), U. Pa., Phila., 1988. Diplomate Am. Bd. Neurology. Intern Hosp. U. Pa., 1975-76, resident in neurology, 1976-79; fellow U. Pa., Phila., 1979-82, NIMR, London, 1981-82; asst. prof. depts. neurology and microbiology U. Pa., Phila., 1982-88, assoc. prof., 1988-94, prof., 1994—. Vice-chair rsch. neurology dept. U. Pa, 1998-99, chair 1999—; co-dir. Pa. Ctr. for HIV and AIDS, 1998—, Pa. Neurosci. Ctr., 2006—; chmn. bd. sci. counselors Nat. Inst. Neurol. Diseases and Stroke, Bethesda, Md., 1993-97, Nat. Adv. Neurol. Diseases and Stroke Coun., 2004—. Assoc. editor Viral Pathogenesis, 1997; editl. bd. Jour. Neurovirology, 1996—, Virus Rsch., 1997—, AIDS, 1995-2002, GLIA, 1999—, Jour. Virology, 2000—, Virology, 2004—. Trustee Swarthmore Presbyn. Ch., 1997-2000, session 2004-07. Harry Weaver scholar Multiple Sclerosis Soc., NYC, 1982-87. Fellow: Phila. Coll. Physicians; mem.: Inst. of Medicine, Am. Soc. Clin. Investigation, Am. Acad. Neurology (mem. sci. issues com. 1985—89, profl. and pub. issues com. 1987—93), Am. Neurol. Assn. (exec. coun. 2001—03, chair sci. profl. com. 2005—), Scroll & Key, John Morgan Soc., Penn Club, Alpha Omega Alpha. Presbyterian. Avocation: photography. Office: U Pa Dept Neurology Hosp U Pa 3 W Gates Bldg Philadelphia PA 19104-4283 Office Phone: 215-662-3360. Business E-Mail: francisco.gonzalez@uphs.upenn.edu.

GONZALEZ-TORNERO, SERGIO, artist; b. Santiago, Chile, May 22, 1927; came to the U.S., 1962; s. Higinio and Rebecca (Tornero) Gonzalez; m. Maxine Adrienne Cullom, 1962; children: Katya, Alicia, Savina. Studies in, Chile, Brasil, U.S., France and Eng., 1959-62; student under S.W. Hayter, Atelier 17, Paris, 1959-62. Exhibitions include Mus. Fine Arts, Santiago, Chile, 1993; one-man exhbns. paintings Haida Gwaii Mus., Qay'Llnagaay, Skidegate, B.C., 1996, Gallery of Tribal Art, Vancouver, 1996, Mus. No. B.C. at Prince Rupert, 1997, Putnam Arts Coun., Mahopac, NY, 1999, Greenhill Invitationals, Yorktown, NY, 2000, Silvermine Galleries, New Canaan, Conn., 2001, 04, Shelnutt Gallery, Rensselaer Polytechnic Inst., Troy, NY, 2001, 04, The Studio, Armonk, NY, 2002, Chappaqua (NY) Libr. Gallery, 2004, Solon Dorblum Gallery, New Canaan, Conn., 2004, Westchester Cmty. Fine Arts Gallery, Valhalla, NY, 2006, Gallery 25N, Peekskill, NY, 2006; retrospective of 218 prints at Antiguo Asilo de Beneficencia, San Juan, 1998; numerous pub. and pvt. collections. Recipient UNESCO prize Internat. Bienial of Prints, Krakow, 1966, 1st prize X Bienial of Prints, L.Am. and the Caribbean, San Juan, P.R., 1993, 26 other prizes, 1960—; NY State Coun. for the Arts fellow, 1987; grantee Adolph and Esther Gottlieb Found., NY, 1990. Mem. Soc. Am. Graphic Artists. Home and Office: 30 Highridge Rd Mahopac NY 10541-2165 Office Phone: 845-628-6571. Personal E-mail: alicia2mil@aol.com.

GOO, ABRAHAM MEU SEN, retired manufacturing executive; b. Honolulu, Hawaii, May 21, 1925; s. Tai Chong and Lily En Wui (Dai) Goo; m. Shin Quon Wong, June 12, 1950; children: Marilynn, Steven, Beverly Cardinal. BSEE, U. Ill., 1951; postgrad., MIT, 1975. With Boeing Co., Seattle, 1951—73; mgr. B-1 avionics program, v.p., gen. mgr. aircraft armament divsn. Boeing Aerospace Co., Seattle, 1974—77; v.p. mil. sys., exec. v.p., pres. Boeing Mil. Airplane Co., Wichita, Kans., 1977—87; pres. Boeing Advanced Sys., Seattle, 1987—89. With USAAF, 1946—47. Recipient Chinese-Am. Engrs. and Scientists of So. Calif. Achievement award, Sci. and Enginrg., 1989, Pioneer award, Unmanned Vehicle Sys., 1989. Mem.: Am. Legion (comdr. 2004—06). Home: 18909 SE 282nd Ct Kent WA 98042-5458 Personal E-mail: amssgg@msn.com.

GOO, JAHYUN, humanities educator; arrived in US, 1996; BAA, Hangyang U., 1993; MBA, SUNY, Buffalo, PhD, 2003. Asst. prof. SUNY, Fredonia, 2001—03, Fla. Atlantic U., Boca Raton, 2003—. Contbr. articles to profl. jours. Mentor coll. group 20' Something, Ft. Lauderdale, Fla., 2004. Sgt. Korean Army, 1985—88. Recipient Best Ph.D. Student Achievement award, SUNY, Buffalo, 2003, Best Paper award, Hawaii Internat. Conf. Sys. Sci., 2007; fellow, SUNY, Buffalo, 1999—2001; grantee, Mark Diamond Rsch. Fund, 2003—04, Can.-Am. Studies Competition, 2003. Office: Florida Atlantic Univ 777 Glades Rd Boca Raton FL 33431 Office Phone: 561-297-2352. Business E-Mail: jgoo@fau.edu.

GOO, JUNG-SUK, semiconductor company research engineer; b. Seoul, Republic of Korea, June 4, 1966; arrived in U.S., 1995; s. Jae-Gyu Goo and Kee-Joon Kim; m. Inseong Kim; children: Timothy, Philip. BS, Yonsei U., Seoul, 1988; MS, Stanford U., 1997, PhD, 2001. Sr. engr. LG Semicon, Seoul, Republic of Korea, 1988—95; analog design and modeling engr. Atheros Comm., Inc., Sunnyvale, Calif., 2001—01; sr. mem. tech. staff Advanced Micro Devices, Sunnyvale, 2001—. Contbr. articles to profl. jours. Mem.: IEEE. Achievements include research in the field of the hot carrier effect, high frequency MOSFET noise, PD-SOI modeling; patents in field; invention of world-record CMOS low-noise amplifier. Home: 1485 Oakhurst Ave Los Altos CA 94024 Office: Advanced Micro Devices One AMD Place PO Box 3453 MS 79 Sunnyvale CA 94088-3453 Personal E-mail: goojs@stanfordalumni.org. Business E-Mail: Jung-Suk.Goo@amd.com.

GOO, VALERIE M., lawyer; BA, U. Calif., LA, 1992, JD, 1996. Bar: Calif. 1996, US Dist. Ct. (ctrl. dist.) Calif., US Ct. Appeals (9th cir.). Sr. assoc. Pillsbury Winthrop Shaw Pittman, LA, 2005—06, ptnr., 2006, Orrick, Herrington & Sutcliffe, LA, 2006—. Mem.: State Bar of Calif. Office: Orrick Herrington & Sutcliffe LLP 777 S Figueroa St Ste 3200 Los Angeles CA 90017 Office Phone: 213-629-2020.*

GOOCH, ANTHONY CUSHING, retired lawyer; b. Amarillo, Tex., Dec. 3, 1937; s. Cornelius Skinner and Sidney Seale (Crawford) G.; m. Elizabeth Melissa Ivanoff, May 27, 1963 (div. Nov. 1983); children: Katherine C., Jennifer C. Gooch Avery, Melissa G., Andrew E.; m. Linda B. Klein, Nov. 7, 1987 (dec. Apr. 25, 2004). BA, U. of South, 1959; diploma, Coll. of Europe, 1960; JD, NYU, 1963, M in Comparative Law, 1964; M in Internat. Affairs, Columbia U., 2005. Bar: N.Y. 1963. Assoc. Cleary, Gottlieb, Steen & Hamilton, NYC, Paris, Brussels, 1963-72, ptnr. Rio de Janeiro, 1973-78, NYC, 1978-99, sr. counsel, 2000—03; ret., 2004; gen. counsel Internat. Inst. Rural Reconstruction, 2000—02, bd. trustees, 2002—, chair, 2006—. Co-author: Loan Agreement Documentation, 1982, 2d edit., 1991, Swap Apreement Documentation, 1987, 2d edit., 1988, Documentation for Derivatives, 1993, Credit Support Supplement, 1995, Cross-Product Risk Mgmt. Supplement, 2000, 4th edit., 2002, Master Agreement Supplement, 2003, Documentation for Loans, Assignments and Participations, 1996, ISDA Master Agreement Supplement, 2004, Supplement on the Cross-Product Master Agreement, 2004; articles editor NYU Law Rev., 1962-63. V.p. planned giving Assoc. Alumni U. of the South, Sewanee, Tenn., 2001—05, bd. trustees, 2006—, Internat. Inst. Rural Reconstruction, 2002—, chmn., 2007—. Mem. ABA, N.Y. State Bar Assn., Assn. Bar City N.Y. Episcopalian. Home: 7 Mine Hill Rd Redding CT 06896-2701 E-mail: tonygooch@aol.com.

GOOD, ALLEN HOVEY, investment banker, real estate broker; b. Boston, July 5, 1930; s. Herbert Shelley Good and Elizabeth (Hovey) Jack; m. Catherine Forrester Campbell, June 25, 1959 (div. June 1975); children: Alison Good Ross, Forrester Hovey; m. Joan Duffey Meyers, June 12, 1976; stepchildren: Robert Whitney Meyers Jr., Mary Meyers. AB in English, Bus. Adminstrn., U. Mass., 1955. Ea. region sales mgr. Sandpaper, Inc., Rockland, Mass., 1956-67; pres. A.H. Good Corp., Summit, N.J., 1967-75, Chemdyne, Inc., Summit, 1975-84; v.p. Mid-Atlantic Bus. Brokers, Florham Park, N.J., 1984-86; pres. Atlantic Nat. Acquisition, Inc., East Hampton, NY, 1987—, Atlantic Nat. Mgmt. Cons., 1995—. Cons. Pfizer, Inc., N.Y.C., 1983; substitute instr. Fairleigh-Dickinson Grad. Sch., Madison, N.J., 1986. Soc. Colonial Wars, 1999—, Presdl. Roundtable, 2001; mem. Lic. Exec. Soc., Norwalk, Conn., 1988-89. Editor Newsletter Summit Tennis Club, 1977; patentee: skin lotion, 1982, skin cleanser, 1985. Mem. Rep. Club, Short Hills, N.J., 1957-59, N.J. Symphony Jr. Com., 1959-60; chmn. spl. projects, 1995—; mem. Images Exec. Com., 1995-2001, N.J. Ctr. for Visual Arts, Summit. Mem.: Short Hills Club. Avocations: tennis, sailing. Office: Atlantic Nat Acquisitions 14 Old Orchard Ln East Hampton NY 11937 Address: 841 Tanbark Dr #204 Naples FL 34108 Office Phone: 973-467-9050. Personal E-mail: allengood@optonline.net.

GOOD, CANDACE R., psychiatrist, educator; BS, Penn State U., Univ. Pk., 1991—95; MD, Penn State U., Hershey, 1995—99. Cert. psychiatrist Am. Bd. Psychiatry & Neurology, 2005. Asst. prof. psychiatry U. Pitts. Med. Ctr., 2004—. Med. dir. Ctr. Children & Families, Pitts. Mem.: Am. Acad. Child & Adolescent Psychiatry, Am. Psychiat. Assn. Office: We Psychiatric Inst & Clinic 3811 O'Hara St Pittsburgh PA 15213 Office Fax: 412-246-5210.

GOOD, EDITH ELISSA (PEARL WILLIAMS), writer; b. Hollywood, Calif., Jan. 10, 1945; d. Jack Brian and Rose Marie (Miller) Good; m. Michael Lawrence Black, Dec. 18, 1986 (dec.). Student, UCLA and U. Calif., Berkeley, 1962—92, Ballet Folklorico, Mex., 1963; BA in English summa cum laude, Calif. State U., Northridge, 1974. Explorer Mayan ruins, Mex., 1963; author, pub. Gull Press, LA, 1990—. Participant numerous dance, art, music, lit., math. and sci. classes; dancer Hajde Dance

Troop, Berkeley, Calif., 1962-66. One-woman shows LA, 1962-95; singer in various langs. at various venues, LA, 1986—; author: (pseudonym Pearl Williams) The Trickster of Tarzana, 1992, Short Stories, 1995, Mad in Craft, 1995, Missives, 1995, Dictionary of Erudition, 1995, others; author numerous poems. Participant Dem. clubs, Calif. and Mex., 1962—; supporter mental health orgns., sensitivity tng. encounter groups, 1962—; participant consciousness raising groups, local convs., fundraiser, canvasser, office worker, driver, participant W.E.B. DuBois Club, Congress Racial Equality, San Francisco, Berkeley, L.A., and Oakland, 1965, Peace in Alliance for Survival, Berkeley, Oakland, L.A., 1964-80, women's rights Westside Women's Ctr., Woman's Bldg., L.A., 1974-80, Environment in Earth Day, L.A., 1977, phys. and mental health VA, cons. book reviewer, tutor, Mental Health Assn., L.A., 1962—; supporter residential collectives, 1985—. Mem. Mensa, Am. Soc. Composers, Authors, and Pubs., Plummer Park Writers, Westside Writers. Achievements include writing chosen by a jury of experts for inclusion in the permanent collecton of the Library of Congress. Home: 1470 S Robertson Blvd Apt B Los Angeles CA 90035-3402 Office Phone: 310-276-8933.

GOOD, ESTELLE M., minister; b. Charleston, SC, Oct. 5, 1927; d. John Wesley and Minnie Estelle Hilton; divorced; children: Raymond L., Lee Good Sanders. BTh, Clarksville Sch. Theology, 1972, ThM, 1975, ThD, 1976, ThD, 1978, B in Sacred Music, 1980; PhD of Christian Psychology, Cornerstone U., 1992. Ordained to preach 1955; cert. hypnotherapist Internat. Assn. Counselors and Therapists, 1994. Organizer, pastor Covenant Life Cathedral, Macon, Ga., 1962—. Pres. Lighthouse Bible Tng. Ctr., 1976—88. Fellow: Nat. Christian Counselors Assn. (diplomate 1993, lic. temperament therapist 1991, Christian counselor and therapist 1992); mem.: Women Preachers Coun. Am., Full Gospel Fellowship of Churches and Ministers Internat. Office: Covenant Life Cathedral 4543 Bloomfield Rd Macon GA 31203

GOOD, IRVING JOHN, statistician, educator, philosopher; b. London, Dec. 9, 1916; arrived in US, 1967; s. Morris Edward and Sophia (Polikoff) Good. ScD, Cambridge U., Eng., 1963; DSc, Oxford U., Eng., 1964. Sci. officer Fgn. Office, Bletchley, England, 1941—45; lectr. math. and electronic computing Manchester (Eng.) U., 1945—48; sr. prin. sci. officer Govt. Comm. Hdqrs., Cheltenham, England, 1948—59; spl. merit dep. chief sci. officer Admiralty Rsch. Lab., Teddington, England, 1959—62; sr. rsch. fellow Trinity Coll., Oxford U. and Atlas Computer Lab., Didcot, England, 1964—67; Univ. disting. prof. stats, adj. prof. philosophy Va. Poly. Inst. and State U., Blacksburg, 1967—, prof. emeritus. Adj. prof. Ctr. Study of Sci. in Society; mem. comm. theory com. Ministry Supply, London, 1953-56; mem. comm. com. electronics rsch. com. Ministry Aviation, London, 1960-62; mem. rsch. sect. com. Royal Statis. Soc., London, 1965-67. *Irving John Good's work cannot be summarized briefly. He showed Tukey a Fast Fourier Transform in 1957. Good used Empirical Bayes (1953), the EM method (1956), the log-linear model, penalized likelihood, maximum entropy, generalized linear models, and hierarchical Bayes, in some cases before they were named. He invented "necessitude and sufficitude" for legal philosophy. Since 1990 he has refuted many attempts to prove the inconsistency of the kinematics of special relativity. This work included a "Swings and Roundabouts" theorem in relation to clock paradoxes. Good early speculated about hierarchical universes, winding space, and about our universe as a rotating black hole in a maternal universe.* Author: Probability and the Weighing of Evidence, 1950, The Estimation of Probabilities, 1965, Good Thinking, 1983; co-author (with Donald Michie and Geoffrey Timms): General Report on Tunny with Emphasis on Statistical Methods, 1945; co-author: (with David B. Osteyee) Information, Weight of Evidence, the Singularity between Probability Measures and Signal Detection, 1974; gen. editor: The Scientist Speculates, 1962, (also French and German translations); contbr. chapters to books, over one thousand articles to profl. jours. Recipient Smith's prize, Cambridge, Eng., 1940, Internat. Order of Merit, 1993, Congl. medal of excellence, 2004; grantee NIH, 1970—89. Fellow Royal Stats. Soc. (hon.), Am. Acad. Arts and Scis., Va. Acad. Scis., Inst. Math. Stats., Am. Statis. Assn.; mem. IEEE Computer Soc. (Pioneer award 1998), Internat. Statis. Inst. (hon.). Home: 1309 Lynn Dr Blacksburg VA 24060-3001 Office: Va Poly Inst and State U Dept Stats Blacksburg VA 24061-0439 Personal E-mail: ijgood@vt.edu.

GOOD, JENNIFER L., pharmaceutical executive; BBA, Pacific Lutheran U. Various positions including audit mgr. Ernst & Young LLP, 1987—93; corp. contr., corp. dir. fin. Penford Corp., 1993—97; CFO Penwest Pharmaceuticals Co., 1997—2005, COO, 2005—06, pres., 2005—, CEO, 2006—. Office: Penwest 39 Old Ridgebury Rd Ste 11 Danbury CT 06810

GOOD, LARRY IRWIN, gastroenterologist, educator; b. NYC, Feb. 8, 1948; s. Samuel and Lillie (Sternlight) G.; m. Judy Chafetz, Aug. 16, 1969; children: Adam Eric, Lauren Elyse, Bryan Scott, Allison Jill. BA, Colgate U., 1969; MD, Med. U. of SC, 1973. Diplomate Am. Bd. Internal Medicine, Am. Bd. Gastroenterology. Intern in medicine Tchg. Hosp. Med. U. of SC, 1973-74, resident in medicine Tchg. Hosp., 1974-75, chief resident in medicine Tchg. Hosp., 1975-76; fellow in gastroenterology U. Pa., 1976-78; with Hempstead (NY) Gen. Hosp., 1978—, Nassau County Med. Ctr., East Meadow, NY, 1978—, South Nassau Cmtys. Hosp., Oceanside, NY, 1978—, chief divsn. gastroenterology dept. medicine, 1989. Asst. prof. Sch. of Medicine, SUNY, Stony Brook, 1978; mem. health adv. bd. Hofstra Health Dome Uniondale, NY, 1983; with Lydia E. Hall Hosp., Freeport, NY, 1978-86, Mercy Hosp., Rockville Centre, NY, 1978-80. Contbr. articles to Am. Jour. Gastroenterology, The Papilla Vateri and its Diseases, Med. Times, New Eng. Jour. Medicine., Gastroenterology, Alpha Omega Alpha. Trustee, dir. Little Village Sch. & House, Garden City, NY, 1985—. Recipient Rsch. Svc. award NIH, 1977. Fellow Am. Coll. Gastroenterology; mem. AMA, ACP, L.I. Gastroenterologic Assn., Am. Gastroenterologic Assn. Jewish. Office: 229 7th St Ste 307 Garden City NY 11530-2913 Home Phone: 516-449-4382; Office Phone: 516-766-0800. Personal E-mail: goodlb@optonline.net.

GOOD, LAURANCE FREDERIC, hospital administrator; b. Wheeling, W.Va., Sept. 26, 1932; s. Sidney Samuel and Jeannette (Berg) G.; m. Barbara S. Mayer, Oct. 18, 1959; children: Philip (dec.), Jay, Paul, Jenny, Heidi. BA, Brown U., 1954; postgrad., U. Va., 1955. CLU, ChFC, cert. employee benefits specialist, CEBS, health ins. assoc.; registered health underwriter, LUTCF. V.p., gen. mdse. mgr. L.S. Good & Co., Wheeling, 1961-80, exec. v.p., 1969-80, vice chmn., sec. bd., 1961-80, Good's of Wheeling, W.Va., Steubenville, Ohio, St. Clairsville, Ohio, Gables, Altoona, Pa., Knapps, Lansing, Miss., Jackson, Miss., Fowler's, Binghamton, NY, Kann's, Wash., DC, Arlington, Va., Purcell's, Lexington, Ky., D.M. Christian Co., Owasso, Mich., Smith-Bridgeman, Flint, Mich., Grand Blanc, Mich., Robinson's Battle Creek, Mich.; pres. Personal History Systems, Inc.; life underwriter Equitable Life Assurance Soc. Am., 1983-89; health and welfare cons. Mockenhaupt, Mockenhaupt, Cowden & Parks, 1989; employee benefit specialist, life underwriter Lincoln Fin. Svcs., Inc., Pitts., 1990; exec. dir. Wheeling Works, Inc., Wheeling, W.Va., 1993-95; dir. Office of Gift Planning Med. Park Found., Wheeling, W.Va., 1995—2006; dir. devel. Wheeling Hosp. Mem. Million Dollar Roundtable, 1985-86; pres. Personal History Systems. Producer: Wheeling Rediscovered; Author: My Lifetime Book. Bd. dirs. Wheeling Symphony Soc., 1964-67, 68-73; with Ohio Valley Indsl. and Bus. Devel. Corp., Wheeling, 1971; chmn. Brown U. Alumni Program, 1954-88, W.Va.; Christmas seals chmn. Tb Assn. Ohio Valley, 1973; co-chmn. United Jewish Appeal, 1971-73; v.p., chmn. fin. com. Temple Shalom, 1986-89; co-founder Good Zoo in memory of eldest son, Philip; co-founder, pres. Good Zoo Friends, 1974-78; chmn. establishment com. Wheeling Devel. Conf.; bd. found. W. Liberty State Coll., 1971; creator Kraft-Good Archives; bd. dirs. Wheeling Hosp., 1972-87, hon. bd. dirs., 1988-96; bd. visitors Bethany Coll., 1972-77; trustee Oglebay Inst., 1972-90; mem. Estate Planning Coun. of Ohio Valley and Pitts.; co-chair Greater Wheeling/Bel-o-Mar Empowerment Zone/Enterprise Community Initiative, 1994; campaign dir. Toward the Next Century, Wheeling Hosp., 1998, dir. capital funds campaign, 2004. With USN, 1955-57. Charter recipient Disting. West Virginian award, 1976; named W.Va. Master Gardener, 2007. Mem. NAACP (charter life mem.), Nat. Retail Mchts. Assn. (dir. merchandising div. 1966-71, del. conf. 1969), Ohio Valley Assn. Life Underwriters (pres. 1987), W.Va. Assn. Life Underwriters (regional dir. 1988). Office: Wheeling Hosp Dir Devel One Medical Pk Wheeling WV 26003 Office Phone: 304-242-1075. Personal E-mail: good-for-you@comcast.com. Business E-Mail: barbaragood@comcast.net.

GOOD, LYNN J., energy executive; BS in Systems Analysis and Acctg., Miami U., Oxford, Ohio. Various positions Arthur Andersen, 1981—2002, ptnr., 1992—2002, Deloitte & Touche, Cin.; v.p. fin. project strategy Cinergy, 2003, v.p., contr., 2003—05, v.p. fin., contr., 2005, exec. v.p., CFO, 2005—06; sr. v.p., treas. Duke Energy, Charlotte, NC, 2006—. Office: Duke Energy 526 S Church St Charlotte NC 28202-1904 Office Phone: 704-594-6200.*

GOOD, MARK, retail executive; BA, U. Calif., Berkeley; MBA, San Francisco State U. Planning engr. The Gap, Inc., 1980—83, tech. services mgr., 1983—85, dir. distbn. planning, 1985—87, dir. internat. expansion, 1987—89; mgr. distbn. centers and transp. centers Cost Plus Imports, Inc., 1989—90; dir. logistics and info. systems A Pea in the Pod, Inc., 1990—94; dir. distbn. Westinghouse Elec. Supply co., 1994—97; v.p., gen. mgr. parts Sears Roebuck and Co., 1997—98, v.p., gen. mgr. parts and carry in svc., 1998—99, exec. v.p., product repair services, 1999—. Mem. Coun. of Logistics Mgmt. Office: Sears Roebuck and Co 3333 Beverly Rd Hoffman Estates IL 60179

GOOD, MARY LOWE, investment company executive, educator; b. Grapevine, Tex., June 20, 1931; d. John W. and Winnie (Mercer) Lowe; m. Billy Jewel Good, May 17, 1952 (dec. 2005); children: Billy, James. BS, Ark. State Tchrs. Coll., 1950; MS, U. Ark., 1953, PhD, 1955, LLD (hon.), 1979; DSc (hon.), U. Ill., Chgo., 1983, Clarkson U., 1984, Ea. Mich. U., 1986, Duke U., 1987, St. Mary's Coll., 1987, Kenyon Coll., 1988; degree (hon.), Stevens Inst. Tech., 1989, Lehigh U., 1989, Northeastern Ill. U., 1989, U. SC, 1989, NJ Inst. Tech., 1989; degree in law (hon.), Newcomb Coll. Tulane U., 1991; LLD (hon.), Coll. William Mary, 1992; DSc (hon.), Manhattan Coll., 1992, Ind. U., 1992, SUNY, Binghamton, 1994, Rensselaer Polytechnic Inst., 1994, Monmouth U., 1995, La. State U., 1995, Ill. Inst. Tech., 1997, Mich. State U., 1997, U. Mich., 1998; DEng (hon.), Colo. Sch. Mines, 2000; DSc (hon.), U. Ctrl. Ark., Conway, 2007. Instr. Ark. State Tchrs. Coll., Conway, summer 1949; from instr. to asst. prof. La. State U., Baton Rouge, 1954—58, Boyd prof., 1978—80; assoc. prof. to Boyd prof. U. New Orleans, 1958—78; pres. Signal Rsch. Ctr. Inc., 1983—85; pres. engineered materials rsch. divsn Allied-Signal Inc., Des Plaines, Ill., 1986—87, sr. v.p.-tech. Morristown, NJ, 1987—93; under sec. of commerce for technology Dept. of Commerce, Washington, 1993-97; mng. mem. Venture Capital Investors LLC, Little Rock, 1997—2005, Fund for Ark., 2005—; Donaghey Univ. prof., dean Coll. Info. Sci. & Systems Engr U. Ark., Little Rock, 1998—. Chmn. Pres.'s Com. for Nat. Medal Sci., 1979-82; adv. bd. NSF Chemistry Sect., 1972-76; com. medicinal chemistry NIH, 1972-76, Office of USAF Rsch., 1974-78, chemist divsn. Brookhaven and Oak Ridge Nat. Labs., 1973-83, chem. tech. divsn. Oak Ridge Nat. Lab., catalysis program Lawrence-Berkeley Lab.; bd. dirs. Delta Bank and Trust, Acxiom Inc.; bd. chem. sci. and tech., Nat. Rsch. Coun., 2003-04, Govt. U., industry roundtable, NRC, 2000-05, Ark. Sci and Tech. Authority, 1998-03, Dialog Com, Am. Chem. Coun., 2002-05. Contbr. articles to profl. jours. Mem. Nat. Sci. Bd., 1980-91, vice chair, 1984-88, chair, 1988-91; mem. Pres.' Coun. Advisors for Sci. and Tech., 1991-93. Recipient Agnes Faye Morgan rsch. award, 1969, Disting. Alumni citation U. Ark., 1973, Scientist of Yr. award Indsl. R&D mag., 1983, Delmer S. Fahrney medal Franklin Inst., 1988, N.J. Women of Achievement award Douglass Coll., Rutgers U., 1990, Indsl. Rsch. Inst. medal, 1991, Disting. Svc. award NSF, 1992, Roe award ASME, 1993, Gold medal SME, 1995, Earle Barnes award ACS, 1996, Priestley medal, 1997, UCLA Glenn T. Seaborg medal, 1996, Nat. Materials Advancement award Fedn. Materials Socs., 1996, Othmer medal award Chem. Heritage Found., 1998, Henry Michel award, Civil Engring. Rsch. Found., 1998, Heinz award for tech. The Economy and Employment, 2000, Vannevar Bush award NSF, 2004; AEC tng. grantee, 1967, NSF Internat. travel grantee, 1968, NSF rsch. grantee, 1969-80, Albert Fox Demers award, 1992. Fellow AAAS (Abelson award 1999, pres. 2000, chmn. bd. dirs. 2001), Am. Inst. Chemistry (Gold medal 1983), Chem. Soc. London, Royal Soc. Chemistry (hon.); mem. NAE, Acad. Arts and Scis, Am. Philos. Soc., Swedish Acad. Engring., Am. Chem. Soc. (1st woman dir. 1972-74, regional dir. 1972-80, chmn. bd. 1978, 80, bd. publs., pres. 1987, mem. bd. pub. 2002-, Garvan medal 1973, Herty medal 1975, award Fla. sect. 1979, Charles Lathrop Parsons award 1991), Internat. Union Pure and Applied Chmistry (pres. inorganic div. 1980-85),Alliance for Sci. and Tech. Rsch. in Am. (chmn. bd. dirs. 2000-), Zonta (past pres. New Orleans club, chmn. dist. status of women com. and nominating com., chmn. internat. Amelia Earhart scholarship com. 1978-88, pres. internat. Found. 1988-93, mem. internat. bd. 1988-90), Rotary Internat., Phi Beta Kappa, Sigma Xi, Iota Sigma Pi (regional dir. 1967-93, hon. mem. 1983), Ark. Women's Forum. Home: 13824 Rivercrest Dr Little Rock AR 72212-1521 Office: U Ark at Little Rock Coll Info Sci/Sys Engring 2801 S University Ave Little Rock AR 72204-1000 Office Phone: 501-569-8189. Personal E-mail: thegoods@aristotle.net. Business E-Mail: mlgood@ualr.edu.

GOOD, RICHARD STANDISH, geologist; b. West Chester, Pa., Sept. 18, 1928; s. Bernard Stafford Good and Marjorie Payne Johnson; m. Edith Read Brodhead, Oct. 15, 1966 (div. Aug. 1982); m. Marsha Wallace, Apr. 29, 2000 (dec. May 31, 2006). BS in Geology and Mineralogy, Pa. State U., 1950, MS in Geology, 1955. Cert. profl. geologist, Va. Chem. analyst Foote Mineral Co., Malvern, Pa., 1951; project engr. Aeroprojects, Inc., West Chester, Pa., 1952-53; rsch. asst. Pa. State U., State College, 1953-55; geologist Geo-Tech Devel. Co., Ltd., Toronto, Ont., Can., 1955-56, Hunting Tech Svcs., Ltd., London, 1957-58; cons., geologist San Francisco, 1958-60; chem. analyst Kawecki Chem. Co., Boyertown, Pa., 1960. Tchg. asst. Bryn Mawr Coll., Pa., 1962-64; geologist, head Geol. Lab, Va. Divsn. of Mineral Resources, Charlottesville, Va., 1966-91; collection mgr. rocks/fossil, Va. Museumont Naturaly History, 1992. Vol. Hospice, Charlottesville, 2001. Fellow NSF, Bryn Mawr, 1963-64. Fellow Assn. Exploration Geochemists; mem. Geol. Soc. Am., Soc. Mining Engrs., Va. Acad. Sci., AAAS, Sigma Xi. Avocations: writing, tennis, hiking, reading. Home: 63 Woodlake Dr Charlottesville VA 22901 Personal E-mail: rsgood28@aol.com.

GOOD, STEVEN LOREN, real estate consultant; b. Tokyo, Nov. 16, 1956; came to U.S., 1957; s. Sheldon F. and Lois (Kroll) G. Student, Oxford U., 1975; BS in Fin., Syracuse U., 1978; JD, DePaul U., 1981; LHD (hon.), Robert Morris Coll., Chgo., 1998. Bar: Ill. 1981, U.S. Dist. Ct. (no. dist.) Ill. 1982, Fla. 1983, U.S. Ct. Appeals (7th cir.) 1983, U.S. Supreme Ct. 2006. Assoc. Sheldon Good & Co., Internat., Chgo., 1978-82; v.p., gen. counsel Sheldon Good & Co., Chgo., 1982-87, pres., 1987—2000, chmn., CEO, 2001—. Instr. FDIC, Washington, 1985, Mo. Auction Sch., Kansas City, 1981-97, Reppert's Sch. Auctioneering, 1998-; bd. dirs. Real Estate Ctr., Kelly Sch. Bus., Ind. U., Sch. Bus. Administrn, Citadel Mil. Coll., Ohn Marshall Law Sch.; lectr., spkr. in field. Author: Churches, Jails, and Gold Mines: Mega-Deals from a Real Estate Maverick, 2003; columnist: Auction World mag., 2004—; contbr. articles. Mem. men's coun. Mus. Contemporary Art, Chgo., 1985-91; vice chmn. real estate divsn. Jewish United Fund, Chgo., 1986, 88, 91; bd. dirs. United Cerebral Palsy, Chgo., 1987-97, chmn. Chgo. telethone, 1996; trustee Robert Morris Coll., Chgo., 1991-96; assoc. trustee U. Chgo. Cancer Rsch. Found., 1989-93, chmn. dean's coun., 1997-2000. Recipient Alumni Service Award for Outstanding Service to the Business Community, DePaul U. Coll. Law, 2001, Infinitec Corporate Leadership award, United Cerebral Palsy Assn., Community Svc. award, Easter Seals, 2003. Mem. ABA, Ill. Bar Assn., Fla. Bar Assn., Chgo. Bar Assn., Nat. Assn. Realtors (dir., chmn. Real Estate Auction Forum, 2004), Ill. Assn. of Realtors (dir. 2000-), Chgo. Assn. Realtors (pres. 2003-2004, instr. 1981—, Realtor of Yr. 2005), Young Pres. Orgn., Standard Club, Lamda Alpha. Avocations: tennis, skiing, shooting skeet, music, theater. Office: Sheldon Good & Co 333 W Wacker Dr Ste 400 Chicago IL 60606-1284 Office Fax: 312-346-0727. Business E-Mail: stevengood@sheldongood.com.

GOOD, WALTER RAYMOND, investment company executive; b. Oak Park, Ill., Sept. 9, 1924; s. Walter William and Elsie Sophia (Lussow) G.; m. Jean W. Stockman, Feb. 5, 1949; children: Elizabeth, Deborah, William. PhB, U. Chgo., 1947, MBA, 1949. Buyer fats and oils Procter and Gamble, Cin., 1949-52; security analyst, dir. research Brown Bros. Harriman, NYC, 1952-70; exec. v.p., dir. Lionel D. Edie, NYC, 1970-80; v.p. Continental Group Inc., Stamford, Conn., 1980-85; mng. ptnr. Actively Managed Universes, Darien, Conn., 1985-86; pres. Mellon Universe Mgmt. Group, Stamford, 1986-90; mng. ptnr. Capital Market Systems, Darien, 1990-98. Mem. investment adv. panel Pension Benefit Guaranty Corp., Washington, 1980-83; dir., mem. exec. com. Retirement Systems for Savs. Instns., NYC, 1985-86; mem. investment adv. council NYC Retirement Funds, 1980-85; mem. Pension Execs. Conf., 1981-85, chmn., 1983, mem. fin. adv. panel The Aerospace Corp., 1986-2006. Author: (with D. Love) Managing Pension Assets: Pension Finance and Corporate Financial Goals, 1990, (with R. Hermansen and J. Meyer) Active Asset Allocation: Gaining Advantage in a Highly Efficient Stock Market, 1993, (with R. Hermansen) Index Your Way to Investment Success, 1998; mem. editl. bd. Fin. Analysts Jour., 1972-97. Served with USAAF, 1943-46. Recipient Graham and Dodd Scroll Fin. Analysts Fedn., 1979. Mem. Inst. Chartered Fin. Analysts (council examiners 1980-86). Personal E-mail: walter_r_good@sbcglobal.net.

GOOD, WILLIAM ALLEN, professional society executive; b. Oak Park, Ill., May 29, 1949; s. Fred Clifton and Dorothy Helen (Stockdale) G.; m. Julianne Doggett, Jan. 8, 1972 (div. Apr. 1980); m. Paulette Edith Gordon, Apr. 23, 1983 (div. Apr. 1991); m. Laura Elizabeth Wellbank, Sept. 25, 1993. MBA, U. Chgo., 1992. Supr. Dun & Bradstreet, Inc., Chgo., 1972-73; gen. mgr. Nat. Roofing Contractors Assn., Chgo., 1973-85, exec. v.p., Rosemont, Ill., 1987—; dir. mktg. Rand Devel. Corp., San Antonio, 1985-86; co-owner GT Communications, Inc., Dallas, 1985-87. Mem. Am. Soc. Assn. Execs. (cert.), Inst. for Orgn. Mgmt. (chmn. 1990-91), Chgo. Soc. Assn. Execs. (pres. 1996-97). Republican. Roman Catholic. Avocations: tennis, photography. Office: Nat Roofing Contractors Assn 10255 W Higgins Rd Rosemont IL 60018-5606 Home Phone: 847-318-5558; Office Phone: 847-299-9070. E-mail: bgood@nrca.net.

GOODACRE, CHARLES J., dean, educator; b. 1946; m. Ruth E. Goodacre. DDS, Loma Linda U., 1971; MSD, Ind. U., Indpls., 1974. Diplomate Am. Bd. Prosthodontics. Prof., chmn. dept. prosthodontics Sch. Dentistry Ind. U., Ind., 1974; prof. Loma Linda U., dean Sch. Dentistry. Contbr. articles to profl. jours.; co-author: (textbook) Johnston's Modern Practice in Fixed Prosthodontics (4th edit.); editor: Internat. Journal of Prosthodontics. Fellow: Acad. Prosthodontics, Am. Coll. Prosthodontics; mem.: Am. Acad. of Fixed Prosthodontics, Am. Bd. Prosthodontics (pres.). Avocations: woodworking, sports, Lionel trains, off-road motorcylcing. Office: Loma Linda Univ Loma Linda CA 92350 Business E-Mail: cgoodacre@llu.edu.

GOODALE, JAMES CAMPBELL, lawyer, television producer, columnist, educator; b. Cambridge, Mass., July 27, 1933; s. Robert Leonard and Eunice (Campbell) G.; m. Toni Krissel, May 3, 1964; children: Timothy Fuller, Ashley Krissel; foster child: Joseph Clayton Akiwenzie. Grad., Pomfret Sch., 1951; BA, Yale U., 1955; JD, U. Chgo., 1958. Bar: N.Y. 1960. Assoc. Lord, Day and Lord, NYC, 1959—63; gen. atty. N.Y. Times Co., 1963—67, gen. counsel, 1967—72, sr. v.p., 1972—73, exec. v.p., 1973—79, vice-chmn., 1979—80; ptnr. Debevoise and Plimpton, 1980—93, founder, head media-comm. and intellectual property sect., 1980—96, mem. exec. com., 1981—84, of counsel, 1994—96; prodr., host Digital Age (formerly The Telecom. and Info. Revolution) Channel 25 WNYE/NYC TV, 1995—. With Cmty. Law Office, East Harlem, 1968-70; vis. lectr. Yale U. Law Sch., 1977-80; adj. prof. NYU Sch. Law, 1983-86, Fordham Law Sch., 1986—; mem. NY State Privacy and Security Com., 1976-79; 2d cir. Commn. Reduction of Burdens and Costs in Civil Litig., 1977-80; vice chmn. NY State Jud. Commn. on Minorities, 1987-90, chmn., 1990-91; bd. dirs. Com. to Protect Journalists, 1989—, chmn., 1989-94; pres., owner Midtown Skating Corp., 1981-90; chmn. bd. Cable TV Law and Fin., 1981-93; trustee NYC Citizens Budget Commn., 1990-98; advisor U.S. Supreme Ct. Jud. Conf. Com. on Judiciary, 1980-89; chmn., founder PLI Comm. Law Seminar, 1972—; sec. NY Observer, 1988-92, Paris Rev. Found., 2001-. Author: All About Cable, 1987; compilor, editor: The New York Times Company vs. U.S., 1971; bd. editors: Media Law Reporter (co-founder), Nat. Law Jour., 1983-90; columnist nat. and N.Y. law jours.; contbr. articles on comms. law to profl. jours. Rules com. Dem. Nat. Conv., 1988; chmn. NY lawyer com. for Dukakis, 1988; former bd. dirs. NY Times, NY Times Neediest Cases Fund, NY Times Found.; former trustee Pomfret Sch., Gunnery Sch., St. Bernard's Sch., Boys' Club NY, Salzburg Seminar, Fed. Bar Coun.; vis. com. U. Chgo. Law Sch., 1977-80; bd. dirs. Human Rights Watch, 1994-96, Sky Rink Scholarship Fund, Inc., 1990-99, Citizens Pub. Utilities, 1996-99, Ice Theatre of NY, Internat. Ctr. Journalists, Paris Rev. Found. With AUS, 1958-59, Res., 1959-64. Named one of 200 Rising Leaders in U.S., Time mag., 1974, with 100 Most Influential Lawyers in U.S., Nat. Law Jour., 1991-97, one of Best Lawyers in Am., 1991-99; William Brinckerhoff Jackson scholar, 1954-55, Nat. Honor scholar U. Chgo. Law Sch., 1955-58. Fellow Inst. Jud. Administrn., N.Y. State Bar Assn. (chmn. spl. com. on pub. access to info. and proc. 1979-84, spl. com. on media law 1985-92); mem. N.Y.C. Bar Assn. (chmn. comm. law com. 1978-83, corp. law com. 1977-81), ABA (governing bd. comm. law forum, comm. on pub. understanding about law 1979-82), Fed. Bar Coun. (trustee 1980-84), Columbia U. Seminars on Media and Society, Yale Club (gov. 1964-67), Century Assn. Club, Economic Club, St. Elmo Club, Elihu Club (gov. 1966-70), Washington Conn. Club (gov. 1972-78). Office: Debevoise & Plimpton 919 3rd Ave Fl 30 New York NY 10022-6225 Office Phone: 212-909-6253.

GOODALE, TONI KRISSEL, research and development company executive; b. NYC, May 26, 1941; d. Walter DuPont and Ricka Krissel; m. James Campbell Goodale, May 3, 1964; children: Timothy Fuller, Ashley Krissel, Clayton A. (Ward). AB cum laude, Smith Coll., Northampton, Mass., 1963; student, U. Geneva, 1962-63; postgrad., Hunter Coll., NYC, 1964-65. Congl. intern Senator Keating U.S. Senate, Washington, 1963; broadcast analyst FCC, Washington, 1963-64; adminstrv. asst., dir. grant rsch. dept. Ford Found., NYC, 1964-67, cons. pub. edn. dept., 1968-69; NY rep. Smith Coll., NYC, 1975-78, asst. dir. devel., 1978-79; pres. Goodale Assocs., NYC, 1979-92, chmn., CEO, 1992—; vice-chmn. Metropolitan Mus. Bus. Com., NYC. Mem. NYC 2000 Millennium Coun.; vis. com. continuing edn. New Sch. Social; mem. bd. advs. First Women's Bank; bd. dirs. NY Outward Bound., mem. exec. com., chmn. alumni com.; lectr., writer in field. Columnist Fund Raising Mgmt., NY Social Diary. Bd. dirs.

NY Pub. Libr.; bd. dirs., mem. exec. com. Pen Am. Ctr., chmn.; mem. Women's Fgn. Policy Group; mem. UNA Chmn. Coun.; lectr. U.S. Naval Acad.; mem. alumnae fund com. Smith Coll., v.p. class, chmn. 25th reunion, Women's Forum; univ. chmn.'s coun., trustee, alumnae fund chmn., mem. alumnae coun.; bd. dirs. Brearley Sch.; mem. exec. com. Parents' Assn., St. Bernard's Sch.; mem. benefit com. NY Philharmonic; trustee, bd. govs. Churchill Sch.; co-chmn. spl. events com. Carnegie Hall, The Joffrey Ballet Opening Gala; chmn. Coro Benefit Dinners; trustee NY Inst. Child Devel.; mem. women's divsn. Legal Aid Soc.; mem. NY com. Joffrey Ballet; mem. benefit com. Grosvenor House; vice chmn. NYC Opera Benefit, Peir Ctr. Benefit; mem. com. Sch. Am. Ballet; active Women's Forum, mem. bus. com. Met. Mus. Mem. Am. Coun. Arts (vice-chmn. bd., exec. com., chmn. nat. patrons commn., chair long range planning com.), Nat. Cultural Alliance (bd. dirs.), Am. Assn. Fund-Raising Counsel (bd. dirs. trust for philanthropy), Nat. Assn. Fund Raising Execs., Assn. Healthcare Philanthropy, Brearley Sch. Alumnae Assn., Smith Coll. Alumnae Assn., Cosmopolitan Club, Smith Club, Washington Club, Seventh Regiment Armory Club, Doubles Internat. Club, Women's Forum (Women's Leadership Forum select cir., transition team, NYC pub. adv.). Office: 52 E 66 St New York NY 10021 Office Phone: 212-759-2999, 212-472-0300. Office Fax: 212-472-0311. Personal E-mail: riowoman@aol.com.

GOODALL, JANE, zoologist; b. London, Eng., Apr. 3, 1934; d. Mortimer Herbert and Vanne (Joseph) Morris-Goodall; m. Hugo Van Lawick, 1964 (div. 1974); one child, Hugo Eric Louis; m. Derek Bryceson, 1975 (dec. 1980). PhD in Ethology, Cambridge U., 1965; degree (hon.), Wesleyan Coll., Macon, Ga., 2000, U. Minn., 2001, U. Buffalo, NYC, 2001, Ryerson U., Toronto, Ont., Can., 2001, Providence U., Taiwan, 2001, Elon U., NC, 2002, Sweet Briar Coll., Va., 2002, U.Ctrl. Lancashire, UK, 2003, Pecs U., Hungary, 2005, Syracuse U., NYC, 2005, Rutgers State U., NJ, 2005, numerous other univs., 1975—99. Asst., sec. to Dr. Louis S. B. Leakey Coryndon Meml. Mus. Nat. History, Olduvai Gorge, Tanzania; rschr. in animal behavior, sci. dir. Gombe Stream Rsch. Ctr., Tanzania, 1960—2003. Vis. prof. psychiatry, human biology Stanford U., 1971-75; hon. vis. prof. zoology U. Dar Es Salaam, Tanzania, 1973—; lectr. Yale U., 1973; adj. prof. dept., environ. studies Tufts U. Sch. Vet. Medicine, 1987-88; assoc. Cleve. Natural History Mus., 1990; disting. adj. prof. occupl. therapy and anthropology U. So. Calif., 1990; Andrew D. White prof.-at-large Cornell U., 1996-2002; Messenger of Peace UN, 2002—; spkr. 20/20, Nightline, Good Morning America. Author: My Friends the Wild Chimpanzees, 1967, In the Shadow of Man, 1971, The Chimpanzees of Gombe, 1986 (R.R. Hawkins award for outstanding tech., sci. or med. book, 1986, Award for Outstanding Pub. in Wildlife Ecology and Mgmt., Wildlife Soc. U.S.A., 1986), The Chimpanzee Family Book, 1989, Through a Window, 1990, Visions of Caliban, 1993 (N.Y. Times "Notable Book", 1993, Libr. Jour. "Best Sci-Tech.Book, 1993), Jane Goodall: With Love, 1994, Dr. White, 1999, 40 Years at Gombe, 1999, Brutal Kinship, 1999, The Eagle and the Wren, 2000, Africa in My Blood: An Autobiography in Letters, 2000, Chimpanzees I Love: Saving Their World and Ours, 2001, Beyond Innocence: An Autobiography in Letters, 2001; author: (with Philip Berman) Reason for Hope, 1999; author: (with Marc Bekoff) The Ten Trusts: What We Must Do To Care for the Animals We Love, 2002; author: (with Gary McAvoy and Gail Hudson) Harvest for Hope: A Guide to Mindful Eating, 2005; contbr. Primate Behavior, 1965, Primate Ethology, 1967, Am. Handbook of Psychiatry, 1976, Understanding Chimpanzees, 1990; author (with H. van Lawick): (children's book) Grub: The Bush Baby, 1972; author: My Life With the Chimpanzees, 1988 (Parenting's Reading-Magic award for outstanding book for children, 1989), The Chimpanzee Family Book, 1989, Jane Goodall's Animal World: Chimps, 1989, Animal Family Series, 1989, With Love, 1994, Dr. White, 1999, The Eagle and the Wren, 2000, Chimpanzees I Love: Saving Their World and Ours, 2001; author: (with Alan Marks) Rickie and Henri: A True Story, 2004; author: (films) Miss Goodall and the Wild Chimpanzees, 1963, Among the Wild Chimpanzees, 1984; author: (with Hugo van Lawick) People of the Forest, 1988; author: Chimpanzee Alert, in the Nature Watch Series, 1990, The Life and Legend of Jane Goodall, 1990, The Gombe Chimpanees, 1990, Jane Goodall: Reason for Hope, 1999, Chimps R Us, 2001, Jane Goodall's Wild Chimpanzees, 2002; contbr. numerous articles to profl. jours. Founder Jane Goodall Inst. for Wildlife Rsch., Edn. and Conservation, 1977—; sci. gov. Chgo. Acad. Scis., 1981—; internat. dir. ChimpanZoo, 1984—; trustee Jane Goodall Inst. U.K., 1988—, Jane Goodall Inst. Can., 1993—; adv. bd. Advocates for Animals, Scotland, 1990—, Albert Schweitzer Inst. for Humanities, 1991—, Trees for Life, 1994—, Dolphin Project Internat. and Dolphin Project Europe, 1995—, Fred Found., Netherlands, 1996—, Lab. Primate Advocacy Group, 2001—, Initiative for Animals and Ethics, Harvard U., 2004—, Friends of Africa Internat., 2005—; mem. internat. adv. bd. Tchrs. Without Borders, 2001—; adv. coun. Cin. Zoo, 2005—. Decorated Dame of Brit. Empire, Legion of Honor (France); named Internat. Patron, Immortal Chaplains Found., 2006; recipient Franklin Burr award, Nat. Geographic Soc., 1963, 1964, Centennial award, 1988, Hubbard medal, 1995, Conservation award, Women's Br. N.Y. Zool. Soc., 1974, Albert Schweitzer award, Internat. Women's Inst., 1987, Kyoto prize, Inamori Found., 1990, Tanzanian Kilimanjaro medal for Contbn. to Wildlife Conservation, Pres. Mwinyi, 1996, Mt. Kilimanjaro award, 1996, Pub. Svc. award, Nat. Sci. Bd., 1998, John Hay award, Orion Soc., 1998, Huxley Meml. medal, Royal Anthrop. Inst. Gt. Britain and Ireland, 2001, 2002, Gandhi/King award for Non-Violence, 2001, Benjamin Franklin medal in Life Sci., 2003, Prince of Asturias award, 2003, Gandhi/King award, Nierenberg Prize for Sci. in the Pub. Interest, 2004, European Heroes award, Time Mag., 2004, President's Medal for Exemplary Achievement, Westminster Coll., 2005, Natura award, Pax, 2005, Gold medal award, UNESCO, 2006, 2007 Women of Discovery: Lifetime Achievement award, Wings WorldQuest, Lifetime Achievement award, Jules Verne Adventures, 2006, numerous others. Fellow: Royal Anthropol. Inst. Gt. Britain and Ireland (hon.); mem.: Academia Scientiarium et Artium Europaea Austria, Deutsche Akademie der Naturforscher Leopoldina (Germany), Soc. Women Geographers, Am. Philos. Soc., Rsch. Ctr. for Human Ethology (fgn.), Am. Acad. Arts and Sci. (hon. fgn.) (hon.), Explorer's Club (N.Y.). Achievements include research in in behavior of free-living chimpanzees in the Gombe National Park, Tanzania; social behavior of the spotted hyena, crocutta crocutta Ngorongoro Conservation Area; on behavior of the olive baboon, Papio anub is, Gombe National Park. Business E-Mail: jginformation@janegoodall.org.

GOODALL, LEONARD EDWIN, public administration educator; b. Warrensburg, Mo., Mar. 16, 1937; s. Leonard Burton and Eula (Johnson) G.; m. Lois Marie Stubblefield, Aug. 16, 1959; children: Karla, Karen, Greg. BA, Ctrl. Mo. State U., 1958; MA, U. Mo., 1960; PhD, U. Ill., 1962; AA (hon.), Schoolcraft Coll., 1977; DHL (hon.), Ctrl. Mo. State U., Warrensburg, 2000. Asst. prof. polit. sci., asst. dir. Bur. Govt. Rsch., Ariz. State U., Tempe, 1962-65, bur. dir., 1965-67; assoc. prof. polit. sci., assoc. dean faculties U. Ill. at Chgo. Circle, 1968-69, vice chancellor, 1969-71; chancellor U. Mich., Dearborn, 1971-79; pres. U. Nev., Las Vegas, 1979-85, prof. mgmt. and pub. administrn., 1985—2000. Cons. Ariz. Acad., Phoenix, 1964-67; dir. Peace Corps tng. program for Chile, 1965; vice chmn. bd. Comml. Bank of Nev., 1993-98; chmn. bd. Colonial Bank Nev., 1998—. Contbg. editor: Can. Moneysaver, 1997—; Author: The American Metropolis: Its Governments and Politics, 1968, rev. edit., 1975, Gearing Arizona's Communities to Orderly Growth, 1965, State Politics and Higher Education, 1976, When Colleges Lobby States, 1987, Managing Your TIAA-CREF Retirement Accounts, 1990, The World Wide Investor, 1991, Nevada Government and Politics, 1996, Reinventing the System, 2001; editor: Urban Politics in the Southwest, 1967. Mem. univ. exec. com. United Fund, 1966-67; v.p. Met. Fund, Inc.; mem. Mich. Gov.'s Commn. Long Range Planning, 1973-75, Tempe Planning and Zoning Commn., 1965-67, New Detroit Com., 1972-79; mem. Wayne County (Mich.) Planning Commn., 1973-79, vice chmn., 1976-79; mem. exec. bd. Clark County chpt. NCCJ, 1979-86; bd. dirs. Nev. Devel. Authority, 1980-86, Boulder Dam coun. Boy Scouts Am., 1980-89; bd. dirs. Nev. Power Co. Consumer Adv. Coun., 1984-90, chmn., 1986-89. Served with AUS, 1959. Kendrick C. Babcock fellow, 1961—62. Mem. Am. Polit. Sci. Assn., Am. Soc. Pub. Administrn. (chpt. pres. 1989-90), Western Govtl. Rsch. Assn. (exec. coun. 1966-68), Clark County Growth Task Force (chmn. 2004-05), Las Vegas Rotary Found. (pres. 2005-06), Dearborn C. of C. (dir. 1974-79), Rotary, Phi Sigma Epsilon, Phi Kappa Phi Found. (bd. dirs. 1994-96). Home: 6530 Darby Ave Las Vegas NV 89146-6518 Office: U Nev Dept Pub Adminstrn Las Vegas NV 89154 Personal E-mail: patgoodall@aol.com.

GOODCHILD, LESTER FRANCIS, higher education educator; b. Lackawanna, NY, Apr. 30, 1948; s. Thomas J. and Mary June (DeVoy) Walczak; m. Wynn Evelyn Johnson, Sept. 20, 1980 BA, U. St. Thomas, 1970; MDiv with high honors, St. Meinrad Sch. Theology, 1975; MA, Indiana U., Bloomington, 1979; PhD, U. Chgo., 1986. Dir. project respond St. Meinrad (Ind.) Seminary, 1971-72; assoc. instr. dept religious studies Ind. U., 1973; supr. pastoral edn. St. Meinrad Sch. Theology, 1973-74, teaching asst. dept. ch. hist., 1974; dir. aged ministry program St. Joseph's Hosp., Huntingberg, Ind., 1973-74; deacon St. Andrew's Ch., Joliet, Ill., 1974, St. Paul the Apostle Ch., Joliet, 1975; cons. residential property ops., regional property mgr., property mgr. Lehndorff Mgmt. U.S.A. Ltd., Chgo., 1976-78; property mgr. The Habitat Co., Chgo., 1979-81; rsch. asst. ctr. for continuing edn. U. Chgo., 1979-81; instr., mentor Sch. for New Learning DePaul U., Chgo., 1981-88, dir. suburban campuses, 1987; asst. prof. higher edn. coll. edn. dept. profl. studies Iowa State U., Ames, 1988-89; adj. rsch. assoc. ctr. for study of higher edn. Pa. State U., University Park, 1989—90; assoc. prof. edn., coord. higher edn. and adult studies program coll. edn. U. Denver, 1990—2003, interim dean, 2000—01; prof. higher edn. U. Mass. Boston Grad. Coll. Edn., 2003—06, dean, 2003—06; prof. edn., dir. higher edn. program Santa Clara U. Sch. Edn., Counseling Psychology, and Pastoral Ministries, Calif., 2006—, dean, 2006—07. Vis. lectr. Loyola U. Sch. Edn., Chgo., 1989-90; vis. scholar, prof. Boston Coll., Pa. State U., 1997, U. Calif. Berkeley, 2002; presenter in field. Co-editor The History of Higher Education, 1989, 3d edit., 2007, Administration as a Profession, 1991, Public Policy and Higher Education, 1997, Rethinking the Dissertation Process: Tackling Personal and Institutional Obstacles, 1997; asst. editor (refereed jour.) Religion & Edn., 1989-94; assoc. editor: Higher Education: Handbook of Theory and Research, 1992-96; mem. editl. bd. Jour. Gen. Edn., 1990-94, Rev. Higher Edn., 1992-95, History of Higher Edn. Ann., 1994—; contbr. articles to profl. jours., chpts. to books. Election judge City of Chgo., 1976. Travel grant U. Notre Dame, 1982, NEH, 1989; mini grant Iowa State U., 1989; Faculty Rsch. grant U. Denver, 1992, Faculty Internat. Rsch. grant Hewlett Found., 1999, Sturm Family Found., 2002, Nellie Mae Found., 2004; scholar Meinrad Sch. Theology, 1971-75, Ind. U., 1973; recipient K-12 Achievement award Boston Mayor, 2004. Mem.: AAUP, Am. Assn. Colls. for Tchr. Edn., Nat. Coun. on Religion and Pub. Edn. (article reviewer 1990—94), Internat. Standing Conf. for History of Edn., Hist. Edn. Soc., Assn. Study Higher Edn. (registration com. 1984, program com. 1987, futures com. 1987—89, welcoming com. 1988—98, chair Dissertation of Yr. award com. 1990, Task Force on Edn. in 21st Century 1990—92, chair curriculum, learning and instrn. com. 1990—96, chair Coun. for Advancement of Higher Edn. Programs, annual conf. evaluation com. 1992, proposal reviewer 1988—), Am. Coll. Pers. Assn., Am. Hist. Assn., Am. Ednl. Rsch. Assn. (proposal reviewer 1985, 1988—96), Am. Cath. Hist. Assn., Am. Assn. Higher Edn. Democrat. Roman Catholic. Avocations: tennis, hiking, skiing. Office: Santa Clara U Sch Edn Counseling Psychology et al 500 El Camino Real Santa Clara CA 95053-0201 Home: 851 Nevada Ave San Jose CA 95125 Office Phone: 408-554-4464. Business E-Mail: lgoodchild@scu.edu.

GOODCHILD, MICHAEL FRANK, geographer, educator; b. Feb. 24, 1944; married; 3 children. BA in Physics, Cambridge U., Eng., 1965; PhD in Geography, McMaster U., Ont., Can., 1969; DSc (hon.), Laval U., Can., 1999, Keele U., 2001, McMaster U., Ont., Can., 2004; LLD (hon.), Ryerson U., Toronto, Can., 2004. Asst. prof. U. Western Ont., 1969—71, assoc. prof., 1971—79, prof., 1979—89; prof. geography U. Calif., Santa Barbara, 1989—. Cons.; vis. prof. McGill U., 1972, U. Iowa, 1973, rsch. assoc., 74, vis. assoc. prof., 74; vis. prof. U. Calif., Santa Barbara, 1978, 79, 1988—89, chair dept. geography, 1998—2000, dir. Ctr. Spatially Integrated Social Sci., 1999—; chmn. dept. geography U. Western Ont., 1982—85, hon. prof., 1989—94; vis. prof. U. Auckland, 1986; vis. scholar Commonwealth Sci. and Indsl. Rsch. Orgn., Canberra, Australia, 1986; mem. adv. bd. Inst. Market and Social Analysis, Toronto, Canada, 1987—89; co-dir. Nat. Ctr. Geog. Info. and Analysis, 1988—91, dir., 1991—96, chair exec. com., 1997—; mem. sci. adv. bd. Internat. Cartographic Assn., 1990—; assoc. dir. Alexandria Digital Libr., 1994—; chair mapping sci. com. NRC, 1997—99; vis. prof. U. London Birkbeck Coll., 1997. Contbr. articles to profl. jours.; mem. adv. editl. bd.: Internat. Jour. Geog. Info. Systems, 1986—; editor: Geog. Analysis, 1987—90; mem. editl. bd.: Operational Geographer, 1989—97, Geog. Systems: The European Jour. Theoretical and Applied Geography, 1990—, Jour. Geog. Systems, 1998—, Cartography and Geog. Info. Systems, 1999—, Geoinformation Sci. Jour., 2005—, Profl. Geographer, 2005—, mem. editl. adv. bd.: Geog. Info. Systems, 1990—, GIS World, 1990—, Geog. Analysis, 1990—, assoc. editor: Annals of the Assn. of Am. Geographers, 1996—2000, editor methods, models and geog. info. scis.:, 2000—. Co-recipient Horwood Critique prize, Urban and Regional Info. Systems Assn., 1993, 1995, Gerald McCalden award, Australasian Urban and Regional Info. Systems Assn., 1994, Intergraph award, Am. Soc. Photogrammetry and Remote Sensing, 1996; named Educator of Yr., Univ. Consortium for Geog. Info. Sci., 2002; recipient Applied Geography Citation award, Assn. Am. Geographers, 1983, Award for Disting. Scholarship, 1996, Scholarly Distinction in Geography award, Can. Assn. Geographers, 1990, Award of Distinction for Exceptional Scholarly Contbns. to Cartography, Can. Cartographic Assn., 1999, Lifetime Achievement award, Environ. Systems Rsch. Inst., 2001, Founder's medal, Royal Geog. Soc., 2003; grantee Leave fellowship, Social Scis. and Humanities Rsch. Coun., 1986. Fellow: Royal Soc. Can. (fgn. fellow), Am. Acad. Arts & Scis.; mem.: NAS. Office: Dept Geography U Calif 5707 Ellison Hall Santa Barbara CA 93106-4060 E-mail: good@ncgia.ucsb.edu.

GOODE, BETTY RUTH, retired social worker; b. Peason, La., Apr. 25, 1926; d. Woodie Watson Goode and Allie Ruth Porter. BA, Fla. State U., 1947; MSW, U. Pitts., 1949. Cert. profl. social worker Acad. Cert. Social Workers. Program worker Homer Toberman Settlement House, San Pedro, Calif., 1949—55; instr. Scarritt Coll. Christian Workers, Nashville, 1956—57; program worker Centenary Meth. Cmty. Ctr., Nashville, 1957—60, program coord., 1964—70; staff campus travel Meth. Bd. Missions, 1960—64; dir. social svcs. Day Care Moore Cmty. House, Biloxi, Miss., 1971—78; program asst. Office Deaconess Home Missionary Svc. Gen. Bd. Global Ministries, NYC, 1978—89; ret., 1989. Bd. dirs. Hope, Inc., Nashville, 1969—70; sec. Matthew Walker Health Coun., Nashville, 1968—70. Deaconess United Meth. Ch., 1952—; pres. United Meth. Women, St. Cloud, Fla., 1997—2000, 2006—. Mem.: AAUW, Nat. Assn. Social Workers (chpt. sec. 1966—67, 1971—74), Philanthropic and Ednl. Orgn. Women (chaplain GO chpt. 2005—, rec. sec. GO chpt. 1993—99), Phi Kappa Phi, Phi Beta Kappa. Democrat. Home: 2825 Vickie Ct Kissimmee FL 34744

GOODE, BOBBY CLAUDE, retired secondary school educator; b. Celeste, Tex., Dec. 10, 1940; s. Claude Elmer and Clarice Edna G.; m. Jean Helen Ames, June 9, 1963; children: James Lonnie, Joel Dietrich, John Shalom. BS, MIT, 1963; MA, Andover Newton Sem., Newton Centre, Mass., 1968; MS, Rensselaer Poly. Inst., 1972. Cert. tchr. sci. and math. Tchr. math. Lawrence D. Bell High Sch., Hurst, Tex., 1966-67; tchr. physics and chemistry Grapevine (Tex.) High Sch., 1967-70; tchr. advanced physics, advanced chemistry, advanced biology South Plainfield (N.J.) High Sch., 1970-96, ret., 1996. Sci. tchr. Princeton (N.J.) U., 1983, Disting. Secondary Sch. Tchg. finalist, 1983. Author: (booklets) Lap Physics, 1973, Stars, Planets, People, 1980, Atoms and Molecules, 1980, Physics Problem Solutions, 1980. Mem. Civil Rights Commn., Piscataway, N.J., 1977, Sr. Citizens Housing Com., Piscataway, 1975; ch. sch. tchr. First Bapt. Ch. of New Market, 1970-96. Named Outstanding Sci. Tchr., Sigma Xi, 1986. Mem. NEA, N.J. Edn. Assn., Am. Assn. Physics Tchrs., Nat. Sci. Tchrs. Assn. (recipient Exemplary Secondary Sci. Tchr. Nat. award 1980). Democrat. Avocations: travel, writing, sports. Home: 129 Stonegate S Boerne TX 78006-3411

GOODE, CONSTANCE LOPER, elementary school principal; b. Camden, NJ, Dec. 8, 1950; d. Joseph R. and Cora F. (Loper) Stallings; m. Thomas L. Goode, Mar. 24, 1973; children: Bryan Thomas, James Robert. BS, Duquesne U., 1973; MEd, Coll. William and Mary, 1989; advanced degree in Adminstrn. and Supervision, George Washington U., 1996. Cert. elem. tchr. Va. Tchr. spl. edn. Las Cruces (N.Mex.) Pub. schs., 1973-74; elem. tchr. Va., 1974-89; elem. counselor Newport News (Va.) Pub. Schs., 1989-91, staff devel. coord., 1991-95; asst. prin. Carver Elem. Sch., Newport News, 1995-97; prin. Briarfield Elem. Sch., Newport News, 1997—2002, Palmer Elem. Sch., 2002—06; ret. Recipient oustanding svc. award; scholar Mennon Co. Mem. Newport News Edn. Assn. (past pres.), Sigma Lambda Delta, Delta Kappa Gamma. Home: 112 Hilda Cir Hampton VA 23666-4723

GOODE, CORALYN, lawyer; b. New Brunswick, NJ, 1956; AB, Georgetown U., 1978; JD, Coll. William & Mary U., 1981. Bar: DC 1981, US Dist. Ct., DC 1993. Ptnr., energy, project finance Squire, Sanders & Dempsey, LLP, Houston, mem. mgmt. com., mng. ptnr.-Houston Office. Fluent in Spanish. Office: Squire Sanders & Dempsey LLP 6250 Chase Tower 600 Travis St Houston TX 77002-3000 Office Phone: 713-546-3355. Office Fax: 713-546-5830. Business E-Mail: cgoode@ssd.com.

GOODE, ERICA TUCKER, internist; b. Berkeley, Calif., Mar. 25, 1940; d. Howard Edwin and Mary Louise (Tucker) Sweeting; m. Bruce Tucker (div. 1971); m. Barry Paul Goode, Sept. 1, 1974; children: Adam Nathaniel, Aaron Benjamin. BS summa cum laude, U. Calif., Berkeley, 1962, MPH, 1967; MD, U. Calif., San Francisco, 1977. Diplomate Am. Bd. Internal Medicine. Chief dietitian Washington Hosp. Ctr., Washington, 1968; pub. health nutritionist Dept. Human Resources, Washington, 1969—73; intern Children's Hosp. (now Calif. Pacific Med. Ctr.), San Francisco, 1977—78, resident, 1978—80, chief med. resident internal medicine, 1979—80; pvt. practice internal medicine San Francisco, 1980—. Expert witness med.-legal issues, Calif., 1990—; lectr., tchr. med. house staff Calif. Pacific Med. Ctr. Hosp., 1982—; assoc. prof. medicine U. Calif., San Francisco, 1984—; apptd. mem. Calif. Commn. on Aging, 2003—. Contbr. articles to profl. publs. Co-chair Physicians for Clinton, No. Calif., 1992, 96 Mem. AMA, ACP, Calif. Med. Assn., Calif. Soc. Internal Medicine, San Francisco Med. Soc. (mem. editl. bd.), U. Calif. Alumni Assn. (del.), Alpha Omega Alpha (named Best Doctor's list 1998-2006). Office: CPMC Inst for Health & Healing Clinic 2300 California St Ste 200 San Francisco CA 94115-2754 Home Phone: 510-233-3819; Office Phone: 415-600-3503. Business E-Mail: goodee@sutterhealth.org.

GOODE, JOHN MARTIN, manufacturing executive; b. Chgo., Sept. 24, 1934; s. Robert C. and Alyce (Belz) G.; children: John Martin, Sue Ellen, James Edward, Leslie Maureen. B Commerce, DePaul U., 1960; MBA, U. Chgo., 1966; EdD, No. Ill. U., 1984. CPA, Ill.; CMA, Ill. Contr. farm equipment div. Allis Chalmers, Milw., 1966-69; v.p., contr. Maremont Corp., Chgo., 1969-73; sr. v.p. Whittakers Corp., Chgo., 1973-75; assoc. dean DePaul U., Chgo., 1976-78, asst. prof., 1975-80; sr. v.p. fin. and corp. planning J.I. Case Co., Racine, Wis., 1980-85; chmn. bd., chief exec. officer Prestolite Electric Inc., Toledo, 1986-91; dean Sch. Mgmt. and Bus. Nat. U., San Diego, 1991-93; investor, 1993—; chmn. bd. dirs., CEO K&W Products, LLC, Bloomington, Ind., 1996-2000. Chmn. bd. dirs., CEO, A.P. Labs, Inc., San Diego, Am. Innotek Inc., San Diego. Mem. San Diego Yacht club, Univ. Club, Del Mar Country Club. Home: PO Box 170 Genoa NV 89411-0170

GOODE, STEPHEN HOGUE, publishing executive; b. Charlotte, NC, Dec. 25, 1924; s. Henry Grady and Marie Louella (Creamer) G.; m. Jean Cameron Advena, Oct. 16, 1953; children: Elizabeth Whitston Joane Downe, Polly Turpin Dulcinea Hogue. BA, U. Md., 1948; MA, U. Pa., 1954, PhD, 1958. Asst. prof. English Rensselaer Poly. Inst., 1958-59; asst. prof. Fairleigh Dickinson U., 1960-65; dir. libraries, assoc. prof. English Russell Sage Coll., 1965-78; pres., chmn. bd. Whitston Pub. Co., Troy, NY, 1968-81, Turpin Book Corp., Troy, 1973-80; pres. Penkevill Pub. Co., Greenwood, Fla., 1982—. Dir. Trenowyth Pub. Co., Penkivil Book Co. Author: Index to Little Magazines, 1943-47, 1965, Index to Little Magazines, 1940-42, 1967, Index to Commonwealth Little Magazines, 1966-67, 68, plus, biennial, Index to American Little Magazines, 1920-39, 1969, 1900-1919, 1974; editor: Studies in 20th Century, 1968-75; founding editor Am. Humanities Index, 1978-82. Served with AUS, 1943-46, 49-52. Decorated Purple Heart, Bronze Star with oak leaf cluster. Mem. MLA, Am. Hist. Assn., Bibliog. Soc. (London), Bibliog. Soc. Am., Bibliog. Soc. U. Va., Index Soc. (London). Clubs: Grolier (N.Y.C.).

GOODE, STEVEN, law educator; b. 1951; BA Polit. Economy with high honours, Williams Coll., 1972; JD, Yale U., 1975. Bar: D.C. 1975, Tex. 1977. Staff atty. Children's Def. Fund, D.C., 1975-77; asst. prof. U. Tex., Austin, 1977-82, assoc. prof., 1982-84, Fulbright and Jaworski prof., 1984—, assoc. dean for academic affairs, 1998—2006, dean, 2006, teaching prof. Lectr. Coll. of Advanced Jud. Studies Tex. Ctr. for Judiciary. Emily Marshall Wulff Cen. faculty fellow 1986-88, recipient Tex. Excellence Teaching award 1992. Mem.: Tex. Bar Found. (life fellow), Acad. of Disting. Teachers U. Tex. 1998., Phi Beta Kappa. Office: U Tex Sch Law 727 E Dean Keeton St Austin TX 78705 Office Phone: 512-232-1331. Office Fax: 512-471-6988. Business E-Mail: sgoode@law.utexas.edu.

GOODE, VIRGIL H., JR., congressman; b. Richmond, Va., Oct. 17, 1946; m. Lucy D. Dodson; 1 child, Catherine S. BA, U. Richmond, 1969; JD, U. Va. Sch. Law, Charlottesville, 1973. Lawyer pvt. practice; mem. Va. State Senate, 1973—96, US Congress from 5th Va. dist., 1997—, mem. appropriations com. Served in Va. Army N.G., 1969—75. Recipient Outstanding Legis. Svc. award Va. State Sheriffs' Assn., Outstanding Svc. award Vol. Rescue Squads, 1994. Mem. Phi Beta Kappa, Omicron Delta Kappa, Lambda Chi Alpha, Phi Alpha Delta. Republican. Baptist. Office: US Ho Reps 1520 Longworth Ho Office Bldg Washington DC 20515-4605 Office Phone: 202-225-4711.*

GOODELL, JOSEPH EDWARD, manufacturing executive; b. El Paso, Tex., Aug. 18, 1937; s. Joseph Edward and Grace Louise (Beck) g.; m. Margaret Rives, Aug. 12, 1961 (di. June 1978); children: Marian, Margaret Trout, MarthaLamanna, Maryellen Olszyk; m. Mary Ellen Hager, Sept. 17, 1993. BSME, MIT, 1959; MBA, Harvard U., 1961. Project engr. Bechtel Corp., San Francisco, 1961-65; mfg. engr. Chase Brass and Copper Co., Cleve., 1965-67; adminstrv. mgr. Montpelier, Ohio, 1967-69, Waterbury, Conn., 1969-71; v.p., gen. mgr. Montpelier, 1971-76; group v.p. Chase Brass and Copper Co., Cleve., 1976-79, Pangborn div. Carborundum, Hagerstown, Md., 1979-81; sr. v.p. Standard Oil Ind. Products, Cleve.,

1981—85; CEO Am. Brass Co., Buffalo, 1985—94; chmn. bd. Empire Steel Co., 1999—2001. Bd. dirs. WNED Pub. Broadcasting Sta., Buffalo, Tech. Bldg. Corp., Boston; owner, operator pvt. railroad car DAGNY Taggart; chmn. bd. West Tex. and Buffalo Steam Ship & Rwy. Co., 1990—. Active Boy Scouts Am., Waterbury, Conn.; past chmn. Buffalo Health Care Coalition; vice chmn. Greater Buffalo Partnership; chmn. Horizons Waterfront Commn.; dir. Downtown Devel., Inc.; dir. Buffalo State Coll. Found.; trustee, past pres., past exec. dir. Buffalo Philharm. Orch., 1995-99; chmn. planning com. Buffalo Pan Am. Expo, 2001; past bd. adv. Symphony Orch. Inst.; past v.p. Sheas Preservation Soc.; past bd. dirs. Kenmore Mercy Hosp. Found.; bd. dirs. Kleinmans Music Hall, Erie County Who Does What Commn., Erie County Exec. Transition Com., Erie County Stabilization Project, 2005; appt. by Gov. Pataki Erie County Fiscal Stabilization Authority, 2006. Recipient Spl. award Buffalo Philharm. Orch., 1999; named Citizen of Yr. Buffalo, 1996. Mem. Buffalo Club, Wanakah Country Club. Home: 6746 Lake Shore Rd Derby NY 14047-9739

GOODELL, ROGER, national football league commissioner; b. Jamestown, NY, Feb. 19, 1959; s. Charles Ellsworth and Jean (Rice) Goodell; m. Jane Skinner; 2 children. BA in Econs., Washington and Jefferson Coll., 1981. Intern NFL Offices, NYC, 1982—83; mem. pub. rels., adminstrn. NY Jets, 1983—84; publ. rels. asst. NFL, NYC, 1984—87, dir. internat. devel., dir. club adminstrn., v.p. ops., bus. devel., sr. v.p. league and football devel., exec. v.p. bus. football devel., exec. v.p. bus., properties, club svcs., exec. v.p., COO, 2001—06, commr., 2006—; asst. to pres. Am. Football Conf. (AFC), 1987—90. Mem. bd. NYC chpt. Big Bros. & Big Sisters. Achievements include helping launch NFL Network. Office: NFL 280 Park Ave New York NY 10017 Office Fax: 212-681-7599.*

GOODEN, BENNY L., school system administrator; Supt. Ft. Smith (Ark.) Pub. Schs. State finalist Nat. Supt. Yr. award, 1993; recipient Phoebe Apperson Hearst Outstanding Educator award Nat. PTA, 1999. Office: Ft Smith Pub Schs 3205 Jenny Lind Rd Fort Smith AR 72901-7101 Office Phone: 479-785-2501.

GOODEN, DREW, professional basketball player; b. Sept. 24, 1981; s. Andrew. Attended, Univ. Kans. Basketball player Memphis Grizzlies, 2002, Orlando Magic, 2002—04, Cleve. Cavaliers, 2004—. Named First-Team All-American, AP, 2002, Player of the Yr., Basketball America, 2002, Power Forward Yr., ESPN Mag., 2002, Pete Newell Big Man Yr., 2002. Office: Cleve Cavaliers Gund Arena One Center Ct Cleveland OH 44115

GOODEN, LINDA R., aerospace transportation executive; b. 1953; Degree in Computer Tech., Youngstown State U., Ohio; BS in Bus. Adminstrn., U. Md. U. Coll.; post-baccalaureate studies, San Diego State U.; D in Pub. Svc. (hon.), U. Md U. Coll., 2005. Software engr. Gen. Dynamics, San Diego; with Lockheed Martin Corp., Bethesda, Md., 1980—, v.p., Software Support Services, 1994—2006, dep. exec. v.p., Info. Tech. Services Cherry Hill, NJ, 2006—07, exec. v.p., 2007—. Mem. exec. bd. A. James Clark Sch. Engring., U. Md., Robert H. Smith Sch. Bus. Ctr. for Electronic Markets & Enterprises, Prince George's Cmty. Coll. Found., Md. Bus. Roundtable for Edn. Named 2006 Black Engr. of Yr., US Black Engr. and IT Mag., 2006 Aiming High honoree, Legal Momentum; named one of Women of Power in Bus. for 2006, Black Enterprise Mag.; named to 1997 Salute to Am.'s Best and Brightest, Dollars & Sense Mag.; recipient Ann. Peat Marwick High Tech Entrepreneur award, 1994, 2002 Fed. 100 Eagle award, Fed. Computer Wk., 2002 Corp. Leadership award, Women in Tech. Mem.: Exec. Leadership Coun. (mem. exec. bd.), Internat. Info. Tech. Assn. of Am. (mem. exec. bd.), Armed Forces Comm. Electronics Assn. (mem. exec. bd.). Office: Lockheed Martin Information and Technology Services 2339 Rt 70 W Cherry Hill NJ 08002*

GOODEN, RANDALL SCOTT, historian, archivist; b. Morgantown, W.Va., July 11, 1962; s. Ronald Leara and Barbara Ellen Gooden; m. Stacy Ann Tregaskes, June 15, 1990; children: Joseph Ephraim, William Randall, Michael Shannon. BA in History, W.Va. U., Morgantown, 1984, MA in History, 1985, PhD in History, 1995. Asst. curator W.Va. and regional history collection W.Va. U., 1992—95; head archives libr. Youngstown Hist. Ctr. Industry and Labor Ohio Hist. Soc., 1995—2001; prin. historian Gooden & Assocs., New Middletown, Ohio, 2001—03; exec. dir. Geauga County Hist. Soc., Burton, Ohio, 2003—04; cir. rider archivist Ga. Archives, Morrow, Ga., 2005—. Adj. faculty Youngstown State U., 1995—96; faculty accelerated program Ursuline Coll., Pepper Pike, Ohio, 2005; asst. prof. history Clayton State U., Morrow, Ga., 2005—. Editor (publisher): (weekly newspaper) New Middletown Postmark. Scoutmaster Boy Scouts Am., Fayetteville, Ga., 2006—06; mem. county ctrl. com. Rep. Party, Waynesburg, Pa., 1994—95, Youngstown, Ohio, 1998—2003, exec. dir. county chpt., 2002—03, mem.exec. com. county, 2002—03; high priest LDS Ch. Mem.: Soc. Ga. Archivists, Mahoning County Rural Rep. Club (sec. 1999—2002). Republican. Lds Ch. Home: 240 Pinewood Dr Senoia GA 30276 Office: Clayton State University 2000 Clayton State Blvd Morrow GA 30260 Home Phone: 770-461-2487; Office Phone: 678-364-3835. Business E-Mail: randallgooden@clayton.edu.

GOODENBERGER, DANIEL MARVIN, medical educator; b. McCook, Nebr., Apr. 24, 1948; s. Marvin Eugene and Mary Ellen (Marshall) Goodenberger; children: James Michael, Katherine Elizabeth. BS, U. Nebr., Lincoln, 1970; MD, Duke U., Durham, NC, 1974. Diplomate Am. Bd. Internal Medicine, Am. Bd. Emergency Medicine (examiner 1983-95), Am. Bd. Pulmonary Disease, Am. Bd. Critical Care Medicine. Intern Peter Bent Brigham Hosp., Boston, 1974-75, resident in internal medicine, 1975-76; clin. assoc. Nat. Cancer Inst., Bethesda, Md., 1976-78; fellow pulmonary and critical care medicine Boston U. Med. Ctr., 1985-88; assoc. dir. emergency dept. Arlington Hosp., Va., 1979-82; edn. dir. emergency dept. Georgetown U. Hosp., Washington, 1982-85; dir. emergency svcs. U. Hosp., Boston, 1986-87; dir. pulmonary and critical care fellowship Washington U. Med. Schs., St. Louis, 1989-93; dir. pulmonary cons. svcs. Barnes Hosp., St. Louis, 1990-93, dir. internal medicine residency program, 1992—2006; assoc. prof. medicine Washington U., St. Louis, 1995-99; dir. divsn. med. edn. Washington U. Sch. Medicine, 1998—2006, prof. medicine, 1999—2006; prof., chair dept. medicine U. Nev. Sch. Medicine, Las Vegas, 2006—. Chief Wood-Moore Firm, Barnes-Jewish Hosp., 1996-2001. Editor Careers, 1996-98. Lt. comdr. USPHS, 1973-78. Winthrop Breon and Am. Coll. Chest Physicians scholar, 1987. Fellow ACP, Am. Coll. Chest Physicians; mem. AMA, Am. Thoracic Soc., Am. Clin. and Climatological Assn., Assn. Program Dirs. Internal Medicine (nominating and publs. com. 1991-98, councillor 2004-07), Assn. Profs. Medicine. St. Louis Met. Med. Soc. (councilor 1997-2000), St. Louis Club, Harbor Point Yacht Club, Phi Beta Kappa, Alpha Omega Alpha. Methodist. Avocations: theater, music, travel, sailing. Home: 372 Arbour Garden Ave Las Vegas NV 89148 Office: U Nevada Sch Medicine 2040 W Charleston Blvd Ste 300 Las Vegas NV 89102 Office Phone: 702-671-2345. Personal E-mail: goodenberger@sbcglobal.net. Business E-Mail: dgoodenberger@unr.edu.

GOODENOUGH, JOHN BANNISTER, engineering educator, physicist, researcher; b. Jena, Germany, July 25, 1922; came to US, 1922; parents Am. citizens. s. Erwin Ramsdell and Helen Meriam (Lewis) G.; m. Irene Johnston Wiseman, June 16, 1951. AB, Yale U., New Haven, Conn., 1943; MS, U. Chgo., 1951, PhD, 1952; DHC (hon.), U. Bordeaux, France, 1967; MA (hon.), Oxford U., Eng., 1976; DHC (hon.), U. Santiago de Compostela, 2002. Registered profl. engr. Rsch. engr. Westinghouse Rsch. Corp., 1951-52; rsch. scientist, group leader Lincoln Lab., MIT, 1952-76; prof., head inorganic chem. lab. U. Oxford, England, 1976-86; Virginia H. Cockrell Centennial Chair and prof. engring. U. Tex., Austin, 1986—. Trustee, fellow Neuroscis. Rsch. Program, 1962-76; Centenary lectr. Royal Soc. Chemistry, 1976; vis. Raman prof. Indian Inst. Sci., 1983; hon. prof. Northwestern U., Changchun, China, 1996, Jilin U., Shenyang, China, 1996; cons. in field Author: Magnetism and the Chemical Bond, 1963, Les Oxydes des métaux de transition, 1973; assoc. editor Materials Rsch. Bull., 1966—, Jour. Solid State Chemistry, 1968—, Structure and Bonding, 1977—, Solid State Ionics, 1980—, Superconductor Sci. and Tech., 1987, Jour. Materials Chem., 1991—, Chem. of Materials, 1989-92; mem. editl. bd. Jour. Applied Electrochemistry, 1982-89, European Jour. Solid State and Inorganic chemistry, 1992; contbr. articles to profl. jours., chpts. to books. Capt. USAAF, 1942-48. Recipient Solid State Chemistry prize Chem. Soc. UK, 1980, Sr. Rsch. award Am.Soc. for Engring. Edn., 1990; professorial fellow St. Catherine's Coll., Oxford U., 1976; recipient medal for disting. achievement U. Pa., 1996, John Bardeen award Minerals, Metals and Materials Soc., 1997, Olin Palladium award Electrochem. Soc., 1999, Japan prize, 2001. Fellow AAAS, Royal Soc. Chemistry, Am. Phys. Soc. (profl.), Indian Acad. Scis. (fgn. assoc.), Nat. Acad. Engring., Acad. Scis. L'Inst. France (fgn. assoc.), Materials Rsch. Soc. (hon.), Acad. Sci. Exactas, Fisicas y Naturales (fgn. assoc.); mem. Am. Chem. Soc., Materials Rsch. Soc. (Von Hippel award 1989), Japanese Phys. Soc., Ashmolean Club (Oxford), Skull and Bones, Phi Beta Kappa, Sigma Xi Episcopalian. Achievements include discovery of cathode materials for lithium rechargable batteries. Office: Mechanical Engineering Dept U Tex ETC 9 184 1 Univ Sta C2200 Austin TX 78712-0292 Office Phone: 512-471-1646. Business E-Mail: jgoodenough@mail.utexas.edu.

GOODENOUGH, OLIVER RAMSDELL, lawyer, educator; b. Phila., Dec. 18, 1952; s. Ward Hunt and Ruth (Gallagher) G.; m. Alison Hudnut Clarkson, Apr. 26, 1955; children: Ward Hunt, William Hudnut Clarkson. BA, Harvard U., 1975; JD, U. Pa., 1978. Bar: Pa. 1978, N.Y. 1980, U.S. Dist. Ct. (so. and ea. dists.) N.Y. 1980. Assoc. Cleary Gottlieb Steen & Hamilton, NYC, 1978-81, Fulop & Hardee, NYC, 1981-82, Kay Collyer & Boose, NYC, 1983-86, ptnr., 1986-90, of counsel, 1991—2003; prof. law Vt. Law Sch., South Royalton, 1991—. Lectr. law U. Pa., Phila., 1988-90; vis. scholar Cambridge U., Eng., 1991, 99-2000; bd. dirs. Vt. Film Commn., Montpelier, 1996-2003; vis. prof. Charité, Humboldt U., Berlin, 2003-06, Dartmouth Coll., NH, 2004-05, adj. prof., 2006-. Author: Privacy and Publicity, 1996; co-author: This Business of Television, 1991, 3d. edit. 2006. Gruter Inst. rsch. fellow, 1994—. Democrat. Episcopalian. Avocation: music. Office: Vt Law Sch Chealsea St South Royalton VT 05068 Home Phone: 802-457-4627; Office Phone: 802-831-1231. Business E-Mail: ogoodenough@vermontlaw.edu.

GOODENOUGH, WARD HUNT, anthropologist, educator; b. Cambridge, Mass., May 30, 1919; s. Erwin Ramsdell and Helen Miriam (Lewis) G.; m. Ruth Gallagher, Feb. 8, 1941, (dec. March 6, 2001); children: Hester G. Goodenough Gelber, Deborah L. Goodenough Gordon, Oliver R., Garrick G. AB, Cornell U., 1940; PhD, Yale U., 1949. Instr. anthropology U. Wis., 1948-49; mem. faculty U. Pa., Phila., 1949—, prof. anthropology, 1962-89, university prof., 1980-89, emeritus univ. prof., 1989—, chmn. dept. anthropology, 1976-82. Vis. prof. Cornell U., Ithaca, N.Y., 1961-62, vis. lectr., summer 1950; vis. lectr. Swarthmore Coll., spring 1955, Bryn Mawr Coll., fall 1955, U. Hawaii, summer 1959, 75-77; vis. prof. U. Wis., Milw., summer 1967, Yale U., New Haven, spring 1969, Colo. Coll., spring 1979, U. Hawaii, 1982-83; anthrop. studies in Truk, 1947, 64-65, Gilbert Islands, 1951, New Guinea, 1951, 54; Pacific Sci. bd. Nat. Acad. Scis.-NRC, 1962-66; standing com. anthropology and social scis. Pacific Sci. Assn., 1962-66; cons. Office Sci. and Tech., 1961-62. Author: Property, Kin and Community on Truk, 1951, Cooperation in Change, 1963, Explorations in Cultural Anthropology, 1964, Description and Comparison in Cultural Anthropology, 1970, Culture, Language and Society, 1971, Trukese-English Dictionary, 1980, 90, Prehistoric Settlement of the Pacific, 1996, Under Heaven's Brow, 2002. Bd. dirs. Human Rels. Area Files, Inc., 1964-86, chmn., 1971-81; bd. dirs. East Rock Inst., 1986-98, sec., 1995-98. With AUS, 1941-45. Fellow Center Advanced Study Behavioral Scis., 1957-58; Guggenheim fellow, 1979-80; Fulbright lectr. St. Patrick's Coll., Ireland, 1987. Mem. NAS, AAAS (v.p., chmn. sect. H 1971, bd. dirs. 1972-75), Am. Philos. Soc., Am. Acad. Arts and Scis., Royal Anthrop. Inst., Am. Anthrop. Assn. (editor 1966-70, Disting. Svc. award 1986), Am. Ethnol. Soc. (pres. 1962), Soc. Applied Anthropology (pres. 1963, Malinowski award 1997), Linguistics Soc. Am., Inst. on Religion in an Age of Sci. (pres. 1987-89), Polynesian Soc., Assn. Social Anthropology in Oceania, Phi Beta Kappa, Sigma Xi, Phi Kappa Phi. Office: Univ Penn Univ Museum Philadelphia PA 19104-6398 Business E-Mail: whgooden@sas.upenn.edu.

GOODENOW, REW R., lawyer; b. Cleve., Sept. 24, 1962; s. Frederick and Margarite (Burgoin) G.; m. Susan Mae Voss, June 8, 1985; children: Sarah, Emily, Allison, Lindsey. BA, Tulane U., 1985; JD, U. Iowa, 1988. Bar: Iowa 1988, U.S. Dist. Ct. (no. dist.) Iowa 1988, Nev. 1989, U.S. Dist. Ct. Nev. 1989, U.S. Ct. Appeals (9th cir.) 1991, U.S. Supreme Ct. 1993. Assoc. Vargas & Bartlett, Reno, 1989-94, Marshall Hill Cassas & de Lipkau, Reno, 1994-95, shareholder, 1995; ptnr. Parsons Behle & Latimer, Reno. Author: Nevada Business Entities, 1997; prin. author Nevada Limited Liability Company Act; contbr. articles to profl. publs; editl. bd. ABA Jour.; editor in chief, Bus. Law Today. Parliamentarian Nev. Rep. Party, Las Vegas, 1994, ctrl. com., 1995, gen. counsel; exec. com. Washoe County Rep. Party, Reno, 1995, first v.p., 1998. Mem. ABA (assembly clk. young lawyers divsn. 1997-98, spkr. 1998), State Bar Nev. (chmn. young lawyers sect. 1991-92, pres. 2006-07); Rotary (pres. Reno) Republican. Presbyterian. Avocations: skiing, golf, hiking. Office: Parsons Behle & Latimer Ste 750 50 Liberty St Reno NV 89501 Office Phone: 775-323-1601. Office Fax: 775-348-7250.

GOODENOW, ROBERT W., lawyer, former sports association administrator; b. Dearborn, Mich., Oct. 29, 1952; BA, Harvard U., Cambridge, Mass., 1974; JD, U. Detroit, 1979. Atty., Detroit; dep. exec. dir. NHL Player's Assn., Toronto, Canada, 1990—92, exec. dir., gen. counsel, 1992—2005.

GOODFELLOW, ROBIN IRENE, surgeon; b. Xenia, Ohio, Apr. 14, 1945; d. Willis Douglas and Irene Linna (Kirkland) G. BA summa cum laude, Western Res. U., Cleve., 1967; MD cum laude, Harvard U., 1971. Diplomate Am. Bd. Surgery. Intern, resident Peter Bent Brigham Hosp., Boston, 1971-76; staff surgeon Boston U., 1976-80, asst. prof. surgery, 1977-80; pvt. practice medicine specializing in surgery Jonesboro, La., 1980-81; practice medicine specializing in surgery Albion, Mich., 1984-87, Coldwater, Mich., 1987—. Bd. Overseers Case Western Res. U., 1977-82. AAUW fellow, 1970. Fellow ACS; mem. AMA, Phi Beta Kappa. Republican. Methodist.

GOODFRIEND, HERBERT JAY, lawyer; b. NYC, Sept. 9, 1926; s. Sidney and Blanche (Prager) G.; m. Barbara Gottlieb, Oct. 12, 1952; children: Sandra, Beth Ann. AB, NYU, 1947, LLB, 1950, LLM in Taxation, 1953. Bar: N.Y. 1950, U.S. Dist. Ct. (so. dist.) N.Y. 1951, U.S. Dist. Ct. (ea. dist.) N.Y. 1952, U.S. Ct. Appeals (2nd cir.) 1953, U.S. Tax Ct. 1954. Assoc. Otterbourg, Steindler Houston & Rosen, NYC, 1950—55, ptnr., 1955—86; counsel Summit, Solomon & Feldesman, 1986-93, NYC, Philips, Nizer, 1993—. Counsel N.Y. Bd. Trade, N.Y.C., 1981-87, bd. dirs., 1982-88; spl. master Supreme Ct. New York County, N.Y.C., 1977-79; vice chmn., bd. dirs. Jones Apparel Group, Inc., 1990-98., sec., 1990-2001. Columnist N.Y. Law Jour., 1977-79, treas. 2001-04. Treas., dir. N.Y.C. Alliance Against Sexual Abuse, 2001—; dir. Cmty. Health Charities N.Y., 2004—. With U.S. Army, 1945-46. Fellow Am. Bar Found., Coll. Law Practice Mgmt.; mem. ABA (chmn. econs. law practice sect. 1984-85, ho. of dels. 1994-97), N.Y. State Bar Assn. (chmn. com. on law office econ. and mgmt. 1983-85), N.Y. County Lawyers Assn. (com. on arbitration 1974-87), NYU Club (v.p. exec. com. 1976-80), Adelphi U. Inst. for Paralegal Tng. (adv. bd. 1976-96), Am. Apparel Mfg. Assn. (fin. mgmt. com. 1980-2001), Tau Delta Phi (nat. pres. 1952-57). Avocations: golf, computers. Home: 176 E 71st St New York NY 10021-5159 Office: Phillips Nizer 666 Fifth Ave New York NY 10103 Home Phone: 212-794-2054; Office Phone: 212-841-0720. Business E-Mail: hgoodfriend@phillipsnizer.com.

GOODHARTZ, GERALD, law librarian; b. NYC, Oct. 23, 1938; s. Jack and Anna (Sperling) G.; m. Carol Scialli, Aug. 18, 1969; children: Joanna, Allison. BSCE, CCNY, 1961; MLS, U. So. Calif., 1970. Night reference asst. Assn. Bar of City of NY, 1956—61; libr. asst. Cravath, Swaine & Moore, NYC, 1961—65; head libr. Rosenman, Colin, Freund, Lewis & Cohen, NYC, 1965—69, Keatinge & Sterling, LA, 1969—70, Kaye, Scholer, Fierman, Hays & Handler, NYC, 1970—98; mgr. info. svcs. Broad and Cassel, Orlando, 1998—99; dir. libr. svcs. Thelen Reid Brown Raysman & Steiner LLP (formerly Brown Raysman Millstein Felder & Steiner LLP), NYC, 1999—, libr., 2007—. Libr. planning cons. Olympic Towers, NYC, 1975; lectr. in field. Mem.: ABA, Mem. ABA, ALA, Am. Assn. Law Librs. (cert.), Law Libr. Assn. Greater NY, Assn. Law Librs. of Upstate NY, Spl. Librs. Assn., Am. Soc. Info. Scientists, Am. Mgmt. Assn., Assn. Info. Mgrs., Nat. Micrographics Assn. Office: Thelen Reid Brown Raysman & Steiner LLP 900 3rd Ave New York NY 10022 Business E-Mail: ggoodhartz@thelen.com.

GOODHEART, EUGENE, literary critic; b. Bklyn., June 26, 1931; s. Samuel and Miriam G.; m. Patricia Somer, Aug. 13, 1960 (div. July 1973); children: Eric, Jessica; m. Joan Bamberger, July 8, 1977. BA, Columbia U., 1953, PhD in English and Comparative Lit., 1961; MA in English, U. Va., 1954; postgrad. (Fulbright fellow), Sorbonne, U. Paris, 1956-57. From instr. to asst. prof. English Bard Coll., 1958-62; asst. prof. U. Chgo., 1962-66; assoc. prof. Mt. Holyoke Coll., 1966-67; from assoc. prof. to prof. MIT, 1967-74; prof., chmn. dept. English Boston U., 1974-83; Edytha Macy Gross prof. emeritus humanities Brandeis U., 1983—2001, emeritus, 2001—. Vis. prof. Wesleyan U. Summer Sch., 1963-64, 66, 69, Columbia U.; Gauss seminarist Princeton U., 1972. Author: The Utopian Vision of D.H. Lawrence, 1963, The Cult of the Ego, 1968, Culture and the Radical Conscience, 1973, The Failure of Criticism, 1978, The Skeptic Disposition in Contemporary Criticism, 1984, Pieces of Resistance, 1987, Desire and Its Discontents, 1991, The Reign of Ideology, 1996, Does Literary Studies Have a Future, 1999, Confessions of a Secular Jew, 2001, Novel Practices: Classic Modern Fiction, 2004. Fellow Am. Coun. Learned Socs., 1965-66, Guggenheim Found., 1970-71, NEH, 1980-81, Nat. Humanities Ctr., 1987—; resident Rockefeller Found., Bellagio. Mem. PEN. Home: 25 Barnard Ave Watertown MA 02472-3412 Office: Brandeis Univ Dept English Waltham MA 02454 Business E-Mail: goodheart@brandeis.edu.

GOODHUE, PETER AMES, obstetrician, gynecologist, educator; b. Ft. Fairfield, Maine, Feb. 26, 1931; s. Lawrence and Zylpha (Ames) G.; m. Edith Ann Helfenstein, June 21, 1958; children: Lisa Grace, Scott Ames. BA, Amherst Coll., 1954; MD, U. Vt., 1958. Diplomate Am. Bd. Ob-Gyn. Intern Bellevue Hosp., NYC, 1958-59; resident Yale-New Haven Med. Ctr., 1959-62; practice medicine specializing in ob-gyn. Stamford, Conn., 1964—. Assoc. clin. prof. ob-gyn. N.Y. Med. Coll., 1984—98; asst. clin. prof. ob-gyn. Columbia Presbyn. Hosp., 1999—2004; mem. Conn. State Maternal Mortality Com., 1971—, chmn., 1981—83. Contbr. articles to profl. jours. Served to capt. USAF, 1962-64. Recipient Carbee prize U. Vt., 1958. Fellow ACOG (chmn. Conn. sect. 1976, pres. Conn. sect. 1973-76), ACS, Am. Fertility Soc., Am. Soc. for Colposcopy and Cervical Pathology, Am. Assn. Gynecologic Laproscopists; mem. Conn. Med. Soc., Conn. Soc. Am. Bd. Obstetricians and Gynecologists (pres. 1973-76), Fairfield County Med. Soc., Fairfield County Gynecol. and Obstet. Soc., Stamford Med. Soc. (pres. 1989-90). Republican. Episcopalian. Office: Stamford Gynecology PC 70 Mill River St Stamford CT 06902-3725 Office Phone: 203-359-3340.

GOODHUE, WILLIAM WALTER, JR., pathologist, military officer, educator; b. St. Louis, Feb. 5, 1945; s. William W. and Rose Marie (Vahousek) Goodhue. BS cum laude, Georgetown U., DC, 1966; MD, Cornell U., Ithaca, NY, 1970. Diplomate Am. Bd. Pathology. Anat. pathology intern N.Y. Hosp.-Cornell Med Ctr., NYC, 1970-71, resident anat. pathology, 1971-74; chief resident pediatric pathology Columbia-Presbyn. Med. Ctr., NYC, 1974-75; resident clin. pathology Tripler Army Med. Ctr., Honolulu, 1976—78, chief pathology grad. med. edn., dir. electron microscopy, 1994—97, asst. chief dept. pathology and area lab. svcs., 1997—2001; first dep. med. examiner, de facto mayoral cabinet mem. City and County of Honolulu, 2001—. Chief dept. pathology U.S. Army Hosp., Ft. Campbell, Ky., 1978—80; chief dept. pathology, med. dir. Sch. Med. Tech., dir. pathology residency tng. Gorgas Army Hosp., Panama; C.Z. and assoc. prof. med. tech. Panama Canal Coll., 1980—82; resident officer U.S. Army Command and Gen. Staff Coll., Ft. Leavenworth, Kans., 1982—83; divsn. surgeon 2d Inf. Divsn., 1983—84; dep. comdr. clin. svcs., chief dept. primary care and cmty. medicine, staff pathologist, acting comdr. Bayne-Jones Army Hosp., Ft. Polk, La., 1984—85; chief dept. pathology and area lab. svcs., dir. pathology residency tng. Dwight David Eisenhower Army Med. Ctr., Ft. Gordon, Ga., 1985—94; clin. assoc. prof. pathology Med. Coll. Ga., Augusta, 1986—94, Sch. Medicine U. Hawaii, Honolulu, 1997—; cons. in pathology Eisenhower Health Svc. Region to Comdg. Gen.; cons. ARC, 1978—80; rep. Alt. Army Med. Dept. Coll. Am. Pathologists Ho. of Dels., Am. Soc. Clin. Pathologist Adv. Coun., 1990—2001; mem. profl. adv. bd. Med. Lab. Observer, 1993—95; Army councillor-at-large Armed Forces Med. Lab. Scientists, 1993—2001; v.p. Land Bd. R.W. Meyer, Ltd. Assoc. editor: Hawaii Med. Jour., 2003—04; contbr. articles to profl. jours. Col. M.C. US Army, 1975—2001. Decorated Order Mil. Med. Merit; recipient Surgeon Gen.'s "A" designator med. splty. excellence, 1997; fellow Rsch., USPHS, 1971—74. Fellow: Coll. Am. Pathologists, Am. Soc. Investigative Pathology, Nat. Assn. Med. Examiners, Am. Soc. Clin. Pathologists (lab. accreditation insp. & accreditation program 1988—), Am. Acad. Forensic Scis.; mem.: AMA (Physicians Recognition award 1976, 1978, 1980, 1982, 1986, 1989, 1992, 1995, 1998, 2001, 2004, 2007), U.S.-Can. Acad. Pathology, Clin. Lab. Mgrs. Assn. (bd. dir. 1989—92), Alliance Française, Assn. U.S. Army, Soc. Armed Forces Med. Lab. Scientists, NY Acad. Sci., Hawaii Soc. Pathologists, Soc. Ultrastructural Pathology, Am. Assn. Blood Banks, Assn. Mil. Surgeons U.S., Med. Assn. Isthmian Canal Zone (v.p. 1980—81), Soc. Pediat. Pathology, Makani Kai Yacht Club, Outrigger Canoe Club, Cornell Club NY. Republican. Roman Catholic. Home: 45-995 Wailele Rd # 52 Kaneohe HI 96744-3041 Office: Dept Med Examiner 835 Iwilei Rd Honolulu HI 96817 Home Phone: 808-247-5607; Office Phone: 808-527-6777. Personal E-mail: wwgjrmd@aol.com. Business E-Mail: wgoodhue@honolulu.gov.

GOODING, CHARLES ARTHUR, radiologist, physician, educator; b. Cleve., Feb. 28, 1936; s. Joseph J. and Florence G. (Pitt) G.; m. Gretchen Wagner, June 19, 1961; children: Gunnar, Justin, Britta. BA, Western Res. U., 1957; MD, Ohio State U., 1961. Intern Ohio State U. Hosp., 1961-62; resident in radiology Peter Bent Brigham Hosp., Children's Hosp. Med. Center, both Boston, 1963-65; rsch. fellow radiology Harvard Med. Sch., Boston, 1962, tchg. fellow, 1965-66; Harvard Med. Sch. fellow Hosp. for Sick Children, London, Karolinska Hosp., Stockholm, 1966; faculty U. Calif. Med. Center, San Francisco, 1967—, prof. radiology and pediatrics, 1976—, exec. vice-chmn. dept. radiology, 1974—2001. Pres. Radiology Rsch. and Edn. Found., 1973-96, Radiology Outreach Found., 1988-2002, pres. emeritus 2002—; hon. mem. faculty Francesco Maroquin U. Sch. Medicine, Guatemala City. Contbr. chpts. to books.; Editor: Pediatric Radiology, 1973—96; editor: Diagnostic Radiology, 1972-92; contbr.

articles to profl. jours. Capt. M.C. USAR, 1967-68. Recipient Outstanding Alumni award Brigham Women's Hosp. Harvard Med. Sch., 1994, Disting. Alumnus award Ohio State U., 1986, Case Western Res. U., 1999, Beclere medal Internat. Soc. Radiology, 1998; named to Disting. Alumni Hall of Fame Cleve. Heights H.S., 1999, Top Pediat. Radiologist San Francisco mag., 2001. Fellow Am. Coll. Radiology, Royal Coll. Radiologists London (hon.), Armenian Radiol. Soc. (hon.); mem. Am. Roentgen Ray Soc., Assn. Univ. Radiologists, European Soc. Pediat. Radiologists (hon.), Pacific Coast Pediat. Radiologists Assn. (past pres.), Radiol. Soc. N.Am., Polish Radiology Soc. (hon.), Hungarian Radiology Soc. (hon.), San Francisco Med. Soc., Soc. Pediat. Radiology (v.p. 1994, pres. 1997 pres. SPR rsch. and edn. found. 1993-96, chmn., bd. dirs. 1998), Rocky Mountain Mountain Radiol. Soc. (hon.), Australian Soc. for Pediatric Imaging (hon.), Chinese Radiol. Soc. (hon.), Swiss Radiol. Soc. (hon.), Malaysian Radiol. Soc. (hon.), Vietnamese Radiol. Soc. (hon.), Thailand Radiology Soc. (hon.), French Soc. Radiology (hon.), Indian Radiol. and Imaging Soc. (hon.), Radiol. Soc. Pakistan (hon.), Indonesian Radiol. Soc. (hon.), Mongolian Nat. Radiol. Assn. (hon.), Nepal Radiol. Soc. (hon.), Armenian Med. Diagnostic Assn. (hon.), Brazilian Coll. Radiology (hon.), Cuban Radiol. Soc. (hon.), Indonesian Pediatric Radiol. Soc. (hon.), Asian and Oceanean Radiol. Soc. (gold medal 2004). Office: U Calif Med Ctr Dept Radiology San Francisco CA 94143-0628 E-mail: charles.gooding@radiology.ucsf.edu.

GOODING, CHARLES THOMAS, psychologist, educator, retired academic administrator; b. Tampa, Fla., Nov. 18, 1931; s. Charles T. and Gladys (Bingman) G.; m. Shirley Ann Puckett, June 7, 1953; children: Steven Thomas, Carol Ann, David Lee, Mark Charles. BA, U. Fla., 1954, M.Ed., 1962, Ed.D., 1964; postgrad., U. Tampa, 1956-58. Tchr. Meml. Sch., Tampa, 1956-58; asst. prin., then prin. St. Mary's Sch., Tampa, 1958-62; grad. fellow U. Fla., Gainesville, 1962-63, instr., 1963-64; assoc. prof., then prof. SUNY, Oswego, 1964-79, prof. psychology, 1980-98, assoc. dean grad. studies, 1982-89, dean grad. studies and rsch., 1989-95, provost, v.p. for acad. affairs, 1995-98, emeritus, 1998—. Vis. prof. U. Liverpool, Eng., 1979-80; mem. SUNY Chancellor's Task Force on Tchr. Edn., 1984. Author: Learning Theories in Educational Practice, 1971; contbg. author: Florida Studies in the Helping Professions, 1969, Questioning and Discussion: A Multidisciplinary Study, 1988, Research Matters to the Science Teacher, 1992; contbr. articles to profl. jours. Trustee U. of South, 2002-05; bd. dirs. Oswego Coll. Found., 1996—. Served to 1st lt. USAR, 1954-56. SUNY Rsch. Found. grantee, 1966, 69-70, NY State Dept. Edn. grantee, 1971-72, 88-94, NSF grantee, 1980-81, 85-88, 90-95. Mem. APA, Ea. Ednl. Rsch. Assn. (v.p. 1979-81, treas., dir. 1983-85, pres.-elect 1987-88, pres. 1989-91, editl. bd. 1991-2000), Am. Ednl. Rsch. Assn. (chair ednl. enterprises SIG, 1994-96). Avocations: antique and classic automobiles, Jaguar sports cars specialist. Home: 603 Wild Pine Way Venice FL 34292-4618 E-mail: tgooding@comcast.net.

GOODING, CUBA, JR., actor; b. Bronx, NY, Jan. 2, 1968; s. Cuba, Sr. and Shirley Gooding; m. Sara (Kapfer) Gooding, Mar. 13, 1994; children: Spencer, Mason, Piper. Films include: Coming to America, 1988, Sing, 1989, Boyz N the Hood, 1991, Gladiator, 1992, A Few Good Men, 1992, Hitz, 1992, Judgement Night, 1993, Lightning Jack, 1994, Losing Isaiah, 1995, Outbreak, 1995, Jerry Maguire, 1996 (Golden Globe nomination, Academy award for Best Supporting Actor, 1997), The Audition, 1996, As Good As It Gets, 1997, What Dreams May Come, 1998, A Murder of Crows, 1999, Instinct, 1999, Menof Honor, 2000 (NAACP Image award nominee), Pearl Harbor, 2001, Rat Race, 2001, In the Shadows, 2001, Snow Dogs, 2002, Boat Trip, 2002, Psychic, 2003, The Fighting Temptations, 2003, Radio, 2003, Home on the Range (voice), 2004, Lightfield's Home Videos, 2005, Shadowboxer, 2005, Dirty, 2005, End Game, 2006, Norbit, 2007; TV movies include: Kill or Be Killed, 1990, Murder with Motive: The Edmund Perry Story, 1992, Daybreak, 1993, Tuskegee Airmen, 1995 (NAACP Image award nominee); (TV appearances) MacGyver, Hill Street Blues, The Untouchables. Office: Endeavor Talent Agy 9701 Wilshire Blvd Fl 10 Beverly Hills CA 90210 also: Rogers Cowan 8687 Melrose Ave Ste G700 West Hollywood CA 90069-5721*

GOODING, DAVID MICHAEL, judge; b. Jacksonville, Fla., June 10, 1952; s. Marion William and Eunice (Drawdy) Gooding; m. Cathy Rhoden, Aug. 3, 1974; children: Sara Lynn, John Thomas. BA, U. Fla., 1974; JD, U. Miami, 1988. Bar: Fla. 1988, U.S. Dist. Ct. (mid. dist.) Fla. 1988. Asst. state atty. Office of State Atty., Jacksonville, Fla., 1988—89; assoc. Penland & Penland, P.A., Jacksonville, 1989—92; shareholder Kent, Ridge & Crawford, Jacksonville, 1992—97, Kent, Crawford & Gooding, Jacksonville, 1997—2002; circuit ct. judge Jacksonville, 2003—. Adult tchr. Christ Ch., 1994—96, nursery vol., 1991—94; elder South Jacksonville Presbyn. Ch., 1991—94; adult tchr. Southside Bapt. Ch., 2002—; bd. dirs. Samaritan Counseling Ctr., Jacksonville, 1990—94, Girls, Inc., Jacksonville, 1997—2001, pres., 1999—2000, endowment trustee, 2000—02; bd. dirs. Southside United Meth. Presch., Jacksonville, 1995—97, Luth. Social Svcs., Jacksonville, 2001—, Family Farm of N.E. Fla., Jacksonville, 2001—, First Coast Christian Outreach, 2002—. Mem.: ABA, Jacksonville Bar Assn., Christian Legal Soc. (trustee 1997—2000), Fla. Bar, York Rite, Shriners (1998 imperial conv. com. 1997—98), Royal Order of Jesters, Scottish Rite, Masons. Bap. Office: Duval County Courthouse 330 E Bay St Rm 107 Jacksonville FL 32202 E-mail: dgooding@coj.net.

GOODING, GRETCHEN ANN WAGNER, physician, educator; b. Columbus, Ohio, July 2, 1935; d. Edward Frederick and Margaret (List) Wagner; m. Charles A. Gooding, June 19, 1961; children: Gunnar Blaise, Justin Mathias, Britta Meghan. BA magna cum laude, Ohio Dominican U., 1957; MD cum laude, Ohio State U., 1961. Diplomate Am. Bd. Diagnostic Radiology. Intern Univ. Hosps., Columbus, 1961-62; rsch. fellow Boston City Hosp., 1962-63, Boston U., 1963-65; with dept. radiology U. Calif., San Francisco, 1975—, assoc. prof. in radiology, 1981-85, prof., vice chmn., 1986—2003; asst. chief radiology VA Med. Ctr., San Francisco, 1978-87, chief radiology, 1987—2003, chief ultrasonography, 1975—. Chair com. acad. pers. U. Calif., San Francisco, 1993-94, bd. dirs. commn. accreditation vascular labs., 1993-96. Co-editor Radiologic Clinics of N.Am., 1993—; mem. editl. bd. San Francisco Medicine, 1986—, Applied Radiology, 1987-89, Current Opinion in Radiology, 1992-93, The Radiologist, 1993—, Emergency Radiology, 1993-2003, Jour. Clin. Ultrasound, 1997—; guest editor Emergency Radiology, 1999; contbr. articles to profl. jours. Recipient Recognition award Inter Societal Commn. for Accreditation of Vascular Labs., 1997, Disting. Alumna award, Ohio State U. Coll. Medicine and Pub. Health, 2001, Alice Ettinger Disting. Achievement award, 2003; named Reviewer Extraordinaire, Jour. Ultrasound in Medicine, 2006. Fellow Am. Coll. Radiology (mem. commn. on ultrasound 1984-2000, chair stds. com. commn. on ultrasound 2004—, chmn. com. practice guidelines and tech. standards 2004—), Am. Inst. Ultrasound in Medicine (bd. govs. 1981-84, chair conv. program 1986-88, Presdl. Recognition award 1984), Am. Soc. Emergency Radiology, Soc. Radiologists U.S.; mem. AMA, San Francisco Med. Soc. (chmn. membership com. 1992-94, bd. dirs. 1996—), RSNA (course com. 1984-88, tech. exhibit com. 1992-96, mem. site med. advisor 2005-06), Bay Area Ultrasound Soc. (pres. 1979-80), Soc. Radiologists Ultrasound (chair membership com. 1991-93, chair corp. com. 1996-97), ARRS, AUR, CRS, Calif. Med. Assn., Am. Assn. Women Radiologists (pres. 1984-85, trustee 1991-94, Alice Ettinger Disting. Achievement award 2003), VA Chiefs of Radiology Assn. (pres.-elect, pres. 1994-95), San Francisco Radiol. Soc. (pres. 1990-91), Hungarian Radiol. Soc. (hon.), Pakistan Radiol. Soc. (hon.), Cuba Radiol. Soc. (hon.). Office: Dept Veteran Affairs Med Ctr Radiology Svc 4150 Clement St San Francisco CA 94121-1545 Home Phone: 415-388-0536.

GOODISH, JOHN H., metal products executive; BSBA, Waynesburg Coll., Pa., 1970. Acctg. mgmt. trainee US Steel, Pitts., 1970—71, jr. auditor, 1971—73, supr. billing Irvin Plant, 1973, various acctg. positions Irvin Plant, 1973—77, with acctg. dept. Homestead Works, 1977—82, gen. supr. line acctg. Clairton Works, 1982, various acctg. and fin. positions, 1982—84, acctg. mgr. mill analysis Gary Works, 1984—87, divsn. mgr. coke and chems., 1987—89, mgr. ops. svcs. Gary Works, 1989, divsn. mgr. 84-inch hot strip mill Gary Works, 1989—90, gen. mgr. Mon Valley Works, 1990—94, gen. mgr. Gary Works, 1994—96, pres. US Steel Kosice, s.r.o., 2000—03, exec. v.p. internat. and diversified businesses, 2003, exec. v.p. ops., 2003—05, exec. v.p., COO, 2005—; pres. USX Engrs. and Consultants, Inc. (now UEC Techs. LLC), 1996—2000. Office: US Steel 600 Grant St Pittsburgh PA 15219-2800 Office Phone: 412-433-1121.*

GOODKIN, MICHAEL JON, publishing company executive; b. NYC, June 10, 1941; s. Harold and Rose (Mostkoff) G.; m. Helen Graham Fairbank, Oct. 1, 1971; children: Graham Laird, Nathalie Fairbank Emami. BA, Harvard U., 1963; postgrad., U. Chgo., 1964. Trainee Random House, NYC, 1964-65; asst. dir. Simulmatics, NYC, 1966-67; account exec. World Book Ency., Inc., Chgo., 1967-70, rsch. dir., 1970-73, v.p. mktg., 1973-76, v.p., gen. mgr. mail order div., 1976-78, pres., chief operating officer, 1978-86, chmn., chief exec. officer, pres., dir., 1983; exec. v.p. World Book Inc., 1978-84, pres., 1984-86, sr. v.p., 1979-80; exec. v.p., corp. dir. mktg., dir. World Book Internat. Inc., 1983-84; dep. dir. World Book Pty. Ltd., Australia, 1983-86; pres. World Book Life Ins. Co., 1983; prin. Chgo. City Capital Group, 1987-91; chmn. Med. Holdings, Inc., Chgo., 1987-91; sr. v.p. mktg. internat. P.F. Collier, NYC, 1992—94, pres., 1994—96; dir. KT holdings, 1996—99; mng. mem. Arlington Haven Partners LLC, 2000—. Bd. dirs. Chgo. Area Project; pres. aux. bd. Art Inst. Chgo., 1975-77, trustee, 1974-99; trustee Modern Poetry Assn., Latin Sch. Chgo., 1983-92, chmn. ednl. policy com., pres., 1990-92, mem. long range com., chmn. mktg. com., 1979-99; trustee DMA Edn. Found., 1983-94, mem. exec. com., 1988-94; mem. vis. com. visual arts U. Chgo., 1990-2002. With Army N.G., 1963-69. Mem. Direct Mktg. Assn. (internat. coun. steering com. 1983), Direct Selling Assn. (internat. com. 1982-86), Racquet Club, Harvard Club (N.Y.C.), Harvard Club (Boston). Business E-Mail: hmgoodkin@worldnet.alt.net.

GOODKIN, ROBERT, neurosurgeon, educator; Diploma, Coll. William and Mary, 1958, NYU, 1960; MD, Chgo. Med. Sch., 1964. Diplomate Nat. Bd. Med. Examiners, 1965, Am. Bd. Neurol. Surgeons, 1973. Intern Bellevue Hosp. Ctr. NYU, NYC, 1964—65, resident in neurology Bellevue Hosp. Ctr., 1965—66, resident in neurol. surgery Bellevue Hosp. Ctr., 1966—71; attending staff Barrow Neurol. Inst., Phoenix, 1971—76; adj. assoc. prof. divsn. neurol. surgery U. Fla., Gainesville, 1976—78; assoc. prof. and chief divsn. neurol. surgery Jacksonville (Fla.) Hosps. Ednl. Program, U. Fla., 1976—78; chief dept. neurol. surgery U. Hosp. Jacksonville, 1976—78; pvt. practice neurosurgery Hollywood, Fla., 1978—81; clin. assoc. prof. dept. neurol. surgery U. Miami, Fla., 1978—82; clin. prof. dept. neurol. surgery U. So. Calif., LA, 1981—2000; dir. dept. neurol. surgery City of Hope Nat. Med. Ctr., Duarte, Calif., 1981—86; assoc. prof. neurol. surgery U. Wash. Med. Sch., Seattle, 1987—2003; chief neurosurgery Madigan Army Med. Ctr., Tacoma, 1987—89; chief neurosurgery sect. VA Puget Sound Health Care Sys., Seattle, 1989—2003; prof. neurol. surgery U. Wash. Med. Sch., Seattle, 2003—. Faculty U. Wash. Med. Sch., Seattle, 1987—; mem. neurosurg. cons. com. surg. svc. VA Ctrl. Office-Hdqrs., Washington, 2000—05, chmn., 2000—03; co-dir. gamma knife radiosurgery ctr. Harborview Med. Ctr., 2004—. Mem. editl. bd.: Surg. Neurology, 2004—. Mem.: Soc. for Neuro-Oncology, Internat. Spinal Cord Soc., Movement Disorder Soc., N.Am. Skull Base Soc., Am. Assn. Stereotactic and Functional Neurosurgery, N.Y. Acad. Scis., Congress Neurol. Surgeons, Neurosurg. Soc. Am. (pres. 1997—98), Am. Paraplegic Soc., World Soc. Stereotactic and Functional Neurosurgery, Am. Assn. Neurol. Surgeons. Office: UWMC-Harborview Medical Center Box 359766 325 9th Ave Seattle WA 98104 Home Phone: 206-364-5088; Office Phone: 206-744-9300.

GOODKIND, CONRAD GEORGE, lawyer; b. Arlington, Va., Aug. 8, 1944; s. Bernard Arthur and Sylvia (Lieber) G.; m. Sandra Timme, Aug. 27, 1966; children: Carley M., Adam B., Erica L., Anne G. BS, U. Wis., 1966, JD, 1969. Bar: Wis. 1969, U.S. Dist. Ct. (ea. and we. dists.) Wis. 1969. Assoc. Kivett & Kasdorf, Milw., 1969-71; counsel Citizens' Study Com. on Jud. Orgn., Madison, Wis., 1971-73; dep. commr. securities State of Wis., Madison, 1973-79; assoc. Quarles & Brady, Milw., 1979-81, ptnr., 1981—, mem. exec. com., 1983—2005. Adj. prof. securities law U. Wis. Law Sch., Madison, 1974-77, Marquette U. Law Sch., Milw., 1981-83; mem. Gov.'s Bus. Cts. Task Force, 1994-98, state regulation com. Nat. Assn. Securities Dealers, Inc., Washington, 1986-92; bd. dirs. Able Distbg. Corp., 1995-2005; bd. dirs., sec. Cade Industries, Inc., 1989-99; sec. Brady Corp., 1999—. Bd. dirs. Milw. Repertory Theatre, 1995-2001, exec. com. mem., 1997-2001; bd. curators Wis. Hist. Soc., 2006-. Mem. ABA (vice chmn. state regulation securities com. 1986-89, chmn. 1989-92, vice chmn. bus. law sect. com. on insts. and seminars 2001-2003, chmn. 2003-2006, coun. mem. sect. bus. law 2006—, standing com. mem. continuing legal edn. 2006—), Wis. Bar Assn. (chmn. securities com. 1981-95, bd. dirs. sect. bus. law 1991-2001, vice chair sect. bus. law 1996-98, chair 1998-2000). Office: Quarles & Brady LLP 411 E Wisconsin Ave Ste 2550 Milwaukee WI 53202-4497 Office Phone: 414-277-5305. Business E-Mail: cgg@quarles.com.

GOODLAD, JOHN INKSTER, education educator, writer; b. North Vancouver, BC, Can., 1920; s. William James and Mary Goodlad; m. Evalene M. Pearson, 1945; children: Stephen John, Mary Paula. BA, U. B.C., 1945, MA, 1946; PhD, U. Chgo., 1949; DPS (hon.), Brigham Young U., 1995; LHD (hon.), Nat. Coll. Edn., 1967, U. Louisville, 1968, So. Ill. U., 1982, Bank Street Coll. Edn., 1984, Niagara U., 1989, SUNY Coll. Brockport, 1991, Miami U., 1991, Linfield Coll., 1993, W.Va. U., 1998; LLD (hon.), Kent State U., 1974, Pepperdine U., 1976, Simon Fraser U., 1983, U. Man., 1992; DEd (hon.), Eastern Mich. U., 1982, U. Victoria, 1998; LittD (hon.), Montclair State U., 1992; PedD (hon.), Doane Coll., 1995; LHD (hon.), U. Nebr., Lincoln, 1999, U. So. Maine, 2001. Cert. tchr. Vancouver Normal Sch., 1939. Tchr. Surrey Schs., B.C., 1939-41, prin., 1941-42; dir. edn. Provincial Sch. For Boys, B.C., 1942-46; cons. curriculum Atlanta Area Tchr. Edn. Service, 1947-49; assoc. prof. Emory U., 1949-50; prof., dir. div. tchr. edn. Agnes Scott Coll. and Emory U., 1950-56; prof., dir. U. Chgo. Center Tchr. Edn., 1956-60; prof., dir. Univ. Elem. Sch. UCLA, 1960-85, dean Grad. Sch. Edn., 1967-83; prof. U. Wash., Seattle, 1985-91; prof. emeritus, 1991—; dir. Ctr. for Ednl. Renewal U. Wash., Seattle, 1986-2000; pres. Inst. for Ednl. Inquiry, Seattle, 1992—. Chmn. Coun. on Coop. Tchr. Edn., Am. Coun. Edn., 1959-62; dir. rsch. Inst. for Devel. of Ednl. Activities, 1966-82; mem. governing bd. UNESCO Inst. for Edn., 1971-79. Author: (with others) The Elementary School, 1956, Educational Leadership and the Elementary School Principal, 1956, (with Robert H. Anderson) The Nongraded Elementary School, 1959, rev. edit., 1963, reprinted, 1987, (with others) Computers and Information Systems in Education, 1966, Looking Behind the Classroom Door, 1970, rev. edit., 1974, Toward a Mankind School, 1974, The Conventional and the Alternative in Education, 1975, Curriculum Inquiry: The Study of Curriculum Practice, 1979, Planning and Organizing for Teaching, 1963, School Curriculum Reform, 1964, The Changing School Curriculum, 1966, School, Curriculum and the Individual, 1966, The Dynamics of Educational Change, 1975, Facing the Future, 1976, What Schools Are For, 1979, A Place Called School, 1983, 2004, Teachers for Our Nation's Schools, 1990, Educational Renewal: Better Teachers, Better Schools, 1994, In Praise of Education, 1997, (with others) Education for Everyone: Agenda for Education in a Democracy, 2004, Romances with Schools: A Life of Education, 2004; author, editor: The Changing American School, 1966, (with Harold S. Shane) The Elementary School in the United States, 1973, (with M. Frances Klein and Jerrold M. Novotney) Early Schooling in the United States, 1973, (with Norma Feshback and Alvima Lombard) Early Schooling in England and Israel, 1973, (with Gary Fenstermacher) Individual Differences and the Common Curriculum, 1983, The Ecology of School Renewal, 1987, (with Kenneth A. Sirotnik) School-University Partnerships in Action, 1988, (with Pamela Keating) Access to Knowledge, 1990, (with others) The Moral Dimensions of Teaching, 1990, Places Where Teachers Are Taught, 1990, (with Thomas C. Lovitt) Integrating General and Special Education, 1992, (with Timothy J. McMannon) The Public Purpose of Education and Schooling, 1997, (with others) Developing Democratic Character in the Young, 2001, (with Timothy J. McMannon) The Teaching Career, 2004; mem. bd. editors Sch. Rev, 1956-58, Jour. Tchr. Edn, 1958-60; contbg. editor: Progressive Edn, 1955-58; mem. editorial adv. bd. Child's World, 1952-80; chmn. editorial adv. bd. New Standard Ency, 1953-; chmn. ednl. adv. bd. Ency. Brit. Ednl. Corp, 1966-69; contbr. chpts. to books, articles to profl. jours. Recipient Disting. Svc. medal Tchrs. Coll., Columbia U., 1983, Outstanding Book award Am. Ednl. Rsch. Assn., 1985, Disting. Contbns. to Ednl. Rsch. award 1993; named Faculty Rsch. Lectr. U. Wash., 1987-88, faculty of High Distinction, UCLA, 1987, Edward C. Pomeroy award, Am. Assn. Coll. Tchr. Edn., 1995, Disting. Svc. award Coun. Chief State Sch. Officials, 1997, Harold W. McGraw, Jr. Prize in Edn., 1999, Edn. Commn. State James Bryant Conant award, 2000, Brock Internat. prize in edn., 2002, NY Acad. Edn. medal, 2003, Am. Edn. award Am. Assn. Sch. Adminstrs., 2004, Disting. Educator award Assn. Tchr. Educators, 2005. Fellow Internat. Inst. Arts and Letters; mem. Nat. Acad. Edn. (charter; sec.-treas.), Am. Ednl. Rsch. Assn. (past pres., award for Disting. Contbns. to Ednl. Rsch. 1993), Nat. Soc. Coll. Tchrs. Edn. (past pres.), Nat. Soc. for Study of Edn. (dir.), Am. Assn. Colls. for Tchr. Edn. (pres. 1989-90). Office: Inst for Ednl Inquiry 124 E Edgar St Seattle WA 98102

GOODLATTE, BOB (ROBERT WILLIAM), congressman, lawyer; b. Holyoke, Mass., Sept. 22, 1952; m. Maryellen Flaherty; children: Jennifer, Robert. BA in Govt., Bates Coll., Lewiston, Maine, 1974; JD, Washington & Lee U. Sch. Law, 1977. Bar: Mass. 1977, Va. 1978, US Ct. Appeals (4th cir.) 1981. Dist. mgr. Staff of US Rep. M. Caldwell Butler, Washington, 1977—79; lawyer pvt. practice, Roanoke, Va., 1979—81; ptnr. Bird, Kinder & Huffman, Roanoke, 1981—93; mem. US Congress from 6th Va. dist., 1993—, co-chair Congl. Internet Caucus, chair Rep. High Tech Working Group, mem. judiciary com.; internet and intellectual property subcom. US Congress from 6th Va. Dist.; ranking rep. mem. agr. com. US Congress from 6th Va. dist., 2003—06. Mem. bldg. better bds. adv. com. United Way of Roanoke Valley, Roanoke, 1988-92; chmn. Roanoke City Rep. Com., 1980-83, 6th Congl. Dist. Rep. Com., Va., 1983-88. Mem. Civitan (pres. Roanoke chpt. 1989-90). Republican. Avocations: tennis, swimming, hiking, reading. Office: US Hep Reps 2240 Rayburn Ho Office Bldg Washington DC 20515-4606 Office Phone: 202-225-5431.

GOODLING, MONICA MARIA, former federal official; b. Aug. 6, 1973; BA in Comm., Messiah Coll., 1995; student, Am. U. Wash. Coll. Law, 1995—96; JD in Law & Pub. Polcy, Regent U. Law Sch., 1999. Opposition rschr. RNC, 2000; joined US Dept. Justice, 2000, dep. dir. Office Pub. Affairs., 2002—05; with Exec. Office US Attorneys, US Dept. Justice, 2005—06; sr. counsel to atty. gen. US Dept. Justice, 2006—07. Republican.*

GOODMAN, ALFRED NELSON, lawyer; b. Jan. 21, 1945; s. Bernard R. and Mildred (Schlanger) Goodman. BS in Mech. and Aerospace Scis., U. Rochester, 1966; JD, Georgetown U., 1969. Bar: N.Y. 1970, D.C. 1971, U.S. Supreme Ct. 1974. Patent examiner U.S. Patent Office, Washington, 1969—71; assoc. Roylance, Abrams, Berdo & Goodman, LLP, Washington, 1971—74, ptnr., 1975—. Mem.: ABA, Bar Assn. D.C. (chmn. patent, trademark and copyright law sect. 1984—85, bd. dir. 1985—86), Am. Patent Law Assn. Home: 4948 Sentinel Dr Bethesda MD 20816-3556 Office: Roylance Abrams Berdo & Goodman LLP 1300 19th St NW Ste 600 Washington DC 20036-1649 Home Phone: 301-229-5774; Office Phone: 202-659-9076. Business E-Mail: agoodman@roylance.com.

GOODMAN, ALLEGRA, writer; b. Bklyn., 1967; married. BA magna cum laude, Harvard Univ., 1989; PhD in English, Stanford Univ., 1996. Author: (short stories) (collection) Total Immersion, 1989, The Family Markowitz, 1996 (NY Times Notable Book Yr., fiction winner First Annual Salon Book awards), (novels) Kaaterskill Falls, 1998, Paradise Park, 2001, Intuition, 2006; contbr. articles New Yorker, Good Housekeeping, Slate, Am. Scholar. Named one of 20 Best Writers under 40, New Yorker Mag.; recipient Whiting award. Mailing: Author Mail Bantam Dell Publ 1745 Broadway New York NY 10019

GOODMAN, ALLEN CHARLES, economist, educator; b. Cleve., Oct. 28, 1947; s. Nathan and Pearl (Dorfman) Goodman; m. Janet Hankin, July 22, 1984; 1 child, Sara. AB, U. Mich., 1969; PhD, Yale U., 1976. Asst. prof. Lawrence U., Appleton, Wis., 1975-78; rsch. scientist Johns Hopkins U., Balt., 1978-86; economist HUD, Washington, 1985-86; assoc. prof. Wayne State U., Detroit, 1986-88, prof. econs., 1988—, chmn. dept., 1988-96. Author: Changing Downtown, 1987, Economics of Housing Markets, 1989, Economics of Health and Health Care, 5th edit., 2006. Mem. Mayor's Coord. Coun. Criminal Justice, Balt., 1984—86. Fellow, Homer Hoyt Advanced Studies Inst., 2002—. Mem.: Internat. Health Econs. Assn., Am. Real Estate and Urban Econs. Assn., Am. Econs. Assn. Office: Wayne State U Dept Econs Detroit MI 48202 Business E-Mail: allen.goodman@wayne.edu.

GOODMAN, ALVIN IRWIN, internist, nephrologist, educator; b. NYC, July 12, 1929; s. Morris and Fanny (Rifkin) G.; m. Suzanna Elizabeth Gebhard; children: Nadine, Derek, Danielle, Leslie, Reva. BA, NYU, 1949; MD, U. Geneva, 1955. Diplomate Am. Bd. Internal Medicine, Am. Bd. Nephrology. Intern Jewish Hosp. Bklyn., 1956, resident in medicine, 1957—58; fellow in medicine Yale U. Sch. Medicine, New Haven, 1960—62, resident in medicine, 1962—63; dir. nephrology and renal ctr. Westchester County Med. Ctr., Valhalla, 1963—2000; prof. medicine, dir. nephrology N.Y. Med. Coll., Valhalla, 1975—2000, prof. med., 1963—2005, prof. med. emeritus, 2005. Dir. endstage renal disease program Bur. Quality Assurance, USPHS, Rockville, Md., 1974-75. Contbr. numerous articles to medl jours. Capt. M.C., U.S. Army, 1958-60. Recipient President's award Nat. Kidney Found., 1977, Cardinal Cook award N.Y. Med. Coll., 1986, Disting. Svc. award N.Y. Med. Coll., 2002. Fellow ACP; mem. Am. Soc. Nephrology, Internat. Soc. Nephrology, Am. Soc. Transplant Physicians, N.Y. Soc. Nephrology (pres. 1980-81), Beta Lambda Sigma. Avocation: travel. Office: Westchester Med Ctr NY Med Coll Valhalla NY 10595 Office Phone: 914-493-7703. Personal E-mail: dralvingoodman@aol.com.

GOODMAN, BARRY JOEL, lawyer; b. NYC, May 28, 1953; s. Walter Louis and Shirley (Lenzer) G.; m. Nicole Goodman; children: Aaron, Rebecca, Noah, Jacob BA, Bradley U., 1974; JD with honors, Stetson U., 1977. Bar: Fla. 1977, US Ct. Appeals 1978, Mich. 1979, US Dist. Ct. (we. dist.) Fla., US Dist. Ct. (ea. dist.) Mich. With Diecidue, Ferlita & Prieto, Tampa, Fla., 1977-78; assoc. Provizer, Eisenberg et al, Southfield, Mich., 1979-82, Thurswell, Chayet & Weiner, Southfield, 1982-87, ptnr., 1987-93; owner Gordon, Goodman & Acker, Southfield, 1993-98, Goodman Acker, Southfield, 1998—. Lectr. Inst. Continuing Legal Edn., Ann Arbor, Mich., Mich. Trial Lawyer's Assn., State Bar of Mich. Officer-at-large Mich. Dem. Party; v.p. Anti-Defamation League, 1983—; bd. dirs. B'nai B'rith Youth Orgn., Mich., 1995—97, West Bloomfield Woods Homeowners Assn.,

Mich., 1980—83. Mem.: State Bar of Mich. (chair negligence sect.), Oakland County Trial Lawyers Assn., Oakland County Bar Assn., Mich. Trial Lawyers Assn. (bd. dirs. 1985—, treas. 1995, sec. 1996, v.p. 1997, pres.-elect 1998, pres. 1999—2000), Am. Assn. Justice. Democrat. Jewish. Avocations: tennis, golf, reading, theater. Office: Goodman Acker PC 17000 W 10 Mile Rd 2nd flr Southfield MI 48075-2945 Office Phone: 248-483-5000. Business E-Mail: bgoodman@goodmanacker.com.

GOODMAN, BARRY MICHAEL, lawyer; b. LA, Nov. 22, 1946; s. Ralph Arthur and Natalie Bell (Hamburger) G.; BA in History, Calif. State U., 1967; JD, U. So. Calif., 1970; m. Susan Lynn Reigrod, June 18, 1969; children: Gregory, Alison. Bar: Calif. 1971, DC 1972. Sr. atty. Office of Chief Counsel, Urban Mass Transp. Adminstrn., Washington, 1971-74; dir. Office Pub. Transp., City of Houston, 1974-78; exec. dir. Met. Transit Authority, Houston, 1978-79; pres. Goodman Corp., Houston, 1979—. Mem. ABA, Calif. Bar Assn., DC Bar Assn., Urban Land Inst., Transp. Research Bd. Jewish. Office: Goodman Corp 3200 TravisSt Ste 200 Houston TX 77006 Home Phone: 713-467-3333; Office Phone: 713-951-7951. E-mail: Barry@thegoodmancorp.com.

GOODMAN, BARRY S., lawyer; b. Jersey City, June 7, 1951; s. Milton and Margaret Goodman; m. Emily J. Reynolds G., Dec. 5, 1982. BA cum laude, Rutgers U., Newark, 1973, JD, 1977. Bar: NJ, US Dist. Ct. NJ, US Ct. Appeals (3rd cir.), US Supreme Ct. Jud. law clk. hon. Eugene L. Lora Superior Ct. NJ Appellate Divsn., Hackensack, 1977—78; atty. Essex-Newark Legal Svcs., Orange, NJ, 1978—79, Crummy, Del Deo, Dolan & Purcell, Newark, 1979—84, Greenbaum, Rowe, Smith & Davis LLP, Woodbridge, NJ, 1984—. Author: (manual) New Jersey Students' Rights, 1977; mem. editl. bd. Rutgers Law Rev., 1976-77; contbr. articles to profl. jours. Vol. atty. Essex-Newark Legal Svcs, 1979—81; mem. Kinoy Fellowship Adv. Com., Newark, 1991—96; mem. 20th reunion conf. com. Rutgers Constnl. Litigation Clinic, Newark, 1991; mem. funds allocation com. United Way Hunterdon County, Clinton, NJ, 1995—, agy. admissions com., 1996, trustee, 1997—2004, treas., 1998—99, exec. com., 1998—2001, spl. gifts com., 1998—2004, cmty. rels. com., 1998—2004, v.p., 1999—2001, pres., 2001—03; mem. Hunterdon County Health and Human Svcs. Adv. Coun., Flemington, 1998—2000; trustee Hunterdon Health Care Sys., 2003—, IOLTA Fund/Bar Assn. NJ, 2003—, treas., 2004—06, chair, 2007; trustee Hunterdon Med. Ctr., 2003—, chair, needs com., 2004—, mem. quality ctrl. com., 2005—, mem. campaign com., 2007—; trustee Hunterdon Regional Cmty. Health, 2003—; co-chair Hunterdon County Dems. for Clinton Com., Flemington, NJ, 1992; mem. Hunterdon County Dem. Com., Flemington, 1994—, mem. exec. com., 1996—2000, 2002—. Mem. ABA (litigation sect., antitrust sect.), Fed. Bar Assn. NJ, NJ State Bar Assn. (civil trial sect., antitrust sect., real property and probate sect.), Trial Attys. NJ (trustee 1996-2004), Middlesex County Bar Assn., Hunterdon County Bar Assn., Rutgers-Newark Sch. Law Alumni Assn. (annual reunion dinner com. 1992, co-chair 1999, annual spring dinner com. 1995-2004, trustee 1999-2007, treas. 1999-2000, sec. 2000-01, v.p. 2001-2002, pres. elect 2002-2003, pres. 2003-04, exec. com. 1999-2005, Meritorious Svc. award 2006), Phi Beta Kappa, Phi Kappa Phi. Office: Greenbaum Rowe Smith & Davis LLP 99 Wood Ave S Iselin NJ 08830-2715 Office Phone: 732-476-2560. Business E-Mail: bgoodman@greenbaumlaw.com.

GOODMAN, BENNETT J., hedge fund executive; b. Apr. 4, 1957; BA in engring., Lafayette Coll., 1979; MBA, Harvard Bus. Sch., 1984. With Drexel Burnham Lambert, 1984—88, Donaldson, Lufkin & Jenrette Inc., 1988—2000, mng. dir. capital markets, 1995—96; mng. dir. high yield bonds Donaldson, Lufkin & Jenrette Inc. (merged with Credit Suisse First Boston in 2000), 1997—2000; mgr. dir. global leveraged fin. Credit Suisse First Boston LLC, 2000—03, chmn. merchant banking and leveraged fin., 2003—04; head, alternative capital div. Credit Suisse First Boston, NYC, 2004; co-founder GSO Capital Partners, 2005—.

GOODMAN, BERNARD, physics professor; b. Phila., June 14, 1923; s. Louis and Fannie (Solomon) G.; m. Joyce Janet Willoughby, Mar. 3, 1950; children— David Nathan, Jonathan Bernard, Mark William AB, U. Pa., 1943, PhD, 1955. Stress analyst Internat. Harvester Co., Chgo., 1947-52; research assoc. U. Mo., 1952, asst. prof. physics, 1954-58, assoc. prof., 1958-64, prof., 1964—; prof. physics U. Cin., 1965-93, prof. emeritus, 1993—. Vis. sci. Argonne Nat. Lab., 1956-57, 61-62, 65-66, 70, Brookhaven Nat. Lab., 1960, Bell Telephone Lab., 1967, Ohio U., 1969; Nordita guest prof. Inst. Theoretical Physics, Uppsala, Sweden, 1962-63, Gothenberg, Sweden, 1971-72; vis. prof. Inst. Theoretical Physics, Gothenberg, 1985. Guggenheim fellow, 1962-63, Gordon Godfrey fellow U. NSW, Sydney, Australia, 1990; Fulbright scholar Inst. Theoretical Physics, Trieste, Italy, 1979-80 Fellow: Am. Phys. Soc.; mem.: AAAS, Phi Beta Kappa, Sigma Xi. Achievements include research in condensed matter theory. Home: 3411 Cornell Pl Cincinnati OH 45220-1501 Office: U Cin Dept Physics Cincinnati OH 45221-0011 Office Phone: 513-556-0537. E-mail: goodman.bernard@gmail.com.

GOODMAN, BRUCE, health products executive; Degree in elec. engring., NYU; postgrad., Stanford U. CLU, chartered fin. cons. Former CEO Prudential Svc. Co., C2K Tech. Ptnrs., Inc., Livingston, NJ; sr. v.p., chief info. officer Humana, Inc., 1999—2002, sr. v.p., chief svc. and info. officer, 2002—. Office: Humana Inc 500 W Main St Louisville KY 40202

GOODMAN, CHARLES DAVID, physicist, researcher; b. NYC, May 9, 1928; s. Jacob and Libby (Freed) Goodman; m. Joan Louise Wright, June 11, 1952; children: Henry N., Diana R. AB, Clark U., Worcester, Mass., 1949; PhD, U. Rochester, NY, 1955. Rsch. scientist Oak Ridge Nat. Lab., Tenn., 1955—80; prof. physics Ind. U., Bloomington, 1980—98, prof. emeritus, 1999—. Vis. scientist Weizmann Inst. Sci., Rehovot, Israel, 1966; vis. prof. U. Colo., Boulder, 1972-73; guest scientist Los Alamos Nat. Lab., N.Mex., 1979-94, Lawrence Berkeley Lab., Calif., 1980—, Lawrence Livermore Lab., Calif., 1980—91, Laboratoire Nat Saturne, Saclay, France, 1982-91; originator, organizer internat. nuc. physics confs., Telluride, Colo., 1979, 82, 85, 88, 91. Contbr. articles to profl. jours. Recipient Humboldt Found. Rsch. award, Germany, 1991. Fellow AAAS, Am. Phys. Soc. (Tom W. Bonner Prize 1983); mem. IEEE, Sigma Xi. Achievements include mapping of Gamow-Teller strength function; patent on neutron detector. Business E-Mail: goodmanc@indiana.edu.

GOODMAN, CHRISTOPHER LAWRENCE, lawyer; b. May 24, 1973; BA summa cum laude, Hamline U., 1995; JD, U. Minn., 1998. Bar: Minn. 1998, US Dist. Ct. (dist. Minn.), US Dist. Ct. (we. dist. Wis.). Ptnr. gen. liability and civil litig., ins. coverage and litig., product liability, and toxic tort and mass litig. practice grps. Foley & Mansfield, P.L.L.P., Mpls., 2001—. Named a Rising Star, Minn. Super Lawyers mag., 2006. Mem.: Def. Rsch. Inst., Minn. State Bar Assn., ABA, Phi Beta Kappa. Office: Foley & Mansfield PLLP 250 Marquette Ave Ste 1200 Minneapolis MN 55401 Office Phone: 612-371-8507. E-mail: cgoodman@foleymansfield.com.*

GOODMAN, COREY SCOTT, neuroscientist, biotechnologist, educator; b. Chgo., June 29, 1951; s. Arnold Harold (dec.) and Florence (Friedman) G.; m. Marcia M. Barinaga, Dec. 8, 1984. BS, Stanford U., Calif., 1972; PhD, U. Calif., Berkeley, 1977. Postdoctoral fellow U. Calif., San Diego, 1979, prof. neurobiology and genetics Berkeley, 1987—2005, co-founder Helen Wills Neurosci. Inst., 1997, Evan Rauch prof. neuroscience, 1999—2001, adj. prof. neurobiology, 2005—; asst. prof. dept. biol. scis. Stanford U., 1979-82, assoc. prof., 1982-87; co-founder Exelixis, Inc., 1995; dir. Helen Wills Neurosci. Inst., 1999—2000; co-founder Renovis Inc., 2000—, CEO, pres., bd. dirs., 2001—. Investigator Howard Hughes Med. Inst., 1988—2001; chair bd. life sci. NRC, 2001—06. Contbr. more than 200 articles to profl. jours. Pres. McKnight Found. Endowment Fund Neurosci., 2000—05, v.p., 2005—. Recipient Charles Judson Herrick award, 1982, Alan T. Waterman award Nat. Sci. Bd., 1983, Javits Neurosci. Investigator award NIH, 1985, 92, NIH Merit award, 1985, Found. IPSEN Neuronal Plasticity prize, 1996, J. Allyn Taylor Internat. prize in medicine, 1996, Gairdner Found. Internat. award for achievement in med. sci., 1997, Ameritec Found. Basic Rsch. Toward Cure Paralysis prize, 1997, Wakeman award for rsch. in neuroscis., 1998, March-Of-Dimes prize in Devel. Biology, 2001. Fellow Am. Acad. Arts and Scis.; mem. NAS, Am. Philos. Soc. Office: Renovis Inc Two Corporate Dr South San Francisco CA 94080 Home Phone: 510-652-9792; Office Phone: 650-266-1476. E-mail: goodman@renovis.com.

GOODMAN, CYNTHIA DIANE, public health physician; b. Odessa, Tex., Oct. 11, 1954; d. Edwin Lloyd and Dorothy Jean Coventon; m. Sanford Jay Goodman, Oct. 26, 2003. BS, Dallas Bapt. U., 1977; MD, U. Tex., San Antonia, 1983; MS, SUNY, Buffalo, 1998. Cert. Am. Bd. Phys. Medicine and Rehab., 1990. Staff physician various NYC hosps., 1983—88; psychiatrist Work Well, Pitts., 1988—89; cons. Dept. Human Svcs., Oklahoma City, 1990—95; fellow preventive medicine SUNY, Buffalo, 1995—98; fellow pub. health HCFA, Dallas, 1998—2000; pub. health physician Pa. Health Dept., Harrisburg, Pa., 2000—. Mem. Kesher Israel Synagogue, Harrisburg, 2000—. Fellow: Am. Coll. Preventive Medicine, Am.-Can. Soc. Preventive Medicine; mem.: Dauphin County Med. Soc., Am. Med. Assn. Republican. Jewish.

GOODMAN, DAVID JOEL, electrical engineering educator, science facility director; b. Bklyn., June 9, 1939; s. Arthur and Martha (Persky) G.; m. Janet Silverman, Sept. 9, 1962 (div. 1977); children: Leila Denise, Alissa Tamar; m. Natalee Woolfolk Everett, Aug. 5, 1980 BEE, Rensselaer Poly. Inst., 1960; MEE, NYU, 1962; PhD, U. London, 1967. Registered profl. engr. Mem. tech. staff AT&T Bell Labs., Murray Hill, NJ, 1967-74, supr., 1975-77, dept. head Holmdel, NJ, 1977-86, 87-88; rsch. mgr. AT&T Internat., London, 1986-87; prof. elec. engring. Rutgers U., New Brunswick, NJ, 1988—, chair dept. elec. and computer engring., 1988-91; dir. Rutgers Wireless Info. Network Lab., Piscataway, NJ, 1989—99; prof., head Dept. Elec. Engring. Polytechnic U., Brooklyn, 1999—. Vis. prof. Imperial Coll. Sci. and Tech., London, 1983-88, Southampton (Eng.) U., 1987—; rsch. visitor Philips Rsch. Labs., Redhill, Eng., 1986-87; rsch. assoc. Program on Info. Resources Policy, Harvard U., 1995. Contbr. numerous articles to profl. jours. Holder 7 patents. Imperial Coll. Sci. and Tech. sr. rsch. fellow, London, 1974-75. Fellow IEEE (1988 Paper of Yr. award), Instn. Elec. Engrs. (Eng.), Keyport (N.J.) Yacht Club, Dorset (Vt.) Field Club. Jewish. Avocations: sailing, cooking, hiking. Home: 7 Parmly St Rumson NJ 07760-1755 Office: Polytechnic U 5 Metrotech Ctr, Rm LC 206 Brooklyn NY 11201 Office Phone: 718-260-3221. E-mail: dgoodman@poly.edu.

GOODMAN, DAVID S., lawyer; b. Cleve., 1952; BA, Oberlin Coll., 1974; JD, Harvard U., 1977. Bar: Ohio 1977. Ptnr. Squire, Sanders & Dempsey LLP, Cleve., chmn., Pub. Securities Practice Group. Mem.: Nat. Assn. Bond Lawyers, Ohio Bar Assn., Cleve. Bar Assn. Fluent in German. Office: Squire Sanders & Dempsey LLP 4900 Key Tower 127 Public Sq Cleveland OH 44114-1304 Office Phone: 216-479-8649. Office Fax: 216-479-8780. Business E-Mail: dgoodman@ssd.com.

GOODMAN, DAVID WAYNE, research chemist, educator; b. Dec. 14, 1945; s. Henry G. and Anniebelle G.; m. Sandra Faye Hewitt, June 9, 1967; 1 child, Jac Hewitt. BS, Miss. Coll., 1968; PhD, U. Tex., 1974. NATO postdoctoral fellow Tech. Hochschule, Darmstadt, Fed. Republic of Germany, 1974-75; NRC postdoctoral fellow NBS, Washington, 1975-76, mem. rsch. staff, 1976-80, Sandia Labs., Albuquerque, 1980-85, head surface sci. divsn., 1985-88; prof. chemistry Tex. A&M U., College Station, 1988-94, head phys. and nuc. divsn., 1991-94, Welch prof., 1994—, Welch chair, 1998—, disting. prof., 2000—. Lectr. Tex. A&M U., 1987, U. Tex., 1990, Northwestern U., 1993; Robert Burwell lectr. N.Am. Catalysis Soc., 1997. Named Langmuir Disting. lectr., 1991, Disting. Alumnus, Miss. Coll., 1992; recipient Yarwood medal, 1994, Humboldt Rsch. award, 1995, Giuseppe Parravano award, 2001, Arthur W. Adamson award, 2002, Disting. Rsch. Visitor award, U. Auckland, 2003, Gabor A. Somorjai award, 2005; Fulbright Disting. scholar, 2002. Mem.: Am. Vacuum Soc. (mem. exec. coun. 1981, 1985—87), Am. Chem. Soc. (treas. divsn. colloid and surf. sci. 1980—83, vice chair 1983, chmn. 1984). Office: Tex A&M U Dept Chem PO Box 30012 College Station TX 77842-3012 Office Phone: 979-845-0214. Business E-Mail: goodman@mail.chem.tamu.edu.

GOODMAN, ELIZABETH ANN, retired lawyer; b. Marquette, Mich., Aug. 11, 1950; d. Paul William and Pearl Marie Goodman; m. Herbert Charles Gardner, Sept. 24, 1977. Student, U. Munich, 1970-71; BA cum laude, Alma Coll., Mich., 1972; JD cum laude, U. Mich., 1977. Bar: Minn. 1978, Mich. 1978, U.S. Dist. Ct. Minn. 1979. Cert. real property law specialist, real property sect. Minn. Bar Assn. High sch. tchr. Onaway (Mich.) High Sch., 1973-74; assoc. Dorsey & Whitney LLP, Mpls., 1978-82; ptnr. Dorsey & Whitney, Mpls., 1983-99; v.p., chief gen. counsel Ryan Cos., 2000—03; ret., 2003.

GOODMAN, ELLEN HOLTZ, journalist; b. Newton, Mass., Apr. 11, 1941; d. Jackson Jacob and Edith (Weinstein) Holtz; m. Robert Levey; 1 dau., Katherine Anne. BA cum laude, Radcliffe Coll., 1963; degree (hon.), Mt. Holyoke Coll., Amherst Coll., U. Pa., U. NH. Researcher, reporter Newsweek Mag., 1963-65; feature writer Detroit Free Press, 1965-67; feature writer columnist Boston Globe, 1967-74, assoc. editor, 1986—2001; syndicated columnist Washington Post Writers Group, 1976—; radio commentator Spectrum, CBS, 1978-80, NBC, 1979-80; commentator NBC Today Show, 1979-81. Vis. prof. Stanford U., 1995. Author: Close to Home, 1979, Turning Points, 1979, At Large, 1981, Keeping in Touch, 1985, Making Sense, 1989, Value Judgments, 1993, (with Patricia O'Brien) I Know Just What You Mean, 2000, Paper Trail, 2004. Trustee Radcliffe Coll.; judge Livingston Awards for Young Journalists, 1986—. Nieman fellow Harvard U., 1974, Lyndhurst fellow, 2000; named New Eng. Newspaper Woman of Year New Eng. Press Assn., 1968; recipient Catherine O'Brien award Stanley Home Products, 1971, Media award Mass. Commn. Status Women, 1974, Columnist of Year award New Eng. Women's Press Assn., 1975, Pulitzer Prize for Commentary, 1980, prize for column writing Am. Soc. Newspaper Editors, 1980, Hubert H. Humphrey Civil Rights award, 1988, William Allen White award 1995. Office: 5 JFK St Cambridge MA 02138 E-mail: ellengoodman@globe.com.

GOODMAN, ERIK DAVID, engineering educator; b. Palo Alto, Calif., Feb. 14, 1944; s. Harold Orbeck and Shirley Mae (Lillie) G.; m. Denise Rowand Dyktor, Aug. 10, 1968 (div. 1976); m. Cheryl Diane Barris, Aug. 27, 1978; 1 child, David Richard. BS in Math., Mich. State U., East Lansing, 1966, MS in Systems Sci., 1968; PhD in Computer Communication Sci., U. Mich., Ann Arbor, 1972; Doctorate (hon.), Dneprodzerzhinsk State Tech U., Ukraine, 1996. Asst. prof. elec. engring. Mich. State U., East Lansing, 1972-77, assoc. prof. elec. engring., 1977-84, dir. case ctr. for computer aided engring. and mfg., 1983—2002, prof. elec. engring., dir., 1984—, prof. mech. engring., 1992—. Dir. Mich. State U. Mfg. Rsch. Consortium, 1993—2003; v.p. Red Cedar Tech., Inc., East Lansing, Mich., 1999-; pres. Tech. Gateway, Inc., East Lansing; cons. Chinese Computer Comms., Inc., Lansing, 1988—; gen. chair First Internat. Conf. on Evolutionary Computation and its Applications, Moscow, 1996, Seventh Internat Conf. on Genetic Algorithms, 1997, Genetic and Evolutionary Computation Conf., 2001; gen. co-chmn. Internat. Computer Graphics Conf., Detroit, 1986; adv. prof. Tongji U., Shanghai, China, 2002—, East China Normal U., 2002-, Shanghai Bus. Sch., Shanghai Maritime U., 2007-. Author: (with others) SYSKIT: Linear Systems Toolkit, 1986; patentee in field. Academician, Internat. Informatization Acad. (Russia), 1993—. Fellow Internat. Soc. Genetic and Evolutionary Computation (sr., exec. com. 2001-04, chair 2001-04); mem. AIAA (chair rsch. and future dirs., subcom. CAD/CAM tech. com. 1987-89, Outstanding Svc. 1990), IEEE Computer Soc., Assn. Computing Machinery (chair SIGEVO, spl. interest group genetic and evolutionary computation 2005—), Soc. Mfg. Engrs., Aircraft Owners and Pilots Assn., Acad. Engring. Scis. Ukraine Avocations: musician, tennis, studying Chinese. Office: Mich State U Dept Elec & Computer Engring 2308M Engineering Bldg East Lansing MI 48824 Business E-Mail: goodman@egr.msu.edu. E-mail: e.goodman@redcedartech.com. *Evolutionary computation is now allowing huge advances in engineering design optimization and design automation of complex structures.*

GOODMAN, ERNEST MONROE, military officer; b. Casper, Wyo., May 14, 1955; s. Gordon Lee and Georgia Lee (Lent) G.; m. Songkran Sana, Sept. 30, 1976 (div. Feb. 1995). BSEE, U. Okla., 1982; MBA in Mgmt., Ctrl. State U., Edmond, Okla., 1986; postgrad., Air U., Maxwell AFB, Ala., 2001, postgrad., 2006. Registered profl. engr., Okla. Avionics technician USAF, N.D., Okla., and S.E. Asia, 1973-78, USAFR, Tinker AFB, Okla., 1978-83; project engr., mgr. engring. Okla. City Air Logistics Ctr., Tinker AFB, 1982-90, 90—; commd. 2nd lt. USAF, 1983, advanced through grades to lt. col.; engring. officer Kirkuk Regional Air Base Iraq USAFR, Offutt AFB, Nebr., 1983—, civil engr. squadron comdr. Kirkuk Regional AFB, Iraq, 2006—. Mem. NSPE, Okla. Soc. Profl. Engrs., Air Force Assn., Res. Officers Assn. (pres. Okla. dept. 1999-2000), Tinker Mgmt. Assn. (pres. 1997-98), Toastmasters Internat. Democrat. Roman Catholic. Avocations: photography, fishing, hunting, hiking, jogging. Home: 1313 SW 22d St Moore OK 73170-7483 Office: USAF 547th Aircraft Sustainment Squadron Tinker AFB OK 73145 Home Phone: 405-912-1069; Office Phone: 405-734-2308. Business E-Mail: ernest.goodman@tinker.af.mil.

GOODMAN, FREDERICK DENIS, retired environmental scientist; b. Altoona, Pa., June 19, 1952; s. Albert Raymond and Winifred Martha Goodman; m. Debra Ann White, Aug. 16, 1975; children: Michael Nelson, Matthew Alan. BS in Biology Edn., Ind. U. Pa., Indiana, 1974, MEd, 1979. Cert. instructional II cert. in biology Pa. Animal lab tech. Ind. U. Pa., 1971—74; sci. educator Derry Area Sch. Dist., 1974—2007; environ. interpretation tech. Pa. D.E.R, Harrisburg, 1974; edn. info. specialist Pa. Fish and Boat Commn., 1983—; chmn. sci. dept. Derry Area Sch. Dist., 1998—2007; ret., 2007. Ednl. cons. Westmoreland Soil and Conservation Dist., 2001—01; curriculum cons. Pa. Fish & Boat Commn., Harrisburg, 1989; mem. adv. coun. Merrill Pub., 1988—89. Councilman Derry Borough Coun., 1979—85; planning commn. Derry Borough, 1986—93; chmn. Zoning Hearing Bd., 1993—98; robotic coach YWCA, Greensburg, 2002—; scoutmaster Westmoreland/Fayette coun. Boy Scouts Am., 1986—. Named Conservation Educator of Yr., 1991, Conservation Vol. of Yr., 1998; recipient District award of Merit, 1999, Daniel Carter Beard Masonic Scouter award, 2002, George Meany award, 2003. Mem.: Shriners, Scottish Rite, La Monte Lodge (sec. 2003—). Conservative. Luthern. Avocations: hiking, camping, bicycling, fishing, photography. Home Phone: 724-694-5166.

GOODMAN, GARY A., lawyer; b. NYC, Mar. 8, 1948; s. Nathaniel and Edith (Rosen) G.; m. Susan Schachter, Aug. 13, 1972; children: Max, Jonah, William, Zachary, Holden. AB in History summa cum laude, Economics with honors, U. Rochester, 1970; JD, NYU, 1973. Bar: N.Y. 1974, U.S. Dist. Ct. (so. dist. and ea. dists.) N.Y. 1974, U.S. Dist. Ct. Guam, 1975, U.S. Ct. Appeals (2d cir.) 1975, Calif. 1996, Tex. 1996. Ptnr. Sonnenschein Nath & Rosenthal LLP, NYC, 2002—. Contbr. numerous articles to profl. jours. Mem. bd. edn. Locust Valley (N.Y.) Ctrl. Sch. Dist., 1995-96, v.p., 1996-97, pres., 1997-98. Mem.: ABA (vice chmn. internat. investment in real estate com. 1983—90, chmn. Pacific Rim trans. subcom. real estate financing com. 1987—88), Am. Coll. Mortgage Attys., Mortgage Bankers Assn. Am., Comml. Mortgage Securities Assn., Assn. Fgn. Investors in Real Estate, Real Estate Bd., Internat. Coun. Shopping Ctrs. (task force environ. issues 1987—90, law com. 1991—94), Assn. Bar of City of N.Y. (uniform state laws com. 1978—80, real property law com. 1991—94, land use com. 1994—97, real property law com. 1997—2000), N.Y. State Bar Assn. (chmn. fgn. investment in U.S. real estate com. 1987—88). Office: Sonnenschein Nath & Rosenthal LLP 1221 Ave of the Americas New York NY 10020 Home Phone: 516-626-3504; Office Phone: 212-768-6916. E-mail: ggoodman@sonnenschein.com.

GOODMAN, GEORGE JEROME WALDO (ADAM SMITH), writer, television journalist, consultant; b. St. Louis, Aug. 10, 1930; s. Alexander Mark and Viola (Cremer) G.; m. Sallie Cullen Brophy, Oct. 6, 1961; children: Alexander Mark, Susannah Blake. AB magna cum laude, Harvard U., 1952; AB Rhodes scholar, Oxford U., Eng., 1952-54. Reporter Barron's, 1957; contbg. editor, assoc. editor Time and Fortune mags., 1958—60; portfolio mgr., v.p. Lincoln Fund, 1960—62; co-founder New York mag., 1967, contbg. editor, v.p., 1967—77; exec. editor, then cons. Esquire, 1978—81; 1st editor, exec. v.p., bd. dirs. Instl. Investor, 1967—72; chmn. Continental Fidelity Group, 1980—98, also dir. Exec. v.p., dir. Instl. Investor Systems, 1969-72; dir. USAIR, Inc., 1978-99, Hyatt Hotels, 1977-81, Cambrex, Inc., 1981-2003, Providentia Ltd., Sweden, 1984-86; mem. dirs. adv. bd. MetLife, 2003—; lectr. Harvard Bus. Sch., Princeton; commentator NBC News, 1974, PBS, 1981—; creator, host, editor-in-chief Adam Smith's Money World, PBS, 1984-97; 1st U.S. pub. affairs TV broadcast in Russia, 1990—; host, editor-in-chief Adam Smith's Money Game, PBS, 1998-99; editl. chmn. N.J. Monthly, 1976-79; adv. com. publs. U.S. Tennis Assn., 1978-83; chmn. Adam Smith Global TV, 1997—; lectr. media and global affairs Princeton U., 2003—. Screenwriter, L.A., 1962-65, screenplay The Wheeler Dealers; author: The Bubble Makers, 1955, A Time for Paris, 1957, Bascombe, The Fastest Hound Alive, 1958, A Killing in the Market, 1958, The Wheeler Dealers, 1959; under pseudonym Adam Smith: The Money Game, 1968 (#1 bestseller), Supermoney, 1971 (#1 bestseller), Powers of Mind, 1975, Paper Money, 1981, The Roaring 80's, 1988; mem. editl. bd. N.Y. Times, 1977; contbr. articles to profl. jours. Trustee Glassboro (N.J.) State Coll., 1967-71, co-chmn. presdl. selection com., 1968; trustee C.G. Jung Found., 1981-88; mem. adv. council econs. dept. Princeton U., 1970-89, chmn., 1975-77; rep. com. on shareholder responsibility Harvard U., 1971-74, mem. vis. com. psychology and social relations dept., 1974-80—, mem. vis. com. Middle East Inst.; mem. adv. council Sloan Fellowships, Princeton U., 1976-79, Ctr. for Internat. Studies, Princeton U., 1990—; trustee The Urban Inst., 1986-96, Found. for Child Devel., 1986-88. Served with AUS, 1954-56. Recipient G.M. Loeb award for disting. achievement bus. and fin. writing U. Conn., 1969, Media award for econ. understanding with TV documentary Amos Tuck Sch., Dartmouth Coll., 1978, Overseas Press award, 1996; Ind. award Brown U., 1993; nominee 8 Emmy awards, 1985-97, winner Best Interview 1995, winner 3 Emmys, graphics, 1985-94, Adam Smith Internat. PBS Documentaries gold medal Houston Internat. Film Festival, 2001, 02. Mem.: Assn. Harvard Alumni (bd. dirs. 1972—75), Authors Guild (bd. dirs. 1975—2006), Authors League Fund (v.p.), Coun. Fgn. Rels., Knickerbocker Club, Century Assn., Harvard Club. Office: Adam Smith Global TV 26 E 63rd St New York NY 10021-8030

GOODMAN, GERTRUDE AMELIA, civic worker; b. El Paso, Tex., Oct. 24, 1924; d. Karl Perry and Helen Sylvia (Pinkiert) G. BA, Mills Coll., 1945. Pres. El Paso chpt. Tex. Social Welfare Assn., 1963-65, bd. dirs. 1965-70, state bd. dirs., 1965-70; state bd. dirs. Pan-Am. Round Table, El Paso, 1966—, bd. dirs. 1970-71, sec., 1973-74, life mem.; founder, 1st chmn. El Paso Mus. Art Mem. Guild, 1962-68; bd. dirs. Mus. Art Assn., 1962-69, also v.p.; chmn. dir. El Paso C. of C. women's Dept., 1976-77; bd. dirs. Rio Grande Food Bank, 1988-94; bd. dirs. El Paso Pub. Libr., 1972-80, pres. bd. dirs., 1978-80; pres. El Paso County Hist. Soc., 1981-82, bd. dirs., 1986-92; mem. planning com. El Paso United Way, 1953—; mem. El Paso Mus. Art Bd. Coun.; pres. Las Comadres, 2000-01. Recipient Hall of Honor award El Paso County Hist. Soc., Nat. Human Rels. award NCCJ, 1981, numerous awards for civic vol. work. Avocations: tennis, travel, art, books. Home: 905 Cincinnati Ave El Paso TX 79902-2435

GOODMAN, HERBERT IRWIN, petroleum company executive; b. Pitts., Mar. 11, 1923; s. Meyer Irwin and Bessie (Crossof) G.; m. Mary Katherine Schilken, Aug. 12, 1978; children: Michael Christopher, Anne Katheryn, Nancy Hjortshoj, Sara Elizabeth, Mary Elien. BS, U. Pitts., 1943; cert., U. Besancon, 1945; MBA, Harvard U., 1949, AM, 1950. Commd. officer U.S. Fgn. Svc., 1951; served in U.S. Embassy, Copenhagen, 1951-53, Vietnam, 1953-54, U.S. Fgn. Service, Kampuchea, 1954-55; intelligence rsch. officer Dept. State, 1956-57; with Gulf Oil Corp., 1957-84, coord. European sales London, 1957-59; gen. mgr. Pacific Gulf Oil, Tokyo, 1960-64, coord. crude oil dept. Pitts., 1964-66, coord. Far East, 1966-70; pres. Gulf Oil Co. South Asia, Singapore, 1970-72, Gulf Oil Trading Co., Pitts., 1972-80, Gulf Trading and Transp. Co., Houston, 1980-84, GOTCO USA, Inc., Houston, 1984-87, SARMAR Corp., Houston, 1987—; chmn. bd. Applied Trading Sys., Houston, 1988-96, IQ Holdings, Inc., Houston, 1996—2004, pepex.net LLC, 2000—05. Bd. dirs. Houston Livestock Show and Rodeo, Brazil Ethanol, Nanodynamics, Genesis Energy L.P.; adv. bd. Pacific Inst. Bd. dirs., chmn. internat. adv. bd. Tex. A&M U.; bd. dirs. U. St. Thomas Sch. Bus., AA Grapevine, Inc.; trustee gen. svc. bd. Alcoholics Anonymous. 1st lt. U.S. Army, 1943-46. Decorated Bronze Star; médaille de la Réconnaissance (France). Mem. Am. Petroleum Inst., Am. Mgmt. Assn., Coun. on Fgn. Rels., Assn. Asian Studies, Mid East Inst., Asia Soc. N.Y. (corp. coun.), Assn. Internat. Petroleum Negotiators, Harvard Club (N.Y.C.), Racquet Club, Petroleum Club. Office: SARMAR Corp One Riverway Ste 1700 Houston TX 77056 Office Phone: 713-840-6499. Personal E-mail: herbg@pepex.net. Business E-Mail: hgoodman@houston.rr.com.

GOODMAN, JEROME DAVID, psychiatrist; b. Chester, Pa., Oct. 23, 1933; s. William Henry and Amelia (Kopl) G.; m. Gail Ann Theis, Feb. 10, 1961; children: David Hammond, Douglas Andrew. BA, Swarthmore Coll., 1955; MD, U. Pa., 1959. Diplomate Am. Bd. Psychiatry and Neurology with subspecialty in child psychiatry. Asst. clin. prof. psychiatry Coll. Physicians and Surgeons Columbia U., NYC, 1964—75; pvt. practice Saddle River, NJ, 1968—. Author: Child Mental Status Examination, 1967, 2d edit., 1998; composer: Sonata for Violin and Piano, 1990, Six Cryptic Rhythms for Chamber Orch., 1992, Montségur Suite, 1993, Symphony # 2, 1994, Violin Concerto, 1995, Concerto for Clarinet, Violoncello and Orch., 1996, Dance Patterns: A Choreographic Poem for Orch., 1997, Stockbridge Overtones: Tone Poem for Orch., 1998, Saddle River Almanac: A Tone Poem for Orchestra, 2002, Saxophone Quartet, 2002, Two Elizabethan Lyrics for Soprano and Piano, 2003, Concert Piece for Piano, Strings, and Percussion, 2003, Vocalise and Lyrical Piece for Unaccompanied Chorus, 2005, Three Preludes for Piano, 2006, Essay for Flute and Piano, 2006. Capt. U.S. Army, 1966-68. Recipient Margaret Fairbanks Jory award, 1992. Jewish. Office: 45 W Saddle River Rd Saddle River NJ 07458-3016 Office Phone: 201-825-0384.

GOODMAN, JERRY L(YNN), judge; b. Mangum, Okla., Apr. 17, 1939; s. A.O. and Viola Louise (Bogart) G.; m. Donna L. Rudy, Dec. 16, 1961; children: Courtney L., Polly K., Mallory E., Benjamin R. BA, U. Tulsa, 1961; JD, Georgetown U., 1964. Bar: Okla. 1964. Law clk. antitrust divsn. Dept. Justice, 1962-63; legis. asst. to U.S. Senator J. Howard Edmondson, 1963-64; assoc. David M. Thornton Atty.-at-Law, 1964-65; asst. city atty. City of Tulsa, Okla., 1965-68; ptnr. Owens & Goodman, Tulsa, 1968-70; gen. counsel OTASCO Stores, Tulsa, 1970-74, v.p., gen. counsel, 1974-85, chmn., CEO, 1985-89; spl. counsel Bank of Okla., 1989-90; pres., gen. counsel The Sigma Asset Mgmt. Group, Inc., 1991-92; sec. policy and mgmt., COO Office of Gov., State of Okla., Tulsa, 1992-94; judge Okla. Ct. Civil Appeals, Tulsa, 1994—. Bd. dirs. United Way, 1984—87; chmn., bd. trustees Univ. Ctr. at Tulsa, 1992. Lt. USNR, 1964—70. Mem.: Tulsa County Bar Assn. (v.p. 1971), Okla. Bar Assn., Okla. Jud. Conf. (pres. 2001), Tulsa C. of C. (chmn. 1988). Presbyterian. Office: Okla Ct Civil Appeals 601 State Office Bldg 440 S Houston Ave Tulsa OK 74127-8922 Office Phone: 918-581-2711. Personal E-mail: jerry.goodman@oscn.net.

GOODMAN, JESSE, physician, director, public health facility administrator, research scientist; BS, Harvard U.; MD, Albert Einstein Coll. of Medicine; MPH, U. Minn. Prof. medicine, dir. US Govt. Interagency Task Force Antimicrobial Resistance, 1998—2000; sr. advisor to commr. FDA, 1998—99, dep. dir. medicine Ctr. Biologics, Evaluation, and Rsch., 1999—2000, dir. Ctr. Biologics, Evaluation, and Rsch., 2003—, prof. medicine, 1997—2001; dir. divsn. infectious diseases U. Minn. Med. Sch., 1998—2001. Adj. prof. medicine U. Minn., Howard U.; attending physician NIH Clin. Ctr. and Walter Reed Army Med. Ctr. Mem.: Inst. Medicine of Nat. Acad. Sci., Am. Soc. for Clin. Investigation. Office: Ctr Biologics Evaluation and Rsch FDA 1401 Rockville Pike Ste 200N Rockville MD 20852-1448

GOODMAN, JOE M., lawyer; b. Columbia, Tenn., July 25, 1950; BS magna cum laude, U. Tenn., 1972, JD, 1974; LLM in Taxation, NYU, 1978. CPA Tenn., 1975; bar: Tenn. 1975, US Tax Ct. 1979, Ky. 1997. Ptnr. transactions and corp. adv. svcs. Adams & Reese, LLP, Nashville. Contbr. articles to profl. jours.; author: Family Bus. Successorship and Continuity, 1995, Estate Planning for Family Bus. Owners, 1999, Rich Widows Live Forever, 2004; co-author: Bus. Succession Planning and Beyond, 1997; mem. editl. bd.: Family Bus. mag. Named one of Nation's Top 100 Most Exclusive Wealth Advs., Worth mag., 2004, Top 100 Attys., 2005—06. Mem.: Attys. for Family-Held Enterprises, Tenn. Soc. CPA, Family Firm Inst., AICPA, ABA, Tenn. Bar Assn., Nashville Bar Assn., Omicron Delta Kappa, Beta Alpha Psi, Beta Gamma Sigma. Office: Adams & Reese Fifth Third Ctr 424 Church St Ste 2800 Nashville TN 37219 Office Phone: 615-259-1011. E-mail: joe.goodman@arlaw.com.

GOODMAN, JOHN, actor; b. St. Louis, June 20, 1952; m. Annabeth Hartzog, 1989; 1 daughter. Student, Meramac CC; BFA in Theater, S.W. Mo. State U., 1975. Performer dinner and children's theater prodns., off-Broadway plays; appeared on Broadway in Loose Ends, 1979, Big River, 1985, Cat on a Hot Tin Roof, 2005; TV credits include Mystery of the Moro Castle, Face of Rage, Heart of Steel, 1983, Moonlighting, Chiefs, 1983, The Paper Chase, Murder Ordained, The Equalizer; series regular, Roseanne, 1988-96 (Emmy award nominations outstanding lead actor in comedy series, 1989, 90, 93, 94), Father of the Pride (voice), 2004, Center of the Universe, 2004-; actor (films) The Survivors, 1983, Eddie Macon's Run, 1983, Revenge of the Nerds, 1984, C.H.U.D., 1984, Maria's Lovers, 1985, Sweet Dreams, 1985, True Stories, 1986, The Big Easy, 1987, Burglar, 1987, Raising Arizona, 1987, The Wrong Guys, 1988, Everybody's All-American, 1988, Punchline, 1988, Sea of Love, 1989, Always, 1989, Stella, 1990, Arachnophobia, 1990, King Ralph, 1990, Barton Fink, 1991, The Babe, 1992, Matinee, 1993, Born Yesterday, 1993, The Flintstones, 1994, Mother Night, 1996, Fallen, 1997, Combat!, 1997, The Borrowers, 1997, The Big Lebowski, 1998, Blues Brothers 2000, 1998, Dirty Work, 1998, The Runner, 1999, Bringing Out the Dead, 1999, Coyote Ugly, 2000, O Brother, Where Art Thou?, 2000, What Planet Are You From, 2000, Hitting the Wall, 2000, My First Mister, 2000, One Night at McCool's, 2000, Emperor's New Groove (voice), 2000, Monsters, Inc. (voice), 2001, Dirty Deeds, 2002, Masked and Anonymous, 2003, The Jungle Book 2 (voice), 2003, Clifford's Really Big Movie (voice), 2004, Beyond the Sea, 2004; actor (TV movies) The Jack Bull, 1999; actor, prodr. (TV movies) Kingfish: A Story of Huey P. Long, 1995; guest star (TV series) The West Wing, 1999; appeared in numerous commls. Office: Creative Artists Agency c/o Fred Specktor 9830 Wilshire Blvd Beverly Hills CA 90212-1825

GOODMAN, JOHN B., heating/air conditioning manufacturing executive; CEO Goodman Mfg., Houston, 1999—. Office: Goodman Mfg 2550 N Loop W Ste 400 Houston TX 77092-8908 Office Fax: (713) 861-2176.

GOODMAN, JOHN M., construction executive; b. Omaha, Apr. 5, 1947; BS in Acctg., Calif. State U., Long Beach, 1970; JD, Pepperdine U., 1974. CPA, Calif.; cert. real estate broker, Calif.; cert. ins. agt., Calif.; lic. contractor, Calif. CFO Lewis Homes Mgmt. Corp., Upland, Calif., 1978—92, sr. v.p., CEO, dir., 1992—. Office: Lewis Operating Corp 1156 N Mountain Ave PO Box 670 Upland CA 91785-0670

GOODMAN, JORDAN ELLIOT, journalist; b. NYC, Sept. 13, 1954; s. Elliot Raymond and Norma (Bromberg) G.; m. Suzanne Kay Koblentz, June 20, 1981; 1 child, Jason Koblentz. Student, London Sch. Econ., 1974-75; BA, Amherst Coll., 1976; MA, Columbia U., 1977. Editor in chief Info Mag., NYC, 1977-79; sr. reporter Money Mag., NYC, 1979-92, Wall St. corr., 1992-97. Commentator Fin. News Network, NYC, 1985—91, Mut. Broadcasting Sys., Washington, 1988—97, Marketplace Pub. Radio Internat., 1988—, Cable News Network, NYC, 1989—90; regional dir. Soc. Profl. Journalists, Chgo., 1989—90; columnist onmoney.com, 2000—02, Moneyanswers.com, 2000—. Author: Dictionary of Finance and Investment Terms, 1986, 7th edit., 2007, Barron's Finance and Investment Handbook, 1987, 7th edit., 2006, Dictionary of Business Terms, 1989, rev., 1998, Everyone's Money Book, 1993, 3rd edit., 2001, Reading Between the Lies, 2003, Everyone's Money Book Series, 2002, Master Your Money Type, 2006. Mem. Common Cause, N.Y.C., 1985—. Mem. Mid-Atlantic Club, N.Y.C. Fin. Writers Assn., N.Y. Deadline Club (pres. 1986-87), Freedom Investment Club Fin. Svcs. (pres. 2006). Democrat. Jewish. Avocation: sailing. Home and Office: 84 Walworth Ave Scarsdale NY 10583-1139 Home Phone: 914-725-6395; Office Phone: 914-722-0032. Personal E-mail: jordan.goodman@verizon.net.

GOODMAN, JOSEPH WILFRED, electrical engineering educator; b. Boston, Feb. 8, 1936; s. Joseph and Doris (Ryan) G.; m. Hon Mai Lam, Dec. 5, 1962; 1 dau., Michele Ann. BA, Harvard U., 1958; MS in E.E., Stanford U., 1960, PhD, 1963; DSc (hon.), U. Ala., 1996. Postdoctoral fellow Norwegian Def. Rsch. Establishment, Oslo, 1962-63; rsch. assoc. Stanford U., 1963-67, asst. prof., 1967-69, assoc. prof., 1969-72, prof. elec. engring., 1972-99; vis. prof. Univ. Paris XI, Orsay, France, 1973-74; dir. Info. Sys. Lab. Elec. Engring. Stanford U., 1981-83, chmn. dept. of elec. engring., 1988-96, William E. Ayer prof. elec. engring., 1988-99, sr. assoc. dean engring., 1996-98, acting dean engring., 1999, prof. emeritus, 2000—. Cons. govt. and industry, 1965—; v.p. Internat. Comm. Optics, 1985-87, pres., 1988-90, past pres., 1991-93; founding chmn. bd. ONI Sys., Inc.; former chmn. bd. Nanoprecision Products Inc.; former bd. mem. E-TEK Dynamics. Author: Introduction to Fourier Optics, 1968, 3d edit., 2005, Statistical Optics, 1985, (with R. Gray) Fourier Transforms: An Introduction for Engineers; editor: International Trends in Optics, 1991, Speckle Phenomena in Optics, 2006; contbr. articles to profl. jours. Recipient F.E. Terman award Am. Soc. Engring. Edn., 1971, Frederic Ives Medal, 1990, Optical Soc. Am., Ester Hoffman Beller award Optical Soc. of Am., 1995. Fellow AAAS, Optical Soc. Am. (dir. 1977-83, editor jour. 1978-83, Max Born award 1983, Frederick Ives award 1990, Esther Hoffman Beller medal 1995, v.p. 1990, pres.-elect 1991, pres. 1992, past pres. 1993), IEEE (edn. medal 1987), Soc. Photo-optical Instrumentation Engrs. (bd. govs. 1979-82, 88-90, Dennis Gabor award 1987, Gold medal 2007), Am. Acad. Arts and Scis.; mem. NAE, Electromagnetics Acad. Home: 570 University Ter Los Altos CA 94022-3523 Office: Stanford U Dept Elec Engring Stanford CA 94305 Business E-Mail: goodman@ee.stanford.edu.

GOODMAN, KAREN LACERTE, financial services executive; b. Mesa, Ariz., Nov. 9, 1946; d. Howard Lee and Margaret (Duncan) G.; m. Grant A. Lacerte, Feb. 1, 1964; children: Arthur Grant Jr., Arcel Leon Rene. Student, George Washington U., 1974-76. Prodn. mgr. Data Corp. of Am., Reston, Va., 1967-73; pres. Transco Leasing Co., Washington, 1974-78; sec., treas. to v.p. Certa Data Corp., Orlando, Fla., 1989—; pres. Fin. Rsch. Assocs., Inc., Orlando, 1979—. Cons. in field, 1979—; dir. statis. seminars in field. Editor, pub.: Financial Studies of the Small Business (annual publ.), 1976—. Mem. Am. Heart Assn., Winter Haven, Fla., MADD, 1985—. Mem. Greater Orlando C. of C. Republican. Home: 6759 Winterset Gardens Rd Winter Haven FL 33884-3154 Office: 203 Ave A NW Ste 202 Winter Haven FL 33881-4503 Home Phone: 863-324-4047; Office Phone: 863-299-2400. E-mail: kgoodman@certipay.com.

GOODMAN, KIM C., credit card and former computer company executive; BA in Polit. Sci., Stanford U., MS in Indsl. Engring.; MBA, Harvard U., 1992. V.p. Bain & Co., Inc.; v.p. bus. devel., exec. asst. to the CEO Dell Inc., v.p., gen. mgr. for networking product group, v.p. pub. sector mktg. & transactional sales, 2003—05, v.p. software & peripherals, 2005—07; exec. v.p. No. Am. merchant services Am. Express, NYC, 2007—. Bd. dirs. AutoNation, Inc, 2007—. Office: American Express World Fin Ctr 200 Vesey St New York NY 10285-5104*

GOODMAN, LARRY J., health facility administrator; b. Detroit, 1950; Degree with distinction, U. Mich., MD, 1976. Diplomate Am. Bd. Internal Medicine, Am. Bd. Infectious Disease. Intern Rush Presbyn.-St. Luke's Med. Ctr., Chgo., 1976—77; resident in internal medicine Rush U. Med. Ctr., Chgo., 1977—79, chief resident, 1979, fellow in infectious disease, 1979—81, mem. faculty and staff, 1981—87, former prof., assoc. dean med. student programs, former dir. divsn. specialized tng. programs, dir. interinstnl. affairs, sr. v.p. for med. affairs, 1998—2002; Henry R. Russe dean, prof. Rush Med. Coll., Chgo., 2000—02; pres., CEO Rush U. Med. Ctr., 2002—; med. dir. Cook County Hosp., Chgo., 1996—98. Pres. Rush U., Chgo.; prin. officer Rush Bd. Trustees; CEO, chmn. bd. dirs. Rush Sys. for Health; mem. site survey team Liaison Com. on Med. Edn. Contbr. articles to profl. jours. Office: Rush U Med Ctr 1650 W Harrison St Chicago IL 60612

GOODMAN, LINDSEY ALAN, furniture manufacturing executive, architect; b. LA, Nov. 17, 1957; s. Ira and Wilma Carolyn (Sanders) G.; m. Joan Frances Radditz, July 7, 1990; children: Alexandra Isabelle, Andrew Nicholas. BA, UCLA, 1980; MArch, Calif. State Poly. U., Pomona, 1983. Registered architect. Project designer Bertram Berenson, Architect, Claremont, Calif., 1983; job capt. Architecture & Planning, San Rafael, Calif., 1985-86, Barry Archtl. Design Group, Santa Barbara, Calif., 1986-87; project architect Architects West, Santa Barbara, 1987-89; prin. L.A. Goodman, Architect, Santa Barbara, 1989-91; v.p. Homtomi Am., Inc., Chino, Calif., 1992—2000, pres., 2000—, also bd. dirs. Bd. dirs. Homtomi Holdings, Inc.; ptnr. Homtomi/Capitel Devel., Chino, 1991—; bd. advisors Human Race, Inc., Santa Barbara, 1997-98; hon. chmn. bus. adv. coun. Nat. Rep. Congl. Com., 2003-06. Author: (poem) The Camargue, 1987. Adv. coun. Santa Barbara Mus. Natural History, 1988-89, 95-96, trustee, 1989-95, v.p. bd. trustees, 96-98, pres., 1998-2001; patron Santa Barbara Civic Light Opera, 1992-2000; mem. Young Pres.'s Orgn., 1996-2002. Mem.: NRCC Bus. Adv. Coun. (hon. chmn. 2003—06), AIA. Avocations: tennis, international travel, reading, attending musicals and plays. Office: Homtomi Am Inc 15044 La Palma Dr Chino CA 91710-9669

GOODMAN, LOUIS ALLAN, lawyer; b. Providence, Nov. 13, 1943; s. Jacob and Frieda (Feldman) G.; m. Phebe Silver, June 9, 1968; children: Jonathan J., Rebecca A. AB, Columbia U., 1965; MA, Harvard U., 1966, JD, 1969. Bar: NY 1970, Mass. 1973. Assoc. Skadden, Arps, Slate, Meagher & Flom LLP, 1970—77, ptnr., 1978—. Home: 59 North St Newton MA 02460-1065 Office: Skadden, Arps, Slate, Meagher & Flom LLP 1 Beacon St Boston MA 02108-3107 Home Phone: 617-964-1978; Office Phone: 617-573-4830.

GOODMAN, MAJOR MERLIN, botanical sciences educator; b. Iowa, Sept. 13, 1938; s. Jarrett Wilson and Mable Ollie (Michael) G.; m. Sheila Balfour Dail; children: Sean Balfour Dail, Andrew Scot Dail. BS, Iowa State U., 1960; MS, N.C. State U., 1963, PhD, 1965. Rsch. asst. N.C. State U., Raleigh, 1960-61, NSF coop. fellow, 1961-65; NSF postdoctoral fellow Inst. de Genetica Escola Superior de Agricultura, Piracicaba, Sao Paulo, Brazil, 1965-67; vis. asst. prof. N.C. State U., Raleigh, 1967-68, asst. prof., 1968-70, assoc. prof., 1970-76, prof. crop sci., statistics, genetics, botany, 1976-88, W.N. Reynolds disting. univ. prof., 1988—. Co-author: Races of Maize in Brazil and Adjacent Areas, 1977; author numerous tech. artilces. Recipient research awards Sigma Xi, 1973, N.C. State U. Alumni Assn., 1982, O.M.Gardner award, 1987, Meyer medal, 2000, Holladay medal, 2003; named Outstanding PhD Phi Sigma and Phi Kappa Phi, 1965. Mem.: Crop Sci. Soc. Am. (Rsch. award 2005), Soc. for Econ. Botany, Nat. Acad. Scis. Achievements include clarification of genetics of numerous isozyme loci in maize including chromosomal localizations; devel. of several commercially used parental inbred lines of corn. Office: NC State Univ Crop Sci Dept PO Box 7620 Raleigh NC 27695-7620 Home Phone: 919-828-4709; Office Phone: 919-515-7039. Business E-Mail: major_goodman@nesu.edu.

GOODMAN, MARK N., lawyer; BA, Prescott Coll., 1973; JD summa cum laude, Calif. Western Sch. Law, 1977; LLM, U. Calif., Berkeley, 1978. Bar: Ariz. 1977, US Dist. Ct. Ariz. 1978, US Ct. Appeals (9th cir.) 1978, US Supreme Ct. 1981. Practice Law Offices Mark N. Goodman, Prescott, Ariz., 1978-79, 81-82, Mark N. Goodman, Ltd., Prescott, 1983—88; ptnr. Alward and Goodman, Ltd., Prescott, 1979-81, Goodman Law Firm, P.C., Prescott, 1988—. Author: The Ninth Amendment, 1981; contbr. articles to profl. jours.; notes and comments editor Calif. Western Law Rev., 1976. Bd. dirs. Yavapai Symphony Assn., Prescott, 1981-84, N. Ariz. chpt. Alzheimer's Assn., 1995-97. Mem.: ABA, Yavapai County Bar Assn. (v.p. 1981—82), State Bar Ariz. (vice chmn. fee arbitration com. 1988—2002). Office: Goodman Law Firm PC PO Box 2489 Prescott AZ 86302-2489 Office Phone: 928-445-3230. E-mail: info@goodmanlaw.com.

GOODMAN, MAX A., lawyer, educator; b. Chgo., May 24, 1924; s. Sam and Nettie (Abramowitz) G.; m. Marlyene Monkarsh, June 2, 1946; children: Jan M., Lauren A. Packard, Melanie Murez. AA, Herzl Jr. Coll., 1943; student, Northwestern U., 1946—47; JD, Loyola U., 1948; LLD (hon.), Southwestern U. Sch. Law, 2000. Bar: Calif. 1948; cert. family law specialist, 1980, 85, 90. Pvt. practice, LA, 1948-53; ptnr. Goodman, Hirschberg & King, LA, 1953-81; prof. Southwestern U. Sch. Law, LA, 1966—2006, prof. emeritus in residence, 2006—. Lectr. Calif. Continuing Edn. of the Bar, 1971—90. Contbr. articles to profl. jours. Served to cpl. U.S. Army, 1943-45. Mem. ABA (chmn. law sch. curriculum com. family law sect. 1987-88, family law sect. 1987-88, 97-98), State Bar Calif. (del. conf. dels. 1972, 80-87, 91, exec. com. family law sect. 1981-85), Los Angeles County Bar Assn. (chmn. family law sect. 1971-72, editor family law handbook 1974-89). Avocation: bridge. Office: Southwestern U Sch Law 3050 Wilshire Blvd Los Angeles CA 90010-1106 Office Phone: 213-738-6823. Business E-Mail: mgoodman@swlaw.edu.

GOODMAN, MICHAEL B(ARRY), communications educator; b. Dallas, July 10, 1949; s. Harold A. and Dora (Einhorn) G.; m. Karen E. Kailenta, June 4, 1977; children: 1 stepchild, Craig Cook, 1 child, John David. BA, U. Tex., 1971; MA, SUNY, Stony Brook, 1972, PhD, 1979. Adj. instr. SUNY, Old Westbury, 1976—79; adj. asst. prof. NY Inst. Tech., NYC, 1976—82, NYU, NYC, 1979—81; asst. prof. SUNY, Stony Brook, 1979—81, Northeastern U., Boston, 1982-86; prof. corp. comm. Fairleigh Dickinson U., Madison, NJ, 1986—2007, dir. MA in Corp. Comm. program, 1996—2002, founder, dir. Corp. Comm. Inst., 1999—; prof. corp. comm. Baruch Coll. CUNY, NYC, 2007—. Cons. in corp. comms. to numerous orgns. in U.S.; condr. seminars and workshops on corp. comm., 1979—; conf. chmn. Internat. Profl. Comm. Conf., Phila., 1993, New Orleans, 1999; founder Ann. Conf. on Corp. Comm., 1988-98, 2002—; adj. prof. Baruch Coll., CUNY, 2004-2007; vis. prof. Bangkok U., 2006—, Hong Kong Poly. U., 2006, Aarhus Sch. Bus., Denmark, 2006, U. Johannesbourg, South Africa, 2007; lectr. in field. Assoc. editor, mem. editl. adv. bd.: Corp. Comm. An Internat. Jour., 2006—. V.p. Friends Sem. PTA, N.Y.C., 1990-91; mem. adv. bd. Bus. Diplomatic Action, 2003—. Named to Resident Faculty Nat. Faculty Excellence in Teaching English Program, Vassar Coll., 1984. Fellow Royal Soc. Encouragement Arts, Mfrs. and Commerce (London), Soc. Tech. Comm.; mem. Profl. Comm. Soc. of IEEE (sr., mem. adminstrv. com., Alfred Goldsmith award 1994), MLA, Nat. Coun. Tchrs. of English, Am. Mgmt. Assn., Assn. Bus. Comm. (v.p. 2005—, bd. dirs. 2005—, chmn. program internat. conv. 2007), Authors Guild, Authors League, Arthur W. Page Soc., Assn. Bus. Comm. (v.p. ea. region U.S., bd. dirs. 2005—), Nat. Investors Rels. Inst. Avocations: hiking, skiing, bicycling. Home: 28 W 38th St Apt 11W New York NY 10018-6287 Office: Dept Comm Baruch Coll CUNY Box 8-240 New York NY 10010 Office Phone: 646-312-3720. Business E-Mail: cci@corporatecomm.org.

GOODMAN, OSCAR BAYLIN, mayor, lawyer; b. Phila., July 26, 1939; s. A. Allen and (Baylin) Goodman; m. Carolyn Goldmark, June 6, 1962; children: Oscar B., Ross C., Eric A., Cara Lee. BA, Haverford Coll., 1961; JD, U. Pa., 1964. Bar: Nev. 1965, US Ct. Appeals. Chief dep. pub. defender Clark County, Nev., 1966—67; sr. ptnr. Goodman, Chesnoff and Keach (formerly Goodman, Stein & Chesnoff), Las Vegas, 1965—; mayor City of Las Vegas, 1999—. Adv. bd. Us. Conf. of Mayors. Guest appearance (films) Casino, 1995, (TV series) CSI: Crime Scene Investigation, 2004. Named one of Best Criminal Defense Attys., Las Vegas Review-Jour., 1999. Mem.: Nat. Assn. Criminal Def. Lawyers (pres. 1983). Democrat. Jewish. Office: City Hall 10th Fl 400 Stewart Ave Las Vegas NV 89101-2927 also: Goodman Chesnoff & Keach 520 S 4th St Las Vegas NV 89101-6524 Office Phone: 702-229-6241, 702-384-5563.*

GOODMAN, RICHARD, food products executive; BA, MA, MBA, PhD, Columbia Univ. Fin. mgmt. positions through corp. v.p. & CFO specialty chemicals W.R. Grace & Co., 1979—92; v.p. corp. strategic planning, CFO KFC Internat. Pepsico, 1992—94, sr. v.p. CFO Taco Bell, 1994—97; exec. v.p. CFO Sunterra Corp., Orlando, Fla., 1998; v.p. gen auditor Pepsico, 2000—01; sr. v.p. CFO Pepsico Beverages Internat., 2001—03, Pepsico Internat., 2003—06; CFO Pepsico, Purchase, NY, 2006—. Office: Pepsico 700 Anderson Hill Rd Purchase NY 10577*

GOODMAN, RICHARD H., biomedical researcher; BS, MIT; MD, PhD, U. Penn., 1976. Trainee Tufts-New England Med. Ctr., Boston, 1976—78; endocrinology fellow New England Med. Ctr., 1978—82, 1978—82; asst. prof. Harvard Med. Sch., 1982; prof. Tufts-New England Med. Ctr., 1983—90, chief of molecular medicine div., 1983—90; prof. Oreg. Health

& Sci. U., Portland, 1990—, dir. Vollum Inst., 1990—. Contbr. scientific papers. Mem.: Inst. Medicine. Office: The Vollum Inst Oreg Health & Sci Univ L474 3181 SW Sam Jackson Pk Rd Portland OR 97239-3098 Office Phone: 503-494-5078. Office Fax: 503-494-4353. E-mail: goodmanr@ohsu.edu.

GOODMAN, RICHARD SHALEM, lawyer, orthopedic surgeon; m. Jemi Horn; children: Lorraine, Carolyn Pianin, Deborah Lieb, Keith London, Evan London. BA, Alfred U., NY, 1955; MD, NYU, 1960; JD, Touro Coll., 1987. Bar: N.Y. 1991, U.S. Ct. Claims 1995, U.S. Ct. Mil. Appeals 1995, U.S. Ct. Appeals 1995, U.S. Supreme Ct. 1995; lic. physician, N.Y., Calif.; diplomate Am. Bd. Orthopedic Surgery. Intern Ind. U. Med. Ctr., Indianapolis, 1960—61; asst. resident in gen. surgery Bronx Mcpl. Hosp. Ctr., 1961—62; resident in orthopedics N.Y.C. Med. Ctr. and various others, 1964—67; attending physician St. Catherine of Sienna Hosp. (formerly St. John's Episcopal Hosp.), Smithtown, NY, 1967—, pres. med. staff, 1978; attending physician Cmty. Hosp. Suffolk, Smithtown, 1967—96; cons. in orthop. LIJ Hosp., New Hyde Park, NY, 1996—; adjunct staff dept. Orthop. Surgery North Shore U. Med. Ctr., 2001—; chmn. clin. dept. surgery Saba U. Med. Sch., 2006—. Asst. prof. dept. anatomy SUNY, Stony Brook, 1971-88, Stonybrook Found. Pres. Marine Scis. Rsch. Ctr., 1984-87; pres. staff Community Hosp. of We. Suffolk, 1977-78; policy advisor Inst. Advancement Health Care Mgmt., U. Albany, SUNY, 1992—; cons. to numerous bus., govt. agys., and ins. cos.; presenter, speaker, and panelist in fields. Co-author: American Jurisprudence Proof of Facts, 3d series, vol. 2 Pelvic Injuries, 1988, Handling Soft Tissue Injury Cases: Medical Aspects, 1988, 2d edit., 1993, Preparing and Winning Medical Negligence Cases, 1989, 2d edit., 1994, Legal Medicine: Legal Dynamics of Medical Encounters, 2d edit., 1990; contbr. articles to med. and lega. jours., chapters to books; mem. editl. bd.: Orthopedics and Orthopedics Today, 1984—87, Med. Malpractice Prevention, bd. editl. cons.:, med. disability advisor: Workplace Guidelines for Disability Duration, 5th edit., vol. 1; contbr. chapters to books. Trustee Alfred U., 1978-84; policy adv. Inst. Advancement Health Care Mgmt. U. Albany; nat. chmn. U. Albany Parents Fund, 1991-94; nat. chmn. U. Albany Parent's Fund, 1991-92; active Arthritis Found. Fellow: Am. Coll. Legal Med. (program chmn. annual meeting 1988—, mem. policy and planning com.), Am. Acad. Orthoped. Surgeons; mem.: Assn. Bar City N.Y., Suffolk County Bar Assn., N.Y. Bar Assn., Internat. Coll. Surgeons, N.Y. State Med. Soc., Suffolk County Med. Soc., Am. Soc. Law and Med., Ea. Orthoped. Assn., Am. Coll. Legal Medicine (chmn. exhibits com. ann. meeting 1989—90, mem. program com. ann. meeting 1989—90, mem. com. to confer with com. Med. Soc. State N.Y. 1991—, co-chmn. exhibitor's com. 1993, mem. rsch. com. 1993, mem. student awards com. 1993, chmn. computer bull. bd. sys. 1995, mem. policy and planning com., assoc. editor Communique and newsbriefs), Bach Aria Group (bd. dirs. 1970—88), NYU Bellevue Alumni Assn., Stony Brook Yacht Club, Univ. Club. Office: 285 E Main St Smithtown NY 11787 also: 743 Columbia Tpke East Greenbush NY 12061 Address: 5 Route 376 Hopewell Junction NY 12533 Office: 350 Fifth Ave Ste 2613 26th Fl New York NY 10118 Office Phone: 631-724-2727. Personal E-mail: RSGMDESQ@aol.com.

GOODMAN, ROBERT MARK, dean, educator; b. NYC, Aug. 14, 1949; s. Morris and Sherry Goodman. BA, Bklyn Coll., 1970; MA, U. Hawaii Manoa, Honolulu, 1975, MPH, 1977; PhD, U. NC, Chapel Hill, 1987. Prof. and chair U. Pitts. GSPH, 2003—07; dean Ind. U. HPER, Bloomington, Ind., 2007—. Usdin family prof. Tulane U., New Orleans, 1997—2003. Recipient Advocacy award, Ctrs. Disease Control and Prevention. Fellow: Soc. Pub. Health Edn.; mem.: APHA (Early Career award). Achievements include Advocacy Award - Centers for Disease Control and Prevention. Home Phone: 412-661-7799; Office Phone: 412-624-3100.

GOODMAN, ROBERT UHLE, lawyer; b. Shreveport, La., Apr. 18, 1929; s. Uhle Slater and Edith (Caskey) Goodman; m. Martha Knox McGuffin, Mar. 22, 1957. BA, Washington and Lee U., 1950; LLB, La. State U., 1953. Bar: La. 1953. Ptnr. Naff, Goodman, and Johns and successor firms, Shreveport, 1956—89; pvt. practice Robert U. Goodman, P.C., Shreveport, 1989—. Former asst. city atty. City of Shreveport; former asst. atty. gen. State of La.; bd. dirs. Pioneer Bank, Aeropres Corp., Sound Fighter Sys., Inc. Gen. counsel Housing Authority City of Shreveport; bd. dirs., former pres. North La. Goodwill Industries Rehab. Ctr., Inc.; former bd. dirs. Salvation Army; chancellor, former vestry mem. St. Mark's Cathedral, 1965—; past pres. Holiday in Dixie. Capt. USAF, 1953—55. Recipient Runner-up Outstanding Man of Yr. Mem.: Housing and Devel. Law Inst., 5th Cir. Bar Assn., Garden of the Gods Club, Ambassadors Club (past chmn.), Cambridge Club, Shreveport Club. Republican. Episcopalian. Office: 416 Travis St Ste 1105 Shreveport LA 71101-5504 Home Phone: 318-868-5848; Office Phone: 318-221-1601. E-mail: rugus@bellsouth.net.

GOODMAN, ROY MATZ, corporate financial executive, former state senator; b. NYC, Mar. 5, 1930; s. Bernard A. and Alice (Matz) G.; m. Barbara Christine Furrer, June 28, 1955; children: Claire Goodman Pellegrini Cloud, Leslie Alice, Randolph Bernard. BA cum laude, Harvard U., 1951, MBA with distinction, 1953; DHL (hon.), Pratt Inst., 1994; LLD (hon.), Baruch Coll. CUNY, 2002. Assoc. buying and new bus. dept. Kuhn, Loeb & Co. Investment Bankers, 1955-60; pres., dir. Drug Devel. Corp., Ex-Lax, Inc., Roycemore, Inc., 1962-71; mem. N.Y. State Senate, 1969—2002; pres., CEO UN Devel. Corp., NYC, 2002—. Dep. majority leader for policy, chmn. investigations, taxation and govt. ops. com.; chmn. Senate spl. com. on arts and cultural affairs; mem. Senate task forces on def. spending, AIDS, vandalism, religious desecration and bigotry, and econ. recovery and devel.; fin., rules, cities, edn., crime and correction and transp. coms., subcom. on librs. chmn. legis. com. on pub. pvt., coop., 1985-88; chmn. housing and urban devel. com., 1968-76; pres. Goodman Family Found.; bd. dirs. 1st Empire State Corp., 1984-2000; mem. adv. bd. Chem. Bank, 1963-65, M & T Bank Corp., 2000- , commr. fin., fin. adminstr. City of N.Y., 1966-68; mem. N.Y.C. Banking Commn., 1966-68; past trustee N.Y.C. Police Pension Fund, N.Y.C. Fire Dept. Pension Fund, 1966-68; mem. Mayor's Cabinet and Supercabinet, 1966-68, N.Y.C. Treas., 1966-68; chmn. State Charter Revision Commn. for N.Y.C., 1972-76; adj. prof. pub. admin. Baruch Coll. CUNY, 1975; mem. Mayor Guiliani Transition Team, 1993; mem. Gov. Pataki Transition Team, 1994. Bd. dirs. Citizens Com. N.Y.C.; past mem. bd. Brotherhood-In-Action; trustee Heart Rsch. Found.; exec. asst. to chmn. N.Y. State Assembly Jud. Com., 1963-64; asst. to atty. gen. State N.Y., 1960; pres. 9th A.D. Rep. Club, 1963-64; del. N.Y. State Rep. Convs., 1966-2000, del. Rep. Nat. Conv., 1968, 72, 76, 80, 84, 88, 92, 96, 2000, 2004, Presdl. Elector, 1984; chmn. N.Y. County Rep. Com., 1981-2002, treas., 1965; mem. N.Y. Rep. State Com., exec. com.; N.Y. State co-chmn. Bush-for-Pres. campaigns, 1988, 92, Bush-Quayle Nat. Fin. Com., 1988, 92; candidate for Mayor of N.Y.C., 1977; trustee Carnegie Hall Soc., Inc., Carnegie Hall Corp., past trustee Columbia Coll. Pharm. Scis., L.I. Coll. Hosp., N.Y. Com. Young Audiences, United Jewish Appeal, Tel Aviv U., Freedom House, Dalton Schs. Brotherhood-In-Action, Heart Rsch. Found.; presdl. appointee to Nat. Commn. Fine Arts, 1985-89, Nat. Endowment Arts Coun., 1989-96, trustee John F. Kennedy Ctr. for Performing Arts, 2002-; amb. arts NEA, 2000; fellow Met. Mus. Art; patron Met. Opera; sponsor N.Y. Philharm. Soc.; mem. Regents vis. com. N.Y. State Mus.; trustee Temple Emanu-El; past bd. dirs. Freedom House; mem. N.Y. Com. for Young Audiences, Harvard Com. on Univ. Resources,; mem. bd. overseers John F. Kennedy Sch. Govt./Harvard U. Lt. USNR, 1953-56. Decorated Adm.'s Meritorious Svc. citation; recipient Disting. Service award Jaycees, 1966, Mt. Scopus citation Hebrew U., Jerusalem, 1968, Scroll of Honor United Jewish Appeal, 1970, Kennedy Ctr. award for Disting. Leadership in Arts-in Edn., Nat. Arts Club Citation of Merit, City U., Medal of Merit, 1972, Man of Yr. award Brotherhood-in-Action, 1972, Humanitarian award Soc. for Prevention Cruelty to Children, 1976, citation for cmty. service Odyssey House, 1976, Our Town newspaper award for leadership in City Charter revision, 1976, Fiorello H. LaGuardia Meml. award, 1979-80, citation for outstanding service N.Y. Young Rep. Club, 1982, Disting. Alumni award Hunter Coll. Elem. Sch. Parents Assn., 1985, Service awards N.Y. Police Found. and N.Y. Fire Safety Found., 1986, Patriotic Service award U.S. Treasury Dept., N.Y. Gov.'s Arts Medal, 2002, Sutton Area Cmty. Svc. Award, 2002, WNYC Radio Arts Award, 2002, U.N. Delegations' Citizen of the World Award, 2002, Alliance of N.Y. Arts Org. Arts Advocate Award, 2002, City Club of N.Y. Disting. New Yorker Award, 2002, Internat. Coun. for Caring Communities Caring Citizen of the Humanities Award, 2003; named to honor scroll Columbia Assn. of N.Y.C. Police Dept., 1979, N.Y. State Rep. of Yr. Ripon Soc., 1972, Cmty. Activist award Lenox Hill Neighborhood Assn., Inc., 1995, Artists fellowship award, John LaFarge Meml. award for interracial justice, Local Hero award Stanley Isaacs Assn., Playwrights Horizon award, 1995, Gari Melchers Meml. medal, 1995, South Street Seaport Mus. award, 1995, Friend of the Arts award Town Hall Found., 1995, Legacy of Hope award N.Y. Foundling Home, Carnegie Hall, 1996, Margaret Sanger award Family Advs. N.Y., 1997; Statesman Father of Yr. award, 1984, named to Econ. Hon. Soc. St. John's U., 1991. Mem. Anti-Defamation League (bd. govs. N.Y.), Am. Young Pres.'s Orgn., Fin. Analysts Fedn., N.Y. Soc. Security Analysts, Council Fgn. Rels., Woodrow Wilson Internat. Ctr. Scholars (mem. adv. group), Assn. Harvard Alumni (past dir.), Harvard Club (gov.), Century Assn., Century Country Club, Dutch Treat Club, Senate Club (pres.), Harvard Bus. Sch., City Club, Omicron Delta Epsilon (hon.). Home: 1035 5th Ave New York NY 10028-0135 Office: 2 UN Plaza 27th Fl New York NY 10017

GOODMAN, SAM RICHARD, electronics executive; b. NYC, May 23, 1930; s. Morris and Virginia (Gross) G.; m. Beatrice Bettencourt, Sept. 15, 1957; children: Mark Stuart, Stephen Manuel, Christopher Bettencourt. BBA, CCNY, 1951; MBA, NYU, 1957, PhD, 1968. Chief acct. John C. Valentine Co., NYC, 1957-60; mgr. budgets and analysis Gen. Foods Corp., White Plains, NY, 1960-63; budget dir. Crowell Collier Pub. Co., NYC, 1963-64; v.p., chief fin. officer Nestle Co., Inc., White Plains, 1964; chief fin. officer Aileen, Inc., N.Y.C., 1973-74, Ampex Corp., 1974-76; exec. v.p. fin. and adminstrn. Baker & Taylor Co. div. W.R. Grace Co., NYC, 1976-79, Magnuson Computer Systems, Inc., San Jose, Calif., 1979-81; v.p., chief fin. officer Datamac Computer Systems, Sunnyvale, Calif., 1981; pres. Nutritional Foods Inc., San Francisco, 1983-84; chmn., chief exec. officer CMX Corp., Santa Clara, Calif., 1984-88; dir., sr. v.p. Masstor Systems Corp., Santa Clara, 1988—; pvt. cons. Atherton, Calif., 1990—; sr. mgmt. cons. Durkee/Sharlit, 1991—; pres. Mayfair Packing Co., 1991—; mng. dir. Quincy Pacific Ptnrs., L.P., 1992—; pres., CEO Mayfair Packing Co., San Jose, Calif., 1991-94; pvt. cons. BMG Assocs., 1994—. Lectr. NYU Inst. Mgmt., 1965-67, U. San Francisco, 2006; asst. prof. mktg. Iona Coll. Grad. Sch. Adminstrn., 1967-69; prof. fin. and mktg. Pace U. Grad. Sch. Bus. Adminstrn., 1969-79, prof. Golden Gate U., 1974—. Author 7 books, including Controller's Handbook; contbr. articles to jours. Lt. (j.g.) USNR, 1951—55. Decorated Korean Occupation Svc. medal Armed Forces Svc., Nat. Def. Svc. medal. Mem. Fin. Execs. Inst., Nat. Assn. Accts., Am. Statis. Assn., Am. Econs. Assn., Planning Execs. Inst., Am. Arbitration Assn., Turnaround Mgmt. Assn. Home and Office: 60 Shearer Dr Atherton CA 94027-3957 Office Phone: 650-207-7411. Personal E-mail: bgoodman@cbnorcal.com.

GOODMAN, SEYMOUR EVAN, computer science and international studies educator, researcher, consultant; b. Chgo., June 19, 1943; s. Paul S. and Shirley (Young) G.; m. Diane Margot Samuel, Dec. 18, 1966; children: Richard Michael, Steven Neal. BS, Columbia U., 1965, MS, 1966; PhD, Calif. Inst. Tech., 1970. Asst. prof. applied math. U. Va., Charlottesville, 1970-75, assoc. prof. applied math. and computer sci., 1975-81; prof. mgmt. info. sys. U. Ariz., Tucson, 1981—2000; prof. Sam Nunn Sch. Internat. Affairs Coll. of Computing, Ga. Inst. of Tech., Atlanta, 1999—; co-dir. Ctr. Internat. Strategy Tech. and Policy, 2000—, Ga. Tech. Info. Security Ctr., 2000—. Vis. prof. pub. and internat. affairs, Princeton U., NJ, 1977-79, rsch. fellow, 1978-79; vis. scholar U. Chgo., 1979; mem. Mid. Ea. Ctr., 1992-00; Carnegie Sci. fellow Ctr. Internat. Security and Arms Control, Stanford U., 1994-97; dir. program info. tech. and nat. security, 1996-98, dir. Consortium for Rsch. on Info. Security and Policy, Stanford U., 1998-2000, vis. prof. dept. engring. econ. sys. and ops. rsch., 1998-99; mem. adv. com. Internat. Trade Adminstrn., Dept. Commerce, 1979-82; mem. adv. com. Def. Sci. Bd., Dept. Def., 1981-84, Def. Intelligence Agy., 1983-87, NRC coms., 1985-92, Dept. State, 1987-89; chmn. NRC com. Internat. Devel. in Computer Sci. and Tech., 1987-88; chmn. computer tech.-subpanel NRC panel on Future Design and Implementation of US Nat. Security Export Controls, 2005-07, chmn. NRC Com. on Improving Cybersecurity Rsch. in the US, 2005-07; cons. govtl. agys. Danforth Assoc., 1977-82; Sesquicentennial Assoc. State of Va., 1977; mem. telecom study panel US Dept. Def., 2003-04, chmn. Com. on cybersecurity rsch. in US, NRC. Editor: Technology and Transnational Political Issues, International Information Systems, 1991-93; adv. bd. PRIISM, 1995-97; adv. editor Jour. Global Info. Tech. Mgmt., 1997-2000; mem. editl. bd. Jour. Info. Tech. in Internat. Devel., 2002-; contbr. numerous articles to profl. jours. NSF grantee, 1978-79, 83, 2001-; numerous grant and rsch. contracts Office Tech. Assessment, U.S. Congress, MacArthur Found., 2003-, Los Alamos Nat. Lab., USAF, Battelle Meml. Labs., IBM, Nat. Coun. for Soviet and East European Rsch., Dept. Commerce, Dept. Def., NSF; U.S. participant U.S.-USSR IREX program, 1988-89. Mem. Assn. for Computing Machinery (nat. lectr. 1981-82, com. computing and pub. policy 1981-83, 93—, contbg. editor Internat. Perspectives, Comms. 1991—), Am. Assn. for Advancement of Slavic Studies, Computer Soc. of IEEE (com. on pub. policy 1987-95), Highlands Forum. Office: Sam Nunn Sch Internat Affairs Coll Computing Ga Inst Tech 781 Marietta Ave NW Atlanta GA 30332-0610 Home Phone: 770-455-7554; Office Phone: 404-385-1461. Business E-Mail: goodman@cc.gatech.edu.

GOODMAN, STANLEY, lawyer; b. Cin., June 16, 1931; s. Sol and Ethel (Barsman) G.; m. Diane Elaine Kassel, Apr. 15, 1956; children: Julie Lerner, Jeffrey Stephen, Richard Paul. BA, U. Cin., 1953, JD, 1955. Bar: Ohio 1955, Ky. 1976. Ptnr. Goodman & Goodman, Cin., 1955—. Dir. Winbco Tank Co., Ottumwa, Iowa; lectr. Ohio Bar Continuing Legal Edn. Series; mediator Am. Health Lawyers Alternative Dispute Resolution Svc.; mediator, arbitrator Thomas H. Crush Dispute Resolution Svc.; dir. Spring Valley Bank, Wyoming, Ohio. Mem. ABA, Am. Health Lawyers Assn., Ohio State Bar Assn. (chair eminent domain com. 1997-2000), Ky. Bar Assn., Cin. Bar Assn., Bankers Club, Ridge Club. Jewish. Office: 123 E 4th St Cincinnati OH 45202-4003 Home Phone: 513-221-4699; Office Phone: 513-621-1505. E-mail: sgoodman@goodlaw.com.

GOODMAN, STEPHEN MURRY, lawyer; b. Phila., Oct. 8, 1940; s. Edward and Jean (Landau) G.; m. Janis Freeman, Jan. 8, 1983; children: Carl, Rachel. BS cum laude, U. Pa., 1962, LLB magna cum laude, 1965. Bar: DC 1967, Pa. 1969. Law clerk to Hon. David Bazelon US Ct. Appeals (DC cir.), Washington, 1965-66; law clk. to Hon. William J. Brennan Jr. US Supreme Ct., Washington, 1966-67; ptnr. Goodman & Ewing, Phila., 1970-83, Wolf, Block, Schorr & Solis-Cohen, Phila., 1983-94, Morgan, Lewis & Bockius LLP, Phila., 1995—. Mem. Order of Coif. Democrat. Jewish. Avocation: profl. jazz pianist. Office: Morgan Lewis & Bockius LLP 1701 Market St Philadelphia PA 19103-2903 Home Phone: 215-922-4154; Office Phone: 215-963-5086. Business E-Mail: sgoodman@morganlewis.com.

GOODMAN, STEVEN MICHAEL, conservation biologist; b. Detroit, Aug. 3, 1957; BS, U. Mich., 1984; PhD, U. Hamburg, 2000; HDR, U. Paris-Sud XI, 2005. Field biologist Field Mus. Natural History, Chgo., 1989—. Prof. U. Autananarivo, Madagascar, 1994—; coord. etology tng. program WWF Madagascar, 1994—. Author: The Birds of Egypt, 1989; editor: Natural Change and Human Impact in Madagasian, 1997; co-editor, lead author The Natural History of Madagascar, 2004. Grantee John and Catherine MacArthur Found., 1995-98, Nat. Geographic Soc.; named MacArthur fellow, John D. and Catherine T. MacArthur Found., 2005. Office: Field Mus of Natural History Roosevelt Rd/Lake Shore Dr Chicago IL 60605

GOODMAN, SYLVIA KLUMOK, film center executive; b. Moorhead, Miss., June 19, 1940; d. Sol Harry and Fannie Ida (Davidson) Klumok; m. Carl Gerald Goodman, June 5, 1960; children: Lisa Wynne Goodman Stone, Gary Steven, Jeffrey David. BS in Zoology with honors, Newcomb Coll., 1962; M in Zoology, Tulane U., 1963; postgrad., Harvard U., 1990. Tchr. Midway Jr. H.S., Shreveport, La., 1963-68; instr. biology La. State U., Shreveport, 1967-68; instr. physiology, asst. coord. plans La. State U. Med. Ctr., Shreveport, 1970-74; chmn. bd. dir. Goldring Woldenberg Inst. So. Jewish Life, 2000—03; pres., CEO Robinson Film Ctr., Shreveport, La., 2004—. Pres. Shreveport Jewish Fedn., 1982—83; mem. C. of C. 100 Women of the Century; chmn. Food Project, Shreveport, 1990—92; chair beautification com. Shreveport Regional Airport, 1990—94, So. Jewish Inst., 2000—; pres. Sci-Port Discovery Ctr., 1993—95; trustee Shreveport-Bossier Cmty. Fedn., chmn., 1993—; vice chmn. Meadows Art Mus., 1995; mem. Shreveport Mayor's Women's Commn., 1986—90; vice-chair La. State Mineral Bd., Baton Rouge, 1988—92; bd. dir. Sci-Port Discovery Ctr., Shreveport, 1990—, Meadows Art Mus., 1991—97, La. Endowment Humanities, 1996—99; bd. dirs. Robinson Film Theater, 2003—, chair capital campaign, 2003, pres., 2005—; mem. chancellor's adv. com. LSU-S, 1996—; chmn. bd. dir. Goldring/Woldenberg Inst. So. Jewish Life, 2000—. Recipient Humanitarian award NCCJ, Humanitarian award Caddo Commn., 1991, Vol. Fundraiser award Nat. Fedn. Fundraising Execs., 1996, Angel award Blue Cross Blue Shield, 1998, award Point of Light Found., 1999, Friend of Edn. award Caddo Assn. Educators, 2001, Heroines award La., 2006, La. Legend award, 2006, Outstanding Leader of 2006 Outstanding Leader award The Times, 2006; named Women Who Made a Difference Shreveport Celebration of Women Week, 1996, Best-Dressed Woman of No. La. Shreveport Times, 1998, Women of Century, Shreveport C.of C. Mem. Jr. League Shreveport (Sustainer of Yr. award 1995, Daily Point of Light 1999), Mensa, Phi Beta Kappa, Alpha Epsilon Phi. Jewish. Avocations: theater, piano, dance, taking courses, movies. Home: 409 Southfield Rd Shreveport LA 71106-2213 E-mail: gigigood@aol.com.

GOODMAN, TOBY RAY, lawyer; b. Wichita Falls, Tex., Nov. 2, 1948; s. Johnnie U. and Opal E. (Johnson) G.; m. Lisa C. Schrader, Sept. 14, 1967 (div. 1982); children; Brian Scott, Lauri Ann; m. Gloria Jean Majors, June 14, 1983; 1 child, Christie Louise. BBA, Tex. Christian U., 1971; JD, Baylor U., 1974. Bar: Tex. 1974, U.S. Dist. Ct. (no. dist.) Tex. 1974, U.S. Ct. Appeals (5th cir.) 1977. Asst. city atty. City of Arlington, Tex., 1974-76; ptnr. Remington & Goodman, Arlington, 1976-84, Goodman & Clark, Arlington, 1984—; state rep. State of Tex. Dist. 93, 1990—. Chair Tarrant 2000 Civil Justice, 1989-90; mem. Rep. Caucus Tex. Ho. Reps. Fellow Tex. Bar Found.; mem. Arlington Bar Assn. (dir.), Tarrant County Bar Assn. (dir.); vice chair house comm. Juvenile and Family Issues. Baptist. Home: 2801 Knotted Oaks Trl Arlington TX 76006-2759 Office: Goodman & Clark 1600 E Lamar Blvd Ste 250 Arlington TX 76011-4588 Office Phone: 817-460-8171. E-mail: toby@goodmanclark.com.

GOODMAN, VALERIE DAWSON, psychiatric social worker; b. Bluefield, W.Va., Feb. 2, 1948; d. Francis Carl and Lesly (Collett) Dawson; m. David William Goodman, June 9, 1985; 1 child, Amanda Lynn. BS, W.Va. U., 1970, MS, 1972; MSW, U. Md., 1980. Lic. clin. social worker, Md. Social worker Md. Children's Aide Family Svcs. Soc., Balt., 1972-78; social worker III Montgomery County Dept. Social Svcs., Rockville, Md., 1980-81; clin. social worker Johns Hopkins Hosp., Balt., 1981-83; pvt. practice Suburban Psychiat. Assoc. Hopkins at Greenspring Station, Balt., 1986—. Supr. Johns Hopkins Hosp., 1983-86, chair Brogden com., 1984-85, spl. events com. depression and related affective disorders dept. psychiatry, 1994; spkr. in field. Parent vol. Park Sch. Mem. Kappa Delta. Avocations: reading, piano, gourmet cooking, weightlifting. Home: 54 Bellchase Ct Pikesville MD 21208-1300 Office: Suburban Psychiat Svc Md Adult Ctr ADD Johns Hopkins at Greenspring Sta Falls Concourse Falls Rd Ste 306 Lutherville MD 21093 Office Phone: 410-583-2723.

GOODMAN, WILLIAM BEEHLER, editor, literary agent; b. Bklyn., July 1, 1923; s. Philip Howard and Anne Louise (Landersman) G.; m. Lorraine Rappaport, Nov. 24, 1948; children: Jonas Robert, Sara Emily. BA, Washington Sq. Coll., NYU, 1948; MA, U. Mich., 1952. Editor coll. and trade Harcourt Brace Jovanovich Inc., NYC, 1956-76; gen. editor Harvard Univ. Press, Cambridge, Mass., 1976-79; editorial dir. David R. Godine Pub., Inc., Boston, 1979-90, editor, lit. agt., 1990—. Tutor history and lit. Harvard U., 1953-54, lectr. in English, 1982-83, 84-85. Contbr.: essay Reading in the 1980's, 1983. Trustee Warner Library, Tarrytown, N.Y., 1973-75. Served with U.S. Army, 1943-44. Mem.: Harvard (N.Y.C.). Home: 53Lyme Rd 36 Hanover NH 03755-1216 Office Phone: 603-643-3237. Personal E-mail: goodbill@comcast.net.

GOODMAN, WILLIAM RICHARD, insurance adjusting company executive; b. Staunton, Va., Sept. 19, 1930; s. Harry and Ruth (Meyer) G.; m. Alice Helene Katzenstein, June 13, 1954; children: Harvey, Laurie, Barry. BS, U. Md., 1952; JD, U. Balt., 1955. Cert. fellow profl. pub. adjuster, sr. profl. pub. adjuster. Pub. ins. adjuster, lawyer Goodman-Gable-Gould Co., Balt., 1952-73, v.p., 1973-85, pres., 1985-97, CEO, 1985—, chmn. bd., 1989—. Chmn. Baltimore County Indsl. Devel. Commn., 1967-69; mem. Met. Transit Authority, Balt., 1969-71, bd. rev. Dept. Transp., Md., 1971-76, Md. Racing Commn., 1984. Mem. Nat. Assn. Pub. Ins. Adjusters (dir., v.p., pres., chmn. bd. dirs., Disting. Svc. award 1987, Man of Yr. 1995, fellow in profession of pub. adjusting), B'nai B'rith (v.p. Menorah Lodge 1992-94, pres. 1996-98). Democrat. Jewish. Avocation: collecting toy trains and antique cars. Home: 7811 Park Heights Ave Baltimore MD 21208-4322 Office: Goodman-Gable-Gould Co Adjusters Internat 6 Reservoir Cir Ste 202 Baltimore MD 21208-7310 Office Phone: 410-602-0800.

GOODMANSON, RICHARD R., chemicals executive; b. Australia, 1947; m. Janet Goodmanson; 2 children. BCE, Royal Mil. Coll. Australia, 1969; B in Commerce and Econs., U. Queensland, Australia, 1979; MBA, Columbia U., 1980. Prin. McKinsey & Co., Inc., 1980-92; sr. v.p. ops. Frito-Lay, Inc., 1992-96; pres., CEO Am. W. Airlines, 1996-99; exec. v.p., COO DuPont, 1999—. Office: E I DuPont de Nemours and Co 1007 Market St Wilmington DE 19898-0001*

GOODNER, NORMAN WESLEY, governmental relations specialist; b. Fort Smith, Ark., Apr. 16, 1969; s. Charles E. and Sharron A. (Langston) G. BS in Pub. Adminstrn., U. Ark., 1990, student, 1991-92. Govt. rels. Auditor of State's Office, Little Rock, 1992—2006, govt. rels. treas., 2006—. Mem. Ark. State Dem. Com., 2002—. Bd. dirs. Scott County Friends of Libr., Waldron, Ark., 1988; asst. coord. Little Rock Town Hall Meeting On Africa, 1997; constituent liaison Ark. Senate Adv. Com., Waldron, 1983-2000; vol. Victims Svcs. Program, 2001; mem. State Dem. Com., Ark., 2002-06. Recipient Capitol citation Ark. Sec. of State, 1986, Jeffrey Ledbetter Meml. award, 2003. Democrat. Methodist. Avocations: hiking, reading. Home: 2501 Riverfront Dr Apt A-108 Little Rock AR 72202-1772

GOODNICK, PAUL JOEL, psychiatrist; b. Phila., Sept. 29, 1950; BA magna cum laude, U. Pa.; MD with honors, SUNY Downstate Med. Ctr., Bklyn. Diplomate Am. Bd. Psychiatry and Neurology. Resident Washington U., St. Louis, Columbia U., NYC; fellow Mt. Sinai Hosp., NYC; asst. prof. psychiatry Wayne State U., Detroit, 1980-81, U. Chgo., 1981-84, Columbia U., NYC, 1984-87, U. Miami, Fla., 1987-89, clin. assoc. prof. psychiatry Fla., 1989-90, assoc. prof. Fla., 1990-93, prof. Fla., 1993—2002, clin. prof. of psychiatry, dir. mood disorders program, dept. psychiatry Fla., 1989—2003; dir. clin. svc. Carrier Clinic, Belle Mead, NJ, 2003—; clin. prof. psychiatry U. Medicine and Dentristry, NJ, 2004—. Dir. outpatient svcs. and affective disorders program Fair Oaks Hosp., Boca/Delray, Fla., 1987-90; cons. APA, 1991. Assoc. editor jour. Lithium, 1989-94; editor: Chronic Fatigue and Related Immune Deficiency Syndromes, 1993, Predictors of Response in Mood Disorders, 1996, Mania, 1998; editor Expert Opinion on Pharmacotherapy, 1999—, Annals of Clinical Psychiatry, 2000-05, Expert Opinion on Drug Safety, 2001—; Therapy, 2005-. Mem. nat. adv. bd. Jerusalem Health Ctr. Recipient Clin. Excellence award N.Y. Alliance for Mentally Ill, 1987, SUNY Downstate award, 2001. Fellow Am. Psychopathol. Assn., Am. Psychiat. Assn., Internat. Soc. Affective Disorders; mem. AAAS, Soc. Biol. Psychiatry, N.Y. Acad. Sci., Am. Acad. Clin. Psychiatry, KP. Office: Carrier Clinic 252 Rte 601 POB 147 Belle Mead NJ 08502 Office Phone: 908-281-1484. Personal E-mail: pgoodnick@aol.com.

GOODNIGHT, JAMES H., software company executive; b. Wilmington, NC, Jan. 6, 1943; m. Ann Goodnight; 3 children. B, M, PhD in Statistics, NC State U., 1972—76. Faculty N.C. State U., 1972-76; co-founder, chmn. SAS Inst. Inc., pres. & CEO Cary, NC, 1976—. Adj. prof. N.C. State U., 1976—. Started SAS inSchool; founder Cary Acad., Cary, NC, 1996. Named one of Forbes' Richest Americans, 1999—, World's Richest People, Forbes mag., 2001—, 20th Century's Great Am. Bus. Leaders, Harvard Bus. Sch., 2004, Am.'s 25 Most Fascinating Entrepreneurs, Inc. mag., 2004. Fellow Am. Statis. Assn. Office: SAS Inst Inc Attn Miranda Drake-Shaw Corp Commn Dept SAS Campus Dr Cary NC 27513 E-mail: software@sas.com.*

GOODNOUGH, ROBERT ARTHUR, artist; b. Cortland, NY, Oct. 23, 1917; s. Leo J. and Hariett (Summers) G. BFA, Syracuse U., 1940; MA, NYU, 1950; student, New Sch. for Social Research, 1949, Ozenfant Sch. Art, 1950-51, Hoffman Sch. Art, 1951. Instr. painting NYU, 1953, Fieldston Sch., Riverdale, NY, 1953-60, Cornell U., 1960. Instr. painting NYU, 1953, Fieldston Sch., Riverdale, NY, 1953-60, Cornell U., 1960 Contbr. articles to nat. mags.; one-man shows: Tibor de Nagy Gallery, NYC, Andre Emmerich Gallery, NYC, Nina Freudenheim Gallery, Bklyn.; work exhibited in permanent collections: Albright Art Gallery, Buffalo, Art Inst. Chgo., Mus. Modern Art, NYC, Whitney Mus., NYC, NYU Mus., R.I. Sch. Design Mus., NC Mus. Art, also pvt. collections. Served with US Army, 1941-45. Recipient award Art Inst. Chgo., 1962; Guggenheim fellow, 1972

GOODPASTURE, PHILIP HENRY, lawyer; b. Lisbon, Portugal, Sept. 16, 1960; s. Henry McKennie and Ellen Ingabor (Moller) G.; m. Paige Everett Hargroves, June 25, 1994. BA with high distinction, U. Va., 1982, JD, 1985. Bar: Va. 1985, U.S. Dist. Ct. (ea. dist.) Va. 1985. Assoc. Christian & Barton and predecessor firm, Richmond, Va., 1985-92, ptnr., 1993—2004, vice-chmn. corp. team, 1994-97, mem. exec. com., 1998; ptnr. Williams, Mullen, P.C., 2004—. Dir. Va. League for Planned Parenthood, Richmond, 1989-95, Downtown Presents Inc., Richmond, 1993-2001, Parliament City of Richmond, 1997-98, Read to Them, 2006-; mem. Leadership Metro Richmond, 1994, Leadership Devel. Coun. ARC, 1995; vol. Emergency Families for Children, Richmond, 1998-2000; mem. vestry St. Thomas Episc. Ch., 2007—. Mem. Va. Bar Assn., Richmond Bar Assn. Office: Williams Mullen 1021 E Cary St Ste 1700 Richmond VA 23219 Office Phone: 804-783-6904. Business E-Mail: pgoodpasture@williamsmullen.com.

GOODRICH, GEORGE HERBERT, retired judge; b. Charleston, W.Va., June 19, 1925; s. Edgar Jennings and Beulah Etta (Lenfest) G.; m. Nancy Ann Needham, Sept. 3, 1949; children: George Herbert, Craig N., Thomas A. BA, Williams Coll., 1949; LL.B., U. Va., 1952. Bar: D.C. 1953, Md. 1958. Gen. practice law, Washington, also, Md., 1953-69; asso. judge D.C. Superior Ct., 1969-91, sr. judge, 1991—2005, ret., 2005; lectr. law Am. U., 1969-74. Pres. Homemakers Service, 1962-63; v.p. Hillcrest Children's Center, 1963-69; mem. community adv. com. Jr. League D.C., 1969-73; bd. dirs. ARC. Served with USNR, 1943-46. Mem. D.C. Bar Assn., Delta Psi. Clubs: Chevy Chase. Republican. Presbyterian. Home: 2600 Barracks Rd Apt C9 Charlottesvle VA 22901-2197

GOODRICH, ISAAC, neurosurgeon, educator; b. Milledgeville, Ga., Sept. 19, 1939; s. Ellis and Frieda (Bergman) G.; m. Dianne L. Brittain, Aug. 28, 1965; children: Mindy Anne, Scott David, Jennifer Gale. AA, Ga. Mil. Coll., 1959; BS, U. Ga., 1961; MD, Med. Coll. Ga., 1964. Cert. Am. Bd. Neurol. Surgery. Intern Columbia-Presbyn. Med. Ctr., NYC, 1964-65; resident in neurosurgery Yale-New Haven Med. Ctr., 1967-71; practice medicine specializing in neurosurgery New Haven, 1971—. Instr. neurosurgery, Yale U. Med. Sch., 1970-71, asst. clin. prof., 1978-86; assoc. clin. prof., 1986—; attending neurosurgeon Yale-New Haven Hosp., 1973—, Hosp. St. Raphael, 1971—; mem. courtesy staff Milford Hosp., 1986—; cons. staff Midstate Med. Ctr., 1986—, VA Hosp., West Haven, 1990—, Griffin Hosp., 1992-99, St. Mary's Hosp., 1995-99, courtesy staff, 1999—. Contbr. articles to profl. jours. Capt. U.S. Army, 1965-67. Decorated Bronze Star, Air Medal; recipient Disting. Alumni award Ga. Mil. Coll., 1980; named Hon. Citizen, Boys Town, Nebr., 1971. Fellow: ACS, Royal Soc. Medicine, Internat. Coll. Surgeons; mem.: AAAS, AMA (Physicians Recognition awards for Continuing Med. Edn.), NY Acad. Scis., New Haven County Med. Assn. (pres. 1998—99), Conn. State Med. Soc. (v.p. 2000—01, pres.-elect 2001—02, pres. 2002—03), Conn. State Neurosurg. Soc. (pres. 2001—03), Am. Assn. Neurol. Surgeons, New Eng. Neurosurg. Soc. (pres. 1997—99), Congress Neurol. Surgeons, Veterans of Fgn. Wars, Soc. 1st Inf. Divsn., New Haven City Med. Assn. (pres. 1989—90), 28th Inf. Assn., Am. Legion. Jewish. Home: 84 Links Way Oxford CT 06478 Office: 330 Orchard St Ste 316 New Haven CT 06511-4430 Office Phone: 203-781-3400.

GOODRICH, JAMES A., veterinarian, researcher; s. Neil E. and Barbara F. (Weeks) G. BS, U. Conn., 1983; DVM, Tufts U., 1988. Diplomate Am. Coll. Lab. Animal Medicine. Assoc. prof. Med. U. SC, Charleston, 1995—2007; assoc. prof., attending vet. U. Wis. Sch. Medicine and Pub. Health, Madison, 2007—. Mem. editl. rev. bd. Comparative Medicine, 2006—, Jour. Am. Assn. Lab. Animal Sci., 2006—; contbr. articles to profl. jours. Eagle Scout Boy Scouts Am., Cheshire, Conn., 1978. Mem. Am. Veterinary Med. Assn., Assn. Primate Veterinarians, S.C. Assn. Veterinarians, Assn. Lab. Animal Practitioners. Office: Univ Wis Rm 2050A MSC 1300 University Ave Madison WI 53706 Office Phone: 608-263-0664. Business E-Mail: jagoodrich@wisc.edu.

GOODRICH, JAMES TAIT, neuroscientist, neurosurgeon; b. Portland, Oreg., Apr. 16, 1946; s. Richard and Gail (Josselyn) Goodrich; m. Judy Loudin, Dec. 27, 1970. Student, Golden West Coll., 1971—72; AA, Orange Coast Coll., 1972; BS cum laude, U. Calif., Irvine, 1974; PhD, Columbia U., 1970, MPhil, 1979; MD, Coll. of Mt. St. Vincent, 1980; DSc honoris causa, Columbia U., 2005. Diplomate Am. Bd. Neurol. Surgery, Am. Bd. Pediatric Neurosurgery. Intern Columbia-Presbyn. Med. Ctr., NYC, 1980—81; resident in neurol. surgery N.Y. Neurol. Inst., NYC, 1981—86; assoc. Montefiore Med. Ctr., Bronx, NY, 1986—; mem. staff Jacobi Med. Ctr., 1986—; assoc. Weiler Hosp. Albert Einstein Coll. Medicine, NYC, 1986—, prof. nuerosurgery, 1998—. Prof. neurosurgery U. Palermo, Sicily, Italy, 1992—. Editor: Jour. Child Nervous Sys., Neurosurgery; contbr. scientific papers to profl. jours. Named Disting. Alumnus, U. Calif., Irvine, 2007, Dep. Comdt.'s Guest of Honor, Evening Parade USMC Barracks, Washington, 2007; named one of Best Med. Drs. in NY, NY Mag., 2006, 2007; named to Guide to Am.'s Top Surgeons, Consumers Coun. Am., 2002, Best Drs. in Am., 2003; recipient Roche Labs. award in Nuersci., 1978, Mead-Johnson award, 1978, Bronze medal, Alumni Assn. Coll. Physicians and Surgeons, 1980, Sandoz award for Outstanding Rsch., 1980, NYC Mayor's award sci. and tech., 2004, Maj. Gen. John L. Russell Leadership award, US Marine Corps U. Found., 2006; Willamette Industries scholar, NIH grantee. Fellow: Royal Soc. Medicine (London); mem.: AMA, AAAS, Dionysius Coun. Presbyn. Hosp. N.Y.C., Les Amis du Vin, Am. Osler Soc., Soc. Ancient Medicine, Columbia Presbyn. Med. Soc., Soc. Bibliography Natural History (London), ISIS History Sci. Soc., Med. History Soc. N.J., Congress Neurol. Surgeons, Am. Assn. Neurol. Surgery (chmn. sect. history neurol. surgery), N.Y. Acad. Scis., Brit. Brain Rsch. Assn., Am. Assn. History Medicine (Sir William Osler medal 1977—78), N.Y. Acad. Medicine (Melicow award 1980), Internat. Soc. Pediat. Neurosurgeons, European Brain Rsch. Assn., Am. Soc. Pediat. Neurosurgeons, Am. Epilepsy Soc., Am. Assn. Neurol. Surgeons, U. Calif. Alumni Assn., Friends Columbia U. Librs., Worshipful Soc. Apothecaries (London), South Coast Wine Explorers Club (past chmn.), Sigma Xi, Alpha Gamma Sigma. Achievements include research in neuronal regeneration, brain reconstruction and craniofacial reconstruction. Home: 125 Tweed Blvd Nyack NY 10960-4913 Office: Albert Einstein Coll Medicine Montefiore Med Ctr Div Pediat Neurosurg 111 E 210th St Bronx NY 10467-2401 Office Phone: 718-920-4197. Business E-Mail: goodrich@aecom.yu.edu.

GOODRICH, JAMES WILLIAM, retired historian executive; b. Burlington, Iowa, Oct. 31, 1939; s. Martin Glenn and Marion Elizabeth (Prasse) G.; m. Linda Marlyse Andreoli, Aug. 31, 1963 (div. Aug. 1989); children: Anne Marlyse, Kimberly Ann. BS in Edn., Cen. Mo. State U., 1962; MA, U. Mo., 1964, PhD, 1974. Archivist Sec. of State, Mo., 1966; asst. then assoc. editor State Hist. Soc. Mo., Columbia, 1967-78, assoc. dir., 1978-85, dir., 1985—, ret., 2004. Cons. USDA Soil Conservation Svc., Columbia, 1976, Mus. History and Sci., Kansas City, Mo., 1978, Mo. State Mus., 1989, Mo. Dept. Conservation, 1990, 91, 95, 97; mem. Mo. Hist. Records Adv. Bd., Jefferson City, 1985—, State Records Commn., Jefferson City, 1984—, Mo. Bd. Geographic Names, 1995--; dir. Western Hist. Manuscript Collection, 1985—; adj. prof. history U. Mo., Columbia, 1988—. Co-author: Historic Missouri, 1988; editor: Report on a Journey to North America, 1980; assoc. editor Mo. Hist. Rev., 1967-85, editor 1985—; co-editor: German-American Experience in Missouri, 1986; co-editor, contbr. Marking Missouri History, 1998; contbr. articles to profl. jours. Mem. Planning and Zoning Commn., Columbia, 1975-77; councilman City of Columbia, 1977-79, 79-81; chmn. city audit com., Columbia, 1981-88; v.p. Friends of Mo. St. Archives, 1989-94; mem. 13th Jud. Cir. Bar Rev. Com., 1991-97; bd. dirs. Mo. Mansion Preservation Inc., 1991—; bd. dirs. Boone County Cmty. Trust, 1992—; mem. exec. com. Mo. State U. Alumni Assn., 1988-92, pres. 1991; mem. 6th Regional Disciplinary Com. Mo. Judiciary, 1997—; mem. Mo. Lewis and Clark Bicentennial Com., 1997—. Mem. Orgn. Am. Historians, Western History Assn., Am. Assn. for State & Local History, Conservation Fedn. Mo., Ducks Unlimited, Mo. Mus. Assn., Mo. Press Assn., Wild Canid Survival and Rsch. Ctr. Avocations: decoy collecting, waterfowl hunting, orinthoscopy. Office: State Hist Soc Mo 1020 Lowry St Columbia MO 65201-7207

GOODRICH, JOHN BERNARD, lawyer, consultant; b. Spokane, Wash., Jan. 4, 1928; s. John Casey and Dorothy (Koll) G.; m. Therese H. Vollmer, June 14, 1952; children— Joseph B., Bernadette M., Andrew J., Philip M., Thomas A., Mary Elizabeth, Jennifer H., Rosanne M. JD, Gonzaga U., 1954. Bar: Wash, 1954, Ill. 1955. Indsl. traffic mgr. Pacific N.W. Alloys, Spokane, 1950-54; asst. to gen. counsel Cromium Mining & Smelting Corp., Chgo., 1954-56; with Monon R.R., 1956-69, atty., gen. solicitor, 1956-66, sec., 1957-69, treas., 1959-66, v.p. law, 1966-69; also dir.; sec.-treas. I.C.G.R.R., Chgo., 1970-79, sec., gen. atty., 1979-85; gen. counsel Ill. Devel. Fin. Authority, Chgo., 1985-92, spl. counsel, 1993; atty., cons. pvt. practice, Park Forest, Ill., 1994—. Mem. Park Forest Traffic and Safety Commn., 1963-66; mem. Park Forest Recreation Bd., 1966-77, chmn., 1969-70; trustee Village of Park Forest, 1977-80; mem. bd. Sch. Dist. 163, 1984-89; pres. South Cook Orgn. for Pub. Edn., 1988-89; conf. and meeting planner The Compassionate Friends, Inc., Oak Brook, Ill., 1991-94; bd. dirs. Park Forest Art Ctr., 1993-95, Ill. Philharm. Orch., 1994-98, treas., 1995-98; mem. adv. bd. Chgo. Self Help Ctr., 1993-94; bd. dirs. Ill Self Help Coalition, 1994-96; treas. Bereaved Parents of the U.S.A., 1995-2000, bd. dirs. 2000-03, Tall Grass Arts Assn., 1999-2003; trustee Chgo. South Suburban Mass Transit Dist., 1996—, treas., 2000-04, vice chmn., 2004—. Inducted into Park Forest Hall of Fame, 1998. Mem. KC, The Parkforesters, Inc. (pres. 1998-2004, dir.), Kiwanis. Roman Catholic. Home and Office: 35 Cunningham Ln Park Forest IL 60466-2094

GOODRICH, KENNETH PAUL, retired dean; b. Elkhorn, Wis., 1933; s. Kenneth Potter and Helene (Keller) G.; m. Elaine L. Ashby, June 12, 1954; children— Laurel Lynn, David Kenneth, Paul Ashby, Karen Elaine. AB Oberlin Coll, 1955; MA, U. Ia., 1958, PhD, 1959. Mem. faculty U. Pa. Phila., 1959-63; lectr., project assoc. U. Wis., Madison, 1963-65; mem. faculty psychology Macalester Coll., St. Paul, 1965-73, chmn. dept. psychology, 1965-67, dean coll., 1967-69, dean and dir. ednl. resources, 1969-71, v.p. for acad. affairs and provost, 1971-73; dean Coll. Arts and Scis., prof. psychology Syracuse (N.Y.) U., 1973-78; provost Ohio Wesleyan U., Del., 1978-83; v.p. acad. affairs, dean of faculty Linfield Coll., McMinnville, Oreg., 1983-94, spl. asst. to pres. for instnl. rsch. and planning, 1994-95. Bd. dirs. Group Health Plan, Inc., St. Paul, 1970-73, Yamhill County (Oreg.) United Way, 1991-95, McMinnville Area Habitat for Humanity, 1993-95; vol. carpenter Greater Columbus Habitat for Humanity, 1995-2004. Personal E-mail: kgoodric@world.oberlin.edu.

GOODRICH, THOMAS MICHAEL, engineering and construction executive, lawyer; b. Milan, Tenn., Apr. 28, 1945; s. Henry Calvin and Billie Grace (Walker) Goodrich; m. Gillian Comer White, Dec. 28, 1968; children: Michael, Braxton, Charles, Grace. BSCE, Tulane U., 1968; JD, U. Ala., 1971. Bar: Ala. 1971. Adminstrv. asst. Supreme Ct. Ala., Montgomery, 1971—72; from various mgmt. positions to CEO BE & K, Inc., Birmingham, Ala., 1989—95, pres., CEO, 1995—, chmn. bd. dir., 2003. Bd. dirs. First Comml. Bank, Energen Corp., Birmingham, Synovus Fin. Corp., Columbus, Ga. Trustee Nat. Bldg. Mus., Elsenhowen Exchg. Fellow. Capt. US Army, 1970—72. Mem.: Constrn. Industry Roundtable, Assn. Builders and Contractors (pres. 1990), Ala. State Bar Assn., ABA, TAPPI. Office: B E & K Inc 2000 Internat Park Dr Birmingham AL 35243

GOODRIDGE, ALLAN D., lawyer; b. Bucharest, Romania, June 12, 1936; s. Benjamin F. and Fanny M. (Weissman) G.; m. Lora, Sept. 12, 1965; children: Jeremy P., Andrew P. BA, Harvard U., 1957; JD, Columbia U., 1960. Bar: N.Y., U.S. Dist. Ct. (so. dist., ea. dist. N.Y.), U.S. Ct. Appeals (2d circuit). Assoc. Wickes, Riddell, Bloomer, Jacobi & McGuire, NYC, 1960-64, Spitzer & Feldman, NYC, 1965, Demov, Morris & Hammerling, NYC, 1965-70, ptnr., 1970-85, Schnader, Harrison, Segal & Lewis, NYC, 1985—. Mem. ABA, N.Y. Bar Assn. Clubs: Harvard (N.Y.C.). Home: 336 Central Park W New York NY 10025-7111 Office: Schnader Harrison Segal & Lewis LLP Ste 3100 140 Broadway New York NY 10005 Office Phone: 212-973-8145. Business E-Mail: agoodridge@schnader.com.

GOODSELL, CHARLES TRUE, public administration educator, researcher; b. July 23, 1932; BA, Kalamazoo Coll., 1954; MPA, Harvard U., 1958, MA, 1959, PhD, 1961. Asst. prof. U. P.R., Rio Piedras, 1961-64; prof. So. Ill. U., Carbondale, 1966-78; prof. pub. adminstrn. Va. Tech., Blacksburg, 1978—2002, prof. emeritus, 2002—. Author: Administration of A Revolution, 1965, American Corporations and Peruvian Politics, 1974, The Public Encounter, 1981, The Social Meaning of Public Space, 1988, Public Administration Illuminated and Inspired by the Arts, 1995, The American Statehouse, 2001, The Case for Bureaucracy, 4th edit., 2004. Recipient Waldo award, Am. Soc. Pub. Adminstrn., 2003. Personal E-mail: goodsell@vt.edu.

GOODSON, RICHARD CARLE, JR., chemist; b. Toledo, June 22, 1945; s. Richard Carle Goodson Sr. and Norma (Buehler) Robinson; m. Deborah Ann Hart, Mar. 29, 1969 (div. Feb. 1978); 1 child, Geoffrey Carle; m. Thelma Agnes Matthews, Nov. 22, 1978. BS in Chemistry, Union Coll., 1967; MS in Inorganic Chemistry, U. Conn., 1970. Dist. engr. Drew Chem. Corp., Boonton, N.J., 1972-74, product supr., 1974-75, regional tech. supr., 1975-76; chief chemist, tech. dir. Environ. Waste Removal, Waterbury, Conn., 1976-79; gen. mgr., dir. tech. lab. Conn. Treatment Corp., Bristol, 1978—82; dir. ops., corp. dir. waste mgmt. and regulatory compliance Hampden Mathieu Chem. Co., Springfield, 1990—2000; pres., owner Goodson Assoc., Farmington, Conn., 1982—. Mem. Am. Chem. Soc. Republican. Avocations: boating, hiking, skiing, bicycling. Home and Office: 2 Azalea Ct Farmington CT 06032-2037 Personal E-mail: richardgoodson@msn.com.

GOODSPEED, KATHRYN ANN, pre-school educator; b. Elgin, Ill., Oct. 2, 1939; d. Earle Muller and Ruby Vera Curtiss; m. Robert Harrison Goodspeed, Feb. 4, 1961; children: Julie, Jill, Jerry, Jeff, Jennifer. BS, No. Ill. U., 1961. Tchr. spl. edn. Sch. of Hope, Rockford, Ill., 1962—65; home day care provider, 1971—78; tchr. presch., dir. Melrose DayCare Ctr., Iowa City, 1978—89; tchr. Blind Children's Learning Ctr., Santa Ana, Calif., 1989—92, dir. early childhood ctr., 1992—2001, asst. exec. dir., 2001—, interim exec. dir., 2004—05. Bd. pres. So. Calif. Network Serving Infants and Preschool Children with Visual Impairments, 1998—; cons. Supporting Early Edn. Delivery Sys. Co-treas. Joint Action Com. Visually Impaired, Calif., 1997—; co-chair Infant Vendor Com., Santa Ana, 2000; mem. adv. bd. Calif. Deaf-Blind Svcs.; edn. commn. head Yorba Linda United Meth. Ch., 1998—2002. Named Laywoman of Yr., Yorba Linda United Meth. Ch., 2000. Mem.: Family Support Network Bd., Assn. Edn. and Rehab. Blind and Visually Impaired, Coun. Exceptional Children, Calif. Transcribers & Educators Multihandicapped Specialist, Calif. First Chance Consortium (co-chair, bd. dir., family support network com., mem. camp TLC). Avocations: reading, cooking, travel, watercolor painting. Home: 856 Amber Ln Anaheim CA 92807 Office Phone: 714-573-8888.

GOODSPEED, LINDA A., manufacturing executive; BSME, Mich. State U., 1984, MA in Bus. Adminstrn., 1989. Engr. Ford Motor Co., 1984—89; with R&D dept. Nissan, 1989—96; with GE, 1996—2001, range product devel. mgr., 1997, gen. mgr. Six Sigma divsn., 1999, product gen. mgr. GE Appliances, 1999—2001; pres., COO Partminer, Inc., 2001; chief tech. officer Lennox Internat., Richardson, Tex., 2001—. Bd. dir. Am. Electric Power, Columbus McKinnon Corp. Office: Lennox Internat 2140 Lake Park Blvd Richardson TX 75080

GOODSTEIN, AARON E., federal magistrate judge; b. Sheboygan, Wis., Apr. 28, 1942; BA, U. Wis. Madison, 1964; JD, U. Wis., 1967. Bar: Wis. 1967, U.S. Dist. Ct. (ea. and we. dists.) Wis. 1967, U.S. Ct. Appeals (7th crct.) 1968. Law clk. to Hon. Myron L. Gordon U.S. Dist. Ct., Ea. Dist. Wis., 1967-68; shareholder Chernov, Croen & Goodstein, S.C., Milw., 1968-79; U.S. magistrate judge Ea. Dist. Wis., Milw., 1979-87, reapptd., 1987—. Panelist Current Issues Relating to the Fourth, Fifth and Sixth Amendments, Jud. Conf. of 7th Cir., 1991; speaker fed. ct.'s class Marquette Law Sch., 1992; moderator probation and pretrial svcs. divsn. U.S. Cts., 1992; chair magistrate judges edn. com. Fed. Jud. Ctr., 1990-98, mem. magistrate judges com. of Jud. Conf. of U.S., 1993-99; adv. com. local rules and practice Ea. Dist. Wis., mem. adv. panel under Civil Justice Reform Act 1990; faculty mem. in field. Prodr: (video) Complaints, Warrants for Arrest and Search Warrants, 1992, Administrative Matters Pertaining to Magistrate Judges and Their Staff, 1993, Social Security: Process and Problems, Parts One and Two, 2000; mem. editl. adv. panel Handbook of Federal Civil Discovery and Disclosure, 1998; contbr. articles to profl. jours. Bd. dirs. Milw. Legal Aid Soc., 1974-79, Milw. Jewish Coun., 1977-79; pres. Milw. Forum, 1979-80, alumni mem.; pres. Congregation Shalom, 1990-92. Recipient Pro Bono award Gene and Ruth Posner Found., 1988 Mem. ABA (former chair magistrate judges com. Nat. Conf. Fed. Trial Judges), Fed. Magistrate Judges Assn. (pres. 2004-05), State Bar Wis. (pres. young lawyers divsn. 1975-76, bd. govs. 1975-77), Milw. Bar Assn. (exec. bd. 1978-79, sec. 1979-82), U. Wis. Law Sch. Alumni Assn. (bd. dirs. 1989-98), Order of Coif, Phi Kappa Phi. Office: US Magistrate Judge 258 US Courthouse 517 E Wisconsin Ave Milwaukee WI 53202-4500 Office Phone: 414-297-3963.

GOODSTEIN, BARNETT MAURICE, lawyer; b. Dallas, Oct. 1, 1921; s. Arthur Louis and Viola Esther (Levy) G.; m. Mira Brodsky, Jan. 26, 1947; children: Pamela Renee, Heather Ann, Robin Leslie. Student, Rice Inst., 1938—40; BA, MA, U. Tex., 1942; postgrad., U. Wis., 1949—51; JD, So. Meth. U., 1957. Bar: Tex. 1957, U.S. Dist. Ct. (no. dist.) Tex. 1963, U.S. Supreme Ct. Acting dir. case analysis Wage Stblzn. Bd., Dallas, 1951-53; practice of law Dallas, 1957—; pres. Goodstein & Starr, P.C., 1977-91, Goodstein, Starr & Pascoe, P.C., 1991—95; adminstrv. law judge City of Dallas, 1994—95; pvt. practice, 1995—. Lectr. econs. So. Meth. U., Dallas, 1946-48, 51-60; lectr. Massey Realty Coll., Real Estate Inst., Dallas; labor arbitrator, 1953—; former permanent arbitrator City of San Antonio, Police Officers' Assn.; mem. permanent arbitration panel Tinker AFB, Okla., 1984-88, Am. Fedn. Govt. Employees, 1984-90, SW Bell Tel., AT&T, CWA, IBEW, 1988—, FAA, 1993—, Nat. Assn. Air Traffic Specialists, 1994—, Ga. Pacific, 1994—, UPIU, 1994—, U.S. Customs and INS, 2001--, also various VA Med. Facilities, paper and copper industries, others; mem. permanent panel Dallas Area Rapid Transit Sys., 1988-90, 94-96; adminstrv. law judge City of Dallas, 1994-96. Hearing officer work suspensions appeals bd. City of Dallas, 1981-83; trustee Dallas County Sch. Bd., 1980-2005, v.p., 1990-91, 2003-2005; past trustee Temple Emanu-El; mem. legal representation com. Nat. Acad. Arbitrators, 1992-96, chmn. legal affairs com. 1997-99. Served with USAAF, 1942-46, China, 1945-46 Mem.: ABA, Am. Arbitration Assn. (Southwestern adv. coun. 1985—92), Indsl. Rels. Rsch. Assn. (pres. North Tex. chpt. 1985—86, neutral mem. bd. dirs. North Tex. chpt. 1990—92), Nat. Acad. Arbitrators (chmn. S.W. region 1987—88), Tex. Bar Assn. Home: 6427 Forest Creek Dr Dallas TX 75230-2814 Office: Law Offices of Barnett M Goodstein Ste 215J 4230 Lyndon B Johnson Fwy Dallas TX 75244-5816 Office Phone: 972-387-4303. Personal E-mail: bgoodm@sbcglobal.net.

GOODSTEIN, DAVID LOUIS, physics professor; b. Bklyn., Apr. 5, 1939; s. Sam and Claire (Axel) G.; m. Judith R. Koral, June 30, 1960; children: Marcia, Mark. BS, Bklyn. Coll., 1960; PhD, U. Wash., 1965. Research instr. U. Wash., Seattle, 1965-66; research fellow Calif. Inst. Tech., Pasadena, 1966-67, asst. prof., 1968-71, asso. prof., 1971-76, prof., 1976—, vice-provost, 1987—2007, Frank J. Gilloon disting. teaching and svc. prof., 1995—. Vis. scientist Frascati Nat. Lab., Italy, 1971—. Author: States of Matter, 1975, (with J. Goodstein) Feynman's Lost Lecture, 1996, Out of Gas, 2004; mem. editl. bd. Il Nuovo Cimento, 1987—; contbr. articles to profl. jours.; project dir., host physics TV course The Mechanical Universe. Bd. dirs. Calif. Coun. Sci. and Tech., 1989—, Sierra Monolithics; sci. adv. com. David and Lucille Packard Found., 1988—. NSF postdoctoral fellow, 1967-68; Sloan Found. fellow, 1969-71; recipient Oersted medal, 1999, John P. McGovern Sci. and Soc. award, 2000. Fellow AAAS; mem. Am. Phys. Soc., Am. Inst. Physics. Office: Calif Inst Tech Dept Physics Pasadena CA 91125-0001 Home: 430 South Parkwood Ave Pasadena CA 91107 Business E-Mail: dg@caltech.edu.

GOODSTEIN, LAURIE BETH, journalist; b. NYC, June 25, 1960; d. Daniel Victor and Joan G. (Waxgiser) G.; m. Peter Grand, June 19, 1993; 1 child, Gabriel. BA, U. Calif. Berkeley, 1984; MFA, Columbia U., 1989. Editl. asst. The Washington Post, 1989-93, staff religion writer, 1993—97; religion reporter New York Times, 1997—. Judge Leslie Sander Social Justice Awards, N.Y.C., 1989—. Named John Templeton Religion Reporter of Yr. Religion Newswriters Assn., 1994-95, Supple Religion Newswriter of Yr., 1994-95, Am. Acad. Religion award, 2004. Jewish. Office: New York Times 229 W 43d St New York NY 10036 Office Phone: 212-556-1854. Office Fax: 212-556-7614.

GOODSTEIN, LES, newspaper publishing executive; b. NYC, 1951; Grad., SUNY. With The Daily News, NYC, 1977—, v.p.-advertising, 1991—95, exec. v.p. assoc. pub., 1995—2000, pres., COO, 2000—05; sr. v.p. News Corp., NYC, 2006—. Office: News Corp Fl 8 1211 Ave of Americas New York NY 10036 Office Phone: 212-852-7000.

GOODSTONE, MICHAEL S., psychology professor, consultant; b. Bklyn., Dec. 8, 1961; s. Edward H. and Harriet J. Goodstone; m. Lori Sprung, Aug. 28, 1983; children: Adam T., Emily S. BS, Syracuse U., 1983; MA, Hofstra U., 1986, PhD, 1989. V.p. Lopez & Assocs., Indsl. Psychologists, Great Neck, NY, 1991—96; assoc. prof. SUNY, Farmingdale, NY, 1996—. Cons. Michael S. Goodstone, PhD, NY, 1996—. Contbr. articles to profl. jours. Recipient Chancellor's Award for Excellence in Tchg., SUNY, 2005, Farmingdale Found. Excellence in Tchg. award, 2003. Mem.: APA, Soc. for Indsl. and Orgnl. Psychology. Avocations: fishing, boating. Office: SUNY - Farmingdale 2350 Broadhollow Rd Farmingdale NY 11735 Home Phone: 516-623-1436; Office Phone: 631-420-2236. Business E-Mail: michael.goodstone@farmingdale.edu.

GOODWICK, DAVID LEE, retired advertising executive; b. Beloit, Wis., Oct. 20, 1954; s. James Lee and Helen Maude (Alton) G.; m. Christie Wren Spencer, Apr. 18, 1981; children: Jesse David, Lindsey Leah, Jamie Christopher. BA in Polit. Sci., U. Wis., Whitewater, 1976, BA in Journalism, 1976. Intern J. Walter Thompson, Chgo., 1975; advt. mgr. LRP, Inc., Lake Geneva, Wis., 1976; mktg. svcs. mgr. Mercury Marine, Fond du lac, Wis., 1976—77; advt. mgr. Johnson Outboards, Waukegan, Wis., 1977—79; advt. account mgr. GE, Fairfield, Conn., 1979—82; ptnr. Profl. Svcs. Assocs., Inc., Newtown, Conn., 1986—91, Hist. Property Preservations, Ltd., Newtown, 1986—91; pres., owner Typ-Hi Printers, Newtown, 1989—92; v.p., ptnr. Best Homes Constrn. Co., Janesville, Wis., 1993—96; pres., owner Goodwick Assocs., Inc., Newtown, 1982—99, Bandwick Prodns., Newtown, 1998—2004; CEO, creative dir. The Leverage Mktg. Svcs., Newtown, 1999—2006; chmn. Goodwick/Liazon Co., Newtown, 1999—2006; ret., 2006. Advisor Insight Assocs., Westport, Conn., 1984-89; press sec. to Gov. Patrick Lucey of Wis., Madison, 1974. Pub.: newspaper The Alternative, 1974—76. Co-prodr. Ox Ridge Charity Horse Show, Darien, Conn., 1984-86; chmn. comms. com. United Way, Danbury, Conn., 1987-88; bus. mem. Newtown H.S. Alliance, Ancell Sch. Bus., Western Conn. State U.; bd. mem. NHS Blue and Gold Booster Club, Newtown H.S. Recipient numerous readership-based and creative competition awards various mags. including Most Significant Ads of the 20th Century award Indsl. Equipment News. Mem. Am. Entrepenurial Assn., Internat. Platform Assn. Avocations: musician, fishing. Home: 201 Hattertown Rd Newtown CT 06470-2451 Home Phone: 203-426-7024. Business E-Mail: david@leverage-marketing.com.

GOODWIN, ALFRED THEODORE, federal judge; b. Bellingham, Wash., June 29, 1923; s. Alonzo Theodore and Miriam Hazel (Williams) G.; m. Marjorie Elizabeth Major, Dec. 23, 1943 (div. 1948); 1 child, Michael Theodore; m. Mary Ellin Handelin, Dec. 23, 1949; children: Karl Alfred, Margaret Ellen, Sara Jane, James Paul. BA, U. Oreg., 1947; JD, 1951. Bar: Oreg. 1951. Newspaper reporter Eugene (Oreg.) Register-Guard, 1947—50; practiced in Eugene until, 1955; circuit judge Oreg. 2d. Jud. Dist., 1955—60; assoc. justice Oreg. Supreme Ct., 1960—69; judge US Dist. Ct. Oreg., 1969—71, US Ct. Appeals (9th cir.), Pasadena, Calif., 1971—88, chief judge, 1988—91, sr. judge, 1991—. Editor: Oreg. Law Rev., 1950—51. Adv. bd. Eugene Salvation Army, 1956—60; chmn., 1959; Bd. dirs. Central Lane YMCA, Eugene, 1956—60, Salem (Oreg.) Art Assn., 1960—69. Capt., inf. AUS, 1942—46, ETO. Mem.: ABA (ho. of dels. 1986—87), Am. Law Inst., Am. Judicature Soc., Order of Coif, Alpha Tau Omega, Sigma Delta Chi, Phi Delta Phi. Republican. Office: US Ct Appeals 9th Cir PO Box 91510 125 S Grand Ave Pasadena CA 91105-1621 Home Phone: 626-441-2797; Office Phone: 626-229-7100. E-mail: alfred_goodwin@ca9.uscourts.gov.*

GOODWIN, ANDREW WIRT, II, radiologist; b. Oil City, Pa., Feb. 4, 1932; s. Frank Bert and Florence Bickford (Green) G.; m. Anita Faye Adkins, May 27, 1987; children: Andrew, Victoria, Mary Elizabeth, Mark H., Martha J., Lisa R. BA, Colgate U., 1953; MD, U. Mich., 1957. Diplomate Am. Bd. Radiology, Am. Bd. Nuclear Medicine. Intern Mary Hitchcock Meml. Hosp., Hanover, NH, 1957-58; resident in radiology Mayo Clinic, Rochester, Minn., 1958-61, resident, 1958-61; radiologist Associated Radiologists, Inc., Charleston, W.Va., 1961-86, Radiol. Physicians Assn., Fairmont, W.Va., 1988—; pvt. practice. Republican. Episc. Home Fax: 304-926-0851. Personal E-mail: agoodwinii@aol.com.

GOODWIN, ANNIE M., state agency administrator; b. Helena, Mont., 1958; BSN magna cum laude, Carroll Coll., Helena, Mont., 1981; JD magna cum laude, U. Mont., Missoula, 1984. Bar: Mont. 1984, US Dist. Ct. (dist. Mont.) 1984, US Ct. Fed. Claims 1990, US Dist. Ct. (dist. DC) 1991. Law clk. Mont. Supreme Ct., 1984; litig. atty. risk mgmt. tort def. divsn. Mont. Dept. Adminstrn.; chief legal counsel Mont. Dept. Commerce, 1988—2001; commr. Mont. Divsn. Banking & Fin. Instns., Helena, 2001—. Bd. dirs. Am. Lung Assn., 1988—91. Office: Mont Divsn Banking & Fin Instns PO Box 200546 Helena MT 59620 Office Phone: 406-841-2920. Office Fax: 406-841-2930. E-mail: angoodwin@mt.gov.

GOODWIN, ANTHONY ROBERT HOLMES, chemist, editor; b. Colchester, Eng., Sept. 7, 1961; BSc in Chemistry, Univ. Coll. London, 1981, PhD in Chemistry, 1987. Guest rschr. Nat. Bur. Stds., Gaithersburg, Md., 1987—88; petroleum engr. BP, Sunbury-on-Thames, England, 1988—91; rsch. chemist Nat. Inst. Stds. and Tech., Gaithersburg, 1991—93; prof. chem. engring. U. Idaho, Moscow, 1993—98; rsch. scientist Schlumberger Cambridge Rsch., England, 1998—2000, prin. rsch. scientist, 2002—04; sr. rsch. scientist Schlumberger-Doll Rsch., Ridgefield, Conn., 2000—02; prin. chemist Schlumberger Product Ctr., Sugar Land, Tex., 2004—. Contbr. articles to profl. jours, books, conf. procs; editor: Experimental Thermodynamics Volume VI, Measurement of the Properties of Single Phases; editor Jour. Chem. Thermodynamics, 2001—05. Grantee, Gas Rsch. Inst., 1993—97, Dept. of Trade and Industry, UK, 2005—, NSF, 1997; Tufnell scholar, U. London, 1984. Fellow: Royal Soc. Chemistry; mem.: Internat. Assn. Transport Properties, Internat. Assn. Chem. Thermodynamics (treas., bd. dirs. 2002—), Am. Chem. Soc. (editor Jour. Chem. Engring. Data 2005—). Achievements include patents for electrostatic transducers and numerous oilfiled related technologies. Office: Schlumberger 125 Industrial Blvd Sugar Land TX 77478 Home Phone: 281-313-2191; Office Phone: 281-285-4962. Personal E-mail: goodwin@jced.com. E-mail: agoodwin@slb.com.

GOODWIN, BEATRICE, nursing educator, consultant; d. David and Myrtle Goodwin. BS in Nursing, Vanderbilt U., 1955; MA, NYU, 1960, PhD, 1970; PhD (hon.), Valparaiso U., 2003. RN NY, 1958. Prof. nursing CUNY, NYC, 1970—98; vis. prof. Catholic U. Chile, Santiago, 1972—73, U. Conception, Chile, 1984—88, U. Los Andes, Santiago, 1999—2000, U. Chile, Santiago, 2006—, U. Andres Bello, Santigo, Chile, 2006—; adj. prof. nursing NYU, NYC, 1998—. External reviewer U. Ottawa, Canada, 1978; cons. clin. nursing Surgeon Gen., US Air Force, DC, 1980—82; cons. curriculum in baccalaureate nursing World Health Orgn., DC, 1986—88; dir. Latin Am. projects NYU Coll. Nursing, NYC, 1998—; keynote spkr. Nat. Colloquium Nursing Rsch., Bogota, Colombia, 2001, Internat. Nursing Conf., Chile, 2002, Colombia, 04; curriculum cons. programs in nursing Colombian Assn. Faculties Nursing, Chile, 2006—; vis. prof. U. Andrés Bello, Santiago, Chile, 2006—, U. Chile, Santiago, 2006—. Founding editor: Jour. Nursing Scholarship. Mem. Career Devel. Bd., US Air Force Nurse Corps, DC, 1979—81, NYU Nurse Alumni Assn., NYC, 2002—. Decorated Meritorious Svc. Medal US Air Force. Mem.: Internat. Ctr. Nursing Rsch., Chilean Assn. Nursing Edn. (hon.), Chilean Assn. Edn. in Nursing (hon.), Sigma Theta Tau (life), Kappa Delta Pi (life). Home: 220 E 65th St Apt 21K New York NY 10065 Home Phone: 212-753-2446. Personal E-mail: beagoodwin@aol.com.

GOODWIN, BECKY K., educational technology resource educator; Sci. tchr. USD 233 Sch. Dist., Olathe, Kans. Christa McAuliffe fellowship grantee State of Kans., 1992, 94, 97; named Kans. Tchr. of Yr., 1995; recipient Presdl. award for Excellence in Sci. and Math. Secondary Sci. for Kans., 1992, Outstanding Biology Tchr. award Nat. Assn. Biology Tchrs., 1992, Sci. Teaching Achievement Recognition Star award NSTA, 1993, Milken Nat. Educator award, 1995, Tandy Tech. Tchr. award, 1998. Office: USD 233 14090 Black Bob Rd Olathe KS 66063

GOODWIN, BEVERLY ANN, elementary school educator; b. Worcester, Mass., May 12, 1952; d. Richard Harvey Bejune; m. Jeffrey Scott Goodwin, June 29, 1974. BS in Edn., Westfield State Coll., Mass., 1974. Cert. elem. tchr. Mass., 1974. Tchg. asst. grades k-5 Agawam Pub. Schs., Mass., 1974—75, second grade tchr., 1975—2005; English Lang. Learners and ESL tchr. Agawam Mid. Sch., 2005—. Vol. Westfield Soup Kitchen, Mass., 2002—05; tchr. rep., coord. parent/tchr./student activities PTO, 1995. ESL Profl. Devel. Leadership grantee, Agawam Pub. Schs., 2006. Mem.: Mass. Teacher's Assn. (licentiate). Republican. Avocations: languages, youth art and academic sponsor, future teacher mentoring, travel. Home: 46 Neptune Ave West Springfield MA 01089 Office: Agawam Mid Sch Main St Agawam MA 01001 Office Phone: 413-789-1400. E-mail: buceojs@aol.com.

GOODWIN, BRUCE T., engineer; BS in Physics, City Coll. NY; MS in Aeronautical and Astronautical Engring., PhD in Aeronautical and Astronautical Engring., U. Ill. Staff mem. Los Alamos Nat. Lab.; with Lawrence Livermore Nat. Lab., 1985—, B Program/B Divsn. leader def. and nuclear tech., 1996—2001, assoc. dir. def. and nuclear tech., 2001—. Recipient Aerospace Laurels Honor, Aviation Week & Space Tech. Mag., 2000, Ernest Orlando Lawrence award, US Dept. Energy, 2002. Office: Lawrence Livermore Nat Lab 7000 E Ave Livermore CA 94550

GOODWIN, CHARLES HUGH, technology education educator; b. Cortland, NY, Feb. 2, 1945; s. Arthur George and Elizabeth Sarah (Pratt) G.; m. Frances Margaret Dunkle, Aug. 18, 1967 (div. June 1979); 1 child, Chad Conlin; m. Barbara Louetta Milan, Aug. 16, 1980. BS, SUNY, Oswego, 1967, MS in Edn., 1973. Cert. tech. tchr. trainer, N.Y. Indsl. arts tchr. Worcester Ctrl. Schs., NYC, 1967-69, Endicott Ctrl. Schs., NYC, 1969-86, tech. edn. tchr., 1986—; chmn. tech. and mgmt. sci. dept. Union-Endicott Ctrl. Schs., 1996—. Applied physics tchr. Broome C.C., Binghamton, N.Y., 1994—; curriculum writer N.Y. State Edn. Dept., Albany, 1983-88, test writer, evaluator, 1978-95, tchr. trainer, 1986-92, sch. quality reviewer, 1992-96; higher edn. com. N.Y. State Strategic Systemic Initiative, 1995; mem. Endicott Sch. Dist. Planning Team, 1992-03; N.Y. State Edn. Assn. adv. coun. chair, 2002-; cons. U. Minn. Educators Study, 2003—, N.Y. State Edn. Dept. Tech. Edn. Delphi study, 2005, N.Y. State Edn. Dept. Tech. Edn. preK-12 framework com., 2006. Contbr. articles to profl. publs. Merit badge counselor Boy Scouts Am., Endicott, 1984—; mem. com., planner Endicott Tech. Ctr., 1993-95; mem. adv. bd. U. Minn. Educator's Study, 2003—; trustee Union-Endicott Edn. Found., 2004—. Named NY State Tech. Tchr. of Yr., Internat. Tech. Edn. Assn., 1986; named Disting. Alumnus, SUNY, Oswego, 1986; named to Elmira Southside H.S. Sports Hall of Fame, 1997; recipient Tech. in Edn. award 8 NY County Tech. Rsch. Com., 1997, Outstanding Educator award NY State Tech. Prep. Conf., 1998, 2003, Citizen of Yr. award NY State Soc. Profl. Engrs., 1999, Outstanding Achievements and Contbns. in the Field of Edn. award, NY State Soc. Profl. Engrs., 2004, Outstanding Contbns. to Broome-Tioga Tech. Prep., 2003. Mem.: NY State Congress Parents and Tchrs. (hon. life), So. Tier Tech. Educators' Assn. (pres. 1974—75, Tchr. of Yr. 1984, 2004), Soc. Plastics Engrs. (pres. 1991—92, 2004—, editor newsletter Perspective, Mem. of Yr. 1991—92, Past Pres. award 1992), NY State Tech. Edn. Assn. (polit. action chmn. 1991—96, pres. 1992—93, authentic assessment chmn. 1994—, chairperson statewide adv. coun. 2002—, chairperson corp. membership 2004—, Exemplary Svc. award 2007, Outstanding Svc. award 1996, Recognition award 2003), Epsilon Pi Tau (Laureate mem. 2006, Laureate citation 2006). Avocations: running, hunting, woodworking, dance. Home: 12 Tudor Dr Endicott NY 13760-4332 Office: Union-Endicott Ctrl Schs 1200 E Main St Endicott NY 13760-5220 Business E-Mail: cgnystea@stny.rr.com.

GOODWIN, CRAUFURD DAVID, economics professor; b. Montreal, Que., Can., May 23, 1934; came to U.S., 1962; s. George G. and Roma (Stewart) G.; m. Nancy Virginia Sanders, June 7, 1958. BA, McGill U., 1955; PhD, Duke U., 1958. Econ. research asst. Courtauld's Can., Ltd., 1955; lectr. econs. U. Windsor, Ont., 1958-59; exec. sec. Commonwealth Studies Center, Duke U., also; vis. asst. prof., 1959-60; hon. rsch. fellow Australian Nat. U., 1960-61; asst. prof. econs. York U., Toronto, 1961-62; asst. prof. econs., asst. to provost Duke U., Durham, N.C., 1962-63, assoc. prof. econs., sec. to Univ., asst. to provost, 1963-64, assoc. prof. econs., sec. Univ., asst. provost, 1964- 66, assoc. prof. econs., asst. provost, dir. internat. studies, 1966-68, prof. econs., vice provost for internat. studies, 1968-69, prof. econs., vice provost, dir. internat., 1969-72, prof. econs., 1971-74, James B. Duke prof. econs., 1974—, dean Grad. Sch., vice provost for rsch., 1980-86, interim chair dept. econs., 2002—03. Smuts fellow Cambridge U., 1967-68; officer in charge European and internat. affairs Ford Found., 1971-76. Author: Canadian Economic Thought: The Political Economy of a Developing Nation 1814-1914, 1961, Economic Enquiry in Australia, 1966, The Image of Australia, 1974, (with M. Nacht) Absence of Decision, 1983, Fondness and Frustration, 1984, Decline and Renewal, 1986, Abroad and Beyond, 1988, Missing the Boat, 1991; editor: (with W.B. Hamilton and Kenneth Robinson) A Decade of the Commonwealth 1955-64, 1966, (with I.B. Holley) The Transfer of Ideas, 1968, (with R.D.C. Black and A.W. Coats) The Marginal Revolution in Economics, 1973, Exhortation and Controls, 1975, Energy Policy in Perspective, 1981, Economics and National Security, 1991, International Investment in Human Capital, 1993, (with Alan Smith, Ulrich Teichler, and Peggy Blumenthal) Academic Mobility in a Changing World: Regional and Global Trends, 1996, (with M. Nacht) Beyond Government, 1995, Talking to Themselves, 1995, Art and the Market, 1998, (with N. Demarchi) Economic Engagements with Art, 2000; editor: (jour.) History of Political Economy, 1969—, (series) Historical Perspectives on Modern Economics, 1981—. Guggenheim fellow, 1967-68 Home: PO Box 957 Hillsborough NC 27278-0957 E-mail: goodwin@econ.duke.edu.

GOODWIN, DAVID B., lawyer; AB, U. Calif., Santa Cruz, 1974; BA, Oxford U., 1976, MA, 1979; JD, Stanford U., 1982. Bar: Calif. Atty., shareholder Heller Ehrman LLP, San Francisco, 1986—, co-chair appeals and strategy. Office: Heller Ehrman LLP 333 Bush St San Francisco CA 94104 Office Phone: 415-775-6319. Fax: 415-772-6268. Business E-Mail: david.goodwin@hellerehrman.com.

GOODWIN, DORIS HELEN KEARNS, historian, writer; b. Bklyn., Jan. 4, 1943; d. Michael Alouisius and Helen Witt (Miller) Kearns; m. Richard N. Goodwin, 1975; children: Richard, Michael, Joseph. BA magna cum laude, Colby Coll., 1964; PhD, Harvard U., 1968. Intern US Dept. State, Washington, 1963, Ho. of Reps., 1965; rsch. assoc. U.S. Dept. Health, Edn., & Welfare, 1966; spl. asst. to Willard Wirtz U.S. Dept. Labor, 1967; staff asst. to President Lyndon B. Johnson The White House, 1968; prof. govt. Harvard U., Cambridge, Mass., 1969—79. Spl. cons. to Pres. Lyndon Johnson, 1969-73; hostess "What's the Big Idea", WGBH-TV, Boston, 1972; polit. analyst news desk, WBZ-TV, Boston, 1972; mem. Women's Polit. Caucus, Mass., 1972, Dem. Party Platform Com., 1972; reg. panelist News Hour with Jim Lehrer; commentator NBC, MSNBC. Author: Lyndon Johnson and the American Dream, 1976, The Fitzgeralds and the Kennedys: An American Saga, 1987, No Ordinary Time: Franklin and Eleanor Roosevelt: The Homefront in World War II, 1994 (Harold Washington Lit. award, New England Bookseller Assn. award, Ambassador Book award, Wash. Monthly Book award, Pulitzer Prize for History, 1995), Wait Till Next Year: A Memoir, 1997, Team of Rivals: The Political Genius of Abraham Lincoln, 2005; numerous articles on politics and baseball; contbr.: Telling Lives: The Biographer's Art, 1979; forward: Mortal Friends: A Novel, 1992, Kennedy Weddings: A Family Album, 1999. Trustee Wesleyan U., Colby Coll., Robert F. Kennedy Found. Named Fulbright fellow, 1966, White House fellow, 1967, recipient: Charles Frankel prize from Nat. Endowment for Humanities, Sara Josepha Hale medal, Lincoln prize, Gettysburg Coll., 2006. Mem. Am. Polit. Sci. Assn., Coun. Fgn. Relations, Women Involved, Group for Applied Psychoanalysis, Signet Soc., Soc. Am. Historians, Am. Acad. Arts & Scis., Harvard U. Bd. Overseers, Phi Beta Kappa (outstanding young women of yr. award 1966), Phi Sigma Iota. Roman Catholic. Office: c/o Dori Lawson Soldier Creek Assoc PO Box 477 Rockport ME 04856

GOODWIN, FRANK ERIK, materials engineer; b. Bethlehem, Pa., Jan. 6, 1954; s. Francis Black and Grethe Julie (Andresen) G.; m. Rosalind Ann Volpe, May 30, 1987; children: Adrian Edmond, Marianna Rose. BS, Cornell U., 1975; ScD, MIT, 1979. Plant engr. Chambersburg (Pa.) Engring. Co., 1979-80; devel. dir. Chromalloy Rsch. & Tech., Orangeburg, NY, 1980-82; mgr. devel. Internat. Lead Zinc Rsch. Orgn., Research Triangle Park, NC, 1982-84, mgr. metallurgy, 1984-86, v.p. materials sci., 1986—2004, exec. v.p., 2004—. Mem. peer review com. on lead Dept. Energy, Washington, 1987-89. Author: Galfan Galvanizing Alloy & Technology, 1984; editor: Stress Calculations for Zinc Die Castings, 1988, Engineering Properties of Zinc Alloys, 1988; contbr. articles to profl. jours., chpts. to books. Mem. ASM, N.Am. Die Casting Assn. (rsch. com.), N.Y. Acad. Scis. Republican. Episcopalian. Achievements include patents (with other) for new aluminum alloy, new lead alloy for batteries. Office: Internat Lead Zinc Rsch Org 2525 Meridian Pky Ste 100 Durham NC 27713-2261

GOODWIN, FREDERICK KING, psychiatrist; b. Cin., Apr. 21, 1936; s. Robert Clifford and Marion Cronin (Schmadel) G.; m. Rosemary Powers, Oct. 19, 1963; children: Kathleen Kelly, Frederick King, Daniel Clifford. BS, Georgetown U., 1958; philosophy fellow, St. Louis U., 1958—59, MD, 1963. Intern medicine and psychiatry SUNY, Syracuse, 1963-64; resident in psychiatry U. N.C., Chapel Hill, 1964-65; commd. med. officer USPHS, 1965; clin. assoc. adult psychiatry br. NIMH, 1965-67; rsch. fellow Lab. Biochemistry, Nat. Heart Inst., NIH, Bethesda, Md., 1967-68; chief sect. on psychiatry NIMH, Bethesda, 1968-73, chief clin. psychobiology br., 1977-81, sci. dir., 1981-88; apptd. by Pres. adminstr. Alcohol, Drug Abuse and Mental Health Adminstrn., Washington, 1988-92; pvt. practice Chevy Chase, Md., 1967—; dir. NIMH, Rockville, Md., 1992-94; dir. Ctr. on Neurosci. Med. Progress and Soc. George Washington U. Med. Ctr., Washington, 1994—. Faculty George Washington U. Sch. Medicine, Washington Sch. Psychiatry, Uniformed U. Sch. Health Scis.; vis. prof. U. Calif., Irvine, U. Wis., Boston U., U. So. Calif., Duke U.; cons. AMA Coun. on Drugs; AIDS coord. Alcohol, Drug Abuse and Mental Health Adminstrn., 1986-90; participant pub. edn. programs on local and network TV and radio. Author: (with K.R. Jamison) Manic-Depressive Illness, 1990 (Best Med. Book award 1990 Assn. Am. Pubsd.); editor-in-chief Psychiatry Research, 1979-97; mem. editl. bd. Archives of Gen. Psychiatry, 1978—, Psychopharmacology, 1976-79; contbr. articles to med. jours.; host (pub. radio program) The Infinite Mind, 1998-2005 (EDI award for excellence in media Easter Seal Soc., 1999); sr. contbr. The Infinite Mind, 2005—. Mem. adv. bd. Max Planck Inst., Munich. Recipient Psychopharmacology Rsch. prize Am. Psychol. Assn., 1970, Internat. Anna-Monika prize for rsch. in depression, 1971, Taylor Manor award, 1976, Adminstrs. award HEW, 1977, Superior Svc. award USPHS, 1980, Strecker award, 1983, Sr. Exec. Svc. Presdl. Meritorious Rank award, 1982, Disting. Rank award, 1986, Disting. Exec. Svc. award Sr. Exec. Assn. Profl. Devel. League, 1986, Best Tchr. in Am. Psychiatry award CME Inc., 1989, Svc. to Sci. award Nat. Assn. for Biomed. Rsch., 1990, Pub. Svc. award. Fed. Am. Socs. for Exptl. Biology, 1990, 1st recipient of Fawcett Humanitarian award NDMDA, 1990, McAlpin award NMHA, 1991, EDI award Easter Seal Soc., 1999, Nola Maddox Falcone prize, 1999; NIMH Spl. fellow, 1967-68. Fellow Am. Psychiat. Assn. (chmn. com. on protection of human subjects, task force on rsch. tng., Hofheimer prize for rsch. 1971, chmn. task force on future of psychiat. rsch.), Am. Coll. Neuropsychopharmacology (chmn. com. on problems of pub. concern); mem. Inst. Medicine, NAS, AAAS, Am. Psychosomatic Soc., Soc. Biol. Psychiatry (A.E. Bennett award 1970), Am. Acad. Psychoanalysis, Soc. for Neurosci., Psychiat. Rsch. Soc. (pres. 1998-2000), Washington Psychiat. Soc. Office: Ctr Neuroscience Med Progress Soc 7500 Old Georgetown Rd Ste 601 Bethesda MD 20814 Business E-Mail: fred@drgoodwin.com, psyfkg@gwumc.edu. *Many aspects of one's innerself contribute to shaping a career, most, I suspect, evolving and changing along the way. For me, one characteristic stands out as unchanging - the capacity to derive genuine pleasure and a special sense of satisfaction from the successes and the growth of those whose careers you have helped - in a sense, your professional "children".*

GOODWIN, GEORGE EVANS, public relations executive; b. Atlanta, June 20, 1917; s. George and Carrie (Clark) G.; m. Lois Milstead, Nov. 2, 1940 (dec. Dec. 2005); children: Clark, Allen. AB with cert. in journalism, Washington and Lee U., 1939, HDL, 1997. Reporter Atlanta Georgian, 1939, Charleston (S.C.) News and Courier, 1940, Washington Times-Herald, 1940-41, Miami Daily News, 1941-42; staff writer Atlanta Jour., 1945-52; exec. dir. Central Atlanta Improvement Assn., 1952-54; v.p. First Nat. Bank of Atlanta, 1954-64; exec. v.p. Bell & Stanton, Inc., 1965-76; mng. dir. Manning, Selvage & Lee, Atlanta, 1976-85, sr. counselor, 1985—. Exec. sec. Ga. Senatorial Transit Study Com., 1954 Chmn. Atlanta Bicentennial Commn., 1974-76; trustee emeritus Oglethorpe U.; life dir. Alliance Theater; elder Presbyn. Ch.; mem. Ga. Citizens Y2K Task Force, 1999-2000. Decorated Purple Heart, Navy Unit Commendation; recipient Pulitzer prize for local reporting, 1948, Sigma Delta Chi award for gen. reporting, 1948, Pall Mall Big Story award, 1949. Mem. SAR, Pub. Rels. Soc. Am., Rotary Internat., Delta Tau Delta, Soc. Profl. Journalists/Sigma Delta Chi (award for gen. reporting on vote fraud 1948), Omicron Delta Kappa. Home: 3302 Ivanhoe Dr NW Atlanta GA 30327-1528 Office: Manning Selvage & Lee Ste 400 1170 Peachtree St NE Atlanta GA 30309 Office Phone: 404-875-1444. Business E-Mail: george.goodwin@mslpr.com.

GOODWIN, IRWIN, journalist, writer; b. Chgo., Aug. 19, 1929; s. Albert and Sarah Esther (Wallen) Goodwin; m. Mary Margaret Revell, Apr. 21, 1966 (div. 1986). AB, Roosevelt U., Chgo., 1948; MA, U. Mich., 1949. Reporter City News Bur., Chgo., 1949-50; reporter, asst. editor Newsweek, Chgo. and NYC, 1952-58; dir. pub. info. Sci. Rsch. Assocs., Chgo., 1958-60; corr. Newsweek, London, 1960-70; Caribbean corr. Washington Post, San Juan, 1970-72; corr. NBC News, 1970—72; spl. asst. to dir. Smithsonian Instn., Washington, 1972-73; sr. editor NAS, Washington, 1973-82; editor Washington bur. Physics Today, Washington, 1983-93, sr. editor Washington bur., 1993-2000; corr. Nature, 2000—. Co-author: Physics and Nuclear Arms Today, 1991; editor: Paying for America's Health Care, 1973, Energy and Environment: Collision of Crises, 1974; book reviewer Chgo. Tribune, 1958-59; contbr. articles to profl. jours. Sgt. maj. U.S. Army, 1950-52. Recipient News Writing award Overseas Press Club, 1971, 72, Pub. Svc. Group Achievement award NASA, 1981. Mem. AAAS, Nat. Assn. Sci. Writers, Fedn. Am. Scientists, Fgn. Affairs Coun., DC Sci. Writers Assn., Nat. Press Club, Union Concerned Scientists, Phi Beta Kappa. Business E-Mail: goodwin@aip.org. E-mail: irwingoodwin@aol.com.

GOODWIN, JAMES E., retired air transportation executive; BBA, Salem Coll. With United Airlines, 1967, sr. v.p. internat., 1992, sr. v.p. N.Am., 1992—98, pres., COO, 1998—99; chmn., CEO UAL Corp., Elk Grove Twp., Ill., 1999—2001; mem. bd. of dir. AAR Corp., Wood Dale, Ill., 2002—. Bd. dir. AAR Corp., Wood Dale, Ill., 2001—, Labe Bank, DBS Commn. Inc. Trustee Lewis U.; bd. dirs. Chgo. Coun. Fgn. Rels. Mem. Exec. Club Chgo. (bd. dirs.), Comml. Club Chgo. (civic com.). Office: AAR Corp One AAR Place 1100 Wood Dale Rd Wood Dale IL 60191

GOODWIN, JANE AYERS, pediatric anesthesiologist; b. Providence, July 27, 1968; d. Robert and Carole Ayers; m. Salvatore Robert Goodwin, Mar. 12, 1994; 1 child, Casey. MD, U. of Fla., Gainesville, 1994. Diplomate anesthesiology Am. Bd. of Anesthesiology. Clin. asst. prof. dept. anesthesiology U. of Fla., Gainesville, 1999—2000; asst. prof., cons. dept. anesthesiology Nemours Children's Clinic, Jacksonville, Fla., 2000—. Contbr. articles to rsch. publs. Mem.: Internat. Anesthesia Rsch. Soc., Soc. for Pediat. Anesthesiology, Am. Soc. of Anesthesiology, Alpha Omega Alpha. Achievements include collaborative research efforts with bioengineering colleagues in Portugal regarding development of fetal, neonatal and infant simulation software and models which may be used for education; research in model for educational simulation of infant cardiovascular physiology. Office: Nemours Children's Clinic 807 Children's Way Jacksonville FL 32207 Office Phone: 904-202-8332. Office Fax: 904-396-1630.

GOODWIN, JEAN MCCLUNG, psychiatrist; b. Pueblo, Colo., Mar. 28, 1946; d. Paul Stanley and Geraldine (Smart) McClung; m. James Simeon Goodwin, Aug. 8, 1970; children: Laura (dec.), Amanda Harding Goodwin, Robert Caleb, Paul Joshua, Elizabeth Cronin Goodwin. BA in Anthropology summa cum laude, Radcliffe Coll., 1967; MD, Harvard U., 1971; MPH, UCLA, 1972. Diplomate Am. Bd. Psychiatry and Neurology, Am. Bd. Forensic Psychiatry, added qualifications in forensic psychiatry Am. Bd. Psychiatry and Neurology, cert. adult psychoanalysis Am. Psychoanalytic Assn. Resident in psychiatry Georgetown U. Hosp., Washington, 1972-74, U. N.Mex. Sch. Medicine, 1974-76, asst. dir., dir. psychiat. residents tng., 1979-85; prof. Med. Coll. Wis., 1985-92, U. Tex. Med. Br., Galveston, 1992-98, prof. clin. psychiatry, 1998—; pvt. practice in gen. psychiatry, psychoanalysis. From instr. to assoc. prof. dept. psychiatry U. N.Mex. Sch. Medicine, 1976-85; cons. protective services Dept. Human Services, N.Mex., 1976-84; faculty Houston-Galveston Psychoanalytic Inst., 1999—; founding bd. dirs. Houston-Galveston Trauma Inst.; lectr. in field Author: Effects of High Altitude on Human Birth, 1969, Sexual Abuse: Incest Victims and Their Families, 1982, 2d edit., 1989, Rediscovering Childhood Trauma: Historical Casebook and Clinical Applications, 1993, Mischief and Mercy, 1993; co-author (with Reina Attias) Splintered Reflections: Images of the Body in Trauma, 1999; mem. editl. bd. Jour. Traumatic Stress, 1985-93, Dissociation, 1988-98, Psychotherapy Rev., 1998-2000, Trauma and Dissociation, 2000—; contbr. articles to profl. jours. Chmn. work group on child sexual abuse Surgeon Gen.'s Conf. on Violence and Pub. Health, Leesburg, Va., 1985; mem. adv. bd. Nat. Resource Ctr. on Child Sexual Abuse, 1989-96. Recipient Esther Haar award Am. Acad. Psychoanalysis, 1990, Cornelia Wilbur award Internat. Soc. for Study of Dissociation, 1994; Nat. Cen. Child Abuse and Neglect grantee, 1979-82, Nat. Inst. Aging grantee, 1980-85. Fellow Internat. Soc. Study Dissociation (exec. com. 1991-96), Am. Psychiat. Assn. (dist. br. treas., sec. N.Mex. br. 1980-82, exhibits and programs subcoms. 1985-91) Democrat. Roman Catholic. Office: 4925 Fort Crockett Blvd Apt 510 Galveston TX 77551-5949 Office Phone: 409-762-1101. Personal E-mail: jmgoodwin@aol.com.

GOODWIN, JOHN P., treasurer; BS in Math. Engring., Loughborough U. Joined Procter & Gamble Co., 1990, asst. treas. investor rels. and shareholder svcs., 2001—04, treas., 2004—. Fellow: Inst. of Chartered Accountants. Office: Procter & Gamble Co One Procter & Gamble Plaza Cincinnati OH 45202*

GOODWIN, JOHN ROBERT, lawyer, educator, writer; b. Morgantown, W.Va., Nov. 3, 1929; s. John Emory and Ruby Iona Goodwin; m. Betty Lou Wilson, June 2, 1952; children: John R., Elizabeth Ann Paugh, Mark Edward, Luke Jackson, Matthew Emory. BS, W.Va. U., Morgantown, 1952, LLB, 1964, JD, 1970. Bar: W.Va., U.S. Supreme Ct. Formerly city atty., county commr., spl. pros. atty.; then mayor City of Morgantown; prof. bus. law W.Va. U., Morgantown, 1964—80; prof. hotel and casino law U. Nev., Las Vegas, 1980—93, prof. emeritus, 1994—; pvt. practice, Morgantown, 1964—. Author: Legal Primer for Artists, Craftspersons, 1987, Hotel Law, Principles and Cases, 1987, Twenty Feet from Glory, 1970, Bus. Law, 3d edit., 1976, High Points of Legal History, 1982, Travel and Lodging Law, 1980, Desert Adventure, Gaming Control Law, 1985; editor Hotel and Casino Letter; past editor Bus. Law Rev., Bus. Law Letter. 1st lt. U.S. Army, Korean War. Named Outstanding West Virginian, State of W.Va.; named Hon. Gen. Gov. of W.Va., 1970. Democrat. Home: Casa Linda 48 5250 E Lake Mead Blvd Las Vegas NV 89156-6751 also: Goodwin Bldg 2d Fl Morgantown WV 26505 Office Phone: 702-452-2380. Personal E-mail: elcampo@att.net.

GOODWIN, JOSEPH ROBERT, judge; b. 1942; BS, W.Va. U., 1965, JD, 1970. Bar: W.Va. 1970. Ptnr. Goodwin & Goodwin, 1970-95; judge U.S. Dist. Ct. (so. dist.) W.Va., Charleston, 1995—. Editor-in-chief W.Va. Law Rev, Order of Coif. Mem. W.Va. U. Bd. Advisors, 1981-86; bd. visitors W.Va. U. Coll. Law, 1995-98, chmn., 1998. With USAR, 1965-67. Mem. ABA, W.Va. State Bar Assn., Jackson County Bar Assn., 4th Cir. Jud. Conf. Office: US Dist Ct So Dist WVa 300 Virginia St Charleston WV 25301 Office Phone: 304-347-3192.

GOODWIN, KELLY DEE, microbiologist, researcher; m. Robert Johnson; 1 child, Kai Johnson. Degree with high honors, U. Fla., 1988; PhD, Calif. Inst. Tech., Pasadena, 1995. Microbiologist, prin. investigator NOAA, Miami, 2003—. Adj. asst. prof. U. Miami. Finalist Techno-Entrepreneurship award, Takeda Found., 2001; fellow, Soroptimist Soc., 1990; Tng. grantee, Nat. Inst. Health Biotech., 1994—95, Postdoctoral Assoc., NRC, 1995—97. Mem.: Phi Beta Kappa, Golden Key. Office: Nat Oceanog and Meteorol Adminstrn 4301 Rickenbacker Causeway Miami FL 33019

GOODWIN, MARTIN BRUNE, retired radiologist; b. Vancouver, BC, Can., Aug. 8, 1921; came to US, 1948; m. Cathy Dennison, Mar. 7, 1980; 1 child, Suzanne; stepchildren: Chuck Glikas, Dianna; 1 child from previous marriage, Nancijane Goodwin Hilling. BSA in Agriculture, U. BC, 1943, postgrad., 1943-44; MD, CM, McGill U. Med. Sch., Montreal, Can., 1948. Diplomate Am. Bd. Med. Examiners, lic. Med. Coun. Can.; cert. diagnostic and therapeutic radiology Am. Bd. Radiology; cert. Am. Bd. Nuclear Medicine. Intern Scott & White Hosp., Temple, Tex., 1948-49; fellow radiology Scott & White Clinic, 1949-52, mem. staff, 1952-53; instr. U. Tex., Galveston, 1952-53; radiologist Plains Regional Med. Ctr., Clovis, N.Mex., Portales, N.Mex., pres. med. staff; chief radiology De Baca Gen. Hosp., Ft. Sumner, N.Mex.; cons. Cannon AFB Hosp., Clovis; pvt. practice radiology Clovis, Portales, Ft. Sumner and Tucumcari, 1955—2005; ret., 2005. Adj. prof. health scis. Ea. N.Mex. U., 1976-77; adj. clin. prof. health scis. We. Mich. U., 1976-78 Apptd. N.Mex. Radiation Tech. Adv. Coun., N.Mex. Bd. Pub. Health; former chmn. N.Mex. Health and Social Svcs. Bd.; mem. Regional Health Planning Coun.; treas. Roosevelt County Rep. Ctrl. Com. Capt. U.S. Army M.C., 1953-55; Col. USAF M.C., 1975-79. Fellow AAAS, Am. Coll. Radiology, Am. Coll. Radiology (past councillor); mem. Am. Soc. Thoracic Radiologists (founder), Radiol. Soc. of N.Am. (past councillor), N.Mex. Med. Soc. (various coms., chmn. joint practice com., councillor bd. dirs.), N.Mex. Radiol. Soc. (past pres.), N.Mex. Thoracic Soc. (past pres.), N.Mex. Med. Review Assn. (bd. dirs. 1970-93), N.Mex. Med. Soc. Found. for Med. Care (bd. dirs. 1975—, former v.p., former treas.), County Med. Soc. (past pres., past v.p., past sec.), Clovis C. of C. (chmn. civic affairs com., bd. dirs.), Clovis Elks Lodge (past exalted ruler), Clovis Noonday Lions Club (past sec.). Republican. Presbyterian. Home: 505 E 18th St Portales NM 88130-9201 Home Fax: 505-356-5035.

GOODWIN, MICHAEL, labor union administrator; b. Staten Island, NY, Oct. 12, 1942; divorced; children: Karen Edmonds, Cherylyn Beckey, Patricia Peters, Donna Carbonaro; m. Patricia Hoffman; children: Anne, Christopher. Elected sec. treas. OPEIU Local 153, 1977, elected v.p., 1979; v.p. The Office and Profl. Employees Internat. Union, 1985—97, pres., 1997—. Mem. exec. council AFL-CIO, also v.p.; v.p. NYC Ctrl. Labor Council; sec.-treas. NY Hotel Trades Council, Coalition of Kaiser Permanente Unions; treas. Alliance for Economic Justice, Wash., DC; chmn. Oversight Panel for referred cases under the Strategic Campaign Registration Program. Recipient Paul Hall Award of Merit, Maritime NY Coun. Greater NY and Vicinity, Ellis Island Medal Honor, 1995, NY State AFL-CIO Labor Recognition, NYC Ctrl. Labor Council Distinguished Services Award, Israel Bonds 50th Anniversary Award, Irish American Labor Coalition Award, Raymond T. McKay Memorial Award, Greater So. Fla. Maritime Trades Coun., Human Rights Award, Jewish Labor Com., 2006. Mem.: New Democracy Project (mem. bd. advisors). Office: Office/Profl Employees Internat Union 265 W 14th St 6th Fl New York NY 10011-5300 Office Phone: 800-346-7348.*

GOODWIN, ROBERT CRONIN, lawyer; b. Cleve., 1941; s. Robert Clifford and Marion Goodwin; m. Judith Mary Baxter, June 7, 1968; children: Anne, Helen, Sharon, Katherine. AB, Fordham U., 1963; JD, Georgetown U., 1969. Bar: D.C. 1970, Md. 1990. Vol. Peace Corps, Thailand, 1964-65; asst. cmty. devel. advisor AID, Thailand, 1965-66; atty. advisor Office Gen. Coun., Dept. Commerce, 1969-74; dep. asst. gen. coun. internat. & resouce devel. programs Fed. Energy Adminstrn., Washington, 1974-77, asst. gen. coun. internat. conservation & resource devel., 1977; asst. gen. coun. internat. trade & emergency preparedness Dept. Energy, Washington, 1977-79; ptnr. Thompson, Hine & Flory, 1979-82; v.p., gen. coun. China Energy Ventures, Washington, 1982-86; ptnr. Goodwin & Soble, 1986-90; pvt. practice, 1990-92; exec. v.p., gen. coun. Chindex Internat., Inc., 1992—2005; prof. U. Md. U. Coll., 2005—, dir. internat. mgmt. program Grad. Sch. Mgmt. and Tech., 2005—. Guest lectr. internat. petroleum contracts East China Petroleum Inst. Beijing, 1985; frequent lectr. on internat. contracts and Chineses legal and bus. issues. Editor-in-chief Law and Policy in International Business, 1968-69; co-editor Legal Environ. for Fgn. Direct Investment in U.S., 1994; contbr. articles to profl. jours. Mem. sch. bd., 1980-83. Recipient cert. of Merit Fed. Energy Adminstrn., 1974, cert. Spl. Acheivement, 1974, 76. Mem. ABA, DC Bar Assn., Thai-Am. Assn. (chmn. bus. com. 1991, pres. 1995), Nat. Coun. US China Trade (chmn. legal com. 1987), Am. Corp. Counsel Assn., Md.-China Bus. Coun. (bd. dirs., v.p. 1999-2005). Home: 3710 Bradley Ln Chevy Chase MD 20815-4257 Office: U Md U Coll 3501 Univ Blvd E Ste 3224 Hyattsville MD 20783-8030

GOODWIN, ROBERT KEER, foundation administrator; b. Nov. 15, 1948; s. Edward L. and Jeanne B. (Osby) Goodwin; m. Ruth Goodwin. BA, Oral Roberts U., 1970; MA in Christian Ethics, San Francisco Theol. Seminary; PhD (hon.), LeMoyne Owen Coll., Ripon Coll., U. Md.-Eastern Shore, U. Notre Dame. Pub. Okla. Eagle, Tulsa, 1973—81; regional sales mgr. Nat. U. Soc., Houston, 1985—87; dir. pub. info. to assoc. v.p. univ. rels. Prairie View A&M U.; asst. dep. chancellor for external affairs Tex. A&M U., 1987—89; exec. dir. White House Initiative on Historically Black Colls. and Univs., US Dept. Edn., 1989—92; exec. v.p., COO Points of Light Found., Washington, 1992—95, pres., 1995—. Founding bd. mem. Am.'s Promise the Alliance for Youth; bd. mem. Generations United, Interdenominational Theol. Ctr., Nat. Assembly, Nat. and Cmty. Svc. Coalition, Nat. Urban Fellows, Inc., Salvation Army, Youth for Understanding. Named Man of Yr., Nat. Coun. of Christians and Jews; recipient Award for Excellence in Nat. Exec. Leadership, Nat. Assembly of Health and Human Svcs. Orgns., 2001, Excellence in Cmty. Svc., 100 Black Men of Am.

GOODWIN, SCOTT CRAIG, interventional radiologist; b. Gardena, Calif., July 15, 1957; s. Alfred Boree Goodwin and Dorothy Tena Curtis; m. Suzie May El-Saden, Aug. 7, 1993; children: Alexander Boree, Adam El-Saden. BS magna cum laude with dept. honors, UCLA, 1979; MD, Harvard U., 1984. Intern in internal medicine St. Luke's Hosps./Wash. U., St. Louis, 1984-85; resident in diagnostic radiology UCLA Med. Ctr., 1985-88, fellowship in cardiovascular and interventional radiology, 1988-89, vis. asst. prof. radiology, 1989, from asst. prof. to assoc. prof., 1989—2001, prof. radiology, 2001—, chief vascular, interventional radiology, 1994-2001, vice chmn. radiology, 2003—; chief angiography and interventional radiology Daniel Freeman Hosp., Inglewood, Calif., 1989-91; vice chmn. imaging svcs. Irvine (Calif.) Med. Ctr., 1991-92; chmn., prof. radiology Wayne State U., Detroit, 2001—02; chmn. radiology Greater L.A. VA Med. Ctr., 2002—; vice chmn. radiology UCLA Med. Ctr., 2002—. Lectr. in field. Author (with others): Uterine Artery Embolization for the Treatment of Uterine Leiomyomata, 1997; contbr. articles to profl. jours. Recipient numerous rsch. grants. Office: Greater LA VA Med Ctr 11301 Wilshire Blvd 500-0608 Los Angeles CA 90073 Office Phone: 310-268-3478. Business E-Mail: scott.goodwin@med.va.gov, sgoodwin@mednet.ucla.edu.

GOODWIN, WILLIAM H., JR., diversified financial services company executive; m. Alice Goodwin. BS, Va. Polytechnic Inst., 1962; MBA, U. Va. Founder, chmn., pres. CCA Industries, Richmond, Va.; CEO, COO The Riverstone Group, LLC, Richmond, Va. Chmn. AMF Bowling; bd. dirs. Wachovia Corp., Charlotte, NC, 1993—. Bd. trustees Darden Found., 1986—95, chmn., 1990—92. Named one of 50 Most Generous Philanthropists, BusinessWeek, 2005; recipient Charles C. Abbott Award. Mem.: Raven Soc. Office: Wachovia Corp One Wachovia Ctr Charlotte NC 28288-0013

GOODWIN, WILLIAM MAXWELL, financial executive; b. Muncie, Ind., Oct. 13, 1939; s. Donald Dunkin and Beth Virginia (Maxwell) G.; m. LaDonna Sherry Erickson, June 9, 1962; children: Lauri Michelle, Lisa Dianne. AB, Ind. U., 1961, MBA, 1966. CPA, Ind. Staff acct., supr. Ernst & Whinney (now Ernst Whinney & Young), Indpls., 1966-72; contr. Lilly Endowment, Inc., Indpls., 1972-82, treas., sec., 1983-95, v.p. cmty. devel., 1996—. Advisor Sch. Bus., Ind. U., Bloomington, Ind., 1980-95; fin. advisor U.S. Gymnastic Fedn., Indpls., 1983-89; treas., dir. Nat. Gymnastics Found. Inc., Indpls., 1988-89. Contbr. articles to profl. jours. Treas., dir. Ind. Sports Corp., Indpls., 1979-88; dir. Youth Works, Inc., Indpls., 1977-85, Greater Indpls. Progress Com., 1996—; treas. Nat. Sports Festival, Indpls., 1982; treas., mem. exec. com. 1987 Pan Am. Games, Indpls.; chmn. AAU Sullivan Award Dinner, Indpls., 1983-94, mem. award selection com., 1993—. Capt. U.S. Army, 1962-64. Mem. AICPA, Ind. Assn. CPAs, Beta Gamma Sigma, Delta Phi Alpha. Republican. Methodist. Home: 3586 Inverness Blvd Carmel IN 46032-9380 Office: Lilly Endowment Inc PO Box 88068 Indianapolis IN 46208-0068 Home Phone: 317-872-5491; Office Phone: 317-924-5471. Business E-Mail: goodwinb@lei.org.

GOODY, JOAN EDELMAN, architect; d. Beril and Sylvia (Feldman) Edelman; m. Marvin E. Goody, Dec. 18, 1960 (dec. 1980); m. Peter H. Davison, Aug. 11, 1984 (dec. 2004). BA, Cornell U.; MArch, Harvard U. Prin. Goody, Clancy & Assocs., Inc., Boston. Asst. prof., design critic Harvard U., Cambridge, Mass., 1973-80, Eliot Noyes vis. critic, 1985; faculty Mayors Inst. for Design, 1989—; lectr. in field. Mem. Boston Landmarks Commn., 1976-87; chair Boston Civic Design Commn., 1994-2005; bd. dirs. Historic Boston. Fellow AIA (design awards), Boston Soc. Archs. (award of honor 2005), Boston Archtl. Ctr. (hon.), Saturday Club, Tavern Club. Office: Goody Clancy & Assocs Inc 420 Boylston St Boston MA 02116-3866

GOODY, RICHARD MEAD, geophysicist; b. Welwyn-Garden-City, Eng., June 19, 1921; came to U.S., 1958, naturalized, 1966; s. Harold Earnest and Lilian (Rankine) G.; m. Elfriede Koch, Sept. 11, 1946; 1 dau., Brigid. PhD, Cambridge U., 1949; MA (hon.), Harvard U., 1958. With Brit. Civil Service, 1942-46; fellow St. John's Coll., Cambridge, 1950-53; reader London U., 1953-58; prof. div. applied scis. Harvard U., 1958-91; dir. Blue Hill Obs., 1958-70, Center for Earth and Planetary Physics, 1970-71. Disting. vis. scientist Jet Propulsion Lab., 1977—. Author: Physics of the Stratosphere, 1947, Atmospheric Radiation, 1964, rev. edit., 1989, Atmospheres, 1974, The Principles of Atmospheric Physics and Chemistry, 1995. Fellow Am. Geophys. Union (William Bowie medal 1998), Am. Meteorol. Soc. (hon., 50th Anniversary medal 1970, Cleveland Abbé award 1977); mem. Royal Meteorol. Soc. (Buchan prize 1955), Nat. Acad. Scis., Am. Philos. Soc., Internat. Radiation Commn. (hon., Gold medal 2004). Home: 101 Cumloden Dr Falmouth MA 02540-1609 E-mail: goody@huarp.harvard.edu.

GOOGASIAN, GEORGE ARA, lawyer; b. Pontiac, Mich., Feb. 22, 1936; s. Peter and Lucy (Chobanian) G.; m. Phyllis Elaine Law, June 27, 1959; children— Karen Ann, Steven George, Dean Michael BA, U. Mich., 1958; JD, Northwestern U., 1961. Bar: Mich. 1961. Assoc. Marentay, Rouse, Selby, Fischer & Webber, Detroit, 1961-62; asst. U.S. Atty. U.S. Dept. Justice, Detroit, 1962-64; assoc. Howlett, Hartman & Beier, Pontiac and Bloomfield Hills, Mich., 1964-81; ptnr. Googasian Hopkins Hohauser & Forhan, Bloomfield Hills, Mich., 1981-96, The Googasian Firm, Bloomfield Hills, 1996—. Mem. bd. law examiners State of Mich., 1997—2002, pres., 2001—02. Author: Trial Advocacy Manual, 1984, West Groups Michigan Practice Torts, vols. 14 and 15, 2001. Pres. Oakland Parks Found., Pontiac, 1984-89; chmn. Oakland County Dem. party, Pontiac, 1964-70; state campaign chmn. U.S. Senator Philip A. Hart, Detroit, 1970; bd. dirs. Big Bros. Oakland County. 1968-73 Fellow Am. Bar Found., Am. Coll. Trial Lawyers, Internat. Acad. Trial Lawyers; mem. ABA (del. 1992-93, exec. com. nat. conf. bar pres. 1993-96), ATLA, Am. Bd. Trial Advocates, State Bar Mich. (pres. elect 1991-92, pres. 1992—), Internat. Soc. Barristers, Oakland County Bar Assn. (pres. 1985-86), Oakland Bar Found. (pres. 1990-92). Clubs: U. Mich. Club Greater Detroit. Presbyterian. Home: 3750 Orion Rd Oakland MI 48363-3029 Office: 6895 Telegraph Rd Bloomfield Hills MI 48301-3138 Office Phone: 248-540-3333.

GOOGINS, SONYA FORBES, state legislator, retired banker; b. New Haven, Nov. 9, 1936; d. Edward and Madeline Forbes; m. Robert Reville Googins, June 21, 1958; children: Shawn W. and Glen R. BE, U. Conn., 1958. Tchr. Manchester (Conn.) High Sch., 1958-61; pres. Colonial Printing Co., Glastonbury, 1971-76; bank officer Conn. Nat. Bank, Hartford, 1982-89; mem. Conn. Ho. of Reps., 1994—2006. Mem. Conn. employment and tng. commn. Greater Hartford United Way, 1995; vice-chair commerce Nat. Conf. State Legislatures; mayor Town of Glastonbury, 1983—85, 1987—91, 1993—95; mem. Town Coun., 1979—94, Rep. Town Com., Capitol Region Coun. Govts., 1983—94, chmn., 1989—94; chair Conn. Adv. Commn. Intergovtl. Rels., 1992—; chair fin. svc. com. Nat. Conf. of State Legislators, 2002—04; advocacy com. Am. Diabetes Assn.; bd. dirs. Conn. Capitol Region Growth Coun., 1994—96, Conn. Audubon Soc., 1997—99, Hartford Symphony Orch., 1997—2006. Recipient Outstanding Svc. award Friends of Glastonbury Youth, 1990, Disting. Svc. award Conn. Capitol Region Coun. Govts., 1994, Svc. award Women's Campaign Sch. at Yale, 2004; named Glastonbury Rep. of Yr., 1992. Mem. Auto Assn. Am. Allied Group Inc. (bd. dirs. 1994—), Glastonbury Bus. and Profl. Women (past pres. and founder, Woman of Yr. 1988), Glastonbury C. of C. (bd. dirs. 1994—), Glastonbury Jr. Woman's Club (past pres.). Roman Catholic. Avocations: golf, tennis, sailing. Home: 21 B Brewster Rd Glastonbury CT 06033 Personal E-mail: sonnygoogins@yahoo.com.

GOOKIN, THOMAS ALLEN JAUDON, civil engineer; b. Tulsa, Okla., Aug. 5, 1951; s. William Scudder and Mildred (Hartman) G.; m. Sandra Jean Andrews, July 23, 1983. BS with distinction, Ariz. State U., 1975. Registered profl. engr., Calif., Ariz., Nev., land surveyor Ariz., hydrologist. Civil engr., treas. Gookin Engrs. Ltd, Scottsdale, Ariz., 1968—. V.p. instl. devel. Am. Inst. Hydrologists, 2006. Chmn. adv. com. Ariz. State Bd. Tech. Registration Engring., 1984—. Recipient Spl. Recognition award Ariz. State Bd. Tech. Registration Engring., 1990. Mem. NSPE, ASCE, Ariz. Soc. Profl. Engrs. (sec. Papago chpt. 1979-81, v.p. 1981-84, pres. 1984-85, named Young Engr. of Yr. 1979, Outstanding Engring. Project award 1988), Order Engr., Am. Inst. Hydrology (nat. v.p.), Ariz. Congress on Surveying and Mapping, Ariz. Water Works Assn., Tau Beta Pi, Delta Chi (Tempe chpt. treas. 1970-71, sec. 1970, v.p. 1971), Phi Kappa Delta (pres. 1971-73). Republican. Episcopalian. Achievements include co-author Globe Equity # 59 Call System. Avocations: disneyana, science fiction, computer gaming. Home: 10760 E Becker Ln Scottsdale AZ 85259-3868 Office: Gookin Engrs Ltd 4203 N Brown Ave Ste A Scottsdale AZ 85251-3946 Office Phone: 480-947-3741. E-mail: water@gookin.biz.

GOOLD, DOUGLAS, think-tank executive; BA, McMaster U.; MA, U. Alta.; PhD in Modern History, Cambridge U. Investment editor, columnist The Globe and Mail newspaper, 1992—97, editor Report on Bus. sect., 1997—2000; editor Report on Bus. Mag., 2000—04; pres., CEO Can. Inst. Internat. Affairs, Toronto, Ont., Canada, 2004—. Author (with Andrew Willis): The Bre-X Fraud; co-author: Peace Without Promise. Killam Postdoctoral fellow, U. B.C. Office: Can Inst Internat Affairs Ste 302 205 Richmond St West Toronto ON Canada M5V 1V3 Home Phone: 416-653-1233; Office Phone: 416-977-9000 ext. 33. Business E-Mail: dgoold@ciia.org.

GOOLDY, PATRICIA ALICE, retired elementary school educator; b. Indpls., Nov. 23, 1937; d. Harold Emanuel and Emma Irene (Wade) VanTreese; m. Walter Raymond Gooldy, May 4, 1968. BS, U. Indpls., 1959; MS, Butler U., 1963. Tchr. Franklin Twp. Cmty. Schs., Indpls., 1959-68, 72-99, USA Dep. Schs., Bad Kreuznach, Germany, 1969-72; ret., 1999. Owner Ye Olde Genealogie Shoppe, Indpls., 1972—; lectr. in field. Author: 21 Things I Wish I'd Found, 1984; editor: Indiana Wills to 1880: Index to Indiana Wills, 1987; co-editor: Indiana Manual For Gen, 1991, Illinois Manual For Gen, 1994. Named Ky. Col., 1995; named one of Outstanding Elem. Tchrs. of Am., 1974. Mem. Franklin Twp. Hist. Soc. (founder), Ind. Geneal. Soc. (chartered). Office: Ye Olde Genealogie Shoppe PO Box 39128 Indianapolis IN 46239-0128 Office Phone: 317-862-3330. Personal E-mail: yogs@iquest.net.

GOOLKASIAN, PAULA A., psychologist, educator; b. Methuen, Mass., Aug. 9, 1948; d. Paul K. and Sadie T. (Touma) G.; m. Francis C. Martin, July 29, 1978; 1 child, Christopher. BA, Emmanuel Coll., 1970; MS, Iowa State U., 1972, PhD, 1974. Asst. prof. U. N.C., Charlotte, 1974-79, assoc. prof., 1979-85, prof. psychology, 1985—, pres. faculty, 1989—. Cons. in field. Exec. editor: Jour. Gen. Psychology. NDEA fellow, 1971-74; grantee NSF, NIH, numerous others. Fellow APA, Assn. Psychol. Scis.; mem. Psychonomics Soc., Soc. for Computers in Psychology (sec.-treas. 1989-91, pres. 1994), Sigma Xi, Phi Kappa Phi. Office: U NC Dept Psychology 9201 University City Blvd Charlotte NC 28223 Home Phone: 704-895-0827; Office Phone: 704-687-4749. Business E-Mail: pagoolka@uncc.edu.

GOOLRICK, ROBERT MASON, management consultant; b. Fredericksburg, Va., Mar. 25, 1934; s. John T. and Olive E. (Jones) Goolrick; m. Audrey J. Dippo (div.); children: Stephanie M., Meade A. BA with distinction, U. Va., 1956, JD, 1959. Bar: Va. 1959, DC 1959, US Dist. Ct. DC 1961, US Ct. Appeals (DC cir.) 1961. Assoc. Steptoe & Johnson, Washington, 1959-65, ptnr., 1965-79; pvt. practice Alexandria, Va., 1979-83; cons. bus., oil and gas fin. Instr. U. Va. Law Sch. Author: Public Policy Toward Corporate Growth, 1978, Corporate Mergers and Acquisitions under Federal Securities Laws, 1978. Mem.: ABA (corps. sect.), Raven Soc., Jefferson Soc., Phi Beta Kappa, Order of Coif. Home: 7462 Cross Gate Ln Alexandria VA 22315-4618 Office: PO Box 150672 Alexandria VA 22315-0672 Office Phone: 703-971-3422. Personal E-mail: rmgoolrick@cox.net.

GOOLSBY, ALLEN CUNNINGHAM, III, lawyer; b. Richmond, Va., Oct. 19, 1939; s. Allen C. Goolsby Jr. and Adelaide Rawles; m. Louanna Godwin. BA, Yale U., 1961; LLB, U. Va., 1968. Bar: Va. 1968, U.S. Dist. Ct. (ea. dist.) Va. Ptnr. Hunton & Williams, Richmond, Va., 1975—. Author: Virginia Corporation Law Practice, 1990, Goolsby on Virginia Corporations, 2002, 2d edit, 2005. Fellow Am. Bar Found., Va. Bar Found. Office: Hunton & Williams Riverfront Plz East Tower PO Box 1535 Richmond VA 23218-1535 Office Phone: 804-788-8289. Business E-Mail: agoolsby@hunton.com.

GOOLSBY, BRYAN L., lawyer; b. Dallas, Dec. 19, 1950; BBA with honors, Texas Tech U., 1973; JD with honors, U. Tex., 1977. CPA Tex., 1977; bar: Tex. 1977. Mng. ptnr. Locke, Liddell & Sapp, LLP, Dallas, 2001—06, chmn., 2007—. Adv. bd. Dallas region JPMorgan Chase & Co.; assoc. mem. bd. govs. Nat. Assn. Real Estate Investment Trusts, Inc. Mem. Dallas Citizens Coun.; bd. mem. Jr. Achievement of Tex.; dir. Med. Properties Trust; dir. assoc. bd. dirs. So. Meth. U. Edwin L. Cox Sch. Bus.; exec. com. mem. U. Tex. Syst. Law Alumni Assn. Mem.: ABA, Pension Real Estate Assn., Nat. Multi-Family Housing Assn., Greater Dallas C. of C., Royal Oaks Country Club, Beta Gamma Sigma, Phi Delta Phi, Phi Kappa Phi. Office: Locke Liddell & Sapp LLP Ste 2200 2200 Ross Ave Dallas TX 75201 Office Phone: 214-740-8550. Office Fax: 214-740-8800. E-mail: bgoolsby@lockeliddell.com.*

GOOLSBY, MICHELLE P., lawyer, food products executive; b. 1958; BBA, JD, U. Tex. Various positions Trammel Crow Co., Winstead Sechrest & Minick, 1988-98; ptnr., chair bus. sect., mem. compensation com.; exec. v.p., gen. counsel, chief adminstrv. officer, sec. Dean Foods Co. (formerly Suiza Foods Corp.), Dallas, 1998—. Mem. ABA. Office: 2515 Mckinney Ave Ste 1200 Dallas TX 75201-1945*

GOOLSBY, O. B., JR., food products executive; V.p., prep. food ops. Pilgrim's Pride Corp., Pittsburg, Tex., 1987—92, sr. v.p., 1992—98, exec. v.p., 1998—2002, pres., COO, 2002—04, pres., CEO, 2004—. Office: Pilgrim's Pride Corp 4845 US Hwy 271 N Pittsburg TX 75686 Mailing: Pilgrim's Pride Corp PO Box 93 Pittsburg TX 75686-0093*

GOON, ARTHUR DAVID, academic administrator, educator; b. NYC, Aug. 29, 1957; s. William and Lily Goon; m. Sue Ann Marshall; children: Brandon, Madison. BSBA, Tenn. Wesleyan Coll., 1979; MS in Edn. Adminstrn and Supervision, SUNY, 1992. Admissions and fin. aid counselor, mens head soccer coach Tenn. Wesleyan Coll., Athens, 1980—84; sr. admissions adv., spl. asst. to pres., mens head soccer coach SUNY, New Paltz, 1986—92; assoc. dir. enrollment mgmt. Arcadia U., Glenside, Pa., 1994—99; from dir. recruitment admissions and records to v.p. coll. rels. and advancement Montgomery County CC, Blue Bell, Pa., 1999—2003; v.p. enrollment mgmt. and student affairs Chestnut Hill Coll., Phila., 2003—. Womens head soccer coach Arcadia U., Glenside, 1995—2003; mens head soccer coach Rutgers U., Newark, 1993—94, U. Tenn., Chattanooga, 1984—86. Named Coach of Yr., Pa. Athletic Conf., 1996, 1998, 2000, Tenn. Intercollegiate Soccer Assn., 1981—83, Dist. Coach of Yr., Nat. Assn. Intercollegiate Athletics, 1982—83; named to Athletic Hall of Fame, Tenn. Wesleyan Coll., 1997. Office: Chestnut Hill Coll 9601 Germantown Ave Philadelphia PA 19118 Business E-Mail: goona@chc.edu.

GOORLEY, JOHN TIMOTHY, nuclear engineer; b. Ft. Campbell, Ky., Apr. 13, 1974; s. John Thomas and Sherrie Goorley. BS in Nuc. Engring., Tex. A&M U., 1996; BS in Radiol. Health Engring., Tex.A&M U., 1996; MS in Nuc. Engring., PhD in Nuc. Engring., MIT, 2002. Tech. staff Los Alamos Nat. Lab., N.Mex., 2002—. Pres.'s Endowed scholar, Tex. A&M U., 1992—96. Mem.: Am. Nuc. Soc., Sigma Xi, Alpha Nu Sigma. Avocations: medieval studies, travel, fencing. Home: 2628 Via Berrenda Santa Fe NM 87505 Personal E-mail: jgoorley@alum.mit.edu.

GOOS, ROGER DELMON, retired mycologist; b. Beaman, Iowa, Oct. 29, 1924; s. Gus and Georgiana Bertha (Witt) Goos; m. Mary Lee Engel, Sept. 21, 1946; children: Marinda Lee, Suzanne Maurine. BA, U. Iowa, Iowa City, 1950, PhD, 1958. Mycologist United Fruit Co., Norwood, Mass., 1958-62; scientist USPHS, NIH, Bethesda, Md., 1962-64; curator of fungi Am. Type Culture Collection, Rockville, Md., 1964-68; assoc. researcher, vis. assoc. prof. botany U. Hawaii, Honolulu, 1968-70; assoc. prof. botany U. R.I., Kingston, 1970-72, chair dept. of botany, 1971-86, prof. botany, 1972-95, prof. emeritus, 1995—. Trustee Am. Type Culture Collection, Rockville, Md., 1977-82; vis. rschr. U. BC, 1977, U. Hawaii, 1977, U. Exeter, UK, 1984, Bishop Mus., 1990. Served with US Army, 1944-46, 50-51. Decorated Bronze Star, Purple Heart, Combat Infantry badge; Indo-Am. fellow, U. Madras, India, 1981; Fulbright scholar U. Lisbon, 1993. Mem. Mycol. Soc. Am. (sec.-treas. 1980-83, v.p. 1983-84, pres.-elect 1984-85, pres. 1985-86), Bot. Soc. Am., Am. Soc. Microbiology, Am. Phytopath. Soc., Mycol. Soc. Japan, Brit. Mycol. Soc. Home: 4 Tanglewood Trl Narragansett RI 02882-1034 Office Phone: 401-874-2630.

GOOSEN, RETIEF, professional golfer; b. Pietersburg, South Africa, Feb. 3, 1969; m. Tracy Goosen; children: Leo, Ella. Profl. golfer PGA European Tour, PGA Tour. Mem. Pres. Cup Team, 2000, 03, 05, World Cup Team, 1993, 95, 2000, 01, Dunhill Cup Team, 1995—2000. Achievements include winning the US Open in 2001 and 2004; 6 career PGA Tour victories; 14 PGA European Tour victories. Office: McCormack House Hogarth Bus Pk Burlington Ln London W4 2TH England Office Phone: +44 208 233 5300.

GOOTEE, CHRISTY BECK, minister, educator; b. New Orleans, Oct. 5, 1951; d. John Warren and Conchita Curranlt Beck; m. Jim Edward Gootee, July 8, 1984; children: Jan, Joe, Joyce, Jeff, Jill, Jason, J.J. BA in French, English with honors, U. New Orleans, La., 1973; MA in Comparative Lit., Ind. U., Bloomington, 1976, PhD in Comparative Lit., 1982. Tchr. comparative arts Ind. U., Bloomington, 1977—79; tchr. ESL Delgado Coll., New Orleans, 1982—83; tchr. freshman composition Tulane U., New Orleans, 1983—84; tchr. world lit. and conversational English Loyola U., New Orleans, 1983—84; co-founder Two Hearts Gospel Ministry, New Orleans, 1984; co-dir. Christos Ho. of Prayer, Gautier, Miss., 1986—98; minister, bd. dirs. Two Hearts Gospel Ministry, Inc., Alexandria, La., 1998—. Retreat dir. Mary Hill Renewal Ctr., Pineville, La., 2002—; spkr. various religious confs. Prodr.: (radio program) Moments of Light, 1985—88; prodr.: (radio program) Moments of Light, 2001—; author: (poetry collection) Winter Arches with Goldenrod, 1972; editor: The Gist of Life, 1974; author: (book on inner healing) Peace Is My Gift, 1992; assoc. editor: Vision mag., 1984. Recipient poem Calvary chosen for The Sound of Poetry collection, Internat. Libr. Poetry, Md., 2001. Mem.: Mensa. Roman Catholic. Achievements include 8th ranked woman chess player in the U.S., 1970. Avocations: art, music, reading, dogs. Office: Two Hearts Gospel Minstry Inc PO Box 7206 Alexandria LA 71306 Personal E-mail: christyg@4isp.com.

GOOTEE, JANE MARIE, lawyer; b. Jasper, Ind., July 5, 1953; d. Thomas H. and Anne M. (Dreifke) G. BA, Ind. U., 1974; JD cum laude, St. Louis U., 1977. Bar: Ind. 1977, Mo. 1978, Mich. 1980, Ohio 1983, US Dist. Ct. (so. dist.) Ind. 1977, US Dist. Ct. (ea. dist.) Mich. 1980, US Ct. Appeals (7th cir.) 1978, US Supreme Ct. 1980, US Ct. Appeals (6th cir.) 1982, US Ct. Appeals (4th cir.) 1986. Dep. atty. gen. Ind., Indpls., 1977-79; corp. atty. Dow Chem. Co., Midland, Mich., 1979-2003, ea. div. counsel, 1981-84, sr. atty., 1984-86, Mich. div. counsel, 1986-90, Dow Europe sr. staff counsel, 1990-94, asst. gen. counsel fin. law, 1994-99, asst. gen. counsel litigation, 1999-2002, dep. dir. global ethics and compliance, 2003; with Stroup, Erhart & Lyons, P.C., 2004—; mem. adv. com. Nat. Chamber Litigation Ctr. Environ. Law, 1985-90; chair Dow Epidemiology Instl. Rev. Bd., 1984-90; pro-bono def. Midland Cir. Ct., 1980-81. Bd. dirs. Big Sisters Midland, 1979-81, 84-86, Big Bros./Big Sisters Midland, 1986-90, also pres., 1988-89; exec. bd. Lake Huron Area coun. Boy Scouts Am., 1988-90, NYC YWCA Acad. of Women Achievers, 1988, mediator No. Cmty. Mediation, Petoskey, Mich., 2004; pres. Charlevoix Country Club, bd. advisors 2005-07. Fellow Mich. State Bar Found., Mo. Bar, Mich. Bar Assn. Office Phone: 231-347-3907.

GOOTNICK, MARGERY FISCHBEIN, lawyer; b. Rochester, N.Y., Oct. 24, 1927; d. Morris R. and Regina (Kroll) Fischbein; m. Lester T. Gootnick, Mar. 1, 1952; children— Jonathon, David, Amy. B.A., Harvard U., 1949; J.D., Cornell U., 1952. Bar: N.Y. 1952. Assoc. Stone & Hoffenberg, Rochester, N.Y., 1952-55; sole practice, Rochester, 1968—; permanent arbitrator Am. Airlines and Assn. Profl. Flight Attendants, NW Airlines and Teamsters Local 2000, Presbyn. Hosp.-N.Y. State Nurses Assn., U. Rochester and U. Rochester Security Guards Union, numerous others; chmn. Fgn. Service Impasse Disputes Panel, Washington, 1983-97; apptd. fgn. svc. grievance bd. U.S. State Dept., 1997; mem. exec. com. N.Y. State Bar, 1998. Mem. Rep. Jud. Screening Com., Rochester, 1976—. Mem. ABA, Fed. Bar Assn., Nat. Acad. Arbitrators (v.p. 1992-94, chair membership com. 1988-91, exec. com. 1987, bd. govs. 1983-86), N.Y. State Bar Assn. (labor and employment sect. chair elect 1994—, exec. com. 1982—), Soc. Fed. Labor Rels. Profls. (1st v.p. 1993—), Am. Arbitration Assn. (upstate N.Y. labor adv. panel). Office e-mail: mornings@ix.netcom.com. Home and Office: 46 Knollwood Dr Rochester NY 14618-3513 E-mail: mgootnich@ix.netcom.com.

GOOTT, ALAN F(RANKLIN), lawyer; b. Washington, Aug. 6, 1947; BA, George Washington U., 1969; JD cum laude, Harvard U., 1973. Bar: N.Y., 1974, U.S. Dist. Ct. (so., ea. dists.) N.Y. 1974, U.S. Ct. Appeals (2d cir) 1974. Assoc. Kaye Scholer LLP, NYC, 1973-82, ptnr., 1982—. Office: Kaye Scholer LLP 425 Park Ave New York NY 10022-3598 Office Phone: 212-836-8157. Business E-Mail: agoott@kayescholer.com.

GOPALAKRISHNAN, KASTHURIRANGAN, civil engineer, research scientist; arrived in US, 1998; s. Ramaswamy and Jayalakshmi Gopalakrishnan. BE with honors, Birla Inst. Tech. Sci., Pilani, India, 1993—97; MS, La. State U., Baton Rouge, 1998—99; PhD, U. Ill., Urbana, 2001—04. EIT La., 1999. Rsch. intern Structural Engring. Rsch. Ctr., Chennai, India, 1997; rsch. asst. La. State U., 1998—99; Eisenhower rsch. fellow Turner-Fairbanks Hwy. Rsch. Ctr., McLean, Va., 2000—01; rsch. asst. U. Ill., 2001—04; post-doctoral rsch. assoc. Iowa State U., Ames, 2005—. Contbr. articles to profl. jours. Mem.: ASCE (assoc.). Avocations: Karate, swimming, music. Home Phone: 515-294-3973.

GOPE, DIPANJAN, computer engineer; b. Calcutta, West Bengal, India, Feb. 22, 1978; s. Diptendu Bikas and Polly Gope; m. Sonia P Parandekar, Dec. 20, 2001. BTech in Electronics and Elec. Comm., Indian Inst. Tech., Kharagpur, 2000; PhD, U. Wash., Seattle, 2005. Registered profl. engr., Wash., 2005. Rsch. asst. U. Wash., Seattle, 2000—05; computer aided design engr. Intel Corp., Santa Clara, Calif., 2005—07; dir. R&D Physware, Inc., Bellevue, Wash., 2007—. Co-recipient Best paper in session award (SRC Techcon), Semiconductor Rsch. Corp., 2003. Mem.: IEEE (assoc.). Achievements include co-development of PILOT, a software tool to predict electrical performance of circuits. Invention disclosed with University of Washington. Office: Physware Inc 411 108th Ave NE Ste 1980 Bellevue WA 98004 also: Intel Corporation 2200 Mission College Blvd Santa Clara CA 95054 Home Phone: 425-205-0925; Office Phone: 425-458-6816. Personal E-mail: dipanjangope@yahoo.com.

GOPHEN, MOSHE, research scientist; b. Kibbutz Afikim, Israel, Dec. 18, 1936; s. Itzchak and Sara (Sheinberger) G.; m. Eva Gophen, May 5, 1998; children from previous marriage: Michal, Yair, Ruth, Rachel. BSc, Hebrew U., Jerusalem, 1963, MSc, 1967, PhD, 1976. H.S. tchr., Beit-Yerach, Israel, 1963-69; sr. scientist Kinneret Limnological Lab., Tiberias, Israel, 1968—; lectr. Hebrew U., 1972-73, Haifa U., Oranim, Israel, 1973-78; sr. scientist Kinneret Limnological Lab., Tiberias, Israel, 1968—2001, dir., 1980-86; rsch. prof. U. Okla., Norman, 1992-94; ret., 2001. Sci. coord. Hula (Israel) Project, 1995—, chmn. Hula com., 1997—; sr. coord. Hula Project MIGAL Galilee Tech. Ctr., 2001—; prof. Tel-Hai (Israel) Coll., 1995—; cons. Ilopango Assn., San-Salvador, El-Salvador, 1995—, Lake Amatitlan Assn., Guatemala City, Guatamela, 1995-96; active Hula Valley Project, 1995—; rsch. lake mgmt. Israel, Egypt, US, Aid, Merc, 2001—; climate change impacts Glowa Found., Germany, 2001—; rsch. projects leader Israel-Egypt-USA Lake Mgmt., 1980-2001, Israel-German Hula Valley Ecology, 2003—; cons. Guanting Reservioir, China, 2005—; sci. coord Hula Valley Ecology USA Forestry Svc., 2005—; tchr. Limnology U., Valdivia, Chile, 2005; spkr. in field. Author: Lake Kinneret, 1992 (Kinneret Authority award 1989); co-author: Scientific Basis for Water Resurces Management, 1985, Large Lakes-Ecological Structure and Function, 1990 (Minerva award 1990), Guidelines of Lake Management, 1995 (Kinneret Lab. award 1995); contbr. numerous articles to profl. jours. Edn. com. Karmiel mcplty., 1979; chmn. Ctrl. Com. for Labor Party, Karmiel, 1987-88; vol. Ecological Com., Karmiel, 1995—. Sgt. Israel mil., 1955-58. Eshkol Found. Water Rsch. fellow Israel Kinneret Inst., 1973, DAAD fellow, Germany, 1982, Minerva fellow, Germany, 1987-88. Mem. Internat. Assn. Limnology, Am. Soc. Limnology and Oceanography, Freshwater Biol. Assn. (life). Avocations: classical music, art, astronomy and universe sciences, nature. Home: Hativat Iftach St 73/1 21197 Karmiel Israel Office: MIGAL POB 831 11016 Kiryat Shmone Israel Office Phone: 972-4-6953556. Business E-Mail: gophen@migal.org.il.

GOPMAN, JONATHAN E., lawyer; b. Aug. 24, 1965; BA, U. South Fla., 1986; JD with high honors, Fla. State U., 1990; LLM in Estate Planning, U. Miami Sch. Law, 1991. Bar: Fla. 1990, NC 1993, US Tax Ct., US Dist. Ct. (we. dist. NC). Ptnr. Cummings & Lockwood, LLC, Naples, Fla. Contbr. articles to profl. publs. Mem. U. Miami Citizens Bd. Named one of Top 100 Attys., Worth mag., 2005. Mem.: Soc. Trust and Estate Practitioners. Office: Cummings & Lockwood LLC 3001 Tamiami Trail N Naples FL 34103 Office Phone: 239-262-8311. E-mail: jgopman@cl-law.com.*

GOPPELT, JOHN WALTER, physician, psychiatrist; b. Saginaw, Mich., Jan. 20, 1924; s. Paul Gustave and Marion LeRoy (Payne) G.; m. Martha Keller Rowland, Mar. 31, 1956; 1 child, Edmund H. S.B., MIT, Cambridge, Mass., 1949; MD, U. Pa., Phila., 1955. Diplomate Am. Bd. Psychiatry and Neurology. Intern Bryn Mawr Hosp., Pa., 1955—56; resident in psychiatry Inst. of Pa. Hosp., Phila., 1956-59; practice medicine, specializing in psychiatry Haverford, Pa., 1959—. Contbr. articles to profl. jours. Chmn. Drug and Alcohol Coun. Del. County, Media, Pa., 1979—83; committeeman Rep. Party, Haverford Twp., Pa., 1980. With US Army, 1943—46. Recipient Legion of Honor award Chapel of Four Chaplains. Mem. AMA, Am. Psychiat. Assn., NY Acad. Scis., Sigma Xi. Avocation: mathematics. Address: 369 Exeter Rd Haverford PA 19041-1084 Office Phone: 610-649-2047. Personal E-mail: mgoppelt@yahoo.com.

GORA, JOANN M., academic administrator; BA, Vassar Coll.; M in Sociology, D in Sociology, Rutgers U. Dean Coll. Arts and Scis., sr. dean Madison campus Fairleigh Dickinson U., 1985—92; provost, v.p. for acad. affairs, prof. sociology Old Dominion U., Norfolk, Va., 1992-01; chancellor U. Mass., Boston, 2001—04; pres. Ball State U., Muncie, Ind., 2004—. Author: The New Female Criminal: Empirical Reality or Social Myth?; co-author: Emergency Squad Volunteers: Professionalism in Unpaid Work; contbr. numerous articles to profl. jours. Office: Ball State U Office Pres AD Bldg 101 Muncie IN 47306 Office Phone: 765-285-5555. Business E-Mail: president@bsu.edu.

GORA, SUSANNAH PORTER MARTIN, journalist, poet; b. NYC, Sept. 4, 1977; d. Joel Mark and Ann Ray Martin Gora; m. Zachary Abella, July 22, 2006. BA in English cum laude with high distinction, Duke U., Durham, NC, 1999. Intern NY1 News, NYC, 1994, CBS News, NYC, 1996, Brillstein-Grey Entertainment, Beverly Hills, Calif., 1998; prodn. asst. ABC TV, NYC, 1999—2000; asst. to the editor Premiere Mag., NYC, 2000—01, assoc. editor, 2001—04; entertainment journalist publs. including Elle, Variety and Woman's Day, 2004—; host, writer Classics on Film, 2005—. Contbr. of entertainment coverage AP Radio, NYC, 2002—05; editor-in-chief Shindigging.com. Author: (poetry) Where Home Is, 1999, numerous poems. E. Blake Byrne scholar, Duke U., 1997. Mem.: The Authors Guild, NY Women in Comm., Inc., Phi Eta Sigma, Kappa Kappa Gamma (life; dir. of pub. rels. 1998—99). Personal E-mail: susannahgora1@aol.com.

GORALSKI, DONALD JOHN, public relations executive, counselor; b. Buffalo, Apr. 21, 1957; s. John Bernard and Irene (Kazmierczak) G. BA, Canisius Coll., 1980. Cmty. svc. rep. we. N.Y. chpt. March of Dimes Birth Defects Found., Buffalo, 1981—82, dir. pub. rels. we. N.Y. chpt., 1982—83, dir. pub. rels. no. Jersey chpt. Fairfield, 1983—84; dir. pub. rels. Ellis Singer, Greve, St. Paul, 1984—87, Buffalo, 1984—87; sr. pub. rels. officer Multidisciplinary Ctr. for Earthquake Engring. Rsch., Buffalo, 1987—. Guest lectr. U. Buffalo, Buffalo State Coll., Medaille Coll., 1984-88, 95, Canisius Coll., 1990, 95, 97, 99, 2000, 01, 05; adj. faculty Canisius Coll, 2005 Mem. spl. events com. Am. Cancer Soc., Western N.Y. chpt., 1985—86; mem. mktg. subcom. St. Mary's Sch. for the Deaf, 1987; mentor Pub. Rels. Student Soc. of Am., Buffalo, 1989—91; mem. Allied Comm. Talent for Literacy, Buffalo, 1990—91; mem. meeting and event planners coun. Univ. at Buffalo, 1992; mem. comm. com. World Assn. Vet. Athletes 1995 Games, 1994—95; mem. Ad Coun. Western N.Y., 1995; mem. comm. com. Buffalo Alliance for Edn., 1993; mem. Mayor's Adv. Com. for a City Vision, Buffalo, 1994—95; trustee Turner/Carroll H.S., 1996—97; mem. Dr. Marilyn G.S. Watt scholarship com. Canisius Coll., 1997—, mem. May C. Randazzo Meml. scholarship com., 1997—; liaison State Employees Federated Appeal/United Way, 1998—; mem. comm. com. ARC Greater Buffalo chpt., 2000—. Mem. Pub. Rels. Soc. Am. (bd. dirs. Buffalo-Niagara chpt. 1987-91, pres.-elect 1992, pres. 1993, past pres. 1994-95, accredited, 1995, assembly del. 1997-2001, N.E. dist. sec./treas. 1999, N.E. dist. chair elect 2000, N.E. dist. chair 2001, N.E. dist. immediate past chair 2002, nat. nominating com. 2001, Cert. Recognition 1993, Nat. Chpt. Banner award Buffalo/Niagara chpt. 1993), Pub. Rels. Assn. We. N.Y. (treas. 1986-87, v.p. 1987-88, pres. 1989), We. N.Y. Pub. Rels. and Comm. (exec. steering com. 1987-90, 92-94, chmn. 1994). Avocations: golf, football, reading, current events. Office: Multidisciplinary Ctr Quake Engring Rsch U Buffalo Red Jacket Quad Buffalo NY 14261 Home: 50 Kemp Ave Cheektowaga NY 14225-4535 E-mail: goralski@buffalo.edu.

GORAN, MARK H., lawyer; BA, Washington U., St. Louis, 1971, JD, 1974; MS, U. Wis., 1973. Bar: Mo. 1975. Ptnr., group leader Health Care Bryan Cave LLP, St. Louis. Office: Bryan Cave LLP One Metropolitan Square 211 N Broadway, Ste 3600 Saint Louis MO 63102 Office Phone: 314-259-2686. E-mail: mhgoran@bryancave.com.

GORBATY, MARTIN LEO, chemist, researcher; b. Bklyn., Nov. 17, 1942; s. Julius and Florence (Birnbach) G.; m. Dianne Morse, June 30, 1968; children: Howard M., Matthew J., Lisa R. BS in Chemistry with honors, CCNY, 1964; PhD in Organic Chemistry, Purdue U., 1969. Rsch. chemist Esso Agrl. Products Lab. Esso Rsch. and Engring. Co., Linden, NJ, 1969-70; sr. rsch. chemist Corp. Rsch. Lab., Exxon Rsch. and Engring. Co., Linden, 1970-73, sr. rsch. chemist Baytown (Tex.) R & D divsn., 1973-75, group head Corp. Rsch. Labs. Linden, 1975-78, lab. dir. corp. rsch., 1978-84; disting. rsch. assoc. Corp. Rsch.-Resource Chemistry Lab., ExxonMobil Rsch. and Engring. Co., Annandale, NJ, 1984—2006. Mem. internat. editorial bd. Fuel, 1983—; chmn. Gordon Conf. Fuel Sci., 1988. Editor 5 books on synthetic crudes and coal sci.; contbr. some 75 articles to profl. jours.; holder more than 50 patents. Recipient R.A. Glenn award Bituminous Coal Rsch., Inc., 1990, Disting. Alumnus award Sch. of Sci. Purdue U., 1993, Disting. Svc. award, Petroleum Chemistry, 2003. Mem. AAAS, Am. Chem. Soc. (chmn. divsn. petroleum chemistry 1983-84, program com. 1978—, councilor 1988-99, 2001—, divsn. fuel chemistry, adv. bd. ACS books 1984-87, editl. bd. Chemtech 1986-99, Henry H. Storch award 1993), N.Y. Acad. Scis., Soc. Sigma Xi, Phi Lambda Upsilon. Achievements include patents in field of of coal and petroleum processing. Office Phone: 908-233-5676. Personal E-mail: mlgorbaty@verizon.net.

GORBATY, NORMAN, graphics designer, artist; b. NYC, Oct. 5, 1932; s. Ben and Rebecca Gorbaty; m. Joy Marks; children: Lisa Haldane, Ben. BA, Amherst Coll., Mass., 1953; MFA, Yale U., New Haven, Conn., 1955. Designer James Eng Assoc., NYC, 1955—56, L.W. Frohlich, NYC, 1956—58; v.p. art group supr. Benton & Bowles Inc, NYC, 1959—68;

pres., designer Norman Gorbaty Design Inc, NYC, 1968—. Instr. Yale Norfolk Art Sch., New Haven, 1955; adj. prof. Cooper Union Sch. Art, NYC, 1961—70; instr. Silvermine Sch. Art, New Canaan, Conn., 1971. Designer (glass design) Design in Glass for Corning, illustrator (over 85 children's books); Represented in permanent collections Smithsonian and Print Rsch. Found. Simpson fellow, Amherst Coll., 1953. Home Phone: 516-482-0587; Office Phone: 203-454-1101.

GORBERG, DAVID J., lawyer; BL, U. Wis., 1985; JD, Southwestern Sch. Law, 1988. Bar: Pa. Mng. atty. David J. Gorberg and Assoc., PC, Phila. Mem.: Phila. Bar Assn., Phila. Trial Lawyers Assn., Pa. Trial Lawyers Assn. Office: David J Gorberg and Assoc PC 1234 Market St Ste 2040 Philadelphia PA 19107 Office Phone: 215-563-7210. E-mail: david@myleman.com.

GORBIEN, MARTIN JOHN, medical educator, geriatrician; b. Chgo., Dec. 24, 1955; MD, Autonomous U., Guadalajara, Mexico, 1983. Cert. internal medicine 1996, geriatric medicine 1998. Intern to resident, geriatric medicine Mercy Hosp. and Med. Ctr., Chgo., 1984—87; fellowship, geriatric medicine UCLA, 1987—89; asst. prof. medicine U. Chgo. Pritzer Sch. Medicine, Chgo., 1994—98; assoc. prof., dir. Rush Med. Coll., St. Lukes Med. Ctr., Geriatric Dept., Chgo., 1998—. Office: Rush U Med Ctr 1725 W Harrison St Ste 955 Chicago IL 60612 Office Phone: 312-942-3362, 312-942-5321. Business E-Mail: mgorbien@rush.edu.

GORBY-SCHMIDT, MARTHA LOUISE, pharmacologist, researcher; d. Charles and Louise Gorby. BS in Nursing, Villanova U., 1983. RN Pa., 1983; cert. paralegal. Clin. rsch. asst. Scirex, Blue Bell, Pa., 1996—97; mgr. data quality compliance Aventis Pharma/Rhone Poulenc Rorer, Bridgewater, NJ, 1998—2001; mgr. clin. data rev. Premier Rsch. Worldwide, Phila., 1997—98; assoc. dir. Yamanouchi Pharma Am., Paramus, NJ, 2001—04; global project data mgr. Merck Rsch. Labs., Blue Bell, 2004—07, sr. clin. rsch. specialist-clin. rsch. oncology, 2007—. Meddra blue ribbon panel Northrup Grumman, Alexandria, Va., 2003; spkr. in field. Editor: Pen and Ink Mag. (Svc. Award, 1979). Office vol. adminstr. Ch. Good Samaritan, Paoli, Pa., 1990—94, 12 step group facilitator, 1990—94, music dir. sch. com., advt. chmn., 1990—94. Mem.: NAFE, AACN, ANA, N.Y. Acad. Scis., Oncology Nurse Soc., Am. Chem. Soc., Am. Heart Assn., Assn. Clin. Rsch. Profls., Soc. Clin. Data Mgmt., Regulatory Affairs Profl. Soc., Drug Info. Assn. (spl. interest action com. 2003—), Am. Soc. Clin. Oncology (assoc.). Episcopalian. Achievements include research in oncology-early to late stage development. Avocations: music, travel, reading, comedy, hiking. Office: Merck Rsch Labs PO Box 1000 UC-72 North Wales PA 19454 Office Phone: 267-305-5896. Personal E-mail: mlgs2327@verizon.net. Business E-Mail: martha_schmidt@merck.com.

GORCHOW, BRUCE D., investment company executive; b. Mpls., Mar. 13, 1958; s. Neil Gorchow, Roslyn Gorchow; m. Marie L. Fioramonti; children: Grace Fioramonti-Gorchow, Sophia Fioramonti-Gorchow, Gabriel Fioramonti-Gorchow. BA, Haverford Coll., 1980; MBA, U. Pa., 1982. Investment mgr. TIAA/CREF, New York, NY, 1982—86; v.p. Equitable Capital Mgmt., Inc., 1987—91; exec. v.p. PPM Am., Inc., Chgo., 1991—2000; pres. PPM Am. Capital Ptnrs., LLC, 2000—. Bd. dirs. PPM Am., Inc.; bd. dir. Global Imaging Systems, Inc., Tampa, Fla., 1996—2002; bd. dirs. Elizabeth Arden Salon and Spa Holdings, Inc, Phoenix, Examination Mgmt. Svcs., Inc, Dallas; Director Tomah Products, Inc, Tomah, WI, 1997—99, Applied Process Solutions, Inc., Tulsa, OK, 1998—2000, Corvest Promotional Products, Miami, FL, 1999—. Mem.: U. Club Chgo., Phi Beta Kappa. Office: PPM Am Capital Ptnrs LLC 225 West Wacker Dr Ste 1200 Chicago IL 60606 Home Phone: 312 482-8756; Office Phone: 312 634-2512.

GORDEN, DAVID LEE, surgeon, educator; children: Isaac William, Eliana Moshe. BA, Brown U., Providence, RI, 1985; MD, Vanderbilt U. Sch. Medicine, Nashville, Tenn., 1990. Diplomate Am. Bd. Surgery, 1999, fellow hepatobiliary surgery and liver transplantation U. Toronto, 2000. Postdoctoral fellow U. Geneva, 1994—96; asst. prof. surgery Vanderbilt U. Med. Sch., Nashville, 2001—07, assoc. prof. surgery and cancer biology, 2007—. Photography exhibition, Dans Un Regard, photography, Working (setting the hair on the hog) (Wash. Post Photography award, 1980). Surgeon Internat. Med. Team, Guatemala; clinic worker Politecnica de Quito, Ecuador, 1985—86. Recipient Tchg. award, AOA Med. Honor Soc., 2005; grantee, NIH, 2005—. Fellow: Am. Coll. Surgeons; mem.: Am. Soc. Transplant Surgeons, Am. Assn. Cancer Rsch.

GORDENKER, LEON, political science professor; b. Detroit, Oct. 7, 1923; s. Samuel and Anna (Posalsky) G.; m. Belia Emilie Strootman, Aug. 16, 1956 (dec. Apr. 1984); children: Robert Jan Mario, Hendrik Willem Paul, Emilie Elise Saskia. AB, U. Mich., 1943; student, Inst. d'Etudes Politiques, Paris, 1951-52; MA, Columbia U., NYC, 1954, PhD, 1958; postgrad., Acad. Internat. Law, Hague, The Netherlands, 1958. Journalist AP, 1943, Detroit Free Press, 1944-45; info. officer Nat. War Labor Bd., 1945; pub. info. officer UN, 1945-53; instr. Dartmouth Coll., 1956-58; mem. faculty Princeton U., 1958—, prof. politics, 1966-86, prof. emeritus, 1986—; prof. Institut Universitaire de Hautes Internationales, Geneva, 1986-89, vis. prof., 1979-80; dir. Centre de Recherches sur les Institutions Internationales, Geneva, 1986-89. Vis. prof. Columbia U., 1961, 67, Makerere U., Uganda, 1969-70, U. Pa., 1971, 74, U. Witwatersrand, South Africa, 1976, Leiden U., 1984-85, 93, Erasmus U., 1985, CUNY, 1989, 90, 92, 95, Inst. Social Studies, The Hague, 1993-97. Author: The United Nations and the Peaceful Unification of Korea, 1959, The UN Secretary-General and the Maintenance of Peace, 1967, The United Nations in the International System, 1971, International Aid and National Decisions, 1976, The International Executive, 1978, (with W.P. Davison) Resolving Nationality Conflicts, 1980, Refugees in International Politics, 1987, (with T.G. Weiss) Soldiers, Peacekeepers and Disasters, 1991, (with P.R. Baehr) The United Nations: Reality and Ideal, 1981, 4th edit., 2005, De Verenigde Naties: Werkelijkheid en Ideaal, 1992, 94, 96, 2005, (with Benjamin Rivlin) The Challenging Role of the UN Secretary-General, 1993, (with others) International Cooperation in Response to AIDS, 1995, (with T.G. Weiss) NGOs, The UN and Global Governance, 1996, The UN Secretary-General and Secretariat, 2005 Fellow The Netherlands Inst. Advanced Study, 1972-73, 96-97. Mem. Acad. Coun. on UN, Princeton Club of N.Y. Office: Princeton U Dept Politics Princeton NJ 08544-0001

GORDER, JOSEPH W., energy executive; BBA, U. Mo., St. Louis; MBA, Our Lady of the Lake U. Dir. info. systems Diamond Shamrock, asst. treas., dir. comml./indsl. sales; v.p. bus. devel. Ultramar Diamond Shamrock; sr. v.p. corp. devel. Valero Corp., San Antonio, 2003, exec. v.p. mktg. and supply. Office: Valero Energy Corpn PO Box 696000 San Antonio TX 78269-6000*

GORDIMER, NADINE, writer; b. Springs, Republic of South Africa, Nov. 20, 1923; d. Isidore and Nan (Myers) Gordimer; m. Reinhold Cassirer, Jan. 29, 1954; children: Oriane, Hugo. Student, Convent Sch., Springs, Republic of South Africa; degree (hon.), Yale U., Harvard U., Columbia U., New Sch. Social Rsch., NYC, U. Leuven, Belgium, U. York, Eng., U. Cape Town, South Africa, Cambridge U., Eng. Author: (collections) Face to Face, 1949, The Soft Voice of the Serpent, 1952, Six Feet of the Country, 1956, Friday's Footprint, 1960 (W.H. Smith and Son Literary award 1961), Not for Publication, 1965, Livingstone's Companions, 1971, Selected Stories, 1975, Some Monday for Sure, 1976, A Soldier's Embrace, 1980, Something Out There, 1984, The Essential Gesture, 1988, Crimes of Conscience, 1991, Jump, 1991, Three in a Bed, 1991, Why Haven't You Written: Selected Stories 1950-1972, 1992, Living in Hope and History: Notes From Our Century, 1999, Beethoven Was One Sixteenth Black, 2007; (novels) The Lying Days, 1953, A World of Strangers, 1958, Occasion for Loving, 1963, The Late Bourgeois World, 1966, A Guest of Honour, 1970 (James Tait Black Meml. prize 1973), The Conservationist, 1974 (Booker prize for Fiction Eng. 1974), Burger's Daughter, 1979, July's People, 1981, A Sport of Nature, 1987, My Son's Story, 1991, None to Accompany Me, 1994, The House Gun, 1998, The Pickup, 2001, Loot, 2003, Get a Life, 2005; (non-fiction) On the Mines, 1973, Lifetimes Under Apartheid, 1986; (literary criticism) The Black Interpreters, 1973, Writing & Being: Charles Eliot Norton Lectures, 1995; (essays) Living in Hope and History: Notes from Our Century, 1999; editor: Telling Tales, 2004; co-editor: (with Lionel Abrahams) Southern African Writing Today, 1967 Decorated comdr. de l'Ordre des Arts et des Lettres (France), 1986, Ordre national de la Légion d'honneur (France), 2007; recipient Thomas Pringle award English Acad. South Africa, 1969, CNA award, 1974, 79, 81, 91, Grand Aigle d'Or, 1975, Disting. Svc. in Lit. Commonwealth award, 1981, MLA award, 1982, Nelly Sachs prize (Germany), 1985, Malaparte award (Italy), 1986, Bennett award, 1986, Internat. Premo Leui award, 2002, Mary McCarthy award, 2003; Benson medal, 1990, Nobel Prize for Literature, 1991; Neil Gunn fellow Scottish Arts Coun., 1981. Fellow Royal Soc. Lit.; mem. AAAS, Com. European Authors, Am. Acad. (hon.), Inst. Arts and Letters (hon.), Internat. PEN (v.p.). Home: Johannesburg South Africa Mailing: care Farrar Straus & Giroux 19 Union Square W New York NY 10003

GORDIS, DAVID MOSES, academic administrator, rabbi; b. NYC, June 4, 1940; s. Robert and Fannie (Jacobson) G.; m. Felice Witztum, Sept. 3, 1962; children: Lisa, Elana. BA, Columbia U., 1960, MA, 1966; MHL, Jewish Theol. Sem., 1962, PhD, 1980. Ordained rabbi, 1964. Dean of students Tchrs. Inst., Jewish Theol. Sem., NYC, 1966-72; exec. dir. Found. for Conservative Judaism, 1981-84; assoc. prof., v.p. U. of Judaism, LA, 1972-84; v.p. Jewish Theol. Sem., NYC, 1981-84; exec. v.p. Am. Jewish Com., NYC, 1984-87; v.p. U. Judaism, LA, 1988-92, dir. Wilstein Inst. of Jewish Policy Studies, 1988—, adj. assoc. prof. Talmud, 1988-92, dir. inst. rsch.; pres. Hebrew Coll., Newton, Mass., 1993—; mem. exec. com. Interreligious Ctr. Pub. Life, 2001—. Mem. editl. bd.: Tikkun. Pres., prof. rabbinics Hebrew Coll., 1993—; exec. com. Am. Found. for Polish-Jewish Studies, 1988—; trustee Am. Jewish Hist. Soc., 1993—, vice-chair Archives for Hist. Documentation, 1995-2000; chair United Synagogue Coun. on Jewish Edn., 1973-82. Mem. Rabbinical Assembly Am., Assn. Colls. Jewish Studies, Nat. Coun. Jewish Pub. Soc. Avocation: cello. Home Phone: 617-244-7316; Office Phone: 617-559-8772. Business E-Mail: dgordis@hebrewcollege.edu.

GORDIS, LEON, physician; b. NYC, July 19, 1934; s. Robert and Fannie (Jacobson) Gordis; m. Hadassah Cohen, June 14, 1955; children: Daniel, Elihu, Jonathan. BA, Columbia, 1954; BHL, Jewish Theol. Sem., 1954; MD, SUNY, 1958; MPH, Johns Hopkins U., 1966, MPH, 1968. Intern, then resident in pediat. Jewish Hosp., Bklyn., 1958—61; fellow in pediat. Sch. Medicine Johns Hopkins U., 1962—66, instr. Sch. Medicine, 1966—68, assoc. prof. epidemiology, Sch. Hygiene and Pub. Health, 1971—73; asst. med. dir. ambulatory care Sinai Hosp., Balt., 1966—68, chief dept. community medicine, 1968—69; prof. epidemiology Johns Hopkins, 1973—, chmn. dept. epidemiology, 1975—93; prof. pediat., 1992—; assoc. dean admissions & Acad. affairs Johns Hopkins Sch. Medicine, 1993—99. Vis. prof. med. ecology Hebrew U., Jerusalem, 1969—71. With USPHS, 1961—65. Fellow: AAAS, Am. Acad. Pediat.; mem.: APHA, Assn. Tchrs. Preventive Medicine, Am. Heart Assn., Soc. Pediatric Rsch., Am. Pediatric Soc., Am. Epidemiol. Soc. (pres. 1983—84), Soc. Epidemiologic Rsch. (pres. 1979—80), Inst. Medicine NAS. Home: 105 Swanhill Ct Baltimore MD 21208-1608 Office: 615 N Wolfe St Baltimore MD 21205-2103 Business E-Mail: lgordis@jhsph.edu.

GORDLY, AVEL LOUISE, state legislator, political organization worker; b. Portland, Oreg., Feb. 13, 1947; d. Fay Lee and Beatrice Bernice (Coleman) G.; 1 child, Tyrone Wayne Waters. BS in Adminstrn. of Justice, Portland State U., 1974; Grad. John F. Kennedy Sch. Govt., Harvard U., 1995; grad., U. Oreg. Pacific Program, 1998. Phone co. clk. Pacific West Bell, Portland, 1966-70, mgmt. trainee, 1969-70; work release counselor Oreg. Corrections Divsn., Portland, 1974-78, parole and probation officer, 1974-78; dir. youth svcs. Urban League of Portland, 1979-83; dir. So. Africa program Am. Friends Svc. Com., Portland, 1983-89, assoc. exec. sec., dir. Pacific N.W. region, 1987-90; freelance writer Portland Observer, Portland, 1988-90; program dir. Portland House of Umoja, 1991; mem. Oreg. Ho. of Reps., Portland, 1991-96, mem. joint ways and means com., adv. mem. appropriations com., rules and reorgn. com., low income housing com., energy policy rev. com., others; mem. Oreg. Senate from 10th dist., Salem, 1997—; mem. crime and corrections com., trades econ. devel. com. Oreg. Senate, 1997, mem. joint ways and means com. on pub. safety, 1997, mem. joint ways and means com. on edn., 1999, emergency bd., co-chair, interim task force on parental and family abductions, 2003—04, mem. joint ways and means pub. safety com., 2005—, mem. joint ways and means edn. com., 2005—, chair, joint ways and means, full com., 2005. Mem. joint ways and means com. on edn., mem. gov. drug and violent crime policy bd., mem. Oreg. liquor control commn. task force, mem. sexual harrassement task force, mem. Hanford waste bd., mem. Gov.'s Commn. for Women, Gov.'s Drug and Violent Crime Policy Bd.; originator, producer, host Black Women's Forum, 1983-88; co-producer, rotating host N.E. Spectrum, 1983-88; assoc. prof. dept. black studies Portland State U., 2006—. Mem. corrections adv. com. Multnomah Cmty.; mem. adv. com. Oregonians Against Gun Violence; mem. Black Leadership Conf.; treas., bd. dirs. Black United Fund; co-founder, facilitator Unity Breakfast Com.; co-founder Sisterhood Luncheon; past project adv. bd. dirs. Nat. Orgn. Victims Assistance; past citizen chmn. Portland Police Bur.; past mem. coordinating com. Portland Future Focus Policy Com.; past coord. Cmty. Rescue Plan; past vice chmn. internat. affairs Black United Front; past sec. Urban League Portland, past vice chmn. and exec. com.; past adv. com. Black Ednl. Ctr.; past vice chmn. Desegregation Monitoring; also past adv. com., past chmn. curriculum com., founder African Am. Leg. Issues Roundtable; founder Black Women Gathering; other past orgn. coms.; elected state senate First African Am. Woman, 1996. Recipient Outstanding Cmty. Svc. award NAACP, 1986, Outstanding Women in Govt. award YWCA, 1991, Girl Scout-Cmty. Svc. award, 1991, N.W. Conf. of Black Studies-Outstanding Progressive Leadership in the African-Am. Cmty. award, 1986, Cmty. Svc. award Delta Sigma Theta, 1981, Joint Action in Cmty. Svc.-Vol. and Cmty. Svc. award, 1981, Quality of Life Photography award Pacific Power & Light Co., 1986, Am. Leadership Forum Sr. fellow, 1988, Equal Opportunity award, Urban League, 1996, Outstanding Alumni, 1996, PSU, Causa '98 En Defensa de la Comunidad award, 1997, Matrix award Assn. for Women in Comm., 1999, Pres.'s award Portland Oreg. Visitors Assn., 1999, Legacy award Black United Fund, 2000, Leadership award Albina Ministerial Alliance, 2000 Mem. NAACP. Avocations: reading, photography, walking. Home: 6805 NE Bradway St Portland OR 97213-5304

GORDON, ALAN LEE, psychiatrist; b. NYC, Nov. 26, 1936; s. Abe and Fan Gordon; m. Lois Goldfein; 1 child, Robert Michael. AB, Columbia Coll., 1957; MD, U. Wis., 1963. Resident Albert Einstein Coll. Medicine, NYC, 1964-66, 68-69; dir. of aftercare Riverdale Mental Health Clinic, NYC, 1969-78; clin. instr. Mt. Sinai Sch. Medicine, NYC, 1982-90; psychiatrist divsn. of post-institutional svcs. Human Resources Adminstrn.-City of N.Y., 1986—; psychiatrist Bowery Residence Com., CSS Program, NYC, 1990—. Lectr. in field; TV, radio interviewer; spkr. in field. Author: American Chronicle: Six Decades in American Life, 1920-79, 1987, American Chronicle: Seven Decades of American Life 1920-89, 1990, Columbia Chronicles of America Life, 1960-92, 1995, American Chronicle: Year by Year through the Twentieth Century, 1999; contbr. poetry to various jours. Capt. US Army, 1966—68. Mem.: Alpha Omega Alpha. Democrat. Jewish. Avocations: history, literature, sports. Office: 300 Central Park W New York NY 10024-1513 Office Phone: 212-362-4011.

GORDON, ALEX JONATHAN, professional baseball player; b. Lincoln, Nebr., Feb. 10, 1984; s. Mike and Leslie Gordon. Attended, U. Nebr. Third baseman Kansas City Royals, 2007—. Named to All-Star Futures Game, Baseball Am. Mag., 2006; recipient Golden Spike award, USA Baseball, 2005, Minor League Player of Yr. award, Baseball Am. Mag., 2006. Office: Kauffman Stadium PO Box 419969 Kansas City MO 64141 Office Phone: 816-921-8000.*

GORDON, ALLEN BARRY, musician, composer; b. LA, Mar. 12, 1950; s. Rubin and Florence Irene G.; m. Susan Sutwarti, Jan. 2, 1976. Studied piano with Antonio Iturioz; student, Santa Monica Coll., 1998. Master jazz pianist. Head pianist Filmex, 1979-81, Jonathan Club, 1989-91; freelance pianist. Instr. piano. Played televised banquet, Biltmore Hotel, Ted Kennedy (US senator), 1981, concert for Mikhail Gorbachev (former Russian Premier), Pheonix Hall Anaheim, 2000, jazz and musical compositions played in 25 countries worldwide. Played concerts for sr. citizens; played concert at VA Hosp. Recipient Pub. Citation award, City of L.A. Mem. ASCAP. Democrat. Jewish. Avocations: playing and listening to music, reading biographies, teaching, coin collecting/numismatics, baseball art. Home: 4140 Grand View Blvd Los Angeles CA 90066-5258 Office Phone: 310-398-1180.

GORDON, ANITRA, librarian; b. Bklyn., July 10, 1936; d. Samuel Frank and Florence (Aronowitz) Sisholce; m. Jesse E. Gordon, Mar. 8, 1956; children: Scott, Jessani, Erica. BA, U. Wis., 1957; MA, Mont. State U., 1961; MA in Library Sci., U. Mich., 1970, PhD, 1985. Tchr. French Ann Arbor Pub. Schs., Mich., 1964-66; librarian Reading is Fundamental Lincoln Consol. Schs., Ypsilanti, 1967—2004. Writer, cons. Sch. Libr. Mgmt. Notebook, 1991; supervising tchr. Ea. Mich. U., Ypsilanti, 1968-80, lectr., 1975-85; supervising tchr. U. Mich., Ann Arbor, 1968-80; workshop presenter various orgns., 1975-2000; editorial advisor Jour. Reading, 1974-75. Author, cons Sch. Libr. Mgmt. Notebook, 2d edit., 1991; contbr. articles and revs. to profl. publs. Recipient Disting. Achievement award Edpress, 1973, Vol. of Yr. award Reading Is Fundamental, NW region, 2004. Mem. Mich. Assn. Media in Edn. (workshop presenter 1974-2000, bd. dirs. 1991-94), Faculty Womens Book Club, Faculty Womens Garden Club, Beta Phi Mu. Democrat. Jewish. Avocations: photography, gardening, travel. Home: 1300 Chalmers Dr Ann Arbor MI 48104-4216 E-mail: agordon@ameritech.net.

GORDON, ANNE KATHLEEN, editor; m. Phillip L. Berman; 1 child, Aaron. BA speech pathology and audiology, U. Denver, 1979; postgrad., Columbia Grad. Sch. Journalism, 1983. Fin. writer Rocky Mountain Bus. Jour., Denver, 1981, Sun-Tattler, Hollywood, Fla., 1982-83, fin. editor, 1983; asst. bus. editor Ft. Lauderdale (Fla.) News, 1983-85; bus. editor The Denver Post, 1985-88, asst. mng. editor, 1988; news cons. Sta. KCNC-TV, Denver, 1988-89, assignment mgr., 1989-90; editor Jackson Hole News, 1990-92; editor Sunday Mag. The Plain Dealer, Cleve., 1993-99; arts and entertainment editor The Phila. Inquirer, 1999—2000, from assoc. mng. editor to dep. mng. editor arts and features, 2000—02, mng. editor, 2002—07; ptnr. Dubilier & Co., Stamford, Conn., 2007—. Comm. dir. Colo. Dem. Party, Clinton presdl. campaign, 1992. Author: A Book of Saints, 1994. Recipient Best of Show award Colo. Press Assn., 1981, 86, Woman of Yr. award Broward County Bus. and Profl. Women's Assn., 1983, 1st Pl. Spot News award Colo. Associated Press, 1986, 1st Pl. Breaking News award Colo. Press Assn., 1986, Gen. Excellence award Wyo. Press Assn., 1991, Gen. Excellence award Nat. Newspaper Assn., 1992; Eisenhower fellow, 2000. Home: 149 Fairview Rd Narberth PA 19072-1330 Office: The Philadelphia Inquirer 400 N Broad St Philadelphia PA 19130-4015 E-mail: agordon@phillynews.com.

GORDON, ARNOLD MARK, arbitrator, educator; b. Norwich, Conn., Oct. 2, 1937; s. Barney and Rose (Bilsky) G.; m. Carolyn. BSBA, Wayne State U., Detroit, 1959, JD, 1962. Bar: Mich. 1962. With Gordon & Gordon P.C. and predecessor firms, Southfield, Mich.; arbitrator Am. Arbitration Assn., 1969—. Lectr. in field. Mem. Am. Coll. Trial Lawyers, State Bar Mich. (chmn. med.-legal com. 1976—, negligence sect. 1977-78, pub. negligence sect. bull.), Detroit Bar Assn. (co-chmn. trial advocacy program continguing legal edn. 1972—), Assn. Trial Lawyers Am. (exec. bd. Mich. 1967—), Mich., Detroit trial lawyers assns., Tau Epsilon Rho. Clubs: Masons. Office: Gordon & Gordon PC Ste A 32781 Middle Belt Rd Farmington Hills MI 48334 Office Phone: 248-855-6975. Personal E-mail: agordon404@aol.com.

GORDON, BARON JACK, stockbroker; b. 1926; m. Ellin Bachrach, Aug. 20, 1954; children: Jonathan Ross, Rose Patricia, Alison. Midshipman, U.S. Naval Acad., 1946; BS, Lynchburg Coll., 1953. Asst. treas. Henry Montor Assocs., Inc., NYC, 1956; v.p., sec. Propp & Co., Inc., NYC, 1957-58; ptnr. Koerner, Gordon & Co., NYC, 1959-62; sr. ptnr. Gordon, Kulman Perry, and predecessor firm, NYC, 1962-71, pres., chmn. bd., 1971-74, Palison, Inc., White Plains, N.Y., 1974—; chmn. bd. Rojon, Inc., Williamsburg, Va., 1979—. Mem. N.Y. Stock Exch., White Plains, N.Y., 1974—. Mem. Harrison (N.Y.) Archtl. Rev. Bd., 1970-72, Harrison Planning Bd., 1975-77; bd. dirs. Montefiore Hosp. Assn., YM-YWHA, Lafayette Ednl. Fund, Inc., 1986-92; internat. adv. coun. Mus. of Am. Folk Art, 1990—. Lt. USNR, 1953—55, U.S.S. Midway, naval aide-de-camp to gov. (rank of capt.), 1989—98, Va. Recipient Wisdom award of honor and eminent wisdom; fellow Wisdom Hall of Fame. Mem. Folk Art Soc. (bd. dirs. 1987-95, mem. nat. adv. bd. 1996—), U.S. Naval Acad. Alumni Assn. (life), Stock Exch. Luncheon Club (N.Y.C.), Buttonwood Club. Home: 113 Elizabeth Meriwether Williamsburg VA 23185-5107 Office: Drawer JG Williamsburg VA 23187 Personal E-mail: ebginwmsbg@aol.com.

GORDON, BARTON JENNINGS (BART GORDON), congressman, lawyer; b. Murfreesboro, Tenn., Jan. 24, 1949; s. Robert Jennings and Margaret Louise (Barton) Gordon; m. Leslie Peyton, 1998; 1 child. BS with honors, Mid. Tenn. State U., 1971; JD, U. Tenn., Knoxville, 1973. Bar: Tenn. 1974. Mem. US Congress from 6th Tenn. dist., 1985—, ranking mem. sci. com., mem. energy and commerce com. Mem. Tenn. Dem. Exec. Com., 1974-83, exec. dir., 1979-81, chmn., 1981-83; bd. dirs. Mid. Tenn. State U. Found.; chmn. Rutherford County United Givers Fund, Rutherford County Cancer Crusade Served in USAR, 1971—72. Mem. Rutherford County C. of C. (bd. dirs.) Democrat. Methodist. Office: US Ho Reps 2304 Rayburn Ho Office Bldg Washington DC 20515-0001 Office Phone: 202-225-4231.*

GORDON, BASIL, retired mathematics professor; b. Balt., Dec. 23, 1932; s. Basil and Helen (Williams) G. MA, Johns Hopkins, 1953; PhD, Calif. Inst. Tech., 1956. Instr. Calif. Inst. Tech., 1956-57; asst. prof. math. U. Calif. at Los Angeles, 1959-63, assoc. prof., 1963-67, prof., 1967-93; prof. emeritus, 1993—. Editor: Pacific Jour. Mathematics, 1969-70, 72-73, Jour. Combinatorial Theory, 1970-2002, Ramanujan Jour., 1997—; contbr. articles to profl. jours. Served with AUS, 1957-59. Alfred P. Sloan fellow, 1962-64 Mem. Math. Assn. Am., Pi Mu Epsilon. Achievements include research in number theory, combinatorics, group theory, and function theory. Home: 526 Palisades Ave Santa Monica CA 90402-2722 Office: 405 Hilgard Ave Los Angeles CA 90095-9000 Business E-Mail: bg@math.ucla.edu.

GORDON, BEN, professional basketball player; b. Apr. 4, 1983; Attended, Univ. Conn. Basketball player Chgo. Bulls, 2004—. Named NBA Sixth Man Yr., 2005, First Team All-Rookie, NBA, 2005. Office: Chgo Bulls United Ctr 1901 West Madison St Chicago IL 60612

GORDON, BENJAMIN DICHTER, pediatrician, educator, health facility administrator; b. Bklyn., Mar. 4, 1927; s. Abraham S. and Selma F. (Dichter) G.; m. Ellen M. Nimaroff, June 10, 1951; children: Wendy, Marcy, Amanda. AB, Amherst Coll., 1947; MD, U. Md., 1951. Diplomate Am. Bd. of Pediatrics. Rotating intern Kings County Hosp., Bklyn., 1951-52, asst. resident in pediatrics, 1953-54, Maimonides Hosp., Bklyn., 1952-53; research fellow Irvington House, Irvington-on-Hudson, NY, 1954-55; practice medicine specializing in pediatrics Stratford & Bridgeport, Conn., 1955-73; assoc. attendant, emergency dept. Bridgeport Hosp., 1973-78; asst. dir. emergency dept. Danbury (Conn.) Hosp., 1978-82; clin. dir. Union Carbide Corp., Danbury, 1982-87; med. dir Chesebrough-Ponds, Inc., Trumbull, Conn., 1987-90. Asst. prof. occupational medicine Yale U.; chmn. Rheumatic Fever com. Conn. State Heart Assn.; cons. to cosmetic industry and product-testing labs.; attending occupl. med. clinic Milton (Mass.) Hosp., Jordan Hosp., Plymouth, Mass.; cons. Clin. Rsch. Ctr. Cape Cod. Author: Practical Guide for New Parents, 1970; contbr. articles to profl. jours. Chmn., Bd. Health, Town of Yarmouth, Mass.; mem. Regional Emergency Planning Com. for Barnstable County. Served with USNR, 1945-46. Fellow: Am. Coll. Occupl. and Environ. Medicine, Am. Acad. Pediats.; mem.: Barnstable Dist. Med. Soc. (com. on violence), Mass. Med. Soc., Occupl. Med. Assn. Conn. (pres. 1987—88), Fairfield County Med. Soc. (past chmn. pub. health com.), Conn. State Med. Soc. (past chmn. comty. pub. health), Williams Club (N.Y.C.). Jewish. Avocations: music, dance, reading, history, golf. Home: 14 Hillsea Rd Yarmouth Port MA 02675-1111 Personal E-mail: b.gordonmd@comcast.net.

GORDON, BERNARD M., computer company executive; b. 1927; B.E.E., MIT, 1948, M.E.E., 1949. Co-founder EPSCO, Inc., 1953—64; founder Gordon Engring. (became Analogic Corp.), 1964—69; founder, pres., CEO, chmn. Analogic Corp., Peabody, Mass., 1969—94, CEO, 1969—2003, chmn., 1969—2004, chmn. emeritus, 2004—; co-founder, pres. Neuro-Logica Corp., Danvers, Mass., 2004—. Founder Gordon Inst. Tufts U., 1984—. Bd. trustees Tufts U., 1996—. Recipient Nat. Medal Tech., 1986, John Fulke Sr. Meml. award, 1993, Benjamin Franklin award for Innovation in Engineering and Technology, Franklin Inst, Walker prize, Museum of Science, 2004; named one of 50 Most Generous Philanthropists, BusinessWeek, 2005. Fellow IEEE (Leadership Recognition award 1992), Am. Acad. Arts & Scis.; mem. Nat. Acad. Engrs, 1991. Achievements include pioneer in high-speed analog-to-digital conversion; patents for over 200 inventions including the first solid state x-ray generator, the first baseband quadrature-detecting ultrasound scanner, the first fetal monitor, and the first instant imaging CT system. Office: Analogic Corp 8 Centennial Dr # B-1 Peabody MA 01960-7987 also: NeuroLogica Corp 14 Electronics Ave Danvers MA 01923*

GORDON, BOBBY G., civilian military employee; b. Laurens, SC, Feb. 21, 1971; s. Robert Earl and Delores Ann Gordon; m. Jennifer Ann King; 1 child, Rion Vincent. Electronic worker SC Army N.G., Columbia, 1990—98, electronic mechanic Laurens, 1998—. V.p. Laborer's Internat. Union of N.Am. Local 117, Eastover, SC, 1996—2006, 3d v.p., 2006—. Sgt. US Army, 2003—04, Iraq. Decorated Unit Citation Gov. of SC, Army Svc. Ribbon Dept. of Army, Nat. Def. Svc. medal, Army Res. Components Achievement medal, Army Commendation medal, Army Achievement medal, Global War on Terrorism Expeditionary medal, Armed Forces Res. Medal with device, Combat Action Badge, SC Palmetto Svc. Ribbon SC Mil. Dept., SC Achievement Ribbon, SC Active State Svc. Ribbon, SC Mobilization Ribbon; recipient Outstanding Guardsman cert., 1999, State Command Sgt. award, 1999, Commendation cert., Dept. of Army and Air Force, 1996, 2001. Mem.: VFW, N.G. Assn. of US, N.G. Assn. of SC (life), Am. Legion. Republican. Avocations: coaching Dixie Youth Baseball, travel, computers. Home: 210 Forest Dr Laurens SC 29360 Office: SC Army NG 4171 Torrington Rd Laurens SC 29360 Home Phone: 864-984-0909; Office Phone: 864-682-3158. Office Fax: 864-682-9797. Personal E-mail: bobbygordon22@yahoo.com. Business E-Mail: bobby.gordon@sc.ngb.army.mil.

GORDON, BRUCE S., civil rights organization executive, former telecommunications company executive; b. Camden, NJ, Feb. 15, 1946; s. Walter and Violet Gordon; m. Genie Alston, Feb. 20, 1970 (div.); 1 child, Taurin; m. Tawana Gordon. BA, Gettysburg Coll., 1968; MS, MIT, 1988. With Bell Atlantic Corp., Arlington, Va., 1968—70, bus. office mgr., 1970—72, sales mgr. mktg., 1972—74, personnel supr., 1974—76, market mgmt. supr., 1976—78, mktg. mgr., 1978—80, divsn. staff mgr., 1980—81, divsn. ops. mgr., 1981, divsn. mgr. phone ctr., 1981—83, mktg. mgr., 1983—84, gen. mgr., mktg./sales, 1985—88, v.p. mktg., 1988—93; group pres. bus. unit Bell Atlantic Corp. (mergered with GTE), 1993—2000; pres. retail markets group Verizon Communications Inc., NYC, 2000—03; pres., CEO NAACP, Balt., 2005—. Bd. dirs. Southern Co., Tyco Internat. Ltd., Office Depot, Bartech Personnel Svcs., Urban League, 1984—86, Innroads of Phila., 1985—88, CBS Corp., 2005—; bd. trustees Gettyworg Coll., Alvin Ailey Dance Found., Lincoln Ctr. Named Exec. of Yr., Black Enterprise Mag., 1998; fellow Alfred P. Sloan, MIT. Office: NAACP National HQ 4805 Mt Hope Dr Baltimore MD 21215

GORDON, CAREY NATHANIEL, lawyer, federal agency administrator; b. Cleve., Mar. 11, 1950; s. Murray Byron and Pearl Miriam (Jackson) Gordon; m. Lois Elizabeth Bradshaw, Nov. 28, 1981. BA, Ohio State U., 1972; MA, U. London, 1973; postgrad., Cambridge U., Eng., 1973-74; JD, Cleve. State U., 1977. Bar: Ohio 1977, DC 1978, US Supreme Ct. 1983. Assoc. Rippner Schwartz & Carlin, Cleve., 1977-80, ptnr., 1980-84; contract advisor U.S. Agy. for Internat. Devel., Khartoum, Cairo, Kinshasa, Islamabad, 1986-94, contracting officer Abidjan, Ivory Coast, 1995-97, Phnom Penh, Cambodia, 1997—2003, Bangkok, 2003—. Vis. lectr. U. Khartoum, 1984—85. Bd. dirs., treas. Internat. Sch. Phnom Penh, 2000—02. Mem.: Cleve. Bar Assn. Office: USAID Am Embassy Bangkok Box 47 APO AP 96546

GORDON, COREY LEE, lawyer; b. Mpls., Aug. 22, 1956; s. Jack I. and LaVerne (Shedlov) G.; m. Ciel Schaeffer, Aug. 29, 1982; children: Jared Isaac, Lian Miriam. BA, Macalester Coll., 1976; JD cum laude, U. Minn., 1980. Bar: Minn. 1980, U.S. Dist. Ct. Minn. 1981, U.S. Ct. Appeals (8th cir.) 1983, U.S. Supreme Ct. 1983, Wis. 1987, U.S. Dist. Ct. (ea. and we. dists.) Wis. 1987, N.Y. 1991, U.S. Dist. Ct. (so. dist.) N.Y. 1991, U.S. Ct. Appeals (3d cir.) 1992, Ill. 1993, U.S. Dist. Ct. (no. dist.) Ill. 1995, Fla. 1995, U.S. Dist. Ct. (we., ea., and no. dists.) N.Y. 1999, U.S. Ct. Appeals (11th cir.) 1999, U.S. Ct. Appeals (7th cir.) 1999, U.S. Dist. Ct. (so. and ctrl. dists.) Ill. 1999, U.S. Ct. Appeals (2d cir.) 1999, U.S. Dist. Ct. (so. and no. dists.) Fla. 2000, U.S. Dist. Ct. (mid. dist.) Fla. 2003. Assoc. Fried, Frank, Harris, Shriver & Jacobson, NYC, 1980-81, Robins, Zelle, Larson & Kaplan, St. Paul, 1986-88; ptnr. Shapiro, Lavintman & Gordon P.A., Mpls., 1982-85, Robins, Kaplan, Miller & Ciresi, Mpls., 1989—2000, Shapiro Gordon LLC, Mpls., 2003—06, Blackwell Burke P.A., Mpls., 2006—; dep. atty. gen. State of Minn., St. Paul, 2001—02; spl. counsel Blackwell Igbanugo, P.A., Mpls., 2002—03. Treas. The H.H.H. Fund, Minn., 1984—89; bd. dirs., sec.-treas. Minn. Humane Soc., 1985—86; chair bd. dirs. Circus Juventas, 2002—07; active Dem. Farm Labor Party; trustee Bet Shalom Synagogue, 1992—93, v.p., 1993—97, pres., 1997—99; bd. dirs. Jewish Family and Children's Svc. of Mpls, 1992—96, Mpls. Fedn. for Jewish Svc., 1994—99, Jewish Vocat. Svc., 2002—05. Mem.: ATLA (co-chair inadequate security litig. group 1992—95,), Rape and Incest Nat. Network (RAINN) (legal adv. bd. 2004—06), Nat. Crime Victim Bar Assn. (adv. bd. 2004—). Jewish. Avocations: folk music, scuba diving, photography. Home: 2640 Glenhurst Pl Minneapolis MN 55416-3957 Office Phone: 612-343-3266. Business E-Mail: cgordon@blackwellburke.com.

GORDON, CRAIG JEFFREY, oncologist, educator; b. Detroit, Feb. 10, 1953; s. Maury Allen and Shirley Phoebe (Jacoby) G.; m. Susan Ann Blase, Aug. 3, 1980; children: Sari, Scott, Brittany. BS, Oakland U., 1978; DO, U. Osteo. Med. and Health Scis, Des Moines, 1983. Diplomate Am. Bd. Internal Medicine, Am. Bd. Med. Oncology. Intern-chief Botsford Gen. Hosp., Farmington Hills, Mich., 1983-84, resident, 1984-87; fellow in hematology and oncology Wayne State Univ. (affiliated Hosp.'s Prog.), Detroit, 1987-90, fellow-chief, 1989-90; clin. asst. prof. dept. medicine Wayne State U., Detroit, 1990—; dir. divsn. hematology and oncology Botsford Hosp., Livonia, Mich., 1992—; med. dir. Angela Hospice, 1993—98; pres. Clin. Oncology Assocs., 1998—. Mem. extrarenal transplantation com. Mich. Dept. Pub. Health; physician advisor Gilda's Club Mich., 1993—2001; mem. Greater Detroit Area Health Care Coun. on Cancer Care. Contbr. articles to profl. jours. Named Intern of the Yr. Botsford Hosp. Staff, 1984, Resident of the Yr., 1985-87; clin. fellow Am. Cancer Soc., 1987-90. Fellow Am. Coll. Osteo. Internists; mem. Am. Osteo. Assn., Mich. Assn. Osteo. Physicians and Surgeons, Mich. Soc. Hematology and Oncology, Assn. Cancer Execs., S.W. Oncology Group, Am. Soc. Clin. Oncologists, Oakland County Osteo. Assn. Avocations: sports, popular music, astronomy, electronics. Office: 30160 Orchard Lake Rd Farmington Hills MI 48334 Home Phone: 248-538-7922. Personal E-mail: gordondo@comcast.net.

GORDON, DAN A., food service executive; Exec. v.p. Gordon Food Svc. Inc., Grand Rapids, Mich., 1989—91, pres., CEO, 1991—. Bd. dir. Internat. Food Svc. Distributors Assn. Bd. dir. Econ. Club of Grand Rapids. Office: Gordon Food Svc Inc 333 5th St SW Grand Rapids MI 49501

GORDON, DANE REX, philosophy educator, minister; b. London, June 15, 1925; came to US, 1954; s. Leonard and Heather (Gibson) G.; m. Elizabeth May Marshall, Aug. 16, 1952 (dec. Apr. 1987); m. Judith Fisher Ward, July 6, 1991. BA, U. Cambridge, 1951, MA, 1958; BD, U. London, 1956; MA in Philosophy, U. Rochester, 1960. Ordained to ministry Presbyn. Ch., 1958. Profl. actor, England, 1938-43; bookseller Hatchards, London, 1946-48; assoc. minister Cen. Presbyn. Ch., Rochester, NY, 1958-61; asst. prof. Rochester Inst. Tech., 1962-71, Danforth assoc., 1967-69, assoc. prof., then prof., chmn. dept., asst. dean, acting dean, 1976-77, assoc. dean Coll. Liberal Arts, 1976-87, prof. philosophy, 1976—2000, chmn. dept. philosophy, 1994, prof. emeritus, 2000. Vis. lectr. in philosophy and religion Adam Mickiewicz U., Poznan, Poland, 1993; Provost fellow for internat. partnerships and vis. disting. lectr., Am. U. in Bulgaria, 1996; Balkan scholar in philosophy Am. U., Bulgaria, 1999-2000. Author: New Way Eng., 1964, Philosophy of Religion Study Guide, 1973, Rochester Institute of Technology: Industrial Development and Educational Innovation in an American City, 1982, rev. edit., 2007, The Old Testament: A Beginning Survey, 1985, Thinking and Reading in Philosophy of Religion, 1994, Philosophy and Vision (Eng. and Polish translation), 1994, The Old Testament in its Cultural, Historical and Religious Context, 1994; author: (with Milford Fargo) A Family Christ Mass, 1973, Away He Run, 1976; editor: Philosophy in Post Communist Europe, 1998; editor: (with Jozef Niznik) Criticism and Defense of Rationality in Contemporary Philosophy, 1998; editor: (with David Durst) Civil Society in Southeast Europe, 2004, A Feeling Intellect and a Thinking Heart, 2002; editor: (with David Suits) Epicurus: His Continuing Influence and Contemporary Relevance, 2003, St. Petersburg: Poems, 2007. Served with Royal Navy, 1943-46 Recipient Eisenhart award Outstanding Teaching, 1996-97. Mem. AAUP, Am. Philos. Assn., Am. Soc. Composers, Authors, Producers, Presbytery of Genesee Valley. Office: Rochester Inst Tech Coll Liberal Arts Dept of Philosophy Rochester NY 14623 Office Phone: 585-475-7182. Fax: 585-475-7120. Business E-Mail: drggla@rit.edu. *As we get older, we understand less and trust more.*

GORDON, DAVID, playwright, theater director, choreographer; b. NYC, July 14, 1936; m. Valda Setterfield; 1 child, Ain. Founder, dir. Pick Up Performance Co., Inc., NYC, 1978—. Playwright, dir. dance, theater, music prodn. The Mysteries and What's So Funny?, 1991; writer, dir. TV program (1992-93) and theatrical work (1996) Punch and Judy Get Divorced; co-writer, dir.: (with Ain Gordon) The Family Business, 1994-95; dir. Shlemiel The First, Am. Repertory Theater, 1994-95; dir., choreographer: The Firebugs, The Guthrie Theater, 1995; co-writer, dir. (with Ain Gordon) First Picture Show, 1999; dir.: Past/Forward with Mikhail Baryshnikov, 2000-01, Autobiography of a Liar, 1999, Private Livees of Dancers, 2001-03, Dancing Henry Five, 2004, The Chairs, 2004. Guggenheim fellow, 1981, 87. Office: Pick Up Performance Co 520 8th Ave Ste 303 New York NY 10018 Office Phone: 212-244-7622. E-mail: pickupperformance@earthlink.net.

GORDON, DAVID, writer, educator; b. LA, Apr. 7, 1948; s. Hyman and Sybil Gordon. BA, UCLA, 1965, MA, 1970, PhD, 1975. Sr. fellow Ludwig von Mises Inst., Auburn, Ala., 1987—. Author: (book) Resurrecting Marx, 1990, Introduction to Economic Reasoning, 2000; co-author (Roberta A. Modugno): Individualismo Metodologico, 2002; contbr. articles to profl. jours. Home and Office: 356 N Hayworth Ave 1 Los Angeles CA 90048 Home Phone: 323-655-8372; Office Phone: 323-655-8372. Business E-Mail: dgordon@mises.org.

GORDON, DAVID A., lawyer; BA, Cornell Univ., 1982; JD, Syracuse Univ., 1986. Bar: Calif. 1986, NY 1995. Mng. ptnr. Latham & Watkins LLP, NYC. Named one of the 45 Elite Lawyers in the US under age 45, Am. Lawyer mag., 2003. Mem.: ABA. Office: Latham & Watkins LLP Ste 1000 885 Third Ave New York NY 10022-4834 Office Phone: 212-906-1251. Business E-Mail: david.gordon@lw.com.

GORDON, DAVID JAMIESON, tenor; b. Phila., Pa, Dec. 7, 1947; s. David William and Lois Irene (Lukens) G.; m. Ginna Bell Bragg, Feb. 14, 2004. Student, Coll. of Wooster, 1965-68, McGill U., Montreal, Que., Can., 1968-70; student of Dale Moore, 1965—. Former faculty Sonoma State U. Debut with Lyric Opera Chgo., 1973; leading tenor Landestheater Linz (Austria), 1975-79; prin. roles with San Francisco Opera, Houston Grand Opera, Met. Opera, Hamburg Staatsoper, Washington Opera, Mostly Mozart Festival, Salzburg Festival; concert soloist with Bach Festivals: Carmel, Calif., Bethlehem, Pa., Festival Casals, Stuttgart, Tokyo, Buenos Aires, Eugene, Oreg., Boston Symphony, Berlin Philharm., Czech Philharmonic, Vienna Symphony, St. Louis Symphony, San Francisco Symphony, LA Philharm., Seattle Symphony, Phila. Orch., Cleve. Orch., Nat. Symphony Washington, Baltimore Symphony; appears in opera, concerts, chamber music, recitals throughout US and Europe as performer, lectr., and tchr.; specialist in music of J.S. Bach; performing artist for Delos, Dorian, Telarc, London Records, Decca Records, Smithsonian Collection of Recs., RCA Red Seal, Nonesuch Records. Home: Po Box 4843 Carmel CA 93921-4843 E-mail: dgordon@spiritsound.com.

GORDON, DAVID ZEVI, retired lawyer; b. Bklyn., Mar. 2, 1943; s. Isidore and Yaffa S. (Stern) G.; m. Karen Baranker, Apr. 25, 1971; children: Ilana, Naomi. BA magna cum laude, Yeshiva U., 1964; JD cum laude, MBA, Columbia U., 1969. Bar: N.Y. 1970, U.S. Dist. Ct. (so. dist.) N.Y. 1973, U.S. Ct. Appeals (2d cir.) 1973. Assoc. Spear and Hill, NYC, 1969-71; sr. assoc. LeBoeuf Lamb Leiby & McRae, NYC, 1971-77; ptnr. Finley Kumble Heine & Underburg, NYC, 1977-78, David Z. Gordon and Assocs., NYC, 1978-81; mng. ptnr. Moroze Sherman Gordon & Gordon, P.C., NYC, 1981-96; ret., 1996. Trustee, exec. com. Stern Coll. for Women, 1990-96; co-chmn. United Jewish Appeal, Operation Exodus, 1991-96, Project Renewal, 1987-96, exec. com. Israel econ. devel.; chmn. Israel Bonds, Bronx, 1988-96; co-chmn. bd. dirs. Am. Com. for Shaare Zedek Med. Ctr., Jerusalem, 2000—. Recipient Heritage award Yeshiva U., 1988, Star of Peace and Hope award Israel Bonds, 2002, Cmty. Svc. award Shaare Zedek Med. Ctr. 2002. Mem. ABA, N.Y. State Bar Assn., N.Y.C. Bar Assn. (mem. com. condemnation and tax certiorari), Real Estate Tax Bar Assn. Democrat. Personal E-mail: flashgordon@peoplepc.com.

GORDON, EDGAR GEORGE, retired lawyer; b. Detroit, Feb. 27, 1924; s. Edgar George and Verna Florence (Hay) G.; m. Alice Irwin, Feb. 4, 1967; children: David A., J. Scott. AB, Princeton U., 1947; JD, Harvard U., 1950. Bar: Mich. 1951, U.S. Supreme Ct. 1953. Assoc. Poole, Warren & Littell, Detroit, 1950-54; ptnr. Poole, Warren, Littell & Gordon, Detroit, 1953-63; gen. counsel Hygrade Food Products Corp., Detroit, 1963-69, sec., 1966-69, v.p., 1968-69; v.p., sec. counsel City Nat. Bank of Detroit, 1969-81; v.p., sec., gen. counsel No. States Bancorp, 1970-81; v.p., sec., counsel First of Am. Bank Corp., Kalamazoo, 1981-84; also ptnr. Howard & Howard, Kalamazoo, 1981-2000; ret., 2000. Dir. First Citizens Bank, Troy, Mich., 1973-81, First Nat. Bank, Plymouth, Mich., 1974-81; pres., chmn. bd. First of Am. Mortgage Co., Kalamazoo, 1978-84. Commr. City of Kalamazoo, 1995-2001. Lt. (j.g.) USN, 1943-46. Mem. ABA, Mich. Bar Assn., Kalamazoo Bar Assn., Country Club of Detroit (Grosse Pointe, Mich.). Republican. Presbyterian. Home: 4339 Lakeside Dr Kalamazoo MI 49008-2802

GORDON, ELLEN RUBIN, candy company executive; d. William B. and Cele H. (Travis) Rubin; m. Melvin J. Gordon, June 25, 1950; children: Virginia, Karen, Wendy, Lisa. Student, Vassar Coll., 1948—50; BA, Brandeis U., 1965; postgrad., Harvard U., 1968. With Tootsie Roll Industries, Inc., Chgo., 1968—, corp. sec., 1970-74, v.p. product devel., 1974-76, sr. v.p., 1976-78, pres., COO, 1978—; v.p., dir. HDI Investment Corp. Mem. coun. on divsn. biol. scis. and Pritzker Sch. Medicine U. Chgo.; mem. med. sch. adv. coun. for cell biology and pathology Harvard U.; mem. bd. fellows Faculty of Medicine, Harvard Med. Sch. Mem. adv. coun. J.L. Kellogg Grad. Sch. Mgmt. at Northwestern U.; mem. univ. resources and overseers com. Harvard U.; mem. bd. advisors Women Inc. Recipient Kettle award, 1985. Mem. Nat. Confectioners Assn. (bd. dirs.). Office: Tootsie Roll Industries Inc 7401 S Cicero Ave Chicago IL 60629-5885

GORDON, ERIN KATHLEEN, elementary school educator; d. Richard Raymond and Patricia Ann Gordon. BS in Edn. magna cum laude, Villanova U., Pa., 2003, BA in Spanish, 2003; M in Ednl. Studies summa cum laude, Johns Hopkins U., Balt., 2006. Cert. ednl. adminstrn. and supervision Johns Hopkins U., 2006, reading Johns Hopkins U., 2006, PhonoGraphix Read Am., 2006, elem. edn. NJ, 2007, adminstr. I Interstate Sch. Leaders Licensure Consortium, 2006, adminstr. II Interstate Sch. Leaders Licensure Consortium, 2007. Focus Eng. Lang. Inst. instr. Choate Rosemary Hall, Wallingford, Conn., 2002—; Spanish instr. St. Paul's Sch., Brooklandville, Md., 2003—06, 4th grade educator, 2006—07; 2nd grade tchr. The Peck Sch., Morristown, NJ, 2007—. Head of house Choate Rosemary Hall, Wallingford, 2002—; dance instr. St. Paul's Sch., Brooklandville, 2004—07, subject area tchr. chairperson, 2005—07, diversity com. co-chairperson, 2005—07; vis. evaluation team mem. Assn. Ind. Md. Schs., 2005; presenter in field. Vol. Habitat for Humanity, New Orleans, 2002—03; vol. tutor Honors Vol. Tutoring Program, Villanova, 2002—03; poll worker Ho. of Dels., Towson, Md., 2006. Recipient Recognition of Excellence, Ednl. Testing Svcs. Mem.: Nat. Soc. Collegiate Scholars, Kappa Delta Pi, Delta Gamma. Avocations: dance, running, community service, higher education, travel. Office: The Peck School 247 South St Morristown NJ 07960

GORDON, EZRA, architect, educator; b. Detroit, Apr. 5, 1921; s. Abraham and Rebecca (Reimer) G.; m. Jeanette Greenberg, Oct. 8, 1942; children: Cheryl P. Gordon Van Ausdal, Rana Gordon Oremland, Judith Gordon Eichhorn. Student, Roosevelt Coll., Chgo., 1946-48; BS in Architecture, U. Ill., Champaign-Urbana, 1951. Draftsman Pace Assos. Architects, 1951-53; sr. planner Chgo. Plan Commn., 1953-54; project architect Harry Weese & Assos., 1954-61; ptnr. Gordon-Levin & Assocs., Chgo., 1961-84, Gordon & Levin, Inc., Chgo., 1984-95; cons. Dept. Urban Renewal City Chgo., Council for Jewish Elderly, Chgo. Jewish Fedn. Prof. emeritus U. Ill.-Chgo. Sch. Architecture; former mem. Mayor's Adv. Coun. on Bldg. Code Amendments; master juror Nat. Coun. Archtl. Registration Bds. Works include Long-Kogan Office Bldg., 1957, 5401 Hyde Park Apt. Bldg., Chgo., 1962, South Commons, Chgo., 1968, The Commons Townhouse Devel., Chgo., 1968, Hyde Park West Apts., Chgo., 1969, IBM Office bldgs., Kalamazoo, 1969, Moline, Ill. 1970, Jefferson City, Mo., Omaha, 1971, Eastwood Tower Apts., Chgo., 1970, Wexler Pavilion and Siegel Inst., U. Chgo. Stats. Lab.-Design & Constrn., 1970, Cardiac Intensive Care Unit and Tumor Clinic, 1971, Michael Reese Hosp., Chgo., 1971, Arbor Trails Apts. and Townhouses, Park Forest, Ill., 1972, Kenmore Plaza Apts. Sr. Housing, Chgo., 1972, Kennaly Sq. Warehouse Apts., Chgo., 1972-74, Pontiac Office Bldg., Mich., 1972, Concourse Office Towers, Skokie, 1972, Belle Plaine Apts., Chgo., 1972, Stats. Lab, U. Chgo., 1972, Newberry Plaza Apts., Chgo., 1973, Greenwood Park Apts., Chgo., 1974, River Plaza Apts., Chgo., 1976, Elm St. Plaza Apts., Chgo., 1976, Dearborn Park, Twin Tower Apts., Chgo., 1979, Huron Plaza Apt., Chgo., 1981, 400 E. Ohio Condominiums, Streeterville, Chgo., 1983, East Bank Club, Chgo., 1983, U. (Champaign) Ill. Speech and Hearing Clinic, 1985, Dearborn-Elm Apts., Chgo., 1986-87; designer World Trade Ctr. Apts., Chgo., 1989, Lachman Montisorri Sch. for Hearing Impaired Children, Deerfield, Ill., 1990, Elm Street Apts., 1990, restoration of 1130 S. Michigan Ave., 1991, Chgo. Montessori Sch. for the Hearing Impaired, 1991, Love residence addition, Glencoe, Ill., 1991, Periodontist offices, Skokie, Ill., 1991, Oral Rehab. Ctr., Skokie, 1992, residence addition, Glencoe, 1998. Former bd. dirs. Hyde Park-Kenwood Cmty. Conf., Chgo., Astor St.-Lake Shore Dr. Assocs., Chgo.; former v.p. Harper Ct. Found., Chgo.; mem. Art Inst. Chgo., Mus. Sci. and Industry, Spertus Mus., Mus. Contemporary Art, Chgo. Hist. Soc.; mem. Landmarks Preservation Coun., Chgo. Archtl. Found.; former v.p. bd. dirs. 1300 Lake Shore Drive Condo Assn., Chgo. Decorated Croix de Guerre with palm; recipient Honor award Dept. Housing and Urban Devel., 1967, Honor award AIA-Chgo. C. of C., 1967, award AIA-House & Home Mag., 1967, Distinguished Bldg. award AIA, 1957, 63, 69, 71, 73, 75, award City of Chgo. Beautification, 1969, 75, award of excellence Concrete Post Tensioning Inst., 1984, Silver Circle award for excellence in teaching U. Ill., Chgo., 1985. Fellow AIA (former bd. dirs Chgo. chpt.); mem. AIA, Peace Now, Am. Jewish Congress, Chgo. Archtl. Found., Lambda Alpha. Clubs: Cliff Dwellers. Jewish. Business E-Mail: egor@uic.edu.

GORDON, FLORENCE IRENE, graphics designer, illustrator; b. LA, Oct. 22, 1928; d. Harry and Etta (Goldstein) Gronoff; widowed; 1 child. Student, Chounard Art Inst., LA, Santa Monica City Coll.; BA, Art Ctr., LA. Graphic artist Ned North Enterprises, LA; artist Hawaii Newspaper, Oahu; tech. illustrator Northrop-Aircraft, LA, McDonnell Douglas, LA. Exhibited in group shows. Art scholar Chounard Art Inst., 1950. Home: 5166 Sepulveda Blvd Apt 208 Culver City CA 90230-5235

GORDON, FRANK JEFFREY, medical educator; b. Washington, Dec. 5, 1948; married; 2 children. Attended, Case Western Reserve U., 1966-69; BS in Biology, N.Mex. State U., 1972, MA in Psychology, 1974; PhD in Biopsychology, U. Iowa, 1980. Interdisciplinary rsch. fellow U. Iowa, Iowa City, 1978-80, postdoctoral rsch. fellow Dept. Internal Medicine, 1980-81, rsch. scientist, 1981-82; asst. prof. dept. pharmacology Emory U. Sch. Medicine, Atlanta, 1982-88, assoc. prof., 1988—. Spkr. in field. Editl. bd.

Am. Jour. Physiology, 1989-93. Mem. com. on risk factors Iowa Heart Assn., 1982. USPHS pre-doctoral fellow, 1978-80, post-doctoral fellow, 1980-82; rsch. starter grantee Pharm. Mfgs. Assn. Found., 1983-85. Fellow Coun. High Blood Pressure Rsch.; mem. Am. Physiol. Soc., Am. Soc. Pharmacology and Exptl. Therapeutics, Am. Heart Assn. (rsch. investigatorship Ga. affiliate 1987-88, AHA established investigator 1989-94), Soc. Neurosci., Sigma Xi. Achievements include research in brain and spinal cord regulation of peripheral cardiovascular systems in normal and pathological states. Office: Dept Pharmacology Rollins Rsch Ctr Rm 5011 Atlanta GA 30322-0001 Office Phone: 404-727-5893.

GORDON, FREDERICK JAMES, orthopedist, surgeon; b. NYC, Apr. 5, 1939; MD, NYU Sch. Med., 1964. Diplomate Am. Bd. Orthopaedic Surgeons. Intern, surgery NYU-Bellevue Med. Ctr., NYC, 1964—65, resident, 1967—70, resident, orthopaedic surgery, 1965—66; orthopaedic fellowship NYU Med. Ctr., NYC, 1966—67; orthopaedic surgeon St. Barnabas Med. Ctr., Livingston, NJ. Orthopaedic cons. NJ Ballet, Kessler Inst., NJ. Fellow: Am. Acad. Orthopaedic Surgeons, ACS. Office: St Barnabas Ambulatory Care Ctr Sports Medicine Inst 200 S Orange Ave Livingston NJ 07039 Office Phone: 973-322-7330.*

GORDON, GILBERT, chemist, educator; b. Chgo., Nov. 11, 1933; s. Walter and Catherine Gordon; m. Joyce Elaine Masura; children: Thomas, Lyndi. BS, Bradley U., 1955; PhD, Mich. State U., 1959. Postdoctoral rsch. assoc. U. Chgo., 1959-60; asst. prof. U. Md., College Park, 1960-64, assoc. prof., 1964-67, prof., 1967; prof. chemistry U. Iowa, Iowa City, 1967-73; prof., chmn. dept. Miami U., Oxford, Ohio, 1973-84, Volwiler Disting. Rsch. prof., 1984—2003, disting. rsch. prof. emeritus, 2003—. Mem. editl. bd. Synthesis Inorganic Metal, Organic Chemistry, Ozone, Sci. and Engring.; contbr. articles to chem. jours. Named Cin. Chemist of Yr., 1981 Mem.: Faraday Soc., Chem. Soc. London, Am. Chem. Soc., Internat. Ozone Assn. (dir. 1995—, treas. 1998—, pres. 2002—04), Phi Kappa Phi, Sigma Xi. Home: 190 Shadowy Hills Dr Oxford OH 45056-1441 Office: Miami U Dept Chemistry Oxford OH 45056 Office Phone: 513-529-3336. Business E-Mail: gordong@muohio.edu. *My objectives have been to investigate meaningful areas of chemistry in an attempt to better understand chemical phenomena affecting our everyday lives (such as better and less expensive ways to purify drinking water), and to work diligently with the public while helping to educate them to be better citizens and aware of the exciting potential of science.*

GORDON, GRANVILLE HOLLIS, church official; b. Picayune, Miss., Oct. 12, 1922; s. Thomas and Eugenia (Landrum) G.; m. Miriam C. Culpepper, Sept. 6, 1942; children: Tessa Eileen, Gerald Keith, Cathy Annette, Connie Jean, Donna Lynn. Student, Jacksonville Bapt. Coll. & Sem., 1950-52. Ordained to ministry Bapt. Ch., 1950. Pastor Friendship Bapt. Ch., Jewett, Tex., 1950-51, Little Flock Bapt. Ch., Jewett, 1950-51, Rural Shade Bapt., Kerens, Tex., 1951-52, Ogden Ave. Bapt., Mobile, Ala., 1952-54, Stanton Way Bapt., Mobile, 1954-58, Creston Hills Bapt., Jackson, Miss., 1958-65, 1st Bapt. Shady Grove, Laurel, Miss., 1965-74, Creston Hills Bapt., Jackson, Miss., 1974-84, Rolling Hills Bapt., Jacksonville, Fla., 1984-86, Temple Bapt. Ch., Lucedale, Miss., 1986-89, Highland Pk. Bapt., Hattiesburg, Miss., 1990-96, Shiloh Bapt. Church, Mt. Olive, Miss., 1996-98; Pastor Pear Orchard Bapt. Ch., Jackson, Miss., 1998—. With USAF, ETO. Mem. Miss. Bapt. Assn. (rec. clk. 1961-70), Bapt. Missionary Assn. (rec. clk. 1975-94). Baptist. Office: Baptist Missionary Assoc of Am 193 Old Canton Hill Dr Jackson MS 39211-3337 Office Phone: 601-957-2086. E-mail: ghggordon@aol.com.

GORDON, HAROLD SONNY, bank executive; b. Montreal, 1937; BA, Sir George Williams U., 1961; BCL, McGill U., 1964, BComm, 1958. Apptd.: Queen's Counsel 1985. Atty. Stikeman Elliott, Montreal, 1967-75, ptnr., 1975-95; vice-chmn. Hasbro, Inc., Pawtucket, RI, 1995—2002; chmn. Dundee Corp., Toronto, 2001—. Bd. dirs. Alliance Atlantis Comms. Inc., Dorel Industries Inc., Dundee Corp., Transcontinental Inc., Madacy Holding, Inc., Pethealth Inc. Office: Dundee Corp 1 Adelaide Street E Toronto ON Canada M5C 2V9 Home: 15695 Collins Av 304 Sunny Isles Beach FL 33160 Office Phone: 416-804-0440. Business E-Mail: hgordon@dundeecorporation.com.

GORDON, HOWARD LYON, advertising and marketing executive; b. Chgo., Oct. 8, 1930; s. Milton Arthur and Bess Z. (Ginsburg) G.; m. Lois Jean Kaufman, Aug. 21, 1955; children: Carolyn Ann, Leslie Meredith. BS, U. Ill., Urbana, 1953; MS, Northwestern U., Evanston, Ill., 1954, MBA, 1962. Mktg. rsch. mgr. Marsteller Inc.; advt. Chgo., 1960-68; v.p. mktg. services Marsteller Inc. and Burson Marsteller, Chgo., 1968-76; dir. client service Britt and Frerichs Inc., mktg. research and advt. cons. Chgo., 1977-78, sr. v.p., 1978—, prin., 1979—, ptnr., 1986—; lectr. advt. and mktg. Northwestern U., 1963—. Vis. prof. Medill grad. studies in advt., 1981—; advt. prof. in residence No. Ill. U., DeKalb, 1974-76; lectr., seminar leader Am. Mgmt. Assn., 1965-72; adj. lectr. Ctr. Intellectual Property Law, John Marshall Law Sch., 2000—; bd. dir. Bus. Advt. Rsch. Coun., 1985—; chmn. life style rsch. com. Advt. Rsch. Found., 1991—; bd. dir. Advt. Rsch. Found., Media Comm. Coun.; mem. alumni awards com. Medill Sch. Northwestern U., 1986, fund-raising com. Kellogg Grad. Sch. Northwestern U., 1986—; presenter 17th World Advt. Congress, Amsterdam, 1992, Kellogg Sch. Leadership Forum, 2005, Evanston; mem. publs. bd. U. Ill., 1997—; amb. U. Ill., 2004—. Author: Know The Buyer Better, 1991; co-author: Marketing Manager's Handbook, 3rd edit., 1994; contbr. articles to profl. publs. and mktg. texts. Regional chmn. Crusade of Mercy, Evanston, Ill., 1969; founding dir. Alumni Assn. Medill Sch., 1984—; adv. council athletic dept. Northwestern U., 1985—. With AUS, 1954-56. Recipient award Dept. Def., 1956, Alumni award Northwestern U., 1989. Mem. Am. Mktg. Assn. (dir., v.p. mktg. mgmt.), Northwestern U. Faculty, Kellogg Alumni Assn. (program com., exec. bd. dirs.), Direct Mktg. Assn., Assn. Consumer Rsch., Am. Assn. Pub. Opinion Rsch., Sigma Delta Chi. Office: 400 E Randolph Dr Chicago IL 60601-7329 Business E-Mail: hgordon@grfltd.com.

GORDON, J. HOUSTON, lawyer, political organization worker; b. Camden, Tenn., Sept. 16, 1946; s. Houston Darnal and Florence Jane (Culvahouse) G.; m. Deborah Watridge; children: Nathan, Baker, Blake. BS in Liberal Arts cum laude, U. Tenn., Martin, 1968; JD, U. Tenn., Knoxville, 1970; LLM in Taxation, George Washington U., 1973. Bar: Tenn. 1970, D.C. 1978. Asst. dist. atty. 16th Jud. Cir. Tenn., 1974-75; county atty. Tipton County, Tenn., 1981-84, delinquent tax atty.; atty. pvt. practice. Mem. dean's alumni adv. council Coll. Law U. Tenn., 1974-87, trustee, 1990-96, vice chair, 1994-95, vis. lectr.; instr. Dyersburg State C.C.; vis. lectr. U. S.C., Memphis State U., U. Ala., Valdosta State Coll. Contbr. articles to profl. jours. Alt. del. Nat. Dem. Conv., 1978 96; Dem. nominee U.S. Senate, Tenn., 1996; chair Tenn. Dem. Party, 1997—. 2d lt. Mil. Police Corps U.S. Army, 1970, capt. JAGC, 1970-74. Named Tenn. Outstanding Young Man, 1978. Fellow Am. Bar Found., Am. Coll. Trial Lawyers; mem. ABA, ATLA, Am. Bd. Trial Advocates (adv.), Tenn. Bar Assn. (advisor young lawyers divsn.), Tenn. Bar Found., Tenn. Trial Lawyers Assn. (bd. govs. 1976-78, 80-96, pres. 1989-90), D.C. Bar Assn., Memphis-Shelby County Bar Assn., Tipton County Bar Assn., U. Tenn. Alumni Assn. (bd. govs. 1976-78). Office: 114 W Liberty Ave PO Box 865 Covington TN 38019-0865

GORDON, JAMES A., investment company executive; B summa cum laude, Northwestern U. With Gordon's Wholesale, 1971—86; founder, mng. ptnr. Edgewater Growth Capital Ptnrs. Treasurer Whitney Mus. Am. Art, trustee; bd. dir. Des Moines Ballet; mem. bd. Grinnell Coll., chmn. investment com.; bd. dir. Chgo. Mus. Am. Art, Northwestern Meml. Found., John F. Kennedy Ctr. Performing Arts, Chgo. Cares Inc., Bankers Trust Co., Methodist Med. Adv.; bd. dir. & former pres. Des Moines Art Ctr.; bd. dir. Iowa Soc. to Prevent Blindness, Des Moines Opera. Office: Edgewater Funds Growth Capital Ptnrs 900 N Michigan Ave Ste 1800 Chicago IL 60611 Mailing: c/o Whitney Mus Am Art 945 Madison Ave New York NY 10021 Office Fax: 312-664-8649. Business E-Mail: jim@edgewaterfunds.com.

GORDON, JAMES S., lawyer, director; b. NYC, Feb. 15, 1941; s. George S. and Sylvia A. (Wolfson) Gordon; m. Marcia G. Gordon, Dec. 22, 1968 (dec.); children: Daniel, Sarah; m. Debbie S. Pase, June 15, 1996. BA with high honors, U. Fla., 1962; LLB, Yale U., 1965. Bar: Ill. 1965, Fla. 1966, U.S. Supreme Ct. 1974. Asst. prof. Ind. U. Sch. Law, Bloomington, 1967-68, assoc. prof., 1969; ptnr. Feiwell, Galper & Gordon, Chgo., 1970-72; pvt. practice Chgo., 1972-80; pres. James S. Gordon, Ltd., Chgo., 1981-93; chmn. Gordon, Glickman, Flesch, & Rosenwein, Chgo., 1994—; dir. Mo. Metals, LLC. Editor: Yale Law Jour., 1963—65; contbr. articles to profl. jours. Ford Found. grantee, 1965—66. Mem.: Order of the Coif, Fla. Blue Key, Birchwood Club (Highland Park, Ill.), Lawyers Club Chgo., Phi Beta Kappa, Phi Alpha Delta. Office: 140 S Dearborn St Ste 404 Chicago IL 60603-5202 Home Phone: 847-441-7848; Office Phone: 312-346-1080. Business E-Mail: jgordon@lawggf.com.

GORDON, JAMES SAMUEL, psychiatrist; b. NYC, Oct. 12, 1941; s. Jules David and Cynthia (Hymanson) G. AB magna cum laude, Harvard U., 1962, MD, 1967. Diplomate Am. Bd. Psychiatry and Neurology. Tchg. fellow gen. edn. Harvard U., Cambridge, Mass., 1963-67; NIH rsch. fellow, tchg. asst. dept. pathology Cornell Med. Coll., NYC, 1964-65; intern Mt. Zion Hosp., San Francisco, 1967-68; resident in psychiatry Albert Einstein Coll. Medicine, Bronx, NY, 1968-70, chief resident, clin. instr. psychiatry, 1970-71; research psychiatrist NIMH, Rockville, Md., 1971-82, cons. alternative forms of svc., 1974-82, dir. spl. study Pres.'s Commn. Mental Health, 1977-78; chief adolescent svcs. St. Elizabeths Hosp., Washington, 1980-82; clin. prof. Georgetown U. Med. Sch., Washington, 1980—; founder dir. Ctr. for Mind-Body Medicine, Washington, 1991—. Chair program adv. coun. Office of Alternative Medicine NIH, 1994-97; sr. cons. L.Am. Youth Ctr., Washington, 1984—; mem. cancer adv. panel NIH, 1998—; chair White House Commn. on Complementary and Alternative Medicine Policy, 2000-02; vis. scholar Aurora Assocs., Washington, 1982-84; rsch. psychiatrist divsn. spl. mental health programs NIMH, 1980-82; med. cons. wellness program Walter Reed Army Med. Ctr., Washington, 1980-82; sr. cons. on adolescence divsn. child and adolescent svcs. St. Elizabeths Hosp., Washington, 1979-80; Blanche Ittleson cons. Group for Advancement of Psychiatry, 1979; dir. spl. study on alternative svcs. Pres.' Commn. on Mental Health, 1977-78; vis. lectr. Cmty. Therapy Tng. Ctr., Washington, 1975, Cath. U. Am., Washington, 1974; lectr. in field. Author: The Golden Guru, 1987, Holistic Medicine, 1988, Stress Managment, 1989, Manifesto for a New Medicine, 1996, Comprehensive Cancer Care, 2000; editor: Health for the Whole Person (Med. Self Care Book award 1980), Mind, Body and Health: Towards and Integral Medicine, 1984; contbr. articles to profl. jours. Comdr. USPHS, 1971-82. Recipient award Ford Found., 1982, O. Spurgeon English Humanitarian award, 2002. Fellow Am. Assn. Social Psychiatry; mem. Am. Psychiat. Assn., Am. Holistic Med. Assn. (founding mem. 1980, trustee 1980-86), Am. Assn. Med. Acupuncture (founding mem. 1987), Physicians for Social Responsibility (exec. com. 1984-86). Office: Ctr Mind Body Medicine Ste 414 5225 Connecticut Ave NW Washington DC 20015-1845 Office Phone: 202-537-6837.

GORDON, JEFF, race car driver; b. Vallejo, Calif., Aug. 4, 1971; m. Brooke Sealy, Nov. 26, 1994 (div. June 2003); m. Ingrid Vandebosch, Nov. 7, 2006; 1 child, Ella Sofia. Stock race car driver Hendrick Motorsports, 1993—. Named Maxx Race Cards Rookie of Yr., 1993, winner, NASCAR Winston Cup, 1994, 1997, 1998, 2001, Busch Clash, 1994, The Winston, 1995, 1997, 2001, Brickyard 400, 1994, 1998, 2001, 2004, Goodwrench 500, 1995, Purolator 500, 1995, Ford City 500, 1995, 1997, 1998, Pepsi 400, 1995, Slick 50 300, 1995, Mountain Dew So. 500, 1995—98, 2002, MBNA 500, 1995, Daytona 500, 1997, 1999, 2005, CMT 300, 1997, Bud at the Glen, 1997, 1998, Calif. 500, 1997, 1999, Pocono 500, 1997, 2007, Coca-Cola 600, 1997, 1998, Goody's 500, 1997, Goodwrench 400, 1997, 1998, Pa. 500, 1998, Pepsi 400, Daytona, 1998, AC Delco 500, 1998, NAPA 500, 1998, Cracker Barrel 500, 1999, Save Mart/Kragen 350 (now Dodge/ Save Mart 350), 1998, 1999, 2006, Frontier at the Glen, 1999, NAPA Autocave 500, 1999, UAW-GM 500, 1999, Die Hard 500, 2000, Chevrolet Monte Carlo 400, 2000, UAW Daimler Chrysler 400, 2001, MBNA Platinum 400, 2001, Kmart 400, 2001, Global Crossing at the Glen, 2001, Protection One 400, 2001, 2002, Va. 500, 2003, Subway 500, 2003, 2005, Subway Fresh Fit 500, 2007, Bass Pro Shops MBNA 500, 2003, Aaron's 499, 2004, 2005, 2007, Advance Auto 500, 2005, USG Sheetrock 400, 2006, Dodge Avenger 500, 2007; named to McDonald's All-Star Team, 1994, 1995. Achievements include 2nd youngest Winston Cup Champion NASCAR ever at age 24. Mailing: Jeff Gordon Network 4345 Papa Joe Hendrick Blvd Charlotte NC 28262 E-mail: JGFAN@Primenet.com.*

GORDON, JEFFREY IVAN, gastroenterologist, educator, molecular biologist, researcher; b. New Orleans, Oct. 4, 1947; BA in Biology, Oberlin Coll.; MD, U. Chicago-Pritzker Sch Medicine, 1973. Intern, medicine Barnes Hosp., St. Louis, 1973—74, jr. asst. resident, medicine, 1974—75, sr. asst. resident. medicine, 1978—79; rsch. assoc. biochemistry lab, gastrointestinal medicine Nat. Cancer Ins., NIH, Bethesda, Md., 1975—78; chief med. resident Wash. U. Medical Service, John Cochran VA Hospital, St. Louis, 1978—79; fellow in medicine, gastroenterology Wash. U. Sch. of Medicine, St. Louis, 1979—81, asst. prof. medicine and biol. chemistry, 1981—84, assoc. prof. medicine and biol. chemistry, 1985—87, prof. medicine and biol. chemistry, 1987—90, head molecular biology & pharmacology dept., 1991—, Robert J. Glaser Disting. U. Prof., 2002—, dir. Ctr. Genome Sciences, 2004—. Contbr. articles to profl. publications. Named Wellcome Vis. Prof. in Basic Med. Sciences, 1998, Horace W. Davenport Disting. Lecturer, Am. Physiological Assn., 2003, Sir Arthur Hurst Lecturer, British Soc. Gastroenterology, 2004; recipient Young Investigator award, Am. Federation Clinical Rsch., 1990, NIDDK Young Scientist award, 1990, Marion Merrell Dow Disting. prize in Gastrointestinal Physiology, 1994, Janssen Sustained Achievement award in Digestive Sciences, 2003, Sr. Scholar award in Global Infectious Diseases, Ellison Medical Found., 2003; John A. & George L. Hartford Found. Fellowship, 1981—84, Established Investigatorship, Am. Heart Assoc., 1985—90. Fellow: AAAS, Am. Acad. Arts and Scis., Am. Acad. Microbiology; mem.: NAS, Am. Gastroenterology Assn. (Morton I. Grossman Disting. Lectr. 1999, Disting. Achievement award 1992, 1992), Assn. Am. Physicians. Achievements include internationally known for research on gastrointestinal development and how gut bacteria affect normal intestinal function and predisposition to health and to certain diseases. Office: Dept Molecular Biology & Pharmacology Wash U Campus Box 8510 4444 Forest Park Saint Louis MO 63108 Office Phone: 314-362-7243. Business E-Mail: jgordon@molecool.wustl.edu.*

GORDON, JEFFREY NEIL, law educator; b. Richmond, Va., June 18, 1949; s. Irving Leonard and Viola Anne (Clayman) G. BA, Yale U., 1971; JD, Harvard U., 1975. Bar: N.Y. 1977, U.S. Dist. Ct. (so. and ea. dists.) N.Y. 1978, U.S. Ct. Appeals (2nd cir.) 1979, D.C. 1981. Reporter Rocky Mount News, Denver, 1971-72; law clk. to judge U.S. Ct. Appeals (10th cir.), Denver, 1975-76; assoc. Cleary, Gottlieb, Steen & Hamilton, NYC, 1976-78; spl. asst. to gen. counsel, atty. advisor U.S. Treasury, Washington, 1978-81; prof. law NYU, NYC, 1982-88, Columbia U., NYC, 1988—, Alfred W. Bressler prof., 1998—. Co-dir. Ctr. Law and Econ. Studies, Columbia U. Contbr. articles to profl. jours. Recipient Exceptional Svc. award U.S. Dept. Energy, 1982. Mem. ABA, Am. Law Inst., Assn. of Bar of City of N.Y., Harvard Club, Phi Beta Kappa. Democrat. Jewish. Home: 410 Riverside Dr Apt 81 New York NY 10025-7923 Office: Columbia Law Sch Ctr Law Econ Studies 435 W 116th St New York NY 10027-7297 Office Phone: 212-854-2316.

GORDON, JENNIFER LYNN, lawyer, administrator; b. Willimantic, Conn., Aug. 14, 1965; BA, Harvard/Radcliff Coll., 1987; JD, Harvard U., 1992. Bar: NY 1992, US Dist. Ct. (ea. dist.) NY 1994. Exec. dir., supervising atty. The Workplace Project, Hempstead, NY, 1992; prof. of law Fordham U Sch. of Law, NYC. Contbr. articles to profl. jours. Office: Fordham U Sch of Law 140 W 62nd St New York NY 10023 Office Phone: 212-636-7444. Office Fax: 212-636-6899. Business E-Mail: jgordon@law.fordham.edu.

GORDON, JOHN CHARLES, forestry educator; b. Nampa, Idaho, June 10, 1939; s. John Nicholas and Ada Elizabeth (Scheuermann) G.; m. Helka Lehtinen, Aug. 6, 1964; 1 child, Sean Nicholas. BS, Iowa State U., Ames, 1961, PhD, 1966; postgrad., U. Helsinki, Finland, 1961-62; MA (hon.), Yale U., New Haven, Conn., 1984; LHD (hon.), Unity Coll., Maine, 2000. Instr. forestry Iowa State U., Ames, 1965-66; plant physiologist US Forest Service, Rhinelander, Wis., 1966-70; prof. forestry Iowa State U., Ames, 1970-77; prof., head dept. forest sci. Oreg. State U., Corvallis, 1977-83; prof., dean forestry and environ. studies Yale U., New Haven, 1983-92, 97-98, Pinchot prof. forestry and environ. studies, 1991—2001, acting dir. Inst. for Biospheric Studies, 1994-95, 96, Pinchot prof. emeritus, 2001—; founding ptnr. Interforest LLC, 1996—; chmn., mem. exec. com. Candlewood Timber Group, 1999—. Chmn. Commn. on Rsch. and Resources Mgmt. in Nat. Pks., 1988—89; bd. dirs. Nat. Commn. on Sci. and Sustainable Forestry, 2000—, chmn., 2000—02; chmn. com. on forestry rsch. NAS, 1989—92; adj. prof. Portland State U., 2004—; lectr. in field. Editor: Symbiotic Nitrogen Fixation, 1983; author: Agroforestry Research, 1991, Environmental Leadership, 1993, Ecosystems, 1998, Forests to Fight Poverty, 1999, Forest Certification, 1999, Buy on the Upside: Stock Investing, 2005, Environmental Leadership Equals Essential Leadership, 2006, Eat Your Spinach: Spend Less and Save More, 2006, Planning Research, 2007; contbr. articles to profl. jours. Bd. dirs. Friends of Gray Towers, Milford, Pa., 1983-87, Yale U. Alumni Fund, 1985-92, Tropical Forest Found., 1991-94, Wintock Internat., 1993-95, Soc. for Protection NH Forests, 2001-05; vis. com. Harvard U., 1985-92; pres. C.V. Riley Found., NYC, 1985, 92-94, Conn. Fund for Environ., 1986-92; mem. rsch. adv. com. US AID, 1988-92; co-chmn. 7th Am. Forest Congress, 1994-97. Fulbright scholar, 1961, 84; hon. sr. fellow U. Glasgow, Scotland, 1975-76; Green vis. prof. U. BC, Vancouver, 1985; named Conservationist of the Yr., Pacific Rivers Coun., 1992; fellow Timothy Dwight Coll., Yale U.; disting. svc. award Am. Forests, 1996. Mem. Soc. Am. Foresters (Gifford Pinchot medal 2005), Am. Forestry Assn. (Disting. Svc. award 1996), Yale Club (NYC), Morys (New Haven), Cosmos Club (Washington), Sigma Xi, Phi Kappa Phi. Presbyterian. Avocations: hiking, fishing, writing short stories. Home: 28072 SW Morgan St Wilsonville OR 97070-6791 Office Phone: 503-956-3574. Personal E-mail: jgordon@iforest.com.

GORDON, JOSEPH ELWELL, university official, educator; b. Deatsville, Ala., July 2, 1921; s. Joseph Elwell and Martha (Berry) G.; m. Doris Elizabeth Smith, June 5, 1948; children— Cecile Lizabeth, Joseph Elwell, Melissa Innes. AB, Birmingham-So. Coll., 1942; MS, Auburn U., 1949; PhD, U. Chgo., 1951. Tchr. math., Montgomery, Ala., 1946-48; instr. math. Auburn U., 1948-49; research asst. North Central Assn. Colls. and Secondary Schs., Chgo., 1949-51; program analyst Air U., Maxwell AFB, 1951-54; mem. faculty Tulane U., 1954—, asst. prof. edn., 1958—, assoc. dir. admissions, 1957-63, dean Coll. Arts and Scis., 1964-84, dir. found. rels., 1984-86, spl. asst. to v.p. devel., 1986-90, univ. historian, 1990-96, vice provost, 1996-97. Author (with Clarence Mohr): Tulane: The Emergence of a Modern University 1945-1980, 2001. Served to lt. USNR, 1942-46. Mem. Omicron Delta Kappa, Phi Delta Kappa, Pi Kappa Alpha. Democrat. Presbyterian. Home: 150 Broadway Apt 706 New Orleans LA 70118

GORDON, JOSEPH HAROLD, lawyer; b. Tacoma, Mar. 31, 1909; s. Joseph H. and Mary (Obermiller) G.; m. Jane Wilson, Sept. 12, 1936 (dec.); children: Joseph H., Nancy Jane; m. Eileen (Rylander) Rademaker, Jan. 7, 1967 (dec. 2001). BA, Stanford U., 1931; LLB, JD, U. Wash., 1935. Bar: Wash. 1935. Sole practice, Tacoma; ptnr. Gordon & Gordon, Tacoma, 1935—50, Henderson, Carnahan, Thompson & Gordon, Tacoma, 1950—57, Carnahan, Gordon & Goodwin, Tacoma, 1957—70, Gordon, Thomas, Honeywell, Malanca, Peterson & Daheim, Tacoma, 1970—. Elder Presbyn. Ch. Mem.: ABA (ho. dels. 1951—, bd. govs. 1962—72, treas. 1965—72), Tacoma Bar Assn. (past pres.), Wash. State Bar Assn., Tacoma Golf and Country Club, Tacoma Club, Rotary. Office: Gordon Thomas Honeywell Malanca Peterson & Daheim PO Box 1157 2200 Wells Fargo Plz Tacoma WA 98401-1157 Office Phone: 253-620-6408. Personal E-mail: gordsr@themetrolink.com, gordsr@gmail.org. Business E-Mail: gordsr@gth-law.com.

GORDON, JULIE PEYTON, foundation administrator; b. Jacksonville, Fla., June 21, 1940; d. Robert Benoist Shields and Bessie (Cavanaugh) Peyton; m. Robert James Gordon, June 22, 1963. BA, Boston U., 1963; MA, Harvard U., 1965, PhD, 1969. Asst. prof. English Ill. Inst. Tech., Chgo., 1968-75, assoc. prof., 1975-77, asst. dean students, 1975-78; asst. dean acad. affairs Northwestern U., Evanston, Ill., 1978-80, lectr. English, Univ. Coll., 1978—2001, assoc. dean Univ. Coll., 1980-85, sec. Econometric Soc., 1975—, exec. dir. Econometric Soc., 1985—. Mem. nat. adv. com. ALA, Chgo., 1983—86; lectr. English Northwestern U., Evanston, 2003—. Author: Seasons in the Contemporary American Family, 1984. Grantee NEH, 1971-73; project scholar NEH, 1983-86. Mem.: Phi Beta Kappa. Avocation: writing. Home: 202 Greenwood Evanston IL 60201-4714 Office: Northwestern U Dept Econs Econometric Soc Evanston IL 60208-2600 Home Phone: 847-869-3544; Office Phone: 847-491-3615. Business E-Mail: jpg@northwestern.edu.

GORDON, JUNE SACAVAGE, art educator; b. Ringtown, Pa. d. Leonard and Violet Sacavage; m. Peter C. Gordon, Aug. 1990. BS in Art Edn., Mansfield U., Pa., 1983; MS in Edn., Elmira Coll., NY, 1987. Art educator Elmira City Sch. Dist., 1983—. Art tchr. summer cleft program, Elmira, 1985—93; coop. tchr. Mansfield U. and Elmira Coll., 1986—; art chair Mid. States Evaluatin Team, NY, 1990. Advisor Elmira Fee Acad Art Club, 1990—. Mem.: Nat. Art Educators Assn., NY State Art Tchrs. Assn. Avocations: photography, hiking, bicycling. Office: Elmira Fee Acad 933 Hoffman St Elmira NY 14905 Office Phone: 607-735-3100.

GORDON, KEVIN DELL, lawyer; b. Oklahoma City, June 23, 1958; s. James Dell and Mary Lurana (Tracewell) G.; m. Janice Linn Mathews, Aug. 4, 1979; children: Tracewell, Elise. BA cum laude, Westminster Coll., 1981; JD, Washington U., 1984. Bar: Okla. 1984, U.S. Dist. Ct. (we., no. and ea. dists.) Okla. 1984, U.S. Ct. Appeals (10th cir.) 1985, U.S. Supreme Ct. Shareholder, dir. Crowe & Dunlevy, Oklahoma City, 1984—. Adj. prof. health law U. Okla. Law Sch., 1997-2002; bd. dirs. Citizen's Policy Ctr. Editor Washington U. Law Quar., 1982-84; contbr. chpts. to books. Trustee, past pres. Youth Svcs. Oklahoma County, 1986-2004; chair adv. com. Okla. Assn. Youth Svcs., 1994-98. Fellow Okla. Bar Found., Litig. Counsel Am.; mem. ABA (ins. coverage com. 1990—), Okla. Bar Assn. (uniform laws com. 1994-97, coord./moderator ann. ins. law update 1999—, mentorship com. 1999—, Outstanding CLE award 1999), Am. Health Lawyers Assn. (HMO and ins. coms. 1998—, HMO and health plans practice, chmn. 2005—), Oklahoma County Bar Assn. (professional com., legal aid com. 1990-98, cmty. svc. com. 1997-99, bd. dirs.), Ruth Bader Ginsberg Am. Inn of Ct. (chair mentoring com. 1996-99, chair membership com. 1999-2000, pres. 2002-04, Master of Yr. 1998), U.S. C. of C. (employee benefits com. 2001-), Order of Coif. Avocations: sports, gardening, guitar, reading. Home: 8309 Glenwood Ave Oklahoma City OK 73114-1111 Office: Crowe & Dunlevy 20 N Broadway Ave Ste 1800 Oklahoma City OK 73102-8273 Office Phone: 405-239-7700.

GORDON, LANA G., state representative; b. Kansas City, Mo., Aug. 20, 1950; m. Arnold Gordon; children: Jennifer, Stacey, Jamie. BS in Edn., U. Kans., 1971. Subst. tchr., Mo., 1971—72; tchr. Lee's Summit (Mo.) Pub. Sch., 1972—73; test adminstr. State of Kans., 1978—80; sec., treas. Cardinal Bldg. Svcs., 1997—2001; office gen. Cardinal DBA/BG Svc. Solution, 2002—; mem. Kans. Ho. of Reps., 2001—. Bd. dirs. Kansas, Inc. Sec. citizens adv. coun. USD 501 Dist., 1982—85; bd. dirs. USD 501 Sch. Found., 1994—97, Vol. Ctr. Topeka, 1998—, Jr. League Topeka, 2002—04, Topeka Conv. and Visitors Bur., Topeka C. of C., 2006—. Republican. Jewish. Address: 5820 SW 27th St Topeka KS 66614

GORDON, LARRY JEAN, sanitarian, environmental health consultant; b. Tipton, Okla., Oct. 16, 1926; s. Andrew J. and Deweylee (Stewart) G.; m. Nedra Callender, Aug. 26. 1950; children: Debra Gordon Dunlap, Kent, Gary. Student, U. Okla., 1943-44; BS, U. N.Mex., 1949, MS, 1951; DHL (hon.), U. N.Mex., Albuquerque, 2007; MPH, U. Mich., 1954. High sch. sci. tchr., N.Mex., 1949-50; various positions N.Mex. Dept. Health, 1950-55; commd. officer USPHS, 1957—, advanced through grades to Dir. Grade (Navy capt.), dir. Albuquerque Environ. Health Dept., 1955-68, 82-86; dir. Environ. Improvement Agy., Santa Fe, 1968-73; adminstr. for health and environ. programs N.Mex. HHS Dept., Santa Fe, 1976-78; dir. N.Mex. Sci. Lab. System, Albuquerque, 1973-76; dep. sec. N.Mex. Health and Environ. Dept., Santa Fe, 1978-82, sec., 1987-88; vis. prof. pub. adminstrn. U. N.Mex., Albuquerque, 1988—, adj. prof. polit. sci., 1997—, sr. fellow Inst. for Pub. Policy, 1997—. Chmn. N.Mex. Water Quality Commn., 1971-73, New Mex. Coal Surface Mining Commn., 1971-73 Asst. editor Jour. Environ. Health, 1975-78; cons. editor Environ. News Digest, 1970-82; editl. cons. Jour. Pub. Health Policy, 1980-96, Underwriters Labs., 1996; contbr. over 240 articles to profl. jours. With USN, 1944—46. Recipient Samuel J. Crumbine award for Outstanding Devel. of Comprehensive Program for Environ. Sanitation, 1959 and 65, Sanitarians Disting. Service award Internat. Assn. Milk, Food, and Environ. Sanitarians, 1962, Outstanding Contrbn. award N.Mex. Assn. Pub. Health Sanitarians, 1967, Boss of Yr. award Santa Fe chpt. Nat. Secs. Assn., 1970, Walter F. Snyder award For Achievement in Environ. Quality, 1978, Commendation for Leadership in Health Care N.Mex. Hosp. Assn., 1981, N.Mex. Outstanding Pub. Svc. award, 1988, Zimmerman award U. N.Mex. Alumni, 1993, L.A. County Breslow award L.A. County Dept. Health Svcs., 1994, Outstanding Leadership in Environ. Adminstrn. award Am. Soc. for Pub. Adminstrn., 1994. Hon. Doctor of Humane Letters award, U. New Mexico Bd. Regents, May 2007 Mem. APHA (exec. bd. 1975-82, pres. 1980-81, John J. Sippy Meml. award 1962, other coms., Sedgwick award 1987), Am. Acad. Sanitarians (founder, David Calvin Wagner Excellence award 1984), N.Mex. Pub. Health Assn. (past pres., Disting. Svc. award 1970, Spl. award, 1978, D.A. Larrazola award 1989), N.Mex. Environ. Health Assn., (past pres.), Am. Lung Assn. N.Mex. (bd. dirs. 1982-94, Clinton P. Anderson award for Oustanding Contbn. to Lung Health 1987), Nat. Accreditation Coun. Environ. Health Curricula, Nat. Audubon Soc. (pres. coun. 1982-86), U. Mich. Sch. Pub. Health Alumni Assn. (bd. govs. 1985-88, Outstanding Alumnus award 1995), Royal Soc. Promotion of Health, London (hon.), N.Mex. Soc. Pub. Adminstrn. (Disting. Pub. Adminstr. award 1996), Delta Omega, Phi Kappa Phi, Phi Sigma. Independent. Avocations: fishing, travel, golf, genealogy. Home: 1674 Tierra Del Rio NW Albuquerque NM 87107-3259 Personal E-mail: 1016Larry@msn.com.

GORDON, LAURIE ANNE, academic director; d. Randolph Orlando and Norma Fay Gordon. BA, NYU, 1993; MA, Fairleigh Dickinson U., 1996; PhD, Lehigh U., 2004. Psychotherapist Florence Child Guidance Ctr., Allentown, Pa., 1998—99; counselor, case mgr. Starting Point, Allentown, 1999—2000; pre-doctoral psychology intern Philhaven Behavioral Healthcare, Mt. Gretna, Pa., 2000—01; program dir. Lancaster Diversion Program, Pa., 2001—03; counselor Elizabethtown Coll., Pa., 2003—06, dir., 2006—. Mem. Single County Authority adv. bd. Lancaster County Drug and Alcohol Commn., 2004—; mem. Susquehanna Valley Consortium for Substance Abuse Prevention, Elizabethtown, 2004—. Mem.: APA. Home: 835 Skyline Dr #A21 Lancaster PA 17601 Office: Elizabethtown College 1 Alpha Dr Elizabethtown PA 17022

GORDON, LEO I., hematologist, oncologist, educator; b. Milw., Nov. 24, 1947; s. Abraham and Fira (Weinstein) G.; m. Linda Robinson; children: Elizabeth, Peter. BA, U. Chgo., 1969; MD, U. Cin., 1973. Diplomate Am. Bd. Internal Medicine, 1976, Am. Bd. Internal Medicine Hematology, 1978, Am. Bd. Internal Medicine Oncology, 1979. Intern in medicine U. Chgo. Hosps., 1973-74, resident in medicine, 1974-76, fellow in hematology/oncology, 1978-79; fellow in hematology U. Minn., Mpls., 1976-78; asst. prof. medicine Northwestern U., Evanston, Ill., 1979-85, assoc. prof., 1985-95, prof. medicine, 1995—. Chief divsn. hematology/oncology, Northwestern U. Med. Sch., Chgo., 1996—. Contbr. over 125 articles and abstracts to profl. jours.; author book. Office: Northwestern U Med Sch 676 N St Clair Ste 850 Chicago IL 60611 Business E-Mail: l-gordon@northwestern.edu.

GORDON, LEO MAURY, federal judge; b. Jan. 18, 1952; BA, U. N.C. Chapel Hill, 1973; JD, Emory U., 1977. Asst. counsel subcom. on monopolies and comml. law, com. on judiciary U.S. Ho. of Reps., 1977—81; asst. clk. U.S. Ct. Internat. Trade, NYC, 1981—99, clerk, 1999—2006, judge, 2006—. Office: US Ct Internat Trade One Federal Plz New York NY 10278-0001

GORDON, LEONARD, retired social sciences educator; b. Detroit, Dec. 6, 1935; s. Abraham and Sarah (Rosen) G.; m. Rena Joyce Feigelman, Dec. 25, 1955 (dec. Nov. 24, 2005); children: Susan Melinda, Matthew Seth, Melissa Gail. BA, Wayne State U., 1957; MA, U. Mich., 1958; PhD, Wayne State U., 1966. Instr. Wayne State U., Detroit, 1960-62; rsch. dir. Jewish Cmty. Coun., Detroit, 1962-64; dir. Mich. area Am. Jewish Com., NYC, 1964-67; asst. prof. Ariz. State U., Tempe, 1967-70, assoc. prof., 1970-77, prof., 1977—, chmn. dept. sociology, 1981-90, assoc. dean for acad. programs Coll. Liberal Arts and Scis., 1990-2001, rsch. prof., 2001—02, prof. emeritus, 2002—, founding mem. emeritus coll. coun., 2005—; dean Ariz. State U. Emeritus Colls., 2007—. Cons. OEO, Maricopa County, Ariz., 1968. Author: A City in Racial Crisis, 1971, Sociology and American Social Issues, 1978, (with A. Mayer) Urban Life and the Struggle To Be Human, 1979, (with R. Hardert, M. Laner and M. Reader) Confronting Social Problems, 1984, (with J. Hall and R. Melnick) Harmonizing Arizona's Ethnic and Cultural Diversity, 1992. Sec. Conf. on Religion and Race, Detroit, 1962-67; mem. exec. bd. dirs. Am. Jewish Com., Phoenix chpt., 1969-70. Grantee NSF, 1962, Rockefeller found., 1970, 84; Recepient James W. Creasman award for Lifetime Achievement, Ariz. State U., 2000. Fellow Am. Sociol. Assn. (chair task force on current knowledge on hate/bias acts on coll. and univ. campuses 2000—, chair ASU emeritus coll. policy com., 2005-) mem. AAUP, Pacific Sociol. Assn. (v.p. 1978-79, pres. 1980-81), Soc. Study Social Problems (chair C. Wright Mills award com. 1988, treas. 1989-96), Ariz. State U. Alumni Assn. (faculty dir. 1981-82, founding mem. emeritus coll. coun., 2005-). Democrat. Jewish. Home: 13660 E Columbine Dr Scottsdale AZ 85259-3753 Office: Ariz State U Emeritus Coll Wilson Hall 101 Tempe AZ 85287-5203 Home Phone: 480-451-7899; Office Phone: 480-965-0002. Business E-Mail: len.gordon@asu.edu.

GORDON, LEONARD H(ERMAN) D(AVID), history educator; b. NYC, Aug. 8, 1928; s. Herman and Ray (Keidan) G.; m. Marjorie J(osephine) Hunt, June 11, 1951; children: Herman, David. BA, Ind. U., 1950, MA, 1953; PhD, U. Mich., 1961. Far Eastern diplomatic historian U.S. Dept. State, Washington, 1961-63; asst. prof. East Asian history U. Wis., Madison, 1963-67; assoc. prof. Chinese history Purdue U., West Lafayette, Ind., 1967-94, chmn. Asian studies program, 1992-94, prof. emeritus Chinese history, 1994—. Mem. preliminary screening com. Am. Coun. Learned Socs., N.Y.C., 1971-72, nat. com., 1972-74, joint com. Social Scis. Rsch. Coun. Editor: Taiwan: Studies in Chinese Local History, 1970; co-editor: Doctoral Dissertations on China, A Bibliography of Studies in Western Languages, 1945-70, 1972, Bibliography of Sun Yat-Sen in China's Republican Revolution, 1985-1925, 1991, 2d edit., 1998; co-author: All Under Heaven: Sun Yat-Sen and His Revolutionary Thought, 1991; author: Confrontation over Taiway: Nineteenth Century China and the Powers, 2007. With U.S. Army, 1953-56. Faculty grantee U. Wis., 1963, 64, Faculty grantee Purdue U., 1968, grantee Am. Philos. Soc., 1963, 67, 80; Fulbright Rsch. fellow, Tokyo, 1959-60; Inter-Univ. fellow for Field Tng. in Chinese, Taipei, 1958-59. Mem. Assn. for Asian Studies (publs. com. 1968-71, editor newsletter). Business E-Mail: lhdgordon@alumni.indiana.edu.

GORDON, LINCOLN, political economist; b. NYC, Sept. 10, 1913; s. Bernard and Dorothy (Lerned) Gordon; m. Allison Wright, June 25, 1937 (dec.); children: Anne, Robert W., Hugh, Amy. AB, Harvard, 1933; DPhil (Rhodes scholar), Oxford U., Eng., 1936; LLD, Fairleigh Dickinson U., 1965, Columbia, 1967, Rutgers U., 1967, U. Md., 1968, Wash. Coll., 1968, U. Del., 1969; LHD, Loyola Coll., Balt., 1968. Instr., faculty instr. govt. Harvard, 1936-41, William Ziegler prof. internat. econ. relations, 1955-61; research technician water, energy resources U.S. Nat. Resources Planning Bd., Washington, 1939-1940; mem. staff requirements com. W.P.B., 1942-45, program vice chmn., 1945; dir. bur. reconversion priorities Civilian Prodn. Adminstrn., 1945-46; assoc. prof. bus. Harvard, 1946-47, prof. govt. and adminstrn., 1947-50; cons. U.S. Rep. UN AEC, 1946, Army and Navy Munitions Bd., Dept. of State, 1947, ECA, 1948; North Atlantic Council Com. of Three on non-mil. aspects of NATO, 1956; dir. program div. Office ECA, spl. rep. in Europe, 1949-50; econ. adviser to spl. asst. to President, 1950-51; asst. dir. Office of Mut. Security, 1951-52; chief Marshall Aid mission and minister econ. affairs in Am. Embassy in London, 1952-55; U.S. amb. Brazil, 1961-66; asst. sec. state for inter-Am. affairs, 1966-67; pres. Johns Hopkins, Balt., 1967-71; vis. prof. polit. economy Sch. Advanced Internat. Studies, Washington, 1971-72; fellow Woodrow Wilson Internat. Center for Scholars, 1972-75; sr. fellow Resources for Future, Washington, 1975-80; mem. sr. rev. panel CIA, 1980-82, nat. intelligence officer-at-large, 1982-83; guest scholar Brookings Instn., 1984—. Author: The Public Corporation in Great Britain, 1938; author: (with M. Fainsod) Government and the American Economy, 1941, rev. edit., 1959; author: Fuel and Power in Industrial Location and National Policy, Nat. Resources Planning Bd., 1942, Representation of the U.S. Abroad (in part), 1956, rev. edit., 1964; author: (with Engelbert L. Grommers) United States Manufacturing Investment in Brazil, 1961; author: A New Deal for Latin America, 1963, Growth Policies and the International Order, 1979; author: (with Joy Dunkerley and others) Energy Strategies for Developing Nations, 1981; author: (with J.F. Brown and others) Eroding Empire: Western Relations with Eastern Europe, 1987; author: (with T. Stanley) Integrating Economic and Security Factors in East-West Relations, 1988; author: Brazil's Second Chance: #En Route toward the First World, 2001, Portuguese translation, 2002; editor: International Stability and Progress: U.S. Interests and Instruments, 1957, From Marshall Plan to Global Interdependence, 1978. Hon. trustee Com. Econ. Devel.; bd. dirs. Atlantic Coun. US. Decorated Grand Cross Order Quetzal Guatemala, Order Cruzeiro do Sul Brazil. Fellow: Am. Acad. Arts and Scis.; mem.: Royal Econ. Soc., Internat. Inst. Strategic Studies, Am. Polit. Sci. Assn., Coun. Fgn. Rels., Cosmos Club Washington, Phi Beta Kappa. Home: 10450 Lottsford Rd Apt 253 Mitchellville MD 20721-3303 Office Phone: 202-797-6259. Business E-Mail: lgordon@brookings.edu.

GORDON, LINDA, history educator; b. Chgo., Jan. 19, 1940; d. Bill and Helen (Appelman) G.; m. Allen Hunter; 1 child, Rosa Gordon Hunter. BA in History magna cum laude, Swarthmore Coll., 1961; MA in History and Russian Studies, Yale U., 1963, PhD in History with distinction, 1970. Prof. history U. Mass., Boston, 1968-84, U. Wis., Madison, 1984-90, Florence Kelley prof. history, 1990—, Vilas disting. rsch. prof., 1993—2004; prof. history NYU, 1999—. Vis. prof. U. Amsterdam, 1984; cons. and lectr. in field. Author: Woman's Body, Woman's Right: A Social History of Birth Control in America, 1976, paperback edit., 1977, 2d rev. edit., 1990, Cossack Rebellions: Social Turmoil in the Sixteenth Century Ukraine, 1983, Heroes of Their Own Lives: The Politics and History of Family Violence, Boston 1880-1960, 1988 (AHA Joan Kelly prize, Wis. Libr. Assn. award, 1988), paperback edit., 1989, Brit. edit., 1989, Pitied But Not Entitled: Single Mothers and the History of Welfare, 1994 (winner Berkshire prize, 1995, Gustavus Myers human rights award, 1995), The Great Arizona Orphan Abduction, 1999 (winner Bancroft and Beveridge prizes), The Moral Property of Women, 2002, Impounded: Dorothea Lange and the Censored Image of Japanese Internment, 2006. NIMH rsch. grantee, 1979-82, Am. Coun. Learned Socs. travel grantee, 1980; Guggenheim fellow, 1983-84, Bunting Inst. fellow, 1983-84, Am. Coun. Learned Socs./Ford Found. fellow, 1985-86, Harry Frank Guggenheim Found. fellow, 1987, Russell Sage Found. fellow, 1997-98, Cullman Ctr. Scholars and Writers fellow, 2004-05; recipient Antonovych prize, 1983, Bird Meml. Lectureship, U. Maine, 1986, Am. Philos. Soc. Rsch. award, 1988-89, Joan Kelly prize, 1988, Berkshire prize, 1994, Bancroft prize, 2000, Beveridge prize, 2000. Mem. Presdl. Adv. Coun. on violence against women, Am. Hist. Assn. (jour. editl. bd. 1990-93), Orgn. Am. Historians (exec. bd. 1991-94, mem. editl. bd. jour. 1994-97), Inst. for Rsch. on Povety (exec. com. 1990-95). Jewish. Office: NYU 53 Washington Sq S New York NY 10012 Office Phone: 212-998-8627. Business E-Mail: Linda.Gordon@nyu.edu.

GORDON, LOIS G., language educator; b. Englewood, NJ; d. Irving David and Betty (Davis) Goldfein; m. Alan Lee Gordon, Nov. 13, 1961; 1 son, Robert Michael. BA (Nat. Merit scholar, Barbour scholar), U. Mich., 1960; postgrad., Columbia U., 1960-61; MA, U. Wis., 1962, PhD (Dissertation Completion fellow), 1966. Teaching asst. U. Wis., 1962-64; lectr. CCNY, 1964-66; asst. prof. U. Mo., Kansas City, 1966-68; asst. prof. English Fairleigh Dickinson U., Teaneck, N.J., 1968-71, assoc. prof., 1971-75, prof., 1975—, chmn. dept. English and comparative lit., 1982-90. Vis. exch. prof. Rutgers U., 1994; cons. U. Mo. Press, 1968-69, Doubleday Inc., 1974, Fairleigh Dickinson U. Press, 1975—, Prentice Hall, 1977—, Duke U. Press, 1986—, U. Wis. Press, Rutgers U. Press, Cambridge U. Press, Harper Collins, The New Yorker. Author: Stratagems To Uncover Nakedness: The Dramas of Harold Pinter, 1969, Donald Barthelme, 1981, Robert Coover: The Universal Fiction-Making Process, 1983, American Chronicle: Six Decades in American Life, 1920-79, 1987, Seven Decades in American Life, 1920-89, 1990, Harold Pinter: A Casebook, 1990, The Columbia Chronicles of American Life, 1910-1992, 1995, The World of Samuel Beckett, 1906-1946, 1996, Chinese edit., 2001, American Chronicle: Year by Year Through the Twentieth Century, 1999, Pinter at 70, 2001, Reading Godot, 2002, Nancy Cunard: Heiress, Muse, Political Idealist, 2007; asst. editor Lit. and Psychology, 1968-71; contbr. book revs. to profl. jours. and newspapers. Research grantee U. Mo., 1968, Fairleigh Dickinson U., 1985, 89, 97, 2001, Disting. scholar, 2001. Mem. MLA, PEN, Internat. Bach Soc., Internat. League Human Rights, Authors Guild, Acad. Am. Poets, So. Poverty Law Ctr., Harold Pinter Soc., Samuel Beckett Soc., U.S. Hist. Landmarks Commn. Jewish. Home: 300 Central Park W New York NY 10024-1513 Office: Fairleigh Dickinson U Dept English Teaneck NJ 07666 Office Phone: 201-692-2263. Personal E-mail: loisgord@aol.com.

GORDON, LONNY JOSEPH, artist, educator, dean; s. Charles Gordon and Ruth Rebecca Lee. BFA, U. Tex., 1965; MFA, U. Wis., 1967; diploma, Nishikawa Sch., Tokyo, 1980. Prof. U. Wis., Madison, 1976—91; chmn. dance U. Nev., Las Vegas, 1991—94, dir. devel. Performing Arts Ctr., 1994—98; dean fine arts Ill. State U., Normal, 2004—. Design artist, concert soloist debut: Toronomon Hall, 1968; internat. concert and lecture tour: US Info. Agy., 1969; solo performer: major concert halls and museums, creator more than 80 art/dance/theater works:, performer: (role of Tamura) Umewaka Noh Theater; cultural reviewer: Asahi Evening News, 1968, Korea Times, 1983, cultural writer: Capital Times; editor: Ency. Britannica. Pres. U. Nev. Las Vegas Faculty Alliance, 1994—96, 1997. Fellow, Japan Found., 1979, Korean Performing Arts Ctr., 1994—95; grantee, Japan Fulbright Hays Found., 1967—70, Mobile Found., 1971—72, Korean Fulbright Found., 1983, Nat. Endowment Arts, 1982—83, Nev. Arts Coun., 1992—2000; Devel. grants, U. Nev., Las Vegas, 1999, 2001. Mem.: Am. Coll. Dance Festival (v.p. 1999—2005). Avocations: gardening, body building, writing, painting.

GORDON, LORI HEYMAN, psychotherapist, author, educator; b. S.I., NY, Jan. 31, 1929; d. Julius and Bertha (Hahn) Heyman; m. Morris Gordon, Sept. 5, 1982 (dec.); children: Beth, Jonathan, David, Seth. BS, Cornell U., 1950; MSW, Cath. U. Am., 1963; PhD, Summit U. La., 1993. Lic. clin. social worker, accredited supr., Va. Founder/dir. Family Rels. Inst., Falls Church, Va., 1969; condr. psychoednl. tng. seminars nat. and internat. PAIRS (Practical Application Intimate Relationship Skills), Falls Church. Instr. family therapy Am. U. Grad. Sch. Counseling Edn., Washington; field supr. Cath. U. Am. Sch. Social Work, Washington; presenter profls. cons. Am. Assn. Marriage and Family Therapy Conf., 1988-91, Va. Assn. Marriage and Family Therapy Conf., 1989, ABA Family Law divsn. ptnrs. program, 1994; founder Ctr. for Separation and Divorce Mediation, 1980; founder, dir. PAIRS Ltd., 1984, PAIRS Inst., 1990; founder, exec. dir. PAIRS Found., Inc., 1991, dir. tng., 1995 Author: Love Knots--How To Untangle Daily Frustrations, 1990, Passage to Intimacy, 1993, rev. edit., 2001, If You Really Loved Me, 1996, Pairs Participant Handbook, Paris Curriculum Guide and Training Manual vol. I, II, revised, 1999, The Peers Experience, 1999, Breaking the Code of Jealousy: Seven Steps to Healing, 2004; co-author: Prepairs, A Guide for Catholic Couples, 1999, Preventive Approaches to Couples Therapy, 1999, Prepairs, A Guide for Jewish Couples, 2001, Prepairs: A Guide for Christian Couples, 2001, Christian Pairs, 2002, Dare to be: The Autobiography of Rabbi Morris Gordon, 2006; contbr. articles to profl. jours. and mags., chpts. to books. Mem. Internat. Human Lng. Resource Network, Avanta-The Va. Satir Tng. Orgn., Inst. Noetic Scis., Coalition Marriage, Family and Couples Edn. (bd. dirs.). Office: PAIRS Found Ltd 1056 Creekford Dr Weston FL 33326-2836 Office Phone: 954-385-1775. Personal E-mail: pairsline@aol.com.

GORDON, LOUIS, retired lawyer; b. Detroit, May 10, 1933; s. Isador and Esther (Kraizman) G.; m. Patricia Janis, Nov. 25, 1973 (div. Mar. 1986); children: Aaron, Marla; m. Johanna C. Gordon, Aug. 15, 1987 (dec.); children: Susan, Laurie. BSBA, Wayne State U., 1955, JD, 1958. Sole practitioner, Detroit, 1959-75; owner Louis Gordon. P.C., Southfield, Mich., 1976—2003; spl. asst. atty. gen. State of Mich., Lansing, 1975—; of counsel Gordon & Pont PC, Southfield, Mich., 2003—. Mem. ABA, Mich. Trial Lawyers Assn., Oakland Bar Assn. Avocations: tennis, golf, sailing, skiing, power boating. Office: Gordon & Pont PC 21700 Northwestern Hwy Ste 1100 Southfield MI 48075-4923 Fax: 248 395 4101. E-mail: Louaag@aol.com, Lawmich@aol.com.

GORDON, MALCOLM STEPHEN, biology professor; b. Bklyn., Nov. 13, 1933; s. Abraham and Rose (Walters) G.; m. Diane M. Kestin, Apr. 16, 1959 (div. Sept. 1973); 1 child, Dana Malcolm; m. Marjorie J. Weinzweig, Jan. 28, 1976 (dec. Mar. 1990); m. Carol A. Cowen, July 19, 1992. BA with high honors, Cornell U., 1954; PhD, Yale U., 1958. Instr. UCLA, 1958-60, asst. prof., 1960-65, assoc. prof., 1965-68, prof. biology, 1968—, dir. Inst. Evolutionary and Environ. Biology, 1971-76, chmn. interdept. com. Environ. Sci. Engring. Program, 1984-88; asst. dir. rsch. Nat. Fisheries Ctr. and Aquarium, U.S. Dept. of Interior, Washington, 1968-69. Vis. prof. zoology Chinese U. Hong Kong, 1971-72; panel on marine biology, panel on oceanography Pres.'s Sci. Adv. Com., 1965-66; nat. adv com. R/V Alpha Helix, Scripps Inst. Oceanography, 1969-73; com. on Latimeria, NAS, 1969-72; mem. tech. adv. com. Santa Monica Bay Restoration Project, EPA, 1988-2006; tech. adv. group on milkfish reprodn. AID, 1984-92; chmn. Commn. on Comparative Physiology, Internat. Union Physiol. Sci., 1993—; co-founder Inst. of Environment, UCLA, 1997; vis. assoc. in bioengring. and aeronautics Calif. Inst. Tech., 2003-06. Author coll. textbooks, technical books; mem. editorial bd. Fish Physiol. Biochem. Jour., 1986—, Jour. Exptl. Zool., 1990-93; contbr. articles to profl. jours. Active cmty. orgns. on environ., civil liberties. NSF fellow Yale U., 1954-57, Fulbright fellow U.K., 1957-58, Guggenheim fellow Italy and Denmark, 1961-62; Sr. Queen's fellow in marine sci. Australia, 1976; Irving-Scholander Meml. lectr., U. Alaska-Fairbanks, 2000. Fellow AAAS; mem. Am. Physiol. Soc. (exec. com. pub. affairs 1989-92, internat. physiol. com. 2002-05), Am. Soc. Ichthyologists and Herpetologists, Soc. Integrative Comparative Biology (chmn. divsn. ecology 1979-80, chmn. divsn. comparative biochem. physiology 1988-89), Soc. Exptl. Biology, Internat. Union Physiol. Sci. (coun. mem. 2005—, treas. 2007—) Home: 2801 Glendower Ave Los Angeles CA 90027-1118 Office: UCLA Dept Ecology Evolutionary Biol PO Box 951606 Los Angeles CA 90095-1606 Office Phone: 310-825-4579. Business E-Mail: msgordon@ucla.edu.

GORDON, MARCUS, judge; b. Union, Miss. s. Marcus Benton and Flossie C. Gordon; m. Polly Gordon; 4 children. Attended, East Central Community Coll.; BA, U. Miss., JD, 1959. Bar: 1959. Private practice with brother Rex Gordon, 1959—71; dist. atty. 8th Circuit Ct. Dist., 1971—77; circuit ct. judge Neshoba County, Miss., 1977—87; private practice with brother Rex and nephew Rex Jr., 1987—90; circuit ct. judge Neshoba County, Miss., 1990—. Served USAF, 1951—53. Achievements include presiding judge over Mississippi versus Ray Edgar Killen, convicted of the 1964 manslaughter of 3 civil rights workers, Andrew Goodman, James Chaney and Michael Schwerner in June 2005. Office: P O Box 220 Decatur MS 39327 Office Phone: 601-635-3540.

GORDON, MARJORIE, lyric-coloratura soprano, music educator, opera producer; b. NYC; d. Theodore and Minnie (Glantz) Fishberg; m. Nathan Gordon; children: Maxine, Peter Jon. BA cum laude, Hunter Coll., NYC. Nat. cert. voice tchr. Prof. voice Duquesne U., 1957-59, Wayne State U., 1961-91, Nat. Music Camp, Interlochen, 1963-65, Meadowbrook Sch. Music, 1966-71, U. Mich., 1970, Mich. State U., 1971; soloist, tchr. Am. U.-Wolf Trap Program, Washington, 1973. Spl. edn. cons. Detroit Grand Opera Assn.; adj. prof. Oakland U., Mich.; pres., gen. dir. Piccolo Opera Co., Inc. Solo debut N.Y. Philharm. Symphony, 1950, soprano soloist, NYC Opera, 1955-57, Chautauqua Opera Co., 1949-61, Pitts. Opera, 1956; dir. Detroit Opera Theatre, 1960-72, Piccolo Opera Co., 1961—; soloist with Chgo. Symphony, Phila. Symphony, Pitts. Symphony, other orchs., opera cos., summer stock, on radio and TV; recitals US, Greece, Europe, Can., Israel; editor: Opera Study Guide, 1968—. Mem. music adv. panel Mich. Arts Coun., 1990-; mem. Palm Beach County Cultural Commn., 1992—; opera prodr. Blue Lake Fine Arts Camp, 1993—. Recipient resolution honoring 25th Anniversary Piccolo Opera Co., Mich. Senate; established voice scholarship in perpetuity Nat. Opera Assn. Mem.:

AFTRA, Nat. Assn. Tchrs. Singing, Met. Opera Guild, Ctrl. Opera Svc., Nat. Opera Assn., Music Tchrs. Nat. Assn., Am. Guild Mus. Artists, Mich. Music Tchrs. Assn. (voice chmn. 1970—76), Fla. Music Tchrs. Assn., Boca Delray Music Soc., Broward County Music Club, Mu Phi Epsilon. Avocations: handcrafts, swimming, reading, sketching. Office Phone: 800-282-3161. Office Fax: 561-394-0520. Personal E-mail: leejon51@msn.com.

GORDON, MARK, II, film producer; b. Oct. 10, 1956; 2 children. Prodr. films including: Sawdust, 1988, Brothers in Arms, 1989, Opportunity Knocks, 1990, traces of Red, 1992, Fly by Night, 1993, Swing Kids, 1993, Speed, 1994, Trial by Jury, 1994, A Pyromaniac's Love Story, 1995, Broken Arrow, 1996, Hard Rain, 1998, Paulie, 1998, Saving Private Ryan, 1998, To the Moon, 1999, The Patriot, 2000, The Day After Tomorrow, 2004, Hostage, 2005, Casonova, 2005, The Hoax, 2006, Talk to Me, 2007; exec. prodr.: The Relic, 1997, Speed2: Cruise Control, 1997, The Jackal, 1997, A Simple Plan, 1998, Black Dog, 1998, Virus, 1999, All the Rage, 1999, The Patriot, 2000, The League of Extraordinary Gentlemen, 2003, The Matador, 2005, Life of the Party, 2005, Prime, 2005, The Painted Veil, 2006; TV films include: Out of Step, 1983, One Too Many, 1983, How to be a Perfect Person in Just Three Days, 1983, War Between the Classes, 1985, Double Switch, 1987, exec. prodr. TV: Lightning Field, 1991, Love Kills, 1991, Past Tense, 1994, The Man Who Wouldn't Die, 1994, Children Remember the Holocaust, 1995, The Ripper, 1997, Footsteps, 2003, LAX, 2004, Grey's Anatomy, 2005, Criminal Minds, 2005, Army Wives, 2007; dir. TV: Good Time Harry, 1980, Children Remember the Holocaust (also prodr.), 1995. Winner Daytime Emmy award for outstanding children's spl. for War Between the Classes, 1985, Motion Picture Prodr. of the Yr. award for Saving Pvt. Ryan, 1999. Office: Mutual Film Co Raleigh Studios Clinton Bldg 650 N Bronson Ave Los Angeles CA 90004-1404*

GORDON, MARK J., real estate company executive; b. 1968; BS, Ithaca Coll.; MS, NYU. Prin. & mng. dir. Sonnenblick Goldman LLC, NYC, 1994—, pres. Internat. Lodging & Leisure group. Named a Rising Star, Real Estate Weekly, 2005, Star to Watch, Comml. Property News, 2002; named one of 40 Under 40, Real Estate NY, 2002, 2003, Crain's NY Bus., 2007. Mem.: Urban Land Inst., NY Hospitality Coun. Office: Sonnenblick Goldman 712 5th Ave New York NY 10019 Office Phone: 212-841-9200. Office Fax: 212-262-4224. E-mail: mgordon@songold.com.*

GORDON, MARSHA L., dermatologist; b. Annapolis, Md., 1958; BA, Rutgers U., 1980; MD, U. Pa., 1984. Diplomate Am. Bd. Dermatology. Intern Cooper Med. Ctr., Camden, 1984—85; resident in dermatology Mt. Sinai Med. Ctr., NYC, 1985—88, chief cons., 1988—, vice chair dermatology, 1996—. Asst. prof. Mt. Sinai Sch. Medicine, NYC, 1988—97, assoc. clin. prof., 1997—. Office: Mount Sinai Med Ctr Box 1048 5 E 98th St New York NY 10029-6501 Office Phone: 212-241-9773.

GORDON, MARVIN F., retired social sciences educator; s. Samuel F. and Lena B. Gordon; m. Lucille S. Gordon, May 27, 1956; children: Stephen E., Margaret J. PhD, Columbia U., NYC, 1956. With U.S. Govt., Washington, 1956—66; v.p. Fgn. Svcs., Inc., 1965—92; prof., chair dept. geography George Washington U., Washington, 1966—91, dir. L.Am. program, 1966—91, prof. emeritus, 1991—. Dir. cultural exch. George Washington U., Cath. U. Peru; mem. editl. staff Jour. Rural Studies, L.Am. Affairs; chmn. Mid-Atlantic divsn. Assn. Am. Geographers; cons., rsch. US State Dept., Washington, US Dept. Def., Def. Intelligence Agy., UN Devel. Programme, UN Population Fund, OAS, Caribbean Cmty. and Common Mkt., Govt. Ethiopia, Govt. Yemem, Govt. Sudan, Govt. Papua New Guinea; cons. US Army Concepts Analysis Agy., Bus. Coun. Internat. Understanding; advisor overseas econ. devel. Gallaudet U., Washington, Catholic U., Washington, Montgomery Coll., Tacoma Park, Md., George Mason U., Fairfax, Va.; vis. lectr. U. Beijing, Kansai U., Osaka, Japan; guest lectr., 1987—2006. Sgt. inf. US Army, 1942—45, ETO. Decorated Bronze Star US Army, Combat Infantryman's Badge; grantee, NEH, 1980—83. Mem.: Population Reference Bur., Population Assn. Am., Mensa, Combat Infantrymen's Assn., Veterans Battle of Bulge. Independent. Avocations: golf, chess. Home: PO Box 13553 Mesa AZ 85216

GORDON, MELVIN JAY, food products executive; b. Boston, Nov. 26, 1919; s. Jacob S. and Sadye Z. (Lewis) G.; m. Ellen Rubin, June 25, 1950; children: Virginia Lynn, Karen Dale, Wendy Jean, Lisa Jo. BA, Harvard, 1941, MBA, 1943. V.p. Clear Weave Hosiery Stores, Inc., Boston, 1945-50, Tenn. Knitting Mills, Inc., Columbia, 1945-56; pres. P.R. Hosiery Mills, Inc., Arecibo, 1956-61; ptnr. Manchester (N.H.) Hosiery Mills, 1946-69; chmn. bd. Tootsie Roll Industries, Chgo., 1962—, pres., 1968-69, 75-78, Hampshire Designers Inc., 1969-77, HDI Investment Corp., 1977—, MJG Inc., 1981—, Ellen Gordon Inc., 1984-88, Lisa Gordon Inc., 1987—, Wendy Gordon Inc., 1989—. Adv. com. Mfrs. Hanover Bank, N.Y.C., 1967-88. Author: Better Than Communism, 1958. Mem. Pres.'s Citizens Adv. com. Fitness Am. Youth, 1957-60, exec. com. 1959-60; del. White House Conf. Youth Fitness, 1962; co-chmn. Com. Support Psychol. Offensive, 1961-63; bd. dirs. mem. exec. com. Coun. World Tensions, N.Y.C., 1960-65; chmn. Mass. Gov.'s Com. Youth Fitness, 1958-64; bd. dirs. New Eng. Econ. Edn. Coun., 1960-63, N.H. Coun. on World Affairs, 1962-65; bd. dirs., chmn. exec. com. Citizen Exchange Corps., N.Y.C., 1964-66, hon. chmn. adv. coun. 1966-67; del. Prime Minister's Econ. Conf., Israel, 1968, 73; bd. overseers Harvard Coll., mem. vis. com. behavioral scis., 1967-71, vis. com. psychology, 1972; vis. com. Russian Rsch. Ctr., 1972-76; dir. Rensselaerville Inst., N.Y., 1966—; chmn. N.E. region m. Com. for Weizmann Inst. Sci. Rehovot, Israel, 1972-73; dir. Am. com., 1973-75; nat. trustee Nat. Symphony Orch., Washington, 1993—. Recipient Dean's award Nat. Candy Wholesalers Assn., 1978 Mem. Chief Execs. Orgn., World Bus. Coun., World Affairs Coun. Boston (treas., bd. dirs. 1966-67, v.p., bd. dirs. 1968-74), New Eng. Soc. N.Y.C., Harvard Varsity Club, Harvard Club (Boston). Clubs: Harvard (Boston); Varsity (Harvard). Office: Tootsie Roll Industries Inc 7401 S Cicero Ave Chicago IL 60629-5885

GORDON, MICHAEL MACKIN, lawyer; b. Boston, Apr. 15, 1950; s. Lawrence H. and Gladys (Mackin) G.; m. Linda Lowry, June 8, 1991; children: Alexandra, Harrison. AB, Vassar Coll., 1972; JD, Columbia U., 1976. Bar: N.Y. 1977, U.S. Dist. Ct. (so. and ea. dists. N.Y. 1977), D.C. 1980, U.S. Ct. Appeals (2d cir.) 1985, U.S. Supreme Ct. 1985, U.S. Claims Ct. 1991, U.S. Ct. Appeals (3d cir.), 1992, U.S. Dist. Ct. (no. dist.), Tex. 1993, U.S. Ct. Appeals (5th cir.) 1995, U.S. Dist. Ct. (ea. dist.) Tex. 1996, U.S. Dist. Ct. (no. dist. N.Y.) 1999. Assoc. Seward & Kissel, NYC, 1977-79, Cadwalader, Wickersham & Taft, NYC, 1979-85, ptnr., 1985—2005, King & Spalding, LLP, NYC, 2005—07, McKee Nelson LLP, NYC, 2007—. Mem.: ABA, N.Y. State Bar Assn., N.Y. County Lawyers Assn., Vassar (N.Y.C.). Home: 12 W 72nd St New York NY 10023-4163 Office: McKee Nelson LLP One Battery Pk Plz New York NY 10004 Office Phone: 917-777-4567. Business E-Mail: mgordon@mckeenelson.com.

GORDON, MILDRED HARRIET GROSS, hospital executive; b. Phila., Mar. 13, 1934; d. Nathan and Kate (Segal) Gross; m. Ivan H. Gordon, June 13, 1954; 1 child, Radene Lara. BS, Kutztown State U., Pa., 1960; MS, Med. Coll. Pa., 1970, PhD in Psychiatry, 1972. Tchr. sci. pub. schs., 1961—66; with Family Guidance Ctr., 1960—70; dir. dept. psychiatry Mental Health Treatment Ctr., Reading Hosp., West Reading, 1972—. Cons. Ctr. Mental Health-Reading Hosp. and Med. Ctr.; clin. instr. dept. psychiatry Med. Coll. Pa., Phila., 1972—78; clin. asst. prof. dept. psychiatry Temple U. Med. Sch.; pvt. practice, Wyomissing, Pa.; mem. Pa. Gov.'s Counl. on Drug and Alcohol Abuse, 1972—78. Bd. dirs. Confront, 1971—73, Coun. on Chem. Abuse, 1971—73. Named to Ct. Hon. Disting. Daus., Phila. H.S. Girls, 2002; recipient Svc. award, Reading Hosp. and Med. Ctr., 2003, Jasper G. Chen See M.D. Healthcare Profl. award, Caron Found., 2003; fellow, Falk Found. Fellow: Am. Coll. Forensic Examiners (diplomate); mem.: APA. Home: 1850 Oak Ln Reading PA 19604-1641 Office: 560 Van Reed Rd Wyomissing PA 19610-1799 Office Phone: 610-988-4947.

GORDON, MORRIS AARON, medical mycologist; b. Waterbury, Conn., Apr. 3, 1920; s. Samuel and Anna (Rubinstein) G.; m. Ruth Kathryn McKee, May 22, 1945 (div. 1970); children: Barbara Jean, David Spencer, Sarah Elizabeth. BS, City Coll. N.Y., NYC, 1940; MS, U. Chgo., 1942; PhD, Duke U., 1949. Diplomate Am. Bd. Microbiology; cert. lab. dir., N.Y. Lab. officer Regional Hosp., U.S. Army, Camp Blanding, Fla., 1945-46; mycologist Communicable Disease Ctr., Atlanta, 1949-54; lectr. Emory U., 1952—53; biol. warfare specialist Chem. Corps Training Command, Fort McClellan, Ala., 1954-55; assoc. prof. microbiology Med. Coll. S.C., Charleston, 1955-59; sr. to prin. rsch. scientist, dir. mycology labs. N.Y. State Dept. Health, Albany, 1959-87, dir. clin. microbiology & mycology labs., 1983-87, dir. emeritus clin. microbiology and mycology labs., 1987—96. Study sect. NIH, Washington, 1971-75; adv. com. Brown-Hazen Awards, N.Y.C., 1974-78; cons. VA Hosp., Albany, 1959-96; rsch. prof. Albany Med. Coll., 1975-90. Author: Laboratory Identification of Pathogenic Fungi, 1970; founder/editor Bull. Med. Mycol. Soc. Ams., 1976-94; contbr. over 150 articles to numerous profl. jours. Lt. comdr. USPHS, 1949-54. Recipient various rsch. grants NIH, teaching fellowship Duke U., 1947-49; Fulbright prof., Uruguay, 1978, Inter-Am. fellow La. State U., 1959. Mem. Med. Mycol. Soc. Ams. (pres. 1978-79, Benham award 1988), Internat. Soc. Human and Animal Mycology (v.p. 1982-85, Georg award 1991), Am. Soc. Microbiology (pres. mycology sect.), Phi Beta Kappa, Sigma Xi (pres. Albany chpt. 1972). Achievements include invention of latex test for cryptococcosis; initiation of diagnostic immunofluorescence for human fungal diseases; cultured pathogenic lipophilic yeasts; establishment of first presence in North America and first presence in humans of Dermatophilus infection. Address: 251 Springmoor Dr Raleigh NC 27615 Office Phone: 919-848-7251. Personal E-mail: gordon251@hotmail.com.

GORDON, NICHOLAS, broadcast and performing arts executive; b. Chgo., Apr. 12, 1928; s. Jacques and Ruth (Janeway) G.; m. Gladys Sack, Apr. 10, 1950 (div. 1976); children: Catherine, Christopher, Susan; m. Julie E. Miles, Aug. 12, 1977 (dec. May 3, 2005); m. Estelle Magowan, Aug. 18, 2006. Ph.B., U. Chgo., 1946. Reporter City News Bur., Chgo., 1948; radio-TV analyst William Weintraub Agy., NYC, 1949-50; dir. rsch. and sales planning Keystone Broadcasting Sys., NYC, 1951-52; with NBC, 1953-74, mgr. rates and program evaluation, 1956-58, mgr. sales devel. NBC-TV Sales, 1959-60, dir. sales devel. NBC-TV Sales, 1960-63, account exec. TV sales, 1964-68, v.p. Ea. sales, 1968-70, v.p. radio network sales NYC, 1970-74; pres. Keystone Broadcasting Sys., NYC, 1974-85, chmn., 1985—. Vice chmn. Riverdale Cmty. Coun., 1968-71; mem. N.Y.C. Planning Bd., Riverdale, 1969-75, vice chmn., 1972-74; pres. Riverdale Cmty. Planning Assn., 1972-76; mem. vol. corps N.Y.C. Dept. Commerce, 1968-70; bd. dirs. Wave Hill Ctr. Environ. Studies, 1969-80, exec. v.p., 1970-80; mem. Bronx Democratic County Com., 1968; bd. dirs. Music Mountain, Inc., Falls Village, Conn., 1970-, pres., 1974-; bd. dirs. Riverdale Neighborhood House, Bronx, N.Y., 1970-74, Bronx Coun. Arts, 1970-72, Phila. Orch. Media Inst., 1998-2003; trustee St. Hilda's and St. Hugh's Sch., 1965-76; justice of peace, Conn., 2004—. Decorated chevalier l'Ordre des Arts et des Lettres (France) Mem. Century Assn., Univ. Club, Explorers Club (N.Y.C.), Tavern Club, Cliff Dwellers Club (Chgo.), East India Club (London). Office: Keystone Broadcasting Syst PO Box 1739 Sharon CT 06069-1739 Office Phone: 860-364-2080. Business E-Mail: ngordon@keystonebroadcasting.com.

GORDON, PAUL JOHN, management educator; b. NYC, Oct. 14, 1921; s. Arthur L. and Georgiana (McDonough) G.; m. Mary Brigid Keany, Jan. 28, 1950; children: Brian Joseph, Peter Christopher, Martha Ann, Hugh John, Paul John. BBA, CCNY, 1945; MBA, Cornell U., 1949; PhD, Syracuse U., 1958. With Brooks Bros., NYC, 1941-43, Lago Oil & Transp. Co., Ltd., Netherlands W. Indies, also Bayway Refinery, Linden, N.J. and Standard Oil Co. N.J., 1943-48; asst. prof. Cornell U., Ithaca, NY, 1949-54; prof., chmn. dept. mgmt. Sch. Bus. Duquesne U., Pitts., 1954-55; rsch. cons. Sloan-Kettering Meml. Ctr. for Cancer, NYC, 1955-56; assoc. prof. bus. adminstrn., planning dir. grad. program hosp. adminstrn. Sch. Bus. Adminstrn. Emory U., Atlanta, 1956—59; assoc. prof. Grad. Sch. Bus. Ind. U., 1959-63, prof., chmn. dept. mgmt. adminstrv. studies Grad. Sch. Bus., 1963-67, prof. mgmt. Grad. Sch. Bus., 1963-89, chmn. adminstrv. and behavioral studies Grad. Sch. Bus., 1980-83, prof. emeritus mgmt. Grad. Sch. Bus., 1989—; disting. prof. mgmt. St. John's U., NYC, 1990-93. Fulbright/FLAD chair in strategic mgmt. Tech. U. Lisbon, Portugal, 1997; chief U.S. Dept. State-Ford Found. party Ljubljana U., Yugoslavia, 1967; vis. prof. Trinity Coll., Dublin, 1967; vis. prof., Fulbright lectr. Instituto Post-Universitario Per Lo Studio Dell Organizzazione Aziendale, Turin, Italy, 1963; Fulbright lectr., cons. Nat. U. Republic Uruguay, 1970; disting. guest Systems Rsch. Inst., Polish Acad. Scis., 1980; vis. Fulbright prof. Helsinki Sch. Econs. and Bus. Adminstrn., Finland, 1990; mem. U.S. AID Mgmt. Edn. Reconnaissance Survey, India, also Pakistan, 1971; cons. IRS, 1956-63, Am. Coll. Hosp. Adminstrs., 1957—; with Inst. Higher Studies of Adminstrn., Caracas, Venezuela, 1973-79. Editor Acad. Mgmt. Jour, 1964-66, mem. editorial bd., 1961-75; editorial cons. adv. bd.: Bus. Horizons, Hosp. Adminstrn, W.B. Saunders Co.; contbr. articles to profl. jours. Mem. Cath. Commn. on Intellectual and Cultural Affairs, 1973—, chmn., 1980-81; chmn. UNESCO multi-nat. bus. conf. Ind. U., 1972; chmn. adv. screening com. in bus. mgmt. Coun. for Internat. Exch. of Scholars, Fulbright-Hays Program, 1979-80, 90-93, chmn., 1991-93; bd. dirs. Ind. Newman Found., 1971-82; mem. adv. bd. Abbey Press, St. Meinrad, Ind., 1991-95. Fellow, IBM, 1964; grantee, Ford Found., 1963, 1966, 1970. Fellow Acad. Mgmt. (v.p. program 1967, pres. 1969, Disting. Svc. award 1992), Internat. Acad. Mgmt., Am. Acad. Med. Adminstrs. (hon.); mem. Fulbright Assn. (life). Home: 1422 S Winfield Rd Bloomington IN 47401-6152 E-mail: pauljgordon@aol.com.

GORDON, PHILLIP, lawyer; b. Potgietersrus, South Africa, July 11, 1943; m. Norma Gordon. BA, U. Witwaterstrand, South Africa, 1964, BA with honors, 1965; BA, Oxford U., 1967; JD, U. Chgo. Law Sch., 1969; MA, Oxford U., 1973. Bar: Ill. 1969, NY 1973 (inactive). Interim gen. counsel Strategic Hotel Capital, Chgo., 1997-98; ptnr. Perkins Coie, LLP, 2003—. Tchg. assoc. Northwestern U. Sch. Law, Chgo., 1967-68. Author: Ill. Practice Consultant, Midwest Transactional Guide, 1981. Dir. Lyric Opera Chgo.; chmn., trustee Spertus Inst. Jewish Studies, Chgo.; advising fellow Oxford U. Ctr. Socio-Legal Studies, London. Mem. ABA, Chgo. Bar Assn., Hotel Devel. Coun., Internat. Coun. Urban Land Inst. Office: Perkins Coie LLP 131 S Dearborn St Ste 1700 Chicago IL 60603-5559 E-mail: pgordon@perkinscoie.com.

GORDON, PHILLIP BRUCE, mayor; b. Chgo., Apr. 18, 1951; s. Sid and Judy Gordon; m. Christa Severns; children: David, Jeff, Rachel, Jacob. BA in History Edn., U. Ariz.; JD cum laude, Ariz. State U. Chmn. Landiscor Aerial Photography Co.; atty. Pearlstein Law Firm; councilman Phoenix (Ariz.) City Coun., 1997—2003; mayor City of Phoenix, 2003—. Founder, chmn. Slumlord Task Force; chmn. Ariz. Child Occupant Protection Task Force, Men's Anti-Violence Network; bd. dir. Voice for Crime Victims; mem Madison Sch. Bd. Bd. dir. Orpheum Theatre Found., Downtown YMCA, Phoenix (Ariz.) Ballet Co., Roosevelt Action Assn. Office: City Hall 200 W Washington St 11th Fl Phoenix AZ 85003-1611*

GORDON, RACHEL SINGER, editor; b. Spokane, Wash., Apr. 16, 1970; d. Gary David and Mary Kiernan Singer; m. Todd Gordon, June 1, 1997; children: Samuel Lee children: Jacob Alexander. BA, Carleton Coll., Northfield, Minn., 1992; MA, Northwestern U., Evanston, Ill., 1994; MLIS, Dominican U. (formerly Rosary Coll.), River Forest, Ill., 1996. Head computer svcs. Franklin Park Libr., Ill., 1999—2002. Consulting editor Info. Today, Inc., Books, Medford, NJ, 2005—; webmaster LISjobs.com, Villa Park, Ill., 1996—; editor, publisher Info Career Trends, 2000—. Author: The NextGen Librarian's Survival Guide, The Accidental Library Manager, The Librarian's Guide to Writing for Publication, The Accidental Systems Librarian, The Information Professional's Guide to Career Development Online, Teaching the Internet in Libraries; author, editor: Information Tomorrow, 2007; columnist Libr. Jour., NYC, 2002—, Emerald, UK, 2004—, Computers in Librs., Medford, NJ, 2006—. Recipient Movers & Shakers award, Libr. Jour., 2002; scholar EBSCO/ALA, 2004. Mem.: ALA, Beta Phi Mu. Jewish. Home: PO Box 6931 Villa Park IL 60181 Home Phone: 630-620-6662. Personal E-mail: rachel@lisjobs.com. Business E-Mail: rgordon@infotoday.com.

GORDON, ROBERT A., food products executive, lawyer; b. 1952; Grad., Yale U., 1973; JD, U. Va., 1976. Litig. ptnr. Pillsbury Madison & Sutro, 1984—99; dep. gen. counsel Safeway, Inc., Pleasanton, Calif., 1999—2000, sr. v.p., gen. counsel, 2000—. Office: Safeway Inc 5918 Stoneridge Mall Rd Pleasanton CA 94588-3229 Office Phone: 925-467-3000. Office Fax: 510-467-3323.*

GORDON, ROBERT DANA, transplant surgeon; b. NYC, Jan. 25, 1945; s. Gerson George and Muriel Ruth (Danish) G.; m. Linda Susan Svirsky, July 9, 1970; children: David Charles, Daniel Lawrence. BA, Amherst Coll., 1966; MD, Cornell U., 1971. Diplomate Am. Bd. Surgery. Intern in surgery Mass. Gen. Hosp., Boston, 1971-72, resident in surgery, 1972-74, 77-78, rsch. fellow Harvard Med. Sch., 1974-76; vis. scientist transplantation biology unit Clin. Rsch. Ctr., Harrow, England, 1974-76; clin. fellow Harvard Med. Sch., Boston, 1977-78; asst. prof. surgery U. Colo., Denver, 1979-83, U. Pitts., 1983-88, assoc. prof., 1988-92; prof. surgery, chief liver transplant svc. Emory U. Sch. Medicine, Atlanta, 1992-98; sr. med. dir. transplantation Roche Labs., Nutley, NJ, 1999—2006; v.p. med. affairs UCB, Inc., Smyrna, Ga., 2006; sr. dir. med. and clin. rsch. LCPharma Inc., Jersey City, 2006—. Attending surgeon Egleston Children's Hosp., Atlanta, 1992-98; attending surgeon, co-dir. organ transplant svcs., Emory U. Hosp., Atlanta, 1992-98; chmn. fgn. rels. com. United Network Organ Sharing, Richmond, Va., 1987-90. Bd. dirs. Pitts. chpt. ARC; mem., chair tng. and edn. com. Corp. of Jackson Lab., Bar Harbor, Maine, 1994—2001. Fellow ACS; mem. Internat. Soc. Cardiovasc. Surgery, Internat. Soc. for Heart and Lung Transplantation, Ctrl. Surg. Assn., Soc. Univ. Surgeons, Am. Soc. Transplant Surgeons, Am. Soc. Transplantation, Transplantation Soc., Internat. Liver Transplantation Soc., Am. Assn. for Study Liver Diseases, Pan Am. Med. Assn. (pres. sect. organ transplantation 1992), Pa. Soc. Biomed. Rsch. (bd. dirs. 1991-92). Avocations: computer science, skiing, hiking, bicycling, flight simulation. Office: 2500 Harborside Fin Ctr Plz 5 25th Fl Jersey City NJ 07311 Home Phone: 404-843-2010. Personal E-mail: robert.gordon@mindspring.com. Business E-Mail: rgo@lcpharma.com.

GORDON, ROBERT EUGENE, lawyer; b. LA, Sept. 20, 1932; s. Harry Maurice and Minnie (Shaffer); 1 child, Victor Marten. BA, UCLA, 1954; LLB, U. Calif., Berkeley, 1959, JD, 1960; cert., U. Hamburg, Germany, 1960. Bar: Calif. 1960. Assoc. Lillick, Geary, McHose, Roethke & Myers, LA, 1960—64, Schoichet & Rifkind, Beverly Hills, Calif., 1964—67; ptnr. Baerwitz & Gordon, Beverly Hills, 1967—69, Ball, Hunt, Hart, Brown & Baerwitz, Beverly Hills, 1970—71; of counsel Jacobs, Sills & Coblentz, San Francisco, 1972—78; ptnr. Gordon & Hodge, San Francisco, 1978—81; pvt. practice San Francisco, 1981—89, Corte Madera, Calif., 1989—2002, Sausalito, Calif., 2002—. Adj. prof. entertainment law Hastings Coll. Law, San Francisco, 1990-91, U. Calif., Berkeley, 1992. Served to 1st lt. U.S. Army, 1954-56. Mem. ABA (forum com. on entertainment and sports law), LA Copyright Soc. (bd. trustees 1970-71), Copyright Soc. of USA. Avocations: bicycling, skiing. Home: 35 Elaine Ave Mill Valley CA 94941-1014 Office: One Harbor Dr Ste 106 Sausalito CA 94965 Office Phone: 415-331-0611. Business E-Mail: lawmuse@pacbell.net.

GORDON, ROBERT JAMES, economics professor; b. Boston, Sept. 3, 1940; s. Robert Aaron and Margaret (Shaughnessy) G.; m. Julie S. Peyton, June 22, 1963. AB, Harvard U., 1962; MA, Oxford U., Eng., 1969; PhD, MIT, 1967. Asst. prof. econs. Harvard U., 1967-68; asst. prof. U. Chgo., 1968-73; prof. econs. Northwestern U., Evanston, Ill., 1973—, Stanley G. Harris prof. social scis., 1987—, chair econs. dept., 1992-96. Rsch. assoc. Nat. Bur. Econ Rsch., 1968—; mem. Brookings Panel Econ. Activity, 1970—; co-chmn. Internat. Seminar Macroecons., 1978-94; mem. exec. com. Conf. Rsch., Income and Wealth, 1978-83; mem. panel rev. productivity measures NAS, 1977-79; cons. bd. govs. Fed. Res. Sys., 1973-83, U.S. Dept. Treasury, 1967-80, U.S. Congl. Budget Office, 1996—, U.S. Bur. Econ. Analysis, 1999—; mem. Nat. Commn. on Consumer Price Index, 1995-97. Author: Macroeconomics, 1978, 10th edit., 2006, Milton Friedman's Monetary Framework, 1974, Challenges to Interdependent Economies, 1979, The American Business Cycle: Continuity and Change, 1986, The Measurement of Durable Goods Prices, 1990, International Volatility and Economic Growth, 1991, The Economics of New Goods, 1997, Inflation, Unemployment and Productivity, 2003; editor Jour. Polit. Economy, 1970-73. Recipient Lustrum prize Erasmus U., 1999; Marshall fellow, 1962-64; Ford Found. fellow, 1966-67; grantee NSF, 1971—2004; Guggenheim Meml. Found. fellow, 1980-81; rsch. fellow German Marshall Fund, 1985-86. Fellow AAAS, Econometric Soc. (treas. 1975—2005); mem. Am. Econ. Assn. (bd. editors 1975-77, mem. exec. com. 1981-83), Phi Beta Kappa Office: Northwestern U Dept Econs Evanston IL 60208-2600 Home Phone: 847-869-3544; Office Phone: 847-491-3616. E-mail: rjg@northwestern.edu.

GORDON, ROBERT JAY, lawyer, educator; b. Miami, Fla., May 10, 1956; s. Jerome B. and Florence (Lipschitz) G.; m. Leslie C. Gottlieb, Sept. 5, 1982. BA with distinction, U. Mich., 1977; JD with honors, George Washington U., Washington, 1980. Bar: Pa. 1980, US Dist. Ct. (ea. dist.) Pa. 1981, US Ct. Appeals (3d cir.) 1984, NJ 1985, US Dist. Ct. NJ 1985, US Supreme Ct., 1986, NY 1987, US Dist. Ct. (so. dist.) NY 1987, US Dist Ct. (ea. dist.) NY 1992. Asst. dist. atty. Phila. Dist. Atty.'s Office, 1980-84; assoc.& ptnr. Greitzer & Locks, Phila., 1984—1991; mem. & chief trial atty. Weitz & Luxenberg, NYC. Adj. prof. Temple U., Phila., 1983-85. Contbr. articles to profl. jours. Named one of Top 40 Lawyers Under 40 Nat. Law Jour., 1995. Mem. Assn. Trial Lawyers Am., ABA, Assn. Bar City of NY, NY State Trial Lawyers Assn., Trial Lawyers for Pub. Justice, Pa. Trial Lawyers Assn., Pa. Bar Assn., Phila. Bar Assn. Democrat. Jewish. Office: Weitz & Luxenberg 180 Maiden Lane New York NY 10038 Office Phone: 212-558-5500. Business E-Mail: rgordon@weitzlux.com.

GORDON, ROMA DIANNE, music educator; b. Cherokee, Iowa, Dec. 23, 1945; d. Clarence Roy and Lillian Mae Wilkie; m. John Kinney Gordon, June 4, 1972; children: Matthew Joseph, Ann Wilkie. B in Music Edn., Drake U., 1968. Lic. Tchg. Wis., 1968, Iowa, 1968. Elem. music tchr. Beloit Pub. Sch., Beloit, Wis., 1968—71; music tchr. Storm Lake Cmty. Sch., Storm Lake, Iowa, 1971—73; elem. music tchr. Meriden-Cleghorn Sch. Dist., Cleghorn, Iowa, 1975—77, Cherokee Cmty. Sch., Cherokee, Iowa, 1986—. Mem. of coop. curriculum devel. project Iowa Western Hills Edn. Assn., Sioux City, Iowa, 1990—93; mem. on the early childhood fine arts del. to the Republic of China People to People, Seattle, 1994—94; mentor for new tchr. Cherokee Cmty. Schs., Cherokee, Iowa, 2003—.

Contbr. scientific papers. Sec., treas. Cedar Cemetery Assn., Larrabee, Iowa, 1985—2005; organist Meml. Presbyn. Ch., Cherokee, Iowa, 1978—; mem. bd. Plains Area Mental Health, Le Mars, Iowa, 1985—87. Mem.: NEA/ISEA (corr.), Music Educators Nat. Conf. (corr.), PEO (corr.; treas. 2001—03). Presbyterian. Avocations: walking, reading, antique dishes. Home: 4688 Old 21 Rd Cherokee IA 51012 Home Phone: 712-225-4638; Office Phone: 712-225-6760.

GORDON, SANDY GALE COMBS, medical/surgical nurse; b. Lafollette, Tenn., Sept. 8, 1950; d. Wise and Edna Leona (Boshears) Combs; m. Ralph William Gordon, Aug. 30, 1975 (dec. Feb. 1998). Diploma, Middletown Hosp., 1971. RN, Ohio. Staff nurse Middletown Hosp., Ohio, 1971—79; pub. health nurse Bur. Pub. Health, Middletown, Ohio, 1979—82, ret., 1982. Founder, pres. Middleton Poetry Circle, 1996. Named Internat. Women of Yr., 1994-95. Mem. Middletown Hosp. Alumni Assn. Home: 1107 Ellen Dr Middletown OH 45042-3341 Personal E-mail: sgordon@erinet.com.

GORDON, SANFORD DANIEL, economics professor; b. Newark, June 23, 1924; s. Harry Louis and Beatrice (Safris) G.; m. Alice Lillian Pressman, May 27, 1948; children— Ellen Ann, Eric Alan. Student, Tulane U., 1942; BS magna cum laude, NYU, 1947, MA, 1948, PhD, 1953. Instr. econ. NYU, 1948-50; mem. faculty State U. Coll., Oneonta, NY, 1950—, prof. econs., 1957—, chmn. dept., 1960—; asst. vice chancellor for policy and planning State U. N.Y. Central Adminstrn., 1972-76, provost for policy analysis, 1976-79; exec. dir. N.Y. State Coun. on Econ. Edn., 1979-89; prof. econs. Russell Sage Coll., 1979-89. Adj. prof. econs. U. So. Fla., 1989-99; lectr. to elder hostels; econ. editor Kennikat Press., Inc., Port Washington, N.Y., 1970—; cons. to govt., industry, banks, pub. schs., 1954—; vis. prof. State U. N.Y., Buffalo, 1965, U. Miami, 1967. Author: (with J. Witchel) An Introduction to the American Economy, 1967, A Visual Analysis of the American Economy, 1968, (with G. Dawson) The American Economy, 1969, Introductory Economics, 1972, 7th edit., 1991; (with Conover and Ramstadder) Business Dynamics, 1982, 2d edit., 1988, The Economy of New York State, 1987, Basic Economic Principles, 1988, Economics U$A: A Resource Guide for Teachers, 1988, (with A. Stafford) Applying Economic Principles, 1994; lectr., writer: pub. TV series The American Economy, Conversations on Economic Issues, 1970—. Mem. Parks Commn., also Charter Revision Commn., Oneonta, 1957—; v.p. Oneonta Brotherhood, 1958; Dem. candidate for 13th Congl. Dist., Fla., for U.S. Ho. of Reps. Served to sgt. USAAF, 1942-44. Recipient Kazajian Found. award, 1967, Bessie B. Moore Service award , 1987. Mem. N.Y. Econ. Assn. (past pres.), AAUP (past pres. N.Y. conf.) Home: 7127 Fairway Bend Ln Sarasota FL 34243-3608 E-mail: Budalice@aol.com. *Success has less to do with innate ability than with self-confidence, motivation, and perhaps most important, resiliancy.*

GORDON, SCOTT (HARRY SCOTT BUEHLMEIER), entertainer, actor; b. Dumont, NJ, Oct. 12, 1949; s. Harry Gordon and Florence Victoria (Bielawski) B.; m. Dian Mary Kenlon, Nov. 10, 1973. Grad. high sch., Mahwah, NJ. Pres. Scott Gordon Enterprises, Inc., Paramus, N.J., 1974—; performer, writer The Uncle Floyd Show, West Orange, N.J., 1976—, Gordon and Rogue, 1993—; ptnr. WWW.PlanetShowbiz.com, 1999—2001; writer Burns and Hope at Madison Sq. Garden, NYC, 1989. Audio cons. Playhouse on the Mall, Paramus, NJ, 1974; make-up cons. Ken's Costumes, Fair Lawn, NJ, 1976—94, SYSOP/Cons. Genie On-Line Svc., 1990—97; rec. artist Mercury Records; comedy team mem. Gordon and Rogue; mem. nominating com. MixMag. TEC Awards, 1998—. Author, editor (Profl. mag.) Psychicos, 1978-80; author (column) Vibrations, 1987; maker radio commls.; San Antonio Rose with Willie Nelson, B-52s, Labour of Lust, First Exposure; enbr. (radio programs) The Italian American Serenade, The Colavita Music Hall, Italian Melodies, Sunday Funnies; air personality Remember When, 1987-98, syndicates 1995; entertainer Nickelodeon Turkey TV; appeared on Broadway with Collinsport Players, 1995; cast mem. Uncle Floyd's Last Authentic American Traveling Burlesque Show, 2005—. Mem. AFTRA, Psychic Entertainers Assn. (bd. dirs. 1978-80, founder), Audio Engrng. Soc., Circle Tri Corbies, The Radio Repertory Co. of Am. Avocations: music, guitar, bass, drums. Office: Scott Gordon Enterprises Inc PO Box 791 Paramus NJ 07653-0791 Office Phone: 201-670-0054. Business E-Mail: info@sge-inc.com.

GORDON, SHARON ANN, mathematics and pre-school educator; b. Newton, NJ, Aug. 8, 1945; d. Kenneth William Gordon and Hazel Emma Pascoe. Attended, Centenary Coll., 1963—64; BA in Math., Chemistry, and History, Drew U., 1967; MEd, Montclair U., 1970. Cert. Secondary Sch. Math. Tchr. (seventh through twelfth grades) NJ Bd. Examiners, 1969. Math. tchr. Sparta HS, NJ, 1968—2000; pre-sch. tchr. aide Cir. Friends Pre-Sch., Sparta, 2000—. Mem. Sparta United Meth. Ch., 1956—. Recipient Creative Writing award, Centenary Coll., 1963. Mem.: NEA, Sussex County Retired Educators Assn., NJ Retired Educators Assn., Jack Russell Terrier Club Am., Phi Theta Kappa. Methodist. Avocations: poetry writing, baking, cooking, counted cross stitch, reading.

GORDON, STEPHEN LOUIS, lawyer; b. Syracuse, NY, Oct. 31, 1956; s. Richard E. and Carole (Silverstein) G.; m. Lorraine (Winheim) Gordon, Oct 24, 1999; children, Samantha and Dana; 2 stepchildren, Matthew Fenster and Emily Fenster. AB, Cornell U., 1978; JD, Harvard U., 1981. Bar: N.Y 1982. Ptnr., tax dept. Cravath, Swaine & Moore LLP, NYC, 1981—. Mem. ABA (tax sect.), N.Y. State Bar Assn. (tax sct.), Assn. of Bar of City of N.Y. Office: Cravath Swaine & Moore 825 8th Ave Fl 38 New York NY 10019-7475 Office Phone: 212-474-1704. Office Fax: 212-474-3700. Business E-Mail: gordon@cravath.com.

GORDON, STEPHEN MAURICE, manufacturing company executive, rancher; b. Chgo., Aug. 20, 1942; s. Milton A. and Elinor (Loeff) G.; m. Helene Lindow, Feb. 11, 1978 (div. Mar. 1998); 2 children: Hallie Lindow, Lacey Edison; m. Marilee Ann Enright, Mar. 21, 1998. Student, Middlebury Coll., 1960-61; BA, U. Chgo., 1964; JD, NYU, 1967; D.I.L., Cambridge U., Eng., 1968. Bar: N.Y. State 1968. Aide to Vice Pres. Hubert Humphrey, Democratic Nat. Com., Washington, 1968; assoc. firm Marshall, Bratter, Greene, Allison & Tucker, NYC, 1968-70; sr. rsch. assoc. Halle & Stieglitz, Inc., NYC, 1970-72, v.p., 1972-75, pres., 1975-79; pres., chief exec. officer Irvin Industries Inc., NYC, 1979-89; pres. Diamond G Ranch Inc., Dubois, Wyo. Chmn. bd. dirs. Vincennes Steel Corp., 1989—97; mem. vis. com. U. Chgo. Mem. Nat. Wildlife Art Mus. (dir., treas.), MacLean-Fogg (dir.), Am. Red Angus Assn., Young Pres.' Orgn., Beta Gamma Sigma, Psi Upsilon. Home: Diamond G Ranch Dunoir Rd Dubois WY 82513 Office: PO Box 1887 Wilson WY 83014

GORDON, STEWART LYNELL, musician, educator; b. Olathe, Kans., Aug. 28, 1930; s. Lynell Frank and Guanetta (Stewart) Gordon. Diploma, State Conservatory Music, 1951; BA, U.Kans., 1954, MA, 1955; D of Musical Arts, Eastman Sch., Rochester, NY, 1965. Asst. prof. music Wilmington (Ohio) Coll., 1957—60; from asst. prof. to assoc. prof. to prof. U. Md., Coll. Park, 1960—86, music dept. chair, 1979—86; v.p. for acad. affairs, provost Queens Coll., Flushing, NY, 1986—89; prof. keyboard studies U. So. Calif., LA, 1989—, chair keyboard studies, dir undergrad. studies, 1996—2004. Adjudicator Gina Bachauer Internat. Piano competition, Canadian Music Competition finals, Gilmore Found. Nominating Com.; touring pianist Europe, 1955—60, N. Am., 1960—80, Middle East, 1968, Asia, 1977—79; founder, dir. Wm. Kapell Internat. Piano Competition, Md., 1970—85, Savannah On Stage Festival and Am. Trads. Competition, 1989—2002, Cultural Heritage and Great Gospel Competitions, Queens, NY, 1990—91. Author: Etudes for Piano Teachers, Essays on the Teachers' Art, 1995, A History of Keyboard Music for the Piano and Its Forerunners, 1996, Mastering the Art of Performance, 2005; co-author (with others): The Well Tempered Keyboard Teacher 2d edit., 1999; composer: Spirit of the Navy, 1955; editor: Beethoven Piano Sonatas, 2002, 2005. Lt. j.g. USN, 1954—57. Recipient Danforth Tchr. Study grant, Danforth Found., 1963—64, Lifetime Achievement award, Md. Music Tchrs. Assn., 1983, Ramo Music Faculty award, U. So. Calif., 2001. Mem.: Calif. Music Tchrs. Assn., Nat. Music Tchrs. Assn. (adjudicator nat. music competition finals), Phi Kappa Phi, Phi Kappa Lambda, Phi Beta Kappa. Avocations: gardening, bull terriers, tropical fish, languages. Home: 3262 Starline Dr Rancho Palos Verdes CA 90275-6308 Office Phone: 213-740-3118. Personal E-mail: stewgor@sbcglobal.net. Business E-Mail: stewartg@usc.edu.

GORDON, STORROW MOSS, lawyer, information technology executive; b. 1952; married; 2 children. BA, U. Tex.; JD, So. Meth. U. Bar: 1978. Ptnr. Johnson & Wortley, P.C.; sr. atty. Electronic Data Sys. Corp., Plano, Tex., 1991, legal mgr., corp. acquisitions and fin., 1992—96, sec. governance com. bd. dirs., 1996—99, dir. bd. ops., 1999—2000, dep. gen. counsel, 2002—05, exec. v.p., gen. counsel, 2005—. Named Super Lawyer, Tex. Monthly mag., 2004, 2005. Office: Electronic Data Sys Inc 5400 Legacy Dr Plano TX 75024 Office Phone: 972-605-6000.*

GORDON, STUART A., lawyer; BA, U. Pa., 1962; JD, NYU, 1965. Bar: NY 1965, US Dist. Ct. So. and Ea. Dists. NY 1966. Mng. ptnr., mem. ops. group Bryan Cave LLP, NYC. Office: Bryan Cave LLP 1290 Ave of the Americas New York NY 10104 Office Phone: 212-541-2060. E-mail: sagordon@bryancave.com.

GORDON, SUSAN C., broadcast executive; B in Econs., Lake Forest Coll., Ill.; M in Accountancy, NYU. CPA. Auditor KPMG Peat Marwick; with Viacom, 1981—2005, contr. Viacom Broadcast Group, 1985—86, v.p. internal audit, 1986—95, CFO Madison Sq. Garden, 1994—95, v.p., contr., chief acctg. officer, 1995—2002, sr. v.p. contr., chief acctg. officer, 2002—05; sr. v.p., corp. contr., chief acctg. officer CBS Corp., 2006—. Office: CBS Corp 51 W 52nd St New York NY 10019-6188 Office Phone: 212-975-4321.*

GORDON, WALTER KELLY, retired academic administrator, retired language educator; b. Bklyn., Jan. 25, 1930; s. William Benjamin and Grace Adele (Kelly) G.; m. Lydia Caroline Fruchtman, Aug. 29, 1959; 1 child, Karyn Gay. AB, Clark U., 1950; MA, U. Pa., 1956, PhD, 1961. Instr. Cedar Crest Coll., 1959-61; faculty Rutgers U., Camden, 1961-97, prof., dean coll., 1974-81, acad. dean, provost Camden campus, 1981-97; ret., 1997. Cons. Campbells Soup Co., 1976-94. Author: (with J.L. Sanderson) Exposition and the English Language, 1963, 2d edit., 1968, Literature in Critical Perspectives, 1969. Bd. dirs. Walt Whitman Internat. Poetry Center, 1974-77. Served to lt. USNR, 1951-56. Recipient Lindback award for disting. teaching, 1970 Home: 2803 Salem Dr Riverton NJ 08077-4027 Office: Rutgers U Camden Coll Arts & Scis 379 Armitage Hall Camden NJ 08102 E-mail: gordonwalterk@comcast.net.

GORDON, WILLIAM BINGHAM (BING GORDON), software marketing executive; b. Detroit, Feb. 5, 1950; s. William Chalmers and Barbara (Bingham) G.; m Debra Radabaugh, Sept. 27, 1980; 1 child Chloe. BA in English, Yale U., New Haven, Conn., 1972; MBA, Stanford Grad. Sch. of Bus., Stanford, Calif., 1978. Actor Actors Equity, NYC, 1973; fisherman Astoria, Oreg., 1974-76; product mktg. Fairchild Test SYstems, San Jose, Calif., 1978-80; acct. exec. Ogilvy and Mather, San Francisco, 1980-81; acct. supr. Ketchum Communication, San Francisco, 1982; dir. mktg. Electronic Arts, San Mateo, Calif., 1982-83, v.p. mktg., 1984-86, v.p. GM Entertainment, 1987-89, sr. v.p. mktg. and planning, 1990—98, exec. v.p., chief creative officer, 1998—. Dir. Electronic Arts Ltd., London, 1990; sec. Debra Radabaugh Assn., Menlo Park, Calif., 1984. Steering com., San Francisco Museum of Mdern Art Archtl. and Design Dept., 1978. Recipient All New England Lacrosse, ECAC, 1972. Avocations: ice hockey, computer games, skiing, travel, parenting. Office: Electronic Arts 1820 Gateway Dr San Mateo CA 94404-4022

GORDON, WILLIAM CHARLES, academic administrator; m. Kathryn Gordon; children: Jason, Scott, Kate, Jonathan. Bachelor's degree, Master's degree, Wake Forest U.; PhD in Exptl. Psychology, Rutgers U. Asst. prof. psychology SUNY, Binghamton, 1973-78; tchr. psychology dept. U. N.Mex., Albuquerque, 1978, chair psychology dept., 1990, interim dean Coll. Arts and Scis., 1992, dean, 1993, provost, v.p. for acad. affairs, 1996, interim pres., 1998—99, pres., 1999—2002; provost Wake Forest U., 2002—. Office: Office of the Provost Wake Forest U 1834 Wake Forest Rd Winston Salem NC 27106 Business E-Mail: gordonwc@wfu.edu.

GORDON, WILLIAM EDWIN, physicist, educator, electrical engineer, academic administrator; b. Paterson, NJ, Jan. 8, 1918; s. William and Mary (Scott) G.; m. Elva Freile, June 22, 1941 (dec. Feb. 2002); children: Larry Scott, Nancy Lynn; m. Elizabeth Bolgiano, Aug. 31, 2003. BA, Montclair State Coll., NJ, 1939, MA, 1942; MS, NYU, 1946; PhD, Cornell U., Ithaca, NY, 1953. Registered profl. engr., Tex. Cons. radio engr. Strumberg Carison G.E. Airforce, NAVY, ARCO, 1950—; cons. engr., 1950—; assoc. prof. Cornell U., 1953-59, prof., 1959-65; Walter R. Read prof. engring. Arecibo Ionospheric Obs., PR, 1965; prof. elec. engring. and space physics and astronomy Rice U., Houston, 1966-86, dean engring. and sci., 1966-75, dean Sch. Natural Scis., 1975-80, provost, v.p., 1980-86, disting. prof. emeritus, 1986—; fgn. sec. NAS, 1986-90. Conceived, directed design and early operation of Arecibo Obs. and 1000 foot antenna, 1960-65 (named Milestone in Elec. Engring. and Landmark in Mech. Engring. 2001); chmn. bd. trustees Upper Atmosphere Rsch. Corp., 1971, 73-78, Univ. Corp. for Atmospheric Rsch., 1979-81, 86-89, 91-92; trustee Cornell U., 1976-80; mem. Arecibo Obs. Adv. Bd., 1977-80, 90-93. Bd. dirs. Taping for the Blind, Houston, 1994-2002. Capt. USAAF, 1942-46. Recipient Balth. Vander Pol award for disting. rsch. in radio sci., 1966; 50th Anniversary medal Am. Meteorol. Soc., 1969, Arktowski medal, 1984, Arecibo Telescope award, 2001; Guggenheim fellow, 1972-73. Fellow IEEE (chmn. profl. group on antennas and propagation 1964-65), Am. Geophys. Union; mem. AAAS, NAS, NAE, Am. Acad. Arts and Scis., Internat. Sci. Radio Union (v.p. 1975-81, pres. 1981-84, hon. pres. 1990—), Internat. Coun. Sci. Unions (v.p. 1988-93), Am. Meteorology Soc., Philos. Soc. Tex., Cosmos Club, Sigma Xi, Tau Beta Pi, Kappa Delta Pi, Sigma Kappa Nu, Phi Kappa Phi. Achievements include research in radio scattering. Personal E-mail: bg72@cornell.edu.

GORDON, WYCLIFFE, trombonist, jazz musician, music educator, composer; b. Waynesboro, Ga., 1967; s. Lucius Gordon. Leader Wycliffe Gordon Quartet; former mem. Wynton Marsalis Septet, 1989, Lincoln Ctr. Jazz Orch., 1989, Gully Low Jazz Band; mem. Jazz Studies Program faculty Juilliard Sch. Composer: (songs) NPR Theme Song, 2003; musician: (albums with Wynton Marsalis, Lincoln Ctr. Jazz include) Crescent City Christmas Card, 1989, original soundtrack from Tune in Tomorrow, 1989, Blue Interlude, 1991, Citi Movement, 1992, In This House, On This Morning, 1992, Joe Cool's Blues, 1994, Blood on the Fields, 1995, Jump Start & Jazz, 1996, Big Train, 1999, Live at the Village Vanguard, 1999, Marciac Suite, 1999, Reeltime, 1999, (solo albums include) Bone Structure, 1996, Slidin' Home, 1999, The Gospel Truth, 2000, The Search, 2000, What You Dealin' With, 2001, We, 2002, The Joyride, 2003, Dig This!!, 2003, In the Cross, 2004, Cone's Coup, 2006, Standards Only, 2006, This Rhythm on My Mind, 2006. Mem. US Statesmen of Jazz. Recipient Critic's Choice award for Best Trombone, Jazz Journalists Assn., 2000, Trombonist of Yr. award, 2001, 2002, Vanguard award, ASCAP Found., 2007. Office: Coup de Cone Music Inc Ste 4 126 W 121 St New York NY 10027 Office Phone: 212-663-6069. Office Fax: 212-864-9789. E-mail: coupdeconebiz@aol.com.*

GORDON-LARSEN, PENNY, nutritionist, educator, researcher; m. Robert A. Larsen; children: Isabella, Frederick. PhD, U. Pa., 1997. Instr. U. Pa., Phila., 1995—98; Dannon postdoctoral fellow U. N.C. Chapel Hill, 1998—2000, asst. prof. nutrition, 2000—. Rev. panels, obesity rsch. NIH, Bethesda, Md., 2003—; sci. meeting planning com. N.Am. Assn. for Study of Obesity, Silver Spring, Md., 2004—, mem. pediat. obesity sect., 2004—; cluster head macro & built environment U. N.C. Chapel Hill, 2004—; mem. editl. bd. obesity rsch. Boston Med. Ctr., 2004; mem. editl. bd. Obesity Rsch., Annals Behavioral Medicine. Mem. editl. bd.: Annals Behavioral Medicine. Chair pers. com. Chapel Hill Day Care Ctr., 2002—03. Recipient Young Investigator Awards, N.Am. Assn. for Study of Obesity; Ind. Rsch. Grants, NIH, 2002—, Dannon Nutrition Inst. Postdoctoral Fellowship Interdisciplinary Rsch., Dannon, 1998—2000. Fellow: Ctr. for Regional and Urban Studies (assoc.), Carolina Population Ctr. (assoc. Fellow 2001-present); mem.: N.Am. Assn. Study Obesity, Obesity Soc. (gov. coun., pediat. gov. coun., sec.- treas. pediat. obesity sect.). Achievements include research in obesity, pediatric and adolescent medicine, interdisiplinary studies, health disparities; development of population-based GIS methods for epidemiologic research. Avocations: running, swimming, cooking. Office: Univ NC-Chapel Hill Univ Sq CPC 123 W Franklin St Chapel Hill NC 27516 Office Phone: 919-843-9966. Office Fax: 919-966-1959. E-mail: pglarsen@unc.edu.

GORDY, BERRY, entrepreneur, film producer, recording industry executive; b. Detroit, Nov. 28, 1929; children from a previous marriage: Berry IV, Hazel Joy, Terry James, Kerry A., Sherry R., Kennedy W., Stefan K., Rhonda Ross-Kendrick. PhD in Music (hon.), Ea. Mich. U., 1971. Founder Motown Record Corp., 1961—; exec. prodr. motion pictures; chmn. bd. dirs. West Grand Media, 1998—; founder Jobete Music Co., Inc., 1997—. Dir.: (films) Mahogany, 1975; exec. prodr.: Lady Sings the Blues, 1972, Bingo Long Traveling All-Stars and Motor Kings, 1975, Berry Gordy's the Last Dragon, 1984; author: To Be Loved: The Music, the Magic, the Memories of Motown, 1994. Named star, Hollywood Walk of Fame, 1996; named to Minority Hall of Fame, Atlanta U. Sch. Bus. Adminstrn., 1981, Leading Entrepreneurs of Nation, Babson Coll., 1978, Rock and Roll Hall of Fame, 1988, Nat. Bus. Hall of Fame, Jr. Achievement, 1998; recipient Bus. Achievement award, Interracial Coun. for Bus. Opportunity, 1967, Golden Mike and MLK, Jr.'s Leadership award, NATRA, 1969, 2d Ann. Am. Music award for outstanding contbn. to music industry, 1975, Whitney M. Young Jr. award, L.A. Urban League, 1980, Trustees award, NARAS, 1991, 20th Century award, Black Radio Exclusive, 1993, Abe Olman Pub. award, Songwriters Hall of Fame, 1993, Livetime Achievement award, Black Bus. Assn., 1993, Generation award, Congl. Black Caucus Found., 1993, Am. Legend award, ASCAP Pop Music Awards, 1998, Lifetime Achievement award, NABOB, 1998, Legend award, BESLA, 1998, A.G. Gaston Lifetime Achievement award, Black Ent./Bank of Am., 2001, Wall St. Project Millennium award, Rainbow/Push, 2000, Legend award, Rainbow/Push Coalition, 2001, Candle award for Lifetime Achievement in Arts and Entertainment, Morehouse Coll., 2005; Gordon Grand fellow, Yale U., 1985. Mem.: NAACP, Acad. Motion Picture Arts and Scis., BMI, Dirs. Guild Am. Office: West Grand Media 9100 Wilshire Blvd Beverly Hills CA 90212-3401

GORE, AL (ALBERT ARNOLD GORE JR.), former Vice President of the United States; b. Washington, Mar. 31, 1948; s. Albert and Pauline LaFon Gore; m. Mary Elizabeth Aitcheson, May 19, 1970; children: Karenna, Kristin, Sarah, Albert III. BA cum laude (U. scholar), Harvard U., 1969; student, Grad. Sch. of Religion, Vanderbilt U., 1971-72, Vanderbilt Law Sch., 1974-76. Investigative reporter, editorial writer The Tennessean, 1971-76; homebuilder and land developer Tanglewood Home Builders Co., 1971-76; livestock and tobacco farmer, 1973—; mem. US Congress from 6th Tenn. dist. (formerly 4th), 1977-85; US Senator from Tenn., 1985-93; v.p. U.S., 1993-2001; Dem. candidate for Pres., 2000; vice chmn. Metropolitan West Fin., Los Angeles, Calif., 2001—; sr. adv. Google, Inc., 2001—; chmn. Generational Investment Mgmt. Inc., London, 2004—; co-founder Current TV, San Francisco, 2005—. Bd. dirs. Apple Computer Inc., 2003—; vis. prof. Columbia U. Sch. Journalism, 2001, Fisk U., Middle Tenn. State U., UCLA, 2001—. Author: Earth in the Balance: Ecology and the Human Spirit, 1992, Let the Glory Out: My South and It's Politics, 2000, An Inconvenient Truth: The Planetary Emergency of Global Warming and What We Can Do About It, 2006 (No. 1 NY Times Paperback Bestseller list, Amazon Bestseller list, Publishers Weekly Bestseller list, 2006, Quills award current events The Quills Literacy Found., 2006), The Assault on Reason: How the Politics of Fear, Secrecy, and Blind Faith Subvert Wise Decision Making, Degrade Our Democracy, and Put Our Country and Our World in Peril, 2007; (children's books) An Inconvenient Truth: The Crisis of Global Warming, 2007; co-author: (with Joseph Kaufman) The World According to Al Gore: An A-To-Z Compilation of His Opinions, Positions, and Public Statements, 2000;(with Tipper Gore) Joined at the Heart: The Transformation of the American Family, 2002; host, co-prodr. (documentary) An Inconvenient Truth (Spl. award, Humanitas Prize Bd., 2006). Served with U.S. Army, 1969-71, Army Journalist, Vietnam. Named Policy Leader of Yr., Scientific Am. mag., 2006; named one of The World's Most Influential People, TIME mag., 2006—07; recipient Webby Lifetime Achievement award, Internat. Acad. of Digital Arts and Sciences, 2005, Founders award, Internat. Acad. TV Arts and Sciences, 2007, Principe de Asturias prize, Fundación Príncipe de Asturias, 2007. Fellow Am. Acad. Arts & Scis.; mem. Farm Bur., Tenn. Jaycees. Clubs: Am. Legion, VFW. Democrat. Baptist. Office: Current TV, LLC 118 King St San Francisco CA 94107*

GORE, GEORGE HENRY, lawyer; b. Oak Park, Ill., June 22, 1923; s. Robert Hayes and Lorena Claire (Haury) Gore; m. Leona M. O'Grady; children: Stephen H., Gregory J., Georgene M. Urbanek, Kathleen M. Whitney. JD, U. Notre Dame, 1948; LLM, NYU, 1950. Bar: Fla. 1948. Assoc. Saunders, Buckley & O'Connell, Fort Lauderdale, Fla., 1950; sole practice Fort Lauderdale, Fla., 1951—54; ptnr. Saunders, Curtis, Ginestra & Gore, Fort Lauderdale, Fla., 1954—2000, of counsel, 2000—. Sec., dir. North Am. Co., Fort Lauderdale, 1950—. Represented in permanent collections U. Notre Dame, Carlow Coll., Holy Cross Hosp. and Convent, Assumption Ch., others. Mem. law adv. coun. U. Notre Dame, Ind., 1965—88; trustee Gore Family Meml. Found., 1973—, Holy Cross Hosp., Inc., Ft. Lauderdale, 1966—96, chmn. bd., 1984—87; mem. coun. Village of Sea Ranch Lakes, Ft. Lauderdale, 1959—63; mem. Fla. Govs. Challenge program, Ft. Lauderdale, 1982; bd. dirs. Ralph J. Baudhuin Oral Sch. of Nova U., Ft. Lauderdale, 1956—88, pres., 1981—88; bd. dirs. Hospice Care of Broward County, Inc., 1981—83. With US Army, 1942—45, ETO. Decorated Purple Heart, Bronze Star. Mem.: Fla Bar (exec. coun. tax sect. 1955—57), Knights of St. Gregory (knight comdr.), Coral Ridge Yacht Club, Tower Club, U. Notre Dame Club. Republican. Roman Catholic. Home: 23 Minnetonka Rd Sea Ranch Lakes FL 33308-2908 Home Phone: 954-946-8966; Office Phone: 954-229-1956.

GORE, SAMUEL MARSHALL, art educator, sculptor; b. Coolidge, Tex., Nov. 24, 1927; s. John Ellis Gore and Mary Letha Pepper; m. Marjorie Bryant Gore; children: Judy Gore Gearhart, Paul Bryant, Jan Gore Mellado, Philip M. BFA, Atlanta Coll. Art, 1950; BA, Miss. Coll., 1952; MA, U. Ala., 1956; EdD, Ill. State U., 1964. Prof., chmn. art dept. Miss. Coll., Clinton, 1951—93, part-time prof., 1993—. Vis. prof. Johnson Atelier, Princeton, NJ, 1975. Represented in permanent collections Miss. Agr. Mus., Miss. Bapt. Med. Ctr., Miss. Vet. Sculpture, Clinton, Miss.

Coll., Chapel of the Cross, Madison, Miss., First Baptist Chs. Jackson and Clinton, Miss., Uptown Baptist Ch., Chgo., Salvation Army Coll., Atlanta, Valley Baptist Med. Ctr., Harlington, Tex., Samuel Marshall Gore Art Galleries, Miss. Coll. Served with USNR, 1946—48, lt. col. USAF, 1972—97. Named Outstanding Citizen of Yr., Clinton C. of C., 2000; recipient Meritorious Svc. award, USAF CAP, 1987, Gov.'s award for excellence, State of Miss., 1997, Miss. Ageless Hero award, Blue Cross-Blueshield, 2002. Baptist. Avocations: beekeeping, gardening. Home: PO Box 608 Clinton MS 39060 Office Phone: 601-925-3231. Personal E-mail: samgore1927@bellsouth.net.

GORE, STEVEN LOWELL, accountant; b. Paducah, Ky., June 22, 1953; *Sister, Marsha and brother-in-law Dale Lampley, electrician, Paducah, Kentucky, have two children, Michael, air force airman, and Melissa Walker, sonographer, Paducah. Melissa has a son, Carson. Sister Sharon, married to brother-in-law Wally Brines, wildlife biologist, Cookeville, Tennessee. Also has a sister, Denise Bradford, Paducah. Brother, Jesse Gore is CEO Genetics Associates, Nashville. His wife is Gloria. They have five children: Jonathan is an electrical engineer with Envision Advantage, Nashville; Benjamin, sales, Ortho Mattress, Nashville; Steven, student at UT Knoxville; Kristen; and Zachary. Benjamin is married to wife Carolyn and they have a daughter, Aliyah.* BS in Acctg., Lipscomb U., Nashville, 1975. CPA Tenn., cert. treasury profl. Analyst fiscal svcs. King Faisal Hosp., Riyadh, Saudi Arabia, 1976—77; facility acct. Am. Retirement Corp., Nashville, 1983; staff auditor Hosp. Corp. Am., Nashville, 1984—87; contr. Sumner Regional Med. Ctr., Gallatin, Tenn., 1987—2003; devel. officer Genetics Assocs., Inc., Nashville, 2003—05; freelance cons. Nashville, 2005—; examiner Dept. Commerce and Ins., Nashville, 2005—. Vol. Margaret Maddox YMCA-East, Nashville, 1997—2000; poll ofcl. Metro-Davidson County Election Commn., Nashville, 1999. Recipient Appreciation Letter for Svc. United Way of Sumner County, 1997-2000. Mem.: IEEE, AAAS, UN Assn. USA, Am. Math. Soc., Math Assn. Am., Nat. Space Soc., Population Reference Bur., World Future Soc., Planetary Soc., NY Acad. Sci., Am. Pub. Health Assn., Am. Chem. Soc. Avocations: fishing, reading, jogging, golf. Office: Tenn Dept Commerce and Ins 500 James Robertson Pkwy Ste 750 Nashville TN 37243-1169 Home: 1413 Clifton Ln Nashville TN 37215-1615 Office Phone: 615-741-2677. Personal E-mail: stevengore@msn.com.

GORE, TIPPER (MARY ELIZABETH GORE), wife of the former Vice President of the United States; b. Washington, Aug. 19, 1948; m. Albert Gore Jr., May 19, 1970; children: Karenna, Kristin, Sarah, Albert III. BA in Psychology, Boston U., 1970; MA in Psychology, Vanderbilt U., 1975. Freelance photographer; photographer Nashville Tennessean. Mental health policy advisor to pres. Author: Raising PG Kids in an X-Rated Society, 1987, Picture This: A Visual Diary, 1996; co-author The Spirit of Family, 2002, Joined at the Heart: The Transformation of the American Family, 2002; co-prodr. (with Nat. Mental Health Assn.) Homeless in America: A Photographic Project. Co-founder Parents Music Resource Ctr., Arlington, Va., 1985; founder Tenn. Voices for Children, 1990; co-chair Am. Goes Back to Sch. Initiative, 1996—; chair Congl. Wives Task Force, 1978-79' co-founder The Climate Project, 2006-. Democrat. Office: 2100 West End Ave Nashville TN 37203*

GORE, TUSHAR, marketing professional; s. Balkrishna and Anuradha Gore; m. Ramya Kumbale, June 10, 1996. BSChemE, Indian Inst. of Tech., Bombay, 1994; PhD in Chem. Engring., U. Minn., 2000. Assoc. cons. McKinsey and Co., Florham Park, NJ, 2000—02; assoc. dir. bus. analyst Novo Nordisk Pharm. Inc., Princeton, NJ, 2003—. Presenter in field. Contbr. articles to profl. publs. Project coord. Am. India Found., NYC, 2001. Grantee, U. Minn. Mem.: NY Acad. Scis. Avocations: scuba diving, model railroad, guitar, photography.

GORELICK, ELLEN CATHERINE, museum executive director, chief curator, artist, educator, civic volunteer; b. Chgo., Jan. 2, 1946; d. Martin Francis and Doris Harriet (Adams) Heckmann; m. Walter Lee Gorelick, Dec. 19, 1970. AA cum laude, Coll. of Sequoias, 1976; BA cum laude, Calif. State U., Fresno, 1979, MA in Art, 1982. Book divsn. corr. Time, Inc., Chgo., 1964-68; accounts receivable supr. Tab Products Co., San Francisco, 1968-69; exec. sec. Foremost-McKesson, Inc., San Francisco, 1969-71, McCarthy Land Co., Visalia, Calif., 1972-74; adminstrv. dir. Creative Ctr. for Handicapped, Visalia, 1979-80; curator Tulare (Calif.) Hist. Mus., 1984-87, dir., curator, 1994—; mem. adj. faculty Coll. of Sequoias, Visalia, 1985-96; gallery dir. Calif. State U., Fresno, 1997—98, adj. faculty, 1998. Bd. dirs. Tulare-Kings Regional Arts Coun., pres., 1989-90, Coll. Sequoias Found. Bd., 2002-05; bd. dirs. Tulare County Art League, pres., 1977-78; bd. dirs. Leadership Tulare, founding CORE com., 1991-93, alumni chair, 1992-93; bd. dirs. Tulare County U. Calif. Campus Expansion task force, Visalia, 1988-91, Tulare City Sch. Dist. Classrooms for Kids Campaign, co-chair, 1989; bd. mem. Tulare City Hist. Soc. long range planning com., 1995; bd. mem. Tulare County Symphony Assn., 1983-86, 1992-95, 2000-03, sec., 1993, adv. bd., 2003-06; founding bd. dirs., v.p., program chair Tulare Cultural Arts Found., 1997—; local legacies Tulare County coord., Libr. Congress, 2000. Named Artist of Yr., Tulare-Kings County Arts Coun., 1988; recipient cert. of appreciation City of Tulare, 1989, Tulare County Bd. Suprs., 1991, Woman of Distinction award Soroptimists, Tulare, 1994, 2003, City of Tulare Woman of Year, 2004, Woman of Year State Calif. 34th Assembly Dist., 2006. Mem. Tulare Palette Club (pres. 1984-85, Artist of Yr. award 1985). Democrat. Roman Catholic. Avocations: photography, travel, gourmet cooking. Office: Tulare Hist Mus 444 W Tulare Ave Tulare CA 93274-3831 Business E-Mail: egorelick@tularehistoricalmuseum.org.

GORELICK, JAMIE SHONA, lawyer; b. NYC, May 6, 1950; d. Leonard and Shirley (Fishman) Gorelick; m. Richard E. Waldhorn, Sept. 28, 1975; children: Daniel H. Waldhorn, Dana E. Waldhorn. BA magna cum laude, Harvard U., 1972, JD cum laude, 1975. Bar: DC 1975, US Dist. Ct. DC 1976, US Tax Ct. 1976, US Ct. Claims 1976, US Ct. Appeals (DC cir.) 1976, US Ct. Appeals (5th cir.) 1977, US Supreme Ct. 1979, US Ct. Appeals (fed. cir.) 1982, US Ct. Internat. Trade 1984, US Dist. Ct. Md. 1985, US Ct. Appeals (4th cir.) 1986, US Ct. Appeals (3d cir.) 1988. With Miller, Cassidy, Larroca & Lewin, Washington, 1975-79, 80-93; asst. to sec., counselor to dep. sec. US Dept. Energy, 1979—80; gen. counsel Dept. Def., 1993—94; dep. atty. gen. Dept. Justice, Washington, 1994-97; vice chair Fannie Mae, Washington, 1997—2003; ptnr. litigation, co-chmn. Nat. Security & Govt. Contracts dept., co-chmn., Public Policy & Strategy group WilmerHale, Washington, 2003—. Mem. chmn.'s adv. coun. US Senate Jud. Com., 1988—93; tchr. Trial Advocacy Workshop Harvard Law Sch., Cambridge, Mass., 1982, Cambridge, 84; vice chair task force evaluation audit investigative inspection components Dept. Def., 1979—80; mem. sec.'s transition team Dept. Energy, 1979; bd. dirs. United Techs. Corp., Schlumberger Ltd., Lucent Govt. Adv. Bd., Best Lawyers Adv. Bd. Mem. editl. bd. Corp. Criminal Liability Reporter, 1986—93; contbr. articles to profl. jours. Mem. nat. security adv. panel CIA, 1997—2005; mem. Pres.'s Intelligence Rev. Panel, 2001—02; threat reduction adv. com. Dept. Def.; co-chair adv. com. Presdl. Commn. Critical Infrastructure Protection, 1997—99; mem. Nat. Commn. Support Law Enforcement, Washington, 1995—97; commr. Nat. Commn. Terrorist Attacks Upon US (9-11 Commn.), 2002—04; bd. dirs. John D. & Catherine T. MacArthur Found., Fannie Mae Found., 1997—2005, Urban Inst., 1999—2003, Am.'s Promise-Alliance Youth, 1997—2004, Nat. Pk. Found., 1997—2004, Carnegie Endowment, 1989—93, Nat. Women's Law Ctr., 1991—93, Washington Legal Clinic Homeless; bd. overseers Harvard Coll., 1998—2004; mem. coun. Am. Law Inst., 1997—2000, DC Bar Found.; mem. selection com. Supreme Ct. Jud. Fellow, 2003—06; bd. dirs. Legal Affairs, 2004—06. Named one of Top 30 Lawyers in Washington, Washingtonian mag., 100 Most Powerful Women, 50 Most Powerful Women in Bus., Fortune mag., America's Top Businesswomen, Forbes, 50 Smartest Women in Money Bus., Money Mag., 50 Most Influential Women Lawyers in Am., Nat. Law Jour., 2007; recipient Corp. Leadership award, DC C. of C., 2003, Aiming High award, NOW Legal Def. & Edn. Fund, 2002, Judge Learned Hand award, Am. Jewish Com., 1999, Wickersham award for exceptional pub. svc., 1998, Outstanding Advocate of the Year, Equal Justice Works, 1997. Fellow: Am. Bar Found. (Star of the Bar award 2003); mem.: ABA (vice-chair complex crimes litig. com. 1983—84, chair complex crimes litig. com. litig. sect. 1984—87, sec. litig. sect. 1988—90, coun. mem. 1990—93, mem. com. profl. discipline, ho. dels. 1991—93, 1997—, Margaret Brent award 1997), Coun. Fgn. Rels., Am. Law Inst. (couns.), Women's Bar Assn. (Lawyer of the Yr. award 1993), DC Bar (pres. 1992—93, bd. govs. 1982—88, sec. bd. govs. 1981—92, bar found. advisors 1985—93, mem. legal ethics com.). Office: WilmerHale 1875 Pennsylvania Ave NW Washington DC 20006 Office Phone: 202-663-6500. Office Fax: 202-663-6363. Business E-Mail: jamie.gorelick@wilmerhale.com.

GOREN, STEVEN ELIOT, lawyer; b. Detroit, Apr. 9, 1960; s. Robert and Judith A. (Wise) G.; m. Eva Calmidis, Sept. 25, 1980; children: Robert C., Sophia J. BA with high distinction, U. Mich., 1981, JD cum laude, 1984. Bar: Mich. 1984, Ohio 2001, U.S. Dist. Ct. (ea. dist.) Mich. 1984. Atty. Dickinson, Wright, Moon, VanDusen & Freeman, Bloomfield Hills, Mich., 1984-86, pvt. practice, Birmingham, Mich., 1986—91. Adjunct prof. U. Detroit Law Sch., 1989-95; med. malpractice task force Mich. Trial lawyers, 1989; mem. litigation adv. com., Inst. Continuing Legal Edn. Contbr. articles to profl. jours. Precinct Del. Democratic Party, Beverly Hills, Mich., 1990-91. Mem.: Mich. Trial Lawyers Assn. (exec. bd. 2000—). Office: 30400 Telegraph Rd Ste 470 Bingham Farms MI 48025-5818

GORENBERG, CHARLES LLOYD, finance company executive; b. Phila., Mar. 1, 1938; s. Abraham and Esther (Freedman) G.; m. Roslyn Grobman, May 22, 1960; children: David M., Kenneth M. BA, Franklin & Marshall Coll., 1960; MS, The Am. Coll., Bryn Mawr, Pa., 1981. Cert. Employee Benefit Specialist, CLU, ChFC, APM. Sales assoc. Landis & Co., Phila., 1960-62; agt. Phoenix Mut. Life, Phila., 1962-64, supr., 1964-67; dir. tng. Rittenhouse Assocs., Phila., 1967-75; exec. v.p. Corp. Pension Actuaries, Phila., 1975-91; pres. Delta Fin. Group, Phila., 1991-97, Chaslyn Fin. Group, Marlton, N.J., 1997—. Co-editor: (book) Planning for Business Owners and Professionals, 1988; contbr. over 35 articles to mags. Mem. Internat. Soc. Cert. Employee Benefit Specialists, Am. Soc. CLUs and ChFCs (various offices), Am. Soc. Pension Actuaries. Avocation: golf. Office: Chaslyn Fin Group 413 Marlton Pike E Ste 100 Cherry Hill NJ 08034-2483 Office Phone: 856-761-1836. Business E-Mail: chuck@chaslynfinancialgroup.com.

GORENCE, PATRICIA JOSETTA, judge; b. Sheboygan, Wis., Mar. 6, 1943; d. Joseph and Antonia (Marinsheck) G.; m. John Michael Bach, July 11, 1969; children: Amy Jane, Mara Jo, J. Christopher Bach. BA, Marquette U., 1965, JD, 1977; MA, U. Wis., 1969. Bar: Wis. 1977, U.S. Dist. Ct. (ea. and we. dists.) Wis. 1977, U.S. Ct. Appeals (7th cir.) 1979, U.S. Supreme Ct. 1980. Asst. U.S. atty. U.S. Atty.'s Office, Milw., 1979-84, 1st asst. U.S. Atty., 1984-87, 89-91, U.S. Atty., 1987-88; dep. atty. gen. State of Wis. Dept. Justice, Madison, 1991-93; assoc. Ginbel, Reilly, Guerin & Brown, Milw., 1993-94; U.S. magistrate judge U.S. Dist. Ct. Wis., Milw., 1994—. Mem. judge adv. com. U.S. Magistrate, 2006—. Bd. dirs. U. Wis.-Milw. Slovenian Arts Coun., 1989—, treas., 1989—, Milw. Dance Theatre, 1993-98; bd. chair Bottomless Closet, 1999-2006. Recipient Spl. Commendation, U.S. Dept. Justice, 1986, IRS, 1988. Mem. ABA, Am. Law Inst., US Magistrate Judges (mem. adv. group 2006-), Fed. Magistrate Judges Assn. (cir. dir. 1997-2000), Milw. Bar Assn. (chair cmty. rels. com. 2000-03, Prosecutor of Yr. 1990, Disting. Svc. award 2003, Wis. Law Jour. Innovator of Yr. award 2003), State Bar Wis. (chair lawyer dispute resolution com. 1986—, chair professionalism com. 1988-00, vice chair legal edn. commn. 1994-96, Pres. award 1995), 7th Cir. Bar Assn. (chair rules and practices com. 1991-95), Ea. Dist. Wis. Bar Assn. (bd. dirs. 2004—), Assn. Women Lawyers, Profl. Dimensions (sec. 1998-00, v.p. adminstrn. 2000-02).

GORENIUC, MIRCEA C. PAUL, sculptor; b. Dec. 12, 1942; At, Acad. Fine Arts, Munich, 1971—72; BA, San Francisco State U., 1974; MA in Art, San Jose State U., Calif., 1975, MFA in Sculpture, 1977. Cert. tchr. jr. coll., univ. Calif., 1978. Tchg. asst. San Jose State U., 1976—77, lectr., 1978; faculty to prof. West Valley Coll., Saratoga, 1981—86. Prin. works include Space Dance for Peace, Beijing, 2002, Rock and Roll for Peace, Concord, 2002 (Peoples Choice award), Space Symphony for Peace, Beijing, 2006, exhibitions include Internat. Sculpture Exhbn. and Symposium, 2002, 2d Internat. Art Biennale, 2005, Beijing Exhbn. Hall, 2006, Romanian Embassy in Beijing, 2006. Mem. com. pub. art City of San Jose, 1985. Recipient prize of Excellence, Chinese Ministry of Culture, 2002. Mem.: Romanian Plastic Artists Union (life), Phi Kappa Phi (life). Personal E-mail: paulgore@ix.netcom.com.

GORENSTEIN, DAVID G., chemistry and biochemistry professor; b. Oct. 6, 1945; s. Ben and Shirley (Adelberg) G.; m. Deborah H. Joseph, June 11, 1967; 1 child, Jennifer. BS in Chemistry, M.I.T., 1966; MA in Chemistry, Harvard U., 1967, PhD in Chemistry, 1969. Asst. prof. U. Ill., Chgo., 1969-73, assoc. prof., 1973-76, prof., 1976-85; prof. chemistry Purdue Univ., West Lafayette, Ind., 1985-94; dir. Purdue Biochem. MRI Lab., West Lafayette, Ind., 1985-94, NSF Nat. Biol. Facilities Ctr., West Lafayette, 1987-93, NMR and Structural Biology Cores, West Lafayette, 1988-94; dep. dir. NIH Designated AIDS Rsch. Ctr., West Lafayette, 1993-94; prof. human biol. chemistry and genetics U. Tex. Med. Sch., Galveston, 1994—; sr. investigator Sealy Ctr. Molecular Sci. U. Tex. Med. Br., Galveston, 1994—; dir. Nuclear Magnetic Resonance Ctr. U. Tex. Med. Br., Galveston, dir. Sealy Ctr. for Structural Biology, 1995—2002, dep. dir. NIEHS Ctr., 1996—2002, Charles Marc Pomerat Disting. Prof. of biology, 1997—, vice chmn. human biol. chem. genetics, 1999—2002, assoc. dean rsch., 2006—. Dir. Gulf Coast NMR Consortium; founder, chmn. AptaMed, Inc., 2003—; vis. assoc. prof. U. Wis., Madison, 1975; vis. prof. Oxford U., 1977-78, U. Calif., San Francisco, 1986; adj. prof. Biomed. Engring. U. Tex., Austin, 1996—; cons. Baxter Travenol, 1985-95, Merck and Co., 1988, Eli Lilly, 1987-89, Ill. Tool Works, 1973-85, Chronomatic Inc., 1973-85, U.S. Dept. of Labor, 1975, Continental Group, Inc., 1982-84, Abbott Corp., 2001- Abbott Diagnostics, 2002; active numerous univ. coms.; lectr. in field. Editor Bull. of Magnetic Resonance, 1982-99; mem. editorial bd. Magnetic Resonance Revs., 1983-93, Jour. Magnetic Resonance, 1992-99, Biophys. Jour., 1992-98; pub. abstracts; contbr. articles to profl. jours. Grantee: NSF, 1987-93, NIH, 1970—, Eli Lilly, 1988-94 and numerous others; tchg. fellow Harvard U., 1966-69, trainee summer fellow NSF, 1966, predoctoral fellow NIH, 1967-69, Alfred P. Sloan fellow 1975-79, Sr. Rsch. fellow Fulbright, 1977-78, Guggenheim fellow, 1986; recipient Internat. Lectr. award Fulbright, 1978. Fellow AAAS; mem. Am. Soc. for Biochemistry and Molecular Biology, Am. Chem. Soc. (program chmn. divsn. biol. chemistry 1985-87, vice chmn. Purdue sect. 1990-91, chmn. 1991-92), Biophys. Soc., Protein Soc., Sigma Xi, Phi Lambda Upsilon. Achievements include patents in process for Preparing Dithiophosphate Oligonucleotide Analogs via Nucleoside Thiophosphoramidite Intermediates and in vivo selection of aptamers; research in proteomics and applications of NMR spectroscopy and other physical techniques to biological systems, theoretical bio-organic chemistry, biomolecular design; cancer and anti-viral drugs development. Address: 3922 Crown Ridge Ct Houston TX 77059-3711 Office: U Tex Med Br Sch Medicine Galveston TX 77555-1157 Business E-Mail: dggorens@utmb.com.

GORENSTEIN, ETHAN EZRA, psychologist, educator; b. NYC, Oct. 29, 1953; s. Samuel and Shirley Gorenstein; m. Margaret Troy, Apr. 6, 1980; children: Eleazer Tyng, Julian Troy. BA with honors, McGill U., Montreal, Can., 1975; PhD, Ind. U., 1981. Lic. psychologist NY, NJ. Psychology intern Lafayette Clinic, Detroit, 1979—80, staff psychologist, 1980—81; asst. prof. dept. psychology Columbia U., NYC, 1981—89, asst. prof. clin. psychology, 1989—2006, clin. dir. behavioral medicine program, 1991—, assoc. clin. prof. behavioral medicine, 2006—; rsch. scientist NY State Psychiat. Inst., NYC, 1997—2002. Author: The Science of Mental Illness, 1992, Case Studies in Abnormal Psychology, 2002; mem. editl. bd. Cognitive and Behavioral Practice, 2001—. Basketball coach Congregation Neve Shalom, Metuchen, NJ, 1999—2006. Recipient B.A. Honors First Class, McGill U., 1975, Dissertation Yr. Award, Ind. U., 1978-1979, Young Faculty Award, Spencer Found., 1983; fellow Predoctoral Tng. Fellowship, NIMH, 1975-1977, Nat. Insitute on Alcoholism and Alcohol Abuse, 1977/1979; scholar, McGill U., 1973. Mem.: APA, Obsessive-Compulsive Found., Assn. Behavioral and Cognitive Therapies. Achievements include research in psychopathology and behavior therapy. Office: Columbia U 622 W 168th St Box 427 New York NY 10032 Home Phone: 732-205-9349; Office Phone: 212-305-9985. Business E-Mail: eeg1@columbia.edu.

GORES, ALEC E., venture capitalist; s. Charlie. BS in Computer Sci., Western Mich. U. Founder Exec. Bus. Systems, 1978—86; founder, chmn. Gores Tech. Grp., LA, 1987—. Named one of Forbes' Richest Americans, 2002, 2004, 2006. Office: Gores Group LLC 18th Fl 10877 Wilshire Blvd Los Angeles CA 90024 Office Phone: 310-209-3010. Office Fax: 310-209-3310.

GORES, CHRISTOPHER MERREL, lawyer; b. NYC, Aug. 27, 1943; s. Guido James and Mary (Callaway) G.; children: Ellen, Eugenia. AB, Princeton U., 1965; LLB, Columbia U., 1968. Bar: N.Y. 1968, Tex. 1973, U.S. Dist. Ct (no. dist.) Tex. 1977. Assoc. Akin, Gump, Strauss, Hauer & Feld, LLP, Dallas, 1973-79, ptnr., 1979—. Bd. dirs. Shakespeare Festival of Dallas, 1982-88. Lt. USNR, 1969-72. Office: Akin Gump Strauss Hauer & Feld LLP 1700 Pacific Ave Ste 4100 Dallas TX 75201-4675 Office Phone: 214-969-2716. Business E-Mail: cgores@akingump.com.

GORES, THOMAS C., lawyer; b. Milw., Sept. 24, 1948; s. Kenneth W. and Carolyn (Camblin) G.; m. Ann P. Pacelli, June 13, 1970; children: Lauren, Jake, Kathryn. BA, U. Notre Dame, 1970, JD, 1973; LLM, U. Miami, 1977. Bar: Wash. 1973, U.S. Tax Ct. 1973. Assoc., then ptnr. Bogle & Gates, Seattle, 1973-78, ptnr., 1978-93, Gores & Blais, Seattle, 1993-2001, Perkins Coie LLP, 2001—. Fellow Am. Coll. Trust and Estate Counsel; mem. Wash. State Bar Assn., Seattle Estate Planning Coun. (pres.). Office: Perkins Coie LLP 1201 3rd Ave Ste 4800 Seattle WA 98101-3099 Office Phone: 206-359-8555. Business E-Mail: tgores@perkinscole.com.

GORES, TOM T., investment company executive; b. Nazareth, Israel, 1964; married; 3 children. BA, Mich. State U. Entrepreneur; founder, chmn., CEO Platinum Equity, LA, 1995—. Bd. dirs. St. Joseph's Hosp., LA, UCLA Med. Ctr. Named one of 400 Richest Ams., Forbes mag., 2006; named to several Forbes' World Billionaires lists. Office: Platinum Equity 360 N Crescent Dr South Bldg Beverly Hills CA 90210 Office Phone: 310-712-1850. Office Fax: 310-712-1848.*

GORE SCHIFF, KARENNA, nonprofit organization administrator, lawyer, writer; b. Tenn., Aug. 6, 1973; d. Al and Tipper Gore; m. Andrew Schiff; children: Wyatt Gore, Anna Hunger. BA, Harvard U., 1995; JD, Columbia U., 2000. With El Pais newspaper, Spain, 2000, Slate mag., Seattle; youth outreach chair Al Gore Presdl. campaign, 2000; atty. Simpson, Thatcher & Bartleet; dir. cmty. affairs Assn. to Benefit Children. Author: (book) Lighting the Way: Nine Women Who Changed Modern America, 2006. Office: Assn to Benefit Children 419 E 86th St New York NY 10028*

GORHAM, BRADFORD, lawyer; b. Providence, Mar. 7, 1935; s. Sayles and Ruth C. (Campbell) G.; m. Diann Gebow, Aug. 1, 1959; children: Christopher, Nicholas, Joshua, Jane, Nancy. Degree, Dartmouth Coll., 1957, Harvard U., 1964. Bar: R.I. 1964. Ptnr. Gorham & Gorham, Scituate, RI, 1964—. State rep. R.I. State Ho. of Reps., Providence, 1969-70, 77-90; state senator R.I. State Senate, Providence, 1991-97. Capt. USMC, 1957-60. Named Legislator of Yr. Nat. Conf. State Legislatures, 1985, Outstanding Legislator Am. Legis. Exch. Coun., 1986. Republican. Home: 11 Cucumber Hill Rd Foster RI 02825-1211 Office: Gorham & Gorham 25 Danielson Pike Scituate RI 02857-1801 Office Phone: 401-647-1400.

GORHAM, EVILLE, retired ecologist; b. Halifax, NS, Can., Oct. 15, 1925; s. Ralph Arthur and Shirley Agatha (Eville) G.; m. Ada Verne MacLeod, Sept. 29, 1948; children: Kerstin, Vivien, Jocelyn, James. BSc in Biology with distinction, Dalhousie U., 1945, MSc in Zoology, 1947, LLD (hon.), 1991; PhD in Botany, U. London, Eng., 1951; DSc (hon.), McGill U., 1993, U. Minn., 1999. Lectr. botany U. Coll., London, Eng., 1951-54; sr. sci. officer Freshwater Biol. Assn., Ambleside, Eng., 1954-58; lectr., asst. prof. botany U. Toronto, 1958-62; assoc. prof. botany U. Minn., Mpls., 1962-65, prof., 1966-75, head dept., 1967-71, prof. ecology, 1975-84, Regents' prof. ecology and botany, 1984-98, Regents' prof. emeritus, 1999—; prof., head dept. biology U. Calgary, Alta., Can., 1965-66. Mem. for Can., Internat. Commn. on Atmospheric Chemistry and Radioactivity, 1959-62; mem. vis. panel to rev. toxicology program NAS-NRC, 1974-75, mem. com. on inland aquatic ecosys. Water Sci. and Tech. Bd., 1994-96, mem. com. to evaluate indicators for monitoring aquatic and terrestrial environments Water Sci. and Tech. Bd., 1997-99, mem. com. on hydrologic sci. bd. on Atmospheric Scis. and Climate, 1998-99; mem. coordinating com. for sci. and tech. assessment environ. pollutants Environ. Studies Bd., 1975-78; mem. com. on med. and biologic effects of environ. pollutants Assembly Life Scis., 1976-77; mem. com. to recommend nat. program for assessing problem of atmospheric deposition (acid rain) President's Coun. on Environ. Quality, 1978; mem. com. on atmosphere and biosphere Bd. Agr. and Renewable Resources, 1979-81; mem. panel on environ. impact diesel impact study com. NAE-NRC, 1980-81; mem. U.S.-Can.-Mex. joint sci. com. on acid precipitation Environ. Studies Bd., NAS-NRC, Royal Soc. Can., Mex. Acad. Scis., 1981-84; mem. health and environ. rsch. adv. com. U.S. Dept. Energy, 1992-94; mem. Water Sci. and Tech. Bd. NAS-NRC, 1996-99; mem. coun. sci. advisors Marine Biol. Lab., Woods Hole, Mass., 1996-99. Mem. editl. bd. Ecology, 1965-67, Limnology and Oceanography, 1970-72, Conservation Biology, 1987-88, Ecol. Applications, 1989-92, Environ. Revs., 1992-2004; contbr. articles on limnology, ecology, and biogeochemistry to profl. jours. Bd. dirs. Acid Rain Found., 1982-87, sec.-treas. 1982-84 Recipient Regents' medal U. Minn., 1984, Benjamin Franklin medal in earth sci. Franklin Inst., Phila., 2000; Royal Soc. Can. rsch. fellow State Forest Rsch. Inst., Stockholm, Sweden, 1950-51; grantee NSF, AEC, NIH, ERDA, NASA, Dept. of Energy, NRC Can., Ont. Rsch. Found., Environment Can., Office Water Resources Rsch., Dept. Interior, Andrew W. Mellon Found., N.Y.C. Fellow AAAS, Royal Soc. Can., Am. Acad. Arts and Scis.; mem. NAS, Am. Soc. Limnology and Oceanography (G. Evelyn Hutchinson medal 1986), Ecol. Soc. Am., Internat. Assn. Theoretical and

Applied Limnology, Soc. Wetland Scientists (Lifetime Achievement award 2005), Swedish Phytogeog. Soc. (hon.), Gown in Town Club. Home: 1933 E River Ter Minneapolis MN 55414-3673

GORHAM, ROBIN WILSON, biology professor; s. James Edgar and Helen Elizabeth Gorham; m. Ollie Jo Burgess, Aug. 16, 1981. PhD, U. Calif., Irvine, 1974. Prof. biology No. Va. C.C., Annandale, 1973—. Home Phone: 703-560-4357; Office Phone: 703-323-3476.

GORHAM, WILLIAM, organization executive; b. NYC, Dec. 14, 1930; s. Jack and Fay (Blank) G.; m. Gail Wiley Finsterbusch, 1973; children from previous marriage: Sarah, Nancy, Kim, Jennifer, Becky (dec.). Student, MIT, 1949-50; BA, Stanford U., 1952; LLD (hon.), Trinity Coll., 1996. Mem. rsch. staff RAND Corp., 1953-62; dep. asst. sec. def. U.S., 1962-65; asst. sec. health, edn. and welfare, 1965-68; co-chmn. (with Daniel Bell) Pres.'s Panel Social Indicators, 1967-68; chmn. Pres.'s Task Force on Child Devel., 1966; founding pres. Urban Inst., Washington, 1968-2000, pres. emeritus, life trustee, 2000—. Bd. dirs. Insituform Group Ltd., 1986-92, chmn., 1987-92; bd. dirs Insituform Techs., Inc., 1992-97, Cesar Chavez Pub. H.S. for Pub. Policy; mem. Internat. Commn. on Edn. for 21st Century, Delors Commn., UNESCO, 1992-97; mem. U.S. adv. com. Internat. Inst. Applied Sys. Analysis, 1974-82; bd. dirs.-at-large Social Sci. Rsch. Coun. Editor: (with Nathan Glazer) The Urban Predicament, 1976; mem. bd. editors Policy Scis, 1969—, Jour. Policy Analysis and Mgmt., 1980—. Bd. dirs. Price Charities, 2000—, San Diego Revitalization Corp., 2002—. Recipient Disting. Civilian Svc. award U.S. Dept. Def., 1965. Mem. Nat. Acad. Pub. Adminstrn., Assn. Pub. Policy Analysis and Mgmt. (policy coun. 1979-85), Cosmos Club (Washington). Office: Urban Institute 2100 M St NW Washington DC 20037-1264 Office Phone: 202-261-5700.

GORIN, STEPHEN H., social worker, educator; b. Providence, Aug. 26, 1946; s. Jeremiah J. and Rosalind Gorin; m. Cynthia Moniz. BA, Boston U., 1965—69; MSW, SUNY, Stony Brook, 1974—76; PhD, Brandeis U., Waltham, Mass., 1976—83. Asst. prof. U. N.H., Durham, 1984—93; prof. Plymouth State U., NH, 1993—. Mem. White Ho. Health Professions Rev. Group, 1993; mem., nat. adv. coun. Ctr. for Mental Health Svcs., U.S. Dept. Health and Human Svcs., 1994—95; del. White Ho. Conf. on Social Security, White Ho. Conf. on Aging, 2005, 1995; mem., coord. coun. Nat. Medicare Edn. Program, U.S. Dept. Health and Human Svcs., 2000; apptd. N.H. Commn. on the Status of Men, 2003—. Co-author: (textbook) Health & Health Care Policy: A Social Work Perspective, 2003; contbr. articles to profl. jours., chapters to books. Chair N.H. Health Care Coalition, Concord, 1989—96; mem. N.H. Assn. for the Elderly, Concord, 1989—98; pres. N.H. Citizens' Alliance, Concord, 1999—2001; vice chair Union Cmty. Fund of N.H., Hooksett, 2002. Grantee Geriatric Enrichment in Social Work Edn. Project, Hartford Found., 2002—04. Mem.: NASW (editor-in-chief Health and Social Work 2007—, exec. dir., N.H. chpt., Social Worker of Yr., N.H. chpt. 1992), Coun. on Social Work Edn. Office: Plymouth State Univ 17 High St Plymouth NH 03264 Office Phone: 603-535-2635. Business E-Mail: sgorin@plymouth.edu.

GORING, DAVID ARTHUR INGHAM, chemist, educator; b. Toronto, Ont., Canada, Nov. 26, 1920; s. George Ingham and Susan Edna (Jones) G.; m. Elizabeth Dodds Haswell, Aug. 24, 1948; children— James, Rosemary, Christopher. B.Sc., U. London, 1942; PhD, McGill U., Montreal, 1949, Cambridge U., 1953. Scientist NRC, Halifax, N.S., Canada, 1951-55; with PAPRICAN, Pointe Claire, Que., Canada, 1955-85, dir. research, 1971-77, v.p. sci., 1977-83, v.p. acad., 1983-85; prof. U. Toronto, 1986—2002, ret., 2002—. Research assoc. McGill U., 1955-69, sr. research assoc., 1969-86 Contbr. chpts. to books and articles to profl. jours. Patentee in field. Served as flying officer RAF, 1943-46 Recipient Le Sueur Meml. Lecture award Can. Sect. Soc. Chem. Industry, 1988, Notable Achievement award Internat. Symposium on Wood and Pulping Chemistry, 2001; named to Paper Industry Internat. Hall of Fame, 2006. Fellow Royal Soc. Can., Chem. Inst. Can., TAPPI (Gunnar Nicholson Gold medal 1986), Internat. Acad. Wood Sci.; mem. Can. Pulp and Paper Assn. (tech. sect., cert. appreciation 1986, John Bates Meml. Gold medal 1995), Am. Chem. Soc. (cellulose paper textile chemistry div., Anselm Payen award 1973). Anglican. Avocations: fishing, music. Home: 14 1/2 Ottawa St Toronto ON Canada M4T 2B6

GOR'KOV, PETER (LEV PETROVICH), biomedical engineer; Imaging hardware designer, Biomedical Magnetic Resonance Lab. U. Ill., Urbana-Champaign; asst. engr. NHMFL Fla. State U., 1999—. Mem.: NAS. Office: Fla State Univ Rm C211-A NHMFL 1800 E Paul Dirac Dr Tallahassee FL 32310 Office Phone: 850-645-3292. Office Fax: 850-644-1366. E-mail: pgorkov@magnet.fsu.edu.

GORLIN, ALEXANDER, architect; Grad., Cooper Union Sch. Architecture, NYC, Yale Sch. Architecture. Critic Yale Sch. Architecture, 1980—92; prin. Alexander Gorlin Archs., NYC, 1987—. Prin. works include Ruskin Place House, Seaside, Fla. (NY State AIA award, 1996, Builder Mag. Grand Prize award, 1996), North Shore Hebrew Acad., King's Point, NY (AIA NY Chpt. Design award, 1998, NY State AIA award, 2001), Gorlin Tower, Miami, Fla., Rocky Mountains House (Colo. State AIA award, 2002, NY State AIA Design Excellence award, 2003, Prism/Archtl. Record Stone in Architecture Awards, 2004), New Ch. Swedenborgian, NYC (Faith and Form Religious Architecture award, 2005). Named one of 30 Deans of Design, Archtl. Digest, 2005; grantee Rome Prize fellowship, Am. Acad. Rome, 1994. Fellow: AIA. Office: Alexander Gorlin Archs 137 Varick St 5th Fl New York NY 10013 Office Phone: 212-229-1199. Office Fax: 212-206-3590. E-mail: agorlin@gorlinarchitects.com.*

GORMAN, CHARLOTTE A., business executive; b. Tuscaloosa, Ala., Apr. 12, 1945; d. Buster and Rosie Gorman; m. C. Curtis Trent, May 5, 1984. BS, Delta State U., Cleve., Miss., 1970; MA, U. Tenn., Knoxville, 1973, Ball State U., Muncie, Ind., 1977, EdD, 1978. Sci. tchr. West Boliver Elem. Sch., Rosedale, Miss., 1970—71; ext. home economist Miss. State U., Starkville, 1973—75; state ext. specialist U. Ark., Little Rock, 1978—84; pres. GT Assocs., Cleburne, Tex., 1985—; ext. agt. U. Ark., Little Rock, 1993—97, Tex. A&M U. Sys., College Station, 1997—2005. Author: The Frugal Mind, 1990 (Book Club selection), The Frugal Mind rev. edit., 1998, The Little Book of Living Frugal, 2001; co-author: Speak for Yourself, 2002. Recipient Charlotte Gorman Day named in her honor, County Judge, Miss. County, Ark., 1993. Mem.: Cleburne C. of C., Cleburne Toastmasters Club. Avocations: garage sales, piano.

GORMAN, COLUM ALPHONSUS, retired endocrinologist; b. Maybridge, No. Ireland, June 27, 1936; arrived in U.S., 1960; s. James and Mary (McCollum) Gorman; m. Una Elizabeth O'Neill, Feb. 9, 1961; children: Kevin, Paul, Fiona, Michael. MB, Bch, BAO, Queens U., Belfast, Ireland, 1959; PhD, U. Minn., 1968. Cons. endocrinology Mayo Clinic, Rochester, Minn., 1966—; from asst. prof. to assoc. prof. Mayo Grad. Sch. Medicine, Rochester, 1971—81, prof., 1981-89; chmn. div. endocrinology Mayo Clinic, Rochester, 1985-92, bd. govs., 1999—2000, acting chair dept. health scis. rsch., 2000—01; assoc. dir. for rsch. devel. Mayo Found., Rochester, 2003—. Cons. in field. Editor, author: book The Eye and Orbit in Thyroid Disease, 1984. Fellow: ACP; mem.: AAAS, Endocrine Soc., Am. Thyroid Assn. (sec. 1984—88, pres. 1995—96). Republican. Avocations: reading, cross country skiing, auto restoration. Home and Office: 2607 Merrihills Dr Rochester MN 55902-1168

GORMAN, GAYLA MARLENE OSBORNE, consumer affairs executive; b. Owenton, Ky., Aug. 9, 1956; d. Frederick Clay and Helen Beatrice (Mason) O. AAS, No. Ky. U., 1982, BS, 1986; cert. in Chinese Mandarin, Def. Lang. Inst., 1975. Pers. clk. Dept. Edn. State Ky., Frankfort, 1974; sec. Dept. Health, Edn., Welfare Nat. Inst. Occupational Safety Health, Cin., 1977-79; specialist sales promotion U.S. Postal Svc., Cin., 1980, coord. customer liaison, task force pub. image, account rep., 1986-87, with stamp distbn. task force, 1993—; reservation sale agt. Delta Airlines, 1987-89. Councilmember Florence City Coun., Ky. 1984-87; vol. Children's Home, Covington, 1982, 87. With USAF, 1974-76. Named to Hon. Order Ky. Cols. Mem. Disabled Am. Veterans, No. Ky. U. Alumni Assn., Nat. Assn. Postmasters U.S., Boone County Fraternal Order Police, Ky. Assn. Realtors, Nat. Bd. Realtors, Women in Mil. Svc. for Am. (charter). Clubs: Fraternal Order Police. Democrat. Baptist. Avocations: horseback riding, travel, organizing seminars. Home: 8395 Juniper Ln Florence KY 41042-9279

GORMAN, GERALD WARNER, lawyer; b. North Kansas City, Mo., May 30, 1933; s. William Shelton and Bessie (Warner) G.; m. Anita Belle McPike, June 26, 1954; children: Guinevere Eve, Victoria Rose AB cum laude, Harvard U., 1954, LLB magna cum laude, 1956. Bar: Mo. 1956. Assoc. firm Dietrich, Tyler, Davis, Burrell & Dicus, Kansas City, 1956-62; ptnr. Dietrich, Davis, Dicus, Rowlands, Schmitt & Gorman, 1963-90; dir. Slagle, Bernard & Gorman, P.C., 1990—. Bd.dirs. Musser-Davis Land Co., Curry Investment Co. Bd. govs. Citizens Assn. Kansas City, 1962—; trustee Harvard/Radcliffe Club Kansas City Endowment Fund, chmn. bd. trustees, 1977-83; trustee Kansas City Mus., 1967-82; chmn. bd. trustees Avondale Meth. Ch., 1969-92, chmn endowment comn., 2001—; mem. Citizens Bond Com. of Kansas City, 1973-2000, chmn. 7th jud. cir. citizens com., 1982-84; chmn. Downtown Coun. Allis Plaza Reconstrn., 1983-85; bd. dirs. Spofford Home for Children, 1972-77, Clay County Econ. Devel. Commn., 1989-94, mem. exec. com., 1991-93, bd. dirs. Jackson County Hist. Soc. 2001-2004, Clay Co. Devel. Disabities Resources Bd., 2002-05. With U.S. Army, 1956-58; capt. USAR, 1958-64. Mem. Lawyers Assn. Kansas City (exec. com. 1968-71), ABA, Mo. Bar Assn., Kansas City Bar Assn., Clay County Bar Assn., Harvard Law Sch. Assn. Mo. (pres. 1973), Harvard Club (pres. 1966), Univ. Club (bd. dirs. 1983-86, 88-93, pres. 1990-91), Kansas City Club (bd. dirs. 1993-97), 611 Club (bd. dirs. 1987-91, pres. 1990), Kansas City Country Club, Old Pike Country Club, River Club, Man-of-the-Month Fraternity. Republican. Home: 917 NE Vivion Rd Kansas City MO 64118-5317 Office: 4600 Madison Ave Ste 600 Kansas City MO 64112-3031 Home Phone: 816-452-4141; Office Phone: 816-410-4604. Business E-Mail: ggorman@sbg-law.com.

GORMAN, JAMES CARVILL, manufacturing executive; b. Mansfield, Ohio, Apr. 16, 1924; s. James Carville and Ruth (Barnes) G.; m. Marjorie Newcomer, Apr. 10, 1950; children: Jeff, Gayle. BS, Ohio State U., 1949. Sales engr. Gorman Rupp Co., Mansfield, Ohio, 1949-58, sales mgr., 1958-64, pres., 1964-89, chmn., CEO, 1989-99, chmn., 1999—. Pres. Manairco, Inc., 1952-85, chmn. bd., 1985—; chmn. Mansfield Airport Commn., 1954-2000; treas. EAA Aviation Found., Oshkosh, Wis., 1973-2003. Capt. USAAF, 1942-46. Mem. Constrn. Industry Mfrs. Assn. Episcopalian. Home: PO Box 2599 Mansfield OH 44906-0599 Office: Gorman Rupp 305 Bowman St Mansfield OH 44903-1600 Office Phone: 419-755-1223. Personal E-mail: mng19sl@aol.com.

GORMAN, JAMES P., finance company executive; b. Australia; m. Penny Gorman; 2 children. Bachelor's Degree, Law Degree, U. Melbourne; MBA, Columbia U. Atty. Phillips Fox & Masel, Melbourne, Australia, 1982—85; ptnr. McKinsey & Co., 1992—97, co-head personal fin. svcs. practice N.Am., 1992—96, chmn. N.Y. pers. oper. com., 1996—99, mem. ptnr. election com., 1997—99, sr. ptnr. NY, 1997—99; chief mktg. officer Merrill Lynch & Co., Inc., 1999, exec. v.p., 1999, head USPC client relationship group, 2000, pres. global pvt. client, 2001—05, exec. v.p. acquisitions, strategy and rsch., 2005; pres., COO global wealth mgmt. Morgan Stanley, NYC, 2005—. Chmn. bd. dirs. Graham-Windham. Office: Morgan Stanley 1585 Broadway New York NY 10036*

GORMAN, JOSEPH GREGORY, JR., lawyer; b. Chgo., Sept. 27, 1939; s. Joseph Gregory and Genevieve C. (Smith) Gorman; m. Mary (Molly) O'Donovan, Mar. 23, 1968 (dec. Aug. 15, 2005); children: Jennifer Ann Gorman Patton, Joseph Gregory III. BA, U. Calif., Berkeley, 1961; MBA, UCLA, 1963, JD, 1966. Bar: U.S. Dist. Ct. (cen. dist.) Calif. 1967, U.S. Ct. Appeals (9th cir.) 1967, U.S. Tax Ct. Atty. Sheppard, Mullin, Richter & Hampton LLP, LA, 1966—. Chair death and gift tax com. LA County Bar Assn., chair probate & trust law sect., 1980-81; chair death and gift tax com. Calif. State Bar, 1976-77; co-founder U. So. Calif. Probate & Trust Conf., 1974—; adv. bd. U. Miami Heckerling Inst. Estate Planning, 1978—. Contbr. articles to profl. jours. Served with USAR, Calif. NG, 1962-68. Fellow Am. Coll. Trust and Estate Counsel, Academician, The Internat. Acad. of Estate and Trust Law. Clubs: Annandale Golf (Pasadena); Jonathan (Los Angeles). Republican. Roman Catholic. Office: Sheppard Mullin Richter & Hampton LLP 333 S Hope St Fl 48 Los Angeles CA 90071-1448 Office Phone: 213-617-4121. Business E-Mail: jgorman@sheppardmullin.com.

GORMAN, KATHLEEN JEAN, performing arts educator, choreographer; b. Mpls., Apr. 9, 1956; d. John William and Ruth Mary Gorman; m. Robert Chetwyn Glise, June 1, 1996; children: Zoe Mei Glise, Annie Li Glise. BA in Dance, Coll. of St. Teresa, Winona, Minn., 1980; MA in Dance Pedagogy, Brigham Young U., Provo, Utah, 1997. Dancer, choreographer Pasticcio Dance Ensemble, Mpls., 1981—83; dance faculty dept. theatre arts Viterbo U., LaCrosse, Wis., 1984—2000; artistic dir., tchr. dance The LaCrosse Dance Ctr., Wis., 1985—2001; artistic dir., choreographer, dancer The LaCrosse Dance Co., Wis., 1985—2001; dance faculty dept. exercise and sports sci. U. Wis., LaCrosse, 1997—, choreographer dept. theatre arts, 1998—. Choreographer numerous musicals and plays, artistic dir., choreographer Nutcracker Ballet, 1990—2000. Office: U Wis 1725 State St La Crosse WI 54601 Home: 902 Oak Timber Dr Onalaska WI 54650 Office Phone: 608-785-8180. Business E-Mail: gorman.kath@uwlax.edu.

GORMAN, MAUREEN J., lawyer; b. Rockford, Ill., Dec. 17, 1955; d. John William and Joanne Mary (Ollman) G.; m. Alan O. Sykes, 1980. BA, Coll. William and Mary, 1978; JD, Yale U., 1981. Bar: DC 1983, Ill. 1987. Law clk. to Hon. Warren W. Eginton US Dist. Ct. Conn., 1981-82; assoc. Caplin & Drysdale, Wash., 1982-85; legis. atty. joint com. on taxation US Congress, Wash., 1985-86; assoc. Mayer, Brown & Platt, Chgo., 1986-88, ptnr., 1988, Mayer, Brown, Rowe & Maw LLP, Palo Alto, Calif. Mem. ABA (chairperson subcom. tech. corrections, employee benefits com., tax sect. 1987-91). Office: Mayer Brown Rowe & Maw LLP 2 Palo Alto Sq Ste 300 Palo Alto CA 94306 Office Phone: 650-331-2000.

GORMAN, MICHAEL JOSEPH, retired library director, educator; b. Witney, Oxfordshire, Eng., Mar. 6, 1941; came to U.S. 1977; s. Philip Denis and Alicia F. (Barrett) G.; m. Anne Gillett, Mar. 6, 1962 (div. 1992); children: Emma, Alice; m. Anne Christine Reuland, June 6, 2003. Student, Ealing Sch. Librarianship, 1964-66. Dir. gen. services dept. Univ. Library U. Ill., Urbana, 1977-88, acting univ. librarian, 1986-87; prof. library adminstrn. U. Ill., Urbana, 1977-88; vis. prof. U. Chgo. Library Sch., 1984, 86-88, U. Calif., Berkeley, 1989-91; dean libr. svcs. Calif. State U., Fresno, 1988—2007; ret., 2007. Vis. lectr. U. Ill. Grad. Sch. Library Sci., Urbana, 1974-75; bibliog. cons. Brit. Library Planning Secretariat, 1972-74; head cataloguing Brit. Nat. Bibliography 1969-72. Author: A Study of the Rules for Entry and Headings in the Anglo-American Cataloguing Rules, 1967, 68, Format for Machine Readable Cataloguing of Motion Pictures, 1973, Concise AACR2, 1980, 4th edit., 2004, Technical Services Today and Tomorrow,1990, 2nd edit., 1998, Future Libraries (with Walt Crawford) 1995, Our Singular Strengths: Meditations for Librarians, 1998, Our Enduring Values, 2000, The Enduring Library, 2002, Our Own Selves, 2005, others; editor: Anglo-American Cataloguing Rules, 2d edit., 1978, rev., 1988, Catalogue and Index, 1973, Non Solus, 1981, Crossroads, 1986, Convergence, 1990; contbr. articles to profl. jours., chpts. to books. Recipient Blackwell scholarship award, 1997. Fellow: Libr. Assn. (Eng.), Brit. Libr. Assn., Chartered Inst. Libr. and Info. Profls. U.K. (hon.); mem.: ALA (mem. coun. 1991—95, 2002—, mem. exec. bd. 2003—07, pres.-elect 2004—05, pres. 2005—06, Margaret Mann citation 1979, Melvil Dewey medal 1992, Highsmith award 2001), Libr. Info. and Tech. Assn. (mem.-at-large exec. bd. 1982—85, pres. 1999—2000). Home Phone: 559-436-0105.

GORMAN, ROBERT SAUL, architect; b. NYC, June 28, 1933; s. Philip and Lillian (Weiss) G.; m. Judith Alice Albaum, July 2, 1965; children: Melissa, Sahsa William Shannon. BArch, MArch, Yale U., 1966. Apprentice to Frank Lloyd Wright, 1953-56; designer Eero Saarinen, Hamden, Conn., 1961-67; architect, planner Victor Gruen Assocs., NYC, 1967-69; Juster/Pope, Architects, Shelburne Falls, Mass., 1977-78; arch. Robert Gorman Assocs., Architects, Planners, Solar Energy, Richmond, NH, 1969-80; founder, prin. Rawson Place Architects, 1980-89, Green River Archs., 1989—. Cons. Bklyn. Coll., 1967-69. Served with AUS, 1956-58. Fellow Frank Lloyd Wright Found., 1953—. Mem. AIA (Design award 1972). Achievements include development of of many original solar applications in environmentally concerned architecture. Office: Green River Architects 935 Green River Rd Brattleboro VT 05301-9202 Home: 83 Oak St Brattleboro VT 05301 E-mail: robert@greenriverarchitects.com.

GORMAN, STEVE M., communications executive; b. 1969; BBA, Rider Coll., Lawrenceville, NJ. Product mgr. BellSouth; dir., Small Bus. Devel. Media One; product mgr., Residential Data Services Cox Comm., Inc., Atlanta, 1999, exec. dir. mktg., High Speed Internet, v.p., Product Mktg. & Mgmt., High Speed Internet, 2003—. Named one of 40 Executives Under 40, Multichannel News, 2006. Office: Cox Communitcations Inc 1400 Lake Hearn Dr Atlanta GA 30319 Office Phone: 404-843-5000. Office Fax: 404-843-5975.

GORMÈZANO, KEITH, small business advisor, arbitrator, writer, web site designer; b. Madison, Wis., Nov. 22, 1954; s. Isadore and Miriam Gormèzano; m. Emma Lee Rogers, Aug. 17, 1986 (div. Nov. 1990). BGS, U. Iowa, 1977, postgrad. in pub. affairs, 1979-80; postgrad. in law, U. Puget Sound, 1984-86. Pub. Le Beacon Presse, Seattle, 1980-89; real estate agt. Jim Stacy Realty, Seattle, 1988-89; owner A Better Temporary, Inc., 2003—; arbitrator Better Bus. Bur. Greater Seattle, 1987-93; ops., office mgr. Stuart Silk Arch., 2000—03; pres. A Better Temporary, 2003—. Arbitrator Op. Improvement Found., 1980—81, Puget Sound Multi-Listing Assn., 1988—89, Nat. Assn. Securities Dealers, 1989—92, 1998—2004, Harborview Med. Ctrs., 1990—91, Ford Consumer Appeals Bd., 1991—93, Harborview Med. Ctrs., 1992—93, N.Y. Stock Exch., 2004—; joint labor mgmt. com. Puget Fin. Svcs., U. Wash. Med. Ctr., 1990—91, 1992—93, pub. info. officer; dir. ACJS, Inc., 1981—82; mem. Fin. Times Investor and Exec. Survey Panel, 2001—, Comm. Experts Adv. Bd., 2001—; adv. bd. Voice Newspaper, 2006—. Editor: M'godolim, 1980—81, Funding Bull. U. Wash. Health Scis. Grantseekers, 1991, (newsletter) Lox of Friends, 2004—06; pub., editor Beacon Rev., 1980—89. Vice chmn. Resource Conservation Commn., Iowa City, 1979—80; vol. VISTA, 1982—83; active Selective Svc. System, 1982—, vice chmn. civilian rev. bd. 742, 1985—; active City of Seattle Animal Control Commn., 1984—86, vice chmn., 1985—86, chmn., 1986; active Wash. State Local Draft Bd. # 18, 1982—84, controlled choice appeals bd. Seattle Sch. Dist., 1989; patient collection rep. U. Wash., 1990—91, Harborview Med. Ctrs., 1990—91, 1992—93; jt. labor-mgmt. com. patient fin. svcs. U. Wash. Med. Ctr., 1990—93; dispute settlement bd. Ford Motor Co., 1991—93, consumer appeals bd., 1991—93; active No Safeword Writers Group, 1996—98, Phinney Neighborhood Assn., 2000—, Group Health Coop., 2000—04, Lox of Friends, 2002—, steering com. mem., 2004—05; active Puget Sound Consumers Coop., 2005—; coord. Seattle BiPolar Support Group, 1992—93; co-facilitator Polyfidelity Group, 1995—98; amb. Wash. State Basic Health Program, 1996—2000; sec. Friends of Cougar Hot Springs, 2005—; active Recreation Equipment Inc., NY Times Insight Panel, 2005—, Seattle Sr. Housing Program Advocates II, 1996—; patron mem. Seattle Art Mus., 2006—07; active Washington Dem. Party, Temple B'nai Torah, 1986—96, Congregation Eitz Or; exec. bd. thirty-something plus Jewish Cmty. Ctr., 1991—92; coord. com. edn. after dark program Jewish Fedn. Greater Seattle, 1991—92, young leadership divsn.; bd. dirs. Seattle Mental Health Inst., 1981—83, Youth Advs., Seattle, 1984, Atlantic St. Ctr., 1984; mem. steering com. Seattle Poly Potlucks Group, 1994—98; active QuickBooks Pro Advisor Program, 2006—; mem. adv. bd. The Voice Newspaper, 2006—. Named Citizen of the Day Radio Sta. KIXI, 1982. Mem. AARP, Am. Assn. for Nude Recreation, Self Help for the Hard of Hearing, The Naturist Soc., Hosteling Internat., League United Latin Am. Citizens Amigos (chmn. 1984-86), U. Iowa Alumni Assn., No Safeword Writers' Group, Wandering Jews Hiking Club, Seattle Cmty. Network Assn., NW Jewish Singles, Mensa, Sierra Club. Democrat. Jewish. Address: 6561 Phinney Ave N #217 Seattle WA 98103-5255 Office Phone: 206-789-8328. Personal E-mail: bb822@scn.org.

GORMLEY, DENNIS MICHAEL, research scholar; b. Meriden, Conn., Feb. 1, 1943; s. Lawrence Edward and Anna (Seitz) G.; m. Elizabeth Carol Festa, Aug. 12, 1967 (div. Sept. 1984); children: Douglas Lawrence, Jennifer Marie; m. Janet Lee Johnson, Mar. 23, 1985 (div. Nov. 2004); m. Sonia Ben Ouagrham, June 4, 2005 BA, U. Conn., 1965, MA, 1966. Advanced through grades to 1st lt. U.S. Army; rsch. specialist fed. civil svc. Army Materiel Command, Washington, 1969-72; chief fgn. intelligence U.S. Army Harry Diamond Labs, Washington, 1972-79; sr. v.p. Pacific-Sierra Rsch. Corp., Arlington, Va., 1979-99; pres. Blue Ridge Consulting Group, Inc., 1999—2003. Cons. Sci. Applications Internat. Corp., 1996—2000, Sandia Nat. Labs., Albuquerque, 1992—99, Rand Corp., Santa Monica, Calif., 1987-90, 2000-02, The Brookings Instn., Washington, 1973-75; govt. adv. com. chmn., mem. Dept. Def., Washington, 1983—; vis. scholar Geneva Ctr. for Security Policy, 1997; sr. fellow Monterey Inst. for Internat. Studies, Ctr. for Nonproliferation Studies, 2003—; sr. lectr. U. Pitts. Grad. Sch. Pub. and Internat. Affairs, 2002— Author: Double Zero and Soviet Military Strategy, 1988, rev. paperback, 1990, Dealing with the threat of Cruise Missiles, 2001; co-author: Controlling the Spread of Land-Attack Cruise Missiles, 1995; contbr. articles, book revs. to profl. jours. and newspapers. Vol. home hospice work. 1st lt. U.S. Army, 1966-69. Rsch. assoc. Internat. Inst. for Strategic Studies, London, 1984, sr. fellow, 2000-02. Mem. AAAS, Internat. Inst. for Strategic Studies, Arms Control Assn., Nat. Liberal Club, London, Phi Alpha Theta. Avocations: fly fishing, marathons, bicycling, volunteer work. Home and Office: 3514 Valley Dr Alexandria VA 22302 Office Phone: 703-472-1888. Personal E-mail: dmgormley@comcast.net.

GORMLEY, KENNETH, lawyer; b. NYC, Mar. 8, 1969; BA, Fordham U., 1991, JD, 1994. Bar: NY 1995, NJ 1995, US Dist. Ct. So., Ea., & No. Districts NY, US Ct. Appeals 2nd Cir., US Supreme Ct. Ptnr. Wilson, Elser, Moskowitz, Edelman & Dicker LLP, NYC. Mem.: NY State Bar Assn. Office: Wilson Elser Moskowitz Edelman & Dicker LLP 23rd Fl 150 E 42nd St New York NY 10017-5639 Office Phone: 212-490-3000 ext. 2328. Office Fax: 212-490-3038. Business E-Mail: gormleyk@wemed.com.

GORMLEY, ROBERT JOHN, retired publishing executive; b. Lynn, Mass., Oct. 14, 1939; s. Ernest Raymond and Catherine Louise (Maitl) G.; m. Beatrice LeCount, Sept. 4, 1966; children: Catherine, Jennifer. BA, Williams Coll., 1961; MA, U. Calif., Berkeley, 1964. With Wadsworth Inc., 1964-85; pres., pub. PWS Pubs. (encompassing various divs. Wadsworth, Inc.), Boston, 1980-85; pres. Duxbury Press, Boston, 1971-80; corp. v.p. Wadsworth, Boston, 1981-83, Ea. group v.p., 1983-85; exec. dir. Orbis Books, Maryknoll, N.Y., 1986-98; pub. Chatham House, NYC, 1998-2001; ptnr. Seven Bridges Press, NYC, 1998-2001; pub. Wiley/Jossey Bass Edn., 2001—; editor-in-chief Northeastern U. Press, 2002—04. Bd. dirs. Mayflower Mental Health Assn.; trustee Duxbury Free Library, Westport Free Libr., 2007; pres. Greater Boston Irish Children's Fund, Inc. Served with U.S. Army, 1964-69. Mem. Cath. Book Pubs. Assn. (pres.). Democrat. Roman Catholic. Home: PO Box 3922 1775 Drift Rd Westport MA 02790-0299

GORN, JANET MARIE, government official; b. Fond du Lac, Wis., Sept. 29, 1938; d. A. Reinhold Walter and Glady Lucille (Schulze) G.; m. Ronald Lee Braun, June 20, 1959 (div. Mar. 1980); children: Suzette Karen Braun Batchelder-Mitchell-Fulton, Gregory Reinhold William. BA, Drew U., 1973; MA, San Jose State U., 1982; postgrad., George Washington U., 1984-86. Policy analyst City of San Jose, Calif., 1975-76; rsch. asst. Brookings Instn., Washington, 1978; rsch. analyst Congl. Rsch. Svc., Washington, 1978-79; program analyst Nuclear Regulatory Commn., Washington, 1980-82, congl. affairs officer, 1982-87, sr. internat. rels. officer, 1988-99; sr. fgn. affairs officer U.S. Dept. of State, 1999—. Staff alt. Presdl. Task Force-State Planning Coun. Radioactive Waste Mgmt., Washington, 1980-82; mem. Internat. Atomic Energy Agy. Com. Devel. Code of Practice Internat. Transfers of Radioactive Waste, 1989-90, U.S. del. Internat. Atomic Energy Agy. Com. Control Radiation Sources and Devices, 1988-96, dep. head del., head of del., 1997—, steering com. Nuclear Energy Agy. Internat. Orgn. Econ. Cooperation and Devel., 1991—, commd. mem. solid waste mgmt. adv. com., 1992-2000, head U.S. delegation spent fuel and radioactive waste convention, 2003, 2006; councilman Quantico Civilian-Mil. Cmty. Rels. Coun., 1995—; mem. adv. coun. Internat. Policy Inst., 1993—; secretariate Internat. Nuc. Regulators Assn., 1997-99; com. mem. Sanitary Landfill Oversight Com. Prince William County, Va., 1990-92; commr. Prince William County Commn. on Future, 1989-90; sub-com. chmn. Prince William County Commn. and Libr. Planning Commn., Va., 1987-88 Author: Analysis of Low-Level Radioactive Waste Burial Site Capacity, 1981. Co-organizer, den mother, coach Pack 124 Cub Scouts Morris-Sussex Area coun. Boy Scouts Am., 1969-73; chairperson State Ad Hoc Com. to Establish Bus. Women and Adv. Bd., N.J., 1971-72; mem. Peralta Adobe Restoration Commn., San Jose, Calif., 1974-76, San Jose Bicentennial Commn., 1974-76, Mayor's Adv. Commn., Vienna, Va., 1978-79; bd. dirs. Prince William Libr. Found., 2004—, pres., 2005— Recipient commendation U.S. Nuclear Regulatory Commn. Chmn., 1990, Superior Honor award U.S. Dept. State, 2003; named Outstanding County Leader, Monmouth County, N.J., 1968, Woman of Yr., Morristown Jr. Woman's Club, N.J., 1969, West Valley Federated Woman's Club, San Jose, 1973; named to State Honor Role, N.J. Federated Woman's Clubs, 1973; acad. scholar Drew U., Madison, N.J., 1969, 70, 71, 72. Mem. AAUW (v.p. chpt. 1978-79), LWV (v.p. chpt. 1966-67, pres. 1968-69), Am. Nuclear Soc., Nuclear Women in Energy, European Nuclear Soc., Women in Energy (nat. v.p. 1984-86), Masons (Demolay club pres. 1978-79), Montclair Property Owners Assn. (bd. dirs. 2000—, pres. 2003-04) Republican. Episcopalian. Office: Nuclear Energy Safety and Security US Dept State Washington DC 20520 Office Phone: 202-647-3331. Business E-Mail: gornjm@state.gov.

GORNEY, JON L., bank executive; m. Nancy Gorney; 3 children. BS in Computer Sci., U. Dayton, Ohio, 1973. With Nat. City Corp., Cleve., 1973—77, mgmt. devel. trainee, systems officer, 1977—81, v.p., 1988—91, sr. v.p., 1991—93, exec. v.p. corp. ops. and info. svcs., 1993—. Bd. mem. Nat. Processing Inc., 2000—, chmn., CEO, 2002—; US region bd. dirs. MasterCard Internat. Trustee Elyria Cath. Found., mem. adv. bd., U. Dayton. Mem.: Bank Adminstrn. Inst., Am. Inst. Banking, KC. Office: Nat City Corp Nat City Ctr 1900 E Ninth St Cleveland OH 44114-3484 Office Phone: 216-222-2000. Office Fax: 216-575-2860.*

GORNEY, RODERIC, psychiatrist, educator; b. Grand Rapids, Mich., Aug. 13, 1924; s. Abraham Jacob Gorney and Edelaine (Roden) Harburg; m. Carol Ann Sobel, Apr. 13, 1986. BS, Stanford U., 1948, MD, 1949; PhD in Psychoanalysis, So. Calif. Psychoanalytic Inst., 1977. Diplomate Am. Bd. Psychiatry and Neurology. Pvt. practice psychiatry, San Francisco, 1952-62; asst. prof. UCLA, 1962-71, assoc. prof., 1971-73, prof. psychiatry, 1980—, dir. psychosocial adaptation and the future program, 1971—85; psychoanalytic mem. emeritus New Ctr. Psychoanalysis, 2005—. Faculty So. Calif. Psychoanalytic Inst. Author: The Human Agenda, 1972. Served with USAF, 1943-46. Fellow AAAS, Acad. Psychoanalysis, Am. Psychoanalytic Assn., Internat. Psychoanalytic Assn., Am. Psychiatric Assn. (essay prize 1971), Group for Advancement of Psychiatry, New Ctr. for Psychoanalysis. Avocation: music. Office: Semel Inst Neurosci and Human Behavior 760 Westwood Plz Los Angeles CA 90095-8353 Business E-Mail: preadapt@ucla.edu.

GORNICK, LONI ERIN, music educator; B Music Edn., U. Wis., Eau Claire, 2003. Orch. dir. Badger HS, Lake Geneva, Wis., 2003—. Recipient Results Plus award, Lake Geneve Sch. Dist., 2005. Mem.: Music Educators Nat. Conf., Am. String Tchrs. Assn.

GORNY, JACOB AARON, religious organization administrator, researcher; b. Edmonton, Alta., Can., Feb. 16, 1974; s. Norman Frank and Bonnie Ann (Mabbott) Gorny. BA in English, Whitman Coll., Walla Walla, Wash., 1996; MDiv, Holy Cross Greek Orthodox Sch. Theology, Brookline, Mass., 2000, ThM, 2004. Project coord. Oreg. Health & Scis. U., Portland, 2001—02; e-business mgr. Greek Orthodox Archdiocese Am., New York, NY, 2002—. Youth ministry leader Holy Trinity Ch., Portland, 2004—07. Mem.: Mensa. Libertarian. Greek Orthodox Christian. Avocations: guitar, biblical studies, photography. Home Phone: 503-449-7720.

GORNY, MARINA DUBINSKY, music educator; b. Sverdlovsk (now Ekaterinburg), Russia, Oct. 8, 1950; d. David and Dina Dubinsky; m. Peter Gorny, Nov. 24, 1994; 1 child, Isaac Alexander Livshetz. Diploma, Sch. of Music & Choral Conducting, 1966—70; M in music, Gnessin Inst. of Music, 1970—75; M in edn., Harvard U., 1986—87. Educator's Certificate Mass. Dept. of Edn., 1995. Music editor Pub. Ho., All-Russia Choral Soc., Moscow, 1977—79; music educator Various Music Schools, Moscow, 1970—79; tchr. self-employed, Moscow, 1979—85; music tchr./ choral dir. Nashoba Brooks Sch. of Concord, Concord, Mass., 1987—; ballet accompanist Emerson Coll., Boston, 1986—87. Editor & transcriber of folk songs Nat. Composers' Alliance, Moscow, 1979—84; mem. of nat. editl. bd. Am. Orff-Schulwerk Assn., Cleve., 1993—2001; writer and reviewer Profl. Publications, Moscow, 1977—84; evaluator of student teams Harvard U., Cambridge, Mass., 1986—87; mem. Zamir Chorale of Boston, Boston, 1990—99. Refusenik Soviet Jewry Alliance, Moscow, Russia, 1978—85. Scholar, Harvard U., 1986, Max Rosenfeld Found., 1987, grant, Nashoba Brooks Sch., 1990, 2001. Mem.: Music Educators Nat. Conf., Am. Kodaly Educators, Am. Orff-Schulwerk Assn., Am. Choral Directors Assn. Jewish. Avocations: travel, reading, music, creative expression. Home: 27 Clarendon Street Newton MA 02460 Office: Nashoba Brooks Schl of Concord 200 Strawberry Hill Rd Concord MA 01742 Home Phone: 617-527-4942; Office Phone: 978-369-4591 195. Personal E-mail: mdgorny@comcast.net. E-mail: marina@nbsc.org.

GOROFF, DAVID B., lawyer; BA summa cum laude, U. Ill., 1982; JD, Columbia U., 1985. Bar: Ill. 1985, US Dist. Ct. (no. dist. Ill.) 1986, US Ct. Appeals (2nd, 6th & 7th cirs.) 1986, US Supreme Ct. 1986. Law clk. to Hon. Richard D. Cudahy US Ct. Appeals (7th cir.), 1985—86; ptnr. Foley & Lardner, LLP, Chgo., co-chmn. appellate practice group. Adj. prof. U. Ill. Coll. Law, Chgo.-Kent Coll. Law; instr. Ill. Inst. CLE, Nat. Inst. Trial Advocacy. Mem.: ABA, ACLU. Office: Foley & Lardner LLP Suite 2800 321 N Clark St Chicago IL 60610 Office Phone: 312-832-5160. E-mail: dgoroff@foley.com.*

GORONKIN, HERBERT, physicist; b. Pitts., Jan. 9, 1936; s. Sander (Tammie) and Mae (Shulman) G.; children: David, Jeffrey, Michael; m. Pamela Louise Cooper, Oct. 4, 1980; children: Rebecca Louise, Theresa Louise, James David. BA, Temple U., 1961, MA, 1962, PhD, 1973. Physicist Internat. Resistance Co., Phila., 1963-65; sr. rsch. physicist Honeywell Inc., Ft. Washington, Pa., 1965-66; sect. head Am. Electronic Labs., Colmar, Pa., 1966-69; project engr. GE, Syracuse, NY, 1969-75; mgr. semiconductor ops. Varian Assocs., Beverly, Mass., 1975-77; from mgr. high speed devices to chief scientist Phoenix corp. rsch. labs. Motorola Inc., Phoenix, 1977-88, mgr. to dir. phys. rsch. lab., 1988-99; v.p. phys. rsch. labs. Phys. Scis. Rsch. Labs., Phoenix, 1999—2003, dir. rsch. activities in molecular electronics, spintronics, biotechnology and nanosci.; pres. Tech. Acceleration Assoc., 2003—; spl. adv. Lux Capital, 2003—. Chmn. Workshop on Compound Semiconductor Microwave Materials and Devices, 1984-86, Quantum Electronics, Quantum Functional Devices and Compound Semiconductor Devices, 1986, Advanced Hetrostructure Workshop, 1994; program chair Internat. Symposium on Compound Semiconductors, 1994, gen. chair, 1997; govering bd. Ctr. of Intergrated Nanosystems, 2003-, co-chmn. NanoBus. Alliance Tech. Adv. Bd., LP Lux Capital, 2005. Guest editor MRS Bull. on Future Memories; contbr. articles to profl. jours., chpts. to books; patentee in field. Served with USAF, 1954-57. Recipient Motorola Disting. Innovator award, 1993, Motorola Master Innovator award, 1995, Motorola Dan Noble fellow, 1996; named IEEE Phoenix Sect. Sr. Engr. of Yr., 1993. Fellow IEEE (IEDM compound semiconductor tech. program com. 1983-86); mem. Am. Phys. Soc., Sigma Xi. Avocations: hiking, japanese, cooking. Home and Office: 8641 S Willow Dr Tempe AZ 85284-2473 E-mail: hgoronkin@cox.net.

GORRELL, J. WARREN, JR., lawyer; b. Lexington, Ky., Feb. 7, 1954; s. John Warren and Geraldine (Standiford) G. AB magna cum laude, Princeton U., 1976; JD, U. Va., 1979. Bar: D.C. 1979, N.Y. 1995. Assoc. Hogan & Hartson, Washington, 1979-85, ptnr., 1986—, chmn., 2001—, mem. exec. com., 1991—93, 1995—97, 1999—2001, dir. corp. and securities group, 1997—. Named Dealmaker of the Year, The Am. Lawyer; named one of D.C. Leading Lawyers: Top 10 Deal-Makers, Legal Times, 2006, 100 Most Influential Lawyers, Nat. Law Jour., 2006. Mem. ABA (bus. sect. 1979—), Nat. Assn. Real Estate Investment Trusts, City Club Washington. Office: Hogan & Hartson LLP 555 13th St NW Washington DC 20004-1161 Office Phone: 202-637-8618. Office Fax: 202-673-5910. Business E-Mail: jwgorrell@hhlaw.com.*

GORRIE, M. MILLER, construction executive; b. Birmingham, Ala. m. Frances Gorrie. BS, Auburn U., Ala., 1957. Chmn., CEO Brasfield & Gorrie LLC, Birmingham, Ala., 1995. Trustee Colonial Properties Trust; bd. mem. Am. Cast Iron Pipe Co., Met. Devel. Bd., Econ. Devel. Partnership of Ala., Ala. Symphony Orch., U. of Ala. at Birmingham Civil Engr. Adv. Bd. Co-founder Cloister Creek Ednl. Ctr. Named to State of Ala. Engring. Hall of Fame; recipient Outstanding Corp. Citizen, Nat. Soc. Fund Raising Execs., Tree of Life award, Jewish Nat. Fund, Hope award, Multiple Sclerosis Soc. Office: Brasfield & Gorrie PO Box 10383 729 30th St S Birmingham AL 35233-2939 Office Fax: 205-251-1304.*

GORRIN, EUGENE, lawyer; b. Irvington, NJ, Apr. 22, 1956; s. Harry and Ruth (Goldberg) G. BA, Rutgers U., 1978; JD, George Washington U., 1981; LLM in Taxation, NYU, 1982. Bar: NJ 1981, US Dist. Ct. NJ 1981, US Tax Ct. 1982, US Supreme Ct. 1985. Assoc. Ozzard, Rizzolo, Klein, Mauro & Savo, Somerville, NJ, 1982-83, Levine, Furman & Davis, East Brunswick, NJ, 1984-88; assoc., ptnr. Cole, Schotz, Meisel, Forman & Leonard, P.A., Hackensack, NJ, 1988—98; v.p., corp. adv. specialist family office group, sr. trust officer, mgr. bus. and real estate groups Merrill Lynch Trust Co., FSB, Pennington, NJ, 1999—2006. Contbr. articles to profl. pubs. Mem. ABA (taxation sect.), NJ Bar Assn. (taxation sect.), Phi Alpha Delta. Home: 2607 Frederick Ter Union NJ 07083

GORRY, JAMES A., III, lawyer; b. Wilmington, Del., Mar. 1, 1939; s. James A. Jr. and Carolyn Allmond Gorry; m. Anne Evans, May 7, 1975; children: Scott Baker, Katherine Gorry Lawson. BA, U. Del., 1961; JD, Washington & Lee U., 1964. Bar: Va. 1964, U.S. Dist. Ct. (ea. dist.) Va. 1968, U.S. Ct. Appeals (4th cir.) 1982, U.S. Supreme Ct. 1982. Atty. U.S. Army-Judge Adv. Gen. Corps, Virginia Beach, Va., 1965-68, Murphy, Bennett & Gorry, Virginia Beach, 1968-72, Broyles, Gorry, Moore & Brydges, Virginia Beach, 1972-82, Taylor & Walker, P.C., Norfolk, Va., 1982-99; ptnr. DMZ Law Group, L.L.P., Norfolk, 1999; gen. counsel, corp. sec. Dollar Tree Stores, Va. Commr. in chancery Virginia Beach Cir. Ct., 1985—. Capt. U.S. Army, 1964-68. Mem. Va. State Bar (bd. govs. civil litigation sect. 1994—), Va. Assn. Def. Attys. (dir. 1993-96), Va. Trial Lawyers' Assn., Va. Bar Assn., Virginia Beach Bar Assn. (pres. 1980), Norfolk-Portsmouth Bar Assn. Avocations: scuba diving, golf, running. Office: Dollar Tree Stores 500 Volvo Parkway Chesapeake VA 23320 Office Phone: 757-321-5419. Office Fax: 757-321-5111.

GORSKE, ROBERT H., lawyer; b. Milw., 1932; m. Antonette Dujick; 1 child, Judith Mary (Mrs. Charles H. McMullen). Student, U. Wis., Milw., 1949-50; BA cum laude, Marquette U., 1953, JD magna cum laude, 1955, MS in Clin. Psychology, 1996; LLM (W.W. Cook fellow), U. Mich., 1959; student, Hague Acad. Internat. Law, The Netherlands, 1981. Bar: Wis. bar 1955, D.C. bar 1975, U.S. Supreme Ct. bar 1970; cert. Gerontology, Marquette U., 2002. Assoc. firm Quarles, Spence & Quarles, Milw., 1955-56; atty. Allis-Chalmers Mfg. Co., West Allis, Wis., 1956-62; instr. law U. Mich. Law Sch., Ann Arbor, Mich., 1958-59; lectr. law Marquette U. Law Sch., Milw., 1963; assoc. firm Quarles, Herriott & Clemons, Milw., 1962-64; atty. Wis. Electric Power Co., Milw., 1964-67, gen. counsel, 1967-94, v.p., 1970-72, 76-94, dir., 1991-94; mem. firm Quarles & Brady, Milw., 1972-76; gen. counsel Wis. Energy Corp., Milw., 1981-94. Tutor in psychiatry Med. Coll. Wis., 1995. Contbr. articles to profl. jours.; Editor-in-chief: Marquette Law Rev, 1954-55. Bd. dirs. Guadalupe Children's Med. Dental Clinic, Inc., Milw., 1976-86; bd. dirs. Milw. Urban League, 1991-94, treas., 1993-94; trustee Ronald McDonald House, Wauwatosa, Wis., 1987-94, St. Mary's Visitation Parish, Elm Grove, Wis., 2003-07. Mem. State Bar Wis., Edison Electric Inst. (vice chmn. legal com. 1975-77, chmn. 1977-79), Am. Arbitration Assn. (panelist comml. arbitrators 1985—), Ctr. for Pub. Resources (com. on alt. dispute resolution 1985-94, exec. com. 1991-94, panel disting. neutrals 1991-94).

GORSKI, WALDEMAR, chemist, educator; MS in Chemistry, Warsaw U., 1980, PhD in Chemistry, 1990. Postdoctoral assoc. Miami U., Oxford, Ohio, 1990—94; vis. scholar U. Fla., Gainesville, 1994—96; from asst. prof. to prof. chemistry U. Tex., San Antonio, 1996—, Welch departmental rsch. grant adminstr., 2002—07, interim dept. chair, 2006—. Co-chmn. tech. session Electrochem. Soc., San Antonio, 1996. Author: (research papers) Published In Premier Scientific Journals; contbr. articles to profl. jours. Grantee NIH, Welch Found., Rsch. Corp. Mem.: Am. Chem. Soc. (organizer, chmn. tech. session 57th SW meeting 2001). Achievements include development of integration of enzymes and electrodes using a biopolymer chitosan; discovery of new synthetic route to catalytic films of mixed metal oxides; invention of new electrocatalytic systems for determination of insulin.

GORSLINE, STEPHEN PAUL, security specialist; b. Washington, Aug. 22, 1954; s. Robert William and Patricia Ann (Ketchum) G. AAS in Criminal Justice, Coll. of Lake County, 1987; BS in Criminal Justice, Madonna U., 1998. Dir. safety ops. Thielenhaus Corp., Novi, Mich., 1998-99; with US Dept. of Def. Vol. Nat. Rep. Com., Washington, 1992. Staff sgt. USAF, 1977-82. Mem. Safety/Security Mgmt. Assn. (exec. dir. 1996-99), Fraternal Order Police. Roman Catholic. Avocations: collecting stamps, old coins and postcards. E-mail: stevegorsline@yahoo.com.

GORSUCH, EDWARD LEE, former chancellor; Degree in Econ. and Cmty. Devel., U. Mo. Dir. Inst. Social and Econ. Rsch., 1976-94; dean Sch. Pub. Affairs U. Alaska, Anchorage, 1988-94, chancellor, 1994—2004. Bd. dirs. Commonwealth North; mem. adv. bd. Alaska Airlines Anchorage Cmty.; mem. civilian adv. bd. ALCOM; mem. Fiscal Policy Coun. Alaska, U.S. Artic Rsch. Com., U.S. MAB; dir. High Latitude Ecosystems. Mem., pres. Alaska Assn. Sch. Bds. Mem.: AAAS (pres. Alaska chpt.). Home Phone: 360-647-5233; Office Phone: 360-647-5233. Business E-Mail: lee.gorsuch@uaa.alaska.edu.

GORSUCH, NEIL MCGILL, federal judge, lawyer; b. Denver, Aug. 29, 1967; s. David Ronald Gorsuch and Anne McGill Burford; m. Marie Louise Burletson, June 22, 1996; children: Belinda Loveday, Emma Louise. BA with honors, Columbia U., NYC, 1988; JD cum laude, Harvard U., Cambridge, Mass., 1991; DPhil, Oxford U., Eng. Bar: NY 1992, Colo. 1994, DC 1997. Law clk. to Hon. David B. Sentelle US Ct. Appeals (DC cir.), Washington, 1991—92; law clk. to Justice Byron R. White & Justice Anthony M. Kennedy US Supreme Ct., Washington, 1993—94; assoc. Kellogg, Huber, Hansen, Todd & Evans, Washington, 1995—97, ptnr., 1998—2005; prin. dep. assoc. atty. gen., acting assoc. atty. gen. US Dept. Justice, Washington, 2005—06; judge US Ct. Appeals (10th cir.), Denver, 2006—. Contbr. articles to profl. jours. Recipient Edmund J. Randolph award for Outstanding Svc., US Dept. Justice, 2006, Joseph Stevens Pub. Svc. award, Harry S. Truman Found.; Marshall scholar, 1992—95, Harry S. Truman scholar, 1987—90. Mem.: Coun. Fgn. Rels., Trout Unltd., Phi Beta Kappa. Avocations: skiing, fly fishing, tennis. Office: US Ct Appeals 10th Cir Byron White Ct House 1823 Stout St Denver CO 80257*

GORT, MICHAEL, economics professor; b. Minsk, USSR, Sept. 30, 1923; came from China to U.S., 1937; m. Elizabeth Ann Mitchell, June 15, 1957; children: William Henry, Adam Michael. AB, Bklyn. Coll., CUNY, 1943; AM, Columbia U., 1951, PhD, 1954. Lectr. in econs. U. Calif., Berkeley, 1951-54; mem. research staff Nat. Bur. Econ. Research, NYC, 1954-57; assoc. prof. fin. U. Chgo., 1957-62; cons. Dept. Commerce, Washington, 1962-63; prof. econs. SUNY, Buffalo, 1963—. Vis. prof. econs. Northwestern U., Evanston, Ill., 1967-68; sr. research staff mem. and dir. research program in indsl. orgn. Nat. Bur. Econ. Research, N.Y.C., 1971-75; pres. Michael Gort Assocs. LLC, Buffalo, 2004— Author: Diversification and Integration in American Industry, 1962, Changes in the Size Standard of Business Firms, 1964; contbr. articles to profl. jours. Mem. adv. com. U.S. Bur. of the Census, 1994-2000. Social Sci. Rsch. Coun. fellow, 1950-51. Mem. Am. Econ. Assn. Home: 71 Smallwood Dr Buffalo NY 14226-4028 Office: SUNY Dept of Econs North Campus Buffalo NY 14260 Business E-Mail: gort@buffalo.edu.

GORTATOWSKI, MELVIN JEROME, retired chemist; b. Chgo., Oct. 30, 1925; s. Walter Harry and Anna Martha (Santowski) Gortatowski. BS, U. Ill., 1950, PhD, 1956; MS, Wash. State U., 1952. Research instr. biochemistry U. Utah, Salt Lake City, 1955-58, research assoc. psychiatry, 1958-59, research instr. biochemistry, chemist VA Hosp., 1959-65; assoc. investigator, asst. rsch. prof. pediatrics, biochemistry U. So. Calif. Children's Hosp., Los Angeles, 1965-71; dir. bur. clin. chemistry Utah State Health Lab., Salt Lake City, 1971-87, safety officer, 1980-87. Contbr. articles to profl. jours. With US Army, 1944—46. Eastman Kodak fellow, U. Ill., 1954. Mem.: Mineral Collectors Utah, Am. Chem. Soc., Utah Numismatic Soc. (bd. dirs. 1976—77), Phi Lambda Upsilon, Sigma Xi. Roman Catholic. Avocations: photography, stamp collecting/philately, music, mineral collecting, swimming. Home: 4045 Foubert Ave Salt Lake City UT 84124-3410

GORTON, MARK HOWARD, information technology executive, entrepreneur; b. NJ, 1967; 3 children. BS in Elec. Engring., Yale U., 1988; MS in Elec. Engring., Stanford U.; MBA, Harvard U., 1993. Elec. engr. Martin Maritta (now Lockheed Martin); fixed income proprietary trader Credit Suisse First Boston, 1993—98; mng. dir. Tower Rsch. Capital LLC, NYC, 1998—; founder & CEO Lime Wire LLC, NYC, 2000—; founder & dir. Lime Brokerage LLC, NYC, 2005—; CEO Lime Group, NYC. Founder & pres. Open Planning Project, NYC, 1999—. Office: Lime Group 11th Fl 377 Broadway New York NY 10013 also: The Open Planning Project 349 W 12th St #3 New York NY 10014 Office Phone: 212-219-6000. Office Fax: 212-219-6006. E-mail: info@limegroup.com.*

GORTON, NATHANIEL M., federal judge; b. 1938; m. Jodi Linnell; 3 children. AB, Dartmouth Coll., 1960; LLB, Columbia U., 1966. Bar: Mass. 1966, US Dist. Ct. Mass. 1967, US Ct. Appeals (5th cir.) 1975, US Ct. Appeals (9th cir.) 1977, US Ct. Appeals (1st cir.) 1979, US Ct. Appeals (11th cir.) 1990. Assoc. Nutter, McClennen & Fish, Boston, 1966-69, Powers & Hall, P.C., Boston, 1970-74, ptnr., dir., 1975-92; judge US. Dist. Ct., Mass., 1992—. Fgn. Intelligence Surveillance Ct., 2001—. Trustee Buckingham Browne & Nichols Sch., Cambridge, Mass., 1984-93, chmn., 1989-93; mem. corp. New Eng. Home for Little Wanderers; mem. Wellesley Town Meeting, 1971-86; sr. warden All Saints Episcopal Ch., Brookline, Mass., 1975-80; apptd. Mass. Citizens Commn. on Gen. Ct., 1976; mem. com. Modern Legis., 1967-69; coach Wellesley Little League and Youth Hockey, 1983-87; bd. dirs. Rep. Club Mass., 1991-92; mem. fin. com. Citizens for Joe Malone, 1989-90; mem. Weld/Cellucci Com., 1989-90. Lt. (j.g.) USNR, 1960-62. Mem. Boston Bar Assn. (law day classroom program, 1987-93, litigation, adminstrn. justice sect.). Avocations: hockey (member Boston Atoms Hockey North America national finalist 1988, 91), tennis, skiing, sailing. Office: US Dist Ct 1 Courthouse Way Ste 3110 Boston MA 02210

GORTON, ROBERT L., retired mechanical engineer; b. Houston, Oct. 19, 1931; s. Lester H. and Frances M. Gorton; m. Rosalind D. Davis, June 11, 1960; children: Elaine F. Kaifes, Catherine M. Hogan, Christine A. Robinson, Robert J. BS, La. Tech U, Ruston, 1953; MS, La. State U., Baton Rouge, 1960; PhD, Kans. State U., Manhattan, 1966. Registered profl. engr., La., 1953, Kans., 1994. Engr. Schlumberger Corp., Morgan City, La., 1955—58; faculty assoc. La. State U., Baton Rouge, 1959—60; prof., mech. engring. Kans. State U, Manhattan, 1960—94, emeritus prof., 1994—. Prin. Gorton Assoc., Manhattan, 1969—2003. Contbr. articles to profl. jours. With US Army, 1953—55. Recipient Halliburton Prof., Kans. State U, 1976—78, Hollis award, Coll. Engring., Kans. State U, 1992, Conoco All U. Tchg. Excellence award, Kans. State U, 1994; fellow, Am. Oil Co., 1965—66. Fellow: ASHRAE (life Distirg. Svc. award), ASME (life). Achievements include research in heat transfer, air conditioning, power plants. Home: 2043 Stephen Ct Manhattan KS 66503 Personal E-mail: gorton@ksu.edu.

GORTON, SLADE (THOMAS SLADE GORTON III), lawyer, former senator; b. Chgo., Jan. 8, 1928; s. Thomas Slade and Ruth (Israel) Gorton; m. Sally Jean Clark, June 28, 1958; children: Tod, Sarah Jane, Rebecca Lynn. AB, Dartmouth Coll., 1950; LLB with honors, Columbia U., 1953. Bar: Wash. 1953. Assoc. law firm, Seattle, 1953—65; ptnr. law firm, 1965—69; atty. gen. State of Wash., Olympia, 1969—81; ptnr. Davis, Wright & Jones, Seattle, 1987—89; senator from Wash. U.S. Senate, 1981—87, 1989—2001; of counsel Preston, Gates & Ellis, Seattle and Washington, 2001—. Mem. Wash. Ho. of Reps., 1959—69, majority leader, 1967—69, nat. Rep. senatorial com., Indian affairs, budget com., appropriations com., commerce/sci. and transp. com., energy and natural resources com.; chmn. commerce, sci. and transp. subcom. on aviation, com. on appropriations subcom. on interior; commr. The Nat. Commn. on Terrorist Attacks Upon the U.S. (The 9-11 Commn.), 2002—04; bd. dirs. IDT Corp., Newark, 2005—. Trustee, founding mem. Pacific Sci. Ctr., Seattle, 1977—78; mem. Pres.'s Consumer Adv. Coun., 1975—77, Wash. State Law and Justice Commn., 1969—80, chmn., 1969—76; mem. State Criminal Justice Tng. Commn., 1969—80, chmn., 1969—76. With US Army, 1946—47, to 1st lt. USAF, 1953—56, col. (ret.) USAF. Mem.: ABA, Nat. Assn. Attys. Gen. (pres. 1976—77, Wyman award 1980), Wash. Bar Assn., Wash. Athletic Club (Seattle), Seattle Tennis Club, Phi Beta Kappa, Phi Delta Phi. Office: Preston Gates & Ellis 925 4th Ave Ste 2900 Seattle WA 98104-1158

GORTON-HORAN, ANN HILBERT, vice principal; b. NYC, Mar. 30, 1937; d. Clarence Webb and Irene Madden Hilbert; children: Gwynne Gorton Zisko, Melissa Gorton Sadin, Lara Leigh Groton. BS in Elem. Edn., SUNY, 1959; MA in devel. reading, Coll. NJ, 1986. Cert. K-8 elem. sch. tchr., NJ tchr. of reading, reading specialist. Tchr. Mamaroneck Sch. Dist., NY, 1959—61, Bridgewater-Raritan Sch. Dist., NJ, 1961—63, Hillsborough Township Sch. Dist., NJ, 1965—76, Branchburg Twp. Sch. Dist., NJ, 1977—98; asst. prin. Whiton Sch., 1998—. Contbr. articles various profl. jours. Mem., v.p. BOE, Hillsborough Twp., NJ, 1972—89. Named Citizen of Yr., Rotary Club, 1974, Media Ctr. named after Ann Hilbert Gorton-Horan, Hillsborought BOE, 1990, Tchr. of Yr., Branchburg Twp. Sch. Dist., 1985, Reading Tchr. of Yr., NJRA Mary Filosa award, 1990. Mem.: Reading Recovery Coun. of N. Am., NJ Prin./Suprv. Assn., Assn. for Suprv. of Curriculum Devel., Nat. Coun. of Tchrs. of English, Ctrl. NJ Reading Coun., NJ Reading Assn., Internat. Reading Assn., Delta Kappa Gamma, Kappa Delta Phi. Avocations: knitting, crewel, reading, travel. Office Phone: 908-371-0842. Office Fax: 908-369-1582. E-mail: aghoran@aol.com.

GOSALIA, KEYOOR CHETAN, electrical engineer; b. Mumbai, Maharashtra, India, June 7, 1978; arrived in U.S., 2000; s. Chetan Shantilal and Jagruti Chetan Gosalia; m. Nupur Keyoor Gosalia, Jan. 22, 2006. BE, Sardar Patel U., India, 1999; MS, NC State U., Raleigh, 2001, PhD, 2004. Trainee engr. Pioneer Furnaces Pvt. Ltd., Vallabh Vidyanagar, Gujarat, India, 1999—2000; rsch. asst. NC State U., Raleigh, 2000—04; rf engr. ii Gen. Dynamics C4 Sys. Satcom Tech., Kilgore, Tex., 2004—06; sr. rsch. engr. Paratek Microwave, Inc., Columbia, Mo., 2007—. Reviewer Antennas and Wireless Propagation Letters. Contbr. articles to profl. jours., chapters to books. Recipient H. A. Wheeler Application prize, IEEE Antennas and Propagation, 2005. Mem.: IEEE (assoc.), Sigma Xi (assoc.), Phi Kappa Phi (assoc.). Achievements include invention of 3 invention disclosures for novel antenna structures; patents pending for bio-implantable micro antenna. Home: 1417-D Skyridge Dr Crystal Lake IL 60014 Home Phone: 919-522-7138. Personal E-mail: keyoor@gmail.com.

GOSAVI, SUCHETA, internist; d. Ashok Dattatrey and Sanjivani Ashok Gosavi. MB, BChir, R.G. Kar Med. Coll., Calcutta, 1989; diploma in tropical medicine and hygiene, Sch. Tropical Coll., Calcutta, 1993; MD in Internal Medicine, Dr Vaishampayan Meml. Med. Coll., Solapur, 1996; MD Internal Medicine in Internal Medicine, U. Mo., Columbia, 2007. Resident in internal medicine R.G. Kar Med. Coll. and Hosp., Calcutta, 1989—90, Seth Sukhlal Karnani Meml. Hosp. Polyclinic, Calcutta, 1991; resident in tropical medicine and hygiene Sch. Tropical Medicine, Calcutta, 1991—93; resident in internal medicine Dr. Vaishampayan M emorial Med. Coll., Solapur, 1993—96; physician critical care unit Maharashtra Med. Found., Pune, India, 1996; sr. med. officer Ctrl. Govt. Health Svc., Pune, 1996—2001; rsch. asst. St. Louis U., 2001—04; resident physician U. Mo., Columbia, 2004—. Contbr. scientific papers, articles to profl. jours. Recipient, R.G.Kar Med. Coll., Calcutta, Govt. of West Bengal, India., 1984. Mem.: ACP, AMA, Assn. Physicians India.

GOSCHKE, LINDA FRY, artist; b. Ridley Park, Pa., July 17, 1957; d. Dale Eugene Fry and Annie Josephine Rhoades; m. John Phillip Goschke, Apr. 7, 1990. BFA in Painting with Distinction, Pa. State U., 1979; MA, Phila. Coll. Art, 1985; tchg. cert., Temple U., 1988; MFA, Pa. Acad. Fine Arts, 2002. Internship Rosenbach Mus. and Libr., 1984; art instr. Del. County CC, Media, Pa., 1986; comml. printing instr. Eastern Montgomery County Vocat.-Tech. Sch., Willow Grove, Pa., 1986—91; art instr. Berkeley Edn. and Tng. Ctr., Bala Cynwyd, Pa., 1990—93, Camden County Coll., Blackwood, NJ, 1991—93, 1995—2000, Holy Family Coll., Phila., 1992—96, Cabrini Coll., Radnor, Pa., 1993; internship Greater Phila. Cultural Alliance, 2001; asst. curator Pa. Acad. of Fine Arts Studio Sch. Gallery, Phila., 2001; art instr. Gloucester County Coll., Sewell, NJ, 2007. Artist, designer Barbara Kates Designs, Bala Cynwyd, 1980—90, 1993—94, NDI Engring. Co., Pennsauken, NJ, 1981—86, Cornerstone Media, Ambler, Pa., 1998, Enterprise Mktg. & Comm., Cherry Hill, NJ, 1999—; set designer, prodn. designer Hatboro-Horsham HS, Pa., 1989—2006; directory artist Pa. Coun. on the Arts, Arts-in-Edn. Artist-in-Residence Program, Harrisburg, 1991—. One-woman shows include Springfield Pub. Libr., Pa., 1979, Benjamin Rush Gallery at Unitarian Universalist House, Phila., 1996, exhibitions include Ctrl. Pa. Festival Arts, HUB Gallery, 1979, University Park, 2001, CAC, Wallingford, Pa., 1980, 1981 (First prize Pastel, 1980, 1981), Terrance Gallery, Palenville, NY, 1981, Rittenhouse Sq. Fine Arts Ann., Phila., 1981, Print Club, 1981, 1982, Provident Nat. bank, 1982, Glassboro State Coll., 1991, People's Republic of China, 1986—87, Allied Artists Winston-Salem, NC, 1992, Woodmere Art Mus., Phila., 1994, Main Line Arts Ctr., Haverford, Pa., 1994, Printmaking Coun. NJ, Somerville, 1996, 1997, 1998 (Johnson & Johnson Purchase prize), Camden County Coll. Art Gallery, 1998, 1999, Pa. Acad. Fine Arts, 2000—02, Mus. Am. Art, Pa. Acad. Fine Arts, Phila., 2002, West Chester Arts Walk, 2004, Jenkins Arboretum Greenhouse Gallery, Devon, Pa., 2005, numerous others. Recipient Images '97 Hon. Mention, Ctrl. Pa. Festival of Arts, 1997, Second prize, Photography, Best of Pa. Artists & Artisans, 2005, First prize in photography, ArtAbility, 2006. Mem.: Nat. Assn. Photoshop Profls. Avocations: travel, sewing, nature. Home: 169 W Abbottsford Ave Philadelphia PA 19144 Office Phone: 215-848-2014. Personal E-mail: lafrites@aol.com.

GOSCIEWSKI, ROBERT LOUIS, logistician; b. Bristol, Pa., Mar. 10, 1957; s. Victor Stanley and Palma Mary Gosciewski; m. Maria Luisa Capasso, May 26, 1984; children: Diana Dawn, Kathryn Kelly. BA, U. Pa., 1979; prof. cert. Italian, Def. Lang. Inst., Monterey, Calif., 1981; MSBA, Boston U., 1985; M of Strategic Studies, U.S. Army War Coll., 2004; grad. def. leadership and mgmt. program, U.S. Dept. Def., 2006. Cert. Army Acquisition Program; profl. logistician Internat. Soc. Logistics Engrs., 3wizard 3com Corp., CTM Toastmasters Internat., program mgmt., life cycle logistics. Instr. Big Bend CC, Vicenza, Italy, 1984-85; cons. engring. Ingegneria Info. S.p.A., Turin, Italy, 1985-86; prodn. mgr. L.F. Lambert Spawn Co., Coatesville, Pa., 1986-89; computer systems analyst Army Legal Svcs. Agy., Falls Church, Va., 1989-92; treas. Valley Ctr. Corp., Parkesburg, Pa., 1989-90; mktg. cons. Conemar, Manassas, Va., 1989-92; computer specialist, engr. Office Dep. Chief of Staff, U.S. Army, Heidelberg, Germany, 1992-93; info. mgmt. officer Office Provost Marshal, HQUSAREUR, Mannheim, Germany, 1993-96; logistics automation specialist Logistics Automation Divsn., Vicenza, Italy, 1996-98; chief Logistics Automation divsn. So. European Task Force, Vicenza, Italy, 1998—2000, 2002—07; chief programs integration and execution, dir. combat devel. Combat Svc. Support, U.S. Army Combined Arms Support Command, 2000—02; dep. SETAF Transformation Team, 2005—06; combat developer, joint and allied futures, concepts and doctrine directorate US Army Combined Arms Support Command, 2007—. Cons. Engring. Ingegneria Informatica S.p.A., Torino, Italy, 1985—86; internet working computer cons., local wide area networking svcs. Army Mgmt. Staff Coll., 1993—98. Mem. West End Fire Co. No. 3, Coatesville, 1989. Capt. inf. US Army, 1979—83. Mem.: Military Officers Assn. Am., Assn. U.S. Army, Internat. Soc. Logistics, Am. Econs. Assn., Beta Theta Pi. Roman Catholic. Avocations: community service, golf, reading, writing. Address: 1606 Berkeley Ave Petersburg VA 23803

GOSFIELD, MARGARET, secondary school educator, school system administrator, consultant, editor; b. Marshall County, Minn., Mar. 9, 1942; d. William Jay and Evelyn Pearl (Anderson) Wayne; m. Amor Gosfield, Aug. 21, 1964. BA in History, U. Calif., Santa Barbara, 1966, secondary tchrs. credential, 1968, MA in Edn., 1976. Cert. tchr. Calif. Tchr. Ventura (Calif.) Unified Sch. Dist., 1969-89, coord. gifted and talented edn. program, 1982-97; cons. gifted edn. Author: (book) History of the Anderson Family, 1981, History of the Wayne Family, 1983; editor: Meeting the Challenge: A Guidebook for Teaching Gifted Students, 1996, Gifted Edn. Communicator, 1998—. Named Calif. Outstanding Educator, Johns Hopkins U., 1994; recipient EdnI. Achievement award, Phi Delta Kappa, 1997. Mem.: Calif. Assn. for the Gifted (regional rep. 1990—94, v.p. 1994—96, pres. 1996—98, Tchr. of the Yr. 1985), Santa Barbara Mus. Art. Avocations: travel, writing, gardening. Home: 3136 Calle Mariposa Santa Barbara CA 93105-2775 Office: 11130 Sun Center Dr Ste 100 Rancho Cordova CA 95670 Office Phone: 916-441-3999. Personal E-mail: gosfield@cox.net.

GOSHORN, RICHARD HENLEY, lawyer; b. Ft. Thomas, Ky. m. Lori Kidder; children: Kendall, Millicent, Leland. BA, Coll. Wooster, 1978; JD, Duke U., 1981. Pvt. practice Frost Brown Todd LLC, Cinn., Gottesman Jones Partners, London; sr. atty. Fort Howard Corp.; sr. v.p. Cable and Wireless Global; various sr. exec. legal positions including gen. counsel Cable and Wireless PLC, 1999—2001; corp. v.p., gen. counsel, sec. Acterna Corp., 2001—04; gen. counsel Akin Gump Strauss Hauer & Feld LLP, 2004—. Office: Akin Gump Strauss Hauer & Feld LLP Robert S Strauss Bldg 1333 New Hampshire Ave NW Washington DC 20036-1564 Office Phone: 202-887-4294. Office Fax: 202-887-4288. E-mail: rgoshorn@akingump.com.

GOSIN, BARRY M., real estate company executive; BA in Econs. and History, Ind. U. Prin. Newmark Knight Frank, NYC, 1978—, CEO, 1979—. Bd. govs. Real Estate Bd. of NY. Trustee Parker Jewish Inst., Pace U.; bd. dirs. Partnership of NYC, NYC and Co.; bd. govs. exec. com. Real Estate Bd. NY; trustee Citizens Budget Com.; bd. dirs., trustee Parker Jewish Geriatric Inst.; trustee and mem. bd. fedn. employment and guidance services Pace U.; bd. dirs. Ctr. for Downtown NY; hon. trustee HS Economics and Fin. Named Entrepreneur of Yr., Ernst & Young, 2002, Man of Yr., Northern Westchester Hosp., 2001; recipient Leadership in Mgmt. award, Pace U., Most Ingenious Deal of Yr., Real Estate Bd. NY. Office: Newmark Knight Frank 125 Park Ave New York NY 10017 Office Phone: 212-372-2000. Business E-Mail: bgosin@newmarkkf.com.*

GOSLEE, DWIGHT J., agricultural products executive; BS in Acctg., U. Minn. CPA. Formerly with Touche Ross & Co.; asst. corp. controller to v.p./controller internat. divsn. ConAgra, Inc., Omaha, 1985—94, sr. v.p. mergers and acquisitions, CIO, 1994—. Office: ConAgra Inc 1 ConAgra Dr Omaha NE 68102

GOSLIN, GERALD HUGH, concert pianist, educator; b. Detroit, Jan. 7, 1947; s. Hugh Jennings and Helen Margaret (Senauit) Goslin. Student, Wayne State U., Detroit, 1966—69. Music tchr. Peralta Music, Farmington, Mich., 1965—80, Hammell Music, Livonia, 1980—83; prof. music Oakland CC, Farmington Hills, 1983—; host The Piano Hour Sta. WHND-AM, Oak Park, 1995; recitalist Allen, Rodgers and Baldwin Organs, Detroit, 1975—90; prof. voice, theory and piano Livonia Conservatory, 1998—. Judge Leontyne Price Vocal Competition, 1986—, Verdi Opera Assn. Vocal Competition, 1995—96. Block capt. Rogers Park Residents Assn., Redford, Mich., 1995—2002; choirmaster, organist Bushnell Congl. Ch., Detroit, 2000—. Mem.: Am. Guild Organists, Am. Choir Dir. Assn., Detroit Fedn. Musicians Local # 5. Home and Office: 22600 Middlebelt Rd C-10 Farmington Hills MI 48336-3672 Home Phone: 248-476-3648; Office Phone: 313-330-3529.

GOSLINE, NORMAN ABBOT, real estate appraiser, consultant; b. Gardiner, Maine, Nov. 6, 1935; s. Arthur N. and Katherine R. (Wadsworth) G.; m. Shirlene Heath Hoch; children: M. Lee (dec.), Jeffrey C., Mark A; stepchildren: Jolene Hoch Collins, Ellen M. Hoch, William K. Hoch Jr. BA, U. Maine, 1957. With Gosline Dairy, Gardiner, 1957—59, Gosline & Co., Gardiner, 1960—. Adj. faculty U. Maine, Augusta, 1973-81; real estate team visit to People's Republic of China, Citizen Amb. Program of People to People, 1995; cons. in field. Past mem. Gardiner Planning Bd. ambulance adv. com. Mem. Am. Inst. Real Estate Appraisers (pres. N.E. chpt. 1985), Soc. of Real Estate Appraisers (pres. Maine chpt. 1975-76, 81-82), Appraisal Inst. (dir. 1993-96), Nat. Assn. Realtors (bd. dirs. 1967), Maine Assn. Realtors (pres. 1967), Am. Soc. Real Estate Counselors, Kennebec Valley Bd. Realtors (pres. 1963-64, Realtor of Yr. 1967), Rotary (Paul Harris fellow), Shrine. Home: 87 W Hill Rd Gardiner ME 04345-1931 Office: PO Box 247 Gardiner ME 04345-0247 Office Phone: 207-582-1100.

GOSLING, JOHN THOMAS, space plasma physicist, researcher; b. Akron, Ohio, July 10, 1938; s. Arthur Warrington and Wilhelmina (Bell) G.; m. Marie Ann Turner, Dec. 21, 1963; children: Mark Raymond, Steven Arthur; m. Margaret Judith Hughes, Jan. 8, 1994. BS in Physics, Ohio U., 1960; PhD in Physics, U. Calif., Berkeley, 1965; postdoctoral studies, Los Alamos Nat. Lab., N.Mex., 1965-67. Staff mem. Nat. Ctr. Atmospheric Research, Boulder, Colo., 1967-75; staff mem., Space Plasma Physics Team Los Alamos Nat. Lab., 1975—2005, fellow; sr. rsch. assoc. Lab. Atmospheric & Space Physics U. Colo., Boulder, 2005—. Mem. Nat. Rsch. Council Com. on Solar-Terrestrial Rsch, 1994-97. Contbr. more than 400 articles to profl. jours. Recipient Tech. Achievement award Nat. Ctr. Atmospheric Research, Boulder, 1974, several Achievement Awards from NASA. Fellow Am. Geophys. Union (pres. space physics and aeronomy sect. 2000-02, John Adam Fleming medal, 2000, Parker Lecture 2004); mem. AAAS, Internat. Astron. Union. Democrat. Avocations: sports, hiking, music. Home: 790 Niwot Ridge Ln Lafayette CO 80026 Office: LASP 1234 Innovation Dr Boulder CO 80303 Business E-Mail: jack.gosling@lasp.colorado.edu.

GOSLING, RYAN (RYAN THOMAS GOSLING), actor; b. Cornwall, Ont., Can., Nov. 12, 1980; s. Thomas and Donna. Actor: (TV series) The Mickey Mouse Club, 1993—94; (films) Frankenstein and Me, 1996, Remember the Titans, 2000, The Believer, 2001, The Slaughter Rule, 2002, Murder By Numbers, 2002, The United States of Leland, 2003, The Notebook, 2004, Stay, 2005, Half Nelson, 2006 (Best Breakthrough Performance - Male Nat. Bd. Review, 2006), Fracture, 2007; (TV films) Nothing Too Good for a Cowboy, 1998, The Unbelievables, 1999; (TV series) Breaker High, 1997—98, Young Hercules, 1998—99. Office: IFA Talent Agy 8730 Sunset Blvd Ste 490 Los Angeles CA 90069*

GOSNELL, DAVINA J., dean, nursing educator; BSN, U. Pitts.; MS, PhD, Ohio State U. Dean Sch. Nursing, prof. Kent (Ohio) State U. Chair Ohio Pub. Health Coun. Recipient U. Pitts. Sch. Nursing Disting. Alumni award. Mem. ONA, NLN, STT, GSA, Delta Kappa Gamma. Office: Kent State U Sch Nursing PO Box 5190 Kent OH 44242-0001 E-mail: dgasnell@kent.edu.

GOSNELL, GUY R., lawyer; b. Kans. City, Mo., Oct. 29, 1965; BSEE, Univ. Mo., 1988, BS in Computer Engring., 1988; JD magna cum laude, St. Louis Univ., 1992. Bar: NC 1992, registered: Patent and Trademark Off. Ptnr., chmn., Intellectual Property - Electronics and Computer Tech. group Alston & Bird LLP, Charlotte, NC. Office: Alston & Bird LLP Ste 4000 Bank of Am Plz 101 S Tryon St Charlotte NC 28280-4000 Office Phone: 704-444-1029. Office Fax: 704-444-1111. Business E-Mail: ggosnell@alston.com.

GOSNELL, NANCI LITTLE, information technology executive, nurse; BS in Nursing, Old Dominion Univ., Norfolk, Va., 1978; MBA, Marymount Univ., Arlington, Va. Staff nurse, emergency dept. and operating room Sibley Mem. Hosp., Washington; mgr., clin. applications Inova Health Sys., Falls Church, Va., 1990—99, asst. v.p., info. svc., 1999—2002, and interim chief info. officer, 2000—02, v.p., info. svc. & chief info. officer, 2002—. Adj. prof. George mason Univ. Mem.: Coll. of Healthcare Info. Mgmt. Executives. Office: VP & CIO Inova Health Sys Ste 200 2990 Telestar Ct Falls Church VA 22042

GOSPER, BRETT, advertising agency executive; b. Melbourne, Australia, June 21, 1959; s. Richard Kevan and Jillian Mary (Galwey) G.; div. Oct. 1994; 1 child, Jonathan Kevan Thomas; m. Elizabeth Bernsen, May 9, 1998; children: Ella Jillian, Matt William Svend. Grad. in econs. and politics, Monash U., Melbourne, 1981. Exec. Ogilvy & Mather, Melbourne, 1981-82, acct. supr. Paris, 1982-86, acct. dir., 1986-89; dir. TBWA/BDDP, Paris, 1989-91, dep. mng. dir., 1991-93, mng. dir., founder Frankfurt, Germany, 1993-94; CEO, chmn. Euro RSCG-Wnek-Gosper Advt., London, 1994—2003; bd. dirs. Euro RSCG Worldwide, London; pres. McCann-Erickson USA, NY, 2003—04, 2005; mem. McCann World-Group Bd., 2005—; dir. Advt. Week NY, NY, 2006; dir.-at-large Am. Assn. Advt. Agys., 2007. Rugby player rep. Victoria, Queensland, Australia, 1982, French Barbarians versus New Zealand All Blacks at Rugby, 1986; capt. Italian Zebras, Monaco Sevens, 1987. Recipient Best Player award Melbourne Rugby Club, 1978, 79, 80. Mem.: Racing Club de France (Best Player award 1987, finalist French championship 1987), Melbourne Cricket Club, Marylebone Cricket Club. Office: McCann-Erickson USA 622 Third Ave New York NY 10017 Business E-Mail: brett.gosper@mccann.com.

GOSS, CURTIS DALE, language educator; s. Benny Adrian and Wanda Joy Goss; m. Margaret Marian Crozier, May 5, 1995; 1 child, Adriana Joy; m. Dialith Odelsa Santos, Jan. 27, 1974 (div. July 19, 1983); children: Virginia Grace White, Dialith Jahel Urista, Suzannah Elaine Herczeg. BA, Tex. Tech U., Lubbock, 1977, MA, 1994. Cert. tchr. Tex. Edn. Agy., 1983. Adminstrn. specialist, sr. pers. clk. US Army, 1978—82; tchr. Spanish Littlefield H.S., Tex., 1984—86, Kermit H.S., Tex., 1986—88; tchg. asst. Tex. Tech U., 1988—94; asst. prof. S.W. Bapt. U., Bolivar, Mo., 1994—. Dir. spanish program dir. S.W. Bapt. U., 1994—, fgn. lang. adj. liaison, 1994—. With US Army, 1978—82. Decorated Achievement medal Sec. US Army, Commendation medal. Mem.: Am. Coun. Tchg. Fgn. Langs., Bolivar Lions Club (pres. 2006—). Green Party. Office: Southwest Baptist Univ 1600 University Ave Bolivar MO 65613 Personal E-mail: candmgoss@hotmail.com. Business E-Mail: cgoss@sbuniv.edu.

GOSS, HOWARD S(IMON), financial executive; b. Nov. 17, 1933; s. Maurice Jack and Sally (Yanov) G.; m. Roberta Jacobs, June 19, 1955; children: Robert, David, Marcy, Scott BS, DePaul U., 1956, PhD, 2005. CPA, Ill. Auditor Steel Channon & Co., Chgo., 1955-60; contr. Transco Inc., Chgo., 1960-67, pres., 1967—, dir., 1980—2002, chmn. bd., 1989, ret. chrmn. cons., 2002—. Dir., Graycor Inc Mem. fin. com. New Trier Rep. Orgn., Winnetka, Ill., 1977-93; chmn. adv. coun. DePaul U. Coll. Commerce, bd. trustees, 1987, trustee DePaul U., 1988, exec. com., 1992; mem. adv. coun. Jewish Vocat. Svc., 1991; bd. dirs. Chgo. Crime Commn., 1993; chmn. alumni forum Coll. Commerce; chief Crusader United Way, Chgo., 1989; trustee Adler Planetarium and Astronomy Mus., 1996, treas., 1997, chmn. bd. trustees, 2000-2002 Recipient Humanitarian award Nat. Jewish Hosp., Denver, 1980, Disting. Alumni award DePaul U., 1993. Mem. AICPA, Ill. Soc. CPAs, Young Pres.'s Orgn., Chgo. Pres.'s Orgn., Std. Club, Econ. Club, Nat. Honor Soc. Commerce, Beta Gamma Sigma Office: Transco Inc 55 E Jackson Blvd Ste 2100 Chicago IL 60604-4166 Home Phone: 847-835-0992; Office Phone: 312-427-2818.

GOSS, JAMES WILLIAM, lawyer; b. London, Ont., Can., Mar. 10, 1941; s. Joseph Allen and Virginia Ruth (Farrah) G.; m. Rita Meyer, Aug. 2, 1969; children: Anne Candace, Jennette Courtney. BBA, We. Mich. U., Kalamazoo, 1966; MS, U. Ill., 1972; JD, Georgetown U., Washington, DC, 1974. Bar: Mich. 1974, US Dist. Ct. (ea. dist.) Mich. 1974, US Ct. Appeals (6th cir.) 1974. Sr. acct. Price Waterhouse & Co., Washington, 1969—71; assoc. Miller, Canfield, Paddock & Stone, Detroit, 1974—82, James W. Goss P.C., Southfield, Mich., 1982—88; ptnr. Dean & Fulkerson, Troy, Mich., 1988—95, James W. Goss P.C., Grosse Pointe Farms, Mich., 1995—. Adj. lectr. U. Mich. Law, Ann Arbor, 1978—82. Mem. Jefferson Ave. Presbyn. Ch.; bd. dirs. Old Newsboys Goodfellow Fund of Detroit, 1990—96, Adrian Coll., 1991—96; bd. dirs., v.p. Svc. to Older Citizens Soc., Grosse Pointe, Mich., 1997—2001; assoc., bd. govs., mem. exec. com. William L. Clements Libr. U. Mich., 1998—. Named Outstanding Goodfellow, Old Newsboys Goodfellows of Detroit, 1991; recipient Disting. Alumni award We. Mich. U., 1995. Mem. Georgetown U. Law Alumni Assn., Grosse Pointe Yacht Club, Georgetown Club of Mich., Commanderie de Bordeaux, Hundred Club, Rotary (Grosse Pointe Rotarian of Yr. 2000-01), Masons. Presbyterian. Avocations: wine collecting, cartographic collecting, book collecting. Home: 398 Rivard Blvd Grosse Pointe MI 48230-1629 Office Phone: 313-885-7500. Personal E-mail: jwgxx@comcast.net.

GOSS, JEROME ELDON, craftsman, retired cardiologist; b. Dodge City, Kans., Nov. 30, 1935; s. Horton Maurice and Mary Alice (Mountain) G.; m. Lorraine Ann Sanchez, Apr. 20, 1986. BA, U. Kans., 1957; MD, Northwestern U., 1961. Diplomate Am. Bd. Internal Medicine, Am. Bd. Cardiology (fellow, bd. govs. 1981-84), fine bookbinding Glasgow Met. Coll., 2004-05. Intern Met. Gen. Hosp., Cleve., 1961-62; resident in internal medicine Northwestern U. Med. Ctr., Chgo., 1962-64; fellow in cardiology U. Colo., Denver, 1964-66; asst. prof. medicine U. N.Mex., Albuquerque, 1968-70; pvt. practice N.Mex. Heart Clinic, Albuquerque, 1970—99, Presbyn. Med. Group, Albuquerque, 2000—02; with Presbyn. Heart Group, Albuquerque, 2003—05; propr. fine bookbinding and repair, 2005—. Bd. alumni counselors Northwestern U. Med. Sch., 1977-89, nat. alumni bd., 1991-97; chief dept. medicine Presbyn. Hosp., Albuquerque, 1978-80, exec. com., 1980-82, dir. cardiac diagnostic svcs., 1970-96. Contbr. articles to profl. jours. Bd. dir. Presbyn. Heart Inst., Ballet West N.Mex., N.Mex. Symphony Orch.; pres. Albuquerque Mus. Found., Corrales Hist. Soc. (pres. 2002-05). Lt. comdr. USN, 1966-68. Nat. Heart Inst. research fellow, 1965-66; named one of Outstanding Young Men Am., Jaycees, 1970; recipient Alumni Service award Northwestern U. Med. Sch.,

1986, Disting. Achievement award Albuquerque Mus. Found., 1997, Sr. Svc. award Presbyn. Healthcare Sys., 1999. Fellow ACP, ACC, Coun. Clin. Cardiology of Am. Heart Assn., Soc. Cardiac Angiography, Am. Soc. of Geriatric Cardiology; mem. Albuquerque-Bernalillo County Med. Soc. (sec. 1972, treas. 1975, v.p. 1980), Alpha Omega Alpha. Republican. Methodist. Office Phone: 505-792-1516. Personal E-mail: jegoss@comcast.net.

GOSS, JOEL FRANCIS, writer; b. Pawnee, Okla., Nov. 15, 1955; s. William Richard and Mary Ann (Webb) G.; m. Cat Guthrie, 1992; 1 child, William Keaton Guthrie-Goss. BA, U. Tenn., 1985. Staff writer Sta. WDXB, Chattanooga, 1970-73, Sta. WGOW, Knoxville, Tenn., 1973-75; writer, dir. V.T. Films, Knoxville, 1974-76; writer Hi-Test Films, Knoxville, 1976; freelance writer NYC, 1976-80; writer, mgr. Improvisation, Inc., NYC, 1980-84; writer, producer CB Prodns., NYC, 1984; mng. dir. Albuquerque '49, NYC, 1983—; v.p. Buster Keaton Archive, NYC, 1985—; founder, pres. Lucid Loving, 2006. Cons. Rohauer Films, London, 1985-88, Am. Theatre Wing, N.Y.C., 1987; film instr. Brown Sch., Knoxville, 1976; chmn. Film com., Knoxville, 1974-76. Author: Albuquerque '49, 1973; author: (with Michael Kaluta) The Shadow, 1992; author: Coils of Leviathan, 1993; author: (with Cat Guthrie) A Day In The Life of a Mother & Wife, 2001; author: Zombie Masters, 2007, (screenplays) The Prairie Traveler, 1986, Manhattan Underground, 1987, Bard of Broadway, 1988, Sandhogs, 1991, Battling Butler, 1991; author: (with Mike Rowe) Warm Toast, 1989; author: (with Eliot Camaren) Good Night Bassington, 2003; translator: (tng. manuals) Construczione Aerounaticle, 1973; co-screenwriter (with Raymond Rohauer), rschr. Buster Keaton-A Hard Act to Follow, 1987; rschr., writer: Buster Keaton Remembered, 2001; writer Spectacular Days of Radio, 1990, (with Martin Connor) Madame Sherry, 1989, Cat Guthrie in Concert, 1992, The Rich Conaty Radio Show, 1992, (with others) The Rocketeer, The Shadow, 1994, The Shadow & the Mysterious 3, 1994, (with M. Kaluta and Gary Gianni) Hell's Heat Wave, 1994, Buster Keaton: Genius In Slapshoes, 1995, Cut To The Chase: Buster Keaton, 1995, The Sound of Buster Keaton, 1995, Complete Films of BK, A Satin Doll Christmas, 2000, Lucid Loving, 2007, (with Carolyn Rossi Copeland) Oh What a Beautiful Evening Revue; dir. co-writer (with Emily Daly): Zombie Master, 2007; restored dialog to film: with Bruce Goldstein The Donovan Affair (1929), 1992, Cliff Edwards--Fascinatin' Rhythm, 1996. Vol. Nat. Music Theatre Network, N.Y.C., Washington, 1985, 87, Nat. Theatre Wing, N.Y.C., 1987, Muscular Dystrophy Assn., N.Y.C., 1987; signings for St. Jude's Children's Hosp., 1994. Grantee U. Tenn., 1975, CB Prodns., 1984. Mem. Buster Keaton Soc. Home Phone: 845-424-4340; Office Phone: 914-420-2339. Personal E-mail: joelgoss@gmail.com.

GOSS, KENT, lawyer; BA in Economics, Occidental Coll., 1983; JD, U. Calif., 1987. Bar: Calif. 1987, US Dist. Ct. (so. dist.) Calif., US Dist. Ct. (ctrl. dist.) Calif., US Dist. Ct. (no. dist.) Calif., US Ct. Appeals (9th cir.). Ptnr. Pillsbury Winthrop Shaw Pittman, Orrick, Herrington & Sutcliffe LLP, LA, 2006—. Mem.: US Trademark Assn., ABA. Office: Orrick Herrington & Sutcliffe LLP 777 S Figueroa St Ste 3200 Los Angeles CA 90017 Office Phone: 213-612-2411.*

GOSS, LAURENCE EDWARD, JR., geographer, educator; s. Laurence Edward and Anna Louise (Oliver) G.; m. Sharon Margaret Ripp, June 9, 1968; children: Laura Marie, Peter Edward. AB, Dartmouth Coll., 1966; MA, U. Wash., 1969, PhD, 1973. Registered planner, Am. Inst. Cert. Planners. Adminstr., lectr. Dartmouth Coll., Hanover, N.H., 1970-71; asst. prof. SUNY, Oswego, 1971-76; asst. dir. Office of State Planning, Concord, N.H., 1976-86; project dir. Provan & Lorber, Inc., Contoocook, N.H., 1986-91; prin. No. Econ. Planners, Concord, 1991—; assoc. prof. Salem State Coll., Mass., 1996—2003, prof., 2003—. Pres. Frontiers of Knowledge Lyceum, Concord, 1996. Lead author: Garvins Falls Devel. Strategy for City of concord, N.H., 1996 (Tech. Merit award for Maine, N.H. and Vt. 1997 No. New Eng. chpt. Am. Planners Assn.). Recipient Letter of Commendation Nat. award HUD, Washington, 1986. Mem. Am. Planners Assn. (pres. no. New Eng. chpt. 1989-91, Profl. Planner of Yr. 1993, Project of Yr. award 1995), New Eng.-St. Lawrence Valley Geog. Soc. (bd. dirs. 1992-94), N.H. Planners Assn. (pres. 1982-83), N.H. Natural Resources Forum (treas. 1993-2000). Congregationalist. Office: Dept Geography Salem State Coll Salem MA 01970 Business E-Mail: lgoss@salemstate.edu.

GOSS, MARY E. WEBER, sociology educator; b. Chgo., May 8, 1926; m. Albert E. Goss, 1945; 1 son, Charles. BA in Sociology with distinction (Univ. Merit scholar 1946-47, Chi Omega Sociology prize 1947), U. Iowa, 1947, MA, 1948; PhD (Gilder fellow 1951-52), Columbia U., 1959. Rsch. asst. U. Iowa, 1947-48, Amherst Coll., 1949; instr. Smith Coll., 1949-50, U. Mass., 1950-51, 55-56, adj. mem. grad. faculty, 1961-66; rsch. assoc. Bur. Applied Social Rsch., Columbia U., 1952-53; cons. sociology, mem. rsch. staff, rsch. coord. N.Y. Hosp.-Cornell U. Med. Center, NYC, 1957-66; mem. faculty dept. medicine Cornell U. Med. Coll., 1959-72, prof. sociology in pub. health, 1973-92, prof. emerita, 1992—. Author: Physicians in Bureaucracy, 1980; also numerous articles; editor: Jour. Health and Social Behavior, 1976-78; co-editor: Comprehensive Medical Care and Teaching: A Report on the N.Y. Hospital-Cornell Medical Center Program, 1967; mem. editorial bd. profl. jours. Fellow APHA, N.Y. Acad. Medicine; mem. AAAS, AAUP, Am. Sociol. Assn., Assn. Tchrs. Preventive Medicine, Acad. Health, Internat. Sociol. Assn., Ea. Sociol. Soc., Phi Beta Kappa, Sigma Xi. Home: 25 Hillcrest Drive Piscataway NJ 08854

GOSS, PORTER JOHNSTON, former CIA director, former congressman; b. Waterbury, Conn., Nov. 26, 1938; m. Mariel Robinson; children: Leslie, Chauncey, Mason, Gerrit. BA in Greek, Yale U., 1960. Clandestine svcs. officer CIA, 1962-71; co-founder Island Reporter, Sanibel, Fla., 1973; mayor City of Sanibel, 1975—77, 1982, coun. mem., 1974—80, 1981—82; commr. County of Lee, Fla., 1983—88, chmn. Fla., 1985—86; mem. U.S. Congress from 14th Fla. dist., 1989—2004; chmn. Perm. Select Com. on Intelligence, 1997—2004; mem. rules com.; mem. Select Com. on Homeland Security; dir. CIA, Washington, 2004—06. Port commr. S.W. Fla. Regional Airport. Dir. Lee County Mental Health Ctr., J.N. "Ding" Darling Found.; dir. chmn. Sanibel-Captiva Conservation Found.; chmn. bd. Canterbury Sch.; mem. S.W. Fla. Mental Health Dist. Bd. Intelligence officer U.S. Army, 1960-62. Republican. Presbyterian.

GOSSARD, ARTHUR CHARLES, physicist, researcher; b. Ottawa, Ill., June 18, 1935; s. Arthur Paul and Mary Catherine (Lineberger) G.; m. Marsha Jean Palmer, Jan. 8, 1965; children: Girard Christopher, Elinore Suzanne. BA, Harvard U., 1956; PhD, U. Calif., Berkeley, 1960. Solid state physicist, disting. mem. tech. staff AT&T Bell Labs., Murray Hill, NJ, 1960-87; prof. materials and electrical and computer engring. U. Calif., Santa Barbara, 1987—. Author tech. papers magnetic resonance, magnetism, transition metals, molecular beam epitaxy, quantum structures, semiconductors. Recipient John Bardeen award TMS, 2005, Newcombe-Cleveland prize AAAS, 2006, 2007; sr. fellow Humboldt Found. Fellow IEEE, Am. Phys. Soc. (Oliver Buckley condensed matter physics prize 1984, James McGroddy prize for New Materials 2001); mem. NAS, Nat. Acad. Engring. Office: U Calif Materials Dept Santa Barbara CA 93106 Business E-Mail: gossard@engineering.ucsb.edu.

GOSSARD, MARCIA NADINE, writer; d. Bettie Josephine and Raymond Hoff (Stepfather); m. Jeffrey Richard Gossard, May. 21, 1988; 1 child, Julian Michael Hill. BA in Psychology, U. Wash., Seattle, 1992; MA in Sociology, Wash. State U., Pullman, 1999, PhD in Sociology, 2004. Freelance sci. writer, editor, Pullman, 2004—. Issue editor Moscow Food Co-op Newsletter, Idaho, 2007—; contbr. articles to profl. jours. Mass Media Sci. & Engring. Summer fellowship, AAAS, 2002.

GOSSELIN, KAREN CHOWNING, music educator; b. Muskogee, Okla., June 16, 1963; d. Eldon Leo and Kathryn Ann Chowning; m. Gregory Scott Gosselin, Sept. 9, 1989; children: Robert Chowning, Kathryn Jean, Stephen Dale. BS in Music Edn., Southeastern Okla. State U., Durant, 1985; MusM, Southwestern Bapt. Theol. Sem., Ft. Worth, 1988. Cert. tchr. Okla., 1985, Ala., 1989. Music tchr. Montgomery County Sch. Systems, Ala., 1989—96; pvt. practice music specialist Panama City, Fla., 1996—2000, Paris, Tex., 2000—03; founder and dir. Capital City Singers Homeschool Choir, Montgomery, 2003—; choral instr. Judson Coll., Marion, Ala., 2006—. Music asst. Ea. Hills Bapt. Ch., Montgomery, 2003—; music clinician Bapt. Gen. Conv. Tex., 2005—. Mem.: Music Educators Nat. Conf., Am. Choral Dirs. Assn., Choristers Guild. Conservative. Baptist. Avocations: travel, scrapbooks. Home: 313 Foxhall Rd Pike Road AL 36064 Office: Judson College 302 Bibb St Marion AL 36756 Home Phone: 334-272-8556; Office Phone: 334-683-5142. Business E-Mail: kgosselin@judson.edu.

GOSSELS, CLAUS PETER ROLF, lawyer; b. Berlin, Aug. 11, 1930; came to US, 1941; s. Max and Charlotte (Lewy) G.; m. Nancy Lee Tuber, June 29, 1958; children: Lisa Rae, Amy Devra, Daniel Joshua. AB, Harvard U., 1951, LLB, 1954. Bar: Mass. 1955, US Dist. Ct. Mass. 1957, US Ct. Appeals (1st cir.) 1957, US Supreme Ct. 1965. Assoc. Sullivan & Worcester, Boston, 1956-65; mem. Zelman, Gossels & Alexander, Boston, 1965-72, Weston, Patrick, Willard & Redding, Boston, 1972—. Master Superior Ct. Mass., 1984—; guardian ad litem, conservator Mass. Probate Family Ct. Co-author, editor: Vetaher Libenu, 1980, Chadesh Yamenu, 1997, Canfey Hashachar, 2003; contbr. articles to profl. jours. Moderator Town of Wayland, Mass., 1982—. With US Army, 1954-56. Mem. Mass. Bar Assn., Boston Bar Assn., Mass. Moderators Assn., Mass. Acad. Trial Lawyers. Jewish. Avocations: reading, tennis, travel, gardening, theater. Home: 32 Hampshire Rd Wayland MA 01778-1021 Office: Weston Patrick 84 State St 11 Fl Boston MA 02109-2299 Office Phone: 617-742-9310. Business E-Mail: pgossels@socialaw.com.

GOSSETT, LOUIS, JR., actor; b. Bklyn., May 27, 1936; s. Louis and Helen (Wray) G.; 1 child, Satie; m. Cyndi Jones-Reese, 1987 (div. 1992); 1 adopted child, Sharron. BA, N.Y. U., 1959; studied with, Frank Silvera, Nola Chilton, Eli Rill, Lloyd Richards. Made Broadway debut in Take a Giant Step; other stage performance include The Charletan; appeared in motion pictures including A Raisin in the Sun, 1961, The Landlord, 1970, The Bushbaby, 1970, Skin Game, 1971, Travels with My Aunt, 1972, The Laughing Policeman, 1973, The White Dawn, 1974, The River Niger, 1976, J.D.'s Revenge, 1976, The Deep, 1977, The Choirboys, 1977, An Officer and a Gentleman, 1982 (Acad. award for Best Supporting Actor), Jaws 3-D, 1983, Finders Keepers, 1984, Enemy Mine, 1984, Iron Eagle, 1985, Firewalker, 1986, The Principal, 1987, Iron Eagle II: Battle Beyond the Flag, 1988, The Punisher, 1990, Cover Up, 1991, Toy Soldiers, 1991, Aces: Iron Eagle III, 1992, Diggstown, 1992, Monolith, 1993, A Good Man in Africa, 1994, Blue Chips, 1994, Iron Eagle IV, 1995, Inside, 1996, Managua, 1996, Legend of the Mummy, 1997, Y2K, 1999, The Highwayman, 2000, Left Behind: World at War, 2005, All In, 2006, Club Soda, 2006, Daddy's Little Girls, 2007; TV films: It's Good to be Alive, 1974, Side Kicks, 1974, Delancey Street: The Crisis Within, 1975, Little Ladies of the Night, 1977, Roots, 1977 (Emmy award Nat. Acad. TV Arts and Scis. 1977), The Critical List, 1978, To Kill a Cop, 1978, This Man Stands Alone, 1979, Backstairs at the White House, 1979, Don't Look Back, 1981, Benny's Place, 1982, Sadat, 1983, The Guardian, 1984, A Gathering of Old Men, 1987, The Father Clements Story, 1987, Roots: The Gift, 1988, Goodbye Miss 4th of July, 1988, El Diablo, 1990, Sudie and Simpson, 1990, The Josephine Baker Story, 1991, Carolina Skeletons, 1991, Keeper of the City, 1992, Father and Son: Dangerous Relations, 1993, Return to Lonesome Dove, 1993, Ray Alexander: A Taste For Justice, 1994, Flashfire, 1994, A Father For Charlie, 1995, Zoo Man, 1995, Curse of The Starving Class, 1995, Captain Heart: The James Mink Story, 1996, In His father's Shoes, 1997, To Dance With Olivia, 1997, Color of Love, 2000, Inspectors 2, 2000, For Love of Olivia, 2001, What About Your Friends: Weekend Getaway, 2002, Jasper, Texas, 2003, Momentum, 2003, Solar Strike, 2005, Lackawanna Blues, 2005; also various TV series, including The Young Rebels, 1970-71, The Lazurus Syndrome, 1979, The Powers of Matthew Star, 1982-83, Gideon Oliver, 1989, (voice) Captain Planet and The Planeteers, 1990, Nitecap, 1992; singer in nightclubs, 1960s. Mem. Acad. Motion Picture Arts and Scis., Actors Equity, Screen Actors Guild, AFTRA, Am. Guild Variety Artists, Am. Fed. Musicians, Negro Actors Guild Am., Alpha Phi Alpha. Office: Writers Artists 360 N Crescent Dr Bldg North Beverly Hills CA 90210-6818*

GOSSETT, PHILIP, musicologist; b. NYC, Sept. 27, 1941; s. Harold and Pearl (Lenkowsky) G.; m. Suzanne Solomon, Aug. 4, 1963; children: David, Jeffrey. BA summa cum laude, Amherst Coll., 1963; student, Columbia U., 1961-62; MFA, Princeton U., 1965, PhD, 1970; LHD, Amherst Coll., 1993. Asst. prof. music and humanities U. Chgo., 1968-73, assoc. prof., 1973-77, prof., 1977-84, Robert W. Reneker Disting. Svc. prof. music, 1984—, dean divsn. humanities, 1989-99. Vis. assoc. prof. Columbia U., 1975, Inst. Musicologie U. Paris, 1988, Gauss seminars, Princeton U., 1991; Hambro prof. opera studies Oxford U., 2001; musicological cons. Verdi Festival, Parma, 2001; prof. U. Rome, 2004—. Gen. editor: The Works of Giuseppe Verdi, Edizione Critica della opere di Gioachino Rossini, 1979—2005, Works of Gioachino Rossini, 2006—; mem. editl. bd. Am. Musicol. Soc., 1972—78; cons. editor: Critical Inquiry, 1974—, Nineteenth Century Music, 1976—2004, Cambridge Opera Jour., 1987—2002, 2007—, Rivista Italiana di Musicologia, 2004—; translator: Treatise on Harmony (Jean-Philippe Rameau); translator: (with Charles Rosen) Early Romantic Opera, Anna Bolena and the Maturity of Gaetano Donizetti, 1985; translator: Il Barbiere di Siviglia, 1993, Don Pasquale, 2000, Divas and Scholars: Performing Italian Opera, 2006, also numerous critical edits.; prepared vocal ornamentation for operas in Milan, Rome, Bologna, Pesaro, Chgo., Miami, St. Louis, NY, Santa Fe, Paris. Trustee Chgo. Symphony Orch., 1991-2001, Ct. Theatre, Chgo., 1994—. Decorated Gold medal 1st class (Italy), 1985, Grande Ufficiale della Rep. (Italy), 1997, Order Rio Branca, Brazil, 1998, Cavaliere di Gran Croce (Italy), 1998; recipient Disting. Achievement award Mellon Found., 2004; Woodrow Wilson fellow, 1963-64, 66-67; Fulbright scholar Paris, 1965-66; Martha Baird Rockefeller fellow, 1967-68; Guggenheim fellow, 1971-72; NEH sr. scholar, 1982-83, Phi Beta Kappa Vis. scholar, 2002-03; Deems Taylor award of ASCAP, 1986. Fellow AAAS, Academia Filarmonica of Bologna (hon.), Ateneo Veneto, Accademia di Santa Cecilia Rom (accademico onorario); mem. Am. Musicol. Soc. (coun. 1972-74, bd. dirs. 1974-76, v.p. 1986-88, Albert Einstein award 1969, pres. 1994-96), Internat. Musicol. Soc. (directorium 2007—), Am. Inst. Verdi Studies (bd. dirs.), Societa Italiana di Musicologia, Soc. Textual Scholarship (pres. 1993-95), Premio Paolo Borciani (pres. 1997, 2002). Office: U Chgo Dept Music Chicago IL 60637 Office Phone: 773-955-3738. Business E-Mail: phgs@uchicago.edu.

GOSSETT, ROBERT FRANCIS, JR., merchant banker; b. San Antonio, Nov. 19, 1943; s. Robert Francis and Anne Elizabeth (Donnell) G.; m. Pauline Washington Gillespie, June 27, 1964; children: Robert Francis III, Frank Morgan Gillespie. BA, U. Tex., 1964; JD, Georgetown U., 1967; MBA, U. Pa., 1969. Assoc., investment bank div. Merrill Lynche, Pierce, Fenner & Smith, NYC, 1969-74; v.p. Oppenheimer Properties, Inc., NYC, 1974-78; exec. v.p., dir. Loeb Rhoades Hornblower Capital Corp., NYC, 1978-81; chmn. bd., pres. Vance Capital Corp., NYC, 1981—. Gen. ptnr. First San Bernardio Assoc., Ltd., Long Beach, Calif., 1979-2004, First Riverside (Calif.) Assoc., 1980-2004, First Portland Assoc., Beaverton, Oreg., 1980-2005, Corp. Realty Income Fund I, Ltd., NYC, 1986-2007, Vance, Teel & Co. Ltd., San Antonio, 1998—; chmn. bd. dirs. 1345 Realty Corp., N.Y.C., 1994-2007, Minn. Street Assoc., Inc., St. Paul, 1988-2006; gen. ptnr. Hoopes Assocs., Ltd., Rockport, Tex., 1989—, Teel Land and Cattle Co., LLC, Yancey, Tex., 1997—. Mem. bd. regents Georgetown U., 1993-99. Mem. Campfire Club, The Mashomack Preserve Club. Office: Vance Capital Corp 406 E 85th St New York NY 10028-6302 Home Phone: 212-744-0853; Office Phone: 212-751-3515. E-mail: rfgossett@aol.com.

GOSTIN, IRWIN, retired lawyer; b. NYC, July 22, 1927; s. Herman and Vera (Ostrinsky) G.; m. Ruth Koenig (div. 1963); children: Theodore David, Leslie Ann Gostin Sikes, Deborah Lynn Gostin; m. Margit Nellaway (div. 1984); m. Mary L. Dekker, Jan. 27, 1990. AB, UCLA, 1948; LLB, Harvard U., 1951, JD, 1967. Bar: Calif. 1952, U.S. Dist. Ct. (cen. dist.) Calif. 1952, U.S. Ct. Appeals (9th cir.) 1952, U.S. Dist. Ct. (so. dist.) Calif. 1957. Pvt. practice, LA, 1952-56; ptnr. Gostin & Katz, San Diego, 1957-70; pres. Gostin & Katz Inc., San Diego, 1971-78, Irwin Gostin, APL, San Diego, 1979-94; admin. sec. Nat. Lawyer's Guild, LA, 1953—56. Mem. legal panel, chmn. ACLU, San Diego, 1958-67, pres., 1968; pres. San Diego Children's Home Soc., 1967; sec.-treas. Breeden-Schmidt Found., 1991—. With U.S. Army, 1945-46. Mem. San Diego County Bar Assn., Assn. Trial Lawyers Am., Calf. Trial Lawyers Assn., San Diego Trial Lawyers Assn. (pres. 1969). Avocation: thoroughbred horse racing. Home: 11216 Pergola Point Ct Las Vegas NV 89144 Personal E-mail: gostin@cox.net.

GOSTIN, LAWRENCE O., lawyer, educator; b. Oct. 19, 1949; s. Joseph and Sylvia (Berkman) G.; m. Jean Catherine Allison, July 30, 1977; children: Bryn Gareth, Kieran Gavin. BA summa cum laude, SUNY, Brockport, 1971; LLD (hon.), SUNY; JD, Duke U., 1974. Bar: N.Y. 1981, Coun. Europe. Legal dir. Nat. Assn. Mental Health, London, 1975-82; vis. fellow U. Oxford Ctr. for Criminol. Rsch., 1982-83; gen. sec. Nat. Coun. Civil Liberties, London, 1983-85; sr. fellow in health law Harvard U. Sch. Pub. Health, 1985—. Vis. prof. social policy McMaster U., Hamilton, Ont., Can., 1978-79; exec. dir. Am. Soc. Law, Medicine, and Ethics, Boston, 1987-94; adj. assoc. prof. Sch. Pub. Health, Harvard U., 1988—, adj. prof., 1990—, lectr. Law Sch., 1990—; vis. prof. Georgetown U. Law Ctr., 1993-94, assoc. prof., 1994-95, prof., 1996—, John Carroll rsch. prof., 2004-05, assoc. dean for rsch. and acad. programs, 2005—; prof. Johns Hopkins Sch. Hygiene and Pub. Health, 1994—; co-dir. Georgetown/Johns Hopkins Program on Law and Pub. Health; dir. CDC Collaborating Ctr. on Law and the Pub.'s Health; legis. coun. U.S. Senate Labor and Human Resources Com., Washington, 1987, 88; bd. dirs., nat. exec. com. Am. Civil Liberties Union, 1987—; assoc. dir. Harvard U. WHO Internat. Collaborating Ctr. on Health Legis., 1989— Western European editor Internat. Jour. Law and Psychiatry, London, 1978-81; editor in chief: Law Medicine & Health Care; exec. editor: Am. Jour. Law and Medicine; sect. editor Jour. AMA; editor: Secure Provision, 1985, AIDS and the Health Care System, 1990, Surrogate Motherhood: Politics and Privacy, 1990, Implementing the Americans with Disabilities Act, 1993; co-editor: Law, Science and Medicine, 2d edit., 1996; author: Human Rights and Public Health in the AIDS Pandemic, 1997, The Rights of Persons with HIV Disease, 1996, Mental Health Services: Law and Practice, 1986, Institutions Observed, 1986, Mental Health: Tribunal Procedure, 1984, 2d edit., 1992, A Human Condition, 1975, 2d vol., 1977, Civil Liberties in Conflict, 1988, Public Health Law: Power, Duty, Restraint, 2000, The AIDS Pandemic: Complacency, Injustice and Unfulfilled Expectations, 2004; editor Public Health law and Ethics: A Reader, 2002, The Human Rights of Persons with Intellectual Disabilities: Different But Equal, 2003. Legal affairs com. Internat. League Socs. for Mentally Handicapped, Brussels, 1980—; trustee Cobden Trust, London, 1983-85; chmn. Advocacy Alliance, London, 1981-84; sec. All Party Parliamentary Civil Liberties Group, London, 1984-85; bd. dirs. ACLU, 1986—, exec. com., 1988—; mem. com. experts drafting conventions on human experientation UN, Siracusa, Italy, 1980-82. Recipient Rosemary Deldridge Meml. award Nat. Consumer Coun. U.K., 1983; fellow Kennedy Inst. Ethics, 1994—, Fulbright fellow U. Oxford, 1974-75. Avocations: climbing, vegetable growing. Home: 10413 Masters Ter Potomac MD 20854-3862 Office: Georgetown U Law Ctr 600 New Jersey Ave NW Washington DC 20001-2075 Business E-Mail: gostin@law.georgetown.edu.

GOTBAUM, BETSY, municipal official; b. NYC; m. Victor Gotbaum; 1 child. Student, Barnard Coll.; BA, George Washington U., 1961; MEd, Columbia U., 1968. English instr. Brazil; asst. edn. City NY; exec. dir. NYC Police Found., 1977-82, Nat. Alliance Against Violence, 1982-86; assoc. Prospect Group, 1986-90; commr. NYC Parks & Recreation, 1990-94; pres. NY Hist. Soc., 1994—2001; public advocate NYC, 2001—. Office: 1 Centre St 15th Fl New York NY 10007

GOTHAM, RICHARD ERNEST, professional sports team executive; b. Norwood, Mass., Aug. 31, 1964; s. Ernest McLain Gotham and Cynthia (Mason) Iadarola; m. Kara Gotham; children: Olivia, Jayne, Trace. BSBA, Providence Coll., 1986. Sales rep. NCR Corp., Milford, Conn., 1986—87, nat. account mgr. Hartford, Conn., 1988—90; regional sales mgr. Process Software Corp., Framingham, Mass., 1990—91, bus. devel. mgr., 1992; v.p. channel sales and market devel. FTP Software, Inc.; v.p. e-commerce sales Lycos, Inc.; positions up to v.p. US sales and corp. devel. Terra Lycos, 1998—2003; exec. v.p. sales, mktg. and corp. devel. Boston Celtics, 2003—06, COO, 2006—07, pres., 2007—. Mem. adv. bd. Nat. Sports Mktg. Network. Mem. Com. for Phys. Fitness and Sport, Mass.; mem. bd. visitors New Eng. Baptist Hosp.; bd. mem. Jr. Achievement of Mass. Republican. Avocations: basketball, surfing, scuba diving. Office: Boston Celtics Fourth Fl 226 Causeway St Boston MA 02114*

GOTHOLD, STUART EUGENE, school system administrator, education educator; b. LA, Sept. 20, 1935; s. Hubert Eugene and Adelaide Louise (Erickson) G.; m. Jane Ruth Soderberg, July 15, 1955; children: Jon Ernest, Susan Louise, Eric Arthur, Ruth Ann. BA, Whittier Coll., Calif., 1956, MA in Edn., 1961, LLD (hon.), 1988; EdD, U. So. Calif., 1974. Tchr. grades 1-9 El Rancho Sch. Dist., Pico Rivera, Calif., 1956-61, prin. jr. h.s., 1961-66; curriculum cons. LA County Office Edn., 1966-70; asst. supt. South Whittier Sch. Dist., Calif., 1970-72, supt. Calif., 1972-77; asst. supt. LA County Office Edn., Downey, 1977-78, chief dep. supt., 1978-79, supt., 1979-94; clin. prof. emeritus U. So. Calif., LA, 1994—. Exec. dir. Edn. Insights, Detroit, 1990—; chmn., bd. dirs. Fedco Found.; co-chmn. LA Music Ctr. Edn. Coun. Author: (book) Inquiry, 1970, Decisions-A Health Edn. Curriculum, 1971. Recipient Alumni Merit award USC, 1993, Alumni Achievement award Whittier Coll., 1986; named Dist. Educator Calif. State U., 1993. Republican. Roman Catholic. Avocations: tennis, singing, photography, hiking. Home: 10121 Pounds Ave Whittier CA 90603-1649 Office: U So Calif WPH 902 C Los Angeles CA 90089-4039 Office Phone: 213-740-3451. Business E-Mail: gothold@usc.edu.

GOTLIEB, ALLAN E., former ambassador; b. Winnipeg, Man., Can., Feb. 28, 1928; s. David Phillip and Sarah (Schiller) G.; m. Sondra Kaufman, Dec. 20, 1955; children: Rebecca, Marcus, Rachel. BA, U. Calif., 1949; LLB, Harvard U., 1954; MA, BCL (Vinerian Law scholar), Oxford U., 1956; LLD (hon.), U. Toronto. Bar: Eng. 1956. Fellow Wadham Coll. and univ. lectr. in law Oxford U., 1954-56; joined Can. Dept. External Affairs, 1957; asst. under sec. for external affairs and legal adviser, 1967-68; dep. minister communications, 1968-73; dep. minister manpower and immigration, 1973-76; chmn. Can. Employment and Immigration Commn., 1976-77, Can. Coun., Ottawa, 1989-94; under sec. Dept. External Affairs, 1977-81; Can. amb. to US, Washington, 1981-89. Vis. fellow All

Souls Coll., Oxford, 1975-76; William Lyon Mackenzie King vis. prof. Harvard U., 1989, Claude Bissell vis. prof. U. Toronto, 1989; sr. fellow Massey Coll.; former gov. Internat. Devel. Rsch. Ctr., Nat. Film Bd.; former pub. Saturday Night Mag.; bd. dirs. Davis and Henderson Income Trust; N.Am. vice chmn. Trilateral Commn.; chmn. Donner Can. Found., Sotheby's Can., The Aurea Found.; sr. advisor Bennet Jones, Toronto; trustee Art Gallery Ont., Gandiver Mus. Author: Disarmament and International Law, 1965, Canadian Treaty-Making, 1968, The Washington Diaries, 1981-96, Impact of Technology on the Development of International Law, 1982, I'll Be With You In A Minute, Mr. Ambassador, 1991; editor: Human Rights, Federalism and Minorities, 1979; editor: Harvard Law Rev., 1950-51. Decorated companion Order of Can.; recipient outstanding achievement award Govt. of Can., 1983, Haas internat. award U. Calif. Bd. Regents, 1985, Woodrow Wilson Pub. Svc. award, Woodrow Wilson Internat. Ctr. Scholars, 2002; hon. fellow Wadham Coll. Oxford. Office: 3400 One First Canadian Pl PO Box 130 Toronto ON Canada M5X 1A4 Business E-Mail: gotlieba@bennettjones.ca.

GOTLIEB, CALVIN CARL, computer scientist, educator; b. Toronto, Ont., Mar. 27, 1921; s. Israel and Jennie G.; m. Phyllis Fay Bloom, June 12, 1949; children: Leo, Margaret, Jane. BA, U. Toronto, 1942, MA, 1944, PhD, 1947; D in Math. (hon.), U. Waterloo, Can., 1968; D in Engring. (hon.), N.S. Tech. U., 1985; LLD (hon.), U. Toronto, 1996. Faculty U. Toronto, 1949—; dir. Inst. Computer Sci., 1962-70, chmn. dept. computer sci., 1964-67, prof. computer sci., 1962—, emeritus, 1986—. Pres. C.C. Gotlieb Cons. Ltd., 1978—; cons. info. scis. to various govts., internat. orgns., indsl. cos., 1969—; McKay vis. prof. U. Calif., Berkeley, 1981; chmn. tech. com. 9 on relationship between computers and soc. Internat. Fedn. for Info. Processing, 1975-81 Author: (with J.N.P. Hume) High-Speed Data Processing, 1958, (with A. Borodin) Social Issues in Computing, 1973, (with L.R. Gotlieb) Data Types and Structures, 1978, Economics of Computers, 1985; editor, editor-in-chief, contbr. various Can., Netherlands, U.S. sci. jours. Recipient Silver Core award Internat. Fedn. of Info. Processing Socs., 1974, Auerbach award, 1994; rsch. grantee Nat. Sci. and Engring. Rsch. Coun. Can., 1955-90, C.M. Order of Can., 1996. Fellow: Assn. Computing Machinery (Pres.'s medal 2002), Brit. Computer Soc., Royal Soc. Can., Can. Info. Processing Soc. (hon.); mem.: Nat. Yacht Club (Toronto), Faculty Club (U. Toronto). Jewish. Home: 19 Lower Village Gate PH 06 Toronto ON Canada M5P 3L9 Office: U Toronto Dept Computer Sci Toronto ON Canada M5S 3G4 Home Phone: 416-482-4509. Business E-Mail: ccg@cs.toronto.edu.

GOTLIEB, JAQUELIN SMITH, pediatrician; b. Washington, Oct. 20, 1946; d. Turner Taliaferro and Lois Barbara (Fisk) Smith; m. Edward Marvin Gotlieb, June 25, 1970; children: Sarah Ruth, Aaron Franklin, David Jacob. BS in Zoology, Duke U., 1968; MD, Med. Coll. Va., 1972. Diplomate Am. Bd. Pediat. Rotating intern Med. Coll. Va. Hosps.-Va. Commonwealth U., Richmond, 1972—73, resident in pediat., 1973—74; pvt. practice Richmond, 1974—75, Stone Mountain, Ga., 1976—86, 1987—; resident in pediat. U. Colo., Denver, 1975—76; med. dir., cons. CIGNA Healthplan Ga., Atlanta, 1986—87. Sch. physician Richmond City Schs., 1974-75. Bd. dirs. Ga. Health Found., Atlanta, 1985-95, 2005-, vice chmn., 1995-99, chmn., 1999-2005.2005 Recipient Tee Rae Dismukes award, 2003. Fellow Am. Acad. Pediat. (Ga. chpt. bd. dirs. 1996-99, coord. state chpt. Pediat. Rsch. in Office Settings, 1996—, mem. steering com. Pediat. Rsch. in Office Settings, 2005—); mem. Med. Assn. Ga., Ga. Perinatal Assn. (bd. dirs. 1994-2002, pres. 1999-2000), DeKalb Med. Soc. (chmn. com. 1976). Office: Pediatric Ctr 5405 Memorial Dr Ste D Stone Mountain GA 30083-3236 Home Phone: 770-564-2339; Office Phone: 404-296-3800.

GOTMAN, JOHN ANDREW, freelance/self-employed journalist; b. Hoboken, NJ, Aug. 28, 1938; s. Thomas Francis Gorman and Edith Rose Ward. BA, Manhattan Coll., NYC, 1960; MA, Johns Hopkins U., Balt., 1961, PhD, 1967; postgrad., U. Freiburg, Germany, 1962—63. Yacht capt. various pleasure craft, 1965—86; asst. prof. German Lamar State U., Beaumont, Tex., 1965—66, U. Miami, Coral Gables, Fla., 1967—74; purser various cruise ships, Miami, Fla., 1976—81; freelance journalist, 1982—2006. Author: The Reception of Federico Garcia Lorca in Germany, 1973, King of the Romans, 1999. Mem.: ACLU, Elks. Libertarian. Avocations: sailing, motorcycling.

GOTO, MIDORI, classical violinist; b. Osaka, Japan, Oct. 25, 1971; Attended, Juilliard Sch. Music; grad., Profl. Childrens Sch., 1990; BA in Psychology and Gender Studies, NYU, 2000. Performer worldwide, 1982—; founder Midori and Friends, 1992; faculty Manhattan Sch. Music, 2001—. Recordings on Philips, Sony Classical, Columbia Masterworks; performed with N.Y. Philharmonic Orch., Boston Symphony Orch.; worldwide performances include Berlin, Chgo., Cleve., Phila., Montreal, London; recordings include Encore, Live at Carnegie Hall; recordings (albums) Paganini: 24 Caprices, 1989, Encore!, 1992, Midori's 20th Anniversary CD, 2001. Named Best Artist of Yr. by Japanese Govt., 1988; recipient Dorothy B. Chandler Performing Arts award, L.A. Music Ctr., 1989, Crystal award Ashani Shimbun Newspaper contbn. arts, Suntory award, 1994. Office: Midori And Friends 352 7th Ave Rm 201 New York NY 10001-5012

GOTO, TOSHIKO, retired art educator; b. San Pedro, Calif., Aug. 19, 1929; d. Kimitaro and Tora Yasui Goto. AA, LA Harbor Jr. Coll., Wilmington, Calif., 1952; BA, Calif. State U., Long Beach, 1954, MA, 1956; postgrad., Sch. Pond Farm Pottery, Guerneville, Calif., 1959—61. Tchr. Long Beach Unified Jefferson, 1961—64; art tchr. Long Beach Unified Jordan HS, 1964—79, Long Beach Unified Milliken HS, 1979—89; part-time art edn. tchr. Long Beach State Coll., 1960—64; part-time pottery tchr. Chapman Coll., Orange, Calif., 1964—73, Long Beach C.C., 1976—2005; ret., 2005. Pres. Art Tchrs. Assn. Long Beach, 1964—76; mem., corr. sec. Calif. Art Educators Assn., LA, 1964—76. Exhibitions include Chapman Coll., Long Beach C.C., Fullerton Art Mus., 2002, Calif. State U., San Bernardino, 2002. Active Higashi Honganji Buddhist Ch., LA. Scholar, Ebell Club, 1953—54, Space Workshop, 1966. Mem.: NEA, Calif. Ret. Tchrs. Assn., Calif. Tchrs. Assn. Avocations: woodblock printing, writing Haiku, pottery. Home: 1431 Fifth Ave Redlands CA 92374

GOTSCH, JOHN WARREN, contemporary arts house director; b. New Rochelle, NY, Feb. 17, 1937; s. Charles Stephen and Alta Margaret (Moore) G.; 1 child, Sybil Gabriella. BA in Sociology and Anthropology, Hobart Coll., 1963. Dir., CEO Ateliers Pro Arts, Budapest, Hungary, 2001—. Ctrl. European venture capital investment cons. Author: (novels) Goethe's Paradigms Afire!, Shinning Moon, Biennale, Anomalies, Amnesia and Burnt Bricks, Magical Stones, Stumbling Dodo Bird, Europe's Salvation: Eurasia and Darwinian Evolution; contbr. articles to profl. jours. Trustee Princeton (N.J.) Pro Musica, 1991, Russian Am. Network, 1996; mem. N.J. Health Planning Coun., Trenton; v.p. Delaware Valley Regional Tourism Coun., Trenton, 1984, Roebling (N.J.) Summit Conf. Com., 1984—, St. Mary's Band Change Ringers, Burlington, N.J., 1995—. Named to Athletic Hall of Fame, Bernard's Sch., 1986; recipient Golden Cross of Merit, Republic of Hungary. Mem. World Future Soc. Republican. Avocations: photography, reading, travel, writing, vol. to non-profits. Office: Ateliers Pro Arts Horanszky Utca 5 1085 Budapest Hungary

GOTSCHLICH, EMIL CLAUS, physician; b. Bangkok, Jan. 17, 1935; arrived in U.S., 1950, naturalized, 1955; s. Emil Clemens and Magdalene (Holst) Gotschlich; m. Kathleen-Anne Haines, May 24, 1975; children: Emil Christopher, Hilda Christina, Emil Chandler, Emily Claire. BA, NYU, 1955, MD, 1959. Intern Bellevue Hosp., NYC, 1959—60; mem. faculty Rockefeller U., NYC, 1960—, prof. microbiology, 1978—, sr. physician, 1978—, prof., v.p. med. sci. Capt. med. corps US Army, 1966—68. Recipient Squibb award, Am. Soc. Infectious Disease, 0197, Lasker award, Albert and Mary Lasker Found., 1978. Mem.: NAS, Am. Soc. Clin. Investigation, Am. Assn. Immunologists, Peripatetic Club, Alpha Omega Alpha, Sigma Xi. Office: Rockefeller U Dept Bacterial Pathogenesis & Immunology 1230 York Ave New York NY 10021-6399

GOTTA, ALEXANDER WALTER, anesthesiologist, educator; b. Bklyn., Apr. 10, 1935; s. A. Walter and Helen C. (Bruskewic) G.; m. Colleen A. Sullivan, July 17, 1965; 1 child, Nancy C. BS summa cum laude, St. John's U., 1956; MD, NYU, 1960. Diplomate Am. Bd. Anesthesiology, Am. Bd. Med. Examiners. Intern U. Chgo., 1960-61; resident in surgery Boston City Hosp., 1961-62; resident in anesthesiology N.Y. Hosp.-Cornell U., NYC, 1962-64; instr. anesthesiology Cornell U., 1965-66; adj. prof. St. John's U., 1977—79; dir. anesthesia St. Mary's Hosp., Bklyn., 1968-78; from asst. prof. to prof. SUNY, Bklyn., 1968—97; prof. emeritus, 1997—; mem. dean's adv. bd. St. John's Coll., 2003—07. Dir. anesthesia L.I. Coll. Hosp., Bklyn., 1983-90, Kings County Hosp. Ctr., 1990-97; spkr. in field. Editor: Anesthesiology Clinics Trauma, 1996; contbr. articles to profl. jours. Capt. U.S. Army, 1966-68, Vietnam. Fellow N.Y. Acad. Medicine (chmn. anesthesia sect. 1990, recognition for svc. to urban medicine 1997), Am. Coll. Anesthesiologists, Am. Soc. Anesthesiologists (ho. dels. 1986-97, chmn. refresher course com. 1995); mem. N.Y. Soc. Anesthesiologists (bd. dirs. 1983-97, chmn. sci. program com. 1991-93, chmn. PGA 1994-96, v.p. 1994, pres.-elect 1995, pres. 1996), N.Y. Soc. Critical Care Medicine (pres. 1985), Assn. Univ. Anesthesiologists, Acad. Anesthesia. Republican. Roman Catholic. Home: 29 Ascot Ridge Rd Great Neck NY 11021-2912 Office: Kings County Hosp Ctr 451 Clarkson Ave Brooklyn NY 11203-2097 E-mail: alexwg@optonline.net.

GOTTA, JOSEPH D., music company executive; Grad. in Piano Tuning and Repair, Ctrl. Piedmont C.C., 1989. Registered piano technician Piano Technicians Guild, 1990. Pres. Charlotte NC chpt. Piano Technicians Guild, 2003—; exec. dir. SE Regional Conf. Piano Technicians Guild, Charlotte, NC, 2006—. Chmn. bd. dirs. Woodberry Forest Neighborhood Assn., 2007—, vice chmn. bd., 2004. Mem.: Piano Technicians Guild (pres. Charlotte chpt. 2003—07), Master Piano Technicians of Am. Home: 7701 Gayle Ave Charlotte NC 28212 Office: A 440 Piano Svc 7701 Gayle Ave Charlotte NC 28212 Home Phone: 704-563-8230. Personal E-mail: tune@a440piano.com.

GOTTESMAN, A(RTHUR) EDWARD, lawyer; b. Hillside, NJ, July 29, 1937; s. Joseph Jack Gottesman, Sadonia Herskowitz; m. Patricia Jo Matson; m. Allison Pierce Coudert (div.); children: Polly Moore, Catherine Coudert. BA, U.Chgo., 1954; LLB, Yale U., 1957. Bar: N.Y. 1959. Ptnr. Coudert Bros., London, 1963—70; sr. ptnr. Gottesman Jones & Partners, London, 1970—. Pres. Am. C. of C., London, 1981—83; chmn. Derby Internat. Corp., Luxembourg, Exeter Internat. Corp., Luxembourg, Prin. Healthcare Fin. Ltd., London. Author: Blueprint for Public Company Reform, World Economics, 2003, Two Myths of Globalization, World Policy Journal, 2006. Dir. London Bach Orch., 1980—89; Member Yale University President's Council on International Activities, New Haven. Private US Army, 1960—61, Fort Dix, N.J. Mem.: Yale Club, Reform Club. Office: 26 Old Bailey EC4M 7HW London England Home Phone: 212-921-3535; Office Phone: 44207-653-6900. Personal E-mail: centenint@aol.com. Business E-Mail: gottesmanjones@aol.com.

GOTTESMAN, DAVID SANFORD, investment company executive; b. NYC, Apr. 26, 1926; s. Benjamin and Esther (Garfunkel) G.; m. Ruth Levy, Aug. 17, 1950; children: Robert, Alice, William. BA, Trinity Coll., 1948; MBA, Harvard U., 1950; LHD (hon.), Yeshiva U., 1988. Sr. mng. dir. First Manhattan Co., NYC, 1964—. Bd. dirs. Berkshire Hathaway, Inc. Vice-chmn., trustee Am. Mus. Natural History; trustee Mt. Sinai Hosp.; chmn. emeritus Yeshiva U., N.Y.C. Mem. The Century Assn., Econs. Club, Harmonie Club, Century Country Club. Office: First Manhattan Co 437 Madison Ave New York NY 10022-7001

GOTTESMAN, IRVING I., psychologist, educator; b. Cleve., Dec. 29, 1930; s. Bernard and Virginia (Weitzner) G.; m. Carol Applen, Dec. 23, 1970; children: Adam M., David B. BS, Ill. Inst. Tech., 1953; PhD, U. Minn., 1960. Diplomate in clin. psychology and psychol. assessment; lic. psychologist Calif., Va. Intern clin. psychology VA Hosp., Mpls., 1959—60; lectr. depts. social rels. and psychology Harvard U., 1960—63; USPHS fellow in psychiat. genetics Inst. Psychiatry, London, 1963—64; assoc. prof. psychiat. & genetics, dept. psychiatry U. N.C., 1964—66; prof. dept. psychology, psychiatry and genetics U. Minn., 1966—80; prof. dept. psychiatry and genetics Washington U., St. Louis, 1980—85; Commonwealth prof. psychology U. Va., Charlottesville, 1985—94, Sherrell J. Aston prof. psychology, prof. clin. pediats., 1994—2001, Sherrell J. Aston prof. emeritus, 2001—; sr. fellow psychology, Drs. Irving and Dorothy Bernstein prof. adult psychiatry U. Minn., 2001—. Cons. NIMH, Washington, 1975-79, 92-96, NIMH Nat. Plan for Schizophrenia, 1988-89; mem. Pres.'s Commn. on Huntington Disease, 1977; tng. cons. VA, Washington, 1968-85, 2001—; fellow Ctr. for Advanced Studies in the Behavioral Scis., Stanford, Calif., 1987-88; Inst. of Medicine Com. cons. Vietnam War Experience Study, 1987-88, Med. Follow-Up Agy., 2000—; NRC cons. Workshop on Schizophrenia, 1995-96; cons. human rights Equal Opportunities Commn., Hong Kong, 1999-2003, 05-06; mem. Inst. Medicine Follow-up Agy., 2000—; chair twins com. Inst. Medicine, 2000-07, mem. com. on genomics and the public's health in the 21st century, 2004-05. Author: Schizophrenia and Genetics, 1972 (Hofheimer prize), Schizophrenia The Epigenetic Puzzle, 1982, Schizophrenia Genesis: The Origins of Madness, 1991 (transl. into Japanese and German, William James Book award, Phi Beta Kappa U. Va. Book award 1992), Schizophrenia and Genetic Risks, 1992, 3d edit., 1999, Schizophrenia and Manic Depressive Disorder: Biological Roots of Mental Illness Revealed by Study of Identical Twins, 1994, transl. into Japanese, 1998, Seminars in Psychiatric Genetics, 1994, Psychiatric Genetics and Genomics, 2002, revised, 2004; editor: Man, Mind and Heredity, 1971, Vital Statistics, Demography and Schizophrenia, 1989. Served with USNR, 1949-53, 56-61; USN, 1953-56. Guggenheim fellow U. Copenhagen, 1972; recipient R. Thornton Wilson prize Ea. Psychiat. Rsch. Assn., 1965, Stanley Dean award Am. Coll. Psychiatrists, 1988, Eric Stromgren medal Danish Psychiat. Soc., 1991, Kurt Schneider prize, Bonn, 1992, Alexander Gralnick prize Am. Assn. Suicidology, 1992, Jonathan Logan award Nat. Alliance for Mentally Ill, 1995; David C. Wilson lectr. U. Va. Sch. Medicine, 1967, Lifetime Achievement award Internat. Soc. for Psychiat. Genetics, 1997; Parker lectr. Ohio State U. Sch. Medicine, 1983, 93, others. Fellow APA (Disting. Scientist award divsn. 12, sect. 3 1994, Disting. Sci. Contbns. award 2001), AAAS, Am. Psychopathol. Assn., Royal Coll. Psychiatrists (hon.), Am. Psychol. Soc. (human capital initiative task force for psychopathology rsch. agenda 1993-96); mem. Minn. Human Genetics League (v.p. 1969-71), Soc. Study Social Biology (v.p. 1976-80), Behavior Genetics Assn. (pres. 1976-77, J. LeJeune lectr. 2007, T. Dobzhansky award 1990), Am. Soc. Human Genetics (editl. bd. 1967-72), Soc. Rsch. in Psychopathology (pres. 1993, Joseph Zubin award 2001), Japanese Soc. Biol. Psychiatry (spl. lecture award 2001), Inst. of Psychiatry (14th Eliot Slater Lectr., 2002), Am. Psychol. Found. (Life Achievement Gold medal, 2007). Home: 5823 Vernon Ln Edina MN 55436 Business E-Mail: gotte003@umn.edu.

GOTTESMAN, MICHAEL MARC, biomedical researcher; b. Jersey City, Oct. 7, 1946; s. Jacob Joseph and Frieda (Shapiro) G.; m. Susan Kemelhor, Feb. 5, 1966; children: Daniel Eric, Rebecca Fran. AB, Harvard Coll., 1966; MD, Harvard Med. Sch., 1970. Diplomate Am. Bd. Internal Medicine. Med. intern then resident Peter Bent Brigham Hosp., Boston, 1970-71, 74-75; rsch. assoc. NIH, Bethesda, Md., 1971-74; asst. prof. dept. anatomy Harvard Med. Sch., Boston, 1975-76; sr. investigator Nat. Cancer Inst., Bethesda, 1976-80, chief molecular genetics sect. Lab. Molecular Biology, 1980-90, chief Lab. Cell Biology, 1990—; acting dir. Nat. Ctr. Human Genome Rsch., 1992—93, acting sci. dir., 1993; dep. dir. intramural rsch. NIH, 1993—. Asst. surgeon gen. (rear adm.), 1997—, USPHS. Recipient Milken Family Found. Award for Cancer Rsch., 1988, C.E. Alken Prize, 1991, Samuel G. Taylor III Award for Excellence in Cancer Rsch., 1991, Jefferson Cancer Inst. Prize, 1991, Rosenthal Found. Award, 1992, Am. Soc. Pharmacology and Exptl. Therapeutics (ASPET) Award, 1997. Fellow: AAAS. Achievements include rsch. on molecular basis of resistance to anti-cancer drugs. Office: Nat Cancer Inst Lab Cell Biology 37 Convent Dr Rm 2108 Bethesda MD 20892-4255 Office Phone: 301-496-1530. Office Fax: 301-402-0450. E-mail: mgottesman@nih.gov.

GOTTESMAN, PATRICIA ANN, marketing executive; b. Feb. 10, 1959; m. Samuel Judah Gottesman, Feb. 14, 2004; 4 children. Grad., Hofstra U., 1979. Prodr. local origination dept., LI system Cablevision Systems Corp., 1979; system mgr., Cablevision Systems Corp, gen. mgr., NJ Bayonne, LI Hauppauge system; v.p. cable ops. Cablevision Systems Corp., 1991—93, sr. v.p. regional ops. in NYC & Conn., v.p. mktg., sr. v.p. consumer product mgmt. & mktg., exec. v.p. product mgmt. & mktg., exec. v.p. digital mktg. & commerce, 2007—. Mem. Nat. Franchising Team, 1981. Named a Woman to Watch, Advt. Age, 2007; recipient Wonder Woman award, Women in Cable & Telecom. (WICT), 2006. Office: Cablevision Systems Corp 1111 Stewart Ave Bethpage NY 11714*

GOTTFRIED, EUGENE LESLIE, physician, educator; b. Passaic, NJ, Feb. 26, 1929; s. David Robert and Rose (Chill) G.; m. Phyllis Doris Swain, Aug. 16, 1957. AB, Columbia U., 1950, MD, 1954. Cert. Nat. Bd. Med. Examiners, Am. Bd. Internal Medicine. Intern Presbyn. Hosp., NYC, 1954-55, asst. resident in medicine, 1957-58; resident Bronx (N.Y.) Mcpl. Hosp. Ctr., 1958-59, fellow in medicine, 1959-60; asst. instr. medicine Albert Einstein Coll. Medicine Yeshiva U., NYC, 1959-60, instr., 1960-61, assoc., 1961-65, asst. prof., 1965-69; assoc. prof. medicine Cornell U. Med. Coll., NYC, 1969-81, assoc. prof. pathology, 1975-81; clin. prof. dept. lab. medicine U. Calif., San Francisco, 1981-93, prof., 1993-99, vice chmn. dept. lab. medicine, 1981-98, prof. emeritus, 1999—. Hosp. appointments include asst. vis. physician Bronx Mcpl. Hosp. Ctr., 1960-66, assoc. attending physician, 1966-69; assoc. attending physician N.Y. Hosp., N.Y.C., 1969-81, assoc. attending pathologist, 1975-81, dir. lab. clin. hematology, 1969-81; chief lab. medicine San Francisco Gen. Hosp. Med. Ctr., 1981-98, dir. clin. labs., 1981-98. Assoc. editor Jour. Lipid Research, 1971-72, 75-77; mem. editorial bd. Jour. Lipid Research, 1972-77. Dir. Rescue One Found., 1998—, Moraga-Orinda Fire Protection Dist., 2002—. Lt. comdr. M.C. USNR, 1955—57, with Ready Res. USNR, 1957—64. Recipient Career Scientist award Health Research Council City of N.Y., 1964-72. Fellow ACP, Am. Soc. Hematology, Internat. Soc. Hematology, Acad. Clin. Lab. Physicians and Scientists, Nat. Com. Clin. Lab. Stds. (chair area com. on hematology 1995-00), Orinda Pub. Safety Adv. Commn., Rotary (pres. Orinda club 2004-05), Phi Beta Kappa, Alpha Omega Alpha. Business E-Mail: eugene.gottfried@ucsf.edu.

GOTTFRIED, IRA SIDNEY, management consulting executive; b. Bronx, NY, Jan. 4, 1932; s. Louis and Augusta (Champagne) G.; m. Judith Claire Rosenberg, Sept. 19, 1954; children: Richard Alan, Glenn Steven, David Aaron. BBA, CCNY, 1953; MBA, U. So. Calif., 1959. Lic. airline transport pilot. Sales mgr. Kleerpak Plastics, North Hollywood, Calif., 1956-57; head sys. and procedures Hughes Aircraft Co., Culver City, Calif., 1957-60; mgr. corp. bus. sys. The Aerospace Corp., El Segundo, Calif., 1960-61; dir. adminstrn. Eldon Industries, Inc., Hawthorne, Calif., 1962; mgr. info. sys. Litton Industries, Inc., Woodland Hills, Calif., 1963-64; exec. v.p. Norris & Gottfried, Inc., LA, 1964-69; pres. Gottfried Cons., Inc., LA, 1970-85; exec. ptnr. PriceWaterhouseCoopers, LLP, LA, 1985-88, ret., 1988. V.p. Cresap/Towers Perrin, 1988-90; pres., dir. Gottfried Cons. Internat. 1990—; vice chmn. ACME Inc., 1984-85; dir., mem. exec. com. Blue Cross of Calif., 1968-77. Contbr. articles to profl. jours. Bd. dirs. ARC, 1988-2003, Westside Amateur Radio Club, Univ. Synagogue, 1986-92. With USNR, 1953-56. Recipient Pres.'s award United Hosp. Assn. Mem. Inst. Mgmt. Cons. (life), Am. Arbitration Assn., Assn. Info. Tech. Profls. (life), Alpha Phi Omega (life), Brentwood Country Club. Jewish. Avocations: radio, flying, model building. Home: 12118 La Casa Ln Los Angeles CA 90049-1530 Office Phone: 310-476-2124.

GOTTFRIED, KEITH EVAN, lawyer; b. Bklyn., Nov. 11, 1966; s. Bertram David and Rosalie (Penso) G.; m. Cindy Goldwasser, Apr. 1, 2005; 1 child, Sophie Regine. BS in Econs. and Acctg., Wharton Sch., U. Pa., Phila., 1987; JD cum laude, Boston U., 1992, MBA with high honors, 1995. Bar: Pa. 1992, NJ 1992, Mass. 1994, NY 1995, Calif., 2001; CPA, Pa. Staff acct., auditor Arthur Young & Co. (now Ernst & Young LLP), Phila., 1987—89; corp. assoc. Blank Rome LLP, Phila., 1992—94; assoc. Skadden, Arps, Slate, Meagher & Flom, LLP, NYC, 1994—2000; sr. v.p., gen. counsel, corp. sec., chief legal officer Borland Software Corp., Scotts Valley, Calif., 2000—03, sr. v.p. corp. affairs, spl. advisor to CEO Cupertino, 2003—04; gen. counsel, chief legal officer US Dept. Housing & Urban Devel., Washington, 2005—06; ptnr. Blank Rome LLP, Washington, 2007—. Spkr. in field; bd. dirs. Bus. Software Alliance; Senate confirmed presdl. appointee George W. Bush Adminstrn., Washington, 2005—06. Delegate Asia-Pacific Econ. Coop. Summits, China, 2001, Mex., 2002, Thailand, 2003; mem. U.S. Dept. Commerce Industry Trade Adv. Com.; mem. state fin. com. Bush-Cheney, 2004; mem. fin. com. Rosario Marin for U.S. Senate, 2004. Recipient Silver award, League Am. Comm. Profls., 2002. Mem.: ABA, Corp. M&A Assn., Republican Nat. Lawyers Assn., U. Pa. Alumni Club, Wharton Alumni Club, Beta Gamma Sigma. Republican. Jewish. Avocations: running, hiking, swimming, politics, reading. Office: Blank Rome LLP Watergate 600 New Hampshire Ave Washington DC 20037 Home Phone: 301-963-4950; Office Phone: 202-772-5887. Office Fax: 202-572-1434; Home Fax: 301-963-4950. Personal E-mail: kgottfri@yahoo.com. Business E-Mail: gottfried@blankrome.com.

GOTTFRIED, MARK ELLIS, accountant, consultant; b. Toledo, Mar. 12, 1953; s. Max and Barbara Alice (Johnston) G.; m. Linda Jean Perkins, Aug. 7, 1976; children: Christopher Ellis, Katharine Powell. BA, Northwestern U., 1975; MBA, U. Chgo., 1980. CPA Ill., Ind., Va. Sr. acct. Deloitte Haskins & Sells, Chgo., 1980-84; corp. mktg. mgr. Micro Data Base Systems, Lafayette, Ind., 1984-85; sr. cons. Deloitte Haskins & Sells, Indpls., 1985-86, mgr., 1986-88; owner Gottfried & Assocs., Indpls., 1988-91; v.p. fin., sec. Trilithic, Inc., Indpls., 1989-92; pres. TriVox Corp., 1990-92, Performance Ptnrs., Inc., 1991-93; CFO Frontier Broadband LLC, Va., 2000—02; prin., owner Gottfried Cons., Va., 1995—2004; corp. contr. Allied Aerospace Industries, Inc., Va., 2004—06; controller Triumph Aerospace Sys., Newport News Inc., 2006—. Bd. dirs., treas. Ptnrs. in Mktg. Inc., 1992-93; bd. dirs. ReproComm. Inc., 1992-95; instr., bus. cons. Premier FastTrac tng. program Va. Peninsula C. of C., 1996-99 Editorial bd. Computers in Acctg., 1984-89. Bd. dirs. Chgo. Theatre Group, 1984; bd. dirs. Ind. Repertory Theatre, mem. fin. com., 1987-92; cons. Jr. Achievement, Indpls., 1986-87. Mem. AICPA, Ind. Soc. CPAs, Va. Soc. CPAs, Inst. Mgmt. Acct., Indpls. C. of C. (govt. com. 1986-89), Ind. Electronics Mfrs. Assn. (v.p. fin. and legal 1989-91), Ind. Small Bus. Coun., U. Chgo. Grad. Sch. Bus. Alumni Assn. (pres. Ind. chpt. 1987-95), Columbia Club. Republican. Episcopalian. Home: 109 William Claiborne Williamsburg VA 23185-6536 Personal E-mail: megottfried@yahoo.com.

GOTTHARDT, MARY JANE, retired religious studies educator; b. Davenport, Iowa, Sept. 22, 1940; d. Harry Claus and Roseanne (Beulah May) Stoltenberg; m. Lawrence John Gotthardt, July 8, 1967; children: Michael John, Paula Formold. BA, DeLourdes Coll., 1987; MAT, Nat. Louis U., 1999. RN Ill. Nurse Resurrection Hosp., Chgo., 1960—70; chmn. pub. rels. Mark Hopkins Sch., Elk Grove, Ill., 1975—78, Transfiguration Night Train, Wauconda, Ill., 1980; tchr. religious edn. Transfiguration Sch., Wauconda, 1979—2002, tchr. and libr. aid, 1979—2000, tchr., 2000—06; tchr. religious edn. St. Peter Ch., Volo, Ill., 1998—2002, dir. religious edn., 2000—06; ret. Co-owner Mannheim Rental Equipment, Franklin Pk., Ill., 1968—. Sec. Homeowner's Assn., Wauconda. Mem.: AAAS, Nat. Mid. Sch. Assn., Pope John Paul II Cultural Ctr., Smithsonian Inst., Gallop Poll, Hist. Ill. Preservation Soc., Phi Delta Kappa. Roman Catholic. Avocation: travel. Office: Transfiguration Sch 316 W Mill St Wauconda IL 60084

GOTTHOFFER, LANCE, lawyer; b. NYC, June 23, 1949; s. Joel Sidney and Muriel (Diamond) G. BA, Monmouth Coll., 1971; JD, Georgetown U., 1974. Bar: N.Y. 1975, U.S. Dist. Ct. (so. dist.) N.Y. 1975, U.S. Ct. Appeals (2nd, 3rd, 5th, 6th and 9th cirs.) 1981, U.S. Ct. Internat. Trade 1986, U.S. Supreme Ct. 1987. Legal asst. Office of N.Y.C. Coun. Pres., NYC, 1970-73; assoc. Mudge, Rose, Guthrie & Alexander, NYC, 1974-77; ptnr. Marks & Murase, NYC, 1977-94, Oppenheimer, Wolff & Donnelly, NYC, 1994—2002, Reed Smith, NYC, 2003—. Guest lectr. Grad. Sch. Bus., Baruch Coll., N.Y.C.; speaker in field. Mem. ABA. Office: Reed Smith 599 Lexington Ave New York NY 10022 Home: 245 E 40th St Apt 32b New York NY 10016-1719 Office Phone: 212-549-0289. Business E-Mail: lgotthoffer@reedsmith.com.

GOTTHOLD, WILLIAM EUGENE, emergency physician; b. Long Beach, Calif., Sept. 20, 1942; BA, Trinity U., 1964; MD, Tulane U., 1969. Cert. emergency medicine. Intern Letterman Army Med. Ctr., San Francisco, 1969-70, resident in gen. surgery, 1970-72; mem. staff Ctrl. Wash. Hosp., Wenatchee, 1978—; med. infomatics officers Wenatchee (Wash.) Valley Clinic. Mem. AMA, Am. Coll. Emergency Physicians, Wash. State Med. Assn., Am. Bd. Emergency Medicine (cert., sr. dir.). Office: Wenatchee Valley Med Ctr 820 N Chelan Ave Wenatchee WA 98801-2028 Office Phone: 509-663-8711. E-mail: wgotthold@wvclinic.com.

GOTTI, VICTORIA, columnist, writer, actress; b. Bklyn., Nov. 27, 1962; d. John J. and Victoria (DiGiorgio) Gotti; m. Carmine Agnello, 1984 (div. Feb. 2002); children: John Gotti Agnello, Carmine Gotti Agnello, Frank Gotti Agnello. BA, St. John's U. Weekly features columnist NY Post; entertainment corr. EXTRA!, 2002; columnist Star mag., exec. editor-at-large; editor-in-chief Red Carpet mag. Actress & exec. prodr. (reality TV series) Growing Up Gotti, A & E, 2004—05; author: Women & Mitral Valve Prolapse: A Comprehensive Guide to Living & Coping With MVP & Its Symptoms, 1995, The Senator's Daughter, 1997 (Mystery of Yr., Mystery Writers Assn.), I'll Be Watching You, 1998, Superstar, 2000, The Fifth Avenue Club, The Loyal Son, Hot Italian Dish: The Victoria Gotti Cookbook, 2006; actor: (plays) We're Still Hot, 2005. Named Woman of Yr., Nat. Chpt. Am. Heart Assn., Writer of Yr., Women's Writer's Guild, Woman of Yr., Women's Coalition for Equal Rights; recipient Outstanding Humanitarian, St. Frances Guild Inc. Mailing: c/o Theatre at St Luke's 308 West 46 St New York NY 10019

GOTTLICH, SCOTT, chef; b. 1975; m. Gina Gottlich. Grad., Coll. Culinary Arts, Johnson & Wales U., Colo. Chef Le Bernardin, NYC, Aubergine, Calif.; cons. Cafe Toulouse, 2005; interim chef Taverna; exec. chef Lola Restaurant, Dallas, Bijoux, Dallas, 2006—. Named one of Dallas' Rising Stars, StarChefs.com, 2007. Office: Bijoux 5450 W Lovers Ln Dallas TX 75209*

GOTTLIEB, ALAN MERRIL, advertising, fundraising and broadcasting executive, writer; b. LA, May 2, 1947; s. Seymour and Sherry (Schutz) G.; m. Julie Hoy Versnel, July 27, 1979; children: Amy Jean, Sarah Merril, Alexis Hope, Andrew Michael. Grad., Inst. on Comparative Political and Economic Sys. at Georgetown U., 1970; BS Nuc. Engring., U. Tenn., 1971. Press sec. Congressman John Duncan, Knoxville, Tenn., 1971; regional rep. Young Am. for Freedom, Seattle, 1972, nat. dir. Washington, 1971-72; nat. treas. Am. Conservative Union, Washington, 1971—, bd. dirs., 1974—; pres. Merril Assoc., 1974—. Chmn. Citizens Com. for Right to keep and Bear Arms, Bellevue, Wash., 1972—, exec. dir., 1973; pres. Ctr. Def. of Free Enterprise, Bellevue, 1976—, Second Amendment Found., Bellevue, 1974—, NoInternetTax.org, 2001—; pub. Gun Week, 1985—, The Gottlieb-Tartaro Report, 1995—; bd. dir. Nat. Pk. User Assn., 1988—; bd. dirs. Am. Polit. Action Com., 1988—; bd. dir. Coun. Nat. Policy, bd. gov., 1985—, Svc. Bur. Assn., pres., dir., 1974—, Chancellor Broadcasting, Inc., Las Vegas, 1990—93; pres. Sta. KBNP Radio, Portland, 1990—, Sta. KITZ Radio, Evergreen Radio Network, Seattle, 1990—93, Westnet Broadcasting Inc., Bellevue, 1990, Sta. KSBN Radio, Spokane, 1995—, KGTK Radio, Olympia, Wash.; chmn. Talk Am. Radio Networks, 1994—2001, Univ. Talk Network, 2002; mem. exec. com. World Forum on the Future of Sport Shooting Activities, 2007. Author: The Gun Owners Political Action Manual, 1976, The Rights of Gun Owners, 1981, rev. edit., 1991, The Gun Grabbers, 1988, Gun Rights Fact Book, 1989, Guns for Women, 1988, The Wise Use Agenda, 1989, Trashing the Economy, 1993, Thinks You Can Do To Defend Your Gun Rights, 1993, Alan Gottlieb's Celebrity Address Book, 1994, 2d edit., 2001, More Things You Can Do To Defend Your Gun Rights, 1995, Politically Correct guns, 1996, She Took a Village, 1998, Double Trouble, 2001, Gun Rights Affirmed, 2001, George W. Bush Speaks to the Nation, 2004, America Fights Back, 2007. With U.S. Army, 1968-74. Recipient Good Citizenship award, Citizens Home Protective Assn., Honolulu, 1978, Cicero award, Nat. Assn. Federally Licensed Firearms Dealers, Fla., 1982, 2d Amendment award, Scope, 1983, 1991, Defender of Freedom award, 2005, Outstanding Am. Handgunner award, Am. Handgunners Award Found., Milw., 1984, Roy Rogers award, Nat. Antique Arms Collectors Assn., Reno, Nev., 1987, Golden Eagle award, Am. Fedn. Police, Washington, 1990, award, Assn. NJ Rifle and Pistol Clubs, 2006. Mem. NRA. Republican. Office Phone: 425-454-7012. Personal E-mail: alangottlieb@aol.com.

GOTTLIEB, ALICE B., dermatologist; PhD in Immunology, Rockefeller U., 1979; MD, Cornell U., 1980. Diplomate Am. Bd. Dermatology, bd. cert. rheumatology and internal medicine. Fellow in rheumatology Cornell U. Hosp. for Spl. Surgery, NYC, 1982—84; resident in internal medicine N.Y. Hosp., NYC, 1980—82, resident in dermatology, 1990—93; chair dermatology, dermatologist-in-chief Tufts-New Eng. Med. Ctr., Boston, 2005—. Office: Tufts-New Eng Med Ctr 750 Washington St Box 114 Boston MA 02111 Office Phone: 617-636-5370.

GOTTLIEB, DANIEL SETH, lawyer; b. LA, Sept. 19, 1954; s. Seymour and Blanche Joyce (Kaufman) G.; m. Marilynn Jeanne Payne, July 21, 1985; children: Gwendolyn Z., Rebecca Lucinda. BA summa cum laude, Columbia U., 1976; JD, Harvard U., 1980. Bar: Wash. 1980, Oreg. 2004, U.S. Dist. Ct. (we. dist.) Wash. 1980. Assoc. Riddell, Williams, Bullitt & Walkinshaw, Seattle, 1980-86, ptnr., 1986-95; prin. Graham & James LLP/Riddell Williams P.S., Seattle, 1996-97; mem. Gottlieb, Fisher & Andrews, PLLC, Seattle, 1997—. Coord. S.E. Legal Clinic, Seattle, 1984—86; mem. Wash. State Access to Justice Bd., 2004—. Mem. Seattle Fremont Adv. Com. Recipient Achievement award Seattle-King County Econ. Devel. Coun., 1990. Mem. ABA, Nat. Assn. Bond Lawyers, Wash. State Bar Assn., King County Bar Assn. (treas. 1993-95, 2d v.p. 1995-96, 1st v.p. 1996-97, pres. 1997-98, bd. dirs. young lawyers divsn. 1987-90, treas. 1987-88, vice-chmn. 1988-89, chmn. 1989-90, chmn. legal info. and referral clinics com. 1986-87, Helen Geisness award 2001), Wash. State Assn. Mcpl. Attys., Wash. State Soc. Healthcare Attys., Bainbridge Island-North Kitsap Jewish Chavurah (v.p. and sec. 1993-95). Jewish. Avocations: tuba, hiking, bicycling. Home: 4880 NE North Tolo Rd Bainbridge Island WA 98110-3461 Office: Gottlieb Fisher & Andrews PLLC Ste 2510 520 Pike St Seattle WA 98101-4006 Home Phone: 206-842-8107; Office Phone: 206-654-1949. Personal E-mail: dan@goandfish.com.

GOTTLIEB, DAVID, mathematics professor; BSc, MSc, Tel-Aviv U., PhD in Applied Math., 1972. Instr., lectr. dept. applied math. MIT, Cambridge, 1972—75; assoc. mem. ICASE NASA Langley Rsch. Ctr., Hampton, Va., 1974—98, rsch. scientist ICASE, 1975—76; sr. lectr. dept. applied math. Tel-Aviv U., 1976—77; assoc. prof., 1978—82, prof., 1982—86, chmn., 1983—85; prof. divsn. applied math. Brown U., Providence, 1985—, Ford Found. prof., 1993—, chair, 1996—99. Contbr. articles to sci. jours.; co-author (with S. Orszag): Numerical Analysis of Spectral Methods/Theory and Applications, 1977; co-author: (with J. Hesthaven and S. Gottlieb) Spectral Methods for Time Dependent Problems, 2006. Mem.: NAS. Office: Brown U Box F Providence RI 02912 Office Phone: 401-863-2266. Office Fax: 401-863-1355. E-mail: David_Gottlieb@brown.edu.

GOTTLIEB, GARY L., hospital administrator; b. May 6, 1955; m. Derri Shtasel; 2 children. BS cum laude, Rensselaer Poly. Inst., 1975; MD, Albany Med. Coll., 1979; MBA Health Care Admin. with distinction, U. Pa., 1985. Diplomate in psychiatry and geriatric psychiatry Am. Bd. Psychiatry and Neurology; lic. physician, Pa., N.Y. Rotating intern NYU Med. Ctr., NYC, 1979-80, resident in psychiatry, 1980-82, chief resident in psychiatry, 1982-83; Robert Wood Johnson Found. clin. scholar U. Pa., Phila., 1983-85; from instr. to assoc. prof. dept. psychiatry U. Pa. Sch. Medicine, Phila., 1985-94, clin. prof. psychiatry, 1994—; assoc. dean for managed care U. Pa. Med. Ctr., Phila., 1992-94, interim chair dept. psychiatry, 1993-94; dir., CEO Friends Hosp., Phila., 1994—2002; prof. psychiatry Harvard Med. Sch., 1998—; pres. Brigham & Women's/Faulkner Hosp., 2002—. Ascher-Globus vis. prof., lectr. dept. psychiatry Cornell U. Sch. Medicine, N.Y.C., 1993. Mem. editorial bd. Internat. Jour. Geriatric Psychiatry, 1988—; asst. editor Am. Jour. Geriatric Psychiatry, 1992—; contbr. articles to profl. jours. Recipient Henry J. Kaiser prize Wharton Grad. Sch., U. Pa., 1985, Earl Bond award for teaching excellence U. Pa., 1989, Christian R. and Mary F. Lindback Found. award for Disting. Teaching, U. Pa., 1991. Mem. Am. Psychiat. Assn., Am. Geriatrics Soc., Am. Assn. Gen. Hosp. Psychiatrists, Alzheimer's Assn., Am. Assn. Geriatric Psychiatry (bd. dirs. 1987-90, pres. 1993-95), Assn. Acad. Psychiatry, Gerontol. Soc. Am., Pa. Psychiat. Soc., Phila. Psychiat. Soc., Soc. for Health and Human Values, Beta Gamma Sigma.

GOTTLIEB, GEOFFREY JON, dermatologist; b. Lowell, Mass., Dec. 28, 1950; m. Alice Surnamer, Aug. 4, 1974; children: Amy Beth, Sarah Jane. AB, Cornell U., Ithaca, NY, 1972; MD, Cornell U., NYC, 1976. Cert. dermatopathology Am. Bds. Pathology and Dermatology, 1982, anatomic pathology Am. Bd. Pathology, 1979. Dir. Ackerman Acad. Dermatopathology, NYC, 2000—. Editor: (book) Kaposi's Sarcoma: A Text and Atlas; co-author: Histologic Diagnosis of Inflammatory Skin Diseases; contbr. articles to profl. jours. Mem.: Phi Beta Kappa, Alpha Omega Alpha. Office: Ackerman Acad Dermatopathology 145 E32nd St New York NY 10016 Home Phone: 914-478-9329; Office Phone: 212-889-6225. Office Fax: 212-889-8267.

GOTTLIEB, JERROLD HOWARD, advertising executive; b. NYC, Aug. 25, 1946; s. Saul and Sylvia (Siegel) G.; m. June L. Brownstein, June 18, 1978; children: Steven Andrew, Melissa Eve. BA, Mich. State U., 1968; MBA, Am. U., 1969. Sales rep. Gen. Foods Corp., White Plains, NY, 1969-71, sr. product mgr., 1976-78; v.p., account mgr. J. Walter Thompson, NYC, 1971-75, sr. v.p. N.Y. office, account dir., 1980-82, sr. v.p. U.S.A., mng. dir., 1982-84, sr. v.p. U.S.A., worldwide mng. dir., 1984-87, sr. v.p. worldwide, dir. account mgmt., 1987-90; v.p., account mgr. Batten, Barton, Durstein & Osborn, NYC, 1978-80; exec. v.p. Backer Spielvogel Bates Inc., NYC, 1991-92, exec. v.p., mng. dir. office of chmn., 1992-94; pres. Lane Gottlieb Advt., NYC, 1994-96; chmn., CEO McCaffery Gottlieb & Lane LLC, NYC, 1997—. Bd. dirs. Advt. Hall of Fame, N.Y.C., U.J.A. Fedn. N.Y. Founder Washington Saturday Coll., 1969; chmn. Am. U. campus, Washington, 1969; mem. adv. coun. ARC, Washington, 1981-86; vice chmn. mktg. UJA Fedn., N.Y.C., 1987-91, chmn., 1992-96, bd. dirs., 1994-2001. Mem.: Metropolis Club (bd. govs., v.p.). Home: 1095 Park Ave New York NY 10128-1154 Office: McCaffery Gottlieb & Lane 370 Lexington Ave New York NY 10017-6503

GOTTLIEB, JONATHAN W., lawyer; b. Washington, June 24, 1959; s. Julius Judah and Charlotte (Papernick) G.; m. Deborah Jo Levine, June 28, 1987; children: Maya Lane, Seth Joseph. BA with honors, DePaul U., 1982; student, Am. U., 1984-85; JD, N.Y. Law Sch., 1985. Bar: Pa. 1986, D.C. 1989, U.S. Ct. Appeals (D.C. cir.) 1990. Trial atty. Fed. Energy Regulatory Commn., Washington, 1987-88; assoc. Wickwire, Gavin & Gibbs, Washington, 1988-89, Ballard Spahr Andrews & Ingersoll, Washington, 1990-92, Reid & Priest, Washington, 1992-94, ptnr., 1995-98, Thelen Reid & Priest, Washington, 1998-99, Baker & McKenzie, Washington, 1999—. Chmn. legal affairs task force Nat. Hydropower Assn., 1992-95; counsel Mid-Atlantic Ind. Power Producers; gen. counsel Power Markets Devel. Co. (PPL Global), 1995-96; adv. bd. Bradley Energy Internat., 1997—; acting gen. counsel Packard Bell NEC, Inc., 1998. Contbg. editor Project Fin. Monthly; editor Competitive Utility, 1993—. Donor mem. Corning Mus. Glass. Mem. Fed. Energy Bar Assn., Pa. Bar Assn., D.C. Bar Assn., Southeastern Energy Soc. Republican. Avocations: glass collecting, stained glass making, gardening. Home: 9317 W Parkhill Dr Bethesda MD 20814-3966 E-mail: jonathan.w.gottlieb@bakernet.com.

GOTTLIEB, JOURDAN, plastic surgeon; BA, Occidental Coll., LA, 1970, Premed study, 1970—71; MD, Case Western Res. U., Cleve., 1976. Lic. Wash., cert. Am. Bd. Surgery, 1982, Am. Bd. Plastic Surgery, 1987. Surgery resident U. Va., Charlottesville, 1976—78, Northwestern U. Med. Sch., Chgo., 1982—85, plastic surgery resident, 1981—85, assoc. in surgery, 1981—85, U. Wash., 1985—86; chief of plastic surgery VA Med. Ctr., Seattle, 1985—90; pvt. practice Elan Plastic Surgery Ctr., Kirkland, Wash., 1990—2002, Plastic Surgery Seattle, 2002—. Adj. attending Northwest Meml. Hosp., Chgo., 1981—82; attending physician U. Wash. Hosps., Seattle, 1985—90, Children's Hosp. & Med. Ctr., 1985—, Providence Hosp., 1990—, Swedish Hosp., 1990—, Seattle Surgery Ctr., 1993—. Contbr. articles to profl. journals. Named one of Puget Sound's Top Doctors for Women, Seattle Mag. Mem.: AMA, Wash. Soc. Plastic Surgeons, Henry N. Harkins Soc., Am. Burn Assn., Wash. State Med. Soc., King County Med. Soc., Am. Soc. Plastic Surgeons, Am. Coll. Surgeons, Omicron Delta Epsilon, Phi Beta Kappa. Office: Plastic Surgery Seattle Ste 501 1600 E Jefferson St Seattle WA 98122 Office Phone: 206-320-2270.*

GOTTLIEB, JULIUS JUDAH, retired podiatrist; b. Jersey City, May 27, 1919; s. Joseph Uziel and Gussie (Farber) G.; m. Charlotte Papernik, Oct. 18, 1942; children: Sheldon, Cynthia, Lorinda, David, Jonathan. Student, NYU, 1938-39, Ill. Coll. Podiatric Medicine, 1940-42; DPM, Ohio Coll. Podiatric Medicine, 1943. Diplomate Am. Podiatric Med. Specialties Bd. Pvt. practice podiatric medicine, Washington, 1943—92; pres. Chevy Chase Prof. Cons., 1993—96; ret., 1996. Past cons. Army Footwear Clinic. Co-inventor fiberglass foot prosthetics and plastic shoe lasts. Podiatry dir. Greater Washington Hebrew Home for the Aged, 1963; pres. Franklin Knolls Citizens Assn., 1963, Ridgefield Citizens Inc., 1994-96, 97-2003; chmn. com. Nat. Capital Area coun. Boy Scouts Am., 1969-73; pres. Active Retirees of Kehilat Shalom, 1996-98. Recipient Shofar award Boy Scouts Am. Fellow Acad. Ambulatory Foot Surgeons (region 8 sci. chmn. 1987-88); mem. Am. Podiatric Med. Assn. (life), Am. Pub. Health Assn., Am. Podiatric Circulatory Soc., Am. Bd. Foot Surgeons (founding diplomate), D.C. Podiatric Med. Soc. (past pres.), Am. Assn. Foot Specialists (past pres., Foot Specialist of the Yr. 1973), Am. Assn. Individual Investors, Am. Physicians Fellowship Inc. for Medicine in Israel, Columbia Heights Bus. Men's Assn. (past pres., Man of Yr. 1964), Parents Assn. U. Md. (co v.p. parents fund 1980-81, co-recipient Outstanding Svc. Award), B'nai B'rith. Republican. Jewish. Home: 15812 Ancient Oak Dr Darnestown MD 20878-2110

GOTTLIEB, LESTER M., entrepreneur; b. NYC, May 3, 1932; s. Samuel and Eva (Schoenfeld) G.; children: Cynthia, Curtis, Mark, Alyssa, Adine. BA, CCNY, 1954; postgrad., NYU, 1956. With IBM, 1956-69, mgr. bus. planning for systems devel. div., 1967-69; pres. Data Dimensions, Inc., 1969-84, vice chmn., 1984-90; pres. CAMAC Securities, Ltd., Greenwich, Conn., 1981-91, also chmn. bd. dirs., 1991—; pres. CAMAC Equities, Ltd., 1981—. Chmn. bd. dirs. Drain King, LLC, New Rochelle, On Track Fitness, NY, Peekskill, NY; adj. asst. prof. econs. U. Bridgeport; lectr. Assn. Computing Machinery; bd. dirs. Ctr. for Internat. Mgmt. Studies. Nat. Bd. YMCA's, 1972-90, Greater N.Y. YMCA; bd. dirs., treas. City Coll. Fund, 1990, v.p., 1996-99. With AUS, 1954-56. Recipient Leo Klauber award, Mark Asa Abbott award; named Vol. of Yr. Greater N.Y. YMCA, 1994. Mem. Am. Arbitration Assn. (comml. arbitrator 1981—), CCNY Alumni Assn. (bd. dirs. 1983, pres. alumni varsity assn. 1987-88, Alumni Svc. award, Athletic Hall of Fame). Republican. Home: 10 Stewart Pl Apt 7 BE White Plains NY 10603

GOTTLIEB, LYNN, engineer; d. Abram Gottlieb and Ruth Goldwater; m. Kenton Bolte, Dec. 20, 1975 (div. Sept. 15, 1989). BSc, U. Wash., Seattle, 1997; MSc, U. Wash., 2002. Systems analyst Pacific NW Bell (now Qwest), Seattle, 1975—87; info. engring. dir. City of Seattle, 1987—91; project mgr. U. Wash., 1993—97; process improvement specialist The Boeing Co., Seattle, 1997—2002; program mgr. Microsoft, Redmond, Wash., 2002—04; chief engr. Gottlieb and Assoc., Seattle, 2004—06; sr. tech. writer Connx Solutions, Redmond, Wash., 2006—. Instr. Bellevue Cmty. Coll., Wash., 2002—. Vol. KPLU, Tacoma, 1989—, Seattle Tilth, 1999—2006, Aboretum Found., 2007—; bd. dirs. Congregation Beth Shalom, Seattle, 1991—93, gabbai, 1993—, mem., 1991—. Recipient Vol. of Yr., KPLU, 1995. Mem.: Soc. for Tech. Commn. (sr.), Assn. Computer Machinery Spl. Interest Group On Human Computer Interaction, Microsoft Alumni Network, U. Wash. Alumni Assn. (life). Jewish. Avocations: hiking, travel, art, gardening. Home Phone: 206-984-0989; Office Phone: 425-519-6600.

GOTTLIEB, MARISE SUSS, epidemiologist, physician; b. N.Y.C., July 16, 1938; d. Lester J. and Fannie (Freeman) Suss; m. A. Arthur Gottlieb, June 8, 1958 (dec.); children: Mindy Cheryl Davidson, Joanne Meredith. AB, Barnard Coll., 1958; MD, NYU, 1962; MPH, Harvard U., 1966. Intern medicine, Mass. Meml. Hosp., 1962-63; resident preventative medicine dept. epidemiology Harvard U. Sch. Pub. Health, 1965-68, instr. dept. medicine, Harvard Med. Sch., Boston, 1969-70, also fellow, asst. in Medicine Peter Bent Brigham Hosp.; dir. chronic disease control N.J. Dept. Health, Trenton, 1970-75; asst. prof. dept. community medicine Rutgers Med. Sch., Piscataway N.J., 1972-75; assoc. prof. dept. medicine Tulane U. Sch. Medicine, New Orleans, 1975-91; assoc. prof. dept. epidemiology Sch. Pub. Health, 1975-80; chief chronic disease control, La. Dept. Health and Human Resources, New Orleans, 1975-85; dir. clin. and regulatory affairs, v.p. med. affairs Imreg Inc., New Orleans, 1985-98; sec. treas. Pres. Endeavor Corp., 1998—; mem. bd. alumni coun. Harvard U. Sch. Pub. Health, 2005—; mem. epidemiology and disease control study sect. NIH, Bethesda, Md., 1982-85. NIH traineeship, 1965-66, spl research fellow Nat. Inst. Arthritis, Metabolism and Digestive Diseases, 1966-68. Diplomate Am. Bd. Preventive Medicine. Fellow Am. Coll. Preventive Medicine, Am. Coll. Epidemiology; mem. Am. Diabetes Assn., Soc. Epidemiol. Rsch., Am. Fedn. Med. Rsch., Am. Pub. Health Assn. Contbr. articles to profl jours. Home: 215 Chestnut Hill Rd Chestnut Hill MA 02467-1313 Business E-Mail: marsgott@massmed.org.

GOTTLIEB, MICHAEL NORMAN, internist, educator, health facility administrator; b. Bklyn., July 26, 1943; s. Louis and Grace Gottlieb; m. Anne A. Appelman, Dec. 25, 1965; children: Brian, Elizabeth. BA, SUNY, Binghamton, 1964; MD, SUNY, Bklyn., 1968. Diplomate Am. Bd. Internal Medicine. Intern Univ. Hosp. U. Calif., San Diego, 1968-69, resident Univ Hosp., 1969-71, clin. fellow in nephrology, 1971-72, 1971-72; rsch. fellow in medicine Harvard Med. Sch., Boston, 1972-73; spl. fellow Peter Bent Brigham Hosp. NIH, Boston, 1972-73; instr. in medicine Peter Bent Brigham Hosp., Harvard Med. Sch., Boston, 1974-77; asst. clin. prof. medicine Harvard Med. Sch., Boston, 1976—; ptnr. Commonwealth Nephrology Assn., Boston, 1977—; assoc. chair dept. medicine Metrowest Med. Ctr., Framingham, Mass., 1992-95, chief med. officer, 1995—. Assoc. in medicine Peter Bent Brigham Hosp., Boston, 1975—82; med. dir. West Suburban Artificial Kidney Ctr., Framingham, Mass., 1980—, The Kidney Ctr., Boston, 2001—04, MetroWest Artificial Kidney Ctr., Waltham, Mass., 1990—2006, active staff, 1992—; assoc. physician Brigham and Women's Hosp., Boston, 1982—; courtesy staff Norwood (Mass.) Hosp., 1994—; bd. dirs. End Stage Renal Disease Network #1. Contbr. to med. textbooks, numerous articles to profl. jours. Mem. AMA, ACP, Am. Soc. Nephrology, Am. Soc. Artificial Internal Organs, Mass. Med. Soc., Am. Soc. Enteral and Parenteral Nutrition, Am. Coll. Physician Execs., Internat. Soc. Artificial Organs. Avocations: boating, sailing. Office: Metrowest Med Ctr 67 Union St Natick MA 01760-6056 Office Phone: 508-650-7155. E-mail: michael.gottlieb@mwmc.com.

GOTTLIEB, PAUL MITCHEL, corporate financial executive; b. NYC, Mar. 30, 1954; s. Henry Gottlieb and Thelma Ethel (Friedman) Miller; m. Helene Manya Roiter, Apr. 3, 1982; children: Jordan Seth, Zachary Michael. BA, Hobart Coll., 1976; JD, MBA, Washington U., St. Louis, 1980. Bar: Ill. 1980, U.S. Dist. Ct. (no. dist. Ill.) 1980, N.Y. 1988; lic. securities series 7, 9, 10, 24 2002. Assoc. Rudnick & Wolfe, Chgo., 1980-81; ind. trader Chgo. Bd. of Trade, 1981—82; staff atty. Chgo. Merc. Exch., 1983-84, v.p. market regulation, 1984—87; commodity counsel Morgan Stanley and Co. Inc., NYC, 1987-89; spl. counsel commodities, futures and derivative products Skadden, Arps, Slate, Meagher & Flom, NYC, 1989-92; ptnr., chair derivative products practice group Seward & Kissel, NYC, 1992-96; dir., sr. counsel structured products & commodities Union Bank of Switzerland, NYC, 1996-98; sr. v.p., dep. gen. counsel PaineWebber Inc., NYC, 1998—2000; exec. dir. UBS Warburg LLC, NYC, 2000-01; mng. dir., COO RBC Capital Mkts. Corp., NYC, 2001—; sr. v.p. Royal Bank of Can., 2001—. Contbr. chpts. to books, articles to profl. jours. Mem.: Securities Industry Assn. (law and compliance divsn.), Chgo. Bd. Trade, Chgo. Mercantile Exch., N.Y. Stock Exch. Jewish. Avocations: coaching youth hockey and lacrosse, golf, skiing. Home: 11 Highpoint Pl West Windsor NJ 08550-5238 Office: RBC Capital Markets Corp 1 Liberty Plz 165 Broadway New York NY 10006-1404

GOTTLIEB, ROBERT ADAMS, editor, dance critic, writer; b. NYC, Apr. 29, 1931; s. Charles and Martha (Keen) G.; m. Maria Tucci, Apr. 26, 1969; children— Roger, Elizabeth, Nicholas. BA, Columbia U., 1952; postgrad., Cambridge U., Eng., 1952-54. Editor-in-chief, v.p. Simon & Schuster, 1955-68; editor-in-chief Alfred A Knopf, Inc., NYC, 1968-87, exec. v.p., 1968-73, pres., 1973-87; editor New Yorker mag., 1987-92. Author: Reading Jazz, 1996, George Balanchine: The Ballet Maker, 2004; co-author: Reading Lyrics, 2000; dance critic N.Y. Observer. Mem. Phi Beta Kappa.

GOTTLIEB, ROBERT GENE, lawyer; b. Newark, May 13, 1951; BA cum laude, Penn. State U., 1973; JD with honors, George Washington U., 1976. Bar: Va. 1976, DC 1978. Ptnr., real estate & taxation Venable LLP, Washington. Adjunct prof. George Washington U., 1985—95, Georgetown U., 1990—. Mem.: ABA (mem. tax section), Am. Coll. Real Estate Lawyers, Va. Bar Assn., DC Bar Assn. Office: Venable LLP 575 7th St NW Washington DC 20004 Office Phone: 202-344-8526. Office Fax: 202-344-8300. Business E-Mail: rggottlieb@venable.com.

GOTTLIEB, ROBERT W., lawyer; b. NYC, Jan. 28, 1942; BA cum laude, Alfred U., 1963; LLB magna cum laude, Columbia U., 1966. Bar: NY 1967, US Ct. Appeals, 2nd Cir., US Dist. Ct., Ea. and So. Dist. NY, US Supreme Ct. Ptnr. Katten Muchin Zavis Rosenman, NYC. Office: Katten Muchin Zavis Rosenman 575 Madison Ave New York NY 10022 Office Phone: 212-940-7090. Office Fax: 212-935-8405. E-mail: robert.gottlieb@kmzr.com.

GOTTO, ANTONIO MARION, JR., internist, educator; b. Nashville, Tenn., Oct. 10, 1935; s. Antonio M. and Reather (Gray) Gotto; m. Anita Louise Safford, July 21, 1959; children: Jennifer, Gillian, Teresa. BA magna cum laude, Vanderbilt U., 1957, MD, 1965; DPhil, Oxford U., Eng., 1961; LLD (hon.), Abilene Christian U., 1979; MD (hon.), U. Bologna, 1982. Diplomate Am. Bd. Internal Medicine. Intern Mass. Gen. Hosp., Boston, 1965—66, resident, 1966—67; practice medicine specializing in internal medicine, 1967—; head molecular disease br. Nat. Heart and Lung Inst. NIH, Bethesda, Md., 1969—71; dir. and prin. investigator Lipid Rsch. Clinic, Houston, 1971—77; prof. medicine, chief dir., arteriosclerosis and lipoprotein rsch. Baylor Coll. Medicine, Houston, 1971—96; dir., prin. investigator specialized ctr. rsch. in arteriosclerosis Nat. Heart, Lung and Blood Inst., 1971—96, dir., prin. investigator Spl. Ctr. Rsch. Arteriosclerosis, 1971—96; J.S. Abercrombie prof. Baylor Coll. Medicine, 1976—96, Disting. Svc. prof., 1985—96; sci. dir. Meth. Hosp. and Baylor Nat. Rsch. and Demonstration Ctr., 1974—83, 1987—90; Bob and Vivian Smith prof. and chmn. dept. medicine Baylor Coll. Medicine, 1977—96; chief internal medicine svcs. The Meth. Hosp., 1977—96; dean Weill Med. Coll., Cornell U., 1997—; provost med. affairs Cornell U., 1997—. Hon. guest lectr. various med. socs., schs. and hosps., 1972—; mem. nat. diabetes adv. bd. HEW (now HHS), 1977—84; mem. steering com. Italian-Am. com. on cardiovascular disease NIH, 1978—; mem. adv. coun. Nat. Heart, Lung and Blood Inst., 1987—91; hon. prof. U. Buenos Aires, 1985. Author (with Michael E. DeBakey): The Living Heart, 1977; author: The Living Heart Diet, 1984, The New Living Heart Diet, 1996, The New Living Heart, 1997; editor: Current Atherosclerosis Reports, 1998—, Current Practice of Medicine, 1999—; co-editor: Atherosclerosis Rev. Series, 1976—92, Jour. Cardiovasc. Risk, 1994—; mem. editl. bd.: Jour. Biol. Chemistry, 1976—81, Advanced in Lipid Rsch., 1973—78, Am. Heart Jour., 1981—, Arteriosclerosis, 1981—89, Circulation Rsch., 1974—79, Cardiovascular Rsch. Ctr. Bull., 1972—; contbr. articles on biochem. and cardiovascular rsch. to profl. publs. Mem. sci. adv. bd. Fondation Cardiologique Princesse Liliane, Brussels, 1976—, Lorenzini Found., Milan, Fritz Thyssen Found., Cologne, Germany; mem. Mission of Houston Econ. Devel. Coun., 1985; walkathon chmn. Juvenile Diabetes Found., 1986. With USPHS, 1967—69. Decorated knight Order of Merit, Italy, Order of the Lion Finland; named hon. cons., Adm. Bristol Hosp., Istanbul, Turkey, Houston Internat. Exec. Yr., 1987; named one of New York's Influentials, New York Mag., 2006; recipient Albert Weinstein award, 1965, Laurea ad Honorem, U. Bologna, Seale Harris award, So. Med. Assn., 1995; grantee, John A. Hartford Found., 1971—75. Fellow: Am. Coll. Cardiology; mem.: Am. Longevity Assn., Am. Assn. Rhodes Scholars, Am. Bd. Internal Medicine, Am. Heart Assn. (pres. 1983—84, past pres. 1984—86, Paul Ledbetter award for disting. svc., Paul Dudley White award for outstanding contbns., Gold Heart award 1989), Am. Diabetes Assn., Am. Soc. Biol. Chemists, Am. Assn. Physicians, Internat. Soc. Atherosclerosis (pres. 1985—, Achievement award 1982), So. Soc. Clin. Investigation, Am. Soc. Clin. Investigation (v.p. 1980—81), Inst. Medicine of NAS, River Oaks Country Club, Alpha Omega Alpha. Presbyterian. Office: Weill Med Cornell U 1300 York Ave Rm F 105 New York NY 10021-4805 Office Phone: 212-746-6005. Business E-Mail: dean@med.cornell.edu.

GOTTS, EDWARD EARL, psychologist, researcher; s. Earl and Norma Noma Gotts; m. Shirley Jean Lund, Sept. 10, 1955; children: Gregory, Gary, Kimberly. BA, Whitworth Coll., Spokane, 1960, MA, 1962; PhD, U. Tex., Austin, 1966. Lic. psychologist Ind., diplomate Am. Bd. Assessment Psychology, Am. Bd. Profl. Psychology. Asst. prof. edn. psychology U. Tex., Austin, 1966—67; rsch. coord., asst. prof. Inst. CLU for the Study Ind. U., Bloomington, 1967—69, prof., psychol. dir. Devel. Tng. Ctr., 1972—74; dir. divsn. childhood & parenting Appalachian Edn. Lab., Charleston, W.Va., 1974—83; chief psychology, clin. prof. Marshall Med. Sch., Huntington, W.Va., 1983—86; chief psychologist, internship dir. Madison State Hosp., Ind., 1986—2003; adj. faculty Mass. Sch. Profl. Psychology, Boston, 2004—. Mem. Child Mental Health Adv. Bd., Indpls., 1968—76, chair, 1973—74; mem. Gov.'s Mental Health Adv. Bd., Indpls., 1974—76, Mental Health & MR Planning Commn., Indpls., 1974—76. Author: The Clinical Application of MMPI Special Scales, 1995, The Clinical Interpretation of the MMPI-2, 2005; gen. editor: The Home Visitor's Kit, 1977. Bd. dirs. First Steps Program, Madison, 1994—97; lay leader, lay spkr. N. United Meth. Ch., Madison, 1999—. Capt. USAF, 1953—57. Fellow, U. Colo. Med. Ctr., 1971—72; USPHS fellow, U. Tex., 1965—67. Fellow: APA; mem.: Soc. Personality Assessment, Ind. Psychol. Assn. (editor 1996—97), Rotary (bd. dirs. Madison chpt. 1989—90). Avocations: travel, gardening, hiking. Office: PO Box 856 Madison IN 47250

GOTTS, ILENE KNABLE, lawyer; b. Phila., Nov. 25, 1959; d. Harry Lee and Ethel Beatrice (Teitelman) Knable; m. Michael D. Gotts, May 25, 1986; children: Isaac, Samuel. BA magna cum laude with hon., U. Md., 1980; JD cum laude, Georgetown U., 1984. Bar: D.C. 1984, N.Y., 1997, U.S. Dist. Ct. D.C. 1986, U.S. Ct. Appeals (D.C. cir.) 1985, U.S. Dist. Ct. Md. 1987, U.S. Ct. Appeals (fed. cir.) 1989, U.S. Supreme Ct. 1988. Staff atty. FTC, 1984-86; assoc. Foley & Lardner, Washington, 1986-92, ptnr., head legis./adminstrv. group, antitrust practice group, 1992-96; ptnr. Wachtell, Lipton, Rosen & Katz, NYC, 1996—. Adj. prof. George Washington U. Law Ctr., 1995-96; trustee U. Md. Found., 2003—06, Nat. Law Alumni Bd., Georgetown U. Law Ctr, 2002-. Mem. editl. bd. Practical Lawyer, 1994-2004, Antitrust Counselor, 1995—; mem. adv. bd. Antitrust Trade and Regulatory Report, 2003-; contbr. articles to profl. jours. Mem. legal adv. bd. Momentum, 2001—. Recipient Sklar award U. Md., 1980; Mary Elizabeth Robey scholar. Mem.: NOW (legal momentum adv. bd. 2001—), FBA (chair health care com. of antitrust sect. 1991—95, chair antitrust and trade regulation sec. 1995—97), ABA (antitrust sect. 1988—, consumer protection com. 1994—96, vice chair intellectual property com. 1994—97, vice chair Clayton Act com. 1997—98, chair 1998—2001, chair merger rev. task force 1998—2003, coun. 2001—04, program officer 2004—05, internat. officer 2005—, editor The Merger Rev. Process, 2d and 3d edits.), Internat. Bar Assn., N.Y. Women's Bar Assn., N.Y. State Bar Assn. (exec. com. antitrust law sect. 2000—, sec. 2003—04, vice-chair 2004—05, chair 2005), Washington Coun. Lawyers (exec. com. and bd. dirs. 1988—97, pres. 1994—95), Am. Law Inst., D.C. Bar (steering com., antitrust and trade regulation com. 1994—95), Phi Beta Kappa, Mortar Board, Phi Alpha Theta, Pi Sigma Alpha, Phi Kappa Phi. Democrat. Jewish. Office: Wachtell Lipton Rosen & Katz 51 W 52d St New York NY 10019 Home Phone: 212-724-1015; Office Phone: 212-403-1000. Business E-Mail: ikgotts@wlrk.com.

GOTTS, LAWRENCE J., lawyer; b. Washington, Apr. 18, 1958; BS summa cum laude, Univ. Md., 1980; JD with high honors, George Washington Univ., 1985. Bar: Va. 1985, DC 1989, US Patent & Trademark Office, US Ct. Appeals (Fed. cir.). Patent examiner US Patent & Trademark Office, 1981—83; ptnr., chmn. Litigation group Pillsbury Winthrop Shaw Pittman, McLean, Va. Mem.: Am. Intellectual Property Law Assn., Am. Soc. Mech. Engineers, Order of the Coif. Office: Pillsbury Winthrop Shaw Pittman 1650 Tysons Blvd Mc Lean VA 22102-4859 Office Phone: 703-770-7604. Office Fax: 703-770-7901. Business E-Mail: larry.gotts@pillsburylaw.com.

GOTTSCHALK, ALEXANDER, radiologist, educator; b. Chgo., Mar. 23, 1932; s. Louis R. and Fruma (Kasden) G.; m. Jane Rosenbloom, Aug. 13, 1960; children: Rand, Karen, Amy. BA magna cum laude, Harvard U., 1954; MD, Washington U., St. Louis, 1958. Diplomate: Am. Bd. Radiology, Am. Bd. Nuclear Medicine. Intern U. Ill. Research and Edn. Hosps., Chgo., 1958-59; resident U. Chgo., 1959-62, asst. prof., 1964-66, assoc. prof., 1966-68, prof. radiology, 1968-74, chmn. dept. radiology, 1971-72; research assoc. Donner Lab., Lawrence Radiol. Lab., Calif., 1962-64; dir. Franklin McLean Meml. Research Hosp., 1967-74; prof. and dir. nuclear medicine Sch. Medicine Yale U., New Haven, 1974-77, acting chmn. radiology, 1980-81, vice-chmn. radiology, 1977-89; prof. radiology Mich. State U., East Lansing, 1990—. Contbr. chpts. to books, articles to publs. in field. Fleischner lectr., 1983 Fellow Am. Coll. Radiology, Am. Coll. Chest Physicians; mem. Radiol. Soc. N.Am. (2d v.p. 1977, Gold medal 2004), Assn. Univ. Radiologists (pres. 1971, Gold medal 1987), Soc. Nuclear Medicine (pres. 1974-75, Cassen prize 2006, Cassen lectr. 2006), Am. Roentgen Ray Soc., Fleischner Soc. (treas. 1978-83, pres. 1989-90), Phi Beta Kappa, Alpha Omega Alpha. Home: 4246 Van Atta Rd Okemos MI 48864-3137 Office: Radiology Bldg Rm 120 Mich State U East Lansing MI 48824-1303 Business E-Mail: alg@rad.msu.edu.

GOTTSCHALK, ALFRED, retired academic and museum administrator; b. Oberwesel, Germany, Mar. 7, 1930; came to U.S., 1939, naturalized, 1945; s. Max and Erna (Trum-Gerson) G.; m. Deanna Zeff, 1977; children by previous marriage: Marc Hillel, Rachel Lisa. AB, Bklyn. Coll., 1952; MA with honors, Hebrew Union Coll.-Jewish Inst. Religion, 1957; PhD, U. So. Calif., 1965, STD (hon.), 1968, LLD (hon.), 1976, U. Cin., 1976, Xavier U., 1981, Mt. St. Joseph Coll., 1995, No. Ky. U., 1996; DHL (hon.), U. Judaism, 1971, Jewish Theol. Sem., 1986, Bklyn. Coll., 1991, Trinity Coll., 1996; LittD (hon.), Dropsie U., 1974, St. Thomas Inst., 1982; D Religious Edn. (hon.), Loyola-Marymount U., 1977; DD (hon.), NYU, 1985. Ordained rabbi, 1957. Dir. Hebrew Union Coll., Jewish Inst. Religion, LA, 1957-59, dean, 1959-71, prof. Bible and Jewish intellectual history, 1965—, pres., 1971-95, chancellor, 1996—2000, chancellor emeritus, disting. prof. emeritus of Jewish Intellectual History, 1995—; pres. Mus. of Jewish Heritage, NYC, 1999—2001; sr. fellow Mus. Jewish Heritage, 2001—. Hon. fellow Hebrew U., Jerusalem, 1972, Oxford Ctr. for Hebrew and Jewish Studies, 1994. Author: Your Future as a Rabbi-A Calling that Counts, 1967, (translator) Hesed in the Bible, 1967, The Man Must be the Message, 1968, Jewish Ecumenism and Jewish Survival, 1968, Ahad Ha-Am, Maimonides and Spinoza, 1969, Ahad Ha-Am as Bible Critic, 1971, A Jubilee of the Spirit, 1972, Israel and the Diaspora: A New Look, 1974, Limits of Ecumenicity, 1979, Israel and Reform Judaism: A Zionist Perspective, 1979, Ahad Ha-Am and Leopold Zunz: Two Perspectives on the Wissenschaft Des Judentums, 1980, Hebrew Union College and Its Impact on World Progressive Judaism, 1980, Diaspora Zionism: Achievements and Problems, 1980, What Ecumenism Means to a Jew, 1981, Introduction: Religion in a Post-Holocaust World, 1982, Problematics in the Future of American Jewish Community, 1982, Introduction to the American Synagogue in the Nineteenth Century, 1982, A Strategy for Non-Orthodox Judaism in Israel, 1982, (in Chinese) Ahad Ha-Am and the Jewish National Spirit, 1982, Our problems and Our Future: Jews and America, 1983, From the Kingdom of Night to the Kingdom of God: Jewish Christian Relations and the Search for Religious Authenticity after the Holocaust, 1983, The Making of a Contemporary Reform Rabbi, 1984, Is Yom Kippur Obsolete?, 1985, Ahad Ha-am: Confronting the Plight of Judaism, 1987, To Learn and To Teach, Your Future as a Rabbi, 1988, Preface to Gezer V: The Field I Caves, 1988, The American Reform Rabbinate Retrospect and Prospect, A Personal View, 1988, The German Pogrom of November 1938 and the Reaction of American Jewry, 1988, Building Unity in Diversity 1989, Ahad Ha'am and the Jewish National Spirit (Hebrew), 1992; contbr. to Studies in Jewish Bibliography, History, and Literature, 1971, The Yom Kippur War: Israel and the Jewish People, 1974, The Image of Man in Genesis and the Ancient Near East, 1976, The Public Function of the Jewish Scholar, 1978, The Reform Movement and Israel: A New Perspective, 1978, The Use of Reason in Maimonides--An Evaluation by Ahad Ha-Am, 1993, Reform Judaism of the New Millenium: A Challenge, 2001, Israel and America: Beyond Survival and Philanthropy, 2000, Life of Reason, Ahad Ha-Am and His Work, 2003; also numerous articles to profl. jours. Mem. Pres. Johnson's Com. on EEO, 1964-66, Gov.'s Poverty Support Corps Program, 1964-66, Pres.'s Commn. on Holocaust, 1979, U.S. Holocaust Meml. Coun., 1980-92, 96-01 (exec. com., 1980-87, 96—, chmn. edn. com., 1986-88, chmn. acad. com., 1988-96, com. on conscience, 1996—); chmn. N.Am. Assoc. Internat. Ctr. Univ. Teaching of Jewish Civilization, 1982-93; bd. trustees Am. Sch. Oriental Rsch., Albright Inst. Archaeol. Rsch., 1972-95; sr. fellow Mus. of Jewish Heritage, N.Y.C., 2001—; bd. govs. Oxford Ctr. for Hebrew and Jewish Studies, 1995—; bd. trustees Mus. Jewish Heritage, N.Y.C., 2001-; exec. com. Nat. Underground Railroad Freedom Ctr., 1997-2000, Nat. Adv. Bd., Nat. Underground Freedom Ctr., 1996—; mem. coun. World Union Jewish Studies, 1997. Recipient award for contbns. to edn. L.A. City Coun., 1971, Human Relations award Am. Jewish Com., 1971, Tower of David award for cultural contbn. to Israel and Am., 1972, Gold medallion Jewish Nat. Fund, 1972, Alumnus of Yr. award Bklyn. Coll., 1972, Myrtle Wreath award Hadassah, 1977, Brandeis award Z.O.A., 1977, Nat. Brotherhood award NCCJ, 1979, Alfred Gottschalk Chair in Communal Svc. HUC, 1979, Jerusalem City of Peace award 1988, Defender of Jerusalem award honoree, 1990, Isaac M. Wise award, 1991, Heritage award Jewish Club of 1933, 1991, Nat. award NCCJ, 1994, Shanghai Acad. Social Scis. award, 1994, others, Xavier Medallion, Xavier U., 1996, Elie Wiesel Holocaust Rememerance award, State of Israel bonds, 2001; grantee State Dept./Smithsonian Instn., 1963, 67.; honoree Assn. Hebrew Union Coll., 1996; recipient Award Svc. to City, Cin. City Council, 2001. Mem. AAUP, NEA, Union Am. Hebrew Congregations and Ctrl. Conf. Am. Rabbis (exec. com., bd. govs. Hebrew Union Coll.), Soc. Study Religion, Am. Acad. Religion, Soc. Bibl. Lit. and Exegesis, Internat. Conf. Jewish Communal Svc., Israel Exploration Soc., So. Calif. Assn. Liberal Rabbis (past pres.), So. Calif. Jewish Hist. Soc. (hon. pres.), World Union Jewish Studies (internat. coun.), World Union Progressive Judaism (hon. life, gov. bd.), Coun. for Initiatives in Jewish Edn. (bd. dirs.), Phi Beta Kappa. Office: Hebrew Union Coll Jewish Inst of Religion One W 4th St New York NY 10012-1186 Office Phone: 212-674-5300. E-mail: agottschalk@huc.edu. *I value the need for the individual to feel unique and for the collective to remain hospitable to diversity. I believe in unity without uniformity and in humanity's capacity to redeem himself.*

GOTTSCHALK, CHARLES M., international energy consultant; b. Bochum, Germany, Feb. 2, 1928; emigrated to US, 1941, naturalized, 1949; s. Josef and Elsbeth Gottschalk; m. Marianne Ida Besser, Dec. 24, 1948; children: Diane Linda, Leslie Anne. B Engring. Scis., Cleve. State U., 1950; MA, Pa. State U., State College, 1951; MLS, Cath. U., Washington, DC, 1966. Research analyst Library of Congress, 1951-54, phys. sci. adminstr., head reference sect., sci. and tech. div., 1956-62, chief stack and reader div., 1962, head systems identification and analysis sect., 1962-63; instrumentation physicist Nat. Bur. Standards, 1954-56; information systems specialist Atomic Energy Comm., 1963-66, dir. libraries, 1966-69; sr. officer Internat. Atomic Energy Agy., Vienna, Austria, 1969-74, Energy Research and Devel. Adminstrn., Washington, 1974-77, Dept. Energy, 1977-79; sr. ofcl. UNESCO, Paris, 1979-88, cons., expert, 1988-94, CMG Internat. Energy Consultancy, Paris and Washington, 1994—. Liaison officer/registrar Internat. Tech. U., London and Paris, 1989-93; liaison officer World Fedn. Engring. Orgns., London and Paris, 1995-96; lectr. Dept. Agr. Grad. Sch., 1964-66; cons. Arctic Inst. N.Am., 1954-59; rsch. asst. Ohio State U., 1958-59; exec. sec. oper. com. Fed. Coun. Sci. and Tech. Com. on Sci. and Tech. Info., 1965, exec. sec. panel edn. and tng., 1965-66, mem. panel info. scis. and tech., 1966-68, mem. nuclear cross sect. adv. group, 1965-69; mem. com. on terminology World Energy Conf., 1980-96. Author articles, monographs. Served with AUS, 1946-47; Served with USMCR, 1947-51. NSF grantee, 1961-62. Mem. World Energy Coun., Assn. Energy Engrs., Diplomatic and Consular Officers Ret., Mensa, Beta Phi Mu. Home Phone: 301-942-3030. E-mail: cmgm@usa.net.

GOTTSCHALK, FRANK KLAUS, real estate company executive; b. Berlin, Jan. 25, 1932; came to U.S. 1947, naturalized 1953; s. Richard and Grete Johanna (Singer) G.; m. Ellen Ruth Meinhardt, June 16, 1957. Student N.Y. Inst. Banking & Fin., N.Y.C., 1952-53, NYU, 1955-56. Lic. comml. real estate broker. Trainee, investment securities Newborg & Co. mem. N.Y. Stock Exchange, N.Y.C., 1951-52; fin. analyst Bendix Luitweiler & Co. Investment Bankers, N.Y.C., 1952-53; assoc. broker, v.p., dir. Peter F. Pasbjerg & Co., Inc., Mortgage Bankers, Newark, N.J., 1955-62; v.p., dir. Baldwin Bros., Inc. Real Estate Investors, Erie, Pa., 1962—; pres., treas., dir. The Baldwin-Gottschalk Group, Investment Real Estate, asset. mgmt. cons., Erie, Pa., Charleston, W.Va., 1994—; pres. Baldwin-Gottschalk, Inc. Real Estate and Mortgage Financing, N.Y.C., Erie, Charleston, 1962—; pres., treas., dir. Baldwin Gottschalk Properties, Erie, 1967—, Balgot Realty Corp., Erie, 1963—, Balgot Bldg. Corp., Erie, 1967—; pres. The Kanawha Realty Investment Group, Investment Real Estate, Charleston, Erie, 1990—; pres., treas., dir. Kanawha Realty & Devel. Corp., Charleston, 1959—, Associated Properties Holdings, Inc., Charleston, 1962—; pres. Assoc. Properties Holdings Pension Trust, Charleston, W. Va., 1982—; pres., dir. APH Securities, Charleston, W. Va., 1990—; trustee Assoc. Properties Holding Retirement Trust, Charleston, 1982—; mng. ptnr. Kanawha-Monarch Holdings, Erie, 1980—, Balgot-Kanawha Holdings, Erie, Pa., 1994—. Trustee, Erie Philharm., 1971-90; corporator Gannon U., 1980—. Served with U.S. Army, 1953-55, ETO. Mem. Internat. Real Estate Inst., Erie Club, Aviation Country Club Erie, Mizner Country Club, Delray Beach, Fla. Office: Baldwin Gottschalk Inc 5 W 10th St Erie PA 16501-1492

GOTTSCHALK, SISTER MARY THERESE, nun, hospital administrator; b. Doellwang, Germany, June 21, 1931; arrived in U.S., 1953, naturalized, 1959; d. John and Sabina (Dietz) G. BS in Pharmacy, Creighton U., 1960; M.H.A., St. Louis U., 1970; DHL (hon.), U. Okla., 2001. Joined Sisters of the Sorrowful Mother, Roman Cath. Religious Order, 1952. Dir. pharmacy St. Mary's Hosp., Roswell, N.Mex., 1960-68, CEO, 1972-74; asst. adminstr. St. John Med. Ctr., Tulsa, 1970-72, pres., CEO, 1974-99, St. John Health Sys., Tulsa, 1982—; pres. Marian Health Sys., Tulsa, 1980—. Recipient Alumni Merit award, Creighton U., 2003. Fellow: Am. Coll. Healthcare Exec.; mem.: Cath. Health Assn. (bd. dirs. 1995—2001), Tulsa C. of C., Okla. Cath. Health Conf. (past pres.), Tulsa Hosp. Coun. (past pres.), Okla. Hosp. Assn. (pres. 1984, Disting. Svc. award 1999), Am. Hosp. Assn. (ho. of dels., regional policy bd., governing coun.). Office: St John Health System 1923 S Utica Ave Tulsa OK 74104-6502

GOTTSCHALK, STEPHEN ELMER, retired lawyer; b. Rochester, Minn., Oct. 9, 1947; s. Elmer H. and Ruth F. (Thurley) G.; m. Lorilyn J. Dopp, Feb. 14, 1970; children: Andrew Stephen, Stephanie Beth, Lorissa Christine, Michael Donald. BS, Valparaiso U., 1969, JD, 1972. Bar: Minn. 1972, U.S. Dist. Ct. (Minn.) 1972. Jud. clk. Minn. Supreme Ct., St. Paul, 1972—73; assoc. Dorsey & Whitney, Minn., 1973—78, ptnr., 1979—2006, co-chmn., employee benefits dept., 1986—91, 1998—2006. Adj. prof. employee benefits Sch. Law U. Minn., 1998—. Bd. dirs. Habitat for Humanity of Minn. Recipient Svc. award Valparaiso Alumni Assn., 1986. Office: Dorsey & Whitney 50 S 6th St Ste 1500 Minneapolis MN 55402-1498 Office Fax: 612-340-2777. E-mail: gottschalk.steve@dorsey.com.

GOTTSCHALK, THOMAS A., automotive executive, lawyer; b. Decatur, Ind., July 5, 1942; s. John Simson and Edith (Liechty) G.; m. Barbara J. Risen, Aug. 28, 1965; children: Deborah, Diane. AB, Earlham Coll., 1964; JD, U. Chgo., 1967. Bar: Ill. 1967, D.C. 1986, U.S. Supreme Ct. Assoc. Kirkland & Ellis LLP, Chgo., 1967-73, ptnr., 1973-94, of counsel Washington, 2007—; sr. v.p., gen. counsel Gen. Motors Corp., Detroit, 1994—2001, exec. v.p., law & public policy, gen. counsel, 2001—06, exec. v.p., law & public policy, 2006—07. Trustee Earlham Coll., Richmond, Ind., 1972—, chmn., 1985-91. Mem. ABA (mem. litigation, antitrust and criminal law sects.), D.C. Bar Assn., Chgo. Coun. of Lawyers, Conf. Bd. Coun. of Chief Legal Officers; mem. bd. of trustees, Am. Univ., Wash., D.C. Office: Kirkland & Ellis 655 Fifteenth St NW Washington DC 20005-5793 Office Phone: 202-879-5000. Office Fax: 202-879-5200.*

GOTTSCHALL, EDWARD MAURICE, editor, writer; b. NYC, Dec. 28, 1915; s. Myer and Stephanie (Kraus) G.; m. Lee Beatrice Natale, Feb. 6, 1943 (dec. 1984); 1 child, Robert J.; m. Alice J. Wise, Jan. 20, 1985. BS, CCNY, 1937; MS, Columbia U. Sch. of Journalism, 1938. Mng. editor Graphic Arts Prodn. Yearbook, Colton Press, 1937-51; editor Art Direction, 1952-69; sr. editor Popular Merchandising Co., Passaic, N.J., 1964-67; co-pub., editorial dir. Advt. Trade Publs., Inc., 1967-69; exec. dir. Am. Inst. Graphic Arts, NYC, 1969-75; exec. v.p. Internat. Typeface Corp., NYC, 1975-86, vice chmn., 1986-90; editor U & lc, 1981-89, cons. editor, 1990—. V.p. Design Processing Internat., Inc., 1977-85; U.S. rep. Assn. Typographique Internat., 1978-89, chmn. world conf. on typographic communication, 1988; lectr. Pratt Inst. Evening Art Sch., 1947-64, N.Y. U., 1955-64 Author: (with F.C. Rodewald) Commercial Art as a Business, 3d edit., 1972; Author: Vision '80s, 1980, Graphic Communication '80s, 1981, Typographic Communications Today, 1988, reprinted 1992; co-editor: Advertising Directions, vols. 1-4, 1960-64, Editor Typographic i, 1969-79; cons. editor: Graphic Arts Manual, 1973-80; contbr. essay to Contemporary Masterworks, 1992. Served with Signal Corps. U.S. Army, 1943-44, USAAF, 1944-45, ETO. Mem. Type Dirs. Club (past pres., Spl. award 1963), N.Y. Club of Printing House Craftsmen (Fellowship award 1993), Masons, Wednesday Sr. Men's Club of Jewish Cmty. Ctr. of Mid-Westchester (pres. 1999, 2000, 04-05), Phi Delta Pi. Home: 63 Highland Ave Eastchester NY 10709-3627 *Knowledge is never enough. One must be able to evaluate, to judge, to have taste, and to make decisions.*

GOTTSCHALL, JOAN B., judge; b. Oak Ridge, Tenn., Apr. 23, 1947; d. Herbert A. and Elaine (Reichbaum) G. BA cum laude, Smith Coll., Mass., 1969; JD, Stanford Univ., Calif., 1973. Bar: Ill. 1973. Assoc. Jenner & Block, 1973-76, 78-81, ptnr., 1981-82; staff atty. Fed. Defender Program, 1976-78, Univ. of Chgo., Office of Legal Counsel, 1983-84; magistrate judge U.S. Dist. Ct. (no. dist.) Ill., Chgo., 1984—96, judge, 1996—. Mem. vis. com., past chair Divinity Sch., U. Chgo., 1984—97. Bd. dirs. Martin Marty Ctr., U. Chgo. Div. Sch., Ill. Humanities Coun. Mem.: ABA, Divinity Sch. (vis. com.), Chgo. Bar Assn. Office: US Dist Ct no dist Ill Everett McKinley Dirksen Bldg 219 S Dearborn St Ste 2356 Chicago IL 60604-1877

GOTTUNG, LIZANNE C., health products executive; m. Mark Gottung; 3 children. Employee rels. counselor Kimberly-Clark Corp., 1981, various positions in labor rels., recruiting, tng. and safety, team leader tissue mfg. Lakeview mill Neenah, Wis., ops. mgr. Badger-Globe facility, feminine care plant mgr. New Milford, Conn., 1993, infant care plant mgr., mgr. Nonwovens mill Corinth, Miss., 1997, v.p. human resources Roswell, Ga., 2001—02, sr. v.p. human resources, 2002—. Office: Kimberly Clark 1400 Holcomb Bridge Rd Roswell GA 30076*

GOTTWALD, FLOYD DEWEY, JR., chemicals executive, director; b. Richmond, Va., July 29, 1922; s. Floyd Dewey and Anne (Cobb) G.; m. Elisabeth Morris Shelton, Mar. 22, 1947 (dec. Dec. 2003); children: William M., James T., John D.; m. Helga Koch Andrews, July 29, 2005. BS, Va. Mil. Inst., 1943; MS, U. Richmond, 1951. With Albemarle Paper Co., Richmond, 1943-62, sec., 1956-57, v.p., sec., 1957-62, pres., 1962; exec. v.p. Ethyl Corp., Richmond, 1962-64, vice chmn., 1964-68, chmn., 1968-94, CEO, 1970-92, chmn. exec. com., 1970-94, vice chmn., 1994-96. Vice-chmn. Albemarle Corp. Past bd. dirs. Nat. Petroleum Coun.; trustee U. Richmond; mem. River Rd. Bapt. Ch.; past trustee V.M.I. Found., Inc.; mem. bd. visitors Coll. William and Mary, 1993-97; pres. bd. trustees Va. Mus. Fine Arts, 1994-96. Decorated Bronze Star, Purple Heart. Mem. NAM (former bd. dirs.), Am. Petroleum Inst. (bd. dirs.), Am. Chem. Coun. (bd. dirs.), Internat. Game Fish Assn. (trustee 1992—), Alfalfa Club, Country Club Va., Commonwealth Club. Office: Albemarle Corp PO Box 1335 Richmond VA 23218-1335

GOTTWALD, WILLIAM M., chemicals executive; Pres. Whitby, Inc. subs., corp. sr. v.p. Ethyl Corp.; v.p. corp. strategy Albemarle Corp., 1996—2001, bd. dirs., 1999—, chmn. bd., 2001—. Bd. dirs. Tredegar Corp., Richmond, Va., 1997—. Office: Albemarle Corp 330 S Fourth St Richmond VA 23219 Office Phone: 843-769-2010, 804-788-6000. Office Fax: 804-788-5688.*

GOUGAR, HANS DAVID, nuclear engineer, director; b. Joliet, Ill., Oct. 12, 1962; s. Harry William and Janet Mae Gougar; m. Mary Lou Dunzik, Oct. 17, 1992; children: Charles Dunzik, Elizabeth Dunzik. BS in Edn., U. Wis., 1985; MS in Nuc. Engring., Pa. State U., 1997, PhD in Nuc. Engring., 2004. Cert. secondary sci. edn. 1985. Engr. Idaho Nat. Lab., Idaho Falls, 1998—2003, mgr. fission and fusion sys. dept., 2003—. Sci. tchr. Parker H.S., Janesville, Wis., 1985—88, Am. Sch. in Switzerland, Eng. Am. Sch., Thorpe, Surrey, 1989—92, Upper Darby H.S., Pa., 1992—94; pres. Snake River Montessori Schs., Idaho Falls, 2001—04. Treas. cmty. theater Stage One, Inc., Janesville, Wis., 1985—88. Scholar, Pitts. sect. Am. Nuc. Soc., 1996. Mem.: Am. Nuc. Soc. (com. chair bylaws and rules, student sects. 1998—2003, chair Idaho chpt. 2006—). Achievements include development of the first modern design technique for pebble-bed nuclear reactors. Home Phone: 208-524-6413; Office Phone: 208-526-2760.

GOUGH, CLARENCE RAY, retired designer, educator; b. Denton County, Tex, Dec. 7, 1919; s. Herman Lang and Gertrude (Page) G.; m. Georgia Belle Leach, Feb. 7, 1975. BS in Art, U. North Tex., Denton, 1940, MS in Art, 1941; BArch, Ill. Inst. Tech., 1950. Art tchr. Edinburg Ind. Sch. Dist., Tex., 1941; interior designer Contemporary House, Dallas, 1950; environ. designer Gough Assoc., Denton, 1951-90; prof. U. North Tex., Denton, 1951-88. Juror Nat. Coun. Interior Design Qualifications, 1983-88; chmn. accreditation com. Found. Interior Design Rsch., 1985-90. Illustrator Modern Dance for the Youth of Am., 1944, photographer (exhibitions) Visual Arts Ctr., Denton, 2001; exhibitions include photography No. Tex. area Art League Exhbn., 2003. Exhbn. chmn. U. North. Tex., Denton, 1950-63; curator exhbns. Greater Denton Arts Coun., 1997-98. Lt. USNR, 1942-46, PTO. Recipient Career Educator award Am. Soc. Interior Designers, 1993, Dallas, Svc. award Gov. Conf. on the Arts, Denton, 1990; Internat. Artist award, North Tex. Area Art League, 2003, Green Glory award, U. North Tex., 2004. Avocations: photography, collecting art. Home: 1813 Willowwood St Denton TX 76205-6992

GOUGH, DENIS IAN, geophysics educator; b. Port Elizabeth, Cape, South Africa, June 20, 1922; came to Can., 1966; s. Frederick William and Ivy Catherine (Hingle) G.; m. Winifred Irving Nelson, June 2, 1945; children— Catherine Veronica, Stephen William Cyprian B.Sc., Rhodes U., Grahamstown, Republic of South Africa, 1943, M.Sc., 1947, D.Sc. (hon.), 1990; PhD, U. Witwatersrand, Johannesburg, Republic of South Africa, 1953. Research officer Nat. Phys. Lab., Johannesburg, S. Africa, 1947, sr. research officer; lectr. Univ. Coll. Rhodesia, Salisbury, 1958, sr. lectr.; assoc. prof. geophysics Southwest Ctr. for Advanced Studies, Dallas, 1964-66; prof. geophysics U. Alta., Edmonton, Can., 1966-87, prof. emeritus, 1987—, dir. Inst. Earth and Planetary Physics, 1975-80. Contbr. numerous articles to profl. jours. Royal Soc. Can. fellow, 1972 Fellow Royal Astron. Soc. (Chapman medal 1988), Am. Geophys. Union; Geol. Assn. Can.; mem. Can. Geophys. Union (past pres., J. Tuzo Wilson medal 1983), Internat. Assn. Geomagnetism and Aeronomy (pres. 1983-87), S. African Geophys. Assn. (Rudolf Krahmann medal 1989). Avocations: reading, music, poetry. Office: Univ Alta Dept Physics Edmonton AB Canada T6G 2J1 E-mail: iangough@incentre.net.

GOUGH, HERBERT FREDERICK, JR., minister; b. Knoxville, Tenn., May 3, 1941; s. Herbert Frederick and Jessie Post Gough; m. Catherine Mauldin Hill, Aug. 6, 1986. Cert., US Army War Coll., Carlisle, Pa., 1990, St. George's Coll., Jerusalem, 1980; BA, U. Chattanooga, 1967; MDiv, Va. Theol. Sem., Alexandria, 1972. Curate Holy Trinity Episcopal Ch., Memphis, 1972—73; vicar St. Mark's Episcopal Ch., Copperhill, Tenn., 1973—76; rector St. Paul's Episcopal Ch., Clinton, NC, 1976—80; asst. rector Emmanuel Episcopal Ch., Athens, Ga., 1980—82; rector St. Barnabas Episcopal Ch., Dillon, SC, 1982—96, St. Matthew's Episcopal Ch., Darlington, SC, 1996—2007. Mem. state ch. com. Diocese of SC, Charleston, 1987—90, mem. coun., 1988—91; chief chaplain SC State Guard, Columbia, SC, 1999—; mem. standing com. Diocese of SC, Charleston, 2000—03. Chmn. Sampson County Assn. for Handicapped, Clinton, 1978—79, SC Foster Care Rev. Bd., Columbia, 1993—95; bd. dirs. SC Mil. Heritage Found., Columbia, 2005—. Col. SC Guard, 1990—. Recipient Knight Grand Cross, Order of White Eagle, Poland, 1990, Knight Grand Officer, Order of Star of Honor, Ethiopia, 2000. Mem.: Sumter Guard Charleston, Imperial Soc. St. George of Lalibela, Order of St. Lazarus (chaplain 2000), Darlington County Hist. Soc. Avocations: travel, archaeology. Home: 110 Circle Dr Darlington SC 29532

GOUGH, JOHN FRANCIS, lawyer; b. Phila., Nov. 28, 1934; s. John Joseph and Honora Veronica (Garrity) G.; m. Natalie Smith, Mar. 8, 1984; children: David, Robert, J. Joseph II, Richard, Jonathan, Kristin. AB cum laude, St. Joseph's U., 1957; JD, Yale Law Sch., New Haven, Conn., 1960. Bar: Pa. 1961, NJ 1994, US Dist. Ct. (ea. dist.) Pa. 1961, US Ct. Appeals (3d cir.) 1966, US Supreme Ct. 1967. Assoc. Erskine, Barbieri & Sheer, Phila., 1960-65, White and Williams, Phila., 1965-68, ptnr., 1968-80, Toll, Ebby & Gough, Phila., 1980-87; ptnr., chmn. corp. dept. Abrahams & Loewenstein, Phila., 1987-88; ptnr. Hoyle, Morris & Kerr, Phila., 1988-92, Montgomery, Mccracken, Walker & Rhoads, LLP, Phila., 1992-98, co-chair bus. bankruptcy sect., 1998; ptnr. Hoyle, Morris & Kerr LLP, Phila., 1998-2000; of counsel Montgomery, McCracken, Walker & Rhoads, LLP, Phila., 2000—05; pvt. practice Phila., 2005—. Exec. com. Ea. Dist Bankruptcy Conf., 1989—; faculty co-chmn. and lectr. Temple Grad. Sch. Law C.L.E. Program, 1989-92; lectr. U. Pa. Grad. Sch., Temple Law Sch., 1990—. Author course materials for profl. and ednl. orgns. Pres. Highfield Sch. PTA, Plymouth, Pa., 1966-68, Greene Towne Montessori Sch., Phila., 1979-80; chmn. Penjerdel region, mem. nat. exec. com. Yale Law Sch. Assn., 2002-; mem. exec. com., sec. Schuylkill River Devel. Corp., 2000—; chmn. Tidal Schuylkill River Master Plan Task Force; pres. Rittenhouse Savoy Owners Assn.; mem. Center City Residents Assn., Phila., 2005—. Mem. Pa. Bar Assn., Am. Law Inst., Phila. Bar Assn. (pres. Jr. Bar Assn. 1964-65), Hosp. Attys. S.E. Pa. (pres. 1977-79), Am. Bankruptcy Inst. (bd. cert. in bus. bankruptcy), Yale Club Phila. Avocations: tennis, gardening, exercise. Office: 123 South Broad St 28th Fl Philadelphia PA 19109 Office Phone: 215-772-5033. Office Fax: 215-772-5034. Business E-Mail: jfg@jgoughlaw.com.

GOUGHER, RONALD LEE, language educator; b. Allentown, Pa., July 27, 1939; s. Samuel Franklin and Beatrice Dorothy (Shanaberger) G.; 1 child, Robert. BA, Muhlenberg Coll., 1961; postgrad., Albright Coll., 1962, Stanford U., 1963; MA, Lehigh U., 1964; postgrad., Harvard U., 1964, U. Pa., 1964—75; advanced cert., Goethe Inst., Munich, 1969. Chmn. fgn. lang. dept. Parkland H.S., Allentown, 1961-65; tchr. German Moravian Sem. for Girls, 1965-69; instr. German Lehigh U., 1965-69; assoc. prof. German West Chester (Pa.) U., 1969—, coord. German studies, 1972—, dir. internat. edn., 1974-83, chmn. dept. fgn. langs., 1977-96, campus dir. Expt. in Internat. Living, 1972-92. Treas. Pa. Consortium Internat. Edn., 1978-83, pres., 1983-86, World Learning Inc., 1992—; coord.-chairperson Assn. Depts. Fgn. Langs., State Sys. Higher Edn., Pa., 1984-88, del. First Joint Conf. Chinese and Am. Edn. Great Hall of People, Beijing, 1992; citizen amb. Linguistics del. to China, 1991-92, lectr. in field, cons. Franklin Mint, 1992—; cons., program dir. Chester Conty Intermediate Unit; guest lectr. Ufa, Ivanova, Russia, 1993, Czestochowa, Poland, Ufa, Russia, Sendai, Japan, Jurmala, Riga, Valmiera, Latvia, 1994-96, Kaunus, Lithuania, 1995; participant Hungarian Parliament Sessions, Budapest, 1994; dir. Am.-European studies program, West Chester U. and Soros Found., Latvia, Lithuania, Czech Republic, Slovakia, Hungary, Romania, Yugoslavia, Bulgaria, Croatia, Slovenia, Macedonia, 1994, Moldova, 1995, Estonia, 1996, Albania, Bosnia, Kyrgystan, Mongolia, 1997—, Kazakhstan, 1998—, Azerbaijan, 1999, Kosovo, 2001-02, Georgia, 2003, China, Haiti, others, 2005; dir. Internat. Sch.-U. Partnership Program, West Chester U. and Chester County Intermediate Unit, 1988—; dir. Internat. Sch.-U. Ptnrs. program Chester County Intermediate Unit and West Chester U., 1991-97. Co-editor, Individualization Fgn. Lang. Learning in Am., 1970-75; author numerous publs. in German lang. and lit., individualizing instrn. in fgn. langs. Bd. dirs. Peters Valley Crafts Ctr., USIA, 1988-95; active Congress-Bundestag Youth Exch. Program, 1988-96, Citizen Amb. Program, China, 1991, 92. Grantee Fulbright Found., 1963, 69, Soros Found., 1990-94, 94—, Fed. Fgn. Lang. Assistance Act, 1992-96, Open Soc., 1994-2005, Immaculata U., 2005; recipient Chapel of Four Chaplains award, 1981. Mem. Am. Assn. Tchrs. German, Am. Coun. Tchg. Fgn. Langs., N.E. Conf. Tchg. Fgn. Langs., Internat. Platform Assn., Smithsonian Instn., Ruffed Grouse Soc., Trout Unlimited, Ducks Unlimited. Republican. Lutheran. Home: 3309 Windsor Ln Thorndale PA 19372-1038 Office: West Chester U Dept Fgn Langs West Chester PA 19380 Personal E-mail: rgougher1@msn.com.

GOUGHNOUR, ROY ROBERT, civil engineer, educator, director; b. Canton, Ohio, May 10, 1928; s. Roy George and Doris Belle (Malone) G.; m. Marilynn Ruth Knoll, Sept. 20, 1948 (div. Mar. 1968); children: Robert Lee, Steven David, Mekyla Ann Goughnour Hart; m. Mary Rosetta Strahan, June 28, 1968. BS, Mich. State U., 1961, MS, 1965, PhD, 1967. Registered profl. engr., Mich. V.p. A.C. Aukerman Co., Jackson, Mich., 1958-64, Aukerman-Goughnour Co., Jackson, 1972-76, Geotechnics Am., Inc., Peachtree City, Ga., 1989—2000; assoc. prof. No. Ariz. U., Flagstaff, 1967-68, Mich. State U., East Lansing, 1968-72; pres. Strahan Mfg. Co., Tampa, Fla., 1976-77; v.p. R & D Vibroflotation Found. Co., Pitts., 1976-86; exec. v.p. GeoSys., Inc., Sterling, Va., 1986-89; mgr. engring. Nilex Corp., Centennial, Colo., 2000—. Cons. Hubbell, Roth & Clark, Bloomfield Hills, Mich., 1989-91, Tensar Corp., Morrow, Ga., 1989-91. Contbr. articles to profl. jours.; patentee slipform and ground improvement fields. Rsch. grantee NSF, 1969, Fed. Hwy. Assn., 1980. Mem. ASCE (assoc.), Internat. Soc. Soil Mechanics and Found. Engring., SE Asian Geotech. Soc. Republican. Avocations: hunting, target shooting. Home: 705 Duff Rd NE Leesburg VA 20176-4907 Office: Nilex Corp 15171 E Fremont Dr Centennial CO 80112 Personal E-mail: bob@goughnour.net.

GOUIN, WARNER PETER, information technology consultant; b. International Falls, Minn., Sept. 14, 1954; s. Joseph Andre and Rose Marie (Grandaw) G.; m. Judith Ann Nelson, Aug. 25, 1979; 1 child, Nicole Renee. AA, Rainy River CC., 1974; BS Mgmt., St. Cloud State U., 1979; BSEE, N.D. State U., 1985, MS in Indsl. Engring. and Mgmt., 1987. Cert. sys. integrator; cert. prodn. and inventory control mgr. Purchasing/prodn. contr. Plastech Rsch., Inc., Rush City, Minn., 1979-80; inventory supr. Aero Sys. Engring., St. Paul, 1980-81; grad. asst. N.D. State U., 1985-87; elec. engr. Marvin Windows, Warroad, Minn., 1987-93, sys. integrator MIS dept., 1993-95, sys. engr., automation sys. acquisition, sr. project engr., 1995-97; sales rep. Digi-Key Corp., Thief River Falls, Minn., 1997; info. tech. specialist 3 Minn. Correctional Facility, Shakopee, 1997—2003; with IT Lifecycle Cons., Eagan, Minn., 2003—. Trainer process reengring. Total Quality Mgmt., Warroad, Minn., 1992-95, customer svc specialist Office Depot, 2007—. Scoutmaster Boy Scouts Am., Warroad, 1989-91. Mem. Office Automation Soc. Internat. (editor 1989-90), Soc. Mfg. Engrs. Avocations: computer integrated manufacturing research, fishing, hunting, walking, guitar. Office: IT Lifecycle Cons 3801 Ballantrae Rd # 3 Eagan MN 55122 Office Phone: 651-452-7733. Business E-Mail: ITLifecycler@comcast.net.

GOULAZIAN, PETER ROBERT, retired broadcasting executive; b. NYC, Apr. 17, 1939; s. G.B. and Alice Goulazian; m. Mary C. Holland, Dec. 19, 1965; children: Cindy Anne, Peter Robert. BA, Columbia U., 1962. With media and programming dept. Dancer-Fitzgerald-Sample, Inc., NYC, 1963-67; v.p., mktg. dir. Katz Communications, Inc., NYC, 1967-79, v.p. broadcasting, 1980-81; pres. Continental TV div., 1981-84, pres. TV group, 1985-91; pres., CEO Katz Media Corp., 1992-94. Bd. dirs. The TV Bur., Seltel Inc., Cable Media Corp., Katz Internat., Petry Media Corp. Chmn. Woodstock Recreation Ctr. Mem. Varsity "C" Club, N.Y. Athletic Club, Nantucket Anglers Club, Columbia U. Club, Woodstock Rotary (dir.), Pentangle Arts Coun. (trustee). Home: PO Box 404 Woodstock VT 05091 E-mail: longlake@valley.net.

GOULD, ALAN BRANT, academic administrator; b. Aug. 2, 1938; m. Mary Nell; children: Adam, Charles, Christopher. BA in History cum laude, Marshall U., 1961, MA in History, 1962; PhD in Am. History, W.Va. U., 1969. Grad. instr., dept. history W.Va. U., Morgantown, 1962-65; instr., dept. history D.C. Tchrs. Coll., 1965-66; asst. prof. history No. Va. Community Coll., 1966-69; prof., dept. history Marshall U., Huntington, W.Va., 1969—, sr. v.p., 1988-89, provost, 1989-92, interim pres., 1990-91, v.p. for acad. affairs, 1991-94, dean Coll. Liberal Arts, 1980-88, acting v.p. acad. affairs, 1984-86, asst. to pres. for spl. projects, 1986, chmn. dept. history, 1977-80, asst. to v.p. acad. affairs, 1976-77, coord. Regents BA degree program, 1976-80, 86-94; exec. dir. John Deaver Drinko Acad., 1994—. Adj. prof. history W.Va. Coll. Grad. Studies, 1976-86; lectr. Ohio U., Ironton, 1970-74; vis. lectr. for Project Newgate, Fed. Youth Correction Inst., Summit, Ky., fall 1970. Contbr. articles to hist. jours, also conf. papers. Chmn. Cabell County Hist. Landmark Commn., 1983-92; trustee Huntington Mus. Art, 1983-93, chmn. edn. com., mem. exec. com.; pres. River Cities Cultural Coun., 1985-91; bd. dirs. W.Va. Humanities Coun., 1986-90, v.p., 1989-91, pres., 1991-94, W.Va. Coalways, Inc., 1987—; mem. Mayor of Huntington's Main St. Project, 1987-92, Marshall U. Rsch. Corp., 1988, mem., 1982-86; mem. W.Va. Antiquities Commn., 1975-77, Cabell County Commn. on Crime, Delinquency and Corrections, 1982-86, statewide steering com. Ideas That Built Am., 1985-86, Carter G. Woodson Meml. Commn., 1986—; mem. steering com. Ethics W.Va. Program, 1983-84, chmn. Great Books Program; mem. affirmative action bd. City of Huntington, 1989-91, mem. Cabell County (W.Va.) hist. landmark commn., 1989-91, 94—; trustee W. Va. Ednl. Found., Inc., 1993-2001; mem. W.Va. Libr. Commn., 1997—. Inducted into Huntington East High Sch. Hall of Fame, Class of 1986, City of Huntington (W.Va.) Wall of Fame, 1997; recipient Charles Daugherty Humanities award W.Va. Humanities Coun., 1996. Mem. Am. Hist. Assn. (com. on status of history in schs. 1974-76), Orgn. Am. Historians (state rep.), W.Va. Hist. Assn. (sec. 1974, v.p. 1975, pres. 1976), W.Va. Assn. Acad. Deans (mem. exec. bd. 1982-86). W.Va. Bd. Regents (univ. rep., acad. affairs adv. com. 1984-86), Soc. Yeager Scholars (steering com. 1986-87), W.Va. Humanities Ctr. (exec. com. 1987—), Gamma Theta Upsilon, Omicron Delta Kappa, Phi Alpha Theta, Phi Eta Sigma, Pi Sigma Alpha. Avocations: tennis, travel. Office: Marshall U John Deaver Drinko Acad One John Marshall Dr Huntington WV 25755-0003 Home Phone: 304-525-1803; Office Phone: 304-696-2739. Business E-Mail: gould@marshall.edu.

GOULD, ALVIN R., manufacturing executive; b. Seattle, May 16, 1922; s. Charlie I. and Laura (Klos) Gould; m. Ruth Nelson, May 25, 1946; children: Stephen Charles, Jon Patrick. Grad. pub. schs. Mem. engring. dept. Pacific Car & Foundry Co., Renton, Wash., 1943-45, asst. mgr. indsl. sales, 1945-48, mgr. indsl. sales, 1948-55, gen. sales mgr., 1956-60, Peterbilt Motors Co., Newark, Calif., 1961-64; v.p., dir., gen. sales mgr. Honolulu Iron Works Co., 1964-66, exec. v.p., dir., chief operating officer, 1966, pres., dir., chief exec. officer, 1968—71; group pres. Food Equipment Group Ward Foods Inc., NYC, 1970-71; v.p. merchandising Dillingham Corp., Honolulu, 1972-73, v.p. mining and merchandising, 1973-75, group v.p., exec. mgmt. com. mining and merchandising; pres. Truck Center Corp., Seattle, 1976-90, co-owner, sec.-treas., 1991-95; pvt. practice in personal investments, 1996—. Mem. nat. export expansion Coun. Dept. Commerce, 1969—74, chmn. regional export expansion coun., 1969—74; mem. Western Regional Export Coun.; chmn. Honolulu Export Coun., 1975—77; chmn. bd. trustees Hawaii Pacific Coll., 1973—77; bd. dirs. Ctr. Internat. Bus. Mem.: Hawaii Assn. Industries (v.p., bd. dirs. 1975—76), Hawaii World Trade Assn. (mem. exec. com. 1968—69), Navy League (bd. dirs.), Hawaii C. of C. (chmn. trade com. 1968—69), Rainier Club, Outrigger Canoe Club, Rotary. Home: 8464 W Mercer Way Mercer Island WA 98040-5633

GOULD, ANDREW, oil industry executive; b. UK, Dec. 17, 1946; married; 3 children. B. with honors, U. Wales. With Ersnt & Young, NYC, Schlumberger Ltd., 1975—77, mem. internal audit dept. Paris, 1977—79, contr. Schlumberger Instrument Velizy, 1979—81, contr. FEA Wireline, 1981—82, contr. Forex Neptune, 1982—84, contr. drilling & prodn. svcs., 1984, v.p. finance Dowell Schlumberger Houston, 1984—85, treas. Atlantic Asia, 1985—86, contr. Wireline & Testing, 1986—90, treas. Schlumberger Ltd. NY, 1990—91, v.p. ops. Sedco Forex, 1991—93, pres. Sedco Forex, 1993—98, pres. Wireline & Testing, 1998—99, pres. Oilfield Svcs. Products, 1999—2002, exec. v.p. Oilfield Svcs. Products, 2002, pres., COO, 2003, chmn., CEO, 2003—. Non-exec. dir. Rio Tinto. Office: Schlumberger Ltd 57th Fl 153 E 53rd St New York NY 10002-4624

GOULD, BRUCE ELLIOTT, physician, medical educator, academic administrator; b. Queens, NY, 1954; BA, Cornell U.; MD, SUNY, Syracuse, 1979. Intern U. Mass. Med. Ctr., Worcester, resident in medicine, fellow in medicine; prof. gen. internal medicine U. Conn. Sch. Medicine, assoc. dean primary care; med. dir. St. Francis Hosp./U. Conn. Primary Care Ctr. Burgdorf /Fleet Health Ctr., Hartford. Dir. Conn. area health edn. ctr. program U. Conn. Sch. Medicine, 1997—, founder, participant Migrant Farm Workers program, 1998—; chair nat. adv. coun. migrant health U.S. Dept. HHS, 2004—. Mem.: AMA Found. (Pride in Profession award 2004). Office: Burgdorf Health Ctr 131 Coventry St Hartford CT 06112 Address: U Conn Health Ctr 263 Farmington Ave Farmington CT 06030-2926 Office Phone: 860-679-4322. Fax: 860-679-1101. E-mail: gould@adp.uchc.edu.

GOULD, CHARLES W., foundation administrator, lawyer; JD, U. Minn. Bar: Minn., DC, Colo. Atty. Arnold & Porter, Washington, Hogan & Hartson, Washington; pres. Vols. of Am. Health Svcs.; pres., CEO Vols. of Am., 1995—. Bd. mem. Nat. Assembly of Health and Human Svc. Orgns., Nat. Affordable Housing Trust, Generations United, Ptnrs. for Livable Cmtys.; mem. nat. adv. bd. Make a Difference Day. Recipient Excellence in Nat. Exec. Leadership Award, Nat. Assembly of Health and Human Svc. Orgns., 2004. Office: Vols of Am 1660 Duke St Alexandria VA 22314 Office Phone: 703-341-5000. Office Fax: 703-341-7000.

GOULD, CHRISTOPHER ROBERT, physics professor; BS, Imperial Coll., London, 1965; MS, PhD, U. Pa., 1969. Rsch. assoc. Duke U., Durham, N.C., 1969-71; asst. prof. N.C. State U., Raleigh, 1971-76, assoc. prof., 1977-83, prof., 1983—, alumni disting. undergrad. prof., 1990, dept. head, 1995—2005, assoc. dean for adminstrn., 2005—. Vis. scientist Inst. for Atomic Energy, Beijing, China, 1984, U. Petroleum, Dhahran, Saudi Arabia, 1987, Los Alamos Meson Physics Facility, N.Mex., 1991; scholar-in-residence Oak Ridge Ctr. for Advanced Studies, 2005. Editor: Tests of Time Reversal Invariance in Neutron Physics, 1987, Time Reversal Invariance and Parity Violation in Neutron Reactions, 1994, Fundamental Physics with Pulsed Neutron Beams, 2001, Astrophysics, Symmetries and Applied Physics at Spallation Neutron Sources, 2002. Humboldt fellow Frankfurt, Germany, 1976-77. Fellow Am. Phys. Soc. Office: NC State Univ PO Box 8202 Raleigh NC 27695-8202

GOULD, DAVID, lawyer; b. LA, Feb. 19, 1940; s. Erwin and Beatrice (Altman) G.; m. Bonnie Becker, Feb. 12, 1967; children: Julie M., Michael. AB, U. Calif., LA, 1962; LLB, U. Calif., Berkeley, 1965. Bar: Calif. 1965, U.S. Dist. Ct. (cen., so., ea. and no. dists.) Calif. 1966, U.S. Ct. Appeals (9th cir.) 1967, U.S. Supreme Ct. 1995. Dep. atty. gen. Calif. Dept. of Justice, LA, 1965-68; assoc. Loeb & Loeb, LA, 1968-73, Danning, Gill, Gould, Diamond & Spector, LA, 1974-76, ptnr., 1976-92, McDermott, Will & Emery, LA, 1992—. Adj. assoc. prof. Southwestern U. Sch. of Law, L.A., 1978-80; adj. prof. Pepperdine U. Sch. of Law, Malibu, Calif., 1982. Co-author: Local Bankruptcy Practice Manual for the Central District of California, 2d edit., 1990—. Fellow: Am. Coll. Bankruptcy; mem.: L.A. Bankruptcy Forum (bd. trustees 1989, sec. 1990—, pres. 1993—94, lawyer rep. ctrl. dist. Calif. to 9th cir. jud. conf.), Calif. Bankruptcy Forum, L.A. County Bar Assn. (fed. cts. com. 1987—, treas. 1998—99, sec. 1999—), Calif. Bar Assn. (debtor/creditor rels. and bankruptcy com. 1984—87, chair 1987—88, advisor 1988—89, uniform comml. code com. 1988—92, bankruptcy cons. group bd. legal specialization 1989—93), ABA (bus. bankruptcy com. sect. on bus. law 1982—, vice chair rules subcom. 1986—92, chair 1992—). Avocation: trap and skeet shooting. Office: McDermott Will & Emery LLP 2049 Century Park E Ste 3400 Los Angeles CA 90067-3208

GOULD, DONALD EVERETT, retired chemical company executive, consultant; b. Concord, NH, May 19, 1932; s. Everett Luther and Gladys (Wilcox) G.; m. Marilyn Bachelder, June 13, 1953; children: Barbara, Allen, Douglas. BS in Chem. Engring., U. NH, 1954; postgrad., Rutgers U., 1955—59. Devel. chem. engr. plastics divsn. Union Carbide Co., Bound Brook, NJ, 1954-59, tech. svc. engr. Bound Brook and Wayne, NJ, 1959-64, mgr. tech. svc. indsl. bag dept. Wayne, 1964-66, mgr. tech. svcs. indsl. fabricated products dept., 1966-67, mktg., mgr. indsl. bags, 1967-69, sr. packaging engr., 1969-72, mgr. packaging, 1972-74, mgr. distbn. safegy and regulations, 1974-79, staff engr. packaging, 1980-85, sr. staff engr. packaging, labeling, 1985-91, prin. engr. packaging, labeling and regulations, 1991-94, cons., 1994—. Contbr. articles to profl. jours.; contbg. author Encyclopedia of Engineering Materials and Processes. Chmn. Andover Planning Bd., NH, 2000—. Mem. Inst. Packaging Profls. (vice chmn. films, foils and laminations com. 1962-64, chmn. 1964-66, sect. leader bottle containers, chmn. bag com. 1975-78, 85-88, exec. com. chem. packaging 1985-94, hon. life mem. 1992), Am. Soc. Quality Control (hon., life), Chem. Mfrs. Assn. (chmn. distbn. work group), Am. Coun. Chem. Labeling, Andover Hist. Soc. (treas.), Andover Planning Bd. (chmn.), Alpha Chi Sigma, Alpha Gamma Rho. Home and Office: 21 Lawrence St PO Box 231 East Andover NH 03231-0231

GOULD, DOROTHY MAE, executive secretary, soprano; b. Bridgeport, Conn., Sept. 9, 1927; d. Clifford Alexander and Mary Irene Hedin; m. John Colquitt Gould, Nov. 26, 1958; children: Natalie Mary, Clifford Gardner, Andrew Woodhouse. BA in English Lit. and Creative Writing, U. Mont., 1997; studied voice with Estelle Liebling, Julliard, 1959—63, studied voice with Bernard Taylor, 1943; studied voice with Alexander Kipnis, Met. Opera, 1968—72; scholar, New Eng. Conservatory. Legal sec. Thompson Knight, Dallas, White, McElroy, Dallas, Gibbons, Tucker, Smith, McEwen, Coxer and Taub, Tampa, Fla., Curtis, Trevethan & Gerety, Bridgeport, Conn., Music Corp. Am., NYC; sec. GE Co., Bridgeport, Columbia Artists Mgmt., NYC, AMF, Greenwich, Conn.; soprano USO, Conn., 1944—45, Tampa Opera, 2002—; oratorio singer, soloist soprano N.Y., Conn., Fla. Sec. Music Corp. Am., NYC. Finalist Barnum Festival Jenny Lind contest, 1948, Stamford Advocate, Greenwich Times contest, 1985—86. Home: 13871 N 91st Ln Peoria AZ 85381 Personal E-mail: colquitt3@msn.com.

GOULD, ELIZABETH, neuroscientist, educator; BA in Psychology, St. John's U., 1984; MA in Behavioral Neuroscience, UCLA, 1986, PhD in Behavioral Neuroscience, 1988; post-Dal fellow in Neuroendocrinology, Rockefeller U., 1989—92. Asst. prof. Rockefeller U., 1993—96, adj. prof., 1997—; asst. prof. dept. psychology Princeton U., 1997—2000, prof., 2000—. Contbr. articles to profl. jours. Recipient Troland Rsch. award NAS, 2000. Office: 1-S-12 Green Hall Dept Psychology Princeton Univ Princeton NJ 08544-1010 Office Phone: 609-258-4483. Business E-Mail: goulde@princeton.edu.

GOULD, ELLIOTT, actor; b. Bklyn., Aug. 29, 1938; s. Bernard and Lucille (Raver) Goldstein; m. Barbra Streisand, Mar. 21, 1963 (div.); 1 son, Jason; m. Jennifer Bogart; children— Molly, Sam. Student, Profl. Children's Sch., NYC, 1955; pupil of, Jerome Swinford, Sonya Box, Bill Quinn, Colin Romoff, Charles Lowe, Eugene Lewis, Matt Mattox. Theatrical appearances include Rumple, 1957, Say, Darling, 1958, Irma La Douce, 1960, I Can Get It For You Wholesale, 1962, On The Town, 1963, The Fantastiks; appeared in films: Bob & Carol & Ted & Alice, 1969, M*A*S*H, 1970 (Best Male Comedy Performance, Golden Laurel award, 1971), I Love My Wife, 1970, Getting Straight, 1970, Move, 1970, The Touch, 1971, Little Murders, 1971, The Long Goodbye, 1973, Spys, 1974, Busting, 1974, California Split, 1974, Nashville, 1975, Whiffs, 1975, I Will, I Will... For Now, 1976, Harry & Walter Go to N.Y, 1976, Mean Johnny Barrows, 1976, A Bridge Too Far, 1977, Capricorn One, 1978, Matilda, 1978, The Silent Partner, 1979, Escape to Athena, 1979, The Lady Vanishes, 1979, The Muppet Movie, 1979, Falling in Love Again, 1980, The Devil and Max Devlin, 1981, Dirty Tricks, 1981, The Brooklyn Bridge, 1984, The Naked Face, 1984, Inside Out, 1987, Dead Men Don't Die, 1989, Strawanser, The Lemon Sisters, 1990, Bugsy, 1991, The Player, 1992, Johns, 1996, American History X, 1998, The Big Hit, 1998, Am. Hist. X, 1998, Playing Mona Lisa, 2000, Picking Up the Pieces, 2000, The Experience Box, 2001, Ocean's Eleven, 2001, Puckoon, 2002, Ocean's Twelve, 2004, Open Window, 2006, Ocean's Thirteen, 2007; TV appearance in Once Upon A Mattress, 1964, Come Blow Your Horn, 1981; star TV series E.R., 1984, Together We Stand, 1986, Friends (15 episodes), 1998, Getting Personal, 1998, It's Like You Know (3 episodes), 1998, Mentors, 1999, Baby Bob, 2002, K Street, 2003, (voice) Kim Possible, 2003-07; other TV appearances include: (film) The Rules of Marriage, Saturday Night Live (6 segments), Shelly Duvall's Fairy Tale Theater prodn. of Jack and the Beanstalk, 1983, Tall Tale of Casey at the Bat, 1986, (film) Vanishing Act, 1986, Sessions, 1991, Bloodlines: Murder in the Family, 1993, Hoffman's Hunger, 1993, The Dangerous, 1995, Touched by an Angel, 1997, The Shining, 1997. Mem. Actor's Equity Assn., AFTRA, SAG. Office: 1900 Ave Of Stars Ste 1640 Los Angeles CA 90067-4407*

GOULD, EMILY, editor; b. 1982; BA, New Sch., NYC, 2004. Editl. asst. Hyperion Books, NYC, 2004—05, asst. editor, 2005—06; co-editor-in-chief Gawker.com, NYC, 2006—. Co-author: Hex Education; author: (blogs) www.EmilyMagazine.com, 2005—. Office: Gawker Media 76 Crosby New York NY 10012 Office Phone: 212-655-9524.*

GOULD, HARRY EDWARD, JR., paper company executive; b. NYC, Sept. 24, 1938; s. Harry Edward and Lucille (Quartucy) Gould; m. Barbara Clement, Apr. 26, 1975; children: Harry Edward III, Katharine Elizabeth. Student, Oxford U., 1958; BA cum laude, Colgate U., 1960; postgrad., Harvard Bus. Sch., 1960—62; MBA, Columbia U., 1964. Assoc. in corp. fin. dept. Goldman, Sachs & Co., NYC, 1961—62; exec. asst. to sr. v.p. ops. Universal Am., NYC, 1964—65; sec., treas. Young Spring & Wire Corp., Detroit, 1965—67, exec. v.p., COO, 1967—69, also bd. dirs.; v.p. adminstrn. and fin. Universal Am. Corp., 1968—69; mem. exec. com., v.p., sec.-treas. Daybrook-Ottawa Corp., Bowling Green, Ohio, 1967—69; dir., mem. exec. com. Am. Med. Ins. Co., NYC, 1966—74; chmn., pres., CEO Gould Paper Corp., NYC, 1969—, also chmn. bd. dirs.; chmn. bd., dir. Vrisimo Mfg., Inc., Ceres, Calif., 1974—99; chmn. bd. Lewis & Gould Paper Co., Inc., Northfield, Ill., 1975—78; chmn., pres., CEO Signature Comm. Ltd., LA and NYC, 1986—; chmn. bd. Legion Paper West Corp., Commerce, Calif., 1997—2003; chmn. Price & Pierce Internat., Inc., Stamford, Conn., 2004, Price & Pierce Finland Oy, Helsinki, Finland, 2004—, Price & Pierce (Asia Pacific) Pte. Ltd., Singapore, 2004—. Chmn. bd. dirs. Samuel Porritt & Co., East Peoria, Ill., 1970—86, Ingalls Mfg., Inc., Ceres, 1974—99, Hawthorne Paper Co., Kalamazoo, 1970—75, Weiss/McNair/Ramacher, Inc., Chico, 1974—; ltd. ptnr. Hardy & Co., NYC, 1973—78; chmn. exec. com., bd. dirs. Richard Lewis Paper Corp., Northfield, 1992—97; bd. dirs., mem. environ. and health and safety com. Domtar, Inc., Montreal, Canada, 1995—2003. Co-chmn. Pacesetters com. Boy Scouts Am., 1966—69; participant as U.S. Pres.'s rep. UN E-W Trade Devel. Commn., 1967; mem. nat. coun. Colgate U., 1973—76, trustee, mem. budget, devel., fin. and student affairs coms., 1976—82; mem. exec. com., chmn. export expansion subcom., mem. export promotion subcom. U.S. Pres.'s Export Coun., 1979—82; nat. trustee, mem. exec. com. Nat. Symphony Orch., Washington, 1978—99; mem. NY Gov.'s Task Force on NY State Cultural Life and Arts, 1975—78; pres. Harry E. Gould Found., NYC, 1971—; mem. bd. govs. Actors Studio Drama Sch. of New Sch. U., 1995—; mem. exec. br. Acad. Motion Picture Arts and Scis., 1985—; trustee Riverdale Country Sch., 1990—98; mem. Dem. Nat. Fin. Coun., 1974—78, vice chmn. exec. com., chmn. budget and audit coms.; treas. NY State Dem. Com., 1976—77; mem. mayor's citizens com. Dem. Nat. Conv., 1976; bd. dirs. United Cerebral Palsy Rsch. and Ednl. Found., 1976—97, Nat. Multiple Sclerosis Soc., 1977—, NYC Housing Devel. Corp., 1977—, USO of Met. NY, 1981—, Housing NY Corp., 1986—, vice chmn., 1987—; bd. dirs., chmn. exec. com. Cinema Group, Inc., LA, 1979—86, chmn., pres., 1982—86; bd. dirs. Residential Mortgage Ins. Corp., 1992—. Mem.: Fin. Execs. Inst., Am. Mgmt. Assn. (trustee, audit com. 1997—2000), Young Pres. Orgn., Paper Distbn. Coun. (chmn. 1993—94), Paper Mchts. Assn. NY (dir. 1972—84), Nat. Paper Trade Alliance (dir., mem. printing paper com. 1973—74), Les Ambassadeurs (London), Paper Club NY, Harvard Club, Friars Club, Pres.'s NY Club (co-chmn. assocs. divsn. 1964—68), Harvard Bus. Sch. Club, Phi Kappa Tau. Office: Gould Paper Corp 1 Madison Ave Fl 14 New York NY 10010-3629 Office Phone: 212-301-0000. *In business the most difficult problem to resolve is blending the profit goals with the dignity of human relations. In the long run, it is probably best to forego some of the profits in order to successfully meld the economic and human sides of business.*

GOULD, HARRY J., III, neurology educator; b. Columbus, Ohio, Mar. 1, 1947; s. Harry J. Jr. and Madeline (Folger) G.; m. Anne Marie Thompson, Jan. 30, 1971; children: Trevor Nicholas, Laura Nicole. BS, SUNY, Stony Brook, 1969; PhD, Brown U., 1974; MD, La. State U., 1990. Asst. prof. Med. Sch. U. Cin., 1974-80; asst. prof. Med. Sch., La. State U., New Orleans, 1980-86, assoc. prof., 1986, resident in neurology, 1990-94; asst. prof. med. sch. La. State U., New Orleans, 1994-98, assoc. prof. neurology, 1998—, Tom Benson prof. neurology, dir. Multidisciplinary Pain Ctr. Contbr. articles to profl. jours. With USAR, 1970-76. NSF grantee, 1986-89. Mem. Internat. Assn. for the Study Pain, Soc. for Neurosci., Am. Acad. Neurology, Am. Pain Soc., Am. Acad. Pain Medicine. Republican. Methodist. Avocations: songwriting, banjo, guitar. Office: La State U Med Ctr Dept of Neurology 533 Bolivar St New Orleans LA 70112-2825 Home: 4848 Windsor Village Dr Unit 77 Baton Rouge LA 70817 Home Phone: 985-643-5460; Office Phone: 504-568-4090. Business E-Mail: hgould@lsuhsc.edu.

GOULD, HOWARD RICHARD, retired physician; b. NYC, May 21, 1931; m. Barbara Ann Paretti, Oct. 6, 1956; children: Susan, Carolyn, Richard, Joanne, Anthony, MaryJean, Eileen, Laura, Margaret. Student, Fordham U., 1949—52; MD, SUNY, 1956. Diplomate Am. Bd. Radiology (examiner oral exams. 1979), Am. Bd. Nuclear Medicine, Nat. Bd. Med. Examiners. Resident in radiology St. Vincent's Hosp., NYC, 1957-60, assoc. dir., 1974-79; chief radiology 811th Med. Group, Loring AFB, Maine, 1960-62, USAF Hosp., Wiesbaden, Germany, 1962-65; radiologist St. Vincent's Hosp., NYC, 1965-79; dir. diagnostic radiology Clin. Sci. Ctr. U. Wis., Madison, 1979-84, U. Tenn. Med. Ctr., Knoxville, 1984-95, sr. radiologist, 1995-99, prof. radiology, 1984-99, prof. emeritus, 2000—. Clin. asst. prof. N.J. Coll. Med., 1965-69; clin. assoc. prof. NYU Sch. Med., N.Y.C., 1969-79; prof. radiology U. Wis., Madison, 1979-84; sec. v.p., pres. elect, pres. med. staff St. Vincent's Hosp., 1969-76; chief staff elect, chief staff U. Tenn. Med. Ctr., 1993, 94; sec. N.Y. Celtic Med. Soc., N.Y.C., 1969-73. Author various book chpts.; contbr. articles to profl. jours. Maj. USAF, 1957-65. Fellow Am. Coll. Radiology; mem. AMA, Radiol. Soc. N.Am., Am. Coll. Radiology, N.Y. Roentgen Soc. (sec., v.p., pres. 1971-78), Assn. Univ. Radiologists, Am. Roentgen Ray Soc., Alpha Omega Alpha. Roman Catholic. Avocations: reading, woodworking. E-mail: drhgould@aol.com.

GOULD, JAMES L., biology professor; b. Tulsa, July 31, 1945; s. James L. and Doris Mae (Frazier) Gould; m. Carol Holly Grant, June 6, 1970; children: Grant Frazier, Clare Holly. BS, Calif. Inst. Tech., 1970; PhD, Rockefeller U., 1975. Asst. prof. Princeton U., NJ, 1975-80, assoc. prof., 1980-84, prof. biology, 1984—. Author: Ethology, 1982, The Honey Bee, 1988, Sexual Selection, 1989, The Animal Mind, 1994, Biological Science, rev. edit., 1996, Biostats Basics, 2001, Animal Architects, 2007; contbr. articles to profl. jours. With US Army, 1967—68. Named Prof. of the Yr., Carnegie Found. NJ, 1996, Tchr. of the Yr., Animal Behavior Soc., 1997; grantee, NSF, 1976, 1979, 1982, 1985, NIH, 1976, Nat. Geographic Soc., 1984; Guggenheim Found. fellow, 1987, AAAS fellow, 1988, Animal Behavior Soc. fellow, 1992. Presbyterian. Achievements include research in animal behavior. Office: Princeton U Dept Ecol Evol Biology Princeton NJ 08544-0001 E-mail: gould@princeton.edu.

GOULD, JOHN PHILIP, economist, educator; b. Chgo., Jan. 19, 1939; s. John Philip and Lillian Gould; children: John Philip III, Jeffrey Hayes; m. Kathleen A. Carpenter. BS with highest distinction, Northwestern U., 1960; MBA, U. Chgo., 1963, PhD, 1966. Faculty U. Chgo., 1965—, prof. econs., 1974—, disting. service prof. econs., 1984—, dean Grad. Sch. Bus., 1983-93, v.p. planning, 1988—91; Steven G. Rothmeier prof., disting. svc. prof. econs., 1996—; exec. v.p. Lexecon Inc., Chgo., 1994—2004; pres. Cardean, Chgo., 1999—2001. Vis. prof. Nat. Taiwan U., 1978; spl. asst. econ. affairs to sec. labor, 1969-70; spl. asst. to dir. Office Mgmt. and Budget, 1970; past chmn. econ. policy adv. com. Dept. Labor; bd. dirs. DFA Investment Dimensions Group, Harbor Capital Advisors, Chgo. bd. of Trade, 1986-89; chmn. Pegasus Funds, 1996-99, Milw. Mutual, 1997—, Unext.com, 1999—2006; mem. adv. com. competitive markets Chgo. Merc. Exch., 2004—; editor Jour. Law and Econs., 2006—. Author: (with E. Lazear) Microeconomic Theory, 6th edit, 1989; contbg. author: Microeconomic Foundations of Employment and Inflation Theory, 1970; editor: Jour. of Bus. , 1976-83, Jour. Fin. Econs., 1976-83, Jour. Acctg. and Econs., 1978-81, Jour. Law and Econs., 2006—; contbr. articles to profl. jours. Bd. dirs. United Way/Crusade of Mercy, 1986-91, Lookingglass Theatre Co., 1994-96. Recipient Wall St. Jour. award, 1960, Am. Marketing Assn. award, 1960; Earhart Found. fellow. Mem. Am. Econs. Assn., Econometric Soc. (chmn. local arrangements 1968), Econ. Club of Chgo., Comml. Club of Chgo., Beta Gamma Sigma. Home: 100 E Huron St Apt 2105 Chicago IL 60611-5903 Office: U Chgo Grad Sch Bus 5807 S Woodlawn Chicago IL 60637-1511

GOULD, KAREN A., lawyer; b. Cleve., Mar. 20, 1954; BA with distinction, U. Va., 1976; JD cum laude, U. SC, 1979. Bar: Va. 1979, SC 1979, Va. Ct. Appeals, Va. Supreme Ct., US Dist. Ct. (We. Dist. Va.), US Dist. Ct. (Ea. Dist. Va.), US Ct. Appeals (4th Cir.), US Supreme Ct. Ptnr. McSweeney Crump Childress & Gould PC, Richmond, Va. Mem.: Met. Richmond Women's Bar Assn., Va. Assn. Def. Attys., John Marshall Inn of Ct., Richmond Bar Assn., SC State Bar, Va. State Bar (pres. 2006—07, coun. mem. 2000—05, mem. budget and fin. com.). Office: McSweeney Crump Childress & Gould PC PO Box 1463 Richmond VA 23218 Office Phone: 804-545-2415. Office Fax: 804-782-2130.

GOULD, KENNETH LANCE, cardiologist, researcher, educator; b. Wilsonville, Ala., Oct. 28, 1938; s. Kenneth Newton and Elizabeth May (Barrett) G.; m. Helene Freiin von Eckardstein, Sept. 28, 1970; 1 son, Stefan Anton. BA in Physics, Oberlin Coll., 1960; MD, Western Res. U., 1964. Intern U. Wash. Hosps., Seattle, 1964-65, resident, 1965-67; instr. medicine U. Wash., Seattle, 1970-72, asst. prof., 1972-76, assoc. prof., 1976-79; prof. dept. internal medicine and cardiology U. Tex., Houston, 1979—, dir. div. cardiology, 1979-85, vice chmn. clin. affairs dept. medicine, 1980-84, dir. Positron Diagnostic and Research Ctr., 1979—97; Martin Buckbaum disting. univ. chmn. Weatherhead P.E.T. Ctr. for Preventing and Reversing Atherosclerosis, 1997—, prof. cardiovascular medicine, 1997—, exec. dir., 1997—. Mem. editorial bd. Circulation, 1988-92, Circulation Res., 1982-87, 2004—, Jour. Am. Coll. Cardiology, 1982-88, 2004—, Am. Jour. Cardiology, 1978-86; assoc. editor Circulation, 1993-2003; contbr. articles to profl. jours Recipient George von Hevesy prize, 1978, ACC Young Investigators award, 1983 Fellow Am. Coll. Cardiology (trustee 1984-89), Am. Heart Assn. (chmn. coun. on circulation, Brown Meml. lectr. 1990); mem. Am. Soc. Clin. Investigation, Soc. Nuclear Medicine, N.Am. Soc. Cardiac Radiology, Am. Physiologic Soc., Assn. Am. Physicians, Assn. Univ. Cardiologists, NIH diagnostic radiol. study sect., Houston Cardiol. Soc. (pres. 1983) Democrat. First to report the concept of coronary flow reserve for defining stenosis severity, quantification of stenosis fluid dynamics in vivo, pharmacologic stress perfusion imaging, experimental and clinical positron emission tomography (PET) of coronary artery stenosis, improved PET perfusion defects in patients with CAD after both short and long term lipid lowering, the basic principles of and mathematical structure of the coronary artery tree, the longitudinal base to apex perfusion abnormality of diffuse coronary atherosclerosis before localized stenosis, the resting perfusion heterogeneity of endothelial dysfunction due to early CAD and an 80% reduction in coronary events in CAD after intense combined pharmacologic and lifestyle treatment compared to usual care. Office: PO Box 20708 Houston TX 77225-0708 Office Phone: 713-500-6611. Business E-Mail: k.lance.gould@uth.tmc.edu.*

GOULD, LAURENCE IRA, physicist; b. Bklyn., May 9, 1941; s. Albert and Anne Irene (Roessler) G. BS, Carnegie-Mellon U., 1964; MA, Temple U., 1975, PhD, 1982. Rsch. assoc., assoc. engr. Machlett Labs., Stamford, Conn., 1967-69; asst. prof. Beaver Coll., Glenside, Pa., 1980; instr. Phila. Coll. Textiles and Sci., 1979-82; vis. asst. prof. Temple U., 1982-85; asst. prof. U. Hartford, West Hartford, Conn., 1985-89, assoc. prof. physics, 1989-94, prof. physics, 1994—. Lectr. in field, on symmetry in art and sci., Albert Einstein, symbolic computations, ontological interpretation of quantum physics as applied to brain processes. Contbr. articles to profl. jours. Fellow, U. Hartford Humanities Ctr.; grantee, 1989—90, NASA Jet Propulsion Lab. Caltech, 2006; vis. fellow, Yale U., 1988—89. Mem. Am. Phys. Soc. (sec./treas. New Eng. sect. 1994-2000, chair 2004), Am. Assn. Physics Tchrs. (mem. com. on women in physics 1989-92), Internat. Symmetry Assn. (chmn. exec. bd. 2003—), Conn. Acad. Arts and Scis., Sigma Xi. (pres. U. Hartford chpt, 1988—), Pi Mu Epsilon. Office: U Hartford Physics Dept West Hartford CT 06117 Office Phone: 860-768-4307. Business E-Mail: lgould@hartford.edu.

GOULD, MARTHA BERNICE, retired librarian; b. Claremont, NH, Oct. 8, 1931; d. Sigmund and Gertrude Heller; m. Arthur Gould, July 29, 1960; children: Leslie, Stephen. BA in Edn., U. Mich., Ann Arbor, 1953; MS in Libr. Sci., Simmons Coll., Boston, 1956; cert., U. Denver Libr. Sch., 1978. Childrens libr. NY Pub. Libr., 1956-58; adminstr. libr. svcs. act demonstration regional libr. project Pawhuska, Okla., 1958-59; cons. N.Mex. State Libr., 1959-60; children's libr. then sr. children's libr. LA Pub. Libr., 1960-72; acctg. dir. pub. svcs., reference libr. Nev. State Libr., 1972-74; pub. svcs. libr. Washoe County Libr., Nev., 1974-79, asst. county libr. Nev., 1979-84, county libr. Nev., 1984-94; ret., 1994. Cons. Nev. State Libr. and Archives, 1996—2003; part-time lectr. libr. adminstrn. U. Nev.; acting dir. Nev. Ctr. for the Book; vice-chair Nat. Commn. in Librs. and Info. Sci., 1993—2000, chair, 2000—03; mem. adv. coun. Nev. Coun. on Librs. and Literacy, 2001—05; mem. adv. bd. Fleischmann Planetarium, 1999—2003. Co-editor: Nevada Women's History Project Annotated Bibliography, 1999; contbr. articles to jours. Exec. dir. Kids Voting/USA, Nev., 1996; treas. United Jewish Appeal, 1981; bd. dirs. Temple Sinai, Planned Parenthood, 1996-97, Truckee Meadows Habitat for Humanity, 1995-98; trustee RSVP, North Nevadans for ERA; No. Nev. chmn. Gov.'s Conf. on Libr., 1990; bd. dir. Campaign for Choice, No. Nev. Food Bank, Nev. Women's Fund (Hall of Fame award 1989); mem. No. Nev. NCCJ, Washoe County Quality Life Task Force, 1992—, Washoe County Elections Taskforce, 1999—; bd. dirs. KUNR Pub. Radio, 1999-00, chair bd. dirs., 2000-04; chair Sierra Nevada Cmty. Access TV; adv. bd. Partnership Librs. Washoe County; co-chair social studies curriculum adv. task force Washoe County Sch. Dist.; mem. Nev. Women's History Project Bd. 1997-99; chair Downtown River Corridor Com., 1995-97; vice chair Dem. Party Washoe County, 1998-00; v.p. Nev. Diabetes Assn. for Children and Adults, 1998-02, pres., 2002-04, mem. adv. bd., 2004-06, sec., 2007—; chair devel. com. Planned Parenthood, 2002-; bd. dir. Washoe Libr. Found., 2003-05; mem. adv. Adv. Coun. on Edn./to the Holocaust, 2000-; chair Washoe County Dem. Women's Club, 2003-05; coord. Diabetes Edn. Prevention Program, Nev., 2005—; chair 2nd Century Endowment for Friends of Washoe County Libr., 2005—; mem. bd. Reno chpt. AAUW, 2006-, Nev. Women's History Project, 2007-. Recipient Nev. State Libr. Letter of Commendation, 1973, Washoe County Bd. Commrs. Resolution of Appreciation, 1978, ACLU of Nev. Civil Libertarian of Yr. 1988, Freedom's Sake award AAUW, 1989, Leadership in Literacy award Sierra chpt. Internat. Reading Assn., 1992, Woman of Distinction award 1992, Cornerstone award Sierra chpt. Assn. Fundraising Profls., 2003, Women Helping Women award Soroptimist Internat., 2005, Alumni Achievement award Simmmons Coll. Grad. Sch. Libr. and Info. Sci., 2006. Mem. ALA (bd. dirs., intellectual freedom roundtable 1977-79, intellectual freedom com. 1979-83, coun. 1983-86), ACLU (bd. dir. Civil Libertarian of Yr. Nev. chpt. 1988, chair gov.'s conf. for women 1989), Nev. Libr. Assn. (chmn. pub. info. com. 1972-73, intellectual freedom com. 1975-78, govt. rels. com. 1978-79, v.p., pres.-elect 1980, pres. 1981, Spl. Citation 1978, 87, Libr. of Yr. 1993). E-mail: mgould@unr.edu.

GOULD, PHILLIP, engineer; b. NYC, Feb. 19, 1940; s. Isaac and Blanche Gould; m. Elizabeth West Ratigan, Nov. 29, 1980; children: David Elliot, Jessica Ann. BSME, CCNY, 1961; MS, MIT, 1963, ScD, 1965. Asst. prof. mech. engring. MIT, Cambridge, 1965-67; mem. staff Inst. for Def. Analyses, Alexandria, Va., asst. dir., 1984—. Dir. Def. Sci. Study Group, 1998—. Fellow, Ford Found., 1965. Fellow: AAAS; mem.: N.Y. Acad. Scis., Internat. Fedn. Secular Humanistic Jews (v.p.), Soc. for Humanistic Judaism (past pres.), Washington Congregation for Secular Humanistic Judaism (past pres.), Sigma Xi. Home: 4590 Indian Rock Ter NW Washington DC 20007-2567 Office: Inst Def Analyses 4850 Mark Ctr Dr Alexandria VA 22311-1882 E-mail: pgould@alum.mit.edu.

GOULD, PHILLIP LOUIS, engineering educator; b. Chgo., May 24, 1937; m. Deborah Paula Rothholtz, Feb. 5, 1961; children: Elizabeth, Nathan, Rebecca, Joshua. BS, U. Ill., 1959, MS, 1960; PhD, Northwestern U., 1966. Structural designer Skidmore, Owings & Merrill, Chgo., 1960-63; prin. structural engr. Westenhoff & Novick, Chgo., 1963-64; NASA trainee Northwestern U., Evanston, Ill., 1964-66; asst. prof. civil engring. Washington U., St. Louis, 1966-68, assoc. prof., 1968-74, prof., 1974—, chmn. dept. civil engring., 1978-98, Harold D. Jolly prof. civil engring., 1981—. Vis. prof. Ruhr U., Fed. Republic Germany, 1974-75, U. Sydney, Australia, 1981, Shanghai Inst. Tech., Peoples Republic of China, 1986; dir. Earthquake Engring. Rsch. Inst., exec. coun. Internat. Assn. for Shell and Spatial Structures, pres. Great Lakes chpt. and New Madrid chpt. Earthquake Engring. Rsch. Inst. Author: Static Analysis of Shells: A Unified Development of Surface Structures, 1977, Introduction to Linear Elasticity, 1984, Finite Element Analysis of Shells of Revolution, 1985, Analysis of Shells and Plates, 1987, 2d edit., 1999; co-author: Dynamic Response of Structures to Wind and Earthquake Loading, 1980; co-editor: Environmental Forces on Engineering Structures, 1979, Natural Draught Cooling Towers, 1985; editor: Engineering Structures, 1979—. Dir. Earthquake Engring. Rsch. Inst., 1993—95; vice chmn. Mo. Seismic Safety Commn., 1998—99, chmn., 2000—01; St. Louis regional dir. Mid-Am. Earthquake Ctr. Recipient Sr. Scientist award Alexander von Humboldt Found., Fed. Republic Germany, 1974-75 Fellow ASCE (bd. dirs. St. Louis sect. 1985-87, Otto Nutli award, Profl. Recognition award); mem. Am. Soc. Engring. Edn., Internat. Assn. Shell Structures, Structural Engrs. Assn. Ill. (Outstanding Engr. in Edn. award), Civil Engring. Alumni Assn. U. Ill., Urbana-Champaign (Disting. Alumnus award). Office: Washington U 1130 Dept Civil Engring 1 Brookings Drive Saint Louis MO 63130-1130 Home Phone: 314-647-0388. Business E-Mail: pgoul@seas.wustl.edu.

GOULD, RONALD MURRAY, federal judge; b. St. Louis, Oct. 17, 1946; s. Harry H. and Sylvia C. (Sadofsky) Gould; m. Suzanne H. Goldblatt, Dec. 1, 1968; children: Daniel, Rebecca. BS in Econs., U. Pa., 1968; JD, U. Mich., 1973. Bar: Wash. 1975, US Dist. Ct. (we. dist.) Wash. 1976, US Ct. Appeals (9th cir.) 1980, US Supreme Ct. 1981, US Dist. Ct. (ea. dist.) Wash. 1982, US Ct. Appeals (fed. cir.) 1986. Law clk. to hon. Wade H. McCree Jr. US Ct. Appeals (6th cir.), Detroit, 1973—74; law clk. to hon. justice Potter Stewart US Supreme Ct., Washington, 1974—75; assoc. Perkins Coie, Seattle, 1975—80, ptnr., 1981—99; judge US Ct. Appeals (9th cir.), Seattle, 1999—. Adj. prof. U. Washington Law Sch., 1986—89. Editor-in-chief: Mich. Law Rev., 1972—73; editor: Washington Civil Procedure Deskbook, 1981. Exec. bd. chief Seattle coun. Boy Scouts Am., 1984—; bd. dirs. econ. devel. coun. Seattle and King County, 1991—94;

citizens cabinet mem. Gov. Mike Lowry, Seattle, 1993—96; bd. trustees Bellevue CC, 1993—99; mem. cmty. rels. coun. Jewish Fedn. of Greater Seattle, 1985—88. Fellow: ABA (antitrust sect., litig. sect.); mem.: Am. Judicature Soc., King County Bar Assn. (Disting. Svc. award 1987), Wash. State Bar Assn. (bd. govs. 1988—91, pres. 1994—95), 9th Jud. Cir. Hist. Soc. (bd. dirs. 1994—), Supreme Ct. Hist. Soc. Jewish. Avocations: reading, chess. Office: US Courthouse 1200 6th Ave Fl 21 Seattle WA 98101-3123*

GOULD, ROY WALTER, engineering educator; b. LA, Apr. 25, 1927; s. Roy Walter Gould and Rosamonde Belle (Stokes) Termain; m. Ethel Stratton, Aug. 23, 1952; children: Diana Stratton, Robert Clarke. BS, Calif. Inst. Tech., 1949, PhD, 1956; MS, Stanford U., 1950. With Calif. Inst. Tech., Pasadena, 1955—, exec. officer for applied physics, 1972-79, chmn. div. engring. and applied sci., 1979-84, Simon Ramo prof. engring., 1979-96, prof. emeritus, 1996—. Dir. div. controlled thermonuclear research U.S. Energy Research Devel. Agy., Washington, 1970-72. Contbr. articles to profl. jours. Served with USN, 1945-46. Fellow IEEE, Am. Phys. Soc. (James Clerk Maxwell prize in plasma physics 1994); mem. NAS, Am. Acad. Arts and Scis., Nat. Acad. Engring. Office: Calif Inst Tech Dept Engring Applied Sci Ms 128 95 Pasadena CA 91125-0001 Business E-Mail: rwgould@caltech.edu.

GOULD, TAFFY, Internet company executive, real estate executive; b. Miami, Fla., Apr. 14, 1942; d. Emil J. and Estelle F. Gould; m. Bernard Arthur Beber, Apr. 5, 1964 (div. Jan. 1975); children: Karen B. Futernick, J. Gregory Beber. BA, Smith Coll., Northampton, Mass., 1963. Cert. real estate broker, Fla. Pres. Housing Engrs. Fla., Inc., Miami, 1977—; chmn. e-Med. Edn., LLC, Fla., 1999—; chmn. coun. Oceania U. Medicine, Samoa; vice chmn. Non-Invasive Monitoring Sys., Inc. Lectr. Potomac Spkrs. Bur., Washington, 1993-98. Author: South Africa: Land of Hope, 1989, White Woman Witchdoctor, 1993 (Best Seller 1994); co-author: Create Your Own Future, 1996; newspaper columnist Miami Today, 1983-88, Miami Today, Miami Herald; radio talk host WINZ, Miami, 1986-88. Mem. nat. com. Zionist Orgn. Am., N.Y., 1995—; bd. dirs. Alexander Muss H.S. in Israel, Miami, 1995—, Cen. Agy. for Jewish Edn.; dir. U. Miami, Miami Hot Glass, Coral Gables, Fla., 1998—; governing coun. Fla. Philharmonic Orch., 1998—; mem. exec. com. Miami Mus. Sci., 2003. Recipient Humanitarian and Arts award Internat. Bolivarian Soc., Miami, 1994, City of the Future award City of Ariel, Israel, 1999, Louis Brandeis award Zionist Orgn. Am., NY, 2000. Mem.: Tribal Arts Soc. (pres.). Avocations: classical music, reading. Home: 10 Edgewater Dr Apt 14F Coral Gables FL 33133-6968 Office Phone: 305-670-8500. Home Fax: 305-668-3298. Personal E-mail: taffyg@bellsouth.net. E-mail: taffygould@taffygould.com.

GOULD, W. SCOTT, financial administrator; b. Boston, July 19, 1957; m. Michèle A. Flournoy; 1 child, Alexander. AB, Cornell U., 1979; MBA, EdD, U. Rochester. Commd. ensign USN, advanced through grades; mgmt. cons. TB&A, 1988-90, mng. assoc., 1990-91; asst. receiver, dir. ops. City of Chelsea, Mass., 1991-93; spl. asst. to chmn. Export-Import Bank of U.S., Washington, 1993-94; spl. asst. White House Chief of Staff, Washington, 1993-94; dep. asst. sec. Dept. Treasury, Washington; CFO, asst. sec. adminstrn. Dept. Commerce, Washington, until 1999; CFO, Exoice Inc., Washington, 1999—. Mem. adv. bd. Simon Sch. Bus.; class agt. Roxbury Latin Sch. Ann. Fund; mentor Cornell U. Extern Program. Comdr. USNR. Mem. Inst. Mgmt. Consultants (assoc.), Kappa Delta Pi. Office: 6725 Honesty Dr Bethesda MD 20817-5516

GOULD, WAYNE, application developer, retired judge; b. New Zealand, 1945; m. Gaye Gould; children: Sally, Scott. Lawyer, Matamata, New Zealand, 1969—82; judge Hong Kong, 1982—93; chief dist. ct. judge, 1993—97. Editor: Su Doku: The Utterly Addictive Number-placing Puzzle, 2005. Named one of 100 Most Influential People, Time Mag., 2006. Achievements include development of Pappocom Sudoku computer program leading to popularization of game worldwide. Home: New Zealand also: United States

GOULD, WILLIAM BENJAMIN, IV, lawyer, federal agency administrator, educator; b. 1936; AB, U. R.I., 1958; LLB, Cornell U., 1961; postgrad., London Sch. Econs., 1962—63; LLD (hon.), U. R.I., 1986, D.C. Sch. Law, 1995, Stetson U., 1996; LLD, Capital U., 1997, Rutgers U., 1998. Bar: Mich. 1962. Asst. gen. counsel UAW, AFL-CIO, Detroit, 1961—62; atty. NLRB, Washington, 1963—65; assoc. Battle, Fowler, Stokes & Kheel, NYC, 1965—68; prof. Wayne State U., Detroit, 1968—71, Stanford U. Law Sch., 1972—, Charles A. Beardsley prof. law, 1984—2002, emeritus, 2002—; William M. Ramsey Disting. Prof. Law Willamette Coll. Law, 2002—04. Chmn. Nat. Labor Rels. Bd., Washington, 1994—98, Coun. Adminstrv. Conf. U.S., Washington, 1994—95; vis. prof. Harvard U., 1971—72; overseas fellow and vis. prof. Churchill Coll., Cambridge, England, 1975; vis. scholar U. Tokyo, 1975, 78; Fulbright-Hays Disting. lectr. Kyoto Am. Studies Summer Seminar; Charles A. Beardsley prof. Stanford Law Sch., 1984; vis. fellow Australian Nat. U. Faculty of Law, 1985; vis. prof. European U. Inst., Florence, Italy, 1988, U. Witwatersrand, Johannesburg, 1991; lectr. Am. and fgn. indsl. rels., labor law U.S., Europe, Japan, S.E. Asia, Africa, Eastern Europe. Author: Diary of a Contraband: The Civil War Passage of a Black Sailor, Labored Relations: Law, Politics and the NLRB- A Memoir, 2000, International Labor Standards: Globalization, trade and Public Policy, 2003, A Primer on American Labor Law, 2004. Fellow, Rockefeller Found., 1975, Guggenheim, 1978. Mem.: ABA (sec. labor and employment law sect.), Internat. Soc. for Labor Law and Social Security (exec. com. U.S. nat. br.), Nat. Acad. Arbitrators. Office: Stanford Law School Crown Quadrangle 559 Nathan Abbot Way Stanford CA 94305-8610

GOULDEN, DAVID, information technology executive; BS in Physics, Durham U., Eng.; exec. MBA, Cranfield Sch. Mgmt., Eng. Various internat. sales and mktg. positions Unisys; with Wang Global, 1990—99, sr. v.p. mktg. and corp. devel., 1997—99, pres. US ops., 1999; mem. bd. mgmt., pres., COO Getronics, 1999—2002; with EMC Corp., Hopkinton, Mass., 2002—, head mktg. and new bus. devel., head worldwide customer ops., exec. v.p., CFO. Office: EMC Corp 176 South St Hopkinton MA 01748 Office Phone: 508-435-1000.*

GOULDEN, JOSEPH CHESLEY, author; b. Marshall, Tex., May 23, 1934; s. Joe C. and Lecta M. (Everitt) G.; m. Leslie Cantrell Smith, 1979; children by previous marriage: Joseph C., Jim Craig. Student, U. Tex., 1952-56. Reporter Marshall News Messenger, 1956, Dallas News, 1958-61, Phila. Inquirer, 1961-68. Dir. media analysis Accuracy in Media, 1989-98. Author: The Curtis Caper, 1965, Monopoly, 1968, Truth Is the First Casualty, 1969, The Money Givers, 1971, Meany, 1972, The Superlawyers, 1972, The Benchwarmers, 1974, The Best Years, 1976, The Million Dollar Lawyers, 1978, Korea: The Untold Story of the War, 1982, Jerry Wurf: Labor's Last Angry Man, 1982, The Death Merchant, 1984, (as Henry S.A. Becket) The Dictionary of Espionage, 1986, Fit to Print: A.M. Rosenthal and His Times, 1988, (with Paul Dickson) There Are Alligators in Our Sewers, 1983, (with Paul Dickson) Myth-Informed, 1993, (with Reed Irvine and Cliff Kincaid) The News Manipulators, 1993, The Money Lawyers, 2006; editor: books include Mencken's Last Campaign, 1976. Served with U.S. Army, 1956-58. Mem.: Internat. Studies Program, Va. Mil. Inst. (bd.), Assn. For Intelligence Officers, Washington Ind. Writers, Tex. Inst. Letters, H.L. Mencken Soc., Cosmos Club, Phi Kappa Tau. Home: 1534 29th St NW Washington DC 20007-3060 Office: Brandt & Hochman 1501 Broadway New York NY 10036-5601 Address: # 206 The Henlopen Rehoboth Beach DE 19971 E-mail: josephg894@aol.com.

GOULDER, GERALD POLSTER, retail executive, management consultant, lawyer; b. Columbus, Ohio, Apr. 30, 1953; s. Norman Ernest and Betty (Polster) G.; children: Gavrielle, Nathaniel. BA, Ohio State U., 1975; JD, Washington U., 1978. Bar: Ohio 1978, N.C. 1985; cert. mediator N.C. Superior Ct., N.C. Indsl. Commn. Spl. prosecutor office state atty. gen. Divsn. Medicaid Fraud Control, Columbus, 1979-80; spl. prosecutor Antitrust Divsn., Columbus, 1981-82; atty. James M. Schottenstein & Assocs., Columbus, 1982-84; chmn., CEO Carolina Drug Distbrs., Inc. and Emporium Stores, Ltd., Greensboro, NC, 1984-96. Mediator Mediation Practice N.C., Bus. Mediation Svc., 2001-03; prin. Equine Dispute Resolution Svc., N.C. Bus. Mediation Coun. Assoc. editor Washington U. Urban Law Ann., 1977-78; contbr. articles to profl. jours. Trustee Wexner Heritage Village, Columbus, 1983-84, bd. dirs. Eastern Music Festival, Greensboro, 1991-94, U. N.C.-Greensboro Spartan Club, 1991-95; v.p. Beth David Synagogue, Greensboro, 1992-95, pres., 1996; participant Leadership Greensboro, 1985, Triad Leadership, 1991; mem. Crime Study Commn., Greensboro, 1992, Greensboro Devel. Corp., 1993-95. Fellow, Inst. of Polit. Leadership, 2004. Mem. Am. Arbitration Assn., Am. Intellectual Property Lawyers Assn., N.C. Bar Assn., Greensboro Bar Assn., Columbus Bar Assn., Ohio Bar Assn., Leadership Greensboro Alumni Assn., Am. Immigration Lawyers Assn. Office: Goulder Immigration Law Firm 3200 Northline Ave Ste 130 Greensboro NC 27408 Home: 12 Wedgewood Ct Greensboro NC 27403-1074 E-mail: ggoulder@triad.rr.com.

GOULDEY, GLENN CHARLES, manufacturing executive; b. NYC, July 28, 1952; s. George Howard and Jeannette Ruth Williamson; m. Leslie Jeanne Ruth, Oct. 2, 1982; children: Jeremy Charles, Nicholas Glenn, Alexander James George. BS in Bus., Coll. N.J., 1976; postgrad., Portland State U., 1980; MBA, Rider U., 1981; postgrad., Dartmouth Coll., 1994—95. Cert. in purchasing mgmt., cert. in prodn. and inventory control. Sr. planner Eaton Corp., Flemington, NJ, 1975-77, pricing mgr., distbn., 1977-79, inventory control mgr., 1979-80, materials mgr., purchasing Beaverton, Oreg., 1980-81, mfg. and materials mgr., 1981-83, mktg. and materials mgr., 1983-87, plant and gen. mgr., 1987-88, v.p. sales and mktg. Carol Stream, Ill., 1988-89, mgr. ops. divsn., 1989-93, gen. bus. mgr., 1993-95, pres., gen. mgr. Lectron Products divsn. Rochester Hills, Mich., 1995-99, v.p., gen. mgr. Actuator Sensor Divsn., 2000—01; v.p. technology, planning strategy IT Eaton Automotive Group Worldwide, Southfield, Mich., 2001—. Patentee in field. Mem. bd. advisors Oakland U. Bus. Sch., Mich. Colls. Found., Albion Coll.-Gerstacker Inst.; bd. dirs., chair Rochester Cmty. Schs. Found.; asst. coach lacrosse Rochester Hills United HS; bd. dirs. Keatering U. Engring. Sch. Mem. SAR, Am. Prodn. Inventory Control Soc., Nat. Youth Sports Coaches Assn. (cert.), Soc. Automotive Engrs. Internat. Republican. Lutheran. Office: Eaton Corp 26201 Northwestern Hwy Southfield MI 48076-3926 Office Phone: 248-226-6776. E-mail: GlennGouldey@eaton.com.

GOULDIN, DAVID MILLEN, lawyer; b. Binghamton, NY, Mar. 8, 1941; s. Paul C. and Virginia M. Gouldin; m. Deborah A. Gouldin, Aug. 20, 1966; children: Robert, Michael, Lauryn, Derek. AB, Princeton U., 1963; JD, Cornell U., 1966. Bar: N.Y., U.S. Dist. Ct. N.Y. Ptnr. Levene, Gouldin & Thompson, LLP, Binghamton, 1966—. Mem. N.Y. State Bd. Law Examiners, 1999—. Author: (with others) Commercial Litigation in New York Courts, 1995. Chmn. Broome County (N.Y.) Arena, 1981; chmn. Broome County Health Fair, 1986-87; gen. chmn. ministry endowment campaign Broome County Coun. Chs., 1986-87; pres. United Way Broome County, 1982-84; mem. United Way N.Y. State, 1985-99, chmn., 1991-92; chancellor Wyo. conf. United Meth. Ch., 1987—; bd. dirs. Roberson Ctr. for Arts, 1983-89, United Health Svcs. Hosps., 1990-2002; bd. dirs. Broome County Urban League, 1994-2000, sec., 1995-2000; trustee Wyo. Sem., 1973-88, Miller S. Gaffney and Adelaide S. Gaffney Found., 1996—; trustee Edwin A. Link and Marion C. Link Found., 1989—, chmn., 1993—, dir. Binghamton U. Found., 2003-, chair, Harpur Forum, 2003-. Recipient Sertoma Svc. to Mankind Dist. award, 1988, Disting. Citizens award Baden-Powell coun. Boy Scouts Am., 1996, Disting. Svc. award Binghamton U., 2004; named to Sect. Four Hall of Fame, 1978, Outstanding Young Men of Am., 1974, Sect. IV Hall of Fame, 1978; named Man of Yr. Post 80 Am. Legion Hall of Fame, 1989. Mem. N.Y. State Bar Assn. (chmn. TICL sect. 1992, Root-Stimson award 1987, John Leach award 1999), Broome County Bar Assn. (pres. 1989), Fedn. Bar 6th Dist. (pres. 1974), Rotary. Republican. Home: 85 Highland Ave Binghamton NY 13905-4039 Office: PO Box F1706 Binghamton NY 13902-0106 Office Phone: 607-584-5706. E-mail: dgouldin@binghamtonlaw.com.

GOULDING, NORA See CLARK, SUSAN

GOULDING, PHILIP L., energy executive; BS, Duke U.; MS, U. Houston. Various sr. level positions Shell Oil Co., 1983—99; v.p., ptnr. L.E.K. Consulting, 1999—2003; v.p. strategic planning, chief comml. officer Allegheny Energy, Inc., Greensburg, Pa., 2003—06, v.p., CFO, 2006—. Office: Allegheny Energy Inc 800 Cabin Hill Dr Greensburg PA 15601 Office Phone: 724-837-3000. Office Fax: 724-838-6764. E-mail: pgouldi@alleghenyenergy.com.

GOULDTHORPE, KENNETH ALFRED PERCIVAL, state official, editor; b. Jan. 7, 1928; came to U.S., 1951, naturalized, 1956; s. Alfred Edward and Frances Elizabeth Finch (Callow) G.; m. Judith Marion Cutts, Aug. 9, 1975; children: Amanda Frances, Timothy Graham Cutts. Student, U. Westminster, 1948-49; diploma, City and Guilds of London, 1949; student, Washington U., 1951—52. Staff photographer Kentish Mercury, London, 1949-50, St. Louis Post-Dispatch, 1951-55, picture editor, 1955-57; nat. and fgn. corr. Life mag., Time, Inc., NYC, 1957-61, Paris Bur., 1961-65, regional editor Australia-New Zealand, 1966-68, editl. dir. Latin Am., 1969-70; editor Signature mag., NYC, 1970-73; mng. editor Penthouse mag., NYC, 1973-76, pub. cons., 1976-79; editor, exec. pub. Adventure Travel mag., Seattle, 1979-80; sr. ptnr. Pacific Pub. Assocs., Seattle, 1979-80; editor, pub. Washington mag., 1984-89; vice-chmn. Evergreen Pub Co., 1984-89; dir. tourism State of Wash., 1989-91. Pub., cons., writer, 1991—; bd. dirs. Grand Fir Pub. Corp., Pacific Pub. Assocs., Seattle; tchr. design, editl. techniques Parsons Sch. Design, N.Y.C.; lectr., contbr. elem. schs. lit. progs. Author: Design for Music, 1998, Seafood Secrets of the Pacific Northwest, 2002; contbr. articles, photographs to nat. mags., books by Life mag. With Royal Navy League Cadet Corps., 1943-45, Sea Service, 1946-48. Decorated Naval Medal and bar; recipient awards of excellence Nat. Press Photographers Assn., AP and UP, 1951-57, Pres.'s medal Ea. Wash. U., 1986; certs. excellence Am. Inst. Graphic Arts, 1971, 72, 73, Comm. Arts, 1980, 81, 84; Spl. award N.Y. Soc. Publs. Designers, 1980; nominated for Pulitzer Prize for coverage of Andrea Doria disaster, 1956. Mem. Regional Pubs. Assn. (v.p., pres., Best Typography award 1985, Best Spl. Issue 1989), Western Publs. Assn. (Best Consumer Mag. award, Best Travel Mag. awards 1980, Best Regional and State Mag. award 1985-86, 88, Best New Publ. award 1985, Best Column award 1985, Best Signed Essay 1986-87, Best Four-Color Layout 1985, Best Four Color Feature Design), City and Regional Mag. Assn. (William Allen White Bronze awards), Time/Life Alumni Soc., Assn. Washington Gens. (gen. of state 1995, bd. dirs.), Medieval Knights of London, Sigma Delta Chi. Episcopalian. Home and Office: 3049 NW Esplanade Seattle WA 98117-2624 Office Phone: 206-782-6658. Personal E-mail: kengouldthorpe@comcast.net.

GOULET, CHARLES RYAN, retired insurance company executive; b. Fond du Lac, Wis., Oct. 13, 1927; s. Charles N. and Irene (Ryan) G.; m. Jeanne Comfort, Aug. 18, 1951; 1 child, Christopher Robert. BA, Beloit Coll., Wis., 1951; MBA, U. Chgo., 1953. Adminstrv. resident Jefferson-Hillman Hosp., Birmingham, Ala., 1952-53; adminstrv. asst., asst. supt. Cleve. City Hosp., 1953-55; asst. prof. U. Pitts., 1955-58; asso. dir. Johns Hopkins Hosp., 1958-62; dir. U. Chgo. Hosps. and Clinics, 1962-69; prof. hosp. adminstrn. U. Chgo., 1962-69, assoc. dir. program in hosp. adminstrn., 1962-69; prin. Cresap, McCormick and Paget, Inc.; mgmt. cons., Chgo., 1969-71; v.p. Blue Cross-Blue Shield, Chgo., 1971-75, exec. v.p., 1975-88; vice chmn., dir. H.M.O. Ill. Inc., 1980-88; exec. sec. Assn. U. Programs in Hosp. Adminstrn., 1962-65, pres. Chgo. Hosp. Council, 1968; pres. HMO Ill., Inc., 1976-82. Treas. Ill. Hosp. Assn., 1969; mem. exec. com. Council Teaching Hosps., Assn. Am. Med. Colls., 1966-69 Mem. adv. coun. Kellogg Found., 1965-67; bd. dirs. Hyde Park Dept. YMCA, 1966-68, Coop. Blood Replacement Plan, Home for destitute Crippled Children, 1965-69, Chgo. Home for Incurables, 1966-69, Harvard-St. George Sch. Chgo., 1968-72, Hosp. Planning Coun. Met. Chgo., 1968-69, Comprehensive Health Planning, Chgo., 1968-71, Ill. Regional Med. Program, 1967-69, Am. Blood Commn., 1976-89, v.p., 1978-83, Geneva Cmty. Chest, Ill., 1990, 93-96, pres., 1975-76; mem. governing commn. Cook County Hosp., 1969-70; mem. Ill. Health Fin. Authority, 1979-82, Ill. Health Care Cost Containment Com., 1984-96; trustee Alexian Bros. Med. Ctr., Elk Grove Village, Ill., 1993-94; bd. govs. Alexian Bros. Health Sys., 1995—; dir. Alexian Bros. Health Providers, 1996—. 1st lt. Med. Adminstrn. Corps AUS, 1946-47. Recipient Bachmeyer award U. Chgo., 1953; Disting. Service award Beloit Coll., 1976 Fellow Am. Coll. Hosp. Adminstrs.; mem. Am. Hosp. Assn., Skyline Club (Chgo.), Big Foot Country Club (Fontana, Wis.), Quadrangle Club (Chgo.), Oasis Country Club (Palm Desert, Calif.), Marrakesh Country Club (Palm Desert), Phi Kappa Phi.

GOULET, DENIS ANDRÉ, development ethicist; b. Fall River, Mass., May 27, 1931; s. Fernand Joseph and Lumena (Bouchard) G.; m. Ana Maria Reynaldo, Nov. 21, 1964; children: Andrea, Sinane. BA in Philosophy, St. Paul's Coll., Washington, 1954, MA in Philosophy, 1956; MA in Social Planning, Institut de Recherche et de Formation en Vue du Développement, Paris, 1960; PhD in Polit. Sci., U. São Paulo, Brazil, 1963. Laborer, France, Spain, Algeria, 1956-59; planning advisor AID, Recife, Brazil, 1964-65; vis. prof. U. Sask., Regina, Canada, 1965-66; assoc. prof. Ind. U., Bloomington, 1966-68; vis. fellow Ctr. for Study of Dem. Instns., Santa Barbara, Calif., 1969; vis. prof. U. Calif., San Diego, 1969-70; sr. fellow Ctr. for Study Devel. and Social Change, Cambridge, Mass., 1970-74; vis. fellow Overseas Devel. Coun./OAS, Washington, 1974-76; sr. fellow Overseas Devel. Coun., Washington, 1976-79; O'Neill chair in edn. for justice, dept. econs. U. Notre Dame, Ind., 1979—2002, O'Neill chair emeritus Ind., 2002—; faculty fellow Kellogg Inst. for Internat. Study, Kroc Inst. for Internat. Peace Studies. Vis. prof. U. Warsaw, Poland, 1989-90. Author: The Cruel Choice, 1971, The Uncertain Promise, 1977, Mexico: Development Strategies for the Future, 1983, Incentives for Development: The Key to Equity, 1989, Development Ethics: A Guide to Theory and Practice, 1995. Editl. bd. Jour. of Health and Population in Developing Countries; internat. adv. coun. TODA Inst. for Global Peace and Policy Rsch.; internat. adv. bd. Internat. Centre for Islamic Political Economy. Decorated chevalier Odre Nat. du Cèdre (Lebanon), 1960; OAS grantee, 1961-62, Fulbright grantee, 1986; recipient Reinhold Niebuhr award U. Notre Dame, 1988. Democrat. Roman Catholic. Avocation: piano. Home: 825 Ashland Ave South Bend IN 46616-1307 Office: U Notre Dame 519 Flanner Hall Notre Dame IN 46556-5677 Business E-Mail: dgoulet@nd.edu.

GOULET, LORRIE, sculptor; b. Riverdale, NY, Aug. 17, 1925; Student, Inwood Potteries Studios, NYC, 1932-36, Black Mountain Coll., NC, 1943-44. Tchr. Mus. Modern Art, 1957, 64, Scarsdale Studio Workshop, 1959, 61, New Sch., 1961—75, Art Students League, 1981—2006. One-woman shows include Clay Club Sculpture Ctr., N.Y.C., 1948, 1955, Cheney Libr., Hoosick Falls, N.Y., 1951, Contemporaries Gallery, N.Y.C., 1959, 1962, 1966, 1968, Rye (N.Y.) Art Ctr., 1966, New Sch. Assocs., N.Y.C., 1968, Temple Emeth, Teaneck, N.J., 1969, Kennedy Galleries, N.Y.C., 1971, 1973, 1975, 1978, 1980, 1982, 1986, Carolyn Hill Gallery, 1988, 1991, Caldwell (N.J.) Coll., 1989, Nat. Mus. Women in the Arts, Washington, 1998, Harmon-Meek Galleries, Naples, Fla., 2000, David Findlay Jr. Gallery, 2001, 2002, 2004, 2005, 2007, exhibited in group shows at Mus. Natural History, 1936, Whitney Mus. Am. Art, N.Y.C., 1948—50, 1953, 1955, Met. Mus. Art, 1951, Detroit Inst. Art, 1960, Pa. Acad., 1950—52, 1954, 1959, 1964, AD, N.Y.C., 1966, 1975, 1977, Corcoran Gallery, Washington, 1966, Hofstra Mus., N.Y.C., 1990, The McNey Mus., 1990, The Copley Soc., Boston, 1991, The Spanish Inst., 1992, Lehigh U. Art Gallery, 1992, Iowa State U. Brunne Gallery, 1992, Paine Art Ctr., Oshkosh, Wis., 1992, Mitchell Art Gallery, St. John's Coll., Annapolis, Md., 1992, Erie (Pa.) Art Mus., 1995, Nat. Sculpture Soc., 2001, Art Students League, N.Y.C., 2003, David Findlay Jr. Gallery, 2005, Reina Sophia Mus., Madrid, 2003, D. Findlay Jr. Gallery, 2007, others, Represented in permanent collections Hunter Mus., Chattanooga, N.J. State Mus., Wichita Mus. Art, Hirschhorn Sculpture Mus., Washington, The Philharm. Ctr., Naples, Fla., Art Students League, N.Y.C., Savannah Coll. Arts. Recipient Malvina Hoffman award Nat. Acad. Design, 2001, others; grantee Fhorsheim Art Fund, 1997. Mem.: NAD (academician 1989, mem. coun. 1994), Fine Arts Fedn. (pres. 1998—2002, hon. v.p. 2003), N.Y. Artists Equity Inc. (pres. 1998—2002), Visual Artists and Galleries Assocs.

GOULIANOS, KONSTANTIN, physicist, educator; b. Thessaloniki, Greece, Nov. 9, 1935; came to U.S., 1958, naturalized, 1967; s. Achilles and Olga G. Student, Aristotelian U. Thessaloniki, 1953—58; PhD, Columbia U., 1963. Research assoc. Columbia U., NYC, 1963-64; instr. physics Princeton U., NJ, 1964-67, asst. prof. NJ, 1967-71; assoc. prof. physics Rockefeller U., NYC, 1971-81, prof., 1981—. Patentee electronic device of analysis of radioactivitively labeled gel electrophoretograms Fulbright scholar, 1958-59 Fellow: Am. Phys. Soc. Home: 11 W 69th St Apt 4A New York NY 10023-4700 Office: Rockefeller U Lab Expt High-Energy Physics 1230 York Ave New York NY 10065-6399 E-mail: dino@rockefeller.edu.

GOUNLEY, DENNIS JOSEPH, lawyer; b. Jan. 29, 1950; s. George Gerard and Elizabeth Mary (Maggioncalda) G.; m. Martha Ann Zatezalo, Sept. 25, 1976. BA, St. Joseph's Coll., Phila., 1971; JD, Dickinson Sch. Law, 1974. Bar: Pa. 1974, U.S. Dist. Ct. (we. dist.) Pa. 1995, U.S. Ct. Appeals (3d cir.) 1976, U.S. Supreme Ct. 1977. Pvt. practice, Greensburg, Pa., 1974-83, 90—; ptnr. Gounley & O'Halloran, Greensburg, 1984-90. Westmoreland County mental health rev. officer, 1991—. Coun. mem. Franklin Towne Condominium Assn., Murrysville, Pa., 1976-79. Mem. Pa. Bar Assn., Westmoreland Bar Assn., Murrysville-Export Rotary Club (pres. 1999-00). Republican. Roman Catholic. Home: 3590 N Hills Rd Murrysville PA 15668-1438 Office: 15 E Otterman St Greensburg PA 15601-2543 Office Phone: 724-834-1320. E-mail: dennis.gounley@verizon.net.

GOURDINE-TYSON, NATACHIA, investment company executive, writer; BSc, Morgan State U.; degree in Justice Adminstrn., Ctrl. Mich. U. Officer spl. projects Nations Bank Corp., Silver Spring, Md., 1992—93; adminstr. Dept. Vets. Affairs, Washington, 1993—96; transp. officer U.S. Army Res., Port Eustis, Va., 1988—98; prin., owner Gourdine Investment Co., Brandywine, Md., 2000—. Adv. Celia & Sons Restaurant, St. Stephen, SC, 2000—03. Author: Legacy of Love, 2001, Legacy of Love, II, 2005. Sec. Am. Assn. Disabled Vets., Washington, 1994—96; vol. Isaac Gourdine County Coun. Campaign, Oxon Hill, Md., 1994—98. Mem.: Internat. Assn. Adminstrv. Profls., Sigma Gamma Rho (sec. 1993—94). Home: 13501 Brandywine Rd Brandywine MD 20613 Office: Gourdine Investment Co PO Box 654 Bowie MD 20718 Personal E-mail: gourdineinvestments@verizon.net.

GOUREVICH, PHILIP, writer, editor; b. 1962; BA, Cornell U., 1986; MFA, Columbia U. Sch. Arts, 1992. NY bur. chief ForeWord, cultural editor, contbg. editor; staff writer New Yorker, 1997—; editor Paris Rev., NYC. Bd. trustees PEN Am. Ctr., NYC, chair internat. com.; sr. fellow World Policy Inst., NYC. Author: We Wish to Inform You That Tomorrow We Will Be Killed With Our Families, 1998 (Nat. Book Critics Cir. award, LA Times Book Prize, George K. Polk award for Fgn. Reporting, PEN/Martha Algrand award for First Nonfiction, NY Pub. Libr. Helen Bernstein award, Guardian First Book award), A Cold Case, 2001. Office: The Paris Review 62 White St New York NY 10013

GOUREVITCH, JACQUELINE, artist; b. Paris, Oct. 28, 1933; came to US, 1940; d. Henry and Sophie (Eliasberg) Herrmann; m. Victor Gourevitch, June 18, 1954; children: Marc, Philip. Student, Black Mountain Coll., NC, 1950; BA, U. Chgo., 1954; student, Art Inst. Chgo., 1955-57. Vis. artist Wesleyan U., Middletown, Conn., 1967-71, Hartford Art Sch., 1973-78; vis. artist, lectr. U. Calif., Berkeley, 1974, Vassar Coll., Poughkeepsie, NY, 1977; prof. painting and drawing Wesleyan U., 1978-89; adj. faculty Cooper Union, NYC, 1989-92; vis. prof. Mt. Holyoke Coll., South Hadley, Mass., 1995. Represented by Mary Ryan Gallery, NYC. Solo exhbns. at Eleanor Rigelhaupt Gallery, Boston, 1967, 69, Tibor de Nagy, NYC, 1971, 72, 73, Wadsworth Atheneum, Matrix Gallery, Hartford, 1975, Gallery Marina Dinkler, Berlin, 1988, New Britain Mus. Am. Art, New Britain, Conn., 1994, Paesaggio Gallery, Conn., 1993, 96, 99, DFN Gallery, NYC, 2000, 02, Mary Ryan Gallery, NYC, 2005; group exhbns. including Invitational, Nat. Acad. Design, NYC, 2002, Watercolor, NY Studio Sch., 2002, Sky/Ground, Paessaggio Gallery, West Hartford, 2003, Modern Shadows, The Painting Ctr., NYC, 2003, Skies and Scapes, DFN Gallery, NYC, 2004, Invitational, Am. Acad. Arts and Letters, NYC, 2004, 181st Ann.: An Invitational Exbhn. Contemporary Art, Nat. Acad. Mus., NYC, 2006; represented in pub. collections at Wadsworth Atheneum, Menil Collection, Houston, De Cordova Mus., Lincoln., Mass., U.Calif., Berkeley, Yale U. Art Gallery, Conn. NEA grantee, 1976; Conn. Commn. Arts grantee, 1983; Tamarind Inst. fellow, 1973; recipient Obrig prize, Nat. Acad. Design, NY, 2002, Academy award, Am. Acad. of Arts and Letters, 2004. Home: 120 Duane St Apt 6 New York NY 10007-1113

GOUREVITCH, PHILIP, editor; b. Phila. Student, Cornell Univ. Sr. fellow World Policy Inst. Contbg. editor Forward newspaper, staff writer New Yorker mag.; editor: Paris Review, 2005—; author: We Wish to Inform You that Tomorrow We Will Be Killed with Our Families: Stories from Rwanda, 1998 (Nat. Book Critics Cir. award for nonfiction, George Polk award for fgn. reporting), A Cold Case, 2001. Recipient Nat. Mag. award for Photojournalism, Am. Soc. Newspaper Editors, 2007. Office: Paris Review 62 White St New York NY 10013-3593*

GOURLEY, DICK R., college dean; b. Franklin, Ky., Dec. 26, 1944; m. Greta Ann Kimbrough, Dec. 7, 1968; 1 child, Kristin Marie. BS in Pharmacy, U. Tenn., 1969, D of Pharmacy, 1970. Lic. pharmacist Tenn. Asst. prof. clin. pharmacy Mercer U., Atlanta, 1970-72, prof., dean., 1984-89, Coll. Pharmacy, U. Tenn., Memphis, 1989—; asst. prof., chmn. dept. pharmacy practice U. Nebr., Omaha, 1972-73, assoc. prof., chmn., 1973-81, prof. chmn., 1981-84. Vis. prof. U. Sydney, Australia, 1978; vis. tutor Ctrl. Inst. Tech., Upper Hutt, New Zealand, 1978; bd. dirs. Internat. Found. for Pharmacy Edn., MERTT, Accredo, Inc.; cons. Eli Lilly Co., 1983-85, Australian Nat. Health and Med. Rsch. Coun., 1982—, Lancaster County Bd. Lancaster Manor Nursing Home, 1981-82, Nebr. State Dept. Pub. Instns., 1976-84, Family Health Care, Inc., Omaha, 1975-84, Tri-County Meml. Hosp., Lexington, Nebr., 1975-76, Pharmacy and Therapeutics Com. Luth. Med. Ctr., Omaha, 1975, Henderson-Floyd Drugs and Shannondale Nursing Home, Knoxville, Tenn., 1971-72, Drs. Meml. Hosp. Atlanta, 1971-72, Ga. Narcotic Treatment Program, 1971-72, Grady Meml. Hosp., Atlanta, 1971-72, and numerous others; active Bd. Pharm Specialists, 1993—, vice chmn., 1994, chair 1995, 96, 97). Author: (with J. McHan) Laboratory Manual for Introductory Pharmacy, Physical Pharmacy and Pharmacy Technology, 1971; (with others) Practicing Pharmacist Handbook: Guidlines for the Establishment of High Blood Pressure Control Services by the Practicing Pharmacist, 1977, various chpts. in Pharmacy Technicians' Manual, 1988, Applied Therapeutics for Clinical Pharmacists, 1983, Clinical Pharmacy and Therapeutics, 1982, Pharmaceutics and Pharmacy Practice, 1981, Sourcebook on Clinical Pharmacy, 1980, Clinical Pharmacy and Therapeutics, 1979, Handbook of Non-Prescription Drugs, 1979, Handbook for Institutional Pharmacy Practice, 1979; editor: A Study Guide for the PCAT Examination, 1983, 3d edit., 1998, 4th edit., 1999, 5th edit., 2000, 6th edit, 2001, 7th edit., 2002, 8th edit., 2004, Comprehensive Review of Pharmacy, 2003, 2nd edit., 2004, 5th edit., 2005; co-editor: Clinical Pharmacy and Therapeutics, 4th edit., 1988, 5th edit., 1992, Textbook of Therapeutics: Drug and Disease Management, 6th edit., 1996, 7th edit., 2000; mem. editorial bds. Topics in Hosp. Mgmt., Clin. Rsch. Practices and Drug Regulatory Affairs, World Pharmacy Sci., Am. Jour. Managed Care; published audio-visual edni. materials; contbr. articles to profl. jours. Chmn. UNMC Coll. Pharmacy United Way Campaign, 1979-81; judge Greater Nebr. Sci. and Engring. Fair, 1973-79. Grantee Eli Lilly and Co., 1996, 97, 98, U. Nebr-Lincoln, 1979, HEW, 1976-80, Area Health Edn. Ctr., 1974, 73, Robert Wood Johnson Found., 1973-76, Novartis, 1994, 95, 96, 97, 98, Schering Plough, 1997, SKB, 1997, Roche, 1997; fellow Internat. Ctr. for Pharmacy Edn. and Rsch., 1988, U. Nebr., 1978. Mem. Am. Coun. Pharm. Edn. (mem. site vis. team), Am. Soc. Hosp., Pharmacists (chmn., vice chmn. ASHP-ANA Joint Com., 1977-79, bd. dirs. 1981-84, del. Ho. Delegates, 1977, 78, 82, 83, 84, bd. liaison Coun. on Legal and Pub. Affairs, 1983-84, Coun. Edn. and Manpower 1982-83, Coun. Organizational Affairs, 1981-82, mem. several other coms.), Am. Assn. Colls. of Pharmacy (chmn. Sect. Teachers of Clin. Instrn. 1977-79, chmn. Coun. of Sects. 1995—, chmn. Standing Rules of Procedure Com., 1974-76, mem. several other coms.), Am. Pharm. Assn. (del. Ho. Delegates, 1977, 88-94), Nebr. Soc. Hosp. Pharmacists (chmn. Program Com. 1979-81, co-chmn. 1976-77, Spl. Svc. to Hosp. Pharmacy award 1984), Ga. Pharmaceutical Assn., Greater Omaha Pharmacists Assn. (bd. dirs. 1974-77), Nebr. Pharmacists Assn., Tenn. Pharmacists Assn., Internat. Found. for Pharmacy Edn. (pres. 1992—), Fedn. Internat. Pharm., Soc. Hosp. Pharmacists Australia, Pan Pacific Found. (program coord. II Conf. 1979-82, III Conf. 1982—, IV Conf. 1987, chmn. V Conf. exec. v.p. 1982-92), public mem. Commn. on Credentialing Pharmacy Residencies, 2003—, mem. bd. pharmacy specialties (chair 1995-97), Blue Lodge, Shriners, Phi Delta Chi (v.p. collegiate affairs 1973-78), Rho Chi (counselor region V 1976-78). Office: U Tenn Coll Pharmacy 847 Monroe Ave Memphis TN 38103-4901 Home Phone: 901-757-5250; Office Phone: 901-448-6036. Business E-Mail: dgourley@utmem.edu. E-mail: dgourley@bellsouth.net.

GOURLEY, JAMES LELAND, editor, publishing executive; b. Mounds, Okla., Jan. 29, 1919; s. Samuel O. and Lodema (Scott) G.; m. Vicki Graham Clark, Nov. 24, 1976; children: James Leland II, Janna Lynn Rousey, Kelly Clark, Brandon Clark. BA in Liberal Studies, U. Okla., 1963. Editor, pub., pres. Daily Free-Lance, Henryetta, Okla., 1946-73; editor, pub. Oklahoma City Friday, 1974—; CEO Nichols Hills Pub. Co., 1974—; pres. Suburban Graphics, Inc., 1991-93. Pres. Central Okla. Newspaper Group, 1987, 90, 93, 96, 98, 99, 2000—; pres. Sta. KHEN, KHEN-FM, Henryetta, 1955-63; pres. Hugo Daily News, Okla., 1953-63; chief of staff gov. Okla., 1959-63; chmn., pres. State Capitol Bank, 1962-69; v.p. sta. KXOJ Sapulpa, 1972-75; treas. Sta. KJEM-FM, Oklahoma City, 1962-67. Mem. Pres. Nat. Pub. Advisory Com. to U.S. Sec. Commerce, 1963-66; exec. dir. Gov's Comm. Higher Edn., 1960-61; Dem. candidate for gov. Okla., 1966. Dist. chmn. Boy Scouts Am., 1963-65; bd. dirs. So. Regional Edn. Bd., 1959-67, Okla. Symphony Soc., 1976-88, Oklahoma City Crimestoppers, 1982—, Salvation Army, Oklahoma City, 1985-87, Okla. Goodwill Industries, 1989-91; mem. Gov.'s Reform Com., 1984; bd. trustees Okla. City Univ., 1993—; bd. dirs. Okla. City Edn. Round Table, 1992—; mem. steering com. Ofcl. Maps for Kids, 2000-2003. Maj. AUS, 1942-46, ETO. Recipient Best Okla. Small Daily newspaper awards, 1949-58, 69-72, Best Large City Weekly newspaper awards, 1977-80, 83-85, 87-91, 94-95, 97, 98, 2004, 05, Rotary Lifetime Achievement award, 2006, Disting. Alumni award, U. Okla., 2007; inducted into Okla. Journalism Hall of Fame, 1980. Mem. UP Internat. Editors Okla. (pres. 1958-59), Okla. Disciples of Christ Laymen (pres. 1964-65), Suburban Newspapers Am. (dir. 1980-89), Nat. Newspaper Assn., Okla. Press Assn. (pres. 1988-89, treas. 1991-93), Oklahoma City C. of C. (dir. 1975—), Henryetta C. of C. (pres. 1955), Oklahoma City Golf and Country Club (bd. dirs. 1991-95), Econ. Club Okla., Oklahoma City Com. of 100, Rotary (pres. Oklahoma City club 1992-93), Okla. Econ. Club, Okla. City Comm. of 100, Fortune Club, Mil. Order of World Wars, Mil. Officers Assn., Pi Kappa Alpha. Republican. Home: 6435 Grandmark Dr Oklahoma City OK 73116-6535 Office: 10801 Quail Plaza Dr Oklahoma City OK 73120-3123 Home Phone: 405-848-4488; Office Phone: 405-755-3311. Business E-Mail: lgourley@okcfriday.com.

GOURLEY, JONATHAN JOSEPH, hydrologist; b. Stillwater, Okla., July 27, 1973; s. Robert Lee and Lana Kay Gourley. BS, U. Okla., Norman, 1996, MS, 1998, PhD, 2003. Rschr. MeteoFrance, Trappes, France, 2003—05; rsch. hydrologist Nat. Severe Storms Lab., Norman, 2005—. Contbr. articles to profl. jours. Recipient Silver medal, Dept. Commerce, 1999; fellow, Coop. Program for Operational Meteorology, Edn., and Tng. and Nat. Weather Svc., 1996—98, Dept. Edn., 1999—2003. Mem.: Am. Meteorol. Soc. (assoc.), Am. Geophys. Union (assoc.), Kappa Sigma (assoc.). Achievements include patents for quantitative precipitation estimation and segregation using multiple sensors. Office: Nat Severe Storms Lab 120 David L Boren Blvd Rm 4745 Norman OK 73072 Home Phone: 405-325-6472; Office Phone: 405-325-6472.

GOURLEY, ROBERT, information technology executive; BS in Chemistry, Middle Tenn. State Univ.; MS in Sci., Tech. Intelligence, Naval Postgraduate Sch.; MS in Military Sci., USMC Univ.; MS in Computer Sci., James Madison Univ. Sr. exec. pvt. industry; intelligence officer US Navy; dir. intelligence, Joint Task Force for Computer Network Def. Dept. Def.; chief tech. officer Def. Intelligence Agy., Washington, 2005—. Named one of Top 25 Chief Tech. Officers, InfoWorld mag., 2007. Office: Chief Tech Officer Def Intelligence Agy 1400 Defense Pentagon Pentagon DC 20301-1400

GOURLEY, SARA J., lawyer; b. 1955; AB cum laude with honors, Ripon Coll., 1977; JD, Univ. Ill., 1980. Bar: Ill. 1980, US Dist. Courts (no. dist. Ill. and dist. of Ariz.), US Ct. of Appeals (4th, 7th, 8th. and 11th circuits). Ptnr. product liability litig. Sidley Austin LLP (formerly Sidley Austin Brown & Wood LLP), Chgo., mem. exec. com., practice area team leader, products & liability. Mem. Univ. Ill. Law Rev., 1978—80. Bd. mem. Family Focus. Mem.: ABA, Def. Rsch. Inst. (steering com., drug and device litigation sect.). Office Phone: 312-853-7694. Office Fax: 312-853-7036. Business E-Mail: sgourley@sidley.com.

GOURVITZ, ELLIOT HOWARD, lawyer; b. Lewiston, Pa., Sept. 21, 1945; s. Louis and Irene (Brass) Gourvitz; m. Bonnie S. Hirsch; children: Evan, Amy, Ross, Ari. BA, Rutgers U., 1966, JD, 1969. Bar: N.J. 1969, N.Y. 1985, U.S. Dist. Ct. N.J. 1969, U.S. Dist. Ct. (ea. dist.) Wis. 1985, U.S. Ct. Appeals (3d cir.) 1972, U.S. Ct. Appeals (2d, 4th, 5th, 7th, 8th, 9th, 10th, and fed. cirs.) 1982, U.S. Tax Ct. 1970, U.S. Ct. Claims 1970, U.S. Ct. Internat. Trade 1985, U.S. Supreme Ct. 1973, cert.: N.J. (matrimonial atty.). Pvt. practice, Short Hills, NJ. Chmn. Early Settlement Panel of Union County, NJ; panelist Essex and Middlesex Counties. Contbr. articles to profl. jours. Named Man of Yr., United Cerebral Palsy League Union County, 1980. Fellow: Internat. Acad. Matrimonial Lawyers, Am. Acad. Matrimonial Attys. (pres. N.J. chpt.); mem.: N.Y. State Bar Assn., N.J. Bar Assn., Am. Coll. Trial Lawyers (diplomate). Business E-Mail: ehg@gourvitz.com.

GOUSE, S. WILLIAM, JR., mechanical engineering executive, researcher; b. Utica, NY, Dec. 15, 1931; s. S. William and Charlotte G.; m. Jacqueline Ann McLaughlin, Aug. 6, 1955; children: Linda Ellen, S. William III. S.B., S.M., Mass. Inst. Tech., 1954, Sc.D., 1958. Instr. mech. engring. MIT, 1956-57, asst. prof., 1957-61, 62-65, assoc. prof., 1965-67, lectr., 1967-68; prof. mech. engring., prin. rsch. engr. Transp. Rsch. Inst., Carnegie-Mellon U., 1967-69; staff mem. Office Sci. and Tech. of Exec. Office of the Pres., Washington, 1969-70; assoc. dean Carnegie Inst. Tech. and Sch. Urban and Pub. Affairs Carnegie-Mellon U., 1971-73, dir. Environ. Studies Inst., 1971-73, adj. prof. engring. and pub. policy, 1980-90; dir. Office R&D, sci. advisor to sec. U.S. Dept. Interior, 1973-75; acting dir. Office Coal Rsch., 1974-75; dep. asst. adminstr. fossil energy ERDA, 1975-77; chief scientist MITRE Corp., 1977-79, v.p., 1979-80, v.p., gen. mgr. Ctr. for Civil Systems, 1980-84, sr. v.p., gen. mgr. Ctr. for Civil Systems, 1984-90, 1990-92, sr. v.p., 1992-94; mng. dir. Energy Sys. and Tech., 1994—. Cons. and mem. panels various industry and govt. agys. including U.S. Dept. Commerce, U.S. Office Sci. and Tech., NSF; mem. rsch. adv. com. Electric Power Rsch. Inst., 1973-76; chmn. rev. adv. bd. on coal liquefaction Internat. Energy Agy., Paris, 1981-82; mem. energy engring. bd. NRC, 1985-88; U.S. rep. to com. energy conservation in indsl. processes World Energy Conf., 1984-89; mem. com. on environ. and energy aspects of waste handling World Energy Coun., vice chmn. com. on efficient use of energy utilization using high tech.; mem. adv. bd. Aspen Inst. Humanistic Studies Com. Pub. Policy Issues Energy and Resources, 1982-95; internat. adv. bd. World Energy Coun.; dir. Colshire Group, 1997; tech. advisor AB Volvo, 1996-2000; tech. adv. bd. Earth First Techs., 2002-03; assoc. dir. Aspen Inst., 1996. Editorial bd. Internat. Jour. Environ. Studies, 1971-81; editor-in-chief Energy Systems and Policy, 1973-93; assoc. editor Energy Sources, 1994-2001; contbr. to books, profl. jours., and congl. testimony. Mem. vis. com. mech. engring. dept. MIT, 1978-85. Served with ordnance AUS, 1961-62. Visking Corp. fellow, 1954-55; GE W. Rice Jr. fellow, 1955-56; recipient Ralph Teetor award Soc. Automotive Engrs., 1966; Sir A.L. Mudslior lectr in tech. Al Alagappa Chettiar Coll. Tech., U. Madras, 1969; Disting lectr. mech. engring. Pa. State U., 1980; recipient Outstanding Svc. award No. Area Environ. Coun., Allegheny County, Pa., 1973, Meritorious Svc. award ERDA, 1976, 60th Lord Melchett Medal Lectr. Inst. Energy London, 1994. Fellow ASME, AIAA (assoc.); mem. AAAS, SAE, U.S. Energy Assn. (bd. dirs. 1987-88, 91-92, audit com. 1992—), Internat. Com. Coal Rsch., Cosmos Club, Explorers Club (steering com., 2001-2004, sec., 2005—, Washington group 2001-03, sec. 2004—), Tower Club. Office Phone: 540-399-9825. Personal E-mail: swgjmg@alum.mit.edu. Business E-Mail: swgjmg@erols.com.

GOUTMAN, LOIS CLAIR, retired drama educator; b. Clairton, Pa., Apr. 14, 1923; m. Dolya Goutman, Mar. 10, 1947; children: Andrew, Christopher, Thomas. BFA in Drama, Carnegie-Mellon U., 1944. Tchr., head drama dept. Baldwin Sch., Bryn Mawr, Pa.; ret. Dir. St. Thomas Players, Circle Theatre, L.A., Carnegie Tech. Drama Sch.; asst. dir. Actors' Lab., L.A., Arlington Films; presenter workshops in field; instr. theatre studies program Rosemont Coll. Forum, Pa. Appeared in various theatrical prodns., including The Tempest; writer, performer of one woman play Edith Wharton; dir. play reading group of srs. Surrey Sr. Svcs., Berwyn, Pa. Stanford U. fellow, Nat. Theatre Conf. alt. fellow, 1947; recipient Olmsted prize Williams Coll., Williamstown, Mass., 1992; holder first Rosamond Cross Chair in Teaching, The Baldwin Sch., 1991; teaching chair endowed in her honor Baldwin Sch. Mem. Am. Edn. Theatre Assn., Am. Alliance for Theatre and Edn., Theatre Edn. Assn., Am. Assn. Univ. Women, Sr. Theatre League Am. Avocations: theater, concerts, reading, art exhibitions. Home: 314 Williams Rd Bryn Mawr PA 19010-1214 Personal E-mail: lcgoutman@comcast.net.

GOUTTIERE, JOHN P., lawyer; b. Toledo, Mar. 18, 1949; BA in Am. Studies, Bowling Green State U., Ohio, 1971; JD, Ohio No. U., Ada, 1974. Bar: Ohio 1974, US Dist. Ct. (no. dist.) Ohio 1975, US Supreme Ct. 1997. Ptnr. Ferstle & Gouttiere, Toledo, 1975—85; pres. John P. Gouttiere Co. LPA, Toledo, 1985—. Adj. prof. U. Toledo Coll. Law Pres. Corp. for Legal Svcs. and Assistance to Poor, 1996-99, Toledo Legal Aid Soc., bd. trustees, 1987-96, pres., 1994-96 Mem. Ohio State Bar Assn., Lucas County Bar Assn. (pres. 1986), Toledo Bar Assn., Comml. Law League Am. Office: 520 Madison Ave Ste 1026 Toledo OH 43604-1341 Office Phone: 419-242-9900. Business E-Mail: johng@gouttierelaw.com.

GOUW, JULIA SURYAPRANATA, bank executive; b. Surabaya, Indonesia, Aug. 22, 1959; came to U.S., 1978; d. Moertopo Suryapranata and Indira (Koelani) Suryapranata; m. Ken Keng-Hok Gouw, June 1, 1981. B.S. with highest honors, U. Ill., 1981. CPA, Ill. Acct., Texaco, Inc., Los Angeles, 1981-83; from asst. acct. to sr. audit mgr. KPMG Peat Marwick, LA, 1983-89; joined East West Bank as v.p., contr., San Marino, CA, 1989, exec. v.p., CFO, East West Bancorp Inc., 1994-, dir., 1997-. Bd. dirs. Huntington Meml. Hosp.; bd. visitors UCLA; bd. overseers LA Philharmonic; mem. Alexis de Tocqueville Soc. United Way. Named Philanthropist of Yr., United Way's Women Leaders for Giving and Nat. Assn. Bus. Owners, 2003, LA Bus. Jour. Women Making a Difference Awards, 2003; Named one of The Top 25 Most Powerful Women in Banking, US Banker mag., 2003, 2005, 2006. Mem. Chinese Am. CPA's, Nat. Assn. Female Execs., Beta Alpha Psi, Fin. Execs. Inst., Calif. Soc. CPA's. Home Phone: 626-793-2428; Office Phone: 626-583-3512, 626-583-3512. Office Fax: 626-799-2799. E-mail: jgouw@eastwestbank.com.*

GOVAN, GLADYS VERNITA MOSLEY, retired critical care nurse, medical/surgical nurse; b. Tyler, Tex., July 24, 1918; d. Stacy Thomas and Lucy Victoria (Whitmill) Mosley; m. Osby David Govan, July 20, 1938; children Orbrenett K. (Govan) Carter, Diana Lynn (Govan) Gray. Student, East Los Angeles Coll., Montebello, Calif., 1951; lic. vocat. nurse, Calif. Hosp. Med. Ctr., LA, 1953; cert., Western States IV Assn., LA, 1978. Lic. vocat. nurse, Calif.; cert. in EKG. Intravenous therapist Calif. Hosp. Med. Ctr., cardiac monitor, nurse; ret. Past pres. PTA, also hon. mem., 1963-2000; charter mem. Nat. Rep. Presdl. Task Force.

GOVAN, MICHAEL, museum director; b. Washington; m. Kathryn Ross. BA in Art History and Studio Art, Williams Coll.; postgrad., U. Calif., San Diego. Acting curator and spl. assts. to the dir. Williams Coll. Mus. Art, Williamstown, Mass.; dep. dir. Solomon R. Guggenheim Mus., NYC; dir. Dia Art Found., NYC, 1994—2006, LA County Mus. Art, 2006—. Fundraiser for Dia Beacon (N.Y.) Mus., 1999—2003; bd. mem. Andy Warhol Mus and Triple Aught Found. Office: LA County Mus Art 5905 Wilshire Blvd Los Angeles CA 90036

GOVE, SAMUEL KIMBALL, retired political science professor; b. Walpole, Mass., Dec. 27, 1923; Student, Mass. State Coll., 1941—43; BS in Econs, U. Mass., 1947; MA in Polit. Sci, Syracuse U., 1951. Research asst. govt. and pub. affairs U. Ill., 1950-51, research asso., 1951-54, mem. faculty, 1954—, prof. polit. sci., 1966-89, prof. emeritus, 1989—; dir. Inst. Govt. and Pub. Affairs, 1967-85, dir. emeritus, 1987—. Staff asst. Nat. Assn. Assessing Officers, 1949; mem. rsch. staff Ill. Commn. Study State Govt., 1950—51; staff fellow Nat. Mcpl. League, 1955—56; exec. asst. Ill. Auditor Pub. Accounts, 1957; program coord. Ill. Legis. Staff Intern Program, 1962—70; mem. com. financing higher edn. Ill. Master Plan Higher Edn., 1963; mem. Ill. Commn. Orgn. Gen. Assembly, 1965—69, 1970—73, Ill. Commn. State Govt., 1965—67; cons. elections ABC, 1964, 66, 68; chmn. Champaign (Ill.) County Econ. Opportunity Coun., 1966—67; state legis. rsch. fellow Am. Polit. Sci. Assn., 1966—68; cons. Am. Council Edn., 1966—67; sec. Local Govts. Commn., 1967—69; staff dir. Ill. Constn. Study Commn., 1968—69; exec. sec. Gov. Ill. Constn. Research Group, 1969—70; mem. Ill. Constn. Study Commn., 1969—70; chmn. Citizens Task Force on Constl. Implementation, 1970—71; mem. Gov. Elect's Task Force on Transition, 1972, 1991—92; adv. coun. Ill. Dept. Local Govt. Affairs, 1969—79, Gov.'s Human Resources, 1991—93, Ill. Commn. on Regulatory Rev., 1994—98, Ill. Bd. Higher Edn., 1998—2005, Ill. Issues Bd., 1974—2003, chmn. bd. dirs., 1974—93. Lt. j.g. USNR, 1943—46. Fellow Nat. Acad. Pub. Adminstrn.; mem. AAUP (past chpt. pres., mem. nat. com. R 1969-75, 78-84, nat. coun. 1978-80), Am. Polit Sci. Assn., Am. Soc. Pub. Adminstrn. (past chpt. chmn.; chmn. univs. govtl. rsch. conf. 1969-71), Govtl. Rsch. Assn. (dir. 1969-71), Ill. Hist. Soc., Midwest Polit. Sci. Assn. (v.p. 1978-80), Nat. Mcpl. League (council 1972-80, 81-84, 85), Nat Civic League (coun. advisors 1987-89), Cosmos Club. Home: 2006 Bruce Dr Urbana IL 61801-6419 Office: 1007 W Nevada St Urbana IL 61801-3812 Personal E-mail: s-gove@uiuc.edu.

GOVE, WALTER R., sociology educator; b. June 8, 1938; married; 2 children. BS, SUNY, Syracuse, 1960; MA in Sociology, U. Wash., 1967, PhD in Sociology, 1968. From asst. prof. to assoc. prof. Vanderbilt U., Nashville, 1968-75, prof. sociology, 1975—, dir. grad. studies, 1985-86. Dir. grad tng. program NIMH, 1972-76; organizer confs., symposia in field; presenter in field. Author: (with Michael Geerken) At Home and at Work: The Family's Allocation of Labor, 1983; (with Michael Hughes) Household Crowding: Social and Structural Determinants of Its Effects, 1983; editor: Deviance and Mental Illness, 1982, co-editor: Labelling Deviant Behavior: Evaluating a Perspective, 1975, 2 edit., 1980, The Fundamental Connection Between Nature and Nurture, 1982, A Feminist Perspective in the Academy, 1983; adv. editor Social Forces, 1971-74; cons. editor Am. Jour. Sociology, 1974-76, Women and Politics, 1978-86; assoc. editor Social Sci. Rsch., 1974—, Social Psychology Quarterly, 1978-80, Jour. Health and Social Behavior, 1981-83, 1997-2003, Jour. Family Issues, 1984-92; contbr. articles to profl., non-profl. jours., book revs. Recipient Reuben Hill award Nat. Coun. Family Rels., 1979, Outstanding Grad. Tchr. award Vanderbilt U., 2001; grantee PHS, 1963-65, 71-76, 79-82, NSF, 1973-77, 93, Dept. Justice, 1984-85, Okla. Dept. Corrections, 1993-94, Ethel Mae Wilson Found., 1980-81, Shell Found., 1974, others. Fellow: AAAS; mem.: So. Sociol. Soc. (pres.-elect 1992—93, pres. 1993—94, exec. coun., program com. 1986), Am. Sociol. Assn. (liaison com. to AAAS 1990—94, Leo Reeder award for disting. svc. to med. sociology 2003), Am. Soc. Criminology, Sociology Rsch. Assn., Soc. Study of Social Problems (Outstanding Scholarship and Svc. to Psychiat. Sociology award 1989). Avocation: numerous first ascents as mountaineer, primarily in Alaska. Home: PO Box 1399 Boulder UT 84716 Home Phone: 435-335-7326. Business E-Mail: walter.r.gove@vanderbilt.edu.

GOVER, ALAN SHORE, lawyer; b. Lyons, NY, Sept. 5, 1948; s. Norman Marvin and Beatrice L. (Shore) Gover; m. Ellen Rae Ross, Dec. 4, 1976 (dec. Jan. 8, 2004); children: Maxwell Ross, Mary Trace. AB, Tufts U., 1970; JD, Georgetown U., 1973. Bar: Tex. 1973, U.S. Dist. Ct. (so. dist.) Tex. 1974, U.S. Ct. Appeals (5th cir.) 1974, U.S. Supreme Ct. 1976, U.S. Dist. Ct. Appeals (DC cir.) 1977, U.S. Ct. Appeals (2d cir.) 1979, DC 1980, U.S. Ct. Appeals (8th, 9th and 11th cirs.) 1981, U.S. Dist. Ct. (no. dist.) Tex. 1988, U.S. Dist. Ct. (ea. dist.) Tex. 1990. Assoc. Baker & Botts, Houston, 1973-80, ptnr., 1981-85, Weil, Gotshal & Manges, Houston, 1985—2001; ptnr., co-chmn. corp. reorganization & bankruptcy group. mem. mgmt. com. Dewey Ballantine LLP, NYC and Houston, 2001—. Co-author: (book) The Texas Nonjudicial Foreclosure Process, 1990; editor, chmn. editl. bd. P. L. I. Oil and Gas Bankruptcy Laws, 1985. Trustee Houston Ballet, 1986—93, 2003—, v.p., 1993—96, 2005—; chmn.

ann. fund St. John's Sch., Houston, 1993—95, trustee, 1996—2004, Retina Rsch. Fund., Houston, 1996—; chmn. East Downtown Mgmt. Dist., Houston, 2000—03; adv. trustee Salvation Army Houston Area Command, 2005—; v.p. Congregation Beth Israel, Houston, 1996—2001, pres., 2001—03; trustee Seven Acres Jewish Home for Aged, 2005—; bd. dirs. Yeshiva Choveve Torah, 2006—. Fellow: Tex. Bar Found.; mem.: N.Y. State Bar, D.C. Bar, State Bar Tex., Houston Bar Assn., ABA, Harmonie Club (N.Y.), Coronado Club Houston, The Argyle (San Antonio). Jewish. Home: 455 Central Park W Apt 21A New York NY 10025 Home Phone: 212-932-2292; Office Phone: 212-259-8600. Business E-Mail: agover@dbllp.com.

GOVER, RAYMOND LEWIS, retired newspaper executive; b. Somerset, Ky., Dec. 5, 1927; s. Raymond Bolen and Leslie Fay (Silvers) G.; m. Frieda Jane McGill, July 27, 1957; children: Janine Gover Park, Mark H., Janet L., Matthew R. BA, U. Mich., Ann Arbor, 1951; PhD (hon.), Shippensburg U., Pa., 1996. Reporter Port Huron Times, Mich., 1951-54; reporter, asst. city editor, city editor The Jour., Flint, Mich., 1954-70, editor, 1976-78; editor, pub. The News, Saginaw, Mich., 1970-76, 78-81; pub. The Patriot News, Harrisburg, Pa., 1981-97; pres. Patriot News Co., Harrisburg, 1997-2001; ret., 2001. Bd. dirs. Milton Hershey Sch., Hershey Trust Co. Bd. dirs. Ctrl. Pa. Hospice, 2000-01, YMCA, Harrisburg, 1984-90, Harrisburg Symphony Orch.; v.p. Tri-County United Way, Harrisburg; bd. adv. Pa. State U., Harrisburg; trustee. v.p. Pa. Newspaper Pubs. Found., pres. 2004—05, Pine St. Presbyn. Ch., Harrisburg, Greater Harrisburg Found. Mem. Newspaper Assn. Am., Pa. Newspaper Assn. (bd. dirs. 1987—, pres. 1990-91), Am. Soc. Newspaper Editors, Mich. Press Assn. (bd. dirs. 1978-81), Soc. Profl. Journalists, West Shore Country Club (mem. bd. govs. 1991-95), Masons. Avocations: golf, fishing, hunting. Home: 905 Grandon Way Mechanicsburg PA 17050-9171 Office: Patriot-News Co PO Box 2265 812 Market St Harrisburg PA 17101-2827 Home Phone: 717-737-2441; Office Phone: 717-728-2711. Personal E-mail: r.gover@verizon.net.

GOVERN, FRANK STANLEY, health facility and research administrator, healthcare educator, writer; b. Plainfield, NJ, May 18, 1951; s. Fred John and Jane Louise (Schweitzer) Govern; m. Patricia Loretta Hermanns, Aug. 19, 1972; children: Jason, Heather. AAS, Middlesex County Coll., 1973; BA, Salem State Coll., 1979; MAS, Johns Hopkins U., 1981; PhD in law, policy, and soc., Northeastern U., 1997. Asst. adminstrn. Circle Terrace Hosp., Alexandria, Va., 1981-84; CEO Tyrone (Pa.) Hosp., 1984—85; pres., CEO Charles River Hosp., Wellesley, Mass., 1985—86; COO Joint Ctr. Radiation Therapy, Boston, 1986—98; dep. dir. radiation oncology scis. program, chief oncology outreach, radiation rsch. Nat. Cancer Inst., Bethesda, Md., 1998—2007; dir. bus. devel. Alliance Oncology, Andover, Maine, 2007—. Sr. instr. Northeastern U., Boston, 1986—98; instr. Harvard Med. Sch., Boston, 1986—98. Author: U.S. Health Policy and Problem Definition: A Policy Process Adrift, 2000; contbr. chapters to books, articles to profl. jours. Founder, pres. Cmty. for Ednl. Excellence, Beverly, Mass., 1991. Capt. USAF, 1974—76. Avocations: bicycling, reading, writing, skiing. Home: 6 Ober St #2 Beverly MA 01915 Office: 600 Federal St Andover MA 01810 Home Phone: 978-766-9609. Business E-Mail: govern@jhu.edu.

GOVIL, NARENDRA KUMAR, mathematics professor; b. Aligarh, India, Jan. 5, 1940; arrived in U.S., 1983; s. Panna Lal and Kamla Devi (Agrawal) G.; m. Urmila Agrawal, Feb. 1, 1964; children: Sanjay, Sandeep. BSc, Agra U., India, 1957; MSc, Aligah Muslim U., India, 1959; PhD, U. Montreal, 1968. Lectr. Concordia U., Montreal, 1967-68, asst. prof., 1968-70, Indian Inst. Tech., New Delhi, 1970-78, assoc. prof., 1978-80, prof., 1980-85; assoc. prof. Auburn (Ala.) U., 1985-86, prof., 1986—. Vis. scientist Dalhousie U., Halifax, Canada, 1980; vis. prof. U. Alta., Edmonton, Canada, 1981, Auburn U., 1983—85; mem. exec. com. Forum Interdisciplinary Math, Delhi, 1989—91; reviewer Math. Reviews. Co-author: Great Mathematician Shrinivas Ramanujan (in Hindi), 2005; editor: Jour. Inequalities in Pure and Applied Math., Australian Jour. Math. Analysis and Applications; co-editor: Fourier Analysis, Approximation Theory and Applications, 1997, Approximation Theory, 1998, Frontiers in Interpolation and Approximation, 2007; assoc. editor: Jour. Inequalities and Applications, 2000—02; mem. editl. bd. Internat. Jour. Math. and Math. Scis., 2000—02; editor: Australian Jour. Math. Analysis and Applications, 2000—02; mem. editl. ed. Jour. Inequalities and Applications, 2000—02, reviewer Math. Reviews; contbr. articles to profl. jours. Mem. exec. India Cultural Assn. East Ala., Auburn, 1986, 96-97. Fellow: Nat. Acad. Scis. India (life); mem.: Indian Math Soc. (life), India Cultural Assn. East Ala. (pres. Auburn 1991). Avocations: music, reading. Home: 523 Owens Rd Auburn AL 36830-2513 Office: Auburn Univ Dept Math Auburn AL 36849 Office Phone: 334-844-6558. Business E-Mail: govilnk@auburn.edu.

GOVINDARAJAN, VIJAY, finance educator; b. Madras, India, Nov. 18, 1949; s. Krishnamachari Vijayaraghavan and Deshikachari Padmasini; m. Kirthi Sundararajan, Feb. 6, 1980; children: Tarunya, Tapasya. BA in Commerce, Annamalai U., Tamil Nadu, India, 1969; Chartered Acct., Inst. of Chartered Accts., Delhi, India, 1972; MBA, Harvard Bus. Sch., Boston, MA, 1976, PhD in Bus., 1978. Mgmt. trainee DCM, Delhi, India, 1972—74; assoc. prof. Indian Inst. of Mgmt., Ahmedabad, India, 1974—80; vis. assoc. prof. Harvard Bus. Sch., Boston, 1980—81; assoc. prof. Ohio State U., Columbus, 1981—85; prof. Dartmouth Coll., Hanover, NH, 1985—. Author: (book) Strategic Cost Management, 1993 (Best Book, 1999), The Quest for Global Dominance, 2001, Management Control Systems, 2001; co-editor: The Many Facets of Leadership, 2002; author: Global Strategy and Organization, 2003, Management Control Systems, 2003, (article) Academy of Management Journal, 1984 (Best Paper, 1986). Named Best Bus. Sch. Prof., Bus. Week, 2001; named to Top 10 Prof., 1993. Mem.: Acad. of Internat. Bus., Strategic Mgmt. Soc., Acad. of Mgmt. Avocation: travel. Home: 13 Rope Ferry Rd Hanover NH 03755 Office: Dartmouth Coll Tuck Sch of Bus 100 Tuck Dr Hanover NH 03755 Business E-Mail: vijay.govindarajan@dartmouth.edu.

GOVINDJEE, SANJAY, engineering educator; b. Urbana, Ill. BS, MIT; MS, PhD, Stanford U. Profl. engr., State of Calif. Prof. U. Calif., Berkeley, 1993—2006, ETH, Zurich, 2006—. Recipient Zienkiewicz medal, Instn. Civil Engrs., London, 1998, Career award, NSF, 1998; Alexander von Humboldt Found. fellow, 1999. Mem.: ASME, Internat. Assn. Computational Mechanics, Am. Acad. Mechanics, US Assn. Computational Mechanics. Office: Univ Calif 709 Davis Hall Berkeley CA 94720

GOVINDJEE, biophysics, biochemistry, and biology professor; b. Allahabad, India, Oct. 24, 1933; arrived in US, 1956, naturalized, 1972; s. Vishveshwar Prasad and Savitri Devi Asthana; m. Rajni Varma, Oct. 24, 1957; children: Anita Govindjee, Sanjay Govindjee. BSc, U. Allahabad, 1952, MSc, 1954; PhD, U. Ill., 1960. Lectr. botany U. Allahabad, 1954-56; grad. fellow U. Ill., Urbana, 1956-58, rsch. asst., 1958-60, USPHS postdoctoral trainee biophysics, 1960-61, mem. faculty, 1961—, assoc. prof. botany and biophysics, 1965-69, prof. biophysics and plant biology, 1969-99, disting. lectr. Sch. Life Scis., 1978, emeritus prof. biophysics, plant biology and biochemistry, 1999—. Author (with E. Rabinowitch): Photosynthesis, 1969; editor: Bioenergetics of Photosynthesis, 1975, Photosynthesis: Energy Conversion by Plants and Bacteria; Carbon Assimilation and Plant Productivity, 2 vols., 1982 (Russian transl. 1987); co-editor: The Oxygen Evolving System of Photosynthesis, 1983, Light Emission by Plants and Bacteria, 1986, Excitation Energy and Electron Transfer in Photosynthesis, 1989, Molecular Biology of Photosynthesis, 1989, Photosynthesis: From Photoreactions to Productivity, 1993, Concepts in Photobiology: Photosynthesis and Photomorphogenesis, 1999, Chlorophyll a Fluorescence: A Signature of Photosynthesis, 2004, Discoveries in Photosynthesis, 2005; editor Hist. Corner: Photosynthesis Rsch., 1989—; guest editor spl. issue Biophys. Jour., 1972, Photochemistry and Photobiology, 1978, Photosynthesis Research, 1993, 96, 2002-04; editor-in-chief Photosynthesis Rsch., 1985-88; series editor: Advances in Photosynthesis and Respiration, vol. 1, 1994, vol. 2, 1995, vols. 3, 4 and 5, 1996, vols. 6 and 7, 1998, vol. 8, 1999, vol. 9, 2000, vols. 10 and 11, 2001, vol. 12, 2002, vol. 13, vol. 14, 2003, vols. 15, 16, 17, 19, 2004, vols. 18, 20, 22, 2005, vols. 21, 23-25, 2006; contbr. articles to profl. jours., also Sci. Am. Recipient Lifetime Achievement award, Rebeiz Found., 2007, Comm. award, Internat. Soc. Photosynthetic Rsch., 2007; Fulbright Scholar, 1956—61, 1996—97. Fellow AAAS, NAS (India); mem. Am. Soc. Plant Biologists, Biophys. Soc. Am., Am. Soc. Photobiology (coun. 1976, pres. 1981), Internat. Photosynthesis Soc. (exec. com., publ. com. 1995-01, hon. pres. 13th Internat. Photosynthesis Congress 2004), Sigma Xi (emeritus). Home Phone: 217-337-0627. Business E-Mail: gov@life.uiuc.edu.

GOW, JOE, academic administrator; BA, Pa. State U., Phd in Speech Comm.; MA in Speech Comm., U. Ala. Dir. Comm. Studies Program Alfred U., 1990—2001, assoc. dean. Coll. Liberal Arts and Scis., 1996—2001; dean Coll. Liberal Arts Winona State U., 2001—04; provost, dean Coll. Liberal Arts and Scis. Nebr. Wesleyan U., Lincoln, 2004—06, interim pres., 2006; chancellor U. Wis., La Crosse, 2007—. Editl. bd. Jour. Popular Music and Soc. Mem.: Nat. Coun. Colls. Arts and Scis. (pres.). Avocation: running. Office: U Wis-La Crosse 1725 State St 135 Graff Main Hall La Crosse WI 54601 Office Phone: 608-785-8004. E-mail: gow.joe@uwlax.edu.

GOW, LINDA YVONNE CARIGNAN CHERWIN, travel executive; b. Plymouth, NH, Dec. 15, 1948; d. Roger and Alice Mary (Theriault) Carignan; m. James T. Gow Jr., Aug. 29, 1987 (dec.); 1 child, Alison. Student, Rivier Coll., 1966-68, Whittemore Sch. Bus., 1976-79. Asst. mgr. Travel New Horizons, Peterborough, N.H., 1972-76; mgr. Garnsey Bros. Travel, Sanford, Maine, 1976-77; gen. mgr. R-W Travel, Dover, NH, 1977—84; pres., owner The Travel Pro, Somersworth, N.H., 1984—. Owner Cruise Quarters, Somersworth, 1988—. Sponsor Internat. Children's Festival, Somersworth, 1985—; mem. Gov.'s Pvt. Industry Council, 1987, 88. The Travel Pro named Bus. of Yr., Somerworth C. of C., 2001. Mem. Am. Retail Travel Agts. Assn., Cruise Lines Internat. Assn., Rochester C. of C., Somersworth C. of C., Seacoast Widowed Persons Assn. (bd. dirs. 2000—), Rotary Internat. (Somersworth chpt., Paul Harris fellow). Office: The Travel Pro 394 High St Somersworth NH 03878-1420 E-mail: lgow@thetravelpro.biz.

GOWA, ANDREW, investor, lawyer; b. NYC, Nov. 6, 1949; s. Everett M. and Louise (Friedman) G.; m. Robin P. Lincoln May 21, 1995; children: Catherine J., Jon T., Timothy M., Melissa Lincoln, Jennifer Lincoln. AB magna cum laude, Tufts U., 1971; JD, U. Pa., 1974. Bar: Pa. 1974, N.Y. 1982. From assoc. to ptnr. Blank, Rome, Comisky & McCauley, Phila., 1974-84; sr. v.p North Atlantic Investment Corp., Phila., 1984-85; pres., chief exec. officer First Equity Devel. Corp., West Chester, Pa., 1984-90; ptnr. Schnader Harrison Segal & Lewis LLP, Phila., 1990—2002; chmn. Gowa Lincoln, PC, Phila., 2002—. Bd. dirs. Equitrust Real Estate Corp., West Chester; developer Brampton Chase, Malvern, Pa., 1988-89; faculty Grad. Builders Inst. Pa. State U., State Coll., 1987-90; faculty Pa. Bar Inst., 1991—; chmn. Allegheny Cardiovascular Inst., 1997, Likoff Cardiovascular Inst., 1995-97. Mem. Tufts U. Alumni Coun., Medford, Mass., 1982-88; bd. overseers Tufts U., Medford, 1988-93; bd. dirs. Kaiserman Ctr. Jewish Cmty. Ctrs. Phila, 1982-88. Recipient Disting. Service medal Tufts U., 1982. Mem. Pa. Bar Assn. (ho. dels. 1983-87), Phila. Bar Assn. (bd. govs. 1985, chmn. real estate sect. 1985, exec. com. real estate sect. 1983-89), Am. Coll. Real Estate Laywers. Avocations: amateur radio, cooking. Office: Gowa Lincoln PC 1525 Locust St Ste 1000 Philadelphia PA 19102 Office Phone: 215-320-9000. Business E-Mail: andy@gowalaw.com.

GOWANS, SIR JAMES LEARMONTH, science administrator, immunologist; b. Sheffield, Eng., May 7, 1924; s. John Gowans and Selma Ljung; m. Moyra Leatham, July 28, 1956; children: William, Jenny, Lucy. MB, BS, U. London, 1947; MA, DPhil, Oxford U., 1953; ScD (hon.), Yale U., 1966; DSc (hon.), U. Chgo., 1971, U. Birmingham, Eng., 1978, U. Rochester, 1987; MD (hon.), U. Edinburgh, Scotland, 1979, U. Sheffield, Eng.; DM (hon.), U. Southampton, Eng., 1987; LLD, U. Glasgow, Scotland, 1988. Rsch. prof. sch. pathology Oxford U., Eng., 1962-77, dir. med. rsch. coun. cellular immunology unit, 1963-77; sec., CEO U.K. Med. Rsch. Coun., 1977-87; cons. WHO Global Program on AIDS, Geneva, Switzerland, 1987-88; rsch. programs adv. com. Nat. Multiple Sclerosis Soc., NYC, 1988-90; sec.-gen. Human Frontier Scis. Program, Strasbourg, France, 1989-93. Chmn. European Med. Rsch. Coun., 1985-87; mem. governing coun. Internat. Agy. for Rsch. on Cancer, Lyon, France, 1980-87; mem. awards assembly GM Cancer Rsch. Found., N.Y.C., 1988-92; dir. European Iniative for Communicators of Sci., Munich, Germany, 1995-99, Charing Cross Sunley Rsch. Ctr., London, 1989-91. Contbr. articles on cellular immunology to profl. jours. Recipient Gairdner Found. award, 1968, Paul Ehrlich prize, 1974, Feldberg award, 1979, Wolf prize in medicine, 1980, Medawar prize, 1990. Fellow Royal Soc. (Royal Medal 1976); mem. NAS (fgn. assoc.), Am. Assn. Immunologists (hon.), Am. Assn. Anatomists (hon.). Avocations: music, gardening, old books. Office Phone: (44) 1865-862304. E-mail: jamesgowans@btinternet.com.

GOWEN, RICHARD JOSEPH, electrical engineer, educator, retired academic administrator; b. New Brunswick, NJ, July 6, 1935; s. Charles David and Esther Ann (Hughes) G.; m. Nancy A. Applegate, Dec. 28, 1955; children: Jeff, Cindy, Betsy, Susan, Kerry. BS in Elec. Engring., Rutgers U., 1957; MS, Iowa State U., 1961, PhD, 1962. Registered profl. engr., Colo. Rsch. engr. RCA Labs., Princeton, NJ, 1957; commd. USAF; ground electronics officer Yaak AFB, Mont., 1957-59; instr. USAF Acad., 1962-63, rsch. assoc., 1963-64, asst. prof., 1964-65, assoc. prof., 1965-66, tenured assoc. prof. elec. engring., 1966-70, tenured prof., 1971-77, dir., prin. investigator NASA instrumentation group for cardiovascular studies, 1968-77; mem. launch and recovery med. team Johnson Space Ctr., NASA, 1971-77; v.p., dean engring., prof. SD Sch. Mines and Tech., Rapid City, 1977-84, pres., 1987—2003, Dakota State U., Madison, 1984-87; exec. dir. Homestate Lab. Conversion Project, Rapid City, SD, 2003—04, SD Sci. Tech. Authority, Rapid City, 2004; ret., 2004. Prin. investigator program in support space cardiovascular studies NASA, 1977-81; co-chmn. Joint Industry, Nuc. Regulatory IEEE, Am. Nuc. Soc. Probabilistic Risk Assessment Guidelines for Nuc. Power Plants Project, 1980-83; mem. Dept. Def. Software Engring. Inst. Panel, 1983; mem. Congl. Web-based Edn. Commn., 1999—; mem. SD Bd. Edn., 2003—; bd. dirs. Mount Rushmore Inst. Contbr. articles to profl. jours.; patentee in field. Bd. dirs. St. Martins Acad., Rapid City, SD, Journey Mus., 1998-2001, Greater Rapid City Econ. Devel. Partnership, 1991-2003, SD Bd. Edn., 2003—; mem. US Web Edn. Commn., 1999-2001. Fellow IEEE (Centennial Internat. pres. 1984, bd. dirs., 1976-75), IEEE Found. (bd. dirs., pres. 2005—), USAB/IEEE Disting. Contbns. to Engring. Professionalism award 1986); mem. Am. Assn. Engring. Socs. (bd. dirs., 1983-87, chmn. 1988), Rapid City C. of C. (bd. dirs. 1998-2003), Rotary, Sigma Xi, Phi Kappa Phi, Tau Beta Phi, Eta Kappa Nu (bd. dirs. 1994, pres. 1998-2000) Pi Mu Epsilon. Roman Catholic. Home: 1609 Palo Verde Dr Rapid City SD 57701-4461 Home Phone: 605-342-5066; Office Phone: 605-484-2763. E-mail: rgower@msn.com.

GOWLER, VICKI SUE, editor-in-chief; b. Decatur, Ill., Apr. 16, 1951; d. Carroll Eugene and Audra Janet (Briggs) G. BS in Journalism, U. Ill., 1973. Reporter Iroquois County Daily Times, Watseka, Ill., 1973-75, Quincy (Ill.) Herald-Whig, 1975-78; from reporter to mng. editor Miami (Fla.) Herald, Stuart, Delray Beach, West Palm Beach, 1089-88; asst. news editor Knight-Ridder Washington Bur., 1988-93; exec. editor Duluth (Minn.) News-Tribune, Knight-Ridder newspaper, 1978—2001, editor and v.p., 1993—97, editor, 2001—; mng. editor Pioneer Press, Knight-Ridder newspaper, 1997—2001, editor, 2001—05; sr. v.p. and editor St. Paul Pioneer Press, Knight-Ridder newspaper, 2001—05; editor & v.p. Idaho Statesman, Boise, 2005—. Recipient numerous awards for journalistic works, including RFK award, state AP awards in all categories. Mem. Am. Soc. Newspaper Editors. Methodist. Avocations: reading, tennis, playing clarinet, travel, visiting with her family. Office: Idaho Statesman PO Box 40 Boise ID 83707 Office Phone: 208-377-6403. E-mail: vgowler@idahostatesman.com.*

GOYAK, ELIZABETH FAIRBAIRN, retired public relations executive; b. Chgo., Oct. 7, 1922; d. Lewis Howard and Berenice Marie (Bowers) Fairbairn; m. Edward Anthony Goyak, May 20, 1951. BEd, So. Ill. U., 1943; MA, No. Ill. U., 1979. Reporter Internat. News Svc., Chgo., 1945-49, Chgo. Tribune, 1949-52; writer Gardner & Jones, Chgo., 1954-59, Aaron Cushman & Assocs., Chgo., 1959-60; v.p. Daniel J. Edelman, Chgo., 1960-76; mgr. pub. rels. Stone Container Corp., Chgo., 1976-82; pres. pub. rels. Firm Chgo. Connection, Matteson, Ill., 1982-98. Dir. pub. rels. Ill. Dem. Women for Adlai Stevenson, 1952; founder, pres. bd. dirs. Matteson Pub. Libr., 1958-87; chmn. Matteson Bicentennial Commn., 1973-76. Mem. Pub. Rels. Soc. Am. (accredited, Silver anvil award 1975), Publicity Club Chgo. (sec., bd. dirs. 1964-76, Golden Trumpet award 1965, 66, 75), Chgo. Jour. Assn. Mem. United Ch. Christ. Home: 9200 Lalique Ln Apt 1503 Fort Myers FL 33919-7408

GOYER, ROBERT ANDREW, pathology educator; b. Hartford, Conn., June 2, 1927; s. Andrew R. and Cecelia P. (Castonquay) G.; m. Mary Ellen Wilke, Feb. 4, 1955; children: Barbara, John, Peter, Ellen. BS, Holy Cross Coll., 1950; MD, St. Louis U., 1955. Diplomate: Am. Bd. Pathology. Intern St. Francis Hosp., Hartford, 1955-56; resident in pathology St. Louis U. Hosps., 1956-60; practice medicine specializing in pathology St. Louis, 1956-65; instr. pathology St. Louis U., 1960-62, asst. prof., 1962-65, Sch. Medicine, U. NC, Chapel Hill, 1965-68, assoc. prof., 1968-71, prof. pathology, 1971-74, adj. prof. pathology, 1979-87; clin. pathologist Cardinal Glennon Meml. Hosp. for Children, St. Louis, 1961-62, dir. labs., 1962-64; staff pathologist NC Meml. Hosp., Chapel Hill, 1965-74; chief pathology U. Hosp., London, Ont., Canada, 1974-79; prof. pathology Health Scis. Centre, U. Western Ont., Canada, 1974-79, 87-92, prof. emeritus, 1992—; dept. dir. Nat. Inst. Environ. Health Scis., Research Triangle Park, NC, 1979-87; pvt. cons. health effects, toxic metals Chapel Hill, 1992—. Nat. assoc. Nat. Acads.; mem. com. WHO/IPCS, NAS, NRC. Contbr. articles to profl. jours.; mem. editl. bd. Yearbook Pathology, 1979-88, AMA Archives of Pathology, 1973-82. Served with USN, 1945-47. Recipient Merit award, Soc. Toxicology, 2004; Nat. Found. fellow, 1959—60. Mem. Coll. Am. Pathology, Am. Assn. Pathologists, Internat. Acad. Pathology, Soc. Exptl. Biology and Medicine, Soc. Toxicology (Merit award 2004). Roman Catholic. Achievements include research in experimental pathology and metal toxicology. Office: 6405 Huntingridge Rd Chapel Hill NC 27517 Office Phone: 919-419-1804. Personal E-mail: robert_goyer@msn.com.

GOYER, ROBERT STANTON, retired communications educator and administrator; b. Kokomo, Ind., Oct. 7, 1923; s. Clarence V. and Genevieve M. (Sober) G.; m. Patricia Ann Stutz, Aug. 12, 1950; children: Karen, Susan, Linda, Amy. BA, DePauw U., 1948; MA, Miami U., Oxford, Ohio, 1950; PhD, Ohio State U., 1955. Instr. Miami U., Oxford, 1949-51; instr., then asst. prof. Ohio State U., Columbus, 1955-58, rsch. assoc., cons. rsch. found., 1956-63; from asst. to assoc. to prof. Purdue U., West Lafayette, Ind., 1958-66; prof. Ohio U., Athens, 1966-81, dir. ctr. communication studies, 1966-74, 79-81, assoc. dean grad. coll., 1978, dean grad. coll., acting dir. rsch., 1979, acting assoc. provost grad. and rsch. programs, 1979, prof. emeritus, 1981—; prof., chmn. dept. communication Ariz. State U., Tempe, 1981-89, prof., 1989-94, prof. emeritus, 1994—. Cons. in field. Author books; contbr. articles to profl. jours. 1st lt. U.S. Army, 1943-46, 52-53. Decorated Bronze Star. Fellow AAAS, Internat. Comm. Assn.; mem. APA, Nat. Comm. Assn. Presbyterian. Home: 517 W Summit Pl Chandler AZ 85225-7799

GOYER, VIRGINIA L., accountant; b. Troy, NY, July 19, 1942; d. Clarence Archie and Edna Alice (Toussaint) G.; m. James Cobb Stewart, May 17, 1986. BS, Rochester Inst. Tech., 1975, MBA, 1976. Tax mgr. Deloitte Haskins & Sells, Rochester, N.Y., 1976-82; pres. Lamanna & Goyer, PC, CPAs, Rochester, 1982-89; owner Goyer & Assocs., CPAs, Rochester, 1989-93; pres. Virginia L. Goyer, CPA, P.C., Rochester, 1993—. Mem. adv. bd. Salvation Army, Rochester, 1985-88, Rochester Inst. Tech. Deferred Giving, 1988-89; mem. bd. Nat. Women's Hall of Fame, 1993-98; bd. dirs., treas. Friends of Women's Rights Nat. Park Inc., 2000-05, pres., 2005—. Mem. AICPA (nat. coun. 1995-98), Fla. Inst. CPAs, N.Y. State Inst. CPAs (bd. dirs. 1990-93, v.p. 1994-95, 1st woman pres. Rochester chpt. 1988-89), Rochester Women's Network, Nat. Assn. Women Bus. Owners (bd. dirs. 1992-93), Estate Planning Coun. (bd. dirs. 1987-89), NOW, Century Club Rochester (bd. dirs., fin. chair 2001-05) Office: 354 Westminster Rd Rochester NY 14607-3233

GOYNE, RODERICK A., lawyer; b. Denver, Aug. 13, 1949; BA with highest honors, hist., U. Tex., Arlington, 1971; JD cum laude, Harvard U., 1974. Bar: Tex. 1974. Ptnr. Baker & Botts LLP, Dallas. Recipient Am.'s Leading Bus. Lawyers, Chambers USA Guide, 2003, Tex. Super Lawyer, Tex. Monthly and Law & Politics, 2003, World's Leading Banking Lawyers, Euromoney's Expert Guide, 2005, Internat. Who's Who of Capital Markets Lawyers, 2005, Best Lawyers in Dallas, D Mag., 2005, Best Lawyers in Am., 2006—07. Mem. ABA, State Bar Tex. (chmn. legal opinions com. bus. law sect. 1992—), Am. Coll. Investment Counsel (trustee 1993—), Tex. Assn. Bank Counsel, Dallas Bar Assn., TriBar Opinion Com. Office: Baker & Botts LLP 2001 Ross Ave Ste 900 Dallas TX 75201-2917 Office Phone: 214-953-6527. Office Fax: 214-661-4527. Business E-Mail: rick.goyne@bakerbotts.com.

GOYOL, APOLLOS BITRUS, education educator; b. Gindiri, Nigeria, June 30, 1960; s. Goyol Bitrus Bakkuk and Rhoda Bitrus Goyol; m. Jemima Apollos Phillip, June 5, 1993; children: Wadelnen Jane, Nenfot Samuel. PhD, Western Mich. U., 1997—2002. Asst. prof. and evaluator U. Ark. for Med. Scis., Little Rock, 2003—05; head dept. Plateau State Poly., Barkin-Ladi, Nigeria, 1984—97; cons. U. Ky., Lexington, 2005—. Dir. planning and implementation Alternative Trade Network of Nigeria, Plateau State, Nigeria, 1995—2002. Author: Adjustment Problems of African Students at Public Universities in America, 2005. Pres. of African student union Western Mich. U., 1999—2001. Recipient Outstanding Cmty. Svc. award, Jack & Jill of Am., Inc, 1998. Mem.: Am. Ednl. Rsch. Assn., Am. Evaluation Assn. (assoc.). Home Phone: 501-960-9761; Office Phone: 859-268-9965. Fax: 501-686-7053. Business E-Mail: apollos.goyol@hotmail.com.

GOZA, FRANKLIN WILLIAM, sociology educator; b. Peoria, Ill., July 19, 1955; s. Franklin Delano Roosevelt and Zona Ann (Challe) G.; m. Lynn Louise Tratnik, Nov. 8, 1986; children: Angelica L., Olivia C. BA magna cum laude, U. Wis., 1980, MS, 1983, PhD, 1987. Vis. prof. demography Fed. U. Minas Gerais, Belo Horizonte, Brazil, 1987-89; asst. prof. sociology Bowling Green (Ohio) State U., 1989-94, assoc. prof., 1994—. Contbr. articles to profl. jours. Rockefeller Found. fellow, 1987-89; sr. Fulbright scholar Brazil, 1992-93. Mem. Am. Sociol. Assn., Population Assn. Am., Brazilian Population Assn., Phi Kappa Phi, Sigma Delta Pi. Avocations: languages, travel. Office: Bowling Green State U Dept Sociology Bowling Green OH 43403-0001

GOZANI, TSAHI, nuclear physicist; b. Tel Aviv, Nov. 25, 1934; came to U.S., 1965; s. Arieh and Rivcca Gozani; m. Adit Soffer, Oct. 14, 1958; children: Mor, Shai Nachum, Or Pinchas, Tal. BSc, Technion-Israel Inst. Tech., 1956, MSc, 1958; DSc, Swiss Fed. Inst. Tech., 1962. Registered profl. nuc. engr., Calif.; accredited nuc. material mgr. Rsch. physicist Israel Atomic Energy Commn., Beer-Sheva, 1962—65; rsch. assoc. nuc. engring. dept. Rensselaer Poly. Inst., Troy, NY, 1965—66; sr. staff scientist Gen.-Atomic & IRT, San Diego, 1966—70, 1971—75; prof. applied physics Tel Aviv U., 1971; chief scientist, divsn. mgr. SAIC, Palo Alto and Sunnyvale, Calif., 1975—84, v.p., chief scientist Sunnyvale, 1984—87, corp. v.p. Santa Clara, Calif., 1987—93, sr. v.p., 1993—97; pres., CEO Ancore Corp., Santa Clara, 1997—2002; pres. Rapiscan Sys. Neutronics and Advanced Tech. Corp., Santa Clara, 2002—07, CEO, pres. emeritus, chief scientist, 2007—. Lady Davis vis. prof. Technion-Israel Inst. Tech., 1983-84; bd. dirs. Radiation Sci. Inst., San Jose State U. Author: Active Non-Destructive Assay of Nuclear Materials, 1981; co-author: Handbook of Nuclear Safeguards Measurement Methods, 1983; contbr. articles to profl. jours., chapters to books. Recipient 1989 Laurel award Aviation Week Jour., R&D 100 award, 1988, Most Innovative New Products. Fellow Am. Nuc. Soc.; mem. Am. Phys. Soc., Inst. Nuc. Materials. Achievements include patents for explosive detection system, explosive detection system using an artificial neural system, multi sensor explosive detection system, composite cavity structure for an explosive detection system, apparatus and method for detecting contraband using fast neutron activation, contraband detection system using direct imaging pulsed fast neutrons; invention of method to measure nuclear reactor's reactivity. Office: Rapiscan Sys Neutronics and Advanced Tech Corp 520 Almanor Ave Sunnyvale CA 94085-3533 Business E-Mail: tgozani@rapiscansystems.com.

GOZON, RICHARD C., retired paper distribution executive; b. Pitts., Oct. 9, 1938; s. Frank J. and Helen (Franklin) G.; m. Fran A. Burmeister, June 21, 1940; children: Cheryl, Michael, Diana. BS in Bus., Valparaiso U., 1960; advanced mgmt. program, Harvard U., 1978. With sales dept. Champion Internat., Hamilton, Ohio, 1959-61; dir. sales Nationwide Papers, Chgo., 1961-72; pres. Rourke Eno Paper Co., Hartford, Conn., 1972-78; exec. v.p. Unisource Corp., Phila., 1978-79, pres., 1979-85; v.p. Alco Standard Corp., Phila., 1982, dir., 1983, exec. v.p., COO, 1987, pres., COO, 1988—93; pres. Alco Paper & Office Products, Phila., 1983, Paper Corp. of Am., Phila., 1985-87; exec. v.p., CEO Alco Standard Corp., Valley Forge, Pa., 1988; exec. v.p. Weyerhaeuser Co., 1994—2002; bd. dir. Amerisource Bergen, 2001—, chmn., 2006—. Trustee Richard Roberts Real estate Growth Trus I, Avon, Conn.; dir. UGI Corp., UGI Utilities, Inc., Triumph Group, Inc. and Amerigas Partners LP. Dir., World Affaris Coun. of Phila. Mem. Sales & Mktg. Execs. Club. Clubs: Merion Golf (Ardmore, Pa.); Pine Valley golf (Clementon, N.J.); Harvard Bus. Sch. Republican. Lutheran. Avocations: golf, tennis, skiing.*

GOZONSKY, EDWIN O. O., investment broker; b. Laconia, NH, Mar. 31, 1930; s. Archie and Ida G.; m. Dorothy Adelson, Feb. 28, 1965; children: Judith, Diane. BA, Yale U., New Haven, Conn., 1952; MBA, Harvard U., Cambridge, Mass., 1954. With Eastman Dillon, Union Securities (merged with Paine Webber 1980), Boston, 1959—, v.p. Boston office, 1971—; pres. Variable Annuities Provide Personal Security, 1979—. Lectr. in retirement income, sales variable annuities, bonds, 1979—; mem. investment coms. Maine and R.I. Founds.; mem. compliance com. New Eng., Nat. Assn. Securities Dealers, 1994-96. With U.S. Army, 1954-56. Mem. Bulldog Soc. (provisional dir.), Harvard Bus. Sch. Alumni (class sec. 1988—). Home: 118 Irving Ave Providence RI 02906-4510 Office: UBS/Paine Webber One Post Office Sq Boston MA 02109

GRAB, FREDERICK CHARLES, lawyer; b. NYC, Aug. 1, 1946; s. Daniel Justin and Elizabeth (Kam) G. BS in Aerospace Engring., Polytech U. N.Y., 1967; JD, U. So. Calif., 1977. Bar: Calif. 1978, U.S. Dist. Ct. (cen. dist.) Calif. 1978, U.S. Supreme Ct. 1988, U.S. Ct. Appeals (9th cir.) 1989. Deputy atty. gen. Calif. Atty. Gen., LA, 1977-2000. Polit. journalist:; contbr. articles to profl. jours. Polit. activist. Avocations: playwright, author, composer, musican.

GRABAR, OLEG, retired art educator; b. Strasbourg, France, Nov. 3, 1929; arrived in US, 1948, naturalized, 1960; s. Andre and Julie (Ivanova) G.; m. Terry Ann Harris, June 9, 1951; children: Nicolas Howard, Anne Louise. BA magna cum laude, Harvard U., Cambridge, Mass., 1950; licence d'Histoire, U. Paris, 1950; PhD, Princeton U., NJ, 1955; D (hon.), U. Mich. Instr. U. Mich., 1954-55, asst. prof., 1955-59, assoc. prof., 1959-64, prof., 1964-69; dir. Am. Sch. of Oriental Rsch., Jerusalem, Jordan, 1960-61, v.p., 1968-75; prof. fine arts Harvard U., 1969-81, Aga Khan prof. Islamic art, 1981-90; with sch. hist. studies Inst. For Advanced Study, Princeton, NJ, 1990-99; ret., 1999. Dir. Mich.-Harvard U. excavations in Syria, 1964-71. Author: Coinage of Tulunide, 1957, Islamic Architecture and Its Decoration, 1967, Sasanian Silver, 1967, The Formation of Islamic Art, 1973, The Alhambra, 1978, City in the Desert, 1978, Epic Images, 1982, Illustrations of the Maqamat, 1984, Islamic Art, 1987, Great Mosque of Isfahan, 1989, The Mediation of Ornament, 1992, The Shape of the Holy, 1996, La Peinture Persane, 1999, Mostly Miniatures, 2000, Islamic Art and Architecture, 660-1250, 2001, Constructing the Study of Islamic Art, 2005—06, The Dome of the Rock, 2006; editor: Ars Orientalis, 1957—71, Muqarnas, 1983—92; contbr. articles to profl. jours. Mem. Coll. Art Assn. (dir. 1968-72), Archeol. Inst. Am., Mediaeval Acad. Am., German Archeol. Inst., Mid. Ea. Studies Assn., Am. Acad. Arts and Scis., Am. Philosophy Soc., Brit. Acad. (hon.), Austrian Acad. (hon.), Acad. Inscriptions et Belles-Lettres (Paris). Home: 43 Maxwell Ln Princeton NJ 08540-4931 Office: Inst for Advanced Study Princeton NJ 08540 Office Phone: 609-734-8310. Business E-Mail: grabar@ias.edu.

GRABENSTEIN, JOHN DOUGLAS, pharmacist, military officer; b. Cumberland, Md., Aug. 12, 1957; s. Herman J. and Irene R. (Ley) G.; m. Laurie Ann Sandquist, Oct. 16, 1982; children: Emily C., Andrea L., Erica K., Peter C. BS in Pharmacy, Duquesne U., Pitts., 1980; EdM with honors, Boston U., 1988; MS in Pharmacy Adminstrn., U. NC, 1991, PhD in Epidemiology, 1999. CPH pharmacist. Commd. officer US Army, 1975, advanced through grades to col., 1979—2006; supr. satellite pharmacies Walter Reed Army Med. Ctr., Washington, 1981-83, chief allergen extract lab., 1983-85; chief pharmacy svc. US Army Hosp., Bremerhaven, 1986-89; resident in pharmacy practice and pharm. care Fitzsimons Army Med. Ctr., Aurora, Colo., 1991-92; chief human subjects protection US Army Clin. Investigation Regulatory Office, Ft. Sam Houston, 1992-96; dir. mil. vaccine program Army Surgeon Gen.'s Office, Falls Church, Va., 1999—2006; dir. scientific affairs Merck Vaccine Divsn., 2006—. Pharmacy rep. influenza and pneumococcal action group Nat. Coalition on Adult Immunization, 1991-99; clin. adv. Inst. Safe Medication Practices, 1995—; mem. adv. bd. Immunization Action Coalition and Hepatitis B Coalition, 1997—2006; chmn. USP Immunology Info. Expert Com., 2005—; presenter in field. Author: ImmunoFacts: Vaccines and Immunologic Drugs, 1993— (named Best New Health Sci. Books of 1993, Doody's Rating Svc.), 2002, Phi Delta Chi: A Tradition of Leaders in Pharmacy, 1995, Pocket ImmunoFacts: Vaccines and Immunologics, 1997, 4th edit. 2002, Immunization Delivery: A Complete Guide, 1997, Pharmacy-Based Immunization Delivery: A National Certificate Training Program, 1997, 8th edit. 2005; author: (with others) American Hospital Formulary Service-Drug Information, 1987, 88, American Society of Hospital Pharmacists, 1987, 2d edit. 1988, Sterile Dosage Forms: Their Preparation and Clinical Application, 3rd edit., 1987, 4th edit., 1994, Nurses Drug Facts, 1996, Guidelines for Pharmacy-Based Immunization Advocacy, 1997; editor, prin. author The Communicator of Phi Delta Chi Pharmacy Frat., 1985-95, Booster Shots, 1994-2001; editor Allergy-Clinical Immunology Specialist Training Manual, 3rd edit., 1984, 4th edit., 1985, Leader-Development Seminar: Facilitator Guide and Participant Syllabus, 1989-92, ImmunoGuide: Response to Disaster, 1993, 3rd edit., 1999; mem. editl. bd. Hosp. Pharmacy, 1990-2002, DRUGDEX Info. Sys., 1992-98, Drug Facts and Comparisons, 1993-2006, ISMP Medication Safety Alert, 1997—, Needle Tips and Hepatitis B News, 1997-2006; contbg. editor Jour. Am. Pharm. Assn., 1998-2002; moderator electronic bull. bd., Internet website; reviewer various pubs.; referee numerous profl. jours.; contbr. articles to profl. jours. Chmn. student-faculty-parent senate Bishop Walsh H.S., Cumberland, Md., 1974-75. Recipient Student Pub. Affairs award Am. Assn. Colls. Pharmacy, 1978, Eli Lilly award for outstanding scholastic and profl. achievement and leadership, 1980, Pharmacy Rsch. award US Army, 1991, Career Achievement award We. Md. Cath. Schs., 1997, Duquesne U. Alumni Achievement award, 1998, Pinnacle award Health Care Quality Alliance, 1998, Du Mez Lectr. award U. Md., 1999, Pharmacy Practice Rsch. award Am. Soc. Health-Sys. Pharmacists, 2002, Rho Chi Nat. Leadership award, 2002, Andrew Craigie Fed. Pharmacy Career Achievement award, 2004, Francke award for mentoring leadership, 2006, ASHP award Sustained Contbn. Lit. and Pharm. Practice, 2006; named Model Mayor of Cumberland, Model City Coun. Bishop Walsh H.S., 1975; named one of Outstanding Young Men in Am., 1980, 96. Fellow Nat. Cath. Pharmacists Guild, Am. Pharm. Assn. (mem. acad. pharmacy practice and mgmt., judge student patient counseling competition 1986, strategic and tactical analysis team on pharmacy payment reform 1995-99, dir. immunication delivery ednl. program 1996—2006); mem. Fedn. Internat. Pharmaceutique, Christian Pharmacists Fedn. Internat., Assn. Mil. Surgeons of US (Andrew Craigie award), Am. Soc. Health-Sys. Pharmacists, Soc. Infectious Disease Pharmacists, Phi Delta Chi (nat. grand pres. 1995-99, dir. pharmacy leadership and edn. inst. 1996—, nat. collegiate v.p. 1983-85, nat. v.p. comm. 1985-95, leader devel. seminars 1989-92), Delta Omega, Rho Chi, Phi Lambda Sigma. Roman Catholic. Avocations: reading, history. Office: Merck Vaccine Divsn PO Box 4 West Point PA 19486

GRABER, DORIS APPEL, political scientist, writer, editor; b. St. Louis, Nov. 11, 1923; d. Ernest and Martha (Insel) Appel; m. Thomas M. Graber, June 15, 1941; children: Lee Winston, Thomas Woodrow, Jack Douglas, Jim Murray, Susan Doris AB, Washington U., St. Louis, 1941, MA, 1942; PhD, Columbia U., 1947. Feature writer St. Louis County Observer, Univ. City Tribune, 1939—41; civilian dir. U.S. Army Ednl. Reconditioning Program, Camp Maxey, Tex., 1943—45; editor legal mags. Commerce Clearing House, Chgo., 1945—46; lectr. polit. sci. Northwestern U., 1948—49, U. Chgo., 1950—51, rsch. assoc. Ctr. for Study Am. Fgn. and Mil. Policy, 1952—71; lectr. polit. sci. North Park Coll., 1952; mem. faculty U. Ill., Chgo., 1964—, assoc. prof. polit. sci., 1964—69, prof., 1970—; editor textbooks Harper & Row, Evanston, 1956—63. Vis. prof. Harvard U., 1996 Author: The Development of the Law of Belligerent Occupation, 1949, 68, Crisis Diplomacy: A History of U.S. Intervention Policies and Practices, 1959, Public Opinion, The President and Foreign Policy, 1968, Verbal Behavior and Politics, 1976, Mass Media and American Politics, 1980, 84, 89, 93, 96, 2001, 2005, Crime News and the Public, 1980, (with others) Media Agenda Setting in a Presidential Election, 1981, Processing the News: How People Tame the Information Tide, 1984, 88, 94, Public Sector Communication: How Organizations Manage Information, 1992; editor, contbr. The President and the Public, 1982; editor, contbr.: Media Power in Politics, 1984, 90, 94, 2000, 2006; editor: Political Comm., 1992-98, founding editor emeritus, 1998—, mem. editl. bd., 2001—; editor: (with others) The Politics of News: The News of Politics, 1998, 2007, Processing Politics: Learning from Television in the Internet Age, 2001 (Goldsmith Book prize 2003), The Power of Communication, 2003; book rev. editor Polit. Psychology, 1998—; mem. editl. bd. Polit. Sci. Quarterly, 1978—, Human Comm. Rsch., 1979-80, Pub. Opinion Quarterly, 1980-84, 93-98, Jour. Comm., 1985-91, 99—, Social Sci. Quarterly, 1989-2003, P.S.: Polit. Sci. and Politics, 1990-93, Discourse and Soc., 1990—, Discourse and Comm., 2006, Orgnl. Comm: Emerging Perspectives, 1994—, Jour. Health Comm., 1995-98, Harvard Internat. Jour. Press/Politics, 1995—, Acta Politica: Internat. Jour. Polit. Sci., 1997—, Comm., Soc. and Politics Series, Cambridge U. Press, 1999—, Polit. Comm., 2001—, Media and Am. Politics Ency., 2003—; contbr. articles to profl. jours Recipient Disting. Alumna award, Washington U., 2001, Univ. Scholar award, U. Ill., Chgo., 2003—. Mem. LWV, Am. Assn. Pub. Opinion Rsch., Midwest Assn. Pub. Opinion Rsch. (coun. 1978-83, program chmn. 1978-79, pres. 1980-81, Career award 1988), Midwest Polit. Sci. Assn. (past pres. 1972-73, coun. 1973-74, program sect. chair 1979, Career award 1994), Am. Polit. Sci. Assn. (coun. 1978-79, v.p. 1980-81, program chmn. 1984, chmn. polit. comm. sect. 1989-91, chmn. editl. bd. Polit. Sci. 1992-94), Internat. Polit. Sci. Assn., Nat. Comm. Assn. (Career award, 2006), Internat. Commn. Assn. (divsn. program chmn. 1978-80, divsn. chmn. 1980-82, chmn. program 1990, chmn. pre-program 2004, Career award 1996), Assn. Edn. for Journalism, Acad. Polit. Sci., Am. Acad. Polit. and Social Sci., Internat. Soc. Polit. Psychology (coun. 1992-93, 95-98, co-program chmn. 1993-94, pres. 1995-96, Career award, 2007), Phi Beta Kappa (pres. Iota of Ill. chpt. 1991-92), Pi Sigma Alpha, Pi Alpha Alpha Home: 2895 Sheridan Pl Evanston IL 60201-1725 Office: U Ill 1007 W Harrison St Chicago IL 60607-7135 Office Phone: 312-996-3108. Business E-Mail: dgraber@uic.edu.

GRABER, ELIZABETH, communications educator, literature educator; b. Salem, Oreg., July 18, 1950; d. Gordon and Virginia Graber; m. Michael Hawfield, July 7, 2001; 1 child, Jennifer Hartman. BA in Secondary English Edn., Oreg. State U., Corvallis, 1972; MA in Tchg. Adult and Cmty. Edn., Alaska Pacific U., Anchorage, 1989; PhD in Rhetoric and Linguistics, Ind. U., Pa., 2002. Tchr. lang. arts Scio Mid. Sch., Oreg.; tchr. English Silverton Union H.S., Oreg.; adj. instr. English Kenai Peninsula coll. U. Alaska, Homer, coord. adult basic edn. Kenai Peninsula coll., prof. English Kenai Peninsula coll., 1989—. Host ann. pub. poetry readings Kenai Peninsula coll. U. Alaska, 1990—. Vol. Homer Coun. Arts, 1995—2006; vol. and mem. Homer Soc. Natural History, Homer, Alaska, 1997—2006. Recipient Chancellor's Tchg. Excellence award, U. Alaska, 1989, James Berlin Outstanding Dissertation award, Conf. Coll. Composition and Comm., 2003. Mem.: Nat. Coun. Tchrs. English. Avocations: african marimba ensemble, camping, kayaking, knitting, travel. Office: Kenai Peninsula Coll 533 East Pioneer Ave Homer AK 99603 Home Phone: 907-235-6078; Office Phone: 907-235-6078.

GRABER, MARK L., internist; m. Deborah Graber; children: Lauren, Emily. BS, Yale U., 1971; MD, Stanford U., 1975. Diplomate Am. Bd. Internal Medicine, 1978. Chief, med. svc. VA Med. Ctr., Northport, NY, 1992—. Prof., vice chair medicine dept. SUNY, Stony Brook. Office: VA Med Ctr Middleville Rd Northport NY 11768

GRABER, RICHARD WILLIAM, ambassador, lawyer; b. Lakewood, Ohio, July 31, 1956; s. Richard Allen and Lynn Carol (Hurschman) G.; m. Alexandria Ahlquist Richardson, Apr. 28, 1984; children: Scott Bailey, Erik Richard. AB magna cum laude, Duke U., 1978; JD, Boston U., 1981. Bar: Wis. 1981. Atty. Reinhart Boerner Van Deuren Norris & Rieselbach, S.C., Milw., 1981—2006, pres., CEO, 2004—06; US amb. to Czech Republic US Dept. State, Prague, 2006—. Bd. governors, Wis. Patient Compensation Fund, 1988-97; chmn., Wis. Rep. Party, 1999-2006, fin. chmn., 1993-99; mem. exec. com. North Shore Rep. Club, Milw., 1988—, Reps. of Wis., 1991; mem. Am. Coun. Young Polit. Leaders, 1990; candidate for Wis. Assembly, 1990; chmn. Kasten for Senate com. 1993; mem. bd. appeals, Village of Shorewood, 1991—, bd. trustees, Medical Coll. Wis., 1997—. Mem. Rotary (pres. Milw. 1988-89, Paul Harris fellow 1990). Avocations: politics, softball, basketball. Office: US Embassy Amb 5630 Prague Pl Washington DC 20521*

GRABER, SAMUEL DAVID, environmental and water resources engineer, consultant; b. NYC, Jan. 12, 1942; s. Sam Mandel Graber and Maud Alice Larson; m. Arlene Jenkins Graber, June 19, 1965; children: Steven David, Brian Earl, Keven Lee, Allen Eben. BSME, U. Miami, 1963; SMME, MIT, 1965, CE, 1966. Profl. engring., N.Y., 1970, Ma., 1975. Project engr. Camp Dresser & McKee Inc, Boston, 1966—67, dir. hydraulic svcs., 1969—74; wastewater tech. dir. Metcalf & Eddy Inc, Boston, 1974—77; cons. engr. Stoughton, Mass., 1977—. Contbr. articles to profl. jours. Scout leader Boy Scouts Am., Stoughton, 1976—, scoutmaster, 1980—94. Capt. US Army, 1967—69, Panama. Recipient Eagle Scout, Boy Scouts Am., 1954. Mem.: ASME, ASCE (urban drainge stds. com. 1993—, Samuel A. Greeley award 1969, J.C. Stevens award 1972, Samuel A. Greeley award 2005), Water Environment Fedn., Tau Beta Pi. Independent. Unitarian Universalist. Avocations: reading, history, genealogy, fishing, travel. Office Phone: 781-341-0390.

GRABER, SUSAN P., federal judge; b. Oklahoma City, July 5, 1949; d. Julius A. and Bertha (Fenyves) Graber; m. William June, May 3, 1981; 1 child, Rachel June-Graber. BA, Wellesley Coll., 1969; JD, Yale U., 1972. Bar: N.Mex. 1972, Ohio 1977, Oreg. 1978. Asst. atty. gen. Bur. of Revenue, Santa Fe, 1972—74; assoc. Jones Gallegos Snead & Wertheim, Santa Fe, 1974—75, Taft Stettinius & Hollister, Cin., 1975—78; assoc., then ptnr. Stoel Rives Boley Jones & Grey, Portland, Oreg., 1978—88; judge pro tem Multonomah County Dist. Ct., 1983—88; arbitrator Oreg. Circuit Ct., 4th Jud. Dist., 1985—88; mediator US Dist. Ct., Dist. Oreg., 1986—88; judge, then presiding judge Oreg. Ct. Appeals, Salem, 1988—90; assoc. justice Oreg. Supreme Ct., Salem, 1990—98; judge US Ct. Appeals (9th cir.), Portland, 1998—. Mem. Gov.'s Adv. Coun. on Legal Svcs., 1979—88; mem. bd. visitors Sch. Law, U. Oreg., 1986—93; bd. dirs. US Dist. Ct. of Oreg. Hist. Soc., 1985—, Oreg. Law Found., 1990—91. Mem.: Am. Law Inst., ABA, Am. Inns of Ct. (master), Oreg. Appellate Judges Assn. (sec.-treas. 1990—91, vice chair 1991—92, chair 1992—93), Oreg. Jud. Conf. (edn. com. 1988—91, program chair 1990), Ninth Cir. Jud. Conf. (chair exec. com. 1987—88), Oreg. State Bar (jud. adminstrn. com. 1985—87, pro bono com. 1988—90), Phi Beta Kappa. Mailing: US Ct Appeals 9th Cir Pioneer Courthouse 555 SW Yamhill St Portland OR 97204*

GRABER, THOMAS M., orthodontist, researcher; b. St. Louis, May 27, 1917; Diplomate Am. Bd. Orthodontics. DMD, Washington U., St. Louis, 1940; MS in Dentistry, Northwestern U., 1946, PhD in Anatomy, 1950; PhD (hon.), U. Gothenberg, 1989; DSc (hon.), Washington U., 1991, U. Mich., 1994, U. Kunming, 1996, Aristotle U., Thessaloniki, Greece, 2005. Diplomate Am. Bd. Orthodontics (Recognition award 1990, Dewel award, 1992). Mem. faculty Northwestern U. Dental Sch., 1946-58, assoc. prof. orthodontics, 1954-58; dir. research Northwestern U. Dental Sch. (cleft lip and palate Inst.), 1947-58; assoc. attending orthodontist Children's Meml. Hosp., Chgo., 1951-58; vis. lectr. U. Mich. Dental Sch., 1958-67; dir. Kenilworth Research Found., Ill., 1967—; prof. orthodontics Zoller Dental Clinic; pediatrics research assoc. prof. anthropology and anatomy U. Chgo., 1969-81, assoc. prof. plastic and reconstructive surgery, 1980-82; research scientist ADA Research Inst., Chgo., 1980-90; dir. G.V. Black Inst. for Continuing Edn., 1967—; vis. prof. U. Mich., 1984-94; clin. prof. orthodontics U. Ill. Coll. Dentistry, Chgo., 1994—. Northcroft lectr., Birmingham, Eng., 1989; cons. in field. Author textbooks, articles; editor-in-chief Am. Jour. Orthodontics, 1985-2000, World Jour Orthodontics, 2000-07. Served as capt. Dental Corps AUS, 1941-45. Decorated Japanese Order of the Sacred Treasure; recipient Alumni Merit award Northwestern U., 1977; named Disting. Alumnus Washington U., 1980; NIH grantee, 1954, 56-60, 76, 77, 79, 80, 85, 86. Fellow Royal Coll. Surgeons (Eng.), Am. Coll. Dentists, Internat. Coll. Dentists; mem. Am. Dental Soc., Ill. Dental Soc., Am. Assn. Orthodontists (gen. chmn. 1960, 77, 80, founding mem., chmn. coun. on orthodontic edn. and audio visual com. 1962, 67, gen. chmn. jour. 1977, trustee, Grieve Meml. award 1964, 84, Disting. Service award 1970, Ketcham award 1975, Salzmann award 1979, 75th Anniversary citation 1990, Mershon award 1989, Horace Hayden award 1991, Jarabak Internat. Teaching and Rsch. award 1994, Heritage award 1998, 99), Internat. Assn. Research (chmn. Chgo. sect. 1973-74), Chgo. Orthodontists Assn. (pres. 1961-62), European Orthodontists Soc.(hon. life), Ill. Orthodontists Soc. (pres. 1969-70, Outstanding Tchg. award 1999), Angle Soc. (pres. 1968), Japan Orthodontists Soc., World Fedn. Orthodontists (hon., Millenium award 2000), Ill. Soc. Orthodontists, SAR. Presbyterian. Home: 2895 Sheridan Pl Evanston IL 60201-1725 Office: U Ill Coll Dentistry 801 S Paulina St # Mc842 Chicago IL 60612-7210 Office Phone: 312-996-2293. Personal E-mail: tmgraber@comcast.net. Business E-Mail: tgraber@uic.edu.

GRABER, WILLIAM RAYMOND, former pharmaceutical executive; b. Vancouver, Wash., Apr. 10, 1943; s. R. Archie and Josephine N. (Martin) G.; m. Mary Lynn McArthur, June 19, 1965; children: Kristine, Kathleen, Timothy. BA in Math., Wash. State U., 1965. Fin. mgr. GE, 1965-91; contr. The Mead Corp., Dayton, Ohio, 1991—99; CFO, sr. v.p. McKesson HBOC, San Francisco, 2000—03. Avocations: golf, jogging.

GRABITSKE, DAVID M., historian; s. Dwight D. and Patricia A. Grabitske. BS, Mankato State U., Minn., 1992; Masters in Non-profit Adminstrn., Met. State U., St. Paul, 2007. Libr. asst. Blue Earth Co. Hist. Soc., Mankato, Minn., 1994—95; historian DAR, Mendota, Minn., 1995—2003; lead guide Minn. Hist. Soc., St. Paul, 1996—99, program officer, 2000—. Bd. chair Living History Soc. Minn., Mendota, 2002—06; vice chair Field Svcs. Alliance, Nashville, 2005—. Trustee Elmhurst Cemetery, St. Paul, 2006—; mem. St. John Luth. Ch., 2003—. Mem.: Am. Assn. State and Local History (awards com. mem. 2004—), WELS Hist. Inst., Nat. Coun. Pub. History. Republican. Lutheran. Avocations: travel, singing, painting.

GRABOFF, MARC, broadcast executive; m. Debi Graboff; children: Jessica, Nicole, Bradley. BA in comm. studies, UCLA, 1977; JD magna cum laude, Loyola Law Sch., 1983. Founding ptnr. Silverberg, Katz, Thompson & Braun; ptnr. Troop, Meisinger, Steuber & Pasich, LA; sr. v.p. CBS Entertainment, 1997—2000; exec. v.p. NBC West Coast, Burbank, Calif., 2000—04, NBC Universal TV Group, 2004—06; pres. NBC Universal TV, West Coast, 2006—07; co-chmn. NBC Universal TV Studio (name changed to Universal Media Studios) & NBC Entertainment, 2007—. Office: Universal Media Studios 100 Universal City Plaza Universal City CA 91608*

GRABOW, RAYMOND JOHN, mayor, lawyer; b. Cleve., Jan. 27, 1932; s. Joseph Stanley and Frances (Kalata) G.; m. Margaret Jean Knoll, Nov. 27, 1969; children: Rachel Jean, Ryan Joseph. BSBA, Kent State U., Ohio, 1953; JD, Western Res. U., Cleve., 1958. Bar: Ohio 1958. Counsel No. Ohio Petroleum Retailers Assn., Cleve., 1965-78; counsel, trustee Alliance of Poles Fed. Credit Union, 1972; also gen. counsel Alliance of Poles of Am., Parma Polish Am. League; councilman City of Warrensville Heights (Ohio), 1962-68, mayor, 1968-98. Sec. Space Comfort Co., S.S.K., Inc.; fed. panelist U.S. Dist. Ct.; active Dem. Exec. Com. Cuyahoga County, 1966—98, precinct com., 1966—80; trustee Brentwood Hosp., Nat. League Cities, Brentwood Found.; bd. govs. Meridia Southpoint Hosp., 1996—99. Mem. cmty. adv. bd. Marymount Hosp. Mem. Ohio Jud. Conf. (life), Ohio State Bar Assn., Cuyahoga County Bar Assn., Cleve. Bar Assn., U.S. Conf. of Mayors, Am. Legion, PLAV Vets, Cleve. Soc., Warrensville Heights C. of C. (trustee 1989-98), Ohio Assn. Pub. Safety Dirs., Ohio Mcpl. League, Mcpl. Treas. Assn., Order of Alhambra, Fraternal Order of Eagles, West Harbor Lagoons Assn. (pres.); bd. dirs. Brentwood Ctr.

Excellence, LLC Southpointe Hosp. Home: 10545 Cambridge Cir Cleveland OH 44133- Office: 5005 Rockside Rd Cleveland OH 44131-2194 Office Phone: 216-447-4496. Personal E-mail: rjggfl@juno.com.

GRABOW, STEPHEN HARRIS, architecture educator; b. Bklyn., Jan. 15, 1943; s. Philip and Ida (England) G.; 1 child, Nicole Elizabeth. BArch., U. Mich., 1965; MArch., Pratt Inst., 1966; postgrad., U. Calif.-Berkeley, 1966-67; PhD, U. Wash., 1973. Architect-planner U.S. Peace Corps, Tunisia, 1967-69; regional planning cons. Teheran, Iran, 1969; asst. prof. architecture U. Ariz., 1969-70; teaching assoc. U. Wash., 1970-72; lectr. town and regional planning Duncan of Jordanstone Coll. Art, U. Dundee, Scotland, 1972-73; asst. prof. architecture and urban design U. Kans.-Lawrence, 1973-76, assoc. prof., 1976-82, prof., 1982—, dir. architecture, 1979-82, 83-86; vis. fellow U. Calif.-Berkeley, 1977; research and design cons. Design Build Architects, Lawrence; bd. dirs. Assn. Collegiate Schs. Architecture, 1982-87. Vis. lectr. Royal Danish Acad. Fine Arts, Copenhagen, 1987-88. Author: Christopher Alexander and the Search for a New Paradigm in Architecture, 1983; mem. editorial bd.: Jour. Archtl. Edn., 1982-84. Recipient award Nat. Endowment for Arts, 1974, citation for excellence in design rsch. NEA, 1980, Biennial Svc. award Denmark's Internat. Studies Program, 1997, Bradley Tchg. award in architecture U. Kans., 1998; Fulbright Scholar award, 1987-88; NEH fellow, 1976-77. Mem. Nat. Archtl. Research Council (appointee 1986-87). Home: 1518 Crossgate Dr Lawrence KS 66047-3504 Office: U Kans Sch Architecture & Urban Design 1465 Jayhawk Blvd Lawrence KS 66045-7614 Office Phone: 785-864-3186. Business E-Mail: sgrabow@ku.edu.

GRABOWSKI, JON, real estate company executive; b. 1981; Sales Johnson & johnson; pres., COO Esquire Properties, Detroit. Named one of 40 Under 40, Crain's Detroit Bus., 2006. Office: Esquire Properties 2900 E Jefferson Detroit MI 48207 Office Phone: 313-580-2200.

GRABOWSKI, MICHAEL JOSEPH, financial executive; b. Milw., Dec. 17, 1961; s. Joseph Casmir and Cecile (Bendyk) G.; m. Denise Marie Krauske, Oct. 19, 1991. BBA in Fin., U. Wis., Milw., 1984; MBA, Keller Grad. Sch. Mgmt., Chgo., 1991. Customer acct. rep. Ford Motor Credit, Milw., 1984-85; fin. planner Capital Concepts Corp., Milw., 1984-87; pres. Michael Properties, Milw., 1987—; corp. controller Leo Lieberman, Inc., Milw., 1991-92; CFO Advance Cleaning Products, Milw., 1992-93; pres., acct., fin. adv. Insight Acctg. and Fin. Cons., Inc., Milw., 1987—. Author: (newsletter) Your Money Management, 1987. Mem. Nat. Assn. Enrolled Agts., Nat. Assn. Tac Prectitioners, Nat. Soc. Pub. Accts., St. Alphonsus Athletic Assn. (bd. dirs.). Avocation: athletic activities. Office: Insight Acctg & Fin Cons Inc 4712 W Forest Home Ave Milwaukee WI 53219-4716

GRABOWSKI, RICHARD JOSEPH, lawyer; b. LA, 1961; BA with gt. distinction, Calif. State U., Long Beach, 1983; JD, U. Calif., LA, 1986. Bar: Calif. 1986, admitted to practice: US Ct. of Appeals, Ninth Cir., US Dist. Courts, Northern, Southern, Eastern, Central Districts of Calif. Ptnr.-in-charge Irvine office Jones Day, Calif. Mem.: Orange County Bar Assn., Fed. Bar Assn., Assn. of Bus. Trial Lawyers (bd. dir.), Order of Coif. Office: Jones Day Ste 1100 3 Park Plz Irvine CA 92614-8505 Office Phone: 949-851-3939. Office Fax: 949-553-7539. Business E-Mail: rgrabowski@jonesday.com.

GRABOWSKI, RODNEY MICHAEL, academic administrator, consultant; b. Syracuse, NY, Aug. 16, 1967; s. Joseph J. and Myra L. Grabowski; m. Julie M. Freeman, Aug. 29, 1992. BA in Internat. Rels., Syracuse U., 1989; MBA in Internat. Bus., U. N. Fla., Jacksonville, 2007. Cert. fundraising exec. Cert. Fundraising Exec. Internat., 2002. Sr. dist. exec. Five Rivers Coun., Boy Scouts Am., Bath, NY, 1990—95; sr. devel. officer Alfred U., NY, 1995—99; exec. dir. devel. Jacksonville U., 1999—2002; assoc. v.p. devel., campaign dir. U. N. Fla., 2002—. Fundraising cons. Meliora Grp., Allegany, NY. Bd. mem. Isle Faith United Meth. Ch., Jacksonville, 2002—04, AFP First Coast Chpt., Jacksonville, 2000—07, pres., 2003; chair AFP Fla. Caucus, 2007. Mem.: Assn. Fundraising Profls. (assoc.; pres., first coast chpt. 2003—03), Rotary (assoc.; bd. mem. 2006—07, 2006). Methodist. Avocations: travel, swimming, camping, bicycling. Home: 13967 Sound Overlook Dr N Jacksonville FL 32224 Office: Univ N Fla 4567 St Johns Bluff Rd S Jacksonville FL 32224 Office Fax: 904-620-2109. Business E-Mail: rod.grabowski@unf.edu.

GRABSTALD, HARRY, urologist, oncologist; b. Hope, Ark., Feb. 17, 1922; s. Meier and Bessie Grabstald; m. Herta Grabstald, July 14, 1979 (div.). BS, So. Meth. U., Dallas, 1942; MD, U. Tex. Southwestern Med. Coll., Dallas, 1945. Diplomate Am. Bd. Urology. Attending surgeon Meml. Hosp. Sloan- Kettering Cancer Ctr., NYC, 1958—80; prof. urology Coll. Medicine Cornell U., 1960—80. Author: History of Urology at Memorial Hospital, 1997; contbr. more than 175 papers to sci. jours. Comdr. USPHS, 1947—53. Fellow: ACS.

GRACA, THOMAS JOHN, education educator, lawyer; b. Chgo., Feb. 7, 1975; s. Mark S. and Linda Mae Graca; m. Clare Elizabeth Bedell, Mar. 30, 1997. BS in Speech Commn., Tex. Christian U., Ft. Worth, 1995, M in Theol. Studies, 2000; MEd, U. Tex., Arlington, 1998; EdD, Tex. A&M U., Commerce, 2004; JD, Southern Meth. U., Dallas, 2004. Bar: Tex. 2004; cert. tchr. Tex., 1998. Asst. prof. U. Tex., Arlington. Contbr. articles to profl. jours. Mem.: ABA, Assn. Study of Higher Edn., Dallas Bar Assn., Edn. Law Assn., Am. Ednl. Rsch. Assn. Office: U Tex UTA Box 19227 Arlington TX 76019-0227 Office Phone: 817-272-0806. Office Fax: 817-272-2530. Business E-Mail: tgraca@uta.edu.

GRACE, DAVID, physician; b. Anchorage, Alaska, May 15, 1954; s. Walter Charles and Marion Grace; m. Lu Ann Watterson, Nov. 12, 1994. BA, North Ctrl. Coll., 1976; MD, U. Ill., Chgo., 1980. Diplomate Am. Bd. Internal Medicine, 1986. Intern, resident U. Ill. St. Francis Hosp., Peoria, 1980—83; ptnr. Pinnacle Med. Group, Bradenton, Fla., 1983—, v.p., 1999—2002. Chief medicine Blake Med. Ctr., Bradenton, Fla., 1991—93, chief staff, 1993—96. Office: Pinnacle Med Group 315 75th St W Bradenton FL 34209 Home Phone: 941-794-3315; Office Phone: 941-792-2211. Personal E-mail: david.grace3@verizon.net.

GRACE, GEORGE H., not-for-profit fundraiser; m. Barbara Grace; 3 children. BS, Tuskegee U.; MS, U. Miami. Cert. Engring. Corp. regional svc. mgr. Bell South, Fla. Mem. Hialeah and Greater Miami C. of C., Dade County Sch. Ptnrs., Dade County Urban League, Dade County Role Models of Distinction, Achievers of Greater Miami, Sweet Home Missionary Bapt. Ch., Dade County Commrs. Round Table. Named one of 100 Most Influential Black Americans, Ebony mag., 2004; recipient City of Miami Disting. Svc. Award, Dade Sch. Ptnrs. Award, 100 Most Influential Black Americans, Ebony mag., 2006. Mem.: Nat. Emergency Network Assn., Dade County NAACP, Omega Psi Phi Fraternity, Inc. (Grand Basileus 2003—06, Immediate Past Grand Basileus 2006—, Chap and Dist. Omega Man of Yr., Superior Svc. Award, Omega Eagle Award). Avocations: travel, golf. Office: Omega Psi Phi Fraternity 3951 Snapfinger Pkwy Decatur GA 30035 Office Phone: 404-284-5533. E-mail: omegagrace@aol.com.

GRACE, JAMES MARTIN, JR., lawyer; b. Columbus, Ohio, Sept. 6, 1967; s. James Martin and Letitia Jean (Stively) G.; m. Michèle Lee Sirna, June 22, 1991. BA, U. Notre Dame, 1989; JD cum laude, U. Houston, 1992. Bar: Tex. Law clk. to Hon. Samuel B. Kent U.S. Dist. Ct. (so. dist.) Tex., Galveston, 1992—93; assoc. Baker Botts, LLP, Houston, 1993—2000; sr. counsel Enron N.Am. Corp., Houston, 2000—01; mgr. Enron Wholesale Svcs., Houston, 2001—02; dir. Tex. state affairs Ctr. Point Energy Inc., Houston, 2002—05; shareholder Winstead, Sechrest & Minick PC, Houston, 2005—. Chmn. state rels. com. Greater Houston Partnership; mem. Maverick PAC of Tex. Mem.: Houston Law Alumni Assn. (dir.), Houston Law Rev. Alumni Assn. (dir.), Houston Bar Assn., State Bar Tex., U. Notre Dame Alumni Assn. (pres. Class of '89), R Club PAC (pres. 2004, dir.), Notre Dame Club Houston (bd. dirs.), Order of the Barons, Phi Delta Phi. Republican. Roman Catholic. Avocations: soccer, football, reading. Office: Winstead Sechrest & Minick PC 910 Travis St Ste 2400 Houston TX 77002 Office Phone: 713-650-2769. Business E-Mail: jgrace@winstead.com.

GRACE, JOHN EUGENE, business company executive; b. Dundee, Ill., Nov. 22, 1931; s. Arnold Victor and Louise Joan (Boncosky) G.; m. Janice Rae Fohey, June 30, 1956; children: Gregory Alan, Michael Brian, Michele Marie. BS in Bus. Adminstrn. with high honors, U. Ill., 1958; MSBA in Fin., No. Ill. U., 1976. Gen. acctg. mgr. Elgin Watch Co., Ill., 1958-60; corp. controller Newell Cos., Freeport, Ill., 1960-68; controller jewelry div. Josten's, Inc., Owatonna, Minn., 1968-71; v.p. fin., chief fin. officer, asst. sec. Duplex Products Inc., Sycamore, Ill., 1971-87, cons., 1987-97. Cons. in field Active local United Fund, Little League, YMCA. Served with USAF, 1951-53. Mem. Fin. Execs. Inst. (past pres., dir. Fox-Rock chpt.), IMA (past dir.), Adminstrv. Mgmt. Soc. (past dir.), Jaycees, C. of C., Beta Alpha Psi. Clubs: Elks. Republican. Methodist. Home and Office: 405 Timber Ln Palm Harbor FL 34683-3737

GRACE, JULIANNE ALICE, retired investment company executive; b. Riverdale, NY, Oct. 29, 1937; d. Arthur Edward and Julia May (McCarthy) Thompson; m. Daniel Vincent Grace, July 2, 1960; children: Daniel Vincent III, Deirdre Elizabeth Beck. BA, Marymount Manhattan Coll., 1959; MA, Fordham U., 1960. Dir. admissions Marymount Manhattan Coll., NYC, 1966-72; mgr. human resources The Perkin-Elmer Corp., Norwalk, Conn., 1972-78, dir. human resources, 1978-81, asst. sr. v.p. semiconductor equipment, 1981-83, asst. pres., 1983-85, v.p., asst. to CEO, 1985-86, v.p. adminstrn., 1986-90, v.p. corp. rels., 1990-95; pres. The Jagcom Group, New Canaan, Conn., 1995—2004; ret., 2004. Bd. dirs. Norwalk and Wilton chpts. ARC, 1975—85, Metropool, 1991—98; pres., bd. dirs. Waveny (Conn.) Care Ctr., 1998—99; bd. dirs. Waveny Network, 1988—; trustee Norwalk YMCA, 1986—94; active Norwalk C.C. Found., 1986—90, Fairfield 2000; mem. corp. cabinet U. Conn. Downstate Initiative, 1995—98, mem. adv. com., lectr. exec. edn. program U. Conn., 1996—2001; bd. dirs. New Canaan Cmty. Found., Conn., 2004—. Fellow Woodrow Wilson Nat. Found., 1959—60. Mem.: Fairfield Pub. Rels. Assn., Nat. Investor Rels. Inst. (sr. exec. roundtable), Econ. Soc. Conn., Saugatuck Harbor Yacht Club (bd. govs., flag officer fleet capt.), Wolfpit Running Club, Sports Car Club Am. Home and Office: 54 Louises Ln New Canaan CT 06840-2120

GRACE, KATHLEEN M, computer scientist, educator, web site designer; b. Malden, Mass. d. Thomas and Barbara Costello; m. James H. Grace; children: Margaret, Mary Kate, James, Paul. MS, U. Mass., Lowell, 2002. Cert. Human Computer Interaction U. Mass., Lowell, 2002. Adj. prof. No. Essex C.C., Haverhill, Mass., 2004—05; web cons. Sonora Designworks, Amesbury, Mass., 2005; client support mgr. Next Eon Com, Inc., Wakefield, Mass., 2005—06, web prodn. mgr., 2006—; adj. prof. Endicott Coll., Beverly, Mass., 2005—. Town meeting mem., Danvers, Mass., 1994—2006. Home: 7 Linden Dr Danvers MA 01923 Office: Endicott Coll 376 Hale St Beverly MA 01915 Home Phone: 978-777-4713; Office Phone: 978-232-5181. Business E-Mail: kgrace@endicott.edu.

GRACE, MAGGIE, actress; b. Columbus, Ohio, Sept. 21, 1983; Actor: (films) Rachel's Room, 2001, Shop Club, 2002, Creature Unknown, 2004, The Fog, 2005; (TV films) Murder in Greenwich, 2002, Twelve Mile Road, 2003; (TV series) Septuplets, 2002, Lost, 2004—05 (Outstanding Performance by an Ensemble in a Drama Series, Screen Actors Guild award, 2006), numerous TV series guest appearances. Mailing: care Innovative Artists 1505 10th St Santa Monica CA 90401

GRACE, MARCIA BELL, advertising executive; b. Pitts., July 29, 1937; d. Daniel Henry and Gertrude Margaret (Loew) Bell; m. Roy Grace, May 16, 1966; children: Jessica Bell, Nicholas Bell. AB, Harvard U., 1959. V.p., assoc. creative dir. Doyle Dane Bernbach, NYC, 1964-77; sr. v.p., creative dir. Wells, Rich, Greene, Inc., NYC, 1977-85, exec. v.p., creative dir., 1986-90; cons. Marcia Grace & Co., NYC, 1990—. Represented in permanent collections Mus. Modern Art. Recipient 1st pl. ANDY award Advt. Club NY, 1968, 70, 72, 75, 1st pl. Gold award One Show, 1973, 78, Hall of Fame award Clio Show, NYC, 1982, 86. Avocations: horseback riding, gardening.

GRACE, NANCY A., news correspondent, former prosecutor; b. Macon, Ga., Oct. 23, 1958; d. Mac and Elizabeth Grace. BA, Mercer U., 1981; JD, Walter F. George Sch. Law, 1984; LLM, NYU. Bar: 1984. Law clk. to fed. ct. judge; practiced law with Fed. Trade Commn.; asst. dist. atty., Fulton County Atlanta, 1987—96; host, Nancy Grace: Closing Arguments Court TV, 2001—07; sub. host Larry King Live, CNN, 2003—05; radio show host Rapid Fire with Nancy A. Grace, Clear Channel's KNEW-AM, 2004—; host CNN Headline News, 2005—. Lit. instr. Sch. Law, Ga. State U.; bus. law instr. Sch. Bus., Ga. State U.; appeared as legal commentator on ABC's The View, The Oprah Winfrey Show and numerous other cable and network programs. Contbr. articles to ABA Jour., various law reviews, and op-eds; author: Objection!: How High-Priced Defense Attorneys, Celebrity Defendants, and a 24/7 Media Have Hijacked Our Criminal Justice System, 2005 (Publishers Weekly Harcover bestseller list, 2005). Staff Atlanta Battered Women's Ctr. Hotline. Mem.: State Bar Ga. Achievements include while at Atlanta Fulton County Dist. Atty. Office, compiled a perfect record of nearly 100 felony convictions at trial and no losses. Office: Court TV 600 Third Ave 3rd Fl New York NY 10016 Office Phone: 212-973-7933.*

GRACE, RICHARD EDWARD, engineering educator; b. Chgo., June 26, 1930; s. Richard Edward and Louise (Koko) Grace; m. Consuela Cummings Fotos, Jan. 29, 1955; children: Virginia Louise, Richard Cummings(dec.). BS in Metall. Engring., Purdue U., West Lafayette, Ind., 1951; PhD, Carnegie Inst. Tech., Pitts., 1954. Asst. prof. Purdue U., West Lafayette, Ind., 1954—58, assoc. prof., 1958—62, prof., 1962—2000, head sch. materials sci. and metall. engring., 1965—72, head divsn. interdisciplinary engring. studies, 1970—82, head freshman engring. dept., asst. dean engring., 1981—87, v.p. student svcs., 1987—95, dir. undergrad. studies program, 1995—2000, prof. emeritus, v.p. emeritus, 2000—. Apptd. Ind. Commn. on Aging by Gov. of Ind., 2005—; cons. to Midwest industries. Author: When Every Day Is Saturday, 2002; contbr. articles to profl. jours. Pres. Lafayette Symphony Found. Bd., 1993-95. Named Sagamore of Wabash, Gov. of Ind., 1995. Fellow Am. Soc. Metals (tchr. award 1962), Am. Soc. Engring. Edn. (Centennial medallion 1993), Accreditation Bd. Engring. and Tech. (past dir. and officer engring. edn. and accreditation com., related engring. com., Grinter award 1989); mem. Minerals, Metals and Materials Soc. (bd. dirs. 1987-90), Lafayette Country Club, Rotary, Elks, Tau Beta Pi, Omicron Delta Kappa, Phi Gamma Delta. Home: 2175 Tecumseh Park Ln West Lafayette IN 47906-2118 Office: Purdue Univ Neil Armstrong Hall Sch Materials Engring 701 W Stadium Ave West Lafayette IN 47907-2045 Office Phone: 765-496-7384. Business E-Mail: regrace@purdue.edu.

GRACE, RICHARD JOHN, history professor; s. Daniel Francis and Anna Winifred Grace; m. Madeleine Paulette Delisle, July 23, 1977; children: Marianne Elizabeth Grace Marino, Benjamin Daniel, Elizabeth Christina. PhD, Fordham U., NY, 1974. Prof. history Providence Coll., 1965—. Contbr. articles to profl. jours. Mem. cathedral choir St. Mary's Cathedral, Fall River, Mass., 1954. Fellow, St. Edmund's Coll., U. Cambridge, 1993. Mem.: Hist. Soc. (assoc.). Roman Catholic. Avocations: gardening, singing. Home: 904 Gardners Neck Rd Swansea MA 02777 Office: History Dept Providence Coll 549 River Ave Providence RI 02918 Home Phone: 508-678-1054; Office Phone: 401-865-2074. Business E-Mail: rjgrace@providence.edu.

GRACE, RYAN THOMAS, lawyer; b. Omaha, Oct. 19, 1976; s. Ted Victor and Irene Kathryn Grace; m. Ellen Rene Colyer, July 17, 2004; 1 child, Savannah Kathryn-Rene. BSCE, U. Nebr., 2000; JD magna cum laude, Creighton U., 2003. Bar: Nebr. 2003, Wash. 2005, U.S. Supreme Ct. Nebr. 2003, U.S. Dist. Ct. Nebr. 2003, U.S. Ct. Appeals (8th cir.) 2003, U.S. Ct. Appeals (fed. cir.) 2003, registered: U.S. Patent & Trademark Office 2003, bar: U.S. Supreme Ct. Wash. 2005. Patent atty., patent agt. Thomte, Mazour & Niebergall, Omaha, 2000—04; patent atty. Mcht. & Gould, Seattle, 2004—. Contbr. articles to profl. jours. Recipient Judge Donald P. Lay award, Creighton U., 2003; scholar, The Windthrop & Francis Ln. Found., 2002—03, The Gail Werner-Robertson and Scott Robertson Found., 2002—03. Mem.: Wash. Software Alliance, Wash. State Bar assn., Am. Intellectual Property Law Assn., Omaha Bar Assn., Nebr. State Bar Assn. Achievements include patents pending for a method of proposing marriage to another individual; a method of expressing gratitude to a benifactor. Avocations: hiking, painting, children's books, travel. Home: 1942 16th CT NE Issaquah WA 98029 Office: Merchant & Gould 701 5th Ave Suite 4100 Seattle WA 98104 Office Phone: 206-342-6200. Office Fax: 206-342-6201. Business E-Mail: rgrace@merchant-gould.com.

GRACE, TOPHER, actor; b. NYC, July 19, 1978; Attended, Groundings Improvisation Sch., Neighborhood Playhouse, U. So. Calif. Actor: (plays) Our Town, Godspell, Lost in Yonkers, A Funny Thing Happened on the Way to the Forum, The Night Before Christmas, The King and I; (TV series) That 70s Show, 1998—2006; (films) Traffic, 2000, (voice) Pinocchio, 2002, Mona Lisa Smile, 2003, Win a Date with Tad Hamilton!, 2004, P.S., 2004, In Good Company, 2004 (Nat. Bd. Rev. award Best Breakthrough Performance by an Actor, 2004), Spider-Man 3, 2007; TV appearances include King of the Hill, 2003.*

GRACE, WILLIAM PERSHING, petroleum geologist, real estate developer; b. Mineral Point, Mo., Sept. 19, 1920; s. William Francis and Bertha Luciel (Nephew) Grace; m. Jeannette Marie Grace, Mar. 28, 1942 (dec.); children: Joyce Medaris, Pamela, Sonia Scott, Patricia Lawser; m. Mary Jeane Tock, June 30, 2003. Student, Corpus Christi U., 1946-47; B in Geology, Tex. Tech. U., 1947-50; student (GRI), U. Colo. Extension, 1968-69. Capt. USAF, 1940-46; regional geologist Anderson-Prichard Oil Corp., San Antonio, Tex., 1950-62; real estate broker Grace Reality, Aurora, Colo., 1963-66; pres. Kimberley Homes, Construction, Aurora, 1966-72; pres., broker Grace-Scott-Cooper Corp., Aurora, 1972—. Pres. Friends of the Aurora Pub. Libr., 1967, trustee mem., 1978; chmn. Adams County Rep. Party, 1970—72; mem. vocat. edn. coun. Sch. Dist. 28J, 1989—. Named Colorado of Yr., Colo. State Libr. Assn., 1988. Mem.: Sixty Five Roses Found., Aurora C. of C. (dir. 1966—68, Man of Yr. 1980), Aurora Bd. Realtors (treas. 1979, Realtor of Yr. 1980), Colo. State Friends and Trustees Assn., Colo. Assn. Realtors, Rocky Mountain Assn. Petroleum Geologists, Nat. Assn. Realtors, Am. Assn. Petroleum Geologists (del., House of Dels. 1961—62), Aurora Kiwainis (internat. del. in Nice, France 1993, lt. gov. Rocky Mountain divsn. 1992, sec. 1965, pres. 1972), Denver Petroleum PioneersClub, Sigma Gamma Epsilon. Lutheran. Avocations: geologic exploration, flying, golf, skiing, travel. Home: 13618 E Bethany Pl 204 Aurora CO 80014 Office Phone: 303-671-4426.

GRACEY, DOUGLAS ROBERT, internist, educator, physiologist; b. Fort Dodge, Iowa, Aug. 7, 1936; s. Warren Robert and Areta Mary (Thompson) G.; m. Edith Ann Haas, Dec. 23, 1961; children— Laura, Douglas Robert BA, Coe Coll., 1958; MD, Northwestern U., 1962; MS, U. Minn., 1968. Diplomate Am. Bd. Internal Medicine. Intern Cook County Hosp., Chgo., 1962-63; resident Mayo Grad. Sch. Medicine, 1963-66, 68-69; asst. prof. medicine Northwestern U. Med. Sch., 1969-75; assoc. prof. medicine Mayo Med. Sch., Rochester, Minn., 1975-83, prof., 1983—, vice chmn. pulmonary div., 1982-87; vice chmn. for practice dept. medicine Mayo Clinic, Rochester, 1983-93, dir. critical care medicine div., 1985-89, chmn. revenue systems com., chmn. divsn. pulmonary and critical care medicine. Author: (with W.W. Addington) Tuberculosis, 1972, Flying Lessons, Ambulances and orther Air Force Vignettes, 2000; editor: Pulmonary Diseases in the Adult, 1981; contbr. articles to profl. jours. Trustee Coe Coll., 1976-92. Served to capt. M.C., USAF, 1966-68 Am. Thoracic Soc. tng. fellow, 1968-69 Fellow ACP, Am. Coll. Chest Physicians, AMA. Lodges: Masons, Shriners. Republican. Office: Mayo Clinic Chmn Div Pulmonary & Critical Care Med Rochester MN 55901 Business E-Mail: dgracey@mayo.edu.

GRACEY, JAMES STEELE, manufacturing executive, director, management consultant; b. Newton, Mass., Aug. 24, 1927; s. Ernest James and Edna Alicia (Steele) G.; m. Dorcas Randall Neal, June 15, 1949; children: Kevin, Cheryl, Pamela BS, U.S. Coast Guard Acad., 1949; MBA, Harvard U., 1956. Commd. ensign USCG, 1949, advanced through grades to adm.; comptr. 2d Coast Guard Dist., St. Louis, 1962—65; dep. Governors' Island project and Coast Guard Base, NY, 1965—69; chief programs divsn. Chief of Staff's Office, Washington, 1969—74; chief of staff 5th Coast Guard Dist., Portsmouth, Va., 1974; comdr. 9th Coast Guard Dist., Cleve., 1974—77; chief of staff Coast Guard Hdqrs., Washington, 1977—78; comdr. Coast Guard Pacific Area and 12th Coast Guard Dist., San Francisco, 1978—81, Coast Guard Atlantic Area and 3d Coast Guard Dist., NYC, 1981—82; commandant USCG, Washington, 1982—86; sr. fellow Inst. for Higher Def. Studies, Capstone, 1986—2001. Chmn. Fed. Exec. Bd. Cleve., 1976-77; coord. regional emegency transp. Fed. Region IX, 1978-81; bd. dirs. Marine Spill Response Corp., chmn. audit com., 1991-2003; bd. dirs. Maguire Group, Inc., Maguire Group Conn., Inc., chmn., 1993-98; advisor New Sulzer Diesel Group, 1991-95; cons. Mitre Corp., 1987-92; vis. lectr. Nat. Def. U., Navy, Air and Army War Colls., Fgn. Svc. Inst., Presdl. Classroom, Sloane Fellows, MIT, Kennedy Sch. Govt., Harvard U., 1982-86; bd. mgrs. Am. Bur. Shipping, 1982-86; leader U.S. del. to Internat. Maritime Orgn., UN Assembly, 1983, 85; bd. visitors Mich. Maritime Acad Mem. world bd. govs. USO, 1982-91; trustee, chmn. Calvary United Meth. Ch., 1988-2001, chmn. ch. coun Decorated Legion of Merit with gold star, D.S.M. with gold star; named Bay Stater of Yr., Maritime Man of Yr., San Diego NL Man of Yr.; recipient Michelob Schooner award, San Francisco Honor medal Mem. Ret. Officers Assn./Mil. Officers Assn. Am. (bd. dirs. 1986-92), Coast Guard Found. (bd. dirs.), Navy League, Nat. Mil. Family Assn. (advisor 1986-2002), Assn. for Rescue at Sea (bd. dirs., vice chmn. 1988-97, chmn. 1997-2003), Army-Navy Country Club Home and Office: 1411 21st St S Arlington VA 22202-1507

GRACEY, PAUL C., JR., lawyer, utilities executive; b. 1959; BBA with distinction, U. Mich., 1981; JD cum laude, U. Calif., 1985; diploma in Sr. Exec. Fin. Progam, Templeton Coll., Oxford, Eng., 1998. Bar: Calif., Ill. V.p., gen. counsel Edison Mission Energy Ltd., London, 1993—2000, Midwest Generation, Chgo., 2000—02; v.p. Nicor Inc. and Nicor Gas, Naperville, Ill., 2002—, gen. counsel, 2002—, sec., 2002—, sr. v.p., 2006—. Mem.: Calif. Bar Assn., Ill. Bar Assn. Office: Nicor Inc 1844 Ferry Rd Naperville IL 60563 Office Phone: 630-983-8676.*

GRACHEK, MARIANNA KERN, healthcare administrator; b. Amsterdam, The Netherlands, Oct. 6, 1949; d. Johannus J. and Paulina G. (DeHaas) Kern; m. Kenneth A. Grachek, June 12, 1971; children: Ellen, Brett. Grad., St. Vincent Med. Ctr., Toledo, 1971; BSN, U. Toledo, 1978; MSN, Med. Coll. of Ohio, 1987. Lic. nursing home adminstr.; cert. gerontol. nurse; cert. DON Nat. Assn. Dirs. of Nursing Adminstrn; cert. nursing home adminstr. and assisted living adminstr., ACHCA. Clinician gerontol. nursing, staff devel. educator St. Vincent Med. Ctr., Toledo, 1982-87; instr. St. Vincent Sch. Nursing, Toledo, 1985; dir. nursing svcs. Lake Park Nursing Care Ctr., Sylvania, Ohio, 1987-90; nursing home adminstr. St. Luke's Transitional Care Ctr., Maumee, Ohio; long term care surveyor Joint Commn. Accreditation Health Care Orgns., Oakbrook, Ill., 1993—97, exec. dir. long term care accreditation program, 1997—2006, pres., 2006—. Recipient Sigma Theta Tau (Zeta Theta Chpt.) Rsch. award, 1987; MCO Satellite scholar, 1986. Mem. Nat. Gerontol. Nursing Assn. (regional bd. dirs. 1988-93), N.W. Ohio Gerontol. Assn. (chair budget com. 1987-91), Alzheimer's Assn. (pres. N.W. Ohio chpt. 1991-93), ALHCA (bd. dirs. 1999-2003), Sigma Theta Tau. Office: Am Coll Health Care Administrators 300 N Lee St Ste 301 Alexandria VA 22314

GRACIN, HANK, lawyer; b. Massapequa Pk., NY, Jan. 27, 1957; s. Bernard Tobias and Ada (Rosenberg) G.; m. Marisol L. Perez, Sept. 9, 1990. BA with honors, SUNY, Binghamton, 1978; JD cum laude, NYU, 1981. Bar: N.Y. 1982, U.S. Dist. Ct. (so. dist.) N.Y. 1982. Assoc. Sullivan & Cromwell, NYC, 1981-83, Schulte Roth & Zabel, NYC, 1983-86, Fulbright Jaworski & Reavis McGrath, NYC, 1986-90; corp. counsel Computer Assocs. Internat., Inc., 1990-94; ptnr. Lehman & Eilen, 1994—. Editor: Private Placements and Restricted Securities, 1981. Mem. South Palm Beach County Bar Assn., Palm Beach Bar Assn., Order of Coif (NYU chpt.). Avocations: bicycling, reading, piano, cigars. Office: Lehman & Eilen LLP Mission Bay Office Plz 20283 State Rd 7 Ste 300 Boca Raton FL 33498 Home Phone: 561-483-2796; Office Phone: 561-237-0804. Business E-Mail: HGracin@Lehmaneilen.com.

GRACY, DAVID BERGEN, II, archivist, information science educator, writer; b. Austin, Tex., Oct. 25, 1941; married; 3 children. BA, U. Tex., Austin, 1963, MA, 1966; PhD in History, Tex. Tech. U., 1971. Cert. archivist. Archivist S.W. Collection Tex. Tech. U., 1966-71; from asst. prof. to assoc. prof. urban life Ga. State U., 1971-77; archivist So. Labor Archives, 1971-77; dir. Tex. State Archives, 1977-86; Gov. Bill Daniel prof. in archival enterprise U. Tex., Austin, 1986—, assoc. dean Grad. Sch. of Libr. and Info. Sci., 1991-95; interim dir. preservation and conservation studies program U. Tex. Grad. Sch. Libr. and Info. Sci.; dir. Ctr. for the Cultural Record, 2000—. Gen. ptnr. David B. Gracy II & Assocs., 1989—; adj. prof. history De Kalb C.C., 1973—74; vis. prof. archival enterprise San Jose State U., 2001, U. Ariz., 2003—04; instr. Ga. Archives Inst., Grad. Sch. Libr. and Info. Sci. U. Tex., Austin, Modern Archives Inst. Nat. Archives of U.S., Rare Books Sch. Columbia U., Soc. Am. Archivists, S.W. Archivists, Spl. Librs. Assn., Tex. State Libr., Trinity U., U.S. Info. Agy. for U. Philippines, Presdl. Commn. on Culture and Arts, Univ. Republic, Uruguay, Utah State Archives, Western Archives Inst.; cons. N.Mex. State Archives and Libr. Bldg. project, 1994—98, Nat. Episc. Ch. Archives, 1978, Oral Roberts U., 1978, Archives Civil Rights, M.L. King Ctr., Atlanta, 1976—81, Am. Heritage Ctr. U. Wyo., 1988—89, San Antonio Pub. Libr., 1988, Nat. Assn. for Preservation and Perpetuation of Storytelling, Jonesborough, Tenn., 1988—89, King Ranch, Kingsville, Tex., 1987, City San Antonio, 2004—; coord. Tex. Hist. Records Adv. Bd., 1979—86; mem. Ga. Hist. Records Adv. Bd., 1976, Nat. Hist. Publs. and Rec. Commn., 1980—85; lectr. U. Tex., Austin, 1980—81, sr. lectr., 1982—86. Author: Littlefield Lands: Colonization on the Texas Plains, 1912-1920, 1968, Archives and Manuscripts: Arrangement and Description, 1977, It's Your Heritage: The Archives of Texas, 1977, An Introduction to Archives and Manuscripts, 1981, Moses Austin: His Life, 1987; co-author: Ships of the Texas Navy, 1979; bibliography advisor The New Handbook of Texas, 1988-94; mem. editl. bd. Libraries and Culture, 1985-05, Am. Archivist, 1976-79; founder, editor Ga. Archive (subsequently Provenance), 1972-76; contbr. to Reflections of Western Historians, 1969; assoc. editor Tex. Mil. History, 1962-88; editor Librs. and the Cultural Record, 2005-; editl. asst. Southwestern Hist. Quar., 1963-66; contbr. articles to profl. jours. Bd. dirs. Nat. Archives Episcopal Ch., 1986—98, vice chair, 1995—98; bd. dirs. Task Force on Preservation Edn., Commn. on Preservation and Access, 1989—90, mem., 1991—97; chmn. task force on archives Summerlee Comm. on Tex. History, 1989—93, Tex. Preservation Task Force, 1988—90; sec. Coun. on Libr. and Info. Resources, 1997—2000. Named Disting. Alumnus Dept. History Tex. Tech. U., 1987; recipient award of merit Am. Assn. for State and Local History, 1969, Disting. Svc. award Organized Labor and Workmen's Circle, Atlanta, 1976, Cert. Merit Soc. Ga. Archivists, 1976, Soc. S.W. Archivists, 1978, Tex. Excellence in Teaching award Grad. Sch. Libr. and Info. Sci. U. Tex. at Austin, 1987, San Jacinto award, 1993. Fellow: Tex. State Hist. Assn., Tex. State Geneal. Soc., Soc. Am. Archivists (v.p., pres. 1982—84, award of merit 1975); mem.: Soc. Ga. Archivists (pres. 1972—74, cert. merit 1976), Acad. Cert. Archivists (bd. regents 1990—93, v.p., pres. 1999—2000), Pan Am. Inst. Geography and History (U.S. rep. archives com. 1982—97), Assn. Records Mgrs. and Adminstrs. (pres. Austin chpt. 1980—81, cert. award 1981), Internat. Coun. Archives (editor Edn. and Devel. News 1989—96, listmaster sect. archival edn. and tng. listserv, 1996—2002, v.p. sect. on archival edn. and tng.), Am. Assn. State and Local History (award of merit 1968), Tex. Bar Hist. Found. Office: U Tex Sch of Info Austin TX 78712-0390 Business E-Mail: gracy@ischool.utexas.edu.

GRACY, ROBERT, science educator; BS in Chemistry and Biol. Scis., Calif. State Polytech U., 1964; PhD in Biochemistry, U. Calif., Riverside, 1968. Postdoctoral fellow, molecular biology, Damon Runyon Cancer Found. Albert Einstein Coll. Medicine, NY, 1968—70; asst. prof. chemistry North Tex. State U., 1970—73, assoc. prof. chemistry and basic health scis., 1973—75; prof., chmn., dept. biochemistry & molecular biology U. North Tex. Health Sci. Ctr., Ft. Worth, 1976—93, assoc. dean for rsch. & biotechnology, prof. biochemistry and molecular biology, 1993—97, dean rsch. and biotechnology, prof. molecular biology and immunology, 1997—2006, acting chmn., dept. microbiology and immunology, 1996—97; v.p. rsch. U Tex., San Antonio, 2006—. Vis. prof., dept. physiol. chemistry U. Würzburg, West Germany, 1975—76, 1990—91; acting chmn., dept. microbiology and immunology Tex. Coll. Osteopathic Medicine, 1986—88; vis. prof. Peoples Republic of China, 1988. Contbr. articles to profl. jours. Recipient NIH Rsch. Career Develop. award, 1972—77, NIH Merit award for rsch. in aging, 1987—97, Wilford I. Doherty award, Am. Chem. Soc. (Dallas/Ft. Worth), 1995; Alexander von Humboldt Found., Germany, 1976—77, 1990—91. Mem.: Nat. Coun. U. Rsch. Adminstrs. Inst. for Internat. Rsch. (Pharm. Divsn.), Tex. Healthcare and Biomedical Inst. Biotechnology Industry Orgn., Assn. U. Tech. Managers Inc., Protein Soc., Tex. Tech. Transfer Assn., Assn. for Gerontology in Higher Edn., Drug Info. Assn. Tech. Transfer Assn., Am. Chem. Soc. Tarrant County Plastic Surgeons' Soc., Am. Assn. U. Professors Tarrant County Dermatology Soc., AAAS Sigma Xi, Am. Soc. Biochemistry and Molecular Biology Nat. Coun. U. Rsch. Adminstrs. Office: U Tex San Antonio Main Bldg MB 2 106 One UTSA Cir San Antonio TX 78249 Office Phone: 210-458-4341. Office Fax: 210-458-7740.*

GRAD, FRANK PAUL, lawyer, educator; b. Vienna, May 2, 1924; came to U.S., 1939, naturalized, 1943; s. Morris and Clara Sophie (Scher) G.; m. Lisa Szilagyi, Dec. 6, 1946; children: David Anthony, Catharine Ann. BA magna cum laude, Bklyn. Coll., 1947; LLB, Columbia U., 1949. Bar: NY 1949. From assoc. in law to prof. emeritus Columbia U. Law Sch., NYC, 1949—95, Joseph P. Chamberlain prof. emeritus legis. and spl. lectr., 1995—; assoc. House, Grossman, Vorhaus & Hemley, 1950—53; legal adv. com. US Council Environ. Quality, 1970-73; mem. N.Y. Deptl. Com. Ct. Adminstrn., Appellate Div., 1st Dept., 1970-74; counsel N.Y. State Spl. Adv. Panel Med. Malpractice, 1975; legal counsel Nat. Mcpl. League, 1967-88. Cons. in field; reporter U.S. Superfund Study group, 1981-82; dir. rsch. N.Y.C. Charter Revision Commn., 1982-83, N.Y. State-City Commn. on Integrity in Govt., 1986; mcpl. codes and state legislation. Author: Public Health Law Manual, 1st edit., 1965, 2d rev. edit., 1990, 3d rev. edit., 2004, The Drafting of State Constitutions, 1963, Environmental law: Sources and Problems, 3d edit., 1985, 4th edit. (with Joel Mintz), 2000, Treatise on Environmental Law, 8 vols., 1973—, (with Robert E. Williams) State Constitutions for the Twenty-First Century, 2006; co-author other legal reports; contbr. articles to profl. jours.; draftsman mcpl. codes and state legislation. With AUS, 1943—46. 10th Horace E. Read Meml. lectr. Dalhousie Law Sch., 1984; Career Accomplishment award Pub. Health Law Assn., 2005 Mem.: APHA, ABA, Internat. Union Conservation of Nature Acad. Law, NY Soc. Med. Jurisprudence, Internat. Coun. Environ. Law, Am. Soc. Law and Medicine, NY Bar Assn., Assn. Bar City of NY, Am. Law Inst. (life), Human Genome Orgn., World Conservation Union (commn. on environ. law 1991—). Office: Columbia U Sch Law 435 W 116th St New York NY 10027-7297 Office Phone: 212-854-2685. Business E-Mail: fgrad@law.columbia.edu.

GRADDICK, CHARLES ALLEN, judge; b. Mobile, Ala., Dec. 10, 1944; s. Julian and Elvera (Smith) G.; m. Corinne Whiting, Aug. 19, 1966; children: Charles Allen, Herndon Whiting, Corinne. JD, Cumberland Sch. Law, 1970. Bar: Ala. 1970. Clk. Ala. Supreme Ct., 1970; asst. dist. atty. County of Mobile, Ala., 1971-75, dist. atty. Ala., 1975-79; atty. gen. State of Ala., Montgomery, 1979-87; ptnr. Thorton, Farish and Gaunt, Montgomery, 1987-89, Anderson, Graddick and Nabors, P.C., Montgomery, 1989-90; dist. atty. Montgomery County, Montgomery County, Ala., 1991-93; ptnr. Graddick & Belser, P.C., Montgomery and Mobile, 1992-99, Sims, Graddick & Dodson, Mobile, 2000—04; presiding cir. judge Mobile County, 2004—. Served with USNG, 1969-96. Named Outstanding Young Man of Mobile, Mobile Jaycees, 1976, State Conservationist of Yr., Ala. Wildlife Fedn.; recipient cert. appreciation Ala. Peace Officers, 1978, Appreciation award Optimists, 1978. Mem. Ala. Bar Assn., Mobile Bar Assn., Nat. Assn. Attys. Gen., Ala. Cir. Judges Assn. Republican. Office: Paul W Brock Inn of Ct Govt Plaza 205 Government St Ct Rm 8600 Mobile AL 36644 Office Phone: 251-574-5639. E-mail: charlie.graddick@alacourt.gov.

GRADDICK-WEIR, MIRIAN, human resources specialist; d. Sam Massenberg. BA, Hampton U.; MS, PhD, Penn State U. With AT&T, Bedminster, NJ, 1981—, various positions in human resources and customer svc., 1981—94, v.p. multimedia products group, exec. v.p. human resources; sr. v.p. HR Merck Inc., Whitehouse Station, NJ, 2006—. Bd. dirs. Harleysville Ins. Cos., Joint Ctr. Polit. and Econ. Studies, Human Resources Policy Assn. Named Human Resources Exec. of Yr., Human Resources Exec. mag., 2000; recipient Disting. Psychologist in Mgmt. award, Soc. Psychologists in Mgmt., 2003. Fellow: Nat. Acad. Human Resources. Office: Merck & Co 1 Merck Dr PO Box 100 Whitehouse Station NJ 08889-0100 Office Phone: 908-221-2000. Office Fax: 908-532-1673.*

GRADE, JEFFERY T., manufacturing executive; b. Chgo., 1943; BS, Ill. Inst. Tech., 1966; MBA, DePaul U., 1972. With Plasto Mfg. Corp., 1965-66, Motorola Inc., 1966-67, Bell and Howell, 1967-68, Ill. Cen. Gulf R.R., 1968-73; v.p. fin. IC Industries, 1973-83; with Harnischfeger Corp., Milw., 1983-99, pres., COO, bd. dirs., 1986—, CEO, 1991-99, also chmn., CEO. Served with USN, 1865-66. Office: Harnischfeger Industries Ste 2780 100 E Wisconsin Ave Milwaukee WI 53202-4127

GRADEL, JAMES D., lawyer; b. Toldedo, Sept. 1, 1954; BBA summa cum laude, U. Cin., 1975; JD with honors, Ohio State U., 1978. Bar: Wash. 1979. Ptnr., Fin. Inst. Practice Area Perkins Coie LLP, Seattle. Named a Wash. Super Lawyer, Washington Law & Politics. Mem.: King County Bar Assn., Wash. State Bar Assn., Beta Gamma Sigma. Office: Perkins Coie LLP 1201 Third Ave Ste 4800 Seattle WA 98101-3099 Office Phone: 206-359-8401. Office Fax: 206-359-9000. Business E-Mail: jgradel@perkinscoie.com.

GRADISON, BILL (WILLIS DAVID GRADISON JR.), former congressman; b. Cin., Dec. 28, 1928; s. Willis David and Dorothy (Benas) G.; m. Helen Ann Martin, June 25, 1950 (div. 1974); children: Ellen, Anne, Margaret, Robin, Beth; m. Heather Jane Stirton, Nov. 29, 1980 (div. 1995); children: Maile Jo, Benjamin David, Logan Jane; m. J. Cari Elliott, Dec. 20, 1995. AB, Yale, 1948; MBA, Harvard, 1951, D.C.S., 1954. With W.D. Gradison & Co., Cin., 1949; research asst., also research assoc. Harvard Bus. Sch., 1951-53; asst. to under sec. US Dept. Treasury, 1953-55; asst. to sec. US Dept Health Edn. & Welfare, 1955-57; gen. partner W.D. Gradison & Co., from 1958; mem. city coun. City of Cin., 1961-74; mayor City of Cin., 1971; mem. US Congresses from Ohio 2nd dist., Washington, 1975—93; sr. pub. policy counselor Patton Boggs LLP, 1999—2002; mem. Pub. Co. Acctg. Oversight Bd., Washington, 2002—, acting chmn., 2005—06. Office: Pub Co Acctg Oversight Bd 1666 K St NW Washington DC 20006

GRADO, ANGELO JOHN, artist; b. NYC, Feb. 17, 1922; s. Pasquale and Rose (Valenti) G.; m. Justine Barbara Johnson, June 26, 1943; children: Barbara, Paul, John, Frank, Richard. Student, Art Students League, Nat. Acad. Design, Frank Reilley Sch. Art. Comml. artist NY Jour.-Am., NYC, 1946-52; art dir. Harrison Publs., NYC, 1952-55; art dir., owner advt. agy. Angelo John Assocs., NYC, 1955-70; artist oils and pastels, 1970—. Tchr. Nat. Art League, NY, Naples Art League, Von Lebig Art Ctr., Naples, Fla.; lectr., Europe and US Author: Mastering the Craft of Painting, 1985; featured in Internat. Artist. Mag., 2004, Pasteagram Mag., 2006. Served with USAAF, 1943-46. Recipient 96 nat. awards, 1957—, Best in Show-Newington award, 1980. Mem.: Degas Pastel Soc. (award 2003), Am. Watercolor Soc., Pastel Soc. Am. (elected master pastelist, Mrs. Pearl Kalikow award 2001, award 2003), Hudson Valley Art Assn. (Best Portrait award 1994), Am. Artists Profl. League (pres. NY 1977—88, pres. emeritus 1988—), Salmagundi Club (Best in Show 2005). Home and Office: 641 46th St Brooklyn NY 11220-1410 Office Phone: 718-853-3244. Personal E-mail: angelograd0@aol.com.

GRADY, DENNIS EDWARD, physicist, researcher; b. San Francisco, June 5, 1940; s. Durward Raymond and Genevieve (Allen) Grady; 1 child, Daniel Raymond. BS in Physics and Math., Lewis and Clark Coll., 1967; PhD in Physics and Math., Wash. State U., 1971. Rsch. scientist Stanford Rsch. Inst., Menlo Park, Calif., 1971-74, Sandia Nat. Labs., Albuquerque, 1974-96; prin. scientist Applied Rsch. Inst., Albuquerque, 1996—. Coeditor: High Pressure Shock Compression of Solids, 1995. With USN, 1958-63. Mem. Am. Phys. Soc. (chmn. topical group on shock compression condensed matter 1990-92, Shock Compression Sci. award 2007), Hypervelocity Impact Soc. (bd. dirs. 1992-98), Internat. DYMAT Assn. (adv. coun. 1986—). Home: 1472 Morning Glory Rd NE Albuquerque NM 87122-1125 Office: Applied Rsch Assocs 4300 San Mateo Blvd NE Albuquerque NM 87110-1229 E-mail: dgrady@ara.com.

GRADY, GREGORY, lawyer, banker; b. Takoma Park, Md., Oct. 10, 1945; s. Francis Joseph Grady and Deane (McGehee) Black; m. Carol Love Harrison, Feb. 25, 1978; children: Olivia Love, Blake McGregor, Harrison Edwards. Diploma, Bullis Sch., 1964; BA in Econs., U. Va., 1969; JD, Tulane U., 1972. Bar: D.C. 1973, U.S. Ct. Appeals (D.C. cir.) 1973, U.S. Ct. Appeals (4th cir.) 1975, U.S. Supreme Ct. 1976, U.S. Ct. Appeals (5th cir.) 1977, U.S. Ct. Appeals (10th cir.) 1979, U.S. Ct. Appeals (11th cir.) 1981, U.S. Ct. Appeals (6th cir.) 1982, U.S. Dist. Ct. 1988. Staff atty., supervisory atty. FPC, Washington, 1972-74; assoc. Littman, Richter, Wright & Talisman, P.C., Washington, 1974-79; mem. Wright & Talisman, P.C., Washington, 1979—, pres., chmn. bd. dirs., chmn. exec. com., 1997-98, mng. mem., 1999—. Bd. dirs. Bank of Franklin, Miss., D.R. McGehee Ins. Agy., Inc., Miss. Mem. Energy Bar Assn., D.C. Bar Assn., The Federalist Soc., Congl. Country Club. Republican. Episcopalian. Home: 666 Live Oak Dr Mc Lean VA 22101-1569 Office: Wright & Talisman PC 1200 G St NW Ste 600 Washington DC 20005-3838

GRADY, JOYCE (MARIAN JOYCE GRADY), psychotherapist, consultant; b. Riverside, NJ, Sept. 27, 1930; d. David and Agnes Marian (Conroy) Lawber; children: Andrea, Christine; m. James F. Moller, June 11, 1983. BA in Clin. Psychology, U. Penna, 1951; M in Social Work, certificate in alcohol studies, Rutgers U., New Brunswick, NJ, 1968; certificate in psychotherapy, Inst. Psychoanalytic Psychotherapy, 1973. Lic. clin. social worker, N.J. Caseworker Upward Bound Program, Rutgers U., New Brunswick, summer 1966; psychiat. social work supr., chief psychiat. social worker Roosevelt Hosp., Edison, N.J., 1968-92, in-svc. educator in nursing and social work, 1972-92, support group caregiver, 1970-92; nursing home cons. Abbot Manor Nursing Home, Plainfield, N.J., 1984-92; pvt. practice psychotherapy, Highland Park, N.J., 1975—. Adj. prof., field instr. grad. sch. social work Rutgers U., New Brunswick, 1970-92; guest lectr. depression and geriatrics Rutgers Sch. Social Work, New Brunswick, 1975-92; cmty. lectr. dying, aging, loss, and depression in long term care; outreach cons. personal assistance and homebound elderly, Middlesex County, N.J., 1975-78; mem. adv. bd., chmn. Middlesex County Adv. Coun. Aging, North Brunswick, N.J., 1973-95. Contbr. papers, panelist in field. Advocate, Middlesex County Adv. Coun. on Aging, North Brunswick, 1970-92; mem. Cmty. Outreach Adv. Coun.; participant seminars svc. providers, Middlesex County, N.J., 1995. Mem.: NASW (guest panel mem., guest spkr. psychotherapy confs.), Rutgers Club, Penn Club N.Y.C. Avocations: writing, decorating, music, computers, gardening. Office: 12 N 4th Ave Highland Park NJ 08904-2736

GRADY, KENNETH ALAN, lawyer, corporate secretary; b. Detroit, Nov. 10, 1956; s. James Valentine and Ellen Hofman Grady; m. June Wojtowicz, May 25, 1985; children: Marie Elizabeth, Erin Margaret, Brendan Connor. BA, Drake U., 1978; M in Mgmt., Northwestern U., 1984, JD, 1984. Bar: Ill. 1984, U.S. Dist. Ct. (no. dist.) Ill. 1984, U.S. Ct. Appeals (7th cir.) 1985, Iowa 1996, Mass. 2004. Assoc. Levin & Funkhouser, Ltd., Chgo., 1984—88, McDermott, Will & Emery, Chgo., 1988—90, ptnr., 1991—94; sr. counsel HON INDUSTRIES Inc., Muscatine, Iowa, 1994—96; v.p., gen. mgr. The HON Co., Cedartown, Ga., 1996—98; group counsel, asst. sec. Payless ShoeSource, Inc., Topeka, 1999—2000, v.p., group counsel, asst. sec., 2000—01; v.p., gen. counsel, sec. KB Toys, Inc., Pittsfield, Mass., 2001—04, exec. v.p. adminstrn., gen. counsel, sec., 2004—05; v.p., gen. counsel., sec. PC Connection, Inc., Merrimack, NH, 2005; pvt. practice North Andover, Mass., 2006; gen. counsel, sec. Wolverine World Wide, Inc., Rockford, Mich., 2006—. Trustee, sec. Sunflower Soccer Assn., Topeka, 2000—01; commr. Pittsfied Mcpl. Airport Commn., 2003—04; dir. Polk Med. Ctr., Cedartown, 1997—98. F.C. Austin scholar, Northwestern U., J.L. Kellogg Grad. Sch. Mgmt., 1980—84. Mem.: ABA, Soc. Corp. Secs. and Governance Profls., Assn. Corp. Counsel. Office: Wolverine World Wide Inc 9341 Courtland Dr Rockford MI 49351 Office Phone: 616-866-7315. Business E-Mail: gradyke@wwwinc.com.

GRADY, KEVIN E., lawyer; b. Charlotte, NC, Jan. 19, 1948; s. Thomas F. and Rosemary (Loughran) G.; m. Mary Beth O'Brien, Dec. 27, 1975; children: Martin E., Donald F. BA, Vanderbilt U., 1969; JD, Harvard U., 1974. Bar: Ga. 1974, U.S. Dist. Ct. (no. dist.) Ga. 1975, U.S. Ct. Appeals (11th cir.) 1981, U.S. Supreme Ct. 1990. Assoc. Jones, Bird & Howell, Atlanta, 1974-76; trial atty. Antitrust divsn. U.S. Dept. Justice, Atlanta, 1976-77; ptnr., antitrust, investigations compliance Alston & Bird LLP, Atlanta, 1977—. Editor: Georgia Hospital Law Manual, 1997; contbr. chpts. to books. Mem. bd. trust Vanderbilt U., 1995-97; hon. consul gen. of Sri Lanka to Georgia, 2000—. Recipient Top Hat award St. Vincent de Paul Soc., 1995. Mem. ABA (chair antitrust sect. 2003-04), Ga. Acad. Healthcare Attys. (pres. 1997-98), Am. Health Lawyers Assn. (vice chair antitrust program 1992-99, chair 1999—2003), Am. Counsel Assn. (dir. 1991-2000, pres. 1995), State Bar Ga. (health law sect., chair 1999-2000), Am. Law Inst. Democrat. Roman Catholic. Avocations: running, reading. Office: Alston & Bird One Atlantic Ctr 1201 W Peachtree St NW Ste 4200 Atlanta GA 30309-3449 Office Phone: 404-881-7164. Business E-Mail: kevin.grady@alston.com.

GRADY, LEE TIMOTHY, pharmaceutical chemist; b. Chgo., Mar. 21, 1937; s. Thomas Aloysius and Lentella Kathryn (Eibel) G.; m. Ann Marie Gill, Aug. 8, 1964; children: Patricia Ann, Meghan Elizabeth. BS in Pharmacy with high honors, U. Ill., 1959, PhD in Chemistry, 1963. Registered pharmacist, Ill., Va., Md. Analyst CIA, Langley, Va., 1963—65; sr. rsch. pharmacologist Merck Inst. Therapeutic Rsch., West Point, Pa., 1965-68; dir. drug standards lab. Am. Pharm. Assn. Found., Washington, 1968-74; dir. drug rsch. and testing lab. U.S. Pharmacopeia, Rockville, Md., 1975-78, v.p., dir. stds. devel., dir. drug stds., 1979-99, v.p., dir. emeritus, 2000—. Expert com. WHO, Geneva, 1980-87; temp. advisor Pan Am. Health Orgn., Washington, 1984; observer Internat. Conf. Harmonization, 1990-2000; mem. Pharmacopeial Discussion group, U.S., Japan, Europe, 1989-2000; cons. in field. Contbr. articles to sci. jours.; sci. editor U.S. Pharmacopeia National Formulary, 1980-2000. Docent Nat. Mus. Am. History, 2000—; vol. Nat. Park Svc, Fairfax County Med. Res. Corp., 2004—. Recipient rsch. award Am. Soc. Hosp. Pharmacists, 1982. Fellow AAAS, Am. Assn. Pharm. Scientists; mem. Am. Pharm. Assn. (J.L. Powers rsch. achievement award 1990), Am. Chem. Soc., Cath. Acad. Scis. U.S. (sec.), Order of Holy Sepulchre, Rho Chi, Phi Kappa Phi, Sigma Chi. Roman Catholic. Avocations: swimming, hiking. Personal E-mail: ltgrady@cox.net.

GRADY, PATRICIA A., federal agency administrator; Diploma in nursing, St. Francis Hosp. Sch. Nursing, 1964; BSN, Georgetown U., 1967; MS in nursing, U. Md., 1968, PhD in physiology, 1977, D (hon.) in Pub. Svc., 1996; cert. in sr. mgrs. in govt., John F. Kennedy sch. Govt., Cambridge, 1994. Instr. Sch. Nursing Washington Hosp. Ctr., 1966-67; from instr. to rsch. asst. prof. Sch. Nursing U. Md., Bethesda, 1968-88, rsch. assoc., 1976-77; health sci. administrator Nat. Inst. Neurol. Disorders and Stroke, NIH, Bethesda, 1988-92, asst. dir., 1992-93, dep. dir., 1993—95, acting dir., 1993-94; dir. Nat. Inst. Nursing Rsch., NIH, Bethesda, 1995—. NIH fellow, 1973-76; NIN(C)DS grantee, 1976-88; recipient Sol Greenberg Award for leadership ability and clin. excellence St. Francis Hosp., 1964, Rozella M. Schlotfeld Disting. Lecture Award Case Western Reserve U., 1996, Centennial Achievement Medal, Georgetown U. Fellow Am. Heart Assn. Stroke Coun. (Excellence in Nursing Lectr. Award 1995); Mem. AAAS, ANA, Am. Acad. Nursing, Am. Lung Assn., Am. Soc. Profl. and Exec. Women, Am. Acad. Neurology (lectr. 1993-95), Am. Neurol. Assn., Soc. Neuroci., NY Acad. Sciences, Neurotrauma Soc., Sigma Theta Tau (award 1966), Inst. Medicine. Office: Nat Inst Nursing Rsch NIH Bldg 31 Rm 5B05 31 Center Dr Bethesda MD 20892-2178 Office Phone: 301-496-8230. Office Fax: 301-594-3405. E-mail: gradyp@mail.nih.gov.

GRADY, SANDRA C., minister, counselor; b. Kinston, NC, July 8, 1941; d. William Devereaux Cobb and Nora Cathleen Davenport; m. Sanders W. Grady; children: Daniel, Dean. BS in Bus. and Eng. Edn., East Carolina u., Greenville, NC, 1963, MS in Counseling and Edn., 1971; ThD, Wagner

Leadership Inst., Colo. Springs, Colo., 2000. School tchr. and counselor, Calif., Conn., and Ark., 1965—94; owner and instr. Grady Studies, Fairfax, Va., 1975—; founder and dir. Va. Prayer Network, Fairfax, Va., 1990—, Master's Keys, Fairfax, Va., 2002—. Prayer coord. Well Builders, Aledo, Tex., 1991—; mid-Atlantic dir. and coord. U.S. Strategic Prayer Network, Washington, 1998—, intercessional counselor Eagles team, 1998—, mem. nat. adv. bd., 2003—; mem. adv. bd. Nat. Coun. Govt. Intercessions, 2005—, Internat. Leadership Embassy, Washington, 2005—; instr. The Citadel, Washington, 2000—, Colombia; internat. spkr. and Biblical counselor, 1990—. Mem.: Nat. Fedn. Music Tchrs., Internat. Coalition of Apostles. Republican. Avocations: writing, composition.

GRADY, WAYNE JOSEPH, retired government official; b. Halifax, NS, Can., Dec. 15, 1943; s. Joseph Myles and Helen Virginia (McNeil) G. B.Comm., St. Mary's U., Halifax, 1973; MHA, U. Alta., Edmonton, 1975. Cons. Health Commn., Halifax, 1975-78; asst. to dep. minister Dept. of Health, Halifax, 1978-87, dep. minister health, 1987-91; dep. minister Dept. of the Environment, Halifax, 1991-96, ret., 1996. Roman Catholic. Personal E-mail: wgrady@hfx.eastlink.ca.

GRAEBNER, CAROL F., diversified financial services company executive, lawyer; b. Ridgway, Pa., Dec. 15, 1953; BA in Internat. Rels. cum laude, Dickinson Coll., 1975; JD, Am. U., 1978. Bar: Pa. 1978, Tex. 1982, N.Mex. 2003. Assoc. Eckert Seamens Cherin & Mellott, Pitts., 1978—82; staff atty. through gen. counsel Global Power subsidiary Conoco Inc., 1982—98; sr. v.p., gen. counsel Duke Energy Internat., 1998—2003; exec. v.p., gen. counsel Dynegy Inc., 2003—06, H&R Block Inc., Kansas City, 2006—. Editor (mng.): Am. Univ. Law Rev. Bd. dir., Houston div. Am. Heart Assn.; bd. dir. Internat. Inst. Edn. Mem.: ABA, Am. Corp. Counsel Assn., State Bar N.Mex., State Bar Tex. Office: H&R Block Inc 1 H&R Block Way Kansas City MO 64105 Office Phone: 816-854-5450. Business E-Mail: carolgraebner@hrblock.com.

GRAEBNER, JAMES HERBERT, transportation executive; b. New Castle, Pa., Aug. 5, 1940; s. Herbert Conrad and Mildred Elizabeth (Fessel) Graebner; children: Karla Elizabeth, Michael Conrad, James Conrad, David Fessel, Mildred Ann. BA, Valparaiso U., 1962; MBA, Case Western Res. U., 1970. Assoc. W. C. Gilman & Co., Inc., Cleve., 1967-71; with Regional Transp. Dist., Denver, 1971-75; gen. mgr. R.I. Pub. Transit Authority, Providence, 1975-78; dir. Santa Clara County Transp. Agy., Calif., 1978-84; dir. product devel. UTDC, 1984-86; pres. Lomarado Group, Denver, 1986—. Vis. prof. Northeastern U., 1979; COO Transit Constrn. Authority, Denver, 1987—89; v.p. San Jose Hist. Trolley Corp.; guest lectr. numerous univs. Bd. dirs. Denver Rail Heritage Soc. Mem.: Denver Union Station Adv. Commn. (co-chair 2003—), Regional Transit Assn. Bay Area LoDo Dist. Inc. (bd. dirs. 1999—, pres. 2002), Calif. Assn. Publicly Owned Transit Sys. (vice chmn. 1984), Am. Pub. Transit Assn. (pres. 1983—84). Lutheran. Office Phone: 303-628-5510. Personal E-mail: carbarn@aol.com.

GRAEBNER, NORMAN ARTHUR, historian, educator; b. Kingman, Kans., Oct. 19, 1915; s. Rudolph William and Helen (Brauer) G.; m. Laura Edna Baum, Aug. 30, 1941; m. Jane Shannon, Jan. 3, 1998 (dec. 2002); m. Mary Moon, July 2, 2004. BS, Milw. State Tchrs. Coll., 1939; MA, U. Okla., 1940; PhD, U. Chgo., 1949; LittD, Albright Coll., 1976; MA, Oxford U., 1978; DHL (hon.), U. Pitts., 1981, Valparaiso U., 1981, Ea. Ill. U., 1986, U. Wis., Milw., 1997; DHL, Averett U., 2003; D of Pedagogy, Marshall U., 1993. Asst. prof. Okla. Coll. for Women, 1942—43, 1946—47; from asst. prof. to prof. Iowa State Coll., 1948—56; prof. history U. Ill., Urbana, 1956—67, chmn. dept. history, 1961—63; Edward R. Stettinius prof. modern Am. history U. Va., 1967—82, Randolph P. Compton prof., Miller Ctr. Pub. Affairs, 1982—. Vis. prof. Stanford U., 1952-53, summers 1959, 72, U. Colo., summer 1968, Concordia Tchrs. Coll., summer 1971, US Mil. Acad., West Point, NY, 1981-82, Beloit Coll., spring 1987, Va. Mil. Inst., fall 1987, Coll. of William and Mary, spring 1988, Marshall U., spring 1989; Commonwealth Fund lectr. U. Coll., London, 1958; Fulbright lectr. U. Queensland, Brisbane, Australia, 1963, U. Sydney, Australia, 1983, U. Heidelberg, Germany, 1998-99; disting. vis. prof. history Pa. State U., 1975-76; Harmsworth prof. Am. history Oxford U., 1978-79; Phi Beta Kappa vis. scholar, 1981-82; Thomas Jefferson vis. scholar Downing Coll., Cambridge U., 1985; disting. vis. prof. Nat. War Coll., 1994-95. Author: Empire on the Pacific, 1955, The New Isolationism, 1956, Cold War Diplomacy, 1962, rev. edit., 1977, The Age of Global Power, 1979, America As a World Power: A Realist Appraisal from Wilson to Reagan, 1984, Foundations of American Foreign Policy: A Realist Appraisal from Franklin to McKinley, 1985, A Twentieth-Century Odyssey: Memoir of a Life in Academe, 2002; co-author: A History of the United States, 2 vols, 1970, A History of the American People, 1970, 2d edit., 1975, Recent United States History, 1972; Editor: The Enduring Lincoln, 1959, Politics and the Crisis of 1860, 1961, An Uncertain Tradition: American Secretaries of State in the Twentieth Century, 1961, The Cold War: A Conflict of Ideology and Power, 1963, rev. edit., 1976, Ideas and Diplomacy, 1964, Manifest Destiny, 1968, Nationalism and Communism in Asia: The American Response, 1977, Freedom in America: A 200-Year Perspective, 1977, American Diplomatic History before 1900, 1978; Traditions and Values: American Diplomacy, 1790-1865, 1985, 1865-1945, 1985; The National Security: Its Theory and Practice, 1945-1960, 1986; contbr. articles to hist. jours. Dir. bicentennial program Pa. State U., 1975-76. Served to 1st lt. US Army, 1943-46. Recipient Thomas Jefferson award, U. Va., 1985. Mem. Am., So. hist. assns., Orgn. Am. Historians, Soc. Am. Historians, Soc. Historians Am., Fgn. Rels. (pres. 1972), Am. Acad. Arts and Scis., Mass. Hist. Soc., Phi Beta Kappa. Home: 1135 Inglecress Dr Charlottesville VA 22901 *One should never demand more of society than society can grant to all without suffering chaos or disintegration.*

GRAEF, LUTHER WILLIAM, civil engineer; b. Milw., Aug. 14, 1931; s. John and Pearl (Luther) G.; m. Lorraine Linnerud, Sept. 18, 1954; children: Ronald, Sharon, Gerald. BCE, Marquette U., 1952; MCE, U. Wis., 1961. Registered profl. engr., Wis., Colo. Engr. C.W. Yoder & Assocs. cons. engrs., Milw., 1956—61; ptnr. Graef Anhalt Schloemer, cons. engrs., Milw., 1961—67; chmn. bd. Graef Anhalt Schloemer Assocs., Inc., Milw., 1978—96. Mem. accreditation bd. for engring. and tech., 1989-95. Active boy Scouts Am.; chmn. bd. assessment City of Milw., 1962-89; bd. dirs. Luther Manor. 1st lt. AUS, 1953-56. Named Disting. Marquette U. Alumnus, 1982, Wis. Profl. Engr. of Yr., 1983. Mem. ASCE (sect. pres. 1968, nat. bd. dirs. 1989-92, nat. v.p. 1993-95, nat. pres. 1997-98), NSPE, Am. Assn. Engring. Soc. (vice chmn. 2000, chmn. 2001), Wis. Soc. Profl. Engrs., Cons. Engrs. Coun. Wis. (pres. 1973-75), Engrs. Scientist Milw. (pres. 1975), World Fedn. Engr. Orgns. (exec. coun. 2001-05), World Fedn. Engring. Socs. (U.S. rep. 2002—). Home: 8503 Country Club Dr Franklin WI 53132-2710 Office: Graef Anhalt Schloemer 125 S 84th St Ste 401 Milwaukee WI 53214-1470

GRAEFF, ALAN S., health association executive; BS in Distributed Sciences, Am. U. Biologist metabolism br. Nat. Cancer Inst., NIH, Bethesda, Md., 1977—81; researcher Nat. Inst. of Allergy and Infectious Diseases, NIH, 1981—87, various IT positions, 1987—95, chief tech. systems sect., 1989—91; chief info. systems dept. NIH Clin. Ctr., 1995-98; dir. Ctr. Info. Tech., NIH, 1998—2005; chief info. officer NIH, 1998—2005; sr. scientist Nat. Ctr. Biotechnology Info. Nat. Libr. Medicine, NIH, 2005—. Office: Nat Libr Medicine Nat Ctr Biotechnology Info Bldg 38A LIster Hill Ctr Rm 8N806 9000 Rockville Pike Bethesda MD 20892 Office Phone: 301-435-5982. Office Fax: 301-480-4559. E-mail: agraeff@ncbi.nlm.nih.gov.

GRAETZ, MICHAEL J., law educator; b. Atlanta, 1944; m. Brett Dignam; children: Lucas, Dylan, Jacob, Sydney, Casey. BBA, Emory U., 1966; LLB, U. Va., 1969; LLD (hon.), Capital U., 1992. Bar: Va. 1969. Advisor tax policy Asst. Sec. Treas., Washington, 1969-72; asst. prof. U. Va., Charlottesville, 1972-74, assoc. prof., 1974-77, prof., 1977-79, U. So. Calif., Los Angeles, 1979-83, Yale U., New Haven, 1983—86, Justus S. Hotchkiss Prof. Law, 1986—; dep. asst. sec. tax policy Dept. Treasury, Washington, 1990-92, asst. to sec., spl. counsel, 1992. Author: Life Insurance Taxation, The Mutual vs. Stock Differential, 1986, The Decline and Fall of the Income Tax, 1997, Foundations of International Income Taxation, 2003, Federal Income Taxation: Principles and Policies, 2005; co-author: Death by a Thousand Cuts: The Fight Over Taxing Inherited Wealth, 2005; contbr. articles to legal and econs. jours. Recipient Exceptional Svc. award Dept. Treasury, 1972; Guggenheim fellow, 1989. Fellow: Am. Acad. Arts and Scis. Office: Yale Law Sch Box 208215 New Haven CT 06520-8215 E-mail: michael.graetz@yale.edu.

GRAF, ALAN B., JR., delivery service executive; b. Evansville, Ind., 1953; BS, MBA, Ind. U. With FedEx Corp., Memphis, 1980—, exec. v.p., CFO, 1996—. Bd. dir. Nike Inc., Kimball Internat., Mid-Am. Apartment Communities, Methodist Healthcare. Mem. Dean's adv. council Kelley Sch. Bus.; trustee Univ. Memphis Herff trust; mem. adv. bd. Univ. Memphis Tiger clubs. Office: FedEx Corp 842 S Shady Grove Rd Memphis TN 38120*

GRAF, HANS, conductor, music director; b. Austria, Feb. 15, 1949; m. Margarita Graf; 1 child, Anna. Studied with Franco Ferrera and Arvid Jansons. Dir. Iraqi Nat. Symphony Orch., Baghdad, Iraq, 1975—76; music coach Vienna State Opera, Austria, 1977—84; music dir. Mozarteum Orch., Salzburg, Austria, 1984-94, Calgary Philharm. Orch., 1995—2003, Orch. Nat. de Bordeaux-Aquitaine and Opera de Bordeaux, France, 1998—, Houston Symphony, 2000—; artist-in-residence Shepard Sch. of Music, Rice Univ., Tex. Guest condr. Vienna Symphony, Vienna Philharm., Orchestre Nat. de France, Leningrad Philharm., Pitts. Symphony, Boston Symphony. Recipient First prize, Karl Bohm Competition, 1979, Chevalier de l'Ordre de la Legion d'Honneur, French Govt., 2002. Avocation: fine wine. Office: Houston Symphony 615 Louisiana St Suite 102 Houston TX 77002*

GRAF, JOHN A., finance company executive; b. Chgo., 1959; BA in Econs., U. Ill., 1981. Sr. v.p. Conseco, Inc.; exec. v.p., chief mktg. officer Western Nat. Life Ins. Co., 1993—97, pres., CEO, 1997—98; vice chmn. We. Nat. Corp., 1996—98; pres., retirement svcs. Am. Gen. Fin. Group, Houston, 1998—2001; pres. We. Nat. Corp., 1998—; sr. vice chmn., asset accumulation Am. Gen. Fin. Group, 2000—01; exec. v.p., retirement savings Amer. Internat. Group Inc., 2002—; vice chmn. AIG SunAmerica Inc., 2001—. Bd. dirs. Jr. Achievement S.E. Tex., Inc., W. Univ. Parks Bd.; vol. St. Vincent de Paul Cath. Ch.; mem. devel. coun. Tex. Children's Hosp. Mem. Young Pres.'s Orgn. Office: Amer Internat Group Inc 70 Pine St New York NY 10270

GRAF, KARL ROCKWELL, nuclear engineer; b. San Diego, Apr. 19, 1940; s. Frederic August and Beatrice (Rockwell) G.; m. Nancy Ann Scott, June 9, 1962; children: Robin Elizabeth, Scott Frederic. BS, U. S. Naval Acad., 1962. Submarine officer USN, 1962-84; comdg. officer USS George Bancroft, 1978—82; dep. comdr. readiness and tng. officer Submarine Squadron One, USN, Pearl Harbor, Hawaii, 1982—84; sr. mgmt. cons. Advanced Sci. and Tech. Assn., Solana Beach, Calif., 1984; dir. nuclear support Ill. Power Co., Decatur, 1985, dir. ops. monitoring, 1986-89, dir. quality assurance, 1990-92, dir. engring. projects, 1992-94, leader life cycle mgmt., 1994-2000; dir. adminstrn. St. Paul's Luth. Ch., Decatur, Ill., 2000—05; dir. fin. Victorious Ministry Through Christ, Winter Park, Fla., 2005—. Founder life cycle mgmt. program Clinton Nuclear Power Sta. Author: Monitoring Manual, 1986. Exec. dir. St. John's Luth. Ch., 1995-97; chmn. zoning bd. Village of Forsyth, Ill., 1988-96, chmn. long-range plan com., 1989-92, mem. long range plan task force, 1999-2002. Mem. U.S. Submarine League, Ret. Officers Assn. Achievements include the development and implementation of an innovative monitoring program at Illinois Power Company's Clinton Nuclear Power Station to monitor, evaluate and trend such things as individual responsibility and professionalism and develop actions to improve performance standards relating to the nuclear reactor, steam turbine and electrical generating systems. Home: 736 Weaver Rd Forsyth IL 62535-9777 E-mail: k4n@insightbb.com. *To determine the right thing to do, and then to really do what is right is a formula that not only defines our integrity, but helps us to avoid many of the pitfalls that can be so destructive to success and meaningful relationships in all aspects of our lives.*

GRAF, PETER GUSTAV, accountant, lawyer; b. Vienna, June 19, 1936; came to U.S. 1940, naturalized, 1945; m. Rosalie Greenbaum, Apr. 6, 1963; 1 child, Paul Evan BS in Econs., U. Pa., 1957; LLB, NYU, 1960, LLM, 1962. Bar: N.Y. 1960; CPA, N.Y. Tax acct. J.K. Lasser & Co., NYC, 1961-62; with Joseph Graf & Co., NYC, 1962-66, ptnr., 1966—. V.p., founder, dir. AGS Computers Inc., N.J., 1967—; ptnr., founder, treas., dir. Nardin Gallery, Inc., Somers, N.Y.; founder Cable Sys. USA Assocs., W.Va., Pa., Ohio, USA Mobile Commn., Inc., Cellular USA Inc., USA Ventures Ltd., MDchoice.com., 1999, Tongue Sys.; chmn. Phonetel Technologies, Inc., 1995-99; founder Congo Inc., Right Angle Rsch. LLC; prin. shareholder ICF Inc. Mem. AICPA, N.Y. State Soc. CPA, N.Y. State Bar Assn. Home: 87 Holly Pl Briarcliff Manor NY 10510-2107 Office: Graf Repetti & Co 1114 Avenue Of The Americas New York NY 10036-7703 Business E-Mail: pggraf@grafrepetti.com.

GRAF, TRUMAN FREDERICK, agricultural economist, educator; b. New Holstein, Wis., Sept. 18, 1922; s. Herbert and Rose (Sell) G.; m. Sylvia Ann Thompson, Sept. 6, 1947; children: Eric Kindley, Siri Lynne, Peter Truman. BS, U. Wis., 1947, MS, 1949, PhD, 1953. Mktg. specialist, coop. agt. USDA and U. Wis., 1948-50; instr. agrl. econs. U. Wis., Madison, 1951-53, asst. prof., 1953-56, assoc. prof., 1956-61, prof., 1961-85, prof. emeritus, 1985—. Expert witness, 1982—; mem. Gov.'s Com. on Wis. Dairy Mktg.; mem. 3-man team to make mktg. analysis in Nigeria, USDA, 1962, made U.S. milk mktg. study, 1971; made mktg. analyses in 13 Carribbean countries, 1964; made mktg. analysis U. Wis., Mex., 1965; made mktg. analyses U.S. Ednl. Found., Finland, 1970, Rumanian Ministry Edn., U.S. Dept. State, Rumania, USSR, 1976, France, 1981, Russia, 1992, Ukraine, 1992, 98, Bulgaria, 1992, 93, Hungary, 1993, Poland, 1993, Zimbabwe, Africa, 1994, Ukraine, 1998, Kazakhstan, 1999, Uganda, 2000, US Treasury Dept., Cuba, 2002, Amenia, 2003, Czech Republic, 2004, Honduras, 2005, others; rschr. in field. Contbr. articles to profl. jours. Active Cub Scouts; bd. dirs. Univ. Houses Assn., 1955-56, Univ. Hill Farm Assn., 1958-59, Univ. Hill Farm Swim Club, 1959-60, Oakwood Retirement Homes, 1992-2001. Recipient Uhlman award Chgo. Bd. Trade, 1952, recipient Man of Yr. award World Dairy Expn., 1976, Disting. Svc. award U. Wis. Extension, 1981, Coop. Builder award Fedn. Coops., 1982, Internat. Trade Spl. award Gov. Wis., 1983. Mem. AARP (econ. security adv. com.), Am. Agrl. Econs. Assn. (Published Rsch. award 1974), Am. Mktg. Assn., Madison Naval Res. Assn. (pres. 1968-72), Am. Econ. Assn., Hist. Soc., United Dairy Industries Assn. (adv. com.), Wis. Fedn. Coops., Lakeshore Federated Dairy Coop., Wis. Ret. Educators Assn. (bd. dirs.), Wis. Coalition of Annuitants (vice chair), Civil War Club, People to People (pres.), Kiwanis (pres. Golden K). Lutheran. Home: 405 Samuel Dr Madison WI 53717-2144 Office: U Wis Dept Agriculture Madison WI 53706

GRAFF, GEORGE LEONARD, lawyer; b. Bklyn., Sept. 6, 1940; s. Charles M. and Nettie (Starr) G.; m. Judith S. Udell, Apr. 20, 1963; children: David, Peter, Matthew. AB, Columbia U., 1962, LLB magna cum laude, 1967. Bar: NY 1967, US Dist. Ct. (so., ea. and no. dists.) NY 1970, US Ct. Appeals (2d, 3rd, 9th and Fed. cirs.) 1975, US Ct. Claims, 1980, US Supreme Ct. 1985. Law clk. to Hon. Stanley H. Fuld NY Ct. Appeals, Albany, 1967-70; assoc. Nickerson, Kramer, Lowenstein, Nessen & Kamin, NYC, 1970-74; member Milgrim, Thomajan & Lee, P.C., NYC, 1974-92; ptnr. Paul, Hastings, Janofsky & Walker, NYC, 1992—2007. Lt. comdr. USNR, 1962-73. Mem. ABA (advisor to drafting com. uniform computer info. transactions act 1994-2003, sci. and tech. sect. 1999-2003, mem. coun.), Assn. of Bar of City of NY (chmn. state legislation com. 1973-75), Intellectual Property Owners Am. (vice chair amicus com.). Home: 112 Holly Pl Briarcliff Manor NY 10510-2107 Office: Paul Hastings Janofsky & Walker LLP 75 E 55th St New York NY 10022 Business E-Mail: georgegraff@paulhastings.com.

GRAFF, GEORGE STEPHEN, aerospace transportation executive; b. NYC, Mar. 16, 1917; s. George Russell and Marjory Eleanor (Dolan) G.; m. Mary Rita Shaughnessy, Oct. 3, 1942 (dec.); children: Mary Ann, George Stephen, James Russell, Thomas Gerald, Maureen Rita; m. Marjory V. Kassabaum, Apr. 4, 1987; stepchildren: Douglas George, Ann Denise, Karen Jane. AB cum laude, DeSales Coll., Toledo, 1939; B.Aero. Engring., U. Detroit, 1942. Draftsman Continental Aviation & Engring. Corp., Detroit, 1940-42; with McDonnell Aircraft Co., 1942-82, dir. system tech., 1961-64, v.p. engring. tech., 1964-68, v.p. engring., 1968-70, exec. v.p., 1970-71, pres., 1971-82, also dir.; v.p. McDonnell Douglas Corp., 1971-82, mem. exec. com., 1974-87, also bd. dirs. Mem. subcom. stability and control NACA, 1951-56; mem. subcom. aerodynamic stability and control NASA, 1956-58, com. missile and spacecraft aerodynamics, 1959-61, com. aircraft aerodynamics, 1964-65, chmn. aircraft aerodynamics com., 1965-67, mem. research and tech. adv. com. on aeros., 1967-71 Mem. industry com. Parks Coll., St. Louis, 1950-58; chmn. bd. trustees Fontbonne Coll., 1977-87; bd. dirs. Jr. Achievement of Mississippi Valley, Inc. Recipient trophy for design excellence Continental Aviation and Engring. Corp., 1942; Outstanding Engring. Alumnus of Yr. award U. Detroit, 1973 Fellow AIAA (regional dir., chmn. com. aircraft design 1964-67, fellow grade com. 1975-76); mem. Nat. Acad. Engring., Tau Beta Pi. Home: 750 S Hanley Rd #38 Saint Louis MO 63105 E-mail: graffgsgxp67@sbcglobal.net.

GRAFF, HARVEY J., history and humanities educator; b. Pitts., June 19, 1949; BA in History with honors, Northwestern U., 1970; MA in History and History of Edn., U. Toronto, 1971, PhD in History and History of Edn., 1975; cert., Newberry Libr. Inst. Instr. summer sch. Northwestern U., 1973; extramural lectr. Ont. Inst. for Studies in Edn., 1974-75; asst. to assoc. to prof. history and humanities U. Tex., Dallas, 1975-98, dir. divsn. behavioral and cultural sci., prof. history San Antonio. Rsch. assoc. Newberry Libr., 1980-81; vis. adj. prof. history Loyola U., Chgo., 1980; vis. prof. English and Edn., English and history summer sch. Simon Fraser U., 1980, 81; cons., reviewer NEH, 1978—, Nat. Inst. Edn., 1980—, Tex. Com. for Humanitites, 1976—; cons.-advisor Tex. local and regional hist. socs. and groups, 1976—; mem. adv. bd. Dallas Jewish Hist. Soc., 1987—; resource person Collaborative Approach to Svcs. for Elderly, U. Tex. Coun. Pres., 1977—; advisor Sta. KERA-TV, Dallas; advisor Handbook on Tex. Women, 1983—, American Teenagers: A Documentary Film, 1997. Author: Children and Schools in Nineteenth-Century Canada/L'ècole Canadienne et L'enfant au Dix-Neuvieme Siecle, 1979, rev. edit., 1993, The Literacy Myth: Literacy and Social Structure in the Nineteenth Century, 1979, rev. edit., 1991, The Legacies of Literacy, 1987, The Labyrinths of Literacy, 1987, rev. edit., 1995, Conflicting Paths: Growing Up in America, 1995, also fgn. transls., others; editor: Growing Up in America: Historical Experiences, 1987; mem. editl. bd. History Edn. Quar., 1975-79, Social Sci. History, 1994—; contbr. articles to profl. jours.; cons. editor Interchange: Quar. Rev. Edn., 1974-78, 94—. NEH fellow The Newberry Libr., 1979-80, Spencer fellow Nat. Acad. Edn., 1979-82, short-term fellow Newberry Libr., 1985-86, Am. Antiquarian Soc./NEH fellow, 1988-89; rsch. grantee U. Tex., Dallas, 1983-85, 87-89, Spencer Found., 1991, 92; recipient Critics Choice award Am. Ednl. Studies Assn., 1987. Mem. Can. Assn. Am. Studies (exec. com. 1972-75, program com. 1974), Am. Ednl. Rsch. Assn. (program com. div. F 1973), Can. Population Studies Group (steering and program coms. 1974-76), History of Edn. Soc. (nominating com. 1976, 79), Women in History Profession (coord. S.W. coordinating com. 1977-79), Social Sci. History Assn. (regional network coor. 1976-84, founding chmn. Allan Sharlin Meml. award com. 1984-85, exec. com. 1987-89), Am. Hist. Assn., Orgn. Am. Historians, Social History Soc. Office: Behavioral and Cultural Scis U Tex 6900 N Loop 1604 W San Antonio TX 78249-1130

GRAFF, HENRY FRANKLIN, historian, educator; b. NYC, Aug. 11, 1921; s. Samuel F. and Florence Babette (Morris) G.; m. Edith Krantz, June 16, 1946; children: Iris Joan (Mrs. Andrew R. Morse), Ellen Toby (Mrs. Martin A. Fox). BSS magna cum laude, Coll. City NY, 1941; MA, Columbia U., 1942, PhD, 1949, LittD (hon.), 2005. Cryptanalyst , Japanese lang. officer AUS, 1942—46; fellow history Coll. City NY, 1941-42, tutor history, 1946; lectr. history Columbia U., NYC, 1946-47, instr. to asso. prof., 1946-61, prof. history, 1961-91, prof. emeritus, 1991—, chmn. dept. history, 1961-64; sr. fellow Freedom Forum Media Studies Ctr., NYC, 1991-92; disting. lectr. Med. Sch. Columbia U., NYC, 1992. Lectr. Vassar Coll., 1953; chmn. advanced placement com. Am. History Coll. Entrance Exam. Bd., 1959-63; presdl. appointee Nat. Hist. Publs. Commn., 1965-71; mem. hist. adv. com. to sec. Air Force, 1972-80; acad. cons. Gen. Learning Corp., Time-Life Books; cons. editor Alfred A. Knopf, Inc.; hist. adviser to CBS for Bicentennial TV Series The American Parade, 1973-76, Presdl. Portraits, 1987-88; disting. spkr. US Air Force Acad., 1980; hist. adviser to ABC for TV series Our World, 1986-87, 20th Century Project, 1993-99; presdl. appointee J.F.K. Assassination Records Rev. Bd., 1993-98; humanities lectr. Med. Sch. Yale U., 1993; Richard W. Cooper lectr. Phi Beta Kappa Assocs., 1996. Author: Bluejackets with Perry in Japan, 1952; author: (with Jacques Barzun) The Modern Researcher, 1957, 2004; author: (with Clifford Lord) American Themes, 1963; author: (with John A. Krout) The Adventure of the American People, 3d edit., 1973; author: The Free and the Brave, 4th edit., 1980, Thomas Jefferson, 1968, American Imperialism and the Philippine Insurrection, 1969, The Tuesday Cabinet, 1970; author: (with Paul J. Bohannan) The Call of Freedom, 1978, The Promise of Democracy, 1978; author: This Great Nation, 1983, The Presidents: A Reference History, 1984, 2d edit., 1996, paperback, 1997, 3d edit., 2002, America: The Glorious Republic, 1985, rev. edit., 1990, Grover Cleveland, 2002; cons. editor Life's History of the United States, 1963—64, Inaugural Addresses of the Presidents, 2005; contbr. articles to profl. jours. 1st lt. AUS, 1942-46. Recipient citation War Dept., 1945, Townsend Harris medal CCNY, 1966, Mark Van Doren award Columbia U., 1981, Gt. Tchr. award Columbia U., 1982, Kidger award New Eng. History Tchrs. Assn., 1990; Am. Coun. Learned Socs. fellow, 1942, Presdl. medal George Washington U., 1997, James Madison award ALA, 1999, Disting. Author award Westchester CC Found., 2000, Kaul Found. Award of Excellence, 2001. Mem. Orgn. Am. Historians, Am. Hist. Assn., Coun. Fgn. Rels., Author's Guild, P.E.N., Soc. Am. Historians, Soc. Historians Am. Fgn. Rels., Mass. Hist. Soc. (corr.), Century Assn. (NYC), Sunningdale Country Club, Phi Beta Kappa (former pres. Gamma chpt.), Phi Beta Assocs. (hon.). Home: 47 Andrea Ln Scarsdale NY 10583-3115

GRAFF, JEFFREY G., emergency physician; b. Chgo., Aug. 25, 1949; MD, U. Ill. Coll. Medicine, 1975. Intern Evanston Hosp., 1975—76, resident in emergency medicine, 1976—78; asst. prof. emergency medicine Northwestern U.; head divsn. emergency medicine Evanston Northwestern

Healthcare; assoc. prof. emergency medicine Northwestern U. Feinberg Sch. Medicine. Bd. mem. Am. Bd. Emergency Medicine, 1996—, pres., 2003—04. Office: 2100 Pfingsten Rd Glenview IL 60025-1301 Office Phone: 847-657-5632.

GRAFF, JOAN MESSING, lawyer; BS, Cornell U.; JD, Columbia U., 1967. Bar: DC 1969, Calif. 1973. Atty. EEOC, 1967—70; vol. atty. Davis, Dunlap and Williams; co-founder, v.p. Equal Rights Advocates (ERA), 1974—81; exec. dir. Legal Aid Soc. of San Francisco-Employment Law Ctr. (LAS-ELC), 1981—. Mem.: State Bar Calif. (Loren Miller Legal Svcs. Award 2006). Office: Legal Aid Soc-ELC 600 Harrison St #120 San Francisco CA 94107 Office Phone: 415-864-8848. Office Fax: 415-864-8199.*

GRAFF, PAT STUEVER, secondary school educator; b. Tulsa, Mar. 24, 1955; d. Joseph H., Sr. and Joann (Schneider) Stuever; m. Mark A. Rumsey; children: Earl, Jr., Jeremy. BS in Secondary Edn., Okla. State U., 1976; postgrad., U. N.M., 1976-87. Cert. tchr. lang. arts, social studies, journalism, French, N.Mex. Substitute tchr. Albuquerque Pub. Schs., 1976-78; tchr. Cleveland Mid. Sch., Albuquerque, 1978-86, La Cueva H.S., Albuquerque, 1986—, co-chair English dept., 1996—, chair sch. restructuring coun., 1999-2001. Adviser award winning lit. mag. El Tesoro, sch. newspapers The Edition, Huellas del Oso; instr. journalism workshops, N.Mex. Press Assn., Ind. U., Bloomington, Nat. Scholastic Press, Mpls., Kans. State U., Manhattan, Interscholastic Press League, Austin, Tex., St. Mary's U., San Antonio, Ala. Scholastic Press Assn., Wash.; keynote spkr. at numerous confs. in Ohio, Ind., Kans., S.C., Utah, La., Okla., Ala., N.Mex., Tex., Wash., Idaho, and N.Y.; reviewer of lang. and textbooks for several cos.; instr. Dial-A-Tchr., N.Mex., 1991-05; texbook evaluator Holt Pub., Inc., 1991; nat. bd. cert. tchr. adolescent/young adult English lang. arts, 2001—; mem. N.Mex. Network of Nat. Bd. Cert. Tchrs., 2002—, 2d v.p., 2003-; state bd. dirs. N.Mex. Coun. for the Social Studies, 1998-2006, chair state conf., 2001, state pres., 2002-03, state treas., 2003-06; comm. officer, sec. ABQ Tchrs. Fedn. 2003-05. Author: Journalism Text, 1983; contbg. author: Communication Skills Resource Text, 1987, Classroom Publishing/Literacy, 1992; contbr. articles to profl. jours. Troop leader Girl Scouts U.S., 1979—90, coord. various programs, asst. program com. chmn. Chaparral Coun., 1988—89, chmn. adult recognition task force, 1991—96, bd. dirs., 1991—98; active PTA Gov. Bent Elem. Sch., 1983—86, v.p., 1985—86, Osuna Elem. Sch., 1986—92, N.Mex. PTA, 1994—2000; pub. various children's lit. mags., 1987—; pub. parent's newsletter, 1986—; newsletter layout editor Albuquerque Youth Soccer Orgn., 1985—88; active YMCA youth and govt. model legis.; faculty advisor La Cueva del., 1986—, press corps advisor, 1987—2001, asst. state dir., 2001—; asst. den. leader Boy Scouts Am., 1987—88, den leader, 1988—91. Recipient Innovative Tchg. award Bus. Week mag., 1990, Svc. commendation Coll. Edn. Alumni Assn., Okla. State U., 1990, Alumni Recognition award, 1993, Mem. Yr. Svc. award Bernalillo County Coun. Internat. Reading Assn., Thanks to Tchrs. award Apple Computers, 1990, Spl. Recognition Albuquerque C. of C., 1992, Disting. Svc. award NCTE, 2002; named one of Gov.'s Outstanding Women in N.Mex., 2004; Spotlighted Mem. Phi Delta Kappa, 1990; Spl. Recognition Advisor Dow Jones Newspaper Fund, 1990; named Nat. H.S. Journalism Tchr. of Yr., 1995, Disting. Advisor, 1991, N.Mex. Pubs. Adviser of Yr., 1991, N.Mex. State Tchr. of Yr., 1993, USA Today All-Am. Tchr., 1999; finalist U.S. West Tchr. Yr. finalist, 1991, Nat. Tchr. of Yr., 1993, Am. Tchr. Awards, Disney, 1998; named to Nat. Tchr. Hall Fame, 2005; grantee Phi Delta Kappa 1989, 91, Geraldine R. Dodge Found., 1990, 92, 95-97, Learn and Serve Am., 1999. Mem.: AAUW (chpt. newsletter editor 1995—2001, local v.p. 1997—99, state program v.p. 1997—99, state media chair 2000—03), ASCD (editor newsletter 1991—92, focus on excellence awards com. 1992—94, state bd. dirs. 2002—, Focus on Excellence award 1990), Albuquerque (N.Mex.) Tchrs. Fedn. (PR and comms. officer 2003—05, sec. 2003—05), N Mex. Coun. for Social Studies (mem. bd. 1999—2002, state v.p. 2001—02, pres. 2002—03), N. Mex. World Class Tchr. Network (state vice-pres. 2002—), N.Mex. Goals 2000 (panel mem. 1994—97), Quill & Scroll (adv. La Cueva chpt. 1986—, judge nat. newspaper rating contest 1988—97), Albuquerque Press Women (v.p. 1994, pres. 1995, Communicator of Achievement award 1993), N.Mex. Press Women (state scholarship chair 1994, publicity chair 1995—96, state treas. 1996—98, state v.p. 1998—99), N.Mex. Scholastic Press Assn. (state v.p. 1985—89, coord. workshop 1986, editor newsletter 1986—89, asst. chair state conf. 1988, 1989, state bd. dirs. 1991—2000, state v.p. 1992—95), N.Mex. Coun. Tchrs. English (regional coord. Albuquerque 1983—86, chair state confs. 1985—87, editl. bd. N.Mex. English Jour. 1986—88, state pres. 1987—88, chair facilities for fall conf. 1988—93, chair English humanities expo com. 1988—99, adv. mgr. 1989—90, editor N.Mex. English Jour. 1999—2003, Svc. award 1989, Outstanding H.S. English Tchr. N.Mex. 1991), Journalism Edn. Assn. (judge nat. contests 1988—, mem. nat. cert. bd. 1989—99, presenter nat. convs. 1989—, cert. journalism educator 1990, nat. bd. 1991—2002, master 1991—), Nat. Fedn. Press Women, Nat. Sch. Pub. Rels. Assn. (issues seminar planning com. 1990, chair 1991, master journalism educator 1991—, nat. conf. chmn. 1997—99, Zia chpt., contest winner 1991—94, Pres.'s award 1993), Nat. Coun. Tchrs. English (nat. chair com. English Tchrs. and Pubs. 1988—91, chair English humanities expo com. 1990—99, standing com. affiliates 1991—94, nat. chair 1995—98, chair English humanities expo com. 2001—03, nat. exec. com. 2001—03, nat. chair assembly for advisors of student pubs., regional rep. Tex., La., N.Mex., chmn. English humanities expo com. 2005—, Disting. Svc. award 2002), Nat. Alliance High Schs. (tchr. rep. 1997—2000), Nat. Assn. Secondary Sch. Prins. (Breaking Ranks tchr. rep.), Phi Delta Kappa (pres. U. N.Mex. br. 2002—), Delta Kappa Gamma (state profl. affairs com. chair 2003—), Pi Lambda Theta (Ethel Mary Moore award Outstanding Educator 1993, Gov.'s Outstanding Women in N.Mex. 2004). Roman Catholic. Avocations: soccer, running, hiking, travel, skiing. Home: 8101 Krim Dr NE Albuquerque NM 87109-5223 Office: La Cueva H S 7801 Wilshire Ave NE Albuquerque NM 87122-2807 Office Phone: 505-823-2327. Personal E-mail: pgraff@aol.com.

GRAFF, RANDY, actress; b. Bklyn., May 23, 1955; Grad., Wagner Coll. Profl. theater debut in Gypsy, Village Dinner Theater, Raleigh, N.C.; appeared in Godspell, Raleigh; other appearances include Pins and Needles, Roundabout Theatre, N.Y.C., 1978, Something Wonderful, Westchester Regional Theatre, Harrison, N.Y., 1979, Sarava, Mark Hellinger Theatre, N.Y.C., 1979, Coming Attractions, Playwrights Horizons, Mainstage Theatre, N.Y.C., 1980, Keystone, McCarter Theatre, Princeton, N.J., 1981, A.My Name is Alice, Village Gate Theatre, N.Y.C., 1984, Amateurs, Playhouse in the Park, Cin., 1985, Fiorello!, Goodspell Opera House, East Haddam, Conn., 1985, Absurd Person Singular, Phila. Drama Guild, Phila., 1986, Les Miserables, Broadway Theatre, N.Y.C., 1987, City of Angels, Va. Theatre, N.Y.C., 1989 (Drama Desk award Featured Actress in Musical 1989, Tony award Supporting of Featured Actress in Musical 1990), Falsettos, 1993, Laughter on the 23rd Floor, 1993, Moon Over Buffalo, Martin Beck Theatre, 1995-96, High Society, St. James Theatre, N.Y.C., 1998, A Class Act, Abmassador Theatre, N.Y.C., 2001, Fiddler on the Roof, Minskoff Theatre, 2004, The Lady with All the Answers, 2005; (TV shows) include Mad About You, Law & Order, Love & War, Pros & Cons; (films) Key's to Tulsa, 1995. Office: TRI Richard Stable 321 W 44th St Ste 805 New York NY 10035-5404

GRAFFAM, WARD IRVING, lawyer; b. Portland, Maine, Sept. 2, 1940; s. Irving Hall and Mary Earl (Williams) G.; m. Linda Lewsen, June 10, 1967; children: Ward Jr., Kristen, Jerome. Bar: Maine 1967, U.S. Dist. Ct. Maine 1967. Lawyer Unum Life Ins. Co., Portland, 1968-70, assoc. counsel, 1970-75, counsel, 1975-80, v.p. ltd. products, 1980-83, v.p. employee benefits mktg., 1983-85, v.p. reins ops., 1985-86, v.p. flexible benefits, 1986—88, v.p. internat. ops., 1988-90; chmn. NEL Britannica Life Assurance, 1990-92; pres., mng. dir. Unum European Holding Co. Ltd. (London), 1990-97; chmn. Unum, Ltd., London, 1990—95; sr. v.p. internat. ops. Unum Life Ins. Co. Am., 1990—97; COO, Young Am. America's Cup Syndicate, 1997-98; co-owner Wayfarer Marine Corp., Camden, Maine, 1997-2000. Bd. dirs. Camden Nat. Corp., Acadia Trust, Montalvo Corp., First Union Life Ins. Co., Maine Med. Ctr., 1st Union Inst. Co.; chmn. Me. Employers Mutual Ins. Co., Waldron Group, ACLI Internat. Life Ins. Coun.; sec. N.E. Health; chmn. bd. dirs. Maine Internat. Trade Ctr., 1995-99, Waldron Group of Cos., 2002—; vice chmn. bd. dirs. Maine World Trade, Internat. Ins. Coun., Found. for Blood Rsch.; bd. visitors U. Maine Law Sch.; chmn., trustee Maine Maritime Acad. Author: (with others) The Mutual Company, 1971; editor-in-chief U. Maine Law Rev., 1966-67. Chmn. bd. South Portland HUD, 1973-75; mem. Gov.'s Coun. on Alcohol and Drug Abuse, Augusta, Maine, 1980-82; bd. dirs. Cumberland unit Am. Cancer Soc., Portland, 1976-78, Vis. Nurses Assn., Portland, 1971-72, YMCA, Portland, 1984-89; bd. dirs. Maine World Affairs Coun., Maine Maritime Mus.; mem. Gov.'s Internat. Adv. Bd., 1995-96; treas., bd. dirs. Maine Maritime Acad., 1997—, Maine Med. Ctr. Recipient 1st Place award Moot Ct. Competition U. Maine Sch. Law, Dist. Alumni award. Mem. ABA, Am. Corp. Counsel Assn., Maine State Bar Assn., Cumberland Bar Assn. (award), London Yacht Club, Portland Country Club, Portland Yacht Club (commodore 1983-84), Masons. Home: 29 Orchard St Portland ME 04102-3613 Office: Graffam & Assocs 29 Orchard St Portland ME 04102

GRAFFEO, MARY THÉRÈSE, music educator, performer; b. Mineola, NY, Jan. 20, 1949; d. Michael Joseph and Florence Marie (Lonette) G. BA in Music Edn., Adelphi U., 1972; MusM in Vocal Performance, Kent State U., 1982. Cert. music tchr. NY. Tchr., therapist Nassau County Bd. Coop. Ednl. Svcs., Westbury, NY, 1972-85; tchr. music, developer curricula Great Neck (N.Y.) Pub. Schs., 1985-87; tchr. music Syosset (N.Y.) Pub. Schs., 1987-88, 89-90, Jericho (N.Y.) Pub. Schs., 1988-89; tchr. music, developer creative programs Lawrence (N.Y.) Pub. Schs., 1990-92; tchr. music Herricks Pub. Schs., New Hyde Park, NY, 1992-93, Hempstead (N.Y.) Pub. Schs., 1993—. Music dir. summer programs Friends Acad., Locust Valley, N.Y., 1989-95. Author: Creative Enrichment Programs/America: The First 300 Years in Song, 1990, (curriculum) Music for the Trainable Mentally Retarded, 1973, Music for the Early Childhood Center of Hempstead Public Schools, 2002, (book) Composing with Kindergarten, 2007; co-author: The Remediation of Learning Discrepancies Through Music, 1980, The Kindergarten Humanities Program, 2007; composer: (plays) Red Riding Hood's Day, 1993, The Bell of Atri, The Children's Song, 1995, Song of the Notes, 2006. Cultural adv. bd. Lawrence Pub. Schs., 1990-92, Hempstead Pub. Schs., 1993—; founding mem. United We Stand Am., Dallas, 1992-93. Scholar Adelphi U., 1968-72, Blossom Festival Sch., Kent, Ohio, 1978-79. Mem. NEA, Am. Fedn. Tchrs., Music Educators Nat. Conf., N.Y. State United Tchrs., N.Y. State Sch. Music Assn., Nassau Music Educators Assn. Democrat. Roman Catholic. Avocations: aviculture, needlecrafts, travel, photography, concerts. Home: 18 Osborne Ln Greenvale NY 11548-1140 Office: Early Childhood Ctr 436 Front St Hempstead NY 11550-4212 Office Phone: 516-489-2424. E-mail: mgraffeo@optonline.net.

GRAFFEO, VICTORIA A., state appeals court judge; BA, State U. Coll., Oneonta, 1974; JD Albany Law Sch., Union U., 1977. Pvt. practice, 1978—82; asst. counsel NY State Divsn. Alcoholism and Alcohol Abuse, 1982—84; counsel to minority leader pro tempore Kemp Hannon NY State Assembly, 1984—89; chief counsel to minority leader Clarence D. Rappleyea Jr. N.Y. State Assembly, 1989—94; solicitor gen. State of NY, 1995—96; justice NY State Supreme Ct. (3rd Jud. Dist.), 1996—98; assoc. justice Appellate divsn., 3rd dept., 1998—2000; assoc. judge NY State Ct. Appeals, Albany, 2000—. Office: NY Ct of Appeals 20 Eagle St Albany NY 12207 Office Phone: 518-285-5050.

GRAFFIS, LEISTER F., retired engineering executive; b. Pekin, Ill., May 7, 1909; s. Runnion Abraham and May (Perdue) Graffis; m. Marian Doris Graffis, Sept. 10, 1943 (dec.); children: Beverly Jean, Elaine Velma. AEE, N.D. State Coll. Sci., 1937; cert. in trade and internat. edn., Colo. State Coll., 1940; cert. in advanced radar and comm. equipment, Harvard U., MIT, 1943. Supt. State Tng. Sch., Mandan, ND, 1937—41; precision assembler Lockheed Aircraft, Burbank, Calif., 1941—42; radio engr. Civil Svc., San Francisco, 1942; staff engr. radio divsn. Bendix, Towson, Md., 1945—50, chief field engr., 1950—57, asst. mgr. field engring., 1957—59, mgr., 1959—62; pres. Bendix Field Engring. Corp., Towson, Md., 1962—70; exec. asst. to corp. v.p. Bendix, Washington, 1970—73; ret., 1973. Contbr. articles to profl. jours. Treas., bd. dirs. Md. Bapt. Children's Aid; mem. Balt. area coun. exec. bd. Boy Scouts Am.; exec. dir. Md. Found.; trustee Golden Gate Bapt. Theol. Sem. Lt. comdr. AC USN, 1942—45, PTO. Named Man of the Yr., Bendix, 1969, Alumnus of the Yr., N.D. State Coll. Sci., 1991; recipient Pub. Svc. award, NASA, 1969, Internat. Honors citation, Epsilon Pi Tau, 1997. Mem.: Masons, Iota Lambda Sigma. Republican. Avocations: science and technology, photography, music. Home: 211 Willow Valley Sq # B204 Lancaster PA 17602

GRAFFMAN, GARY, academic administrator, pianist, music educator; b. NYC, Oct. 14, 1928; s. Vladimir and Nadia (Margolin) G.; m. Naomi Helfman, Dec. 5, 1952. Student, Curtis Inst. Music, 1936-46, Columbia U., 1947-48; studied with Vladimir Horowitz, Rudolf Serkin, Isabelle Vengerova; MusD (hon.), Trinity Coll., 1986, Juilliard Sch., 1993; MusD, Moravian Coll., 1995; MusD (hon.), St. Josephs U., 1996, Univ. Pa., 1997, New Eng. Conservatory Music, 2003. Dir. Curtis Inst. Music, Phila., 1986-95, pres., dir., 1995—. Soloist debut, Phila. Orch, 1947; first tours U.S., 1951, S.Am., 1955, Europe, 1956, Asia-Australia, 1958, South Africa, 1961; solo appearances with N.Y. Philharmonic, Boston, Chgo., Cleve., San Francisco, Los Angeles, London, Cape Town symphony orchs., Philharmonia London, Halle Orch. of Manchester, Royal Liverpool, Berlin, Lisbon, Oslo, Warsaw philharmonic orchs., Johannesburg, Sydney, Melbourne orchs., others; rec. artist with N.Y., Phila., Boston, Cleve., Chgo., San Francisco orchs., also solo recs.; author: I Really Should Be Practicing, 1981. Fulbright scholar, 1950; Ford Found. fellow, 1962; recipient Rachmaninoff Fund. spl. award, 1948, Leventritt award, 1949, Pa. Gov. Excellence in Arts award, 1991. Office: Curtis Inst Music Office of Director 1726 Locust St Philadelphia PA 19103-6187 also: ICM Artists Ltd 40 W 57th St Fl 16 New York NY 10019-4001

GRAFSTEIN, BERNICE, physiology and neuroscience educator, researcher; BA, U. Toronto, Ont., Can., 1951; PhD, McGill U., Montreal, Que., Can., 1954. Prof. physiology and biophysics Cornell U. Med. Coll., NYC, 1973—, disting. prof. neurosci., 1984—. Office: Cornell U Weill Med Coll Dept Physiology New York NY 10021 Office Phone: 212-746-6364. E-mail: bgraf@med.cornell.edu.

GRAFSTEIN, JOEL M., lawyer; b. NYC, May 27, 1948; s. Max G. and Lillian (Weisner) G.; m. Andree M. Clement, Aug. 4, 1974; 1 son, Michael Louis. BS, U. Bridgeport, 1970; JD, NY Law Sch., 1973; LLM, NYU, 1974. Bar: NY 1973, Conn. 1973, U.S. Dist. Ct. Conn. 1973, U.S. Tax Ct. 1973. Assoc. Rome & Case, Bloomfield, Conn., 1974-82, Albrecht, Zelman, Hartford, Conn., 1982-83; ptnr. Lublin, Wolfe, Kantor & Silver, East Hartford, Conn., 1984—1989. Author: Connecticut Collection Law, 1982, 83, 2005; Connecticut Foreclosure Law, 1984, 87; Bankruptcy: A Primer, 1984, 2d edit., 1987; The Connecticut Unfair Trade Practices Act, 1986, Problem Loans in Connecticut, 1988, Connecticut Forclosure Law, 2001. Chmn. Republican Town Com., Barkhamstead, Conn., 1980-82; region chmn. Disaster Relief Com., Hartford, 1978-83. Mem. ABA, Conn. Bar Assn. (exec. com. 1978-83), Lions (treas. 1976-80) (Bloomfield, Conn.). Office: Grafstein & Assoc 10 Melrose Dr Farmington CT 06034 Home: 17 Applewood Ln Avon CT 06001-4503 Office Phone: 860-674-8003.

GRAFTON, ANTHONY THOMAS, history professor; b. New Haven, May 21, 1950; s. Samuel and Edith (Kingstone) G.; m. Louise Erlich, May 13, 1972; children: Samuel David, Anna Temma Rachel. BA, U. Chgo., 1971, MA, 1972, PhD, 1975; Doctorate (hon.), U. Leiden, 2006. Instr. Cornell U., Ithaca, NY, 1974-75; from asst. prof. to assoc. prof. Princeton (N.J.) U., 1975-85, prof., 1985—, Andrew Mellon prof., 1988-93, Dodge prof. of history, 1993-2000, Henry Putnam prof., 2000—. Meyer Schapiro lectr. Columbia U., 1996-97; exhibit curator N.Y. Pub. Libr., N.Y.C., 1992, Libr. of Congress, Washington, 1993. Author: Joseph Scaliger, 1983-93, Defenders of the Text, 1991, New Worlds, Ancient Texts, 1992, The Footnote: A Curious History, 1997, Commerce with the Classics, 1997, Cardano's Cosmos, 1999, Leon Battista Alberti, 2000, Bring Out Your Dead, 2001. Recipient L.A. Times prize for history, 1993, Balzan prize for History of Humanities, 2002, Mellon Disting. Achievement award, 2003; Danforth fellow, 1971-75, Guggenheim fellow, 1988-89, Fairchild fellow Calif. Tech. Inst., 1988-89, Behrman fellow Princeton U., 1994-95. Mem. Am. Philos. Soc., Brit. Acad., Berlin-Brandenburgische Akad. der Wissenschaften (corr.). Democrat. Jewish. Avocations: walking, reading. Office: Princeton U Dickinson Hall History Dept Hl Princeton NJ 08544-0001 Home Phone: 604-921-1919; Office Phone: 609-258-9182. Business E-Mail: grafton@princeton.edu.

GRAFTON, BETH P., music educator; b. Altoona, Pa., Dec. 16, 1957; d. Robert R. Reifsteck, Sally A. Reifsteck; m. Dirk S. Grafton; children: Christopher, Diana. MA in Music Edn., Indiana U. of Pa., 1994. Cert. Instrnl. II Pa., 1979. Tchr. music Indiana Area Sch. Dist., Indiana, Pa., 1979—; violist Altoona Symphony Orch., Altoona, Pa., 1975—94. Violist Johnstown Symphony Orch., Johnstown, Pa., 1979—99. Musician (condr., dir.): Indiana Area H.S. Pit Orch. V.p. Zion Luth. Ch. Coun., Indiana, 1998—2000. Mem.: Pa. State Edn. Assn., Pa. Music Educators Assn., Kappa Delta Pi (life), Delta Omicron (life). Lutheran. Home Phone: 724-349-3376.

GRAFTON, SUE, novelist; b. Louisville, Apr. 24, 1940; d. Cornelius Warren and Vivian Boisseau (Harnsberger) G.; children: Leslie, Jay, Jamie; m. Steven Humphrey, Oct. 1, 1978. BA, U. Louisville, 1961. Lectr. L.A. City Coll., Long Beach (Calif.) City Coll., U. Dayton (Ohio) Writers Conf., Midwest Writers Conf., Canton, Ohio, Calif. Luth. Coll., Thousand Oaks, Santa Barbara (Calif.) Writers Conf., L.A. Valley Coll., Antioch Writers Conf., Yellow Springs, Ohio, S.W. Writers Conf., Albuquerque, Smithsonian Campus on the Mall, Washington, and others. Author: (novels) Keziah Dane, 1967, The Lolly-Madonna War, 1969, "A" is for Alibi, 1982 (Mysterious Stranger award 1982-83), "B" is for Burglar, 1985 (Shamus award 1986, Anthony award 1987), "C" is For Corpse, 1986, "D" is for Deadbeat, 1987, "E" is for Evidence, 1988 (Doubleday Mystery Guild award 1989), "F" is for Fugitive, 1989 (Doubleday Mystery Guild award 1990, The Falcon award 1990), "G" is for Gumshoe, 1990 (Doubleday Mystery Guild award 1991, Anthony award 1991, Shamus award 1991), "H" is for Homicide, 1991 (Doubleday Mystery Guild award 1992), "I" is for Innocent, 1992 (Doubleday Mystery Guild award 1992, Mystery Scene Am. Mystery award 1993), Kinsey and Me, 1992, "J" is for Judgement, 1994, "K" is for Killer, 1994 (Shamus award 1994), "L" is For Lawless, 1995, "M" is For Malice, 1996, "N" is for Noose, 1998, "O" is for Outlaw, 1999, "P" is for Peril, 2001, "Q" is for Quarry, 2002, "R" is for Ricochet, 2004, "S" is for Silence, 2005; editor: Writing Mysteries, 1992; author short fiction, short stories, screenplay, teleplay TV episodes. Named to, Am. Acad. Achievement, 2000. Mem. Writers Guild Am. West, Mystery Writers Am. Inc. (pres. 1994), Private Eye Writers Assn. (pres. 1989-90, Life Achievement award 2003), Crime Writers Assn. Address: Penguin/Putnam 375 Hudson St New York NY 10014-3672

GRAGG, KARL LAWRENCE, lawyer; b. Watertown, NY, Sept. 25, 1946; s. Karl Lawrence and Pauline (Sykes) G.; m. Maureen Gilluly, Dec. 13, 1975; children: Meaghan Christina, Erika Lawrence, Jenny Camille. BS, Fla. State U., 1968; JD, U. Fla., 1974, LLM in Taxation, 1975. Bar: Fla. 1975, U.S Dist. Ct. (so. dist.) Fla., U.S. Tax Ct., U.S. Ct. Appeals (5th cir.). Assoc. Mershon, Sawyer, Johnson, Dunwoody & Cole, Miami, Fla., 1975-80, ptnr., 1980-82, Gunster, Yoakley, Criser & Stewart, Palm Beach, Fla., 1982-84, Walker Ellis Gragg & Deaktor, Miami, 1984-86, White & Case, LLP, Miami, 1987—. Adj. prof. law U. Miami, 1978-89; mem. tax com. Fla. Ho. of Reps., Tallahassee, 1983. Contbr. articles to U. Fla. Law Rev. Vol. Miami United Way, 1977-80; bd. dirs. New Word Sch. of the Arts Found., 1998—, Bapt. Health Sys. Found., 2004—; trustee U. Fla. Law Sch. Found., 2004—. Mem. ABA (taxation sect.), Nat. Assn. State Bar (chmn. 1986), Am. Coll. Tax Counsel, Fla. Bar Assn. (tax sect., chmn. tax sect. 1991, chmn. coun. of sect.), Nat. Assn. Indsl. and Office Parks (bd. dirs. 1989-91), Ctr. for Health Techs., Inc. (bd. dirs. 1992-98), Japan Soc. South Fla. (bd. dirs. 1990-98), Miami City Club (bd. dirs. 2004—). Office: White & Case LLP 200 S Biscayne Blvd Ste 4900 Miami FL 33131-2352 Office Phone: 305-371-2700. E-mail: LGragg@whitecase.com.

GRAGLIA, LINO ANTHONY, lawyer, educator; b. Bklyn., Jan. 22, 1930; s. Pasquale and Antoinette (Romeo) G.; m. F. Carolyn Pennington, July 17, 1954; children: Donna, Carol, Laura. BA, CCNY, 1952; LLB, Columbia U., 1954. Bar: N.Y. 1954, D.C. 1957, Tex. 1980, U.S. Supreme Ct. Atty. U.S. Dept. Justice, Washington, 1954-57; pvt. practice law Washington and NYC, 1957-66; prof. law U. Tex., Austin, 1966—. Author: Disaster by Decree: The Supreme Court Decisions on Race and the Schools, 1976. Recipient George Washington medal Freedoms Foundation at Valley Forge, 1989. Republican. Avocations: tennis, biking, hiking, billiards. Office: U Tex Sch Law 727 E 26th St Austin TX 78705-3224 Office Phone: 512-232-1363. Business E-Mail: lgraglia@law.utexas.edu.

GRAHAM, ALAN MORRISON, surgeon; b. Perth, Scotland, Mar. 23, 1953; m. Michiko P. Graham; children: George A., Mie I, Fraser S., Queen's U., Kingston, Ont., 1973-75, MD, 1979. Diplomate Am. Bd. Surgery, Am. Bd. Gen. Surgery and Vascular Surgery. Internship Kingston Gen. Hosp. Queen's U., 1979—80; residency Royal Victoria Hosp. McGill U., 1980—84; fellowship U. Chgo., 1984—85; asst. prof. dept. surgery Royal Victoria Hosp., 1985-91, McGill U., 1985—91, assoc. prof., 1991—92; assoc. prof. dept. surgery Royal Victoria Hosp., 1991—92; prof., chief div. vascular surgery Robert Wood Johnson Med. Sch., 1992—, program dir. vascular fellowship program, 1992—, Ruth and Norman Rosenberg chair in vascular surgery, 2002—, vice chmn., 2003—. Author numerous book chapters; contbr. articles to profl. jours. Recipient Edgar Forrester scholarship, 1977, W.W. Near scholarship, 1977, Alice Pierce Waddington scholarship, 1977, Prof. prize in Surgery, 1979, Neil Currie Polson Meml. prize, 1979, Outstanding Tchr. award U. Chgo., 1985, E.J. Wylie Travelling fellowship, 1989, numerous grants. Fellow ACS, Royal Coll. Physicians and Surgeons; mem. Soc. Univ. Surgeons, Soc. Vascular Surgery, Ea. Vascular Soc., Can. Assn. Gen. Surgeons, Assn. Acad. Surgeons, Assn. Internat. Vascular Surgery, Can. Soc. Vascular Surgery, Peripheral Vascular Surgery Soc., Internat. Soc. Cardiovascular Surgery, Soc. Clin. Vascular Surgery, Phoenix Alliance, Inc., Vascular Soc. N.J. (pres.), Internat. Fedn. Surg. Colls., Soc. of Surgeons of N.J. Office: Robert Wood Johnson Med Sch 1 Robert Wood Johnson Pl New Brunswick NJ 08901-1928 Office Phone: 732-235-7816. Business E-Mail: grahamal@umdnj.edu.

GRAHAM, ALMA ELEANOR, editor, writer, educational consultant; b. Raleigh, NC, Nov. 13, 1936; d. David Robert and Irene G. (Knott) G. BA in English with honors, U. N.C., 1958; MA in Contemporary Lit., Columbia U., 1970. Exec. editor Am. Heritage Dictionary, 1970—75; editl. mgr., exec. editor McGraw-Hill, 1976—87; free-lance author, corp. cons., 1987—90; editor New World Outlook mag. United Meth. Ch., NYC, 1991—2001; ret., cons. NYC, 2001—. Cons. in bias-free lang. and images; cons. USIA, 1978-80. Author: Our Nation, Our World, 1983, 86, 88, McGraw-Hill Educational Software, 1988, North Carolina: The Land and Its People, 1988, Basic Map Skills, 1991; co-author: Success With Words, 1983, Bridging Worlds Through General Semantics, 1984. Pres. Laymen's Club, trustee Cath. Ch. St. John the Divine, N.Y.C., 1994-99. Named one of 50 Extraordinary Women of Achievement, N.Y. region NCCJ, 1978; Woodrow Wilson fellow, 1958-59. Mem. NOW, Associated Ch. Press, Nat. Coun. for Social Studies, Org. for Equal Edn. the Sexes, Phi Beta Kappa. Achievements include first lexicographer to put courtesy title Ms. into dictionary, 1972. Home: 380 Riverside Dr New York NY 10025-1819 Home Phone: 212-749-6083. E-mail: montsea@aol.com.

GRAHAM, ANNA REGINA, pathologist, educator; b. Phila., Nov. 1, 1947; d. Eugene Nelson and Anna Beatrice (McGovern) Chadwick; m. Larry L. Graham, June 29, 1973; 1 child, Jason. BS in Chemistry, Ariz. State U., 1969, BS in Zoology, 1970; MD, U. Ariz., 1974. Diplomate Am. Bd. Pathology. With Coll. Medicine U. Ariz., Tucson, 1974—, asst. prof. pathology, 1978-84, assoc. prof. pathology, 1984-90, prof. pathology, 1990—. Fellow Am. Soc. Clin. Pathologists (bd. dirs. Chgo. chpt. 1993-2003, sec. 1995-99, v.p. 1999-2000, pres.-elect 2000-01, pres. 2001-02), Internat. Acad. Pathology, Am. Telemedicine Assn., Coll. Am. Pathologists; mem. AMA (alt. del. Chgo. chpt. 1992-99, del. Chgo. chpt. 1999-2004), Ariz. Soc. Pathologists (pres. Phoenix chpt. 1989-91), Ariz. Med. Assn. (treas. Phoenix chpt. 1995-97). Republican. Baptist. Avocations: motorcycles, piano, choir. Office: Ariz Health Scis Ctr Dept Pathology 1501 N Campbell Ave Tucson AZ 85724-5108 Office Phone: 520-626-6828. Business E-Mail: agraham@umcaz.edu.

GRAHAM, BERTA, humanities educator, researcher; b. Beloit, Kans., Apr. 28, 1950; d. Paul and Virginia (McKelvey) Bohning; m. Gregory Graham, June 6, 1970; children: Della, Samuel. BA in Sociology, Drake U., 1978; MA in Selected Studies, U. S.D., 1994; AA in Journalism, Harper Coll., Palatine, Ill., 2004. Adj. faculty Dordt Coll., Sioux Center, Iowa, Morningside Coll., Sioux City, Iowa, Northwestern Coll., OrangeCity, Iowa, 1992—2002. Author: Democracy in Lebanon, Vol I: Reconstruction, Democracy in Lebanon, Vol II: Relativity. Home: 436 Park Ln Barrington IL 60010-3338 Home Phone: 224-558-9191.

GRAHAM, BILLY (WILLIAM FRANKLIN GRAHAM), evangelist; b. Charlotte, NC, Nov. 7, 1918; s. William Franklin and Morrow (Coffey) G.; m. Ruth McCue Bell, Aug. 13, 1943 (dec. June 14, 2007); children: Virginia Leftwich, Anne Morrow, Ruth Bell, William Franklin, Nelson Edman. BA, Wheaton Coll., Ill., 1943; ThB, Fla. Bible Inst., Tampa, 1940; ThB numerous hon. degrees, including Houghton Coll., NY, Baylor U., The Citadel, William Jewell Coll. Ordained to ministry So. Baptist Conv., 1939; minister First Bapt. Ch., Western Springs, Ill., 1943-45; 1st v.p. Youth for Christ, Internat., 1945-50; pres. Northwestern Coll., Mpls., 1947-52; founder World Wide Pictures, Inc., Burbank, Calif.; worldwide evangelistic campaigns, 1949—; speaker weekly Hour of Decision radio program, 1950—; also periodic Crusade Telecasts; founder Billy Graham Evangelistic Assn., 1950; hon. chmn. Lausanne Congress World Evangelization, 1974. Author: Peace with God, 1953, World Aflame, 1965, The Jesus Generation, 1971, Angels: God's Secret Agents, 1975, How To Be Born Again, 1977, The Holy Spirit, 1978, Till Armageddon, 1981, A Biblical Standard for Evangelists, 1984, Approaching Hoofbeats, 1983, Unto the Hills, 1986, Facing Death and The Life After, 1987, Answers to Life's Problems, 1988, Hope for the Troubled Heart, 1991, Storm Warning, 1992, Angels: God's Secret Agents, 1995, Just As I Am: The Autobiography of Bill Graham, 1997, Hope for Each Day: Words of Wisdom and Faith, 2002, Living in God's Love: The New York Crusade, 2005, The Journey: How to Live by Faith in an Uncertain World, 2006; also writer of daily newspaper column. Recipient numerous awards, including Bernard Baruch award, 1955, Humane Order of African Redemption, 1960, Gold award George Washington Carver Meml. Inst., 1964, Horatio Alger award, 1965, Internat. Brotherhood award NCCJ, 1971, Sylvanus Thayer award Assn. Grads. U.S. Mil. Acad., 1972, Franciscan Internat. award, 1972, Man of South award, 1975, Liberty Bell award, 1975, Templeton prize for Progress in Religion, 1982, Presdl. Medal of Freedom, 1983, William Booth award Salvation Army, 1989, Congl. Gold Medal, 1996; Freedom award Ronald Reagan Presdl. Found., 2000, Hon. Knight Comdr. Order British Empire, 2001; named to the Gospel Music Hall of Fame, Gospel Music Assn., 1999. Baptist. Office: Billy Graham Evangelistic Assn PO Box 1270 Charlotte NC 28201-1270 Address: Billy Graham Evangelistic Assn 1 Billy Graham Pkwy Charlotte NC 28201*

GRAHAM, BOB (DANIEL ROBERT GRAHAM), former senator, former governor; b. Coral Gables, Fla., Nov. 9, 1936; s. Ernest R. and Hilda Simmons Graham; m. Adele Khoury, 1959; children: Gwendolyn Patricia, Glynn Adele, Arva Suzanne, Kendall Elizabeth. BA, U. Fla., 1959; LLB, Harvard U., 1962. Atty.; cattle and dairy farmer; real estate developer; mem. Fla. Ho. of Reps., 1966-70, Fla. Senate, 1970-78; gov. State of Fla., Tallahassee, 1978-86; U.S. senator from Fla., 1987—2005. Chmn. Edn. Commn. of the States, 1980-81, Caribbean/Central Am. Action, 1980-81, U.S. intergovtl. adv. council on edn.; mem. So. Growth Policies Bd., chmn., 1982-83; chmn. So. Govs.' Assn.; chmn. com. trade and fgn. affairs Nat. Govs.' Assn.; energy & natural resources, environ. & pub. works com., fin. com., VA affairs/intelligence com., senate Dem. steering & coord. com.; ranking mem. long-term growth, debt and deficit reduction com., com. on fin., 1997-2005; mem. com. environment and pub. works, ranking mem. clean air, wetlands, pvt. property and nuc. safety com., 1995-2005; mem. com. energy and natural resources, ranking mem. energy rsch., devel., prodn. and regulation subcom., 1997-2005; sr. fellow, John F. Kennedy Sch. Govt., Harvard Univ.; bd. dir. WellCare Plans Inc., 2007-. Co-author: (with Jeff Nussbaum) Intelligence Matters: The CIA, the FBI, Saudi Arabia, and the Failure of America's War on Terror, 2004. Active 4-H Youth Found., Nat. Commn. on Reform Secondary Edn., Nat. Found. Improvement Edn., Nat. Com. for Citizens in Edn., Sr. Centers of Dade County, Fla.; chmn. So. Regional Edn. Bd., 1979-81 Named one of 5 Most Outstanding Young Men in Fla. Fla. Jaycees, 1971; recipient Allen Morris award for outstanding 1st term mem. senate, 1972, Allen Morris award for most valuable mem. senate, 1973, Allen Morris award for 2d most effective senator, 1976, named to Fla. Housing Hall of Fame, 2005. Mem. Fla. Bar Assn. Democrat. Mem. United Ch. Of Christ.*

GRAHAM, BRUCE S., dean, educator; b. Windsor, Ont., Can. naturalized, U.S. m. Linda Graham; children: Todd, Beth. Student, U. Windsor, 1966; DDS, U. Toronto, 1970; MS, cert. in prosthodontics, Ohio State U., 1974; MEd, Dalhousie U., 1989. Instr. Ohio State U. Coll. Dentistry, U. Toronto; asst. to assoc. dean acad. affairs Dalhousie U., Halifax, Nova Scotia, Canada; dean, prof. restorative dentistry U. Detroit-Mercy Sch. Dentistry, 1992—2000; dean U. Ill. Chgo. Coll. Dentistry, 2000—. Spkr. in field; bd. dirs. Friends of the Nat. Inst. of Dental and Craniofacial Rsch., 2005—. Fellow: Am. Coll. Dentists; mem.: Internat. Assn. Dental Rsch., Am. Assn. Dental Rsch., ADA. Office: 801 South Paulina Chicago IL 60612 Office Phone: 312-996-1040. Office Fax: 321-996-1022. Business E-Mail: bgraham@uic.edu.

GRAHAM, DAVID ANTONY, lawyer; b. NYC, Feb. 3, 1953; s. Lorenz Bell Jr. and Adele (Hersher) G.; children: Xochitl, Joaquin, Esmeralda, Erica, Julian, Miguel. AA, Community Coll., Denver, 1976; BA in Econs., U. Denver, 1978; JD, U. N.Mex., 1981. Bar: Colo. 1981, N.Mex. 1982, Alaska 1997, U.S. Dist. Ct. Colo. 1981, U.S. Ct. Appeals (10th cir.) 1981, U.S. Dist. Ct. N.Mex. 1982. Ptnr. Graham & Graham, Denver, 1981-82, San Luis, Colo., 1982-85, Lopez, Chavez & Graham, Taos, N.Mex., 1985-88; pvt. practice Taos, 1988—. City atty. Municipality of San Luis, 1983-94. Capt. CAP. Fellow HEW, 1978-81; grantee U. Denver, 1976-78. Mem. Assn. Trial Lawyers Am., N.Mex. Trial Lawyers Assn., Aircraft Owners and Pilots Assn. Office: 408 Lake St Sitka AK 99835-7469 Office Phone: 907-747-7140. Personal E-mail: dgsitka@att.net.

GRAHAM, DAVID BOLDEN, food products executive; b. Miami Beach, Fla., Feb. 10, 1927; s. Robert Cabel and Bertha Eugenia (Hack) G.; m. Stuart Hill Smith, Sept. 1, 1956; children: Bird, Ellen, Darnall, Lamar, Lyle, Gerard, Barbara, David Bolden. Student, Colegio de san Bartolome, Bogota, Colombia, 1946; BS, Georgetown U., 1949; postgrad., Harvard Bus. Sch., 1950. Chmn. Graham Farms, Inc., Washington, Ind., 1950-99, Graham Cheese Corp., Washington, 1950-99; sec. Bal Harbour Square, Fla., 1956-57, Graham Bros., Inc., Washington, 1950-72. Contbr. articles on agr., transp. and early fur traders to various publs. Past pres. Washington Planning Commn., Regional Planning Commn.; past bd. dirs. Hist. Landmarks Found., Ind.; mem. revolving fund com., mem. rural preservation com.; past mem. Ind. Agrl. Adv. Coun.; past mem. adv. coun. Bur. Water and Mineral Resources; past mem. Natural Resources Commn.; mem. various Meth. awareness coms.; dir. Ind. Regional Hwy. Coalition; v.p. I-69 Mid-Continent Hwy. Coalition; past pres. Nat. Turkey Fedn.; mem. Olympic Yachting Staff, 1996; active Coast Guard Aux., Lic. Master Great Lakes or Inland Waters, FCC Marine Radio Lic. Lt. col. USAF Res., 1949-77. Mem. Columbia Club (Indpls.), Rotary (hon., past pres., Paul Harris fellow), Atlantic Cruising Club, Inland Yacht Club, Elks, Soc. of Children's Book Writers, N.Am. Fishing Club (life). Republican. Roman Catholic. Home and Office: Graham Farms PO Box 391 Washington IN 47501-0391

GRAHAM, DAVID BROWNING, lawyer; b. Wildwood, NJ, Dec. 20, 1942; s. William Browning and Mary Graham; m. Linda Lea Beasley, Feb. 20, 1971; children: Owen, Mary. BS, La. State U., 1966, JD, 1969. Bar: La. 1969, D.C. 1972, Va. 2003, U.S. Ct. Appeals (D.C. cir.) 1974, Ill. 1980, Ohio 1999, Va. 2004. Atty. U.S. EPA, Washington, 1972-73; corp. counsel Nat. Rural Elec. Coop. Assn., Washington, 1973-77; dir. office hearing and appeals U.S. Dept. Interior, Arlington, Va., 1977-79; dep. gen. counsel Velsicol Chem. Corp., Chgo., 1979-84; ptnr. Freedman, Levy, Kroll & Simonds, Washington, 1984-89, Kaye, Scholer, Fierman, Hays & Handler, Washington, 1989-92, Howrey & Simon, Washington, 1992-98, Baker & Hostetler, Cleve., 1998—2003, Kaufman & Canoles, Williamsburg, Va., 2003—. Mem. bd. advisors Toxics Law Reporter, Washington, 1987—, Chem. Waste Litigation Reporter, Washington, 1986—. Co-author: New Approaches to Environmental Law and Agency Regulation: The Daubert Litigation Approach, 2000, Emergency Response Planning--A Critical Investment, 2006; contbr. articles to profl. jours. Mem. ABA (former officer sect. environ., energy and environ. law), Va. Bar Assn. (environ. law bd. govs.). Presbyterian. Avocations: running, skiing. Home: 221 William Claiborne Williamsburg VA 23185

GRAHAM, DAVID E., librarian; b. Lancaster, Pa., Sept. 15, 1950; s. Robert L. and Marguerite H. (Wallick) Graham; life ptnr. Carter W. McFall. BS in Edn., Millersville U., Pa., 1971; MLS, U. Md., College Park, 1987. Libr. NIH/Nat. Inst. Neurol. Disorders and Stroke, Bethesda, Md., 1984—95, US FDA/Ctr. for Drug Evaluation Rsch., Rockville, Md., 1995—2000, collections mgmt. team leader, 1995—2000; asst. libr., collections mgmt. and preservation US Libr. Supreme Ct., Washington, 2000—. Recipient Spl. Achievement Award, FDA/Ctr. for Drug Evaluation Rsch., 1997, 1998. Mem.: Soc. Am. Archivists, Spl. Libraries Assn. Avocation: travel. Home: 4204 31st St Mount Rainier MD 20712 Office: US Supreme Ct 1 First St NE Washington DC 20543 Home Phone: 301-864-7971; Office Phone: 202-479-3176.

GRAHAM, DAVID F., lawyer; b. Chgo., Sept. 14, 1953; BA with high honors, Haverford Coll., 1975; JD, U. Chgo., 1978. Bar: Ill. 1978. Law clk. to Hon. Charles Levin Mich. Supreme Ct., 1978-79; Bigelow teaching fellow, lectr. on law U. Chgo., 1979-80; with Sidley Austin Brown & Wood LLP, Chgo., 1980—, ptnr. comml. litig., 1986—, and mem. exec. com. Past gen. counsel Chgo. Coun. of Lawyers. Adv. bd. Legal Aid Soc., Chgo. Mem.: Phi Beta Kappa. Office Phone: 312-853-7596. Office Fax: 312-853-7036. Business E-Mail: dgraham@sidley.com.

GRAHAM, DAVID G., preventive medicine physician, psychiatrist; b. Nov. 17, 1949; s. Thomas and Catherine G.; m. Katherine A. Graham; children: Brigitte, John. BA magna cum laude, Walsh U., 1971; MD, U. Puerto Rico, 1980; MPH, Columbia U., 1985. Diplomate Am. Bd. Preventive Medicine, Am. Bd. Clin. Psychiatry. Intern, then resident in psychiatry SUNY, Stony Brook, 1980-84, resident in preventive medicine, 1984-86, asst. prof. preventive medicine, 1985—; attending physician VA Med. Ctr., Northport, NY, 1985—; dir. pub. health Suffolk County (N.Y.) Dept. Health Svcs., 1986—, chief dep. health commr., 2005—. Author: Medieval Minds, 1985, Profiles in Protest, 1987, Statistics, 1987, Mental Status Manual, 1989. Fellow Am. Coll. Preventive Medicine; mem. APHA, Am. Psychiatric Assn., Am. Assn. Pub. Health Physicians, Alumni Assn. Columbia U. Avocations: gardening, antiques, tennis, reading, outdoor recreation. Office Phone: 631-484-0996.

GRAHAM, DAVID RICHARD, orthopedic surgeon; b. Detroit, May 15, 1940; s. Lewis J. and Elberta Y. Graham; m. Dorothy T. Young, June 11, 1966; children: Rebecca, Jeffrey. BA cum laude, Harvard U., 1962; MD, U. Rochester, 1966. Diplomate Am. Bd. Orthop. Surgery. Intern Highland Hosp., Rochester, NY, 1966—67, resident in surgery, 1967—68; resident in orthopaedic surgery Henry Ford Hosp., Detroit, 1970—72; orthopaedic surgeon Elmira (N.Y.) Orthopaedic Assocs., P.C., 1972—2001, pres., 1992—2001. Pres. Arnot Ogden Med. Staff, Elmira, 1990; clin. assoc. Sch. Medicine & Dentistry U. Rochester, 1992—. Lt. comdr. U.S. Navy, 1968-70. Fellow Am. Coll. Surgeons, Am. Acad. Orthop. Surgeons; mem. AMA, Med. Soc. State N.Y., Ea. Orthop. Assn., Am. Coll. Sports Medicine, Chemung County Med. Soc. (pres. 1993-94), Elmira Torch Club (pres. 1990). Republican. Presbyterian. Home and Office: 690 W Clinton St Elmira NY 14905-2226

GRAHAM, DAVID YATES, gastroenterologist; b. Balboa, Panama, Dec. 24, 1940; came to U.S., 1941; s. Harry Edward and Helen Graham; m. Janet Susan Butel, Mar. 31, 1967; children: Kathleen, David. BS, U. Notre Dame, 1963; MD with honors, Baylor U., 1966. Diplomate Am. Bd. Internal Medicine, Am. Bd. Gastroenterology. Intern Ban Taub Gen. Hosp., VA Hosp., Houston, 1966-67; resident internal medicine Baylor Affiliated Hosps., Houston, 1969-71, fellow gastroenterology, 1972-73; from asst. prof. to prof. medicine Baylor Coll. Medicine, Houston, 1973—, chief gastroenterology sect. VA Med. Ctr., 1976—, from assoc. prof. to prof. virology, 1981-89, prof. molecular virology, 1989—; chief gastroenterology sect. Meth. Hosp., Houston, 1988—. Dir. gastroenterology fellowship program Ben Taub Gen. Hosp., Houston, 1975-80, 88—; chief div. digestive disease dept. medicine Baylor Coll. Medicine, Houston, 1988—; planning com. 10th World Congresses of Gastroenterology, 1991-94; advisor to Japanese Rsch. Soc. for Helicobacter pyloria Related Gastroduodenal Diseases, 1995; editor-in-chief of jour. Helicobacter. Contbr. 60 chpts. in 28 books, numerous articles to profl. jours. With U.S. Army, 1967-69. Recipient Joseph B. Kirsner award Am. Gastroenterology Assn., 1994, Michael E. DeBakey, M.D. award for Excellence in Rsch., 1994, Janssen award for Special Achievement in Gastroenterology, 1995, Frank Brown Berry prize in Fed. Medicine, 2000. Fellow AASS, Am. Coll. Physicians, Am. Coll. Gastroenterology (Henry Baker Lecture award 1983, pres. 1990-91), Am. Acad. Microbiology, Infectious Diseases Soc. Am., World Innovation Found.; mem. Am. Gastroent. Assn., Am. Soc. Gastrointestinal Endoscopy, Tex. Soc. for Gastrointestinal Endoscopy, Houston Gastroent. Soc., Gastrointestinal Rsch. Group, Alpha Omega Alpha. Office: Vet Affairs Med Ctr 2002 Holcombe Blvd Houston TX 77030-4211 E-mail: dgraham@bcm.tmc.edu.

GRAHAM, DIANE E., newspaper editor; b. Gary, Ind., June 29, 1953; d. William M. and Mary Jane (Shreve) Graham; m. Daniel Kevin Miller, Oct. 18, 1986. B, Drake U., 1974. Reporter Des Moines Tribune, 1974—78, Des Moines Register, 1978—84, bus. editor, 1984—86, dep. mng. editor, 1986—95, mng. editor, 1995—. Pres. Iowa Freedom of Info. Coun., Des Moines, 1992—93; chair adv. bd. Drake U. Sch. Journalism, Des Moines, 1995—. Recipient Davenport fellow for bus./econ. reporting, U. Mo., 1983. Avocations: playing pipe organ, gardening. Office: Des Moines Register 715 Locust St Des Moines IA 50309-3767

GRAHAM, DONALD EDWARD, publishing company executive; b. Balt., Apr. 22, 1945; s. Philip L. and Katharine (Meyer) Graham; m. Mary L. Wissler, Jan. 7, 1967; 4 children. BA, Harvard U., 1966. Patrolman Washington Met. Police Dept., 1969—70; formerly with Newsweek mag.; with The Washington Post, 1971—, asst. mng. editor sports, 1974—75, asst. gen. mgr., 1975—76, exec. v.p., gen. mgr., 1976—79, pub., 1979—2000, chmn., 1993—; pres. The Washington Post Co., 1991—93, CEO, 1991—, chmn., 1993—, also dir., 1974—. Mem. Pulitzer Prize Bd., 1999—; dir. BrassRing, Inc. Trustee Fed. City Coun.; pres. DC Coll. Access Program; bd. dirs. The Summit Fund of Washington. Info. specialist 1st Cavalry Divsn. US Army, 1967—68, Vietnam. Mem.: Am. Antiquarian Soc. Office: Washington Post 1150 15th St NW Washington DC 20071-0002*

GRAHAM, DONALD JAMES, food technologist, hygienic design consultant; b. York, NY, Sept. 24, 1932; s. Howard Alexander Graham and Naomi Irene (Fletcher) Graham Horgan; m. Dorothy Jane Schroeder, Jan. 1, 1965; children: Christopher Howard, Jonathan Edward. AAS, N.Y. State Agrl. Tech. Inst., 1952; BS with honors, Mich. State U., 1958, MS, 1959; postgrad., Oreg. State U., 1959-62. Cert. quality control sanitarian Am. Inst. Baking. Profit planning dir. Green Giant Co., LeSueur, Minn., 1962-67; dir. tech. svc. Green Giant of Can., Windsor, Ont., 1967-77; dir. quality assurance William Underwood Co., Westwood, Mass., 1977-83; internat. tech. dir. Pet, Inc., St. Louis, 1983-87; sr. food technologist, food sanitation cons., lectr., fellow Sverdrup Corp., St. Louis, 1988-99; pres. Graham Sanitary Design Consulting, Ltd., Jackson, Mich., 1999—. Faculty, com. mem. Food Processors Inst., Washington, 1980-92. Contbr. articles to tech. pubs. Troop com. chmn. Boy Scouts Am., Medfield, Mass., 1979-82, treas., Chesterfield, Mo., 1984-89; mem. Minn. Rep. Com., 1965-67. Served US Army, 1952—54, Med. and Veterinary Corp., Korea. Mem. Inst. Food Technologists, Internat. Assn. for Food Protection, Inst. Thermal Processing Specialists (bd. dirs. 1980-82), Mo. Food Processors Assn. (bd. dirs. 1992-2003, pres. 1994, 95, 96, exec. v.p. 1997-), Am. Soc. Quality Control, Alpha Zeta (chancellor Kedzie chpt. 1957-58). Avocations: photography, videotaping, genealogy. Home and Office: 66 Wildflower Way Jackson MI 49203 Office Phone: 517-796-1733. Personal E-mail: grahamdj@prodigy.net.

GRAHAM, DOROTHY E., elementary school educator; b. Orangeburg County, SC, Jan. 13, 1941; d. Benjamin Howard Easterlin and Charlie Belle Murray; m. Thomas Wayne Graham, Sept. 3, 1959; children: Janet Elizabeth, Katherine Elaine. BA with hon., McNeese State U., 1967; diploma in religious edn., New Orleans Bapt. Theol. Sem., 1963; diploma in Japanese lang. and culture, Kansai Gakuin U., 1971. Cert. tchr. State of Fla., 1996. Elem. sch. tchr. Lake Charles Sch. Dist., La., 1967—68; missionary, tchr. Japan Bapt. Conv., Kobe, 1968—94; min. children First Bapt. Ch., Ft. Myers, Fla., 1994—96; tchr. elem. sch. Lee Dist. Sch., 1996—. Dir., organizer 100 Voice Children's Chorus, Cape Coral, 2000—06, After Sch. Arts Programs Children, Cape Coral, Fla., 2000—04, Japanese Children's Chorus, Kobe, 1986—93; choral dir., organizer City Wide Cmty. Chorus, Kobe, 1980—94; dir., organizer. sr. chorus First Bapt. Ch., Ft. Myers, 1994—96. Recipient Mayor's award for Outstanding Cmty. Svc., City Kobe, Japan Mayor Miyazaki, 1992, Outstanding Tchr. award, C. of C., 2000—01, 2001—02, Sam's Club Outstanding Tchr. Yr., Sam's Club Stores, Ft. Myers, Fl, 2003. Mem.: Fla. Music Educator's Assn. Avocations: travel, reading, classical music. Home: 1230 Braman Avenue Fort Myers FL 33901 Office: Cape Elementary School 4519 Vincennes Blvd Cape Coral FL 33904 Personal E-mail: grahamprs@aol.com.

GRAHAM, ELEANORE DAVIS, elementary school educator; b. Seville, Fla., Feb. 3, 1954; d. Nathaniel Williams and Virginia Hildajean Hightower; m. LaGoge Wick Graham, May 8, 1976; children: Jeneen Alicia, Janelle Nichole, Kayla Janae, LaGoge Donovan. BS, NC A&T U., Greensboro, 1976; MA, SC State U., Orangeburg, 1980; postgrad., Union Inst. & U., Cin., 2000—. Cert. tchr. Tex., Fla. Pub. health nutritionist Sumter County (SC) Health Dept., 1976—80; pediat. dietitian St. Joseph Hosp., Omaha, 1981—84; tchr. secondary math. and sci. Dept. Def. Dependent Schs., Kaiserslautern, Germany, 1985—90; elem. tchr. San Antonio Ind. Sch. Dist., 1991—96, Orange County Pub. Schs., Orlando, Fla., 1996—. Cons. Gordon Learning Ctr., Orlando, 2005—. Contbr. articles to jours. Mem. bus. adv. coun. Women of Renewing Minds, Sanford, Fla., 2002—03; internet voting poll attendant Orange County, Orlando, 2003—04; mem. bus. adv. coun. Nat. Rep. Congressional Com., Washington, 2005—; liaison United Meth. Ch., Casselberry, Fla., 2003—; bus. dir. Cmty. Options of Ctrl. Fla., Orlando, 2004—. Named Silver Medal Universal Literacy Tchr., 2002—03, Gold Medal Universal Literacy Tchr., 2004—05, Outstanding Bus. Woman, Nat. Rep. Congressional Com., 2005—06. Mem.: NAFE, AAUW, Nat. Alliance Black Educators. Avocations: reading, arts and crafts, travel, dance, music. Home: 1361 Cree Trl Casselberry FL 32707 Office: Cmty Options of Ctrl Fla Inc 1310 W Colonial Ste 8 Orlando FL 32804 Office Phone: 407-999-9039. Office Fax: 407-999-5608. Personal E-mail: onegram50@aol.com.

GRAHAM, FRANKLIN (WILLIAM FRANKLIN GRAHAM III), evangelist, missionary; b. Asheville, NC, July 14, 1952; s. Billy and Ruth Bell Graham; m. Jane Austin Cunningham, 1974; children: William Franklin IV, Roy, Edward, Jane Austin. BA, Appalachian State U., 1978. Bd. mem. Samaritan's Purse, 1978—, pres., 1979—; first vice chmn. Billy Graham Evangelistic Assn. (BGEA), 1995—, CEO, 2000—, pres., 2002—. Author: Rebel with a Cause, 1997, Living Beyond the Limits, 1998, The Name, 2002, It's Who You Know: The One Relationship that Makes All the Difference, 2002; co-author: All For Jesus: A Devotional, 2004. Office: BGEA 1 Billy Graham Pky Charlotte NC 28201 also: Samaritan's Purse PO Box 3000 Boone NC 28607 Office Phone: 704-401-2432, 828-262-1980. Office Fax: 828-266-1053.*

GRAHAM, FRED PATTERSON, news correspondent, journalist; b. Little Rock, Oct. 6, 1931; s. Otis Livingstone and Lois (Patterson) G.; m. Lucile McCrea, Dec. 28, 1961 (div. March 1982); children— Grier, David Silliman, Alyse; m. 2d Skila Harris, Sept. 11, 1982. BA, Yale U., 1953; LL.B., Vanderbilt U., 1959; diploma in law, Oxford U., 1960. Bar: Tenn., 1959, D.C., 1974. Atty. Trabue, Sturdivant & Harbison, Nashville, 1960-63; chief counsel subcom. constl. amendments U.S. Senate, Washington, 1963; spl. asst. to sec. US Dept. Labor, Washington, 1964-65; Supreme Ct. corr. N.Y. Times, NYC, 1965-72; law corr. CBS News, Washington, 1972-87; anchor, sr. editor Sta. WKRN-TV, Nashville, 1987-89; anchor Court TV Network, NYC, 1991, chief anchor and mng. editor, host, Open Ct., sr. editor. Regents lectr. Boalt Sch. Law, U. Calif., Berkeley, 1982. Author: The Self Inflicted Wound, 1970, Press Freedom Under Pressure,

1972, The Alias Program, 1977, Happy Talk, 1990. Mem. bd. Boalt Hall Trust, 1985-90; bd. dirs. Nat. Constitution Ctr., 1987-90; trustee Reporters Com. for Freedom of Press, 1969-77, 87—. 1st lt. USMCR, 1953-56 Recipient George Foster Peabody award, 1975, 3 Emmy awards Am. Acad. TV Arts and Scis., 1974; Fulbright scholar, 1960; named Disting. Alumnus of the Year, Vanderbilt U., 1992 Office: Courtroom TV Network 600 3rd Ave New York NY 10016-1901

GRAHAM, GARTH N., public health service officer, medical educator; s. Glen Graham. BSc in Biology, Fla. Internat. U., Miami, 1996; MPH, Yale U., New Haven, Conn., 1999, MD, 2001. Diplomate Am. Bd. Internal Medicine, 2007. Intern, resident Mass. Gen. Hosp., 2001—03; spl. asst. US Dept. Health of Human Svcs., Washington, 2003—04, dep. asst. sec. minority health, 2004—. Vis. scientist sch. pub. health Harvard U., Boston, 2003—04; lectr. in field. Editor: Jour. Pub. Health Reports, 2004—; mem. editl. bd.: Yale Jour. Health Policy, Law and Ethics, 1999—2001; contbr. articles to profl. jours. Vol. Big Bros. Big Sisters, Washington; mem. Nat. Rural Health Task Force, Washington, 2004. Lt. comdr. USPHS, 2004. Named one of 40 Leaders Under 40, Time Warner Bus. Network Mag., 2005; recipient Leadership award, AMA Found., 2004, award, Internat. Acad. Achievement, 2004, Kaiser Permanente, 2006. Mem.: ACP (assoc.), Physicians Human Rights (bd. dirs. 2002—04). Office Phone: 240-453-2882.

GRAHAM, GEORGE ANDREW, JR., psychologist, consultant; b. Bakersfield, Calif., Dec. 7, 1930; s. George Andrew Graham and Mary Pearl Sandidge; m. Patricia Anne Phillips, June 19, 1953; children: G. Andrew III, Ronald Glen, Holly Anne Meikle. BA, U. Redlands, 1952; BD, Andover Newtown Theol. Sch., 1956; MA, Boston U., 1956; M in Sacred Theology, Union Theol. Sch., NYC, 1957; postgrad., U. Chgo., 1957-60, 69-70; PhD, Marquette U., 1974. Lic. psychologist, Wis. Min. young adults Old S. Ch., Boston, 1952-55; min. youth 1st Bapt. Ch., Mt. Vernon, NY, 1955—57, min., chaplain Iowa City, 1960-63; lab sch. psychologist U. Chgo., 1957-60; chaplain U. Redlands, Calif., 1963-70; assoc. McGinley & Co., Milw., 1970-73; asst. v.p. personnel divsn. 1st Wis. (became Firstar, then US Bank), Milw., 1973-75, dir. employment and devel., 1975-77, v.p., 1977-81, 1st v.p., 1981-85, dir. employment, counseling, devel. and tng., 1985-88; 1st v.p. Firstar Corp., 1988-92; pres. Graham Consulting, Waukesha, Wis., 1992—. Adj. prof. U. Wis., Milw., 1978-88. Pres. Wis. chpt. Leukemia Soc. Am., Wis. Epilepsy Assn., Lad Lake; bd. dirs. Wis. Sch. Profl. Psychology, Wis. Conservatory Music, Wis. Coun. Econ. Edn.; personnel com. ARC; chmn. pers. com. United Way, Milw.; exec. com. Potawatomi Area coun. Boy Scouts Am. Recipient Silver Beaver award Boy Scouts Am., 1988. Mem. Am. Psychol. Assn., Soc. Indls. and Orgnl. Psychologists, Univ. Club Milw. Republican. Home and Office: N8W30095 Woodcrest Dr Waukesha WI 53188 Office Phone: 262-968-5814. E-mail: g1207@msn.com.

GRAHAM, GINGER L., pharmaceutical executive; b. Springdale, Ark., Nov. 18, 1955; m. John Graham; 3 stepchildren. BS in Agrl. Economics, U. Ark., 1979; MBA, Harvard U., 1986. With Elanco Eli Lilly and Co., 1979—92, pres., CEO Advanced Cardiovascular Systems, 1993—2000; group chmn., Office of Pres. Guidant Corp., 2000—03; CEO Amylin Pharmaceuticals Inc., 2003—, pres., 2003—, mem. fin. com. Bd. dirs. Amylin Pharmaceuticals Inc., 1995—, Pharmaceutical Rsch. and Manufacturers of Am., Calif. Coun. on Sci. and Tech.; adv. bd. Kellogg Ctr. for Exec. Women; bd. dean's adv. Harvard Bus. Sch., health industry alumni bd.; health sciences adv. bd. U. Calif. San Diego; spkr. in field. Recipient Emerging Co. Exec. of Yr. award, Pharm. Achievement Awards, 2005. Office: Amylin Pharmaceuticals Inc Ste 110 9360 Towne Centre Dr San Diego CA 92121

GRAHAM, GLORIA FLIPPIN, dermatologist; b. Durham, NC, Mar. 3, 1935; d. James Meigs and Ida Mae (Boyd) F.; m. Douglas Graham (div.); 1 child, Wayne Meigs Graham; m. James Herbert Graham, July 29, 1989. BS, Wake Forest U., Winston-Salem, NC, 1957; MD, Bowman-Gray Sch. Medicine, 1961. Diplomate Am. Bd. Dermatology. Intern Sch. Medicine Vanderbilt U., Nashville, 1961—62; resident dermatology U. Va. Med. Ctr., Charlottesville, 1962—65; pvt. practice Columbia, SC, 1965—66; physician, owner Wilson Dermatology Clinic, NC, 1966—94; physician, dermatologist Grahams' Dermatology Svcs., Morehead City, 1992—2005; attending physician Crystal Coast Dermatology Svcs., P.A., Morehead City, 2000—01; physician, dermatologist Down East Med. Assocs., Morehead City, 2005—. Cons. Carteret Gen. Hosp., Morehead City, 1986-2000; clin. attending prof. Bowman Gray Sch. Medicine, Winston-Salem, NC, 1991-2000; adj. clin. prof. U. NC Sch. Medicine, Chapel Hill, 1995-2001; assoc. prof. dermatology Wake Forest U. Med. Sch., 2001-20, bd. visitors, 2003—. Co-exhibitor: Two Hereditary Osseocutaneous Syndromes, Acad. Dermatology, 1965 (Silver award), So. Med. Assn. Exhibit Hereditary Acrokeratotic Poikiloderma, 1970 (3d Pl. award). Named Woman of Yr., Women's Residence Coun. Wake Forest U., 1982, Practitioner of Yr., Dermatology Found., 1998. Mem.: Internat. Soc. Cryosurgery (v.p. 2001—05, honorary mem. 2005), Women's Dermatologic Soc. (pres. 1997—98, Rose Hirschler award 2001), Am. Dermatologic Assn. (elect), Am. Acad. Dermatology (bd. dirs. 1991—96, audit com. 1996—2000, ethics com. 1996—2001, nominating com. 2002—, chair nominating com. 2003, honorary mem. 2005, Fox award 2003), N.Am. Clin. Dermatologic Soc. (bd. dirs. 1995—2001), World Congress Dermatology (co-chmn. cryosurgical symposium 1997, 2001), Wake Forest U. Sch. Medicine Alumni Assn. (bd. dirs. 2003—06, Disting. Achievement award 2007). Avocations: travel, fishing. Home: 106 Cypress Dr Pine Knoll Shores NC 28513-6706 Personal E-mail: ggfgraham@aol.com.

GRAHAM, H. DILLON, III, lawyer; b. Jacksonville, Apr. 18, 1957; s. Horace, Jr. D. Graham and Dorothy Lee McDaniel-Stein, M. Berman Stein (Stepfather); m. Ellen Beth Warner, June 23, 2001; children: Lea Beth, Lucas Dillon. BBA, U. Miami, Fla., 1980; JD, Nova SouthEastern U., Ft. Lauderdale, Fla., 1983. Bar: Fla. 1983, US Dist. Ct. (so. dist.) Fla. 1984, US Dist. Ct. (mid. dist.) Fla. 1985, US Ct. Appeals (11th cir.) 1986, US Supreme Ct. 2006. Assoc. atty. Mitchell, Harris, Canning & Murry, Miami, 1983—88; sr. assoc. atty. Taylor, Brion, Buker & Greene, Miami, 1988—94; sr. ptnr. Graham & Assocs., P.A., Miami, 1994—. Mem. team in tng. Leukemia and Lymphoma Soc., Miami, 2006—07. Recipient Book award, Fla. Constl. Law, 1982, Legal Process, 1982. Mem.: Guardian Ad Litem Program, N.Am. Brain Injury Assn., Brain Injury Assn. Fla., Brain Injury Assn. Am., Nat. Assn. Personal Injury Lawyers, Dade County Bar Assn., Miami-Dade Justice Assn., Fla. Justice Assn., Am. Justice Assn. Avocation: running. Office: Graham and Assocs PA 2222 Ponce de Leon Blvd Ste 210 Coral Gables FL 33134 Office Phone: 305-445-9185. Office Fax: 305-444-8015.

GRAHAM, HAROLD STEVEN, lawyer; b. Kansas City, Mo., Feb. 1, 1950; s. Martie Sydney and Elsie Helen (Bradford) G.; m. Deborah Ruth Glick, Apr. 8, 1973; children: Elizabeth, Jonathan, Joshua, Lauren. BS, U. Wis., 1972; JD, U. Chgo., 1976. Bar: Mo. 1976. Assoc. Lathrop, Koontz & Norquist, Kansas City, 1976-81; mem. Lathrop & Norquist, L.C., Kansas City, 1982-95, Lathrop & Gage L.C., Kansas City, 1996—. Active Kansas City Tomorrow Alumni Assn. Year X; bd. dirs. Hyman Brand Hebrew Acad., Kansas City, 1985-99, Beth Shalom Synagogue, Kansas City, 1983-88, Jewish Cmty. Campus, 1992-98, Congregation BIAV, Kansas City, 2004—. Mem. ABA (sect. on real property and trust law, sect. on bus. law), Assn. Corporate Growth, Mo. Bar Assn. (property law com.), Kansas City Met. Bar Assn. Avocations: tennis, running. Office: Lathrop & Gage LC 2345 Grand Blvd Ste 2600 Kansas City MO 64108-2617

GRAHAM, HEATHER, actress; b. Milw., Jan. 29, 1970; Film appearances include License to Drive, 1988, Drugstore Cowboy, 1989, I Love You to Death, 1990, Guilty as Charged, 1991, Diggstown, 1992, 6 Degrees of Separation, 1993, Don't Do It, 1994, Swingers, 1996, Boogie Nights, 1997 (MTV movie award 1998), Scream 2, 1997, Austin Powers: The Spy Who Shagged Me, 1999, Bowfinger, 1999, Kiss & Tell, 2000, Sidewalks of New York, 2001, From Hell, 2001, Killing Me Softly, 2002, The Guru, 2002, Aliene Love Triange, 2002, Anger Management, 2003, Hope Springs, 2003, Blessed, 2004, Gray Matters, 2005, Mary, 2005, Cake, 2005, Mary, 2005, The OH in Ohio, 2006, Bobby, 2006, Grey Matters, 2006; (TV series) Emily's Reasons Why Not, 2006; (TV appearances) Growing Pains, 1987, Twin Peaks, 1991, Fallen Angels, 1995, The Outer Limits, 1996, Fantasy Island, 1998, Sex in the City, 2002, Arrested Development, 2004, Scrubs, 2004, 2005. Recipient ShoWest award for Female Star of Tomorrow, 1999. Office: Creative Artists Agency 9830 Wilshire Blvd Beverly Hills CA 90211*

GRAHAM, HOWARD BARRETT, publishing company executive; b. Boston, Dec. 7, 1929; s. Robert M. and Belle (Brown) G.; m. Rita J. Mahony; children: Ronni M., Erica. BA, Syracuse U., 1951. Gen. mgr. sch. supply div., sales mgr. ednl. div. Milton Bradley Co., Springfield, Mass., 1954-63; gen. mgr. jr. book div. McGraw-Hill Co., 1964-69; pres., dir. Franklin Watts Inc., NYC, 1970-87; also chmn. bd. Franklin Watts Ltd.; sr. v.p. mktg/product devel., dir. Grolier, Inc., 1983-89, exec. v.p., 1988-89; pres. Grolier Internat., 1986-89; chmn., chief exec. officer Graham Internat. Pub. and Rsch., Inc., 1989—; ptnr. SMG Assocs., 1990; dir., v.p. The Millbrook Press, 1990-96, chmn. bd. dirs., 1997—; pres., CEO Chambers Kingfisher Graham, Publishers Inc., 1994-96. Mem. adv. bd. Internat. Exec. Svc., 1994-98. Served with USAF, 1951-53. Mem. Mensa, Save the Children (adv. bd. mem. 1994-98). Home: PO Box 77 Sagaponack NY 11962-0077 E-mail: gipr2@aol.com.

GRAHAM, HOWARD LEE, SR., finance company executive; b. Monroe, Mich., May 26, 1942; s. Carl Lee and Myrtle Leota (Manis) G.; m. Bobbie Jo Hamilton; children: Kimber Lee, Howard Lee Jr., Jacquelyn Leota, John-Nathan Howard. Grad., Dake Bible Sch., Atlanta, 1960-62; student, Cen. Bible Coll., Springfield, Mo., 1964-67; grad., Internat. Sem., 1993, DD, 1996. Debit agt. Met. Life Ins. Co., Colorado Springs, Colo., 1963-64, agt. Allen Park, Mich., 1964-67, 68; agy. mgr. Preferred Risk Life Ins. Co., Allen Park, 1968-72; agy. owner Howard Graham Ins. Agy., Taylor, Mich., 1972-85; spl. agt., rep. Prudential Ins. Co., Cleve., 1985-89; regional mgr. Primerica Fin. Svcs., Abingdon, Va., 1995—; pres. Graham & Graham Canvas Shoppe, Inc., 1976-95, CEO, 1995—. Pres. Graham Enterprises, Cleve., 1985—; CEO Graham & Graham Canvas Shoppe, Inc., 1976; nat. and regional sales leader Preferred Risk Ins. Co., Des Moines, 1969-72. Life mem. Full Gospel Bus. Men's Fellowship, Detroit, 1963—, officer, 1974-80, officer, Cleve., 1985—; active Gideons Internat., Cleve., 1963—; pres. Truth Alive, Inc., 1988—; Bible tchr., missionary. Named Central Region Agt. of Yr., Prudential Ins. Co., 1985; admitted to Million Dollar Round Table, 1985, Hall of Honor, 1986. Mem. Indsl. Fabrics Assn. Internat., Am. Coll., Nat. Assn. Life Underwriters, Internat. Platform Assn. Republican. Mem. Pentecostal Ch. Avocations: sports, bible research.

GRAHAM, JAMES HERBERT, retired dermatologist; b. Calexico, Calif., Apr. 25, 1921; s. August K. and Esther P. (Choudoin) G.; m. Anna Kathryn Luiken, June 30, 1950 (dec. May 1987); children: James Herbert, John A., Angela Joann; m. Gloria Boyd Flippin, July 29, 1989. Student, Brawley Jr. Coll., 1941—42; AB, Emory U., 1945; MD, Med. Coll. Ala., 1949. Diplomate: Am. Bd. Dermatology (dir. 1977-87, v.p. 1985-86, pres. 1986-87, Disting. Svc. medal 1987), in dermatopathology Am. Bd. Dermatology and Am. Bd. Pathology. Intern Jefferson-Hillman Hosp., Birmingham, Ala., 1949—50; resident dermatology VA Ctr. and UCLA Med. Center, 1953—56; clin. asst. instr. medicine UCLA, 1954—56; Osborne fellow and NRC fellow dermatopathology Armed Forces Inst. Pathology, Washington, 1956—58, vis. scientist, 1958—69; prof. medicine, chief divsn. dermatology, prof. pathology, dir. sect. dermal pathology and histochemistry U. Calif., Irvine, 1969—78; prof. emeritus Coll. Medicine, U. Calif., 1978—. Chmn. dept. dermatopathology Armed Forces Inst. Pathology, Washington, 1980—88, registrar registry dermatopathology, 1980—88, program dir. dermatopathology, 1979—88, Walter Reed Army Med. Ctr., Washington, 1979—88; asst. prof. dermatology and pathology Temple U., Phila., 1958—61, assoc. prof., 1961—65, prof. dermatology, 1965—69, assoc. prof., prof. pathology, 1965—69; chief dermatology U. Calif. Med. Ctr., Irvine, 1977—78; head sect. dermatology Orange County Med. Ctr., Calif., 1969—73; cons. dermatology VA Hosp., Long Beach, Calif., 1969—73, chief dermatology sect., 1973—78, acting chief med. svcs., 1976; eminent physician VA Physician and Dentist-in-Residence Program, 1980—88; mem. orgnl. com. Am. Registry Pathology Armed Forces Inst. Pathology, Washington, 1976—77, mem. exec. com., 1977—78; prof. dermatology, clin. prof. pathology Uniformed Svcs. U. Health Scis., Bethesda, Md., 1979—88, prof. emeritus, 1989—; program dir. dermatopathology Naval Hosp. and Scripps Clinic and Rsch. Found., San Diego, 1991—94; head divsn. dermatopathology, dept. pathology Scripps Clinic and Rsch. Found., LaJolla, Calif., 1988—94, ret., 1994; cons. in field. Sr. author: Dermal Pathology, 1972; contbr. articles to profl. publs. Served with M.C. USNR, 1949-53. Named Disting. Alumnus, Med. Coll. Ala., 1994; recipient ASDP 3d ann. Walter R. Nickel Award Excellence Tchg. Dermatopathology, Hilton La Jolla Torrey Pines Hotel, 1999, Disting. Achievement award Med. Alumni Assn. Wake Forest U. Sch. Medicine, 2007. Mem. AMA (accreditation coun. grad. med. edn., 1977-87, residency rev. com. dermatology 1977-87, chmn. 1984-87, cert. merit 1960), Soc. Investigative Dermatology (life), U.S. and Can. Acad. Pathology (life), Am. Soc. Investigative Pathology (life, emeritus 1995), Am. Dermatol. Assn. (hon., v.p. 1986-87, Essay award 1958), Am. Soc. Dermatopathology (hon., pres. 1975-76, Founder's award 1990, rep. to bd. dirs. Am. Registry Pathology 1988-92), Dermatopathology Club (pres. 1980-81), Assn. Mil. Dermatologists (life), Am. Acad. Dermatology (life, dir. 1974-77, 82, v.p. 1980-81, rep. to bd. dirs. Am. Registry Pathology 1977-78, hon. San Francisco 2000), N.Am. Clin. Dermatologic Soc. (hon.), 1973, Pa. Acad. Dermatology, Pacific Dermatol. Assn. (dir. 1972-75, hon. 1981), Dermatology Found. (Leader's Soc. and Annenberg Cir.), Washington Dermatol. Soc. (spl. hon.), Phila. Dermatol. Soc. (pres. 1967-68, hon 1994), San Diego Dermatol. Soc., Cutaneous Therapy Soc., Cosmos Club, Alpha Omega Alpha *I have achieved far more than I dreamed possible but it could only happen in America. Being generally optimistic, enthusiastic and persistent has resulted in my serving society in a positive way.*

GRAHAM, JAMES MICHAEL, orthopedic spine surgeon, educator; b. Dallas, Tex., Nov. 1, 1951; BA in Psychology, U. Tex., Austin, 1975, PhD in Physiology, 1980; MD, U. Tex. Med. Sch., Houston, 1984. Cert. Am. Bd. Orthop. Surgeons. Intern, gen. surgery U. Tex. Med. Sch., Houston, 1984—85; fellow, spine surgery Baylor Coll. Medicine, Houston, 1989—90; resident, orthop. surgery U. Tex. Med. Sch., Houston, 1985—89; private practice, orthop. surgery and spinal surgery Northwest Spine Ctr., The Woodlands, Tex., 1992—. Chmn. surgery com. Houston Northwest Med. Ctr., 2000—01. Contbr. articles to profl. jours. Named one of Golf Digest 2006 Top Golf Doctors in Am. Fellow: Am. Acad. Orthop. Surgeons; mem.: Houston Orthop. Soc., Harris County Med. Soc., Tex. Orthop. Assn., Tex. Spine Soc. (pres. 2000—01), Tex. Med. Assn., N.Am. Spine Soc., AMA. Achievements include being the first physician in Houston to use Infuse, an advanced new technology so patients no longer have to undergo the bone grafting harvesting procedure. Office: Northwest Spine Ctr 9200 Pinecroft Ste 280 The Woodlands TX 77380 Office Phone: 281-296-9444.*

GRAHAM, JANET LORRAINE, music educator; b. Halifax, NC, Jan. 15, 1947; d. Lloyd Cartez and Waline Wilkins; m. Aaron Richard Graham, June 21, 1969; children: Andrea Yvonne, Aaron Richard II. BA, NC Ctrl. U., 1969. Cert. music tchr. N.C., Ohio, N.J. 4th grade tchr., H.S. chorus dir. Scotland Neck (NC) Schs., 1969; elem./jr. high music tchr. Akron (Ohio) schs., 1969—71; gen. music tchr. grades K-6 Bergenfield (NJ) schs., 1971—. Composer: (songs) Lessons for Kindergarten, 2005. Bd. dirs. Bergen Philharm., Englewood, NJ, 1997—. Named Tchr. of Yr., State of NJ Dept. Edn., 1994. Mem.: NEA, No. NJ Orff Schulwerk Assn. (pres. 1999—2002), Bergenfield Edn. Assn., Tri-M Music Honor Soc. (life). Achievements include featured in music textbooks on music methods. Avocations: travel, reading, dance. Home: 86 Church St Teaneck NJ 07666 Personal E-mail: Janyvo25@yahoo.com.

GRAHAM, JEWEL FREEMAN, social worker, lawyer, educator; b. Springfield, Ohio, May 3, 1925; d. Robert Lee and Lula Belle Freeman; m. Paul N. Graham, Aug. 8, 1953; children: Robert, Nathan. BA, Fisk U., 1946; student, Howard U., 1946-47; MS in Social Svc. Adminstrn., Case Western Res. U., 1953; JD, U. Dayton, 1979; LHD (hon.), Meadville-Lombard Theol. Sch., 1991. Bar: Ohio; cert. social worker. Assoc. dir. teenage program dept. YWCA, Grand Rapids, Mich., 1947-50, coord. met. teenage program Detroit, 1953-56; dir. program for interracial edn. Antioch Coll., Yellow Springs, Ohio, 1964-69, from asst. prof. to prof., 1969-92, prof. emeritus, 1992—. Mem. Ohio Commn. on Dispute Resolution and Conflict Mgmt., 1990-92. Mem. exec. com. World YWCA, Geneva, 1975-83, 87—, pres., 1983; bd. dirs. YWCA of the U.S.A., 1970-89, pres., 1979-85; bd. dirs. Antioch U., 1994-96. Named to Greene County Women's Hall of Fame, 1982, Ohio Women's Hall of Fame, 1988; named 1 of 10 Outstanding Women of Miami Valley, 1987; recipient Ambassador award YWCA of the U.S.A., 1993. Mem. ABA, Nat. Assn. of Social Workers (charter), Nat. Coun. of Negro Women (life), Alpha Kappa Alpha. Democrat. Unitarian Universalist. Avocations: bicycling, swimming, walking, needlecrafts. E-mail: jewelg@aol.com.

GRAHAM, JOHN H., IV, association executive; BA, Franklin and Marshall Coll., 1971. Mem. Valley Forge coun. Boy Scouts Am., 1971—79; exec. dir. Am. Diabetes Assn., Phila., 1979—83, dir. devel. divsn. NYC, 1983—85, asst. exec. v.p. Alexandria, Va., 1985—88, dep. exec. v.p., 1988—90, CEO, 1990—2003; pres., CEO Am Soc. Assn. Executives, 2003—. Mem.: Combined Health Appeal, Independent Sector, Greater Washington Soc. Assn. Execs., Nat. Health Coun., Am. Soc. Assn. Execs. Office: Am Society of Assn Executives 1575 I St NW Washington DC 20005

GRAHAM, JOHN L., lawyer; Grad. with honors, Princton U., 1985; JD cum laude, U. Tex., 1988. Ptnr. King & Spaulding, NYC, co-head mergers & acquisitions; ptnr. Clifford Chance, NYC, 2006—. Mem.: Order of the Coif. Office: Clifford Chance 31 W 52nd St New York NY 10019-6131 Office Phone: 212-878-4955. Office Fax: 212-878-8375. E-mail: John.Graham@cliffordchance.com.

GRAHAM, JOHN ROBERT, JR., financial executive; b. Chgo., Oct. 11, 1930; s. John Robert and Grace Beatrice (Strangeman) G.; m. Bettina Abigail Hoffman, Sept. 6, 1958 (div. June 1975); children: Jonathan, Karl; m. Beverly Criley, Dec. 31, 1975. BS, U.S. Mcht. Marine Acad., 1952; MBA, Harvard U., 1959. Ship officer Moore-McCormack Lines, NYC, 1952-53, 55-58; asst. v.p., loan officer Hartford Nat. Bank, Conn., 1959-67; asst. treas. Heublein, Inc., Hartford, 1967-68, treas., 1968-74; sr. v.p. fin. and adminstrn. Sikorsky Aircraft Co., Stratford, Conn., 1974-80; v.p. fin., CFO Planning Rsch. Corp., Washington, 1980-82; v.p., CFO Uniroyal Inc., Middlebury, Conn., 1982-88, Uniroyal Holding, Inc., Waterbury, Conn., 1982-88, also bd. dirs.; v.p. fin., CFO, treas., dir. Healthware Corp., Seattle, 1989-92. Bd. dirs. Uniroyal Goodrich Tire Co., Akron, Ohio, U.S. Mcht. Marine Acad. Found.; trustee CDU Holding, Inc. Liquidating Trust, N.Y.C., 1986—. Co-author: Nonwoven Textiles-An Unbiased Appraisal, 1959. Corporator Middlesex Hosp., Middletown, Conn., 1964-85; v.p., treas. Conn. Valley YMCA, Deep River, 1962-64; pres. Essex (Conn.) Bus. Assn., 1964-65; bd. dirs. U.S. Mcht. Marine Acad. Found., 1987—. Lt. (j.g.) USNR, 1953-55, PTO, Korea. Mem. Harvard Club (N.Y.C.), Masons. Avocations: sailing, skiing. Home: 1806 Bellevue Way NE Bellevue WA 98004 Office Phone: 203-720-1427. Personal E-mail: cascade82@aol.com.

GRAHAM, JONATHAN P., lawyer; BA, Pitzer Coll., 1982, JD, 1987. Bar: Calif. 1985. Law clerk Judge Joseph Sneed U.S. Ct. Appeals, San Francisco, 1985—88; atty. Williams & Connolly, 1988—2004, ptnr., 1996—2004; v.p. litig. and policy gen. electric Dahaner Corp., 2004—06; sr. v.p., gen. counsel Danaher Corp., 2006—. Spkr. in field; leader sponsor Equal Justice Works awards Banquet, 2006. Former ed.-in-chief: Tex. Jour. Law Review. Office: Danaher Corp 2099 Pennsylvania Ave NW Washington DC 20006*

GRAHAM, JORIE, writer, educator; b. NYC, May 9, 1951; d. Curtis Bell and Beverly (Stoll) Pepper; m. James Galvin. BFA, NYU, 1973; MFA, U. Iowa, 1978. Asst. prof. Murray (Ky.) State U., 1978-79, Humboldt State U., Arcata, Calif., 1979-81; instr. Columbia U., NYC, 1981-83; mem. staff U. Iowa, Iowa City, 1983—99, prof. English, dir. Writer's Workshop, 1999; Boylston Prof. of Oratory and Rhetoric Harvard U., 1999—. Poetry editor Crazy Horse, 1978-81; chancellor Acad. Am. Poets, 1997-2003. Author: Hybrids of Plants and of Ghosts, 1980 (Great Lakes Colls. Assn. award 1981), Erosion, 1983, The End of Beauty, 1987, Region of Unlikeness, 1991, Materialism, 1993, The Dream of the Unified Field: Selected Poems 1974-94, 1995, The Errancy, 1997, Swarm, 1999, Never, 2002, Overlord, 2005; editor: Earth Took of Earth: 100 Great Poems of the English Language, 1996; co-editor: The Best American Poetry 1990. Recipient Am. Acad. Poets award, 1977, Young Poet prize Poetry Northwest, 1980, Pushcart prize, 1980, 82, American Poetry Review prize, 1982, Pulitzer prize in poetry, 1996, Lavan award Acad. Am. Poets, 1991, Martin Zaubel award Acad. and Inst. of Arts and Letters, 1992; Bunting fellow Radcliff Inst., 1982, Guggenheim fellow, 1983, John D. and Catherine T. MacArthur Found. fellow, 1990; grantee Ingram-Merrill Found., 1981. Office: Harvard U English Dept Barker Cntr 12 Quincey St Cambridge MA 02138

GRAHAM, K(ATHLEEN) M. (K. M. GRAHAM), artist; b. Hamilton, Ont., Can., Sept. 13, 1913; d. Charles and G. Blanche (Leitch) Howitt; m. J. Wallace Graham, Dec. 17, 1938; children: John Wallace, Janet Howitt. BA, U. Toronto, Ont., 1936. (one-woman shows) Carmen Lamanna Gallery, Toronto, 1967, Trinity Coll., U. Toronto, 1968, Founders Coll., York U., Toronto, 1970, Pollock Gallery, Toronto, 1971,73,75, Art Gallery Coburg, Ont., 1973, City Hall, Toronto, 1974, David Mirvish Gallery Gallery, Toronto, 1976, Klonaridis, Inc., Toronto, 1978, Watson-Willour Gallery, Houston, 1980, Downstairs Gallery, Edmonton, Alta., 1980, 82, Lillian Heidenberg Gallery, N.Y.C., 1981,86, Klonaridis, Inc., Toronto, 1981-85, 87, 88, 90, ELCA London Gallery, Montreal, Que., Can., 1983, MacDonald-Stewart Art Centre, Guelph, Ont., 1984, Glenbow Mus., Calgary, 1984, Concordia Gallery, Montreal, 1984, Hart House Gallery, Toronto, 1985, Lillian Heidenberg Gallery, N.Y.C., 1986, Klondaridis Inc., Toronto, 1985, 87, 88, 90, 91, Feheley Fine Arts, Toronto, 1989, Douglas Udell Gallery, Vancouver, 1993, Meml. Art Gallery, St. Johns, N.F., 1994, Beaverbrook Gallery, Fredericktonm, N.B., 1994, Costin and Klintworth, Toronto, Ont., 1994, 95, The Art Gallery of Ont., 1997, The Moore Gallery, Toronto, 2000, 2001, (group shows) Montreal Mus. Fine Arts, 1976, Hirshhorn Mus., Washington, 1977, Edmonton (Alta., Can.) Art Gallery, 1977, Norman MacKenzie Art Gallery, Regina, Sask., Can., 1977, David Mirvish Gallery, Toronto, Watson De Nagy Gallery, Houston, Galerie Wentzel, Hamburg, Fed. Republic Germany, Beaverbrook Gallery, Fredericton, N.B., Associated Am. Artists, N.Y.C., 1986, 88, Elca London,

Montreal, 1987, Klondaris Inc., Toronto, 1987, 91, Douglas Udell Gallery, Vancouver, 1987, Associated Am. Artists, N.Y.C., 1988, Feheley Fine Art, Toronto, 1989, (other) (traveling shows) CanadaxTen, 1974, The Can. Canvas, 1975-76, Changing Visions, 1976-77, The Shell Canada Collection, 1977, The Fauve Heritage, 1997, 14 Canadians Hirschborn Mus., Washington, 1977, Certain Traditions, 1978, 79, (travelling shows), (permanent collections) Nat. Gallery Can., Ottawa, Edmonton Art Gallery, Art Gallery Ont., Art Gallery Hamilton, Ont., MacDonald-Stewart Art Gallery, Guelph, Ont., Toronto City Hall, The Brit. Mus., London, Art Gallery Vancouver, Agnes Etherington Art Centre, Kingston, Ont., Can., Musee d'Art Contemporarin Montreal, Beaverbrook Art Gallery, Frederickton, N.B., Art Gallery Nfld.and Labrador, Art Gallery, Peterborough, Ont., Robert McLaughlin Gallery, Oshawa, Ont., Kitchener Waterloo Art Gallery, McMichael Can. Art Gallery, Hart House Art Gallery, Toronto, also numerous corp. collections. Hon. fellow Trinity Coll., U. Toronto, 1988. Mem. Royal Can. Acad.

GRAHAM, KENNETH ROBERT, psychologist, educator; b. Phila., June 5, 1943; s. Edgar and Margit (Leafgreen) Graham; m. Michele Carolyn Monroe, Aug. 10, 1968; children: Mark Andrew, Richard Alan. BA, U. Pa., 1964; PhD, Stanford U., 1969. Lic. psychologist, Pa. Asst. prof. Muhlenberg Coll., Allentown, Pa., 1970-77, assoc. prof., 1977-84, prof., 1984-99, emeritus prof., 1999—, head psychology dept., 1984-93; rsch. psychologist Unit for Exptl. Psychiatry Inst. of Pa. Hosp., Phila., 1969-70; adj. asst. prof. U. Pa., Phila., 1969-70. Cons. smoking cessation various hosps., 1985-1999. Author: (text) Psychological Research, 1977; asst. editor Am. Jour. Clin. Hypnosis, 1974-95; contbr. over 30 articles to profl. and sci. jours. Bd. dirs., pres. Lehigh Valley Child Care, Allentown, 1979-85; advisor Pathways (Conf. of Chs.), Allentown, 1989-98, N.E. Pa. Synod Luth. Ch. in Am., Wescosville, Pa., 1989-93. Mem. APA (pres. divsn. psychol. hypnosis 1980-81), European Soc. Hypnosis in Psychotherapy and Psychosomatic Medicine, Kiwanis (pres. Allentown chpt. 1991-92, lt. gov. Pa. dist. 1994-95). Democrat. Avocations: swimming, collecting glass paperweights and signatures of 19th century explorers. Office: Muhlenberg Coll Psychology Dept Allentown PA 18104 Personal E-mail: krg6543@aol.com.

GRAHAM, LANIER, art historian, curator; b. Shawnee, Okla., Mar. 6, 1940; s. Floyd and Martha Graham; m. Gloria K. Smith; 1 child, Jennifer R. Ulrich. BA in Internat. Polit. & Cultural Rels., Am. U., 1963; MA in Art History, Columbia U., 1966. Planner cultural instns., 1965—; assoc. curator architecture and design Mus. Modern Art, NYC, 1965—70; curator of paintings and sculpture, renaissance to modern Fine Arts Mus., San Francisco, 1970—76; curator Cultural Resource Mgmt. Ctr., San Francisco, 1976—83; curator of prints and books Australian Nat. Gallery, Canberra, 1984—87; curator of paintings, sculpture and prints, renaissance to modern Norton Simon Mus. Art, Pasadena, Calif., 1987—91; dir. Art Info. Ctr. - An Info. Svc., Northbank, Calif., 1991—97; dir. Art Gallery Calif. State U., Hayward, 1998—. Art history lectr., religious studies, mus. studies educator U. Calif., Berkeley, John F. Kennedy U., Calif. Inst. Asian Studies, Naropa Inst., Boulder, Humboldt State U., Arcata, Calif. State U., Hayward, 1977—. Author: Leonardo's Book Illustrations, 1961, Botticelli's Dante, 1963, Mies van der Rohe Drawings, 1966, The Architecture of Louis I. Kahn, 1966, Chess Sets, 1968, Hector Guimard, 1970, Three Centuries of American Painting, 1971, Three Centuries of French Art, vol. 1, 1973, vol. 2, 1975, Claude Monet, 1974, Brother Sun & Sister Moon: Alchemical Symbols in Traditional and Modern Art, 1979, Illustrated Books of Henri Matisse, 1979, Leonardo & the Androgyne: Nonduality in World Art, 1980, Decades of Light: Early Modern French Painting, 1980, The Spontaneous Gesture: Prints and Books of the Abstract Expressionist Era, 1987, Vincent Van Gogh: Painter, Printmaker, Collector, 1990, The Prints of Willem de Kooning: A Catalogue Raisonné, vol. 1, 1991, Impossible Realities: Marcel Duchamp and the Surrealist Tradition, 1991, Sacred Visions: A Survey of World Art and Architecture, vol. 1, 1991, vol. 2, 1992, The Double Serpent: Symbol of Transformation in World Art, 1993, Rhythms and Reverberations: Multicultural Art in the United States and its Development from the Tribal World, 1993, Solidity and Infinity: The Symbolism of the Circle and Square in World Architecture, 1995, Goddesses in Art, 1997, Life, Death and Laughter: The Art of Masami Teraoka, 1998, The Art of the Book: The Modern Livre d'Artiste, 1999, Duchamp and Androgyny: Art, Gender, and Metaphysics, 2003, Robert Rauschenberg, Artist-Citizen, 2004, Flaming Pages: The Illuminated Books of William Blake, 2005, Global Vision: A Survey of World Art, 2006, The Spirit of the Renaissance: A Recreation of the Studiolo of Urbino around 1500, 2007; collections of poetry include Nature Poems, 1958, The Sin of 100 Debts, 1967, Heavy Light: Haiku on the Theme of Modern Physics & Ancient Wisdom, 1978, Electro-Magnetism: Poems on the Theme of Complementarity, 1982, Fragments of Feelings: Selected Poems, 1994, Undulations of Eternity: Collected Poems, 1994; gen. editor: The Rainbow Book: Color.from Ancient to Modern Times, 1975, 76, rev. edit., 1979, Rodin Graphics: A Catalogue Raisonné, 1975, American Art from the Collection of Mr. and Mrs. John D. Rockefeller 3d, 1976, Giorgione & the Experts: A Documentary Exhibition of the Three Ages of Man & the Process of Authentication, 1993, 94, Leonardo's Light in the Last Supper and Christ among the Doctors, 1995; co-author Code of Ethics for Australian Assn. Mus., 1970-87; author studies in renaissance and modern art from Impressionism to Contemporary Art; rsch. in relationships between modern and traditional art, particularly symbols of the sacred; editor BOA: Bull. of Archives of Art Info. Ctr., 1960—, Renaissance Studies, 1963—, Muse: Newsletter of Visual Edn. and Cultural Planning, 1969—, Bi-Singularity: Double Images of Nonduality in World Art, 1979—, Leonardo Studies, 1980—, Sacred Spaces: World Architecture & Symbolism, 1976—, Poësis: A Rev. of Poetry by Artists, 1987-93, Iconography of Infinity: Essays on Art and Philosophy, 1992—; planner various cultural instns. including Internat. Study Ctr., N.Y.C., Mus. Modern Art, Greenwich Village Hist. Preservation Dist., N.Y.C., Fine Arts Mus., San Francisco, Urban Planning Think Tank, San Francisco, Exploratorium, San Francisco, Bay Area Conservation Ctr., San Francisco, Archives Am. Art, San Francisco, Ft. Mason Ctr., San Francisco, Headlands Ctr. Arts, Golden Gate Nat. Recreation Area, Nat. Pk. Svc., Sausalito, Yerba Buena Ctr. Arts, San Francisco, J. Paul Getty Mus., Malibu, Louvre Mus., Paris, Morris Graves Art Mus., Eureka, Calif. Indian Mus. and Cultural Ctr., Golden Gate Nat. Recreation Area, Nat. Park Svc., San Francisco. Mem. Soc. of Archtl. Historians, Nat. Soc. of Lit. and the Arts, World Print Coun. (adv. com. we. region), Archives of Am. Art, Smithsonian Instn., Internat. Soc. Poets., Inst. for Aesthetic Devel. Avocations: printmaking, poetry, publishing private press editions, box art. Business E-Mail: lanier.graham@csueastbay.edu.

GRAHAM, LAUREN, actress; b. Honolulu, Mar. 16, 1967; d. Lawrence Graham and Donna Grant. BA in English, Barnard Coll., Columbia U.; MFA in acting, So. Meth. U., 1992. Founder Good Game prodn. co. Actor: (TV series) Good Company, 1996, Townies, 1996, Conrad Bloom, 1998, M.Y.O.B., 2000, Gilmore Girls, 2000—07; (films) Nightwatch, 1997, Confessions of a Sexist Pig, 1998, One True Thing, 1998, Dill Scallion, 1999, Sweet November, 2001, Chasing Destiny, 2001, Bad Santa, 2003, Lucky 13, 2004, Seeing Other People, 2004, The Moguls, 2005, The Pacifier, 2005, Gnome, 2005, Because I Said So, 2007, Evan Almighty, 2007; prodr.: Something More, 2003; actor(guest appearance): (TV series) Caroline in the City, 1995—96, 3rd Rock from the Sun, 1996, Law & Order, 1997, Seinfield, 1997, NewsRadio, 1997. Office: ICM 8943 Wilshire Blvd Beverly Hills CA 90211-1934*

GRAHAM, LAURIE, editor, writer; b. Evanston, Ill., Nov. 22, 1941; d. Thomas Harlin and Mary Elisabeth (Stoner) Graham; m. George McKay Schieffelin, Dec. 12, 1980 (dec. Jan. 1988); m. Robert Dale Shearer, Apr. 6, 1994 (dec. Nov. 2002). Student, Mt. Holyoke Coll., 1959-61; BA, U. Colo., 1963. Editor Charles Scribner's Sons, NYC, 1969-87. Originator, co-project dir. The Greater Pitts. Poem Chase, 2001; bd. dirs. Pitts. Arts and Lectures. Author: Rebuilding the House, 1990, Singing the City, 1998, In Other Words, 2007; mem. editl. bd. Creative Nonfiction, 1994—, (press series) Emerging Writers in Creative Nonfiction, Duquesne U., 1994—; contbg. author: Pittsburgh Sports, 2000, Creative Nonfiction, 2003, 2005. Mem.: PEN, NY Jr. League, Colony Club. Personal E-mail: lauriegraham@comcast.net.

GRAHAM, LAWRENCE OTIS, lawyer, writer, television commentator; b. NYC, Dec. 25, 1961; s. Richard Charles and Betty Johnyce (Walker) G.; m. Pamela Alexis Thomas, Feb. 15, 1992. AB, Princeton U., 1983; JD, Harvard U., 1988. Bar: NY. Corp. atty. Weil, Gotshal & Manges, NYC, 1988-93; pres. Progressive Mgmt. Assocs., Inc., Chappaqua, NY, 1993; author NYC. Asst. prof. Fordham U., NYC, 1993—; legal corr. Sta. WNBC-TV, NYC., 1994; adj. lectr. Dutchess C.C., Poughkeepsie, NY, 1997—. Author: 10 Point Plan for College Acceptance, 1980, Jobs in the Real World, 1981, Conquering College Life, 1982, Your Ticket to Law School, 1983, Your Ticket to Business School, 1984, Your Ticket to Medical School, 1984, Flyers: Fun Loving Youth En Route to Success, 1985, (with Betty Graham) Teenager's Ask and Answer Book, 1986, (with Lawrence Hamdan) YouthTrends, 1987, Best Companies for Minorities, 1993, Member of the Club, 1995, Proversity: Getting Past Face Value, 1997, Our Kind of People: Inside America's Black Upper Class, 1999, The Senator and The Socialite: the true Story of America's First Black Dynasty; columnist Gannett Westchester Newspapers, White Plains, 1988-91; contbg. editor U.S. News and World Report, 1997—; assoc. prodr. Warner Bros. Studios, Burbank, Calif. Bd. dirs. Princeton (N.J.) Ctr. for Leadership Tng., 1993—, Westchester County African Am. Adv. Bd., White Plains, 1994-96, Manhattanville Coll. Entrepreneurial Inst., Purchase, N.Y., 1987-91, White Plains br. NAACP, 1990-93, Westchester Civil Liberties Union, 1994-96, Westchester Holocaust Commn., 1996—, White Plains Pub. Libr., 1995—, Coun. on Economic Priority, N.Y.C., 1996—; mem. Coun. of Fgn. Rels., Urban League, 1996—; chair Westchester County Police Bd.; pre-law adv. bd. Marist Coll. Named one of 10 Most Interesting Young Men in Am. by Mademoiselle Mag., 1985. Mem. ABA, Nat. Bar Assn. (Young Lawyer of Yr. 1993), NY State Bar Assn., Assn. Bar City NY, Westchester County Bar Assn., Harvard Club (NYC). Home: 233 S Greeley Ave Chappaqua NY 10514-3336

GRAHAM, LAWRENCE SHERMAN, political science educator, management consultant; b. Daytona Beach, Fla., July 12, 1936; s. Marion Webster and Mary Virginia (Sherman) G.; m. Jane Sharp Merrell, June 8, 1961; children: Merrell Anne Shearer, Virginia Carroll, Lauren Richards, Katherine Lugar. BA, Duke U., 1958; MA, U. Wisc., 1961; PhD, U. Fla., 1965. Prof. govt. U. Tex., Austin, 1965—, assoc. v.p. internat. programs, 2000—04. Exch. scholar NRC-NAS, Romanian Acad., 1977-78, Yugoslav Acad., 1981; cons. mgmt. devel. program UN Devel. Program, N.Y.C., 1989-93, dir. Brazil Ctr., U. Tex., 1995-2000; adv. pub. adminstrn. Inst. Pub. Adminstrn., Lima, Peru, 1967-68. Author: Romania: A Developing Socialist State, 1982, The State and Policy Outcomes in Latin America, 1990, The Portuguese Military and the State, 1993, Politics and Government: A Brief Introduction, 1994, The Politics of Governing: A Comparative Introduction, 2006; editor: In Search of Modern Portugal: The Revolution and Its Consequences, 1982, The Polish Dilemma: Views from Within, 1987, The Political Economy of Brazil, 1990. Recipient Rsch. award Calouste Gulbenkian Found., Portugal, 1971, 79-80, Angola and Mozambique, 1972, Hoover Inst., Stanford, 1988; collaborative projects grantee Internat. Rsch. and Exchs. Bd., Poland, 1984, Ford Found., 1986, 96-2001, Rockefeller Found., 1993, 96; rsch. fellow NATO, 1993. Mem. Am. Soc. Pub. Adminstrn. (pub. adminstrn. review bd. 1973-77, chair internat. and comparative adminstrn. 1981-82, 89-90), Am. Polit. Sci. Assn., Internat. Polit. Sci. Assn., Internat. Acad. of Portugese Culture (corrs. mem.), Portuguese-Am. Leadership Coun. (mem. adv. bd.). Episcopalian. Home: 3404 Mt Barker Dr Austin TX 78731-5725 Office: Univ Tex Dept Of Govt Austin TX 78712

GRAHAM, LINDSEY OLIN, senator; b. Seneca, SC, July 9, 1955; s. E. J. and Millie Graham. BS in Psychology, U. SC, 1977, MPA, 1978, JD, 1981. Area def. counsel Shaw AFB, 1982-84; cir. trial counsel USAF Europe, 1984-88; asst. county atty. County of Oconee, SC, 1988-92; pvt. practice, 1988-94; city atty. Central, SC, 1990-94; mem. SC Ho. of Reps., 1992—95, US Congress from 3d SC dist., 1995—2001; US Senator from SC, 2002—. Mem. com. armed svc. US Senate, com. budget, com. judiciary, com. veterans affairs. Bd. dirs. Rosa Clark Free Med. Clinic, Seneca, SC. Served as Major with SC Air N.G., 1989—95, Desert Shield/Desert Storm, served with USAF Res., 1995—2004, col. USAF Res., 2004—. Decorated Meritorious Svc. medal; recipient Minuteman of Yr. award, Res. Officers Assn., 2004. Mem.: Retired Officers Assn., Am. Cancer Soc. (Oconee County Chpt. fundraising chmn.). Republican. Baptist. Office: US Senate 290 Russell Senate Ofc Bldg Washington DC 20510 also: District Office Ste B 135 Eagles Nest Dr Seneca SC 29678 Office Phone: 202-224-5972, 864-888-3330. Office Fax: 202-224-4003, 864-888-3335.*

GRAHAM, LOREN RAYMOND, historian, educator; b. Hymera, Ind., June 29, 1933; s. Ross Raymond and Hazel Mae (McClanahan) G.; m. Patricia Parks Albjerg, Sept. 6, 1955; 1 child, Marguerite Elizabeth. BS, Purdue U., 1955, LLD (h.c.), 1986; MA, Columbia U., NYC, 1960, PhD, 1964; postgrad., Moscow U., 1960-61. Gandy-dancer Pa. R.R., 1950-51; research chem. engr. Dow Chem. Co., 1955; lectr. dept. history Ind. U., 1963-64, asst. prof., 1965-66; vis. asst. prof. dept. public law and govt. Columbia U., 1965-66, assoc. prof., dept. history, 1967-72, prof., 1972-78, adj. prof., 1978-89; mem. Russian Inst., 1966-78; assoc., mem. exec. com. Davis Ctr. for Russian and Eurasian Studies/Harvard U., 1980—; acting dir. Davis Ctr. for Russian Studies/Harvard U., 1995-96; vis. prof. dept. history of sci. Harvard U., 1985-99; prof. MIT, 1978—2006. Vis. scholar U. Chgo., 1991-92; faculty assoc. Harvard U., 1999—; mem. adv. bd. Internat. Sci. Found., 1992-96; mem. adv. coun. U.S. Civilian R&D Found., 2002—. Author: The Soviet Academy of Sciences and The Communist Party, 1967, Science and Philosophy in the Soviet Union, 1972, Between Science and Values, 1981, Sci. Philosophy and Human Behavior in the Soviet Union, 1987, Science in Russia and the Soviet Union: A Short History, 1993, The Ghost of the Executed Engineer: Technology and the Fall of the Soviet Union, 1993, A Face in the Rock: Tale of a Grand Island Chippewa, 1995, What Have We Learned About Science and Technology From the Russian Experience?, 1998, Moscow Stories, 2006; editor (with others) Functions and Uses of Disciplinary History, 1983, (with R. Stites) Red Star: The First Bolshevik Science Utopia, 1983, Science and the Soviet Social Order, 1990; contbr. numerous articles to profl. jours.; narrator, cons. Nova TV, 1987 Trustee European U., St. Petersburg, Russia, 2000—06, Nat. Lighthouse Mus., 1997—. Served with USN, 1955-58, Coast Guard Aux., 1979—. Recipient Gross award Saginaw Valley State U., 2003; Woodrow Wilson fellow, 1958-59; Danforth fellow, 1958-63; Fulbright Hayes fellow, 1966; Guggenheim fellow, 1969-70; Rockefeller fellow, 1976-77; Smithsonian Instn. fellow, 1981-82. Fellow AAAS, Am. Acad. Arts and Scis., Am. Philos. Soc.; mem. Acad. Natural Scis. (fgn.; Moscow), Acad. Humanitarian Scis. (fgn.; Moscow), Am. Hist. Assn., Am. Assn. Advancement of Slavic Studies, History of Sci. Soc. (Sarton medal 1996), Soc. History of Tech., Soc. Social Study of Sci., Mich. Hist. Soc. (Follo award 2000). Home: 7 Francis Ave Cambridge MA 02138 Office: Harvard Univ CGIS Rm S321 1730 Cambridge St Cambridge MA 02138 Business E-Mail: lrg@mit.edu.

GRAHAM, MICHAEL HAW, orthopedist; b. Des Moines, Mar. 18, 1938; s. William Walter and Katherine Elizabeth (Haw) Graham; m. Nancy Ann Kramer, Aug. 14, 1962; children: Christopher Kramer, Kevin Corkhill. BS in Math., Iowa State U., 1960; MD, State U. Iowa, 1964. Diplomate Am. Acad. Orthop. Surgeons, 1971, lic. Oreg., 1965, Iowa, 1965, diplomate Nat. Bd. Med. Examiners, 1965, lic. Calif., 2004. Internship U. Oreg. Hosp. and Clin., 1964—65, orthop. residency, 1965—69; clin. instr. orthop. Oreg. Health Scis. U., 1971—78, asst. clin. prof. orthop. and rehab., 1979—2002; assoc. staff Good Samaritan Hosp., Portland, Oreg., 1971—73, active staff, 1973—92, Legacy Downtown Hosp., 1992—2002. Orthop. cons. Oreg. Med. Profl. Review Organ., 1998—, Oreg. Medicare, 1998—, Emcompass, 2000—06; assoc. med. dir. Qmedtrix Sys., Inc., Portland, 2001—04. Contbr. articles various profl. jours. Peer reviewer Various Med. Facilities, 1992—. Maj. USAF, 1971, Fla. Recipient Borden Rsch. award, State U. Iowa, 1964. Mem.: Am. Acad. Orthop. Surgeons, Oregon Assn. Orthop. (pres.-elect 1991—92, pres. 1992—2002), Western Orthop. Assn., Am. Coll. Sports Medicine, Multnomah County Med. Soc., Oreg. Med. Edn. Found. (v.p. 1998—2003, pres. 2003—06), Oreg. Med. Assn. (sec., treas. 1987—89, pres.-elect. 1989—90, pres. 1990—91), AMA, Pumpkin Ridge Golf Club, Omicron Delta Kappa, Alpha Omega Alpha, Sigma Alpha Epsilon. Avocations: genealogy, golf, wine. Personal E-mail: michaelhgraham@comcast.net.

GRAHAM, OLIVE JANE, retired medical/surgical nurse; b. Waterford, Wis., Mar. 23, 1932; d. Theodore Joseph Auterman and Edna Wilhelmina Sophia Boldt-Auterman; m. Charles E. Briggs (div.); children: Charles E. Briggs Jr., Joette A. O'Neill, Michael W. Briggs; m. Albert Frank Graham, Sept. 1, 1986. Diploma, St. John's Sch. Nursing, 1952. Cert. oper. room nurse, in oper. room tech., Johns Hopkins Hosp., 1953. Staff nurse Gibson Cmty. Hosp., Gibson City, Ill., 1952—53, Wesley Mem. Hosp., Chgo., 1953—54, Mercy Hosp., Champaign, 1954—55, Ho. Good Samaritan Hosp., Watertown, 1955; oper. rm./emergency rm. supr. Gibson Comty., Gibson City, 1956—58; staff nurse Cole Hosp., Champaign, 1958—59; office nurse Dr. Paul Sunderland, Gibson City, 1960—61; staff nurse Jefferson County Hosp., Ft. Atkinson, Wis., 1962—63, Charleston Meml. Hosp., Ill., 1964—68; tchr. Lamaze Dr. Pearman, Dr. Ferneau, Columbia, Mo., 1968—69; staff nurse Boone Hosp. Ctr., 1969—72, Harry S. Truman Meml. VA, 1972—92; ret. Co-dir.: (video) Pre-Operative Visit, 1982. Asst. leader Green Meadows Coun. Girl Scouts Am., Gibson City, 1958—59, neighborhood chmn., 1959—60; mem. Federated Jr. Womans Club, 1955—61, v.p. 17th dist., 1961—62; vol. blood drives ARC, 1993—2000; mem. bd. Rainbow Ho., Temporary Home for Children in Crisis, Columbia, 1996—2005, pres., 1998—99; mem. Lois Mikeut Century Cir. Internat. ORder King's Daus. and Sons., Inc., 1997—; mem. bd. King's Daus. Home, Mexico, 2001—03; docent Boone County Hist. Mus., 1995—; mem. U. Mo. Ext. Wives, 1993—2006; vol. Mo. State Show-ME Games, 1995—; candidate Columbia City Coun., 1977; mem. choir, prayer chain, care givers Trinity Luth. Ch., Columbia, 1968—; mem. United Meth. Women, 1993—2001. Mem.: Nat. Assn. Fed. Retirees, U. Mo. Alumni Assn., U. Mo. Quarterback Club, Beta Kappa (master), Beta Sigma Phi (charter pres. Xi Epsilon Theta, coun. pres., Girl of Yr. 1984). Lutheran. Avocations: walking, reading, bridge.

GRAHAM, PAMELA SMITH, artist, educator; b. Winona, Miss., Jan. 18, 1944; d. Douglas LaRue and Dorothy Jean (Hefty) Smith; m. Robert William Graham, Mar. 6, 1965 (div. 1974); children: Jennifer Courtney, Eric Douglas; m. Thomas Paul Harley, Dec. 4, 1976 (div. 2000). Student, U. Colo., 1962-65, U. Cin., 1974-76. Profl. artist, craft tchr., 1968—; property mgmt. and investor Cin., 1972-77; acct., word processor Borden Chem. Co. divsn. Borden, Inc., Cin., 1974-78; owner, pres. Hargram Enterprises, Cin., 1977-81; owner Sagebrush Studio, 1985—, Graham & Harley Enterprises, 1981-99; art tchr., dean of ceremonial art Coll. of Transformative Wisdom, 1999—2001; webpage designer dept. pharmacy U. Colo. Hosp., 1998-2000. Tchr.; cons. County committeewoman Bergen County, N.J., 1972, clk. of session, 1975-79, conv. chmn., 1981; campaign chmn. United Appeal, 1977; lifeline telephone counselor Suicide Hotline, 1985-90; coord. program svcs. and victim advisor Abusive Men Exploring New Directions, 1986-91 One woman shows include U. Colo. Health Scis. Ctr. Denison Libr., 1992—, Jefferson County Nature Ctr., 1990, Mt. Vernon Country Club, 1998-99, Colo. Symphony, 1998; exhibited in group shows at Colo. Audubon Soc., 1989, Evergreen Artists Assn. Fine Arts Fair, 1988-95, River Sage, 1989, Evergreen Naturalists Audubon Soc., 1988-91, Foothills Art Ctr., 1989, 93, Rocky Mountain PBS Annual Auction, 1991-, Gilpin County Arts Assn., 1989-94, Glenwood Springs Art Guild, 1989-90, Hilton Head Art League, 1999, Red Rocks Trading Post, 2004; featured in Spree mag., 1989, Weekend Arts sect. Denver Post, 1998; included in Ency. of Living Artists, 11th edit., 1999; represented in permanent collections at U. Hosp., AMEND, U. Colo. Health Scis. Ctr. Chancellor's Office, U. Colo., Boulder Wardenburg Health Ctr., Willis Corroon Corp., Dean Witter Reynolds, Inc., others Recipient People's Choice award Evergreen Artists Assn. Mem. NAFE, AARP, Profl. Artists Assn., Nat. Assn. Fine Artists, Denver Art Mus., Denver Mus. Nature and Sci., Mus. Modern Art N.Y., United Sales Leaders Assn., Nat. Mus. Women in Arts, Colo. Artists Assn., Evergreen Artists Assn. (bd. dirs., pres. 1990-91, People's Choice award 1993), Hilton Head Art League, Ocean Journey Aquariaum, Colo. Calligraphers Guild, Nat. Women's History Mus., Gilpin County Arts Assn., Continental Divide Trail Alliance, Friends of Denver Pub. Libr. Assn., Foothills Art Ctr., Assn. Humanistic Psychology, Assn. of Rsch. Enlightenment, Hemlock Soc., Smithsonian Instn., Mt. Vernon Country Club, Queen City Racquet Club, Alpha Gamma Chi, Kappa Kappa Gamma. Studio: Sagebrush Studio 818 Logan St # 903 Denver CO 80203-3123 Office Phone: 303-832-0043. Personal E-mail: sagebrushstudio@yahoo.com. Business E-Mail: graham@sagebrushstudios.com.

GRAHAM, PATRICIA ALBJERG, education educator; b. Lafayette, Ind., Feb. 9, 1935; d. Victor L. and Marguerite (Hall) Albjerg; m. Loren R. Graham, Sept. 6, 1955; 1 child, Marguerite Elizabeth. BS, Purdue U., 1955, MS, 1957, DLett (hon.), 1980; PhD, Columbia U., 1964; MA (hon.), Harvard U., 1974; DHL (hon.), Manhattanville Coll., 1976; LLD (hon.), Beloit Coll., 1977, Clark U., 1978; DPA (hon.), Suffolk U., 1978, Ind. U., 1980; DLitt (hon.), St. Norbert Coll., 1980; DH (hon.), Emmanuel Coll., 1983; DHL (hon.), No. Mich. U., 1987, York Coll. of Pa., 1989, Kenyon Coll., 1991, Bank St. Coll. Edn., 1993; LLD (hon.), Radcliffe Coll., 1994, Salem State Coll., 1998; LLD (hon.), DePaul U., 2006. Tchr. high sch., Norfolk, Va., 1955-56, 57-58, NYC, 1958-60; lectr., asst. prof. Ind. U., 1964-66; asst. prof. history of edn. Barnard Coll. and Columbia Tchrs. Coll., NYC, 1965-68, assoc. prof., 1968-72, prof., 1972-74; dean Radcliffe Inst., 1974-77; also v.p. Radcliffe Coll., Cambridge, Mass., 1976-77; prof. Harvard U., Cambridge, Mass., 1974-79, Warren prof., 1979—2001, Warren Rsch. prof., 2001—06, dean Grad. Sch. Edn., 1982—91, emerita, 2006—; pres. Spencer Found., Chgo., 1991-2000. Author: Progressive Education: From Arcady to Academe, 1967, Community and Class in American Education: 1865-1918, 1974, S.O.S. Sustain Our Schools, 1992, Schooling America, 2005. Bd. dirs. Dalton Sch., 1973-76, Josiah Macy, Jr. Found., 1976-77, 79—; trustee Beloit Coll., 1976-77, 79-82, Northwestern Mut. Life, 1980-2005, Found. for Tchg. Econs., 1980-87; bd. dirs. Spencer Found., 1983-2000, Johnson Found., 1983-2001, Hitachi Found., 1985-2004, Carnegie Found. for Advancement of Tchg., 1984-92, Ctrl. European U., Budapest, 2002—, Apache, 2002—. Mem.: AAAS (coun. 1993—96, v.p. 1998—2001), Ctr. for Advanced Study in the Behavioral Scis. (bd. dirs. 2001—07), Am. Philos. Soc., Am. Hist. Assn. (v.p. 1985—89), Nat. Acad. Edn. (pres. 1984—89), Sci. Rsch. Assocs. (dir. 1980—89), Phi Beta Kappa. Episcopalian. Office: Harvard U Grad Sch Edn Cambridge MA 02138

GRAHAM, PAUL, Internet company executive, writer; AB, Cornell Univ.; PhD in Computer Sci., Harvard Univ.; student, RI Sch. Design, Accademia di Belle Arti, Florence, Italy. Co-founder Viaweb (sold to Yahoo), 1995—98; creator Bayesian spam filter, 2002; founding ptnr. Y Combinator. Author: On Lisp, 1993, ANSI Common Lisp, 1995, Hackers & Painters, 2004. Named one of 50 Who Matter Now, Business 2.0, 2007. Office: Y Combinator 320 Pioneer Way Mountain View CA 94041*

GRAHAM, R(ICHARD) NEWELL, soft drink bottling company executive; b. Union City, Tenn., June 15, 1947; s. Hardy Moore and Cola Lee (Poindexter) G.; m. Bettie Rene Young, Dec. 28, 1968; children: Richard, Stanford. BA, U. Miss., 1969. Operating ptnr., chief exec. officer Union City Coca-Cola Bottling Co., 1972—; sec., treas. C.C. Coin Caterers Corp., Union City, 1972-93, pres., 1993—, ReelFoot Ordnance Inc., 1996—. Bd. dirs. First State Bank, Union City, chmn. exec. bd.; bd. dirs. Meridian Coca-Cola Bottling Co., Miss., 1st v.p., 2005; chmn. bd. Cmty. First Bankshares, 2007-. Pres. Union City Arts Coun., 1978-79; mem. devel. com. U. Tenn., Martin, 1980-95, vice chmn. devel. coun., 1990-93; treas. St. James Episcopal Ch., Union City, 1987—. With USN, 1969-72. Recipient Project of Yr. award Tenn. Jaycees, Nashville, 1974, Friend of Edn. award Obion County Schs., Union City, 1980. Mem. Assn. Coca-Cola Bottlers Tenn. (pres. 1989-91), Tenn. Soft Drink Assn. (bd. dirs. 1985—), Obion County C. of C. (bd. dirs. 1989-93), Union City Jaycees (pres. 1975, Outstanding Young Man award 1976), Chaine des Rotisseurs (chavalier 1989—), Union City Rotary Club (Paul Harris fellow 1999). Republican. Avocations: wine, food, hunting, military weapons, gardening. Office: Union City Coca-Cola Bottling Co 1915 E Reelfoot Ave Union City TN 38261-6007

GRAHAM, ROBERT ALBERT, physicist, researcher, curator; b. Dallas, Feb. 11, 1931; s. John Mark and Eleanor Ball (Evans) Graham; m. Lettie Barbara Umphres, Sept. 1, 1951 (dec.); children: Stephanie Ann Graham Farrow, Mark Lee, Stuart Russell; m. Nell Heard Griffin, Apr. 6, 1996. AA, Allen Jr. Coll., 1951; BSCE, U. Tex., 1954, MS in Engring. Mechanics, 1958; DSc in Materials Sci. and Engring., Tokyo Inst. Tech., 1990. Rsch. engr. S.W. Rsch. Inst., San Antonio, 1956-57; staff mem. Sandia Nat. Labs., Albuquerque, 1958-83, disting. mem. tech. staff, 1983-96; dir. rsch. Tome Group, 1996—. Adviser NAS, Washington, 1982—, Ctr. Explosives Tech. Rsch., Socorro, N.Mex., 1983—88, U. N.Mex, Albuquerque, 1988—; lectr. in field. Editor: Proc. 1981 Shock Conference, Proc. 1983 Shock Conference, N.Mex. Genealogist, 1974—75, High Pressure Exptl. Processing of Ceramic Trans. Tech., 1987; co-editor: Shock Waves in Condensed Matter, 1982, 1983, 1984, High Pressure Explosive Processing of Ceramics, 1987; editor-in-chief Springer-Verlag book series on Shock Compression of Condensed Matter, 1988—96; mng. editor: Shock Waves Internat. Jour., 1991—96, The Heard Family of Uvalde County, Texas, 2005; author: Solids Under High Pressure Shock Compression: Mechanics, Physics and Chemistry, 1993, 3 Families in the Westward Expansion, 2004; contbr. articles to profl. jours. V.p. Amigos de las Ams., Albuquerque, 1968—70; host family Am. Field Svc., Albuquerque, 1969; active Uvalde County Tex. Hist. Commn. 1st lt. US Army, 1954—56. Recipient Excellence award, Dept. Energy, 1983, G. B. Sawyer Meml. award, Sawyer Rsch. Products, 1984, Shock Compression Sci. award, Am. Phys. Soc., 1993. Fellow: AAAS, Am. Phys. Soc. (organizing com. 1979, 1983, topical conf. 1993); mem.: IEEE (sr.; local arrangements chmn. 1975), Am. Chem. Soc., Materials Rsch. Soc., Phi Theta Kappa, Chi Epsilon, Tau Beta Pi. Achievements include patents in field. Home and Office: 608 Cenizo Blvd Uvalde TX 78801-4009 Personal E-mail: tomecenizo@aol.com.

GRAHAM, ROBERT CLARE, III, lawyer; b. Albuquerque, Mar. 24, 1955; s. Robert C. Jr. and Helen (Hoagland) G.; children: Jennifer, Jessica, Kourtney, Kate. BA, DePauw U., 1977; JD magna cum laude, Pepperdine U., 1980. Bar: Mo. 1980, Ill. 1981, U.S. Dist. Ct. (ea. dist.) Mo. 1981. Assoc. Shephard, Sandberg & Phoenix, St. Louis, 1980-82, Suelthaus & Kaplan, PC and predecessors, St. Louis, 1982-91, Armstrong Teasdale, LLP, St. Louis, 1991—. Chmn. Kirkwood (Mo.) Greentree Festival, 1985. Named one of Outstanding Young Men in Am. Jaycees, 1981; recipient Outstanding Service to the Community of Kirkwood award. Mem. ABA, Ill. Bar Assn., Mo. Bar Assn., Bar Assn. Met. St. Louis, St. Louis County Bar Assn. Republican. Presbyterian. Office: Armstrong Teasdale LLP 1 Metropolitan Sq Ste 2600 Saint Louis MO 63102-2740 Office Phone: 314-621-5070. Business E-mail: rgraham@armstrongteasdale.com.

GRAHAM, ROGER JOHN, photography and journalism professor; b. Phila., Feb. 16; s. William K. and Peggy E. (Owens) G.; divorced; children: John Roger, Robb Curt; m. Debbie Kenyon, Dec. 28, 1991. AA, LA Valley Coll., 1961; BA, Calif. State U., Fresno, 1962, MA, 1967; postgrad, UCLA, 1976. Cert. in elem., jr. high, HS, CC, counseling and adminstrn. Tchr. Riverdale Sch., Calif., 1963, Raisin City Sch., Calif., 1964; tchr., counselor Calif. State Prison, Jamestown, 1966; tchr. trainer UCLA's Western Ctr. War on Poverty, 1967; chmn. media arts dept. LA Valley Coll., Van Nuys, Calif., 1968—, prof. emeritus, 1999—. Vis. prof. Pepperdine U., Malibu, Calif., 1976, Calif. Luth. Coll., Thousand Oaks, 1973, South Africa, 1997; vis. prof. Chapman U., Orange, Calif., 1996, GAIN prof., 1998; del. Calif. Fedn. Tchrs. Conv., 1997; dir. Photography Seminar, Spain, summer 1990. Co-author: Observations on the Mass Media, 1976; author: Our Lives in Bits and Pieces, 1998, Patchwork of Life, 2001, L.A. to Philly - Looking Back, 2002, L.A. to Philly - Looking Back: Again, 2005, (jour.) Jr. Coll. Jour., 1972; co-author: We Remember WW II, 2003, L.A. Valley College History, 2005, The Story Behind the Picture, 2006; photo illustrator: The San Fernando Valley, 1980, display advertiser: Turlock (Calif.) jour., 1962, Fresno Guide, 1963; contbr. articles to profl. jours. Mem. Tom Hayden's Com. for Schs., Santa Monica, Calif., 1984; pres. Pacific Palisades Dem. Club, 1992; rep. to 41st assembly dist. Calif. Dem. Party State Ctrl. Com., 1993, sec. srs. caucus, 1993—. With USN, 1957. NEH scholar 1981; recipient Mayor's Outstanding Citizen award LA Mayor's Office, 1974, Extraordinary Svc. award UCLA, 1971; named one of Outstanding Young Men Am., 1971. Mem. ACLU, CC Journalism Assn. (nat. pres. 1978—, Nat. Dedication Journalism award 1972-76), Journalism Assn. CC (pres. Calif. sect. 1972—), Calif. Srs. Caucus (state sec. 1993—), LA Profs. Club, Dem. Club Pacific Palisades (pres. 1992-93), Patrons Assn. (bd. dirs. 2000—), LA Valley Coll. Retirees Assn. (Outstanding Alumnus award 1999, pres. 1999), Am. Legion (sgt. at arms 1986—, Palisades chpt. adminstrv. officer 1996—), Patrons Assn. (bd. dirs. 2000), LA Westside Geneal. Soc. (exec. bd. 2007), Sons of the Desert, Sons Revolution, Sigma Delta Xi, Phi Delta Kappa, Pi Lambda Theta. Avocation: scuba diving. Home: 7878 Naylor Ave Los Angeles CA 90045-2909 Office: LA Valley Coll 5800 Fulton Ave Van Nuys CA 91401-4096

GRAHAM, SELDON BAIN, JR., lawyer, engineer; b. Franklin, Tex., Apr. 14, 1926; s. Seldon Bain and Lillian Emma (Struwe) G.; m. Patricia Gene Noah, Feb. 14, 1953; children: Seldon Bain (dec.), Kyle, Laurie. BS, U.S. Mil. Acad., 1951; JD, U. Tex., 1970. Cert. petroleum. engr., Tex. Bar: Tex. 1970, U.S. Dist. Ct. (so. dist.) Tex. 1980, U.S. Ct. Appeals (5th cir.) 1983; cert. in oil, gas and mineral law Tex. Bd. Legal Specialization, 1986-2001. With U.S. Army, 1944, advanced through grades to col., 1979; with Office of Dep. Chief of Staff for Pers., 1979, ret., 1979. Area reservoir engr. ARCO, Okla., 1954-60; div. regulatory engr. Mobil Oil Co., Corpus Christi, 1961-67; counsel Exxon Co. USA, Houston, 1970-85. Author: Why Your Gasoline Prices are High, 2005. Decorated Legion of Merit. Mem. Soc. Petroleum Engrs. Methodist. Home and Office: 4713 Palisade Dr Austin TX 78731-4516 Office Phone: 512-452-4000. Personal E-mail: selgraham@austin.rr.com.

GRAHAM, STEPHEN MICHAEL, lawyer; b. Houston, May 1, 1951; s. Frederick Mitchell and Lillian Louise (Miller) G.; m. Joanne Marie Sealock, Aug. 24, 1974; children: Aimee Elizabeth, Joseph Sealock, Jessica Anne. BS, Iowa State U., 1973; JD, Yale U., 1976. Bar: Wash. 1977. Assoc. Perkins Coie, Seattle, 1976-83, ptnr., 1983-2000, Orrick, Herrington & Sutcliffe LLP, Seattle, 2000—, practice leader corp. div. Bd. dirs. Wash. Spl. Olympics, Seattle, 1979—83, pres., 1982—83; trustee Friends of the Children of King County, 2002—; mem. Seattle Fair Campaign Practices Commn., 1982—88; trustee Cornish Coll. Arts, 1986—91, mem. exec. com., 1989—91; trustee Seattle Repertory Theatre, 1993—95, Seattle Children's Theatre, 1996—98, mem. exec. com., 1997—98; trustee Fred Hutchinson Cancer Rsch. Ctr., 1999—2005; bd. dirs., mem. exec. com. WSA, 2002—05; trustee Arboretum Found., 1994—96; mem. Seattle Bd. Ethics, 1982—88, chmn., 1983—88; mem. exec. com. Sch. Law Yale U., 1988—92, 1993—97; bd. dirs. Wash. Biotech. and Biomed. Assn., 1996—, mem. exec. com., 1997—. Mem.: ABA, Wash. State Bar Assn., Rainier Club, Wash. Athletic Club. Episcopalian. Office: Orrick Herrington & Sutcliffe Ste 900 719 Second Ave Seattle WA 98104-7063 Home Phone: 206-329-5242; Office Phone: 206-839-4320. Business E-Mail: sgraham@orrick.com.

GRAHAM, STUART EDWARD, construction company executive; b. Wilkes Barre, Pa., Feb. 17, 1946; s. Stuart E. Graham; m. Kathryn Virginia; children— Cameron, Stuart E. Jr., Devon BS in Econs., Holy Cross Coll., 1967. Supt. Sordoni Constrn. Co., Parsippany, NJ, 1969-72, project mgr., 1972-75, v.p. ops., 1975-78, pres., 1978—. Mem. Young Pres. Orgn. Clubs: Westmoreland (Wilkes-Barre, Pa.), University (NYC). Republican. Roman Catholic.

GRAHAM, SUSAN LOIS, computer scientist, consultant; b. Cleve., Nov. 16, 1942; m., 1971 AB in Math., Harvard U., 1964; MS, Stanford U., 1966, PhD in Computer Sci., 1971. Assoc. rsch. scientist, adj. asst. prof. computer sci. Courant Inst. Math. Sci., NYU, 1969-71; asst. prof. computer sci. U. Calif., Berkeley, 1971-76, assoc. prof., 1976-81, prof. computer sci., 1981—2004, Chancellor's prof., 1997—2000, Pehong Chen disting. prof., 2001—06; Pehong Chen disting. prof. emeritus, 2006—; prof. U. Calif., 2004—; chief computer scientist NSF Nat. Partnership for Advanced Computational Infrastructure, 1997—2005; sr. scientist Lawrence Berkeley Nat. Lab., Calif., 1999—. Vis. scientist Stanford U., 1981; mem. adv. com. div. computer and computation rsch. NSF, 1987-92, mem. program sci. and tech. ctrs., 1987-91, Alan T. Waterman award com., 2001-04; mem. vis. com. elec. engring. and computer sci. MIT, 1989—; mem. vis. com. for engring. and applied sci. Calif. Inst. Tech., 1994-99; mem. vis. com. applied scis. Harvard U., 1995—; mem. commn. on phys. sci., math. and applications NRC, 1992-95; mem. Pres.'s Com. on Nat. Medal Sci., 1994-00; mem. Pres.'s Info. Tech. Adv. Com., 1997-03; bd. dirs. Harvard Alumni Assn., 1997-2000; mem. bd. overseers Harvard U., 2001-, pres., 2006-07; co-chair Nat. Rsch. Coun. Study Future Supercomputing, 2002-04. Co-editor: Comms. ACM, 1975—79; editor: ACM transactions on Programming Langs. and Systems, 1978—92. Mem. bd. trustees Calif. Performances, 2005-. NSF grantee. Fellow AAAS, Assn. for Computing Machinery, Am. Acad. Arts and Sci.; mem. IEEE, NAE. Office: U Calif-Berkeley Computer Sci Div EECS 771 Soda Hall 1776 Berkeley CA 94720-1776 Office Phone: 510-642-2059. Business E-Mail: graham@CS.Berkeley.edu.

GRAHAM, SUSETTE RYAN, retired English educator; b. Plattsburgh, NY, Aug. 31, 1929; d. Andrew Warren Ryan and Lillian Grace MacDougall; m. James H. Graham, July 1, 1950; children: Marguerite, Andrea, James Jr., Martha, Amy, Matthew. BA, Wellesley Coll., 1950; MA, U. Rochester, 1967, PhD, 1987. Prof. English Nazareth Coll., Rochester, N.Y., 1963-93, prof. emerita, 1993; ret. Contbr. articles, revs. to profl. jours. Fulbright sr. lectr., Poland, 1992-93. Mem. AAUW, MLA, Am. Acad. Poets. Democrat. Avocations: travel, reading, genealogical research.

GRAHAM, THOMAS, JR., lawyer; b. Louisville, Oct. 9, 1933; s. Thomas and Charlotte (Henriques) G.; m. Clover Nicholas, Aug. 10, 1968 (div. Dec. 1982); children: Elizabeth Malcolm, Thomas Lawrence, Clover Chace; m. Christine Coffey Ryan, Sep. 26, 1983; stepchildren: Thomas Coffey Ryan, Mary Christine Ryan. AB, Princeton U., 1955; postgrad., L'institute des Sciences Politiques, 1955-56; JD, Harvard U., 1961. Bar: Ky. 1961, DC 1963, NY 1966. Law clk. U.S. Cir. Ct. Appeals (D.C. cir.), 1961-62; chief counsel U.S. Ho. Reps. Com. on Banking and Currency, Washington, 1962-63; counsel to compt. of currency Treasury Dept., Washington, 1963-64; assoc. Wyatt, Grafton & Sloss, Louisville, 1964-66, Shearman & Sterling, NYC, 1966-69; lawyer Office of Sec. USAF, Washington, 1969-70; asst. gen. counsel U.S. Arms Control and Disarmament Agy., Washington, 1970-73, dep. gen. counsel, 1973-77, gen. counsel, 1977—81, 1983—93, dir. Congl. rels. and pub. affairs, 1981-83, acting dir., 1993, acting dep. dir., 1993-94; spl. rep. of Pres. (amb.) Arms Control, Non-Proliferation and Disarmament, 1994-97; ret., 1997. Legal advisor US SALT II del., Geneva, 1974-79; legal advisor US. del. to rev. conf. Nonproliferation Treaty, Geneva, 1980; sr. arms control advisor US del. to negotiations on Intermediate Range Nuclear Forces, 1981-82; legal advisor US del. to Conf. Disarmament, Geneva, 1985; legal advisor US del. to negotiation on nuc. and space arms, Geneva, 1985-88, US del. to ABM Treaty Rev. Conf., Geneva, 1988; sr. arms control advisor, legal advisor US del. Conventional Armed Forces in Europe negotiation, 1989-90; legal advisor US del. START Negotiation, 1991, START II Negotiation, 1992-93; chmn. US del. ABM Treaty rev. conf., 1993, US rep. Nonproliferation Treaty Ext. Conf., 1993-95; chmn. U.S. Del. Conventional Armed Forces Europe rev. com., 1996; chmn. bd. dirs. Mex. Energy Corp., 1997—, Cypress Fund for Peace and Security, 2005—; lectr. U. Va. Law Sch., 1984-91; adj. prof. Georgetown U. Law Ctr., 1991-93, Georgetown Sch. Fgn. Svc., 1991-94, Stanford U., 1999-, U. Washington, 2002-; pres. Lawyers Alliance for World Security, Washington, 1997-2002, chmn. bd. dirs., 2002-05, spl. counsel Morgan, Lewis and Bockius, Washington, 2002-04, sr. counsel, 2004-05; chmn. bd. dirs. Novastar Resources (Thorium Power Ltd), 2006-, exec. chmn., 2007—; bd. dirs. Thorium Power Inc., 1997-2006; sr. cons. Eisenhower Inst., Washington, 2002-04, sr. cons., fellow, 2004-. Author: Disarmament Sketches, Thirty Years of Arms Control and International Law, 2002; author: (with Damien La Vena) Cornerstones of Security, Arms Control Treaties in the Modern Era, 2003; author: Common Sense on Weapons of Mass Destruction, 2004; author: (with Keith Hanson) Spy Satellites and Other Intelligence Technologies that Changed History, 2007. Spl. asst. to chmn. United Citizens for Nixon-Agnew, Washington, 1968. With U.S. Army, 1956-58, 1st lt. U.S. Army Res., 1958-61. Recipient Trainor Excellence in Diplomacy award, Georgetown U., 1995. Mem. ABA (chmn. com. on arms control 1986-94, World Order Under Law award Internat. sect. 2006), D.C. Bar Assn., N.Y. State Bar Assn., Ky. Bar Assn., Coun. on Fgn. Rels., Chevy Chase Club, Cosmos Club, Met. Club, Louisville Country Club, Ausable Club. Republican. Episcopalian. Avocations: tennis, golf, skiing, hiking. Home: 7609 Glenbrook Rd Bethesda MD 20814 Office: Thorium Power Ltd 8300 Greensboro Dr Ste 800 Mc Lean VA 22102 Office Phone: 703-918-3943. Personal E-mail: tgraham@cypressfund.org.

GRAHAM, THOMAS RICHARD, lawyer; b. Shelbyville, Ind., Nov. 23, 1942; s. Kermit A. and Esther L. (Thompson) G.; m. Rosemond Eve Toner, June 12, 1965; children: Rachel Graham Cody, Thomas Ian. BA, Ind. U., 1965; JD, Harvard U., 1968. Bar: DC 1970, US Supreme Ct. 1973. Exec. asst. to pres. Ford Motor de Venezuela, Caracas, 1968-70; vis. prof. law U. Catolica Andres Bello, Caracas, 1968-70; legal officer UN, Geneva, 1970-73; dep. gen. counsel Office U.S. Trade Rep., Washington, 1974-79; vis. prof. U. N.C., Chapel Hill, 1979-80; assoc. Patton, Boggs & Blow, Washington, 1980-81; counsel, ptnr. Kilpatrick & Cody, Washington, 1981-85; ptnr. Skadden, Arps, Slate, Meagher & Flom, Washington, 1985-2000, King & Spalding, Washington, 2000—05, of counsel, 2005—. Adj. prof. law Georgetown U., Washington, 1977-85, 95-98; vis. fellow Brookings Instn., Washington, 1978-79; sr. assoc. Carnegie Endowment, Washington, 1979-80. Co-editor: Managing Trade Relations in the 1980's, 1983, Trade and Environment, 1982; contbr. articles to profl. jours. Chief advisor on internat. trade John Glenn Presdl. Campaign, 1984. Mem. ABA (chmn. subcom. exports 1985-89), Am. Soc. Internat. Law (chmn. internat. econ. law sect. 1981-83). Avocations: history, sports. Home: 6115 33rd St NW Washington DC 20015-2403 Office: King Spalding Llp 1700 Pennsylvania Ave NW Ste 200 Washington DC 20006-4707 Office Phone: 202-626-5609. Personal E-mail: tomrgraham@aol.com. Business E-Mail: tgraham@kslaw.com.

GRAHAM, VICARY M., trust company executive; b. Fitchburg, Mass., Mar. 27, 1960; d. David and Caroline Ruby (Gratton) G. BA, Skidmore Coll., 1982. Account mgr. Bank of New Eng., Boston, 1983; v.p. Boston Safe Deposit & Trust Co., 1983—. Mem. Mortgage Bankers Assn.

GRAHAM, WALLACE KARL, chemicals executive; b. NYC, Sept. 12, 1928; s. Samuel and Mildred G.;/ m. Ruth R. Winer, July 29, 1950; children: James (dec.), Steven L., Eric P. BSChemE, Columbia U., 1950; MS, NYU, 1954. With Nat. Starch and Chem. Corp., 1950-93, corp. v.p., gen. mgr. adhesive div. Bridgewater, NJ, 1972-77, group v.p., 1977-78, pres., chief operating officer, dir., 1978-83, pres., chief exec. officer, 1983-84, chmn., chief exec. officer, 1984-85; group head chems. Unilever PLC and Unilever NV, 1986-91, also bd. dirs., 1986-91. Bd. dirs. Courtalds plc, 1991-98, Jorin Ltd., UK, 1999-. Fellow Instn. Chem. Engrs. London; mem. Soc. Chem. Industry, Am. Inst. Chem. Engrs., Princeton Club, Mid-Ocean (Bermuda) Club, Wentworth Golf Club (Eng.), Algonquin Club.

GRAHAM, WARREN KIRKLAND, dentist; b. Albuquerque, July 22, 1938; s. Warren Reno and Alice Barbara (Eller) G.; m. Nancy Lou White, Apr. 2, 1966; children: John Warren, Jason Kirkland. BS, U. N.Mex., 1960; DDS, Baylor U., 1964. Pvt. practice dentistry, Albuquerque, 1965-89; dental dir. Farmington Cmty. Health Ctr., 1989—; corp. dental dir. Presbyn. Med. Svcs., 1994—; adj. asst. prof. Coll. Dentistry, Baylor U., 1995—2000; adj. asst. prof. dental programs U. N.Mex., 1996-2000, U. Mo. Dental Sch., Kansas City, 2000—02. Mem. N.Mex. Bd. Dental Health Care, 1997-2002, chmn., 2000-02; bd. dirs., examiner Western Regional Exam Bd., 1998-2002; founder Albuquerque (N.Mex.) sr. citizens' dental program, 1985. Bd. dirs. N.Mex. Coun. on Smoking and Health, 1969-71; mem. N.Mex. Medicaid Adv. Bd., 1972-77, Mid Rio Grande Health Planning Coun., 1972-76; chmn. N.Mex. Health Sys. Agy. Subarea Coun., Dist. II, 1977-78. Capt. USAF, 1964-65. Fellow Am. Coll. Dentists, Internat. Coll. Dentists, Acad. Gen. Dentistry, Pierre Fauchard Acad.; mem. ADA, N.Mex. Acad. Gen. Dentistry (pres. 1990-91), N.Mex. Dental Assn. (sec.-treas. 1982-86, v.p. 1986-87, pres. 1988-89), Albuquerque Dist. Dental Soc. (pres. 1976), Am. Assn. Pub. Health Dentistry, Nat. Network Oral Health Access, Am. Assn. Dental Examiners, Sigma Chi, Delta Sigma Delta. Republican. Mem. Lds Ch. Office: Presbyn Med Svcs Farmington Cmty Health Ctr PO Box 3239 Farmington NM 87499-3239

GRAHAM, WILLIAM ALBERT, religious studies and history educator; b. Raleigh, NC, Aug. 16, 1943; s. William Albert and Evelyn (Powell) G.; m. Barbara Stecconi, Aug. 26, 1983; 1 child, Powell Louis. Student, U. Goettingen, Fed. Republic Germany, 1964—65; BA summa cum laude, U. NC, 1966, DHL (hon.), 2004; AM, Harvard U., 1970, PhD, 1973; DHL (hon.), Lehigh U., 2005. Lectr. Islamic religion Harvard U., Cambridge, Mass., 1973-74, asst. prof., 1974-79, Allston Burr sr. tutor, 1975-77, assoc. prof., 1979-81, sr. lectr. history of religion, 1981-85, prof. history of religion and Islamic studies, 1985—2001, chmn. Study of Religion, 1987-90, Murray A. Albertson prof. Middle Eastern studies, 2001—, dir. Ctr. for Middle Eastern Studies, 1990-96, chmn. Near Eastern Langs. and Civilizations, 1997—2002; master Currier House Harvard Coll., 1991—2003; dean and John Lord O'Brian prof. divinity Harvard Div. Sch., 2002—. Chmn. Coun. on Grad. Studies in Religion, 1993-96; vis. lectr. Friedrich-Wilhelms U., Bonn, 1982-83. Author: Divine Word and Prophetic Word in Early Islam, 1977 (Am. Coun. Learned Socs. book prize 1978), Beyond the Written Word, 1987, 93; co-author: Heritage of World Civilizations, 1986, 7th edit., 2005, Three Faiths, One God, 2002; co-editor: Islamfiche: Readings from Islamic Primary Sources, 1987; mem. editl. bd. jours. and ency.; contbr. articles to profl. jours. Woodrow Wilson Found. grad. fellow Harvard U., 1966-67, Danforth Found. grad. fellow Harvard U., 1966-73, John Simon Guggenheim Found. fellow, India, 1982-83, Alexander von Humboldt Found. fellow, Germany, 1982-83, IRCICA quinquinnial award for excellence in rsch. Islamic Studies, Orgn. of the Islamic Conf., 2000. Fellow AAAS; mem. Am. Soc. for Study of Religion, Am. Acad. Religion, Middle East Studies Assn., Am. Oriental Soc., Am. Alpine Club, Phi Beta Kappa; fellow Am. Acad. Arts & Scis. Democrat. Avocations: mountain climbing, running. Home: 44 Francis Ave Cambridge MA 02138 Office: Harvard Divinity Sch 45 Francis Ave Cambridge MA 02138

GRAHAM, WILLIAM EDGAR, JR., lawyer, utilities executive; b. Jackson Springs, NC, Dec. 31, 1929; s. William Edgar and Minnie Blanch (Autry) G.; children: William McLaurin, John McMillan, Sally Faircloth. AB, U. N.C., 1952, JD with honors, 1956. Bar: N.C. bar. Law clk. U.S. Ct. Appeals 4th Circuit, 1956-57; individual practice law Charlotte, N.C., 1957-69; judge N.C. Ct. Appeals, 1969-73; sr. v.p., gen. counsel Carolina Power & Light Co., Raleigh, N.C., 1973-81, exec. v.p., 1981-85, vice chmn., 1985-93; counsel Hunton & Williams, 1994—. Served with USAF, 1952-54. Mem. ABA, N.C. Bar Assn., Wake County Bar Assn. Presbyterian. Office: Hunton & Williams PO Box 109 Raleigh NC 27602-0109 E-mail: dgraham@hunton.com.

GRAHAM, WILLIAM HENRY, lawyer; b. Newark, Jan. 6, 1946; s. Robert and Ruth Ellen (McElroy) G.; m. Lorraine Majeski, Mar. 23, 1969; 1 child, Allison. BA, Ohio State U., 1968; JD, Rutgers U., 1973; LLM in Corp. Law, NYU, 1978, LLM in Trade Regulation Law, 1980. Law clk. Connell Foley & Geiser, Roseland, N.J., 1971-73, atty., 1973-77, Bethlehem (Pa.) Steel Corp., 1977-79, sr. atty., 1979-81, gen. atty., 1981-85, asst. gen. counsel, 1985-89, asst. gen. counsel, asst. sec., 1989-92, gen. counsel, 1992-95, v.p., gen. counsel, sec., 1995-2000, sr. v.p., gen. counsel, sec., 2000—. Bd. dirs. Atlantic Legal Found., N.Y.C., 1986—; bd. mem. Pa. Civil Justice Coalition, Harrisburg, Pa., 1987—; chmn. Pa. Task Force on Product Liability, Harrisburg, 1989—. 1st lt. U.S. Army, 1969-71, Vietnam. Mem. ABA, N.J. Bar Assn., Pa. Bar Assn., Trial Attys. N.J., Am. Iron and Steel Inst., Assn. Gen. Counsel. Lutheran. E-mail: william.graham@bethsteel.com.

GRAHAM, WILLIAM JAMES, packaging company executive; b. Johnstown, Pa., Sept. 20, 1923; s. John Ellis and Margaret (Euwer) G.; m. Natalie Joan Stolk, Feb. 17, 1951; children: Susan, Margaret, John, Elizabeth, Joan, Catherine. BA cum laude, Amherst Coll., 1948. Salesman, Owens-Ill., Inc., 1953-60, closure sales mgr., 1960-66, v.p. sales Pacific region, 1966-69, v.p., gen. mgr. Pacific region, 1969-72, v.p. sales and mktg., 1972-75, v.p., gen. mgr. plastic products div. Toledo, 1975-82, group v.p. plastics and closures, 1982-85, sr. v.p. West, 1985-88, ret., 1988. Bd. dirs. G.W. Plstics, Garden Grow Co., Inc. Trustee, pres. Filoli, 1990-96; trustee Strybing Arboretum, 1996-2002. 1st lt. U.S. Army, 1943-46, 50-51. Mem. Soc. Plastics Industry (dir.-at-large, exec. com.), Plastic Bottle Inst. (chmn. 1983-86), Mgmt. Policy Council (exec. com.), Menlo Country, Foothills Tennis, Eastman (N.H.) Golf Club. Republican. Presbyterian. Home: 8 Hawk View St Portola Valley CA 94028 E-mail: wjgra@aol.com.

GRAHAM, WILLIAM THOMAS, lawyer; b. Waynesboro, Va., Oct. 24, 1933; s. James Monroe and Margaret Virginia (Goodwin) G.; m. Kent Hill, Feb. 1, 1958; children: Ashton Cannon, William Thomas Jr. AB in Econs., Duke U., 1956; JD, U. Va., 1962. Bar: NC 1962, Va. 1962, DC 1970, US Supreme Ct. 1970. Assoc. Craige, Brawley and predecessor firms, Winston-Salem, NC, 1962-64; ptnr. Craige, Brawley, Horton & Graham, Winston-Salem, 1965-69; asst. gen. counsel HUD, Washington, 1969-70; ptnr. Billings & Graham, Winston-Salem, 1971-75; judge N.C. Superior Ct., 1975-79; pvt. practice Winston-Salem, 1981-87; commr. of banks State of N.C., Raleigh, 1987-95; counsel Patton Boggs, LLP, Raleigh, 1995-98; pvt. practice William T. Graham Law Office, Raleigh and WinstonSalem, 1999—. Chmn. N.C. Inst. for Constl. Law, 2003—. Chmn. Forsyth County Reps., Winston-Salem, 1966-69, 73-75, George Bush for Pres., NC, 1988. With US Army, 1957-58. Mem. Old Town Club. Republican. Methodist. Avocation: travel. Home: 465 Sheffield Dr Winston Salem NC 27104 Office Phone: 336-725-3884. E-mail: wtggtw@aol.com.

GRAHAME, HEATHER H., lawyer; b. 1955; BA in Human Biology, Stanford U., 1978; JD, U. Oreg., 1984. Bar: Alaska 1984. Atty. Bogle & Gates PLLC, Anchorage; ptnr., co-chair, telecom. practice group Dorsey & Whitney LLP, Anchorage. Editor-in-chief Oreg. Law Rev., 1983—84. Pres. Alaska Dance Theatre, 2002—. Named Assoc. Mem. Yr., Alaska Telephone Assn., 1993. Mem.: ABA, Alaska Bar Assn., Federal Comm. Bar Assn. (Pacific NW chapt.). Achievements include Sixth place, US Cycling Team Time Trial Championships, 1988; Seventh place, Women's World Championship Sled Dog Race, 2002. Avocation: dog sledding. Office: Dorsey & Whitney LLP Ste 600 1031 W Fourth Ave Anchorage AK 99501-5907 Office Phone: 907-257-7822. Office Fax: 907-276-4152. Business E-Mail: grahame.heather@dorsey.com.

GRAHAM-HUTCHINSON, JOANNA, counselor, minister; b. Ocala, Fla., Nov. 7, 1952; d. Percy Wingo and Louise Brown Wingo; m. Jimmy Graham (div.); children: Ira Stafford, Joseph A. Williams Jr., Juanita Graham Burch, Jennifer Graham, Jacquelyn Graham; m. Randolph Hutchinson (div.); children: Randi Hutchinson, Stephen Hutchinson. AA, Ctrl. Fla. CC, Ocala; BA, St. Leo Coll., Fla.; MS, Nova Southea. U., Ft. Lauderdale, Fla.; MA, Bethany Bible Coll., Dothan, Ala. Case mgr. Dept. Children and Families, Gainesville, Fla.; pub. sch. tchr. Alchua County, Gainesville, drug counselor; founder, family counselor Elnathan Haven of Hope, Gainesville, 2004—. Min. Showers of Blessings Ch., 1999—; spkr. in field. Author: I Remember What Grandma Said, 2007. Tchr. Women's Covenant Group, Gainesville, 2006; founder Victory Chapel Ch., Gainesville, 1986. Mem.: Nat. Christian Counselors Assn. (cert.). Avocations: reading, research, religious activities. Office: Elnathan Haven of Hope PO Box 5041 Gainesville FL 32627 Office Phone: 352-377-8669. Office Fax: 352-377-8669. Personal E-mail: b4real377@yahoo.com.

GRAHMANN, CHARLES V., bishop; b. Halletsville, Tex., July 15, 1931; Student, Assumption-St. John's Sem., Tex. Ordained priest Roman Cath. Ch., 1956. Ordained titular bishop Equilium and aux., San Antonio, 1981—82; 1st bishop Victoria, Tex., 1982—89; coadjutor biship Dallas, 1990; bishop Diocese of Dallas, 1990—. Office: Diocese of Dallas Chancery Office PO Box 190507 Dallas TX 75219-0507

GRAHN, ANN WAGONER, retired science administrator; b. Phila., Feb. 28, 1932; d. George and Marjorie Sharps (Jefferies) W.; m. Douglas Grahn, May 19, 1973. BA magna cum laude with honors, Bryn Mawr Coll., Pa., 1953; MA, Middlebury Coll., Vt., 1954; MBA with distinction, Keller Grad. Sch., Chgo., 1986; DHL (hon.), Hanover Coll., Ind., 2004. Asst. to dir. overseas programs Am. Coun. Edn., Washington, 1955-56; asst. to dir. mat. dist. div. Dem. Nat. Com., Washington, 1956; with geophysics and space sci. NAS, Washington, 1956-70, staff dir. coms. of space sci. bd., 1970-74; coord. Ctr. Policy Studies, assoc. dir. devel. U. Chgo., 1974-79; exec. officer Argonne Univs. Assn., Argonne Nat. Lab., 1979-82, U. Chgo. Office at Argonne Nat. Lab., Argonne, 1982-83. Editor: The Windows of Christ Church, Madison, 2006; spl. editor jour. Perspectives in Biology and Medicine, 1980; editor numerous books and reports. Bd. dirs., founding exec. dir. Community Found. of Madison and Jefferson County, 1992-96; mem. City of Madison Port Authority; adminstr. Christ Episcopal Ch., 1996-98, coord., Collaborative Mktg. Project of Jefferson Cty., 1999-03, bd. dirs., Madison-Jefferson Cty. Econ. Devel. Corp. 1997-, chair, Info. Tech. Infrastructure Task Group, 2003-. Fulbright scholar, 1953-54; recipient NASA Pub. Svc. award Nat. Acad. Scis. Space Medicine Com., 1974, Cmty. Svc. award, C. of C., 2000. Mem. Jefferson County Hist. Soc. (bd. dirs. 1989-92). Republican. Episcopalian. Home: 218 Walnut St Madison IN 47250-3556

GRAIF, JOSEPH NICHOLAS, musician; s. Adolph John and Frances Theresa Graif; m. Susan Anne Mulgrew, Feb. 18, 2006; children: Jeffrey Paul Mulgrew, Heather Anne Mulgrew, Theresa May. BA, Columbia U., NYC, 1976, MBA, 1978; degree, Pace U., NYC, 1983. Dir. music ministries Our Lady Of Good Counsel Cath. Ch., Vienna, Va., 2001—03; pastoral assoc. music and liturgy St. Philip Cath. Ch., Falls Church, Va., 2004—. Mem.: Am. Guild Of Organists (choirmaster 2006, registrar No. Va. chpt. 2006—). Office: Saint Philip Catholic Church 7500 Saint Philip Ct Falls Church VA 22042 Home Phone: 703-385-3915; Office Phone: 703-573-3940. Business E-Mail: st.philipmusic@netzero.net.

GRAINGER, AMANDA R., lawyer; b. Little Rock, Sept. 2, 1973; BS, Cornell U., 1995; MBA, JD, Emory U., 1999. Bar: Tex. 1999. Assoc. Winstead, Sechrest & Minick, Dallas, 1999—2004; assoc., pub. law & policy strategies group Sonnenschein Nath & Rosenthal LLP, Washington, 2004—. Office: Sonnenschein Nath & Rosenthal LLP Ste 600, E Tower 1301 K St NW Washington DC 20005 Office Phone: 202-408-3223. Office Fax: 202-408-6399. Business E-Mail: agrainger@sonnenschein.com.

GRAINGER, JOHN R., medical association administrator; COO Laidlaw, 1997-99; pres., CEO Am. Med. Response, Aurora, Colo., 1999—. Office: Am Med Response Inc 6200 S Syracuse Way Ste 200 Greenwood Village CO 80111-4739

GRALLA, EUGENE, natural gas company executive; b. NYC, May 3, 1924; s. Jacob and Anna Ruth (Kleiman) G.; m. Beverly Dorman, Apr. 7, 1946; children: Rhona Gralla Spilka, Steven Stuart. BS, U.S. Naval Acad., 1945; MBA, Harvard U., 1947. Commd. ensign USN, 1945, advanced through grades to comdr., 1961; served sea duty, 1947-49, 54-56; control officer (Naval Supply Depot, Guantanamo Bay), Cuba, 1959-61; with (Office Asst. Sec. Def. for Installations and Logistics), 1961-64; ret., 1966; dir. data systems planning Trans World Airlines, NYC, 1966-68; corp. dir. mgmt. info. systems Internat. Paper Co., NYC, 1968; v.p. electronic data processing Columbia Gas System Service Corp., Wilmington, Del., 1969-73; sr. v.p. Columbia Gas Distbn. Cos., Columbus, Ohio, 1973-86, pres., 1986-89, ret., 1989. Mem. Harvard Bus. Sch. Club, Palm Beach Club, Mil. Officers Assn. Am., Masons. Home: 7641 La Corniche Cir Boca Raton FL 33433-6007 Personal E-mail: bevandgene@aol.com.

GRALLA, LAWRENCE, publishing company executive; b. Bronx, NY, June 24, 1930; s. Meyer and Julia (Barnett) G.; m. Yvette Glickenstein, Dec. 24, 1952; children— Adele, Heidi. BS, CCNY, 1951, LHD (hon.), 2007. V.p. Nationwide Trade News Service, NYC, 1951-55; pres. Gralla Publs., NYC, 1955-87, exec. cons., 1987-2001; founding pub. Kitchen Bus., 1955, Bank Systems & Equipment, 1964, Multi-Housing News, 1966, Meeting News, 1977, Comml. Property News, 1988. Pres. Woodlands Community Temple, White Plains, N.Y., 1979-81. Recipient Govt. Israel Spl. Trade award 1980, Townsend Harris medal CCNY, 2002; named to Comm. Alumni Hall of Fame C.C.N.Y., 2000. Jewish.

GRALLA, MILTON, retired publisher; b. Bklyn., Jan. 28, 1928; s. Meyer and Julia (Barnett) G.; m. Shirley Edelson, Aug. 31, 1950; children— Edward, Karen, Dennis. BA in Journalism, CCNY, 1948; LHD (hon.), Yeshiva U., 1991. News reporter, 1948-51; co-founder nat. bus. news agy. NYC, 1951-55; co-founder, exec. v.p. Gralla Pubs., NYC, 1955-93; ret., 1993. Adj. prof. journalism NYU, Ramapo Coll., Yeshiva U., 1989—; del. leader Reawakening 1990-91, Moscow, 1990. Author: How Good Guys Grow Rich, 1995. Candidate for Congress, N.J., 1974; chmn. Israel Salute parade, 1993-94. Recipient major awards (trade) Govt. of Israel, (community service) Brandeis U., United Jewish Appeal, Orgn. Rehab. Through Tng., NCCJ, medal of honor Ellis Island. Mem. Friars Club, 24 Karat Club. Republican. Jewish. Personal E-mail: mittandshirley@aol.com.

GRAMES-LYRA, JUDITH ELLEN, artist, educator, municipal official; b. Inglewood, Calif., Feb. 7, 1938; d. Glover Victor and Dorothy Margaret (Burton-Bellingham) Hendrickson and Carolyne Marie Carrick Hendrickson (stepmother); children: Nanséa Ellen Ryan, Amber Jeanne Shelley-Harris, Carolyn Jane Angel Longmire, Susan Elaine Gomez, Robert Derek Shallenberger; m. Jon Robert Lyra, Feb. 14, 1997. Cert in journalism, Newspaper Inst. Am., NYC, 1960; AA, Santa Barbara City Coll., 1971; BA, U. Calif., Santa Barbara, 1978. Cert. tchr. Calif., 1979, tchr. K-12 adult 1983, bldg. insp., plumbing insp. Calif. Editor, reporter, photographer Goleta Valley Sun Newspaper, Santa Barbara, 1968-71; editor, team asst. Bur. of Ednl. Rsch. Devel., Santa Barbara, 1971; bus. writer, graphics cons. Santa Barbara, 1971-77; art and prodn. dir. Bedell Advt. Selling Improvement Corp., Santa Barbara, 1979-81; secondary sch. tchr. Coalinga Unified Sch. Dist., Calif., 1981-83; bldg. insp. aide Santa Barbara County, Lompoc, 1983-88, from bldg. engring. inspector I to III, 1988-99, asst. plans examiner, 1999—2003. Exhibited in group shows at Foley's Frameworks and Interiors, 1984, Grossman Gallery, 1984, 98, Lompoc Valley Art Assn., 1984— (Best of Show 1985, 1st pl. 1984, 94, 2002, 04, 05, 2d pl. 1984, 86, 88, 96-97, 99, 2007, 3d pl. 1987, 89, 97, 2003-05, Judge's Choice award 2004, others), Brushes and Blues Invitational, 1998; featured artist Harvest Arts Festival, 1989, Cypress Gallery, 1994, 2004; author numerous poems Mem. disaster response team Calif. Bldg. Ofcl., 1992-2003, cmty. emergency response team; exec. bd. dir. Lompoc Mural Soc., 1991-2003; planning commr. City of Lompoc. Recipient scholarship, Delta Kappa Gamma. Mem. NOW, Nat. Abortion Rights Action League, Nat. Mus. of Women in the Arts (charter), Nat. Womens History Mus. (charter), Lompoc Valley Art Assn. (bd. dirs.), Cypress Art Gallery (dir.), Toastmasters Internat. (Outstanding Spkr. award 1991-93). Avocations: painting, illustrating note cards, creative writing, home improvement.

GRAMLICH, EDWARD MARTIN, public policy educator, former federal official; b. Rochester, NY, June 18, 1939; s. Jacob Edward and Harriet (Williams) G.; m. Ruth Brown, Aug. 29, 1964; children: Sarah, Robert. BA in economics, Williams Coll., 1961; MA in economics, Yale U., 1962, PhD in economics, 1965. Mem. staff Fed. Res. Bd., 1965-70; dir. policy rsch. divsn. Office Econ. Opportunity, 1971—73; sr. fellow The Brookings Instn., 1973-76; prof. economics and pub. policy U. Mich., 1976—97, dir. Inst. Pub. Policy Studies, 1979-83, 1991—95, chmn. economics dept., 1983—86, dean Sch. Public Policy, 1995—97, interim provost & exec. v.p. acad. affairs, 2005—06, Richard A. Musgrave Collegiate Prof. Pub. Policy, 2005—06, prof. emeritus, 2006—; mem. bd. govs. Fed. Res. Sys., 1997—2005; Richard B. Fisher Sr. Fellow The Urban Inst., Washington, 2006—. Vis. lectr. Monash U., Australia, 1970, Stockholm U., 1979; adj. prof. George Washington U., 1974-75; vis. prof. Cornell U., 1975-76; cons. Res. Bank of Australia, 1970, Nat. Inst. Edn., 1973-75, US Dept. Labor, 1973-75, Health Edn. & Welfare, 1974—, Congl. Budget Office, 1975-78, Senate of Puerto Rico, 1975, Collier's Encyclopedia, 1975-79, Indsl. Research Inst., Sweden, 1979-81, Abt Assocs., 1979-80, Minimum Wage Study Commn., 1981, Fed. Res. Bd. Acad. Cons., 1981. Author: Savings Deposits, Mortgages and Housing in the FRB-Mit-Penn Econometric Model, 1972, Educational Performance Contracting: An Evaluation of an Experiment, 1975, Setting National Priorities: The 1975 Budget, 1974, Setting National Priorities: The 1976 Budget, 1975, Benefit-Cost Analysis of Governmental Programs, 1981, Tax Reform: There Must Be A Better Way, 1982. Editorial bd. National Tax Jour., 1970-73, Jour. Policy Analysis and Mgmt., 1980, Evaluation Review, 1980-83, Jour. Econ. Lit., 1981—. Contbr. articles to profl. jours. Mem. Brookings Panel on Economic Activity, 1973—, Brookings Panel on Social Experimentation, 1973-74, White House Summit Conf., 1974, Econ. Adv. Panel Nat. Inst. of Edn., 1973-74, Edn. Grants Panel, Nat. Inst. Edn., 1973-74, Edn. and Human Resources Adv. Bd., Rand Corp., 1975-78, Com. on Evaluation Research, Social Sci. Research Council, 1977-79, N.Y. State Productivity Commn., 1977-79, Assn. for Pub. Policy and Mgmt. (policy council 1979-84, v.p. 1979-80, program chmn. 1981), Nat. Acad. of Scis. Edn. Research Found., 1980—, State of Mich. Com. on Prof. and Occupational Licensure, 1981-82, Sime-Dime Rev. Panel, US Dept. Health & Human Services, 1980-81, Vis. Com. Albion Coll. Pub. Policy Sch., 1981—, Truman Scholarship Selection Panel, Michigan-Ohio, 1982—, Review Com., Md. Econs. Dept., 1993—, Chmn., Nat. Inst. of Edn. Policy Study Group, 1983. Office: The Urban Inst 2100 M St NW Washington DC 20037 also: U Mich 3074 Fleming Adminstrn Bldg Ann Arbor MI 48109-1340*

GRAMLICH, LARRY E., lawyer; b. Independence, Mo., 1961; BA, Valparaiso Univ., 1983; JD, Duke Univ., 1986. Bar: Ga. 1986. Assoc. Troutman Sanders LLP, Atlanta, 1986—94, ptnr., real estate fin., 1995—, practice leader, comml. develop. and real estate investments, 1998—2000, hiring ptnr., 2000—01. Mem.: ABA, Nat. Assn. Office and Industrial Properties, Atlanta Bar Assn., State Bar Ga. Office: Troutman Sanders LLP One Logan Sq Ste 5200 600 Peachtree St NE Atlanta GA 30308-2216 Office Phone: 404-885-3607. Office Fax: 404-962-6573. Business E-Mail: larry.gramlich@troutmansanders.com.

GRAMMER, KELSEY, actor; b. St. Thomas, V.I., Feb. 21, 1955; s. Sally and Allen Grammer; m. Camille Donatacci, Aug. 2, 1997; children: Mason Olivia, Jude Gordon; m. Doreen Alderman, May 30, 1982 (div. 1990); 1 child; m. Leigh-Anne Csuhany, Sept. 11, 1992 (div. 1993). Studied, Juilliard Sch., NYC. Actor (films) Toy Story 2 (voice), 1999, 15 Minutes, 1999, New Jersey Turnpikes, 1999, Standing on Fishes, 1999, The Real Howard Spitz, 1998, Down Periscope, 1996, (voice) Anastasia, 1997, X-Men: The Last Stand, 2006, (TV series) Cheers, 1984-93, Frasier, 1993-2004 (Best New Comedy award Viewers Quality TV, Favorite Male in New TV Series award 20th Ann. People's Choice Awards, Lead Actor Emmy award - Comedy Series, 1994, 1995, 98, Best Actor in TV Series Golden Globe award 1996, 2000, Emmy award Outstanding Lead Actress in a Comedy Series, 2004, other awards), 15 Minutes, 2001, Even Money, 2006; appeared in (Off-Broadway prodns.) Plenty, A Month in the Country, Sunday in the Park with George, Quartermaine's Terms, (Broadway prodns.) Macbeth, Othello, TV appearances include Kate and Allie (premiere episode), Wings, Tracy Ullman Show, The Simpsons, mini-series include Kennedy, 1983, George Washington, 1984, Crossings, 1986; TV movies include Dance 'til Dawn, 1988, Beyond Suspicion, 1993, (also exec. prodr.) The Innocent, 1994, London Suite, 1996, The Pentagon Wars, 1998, The Sports Pages, 2001; exec. prodr. (TV series) Fired Up, 1997, In-Laws, 2002, Gary the Rate, 2003, Medium, 2005-, Kelsey Grammer Presents: The Sketch Show, 2005; voice (video) Bartok the Magnificent, 1999, (TV) Animal Farm, 1999, The Hand Behind the Mouse: The Ub Iwerks Story, 1999; guest appearance Stark Raving Mad, 1999; dir.: (TV series) Out of Practice, 2005- Recipient SAG award, 2000. Office: The Artists Agency Ste 301 1180 S Beverly Dr Los Angeles CA 90035-1154*

GRAMMIG, ROBERT JAMES (BOB GRAMMIG), lawyer; b. Oceanside, Calif., June 15, 1956; s. Richard Adolf and Mary Elizabeth (Spisak) G.; m. Laurel Jean Lenfestey, Aug. 10, 1996; children: Clare Marie, James Richard, Grace Caroline, Julia Laurel. BA summa cum laude, U. Pa., 1978, MA, 1978; JD, Harvard U., 1981. Bar: Fla. 1982, DC 1986, US Dist. Ct. (mid. dist.) Fla. 1982, US Ct. Appeals (11th and 5th cirs.) 1982, US Supreme Ct. 1985. Law clk. to Hon. Thomas A. Clark US Ct. Appeals (5th and 11th cirs.), Atlanta, 1981-82; assoc. Holland & Knight LLP, Tampa, Fla., 1982-88, ptnr., 1989—, mem. dir. com., 1993—99, 2004—, nationwide practice group leader, securities law and pub. companies. Contbr. articles to profl. jours. Bd. dirs. Child Abuse Coun., Tampa, 1993-97; bd. govs. Crisis Ctr. Tampa Bay, 2006-; mem. Leadership Tampa, 1994-95; sec. Tampa Bay Internat. Trade Coun., 1994, vice chmn., 1995. Mem. Hillsborough County Bar Assn., Tampa Bay Coun. on Fgn. Rels., German Am. C. of C., US-Austrian C. of C., Phi Beta Kappa. Republican. Roman Catholic. Home: 21 Bahama Cir Tampa FL 33606-3317 Office: Holland & Knight LLP 100 N Tampa St Ste 4100 Tampa FL 33602-4322 Office Phone: 813-227-8500. Business E-Mail: rgrammig@hklaw.com.

GRANA, WILLIAM A., orthopedist, surgeon; m. Susan E. Eschrich, Aug. 21, 1965; children: William A. Jr., Beth L. Wing. MD, Harvard U., Cambridge, Mass., 1968; MPH, U. Okla., Oklahoma City, 1995. Dir. orthopaedic sports medicine Okla. Health Sciences Ctr., Oklahoma City, 1978—2000; med. dir. HCA/Okla. Ctr. Athletes, Oklahoma City, 1983—2000; orthopaedic surgeon, pres. Okla. Orthopaedics, Inc., Oklahoma City, 1995—2000; dir. rsch. orthopaedic surgery and reahab. U. Okla., Coll. Medicine, Oklahoma City, 1998—2000; orthopaedic surgeon U. Physicians Healthcare, Tucson, 2000—06; head dept. orthopaedic surgery U. Ariz., Tucson, 2000—. Contbr. articles to profl. jours. With USAF, 1970—72. Fellow: Am. Acad. Orthopaedic Surgeons (editor in chief Orthopaedic Knowledge Online 2001—); mem.: Arthroscopy Assn. N.Am., Am. Orthopaedic Soc. Sports Medicine (pres. 1995—96). Office: U of AZ Dept of Orthopaedic Surgery PO Box 245064 Tucson AZ 85724-5064 Office Phone: 520-626-4024.

GRANADE, CALLIE VIRGINIA SMITH, federal judge; b. Lexington, Va., Mar. 7, 1950; d. Milton Hannibal and Callie Dougherty (Rives) Smith; m. Fred King Granade, Oct. 9, 1976; children: Taylor Rives, Milton Smith, Joseph Kee. BA, Hollins Coll., 1972; JD, U. Tex., 1975. Bar: Tex. 1975, Ala. 1976, U.S. Ct. Appeals (5th cir.) 1976, U.S. Dist. Ct. (so. dist.) Ala. 1977, U.S. Supreme Ct. 1980, U.S. Ct. Appeals (11th cir.) 1981. Law clk. to chief judge John Godbold US Ct. Appeals (5th cir.), Montgomery, Ala., 1975-76; asst. US atty. US Dept. Justice, Mobile, 1977, sr. litigation counsel, 1987-90; chief criminal sect. US Atty.'s Office, Mobile, 1990-97; 1st asst. US Atty. Southern Dist. of Ala., 1997—2001, interim US Atty., 2001—02, judge, 2002—, chief judge, 2003—. Mem. ABA, Fed. Bar Assn., Ala. State Bar Assn., Tex. State Bar Assn., Mobile Bar Assn., Am. Coll. Trial Lawyers. Presbyterian. Office: US Courthouse 113 St Joseph St Mobile AL 36602

GRANAT, RICHARD STUART, lawyer, educator; b. NYC, Nov. 11, 1940; s. George and Judith G.; m. Nancy Ruth Wruble, Dec. 23, 1962; children: Lisa, Hilary, Peter, David. BA, Lehigh U., 1962; JD (Harlan Fiske Stone scholar), Columbia U., 1965. Bar: Md. 1966, D.C. 1977. Asst. counsel U.S. OEO, Washington, 1965-67, dir. housing programs, 1967-78; asst. dir. Model Cities Agy. Office of Mayor, Balt., 1968-69; dir. Cmty. Planning and Evaluation Inst., Balt., 1970-71; pres. Univ. Rsch. Corp. Mgmt. Svcs. Corp., Balt., 1970-77; pvt. practice Washington and Md., 1969—. Pres. Automated Lagal Systems, Inc., Phila., 1984—89; dir. MA in Legal Studies Program, Antioch Sch. Law, 1979—83; pres., chmn. bd. Ctr. for Legal Studies, Washington, 1979—89; chmn. bd. dirs. Ctr. Sch., Rockville, Md.; pres. Inst. Paralegal Tng., Inc., Phila., 1982—89, The Phila. Inst., 1987—89, Inst. for Employee Benefits Tng., 1986—89, The Inst. for Law and Tech., Phila., 1990—92, Interactive Legal Media, Inc., 1992—96; instr. Rutgers Sch. Law, Camden, NJ, 1992—94, Sch. Lang., U. Balt., 1995—96; adj. prof. Sch. Law, U. Md., 1994—96, dir. Ctr. for Law Practice Tech., 1994—, dir. Peoples Law Libr., 1996—2000, dir. Ctr. for On-Line Mediation, Inc., 1996—2000; pres. The Granat Group, LLC, Am. Law On Line, Inc., 2001—. Fellow Am. Bar Found., Coll. Law Practice Mgmt.; mem. ABA, Md. Bar Assn., D.C. Bar Assn. Home: 112 Via Condado Way Palm Beach Gardens FL 33418 Office: 800 Village Sq Ste 318 Palm Beach Gardens FL 33418 Office Phone: 561-214-1306, 561-656-2800. Personal E-mail: rgranat11@gmail.com. Business E-Mail: rgranat@mylawyer.com.

GRANATH, HERBERT A., television industry executive; b. NYC, 1928; Grad., Fordham U., 1954. Pres. Capital Cities/ABC Video Enterprises, Inc., NYC; chmn. ESPN Cable Network, Arts & Entertainment Cable Network, Lifetime Cable Network, Biography Channel, History Channel; founding ptnr. Eurosport; vice-chmn. TV Acad. Trustee Am. Mus. Moving Image; bd. dirs. Ctrl. European Media, Crown Media, Intl. Radio and TV Soc., others. Named to Rose d'Or Hall of Fame, 2005; recipient Two Tony awards, Emmy award, Lifetime Achievement in Sports TV, Lifetime Achievement in Intl. TV. Mem.: League NY Theater Owners & Producers, Trans-Atlantic Dialogue European Comm. Office: Capital Cities/ABC Video Enterprises Inc 77 W 66th St New York NY 10023-6201

GRANATI, DIANE ALANE, retired ophthalmic nurse; b. Bethlehem, Pa., Sept. 23, 1952; d. William Edward and Martha Lou (Bradford) Reichard; m. Joseph P. Granati, June 15, 2000. Diploma, Abington Meml. Hosp., Pa., 1973. Cert. RN in ophthalmology, Nat. Certifying Bd. Ophthalmic Registered Nurses, ophthalmic exec., Nat. Bd. Certification Ophthalmic Execs. Med.-surg. nurse St. Luke's Hosp., Bethlehem, 1973-76; ophthalmic nurse physician's office, Pitts., 1976-77, Everett & Hurite Ophthalmic Assocs., Pitts., 1977-80; exec. dir. Assocs. in Ophthalmology, Inc., Pitts., 1980—2005. Speaker in field. Contbr. articles to profl. jours. Mem. NAFE, Founders Soc., Am. Soc. Ophthalmic Registered Nurses, Abington Nurses Alumnae, Am. Soc. Ophthalmic Adminstrs. Home: 109 BEnt Birch Ln Beaver Falls PA 15010 Office: 500 Lewis Run Rd Ste 218 Pittsburgh PA 15122-3057 also: 125 Daugherty Dr Ste 320 Monroeville PA 15146-2749 also: 2 W Main St Ste 508 Uniontown PA 15401-3403 Address: Ste 230 300 Belmar Dr Pittsburgh PA 15205 also: 2000 Tower Way Ste 2037 Greensburg PA 15601 Personal E-mail: spacesongs@aol.com.

GRANATO, ANDREW VINCENT, physics professor, researcher; b. Cleve., May 9, 1926; s. Salvatore and Frances Granato; m. Pauline Brassard, June 21, 1956; children: Samuel, Andrea, Sarah, Ann. BS in Physics, Rennselaer Polytechnic Inst., Troy, NY, 1948, MS in Physics, 1950; PhD in Applied Math., Brown U., Providence, RI, 1955. Rsch. assoc. Brown U., 1955—57; rsch. asst. prof. U. Ill., Urbana, Ill., 1957—59, assoc. prof., 1961—64, prof., 1964—; vis. prof. Tech. Hsch Aachen, Germany, 1959—61. Contbr. articles to profl. jours. Recipient Zener medal, 1996; grantee, Guggenheim Found., 1960, Humboldt Found., 1976; Bernard T. Matthias scholar, 1987—88. Fellow: Am. Phys. Soc., Acoustical Soc. Am. (exec. com. divsn. condensed matter physics 1983—85). Home: 1917 Moraine Dr Champaign IL 61822 Office: Physics Dept Univ Ill 1101 W Green St Urbana IL 61801

GRANATO, CATHERINE (CAMMI GRANATO), former olympic athlete, sports association executive; b. Downers Grove, Ill., Mar. 25, 1971; d. Natalie and Don Granato; m. Ray Ferraro, Sept. 4, 2004. B in Social Sci.,

Providence Coll., 1993; student, Concordia U., 1994-97. Center US Nat. Women's Hockey Team, 1992—2005. Radio broadcaster LA Kings, 1998—99; rinkside reporter NHL on NBC, 2005—06; dir. devel. for women's hockey FASTHockey, Brookline, Mass., 2007—. Founder Golden Dreams for Children Found., 1999. Recipient Gold Medal, Women's Ice Hockey, Nagano Olympic Games, 1998, Silver Medal, Salt Lake City Olympic Games, 2002.*

GRANATSTEIN, JACK LAWRENCE, historian; b. Toronto, May 21, 1939; s. S. Benjamin and Shirley (Geller) G.; m. Mary Elaine Hitchcock, 1961; children: Carole, Michael (dec.) BA, Royal Mil. Coll., Kingston, Ont., 1961; MA, U. Toronto, 1962; PhD, Duke U., 1966; DLitt (hon.), Meml. U., 1993; LLD (hon.), U. Calgary, 1994, Ryerson Polytech. U., 1999, U. We. Ont., 2000, McMaster U., 2000, Niagara U., 2004. Historian Dept. Nat. Def., Ottawa, Ont., 1965-66; prof. history York U., 1966-95, Disting. rsch. prof. history emeritus, 1995—; Rowell Jackman fellow Canadian Inst. of Internat. Affairs, 1995-98; commr. Spl. Commn. on the Restructuring of the Can. Forces Reserves, 1995; CEO, dir. Can. War Mus., 1998-2000; chair Coun. for Can. Security in 21st Century, 2001—05. Author: Politics of Survival, 1967, Canada's War, 1975, Broken Promises, 1977, Ties That Bind, 1977, American Dollars-Canadian Prosperity, 1978, A Man of Influence, 1981, The Ottawa Men, 1982, Twentieth Century Canada, 1983, The Great Brain Robbery, 1984, Canada 1957-67, 1986, Sacred Trust? Brian Mulroney and the Conservatives in Power, 1986, The Collins Dictionary of Canadian History, 1988, Marching to Armageddon, 1989, How Britain's Weakness Forced Canada into the Arms of the United States, 1989, A Nation Forged in Fire, 1989, Pirouette: Pierre Trudeau and Canadian Foreign Policy, 1990, Mutual Hostages: Canadians and Japanese in the Second World War, 1990, Spy Wars, Espionage and Canada from Gouzenko to Glasnost, 1990, For Better or Worse: Canada and the U.S. to the 1990's, War and Peacekeeping, 1991, English Canada Speaks Out, 1991, Oxford Dictionary of Canadian Military History, 1992, The Generals: The Canadian Army's Senior Commanders in the Second World War, 1993, Empire to Umpire: Canada and the World to the 1990's, 1994, The Good Fight: Canadians and World War II, 1995, Victory 1945: Canadians From War to Peace, 1995, Yankee Go Home? Canadians and Anti-Americanism, 1997, The Canadian 100, 1997, Petrified Campus: The Crisis of Canada's Universities, 1997, The Veterans Charter and Post World War II Canada, 1998, Who Killed Canadian History?, 1998, Trudeau's Shadow, 1998, Prime Ministers, 1999, Our Century, 2000, Canada's Army, 2002, First Drafts, 2002, Importance of Being Less Earnest, 2003, Who Killed the Canadian Military?, 2004, Hell's Corner, 2004, Battle Lines, 2005, The Last Good War, 2005, The Land Newly Found, 2006, Whose War Is It?, 2007. Bd. govs. Royal Mil. Coll., 1996-2005, Can. Def. and Fgn. Affairs Inst., 2004—. Served to lt. Can. Army, 1956-66. Recipient Tyrrell medal for Can. history, 1992, J.W. Dafoe prize, 1993, medal for biography U. B.C., 1993, Vimy award Conf. Def. Assns. Inst., 1996, Pierre Berton prize 2004, Lela Common award, 2005; Killam rsch. fellow Can. Coun., 1982-84, 91-93; rsch. grantee Can. Dept. External Affairs, 1978-80, Can. Dept. Nat. Def., 1987-88, Social Sci. and Humanities Rsch. Coun. Can., 1978-79, 82-84, 85-89, 91-97; named officer Order of Can., 1997. Fellow Royal Soc. Can. Home: 52 St Andrews Gardens Toronto ON Canada M4W 2E1 Home Phone: 416-923-5521. Personal E-mail: jgranatstein@bellnet.ca.

GRANATSTEIN, VICTOR LAWRENCE, electrical engineer, educator; b. Toronto, Ont., Can., Feb. 8, 1935; s. Charles Samuel and Bella (Godfrey) G.; m. Bethie Mills, Sept. 4, 1955; children: Rebecca Miriam, Abraham Solomon, Annie Sara Khaya. BS, Columbia U., 1960, MS, 1961, PhD, 1963. Rsch. staff physicist Bell Tel. Labs., Murray Hill, NJ, 1964-72; head high power electromagnetic radiation br. Naval Rsch. Lab., Washington, 1972-83; prof. elec. engring. U. Md., College Park, 1983—, acting dir. Inst. for Plasma Rsch., 1986-88, dir., 1988-98. Vis. lectr. Hebrew U., Jerusalem, 1969—70; vis. prof. Tel Aviv U., 1994, 2003, Sackler prof. of spl. standing, 2004—; cons. BDM Corp., McLean, Va., 1981—83, Sci. Applications Corp., McLean, Va., 1983—, Omega-P Inc., New Haven, 1983—2000, Pulse Scis. Inc., San Leandro, Calif., 1985—88, Jet Propulsion Lab., Pasadena, Calif., 1987—91, Mission Res. Corp., Newington, Va., 2001—06, BAE Sys., Inc., Washington, 2006—. Author: Physical Principles of Wireless Communications, 2007; editor: Wave Heating and Current Drive in Magnetic Plasmas, 1985, High Power Microwaves, 1987, Applications of High Power Microwaves, 1994; contbr. articles to profl. jours.; patentee microwave devices. Pres. Bethesda-Chevy Chase Jewish Cmty. Group, 1983—84. Recipient R.D. Conrad award Sec. Navy, 1981, Superior Civilian Svc. award Office Naval Rsch., 1980, E.O. Hulbert award Naval Rsch. Lab., 1980, Robert L. Woods award Sec. Def., 1998; Fulbright sr. scholar, 1993-94, Fulbright sr. specialist, 2003, 2004-05. Fellow IEEE (life, vice chmn. plasma sci. com. 1984-85, Plasma Sci. and Applications award 1991), Am. Phys. Soc. Democrat. Avocations; folk dancing, swimming. Home: 13508 Rippling Brook Dr Silver Spring MD 20906-3177 Office: U Md Inst Rsch in Electronics and Applied Physics College Park MD 20742-3511 Office Phone: 301-405-4956. Business E-Mail: vlg@umd.edu.

GRANBERRY, EDWIN PHILLIPS, JR., safety engineer, consultant; b. Orange, NJ, Aug. 20, 1926; s. Edwin Phillips Sr. and Mabel (Leflar) G.; m. Joanne Park, June 15, 1991; children: Melissa, Edwin Phillips III, James, Jennifer, Claudia. BS, Rollins Coll., 1950; MBA, Embry Riddle Aero. U., 1985. Cert. profl. chemist. Weapons sys. engr. Martin Co., Orlando, Fla., 1958-62; supt. indsl. safety Guided Missiles Range divsn. Pan Am. World Airways, Cape Canaveral, Fla., 1962-72; mgr. indsl. hygiene/safety engring. Pratt & Whitney Aircraft, West Palm Beach, Fla., 1972-88; mgr. indsl. and sys. safety engring. Chem. Sys. divsn. United Tech. Corp., San Jose, Calif., 1988-89; pres. Granberry & Assocs. Inc., Winter Park, Fla., 1989—. Adj. faculty Valencia C.C., Orlando; mem. Fla. State Toxic Substances Adv. Coun., 1984-88, Fla. State Emergency Response Commn., 1988, Fla. Divsn. Safety Customer Adv. Coun.; mem. restoration adv. bd. U.S. Naval Tng. Sta., Orlando, 1996—. Scoutmaster Boy Scouts Am., 1946-74, dist. chmn. Wekiwa dist. Ctrl. Fla. coun., 1946-74, also coun. commr. Served with USNR, 1944-54, PTO. Recipient Silver Beaver award Boy Scouts Am., 1960. Fellow Am. Inst. Chemists; mem. ASTM, Welding Soc., Am. Chem. Soc., Am. Bd. Forensic Examiners, Am. Nat. Stds. Inst., Nat. Fire Protection Assn., Rollins Coll. Alumni Assn. (bd. dirs. 1958-61), Am. Soc. Safety Engrs. (chmn. Gold Coast chpt. 1979-90, pres. 1981-84, regional v.p. 1984-88, 94—, v.p. divsns. 1988-90, adminstr. environ. divsn. 1992—, nat. bd. dirs. 1984-90, 94—), Am. Soc. Safety Engrs. Found. (chmn. 1997—, Saftey Profl. of Yr. Fla., Ga., P.R. chpts., 1985, Saftey Profl of Yr. divs., 1991, Saftey Profl. of Yr. Environ. Divsn. 1995-96), Safety Coun. Palm Beach County (pres. 1981-82, chmn. bd. 1983, treas. 1984). Home: 521 Langholm Dr Winter Park FL 32789-5251 Office: Granberry & Assocs Inc 2431 Aloma Ave Ste 276 Winter Park FL 32792-2566

GRAND, MARCIA, civic worker; b. NYC, Aug. 9, 1933; d. Irving and Dorothy (Miller) Kosta; m. Richard Grand, Jan. 27, 1952. Student, U. Ariz., 1950-52, 59-60. Docent, coord., docent trainer Tucson Mus. Art, 1965-71, bd. dirs., 1972-79, chmn. edn. com., 1975-79; v.p., sec. Richard Grand Found., 1966-80, pres., 1980—. Bd. dirs., sec. U. Ariz. Found., 1979-80, v.p., 1986-87, chmn. exec. com., 1986-87; mem. spl. com. office of chair U. Ariz., 1987-92; bd. dirs. Tucson Airport Authority, Greenfield Schs., 1977-82; bd. fellows Ctr. Creative Photography, 1984-98, chmn., 1993-98, mem.-at-large, bd. dirs. Tucson Mus. Art League, 1977-78; bd. trustees San Francisco Art Inst., 1995-2003. Nominated for YWCA Woman on the Move award, 1982; recipient Cmty. Svc. award Mortar Bd., 1978, Disting. Citizen award U. Ariz. Coll. Fine Arts, 1979. Office: 6870 N Andrea Doria Dr Tucson AZ 85704 Personal E-mail: rg@rgrand.com.

GRAND, RICHARD D., lawyer; b. Danzig, Feb. 20, 1930; came to U.S., 1939, naturalized, 1944; s. Morris and Rena Grand; m. Marcia Kosta, Jan. 27, 1952. BA, NYU, 1951; JD, U. Ariz., Tucson, 1958. Bar: Ariz. 1958, Calif. 1973, U.S. Supreme Ct. 1973; cert. specialist in injury litigation Ariz. Bd. Legal Specialization. Dep. atty., Pima County, Ariz., 1958-59; pvt. practice trial law Tucson, 1959—; founder, 1st pres. Inner Circle Advocates, 1972-75; founder Richard Grand Found., 1966, now chmn.; hon. pres. Richard Grand Soc., 1997—. Contbr. articles to legal publs. Mem. bd. visitors law sch. Ariz. State U. Recipient citation of honor Lawyers Coop. Pub. Co., 1964, Profl. Achievement award U. Ariz., 2002. Fellow Am. Acad. Forensic Scis., Internat. Soc. Barristers; mem. Internat. Med. Soc. Paraplegia (assoc.), Am. Coll. Legal Medicine (assoc.), ABA, Pima County Bar Assn., Am. Bd. Trial Advs. (cert. in civil trial advocacy), Brit. Acad. Forensic Scis., Richard Grand Soc. (hon. pres.), Bohemian Club. Office: 6870 N Andrea Doria Dr Tucson AZ 85704 Office Phone: 520-622-8855. Business E-Mail: RG@rgrand.com. *His thinking is his passport. Dream—there is no charge for alterations. The Jury grows a communal nose with which it smells out the strengths and weaknesses of a case.*

GRANDI, ATTILIO, engineering consultant; b. La Spezia, Italy, Sept. 24, 1929; s. Luigi and Egle (Canese) G.; m. Maria Teresa Berti, Apr. 23, 1962; 1 child, Giovanni Maturita scientifica, Liceo Scientifico Pacinotti, La Spezia, 1949; univ. degree in aero. engring., Pisa U., Italy, 1958. Project engr. S.p.A. Piaggio, Pontedera, Italy, 1959-60, Termomeccanica Italiana, La Spezia, 1960-71, tech. mgr., 1971-85, rsch. and mktg. mgr., 1985-88; cons. hydraulic machinery refrigeration and marine propulsive systems, 1988—. Patentee in field Mem. Italian Standard Hydraulic Machinery Roman Catholic. Avocations: mathematics, old languages, fishing.

GRANDI, LOIS A., theater director, choreographer, actor; b. Phila., June 9, 1941; d. John R. and Rosina H.R. Grandinetti; m. Robert Leonard Sieben (div.); children: Laurey Dawn Heinrich, Paul Leonard Sieben. Student, Keith Davis Voice Studio, NYC, 1963—70, Neighborhood Playhouse, 1964—70, Met. Opera Ballet. Actress PBS, San Francisco, 1983; acting tchr. Performing Arts Acad., Walnut Creek, Calif., 1984—; dir. Willows Theatre Co., Concord, Calif., 1990—91, Calif. Conservatory Theatre, San Leandro, Calif., 1992—94; artistic dir. Playhouse West, Walnut Creek, 1995—. Music Man, Merry Widow, Little Me, The Rainmaker, The World Goes 'Round; dir., dir.: The Boy Friend, (Best Entire Prodn., Best Dir. awards), Betrayal, After the Fall, New Wrinkles (3 Critic's Cir. awards), Force of Nature, Taking Sides, Proof (Best Dir., 03), Whispers on the Wind (Best Dir., Critic's Cir.); actor: Light Sensitive (Best Actress Critic's Cir., 00), Lovers and Other Strangers, Two For the Seesaw, Smile, Oklahoma!, Carousel, The Sound of Music; actor, actor: The Boy Friend, (Best Entire Prodn., Best Dir. awards), He Who Gest Slapped, Very Good Eddie, Finian's Rainbow, West Side Story, (PBS TV series) Up and Coming, numerous training and indsl. films, commls.; guest dancer The White House. Recipient recognition, Arts and Culture Commn. Contra Costa County, 1998, 10 Drama-Logue awards, 1997; honored by State Sen. Tom Torlakson and Assemblywoman Lynne Leache for contbn. to arts, 2002. Mem.: SAG, AFTRA, Actors Equity Assn. (mem. adv. bd. 1975). Democrat. Avocations: classical music, piano. Home: 2245 Gladwin Dr Walnut Creek CA 94596

GRANDIN, TEMPLE, industrial designer, science educator; b. Boston, Aug. 29, 1947; d. Richard McCurdy and Eustacia (Cutler) Grandin. BA in Psychology, Franklin Pierce Coll., 1970; MS in Animal Sci., Arizona State U., 1975; PhD in Animal Sci., U. Ill., Urbana, 1989; D (hon.), McGill U., 1999. Livestock editor Ariz. Farmer Ranchman, Phoenix, 1973-78; equipment designer Corral Industries, Phoenix, 1974-75; ind. cons. Grandin Livestock Systems, Urbana, 1975-90, Fort Collins, Colo., 1990—; lectr., prof. animal sci. dept. Colo. State U., Fort Collins, 1990—. Chmn. handing com. Livestock Conservation Inst., Madison, Wis., 1976—; surveyor USDA. Author: Emergence Labelled Autistic, 1986, Recommended Animal Handling Guidelines for Meat Packers, 1991, Livestock Handling and Transport, 1993, 3d edit., 2007, Thinking in Pictures, 1995, Genetics and the Behavior of Domestic Animals, 1998, Beef Cattle Behavior Handling and Facilities Design, 2000, Animals in Translation, 2005 (One of Top Sci. Books of Yr., 2005), Developing Talents, 2005, Unwritten Rules of Social Relationships, 2005; contbr. articles to profl. jours. Named Woman of Yr. in Svc. to Agr. Progressive Farmer, 1999; named one of Processing Stars of 1990, Nat. Provisioner, 1990; recipient Meritorious Svcs. award Livestock Conservation, Madison, Wis., 1986, Disting. Alumni award Franklin Pierce Coll., 1989, Industry Innovators award Meat Mktg. and Tech. Mag., 1994, Brownlee award for internat. leadership in sci. publ. promoting respect for animals Animal Welfare Found. of Canada, 1995, Harry Roswell award Scientists Ctr. for Animal Welfare, 1995, Humane Ethics in Action award Geraldine R. Dodge Found., 1998, Forbes award Nat. Meat Assn., 1998, Founders award Am. Soc. Prevention Cruelty Animals, 1999, Humane award Am. Vet. Med. Assn., 1999, Joseph Wood Krutch award, Humane Soc. of U.S., 2001, Knowlton Innovation award in Meat Mktg. and Tech. Mag., 2001, 2002, Animal Welfare award, Brit. Soc. Animal Sci. and Royal Soc. Prevention Cruelty to Animals, 2002, Pres.'s award, Nat. Inst. Animal Agr., 2004. Mem.: Am. Soc. Agrl. Cons. (bd. dirs. 1981—83), Am. Registry Profl. Animal Scis., Am. Meat Inst. (supplier mem., Industry Advancement award 1995), Am. Soc. Agrl. Engrs., Am. Soc. Animal Sci. (Animal Mgmt. award 1995, Disting. Svc. award We. sect. 2003), Autism Soc. Am. (bd. dirs. 1988—, Trammel Crow award 1989). Republican. Episcopalian. Achievements include patents in field; design of stockyards and humane restraint equipment for major meat packing companies in the U.S., Canada and Australia; development of objective scoring system used for monitoring animal welfare in slaughter plants. Office: Colo State U Animal Sci Dept Fort Collins CO 80523-0001 Office Phone: 970-229-0703.

GRANDISON, TYRONE WILBERFORCE ANDRÉ, systems administrator; b. Kingston, Jamaica, June 15, 1976; s. Lloyd and Pearline Grandison. BSc in Computer Studies and Econs., U. WI, Mona, Jamaica, 1997, MSc in Software Engring., 1998; PhD in Security and Trust Mgmt. for Distributed Sys., Imperial Coll. Sci., Tech. and Medicine, London, 2003. Cert. Internat. Sch. Foundations Security Analysis and Design, 2003, relational database sys. developer Brainbench, 1999; exec. MBA IBM Acad. Edn., IBM T J. Watson Ctr., 2005. Lectr. U. WI, 1999; tutor, tchg. asst., technician Imperial Coll., 1999—2002; internat. intern Distributed Systems Tech. Ctr., U. Queensland, Brisbane, Australia, 2002; sr. software engr. IBM Almaden Rsch. Ctr., San Jose, Calif., 2003—05, mgr, data disclosure rsch., 2005—. Reviewer NSF, Arlington, Va., 2006—. Author: numerous poems; contbr. chapters to books. V.p. IBM Silicon Valley Black Employee Network, San Jose, 2007. Scholar Overseas Rsch. award, Brit. Govt., 1999—2003, Microsoft, 1999—2002; Caribbean Grad. scholar, ScotiaBank, 1999—2003. Mem.: IEEE, Internat. Assn. Privacy Profls., Healthcare Info. and Mgmt. Systems Soc., Am. Med. Informatics Assn., Nat. Soc. Black Engrs., Assn. Computing Machinery. Achievements include research in data disclosure management relevant and applicable to industry verticals; privacy-preserving data management of distributed RFID data sources; privacy-preserving data management and application deployment for mobile devices. Office: IBM Almaden Rsch Ctr 650 Harry Rd San Jose CA 95120 Office Phone: 408-927-1951. Office Fax: 408-927-3215. Business E-Mail: tyroneg@us.ibm.com.

GRANDMAISON, J. JOSEPH, federal agency administrator; b. Nashua, NH, May 19, 1943; s. Oscar N. and Irene P. (Bouchard) G. BA, Burdett Coll., 1963. Campaign dir. Dukakis for Gov., Boston, 1973-74; dir. fed. state relations Commonwealth of Mass., Washington, 1975—; Dem. candidate U.S. Ho. of Reps., 1976; fellow John F. Kennedy Inst. Politics Harvard U., 1976—; fed. co-chmn. New Eng. Regional Commn., Washington, 1977-81; econ. devel. and polit. cons. Augusta, Maine, 1981—93; v.p. Weil & Howe, Augusta, 1983—93; commentator, polit. analyst Sta. WMUR-TV, Manchester, 1986—; dir. U.S. Trade and Devel. Agy., Washington, 1993—2001. Adj. prof. Boston U. Coll. Communications; co-host Focus N.H., 1987-90; bd. dirs. U.S. Export-Import Bank. Mem. bd. aldermen, Nashua, NH, 1970—71; chair N.H. Dem. Party, 1987—90; dem. nominee Gov. of N.H., 1990. Democrat. Roman Catholic. Office: US Export Import Bank Bd of Dir 811 Vermont Ave NW Washington DC 20571-0001 Office Phone: 202-565-3530.

GRAND-MAITRE, JEAN, performing company executive; b. Hull, Quebec; Studied at, York U., Montreal's L'Ecole superieure de danse du Quebec, 1983—86. Ind. choreographer Can. and Europe, 1990—2002; artistic dir. Alberta Ballet, 2002—. Danced with Theatre Ballet of Can., 1987—89, Les Ballets de Montreal Eddy Toussaint, 1990, Ballet British Columbia, 1991; artist in residence Bayerisches Staatsballet, 1998—99, Nat. Norwegian Ballet, 1999—2000. Major commissions include La Veglia degli Angeli, Teatro all Scala, Milan, 1995, Exilium, Stuggart Ballet, 1997, Eja Mater, Paris Opera Ballet, 1997, Ecclesia and Emma B., Bavarian State Ballet, Munich, 1998, 1999, Liaisons Dangereuses, Nat. Ballet of Norway, 2000, Frames of Mind, Hartford Ballet, 1995, Ancient Airs and Uroboros, 1996, 1999, Romeo and Juliet, Dance Conneticut, 2000, The Winter Room, Ballet BC, 1995, Boy Wonder, 1996, Tema Celeste, 2000, La Memoire de l'eau, Les Grand Ballets Canadiens, 1997, Carmen, 2002, Cinderella, 2004, Alberta Ballet, Vigil of Angels, 2004, Dangerious Liasons, 2004, Romeo and Juliet, 2005. Nominee Dora Mavor Moore award. Office: Alberta Ballet Nat Christie Ctr 141-18 Ave South West Calgary AB T2S 0B8 Canada Office Phone: 403-245-4222 ext. 523. Business E-Mail: jeang@albertaballet.com.

GRANDMASTER FLASH, (JOSEPH SADDLER), disc jockey; b. Bridgetown, Barbados, Jan. 1, 1958; Founder Grandmaster Flash & the Furious Five. Musician: (albums) The Message, 1982, Greatest Messages, 1983, They Said It Couldn't Be Done, 1985, The Source, 1986, Ba Dop Boom Bang, 1987, On the Strength, 1988, Old School Rap 3, 1996, Sal Soul Jam 2000, 1997, Essential Mix: Classic Edit., 2002, The Official Adventures of Grandmaster Flash, 2004, Mixing Bullets & Firing Joints, 2005; mus. dir. (TV series) The Chris Rock Show, 1998—2002; performer: Super Bowl, 1998, Commonwealth Games, Manchester, Eng., 2002. Named to Bronx Walk of Fame, with the Furious Five, 2004, Rock & Roll Hall of Fame, with the Furious Five, 2007; recipient Pioneer award, Source mag., New Music Seminar Hall of Fame award, DMC Hall of Fame award, Diamond award, BET (Black Entertainment TV), DJ Vanguard award, 2004, Key to the City, Cin., OH, 2004, Blast Cmty. award, 2004, Lifetime Achievement award, RIAA, 2005, VHI's Hip Hop honors, with the Furious Five, 2005, I AM HIP HOP Lifetime Achievement award, BET Hip-Hop Awards, 2006. Achievements include pioneer in the development of the Hip-Hop musical genre; first DJ to use turntables as musical instruments; development of DJ techniques including cutting, Quick Mix Theory, Fake Phasing, and Clock Theory; first DJ and Hip-Hop artist to be inducted into the Rock & Roll Hall of Fame. Office: Grandmaster Flash Enterprises Ste E7 600 Johnson Ave Bohemia NY 11716 Office Phone: 613-218-2942. Office Fax: 613-218-2619.*

GRANDMASTER MELLE MEL, See GLOVER, MELVIN

GRANDSAERT, JOHN LEO, judge; b. San Francisco, Dec. 2, 1952; s. Alphonse Ramond and Jeannette Christine (Van Workum) G.; m. Regina Kathryn Geraty (dec. 2004), Mar. 22, 1980; children: John C., Katie M., Patrick J. BSBA, U. San Francisco, 1974; JD, U. Calif., San Francisco, 1977; LLM in Taxation, Golden Gate U., 1981. Bar: Calif. 1977, U.S. Dist. Ct. (no. dist.) Calif. 1977, U.S. Dist. Ct. (ctrl. dist.) Calif. 1984. Assoc. Hunt & Hunt, San Francisco, 1977-84; dep. dist. atty. Riverside County, Riverside, Calif., 1984-87, San Mateo County, Redwood City, Calif., 1987—2004; judge San Mateo County Superior Ct., 2004—. Contbg. author: Criminal Law and Procedure, 2d edit., 1994, 3d edit., 1997. Maj. USAR, 1978-93. Mem. Calif. State Bar (adminstrn. of justice com. 1987-89), San Mateo County Bar Assn., Redwood City C. of C., Alpha Sigma Nu. Republican. Roman Catholic. Office: San Mateo County Superior Ct Presiding Criminal Judge 400 County Ctr Redwood City CA 94062 Office Phone: 650-877-5769.

GRANDY, WALTER THOMAS, JR., physicist, researcher; b. Phila., June 1, 1933; s. Walter Thomas and Margaret Mary (Hayes) G.; m. Patricia Josephine Langan, Dec. 27, 1955; children: Christopher, Neal, Mary, Jeanne. BS, U. Colo., 1960, PhD, 1964. Physicist Nat. Bur. Standards, Boulder, Colo., 1958-63; mem. faculty U. Wyo., Laramie, 1963—, prof. physics, 1969-98, head dept., 1971-78; prof. emeritus, 1998—. Fulbright lectr. U. Sao Paulo, Brazil, 1966-67, vis. prof., 1982; vis. prof. U. Tubingen, W. Germany, 1978-79, U. Sydney, Australia, 1988. Author: Introduction to Electrodynamics and Radiation, 1970, Foundations of Statistical Mechanics: Volume I, Equilibrium Theory, 1987, Vol. II, Nonequilibrium Phenomena, 1988, Relativistic Quantum Mechanics of Leptons and Fields, 1991, Scattering of Waves from Spherical Targets, 2000. Served with USNR, 1953-57. Fellow AAAS; mem. Am. Phys. Soc., Brasilian Phys. Soc., Am. Assn. Physics Tchrs., Sigma Xi, Sigma Pi Sigma. Achievements include rsch. on statis. mechanics, electrodynamics, quantum theory. Business E-Mail: wtg@uwyo.edu.

GRANGER, CLIVE WILLIAM JOHN (SIR CLIVE GRANGER), retired economist; b. Swansea, Wales, Sept. 4, 1934; arrived in U.S., 1974; s. Edward John and Evelyn Agnes (Hessey) G.; m. Patricia Anne Loveland, May 14, 1960; children: Mark, Claire. BA, U. Nottingham, Eng., 1955, PhD in Stats., 1959, DSc, 1992; DSc (hon.), Carlos III, Madrid, 1997; D in Econs. (hon.), Stockholm Sch. Econs., 1998; DSc (hon.), Loughborough U., 2002. Lectr. in math. U. Nottingham, 1956—64, prof. stats., 1964—74; prof. econs. U. Calif., San Diego, 1976—2002, chancellor's assoc. chair, 1994—2002; ret., 2003. Author: Forecasting Stock Markets, 1970; editor: Commodity Markets, 1973. Decorated knight bachelor Royal Order Queen Elizabeth of Britain, 2005; fellow Harkness Fund, 1959-60, Econometric Soc., 1973, Guggenheim Found., 1988, recipient Nobel Prize in Econs., 2003. Fellow: Am. Econ. Soc. (Disting.), Am. Acad. Arts and Scis., Brit. Acad. (corr.). Avocations: hiking, swimming, travel, reading. Office: U Calif San Diego Econs Dept D-008 La Jolla CA 92093 Office Phone: 858-534-3856. Business E-Mail: cgranger@ucsd.edu.

GRANGER, DAVID, editor; b. Oct. 31, 1956; married. BA, U. Tenn.; MA in Eng., U. Va. Formerly with Muppet Mag., Family Weekly, Sport Mag., Sports Inc., Nat. Sports Daily, Adweek/Mediaweek, Gentleman's Quarterly; editor-in-chief Esquire Mag. Recipient Nat. Magazine award for Writing, Am. Soc. Mag. Editors, 2007. Office: Esquire Inc 21241 Bentura Blvd Woodland Hills CA 91364*

GRANGER, HARVEY, JR., retired manufacturing executive; b. Savannah, Ga., Sept. 9, 1928; s. Harvey and Marion (Rauers) G.; m. Barbara Brandt, Sept. 8, 1951; children: Harvey, Matthew Brandt, Barbara James. B in Indsl. Engring., Ga. Inst. Tech, 1951. Indsl. engr. Union Camp Paper Co., Savannah, 1950-56, Great Dane Trailers, Savannah, 1956-61, plant mgr., 1961-71, v.p. mfg., 1971-78, exec. v.p., chief operating officer, 1978-84, pres., chief exec. officer, 1984-91; cons. Savannah, 1992-96; ret., 1996. City adv. bd. dirs. Nations Bank, Savannah, 1979-95. Mem. adv. bd. Sch. Engring. Ga. Inst. Tech., 1985-91; mem. bd. trustees St. Joseph's Hosp., Savannah, 1988-97, vice-chmn. 1995, chmn. 1996-97; chmn. bd. trustees St. Joseph's-Candler Health Sys., Savannah, 1997-2000, vice chmn., 2000—03; dir. vol. trustees Not-For-Profit Hosps., Washington,

1995—2003, mem. exec. com., 1997, sec., 1998, vice chmn., 1999—2003. With USN, 1945-47. Mem. Truck Trailer Mfrs. Assn. (chmn. 1986-87). Clubs: Oglethorpe (Savannah) (pres. 1984-85), Savannah Golf. Avocations: golf, fishing. Home: 405 Coveview Dr Savannah GA 31406-3204

GRANGER, KAY, congresswoman; b. Greenville, Tex., Jan. 18, 1943; children: John Dean, Chelsea, Brandon. BS magna cum laude, Tex. Wesleyan U., 1965, DHL (hon.); D in Pub. Svc. (hon.), Tenn. Wesleyan Coll. Prin., owner G&R Ins. Agy., Ft. Worth, Kay Granger & Assocs.; mem. zoning com. City of Ft. Worth, 1981—89; mem. pvt. industry coun., 1988-89; mem. City Coun., Ft. Worth, 1989-91; mayor Ft. Worth, 1991-95; mem. US Congress from 12th Tex. dist., 1997—, dep. majority whip, mem. appropriations com. Bd. visitors USAF Acad.; bd. trustees Southwestern U. Author: What's Right About America?, 2006. Recipient Woman of Yr. award, 1987, Bus. and Profl. Woman award, 1987, YMCA Congl. award, 2004, Nat. Assn. Mfrs. award, PE4LIFE Legislator of Yr. award, 2004, Cmty. Health Defender award Nat. Assn. Cmty. Health Ctrs., 2006; named Exec. of Yr., Ft. Worth Bus. Hall of Fame, 1999; inductee Tex. Women's Hall of Fame, 1999. Mem. Am. Planning Assn., Internat. Sister Cities Assn., Women's Policy Forum (bd. dirs.), East Ft. Worth Bus. and Profl. Assn. (bd. dirs.), Ft. Worth Bus. and Estate Planning Coun., Meadowbrook Bus. and Profl. Womens Assn., East Ft. Worth C. of C. (vice chmn.). Republican. Methodist. Office: US Ho Reps 440 Cannon Ho Office Bldg Washington DC 20515 Office Phone: 202-225-5071.*

GRANGER, PHILIP RICHARD, minister; b. Detroit, June 19, 1943; s. Myrl Richard and Alvirta May (Kling) Granger; m. Karen Elizabeth Draper, Feb. 20, 1965 (div. 1972); children: Mark, Leslie; m. Susan Kay Alderfer, Mar. 4, 1973; children: Randall, Candace. AA, Jackson Jr. Coll., 1963; BA, MBA, Mich. State U., 1965-67; MDiv, No. Bapt. Theol. Sem., Lombard, Ill., 1978; D in Ministry, Oral Roberts U., 1986. CPA Mich.; ordained deacon United Meth. Ch., 1977, ordained elder United Meth. Ch., 1980. Audit staff, cons. Ernst & Ernst, Detroit, 1967-71; mem. contrs. staff Assocs. Corp., South Bend, Ind., 1971-73; v.p., contr. 1st Fed. Savs. and Loan, Chgo., 1973-76; pastor Mokena (Ill.) United Meth. Ch., 1976-82; dir. fin. No. Ind. Conf. United Meth. Ch., Marion, 1982-86; sr. pastor St. Lukes United Meth. Ch., Kokomo, Ind., 1986-89, Trinity United Meth. Ch., Huntington, Ind., 1989-94; dist. supt. Kokomo (Ind.) Dist. United Meth. Ch., 1994-99; sr. pastor Coll. Ave. United Meth. Ch., Muncie, Ind., 1999—2001; pres., CEO Mission Soc., 2001—. New life missioner Gen. Bd. Discipleship, Nashville, 1980—; mem. adj. faculty Huntington Coll., 1990—94; past chmn. bd. dirs. Good News, Wilmore, Ky., Samaritan Ctr., Inc., Huntington Found. Mission and Ministry, Inc., Marion; del. gen. conf. United Meth. Ch., 1988, 92, 96, 2000; bd. dirs. Ch. & Soc., Washington, 1996—2004. Author: Discerment Planning, 1986. Founding mem. Tri-Village Crisis Intervention Ctr., Mokena, 1978—81; bd. dirs. Mental Health Assn. Ill., Chgo., 1974—75; treas. Village of Mokena, 1978—82. Mem.: Am. Assn. Christian Counselors, Rotary, Beta Alpha Psi, Beta Gamma Sigma, Delta Sigma Pi. Avocations: reading, travel, computers. Office: Mission Soc 6234 Crooked Creek Rd Norcross GA 30092 Home: 228 Brookcliff Dr Sugar Hill GA 30518-8197 Business E-Mail: pgranger@msum.org. *To experience life requires more than experiencing the simple joys and pleasures that life provides. To really experience life is to experience the Christian community of caring and sharing that only occurs when we are truly one in Christ.*

GRANGER, RANDY WILLIAM, art educator, consultant; b. Point Pleasant, NJ, May 13, 1948; s. Charles William Granger and Dorothy Marie Wright; m. Irene Elizabeth McHenry, Oct. 4, 2003; children: Fletcher, Michael, Gordon, Willa. BFA, Phila. Coll. Art, 1970; postgrad., NYU, 1973—74. Cert. permanent art edn. N.J., Pa., early adolescence, young adulthood art Nat. Bd. Certification. Instr. visual arts dept. Summit Pub. Schs., 1972—73, founding chair dept. photography, 1974—75; instr. visual arts dept. William Penn Charter Sch., 1975—2007, beach wheelchair project dir., 2001—05, chair visual arts dept., 1981—2006; chair dept. art edn. and art therapy, dir. grad. program art edn. U. the Arts, Phila., 2006—. Project dir. William Penn Charter Sch., Phila., 2000—; part-time instr. visual arts Phila. Parkway Program, 1969—70; instr. design, continuing edn. program Phila. U., 2003—04; adj. asst. prof. grad. art edn. dept. U. of the Arts, 2004—06. With USNR, 1966—72. Named Randy W. Granger Chair in Visual Arts in his honor, 1994, Randy Granger endowed scholarship in his honor, U. Arts, 2003; named to Hall of Fame, Pt. Pleasant Beach Pub. Edn. Assn., 2004, Nat. Tchrs. Hall of Fame, 2005, All-USA Tchr. Team, USA Today, 2005; recipient Nat. Disney Tchr. award, 2005, John F. Gummere Disting. Tchg. award, 1988. Mem.: Citizens for the Arts in Pa., Nat. Art Edn. Assn., Pa. Art Edn. Assn. (pres.-elect 2002—04, pres. 2004—06, Pa. Outstanding Secondary Art Educator award 1998, Pa. Art Educator Yr. 2005, Pa. First Nat. Bd. Cert. Art Tchr. 2001). Achievements include patents for beach wheelchair. Office: Univ of the Arts Dept Art Edn and Art Therapy 320 S Broad St Philadelphia PA 19102

GRANGER, ROBERT ALAN, mechanical and aerospace engineering educator; b. Evanston, Ill., Aug. 7, 1928; s. Robert Alan and Kathleen (Buehr) G.; m. Ruth Nickerson, Oct. 7, 1951; children: Eric Carl, Erin Alyson. BA, Pomona Coll., 1955; MS, Drexel Inst. Tech., 1959; PhD, U. Md., 1970. Sr. rsch. scientist Martin Co., Balt., 1955-60; prin. engr. Boeing Co., Renton, Wash., 1975; prof. mech. and aerospace engring. U.S. Naval Acad., Annapolis, Md., 1960-98, discipline dir., 1972-75; ret., 1998. Prof. emeritus U.S. Naval Acad., Annapolis, 2001; adj. prof. LSC Coll., 1999, lectr., U. Cambridge (Eng.), 2000—; fellow (hon.) Cambridge (England) U., 1991; pub., CEO Sci. Archives, Inc., 1997; sci. contbr. editor Daily Sun newspaper, 1999; cons. NASA, Boeing Co.; vis. prof. U. Petroleum and Minerals, Saudi Arabia, 1977-79, U. Zurich, Switzerland, 1978, Yale U., 1989; dir. Vortex Dynamics Symposium von Karman Inst., Brussels, Belgium; dir., prin. lectr. Introduction to Wing Flutter Symposium, 1991. Author: Fluid Mechanics, 1985, Unified Method of Aeroelasticity, 1986, Experiments in Fluid Mechanics, 1986, Design of Spacecraft, 1988, Introduction to the Flutter of Winged Aircraft, 1992, Experiments in Heat Transfer and Thermodynamics, 1994, Fluid Mechanics, 1994, Life on Mars, 1997, One is Infinity, 2007; contbr. over 800 articles to profl. publs. Served with U.S. Army, 1950-52, Korea. Ford Found. fellow, 1965; recipient USN Meritorious Civilian award, 1996, Euler Math. prize, 1999. Hon. mem. Inst. Modern Physics (Athens, Greece); mem. AIAA, Kappa Mu Epsilon, Alpha Gamma Sigma. Republican. Avocations: composing, mountain climbing, writing, tennis, swimming. Home: 31 Hickory Head Hammock Lady Lake FL 32159-8868 Personal E-mail: ragranger@thevillages.net.

GRANGER, STEVEN TANDVIG, archivist, consultant; b. Duluth, Minn., Feb. 25, 1949; s. Harold Elmer Granger and Dorothy Estelle (Tandvig) Granger; m. Susan Kay Hakomaki, Nov. 23, 1973; children: Andrew Hakomaki, Carla Hakomaki. BA cum laude, U. Minn., 1971, MA, 1980. Cert. Acad. Cert. Archivists, 1990. Collectiions mgr. Waseca County Hist. Soc., Waseca, Minn., 1987—89; acting archivist Carleton Coll., Northfield, Minn., 1989—90; collections processor Humphrey Papers Minn. Hist. Soc., St. Paul, 1990—91; archivist Archdiocese of St. Paul and Mpls., 1992—. Adv. bd. mem. North Star Scouting Mus., St. Paul, 1996—2000; cons. Mpls. Pk. and Recreation Bd., 2001—05. Prodr.: (video) Lines of Beauty. Mem.: Twin Cities Archives Round Table (pres. 1994—95), Plastics Hist. Soc., Soc. Am. Archivists. Avocations: bicycling, camping, antique radio repair, photography. Office: Archdiocese of St Paul and Mpls 226 Summit Ave Saint Paul MN 55102 Home Phone: 651-647-0407; Office Phone: 651-291-4485. Office Fax: 651-290-1629. E-mail: grangers@archspm.org.

GRANHOLM, JENNIFER MULHERN, governor; b. Vancouver, BC, Can., Feb. 5, 1959; arrived in U.S., 1962; d. Civtor Ivar and Shirley Alfreda (Dowden) Granholm; m. Daniel Granholm Mulhern, May 23, 1986; children: Kathryn, Cecelia, Jack. BA, U. Calif., Berkeley, 1984; JD, Harvard U., 1987. Bar: Mich. 1987, U.S. Dist. Ct. (ea. dist.) Mich. 1987, U.S. Ct. Appeals (6th cir.) 1987. Jud. law clk. 6th Cir Ct. Appeals, Detroit, 1987—88; exec. asst. Wayne County Exec., Detroit, 1988—89; asst. U.S. atty. (ea. dist.) Mich. US Dept. Justice, Detroit, 1990—94; corp. counsel Wayne County, Detroit, 1994—98; atty. gen. State of Mich., Lansing, 1999—2002, gov., 2003—. Gen. counsel Detroit/Wayne County Stadium Authority, 1996—98. Contbr. articles to profl. jours. Commr. Great Lakes Comm.; mem. bd. Cyberstate.org YWCA. Mem.: Inc. Soc. Irish Lawyers, Women's Law Assn., Detroit Bar Assn. Democrat. Roman Catholic. Avocation: running. Office: Gov Office PO Box 30013 Lansing MI 48909 Office Phone: 517-335-3400. Office Fax: 517-335-6949.*

GRANICK, MARK S., medical educator; b. New York, NY, July 7, 1951; m. Carol Singer, Feb. 17, 1994. BA, Cornell U., 1973; MD, Harvard Med. Sch., 1977. Cert. Am. Bd. of Plastic Surgery, 1984. Resident Harvard U., U. Pitts., 1977—82; prof. surgery Allegheny U., 1982—2001, N.J. Med. School-UMDNJ, Newark, 2001—. Fellow: ACS. Office: NJ Med Sch UMDNJ 90 Bergen St Ste 7200 Newark NJ 07103 also: 290 South Livingston Ave Livingston NJ 07039 Office Phone: 973-972-8092.

GRANIK, RUSS (RUSSELL T. GRANIK), financial advisory firm executive, former sports association executive; b. July 10, 1948; m. Joyce A. Granik; children: Daniel, Erynn. Grad. magna cum laude, Dartmouth Coll., 1969; law degree cum laude, Harvard U., 1973. With Breed, Abbott & Morgan, NYC; staff atty. NBA, 1976-78, asst. gen. counsel, 1978-80, gen. counsel, 1980-84, exec. v.p., 1984-90, dep. commr., 1990—2006, sr. adv. to dep. commr., 2006; vice chmn. Galatioto Sports Partners, NYC, 2006—. V.p. USA Basketball, 1989-96, pres. 1996-2000; chmn. bd. trustees, Naismith Meml. Basketball Hall of Fame, 2003-. Named to Naismith Basketball Hall of Fame, 2006; recipient Edwards S. Steitz award, 2005. Mem.: Phi Beta Kappa.*

GRANIK, VLADIMIR, mechanic engineering educator, researcher; b. May 16, 1934; arrived in US, 1991, naturalized, 1996; m. Galina Gaevskaya, Apr. 28, 1957; children: Yuri, Tanya. BS summa cum laude, Civil Engring. Inst., Odessa, USSR, 1957; PhD, Ctrl. Rsch. Inst. Concrete, Moscow, 1967; Assoc. Prof. Strength of Materials, Higher Exam. Bd. USSR, Moscow, 1970, D Tech. Scis., 1990. Rsch. engr. Ctrl. Rsch. Inst. Structural Mechanics, Moscow, 1957-66; assoc. prof. Civil Engring. Inst., Odessa, 1966-69; assoc. prof. structural mechanics Mil. Engring. Acad., Odessa, 1969-72, prof. continuum mechanics, 1972-88; prof. strength of materials Maritime Engring. Inst., Odessa, 1988-91; rsch. fellow in continuum mechanics U. Calif., Berkeley, 1991-93, rsch. assoc. continuum mechanics, 1993—98, prof. cons. strength of materials and structural mechanics, 1998—. Head optimization theory dept. Rsch. Inst. Automation, Odessa, 1985-88; founder Doublet Mechanics. Co-author, co-editor: Advances in Doublet Mechanics, 1997; contbr. articles to profl. jours.; assoc. mem., reviewer Jour. Structural Mechanics and Structure Design, 1981-91. Recipient First Prize Queueing Theory Application award Ministry Def., Moscow, 1976, Academician Gadolin medal Ministry Def., 1984. Achievements include rsch. in doublet mechanics; microstructural mechanics of granular media; stochastic dynamics of granular flows in tall shells (silos); reassessment of classical theory of plasticity and yield criteria; stochastic dynamics of supply and demand in a single market; a new theory of osmotic pressures in non-electrolytic solutions of any concentration. Home: 282 18th Ave Apt 3 San Francisco CA 94121-2328 E-mail: vtgranik@peoplepc.com.

GRANIRER, EDMOND ERNEST, mathematician, educator; b. Constanza, Romania, 1935; s. Jacob G. MSc, Hebrew U., Jerusalem, 1959, PhD, 1962. Mem. faculty dept. math. U. Ill., 1962-64, Cornell U., 1964-65, U. B.C., Vancouver, Canada, 1965—66, 1967—, prof. math., 1970-97, prof. emeritus, 1997—; faculty U. Montreal, Canada, 1966-67. Contbr. articles to profl. jours. Grantee NSERC, 1996. Fellow Royal Soc. Can.; mem. Can. Math. Soc., Am. Math. Soc. Office: U BC Dept Math Vancouver BC Canada V6T 1Z2 Home Phone: 604-224-6785. Business E-Mail: granirer@math.ubc.ca.

GRANITE, EDWIN L, oral surgeon; b. Phila., July 27, 1933; DMD, Temple U., Phila., 1957. Diplomate Am. Bd. Oral and Maxillofacial Surgery (scholar), 1965. Chmn., oral and maxillofacial surgery Christiana Care Health Svcs., Wilmington, Del., 2002—. Lt. (sr. grade) USNR, 1957—59, Quantico, Va. Fellow: Am. Coll. Dentists (hon.); mem.: Del. Acad. Medicine. Office: Christiana Care Health Svcs Wilmington Hospital 501 W 14th St Wilmington DE 19801 Home Phone: 610-459-8855; Office Phone: 302-428-6458. Office Fax: 302-428-6822. Business E-Mail: egranite@christianacare.org.

GRANITO, FRANK HENRY, III, lawyer; b. NYC, Jan. 25, 1959; s. Frank H. Jr. and Helen Elizabeth (Altieri) G.; m. Monica Ann Marino, July 8, 1989; 1 child, Frank H. IV. BA, Franklin & Marshall, 1981; JD, St. John's U., 1987. Bar: N.Y. 1987, N.J. 1988; U.S. Dist. Ct. (ea. and so. dists.) N.Y. 1988, U.S. Dist. Ct. N.J. 1988. Regional mgr. Pilgrim Airlines, NY, 1982-84; assoc. Bower & Gardner, NYC, 1987-88, Speiser, Krause & Madole, NYC, 1988; ptnr. Speiser Krause Nolan & Granito, NYC. Mem.: ATLA, ABA (Com. on Aeronautics, Litig. Sect. 1991—, chmn., Com. on Aeronautics, Litig. Sect. 2000—01, co-chmn, Aviation Litig. Com.), Lawyer-Pilots Bar Assn., NY State Trial Lawyers Assn., Assn. Bar City NY. Roman Catholic. Office: Speiser Krause Nolan & Granito 34th Fl Two Grand Central Tower 140 E 45th St New York NY 10017 Home Phone: 203-966-6377; Office Phone: 212-661-0011. Office Fax: 212-953-6483. E-mail: f3g@ny.speiserkrause.com.

GRANN, PHYLLIS E., editor, former publisher executive; b. London, Sept. 2, 1937; d. Solomon and Louisa (Bois-Smith) Eitingon; m. Victor Grann, Sept. 28, 1962; children: Allison, David, Edward. BA cum laude, Barnard Coll., 1958. Sec. Doubleday Pubs., NYC, 1958-60; editor William Morrow Inc., NYC, 1960-62, David McKay Co., NYC, 1962-70; sr. editor Simon & Schuster Inc., NYC, 1970—74, editor-in-chief, Pocket Books paperbacks divsn., 1974—76; editor-in-chief G.P. Putnam's & Sons, NYC, 1976—79, editor-in-chief, pub., 1979—84, pub., pres., 1984—86; pres. Putnam Berkley Group, NYC, 1986—87, pres., CEO, 1987—91, chmn., CEO, 1991—96; pres., CEO Penguin Putnam, Inc., 1996—2001; vice chmn. Random House, 2002, sr. editor, Doubleday Broadway Publishing Co., 2003—. Adj. asst. prof. fin. and economics Columbia Bus. Sch., NYC, 2003—; bd. dirs. Warner Music Group Corp., 2006—. Co-founder Victor & Phyllis Grann Family Found.

GRANNIS, PETE (ALEXANDER BANKS GRANNIS), state official, former state legislator; b. Chgo., Jan. 6, 1942; s. Uri B. and Margorie (Banks) G.; m. Ainslie Dinwiddie, 1971; 1 child, Wilcox Snellings. BA, Rutgers U., 1964; LLB, U. Va., 1967. Mem. staff Parker, Duryee, Zunino, Malone & Carter, NYC, 1967-70; compliance & spl. asst. commr. NY State Dept. Environ. Conservation, 1970-72; mem. staff Berle, Butzel & Kass, 1972-74; mem. NY State Assembly, Dist. 65, 1974—2007; commr. NY State Dept. Environ. Conservation, Albany, 2007—. Mem. ways and means com., environ. conservation, health com., judiciary com. Del. Dem. Nat. Conv., 1976. 80; founder, bd. dirs. Environ. Action Coalition, 1970—; gen. counsel, mem. exec. com. Coun. Environment, 1973—. Named Legislator of Yr., Environ. Planning Lobby, 1981, 88. Mem. Yorkville Alliance Block Assn. (bd. dirs. 1974—), City Club N.Y.C. (mem. housing com. 1974—), Pi Delta Epsilon, Delta Phi. Office: NY State Dept Environ Conservation 625 Broadway Albany NY 12233

GRANOF, MICHAEL H., finance educator, department chairman; b. NYC, June 16, 1942; s. David H. and Diana (Simon) G.; m. Dena Gloria Hirsch, Aug. 27, 1972; children: Leah, Joshua AB, Hamilton Coll., 1963; MBA, Columbia U., 1965; PhD, U. Mich., 1972. CPA, Tex. Sr. acct. Coopers & Lybrand, NYC, 1966-68; asst. prof. to prof. acctg. U. Tex., Austin, 1972-84, chmn., acctg. dept., 1984—88, Ernst & Young disting. centennial prof., chmn. acctg. dept., 1984—, and prof., LBJ sch. pub. affairs, 1999—. Mem. Nat. Coun. on Govtl. Acctg., 1982-84, Govtl. Acctg. Stds. Adv. Coun., Norwalk, Conn., 1984-90; Fulbright prof. Coun. for Internat. Exch. Scholars, Hebrew U., Jerusalem, 1978-79; edn. adv. com. U.S. Comptr. Gen., 2001—, adv. coun. on govtl. auditing stds., 2005—; vis. prof. U. Tel Aviv, 1981; bd. trustees Assn. Govt. Accts. Acad. for Govtl. Accountability, 2005—. Author: How To Cost Your Labor Contract, 1973, Financial Accounting: Principles and Issues, 1977, 4th edit., 1990, Accounting for Managers and Investors, 1983, 2d edit., 1993, Government and Not-for-Profit Accounting, 1998, 3d edit., 2005, Core Concepts in Government and Not-for -Profit Accounting, 2003; co-editor: Government Accounting and Auditing Update, 1989-97. Co-pres. Congregation Agudas Achim; treas. Austin Area Urban League. With USCG, 1965-66 Erskine fellow U. Canterbury, Christchurch, N.Z., 1983 Mem. AICPAs (com. on govt. acctg. and auditing), Am. Acctg. Assn. (chmn. pub. sector sect. 1981-82), Tex. Soc. CPAs (chmn. govt. acctg. standards com.), Govt. Fin. Officers Assn., Assn. Govt. Accts. Jewish. Home: 7310 Valburn Dr Austin TX 78731-1146 Office: U Tex Dept Acctg CBA 4M 202 Austin TX 78712 Business E-Mail: michael.granof@mccombs.utexas.edu.

GRANOFF, GARY CHARLES, lawyer, investment company executive; b. NYC, Feb. 2, 1948; s. N. Henry and Jeannette (Trum) G.; m. Leslie Barbara Resnick, Dec. 21, 1969; children: Stephen, Robert, Joshua. BBA in Acctg., George Washington U., 1970, JD with honors, 1973. Bar: N.Y. 1974, Fla. 1974, U.S. Dist. Ct. (so. dist.) N.Y. 1976. Assoc. Dreyer & Traub, NYC, 1973-75; ptnr. Ezon, Langberg & Granoff, NYC, 1975-78, Granoff & Walker, NYC, 1982-92, Granoff, Walker & Forlenza PC, NYC, 1993—; pvt. practice NYC, 1978-81; pres., also bd. dirs. Elk Assocs. Funding Corp., NYC, 1979—, GCG Assocs., Inc., NYC, 1982—; pres., dir. Gemini Capital Corp., 1996—; pres., chmn., CEO, Ameritrans Capital Corp., 1999—. Atty. del. to U.S.-China Joint Session on Trade, Investment and Econ. Law, Beijing, 1987; dean's adv. bd. George Washington U. Law Sch., 1993-2006. Campaign vol. Mondale for Pres., NYC, 1984; fundraiser Robert Garcia for Congress, Dem. Senatorial Campaign Com., NYC, 1987—88; active N.Y. Lawyers for Dukakis Com., 1988; chmn. N.Y.C. chpt. George Washington U. Nat. Law Ctr. Leadership Gifts Com., 1998—; trustee George Washington U., 1998—2003, 2005—, chmn. fin. com., 2001—02, sr. advisor investment com. bd. trustees, 2003—; trustee Parker Jewish Inst. for Health Care and Rehab., 2001—, chmn. investment com., 2005—, vice chmn. bd., 2006; commr. Village of Kings Point Zoning Bd. Appeals; fundraiser John F. Kerry for Pres., 2004. Recipient Jacob Burns award, George Washngton U. Law Sch., 1998. Mem. N.Y. State Bar Assn., Fla. Bar Assn., Assn. Bar City N.Y., People to People Internat., Nat. Assn. Investment Cos. (legis com.), George Washington U. Alumni Assn. (chmn. N.Y.C. chpt., bd. dirs. law sch. alumni assn., alumni com. 21 century, trustee, Alumni Svc. award 2005), North Shore Country Club (chmn. legal com., bd. govs. 1994-96, 98-2001, chmn. admissions com. 1999-2001, chmn. nominating com. 2004), Fresh Meadow Country Club. Avocations: golf, tennis, skiing. Office: Granoff Walker & Forlenza PC 747 3rd Ave Fl 4 New York NY 10017-2803

GRANOTT, NIRA, psychologist, researcher; b. Petah-Tikva, Israel; came to U.S., 1987; d. Jacob and Celia Granott; children: Guy A. Farber, Bali Farber MA, Tel Aviv U., 1983; EdM, Harvard U., 1988; PhD, MIT, 1993. Dir. multi-media project Edn. TV, Tel-Aviv, 1974—80; sr. analyst, software developer Control data Corp., Tel-Aviv, 1983—86; asst. prof. psychology U. Tex. Dallas, Richardson, 1993—95, dir. microdevel. lab., 1993—2002, asst. prof. psychology, 1997—2002; co-founder, pres. OORIM, LLC, 2000—. Vis. prof. psychology and lectr. edn. Harvard Grad. Sch. Edn., Cambridge, Mass., 1996-97; grant cons. Harvard U., 1995-96. Editor: (spl. issue) New Ideas in Psychology, 2005—06. Rsch. grantee NSF, 1999, Tex. Higher Edn. Bd., 2000, Timberlawn Rsch. Found., 1999; vis. scholar Tufts U., 2002-04, 05-06. Mem. Am. Psychol. Soc., Soc. for Rsch. on Child Devel Avocations: painting, photography, dance, yoga. Personal E-mail: ngranott@aol.com.

GRANOWSKY, ALVIN, writer, educator; b. Bklyn., June 27, 1936; s. Samuel and Helen Golden Granowsky; m. Seena Abramsky (div.); children: Eric Stuart, Sedra Diane, Richard Tod. BA, Colgate U., 1958; MA in Tchg., Harvard U., 1959; EdD, U. Pa., 1971. Tchr. English Monroe-Woodbury (N.Y.) Ctrl. Sch., 1959—60; asst. editor Miller-Freeman Pubs., NYC, 1960—62; tchr. English Poughkeepsie (N.Y.) H.S., 1962—65, Spackenkill (N.Y.) Jr. H.S., 1965—69; rsch. assoc. Rsch. Better Schs., Phila., 1970—73; dir. reading and lang. arts Greensboro (N.C.) Pub. Schs., 1974—76, Dallas Pub. Schs., 1976—81; v.p. edn. World Book, Inc., Chgo., 1987—2000; freelance spkr. and author Dallas, 2000—. Adv. bd. Tex. State Learning Disability Assn., Austin, Tex., 2002—05; cons. in field. Author: Point of View, 1992, All-Star Phonics, 2003, Beauty, The Beast, and the Sisters--A Thrice-Told Tale, 2006, How to Start Your Own Business, 2006. Mem.: Internat. Reading Assn., Phi Delta Kappa. Home: 6924 Desco Dr Dallas TX 75225 Office Phone: 469-232-9252. Personal E-mail: algranowsky@hotmail.com.

GRANT, ALAN J., business executive, educator; b. Chgo., Dec. 18, 1925; s. Hugo Bernard and May (Gardner) G.; m. Margaret Stewart, Dec. 21, 1946; children: Pamela Rose, Deborah May, Bruce David. BSEE, Ill. Inst. Tech., 1946, MSEE, 1948; EdD, U. San Diego, 1992. Cert. instr. math. H.S. Calif., 2004. Instr. elec. engring. Ill. Inst. Tech., Chgo., 1946-49; with N.Am. Aviation, Inc. (Autonetics), Anaheim, Calif., 1949-64, v.p., gen. mgr. computer and data systems div., 1962-64; pres. Lockheed Electronics Co. div. Lockheed Aircraft Corp., Plainfield, N.J., 1965-69; also v.p. parent co.; exec. v.p. Aerojet-Gen. Corp., El Monte, Calif., 1970-74; chmn., pres. Wavecom Industries, Sunnyvale, Calif., 1974-78, Primark Corp., San Mateo, Calif., 1975-80; chmn., chief exec. officer Internat. Rotex, Inc., Reno, Nev., 1980-86; dir. UNC Resources Inc, Falls Church, Va., 1974-81; chmn. Atasi Corp., San Jose, Calif., 1982-85; gen. ptnr. EMC Venture Ptnrs., San Diego, 1984-86; pres. Grant Venture Mgmt. Co., Coronado, Calif., 1986-96; chmn. Am. Innovision, San Diego, 1986-92, SalePoint Systems Corp., San Diego, 1987-92. Adj. prof. managerial scis. U. Nev., Reno, 1979—84; mgmt. San Diego State U., 1986—90; pres. Corp. Mgmt. Assocs., 1996—; adj. prof., dir. Ctr. for Entrepreneurship, Calif. State U., Long Beach, 1999—2001; adj. prof. entrepreneurship Calif. State U., Hayward, 2001—03. Paul T. Babson prof. entrepreneurship Babson Coll., Babson Park, Mass., 1992-94. Mem. Am. Electronics Assn. (chmn. 1973, dir. 1970-74). Home: 4523 Calaveras Ave Fremont CA 94538-1121 Personal E-mail: agrant105@comcast.net.

GRANT, ALEXANDER MARSHALL, retired ballet director; b. Wellington, New Zealand, Feb. 22, 1925; s. Alexander Gibb and Eleather May (Marshall) G. Student, Wellington Coll., Sadler's Wells Sch., London, 1946-46. Mem. Sadler's Wells Ballet (now Royal Ballet), London, 1946-76, prin. dancer, 1950-76, co-dir. Ballet for All touring co., 1970-71, dir., 1971-76; artistic dir. Nat. Ballet Can., 1976-83, ret. Judge internat. ballet competitions, Jackson, Miss., Moscow, Varna, Bulgaria, Helsinki, Paris, Budapest, Hungary. Prin. dancer London Festival Ballet (now English Nat.

Ballet), 1985-91; guest artist Royal Ballet, Joffrey Ballet, English Nat. Ballet; numerous leading roles on stage, also in film Tales of Beatrice Potter, others; staged La Fille Mal Gardeé, Facade, various cities, 1988—, Icon Arts Found. New Zealand, 2005. Scholar Royal Acad. Dance, 1944; Decorated comdr. Brit. Empire; recipient New Zealand Icon award, 2005.

GRANT, AMY, singer, songwriter; b. Augusta, Ga., Nov. 25, 1960; d. Burton and Gloria Grant; m. Gary Chapman, 1983 (div. 1999); children: Matthew Chapman, Millie Chapman, Sarah Chapman; m. Vince Gill, 2000; 1 child, Corrina Grant Gill. Student, Furman U., Vanderbilt U., Coll. Arts & Sci., 1982. Albums include Amy Grant, 1977, My Father's Eyes, 1979, Never Alone, 1980, Amy Grant in Concert, 1981, Amy Grant in Concert II, 1981, Age to Age (Grammy award), 1982, A Christmas Album, 1983, Straight Ahead, 1984, Unguarded (Grammy award), 1985, The Collection, 1986, Lead Me On (Grammy award), 1988, Heart in Motion, 1991, Home for Christmas, 1992, House of Love, 1994, Behind the Eyes, 1997, A Christmas to Remember, 1999, Legacy Hymns & Faith, 2002, Simple Things, 2003, Greatest Hits 1986-2004, 2004, Rock Of Ages.Hymns & Faith, 2005; host (TV series), Three Wishes, 2005. Recipient 24 Dove awards Gospel Music Assn., Grammy award contemporary album, 1983, Grammy award best gospel performance, 1984-86, Grammy award best contemporary album, 1988; honored Walk of Fame, 2001; named to Music Hall of Fame, 2005. Office: c/o Blanton Harrell Cooke & Corzine Ste 100 5300 Virgina Way Brentwood TN 37027 also: Sparrow Records Group PO Box 5010 Brentwood TN 37024-5010 Office Phone: 615-627-0450.

GRANT, ARTHUR GORDON, JR., lawyer, educator; b. New Orleans, May 16, 1945; s. Arthur Gordon and Martha (McCutchon) G.; children: Arthur Gordon III, Kathryn S., Douglas M. BA, U. N.C., 1967; JD, Tulane U., 1970. Bar: La. 1970, U.S. Ct. Appeals (5th cir.) 1970, U.S. Dist. Ct. (ea. and mid. dists.) La. 1970, U.S. Dist. Ct. (we. dist.) La. 1970, U.S. Ct. Appeals (11th cir.) 1981, U.S. Supreme Ct. 1990, U.S. Dist. Ct. (so. dist.) Tex. 1998. Assoc. Montgomery, Barnett, Brown, Read, Hammond & Mintz, New Orleans, 1970-73, ptnr., 1973—. Admiralty and maritime law instr. U. New Orleans Sch. Naval Architecture, 1990—; bd. dirs. Am. Boat and Yacht Coun., 1990-98, 2002-05 Author: Recreational Craft, Jurisdiction, Claims and Coverage, 1989; contbg. author: Recreational Boating Law, 1992, Benedict on Admiralty, Vol. 8, 7th edit., 1995. Fellow La. Bar Found.; mem. Fed. Bar Assn., Navy League of U.S., La. Bar Assn., Soc. Naval Architects and Marine Engrs., Maritime Law Assn. U.S. (vice chmn. recreational boating com. 1990-94), Bar Assn. 5th Fed. Cir., Southeastern Admiralty Law Inst.(bd. dirs. 2002), U.S. Assn. Average Adjusters, So. Yacht Club, Propellor Club Port, New Orleans. Episcopalian. Avocations: hunting, fishing, boating, civil war history. Office: Montgomery Barnett Brown Read Hammond & Mintz 3200 Energy Ctr New Orleans LA 70163 Home Phone: 504-833-2078; Office Phone: 504-585-7681. Business E-Mail: ggrant@monbar.com.

GRANT, BARBARA, venture capitalist; PhD in Organic Chemistry, Stanford U., 1974. Rsch. scientist rsch. divsn. IBM, 1975-86; product mgr. IBM Sys. Printer Products, 1986-91; dir. IBM Storage Divsn. Magnetic Recording Head Bus. Unit, 1991-94; v.p. bus. devel. IBM Storage Sys. Divsn., 1994-95, v.p., gen. mgr. Removable Media Storage Solutions Bus. Unit, 1995—96; pres., CEO Siros Technologies, 1996—2004; exec.-in-residence Amer. River Ventures, 2004—. NSF fellow. Office: Amer River Ventures 2270 Douglas Blvd Ste 212 Roseville CA 95661

GRANT, BARBARA ROSEMARY, science educator, researcher; b. Arnside, Eng., Oct. 8, 1936; d. Alexander and Hilda Gwendoline (Peace) Matchett; m. Peter R. Grant, Jan. 4, 1962; children: Nicola, K. Thalia. BSc with honors, U. Edinburgh, Scotland, 1960; PhD, Uppsala U., Sweden, 1985; DSc (hon.), McGill U., Montreal, Can., 2000, U. San Francisco, Quito, Ecuador, 2005. Rsch. assoc., lectr. U. BC, Vancouver, Canada, 1960—64; rsch. assoc. Yale U., New Haven, 1964—65, McGill U., 1973—77, U. Mich., Ann Arbor, 1977—85; sr. rsch. scholar Princeton U., 1987—, prof. dept. ecology and evolutionary biology. Vis. prof. U. Zurich, Switzerland, 2002. Author: Evolutionary Dynamics of a Natural Population, 1991 (Wildlife Publ. award, 1991); contbr. articles to profl. jours. Recipient Leidy medal, Acad. Natural Scis., Phila., 1994, E.O. Winslow prize, Am. Soc. Naturalists, 1998, Darwin medal, Royal Soc., London, 2002, Miller award, 2003, Grinnell medal, 2003, Balzan prize, 2005. Fellow: Royal Soc. UK, Royal Soc. Can. (fgn.), German Ornithology Assn. (hon.); mem.: Am. Acad. Arts and Scis. Office: Dept Ecology and Evolutionary Biology Princeton U 106a Guyot Hall Princeton NJ 08544-1003 Office Phone: 609-258-6290. Office Fax: 609-258-1334. E-mail: rgrant@princeton.edu.*

GRANT, BRIAN WADE, professional basketball player; b. Columbus, Ohio, Mar. 5, 1972; Degree in Organizational Comms., Xavier, 1994. Forward Sacramento Kings, 1994-97, Portland TrailBlazers, 1997-99, Miami Heat, 2000—04, LA Lakers, 2004—05, Phoenix Suns, 2005—. Active Portland cmty., B. Grant Found. Recipient J. Walter Kennedy Citizenship award NBA, 1999. Avocation: watching movies.

GRANT, BURTON FRED, lawyer; b. Chgo., Mar. 16, 1938; s. Louis Z. and Ruth (Kaplan) G.; m. Joan Carolyn Friedman, July 11, 1965; children: Robin, Steven, Lauren. BA, De Paul U., 1959, JD, 1962; LLM, John Marshall U., 1965. Bar: Ill. 1963, U.S. Dist. Ct. (no. dist.) Ill. 1963. Sole practice, Chgo., 1963-73; ptnr. Grant, Kaplan & Grant, Chgo., 1973-76, Grant, Grant & Stein, Chgo., 1977-81; prin. Grant & Grant, Chgo., 1981—. Adj. prof. De Paul U. Sch. Law, Chgo., 1979-83. Contbr. articles to profl. jours. Named one of Leading Attorneys at Law in Family Law in State of Ill., (pub.) Law and Leading Attorneys, one of 20 Top Divorce Lawyers North Shore Mag., 1997. Fellow Am. Acad. Matrimonial Lawyers (cert.); mem. ABA, Ill. Bar Assn., Chgo. Bar Assn., N.W. Suburban Bar Assn. (cert. appreciation 1986), North Suburban Bar ASsn. (bd. mgrs. 1992—), Lake County Bar Assn., Phi Alpha Delta. Avocations: travel, photography. also: 707 Skokie Blvd Ste 600 Northbrook IL 60062-2841 Office: Grant & Grant 30 N La Salle St #29 Chicago IL 60602-2511 Home Phone: 847-433-5213; Office Phone: 847-641-3600. Business E-Mail: fmlylaw@aol.com.

GRANT, CARL N., communications executive, sales executive; b. Sharon, Pa., July 10, 1939; s. Carl and Hedwig Theresa Nothhaft; m. Carol Ann Pasacic, June 12, 1965; children: Carl, Kevin, Heather Lee. BA, Kent State U., 1963, MA, 1966; PhD, Ohio State U., 1972. With various radio, TV stas., Ohio and Mich., 1962-67; asst. news dir. Sta. WLWC-TV, Columbus, Ohio, 1967-69; news and pub. affairs dir. Sta. WKBS-TV, Phila., 1969-72; exec. staff dir., nat. com. employer support and guard Dept. Def., Washington, 1972-73; dir. Pres. Com. on White House Fellows, Washington, 1973-74; dir. news and pub. affairs Kaiser Broadcasting Corp., Washington, 1974; assoc. dir. and editor Def. Manpower Commn., Washington, 1974-76; dir. pub. affairs Gen. Svcs. Adminstrn., Washington, 1976-77; sr. v.p., exec. counselor to pres. U.S. C. of C., Washington, 1977—. Brig. gen. Army Nat. Guard, ret. 1999. Recipient Investigative Reporting award AP, 1968, 69, Emmy award nomination NATAS, 1968, George Washington medal Freedoms Found., 1989, William Taylor Disting. Alumnus award Kent State U., 1991, Legion of Merit award, 1994. Avocations: running, weight training, golf, bicycling. Office: US C of C 1615 H St NW Washington DC 20062-0001

GRANT, CARMEN HILL, psychologist, psychotherapist; b. Denver, Feb. 10, 1935; d. Floyd Vernon Hill and Ena Celeste Turner; m. Donald Roger Grant, Aug. 4, 1964; stepchildren: Roger W., David M. BA, U. Colo., 1957; PhD, U. Nebr., 1967. Diplomate in clin. psychology Am. Bd. Profl. Psychology, 1977, cert. Nebr. State Bd. Examiners Psychologists, Colo. State Bd. Examiners Psychologists. Clin. psychology intern Southwestern Med. Sch., Dallas, 1960—61; psychology trainee VA Hosp., Omaha, 1962—64; asst. clin. psychologist Nat. Jewish Hosp., Denver, 1962; clinic asst. U. Nebr., Lincoln, 1963—64; staff psychologist U. Health Ctr., U. Nebr., Lincoln, 1964—67, clin. psychologist and clinic coord., 1967—70, clin. psychologist/outreach staff coord., 1970—78; pvt. practice Lincoln, 1978—. Mem. U. Nebr. Task Force on Drug Edn., 1972—75; commr. and health com. chair Lincoln-Lancaster Commn. on Status of Women, 1976—80; sports psychology cons. U. Nebr., 1980—86; pres., sec., bd. dirs. Nebr. Soc. Profl. Psychologists, Lincoln, 1985—88; vice chair, mem. State Bd. Psychologists, 1997—2004; co-developer program on wellness lifestyles U. Health Ctr., Lincoln; presenter in field. Contbr. articles to jour.; co-author: (NETV videotape) Nonverbal Comm. in Counseling, 1974. Co-founder Lincoln Personal Crisis Svc., Inc., 1970—74, v.p., 1970—74, sec., 1970—74, bd. dirs., 1970—74; pres. Lancaster Co. Assn. Mental Health, Lincoln, 1972—75, bd. dirs., 1972—75, profl. adv. bd., 1972—75; com. mem. Mayor's Task Force: Domestic Violence, Lincoln, 1980. Recipient A Peer Group Approach to a Smoking Edn. Program in U. Setting award, Nat. Clearinghouse on Smoking and Health, USPHS Contract, U. Health Ctr., Lincoln, Nebr., 1966—69. Fellow: Acad. Clin. Psychology; mem.: APA, Nebr. Psychol. Assn. (pres./officer/bd. dirs. 1991—96, liaison to State Bd. Examiners of Psychologists 1995—97), Sigma Xi. Avocations: books, travel, tennis, golf, landscape gardening.

GRANT, CYNTHIA D., writer; b. Brockton, Mass., Nov. 23, 1950; d. Robert Cheyne and Jacqueline Ann (Ford) G.; m. Daniel Heatley; 1 child: Morgan; m. Erik Neel; 1 child, Forest. Author: Joshua Fortune, 1980 (Woodward Park Sch. annual book award 1981), Summer Home, 1981, Big Time, 1982, Hard Love, 1983, Kumquat May, I'll Always Love You, 1986, Phoenix Rising, 1989 (Mich. Libr. Assn. Young Adult Caucus best book of yr. 1990, PEN/Norma Klein award 1991, Detroit Pub. Libr. Author Day award 1992), Keep Laughing, 1991, Shadow Man, 1992, Uncle Vampire, 1993 (ALA best books for young adults list 1994), Mary Wolf, 1995, The White Horse, 1998, The Cannibals, Starring Tiffany Spratt, 2002. Recipient Book of Distinction award Hungry Mind Review, 1993, 94. Mem.: PEN (Norma Klein award 1991). Avocations: reading, volunteer work, Cloverstock. Home: PO Box 95 Cloverdale CA 95425-0095 Office: Writers House LLC 21 W 26th St New York NY 10010

GRANT, DANIEL GORDON, information technology executive; b. Taplow, Bucks, Eng., June 28, 1957; came to U.S., 1981; s. Victor Daniel and Annie (McKeown) G.; m. Gaynor Kerry Swainson, Aug. 8, 1981; children: Andrew Douglas, Alexander Daniel, Megan Louise. BS in Computer Sci. with commendation, Portsmouth Poly., Eng., 1979; post-grad., Carnegie Mellon U., 1994-95. Chartered engr. info. scis.; cert. EMT, Nat. EMS registry. Cons. in computers, London, 1979-80; applications cons. Tymshare, U.K., London, 1980-81; from cons. to dep. pres. Tangent Internat., NYC, 1981-90, pres., 1990—, pres., CEO, 1991-94, also bd. dirs.; owner, pres., COO DXI Inc., Pitts., 1994-95, also bd. dirs.; CEO, bd. dirs. Lecor Inc, Pitts., 1995-96; owner, pres., CEO Parallel Tech. Corp., Livingston, N.J., 1996—. Contbr. articles to profl. jours. V.p. Upper Saddle River Vol. Ambulance Corps. Named Chevalier, Conte de Poznan, 1986, Hon. Col. U.S. Army, 1986. Mem. Brit. Computer Soc., Knights of St. John of Jerusalem. Clubs: Franklin Lakes Rangers (N.J.) (capt. 1981). Roman Catholic. Avocations: basketball, soccer, scottish history, pittsburgh dynamos. E-mail: dgrant@2lines.com.

GRANT, DANIEL ROSS, retired academic administrator; b. Little Rock, Aug. 18, 1923; s. James Richard and Gracie (Sowers) Grant; m. Betty Jo Oliver, June 17, 1947; children: Carolyn, Shirley, Ross. BA, Ouachita Bapt. U., 1945; MA, U. Ala., 1946; PhD, Northwestern U., 1948. Asst. prof. polit. sci. Vanderbilt U., 1948-54, assoc. prof., 1954-63, prof., 1963-70, dir. Urban and Regional Devel. Ctr., 1968-70; pres. Ouachita Bapt. U., Akadelphia, Ark., 1970-88, pres. emeritus, 1988—. Assoc. dir. Harris County Home Rule Commn., Houston, 1957; vis. prof. mcpl. govt. and planning Thammasat U., Bangkok, 1958—59; cons. U.S. Adv. Commn. Intergovernmental Rels., 1962—67; mem. adv. com. federalism and met. govt. Nat. Com. Econ. Devel., 1969—73. Author (with others): (book) Plan of Metropolitan Government for Nashville and Davidson County, 1956, Metropolitan Surveys: A Digest, 1958, The States and Metropolis, 1968, Government and Politics: An Introduction to Political Science, rev. edit., 1971; author: The Christian and Politics, 1968; author: (with Lloyd Omdahl) State and Local Government in America, 6th edit., 1993. Chmn. Coop. Svcs. Internat. Edn. Consortium (name now Consortium Global Edn.), 1987—88, cons., 1988—90, pres., 1990—98; active So. Bapt. Found., 1959—60, Ark. Bapt. Found., 1991—97, vice chmn., 1995—96, chmn., 1996—97; mem. regional rev. panel Harry S Truman Scholarship Found., 1982—96, chmn., 1984—96; active Ark. Postsecondary Edn. Planning Commn., 1980—89; mem. Ark. Higher Edn. Coordinating Bd., 1997—, vice chmn., 2002—04; mem. commn. religious liberty and human rights Bapt. World Alliance, 1971—95, vice chmn., 1985—90; mem. edn. commn. So. Bapt. Conv., 1973—80, chmn., 1978—80; 1st v.p. Ark. Bapt. State Conv., 1989—91; pres. Assn. So. Bapt. Colls. and Schs., 1984—85. Mem.: Am. Soc. Pub. Adminstrn., Ark. Polit. Sci. Assn., Am. Polit. Sci. Assn., Arkadelphia C. of C. (bd. dirs. 2000—02), Rotary (pres. 1986—87). Home: 4 Glendale Pl Arkadelphia AR 71923-3529 Office: Ouachita Bapt Univ PO Box 3636 Arkadelphia AR 71998-3636 E-mail: dangrant@iocc.com.

GRANT, EDWIN RANDOLPH, retail executive, manufacturing executive; b. Stoneham, Mass., Oct. 6, 1943; s. Lauris Levi and Dorothy Hall (Lewis) Grant; m. Ruth Louise Kennedy, June 24, 1967; children: Randolph T., George C. BFA, Denison U., 1966; MBA, Syracuse U., 1969. Trainee Sears, Roebuck & Co., Springfield, Mass., 1968—69; asst. to pres. Kennedy Bros., Inc., Vergennes, Vt., 1969—70, v.p., 1970—72, exec. v.p., 1972—74, pres., treas., 1974—; corp. sec. Porter Med. Ctr., Inc., 1997—. Bd. dir. Porter Med. Ctr., Inc.; ptnr. Vergennes (Vt.) Shopping Ctr., 1974—82; exec. bd. Chittenden Trust Co., Vergennes, 1980—94; chmn. bd. Burlington Coll., Vt., 1983—85; commr. Commn. Status of Women, 1984—85; devel. founder Kennedy Bros. Factory Marketplace, Vergennes, 1987; chair Porter Health Sys., Inc. subs. Porter Med. Ctr., Inc., Middlebury, Vt., 1996—2002. Com. chmn. Cub Scout Pack 539, 1987—96; mem. com. Boy Scout Troop 539, 1991—2000, chair, 1997—2000; active Boy Scouts Am., Vergennes; bd. dirs. Addison County (Vt.) Career Devel. Ctr., 1994—97, Friends of Vergennes Opera House, 1993—2004, pres., 2000—02, chmn., 2000—03. Mem.: Vt. Attractions Assn. (pres. 1978—80), Vt. Retail Assn., Lake Champlain C. of C. (bd. dirs. 1977—81), Addison C. of C. (bd. dirs. 1975—76, 1986—93, Bus. of the Yr. award 1990), Vt. State C. of C. (bd. dirs. 1977—78), Vergennes Area C. of C. (pres. 1976—81), Lake Champlain Yacht Club (bd. govs. 1989—94), Green Mountain Transp. Club (pres. 1976—77), Rotary. Home and Office: 11 N Main St Vergennes VT 05491

GRANT, HUGH, actor; b. London, Sept. 9, 1960; BA in English Lit. with honors, Oxford U., Eng., 1982. Formed Simian Films. Debuted on stage at Nottingham Playhouse; formed revue group The Jockeys of Norfolk, 1985; appearences include (films) Privileged, 1982, Maurice, 1987, White Mischief, 1988, The Lair of White Worm, 1988, The Dawning, 1988, Remando al Viento, 1988, La Nuit Bengali, 1988, Impromptu, 1991, Crossing the Line, 1991, Bitter Moon, 1992, The Remains of the Day, 1993, Four Weddings and a Funeral, 1994 (Golden Globe award best actor, 1994, BAFTA award best actor, 1994), Sirens, 1994, Restoration, 1994, The Englishman Who Went Up a Hill But Came Down a Mountain, 1995, Nine Months, 1995, An Awfully Big Adventure, 1995, Sense and Sensibility, 1995, Extreme Measures, 1996, Notting Hill, 1999, Mickey Blue Eyes, 1999, Small Time Crooks, 2000, Bridget Jones's Diary, 2001, About a Boy, 2002, Two Weeks Notice, 2002, Love Actually, 2003, Bridget Jones: The Edge of Reason, 2004, Travaux on sait quand ça commence, 2005, American Dreamz, 2006, Music and Lyrics, 2007; guest appearances include A Very Peculiar Practice, 1986. Stanley Kubrick Britannia award for excellence in film, BAFTA, 2003. Office: Creative Artists Agency c/o Josh Lieberman 9830 Wilshire Blvd Beverly Hills CA 90212-1825 also: Simian Films 335 North Maple Dr Ste 350 Beverly Hills CA 90210*

GRANT, HUGH, agricultural products executive; b. Mar. 1958; BS in Molecular Biology and Agrl. Zoology with honors, Glasgow U., Scotland; MS, Edinburgh U., Scotland; MBA, Internat. Mgmt. Ctr., Buckingham, Eng. Co-pres. agrl. sector Pharmacia Corp., 1998; v.p., COO Monsanto Co., 2000, exec. v.p., COO, 2000—03, chmn., pres., CEO, 2003—. Mem. exec. com. Microedit Summit Campaign; mem. internat. adv. bd. Scottish Enterprise. Bd. govs. United Way St. Louis; bd. trustee Donald Danforth Plant Sci. Ctr.; mem. Civic Progress. Mem.: Biotechnology Industry Orgn., Internat. Policy Coun. on Agr., Food and Trade, CropLife Internat. (mem. of the President's adv. group). Address: Monsanto Co 800 N Lindbergh Blvd Saint Louis MO 63167*

GRANT, ISABELLA HORTON, retired judge; b. LA, Sept. 24, 1924; d. John Daniel and Hannabelle (Horton) Grant. BA, Swarthmore Coll., 1944; MA, UCLA, 1946; JD, Columbia U., 1950; LLD (hon.), Molloy Coll., 1976. Jr. profl. asst. OSS, Washington, 1944-45; economist Inst. Indsl. Rels., UCLA, 1946-47, Office Price Stblzn., LA, 1951-52; ptnr. Livingston, Grant, Stone & Kay, San Francisco, 1953-79; judge Mcpl. Ct., San Francisco, 1979-82, Superior Ct., San Francisco, 1982-97; ret., 1997. Bd. dirs. Kid's Turn, Pocket Opera; mem. San Francisco Ethics Commn., 1997-2002, chair, 2001. Fellow ABA; mem. Am. Arbitration Assn., Action Dispute Resolution, Resolution Remedies, San Francisco Bar Assn. (bd. dirs. 1978-79), Acad. Matrimonial Lawyers (pres. No. Calif. chpt. 1976), Assn. Family and Conciliation Cts. (pres. Calif. chpt. 1987-89), Nat. Coll. Probate Judges (William W. Treat award 2000), Queen's Bench (pres. 1964), Calif. Tennis Club, Phi Beta Kappa. E-mail: ihortongrant@cs.com.

GRANT, J. KIRKLAND, lawyer, educator; b. Monroe, Mich., Feb. 14, 1943; s. Stanley Gordon and Neva Alene (Piper) G.; 1 child, Alexandra. BBA, U. Mich., 1965, JD cum laude, 1967. Bar: Mich. 1968, NY 1970, SC 1975, US Supreme Ct. 1979. Acct. Peat Marwick Mitchell, Detroit, 1964-65; asst. prof. Ga. State U., 1967-70, U. Toledo, 1970-71; assoc. coun. Sullivan & Cromwell, NYC, 1970-72; prof. U. SC, 1972-80; dean, prof. Del. Law Sch., Wilmington, 1980-83; assoc. counsel Bingham, Dana & Gould, Boston, 1983-84; prof. law Touro Law Sch., Huntington, NY, 1984—2006, emeritus prof., 2006—; academic dean Touro Law Ctr., Huntington, NY, 1984-85; pvt. practice Charleston, SC, 1987—, Huntington, NY, 1984—2006. Vis. scholar Columbia U., 1980, Harvard U., 1982-83; chair com. on legal edn. NY State Bar Assn, 1992-95; disting. vis. prof. Charleston Sch. Law, 2005-; cons. in the field; comml. and securities arbitrator; arbitrator, mediator U.S. Dist. Ct. Author: Securities Arbitration, 1994; reporter Revision of SC Bus. Corp. Law, 1981; editor: Lexis Nexis NY Corp. Law Handbook, 1986—; contbr. articles to profl. jours. Mem. ABA, Am. Law Inst. (life), Scribes, Alexander Hamilton Inn of Ct. (pres. 1998-2000, 2002—06), Harvard Club (NY), Sand Dollar Club (Folly Beach). Office: Charleston Sch Law 83 Mary St Charleston SC 29402 Home: 24 Wentworth St Charleston SC 29401 Office Phone: 843-377-2416. Business E-Mail: grantlaw@usa.com.

GRANT, JOAN JULIEN, artist; b. Cornwall, Ont., Can., Apr. 15, 1934; d. John Duncan Julien and Winnifred Josephine McCormick; m. Douglas MacDougal Grant, Sept. 24, 1955; children: Stephen John, Ann Elizabeth, Abigail Jennifer, David King. AA, West LA C.C., 1975; BFA, Otis Art Inst., 1977, MFA, 1979. Instr. Plymouth State Coll., NH, 1998; pvt. art instr. Represented in permanent collections; author, editor: Terrestis, 1995, Flight of the Muse, 2002. Active Citizens for a Livable Culver City, 1998—2000. Avocations: reading, book discussion groups, walking, hiking. Home: 4274 LeBourget Ave Culver City CA 90232 Personal E-mail: joan.grant@earthlink.net.

GRANT, JOI ODOM, mathematics educator; b. Boynton Beach, Fla., May 8, 1967; d. Eddie Odom, Jr. and Yvonne Lee Odom; m. Troy Jennings Grant, June 19, 1993; children: Tyler Joy, Troi Ashlee. Degree in elem. edn., Bethune-Cookman Coll., Daytona Beach, Fla., 1989; MS in Elem. Edn., Nova U., Ft. Lauderdale, Fla., 1992, EdS in Ednl. Leadership, 2006. Tchr. Palm Beach County Sch. Dist., Fla., 1985—2001, math. coach, 2002—05, math. adminstr., 2005—. Mem.: Fla. Assn. of Math. Suprs. (assoc.), Palm Beach County Coun. Tchrs. of Math. (assoc.), Delta Sigma Theta (assoc.). Independent. Baptist. Avocations: relaxing on the beach, motivating others. Home: 5705 N Sable Cir Margate FL 33063 Office: Palm Beach County Sch Dist 3300 Forest Hill Blvd West Palm Beach FL 33406-5813 Home Phone: 954-969-7707; Office Phone: 5614348049. Office Fax: 5614348091.

GRANT, JOSEPH MOORMAN, finance company executive; b. San Antonio, Oct. 30, 1938; s. George William and Mary Christian (Moorman) G.; m. Sheila Ann Peterson, Aug. 26, 1961; children: Mary Elizabeth, Steven Clay. BBA, So. Meth. U., 1960; MBA, U. Tex., 1961, PhD, 1970. Banking officer Citibank, NYC, 1961-65; sr. v.p., economist Tex. Commerce Bank (N.A.) also Tex. Commerce Bancshares, Houston, 1970-73; pres., dir. Tex. Commerce Bank, Austin, 1974-75; chmn., CEO Tex. Am. Bankshares/Ft. Worth, 1986-89; pres. Tex. Am. Bank/Ft. Worth, 1976-89, chmn., CEO, 1983-89; exec. v.p., CFO Electronic Data Systems, Dallas, 1990-98; chmn., CEO Tex. Capital Bancshares, 1998—. Bd. dirs. Vignette Corp., Wingate Ptnrs., Chaparral Steel. Author: (with Lawrence L. Crum) The Development of State-Chartered Banking in Texas, 1978, The Great Texas Banking Crash, 1996. Trustee Tex. Christian U., 1989-94, So. Meth. U., 1980-89; chmn. adv. coun. Coll. Bus. Adminstrn. Found., U. Tex., Austin; trustee Dallas County C.C.; bd. dirs. North Tex. Commn., 1976-86, chmn., 1981-82; trustee Paul Quinn Coll., 1995-98; bd. dirs. Communities Found. Tex., KERA; chmn. Woodall Rodgers Park Found. Recipient Man of Yr. award Anti-Defamation League B'nai B'rith, 1988, Banker of the Year award Am. Banker, 2001; named to Disting. Alumni, U. Tex. at Austin, Coll. Bus. Adminstrn., 1982, Hall of Fame U. Tex. Coll. Bus. Adminstrn., Austin, 1999, Am. Banker, 2001, Ernst & Young's Entrepeneur of Yr. fin. svs., 2002, Dallas Citizen's Coun., 2002. Mem. Ft. Worth C. of C. (past chmn.), Dallas C. of C., Young Pres. Orgn. (bd. dirs. 1980-89, internat. pres. 1987-88, exec. com.), Blue Key, World Presidents Ogrn., Exch. Club, Sigma Alpha Epsilon. Episcopalian. Home: 4305 Overhill Dallas TX 75205 Office Phone: 214-932-6610.

GRANT, LEONARD TYDINGS, clergyman; b. Lakewood, NJ, May 8, 1930; s. Allaire Harrison and Edith Dorothy (MacEntee) Grant; m. Nancy Elisabeth MacKerell, June 21, 1958; children: Scott Alexander, Elisabeth Tydings, Constance Allaire. BA, Rutgers U., 1952; BD, Princeton Theol. Sem., 1955; STM, Temple U., 1958; PhD, U. Edinburgh, 1961; LHD (hon.), Elmira Coll., 1987. Ordained Presbyn. Ch. U.S.A., 1955. Pastor 4th Presbyn. Ch., Camden, NJ, 1955-58, Meml. Presbyn. Ch., Wenonah, NJ, 1961-65; instr. Rutgers U., 1956-58; lectr. Conwell Sch. Theology, Phila., 1962-65; prof. history Indpls. Univ., 1965-76; grad. dean Indpls. U., 1966-76, acad. dean, 1974-76; pres. Elmira (N.Y.) Coll., 1976-87; pres. emeritus, 1987—; pres. Independent Coll. Fund N.Y., 1987-95; interim assoc. pastor Presbyn. Ch., Westfield, NJ, 1995-97; assoc. pastor Ctrl. Presbyn. Ch., Summit, NJ, 1997—2002, dir. planned giving, 2003—. Author: Prayers and Devotions of Richard Baxter, 1965; contbr. articles on edn., history and religion to jours. Former mem. adv. com. Am. Inst.

Banking, Arnot-Ogden Hosp., Coun. Ind. Coll., Ind. Coll. Fund N.Y.; former mem. adv. com. Sullivan Trail Coun. Boy Scouts Am.; former mem. adv. com. Coun. Elizabeth Presbytery, Found. for Ind. Higher Edn.; trustee mem. Permanent Jud. Com.; active Elizabeth Presbytery. Mem.: Princeton Club N.Y.C., Rotary, Phi Delta Kappa, Phi Alpha Theta, Alpha Sigma Lambda. Presbyterian. Office Phone: 908-273-0441 ext. 29. Business E-Mail: Lgrant@centralpres.org.

GRANT, LEWIS O., agricultural products executive, meteorology educator; b. Washington, Pa., Mar. 29, 1923; s. Lewis F. and Rita J. (Jacqmain) G.; m. Patricia Jean Lovelock, July 23, 1949; children: Ann, Nancy, Brenda, Andrew, Laura. BS, U. Tulsa, Okla., 1947; MS, Calif. Inst. Tech., Pasadena, 1948. Meteorological cons. Water Resources Devel. Corp., Pasadena, Calif., 1948-54, Denver, 1948-54; rschr. and rsch. dir. Am. Inst. Aerological Rsch., Denver, 1954-59; asst. prof., assoc. prof., prof. atmospheric sci. dept. Colo. State U., Ft. Collins, 1959-93, emeritus prof., 1993—; pres. Piedmont Farms, Inc., Wellington, Colo., 1975-98; sr. cons. Grant Family Farms, Wellington, 1998—. Cons. Colo. Legis., Denver, 1971-73; bd. dirs. adv. com. Integrated Pest Mgmt. Contb. to profl. jours. Scout master, com. chmn. Boy Scouts of Am.; pres. Partner Communities, Ft. Collins, Colo., 1988; elder Presbyn. Ch., 1980—; 1st lt. U.S. Field Artillery and USAF, 1943-46. Recipient Vincent J. Schaefer award Weather Modification Assn., 1991, Soil and Water Conservation award Ft. Collins Soil Conservation Dist., 1994. Fellow Am. Meterological Assn.; mem. NAS (sect. chmn. 1975-76, mem. climate com.), Organic Farming Rsch. Found. (bd. mem. 1995-2001). Republican. Presbyterian. Avocation: gardening. Office: Grant Family Farms 1020 W County Road 72 Wellington CO 80549-1912 also: Colo State U Dept Atmospheric Sci Fort Collins CO 80523-0001 Personal E-mail: lgrant3309@aol.com.

GRANT, M. DUNCAN, lawyer; b. Madison, Wis., Apr. 22, 1950; s. David Evans and Margaret Jane (Bloomfield) G.; m. Marcia Joan Cox, Sept. 18, 1970 (div. Dec. 1975); 1 child, Thomas David; m. Margaret Ann MacDonald, Mar. 24, 1990 (div. Jan. 1995); m. Victoria Lynn Nichols, Oct. 14, 2000. AB, Princeton U., 1972; JD, U. Pa., 1975. Bar: Pa. 1975, Del. 1991, U.S. Dist. Ct. (ea. dist.) Pa. 1976, U.S. Ct. Appeals (3d cir.) 1977, U.S. Supreme Ct. 1980, U.S. Dist. Ct. (Del.) 1992, U.S. Ct. Appeals (10th cir.) 1986, U.S. Ct. Appeals (11th cir.) 1996, U.S. Ct. Appeals (fed. cir.) 2002. Law clk. to judge U.S. Ct. Appeals (3d cir.), Phila., 1975-76; assoc. Pepper Hamilton LLP, Phila., 1976-83, ptnr., 1983—. Ed. in chief U. Penn Law Review. Am. fellow, Salzburg Seminar, 1986. Mem. ABA, Pa. Bar Assn., Phila. Bar Assn., Del. State Bar Assn. Democrat. Avocations: baseball, wine, golf. Home: 415 Gate Ln Philadelphia PA 19119-2815 Office: Pepper Hamilton LLP 3000 Two Logan Sq 18th & Arch Sts Philadelphia PA 19103-1083 Office Phone: 215-981-4343. Business E-Mail: grantm@pepperlaw.com.

GRANT, MARK ANTONIO, organization administrator; b. Newark, June 16, 1954; s. Louis Wallace and Mary Louise (Bantum) G. Student, Glassboro State Coll., 1972—75; BA, William Paterson U., 1977; postgrad., UCLA, 1984. Film editor ABC, Hollywood, Calif., 1978—81, video engr., 1981—84; pub. info. specialist United Way LA, 1984—85; blood cons. ARC, Santa Monica, Calif., 1985—86, dir., 1986—89; project coord., spokesman South Coast Air Quality Mgmt. Dist., 1989—91; coord. nat. youth Best Campaign for Drug Free Tomorrow, Sherman Oaks, Calif., 1991—; aide State Senator Ronald L. Rice, NJ, 1992—95; prodr. KLCS-TV LA Unified Sch. Dist., 1995—98, coord. spl. projects, 1998—; cmty. liaison The Children's Collective, Inc., LA, 2001—03; internat. liaison Future Schs., Gosford City, Australia, 2003—05; dep. spl. projects Dist. and Dir. Councilman Bill Rosendahl, LA, 2005—. Mem. Emergency Ops. Ctr., Santa Monica, 1986—; assoc. dir. Ednl. Ctr. Tchg. and Tng., Torrance, Calif., 2005— Bd. dirs. UN Assn., West Los Angeles, 1987—; mem. adv. bd. vol. ctr. West Los Angeles, 1988. Named Outstanding Young Man Am., 1982, 84, 88, Emmy award nominee, 1997. Mem.: Kiwanis. Democrat. Episcopalian. Avocations: running, bicycling, basketball, reading. Office Phone: 310-568-8772. Personal E-mail: mgxnj@yahoo.com.

GRANT, MERRILL THEODORE, television producer; b. NYC, July 9, 1932; s. Samuel and Rae (Renko) G.; m. Barbara Rosner, May 24, 1961; children: Andrea, Jonathan Samuel. BBA, CCNY, 1953; MS, Columbia U., 1954. V.p., dir. programming Benton & Bowles, NYC, 1957-70; sr. v.p., dir. radio and TV Grey Advt., NYC, 1970-72; v.p. Viacom Internat., NYC, 1972-74; pres. Don Kirshner Prodns., NYC, 1974-78, Grant Case McGrath, NYC, 1978-79, Grant-Reeves Entertainment, NYC, 1979-85; chmn., CEO Reeves Entertainment, NYC, 1985-93. Served with AUS, 1954-56.

GRANT, MERWIN DARWIN, lawyer; b. Safford, Ariz., May 7, 1944; s. Darwin Dewey and Erma (Whiting) G.; m. Charlotte Richey, June 27, 1969; children: Brandon, Taggart, Christian, Brittany. BA in Econs., Brigham Young U., 1968; JD, Duke U., 1971. Bar: Ariz. 1971, U.S. Dist. Ct. Ariz., U.S. Dist. Ct. (we. dist.) Tex., U.S. Ct. Appeals (5th, 7th, 8th, 9th and 10th cirs.), U.S. Tax Ct., U.S. Supreme Ct. Pres. Merwin D. Grant, P.C., Phoenix, 1977—; ptnr. Beus, Gilbert & Morrill, Phoenix, 1984—93; pres. Grant Williams P.C., Phoenix, 1994—, Grant & Vaughn P.C., 2003—. Guest condr. Phoenix Symphony Orch., 1989. Mem. Ariz. Joint Ho./Senate Ad Hoc Com. on Health Care Dists., 2001; vice chmn. Ariz. Joint County Tobacco Revenue Use and Security Charitable Trust, 2000—; chmn. Citizens' Task Force, Maricopa County Hosp., 2002—; Dist. 2 rrep. Indsl. Devel. Authority; charter mem. Rep. Presdl. Task Force, Washington, 1984—; bd. dirs. Grand Canyon coun. Boy Scouts Am., Phoenix, 1974—76, Maricopa Hosp., Health Sys. Bd., 1997—, Ariz. Motorsports Charitable Found.; pres., bd. dirs. Golden Gate Settlement, Phoenix, 1975—80, 1984—88, Phoenix Internat. Raceway Charities, Ariz. Acad. Decathalon Assn., exec. com., 1999—2002. Fellow: Ariz. Bar Found.; mem.: YMCA, ATLA, ABA (litig. sect.), Am. Paint Horse Assn., Am. Quarter Horse Assn., Kiwanis (bd. dirs. Phoenix chpt. 1972—79). Office: Grant & Vaughn PC 6225 N 24th St Ste 125 Phoenix AZ 85016 Office Phone: 602-393-4322. E-mail: grant@phxlaw.com.

GRANT, MICHAEL ERNEST, educational administrator, management educator; b. LA, June 6, 1952; s. Ernest Grant and Shirley Ruth (George) G. BA in Spanish, Calif. State U., Long Beach, 1974, MA in Edn. Adminstrn., 1978; EdD, Pepperdine U., 1984. Cert. elem., secondary, and cmty. coll. tchr., bilingual and cross-cultural edn., adminstr. Tchr. kindergarten through adult edn. Long Beach Unified Sch. Dist., Calif., 1975—83, tchr. 5th grade, 1975, tchr. 6th grade, 1975—76, bilingual multicultural specialist k-6, 1976—78, tchr. 6th-8th grade Spanish, 1978—79, mgmt. program specialist, 1979—80, adminstr., program specialist, 1980—81, vice prin., 1981—83; asst. prof. tchr. edn. Calif. State U., San Bernardino, 1986—88, prin. dir. IMPACT/TEACH, assoc. prof. ednl. psychology and adminstrn. Long Beach, 1988—91; pres., founder Mykulphone-An Empowerment Through Edn. Project, Beverly Hills, Calif., 1991—; instr. Spanish Calif. Disting. Sch., Beverly Hills, 1993—; founder, pres. Dr. Michael Grant Enterprises, 2004—. Asst. instr. tchr. edn. Grad. Sch. Edn., Calif. State U., Long Beach, 1983-86; pres., CEO Mykulphone, Real Estate Developer, 1999—; v.p. recognition bd. World Congress Arts, Scis. and Comm., 2007; lectr. in field. Exec. prodr., dancer, singer, songwriter (3D animated music video) The Flashy Dancer, 2004; contbr. articles to profl. jours. Grantee, Calif. State U., 1988—91; scholar, Pepperdine U., 1983—84. Mem. ASCAP, NEA, Am. Coun. Tchg. Fgn. Langs., Assn. Calif. Sch. Adminstrs., Nat. Assn. Tchr. Educators, Nat. Coun. States In-Svc. Edn., Nat. Black Congress Faculty, Calif. Faculty Assn., Calif. State Intersegmental Coordination Coun., Calif. Black Faculty and Staff Assn., Calif. Assn. Tchr. Educators, Calif. Edn. Rsch. Assn., Calif. Lang. Tchrs. Assn., Intersegmental Coordinating Coun. Democrat. Baptist. Avocations: shotokon karate (black belt), acting, dance, singing, songwriting. Home and Office: No 911 9663 Santa Monica Blvd Beverly Hills CA 90210-9999 Personal E-mail: drmichaelgrant@verizon.net.

GRANT, PATRICK ALEXANDER, lawyer; b. Denver, Nov. 14, 1945; s. Edwin Hendrie and Mary Belle (McIntyre) G.; m. Carla Clyde Yancey, Aug. 16, 1975; children: Mary Cameron, Sara Mansur, Alexis Hendrie. BA with honors, Colgate U., Hamilton, NY, 1967; MBA, Denver U., 1973; JD, Drake U., Des Moines, 1976. Bar: Colo. 1977. Law clk. to Judge Donald P. Smith, Jr. Colo. Ct. Appeals, Denver, 1976—77; assoc. Grant, McHendrie, Haines & Crouse, PC, Denver, 1977—83, ptnr., v.p., 1984—91, bd. dirs.; state rep. Colo. Gen. Assembly, Denver, 1984—92, vice-chmn. fin. com., 1987—88, chmn. audit com., 1989—90, chmn. judiciary com., 1988—92, chmn. legal svcs. com., 1988—89. Mem. Colo. Coun. Elected Ofcls. for Soviet Jewry, Denver, 1985-92, Colo. Spl. Task Force Tort Liability and Ins., Denver, 1985, Local U.S. Bank Bd., 2003—04; bd. dirs. Colo. Sports Hall of Fame, 1992-98, Colo. State U. Livestock Leader Coun. Kent Denver Leadership Fund, 1996-97, upper sch. chmn. parents divsn.; mem. Denver Cmty. Mental Health Commn., 1985-86; mem. exec. coun., planning com. St. Joseph Hosp., Denver, 1985-88; mem. Denver Bd. for Developmentally Disabled, 1987-88; vestryman, jr. warden St. Barnabas Parish, Denver, 1979-84; adv. com. Nat. Ctr. Preventive Law, 1987-90; bd. dirs. Colo. Jud. Inst., 1990-96, Denver Metro Conv. and Visitors Bur., 2001-, chmn. search com., 2004, chmn. Govt. Affairs com., 2004, exec. com. 2004; chmn. nominating com., mem. exec. com., 2006, bd. dirs. Mountain States Employers Coun, 2006—; exec. bd. Parents Assn., Gettysburg (Pa.) Coll., 1997-2001, chmn. parents fund, 2000-01, nat. campaign steering com., 2000-01; mem. steering com. Colgate U. (NY) Soc. of Families, 2001-04; exec. bd. Denver coun. Boy Scouts Am., scout show chmn., 1997—; mem. Colo. Revised Statutes Adv. Group, 1999, Roundup Riders of Rockies, 1989—; mem. bd. govs. Colo. State U. Sys., 2001—, mem. exec. com., 2003-05, sec., 2004, chmn., 2005-07; bd. dirs. Urban Farm, 2007—. Gates Found. fellow John F. Kennedy Sch. Govt. Harvard U., 1985, Toll Fellow Coun. of State Govts., 1987; recipient Outstanding Alumni award Kent Denver Country Day Sch., 1986, 2005, Colo. Wildlife Fedn. Appreciation award, 1987, Disting. Svc. to Higher Edn. award U. Denver, 1988, Bus. Legis. of Yr., award Colo. Pub. Affairs Coun., 1989, Outstanding Achievement award EPA, 1989, award of honor Hist. Denver, 1989, Stephen H. Hart award Colo. Hist. Soc., 1990, Spl. Recognition award AIA, Gen. Heritage award for Former Legislator, 1997, Disting. Alumni award Kent Denver Sch., 2005, Ellis Island medal of honor, 2007; named one of Outstanding Young Men in Am., US Jaycees, 1980, Legislator of Yr. Associated Builders and Contractors, 1991, Family Citizen of West, 2000; named to Denver Metro Conv. and Visitors Bur. Found. Tourism Hall of Fame, 2005; U. Colo. Health Scis. Ctr. Chancellor Soc. Lunch honoree, 2003. Mem. Colo. Med. Soc. Found. (bd. dirs., pres. 1997-99, pres. emeritus 1999—), Western Stock Show Assn. (exec. com., bd. dirs., exec. v.p., CEO 1990-91, pres., CEO 1991—), Metro Denver C. of C. (bd. dirs., chmn. econ. devel. coun. 1995-96, co-chmn. pub. affairs coun. 1999-2000, co-chmn. entrepreneurship coun. 2001-02), Assn. Rodeo Coms. (bd. dirs., chmn., 2005—). Republican. Episcopalian. Avocations: wood chopping, horseback riding. Home: 3777 S Dahlia St Englewood CO 80113-4215 Office: 4655 Humboldt St Denver CO 80216-2818

GRANT, PAUL, chemical engineer, real estate broker, lawyer; b. Patuxent River, Md., May 19, 1949; s. Ralph F. and Elizabeth (Payne) G. BS in Chem. Engring., Auburn U., Ala., 1971; MS in Chem. Engring., U. Md., College Park, 1975; Cert. Hungarian linguist, U.S. Army, 1972; JD U. Denver, 1995. Lic. real estate broker. Sales engr. Mixing Equipment Co., Rochester, N.Y., 1976-78; precious metals salesman James U. Blanchard & Co., New Orleans, 1979; owner, operator PK Grant & Co., Lakewood, Colo., 1979—; atty.; criminal def., comml., and civil litigator Denver, 1995—. Instr. Jr. Achievement Project Bus., Lakewood, Colo., 1984; state chmn. Libertarian Party, La., 1979, Libertarian Party candidate for gov. Colo., 1982, nat. chmn. Libertarian Party, 1983-85. Served with U.S. Army, 1971-74 Basketball scholar Pensacola Jr. Coll., Fla., 1967-69; named Nat. Merit scholar Auburn U., 1969-71; recipient Outstanding Translator award U.S. Army Def. Intelligence Agy., 1974 Office: 6053 S Quebec St #101 Centennial CO 80111 Office Phone: 303-771-1908.

GRANT, PAULA DIMEO, lawyer, mediator, nursing educator; b. Bridgeport, Conn., Aug. 3, 1943; d. Samuel Peter and Emilie Alyce (DiChiera) DiMeo; m. James Mullett Grant, Nov. 26, 1975. AS in Nursing, U. Bridgeport, 1973; BSN cum laude, Boston Coll., 1975; JD, No. Va. U., 1982; MA in Nursing, NYU, 1994. Bar: D.C. 1985, U.S. Ct. Appeals (D.C.) 1985, U.S. Dist. Ct. D.C. 1985, U.S. Supreme Ct. 1989, U.S. Dist. Ct. Md. 1995. RN, Conn. Coronary care nurse Cornell Med. Ctr., NYC, 1969-70; with Trans World Airlines, Chgo. and NYC, 1980—84; pvt. practice Washington, 1986-98; of counsel Ross & Hardies, Washington, 1998—2004; pvt. practice Washington, 2004—06; pntr. DiMeo and Grant Law Firm, 2006—. Mediator Superior Ct. D.C., 1991—2003; clin. asst. prof. cmty. and preventive medicine N.Y. Med. Coll., 1992—96; adj. prof. dept. nursing Columbia U. Tchrs. Coll., NYC, 1993, 94; adj. asst. prof. nursing Sacred Heart U., Fairfield, Conn., 1998—99, mem. adv. coun., 1998—2000; co-chair Annual TAANA Conf., Washington, 2003; adj. faculty Mercy Coll., White Plains, NY, 2001—; vis. asst. prof. Framingham Coll., Mass., 2005—06. Mem. task force for women Boston Coll., 2003. Mem. ABA, D.C. Bar Assn., Am. Assn. Nurse Attys., Inc. (co-chmn. legis. affairs com. 1987-91, bd. dirs. N.Y. Met. chpt. 1986-88, 2005-06, sec. 1986-87, nat. bd. dirs. 1996-2000, 04-07), Conn. Nurses Assn. (chmn. cabinet on econ. and gen. welfare 1985-88), Assn. Bar City N.Y., N.Y.U. Alumni Assn., The Am. Assn. Nurse Atty. Found. (pres., 1998-2001), Sigma Theta Tau (Cynthia Ellen Northrop award 2001). Roman Catholic. Avocations: reading, theater, music. Office: South Bldg 601 Pennsylvania Ave NW Ste 900 Washington DC 20004 Office Phone: 202-638-6956. Personal E-mail: pdmgrant@aol.com.

GRANT, PETER RAYMOND, biologist, researcher, educator; b. London, Oct. 26, 1936; came to U.S., 1978; m. B. Rosemary Matchett, Jan. 4, 1962; children: Nicola, Thalia. BA with honors, Cambridge U., Eng., 1960; PhD, U. B.C., Vancouver, Can., 1964; PhD (hon.), U. Uppsala, 1986; DSc (hon.), McGill U., 2000, U. San Francisco, Quito, 2005. Prof. McGill U., Montreal, 1965-78, U. Mich., Ann Arbor, 1978-85, Princeton (N.J.) U., 1985—. Author: Ecology and Evolution of Darwin's Finches, 1986, 99; co-author: Evolutionary Dynamics of a National Population, 1989; editor; Evolution on Islands, 1998; co-editor: Molecules, Molds and Metazoa, 1992. Fellow AAAS, Royal Soc. London, Royal Soc. Can.; mem. Am. Philos. Soc., Nat. Acad. Sciences (fgn. assoc.). Office: Princeton U Dept Ecol Evol Biology Princeton NJ 08544-1003

GRANT, RICHARD EARL, retired medical and legal consultant; b. Spokane, Wash., Aug. 27, 1935; s. Conrad Morrison and Sylva Celeste (Sims) G.; m. Susan Kimberly Hawkins, Mar. 17, 1979; children: Paaqua A., Camber Do'otsie O. BSc cum laude, U. Wash., 1961; MEd, Whitworth Coll., 1974; PhD, Wash. State U., 1980. Cert. disability mgmt. specialist; cert. case mgr. Supr. nursing Providence Hosp., Seattle, 1970-72; asst. prof. nursing Wash. State U., Spokane, 1972-78; dir. nursing Winslow (Ariz.) Meml. Hosp., 1978-79; adminstr. psychiat. nursing Ariz. State Hosp., Phoenix, 1979-80; asst. prof. Ariz. State U., Tempe, 1980-83; assoc. prof. Linfield Coll., Portland, Oreg., 1983-86, Intercollegiate Ctr. for Nursing Edn., Spokane, 1986-88; sr. med. care coord. Fortis Corp., Spokane, 1988-92; med. svcs. cons. CorVel Corp., Spokane, 1992-94; owner Richard Grant & Assoc., Spokane, 1995-99; med., vocat. case mgr. Genex Svcs., Seattle, 1999—2003; ret., 2003; cons. Assurance Case Mgmt., 2004—05; med. care cons. Alaska Nat. Ins. Co., 2005—. Cons. Ariz. State Hosp., 1980-82, Pres.'s Commn., Washington, 1981-83, U. No. Colo., Greely, 1985-86, Assurance Case Mgmt., 2004-05; area med. svcs. cons., 1992—. Author: The God-Man-God Book, 1976, Publications of the Membership (Conaa), 1983, 4th rev. edit., 1988, Predetermined Careplan Handbook-Nursing, 1988, Duhikya: The Hopi Healer, 1996; contbr. articles to profl. jours. Judge Student Space Shuttle Project, Portland, 1983, N.W. Sci. Expo, Portland, 1983. With U.S. Army, 1953-56. Grantee NIMH, U. Wash., 1961; named one of top Hopi Scholars, Hopi Tribe, Second Mesa, Ariz., 1981. Mem. AAAS, Nat. League for Nursing, Wash. League for Nursing (v.p. 1988-90), Coun. on Nursing and Anthropology (editor 1982-90), N.Y. Acad. Scis., Case Mgmt. Soc. Am., Sigma Theta Tau. Avocations: painting, scuba diving. E-mail: dr.regrant@comcast.net.

GRANT, ROBERT MCQUEEN, humanities educator; b. Evanston, Ill., Nov. 25, 1917; s. Frederick Clifton and Helen McQueen (Hardie) G.; m. Margaret Huntington Horton, Dec. 21, 1940; children: Douglas McQueen, Peter Williams, Susan Hardie, James Frederick. AB, Northwestern U., 1938; postgrad., Episcopal Theol. Sch., 1938-39, Columbia U., 1939-40; BD, Union Theol. Sem., 1941; STM, Harvard U., 1942, ThD, 1944; DD, Seabury-Western Theol. Sem., 1969, U. Glasgow, 1979; LHD, Kalamazoo Coll., 1979; DD, Ch. Div. Sch. Pacific, 1992. Ordained to ministry Episcopal Ch., 1942. Minister St. James Ch., South Groveland, Mass., 1942-44; instr. to prof. N.T. U. of South, 1944-53, acting dean, 1947; vis. lectr. U. Chgo., 1945, research assoc., 1952-53, assoc. prof., 1953-58, prof., 1958-87, emeritus, 1988—, Carl Darling Buck prof. humanities, 1973-87, Carl Darling Buck prof. emeritus, 1988—. Vis. lectr. Vanderbilt U., 1945-47, Seabury-Western Theol. Sem., 1954-55, 89, Augustinianum (Rome), 1990; lectr. Am. Council Learned Socs., 1957-58; vis. prof. Yale U., 1964-65, Fla. State U., 1989. Author: Second-Century Christianity, 1946, 2d edit., 2003, The Bible in the Church, 1948, rev. edit. (with David Tracy), 1984, Miracle and Natural Law, 1952, The Sword and the Cross, 1955, The Letter and the Spirit, 1957, Gnosticism and Early Christianity, 1959, 63, Gnosticism: An Anthology, 1961, The Earliest Lives of Jesus, 1961, Historical Introduction to the New Testament, 1963, The Apostolic Fathers, vol. I, 1964, vol. II (with H. H. Graham), 1965, vol. IV, 1966, U-Boats Destroyed 1914-1918, 1964, 2002, The Formation of the New Testament, 1965, History of Early Christian Literature (revision from E. J. Goodspeed), 1966, The Early Christian Doctrine of God, 1966, After the New Testament, 1967, U-Boat Intelligence 1914-1918, 1969, 2002, Augustus to Constantine, 1970, new edit., 2004, Theophilus of Antioch Ad Autolycum, 1970, Early Christianity and Society, 1977, Eusebius as Church Historian, 1980, Christian Beginnings: Apocalypse to History, 1983, Gods and the One God, 1986, Greek Apologists of the Second Century, 1988, Jesus after the Gospels, 1989, Heresy and Criticism, 1993, Irenaeus of Lyons, 1997, Early Christians and Animals, 1999, Paul in the Roman World, 2001, U-Boat Hunters, 2003; (with D. N. Freedman) The Secret Sayings of Jesus, 1960, (with G. Menzies) Joseph's Bible Notes, Hypomnestikon, 1996. Fulbright research prof. U. Leiden, 1950-51; Guggenheim fellow, 1950, 54, 59. Fellow Am. Acad. Arts and Scis.; mem. Soc. Bibl. Lit. (pres. 1959), Am. Soc. Ch. History (pres. 1970, co-editor 1962-87), Chgo. Soc. Bibl. Research (pres. 1963-64, editor 1956-61), Phi Beta Kappa. Home: 5807 Dorchester Ave 11E Chicago IL 60637

GRANT, ROBERT NATHAN, lawyer; b. Newburgh, NY, Mar. 7, 1930; m. Barbara Weil, Feb. 10, 1952; children— Susan, Elizabeth Grant Ellerton, Nancy Grant Gray. BA, Yale U., 1951; LLB, Harvard U., 1956. Bar: Ill. 1956, N.Y. 1990. Assoc. Sonnenschein Nath & Rosenthal, Chgo., 1956-65; ptnr. Sonnenschein, Nath & Rosenthal, Chgo., 1965—. Contbr. articles to profl. jours. Pres. Legal Aid Soc. Ill., 1988—94; founding chmn. Winnetka (Ill.) Pub. Schs. Found., 1995—98, Winnetka Cmty. House, 2000—01; pres. Winnetka Bd. Edn., 1980—81, mem., 1974—81, Winnetka Planning Commn., 1975—77, New Trier Twp. Caucus, 1974; bd. dirs. United Charities, 1984—94, mem. legal aid com., 1982—, vice chmn., 1986—87, chmn., 1987—94; founding chmn. New Trier HS Ednl. Found., 2000—03, chmn., 2001—05. 1st lt. USAF, 1951—53. Recipient William H. Avery award for 10 yrs. svc. as chmn. Legal Aid Soc., 1994. Mem. ABA (vice-chmn. commercial leasing com.), Scholarship and Guidance Assn. (bd. dirs. 1968-92, pres. 1979-83), Harvard Law Sch. Spl. Gifts, Yale Alumni Recruiting Com., Standard Club, Yale Club (N.Y.C.), Phi Beta Kappa. Avocations: tennis, jogging, travel, reading. Home: 1165 Hamptondale Ave Winnetka IL 60093-1811 Office: Sonnenschein Nath & Rosenthal 233 S Wacker Dr Ste 8000 Chicago IL 60606-6491 Office Phone: 312-876-8072. E-mail: rgrant@sonnenschein.com.

GRANT, ROBERT ULYSSES, retired manufacturing executive; b. Laramie, Wyo., Sept. 19, 1929; s. Guy Reid and Martha Clotilda (Krehmke) G.; m. Patricia Anne Towle, Feb. 12, 1955; children— Elizabeth, Sheila, Guy, Wilson, Mary BS in Civil Engring., U. Wyo., 1951; MBA, Harvard U., 1957. Fin. analyst, dir. acquisition analysis, v.p. mgmt. services, sr. v.p. corp. devel. Lear Siegler, Inc., Santa Monica, Calif., 1964-87. Served to lt. USNR, 1952-55 Mem.: Jonathan (Los Angeles), Masons. Democrat. Lutheran. Avocations: sailing, jogging. Home: 6549 Via Lorenzo Palos Verdes Peninsula CA 90275-6571 Personal E-mail: rugrant@earthlink.net.

GRANT, RONALD ALFRED, psychiatrist, pastoral counselor, psychoanalyst; b. Providence, May 28, 1938; s. Alfred Edward and Althea G.; children: Andrew Edward, Kathryn Caroline. AB, Tufts U., 1959; MDiv, Andover Newton Theol. Sem., 1963, STM, 1964, D in Ministry, 1972; MD, Boston U., 1969. Cert. psychoanalysis, med. psychotherapy, group therapy. Intern Mary Imogene Bassett Hosp. (affiliate Columbia U. Med. Ctr.), Cooperstown, NY, 1969—70, resident, 1970—71, N.Y. State Psychiat. Inst. and Columbia Med. Ctr., NYC, 1971—73; pvt. practice pastoral counselor, 1972—; pvt. practice psychiatry, Westport, Greenwich, Conn., 1973—; pvt. practice psychoanalysis, 1981—. Mem. faculty, tng. and supervisory analyst C.G. Jung Inst. N.Y., 1981—, med. dir., 1983—87; psychiat. cons. Montessori Sch., Wilton, Conn., 1987—97; staff psychiatrist, supr. Temenos Inst., Westport, Conn., 1987—, med. dir., 1998—2000; mem. adj. faculty Andover Newton Theol. Sem., 1991—98. Mem. editorial bd. Human Devel. Jour., 1986-94. Named one of Outstanding Young Men in Am., 1970. Mem. AMA, Am. Psychiat. Assn., Am. Inst. Homeopathy, N.Y. Assn. Analytical Psychology, Internat. Assn. Analytical Psychology. Avocations: stamp collecting/philately, sports, reading, skiing, golf. Office: 45 E Putnam Ave Greenwich CT 06830-5438 also: 1465 Post Rd E Westport CT 06880

GRANT, RONALD E., Internet company executive; m. Ashley Grant; 3 children. BA in Econs., Dartmouth Coll., Hanover, NH; MBA in Fin. and Internat. Bus., Columbia Bus. Sch., NYC. Dir. internat. bus. devel. NYNEX; ptnr. Mercer Mgmt. Consulting; sr. v.p. bus. affairs and devel. AOL, 1997, pres., COO, 2006—; sr. v.p. ops. Time Warner. Non-exec. dir Music Choice Europe P.L.C., 2004. Office: AOL LLC 22000 AOL Way Dulles VA 20166*

GRANT, RUSSELL PORTER, JR., lawyer, petroleum landsman; b. Ft. Sill, Okla., Nov. 5, 1943; s. Russell Porter and Jimmie (Bell) G.; m. Janice Rae Lockley, Nov. 19, 1966; 1 child, Russell Porter III. BS, US Mil. Acad., West Point, NY, 1966; JD, U. Miss., 1974. Bar: Miss. 1974, US Dist. Ct. (no. dist.) Miss. 1974, US Ct. Appeals (5th cir.) 1980, US Dist. Ct. (so. dist.) Miss. 1992. Ptnr. Patterson & Patterson, Aberdeen, Miss., 1974-80; petroleum landman Aberdeen, 1980-81; ops. landman Hughes & Hughes Oil and Gas, Jackson, Miss., 1981-84; mgr. gas contracts Hughes Ea. Petroleum, Ltd., Jackson, 1984-88; corp. counsel Hughes Ea. Petroleum, Inc., Jackson, 1988-89; pvt. practice Jackson, 1989-90, 91; assoc. Overstreet & Kuykendall, Jackson, 1990-91; ptnr. McKibben, Grant & Assocs., Jackson, 1991-95; pvt. practice Jackson, 1995-2000; petroleum landman, 2000—. Mem. legal com. Interstate Oil and Gas Compact Commn.,

Oklahoma City, 1992—; speaker Oil and Gas Inst., U. Ala., 1990, natural gas seminar Miss. Natural Gas Assn., 1986. Co-chair exec. com. Monroe County Rep. Party, Aberdeen, 1980; pres. Aberdeen Exch. Club, 1978-79; mem. Monroe County (Miss.) Port Authority, 1979-80. Capt. US Army, 1966-72. Named Outstanding Com. Chair, Aberdeen C. of C., 1979. Mem. Miss. Oil and Gas Lawyers (pres. 1986-87), Miss. Assn. Petroleum Landmen (v.p. 1987-88, pres. 1994-95), Miss. Bar (chmn. natural resources sect. 1988-89), Am. Assn. Profl. Landmen (cert. profl. landman), The Federalist Soc., Nat. Lawyers Assn. Episcopalian. Avocations: art, architecture, gardening, music, history. Home and Office: 36 Wintergreen Rd Madison MS 39110-9614 Personal E-mail: russellpjr_grant@bellsouth.net.

GRANT, S. G., education educator; b. Quonset Point, RI, May 10, 1955; s. Donald C. and Gayle P. Grant; m. Anne E. McManus, July 12, 1975; children: Alexander M., Claire E. BS, U. Maine, 1977, MEd, 1981; PhD, Mich. State U., 1994. Social studies tchr. Boothbay Regional HS, Boothbay Harbor, Maine, 1981—86; social studies cons. Maine Dept. Edn., Augusta, 1986—88; dir. grad. edn. U. So. Maine, Gorham, 1988—89; rsch. asst. Mich. State U., East Lansing, 1989—93; assoc. prof. SUNY, Buffalo, 1993—. Curriculum cons. Buffalo Pub. Schs., 2004—, Save Our History, Washington, 2005—, Harcourt Pub., Orlando, Fla., 2005—. Mem.: Nat. Coun. Social Studies, Am. Ednl. Rsch. Assn. Office: SUNY Buffalo 517 Baldy Hall Buffalo NY 14260 Office Phone: 716-645-2455. Business E-Mail: sggrant@buffalo.edu.

GRANT, SUSAN, television executive; b. Boston, Dec. 23, 1954; d. Robert Nathan and Barbara (Weil) G.; m. Steven W. Korn, June 17, 1976 (div. Apr. 1982). AB, Vassar Coll., 1976. Rsch. asst. corp. devel. Cornell U., Ithaca, N.Y., 1976-78; asst. to v.p. fin. dept. Turner Broadcasting System, Atlanta, 1978-79; dir. pub. rels., regional sales mgr. Turner Cable News Network, 1979-81, dir regional sales and mktg., nat. sales mgr., 1982-85; v.p. sales Magnicom Systems, Inc., Stamford, Conn., 1985; dir. nat. accounts Intec Systems, West Palm Beach, Fla., 1985; account exec. Columbia Pictures TV, Atlanta, 1986-88, v.p. syndication S.E. region, 1989—94; pres. Turner Program Services, 1994, CNN Newsource Sales and Turner Living; exec. v.p. CNN News Services. Bd. dirs. Zoo Atlanta; bd. dirs. mng. com. Literacy Action, Inc. Named Woman of Yr. Tech. (enterprise bus.), (WIT) Women in Tech., 2006. Mem.: Women in Cable (pres. 1980). Office: CNN News Services One CNN Ctr Atlanta GA 30303

GRANT, SYDNEY R., education educator, consultant; b. NYC, Feb. 3, 1926; s. Herman S. and Ethel H. G.; m. Margarita Henderson, Sept. 4, 1951. BS in Edn. cum laude, CCNY, 1950; MA in Spanish Letters, Nat. U. Mex., Mexico City, 1951; EdD, Columbia U. Tchrs. Coll., 1961. Program asst. Sch. Gen. Studies CCNY, 1951-52, instr. Spanish Sch. Gen. Studies evening program, 1952-64; tchr. Spanish and common brs., cons. The P.R. study N.Y.C. Bd. Edn., 1952-60; dir. of instrn. K-12 Verona (N.J.) Pub. Schs., 1961-64; assoc. chief of party, assoc. prof. Columbia U. Tchrs. Coll., US./AID contract team, Lima, Peru, 1964-68; assoc. supt. for curriculum Bellevue (Wash.) Pub. Schs., 1968-69; dir. office internat. edn. Coll. Edn. Fla. State U., Tallahassee, 1969-72, assoc. prof., dir. Ctr. for Ednl. Tech., 1972-75, assoc. dean for grad. studies Coll. Edn., 1975-78, prof. Coll. Edn., 1972—, prof., head dept. ednl. founds. and policy studies, 1986-89, prof. internat.-intercultural devel. edn., 1979-85, prof. emeritus, 1994—. Cons. U.S./AID, UN Devel. Program, UNESCO, Fundacion Natura, Fla. State U., Latin Am., S.E. Asia, Africa, 1969-90; sr. resident tech. adv. Min. Edn. and Culture for Fla. State U. in Windhoek, Namibia, 1991-93. With U.S. Army, 1944-46, ETO. Recipient Esso award Esso Standard Oil Co., 1960, Palmas Magisteriales Peruvian Ministry of Edn., 1967, Pres.'s Teaching award Fla. State U., 1978; Downer scholar CCNY, 1950. Mem. Nat. Soc. for Study Edn., Comparative and Internat. Edn. Soc., Common Cause, Amnesty Internat. Avocations: short wave radio, reading. Home: 1503 Belleau Wood Dr Tallahassee FL 32308-0911 Office Phone: 850-531-0448.

GRANT, VERNE EDWIN, biology professor; b. San Francisco, Oct. 17, 1917; s. Edwin and Bessie (Swallow) G.; m. Alva Day, June 12, 1946 (div. Aug. 1959); children: Joyce Grant Mixon, Brian, Brenda; m. Karen Alt, Nov. 3, 1960. AB, U. Calif., Berkeley, 1940, PhD, 1949. Teaching asst. botany U. Calif., Berkeley, 1946-49; NRC fellow Carnegie Inst., Stanford, Calif., 1949-50; geneticist Rancho Santa Ana Bot. Garden, Claremont, Calif., 1950-67; asst. prof. Claremont Grad. Sch., 1951-53, assoc. prof., 1953-57, prof., 1957-67; prof. biology Inst. Life Sci., Tex. A&M U., College Station, 1967-68; prof., dir. Boyce Thompson Southwestern Arboretum U. Ariz., Superior, 1968-70; prof. botany U. Tex., Austin, 1970-87, prof. emeritus, 1987—. Author: Natural History of the Phlox Family, 1959, The Origin of Adaptations, 1963, The Architecture of the Germplasm, 1964, (with Karen Grant) Flower Pollination in the Phlox Family, 1965, (with Karen Grant) Hummingbirds and Their Flowers, 1968, Plant Speciation, 1971, 2d edit., 1981, Genetics of Flowering Plants, 1975, Organismic Evolution, 1977, The Evolutionary Process, 1985, 2d edit., 1991, The Edward Grant Family and Related Families in Massachusetts, Rhode Island, Pennsylvania, and California, 1997; mem. editl. bd. Ency. Americana, 1955-64, Brittonia, 1957-62, Evolution, 1960-62, Am. Naturalist, 1964-67, Biologisches Zentralblatt, 1974-97; contbr. articles to profl. jours. Recipient Sci. award Phi Beta Kappa, 1964 Fellow Am. Acad. Arts and Scis.; mem. NAS, Soc. for Study of Evolution (pres. 1968), Bot. Soc. Am. (cert. of merit 1971), Internat. Soc. Plant Taxonomists, Am. Soc. Plant Taxonomists, Acad. Medicine, Engring. and Sci. of Tex. Home: 2811 W Fresco Dr Austin TX 78731-5028 Office: U Tex Sect Integrative Biology Austin TX 78712

GRANT, WALTER MATTHEWS, retired lawyer; b. Winchester, Ky., Mar. 30, 1945; s. Raymond Russell and Mary Mitchell (Rees) G.; m. Ann Carol Straus, Aug. 5, 1967; children: Walter Matthews II, Jean Ann, Raymond Russell II. ABJ, U. Ky., Lexington, 1967; JD, Vanderbilt U., 1971. Bar: Ga. 1971, Tenn. 1992. Assoc. Alston & Bird, Atlanta, 1971-76, ptnr., 1976-83; v.p., gen. counsel, sec. Contel Corp., Atlanta, 1983-91; sr. v.p., gen. counsel Smith & Nephew Inc., Memphis, 1991-93; sr. v.p., gen. counsel, sec. The Actava Group Inc., Atlanta, 1993-96, Bruno's Supermarkets, Inc., Birmingham, Ala., 1996—2002. Editor in chief Vanderbilt Law Rev., 1970-71, Ga. State Bar Jour., 1979-82. Baptist.

GRANT, WILLIAM FREDERICK, geneticist, educator; b. Hamilton, Ont., Can., Oct. 20, 1924; s. William Aitken and Myrtle Irene (Taylor) Grant; m. Phyllis Kemp Harshaw, July 23, 1949; 1 child, William Taylor. BA, McMaster U., Hamilton, 1947, MA, 1949; PhD, U. Va., Charlottesville, 1953; DSc (hon.), McMaster U., 2000. Botanist, geneticist under Colombo Plan to Dept. Agr., Malaysia, 1953-55; asst. prof. McGill U., Montreal, Que., 1955-61; assoc. prof., 1961-66, prof. depts. plant sci. and biology, 1967-90, prof. emeritus, 1990—. Mem joint WHO and Int Program Chemical Safety Collaborative Study on Short Term Tests for Genotoxicity and Carcinogenicity, 1984—94; environ contaminants adv comt Ministers Environ and Nat health and Welfare, Ottawa, Ont, Canada, 1978—86; co-dir workshop higher plant mutagen bioassays UN Environ Program Quingao Ocean Univ, China, 1995. Editor: Lotus Newsletter, 1970—85, Can Jour Genetics and Cytology, 1974—82; mem ed bd: Mutation Research, 1978—85, Plant Species Biol, 1985—92, Revista Internacional de Contaminacion Ambiental, 1991—; editor (hon ed): Plant Species Biol, 1993—. Named to Alumni Gallery, McMaster U., 1996, Wall of Distinction, Westdale Secondary Sch. , Hamilton, Ont., 2006; recipient Andrew Fleming award, 1953, Gov. Gen. Silver medal, 1977, Distinguished Alumni/Alumnae Scholar award, McMaster U., 1990, award of Excellence, Grant- Moens, 2004; fellow, Blandy Rsch., 1950—53. Fellow: AAAS, Royal Soc Can, Linnean Soc London; mem.: Biol Coun Can (treas 1974—78), Soc Study Evolution (vpres 1972), Am Soc Plant Taxonomists, Int Orgn Plant Biosystematists (life; pres 1981—86), Can Botany Asn (George Lawson medal 1989), Environ Mutagen Soc, Genetics Soc Can (pres 1975, archivist 1984—, Predsl citation 1991, Lifetime Achievement award 2007), Sigma Xi (chpt pres 1975). Home: 43 St Andrews Rd Baie d'Urfe QC Canada H9X 2T9 Office: McGill U Macdonald Campus Dept Plant Sci Box 4000 Sainte Anne de Bellevue QC Canada H9X 3V9 Office Phone: 514-398-7863. Business E-Mail: william.grant@mcgill.ca.

GRANT, WILLIAM JOSEPH, retired judge; b. Nov. 18, 1922; BS, US Naval Acad., Annapolis, Md., 1946; JD, Gonzaga U., Spokane, 1954. Bar: Wash. 1954. Commd. ens. USN, 1946, advanced through grades to lt.; instr. seamanship and navigation US Naval Acad., 1949—50; dep. prosecuting atty. Spokane County, 1954—56; ptnr. Dellwo, Rudolf & Grant, Spokane, 1956—73; judge Wash. State Superior Ct., Spokane, 1973—92; ret., 1992. Instr. creditors rights Gonzaga U. Sch. Law, 1960—72. Recipient Disting. Jud. Svc. award, Gonzaga U. Sch. Law, 1993. Home: 2929 S Waterford Dr Apt 323 Spokane WA 99203-4400

GRANT, WILLIAM WEST, III, banker; b. NYC, May 9, 1932; s. William West and Katherine O'Connor (Neelands) G.; m. Rhondda Lowery, Dec. 3, 1955. BA, Yale U., 1954; postgrad., NYU Grad. Sch. Bus., 1958, Columbia U. Grad. Sch. Bus., 1968, Harvard U. Grad. Sch. Bus., 1971. With Bankers Trust Co., NYC, 1954-58, br. credit adminstr., 1957-58; with Colo. Nat. Bank, Denver, 1958-93, pres., 1975-86, chmn. bd., 1986-93. Chmn. bd. Colo. Capital Advisors, 1989-94; mem. adv. bd. Bancorp., Colo., 1993-99. With Nat. Trust Hist. Preservation; trustee Rocky Mountain Nat. Park Assocs., Estes Pk., Midwest Rsch. Inst., Kansas City; mem. adv. bd. Rocky Mtn. Pub. Broadcasting Sys.; dir. Colo. Energy Sci. Ctr., Four Mile Hist. Pk. Mem.: Colo. Symphony Found., Denver Country Club. Episcopalian. Home: 545 Race St Denver CO 80206-4122 Office Phone: 303-321-1566. Business E-Mail: petergrant1155@comcast.net.

GRANT GOLDMAN, PAMELA, journalist, writer; b. NYC, Sept. 2, 1961; d. Daniel B. and Shirley (Dworsh) G.; m. Joel S. Telpner, Oct. 29, 1995. BA in Polit. Sci., SUNY, Binghamton, 1984; MA in Journalism, Columbia U., 1990. With Sportset Inc., Syosset, N.Y., 1984-87; page NBC TV, Manhattan, N.Y., 1988; researcher NBC News, 1989, David W. Jayne meml. fellow, 1989-90, fgn. desk editor, field producer, 1990-91; freelance journalist Barcelona, 1991-92; assoc. prodr. The Brokaw Report, 1992-93; writer NBC Nightly News, 1993-95; freelance writer and prodr., 1996—. Writer/prodr. Who's Going to Care For These Kids, 1991 (Emmy award for News & Pub. Info. Programming). Recipient Emmy award for news and pub. info. category, 1991. Mem. Soc. Profl. Journalists, N.Y. Deadline Club. Avocations: exercise, travel, reading. Home: 111 E 30th St Apt 15a New York NY 10016-7368

GRANTHAM, CAMILLE RENEE THERIOT, high school librarian, media specialist; b. Lake Charles, La., Nov. 23, 1958; d. George Joseph Jr. and Pattia Jean (Hoppe) Theriot; m. John Steven Grantham, June 27, 1981; 1 child, Laura Lynn. BS, McNeese State U., Lake Charles, 1980, MEd, 1990; M in Libr. and Info. sci., La. State U., 2003. Cert. tchr., La. Bus. tchr. St. Louis H.S., Lake Charles, 1980-84, Sulphur (La.) H.S., 1984-86; libr. A.A. Nelson Elem. Sch., Lake Charles, 1986-87, D.A. Combre Elem. Sch., Lake Charles, 1987-88, Gillis Elem. Sch., Lake Charles, 1988-89, Westlake (La.) H.S., 1989—; vis. libr. dept. tchr. edn. McNeese State U., 2000—05, 2007—. Mem. exec. bd. La. Assn. Student Couns., 1998. Bd. dirs. Children's Theatre Co., Lake Charles, 1996-98, Jr. League of St. Charles, 2003—. Named Libr. of Yr., Calcasieu Parish Reading Coun., 1994-95; named to Outstanding Young Women of Am., 1983; Ray Broussard grantee, 1993-94. Mem. ALA, La. Libr. Assn., Am. Assn. Sch. Librs., La. Assn. Sch. Librs., Profl. Educators of Reading (v.p.), Alpha Delta Kappa (chpt. pres., dist. chmn.). Roman Catholic. Avocations: reading, gardening, scrapbooks, genealogy. Home: 5705 Stonehaven Ln Lake Charles LA 70605-7177 Office: Westlake HS 1000 Garden Dr Westlake LA 70669-2502 Office Phone: 337-433-6866 x16. Personal E-mail: rtgrantham@msn.com.

GRANTHAM, DON, information technology executive; married; 2 children. Semi-profl. soccer player; various leadership roles in sales, mktg. and ops. IBM, head server product mktg. Europe, Mid. East and Africa, head svcs. sales No. Europe; with Sun Microsystems, Inc., 1999—, head worldwide sales ops., exec. v.p. svcs., exec. v.p. global sales and svcs., mem. exec. mgmt. group. Office: Sun Microsystems Inc 4150 Network Cir Santa Clara CA 95054 Office Phone: 650-960-1300.*

GRANTHAM, JARED JAMES, nephrologist, educator; b. Dodge City, Kans., May 19, 1936; married, 1958; 4 children. AB, Baker U., 1958; MD, U. Kans., 1962. Assoc. prof. med. U. Kans., Kansas City, 1969-76, head nephrology sect., 1970-96, prof., 1976-96, disting. prof., 1996—. Founder and chmn. Polycystic Kidney Rsch. Found.; dir. Kidney Inst., 2000. Fellow NIH, 1964-66; grantee Nat. Inst. Diabetes Digestive and Kidney Diseases, 1969-03; recipient Homer Smith award Am. Soc. Nephrology and Am. Heart Assn., 1992, David Hume award Nat. Kidney Found., 1998. Mem. Am. Soc. Nephrology, Am. Soc. Clin. Investigation, Am. Physiol. Soc., Am. Fedn. Clin. Rsch., Assn. Am. Phys. Achievements include research in fluid and electrolyte metabolism, electrolyte transport, mechanism of action of antidiuretic hormone and polycystic kidney disease. Office: U Kans Dept Medicine/ Nephrology 3901 Rainbow Blvd Kansas City KS 66160-0001 E-mail: jgrantha@kumc.edu.

GRANTHAM, JOYCE CAROL, small business owner, music educator; b. Alameda, Calif., Jan. 4, 1940; d. John Charles and Shirley Anne (Maze) G. AB in Music Composition, Mills Coll., 1961; student, LaSalle Extension U., 1965-69; MBA in Gen. Mgmt., Golden Gate U., 1980. Various secretarial and supervisory positions UNIVAC div. Sperry Rand Corp., San Francisco, 1962-68; various mgmt. positions Decimus Corp., San Francisco, 1969-77, sec. policy rev. com., 1976-81, v.p. personnel, 1977-81; product mgr. Bank of Am., San Francisco, 1981-83, asst. v.p., mgr. ops., mktg. and product mgmt., 1984-85; owner Grantham Assocs./White Rabbit Bus. Graphics, Walnut Creek, Calif., 1985—99. Tchr. piano Joyce Grantham Piano Studio, Walnut Creek, 1985—. Composer (piano piece) Sarabande, 1959, (song cycle) Sing the Forsaken, 1960, String Trio, 1961 (Elizabeth Mills Crothers prize, 1961); concert pianist, soloist Oakland and San Francisco Symphonies; radio and TV appearances and collaborative performances, Calif., Hawaii, NY and Brussels, 1952-. Bd. dirs. San Leandro Symphony Assn., 1965-66. Francis J. Hellman scholar, 1957, Calif. State scholar, 1957; recipient and winner Flora Boyd award piano performance Mills Coll., 1958, Mozart concerto competition, 1960. Mem. Nat. Guild of Piano Tchrs. (scholar 1957), Am. Coll. of Musicians, Calif. Assn. Profl. Music Tchrs. (bd. dirs. 1998—, v.p. membership 2000-02, v.p. dists. and chpts. 2004—), Music Tchrs. Nat. Assn., Music Tchrs. Assn. Calif. Democrat. Episcopalian. Avocations: gardening, collecting art and antiques. Office Phone: 925-938-5284.

GRANTHAM, RICHARD ROBERT, financial consultant; b. Ogden, Utah, July 25, 1927; s. Arthur and Dorothy (Taylor) G.; m. Charlotte Blackwood, Aug. 10, 1951; children: Robert Arthur, Scott Ford, Ann Margaret, Susan Marie. BS magna cum laude, Claremont Men's Coll., Calif., 1950. C.P.A., Calif. Acct., Price Waterhouse & Co., Los Angeles, 1950-57; asst. controller Cyprus Mines Corp., Los Angeles, 1957-64, div. controller, 1964-65, budget dir., 1965-72, v.p., treas., 1972-74, sr. v.p., treas., 1975-79, sr. v.p., controller, 1979-81; controller Amoco Minerals Co., Denver, 1980-81; sr. v.p., treas. Trust Co. of the West, LA, 1982-88; sec., treas. TCW Convertible Securities Fund, Inc., 1986-89; mng. dir. Trust Co. of the West, LA, 1989, cons. on oil and gas matters, 1989-92; sr. ptnr., chief adminstrv. officer TCW Realty Advisors, 1989-95; cons. earthquake repair and ins. matters Westmark Realty Advisors, 1995-99; fin. cons. San Marino, Calif., 1999—. Lectr. in field. Trustee Claremont McKenna Coll., 1953-54, 65-68, 74—, vice chmn., 1976-96; dir. Pasadena (Calif.) Symphony Assn., 1993-2004, v.p. fin., 1996-99, exec. v.p., 1999-2000, pres., 2000-02, mem. adv. bd., 2004-06. Mem. AICPA, San Marino Men's Republic Club (pres. 1967), Calif. Soc. CPAs, Claremont Men's Coll. Alumni Assn. (pres. 1953-54), Republican Assocs. Clubs: California. Home: 1660 Oak Grove Ave San Marino CA 91108-1109 Fax: 626-552-7100. E-mail: rgrantham1@socal.rr.com.

GRANTS, VALDIS, engineering manager; b. Liepaja, Latvia, Mar. 5, 1942; came to U.S., 1949, naturalized, 1955; s. Karlis Valdemars and Meta Mudite (Greenvalds) G.; m. Yvette Marie Guhl, June 18, 1966; children: Kristine Marie, Carl Raymond. BS in Sci. Engring., U. Mich., 1964, BS in Engring. Maths., 1965, MS in Elec. Engring., 1967. Rsch. engr. U. Mich., Ann Arbor, 1965-70; sr. design engr. Info. Instrn., Inc., Ann Arbor, 1970-71, Allen-Bradley Co., Highland Heights, Ohio, 1971-76, engring. supr., 1976-77, engr. mgr., 1977-95; mgr. product safety Rockwell Automation, Mayfield Heights, Ohio, 1995. Patentee in field. Mem. IEEE, Am. Soc. for Quality, Tau Beta Pi, Eta Kappa Nu, Phi Kappa Phi. Avocations: astronomy, photography, personal computers, jogging, reading. Office: Rockwell Automation 1 Allen-Bradley Dr Mayfield Heights OH 44124-6118 Office Phone: 440-646-3428. Personal E-mail: val-yvette.grants@prodigy.net. Business E-Mail: vgrants@ra.rockwell.com.

GRAPHIA, GARY P., lawyer; b. Baton Rouge, Sept. 4, 1962; m. Rene Graphia. Degree in fin., La. State U., JD, 1991. Various positions to asst. v.p. Tex. Commerce Bank, Houston; assoc. Phelps Dunbar LLP, Kean, Miller, Hawthorne, D'Armond, McCowan & Jarman LLP, Baton Rouge, 1995—99, ptnr., 1999; sec., gen. counsel The Shaw Group Inc., Baton Rouge, 1999—. Bd. trustees La. Arts & Sci. Mus., 2002—, La. State U. Paul M. Hebert Law Ctr., 2003—. Named one of "40 under 40", Baton Rouge Bus. Report, 2001. Office: The Shaw Group Inc 4171 Essen Ln Baton Rouge LA 70809*

GRAPIN, JACQUELINE G., economist; b. Paris, Dec. 15, 1942; came to U.S., 1985; d. Jean and Raymonde (Ledru) G.; m. Michel Le Goc, June 4, 1971; children: Claire, Julien. Degree, Institut d'Etudes Politiques, Paris, 1966; Degree in Law, U. Paris, 1967; Auditeur, Inst. des Hautes Etudes de Def. Nat., Paris, 1980. Staff writer LeMonde, Paris, 1967-81; dir.-gen. Interavia Pub. Group, Geneva, 1982-86; pres. The European Inst., Washington, 1989—2006, chmn., 2006—; assoc. prof. Am. U. Econ. corr. Le Figaro, Washington, 1987—; prof. Inst. d'Etudes Politiques, Paris, 1974-77. Author: Guerre Civile Mondiale, 1977, Radioscopie des Etats-Unis, 1980, Fortress America, 1984, Pacific America, 1987, Transatlantic Interoperability in Defense Industries, 2002; pub. European Affairs; contbr. articles to profl. jours. Trustee Aspen Inst. for Humanistic Studies, NYC, 1981—96; bd. dirs. French Am. C. of C., Washington, Internat. Action Against Hunger. Recipient Prix Vauban Inst. des Hautes-Etudes, Paris, 1977, Officer in Order of Legion of Honor, 2001. Mem.: Internat. Inst. Strategic Studies, Cosmos Club, Nat. Press Club, Pen Club. Home: 4201 Cathedral Ave NW Apt 415W Washington DC 20016 Office: The European Inst 1001 Ct Ave NW Ste 220 Washington DC 20036 Office Phone: 202-895-1670.

GRASMICK, NANCY S., school system administrator; b. Balt. m. Louis J. Grasmick. BS in Elem. Edn., Towson State U., Balt., Md., 1961; MS in Deaf Edn., Gallaudet U., Washington, DC, 1965; PhD in Communicative Scis. with distinction, Johns Hopkins U., 1979; LHD (hon.), St. Mary's Coll., Towson State U., 1992, Goucher Coll., 1992, U. Balt., 1996, Villa Julie Coll., 1998. Tchr. deaf William S. Baer Sch., Balt., 1961-64; tchr. hearing and lang. impaired children Woodvale Sch., Balt., 1964-68; supr. Office Spl. Edn. Balt. County Pub. Schs., Md., 1968-74; prin. Chatsworth Sch., Balt., 1974-78; asst. supt. Balt. County Pub. Schs., Md., 1978-85, assoc. supt. Md., 1985-89; sec. juvenile svcs. Dept. Juvenile Svc., Balt., 1991; spl. sec. children, youth and families Gov.'s Exec. Office, Balt., 1989-94; supt. schs. Md. Dept. Edn., Balt., 1991—. Mem., chmn. interagy. com. on sch. constrn. Gov.'s Subcabinet for Children, Youth and Families; mem. Gov.'s Workforce Investment Bd., Profl. Stds. and Tchr. Edn. Bd. Md. Assocs. for Dyslexic Adults and Youth, State Bd. Edn. profl. adv. bd. Met. Balt. Assn. Learning Disabled Children, Md. Bus. Roundtable for Edn.; Trustee Md. Retirement and Pension Sys.; mem. adv. coun. Scholastic, Inc. Guest columnist Education Week, Educational Leadership and School Administrator, featured stories in the Wall Street Journal and on BBC. Bd. visitors US Army War Coll., Towson U., U. Md., Coll. Edn.; pres. Child Care Found. Recipient Medallion award Jimmy Swartz Found., 1989, Louise B. Makofsky Meml. award Md. Conf. Social Concern, 1990, Child Advocacy award Am. Acad. Pediat., 1990, Humanitarian award March of Dimes, 1990, Disting. Citizen's award Md. Assn. Non-pub. Spl. Edn. Facilities, 1991, Women of Excellence award Nat. Assn. Women Bus. Owners, 1991, Andrew White medal Loyola Coll., 1992, Nat. Edn. Adminstr. of Yr. award Nat. Assn. Ednl. Office Profls., 1992, Nat. award computing to asst. persons with disabilities Johns Hopkins U., 1992, Vernon E. Anderson Disting. Lecture award for outstanding leadership in edn. Coll. Edn., U. Md., 1992, DuBois Circle Award of Honor, 1992, Disting. Alumna of Yr. award Johns Hopkins U., 1992, Pub. Affairs award Md. C. of C., 1994, Speaker's award and medallion, Md. House Delegates, Profl. Legal Excellence-Advancement of Pub. Understanding of Law award Md. Bar Found., Inc., Pressley Ridge award, Victorine Q. Adams Humanitarian award, Cmty. Honoree 9th Ann. Heartfest Johns Hopkins Hosp., 1999, President's award, Coun., Ednl. Administrv. & Supervisory Organization Md., 2000, Engring. Edn. Leadership award, Engring. Soc. Balt., 2000, Outstanding Advocate award, Nat. Assn. Sch. Psychologists, 2000, President's award, Nat. Assn. Private Schools for Exceptional Children, 2000, Harold W. McGraw, Jr. Prize in Edn., 2000, Louis V. Koerber award, Nat. Flag Day Found., Inc., 2001, Ronald McDonald Foundation's Spirit of Children award, 2001, 2003, Cmty. Svc. award, Md. State Conf. NAACP, 2001, Md. Spirit Pub. Rels. award, Md. Chpt. Pub. Rels. Soc. Am., 2002, Sonya award, Carson Scholars Fund, 2002, John R. Calverti Meml. award, Cable Telecommunications Assn. Md., Del., and DC, 2003, Comm. and Leadership award, Toastmasters Internat. Region VII, 2003, Breath of Life award, Am. lung Assn. Md., Inc., 2003, Woodrow Wilson award for Disting. Govt. Svc., John Hopkins U. Alumni Assn., 2004, Md. Women's Hall of Fame, Md. Commn. for Women, 2004, 2004, President's award for K-12 Leadership Coll. Bd., 2004, Outstanding Achievement award, Better Bus. Bur. Greater Md., 2005, Joan S. Korenman award, Ctr. for Women and Info. Tech., 2006, Disting. Alumni award, Towson U., 2006, James Bryant Conant award, Edn. Commn. of the States, 2006; named Communicator of Yr. by Speech and Hearing Agy., 1990, Marylander of Yr., Advt. and Profl. Club of Balt., 1990, Most Disting. Woman Girl Scouts Ctrl. Md., 1994, Educator of Yr., Am. Coun. on Rural Spl. Edn., Balt. Most Influential, Balt. Bus. Jour., Marylander of Yr. by The Balt. Sun, 1997, Innovator of Yr., Daliy Record, 2004, 2005; selected as one of Md.'s Top 100 Women, Warfields Bus. Record, 1996, 98, 2000; inducted in the Circle of Excellence, 2000, Hall of Fame, Md. Commn. for Women, 2005. Fellow Nat. Assn. Pub. Adminstrs.; mem. Women Executives in State Govt., Phi Delta Kappa (Excellence in Edn. award), Pi Lambda Theta. Office: Md Dept Edn 200 W Baltimore St Baltimore MD 21201-2595*

GRASS, ALEXANDER, retail executive; b. Scranton, Pa., Aug. 3, 1927; s. Louis and Rose (Breman) G.; m. Lois Lehrman, July 30, 1950; children: Linda Jane, Martin L., Roger L., Elizabeth Ann; m. Louise B. Gurkoff, Apr. 26, 1974. LLB, U. Fla., Gainesville, 1949; D (hon.), Hebrew U., 2000, Doctorate (hon.) of Philosophy, 2000. Bar: Fla. 1949, Pa. 1953. Pvt.

practice, Miami Beach, Fla., 1949-51; v.p. Rite Aid Corp., Shiremanstown, Pa., 1952—62, pres., 1966-69, 77-89, chmn., chief exec. officer, 1969-95, chmn. exec. com., 1995-99; chmn., CEO Super Rite Foods, Inc., 1983-95. Chmn. bd. govs. Hebrew U. of Jerusalem, 1996-99, exec. com. mem., 1999-. Nat. exec. com. United Jewish Appeal, 1968-79, nat. vice chmn., 1970-79, gen. chmn., 1984-86, chmn. bd. trustees, 1986-88, bd. trustees, 1988-99; pres. Harrisburg Jewish Fedn., Pa., 1970-72; chmn. Israel Edn. Fund, 1975-78; bd. dirs. Pa. Right to Work Found., 1972-74, Harrisburg Hosp., 1977-81, Nat. Mus. Am. Jewish History, 2007; vice chmn. Harrisburg Hosp., 1988-95; bd. dirs. Pinnacle Health Sys., 1995-2001; active Pa. Coun. Arts, 1982; bd. dirs. Keystone State Games, 1982-92, Israel Ctr. Social and Econ. Studies, 1983; trustee Jerusalem Inst. Mgmt., 1983; exec. com. Jewish Agy. for Israel, 1984-88, bd. govs. 1984-90, chmn. bd. govs., 1999-2003, exec. com., 2003-; treas. United Israel Appeal, 1986-90. With USNR, 1945-46. Recipient Disting. Alumnus award U. Fla., 1992, Nat. Scopus award Hebrew U., 1993, Americanism award Anti Defamation League, 1995. Mem. Nat. Am. Wholesale Grocers Assn. (bd. dirs. 1971-73), Nat. Assn. Chain Drug Stores (bd. dirs. 1972-95, chmn. 1985-86, Nat. Achievement award 1995). Jewish (dir. temple). Office: Grass Cos 1000 N Front St Ste 503 Wormleysburg PA 17043-1043 Personal E-mail: agrass2140@aol.com.

GRASSANO, THOMAS DAVID, minister; b. Greenwood, SC, June 19, 1961; s. Thomas and Atha Elizabeth (Watts) G.; m. Lidia Angélica Minay, Aug. 20, 1983; children: Gabrielle Angélica, Thomas David Jr. MusB, Furman U., 1983; MusM, U. S.C., 1984; MusD, Fla. State U., 1988. Ordained to ministry Ch. of God, 1981, bishop, 1990. Evangelist Ch. of God, 1980-85; assoc. pastor Pkwy. Ch. of God, Tallahassee, Fla., 1985-86; instr. music Fla. State U., Tallahassee, 1986-88, campus min., 1986-88; min. youth and music Br. St. Ch. of God, Tallahassee, 1987-88; dir. worship, campus pastor Univ. Ch. of God, Tampa, Fla., 1988-89; coord. short-term missions and collegiate ministry internat. dept. youth and Christian edn. Ch. of God, 1989-94; founder, dir. Urban Harvest Ministries, NYC, 1994—; pastor Harvest Ch., Bronx, N.Y., 1995—. Lectr. Internat. Bible Schs., Mex., Guatemala, Chile, Argentina, Cuba, 1981—; founder Alpha Omega Campus Outreach Ministry, Ch. of God. Cmty. svc. chaplain, 1996—; dir. Exodus Drama Ministry, 1996—; mem. Nat. Youth Leaders Assn., Ctr. Cmty. Devel.; activist, lectr. empowering urban poor, 2003—. Mem. Southeastern Composers League, Nat. Assn. Composers, Promise Keepers, March for Jesus. Republican. Office: Urban Harvest Ministries PO Box 763 Bronx NY 10455 Business E-Mail: tgrassano@uhm.cc. *Your name, and Your renown, O Lord, are the desire of my heart.*

GRASSE, WANDA GENE, lawyer, writer; b. Baird, Tex., July 28, 1940; d. William Eugene and Alta Roberta (Dickerson) George; m. Weldon Morris Carriker, Jan 27, 1960; div. 1968; 1 child, Conrad Ray; m. 2d, John Lee Grasse, Mar. 28, 1970; 1 child, Karen Diane. LLB, LaSalle-Whittier Coll. Law, LA, 1977; postgrad. entertainment law studies, U. So. Calif., 1983. Bar: Calif. 1978, US Tax Ct. 1981, US Supreme Ct. 1987. Continuity dir. Sta. KLBK-TV and WTTN, Lubbock, Tex., 1960-66; promotion writer, dir. KTTV and KCOP, LA, 1966-72; sole practice law, LA, 1978-81; assoc. Laurence E. Clark, Law Corp. Monterey Park, Calif., 1981—. Mem. LA County Bar Assn., San Gabriel Valley Bar Assn., ABA. Republican. Mem. Sci. Mind, Mensa. Club: Bus. and profl. Women's (v.p. 1980-81, woman achievement award 1980, LA. Home: 1300 Fulton Ave Monterey Park CA 91755-4014 Office: Laurence E Clark Law Corp 631 S Atlantic Blvd Monterey Park CA 91754-3817 Personal E-mail: wandagrasse@sbcglobal.net.

GRASSELLI, MARGARET MORGAN, curator; b. Worcester, Mass., Mar. 1, 1951; d. Paul Shepard and Anne Piersol (Murray) Morgan; m. Nicholas Eugene Grasselli, May 24, 1981; children: James, Juliana, Anne Regina. AB magna cum laude, Radcliffe Coll., 1973; AM in Fine Arts, Harvard U., 1977, PhD, 1987. Curatorial asst. drawing dept. Fogg Art Mus., Cambridge, Mass., 1974-75, curatorial asst. print dept., 1977-78; asst. curator prints and drawings Nat. Gallery of Art, Washington, 1984-89, curator of Old Master Drawings, 1989—. Tutor fine arts dept. Harvard U., Cambridge, Mass., 1977; guest curator exhbn. Nat. Gallery of Art, Washington, 1980-84; professorial lectr. Georgetown U., Washington, 1988. Author: (exhbn. catalogs) Eighteenth-Century Drawings from the Collection of Mrs. Gertrude Laughlin Chanler, 1982, Colorful Impressions: The Printmaking Revolution in Eighteenth-Century France, 2003; co-author: (exhbn. catalogs) Renaissance and Baroque Drawings from the Collection of John and Alice Steiner, 1977, Old Master Drawings and Bronzes from the Cottonian Collection, 1979, Watteau 1684-1721, 1984-85, Master Drawings from the Armand Hammer Collection, An Inaugural Celebration, 1989, Art for the Nation, Gifts in Honor of the 50th Anniversary of the National Gallery of Art, 1991, Dürer to Diebenkorn: Recent Acquisitions of Art on Paper, 1992, Drawings from the O'Neal Collection, 1993, The Touch of the Artist: Master Drawings from the Woodner Collections, 1995, Mastery and Elegance: Two Centuries of French Drawings from the Collection of Jeffrey E. Horvitz, 1998, The Drawings of Annibale Carracci, 1999; Private Treasures: Four Centuries of European Master Drawings, 2007; mem. editl. bd. Master Drawings, 1994—; contbr. articles to profl. jours. Agnes Mongan Travelling fellow Harvard U., 1978-79, Samuel H. Kress Pre-doctoral fellow Samuel H. Kress Found., 1979-80, Ailsa Mellon Bruce Curatorial fellow Ctr. for Advanced Study in Visual Arts, 1989-90. Mem. Print Coun. Am. (bd. dirs. 1993-96). Office: Nat Gallery of Art 2000B S Club Dr Landover MD 20785-0001

GRASSER, GEORGE ROBERT, lawyer, real estate developer, consultant; b. SI, NY, Oct. 21, 1939; s. George J. and Anita F. (Spinetta) G.; m. Cecelia Frizziola, July 13, 1968; children: Mark, Eric. BBA, Iona Coll., 1960; JD, Fordham U., 1964. Asst. office mgr. Chgo. Title Ins. Co., NYC, 1966-67; assoc., then ptnr. Moot & Sprague, Buffalo, 1967-75; ptnr. Willig, Grasser & Sheffer, Williamsville, NY, 1975-77; prin. Albrecht, Maguire, Heffern & Gregg, Buffalo, 1977-85, Law Offices of George R. Grasser, Buffalo, 1985-87; ptnr. Phillips, Lytle, Hitchcock, Blaine & Huber, LLP, Buffalo, 1987—2002; prin. Grasser & Assocs., LLC, Buffalo, 2002—. Mem. adv. bd. Ticor Title Ins. Co., Buffalo, 1981— Author: Property Taxes and Homeowners Associations, 1980, 94, 95, 2002; contbg. author: Condominium Development, 1990; bd. editors N.Y. Land Report, Albany, 1980-83; contbr. articles to profl. jours. Pres. Ptnrs. for Livable Western N.Y., 2001—; mem. bd. advisors Friends of Sch. of Architecture and Urban Planning SUNY at Buffalo, 1999—2003; mem. bd. advisors Daemen Coll. Ctr. for Sustainable Communities and Civic Engagement, 2002—; bd. dirs. Baker Victory Svcs., 2004—. Recipient Cmty. Svc. award, AIA, 2001, Citizen of Achievement award, NY State LWV, 2004, Exemplary Civic Action award, Buffalo Niagara Region All Am. City Com., 2004, Burchfield-Penney Art Ctr. Espirit de Corps award, 2004. Mem. Am. Planning Assn. (Disting. Citizen Planner award Upstate NY chpt., 2006), NY State Bar Assn. (condominium and coop. com. 1978—, co-chmn. 1990-96, unlicensed practice of real estate law com. 1999-2002, co-chmn. 1999-2002), NY State Builders Assn. (trustee legal def. fund 1987-2000, dir. 1989-2000), Erie County Environ. Mgmt. Coun. (Friend of Environment award 2002), Erie County Bar Assn. (chmn. real estate com. 1978-82), Niagara Frontier Builders Assn. (bd. dirs. 1978-80, 89-99, sec. 1980-81, v.p. 1981, Svc. award 1977-98), Cmty. Assns. Inst. (trustee 1988-90, Svc. award 1986), Coll. Cmty. Assn. Lawyers (bd. govs. 1996-99), Buffalo Niagara Partnership (Pres.'s award 2000). Roman Catholic. Office: Grasser & Assocs LLC 11 Summer Street Buffalo NY 14209 Home Phone: 716-741-4650; Office Phone: 716-883-5070. Business E-Mail: ggrasser@irdprojectmanagers.com.

GRASSI, JOSEPH F., lawyer, mediator, arbitrator; b. NYC, Dec. 6, 1949; BA, Queens Coll., 1970; JD, NYU, 1974. Bar: NY 1974, U.S. Dist. Ct. (so. and ea. dists.) NY 1977, U.S. Ct. Appeals (2d cir.) 1975, U.S. Claims Ct. 1996. Law asst. appellate divsn., 2d judicial dept. Supreme Ct. State of NY, 1975-76; assoc. Milbank, Tweed, Hadley & McCloy, NYC, 1976-79; asst. corp. counsel Corp. Counsel of NYC, 1979-83; pvt. practice NYC, 1983—. Mem.: ABA, Assn. Bar City NY. Office: 100 Park Ave 20th Fl New York NY 10017 Office Phone: 212-983-3274. Personal E-mail: jfgrassi@aol.com.

GRASSIA, THOMAS CHARLES, lawyer, educator, writer; b. Westfield, Mass., Aug. 26, 1946; s. Thomas C. and Assunta (Abatiell) Grassia; m. Judith Chace Cranshaw, Aug. 15, 1970; children: Susan C., Joseph C. BA, Boston U., 1968; JD, Suffolk U., 1974. Bar: Mass. 1974, US Dist. Ct. Mass. 1976, US Supreme Ct. 1980. Asst. v.p. Plymouth Rubber Co., Canton, Mass., 1969-71; ptnr. P.T.S. Computer Svcs., Waltham, Mass., 1971-81, D'Angio & Grassia, Waltham, 1974-85, Grassia & Assocs., P.A., Natick, Mass., 1985—98, Grassia, Murphy & Whitney, P.A., Natick, 1998—2002, Grassia, Murphy & Lupan, P.A., Natick, 2002—. Agt. Lawyers Title Ins. Co., First Am. Title Ins. Co., Stewart Title Ins. Co.; bd. dirs. regional corps.; pres., treas., bd. dirs. Lender's Title & Abstract Co. Ltd., Natick; pub. spkr. and lectr. in field. Author: Campfires, 2000; contbr. articles to profl. publs. Mem., team leader Sherborn Fire and Rescue Dept., 1974—; bd. health City of Sherborn, Mass., 1976—81, bd. selectmen, 1981—85, mem. police chief selection com.; mem. Met. Boston Hosp. Coun., Burlington, Mass., 1983—84; former mem. long planning com. Sherborn Sch. Bd.; mem. Sherborn Emergency Med. Com.; trustee Leonard Morse Hosp., Natick, 1981—84; bd. mem. Salvation Army, Framingham, Mass. Mem.: ABA, New Eng. Spkrs. Bur., Am. Arbitration Assn. (comml. arbitration bd.), Mass. Conveyances Assn., Mass. Bar Assn., Helicopter Assn. Internat. (Augusta Cmty. Svc. award 2003), New Eng. Helicopter Pilots Assn. (past pres., chmn. bd. dirs.). Office: Grassia Murphy and Lupan PA 5 Commonwealth Rd Natick MA 01760-1526 Office Phone: 508-650-9252. Business E-Mail: tgrassia@gmllaw.com.

GRASSLEY, CHUCK (CHARLES ERNEST GRASSLEY), senator; b. New Hartford, Iowa, Sept. 17, 1933; s. Louis Arthur and Ruth (Corwin) Grassley; m. Barbara Ann Speicher, 1954; children: Lee, Wendy, Robin, Michele, Jay. BA, U. No. Iowa, 1955, MA in Polit. Sci., 1956; postgrad., U. Iowa, 1957-58. Farmer; instr. polit. sci. Drake U., 1962, Charles City Community Coll., 1967-68; mem. Iowa Ho. of Reps., 1959-75, U.S. Ho. Rep. 94th-96th Congresses from 3d Iowa Dist.; US Senator from Iowa, 1981—. Mem. com. agr., nutrition and forestry US Senate, com. budget, chmn. com. fin., ranking minority mem. com. fin., 2007—, com. judiciary, chmn. com. tax. Recipient Congressional award, Cmty Anti-Drug Coalitions of Am., 1997, Excellence in Health Svc. award, Nat. Assn. Cmty. Health Centers, 1998, Ester Peterson Sr. Advocate award, United Seniors Health Coop., 2000, Am. Fin. Leadership award, Fin. Services Roundtable, 2001, Bipartisan Hero award, Nat. Assn. Pediatric Nurse Assoc. and Practitioners, 2001, Excellence in Public Svc. award, Am. Acad. Pediatrics, 2001, Patients' Champions award, Am. Chiropractic Assn., 2001, Nat. Leadership award, Nat. Citizens' Coalition Nursing Home Reform, 2002, Legis. of Yr., Biotechnology Industry Orgn., 2003, Nat. Energy Leadership award, Nat. Bio-Diesel Bd., 2003. Mem. Am. Farm Bur., Iowa Hist. Soc., Black Hawk County Hist. Soc., Masons, Pi Gamma Mu, Kappa Delta Pi. Republican. Baptist. Office: US Senate 135 Hart Senate Bldg Washington DC 20510-0001 also: Federal Bldg Rm 120 210 Walnut St Des Moines IA 50309 Office Phone: 202-224-3744, 515-288-1145. Office Fax: 202-224-6020.*

GRASSMID, RONALD JAY, elementary school educator; b. Grand Rapids, Mich., Aug. 12, 1946; s. Joe and Florence Grassmid; m. Ruth Elaine Gebben, Aug. 18, 1967; children: Travis, Sheila, Kathy. BA in Elem. Edn., Calvin Coll., Grand Rapids, 1967. Cert. CPR instr. Elem. tchr. Moline Christian Sch., Ill., 1967—91, adminstr., 1991—97, mid. sch. tchr., 1997—. EMT Wayland Area EMS, Mich., 1984—99. Mem.: Nat. Mid. Sch. Assn. Avocations: travel, camping, gardening. Office: Moline Christian Sch 1253-144th Box 130 Moline MI 49335

GRASSO, DICK (RICHARD A. GRASSO), former stock exchange executive; b. Queens, July 26, 1946; m. Lorraine Grasso. D in Comml. Sci. (hon.), Pace U., NYU; cert. advanced mgmt., Harvard U., 1985; JD (hon.), Fordham U., Pepperdine U. Graziadio Sch. Bus., LaSalle U. Mem. staff NY Stock Exch., 1968-73, dir. listing and mktg., 1973-77, v.p. corp. svcs., 1977-81, sr. v.p. corp. svcs., 1981-83, exec. v.p. mktg. group, 1983-86, exec. v.p. capital markets, 1986-88, pres., COO, 1988-93, exec. vice-chmn., pres., 1993-95, chmn., CEO, 1995—2003. Overseer ops. N.Y. Future Exchange; coord. Depository Trust Co., Nat. Securities Clearing Corp.; bd. dirs. Securities Industry Automation Corp. Past chmn. bd. trustees Jr. Achievement N.Y; trustee Securities Industry Found. Econ. Edn., N.Y.C. Police Found., Inc., YMCA Greater N.Y.; bd. dirs. Nat. Italian Am. Found., Police Found., Washington, Centurion Found., Lower Manhattan Development Corp., Twin Towers Fund; metro N.Y. regional chmn. U.S. Olympic Com.; chmn. N.Y.C. Columbus Quincentennial Commn., 1992; hon. chmn. Friends of Statue of Liberty Nat. Monument/Ellis Island Found. Served US Army, 1966—68. Recipient Humanitarian of Yr. award Tomorrows Children's Fund, Spl. Achievement award Nat. Italian Am. Found., Ellis Island medal of honor Nat. Ethnic Coalition of Orgs., Good Scout award Greater N.Y. Couns. Boy Scouts Am., Brotherhood award NCCJ; named Man of Yr., Cath. Big Brothers, 1994.

GRASSO, JAMES ANTHONY, public relations executive, educator; b. Providence, Jan. 12, 1954; s. Forte T. and Eleanor Marie (D'Angelo) Grasso; m. Kimberly I. Maher, Sept. 14, 1986; children: Lauren Patricia, James A. Jr., Michael Robert. BS in Pub. Communication cum laude, Boston U., 1976, MS in Pub. Relations, 1983. Land and pub. relations rep. Algonquin Gas Transmission Co., Boston, 1978-83, asst. mgr., 1983-85, mgr. land, pub. relations, govt. relations, 1985-94, dir. pub. & govt. rels., 1994-97; v.p. pub. & govt. affairs, investor rels. Providence Energy Corp./Providence Gas Co., 1997—2000; v.p. pub. and govt. affairs New England divsn. So. Union Co., 1999—2000; pres., CEO Grasso Assocs., LLC, Needham, Mass., 2001—. Mem. adj. faculty Coll. Comm. Boston U., 1987—98. Bd. dirs. Ctrl. RI Devel. Corp., mem. exec. com.; mem. exec. com. Narragansett Coun. Boy Scouts Am.; bd. dirs. Beth Israel Deaconess Med. Ctr., Needham, New Eng. Coun., New Eng. Can. Bus. Coun., RI Conf. Cmty. and Justice; mem. exec. com. Narragansett coun. Boy Scouts Am. Mem.: New Eng. Gov.'s conf., Northeast Gas Assn., Pub. Rels. Soc. Am., Greater Boston C. of C., Greater Providence C. of C., Univ. Club R.I., Capitol Hill Club. Roman Catholic. Office: Grasso Assocs LLC 17 Avery Sq Needham MA 02494 Office Phone: 781-455-0220. Business E-Mail: jgrasso@grassoassociates.net.

GRATALO, JOHN, JR., banker, small business owner; b. Sommerville, NJ, May 2, 1963; s. John and Minica Villanueva Gratalo. BS in Fin., DePaul U. Banker Sears Mortgage Corp., Libertyville, Ill., 1987—94; sr. loan officer Lincoln Home, Bloomingdale, Ill., 1994—99, United Banc, Northbrook, Ill., 1999—. Owner The Cichild Hideout, Northbrook, Ill.; owner, specialist Loan Origination, 2004—; loan officer First Chgo. Mortgage, 1994—; with Focus Entertainment Inc., 2007—. Mem.: Philipino-Am. C. of C. (officer 1996—). Roman Catholic. Avocations: rare exotic tropical fish, fishing. Office: Loan Origination 1108 Whitfield Rd Northbrook IL 60062-3947 Office Phone: 800-678-5705. Personal E-mail: jgratalo@comcast.net.

GRATCH, SERGE, retired mechanical engineering educator; b. Monte San Pietro, Italy, May 2, 1921; s. Isaak F. and Tatiana (Dermaner) G.; m. Rosemary Delay, June 30, 1951; children: Susan, Mary, Lucia, Karen, Elizabeth, Ann, Barbara, Amy, Ellen, Thomas Charles. BSChemE, U. Pa., 1943, MS, ME, 1945, PhD, ME, 1950. Instr., U. Pa., 1943-45, asst. prof., 1945-50, assoc. prof., 1950-51; rsch. scientist Rohm & Haas Co., Phila., 1951-59; assoc. prof. mech. engring. Northwestern U., Evanston, Ill., 1959-61; supr. processes and devices Ford Motor Co., Dearborn, Mich., 1961-62, mgr. chem. processes and devices, 1963-69, asst. dir. engring. sci., 1969-72, dir. chem. sci. lab., 1972-85, dir. vehicles and component rsch. lab., 1985-86; prof. mech. engring. GMI Inst., Flint, Mich., 1986-96; prof. emeritus Kettering U. (formerly GMI Inst.), Flint, 1999—; ret. Mem. adv. bd. Coll. Engring. U. Iowa, 1969-73, Coll. Engring. U. Detroit, 1971-88; adv. bd. dept. mech. engring. U. Pa., 1973-88; chmn. air pollution rsch. adv. com. Coord. Rsch. Coun., 1983-85; mem. Nat. Alcohol Fuels Commn., 1979-81. Regional editor Internat. Jour. Fracture, 1965-91; contbr. articles to profl. jours. Mem. ASME (hon., past v.p. rsch., past pres., John Fritz medal 1992, Internal Combustion Engine award 1999), NAE, AAAS, Am. Soc. Engring. Edn., Am. Chem. Soc., Engring. Soc. Detroit (past pres.), Soc. Automotive Engrs. (chmn. lubricant rev. bd. 1982-83), Sigma Xi, Tau Beta Pi, Sigma Tau. Roman Catholic. Home: 32475 Bingham Rd Bingham Farms MI 48025-2427 Personal E-mail: sgratch112358MI@comcast.net.

GRATTON, PATRICK JOHN FRANCIS, oil industry executive; b. Denver, Aug. 28, 1933; s. Patrick Henry and Lorene Jean (Johnson) G.; m Jean Marie McKinney, June 10, 1955; children: Sara, Vivian, Patrick, Lizabeth (dec.). BS in Geology, U. N.Mex., 1955, MS in Geology, 1958. Geologist Westvaco Mineral Devel. Corp., Grants, N.Mex., 1955; mining engr. Utah Internat., Denver, 1956; geologist Shell Oil Co., Roswell, N.Mex. and Tyler, Tex., 1957-62; adminstrv. asst. Delhi-Taylor Oil Corp., Dallas, 1962-64; exploration mgr., ptnr. Eugene E. Nearburg, Dallas, 1965-70; ind. geologist Dallas, 1970—; pres. Patrick J.F. Gratton, Inc., Dallas, 1976—. Contbr. articles to profl. jours. Bd. dir. U. N.Mex. Found., 1992-2000. bd. dir. Caswell Silver Found, 1984-89, 1995-2003, With USCG, 1951-53, US Army, 1956-57. Named Disting. Alumnus in Geology, U. N.Mex., 1989; recipient Diplomacy and Innovation Spl. award, Assn. Engring. Geologists, 1991. Mem.: Dallas Geol. Soc. (hon. life 1999, Pub. Svc. award 1985, Profl. Svc. award 1992, Outstanding Svc. award 2002), Tex. Ind. Prodrs. and Royalty Owners Assn. (exec. com. 1985—97, 1999—2004), Soc. Ind. Profl. Earth Scientists (v.p. 1976—77, pres. 1977—78, Outstanding Svc. award 1990, hon. 1998), Am. Assn. Petroleum Geologists (hon. v.p. S.W. sect. 1976—77, del. 1978—81, pres. profl. affairs 1989—90, del. 1991—2002, hon. life profl. affairs 1993, adv. bd. divsn. environ. geoscientists 1993—96, chair ho. of dels. 1996—97, hon. ho. of dels. 2000, pres. 2004—05, chair adv. coun. 2005—06, Disting. Svc. award 1998), N.Y. Athletic Club, Explorers Club (Tex. chpt. chmn. 1987—88), Petroleum Club Dallas. Roman Catholic. Office: 3232 McKinney Ave # LB54/Ste 895 Dallas TX 75204-2429

GRATTON, ROBERT, diversified financial services company executive; b. Montreal, Que., Can., Oct. 23, 1943; s. Bernard and Judith (Dufour) G.; m. Nicole Marcil, Aug. 1966; 3 children. LLL, U. Montreal; LLM, London Sch. Econs. & Polit. Sci.; MBA, Harvard U. Asst. to Hon. Paul Gérin-Lajoie, Quebec City, 1966—68; COO Credit Foncier, 1971—79, pres., CEO, 1979—82; chmn., pres., CEO Montreal Trust, 1982—89; pres., CEO Power Fin. Corp., Montreal, 1989—2005, chmn. bd. dirs., 2005—. Chmn., bd. dirs. Great-West Life & Annuity, U.S., IGM Fin., Inc., Great-West Life, London Ins. Group, London Life Assurance Co., Can. Life Assurance Co., Can. Life Fin. Corp.; bd. dirs. Power Corp. Can., Power Fin. Corp., Pargesa Holding S.A. Mem. Mt. Royal Club, St.-James's Club, St.-Denis Club. Office: Power Fin Corp 751 Victoria Sq Montreal PQ Canada H2Y 2J3

GRATWICK, JOHN, management consulting executive, writer, consultant; b. Langley, Eng., Mar. 2, 1923; emigrated to Can., 1956, naturalized, 1970; s. Ernest Frank and Doris Hilda (Shepherd) G.; m. Dorothy Shirley Vincent, Aug., 1945 (div. 1957); children: Jane Mary, Paul; m. Gwendoline Johnston, Mar. 23, 1957; 1 son, Adrian. Cert. in Physics, London U., 1942, B.Sc., 1948. Chmn. Transp. Devel. Agy., Montreal, 1970-72; v.p. research and devel. Canadian Nat., Montreal, 1972-76, corp. v.p., 1980-82; pres. CN Marine, Montreal, 1976-80; prof. Sch. Bus. Adminstrn. Dalhousie U., Halifax, N.S., 1983-87, dir. Can. Marine Transp. Ctr., 1983-86, exec. dir. Internat. Inst. Transp. & Ocean Policy Studies, 1986-88; chmn. Halifax Industries Ltd., 1978-84; pres. Gratwick Hickling Inc., 1985-98; dir. Oceans Inst. Can., 1989-91. Chmn. Ctr. for Marine Vessel Design and Rsch., Tech. U. N.S., 1989-91; chmn. Halifax-Dartmouth Port Devel. Commn., 1991-96. Gov. Mt. St. Vincent U., 1989-98; mem. Nat. Transp. Act Rev. Commn., 1992-93. Recipient Achievement award Nat. Transp. Week, 1990. Fellow Royal Statis. Soc., Chartered Inst. of Transport; mem. Can. Operational Rsch. Soc. (pres. 1969-70), Can. Transp. Rsch. Forum (hon. life mem., pres. 1971-72), Internat. Fedn. Operational Rsch. Socs. (v.p. 1977-79). Home: 984 Bellevue Ave Halifax NS Canada B3H 3L7 E-mail: johngrat@eastlink.ca.

GRATZ, JAY M., b. NYC; m. Pam Gratz; 1 child, Kimberly. B in Econ. and Chemistry, SUNY, Buffalo, 1973; M of Mgmt. in Fin. and Acctg., Northwestern U., 1975. CPA, Ill. Various positions Inland Steel Industries, Inc., Chgo., 1975-81, asst. mgr., 1981-84, asst. mgr. cash and investments, 1984-86, mgr. fin. planning and analysis, 1986, v.p. fin., v.p. fin. Ryerson Tull, Inc., 1994-96; v.p., CFO Ryerson Inc., Chgo., 1996—98, exec. v.p., CFO, 1999—. Office: Ryerson Inc 2621 W 15th Pl Chicago IL 60608*

GRAU, JOHN MICHAEL, trade association executive; b. St. Joseph, Mich., May 22, 1952; s. Otto R. and Esther P. (Spitzer) G.; m. Gayle Luedeman, May 7, 1983 (div. Nov. 1996); m. Kristine Sweeney, Aug. 30, 1997; 1 child, Brendan Sweeney. BBA, U. Mich., 1974. Realty specialist HUD, Washington, 1974-75; field rep. Nat. Elec. Contractors Assn., San Mateo, Calif., 1975-76, chpt. mgr., Milw. chpt., 1976-85, asst. exec. v.p., Bethesda, Md., 1985-86, exec. v.p., CEO, 1986—2003, CEO, 2004—. Chmn., trustee Nat. Elec. Benefit Fund, Washington, 1986-2002; co-chmn. Coun. Indsl. Rels., Washington, 1986—; bd. mem. Plan for Settlement Jurisdictional Disputes in Constrn. Industry, Washington, 1986—; co-chmn. Nat. Joint Apprenticeship and Tng. Com. for Elec. Industry, Washington, 1986—; trustee Associated Specialty Contractors, Washington, 1987—. V.p. Electri Internat., Bethesda, 1989—, vice chmn., 1999—; bd. dir. Underwriters Lab., Northbrook, Il., 2000-, Elec. Safety Found. Internat., Rosslyn, Va., 1996—, treas., 1996-98, 2001-04; trustee Nat. Labor-Mgmt. Coop. Com., Washington, 1997, Helmets to Hardhats, 2004—. Fellow Acad. Elec. Contracting (bd. dir. 1986—); mem. Am. Soc. Assn. Execs. (key industries assn. com. 1987—, chmn. 2003-04), Am. Soc. Assn. Execs. Found. (bd. dir. 2001-04), Internat. Assn. Elec. Contractors (assoc. bd. dir. 1993—), US C. of C. (Com. of 100 1990—), Ctr. Assn. Leadership (bd. dir. 2004-06). Lutheran. Home: 4805 Jamestown Rd Bethesda MD 20816-2710 Office: Nat Elec Contractors Assn 3 Bethesda Metro Ctr Ste 1100 Bethesda MD 20814-6302

GRAU, MARCY BEINISH, real estate broker, former investment banker; b. Bklyn., Aug. 7, 1950; d. Joseph Beinish and Gloria (Rosenbaum) Bennett; m. Bennett Grau, Nov. 19, 1978; 3 children. AB with high honors, U. Mich., 1971; postgrad., Columbia U., 1972, N.Y. Inst. Fin., 1973. Asst. to chmn. Bancroft Convertible Fund, NYC, 1973-75; precious metals trader J. Aron & Co., NYC, 1975-81, mgr. metals mktg., 1981-83; v.p. Goldman, Sachs & Co/J. Aron, NYC, 1983-88; investment banking cons. NYC, 1988-90; real estate broker Fox Residential Group, 1998-99, Stribling & Assoc., NYC, 1999—2004, v.p., 2004—05, sr. v.p., 2005—. Editor Precious Metals Rev. and Outlook, 1980—; contbr. article to profl. jours. Vol. worker pediatrics dept. Lenox Hill Hosp., N.Y.C., 1978-79; asst. The Holiday Project, The Hunger Project, N.Y.C., 1978-83; vol. Yorkville

Common Pantry, N.Y.C., 1984; tutor Yorkville Neighborhodd Assn., N.Y.C., 1984; assoc. Child Devel. Ctr., N.Y.C.; trustee Congregation B'nai Jeshurun, 1989—, pres., 1991-94, chair, 1994-97; trustee Ethical Fieldston Fund, 1994-2000. Mem. Phi Beta Kappa. Avocations: interior design, fashion, cooking, piano. Home: 300 West End Ave New York NY 10023-8156 Office: 924 Madison Ave New York NY 10021-3577 Office Phone: 212-452-4361. Personal E-mail: marcyg300@aol.com.

GRAU, SHIRLEY ANN (MRS. JAMES KERN FEIBLEMAN), writer; b. New Orleans, July 8, 1929; d. Adolph and Katherine (Onion) G.; m. James Kern Feibleman, Aug. 4, 1955; children: Ian, James, Nora Miranda, William, Katherine. BA, Tulane U., 1950. Author: (short stories) The Black Prince and Other Stories, 1955, The Hard Blue Sky, 1958, The House on Coliseum Street, 1961, The Keepers of the House, 1964 (Pulitzer prize for fiction 1965), The Condor Passes, 1971, The Wind Shifting West and Other Stories, 1973, Evidence of Love, 1977, Nine Women, 1986, Roadwalkers, 1994, Selected Short Stories, 2004; writer publs. including Holiday, New Yorker, New World Writing, Mademoiselle, Saturday Evening Post, Atlantic, The Reporter, 1954—. Mem. Phi Beta Kappa. Office: PO Box 9058 Metairie LA 70055-9058 Personal E-mail: shirleygrau@bellsouth.net.

GRAUBARD, STEPHEN RICHARDS, historian, educator, editor; b. NYC, Dec. 5, 1924; s. Harry and Rose (Polk) G.; m. Margaret Cavendish-Bentinck Georgiades, Aug. 5, 1978; stepsons: William J. Georgiades, David C. Georgiades. AB, George Washington U., 1945; AM, Harvard U., 1946, PhD, 1951; DHL, Providence Coll., 1971, Suffolk U., 1984, Union Coll., 1987; DLitt, U. Vt., 1990. Instr. history and gen. edn. Harvard U., 1952-55, asst. prof., 1955-60, lectr., 1960-63, exec. sec. com. on gen. edn., 1952-59, research assoc. in internat. affairs, 1963-65; vis. prof. history Brown U., 1965-66, prof. history, 1966-94, prof. history emeritus, 1994—; mng. editor Daedalus, 1960-61, editor, 1961-2000; asst. editor Confluence, 1952-55; dir. studies Assembly on Univ. Goals and Governance, 1969-75. Author: British Labour and the Russian Revolution, 1956, Burke, Disraeli and Churchill: The Politics of Perseverance, 1961, Kissinger, Portrait of a Mind, 1973, Mr. Bush's War: Adventures in the Politics of Illusion, 1992, Command of Office: How War, Secrecy, and Deception Transformed the Presidency from Theodore Roosevelt to George W. Bush, 2004, The Presidents: The Transformation of the Presidency from Theodore Roosevelt to George W. Bush, 2005; editor: (with G. Holton) Excellence and Leadership in a Democracy, 1962, A New Europe?, 1964, (with G. Ballotti) The Embattled University, 1970 (with F. Gilbert) Historical Studies Today, 1972, (with S.N. Eisenstadt) Intellectuals and Tradition, 1973, (with F. Cavazza) Il Caso Italiano, 1974, A New America?, 1979, Generations, 1979, The State, 1980, Reading in the 1980s, 1983, Australia: The Daedalus Symposium, 1985, Art and Science, 1987, The Artificial Intelligence Debate, 1989, In Search of Canada, 1990, Living with Aids, 1990, Showa: The Japan of Hirohito (with Carol Gluck), 1992, The Research University in a Time of Discontent (with Jonathan R. Cole and Elinor G. Barber), 1994, (with Daniel Bell) Toward the Year 2000, 1997, A New Europe for an Old, 1998. Served with AUS, 1943. Social Sci. Rsch. Coun. fellow, 1948-50, Acad. fellow Carnegie Corp., 1999—. Fellow: Mass. Hist. Soc., Coun. Fgn. Rels., Am. Acad. Arts and Scis. (editor 1963—2000); mem.: Beefsteak Club, Signet Club, Century Club. Home: 22 Elm Park Gardens London SW10 9NY England Home Phone: 44-1832 720 427; Office Phone: 44-1832 720 636. Personal E-mail: stephengraubard@aol.com.

GRAUER, DAVID W., lawyer; b. Marysville, Kans., 1954; BS in Pharmacy, U. Kans., 1977; MS, Ohio State U., 1982; JD, Capital U., 1984. Bar: Ohio 1984. Pharmacist; ptnr. Squire, Sanders & Dempsey LLP, Columbus, Ohio, co-chmn., Health Care Strategic Bus. Unit & Health Care Practice Group. Mem.: Nat. Health Lawyers Assn., Ohio State Bar Assn. (health care law com.). Office: Squire Sanders & Dempsey LLP 1300 Huntington Ctr 41 South High St Columbus OH 43215-6197 Office Phone: 614-365-2786. Office Fax: 614-365-2499. Business E-Mail: sgrauer@ssd.com.

GRAUER, SHERRARD, artist; b. Toronto, Ont., Can., Feb. 20, 1939; d. Albert Edward and Shirley (Woodward) G.; m. John Keith-King, Feb. 12, 1971; children: Callum, Jonathan, Max. Student, Wellesley Coll., 1956-60, Ecole du Louvre, Paris, 1958-59; BFA, San Francisco Art Inst., 1964. One-woman shows include Mary Frazee Gallery, West Vancouver, Can., 1964, Bau-Xi Gallery, 1965, 67, 68, 70, 75, 76, 80, 83, 85, 87, 89, 90, 92, 97, 2001, Loyola Bonsecours Ctr., Montreal, Can., 1968, Jerrold Morris Gallery, Toronto, 1969, Surrey (B.C.) Art Gallery, 1980, Women in Focus Gallery, Vancouver, 1987, Art Gallery of the So. Okanagan, 1987, Churchill Coll., Cambridge, Eng., 2001, Moore Gallery, Victoria, Can., 2006, Union Club BC, 2007; group exhbns. include Can. Group Painters, 1965-68, Montreal Mus. Fine Arts and Can. Pavilion Expo, 1978, Nine out of Ten Hamilton Art Gallery, 1973, Nat. Gallery Can, 1975, B.C. Prov. Coll., 1978-79, Vancouver Art Gallery, 1986, 2001, Charles H. Scott Gallery, Vancouver, 1985, ARTROPOLIS, Vancouver, 1993, Art Gallery of Greater Victoria, B.C., 2001; commns. include World Wide Internat. Travel Office, Vancouver, 1969, U. B.C., 1972, Dept. Pub. Works Ottawa, 1976, Can. Tng. Inst., 1978, Foreshore Projects, Vancouver, 1990, 2001; represented in various pub. and pvt. collections include Vancouver Art Gallery, Can. Coun. Art Bank, Musée d'Art Contemporain, Montreal, Nat. Gallery Can. Trustee Vancouver Art Gallery, 1974-76, hon. sec., 1975-76; founding bd. mem. Arts, Scis. and Tech. Ctr., Vancouver, 1980-83. Mem. Royal Can. Acad. Arts, Can. Artists' Rep./Front des Artistes Canadiens, Can. Conf. Arts. Avocation: reading. Address: 4160 Hillbank Rd Cowichan Station BC Canada V9L 6MI E-mail: info@sherrardgrauer.com.

GRAULTY, ROBERT THOMAS, engineer, consultant; b. Troy, NY, July 22, 1928; s. Thomas Joseph and Elsie (Connor) Graulty; m. Jacqueline Anne Shields, Feb. 18, 1950; children: Kevin, James, Mark, Karen, Dianne, Daniel, John. BS, U.S. Merchant Marine Acad., Kings Point, NY, 1949; diploma, Westinghouse Mgmt. Program, U. Pitts., 1959. Registered profl. engr., Pa., 68, S.C., 86. Diesel engr. Am. Locomotive Co., Schenectady, NY, 1949—55; nuc. engr. Westinghouse Bettis Lab., Pitts., 1955—69, mgr., reactor engring., 1969—73, mgr., core mfg., 1977—82; spl. assignment to Adm. H.G. Rickover U.S. Navy, Naval Reactors Br., 1973—77; mgr., fuel mfg. Westinghouse Elec. Corp., Columbia, SC, 1982—86; cons. Columbia, SC, 1986—. Instr. Midlands Tech. Coll., Columbia, SC, 2002—. Author: (design manual) Shock and Vibration Design, 1966. Midshipman USNR, 1945—49, Atlantic. Mem.: Soc. Mfg. Engrs. (sr.). Achievements include patents in field. Home: 109 Miles Rd Columbia SC 29223

GRAUSMAN, PHILIP, sculptor; b. NYC, July 16, 1935; 1 child, David. Student, Sch. Painting and Sculpture, Skowhegan, Maine, 1956-57; BA cum laude, Syracuse U., 1957; student, Art Students' League, 1959; MFA, Cranbrook Acad. Art, 1959. Critic of archtl. drawing Grad. Sch. Architecture, Yale U., New Haven, 1974—. Instr. design Cooper Union, 1965-67; instr. design and drawing Pratt Inst., 1965-69; artist-in-residence Dartmouth Coll., 1972; instr. sculpture and drawing Skowhegan Sch. Painting and Sculpture, 1973; vis. asst. prof. art Yale U., 1974-76. Solo exhbns. include Frederik Meijer Gardens and Sculpture Park, Grand Rapids, Mich., 2001, Ice Gallery, N.Y.C., 1998, Borgenicht Gallery, N.Y.C., 1966, 74, 79, Alpha Gallery, Boston, 1968, 75, Dartmouth Coll., Hanover, N.H., 1972, U. Conn., 1976, Pa. State U., 1977, Washington Art Assn., Washington Depot, Conn., 1978, 82, Robert Schoelkopf Gallery, N.Y.C., 1983, 87, Babcock Galleries, N.Y.C., 1993, 2000, Tremaine Gallery, Conn., 1997, Ice Gallery, NY, 1998, Nat. Acad. Art and Design, 173rd Ann. Exhbn., NY, 1998, (Alex Ettl Award), 174 Ann. Exhbn., 1999, Ctrl. Conn. State U., 1999, Aldrich Mus., Figure Show, Conn., 1999, Sculpture Exbhn, Pier Walk, Navy Pier, Chgo., 2000, Meijers Gardens and Sculpture Park Mich., 2001, Chesterwood Nat. Trust, Mass., 2001, Art Omi, The Fields Sculpture Park, Ghent NY, 2003, Lohin Geduid Gallery, N.Y.C., 2006; exhibited in group shows at The Aldrich Mus., Whitney Mus. Am. Art, Am. Acad. in Rome, Nat. Acad. Design, Art OMI Internat. Arts Ctr., Ohio State U., Boston Coliseum, Wadsworth Atheneum, Chgo. Arts Club, Fine Arts Mus. San Diego, U. N.C., Paris/N.Y./Kent Gallery, Kent, Conn., numerous others; represented in collections at Vassar Coll., U. Mich., U. Mass., U. Conn., Newark Mus., Met. Mus. Art, Jewish Mus., N.Y.C., De Cordova Mus. Art, Lincoln, Mass., Cornell U., Bklyn. Mus., Rose Art Mus./Brandeis U., Balt. Mus. Art, Akron Art Mus., others. Recipient Gold medal of honor in sculpture Audubon Artists, 1956, Alfred G.B. Steel Meml. prize Pa. Acad. Fine Aarts, 1962, Solon H. Borglum award Silvermine Guild, Conn., 1980, Albert Jacobson Meml. award Silvermine Guild, 1984, Alex Ettel award, Nat. Acad. of Design, 1998, others; Huntington Hartford fellow, 1957, Louis Comfort Tiffany Found. grantee, 1959, Nat. Inst. Arts and Letters grantee, 1961, Prix de Rome fellow, 1962-65. Fellow Am. Acad. in Rome; mem. NAD (Dessie Greer prize 1981, Gold medal in sculpture 1988, cert. of merit in sculpture 1993). Office: Yale U Sch of Architecture New Haven CT 06520

GRAUSTARK, BARBARA, editor; Assoc. editor Newsweek, 1977—93; House & Home sect. editor NY Times, Style sect. editor, 2001—06, editor-at-large, 2006—. Copy editor Newsweek Condensed Books, 1973; co-author: John Lennon & the Beatles Forever, 1978, Strawberry Fields Forever: John Lennon Remembered, 1980; author: (article) Ono Remembers, Rolling Stone, 1981; writer, prodr., & dir.: (documentary) Yoko Ono: Then & Now, 1984, contbr. (book) The Rock Musician, 1993. Office: NY Times Style Desk 229 W 43rd St New York NY 10036 Office Phone: 212-556-1433. Office Fax: 212-556-5999.

GRAVEL, MIKE (MAURICE ROBERT GRAVEL), former senator; b. Springfield, Mass., May 13, 1930; s. Alphonse and Maria (Bourassa) Gravel; m. Rita Jeannette Martin, 1959 (div.); m. Whitney Stewart, 1984; children: Martin Anthony, Lynne Denise. Student, Am. Internat. U., 1950—51; BS, Columbia U., 1956. Mem. Alaska Ho. Reps., 1962—66, spkr., 1965—66; US Senator from Alaska, 1969—81; mem. environ. & pub. works, fin. & interior com. Founder, pres. The Democracy Found., 1989. Author: Jobs and More Jobs, 1968, Citizen Power: A People's Platform, 1972. Special adjutant in the Communication Intelligence Services and as a Spl. Agent in the Counter Intelligence Corps. US Army, 1951—53. Democrat. Unitarian. Office: Mike Gravel for Pres PO Box 948 Arlington VA 22216*

GRAVELY, MARY JEANE, volunteer; b. East Orange, NJ, July 15, 1920; d. William Chauncey and Marguerite (Guilbert) Ripley; m. Herbert Carlyle Gragely Sr., Sept. 18, 1943; children: Cynthia, David, Carlyle, Marshall, Peter. Student, Wells Coll., 1941. Bd. dirs. York Pl. Children's Home, 1980-85; vol. Grand Stand Humane Soc., Myrtle Beach, S.C., 1985-95; mem. diocesan coun. Episcopal. Ch., Charleston, S.C., 1985-86; pres. ch. women Trinity Ch., Myrtle Beach, 1983-84, vestry, 1986-89. Republican. Home: 5004 Pine Lake Dr Myrtle Beach SC 29577-2437

GRAVER, JACK EDWARD, mathematics professor; b. Cin., Apr. 13, 1935; s. Harold John and Rose Lucille (Miller) G.; m. Yana Regina Hanus, June 3, 1961; children: Juliet Rose, Yana-Maria, Paul Christopher. BA in Math., Miami U., Oxford, Ohio, 1958; MA in Math., Ind. U., 1961, PhD in Math., 1964. Instr. Ind. U., Bloomington, 1964; John Wesley Young Rsch. instr. Dartmouth Coll., Hanover, NH, 1964-66; asst. prof. math. Syracuse (N.Y.) U., 1966-69, assoc. prof., 1969-76; vis. prof. U. Nottingham (Eng.), 1971-72; prof. math. Syracuse U., 1976—, chmn. dept. math., 1979-82. Co-author: (books) (with M. Watkins) Combinatorics with Emphasis on Graph Theory, 1977, Locally Finite, Planar, Edge-Transitive Graphs, 1997, (with J. Baglivo) Incidence and Symmetry in Design and Architecture, 1982, (with B. and H. Servatius) Combinatorial Rigidity, 1993, Counting on Frameworks, 2001; contbr. articles to profl. jours. With USN, 1953—55. Fellow Inst. Combinatories and its Applications; mem. Soc. Indsl. and Applied Math., Nat. Coun. Tchrs. of Math., Assn. Math. Tchrs. N.Y. State, Math. Assn. Am. (bd. govs. 1985-88, Seaway sect. chair 1995-97), Am. Math. Soc. Home: 871 Livingston Ave Syracuse NY 13210-2935 Office: Syracuse Univ Dept Math Syracuse NY 13244-1150 Home Phone: 315-472-5306. Business E-Mail: jegraver@syr.edu.

GRAVER, LAWRENCE STANLEY, language educator; b. NYC, Dec. 6, 1931; s. Louis and Rose (Pearlstein) G.; m. Suzanne Levy, Jan. 28, 1960; children: Ruth, Elizabeth. BA, CCNY, 1954; MA, U. Calif., Berkeley, 1959, PhD, 1961. Asst. prof. English UCLA, 1961-64, Williams Coll., Williamstown, Mass., 1964-67, assoc. prof. English, 1967-72, prof. English, 1972—, William R. Kenan, Jr. prof. English, 1977-81, John H. Roberts prof. English, 1981-97, Roberts prof. emeritus English, 1997—. Author: Conrad's Short Fiction, 1969, Carson McCullers, 1969; editor: Mastering the Film, 1977, Samuel Beckett, 1979, (Landmarks of World Lit. series) Waiting for Godot, 1989, 2d edit., 2004, An Obsession With Anne Frank: Meyer Levin and the Diary, 1995; asst. editor: Columbia Companion to the Twentieth Century American Short Story, 2001. Served with U.S. Army, 1954-56. NEH fellow, 1980-81. Mem. MLA, AAUP. Democrat. Home: 117 Forest Rd Williamstown MA 01267-2028 Office: Williams Coll Dept English Williamstown MA 01267 E-mail: lgraver@williams.edu.

GRAVER, SUZANNE LEVY, English literature educator; b. NYC, Aug. 17, 1936; BA summa cum laude, CUNY, 1958; MA, U. Calif., Berkeley, 1960; PhD, U. Mass., 1976. Tchr. English Berkeley HS, 1960-61, Culver City HS, 1961-62; asst. prof. Berkshire CC, 1966-72; vis. asst. prof. Tufts U., 1976-78; assoc. ind. study Empire State Coll., SUNY, 1978; lectr. Williams Coll., Williamstown, Mass., 1976, 78-82, coord. writing workshop, 1981-85, asst. prof., 1983-87, chair dept. women's studies, 1988-89, assoc. prof. English, 1988-91, assoc. dean faculty, 1990-91, dean of faculty, 1991-94, prof., 1991—2002, John Hawley Roberts prof. English prof. emerita, 2002—, vis. prof. English, 2003—05. Manuscript reader Ind. U. Press, Victorian Studies, Victorian Periodicals Review, PMLA; fellowship and grants application reader NEH, Nat. Humanities Ctr., The Grad. Ctr., CUNY; Andrew W. Mellon emeritus fellow, 2005-07. Author: George Eliot and Community: A Study in Social Theory and Fictional Form, 1984, and numerous essays and revs. in Victorian lit. and culture. U. fellow U. Mass., Amherst, 1974-76, Am. Coun. Learned Socs. fellow, 1985-86, 89-90, Nat. Humanities Ctr. fellow, 1989-90, NEH fellow, 1995-96, Andrew W. Mellon Emeritus fellow, 2005-07. Mem. AAUP, ACLU, NOW, MLA (rep. to del. assembly 1988-91), Amnesty Internat., Wilderness Soc., N.E. MLA (chair English novel sect. 1980). Office: Williams Coll Stetson Hall Williamstown MA 01267-0141 Office Phone: 413-597-2559. Business E-Mail: sgraver@williams.edu.

GRAVES, ANNA MARIE, lawyer; b. Arlington, Va., Sept. 26, 1959; d. George W. and Anna (Czikora) G. AB cum laude, Cornell U., 1981; JD, U. Va., 1985. Bar: Calif. 1985, U.S. Dist. Ct. (cen. dist.) Calif. 1986. Corp. assoc. Memel, Jacobs, Pierno, Gersh & Ellsworth, LA, 1985-87, Stroock & Stroock & Lavan, LA, 1987—96; ptnr., co-chmn. Restaurant Food & Beverage industry group Pillsbury Winthrop Shaw Pittman, LA, 1989—2001. Chmn. UCLA Extension Calif. Restaurant Industry Conf. Named a So. Calif. Super Lawyer, LA Mag., 2004. Mem. ABA, Beverly Hills Bar Assn., Calif. Women Lawyers. Democrat. Office: Pillsbury Winthrop Shaw Pittman 725 S Figueroa St Los Angeles CA 90017 Office Phone: 213-488-7164. Office Fax: 213-226-4017. Business E-Mail: anna.graves@pillsburylaw.com.

GRAVES, BENJAMIN BARNES, business administration educator; b. Jones County, Miss., Nov. 5, 1920; s. Thomas Cannon and Velma (Barnes) G.; m. Hazeline Wood, May 25, 1946; children— Benjamin Barnes, Janis Elizabeth, Cynthia Wood. BA, U. Miss., 1942; MBA, Harvard, 1947; PhD, La. State U., 1961; LL.D., U. Ala., 1970. Staff and supervisory positions Exxon Co., 1947-60; spl. lectr. Coll. Bus. Adminstrn., La. State U., 1959-60, asst. prof., 1960-62; assoc. prof. U. Va., 1962-64; Milner prof. indsl. econs. U. Miss., 1964-65; pres. Millsaps Coll., Jackson, Miss., 1965-70; prof. bus. adminstrn. U. Ala. in Huntsville, 1970-90, pres., 1970-79, prof. emeritus, 1990—. Guest lectr. Mid-South Exec. Devel. Program, La. State U., 1962-68, also asso. dir. program, 1961-62; guest lectr. mgmt. program Natural Resources Mgrs., Pa. State U., 1962-72, Va.-Md. Sch. Banking, U. Va., 1962-73; vis. prof. bus. adminstrn. U. N.C. at Charlotte, 1976-77 Author articles in field. Pres. Miss. Found. Ind. Colls., 1967-68; mem. com. human investigation U. Miss. Sch. Medicine, 1964-70; v.p. Miss. Jr.-Sr. Coll. Conf., 1968-69; pres. Miss. Assn. Colls., 1969-70; mem. exec. com. Ind. Coll. Funds Am.; mem. adv. com. Am. Council on Edn.'s Inst. for Coll. and U. Adminstrs.; mem. Am. Assn. Schs. and Colls. univ. pres.'s del. to People's Republic of China, 1975, Republic of China, 1976; Pres. Huntsville Research Park Adv. Bd., 1973; Mem. exec. bd. Andrew Jackson council Boy Scouts Am., 1966—; bd. dirs. Jackson Symphony Assn., 1965-70; mem. pres.'s coun. U. Ala., Huntsville. Served to lt. (s.g.) USNR, 1942-46. Recipient Humanitarian of Yr. award The Arthritis Found. of Ala., 1999. Mem. Acad. Mgmt., Am. Mktg. Assn., Southwestern Social Sci. Assn., So. Econ. Assn., A.I.M. (pres.'s council), Jackson C. of C., Pi Kappa Alpha (mem. centennial com. 100), Phi Kappa Phi, Omicron Delta Kappa, Rotary (Paul Harris fellow; Vocat. Excellence award 2001). Clubs: Rotarian (dir. Huntsville 1973). Methodist. Home: 1317 Carlton Cove Blvd Huntsville AL 35802

GRAVES, DANIEL EDWARD, medical association administrator, researcher; s. Maurice Eugene Graves and JoAnn Voss; m. Debbra Lynn Currier, Nov. 16, 1996; children: Danielle Lynn Currier-Graves, Kaitlyn Nicole Currier-Graves. BS, U. Houston, 1989, MEd, 1996, PhD, 2001. Asst. prof. Baylor Coll. Medicine, Houston, 1993—; dir. spinal cord injury rsch. Inst. Rehab. and Rsch., Houston, 1996—. Mem. at large Am. Congress Rehab. Medicine, Chgo., 2003—06. Recipient Marcus J. Fuhrer Rsch. Achievement award, Baylor Coll. of Medicine, U. Tex. Health Sci. Ctr., Houston Phys. Medicine and Rehab. Alliance, 2004. Mem.: Psychometric Soc., Am. Congress Rehab. Medicine, Am. Spinal Injury Assn., Internat. Spinal Cord Soc. Avocations: destination imagination team leader, fishing. Office: Baylor Coll Medicine 1333 Moursund A-222 Houston TX 77030 Home Phone: 281-704-4400; Office Phone: 713-799-5023. Office Fax: 713-799-5030. Business E-Mail: dgraves@bcm.tmc.edu.

GRAVES, EARL G., JR., (BUTCH GRAVES), publishing executive; s. Earl G. and Barbara Graves; m. Roberta Graves; 4 children. BA, Yale U., 1984; MBA, Harvard U., 1988. Investment banker Morgan Stanley; v.p. advertising Earl G. Graves Pub. Co., 1988—91, sr. v.p. marketing, 1991—95, exec. v.p., COO, 1995—98, pres., COO, 1998—2006, CEO Black Enterprise mag., 2006—. Office: Earl G Graves Pub Co 130 5th Ave Fl 10 New York NY 10011 Office Phone: 212-242-8000.

GRAVES, EARL GILBERT, publishing executive; b. Bklyn., 1935; s. Earl Godwin and Winifred (Sealy) G.; m. Barbara Kydd, July 2, 1960; children: Earl Gilbert, John, Michael. BA in Econs., Morgan State U., Balt., 1958, LLD (hon.), 1973, Rust Coll., 1974, Wesleyan U., 1982; LHD (hon.), Dowling Coll., 1980; LLD (hon.), Va. Union U., 1976, Fla. Meml. Coll., 1978, J.C. Smith U., 1979; LittD (hon.), Hampton Inst., 1979; PhDBA (hon.), Bryant Coll., 1983; LLD (hon.), Talladega Coll., 1983, Baruch Coll., 1984; LittD (hon.), St. Josephs, NYC, 1985; LLD (hon.), Ala. State U., 1985; HHD (hon.), Morehouse Coll., 1986; LLD (hon.), Mercy Coll., 1986, Iona Coll., 1987, Elizabeth City State U., 1987; DCS (hon.), Suffolk U., 1987; LLD (hon.), Brown U., 1987, Lincoln U., 1988, Cen. State U., 1988; LittD (hon.), Meharry Med. Coll., 1989; LLD (hon.), Howard U., 1989, Livingstone Coll., 1989, Northwood Inst., 1991, U. D.C., 1991, Tougaloo U., 1992; DCL (hon.), Univ. South, 1993, U. Vt., 1994; degree (hon.), N.C. Ctrl. U., 1997, Manhattanville Coll., 1998. Adminstrv. asst. to Senator Robert F. Kennedy, 1965-68; owner mgmt. cons. firm, 1968-70; founder, CEO Black Enterprise Mag., NYC, 1970—2005, chmn., publisher, 2006—. Chmn., CEO Pepsi-Cola of Washington, L.P., chmn. customer adv. and ethnic mktg. com.; pres. Earl G. Graves Pub. Co., Inc., 1998-; bd. dirs. Rohm & Haas Corp., DaimlerChrysler Corp., Mag. Pub. Assn., N.Y. State Urban Devel. Corp., Nat. Supplier Devel. Coun., New Am. Schs. Devel. Corp., Glass Ceiling Commn., TransAfrica Forum, Aetna Life & Casualty Co., Federated Dept. Stores, Inc., AMR Corp. (Am. Airlines); keynote spkr. for small and large corps., pub. and non-profit sectors of bus. in Am. Author: How to Succeed in Business Without Being White, 1997 (finalist Fin. Times/Booz-Allen & Hamilton Global Bus. Book award 1997). Mem. adv. coun. Character Edn. Partnership; bd. dirs. New Am. Schs. Devel. Corp., TransAfrica Forum, Steadman-Hawkins Sports Medicine Found., Am. Mus. Natural History and Planetarium, trustee; nat. commr. scouting Boy Scouts Am.; bd. trustees Howard U., Washington; mem. vis. com. Harvard U. John F. Kennedy Sch. Govt.; mem. Pres.'s Com. Small and Minority Bus.; mem. nat. adv. bd. Nat. Underground R.R. Freedom Ctr.; trustee Howard U., Com. for Econ. Devel.; mem. pres.'s coun. for bus. adminstrn. U. Vt. Capt. U.S. Army, 1958-60. Recipient Silver Beaver award Boy Scouts Am., 1969, Scroll of Honor, Nat. Med. Assn., 1971, Nat. award of excellence U.S. Dept. Commerce, 1972, Pub. for Freedom award Operation PUSH, Black Achiever award Talk mag., 1972, Key award Nat. Assn. Black Mrs., 1972, Chgo. Econ. Devel. Corp. award, 1974, Nat. Alliance Black Sch. Educators award, 1974, Silver Antelope award Boy Scouts Am., 1988, Silver Buffalo award Boy Scouts Am., 1988, Free Enterprise award Internat. Franchise Assn., 1991, Entrepreneurial Excellence award Dow Jones & Co., 1992, Ernst & Young N.Y.C. Entrepreneur of Yr. award, 1995, Sci. and Industry Divsn. award Bklyn. Pub. Libr.'s Centennial Celebration, 1997, award DRUM Orgn./Bell Atlantic Corp., 1998, Marietta Tree award for pub. svc., Citizens Com. for N.Y.C., Inc., 1998, Charlse Evans Hughes gold medal NCCJ, 1998, Ronal H. Brown Leadership award Dept. Commerce Minority Bus. Devel. Agy., 1998, N.Y. Black 100 award Schomburg Ctr. for Rsch. in Black Culture/Black New Yorkers/Black N.Y. Consortium, 1998, Merrick-Moore Spaulding Nat. Achievement award N.C. Mut. Life Ins. Co.-100th Anniversary, 1998, Legacy award Rush Philanthropic Arts Found./Rush Comm., 1998; named one of Ten Most Outstanding Minority Businessman in Country by Pres. U.S., 1973, Outstanding Citizen of Yr., Omega Psi Phi, 1974, also one of 200 Future Leaders of Country, Time mag., Outstanding Black Businessman, Nat. Bus. League, one of 100 Most Influential Black Americans, Ebony mag., 2006; Poynter fellow Yale U., 1978; inducted Nat. Sales Hall of Fame, 1995, Morgan State U. Hall of Fame, 1998. Mem. NAACP (bd. dirs. spl. contbns. fund, Spingarn medal 1999), SCLC, Am. Inst. for Pub. Svc. (bd. selectors), Interracial Coun. Bus. Opportunity (award), Young Pres. Orgn., Mag. Pubs. Assn. (dir.), Advt. Coun., Bus. Mktg. Corp. N.Y.C., N.Y. Econs. Club (trustee), Sigma Pi Phi, Omega Psi Phi. Clubs: N.Y. Econ. (trustee). Democrat. Episcopalian. Office: Black Enterprise Mag and Earl G Graves Pub Co Inc 130 5th Ave Fl 10 New York NY 10011-4399

GRAVES, EARL WILLIAM, JR., journalist; b. Kodiak, Alaska, June 30, 1950; s. Earl William Graves, Sr. and Lola (Olson) Raab; m. Karin Ann Steichen, July 30, 1972; children: Emma, Mark, Max. BA in English with honors, U. Puget Sound, 1972; MA in English, Western Wash. State U., 1976. Tchr. English Naselle (Wash.) High Sch., 1972-74, Clatskanie (Oreg.) High Sch., 1975-77; police reporter Coeur d'Alene (Idaho) Press, 1978-79, city editor, 1980-82, mng. editor, 1983-84; sr. reporter Bulletin, Bend, Oreg., 1984-86; edn. reporter News and Observer, Raleigh, N.C.,

1986-87; state edn. reporter News and Observer/Raleigh Times, 1987-89; edn. reporter The Oregonian, Portland, 1990—. Author: Poisoned Apple, 1995. Recipient Outstanding Svc. award N.C. chpt. Phi Delta Kappa, 1988, Third Prize So. Journalism Feature Reporting award Inst. for So. Studies, 1989, N.C. Sch. Bell award N.C. Assn. Educators, 1989, Benjamin Fine award Nat. Assn. Secondary Sch. Prins., 1989, First Pl. Gen. News Reporting award N.C. Press Assn., 1990, First Pl. Edn. Reporting award Pacific Northwest Excellence in Journalism, Soc. Profl. Journalists, 1991, 92, 2001, Media award Assn. Retarded Children Oreg., 1992, Seconad Pl. Spot News Reporting award Best of West, 1992, Second Pl. Best Writing award Oreg. Newspaper Pubs. Assn., 1993, Excellence in Edn. award Oreg. Assn. Supervision and Cirriculum Devel., 1993; Nieman fellow Harvard U., 1998-99. Mem. Edn. Writers Assn. (pres., sec., bd. dirs. 1990—, Spl. Citation Nat. Awards for Edn. Reporting 1987, 91, Second Pl. Newspaper Series award 1989, Second Pl. Nat. Awards Edn. Reporting 1989). Democrat. Avocations: gardening, photography, outdoors, running, travel. Office: Oregonian 1320 SW Broadway Portland OR 97201-3499

GRAVES, ERNEST, JR., retired army officer, consultant, engineer; b. NYC, July 6, 1924; s. Ernest and Lucy (Birnie) G.; m. Nancy Herbert Barclay, May 12, 1951; children: Ralph Henry, Robert Barclay, William Hooper, Emily Birnie. BS, U.S. Mil. Acad., 1944; PhD, M.I.T., 1951; postgrad., Engr. Sch., Ft. Belvoir, Va., 1954-55, Command and Gen. Staff Coll., Ft. Leavenworth, Kans., 1957-58, Army War Coll., Carlisle Barracks, Pa., 1964-65, Harvard Bus. Sch., 1968. Commd. 2d lt. U.S. Army, 1944, advanced through grades to lt. gen., 1978, ret., 1981; with (SHAPE), Paris, 1951-54, (Army Package Power Reactor), Ft. Belvoir, 1955-57; comdr. (44th Engr. Constrn. Bn.), Korea, 1958-59; dir. (Army Nuclear Cratering Group, Lawrence Radiation Lab.), Livermore, Cal., 1962-64; exec. to sec. army Washington, 1967-68; comdr. (34th Engr. Group), Vietnam, 1968-69; div. engr. (U.S. Army Engr. Div., N. Central), Chgo., 1970-73; asst. gen. mgr. for mil. application U.S. AEC, Washington, 1973-75; dir. civil works Office Chief Engrs., Washington, 1975-77, dep. chief engr., 1977-78; dir. Def. Security Assistance Agy., Washington, 1978-81; sr. advisor Ctr. for Strategic and Internat. Studies, Washington, 1982-99. Contbr. articles to profl. jours. Decorated D.S.M., Legion of Merit, Bronze Star, Air medal. Mem. Soc. Am. Mil. Engrs. Home: 2328 S Nash St Arlington VA 22202-1548

GRAVES, JAMES E., state supreme court justice, educator; BA in Sociology, Millsaps Coll.; JD, Syracuse U.; MPA, Syracuse U. Maxwell Sch. Citizenship & Public Affairs; LLD (hon.), Millsaps Coll. Clerk Dept. of Community Devel., Syracuse, NY, 1978—79; staff atty. Central Miss. Legal Services, Jackson, Miss., 1980—83; ptnr. Murrain and Graves, 1983—84; assoc. atty. Walker and Walker, 1984—86; legal counsel Health Law Div., Miss. Atty. Gen. Office, 1986—89, Human Services Div., Miss. Atty. Gen. Office, 1989—90; special asst. atty. Miss. Atty. Gen. Office, 1986—90; dir. child support enforcement div. Miss. Dept. Human Services, 1990—91; cir. ct. judge 7th Cir. Dist., 1991—2001; justice Miss. Supreme Ct., 2001—. Adj. prof. media and civil rights law Jackson State U., 1980—97; instr. trial advocacy Harvard Law Sch., 1998—2000. Active pub. sch. activities; coach student mock trial teams. Named Parent of Yr., 2000—01; recipient Judge of Yr. award, Nat. Conf. Black Lawyers, 1992, Thurgood Marshall award, Jackson's Martin Luther King Celebration, 1994, 2002, Commissioner's award, US Dept. Health & Human Services, 2001, Special Achievement award, Jackson Federal Exec. Assn., 2002, Humanized Ed. award, Miss. Assn. of Educators, 2002. Mem.: Miss. Bar Found. (Law-Related Public Ed. award 2002), Magnolia Bar Assn. (Govt. Service award 1993, R. Jess Brown award 1994, Govt. Service award 1998), Hinds County Bar Assn. (Innovation award 2000), Nat. Bar Assn. (Disting. Jurist award 1996). Office: PO Box 249 Jackson MS 39205*

GRAVES, JOHN WILLIAM, historian; b. Little Rock, June 25, 1942; s. William A. and Mabel (Morehart) G. BA in History, U. Ark., 1964, MA, 1967; PhD in History, U. Va., 1978. Grad. tchg. asst. U. Ark., 1965-66; instr. history U. S.W. La., LaFayette, 1966-68; rsch. asst. U. Va., Charlottesville, 1971-72; instr. history S.W. Tex. State U., San Marcos, 1972-77; coll. assistance migrant program, freshman studies coord., basic skills specialist, lectr. St. Edward's U., Austin, Tex., 1979—85; assoc. prof. then prof. history Henderson State U., Arkadelphia, Ark., 1985—, chmn. dept. social scis., 2002—. Rep. Sch. Liberal Arts Faculty Senate, 1987-88; Rep., Dept. Social Sci. Faculty Senate, 2002-03. Author: Town and Country: Race Relations in an Urban-Rural Context, Arkansas, 1865-1905, 1990 (Arkansiana award Ark. Libr. Assn. 1991, Commendation award Am. Assn. for Study of State and Local History 1993); contbr. articles to profl. jours. Bd. dirs. Soc. for Preservation of Mosaic Templars of Am. Bldg., Hillcrest Residents Assn., Little Rock, Black History Adv. Com. State of Ark.; adv. bd. dept. Ark. heritage Mosaic Templars Am. Ctr.; rep. Coalition of LIttle Rock Neighborhoods. Recipient Disting. Svc. award Henderson State U., 1999-2000, Disting. Rsch. award Henderson State U., 2001-2002; Stonewall Jackson Meml. fellow Ark. History Commn., 1965, Philip Francis DuPont fellow U. Va., 1969-71. Mem. AAUP (pres. chpt. 1999-2001), So. Hist. Assn., Ark. Hist. Assn. (v.p. 1987-92, pres. 1992-96), Ark. History Coun. (Ark. sec. of state), Audubon Soc. (pres. Bastrop County Tex. 1985), Defenders of Wildlife, Environ. Def. Fund, Ark. Nature Conservancy, Nat. Trust for Hist. Preservation, Hist. Preservation Alliance Ark., Quapaw Qtr. Assn., Student Sen. U. Ark. (grad. sch. rep. 1965-66), Tau Kappa Epsilon (pres. 1964), Phi Alpha Theta. Home: 5218 G St Little Rock AR 72205-3517 Office: Henderson State U Dept History Arkadelphia AR 71999-0001 Fax: (870) 230-5144. E-mail: johnwgrav@aol.com, gravesj@hsu.edu.

GRAVES, JOHN WILLIAM, state supreme court justice; b. Paducah, Ky., Oct. 17, 1935; m. Mary Ann Breivo; children: James Anthony, Kevin Andrew. BS, U. Notre Dame, 1957; postgrad., U. Louisville Sch. of Medicine, 1957—58; JD, U. Ky., 1963; attended, Command & Gen. Staff Coll., Airwar Coll., Nat. Defense U. Bar: Ky. 1963. Jud. law clerk to Judge James B. Milliken Ky. Ct. of Appeals, 1963—64; atty. priv. practice, Ky., 1964—84; judge Ky. Dist. Ct., 1984—88; circuit ct. judge McCracken Cir., 1989-95; justice Ky. Supreme Ct., 1995—2006. Colonel USAR. Decorated Army Commendation medal, Army Meritorious Service medal, Defense Meritorious Service medal. Office Phone: 270-575-7039.

GRAVES, JUDSON, lawyer; b. Jacksonville, Fla., Dec. 13, 1947; s. A. Judson and Martha A. (Lively) G.; children: Ashley, Judson, Mallory. AB in Psychology, Dartmouth Coll., 1969; JD with distinction, Emory U., 1975. Bar: Ga. 1975, Fla. 1975. Assoc. Jones Bird & Howell, Atlanta, 1975-80, ptnr., 1980-83; ptnr., prod. liability group Alston & Bird LLP, Atlanta, 1983—. Lt. USN, l969-72. Mem. Lawyers Club Atlanta, Am. Coll. Trial Lawyers, Order of Coif. Office: Alston & Bird LLP 1 Atlantic Ctr 1201 W Peachtree St NW Atlanta GA 30309-3424 Office Phone: 404-881-7279. Office Fax: 404-881-7777. Business E-Mail: jgraves@alston.com.

GRAVES, LORRAINE ELIZABETH, dancer, educator, coach; b. Norfolk, Va., Oct. 5, 1957; d. Thomas Edward and Mildred Fayette (Odom) G. BS, Ind. U., 1978. Dancer, Regisseuse Dance Theatre of Harlem, NYC, 1978—, ballet mistress, 1980—, prin. dancer, 1980, artistic asst., 1998—. Artistic advisor Va. Ballet Theatre, 1997—; tchr./coach Dance Theatre of Harlem, 1998-99, 2001, guest ballet mistress, 2001—; guest tchr. N.C. Sch. of Arts, Winston-Salem, 1987, 93, Gov.'s Sch. for Arts, U. Richmond, 1990—, Carlton Johnson Acad. of Dance, 1991-95, Okla. Summer Arts Inst., 1993-94, The Flint Sch. Performing Arts, Flint Youth Ballet, 2001—, Dance Theatre of Harlem, Kennedy Ctr. Residency Program, 1993-95, 98—, Worcester Sch. Performing Arts, 1997, Greenville Ballet, 2001; resident guest tchr. Gov.'s Sch. for Arts, Norfolk, Va., 1988-91, mem. faculty, 1996—; guest tchr. Worcester Sch. Performing Arts, 1997; resident guest tchr. S.C. Gov.'s Sch. for Arts, 1995-97; guest tchr. Va. Ballet Theatre, 1996—, artistic advisor, 1998—; guest tchr. Va. Sch. for the Arts, 1997—, resident guest tchr., 2003—; educator, judge Dance Olympus, 1997—; judge Internat. Dance Challenge, 1998—; guest faculty Mid-States Regional Dance Festival, 1999; mem. faculty SERBA Festival, Roanoke, Va., 2003. Dancer Dance Theatre of Harlem as Princess of Unreal Beauty in live TV prodn. of Firebird, 1982, as Myrta, Queen of the Willis in NBC prodn. of Creole Giselle, 1987, performed at White House, 1981, also at the closing ceremonies of the 1984 Olympics, toured with Dance Theatre of Harlem, USSR, 1988, South Africa, 1992, guest artist Young People's Concert series, N.Y. Philharm., 1988, Detroit Symphony, 1989, River City Ballet, Memphis, 1991, 1992, N.W. Fla. Ballet, 1994, prin. dancer Va. Ballet Theatre, Norfolk, 1996—, Dance Theatre of Harlem, 1999, guest ballet mistress, 1999—, regisseuse Dance Theatre of Harlem, 1989—96. Mem. artistic com. Young Audiences of Va.; sec. Norfolk Commn. on the Arts and Humanities, 2002—; mem. program com. Young Audiences Va.; sec., treas. Graves Funeral Home, Inc. Fellow Am. Guild Mus. Artists. Episcopalian. Avocations: modeling, teaching younger dancers.

GRAVES, MICHAEL, architect, educator; b. Indpls., July 9, 1934; s. Thomas Browning and Erma Sanderson (Lowe) Graves; children from previous marriage: Sarah Browning, Adam Daimhin, Michael Sebastian Min. BS in Architecture, U. Cin., 1958; MArch, Harvard U., 1959; acad. fellow, Am. Acad. Rome, 1960—62; DFA (hon.), U. Cin., 1982; LHD (hon.), Boston U., 1984; HHD (hon.), Savannah Coll. Art and Design, 1986; DFA (hon.), RI Sch. Design, 1990, NJ Inst. Tech., 1991; LHD (hon.), Rutgers U., NJ, 1994, U. Colo., 1995; PhD (hon.), Internat. Fine Arts Coll., 1996, Pratt Inst., 1996, Drexel U., Phila., 2000. Lectr. architecture Princeton U., NJ, 1962—67, assoc. prof., 1967—72, Schirmer prof. architecture, 1972—2001, emeritus prof., 2001—; pres. Michael Graves & Assocs., Princeton, 1964—. Arch. in residence Am. Acad. Rome, 1979. Exhibited in group shows including Mus. Modern Art, NYC, 1967, 68, 75, 78, 79, 80, 81, 84, Cooper-Hewitt Mus., 1976, 78, 79, 80, 82, 85, 87, Triennale, Milan, Italy, 1973, 85, Roma Interrotta, Rome, 1978, Venice Biennale, Italy, 1980, Met. Mus. Art, 1985, 86, 87, Emory U. Mus. Art and Archaeology, Atlanta, 1985, Denver Art Mus., 2002; one-man shows include U. So. Calif., 1981, No. Ill. U., 1982, Inst. Architecture and Urban Studies, NYC, 1982, Colby Coll., Maine, 1982, Moore Coll. Art, Phila., 1983, Fla. Internat. U., Miami, 1983, Pa. State U., Univ. Pk., 1984, Royal Inst. Brit. Archs., Heinz Gallery, London, 1984, Wadsworth Athenaeum, Hartford, Conn., 1984, Carleton Coll., Northfield, Minn., 1986, W.Va. U., 1986, Hamilton Coll., Clinton, NY, 1987, Archivolto Gallery, Milan, Italy, 1987, U. Va., Charlottesville, 1987, U. Md., College Park, 1988, Duke U. Mus. Art, Durham, NC, 1988, Butler Inst. Art, Youngstown, Ohio, 1989, 1989, Deutsches Architekturmuseum, Frankfurt, German Dem. Republic, 1989, Washington Design Ctr., 1989, Syracuse U. Sch. Architecture, 1990, Kunstemes Hus, Oslo, 1990, Mikimoto Hall, Tokyo, 1992, Pitts. Cultural Trust, 1993, Richard Stockton Coll., 1993, Clark County Libr., 1994, Thessaloniki Design Mus., Greece, 1996, The Min. Bldg., Seoul, Korea, 1996, Princeton Arts Coun., 1996, 99, U. Conn. Aronoff Ctr. Design and Art, 1996, NJ Sch. Arch., NJ Inst. Tech., 2000; prin. works include Hanselmann House, 1967 (AIA Nat. Honor award, 1975), Newark Mus., 1968, Rockefeller House, 1969 (Progressive Architecture Design award, 1970), Gunwyn Ventures Office, 1971 (AIA Nat. Honor award, 1979), Snyderman House, 1972, Crooks House, 1976 (Progressive Architecture Design award, 1977), Schulman House, 1976, (AIA Nat. Honor award, 1982), Fargo-Moorhead Cultural Ctr., 1977-79 (Progressive Architecture Design award, 1978), Plocek House, 1978 (Progressive Architecture Design award, 1979), pvt. residence in Green Brook, NJ, 1978 (Progressive Architecture Design award, 1980), Sunar showrooms NYC, 1979, 81 (Interiors award, 1981), Chgo., 1979, Houston, 1980, LA, 1980, London, 1985, Loveladies Beach House, 1979 (Progressive Architecture Design award, 1979) Environ. Edn. Ctr., 1980 (Progressive Architecture award, 1983), Portland Bldg., 1980 (AIA Nat. Honor award, 1983), San Juan Capistrano Pub. Libr., Calif., 1980 (AIA Nat. Honor award, 1985), Newark Mus. Master Plan and Renovation, 1982 (AIA Nat. Honor award, 1992), Human Bldg., Louisville, 1982 (Interiors award, 1985, AIA NAt. Honor award, 1987), Emory U. Mus. Art and Archaeology, 1982 (Interiors award 1985, AIA Nat. Honor award, 1987), Riverbend Music Ctr., 1983, Whitney Mus. Am. Art, N.Y.C., 1984, Diane Von Furstenburg Boutique, 1984, Clos Pegase Winery, Calif., 1984 (AIA Nat. Honor award, 1990), Sotheby's Tower, N.Y.C., 1985, Warehouse Renovation (Graves House), 1985 (Progressive Architecture Design award, 1978), Aventine Devel., La Jolla, Calif., 1985, Shiseido Health Club, Tokyo, 1985, Disney Co. Corp. Office Bldg., Burbank, Calif., 1985, Crown Am. Hdqs., Johnston, Pa., 1985, Walt Disney World Dolphin and Walt Disney World Swan hotels, Fla., 1986 (Progressive Architecture award, 1989), Youngston (Ohio) Hist. Ctr. Industry and Labor, 1986 (Progressive Architecture Design award, 1987), 10 Peachtree Pl., Atlanta, 1987, Henry House, Rhinebeck, NY, 1987 (Progressive Architecture award, 1989), U. Va. Arts. and Scis. Bldg., Charlottesville, 1987, Portside Dist. Condominium Tower, Yokohama, Japan, 1987, Momochi Dist. Apt. Bldg., Fukuoka, Japan, 1987, Metropolis Master Plan LA, 1988, stores and galleries for Lenox, Tysons Corner, Va., 1988, Palm Beach, 1988, N.Y.C., 1988, Mpls., 1988, Costa Mesa, 1989, Frankfurt, 1989, Phila., 1989, Nashville, 1989, Midousuji Minami Office Bldg., Osaka, 1988, Tajima Office Bldg., Tokyo, 1988, Hotel NY, 1988, Euro Disneyland, France, 1988, Inst. for Theoretical Physics, U. Calif., Santa Barbara, 1989, Detroit Inst. of Arts Master Plan, 1989, Indpls. Art Ctr., 1989, Emory U. Mus. Art and Archaeology Addition, 1989, Fukuoka Internat. Office Project, 1990, Kasumi Group Rsch. and Tng. Ctr., Tsukaba City, Japan, 1990, Clark County Libr., Las Vegas, 1990, U. Cin. Sci. and Engring. Rsch. Ctr., 1990, Richard Stockton Coll. Arts and Scis. Bldg., Pomona, NJ, 1991, Denver Ctrl. Libr., 1991 (AIA-NJ Design award, 1992, 95, AIA Nat. Honor award for Interior Architecture, 1998, AIA and Am. Libr. Assn. Excellence award, 2001), Astrid Park Plz. Hotel and Bus. Ctr., Antwerp, Belgium, 1992, Thomson Consumer Electronics Hdqs., Indpls., 1992 (AIA-NJ Design award, 1994), Rome Reborn Vatican Exhibit, Libr. Congress, 1992 (Casebook award Print Mag., 1993), Pitts. Cultural Trust Theater and Office Bldg., 1992, Taiwan Mus. Pre-History, Taipei, 1993 (AIA-NJ Design award, 1994), Archdiocesan Ctr., Newark, 1993, Internat. Fin. Corp. Hdqs., Washington, 1993 (AIA-NJ Design award, 1997), 1500 Ocean Dr. Condominiums, Miami, 1994, Del. River Port Authority Hdqs., Camden, NJ, 1994 (AIA-NJ Design award, 1998), St. Martin's Coll. Libr., Lacey, Wash., 1994, Topeka (Kans.) and Shawnee County Pub. Libr., 1995, Miramar Hotel, Egypt, 1995 (AIA-NJ Design award, 1996), NJ Inst. Tech. Residence Hall, 1995, Jiang-to Blvd. Master Plan, Xiamen, China, 1995, Alexandria (Va.) Ctrl. Libr., 1996, U.S. Courthouse Annex, Washington, 1996, Life Mag. Dream House, 1996, Lake Hills country Club, Seoul, Korea, 1996, World Trade Exch., Manila, 1996, new residence Hall, Drexel U., Phila., 1997, Miele Appliances Americas Hdqs. Bldg., Princeton, 1997 (AIA-NJ Design award, 2002), NovaCare Sports Training Facility, 1997 (AIA-NJ Design award, 2002), El Gourna Golf Villas, Egypt, 1997 (AIA-NJ Design award, 2002), French Inst. Libr, N.Y.C., 1997, Hyatt Regency Taba Heights Hotel, Egypt, 1997, St. Mary's Ch., Rockledge, Fla., 1998, Rice U. Master Plan, Houston, 1998, The Impala Bldg., N.Y.C., 1998, Wash. Monument Restoration Scaffolding, 1998 (AIA-NJ Design award, 1998), Rolex Watch Technicum Tng. and Svc. Ctr., Lancaster County, Pa., 1999, Theater Square: Pitts. Cultural Trust Svc. Ctr., 1999, Mus. Shenandoah Valley, Winchester, Va., 1999, 425 Fifth Ave. Tower, N.Y.C., 2000, Mahler IV Mixed-Use Bldg., Amsterdam, 2000, Fed. Res. Bank Dallas: Houston Br., 2000, Famille-Tsukishima Bldg., Tokyo, 2000, U.S. Embassy, Seoul, 2000, Dept. Transp. Hdqs., Washington, 2001, Detroit Inst. Arts, 2001, St. Coletta's Sch., Washington, 2002, NJ City U. Arts and Scis. Bldg., 2002, Nat. Automobile Mus., The Netherlands, 2003, U.S. Courthouse, Nashville, 2003; designer furniture, artifacts, textiles, and consumer products, V'Soske, 1979-80, Sunar, 1980-83, Alessi, 1981—Baldinger Archtl. Lighting, 1983—, Swid Powell, 1985—, Steuben, 1986—, Munari, 1986—Tajima, 1987-88, WMF, 1987—, Atelier Internat., 1987—Vorwerk, 1987—, Lenox Inc., 1988—, Markuse Corp., 1989—, Dunbar Furniture, 1989—, Arkitektura, 1989—, Moeller Internat. Design, 1992—, Target Stores, 1997—, Glen Eden Wool Carpet, 2002—, Delta Faucets, 2003—; monographs include: Five Architects, 1972, Michael Graves, Academy Editions, 1979, Michael Graves: Buildings and Projects 1966-1981, 1981, Michael Graves: Buildings and Projects 1982-1989, 1990, Michael Graves: Buildings and Projects 1990-1994, 1995, The Master Architect Series III: Michael Graves: Selected and Current Works, 1999, Michael Graves: Buildings and Projects 1995-2002, 2003. Named Designer of Yr., Interiors, 1981; recipient Arnold W. Brunner Meml. prize in Architecture, 1981, 61 awards, NJ Soc. Archs., Euster award, 1984, Ind. Arts award, 1984, Henry Hering Meml. medal, Am. Sculpture Soc., 1986, profile Best Archs. and Designers Working Today, Archtl. Digest, 1990, 1995, 2000, Nat. Medal Arts, Nat. Endowment Arts, 1999, Frank Annunzio award, 2001, AIA Gold medal, Sigma Tau Delta, 2003. Fellow: AIA (Gold medal, 2001); mem.: NY Sch. Interior Design (bd. trustees), Mus. Arts and Design (bd. trustees), Am. Acad. Rome (bd. trustees, Rome prize 1960—62), Am. Acad. Arts and Letters. Office: Michael Graves & Assoc 341 Nassau St Princeton NJ 08540 also: Michael Graves Architect 560 Broadway Ste 401 New York NY 10012 Office Phone: 609-924-6409. Office Fax: 609-924-1795. E-mail: info@michaelgraves.com.

GRAVES, PATRICK LEE, lawyer; b. Pasadena, Calif., Sept. 16, 1945; s. James Edward and Virginia (Dudley) G.; married; children: Carrie Kathleen, Michael Patrick. AS, Citrus Jr. Coll., Glendora, Calif., 1969; BS, Calif. State Polytechnic U., Pomona, 1973; BS in Law, Western State U., 1973, JD, 1975. Bar: Calif. 1975, US Dist. Ct. (cen. dist.) Calif. 1976, US Ct. Appeals (9th cir.) 1978, US Supreme Ct. 1980. Assoc. Lynberg & Watkins, Los Angeles, 1975-80, ptnr., 1981-93, Graves & King, Irvine, Calif., 1993—. Settlement officer LA Superior Ct., 1988—, arbitrator, 1981—, mediator, 1993-; arbitrator San Bernardino Superior Ct., 1990—; mediator Riverside Superior Ct., 1996—, AAA-Inland Empire, 1996—. Judge pro tem L.A. Superior Ct., 1992—. Sustaining mem. Rep. Nat. Com., Washington, 1979—; mem. Nat. Rep. Congl. Com., 1980—. Mem. ABA, San Bernardino County Bar Assn., Assn. So. Calif. Def. Counsel (chmn. 1988, bd. dirs. 1996—), Def. Rsch. Inst., Upland (Calif.) C. of C. Avocations: fly fishing, golf. Home: 32302 Alipaz St 135 San Juan Capistrano CA 92672 Office: Graves & King 31815 Camino Capistrano Ste 26 San Juan Capistrano CA 92675 Office Phone: 949-234-0114. Business E-Mail: plgraves@gravesandking.com.

GRAVES, RAY REYNOLDS, retired judge; b. Tuscumbia, Ala., Jan. 10, 1946; s. Isaac and Olga Ernestine (Wilder) Graves; children: Claire Elise, Reynolds Douglass. BA, Trinity Coll., Hartford, Conn., 1967; JD, Wayne State U., 1970. Bar: Mich. 1971, U.S. Dist. Ct. (ea. dist.) Mich. 1971, U.S. Ct. Appeals (6th cir.) 1972, U.S. Supreme Ct. 1976, D.C. 1977. Defender Legal Aid and Defender Assn., Detroit, 1970-71; assoc. Liberson, Fink, Feiler, Crystal & Burdick, 1971-72, Patmon, Young & Kirk, 1972-73; ptnr. Lewis, White, Clay & Graves, 1974-81; mem. legal dept. Detroit Edison Co., 1981; judge U.S. Bankruptcy Ct., Ea. Dist. Mich., Detroit, 1982-2002; chief judge U.S. Bankruptcy Ct., 1991-95; prin. BBK, Ltd., Southfield, Mich., 2002—. Mem. U.S. ct. com. State Bar Mich. Trustee Mich. Opera Theatre, 1986—88; vestry Christ Ch. Episcopal, Grosse Pointe, Mich., 1994—97; del Diocesan Conv. Episcopal Ch., Mich., 1997; bd. dirs. Mich. Cancer Found. Fellow: Am. Coll. Bankruptcy; mem.: D.C. Bar Assn., Detroit Bar Assn., Wolverine Bar Assn., Assn. Black Judges Mich., World Peace Through Law Conf., World Assn. Judges, Nat. Conf. Bankruptcy Judges (bd. govs. 1984—88), Iota Boulè (Sire Archon 1999—2001), Sigma Pi Phi, Delta Kappa Epsilon. Episcopalian. Office: BBK 300 Galleria Officentre # 103 Southfield MI 48034 Home Phone: 313-567-0458; Office Phone: 248-603-8373. Business E-Mail: rgraves@e-bbk.com.

GRAVES, SAMUEL B., JR., congressman, retired state legislator; b. Fairfax, Mo., Nov. 7, 1963; m. Lesley Graves; 3 children. BS in Agronomy, U. Mo., Columbia, 1986. Mem. Mo. Ho. Reps. from Dist. 4, 1993—95, Mo. State Senate from Dist. 12, 1995—2000, US Congress from 6th Mo. dist., 2001—. Mem. agr. com. US Congress, mem. small bus. com., mem. transp. and infrastructure com. Mem. agrl. adv. com. N.W. Mo. State U., mem. univ. ext. coun. Recipient Outstanding Young Farmer in Mo., Mo. Farm Bur., 1990, Outstanding Young Farmer in US, Farm Bur., 1991, Tarkio, Mo. Cmty. Betterment award, 1995, Outstanding Young Farmer in US, Mo. Jr. C. of C., 1996, Mo. Phys. Therapy Assn. award, 1997, Voice of Mo. Bus. award, Associated Industries, 1999. Mem.: Farm Bur., Rotary. Republican. Baptist. Office: US House Reps 1415 Longworth House Office Bldg Washington DC 20515 Office Phone: 202-225-7041. Office Fax: 202-225-8221. E-mail: sam.graves@mail.house.gov.*

GRAVES, TODD PETERSON, lawyer, former prosecutor; b. 1965; m. Tracy Graves; 4 children. BA summe cum laude, U. Mo., 1988; MS, JD, U. Va., 1991. Bar: Mo. 1991, cert.: US Dist. Ct. Mo. 1991, US Ct. Appeals (8th Cir.) 1993. Assoc. Skadden Arps, NYC; asst. atty. gen. State of Mo., 1991; assoc. Bryan Cave law Firm, 1992—94; prosecutor Platte County Ct., Mo., 1994—2001; US atty. (we. dist.) Mo US Dept. Justice, 2001—06; ptnr. Graves Bartle & Marcus LLC, Kans. City, 2006—. Republican. Office: Graves Bartle & Marcus LLC 100 Main St Ste 2600 Kansas City MO 64105 E-mail: todd.graves@pobox.com.*

GRAVES, WALLACE BILLINGSLEY, retired university executive; b. Ft. Worth, Feb. 10, 1922; s. Ellery George and Edith (Billingsley) G.; m. Barbara Jeanne Abey, Nov. 20, 1943; children: David W., Emily Graves Mc Donald, John R., Julie Graves Williams. BA, U. Okla., 1943; MA, Tex. Christian U., 1947; PhD, U. Tex., 1953; LLD (hon.), Ind. State U., 1970, Valparaiso U., 1972; LHD (hon.), Morningside Coll., 1971, U. Evansville, 1989. Teaching fellow Tex. Christian U., Ft. Worth, 1946-47, U. Tex., Austin, 1947-50; prof. polit. sci. DePauw U., Greencastle, Ind., 1950-58; Armstrong prof. govt., dean of men Tex. Wesleyan Coll., Ft. Worth, 1958-63, asst. to pres., 1963-65; acad. v.p. U. Pacific, Stockton, Calif., 1965-67; pres. U. Evansville, Ind., 1967-87, chancellor Ind., 1986-89, pres. emeritus, 1989—. Vis. prof. Butler U., summer 1956; bd. dirs. Citizens Nat. Bank, Evansville, Herrburger Brooks P.L.C., Nottingham, Eng. Author: The United Nations, Great Britain and the British Non-Self Governing Territories, 1954, The One Semester Course in International Relations, 1956, Harlaxton College: The Camelot of Academe, 1990; contbr. articles to profl. jours. Mem. exec. bd. Tarrant County chpt. ARC, 1960-65, chmn. home svc. com.; chmn. ARC of Southwestern Ind., 1994—; midwest region com. ARC, 2000-02; bd. dirs. Ft. Worth Assn. Retarded Children, 1963-65; mem. Met. Ft. Worth Devel. Coordinating Com., World Affairs Coun., Chgo. and Stockton, adv. bd. Supplementary Edn. Ctr., Stockton; v.p. Buffalo Trace coun. Boy Scouts Am., Evansville, 1968, exec. bd., 1968-74, adv. coun, 1974—; bd. dirs. Jr. Achievement Inc., Evansville, 1968-73; mem. commn. ecumenical affairs United Meth. Ch., Evansville, 1968-72, univ. senate, 1972-76, Ind. area study commn., 1972-74; bd. dirs. Evansville Day Sch., 1967-76; mem. Ind. State Scholarship Commn., 1969-77, adv. bd. St. Mary's Med. Ctr., Evansville, 1970—, Evansville's Future Inc., 1967—, pres., 1974-77; bd. dirs. Ind. Health Careers Inc., 1974-75; mem. Govs. Adv. Com. Pub. Health, 1971-72; bd. dirs. Leadership Evansville, 1975-71, Evansville Mus., 1978—, Lincolnland Hist. Trust, 1978—; pres. Beethoven Found., Indpls., 1980-88; mem. organizing com. Pan Am. Games, 1987; bd. dirs. Sta. WNIN Pub. TV, Evansville, 1973—, chmn. bd., 1982-84. With U.S. Army, 1943. Recipient Best Tchr. award DePauw U., 1954, medal of honor U. Evansville, 1977, medal of merit Govt. Thailand, 1984, medal of honofr DAR, 1999; Wallace B. Graves Day named in his honor Office Mayor City Evansville, 1977; rsch. scholar U. Tex., 1947; Ford Found. fellow, summer

1951, 55; Paul Harris (Rotary) fellow, 1995. Mem. AAUP, Am. Assn. Acad. Deans, Am. Coll. Pub. Relations Assn., Am. Polit. Sci. Assn., Ind. Colls. and Univs. Ind. Inc. (pres. 1970-71, 76-77), North Cen. Assn. Colls. and Secondary Schs. (cons., investigator), Am. Assn. Pres. Ind. Colls. and Univs. (exec. com. 1969-70), Am. Assn. Colls. (various coms.), Associated Colls. Ind. (pres. 1972-74), Carl Duisberg Soc. (pres. Am. assn. 1973-74), Internat. Assn. Univ. Pres. (bd. dirs. N.Am. council 1975-87), Ind. Consortium Computer and High Tech. Edn., Ft. Worth C. of C. (chmn. econ. edn. com. 1963-64), Gold Key, Blue Key, Phi Kappa Phi, Phi Mu Alpha, Alpha Sigma Lambda, Pi Sigma Alpha, Sigma Nu. Clubs: Knife and Fork (pres. 1964-65) (Ft. Worth); Commonwealth (San Francisco); Columbia (Indpls.); Petroleum; Evansville Country, Kennel (Evansville). Lodges: Rotary (pres. Ft. club 1964-65). Personal E-mail: wexprex@aol.com.

GRAVES, WILLIAM PRESTON, former governor; b. Salina, Kans., Jan. 9, 1953; s. William Henry and Helen (Mayo) G.; m. Linda Richey, Apr. 1990; 1 child, Katie. BBA, Kans. Wesleyan U., Salina, 1975; postgrad., U. Kans., 1978-79. Dep. asst. sec. of state State of Kans., Topeka, 1980-85, asst. sec. of state, 1985-87, sec. of state, 1987-95, gov., 1995—2003. Former mem. Competitiveness Policy Coun. Mem. Kans. Cavalry; trustee Kans. Wesleyan U., 1987—; bd. trustes Sunflower State Games, Harry S. Truman Scholarship Found., 2003—. Named Outstanding Young Alumnus, Kans. Wesleyan U., Salina, 1975, Outstanding Young Kansan, Salina Jaycees, 1986, Kans. Jaycees, 1986, Outstanding Kans. Citizen, Jayhawk area BSA, 2002; named to Athletic Hall of Fame, Kans. Wesleyan U., Salina, 1986. Mem. Kans. C. of C. and Industry. Republican. Methodist. Avocations: running, reading, travel.*

GRAVING, RICHARD JOHN, law educator; b. Duluth, Minn., Aug. 24, 1929; s. Lawrence Richard and Laura Magdalene (Loucks) G.; m. Florence Sara Semel; children: Daniel, Sarah. BA, U. Minn., 1950; JD, Harvard U., 1953; postgrad., Nat. U. Mex., 1964-66. Bar: Minn. 1953, N.Y. 1956, U.S. Dist. Ct. (so. dist.) N.Y. 1956, Pa. 1968, U.S. Dist. Ct. (we. dist.) Pa. 1968, Tex. 1982, U.S. Dist. Ct. (so. dist.) Tex. 1982. Assoc. Reid & Priest, NYC, 1955-61, Mexico City, 1961-66; v.p. Am. & Fgn. Power Co., Inc., Mexico City, 1966-68; atty. Gulf Oil Corp., Pitts., 1968-69, Madrid, 1969-73, London, 1973-80, Houston, 1980—82; pvt. practice London, 1982—84; prof. law South Tex. Coll., Houston, 1983—; prof. Bush Grad. Sch. Tex. A&M U., Coll. Sta., 2001—05. With U.S. Army, 1953-55. Mem. Am. Soc. Internat. Law. Home: 8515 Ariel St Houston TX 77074-2806 Office: 1303 San Jacinto St Houston TX 77002-7000 Office Phone: 713-646-1827. Business E-Mail: rgraving@stcl.edu.

GRAVITTE, DEBBIE SHAPIRO (LYNN SHAPIRO), singer, actress, dancer; b. Santa Monica, Calif., Sept. 29, 1954; d. Morton Harold and Anne (Lipsman) S.; m. Beau Gravitte, Sept. 21, 1986; 3 children. Appeared in Broadway shows including Perfectly Frank (Drama Desk nomination), They're Playing Our Song, 1979, Blues in the Night, 1982, Zorba, 1983, Jerome Robbins' (Tony award 1989, N.Y. Women Showstopper award 1989), Ain't Broadway Grand, 1993, Annie Get Your Gun, Spotlight, Swing, King's Tapestry, Berlin to Broadway, Gentleman Prefer Blondes, Mack and Mabel, Chicago, Les Miserables; (ballet) Thou Swell; (NY theatre) The Boys From Syracuse, 1997, Tenderloin, Carnival, Big Band Broadway; (film) Isn't She Great? (TV shows) Broadway Plays Washington, CBS Cable Songwriters Series, Trial and Error; (TV appearances) Pat Sajak, Merv Griffin Show; recs. include Mack and Mabel in Concert, The Songs of Stephen Sondheim, The Songs of N.Y., The First Nudie Musical; (albums) The MGM Album, 1997, Part of Your World, The Alan Menken Album, 1994, Defying Gravity; nightclubs acts include Sands Hotel, Atlantic City, Harrah's, Atlantic City, Freddy's Supper Club, N.Y.C., Rainbow and Stars, Rockefellar Ctr., N.Y.C., Les Mouches, N.Y.C., The St. Regis Hotel, N.Y.C., others.*

GRAVLEE, GLENN P(AGE), anesthesiologist, educator, director; b. Birmingham, Ala., Aug. 15, 1950; BS in Medicine, Northwestern U., 1972, MD, 1974. Diplomate Am. Bd. Anesthesiology, Nat. Bd. Echocardiography. Intern Hartford Hosp., Conn., 1974—75; resident anesthesiology Mass. Gen. Hosp., Harvard Med. Sch., Boston, 1975—77, chief resident, cardiac anesthesia fellow, 1977—78, instr., 1978—79; from asst. prof. to prof. Wake Forest U., 1978—94; prof. Allegheny U. Health Scis., Pitts., 1994—99, chair, 1994—99; prof. dept. anesthesiology Coll. Med. and Pub. Health, Ohio State U., Columbus, 1999—, chmn. dept. anesthesiology Coll. Med. and Pub. Health, 1999—2002, vice chmn., 2002—06; prof. Health Scis. Ctr. U. Colo., 2006—, dir. edn. Dept. Anesthesiology Health Scis. Ctr., 2006—. Editor: Cardiopulmonary Bypass: Principles and Practice, 1994, 2000; co-editor: A Practical Approach to Cardiac Anesthesia, 2003, Year Book of Anesthesia, 2004; contbr. articles to profl. jours. Mem.: Am. Soc. Anesthesiologists, Internat. Anesthesiology Rsch. Soc., Soc. Cardiovasc. Anesthesiologists (pres. 2003—05), Am. Bd. Anesthesiologists (dir. 1999—). Office: Univ Colo Health Scis Ctr Dept Anesthesiology 4200 E 9th Ave B113 Denver CO 80262 Business E-Mail: glenn.gravlee@uchsc.edu.

GRAY, ALLEN (ERNEST BUNGAARD), communications executive; b. Council Bluffs, Iowa, Nov. 13, 1920; s. Jeppe and Martha (Petersen) Bundgaard; m. Mary Lee Burden; children; Bruce Burden, Kurt Jepson (dec.), Robert Lee. BA in Speech and Radio Broadcasting, U. Iowa, 1943. Announcer Sta. KFAB, Omaha, 1947-50; dir. Housewives Protective League Sta. WCCO (CBS), Mpls., 1951-58, Sta. WCBS, NYC, 1959-63; owner Food Brockerage Co., Mpls., 1963-71; freelance broadcaster, creator Coffee Breaks various stas., Mpls., 1971-77; owner Advt. Agy., Mpls., 1978-84; owner, founder, chmn. bd. Lakes Broadcasting Group, Sta. KLKS-FM, Breezy Point, Minn., 1984—. Author: The Lore of Uncle Fogy, 1971; creator, dir.: (cassette) Uncle Fogy's Bird Calls, 1974, (album) Nature's Choir, 1979. Founder Uncle Fogy Conservation Found., Mpls., 1973, hon. chmn. for life, 1983—. 1st lt. inf. US Army, 1943—46, ETO. Recipient Minn. Pioneer Broadcaster of Yr. award Minn. Broadcasters Assn., 1997; inducted into Pavek Mus. Broadcasters Hall of Fame, 2001. Mem.: Pres. Club U. Iowa, The 1847 Soc. U. Iowa. Avocation: outdoor activities. Home: 8477 Dove St Breezy Point MN 56472 Office: Sta KLKS-FM PO Box 300 Pequot Lakes MN 56472-0300 Office Phone: 218-562-4884.

GRAY, AMY CASTLE, lawyer; b. Austin, Tex., July 14, 1967; BA in Spanish, Vanderbilt U., 1989; JD, So. Meth. U., 1993. Bar: Tex. 1993. Assoc. Godwin, Pappas, Langley & Ronquillo, L.L.P., Dallas. Named a Rising Star, Tex. Super Lawyers mag., 2006.*

GRAY, ANTHONY ROLLIN, retired finance company executive; b. Des Moines, Nov. 26, 1939; s. James W. and Pauline (Frink) G.; m. Janet Eicher, June 26, 1971 (div. Mar. 1987); m. Barbara Lacey Whittaker, June 14, 1991. BA, Grinnell Coll., 1961; MS, U. Iowa, 1963. Securities analyst Lincoln Nat. Life Ins. Co., Ft. Wayne, Ind., 1966—69; dir. rsch. 1st Wis. Trust, Milw., 1969—71; chief investment officer Oak Park (Ill.) Trust, 1971—74; asst. v.p. Union Ctrl. Life Ins. Co., Cin., 1974—79; dir. rsch. Sun Banks, Orlando, Fla., 1979—85; past pres. Sun Bank Capital Mgmt. Co., Orlando, past chmn. bd., CEO, 1985—2000; ret., 2002. Founder, ptnr. Graybeard Capital LLC, 2002—. Capt. USPHS, 1963-66. Avocations: biking, golf. Office: Graybeard Capital LLC 1211 Orange Ave #101 Winter Park FL 32789 Office Phone: 407-622-5925.

GRAY, BARBARA L., assistant principal, tax specialist; b. Memphis, Aug. 3, 1947; d. Willie Odum Register and Virginia Adline Garcia; children: Bryant, Yolanda, LoMay. BS in Chemistry, LeMoyne Owen Coll., Memphis, 1972; MEd, Memphis State U., 1989. Tchr. math and sci. Shelby County Schs., 1972—97, asst. prin., 1987—; tax specialist H & R Block, Millington, Tenn., 1998—. Mem. City of Millington Appeal and Grievance Bd., 2001—, City of Millington Mcpl. Airport Auth., 2002—04, Pulvair Site Citizens Advisory Group, 2004—. Mem.: ASCD, Shelby County Edn. Assoc. (pres. 2005—07), Nat. Coun. of Tchrs. of Math., Nat. Sci. Tchrs. Assn. Church Of Christ. Avocations: reading, exercise, walking. Home: 7709 Tecumseh Millington TN 38053 Office: Shelby County Schs 5885 Woodstock-Cuba Millington TN 38053 Office Phone: 901-386-8771. Personal E-mail: bgray901@aol.com, sceapres@bellsouth.net.

GRAY, C. BOYDEN (CLAYLAND BOYDEN GRAY), ambassador, lawyer; b. Winston-Salem, NC, Feb. 6, 1943; s. Gordon and Jane (Craige) Gray. BA magna cum laude in Hist., Harvard U., 1964; JD with high honors, U. NC, 1968. Bar: DC 1970, NC. Law clk. to Chief Justice Earl Warren US Supreme Ct., Washington, 1968; assoc. Wilmer Cutler Pickering LLP, Washington, 1969, ptnr., 1976-81, 1993—2005; legal counsel & dep. chief of staff to v.p. The White House, Washington, 1981-85, counselor to v.p., 1985-89, counsel to the Pres., 1989-93; US amb. to European Union US Dept. State, Brussels, 2006—. Chmn. Citizens for a Sound Economy, 1993-2000, Summit Comm., Inc., Atlanta, 1982-89. Mem. com. to visit coll. and com. on univ. devel., Harvard U. Served in USMC, 1964—70. Recipient Presdl. Citizens medal, Disting. Alumnus award, U. NC Law Sch. Mem. ABA (chmn. adminstrv. law and regulatory practice sect., 2000-02), DC Bar Assn., NC Bar Assn., Fed. Bar Assn., Met. Club, Chevy Chase Club, Alibi Club. Republican. Episcopalian. Office: European Union Zinnerstrat 13 Rue Zinner B 1000 Brussels Belgium*

GRAY, CAMPBELL, museum director; Degree in Art, Sydney Coll., Alexander Mackie Coll.; PhD in Art History, U. Sussex, Eng. Faculty mem., coord. postgraduate studies visual arts & art hist. U. Western Sydney; dir. Brigham Young U. Mus. Art, Provo, Utah, 1996—. Office: Mus Art Brigham Young U Provo UT 84602 Office Phone: 801-422-8257.

GRAY, CARLOS GIBSON, restaurant manager, agricultural products supplier, entertainer, television producer; b. Shelbyville, Ind., Sept. 5, 1937; s. Gibson Tull and Edna Frances (Wicker) G.; m. Elizabeth Vivian Stickrod, Aug. 30, 1959 (div. 1971); children: Carla Elizabeth Christine Gray Stokes, Zarrell Thomas Gibson Gray; m. Carolyn June Breeden, 1971. BSEE, Purdue U., 1960. Cert. secondary tchr. Ind. Tchr. math. Reynolds H.S., Ind., 1960—61, Jefferson H.S., Lafayette, Ind., 1961—63, Warren Ctrl. H.S., Indpls., 1963—64; sys. engr. IBM, Indpls., 1964—67, mktg. rep., 1967—69; asst. v.p., mgr. data processing Aero Mayflower Transit Co., Indpls., 1969—74; asst. v.p. application devel. Ind. Nat. Bank, Indpls., 1974—76; co-owner Gray's Seed, Inc., Fairland, Ind., 1976—; owner Boggstown Inn and Cabaret-TDCC, Corp., Ind., 1984—99; co-owner Jacray Corp., 1994—98, Branson Stage Theatre Corp., 1996—97; owner, dir. Ind. Receptive Co., 1998—2002. Data processing cons. Meth. Hosp., Indpls., 1968, Ford Motor Corp., Dearborn, Mich., 1967, Army, Naval Class of Indsl. Coll. Nat. Security, Indpls., 1967; pilot Angel Flights. Ragtime music video and audio cassettes This is Boggstown, 1986; prodr., dir. Ragtime Lil & Banjo-Banjo, Branson, Mo., 1994-97. Active Hoosier Internat. Ragtime Soc. (developed home for preservation and promotion of Am.'s ragtime music), Boggstown, 1986, U.S. C.G. Aux., 2003. Mem. Fretted Instrument Guild Am., Exptl. Aircraft Assn.(chpt. 565 pres. 2006—), Purdue Pilots, Inc. (pres. 1959-60), Angel Flight, Fla. Aviation Expo (chmn.) Avocations: multi-engine, instrument rated pilot, scuba diving, entertaining. Home: 2410 Palo Duro Blvd Herons Glen North Fort Myers FL 33917 Office Phone: 239-989-1109. Business E-Mail: carlos@ragtimepilot.com.

GRAY, CHARLES AUGUSTUS, banker; b. Syracuse, NY, Sept. 16, 1928; s. Charles William and Elizabeth Marie (Koch) G. Cert., Am. Inst. Banking, 1958, Sch. Bank Adminstrn., 1961. Cert. internal auditor. With Mchts. Nat. Bank & Trust Co. of Syracuse, 1946-77, auditor, 1959-77, v.p., 1970-77; N.Y. State dir. Bank Adminstrn. Inst., 1970-72; regional auditor cen. N.Y. region Irving Bank Corp., 1977-82, v.p. cen. N.Y. region, 1982-89. Author: A History of Brantingham, 2000. Treas. Upper N.Y. Synod, Luth. Ch. in Am., 1966-87, Upstate N.Y. Synod, Evang. Luth. Ch. in Am., 1988-2002, Meml. Masonic Temple Corp., 1996—, Luth. Found. Upstate N.Y., 1977-78, bd. dirs., 1980—; pres. Interfrat. Alumni Coun., Syracuse U., 1980-83; treas. N.Y. State Coun. Deliberation, 1997—. Mem. Bank Adminstrn. Inst. (pres. central N.Y. chpt. 1970-72), Inst. Internal Auditors (treas. cen. N.Y. chpt. 1974-76, pres. 1985-86), Lions (pres. local club 1973-75), Masons, Shriners. Republican. Home and Office: 1321 Westmoreland Ave Syracuse NY 13210-3436

GRAY, CHARLES ELMER, lawyer, rancher, investor; b. Elvins, Mo., July 23, 1919; s. Grover P. and Martha Elizabeth (Sullivan) G.; m. Beulah Henrich Gray, July 4, 1942; children— Karen Lee, Cecilia Jean, Bette Sue, Marsha Dawn. Student, Flat River Jr. Coll., 1937-38, U. Hawaii, 1940-41; LL.B., Washington U., St. Louis, 1947. Bar: Mo. 1947. Pvt. practice, St. Louis, 1947—; ptnr. Gray and Ritter. Gen. counsel, dir. United Mo. Bank, St Louis; mem. Mo. Appellate Jud. Commn.; mem. rules com. Supreme Ct. Mo., 1970-81 Served to capt. USAF, 1939-45. Fellow Internat. Acad. Trial Lawyers (dir.), Am. Coll. Trial Lawyers, Internat. Soc. Barristers (state chmn., dir.); mem. ABA, Mo. Bar Assn., St. Louis Bar Assn., Lawyers Assn. St. Louis (v.p. 1954, bd. govs., Honor award 1977), Harbour Ridge Yacht Club (commodore 1991-92), Phi Delta Phi. Home: PO Box 709 Farmington MO 63640-0709 Office: Gateway One on the Mall 701 Market St Fl 8 Saint Louis MO 63101-1850 also: Apt 312 4800 Highway A1A Vero Beach FL 32963 Personal E-mail: cgray34957@aol.com.

GRAY, CHARLES ROBERT, lawyer; b. Kirksville, Mo., Aug. 22, 1952; s. George Devon and Bettie Louise (McCormick) G.; m. Dana Elizabeth Kehr, June 1, 1974; children: Jennifer, Jessica, Marcus, Gregory, Victoria. BS, N.E. Mo. State U., 1974; JD, U. Mo., Kansas City, 1978. Bar: Mo. 1978, Va. 1993, U.S. Dist. Ct. (we. dist.) Mo. 1978, U.S. Ct. Appeals (fed. cir.) 1992, U.S. Ct. Appeals (4th cir.) 1995, U.S. Supreme Ct. 1981; cert. mediator; cert. hearing officer Va. Supereme Ct., 1997. Pvt. practice, Parkville, Mo., 1978-81; asst. pub. defender 5th Jud. Cir. Ct. Mo., St. Joseph, 1978-79; pub. defender 6th Jud. Cir. Ct. Mo., Platte City, 1981; asst. dist. counsel Army Corps of Engrs., Kansas City, 1981-82, Vicksburg, Miss., 1982-83; chief counsel space shuttle, MX missile U.S. Army, Vandenberg AFB, Calif., 1983-85, chief counsel troop support agy. Ft. Lee, Va., 1985-87; fraud counsel Def. Gen. Supply Ctr. Dept. of Def., Richmond, Va., 1987-93; pvt. practice, Chester, Va., 1993-99; asst. atty. gen. Atty. Gen.'s Office State of Va., 1999—, sr. asst. atty. gen., 2005—; owner Pvt. Jud. Svcs., Inc., Chester, 1993—. Adj. prof. St. Leo Coll., Ft. Lee, 1986-91, John Tyler Coll., Chester, Va., 1994—; mem. dispute resolution coun. VA, 2002, mem. adv. oversite panel. Mem. Selective Svc. Draft Bd., Brookfield, Mo., 1972-74; pres. Old Towne Parkville Assn., 1979-81, Chester (Va.) Youth Sports Boosters, 1989-91; den leader Boy Scouts Am., Chester, 1991—. Victor Wilson honor scholar, 1977; recipient Am. Jurisprudence award Coop-Bancroft-Whitney, 1989. Mem. ATLA, Am. Arbitration Assn. (mem. nat. panel arbitrators 1994—, mem. govt. disputes panel 1995—, mem. constrn. panel 1995—, mem. comml. panel 1995—), Def. Rsch. Inst. (approved mem. panel on mediation and arbitration), Mo. Bar Assn., Va. Bar Assn., Va. Trial Lawyers Assn. Methodist. Avocations: coaching youth sports, cub scouts, softball, tennis, basketball. Home: 3813 Terjo Ln Chester VA 23831-1839 Office: Pres Presiding Ofcl PO Box 34386 Chester VA 23834 Office Phone: 804-748-3984. Personal E-mail: charleschuckgray@gmail.com.

GRAY, CHARNELDA L., pharmacist; d. Bennie Earl and Gloria Graham Gray. Attended, Ga. Tech. U., 1995—97; PharmD, Mercer U., Atlanta, 2001. Registered pharmacist Ga. Bd. Pharmacy. Med. info. assoc. Solvay Pharms., Marietta, Ga., 2002—03; clin. info. pharmacist Affiliated Computer Svcs. State Healthcare, Atlanta, 2003—04; clin. pharmacy specialist Kaiser Permanente, Atlanta, 2003—04, drug info. specialist, 2005—06, asst. mgr., clin. pharmacy, 2006—. Contbr. articles to profl. jours. Named a High Quality Peer Reviewer, Jour. Managed Care Pharmacy, 2006. Mem.: Am. Coll. Clin. Pharmacy, Am. Soc. Health-Sys. Pharmacists. Baptist. Avocations: sewing, running, bowling. Office: Kaiser Permanente 3495 Piedmont Rd NE Bldg 9 Atlanta GA 30305 Office Phone: 404-364-7085. Business E-Mail: charnelda.l.gray@kp.org.

GRAY, DONALD MELVIN, molecular and cell biology educator; b. Milton, Pa., Apr. 4, 1938; s. Harry Seal and Edith Sophia (Larrison) G.; m. Carla Christine Winlund, Sept. 10, 1970. BA, Susquehanna U., 1960; MS, Yale U., 1963, PhD, 1967. Postdoctoral fellow U. Calif., Berkeley, 1967—70; asst. prof. molecular and cell biology U. Tex. at Dallas, Richardson, 1970—76, assoc. prof., 1976—83, prof., 1983—, program head, 1989—95, 2004—. Contbr. articles to profl. jours. Fogarty Sr. Internat. fellow European Molecular Biology Lab., Heidelberg, Fed. Republic of Germany, 1977-78; NIH grantee U. Tex. at Dallas, 1972-93, NSF grantee, 1994-98, Welch Found. grantee, 1972—. Fellow AAAS; mem. Am. Chem. Soc., Biophys. Soc. Office: Univ Tex at Dallas Molecular and Cell Biology PO Box 830688 Richardson TX 75083-0688

GRAY, DONNA LEA, small business owner; b. Snyder, Tex., Sept. 5, 1937; d. Dee Roy Chapman and Esther Weaver; m. C. D. Gray, Jr., Dec. 27, 1953; children: Donna Faye Gray Rosson, Cassandra L. Gray-Ratliff. Asst. postmaster USPS, Dunn, Tex., 1955—58; clk. J.C. Penney, Snyder, 1958—59, Fabric Mart, Snyder, 1959—60; owner, operator Donna's Beauty Shop, Snyder, 1963—65; owner, mgr. La Charme' Health Spa, Snyder, 1968—75, Snyder Bookstore and Gift Shop, 1978—90; part-owner, sec. Ice Melt Products LLC, Snyder, 1992. Active United Way, Heart Assn., Am. Cancer Soc., Snyder; dist. chmn. March of Dimes, Snyder, 1984; bd. dirs. Scurry County Fair Assn., Scurry County Hist. Commn.; bd. dirs., treas. Scurry County Child Welfare Bd. Recipient Soze,pre award, 1994, 1997, 1999. Mem.: Goldcoat Orgn., Snyder C. of C. Office: 8860 Road Runner Path Snyder TX 79549-1110 Office Phone: 325-573-6373.

GRAY, DOUGLAS D., child and adolescent psychiatrist; b. Dickinson, ND, Mar. 18, 1955; s. Darrold and Darlene Gray; m. Anne S. Stouffer, Nov. 26, 1983; children: Stacy, Matthew, Melissa. BS in Bioengring., U. Colo., 1978, MD, 1985. Diplomate Am. Bd. Psychiatry with subspecialty in child and adolescent psychiatry. Intern in pediat. U. Utah, Salt Lake City, 1985—86, resident in child psychiatry, 1986—88; resident in gen. psychiatry U. Colo., 1988—90; med. dir. Primary Children's Ctr. Counseling, Salt Lake City, 1990—98; med. dir. child and adolescent psychiatry Nelson, New Zealand, 1998—99; dir. Splty. Clinic, U. Utah, Salt Lake City, 1999—2004, residency tng. dir. child psychiatry programs and triple bd. program, 1999—. Assoc. clin. prof. medicine U. Utah, 1990—; prin. investigator Utah Youth Suicide Stidy, Salt Lake City, 1994—; chmn. Utah Youth Suicide Prevention Task Force, Salt Lake City, 1997—2004; cons. in field. Contbr. articles to profl. jours. Mem. adv. coun. Allies for Families, Salt Lake City, 1993—94. Named one of Best Pediat. Drs. in Salt Lake City, Salt Lake Mag., 2000, Best Doctors, Best Drs. Inc., 2001; recipient Ebaugh award, U. Colo. Med. Sch., 1985. Mem.: Am. Acad. Child and Adolescent Psychiatry, Nat. Alliance for the Mentally Ill, Am. Assn. of Suicidology. Avocations: skiing, hiking, basketball, music, art. Office: 650 S Komas Dr Ste 208 Salt Lake City UT 84108 Office Phone: 801-585-1212. Business E-Mail: douglas.gray@hsc.utah.edu.

GRAY, D'WAYNE, retired marine corps officer; b. Navarro County, Tex., Apr. 9, 1931; s. Henry Oliver and Myrtle Daisy (Lee) G.; m. Mary Joan Sobieck, Oct. 11, 1955; children: Stephen D'Wayne, Elizabeth Joan Gray Hendrickson, Theresa Mary Gray Croghan. Student, N. Tex. Agrl. Coll., 1948-49; BA, U. Tex., 1952; MS in Internat. Affairs, George Washington U., 1971; postgrad., Naval War Coll., 1970-71, Harvard U., 1980. Commd. 2d lt. USMC, 1952, advanced through grades to lt. gen., 1983; combat svc. in Korea, 1953, in Vietnam, 1965, 71-72; asst. div. comdr. 1st Marine Div. Camp Pendleton, Calif., 1977-79; dir. plans Hdqrs. Washington, 1979-80; dir. ops. Hdqrs., 1980-81; dir. personnel mgmt. Hdqrs., 1981-83; chief of staff Hdqrs., 1983-85; comdg. gen. Fleet Marine Force, Pacific; comdr. Marine Corps Bases, Pacific, Camp H.M. Smith, Hawaii, 1985-87; ret., 1987; ind. cons., 1987-89; exec. dir. Montgomery County Revenue Authority, Rockville, Md., 1989-90; undersec. veterans affairs for benefits Dept. Vet. Affairs, Washington, 1990-93. Chmn. bd. dirs. TROA EdPlus, Inc., Alexandria, Va., 2000—; del. Inter-Am. Def. Bd., 1980; bd. dirs. U.S. Naval Inst., 1980-85; mem. bd. govs. Uniformed Svcs. Benefit Assn. Kansas City, 1982-83, 85-88; mem. sec. of state's Adv. Panel on Overseas Security, 1984-85. Chmn. editorial bd., U.S. Naval Inst., 1980-83. Mem. maritime policy study group Ctr. for Strategic and Internat. Studies, Georgetown U., 1981-85. Decorated D.S.M., Legion of Merit with gold star and V, Bronze Star medal with V., Meritorious Svc. medal with gold star, Air medal with bronze numeral 5, Joint Svc. Commendation medal with V, Navy Commendation medal with V. Mem. Marine Corps Assn., U.S. Naval Inst., Marine Corps Heritage Found., Army and Navy Club, Marine Corps Scholarship Found., Mil. Officers Assn. Am. (bd. dirs. 1994-2000, 1st vice chmn. 1998-2000), Cath. War Vets., Disabled Am. Vets., Order St. Crispin. Roman Catholic. Home: 3423 Barger Dr Falls Church VA 22044-1202 *The military way of life is not for everyone. But, to those for whom it is right, it offers an unequalled opportunity for both personal adventure and service to one's fellow Americans. I wish I could do it all again!.*

GRAY, ELIZABETH VAN DOREN, lawyer; b. Columbia, SC, Jan. 3, 1949; d. Robert Lawson and Elizabeth Dacus (Gaines) Van Doren; m. James Cranston Gray, Jr., Apr. 30, 1982; children: James Cranston III, Elizabeth Gaines. BA in Internat. Studies, U. S.C., 1970, JD cum laude, 1976; student, St. Mary's Coll., Raleigh, NC, 1966-67. Bar: S.C. 1977, U.S. Dist. Ct. S.C. 1977, U.S. Ct. Appeals (4th cir.) 1980, U.S. Ct. Appeals (6th cir.) 1989, U.S. Supreme Ct. 1998. Assoc. McNair Law Firm, PA, Columbia, 1977-82, shareholder, 1982-87; ptnr. Glenn Irvin Murphy Gray & Stepp, Columbia, 1987—2000; now ptnr. Sowell Gray Stepp & Lafitte, LLC, Columbia. Contbr. articles to profl. jours. Mem. ABA, Am. Coll. Trial Lawyers, John Belton O'Neal Inn of Ct., S.C. Bar (pres. 2001-02), S.C. Women Lawyers Assn. (bd. dirs. 1995-99, sec. 1997-98), Richland County Bar Assn. Episcopalian. Office: Sowell Gray Stepp & Lafitte LLC PO Box 11449 Columbia SC 29211 Home: 8 Mahalo Ln Columbia SC 29204-3380

GRAY, FARRAH, entrepreneur, writer; LHD (hon.), Allen U., 2006. Co-host Backstage Live radio show, Las Vegas; founder Farr-Out Foods, NYC, New Early Entrepreneur Wonders; owner INNERCITY mag. Founder Urban Neighborhood Econ. Enterprise Club; cons. Minority Bus. Devel. Agency U.S. Dept. Commerce; bd. dirs. Nat. Assn. Real Estate Brokers, Inc.; spkr. in field. Author: (book) Reallionaire: Nine Steps to Becoming Rich from the Inside Out, 2005; contbg. author: book Chicken Soup for the African-American Soul; guest appearances Good Morning America, Tom Joyner Radio Show, Tavis Smiley Radio Show. Bd. dirs. United Way So. Nev.; bd. advisors Las Vegas C. of C. Achievements include acquiring millionaire status at the age of 14 through 1.5 million in sales of Farr-Out Food product. Office: Farrah Gray Found 67 Wall St Ste 2212 New York NY 10005 also: Farrah Gray Found PO Box 11351 Las Vegas NV 89111-1351 Office Phone: 212-859-5028. Office Fax: 702-926-9662. E-mail: fg@farrajgrayfoundation.org, farrahgray@aol.com.

GRAY, FESTUS GAIL, electrical engineer, educator, researcher; b. Moundsville, W.Va., Aug. 16, 1943; s. Festus P. and Elsie V. (Rine) G.; m.

Caryl Evelyn Anderson, Aug. 24, 1968; children: David, Andrew, Daniel. BSEE, W.Va. U., 1965, MSEE, 1967; PhD, U. Mich., 1971. Instr. W.Va. U., Morgantown, 1966-67; asst. prof. Va. Poly. Inst. and State U., Blacksburg, 1971-77, assoc. prof., 1977-82, prof., 1983—2003, prof. emeritus, 2003—. Vis. scientist Rsch. Triangle Inst., N.C., 1984-85; faculty fellow NASA, 1975; cons. Inland Motors, Radford, Va., 1980, Rsch. Triangle Inst., 1987—; researcher Rome Air Devel. Ctr., N.Y., 1980-81, Naval Surface Weapons Ctr., Dahlgren, Va., 1982-83, Army Rsch. Office, 1983-86, NSF, 1991-93, 98-2001, ARPA, 1993-96, Wright-Patterson AFB, 1995-99; publs. chmn. Internat. Symposium on Fault Tolerant Computing, Ann Arbor, Mich., 1985. Co-author: Structured Logic Design with VHDL, 1993, VHDL Representation and Synthesis, 2d edit., 2000; contbr. articles to sci. jours. Assoc. treas. Northside Presbyn. Ch., Blacksburg, 1986—, bd. deacons, 1980-83; coach S.W. Va. Soccer Assn., Blacksburg, 1980-86; asst. scoutmaster Boy Scouts Am., 1990—. Grantee NSF, Office Naval Rsch., NASA, Adv. Rsch. Projects Agy; Teaching fellow U. Mich., 1967-70. Mem. IEEE (chpt. chmn. 1979-80), Computer Soc. IEEE, Sigma Xi. Democrat. Achievements include research on fault tolerance, diagnosis, testing and reliability issues for VLSI, distributed and multiprocessor computer architectures, modeling and synthesis with VHOL, modeling and design with hardware description languages. Home: 304 Fincastle Dr Blacksburg VA 24060-5036 Office: Va Poly Inst and State U Blacksburg VA 24061-0111

GRAY, FRANCINE DU PLESSIX, writer; b. Warsaw; came to U.S., 1941, naturalized, 1952; d. Bertrand Jochaud and Tatiana (Iacovleff) du Plessix; m. Cleve Gray, Apr. 23, 1957; children: Thaddeus Ives, Luke Alexander. BA, Barnard Coll., 1952; Litt.D. (hon.), CUNY, Oberlin Coll., U. Santa Clara, St. Mary's Coll., U. Hartford. Annenberg fellow Brown U., 1997. Disting. vis. prof. CCNY, 1975; vis. lectr. Yale U., New Haven, 1981-82; Ferris prof. Princeton U., 1986; Disting. vis. prof. Vassar Coll., 1999. Author: Divine Disobedience: Profiles in Catholic Radicalism, 1970 (Nat. Cath. Book award), Hawaii: The Sugar-Coated Fortress, 1972 , Lovers and Tyrants, 1976, World Without End, 1981, October Blood, 1985, Adam & Eve and the City, 1987, Soviet Women: Walking the Tightrope, 1989, Rage and Fire: A Life of Louise Colet, 1994, At Home with the Marquis de Sade: A Life, 1998, Simone Weil, 2001, Them: A Memoir of Parents, 2005 (Nat. Book Critics Cir. award for autobiography, 2005). Guggenheim Found. fellow, 1991-92. Fellow, Am. Acad. Arts & Sci.;mem. Am. P.E.N., Am. Acad. Arts and Letters. Democrat. Roman Catholic.

GRAY, FRANK TRUAN, lawyer; b. Prince Frederick, Md., Oct. 22, 1920; s. John B. and Aimèe Atlee (Truan) Gray; m. Sally A. Jackson, Dec. 31, 1976; children: John W., Edward A., Philip L., Theodora R. AB, Princeton U., 1942; student, Cambridge U., Eng., 1945; LL.B., Harvard U., 1948. Bar: Md. 1949. Assoc. firm Piper & Marbury, Balt., 1948-56, ptnr., 1957-90. Asst. atty. gen. State Md., 1955—56; pres. Balt. Estate Planning Coun., 1975—76. Editor: Harvard Law Rev., 1947—48. Pres. Citizen's Planning Housing Assn., Balt., 1960—62; bd. dirs. Balt. Neighborhoods, Inc., 1959—85, Balt. Bar Found., 1985—93; trustee Provident Hosp., Inc., 1961—74, Leonard and Helen R. Stulman Charitable Found., 1991—. Fellow: Md. Bar Found., Am. Bar Found. (chmn. Md. 1993—98); mem.: ABA, Balt. Bar Assn., Md. Bar Assn., Am. Law Inst. Office: DLA Piper LLP 111 S Calvert St Ste 1950 Baltimore MD 21202-6193

GRAY, FRED DAVID, lawyer; b. Montgomery, Ala., Dec. 14, 1930; s. Abraham and Nancy G.; m. Bernice Hill, June 17, 1956; children: Deborah R., Vanessa, Fred D., Stanley F. BS, Ala. State U., 1951; JD, Case Western Res. U., 1954. Bar: Ala. 1954, Ohio 1954, U.S. Dist. Ct. (mid. dist.) Ala. 1955, U.S. Supreme Ct. 1956, U.S. Ct. Appeals (5th cir.) 1958, U.S. Dist. Ct. (no. dist.) Ala. 1963, U.S. Tax Ct. 1968, U.S. Ct. Appeals (11th cir.) 1982. Sr. ptnr. Gray, Langford, Sapp, McGowan, Gray & Nathanson, Montgomery and Tuskegee, Ala., 1983—. Vis. prof., Charles Hamilton Houston Chair N.C. Central Univ. Sch. of Law, Durham, NC. Author: (book) Bus Ride to Justice, 1995, The Tuskegee Syphilis Study, 1998. City atty. City of Tuskegee, 1965—; cooperating atty. NAACP Legal Def. Fund, Inc.; local gen. counsel Tuskegee U.; spl. asst. to atty. gen. State of Ala., 1975; past mem. Ala. Adv. Com. U.S. Commn. on Civil Rights; mem. Tuskegee Civic Assn. (life, award 1981); elder Tuskegee Ch. of Christ; chmn., trustee Southwestern Christian Coll., Terrell, Tex. Recipient Constl. Law award Ala. Civil Liberties Union, 1968, Disting. Alumni award Ala. State U., 1974, Social Engr.'s citation, 1975, Martin Luther King, Jr. Meml. Drum Major award So. Christian Leadership Conf., 1980, Black Achievers award, Ala. chpt. SCLC 1981, Fletcher Reed Andrews Grad. Yr. award Case Western Res. U., 1985, Man Yr. award Southwestern Christian Coll., 1986, Charles Hamilton Medallion of Merit Washington Bar Assn., 1986; honored by Miller Brewing Co. Gallery of Greats: Black Attys. Counsels for the Cause, 1989. Mem. ABA, Assn. Trial Lawyers Am., Ala. Trial Lawyers Assn., Ala. State Bar Assn. (pres.-elect 2001-02, pres. 2002-03), Nat. Bar Assn. (pres. 1985-86, 1st Ann. Equal Justice award 1977), Macon County Bar Assn. (past pres.), Nat. Bar Inst., NAACP (life), Soc. Benchers, Omega Psi Phi, Sigma Pi Phi. Represented Rosa Parks when she was arrested for not giving up her seat on a Montgomery bus, 1955. Office: Gray Langford et al PO Box 830239 Tuskegee AL 36083-0239 also: 400 S Union St Ste 205 Montgomery AL 36104-4316

GRAY, FREDERICK THOMAS, JR., (RICK GRAY), journalist, actor, educator; b. Hopewell, Va., Mar. 22, 1951; s. Frederick Thomas and Evelyn (Helms) Johnson Gray. BA with distinction, U. Va., 1972, JD, 1975, MEd, 1990, postgrad., 1991-94, U. Richmond, 1981-82. Bar: Va. 1976. Law clk. Williams, Mullen & Christian, Richmond, Va., 1975-76, assoc., 1976-78; sec. Commonwealth of Va., Richmond, 1978-81; high sch. tchr., 1982—89, 1999—2000, 2002—04; asst. prin., 1991—92; op-ed columnist, 2004—. Appeared in TV series In the Heat of the Night, 1993, profl. stage prodns. My Fair Lady, 1995-96, Macbeth, 1996, To Kill a Mockingbird. 1995, others Mem. SAG, Raven Soc. (U. Va.). Address: 4701 Bermuda Hundred Rd Chester VA 23836-3257 Office Phone: 804-530-2231. Personal E-mail: deinikes@yahoo.com.

GRAY, GEORGE M., federal agency administrator; m. Ann Gray; 2 children. BS, U. Mich., 1985; MS, U. Rochester, 1988, PhD, 1989. Rsch. fellow Harvard U. Sch. Pub. Health, Boston, 1989—91, rsch. assoc. ctr. risk analysis, 1991—94, instr. risk analysis, 1994—99; acting dir. Harvard Ctr. Risk Analysis, 2001—03, exec. dir., 2003—05; asst. adminstr. office rsch. & devel. EPA, Washington, 2005—. Mem. food advisory com. Ctr. Food Safety and Applied Nutrition FDA; mem. nat. advisory health sci. coun. NIEHS; mem. risk assessment task force Soc. Toxicology; bd. dirs. Found. Rsch. on Econ. and Environ. Office: EPA 1200 Pennsylvania Ave NW MC 8101 R Washington DC 20460

GRAY, GLORIA MEADOR, librarian; b. Marshall, Tex., Aug. 24, 1935; d. Alfred E. and Julia (Whitfield) Meador; m. Philip R. Gray, Mar. 23, 1955; children: Brian, David, Gordon. BA, U. North Tex., 1970, MLS, 1974. Libr. Richardson (Tex.) Ind. Sch. Dist., 1971-91. Mem.: ALA, Tex. Libr. Assn. Democrat. Methodist. Avocations: reading, skiing, community volunteering.

GRAY, GORDON L., communications educator; b. Hampton, Iowa, May 18, 1924; s. Leroy Ernest and Arianna (Oldham) G.; m. Barbara Ann Smith, Feb. 5, 1949; children: David Gordon, Jonathan William. BA, Cornell Coll., 1948; MA, Northwestern U., 1951, PhD, 1957. Radio announcer and newsman, 1948-50; broadcast coordinator NBC-TV, Chgo, 1951; instr. to asso. prof. television and radio Mich. State U., 1953-67; prof. communications Temple U., Phila., 1967-96, prof. emeritus, 1996—, chmn. dept. radio, TV, and Film, 1967-74, 78-82, 1994-95. Program assoc. Ednl. TV and Radio Ctr., Ann Arbor, Mich., 1956-57. Served to staff sgt. AUS, 1943-46. Fulbright scholar Inst. Edn. U. Leeds, U.K., 1965-66

GRAY, HANNA HOLBORN, historian, educator; b. Heidelberg, Germany, Oct. 25, 1930; d. Hajo and Annemarie (Bettmann) Holborn; m. Charles Montgomery Gray, June 19, 1954. AB, Bryn Mawr Coll., 1950; PhD, Harvard U., 1957; MA, Yale U., 1971, LLD, 1978; LittD (hon.), St. Lawrence U., 1974, Oxford U., Eng., 1979; LLD (hon.), Dickinson Coll., 1979, U. Notre Dame, 1980, Marquette U., 1984; LittD (hon.), Washington U., 1974; HHD (hon.), St. Mary's Coll., 1974; LHD (hon.), Grinnell Coll., Iowa, 1974, Lawrence U., 1974, Denison U., 1974, Wheaton Coll., 1976, Marlboro Coll., 1979, Rikkyo U., Japan, 1979, Roosevelt U., 1980, Knox Coll., 1980, Coe Coll., 1981, Thomas Jefferson U., 1981, Duke U., 1982, New Sch. for Social Research, 1982, Clark U., 1982, Brandeis U., 1983, Colgate U., 1983, Wayne State U., 1984, Miami U., Oxford, Ohio, 1984, So. Meth. U., 1984, CUNY, 1985, U. Denver, 1985, Am. Coll. Greece, 1986, Muskingum Coll., 1987, Rush Presbyn. St. Lukes Med. Ctr., 1987, NYU, 1988, Rosemont Coll., 1988, Claremont U. Ctr. Grad Sch., 1989, Moravian Coll., 1991, Rensselaer Poly. Inst., 1991, Coll. William and Mary, 1991, Centre Coll., 1991, Macalester Coll., 1993, McGill U., 1993, Ind. U., 1994, Med. U. of S.C., 1994; LLD (hon.), Union Coll., 1975, Regis Coll., 1976, Dartmouth Coll., 1978, Trinity Coll., 1978, U. Bridgeport, 1978, Dickinson Coll., 1979, Brown U., 1979, Wittenburg U., 1979, Dickinson Coll., 1979, U. Rochester, 1980, U. Notre Dame, 1980, U. So. Calif., 1980, U. Mich., 1981, Princeton U., 1982, Georgetown U., 1983, Marquette U., 1984, W.Va. Wesleyan U., 1985, Hamilton Coll., 1985, Smith Coll., 1986, U. Miami, 1986, Columbia U., 1987, NYU, 1988, Rosemont Coll., 1988, U. Toronto, Can., 1991; LDH, LHD, Haverford Coll., 1995; LDH (hon.), Tulane U., 1995; LLD (hon.), Harvard U., 1995; LHD (hon.), McGill U., 1993, Macalester Coll., 1993, Ind. U., 1994, Med. U. S.C., 1994, Haverford Coll., 1995, Tulane U., 1995; LLD (hon.), Harvard U., 1995, U. Chgo., 1996; DL (hon.), Pontifical Inst. Mediaeval Studies, Toronto, 2005. Instr. Bryn Mawr Coll., 1953—54; tchg. fellow Harvard U., 1955—57, instr., 1957—59, asst. prof., 1959—60, vis. lectr., 1963—64; asst. prof. U. Chgo., 1961—64, assoc. prof., 1964—72; dean, prof. Northwestern U., Evanston, Ill., 1972—74; provost, prof. history Yale U., 1974—78, acting pres., 1977—78; pres. U. Chgo., 1978—93, prof. dept. history, 1978, Harry Pratt Judson disting. svc. prof. history, 1994, prof. emeritus. Fellow Ctr. for Advanced Study in Behavioral Scis., 1966—67, vis. scholar, 1970—71; vis. prof. U. Calif., Berkeley, Calif., 1970—71. Co-editor (with Charles Gray): Jour. Modern History, 1965—70; contbr. articles to profl. jours. Active Nat. Coun. on Humanities, 1972—78; trustee Yale Corp., 1971—74; past bd. regents Smithsonian Instn.; past chmn. bd. Andrew W. Mellon Found.; chmn. bd. Howard Hughes Med. Inst.; mem. Harvard Corp., 1997—2005; chmn. bd. Marlboro Sch. Music. Decorated Grosse Verdienstkreuz Germany; named Pontifical Justice Medieval Studies, Toronto, Can., 2005; recipient Grad. medal, Radcliffe Coll., 1976, Yale medal, 1978, Medal of Liberty award, 1986, Laureate Lincoln Acad. Ill., 1988, Medal of Freedom, 1991, Frontrunner award, Sara Lee, 1991, Charles Frankel prize, 1993, Centennial medal, Harvard U., 1994, Disting. Svc. award in edn., Inst. Internat. Edn., 1994, Medal of Distinction, Barnard Coll., 2000, Fritz Redlich Disting. Alumni award, Internat. Inst. Edn., 2004, The Newberry Libr. award, 2006, Gold medal, Nat. Inst. Social Scis., 2006; fellow Newberry Libr., 1960—61, St. Anne's Coll., Oxford U., 1978—; Fulbright scholar, 1950—51. Fellow: Am. Acad. Arts and Scis.; mem.: Coun. Fgn. Rels. N.Y., Coun. Fgn. Rels. Chgo., Nat. Acad. Edn., Am. Philos. Soc. (Jefferson medal 1993), Renaissance Soc. Am., Phi Beta Kappa (vis. scholar 1971—72). Office: U Chgo Dept History 1126 E 59th St Chicago IL 60637-1580 Business E-Mail: h-gray@uchicago.edu.

GRAY, HARRY BARKUS, chemistry professor; b. Woodburn, Ky., Nov. 14, 1935; s. Barkus and Ruby (Hopper) Gray; m. Shirley Barnes, June 2, 1957; children: Victoria Lynn, Andrew Thomas, Noah Harry Barkus. BS, Western Ky. U., 1957; PhD, Northwestern U., 1960, DSc (hon.), 1984, U. Chgo., 1987, U. Rochester, 1987, U. Paul Sabatier, 1991, U. Göteborg, 1991, U. Firenze, 1993, Columbia U., 1994, Bowling Green State U., 1994, Ill. Wesleyan, 1995, Oberlin Coll., 1996, U. Ariz., 1997, Carleton U., 2001, U. SC, 2003, U. Copenhagen, 2003, U. Edinburgh, 2006. Postdoctoral fellow U. Copenhagen, 1960—61; faculty Columbia U., 1961—66, prof., 1965—66; prof. chemistry Calif. Inst. Tech., Pasadena, 1966—, now Arnold O. Beckman prof. chemistry and founding dir. Beckman Inst. Vis. prof. Rockefeller U., Harvard U., U. Iowa, Pa. State U., Yeshiva U., U. Copenhagen, U. Witwatersrand, Johannesburg, South Africa, U. Canterbury, Christchurch, New Zealand, U. Hong Kong; George Eastman prof. Oxford (Eng.) U., 1997—98; cons. govt., industry; Kistiakowsky lectr. Harvard U., 1999. Author: Electrons and Chemical Bonding, 1965, Molecular Orbital Theory, 1965, Ligand Substitution Processes, 1966, Basic Principles of Chemistry, 1967, Chemical Dynamics, 1968, Chemical Principles, 1970, Models in Chemical Science, 1971, Chemical Bonds, 1973, Chemical Structure and Bonding, 1980, Molecular Electronic Structures, 1980, Braving the Elements, 1995. Named Calif. Scientist of Yr., 1988, Achievement Rewards for Coll. Scis. Man of Sci., 1990; recipient Franklin Meml. award, Stanford U., 1967, Fresenius award, Phi Lambda Upsilon, 1970, Shoemaker award, U. Louisville, 1970, award for excellence in tchg., Mfg. Chemists Assn., 1972, Centenary medal, Royal Soc. Chemistry, 1985, Nat. medal of Sci., 1986, Alfred Bader Bioinorganic Chemistry award, 1990, Gold medal, Am. Inst. Chemists, 1990, Linderstrom-Lang prize, 1992, Priestly award, Dickinson Coll., 1991, Chandler medal, Columbia U., 1999, Harvey prize, Technion Israel Inst. Tech., 2000, Benjamin Franklin medal in Chemistry, Franklin Inst., 2004, Wolf prize in chemistry, Wolf Found., Israel, 2004; Guggenheim fellow, 1972—73, Phi Beta Kappa scholar, 1973—74. Fellow: AAAS; mem.: NAS (Nichols medal 2003, award in chem. scis. 2003), Royal Danish Acad. Scis. and Letters, Am. Philos. Soc., Royal Soc. (London), Royal Swedish Acad., Am. Chem. Soc. (award pure chemistry 1970, Harrison Howe award 1972, award inorganic chemistry 1978, Remsen Meml. award 1979, Tolman medal 1979, award for disting. svc. in advancement of inorganic chemistry 1984, Pauling medal 1986, Priestley medal 1991, Willard Gibbs medal 1992, Wolf prize for chemistry 2004, Benjamin Franklin medal in chemistry 2004, City of Florence prize in molecular scis. 2006), Phi Lambda Upsilon, Alpha Chi Sigma. Office: Calif Inst Tech 408 Beckman MC 127-72 1200 E California Blvd Pasadena CA 91125-0001

GRAY, HAZEL IRENE, retired special education educator, counselor, consultant; b. Van Nuys, Calif., July 2, 1921; d. Charles Clayton Cramer and Ida Mae (Leffler); m. Reed A. Gray; children: Mildred Lorene(dec.) , Paul Charles; m. Neil Chapin Smith (dec.). BA, San Jose State Coll., Calif., 1964, MA, 1968; EdD, U. So. Calif., LA, 1977. Itinerant tchr. hearing impaired Santa Cruz County Office of Edn., 1964—66; resource specialist Santa Cruz Pub. Schools, 1966—68; psychologist Santa Cruz County Office of Edn., 1968—71; psychologist, cons. and parent counselor Project Idea, San Jose, 1971—72; dir. spl. edn. Live Oaks schs. Santa Cruz County Office of Edn., 1972—74; cons. Calif. State Dept. of Edn., Sacramento, 1975—76; adminstr. San Jose City Coll., 1976—78; dir. pupil pers. Campbell Union Sch. Dist., Calif., 1978; pvt. practice marriage counseling, 1971—. Cons. Catholic Pre-Sch., LA; lectr. Calif. State U, San Jose, U. Calif., Santa Clara, Santa Cruz; with Med. Info. Svcs. Co-author: (book) Behavior Modification, 1971. Mem. rescue team Calif. Coast Guard, 1971—76; team mem. marriage family and child counseling license rev. Calif. State Dept. of Licensing, Sacramento. Mem.: San Jose Movie and Video Club, Camera Club. Republican. Mem. Lds Ch. Avocations: travel, photography.

GRAY, HELEN THERESA GOTT, editor; b. Jersey City, July 2, 1942; d. William E. and Cynthia B. Gott; m. David L. Gray, Aug. 15, 1976; 1 child, David Lee Jr. BA, Syracuse U., 1963; M in Internat. Affairs, Columbia U., 1965. Editor religion sect. The Kansas City (Mo.) Star, 1971—. Tchr. Bible sch. Pleasant Green Bapt. Ch., Kansas City, Kans., 1975—, counselor, 1978—; former owner of a Christian book store. Co-author, editor several books; contbr. articles to profl. jours. Recipient writing award Valley Forge Freedom Found., 1967; John Hay Whitney Found. grantee, 1963-64; named 100 Most Influential African Ams. in Greater Kansas City. Mem. Religion Newswriters Assn., Kansas City Assn. Black Journalists (Life Achievement award 1998). Baptist. Office: The Kansas City Star 1729 Grand Blvd Kansas City MO 64108-1458 Office Phone: 816-234-4446. E-mail: hgray@kcstar.com.

GRAY, INA TURNER, fraternal organization administrator; b. Eagleville, Mo., July 25, 1926; d. Farris T. and Teloir (Anderson) Turner; m. Wallace G. Gray Jr., Dec. 18, 1948; children: Toni Jo, Tara Joy BS with high honors, Cen. Meth. Coll., 1948; MA, Scarritt Coll., 1952; postgrad., U. Hawaii, 1969. Tchr. Rutherford-Met. Sch. Bus., Dallas, 1948-49; dir. Christian edn. 1st Meth. Ch., Lawton, Okla., 1953-54, Winfield, Kans., 1957-58; dir. religious life Southwestern Coll., Winfield, 1958-59; dir. commn. on archives and history Kans. West Conf., Winfield, 1960-78; exec. dir. Pi Gamma Mu, Winfield, 1976-96. English tchr. JoGakuin Jr. High, Hiroshima, Japan, 1971-72, Kitakyushu U., Japan, 1997-98 Mem. editorial bd. Fire on the Prairie, 1961-69; mem. editorial and pub. coms. The Lure of Kansas, 1990 Bd. dirs. Cowley County Hist. Soc., 2004—. Named to Hall Fame, Pi Gamma Mu, 2005. Mem. Assn. Coll. Honor Socs. (del. 1986-96), Commn. Archives and History (local Ch. History award 1982—), Kans. State Assn. Parliamentarians (v.p. Walnut Valley unit 1991-92, 99-2000), Faculty Dames (pres. 1981-82). Republican. Avocations: travel, historical research, Japanese flower arranging. Home: 1701 Winfield Ave Winfield KS 67156-1919 Personal E-mail: gray@sckans.edu.

GRAY, J. CHARLES, lawyer, cattle rancher; b. Leesburg, Fla., Mar. 26, 1932; s. G. Wayne and Mary Evelyn (Albright) G.; m. Saundra Hagood, Aug. 18, 1955; children: Terese Ren. John Charles Jr., Lee Jerome. BA, U. Fla., 1955, JD, 1958. Bar: Fla. 1958. County atty. Orange County, Fla., 1977—85; founder, chmn. Gray Robinson, P.A., Attys. Chmn. Fla. Turnpike Authority, 1965-67; city solicitor City of Orlando (Fla.), 1960-61; pres. Santa Gertrudis Breeders Internat., 1981-83; dir. Nat. Cattleman's Assn., 1981-83. Chmn. pres.'s coun. advisors U. Ctrl. Fla., 1978-84; pres. U. Ctrl. Fla. Found., 1990-91, dir. emeritus; past pres. Orange County U. Fla. Alumni Assn., Pi Kappa Alpha Alumni Assn.; past dist. v.p. U. Fla. Alumni Assn.; mem. U. Fla. Pres.'s Coun.; mem. Com. of 100; founding bd. dirs. Fla. Epilepsy Found.; chmn. Econ. Devel. Commn. Mid. Fla., 1987-89; mem. Fla. Econ. Devel. Adv. Coun. Recipient J. Thomas Guerney Lifetime Svc. award, James B. Green award for Econ. Devel., Legacy award Greater Orlando Leadership Found., 2005; inducted into U. Fla. Hall of Fame, Fla. Blue Key, Roast & Toast Fla. Pub. Rels. Assn., J.A. Lauriet Hall of Fame. Mem. ABA, Fla. Bar Assn., Orange County Bar Assn., Citrus Club of Orlando (past dir.), Univ. Club of Orlando (past dir.), Seven Seas Cruising Assn. (commodore, World Circumnavigator award, bd. dirs. O'Force, adv. bd. "Seeds of Peace"). Republican. Episcopalian. Office: Ste 1400 301 E Pine St Orlando FL 32801-2725 Office Phone: 407-843-8880. Personal E-mail: cgray4@cfl.rr.com. Business E-Mail: cgray@gray-robinson.com.

GRAY, JAMES, English literature educator; b. Montrose, Scotland, May 11, 1923; s. James and Matilda (Smythe) G.; m. Pamela Doris Knight, July 26, 1947; 1 child, Caroline Gordon. MA, U. Aberdeen, 1946; BA with honours, U. Oxford, Eng., 1948, MA, 1951; PhD, U. Montreal, 1970. Prof. English Bishops U., Lennoxville, Que., Can., 1948-72, chmn. humanities div., 1971-72; prof., chmn. dept. English Dalhousie U., Halifax, N.S., 1972-75, dean Faculty Arts and Sci., 1975-80, Thomas McCulloch prof. English, 1980-88, prof. emeritus, 1988—. Mem. Humanities Rsch. Coun. Can.; vis. prof. Queen's U., Kingston, Ont., 1955, 70, U. B.C., 1958, Acadia U., 1991. Author: The Sermons of Samuel Johnson: A Study, 1972, Dr. Johnson's French, 1986, Miracles in the 18th Century, 2002, Dr. Johnson's Oxford, 2003; co-editor: The Religious Writings of Samuel Johnson, 1978; mem. editl. bd. Yale U. Press edit. Works of Samuel Johnson, The Age of Johnson; contbr. articles to profl. jours. With Brit. and Indian Armies, 1942—46. Recipient Queen Elizabeth II Coronation medal, Jubilee medal. Fellow Royal Soc. Arts, Royal Soc. Can.; mem. Can. Inst. Internat. Affairs (br. pres.), MLA, English Inst., Am. Assn. for Eighteenth Century Studies, Can. Assn. for Eighteenth Century Studies, Internat. Assn. for Eighteenth Century Studies, Assn. Can. Univ. Tchrs. English (pres. 1982-84), Humanities Assn. Can. (past pres.) Mem. Liberal Party. Presbyterian. Club: University Faculty. Home: Ward MTN RR 2 3856 Prospect Rd Kentville NS Canada B4N 3V8 Office: Dalhousie U Dept English Halifax NS Canada B3H 3J5 Home Phone: 902-679-0574; Office Phone: 902-494-3384. Personal E-mail: jgray000@ns.sympatico.ca.

GRAY, JAMES L., investment company executive; b. Jackson, Mich., Apr. 10, 1948; s. Biscoe LaFayette, Jr. and Margaret Anne (Hurley) G.; M. Mary Elizabeth Gaynon, Mar. 2, 1968 (div. July 1978); 1 child, Bennett Lee; m. Christine J. Smith, July 16, 1994. BA in History, U. Wis., 1972, MA in History, 1974, MA in Libr. Sci., 1975; MBA, Am. Grad. Sch. of Internat. Mgmt., Glendale, Ariz., 1977; JD, So. Tex. Coll. Law Texas A&M U., Houston, Tex., 1986. Trust officer Southwest Fla. Banks, Inc., Fort Myers, Fla., 1977-80; assoc. nat. trust examiner U.S. Treasury Dept./Comptroller of the Currency, Washington, 1980-82; asst. v.p. First City Nat. Bank of Houston, 1982-88; sr. v.p., mgr. trust divsn. First Nat. Bank in Albuquerque, 1988-92; chief operating officer MFR, Inc., NYC, 1992-94; 1st v.p. Concord Holding Corp., NYC, 1994-95; sr. v.p. Schroder Fund Advisors, NYC, 1995-99; v.p. Schroder Capital Mgmt./Internat. Inc.; sr. v.p. Brandywine Asset Mgmt., Inc., Wilmington, Del., 1999-2000; mng. dir. Scudder pvt. investment counsel Deutsche Investment Mgmt., NYC, 2000—05; mng. dir. Legg Mason Investment Counsel, NYC, 2005—. Author: The Southwest Securities Transfer Association Reference Manual, 1985. Bd. dirs. Presbyn. Healthcare Found., Albuquerque, 1990-92, N.Mex. Repertory Theater, Albuquerque, 1989-92; trustee Legg Mason Charitable Gift Trust, 2006—. Mem. SR, SAR (treas. N.Y. treas. 1997-2005), Pilgrims of U.S., St. Georges Soc., Union Club/N.Y., West Side Tennis Club, River Club, Southampton Club. Episcopalian. Avocations: tennis, swimming, golf, gardening, history. Home: 240 E 47th St Apt 31E New York NY 10017-2138 also: 59 Pheasant Close W Southampton NY 11968-3062 Office: Legg Mason 640 Fifth Ave New York NY 10019 Office Phone: 212-554-7125. Business E-Mail: jlgray@leggmason.com.

GRAY, JAMES LARRY, international business executive; b. Southmayd, Tex., Dec. 17, 1932; s. Cecil Lawray and Coquese Adeline (Coe) G. Student, Tex. Tech. U., 1954, So. Meth. U., 1956; MBA, Pepperdine U., 1978. Sales engr. Simplex Wire & Cable, Cambridge, Mass., 1958—96; pres. Integral Corp., Dallas, 1996—2000, Cern Internat. Corp., 1997—; CEO Zylec Corp., 2000—. Served with U.S. Army, 1956-58. Mem. IEEE, Sigma Alpha Epsilon. Clubs: Toastmasters (pres. 1966-67), Jaycees (v.p. 1969-70). Republican. Office: 3818 Cedar Springs Rd Box 101-434 Dallas TX 75219-4731 Business E-Mail: jlgray@zylec.com.

GRAY, JAMES N., computer scientist; BS in Math. and Engring., U. Calif., Berkeley, 1966, PhD in Computer sci., 1969; D of Natural Sci. (hon.), U. Stuttgart, Germany, 1990. Sys. rschr. Bell Labs, Whippany, NJ, 1966—67; rsch. asst., computer sci. U. Calif., Berkeley, Calif., 1967—69; ops. sys. rschr. T.J. Watson Rsch. Lab IBM, Yorktown Heights, NY, 1971—72; UNESCO expert Polytech. Inst., Bucharest, Romania, 1972; database rschr. IBM, San Jose, Calif., 1972—80; rschr. Tandem Computers, Cupertino, Calif., 1980—90; corp. cons. engr. Digital Equipment Corp., 1990—94; sr. rschr. Microsoft Corp., 1995—; founder, mgr., disting. engr. Scaleable Servers Rsch. Group Microsoft Bay Area Rsch. Ctr., San Francisco, 2000—; Missing since Jan. 28, 2007 after a weekend sailing trip to scatter mother's ashes in the waters off Northern Calif.; Coast Guard called off search on Feb. 1, 2007. Vis. scholar U. Calif., Berkeley; pres. Adv. Com. on Info. Tech.; mem. adv. bd. Sch. Engring., Stanford U. Editor: Morgan Kaufmann Data Management Series, Data Mining and Knowledge Discovery; moderator database sect. Computer Sci. Online Rsch. Repository; past editor in chief and endowment bd. VLDB Jour. Recipient A.M. Turing award Assn. Computer Machinery, 1998, Phi Beta Kappa, Sigma Chi. Fellow Assn. Computing Machinery; mem. NAE, NRC (mem. computer sci. and telecomm. bd.).

GRAY, JAN CHARLES, lawyer, business owner; b. Des Moines, June 15, 1947; s. Charles Donald and Mary C. Gray; 1 child, Charles Jan. BA in Econs., U. Calif., Berkeley, 1969; MBA, Pepperdine U., 1986; JD, Harvard U., 1972. Bar: Calif. 1972, D.C. 1974, Wyo. 1992. Law clk. Kindel & Anderson, LA, 1971-72; assoc. Halstead, Baker & Sterling, LA, 1972-75; sr. v.p., gen. counsel and sec. Ralphs Grocery Co., LA, 1975-97; pres. Am. Presidents Resorts, Custer, S.D., Casper/Glenrock, Wyo., 1983—; owner Big Bear (Calif.) Cabins-Lakeside, 1988—; pres. Mt. Rushmore Broadcasting, Inc., 1991—; owner Sta. KGOS/KERM, Torrington, Wyo., 1993—, Sta. KRAL/KIQZ, Rawlins, Wyo., 1993—, Sta. KZMX, Hot Springs, SD, 1993—, Sta. KFCR, Custer, SD, 1992—, Sta. KQLT-FM, Casper, Wyo., 1994—, Sta. KASS-FM, Casper, 1995—, Sta. KVOC-AM, Casper, 1997—, KAWK-FM, Rapid City, SD, 1997—, KHOC, Casper, Wyo., 1998—, KMLD, Casper, Mt. Rushmore Farms Horse Racing, 1999—. Judge pro tem L.A. Mcpl. Ct., 1977-85; instr. bus. UCLA, 1976-85, Pepperdine MBA Program, 1983-85; arbitrator Am. Arbitration Assn., 1977-97; media spokesman So. Calif. Grocers Assn., 1979-90, Calif. Grocers Assn., 1979-97, Calif. Retailers Assn., 1979-97; real estate broker, Calif., 1973—. Contbg. author: Life or Death, Who Controls?, 1976; contbr. articles to profl. jours. Trustee South Bay U. Coll. Law, 1978-79; mem. bd. visitors Southwestern U. Sch. Law, 1983—; mem. L.A. County Pvt. Industry Coun., 1982-96, exec. com. 1984-88, chmn. econ. devel. task force, 1986-89, chmn. mktg. com. 1991-93; mem. L.A. County Martin Luther King, Jr. Gen. Hosp. Authority, 1984—94; mem. L.A. County Aviation Commn, 1986-92, chmn., 1990-91; L.A. Police Crime Prevention Adv. Coun., 1986—97; Angelus Plaza Adv. Bd., 1983-85; bd. dirs. RecyCAL of So. Calif., 1983-89; trustee Santa Monica Hosp. Found., 1986-91, adv. bd., 1991—94; mem. L.A. County Dem. Cen. Com., 1980-90, L.A. City Employees' Retirement System Commn., 1993—; del. Dem. Nat. Conv., 1980. Recipient So. Calif. Grocers Assn. award for outstanding contbns. to food industry, 1982, appreciation award for No on 11 Campaign, Calif./Nev. Soft Drink Assn., 1983; Tyler Price Meml. award Mex.-Am. Grocers Assn., 1995, Radio Affiliate of Yr.-Classic Rock ABC, 1998. Mem.: ABA, Harvard Club of So. Calif., U. Calif. Alumni Assn., Town Hall L.A., Food Mktg. Inst. (govt. rels. com. 1977—97, chmn.lawyers, economists 1993—95, benefits coun. 1993—97), Calif. Retailers Assn. (supermarket com.), L.A. World Affairs Coun., L.A. Pub. Affairs Officers Assn., San Fernando Valley Bar Assn. (chmn. real property sect. 1975—77), L.A. County Bar Assn. (exec. com. corp. law depts. sect. 1979—2000, exec. com. barristers sect. 1974—75, exec. com. corp. law depts. sect. 1974—76, exec. com. barristers sect. 1979—81, chmn. 1989—90, trustee 1991—93, jud. evaluation com. 1993—96, nominating com. 1994), Calif. Bar Assn., Ephebian Soc. L.A., So. Calif. Bus. Assn. (bd. dirs. 1981—99, mem. exec. com. 1982—99, sec. 1986—91, chair 1991—98), Casper Country Club, L.A. Athletic Club, Phi Beta Kappa. Office: PO Box 826 Los Angeles CA 90078 Personal E-mail: jcg4321@aol.com.

GRAY, JANET ETHEL, elementary school educator; b. Snyder, Tex., Dec. 15, 1942; d. James Lavern and Irene McClain (Brown) Cotton; m. Richard Lee Gray, June 24, 1960; children: Melinda, Eric, Heidi, Keith. BS in Edn., Abilene Christian U., 1964; degree in kindergarten-early childhood, Tex. Christian U., 1972. Tchr. Abilene Pub. Schs., Tex., 1964—67, Castleberry Ind. Sch., Fort Worth, 1967—84, Conroe Ind. Sch., Tex., 1984—2002. Tech Elem. Coord. Conroe ISD, 2002—03. Recipient Presdl. award for excellence in sci. and math. teaching NSF, 1994, Presdl. award for excellence in sci., Tex., 1994. Mem. Sci. Tchrs. Assn. Tex., Nat. Sci. Tchrs. Assn., Soc. Elem. Presdl. Awardees, Coun. for Elem. Sci. Internat., Tex. State Tchrs. Assn. (bldg. rep. 1992-95), ASCD. Office: Anderson Elem Sch 1414 E Dallas St Conroe TX 77301-2100 Business E-Mail: jgray@conroeisd.net.

GRAY, JEREMY J.F., lawyer; b. Oxford, Eng., July 17, 1961; BA, Concordia Coll., 1984; JD magna cum laude, Loyola University, LA, 1990. Bar: Calif. 1990. Assoc. Irell & Manella, England, Whitfield, Schroeder & Tredway; ptnr. Katten Muchin Zavis Rosenman, LA. Mem.: ABA, LA County Bar Assn. Office: Katten Muchin Zavis Rosenman Ste 2600 2029 Century Park E Los Angeles CA 90067 Office Phone: 310-788-4592. Office Fax: 310-712-8452. E-mail: jeremy.gray@kmzr.com.

GRAY, JERRY, editor; Reporter & editor, metro desk New York Times, continuous news editor, 1999—2003, weekend editor, nat. desk, 2003—. Office: New York Times 229 W 43d St New York NY 10036 Office Phone: 212-556-7356. Office Fax: 212-556-7614.

GRAY, JONATHAN DAVID, real estate company executive; b. 1970; s. Allen and Susan (Florsheim) Gray; m. Mindy Basser, July 2, 1995. BA magna cum laude in English, U. Pa., Phila., BS in Econs. Positions up to sr. mng. dir., co-head US real estate grp. The Blackstone Grp., NYC, 1992—. Chmn. bd. Extended Stay Hotels, LXR Luxury Resorts. Named one of 25 Most Influential People in the Meetings Industry, MeetingNews, 2006; David Rockefeller fellow, Partnership for NYC, 2004—05. Mem.: Phi Beta Kappa. Office: The Blackstone Grp 345 Park Ave New York NY 10154 Office Phone: 212-583-5000. Office Fax: 212-583-5712.*

GRAY, KARLA MARIE, state supreme court justice; b. Escanaba, Mich., May 10, 1947; BA, Western Mich. U., MA in African History; JD, Hastings Coll. of Law, San Francisco, 1976. Bar: Mont. 1976, Calif. 1977. Law clk. to Hon. W. D. Murray U.S. Dist. Ct., 1976-77; staff atty. Atlantic Richfield Co., 1977-81; pvt. practice law Butte, Mont., 1981-84; staff atty., legis. lobbyist Mont. Power Co., Butte, 1984-91; justice Mont. Supreme Ct., Helena, 1991-2000, chief justice, 2000—. Mem. Mont. Supreme Ct. Gender Fairness Task Force. Fellow Am. Bar Found., Am. Judicature Soc., Internat. Women's Forum; mem. State Bar Mont., Silver Bow County Bar Assn. (past pres.), Nat. Assn. Women Judges. Avocations: travel, reading, piano, genealogy, cross country skiing. Office: Supreme Ct Mont PO Box 203001 Helena MT 59620-3001*

GRAY, KRIS DIANE, nursing consultant, forensic specialist; ASN, Fresno C.C., 1993; BA in Biology, Calif. State U., 1985. Diplomate Am. Bd. Medicolegal Death Investigators (registered), lic. paramedic Calif., cert. emergency nurse Bd. Cert. Emergency Nursing, flight nurse Bd. Cert. Emergency Nursing; RN Calif. Cardiac rsch. assoc. U. Calif. San Francisco, Fresno, 1984—85; paramedic Fort Bend County Emergency Svcs., Rosenberg, Tex., 1987—90, Am. Med. Svcs., Fresno, 1990—94; RN Sierra View Dist. Hosp., Porterville, Calif., 1994—2004; instr. Porterville C.C., 1994—95; RN Holland Am.-West Tours Inc., Seattle, 1996—2000; owner Gray Forensics and Consulting, Visalia, Calif., 2003—; co-owner Mobile Blood Draws, Visalia, Calif., 2007—. Peer counselor Ctrl. Valley Emergency Svcs. Support Team, Fresno, 1990—95; forensic autopsy asst. Tulare County Sheriff's Office, Visalia, 1998—; safety officer Disaster Mortuary Ops./Recovery Team, Washington, 2002—; founding mem. Dept. Homeland Security U.S. Govt.; presenter in field. Rschr. (book) Visalia's Fabulous Fox, 2000, unit prodn. mgr. (feature film) Legend of Jake Kincaid, 2001, interviewer (oral history project) Tulare County and WWII, 2004. Crisis counselor Help in Emotional Trouble, Fresno, 1983—85; bd. dirs. Citizens Adv. Bd., Visalia, 1987. Mem.: Western Pacific Forensic Response Inst. (bd. mem. 2007—), Am. Bd. Forensic Nurses, Air and Surface Transport Nurses Assn., Am. Bd. Forensic Examiners (cert. med. investigator), Am. Assn. Legal Nurse Consultants, Calif. State Coroners Assn. (assoc.). Avocations: golf, snorkeling, guitar. Office: Gray Forensics and Consulting 2115 S Ashton Ct Visalia CA 93277 Office Phone: 559-734-3980, 559-901-6546. Personal E-mail: kgraybar@sbcglobal.net.

GRAY, LAURA B., psychology professor, counselor; d. Harold Herman and Deborah Bowman; m. Philip Lempert, Feb. 24, 1991; 1 child, Jermey. BS, Cornell U., Ithaca, NY, 1966, MA, 1967; post grad., Phillips Inst., Encino, Calif. Lic. perm. tchr. NY State, tchr. Calif., cert. child devel. dirs. Calif., career devel. NJ. Cons., 1982—92; dir. training and devel. Age Wave Inc., Emertville, Calif., 1992—94; v.p. edn. Hosp. Coun., Pleasanton, Calif., 1992—94; v.p. career svcs. Right Mgmt. Cons., LA, 1996—99; dir. career devel. Pepperdine U., Mailbu, Calif., 1999—2001; assoc. prof., counselor Harbor Coll., Wilimington, Calif., 2001—. Bd. dirs. Nat. Employment Counseling Assn., 2002—04, Coll. Human Ecology Cornell U., 2006—; presenter ann. symposium Am. Coll. Pers. Assn., 2002. Adv. bd. Powerhouse Theater, Venice, Calif., 2001—04; recruitment bd. mem. Cornell U. Alumni Amb., LA, 2003—; trustee Cornell U., Ithaca, NY, 2006—; bd. dirs. Cornell U. Coll. Human Ecology, Ithaca, NY, 2006—. Named Outstanding Performer in Training Mgmt., Training Dirs. Forum, 1993. Mem.: Nat. Assn. Edn. of Young Children, Nat. Career Devel. Assn., Am. Counseling Assn. Avocations: ballet, photography, hiking, swimming. Office: 3015 Main St Ste 320 Santa Monica CA 90405

GRAY, LUKE ALEXANDER, artist; b. NYC, Apr. 3, 1961; s. Cleve and Francine du Plessix Gray; m. Dorke Katharina Poelz; children: Jordan Jacob, Pico Sophia. BA in Fine Arts and Lit., U. Pa., Phila., 1982; student, RISD, Providence, 1978, Skowhegan Sch. Painting and Sculpture, Maine, 1979. One-man shows include Galerie Ludwig, Krefeld, Germany, 1996, Thomas Erben Gallery, NYC, 1996, Gary Snyder Fine Art, 1996, 1998, 2002, Addison-Ripley Fine Art, Washington, 1997, 2000, Hunter Gallery, William H. Drury and Richard Grosvenor Ctr. Arts, Newport, RI, 2001, Tremaine Gallery, Lakeville, Conn., 2004, numerous others, exhibited in group shows at Levantehaus, Hamburg, Germany, 2003, J. Johnson Gallery, Jacksonville Beach, Fla., 2004, Alva Gallery, New London, Conn., 2006. Personal E-mail: spacecollector@yahoo.com.

GRAY, LYONS, federal agency administrator; b. Winston-Salem, NC, Oct. 28, 1942; s. Bowman and Elizabeth Christian Gray; m. Constance Fraser, 1971; children: Charlotte, Fraser. Grad., U. NC, 1967. State rep. Dist. 5, NC, 1989—92, Dist. 39, NC, 1993—2002; pres. Salem Sys., Inc., Downtown Winsten-Salem Partnership; chmn. environ. fin. adv. bd. EPA, 2003—05, CFO, 2005—. Served on various coms. in NC gen. assembly including fin., tech., travel and tourism, and pensions and retirement coms.; vice chmn. State Parks and Properties com.; mem. select com. on tobacco settlement. Served with U.S. Coast Guard, 1964—70. Mem.: Rotary Club. Episcopalian. Office: EPA 1200 Pennsylvania Ave NW Washington DC 20460

GRAY, MARVIN LEE, JR., lawyer; b. Pitts., May 9, 1945; s. Marvin L. and Frances (Stringfellow) G.; m. Jill Miller, Aug. 14, 1971; children: Elizabeth Ann, Carolyn Jill. AB, Princeton U., 1966; JD magna cum laude, Harvard U., 1969. Bar: Wash. 1973, U.S. Supreme Ct. 1977, Alaska 1984. Law clk. to judge U.S. Ct. Appeals, NYC, 1969-70; law clk. to justice U.S. Supreme Ct., Washington, 1970-71; asst. U.S. atty. U.S. Dept. Justice, Seattle, 1973-76; ptnr. Davis Wright Tremaine, Seattle, 1976—, mng. ptnr., 1985-88. Staff counsel Rockefeller Commn. on CIA Activities in U.S., Washington, 1974; lectr. trial practice U. Wash. Law Sch., Seattle, 1979-80. Lay reader Episcopal Ch. of Ascension, Seattle, 1982-94. Capt. USAF, 1971-73. Fellow Am. Coll. Trial Lawyers; mem. ABA, Am. Law Inst. Office: Davis Wright Tremaine 1201 3rd Ave Ste 2200 Seattle WA 98101-3045 Business E-Mail: montygray@dwt.com.

GRAY, MARY JANE, retired obstetrician, gynecologist; b. Columbus, Ohio, June 13, 1924; BA, Swarthmore Coll., 1945; MD, Wash. U., 1949; DS, Columbia U., 1954. Diplomate Am. Bd. Ob-Gyn. Intern Barnes Hosp., St. Louis, 1949-50; resident in ob-gyn. Presbyn. Hosp., NYC, 1950-56; fellow Columbia U., 1953—54, instr., 1956-60; asst. prof. ob-gyn. Coll. Medicine U. Vermont, 1960-63, assoc. prof., 1963-69, prof., 1969-76; adj. prof. U. N.C., 1976-85, prof., asst. dean Coll. Medicine, 1985-90, prof. emeritus ob-gyn., 1990—; ret., 1996. Mem. AMA, Am. Coll. Ob-Gyn., Soc. Gynecol. Investigation.

GRAY, MARY WHEAT, statistician, lawyer; b. Hastings, Nebr., 1939; d. Neil C. and Lillie W. (Alves) Wheat; m. Alfred Gray, Aug. 20, 1964. AB summa cum laude, Hastings Coll., 1959; postgrad., J.W. Goethe U., Frankfurt, Fed. Republic Germany, 1959-60; MA, U. Kans., 1962, PhD, 1964; JD summa cum laude, Am. U., 1979; LLD (hon.), U. Nebr., 1993; LHD (hon.), Hastings Coll., 1996. Bar: D.C. 1979, U.S. Supreme Ct. 1983, U.S. Dist. Ct., D.C. 1980. Physicist Nat. Bur. Standards, Washington, summers 1959-63; asst. instr. U. Kans., Lawrence, 1963-64; instr. dept. math. U. Calif., Berkeley, 1965; asst. prof. Calif. State U., Hayward, 1965-67, assoc. prof., 1967-68; assoc. prof. dept. math., stats. and computer sci. Am. U., 1968-71, prof., 1971—, chmn. dept., 1977-79, 80-81, 83—; statis. cons. for govt. agys., univs. and pvt. firms, 1976—. Vis. prof. King's Coll., London, 2004. Author: A Radical Approach to Algebra, 1970; Calculus with Finite Mathematics for Social Sciences, 1972; contbr. numerous articles to profl. jours. Nat. treas., dir. Women's Equity Action League, from 1981, pres., from 1982; bd. dirs. treas. ACLU, Montgomery County, Md.; mem. adv. com. D.C. Dept. Employment Services, 1983—; dir. Amnesty Internat. USA, 1985—, treas., 1988-93, chair, 1993-95; mem. Commn. on Coll. Retirement, 1984-86; bd. dirs. Am.-Middle East Edn. Found., 1983—, chair, 1998--. Recipient U.S. Presdl. award for excellence in sci., engring. and math. mentoring, 2001; Fulbright grantee, 1959-60; NSF fellow, 1963-64, NDEA fellow, 1960-63 Fellow AAAS (chmn. com. on women, com. on investments, com. on sci. freedom and responsibility, Lifetime Mentoring award 1995), Am. Statis. Assn.; mem. AAUP (regional counsel 1984—, com. on acad. freedom 1978—, dir. Legal Def. Fund 1974-78, bd. dirs. Exxon Project on Salary Discrimination 1974-76, com. on status of women 1972-78, Georgina Smith award), Am. Math. Soc. (v.p. 1976-78, coun. 1973-78), Amnesty Internat. (internat. treas. 1995-2001, chair USA 1993-95), Conf. Bd. Math. Scis. (chmn. com. on affirmative action 1977-78), Math. Assn. Am. (chmn. com. on sch. lectrs. 1973-75, vis. lectr. 1974—), Assn. for Women in Math (founding pres. 1971-74, exec. com. 1974-80, gen. counsel 1980—), DC Bar Assn., ABA, Am. Soc. Internat. Law, London Math. Soc., Societe de Mathematique de France, Brit. Soc. History of Math., Can. Soc. History of Math., Assn. Computing Machinery, NY Acad. Scis., Phi Beta Kappa, Sigma Xi, Phi Kappa Phi, Alpha Chi, Pi Mu Epsilon. Home: 6807 Connecticut Ave Chevy Chase MD 20815-4937 Office: Am U Math & Stats Dept Washington DC 20016 Office Phone: 202-885-3171. Business E-Mail: mgray@american.edu.

GRAY, NANCY ANN OLIVER, academic administrator; b. Dallas, Apr. 23, 1951; d. Howard Ross and Joan (Dawkins) Oliver; m. David Nelson Maxson, Oct. 5, 1985; children by previous marriage: Paul, Jeff, Scott. BA, Vanderbilt U., 1973; MEd, North Tex. State U., 1975; postgrad., Vanderbilt U., 1976-79; PhD (hon.), Presbyterian Coll., 2002. Cert. fund raising exec. Tchr. Highland Park High Sch., Dallas, 1973-75; chmn. drama dept. Harpeth Hall Sch., Nashville, 1975-77; assoc. dir. devel. Vanderbilt U., Nashville, 1977-78, assist. dean students, 1978-80; dir. spl. gifts U. Louisville, 1982-86; dir. major gifts Oberlin Coll., Ohio, 1986-90; dir. capital programs The Lawrenceville Sch., NJ, 1990-91; v.p. devel. and univ. rels. Rider U., Lawrenceville, 1991-98; v.p. sem. rels. Princeton Theol. Sem., NJ, 1998-99; pres. Converse Coll., Spartanburg, SC, 1999—2004, Hollins U., Roanoke, Va., 2005—. Trustee Princeton Theol. Sem., 2000—, Spartanburg Day Sch., 2000-2002, Vanderbilt U., Nashville, 1973-77, Found. Ind. Higher Edn., 2006-; bd. dirs. Brevard Music Ctr., 1999—2005, Wye Faculty Seminar, 2000-04, Women's Coll. Coalition, 2006-; sec. Coun. Independent Colls. Va., 2007-. Home: Hollins U PO Box 9630 Roanoke VA 24020 Office: Hollins U PO Box 9625 Roanoke VA 24020 Office Phone: 540-362-6321. Business E-Mail: ngray@hollins.edu.

GRAY, OSCAR SHALOM, lawyer; b. NYC, Oct. 18, 1926; BA, Yale U., New Haven, 1948, JD, 1951. Bar: Md. 1951, D.C. 1952, U.S. Supreme Ct. 1952. Atty.-adviser legal adviser's office U.S. Dept. State, Washington, 1951-57; sec. Nuclear Materials and Equipment Corp., Apollo, Pa., 1957-64, treas., 1957-67, v.p., 1964-71, dir., 1964-67; spl. counsel Presdl. Task Force on Communications Policy, Washington, 1967-68; cons. U.S. Dept. Transp., Washington, 1967-68, acting dir. office environ. impact, 1968-70; sole practice Washington, 1970—, Balt., 1971—. Adj. prof., professorial lectr. Law Ctr. Georgetown U., Washington, 1970-71; lectr. Cath. U. Am., Washington, 1970-71; assoc. prof. U. Md., Balt., 1971-74, prof., 1974-93, Jacob A. France prof. of torts, 1993-96, prof. emeritus, 1996—; vis. prof. U. Tenn., 1977. Author: Cases and Materials on Environmental Law, 1970, 2d edit., 1973, supplements, 1974, 1975, 1977; author: (with F. Harper and F. James Jr.) The Law of Torts, 2d edit., 1986; author: Harper, James and Gray on Torts, 3d edit., Vols. 1-2, 2006, Harper, James and Gray on Torts, 3d edit., Vols. 3-4, 2007; author: (with H. Shulman and F. James Jr.) Cases and Materials on the Law of Torts, 1976; author: (with D. Gifford) Cases and Materials on the Law of Torts, 4th edit., 2003; contbr. articles to profl. legal jours. Mem.: ABA, D.C. Fedn. of Civic Assns. (parliamentarian 1991—99, 2000—04), D.C. Bar, Am. Law Inst. (adviser Restatement of the Law, Third, Torts: Products Liability), Selden Soc. (state correspondent Md.), Phi Beta Kappa, Order of Coif. Office: 500 W Baltimore St Baltimore MD 21201-1602 Office Phone: 410-706-7174. Business E-Mail: ogray@law.umaryland.edu.

GRAY, PAUL EDWARD, academic administrator; b. Newark, Feb. 7, 1932; s. Kenneth Frank and Florence (Gilleo) G.; m. Priscilla Wilson King, June 18, 1955; children: Virginia Wilson, Amy Brewer, Andrew King, Louise Meyer. SB, MIT, 1954, SM, 1955, DSc, 1960. Mem. faculty MIT, 1960-71, 90—, Class of 1922 prof. elec. engring., 1968-71, dean Sch. Engring., 1970-71, chancellor, 1971-80, pres., 1980-90; mem. MIT Corp., 1971—, chmn., 1990-97. Trustee Wheaton Coll., Norton, Mass., 1971-97, trustee emeritus 1997—2005, chmn. bd. trustees, 1976-87, life trustee, 2005—. 1st lt. AUS, 1955-57. Fellow IEEE (life, publs. bd. 1969-70), Am. Acad. Arts and Scis.; mem. NAE (treas. 1994-01), AAAS, Mex. Nat. Acad. Engring. (corr.), Sigma Xi, Eta Kappa Nu, Tau Beta Pi, Phi Sigma Kappa. Mem. United Ch. Christ Office: MIT Dept Elec Engring Rm 38-344 77 Massachusetts Ave Cambridge MA 02139-4307 Office Phone: 617-253-4665. Business E-Mail: pogo@mit.edu.

GRAY, PAULETTE STYLES, federal agency administrator, biologist; b. Chattanooga, Feb. 21, 1944; d. Paul Styles and Louise (Hill) Dennis; m. Walter Leonard, May 10, 1964; children: Walter Leonard Jr., Daniel Allen. BS in biology, Tuskegee Inst., 1966; MS in mycology, Atlanta U., 1976, PhD in cellular and devel. biology, 1978. Asst. prof., dir. electron microscopy lab. Atlanta U., 1978-79; research assoc. U. Kaiserslautern, Germany, 1979-81; instr. U. Maryland, Kaiserslautern, 1980-82; supr. clin. microbiology sect. Landstuhl Army Regional Med. Ctr., Germany, 1981-82; exec. sec. Divsn. Extramural Activities, Nat. Cancer Inst., Bethesda, Md., 1983-84, spl. review officer, 1984, chief rev. logistics br., 1988, assoc. dir. extramural applications, dep. dir., 1997—2005, acting dir., 2003—05, dir., 2005—. Tchr. Sun. Sch. Alfred St. Bapt. Ch., Alexandria, Va., 1982-89, supt., 1988-89; judge sci. and engring. fair Fairfax County pub. schs., 1984-89; speaker Med. Coll. Ga., Augusta, 1985. Recipient Lederle Labs. award, 1977, H.E. Finley Meml. award Atlanta U., 1978, Outstanding Performance award Nat. Cancer Inst., 1983; Josiah Macy Jr. fellow, 1979, Hon. Fulbright Hays fellow, 1979-81, Spl. Act. of Achievement award, 1992, 93, EEO Spl. Recognition award, 1991, NIH Dir.'s award, 1990, Cert. Recognition and Spl. Achievement award, HHS, 1988-93. Mem. Am. Soc. Zoology, Nat. Inst. Sci., Atlanta U. Ctr. Honor Soc. (biology), Am. Assn. Cancer Rsch., Inc., Am. Assn. Cell Biology, Internat. Platform Assn., Women in Cancer Rsch., Assn. Women in Govt., Nat. Assn. Exec. Women. Avocations: cooking, reading, jogging, writing. Office: Nat Cancer Inst Divsn Extramural Activities 6116 Executive Blvd Rockville MD 20852 Office Phone: 301-496-5147. E-mail: pg36f@nih.gov.

GRAY, PHIL R., band director, musician; b. Clearwater, Fla., Sept. 5, 1965; s. Howard and Janet Gray; m. Christine Gray, Aug. 3, 1995; 1 child, Nicholas. AA in Performance, Hillsborough C.C., 1991; BA in Music Edn., Five Towns Coll., 1994; MA in Composition and Music Performance, C.W. Post Coll., 1996. Freelance musician, Tampa, Fla., 1990—94; band dir., brass instr. Seaford (N.Y.) H.S., 1994—97, Island Lakes Unified Sch. Dist., Levittown, NY, 1997—2000, Cold Spring Harbor (N.Y.) Cen. Sch. Dist., 2000—. Brass adjudicator NYSSMA, NYC, 1995—. Editor: (book) Daily Chap Maintenanace, 2004. With USAF, 1985—89. Mem.: Nassau Music Educators Assn. (v.p. 1999—2002), Internat. Trumpet Guild, Internat. Assn. Jazz Edn. Avocations: golf, fishing. Home and Office: 47 Harvard St Garden City NY 11530-4003 Home Phone: 516-398-1823; Office Phone: 516-398-1823. Personal E-mail: pgjazz65@optonline.net.

GRAY, PHILIP HOWARD, former psychologist, writer, educator; b. Cape Rosier, Maine, July 4, 1926; s. Asa and Bernice (Lawrence) G.; m. Iris McKinney, Dec. 31, 1954; children: Cindelyn Gray Eberts, Howard. MA, U. Chgo., 1958; PhD, U. Wash., 1960. Asst. prof. dept. psychology Mont. State U., Bozeman, 1960—65, assoc. prof., 1965—75, prof., 1975—92; ret., 1992. Vis. prof. U. Man., Winnipeg, Can., 1968-70, U. N.H., 1965, U. Mont., 1967, 74, Tufts U., 1968, U. Conn., 1971; pres. Mont. Psychol. Assn., 1968-70 (helped write Mont. licensing law for psychologists); chmn. Mont. Bd. Psychologist Examiners, 1972-74; spkr. sci. and geneal. meetings on ancestry of U.S. presidents; presenter, instr. grad. course on serial killers and the psychopathology of murder; founder Badger Press of Mont., 1998. Organizer folk art exhbns. Mont. and Maine, 1972-79; author: The Comparative Analysis of Behavior, 1966, (with F.L. Ruch and N. Warren) Working with Psychology, 1963, A Directory of Eskimo Artists in Sculpture and Prints, 1974, The Science That Lost Its Mind, 1985, Penobscot Pioneers vol. 1, 1992, vol. 2, 1992, vol. 3, 1993, vol. 4, 1994, vol. 5, 1995, vol. 6, 1996, Mean Streets and Dark Deeds: The He-Man's Guide to Mysteries, 1998, Ghoulies and Ghosties and Long-leggety Beasties: Imprinting Theory Linking Serial Killers, Child Assassins, Molesters, Homosexuality, Feminism and Day Care, 1998, Egoteria of a Psychologist: Poetry, Letters, Memos from Nether Montana, 2001, Classic Inuit Artists: A Critique and Directory of 500 Eminent Artists in Sculpture and Prints, 2006; contbr. numerous articles on behavior to psychol. jours.; contbr. poetry to lit. jours. With US Army, 1944—46. Decorated EAME medal Ctrl. Europe and Rhineland Campaigns, Victory medal WWII, Presdl. Unit citation; recipient numerous rsch. grants. Fellow: APA, AAAS, Internat. Soc. Rsch. on Aggression, Am. Psychol. Soc.; mem.: SAR (trustee 1989, v.p. Sourdough chpt. 1990, pres. 1991—2006, v.p. gen. intermountain dist. 1997—98, pres. state soc. 1998—99, trustee 2001—, v.p. gen. intermountain dist. 2003—04), NRA (life), Order of the Crown of Charlemagne, Gallatin County Geneal. Soc. (charter, pres. 1991—93), Nat. Geneal. Soc., 78th Divsn. Vets. Assn. (life), Vets. of the Battle of the Bulge WWII (life), New Eng. Hist. Geneal. Soc.,

Deer Isle-Stonington Hist. Soc., Flagon and Trencher, Order Descs. Colonial Physicians and Chirugiens, Internat. Soc. Human Ethology, Descs. Illegitimate Sons and Daus. of Kings of Britain, Bozeman Rifle and Pistol Club. Republican. Avocations: collecting folk art, first and signed editions of novels, pistol shooting. Home: 1207 S Black Ave Bozeman MT 59715-5633 E-mail: phgray@mac.com. *We are human to the extent that we have bondings and the more bondings we have the more human we are. These attachments include familial bonding (imprinting), friendship bonding, marital bonding, ethnic-religious bonding, possession and goal bondings, and bonding to the land and ocean. My life's work is the study of these bondings and I am thereby more firmly connected to the human race.*

GRAY, PHILLIP LEE, religious studies educator, pastor; b. Geneva, Pa., Nov. 30, 1953; s. Miles Eward and Ruth Beverly Gray; m. Carolyn Sue Urey, June 1, 1974; children: Phillip Lee II, Mathew Lewis, Carole Lynn. B of Theology, Clarksville Sch. Theology, Tenn., 1980, M of Theology, 1986; D of Ministry with highest honors, Am. Christian Coll. and Seminary, Oklahoma City, 2003. Dir. adminstrv. svcs. Hobe Sound Bible Coll., Fla., 1994—2005; pres., dir. Christian Crisis Counseling Svc., Ft. Lauderdale, Fla., 2003—; sr. pastor First Wesleyan Ch., Ft. Lauderdale, 2000—. Adj. prof. Wesleyan Bible Coll., Georgetown, Guyana, 2003—; cons. Caribbean Wesleyan Bible Coll., Savannah Lamar, Jamaica, 2003—. Author: (books) Emergency Preparedness For Schools and Colleges, 2005. Coord. gifts and supplies, fin. assistance vol. Wesleyan Bible Coll., Georgetown, Guyana, 2003—. Mem.: Internat. Critical Incident Stress Found., Am. Assn. Christian Counselors, Am. Assn. Pastoral Counselors. Avocations: reading, travel, fishing. Office: First Wesleyan Ch 1545 N Andrews Ave Fort Lauderdale FL 33311

GRAY, RICHARD ALEXANDER, JR., retired chemical company executive; b. Pitts., Apr. 28, 1927; s. Richard Alexander and Margaret Katheryn Gray; m. Lucia I. Long, Sept. 8, 1956; children: Richard Alexander III, James W. Midshipman, U.S. Mcht. Marine Acad., 1945-47; BA, Princeton U., 1950; LL.B., Harvard U., 1954; postgrad., Univ. Coll., Southampton, Eng., 1949. Bar: Pa. bar 1955, U.S. Supreme Ct. bar 1975. Asso. firm Reed Smith Shaw & McClay, Pitts., 1954-62; with Air Products and Chems., Inc., Allentown, Pa., 1962-90, asst. gen. counsel, 1976-78, corp. sec., 1978-90, assoc. gen. counsel, 1980-84, v.p., 1984-90. Trustee Kutztown (Pa.) U., 1988-96, chmn., 1995-96; mem. bd. regents Mercersburg (Pa.) Acad., 1971-80. Trustee First Presbyn. Ch. of Allentown. Served to lt. (j.g.) USNR, 1950-51. Mem. ABA, Am. Soc. Corp. Secs. (bd. dirs. 1985-89), Lehigh Country Club (bd. govs. 1993-96). Personal E-mail: ragjr28hh@aol.com.

GRAY, RICHARD ARDEN, retired transportation executive; b. Ft. Bragg, Calif., Oct. 29, 1935; s. Arden Howard and Marion Florence (Coolidge) G.; m. Roberta Jeanne Montna, Feb. 5, 1955; children: Mark Alan, Laura Ann, Deborah Marie, Lisa Lynn. AA, Yuba Coll., 1955; BA, Calif. State U., 1957. Cert. coll. instr., Calif. Dep. sheriff Yuba County Sheriffs Dept., Marysville, Calif., 1957; traffic officer Calif. Hwy. Patrol, Ventura, 1958—60, Yuba City, 1961—68, sgt. field ops. officer Gardena, 1969—71, lt. exec. officer Van Nuys, 1972—76, lt. area comdr. Chico, 1977—88; wholesale, retail distbr. Dick Gray Enterprises, Chico, 1989—94, 1995—2000, 2006—; home-based bus. entrepreneur, 2006—; rschr. alternative cancer treatments, 2000—; property developer, 2000—05. Instr. Yuba Coll., Marysville, 1965-67, Calif. fish and game hunter safety program, Chico, 1982-86; profl. driver, transporter motor homes, 1989-2000, 04-06. Chmn. citizen rev. com. United Way of Butte County, Chico, 1984 (outstanding achievement 1984-86), fundraising campaign chmn. 1986, pres. bd. dirs. 1985; pres., bd. dirs. No. Calif. Counties Exch. Club Child Abuse Prevention Ctr., Chico, 1987-91; mem. Ronald Reagan Presdl. Found., 2001—, Nat. Law Enforcement Mus., 2002—. With USNR, 1953-61. Recipient Individual Excellence Outstanding Cmty. Svc. award United Way Butte and Glenn Counties, 1994-95. Mem. Calif. Hwy. Patrolmen Assn., Mt. Vernon Ladies Assn., US Golf Assn., Oxford Club (dirs. cir. 1998—), Heritage Found. Leader's Club, RV Club, Elks (honors 1988, pres. 1988-89), Breakfast Exch. Club (pres., bd. dirs. 1980-81), Exch. Club Greater Chico (sponsor 1983). Republican. Avocations: traveling in recreational vehicle, tennis, golf. Home Phone: 530-342-9185.

GRAY, RICHARD MOSS, retired college president; b. Washington, Jan. 25, 1924; s. Wilbur Leslie and Betty Marie (Grey) G.; m. Catherine Claire Hammond, Oct. 17, 1943; children: Janice Lynn Gray Armstrong, Nancy Hammond Gray Schultz. BA, Bucknell U., 1942; MDiv summa cum laude, San Francisco Theol. Sem., 1961; PhD, U. Calif., Berkeley, 1972; doctorate degree (hon.), World Coll. West, 1988. Writer, creative dir. N.W. Ayer & Son, Phila., 1942-58; univ. pastor Portland State U., Oreg., 1961-68; founder, pres. World Coll. West, Petaluma, Calif., 1973-88, pres. emeritus, 1988—. Bd. dirs. World Centre, San Francisco, Life Plan Ctr.; founder Presidio World Coll., 1992—. Author poetry Advent, 1989. Bd. dirs. Citizens Found. Marin, San Rafael, Calif., 1988—, Marin Ednl. Found.; ruling elder Presbyn. Ch. U.S.A. Named Disting. Alumnus of Yr. San Francisco Theol. Sem., 1988, Marin Citizen of Yr. Citizens Found., 1988; recipient Svc. to Humanity award Bucknell U., 1992. Mem. Phi Beta Kappa. Avocations: song-writing, poetry.

GRAY, ROBERT F., JR., lawyer; BBA, U. Mich., 1972, MBA, 1974; JD, U. San Diego, 1977; LLM, NYU, 1978. Bar: Calif. 1977, Tex. 1978, DC 1979. With Fulbright & Jaworski LLP, Houston, 1978—2005; ptnr. and head global energy practice group Mayer, Brown, Rowe & Maw LLP, Houston, 2005—. Bd. dir. Jr. Achievement of Houston/Gulf Coast, 1996—2001; adv. bd. dir. Houston Tech. Ctr., 2000—; bd. dir. Houston Entrepreneur's Found., 2000—; bd. mgrs. Cougar Investment Fund, 2001—; dean's adv. bd. Univ. Houston C.T. Bauer Coll. Bus., 2002—. Named a Tex. Super Lawyer, Tex. Monthly Mag., 2003. Fellow: Tex. Bus. Law Found.; mem.: ABA (Tex. State Liaison, com. on corp. laws 1990—98), State Bar Tex. (chmn. bus. law sect. 1995—96), State Bar of Calif., Houston Bar Assn., DC Bar. Office: Mayer Brown Rowe and Maw LLP 700 Louisiana Ste 3600 Houston TX 77002 Office Phone: 713-238-2600. Business E-Mail: rgray@mayerbrown.com.

GRAY, ROBERT MOLTEN, electrical engineering educator; b. San Diego, Nov. 1, 1943; s. Augustine Heard and Elizabeth DuBois (Jordan) G.; m. Arlene Frances Ericson; children: Timothy M., Lori A. BSEE, MSEE, MIT, 1966; PhD in Elec. Engring., U. So. Calif., LA, 1969. Elec. engr. US Naval Ordnance Lab., White Oak, Md., 1963-65, Jet Propulsion Lab., Pasadena, Calif., summers 1966, 67; lectr. U. So. Calif., 1969; asst. prof. elec. engring. Stanford U., 1969-75, assoc. prof., 1975-80, prof., 1980—, dir. Info. Systems Lab., 1984-87, vice chair dept. elec. engring., 1993—2005, Lucent Technologies prof. engring., 2004—. Author: Probability, Random Processes and Ergodic Properties, 1988, Source Coding Theory, 1990, Entropy and Information Theory, 1990; co-author: Random Processes, 1986, Vector Quantization and Signal Compression, 1992, Fourier Transforms, 1995; contbr. articles to profl. jours., chtps. to books. Fireman La Honda Vol. Fire Brigade, Calif., 1970-80, pres., 1971-72; coach Am. Youth Soccer Orgn., La Honda, 1971-78, commr., 1976-78. Japan Soc. for Promotion Sci. fellow, 1981, Guggenheim fellow, 1982, NATO/CNR fellow, 1990. Fellow IEEE (Centennial medal 1984, 3rd Millennium medal 2000), Inst. Math. Stats.; mem. Info. Theory Soc. IEEE (assoc. editor Trans. 1977-80, editor-in-chief 1980-83, paper prize 1976, Golden Jubilee award for technol. achievement 1998), Signal Processing Soc. IEEE (Sr. award 1983, Soc. award 1993, prog. co-chmn. 1997 Internat. Conf. on Image Processing, Tech. Achievement award 1998, Presdl. Mentoring award 2002, Disting. Alumni award U. SC 2003, Meritorious Svc. award 2006), NAE. Avocations: maritime and gilded age history, hiking, computers. Office: Stanford U Dept Elec Engring 161 Packard Bldg 350 Serra Mall Stanford CA 94305-9505 Office Phone: 650-723-4001. Office Fax: 650-723-8473. E-mail: rmgray@stanford.edu.*

GRAY, ROBERT STEELE, publishing executive, editor, writer; b. Beaumont, Tex., Oct. 6, 1923; s. Fred and Ruth Louise (Lewelling) G.; m. Nellie Frances McGuinness, July 3, 1945; children: Robert Steele, Laura, Ruth Ellen (Mrs. Sommy L. Ham). BS, U. Houston, 1954. Newscaster Sta. KPRC-AM, Houston, 1947; news dir. Sta. KNUZ, Houston, 1948-49; reporter Citizens Papers, Houston, 1950; newsfilm dir. Sta. KPRC-TV, 1951-56; writer Houston Post, 1956-60; founder, pub. editor Cordovan Corp., Houston, 1960—, chmn. bd., 1982—; pub. Cordovan Bus. Jours., Houston, 1971; co-founder Golfer Mags., Inc., 1984—. Author: Survivor, 1998. 2nd lt. USMCR, 1942-46, to 1st lt. 1951-52, Korea. Mem.: Soc. Profl. Journalists. Home and Office: 5815 Pebble Springs Dr Houston TX 77066-2310

GRAY, ROBERT WARD, art association administrator; b. Tallahassee, Fla., June 26, 1916; s. Joseph Henry and Welia (Ward) Gray; m. Lenorma Verdelle Connell, Dec. 15, 1943. Studies in civil engring., U. Fla., Tri-State Coll., Sch. for Am. Craftsmen, 1949. Project engr. Fla. State Highway Dept., Fla., 1946—47; mgr. Pottery Shop, Old Sturbridge Village, 1949—51; coord. of craft program Old Sturbridge Village, 1951; dir. Worcester Craft Ctr., 1951—61; exec. dir. Southern Highland Craft Guild, Asheville, NC, 1961—80, dir. emeritus, 1980, dir. devel., 1980—83. Charter mem. bus. cabinet Ga. State Coll., Milledgeville, Ga., 1974—77; fellow Am. Craft Coun., NYC, 1980. Pres. Asheville Tourism Assn., Asheville, NC, 1975—76; adv. coun. Haywood C.C., Clyde, NC, 1975; honoarary lifetime mem. Asheville Tourism Assn., Asheville, NC, 1985. Tech. sgt. USMC, 1942—46. Recipient Dist. Svc. award, Asheville Tourism Assn., 1985, Lifetime Achieve. award, Southern Highland Craft Guild, 1980, Fine Art's award, Gov. of NC, 1998.

GRAY, SHAWN SCOTT, social services administrator; s. Lester Gerald and Anna Jane Gray. A, Vernon Coll., Tex., 1989; B, Midwestern State U., Wichita Falls, Tex., 2003. Commd. 2d lt. USAF, 1982, advanced through grades to sgt., ret., 2002—; disabled vets. outreach specialist Tex. Vets. Commn., Corpus Christi, 2005—. Mem. Vets. Summit Com., Corpus Christi, 2006—. Mem.: Disabled Am. Vets., VFW. Democrat. Methodist. Avocations: golf, baseball, camping.

GRAY, SHEILA HAFTER, psychiatrist, researcher; b. NYC, Oct. 19, 1930; MD, Harvard U., 1958. cert. Washington Psychoanalytic Inst., 1969. Intern St. Elizabeths Hosp., Washington, 1958-59; resident McLean Hosp., Belmont, Mass., 1959-61; clin. and rsch. fellow Mass. Gen. Hosp., Boston, 1961-62; staff psychiatrist Chestnut Lodge, Inc., Rockville, Md., 1962-64; practice medicine, specializing in psychiatry and psychoanalysis Washington, 1964—; clin. asst. prof. psychiatry U. Md. Sch. Medicine, Balt., 1968-75, clin. assoc. prof., 1975-83, clin. prof., 1983-96; instr. Washington Psychoanalytic Inst., 1971-75, tchg. analyst, 1975-96, Balt.-Washington Inst. for Psychoanalysis, 1996—; clin. prof. psychiatry Uniformed Svcs. U. Health Scis., 1997-99, adj. prof. psychiatry, 1999—. Staff U. Md. Hosp., Balt., 1970-96; physician mem. Commn. on Mental Health, Superior Ct. of D.C., 1972-98; bd. govs. Nat. Capital Reciprocal Ins. Co., 1981-98; treas. NCRIC Physicians Orgn., 1994-97; cons. Walter Reed Army Med. Ctr., Washington, 1983—. Active Mayor's Adv. Com. on Mental Health Svcs. Reorgn., Washington, 1984; adv. panel Mayor's Environ. Design Awards Program, 1988-89; exec. com. D.C. Fedn. Civic Assns., 1984—, asst. rec. sec., 1985, rec. sec., 1986-88, 2d v.p., 1989-90, pres., 1991-92, del.-at-large, 1993—; v.p. programs Women's Equity Action League Met. D.C., 1986; commr. D.C. Adv. Neighborhood Commn., 1986-88; mem. Met. Washington Coun. of Govt.'s Partnership for Regional Excellence, 1992; trustee Accreditation Coun. for Psychoanalytic Edn., Inc., 2002—, sec., 2004—. Fellow: Am. Psychiat. Assn. (chair com. quality assurance and improvement, Coun. on Econ. Affairs, 1996—97, disting. life fellow); mem.: Washington Psychoanalytic Soc. (chmn. bd. dirs. psychoanalytic clinic and councillor ex officio 1987—90), Med. Soc. D.C. (exec. bd. 1982, ho. dels. 1992—97), Washington Psychiatric Soc. (councillor 1981—83), Am. Acad. Psychoanalysis (trustee 1996—99, pres.-elect 1999—2000, pres. 2000—01, editl. bd. jour. 2002—), Am. Psychoanalytic Assn. (parliamentarian 2006—, diplomate Bd. Profl. Stds.), Palisades Citizens Assn. (bd. dirs. 1980—, treas. 1983—84, pres. 1984—86). Office: PO Box 40612 Palisades Sta Washington DC 20016 Office Phone: 202-338-1955.

GRAY, SIMON JAMES HOLLIDAY, writer, educator; b. Oct. 21, 1936; s. James Davidson Gray and Barbara Cecelia Mary (Holliday) Davidson; m. Beryl Mary Kevern, 1965 (div. 1997); 2 children; m. Victoria Rothschild, 1997. Student, Westminster Sch., Dalhousie U., Halifax, N.S.; MA, U. Cambridge. Supr. English U. B.C., 1960-63. Sr. instr., 1963-64; lectr. Queen Mary Coll., U. London, 1965-84. Author: (novels) Colmain, 1963, Simple People, 1965, Little Portia, 1967, A Comeback for Stark, 1968, Breaking Hearts, 1997, (non-fiction) An Unnatural Pursuit and Other Pieces, 1985, How's That For Telling 'Em Fat Lady, 1988, Fat Chance, 1995, Enter a Fox, 2001, The Smoking Diaries, 2005, The Year of the Jouncer, 2006, (plays) Wise Child, 1968, Sleeping Dog, 1968, Dutch Uncle, 1969, The Idiot, 1971, Spoiled, 1971, Butley, 1971 (Evening Std. award), Otherwise Engaged, 1975 (Best Play, N.Y. Drama Critics Cir., Evening Std. award), Plaintiffs and Defendants, 1975, Two Sundays, 1975, Dog Days, 1976, Molly, 1977, The Rear Column, 1978, Close of Play, 1979, Quartermaine's Terms, 1981, Tartuffe, 1982, Chapter 17, 1982, The Common Pursuit, 1984, Plays One, 1986, Melon, 1987, Hidden Laughter, 1991, The Holy Terror, 1992, Cell Mates, 1995, Simply Disconnected, 1996, Life Support, 1997, Just the Three of Us, 1997, The Late Middle Classes, 1999, Japes, 2000, Old Masters, 2004, Little Nell, 2007, (TV movies) After Pilkington, 1987, Quartermaine's Terms, 1987, Old Flames, 1990, They Never Slept, 1991, The Common Pursuit, 1992, Running Late, 1992, Unnatural Pursuits, 1993, Femme Fatale, 1993, (film) A Month in the Country, (radio plays) The Holy Terror (rev.), 1989, The Rector's Daughter, 1992, With a Nod and a Bow, 1993, Suffer the Little Children, 1993, Little Nell, 2006. Mem. Dramatists Guild. Mailing: c/o Angela Rose/Granta Agy 2/3 Hanover Yard Noel Rd London N1 8BE England

GRAY, STACEY M., lawyer; BA, Duke U., 1995; JD, U. Calif., Berkeley, 1998. Prin., founder Stacey M. Gray, P.C., NYC, 1999—. Regular legal expert Ct. TV. Leaderships gifts co-chair alumni affairs Duke U., 2004—05. Mem.: Fed. Bar Coun., Duke U. Alumni Assn. (bd. dirs. 2005—). Office: 55 Broad St Ste 2901 New York NY 10004

GRAY, THOMAS ALVA, JR., writer, minister, retired protective services official; b. Ridgeway, Mo., Mar. 2, 1935; s. Thomas Alva and Claudia Ladine (Brown) Gray; m. Barbara Elisabeth Locke (Haug), Jan. 18, 1974; children: Paul David, Daniel Lawrence, Douglas Eric 1 stepchild, Derek Brundage Locke. BA in Sociology, Northwestern U., Evanston, Ill., 1961; MDiv magn cum laude, Nazarene Theol. Sem., Kansas City, 2003. Lic. min. Ch. of Nazarene, 2002. Pres. Gray Furniture, Inc., Smithville, Mo., 1961—65; spl. agt. FBI, 1966—86; pvt. investigator Clarence M. Kelley & Assocs., Kansas City, 1987—89; tchg. asst. Nazarene Theol. Sem., Kansas City, 2000—01; pastor Freeman Christian Ch., Mo., 2002; writer Leawood, Kans. Columnist (Little Known Facts About Authors): Potpourri Lit. Mag., 1991—96; editor: Red Herring Mystery Mag., 1996, The Seedling, 1996—99; author: (short stories) Handprint in the Woods, 1997, Mobius, The Journal of Social Change, 1996; author, editor: A Journey of Faith, 2005. Vol. assoc. chaplain Kingswood Manor Retirement Ctr., Kansas City; vol. tutor Vanderberg Youth Ctr., City Union Mission, Kansas City; vol. Leawood (Kans.) Pioneer Libr., 2006; exec. v.p. adminstn. bd. Nazarene Theol. Sem. Student Assn., Kansas City, 2000—01; sec. World Mission Fellowship coun. Nazarene Theol. Sem., Kansas City, 2001—02, treas. Women in Ministry coun., 2002—03; founding mem., bd. dirs. Arts and Humanities Assn. Johnson County, Overland Park, Kans.; bd. dirs. Friends of Powell Gardens, Inc., Kingswood, Mo. With US Army, 1958—61. Mem.: Phi Eta Sigma. Baptist. Avocations: reading, travel, volunteer work, golf. Home: 2007 Condolea Dr Leawood KS 66209 Office Phone: 913-663-1045.

GRAY, THOMAS KNOX, film producer; b. NYC, July 01; BA, U. Ariz.; postgrad., Thunderbird Sch. Mgmt., Phoenix. Mgmt. trainee United Artists, Spain, 1970, mng. dir. Chile, New Zealand, Colombia and Africa, 1971-74; sr. v.p. prodn. Golden Harvest Films, Beverly Hills, Calif., 1984—; exec. asst. to co-chmn. Cinema Internat. Corp., London, 1974-76; mng. dir. Cinema Internat. Corp./Warner, South Africa, 1976-77; v.p. Far East, Latin Am., Africa, Australia United Artists, 1977-80; v.p. fgn. sales Golden Communications Overseas Ltd., London, 1980-84; pres., CEO RIM Film Distbn. Inc., Beverly Hills, 1992—. Exec. in charge of prodn. feature films: Flying, 1984, Protector, 1985, China O'Brien I, 1986, China O'Brien II, 1986, Best of Martial Arts, 1988, Show of Force, 1990, Teenage Mutant Ninja Turtles, 1990; prodr. Teenage Mutant Ninja Turtles II: The Secret of the Ooze, 1991, Teenage Mutant Ninja Turtles III, 1993, TMNT, 2007. Office: # 191 9899 Santa Monica Blvd Beverly Hills CA 90212-1672*

GRAY, THOMAS STEPHEN, writer; b. Burbank, Calif., Aug. 22, 1950; s. Thomas Edgar and Lily Irene (Ax) G.; m. Barbara Ellen Bronson, Aug. 27, 1977; children: Jonathan Thomas, Katherine Marie. BA, Stanford U., 1972; MA in English, UCLA, 1976. Tchg. assoc. UCLA, 1976-77; reporter LA Daily News, 1977-79, editl. writer, 1979-84, editl. page editor, 1984-95; sr. editor Investor's Bus. Daily, LA, 1995-98; v.p. and account group mgr. Investor Rels. Internat., 2003—. Author: Teach Yourself Investing Online, 1999, Investing Online for Dummies-Quick Reference, 2000, Online Investing Bible, 2001; contbg. writer: Convergence: Mag. of Sci. and Engring., UC Santa Barbara. Recipient 1st Place award Editl. Writing Greater LA Press Club, 1988, Inland Daily Press Assn., 1993. Office Phone: 818-889-4799. E-mail: tsgray@sbcglobal.net.

GRAY, VIRGINIA HICKMAN, political science professor; b. Camden, Ark., June 10, 1945; d. George Leonard and Ethel Massengale (Bell) Hickman; 1 child, Brian Charles. BA with honors, Hendrix Coll., 1967; MA, Washington U., St. Louis, 1969, PhD, 1972. Asst. prof. polit. sci. U. Ky., Lexington, 1971-73; from asst. prof. to assoc. prof. U. Minn., Mpls., 1973-83, prof., 1983-2000, chairperson dept. polit. sci., 1985-88; Winston Disting. prof. polit. sci. U. N.C., Chapel Hill, 2001—. Guest scholar Brookings Inst., Washington, 1977-78; vis. prof. U. Oslo, 1985, Nankai U., 1988, U. B.C., 1992, U. N.C., 1993-94; NSF vis. prof. for women, 1993-94. Co-author: The Organizational Politics of Criminal Justice, 1980, Feminism and the New Right, 1983, Politics in the American States, 1983, 8th edit., 2004, American States and Cities, 1991, 2d edit., 1997, The Population Ecology of Interest Representation, 1996, Minnesota Politics and Government, 1999. Bd. dirs. Health Ptnrs. Inc., 1992-2001, chair, 1999-2001. Fellow Woodrow Wilson Found., 1970, NDEA, 1969-70; grantee Swedish Bicentennial Found., 1985; recipient rsch. assistantship NSF, 1968-69, rsch. grant NSF, 1997-2001; scholar in residence Rockefeller Ctr., Bellagio, Italy; Investigator award Robert Wood Johnson Found., 2003-06; named Disting. Alumnus Hendrix Coll., 2005. Mem. Am. Polit. Sci. Assn. (coun. 1990-92), Midwest Polit. Sci. Assn. (coun. 1984-86, v.p. 1997-99, pres. 2003-2004), Policy Studies Orgn. (coun. 1977-79), So. Polit. Sci. Assn., Western Polit. Sci. Assn. Democrat. Office: U NC Dept Polit Sci CB 3265 Hamilton Hall Chapel Hill NC 27599-3265 Office Phone: 919-843-5602. E-mail: vagray@email.unc.edu.

GRAY, WALTER P., III, historian, archivist, consultant; b. San Francisco, Aug. 8, 1952; s. Walter Patton II and Elsie Josephine (Stroop) G.; m. Mary Amanda Helmich, May 23, 1980. BA in History, Calif. State U., Sacramento, 1976. Rschr. Calif. State R.R. Mus., Sacramento, 1977-80, curator, 1980-81, 85-90, archivist, 1981-85, mus. dir., 1990-98; Calif. state archivist, 1998—2004; state hist. records coord., 1999—2004; chief archeology, history and museums divsn. Calif. State Parks, 2004—. Trustee Golden State Mus., 2003-04; cons. in field, 1976—. Contbr. articles to profl. jours. Buddhist. Avocations: woodworking, antique automobiles, photography. Office: California State Parks 1416 9th St Ste 905 Sacramento CA 95814 Home Phone: 916-455-6864; Office Phone: 916-653-9946. E-mail: wgray@parks.ca.gov.

GRAY, WHITMORE, lawyer, educator; b. 1932; AB, Principia Coll., 1954; JD, U. Mich., 1957; postgrad., U. Paris, 1957—58, U. Munich, 1962; LLD, Adrian Coll., 1982. Bar: Mich. 1958. Assoc. Casey, Lane & Mittendorf, NYC, 1958—60; asst. prof. U. Mich., 1960—63, assoc. prof., 1963—66, prof., 1966—93; assoc. Cleary, Gottlieb, NYC, 1981; of counsel LeBoeuf, Lamb, Greene & MacRae, NYC, 1994—2001. Mem. adv. bd. Bull. on Rsch. in Soviet Law and Govt. and Soviet Statutes and Decisions; lectr. contract law Chinese Acad. Social Scis., 1982; summer faculty Jilin U., China, 1985; vis. prof. Fordham Law Sch., NY, 1989—; advisor on contract and arbitration law, Thailand, 1993, Cambodia, 94, Indonesia, 1995—96. Contbr. articles on comml. arbitration and alternative dispute resolution to profl. jours.; translator: Russian Republic Civil Code, General Principles of Civil Law of People's Republic of China; past editor-in-chief: Mich. Law Rev. Japan Found. fellow, U. Tokyo, 1977—78. Mem.: Japanese-Am. Soc. Legal Studies (bd. dirs.), Internat. Acad. Comparative Law, Am. Fgn. Law Assn. (dir.), Am. Assn. Law Schs. (past chmn. comparative law sect.). Home: 150 S 5th Ave Ann Arbor MI 48104 Office: U Mich Law Sch 625 S State St Ann Arbor MI 48109-1215 also: Fordham U Law Sch 271 W 47th St 30G New York NY 10036 Office Phone: 212-757-9264. Personal E-mail: whitgray@aol.com.

GRAY, WILLIAM GUERIN, engineering educator; b. San Francisco, Jan. 9, 1948; BS, U. Calif., 1969; MA, Princeton U., 1971, PhD, 1974. Asst. prof. dept. civil engring. Princeton U., N.J., 1975-80, dir. grad. studies dept. civil engring. N.J., 1977-84, assoc. prof. dept. civil engring. N.J., 1980-84; prof. dept. civil engring. U. Notre Dame, Ind., 1984-88, chmn. civil engring., geol. scis. Ind., 1984-95, Massman prof. civil engring. and geol. scis. Ind., 1988—. Office: U Notre Dame Dept Civil Engring Sc Notre Dame IN 46556 Home: 759 Pyrula Ave Sanibel FL 33957-6604

GRAY, WILLIAM R., lawyer; b. Peoria, Ill., Aug. 25, 1941; s. John J. and Alverna K. (Kennedy) G.; m. Tiana M. Yeager, June 12, 1982; children: Ann Katherine, Thomas William. BA, U. Colo., 1963, JD, 1966. Bar: Colo. 1966; U.S. Dist. Ct. Colo. 1966; U.S. Ct. Appeals (10th cir.) 1976. Dep. dist. atty. Dist. Atty.'s Office/10th Jud. Dist., Pueblo, Colo., 1967-69, Dist. Atty.'s Office/20th Jud. Dist., Boulder, Colo., 1969-70; dep. state pub. defender Colo. State Pub. Defender, Boulder, 1970-72; ptnr. Miller & Gray, Boulder, 1973-85, Purvis, Gray, Murphy, LLP, Boulder, 1985—. Mem./vice chair, chmn., Colo. Supreme Ct. grievance com., 1983-88, mem. criminal rules com., 1982-84; adj. prof. law U. Colo. Sch. of Law, Boulder, 1984. Bd. dirs. Mental Health Ctr. of Boulder County, 1972—78. Fellow Am. Coll. Trial Lawyers (Courageous Advocacy award 1985), Internat. Soc. Barristers (bd. govs. 2004—), Internat. Acad. Trial Lawyers, Am. Bar Found., Colo. Bar Foun., Colo. Bar Assn. (Professionalism award 1995), Am. Bd. Trial Advs. (Colo. chpt. pres. 2003-04), Am. Counsel Assn. Democrat. Office: Purvis Gray Murphy LLP Ste 501 1050 Walnut St Boulder CO 80302-5144 Office Phone: 303-442-3366. Business E-Mail: bgray@purvisgray.net.

GRAYBEAL, BARBARA, editor, writer; b. Mountain City, Tenn., Sept. 21, 1935; d. Claude Harold and Ruby Lucille (Hodge) G.; m. Lewis N. Kremer, June 7, 1958 (div.); m. Charles L. Ring, May 8, 1982(div.). BA magna cum laude, Marietta Coll., 1957; grad. Pub. Procedures Course, Radcliffe Coll., 1957. With New Yorker mag., NYC, 1957-58; assoc. editor Saturday Evening Post, Phila., 1958-62, Voter Registration in Mississippi, 1964, Episc. mag., Phila., 1962-69; asst. editor Luth. mag., Phila., 1971-72; instr. journalism Temple U., Phila., 1972-81; founding editor CGA World mag., 1980-82, sr. editor, 1982-83. Editor, writer: Fast and Fresh (by Julie Dannanbaum), 1981, The CGA Cookbook, 1984; editl. cons. Good Ideas for Decorating; contbr. articles, photographs and poetry to various publs. Mem. com. interpretation and promotion, dept. overseas missions Nat. Coun. Chs., 1966-68; mem. Phila. Dem. Com., 1968; bd. dirs., sec. Friends of Free Libr. Phila.; bd. dirs. N.C. Sch. Arts, The Assocs. of N.C. Sch. Arts, 1983-86; lay reader Episc. Ch.; vol. 1964 Miss. Freedom summer, Registration Project, Hattiesburg, Miss. Mem. AAUW (pres. br.), Women in Comms. (v.p. chpt.), Marietta Coll. Alumni Assn., Internat. Platform Assn., Phi Beta Kappa, Sigma Delta Chi, Alpha Xi Delta. Address: 1525 Woods Rd Apt 106 Winston Salem NC 27106-3135 Home Phone: 336-924-6913; Office Phone: 336-924-6913. Fax: 336-922-0261.

GRAYBEAL, JACK DANIEL, chemist, educator; b. Detroit, May 16, 1930; s. Paul Herman and Polly Dale (McClintic) G.; m. Evelyn Alice Nicolai, June 13, 1954; children: Daniel Lee, David Eugene, Dale Kevin. BS in Chemistry, W.Va. U., 1951; MS in Chemistry, U. Wis., 1953, PhD in Chemistry, 1955. Mem. tech. staff Bell Tel. Labs., Holmdel, NJ, 1955-57; asst. prof. chemistry W.Va. U., Morgantown, 1957-63, assoc. prof., 1963-68; assoc. prof. chemistry Va. Poly. Inst. and State U., Blacksburg, 1968-69, prof., 1969-97, assoc. head dept., 1975-95, prof. emeritus, 1997—. Author: Molecular Spectroscopy, 1988; contbr. articles to profl. jours. Mem. Am. Chem. Soc., Phi Lambda Upsilon (nat. editor 1981-87, nat. sec. 1987-96, nat. pres. 1996-2002, nat. historian 2002—), Sigma Xi. Avocations: stamp collecting/philately, photography. Home: 312 Apperson Dr Blacksburg VA 24060-3641 Office Phone: 540-552-4073. E-mail: graybealjd@verizon.net.

GRAYCAR, ADAM, dean, former Australian government official; b. Oct. 29, 1946; m. Elizabeth Percival, 1987; 2 children. BA with honors, U. NSW, Sydney, Australia, 1968, PhD in Pub. Policy, 1974, DLitt in Social Policy, 1991. Lectr. polit. sci. U. New South Wales, Sydney, 1970-72; sr. lectr. social adminstrn. Flinders U., Adelaide, Australia, 1973-80; dir. social policy rsch. ctr. U. New South Wales, Sydney, 1980-85; commr. for aging Govt. South Australia, Adelaide, 1985-90, CEO ministry of higher edn., 1990-94, head Cabinet Office, 2003—07; dir. Australian Inst. Criminology Fed. Govt. Australia, Canberra, 1994—2003; dean Rutgers U. Sch. Criminal Justice, Newark, 2007—. Invited expert Social Policy and Labour Mkt. Workshop, Paris, 1991; chair Australian Heads of Govt. Violence Prevention Awards, 1994. Author: Social Policy: An Australian Introduction, 1977, (with Adam Jamrozik) How Australians Live: Social Policy in Theory and Practice, 1989, 2d edit., 1993, (with Satyanshu Mukherjee) Crime and Justice in Australia, 1997, others; editor: Money Laundering: Risks and Countermeasures, 1996, Protecting Superannuation from Criminal Exploitation, 1996; contbr. more than 100 articles to profl. jours. Fellow Australian Inst. Mgmt., Acad. Social Scis. Avocations: walking, reading. Office: Rutgers U Sch Criminal Justice 123 Washington St Newark NJ 07102 Office Phone: 973-353-3292.*

GRAYER, ELIZABETH L., lawyer; b. Boston, June 19, 1964; BA magna cum laude, Amherst Coll., 1986; JD cum laude, Harvard Univ., 1989. Bar: NY 1990. Law clk., Hon. Miriam Goldman Cedarbaum US Dist. Ct., So. Dist. NY; assoc. Cravath Swaine & Moore LLPq, NYC, 1990—97, ptnr., litig., 1997—. Mem.: ABA, Assn. of Bar of City of NY, NY State Bar Assn., Phi Beta Kappa. Office: Cravath Swaine & Moore LLP Worldwide Plz 825 Eighth Ave New York NY 10019-7475 Office Phone: 212-474-1604. Office Fax: 212-474-3700. Business E-Mail: egrayer@cravath.com.

GRAYER, JONATHAN, education company executive; AB, Harvard Coll.; MBA, Harvard U., 1990. Mktg. dir. Newsweek, Inc., 1990; regional ops. dir. Kaplan, Inc., NYC, 1991—94, pres., CEO, 1994—2002, chmn., CEO, 2002—. Bd. mem. BrassRing Inc., NYC Partnership, New Sch. U. Mem. Sec. of Edn.'s Commn. on Future of Edn., 2005. Named one of Nation's Best Managers, BusinessWeek. Mem.: Harvard Bus. Sch. Club NY. Office: Kaplan Inc 888 7th Ave New York NY 10106*

GRAY-FUSON, JOAN LORRAINE, lawyer; b. Glendale, Calif., Mar. 25, 1938; d. Stanley Wayne Brune and Maxine Lorraine (Falconer) Talkin; m. Darrell Herbert Gray, June 26, 1959 (div. 1972); children: Michael Herbert Gray, Thomas Edward Gray; m. Arnold Max Fuson, Dec. 18, 1977; stepchildren: Marie Fuson Hudson, Karen Fuson, Gregory J. Fuson. BA in Edn., Calif. State U., 1960; JD, U. of the Pacific, 1978. Bar: Calif. 1978, U.S. Dist. Ct. (ea. dist.) Calif. 1978. Tchr. Rio Linda Union Sch. Dist., Sacramento, Calif., 1960-65; pvt. practice Sacramento, 1978-81; staff counsel State of Calif. Water Resources Control Bd., Sacramento, 1982-91; sr. staff counsel State of Calif. Dept. of Conservation, Sacramento, 1991—. Elder on session Fremont Presbyn. Ch., Sacramento, 1995-97. Avocations: gardening, folk dancing, exercise. Office: Dept of Conservation 801 K St # Ms24-3 Sacramento CA 95814-3500

GRAYSHAW, JAMES RAYMOND, judge; b. Cleve., Apr. 3, 1948; s. Thomas J. and Bettie Lee Grayshaw; m. Susan Hancher, Oct. 15, 1980; 1 child, John H. BA, L.I. U., Bklyn., 1970; JD, Bklyn. Law Sch., 1975. Legal asst. Cadwalader, Wickersham & Taft, NYC, 1975-77; law asst. Civil Ct., City N.Y., 1977-80; sr. law asst. Supreme Ct., State N.Y., 1980-82; judge housing part Civil Ct., City N.Y., 1983—. Judge advocate Cmty. Advocacy Ctr., N.Y.C., 1996. Sgt. U.S. Army, 1970-72. Mem. Queens Bar Assn., Protestant Lawyers N.Y.C. (dir. 1980—), Vietnam Vets. Am., 16th Inf. Reg. Assn., Masons, Sovereign Mil. Order of Temple of Jerusalem. Democrat. Episcopalian. Home: 215-36 40th Ave Bayside NY 11361-2300 Office: Civil Ct City NY 89-17 Sutphin Blvd Jamaica NY 11435 Office Phone: 718-262-7313. E-mail: jgraysha@courts.state.ny.us.

GRAYSMITH, ROBERT, political cartoonist, author; b. Pensacola, Fla., Sept. 17, 1942; s. Robert Gray and Frances Jane (Scott) Smith; m. Melanie Krakower, Oct. 15, 1975 (div. Sept. 1980); children: David Martin, Aaron Vincent, Margot Alexandra. BA, Calif. Coll. Arts and Crafts, 1965. Polit. cartoonist: Oakland (Calif.) Tribune, 1964—65, Stockton (Calif.) Record, 1965—68, San Francisco Chronicle, 1968—83; author: Zodiac, 1986, Trailside, 1986, The Sleeping Lady, 1990, The Murder of Bob Crane, 1993, Unabomber: A Desire to Kill, 1997, The Bell-Tower, A True Detective Story of Gas-Lit San Francisco, 1999, Ghost Fleet, 1999, Zodiac Unmasked, 2002, Amerithrax: The Hunt for the Anthrax Killer, 2003, (films) Auto-Focus, 2002, Zodiac, 2006; cons. Zodiac, Phoenix Pictures, 2004; illustrator: I Didn't Know What to Get You, 1993. Recipient 2d place Fgn. Press Awards 1973, World Population Contest 1976. Democrat. Presbyterian. Office: San Francisco Chronicle 901 Mission St San Francisco CA 94103-2905 Office Phone: 415-731-4069.

GRAYSON, ALBERT KIRK, social studies educator; b. Windsor, Ont., Can., Apr. 1, 1935; s. Albert Kirk and Helen (Smith) Grayson'; m. Eunice Marie Service, Aug. 3, 1956; children: Vera Lorraine, Sally Frances. BA, U. Toronto, Ont., 1955; MA, U. Toronto, 1958; postgrad., U. Vienna, Austria, 1959-60; PhD, Johns Hopkins U., 1962. Research asst. Chgo. Assyrian Dictionary Oriental Inst., Chgo., 1962-63; asst. prof. history Temple U., Phila., 1963-64; asst. prof. Near Eastern studies U. Toronto, 1964-67, assoc. prof., 1967-72, prof., 1972-2000, prof. emeritus, 2000—. Dir. Royal Inscriptions of Mesopotamia project, 1981—2007; vis. lectr. U. Pa., Phila., 1963-64; spl. asst. dept. Western Asiatic Antiquities Brit. Mus., London, intermittently, 1967-76; invited lectr. various univs., mus., U.S., Germany, Iraq, Eng., Austria, Italy, Finland, Japan. Author: Assyrian Royal Inscriptions vol. I, 1972, Assyrian Royal Inscriptions vol. II, 1976, Assyrian and Babylonian Chronicles, 1975, Babylonian Historical-Literary Texts, 1975, Assyrian Rulers of the Third and Second Millennia, B.C. 1987, Assyrian Rulers of the Early First Millennium BC I-II, 1991-96; contbr. chpts. to books. Can. Council fellow, 1959-61; Samuel S. Fels Fund fellow, 1961-62; Social Scis. and Humanities Research Council Can. editorial grantee, 1981—2007. Fellow Royal Soc. Can. (hon. sec. 1989-92); mem. Soc. Mesopotamian Studies (pres. 1980-92), Fondation Assyriologique Georges Dossin (Belgium), Oriental Club Toronto (sec. 1969-70, pres. 1979-80), Rencontre Assyriologique Internationale (sessional chmn. Berlin 1978, Vienna 1980, Leiden, Netherlands 1983), Am. Oriental Soc. (sec. Midwest br. 1965-68). Mem. Anglican Ch. of Canada. Office: 56 Rathnelly Ave Toronto ON Canada M4V 2M3

GRAYSON, DAVID S., paper company executive; b. Binghamton, NY, Oct. 16, 1943; s. Milton M. and Helen A. (Oretskin) G.; m. Wendy W. Grayson (div. June 1986); children: Natalie, Marc, Dayne. BS, Coll. Forestry, Syracuse, NY, 1965; MS, Rensselaer Poly., 1967. Various positions Riegel Paper div. James River Co., Milford, N.J., 1967-80; sales mgr. Kerwin Paper, Appleton, Wis., 1980-81; pres., founder Am. Fine Paper, Appleton, 1981—. Jewish. Office: Am Fine Paper PO Box 2638 Appleton WI 54912-2638 Office Phone: 920-733-6100. Business E-Mail: david@americanfinepaper.com.

GRAYSON, GERALD HERBERT, economist, educator, arbitrator, writer; b. Bklyn., June 23, 1940; s. Frank and Sylvia (Cohen) G.; m. Florence M. Herbstman, Dec. 27, 1964; children— Todd Zachary, Douglas Philip. BA, Bklyn. Coll., 1961; MA, U. Ill., 1963; PhD, N.Y. U., 1973. With Dept. Labor, Washington, 1963; labor economist N.Y.C. Bd. Edn., 1963-66; prof., chmn. Dep. Social Sci. N.Y.C. Coll. Tech., 1966—98; pub., editor Labor Edn. Pub. Co., NYC, 1995—. Adj. prof. Adelphi U., Garden City, NY, 1974-81, Farmingdale State, 2002—; exec. dir. NY State Conf. AAUP, 1992-2002; labor arbitrator Fed. Mediation and Conciliation Svc., NY State Employees Rels. Bd., Suffolk Pub. Employees Rels. Bd., 2002-; securities arbitrator NASD. Served with USAR, 1962-68. Mem. Am. Arbitration Assn., Labor and Employment Rels. Assn. Jewish. Home: 43 Northcote Dr Melville NY 11747-3924 Office Phone: 931-920-7201. Personal E-mail: jerryarb@optonline.net.

GRAYSON, JOANN HESS, psychology professor; m. Phillip Grayson; 2 children. PhD, Washington U., St. Louis. Asst. prof. to prof. psychology James Madison U., Harrisonburg, Va., 1976—. Past chair Gov.'s Adv. Bd. on Child Abuse and Neglect, Va. Contbr. articles to profl. jours.; editor, pub.: Va. Child Protection Newsletter, 1981—. Recipient TIAA-CREF Va. Outstanding Faculty award, State Coun. Higher Edn. Va., 2004, Commr.'s award for Va., Adminstrn. Children, Youth and Families, US HHS Adminstrn. Children and Families, 2005, Champion for Children award, Prevent Child Abuse Va., 2006, US Prof. of Yr. award, Carnegie Found. for Advancement of Tchg. and Coun. for Advancement and Support of Edn., 2006. Office: Dept Psychology James Madison U MSC 7401 Harrisonburg VA 22807 Office Phone: 540-568-6771. E-mail: graysojh@jmu.edu.*

GRAYSON, TREY (C.M. GRAYSON), state official; b. Ky., Apr. 18, 1972; m. Nancy Humphrey; children: Alexandra, Kate. BA in Govt., Harvard U., 1994; MBA, JD, U. Ky., 1998. Chmn. Young Profls. for Bush/Cheney in Ky., 2000; atty. Keating, Muething and Klekamp, 2001—03; sec. state Commonwealth of Ky., Frankfort, 2004—. Adv. bd. Just Democracy, Inc.; adv. mem. HelpingAmericansVote.org. Named one of 44 Ky. Leaders for New Century, Ky. Press Assn. & Shakertown Roundtable, 1999; Toll Fellowship, Coun. State Govt., 2004. Mem.: Nat. Assn. of Secretaries of State (vice chmn., com. voter participation, election com., bus. svcs. com., subcom. presidential primaries). Republican. Office: Office Sec State State Capitol Ste 152 700 Capitol Ave Frankfort KY 40601 Office Phone: 502-564-3490. Office Fax: 502-564-5687. E-mail: tgrayson@kysos.com.*

GRAYSON-JORDAN, CARRIE See JORDAN, CARRIE

GRAZER, BRIAN, film company executive; b. LA, July 12, 1951; m. Gigi Levangie, 1997 (separated); children: Patrick, Thomas. Grad., U. So. Calif., 1974. Co-founder, co-chair Imagine Films Entertainment, 1986—. Prodr. films including: Night Shift, 1982, Splash, 1984, Real Genius, 1985, Spies Like Us (with George Folsey Jr.), 1985, Armed & Dangerous (with James Keach), 1986, Like Father, Like Son (with David Valdes, 1987, Parenthood, 1989, Cry Baby (with Jim Abrahams, 1990, Kindergarten Cop (with Ivan Reitman), 1990, Closet Land (with Ron Howard), 1991, The Doors (with Nicholas Clainos & Mario Kassar), 1991, Backdraft (with Raffaella DeLaurentiis), 1991, My Girl, 1991, Far and Away (with Ron Howard), 1992, Boomerang (with Warrington Hudlin), 1992, Housesitter, 1992, CB4 (with Sean Daniel), 1993, For Love or Money, 1993, The Paper (with Frederick Zollo), 1994, My Girl 2, 1994, Greedy, 1994, The Cowboy Way, 1994, Apollo 13 (with Ron Howard), 1995 (Daryl F. Zanuck Motion Picture Prodr. of the Yr. award, Acad. Award Nom. Best Picture, 1996), Sgt. Bilko, 1996, Ransom, 1996, Bowfinger, 1999, Beyond the Mat, 1999, Curious George, 2000, Nutty Professor II: The Klumps, 2000, How the Grinch Stole Christmas, 2000, A Beautiful Mind, (with Ron Howard), 2001, (Acad. Award Best Picture, 2002), Undercover Brother, 2002, Blue Crusch, 2002, 8 Mile, 2002, Intolerable Cruelty, 2003, The Cat in the Hat, 2003, The Missing, 2003, Friday Night Lights, 2004, Inside Deep Throat, 2005, Cinderella Man, 2005, Flightplan, 2005, Fun with Dick and Jane, 2005, Inside Man, 2006, The Da Vinci Code, 2006, American Gangster, 2007, Kids in America, 2008; prodr. TV miniseries: From the Earth to the Moon, 1998 (Emmy Outstanding Miniseries) exec. prodr. TV series: The PJs, 1999, Wonderland, 2000, "24", 2001-, The Beast, 2001, Miss Match, 2003-2005, Arrested Development, 2003-2005 (Emmy award for Outstanding Comedy Series 2004), The Big House, 2004, The Inside, 2005, Treasuer Hunters, 2006, Bra Boys, 2007, Friday Night Lights, 2007, Shark, 2006-2007 Named one of 50 Most Powerful People in Hollywood, Premiere mag., 2004—06, The World's Most Influential People, TIME mag., 2007, 100 Most Powerful Celebrities, Forbes.com, 2007; recipient David O. Selznick Lifetime Achievement award, Prodr. Guild Am., 2001, Lifetime Achievement award, ShoWest, 2003. Office: Imagine Films Entertainment 9465 Wilshire Blvd Fl 7 Beverly Hills CA 90212-2606*

GRAZIANI, LEONARD JOSEPH, pediatric neurologist, researcher; b. Phila., Nov. 17, 1929; m. Amelia Honeyford, June 29, 1956; children: Paul, Amy, Virginia, David. BA, LaSalle Coll., Phila., 1951; MD, Jefferson Med. Coll., Phila., 1955. Diplomate Am. Bd. Pediat., Am. Bd. Psychiatry and Neurology. Intern Valley Forge (Pa.) Army Hosp., 1956; resident Brooke Army Hosp., San Antonio, 1959; chief pediatric svc. Ireland Army Hosp., Ft. Knox, Ky., 1960-61; neurology fellow Bronx Mcpl. Hosp. Ctr., 1961-64; interdisciplinary fellow Albert Einstein Coll. Medicine, Bronx, 1964-66, asst. prof. pediat. and neurology, 1964-68; career scientist Health Rsch. Coun., NYC, 1967-68; attending pediatrician, neurologist Thomas Jefferson U. Hosp., Phila., 1968—2004; chief div. pediatric neurology dept. pediat. Jefferson Med. Coll., Thomas Jefferson U., Phila., 1974-99, vice chair dept. pediat., 1988-96, prof. pediat., neurology, 1968—. Cons. neurologist Woods Svcs., Langhorne, Pa., 1968—; staff E.I. duPont Inst., Wilmington, 1984-2004. Contbr. articles to prof. jours. Capt. U.S. Army, 1955-61. Fellow Am. Acad. Neurology, Am. Acad. Pediat.; mem. Am. Pediatric Soc., Soc. Pediatric Rsch., Child Neurology Soc., Alpha Omega Alpha, Sigma Xi.

GRAZIANO, CRAIG FRANK, lawyer; b. Des Moines, Dec. 7, 1950; s. Charles Dominic and Corrine Rose (Comito) G. BA summa cum laude, Macalester Coll., 1973; JD with honors, Drake U., 1975. Bar: Iowa 1976, U.S. Dist. Ct. (no. and so. dists.) Iowa 1978, U.S. Ct. Appeals (8th cir.) 1977, U.S. Supreme Ct. 1988. Law clk. to Hon. M. D. Van Oosterhout U.S. Ct. Appeals (8th cir.), Sioux City, Iowa, 1976-78; pvt. practice Dickinson, Mackaman, Tyler & Hagen, PC, Des Moines, 1978-98; with Office of Consumer Advocate, Iowa Dept. Justice, Des Moines, 1999—. Mem. Gov.'s Task Force on Quality and Efficiency in Govt., 1999—2000. Mem. Iowa Bar Assn. (chair specialization com. 1993-96, chair adminstrv. law sect. 1996-99), Order of Coif, Phi Beta Kappa. Home: 500 44th St Des Moines IA 50312-2408 Office: 310 Maple St Des Moines IA 50319-0063 E-mail: craig.graziano@mchsi.com, cgraziano@mail.oca.state.ia.us.

GRAZIANO, FRANK MICHAEL, medical educator, researcher; b. Easton, Pa., June 5, 1942; s. Michael and Grace (Farace) G.; m. Mary Helen Ashton, Feb. 4, 1967; children: Teresa Ann, Frank Jr., Alicia Grace. BS, St. Joseph's Coll., 1964; MS, Villanova Univ., 1967; PhD, Univ. Va., 1970, MD, 1973. Diplomate Am. Bd. of Internal Medicine, Am. Bd. of Allergy and Clinical Immunology. Internship Univ. Wis. Hosp., Madison, 1973-74; residency in medicine Univ. Wis., Madison, 1974-76, asst. prof., 1978-84, assoc. prof., 1984-89, prof. medicine, 1989—, chief section of Rheumatology, 1989—. Author numerous books, articles, papers in field. Admissions com. Univ. Wis. Medical Sch., 1983-86, Minority subcom. chmn., 1985-86; medical and scientific com. Wis. Arthritis Found., 1979-80, Univ. Wis. Madison AIDS Task Force Com., 1986-89; Bd. dirs. Wis. Arthritis Found., 1990—, Wis. Com. Based Rsch. Consortium, 1990—. Recipient Am. Acad. Travel grant, 1978, NIH Young Investigator award, 1980, NIH Allergic Disease Acad. award, 1985. Fellow Am. Acad. Allergy/Immunology, Am. Coll. Physicians; mem. Am. Assn. Immunologists, Am. Assn. Advancement of Sci., Am. Thoracic Soc., Am. Coll. Pheumatology, Clinical Immunology Soc., Wis. Allergy Soc., Wis. Rheumatism Assn., Sigma Xi. Home: 853 Tipperary Rd Oregon WI 53575-2641 Office: Univ Wis Hosp & Clinics 600 Highland Ave # H6 363 Madison WI 53792-0001

GRAZIANO, MARGARET A., chaplain, recreational therapist, educational consultant, volunteer; b. Portland, Ore., Nov. 25, 1916; d. Agostino Graziano and Madeline Rinella; children: Vincent, Margaret, Salvatore, Anne, Agatha, Prudence, Rosemary, Joseph. BA, Holy Names Coll., 1946; BM, Maryhurst Coll., 1951; MEd, U. Portland, 1961. Cert. correctional chaplain Am. Correctional Cath. Chaplains Assn., Am. Correctional Chaplains Assn., 2000, alcohol counselor Oreg., in adminstrn. and supervision U. Portland. Tchr. Sister of the Holy Names, Ore., 1937—75; music tchr. Montessori, Eugene, Oreg., 1974—76; young musicians artist camp Maryhurst Coll., 1972—73; specialized counselor Triple H. Ranch, Jasper, Oreg., 1972—74; chem. dependancy counselor Treatment Ctr. Youth, Eugene, Oreg., 1975—79; asst. vol. coord. Lane County Adult Corrections, Eugene, Oreg., 1976—2006, chaplain, 1995—2006; recreational therapist Johnson Unit, 2004—05. Chem. dependency facilitator Intensive Treatment Program, Eugene, Oreg., 1997—2007; pres. Internat. Correctional Arts Network, 2000—06. Co-editor (with Susan Clayton): Best in the Business-Corrections Today, 1999. Vol. St. Vincent de Paul Soc. Lane County, 2006; bd. dirs. Committed Ptnrs. for Youth, 2000—06, Cath. Worker John Bosce House, 2000—07; rep. Lane County Human Potential Workshop, Eugene, Oreg., 1970; chmn. Governors Task force on Vol., 1965; cmty. svc. Inner City Burnside Area, Portland, Oreg., 1972; mem. planning com. Seattle Diocese against Death Penalty, 1968. Named one of four honorees, Newman Ctr./ U. Ore., 2005; recipient Alumni award, St. Mary's Acad., 2005, E.R. Cass award, ACA, 2003, Murname Soc. Justice award, Cath. Cmty. Svc., 2004. Mem.: Willamette Bus. Leaders, Sisters of the Holy Names (superior 1958), Sons of Italy (trustee/chaplain 1998—2007, bd. dirs. 2007). Roman Catholic. Avocations: travel, art, music, drama, films. Home: 100 E 11th Ave Apt 208 Eugene OR 97401 Office: Lane County Adult Corrections 101 W 5th Ave Eugene OR 97401 Office Phone: 541-682-2174.

GREALY, MARY R., medical association administrator; b. Ft. Lauderdale, Fla. B, Mich. State U.; JD, Duquesne U. Speech and hearing pathologist; COO & exec. counsel Fedn. Am. Hospitals; sr. Washington counsel Am. Hosp. Assn., 1996—99; pres. Healthcare Leadership Coun., Washington, 1999—. Office: Healthcare Leadership Coun 1001 Pennsylvania Ave NW Ste 550 S Washington DC 20004 Business E-Mail: mgrealy@hlc.org.

GREANEY, JOHN M., state supreme court justice; b. Westfield, Mass., Apr. 8, 1939; s. Patrick Joseph and Margaret Irene (Fitzgerald) G.; m. Susan H. Greaney, Nov. 23, 1967. 1 child, Jessica S. BA summa cum laude, Holly Cross Coll., 1960; JD, NYU, 1963; LLD (hon.), Westfield State Coll., 1967, Western New England Coll., 1969; LLD, New England Law Sch., 1991. Bar: Mass., Supreme Judicial Ct., U.S. Dist. Ct., U.S. Supreme Ct. Ptnr. Ely & King, Springfield, Mass., 1963-73; presiding judge Hampden County Housing Ct., Springfield, Mass., 1973-75; assoc. judge Mass. Superior Ct., Boston, 1975-76; assoc. justice Mass. Appeals Ct., Boston, 1976-84, 1976-84, chief justice, 1984-89; assoc. justice Mass. Supreme Jud. Ct., Boston, 1989—. Former faculty mem. Western New England Law Sch., Westfield State Coll.; co-chair. Supreme Judicial Ct's Gender Bias Study Commn; mem. bd. Tribunes WGBY-Channel 57. Former assoc. editor Mass. Law Review. Trustee, dir. Westfield Atheneum, participant Child and Family Svcs. Program. Fellow Am. Bar Found.; mem. ABA (litigation, judicial adminstrn. section), Hampden County Bar Assn.(former mem. exec. com., grievance com., treas.), Mass. Bar Assn. (former chmn. Young Lawyers section, bd. delegates, exec. com., grievance com., legal svc. com., civil litigation, criminal law sections), Am. Law Inst. Avocations: competitive running, reading. Office: Supreme Judicial Court 1 Pemberton Sq Ste 2-500 Boston MA 02108-1717*

GREANEY, MICHAEL E., lawyer; b. June 15, 1952; BA, Loyola Univ., 1974; JD, Univ. So. Calif., 1977. Bar: Calif. 1977, NY 1999. Former co-ptnr.-in-charge NYC office Gibson Dunn & Crutcher LLP, NYC, now ptnr. corp. transactions and securities. Mem. exec. com. Gibson Dunn & Crutcher. Mem. Univ. So. Calif. Law Rev., 1975—76. Mem.: ABA (fed. regulation of securities com.). Office: Gibson Dun & Crutcher LLP 47th fl 200 Park Ave New York NY 10166-0193 Office Phone: 212-351-4065. Office Fax: 212-351-5260. Business E-Mail: mgreaney@gibsondunn.com.

GREANEY, THOMAS L., lawyer, educator; BA magna cum laude, Wesleyan Univ., 1970; JD, Harvard Univ., 1973. Legis. asst. U.S. Rep. Elizabeth Holtzman, Washington, 1973—74; law clk. FCC, Washington, 1974—76; sr. trial atty. U.S. Dept. Justice, Antitrust div., Washington, 1976—81, asst. chief, 1982—85; Victor Kramer vis. fellow Yale Univ., 1985—86, NIMH fellow, 1986—87, lectr., Law Sch., 1986—87; prof., Sch. Law Saint Louis Univ., 1987—, assoc. prof., Sch. Pub. Health, 1987—; dir. Ctr. for Health Law Studies, Saint Louis Univ., 1987—. Vis. prof. Universite d'Orleans, France, 2001—02; Merck vis. scholar Seton Hall Univ., 2002, vis. prof., 04. Author: Bioethics, Liability; co-author: Health Law: Cases, Materials and Problems, Internat. Ency. Laws, Medical Law, U.S. Nat. ed., Health Law Statutes & Regulations. Fulbright Fellow, European Cmty. Rsch. Program, Brussels, Belgium, 1993—94. Mem.: Phi Beta Kappa. Office: Saint Louis University School of Law 3700 Lindell Blvd Saint Louis MO 63108 Office Phone: 314-977-2766. Business E-Mail: greanetl@slu.edu.*

GREAR, EFFIE CARTER, educational administrator; b. Huntington, W.Va., Aug. 15, 1927; d. Harold Jones and Margaret (Tinsley) Carter. MusB, W.Va. State Coll., 1948; MA, Ohio State U., 1955; EdD., Nova U.,

1976; m. William Alexander Grear, May 16, 1952; children: Rhonda Kaye, William Alexander. Band dir. Fla. A&M HS, Tallahassee, 1948-51, Smith-Brown HS, Arcadia, Fla., 1951-56; band dir. Lake Shore HS, Belle Glade, Fla., 1956-60, dean of girls, 1960-66, asst. prin., 1966-70; asst. prin. Glades Central HS, Belle Glade, Fla., 1970-76, prin., 1976—. Author: Up From the Muck. Bd. dirs. Palm Beach County Mental Health Assn. Recognized for outstanding achievement by Fla. Sugar Cane League, 1985; recipient Community Svc. award ElDorado Civic Club, Martin Luther King Jr. Humanitarian award Palm Beach County Urban League, 1988, Community Svc. award West Palm Br. NAACP, 1989, Ida S. Baker Disting. Black Educator Recognition award Fla. Dept. Edn., 1992. Mem. Nat. Assn. Secondary Sch. Prins. (Excellence in Edn. award 1991, Fla. Secondary Prin. of Yr. (with Burger King Corp.) 1991), Nat. Cmty. Sch. Edn. Conf., Nat. Sch. Pub. Rels. Assn., Assn. Supervision and Curriculum Devel., Fla. Assn. Secondary Sch. Prins. (Prin. of Excellence 1991-92), Palm Beach County Sch. Adminstrs. Assn., Belle Glade Assn. Women's Clubs (pres.), Belle Glade C. of C. (chmn. beautification Com., citizen yr. 1986), Phi Delta Kappa, Alpha Kappa Alpha, Omega Psi Phi (West Palm Beach chpt. Citizen of Yr. 1990), Elite Community Club, Women's Civic Club. Office: Glades Cen HS 425 W Canal St N Belle Glade FL 33430-3086 Personal E-mail: efgrear@bellsouth.net.

GREASER, CONSTANCE UDEAN, communications executive, researcher; b. Jan. 18, 1938; d. Lloyd Edward and Udean Greaser. BA, San Diego State Coll., 1959; postgrad., U. Copenhagen Grad. Sch. Fgn., 1963, Georgetown U. Sch. Fgn. Svc., 1967; MA, U. So. Calif., 1968; exec. MBA, UCLA, 1981. Advt., publicity mgr. Crofton Co., San Diego, 1959-62; supr. Mercury Publs., Fullerton, Calif., 1962-64; supr. engring. support svcs. divsn. Arcata Data Mgmt., Hawthorne, Calif., 1964-67; mgr. computerized typesetting dept. Continental Graphics, LA, 1967-70; v.p., editl. dir. Sage Publs., Inc., Beverly Hills, Calif., 1970-74; head publs. RAND Corp., Santa Monica, Calif., 1974-90; mgr. svc. comms. Am. Honda Motors Co., Torrance, Calif., 1990—2002; ret., 2002. Co-author: Quick Writer-Build Your Own Word Procesing Users Guide, 1983, Quick Writer-Word Processing Center Operations Manual, 1984; editor: Urban Research News, 1971-74; mng. editor: Comparative Polit. Studies, 1971-74; contbr. articles to profl. jours. Nat. com. Million Minutes of Peace Appeal, 1986, Nat. Info. Stds. Orgn., 1987-93, Global Cooperation for Better World, 1988. Recipient Berber award Graphic Arts Tech. Found., 1989. Mem.: Soc. Tech. Comm., Women in Comm., Soc. for Scholarly Pubs. (nat. bd. dirs.), Graphic Comm. Assn. (bd. dirs. 1994—99), Women in Bus. (pres. 1977—78), So. Calif. Women for Understanding (chair LA/Valley chpt. 2004—06).

GREASER, MARION LEWIS, science educator; b. Vinton, Iowa, Feb. 10, 1942; s. Lewis Levi and Elisabeth (Sage) G.; m. Marilyn Sue Pfister, June 12, 1965; children— Suzanne, Scott BS, Iowa State U., 1964; MS, U. Wis., 1967, PhD, 1969. Postdoctoral fellow Boston Biomed. Research Inst., 1968-71; asst. prof. sci. U. Wis., Madison, 1971-73, assoc. prof., 1973-77, prof., 1977—, Cambell-Bascom prof., 2004—. Contbr. articles to profl. jours. Recipient Outstanding Researcher award Am. Heart Assn.-Wis., 1985 Mem. AAAS, Am. Soc. Biochem. Molecular Biology, Biophys. Soc., Am. Meat Sci. Assn. (Disting. Rsch. award 1981), Am. Soc. Animal Sci. (Meat Rsch. award 2000). Home: 2374 Branch St Middleton WI 53562-2809 Office: U Wis Muscle Biology Lab 1805 Linden Dr W Madison WI 53706-1110 Business E-Mail: mgreaser@ansci.wisc.edu.

GREASON, ARTHUR LEROY, JR., retired university administrator; b. Newport, RI, Sept. 13, 1922; s. Arthur LeRoy and Pauline (Brown) G.; m. Pauline Schaaf, Dec. 29, 1945; children— Randall Mark, Katherine, Douglas Bradford. BA, Wesleyan U., Middletown, Conn., 1945; MA, Harvard U., Cambridge, Mass., 1947, PhD, 1954; LittD (hon.), Wesleyan U., Middletown, Conn., 1987; LHD (hon.), Colby Coll., Waterville, Maine, 1989; LHD, Bowdoin Coll., Brunswick, Maine, 1990, Bates Coll., Lewiston, Maine, 1990, U. Maine, Bangor, Maine, 1992; LHD (hon.), U. New Eng., Biddeford, Maine, 2006. Asst. to dean Wesleyan U., 1945-46; teaching fellow English Harvard, 1948-52; mem. faculty Bowdoin Coll., 1952-90, assoc. prof. English, 1961-66, prof., 1966-90, dean students, 1962-66, dean of coll., 1966-75, acting pres., 1981, pres., 1981-90. Driver, companion Neighbors, Inc., Brunswick; trustee Portland Stage Co., 1991-97, Westbrook Coll., 1992-96, Maine Hist. Soc., 1994-97, U. New England, 1996—2004, Maine Bd. Bar Examiners, 1997—2003, DLF Charitable Found., 1997—. Kent fellow Soc. Religion Higher Edn., 1946 Mem. Maine Bar Assn. (fee arbitration commn. 1997-2002), Phi Beta Kappa. Congregationalist. Home: 20 Birch Meadow Brunswick ME 04011-2955 Personal E-mail: algreason@gwi.net.

GREASON, MURRAY CROSSLEY, JR., lawyer; b. Wake Forest, NC, Dec. 12, 1936; s. Murray Crossley and Evelyn Elizabeth (Hackney) G.; m. Joan Millicent Wilder. BS magna cum laude, Wake Forest U., 1959, JD magna cum laude, 1962. Bar: N.C. 1962. Assoc. firm Womble Carlyle Sandridge & Rice, PLLC, Winston-Salem, NC, 1965-70; mem. firm Womble Carlyle Sandridge & Rice, Winston-Salem, NC, 1970—; mng. ptnr. firm Womble Carlyle Sandridge & Rice, PLLC, Winston-Salem, 1988-96. Vis. lectr. Wake Forest U., 1972-74. Pres. Winston-Salem Estate Planning Coun., 1973; trustee Denmark Loan Fund, scholarships to Wake Forest U.; bd. visitors Wake Forest Law Sch., 1983—, chmn. 1994-2000; trustee Wake Forest U., 1990, vice chmn., 1997-2002, chmn., 2003-05, vice chmn., 2005-06; chmn. N.W. N.C. chpt. ARC, 1996; chmn. bd. United Way Forsyth County, 1995; mem. Commn. on Ministry Episcopalian Diocese N.C., 1983-93; bd. dirs. Winston-Salem Alliance, 2000-05, Ideal-liance, 1998—, Wake Forest U. Health Scis., 2000—, Cmty. Care Clinic, 2004—, The NC Railroad Co., 2004—; adv. bd. The Wachovia Corp., 1999—2006, chmn 2003-06; adv. bd. Amarr Co., 2000—. Capt. JAG, AUS, 1962-65. Fellow Am. Coll. Tax Coun.; mem. ABA, N.C. Bar Assn. (I. Beverly Lake Pub. Svc. award 2005), Forsyth County Bar Assn. (pres. 1986-87), Winston-Salem C. of C. (bd. dirs., vice chmn. 2001, chmn. 2002), Wake Forest U. Alumni Assn. (pres. 1973), Forsyth Country Club, Phi Beta Kappa, Omicron Delta Kappa. Episcopalian. Home: 745 Arbor Rd Winston Salem NC 27104-2209 Office: Womble Carlyle Sandridge PLLC One W 4th St Winston Salem NC 27101 Office Phone: 336-721-3616. Business E-Mail: mgreason@wcsr.com.

GREATBATCH, WILSON, biomedical engineer; b. Buffalo, Sept. 6, 1919; married; 5 children. BEE, Cornell U., 1950; MSEE, U. Buffalo, 1957; ScD (hon.), Houghton Coll., 1971, SUNY, Buffalo, 1984, Clarkson U., 1987, Roberts Wesleyan Coll., 1988, D'Youville Coll., 2002. Project engr. Cornell Aeronaut Lab. Inc., 1950—52; asst. prof. elec. engring. U. Buffalo, 1952—57; mgr. electronics div. Taber Instrument Corp., 1957—60; v.p. Mennen Greatbatch Electronics Inc., 1962—78. Adj. prof. elec. engring. SUNY, Buffalo, 1981—; adj. prof. engring. Cornell U., Ithaca, NY, 1989—; adj. prof. physical scis. Houghton (N.Y.) Coll., 1978—; adj. prof. phys. scis. Kingston U., Niagara Falls, Ont., Canada, 2001—. Contbr. over 100 articles to sci. jours.; holder over 320 U.S. and fgn. patents. Named Paul Harris fellow, Rotary Internat., 1993; named to, Nat. Inventors Hall of Fame, 1986, U.S. Space Tech. Hall of Fame, 1993, Sci. and Engring. Hall of Fame, 1997; recipient Holley medal, ASME, 1986, Chancellor Morton medal, U. Buffalo, 1990, disting. svc. award, NSPE, 1984, Pacemaker award, Prince Rainier of Monaco, 1988, Nat. Medal of Tech., Pres. Bush, 1990, Vladimir Karapetoff award, Eta Kappa Nu, 1992, Washington award, Western Engring. Soc., Chgo., 1995, Lemelson/MIT Career Achievement award, 1996, Russ Prize, Nat. Acad. Engring., 2001. Fellow: ASME, IEEE, AAAS, N.Y. Acad. Scis., Am. Inst. Med. and Biol. Engring. (founder), Am. Soc. Angiology, Am. Coll. Cardiology, Royal Soc. Health; mem.: NAE (Russ prize 2001), Assn. Advancement Med. Instrumentation (Laufman award 1982), Eta Kappa Nu., Tau Beta Pi, Sigma Xi. Achievements include invention of implantable cardiac pacemaker; research in implantable power supplies for medical uses, biomass energy, genetic engineering. Office: Greatbatch Technologies Inc 9645 Wehrle Dr Clarence NY 14031

GREAUX, CHERYL PREJEAN, federal agency administrator; b. Houston, July 30, 1949; m. Robert Bruce Greaux. BA, Tex. So. U., 1967; MA, U. Tex., 1973. Mgr. compliance programs Dept. Labor, NYC, 1973-80; corp. human resources mgr. Allied Signal Inc., Morristown, NJ, 1980-85; account exec., sourcing specialist Dean Witter Reynolds, NYC, 1986-88; dir. civil rights staff USDA Rural Devel., Washington, 1994—. Cons. Seagrams, NYC, 1984, Gen. Foods, White Plains, NY, 1985. Author: Struggling Within or Success from Within?, 1973. Lectr. Nat. Urban League, 1980—; cons. Nat. Urban Affairs Coun., NY, 1981—86; bd. dirs. Ednl. Opportunity Fund, NJ, 1985—87. Mem.: Edges Group, Delta Sigma Theta. Office: Dept Agr 14th And Independence SW Washington DC 20250-0001 Office Phone: 202-692-0204. Business E-Mail: cheryl.greaux@usda.gov.

GREAVER, HARRY, artist; b. LA, Oct. 30, 1929; s. Harry Jones and Lucy Catherine (Coons) G.; m. Hanne Synnestvedt Nielsen, Nov. 30, 1955; children: Peter, Paul, Lotte. BFA, U. Kans., Lawrence, 1951, MFA, 1952. Assoc. prof. art U. Maine, Orono, 1955—66; exec. dir. Kalamazoo Inst. Arts, 1966—78; dir. Greaver Gallery, Cannon Beach, Oreg., 1978—. Mem. visual com. Mich. Coun. Arts, 1976-78. One-man exhbns. include Baker U., Baldwin, Kans., 1955, U. Maine, Orono, 1958, 59, Pacific U., 1985; group exhbns. include U. Utah Mus. Fine Arts, 1972-73, Purdue U., 1977, Drawings, USA, St. Paul, 1963, San Diego Mus., 1971, Rathbun Gallery, Portland, Oreg., 1988; 10-yr. print retrospective Cannon Beach Arts Assn., 1989, 20-yr. retrospective, 1998, 25th Anniversary exhibt. Mem. adv. bd. Haystack Ctr. for the Arts, Cannon Beach, 1988-91. Recipient Purchase award Nat. Endowment Arts, 1971; grantee U. Maine, 1962-64. Address: PO Box 120 Cannon Beach OR 97110-0120

GREAVER, JOANNE HUTCHINS, mathematics educator, writer; b. Louisville, Aug. 9, 1939; d. Alphonso Victor and Mary Louise (Sage) Hutchins; 1 child, Mary Elizabeth. BS in Chemistry, U. Louisville, 1961, MEd, 1971; MAT in Math., Purdue U., 1973. Cert. tchr. Pres. Math Mentors Inc., 1962—. Part-time faculty Bellarmine Coll., Louisville, 1982-2002, U. Louisville, 1985—; project reviewer NSF, 1983—; advisor Council on Higher Edn., Frankfort, Ky., 1983-86; active regional and nat. summit on assessment in math., 1991, state task force on math., assessment adv. com., Nat. Assessment Ednl. Progress standards com.; charter mem. Commonwealth Tchrs. Inst., 1984—; mem. Nat. Forum for Excellence in Edn., Indpls., 1983; metric edn. leader Fed. Metric Project, Louisville, 1979-82; mem. Ky. Ednl. Reform Task Force, Assessment Com., Nat. Framework, Nat. Assessment Ednl. Progress Rev. Com.; lectr. in field. Author: (workbook) Down Algebra Alley, 1984; co-author curriculum guides. Named Outstanding Citizen, SAR, 1984; named to Hon. Order Ky. Cols.; recipient Presdl. award for excellence in math. tchg., 1983; grantee, NSF, 1983, Louisville Cmty. Found., 1984—86. Mem. Greater Louisville Coun. Tchrs. of Math. (pres. 1977-78, 94-95, Outstanding Educator award 1987), Nat. Coun. Tchrs. of Math. (reviewer 1981—), Ky. Coun. Tchrs. of Math. (pres. 1990-91, Jefferson County Tchr. of Yr. award 1985), Math. Assn. Am., Phi Delta Kappa Internat., Kappa Delta Pi, Delta Kappa Gamma, Zeta Tau Alpha. Democrat. Presbyterian. Avocations: tropical fish, gardening, handicrafts, travel. Home: 11513 Tazwell Dr Louisville KY 40241 E-mail: jogreaver@aol.com.

GREAVES, JOHN ALLEN, lawyer; b. Kansas City, Mo., Feb. 18, 1948; s. John Allen Greaves and Nancy Lee (Farmer) Greaves-Meltzer; m. Sharon Louise Peace Ventura, Dec. 23, 1967 (div. Mar. 1971); 1 child, Karen Christine Greaves Calogne; m. Jerri Lynn Crawford, Sept. 5, 1981. BA in Polit. Sci., U. Mo., 1976; MPA, JD with honors, Drake U., 1992. Bar: Iowa 1992, U.S. Dist. Ct. (so. dist.) Iowa 1992, Calif. 1994, U.S. Dist. Ct. (no. and ctrl. dists.) Calif. 1994, U.S. Dist. Ct. (so. and ea. dists.) Calif. 1995, U.S. Ct. Appeals (9th cir.) 1995, U.S. Dist. Ct. (no. dist.) N.Y. 1996, U.S. Dist. Ct. S.C. 1995, U.S. Ct. Appeals (4th and 10th cirs.) 1996, U.S. Dist. Ct. (no. dist.) Ill. 2000, D.C. 2001, U.S. Dist. Ct. (so. and ea. dists.) N.Y. 2002, Mo. 2004; Judge pro tem, lic. airline transport pilot. Pres., CEO VIPilot Svcs., Inc., Kansas City, 1980-83; pilot Air Illinois, Carbondale, Ill., 1983-84, Wright Airlines, Cleve., 1983-84, ComAir Airlines, Cin., 1984-88; jud. law clk. to Hon. Arthur E. Gamble Iowa Dist. Ct., Des Moines, 1990-91; pvt. practice Des Moines, 1992—94; shareholder Baum, Hedlund, Aristei, Goldman & Menzies, PC, LA, 1994—. Mem. plaintiffs' steering com. Atlantic S.E. Airlines crash, Carrollton, Ga., 1995, Singapore Airlines crash, Taipei, Taiwan, 2000, MDL-1448 Am. Airlines 587 crash, Belle Harbor (Queens), N.Y., 2001; mem. plaintiffs' exec. com. Sept. 11, 2001 Tort Litig.; lectr. in field. Recipient Safety award, Nat. Air Disaster Found., 2002. Mem. ABA (mem. forum on air and space com., mem. litig. sect., mem. tort trial and ins. practice sect.), Am. Assn. for Justice (mem. aviation law sect.), Air Line Pilots Assn. (mem. coun. 37, chmn. contract adminstrn. com. 1985-87, Disting. Svc. award), Lawyer/Pilot Bar Assn., State Bar Calif., State Bar Iowa, DC Bar Assn., State Bar Mo., Iowa Trial Lawyers Assn., Inn Ct., Delta Theta Phi. Avocations: aviation, snow and water skiing, boating and sailing, tennis, golf. Office: Baum Hedlund Aristei Goldman and Menzies Ste 950 12100 Wilshire Blvd Los Angeles CA 90025-7107 Office Phone: 310-207-3233. Business E-Mail: jgreaves@baumhedlundlaw.com.

GREAVES, ROGER F., health and medical products executive; b. 1937; BA, Calif. State U., Long Beach, 1962. With Allstate Ins. Co., Chgo. and Pasadena, Calif., 1962-68; various positions, then v.p. human resources Blue Cross So. Calif., 1968-82; pres., CEO Health Net, Inc., Woodland Hills, Calif., 1982—91, chmn. bd., 1989—; co-chmn bd., co-pres., co-CEO Health Systems Internat., Woodland Hills, 1991-95, non-exec. bd. dir., 1996—2004, non-exec. chmn., 2004—. Mem. Calif. Wellness Found. (bd. dirs.). Office: Health Net Life Insurance Co 21281 Burbank Blvd Woodland Hills CA 91367-6607*

GREAVES, WILLIAM WEBSTER, chemist; b. Queenstown, Md., Jan. 10, 1951; s. William Emory and Mary Elizabeth (Wood) G. BS in Chemistry, Bucknell U., 1973; PhD in Inorganic Chemistry, Iowa State U., 1978. Tech. publ. editor Standard Oil of Ind., Naperville, Ill., 1978-81, rsch. info. scientist, 1981-84; assoc. editor Science mag., Washington, 1984-86; supr. chem. data systems SK&F Labs., Upper Merion, Pa., 1986-88; sr. patent searcher Abbott Labs., Abbott Park, Ill., 1988-90; patent analyst Amoco Corp., Chgo., 1990-99; sr. staff chemist ExxonMobil Rsch. and Engring. Co., 1999—2002. Dir., cmty. liaison Chgo. Adv. Coun. on Lesbian, Gay, Bisexual and Transgender Issues, 2000—. Contbr. articles to profl. publs.; contbr. revs. to Lambda Book Report. Active Frontrunners Chgo., 1988—, sec., 1991, v.p., 1992, pres., 1993, past pres., 1994, Proud to Run com., 1996-99; active D.C. Front Runners, 1984—; mem. Chgo. Adv. Coun. on Gay and Lesbian Issues, 1994-99; Chgo. coord. track and field and marathon events Gay Games IV, NYC, 1994; mem. hon. bd. Gay Games VII, 2000-02; trustee Adler Sch. Profl. Psychology, Chgo., 2005—. Mem. AAAS, Am. Chem. Soc. (sec. chem. info. divsn. 1994-96, edn. com. Chgo. chpt. 1981-84, mgr. Chgo. chpt. student symposium 1982), Patent Info. Users Group, Soc. Tech. Comm. (sr., sec. Chgo. chpt. 1983), USA Track and Field, Chgo. Area Runners Assn., Stockton (N.J.) Runners Club, Sigma Xi. Office: Chgo Commn on Human Rels 740 N Sedgwick St Ste 300 Chicago IL 60610

GREBENC, JANE, bank executive; B in Econs., John Carroll U., Cleve.; MBA, Case Western Res. U., Cleve. Mgmt. trainee Br. Network Nat. City Corp., Cleve., 1982, br. mgr., lending officer, various leadership positions in sales mgmt., small bus. lending and mktg., sr. v.p., 1994—, exec. v.p. retail banking group Nat. City Bank Cleve., 1995, head comml. and consumer loan svcs. groups, 2003, nat. sales mgr. Pvt. Client Group. Bd. trustees The Gathering Pl. Office: Nat City Corp Nat City Ctr 1900 E Ninth St Cleveland OH 44114-3484 Office Phone: 216-222-2000.*

GREBNER, BERNICE PRILL, author, astrological counselor; b. Peoria, Ill. d. John Elmer and Emma (Duhs) Prill; m. Arthur Conrad Grebner (div. 1974); children: David Arthur, Marjorie Welsch. Astrological counsellor. Pres. Grebner Books Pub. Author: Lunar Nodes, 1980, The Decannates, 1980, Everything Has a Phase, 1982, Mercury, The Open Door I, 1988, Mercury, The Open Door II, 1990, Day of Your Birth, 1990, Bee's Flight, 1991, ABCs of Astrology and Astronomy, 1993; author of poetry. Chmn. Woodford County (Ill.) Citizens for John Kennedy. Mem. Am. Fedn. Astrologers (accreditd profl.). Avocation: music; composing and performing for audiences. Home and Office: 5137 N Montclair Ave Peoria IL 61616-5221

GREBNEV, IGOR, application developer; b. Petersburg, Russia, June 22, 1966; arrived in US, 1998; s. Vadim Grebnev and Aysa Skal; m. Lyana Mankin, Sept. 10, 1996. Undergrad., St. Petersburg U., 1987, MS (hon.) in Physics, 1989. Software developer Audible Inc., Wayne, NJ, 1998—2006, Microsoft Inc., Redmond, Wash., 2006—07. Avocation: acting. Home: 4306 156th Ave NE Apt OO241 Redmond WA 98052 Business E-Mail: igrebnev@microsoft.com.

GREBOW, EDWARD, finance company executive; b. Lakewood, NJ, July 17, 1949; s. Benjamin and Ruth (Blume) G.; m. Cynthia Miller, Feb. 23, 1985. BBA, George Washington U., 1971; postgrad., George Washington, 1972. V.p. Morgan Guaranty Trust Co., NYC, 1972-80, J.P. Morgan & Co., Inc., NYC, 1980-85; exec. v.p. Bowery Savs. Bank, NYC, 1985-88; sr. v.p. CBS, Inc., NYC, 1988-94, exec. v.p., 1994-95; pres. Tele-TV Sys., Reston, Va., 1995-97, Sony Electronics Broadcast and Profl. Co., 1999—2002, Met. TV Alliance, NYC, 2002—04, Ullico, Inc., Washington, 2003, Union Labor Life Ins. Co., 2003—06; pres., CEO Chyron Corp., Melville, NY, 1997-99; dep. pres. Sony Electronics, Inc., 2000—02; mng. dir. Tri-artisan Ptnrs., 2006—; operating ptnr. J.C. Flowers & Co., 2007—. Chmn. Morgan Data Svcs. Inc., Wilmington, Del., 1981-84; pres. J.P. Morgan Lease Funding Corp., NYC, 1982-84; bd. dirs. CBS Studio Ctr. Inc., Panavision, Inc. Bd. dirs., treas. Theater Devel. Fund, George Washington U., Ave of Americas Assn., Delaware Valley Opera, Am. Film Inst.; mem. N.Y. Hosp. Rev. and Planning Coun. Mem. Nat. Assn. Bank Cost and Mgmt. Acctg. Avocation: deep sea fishing. Home: 1136 Fifth Ave New York NY 10128-0122 Office Phone: 212-610-1525. Business E-Mail: egrebow@tri-artisan.com.

GREBSTEIN, SHELDON NORMAN, academic administrator; b. Providence, Feb. 1, 1928; s. Sigmund and Sylvia (Skotkin) G.; m. Phyllis Strumar, Sept. 6, 1953; children: Jason Lyle, Gary Wade. BA cum laude, U. So. Calif., 1949; MA, Columbia U., 1950; PhD, Mich. State U., 1954. Instr. then asst. prof. English U. Ky., 1953-62; asst. prof. U. South Fla., 1962-63; mem. faculty SUNY, Binghamton, 1963-81, prof. English, 1968-81, asst. to pres., 1974-75; dean arts and scis. Harpur Coll., 1975-81; pres. SUNY, Purchase, 1981-93, univ. prof. of lit., 1993-95; dir. edn. Holocaust and Human Rights Edn. Ctr., 1994—2007. Fulbright-Hays lectr. U. Rouen, France, 1968-69; vis. lectr. Caen U., Hull U., and Edinburgh U., 1969. Author: Sinclair Lewis, 1962, John O'Hara, 1966, Hemingway's Craft, 1973; Editor: Monkey Trial, 1960, Perspectives in Contemporary Criticism, 1968, Studies in For Whom The Bell Tolls, 1971; editorial cons. univ. presses, publishers.; Contbr. articles to profl. jours. E-mail: shelgreb28@aol.com.

GRECO, CHRISTOPHER JON, musician, composer, educator; b. Inglewood, Calif., July 19, 1959; s. Donald Rudolph and Sharon Marie Greco; m. Yvette Marcia Ybarra, Dec. 26, 1995. MusB, Calif. State U., LA, 1990—93, MA in Composition, 1993—95; D Musical Arts, UCLA, 2006. Free-lance performer/rec. artist- woodwinds, LA, 1982—; leader of ensembles (duo, trio, quartet, quintet, sextet), 1985—; composer Am. Soc. of Composers, Authors and Publishers, 1988—, pub. (pleiadian music), 1995—; rec. artist (composer/woodwinds) GWSFourwinds Records, Pasadena, 1995—; featured artist, Sept. Euro Club de Jazz, England, 2003. Composer: (compact disc) Trane of Thought, Pleiadian Call/Music for Trio; musician: Well You Needn't/Standards. Named dedication, A Stroll Down the Free Jazz/Avant-Garde Ave., All About Jazz, 2003; recipient Highly Recommended Performances, LA Weekly, 1990, 1991, 1992, 1993, 1994, 1996, Julius Hemphill Composition Award, Jazz Composers Alliance, 2001, Critics' Choice Performance, LA Reader, 1994, 1995, 1996, Recommended Performance, LA Times, 1997, Highly Recommended CD Rev., Jazz Jour. Internat., London U.K., 1996. Mem.: ASCAP (Plus award 2002, 2003, 2004, 2005, 2006), The Coll. Music Soc., Am. Music Ctr. Avocations: walking, gardening. Home Phone: 410-749-7542. Personal E-mail: c.j.greco@worldnet.att.net.

GRECO, JOSEPH A., lawyer; b. Sacramento, May 12, 1957; s. Joseph A. Greco Sr. and Shirley M. Greco; m. Roslyn M. Moschan, Jan. 24, 1981; children: Jason A., Justin A. AB magna cum laude, Dartmouth Coll., 1979; JD, Stanford Law Sch., 1982. Bar: Calif. 1982. Assoc. Fenwick, Davis & West, Palo Alto, Calif., 1982—86, Skjerven, Morrill, MacPherson, Franklin & Friel, San Jose, Calif., 1986—89, ptnr., 1989—97; dir. Howard, Rice, Nemerovski, Canady, Falk & Rabkin, Palo Alto, 1997—2001; of counsel Skjerven Morrill LLP, San Jose, 2001—03; spl. counsel Townsend and Townsend and Crew LLP, Palo Alto, 2003—05, ptnr., 2006—. Author: (essay) The California Droit de Suite Law (Nathan Burkan Meml. Competition, Stanford Law Sch., First Prize award, 1982). Recipient Order of the Coif award, Stanford Law Sch., 1982, Rufus Choate scholar, Dartmouth Coll., 1976—79, No. Calif. Super Lawyer award, Law & Politics Mag., 2005—07. Master: San Francisco Bay Area Intellectual Property Inn Ct.; mem.: ABA, Santa Clara County Bar Assn., Fed. Circuit Bar Assn., Phi Beta Kappa. Home: 1031 Estrellita Way Los Altos CA 94022 Office: Townsend and Townsend and Crew LLP 379 Lytton Ave Palo Alto CA 94301 Office Fax: 650-326-2422. Personal E-mail: jgreco57@yahoo.com. Business E-Mail: jagreco@townsend.com.

GRECO, MICHAEL S., lawyer; b. Rende, Cosenza, Italy, Nov. 22, 1942; came to U.S., 1950; s. Raphael and Rose (Felicetti) G.; children: Christian Raphael, Jordan Phillip, Elizabeth Elena. AB in English, Princeton U., NJ, 1965; JD, Boston Coll., 1972. Bar: Mass. 1972, U.S. Supreme Ct. 1979, U.S. Ct. Appeals (1st Cir. & Armed Forces), U.S. Tax Ct., U.S. Dist. Ct. (Mass. Dist.). Clk. U.S. Ct. Appeals for 2d Circuit, NYC, 1972-73; assoc. Hill & Barlow, Boston, 1973-79, ptnr., 1979—2003, Kirkpatrick & Lockhart Preston, Gates, Ellis LLP, 2003—. Mem. Mass. Bd. Bar Overseers, 1978-81, vice chmn., 1980-81; spl. asst. atty. gen. Dorchester Ct. Case, 1988-90; charter mem. overseers Mass. Supreme Jud. Ct. Hist. Soc., 1989—; mem. adv. com. Mass. Supreme Jud. Ct., 1990-93; mem. exec. com. Jud. Nominating Coun. Commonwealth of Mass., 1990-98; mem. acad. com. Flaschner Jud. Inst., 1990—; mem. Kennedy Commn. on Fed. Jud. Appointments, 1993; pres. Mass. Continuing Legal Edn., Inc., 1994-96. Editor-in-Chief Boston Coll. Law Rev., 1971-72 Mem. permanent sch. accommodations com. Wellesley, Mass., 1980-83; bd. overseers Newton (Mass.)-Wellesley Hosp., 1990-2000; founder Mass. Gov.'s Commn. on Unmet Legal Needs of Children, 1986-89; chmn. Mass. Legal Svcs. for the Poor Plan for Action, 1986-89; co-founder, co-chmn. Nat. Bar Leaders for Preservation Legal Svcs. for the Poor, 1986. Fellow Inst. Comparative Law, U. Florence, Italy, 1974. Fellow Am. Bar Found. (life), Mass. Bar Found. (treas., trustee 1982-90), ABA (chmn. standing com. on fed. judiciary 1998-99, mem. standing com. on law and nat. security

1991-93, Mass. state del. 1993—, chmn. IRR sect. 2000-01, mem. standing com. pres.-elect 2002-05, pres. 2005-06, past pres. 2006-2007); mem. Am. Law Inst., Am. Judicature Soc. (bd. dirs. 1988-92), New Eng. Bar Found. (pres. 1987-92), New Eng. Bar Assn. (pres. 1986-87), Mass. Bar Assn. (pres. 1985-86), Mass. Lawyers Alliance for Nuclear Arms Control (pres. 1988-91), Boston Coll Law Sch. Class of 1972 (law rev. editor in chief, pres.), Princeton U. Class of 1965 (v.p. 1985-90), Princeton Club (NYC), Wellesley Club. Democrat. Office: Kirkpatrick & Lockhart Preston, Gates, Ellis LLP State Street Financial Ctr One Lincoln St Boston MA 02111 Office Phone: 617-261-3232. Business E-Mail: michael.greco@klgates.com.

GRECO, RICHARD, JR., former civilian military employee; b. Mar. 5, 1969; m. Maria Greco; 4 children. BS summa cum laude, Fordham U.; MA, Johns Hopkins U.; MBA, U. Chgo. Assoc. Scowcroft Group; v.p., mng. dir. Stern Stewart & Co., 1997—2002; White House fellow, spl. asst. Immediate Office of Sec. Def., 2002—03; acting dir. pvt. sector devel. for Iraq Coalition Provisional Authority Rep. Office; asst. sec. (fin. mgmt. & comptr.) Dept. Navy, US Dept. Def., 2004—06. Mem. Coun. Fgn. Rels., 2001; mem. exec. steering group U.S. Naval Acad., Acquisition Integrity Bd.; lectr. in field. Contbr. articles to profl. jours. Founder, pres., chmn. bd. Montfort Acad. Named Man of Yr., Nat. Fedn. Italian-Am. Societies, 2004; recipient Ellis Island Medal of Honor, 2004.*

GRECO, RICHARD JUDE, plastic and reconstructive surgeon; b. Hazleton, Pa., Jan. 8, 1960; s. Victor Frank and Mary Jean Greco; m. Robin Emma Robinson, Jan. 30, 1981; children: Richard, Blake, Apryl, Dean. BS in Biology summa cum laude, Ursinus Coll., Collegeville, Pa., 1979; MD magna cum laude, Thomas Jefferson Med. Coll., Phila., Pa., 1983. Diplomate Am. Bd. Plastic Surgery, Am. Bd. Gen. Surgery; cert. Hand Surgery. Resident in gen. surgery Thomas Jefferson U. Hosp., Phila., 1983-88; fellow, hand surgery Hand Ctr., Phila., 1986—87; fellow, plastic surgery U. Pitts., 1988—90; asst. prof. surgery U. Pitts. Sch. Medicine, 1990—93; fellow, aesthetic surgery Manhattan Eye and Ear Hosp., NYC, 1990; dir. Telfair Breast Ctr. Candler Hosp., Savannah, Ga., 1993-97; CEO, pvt. practice Ga. Inst. for Plastic Surgery, Savannah, 1998—. Adv. bd. Consumer Guide to Plastic Surgery; hosp. appointment Meml. U. Hosp., Candler/St. Joseph Healthcare Sys.; presenter in field. Editor: Emergency Plastic Surgery, 1993; contbr. articles to profl. jours.; author med. text-books; featured in Allure, Wall St. Jour., London Times, Oprah mag., Cosmopolitan and others. Polit. adv. People for Pub. Edn., Savannah, 1997. Burroughs Welcome-AMA fellow, 1991. Fellow ACS; mem. AMA, Am. Soc. Plastic Surgery (past chmn. Pub. Edn. Com., mem. new device and tech. com., mem. online com.mem. adv. com. pub. edn. campaign), Am. Soc. Aesthetic Surgery (vice-chmn. pub. edn. com.), Lipoplasty Soc., Am. Soc. for Surgery Hand, Ga. Med. Soc., Jefferson Hand Club, Alpha Omega Alpha. Republican. Roman Catholic. Holds two patents relating to surg. practices. Office: Ga Inst Plastic Surgery 5361 Reynolds St Savannah GA 31405-6014 Office Phone: 800-260-7135. E-mail: plastxdoc@aol.com, greco@mycosmeticsurgeon.md.*

GREDEN, JOHN FRANCIS, psychiatrist, educator; b. Winona, Minn., July 24, 1942; m. Renee Mary Kalmes; children: Daniel John, Sarah Renee, Leigh Raymond. BS, U. Minn., 1965, MD, 1967. Diplomate Am. Bd. Psychiatry and Neurology. Assoc. dir. psychiat. rsch. Walter Reed Army Med. Ctr., Washington, 1972-74; asst. prof. dept. psychiatry U. Mich., Ann Arbor, 1974-77, assoc. prof., 1977-81, dir. clin. studies unit for affective disorders, 1980-85, prof., 1981—, chmn., prof., 1985—, chmn. faculty group practice, 1996—98, exec. dir. Depression Ctr., 2001—. Editor 3 books; contbr. more than 200 articles to profl. jours., more than 30 chpts. to books. Served to maj. U.S. Army, 1969-74. Recipient A.E. Bennett research award Cen. Neuropsychiat. Found., 1974, Nolan D.C. Lewis Vis. Scholar award Carrier Found., 1982. Fellow Am. Psychiat. Assn. (chair coun. on rsch. 2000—); mem. AAAS, Soc. Biol. Psychiatry (past pres., co-editor-in-chief Jour. Psychiatry Rsch. 1984-2000), Am. Coll. Neuropsychopharmacology (coun. 2001—, Psychiat. Rsch. Soc. (past pres.). Office: U Mich Med Ctr Dept Psychiatry 1500 E Medical Center Dr Ann Arbor MI 48109-0295

GREDZENS, SANDRA MAY PILLSBURY, art educator; b. Mpls., Sept. 30, 1949; d. Robert Kinsey and Elizabeth Anne (Massie) Pillsbury; m. David Inesis Gredzens, Nov. 25, 1989; stepchildren: Tabatha, Alex. AA, Stephens Coll., 1971; BFA, U. Calif. Santa Cruz, 1980; MEd, Hamline U., 1995. Cert. elem. and secondary educator. Lay-out artist Monterey (Calif.) Peninsula Herald, 1973-75; tchr.'s aide spl. edn., substitute tchr. Pacific Grove (Calif.) Unified Sch. Dist., 1978-82; educator art Shattuck-St. Mary's Sch., Faribault, Minn., 1982-84; tchr. elem. Woods Acad., Maple Plain, Minn., 1986-87; tchr. elem. art, art cons. Anoka (Minn.)-Hennepin Ind. Sch. Dist., 1987-97; art tchr. Lake Superior Sch. Dist., Two Harbors, Minn., 1997—2000. Exhibited in group shows at Grant Marais Art Colony, 1986—98, 2001—06, Itasca Art Assn. Exhbn., 1996, 1999, 2001, 2003, 2004, Sally Brown Collaborative Art Exhbn., 1995, Union St. Gallery, Chicago Heights, Ill., 2000, Duluth Art Inst., Minn., 2002—07, Lake County Ct. House Atrium, 2002, Vanilla Bean Bakery and Café, 2003, Johnson Heritage Post, Grand Marais, Minn., 2004, 2006, Schroeder Heritage Ctr., Minn., 2004—07. Mem. Nat. Art Educators Am., Art Educators Minn., Delta Phi Delta. Democrat. Lutheran. Avocations: painting, hiking, church activities, photography, gardening. Office Phone: 218-834-8201 ext 8313.

GREEF, CHARLES E. (STORMY GREEF), lawyer; b. Amarillo, Tex., Jan. 16, 1949; AB, Yale U., 1971; JD, U. Tex., 1974. Bar: Va. 1975, Tex. 1976. Shareholder Jenkens & Gilchrist, P.C., Dallas, firm leader fin. institutions practice group. Mem.: Va. State Bar Assn., Tex. State Bar Assn. Office: Jenkens & Gilchrist PC Ste 3200 1445 Ross Ave Dallas TX 75202-2799 Office Phone: 214-855-4337. Office Fax: 214-855-4300. Business E-Mail: cgreef@jenkens.com.

GREEFF, DOUGLAS HAVEN, cosmetics executive; b. NYC, Jan. 18, 1956; BA in Econs., Williams Coll., 1978; MS in Acctg., NYU, 1979. CPA, 1978. V.p. leverage capital dept. and global loans Citibank N.A., 1986-98; mng. dir. fixed income global loans Salomon Smith Barney, 1998-2000; CFO, exec. v.p. Revlon Inc., NYC, 2000—03; exec. v.p. Strategic Fin., 2004—. Office: Revlon Inc 237 Park Ave New York NY 10017 Home Phone: 917-692-9555; Office Phone: 212-527-6455. Business E-Mail: douglas@greeff.us.

GREEGARD, LESLIE F., mathematics professor; BA, Wesleyan U., 1979; MD, Yale U., PhD in Computer Sci., 1987. Prof. math. Courant Inst. of Math. Sci., NYU, NYC, 1989—. Editl. bd. SIAM Jour. Sci. Computing, Applied and Computational Harmonic Analysis, Computers and Math. with Applications; contbr. articles to profl. jours. Recipient Presdl. Young Investigator Award, NSF, 1990, Leroy P. Steele Prize, 2001; grantee Packard Found. Fellow, 1990. Mem.: NAE, Am. Math. Soc., Soc. for Industrial and Applied Math. Office: Courant Inst NYU 251 Mercer St New York NY 10012 Office Phone: 212-998-3306. Office Fax: 212-995-4121. E-mail: greengard@cims.nyu.edu.

GREEHEY, WILLIAM EUGENE (BILL GREEHEY), energy executive; b. Ft. Dodge, Iowa, 1936; married. BBA, St. Mary's U., San Antonio, 1960. Auditor Price Waterhouse & Co., 1960-61; sr. auditor Humble Oil and Refining Co., 1961-63; sr. v.p. fin. Coastal Corp. (and predecessor), 1963-74; with Valero Energy Corp., San Antonio, 1974—, chmn., CEO, 1979—2005, pres., 1998—2003, chmn., 2006—, Valero L.P., 2006—, Valero GP Holdings LLC, 2006—.*

GREEK, DAROLD I., lawyer; b. Kunkle, Ohio, Mar. 30, 1909; s. Albert F. and Iva (Shaffer) G.; m. Catherine Johnson, Oct. 12, 1935 (dec. 1962); 1 child, Darold I (dec.); m. Elizabeth Tracy Ridgley, Sept. 18, 1970 (dec. May 1972); stepchildren— Thomas B., David Ridgley; m. Nadine Berry Weisheimer Bivens, Dec. 23, 1976; stepchildren— Richard A. Weisheimer, Jon B. Weisheimer. Student, Bowling Green State U., 1926-28; LL.B., Ohio State U., 1932. Bar: Ohio 1932. Treas., Williams County, Ohio, 1932-33; atty. Ohio Dept. Taxation, 1934-36; practiced in Columbus, 1937-89; ptnr. George, Greek, King, McMahon & McConnaughey (and predecessors), 1937-79; of counsel Baker & Hostetler, 1979-89. Mem. Ohio Bar Assn., Columbus Bar Assn. (pres. 1966-67), The Golf Club, Naples Yacht Club, Hole in the Wall Golf Club. Presbyterian. Home (Summer): 6635 Lake of Woods Pt Galena OH 43021 Office Phone: 614-228-1541.

GREELEY, ANDREW MORAN, sociologist, writer; b. Oak Park, Ill., Feb. 5, 1928; s. Andrew T. and Grace G. AB, St. Mary of Lake Sem., 1950, STL, 1954; MA, U. Chgo., 1961, PhD, 1962; LHD (hon.), Bowling Green State U., 1986, No. Mich., 1993; HHD (hon.), St. Louis U., 1991; LHD, LLD, Ariz. State U., 1998; LHD (hon.), U. San Francisco, 2002, Bard Coll., 2002; LLD (hon.), Nat. U. Ireland, Galway, 2003. Ordained priest Roman Cath. Ch., 1954. Asst. pastor Ch. of Christ the King, Chgo., 1954-64; sr. study dir. Nat. Opinion Rsch. Ctr., Chgo., 1962-68; dir. Ctr. for Study Am. Pluralism, from 1973; lectr. sociology U. Chgo., 1963-72; prof. sociology U. Ariz., Tucson, from 1978, now adj. prof.; prof. social sci. U. Chgo., 1991—. Cons. Hazen Found. Commn. Columnist Daily Southtown; guest columnist Chgo. Sun Times, 1985—; Author: The Church and the Suburbs, 1959, Strangers in the House, 1961, Religion and Career, 1963, (with Peter H. Rossi) Education of Catholic Americans, 1966, Changing Catholic College, 1967, Come Blow Your Mind With Me, 1971, Life for a Wanderer: A New Look at Christian Spirituality, 1971, The Denominational Society: A Sociological Approach to Religion in America, 1972, Priests in the United States: Reflections on A Survey, 1972, That Most Distressful Nation, 1972, New Agenda, 1973, Jesus Myth, 1971, Unsecular Man, 1974, Ethnicity in the United States: A Preliminary Reconnaissance, 1974, Ecstasy: A Way of Knowing, 1974, Building Coalitions: American Politics in the 1970's, 1974, Sexual Intimacy, 1975, Denomination Society, 1975, The Great Mysteries: An Essential Catechism, 1976, The Communal Catholic: A Personal Manifesto, 1976, Death and Beyond, 1976, The American Catholic: A Social Portrait, 1977, The Making of the Popes, 1978, 79, The Magic Cup: An Irish Legend, 1979, Women I've Met, 1979, Why Can't They Be Like Us?, 1980, Death In April, 1980, The Cardinal Sins, 1981, Religion: A Secular Theory, 1982, Thy Brother's Wife, 1982, Ascent Into Hell, 1983, Lord of the Dance, 1984, Virgin & Martyr, 1985, Piece of My Mind on Just About Everything, 1985, Happy are the Meek, 1985, The Magic Cup, 1985, God Game, 1986, Happy Are the Clean of Heart, 1986, Confessions of a Parish Priest, 1986, Patience of a Saint, 1987, Rite of Spring, 1987, Angels of September, 1986, Happy Are Those Who Thirst For Justice, 1987, The Final Planet, 1987, Angel Fire, 1988, (photography) Andrew Greeley's Chicago, 1989, Love Song, 1989, St. Valentine's Night, 1989, The Bible and Us, 1990, The short stories All About Women, 1990, (photography) The Irish, 1990, The Catholic Myth: The Behavior and Beliefs of American Catholics, 1990, The Cardinal Virtues, 1990, Faithful Attraction: Discovering Intimacy, Love, and Fidelity in American Marriage, 1991, The Search for Maggie Ward, 1991, An Occasion of Sin, 1991, Happy Are the Merciful, 1992, Wages of Sin, 1992, Fall from Grace, 1993, Sacraments of Love: A Prayer Journal, 1994, Irish Gold, 1994, Happy are the Poor Spirit, 1994, Happy are Those Who Mourn, 1995, Angel Light: An Old-Fashioned Love Story, 1995, Windows: A Prayer Journal, 1995, Religion as Poetry, 1995, Sociology and Religion, 1995, White Smoke, 1996, Irish Lace, 1996, Happy Are The Oppressed, 1996, (with J. Neusner) Common Ground: A Priest and a Rabbi Read Scripture Together, 1996, Summer at the Lake, 1997, Star Bright!, 1997, The Bishop at Sea, 1997, I Hope You're Listening, God: A Prayer Journal, 1997, Irish Whiskey, 1998, Contract with an Angel, 1998, The Bishop and the Three Kings, 1998, A Mid-Winter's Tale, 1998, Furthermore! Memories of a Parish Priest, 1999, 2000, The Bishop and the Missing L Train, 2000, Christmas Wedding, 2000, Irish Love, 2001, The Bishop and the Begger Girl of St. Germain, 2001, September Song, 2001, Irish Stew, 2002, The Bishop in the West Wing, 2002, The Bishop Goes to the University, 2003, Irish Cream, 2005, The Making of the Pope 2005, 2005, The Bishop in the Old Neighborhood: A Blackie Ryan Story, 2005, Irish Crystal, 2006, (with Mary Durkin) The Book of Love, 2002, The Bishop Goes to The University, 2003; (with Chilton, Green, and Neusner) Forging a Common Future, 1996, The Catholic Imagination, 2000, (with Albert Bergesen) God in the Movies, 2000, My Love: A Prayer Journal, 2001, Letters to a Loving God, 2002, Second Spring, 2003, Religion in Europe at the End of the Second Millennium, 2003; The Catholic Revolution: New Wine, Old Wineskins, and the Second Vatican Council, 2004; Priests: A Calling in Crisis, 2004; The Priestly Sins, 2004; editor: Emerald Magic, 2004, Golden Years, 2004, Making of the Pope 2005, 2005; contbr. articles to profl. jours. Recipient Cath. Press Assn. award for best book for young people, 1965, Thomas Alva Edison award for radio broadcast, 1962, C. Albert Kobb award Nat. Cath. Edn. Assn., 1977, Mark Twain award Soc. Study Midwestern Lit., 1987, Popular Culture award Ctr. Study of Popular Culture, 1988, Freedom to Read award Friends Chgo. Pub. Libr., 1989, U.S. Cath. award, 1993, Ill. Outstanding Citizen award Coll. Lake County, 1993, Quigley Disting. Alumni award, 1997; named to Top 100 Irish Ams. Irish Am. Mag, 1992, named Irish Am. of Century Irish Am. Mag., 1999. Mem. Am. Sociol. Assn., Soc. for Sci. Study Religion, Religious Research Assn. Office Phone: 773-256-6281.

GREELEY, BURNHAM H., lawyer; b. Mapleton, Minn., Feb. 13, 1934; BA, Grinnell Coll., 1956; LLB, Harvard U., 1959. Bar: Hawaii 1960. Ptnr. Greeley Walker & Kowen, Honolulu. Bd. dir. Kuakini Medical Ctr.; mem. Hawaii Federal Jud. Selection comm. Fellow Am. Bar Found.; mem. ABA (ho. of dels. 1989-91, bd. gov. 2003-2006, chmn. Coalition for Justice comm.), Hawaii State Bar Assn. (pres. 1987), Am. Inn of Ct. IV Hawaii chptr., Am. Judicature Soc. Hawaii chptr. (dir., chmn. Civil Justice comm.). Office: Burnham H Greeley 4189 Round Top Dr Honolulu HI 96822-5039*

GREELY, HANNAH, artist; BA, U. Calif., LA, 2002. One-woman shows include Andrea Rosen Gallery, 2004—05, exhibited in group shows at Sentimental Education, Deitch Projects, NYC, 2000, Drawing Show, Black Dragon Soc., Vienna, 2001, Julius Hummel Gallery, Vienna, 2002, Spoils, Coleman Gallery, LA, 2001, Face Off, The Smell, LA, 2001, Something of that Nature, Black Dragon Soc., LA, 2001, Clandestine, Venice Biennial, 2003, Trance Plants, Latch Gallery, LA, 2003, Another Sculpture Show, Angstrom Gallery, Dallas, 2003, Black Dragon Soc., apex Art, NYC, 2004, Waste Material, The Drawing Room, London, 2005, Day for Night, Whitney Biennial, 2006. Office: Andrea Rosen Gallery 525 W 24th St New York NY 10011*

GREELY, HENRY T. (HANK), law educator; b. 1952; AB in Polit. Sci., Stanford U., 1974; JD, Yale U., 1977. Law clk. to Hon. John Minor Wisdom US Ct. Appeals 5th Cir., 1977—78; law clk. to Hon. Potter Stewart US Supreme Ct., 1978—79; spl. asst. to gen. counsel Deanne C. Siemer US Dept. Def., 1979; staff asst. to Sec. Energy Charles W. Duncan, Jr., 1979—81; assoc. Tuttle & Taylor, LA, 1981—84, ptnr., 1984—85; assoc. prof. Stanford Law Sch., 1985—92, prof., 1992—, C. Wendell and Edith M. Carlsmith prof. law, 2002—04, Deane F. and Kate Edelman Johnson prof. law, 2004—; dir. Stanford Program in Law, Sci. & Tech., 2000—01; co-dir. Stanford Program on Genomics, Ethics, and Soc., 1995—2000; dir. Stanford Ctr. for Law and Biosciences, Stanford Program on Stem Cells & Soc., 2005—. Mem. Calif. Adv. Com. on Human Cloning, 1999—, Calif. Adv. Com. on Human Stem Cell Rsch., 2005—. Office: Stanford Law Sch Crown Quadrangle 559 Nathan Abbott Way Stanford CA 94305-8610 Business E-Mail: hgreely@stanford.edu.

GREEN, ADELE C., educator; b. Boston, Oct. 20, 1938; d. Benjamin and Leona (Rick) Cohen: m. Leonard N. Green, June 25, 1960; children: Lawrence Jeffrey, Stuart Avery, Joshua Steven. BE, Boston State Coll., 1960; MA, Hunter Coll., 1963; PhD, Kent State U., 1985. Instr. ESL Youngstown (Ohio) Internat. Inst., 1964-83, curriculum developer ESL, 1973-85; lectr., cons. ESL Youngstown (Ohio) Bd. Edn., 1985—; instr. psychology Youngstown State U., 1985—. Presenter of papers conf. in ESL and newropsychology North America., 1978—. Author: Becoming Fluent in English, 1974; co-author Situational Exercises in Cross-Cultural Awareness; researcher/author chpts. in textbooks, reviewer. Trustee and founder Liberty Edn. Endowment, Inc. Liberty Twp., Ohio, 1979—, Youngstown Internat. Inst., women's div. Youngstown Jewish Fedn., v.p. 1979-81, Akiva Acad., Youngstown, 1986. Grantee cons. Youngstown State U. and U. Del., 1987—. Mem. Internat. Neuropsychol. Soc., Am. Psychol Assn., Am. Edn. Rsch. Assn., Tchrs. English to Speakers of Other Langs., Sigma Xi, Kappa Delta Pi. Avocation: aerobics. Office: Youngstown State U Psychology Dept Debartolo Bldg Youngstown OH 44555-0001

GREEN, AHMAN RASHAD, professional football player; b. Omaha, Nebr., Feb. 16, 1977; m. Heather Green; children: Ahmani, Myahni. BS in Geology, U. Neb., 1998. Running back Seattle Seahawks, 1998—2000, Green Bay Packers, 2000—06, Houston Texans, 2007—. Founder Ahman Green Foundation for Youth Development, 2001. Named to Nat. Football Conf. (NFC) Pro-Bowl Team, 2001—04. Office: Houston Texans 2 Reliant Pk Houston TX 77054*

GREEN, AL, congressman; b. New Orleans, Sept. 1, 1947; Student, Fla. A&M U., 1971, Tuskegee Inst. Tech.; JD, Tex. So. U. Thurgood Marshall Sch. Law, 1974. Founder, mng. ptnr. Green, Wilson, Dewberry & Fitch, Houston, 1974; justice of peace Precinct 7 Position 2, Houston, 1977—2004; mem. US Congress from 9th Tex. dist., 2005—, mem. fin. svcs. com., mem. sci. com. Past pres. Houston Br. NAACP. Named one of 100 Most Influential Black Americans, Ebony mag., 2006; recipient Disting. Svc. award, Houston Citizens C. of C., 1978, Outstanding Leadership award, Black Heritage Soc., 1981, Citation for Svc., Am. Fedn. Tchrs., 1983. Democrat. Baptist. Office: US Ho Reps 1529 Longworth Ho Office Bldg Washington DC 20515-4309 Office Phone: 202-225-7508.*

GREEN, ALEX EDWARD SAMUEL, physicist, mechanical engineering educator; b. NYC, June 2, 1919; s. Joseph Marvin and Celia (Kahn) G.; m. Freda Kaplow, June 2, 1946; children: Bruce, Deborah, Marcia, Linda, Tamara. BS in Physics, CCNY, 1940; MS, Calif. Inst. Tech., 1941; PhD, U. Cin., 1948. Exptl. physicist Calif. Inst. Tech., Pasadena, 1940-43; assoc. prof. U. Cin., 1946-53; prof. and dir. nuclear sci. Fla. State U., Tallahassee, 1953-59; mgr. space sci. lab. Convair, San Diego, 1959-63; grad. research prof. U. Fla., Gainesville, 1963—, dir. Interdisciplinary Ctr. for Aeronomy and (other) Atmospheric Scis., 1970—; cons. in field. Author: Nuclear Physics, 1955, Atomic and Space Physics, 1965, Nuclear Shell and Optical Model, 1968; editor, contbg. author: Middle Ultraviolet, 1966, Medical Waste Incarceration, 1992, Defense Conversion, 1995; assoc. editor Internat. Jour. Power and Energy Sys. Served with USAF, 1944-45, Asia, Mariannas. Decorated Medal of Freedom; recipient citation for outstanding overseas service War Dept., 1945; named Outstanding Scientist of Fla., Fla. Acad. Sci., 1975 Fellow Am. Phys. Soc., Optical Soc. Am.; mem. Am. Legion. Democrat. Office: ICAAS U Fla PO Box 112050 Gainesville FL 32611-2050 E-mail: aesgreen@ufl.edu.

GREEN, ALVIN, lawyer, consultant; b. Elgin, Ill., Mar. 13, 1931; s. Samuel and Rose (Brustein) G.; m. Miriam E. Blau, June 13, 1954 (dec.); children: Andrew, Marie, Jennifer. BA, U. Mich., 1953, MA, 1954; LLB, Harvard U., 1957. Bar: NY. Atty. Eastern Air Lines, Inc., NYC, 1957-65; asst. to gen. counsel C.I.T. Corp., NYC, 1965-70, gen. counsel, 1970-72; v.p. Condren, Walker & Co., NYC, 1972-75; v.p., gen. counsel, sec. Seatrain Lines, Inc., NYC, 1975-81, exec. v.p., co-CEO, sr. counsel, 1981-90; exec. v.p. Seatrain Tankers Inc., 1987-90, Bay Tankers Inc., 1981-90, Bay Ocean Mgmt. Inc., 1990—95. Arbitrator Nat. Assn. Securities Dealers, Nat. Futures Assn.; chmn., of counsel Seham, Seham Meltz & Petersen; cons. in field. Bd. dirs. Inst. for Child, Adolescent and Family Studies, NYC, Learning Leaders, NYC, Gray Matters. Woodrow Wilson fellow, 1953—54. Mem.: ABA, Am. Bur. Shipping, Assn. of Bar of City of N.Y. (mem. com. on admiralty), Harvard Club (N.Y.C.), Phi Beta Kappa, Phi Kappa Phi. Home and Office: 145 E 48th St 5F New York NY 10017 Office Phone: 212-644-3707. Personal E-mail: green_alvin@hotmail.com.

GREEN, ANGEL YVONNE, literature educator; b. NYC, Oct. 24, 1955; d. Henry Arthur Moss and Lillie Vera Harris; m. Joseph Cecil Green, Nov. 18, 1975 (div. Feb. 1979); 1 child, Gabriel Veran. Baccalaureate English, U. R.I., 1986, Masters English, 1997, PhD English, 2001; Baccalaureate Psychology, Coll. Continuing Edn./U. R.I., Providence, 1995. On-call police matron Newport and Jamestown Police Depts., RI, 1986—95; tchg. asst. U. R.I., Kingston, 1995—2000, fellow Grad. Sch., 2000—01, adj. faculty, 2001—. Vol. Literacy Vol. Am., Newport, RI, 1995—2002; enrichment instr. Talent Devel., U. R.I., Kingston, 1996—2002. Author short stories. Bd. mem. Wahid, Newport, 1986—90, First Step Newport County, Newport, 1990—95. With USN, 1973, with USNR, 1976—98. Recipient MLK Scholarship award, Providence Pub. Schs., 1995—98. Mem.: MLA, NAACP, Mensa. Home: 21-E Rolling Green Rd Newport RI 02840 Office: Univ RI Feinstein Coll Continuing Edn 80 Washington St Providence RI 02903 Personal E-mail: blublocker21@aol.com.

GREEN, ASA NORMAN, academic administrator; b. Mars Hill, Maine, July 22, 1929; s. Clayton John and Annie Glenna (Shaw) G.; m. Elizabeth Jean Zirkelbach Ross, May 27, 1965; 1 son, Stephen Richard Ross. AB cum laude, Bates Coll., Lewiston, Maine, 1951; MA, U. Ala., 1955; LL.D., Jacksonville U., Ala., 1975. Rsch. dir. Ala. League Municipalities, Montgomery, 1955-57; city mgr. Mountain Brook, Ala., 1957-65; exec. sec. Ala. Assn. Ins. Agts., 1965-66; dir. devel. Birmingham-So. Coll., 1966-71; dir. devel. and communications Dickinson Coll., Carlisle, Pa., 1971-73; pres. Livingston (Ala.) U., 1973-93; pres. emeritus Livingston U., 1993—; pres. U. So. Ala. Found., 2004—. Cons. NCAA Pres.'s Commn., 1993—99; instr. polit. sci. U. Ala. Ext. Ctr., Montgomery and Birmingham, 1955—57, 1958—60. Author: Revenue for Alabama Cities, 1956. Mem. adminstrv. bd. Livingston United Methodist Ch., 2005—; bd. dirs. U. South Ala. Found., 1997—, pres. Ala., 2004—. With CIC US Army, 1952—54. Grad. fellow So. Regional Tng. Program in Pub. Adminstrn., 1951 Mem.: Phi Beta Kappa. Independent. Methodist. Office: PO Box 1466 Livingston AL 35470-1620

GREEN, BARTH, neurosurgeon; b. Shoemaker, Calif., 1945; m. Kathy Green; children: Jeremy, Jared, Jenna. BA, Ind. U., 1966; MD, Ind. U. Sch. Medicine, 1969. Diplomate Am. Bd. Neurological Surgeons. Intern, general surgery Henry Ford Hosp., Detroit, 1969—70; resident, neurosurgery Northwestern U. Sch. Med., Chgo., 1970—75; joined U. Miami Med. Ctr., 1975; prof., chmn., dept. neurological surgery U. Miami Sch. Medicine, prof. orthopedics and rehabilitation; chief neurosurgery Jackson Meml. Hosp., VA Med. Ctr., Miami. Vis. prof. at several Am. and internat. universities and med. schools. Mem. editl. bd. Spine Universe. Pres., bd. dir. Ctr. for Haitians Studies and Health Services; co-founder, chmn. bd. Shake-a-Leg, Miami, 1995—; co-founder Miami Project to Cure Paralysis, 1985—, past pres.; co-founder Project Medishare, Haiti. Lt. Col. US Army Med. Reserve. Named to Spinal Cord Injury Hall of Fame, Nat. Spinal

Cord Injury Assn., 2006; recipient Spirit Excellence award, Miami Herald, Spl. medal, Soviet Acad. Sciences, Health Care Hero award, New Miami Mag., St. Marten De Porres Social Justice award, Southern Dominican Order of Preachers, Joseph R. Narot award for Cmty. Svc., Temple Israel, Karolinska Inst. Large Silver medal, Stockholm. Fellow: Am. Coll. Surgeons. Office: U Miami Dept Neurological Surgery 1095 NW 14th Terr Miami FL 33136 Office Phone: 305-243-3254.

GREEN, BERT FRANKLIN, JR., retired psychology professor; b. Honesdale, Pa., Nov. 5, 1927; s. Bert Franklin and Emily May (Brown) Green; m. Hasseltine Beck Robinson, Apr. 29, 1961 (div. 1974); children: Malcolm, Edward. AB, Yale, 1949; MA, Princeton, 1950, PhD, 1951. Mem. psychology group Lincoln Lab., MIT, 1951-62, leader, 1958-62; cons. RAND Corp., 1961; prof. psychology Carnegie Inst. Tech., Pitts., 1962-69, head psychology dept., 1962-67; prof. Johns Hopkins, Balt., 1969-98, prof. emeritus, 1998—. Author: Digital Computers in Research, 1963. Mem.: APA, Am. Edn. Rsch. Assn. (Lindquist award for Excellence Rsch. Measurement 2001), Psychometric Soc., Am. Statis. Assn. Home: 311 Eastway Ct Baltimore MD 21212-4710 Office Phone: 410-516-7074. Personal E-mail: bfgreen@verizon.net. Business E-Mail: bfgreen@jhu.edu.

GREEN, BETTY NIELSEN, education educator, consultant; b. Copenhagen, Apr. 30, 1937; came to U.S., 1979; d. Alfred Christian Josef and Lilly Nielsen; m. Philip Irving Green, Apr. 16, 1962; children: Ruth, Erik, Nils. AA in Fgn. Lang., Daytona Beach C.C., 1981; BA in Liberal Arts, U. Ctrl. Fla., 1986; MS in TESOL, Nova Southeastern U., 1988; EdD in Curriculum and Instrn., U. Ctrl. Fla., 1994. Cert. tchr., Fla.; cert. TESOL trainer, Fla. Tchr. TESOL, program mgr. English Lang. Inst. Daytona Beach CC, Fla., 1986—91; tchr. TESOL, fgn. lang. specialist Volusia County Schs., Daytona Beach, 1991—; tchr. trainer, facilitator Nova Southeastern U., Ft. Lauderdale, Fla., 1991—. Cons. TESOL, Ormond Beach, Fla., 1991; adj. faculty, Daytona Beach, 1997—; chair Fla. Consortium Multilingual-Multicultural Edn., 2001— Author, editor Teaching Assistant Manual, 1987; editor Unitarian Universalist Soc. newsletter, 1987—, religious editl. dir., 1996—; editor UN Local Chptr. News Letter, 2006—. Pres. Unitarian Universalists, Ormond Beach, 1982-84, NE Cluster Unitarian Universalists, Volusia, 1982-86; pres., v.p. S.E. Unitarian Universalists Sem. Inst., Blacksburg, Va., 1985-89. Mem. TESOL, ASCD, Sunshine State TESOL (mem.-at-large 1999—, 2d v.p., 1st v.p., pres. 2003-04, editor messenger newsletter), N.E. Fla. TESOL (pres. 1995—, editor newsletter 1998—), Nat. Coun. Tchrs. English, Fla. Fgn. Lang. Assn. (membership bd., editor Fla. Fgn. Lang. jour. 2001—), Fgn. Lang. Adminstrn. and Mgmt. Edn. (sec. 1995-97, pres. 1998, Supr. of Yr. 2006), Fla. Assn. Bilingual Edn. Suprs. (sec. 1995), Fla. Consortium on Multicultural Edn. (chair), Phi Kappa Phi, Kappa Delta Pi, Pi Delta Kappa, Phi Delta Kappa Democrat. Avocations: foreign languages, research on second language and multi-cultural educations, music, travel. Home: 771 W River Oak Dr Ormond Beach FL 32174-4641 Office: Volusia County Schs 729 Loomis Ave Daytona Beach FL 32114-4723 Office Phone: 386-255-6475 ext 60147. Personal E-mail: bngreen@fastmail.us. Business E-Mail: bngreen@volusia.k12.fl.us.

GREEN, CAROL H., lawyer, educator; b. Seattle, Feb. 18, 1944; BA in History/Journalism summa cum laude, La. Tech. U., 1965; MSL, Yale U., 1977; JD, U. Denver, 1979. Reporter Shreveport (La.) Times, 1965-66, Guam Daily News, 1966-67; city editor Pacific Jour., Agana, Guam, 1967-68, reporter, editl. writer, 1968-76, legal affairs reporter, 1977-79; asst. editor editl. page Denver Post, 1979-81, house counsel, 1980-83, labor rels. mgr., 1981-83; assoc. Holme Roberts & Owen, 1983-85; v.p. human resources and legal affairs Denver Post, 1985-87, mgr. circulation, 1988-90; gen. mgr. Distbn. Systems Am., Inc., 1990-92; dir. labor rels. Newsday, 1992-95, dir. comm. and labor rels., 1995—96; v.p. Weber Mgmt. Cons., 1996—98; v.p. human resources and labor rels. Denver Post, 1998—2000; v.p. human resources, labor rels. Denver Newspaper Agy., 2001—06, sr. v.p., labor rels. and legal affairs, 2006—. 1985 speaker for USIA, India, Egypt; mem. Mailers Tech. Adv. Com. to Postmaster Gen., 1991-92. Recipient McWilliams award for juvenile justice, Denver, 1971, award for interpretive reporting Denver Newspaper Guild, 1979. Mem.: ABA, Soc. Human Resources Mgmt., Colo. and Internat. Women's Forum, Denver Bar Assn. (co-chair jud. selection and benefits com. 1982—85, 2nd v.p. 1986), Newspaper Assn. Am. (mem. human resources and labor rels. com.), Colo. Bar Assn. (bd. govs. 1985—87, chair BAR-press com. 1980), Leadership Denver. Episcopalian.

GREEN, CAROLE L., lawyer; b. Queens, NY, Mar. 17, 1959; d. Gerald Harry and Mary (Clark) Green. AB cum laude with distinction, Dartmouth Coll., 1980; JD, Harvard Law Sch., 1983. Bar: NY. Congl. aide to rep. John Conyers U.S. House of Reps., Washington, 1980; assoc. real estate Kaye Scholer LLP, NY, 1983—85, Richards & O'Neil, NYC, 1985—87; gen. counsel Petrie Stores Corp., Secaucus, N.J., 1987-88; assoc. counsel Mfrs. Hanover Trust Co. (now JP Morgan Chase Bank), NYC, 1988-91; v.p., asst. gen. counsel Chem. Bank (now JP Morgan Chase Bank), NYC, 1991-96; contract atty. NYC, 1996—; pub. arbitrator NASD Dispute Resolution, 1996—. Mem.: ABA, Practicing Attys. for Law Students, Inc. (founding mem. 1986—95, bd. dirs. 2004—), Assn. Bar City N.Y., N.Y. State Bar Assn., Black Alumni of Dartmouth Assn. Avocations: travel, jazz, reading. Office Phone: 212-613-0099.

GREEN, CATHERINE COOPER, artist; b. Bozeman, Mont., Oct. 2, 1948; d. David Lawrence and Mary Francis Cooper; m. Timothy Haskell Green, June 14, 1970. BFA, Temple U., 1970. Art tchr. Rumford (Maine) Sch. Sys., 1970-72, Newburyport (Mass.) Sch. Sys., 1972-86; instr. divsn. continuing edn. U. N.H., Durham, 1979-89; artist Stratham, NH, 1989—. Yankee Mag., 1985, exhibited in group shows at Westfield Art Festival, 1993, Stamford Art Festival, 1993, On the Green Art Show, 1994, 1995, Nat. Print Biennial, 1996, Nat. Print Competition Artlink, Ft. Wayne, 1997, 1998, 2000—05, Calif. State U., 1997, 2002, Works on Paper, U. W. Fla., 2000, Prescott Park Arts Festival, 2005 (Hon. mention, 2005, 2006). Recipient Yankee Print award, Yankee Mag., 1983, Most Creative Print award, League of N.H. Craftsmen, 2005. Mem.: Newburyport Art Assn., NH Art Assn., League NH Craftsmen (mem. stds. com. 1988—, print jury mem. 1989—, v.p. bd. trustees, stds. and edn. mgr.), Exeter League NH Craftsmen Jury (chair 1989—95). Avocations: sailing, racquetball, organic gardening, tai chi, cooking. Home: 128 Bunker Hill Ave Stratham NH 03885-2411 Business E-Mail: info@catherinegreenart.net.

GREEN, CLAUDE, information company executive; b. Jan. 14, 1950; B. in Economics, Kings Coll., Cambridge, Eng. Qualified acct., 1975. Joined Reuters, 1978, various fin. mgmt. positions in the UK, France, Switzerland, and the Nordic countries, internat. sales develop. mgr. historical info. products, mng. dir. Reuters UK and Ireland's Internat. div., 1996, mng. dir. Reuters Health Info., 1998; deputy CEO Factiva, 1999—2006, interim CEO, 2006—. Office: Factiva PO Box 300 Princeton NJ 08543-0300 Business E-Mail: claude.green@factiva.com.

GREEN, DAN, publishing executive; b. Passaic, NJ, Sept. 28, 1935; s. Harold and Bessie (Roslow) G.; m. Jane Oliphant, Sept. 20, 1959; children— Matthew Kenan, Simon Pom. BA, Syracuse U., NY, 1956. Publicity dir. Dover Press, 1957-58, Sta. WNAC-TV, 1958-59, Bobbs-Merrill Co., 1959-62; with Simon & Schuster Inc., 1962-85, assoc. publisher, 1976-80, v.p., pub., 1980-84, pres. trade pub. group, 1984-85; founder, pub. Kenan Press, 1979-80; chief exec. officer Wheatland Pub., NYC, 1985-89; pub. Weidenfeld & Nicolson N.Y., 1985-89; chief exec. officer Grove Press, Inc., NYC, 1985-89; pres. Kenan Books, NYC, 1989—. Pres. Pom Literary Agy., 1989. Office: Pom Inc 611 Broadway Rm 907B New York NY 10012-2608 Home Phone: 516-487-3441; Office Phone: 212-673-3835. Personal E-mail: pominc@verizon.net.

GREEN, DANA I., lawyer, human resources specialist; b. 1949; BA, Ind. U., 1971, JD, 1974; LLM in Taxation, DePaul U., 1990. Bar: Ill. 1974. Atty. through dept. dir., employee rels. Walgreen Co., 1974—98, div. v.p., employee rels., 1998—2000, corp. v.p., human resources, 2000—04, sr. v.p., 2004—05, sr. v.p., gen. counsel, corp. sec., 2005—. Office: Walgreen Co 200 Wilmot Rd Deerfield IL 60015 Office Phone: 847-914-2500. Office Fax: 847-914-2804. E-mail: dana.green@walgreens.com.*

GREEN, DAVID, hematologist; b. Phila., 1934; AB, U. Pa., 1956; MD, Jefferson Med. Coll., 1960; PhD, Northwestern U., 1974. Cert. Am. Bd. Internal Medicine, 1967, in Hematology 1972. Intern Cook County Hosp., Chgo., 1960—61; resident, internal medicine Jefferson Hosp., Phila., 1961—63, fellow, hematology, 1963—64; attending physician Northwestern Meml. Hosp., Chgo., 1975—, 1993—; prof. Northwestern U., 1975—. Office Phone: 312-695-0990.

GREEN, DAVID, nonprofit organization administrator; b. 1956; m. Tanya Shaffer; 1 child, Tavi. BA, U. Mich., 1978, MPH, 1982. With Seva Found. Aravind Eye Hosp., Madurai, India, 1983—2000, founder Aurolab, 1992; founder, CEO Project Impact, Inc., 2000—. Named MacArthur Fellow, John D. and Catherine T. MacArthur Found., 2004, Ashoka Fellow. Achievements include first to establish a non-profit manufacturing facility in a developing country which produces, manufactures and distributes affordable medical technologies. Office: Project Impact 1782 Fifth St Berkeley CA 94710 Office Phone: 510-981-1103. Office Fax: 313-668-6861.

GREEN, DAVID EDWARD, retired librarian, priest, translator; b. Adrian, Mich., June 22, 1937; s. Edward Robert Alexander and Fannie Amelia (Nadler) G.; m. Sharon Weiner, June 1, 1961; children: Alexis Ann, Philip DeWitt. BA, Harvard U., 1960; BD, Ch. Div. Sch. of Pacific, Berkeley, Calif., 1963; MLS, U. Calif., Berkeley, 1970. Ordained priest Episc. Ch., 1964. Assoc. librarian Grad. Theol. Union, Berkeley, 1970-82; libr. dir. Gen. Theol. Sem., NYC, 1982—2002. Translator many German theol. works. Mem. Am. Theol. Libr. Assn., N.Y. Area Theol. Libr. Assn., Beta Phi Mu. Avocation: English country dancing. Office: 6103 Harwood Ave Oakland CA 94618 E-mail: degreen@post.harvard.edu.

GREEN, DAVID WILLIAM, chemist, educator; b. Hudson, Mich., Nov. 19, 1942; s. Francis Harger and Dorotha Louise (Onweller) G.; m. Mary Sarah McCullough, July 8, 1967; children: Laura, Brenda, Mark, Brian, William. BA, Albion Coll., 1964; PhD, U. Calif., Berkeley, 1968; MBA, U. Chgo., 1985. Instr. U. Calif., Berkeley, 1968; rsch. assoc. U. Chgo., 1968-71; asst. prof. Albion (Mich.) Coll., 1971-75; chemist Argonne (Ill.) Nat. Lab., 1975-82, mgr. analytical chemistry, 1982—2001; prof. chemistry Coll. DuPage, Glen Ellyn, Ill., 1991-93. Vis. prof. chemistry Albion Coll., 2001—06; instr. DuPage Coll., 2006, Benedictine U., Lisle, Ill., 2006. Editor Mng. the Modern Lab, 1995-2003, mem. editl. bd., 1994—. Pres. Dist. 58 Bd. Edn., Downers Grove, Ill., 1976-79. Mem. Analytical Lab. Mgrs. Assn. (pres. 1986-87, treas. 1989, exec. dir. 2007—). Home: 5625 Carpenter Downers Grove IL 60516 Personal E-mail: dwgreen@albion.edu.

GREEN, DENNIS E., former professional football coach; b. Harrisburg, Pa., Feb. 17, 1949; m. Marie L. Green; children: Patti, Jeremy, Vanessa, Zachary. BS in Edn., U. Iowa, 1971. Profl. football player, Can. Football League BC Lions, 1971; grad. asst. U. Iowa, 1972, quarterbacks & receivers coach, 1974—76; receivers coach U. Dayton, 1973; asst. coach Stanford U., 1977-78, 80; head coach Northwestern U., 1981-85; asst. coach San Francisco 49ers, 1979, receivers coach, 1986-88; head coach Stanford U., 1989-91, Minn. Vikings, 1992—2002, Ariz. Cardinals, 2004—07. Co-author (with Gene McGivern): No Room for Crybabies, 1997. Named Big-Ten Conf. Coach of Yr., 1982, Nat. Football Conf. Coach of Yr., Coll. & Pro Football News Weekly, 1992, United Press Internat., 1992, NFL Coach of Yr., Washington Touchdown Club, 1992, Pro Coach of Yr. in Upper Midwest, Midwest Sports Channel, 1998, Coach of Yr., Sports Illustrated, 1998, Maxwell Club, 1998, Cmty. Coach of Yr., World Sports Humanitarian Hall of Fame, 2001; recipient Pop Warner Golden Football award, 1993.*

GREEN, DENNIS JOSEPH, retired lawyer; b. Milw., Sept. 28, 1941; m. Janet McQueen; children: Karla Pope, Cheryl Ashley, Deborah Relihan. BS in Mgmt., U. Ill., 1963, JD, 1968. Bar: Ill. 1968, Mo. 1968. Atty. Monsanto Co., St. Louis, 1968-75, asst. co. counsel, 1975-76, counsel, 1976-79; gen. counsel, sec. Fisher Controls Internat. Inc., Clayton, Mo., 1979-85, v.p., gen. counsel, sec., 1985-93; v.p. Emerson Electric Co., St. Louis, 1999—, assoc. gen. counsel, 1999—2004, dep. gen. counsel, 2004—06; ret., 2006. 1st lt. U.S. Army, 1963-65. Office: Emerson Electric Co PO Box 4100 8000 W Florissant Ave Saint Louis MO 63136-1494 E-mail: dennis.green@emrsn.com.

GREEN, DOLORES L., medical association administrator; Exec. dir. Riverside County Med. Assn., Calif., 1983—. CFO Calif. Found. Med. Care; CEO Inland Empire Found. Med. Care. Recipient Med. Exec. Achievement award, AMA, 2005. Office: Riverside County Med Assn 3993 Jurupa Ave Riverside CA 92506 Office Phone: 951-686-9049. Office Fax: 951-686-1692. Business E-Mail: dgreen@rcmanet.org.*

GREEN, DON WESLEY, chemical and petroleum engineering educator; b. Tulsa, July 8, 1932; s. Earl Leslie and Erma Pansy (Brackins) G.; m. Patricia Louise Polston, Nov. 26, 1954; children: Guy Leslie, Don Michael, Charles Patrick. BS in Petroleum Engring., U. Tulsa, 1955; MSChemE, U. Okla., 1959, PhD in Chem. Engring., 1963. Rsch. scientist Continental Oil Co., Ponca City, Okla., 1962-64; asst. to assoc. prof. U. Kans., Lawrence, 1964-71, prof. chem. and petroleum engring., 1971-82, chmn. dept. chem. and petroleum engring., 1970-74, 96-200, co-dir. Tertiary Oil Recovery project, 1974—, Conger-Gabel Disting. prof., 1982-95, Deane E. Ackers Disting. prof., 1995—. Faculty rep. to NCAA. Editor: Perry's Chemical Engineers' Handbook, 1984, 1997; co-author: Enhanced Oil Recovery, 1998; contbr. articles to profl. jours. 1st lt. USAF, 1955-57. Fellow Am. Inst. Chem. Engrs.; mem. Soc. Petroleum Engrs. (Disting. Achievement award 1983, chmn. edn. and accreditation com. 1980-81, Disting. mem. 1986, Disting. lectr. 1986). Democrat. Avocations: handball, baseball, hiking. Home: 1020 Sunset Dr Lawrence KS 66044-4546 Office: U Kans Dept Chem & Petroleum Engring 4008 Learned Hall Lawrence KS 66045-7526 E-mail: dgreen@ku.edu.

GREEN, DONALD HUGH, lawyer; b. Elizabeth, NJ, May 26, 1929; s. Mortimer Jordan and Edna (Reinherz) G.;m. Carol Margaret Medsger, Sept. 20, 1960; children: Michael, Margaret, Matthew, Mark. AB, Syracuse U., 1951; LLB, Harvard U., 1954. Bar: Fla. 1956, N.Y. 1957, D.C. 1960. Atty. Office of Legal Counsel, U.S. Dept. Justice, Washington, 1958-60, atty. civil div., 1960-61; assoc. Bergson & Borkland, Washington, 1961-65; ptnr. Wald, Harkrader & Ross, Washington, 1966-87; vice chmn. exec. com. mng. ptnr., of counsel Pepper, Hamilton LLP, Washington, 1987—, mem. exec. com., mng. ptnr. DC office, 1995—2000. Mem. faculty curriculum com. Legal Edn. Inst., U.S. Dept. Justice, Washington, 1985-92; lectr. Georgetown Law Ctr., Washington, 1981—, various symposia D.C. Bar; adj. prof. Georgetown Law Ctr., 1992-03; apptd. def. adv. com. on women in the svcs. Sec. of Def., 1999, exec. com. 1999-01. Contbr. articles to profl. jours. Mem., chmn. trustees Cedar Lane Unitarian Ch., Bethesda, 1972-75; coxswain USCG Aux., 2001—. Col. USMCR, 1954-85. Decorated Legion of Merit. Mem. ABA, Internat. Assn. Women Judges (mem. bd. mng. trustees 2002—), Fed. Bar Assn., Am. Arbitration Assn., Joint Svcs. Com. on Profl. Ethics, Nat. Panel Arbitrators, Fed. Am. Inn of Ct. (pres. 1994-95). Democrat. Avocations: painting, boating, tennis. Home: 5610 Wisconsin Ave Apt 18A Chevy Chase MD 20815-4415 Office: Pepper Hamilton LLP Hamilton Sq 600 14th St NW Washington DC 20005-2008 Home Phone: 301-654-7737; Office Phone: 202-220-1213. Business E-Mail: greendh@pepperlaw.com.

GREEN, DONALD PHILIP, political scientist, educator; b. Chgo., June 23, 1961; s. Burton and Isabel (Engelhardt) G.; m. Ann Gerken, June 18, 1989; children: Aaron, Rachel. BA in Polit. Sci., UCLA, 1983; MA in Polit. Sci., U. Calif., Berkeley, 1984, PhD, 1988. From asst. to assoc. prof. dept. polit. sci. Yale U., New Haven, 1989-94, prof., 1994—, dir. Instn. for Social and Policy Studies, 1996—, A. Whitney Griswold chair, 2001. Author: Pathologies of Rational Choice Theory, 1994, Partisan Hearts and Minds, 2002, Get Out the Vote, 2004; contbr. articles to profl. jours.; inventor abstract strategy games. Recipient Nat. Young Investigator award NSF, 1993—. Fellow: AAAS. Office: Yale Univ 77 Prospect St New Haven CT 06520-8209 Home Phone: 203-497-9875; Office Phone: 203-432-3237. Business E-Mail: donald.green@yale.edu.

GREEN, DOUGLAS ALVIN, retired library director; b. Gilmer, Tex., Feb. 17, 1925; s. Arthur Elmer and Evalena (Loyless) G.; m. Clovis Wayne Elwell, Dec. 15, 1945; 1 child, Danis (dec.). BA, U. N. Tex., 1950; MA, East Tex. State U., 1951, EdD, 1980; MS, La. State U., 1968. Chief bibliographer U. Ark. Gen. Libr., Fayetteville, 1963-67; libr. dir. Bee County Coll., Beeville, Tex., 1968-73; chmn. learning resources Richland C.C., Decatur, Ill., 1973-75; libr. dir. Laredo (Tex.) State U., 1975-76, Amb. Coll., Big Sandy, Tex., 1976-77, Pasadena, 1977-78, U. Ctrl. Ark., Conway, 1981-84; ret. Ark. State U., Beebe, 1990. Author: An Index to Collected Essays on Educational Media and Technology, 1982; contbg. author: The Smaller Academic Library - A Management Handbook, 1988. With USNR, 1943-46. HEA Title II scholar, 1967-68. Avocations: piano, organ, keyboards, fishing. Home: 3500 S Vine Ave Apt 328 Tyler TX 75701

GREEN, DOUGLAS G., lawyer; MA with honors, Bowdoin Coll., 1968; MA in English, U. Va., 1969; JD, Georgetown U., 1973. Bar: DC 1973. Ptnr. & vice chmn., Electric Power, Antitrust, Toxic Torts & Comml. Litig. Steptoe & Johnson LLP, Washington, mem. exec. com. Spkr. in field; editor: Georgetown Law Jour.; contbr. articles to jour. Office: Steptoe& Johnson LLP 1330 Connecticut Ave NW Washington DC 20036 Office Phone: 202-429-6212. Office Fax: 202-429-3902. Business E-Mail: dgreen@steptoe.com.

GREEN, EDWARD CROCKER, research scientist; b. Washington, Nov. 29, 1944; s. Marshall and Lispenard Seabury (Crocker) G.; m. K. Shannon McCaffray, Sept. 22, 1967 (div. 1977); 1 child, Timothy A.; m. M. Sue McLaughlin, Feb. 22, 1998. BA, George Washington U., 1967; MA, Northwestern U., 1968; PhD, Cath. U. Am., 1974; postgrad., Vanderbilt U., 1978—79. Asst. prof. W.Va. U., Morgantown, 1976—78; pvt. practice devel. cons. various orgns., Washington, 1979—; mgr. internat. programs John Short & Assocs., Columbia, Md., 1986—88; social scientist Acad. for Ednl. Devel., Swaziland, 1981—84; contractor personal svcs. U.S. AID, Swaziland, 1984—85; advisor Mozambique Govt., 1994—95; mgr., rschr. The Futures Group, Washington, 1988—89; sr. rsch. fellow in internat. health Harvard U., Cambridge, Mass., 2001—02, sr. rsch. scientist Sch. Pub. Health, 2002—. Author: Planning Psychiatric Services for Southern Africa, 1979, Practicing Development Anthropology, 1986, AIDS and STDs in Africa, 1994, Indigenous Healers and The African State, 1996, Indigenous Theories of Contagious Disease, 1999, Rethinking AIDS Prevention, 2003; contbr. over 200 articles to profl. jours. Bd. dirs., mem. presdl. adv. bd. HIV/AIDS; mem. adv. bd. NIH, HIV/AIDS orgn. Recipient Mozambique Govt. award for health rsch., 1992, Praxis award Washington Assn. Profl. Anthropologists, 1982, 83; NIMH postdoctoral fellow, 1978-79; Sigma Xi rsch. grantee, 1971; Takami fellow Harvard U., 2001-02. Mem. Am. Anthrop. Assn., Soc. Applied Anthropology, Soc. Med. Anthropology, Global Initiative Traditional Sys. Health (bd. dirs.). Avocation: folk music. Home: 44 Pocahontas Rd Kittery Point ME 03905-5305 Office Phone: 617-495-3014.

GREEN, ELBERT P., retired academic administrator; b. Laneview, Va., June 9, 1935; s. James H. and Levallia C. (DeLeaver) G.; m. Mary M. Green, July 6, 1961; children: Mark B., Marsha B. BS, Va. State Coll., 1957; BD, Felix Adler Meml. U., Chapel Hill, NC, 1969; MS in Edn., Troy State U., Montgomery, Ala., 1988; MBph, Am. Bible Sch., Kansas City, Kans., 1968; PhD, S.W. U., New Orleans, 1991. Cert. tchr., Ala., cert. hypnotherapist; ordained minister. 2d lt. U.S. Army, 1958, advanced through grades to maj.; ret., 1979; dir. jr. ROTC, Indianola (Miss.) City Schs., Macon County (Ala.) Schs.; dir. residence hall Tuskegee (Ala.) U. Author: Poetry Is Soul, 1988, Poetry Is Gold, 1982, The Light of the World Is Poetry, 1995, Daily Bread for Living, 2004; contbr. articles to newspapers. Inductee Internat. Poetry Hall of Fame, 1997, Who Is Who of Contemporary Achievers Hall of Fame, 1997, Phi Beta Sigma Hall of Fame, 1999, Am. Biographical Inst. Hall of Fame, 2002. Mem. Internat. Soc. of Poets, Profl. Educators Orgn., Am. Legion, Lions Internat., Scabbard and Blade, Phi Beta Sigma, Phi Delta Kappa, Gamma Beta Phi. Home: 2910 W Martin L King Hwy Tuskegee AL 36083

GREEN, ELEANOR MYERS, veterinarian, educator; b. Phila., Feb. 10, 1948; d. Wade Cooper and Eleanor Ruth (McWherter) Myers; children: George Ashby Jr., Stacy Elizabeth, William Wade. Student, U. South Fla., 1965-67, U. Fla., 1967-69; DVM, Auburn U., 1973. Diplomate Am. Coll. Vet. Internal Medicine, Am. Bd. Vet. Practitioners (pres. 1993-95, past pres. 1995-96). Ptnrship, owner Guntown (Miss.) Vet. Clinic, 1973-76; asst. prof. Miss. State U., Starkville, 1976-84; assoc. prof. U. Mo., Columbia, 1984-91; prof. U. Tenn., Knoxville, 1991-96; prof., chair dept. U. Fla., Gainesville, 1996—. Named Disting. Practitioner Nat. Acads. of Practice, Coll. Agrl. and Life Scis. award of distinction, 2004. Mem. Am. Assn. Equine Practitioners (bd. dirs. 1997-99, pres.-elect), Fla. Vet. Med. Assn., Am. Vet. Med. Assn., Am. Assn. Vet. Clinicians (Faculty Achievement award 1999, pres. 1995-96, past pres. 1996-97), Nat. Acad.'s Practice (Disting. Practitioner 1998—), Fla. Thoroughbred Owners and Breeders Assn., Fla. Quarter Horse Assn. (bd. dirs.), Rotary Internat.(pres. 2006-07, past pres. 2007—). Presbyterian. Avocations: horseback riding, tennis, painting. Office: U Fla Coll Vet Medicine Dept Large Animal Clin Scis Gainesville FL 32610-0136 E-mail: greene@mail.vetmed.ufl.edu.

GREEN, ERIC HOWARD, lawyer; b. NYC, Jan. 5, 1950; s. Bernard and Edith Green; m. Mona M. Green, July 10, 1982; children: Zachary Samuel, Shawn Alexander. BA, SUNY, Buffalo, 1972, JD, 1976. Bar: N.Y. 1977, U.S. Dist. Ct. (so. and ea. dist.) N.Y. 1979, U.S. Supreme Ct. 1985. Assoc. Pops & Estrin, NYC, 1976-77, Karp & Silver, Queens, N.Y., 1977-81, Edward Leshaw, Esq., NYC, 1981-82; mng. ptnr. Eric H. Green, Esq., NYC, 1982—. Instr. Nat. Inst. of Trial Advocacy, Cardoza Law Sch., N.Y.C., 1987—, U. Buffalo, coll. of Urban Studies, 1974-76; lectr. NYU, Sch. Continuing Edn., N.Y.C., 1986-90; arbitrator Am. Arbitration Assn., 1987—. Mem. N.Y. Dem. Judicial Screening Panel, N.Y.C., 1989; advisor, vol. N.Y.C. Open Doors Edn. Program, 1985-89. Mem. ATLA, N.Y. County Lawyers Assn., N.Y. State Bar Assn., N.Y. State Trial Lawyers Assn. (bd. dirs., speaker cmty. speakers bur. 1988—), N.Y. County Lawyers Assn. (fee dispute com., Supreme Ct. com.), Assn. Bar City N.Y. (tort litigation com., chmn. mediation subcom.). Avocations: sports, theater, antiques. Office: 295 Madison Ave New York NY 10017-6304 E-mail: greenlegal@msn.com.

GREEN, EVA GAELLE, actress; b. Paris, July 5, 1980; d. Walter Green and Marlène Jobert. Attended, Webber Douglas Acad. Dramatic Art, London. Actor: (films) The Dreamers, 2003, Arsène Lupin, 2004, Kingdom of Heaven, 2005, Casino Royale, 2006. Recipient Orange Rising Star Award, Brit. Acad. Film and TV Arts, 2007.*

GREEN, FRANCIS WILLIAM, investment consultant, former missile scientist; b. Locust Grove, Okla., Mar. 17, 1920; s. Noel Francis and Mary (Lincoln) G.; m. Alma J. Ellison, Aug. 26, 1950 (dec. Sept. 1970); children: Sharmon, Rhonda; m. Susan G. Mathis, July 14, 1973 (div. July 1979). BS, Phoenix U., 1955; MS in Elec. Engring., Minerva U., Milan, Italy, 1959; MS in Engring., West Coast U., LA, 1965; cert., Indsl. Coll. Armed Forces, 1967. With Guided Missile Program USN, 1945-49; design and electronic project engr. Falcon missile program Hughes Aircraft Co., Culver City, Calif., 1949-55; sr. electronic engr. Atlas missile program Convair Astronautics, San Diego, 1955-59; sr. engr. Polaris missile program Nortronics divsn. Northrop, Anaheim, Calif., 1959-60; chief, supr. electronic engring. data sys. br. Tech. Support Divsn. Rocket Propulsion Lab. USAF, Edwards AFB, Calif., 1960-67, dep. chief tech. Tech. Support Divsn. Rocket Propulsion Lab., 1967-69, tech. advisor Missile Devel. Ctr. Holloman AFB, N.Mex., 1969-70, tech. advisor 6585 test group Spl. Weapons Ctr., 1970-78; pvt. investment cons., 1978—. Bd. examiners U.S. CSC; mem. Pres.'s Missile Site Labor Rels. Com.; cons. advanced computer and data processing tech. and systems engring.; mem. USAF Civilian Policy Bd. and Range Comdrs. Coun.; maj. gen., comdr. 2d brigade N.Mex. State Milit. Forces; comdr. N.Mex. State Mil. Forces, 1989-99, maj. gen. ret. Contbr. articles to profl. jours. Served as pilot, asst. engring. officer USAAF, 1941-47. Fellow AIAA; mem. IEEE (sr.), Nat. Assn. Flight Instrs., Res. Officers Assn. U.S. Home and Office: 5004 Oso Grande Ct NE Albuquerque NM 87111

GREEN, FRANK EARL, retired civil engineer; b. Joplin, Mo., Nov. 24, 1931; s. Lloyd Cuthbertson and Gladys Alberta (Kennedy) G.; m. Joan Imogene (Wheeler)July 25, 1953; children: Kevin Joe, Keely Sue Green LaNoue. BS in Math., SW Mo. State U., 1953; BSCE, Kans. State U., Manhattan, 1958. Registered profl. engr., Mo., land surveyor, Mo. Hwy. designer Mo. Hwy. and Transp. Dept., Kansas City, 1958-61, sr. hwy. designer, 1962-65, dist. hwy. design engr., 1966-96; ret., 1996. Usher, mem. Grandview United Meth. Ch., Mo., 1970—. With Army Corps. of Engrs., 1953-55. Mem. ASCE (life, bd. dirs. Kansas City sect. 1987-91, sec.-treas. and pres.-elect 1992, pres. 1993), Nat. Soc. Profl. Engrs. (life), Mo. Soc. Profl. Engrs. (bd. dirs. Western chpt. 1985-91). Republican. Home: 5608 E 100th Ter Kansas City MO 64137-1312

GREEN, FRED L., III, bank executive; BS in Fin., U. SC, Columbia, 1979, MBA, 1983. With C&S Nat. Bank, SC; exec. v.p., regional exec. Nat. Bank SC, 1991—95, sr. exec. v.p., 1995—98; pres., CEO Nat. Bank SC Synovus Fin. Corp. (acquired Nat. Bank SC in 1995), 1998—2003, chmn. Nat. Bank SC, 2001—03; vice chmn. Synovus Fin. Corp. (acquired Nat. Bank SC), 2003—06, pres., COO, 2006—. Mem. Fed. Adv. Coun. Fed. Res. Bd. Govs. Bd. mem., treas. U. SC Ednl. Found. Named Outstanding Young Banker, SC Bankers Assn., 1994, Disting. Young Alumnus, U. SC Darla Moore Sch. Bus., 1999. Mem.: Fin. Svcs. Roundtable. Office: Synovus Fin Corp PO Box 120 Columbus GA 31902 Office Phone: 706-649-2311.*

GREEN, GARY JULE, lawyer; b. Mpls., Nov. 22, 1934; s. Jule Wallace Green and Ellen Edna Shawbold; m. Dolores Ann Jones, Nov. 10, 1964; children: Barbara, Linda. BS, U. Minn., Mpls., 1953, MA, 1957; JD, U. Minn., St. Paul, 1973. Bar: Minn. 1973, Ark. 1990, US Surpeme Ct. 1975. Tchr. Minot Sch. Dist., SD, 1957—64, St. Paul Sch. Dist., 1964—73; lawyer Minn. Edn. Assn., St. Paul, Minn. Nurses Assn., St. Paul, Ark. Edn. Assn. Chair social studies dept. St. Paul Pub. Schs., 1964—73; substitute tchr. numerous schs., St. Paul, Oakdale, Minn., Maplewood, Minn.; journalist, photographer Hot Springs Village Voice, Ark. Lobbyist for handicapped edn. St. Paul Pub. Schs., 1964—73; bd. dirs. Parl Hot Springs Village, 1995—2005; pro bono lawyer St. Paul, Hot Springs Village; pres. ch. coun. Christ Luth. Ch., Minnehaha, Minn., 1953; pres. ch. choir CLL, 2000—04. Recipient fundraising leadership plaques, YMCA, St. Paul, 1986—88. Mem.: ABA. Democrat. Lutheran. Avocations: photography, fishing, golf. Home: 1348 Phalen Blvd Saint Paul MN 55106

GREEN, GENE (RAYMOND EUGENE GREEN), congressman; b. Houston, Oct. 17, 1947; s. Garland B. and Evelyn (Clark) Green; m. Helen Lois Albers, 1970; children: Angela, Christopher. BBA, U. Houston, 1971; student, U. Houston Bates Coll. Law, 1973—77. Bar: Tex. 1977. Mgr. printing co.; atty.; mem. Tex. State Ho. Reps., 1973-85, Tex. State Senate, 1985-92, US Congress from 29th Tex. dist., 1993—, mem. energy and commerce com., mem. standards of ofcl. conduct com., mem. fin. svcs. com., sr. dep. whip, regional whip. Recipient Outstanding Legis. award Houston Pk. Police Assn., Appreciation award Dem. Nat. Com., Appreciation award Harris County Sheriff's Deputy Assn., Legis. Support award AFL-CIO, Support award Tex. Dem. Party, Fiestas Patrias Mexicano de Corazon award, US Oncology Medal of Honor, 2003, Disting. Cmty. Health award Nat. Assn. Cmty. Health Care Ctrs., Inc., 2003, Legis. Open Door award Nat. Assn. Credit Mgmt., 2003, Alfred K. Whitehead Legis. award Internat. Assn. Fire Fighters, 2004. Mem. Baytown C. of C., Tex. Hist. Soc., Coastal Conservation Assn., League of United Latin Am. Citizens (hon.) Democrat. Methodist. Office: US Ho Reps 2335 Rayburn Ho Office Bldg Washington DC 20515-4329 Office Phone: 202-225-1688.*

GREEN, GEORGE JOSEPH, publishing executive; b. NYC, May 6, 1938; s. Monroe and Ruth (Gast) G.; m. Wilma H. Jordan. BA, Yale U., 1960. Trainee advt. dept. Burlington Industries, NYC, 1961-62; with The New Yorker Mag., 1962-84, salesman retail advt. N.Y.C. div., 1962-64, salesman advt. Atlanta div., 1964-66, salesman advt. N.Y.C. div., 1966-67, asst. treas., 1967-71, dir. circulation, v.p., 1971-75, pres., 1975-84; exec. v.p. Hearst Mags., NYC, 1984—; pres. Hearst Mags. Internat., NYC, 1989—. Bd. dirs. Nat. Magazine Co. Served with USAR, 1960-65. Mem. Mag. Publs. Assn. (bd. dirs.). Office: Hearst Mags 300 W 57th St New York NY 10019-3795 E-mail: ggreen@hearst.com.

GREEN, GERALD B., state legislator; Freeholder Union County; assemblyman dist. 22 N.J. State Assembly. Chmn. fin. Union County Freehold, 1991, chair bd. dirs., 1990. Pvt. industry coun. Union County Coll. Bd. Sch. Estimate. Mem. Union County Police Chiefs Assn. Office: 17 Watchung Ave Plainfield NJ 07060-1228 Office Phone: 908-561-5757. Business E-Mail: asmgreen@njleg.org.

GREEN, GERARD LEO, priest, educator; b. Batavia, NY, July 27, 1928; s. George Leo and Marian (Powers) G. BS, Mt. St. Mary's Coll., 1952; MA, St. Bonaventure U., 1958; postgrad., U. Notre Dame, 1961—62, U. Buffalo, 1965—66; EdM, SUNY, 1968. Ordained priest Roman Catholic Ch., 1956. Lab technician Eastman Kodak Co., 1947—48; chemist Xerox Co., 1952; parish asst. Diocese Buffalo, 1956—59; instr. chemistry Bishop Turner H.S., Buffalo, 1959—74, dir. sci., 1959—70, 1972—74; adminstr. Our Lady of the Rosary Parish, Wilson, NY, 1968, St. Barnabas Parish and Sch., DePew, NY, 1973—75, pastor, 1976—90; prelate of honor, 1984; mem., supr., leader tng. team, 1979—90; pastor Sts. Peter and Paul Parish, Hamburg, NY, 1990—99; rector pro tem St. Joseph's Cathedral, Buffalo, 2001. Mem. sci. curriculum com. Dept. Edn. Diocese Buffalo, 1960-70, chmn. diocesan chemistry textbook evaluation com., 1961-70, mem. diocesan pastoral coun. for handicapped, 1976-82, sec. 1978-79, diocesan regional coord., 1979-80, mem. diocesan fin. com., 1984-94, diocesan priests coun., 1990-99, 2003—, mem. diocesan coll. of consultors, 1994-99; active Diocesan Cons. Parish Computers, 1983-98, Diocesan Bd. Priests Retirement, 1985-91, 99—, Diocesan Cemetary Bd., 1994—, Sch. Bd. St. Francis H.S., 1992-98; diocesan bd. dirs. for TV prodn. 1986-94; chaplain Hyview Fire Co., 1976-81, Cheektowaga Police PBA, 1976-90, West End Fire Co., 1977-90, Depew Village Fire Co., 1980-88. Contbr. articles to profl. publs. Mem. We. N.Y. Sci. Congress Com., 1960-74, sec., 1968, co-chmn. 1969, chmn. 1972-73, state chmn. 1970; mem. gen. chemistry exam. com. N.Y. State Edn. Dept., 1970-73; mem. Maryvale Schs. Planning Bd., 1977-79; cons. sci. facilities in secondary schs.; mem. local IUE-AFL-CIO Scholarship Fund Com., 1968-71; mem. dist. com. Boy Scouts Am., Buffalo, 1957-74; bd. dirs. Tifft (Conservation) Farm, 1978-82, Hamburg Meals on Wheels, 1999-00; active N.Y. State Fire Chaplains. With AUS, 1946-47 Recipient Disting. Svc. award in sci. edn., 1975, Justice and Charity award First Cath. Charities, 1999, Cure of ARS award Outstanding Priest, 1999, Eagle Scout, Order of Arrow Boy Scouts Am. Mem. Sci. Tchrs. Assn. N.Y. (dir. 1971-73), Nat. Cath. Edn. Assn., KC 4th degree past grand knight), VFW. Address: 9686 Oak Grove Dr Angola NY 14006-8904 E-mail: msgrgreen@hotmail.com.

GREEN, GRANT S., JR., former federal agency administrator; b. Seattle, June 16, 1938; s. Grant S. and Eveleth (Solberg) G.; m. Virginia Dondy; children: Kelley, Shelley, Tana. BA, U. Ark., 1960; MS, George Washington U., 1978. Commd. 2d lt. U.S. Army, 1961, advanced through grades to col., ret., 1983; various mgmt. positions Sears World Trade, Washington, 1983-86; spl. asst. to pres. for nat. security affairs NSC, Washington, 1986-87; asst. sec. def. Office Sec. Def., Washington, 1987-88; v.p. IPAC, Washington; chmn. & pres. GMD Solutions; under sec. for mgmt. U.S. Dept. State, Washington, 2001—05. Cons. Carlyle Group, Washington, 1988—; mem. bd. USO, Nat. Def. Univ., 1987—. Decorated Bronze Star, DFC, DDSM, DSSM, others; recipient Disting. Pub. Svc. award Dept. of Def., several fgn. awards. Mem. World Affairs Coun., Ctr. for Excellence in Govt., Assn. U.S. Army, Army Aviation Assn., Ret. Officers Assn., Am. Legion. Republican. Avocations: antique cars, boating, golf, skiing.

GREEN, HARRY WESTERN, II, geology and geophysics educator; s. Harry Buetel and Mabel (Hendrickson) G.; children from previous marriage: Mark, Stephen, Carolyn, Jennifer; m. Maria Manuela Marques Martins, May 15, 1975; children: Alice, Miguel, Maria. AB in Geology with honors, UCLA, 1963, MS in Geology and Geophysics, 1967, PhD in Geology and Geophysics with distinction, 1968. Postdoctoral rsch. assoc. materials sci. Case Western Res. U., Cleve., 1968-70; asst. prof. geology U. Calif., Davis, 1970-74, assoc. prof., 1974-80, prof., 1980-92, chmn. dept., 1984-88, prof. geology and geophysics Riverside, 1993-99, disting. prof. geology and geophysics, 1999—, dir. Inst. Geophysics and Planetary Physics, 1993-95, 2001, dir. analytical electron microscopy facility, 1994—2000, vice chancellor for rsch., 1995-2000, dir. ctrl. facility advanced microscopy and microanalysis, 2000—, acting chair dept. earth sci., 2005, vice chair, 2005—. Exch. scientist U. Nantes, France, 1973, vis. prof., 1978-79; vis. prof. Monash U., Melbourne, Australia, 1984; specialist advisor World Bank Program, China U. of Geoscis., Wuhan, 1988; adj. sr. rsch. scientist Lamont-Doherty Earth Obs., Columbia U., 1989-95, Vetlesen vis. prof., 1991-92; expert advisor geophysics rev. panel NSF, 1991-94; co-founder Gordon Conf. on Rock Deformation, 1995, chmn. 2d conf., 1997; hon. faculty China U. Geoscis., Wuhan, 1998—; vis. scientist Carnegie Inst. Washington, 2000—, Abelson lectr., 2000, vis. rev. com., 2004; faculty rsch. lectr. U. Calif., Riverside, 2002-03; mem. facilities com. Consortium for Materials Properties Rsch. in Earth Scis., 2002-04, chmn. exec. com., 2004-07, vis. prof. Stanford U., 2007, Alan Cox fellow, 2007-. Contbr. articles to books and profl. jours. Grantee NSF, 1969—, Dept. Energy, 1988-94. Fellow AAAS, Mineral Soc. Am., Am. Geophys. Union (N.L. Bowen award 1994, Francis Birch lectr. 1995); Cosmos Club (Washington), Sigma Xi. Achievements include discovery and characterization of new mechanisms of deep earthquakes; discovery of exhumation of rocks from hundreds of km depth in subduction zones. Office: U Calif Earth Scis 900 University Ave Riverside CA 92521 Office Phone: 951-827-4505. Business E-Mail: harry.green@ucr.edu.

GREEN, HOLCOMBE TUCKER, JR., investment company executive; b. Atlanta, Sept. 29, 1939; s. Holcombe Tucker and Mary Katherine (Woltz) Green; m. Nancy Reade Hall, June 18, 1966. AB, Yale U., 1961; LLB, U. Va., 1967; DBA (hon.), Piedmont Coll., 1995. Bar: Ga. 1967. Assoc. firm Hansell & Post, Atlanta, 1967-70, mem. firm, 1970-87, mgmt. com., 1980-87; CEO Green Capital Investors L.P., Atlanta, 1987—2004; chmn., CEO WestPoint Stevens, Inc., 1992—2003; prin. Access Investors LLC. Bd. dirs. Vytech Industries, Inc., Access Integrated Networks, Inc., Cumulus Media Partners; bd. dirs., chmn. Rhodes, Inc., 1988—96; chmn. HBO & Co., 1990—98. Bd. dirs. Child Svc. and Family Counseling Ctr., 1972—85, pres., 1982—84; active Leadership Atlanta, 1974—75; trustee Atlanta Bot. Garden, 1976—92, pres., 1982—84; bd. dirs. High Mus. Art, 1982—96, Yale U. Art Gallery, 1992—, Atlanta Ballet, 1987—89, Atlanta Hist. Soc., 1993—96; trustee Taft Sch., 1987—2000; trustee, vice chmn. investments Woodruff Arts Ctr., 1990—98; chmn. Yale Devel. Bd., 1998—2005; fellow Yale Corp., 1999—2005; hon. Swedish consul State of Ga., 1988—96. Served to lt. (j.g.) USN, 1961—64. Mem.: Raven Soc. Va., Ocean Forest Golf Club, Doubles Club, Chatooga Club, Wade Hampton Golf Club, Capital City Club, Piedmont Driving Club, Nine O'Clocks Club, Homosassa Fishing Club, Royal Order Polar Star, Order Coif. Democrat. Presbyterian. Home: 2774 Andrews Dr #9 Atlanta GA 30305 Office Phone: 706-926-2211. Personal E-mail: holcombegreen@yahoo.com.

GREEN, HUBERT, professional golfer; b. Birmingham, Ala., Dec. 28, 1946; BS in Mktg., Fla. State U., 1968. Profl. golfer, 1969—; winner Houston Champions Internat., 1971, Tallahassee Open, 1973, BC Open, 1973, Bob Hope Desert Classic, 1974, Greater Jacksonville Open, 1974, 1976, IVB-Phila. Golf Classic, 1974, Walt Disney World Nat. Team Championship (with Mac McLendon), 1974, So. Open, 1975, 1984, Doral Ea. Open, 1976, Sea Pines Heritage Classic, 1976, US Open Championship, 1977, Hawaiian Open, 1978, 1979, Heritage Classic, 1978, First NBC New Orleans Open, 1979, Sammy Davis Jr.-Greater Hartford Open, 1981, PGA Championship, 1985, Bruno's Meml. Classic, 1998, Audi Sr. Classic, 2000, Kroger Sr. Classic, 2000, Lightpath LI Classic, 2002; mem. Champions Tour, 1997—. Winner Dunlop Phoenix, Japan, 1975, Irish Open, 1977. Named Rookie of Yr., 1971; named to World Golf Hall of Fame, 2007. Mailing: Champions Tour 112 PGA TOUR Blvd Ponte Vedra Beach FL 32082*

GREEN, JAMES FRANCIS, lawyer, consultant; b. Pittsfield, Mass., Oct. 1, 1948; s. Earl Levi and Frances Eleanor (Walshi) G.; m. Eileen Mary Kelly, July 31, 1971; childen: Michael Walshe, Maura Kelly, Kelsey Kathryn. BA, St. Anselm Coll., 1970; JD, Suffolk U., 1973. Bar: Mass 1973, U.S. Dist. Ct. Mass. 1874, U.S. Ct. Appeals (D.C. cir.) 1975, U.S. Dist. Ct. D.C. 1975, U.S. Supreme Ct. 1977, U.S. Ct. Appeals (4th cir.) 1978. Rsch. counsel Joint Com. on Jud. Reform of Joint Jud. Com. of Gen. Ct. Commonwealth of Mass., Boston, 1973-74; ptnr. Drucas, Edgerton & Green, Salem, Mass., 1974; sr. ptnr. Ashcraft & Gerel, Washington, 1975—, Herman, Mathis, Casey, Kitchens and Gerel. Presdl. appointment Nat. Ad Hoc Com. on Disability. Named to, Best Lawyers in Am., 2006. Mem. Mass. Bar Assn., Boston Bar Assn., Fed. Bar Assn. (bd. dirs. Washington chpt. 1985-86, internat. law com.), Bar Assn. D.C., D.C. Bar Assn., ABA (torts and ins. practice law sects., vice chmn. nat. com. on liaison with the jud. adminstrn.), Assn. Trial Lawyers Am. (sect. chmn. nat. com. workers compensation 1989-90), Am. Soc. Law and Medicine. Democrat. Roman Catholic. Home: 6522 Heather Brook Ct Mc Lean VA 22101-1607 Office: Ashcraft & Gerel 2000 L St NW Ste 400 Washington DC 20036 Office Phone: 202-783-6400.

GREEN, JAMES SAMUEL, lawyer; b. Berwick, Pa., May 24, 1947; m. Carla Eyer; children: Jennifer, Emily, James Samuel Jr., Jared. AB, Princeton U., 1969; JD, Villanova U., 1972. Bar: Del. 1972, Pa. 1973, U.S. Dist. Ct. Del. 1973, U.S. Ct. Appeals (3d cir.) 1981, U.S. Supreme Ct. 1990. Assoc. Connolly, Bove, Lodge & Hutz, Wilmington, Del., 1972-74, ptnr., 1977-90; dep. atty. gen. State of Del., Wilmington, 1975-76; ptnr. Duane Morris & Heckscher, Wilmington, 1990-99, Seitz, Van Ogtrop & Green, P.A., Wilmington, 1999—. Bd. dirs. David Wellborn Found.; del. Bd. Unauthorized Practice of Law, chmn., 1994—99. Fellow Am. Coll. of Trial Lawyers, Internat. Acad. Trial Lawyers; mem. ABA, Am. Bd. Trial Advocates (nat. bd. dirs. 1991-2000), Del. Bar Assn. (treas. 1980-81, chmn. litigation sect. 1988-91), Ivy Club (Princeton), Wilmington Country Club, Princeton Club NY. Home: 2603 W 17th St Wilmington DE 19806-1108 Office: Seitz Van Ogtrop & Green PA PO Box 68 Wilmington DE 19899-0068 Office Phone: 302-888-7603. E-mail: jgreen@svglaw.com.

GREEN, JAMES WYCHE, sociologist, anthropologist, consultant, psychotherapist; b. Alton, Va., Aug. 5, 1915; s. William Ivey and Mary (Crowder) G.; m. Pearl O'Neal Cornett, Mar. 2, 1940 (dec. 1982); 1 child, Margaret Lydia.; m. Arlene Borkenhagen, Mar. 26, 1983. BS with honors, Va. Poly. Inst., 1938, MS, 1939; postgrad., Duke U., 1947—48; PhD, U. N.C., 1953; postgrad., Sch. Advanced Internat. Studies, Johns Hopkins U., 1959. Rsch. fellow Va. Poly. Inst., 1938—39; rsch. field supr. Va. Expt. Sta., 1939; asst. specialist program planning N.C. State Coll. Extension Svc., 1939—42; v.p. Greever's, Inc., 1946; tchr. h.s., farm operator, 1946—47; asst. prof. rural sociology N.C. State Coll., 1949—54; from assoc. chief to chief cmty. devel. adv. Govt. of Pakistan, Karachi, 1954—59; prof. rural sociology dept. Cornell U., Ithaca, NY, 1960; cmty. devel. adviser Govt. of So. Rhodesia, AID, 1960—64; chief cmty. devel., local govt. adviser Govt. of Peru, 1964—67; chief urban cmty. devel. adviser Govt. of Panama, 1967—69; prof., chmn. dept. sociology and anthropology U. N.C., Charlotte, 1969—70; chief methodology divsn. Bur. Tech. Assistance, AID, Washington, 1970—74; sociologist/anthropologist cons. AID, Washington, 1974—75, contractor Yemen, 1975; pvt. practice cons., 1975—. Author: Integrative Meditation: Towards Unity of Mind/Body/Spirit, 1994, And It Was Never Dull: A Memoir, 2003, Publications and Writings of James Wyche Green, 30 vols., 2003 (Libr. of Congress permanent collection, 2004); author monographs; contbr. chpts. to books and articles to profl. jours. Served from 1st lt. to capt. AUS, 1942-46; lt. col. Res. ret. 1975. Decorated Croix de Guerre with Silver Star France; Croix de Guerre with Palm Belgium; Bronze Star with cluster; named Outstanding Alumnus Hargrave Mil. Acad., 1979 Fellow Am. Anthrop. Assn., AAAS, Soc. Applied Anthropology; mem. Res. Officers Assn., Public Citizen, ACLU, Common Cause, Amnesty Internat., Omicron Delta Kappa, Alpha Zeta, Phi Kappa Phi. Democrat. Lutheran. Home and Office: 6430 Lily Dhu Ln Falls Church VA 22044-1409 Office Phone: 703-941-6536. *I have found few joys in life which are as deep and lasting as "cracking a culture," i.e. understanding how it really works, and then using that understanding for its people's good as they see the good.*

GREEN, JEFFREY C., lawyer; b. Newark, July 6, 1941; s. Albert and Mildred (Rosenberg) G.; m. Iris Landow, Aug. 23, 1964; children: Michelle, Marlene. BA, Rutgers U., 1963, JD, 1966; postgrad., Nat. Coll. State Judiciary, Reno, 1974-75. Bar: N.J. 1966, U.S. Dist. Ct. N.J. 1966. Law clk. to judge N.J. Superior Ct., Middlesex County Ct., New Brunswick, 1966-67; assoc. Toolan, Romond & Burgess, Perth Amboy, N.J., 1967-68; ptnr. Green & Green and predecessors, Somerset, N.J., 1968—. Prosecutor Franklin Twp. Mcpl. Ct., Somerset, 1969-70, mcpl. judge, 1970-76, 97—; judge Millstone (N.J.) Mcpl. Ct., 1970-76, Manville (N.J.) Mcpl. Ct., 1972-73; atty. Cranbury (N.J.) Bd. Adjustment, 1978-2006. Trustee Jersey Legal Svcs., Inc., 2003—; legal counsel Temple Beth El, Somerset, 1974—; bd. dirs. Ctrl. NJ Legal Svcs. Corp., New Brunswick, 1983—. Named Man of Yr., Temple Beth El, 1984; recipient Pro Bono Achievement award Middlesex County Legal Svcs. Corp., 1985, 87, Profl. Lawyer of Year award NJ Commn. Professionalism in Law, 2006. Mem. N.J. State Bar Assn. (trustee 1997-2003, Gen. Practitioner of Yr. award 1997), Middlesex County Bar Assn. (pres. 1985-86), Middlesex County Bar Found. (trustee 1990—, pres. 1994-95), Franklin Twp. Jaycees (pres. 1970-71), Lions Club. Democrat. Home: 3 Denise Ct Somerset NJ 08873-2834 Office: Green & Green PO Box 5321 Somerset NJ 08875-5321 Home Phone: 732-873-2648; Office Phone: 732-247-0770.

GREEN, JERSEY MICHAEL-LEE, lawyer; b. Washington, Feb. 29, 1952; BA in criminology, U. Md., 1976; JD, Syracuse U., 1983. Bar: Colo, 1983, U.S. Dist. Ct. Colo. 1983, U.S. Ct. Appeals (10th cir.) 1983, U.S. Tax Ct. 1983, U.S. Ct. Appeals (9th cir.) 1987, U.S. Supreme Ct. 1988, U.S. Ct. Appeals (2d cir.) 1990, U.S. Dist. Ct. Ariz. 1994. Atty. Wagner & Waller, P.C., Denver, 1983-86, Waller, Mark & Allen, P.C., Denver, 1986-89, Orten & Hindman P.C., Denver, 1989-90, Elrod, Katz, Preeo, Look, Moison & Silverman, P.C., Denver, 1990-97, Preeo, Silverman & Green, P.C., Denver, 1998-99, Preeo, Silverman, Green & Egle, P.C., Denver, 1999—. Mem. exec. com. staff Lawyers for Romer, Denver, 1986; precinct committeeman, 1989-92. Recipient Syracuse (N.Y.) Def. Group scholarship, 1982. Mem. ATLA, Colo. Trial Lawyers Assn., Arapahoe County Bar Assn., Syracuse U. Alumni Assn. (pres. Colo. 1987-89). Democrat. Avocations: mountain climbing, hunting, physical fitness. Office: Preeo Silverman Green & Eagle PC 1401 17th St Ste 800 Denver CO 80202-1246 E-mail: Jersey@preeosilv.com.

GREEN, JODY, real estate company executive, real estate broker; b. Iowa City, Nov. 13; d. George A. and Clare Walton (Wiggs) Olson; m. Samuel C. Wolgemuth, 1964 (div. 1976); children: Amy Clare Wolgemuth-Bordoni, George Robert Wolgemuth; m. John I. Green, 1977. Student, Greenville Coll., 1961—63, Taylor U., Upland, Ind., 1963—64. Lic. real estate broker Ill., Mich. Real estate sales Dixon Gallery Homes, Glen Ellyn, Ill., 1974—75, real estate mgr., 1975—77; real estate sales Coldwell Banker, Wheaton, Ill., 1977—82; real estate recruiter Westdale Better Homes & Gardens, Grand Rapids, Mich., 1985—96, real estate sales trainer, 1992—96; real estate recruiter and trainer Coldwell Banker Schweitzer, Sterling Heights, Mich., 1996—99; real estate sales Keller Williams Realty, Northville, Mich., 1999—. Spkr. in field; mem. Agent Leadership Coun., 1999—. Vol. Wheaton (Ill.) Ctrl. Hosp., 1974—79, Butterworth Hosp., Grand Rapids, 1985—95; established scholarship fund George Olson Meml. Fund Wheaton Coll., Ill., 2002. Mem.: Hosp. Guild (sec. 1982—84), Homeowners Assn. (v.p. 1992—2000, 2004—). Independent. Avocations: reading, boating, travel. Office: Keller Williams Realty Ste 250 22260 Haggerty Northville MI 48167 Office Phone: 248-380-8800.

GREEN, JOHN, radio broadcast editor and author; Former contbr. WBEZ Pub. Radio, NPR's All Things Considered; prod. editor NPR. Author: (novels) Looking for Alaska, 2005 (Named Top Ten Best Books for Teens, 2005, Michael L. Printz award, ALA, 2006), An Abundance of Katherines, 2006.*

GREEN, JOHN F., headmaster; m. Alison Zaeder; 3 children. BA, Wesleyan U.; MEd, Harvard U. Various positions including prof. history, admissions dir., interim head of history dept. and dean of faculty St. Paul's Sch., 1986—2001; head of sch. Peddie Sch., Hightstown, NJ, 2001—. Office: Peddie Sch PO Box A S Main St Hightstown NJ 08520-1010*

GREEN, JOHN LAFAYETTE, JR., strategic planning executive, former educational association administrator; b. Trenton, NJ, Apr. 3, 1929; m. Harriet Hardin Hill, Nov. 8, 1962; 1 child, John Lafayette III. BA, Miss. State U., 1955; MEd, Wayne State U., 1971; PhD, Rensselaer Poly. Inst., 1974. Asst. to treas. Internat. Paper Co., 1955-57; mem. faculty U. Calif., Berkeley, 1957-65; v.p. U. Ga., Athens, 1965-71, Rensselaer Poly. Inst.,

Troy, NY, 1971-76; exec. v.p. U. Miami, 1976-80; sr. v.p. U. Houston, 1980-81; pres. Washburn U., Topeka, 1981-88; founder, exec. dir. Assn. Collegiate Bus. Schs. and Programs, Overland Park, 1988—95; pres., chmn. bd. dirs. Strategic Planning/Mgmt. Assocs., Inc., Overland Park, 1981—. Founder, pres. emeritus Internat. Assembly Collegiate Bus. Edn., Overland Park, 1997—2006; past. pres. Kansas City and Topeka chpts. Planning Forum; chmn. bd. Americans 50 Plus, 2005—. Author: Budgeting, 1967, (with others) Cost Accounting, 1969, Administrative Data Processing, 1970, Strategic Planning, 1980, Strategic Planning: A System for Businesses, 1986, A Strategic Planning System for Higher Education, 1987, Strategy Development and Implementation for Banks, 1988, co-author: Outcomes Assessment in Higher Education Linked to Strategic Planning and Budgeting, 1997, Outcomes Assessment in Higher Education, 2002. Bd. dirs. Boy Scouts Am., Topeka, 1983-85. With U.S. Army 1951-53. Recipient Disting. Kansan of Yr. in Pub. Adminstrn. award Topeka Capital Jour., 1984, Kans. Pub. Adminstr. of Yr. award Am. Soc. Pub. Adminstrn., 1984, Disting. Exec. award Mktg. Exec. Kans., 1984, Edn. Leader's Hall of Fame award, 1995. Mem. AAUP, Conf. Bd., Am. Mgmt. Assn., Fin. Execs. Inst., Demographics Inst., Masons, Scottish Rite, Shriners, Royal Order of Jesters, Phi Delta Kappa, Beta Alpha Psi, Phi Kappa Phi, Pi Kappa Alpha, Delta Sigma Pi. Republican. Presbyterian. (elder, deacon). Avocations: golf, tennis. Office: PO Box 23796 Overland Park KS 66283 Home: 7895 W 157 Terr Overland Park KS 66223 Office Phone: 913-262-6040. Personal E-mail: jlgreen@kc.rr.com.

GREEN, JOHNNIE D., loan officer; b. Malvern, Ark., Feb. 5, 1961; s. Edward and Edessia Green. AAS, Vincennes U., 1998; BBA, Ark. Bapt. Coll., 1999; MBA, Webster U., 1999, MA in Internat. Bus. and Fin., 2000. Admin., fin. and personnel specialist U.S. Army, 1981—84; asst. br. mgr. Twin City Bank, North Little Rock, Ark., 1984—94; asst. v.p., loan officer Bank of Malvern, Ark., 1994—95; comml. loan officer U.S. SBA, Little Rock, 1995—. Adj. prof. Vincennes U., North Little Rock, Ark., 2000—; CEO, chmn. Ark. Cmty. Recreational Svcs.; adj. prof. Webster U., Memphis, 2000—, Embry Riddle Aeronautical Univ. Little Rock AFB, Jacksonville, Ark., 2001—, Ctrl. Bapt. Coll., Conway, Ark., 2001—, Philander Smith Coll., Little Rock, 2002—, Nova Southeastern U., Ft. Lauderdale, Fla., 2003—. Past pres. Malvern Stella Smith Boys and Girls Club; bd. dirs. Teen Promise, Inc.; CEO, chmn. Ark. Cmty. Recreation Svcs. E-5 N.G. US Army, 1987—2002. Decorated Meritorious Svc. Medal; recipient Cert. of Appreciation, Ark. N.G., 2002, Cert. of Svc. award, Ark. Guard Bur., 2002, Commendation medal, State of Ark., 2002. Mem.: ACLU, NAACP, Assn. for Fin. Profls., Fin. Mgmt. Assn. Internat., Nat. Assn. Urban Bankers, Acad. of Mgmt., Non-Commn. Officers Assn., Little Rock Club. Home: 507 Maurice Dr Malvern AR 72104 Office: US SBA 2120 Riverfront Dr Ste 100 Little Rock AR 72202 Office Phone: 501-324-5871 233. Business E-Mail: johnnie.green@sba.gov.

GREEN, JONATHAN H., lawyer; b. Miami Beach, Fla., Apr. 13, 1954; BBA, U. Miami, 1977; JD, Nova U., 1980; LLM in Taxation, U. Miami, 1982. Bar: Fla. 1980, US Tax Ct. 1981. Gen. counsel Wolper, Ross, Ingham & Co., 1987—88; prin. Jonathan H. Green & Assocs., P.A., Miami, Fla. Adj. prof. law Master's prog. in taxation U. Miami Sch. Law, 1985—87. Contbr. articles to profl. publs. Named one of Top 100 Attys., Worth mag., 2005. Mem.: Greater Miami Estate Planning Coun., Greater Miami Tax Inst., South Fla. Employee Benefits Coun. (pres. 1993—94). Office: Jonathan H Green & Assocs PA 799 Brickell Plz Ste 700 Miami FL 33131*

GREEN, JOSHUA, III, foundation administrator, retired bank executive; b. Seattle, June 30, 1936; s. Joshua, Jr. and Elaine (Brygger) G.; m. Pamela K. Pemberton, Nov. 1, 1974; children: Joshua IV, Jennifer Elaine, Paige Courtney. BA in English, Harvard U., 1958. With Peoples Nat. Bank Wash., Seattle, 1960-88, exec. v.p., 1972-75, pres., 1975—77, CEO, 1977-78, chmn. bd., 1979-88, US Bank Washington (merger PeoplesBank and Old Nat. Bank), 1988-96; chmn. Joshua Green Corp., Seattle, 1996—. Bd. dirs., chmn., CEO Far Bank Enterprises, Inc., Fourth Ave. Investments Co., Pacific Sci. Ctr., Joshua Green Corp., Safeco, Port Blakely Tree Farms, Rio Products Internat., Inc., Sage Mfg., U. Wash. Bus. Sch., U. Wash. Found., Va. Mason Hosp. Found., Va. Mason Hosp. Rsch.; dir. Pacific Sci. Ctr., Va. Mason Health Sys. Bd. dirs. Rhododendron Species Found.; trustee Downtown Seattle Assn., ArtsFund (formerly known as Corp. Coun. Arts). Mem. Univ. Club, Rainier Club, Seattle Tennis Club, Wash. Athletic Club. Home: 414 McGilvra Blvd E Seattle WA 98112-2308 Office: 1425 4th Ave Ste 420 Seattle WA 98101-2218 also: PO Box 21829 Seattle WA 98111-3829 Personal E-mail: jiiigreen@aol.com.

GREEN, JOYCE HENS, federal judge; b. NYC, Nov. 13, 1928; d. James S. and Hedy (Bucher) Hens; m. Samuel Green, Sept. 25, 1965 (dec.); children: Michael Timothy, June Heather, James Harry. BA, U. Md., 1949; JD, George Washington U., 1951, LLD, 1994. Practice law, Washington, 1951-68, Arlington, Va., 1956-68; ptnr. Green & Green, 1966-68; assoc. judge Superior Ct., D.C., 1968-79; judge U.S. Dist. Ct. for D.C., 1979—; judge presiding U.S. Fgn. Intelligence Surveillance Ct., 1988-95. Bd. advisors George Washington U. Law Sch., 1991-2001; jud. br. com. Jud. Conf. U.S., 1995-2001. Co-author: Dissolution of Marriage, 1986, supplements, 1987-89, Marriage and Family Law Agreements, 1985, supplements, 1986-89. Chair Task Force on Gender, Race and Ethnic Bias for the D.C. Cir. Recipient Alumni Achievement award George Washington U., 1975, Profl. Achievement award, 1978, Outstanding Contbn. to Equal Rights award Women's Legal Def. Fund, 1976, hon. doctor of Laws George Washington U., 1994, U.S. Dept. Justice Edmund J. Randolph award, 1995, Professionalism award D.C. Cir., Am. Inns Ct., 2004. Fellow Am. Bar Found.; ABA (jud. adminstrn. divsn., chair nat. conf. fed. trial judges 1997-98), Fed. Judges Assn., Nat. Assn. Women Judges, Va. Bar, Bar Assn. D.C. (jud. honoree of Yr. 1994), D.C. Bar, D.C. Women's Bar Assn. (pres. 1960-62, woman lawyer of yr. 1979), Exec. Women in Govt. (chmn. 1977), Woman's Forum of Washington D.C. Office: US Dist Ct E Barrett Prettyman US Courthouse 333 Constitution Ave NW Washington DC 20001-2802

GREEN, JUDSON C., marketing agency executive; Pres. Attractions Divsn. Walt Disney Co., Burbank, Calif., 1991-98, chmn. Attractions Divsn., 1998-2000; pres., CEO Navigation Techs. Corp. (now NAVTEQ), Chgo., 2000—. Office: NAVTEQ Ste 900 222 Merchandise Mart Chicago IL 60654

GREEN, KAREN F., lawyer; b. 1956; AB magna cum laude, Radcliffe Coll., 1978; JD cum laude, Harvard Univ., 1981. Bar: Mass. 1981. Law clk. Judge W. Arthur Garrity, US Dist. Ct. (Mass. dist.), 1981—82; assoc. Hale & Dorr, Boston, 1982—84; asst. U.S. atty. civil div., U.S. Dept. of Justice, Boston, 1984—86; assoc. Hale & Dorr, Boston, 1987—88, jr. ptnr., 1988—90, sr. ptnr., 1990—93; chief of staff Mass. Gov. William F. Weld, 1993; dep. U.S. atty. U.S. Dept. of Justice, Boston, 1994—96; sr. ptnr. Hale & Dorr, Boston, 1996—2004; ptnr., co-chmn. Litigation dept., mem. exec. com. Wilmer Cutler Pickering Hale & Dorr, Boston, 2004—. Co-chmn., transition team for exec. office of health & human svc. Mass. Gov.-elect William F. Weld, 1990—91; bd. dir. Fiduciary Trust Co.; mem. spl. commn. on Suffolk County Sheriff's Dept. for Mass. acting Gov. Jane Swift; vice chmn. com. on pro bono legal svc. Mass. Supreme Judicial Ct.; mem. gender bias com. US Ct. Appeals (1st cir.); mem. com. to revise local criminal rules & com. on alternative dispute resolution US Dist Ct. (Mass. dist.); instr. Harvard Law Sch. Trial Advocacy Workshop, U.S. Atty. Gen. Advocacy Inst. Mem. exec. com. Mass. Judicial Nominating Council; dir. Children's Trust Fund. Named one of Boston's Top Women Lawyers, Boston Globe, 1996, Top 100 Mass. Super Lawyers & Top 50 Female Mass. Super Lawyers, Boston Mag., 2004; recipient award for Outstanding Svc. to City of Boston, Park St. Forum, 1997, Leading Women award, Patriot's Trail Girl Scout Council, 2000, Women's Bus. Hall of Fame award, 2001, honoree for pro bono legal work, Granada House, 2002. Mem.: Boston Bar Found. (trustee), Boston Bar Assn. (council mem. & chmn. Fed. Practice & Procedure com.), Boston Club (dir.), Phi Beta Kappa. Office: Wilmer Cutler Pickering Hale & Dorr 60 State St Boston MA 02109 Office Phone: 617-526-6207. Office Fax: 617-526-5000. Business E-Mail: karen.green@wilmerhale.com.

GREEN, LINDA KATHLEEN, pathologist, educator; b. Landstuhl, Germany, Jan. 6, 1956; d. Gordon Lyle and Nancy Green; m. Chris Chrisopoulos; 1 child, Georgio Gordon Chrisopoulos. MD, U. Tex. Health Sci. Ctr., San Antonio, 1982. Physician in charge cytology and flow cytometry ME DeBakey VA Med. Ctr., Houston, 1987—; prof. pathology Baylor Coll. Medicine, Houston, 2002—07. V.p. Daus. of Penelope, Houston, 2002—04. Fellow, Am Cancer Soc., 1986. Mem.: Am. Soc. Clin. Pathologists, Tex. Soc. Cytology (assoc.; pres. 1996—97), Hosuton Soc. Clin. Pathologists (assoc.; pres. 1997—98), Am. Soc. Cytology (assoc.; chmn. new techs. 2000—03), USCAP (assoc.), Alpha Omega Alpha. Avocation: art and jewelery design. Office: ME DeBakey VA Med Ctr 2002 Holcombe Blvd Houston TX 77030 Home Phone: 713-794-7266; Office Phone: 713-794-7266. Office Fax: 713-794-7657; Home Fax: 713-794-7657. Personal E-mail: linda.green2@med.va.gov. E-mail: linda. green2 @med.va.gov.

GREEN, LISA CANNON, editor; b. Marshall, Ky., May 7, 1962; d. Walter L. and Phyllis (Jones) Cannon; m. Bob Dale Green, May 31, 1980; children: Emily, Ethan. BA in Journalism and English, Murray State U., 1983. With The Post-Intelligencer, Paris, Tenn., 1983-84, The Jackson (Tenn.) Sun, 1984-90; data desk editor The Tennessean, Nashville, 1990—. Office: The Tennessean 1100 Broadway Nashville TN 37203-3134 Office Phone: 615-259-8275. Business E-Mail: lgreen@tennessean.com.

GREEN, MADELEINE F., educational association administrator; BA magna cum laude, Harvard U.; PhD Columbia U. V.p., dir. ctr. instl. and internat. initiatives Am. Coun. Edn. Interim pres. Mt. Vernon Coll., Washington, 1990—91; mem. bd. trustees Wilson Coll., Pa., 1988—93, Sweet Briar Coll., Va., 1994—2002; bd. dirs. Juniata Coll., Pa.; mem. adminstrv. bd. Internat. Assn. Univ., 2000—, v.p., 2004—. Co-author: Internationalizing the Campus: A User's Guide, On Change series, The American College President: 2000 Edition; editor: Leaders for a New Era: Strategies for Higher Education, 1988, Minorities on Campus: A Handbook for Enhancing Diversity, 1989, Investing in Higher Education: A Handbook of Leadership Development, 1991, Transforming Higher Education: Views from Leaders Around the World, 1997. Office: Am Coun Edn One Dupont Cir NW Washington DC 20036 Office Phone: 202-939-9418.

GREEN, MARK ANDREW, former congressman; b. Boston, June 1, 1960; s. Jeremy Raleigh and Elizabeth Pamela (Roome) Green; m. Susan Keske, Aug. 5, 1985; children: Rachel Eve Libinu, Anna Faith Kitali, Alexander Mark Amutavi. BA, U. Wis., Eau Claire, 1983; JD, U. Wis., Madison, 1987. Bar: Wis. 1987. Tchr., intern World Teach Project, Kakamega, Kenya, 1987-88; counsel Godfrey & Kahn, S.C., Green Bay, Wis., 1989-98; mem. Wis. State Assembly, Madison, 1992-98, chmn. assembly majority caucus, 1994-98, chmn. assembly judiciary com., 1994—98; state chmn. Am. Legis. Exch. Coun.; mem. US Congress from 8th Wis. dist., 1999—2007, mem. judiciary com., mem. internat. rels. Legal counsel Rep. Assembly Campaign Com., Madison, 1993. Chmn. mcpl. affairs Brown County Taxpayers Assn., Green Bay, 1990-92; chmn. Brown County Rep. Party, 1991-92; bd. dirs. Nat. R.R. Mus., Green Bay, 1992—; chmn. resolutions com. Wis. Rep. Conv., Milw., 1993. Named Wis. Outstanding Legislator, Wis. Builders Assn., 1995, Healthcare Leader of Wis., State Med. Soc., 1996, Small Bus. Adv., Small Bus. Survival Com., 1999, Super Friend of Srs., 60 Plus Assn., 1999, Friend of the Farm Bur., Am. Farm Bur. Fedn., 2000; recipient Wis. award, Ind. Bus. Assn., 1996, Legislator of Yr. award, Wis. Am. Legion, Spirit of Enterprise award, US C. of C., Mfg. Legis. Excellence award, Nat. Assn. Mfrs., Sr. Legis. Achievement award, Srs. Coalition, 1999—2000, Golden Bulldog award, Watchdogs of the Treas., 2000, Friend of the Family award, Christian Coalition, 2000, Award for Mfg. Excellence, Nat. Assn. Mfrs., 2000, Tax Fighter award, Nat. Tax Limitation Com., 2000, Guardian of Small Bus. award, Nat. Fedn. Ind. Bus., 2000, Thomas Jefferson award, Food Distbrs. Internat., 2000, Hero of the Taxpayer award, Ams. for Tax Reform, 2000, Small Bus. Survival Com. award, 2000, Yr. of the Sr. award, 60 Plus Assn., 2000, Friend of the Shareholder award, Am. Shareholders Assn., 2000. Mem. ABA, Wis. Bar Assn., Am. Legis. Exch. Coun., Nat. Conf. State Legislators, Brown County Home Builders Assn., Kiwanis. Republican.

GREEN, MARK JOSEPH, lawyer, author; b. Bklyn., Mar. 15, 1945; s. Irving Arthur and Anna Constance (Suna) G.; m. Denisse Michele Frand, Aug. 13, 1977; children— Jenya Frand Green, Jonah Frand Green. BA magna cum laude, Cornell U., 1967; JD cum laude, Harvard U., 1970. Bar: D.C. 1971, N.Y. 1988. Dir. Corp. Accountability Research Group, Washington, 1970-76, Public Citizen's Congress Watch, Washington, 1977-80; founding pres. Democracy Project, NYC, 1981-90; commr. consumer affairs City of NY, 1990-93, pub. adv., 1994; hon. chmn. Democracy Project, NYC. Author: (with others) The Closed Enterprise System, 1972, The Other Government: The Unseen Power of Washington Lawyers, 1975, (with R. Nader and J. Seligman) Taming the Giant Corporation, 1976, Who Runs Congress?, 1972, 4th edit., 1984, (with Gail MacColl) Reagan's Reign of Error, 1983, (with J. Berry) The Challenge of Hidden Profits, 1985, America's Transition: Blueprints for the 1990s, 1989, The Consumer Bible, 1995, 2d edit., 1999. Dem. nominee for U.S. Senate, N.Y., 1986. Democrat. Jewish. Office: New Democracy Project 420 Lexington Ave Rm 555 New York NY 10170-0555 Office Phone: 212-490-0001.

GREEN, MARTIN LINCOLN, retired medical products executive; b. Des Plaines, Ill., Feb. 22, 1940; s. Martin Lincoln and Madelyne Mae (Larson) G.; m. Carolyn Elizabeth Johnson, Jan. 19, 1968; children: Peter Cranston, Edward Reavy. BA in Econs., Lawrence U., 1963; MBA, U. Chgo., 1977. News asst. NY Times, NYC, 1963—64; reporter Sheffield Telegraph, England, 1964—66, Balt. Sun, 1966—67; sales rep. 3M Co., Chgo., 1967—70; stockbroker Bache & Co., Chgo., 1970—71; sales mgr. Xerox Corp., Chgo., 1971—77, mgr. strategic planning Rochester, NY, 1977—81; dir. sales, mktg. Bausch & Lomb, Inc., Rochester, 1981—84, v.p. sales, mktg., 1984—87; v.p. strategic planning Cambridge Instruments, Buffalo, 1987—88, pres. Ophthalmic Inst. divsn., 1988—97, Leica, Inc., Buffalo, 1988—97; pres. Thornell Inst., Pittsford, NY, 1998—2002; ret., 2002. Republican. Avocations: investing, walking, reading, weightlifting, writing. Home: 16 Forest Knoll Pittsford NY 14534-3602

GREEN, MAURICE, molecular biologist, educator, virologist; b. NYC, May 5, 1926; s. David and Bessie (Lipschitz) G.; m. Marilyn Glick, Aug. 20, 1950; children: Michael Richard, Wendy Allison Green Lee, Eric Douglas. BS in Chemistry, U. Mich., 1949; MS in Biochemistry and Chemistry, U. Wis.-Madison, 1952, PhD in Biochemistry and Chemistry, 1954. Instr. biochemistry U. Pa. Med. Sch., Phila., 1955-56; asst. prof. St. Louis U. Health Scis. Ctr., 1956-60, assoc. prof., 1960-63, prof. microbiology, 1963-77; prof., chmn. Inst. for Molecular Virology, 1964—. Office: St Louis U Health Sci Ctr Inst for Molecular Virology 3681 Park Ave Saint Louis MO 63110-2511 Business E-Mail: green@slu.edu.

GREEN, MAURICE RICHARD, neuropsychiatrist; b. Chgo., Oct. 28, 1922; divorced; children: Melissa, Suzanne, Constance. BS, Northwestern U., 1942; BM, Northwestern U. Med. Sch., 1945, MD, 1946; cert. in Psychoanalytic Tng., William Alanson White Inst., NYC, 1954. Diplomate Am. Bd. Psychiatry and Neurology. Intern Passavant Hosp., Chgo., 1945-46; resident in psychiatry Bronx (N.Y.) VA Hosp., 1948-51; cons. psychiatrist Brookwood Hall, East Islip, L.I., N.Y., 1955-58; staff psychiatrist Psychiatric Clinic Ct. Spl. Sessions, 1956-60; cons. psychiatrist Bleuler Psychotherapy Ctr., Queens, N.Y., 1956-68; rsch. psychiatrist, mem. psychiat. epidemiology sect. William Alanson White Inst., NYC, 1968-72; attending geriat. psychiatrist Albert Einstein Med. Sch., 1974-76; attending child and adolescent psychiatry Harlem Hosp. of Columbia Presbyn. Med. Ctr., NYC, 1974-75; med. dir. geriat. and family psychiatry Lincoln Hosp., 1974-76; chief psychiatrist Family Ct. Svcs. divsn. South Beach Psychiat. Ctr., SI, N.Y., 1976-80; sr. attending psychiatrist Columbia-Presbyn. at St. Luke's-Roosevelt Hosp., NYC, 1978—; cons. psychiatrist Liaison-Consultation Svc. NYU Med. Ctr., NYC, 1985-86; psychiatrist spl. evaluation and treatment unit Rockland Psychiat. Ctr., 1985-87. Mem. faculty William Alanson White Inst., N.Y.C., 1957—; cons. Goddard Coll., 1961-68; assoc. attending psychiatrist Bellevue Hosp., 1962-85, presently attending physician; supervisory and tng. analyst William Alanson White Inst., 1962—2003; clin. prof. psychiatry NYU Med. Sch., 1964—2003; mem. med. bd. Roosevelt Hosp., 1965-76; prin. investigator Diamox-Thiamine Research Unit Nathan S. Kline Research Inst., 1987; project dir. Brain Chemistry of Schizophrenia at Nathan Kline Inst., 1988-93; med. dir. Neurologic Sys., Inc., 1987; presidium Inst. for Brain Function Rsch., Inc., 1987; mem. Treatment Innovations Task Force-Soc. for Traumatic Stress Studies, 1987. Author: Interpersonal Psychoanalysis: Selected Papers of Clara Thompson, 1971, Psicoanalisi interpersonale, 1972, L'Esperiencze Prelogica, 1972, Violence and the Family, 1980; (with Edward S. Tauber) Prelogical Experience, 1959; assoc. editor Contemporary Psychoanalysis jour., 1968-80; contbr. articles to profl. jours. Project dir. Nathan Kline Rsch. Inst., 1988—. Fellow: N.Y. Acad. Medicine, Am. Acad. Child and Adolescent Psychiatry (com. on hospitalization of children, nat. legis. network 1982—86), Am. Psychiat. Assn. (com. on aging N.Y. Dist. br.), Am. Orthopsychiat. Assn. (publs. com. Anniversary Vol. 1968—71); mem.: Am. Assn. Geriat. Psychiatry, Internat. Soc. Psychoneuroendocrinology, Am. Assn. Psychosocial Rehab., Soc. Biol. Psychiatry, Nat. Assn. Patients Rights and Advocacy, Physicians for Social Responsibility, William Alanson White Psychoanalytic Soc., N.Y. Soc. Clin. Psychiatry, N.Y. Coun. Child Psychiatry. Home and Office: 275 Central Park W Apt 15 D New York NY 10024-3058 Office Phone: 212-595-9774. Personal E-mail: mauriegreen@msn.com. *We are all much more simply human than otherwise; what enhances our individual humanity will also enhance the common humanity of those around us.*

GREEN, MICAH S., trade association administrator; BBA, George Washington U., 1979, JD, 1984. Asst. dir, legis. liaison Nat. Assn. Realtors, 1981—83; legis. asst. to rep. Ronald Sarasin U.S. Ho. of Reps., staff dir., gen. counsel subcom. on human resources, com. on post office and civil svc., 1983—85; tax legis. counsel MCI Comm. Corp., 1985—87; exec. v.p. The Bond Market Assn., COO, 1999—2001, pres., CEO, 2006—. Office: The Bond Market Assn 360 Madison Ave 18th Fl New York NY 10017-7111 Office Phone: 646-637-9200. Office Fax: 646-637-9126.

GREEN, MONICA H., history professor; BA, Barnard Coll., 1978; MA, Princeton U., 1981; PhD in History of Sci., Princeton U., NJ. Fellow U. N.C., Chapel Hill; assoc. prof. history Duke U.; prof. history Ariz. State U., Tempe, 2001—. Author: (essays) Women's Helathcare and the Medieval West: Texts and Contexts, 2000; contbr. articles; editor, translator: The Trotula: A Medieval Compendium of Women's Medicine, 2001. Fellow, NEH, Inst. Advanced Study, Princeton U., Nat. Humanities Ctr., John Simon Guggenheim Meml. Found., 2003. Office: Ariz State U Dept History PO Box 872501 Tempe AZ 85287-2501

GREEN, MORRIS, retired pediatrician, educator; b. Indpls., May 27, 1922; s. Coleman and Rebecca (Oleinick) Green; m. Janice Barber Gorton, Mar. 11, 1955; children: David Schuster, Alan Coleman, Carolyn Ann, Susan Elaine, Marcia Ruth, Sylvia Rebecca. AB, Ind. U., 1942, MD, 1944. Intern Ind. U. Med. Ctr., 1945; resident pediat. U. Ill. Rsch. and Ednl. Hosps., 1947—49; instr. pediat. U. Ill. Coll. Medicine, 1949—52; asst. prof. Yale Sch. Medicine, 1952—57; faculty Ind. U. Sch. Medicine, Indpls., 1957—, Perry W. Lesh prof. pediat., 1963—; chmn. dept. pediat., physician-in-chief James Whitcomb Riley Hosp. for Children, Indpls., 1967—88; ret. Commr. health State of Ind., 1990—91. Author: Pediatric Diagnosis, 6th edit., 1998; co-editor: Ambulatory Pediatrics, 1968, 5th edit., 1999, Bright Futures, 2d edit., 2000; mem. editl. bd.: Pediat. Rev., Contemporary Pediat., Current Problems Pediat., Jour. Devel. Behavioral Pediat., Jour. Ambulatory Pediat. Assn., Social Work in Health Care, nat. adviser: Children Today. Served to capt. M.C. US Army, 1945—47. Recipient George Armstrong award in ambulatory pediat., 1971, C. Anderson Aldrich award in child devel., 1982, Irving S. Cutter award, Phi Rho Sigma, 1984, Ross award for pediat. edn., 1985, Simon Wile award, Am. Acad. Child and Adolescent Psychiatry, 1990, Joseph W. St. Geme award, Fedn. Pediat. Orgns., 1992, Disting. Career award, Ambulatory Pediat. Assn., 1996, Lifetime award for disting. svc. in years of health advancement, Ind. Pub. Health Found., 2003. Mem.: AMA (Abraham Jacobi award 1990), Soc. Rsch. Child Devel., Inst. Medicine, Am. Orthopsychiat. Assn., Am. Acad. Pediat. (Abraham Jacobi award 1990), Am. Fedn. Clin. Rsch., Soc. Pediatric Rsch., Am. Pediatric Soc., Alpha Omega Alpha, Sigma Xi, Phi Beta Kappa. Home Phone: 301-869-2978. Personal E-mail: maunderw@iupui.edu.

GREEN, NANCY LOUGHRIDGE, publishing executive; b. Lexington, Ky., Jan. 19, 1942; d. William S. and Nancy O. (Green) Loughridge. BA in Journalism, U. Ky., 1964, postgrad., 1968; MA in Journalism, Ball State U., 1971; postgrad., U. Minn., 1968; EdD, Nova Southeastern U., 2003. Tchr. English, publs. adv. Clark County H.S., Winchester, Ky., 1965-66, Pleasure Ridge Park H.S., Louisville, 1966-67, Clarksville (Ind.) H.S., 1967-68, Charleston (W.Va.) H.S., 1968-69; asst. publs., pub. info. specialist W.Va. Dept. Edn., Charleston, 1969-70; tchr. journalism, publs. dir. Elmhurst H.S., Ft. Wayne, Ind., 1970-71; adviser student publs. U. Ky., Lexington, 1971-82; gen. mgr. student publs. U. Tex., Austin, 1982-85; pres., pub. Palladium-Item, Richmond, Ind., 1985-89, News-Leader, Springfield, Mo., 1989-92; asst. to pres. newspaper divsn. Gannett Co., Inc., Washington, 1992-94; exec. dir. advancement Clayton State Coll., Morrow, Ga., 1994-96; v.p. advancement Clayton Coll. & State U., Morrow, Ga., 1996-99; v.p. comm. Ga. GLOBE U. Sys., 1999-2000; dir. circulation/distbn., sales & mktg. Lee Enterprises, Davenport, Iowa, 2000—02; v.p. circulation LEE Enterprises, Davenport, 2002—; pub. The Courier, 2004—. Dir. Dow Jonesurban journalism program Harte-Hanks, 1984, Louisville Courier-Jour. and Lexington Herald-Leader, 1976-82; pres. Media Cons., Inc., Lexington, 1980; sec. Kernel Press, Inc., 1971-82. Contbr. articles to profl. jours. Bd. dirs. Studen Press Law Ctr., 1975-2005, Richmond Cmty. Devel. Corp., 1987-89, United Way of the Ozarks, 1990-92, ARC, 1990-92, Springfield Arts Coun., 1990-91, Bus. Devel. Corp., 1991-92, Bus. Edn. Alliance, 1991-92, Caring Found., 1991-92, Cox Hosp. Bd., 1990-92, Springfield Schs. Found., 1964-82, Jr. League, Lexington, 1971-82, Manchester Ctr., 1978-82, pres., 1979-82; chmn. Greater Richmond Progress Com., 1986-87, bd. dirs., 1986-89; pres. Leadership Wayne County, 1986-87, bd. dirs. 1985-89; adv. bd. Ind. U. East, 1985-89, Richmond C. of C., 1987-89, Ind. Humanities Coun., 1988-89, Youth Comm. Bd., 1988-92, Opera Theatre No. Va., 1992-94, Atlanta chpt. AIWF, 1995-2000. Recipient Coll. Media Advisers First Amendment award, 1987, Disting. Svc. award Assn. Edn. Journalism and Mass Comm., 1989; named to Journalism Hall of Fame, Ball State U., 1988, Hall Fame, Coll. Media Advisors, 1994, Journalism Hall of Fame, Ky., 2007. Mem. Student Press Law Ctr. (bd. dirs. 1975-05, pres. 1985-87, 94-96, v.p. 1992-94), Assoc. Collegiate Press, Journalism Edn. Assn. (Carl Towley award 1988), Nat. Coun. Coll. Publs. Advs./Coll. Media Advisers (pres. 1979-83, Disting. Newspaper Adv. 1976, Disting. Bus. Adviser 1984), Columbia Scholastic Press Assn. (Gold Key 1980), So. Interscholastic Press Assn. (Disting. Svc. award 1983), Nat. Scholastic Press Assn. (Pioneer award 1982), Soc. Profl. Journalists, Internat. Newspaper Mktg. Assn. N.Am. (bd. dirs. 2002—07), Newspaper Assn. Am. (postal com. 2001—, readership adv. group 2002—, diversity subcom. 1991-05, circulation fed. bd. 2002-07, 2d v.p. 2006, 1st v.p. 2007), Clayton County C. of C. (adv. bd. 1995-99, chmn. internat. com. 1996-98), Cedar Falls C. of C. (bd. dirs. 2005—) Office: The Courier 501 Commercial St Waterloo IA 50701 Office Phone: 563-383-2126, 319-291-1500. Business E-Mail: nancy.green@lee.net. *An opportunity each day to make the best of every situation to help others, your community, your profession and employees to be successful.*

GREEN, NANCY SUE, pediatrician, health science association administrator; b. 1957; Undergraduate degree in chemistry magna cum laude, Tufts U., Mass.; MD, Columbia U. Coll. Physicians and Surgeons, 1983. Cert. Pediatrics, 1988, Pediatric Hematology-Oncology, lic. NY. Clin. tng. in pediatrics and pediatric hematology-oncology Columbia-Presbyn. Med. Ctr., Barnes Hosp., NY; post-doctoral fellowship, cell biology Albert Einstein Coll. Medicine, Yeshiva Univ., asst. prof., cell biology NY, assoc. clin. prof., dept. pediatrics NY, assoc. clin. prof., dept. obstetrics & gynecology and women's health NY; practices pediatric hematology/oncology and pediatrics Hastings on Hudson, NY; attending physician in pediatric hematology-oncology Montefiore Hosp. Acting med. dir. March of Dimes, med. dir., 2002—. Author: of numerous papers on pediatric hematology, oncology and immunology. Fulbright Scholar, 1986—87. Mem.: Am. Soc. Hematology, Am. Assn. Immunology, Eastern Soc. Pediatric Rsch. (coun. mem.). Office: 31 Hopke Ave Hastings On Hudson NY 10706 Address: March of Dimes 1275 Mamaroneck Ave White Plains NY 10605 Office Phone: 914-997-4649. Business E-Mail: ngreen@modimes.org.

GREEN, PATRICIA PATAKY, school system administrator, consultant; b. NYC, June 18, 1949; d. William J. and Theresa M. (DiGianni) P.; m. Stephen I. Green, Dec. 7, 1975. BS, U. Md., 1971, MEd, 1977, PhD, 1994. Tchr. Prince George's County Pub. Sch., Md., 1971-83; elem. instrnl. adminstrv. specialist Thomas Stone Sch., Mt. Ranier, Md., 1984-85, Glenridge Sch., Lanham, Md., 1984, Greenbelt Ctr. Sch., Md., 1983-84, Prince George's County Pub. Schs., 1985-91; prin. Columbia Pk. Sch., Landover, Md., 1985-91; asst. supt. Prince George's County Pub. Sch., 1991-95, assoc. supt., chief divsn. adminstr., 1995-99, assoc. supt. for pupil svc., 1999—2001, acting dep. supt. for instrn., 2000—02, fellow Broad Ctr. Supt., Bd. Found., 2002; supt. sch. North Allegheny Sch. Dist., Pitts., 2002—. Exec. dir. North Allegheny Found., excellence bd. trustees, 2002—; cons. nationwide sch. systems; presenter in field; spkr. in field. Featured in numerous mag. and on TV shows; contbr. articles to profl. jour. Apptd. commr. Prince George's Comm. for Children, Youth and Families; mem. Prince George's County Cmty. in Sch., 1998—2002; trustee North Allegheny Found., 2002, exec. dir., 2002—. Recipient Nat. Sch. Recognition award US Dept. Edn., 1988, Outstanding Adminstr. award Prince George's County C. of C., 1990, Outstanding Rsch. award Md. Assn. Supervision and Curriculum Devel., 1995, Outstanding Educator award Prince George's County, 1983, Spotlight on Prevention award Md. State Atty. Gen., 1998, Disting. Achievement award North Allegheny Sch. Dist., 2002, Outstanding Profl. award U. Md. Coll. Edn., 2003. Mem. NAESP (Excellence of Achievement award 1988), ASCD, Am. Assn. Sch. Adminstrs., Pa. Assn. Sch. Adminstrs., Pa. Assn. Surp. and Curriculum Devel., Pa. Sch. Bds. Assn., Phi Kappa Phi. Kappa Delta Pi. Avocations: landscape gardening, photography, reading, writing, bicycling. Business E-Mail: pgreen@northallegheny.org.

GREEN, PAUL ELIOT, JR., retired optical engineer; b. Durham, NC, Jan. 14, 1924; s. Paul Eliot and Elizabeth Atkinson (Lay) G.; m. Dorrit L. Gegan, Oct. 30, 1948; children: Dorrit Green Rodemeyer, Nancy E., Judith Green Godin, Paul M., Gordon M. AB, U. N.C., 1943; MS, N.C. State U., 1948; ScD, MIT, 1953. Group leader MIT Lincoln Lab., Lexington, 1951-69; sr. mgr. rsch. divsn. IBM, Yorktown Heights, NY, 1969-97; dir. optical networking tech. Tellabs, Hawthorne, NY, 1997-2000. Radio engring. adv. com. USIA, 1984—93; panel on survivable comm. NRC, 1982—89. Author: Fiber Optic Networks, 1992; co-editor: Computer Communications, 1974; editor: Computer Network Architectures and Protocols, 1982, Network Interconnection and Protocol Conversion, 1988. Served to lt. comdr. USNR, 1943—60, ret. Named Disting. Engring. Alumnus N.C. State U., 1983; recipient Data Comm. award Assn. Computing Machinery, SIGCOM, 1994. Fellow: IEEE (chmn. info. theory group 1960, pres. Comm. Soc. 1992—93, Aerospace Pioneer award 1981, E.H. Armstrong award 1989, Simon Ramo medal 1991); mem.: NAE, Russian Popov Soc. (hon.). Home: 1921 S Lakeshore Dr Chapel Hill NC 27514 Personal E-mail: pegreen@earthlink.net.

GREEN, PAUL WARREN, state supreme court justice; b. San Antonio, Mar. 6, 1952; s. Hubert William and Leah (Tritt) G.; m. Judith Ellen Keppler, Aug. 4, 1973; children: W. Paul, John K. BBA, U. Tex., 1974; JD, St. Mary's U., San Antonio, 1977. Bar: Tex. 1977, U.S. Dist. Ct. (we. dist.) Tex. 1982, U.S. Ct. Appeals (5th cir.) 1985, U.S. Dist. Ct. (so. dist.) Tex. 1990. Ptnr. Green, McReynolds & Reed, San Antonio, 1977—95; judge San Antonio Ct. of Appeals, 1995—2004; justice Tex. Supreme Ct., 2005—. Bd. dirs., Halfway House of San Antonio, 1978-90, pres., 1985. Fellow Tex. Bar Found., San Antonio Bar Found.; mem. ABA (mem. house of delegates 1991-93), State Bar Tex. (dir. 1993-94), San Antonio Bar Assn. (pres. 1991-92). Avocations: golf, sailing, hunting. Office: Tex State Supreme Court PO Box 12248 Austin TX 78711*

GREEN, PETER CARLYLE, retired physician, farmer; b. Roberts, Idaho, Mar. 1, 1922; s. Luman Peter and Reda Jane (Walker) Green; m. Joy Spencer Green, Apr. 11, 2000; m. Mary L. Olson (div.); m. Martha Orr (dec.); children: James C., Mary Louise Nelson, Evelyn Caldwell, Barbara Bale, Thomas. BS, U. Utah, Salt Lake City, 1944, MD, 1947. Dir. Good Samaritan Hosp., Portland, 1976—82. Bd. mem. Molalla City Band, Oreg., 1975—77. Capt. US Med. Corps. Mem.: Oreg. Med. Soc. Republican. Mem. Lds Ch. Avocations: music, tennis. Home: 82 Redbluff Dr Hurricane UT 84737-3185

GREEN, PETER MORRIS, classics educator, writer, translator; b. London, Dec. 22, 1924; came to U.S., 1971; s. Arthur and Olive Emily (Slaughter) G.; m. Lalage Isobel Pulvertaft, July 28, 1951 (div.); children: Timothy Michael Bourke, Nicholas Paul, Sarah Francesca; m. Carin Margreta Christensen, July 18, 1975. BA, Cambridge U., 1950, MA, PhD, Cambridge U., 1954. Dir. studies in classics Selwyn Coll., Cambridge, Eng., 1952-53; freelance writer, journalist, translator, London, 1954-63; lectr. Greek history and lit. Coll. Yr. in Athens, 1966-71; prof. classics U. Tex., Austin, 1971-97, James R. Dougherty Centennial prof., 1982-97, prof. emeritus, 1997—. Vis. prof. classics UCLA, 1976; vis. prof. history U. Iowa, 1997-98, adj. prof. classics, 1998—; vis. prof. history, Athens, 1999; Mellon chair in humanities Tulane U., 1986; vis. fellow, writer-in-residence Hellenic studies program Princeton U., 2001; King Charles II Disting. vis. prof. classics and ancient history East Carolina U., 2004 Whichard vis. prof. classics and ancient history, 2006. Fiction critic: Daily Telegraph, London, 1954-63; sr. cons. editor: Hodder & Stoughton Ltd., London, 1959-63; cons.: (Odyssey project) Nat. Radio Theatre, Chgo., 1980-81; author: The Sword of Pleasure, 1957 (Heinemann award for Lit. 1957), The Laughter of Aphrodite, 1965, Armada from Athens, 1970, The Shadow of the Parthenon, 1972, Alexander of Macedon 356-323 BC: A Historical Biography, 1974, 2d edit., 1991, Classical Bearings, 1989, ed edit., 1998, Alexander to Actium: The Historical Evolution of the Hellenistic Age, 1990, rev. edit., 1993, The Greco-Persian Wars, 1996, From Ikaria to the Stars, 2004, The Hellenistic Age: A Short History, 2007; translator, editor: Juvenal, The Sixteen Satires, 1967, 3d edit., 1998, Ovid: The Erotic Poems, 1982, Yannis Ritsos: The Fourth Dimension, 1993, Hellenistic History and Culture, 1993, Ovid: The Poems of Exile, 1994, rev. edit., 2005, Apollonios Rhodios, The Argonautika, 1997, The Poems of Catullus, bilingual edit., 2005, Diodorus Siculus 11-12.37.1: Greek History 480-431 B.C.: The Alternative Version, 2006; editor-in-chief Syllecta Classica, 1999—. Served to sgt. RAF, 1943-47. NEH fellow, 1983-84; Craven scholar Cambridge U., 1950; Obermann Ctr. for Advanced Rsch. fellow U. Iowa, 1997; recipient 1st prize Nat. Poetry Libr., 1997. Fellow Royal Soc. Lit. (council 1959-63); mem. Soc. for Promotion of Hellenic Studies (U.K.), Classical Assn. (U.K.), Am. Philol. Assn., Archaeol. Inst. Am., Mem. Liberal Party. Club: Savile (London). Office: Dept Classics U Iowa Iowa City IA 52242 Office Phone: 319-341-6573. Business E-Mail: peter-green-1@uiowa.edu. *Prime aims, then, now always; to have maximum possible time for writing, travel, sport, relationships; to avoid any job that threatens my solitude or independence; to shun mature opinions; to go on, forever if possible, finding every day exciting, new, a fresh challenge, mentally and physically; to love and be loved always, to write all the books I have in me, and be healthy in mind and body until I die, preferably at well over the century, in Greece.*

GREEN, RAYMOND FERGUSON ST. JOHN, marketing and advertising executive; b. Phila., Aug. 15, 1950; Raymond Silvernail and Rose Dorathea (Basile) G.; BA in Psychology, Lafayette Coll., 1972; postgrad. Temple U., 1972-75; m. Lisa Rose Wardzinski, June 24, 1972; children: Katharine Amanda, Ian Ferguson Paul. Prodn. asst. Franklin Broadcasting Co., Phila., 1972-73, asst. sec., 1973-75, v.p. corp. affairs, 1975-78, exec. v.p., 1978-84; pres., gen. mgr., COO Franklin Broadcasting Co., 1983-88, pres. Magnetik Prodns., Inc., 1982-88; pres. Greenrose Corp., 1988—, also bd. dirs.; pres. Greenrose Broadcasting Svcs., WWPR Bradenton, Fla., 1996—; sec./treas. Liebert & Co.; bd. dirs. Young Audiences Eastern Pa., co-chmn., 1989-90. Associated Bio-Med. Svcs.; dir. Northwestern Corp., 1988-93; v.p. Amica Co., 1985-93; treas. NW Ctr. MH/MR, 1986-93. Mem. adv. bd. Phila. Boys Choir & Chorale, 1986—, Musical Fund Soc. of Phila. Mem. Northwest Center; mem. Musical Fund Soc. Phila., Phila. Art Alliance; dir. choral Arts Soc. of Phila., 1991-98, v.p., 1995-97, pres., 1997-98. Mem. Internat. Soc. Bacchus (trustee, chmn. Phila. chpt. 1988-91), Center Internat. Gastronomic Studies (trustee), Union League Club, Commonwealth Club, Rotary. Roman Catholic. Office: 5910 Carter Rd West Ste 130 Bradenton FL 34210

GREEN, RICH, information technology executive; Mgr. software tools divsn. Sun Microsystems, Inc., Santa Clara, Calif., 1989, v.p., gen. mgr. Solaris products orgn., v.p., gen. mgr. Java orgn., exec. v.p. software, 2006—; exec. v.p. products Cassatt Corp., San Jose, Calif., 2004—06. Office: Sun Microsystems Inc 4150 Network Cir Santa Clara CA 95054 Office Phone: 650-960-1300.*

GREEN, RICHARD ALAN, retired lawyer; b. Springfield, Mass., Apr. 25, 1926; s. Herman and Emma (Rudnick) Green; m. Lorna H. Paul, Sept. 6, 1957; children: Charles C., Thomas F. AB cum laude, Harvard U., 1947, LL.B., 1952. Bar: NY 1954, DC 1975, Md. 1987. Assoc. Steinberg & Patterson, NYC, 1954-57; asst. U.S. atty. So. Dist. NY, 1957-59; 1st asst. counsel NY State Commn. Investigation, 1960; individual practice law NYC, 1961-64; dir. ABA Project on Standards for Criminal Justice, 1964-73; dep. dir. Nat. Commn. on Reform of Fed. Criminal Laws, 1967-71; lectr. U. Va. Sch. Law, 1971; dep. dir. Fed. Jud. Center, Washington, 1971-74; partner Rowley and Green, Washington, 1974-80, Stohlman, Beuchert, Egan & Smith, Washington, 1981-2000; ret., 2000. Served with USN, 1944-46. Mem. ABA, Am. Law Inst., DC Bar Assn., Assn. of Bar of City of NY, Harvard (NYC) Club. Home: 1050 N Stuart St Apt 714 Arlington VA 22201-5749

GREEN, RICHARD C., lawyer; b. Phoenix, 1944; BA, Yale U., 1966; JD, Georgetown U., 1976. Bar: Md. 1976, DC 1980. Of counsel, Energy Transactions Andrews Kurth LLP, Washington, mng. ptnr. DC office. Mem. Georgetown Law Jour., 1975—76. Mem.: Fed. Energy Bar Assn., Bar State Md., DC Bar.

GREEN, RICHARD CALVIN, JR., electric power and gas industry executive; b. Kansas City, Mo., May 6, 1954; s. Richard C. and Ann (Gableman) G.; m. Nancy Jean Risk, Aug. 6, 1977; children: Allison Thompt, Ashley Jean, Richard Calvin III. BSBA, So. Methodist U., 1976. With Mo. Pub. Service, Kansas City, 1976-85, exec. v.p., 1982-85; pres., CEO UtiliCorp. United Inc., Kansas City, 1985—89, Aquila, Inc., Kansas City, 1985—96, CEO, 1996—2001, pres., CEO, 2002—, chmn., 1989—. Bd. dirs. Midwest Rsch. Inst., The BHA Group, Inc., Urban Inst. Washington. Office: Aquila Inc 20 W 9th St Kansas City MO 64105-1704*

GREEN, RICHARD FREDERICK, astronomer; b. Omaha, Feb. 13, 1949; m. Joan Auerbach; children: Alexander Simon, Nathaniel Martin. AB in Astronomy magna cum laude, Harvard U., 1971; PhD in Astronomy, Calif. Inst. Tech., 1977. Physics lab instr. Harvard U., Cambridge, 1970-71; NSF trainee Calif. Inst. Tech., Pasadena, 1971-72, grad. teaching asst. in astronomy, 1972-74, grad. rsch. asst. in astronomy, 1974-77, rsch. fellow in astronomy, 1977-79; asst. astronomer Steward Observatory, U. Ariz., Tucson, 1979-83, Kitt Peak Nat. Observatory, Tucson, 1983-85, assoc. astronomer, 1986-90, astronomer, 1990—, dir., 1997—2005; acting dir. Nat. Optical Astronomy Observatories, Tucson, 1992-93, acting dep. dir., 1993-94, dep. dir., 1994-99; dir. Large Binocular Telescope Obs. U. Ariz., Tucson, 2005—. Rsch. asst. Smithsonian Astrophys. Observatory, 1970-71; adj. asst. prof. Steward Observatory, U. Ariz., 1983-85, adj. assoc. astronomer and prof., 1986-90, adj. astronomer, 1990—; mem. users' com. Internat. Ultraviolet Explorer Satellite, NASA, 1979-81, chair proposal rev. panel, 1986-88, 93, final sci. program com., 1993, mem. sci. team Far Ultraviolet Spectroscopic Explorer Satellite, 1981—, Space Telescope Imaging Spectrograph, 1982—, guest observer working group Extreme Ultraviolet Explorer Satellite, 1988-92, chair proposal rev. panel ROSAT Guest Observer Program, 1989, 92, ROSAT Users' Coms., 1990-93, chair HST Cycle 2 Porposal Rev. Panel, mem. time allocation com., 1991, STSDAS users' com., 1991-92, Hubble Space Telescope Program Rev., 1997; mem. panel ultraviolet and optical astronomy from space, astronomy survey com. Nat. Acad. Scis., 1989-90; mem. panel HST and Beyond AURA, 1994-95; mem. proposal rev. panels NSF, 1996-97; instrument scientist Gemini 8-m Telescopes Project, 1991-92; mem. U.S. Gemini sci. adv. com., Gemini (Internat.) sci. com. U.S. Gemini Project Office, 1991-93, acting U.S. Gemini Project scientist, 1992-93, mem. instrument forum, optical instrumentation sci. working group, chair multi-object spectrograph critical design rev., 1997. Nat. Merit scholar; Hon. scholar Harvard U. Mem. AAAS (astronomy divsn. nominating com. 1992, coun. astronomy rep. com. coun. affairs 1995-97), Am. Astronomical Soc., Internat. Astronomical Union, Astronomical Soc. of the Pacific, Phi Beta Kappa. Office: U Ariz Steward Obs PO Box 210065 933 N Cherry Ave Tucson AZ 85721 Office Phone: 520-626-7088.

GREEN, RICHARD JOHN, architect; b. Painesville, Ohio, Mar. 14, 1944; s. Robert Franklin and Hazel (Ruble) Green; m. Judith Marie Ellen Niemi, Aug. 25, 1965 (div. 1985); children: Kevin Ward, Tyler Andrew. BArch with honors, NC State U., 1968. Registered arch., Mass., Calif., Pa., Ill., Ind., NH, NC, Conn., Minn., NY, Mich. Project designer Stubbins Assocs., Inc., Cambridge, Mass., 1968-74, assoc., 1974-77, v.p. design, 1977-83, pres., COO, 1983-92, chmn., pres., 1992—2003, consulting prin., 2004—07; dir. scis. group CBT Archs., Boston, 2004—. Instr. Boston Archtl. Ctr., 1971—72, 1975—76; vis. instr. Calif. State Poly. U., Pomona, 1980—84; vis. lectr. Nat. U. Mex., Mexico City, 1981; thesis advisor Harvard U., Cambridge, 1981—82; part-time adj. faculty dept. arch. NC State U., 1998; adj. prof. arch. U. Hawaii, 1998—. Bd. dirs. Sch. Design Found., NC State U. Fellow: AIA (mem. internat. com., corr. mem., mem. com. design and urban design and planning, cert. of Merit 1968, Rotch Travelling scholar 1972); mem.: Archtl. League NY, Nat. Coun. Archtl. Registration Bds., AIA Mass., Boston Soc. Archs., Corinthian Yacht Club. Avocations: athletics, travel, sailing, Tae Kwon Do. Home: 22 Oak St Marblehead MA 01945-1947 Office Phone: 617-646-5116.

GREEN, RICHARD K., real estate company executive; b. NYC, Apr. 22, 1959; m. Patricia Flora Harris; children: Hannah Harris Green, Morgan Harris Green. AB in Economics, cum laude, Harvard U., 1980; MS in Economics, U. Wis., Madison, 1986, PhD in Economics, 1990. V.p. rsch. and fin. Wis. Realtors Assn., 1987—90; asst. prof. Real Estate and Urban Land Economics U. Wis. Sch. of Bus., Madison, 1990—96, assoc. prof., 1996—2001, prof., 2001—03; chmn. and Wangard Faculty Scholar, Real Estate and Urban Land Economics U. Wis., Madison, 1999—2002; prin. economist Freddie Mac, 2002—03, dir. fin. strategy and policy analysis, 2003; vis. prof. real estate Wharton Sch., U. Pa., 2004, adj. prof. real estate, 2006—; Oliver T. Carr chair of real estate and fin., prof. fin. George Washington U., Washington, 2004—, assoc. dean grad. programs, 2005—, dir. Ctr. Washington Area Studies. Faculty assoc. Lincoln Inst. for Land Policy, 1997—; fellow U. Wis. Tchg. Acad., 1997—2003; Wangard faculty scholar U. Wis., 1998—2003; spl. assoc. mem. Conf. Bus. Economists, 2001—02; postdoctoral fellow Homer Hoyt Inst., 1995, fellow, 2003—; dep. North American editor Jour. Property Rsch., 1995—2002; edit. bd. Jour. Real Estate, Fin. and Economics, 1998—2003, Jour. Housing Economics, 2002—, Jour. Property Rsch., 2002—. Affiliate Inst. for Rsch. on Poverty, U. Wis., 1999—. Recipient Tchr. of Yr. award, U. Wis. Grad. Bus. Assn., 1995. Master: Nat. Assn. Industrial and Office Properties; fellow: Ctr. Urban Land Economics Rsch.; mem.: Am. Real Estate and Urban Econ. Assn. (first v.p. 2005). Office: George Washington Univ Duques Hall 550 H 2201 G St NW Washington DC 20052 Office Phone: 202-994-2377. Business E-Mail: drgreen@gwu.edu.*

GREEN, RIVA LEE, social worker, minister; b. Denmark, SC, May 18, 1953; d. Rious and Elizzillia (Banks) G.; m. George E. Collins, June 19, 1974 (div. June 1985); children: Corey E., Kevin L., Monique N. AAS, Cumberland County Coll., Vineland, NJ, 1992. Ordained to ministry Jamison Sch. Ministry, Phila., 1995. Caseworker Salem County Women's Svcs., Salem, NJ, 1992-97; family non-violence training U.S. Army, Ft. Dix, NJ, 1995—; family svc. specialist III State of N.J. Divsn. Youth and Family Svcs., Camden, 1997—. Pastor Strings of Faith ministry, Seabrook, N.J. Active NAACP (area coord. Bridgeton, N.J., 1995, 1st v.p. Cumberland County, 1995—); adv. bd. Maple Garden Tenant Assn., 1991-93; natural leader Martin Luther King Academy, 1995—; mem. C.O.R.E. Mem. C.O.R.E. Home: 32 Tower Ln Willingboro NJ 08046-4114

GREEN, ROBERT EDWARD, JR., physicist, researcher; b. Clifton Forge, Va., Jan. 17, 1932; s. Robert Edward and Hazle Hall (Smith) G.; m. Sydney Sue Truitt, Feb. 1, 1962; children: Kirsten Adair, Heather Scott. BS, Coll. William and Mary, 1953; PhD, Brown U., 1959. Physicist underwater explosions rsch. divsn. Norfolk Naval Shipyard, Va., 1959; asst. prof. mechanics Johns Hopkins U., Balt., 1960-65, assoc. prof., 1965-70, prof., 1970—2006, prof. emeritus, 2007—, chmn. mechanics dept., 1970-72, chmn. mechanics and materials sci. dept., 1972-73, chmn. civil engring./materials sci. and engring. dept., 1979-82, chmn. materials sci. and engring. dept., 1982-85, 91-93, dir. ctr. for nondestructive evaluation, 1985—2002. Ford Found. resident sr. engr. RCA, Lancaster, Pa., 1966-67; cons. U.S. Army Ballistic Rsch. Labs., Aberdeen Proving Ground, Md., 1973-74; physicist Ctr. for Materials Sci., U.S. Nat. Bur. Standards, Washington, 1974-81; program mgr. Def. Advanced Rsch. Projects Agy., 1981-82; spkr., presenter in field Contbr. articles to profl. jours. Fulbright grantee. Mem. ASM Internat., Am. Phys. Soc., Acoustical Soc. Am., Met. Soc. AIME, Am. Soc. Nondestructive Testing, Soc. for the Advancement of Material and Process Engring., Materials Rsch. Soc., Sigma Xi, Tau Beta Pi, Alpha Sigma Mu, Sigma Nu. Methodist. Achievements include research in recovery, recrystallization, elasticity, plasticity, crystal growth and orientation, X-ray diffraction, electro-optical systems, linear and non-linear elastic wave propagation, light-sound interactions, high-power ultrasonics, ultrasonic attenuation, dislocation damping, fatigue, acoustic emission, non-destructive testing, polymers, biomaterials, synchrotron radiation, composites, sensors and process control. Office: Johns Hopkins Univ Materials Sci and Engring Dept 103 Maryland Hall 3400 N Charles St Baltimore MD 21218-2689 Business E-Mail: robert.green@jhu.edu.

GREEN, RONALD MICHAEL, bioethics educator; b. NYC, Dec. 16, 1942; s. Daniel David and Beatrice (Friedlander) G.; m. Mary Jean Matthews, June 25, 1965; children— Julie Elisabeth, Matthew Daniel AB, Brown U., 1964; PhD, Harvard U., 1973. Instr. Dartmouth Coll., Hanover, NH, 1969-73, asst. prof., 1973-79, assoc. prof., 1979-85, John Phillips prof. of religion, 1985-98, chmn. dept. religion, 1980—83, 1985, 2000—, adj. prof. Amos Tuck Sch. Bus. Adminstrn., 1985-92, Cohen prof., 1998—. Vis. assoc. prof. Stanford U., Calif., 1984-85; adj. prof. dept. cmty. medicine Dartmouth Med. Sch., 1980—; dir. Dartmouth Ethics Inst., 1993—, Office of Genome Ethics Nat. Human Genome Rsch. Inst. NIH, 1996-97; human embryo rsch. panel NIH, 1994; chmn. ethics adv. bd. Advanced Cell Tech. Author: Population Growth and Justice, 1975, Religious Reason, 1978, Religion and Moral Reason, 1988, Kierkegaard and Kant, 1992, The Ethical Manager, 1994, The Human Embryo Research Debates, 2001, Babies by Design, 2007; assoc. editor Jour. Religious Ethics, 1973-91, mem. editorial bd., 1991—; mem. editorial bd. Jour. Am. Acad. Religion, 1985-91. Kent fellow, 1965-69, Guggenheim fellow, 2005-; recipient Fulbright award, 1964-65, Dartmouth Disting. Teaching award, 1978 Mem. Am. Acad. Religion (sec. 1995—), Soc. Christian Ethics (bd. dirs., v.p. 1997-98, pres. 1998-99), Soc. Bus. Ethics, Am. Soc. for Study Religion. Jewish. Office: Dartmouth Coll Dept Religion Hanover NH 03755 Office Phone: 603-646-1263. Business E-Mail: ronald.m.green@dartmouth.edu. *I continue to believe in the ideals of the enlightenment: that human beings can use their reason to expand opportunity, freedom and community.*

GREEN, RUTHANN, marketing and management consultant; b. Streator, Ill., July 14, 1935; d. John Joseph and Edna Marie (Peters) G. BS in Edn., U. Ill., 1957. Elem. tchr. Jefferson Sch., Davenport, Iowa, 1957-59; tchr. Hinsdale (Ill.) Jr. High Sch., 1959-62; ednl. cons. Harcourt Brace & World, Chgo., 1962-63; exec. sec. Everpure, Inc., Oakbrook, Ill., 1963-68; ednl. cons. Houghton Mifflin Co., Europe, 1968-69, Palo Alto, Calif., 1969-77, sr. mktg. mgr. Boston, 1977-87; v.p., nat. sales mgr. Riverside Pub. Co., Chgo., 1987-89; v.p., dir. mktg. McDougal, Littell & Co., Evanston, Ill., 1990-92; v.p., gen. mgr. Open Court Pub. Co., Chgo., 1992-94; pres. Peters & Green, Inc. Mktg. Svcs. and Bus. Devel., Chgo., 1994—. Author: WSIL: Why Should I Listen, 1987, 1993, 2004, 2007, A Garfield Memoir, 1995. Recipient Svc. award Am. Arbitration Assn., 1987, Golden Reel of Excellence Internat. TV Assn., 1983. Mem. ASCD, Internat. Reading Assn., People for Am. Way, Am. Arbitration Assn., Achievement Rewards for Coll. Scientists Found., Urban Gateways (v.p. bd. dirs.), Ritchie Tower Condo Assn. (bd. dirs., sec.), Phi Mu. Avocations: reading, fitness activities, travel, art. Home and Office: 1310 N Ritchie Ct Apt 21A Chicago IL 60610-8405 Office Phone: 312-787-2767. E-mail: petersgreen@att.net.

GREEN, SHIRLEY MOORE, retired communications executive, public information officer; b. Graham, Tex., Dec. 21, 1933; d. N. Edgar and Cora Day (Morrow) Moore; m. Paul M. Green, Aug. 26, 1967 (div. 1981); children: Ruth Lynn, Tracy Moore Anderson. Student, Midwestern U.,

Wichita Falls, Tex., 1952; BBA, U. Tex., 1956. Staff asst. Rep. Party, Austin, Tex., 1965-67; press asst. Bob Price U.S. Rep., Washington, 1967; coordinator Tex. and Ark. Bush for Pres. Campaign, Houston, 1979-80; dep. press sec. V.p. Bush, Washington, 1984, acting press sec., 1983; dir. pub. affairs NASA, Washington, 1985-86, dep. assoc. adminstr. communications, 1987-89; spl. asst. to the Pres. White House, Washington, 1989-92, dep. asst. to Pres., 1992; dir. Pres. Bush Transition Office, Washington, 1993; dir. program support Internat. Rep. Inst., Washington, 1993-96; dir. corr. and constituent svcs. Gov. George W. Bush, Austin, 1996-2001; dir. comm. svcs. Atty Gen. John Cornyn, 2001—03. Local chair Jim Baker for Atty. Gen., 1978, Pres. Ford Com., San Antonio, 1976; trustee S.W. Found. Forum, San Antonio, 1974-78; bd. dirs. Child Welfare Bd. Bexar County, 1975-79; vice-chair J. William Fulbright Scholarship Bd., 2005—. Recipient Exceptional Svc. medal NASA, 1989. Mem.: Tex. Fedn. Rep. Women (editor Partyline mag. 1969—72, one of 10 Outstanding Rep. Women Tex. 1979). Presbyterian. Avocations: reading, travel. Home: 1513 W 30th St Austin TX 78703-1403

GREEN, STEPHANIE, lawyer; b. Coral Gables, Fla., Oct. 6, 1950; d. Thomas Robert and Nilda (Lopez) Green; m. Gerald McBride, Dec. 2, 1978 (div. 1980); m. Terence Murphy, Feb. 8, 1986 (div. 2000); 1 child, T. Maxwell. B.A., U. Fla., 1973; J.D., U. Miami, 1978. Bar: Fla. 1980. Atty. firm Paige & Catlin, Miami, Fla., 1978-80; adminstrv. mgr. internat. div. Aeromexico, Miami, 1980-82, legal counsel internat. div., 1982-87; prin. Law Offices of Stephanie G. Murphy, Coral Gables, Fla., 1987—; staff counselor labor rels. Eastern Air Lines, 1990-91; legal counsel Fla. Internat. U.- Human & Labor Rights Inst., 1995—. Active Dade County Commn. on the Status of Women, 1990-91. Mem. Am. Immigration Lawyers Assn., Fla. Bar Assn. Democrat. Roman Catholic. Home: 4920 SW 60th Pl Miami FL 33155-6218 Office: 815 Ponce De Leon Blvd Ste 308 Coral Gables FL 33134 Home Phone: 305-667-9098; Office Phone: 305-445-8788. E-mail: sgreeninslaw@aol.com.

GREEN, STEPHEN L., real estate developer; b. Bklyn. s. Irving Arthur and Anna Constance (Suna) Green; m. Nancy A. Peck. BA, Hartwick Coll., 1959; JD, Boston Coll. Founder S.L. Green Real Estate, 1980; CEO SL Green Realty Corp., 1997—2004, chmn., 1997—. Bd. dirs. Urecoats Industries Inc., 2002. Co-recipient with Nancy A. Peck, Starlight Children's Found., 2000. Mem.: Real Estate Tax Fairness Coalition (co-chmn.), Real Estate Bd. NY (gov., at large mem. exec. com. bd. governors). Office: SL Green Realty Corp 420 Lexington Ave New York NY 10170*

GREEN, STUART PAUL, law educator; b. Phila., Nov. 29, 1961; s. Stanley and Lola (Apothaker) G.; m. Jennifer Moses; children: Samuel, Rose, Jonathan. BA, Tufts U., 1983; JD, Yale U., 1988. Bar: Pa. 1990, DC. 1991, U.S. Dist. Ct. D.C. 1991, U.S. Ct. Appeals (D.C. cir.) 1993, U.S. Supreme Ct. 1994. Law clk. to Hon. Pamela Rymer U.S. Dist. Ct., LA, 1988-89, U.S. Ct. Appeals (9th cir.), LA, 1989; assoc. Wilmer, Cutler & Pickering, Washington, 1990-95; prof. law La. State U. Law Sch., Baton Rouge, 1995—. Vis. prof. U. Mich. Law Sch., 2005. Author: Defining Crimes: Essays on the Special Part of the Criminal Law, 2005, Lying, Cheating, and Stealing: A Moral Theory of White Collar Crime, 2006. Fulbright Disting. scholar, Eng., 2002—03. Office: LSU Law School East Campus Dr Baton Rouge LA 70803 Office Phone: 504-578-8715. Business E-Mail: stuart.green@law.lsu.edu.

GREEN, THOMAS ANDREW, lawyer, educator; b. 1940; AB, Columbia U., 1961, MA, 1962, PhD, 1970; JD, Harvard U., 1972. Asst. prof. Bard Coll., Annandale, NY, 1967—69; prof. law and hist. U. Mich. Law Sch., Ann Arbor, John P. Dawson Collegiate Prof. Law. Vis. prof., Harvey and Susan Perlman Disting. Vis. Prof. Law U. Nebr., 2003. Co-editor: Studies in Legal History, 2003; mem. editl. bd. Am. Jour. of Legal History, Jour. of British Studies, and Law and Soc. Review; contbr. articles to law jours. Mem.: Am. Soc. Legal History (pres. 2000—01), Am. Hist. Assn., Selden Soc. Office: U Mich Law Sch 342 Hutchins Hall 625 S State St Ann Arbor MI 48109-1215 Office Phone: 734-764-1457. Office Fax: 734-763-9395. E-mail: tagreen@umich.edu.

GREEN, THOMAS CHARLES, lawyer; b. Mpls., Feb. 7, 1941; s. Myron Bernard and Donna (Lavine) G.; m. Rochelle K. Green (div. 1974); children: Joshua L., Marisa A.; m. Pamela Kellogg, Aug. 31, 1979; children: David Swiler, Michael Curtis. AB, Dartmouth Coll., 1962; LLB, Yale U., 1965. Bar: Minn. 1965, D.C. 1967, U.S. Supreme Ct. 1968, U.S. Ct. Military Appeals. Asst. U.S. atty., Washington, 1967-70; pvt. practice, 1967—90; sr. litigation ptnr. Sidley & Austin (now Sidley, Austin, Brown & Wood LLP), Washington, 1990—, head, white collar criminal def. practice. Instr. civil and criminal trial practice various law schs., bar assnsn., Nat. Inst. Trial Advocacy; lectr., panelist various profl. programs. Capt. and arty. battery commdr. U.S. Army, 1965-67; attached 1st Air Cavalry Divsn., Vietnam. Named one of Top 10 Litigators, Nat. Law Jour., 2003, 75 Best Lawyers in Washington, Washingtonian survey mag. Fellow: Am. Coll. Trial Lawyers; mem.: Nat. Assn. Criminal Def. Lawyers (past. chmn. com. on environ. crime), Asst. U.S. Attys. Assn. (past pres.). Democrat. Jewish. Avocations: sailing, tennis, bicycling. Office: Sidley Austin Brown & Wood LLP 1501 K St NW Washington DC 20005 Office Phone: 202-736-8069. Office Fax: 202-736-8711. Business E-Mail: tcgreen@sidley.com.

GREEN, TIM M., mathematics educator; b. Bradley, Ill., Mar. 16, 1971; s. Melton T. and Barbara E. Green; m. Lynnette D. Dunlap, July 11, 2004; children: Jade children: Jordan. BS in Math. Edn., U. Ill., Urbana-Champaign, 1993. Food svc. dir. ARAMARK, Chico, Calif., 1994—99; math. educator Lindhurst H.S., Olivehurst, Calif., 1999—. Presenter/instr. Chico Math. Project - North State Math. Partnership, Red Bluff, Calif., 2005—06; particpant Chico Math. Project - Tchr. Leadership Acad., 2003; participant Profl. Devel. Inst. - Secondary (Geometry), Chico, 2002, Chico Math. Project - Algebra I, 2001; presenter Mt. Lassen Math Conf., Chico, 2003, Redding, Calif., 01. Sunday sch. tchr. Neighborhood Ch., Chico, 2005—06, Orchard Ch., Chico, 2003—04. Grantee (2) Classroom Minigrantee, Calif. Math Coun. - No. Region, 2005—06, EAST Initiative, 2003—05, Jordan Fundamentals grantee, NIKE Found., 2002. Mem.: Nat. Coun. of Tchrs. Math., Calif. Math Coun. Avocations: softball, basketball, fantasy sports, travel. Home: 2754 San Jose St Chico CA 95973 Office: Lindhurst High School 4446 Olive Ave Olivehurst CA 95961 Home Phone: 530-892-0345; Office Phone: 530-741-6150. Office Fax: 530-741-6141. Personal E-mail: looneytunes316@sbcglobal.net.

GREEN, TRAVIS, professional hockey player; b. Castlegar, BC, Can., Dec. 20, 1970; m. Sherry Ragan, July 18. Center NY Islanders, 1989-98, Anaheim Ducks (formerly Mighty Ducks of Anaheim), 1998-99, 2006—, Phoenix Coyotes, 1999—2001, Toronto Maple Leafs, 2001—03, Boston Bruins, 2003—06. Mem. Team Canada at World Championships, Vienna, 1995-96/ Office: Anaheim Ducks 2695 E Katella Ave Anaheim CA 92806

GREEN, TRENT JASON, professional football player; b. Cedar Rapids, Iowa, July 9, 1970; m. Julie Green; children: T.J., Derek Green. Degree in Bus., Ind. U. Quarterback San Diego Chargers, 1993, Washington Redskins, 1995—99, St. Louis Rams, 1999—2001, Kans. City Chiefs, 2001—07, Miami Dolphins, Fla., 2007—. Established Trent Green Family Found., 1999; supporter Star Bright Rm. at Kans. Children's Mercy Hosp. Named to AFC Pro-Bowl Team, 2003, 2005. Avocations: basketball, golf, hunting, fishing. Mailing: Miami Dolphins 7500 SW 30th St Davie FL 33314*

GREEN, WAYNE HUGO, psychiatrist, psychoanalyst; b. Schenectady, NY, July 23, 1941; s. Albert George and Mildred (Hugo) G. AB, U. Chgo., 1963; MD, NYU, 1967. Diplomate Am. Bd. Psychiatry and Neurology, cert. in psychiatry Am. Bd. Psychiatry and Neurology, 1975, in child psychiatry Am. Bd. Psychiatry and Neurology, 1978, in psychoanalysis William Alanson White Inst. Psychiatry, Psychoanalysis, and Psychology, 1977. Intern Lenox Hill Hosp., NYC, 1967-68; resident in psychiatry NYU-Bellevue Med. Ctr., 1970-72, fellow in child psychiatry, 1972-74; asst. dir. Children's Mental Hygiene Clinic-Bellevue Psychiat. Hosp., NYC, 1974-77; unit chief Children's Psychiat. Inpatient Svc.-Bellevue Hosp., NYC, 1978-86, unit chief child and adolescent outpatient clinic, 1986—2000; asst. clin. prof. psychiatry NYU, 1977—79, asst. prof. psychiatry, 1979—85, assoc. prof. clin. psychiatry, 1985—2000; chief psychiatrist Children's Aid Soc., NYC, 2001—06, dir. psychiatry, 2006—. Asst. attending psychiatry NYU Med. Ctr., U. Hosp., N.Y.C., 1974-2000; asst. attending psychiatrist Bellevue Hosp. Ctr., N.Y.C., 1974-2000; dir. tng. & edn. NYU Residency in Child and Adolescent Psychiatry, 1995-99. Sr. editor Jour. Child & Adolescent Psychopharmacology, 1998-; author: Child and Adolescent Clinical Psychopharmacology, 4th edit., 2007; contbr. more than 50 articles to profl. jours.; contbr. chapters to books. With USPHS, 1968-70. Fellow Am. Acad. Child Psychiatry. Office: Children's Aid Soc 150 E 45th St New York NY 10017 Office Phone: 917-612-2986.

GREEN, WILLIAM D., management consulting firm executive; married; 2 children. BS, MBA, Babson Coll. With Accenture, NYC, 1977—, ptnr., 1986—, mng. ptnr. New England, head mfg. ind. group, 1994—97, group chief exec. resources group, 1997—99, group chief exec. comm. & high tech., 1999—2003, mng. dir. U.S., 2000—04, bd. dir., 2001—, COO client services, 2004, CEO, 2004—, chmn., 2006—. Mem. exec. com. Council on Competitiveness; mem. Bus. Roundtable, G100. Trustee Dean Coll. Office: Accenture 1345 Ave of the Americas New York NY 10105*

GREEN, WILLIAM L., lawyer; b. Syracuse, NY, Oct. 13, 1954; BA in Polit. Sci. cum laude, Middlebury Coll., 1976; JD magna cum laude, Boston Coll., 1980. Bar: Mass. 1980, NY 1981, Wash. 1986. Assoc. Quint, Marx, Chill & Greene, NY, 1980—82, Skadden, Arps, Slate, Meagher & Flom, NY, 1982—86; ptnr. real estate group Perkins Coie LLP, Seattle, 1986—. Limited Practice Bd. Wash. State Supreme Ct., 1993—2000; trustee Intiman Theatre Co., 1996—2002. Mem.: Wash. State Bar Assn. (Real Property, Probate & Trust Sect 1995—97), Mt. Baker Cmty. Club (pres. 1993—95). Office: Perkins Coie LLP 1201 Third Ave Ste 4800 Seattle WA 98101-9000 Office Phone: 206-359-8513. Office Fax: 206-359-9513. Business E-Mail: wgreen@perkinscoie.com.

GREEN, WILLIAM PORTER, lawyer; b. Jacksonville, Ill., Mar. 19, 1920; s. Hugh Parker and Clara Belle (Hopper) G.; m. Rose Marie Hall, Oct. 1, 1944; children: Hugh Michael, Robert Alan, Richard William. BA, Ill. Coll., 1941; JD, Northwestern U., Evanston, Ill., 1947. Bar: Ill. 1947, Calif. 1948, U.S. Dist. Ct. (so. dist.) Tex. 1986, U.S. Ct. Customs and Patent Appeals, U.S. Patent and Trademark Office 1948, U.S. Ct. Appeals (fed. cir.) 1982, U.S. Ct. Appeals (5th and 9th cir.), U.S. Supreme Ct. 1948, U.S. Dist. Ct. (cen. dist.) Calif. 1949, (so. dist.) Tex.1986. Pvt. practice, LA, 1947—; mem. Wills, Green & Mueth, LA, 1974-83; of counsel Nilsson, Robbins, Dalgarn, Berliner, Carson & Wurst, LA, 1984-91; of counsel Nilsson, Wurst & Green LA, 1992—. Del. Calif. State Bar Conv., 1982—, chmn., 1986. Bd. editors Ill. Law Rev., 1946; patentee in field. Mem. L.A. world Affairs Coun., 1975—; deacon local Presbyn. Ch., 1961-63. Mem. ABA, Calif. State Bar, Am. Intellectual Property Law Assn., L.A. Patent Law Assn. (past sec.-treas., mem. bd. govs.), Lawyers Club L.A. (past treas., past sec., mem. bd. govs., pres. 1985-86), Los Angeles County Bar Assn. (trustee 1986-87), Am. Legion (past post comdr.), Northwestern U. Alumni Club So. Calif., Big Ten Club So. Calif., Town Hall Calif. Club, PGA West Golf Club (La Quinta, Calif.), Phi Beta Kappa, Phi Delta Phi, Phi Alpha. Republican. Home: 3570 Lombardy Rd Pasadena CA 91107-5627 Office: 707 Wilshire Blvd Ste 3200 Los Angeles CA 90017-3514 Home Phone: 760-777-1886; Office Phone: 213-362-9501. Personal E-mail: wpgreen@aol.com.

GREENAMYRE, JOHN TIMOTHY, medical educator; BS, Mich. State U.; MD, PhD, U. Mich. Cert. Am. Bd. of Psychiatry & Neurology. Prof. U. Rochester, 1990, Emory U., 1995, U. Pittsburgh, 2005—; chair & chief Movement Disorders; dir. Pittsburgh Inst. for Neurodegenerative Diseases, Am. Parkinson Disease Assn. Advanced Ctr. for Parkinson's Disease Rsch. at U. Pittsburgh. Mem. of sci. adv. bd. Michael J. Fox Found.; mem. sci. adv. com. Cure Parkinson's Project, Parkinson's Disease Found.; past chmn. Huntington's Disease Soc. of Am. rsch. grants subcommittee; mem. NIH Parkinson's disease rsch. agenda planning com., Parkinson's disease implementation com., Neurological Sciences and Disorders B study section of NINDS. Named a Mallinckrodt Scholar, 1994—97; recipient Roland B. Mackay Award, 1986, rsch. fellowship award, Am. Acad. of Neurology, 1990—93, Langston Award, Michael J. Fox Found. Mem.: Soc. for Neuroscience, Parkinson Study Group, Movement Disorders Soc., Huntington Study Group, Am. Neurological Assn., Am. Acad. of Neurology. Office: Department of Neurology 811 Kaufmann Medical Building 3471 Fifth Avenue Pittsburgh PA 15213 Office Phone: 412-648-9793. E-mail: greenamyrejt@upmc.edu.*

GREENAWALT, PEGGY FREED TOMARKIN, advertising executive; b. Cleve., Apr. 27, 1942; d. Bernard H. and Gyta Elinor (Arsham) Freed; m. Gary Tomarkin, Aug. 7, 1966 (div. 1981); children: Craig William, Eric Lawrence; m. William Sloan Greenawalt, Oct. 31, 1987. BS, Simmons Coll., 1964. Asst. account exec. Howard Marks/Norman, Craig & Kummel, Inc., NYC, 1964-66; account exec. Shaw Bros. Advt. Co., NYC, 1966-67; copywriter Claire Advt. Co., NYC, 1967; ptnr. Copywriters Coop., Hartsdale, N.Y., 1970-73; copy chief Howard Marks Advt., NYC, 1973-80; sr. copywriter Wunderman, Ricotta & Kline, NYC, 1980-82; v.p., assoc. creative dir. Ayer-Direct (N.W. Ayer), NYC, 1982-84; sr. v.p. creative dir. D'Arcy Direct (D'Arcy MacManus & Masius), NYC, 1984-86; pres. Tomarkin/Greenawalt, Inc., NYC, 1986—. Judge Echo Awards, Caples Awards, Fin. Comm. Soc. Awards. Author: Kiss, The Real Story, 1980. Dem. dist. leader. Mem. Direct Mktg. Assn., Women in Comms., Direct Mktg. Club N.Y., Westchester Assn. Women Bus. Owners (past pres.). Office: 24 Lewis Ave Hartsdale NY 10530 Home Phone: 914-683-5977; Office Phone: 914-683-8833. E-mail: pegdirect@aol.com.

GREENAWALT, ROBERT KENT, lawyer, educator; b. Bklyn., June 25, 1936; s. Kenneth William and Martha (Sloan) G.; m. Sanja Milic, July 14, 1968 (dec. Nov. 1988); children: Robert Milic, Alexander Kent Anton, Andrei Milenko Kenneth, Sarah Pagels, David Pagels. AB with honors, Swarthmore Coll., Pa., 1958; BPhil; Keasbey fellow, Oxford U., Eng., 1960; LLB; Kent scholar, Columbia U., NYC, 1963. Bar: NY 1963. Law clk. to Justice Harlan, US Supreme Ct., 1963-64; spl. asst. AID, Washington, 1964-65; mem. faculty Columbia U. Law Sch., 1965—, prof. law, 1969—, Cardozo prof., 1979—, Univ. prof., 1990—. Dep. solicitor gen. US, 1971-72; assoc. dir. NY Inst. Legal Edn., 1969; vis. prof. Stanford U. Law Sch., 1970, Northwestern U. Law Sch., 1983, Marshall-Wythe Sch. Law, 1985, N.Y.U. Law Sch., 1989-90; atty. Lawyers Com. Civil Rights, 1965, trustee, 1992; mem. staff Task Force Law Enforcement NYC, 1965; vis. fellow All Souls Coll. Oxford U., Eng., 1979 Co-author: The Sectarian College and The Public Purse, 1970; author: Legal Protections of Privacy, 1976, Discrimination and Reverse Discrimination, 1983, Conflicts of Law and Morality, 1987, Religious Convictions and Political Choice, 1988, Speech, Crime and the Uses of Language, 1989, Law and Objectivity, 1992, Private Consciences and Public Reasons, 1995, Fighting Words, 1995, Statutory Interpretation: Twenty Questions, 1999, Does God Belong in Public Schools?, 2005, Religion and the Constitution, Volume I Fairness and Free Exercise, 2006; editor-in-chief Columbia U. Law Rev., 1962-63; contbr. articles to legal jours. Recipient Ivy award Swarthmore Coll., 1958; fellow Am. Council Learned Soc., 1972-73. Fellow Am. Acad. Arts and Scis.; mem. Am. Philos. Soc., Am. Law Inst., Am. Soc. Polit. and Legal Philosophy (pres. 1992-93). Office: Columbia U Law Sch 435 W 116th St New York NY 10027-7201 Home Phone: 212-749-4701; Office Phone: 212-854-2637. Business E-Mail: kgreen@law.columbia.edu.

GREENAWALT, WILLIAM SLOAN, lawyer; b. Bklyn., Mar. 4, 1934; s. Kenneth William and Martha Frances (Sloan) G.; m. Jane DeLano Plunkett, Aug. 17, 1957 (div. May 1986); m. Peggy Ellen Freed Tomarkin, Oct. 31, 1987; children: John DeLano, David Sloan, Katherine Downs. AB, Cornell U., 1956; LLB, Yale U., 1961. Bar: NY 1962, US Dist. Ct. (so. and ea. dists.) NY 1962, US Ct. Appeals (2d cir.) 1962, US Supreme Ct. 1966. Assoc. Sullivan & Cromwell, NYC, 1961—65; dir. N.E. regional legal svcs. U.S. Office Econ. Opportunity, NYC, 1965—68; assoc. Rogers & Wells, NYC, 1968—69, ptnr., 1969—77, sr. ptnr., 1977—81, Halperin, Shivitz, Eisenberg, Schneider & Greenawalt, NYC, 1981—86, Eisenberg Honig Fogler Greenawalt & Davis, NYC, 1986—91, Bangser Klein Rocca & Blum, NYC, 1991—93, Loselle Greenawalt Kaplan Blair & Adler, NYC, 1993—97, Loselle Greenawalt Kaplan & Blair, NYC, 1997—99, Meyer Greenawalt Taub & Wild, LLP, NYC, 1999—2001; pvt. practice NYC, 2001—05; counsel McCarthy Fingar LLP, 2005—. Lectr. in field. Bd. editors: Yale Law Jour., 1959-61; contbr. articles in field to profl. jours. Chmn. bd. dirs. Applied Resources, Inc., NYC, 1968-70; chmn. Nat. Coun. Crime and Delinquency, Westchester, 1970-71, Cmty. Aid Employment Ex-Offenders, Westchester, NY, 1971; pres. Legal Svcs. of Hudson Valley (formerly Westchester-Putnam Legal Svcs.), 1971-74, bd. dirs., 1975-91, Farrel Corp., 2005-07; mem. NY State Gov.'s Task Force on Elem. and Secondary Edn., 1974-75; mem. Pres. Carter's Task Force on Criminal Justice, 1976; adv. coun. NY State Senate Dems., 1978—; asst., acting treas. NY State Dem., 1990-96, vice chair, 1996-2000, 9th jud. dist. rep. 2002—, state com., 1974—, exec. com. 1990-2000, 02-; chair Greenburgh Dem., 1997-2002; mem. Greenburgh Recreation Commn., 1976-83, Dem. Statewide Spl. Commn. on Polit. Ethics, 1986-87, Statewide Spl. Commn. on Election Law and Campaign Spending Reform, 1989-95; pres. Westchester Crime Victims Assistance Agy., 1981-82; commr. Taconic State Pk., Recreation and Hist. Preservation Commn., 1984-96, 2004—, chmn., 1989-96; vice chmn. NY State Coun. on Pk., Recreation and Hist. Preservation, 1989-94; NY State Recreation and Pk. Soc., 1998—; moderator Scarsdale Congl. Ch., 1988-90; mem. Westchester County Parks, Recreation and Conservation Bd., 1998—, vice chmn., 1999-2004, chmn. 2004—, Westchester White-Tailed Deer Impact and Forest Regeneration Citizens' Task Force, 2006—; mem. Westchester County Execs. Transition Team on Planning, 1997. Lt. comdr. USN, 1956-58, with Res., 1961-68. Fellow NY Bar Found.; mem. ABA, Am. Arbitration Assn. (panel comml. arbitrators 1977—), Nat. Recreation and Pk. Assn., NY State Bar Assn. (chmn. com. on availability of legal svcs. 1968-70, chmn. action unit 3 1979-81, chmn. spl. commn. on alternatives to jud. resolution of disputes 1981-85), Westchester County Bar Assn., Assn. of Bar of City of NY, Nat. Legal Aid and Defenders Assn., Sphinx Head, Aleph Samach, US Tennis Assn., County Tennis Club Westchester (Scarsdale, NY, pres. 1979-80), Yale Club, Phi Alpha Delta, Chi Psi. Democrat. Congregationalist. Home: 24 Lewis Ave Hartsdale NY 10530 Office: McCarthy Fingar LLP 11 Martine Ave White Plains NY 10606 Office Phone: 914-946-3700. Office Fax: 914-946-0134. Personal E-mail: wsgreenawalt@aol.com. Business E-Mail: wgreenawalt@mccarthyfingar.com.

GREENAWAY, JOSEPH ANTHONY, JR., judge; b. London, Nov. 16, 1957; came to U.S., 1959; s. Joseph Anthony Sr. and Brucel May (Lynch) G BA in History, Columbia U., 1978; JD, Harvard U., 1981. Law clk. to Hon. Vincent L. Broderick U.S. Dist. Ct. (so. dist.) N.Y., 1982—83; lawyer Kramer, Levin, Nessen, Kamin & Frankel, NYC, 1981-82, 83-85; chief narcotics divsn., asst. U.S. atty. Dept. Justice, Newark, 1985-90; in-house counsel Johnson & Johnson, New Brunswick, NJ, 1990-96; dist. judge U.S. Dist. Ct., Newark, 1996—. Weintraub lectr. Rutgers U. Law Sch., 1998; adj. prof. law sch. Rutgers U., 2002-06, Cardozo Sch. Law, 2006—, Columbia Coll., 2007—. Presenter in field. Past sec. Columbia U. Alumni Assn., bd. dirs., N.Y.C.; bd. dirs. Columbia U. Nat. Coun.; chair emeritus Columbia Coll. Black Alumni Coun.; bd. visitors Columbia Coll. Named Minority Achiever of Yr. East Orange YMCA, 1997; recipient proclamation Newark City Coun., 1990, medal of excellence Columbia U., 1997, John Jay award Columbia U., 2003, Excellence award Thurgood Marshall Coll. Fund, 2007; Earl Warren Legal scholar. Mem. ABA, Nat. Bar Assn., Garden State Bar Assn., Fed. Judges Assn., Am. Corp. Counsel Assn. (Disting. Svc. award 1997), Garden State Bar Assn. (Disting. Jurist award 1999, Roger M. Yancey award 2007), Columbia Coll. Alumni Assn. Avocation: golf. Office: US Post Office and Courthouse PO Box 999 Newark NJ 07101-0999

GREENBAUM, LEWIS, lawyer; b. NYC, July 29, 1948; BA with honors, NYU, 1970; JD, Georgetown U., 1973. Bar: NY 1974, Ill. 1978. Ptnr. pub. fin. Katten Muchin Zavis Rosenman, Chgo. Office: Katten Muchin Rosenman 525 W Monroe St Ste 1900 Chicago IL 60661 Office Phone: 312-902-5418. Office Fax: 312-577-8960. Business E-Mail: lewis.greenbaum@rattenlaw.com.

GREENBAUM, STUART I., economist, educator; b. NYC, Oct. 7, 1936; s. Sam and Bertha (Freimark) G.; m. Margaret E. Wache, July 29, 1964; children: Regina Gail, Nathan Carl. BS, NYU, 1959; PhD, Johns Hopkins U., 1964. Fin. economist Fed. Res. Bank of Kansas City, Mo., 1962-66; sr. economist Office of the Comptroller of the Currency, Washington, 1966-67; assoc. prof. econs. U. Ky., Lexington, 1968-74, prof., 1974-76, chmn. dept. econs., 1975-76; vis. prof. fin. Kellogg Grad. Sch. Mgmt., Northwestern U., Evanston, Ill., 1974-75, prof. fin., 1976-78, Harold L. Stuart prof. banking and fin., 1978-83, Norman Strunk disting. prof. fin. instns., 1983-95, dir. Banking Research Ctr., 1976-95, assoc. dean for acad. affairs, 1988-92, vis. prof., 2006—; dean John M. Olin Sch. of Bus., Washington U., St. Louis, 1995—2005, Bank of Am. prof. managerial leadership, 2000—07, prof. emeritus, 2007—. Cons. Fed. Res. Bank Chgo., 1994-95, 2005-; mem. Fed. Savs. and Loan Adv. Coun., 1986-89; vis. prof. banking and fin. Leon Recanati Grad. Sch. Bus. Adminstrn., Tel Aviv (Israel) U., 1980-81; vis. scholar E.M. Kauffman Found., 2005-06. Assoc. editor Nat. Banking Rev., 1966-67, So. Econ. Jour., 1977-79, Jour. Fin., 1977-83, Jour. Banking and Fin., 1980-92, Jour. Fin. Rsch., 1981-87, Fin. Rev., 1985-89, Managerial and Decision Econs., 1989-94, Jour. Econs., Mgmt. and Strategy, 1991-95; founding and mng. editor Jour. Fin. Intermediation, 1989-96, mem. editl. adv. com., 2004—. With US Army, 1958—64. Mem.: Am. Econ. Assn. Office: Washington U Campus Box 1133 One Brookings Dr Saint Louis MO 63130-4899 Business E-Mail: greenbaum@wustl.edu.

GREENBAUM, YVONNE LEE, medical/surgical nurse; b. Argentina, Nfld., Can., Sept. 2, 1949; d. Elzie Lee and Olive Marie (Morgan) Gadberry; m. James D. Greenbaum (div.); children: Benjamin, Jonathan, Rachel. BS, San Diego State U., 1972. RN Tex. Nurse Scripps Meml. Hosp., La Jolla, Calif., Norfolk Gen. Hosp., Va., Met. Meth., San Antonio. Home: 1168 Garrary Rd San Antonio TX 78209-6015

GREENBERG, ALAN COURTNEY (ACE LEV PETROVICH), diversified financial services company executive; b. Wichita, Kans., Sept. 3, 1927; s. Theodore H. and Esther (Zeligson) G.; m. Kathryn Olson, June 27, 1987; children: Lynn, Theodore. Student, U. Mo., 1949. With Bear Stearns & Co., NYC, 1949—, gen. ptnr., 1958—, chmn. bd., CEO, 1978-93, chmn. bd., 1993—2001, chmn. exec. com., sr. mng. dir., 2001—. Bd. dirs.

Viacom, 2003—. Winner Nat. Bridge Championship, 1977; recipient Horatio Alger award, 1997. Mem. Soc. Am. Magicians, Harmonie Club, Bond Club, Deep Dale Club. Office: Bear Stearns 383 Madison Ave New York NY 10179*

GREENBERG, ALBERT, art director; b. NYC, Mar. 15, 1924; s. Samuel David and Mary (Miller) G.; m. Marilyn Hoffner, May 29, 1949; children: Doren Roe, Peter Cooper. BFA, Cooper Union, 1948. Art editor Gentry, Am. Fabric Mags., NYC, 1951-56; art dir. Gentlemen's Quar. Mag., Esquire, Inc., NYC, 1956-70; sales promotion art dir. Lampert Agy., NYC, 1970-71; v.p., sales promotion art dir. Wells Rich Greene Inc., NYC, 1971-83; chmn. dept. comms. design Parsons Sch. Design, NYC, 1983-94. Tchr. Pratt Inst., 1964-65, 73-74, Cooper Union, 1967-68, Finch Coll., 1973-75, Manhattanville Coll., 1974-75, Parsons Sch. Design, 1975-82. Contbg. editor: Typographic Directions, 1964, Advertising Directions, Photography, 1962, Advertising Directions, Visual Advertising, 1961. Trustee Cooper Union, 1979-82. Served with USAAF, 1943-45, ETO. Decorated air medal with silver oak leaf cluster; named Alumnus of Yr., Cooper Union, 1968; recipient more than 100 profl. awards including Gold medal, Art Dirs. Club, 1979, Pres.'s citation for profl. achievement, Cooper Union, 1982, Alumni Assn. St. Gauden's medal for profl. achievement in art, 2006. Mem. Art Dirs. Club N.Y. (designer 43d ann.), Cooper Union Alumni Coun. (1st v.p. 1970-71, pres. 1971-73). Home Phone: 212-675-1958, 845-229-8469; Office Phone: 845-229-8469. Personal E-mail: cu1948@aol.com.

GREENBERG, ALLAN, advertising and marketing research consultant; b. NYC, Dec. 8, 1917; s. Solomon and Rose (Honik) G.; m. Rosalie Katz, Nov. 7, 1943; children— Barbara L. Gutman, Roy J. BS, CCNY, 1942; postgrad., U. Wis., 1944, New Sch. for Social Rsch., 1946—54. Assoc. Psychol. Corp., NYC, 1937—38; rsch. analyst Serutan, Inc., Jersey City, 1939—41; rsch. mgr./asst. dir. rsch. Grey Advt., Inc., NYC, 1948—55; sr. v.p., dir. rsch. and planning Doyle Dane Bernbach, Inc., NYC, 1955—74; rsch. cons. to advt. agys. and mfrs., 1974—. Former chmn. tech. rsch. com. Advt. Rsch. Found.; former pres. joint coun. Empire Blue Cross/Blue Shield-HMO. Author: (with Mary Joan Glynn) A Study of Young People; booklet, 1966; contbr. articles to profl. jours. Former pres. mems. coun. Cmty. Health Program Queens-Nassau; mem. Profls. and Execs. in Retirement Group at Hofstra U. With AUS, 1942-45. Mem.: B'nai Zion (past mem. nat. exec. bd.; past pres. L.I. region). Home and Office: 5333 Zelzah Ave Apt 140 Encino CA 91316-2207 Home Phone: 818-708-2530.

GREENBERG, ANGELA BARMBY, lawyer; b. Kansas City, Mo., 1969; m. Andrew Greenberg; 1 child. BA, U. Kans., Lawrence, 1992; JD, U. Tulsa Coll. Law, 1996. Bar: Tex. 1997. Assoc. Lanier Law Firm, Houston, 2000—. Mem. editl. bd.: Energy Law Jour., 1996. Named a Rising Star, Tex. Super Lawyers mag., 2006. Mem.: Trial Lawyers for Pub. Justice, Assn. Trial Lawyers of Am., Houston Young Lawyers Assn., ABA, Houston Bar Assn. Office: Lanier Law Firm PC 6810 FM 1960 West Houston TX 77069 Office Phone: 713-659-5200.*

GREENBERG, BARRY, physician; b. Bklyn., June 24, 1944; s. Reuben and Blanche (Ross) G.; m. Jennifer Keithly, Feb. 18, 1984; children: Lauren, Miranda. BA, Bklyn. Coll., 1966; MD, SUNY, Syracuse, 1970. Diplomate in internal medicine and cardiovascular diseases Am. Bd. Internal Medicine. Prof. medicine Oreg. Health Scis. U., Portland, 1977-95; prof. medicine, dir. advanced heart failure treatment program U. Calif., San Diego, 1995—. Editor: Valvular Heart Disease, 1987, Congestive Heart Failure, 2001. Mem.: HFSA (pres.), ACC, AHA. Office: U Calif San Diego 200 W Arbor Dr San Diego CA 92103-8411 Office Phone: 619-543-7751. E-mail: bgreenberg@ucsd.edu.

GREENBERG, BARRY MICHAEL, talent executive; b. Bklyn., Nov. 9, 1951; s. Aaron Herbert and Alice Rhoda (Strauss) Greenberg; m. Julie Marie Greenberg, Oct. 9, 2005; children: Samuel Jacob, Seth Grahame-Smith. BA, Antioch Coll. (previously known as Antioch U.), 1979. Dir. B'nai B'rith, Phila., 1976-80; acting dir. Jewish Nat. Fund, LA, 1980-81; chmn. Celebrity Connection, LA, 1981—. Co-founder Beverly Hills Air Force Co.; adj. faculty U. So. Calif. Annenberg Sch. Journalism. Emeritus mem. Air Force adv. bd. USAF; Wilshire cmty. police adv. bd. L.A. Police Dept.; fin. co-chair, past chair Cmty.-Police Adv. Bd. Summit; 50th Anniversary of WWII com. U.S. Dept. Def.; pub. safety steering com. L.A. 4th Councilmanic Dist.; exec. bd. CDC Bus. Responds to AIDS program; co-founder Windsor Watch; adv. bd. Windsor Sq. Assn.; charter past pres. entertainment industry unit B'nai B'rith; past pres. Temple Israel of Hollywood Men's Club; past bd. mgrs. Hollywood-Wilshire YMCA; treas. Fuller Ave. Sr. Housing. Recipient Chief of Chaplains Meritorious Svc. award, USAF. Mem. Def. Orientation Conf. Assn., Air Force Pub. Affairs Alumni Assn. Jewish. Avocations: flying, music. Office: Celebrity Connection 2208 Patricia Ave Los Angeles CA 90064 Home: 2208 Patricia Ave Los Angeles CA 90064 Office Phone: 323-650-0001. Business E-Mail: info@celebconn.com.

GREENBERG, BENJAMIN, physician; b. NYC, Sept. 10, 1914; s. Moses and Beatrice (Kasten) G.; children: William Michael, Harvey Herman, Barry Edward. BA, Ind. U., 1936; MD, U. Edinburgh, Scotland, 1941. Intern Maimonides Hosp., NYC, 1942-43; resident in surgery Maimonide Hosp., NYC, 1943-44; pvt. practice NYC, from 1946. Contbr. articles to profl. jours. Bd. dirs. Rockwood Park Security Assn.; chmn. adv. bd. Rep. Party; mem. Inner Circle Nat. Rep. Party, mem. Round Table; mem. Citizens Ambassador Program. Recipient Medal of Freedom award Sen. Rep. Party, 1994; named Comdr. of Honor, Eng. Mem. AMA, Am. Acad. Family Practice, Am. Acad. Sports Medicine and Rsch., Rockwood Park Civic Assn. (bd. dirs. 1960-70), Poan Am. Med. Assn., N.Y. State Med. Assn., Queens County Acad. Medicine. Republican. Jewish. Avocations: tennis, golf, photography. Address: 132 W 31st St Fl 15 New York NY 10001-3406

GREENBERG, BERNARD, retired entomologist; b. NYC, Apr. 24, 1922; s. Isidore and Rose (Gordon) Greenberg; m. Barbara Muriel Dickler, Sept. 1, 1949; children: Gary, Linda, Deborah, Daniel. BA, Bklyn. Coll., 1944; MA, U. Kans., 1951, PhD, 1954. Asst. prof. biology U. Ill. Med. Ctr., Chgo., 1954-61, assoc. prof., 1961-66, prof. geophys. scis., 1966-90, prof. emeritus, 1990—. Vis. scientist Istituto Superiore di Sanita, Rome, 1960—61, Fulbright-Hays sr. rsch. scholar, 1967—68; vis. scientist Instituto de Salubridad y Enfermedades Tropicales, Mexico City, 1962, Mexico City, 63; pres. Bioconcern; nat. lectr. Sigma Xi, 1996—; cons. in field; expert witness forensic entomology. Author: Flies and Disease, vol. 1, 1971, Flies and Disease, vol. 2, 1973, Entomology and the Law: Flies as Forensic Indicators, 2002; contbr. articles to profl. jours. With USAF, 1944—46. NSF grantee, 1959—60, 1979—81, NIH grantee, 1960—67, U.S. Army Med. R & D Command grantee, 1966—72, Electric Power Rsch. Inst. grantee, 1976—85, Office Naval Rsch. grantee, 1977—78. Fellow: AAAS; mem.: Chgo. Acad. Sci. (sci. gov. 1981—91), Entomol. Soc. Am. Home: 1463 E 55th Pl Chicago IL 60637-1875 Office: Dept Biol Scis M/C 066 U Ill Chgo Chicago IL 60607 Office Phone: 312-996-3103. Personal E-mail: barnbern@hotmail.com. Business E-Mail: bugaboo@uic.edu.

GREENBERG, BRADLEY SANDER, communications educator; b. Toledo, Aug. 3, 1934; s. Abraham and Florence (Cohen) G.; m. Delight Thompson, June 7, 1959; children: Beth, Shawn, Debra. BA in Journalism; Univ. scholar, Bowling Green State U., 1956; MS in Journalism; Univ. fellow, U. Wis., 1957, PhD in Mass Communication, 1961. Postdoctoral fellow Mass. Comms. Rsch. Ctr., 1960-61; research asso. Inst. Communication Research, Stanford U., 1961-64; asst. prof. Mich. State U., East Lansing, 1964-66, assoc. prof., 1966-71, prof. dept. communication, 1971—2004, Univ. Disting. prof., 1990, chmn. dept., 1977-84, prof. telecommunication, 1975—2004, chmn. dept., 1984-90. Vis. prof. U. Mich., 2004, U. Ga., Athens, 1999, U. Calif., Berkeley, 1992; fellow Ctrs. Disease Control and Prevention, Atlanta, 1999; sr. fellow East-West Ctr., Comms. Inst., Honolulu, 1978-79, 81; rsch. fellow Ind. Broadcasting Authority, London, 1985-86; cons. Pres.'s Commn. on Causes and Prevention Violence, 1968-69, Surgeon Gen.'s Sci. Adv. Com. on TV and Social Behavior, 1970-72, 82. Author: The Kennedy Assassination and the American Public: Social Communication in Crisis, 1965, Use of Mass Media by the Urban Poor, 1970, Life on Television, 1980, Mexican Americans and the Mass Media, 1983, Cableviewing, 1988, Teletext in the U.K., 1988, Mass Media, Sex and the Adolescent, 1993, Desert Storm and the Mass Media, 1993, The Alphabet Soup of TV Ratings, 2001, Communication and Terrorism, 2003. Served to maj. U.S. Army Res., 1973. Recipient Chancellors award for disting. svc. in journalism U. Wis., 1978, disting. faculty award Mich. State U., 1979; named to Journalism Hall of Fame Bowling Green State U., 1980; rsch. grantee NIH, NSF, USPHS, Carnegie Corp., Hoso Bunka Found., Nat. Assn. Broadcasters. Fellow Internat. Comm. Assn. (pres. 1994-95); mem. Assn. for Edn. in Journalism, Phi Kappa Phi (pres. 1993-94). Home: 350 Winterberry Ln Okemos MI 48864-4166 Office: Mich State U Dept Telecommunication 569 Communication Arts Sci East Lansing MI 48824-1212 Office Phone: 517-353-6629. E-mail: bradg@msu.edu.

GREENBERG, BYRON STANLEY, newspaper and business executive, consultant; b. Bklyn., June 17, 1919; s. Albert and Bertha (Getleson) G.; m. Helena Marks, Feb. 10, 1946; children: David, Eric, Randy. Student, Bklyn. Coll., 1936-41. Circulation mgr. N.Y. Post, 1956-62, circulation dir., 1962-63, bus. mgr., 1963-72, gen. mgr., COO, 1973-79; sec., dir. N.Y. Post Corp., 1966-75, treas., dir., 1975-76, v.p., 1976-81. V.p., dir. Leisure Systems, Inc., 1978-80; pres., chief exec. officer, dir. Games Mgmt. Services, Inc., 1979-80 Bd. dirs. 92d St YMHA, 1970-71, Friars Nat. Found., 1981-82. Served with AUS, 1942-45. Mem. Friars Club. Home and Office: 2560 S Grade Rd Alpine CA 91901-3612 Home Phone: 619-445-8559. E-mail: slugger19@cox.net.

GREENBERG, CAROLYN PHYLLIS, retired anesthesiologist; b. San Francisco, July 7, 1941; AB, Stanford U., 1962; MD, U. Calif., San Francisco, 1966. Diplomate Am. Bd. Anesthesiology. Rotating intern L.A. County Hosp., 1966-67; resident in anesthesiology Presbyn. Hosp., NYC, 1967-69, vis. fellow in anesthesiology, 1969-70, asst. attending anesthesiologist, 1971-90, assoc. attending anesthesiologist, 1990-99, med. dir. ambulatory surgery, 1986-96, attending anesthesiologist, 1999; asst. attending anesthesiologist NY Hosp., 1970-71; attending anesthesiologist NY Presbyn. Hosp., 1999—2006; ret., 2006. Instr. anesthesiology Cornell Med. Sch., 1970—71; assoc. anesthesiology Columbia U., NYC, 1971—74, asst. prof. clin. anesthesiology, 1974—90, assoc. prof. clin. anesthesiology, 1990—99, prof. clin. anesthesiology, 1999, prof. emerita anesthesiology, 1999—; clin. prof. anesthesiology Cornell Med. Sch., 1999—2006. Contbr. book chpts., articles to profl. jours. Mem. Am. Soc. Anesthesiologists, NY State Soc. Anesthesiologists (Media award 1992), Med. Soc. NY, Soc. Ambulatory Anesthesia (treas. 1994-98, 2nd v.p. 1998-99, 1st v.p. 1999, Ambulatory Anesthesia Rsch. Found. award 1992), Malignant Hyperthermia Assn. of US (hotline cons. 1983-99, partnership award 1996). Jewish. Avocations: swimming, reading, piano, travel. Personal E-mail: cgfcalvin@yahoo.com.

GREENBERG, DANIEL LAWRENCE, lawyer; b. Bklyn., Oct. 14, 1945; s. Irving and Beatrice (Rabinowitz) G.; m. Karen R. Nelson, Apr. 4, 1987; children: Ilana Nelson-Greenberg, Mara Nelson-Greenberg. BA, Bklyn. Coll., 1966; JD, Columbia U., 1969; Fellow (hon.), U. Pa. Law Sch., 1996. Elem. tchr. N.Y.C. Pub. Sch. 208, 1969—71; atty. MFY Legal Svcs., NYC, 1971—73, mng. atty., 1973—87; dir. clin. edn. Harvard U. Law Sch., Cambridge, Mass., 1987—94; pres./atty.-in-chief The Legal Aid Soc., NYC, 1994—2004; spl. counsel pro bono initiatives Schulte Roth & Zabel LLP, NYC, 2005—. Bd. visitors CUNY Law Sch., Queens, 1989—, Columbia Law Sch., 1995—, Boston Coll. Law Sch., 1996—; Sibley lectr. U. Ga. Sch. Law, 1999; disting. visitor, NYU Sch. Law, 2004-05; cons. to Justice Minister, Govt. of Vietnam, 2005. Contbr. guest editls. N.Y. Times, Daily News, 1989-97. Mem bd. advisors The Workplace Project, Hempstead, N.Y., 1995—, Programs on the Legal Profession of the Open Soc. Inst., 1997-2000, Stein ethics program, Fordham Law Sch., 1996—; mem. selection panel Root-Tilden Project NYU Law Sch., 1997. Recipient First Ann. Pub. Interest Honoree award Columbia U. Law Sch., 1991, Disting. Pub. Interest Lawyer in Residence award Touro Coll. Sch. of Law, 1998, Emory Buckner award for pub. svc. Fed. Bar Coun. 2002. Mem. Nat. Lawyers Guild (pres. NYC chpt. 1985-87, Ann. award 2001), Assn. of the Bar of the City of N.Y., N.Y. County Lawyers, N.Y. State Bar Assn. Dem. Jewish. Office: Schulte Roth & Zabel LLP 919 Third Avenue New York NY 10022 Office Phone: 212-756-2069. Office Fax: 212-593-5955. E-mail: danny.greenberg@srz.com.

GREENBERG, DAVID BERNARD, chemical engineering educator; b. Norfolk, Va., Nov. 2, 1928; s. Abraham David and Ida (Frenkil) G.; m. Helen Muriel Levine, Aug. 15, 1959 (div. Aug. 1980); children: Lisa, Jan, Jill BS in Chem. Engring., Carnegie Inst. Tech., 1952; MS in Chem. Engring., Johns Hopkins U., 1959; PhD, La. State U., 1964. Registered profl. engr., La. Process engr. U.S. Indsl. Chem. Co., Balt., 1952-55; project engr. FMC Corp., Balt., 1955-56; asst. prof. U.S. Naval Acad., Annapolis, Md., 1958-61; from instr. to prof. La. State U., Baton Rouge, 1961-74; prof. chem. engring. U. Cin., 1974—, head dept., 1974-81. Program dir. engring. divsn. NSF, Washington, 1972-73, chem. and thermal scis. divsn., 1989-90; sr. scientist Chem. Sys. Lab., Dept. Army, Edgewood, Md., 1981-83; cons. Burk & Assocs., New Orleans, 1970-78. Contbr. numerous articles on chem. engring. to profl. jours. Mem. Cin. Mayor's Energy Task Force, 1981—. Served to lt. USNR, 1947-52 Esso research fellow, 1964-65, NSF fellow, 1961 Fellow Am. Soc. for Laser Medicine and Surgery; mem. Am. Inst. Chem. Engrs., Am. Chem. Soc., Am. Soc. for Engring. Edn., Sigma Xi, Tau Beta Pi, Phi Lambda Upsilon. Jewish. Home: 8547 Wyoming Club Dr Cincinnati OH 45215-4243 Office: Univ Cincinnati Dept Chem and Materials Engring PO Box 210012 Cincinnati OH 45221-0012 Home Phone: 513-821-1868. Business E-Mail: david.greenberg@uc.edu.

GREENBERG, DAVID ETHAN, communications consultant; b. NYC, Oct. 8, 1949; s. Abraham M. and Norma B. (Jacovitz) G.; m. Kerri Shwayder, Apr. 24, 1983; children: Alison Leigh, Zachary Scott. BA cum laude, Columbia U., 1971; JD, Harvard U., 1975. Bar: Colo. 1975. Speechwriter Gov. Richard D. Lamm, Denver, 1977-78, legal counsel, 1978-79; dir. mktg. Colo. Ski Country U.S.A., Denver, 1979-82; founder and mng. ptnr. GBSM, Denver, 1982; sec. of bd. & founder Denver Sch. of Sci. and Tech., Denver. Adj. assoc. prof. U of Colo., Denver, 1984-89. Columnist, The Denver Post, 1985-88. Spl. asst. to adminstr. for communications EPA, Wash. 1989; pres. Children's Mus. Denver, 1988; vice chair Colo. Ocean Journey Aquarium, 1994—; mem. Colo. Commn. Higher Edn., 1993-2003, trustee Clayton Coll. Found. Nat. Merit Scholar, NYC, 1967, fellow White House, 1988-89. Office: Denver Sch of Sci and Tech 2000 Valentia St Denver CO 80238 Office Phone: 303-320-5570. Office Fax: 303-377-5101.

GREENBERG, DAVID I., consumer products company executive; Grad., Williams Coll.; JD, MBA, U. Chgo., 1981. Legis. rep. Staff of Ralph Nader, 1975—77; legis. dir., gen. counsel Consumer Fedn. Am., 1981—84; ptnr. Arnold & Porter, 1984—88; staff v.p. Washington rels. Philip Morris Mgmt. Corp., 1988—90, v.p. corp. affairs strategy and devel. NYC, 1998—99; v.p. govt. affairs Philip Morris Cos., 1990—92; v.p. corp. affairs Europe Philip Morris Internat., Brussels, 1992—98, sr. v.p. corp. affairs, 1999—2001; sr. v.p., chief compliance officer Altria Grp., Inc., NYC, 2001—. Mem.: Phi Beta Kappa. Office: Altria Group Inc 120 Park Ave New York NY 10017-5592 Office Phone: 917-663-3620. Business E-Mail: david.greenberg@altria.com.

GREENBERG, E. PETER, microbiologist; BA in Biology, Western Wash. U.; MS in Microbiology, U. Iowa; PhD in Microbiology, U. Mass., 1977. With Cornell U., U. Iowa, 1988—2004, Sheppard prof. molecular pathogenesis; chair dept. microbiology U. Wash. Sch. Med., 2005—07, prof. microbiology, 2007—. Sci. advisor Integrated Genomics Inc.; chief sci. officer Quorum Scis., 1998—2000. Editor: Jour. Bacteriology; assoc. editor Annual Reviews Microbiology. Mem.: Am. Acad. Microbiology, AAAS, NAS. Office: U Wash Sch Medicine Dept Microbiology 1959 NE Pacific St Box 357242 HSB G-328 Seattle WA 98195-7242 Office Phone: 206-616-2881. Business E-Mail: epgreen@u.washington.edu.

GREENBERG, EDWARD SEYMOUR, political science professor; b. Phila., July 1, 1942; s. Samuel and Yetta (Kaplan) G.; m. Martha Ann Baker, Dec. 24, 1964; children: Joshua, Nathaniel. BA, Miami U., Ohio, 1964, MA, 1965; PhD, U. Wis., 1969. Asst. prof. polit. sci. Stanford (Calif.) U., 1968-72; assoc. prof. Ind. U., Bloomington, 1972-73; prof. U. Colo., Boulder, 1973—, dir. research program polit. and econ. change Inst. Behavioral Sci., 1980—, chair dept. polit. sci., 1985-88. Author: Serving the Few, 1974, Understanding Modern Government, 1979, Capitalism and the American Political Ideal, 1985, The American Political System, 1989, Workplace Democracy, 1986 (Dean's Writing award Social Scis. 1987), The Struggle for Democracy, 1993, 8th edit., 2007, 4th brief edit., 2002, The American Democratic Republic, 2005, 2d edit., 2007; contbr. articles to profl. jours. Recipient fellowship In Recognition of Disting. Tchg., 1968, Jeffrey Pressman award Policy Studies Assn.; grantee Russell Sage Found., 1968, U. Wis., 1968, NSF, 1976, 82, 85, NIH, 1991-94, 96-2001. Mem.: Internat. Polit. Sci. Assn., Am. Polit. Sci. Assn., Western Polit. Sci. Assn. (mem. exec. bd. 1986—89). Avocations: reading, bicycling, travel, golf, skiing. Home: 755 11th St Boulder CO 80302-7512 Office: U Colo Inst Behavioral Sci PO Box 487 Boulder CO 80309-0487 Home Phone: 303-443-8517; Office Phone: 303-492-2141. Business E-Mail: edward.greenberg@colorado.edu.

GREENBERG, ELINOR MILLER, director, consultant; b. Bklyn., Nov. 13, 1932; d. Ray and Susan (Weiss) Miller; m. Manuel Greenberg, Dec. 26, 1955; children: Andrea, Julie, Michael. BA, Mt. Holyoke Coll., South Hadley, Mass., 1953; MA, U. Wis., Madison, 1954; EdD, U. No. Colo., Greeley, 1981; LittD (hon.), St. Mary-of-the-Woods, Ind., 1983; LHD (hon.), Profl. Sch. Psychology, Calif., 1987. Speech pathologist various orgns., 1954—69; mem. faculty U. Colo., 1967—69, exec. dir., Arapahoe Inst. for Cmty. Devel., 1969—71; founding dir., nat. coord. Univ. without Walls, Loretto Heights Coll., Denver, 1971—79, asst. acad. dean, 1982—84, asst. to pres., 1984—85; regional exec. officer Coun. for Adult and Experiential Learning, Chgo., 1979—91; founding exec. dir. US West Comm.-CWA, Pathways to the Future, 1986—91; rsch. assoc. Inst. Rsch. on Adults in Higher Edn., U. Md., U. Coll., 1991; exec. dir. Project Leadership, 1986—. Project dir. Healthcare Seminars, Colo. Rural New Economy Initiative, 2000-02; pres., CEO EMG and Assocs., 1991—; cons. US West Found., No. Telecom, Rose Found., U. Colo. at Denver, Cogeoinfo., 1992-96, NEON Project, State Scholars Initiative, Western Interstate Commn. Higher Edn., 2003—06, NEAT Project, U. Wis., 2003—2006, Colo. Dept. Labor and Employment, 2004-05, Colo. AHEC Sys., U. Colo. Health Scis. Ctr., 2004-05, U. Memphis Leadership Inst. for Jud. Edn., 2007; founding regional coord. Mountain and Plains Partnership, 1996-02; adminstr. Visible Human Project-Undergrad., 2002-04. Co-editor, contbr.: Educating Learners of All Ages, 1980; co-author: Designing Undergraduate Education, 1981, Widening Ripples, 1986, Leading Effectively, 1987, In Our Fifties: Voices of Men and Women Reinventing Their Lives, 1993, MAPP Online Voices, 2000; editor, contbr.: New Partnerships: Higher Education and the Nonprofit Sector, 1982, Enhancing Leadership, 1989; author: Weaving: The Fabric of a Woman's Life, 1991, Journey for Justice, 1993; guest editor Liberal Edn. Jour.; gen. editor Seven MAPP Studies, 2002; feature writer Colo. Woman News, 1993-96, Women's Bus. News, 1995-96; contbr. Sculpting The Learning Organization, 1993, A Snapshot: Americans in Cuba-Villager Newspaper, 2007; contbr. articles to profl. jours. Bd. dirs., exec. com. Anti Defamation League of B'nai B'rith, Denver, 1981-99, chair women's leadership com., 1991-93, bd. dirs., 1985-95; mem. Colo. State Bd. C.C. and Occupl. Edn., 1981-86, vice-chair, 1984-85; bd. dirs. Internat. Women's Forum, 1986-88, Internat. Women's Forum Leadership Found., 1991-95, Griffith Ctr., Golden, Colo., 1982-86, Colo. Bd. CLE and Jud. Edn., 1984-96; bd. dirs. Colo. Jud. Inst., 2004—, vice chair, 2005-; mem. Women's Forum Colo., 1981-, pres. 1986; v.p. Women's Forum Colo. Found., 1987; adv. bd. Anchor Ctr. Blind Child, Colo. Coalition Prevention Nuclear War, Mile Hi Girl Scouts, Nat. Conf. on Edn. Women's Devel.; cmty. adv. bd. Colo. Woman News; adv. com. Colo. Pvt. Occupl. Sch., 1990-98, Colo. Cmty. Incentive Fund; co-chair Gov.'s Women's Econ. Devel. Taskforce, Women's Econ. Devel. Coun., 1988-96; bd. visitors U. Hosp., U. Colo., 1990-91, gov. apptd. Colo. Math., Sci. and Tech. Commn., chair, 1991-93, co-telecom. adv. commn. TAC 14, chair, 1993-95; founding steering com. Colo. Women's Leadership Coalition, 1988-96; mem. interdisciplinary telecomm. program, exec. bd. U. Colo., 1992-03; U.S. Dept. Edn., mem. Tech. Panels, 1991—, mem. Expert Panel on Lifelong Learning, 1999-02, Western AHEC Reg. Learning System, chair, coursework com., 1998; bd. dirs. Colo. Rural Tech. Program, 1996-00, Housing for All/Metro Denver Fair Housing Ctr., 1999-03, chair, 2002-03; chair Colo. Coalition for the Advancement of Telehealth, 2002-03; co-chair Colo. Coun. on Telehealth, 2003; mem. U. Physicians Inc. Task Force on Telehealth, 2003; mem. industry adv bd. MESA, 2002-05, bd. dirs., 2005-; mem. planning com. Colo. Women's Health Rsch. Symposium, 2004-05; mem. resource devel. com., program com. Health Careers Initiative Tracks, 2005—. Named Citizen of Yr., Omega Psi Phi, Denver, 1966, Woman of Decade Littleton Ind. Newspapers, 1970; recipient Sesquicentennial award Mt. Holyoke Coll. Alumni Assn., 1987, Minoru Yasui Cmty. Vol. award, 1991, Women of Excellence award Colo. Women's Leadership Coalition, 1996, Founding Mothers award, 1997, Woman of Dist., Mile High Girl Scouts, 1997, Martin Luther King Disting. Svc. award to Littleton Coun. for Human Rels., Arapahoe CC, 2003, 06, Arthur and Bea Branscombe Meml. award Housing for All: The Metro Denver Fair Housing Ctr., 2003, Martin Luther Kind Disting. Svc. award, Araphoe CC, 2006, MESA Disting. Svc. award, 2006, 07; grantee W. K. Kellogg Found., 1982, Weyerhaeuser Found., 1986, Fund for Improvement of Post Secondary Edn., 1977, 80, Robert Wood Johnson Found., 1997-2002. Mem. Kappa Delta Pi. Democrat. Jewish. Home: 6725 S Adams Way Littleton CO 80122-1801 Office Phone: 303-771-3560. Business E-Mail: ellie.greenberg@uchsc.edu.

GREENBERG, EVA MUELLER, retired librarian; b. Vienna, July 19, 1929; came to U.S., 1939; d. Paul and Greta (Scheuer) Mueller; m. Nathan Abraham Greenberg, June 22, 1952; children: David Stephen, Judith Helen, Lisa Pauline. AB, Harvard/Radcliffe Coll., 1951; MLS, Kent State U., 1975. Head reference McIntire Libr., Zanesville, Ohio, 1978; with Lorain (Ohio) Pub. Libr., 1978-81; head reference Elyria (Ohio) Pub. Libr., 1981-82; reference libr. adult svcs. Cuyahoga County Pub. Libr., Strongsville, Ohio, 1983-89; head adult svcs. Oberlin (Ohio) Pub. Libr., 1989—2004; ret., 2005. Contbr. articles to profl. jours. Grantee Ohio

Humanities Coun. for Pub. Programs; named Libr. of Yr., Ohio Support Svcs., 2000. Mem. ALA, Ohio Libr. Assn. (coord. cmty. info. task force). Home: 144 Kendal Dr Oberlin OH 44074-1906 Personal E-mail: evagreenberg@usa.net.

GREENBERG, GARY HOWARD, lawyer; b. NYC, Mar. 2, 1948; s. Leo and Elizabeth P. (Weissman) G.; m. Sherri Snyder, June 21, 1987; children: Benjamin, Laura, Nicholas. BA, Johns Hopkins U., 1970; JD, N.Y.U., 1974. Bar: N.Y. 1975, U.S. Dist. Ct. (so. dist.) N.Y. 1975, U.S. Dist. Ct. (ea. dist.) N.Y. 1975, U.S. Ct. Appeals (2nd cir.) 1984. Assoc. Orans, Elsen & Lupert, NYC, 1975—83, ptnr., 1983—2002; of counsel Vinson & Elkins LLP, NYC, 2002—04. Instr. trial acad. direct and cross exam. skills N.Y. County Lawyers' Assn.-Nat. Inst. of Trial Advocacy, 1995. Mem. ABA, Assn. of Bar of City of N.Y. (mem. com. on fed. legis. 1983-86), N.Y. State Bar Assn., N.Y. County Lawyers' Assn. (chair appellate cts. com. 1996-99).

GREENBERG, GORDON ALAN, lawyer; b. Chgo., July 2, 1954; s. Henry and Ruth (Bluestien) G.; m. Patricia L. Collins; children: Haley, Danielle. BA, U. Ill., 1976; JD with honors, Ill. Inst. Tech./Chgo.-Kent, 1980. Bar: Ill. 1980, U.S. Dist. Ct. (no. dist.) Ill. 1980, U.S. Ct. Appeals (7th cir.if. 1980, Calif. 1984, U.S. Ct. Appeals (9th cir.) 1984. Asst. state atty. Cook County, Chgo., 1980-83; spl. asst. U.S. atty. No. Dist. Ill., Chgo., 1982-83; asst. U.S. atty., chief Fin. Investigations Unit L.A. U.S. Atty. Office, 1983-89; ptnr. Sheppard, Mullin, Richter & Hampton, LA, 1989—; ptnr.-in-charge L.A. Office McDermott Will & Emery LLP, L.A. Instr. U.S. Dept. Justice, 1985-89, lawyer rep. 9th cir., L.A., 1993-96. Contbr. articles profl. jours. Named one of top 50 trial lawyers in L.A., L.A. Bus. Jour. Mem. ABA, State Bar Assn. Calif., L.A. County Bar Assn. (chmn. White Collar Def. Com.). Office: McDermott Will & Emery 2049 Century Park E Fl 34 Los Angeles CA 90067-3101 Office Phone: 310-551-9398. Office Fax: 310-277-4730. Business E-Mail: ggreenberg@mwe.com.

GREENBERG, HINDA FEIGE, library director; b. Bayreuth, Germany, Feb. 26, 1947; arrived in U.S., 1951; d. Samuel Leon and Sima (Schampagnere) F.; m. Joseph Lawrence, July 6, 1968; children: David Micah, Jacob Alexander. BA, Temple U., 1969; MLS, Rutgers U., 1981; PhD, Drexel U., 1999. Assoc. librarian Ednl. Testing Svc., Princeton, NJ, 1981-86; dir. info. ctr. Carnegie Found., Princeton, 1986-97, Robert Wood Johnson Found., Princeton, 1997—. Former pres. Consortium of Found. Librs. Avocation: travel.

GREENBERG, HOWARD, publishing executive; married. With Sun-Sentinel Co., Ft. Lauderdale, 1984—, circulation mktg. mgr., vp. & dir. devel., v.p. & circulation dir., sr. v.p./mng. dir., sr. v.p./gen. mgr., 2005—07, pres. & CEO, 2007—; pub. South Fla. Sun-Sentinel, Ft. Lauderdale, 2007. Active in Broward Alliance, chmn., 2004—05. Office: Sun-Sentinel 200 E Las Olas Blvd Fort Lauderdale FL 33301 Office Phone: 954-356-4229. E-mail: hgreenberg@sun-sentinel.com.*

GREENBERG, IRA ARTHUR, psychologist; b. Bklyn., June 26, 1924; s. Philip and Minnie (S.) G.; m. Martha Estella Cantrell, 1949 (div. 1950); m. Judith Linda Burgard-Rials, 1952 (div. 1954); m. Monita Ruth Niborod, 1961 (div. 1965). Grad. Scouts and Raiders Sch., US Naval Amphibious Tng. Base, 1944; BA in Journalism, U. Okla., 1949; MA in English, U. So. Calif., 1962; MS in Counseling, Calif. State U., LA, 1963; PhD in Psychology, Claremont Grad. Sch., 1967; Grad., Marine Corps Inst.'s Command and Staff Coll., 1992. Editor Ft. Riley Guidon, Kans., 1950—51; copy editor, reporter Columbus Enquirer, Ga., 1951—55; reporter Louisville Courier-Jour., 1955—56, LA Times, 1956—62; free-lance writer LA, Montclair, Camarillo, Calif., 1960—69, 1976—. Counselor Claremont Coll. Psychol. Clinic and Counseling Ctr., 1964-65; lectr. psychology Chapman Coll., Orange, Calif., 1965-66; psychologist Camarillo State Hosp., 1967-69, supervising psychologist, 1969-73, clin. psychologist, 1973-93; asst. prof. edn. San Fernando Valley State Coll., Northridge, Calif., 1967-69, lectr. psychodrama, social welfare U. Calif. Extension Divsn., Santa Barbara, 1968-69; vis. prof. edn. U. Nev., Reno, 1977—; vol. psychologist Free Clinic, LA, 1968-70; staff dir. Calif. Inst. Psychodrama, 1969-71; tng. cons. Topanga Ctr. for Human Devel., 1970-75; faculty Calif. Sch. Profl. Psychology, 1970-80; founder, exec. dir. Behavioral Studies Inst., mgmt. cons., LA, 1970—; founder, exec. dir. Psychodrama Ctr. for LA, Inc., 1971—, Group Hypnosis Ctr., LA, 1976—; prodr., host TV talk show Crime and Pub. Safety, Time Warner Cable, 1983—; cons. in field. Author: Psychodrama and Audience Attitude Change, 1968; editor (author): Psychodrama: Theory and Therapy, 1974, Group Hypnotherapy and Hypnodrama, 1977, The Hebrew National Orphan Home: Memories of Orphanage Life, 2001. Vol. humane officer State of Calif., 1979-89; res. officer LA Police Dept., 1980-86; bd. dirs. Humane Educators Coun., 1982-86; active Nat. Coun. Employer Support of Guard and Res., 1998—. With AUS 78th inf. divsn., 1943, army specialized tng. program, 1944, 11th engr. combat battalion XXI corps 7th Army, ETO, 1944-46; USAR, 1950-51, sgt. 1st class; capt. Calif. State Mil. Res., 1986-93, maj., 1993-2000; lt. col. US Svc. Command, 2000-02; col. Emergency Disaster Assistance Corps, 2002—; col. Am. Vol. Res., 2006—. Fellow Am. Soc. Clin. Hypnosis, Am. Soc. Group Psychotherapy and Psychodrama; mem. APA, Calif. Psychol. Assn., LA County Psychol. Assn., So. Calif. Soc. Clin. Hypnosis (pres. 1977-78), Group Psychotherapy Assn. So. Calif. (pres. 1987-88), So. Calif. Psychotherapy Affiliation (dir. 1976-85), Am. Soc. Psychical Rsch., Assn. Rsch. and Enlightenment, Peace Officers Assn., LA County; Acad. TV Arts and Scis., Nat. Acad. Cable Programming, UDT/SEAL Assn., Navy Amphibious Scouts and Raiders Assn., 11th Engr. Combat Battalion Assn., 78th Infantry Divsn. Assn., VFW, Am. Legion, Jewish War Vets., State Def. Forces Assn. Am., State Def. Forces Assn. Calif., Mensa, Am. Zionist Fedn., NRA, Calif. Rifle and Pistol Assn., SW Pistol League, Animal Protection Inst. Am., LA SPCA, Hebrew Nat. Orphan Home Alumni Assn., Sigma Delta Chi, Sierra Club, Greater LA Press Club, B'nai B'rith Club, Beverly Hills Gun Club Office Phone: 310-472-2662.

GREENBERG, IRA GEORGE, lawyer; b. NYC, May 8, 1946; s. Julius M. and Florence Greenberg; children: Amanda, Glenn. AB, Harvard U., 1968, JD, 1971. Bar: NY 1972. Asst. to gen. counsel Office of Sec. of Army, Washington, 1971-74; assoc. Dewey Ballantine, NYC, 1974-81, Summit Solomon & Feldesman and predecessor firms, NYC, 1981-83, ptnr., 1983-92, Edwards Angell Palmer & Dodge LLP and predecessor firm, NYC, 1992—. Capt. U.S. Army, 1971-74. Mem. ABA, N.Y.C. Bar Assn. (judiciary com.). Democrat. Office: Edwards Angell Palmer & Dodge LLP 750 Lexington Ave New York NY 10022-1200 Office Phone: 212-912-2756. Business E-Mail: igreenberg@eapdlaw.com.

GREENBERG, IRVING, rabbi; b. Bklyn., May 16, 1933; s. Elias and Sonya G.; m. Blu Genauer, June 23, 1957; children: Jeremy, David, Deborah, Jonathan, Judith. BA summa cum laude, Bklyn. Coll., 1953; MA, Harvard U., 1954, PhD, 1960, Brandeis U., 1986. Ordained rabbi, 1953. Rabbi Riverdale Jewish Ctr., Riverdale, N.Y., 1965-72; assoc. prof. history Yeshiva U., NYC, 1964-72, asst. prof. history, 1959-64; prof. dept. Jewish studies CUNY, 1972-79; pres. The Nat. Jewish Ctr. for Learning and Leadership, NYC, 1974—97; co-founder, pres. Jewish Life Network, 2000—07, chmn., 2000—02. Bd. dirs. Student Struggle for Soviet Jewry, SAR Acad., Riverdale, N.Y.C. Mus. Jewish Heritage, Am. Jewish Joint Distbn. Committed, Am. Assn. for Ethiopian Jewry, others. Author: The Jewish Way: Living the Holidays, 1988, Theodore Roosevelt and Labor: 1900-1918, 1988; co-editor: Confronting the Holocaust: The Impact of Elie Wiesel, 1978; contbr. articles to profl. jours. Recipient Rothberg award, Hebrew U., 1990, Smolar award, 1983, Akiba award, 1991; named one of The Top 50 Rabbis in America, Newsweek Mag., 2007. Mem. Am. Acad. Religion, Am. Jewish Hist. Soc., Assn. for Jewish Studies, Religious Edn. Assn., Religious Rsch. Assn., Rabbinical Coun. of Am. Fax: 212-279-1155.

GREENBERG, JACK, lawyer, educator; b. NYC, Dec. 22, 1924; s. Max and Bertha (Rosenberg) G.; m. Sema Ann Tanzer, 1950 (div. 1970); children: Josiah, David, Sarah, Ezra; m. Deborah M. Cole, 1970; children: Suzanne, William Cole. AB, Columbia U., 1945, LLB, 1948, LLD, 1984, Morgan State Coll., Central State Coll., 1965, Lincoln U., 1977, John Jay Coll. Criminal Justice, 1983, De Paul U., 1994, Howard U., 2004, Notre Dame, 2005. Bar: NY 1949. Rsch. asst. N.Y. State Law Revision Commn., 1949; asst. counsel NAACP Legal Def. and Ednl. Fund, 1949-61, dir.-counsel, 1961-84; argued in sch. segregation, sit-in, employment discrimination, poverty, capital punishment, other cases before U.S. Supreme Ct.; adj. prof. Columbia U. Law Sch., 1970-84, prof., vice-dean, 1984-89, prof. NYC, 1993—2006, Alphonse Fletcher Jr. prof. law, 2007—; dean Columbia Coll., 1989-93. Cons. Ctr. Applied Legal Studies, U. Witwatersrand, 1978; vis. lectr. Yale U. Law Sch., 1971; vis. prof. CCNY, 1977, Tokyo U., 1993-94, 99, St. Louis U. Law Sch., 1994, Lewis and Clark Law Sch., 1994-98, Princeton U., 1995, U. Munich, 1998; lectr. Harvard U. Law Sch., 1983, Hebrew U., 2005; disting. lectr. humanities Columbia Coll. Physicians and Surgeons, 1998, U. Nurenberg-Erlangen, 1999, Hebrew U., 2005, U. Auckland, New Zealand, 2005 Author: (with H. Hill) Citizens Guide to Desegregation, 1955, Race Relations and American Law, 1959, Judicial Process and Social Change, 1976, (with James Vorenberg) Dean Cuisine or the Liberated Man's Guide to Fine Cooking, 1990, Crusaders in the Courts, 1994, Crusaders in the Courts: Legal Battles of the Civil Rights Movement, 2004, Brown v. Board of Education: Witness to a Landmark Decision, 2004; contbg. author: Race, Sex and Religious Discrimination in International Law, 1981; contbr. articles to profl. jours. Bd. dirs. NYC Legal Aid Soc., Internat. League for Human Rights, Mex.-Am. Legal Def. Fund, 1968-75, Asian Am. Legal Def. Fund, 1980—, Human Rights Watch, 1978-98, NAACP Legal Def. and Ednl. Fund. Co-recipient Grenville Clark prize, 1978; Shikes fellow, Harvard Law Sch., 1981, hon. fellow, U. Pa. Law Sch., 1975. Fellow AAAS, Am. Coll. Trial Lawyers; mem. ABA (commn. to study FTC, adv. com. to spl. com. on crime prevention, sect. on individual rights and responsibilities, Silver Gavel award, Thurgood Marshall prize, Presdl. Citizens medal 2001), NY State Bar Assn. (exec. dir. spl. com. study state antitrust laws 1956), Am. Law Inst., Bar Assn. City NY (Cardozo lectr. 1973) Adminstrv. Conf. U.S. Home: 118 Riverside Dr New York NY 10024-3708 Office: Columbia Law Sch 435 W 116th St New York NY 10027-7297 Office Phone: 212-854-8030. Business E-Mail: jg25@columbia.edu.

GREENBERG, JACK M., former food products executive; b. Sept. 28, 1942; s. Edith S. Scher; m. Donna Greenberg; children: David, Ilyse, Allison. BSc in Acctg., DePaul U., Chgo., 1964, JD, 1968. CPA Ill.; bar:. With Arthur Young & Co., 1964-82; vice chmn., CFO McDonald's Corp., Oak Brook, Ill., CFO, exec. v.p., 1982, vice chmn., CFO, 1992, vice chmn., 1991—98, pres., 1998—99, pres. US Bus., 1997, CEO, 1998—2002, chmn., 1999—2002. Bd. dirs. Abbott Labs, Abbot Park, Ill., Allstate Corp., Northbrook, Ill., Hasbro, Inc., Pawtucket, RI, Manpower Inc., Milw., Innerworkings, Inc., Chgo.; chmn. Western Union. Bd. dirs. DePaul U. Field Mus., Inst. Internat. Edn., Chgo. (Ill.) Cmty. Trust. Mem.: AICPA, Ill. Inst. Cert. Pub. Accts. Office Phone: 312-368-7001. E-mail: jack.greenberg@us.mcd.com.

GREENBERG, JACOB, biochemist, educator, consultant; b. Haifa, Israel, Mar. 10, 1929; came to U.S., 1961; s. Shlomo and Temima Greenberg; m. Esther Kahana, May 19, 1957; children: Abraham, Daphne. PhD, Hebrew U., Jerusalem, 1958. Assoc. rsch. biochemist biochem. dept. NYU, 1962—67, assoc. rsch. scientist Sch. Medicine, 1969—71; assoc. rsch. scientist Mt. Sinai Med. Sch., NYC, 1967—68; asst. prof. N.Y. Med. Coll., 1972—76; dir. R&D quality assurance Advanced Biofactures, NYC, 1971—83; dir. R&D Protos, NYC, 1983—. Cons. Columbia U., N.Y.C., 1965-67. Editor Autism Now; contbr. articles to profl. jours. Mem. White House Inner Cir., Washington, 1984-93, Autistic Soc. NIH fellow, 1961-62, grantee, 1972-76. Mem. AAUP, Internat. Congress Biochemistry, Am. Chem. Soc. (grantee 1967), N.Y. Acad. Scis. Avocations: swimming, chess, writing. Office: Protos A Co 130-16 Francis Lewis Blvd Jamaica NY 11413-1841 Home Phone: 718-276-6090. Personal E-mail: jacobautie@aol.com.

GREENBERG, JERRY A., information technology executive; b. NJ; Degree in Econs., Harvard U. With Cambridge Technology Inc.; co-founder, co-chmn., co-CEO Sapient Corp., Cambridge, Mass., 1991—. Spkr. in field. Named one of Top 25 Most Influential Consultants, Consulting mag., 2005. Office: Sapient Corp 25 First St Cambridge MA 02141

GREENBERG, JOEL I., lawyer; BS, NYU, 1967; JD, Yale U., 1974. Bar: NY 1974. Ptnr., co-chair Corp. & Fin. Dept. Kaye Scholer LLP, NYC. Mem.: ABA, Assn. Bar of City NY. Office: Kaye Scholer LLP 425 Park Ave New York NY 10022 Office Phone: 212-836-8201. E-mail: jigreenberg@kayescholer.com.

GREENBERG, JUDITH HOROVITZ, geneticist; b. Phila., Apr. 2, 1947; d. Monty B. and Evelyn (Cohen) Horovitz; m. Warren Greenberg, June 8, 1969; 1 child, Elyssa H. BS in Biology, U. Pitts., 1967; MA in Biology, Boston U., 1970; PhD in Biology, Bryn Mawr Coll., 1972. Rsch. assoc. ARC, Bethesda, Md., 1971—74; postdoctoral fellow NIH, Bethesda, 1974—75, sr. staff fellow, 1975—81, health scientist adminstr., 1981—88; dir. divsn. genetics and devel. biology NIH, Nat. Inst. Gen. Med. Scis., Bethesda, 1988—; acting dir. Nat. Inst. Gen. Med. Scis. NIH, Bethesda, 2002—03. Recipient Pub. Health Svc. Spl. Recognition award, 1991, Presdl. Meritorious Exec. award, 1999, NIH Dirs. award, 2004, 06. Mem. Soc. Devel. Biology, Am. Soc. Cell Biology, Am. Soc. Human Genetics, AAAS, Sigma Xi. Office: NIGMS NIH 45 Center Dr Bldg 45 Bethesda MD 20892-6200 E-mail: greenbej@nigms.nih.gov.

GREENBERG, LENORE, public relations professional; b. Flushing; d. Jack and Frances Orenstein. BA, Hofstra U.; MS, SUNY. Dir.pub. rels. Bloomingdale's, Short Hills, N.J., 1977-78; dir. comms. N.J. Sch. Bds. Assn., Trenton, 1978-82; dir pub. info. N.J. State Dept. Edn., Trenton, 1982-90; assoc. exec. dir. Nat. Sch. Pub. Rels. Assn., Arlington, Va., 1990-91; pres. Lenore Greenberg & Assocs., Inc., 1991—. Adj. prof. pub. rels. Rutgers U. Freelance feature writer N.Y. Times. Mem. bd. assocs. McCarter Theatre, Princeton, N.J.; mem. Franklin Twp. Zoning Bd. Adjustment; mem. Franklin Twp. Human Rels. Commn.; chair Somerset County LWV; instr. Bus. Vols. for the Arts. Recipient award Am. Soc. Assn. Execs., award Women in Comms., award Internat. Assn. Bus. Communicators; Gold Medallion awrd Nat. Sch. Pub. Rels. Assn. Mem. Pub. Rels. Soc. Am. (accredited; pres. N.J. State chpt., nat. nominating and accreditation coms., Silver Anvil award), Nat. Health/Edn. Consortium. Home and Office: 30971 Carrara Rd Laguna Niguel CA 92677-2757

GREENBERG, LINDA GARRETT, education educator, volunteer, singer; b. Hanover, Pa., June 8, 1941; d. Richard Barnhart and Lillian (Shaffer) Garrett; m. Frederic Greenberg, Apr. 2, 1966; children: Timothy, Richard, Joshua. BA, Bucknell Univ., Lewisburg, Pa., 1963; MA, Columbia Univ., NY, NY, 1964. Asst. prof., speech and theatre Montclair State Coll., Montclair, NJ, 1964—70; actor, children's theatre Pushcart Players, Caldwell, NJ, 1972—73; tchr. John Robert Power Sch., NYC, 1964—67, NY Bus. Sch., NYC, 1967—68; adj. prof. Fairleigh Dickinson Univ., Rutherford, NJ, 1991—93, Montclair State Univ., Montclair, NJ, 1993—99, ret., 1999. Singer: (oratorio) NY Oratorio Soc., 1964—69; performer: (plays) Caldwell Players, 1970—74; singer: (oratorio) NJ Oratorio Soc., 1970—74; performer: (plays) Caldwell Players, 1980, Glen Ridge Cmty. Players, 1991; soloist: Keys Chorale (Key West). Trustee Bucknell Univ., Lewisburg, Pa., 1995—, alumni bd. dir., 1991—95; mem. mktg. com. Cmty. Found., Key West; bd. mem. The Actors Co. Theatre, NYC, 2005—; bd. dirs. Founders Soc., Key West, 2005—. Mem.: ednl. organizations (v.p.), Key West Arts and Hist. Soc. (soloist), Assn. of Gov. Bd. (AGB), Assn. of Univ. Women (AAUW), Turnip Theatre (bd. mem. 1990—2000), Arts Coun. of the Essex Area (v.p. 1973—80), Jr. League of Montclair (pres. 1976—78), art organizations (v.p.). Jewish. Avocations: singing, travel, reading, attending concerts and theatre, museums. Home (Winter): 17027 Flying Fish Lane Sugarloaf FL 33042 Home (Summer): 45 E 89th St Apt 31E New York NY 10128 E-mail: lgreenb@msn.com.

GREENBERG, LON RICHARD, energy executive, lawyer; b. NYC, Sept. 4, 1950; s. Ralph Austin and Miriam (Kenner) G.; m. Bonnie Small, June 25, 1972; children: Jody B. Scott B., Daniel A. BS, U. Pa., 1972; JD, Villanova U., 1975; postgrad., Harvard U., Boston, 1994. Bar: Pa. 1975. Law clk. to Hon. J. Sydney Hoffman, Superior Ct. Pa., Phila., 1975-76; assoc. Morgan, Lewis & Bockius, Phila., 1976-80; corp. devel. counsel UGI Corp., Valley Forge, Pa., 1980-82, corp. sec., 1982-87, v.p., gen. counsel, 1983-87, v.p. legal and corp. devel., 1987-89, sr. v.p. legal and corp. devel., 1989-94, pres., 1994-95, pres., CEO, 1995-96, chmn., pres., CEO, 1996—2005, chmn., CEO, 2005—, also bd. dirs. Chmn. bd. dirs. World LP Gas Assn.; bd. dirs. AmeriGas Propane, Inc., chmn., 1996—; bd. dirs. Aqua Am., Inc., Temple U. Health Sys. Bd. dirs., mem. fin. com., chmn. investment com., mem. nominating com. Reading Is Fundamental, Washington, 1995—; mem. policy com. Pa. Bus. Roundtable, Harrisburg, 1995—, chmn., 2005—06; former bd. trustees Chestnut Hill Healthcare; former mem. opportunities Industrialization Ctrs. Am.; former mem. task force com. United Way Leadership Giving Southeastern Pa., Phila.; bd. dirs. United Way Southeastern Pa., Phila., gen. campaign chair, 2006; coach Chestnut Hill Fathers Club, Phila.; adv. bd. Ea. Pa. chpt. Arthritis Found.; bd. dirs. Greater Phila. C. of C., CEO Coun. on Growth. Recipient Good Samaritan award N.W. Victim Svcs., 1994, Disting. Svc. award Chestnut Hill Cmty. Assn., 1994. Mem.: ABA, Pa. Bar Assn. Avocations: swimming, tennis, golf. Office: UGI Corp 460 N Gulph Rd King Of Prussia PA 19406

GREENBERG, MARK, television producer; Prodr.: (TV series) Entourage, 2004— (Producers Guild award, 2006). Mailing: Home Box Office Entourage 1100 Ave of the Americas New York NY 10036

GREENBERG, MARTIN ALAN, criminologist, educator; b. NYC, June 29, 1944; s. Irving Joseph and Martha Greenberg; m. Ellen Carol Wertlieb, Oct. 9, 1979; 1 child, Edward W. AA, Queens Coll., NYC, 1965; BA, Queens Coll., 1966; MA, John Jay Coll. of Criminal Justice, NYC, 1970; JD, N.Y. Law Sch., NYC, 1969; PhD, CUNY, 2001. Cert. protection profl. ASIS Internat./VA, 1986. Sch. security aide Jamaica HS, NYC, 1963—65; sr. ct. officer Unified Ct. Sys./Supreme Ct., NYC, 1970—77; coord./instr. of criminal justice Hawaii CC, Hilo, 1977—81; asst. prof. of law enforcement Ark. State U., Jonesboro, 1981—83; asst. prof. of criminal justice Castleton State Coll., Vt., 1984—85; probation officer Tompkins County, Ithaca, NY, 1986—87; coord./chair, criminal justice program/dept. Ulster County CC, Stone Ridge, NY, 1988—2003; dir., grad. program in criminal justice adminstrn. Point Pk. U., Pitts., 2003—06; chair criminology/criminal justice dept. Va. Union U., Richmond, 2006—07; asst. prof. criminal justice Coll. St. Rose, Albany, NY, 2007—. Aux. dep. insp. NYC Police Dept., 1965—77; pres. Aux. Police Benevolent Assn. of the City of NY, Inc., 1973—74. Author: (books) Auxiliary Police: The Citizens Approach to Public Safety, Prohibition Enforcement: Charting a New Mission, Citizens Defending America: From Colonial Times to an Age of Terrorism. Chair Security and Crime Prevention Sect., Acad. of Criminal Justice Sci., 2006. Recipient Am. Jurisprudence award for Trials and Appeals, NY Law Sch., 1969; Arthur Niederhoffer Meml. fellow, John Jay Coll. of Criminal Justice, 1988. Fellow: Criminal Justice Educators Assn. of N.Y. State (life); mem.: Acad. of Criminal Justice Sci. (life), Aux. Police Benevolent Assn. of the City of N.Y. (hon.). Office: Coll St Rose 432 Western Ave Albany NY 12203 Home: 955 Inman Rd Niskayuna NY 12309 Home Phone: 412-344-1301. Business E-Mail: greenbem@strose.edu.

GREENBERG, MAURICE RAYMOND (HANK), retired insurance company executive; b. NYC, May 4, 1925; s. Jacob and Ada (Rheingold) G.; m. Corinne Phyllis Zuckerman, Nov. 12, 1950; children: Jeffrey W., Evan G., L. Scott, Cathleen J. Pre-law cert., U. Miami, Fla., 1948; LLB, NY Law Sch., 1950, JD (hon.), New Eng. Sch. Law, 1970, Bryant Coll., Middlebury Coll., Brown U., Pace U. Bar: NY 1953. With Continental Casualty Co., 1952-60, Am. Internat. Group Inc., NYC, 1960—2005, pres. subs. Am. Home Assurance Co., 1962-67, pres., CEO, 1967—89, chmn. bd., CEO, 1989—2005, non-exec. chmn., 2005; v.p. C.V. Starr & Co., NYC, 1960—65, dir., 1965—68, pres., CEO, 1968—2005, chmn., CEO, 2005—. Mem. Bus. Roundtable, pres.'s adv. com. Trade Policy and Negotiations; vice-chmn. Ctr. for Strategic and Internat. Studies; chmn. US-China Bus. Coun., US-Korea Bus. Coun., US-ASEAN Bus. Coun.; hon. vice-chmn. Coun. on Fgn. Rels.; founding chmn. US-Philippine Bus. Com.; former chmn., dep. chmn., dir. Fed. Res. Bank NY. Bd. govs. NY Hosp.; mem. Pres.'s adv. com. on trade negotiations Ctr. for Strategic and Internat. Studies, mem. bus. roundtable; chmn. emeritus NY Presbyn. Hosp., 1995, NY Presbyn. Hosp. Found. Inc.; mem. bd. overseers Weill Med. Sch, Cornell U.; trustee Am. Mus. Nat. History; trustee emeritus Rockefeller U.; life trustee NYU; trustee Sch. Risk Mgmt., Ins., Actuarial Sci.; hon. trustee Mus. Modern Art; chmn. Acad. Medicine Devel. Co.; bd. dirs. Internat. Rescue Com. Capt. US Army, ETO, Korea. Decorated Bronze Star; named one of Forbes' Richest Americans, 1999—, World's Richest People, Forbes mag., 1999—, New York's Influentials, New York Mag., 2006. Mem. NY Bar Assn., The Asia Soc. (chmn.), Police Athletic League, Lotos Club, Harmonie Club. Office Phone: 212-759-5999. Business E-Mail: maurice.greenberg@cvstarrco.com.*

GREENBERG, MICHAEL RICHARD, urban studies and community health educator; b. NYC, Aug. 22, 1943; s. Sidney Saul and Mildred (Saletra) Greenberg; m. Gwendolyn Barker, Jan. 19, 1978; children: Seana Pappas, Heather Wilkerson, Joshua Suggs, Alexandra Greenberg. BA, CUNY, 1965; MA, Columbia U., 1966, PhD, 1969. Asst. prof. Columbia U., NYC, 1969-71; assoc. prof. Rutgers U., New Brunswick, NJ, 1971-73, prof., 1973-78, disting. prof., 1978-82, prof. urban studies and cmty. health, 1982—, assoc. dean faculty, 2000—. Co-dir. pub. health N.J. Grad. Progam in Pub. Health, New Brunswick, 1983—. Author: Urbanization and Cancer Mortality, 1983, Public Health and the Environment, 1988, Environmental Risk and the Press, 1989 (award 1988), Environmental Reporter's Handbook (award 1989), Environmentally Devastated Neighborhoods, 1996, Restoring America's Neighborhoods, 1999. Recipient Spl. Merit award, EPA, 1977, Dennis Sullivan award, Pub. Health Assn., 2001. Mem. APHA, Assn. of Am. Geographers (Disting. Scholars award 1997 Disting. Achievement award 2003), Soc. for Risk Analysis. Avocation: walking. Office: Rutgers U Dept Urban Studies Civic Sq Bldg 33 Livingston Ave Ste 100 New Brunswick NJ 08901-1900 E-mail: mrg@rci.rutgers.edu.

GREENBERG, MIKE, sportscaster; b. Aug. 6, 1967; Graduate, Northwestern Univ. Medill Sch. Journalism, 1989. Sports anchor, reporter WMAQ-Radio, Chgo., 1989—92; syndicated sports columnist Copley News Svc., Calif., 1993—95; sports reporter Sports Channel Chgo., 1994—95, WSCR-Radio, Chgo., 1992—96; anchor, ESPN News, 1996—99; anchor, Sportscenter ESPN, 1999—; co-host, Mike and Mike in the Morning ESPN Radio. Contbr. articles to ESPN The Mag.; author: (sports book) Why My Wife Thinks I am an Idiot, 2006. Office: ESPN Plz 935 Middle St Bristol CT 06010 E-mail: mikeandmike@espnradio.com.

GREENBERG, MORTON IRA, federal judge; b. Phila., Mar. 20, 1933; s. Harry Arnold and Pauline (Hofkin) Greenberg; m. Barbara-Ann Kissel, May 29, 1987; children from previous marriage: Elizabeth, Suzanne, Lawrence. AB, U. Pa., 1954; LLB, Yale U., 1957. Bar: NJ 1958, US Dist. Ct. NJ 1958, US Ct. Appeals (3d cir.) 1972, US Supreme Ct. 1973. Law clk.office of atty. gen. State of NJ, Trenton, NJ, 1957—58, dep. atty. gen., 1958—60, asst. atty. gen., 1971—73; pvt. practice Cape May, 1960—71; judge law div. Superior Ct. NJ, New Brunswick, 1973—76, judge chancery and gen. equity divs. Trenton, 1976—80, judge appellate div., 1980—87; judge US Ct. Appeals (3d cir.), Trenton and Phila., 1987—2000, sr. judge, 2000—. Office: US Ct Appeals US Courthouse Rm 219 402 E State St Trenton NJ 08608-1507*

GREENBERG, MORTON PAUL, lawyer, consultant, life settlement broker; b. Fall River, Mass., June 2, 1946; s. Harry and Sylvia Shirley (Davis) Greenberg; m. Louise Beryl Schindler, Jan. 24, 1970; 1 child, Alexis Lynn. BSBA, NYU, 1968; JD, Bklyn. Law Sch., 1971. Bar: N.Y. 1972; CLU Am. Coll., 1975. Atty. Hanner, Fitzmaurice & Onorato, NYC, 1971—72; dir., counsel, cons. on advanced underwriting The Mfrs. Life Ins. Co., Toronto, 1972—98; mng. gen. agt. for life settlements Viaticus, Inc., Chgo., 1999—2001; prin. life settlement broker Parker, Co., 1998—. Mem. sales ideas com. Million Dollar Roundtable, Chgo., 1982—83, 4th ann. George M. Graves meml. lectr., 1991; mem. adv. bd. Keeping Current, 1999—; bd. dirs. Biosafe, Inc., Pitts.; spkr. on law, tax, life settlements, and advanced underwriting various profl. groups. Contbr. articles to profl. jours.; author: (tech. jour.) ManuBriefs. Mem. bd. dir. Biosafe Inc., Pitts., 2005—. Mem.: ABA, Soc. Fin. Svcs. Profls., Nat. Assn. Ins. and Fin. Advisors, Internat. Platform Assn., Assn. for Advanced Life Underwriting (mem. bus. ins. and estate planning steering com. 1989—93), N.Y. State Bar Assn., Stern Sch. Bus. Alumni Assn., NYU Alumni Assn. Office Phone: 303-841-0891. Business E-Mail: mortgreenberg@mpgjd.com.

GREENBERG, MYRON SILVER, lawyer; b. LA, Oct. 17, 1945; s. Earl W. and Geri (Silver) G.; m. Shlomit Gross; children: David, Amy, Sophie, Benjamin. BSBA, UCLA, 1967; JD, 1970. Bar: Calif., 1971, U.S. Dist. Ct. (middle dist.) Calif. 1971, U.S. Tax Ct. 1977; cert. splst. in taxation law bd. legal specialization State Bar Calif.; CPA, Calif. Staff acct. Touche Ross & Co., LA, 1970-71; assoc. Kaplan, Livingston, Goodwin, Berkowitz, & Selvin, Beverly Hills, Calif., 1971-74; ptnr. Steefel, Levitt, & Weiss, 1975—82, Myron S. Greenberg, a Profl. Corp., Larkspur, Calif., 1982—. Professorial lectr. tax. Golden Gate U.; instr. estate planning U. Calif., Berkeley, 1989-2003. Author: California Attorney's Guide to Professional Corporations, 1977, 79; bd. editors UCLA Law Rev., 1969-70. Mem. San Anselmo Planning Commn., 1976-77; mem. adv. bd. cert. program personal fin. planning U. Calif., Berkeley, 1991-2003; bd. dirs. Marin County Estate Planning Coun., 2001—06, pres., 2004. Mem.: ABA, AHA (bd. dirs. Marin county chpt. 1984—90, pres. 1988—89), Calif. Bd. Legal Specialization (mem. tax commn. 1998—2001, chmn. tax. commn. 2001, bd. dirs. 2003—, chair bd. 2006—), Real Estate Tax Inst. Calif. Cont. Edn. Bar (planning com.), Marin County (Calif.) Bar Assn. (bd. dirs. 1994—2007, pres. 1999), Larkspur C. of C. (bd. dirs. 1985—87). Democrat. Jewish. Office: # 205 700 Larkspur Landing Cir Larkspur CA 94939-1711 Office Phone: 415-461-5844. Business E-Mail: msg@eplaw.com.

GREENBERG, NATHAN, accountant; b. Worcester, Mass., May 17, 1919; s. Samuel and Ida (Katz) G.; m. Mimi Aaron, Mar. 12, 1950 (dec.); children: Henry Aaron, Ruthanne; m. Barbara Rudnick, Feb. 9, 1979. BS in Bus. Adminstrn, Boston U., 1942. CPA, Mass. With IRS, 1945-47; v.p. finance, dir. Gt. Am. Plastics Co., Fitchburg, Mass., 1948-68, Gt. Am. Chem. Corp., Fitchburg, 1968-80; founder Greenberg, Rosenblatt, Kull & Bitsoli, P.C., Worcester, 1958—. Bd. dirs. Xsirius, Inc., Kleinert's, Inc. Trustee Nathan and Barbara Greenberg Charitable Trust, Jewish Home for Aged, Jewish Community Center, Jewish Fedn. Served with AUS, 1942-45, ETO. Decorated Bronze Star. Fellow AICPA, Mass. Soc. CPA's, Fla. Soc. CPA's, Controllers Inst. Am.; mem. Mu Sigma. Home: 19 Sloans Curve Dr Palm Beach FL 33480 Office: The Day Bldg 306 Main St Worcester MA 01608-1550 Office Phone: 508-791-0901. Personal E-mail: barbnate@aol.com.

GREENBERG, OSCAR WALLACE, physicist, researcher; b. NYC, Feb. 18, 1932; s. Joseph Jacob and Betty Greenberg; m. Yael Shapiro, May 27, 1969 (div. Apr. 1997); children: Joshua Daniel, Jeremy Hillel, Benjamin Gideon; m. Pearl Katz, June 27, 1999. BS, Rutgers U., 1952; A.M., Princeton U., 1954, PhD, 1957. Instr. Brandeis U., 1956-57; NSF postdoctoral fellow MIT, 1959-61; mem. faculty U. Md., College Park, 1961—, prof. physics, 1967—. Mem. Inst. Advanced Study, 1964-65; vis. assoc. prof. Rockefeller U., 1965-66; vis. prof. Tel-Aviv U., 1968-69, Johns Hopkins U., fall, 1977, NASA/Goddard Space Flight Center, spring 1978; vis. scientist Fermilab, 1984-85; vis. scholar U. Chgo., 1984-85; Fulbright scholar Dublin Inst. for Advanced Studies, 2006-07. Divisional assoc. editor: Phys. Rev. Letters, 1976-78. Served to 1st lt. USAF, 1957-59. Recipient award in phys. scis. Washington Acad. Scis., 1971; Sloan research fellow, 1964-66; Guggenheim fellow, 1968-69 Fellow Am. Phys. Soc. Home: 9404 Saint Andrews Way Silver Spring MD 20901-4859 Office: Univ Md Dept Physics College Park MD 20742-4111 Office Phone: 301-405-6014. Business E-Mail: owgreen@umd.edu.

GREENBERG, PAUL, editor; b. Shreveport, La., Jan. 21, 1937; s. Ben and Sarah (Ackerman) G.; m. Carolyn Levy, Dec. 6, 1964; children: Daniel, Ruth Elizabeth. BA Journalism, U. Mo., Columbia, 1958, MA in History, 1959; student, Columbia Grad. Sch., NYC, 1960—62; LittD, Rhodes Coll., Memphis, 1995; DHL, Lyon Coll., Batesville, Ark., 2007. Lectr. Am. history Hunter Coll., 1962; editorial page editor Pine Bluff (Ark.) Comml., 1962-66, 67-92; syndicated columnist, 1970—; editorial page editor Ark. Dem. Gazette, Little Rock, 1992—. Editl. writer Chgo. Daily News, 1966-67; adj. faculty history U. Ark., Pine Bluff, 1978-82, vis. Fulbright fellow, 1985, mem. faculty in journalism, 1991; commentator BBC, 2004; media fellow Hoover Inst., 2005. Author: Resonant Lives, 1991, Entirely Personal, 1992, No Surprises, 1996, To Life, 1999. Served to capt. U.S. Army, 1969. Recipient Grenville Clark award for best editl., 1964, Pulitzer prize editl. writing, 1969, award Nat. Newspaper Assn., 1968, U. Mo. Sch. Journalism award, 1983, Walker Stone award for editl. writing, 1985, 86, Pulitzer Prize finalist for editl. writing, 1986, H.L. Mencken Writing award, 1987, William Allen White Journalism award U. Kans., 1988, Green Eyeshade award, 1997, 2005, Katie award Dallas Press Club, 1999, 2000, Carmage Walls award, 2003. Jewish. Office: Arkansas Democrat Gazette Capitol at Scott Little Rock AR 72202

GREENBERG, PETER S., travel editor, news correspondent, writer; West Coast corr. Newsweek, LA; v.p. TV develop. Paramount; head creative team MGM; travel corr. ABC's Good Morning Am., 1985; travel editor NBC's Today Show, CNBC, MSNBC, 1995—; chief corr. Travel Channel, 1999—2005; contbg. editor AOL, Men's Health mag. Host Peter Greenberg Worldwide Radio show. Creator, co-exec. prodr. The Crash of Flight 191, History Channel, Secrets of the Black Box, History Channel, prodr., co-host The Royal Tour, creator, exec. prodr., host Inside American Airlines: A Week in the Life, CNBC; author: The Travel Detective, 2005, The Traveler's Diet: Eating Right and Staying Fit on the Road, 2006, Flight Crew Confidential, Hotel Secrets. Recipient Emmy Award. Office: NBC News Today Show 30 Rockefeller Plz Fl 3D New York NY 10112*

GREENBERG, PHILIP ALAN, lawyer; b. Bklyn., Aug. 2, 1948; s. Harry and Jeannette (Nataf) G. BA cum laude, Bklyn. Coll., 1970; JD, N.Y.U., 1973. Bar: N.Y. 1974, U.S. Dist. Ct. (ea. and so. dists.) N.Y. 1975, U.S. Ct. Appeals (2d cir.) 1975, U.S. Supreme Ct. 1977 N.J. 1988. Assoc. Kamerman & Kamerman, NYC, 1973-78, ptnr., 1978-82, Segal, Liling, Erlitz & Greenberg, NYC, 1982, Segal, Liling & Greenberg, NYC, 1982-84, Segal & Greenberg, NYC, 1984; mng. ptnr. Segal, Post, DeMott & Crow, NYC, 1985, Segal, Greenberg, McDonald & Maher, NYC, 1985-86, Segal, Greenberg & McDonald, NYC, 1986-87, Segal & Greenberg, NYC, 1987-93, Bizar & Martin, NYC, 1993-95; ptnr. Wallman Greenberg Gasman & McKnight, NYC, 1995-2000, pvt. practice, NYC, 2000—. Mem. faculty para legal Sobelsohn Sch., 1988-2000. Trustee Congregation Emunath Israel, 1984-99, chmn. law and ins. com., 1987-99. Mem. ABA (com. mem., lit. mem.), N.Y. Bar Assn., Assn. of Bar of City of N.Y., Mason (Maimonides-Marshall #739, master), Masters and Wardens Assn. (past pres. 6th Manhattan 1990-91, sec. 2000-03, pres. 2003-05), Internat. Assoc. Tribune (internat. exec. bd., 2004-06), Phi Alpha Delta. Democrat. Jewish. Home: 7 Francisco Ave Little Falls NJ 07424-2316 Office: 10 Park Ave Ste 2A New York NY 10016 Personal E-mail: lawman802@aol.com.

GREENBERG, RAYMOND SETH, academic and health facility administrator, educator; b. Chapel Hill, NC, Aug. 10, 1955; s. Bernard George and Ruth Esther (Marck) G.; m. Leah Daniella Dacus, Oct. 23, 1988. BA in Chemistry, U. N.C., 1976, PhD in Epidemiology, 1983; MD, Duke U., 1979; MPH, Harvard U., 1980; DMS (hon.), The Citadel, 2001; DS (hon.), Simpson Coll., 2002. Asst. prof. sch. medicine Emory U., Atlanta, 1983-86, assoc. prof., 1986-90, dep. dir. Winship Cancer Ctr., 1985-90, chair epidemiology/ biostat., 1988-90, prof., dean sch. pub. health, 1990-95; v.p. for acad. affairs, provost Med. U. SC, Charleston, 1995-99, pres., 2000—. Chair preventive medicine Nat. Bd. Med. Examiners, Phila., 1991-93; chair epidemiology study sect. NIH, Bethesda, Md., 1992-94; bd. sci. counselors Nat. Inst. for Dental and Craniofacial Rsch., Bethesda, 1994-99, mem. blue ribbon panel on rsch. tng. and career devel., 1999; chair adv. coun. Prudential Ctr. for Health Care Rsch., Atlanta, 1994-96; chair Harvard Adv. Com. on Electromagnetic Fields and Human Health, Boston, 1994-98; adv. com. on rsch. and med. grants, Am. Cancer Soc., Atlanta, 1994-96; breast and cervical cancer early detection and control adv. com., Ctrs. for Disease Control and Prevention, Atlanta, 1996-2000; adv. com. on agrl. health risks, Harvard Ctr. for Risk Analysis, Boston, 1996-99; clin. adv. bd. Deloitte and Touche Healthcare Consulting Group, 1997-99; chair sci. adv. panel 3M Corp., 1998-2002; chair bd. trustees S.C. Gov.'s Sch. Sci. and Math., 2004—; bd. sci. counselors Nat. Ctr. Health Stat., 2004—; mem. adv. bd. McKesson Corp., 2005—, Soc. Fellows and Scholars, Nat. Ctr. Minority Health; mem. S.C. Commn. on Healthcare Access, 2004-05. Author: Medical Epidemiology, 1993, 4th edit., 2005, Epidemiologia Medica, 1995, 3d edit., 2004; contbr. articles to profl. jours. Bd. dirs. Ga. divsn. Am. Cancer Soc., 1987-93, Carolina Art Assn., 1996-98, Trident United Way, 1999-2002, Trident Urban League, 2006—; mem. Gov.'s Task Force on Higher Edn., 2006. Named hon. alumnus, Med. U. S.C. Coll. Medicine Alumni Assn., 2006; recipient SC Order of Palmetto, 2005. Fellow Am. Coll. Epidemiology (pres. 1990-91); mem. APHA, Am. Epidemiology Soc. Democrat. Jewish. Office: Med U SC Colcock Hall 179 Ashley Ave Charleston SC 29425 Office Phone: 843-792-9005. Business E-Mail: greenber@musc.edu.

GREENBERG, RICHARD T., lawyer; b. Bklyn., June 10, 1952; s. Melvin David and Dolores Ruth (Siegartel) Greenberg; m. Kara M. Friedman; children: Brett, Matthew, Jodi, Noah. BA with distinction, Northwestern U., 1974; JD, NYU, 1977. Bar: Ill. 1977, U.S. Dist. Ct. (no. dist.) Ill. 1977, U.S. Dist. Ct. (ctrl. dist.) Ill. 2005, U.S. Dist. Ct. (ea. dist.) Wis. 2005, US Ct. Appeals 7th Cir. 1982. From assoc. to ptnr. Peterson & Ross, Chgo., 1977-87; ptnr. McCullough, Campbell & Lane, Chgo., 1987-96, Ross & Hardies, Chgo., 1996—2003, McGuireWoods LLP, Chgo., 2003—, mng. ptnr. Chgo. office, 2004—. Bd. dirs. Temple B'nai Torah, Highland Park, Ill., 1995-98. Mem. ABA, Ill. Bar Assn., Chgo. Bar Assn. Avocations: reading, politics, running. Office: McGuireWoods LLP Ste 4100 77 W Wacker Dr Chicago IL 60601-1818 Office Phone: 312-750-5755. Office Fax: 312-558-4377. Business E-Mail: rgreenberg@mcguirewoods.com.

GREENBERG, ROBERT JAY, law educator; b. NYC, Nov. 22, 1959; s. Murray Louis and Jeanette (Adams) G.; m. Dafna Rena Fuerst, June 29, 1993; children: Ashira Esther, Aliza Gila, Leora Adina. BA, Yeshiva U., 1981, JD, 1984, LLM, 2000. Bar: N.Y. 1986, U.S. Dist. Ct. N.Y. (ea. and so. dists.) 1986, U.S. Supreme Ct. 1989, U.S. Ct. Appeals (2d cir.) 1998, N.J. 2000, U.S. Dist. Ct. N.Y. (no. and we. dists.) 2000, U.S. Dist. Ct. N.J. 2000, D.C. 2001, U.S. Ct. Appeals (fed. cir.) 2001, Conn. 2001, U.S. Ct. of Internat. Trade 2002, Wyo. 2003; lic. real estate broker N.Y., notary public N.Y., N.J. Asst. to judge N.Y.C. Civil Ct., Bklyn., 1982; assoc. Simon, Meyrowitz, Meyrowitz and Schlussel, NYC, 1983-86; instr. Bruriah High Sch. for Girls, Elizabeth, N.J., 1985-87; lectr. Nat. Acad. for Paralegal Studies, Mahwah, N.J., 1987-88; sr. legal editor Matthew Bender and Co., Inc., NYC, 1987-94. Adj. asst. prof. bus. law Yeshiva U., NYC, 1994-98, asst. prof., 1998-2004, vis. asst. prof. 2004-06, vis. assoc. prof. 2006-; lectr. NYU Inst. Paralegal Studies, NYC, 1994-2000, adj. assoc. prof., 2001—; instr. dept. paralegal studies Queens College CUNY, 1994-; adj. asst. prof. bus. law Queens Coll., CUNY, 2001-. Asst. to author: Judaism and Vegetarianism, Judaism and Global Survival. Lectr. in Jewish law Young Israel of Staten Island, 1976—93, Congregation Beth Yehuda, Staten Island, 1980—93, Young Israel of Forest Hills, Queens, 1993—2003, Queens Jewish Ctr., 2000—03, Congregation Ohr Moshe, Queens, 2003—. Recipient Disting. Svc. award Congregation Beth Yehuda, 1988, Outstanding Svc. award, 1991. Mem.: ABA, Acad. of Legal Studies in Bus., N.Y. County Lawyers Assn., N.Y. State Bar Assn. Democrat. Office: 75-27 171st St Fresh Meadows NY 11366-1416 Office Phone: 917-854-8426. Personal E-mail: robert.greenberg@worldnet.att.net.

GREENBERG, RONALD DAVID, lawyer, educator; b. San Antonio, Sept. 9, 1939; s. Benjamin and Sylvia (Ghetlzer) G. BS, U. Tex., 1957; MBA, Harvard U., 1961, JD, 1964. Bar: N.Y., 1966, U.S. Dist. Ct. (ea. and so. dists.) N.Y. 1970, U.S. Ct. Appeals (2d cir.) 1975, U.S. Supreme Ct. 1975. Engring. lab. instr. U. Tex., 1957; engr. Redstone Arsenal, Army Ballistic Missile Agy., 1957; engr., bus. analyst Exxon Corp., NYC, 1957-64; rsch. asst. Harvard Bus. Sch.; with Smithsonian Astrophys. Observatory and Ednl. Testing Svc., NJ, 1961-62; atty., engr. Allied Corp., NYC, 1964-67; assoc. Arthur, Dry, Kalish, Taylor & Wood, NYC, 1967-69, Valicenti, Leighton, Reid & Pine, NYC, 1969-70; instr. faculty Columbia U., NYC, 1972-81, adj. prof. bus. law and taxation, 1970-71, 82-98; of counsel Delson & Gordon, NYC, 1973-87; sole practitioner Harrison, NY, 1988—. Lectr., cons. AICPA, Inst. Internal Auditors, New Haven C. of C., Citibank, Mfrs. Hanover Trust Co., Harcourt, Brace, Jovanovich, Inc., Prudential-Bache, Drexel, Burnham & Lambert, E.F. Hutton; vol. instr. vol. income tax program, Columbia U., N.Y.C., 1991-92; vis. prof. Stanford U., Palo Alto, Calif., 1978, Harvard U., Boston, 1981; adv. bd. Am. Law Rev, 2004— Author: Business Income Tax Materials, 1994; co-author: Business Organizations: Corporations, General Practice in New York, 1998, Business/Corporate Law and Practice, 8th edit., 2006; editor: The Compleat Lawyer, 1985-88, Tax Lawyer, 1982-95; editor-in-chief: NY Internat. Law Rev., 1988-91, chair adv. bd., 1992—; editor-in-chief: Internat. Law Practicum, 1987-91; mem. adv. bd. Am. Law Rev., 2004-; contbr. chpts. to books, articles to profl. jours. Cons. coun. City of N.Y., 1971-72, Manhattan C.C., 1974-76. Lt. USNR, 1957-59. Recipient Outstanding Prof. award Columbia U. Grad. Sch. Bus., 1973, MIT fellow Mech. Engring. Dept., 1959, Harvard U., Teagle Found., 1959-61; grantee Ford Found., 1977, Columbia U. Ctr. Internat. Studies, Sch. Internat. Pub. Affairs, 1992, Columbia Bus. Sch., 1976, 92-94. Mem. AAAS, ABA (chmn. com. on taxation gen. practice sect. 1978-83, chmn. com. on corp. banking and bus. law. gen. practice sect. 1985-87, moderator, chair profl. edn. programs 1986, 87), ASME, NSPE, N.Y. State Bar Assn. (gen. practice sect., chmn. tax law com. 1983-92, chmn. bus. law com. 1985-88, internat. law & practice sect., chmn. pubs. com. 1988-91, coord. study com. on med. malpractice legislation, 1980-82), Assn. Bar City N.Y., N.Y. Acad. Scis., Mensa, Tau Beta Pi, Pi Tau Sigma, Phi Eta Sigma, Am. Assn. for the Advancement of Sci. E-mail: rdgreenberg@hotmail.com.

GREENBERG, ROSALIE, child psychiatrist; b. Bklyn., Dec. 21, 1950; d. Sam and Molly G.; BA, NYU, 1972; student Upstate Med. Ctr., Syracuse, 1972-73; MD, Columbia U., 1976. Intern Overlook Hosp., Summit, N.J., 1976-77; resident in gen. psychiatry Columbia Presbyn. Med. Ctr., N.Y. State Psychiatric Inst., N.Y.C., 1977-80, fellow in child and adolescent psychiatry, 1979-81, dep. dir. pediatric psychiatry outpatient clinic, 1981-82; dir. child and adolescent outpatient services Fair Oaks Hosp., Summit, N.J., 1982—; instr. Columbia U., 1981—. Mem. Am. Psychiat. Assn., Am. Acad. Child and Adolescent Psychiatry, AMA. Office: Fair Oaks Hosp 19 Prospect St Summit NJ 07901-2531

GREENBERG, SARAH, film company executive; Exec. v.p. publicity Lionsgate Films, Santa Monica, Calif., 2004—06, co-pres. film mktg., 2006—. Prodr.: (films) Leonard Cohen: I'm Your Man, 2005, The US vs. John Lennon, 2006. Named one of 100 Most Powerful Women in Entertainment, Hollywood Reporter, 2006. Office: Lions Gate TV Corp 2700 Colorado Blvd Santa Monica CA 90404 Office Phone: 310-449-9200. Office Fax: 310-225-3870.*

GREENBERG, STEPHEN TODD, plastic surgeon; b. Manhasset, NY, Sept. 22, 1962; BS, George Washington U., DC, MD, 1988. Diplomate Nat. Bd. Med. Examiners. Resident in surgery NY Hosp.-Cornell U. Med. Ctr., NYC, 1989—93; resident in plastic surgery Hosp. of U. Pa., Phila., 1993—95, fellow, 1996; dir. NY Premier Plastic Surgery, NYC and Woodbury, NY. Asst. clin. prof. surgery. Fellow: Am. Coll. Surgeons; mem.: AMA, Nassau County Med. Soc., NY Med. Soc., Am. Cleft Palate-Craniofacial Assn., Am. Soc. Plastic and Reconstructive Surgeons. Office: NY Premier Plastic Surgery 195 Froelich Farm Blvd Woodbury NY 11797 Home Phone: 516-364-1400; Office Phone: 516-364-4200. E-mail: docstg@aol.com.

GREENBERG, STEVE, music company executive; Founder, pres. S-Curve Records, 2000—05; pres. Columbia Records, 2005—07; pres., CEO S-Curve Records, 2007—. Chmn. Nabbr. Office: S-Curve Records 150 Fifth Ave 9th Fl New York NY 10011*

GREENBERG, STEVEN M., physician; b. NYC, June 26, 1956; s. Nathan and Jean Greenberg; m. Elizabeth Anne Attanasio, June 6, 1999; children: Aaron, Adam, Lauren. BS, SUNY, 1977; MD, Albany Med. Coll., 1983. Lic. N.Y., 1984, diplomate Nat. Bd. Med. Examiners, 1983, Am. Bd. Internal Medicine, 1986, Am. Bd. Internal Medicine Subspecialty in Cardiovasc. Disease, 1989, cert. NASPE, 1994. Intern, resident internal medicine Bronx Med. Hosp. and Hosp. of Albert Einstein Coll. of Medicine, 1983—86; dir. clin. evaluation unit Weiler Hosp. of Albert Einstein Coll. of Medicine, Bronx, 1986, asst. attending physician, 1986; rsch. fellow cardiology Albert Einstein Coll. of Medicine, Bronx, 1986—87; asst. attending physician Queens Hosp. Ctr., 1986—89, Bronx Mcpl. Hosp. Ctr., 1986—90; fellow cardiology Mt. Sinai Hosp., NYC, 1987—90, attending physician NY, 1989—90, St. Francis Hosp., Roslyn, NY, 1990—, co-dir., pacemaker ctr., 1990—, coord., pacemaker ctr. Roslyn, NY, 1991, dir. CCU, 1994—. Cons. in field. Co-author articles in numerous profl. jours. Fellow: Heart Rhythm Soc., Am. Coll. Physicians, Am. Coll. Cardiology. Avocations: kayaking, coin collecting/numismatics. Office: St Francis Hosp PO Box 9000 Roslyn NY 11576-9000

GREENBERG, STEVEN MOREY, lawyer; b. Jersey City, Apr. 9, 1949; s. Joseph and Rhoda (Weisenfeld) Greenberg. AB cum laude, Syracuse U., 1971; JD, U. Pa., 1974. Bar: N.J. 1974, U.S. Dist. Ct. N.J. 1974, N.Y. 1980, U.S. Dist. Ct. (so. and ea. dists.) N.Y. 1986, U.S. Ct. Appeals (3d cir.) 1987, U.S. Ct. Fed. Claims 1989. Assoc. Carpenter, Bennett & Morrissey, Newark, 1974—77, Cole, Berman & Belsky, Rochelle Park, NJ, 1977-79; pvt. practice Hackensack, NJ, 1979—94; atty. Bergenfield (N.J.) Rent Leveling Bd., 1985-89, 92-93, 99, Bergenfield Planning Bd., 1993-96; ptnr. Greenberg & Marmorstein, Hackensack, 1994-97, Greenberg & Lanz, Hackensack, 1997—. Numerous offices Jewish Ctr. Teaneck, NJ, 1978—, Jewish Home and Rehab. Ctr., Jersey City, River Vale, NJ, 1982—; active United Jewish Appeal Fedn., Bergen County, N. Hudson, 1997—2004; com. mem. Jewish Home, Rockleigh, NJ, 1999—, v.p., 2003—; pres. Jewish Inst. Bioethics, NYC, 1998—2004, bd. dirs., 1998—; active NJ Leadership Think Tank Allen and Joan Bildner Ctr. Study Jewish Life Rutgers U., New Brunswick, 2001—04, Jewish Cmty. Rels. Coun. No. N.J., 1986—93, 1999—2007; governing body Jewish Home Found. North Jersey, Inc., NJ, 2003—, sec., 2005—; dir. Union Traditional Judaism, 1993—97; active Jewish Family Svc., Inc., 1986—96, 2005—, v.p., 2007—; mem. NJ regional adv. bd. Anti-Defamation League, 1989—; bd. trustees United Jewish Appeal Fedn. No. N.J., 2004—, treas., 2004—05, campaign chair, 2004—05, v.p., 2005—; trustee Jewish Assn. Devel. Disabilities, 1999—, Bergen County HS Jewish Studies, 2000—05, Assn. Jewish Fedns., 2002—03, exec./ops. com., 2002—03; trustee Am. Soc. Protection of Nature in Israel, 2006—; bd. govs. Jewish Home Assisted Living, 2007—, Jewish Home Family, Inc., 2007—. Recipient Second Century award, Jewish Theol. Sem. Am., 1988, Cmty. Svc. award, Friends Lubavitch, 1997, Jewish Ctr. Teaneck award, 1997, Ma'Ayanot Yeshiva HS Girls award, 2001, Americanism award, Anti-Defamation League, 2003, Gates of Jerusalem award, Boys Town Jerusalem, 2004. Mem.: ABA, N.Y. State Bar Assn., Bergen County Bar Assn., N.J. Bar Assn., Pi Sigma Alpha, Phi Kappa Phi. Home: 96 Westminster Ave Bergenfield NJ 07621-3916 Office: 2 University Plz Hackensack NJ 07601-6202 Office Phone: 201-487-7755. Business E-Mail: smg@greenberglanz.com.

GREENBERG, WILLIAM MICHAEL, psychiatrist; b. Bklyn., Oct. 19, 1946; s. Benjamin Greenberg and Marilyn (Berger) Hamberg; m. Wendy Faith Megerman, June 14, 1992. BA, Queens Coll., 1968; postgrad., U. Medicine & Dentistry N.J., 1974—76; MD, Albert Einstein Coll. Medicine, 1978. Diplomate Am. Bd. Psychiatry Neurology, Am. Bd. Geriatric Psychiatry, Am. Bd. Forensic Psychiatry, Am. Bd. Addiction Psychiatry, cert. clin. psychopharmacology. Computer programmer We. Electric Co., NYC, 1970—73; rsch. asst. Bklyn. Jewish Hosp., 1973—74; resident psychiatry Bronx Mcpl. Hosp. Ctr., NY, 1978—83, pres. house staff, 1981—82; acting med. dir. Met. Ctr. Mental Health, NYC, 1983; staff psychiatrist Bronx Psychiat. Ctr., 1983—84; dir. psychiatry clinic North Ctrl. Bronx Hosp., 1984—88; psychiatrist, cons. Montefiore Mental Health Svcs. Rikers Island, East Elmhurst, NY, 1985—86; pvt. practice Bronx, NY, 1985—88, NJ, 1997—; mem. spkr.'s bur. Bergen Pines County Hosp. (now Bergen Regional Med. Ctr.), Paramus, NJ, 1988—2000; chief psychiatrist, attending staff mem. Bergen Regional Med. Ctr., Paramus, 1988—96, dir. psychiat. rsch., 1993—2000, interim med. dir. psychiatry, 1996—98, dir. psychiatry residency tng. program, 1997—2000, chmn. instrnl. rev. bd., 1996—2000; dir. outpatient rsch. ctr. Nat. Kline Inst., Orangeburg, NJ, 2001—. Asst. clin. prof. Albert Einstein Coll. Med., Bronx, NY, 1988—90; vis. asst. prof. Med. Coll. Pa., 1990—94, adj. asst. prof., 1994—2000; adj. assoc. prof. Drexel U. Coll. Medicine, 2000—04; adj. assoc. prof. environ. medicine NYU Sch. Medicine, 2001—02; prin. investigator clin. drug trials; clin. assoc. prof. psychiatry NYU Sch. Medicine, 2002—. Editor: N.J. Psychiatrist, 2001—; asst. editor: Cmty. Psychiatrist, 1985—89, mem. editl. bd.: Einstein Quar. Jour. Biology and

Medicine, 1987—2000; contbr. articles to profl. jours. Union rep. Cmty. Interns Residents, NYC, 1979—81; spkr.'s bur. Physicians Social Responsibility, NYC, 1982—84. Recipient Psychiatrist Recognition award, NJ Alliance Mentally Ill, 1996; scholar Rock Sleyster Mem., AMA, 1977. Mem.: AAAS, NJ Psychiat. Assn. (pres. 2004—05), Assn. Advancement Philosophy Psychiatry, Am. Psychiat. Assn. (pres. 2004—, assembly mem., Bruno Lima Disaster Psychiatry award 2007). Avocations: analytic philosophy, meditation, computers, photography. Office: Nathan S Kline Inst Psychiatry Outpatient Rsch Orangeburg NY 10962

GREENBERGER, HOWARD LEROY, lawyer, educator; b. Pitts., July 16, 1929; s. Abraham Harry and Alice (Levine) G.; m. Bette Jo Bergad, June 15, 1959. BS magna cum laude, U. Pitts., 1951; JD cum laude, NYU, 1954; diploma in law (Fulbright scholar), Oxford U., Eng., 1955. Bar: Pa. 1955, D.C. 1954, N.Y. 1969, U.S. Supreme Ct. 1964. Law clk. U.S. Ct. Appeals (3d cir.), 1958-60; assoc. Kaufman & Kaufman, Pitts., 1960-61; assoc. prof. law NYU, 1961-65, prof., 1965—2001, prof. emeritus, 2001—; assoc. dean NYU Sch. Law, 1968-72; dean and dir. Practising Law Inst., 1972-75; senator NYU, 1994—. Cons. in field.; v.p. Nat. Ctr. Para-Legal Tng.; pres. Early Am. Industries Assn., 1979-82; chmn. Commn. on Fgn. Grad. Study, AALS. Author: (with G. Cole) The Meriden Experiment, 1973; Study of the Quality of Continuing Legal Education in the U.S, 1980; contbr. articles to legal publs.; chmn. editorial bd. Jour. Legal Edn, 1974-77. Pres. N.Y.C. chpt. Am. Jewish Com., 1977-79, nat. bd. govs., 1979-85; vice chmn., gen. counsel Coalition to Free Soviet Jews, 1977—; trustee Law Ctr. Found., 1973-91, Am. Friends of Hebrew U. Jerusalem, 1986—; chair New Amsterdam dist. Boy Scouts Am., 1990—, Ctr. on Social Welfare Policy and Law, 1991—, Blaustein Inst. on Human Rights, 1992—; mem. Boy Scouts Am. Capt. JAGC, U.S. Army, 1955-58. Recipient Alumni Meritorious Svc. award NYU, 1977, Stanley Isaacs award Am. Jewish Com., 1982, Gt. Tchr. award NYU, 1993, Friendship award Govt. of Germany, 1988, Robert B. McKay Disting. Svc. award N.Y.U. Sch. of Law, 1997, Great Tchr. award 1999; Root-Tilden grantee NYU, 1954. Fellow Am. Bar Found.; mem. ABA, Assn. of Bar of City of NY, NY County Lawyers Assn. (bd. dirs. 1990—), Am. Law Inst., Assn. Am. Law Schs., NYU Club (pres. 1981-83, Masons, Sojourners, Vigil Hon. Order Arrow, Order of Coif, Phi Epsilon Pi. Democrat. Jewish. Home: 70 E 10th St Apt 16BApt 16 New York NY 10003 Office: NYU Sch Law Vand Hall 40 Washington Sq S New York NY 10012-1005 Office Phone: 212-998-6221.

GREENBERGER, I. MICHAEL, lawyer; b. Scranton, Pa., Oct. 30, 1945; s. David and Betty (Kabatchnick) G.; m. Marcia Devins, July 19, 1969; children: Sarah Devins, Anne Devins AB, Lafayette Coll., 1967; JD, U. Pa., 1970. Bar: D.C. 1971, U.S. Dist. Ct. D.C. 1971, U.S. Ct. Appeals (D.C. cir.) 1971, U.S. Supreme Ct. 1975. Law clk. to Judge Carl McGowan U.S. Ct. Appeals for D.C. Cir., Washington, 1970—71; legis. asst. U.S. Congresswoman Elizabeth Holtzman, 1972—73; atty., advisor Office of Criminal Justice, Office U.S. Atty. Gen., 1973; assoc. Shea & Gardner, Washington, 1973—77, ptnr., 1977—97; dir. divsn. of trading and markets U.S. Commodity Futures Trading Commn., 1997—99; counselor U.S. Atty. Gen., 1999, prin. dep. assoc., atty. gen., 1999—2001; vis. prof. U. Md. Law Sch., 2001—02, prof., 2002—; dir. U. Md. Ctr. for Health and Homeland Security, 2002—. Bd. govs. D.C. Bar, 1995—98, com. on legal ethics, 1993—95; mem. D.C. Cir. Adv. Com. on Procedures, 1983—89; mem. steering com. D.C. Pro Bono Partnership, 1994—97, Lafayette Coll. Leadership Coun., 1994—99; mediator office of cir. exec. U.S. Cts. for D.C., 1989—97; mem. D.C. Cir. Jud. Conf., 1983—; legal cons. Software Engring. Inst. Carnegie-Mellon U., Pitts., 1986—87; mem. steering com. Pres.'s Working Group on Fin. Markets, 1997—99; mem. hedge fund task force Internat. Orgn. Secs. Commrs., 1999. Editor-in-chief U. Pa. Law Rev., 1969-70; contbr. articles to profl. jours. Bd. dirs. Washington Legal Clinic for the Homeless, 1993-98, Am. Rivers, 1993-98, sec., 1995-98; bd. dirs. MIT Enterprise Forum Washington, 1984-87, Advanced Tech. Assn. Md., 1985-87, D.C. Prisoners' Legal Svc. Project, 1997-98. Fellow: Am. Bar Found.; mem.: Am. Law Inst., Phi Beta Kappa. Address: 2757 Brandywine St NW Washington DC 20008-1041 E-mail: mgreenberger@law.umaryland.edu.

GREENBERGER, MARCIA DEVINS, lawyer; b. Apr. 24, 1946; AB, U. Pa., 1967, JD, 1970; LLD (hon.), Lafayette U., 2000. Bar: D.C. 1970. Atty. Caplin & Drysdale, Washington, 1970—72; dir. Women's Rights Project Ctr. Law and Social Policy (now Nat. Women's Law Ctr.), 1972—81, co-pres. Named Woman Lawyer of Yr., DC Women's Bar Assn., 1996; named one of 25 Heroines, Working Women Mag.; recipient Woman of Distinction award, Soroptimist Internat., 2000, William J. Brennan award, DC Bar, 1994. Fellow: Am. Bar Found.; mem.: ABA (coun. individual rights and responsibilities sect.), Am. Law Inst. Office: Nat Womens Law Ctr Ste 800 11 Dupont Cir NW Washington DC 20036 Office Phone: 202-588-5180.

GREENBERGER, MARTIN, biotechnologist, information scientist, educator; b. Elizabeth, NJ, Nov. 30, 1931; s. David and Sidelle (Jonas) G.; m. Ellen Danica Silver, Feb. 2, 1959 (div. June 1974); children: Kari Edwards, David Silver; m. Liz Attardo, Dec. 11, 1982; children: Beth Jonit, Jonah Ben, Jilly Sal. Grad. with hons., USAF Officer Candidate Sch., 1953; AB, Harvard U., 1955, AM, 1956, PhD, 1958. Teaching fellow, resident adviser, staff mem. Computation Lab., Harvard U., Cambridge, 1954-58; mgr. applied sci. Cambridge IBM, 1956-58; asst. prof. mgmt. Mass. Inst. Tech., Cambridge, 1958-61, assoc. prof., 1961-67; prof., chmn. computer sci., dir. info. processing Johns Hopkins U., Balt., 1967-72; prof. math. scis., sr. research assoc. Center for Met. Planning and Research, 1972-75, prof. math. scis., 1978-82; IBM chair in tech. and info. systems UCLA Anderson Grad. Sch. Mgmt., 1982—; dir. UCLA Ctr. Digital Media, 1995-2000; pres. Council for Tech. and the Individual, 1985—; sr. fellow Milken Inst., 1999—. Mgr. systems program Electric Power Research Inst., Palo Alto, Calif., 1976-77; Isaac Taylor vis. prof. Technion-Israel Inst. Tech., Haifa, 1978-79; vis. prof. Internat. Energy Program, Grad. Sch. Bus., Stanford U., 1980, MIT Media Lab., 1988-89, Harvard U., 2001; computer sci. and engring. bd. NAS, 1970-72; chmn. COSATI rev. group NSF, 1971-72; evaluation com. Internat. Inst. for Applied Systems Analysis, Laxenburg, Austria, 1980; adv. panels, Office Tech. Assessment, GAO, U.S. Congress; adv. com. Getty Info. Inst.; cons. IBM, AT&T, CBS, Rand Corp., Morgan Guaranty, Arthur D. Little, TRW, Munger Tolles, Bolt, Beranek & Newman, Brookings Inst., Resources for Future, Electric Power Rsch. Inst., Atlantic Richfield, Rockwell Internat., Security Pacific Corp., John F. Kennedy Sch. of Govt. Harvard U., Bell Atlantic Corp., Sony Corp., Applied Minds, Mitchell Silberberg and Knupp, Am. Online, Kirkland and Ellis, Vertex Pharmaceuticals, Nat. Cancer Inst. Author: (with Orcutt, Korbel and Rivlin) Microanalysis of Socioeconomic Systems: A Simulation Study, 1961; (with Jones, Morris and Ness) On-Line Computation and Simulation: The OPS-3 System, 1965; (with Crenson and Crissey) Models in the Policy Process: Public Decision Making in the Computer Era, 1976; (with Brewer, Hogan and Russell) Caught Unawares: The Energy Decade in Retrospect, 1983; editor: Management and The Computer of the Future, 1962, republished as Computers and the World of the Future, 1964; Computers, Communications, and the Public Interest, 1971; (with Aronofsky, McKenney and Massy) Networks for Research and Education, 1973; Electronic Publishing Plus: Media for a Technological Future, 1985, Technologies for the 21st Century, Vol. 1, On Multimedia, 1990, Vol. 3, Multimedia in Review, 1992, Vol. 5, Content and Communication, 1994, Vol. 7, Scaling Up, 1996. Mem. overseers' vis. com. Harvard U., 1975-81; founder and mem. working groups Energy Modeling Forum, Stanford U., 1978-81; mem. adv. com. Nat. Center Analysis of Energy Systems Brookhaven Nat. Lab., 1976-80, chmn., 1977; mem. rev. com. Energy and Environment div. Lawrence Berkeley Lab., 1983, applied sci. div., 1986-88; chmn. forum on electronic pub. Washington program Annenberg, 1983-84; co-founder ICC Forum, 1985; chmn. CTI Roundtable Digital Media, 1990-99; chmn. CTI Roundtable Healthy Aging, 2006; trustee Educom, Princeton, N.J., 1969-73, chmn. council, 1969-70. With USAF, 1952-54, USAFR, 1954-60. Named a Disting. Grad. Officer Candidate Sch., USAF, 1953; NSF fellow, 1955-56; Guggenheim fellow U. Calif., Berkeley, 1965-66. Fellow: AAAS (v.p., chmn. sect. T 1973—75); mem.: Sigma Xi, Phi Beta Kappa. Office: UCLA Anderson Grad Sch Mgmt Los Angeles CA 90095-1481

GREENBERGER, PAUL ALLEN, allergist, immunologist, educator, medical researcher; b. Pitts., May 28, 1947; s. Lawrence Fred and Jean (Half) G.; m. Rosalie Simon, Dec. 29, 1974; children: Rachel, Daniel. BS, Purdue U., 1969; MD, Ind. U., 1973. Intern Meth. Hosp., Indpls., 1973; resident in medicine Washington U., St. Louis, 1974-76; allergy, immunology fellow Northwestern U., Chgo., 1976-78, asst. prof. medicine, 1979-83, assoc. prof., 1983-88, prof., 1988—. Contbr. articles to profl. jours. Fellow ACP, Am. Thoracic Soc., Am. Coll. Chest Physicians, Am. Acad. Allergy and Immunology, Am. Coll. Allergy Asthma and Immunology, Cen. Soc. for Clin. Rsch. Office: Northwestern U Dept Medicine 676 N St Clair St #14018 Chicago IL 60611 Office Phone: 312-695-4000. Business E-Mail: p-greenberger@northwestern.edu.

GREENBERGER, RONI SUSAN, elementary school educator; b. Bklyn., May 16, 1950; d. Sidney and Lillian Greenfader; m. Samuel Greenberger, May 29, 1972; children: Brett Ivan, Dara Hope. BS magna cum laude, Adelphi U., Garden City, NY, 1972; postgrad., Queens Coll., NY, 1972—74; AS, Nassau CC, Garden City, 1970. Cert. elem. edn. tchr., health edn. K-12 NY State, 1974. Health educator Park Ave. Sch., Westbury, NY, 1972—75; substitute educator Jericho Pub. Schs., Jericho, NY, 1980—81; head counselor Pierce Country Day Camp, Roslyn, NY, 1982—94; fifth grade tchr. Bowling Green Elem. Sch., Westbury, NY, 1984—. Sch. rep. Human Diginity Com., East Meadow Schs., NY, 2004—; coord. Sharing is Caring / Bowling Green, Westbury, NY, 2005—; grade level chairperson Bowling Green Sch., 1984—96, founding mem. of PMT, 1990—97, grad. chair, 1990—2000. Charter mem. U.S. Holocaust Meml. Mus., Washington, 1993; fundraising v.p. East Meadow Hadassah, East Meadow, NY, 1980—82, edn. v.p., 1978—80; mem. East Meadow Jewish Ctr., 1978. Mem.: East Meadow Tchrs. Assn., NY State United Tchrs., Am. Fedn. Tchrs., So. Poverty Law Ctr. Democrat. Jewish. Avocations: reading, travel, walking, ballet. Office: Bowling Green Elementary School 2340 Stewart Ave Westbury NY 11590 Home Phone: 516-486-5586; Office Phone: 516-876-7480.

GREENBLATT, DAVID J., pharmacologist; b. Boston, Apr. 8, 1945; s. Milton and Gertrude A. (Rogers) G.; m. Lisa L. von Moltke, Nov. 29, 1991. BA, Amherst Coll., 1966; MD, Harvard Med. Sch., 1970. Diplomate Am. Bd. Clin. Pharmacology. Intern in medicine Montefiore Hosp., Bronx, NY, 1970-71; resident in medicine Harvard Med. Svc. Boston City Hosp., 1971-72; fellow clin. pharmacology Mass. Gen. Hosp., Boston, 1972-74, mem. staff clin. pharmacology unit, 1974-76, chief clin. pharmacology unit, 1976-79; dir. clin. pharmacology program Tufts-New England Med. Ctr., Boston, 1979—; prof. pharmacology/exptl. therapeutics, psychiatry, medicine, anesthesia Sch. Medicine, Tufts U., Boston, 1979—; chmn. dept. pharmacology and exptl. therapeutics Sch. Medicine, Tufts U., Boston, 1994—, Louis Lasagna chair in pharmacology and exptl. therapeutics, 1997—. Author, co-author 11 books; contbr. over 800 articles to profl. jours. Recipient T. George Bidder award UCLA, 1988. Fellow Am. Coll. Clin. Pharmacology (bd. regents 1987-91, McKeen-Cattell award 1985, Disting. Svc. award 2001, pres.-elect 1994-96, pres. 1996-98, Dist. Investigator award 2002); mem. Am. Soc. Clin. Pharmacology and Therapeutics (bd. dirs. 1983-85, Rawls-Palmer award 1980), Am. Soc. Clin. Investigation, Am. Coll. Neuropsychopharmacology, Am. Assn. Pharm. Scientists (Clin. Scis. Rsch. Achievement award 2005) Avocation: baseball. Office: Tufts U Sch Medicine 136 Harrison Ave Boston MA 02111-1817 Office Phone: 617-636-6997. Business E-Mail: dj.greenblatt@tufts.edu.

GREENBLATT, HELLEN CHAYA, immunologist, microbiologist; b. Frankfurt au Main, Germany; came to U.S., 1948; d. Gedaljie and Sara (Glass) Greenblatt. BA, CCNY, 1968; MS, U. Okla., 1971; PhD, SUNY Downstate Med. Ctr., Bklyn., 1977. Microbiologist Walter Reed Army Inst., Washington, 1978-80; sr. rsch. immunoparasitologist Merck Sharp & Dohme, Rahway, NJ, 1980-81; assoc. Albert Einstein Coll. Medicine, Bronx, NY, 1981-84; dir. rsch. and devel. Clin. Scis. Inc., Whippany, NJ, 1984-86, dir. new bus. and sci. devel., 1986-88; sr. devel. virology E.I. DuPont, Wilmington, Del., 1988-90; mng. dir. M-CAP Techs. Internat./DCV, Wilmington, 1990-93; tech. rep. BTR Separations, Wilmington, 1993-94; v.p. R & D, DCV Biol. Scis., Wilmington, 1994-97; v.p. devel. Life Scis. divsn. DCV BioNutrition, Wilmington, 1997-2000; v.p. Legacy USA, Melbourne, Fla., 1999—2002; exec. v.p. Legacy for Life, 2002—04, chief sci. officer, 2004—. Numerous internat. and domestic tech. presentations in field. Contbr. chpt. to book, numerous articles to peer-review profl. jours. Tutor Lit. Vols. Am., 1992—97; bd. dirs. Interfaith Housing of Del., 1993—97. Recipient Outstanding Young Woman award Competitive Resident Rsch. Coun., Washington, 1978; grantee NRC, 1978-80; fellow NRC. Mem.: NY Acad. Scis., Am. Acad. Anti-Aging Medicine. Achievements include patents for gastroprotective, anti-inflammatory and anti-diarrheal properties of immune egg; among the foremost authorities on polyvalent hyperimmune egg (PHIE) for human and pet applications. Office: Legacy for Life 2725 Ctr Pl Melbourne FL 32940 Office Phone: 800-746-0300. Business E-Mail: hgreenblatt@legacyforlife.net.

GREENBLATT, MIRIAM, writer, editor, educator; b. Berlin; d. Gregory and Shifra (Zemach) Baraks; m. Howard Greenblatt (div.). BA magna cum laude, Hunter Coll.; postgrad., U. Chgo. Editor Am. People's Ency., Chgo., 1957-58, Scott Foresman & Co., Chgo., 1958-62; pres. Creative Textbooks, Chgo., 1972—. Tchr. New Trier (Ill.) HS, 1978—81. Author (with Chu): The Story of China, 1968; author: (with Cuban) Japan, 1971; author: The History of Itasca, 1976; author: (with others) The American People, 1986; author: James Knox Polk, 1988, Franklin Delano Roosevelt, 1989, John Quincy Adams, 1990; author: (with Welty) The Human Expression, 1992; author: Cambodia, 1995; author: (with Jordan and Bowes) The Americans, 1996; author: Hatshepsut and Ancient Egypt, 2000, Alexander the Great and Ancient Greece, 2000, Augustus and Imperial Rome, 2000, Peter the Great and Tsarist Russia, 2000, Genghis Khan and the Mongol Empire, 2002, Elizabeth I and Tudor England, 2002, The War of 1812, 2003, Iran, 2003, Charlemagne and the Early Middle Ages, 2003, Suleyman the Magnificent and the Ottoman Empire, 2003, Lorenzo de Medici and Renaissance Italy, 2003, Afghanistan, 2003, Julius Caesar and the Roman Republic, 2005, Han Wu Di and Ancient China, 2005, Napoleon Bonaparte and Imperial France, 2005; author: (with Lemmo) Human Heritage, 2006; editl. cons. Peoples and Cultures Series, 1976—78, subject area cons. World Geography and Cultures, 1994; contbg. editor: A World History, 1979. Mem. nat. exec. coun. Am. Jewish Com., 1980—84, v.p. Chgo chpt., 1977—79; treas. Glencoe Youth Svcs., 1981—83. Mem.: Cliff Dwellers. Jewish. Address: 2754 Roslyn Ln Highland Park IL 60035-1408

GREENBLATT, RAY HARRIS, lawyer; b. Milw., June 29, 1931; s. Charles and Ethel (Harris) G.; m. Betty Goldsmith, July 11, 1955 (dec. Mar. 1967); children: Walter, Robert, Edward; m. Helen Judith Pick, Mar. 29, 1969 (div. Dec. 1969). BS in Econs., U. Pa., 1953; JD magna cum laude, Harvard U., 1956. Bar: Ill. 1956. Assoc. Mayer, Brown, Rowe & Maw , 1956-64, ptnr., 1965-94. Arbitrator, mediator Am. Arbitration Assn., 1970-96; hearing officer Ill. State Banking Bd., 1989; lectr. Sch. for Bankers U. Wis., Madison, 1964, 73, Ill. Inst. Continuing Legal Edn., 1973. Contbr. articles to profl. jours. Pres. Winnetka (Ill.) Bd. Edn., 1973-74, mem. 1969-75; vol. tchr. economics, poetry and debate, Providence-St. Mel Sch., Chgo., 1994-98. Mem. Chgo. Literary Club (pres. 2000-01), Cliff Dwellers Club, Lake Shore Country Club. Jewish. Home: 1003 Westmoor Rd Winnetka IL 60093-1855 E-mail: rayofsunsh@aol.com.

GREENBLATT, STEPHEN JAY, literature and language professor, writer; b. Cambridge, Mass., Nov. 7, 1943; s. Harry J. and Mollie (Brown) G.; m. Ramie Targoff; children: Joshua, Aaron, Harry. BA, Yale U., 1964, MPhil, 1968, PhD, 1969; BA, Cambridge U., England, 1966, MA, 1969. Asst. prof. Dept. English U. Calif., Berkeley, 1969—74, assoc. prof., 1974—79, prof., 1979—97, The Class of 1932 Prof., 1984—97; Harry Levin Prof. Lit. Harvard U., Cambridge, Mass., 1997—2000, John Cogan U. Prof. of the Humanities, 2000—. Non-resident permanent fellow, Wissenschaftskolleg zu Berlin, vis. prof. 1996-97, 2003-04, U. Calif. Santa Cruz, 1981, Peking U., Beijing, 1982, Northwestern U., 1984, U. Bologna, Italy, 1988, U. Chgo., 1989, Ecole des Hautes Etudes en Sciences Sociales, Paris, 1989, Harvard U., 1990, 91, 93, 94, U. Trieste, 1991, Dartmouth U., 1992, U. Florence, 1992, 96, U. Torino, 1998, Kyoto U., 1998, Queen Mary and Westfield Coll., U. London, 1999; sr. fellow Soc. for the Humanities, Cornell U., 1983. Author: Three Modern Satirists: Waugh, Orwell, and Huxley, 1965 (Lloyd Mifflin Prize), Sir Walter Raleigh: The Renaissance Man and His Roles, 1973, Renaissance Self-Fashioning: From More to Shakespeare, 1980 (Brit. Coun. Prize in the Humanities), Shakespearean Negotiations: The Circulation of Social Energy in Renaissance England, 1988 (James Russell Lowell Prize, MLA, 1989), Learning to Curse: Essays in Early Modern Culture, 1990, Marvelous Possessions: The Wonder of the New World, 1991, Hamlet in Purgatory, 2001 (Erasmus Inst. Book Prize, 2002), Will in the World: How Shakespeare Became Shakespeare, 2004; co-author (with Catherine Gallagher): Practicing New Historicism, 2000; editor: Allegory and Representation: Selected Papers from the English Institute, 1979-80, 1981, The Power of Forms in the English Renaissance, 1982, Representing the English Renaissance, 1988, New World Encounters, 1993; co-editor (with Giles Gunn): Redrawing the Boundaries: The Transformation of English and American Literary Studies, 1992; co-editor: The Norton Shakespeare, 1997; co-editor: (with M.H. Abrams) Norton Anthology of English Literature, 7th edit., 1999; gen. editor: Norton Anthology of English Literature, 8th edit., 2006. Recipient Mellon Disting. Humanist Award, 2002; fellow, Rockefeller Found. Study and Conf. Ctr., Bellagio, 1999; NDEA Title IV Fellowship, 1966—69, Robert C. Bates Fellowship, 1967—68, Sterling Fellowship, 1968—69, Fulbright Scholarship, 1964—66, NEH Fellowship for Younger Humanists, 1971—72, Howard Found. Fellowship, 1978, Humanities Rsch. Fellowship, 1978, 1983, Guggenheim Fellowship, 1975, 1983, Am. Coun. Learned Societies Travel Grant, 1986. Fellow: Am. Acad. Arts and Sciences. Office: Harvard U Dept English and Am Lit and Lang Barker Ctr 12 Quincy St Cambridge MA 02138 E-mail: greenbl@fas.harvard.edu.

GREENBURG, DAN, author; b. Chgo., June 20, 1936; s. Samuel and Leah (Rozalsky) G.; m. Nora Ephron, Apr. 9, 1967 (div.); m. Suzanne O'Malley, June 28, 1980 (div.); m. Judith Wilson, Oct. 17, 1998. BFA, U. Ill., 1958; MFA, UCLA, 1960. Copywriter Lansdale Co., Los Angeles, 1960-61, Carson Roberts Advt., Los Angeles, 1961-62; mng. editor Eros mag., NYC, 1962-63; copywriter Papert, Koenig, Lois (advt.), NYC, 1963-65; freelance writer NYC, 1965—. Author: How to Be a Jewish Mother, 1964, Kiss My Firm but Pliant Lips, 1965, How to Make Yourself Miserable, 1966, Chewsday: A Sex Novel, 1968, Jumbo the Boy and Arnold the Elephant, 1969, 89, Philly, 1969, Porno-Graphics, 1969, Scoring: A Sexual Memoir, 1972, Something's There: My Adventures in the Occult, 1976, Love Kills, 1978, What Do Women Want?, 1982; (with Suzanne O'Malley) How to Avoid Love and Marriage, 1983, True Adventures, 1985, Confessions of a Pregnant Father, 1986, How to Make Yourself Miserable for the Rest of the Century, 1987, The Nanny, 1987, Exes, 1990, The Guardian, 1990, The Bed Who Ran Away From Home, 1991, Young Santa, 1991, Great Grandpa's in the Litter Box, 1996, A Ghost Named Wanda, 1996, Through the Medicine Cabinet, 1996, Zap! I'm a Mind-Reader, 1996, Moses Supposes, 1997, Dr. Jekyll, Orthodontist, 1997, I'm Out of My Body, Please Leave a Message, 1997, My Son, the Time Traveler, 1997, Never Trust a Cat Who Wears Earrings, 1997, The Volcano Goddess Will See You Now, 1997, Bozo the Clone, 1997, How to Speak Dolphin in Three Easy Lessons, 1997, Now You See Me, Now You Don't, 1998, The Misfortune Cookie, 1998, Elvis the Turnip and Me, 1998, Hang a Left at Venus, 1999, Evil Queen Tut and the Great Ant Pyramids, 1999, Yikes! Grandma's a Teenager, 1999, How I Fixed the Year 1000 Problem, 1999, The Boy Who Cried Bigfoot, 2000, The Day I Went from Bad to Verse, 2000, Don't Count on Dracula, 2000, This Body Isn't Big Enough for Both of Us, 2000, Greenish Eggs and Dinosaurs, 2001, My Grandma, Major League Slugger, 2001, How I Became a Superhero, 2001, The Day Everything Tasted Like Broccoli, 2001, Invasion from the Planet of the Cows, 2001, Maximum Girl Unmasked, 2002, Attack of the Soggy Underwater People, 2002, Trapped in the Museum of Unnatural History, 2002, Me and My Mummy, 2002, Meet Super Sid, Crime-Fighting Kid, 2002, My Teacher Ate My Homework, 2002, If You Tell a Lie, Your Butt Will Grow, 2002, The Worst Bully in the Entire Universe, 2003, Just Add Water and Scream, 2003, It's Itchcraft, 2003, The Onts, 2005, Treachery and Betrayal at the Jolly Days Orphanage, 2005, The Vampire's Curse, 2006, Fall of the House of Mandible, 2006, Dude, Where's My Spaceship, 2006, Lost in Las Vegas, 2006, The Shluffmuffin Boy is History, 2006, Attack of the Giant Octopus, 2006, Chilling with the Great Ones, 2006, Attack of the Evil Elvises, 2006, Claws, 2006, Please Don't Eat the Children, 2007, When Bad Snakes Attack Good Children, 2007; (films) I Could Never Have Sex with Any Man Who Has So Little Regard for My Husband, 1973, Private Lessons, 1981; (with Suzanne O'Malley) Private School, 1983, The Guardian, 1990; (plays) Arf, 1969, The Great Airplane Snatch, 1969; contbr. to Broadway revue Oh, Calcutta, 1969. Recipient Silver Key award Advt. Writers Assn., N.Y.C., 1964, Playboy Humor award, 1964, 72, 76. Mem. Dramatists Guild, Authors Guild Am., AFTRA, Screen Actors Guild, Writers Guild Am., Mystery Writers Am. E-mail: dan@dangreenburg.com.

GREEN-DORSEY, JEAN AUDREY, information technology executive; b. Cleve., Oct. 27, 1940; d. Sydney Howard and Bennie Irene (Blake) Green; m. William R. Dorsey, Nov. 1, 1980. BA, L.I. U., 1962. With IBM, NYC, 1966-72; mktg. mgr. office automation Olivetti, NYC, 1972-80; dep. dir. N.Y.C. Mgmt. Info. Sys., 1981-85; computer sys. mgr. Inter-agy. Task Force, NYC, 1985-86; pres. Inst. Mgmt. Devel., NYC, 1986—. Dir. PolySoft Systems Inc.; sr. cons. Inst. Mgmt. Devel., 1980—; exec. prodr., host Management Matters, 1998—; founder Managementmatters.org, Inc., 2000; adv. editor Hearst Pubs., 1981—, Today's Office, 1986—, others; lectr. in field; bd. dirs. Nat. Inst. Mgmt.; bd. dirs., tech. advisor Am. Inst. Urban Psychol. Studies, 1996—; mem. task force on supplementary edn. Tchrs. Coll. Columbia U., 2004. Bd. dirs. Fair Harbor Com. Assn., 1981—; co-dir. Westgate Tenants Assn., co-chair legal com., 1998—, chair, 1999; leader Citizen Amb. Program People to People office automation del. to People's Rep. China, 1988; mem. exec. bd. Cmty. Bd. #7; v.p. Preserve West Parknorth, 2006. Recipient WESTY award for work to save affordable housing, 2003. Mem. Assn. Computing Machinery, Assn. Info. Sys. Profls. (pres. N.Y.C. chpt., leader sci. and technology del. to People's Rep. China 1988). Clubs: Soroptomists Internat., The Club at N.Y. World Trade Ctr. Office: Managementmatters Orgn Inc Westgate 160 W 97th St New York NY 10025 E-mail: dorsey@managementmatters.org.

GREENE, ADDISON KENT, lawyer, accountant; b. Cardston, Alta., Can., Dec. 23, 1941; s. Addison Allen and Amy (Shipley) G.; m. Janice Hanks, Aug. 30, 1967; children: Lisa, Tiffany, Tyler, Darin. BS in Acctg.,

Brigham Young U., 1968; JD, U. Utah, 1973. Bar: Utah 1973, Nev. 1974, U.S. Tax Ct. 1979. Staff acct. Seidman and Seidman, Las Vegas, Nev., 1968-69, Peat Marwick Mitchell, Los Angeles, 1969-70; atty. Clark Greene & Assocs., Ltd., Las Vegas, 1973—. Instr. Nev. Bar Rev., Las Vegas, 1975-78; bd. dirs. Cumorah Credit Union. Mem. Citizen's for Responsible Gov't, Las Vegas, 1979—; asst. dist. com. mem. Boy Scouts Am., Las Vegas, 1985—. Mem. ABA, Utah Bar Assn., Nev. Bar Assn., Nev. Soc. CPA's (assoc.), Am. Assn., Pension Actuaries (assoc.). Republican. Mem. Lds Ch. Avocations: golf, skiing. Office: Clark Greene & Assocs Ltd 3770 Howard Hughes Pkwy Ste 195 Las Vegas NV 89109-0976 Office Phone: 702-369-2900. Personal E-mail: akgreene@earthlink.net.

GREENE, ALBERT LAWRENCE, healthcare executive; b. NYC, Dec. 10, 1949; s. Leonard and Anne (Birnbaum) G.; m. Jo Linda Anderson, Sept. 3, 1972; children: Stacy, Jeremy. BA, Ithaca Coll., 1971; MHA, U. Mich., 1973. Adminstrv. asst. Harper Hosp., Detroit, 1973-74, asst. adminstr., 1974-77, assoc. adminstr., 1977-80; adminstr. Grace Hosp., Detroit, 1980-84, Harper Hosp., Detroit, 1984-87; pres., CEO Sinai Samaritan Med. Ctr., Milw., 1988-90, Alta Bates Med. Ctr., Berkeley, Calif., 1990-98; CEO Sutter Health East Bay Svc. Area, Berkeley, Calif., 1998-99, HealthCtrl., Emeryville, Calif., 1999—2001, Hollywood Presbyn. Med. Ctr., LA, 2002—06, Valley Presbyn. Hosp., 2006—. Bd. dirs. Sierra Health Svcs.; chmn. Calif. Assn. Hosps. and Health Sys., 1998. Trustee Huron Valley Hosp., Milford, Mich., 1984-87. Mem.: Am. Coll. Healthcare Execs., World Pres. Orgn., Calabasas Country Club. Avocations: tennis, golf. Home: 25948 Wellington Ct Calabasas CA 91302 Office: Valley Presbyn Hosp 15107 Vanowen St Van Nuys CA 91405

GREENE, ALISON DE LIMA, curator; b. Princeton, NJ, Oct. 17, 1956; d. Stephen Greene and Sigrid de Lima. BA cum laude, Vassar Coll., Poughkeepsie, NY, 1978; MA, NYU, NYC, 1981. Curator Mus. Fine Arts, Houston, 1984—. Author: (catalogue) Texas: 150 Works from the Museum of Fine Arts Houston. Office: Museum Fine Arts Houston PO Box 6826 Houston TX 77265

GREENE, ALVIN, management consultant; b. Aug. 26, 1932; s. Samuel David and Yetta Kroff Greene; m. Louise Sokol, Nov. 11, 1977; children: Sharon, Aaron, Ami, Ann, Daniel. BA, Stanford U., 1954, MBA, 1959. Asst. to pres. Narmco Industries, Inc., San Diego, 1959—62; adminstrv. mgr., mgr. mktg. Whittaker Corp., LA, 1962—67; sr. v.p. Cordura Corp., LA, 1966—75; chmn. bd. Sharon-Sage, Inc., LA, 1975—79; exec. v.p., COO Republic Distbrs., Inc., Carson, Calif., 1979—81, also dir.; COO Memel, Jacobs & Ellsworth, 1981—87, 1987—; pres. SCI Cons., Inc. Bd. dirs. Sharon-Sage Inc., True Data Corp.; vis. prof. Am. Grad. Sch. Bus., Phoenix, 1977—81. Chmn. bd. commrs. Housing Authority City of L.A., 1983—88; tchr., mentor Anderson Grad. Sch. Bus., UCLA, 2002—; bd. dirs. Spl. Olympics, 2003; dir. Industry Coun., City of Hope. 1st lt. US Army, 1955—57. Mem.: Bradley Group, Safety Helmet Mfrs. Assn., Direct Mail Assn.

GREENE, BERNARD HAROLD, lawyer; b. Bklyn., Sept. 21, 1925; s. Max and Clara (Pasweg) G.; m. Magda C. Schwartz, Sept. 19, 1948; children: Michael, Edith, Susan, Jonathan, David. BBA magna cum laude, CCNY, 1948; LLB cum laude, Yale U., 1951. Bar: NY 1952. Assoc. Paul, Weiss, Rifkind, Wharton & Garrison, NYC, 1951-60, ptnr., 1960-94, of counsel, 1995—. Vis. lectr. Yale Law Sch., New Haven, 1972-78, 81-83; adj. prof. N.Y. Law Sch., N.Y.C., 1985-88. Chmn. deferred giving and estate planning com. Cmty. Svc. Soc., N.Y.C., 1975-82. 1st lt. U.S. Army, 1943-47. Mem.: Assn. Bar City N.Y. (mem. surrogate's ct. com. 1958—61). Home: 153 Union St Montclair NJ 07042-2102 Office: Paul Weiss Rifkind Wharton & Garrison Rm 200 1285 Avenue of the Americas New York NY 10019-6065

GREENE, CHARLES M., federal agency administrator; 2 children. BA, Va. Union U. Clk. VA; case worker Pa. Dept. Pub. Welfare, Pa. Redevelopment Authority; chief devel. officer Opportunities Industrialization Ctr., Phila.; asst. v.p. devel. Howard U., 1971—73; second-level mgr. Bell of Pa., 1973; dep. mayor for intergovernmental rels. Office of Mayor, City of Phila., 1992—94; regional v.p. Lockheed Martin, 1996—99; pres., CEO Partnership for Advancement of Self-Sufficient Inc., Phila., 1999—2002; dir. cmty. and econ. devel. for Senator Rick Santorum, Pa.; exec. dir. White House Initiative on Historically Black Colls. and Univs. US Dept. Edn., Washington, 2006—. Office: US Dept Edn 400 Maryland Ave, SW Washington DC 20202 Office Phone: 202-502-7900.*

GREENE, CLAYTON, JR., judge; b. Glen Burnie, Md., Jan. 22, 1951; s. Clayton Sr. and Evelyn Greene; m. Janice Elizabeth Butler, Dec. 21, 1974; children: Clayton III, Jonathan. BA in History, U. Md., 1973, JD, 1976. Bar: Md. 1977, Ct. Appeals, Md., 1977, U.S. Bankruptcy Ct., 1978, U.S. Dist. Ct., Md., 1978, Supreme Bench Balt. City, 1978, Anne Arundel County Bar Assn., Md., 1978, D.C. 1980, Ct. Appeals D.C., 1980. Law clerk Anne Arundel County Pub. Defender T. Joseph Touhey Jr., Md., 1974-76, various firms, Md., 1976-77; asst. county solicitor Anne Arundel County, Md., 1977-78; sole practioner Md., 1977-88; asst. pub. defender Anne Arundel County, 1978-85, dep. pub. defender, 1985-88, assoc. judge dist. ct., 1988-90, adminstrv. judge dist. ct., 1990-95, assoc. judge circuit ct., 1995-96, adminstrv. judge 5th Jud. Cirduit, 1996—2002; judge Ct. Special Appeals, 5th Appellate Circuit, 2002—04, Md. Ct. of Appeals, 2004—. Bd. dirs. Anne Arundel County Offender Aid and Restoration, Md., 1978-79; title ins. agent, 1980-88; mock trial judge citizenship law related edn. program, 1988-93; tchr. MICPEL trial adv. course, trial procedures for law enforcement officers, 1990-95; lectr. Anne Arundel C.C., Md., 1990-98, Jud. Inst. Md.; mem. standing com. practice and procedures Ct. Appeals, 1991-95; ex-oficio mem. Anne Arundel County Criminal Justice Coordinating Coun., 1993-95; co-chmn. Ad Hoc com. for implementation of family law divsn., 1997-2002; mem. Public Awareness Com., Md. Jud. Conference, 2000-02; spkr. in field. Asst. coach St. Jane Frances Clinic Soccer League, 1986, Arthur Slade basketball, 1988, Severna Park Green Hornets basketball, 1988, coach Arthur Slade basketball, 1994; mem. Gender Equality Com., 1990-92. Recipient Pub. Svc. award U. Md., 1987, Govs. Citation, 1988, Civic Betterment award Frontiersmen's Internat., 1989, cert. appreciation Kiwanis Club of Odenton, Morris H. Blum Humanitarian award, 1995, Morris H. Blum Humanitarian award Dr. Martin Luther King, Jr. Awards Dinner Foundation, 1995, Donald C. Roane award for Public Service NAACP, 1998. Mem. Hall United Meth. Ch. (bd. dirs. 1978-86, mem. bldg. com. 1984-87, trustee 1978-86), Anne Arundel County Bar Found., Md. (dir. 1993). Avocations: tennis, basketball, alto-saxaphone, clarinet. Office: Md Ct Appeals Robert C Murphy Bldg 361 Rowe Blvd Annapolis MD 21401*

GREENE, DAVID, surgeon, researcher; b. NYC, Nov. 15, 1966; s. Martin and Carole Greene; m. Denise Altman; children: Rachael children: Jonathan. BA magna cum laude, Harvard U., 1989; MD, Yale U., 1993. Diplomate Am. Bd. Med. Examiners, Am. Bd. Otolaryngology, Am. Bd. Facial Plastic Surgery. Rsch. fellow NIH, Bethesda, Md., 1990—90; resident otolaryngology head and neck surgery U. Calif., San Francisco, 1993—98, chief resident head and neck surgery, 1997—98; fellow facial plastic surgery Stanford U., Calif., 1998—99; clin. instr. facial plastic surgery Stanford U. Med. Ctr., 1998—99; staff surgeon Palo Alto Vets. Health Sys., 1998—99; staff otolaryngologist, head and neck surgeon Physicians Regional Med. Ctr. (formerly Cleveland Clinic), Naples, Fla., 1999—, chmn., 2001—. Contbr. articles to profl. jours. Named one of Best Physicians Am., Castle-Connelly's Best Doctors; recipient Spl. Thanks and Recognition award, VA, 1999, Physician Recognition award, AMA, 2001; John Harvard scholar, Harvard U., 1986, Harvard Coll. scholar, 1986. Fellow: Am. Rhinologic Soc., Am. Acad. Otolaryngology (Achievement award 2001); mem.: Am. Acad. Facial Plastic Surgery (Best Clin. Rsch. Paper award 1999), Phi Beta Kappa. Office: Physicans Regional Med Ctr 6101 Pine Ridge Rd Naples FL 34119 Office Phone: 239-348-4400.

GREENE, DIANE, information technology executive; m. Mendel Rosenblum. BS in mech. engring., U. Calif., Berkeley; M in computer sci. and naval architecture, MIT. Joined Sybase, 1986; various tech. leadership positions Tandem, Silicon Graphics Inc.; co-founder, CEO Vxtreme (sold to Microsoft Corp.), Palo Alto, Calif., 1995—98; founder, pres. VMware (sub. of EMC), 1998—. Bd. dirs. Intiut. Named one of 50 Most Powerful People in Networking, Network World mag., 2003. Office: VMware Inc 3145 Porter Dr Palo Alto CA 94304 Office Phone: 650-475-5000, 877-486-9273. Office Fax: 650-475-5005.*

GREENE, DONALD RICHARD, dermatologist, educator; b. Buffalo, Aug. 20, 1947; s. Norman Sanborn and Helen Jean (Second) Powers; m. JoAnne D'Amico, Mar. 5, 1982; children: Patrick Ryan, Claire Elizabeth. BA, SUNY, Buffalo, 1970, MD, 1974. Diplomate Am. Bd. Dermatology. Intern Buffalo Gen. Hosp., 1974-75; resident Hosp. of U. Pa., Phila., 1975-76, Yale-New Haven Hosp., 1976-79, chief resident, 1978-79; clin. instr. Yale U. Sch. Medicine, New Haven, 1979-82, clin. asst. prof., 1982—. Attending physician Yale-New Haven Hosp., Hosp. St. Raphael, 1979—; med. bd. Branford (Conn.) Health Care Ctr., 1983—. Grantee, Am. Cancer Soc., 1972. Fellow Am. Acad. Dermatology (Leadership Cir. for Volunteerism); mem. AMA, Conn. State Med. Soc. (pres. dermatology sect. 1984-85), New Haven County Med. Assn., New Haven City Med. Assn., New Eng. Dermatologic Soc., Dermatology Found. (Leaders Soc.), NY Acad. Sci., Assn. Attendings at Yale U. Sch. Medicine, Mensa, Yale Club New Haven, Penn Club NY, Madison Winter Club, Mory's Assn. Episcopalian. Office Phone: 203-481-3419.

GREENE, ELLIN, library service educator; b. Elizabeth, NJ, Sept. 18, 1927; d. Charles M. and Dorothea (Hooton) Peterson. A.B., Rutgers U., 1953, M.L.S., 1957, Ed.D., 1979. Children's librarian Free Pub. Library, Elizabeth, 1953-57, specialist in group work with children, 1957-59; asst. group work specialist NY Pub. Libr., NYC, 1959-64, supervising children's librarian, Bronx, 1964, asst. coord. children's services, 1965-67, dir. Early Childhood Project, NY Pub. Libr., 1986-89; adj. faculty Rutgers U. Grad. Sch. Libr. and Info. Studies, New Brunswick, NJ, 1968-97; vis. prof. Nat. Coll. Edn.-McGaw Grad. Sch., Chgo., 1976-77; dean students U. Chgo. Grad. Libr. Sch., 1980-82, assoc. prof., 1980-85; cons. libr. svcs. to children, 1985—; vis. prof. U. Ill. Grad. Sch. Libr. and Info. Sci., 1979; adv. com. NY Pub. Libr. Early Childhood Resource & Info. Ctr., 1982—89; adv. bd. Nat. Clearing House for Info. on Storytelling, 1986-88. Author: Recordings for Children, 1964; A List of Stories to Tell and to Read Aloud, 1965; Films for Children, 1966; (with Augusta Baker) Storytelling: Art and Technique, 1977, 3d edit., 1996; (with Madalynne Schoenfeld) A Multimedia Approach to Children's Literature, 1972, 2d edit., 1977; (with George Shannon) Storytelling: A Selected Annotated Bibliography, 1986, Books, Babies, and Libraries: Serving Infants, Toddlers, Their Parents and Caregivers, 1991; Roger Duvoisin: The Art of Children's Books, 1989, Read Me a Story: Books & Techniques for Reading Aloud and Storytelling, 1992; (with others) Best-Loved Stories Told at the National Storytelling Festival, 1992; mem. editl. bd. Arrow Book Club, 1975-85; contbr. articles to profl. jours., chpts. to books; adv. com. Bull. of Ctr. for Children's Books, 1980-85; mem. editl. bd. Library Quar., 1980-85; editl. coun. Nat. Storytelling Jour., 1983—85. Books for children include: The Pumpkin Giant, 1970; Princess Rosetta and the Popcorn Man, 1971; The Rat-Catcher's Daughter: A Collection of Stories by Laurence Housman, 1974; Clever Cooks, 1973, 1977; Midsummer Magic, 1977, The Legend of the Christmas Rose, 1990, The Legend of the Cranberry, 1993, Billy Beg and His Bull, 1994, Li-Ling and the Phoenix Fairy, 1996, The Little Golden Lamb, 2000. Acad. specialist grantee U.S. Info. Agy. Bur. Ednl. and Cultural Affairs, 1989. Recipient Lifetime Achievement award Nat. Storytelling Network Oracle, 2002. Mem. ALA, Assn. Libr. Svc. to Children, Authors Guild Inc., Nat. Storytelling Network, Soc. Children's Book Writers and Illustrators, Douglass Soc., Psi Chi Office: 113 Chatham Ln Point Pleasant NJ 08742-2005

GREENE, FRANK EDWARD WADE, foundation administrator, writer; b. Syracuse, NY, Jan. 17, 1933; s. Melville Hart Greene and Nan Wade Pearson; m. Susanne Cavanagh, Apr. 1, 1966; children: Nathanael Wade, Jennifer Robin. AB, Princeton U., 1956; MS, Columbia U., 1962. Reporter Hartford Courant, Conn., 1956-57; writer Look Mag., NYC, 1958-59; editor Am. Heritage, NYC, 1962-64, Newsweek, NYC, 1964-69, Saturday Rev., San Francisco, 1972-73; writer, editor Commn. Pvt. Philanthropy and Pub. Needs, Washington, 1975-76; editor N.Y. Times Mag., NYC, 1976-77; philanthropy adviser Rockefeller Family and Assocs. , NYC, 1979—. Bd. dirs. Environ. Media Svcs., Washington. Author: Disarmament, Challenge of Civilization, 1966, Giving in America, 1976. Liaison Pres.'s Coun. Sustainable Devel., Washington, 1993—95; mem. Coun. Fgn. Rels., 1994—, League Conservation Voters, Washington, 1995—; trustee Whitehead Found., NYC, 1999—, Beldon Fund, NYC, 2000—, Nantucket Sustainable Devel. Corp., 2000—, Nantucket Land Coun., 2001—. With US Army, 1953—55, Korea. Recipient Eleanor Roosevelt Peace award Peace Action, 1997; Profl. Journalism fellow Stanford U., 1967-68, Alicia Patterson fellow Alica Patterson Found., 1977-78. Mem.: Century Assn. Office: Rockefeller Family and Assocs 30 Rockefeller Plz New York NY 10112

GREENE, FRANK SULLIVAN, JR., investment company executive; b. Washington, Oct. 19, 1938; s. Frank S. Sr. and Irma O. Greene; m. Phyllis Davison, Jan. 1958 (dec. 1984); children: Angela, Frank. BS, Washington U., St. Louis, 1961; MS, Purdue U., 1962; PhD, U. Santa Clara, Calif., 1970. Part-time lectr. Washington U., Howard U., Am. U., 1959-65; pres., dir. Tech. Devel. Corp., Arlington, Tex., 1985-92; pres. Zero One Systems Inc. (formerly Tech. Devel. of Calif.), Santa Clara, Calif., 1971-87, Zero One Systems Group subs. Sterling Software Inc., 1987-89. Asst. chmn., lectr. Stanford U., 1972—74; mng. mem. New Vista Capital, LLC, Palo Alto, Calif., 1993—; pres. Networked Picture Sys. Inc., 1989—91, chmn., 1991—94; bd. dirs. Reach Comms., Compliance Coach; observer ZNYX. Author two indsl. textbooks; also articles; patentee in field. Bd. dirs. NCCJ, Santa Clara, 1980—2005, NAACP, San Jose chpt., 1986-89, Am. Musical Theatre of San Jose, 1995—2005; bd. regents Santa Clara U., 1983-90, trustee, 1990-2000; mem. adv. bd. Urban League, Santa Clara County, 1986-89, East Side Union High Sch., 1985-88. Capt. USAF, 1961-65. Mem IEEE, IEEE Computer Soc. (governing bd. 1973-75), Assn. Black Mfrs. (bd. dirs. 1974-80), Am. Electric Assn. (indsl. adv. bd. 1975-76), Fairchild Rsch. and Devel. (tech. staff 1965-71), Bay Area Purchasing Coun. (bd. dirs. 1978-84), Security Affairs Support Assn. (bd. dirs. 1980-83), Sigma Xi, Eta Kappa Nu, Sigma Pi Phi. Business E-Mail: fgreene@nvcap.com.

GREENE, FREDERICK DAVIS, II, chemistry professor; b. Glen Ridge, NJ, July 9, 1927; s. Phillips Foster and Ruth (Altman) G.; m. Theodora Elizabeth Whatmough, June 5, 1953; children— Alan, Carol, Elizabeth, Phillips. Grad., Phillips Andover Acad., 1944; BA, Amherst Coll., 1949, D.Sc. (hon.), 1969; PhD, Harvard, 1952. Research assoc. U. Calif., Los Angeles, 1952-53; instr. dept. chemistry Mass. Inst. Tech., Cambridge, 1953-55, asst. prof., 1955-58; assoc. prof. MIT, 1958-62, prof., 1962-95; prof. emeritus, 1995—. Editor-in-chief: Jour. Organic Chemistry, 1962-88; contbr. articles to sci. jours. Served with USNR, 1945-46. Alfred P. Sloan fellow, 1958—62, NSF Sr. Postdoctoral fellow, 1965—66. Fellow AAAS; mem. Am. Chem. Soc., Royal Soc. Chem. (U.K.), Am. Acad. Arts and Scis., Phi Beta Kappa. Office: Mass Inst Tech Dept Chemistry Bldg 18-297 77 Massachusetts Ave Cambridge MA 02139-4301

GREENE, HARRY W., biology professor; b. Detroit, Sept. 26, 1945; BS in Biology, Tex. Wesleyan Coll., 1968; MA in Biology, U. Tex., Arlington, 1973; PhD in Zoology, U. Tenn., 1977. Asst. prof. anatomy Sch. Vet. Medicine U. Pa., 1977—78; asst. prof. zoology, asst. curator herpetology Mus. Vertebrate Zoology U. Calif., Berkeley, 1978—83, assoc. prof. zoology, assoc. curator herpetology Mus. Vertebrate Zoology, 1983—92, prof. integrative biology, curator herpetology Mus. Vertebrate Zoology, 1992—98; prof. ecology and evolutionary biology, faculty curator amphibians and reptiles Cornell U., Ithaca, 1999—. Vis. faculty Orgn. Tropical Studies, 1982—91; rsch. assoc. dept. herpetology Calif. Acad. Scis., 1986—; bd. dirs. Orgn. Tropical Studies, 1989—98. Contbr. articles to sci. jours., chapters to books; mem. editl. bd.: Herpetological Natural Hist., 1994—99, Revista de Biologia Tropical, 1995—, BioScience, 2001—03, consulting editor: Organisms and Environments, 1996—, assoc. editor: Integrative Biology, 1997—99, Am. Naturalists, 2002—; author: Snakes: The Evolution of Mystery in Nature, 1997 (named one of 100 Noteworthy Books, NY Times, 1997, Silver medal, Commonwealth Club of Calif., 1998, PEN Ctr. USA West Literary award, 1998). Medic US Army, 1968—71. Co-recipient Outstanding Publ. award, US Fish and Wildlife Svc., 1981; recipient Josef Laszlo Meml. award, Internat. Herpetological Symposium, 1998, Edward Osborne Wilson award, Am. Soc. Naturalists, 2000, Henry S. Fitch award, Excellence in Herpetology, Am. Soc. Ichthyologists and Herpetologists, 2004. Fellow: Calif. Acad. Scis., AAAS. Office: Dept Ecology and Evolutionary Biology Cornell U E251 Corson Hall Ithaca NY 14853 E-mail: hwg5@cornell.edu.

GREENE, HERBERT BRUCE, lawyer, investor, entrepreneur; b. NYC, Apr. 13, 1934; s. Joseph Lester and Shirley (Kasen) G.; m. Judith Jean Metricks, Dec. 31, 1958; children: Pamela S., Scott L. AB, Harvard U., 1955; JD, Columbia U., 1958. Bar: N.Y. 1959, Conn. 1975. Asst. U.S. atty So. Dist. N.Y., Dept. Justice, NYC, 1958-61; assoc. Kaye, Scholer, Fierman, Hays & Handler, NYC, 1961-66; asst. to gen. counsel CIT Fin. Corp., NYC, 1966-67; group gen. counsel Xerox Corp., Rochester, NY, 1967-68, v.p. adminstrn., 1968-71; sr. v.p. Xerox Edn. Group, Stamford, Conn., 1971-75; v.p., gen. counsel, sec. Lone Star Industries, Inc., Greenwich, Conn., 1976-79, sr. v.p., asst. to chmn., 1979-82; chmn., CEO Earle and Greene & Co., Westport, 1982-96, Portland, Oreg., 1997—. Mem. Phi Delta Phi. Republican. Home and Office: Herbert B Greene & Co 4233 W Redondo Ave Portland OR 97239

GREENE, IRA S., lawyer; b. NYC, Nov. 21, 1946; s. Melvin and Syd (Semmelman) G.; m. Robin Colin, Dec. 29, 1973; children: Jessica, Alexander. BA, Syracuse U., 1968; postgrad., U. Buffalo, 1968-69; JD, N.Y. U., 1971. Bar: N.Y. 1972, U.S. Dist. Ct. (so. and ea. dists.) N.Y. 1972, U.S. Ct. Appeals (2d cir.) 1974. Counsel Gainsburg, Gottlieb, Levitan & Cole, NYC, 1982—84; ptnr. Gainsburg, Gottlieb, Levitan, Greene & Cole, NYC, 1984—86, Gainsburg, Greene & Hirsch, Purchase, NY, 1986—91, Squadron, Ellenoff, Plesent & Sheinfeld, NYC, 1991—2002, Hogan & Hartson, NYC, 2002—. Lectr. in field. Mem. Assn. Comml. Fin. Attys., Bank Lawyers Conf., Bankruptcy Lawyers Bar Assn., Assn. of Bar of City of N.Y. Office: Hogan & Hartson LLP 875 Third Ave New York NY 10022

GREENE, JACK PHILLIP, historian, educator; b. Lafayette, Ind., Aug. 12, 1931; s. Ralph Beamon and Nellie (Miller) G.; m. Sue Lucille Neuenswander, June 27, 1953 (div. Aug. 1990); children: Jacqueline Megan, Granville; m. Amy Turner Bushnell, Aug. 29, 1990. AB, U. N.C., 1951; MA, Ind. U., 1952, Litt.D. (hon.), 1977; postgrad., U. Nebr., 1952-53, 54-55, Bristol U., Eng., 1953-54; PhD, Duke, 1956. Instr. history Mich. State U., 1956-59; asst. prof. Western Res. U., 1959-62, assoc. prof., 1962-65; vis. assoc. prof., also vis. editor William and Mary Quar., Coll. William and Mary, 1961-62; vis. assoc. prof. Johns Hopkins U., 1964-65; assoc. prof. U. Mich., 1965-66; prof. history Johns Hopkins U., 1966-75, Andrew W. Mellon prof. humanities, 1976—2005, Andrew W. Mellon prof. in humanities emeritus, 2005—, chmn. dept. history, 1970-72; Disting. prof. U. Calif., Irvine, 1990-92. Mem. Inst. Advanced Study, 1970-71, 85-86; vis. prof. Columbia, 1973-74, 77, Harmsworth prof. Oxford (Eng.) U., 1975-76, Fulbright prof. Hebrew U., Jerusalem, 1979, Fulbright Disting. Bicentennial prof. École des Hautes Études en Scis. Sociales, 1986-87, Freeman prof. U. Richmond, 1996; sweet prof. Mich. State U., 1997. Author: The Quest for Power: The Lower Houses of Assembly in the Southern Royal Colonies, 1689-1776, 1963, The Diary of Colonel Landon Carter of Sabine Hall, 1752-1778, 2 vols, 1965, Settlements to Society, 1584-1763, 1966, Colonies to Nation, 1763-1789, 1967, The Reappraisal of the American Revolution in Recent Historical Literature, 1967, The Ambiguity of the American Revolution, 1968, The Reinterpretation of the American Revolution, 1968, The American Colonies in the Eighteenth Century 1689-1763, 1969, Great Britain and The American Colonies 1606-1763, 1970, The Nature of Colony Constitutions, 1970, The First Continental Congress: A Documentary History, 1974, All Men are Created Equal, 1976, Encylopedia of American Political History, 1984, Political Life in Eighteenth Century Virginia, 1986; Peripheries and Center, 1986, A Bicentennial Bookshelf, 1986, The Intellectual Heritage of the Constitution, 1986, The American Revolution: Its Character and Limits, 1987, Pursuits of Happiness, 1988, Selling the New World, 1989, Imperatives, Behaviors & Identities, 1992, Intellectual Construction of America, 1993, Negotiated Authorities, 1994, Understanding the American Revolution, 1995, Interpreting Early America, 1996; joint editor: Preconditions of Revolution in Early Modern Europe, 1971, Neither Slave nor Free: The Freedmen of African Descent in the Slave Societies of the New World, 1972, Interdisciplinary Studies of the American Revolution, 1976, British Colonial America: Essays in the New History of the Early Modern Era, 1983, Magna Charta for America, 1986, Encyclopedia of the American Revolution, 1991. Served with AUS, 1957. Fulbright fellow U.K., 1953-54; Lilly Found. fellow Clements Library, 1964; Guggenheim fellow, 1964-65; John Carter Brown Library fellow, 1969; fellow Woodrow Wilson Internat. Center for Scholars, 1974-75, Center for Advanced Study Behavioral Scis., 1979-80, Churchill Coll., Cambridge U., Eng., 1986, Nat. Humanities Ctr. 1987-88, Mellon fellow John Carter Brown Libr., 1999-2000. Fellow Royal Hist. Soc. (corr.), Brit. Acad., Am. Acad. Arts & Sciences; mem. Am. Antiquarian Soc., Am. Hist. Assn., Orgn. Am. Historians, So. Hist. Assn., Am. Philos. Soc., Mass. Hist. Soc., Soc. of Am. History, Colonial Soc. Mass., Phi Beta Kappa. Home: 1974 Division Rd East Greenwich RI 02818

GREENE, JAMES K., military officer, educator; b. Bloomington, Ind., Aug. 8, 1956; s. George E. and Vera W. Greene; children: Steven E., Andrew J. BS in Criminal Justice, Ind. U., Bloomington, 1974—79; MS in Nat. Security, Naval War Coll., Newport, RI, 1990—91. Commdg. officer Fighter Squadron 103, Va. Beach, 1996—98, Carrier Air Wing Eleven, Lemoore, Calif., 2001—04; war on terror br. head Office of Chief of Naval Ops., DC, 2004—06; prof. naval sci. U. Ill., Champaign, 2006—. Navy fellow 43rd sr. seminar Dept. State, Arlington, Va., 2000—01. Capt. USN, 1979—2006, Champaign. Office: Univ Ill 505 E Armory Blvd Rm 236 Champaign IL 61822 Home Fax: 217-898-7669. Business E-Mail: meanjim@mac.com.

GREENE, JAMES S., III, school administrator; b. Harlan, Ky., Nov. 10, 1943; s. James S. Jr. and Elizabeth (Howard) G.; m. Glenda Hollors, Feb. 2, 1968; children: Laurel Elizabeth, Amy Janine, James McKeehan. Postgrad., U. N.C., 1961-62; BS in Edn. French and History, U. Wis., 1965; MA in Edn., Union Coll., Barbourville, Ky., 1973; PhD in Edn., Ohio State U., 1982. Cert. tchr. secondary edn., sch. adminstrn. and supervision, Ky. Tchr. French and History Harlan H.S., 1965-83; supr. instrn. Harlan Ind. Sch. Dist., 1983—. Adj. instr. history S.E. Cmty. Coll., Cumberland, Ky., 1977-83; humanities scholar multimedia project The Lynch Legacy Project, 1987. Reviewer The History Tchr., 1973-83; contbr. (book): The Kentucky Ency., 1992. Bd. dirs. Southeastern Ky. Spl. Edn. Coop., Harlan,

1983-88; mem. adv. coun. Stokely Inst. for Liberal Arts Edn., U. Tenn., Knoxville, 1982-89; trustee Pine Mountain (Ky.) Settlement Sch., 1989—; coord. Harlan Christian Arts Festival, 1973, 76; mem. Ky. Bicentennial Commn., Frankfort, 1988-93; pres. bd. dirs. Romance of the Hills Corp., Harlan, 1992-93; elder First Presbyn. Ch., Harlan, 1968-73, 80-83, 90-95, 97-2003, 2006—, organist, 1982—; mem. Ky. State Hist. Records Adv. Bd., 1996—; curriculum advisor Am. Legacies Project, 2002—; mem. Harlan Revitalization Bd., 2006—. Recipient Award for Outstanding Contbns. to Math. Edn., Ky. Coun. Tchrs. Math., 1992; Humanities scholar So. Mountains Settlement Symposium, 1999-2000. Avocation: composing and choral arranging. Office: Harlan Ind Sch Dist 420 E Central St Harlan KY 40831-2372 E-mail: james.greene@harlanind.kyschools.us.

GREENE, JERRY GEORGE, retired physician; b. Regina, Sask., Can., May 13, 1937; came to U.S., 1962, naturalized, 1981; s. David Robert and Fae (Woodman) G.; m. Waltra Laguniak, Feb. 27, 1960; children: Deidre, Cheryl, Michael. MD, U. Man., 1960. Diplomate: Am. Bd. Internal Medicine. Rotating intern St. Boniface Hosp., Winnipeg, Man., Canada, 1960-61, jr. asst. resident medicine, 1961-62; teaching fellow U. Man., 1961-62; fellow in medicine Mayo Clinic, 1962-66, asst. in pulmonary diseases, 1966; chief pulmonary lab. St. Joseph's Hosp., St. Paul, 1966-69; asst. prof. medicine U. Minn. St. Paul, 1968-71; practice medicine specializing in internal medicine, 1966-68, Med. Assos. Saranac Lake, NY, 1972-78; asso. cardiac catheterization lab. St. Mary's Hosp., Mpls., 1967, dir. inhalation therapy program, 1967; chief pulmonary disease St. Paul Ramsey Hosp., 1968-71; med. dir. Will Rogers Hosp., Saranac Lake, NY, 1971-72; chief dept. medicine Saramac Lake Gen. Hosp., 1977-78; chief pulmonary disease sect. VA Hosp., Fargo, ND, 1978-90; clin. assoc. prof. Mt. Sinai Sch. Medicine, 1991—. Asst. prof. medicine in internal medicine U. Minn., 1968-71; prof. medicine U. ND Sch. Medicine; chief pulmonary svc. VA Hosp., Fargo, 1978-91; chief of staff VAMC, Castle Point, NY; past med. dir. VA Upstate NY Healthcare, NY; cons. ND Lung Assn., PSRO, Blue Cross/Blue Shield ND; adv. com. med. edn. NIH 1980—, pulmonary acad. award com. on pulmonary testing 1979-84; comdr. 105th USAF Clinic, Stewart Field, Newburgh, NY. Assoc. editor RT mag.; contbr. articles to profl. jours. Bd. dirs. ND Lung Assn., 1979. Served with RCAF, 1960-62; to lt. col. M.C., USAF, Air N.G., 1982, comdr. Air Nat. Guard, 2000-04, ret. col. USAF, 2004. Recipient Recognition award Mayo Clin. Fellow's Assn., 1966, Pulmonary Acad. award NIH, 1978 Fellow A.C.P., Am. Coll. Chest Physicians (com. on respirator pathophysiology); mem. VA Pulmonary Physicians, Mayo Clinic Alumni Assn.

GREENE, JESSE J., JR., former computer company executive; b. NYC, Mar. 7, 1945; s. Jesse Johnson and Ann (Cox) G.; m. Christine Sofijczuk, Aug. 6, 1972; children: Bryan Michael, Colin Jesse. BSME, NYU, 1969, MSME, 1971; JD and MBA in Bus., Columbia U., 1975. Engr. Grumman Aerospace, Bethpage, N.Y., 1969, IBM Corp., Yorktown Heights, N.Y., 1971-72, tax atty. Armonk, N.Y., 1975-83, IBM Credit Corp., Stamford, Conn., 1983-86, dir. taxes, 1989-91; asst. treas. IBM Corp., Armonk, N.Y., 1991—; CFO, sen. v.p. Compaq Computer Corp., Houston, 2000—01, senior v.p. strategic planning, 2001. NDEA fellow NYU, 1970; N.Y. State Regents scholar, 1963. Mem. ABA, ASME, N.Y. State Bar Assn. Avocations: aviation, boating, fishing, autos, woodworking. Home: 11 Overlook Dr Bedford Corners NY 10549-4908

GREENE, JO, school system administrator; d. Thomas Elmo McKee and Elizabeth Louise McKee-Puckett; m. Allan Robert Greene, Aug. 10, 1976; 1 child, Jennifer Lynn. BS in Elem. Edn., Northwestern Okla. State U., Alva, 1977; M in Elem. Admin., Ctrl. Mo. State U., Warrensburg, 1995; cert. edn. Specialist in elem. adminstrn., Ctrl. Mo. State U., 1997. Lifetime cert. elem. edn. K-8 Mo., cert. admin. II, prin. K-8 Mo., admin. II, prin. 4-8 Mo. Reading tchr., basketball/track coach Prog. Sch., Fairmount, Okla., 1977—78; 3d grade tchr. Yuma Pub. Schs.-Roosevelt, Ariz., 1978—82; 6th grade sci./math tchr. Ft. Osage Schs.- Mid. Sch., Independence, Mo., 1982—89; 3d grade tchr. Ft. Osage Schs.-Blue Hills, Independence, 1989—95; vice prin. Ft. Osage Schs.-Cler-Mont, Independence, 1995—97; prin. Grain Valley Schs.-Matthews, Mo., 1997—2000; instrnl. coach Kansas City Sch. Dist., 2000—. CARE team mem. Ft. Osage Schools/Kansas City Mo. Sch. Dist., 1978—2007; mem. profl. devel. com. Ft. Osage Schs., 1983—94; computer curriculum cons. Pearson Edn., Inc., Chgo., 2000; assessment coord. Kans. City Mo. Schs., 2000—07. Mem. Jackson County Crisis Team, Mo., 1997—2000. Named Ft. Osage Mid. Sch. Educator of Yr., 1987, Independence Mentor of Yr., 1988; recipient Very Influential Person award (6 times), Ft. Osage Schs., 1987—93. Mem.: Phi Delta Kappa. Avocations: travel, sports, writing, music, hunting. Home Phone: 816-229-7281; Office Phone: 816-418-4962.

GREENE, JOHN CLIFFORD, dentist, retired dean; b. Ashland, Ky., July 19, 1926; s. G. Norman and Ella R. Greene; m. Gwen Rustin, Nov. 17, 1957; children: Alan, Lisa, Laura. AA, Ashland Jr. Coll., 1947; student, Marshall Coll., 1948; D.MD, U. Louisville, 1952, Sc.D. (hon.), 1980; M.P.H., U. Calif., Berkeley, 1961; Sc.D. (hon.), U. Ky., 1972, Boston U., 1975. Diplomate Am. Bd. Dental Pub. Health. Intern USPHS Hosp., Chgo., 1952-53, staff San Francisco, 1953-54; asst. regional dental cons. Region IX, San Francisco, 1954-56; asst. to chief dental officer USPHS, Washington, 1958-60; chief epidemiology program Dental Health Center, 1961-66; dep. dir. Div. Dental Health, 1966-70, acting dir., 1970, dir., 1970-73; acting dir. Bur. Health Resources Devel., 1973-74, dir., 1974-75; chief dental officer USPHS, 1974-81, dep. surgeon gen., 1978-81; with Epidemic Intelligence Service, Communicable Disease Center, Altanta and Kansas City, Mo., 1956-57; epidemiology and biometry br. Nat. Inst. Dental Research, NIH, Bethesda, Md., 1957-58; prof. and dean sch. dentistry U. Calif., San Francisco, 1981-94; prof. and dean emeritus, 1994—. Spl. cons. WHO, India, 1957; mem. adv. com. rsch. women's health NIH, Bethesda, Md., 1995—97. Contbr. articles to profl. jours. With USN, 1945—46. Recipient citation, Sch. Grad. Dentistry Boston U., 1971, U. of the Pacific, 1977, Meritorious and Disting. Svc. awards, HEW, 1972, 1975, Outstanding Alumnus award, U. Louisville, 1980, award of merit, FDI, 1978, Alumnus of Yr. award, U. Calif. Sch. Pub. Health, Berkeley, 1984, John W. Knutson award, APHA, 1997, U. Calif. San Francisco medal, 1999, Disting. Svc. award, Am. Dental Edn. Assn., 2001, Bill Tuttle award, 2002. Fellow: Am. Coll. Dentists, Internat. Coll. Dentists; mem.: ADA, Inst. of Medicine of NAS, Am. Assn. Pub. Health Dentistry (Disting. Svc. award 1996), Am. Assn. Dental Schs. (former v.p., chair coun. of deans), Am. Assn. Pub. Health Dentistry, Am. Assn. Dental Rsch. (past pres.), Internat. Assn. Dental Rsch. (past pres.), San Francisco Dental Soc., Calif. Dental Assn., Delta Omega, Omicron Kappa Upsilon. Home: 103 Peacock Dr San Rafael CA 94901-1551

GREENE, JOHN COLTON, retired historian; b. Indpls., Mar. 5, 1917; s. Edward Martin and Helen (Carter) G.; m. Ellen Wiemann Greene, Nov. 3, 1945; children: Ruth, Ned, John David. BA, U. S.D., 1938, DHL (hon.), 1986; MA, Harvard U., 1939, PhD, 1952. Instr. U. Chgo., 1948-52; asst. prof. U. Wis., Madison, 1952-56; from assoc. prof. to prof. Iowa State U., Ames, 1956-62; vis. prof. U. Calif., Berkeley, 1962-63; prof. U. Kans., Lawrence, 1963-67, U. Conn., Storrs, 1967-87, prof. emeritus, 1987—. Author: The Death of Adam, 1959, Darwin and the Modern World View, 1961, Science, Ideology and World View, 1981, American Science in Age of Jefferson, 1984, paperback edit., 2004, Debating Darwin: Adventures of a Scholar, 1999, A Scholar Goes to War, 2005. Capt. U.S. Army, 1942-46. Jr. fellow Harvard U., 1941-42, 46-48, Guggenheim fellow, 1966-67, Am. Antiquarian Soc. fellow, 1983—; vis. scholar Cambridge U., 1974. Mem. AAUP, History of Sci. Soc. (sec. 1960-70, pres. 1975-77, George Sarton medal 2002), Midwest Junto History of Sci. (pres. 1961-62), Internat. Acad. History of Sci. (corr.). Democrat. Episcopalian. Avocation: singing.

GREENE, JOHN JOSEPH, lawyer; b. Marshall, Tex., Jan. 19, 1946; s. William Henry and Camille Anne Greene. BA, U. Houston, 1969, MA, 1974; JD, South Tex. Coll., 1978. Bar: Tex. 1978, US Supreme Ct. 1982. Asst. atty. City of Amarillo, Tex., 1978-79, Harris County, Tex., 1979-83; pvt. practice, 1983—; city atty. City of Conroe, Tex., 1983-89; sr. asst. city atty. City of Austin, Tex., 1990—2006; pvt. practice, 2006—. Served to capt. USAR, 1969—76. Decorated Bronze Star, Air medal. Roman Catholic.

GREENE, JOHN THOMAS, judge; b. Salt Lake City, Nov. 28, 1929; s. John Thomas and Mary Agnes (Hindley) G.; m. Dorothy Kay Buchanan, Mar. 31, 1955; children: Thomas Buchanan Greene, John Buchanan Greene, Mary Kay Greene Platt. BA in Polit. Sci., U. Utah, 1952, JD, 1955. Bar: Utah 1955, U.S. Dist. Ct. (10th cir.) 1955, U.S. Supreme Ct. 1966. Pvt. practice, Salt Lake City, 1955-57; asst. U.S. atty., 1957-59; ptnr. Marr, Wilkins & Cannon (and successor firms), Salt Lake City, 1959-75; ptnr., pres., chmn. bd. dirs. Greene, Callister & Nebeker, Salt Lake City, 1975-85; judge U.S. Dist. Ct., Salt Lake City, 1985—. Author: (manual) American Mining Law, 1960; contbr. articles to profl. jours. Chmn. Salt Lake City Cmty. Coun., 1970-75, Utah State Bldg. Authority, Salt Lake City, 1980-85; Regent Utah State Bd. Higher Edn., Salt Lake City, 1982-86. Recipient Order of Coif U. Utah, 1955, Merit of Honor award, 1994, Utah Fed. Bar Disting. Svc. award, 1997. Fellow ABA Found. (life); ABA ho. of dels. 1972-92, bd. govs. 1987-91; mem. Dist. Judges Assn. (pres. 10th cir. 1998-2000), Utah Bar Assn. (pres. 1971-72, Judge of Yr. award 1995), Am. Law Inst. (life, panelist and lectr. 1980-85, advisor 1986-98); Phi Beta Kappa. Mem. Lds Ch. Avocations: travel, reading, tennis. Office: US Dist Ct 350 S Main St Ste 447 Salt Lake City UT 84101-2180 Home Phone: 801-322-2301; Office Phone: 801-524-6180. Personal E-mail: JTGJR@hotmail.com. Business E-Mail: Thomas_Greene@utd.uscourts.gov.

GREENE, JOSEPH E., material science researcher; PhD in Materials Sci., U.S.C., 1971. Prof. U. Ill., 1971—; Erlander prof. Physics Linkping U., Sweden. Editor: CRC Critical Revs. in Solid State and Materials Sci., Thin Solid Films. Recipient Tage Erlander Physics prize 1992-95, Tech. Excellence award Semiconductor Rsch. Corp. 1994, Dept. Energy Sustained Outstanding Rsch. award 1996, David Adler Lectrship. award 1998. Mem. Am. Vacuum Soc. (bd. dirs., pres.), Am. Inst. Physics (gov. bd. mem.), Am. Physical Soc., AVS, TMS, MRS. Office: Dept Materials Sci and Engring U Ill 1101 W Springfield Ave Urbana IL 61801-3005

GREENE, JULE BLOUNTE, lawyer; b. Dublin, Ga., Aug. 15, 1922; s. Jule B. and Bette (O'Neal) G.; m. George Williams, Aug. 22, 1952; children: James Herschel, Bradley O'Neal. AB, Mercer U., 1949, LL.B., 1950. Bar: Ga. 1950, U.S. Supreme Ct. 1960. Atty. SEC, Atlanta, 1950-53, Washington, 1956-58, atty.-in-charge Miami, Fla., 1958-69, regional adminstr. Atlanta, 1969-82; regional counsel Nat. Assn. Securities Dealers, Atlanta, 1982-90; pvt. practice law Macon and Waycross, Ga., 1953-56, Dublin, Ga., 1990—. Former mem. Atlanta Fed. Exec. Bd., Interagy. Bd. U.S. Civil Service Examiners; former v.p., dir. Peachtree Fed. Credit Union.; former treas., dir. Mental Health Assn. Met. Atlanta. Served with A.C. AUS, 1942-46. Recipient award for exemplary achievement in pub. adminstrn. William A. Jump Meml. Found., 1958 Methodist.

GREENE, KAREN SANDRA, actress, educator, singer; b. NYC, Jan. 7, 1942; d. Nathan and Natalie (Barashick) Stein; m. Richard Greene, July 1, 1962 (div. 1980); children: Barry Randall and Lauren Jennifer. BA, U. Conn., Storrs, 1988. Singer, dancer, Broadway actress, NYC, 1960—62; pres., educator Karen Greene Studios, A Class Act, Tigre Prodn., Norwalk, Conn., 1962—; dir., educator theater arts Westport YMCA, Conn., 1981—85; pres., dir. voice On Stage Acad., Ltd., Westport, Conn., 1982—84; pres. Front Row Ctr. for Performing Arts, 1993—; educator voice Norwalk Cmty. Coll., Conn. Educator Temple Shalom, Norwalk, 1975-87; dir. theater arts Bridgeport, Conn. Jewish Ctr., 1985; dir. Norwalk Jewish Ctr., 1985, Wilton, Conn. Children's Theater, 1988-90; educator music and drama St. Luke's Sch., New Canaan, Conn., 1989-90; educator voice, acting, adult edn. Norwalk and Westport, Conn.) Bd. Edn., 1974—; dir., educator Curtain Call, Stamford, Conn., 1996—, dir. instr. voice, Norwalk Cmty. Coll., 2004. Voiceover artist nat. performing tours; dir., vocalist soc. band Shades of Green; dir. Grease, Norwalk C.C., 1993, Pippin, 1994. Founding mem., chmn. Norwalk Soc. for Arts, 1999; coord. Southwestern Conn. Women's Issues Conf., 1988; active women's equal rights, pro-choice, NOW, Women's Empowerment, Fairfield County, Conn.; active animal rights advocate; Conn. rep. Friends of Animals, others; founding mem., sec. The Greater Norwalk Coun. of the Arts, Conn., 1996—; dir., educator improvisation conquering stage fright program Norwalk H.S., 1999—; educator, dir. Westpor, Conn. Summer Teen Mus. Theater, 1990—, Greenwich, Conn. Acad., 1997—, Norwalk Cmty. Coll.; voice tchr. Norwalk, Conn. C.C., 2004-. Mem. NOW, AFTRA, SAG, Actor's Equity Assn., Internat. Platform Assn., Internat. TV Assn., Women's Empowerment, N.E. Anti-Vivisect. Soc. (Conn. rep.), People for the Ethical Treatment of Animals (Conn. rep.), Greenpeace (Conn. rep.), Best Friends Animal Sanctuary. Avocations: art, animals, holistic healing, reiki ii, mariel. Home: 238 Fillow St Norwalk CT 06850 Personal E-mail: solatido5678@yahoo.com.

GREENE, KEVIN C., lawyer; b. Cheverly, Md., Oct. 4, 1952; BA with highest honors, U. Md., 1974; JD, Cath. U. Am., 1977. Bar: Ga. 1977, D.C. 1979, U.S. Dist. Ct. (no. dist.) Ga., 1979. Law clk. to Hon. Charles A. Moye, Jr. U.S. Dist. Ct. (no. dist.) Ga., 1977-79; assoc. Troutman Sanders LLP, Atlanta, 1977—85, ptnr., 1986—, group co-leader, energy dept. Named a Super Lawyer, Atlanta Mag., 2004. Mem. ABA, D.C. Bar, State Bar Ga. Office: Troutman Sanders LLP 600 Peachtree St NE Ste 5200 Atlanta GA 30308-2216 Office Phone: 404-885-3146. Office Fax: 404-962-6575. Business E-Mail: kevin.greene@troutmansanders.com.

GREENE, LAURA HELEN, physicist; b. Cleve., June 12, 1952; d. Sam and Frances (Kain) G.; children: Max Greene Giannetta, Leo Greene Giannetta. BS cum laude in Physics, Ohio State U., 1974, MS in Physics, 1978; MS in Exptl. Physics, Cornell U., 1980, PhD in Physics, 1984. Mem. tech. staff Hughes Aircraft Co., Torrance, Calif., 1974-75; tchg. asst. Ohio State U., Columbus, 1975-76, rsch. asst., 1976-77; tchg. asst. Cornell U., Ithaca, NY, 1977-79, rsch. asst., 1979-83; postdoctoral mem. tech. staff Bellcore (formerly Bell Labs.), Red Bank, NJ, 1983-85, Murray Hill, NJ, 1983-85, mem. tech. staff Red Bank, NJ, 1985-92; prof. dept. physics U. Ill., Urbana, 1992—, Swanlund endowed chair, 2000—. Beckman assoc. Ctr. Advanced Study U Ill. at Urbana-Champaign, 1996-97, mem. provost's com. on sexual harassment edn., 1999-2001, mem. physics adv. com., 1999—; mem. McMillan award com. 1994-96, chair, 1995-97; co-chair Gordon Rsch. Conf., 1996, chair, 1998; mem.-at-large Coun. Gordon Rsch. Confs., 1999—, mem. schedule and selection com.; mem. Basic Energy Scis. Adv. Com., 2000; interim and founding bd. trustee Inst. for Complex and Adaptive Materials, Los Alamos and U. Calif.; mem. various rev. panels and workshops NSF and Dept. Energy; presenter in field; resident assoc. ctr. for advanced study U. Ill., Urbana, Ill., 2000-2001; rev. panel Can. Inst. Advanced Rsch., Superconductivity Rev., 2002; mem. oversight com. for vice chancellor rsch., U. Ill., 2001-2002, Sloan Found. Selection Com. for Physics, 2001—; adv. com. Sec. of Energy Bill Richardson, 2000—; chair external rev. panel, mem. bd. trustees Ctr. Integrated Nanotechnologies Nat. Lab., Los Alamos Nat. Lab., Sandia Nat. Lab. Contbr. over 200 articles to profl. jours.; presenter over 150 domestic and internat. invited talks. Recipient Beckman award U. Ill. Campus Rsch. Bd., 1993, E.O. Lawrence award Dept. Energy, 1999, 2001; rsch. grantee NSF, 1991—, ONR, 1995—, Dept. Energy, 1995—. Fellow AAAS (electorate nominating com. of sect. B physics 2000—, chmn. nominating com. for physics, 2001-02), Am. Acad. Arts and Scis., Am. Phys. Soc. (gen. councilor 1992—, congl. fellow screening com. 1993, exec. bd. 1995—, com. on coms. 1995—, chair 1997, search com. The Phys. Rev. 1996, nominating com. divsn. condensed matter physics 1998—, Maria Goeppert-Mayer award 1994, Centennial Spkr. 1997); mem. Materials Rsch. Soc. (symposium chair 1992), Am. Assn. Physics Tchrs., Internat. Union Pure and Applied Physicists (commr., U.S. liaison com. 1996—, U.S. del. to Low-Temperature Physics Commn. 1996—), Phi Kappa Phi, NAS. Avocations: physics, exercise, music. Office: U Ill Loomis Lab Physics 1110 W Green St Urbana IL 61801-9013 E-mail: lhg@uiuc.edu.

GREENE, LILIANE, literature and language educator, editor; b. Salonica, Greece, Oct. 10, 1928; came to U.S., 1941; d. Maurice and Daisy (Kohn) Massarano; m. Thomas McLernon Greene, May 20, 1950; children: Philip James, Christopher George, Francis Richard BA, Hunter Coll., 1948; MA, Columbia U., 1949; PhD, Yale U., 1969. Asst. in instrn. French Yale U., New Haven, 1964-65, instr., 1967-68, lectr., mng. editor Yale French Studies, 1980-94 (ret.); instr. Conn. Coll., New London, 1968-69, asst. prof., 1970-75. Contbr. articles to profl. jours. Fullbright fellow, 1949-50. Mem. MLA, Am. Assn. Tchrs. French, Ctr. Ind. Study (founding mem., pres. 1978-79, bd. dirs. 1977-89), Conn. Acad. of Arts and Scis. Democrat. Avocations: travel, theater. Home: 125 Livingston St New Haven CT 06511-2428

GREENE, MARK I., lawyer; b. Neponsit, NY, July 18, 1967; BA, Cornell U., 1989; JD, U. Pa., 1993. Bar: NY 1995. Law clk., Hon. Charles A. Legge US Dist. Ct. (no. dist.), Calif.; assoc. Cravath Swaine & Moore LLP, NYC, 1994—2001, ptnr., corp, 2001—. Mem.: ABA, Internat. Bar Assn., Assn. of Bar of City of NY (European Affairs Com.), NY State Bar Assn. Office: Cravath Swaine & Moore LLP Worldwide Plz 825 Eighth Ave New York NY 10019-7475 Office Phone: 212-474-1150. Office Fax: 212-474-3700. Business E-Mail: mgreene@cravath.com.*

GREENE, MARY KATHERINE, lawyer; b. Atlanta, May 1, 1968; BA, UNC, Chapel Hill, 1990; JD cum laude, Mercer Univ. Walter F. George Sch. Law, 1993. Bar: Ga. 1993. Ptnr. Carlock, Copeland, Semler & Stair, LLP, Atlanta. Spkr. in field. Contbr. articles to numerous profl. jours. Named Rising Star, Ga. SuperLawyers Mag., 2005. Mem.: ABA, Ga. Bar Assn., Atlanta Bar Assn. Office: Carlock Copeland 2600 Marquis Two Tower 285 Peachtree Ctr Av Atlanta GA 30303

GREENE, MAURICE, Olympic athlete, track and field athlete; b. Kansas City, Kans., July 23, 1974; Gold medalist 100m and 4x100m, 2000; U.S. indoor 60m champ, 2001; world indoor 60m champion, 1999; placed 1st at Home Depot invitational outdoors, 2003; placed 1st in Athens, 2002; placed 1st in Monaco, 2002; won3rd US 100m title, 2002; ranked #3 in the world (#2 in US) T&FN, 2002. Recipient USATF's Visa Humanitarian of the Yr. award, 2001, Jesse Owens award, 1999. Holder record time Grand Prix meet, Athens, 1999, world's fastest man, Sydney, 2000; became first man to win both 100 and 200 meter races at World Championship, 1999. Office: USA Track and Field Team One RCA Dome Ste 140 Indianapolis IN 46225

GREENE, RICHARD H., journalist, writer, policy analyst; b. Milford, Conn., Aug. 12, 1955; s. Eugene Harold and Bebe (Bender) G.; m. Katherine Barrett, Feb. 21, 1982; children: Benjamin, Sandra. BS in Journalism, Northwestern U., 1977. Rschr. Forbes mag., NYC, 1977-79, reporter, 1979-81, staff writer, 1981-82, assoc. editor, 1982-84, contbg. editor, 1984-89; freelance writer NYC, 1984—; pres. Barrett & Greene, NYC, 1996—. Sr. project coord. Pew Ctr. on the States, 2005—; corr. Governing mag.; founding editor B and G Report; spkr. in field. Author (with Katherine Barrett): The Man Behind the Magic, 1991, Frankly My Dear., 1996, Powering Up, 2000, Inside the Dream, 2001; co-prodr. Walt Disney biographical CD-ROM; co-prodr., writer TV documentary Walt: The Man Behind the Myth; contbr. articles to mags., including Newsweek, Glamour, Ladies' Home Jour., Reader's Digest, Redbook, Working Woman, others. Curator Walt Disney Family On-line Mus. Recipient Amos Tuck award, Dartmouth Coll., 1978, award for excellence in fin. journalism, N.Y. Soc. CPAs, 1984, 1991, cert. of merit, 1987, Children's Choice award, Internat. Reading Assn., 1992, Wash. Monthly Journalism award, 1999, Folio Editl. Excellence award, 2002, Excellence in Health Case Reporting award, Nat. Inst. Health Care Mgmt., 2005. Home and Office: 25 Waterside Plz Apt GG New York NY 10010-2621 E-mail: greenebarrett@gmail.com.

GREENE, ROBERT (BOB) BERNARD, JR., news correspondent, journalist, writer; b. Columbus, Ohio, Mar. 10, 1947; s. Robert Bernard and Phyllis Ann (Harmon) G.; m. Susan Bonnet Koebel, Feb. 13, 1971; 1 dau., Amanda Sue. BS, Northwestern U., 1969. Reporter Chgo. Sun-Times, 1969-71, columnist, 1971-78; syndicated columnist Field Newspaper Syndicate, Irvine, Calif., 1976-81, Tribune Co. Syndicate, NYC, 1981—2002; contbg. corr. ABC News Nightline, from 1981; columnist Chgo. Tribune, 1978—2002. Lectr. fine arts U. Chgo. Contbg. editor: Esquire Mag., 1980—; books include We Didn't Have None of Them Fat Funky Angels on the Wall of Heartbreak Hotel and Other Reports from America, 1971; Running: A Nixon-McGovern Campaign Journal, 1973, Billion Dollar Baby, 1974, Johnny Deadline, Reporter: The Best of Bob Greene, 1976, (with Paul Galloway) Bagtime, 1977, American Beat, 1983, Good Morning, Merry Sunshine, 1984, Cheeseburgers, The Best of Bob Greene, 1985, Be True to Your School, 1987, Homecoming: When the Soldiers Returned From Vietnam, 1989, Hang Time: Days and Dreams With Michael Jordan, 1992, All Summer Long, 1993, Once Upon a Town: The Miracle of the North Platte Canteen, 2002, And You Know You Should Be Glad, 2006. Recipient Nat. Headliner award for best newspaper column in U.S., 1977, Peter Lisagor award, 1981

GREENE, ROBERT MICHAEL, lawyer; b. Buffalo, Jan. 14, 1945; s. Gerald Henry and Dorothy Louise (Doll) Greene; m. Catherine Ellen Ostanski, Sept. 28, 1974; children: Amy, Megan, Timothy, Daniel. BA, Canisius Coll., 1966; JD, U. Notre Dame, 1969; LLM, NYU, 1971; LHD (hon.), Canisius Coll., 2005. Bar: NY 1970, U.S. Dist. Ct. (we. dist.) NY 1970, U.S. Ct. Appeals (2d cir.) 1970. Atty. VISTA, NYC, 1969-71; assoc. Phillips Lytle LLP, Buffalo, 1971-75, ptnr., 1976—, mng. ptnr., 1982—95, CEO, 1982—2003. Del. White House Conf. on Small Bus., 1986; bd. dirs. Cello Pack Corp., Gioia Mgmt., Inc. Author: Managing Partner 101: A Primer on Law Firm Leadership, 1990, Making Partner, A Guide for Law Firm Associates, 1992; co-author: Summary of Land Use Regulation in the State of New York and State Land Use Programs, 1974; editor: The Quality Pursuit: Assuring Standards in the Practice of Law, 1989; bd. editors Law Practice Mgmt. mag., 1989-93, articles editor, 1992-93. Trustee Canisius Coll., 1971-77, 92-2000, chmn. 1993-97; chmn. Shea's Ctr. for Performing Arts, Buffalo, 1981-85; chmn. Zool. Soc. of Buffalo, 1987-92; chmn. Buffalo Philharm. Orch., 1997-99; pres. bd. Cath. Edn. Diocese of Buffalo, 1987-97; trustee Western NY Pub. Broadcasting Assn., 1984—, chmn. 1993-96; Greater Buffalo Devel. Found., 1992-93; bd. dirs. Greater Buffalo Partnership, 1993-2000, sec. 1996-2000; trustee Buffalo Philharm. Orch. Found., 2001-04, chmn., 2003-04; trustee Found. of Diocese of Buffalo, 2000—, Zool. Soc. Buffalo Found., 1999—, WNED Found., 2001—; bd. dirs. Albright-Knox Art Gallery, 2000—. Recipient LaSalle award Canisius Coll., 1980, Bd. Regents Dist. Citizens Achievement award, 1987, Disting. Alumni award 1991, Signum Fidei award St. Joseph's Collegiate Inst., 1990, Golden Marquee award Shea's Buffalo Theatre, 1984, Theodore Roosevelt Exemplary Citizen award, 1993, Person of Yr. award Notre Dame Club of Buffalo, 1994, Brotherhood award Nat. Conf., 1997, Chmn.'s award Buffalo Niagara Partnership, 1999, Humanitarian award Niagara Luth. Health Found., 2000, Caritas award St. Joseph Hosp. Found.,

2002, Reflections award Trocaire Coll., 2003, Bishop's medal, Diocese Buffalo, 2005, Cmty. Service award, D'Youville Coll., 2006; named to Jr. Achievement Hall Fame Laureate, 2006. Mem. NY State Bar Assn., Erie County Bar Assn., U. Notre Dame Law Assn. (bd. dirs. 1988—, pres. 2003-04), Buffalo Club (bd. dirs. 1997-2000, 2005-), Cherry Hill Club. Democrat. Roman Catholic. Office: Phillips Lytle LLP 3400 HSBC Ctr Buffalo NY 14203-2887 Home Phone: 716-838-6766; Office Phone: 716-847-7038. Office Fax: 716-852-6100. Business E-Mail: rgreene@phillipslytle.com.

GREENE, ROBERT WILLIAM, communications educator, media consultant; b. Jamaica, NY, July 12, 1929; s. Francis McLaughlin and Mary Virginia (Clancy) G.; m. Kathleen A. Greene, Jan. 28, 1951; children: Robert William, Lea Marie (dec.). Student, Fordham U., 1947-50. Reporter Jersey Jour., 1949-50; sr. investigator N.Y.C. Anti-Crime Com., 1950-55; reporter Newsday, Garden City, NY, 1995, leader investigative team, 1967-73, sr. editor, 1970-92, Long Island editor, 1972-78, asst. mng. editor, 1978-93; Disting. Stessin prof. , chair dept. journalism and mass media studies Hofstra U., 1995—2003; ret., 2003. Staff investigator US Senate Select Com. on Unfair Practices in Labor/Mgmt. Field, 1957; dir. Ariz. Project, 1976-77; pres., CEO Greene Assocs.; journalism program coord. SUNY, Stony Brook, 1986-95; vis. prof. journalism Stony Brook U., 2006—; cons., lectr. in field. Author: Naked Came the Stranger, 1969, The Heroin Trail, 1973, The Sting Man, 1981. Chmn. publicity Smithtown Tercentenary, 1967; founding mem., bd. dirs. Suffolk County Happy Landings Fund; bd. visitors Inst. on Polit. Journalism Georgetown U.; bd. dirs. Smithtown Hist. Soc., Mus. at Stony Brook, Cleary Sch. for Deaf; founder, former pres. L.I. Press Club; founder St. Anthony's Gridiron Club; mem. Pres.' Coun. Xavier H.S.; chmn. Mollenhoff Journalism Award Comn. Named Hon. mem. Class of 1996, U. Md. Coll. Journalism, Hon. Alumnus, Hofstra U., 1999, Tchr. of Yr., 2000, hon. pres., Norwegian Investigative Reporters, Oslo, 1991; named to, L.I. Hall of Fame, 1991; recipient George Polk award, L.I. U, Peter Zenger award, U. Ariz., James Wright Brown award, Gold Medal Pulitzer prize, 1970, 1974, Mo. medal for disting. svc. to Am. journalism, 1979, Front Page award, 1982, Edgar award, Mystery Writers Am., 1982, Disting. Achievement award, Fordham U. Grad. Sch. Edn., 1994, Pres.'s medal, Hofstra U., 2001. Fellow Soc. Profl. Journalists; mem. Investigative Reporters and Editors Group (pres. 1976-77, chmn. exec. bd.), Assn. Edn. Journalism & Mass Comms., Radio & TV News Dirs.'s Assn. Clubs: Hofstra Univ. Club, L.I. Press (pres. 1976). Republican. Roman Catholic. Office: 4 Ardmore Pl Kings Park NY 11754-4002 Home Phone: 631-360-8868. Personal E-mail: rgreene455@aol.com.

GREENE, SHEREE' JEANE, elementary school educator, consultant; d. Floyde Eugene and Betty Etheridge Greene. B in Early Childhood Edn., Wesleyan Coll., 1984; M in Early Childhood Edn., Piedmont Coll., 1996. In-Tech Certification Ga. State Bd. Edn., 2005; PBT-5 tchg. cert. in early childhood edn. Ga. State Bd. Edn., 2005, cert. tchr. support specialist Ga. State Bd. Edn., 1997. Elem. educator Northside Elem. Sch., Griffin, Ga., 1984—86; receptionist/sec. Athens (Ga.) Regional Youth Devel. Ctr., 1986—87; elem. educator Ila (Ga.) Elem. Sch., 1987—. Motivational spkr./cons. Nat. and State Inclusion Confs., Athens, 1992—; ednl. rsch. cons. U. Ga. Sch. Edn., Athens, 1993—94, vol. mentor (open door classroom observations), 1994—96; ednl. rsch. cons. U. Ga., Athens, 1994—95; portfolio evaluator Madison County Tchr. of the Yr. Evaluation Com., Danielsville, Ga., 1996—97; so. accreditation of colleges and schools steering com. co-chairperson Ila Elem. Sch., 1999—2004; motivational spkr. Emmanuel Coll., Franklin Springs, Ga., 2003—. Composer: (written lyrics and melody) Single Married Man (Ga. Songwriters Association's Top Ten Songwriters, 1992). Exec. com. co-chairperson/social events coord. Friends of the Madison County Libr., Danielsville, Ga., 1994—96; motivational spkr./singer various chs., Ga., 2004—. Recipient Leadership/Future Tchr. award, Alpha Delta Kappa, 1980, Tchr. of Yr. Cmty. award, Madison County Optimist Club, 1996, Tchr. of the Yr., Ila Elem., 1995, Madison County Sch. Sys., 1996; Future Tchr. scholar, Kappa Delta Epsilon, 1980. Avocations: songwriting, singing, gardening, creative writing, event planning. Office: Ila Elementary School 150 Sewell Mill Rd Ila GA 30647 Home Phone: 706-548-8928; Office Phone: 706-789-3445. Business E-Mail: sgreene@madison.k12.ga.us.

GREENE, STEPHEN CRAIG, lawyer; b. Watertown, NY, Apr. 27, 1946; s. Harold Adelbert and Mildred Esther (Baker) G.; m. Nancy Jean Adams, Mar. 28, 1965; children: Kathryn, Stephen, Hilary. AB, Syracuse U., 1967, JD, 1970. Bar: NY 1971, US Tax Ct., 1977. Asst. to pres. SUNY, Oswego, NY, 1970-73; assoc. firm Leyden E. Brown, Oswego, NY, 1973-75; ptnr. Brown and Greene, 1976-81; pvt. practice law, 1981—. Bd. dirs. Found. Corp. Legal Studies, Inc., 1968-70, United Way of Oswego County, Inc., 1985-88, Campbell's Point Assn., 1994-96; bd. dir. Oswego Hosp., 1981-2000, mem. exec. com., 1985-2000, pres., 1996-98; bd. dirs. Oswego Health, Inc., 1997—, pre, 1997-02; town atty. Oswego, 1972—; counsel Oswego County Bd. Realtors, 1978—; mem. Oswego County Rep. Com., 1974-85, counsel, 1980-83; gen. counsel Express Abstract Co., 1992-95; mem. Oswego coll. coun. SUNY, Oswego, 2007—. Recipient Inst. Counsel, 1970. Mem. ABA, NY Bar Assn., Oswego County Bar Assn., Greater Oswego C. of C. (bd. dir. 1980-87), Oswego Country Club (counsel 1977-81), Masons, Shriners, Phi Delta Phi. Home: 611 W 1st St Oswego NY 13126-4137 Office: 85 W Bridge St Oswego NY 13126-2011

GREENE, TENA LORRAINE, singer, educator, actor; d. Roy and Kathryn Correen (Case) Greene. MusM in Voice Performance, Converse Coll., Spartanburg, SC, 2001. Voice tchr. Limestone Coll. Acad., Gaffrey, SC, 1995—97, Converse Pre-Coll., Spartanburg, 1999—2002, U. S.C., Spartanburg, 1999—2003, Mars Hill (N.C.) Coll., 2003—. Singer: various local cmty. theater and opera cos. Sec. bd. dirs. Tryon Little Theater, 1993—, fund raising performer, ARC, Tryon, Columbus, NC, 2000—05. Named Dist. winner, Nat. Assn. Tchrs. Singing, 2001; A. J. Fletcher Found. scholar, Gardner-Webb U., 1987. Mem.: Foothills Music Club. Home: 49 Locust St Columbus NC 28722 Office: Mars Hill Coll Music Dept PO Box 370 Mars Hill NC 28754-0370

GREENE, THOMAS HARDY, architect; b. Washington, Apr. 19, 1948; s. Thomas Elbert and Marie Dabney (Sitton) G.; m. Linda Louise Weaver, June 16, 1978. Student, Montgomery Coll., 1966-68, 72-73; BArch cum laude, U. Md., 1979. Registered arch., D.C., Md., Tex., Wis., Va., Mass., N.Y., Fla., Conn., Calif., Okla., Pa., N.C., S.C, Nev.; cert. cert. NCARB, LEED Accredited Profl. Archtl. designer, technologist Clifton B. White, Silver Spring, Md., 1965, Cohen, Haft & Assocs., Silver Spring, Md., 1966-69, 70-72, Sullivan, Clark, Almy & Savage, Bethesda, Md., 1973; archtl. model builder Roger Lewis & Assocs., Washington, 1974-75; archtl. designer Thomas H. Greene Design, Chevy Chase, Md., 1976; designer, technologist David M. Schwarz Archtl. Svcs., Washington, 1976-78; architect, chmn. bd. dirs. David M. Schwarz Archtl. Svcs., Inc., Washington, 1978—; ptnr. David M. Schwarz & Ptnrs., Washington, 1990—. Bd. dirs. Glen Briar Condominium Owners' Assn., Silver Spring, 1982, pres., 1983. Recipient U. Md. Divsn. Arts and Humanities cert. scholarship, 1977. Mem. AIA, Nat. Fire Protection Assn., Nat. Trust Hist. Preservation, Internat. Code Coun., Amnesty Internat., U. Md. Alumni Assn., Phi Kappa Phi. Avocations: travel, photography, t'ai chi chuan, reading. Home: 2304 Ashboro Dr Chevy Chase MD 20815-3048 Office: David M Schwarz Archtl Svcs Inc 1707 L St NW Ste 400 Washington DC 20036 Office Phone: 202-862-0777. Business E-Mail: thg@dmsas.com.

GREENE, TIMOTHY JAMES, industrial engineering educator; b. Lafayette, Ind., Oct. 18, 1952; s. James H. and Barbara H. (Holt) G.; m. Nancy E. Van Kuren, Nov. 16, 1996. BS in Aero. and Astron. Engring., Purdue U., 1975, MS in Indsl. Engring., 1977, PhD, 1980. Instr., rsch. asst. sch. indsl. engring. Purdue U., West Lafayette, Ind., 1975-80; asst. prof. indsl. engring. Va. Tech., Blacksburg, 1980-85, assoc. prof. indsl. engring., 1985-91, asst. head dept. indsl. engring., 1986-91; prof., head dept. indsl. engring. and mgmt. Okla. State U., Stillwater, 1991-96, assoc. dean for rsch. Coll. Engring., Arch. and Tech., 1995-99; dean coll. engring. U. Ala., Tuscaloosa, 2000—04, asst. v.p. rsch. and acad. affairs, 2004—. Contbr. 5 chpts. to books, over 30 articles to profl. jours. Fellow Inst. Indsl. Engrs. (trustee 1991-99, sr. v.p. tech. ops. 1994-96, sr. profl. devel. 1992-94, Outstanding Young Indsl. Engr. 1987, pres. elect 1996-97, pres., 1997-98, past pres. 1998-99), Soc. Mfg. Engrs. (Outstanding Young Mfg. Engr. 1986); mem. Am. Soc. Engring. Educators. Home: 8151 Brandon Cir Mattawan MI 49071-8415

GREENE, WARNER CRAIG, medical educator, administrator; b. Mexico, Mo., June 13, 1949; Lic. physician Md., N.C., Calif., diplomate Am. Bd. Allergy and Immunology, Am. Bd. Internal Medicine. Investigator metabolism br. Nat. Cancer Inst., NIH, Bethesda, Md., 1979—83, sr. investigator metabolism br., 1983—86; investigator Howard Hughes Med. Inst., Chevy Chase, Md., 1987—92; prof. medicine Duke U. Sch. Medicine, Durham, NC, 1987—92; prof. medicine, microbiology and immunology U. Calif., San Francisco, 1992—, dir. & sr. investigator Gladstone Inst. for Virology and Immunology Ctr. for AIDS Rsch., 1992—, co-dir. Gladstone Inst. for Virology and Immunology Ctr. for AIDS Rsch., 1994—. Cons. Merck Pharms., Whitehouse Station, NJ, Eli Lilly Inc., Indpls., Abbott Pharms., Abbott Park, Ill., Hoffman LaRoche, Nutley, NJ, Sagres Pharm., Alliance Pharms., Inc., San Diego, Pfizer, Inc., NYC; mem. Nat. Inst. Allergy and Infectious Diseases, AIDS Rsch. Rev. Com., 1988—90; co-chair Keystone AIDS Symposium, 1995; mem. postdoctoral fellowship rev. com. Pfizer, 1995—; mem. adv. bd. exec. com. Inst. Human Virology, 1999—; Syntex lectr. Laurentian Hormone Conf., 1987; Kroc vis. prof. rheumatology UCLA, 1989; Plenary lectr. Sandoz Symposium on Human Retroviruses, 1990; keynote address Calif. Acad. Scis., 1994. Assoc. editor: Jour. of Acquired Immune Deficiency Syndromes, mem. editl. bd.: Cytokine, Growth Factors, 1987, Blood, others, 1987, assoc. editor: Jour. of Immunology, 1984—88. Named one of 100 Most Cited Scientists, Inst. for Sci. Info., 1981—88; recipient rsch. grants in field, Washington Acad. of Scis. Award in Biol. Scis., 1984. Fellow: Am. Rheumatism Assn. (Young Investigator award 1988); mem.: ACP, Inst. Medicine, Assn. Am. Physicians, Calif. Acad. Medicine, Am. Soc. for Clin. Investigation (v.p. 1993—94), Am. Assn. Immunologists, Am. Fedn. for Clin. Rsch. (Outstanding Investigator award 1987), Alpha Omega Alpha, Sigma Xi. Achievements include research in basic scientific studies aimed at further understanding how HIV grows and interacts with its cellular host; biology of NF-kB, an inducible eukaryotic transcription factor that is capable of activating HIV replication.

GREENE, WILLIAM P., JR., federal judge; b. Bluefield, W.Va., 1943; m. Madeline Sinkford; children: William Robert, Jeffrey. BA, W. Va. State Coll., 1965; JD, Howard U., 1968; attended, Judge Adv. Gen. Sch., Charlottesville, Va., U.S. Army Command & Gen. Staff Coll., Fort Leavenworth, Kans., U.S. Army War Coll., Carlisle, Pa. Bar: W. Va. 1968. Immigration judge US Dept. Justice, Washington, 1993—97; judge US Ct. Appeals Vets. Claims, 1997—2005, chief judge, 2005—. Colonel Judge Adv. Gen. Corps US Army, 1968—93. Decorated Legion of Merit (3 awards); named Hon. Col. Judge Adv. Gen. Corps, 1997, Disting. Mem. Judge Adv. Gen. Corps, 2000, Disting. Mem. U.S. Army Judge Adv. Gen. Corps. Mem.: Nat. Bar Assn. (co-founder Mil. Law sect., NBA Mil. Law Hall of Fame 2002). Office: US Ct Appeals Vets Claims Ste 900 625 Indiana Ave NW Washington DC 20004-2950

GREENEBAUM, LEONARD CHARLES, retired lawyer; b. Langgoens, Germany, Feb. 6, 1934; arrived in U.S., 1937, naturalized, 1952; s. Norbert and Henny Lisa (Greenbaum) Greenebaum; m. Barbara Rosendorf, Feb. 10, 1957; children: Beth Lynn, Cathy Sue, Steven I. BS Commerce cum laude, Washington and Lee U., 1956, JD cum laude, 1959. Bar: DC 1959, Va. 1959, Md. 1965. Atty. Sachs, Greenebaum & Tayler and predecessor firms, Washington, 1959—64, ptnr., 1964—75, mng. ptnr., 1975—89; ptnr., D.C. coord. litig. Baker & Hostetler, Washington, 1990—95, chair firmwide litig. group, 1992—2000; ret., 2001. Arbitrator Am. Arbitration Assn., Washington, 1975—2000; mem. law coun. Washington and Lee U.; mem. bd. mentors Citadel Mil. Coll. SC, 2002—; mem. citizens adv. bd. Hollins Cancer Ctr. Med. U. SC, 2003—06. Chmn. bd. dirs. Davis Meml. Goodwill Industries, Washington, 1979—82; bd. dirs. Coun. Ct. Excellence, Cold War Submariner Meml. Found., Charleston; dir. Cold War Sub. Meml. in Charlston Habor and Found.; bd. mem. visitors of Roper St. Francis Hosp. Sys., 2006—. Capt. US Army, 1957. Recipient Svc. to Handicapped award, Davis Meml. Goodwill Industries, 1982. Fellow: Am. Bar. Found. (life); mem.: Va. State Bar Assn., Montgomery County Bar Assn., D.C. Bar Assn., Biltmore Forest Country Club, County Club Estates Cmty. Assn. (bd. dirs.), Country Club of Charleston. Jewish. Personal E-mail: curlyccc@comcast.net.

GREENER, SIR ANTHONY, educational association administrator; b. 1940; Dir. Reed Internat., 1990-98, Reed Elsevier, 1993-98; chmn. Guinness plc, 1993—97, Diageo plc, 1997-2000, Uf Industry Ltd., London, 2000—04, Robert Mondavi, 2000—04, Qualifications and Curriculum Authority, London, 2002—; dep. chmn. Brit. Telecom, 2001—06; bd. dir. United Learning Trust, 2005—, Williams Sonoma, 2007—, WNSGS, 2007—. Office: Qualifications and Curriculum Authority 83 Piccadilly London W1J 8QA England Office Phone: 02075095555. Office Fax: 02075096975.

GREENER, RALPH BERTRAM, lawyer; b. Rahway, NJ, Sept. 23, 1940; s. Ralph Bertram and Mary Ellen (Esch) G.; m. Jean Elizabeth Wilson, Mar. 21, 1964; children: Eric Wilson, Erin Hope, Nicholas Christian. BA, Wheaton Coll., 1962; JD, Duke U., 1968. Bar: Minn. 1969. With Fredrikson & Byron P.A., Mpls., 1969—. Chmn. bd. Minn. Lawyers Mutual Ins. Co., Mpls. 1981—. 1st Lt. USMCR, 1962-65. Recipient award of profl. excellence Minn. State Bar Assn., 1993. Mem. Rotary Club (pres. Mpls. 2002-03). Office: Fredrikson & Byron PA 200 S 6th St Ste 4000 Minneapolis MN 55402-1425 Home Phone: 1314 Marquette Ave #2402 Minneapolis MN 55403 E-mail: rgreener@fredlaw.com.

GREENES, ROBERT A., medical educator; MD, Harvard U., 1966, PhD, 1977. Prof. radiology Med. Sch. Harvard U., Boston, prof. health scis. and tech., prof. health policy and mgmt. Sch. Pub. Health. Contbr. articles to profl. jours. Mem.: NIH. Office: Brigham and Women's Hosp Dept Radiology 75 Francis St Boston MA 02115-6106 Fax: 617-732-6317. E-mail: greenes@harvard.edu.

GREENFIELD, DAVID W., lawyer; b. Greenville, Pa., May 6, 1950; m. Carla Greenfield; 2 children. BA magna cum laude, U. Pitts., 1972; JD, Wake Forest U., 1975. Bar: Pa. 1975, US Dist. Ct. (we. dist.) Pa. 1975, US Supreme Ct. 1984. Atty. G.C. Murphy Co., 1975—79; counsel, asst. sec. Westinghouse Electric Corp., 1979—82; asst. gen. counsel Rockwell Internat. Corp., 1982—95, assoc. gen. counsel, 1995—97; sr. v.p., gen. counsel, sec. Meritor Automotive, Inc. (now ArvinMeritor, Inc.), 1997—99, ptnr., 1999—2000; with Buchanan Ingersoll PC, Pitts., 2000—07; v.p., sec., gen. counsel Kennametal, Inc., Latrobe, Pa., 2001—. Mem.: Am. Corp. Counsel Assn., Soc. Corp. Secretaries and Governance Profls. Office: Kennametal Inc 1600 Technology Way PO Box 231 Latrobe PA 15650-0231 Office Fax: 724-539-3839.

GREENFIELD, GEORGE B., radiologist; b. NYC, May 4, 1928; s. Jacob and Rose (Wolf) G.; m. Barbara Anne O'Driscoll, Mar. 3, 1956; children: Edward James, Sheelagh Anne. BA, NYU, 1949; MD, State U. Utrecht, Netherlands, 1956. Diplomate: Am. Bd. Radiology, Am. Bd. Nuclear Medicine. Intern Bridgeport (Conn.) Hosp., 1956-57; resident radiology Presbyn.-St. Lukes Hosp., Chgo., 1957-60; practice medicine, specializing in radiology Chgo., 1960—; radiologist Cook County Hosp., 1961-66, asst. dir. diagnostic radiology, 1966-69; assoc. prof. radiology U. Ill., 1966-69; prof., chmn. dept. radiology Chgo. Med. Sch., 1969-74, Mt. Sinai Hosp. Med. Center, 1969-89; prof. diagnostic radiology Rush Med. Coll., 1975-87; pres. med. staff Mt. Sinai Hosp. Med. Center, 1983-85; prof. radiology Cook County Grad. Sch. Medicine., Chgo. Med. Sch., 1987-89, vice chmn. dept. radiology, 1988-89; prof. radiology U. South Fla., Tampa, 1989—2003, prof. emeritus, 2004—. Attending radiologist H. Lee Moffitt Cancer Ctr. and Rsch. Inst., Tampa. Author: Radiology of Bone Diseases, 5th edit., 1990; sr. author: A Manual of Radiographic Positioning, 1973, Computers in Radiology, 1985, Imaging of Bone Tumors, 1995 Imaging of Arthritis, 2001; contbr. articles to profl. jours. Trustee Mt. Sinai Hosp., 1986-89. Served with U.S. Army, 1951. Fellow Am. Coll. Radiology; mem. AMA, AAAS, Chgo. Med. Soc., Chgo. Roentgen Soc., Am. Roentgen Ray Soc., Radiol. Soc. N.Am., Inst. Medicine Chgo., Internat. Skeletal Soc., Soc. Skeletal Radiology, Sigma Xi. Office: Moffitt Cancer Ctr & Rsch Inst PO Box 17 Tampa FL 33601-0017 Home Phone: 727-360-8021. Personal E-mail: gbgreenfield@worldnet.att.net.

GREENFIELD, JAMES ROBERT, lawyer; b. Phila., Mar. 31, 1926; s. Milton and Katherine E. (Rosenberg) G.; m. Phyllis Chaplowe, Aug. 17, 1947 (dec. May 1978); m. Joyce MacDonald Koehler, Mar. 22, 1980. BS, Bates Coll., 1947; JD, Yale U., 1950. Bar: Conn. 1950, U.S. Dist. Ct. Conn. 1951, U.S. Ct. Appeals (2d cir.) 1966, U.S. Supreme Ct. 1959. Atty. Chaplowe & Greenfield, 1950-54, Markle & Greenfield, New Haven, 1954-58; sr. ptnr. Lander, Greenfield & Krick, New Haven, 1958-80, Greenfield, Krick & Jacobs, New Haven, 1980-90, Greenfield & Murphy, New Haven, 1990-98; of counsel Tyler Cooper & Alcorn, New Haven, 1998—. Lectr. U. Conn. Law Sch., 1966-67, 71-72, 75-76. Mem. editl. bd. Conn. Bar Jour., 1963-77. Pres. New Haven Symphony, 1976-78, Conn. Bar Found., 1976-77; bd. dirs. Nat. Jud. Coll., 1978-84. With USNR, 1944-46. Fellow Am. Bar Found. (state chmn. 1985-90); mem. ABA (state del. 1975-78, bd. govs. 1978-81, ho. of dels. 1972-83, spl. com. on goverance 1983-84, chmn. various coms.), Conn. Bar Assn. (pres. 1973-74, Disting. Profl. Svc. award 1989), Am. Judicature Soc. (bd. dirs. 1983-87, 2002-03), Am. Law Inst., Am. Acad. Matrimonial Lawyers (pres. Conn. chpt. 1993-94, Lifetime Achievement award 2007), Internat. Acad. Matrimonial Lawyers, New Haven County Bar Assn. (pres. 1969-70, Lifetime Achievment award 1993, Conn. Law Tribune Svc. to the Profession award 2002), Yale Law Sch. Assn. (sec. 1977-80), Quinnipiack Club, Mory's. Office: Tyler Cooper & Alcorn LLP 555 Long Wharf Dr 8th Fl New Haven CT 06511 Office Phone: 203-784-8200. Business E-Mail: greenfield@tylercooper.com.

GREENFIELD, (HENRY) JEFF, news analyst; b. NYC, June 10, 1943; s. Benjamin and Helen Evelyn (Greenwald) Greenfield; m. Carrie Carmichael, May 11, 1968 (div. 1993); children: Casey Carmichael, David Carmichael; m. Karen Gannett, 1993 (div. 1997); m. Dena Sklar, June 21, 2002. BA with honors, U. Wis., 1964; LLB cum laude, Yale U., 1967. Legis. aide to Senator Robert F. Kennedy, Washington, 1967-68; speechwriter to Mayor John V. Lindsay, NYC, 1968-70; media critic CBS News, NYC, 1979-83; polit. media analyst ABC News, NYC, 1983-97; sr. analyst CNN, NYC, 1998—2007; sr. polit. corr. CBS News, 2007—. Contbr. Inside Politics with Judy Woodruff, American Morning and NewsNight with Aaron Brown; host Greenfield at Large, CNN, CEO Exchange, PBS; guest host Larry King Live; moderator CNN town hall meeting Investigating the President: Media Madness?, 1998, Listening after Littleton, 1999. Columnist Universal Press Syndicate, 1981—96, Time mag., 1996—; contbr. articles to NY Times, Esquire and Nat. Lampoon; co-author: The Advance Man, 1971, A Populist Manifesto, 1972; author: No Peace, No Place, 1973, The World's Greatest Team, 1975, Television: The First 50 Years, 1977, Playing to Win, 1980, The Real Campaign, 1982, The People's Choice, 1995, Oh Waiter! One Order of Crow!, 2001. Recipient Emmy Award, NATAS, 1986, 1991, 1993, 1999, Quill Award for Profl. Achievement, 2002. Office: CBS 51 W 52nd St New York NY 10019*

GREENFIELD, JOHN CHARLES, biochemist, professional society administrator; b. Dayton, Ohio, 1945; s. Ivan Ralph and Mildred Louise (House) Greenfield; m. Liga Miervaldis, Aug. 20, 1980; children: John Hollen, Mark Richard. BS cum laude, Ohio U., 1967; PhD, U. Ill., 1974. Instr. sci. area HS, Dayton, 1968-71; grad. rsch. asst. U. Ill., 1971-74; postdoctoral rsch. fellow Swiss Fed. Inst. Tech., Zurich, 1975-76; rsch. chemist infectious diseases rsch. Upjohn Co., Kalamazoo, 1976-82, sr. rsch. scientist drug metabolism rsch., 1982-93; sr. project mgr. Upjohn Labs., Kalamazoo, 1993-95, Pharmacia & Upjohn Inc., Kalamazoo, 1995-96; acquisitions review specialist, bus. devel. Pharmacia and Upjohn, Inc., Kalamazoo, 1996-98, clin. monitor, US market co. med. affairs, 1998-2000; dir. global med. svcs. Pharmacia Inc., Kalamazoo, 2000—03, Pfizer, Inc., Kalamazoo, 2003—04; v.p. bus. devel. Biomedical and Pharmaceutical Info. Solutions, Kalamazoo, 2004—07; exec. dir. Mich. Core Tech. Alliance, Grand Rapids, Mich., 2007—. Contbr. articles to profl. jours. Adult leader Boy Scouts Am. Am.-Swiss Found. Sci. Exch. fellow, 1975, NSF-NATO postdoctoral fellow, 1975—76. Mem.: AAAS, Drug Info. Assn., Am. Assn. Microbiology, Am. Assn. Pharm. Scientists, Am. Chem. Soc., Sigma Xi, Delta Tau Delta, Phi Lambda Upsilon, Blue Key, Phi Eta Sigma. Achievements include patents in field; identification, evaluation and management of worldwide research and development projects for new pharmaceutical agents. Home: 6695 E E Ave Richland MI 49083-9471 Office: Van Andel Inst 333 Bostwick Ave NE Grand Rapids MI 49503 Office Phone: 616-234-5516. Business E-Mail: john.greenfield@vai.org.

GREENFIELD, JOSEPH CHOLMONDELEY, JR., physician, educator; b. Atlanta, July 20, 1931; s. Joseph Cholmondeley and Agnes (Game) Greenfield; m. Mary Ruth Fordham, Aug. 13, 1955; children: Mary Agnes, Ruth Ann, Susan Lee. AB in History, Emory U., 1954, MD, 1956. Intern, resident in medicine Duke Med. Ctr., Durham, NC, 1956—59, mem. staff, 1962—2001, asst. prof. medicine, 1962—65, assoc. prof. medicine, 1965—70, prof. medicine, 1970—, dir. heart sta., 1972—2001, James B. Duke disting. prof., 1981—, chief cardiovasc. divsn., 1981—89, chmn. dept. medicine, 1983—95; staff., dir. heart sta. VA Med. Ctr., Durham, 1962—; clin. assoc. NIH, USPHS, 1959—62, mem. cardiovasc. and pulmonary study sect., 1974—78, chmn., 1975—78. Author: A Quail Hunter's Odyssey, 2004, Duke Cardiology Fellows Training Program, Origin to the Present, 2004, Bawna Babu, 2005, Duke Chief Medical Residents, 2005; contbr. 200 articles to profl. jours. Fellow: ACP, Am. Coll. Cardiology (disting. sci. award 1985); mem.: NRA (life), Inst. Medicine, Assn. Am. Physicians, Am. Physiol. Soc., Am. Soc. Clin. Investigation, SCV, Safari Club Internat., Kappa Alpha, Alpha Omega Alpha, Phi Beta Kappa. Methodist. Home: 1212 Virginia Ave Durham NC 27705-3264 Office: Duke U Med Ctr PO Box 3246 Durham NC 27715-3246 Office Phone: 919-286-6951. Business E-Mail: green045@mc.duke.edu.

GREENFIELD, LAZAR JOHN, surgeon, educator; b. Houston, Dec. 14, 1934; s. Robert G. and Betty B. (Greenfield) Heath; m. Sharon Dee Bishkin, Aug. 29, 1956; children: John, Julie, Jeff. Student, Rice U., 1951-54; MD, Baylor U., 1958. Diplomate: Am. Bd. Surgery (dir. 1976-82), Am. Bd. Thoracic Surgery, cert. gen. vascular surgery, 1991. Intern Johns Hopkins Hosp., Balt., 1958-59, resident, 1961-66; chief surgery VA Hosp., Oklahoma City, 1966-74; prof. dept. surgery U. Okla. Med. Center, 1971-74; Stuart McGuire prof., chmn. dept. surgery Med. Coll. Va., Richmond, 1974-87; F.A. Coller prof., chmn. dept of surgery U. Mich., 1987—2002; CEO U. Mich. Health System, 2002—03; interim exec. v.p. med. affairs U. Mich. Med. Sch., 2002—03; sabbatical FDA, 2003—04. Mem. surgery A study sect. NIH. Author: Surgery in the Aged, 1975; editor-in-chief Surgery, Scientific Principles and Practice, 1993, 96, 3d edit., 2001, Surgery News, 2004-; editor Complications in Surgery and Trauma, 1983, 2d edit., 1990; contbr. to profl. publs. Served with USPHS, 1959-61. Recipient Disting. Alumni award Rice U., 1999; Thomas R. Franklin scholar, 1952, John and Mary Markle scholar in med. sci., 1968-73. Mem. Inst. of Medicine of NAS, Am. Surg. Assn., Am. Assn. Thoracic Surgery, Assn. Acad. Surgery, Soc. Univ. Surgeons, Johns Hopkins Soc. Scholars, Phi Delta Epsilon. Home: 505 E Huron St Ann Arbor MI 48104-1573 Office: UMMC Surgery 1327 Jones Dr # 201 Ann Arbor MI 48105 Home Phone: 734-668-7571; Office Phone: 734-936-6398. E-mail: lazarg@umich.edu.

GREENFIELD, LEE, state legislator; b. Bklyn., July 29, 1941; s. Solomen and Edith (Herschman) G.; m. Marcia Greenfield, Nov. 25, 1965. BS in Physics, Purdue U., West Lafayette, Ind., 1963; postgrad., U. Minn., 1963-73. Instr. applied math. U. Minn., Mpls., 1964-73; prin. asst. Hennepin County Bd. Commrs., Mpls., 1975-77; mgmt. analyst Office of Planning & Devel., Hennepin County, Mpls., 1977; rep. Minn. Ho. of Reps., St. Paul, 1979-2000; prin. adminstrv. asst. Hennepin County Dept. Human Svcs. and Pub. Health, 2001—. Mem. steering com. Reforming State Group, N.Y.C., 1993—, chmn., 1994-96. Bd. dirs. Twin City Cmty. Program for Affordable Health Care, Mpls., 1982-84, Arthritis Found., Mpls., 1988-90, Minn. Aids Project Mpls., 2002-, Minn. Vis. Nurse Agy., Mpls., 2003-, Ams. for Dem. Action, Mpls., 1979—, v.p., 1976-78. Recipient Dwight V. Dixon award Mental Health Assn. Minn., 1994. Mem. Mental Health Assn. Minn. (Disting. Svc. award 1987), Planned Parenthood of Minn. (Pub. Svc. award 1993). Dfl. Jewish. Office: Hennepin County Health Policy Ctr A-1702 Government Center Minneapolis MN 55487-0172 Home Phone: 612-724-7549; Office Phone: 612-348-3553. Business E-Mail: lee.greenfield@co.hennepin.mn.us.

GREENFIELD, LINDA SUE, nursing educator; b. Dover, Del., Aug. 5, 1950; d. Norman Raymond and Eleanor Henrietta (Harmon) Connell; m. Douglas Herman Greenfield, Dec. 27, 1976; children: Leah, Paige. BSN, Cath. U., 1972; MSN cum laude, Boston U., 1977; postgrad., Coll. New Rochelle, 1986-88; PhD, Adelphi U., 1998. RN, N.Y. Staff nurse emergency rm. and ICU Washington Hosp. Ctr., 1974-75; operating rm. nurse Mass. Eye & Ear, Boston, 1975; ICU nurse Peter Bent Brigham Hosp., Boston, 1975-76; surg. nurse practitioner Kingsbrook Jewish Hosp., Bklyn., 1976-79; nurse anesthetist student Metropolitan Hosp., 1979—81; cert. registered nurse anesthetist Brookdale Hosp., Bklyn., 1981-92, Winthrop U. Hosp., Mineola, N.Y., 1992-94; adj. prof. Adelphi U., Garden City, N.Y., 1995-99; adj. prof. nursing N.Y. Inst. Tech., Old Westbury, 1998-99; clin. supr. Midtown Ctr. Complementary Care, NYC, 1999-2000; clin specialist St. Francis Hosp., Roslyn, N.Y., 2000-01; assoc. prof. nursing Adelphi U., 2001—. Bd. officer Manhasset Newcomers, N.Y., 1988-90; bd. dirs. Friends of Manhasset Libr., N.Y., 1990-94; mem. Make a Wish Found., Port Washington, N.Y., 1990—. Lt. U.S. Army, 1970-74. Mem.: ANA, Nat. Assn. U. Women, Nat. Assn. for Holistic Nurses, Nat. Assn. Homeopathy, Noetic Soc., Sch. Cmty. Assn., Am. Assn. Nurse Anesthetists, Sigma Theta Tau. Avocations: skiing, sailing, dance. Office Phone: 516-877-4515. Personal E-mail: doclsg@aol.com. Business E-Mail: greenfi2@adelphi.edu.

GREENFIELD, LUCILLE JEAN, music educator, composer; b. NYC, Feb. 24, 1929; d. William Horace and Minnie Greenfield. BS in Music, Columbia U., NYC, 1959. Music tchr. Ctrl. Park Sch., NYC, 1964—81, East Manhattan Sch. for Bright and Gifted Children, NYC, 1981—89. Composer: (symphony) 20th Century Wars, 1998, Catch a Falling Star, 1989, various scores for musicals. Recipient awards for musical shows, ASCAP, 1978—2007. Mem.: Composers Authors and Artists Am. (sec. 1999—2000, pres. 2000—01). Avocation: working with animals. Home: 338 W 15th St Apt 1 New York NY 10011-5901 Home Phone: 212-243-0122.

GREENFIELD, NORMAN SAMUEL, psychologist, educator; b. NYC, June 2, 1923; s. Max and Dorothy (Hertz) G.; m. Marjorie Hanson Klein, May 17, 1969; children— Ellen Beth, Jennifer Ann, Susan Emery. BA, NYU, 1948; MA, U. Calif., Berkeley, 1951, PhD, 1953. Fellow med. psychology Langley Porter Clinic, U. Calif. Med. Center, 1949-50; VA Mental Health Clinic trainee San Francisco, 1950-53; instr. clin. psychology U. Oreg. Med. Sch., 1953-54; from asst. prof. to prof. psychiatry U. Wis. Med. Sch., Madison, 1954—2005, emeritus prof. psychiatry, 2006—; assoc. dir. Wis. Psychiat. Inst., U. Wis. Ctr. for Health Scis., 1961-74. Emeritus prof. psychiatry, 1991—. Co-editor: The New Hospital Psychiatry, Handbook of Psychophysiology, Psychoanalysis and Current Biological Thought; contbr. articles to profl. jours. Served with USAAF, 1943-46. Mem. AAUP, Am. Psychol. Assn., Soc. Psychophysiol. Rsch., Am. Psychosomatic Soc. Office: U Wis Psychiat Inst 6001 Research Park Blvd Madison WI 53719-1176 E-mail: ngreen5921@aol.com.

GREENFIELD, ROBERT KAUFFMAN, retired lawyer; b. Phila., Mar. 30, 1915; s. William I. and Bertha (Kauffman) G.; m. Louise Rose Stern, June 20, 1937; children: Linda Greenfield Baldwin, Mary Greenfield Davenport, William Stern, James Robert. AB, Swarthmore Coll., 1936; JD, Harvard U., 1939; LHD (hon.), Pa. Coll. Podiatric Medicine, 1990. Bar: Pa. 1939. Pvt. practice, Phila., 1939-87; with firm Goodis, Greenfield, Henry & Edelstein (and predecessors), 1939-77; of counsel Montgomery, McCracken, Walker & Rhoads, 1977-87; ret. Chmn. bd. Phila. Theatre Co., 1983-85. Bd. dirs. Conv. and Tourist Bur., Phila., 1942-84; commr., v.p. Phila. Fellowship Commn., 1965-74; pres. Jewish Comty. Rels. Coun., 1962-65; chmn. bd. Moss Rehab. Hosp., 1974-77; pres. Alexis Rosenberg Found., 1983-91; fin. chmn. Inst. Contemporary Art, 1974-83; exec. com. Coun. Performing Arts, 1964-70; v.p. Nat. Comty. Rels. Adv. Coun., 1965-68; pres. Phila. chpt. Am. Jewish Com., 1966-68; trustee Pa. Coll. Podiatric Medicine, 1967-91, chmn., 1989-90; pres. Greenfield Found., 1991-05; dir. Asolo Theatre Co. , 1997-02, v.p. 1999-01; trustee Asolo Endowment Fund, 2003-06, Hermitage Artist Retreat, 2004—. Mem. Landings Racquet Club (pres. 1994-96), Phi Beta Kappa. Home: 1650 Landings Blvd Sarasota FL 34231-3223 Personal E-mail: rkg1650@comcast.net.

GREENFIELD, SARAH, photo editor; Studio mgr. Kenji Toma Studio; photo editor CITY Mag., NYC, 2006—. Recipient Nat. Mag. award for Photo Portfolio, CITY Mag., Am. Soc. Mag Editors, 2007. Office: CITY Mag 151 Mercer St New York NY 10012 Office Phone: 212-965-9484. Office Fax: 212-966-3329.*

GREENFIELD, VAL SHEA, ophthalmologist; b. NYC, Apr. 20, 1932; s. Frank Lynne and Helen (Meyers) G. Student, Brown U., 1948-49, 50-51, St. John's U., 1949; BA cum laude, Bklyn. Coll., 1952; MD, Yale U., 1956. Diplomate Am. Bd. Ophthalmology. Intern Walter Reed Army Hosp., Washington, 1956-57; asst. chief U.S. Army Dispensary, Phila., 1957-59, chief, 1959-60; postgrad. preceptorship in ophthal. under co-chief ophthal. Presbyn.-U. Pa. Med. Ctr., Phila., 1963-66; practice medicine specializing in obstetrics Phila., Riveride, NJ, 1960-63; practice medicine specializing in ophthalmology Phila., 1966—. Assoc. dir., lectr. in neuro-ophthalmology Hahnemann U., Phila., 1978—, from asst. prof. to assoc. prof. ophthalmology Sch. Medicine, 1977-88; assoc. clin. prof. Robert Wood Johnson Med. Sch.-N.J. U. Medicine and Dentistry, 1988—; attending surgeon in ophthalmology Frankford and Rolling Hills Hosps., Phila., 1970—; lectr. Bibl. topics U.S., Israel, Europe, New Zealand, USSR; guest speaker TV stas. and clubs; speaker, Gideons Internat. Gospel Soc. Internat., 2001. Contbr. articles to profl. jours., chpts. to textbooks. Mem. bd. deacons Cmty. Ch., Mt. Laurel Chapel and Fellowship, 1970—; bd. dirs. Hebrew Christian Outreach of Ch. of Our Lord Jesus Christ, 1958—; v.p. NJ MOorestown Camp of Gideons Internat. Bible Distbn. and Lectr. Soc., 2004—; spkr. ann. meeting G.I. Gospel Soc. Internat., 2001; trustee The Delaware Valley Pa. Vision Rsch. Charitable Trust, Cornell Inst. for Med. Rsch., Red Cross, Fedn. Allied Jewish Appeal, 2003—. Served to capt. M.C., U.S. Army, 1955-60. Inducted into Chapel of 4 Chaplains, Temple U., 1981; inducted Hon. Brave Cherokee Indians by Chief Rising Sun, Chief and High Priest of N.Am. and S.Am. Indian Tribes and Couns., 1947; recipient AMA Physicians Recognition award in med. edn., tri-annually, 1974—. Fellow ACS, ACP, Am. Geriatrics Soc., Phila. Coll. Physicians; mem. AMA, Pa. Med. Soc., Phila. County Med. Soc., Am. Acad. Ophthalmology, N.Y. State Ophthal. Soc., Pa. Acad. Ophthalmology, Pan-Am. Soc. Ophthalmology, Soc. Contemporary Ophthalmology, Christian Med. Soc., Am. Soc. Cataract and Refracture Surgery, Internat. Platform Soc., Am. Judeo-Christian Fellowship, Alpha Kappa Kappa. Avocations: book collecting, bible lectures and writings. Home Phone: 856-234-7268; Office Phone: 856-234-7268. Personal E-mail: greenfieldv@aol.com. *In over fifty years of studying and applying the principles of medicine to my patients, I have seen the devastating toll that anger, hatred, fear, doubt, anguish, inordinate lust and jealousy have taken on men's and women's bodies and souls. I continually advise my patients that conventional medicines and therapies alone cannot heal or cure these "spiritual diseases". I add to my therapeutic armamentarium the concepts of the Ten Commandments and the Sermon on the Mount, which I suggest that my patients apply to their daily lives. The happiest moments in my professional life have been when I observe the salubrious effects that faith, hope and love have upon my patients' afflictions. Jesus, the Annointed One of God, prophetically called "The Mighty God, the Everlasting Father, the Prince of Peace", summed up His whole religion, which I heartily recommend to my patients, colleagues, friends, as well as to myself, as follows: "Thou shalt love The Lord thy God with all thy heart and with all thy soul and with all thy mind. Thou shalt love thy neighbor as thyself. On these two commandments hang all the law and Prophets." Unless mankind in general, and each and every man and woman in particular, appropriate and follow these commandments, then we will face the dire consequences that are already evolving worldwide: the scourges of war, pestilence and famine.*

GREENGARD, LESLIE F., mathematician, educator; b. London; BA in Math., Wesleyan U., 1979; MD, Yale U., 1987, PhD in Computer Sci., 1987. Assoc. rsch. scientist dept. computer sci. Yale U., 1987—89; asst. prof. math. NYU Courant Inst. Math. Scis., 1989—92, assoc. prof., 1992—95, prof., 1995—, dir., 2006—. CEO, chief tech. officer MadMax Optics, Hamden, Conn., 2001—04; mem. sci. adv. coun. UTEK Corpn. Contbr. articles to profl. jours.; mem. editl. bd.: Jour. Sci. Computing, Applied and Computational Harmonic Analysis, Computers and Math. with Applications. Recipient Nat. Rsch. Svc. award, Pub. Health Svc., 1979—86, Presdl. Young Investigator award, NSF, 1990, Leroy P. Steele prize, Am. Math. Soc., 2001; grantee Postdoctoral fellowship, NSF, 1987—89, Packard Foundation fellowship, 1990. Mem.: NAE, NAS, Am. Math. Soc., Soc. Indsl. and Applied Math. Office: Courant Inst NYU 251 Mercer St New York NY 10012

GREENGARD, PAUL, neuroscientist, educator; b. NYC, Dec. 11, 1925; married; 3 children. AB, Hamilton Coll., 1948; PhD, Johns Hopkins U., 1953. NSF fellow in neurochemistry U. London (Eng.)Inst. Psychiatry, 1953—54; Nat. Found. Infantile Paralysis fellow U. Cambridge (Eng.) Molteno Inst., 1954—55; Paraplegia Found. fellow Nat. Inst. Med. Rsch., England, 1955—56; fellow Nat. Inst. Neurological Diseases and Blindness, 1956—58; dir. biochemistry dept. Ciba-Geigy Rsch. Labs., 1958—67; prof. pharmacology and psychiatry Yale U. Sch. Medicine, New Haven, 1968—83; Andrew D. White prof.-at-large Cornell U., Ithaca, NY, 1981—87; Vincent Astor prof., dept. Neuroscience Rockefeller U., NYC, 1983—. Vis. scientist Nat. Heart Inst., 1958—59; vis. assoc. prof. Albert Einstein Coll. Medicine, 1961—68, vis. prof., 1968—83, Vanderbilt U., 1967—68; Harvey Soc. lectr., 1980; lectr. in field. Recipient Dickson prize and medal in medicine, U. Pitts., 1977, Ciba-Geigy Drew award, 1979, Biol. and Med. Scis. award, N.Y. Acad. Scis., 1980, 3M Life Scis. award, Fedn. Am. Socs. Exptl. Biology, 1987, Bristol-Myers award for disting. achievement in neurosci. rsch., 1989, Goodman and Gilman award in receptor pharmacology, 1992, Karl Spencer Lashley prize, Am. Philos. Soc., 1993, Biochem. Soc. Thudichum medal, 1996, Charles A. Dana Found. award for pioneering achievements in health, 1997, Met. Life Found. award for excellence in sci. and tech., 1999, Nobel prize in physiology or medicine, 2000. Mem.: NAS (award in neurosci. 1991), Nat. Alliance for Rsch. on Schizophrenia and Depression (Lieber prize Outstanding Achievement Schizophrenia Rsch. 1996), Soc. for Neurosci. (Grass lectr. 1986, Gerard prize 1994), Am. Acad. Arts and Scis., Am. Neurol. Assn. (hon.). Office: Rockefeller U 1230 York Ave New York NY 10021-6399

GREENGRASS, PAUL, film director; b. Cheam Surrey, Eng., Aug. 13, 1955; Attended, Cambridge U. Dir., writer: (TV films) Open Fire, 1994; The One That Got Away, 1996; The Fix, 1997; The Murder of Stephen Lawrence, 1999; Bloody Sunday, 2002; writer, prodr. Omagh, 2004; dir.: (films) Resurrected, 1989, The Theory of Flight, 1998, The Bourne Supremacy, 2004, The Bourne Ultimatum, 2007; writer, dir. (films) United 93, 2006 (Best Dir., LA Film Critics Assn., 2006, Best Picture of the Yr., NY Film Critics Circle award, 2006, Best Director, Nat. Soc. Film Critics, 2007, David Lean award for Achievement in Direction, Brit. Acad. Film and TV Arts, 2007); dir.: (TV films) When the Lies Run Out, 1993; (TV series) Kavanagh QC, 1995—2001; co-author: (book) Spycatcher, 1988.*

GREENGUS, SAMUEL, academic administrator, theology studies educator; b. Chgo., Mar. 11, 1936; s. Eugene and Thelma (Romirowsky) G.; m. Lesha Bellows, Apr. 30, 1957; children: Deana, Rachel, Judith. Student, Hebrew Theol. Coll., Chgo., 1950-58; MA, U. Chgo., 1959, PhD, 1963. Prof. semitic langs. Hebrew Union Coll.-Jewish Inst. Religion, Cin., 1963-89, Julian Morgenstern prof. bible and near eastern lit., 1989—, dean rabbinic sch., 1979-84, dean Cin. campus, 1985-87, dean sch. grad. studies, 1985-90, dean faculty, 1987-98, v.p. for Acad. affairs, 1990-96. Vis. lectr. U. of Dayton, Ohio, 1964-69, Leo Baeck Coll., London, 1976-77; area supr. Tel Gezer Excavation, Israel, 1966-67; mem. bd. editors Hebrew Union Coll. Ann. Author: Old Babylonian Tablets from Ishchali and Vicinity, 1979, Studies in Ishchali Documents, 1986; mem. bd. editors Zeitschrift fur Altorientalische und Biblische Rechtsgeschichte; contbr. articles to profl. jours. Mem. Cin. Community Hebrew Schs. Bd., 1970-75; mem. vis. com. Sch. for Creative and Performing Arts, Cin., 1980-82; chmn. acad. officers, Greater Cin. Consortium Colls. and Univs., 1984-85, mem. exec. com., 1989-96. Am. Council Learned Socs. fellow, 1970-71, Am. Assn. Theol. Schs. fellow, 1976-77. Mem. Am. Oriental Soc., Assn. Jewish Studies, Soc. Bibl. Lit., Phi Beta Kappa. Jewish. Office: Hebrew Union Coll Jewish Inst Religion 3101 Clifton Ave Cincinnati OH 45220-2404 Home Phone: 513-281-4567; Office Phone: 513-221-1875. Business E-Mail: sgreengus@huc.edu.

GREENHALGH, PAUL, academic administrator; b. Bolton, Eng. Degree, U. Reading, 1978; M in Art History, specializing in design, Courtauld Inst. Art, 1980. Tutor Royal Coll. of Art; head art history Camberwell Coll. of Arts, London; dep. keeper of ceramics and glass Victoria and Albert Mus., London, head of rsch.; pres. Nova Scotia Coll. Art and Design, 2001—05; dir. & pres. Corcoran Gallery of Art and Coll. of Art and Design, Washington, 2006—. Chief organizer, Art Nouveau exhbn. Nat. Gallery Art, Washington, 2000. Author: Ephemeral Visitas, 1988, Modernism in Design, 1990, Quotations and Sources on Design and Decorative Arts 1800-1990, 1994, The Essential Art Nouveau, 2000, Art Nouveau 1890-1914, 2000, The Persistence of Craft, 2002, The Modern Ideal: The Rise and Collapse of Idealism in the Visual Arts from the Enlightenment to Postmodernism, 2005. Avocation: collecting ceramics. Office: Corcoran Coll Art and Design 500 17th St NW Washington DC 20006-4804*

GREENHAW, (HAROLD) WAYNE, writer; b. Sheffield, Ala., Feb. 17, 1940; s. Harold and Myrtie Lee Greenhaw; m. Sally Maddox, Aug. 26, 1972. BS in English, U. of Ala., 1966; Nieman Fellowship, Harvard U., 1973. Editor, pub. Ala. Mag., Montgomery, 1982—86; dir. State Bur. of Tourism, Montgomery, Ala., 1993—94. Author: (novels) The Golfer, 1968 (Hector award for Outstanding Journalism, 1990), King of Country, 1994, Beyond the Night: A Remembrance, 1999, The Long Journey, 2002, (non-fiction) The Making of a Hero: Lt. William Calley and the My Lai Massacre, 1971, Watch out for George Wallace, 1976, Elephants in the Cottonfields: Ronald Reagan and the New Republican South, 1982, Flying High: Inside Big-Time Drug Smuggling, 1984, Alabama on my Mind, 1987, Alabama: A State of Mind, 2000, My Heart is in the Earth: True Stories of Alabama and Mexico, 2001, Montogomery: The River City, 2002, The Thunder of Angels: The Montgomery Bus Boycott and the People Who Broke the Back of Jim Crow, 2005, (fiction collections) Tombigbee and Other Stories, 1991, The Spider's Web: A Novella and Other Stories, 2003, (plays) Rose: A Southern Lady; The Spirit Tree, (screenplay) The Long Journey; co-author (with Kathy Holland): (non-fiction) Montgomery: Center Stage in the South, 1990. Sec. Ala. Humanities Found., Birmingham, 2000—03. Named Travel Writer of the Yr., Southern Tourism Soc., 1995; recipient Harper Lee award, 2006. Mem.: Author's Guild. Democrat. Avocation: traveling to Mexico. Home: San Miguel de Allende Mexico Office: PR Assocs Inc PO Drawer 6161 Montgomery AL 36106 Home Phone: 334-265-7154. Personal E-mail: wgreenhaw@mindspring.com.

GREENHILL, JOE ROBERT, retired judge, lawyer; b. Houston, July 14, 1914; s. Joe R. Jr. and Violet (Stanuell) G.; m. Martha Shuford, June 15, 1940; children: Joe IV, William D. BBA, BA, U. Tex., 1936, LLB, 1939; LLD (hon.), So. Meth. U., 1977. Briefing atty. for chief justice Alexander Tex. Supreme Ct., Austin, 1941, 46; 1st asst. atty. gen. Tex. Austin, 1947-50; co-founder Graves, Dougherty & Greenhill, Austin, 1950-57; justice Supreme Ct. of Tex., Austin, 1957-72, chief justice, 1972-82; of counsel Baker & Botts, Austin, 1982—. Co-incorporator Tex. Ctr. for Professionalism and Ethics, Austin, 1991—; pres. elect Conf. Chief Justices and Nat. Ctr. for State Courts, Williamsburg, Va., 1982. Editor Tex. Law Rev., 1937-39 (Outstanding Ex-Editor 1975). Lt. USNR, 1942-46, PTO. Named Disting. Alumnus U. Tex., 1974, Disting. Alumnus U. Tex. Law Sch., 1977, Disting. Alumnus U. Tex. Coll. Bus. Adminstrn., 1974. Fellow Tex. Bar Found. (life, Outstanding 50 yr. lawyer 1989, exec. dir. 1984—), Am. Bar Found. (life); mem. Masons (33 degree). Office: Baker & Botts 98 San Jacinto Blvd Ste 1600 Austin TX 78701-4078

GREENHILL, ROBERT FOSTER, investment banker; b. Mpls., June 20, 1936; s. J. Raymond and Mary (Foster) G.; m. Mary Gayle Gussett, Sept. 13, 1958; children: Sarah B., Robert Foster, Mary B. AB, Yale U., 1958; MBA, Harvard U., 1962. Assoc. Morgan Stanley & Co., Inc., NYC, 1962-70, mng. dir., 1970-93, pres., 1991-93; chmn., CEO Smith Barney Shearson, Inc., NYC, 1993-96, Greenhill & Co., LLC, NYC, 1996—. Trustee Am. Enterprise Inst. Served to lt. (j.g.) USNR, 1960-62. Mem. Ausable Club (Keene Valley, N.Y.), Field Club, Links Club, River Club. Clubs: Ausable (Keene Valley, N.Y.); Field (Greenwich); Links; River (N.Y.C.). Office: Greenhill & Co LLC 300 Park Ave New York NY 10022 Office Phone: 212-389-1510.

GREENHOUSE, LINDA JOYCE, journalist; b. NYC, Jan. 9, 1947; d. Herman Robert and Dorothy Eleanor (Greenlick) Greenhouse; m. Eugene R. Fidell, Jan. 1, 1981; 1 child, Hannah Margalit Fidell. BA, Radcliffe Coll., 1968; M of Studies in Law, Yale U., 1978; DHL (hon.), Brown U., 1991, Binghamton U., 2006; LLD (hon.) (hon.), Colgate U., 1993, Northeastern U., 1997, CUNY, 1997; LLD (hon.), U. Miami, 2004, Georgetown U., 2004, Skidmore Coll., 2007. Asst. to James Reston The N.Y. Times, NYC, 1968—69, met. reporter, 1970—74, state polit. reporter, 1974—77, supreme ct. corr. Washington, 1978—85, 1988—, congl. corr., 1986—88. Author: Becoming Justice Blackmun: Harry Blackmun's Supreme Court Journey, 2005. Adv. com. Schlesinger Libr. on the History of Women in Am., Radcliffe Coll., 1995—2002; mem. Schlesinger Libr. Coun., 2003—; bd. dirs. Yale Law Sch. Fund, New Haven, 1984—91. Recipient Pulitzer prize in journalism for beat reporting, 1998, Carey McWilliams award, Am. Polit. Sci. Assn., 2002, Henry J. Friendly medal, Am. Law Inst., 2002, Golden Pen award, Legal Writing Inst., 2002, Goldsmith Career award, John F. Kennedy Sch. Govt., Harvard U., 2004, Pres.'s Spl. award, N.Y. Women's Bar Assn., 2004, John Chancellor award for excellence in journalism, 2004, Anvil of Freedom award, Estlow Internat. Ctr. for Journalism and New Media, U. Denver, 2005, William Green award Profl. Excellence, U. Richmond Law Sch., 2005, medal of distinction, Barnard Coll., 2006, medal, Radcliffe Inst., 2006. Fellow: Am. Acad. Arts and Scis. (mem. coun. 2004—); mem.: Women's Forum of Washington (v.p. 2003—05), Yale Law Assn. (exec. com. 1993—97), Am. Law Inst. (hon.), Am. Philos. Soc., Harvard Club of Washington (bd. dirs. 1989—92), Phi Beta Kappa (vis. scholar 2004—06). Office: The NY Times 1627 I St NW Washington DC 20006-4007 Home Phone: 301-229-1684; Office Phone: 202-862-0371. Business E-Mail: ligree@nytimes.com.

GREENHUT, MELVIN LEONARD, economist, educator; b. NYC, Mar. 10, 1921; s. Ab and Lillian (Frudman) G.; m. Elmara Margaret Griffith, Mar. 24, 1944; children: Margaret Lee, Pamela Jo, John Griffith, Patricia Lynn. PhD, Washington U., 1951. Prof. econ. various univ., 1948-62; prof., head dept. econ. Tex. A&M U., Coll. Sta., 1966-69, disting. prof. econ., 1969—, alumni disting. prof. econ., 1980-85, Abell Prof. Liberal Arts, disting. prof. econ., 1986—, Abell Prof. Liberal Arts, disting. prof. econ. emeritus, 1992—, chmn. disting. prof., 1988-89. Vis. prof., lectr. in field. Co-author (with John Greenhut): (book) Sci. and God, 2002, Our Teleological Econ. World, 2002; author: 19 books; contbr. articles to profl. jour. Mem. nat. econ. policy com. and econ. adv. coun. US C. of C., 1960-63. Maj. US Army. Mem. Am. Econ. Assn., So. Econ. Assn. (past v.p.), Regional Sci. Assn. (councillor), Royal Econ. Soc., Econometric Soc., Delta Chi, Omicron Delta Gamma. Lutheran. Home: 5814 Constellation Cir Rockwall TX 75032-5770 Office: Tex A&M U Dept Econs College Station TX 77843-0001

GREENLAND, LEO, advertising executive; b. NYC, Mar. 4, 1920; s. Jack and Ida (Abrams) G.; m. Rita Levine, June 29, 1955 (dec. Sept. 7, 1991); m. Eileen Ludwig, Feb. 2, 2004 children: Seth, Andrew. Student, New Sch. for Social Rsch., 1945—47. Pres. Sherwood Prodns., 1949-52; exec. various advt. agys., 1952-59; pres. Smith/Greenland Co., Inc., NYC, 1959—, chmn., CEO, 1974—. Guest lectr. Fordham U. Sch. Communication Arts, 1967-, Cornell Sch. Hotel Mgmt., NYU. Nat. commr. Anti-Defamation League, chmn. radio-TV dept.; bd. dirs., pres. Friars Found.; trustee ADL Found., hon. vice-chmn.; hon. chief N.Y.C. Fire Dept.; mem. adv. bd. bus. coun. UN; mem. Am. Forces Info. Svc. Task Force; bd. dirs. Nat. Libr. Mus., Phila., Am. Interfaith Inst. Served with AUS, 1943-46. Mem. Am. Advt. Agys. (bd. govs. N.Y.), Nat. Advt. Rev. Bd., Am. Mgmt. Assn. (lectr. 1969—), Am. Arbitration Assn., Nat. Businessmen's Coun., Fgn. Policy Assn. Interracial Businessmen's Coun., Ea. Frosted Foods Assn. (pres. 1965-67, bd. dirs.), Chief Execs. Orgn., Met. Pres. Orgn., Sales

Execs. Club N.Y., Newcomer Soc. N.Am., Def. Orientation Conf. Assn., Am. Forces Info. Svc. Task Force, Young Presidents Orgn., World Bus. Coun., Sierra Club, Econs. Club, Gilda's Club (founding mem.), Rockrimmon Country Club, Friars Club (pres. found.), Palm Beach Round Table. Home: PO Box 806 Bedford NY 10506-806 Office: Smith/Greenland Inc 1056 5th Ave # 10A New York NY 10028-0112 Office Phone: 646-672-9233. Personal E-mail: leobald@aol.com.

GREENLAW, MARILYN JEAN, retired adult education educator; b. St. Petersburg, Fla., Apr. 1, 1941; d. Hinckley and Dorothy Rebecca (Ball) G. BA, Stetson U., 1962, MA, 1965; PhD, Mich. State U., 1970. Elem. tchr. Broward County schs., Ft. Lauderdale, Fla., 1962-64; ele. cons. Harper and Row Publs., Evanston, Ill., 1965-69; from asst. to assoc. prof. U. Ga., Athens, 1970-78; from assoc. to full prof. U. North Tex., Denton, 1978-87, regents prof., 1987—2005, ret., 2005. Cons. Scholastic Publs., N.Y.C., 1978-87, Houghton Mifflin Co., Boston, 1984-94, Tex. Instruments, Dallas, 1981-85, Coordinating Bd., Austin, Tex., 1987-91. Author: Ranch Dressing: The Story of Western Wear, 1993, Welcome to the Stock Show, 1997; co-author: Storybook Classrooms, 1985, Educating the Gifted, 1988; editor book rev. column Jour. Reading, 1981-84, The New Adv., 1987-94. Mem. Friends of the Denton Pub.Libr., 1984—, pres., 1995-97, 2001-, Keep Denton Beautiful, pres., 2003; bd. dirs. Denton Libr., 1992-97, chair, 1995-96. Recipient Arbuthnot award, 1992, Disting. Svc. award Tex. State Reading Assn., 1996, Pres.'s Coun. Disting. Svc. award U. North Tex., 1996. Mem.: ALA (com. chairperson 1984—85), Internat. Reading Assn. (com. chairperson 1980—90, Arbuthnot award 1992), Nat. Coun. Tchrs. of English (com. chairperson 1980—, Outstanding Leadership in Edn. award 1976), Kiwanis (pres. 2002—), Phi Kappa Phi (v.p. 1986—87), Phi Delta Kappa (pres. 1982—83, Outstanding Young Educator award 1981). Republican. Avocations: reading, gardening, photography. Home: 2600 Sheraton Rd Denton TX 76209-8620

GREENLEAF, JAMES FOWLER, biophysics educator; b. Salt Lake City, Feb. 10, 1942; s. Harold S. and Mildred (McCullough) G.; m. Suzanne Gruhlke, Aug. 20, 1977; children: William James, Stephanie. BS in Engring. Sci., U. Utah, 1964; MS, Purdue U., 1968; PhD, Purdue U. and Mayo Grad. Sch. Medicine, 1970. Rsch. technician Upper Air Rsch. Lab., Salt Lake City, 1962-64, Latter-day Saints Hosp., Salt Lake City, 1966; rsch. technician dept. physiology and biophysics Mayo Clinic, Rochester, Minn., 1967; predoctoral rsch. asst. dept. physiology and biophysics Mayo Grad. Sch. of Medicine and Purdue U., Rochester and W. Lafayette, Ind., 1969-70; postdoctoral rsch. asst. Mayo Grad. Sch. of Med., Rochester, 1970-72; rsch. assoc. Mayo Found., Rochester, Minn., 1973; instr. in physiology Mayo Med. Sch., Mayo Clinic, Rochester, 1973-74, asst. prof. physiology, 1974-77, asst. prof. biophysics and medicine, 1977-78, assoc. prof. biophysics and medicine, 1978-83, prof. biophysics and assos. prof. medicine, 1983—. Dir. Ultrasound Rsch. Lab., Mayo Clinic, Rochester, 1973—; assoc. cons. physiology and biophysics and cardiovascular diseases and medicine Mayo Found., Rochesterm 1973-74, cons. biodynamics rsch. unit, 1974—; cons. Cardiovascular Rsch. Lab., Mayo Clinic, 1983—; vis. prof. radiol. sci. U. Pa. Hosp., Phila., 1988-89. Editor: Computer Aided Tomography and Ultrasonics in Medicine, 1979, Acoustical Imaging, 1984, Tissue Characterization with Ultrasound, 1986; patentee in field. 1st lt. U.S. Army, 1970. Recipient Career Devel. award Nat. Heart, Lung, and Blood Inst., 1975-80, Rsch. Career Investigator award NIH, 1976-81; Career Investigator Rsch. fellow Am. Heart Assn., 1971-73. Fellow IEEE (Achievement award, 2003), Am. Inst. Ultrasound in Medicine (Joseph H. Holmes Pioneer award 1986, Willam F. Frey Meml. Lect. award, 1986); mem. Am. Physiol. Soc., Biomedecial Engring. Soc., Acoustical Soc. Am., Coun. on Circulation of the Am. Heart Assn., AAAS, Sigma Xi. Avocations: racquetball, skiing. Office: Mayo Clinic 200 1st St SW Rochester MN 55905-0002 Office Phone: 507-284-3703. Office Fax: 507-266-0361. E-mail: jfg@mayo.edu.

GREENLEAF, JOHN EDWARD, human research consultant; b. Joliet, Ill., Sept. 18, 1932; s. John Simon and Julia Clara (Flint) G.; m. Carol Lou Johnson, Aug. 28, 1960. MA, N.Mex. Highlands U., 1956; BA in Phys. Edn., U. Ill., 1955, MS, 1962, PhD in Physiology, 1963. Tchg. asst. N.Mex. Highlands U., Las Vegas, 1955-56; engring. draftsman Allis-Chalmers Mfg. Co., Springfield, Ill., 1956-57; tchg. asst. in phys. edn. U. Ill., Urbana, 1957-58, rsch. asst. in phys. edn., 1958-59, tchg. asst. in human anatomy and physiology, 1959-62; summer fellow NSF, 1962; pre-doctoral fellow NIH, 1962-63; rsch. physiologist Life Scis. Directorate, NASA, Ames Rsch. Ctr., Moffett Field, Calif., 1963—66; rsch. physiologist Space Scis. directorate NASA/Ames Rsch. Ctr., Moffett Field, Calif., 1967—2002; postdoctoral fellowship Karolinska Inst., Stockholm, 1966-67. Adj. prof. biology dept. San Francisco State U., 1988-2002; adj. prof. dept. exercise sci. U. Calif., Davis, 1996-01; adj. prof. dept. human performance San Jose State U., 2002—; Japan Soc. for Promotion of Sci. vis. prof. Kyoto Prefectural U. Medicine, 1997; mem. internat. adv. bd. Medicina Sportiva. Mem. editorial bd. Jour. Applied Physiology, 1989-99, Med. Sci. Sports Exercise, 2000-02; contbr. articles to profl. jours. Pub. dir. N.Mex. Highlands U. Found., 1999—. Served with U.S. Army, 1952-53. Recipient Disting. Alumni award N.Mex. Highlands U., 1990, Disting. Alumni award dept. molecular and integrative physiology U. Ill., 1998, Am. Coll. Sports Medicine Citation award, 1999, Water and Medicine prize Internat. Cannes and Nestle Water Inst., 2003; exch. fellow NAS, 1973-74, 77, 89, NIH, 1980; named to Springfield (Ill.) H.S. Hall of Fame, 2005. Fellow AIAA (assoc.), Am. Coll. Sports Medicine (trustee 1984-87), Aerospace Med. Assn. (Harold Ellingson award 1981-82, Eric Liljencrantz award 1990), NASA Ames Assn. (assoc.); mem. Am. Physiol. Soc. (mem. com. on coms. 1984-87, long range planning com. 1987-90, internat. physiol. com. 1997-00, environ. and exercise physiology sect. Honor award, 2004), Polish Soc. Sports Medicine (hon.), Shooting Sports Rsch. Coun. (internat. shooters devel. fund 1984), Sigma Xi. Achievements include patents in field. Home: 12391 Farr Ranch Ct Saratoga CA 95070-6527 Office Phone: 408-867-5680.

GREENLEAF, VIRGINIA M. See KOCH, VIRGINIA

GREENLEE, JIM MING, prosecutor; B in Engring., U. Miss., JD. Atty. Taylor and Whitwell, 1981—85; ptnr. Taylor, Jones, Alexander, Greenlee, Seale and Ryan, 1985—87; asst. US atty. (no. dist.) Miss. US Dept. Justice, 1987—2001, US atty. (no. dist.) Miss., 2001—. Office: US Attys Office 900 Jefferson Ave Oxford MS 38655 Office Phone: 662-234-3351.*

GREENLER, ROBERT GEORGE, physics professor, researcher; b. Kenton, Ohio, Oct. 24, 1929; s. Dallas George and Ruth Edna (Mallett) G.; m. Barbara Stacy, May 30, 1954; children: Leland S., Karen R., Robin A. BS in Physics, U. Rochester, 1951; PhD in Physics, Johns Hopkins U., 1957. Rsch. scientist Allis-Chalmers Mfg. Co., Milw., 1957-62; assoc. prof. physics U. Wis., Milw., 1962-67, prof., 1967-91, adj. prof., 1991-98, prof. emeritus, 1998—. Sr. vis. fellow U. East Anglia, Norwich, Eng., 1971-72; traveling lectr. Optical Soc. Am., 1973-74; lectr. Coop. Edn. Program, Malaysia, 1990-91; organizer pub. outreach program Sci. Bag; prodr. 25 ednl. videos; did field rsch. on optical atmospheric effects at U.S. Antarctic Rsch. Station, South Pole, 1976-77, 97-98, 98-99. Author: Rainbows, Halos and Glories, 1980, Chasing the Rainbow: Recurrences in the Life of a Scientist, 2000; contbr. 90 articles to profl. jours. Grantee, NSF, Petroleum Rsch. Fund, Am. Chem. Soc.; Sr. Fulbright scholar, Fritz Haber Inst. of Max Planck Soc., West Berlin, 1983. Fellow AAAS, Optical Soc. Am. (v.p. 1985, pres.-elect 1986, pres. 1987, 1st Esther Hoffman Beller award 1993); mem. Am. Assn. Physics Tchrs. (Milikan Lectr. award 1988). Achievements include research in surface science, infrared spectroscopy of absorbed molecules, meteorological optics, irridescent colors in biological systems. Home: 6225 Mineral Point Rd Apt 17 Madison WI 53705 Business E-Mail: greenler@uwm.edu.

GREENLEY, BEVERLY JANE, lawyer, educator; b. Cleve., Sept. 24, 1947; d. Gaylord H. and Joan C. G. BA, Principia Coll., 1969; JD, U. Mo., 1976; LLM, Washington U., 1981. Bar: Mo. 1976, Ill. 1977, U.S. Tax Ct. 1979. Ptnr. McCarter & Greenley, St. Louis, 1976—81, McCarter, Snyder & Greenley, St. Louis, 1981—85; assoc. prof. law Stetson U. Coll. Law, St. Petersburg, Fla., 1981—85; ptnr. Gage & Tucker, St. Louis, 1985—87, Husch, Eppenberger, Donohue, Cornfeld & Jenkins, St. Louis, 1987—90, McCarter & Greenley, LLC, St. Louis, 1990—. Estate planning lectr. for CLE programs, 1997—; estate planning expert witness, 2000—. Co-author: Missouri Lawyer's Guide, 1984. Mem. Bd. St. Louis Estate Planning Coun., 2007—. Mem.: Ill. Bar Assn., Mo. Bar Assn. Office: 1 Metropolitan Sq Ste 2100 Saint Louis MO 63102-2797 E-mail: bgreenley@mccartergreenley.com.

GREENLY, COLIN, artist; b. London, Jan. 21, 1928; came to U.S., 1939, naturalized, 1948; s. Arthur John and Caroline Matilda (Fantini) G.; m. Laurie Ann Zadek, May 8, 1976; 1 child, Katharine Lydia Caro Herman. AB, Harvard Coll., 1948; student, Columbia U. Sch. Painting and Sculpture, 1951-53; attended Grad. Sch. Fine Arts, Am. U., 1956. Dir. art Madeira Sch., Greenway, Va., 1955-68; Dana prof. fine arts Colgate U., 1972-73; vis. artist numerous colls., univs. One-man shows Corcoran Gallery of Art, Washington, 1968, Royal Marks Gallery, N.Y.C., 1968, 70, Everson Mus., Syracuse, N.Y., 1971, Andrew Dickson White Mus. (now Herbert F. Johnson Mus.), Cornell U., 1972, Picker Gallery, Colgate U., 1973, Finch Coll. Mus., N.Y.C., 1974; group shows include Mus. Modern Art, N.Y.C., 1953, 73, De Cordova Mus., Lincoln, Mass., 1965, Des Moines Art Ctr., 1967, Nat. Collection Fine Arts, Washington, 1968, Krannert Art Mus., Champaign, Ill., 1969, 74, Emmerich Gallery Downtown, N.Y.C., 1972, John Weber Gallery, N.Y.C., 1975, Whitney Mus. Am. Art, N.Y.C., 1978, N.Y. State Mus., Albany, 1981; represented in permanent collections Albright Knox Art Gallery, Buffalo, Corcoran Gallery Art, Des Moines Art Ctr., Everson Mus., High Mus. Art, Atlanta, Mus. Modern Art, N.Y.C., Phila. Mus. Art, Nat. Gallery Art, Washington, Nat. Collection Fine Arts (now Smithsonian Am. Art Mus.), Washington, Herbert F. Johnson Mus., Ithaca, N.Y.; restoration and contemporary adaptation of Hulse Barn, Campbell Hall, N.Y.; contbr. to World Trade Ctr. Site Meml. Competition, 2003; contbr. works of art, videos, photographs to CDROM Images of the Whole, 1998; contbr. articles to profl. jours. Ptnr. Leaning Post Prodns. Grantee Nat. Endowment for Arts, 1967, Com. for Visual Arts, 1974, Creative Artists Pub. Svc. Program, 1972, 78, N.Y. State Coun. on Arts, 1993; named winner nat. competition playground sculpture Art in Am. and Corcoran Gallery Sch. Art, 1967. Mem. Nat. Audobon Soc., Nature Conservancy, Wilderness Soc., Nat. Trust for Hist. Preservation, Sierra Club. Achievements include incorporating the characteristics of a circle and a square into a single image, thereby discovering an effective visual symbol for the concepts of transition and change, 1964; Intangible Sculpture. Address: 487 Hulsetown Rd Campbell Hall NY 10916-3201 Home Phone: 845-496-4709. Personal E-mail: greenly@leaningpost.com. *Developing one's abilities may require a measure of commitment and excellence, but committing excellence to indiscriminate ends is artless. The synthesis of life and art is art.*

GREENMAN, FREDERICK F., JR., lawyer; b. NYC, Feb. 22, 1933; s. Frederick F. and Mildred G.; m. Angela Lancieri; children: Paul Rudolph, Jodi La Bourene. BA, Harvard U., 1954, LLB, 1961, LLM, 1963. Bar: NY 1962. Assoc. Hays, Sklar & Herzberg, NYC, 1962—66; asst. U.S. atty. So. Dist. NY, 1966—69; assoc. Linden and Deutsch, 1969—70; ptnr. Deutsch Klagsbrun & Blasband (and predecessor firm), 1971—2001; lawyer pvt. practice, 2001—. Legal and investment advisor Am. Adoption Congress; bd. dirs., treas. Evan B. Donaldson Adoption Inst. Mem. Assn. Bar City of N.Y., N.Y. State Bar Assn. Jewish. Office: 21st Fl 641 Lexington Ave New York NY 10022-4503 Office Phone: 212-758-1158. E-mail: FFGreenman@aol.com.

GREENMAN, JANE FRIEDLIEB, lawyer, human resources executive; b. NYC, Sept. 9, 1950; d. Morton Jerome and Isabelle Irene (Bisgyer) F.; m. Charles P. Greenman, Nov. 23, 1975; children: Margot, Jaclyn, Danielle. BS, Cornell U., 1972; JD, NYU, 1975, LLM in Labor Law, 1981. Bar: NY 1976, NY 1986. Assoc. Wolf Haldenstein, NYC, 1975-79; faculty NYU Law Sch., 1979-81, Bklyn. Law Sch., 1981—82; assoc., counsel Hughes Hubbard & Reed, NYC, 1982-91, ptnr., chair employee benefits dept., 1991-96; v.p., dep. gen. coun. human resources Honeywell Internat., Inc., Morristown, NJ, 1996—2003; v.p. compensation, benefits and labor rels. Tyco Internat., NYC, 2003—. Adj. prof. Bklyn. Law Sch., 1982-92, 95, Hofstra U.; bd. dirs. Women's Fund of N.J., NYC Bound Outward. Mem. Religious Action Ctr. Commn. for Social Action. Mem. ABA, N.Y.C. Bar Assn., N.Y. State Bar Assn. Jewish. Office: Tyco International PO Box 5260 Princeton NJ 08543-5260 Personal E-mail: jgreenman@aol.com.

GREENMAN, JOSH, editor; Spl. asst. to dep. mayor for planning, ed. & cultural affairs, NYC, 2000—01; comm. advisor US Senator Joseph Lieberman, 2001—03, chief speechwriter, 2003—04; dir. strategy & comm. The Teaching Commn., NYC, 2004—06; opinion editor NY Daily News, NYC, 2006—. Office: The Teaching Commission Ste 6200 365 5th Ave New York NY 10016 also: NY Daily News 450 W 33rd St New York NY 10001-2681

GREENMAN, PAULA S., lawyer; b. Putnam, NY, 1951; BA cum laude, Yale U., 1972; JD, Boston Coll., 1976. Bar: Conn. 1976, N.Y. 1995. Atty. Skadden, Arps, Slate, Meagher & Flom LLP, NYC, ptnr., 2001—. Office: Skadden Arps Slate Meagher & Flom LLP Four Times Sq New York NY 10036

GREENMAN, STEVEN MARK, musician; b. Pitts., Dec. 11, 1966; s. Elliot Howard and Judith Rita Greenman. MusB in Violin Performance, Cleve. Inst. Music, 1989, M in Violin Performance, 1991. Internat. performer various, 1995—; violin soloist Cleve. Pops Orch., 1997—2005. Violin faculty KlezKanada, Lantier, Quebec, Canada, 1999—, Living Traditions, KlezKamp, Parksville, 1995, Parksville, 96, Parksville, 97, Cherry Hill, NJ, 2002, KlezFest, London, 2002, Yiddish Summer Weimar, Germany, 2005, 07, 10th Internat. Klezmer Festival Fuerth, Fuerth, Bavaria, Germany, 2007; Klezmer music storyteller Cleve. Orch. Ednl. Dept., 2001—. Exec. prodr., composer (studio recording) Stempenyu's Dream; musician: (studio recording) Budowitz - Mother Tongue; co-prodr. (studio recording) Khevrisa - European Klezmer Music, Smithsonian Folkways; performer: Ashkenaz: A Festival of New Yiddish Culture, 1995, 1997, 1999, 2002, 2004, Jewish Culture Festival in Krakow, 2001, 2002, 2005, 2006. Home: 818 S Green Rd Apt 4 South Euclid OH 44121 Home Fax: 216-382-5644. Personal E-mail: greenfidl@sbcglobal.net.

GREENOUGH, WILLIAM BATES, III, medical educator; b. Providence, Jan. 3, 1932; s. William Bates Jr. and Dorothy Garrison (Rand) G.; m. Jane Cheney Woodruff, Aug. 14, 1954 (dec. 1964); children: William Beckley, Kate, Thomas Clark, Elisabeth Bates; m. Quaneta Ahmed, 1965; 1 child, Zarin Farah Naz. BA magna cum laude, Amherst Coll., 1953; MD cum laude, Harvard U., 1957. Intern, asst. resident Columbia U. Coll. Physicians and Surgeons, NYC, 1957-59; sr. rsch. fellow Mary Imogene Bassett Hosp., Cooperstown, NY, 1959-61; sr. resident Peter Bent Brigham Hosp., Boston, 1961-62; staff assoc. Nat. Heart Inst. Cholera Rsch. Lab., Dhaka, Bangladesh, 1962-65; chief infectious diseases div. Johns Hopkins U. Sch. Medicine, Balt., 1970-76, dir. Robert Wood Johnson Clin. Scholars Program, 1974-77, prof. medicine, 1983—, prof. internat. health sch. pub. health, 1985—; dir. Internat. Ctr. for Diarrhoeal Disease Rsch., Dhaka, Bangladesh, 1979-85; mem. geriatric medicine div. Johns Hopkins U., 1985—. Mem. bacteriology and mycology study sect. NIH, 1972-76, chmn., 1974-76; ad hoc study group on enteric disease Walter Reed Army Inst. Rsch., 1975-77; pres. Bangladesh Info. Ctr., Washington, 1971-84; adv. coun. Bangladesh Found., Chgo., 1972; active Md. Gov.'s Commn. on Phys. Fitness and Marathon Commn., 1971-77; pres., chmn. bd., trustee Internat. Child Health Found., Columbia, Md., 1985-95, pres., 1998—; chmn. Internat. Ctr. for Diarrhoeal Disease Rsch., Bangladesh Endowment Fund, 1997—; cons. Cera Products Inc., 1993—, chmn. sci. adv. bd., 2002—; cons. in field. Editor Infection and Immunity, 1975-78, Topics in Infectious Disease, 1976—, Jour. Diarrhoeal Disease Rsch., 1983-85, 93-2000; internat. adv. Kuwait Med. Jour., Jour. Health Population and Nutrition, 2000-; contbr. articles to profl. jours., chpts. to books Sr. surgeon USPHS, 1962-67. Recipient Internat. prize in medicine, King Faisal Found., 1984, Maurice Pate prize UNICEF, 1984, recognized for svc. to children, 1983; Howard Florey Meml. lectr. U. Adelaide, 2001, Paul G. Rogers Soc. Ambassador Global Health Rsch., 2006. Fellow: ACP, AAAS, Infectious Diseases Soc. Am. (mem. internat. affairs com. 2000—03); mem.: Bangladesh Med. Soc., Am. Soc. Microbiology, Bangladesh Assn. for Advancement Scis., Am. Geriatric Soc., Am. Soc. for Clin. Investigation, Assn. Am. Physicians. Muslim. Achievements include patents in field. Home: 1300 Hollins Ln Baltimore MD 21209-2237 Office: Johns Hopkins Geriatrics Ctr 5505 Hopkins Bayview Cir Baltimore MD 21224-6822 Office Phone: 410-550-0782. Personal E-mail: wgreenou@hotmail.com. *"Assuredly The Creation of The Heavens And The earth Is a greater matter Than The creation of man: Yet most men understand not.".*

GREENOUGH, WILLIAM TALLANT, psychobiologist, educator; b. Seattle, Oct. 11, 1944; s. Harrison and Maryon C. (Whitten) G.; 1 dau., Jennifer Anne. BA, U. Oreg., 1964; MA, UCLA, 1966, PhD, 1969. Instr. U. Ill., Urbana-Champaign, 1968-69, asst. prof., 1969-73, assoc. prof., 1973-77, chair neural and behavioral biology program, 1977-87, prof. psychology, psychiatry, cell and devel. biology, 1978—, dir. neurosci. program, 1999—2001, dir. Ctr. Advanced Study, 2000—; assoc. dir. Beckman Inst. for Advanced Sci. and Tech., 1987-91; prof. U. Ill. Ctr. Advanced Study, 1997—, Swanlund prof. psychology, psychiatry, cell and devel. biology, bioengineering, 1998—. Vis. prof. psychobiology U. Calif., Irvine, 1972; vis. prof. psychology U. Wash., 1975-76; program chmn. Winter Conf. on Brain Rsch., 1984-85, conf. chair, 1994-95; panel mem. integrative neural sys. NSF, 1987-91; dir. NSF Ctr. of Neurobiology of Learning and Memory, 1989-94; v.p., exec. com. Forum on Rsch. Mgmt., Fed. Behavioral, Psychol. and Cognitive Sci., 1991-93; mem. sci. adv. bd. Am. Psychol. Assn. Sci. Directorate; mem. NSF Biol. Sci. Directorate Adv. Com. Editor: (with R.N. Walsh) Environments as Therapy for Brain Dysfunction, 1976, (with J.M. Juraska) Developmental Neuropsychobiology, 1987; co-editor jour. Neurobiol. Learning and Memory, 1984-2004; contbr. numerous articles to profl. jour. Recipient William Rosen award for rsch. Nat. Fragile X Found., 1998; Cattell Found. fellow, 1975-76; USPHS and NSF grantee, 1969—; U. Ill. sr. scholar, 1985-88. Fellow AAAS (chair sect. I, Psychology 2001-02), Soc. for Rsch. into Child Devel. (disting. Sci. Contbn. award 2003, APA (Disting. Sci. Contbn. award 1999), Am. Psychol. Soc. (William James Fellow award 1998), Soc. Exptl. Psychology, Am. Acad. Arts & Sciences; mem. NAS, Soc. Neurosci. (councilor 1990-94, treas. 2003-05), Soc. Devel. Neurosci., Soc. Devel. Psychobiology (bd. dirs. 1977-80), Sigma Xi. Achievements include rsch. interests in morphological plasticity of cerebellum, experience and learning-based synapse formation, molecular mechanisms of mental retardation, and plasticity of glial cells. Office: U Ill Beckman Inst 405 N Mathews Ave Urbana IL 61801-2325 Office Phone: 217-333-4472. E-mail: wgreenou@uiuc.edu.

GREENSLADE, THOMAS BOARDMAN, JR., physics educator; b. Staten Island, NY, Dec. 23, 1937; s. Thomas Boardman and Mary (MacWilliam) G.; m. Sonia Catherina Burggraf, June 20, 1959; children: Thomas Boardman III, Russell M. BA in Physics, Amherst Coll., Mass., 1959; MS in Physics, Rutgers U., 1961, PhD in Physics, 1965. From instr. to assoc. prof. physics Kenyon Coll., Gambier, Ohio, 1964-88, prof. physics, 1988—. Lectr. in physics U. of the W.I., Jamaica, 1972-73; vis. assoc. prof. physics Kans. State U., Manhattan, 1985-86. Contbr. numerous articles to profl. jours. Mem. Am. Assn. Physics Tchrs. (Disting. Svc. citation 1988), Sigma Xi. Business E-Mail: greenslade@kenyon.edu.

GREENSPAN, ALAN, former Chairman of the Board of Governors of the Federal Reserve System, economist; b. NYC, Mar. 6, 1926; s. Herman Herbert Greenspan and Rose Goldsmith; m. Andrea Mitchell, Apr. 6, 1997. BS summa cum laude, NYU, 1948, MA, 1950, PhD, 1977; degree (hon.), Harvard U., Yale U., U. Notre Dame, Wake Forest U., Colgate U., U. Pa., U. Leuven, Belgium. Rsch. assoc. Nat. Indsl. Conf. Bd., NYC, 1948—53; pres., CEO Townsend-Greenspan & Co., Inc., NYC, 1954-74, 77-87; cons. Coun. Econ. Advisors, Exec. Office of the Pres., 1970-74, chmn., 1974-77; cons. Congressional Budget Office, 1977-87; chmn. bd. govs. Fed. Res. Sys., 1987—2006; spl. cons. Pacific Investment Mgmt. Co, Newport Beach, Calif., 2007—; sr. adv. Deutsche Bank AG, Frankfurt am Main, 2007—. Mem. Pres.'s Econ. Policy Adv. Bd., 1981-87; chmn. Nat. Commn. on Social Security Reform, 1981-83; mem. Task Force on Econ. Growth, 1969, Pres.'s Fgn. Intelligence Adv. Bd., 1983-85; commn. on an All-Vol. Armed Force, 1969-70; commn. on Fin. Structure and Regulation, 1970-71; sr. adv. panel on econ. activity Brookings Instn., 1970-74, 77-87; mem. bd. economists Time mag., 1971-74, 77-87, bd. dirs. Aluminum Co. of Am., Automatic Data Processing, Inc., Capital Cities/ABC, Inc., General Foods, Inc., J.P. Morgan & Co., Inc., Morgan Guarantee Trust Co. of N.Y., Mobil Corp., The Pittston Co.; bd. trustees, Rand Corp., chmn., Fed. Open Market Com., US alt. gov., IMF, 1987-2006 Author: The Age of Turbulence: Adventures in a New World, 2007. Bd. overseers Hoover Instn. on War, Revolution and Peace, 1973—74, 1977—87. Recipient John P. Madden medal, 1975, Pub. Svc. Achievement award, 1976, William Butler Meml. award, 1977, Comdr. Legion of Honor (France), 2000, Hon. Knight Comdr. of the British Empire, 2002, Gerald R. Ford medal for Disting. Pub. Svc., 2003, Presdl. Medal of Freedom, The White House, 2005. Fellow: Am. Statis. Assn., Nat. Assn. Bus. Economists (past pres.); mem.: Harmonie Club.*

GREENSPAN, DEBORAH, dental educator; BDS, U. London, 1960, BDS, 1964; LDS, Royal Coll. Surgeons, Eng., 1964; ScD (hon.), Georgetown U., 1990; DSc, U. London, 1991. Registered dental practioner, U.K.; diplomate Am. Bd. Oral Medicine. Vis. lectr. oral medicine U. Calif., San Francisco, 1976-83, asst. clin. prof., 1983-85, assoc. clin. prof., 1985-89, clin. prof., 1989-96, prof. clin. oral medicine, 1996—, interim chair dept. orofacial scis. Sch. Dentistry, 2004—, interim chair dept. orofacial scis., 2004—. Lectr. in oral biology, U. Calif., San Francisco, 1972, clin. dir. Oral AIDS Ctr., 1987—, active Sch. Dentistry coms. including admissions com., 1985—, chair task force on infection control, 1987—; cons. Joint FDI/WHO Working Group on AIDS, 1989—, EEC, 1990, WHO, 1990, 91, Dept. Health State Calif., 1991, others; ad hoc reviews Epidemiology and Disease Control Sect. Div. Rsch. Grants NIH, 1987—; mem. programs adv. com. Nat. Inst. Dental Rsch., 1989—, mem. spl. ad hoc tech. rev. panel, 1991, mem. panel Fed. Drug Adminstrn., 1991-94; other svc. to govtl. agys.; participant numerous sci. and profl. workshops, meetings, and continuing edn. courses, numerous radio, TV, and press interviews concerning AIDS and infection control in dentistry. Author: (with J.S. Greenspan, Pindborg, and Schiødt), AIDS and the Dental Team, 1986 (transl. German, French, Italian, Spanish, Japanese), AIDS and the Mouth, 1990, (with others) San Francisco General Hospital AIDS Knowledge Base, 1986, Dermatologic Clinics, 5th edit., 1987, Infectious Disease

Clinics of North America, 2nd. edit., 1988, Oral Manifestations of AIDS, 1988, Contemporary Periodontics, 1989, Opportunistic Infections in AIDS Patients, 1990, AIDS Clinical Review, 1990, Oral Manifestations of Systemic Disease, 1990, others; mem. editl. bd. rev. Jour. Am. Coll. Dentists, 1991; mem. editl. bd. Oral Diseases, 1999; ad hoc referee Jour. Oral Pathology, 1983—, Cancer, 1985—, Jour. Acad. Gen. Dentistry, 1986—, European Jour. Cancer & Clin. Oncology, 1986, Archives of Dermatology, 1988—, Jour. AMA, 1988—, AIDS, 1991; contbr. numerous articles to profl. jours. Mem. dental subcom. of profl. edn. com. Calif. div. Am. Cancer Soc., 1982-90, profl. health care providers task force, 1991. Nat. Cancer Inst. fellow, 1978-79, Am. Coll. Dentists fellow, 1988; recipient Woman of Distinction award, London, 1986, Commendation cert. Asst. Sec. for Health, 1989; named Seymour J. Kreshover lectr. Nat. Inst. Dental Rsch., 1989, Hon. Lectr. United Med. and Dental Schs. of Guys and St. Thomas Hosps., U. London, 1991. Fellow AAAS, Royal Soc. Medicine, Royal Coll. Surgeons; mem. ADA (vis. lectr. speaker's bur. 1988—, cons. coun. on dental therapeutics 1988—, mem. coun. sci. affairs 1999—), Am. Assn. Dental Rsch. (session chair 1986-87, constitution com. 1988-91, chair 1990-91, pres. San Francisco sect. 1990—, treas. 1992—), Am. Acad. Oral Pathology, Am. Soc. Microbiology, Am. Assn. Women Dentists, Am. Acad. Oral Medicine, Am. Assn. Dental Schs., Internat. Assn. Dental Rsch. (pres. exptl. pathology group 1989-90, v.p. 2004-05, other coms. and offices), Internat. Assn. Oral Pathologists, Internat. Assn. for Dental Rsch. (v.p. 2005—), Internat. Dental Assn. for Dental Rsch. (pres.), Calif. Dental Assn., San Francisco Dental Soc., Internat. AIDS Soc., Inst. of Medicine. Achievements include rsch. on oral candidiasis in HIV infection, on HIV-associated salivary gland disease, on oral hairy leukoplakia, and on the prevalence of HIV-associated gingivitis and periodontitis in HIV-infected patients. Office: U Calif Sch Dentistry Dept Orofacial Scis S 612 513 Parnassus Ave Box 0422 San Francisco CA 94143-0422

GREENSPAN, FRANCIS S., physician; b. Perth Amboy, NJ, Mar. 16, 1920; s. Philip and Francis (Davidson) G.; m. Bonnie Jean Fisher, Oct. 25, 1945; children: Richard L., Robert H., Susan L. BA, Cornell U., 1940, MD, 1943. Diplomate Am. Bd. Internal Medicine. Mem. endocrinology staff U. Calif.-San Francisco; chief endocrinology Stanford (Calif.) Hosp., 1949-59; chief thyroid clinic U. Calif. Med. Ctr., San Francisco, 1959—, now clin. prof. medicine and radiology; practice medicine specializing in endocrinology San Francisco; chief of staff U. Calif. Hosps. and Clinics, San Francisco, 1976-78. Editor: Textbook of Endocrinology; contbr. articles to med. jours. Served with USNR, 1944-45. Mem. San Francisco Med. Soc., Calif. Med. Assn., AMA, Endocrine Soc., Am. Thyroid Assn., Western Soc. Clin. Rsch., Western Assn. Physicians, Calif. Acad. Medicine. Office: U Calif Med Ctr Ste 553 400 Parnassus Ave San Francisco CA 94143-1222 Home Phone: 415-751-7570; Office Phone: 415-353-2350. Business E-Mail: frankg@medicine.ucsf.edu.

GREENSPAN, HARVEY PHILIP, applied mathematician, educator; b. NYC, Feb. 22, 1933; s. Louis and Jessie (Scholnick) G.; m. Mirian Gordon, Sept. 6, 1953; children— Elizabeth, Judith. BS, CCNY, 1953; MS, Harvard U., 1954, PhD, 1956; D Tech. (hon.), Royal Inst. Tech., Stockholm, 1991. Asst. prof. applied math. Harvard, 1957-60; faculty MIT, Cambridge, 1960—, prof. applied math., 1964—2002, prof. emeritus, 2002—. Author: Theory of Rotating Fluids, 1968, Calculus: An Introduction to Applied Mathematics, 1973; editor: Studies in Applied Mathematics, 1969; patentee centrifugal spectrometer. Home: 15 Chatham Cir Brookline MA 02446-5410 Office: Mass Inst Tech 77 Massachusetts Ave Cambridge MA 02139-4301 Office Phone: 617-253-4982. Business E-Mail: hpg@math.mit.edu.

GREENSPAN, JAY SCOTT See **ALEXANDER, JASON**

GREENSPAN, JEFFREY DOV, lawyer; b. Chgo., July 19, 1954; s. Philip and Sylvia (Haberman) G.; m. Eleanor Helen Goldman, Aug. 28, 1983. BS in Econs., U. Ill., Urbana, 1976; JD, Ill. Inst. Tech., 1979. Bar: Ill. 1979, U.S. Dist. Ct. (no. dist.) Ill. 1979, U.S. Ct. Appeals (7th cir.) 1979. Atty. Govs. Office Consumer Svcs., Chgo., 1978-80; asst. pub. defender Cook County Pub. Defenders Office, Chgo., 1980-81; asst. corp. counsel Village of Skokie, Chgo., 1981-91; of counsel Fioretti & Des Jardins, Chgo., 1990-91; with Ancel, Glink, Diamond, Cope & Bush, P.C., Chgo., 1991-99, Fioretti & Des Jardins, Chgo., 1999-2001; gen. counsel, dir. land acquisition CorLands, Chgo., 2001—03; sr. project mgr. Trust Pub. Land, Chgo., 2003—. Sec., treas. Polit. Cons., Inc., Skokie, 1984-88. Author polit. computer software Master Campaigner, 1984. Mem. Niles (Ill.) Twp. Dem. Orgn., 1976—; chmn. Niles Twp. Com. on Youth, 1982-85, TRY-Citizens for Drug Awareness, Niles, 1983-84; mem. Centereast Bd. Authority, 1998—; bd. dirs. Niles Twp. H.S., 1999—. Mem. Chgo. Bar Assn. (chmn. devel. of law com. 1990-91, chmn. local govt. law com. 1992-93). Home: 9445 Keeler Ave Skokie IL 60076-1442 Office: Ste 815 53 E Jackson Chicago IL 60604 Office Phone: 312-427-1979. Business E-Mail: jeff.greenspan@tpl.org.

GREENSPAN, JOHN S., dental and medical educator, researcher, academic administrator; b. London, Jan. 7, 1938; came to U.S., 1976; s. Nathan and Jessie (Dion) G.; m. Deborah, Dec. 1962; children: Nicholas J., Louise C. BSC in Anatomy with 1st class honors, U. London, 1959, B in Dental Surgery, 1962, PhD in Exptl. Pathology, 1967; ScD (hon.), Georgetown U., 1990. Licentiate in dental surgery Royal Coll. of Surgeons of Eng. Asst. house surgeon in conservation and periodontology Royal Dental Hosp. London, 1962; asst. lectr. oral pathology Sch. of Dental Surgery Royal Dental Hosp. of London, U. London, 1963-65, lectr. oral pathology Sch. of Dental Surgery, 1965-68, sr. lectr. oral pathology Sch. of Dental Surgery, 1968-75; prof. oral biology and oral pathology Sch. of Dentisty, U. Calif., San Francisco, 1976—, vice chmn. dept. oral medicine and hosp. dentistry, 1977-82, chmn. div. oral biology, 1981-89, coord. basic scis., 1982-96; chmn. dept. stomatology Sch. of Dentistry, U. Calif., San Francisco, 1989—2000, dean rsch., 2001—; dir. AIDS Rsch. Inst. U. Calif., 2004—. Cons. oral pathology St. John's Hosp. and Inst. of Dermatology, London, 1973-76; cons. dental surgeon St. George's Hosp., 1972-76; prof. dept. pathology Sch. Medicine U. Calif., San Francisco, 1976—; dir. U. Calif. AIDS Specimen Bank, San Francisco, 1982—, U. Calif. Oral AIDS Ctr., San Francisco, 1987—; assoc. dir. dental clin. epidemiology program U. Calif., San Francisco, 1987-95; dir. U. Calif. AIDS Clin. Rsch. Ctr., San Francisco, 1992-2005; Burroughs Wellcome vis. prof. Royal Soc. Medicine, U.K., 1996-97; dir. UCSF Aids Rsch. Inst., 2004—; fellow Kings Coll., London, Eng., 2003; presenter, lectr. in field. Author: (with others) Opportunistic Infections in Patients with the Acquired Immunodeficiency Syndrome, 1989, Contemporary Periodontics, 1989, Gastroenterology Clinics of North America, 1988, Perspectives on Oral Manifestations of AIDS, 1988, AIDS: Pathogenesis and Treatment, 1988, others; contbr. articles to profl. jours.; editorial cons. Achives of Oral Biology, 1968—, Jour. of Calif. Dental Assn., 1980—; editoral adv. bd. Jour. of Dental Rsch., 1977—; editorial bd. AIDS Alert, 1987-89, Brit. Dental Jour., 1998—; sr. editor Oral Diseases, 1994-98. Rsch. grantee NIH-Nat. Inst. Dental Rsch., 1978-82, 86—, U. Calif. Task Force on AIDS, 1983—, rsch. com. Royal Dental Hosp., London, 1964-76, Med. Rsch. Coun. of U.K., 1974-77, chmn. U. Calif. San Francisco Acad. Senate, 1983-85; Nuffield dental scholar, 1958-59; fellow Am. Coll. Dentists, 1982—, AAAS, 1985—; recipient Seymour J. Kreshover Lecture award Nat. Inst. Dental Rsch., NIH, 1989, Rsch. in Oral Biology award Internat. Assn. Dental Rsch., 1992. Fellow: Royal Coll. Surgeons Faculty of Dental Surgery, Royal Coll. Pathologists; mem.: AAAS, ADA, King's Coll. London, Am. Assn. Pathologists, Calif. Soc. Oral Pathologists Histochem. Soc., Calif. Dental Assn., San Francisco Dental Soc., Internat. Assn. Oral Pathologists, Bay Area Tchrs. Oral Pathology, Am. Acad. Oral Pathology, Oral Pathology Soc. (U.K.), Pathological Soc. (U.K.), Royal Soc. Medicine (U.K.), Internat. Assn. Dental Rsch. (pres. 1996—97), Am. Assn. Dental Rsch. (pres. 1988—89), Inst. Medicine of Nat. Acad. Scis. Avocations: skiing, gardening, travel, wine. Office: U Calif PO Box 422 San Francisco CA 94143-0422 Office Phone: 415-476-2220. Business E-Mail: john.greenspan@ucsf.edu.

GREENSPAN, LEON JOSEPH, lawyer; b. Phila., Feb. 10, 1932; s. Joseph and Minerva (Podolsky) G.; m. Irene Gordon, Nov. 2, 1958; children: Marjorie, David, Michael, Lisa. AB, Temple U., 1955, JD, 1958. Bar: N.Y. 1959, N.J. 1985, Fla. 1985, Pa. 1986, Conn. 1991, U.S. Tax Ct. 1973, U.S. Supreme Ct. 1969. Pvt. practice law, White Plains, NY, 1959-64; ptnr. Greenspan and Aurnou, White Plains, 1964-77, Greenspan, Jaffe & Rosenblatt, White Plains, 1987-91, Greenspan & Greenspan, White Plains, 1992—. Counsel Brown, Boston; lectr. Fla. Bar CLER Program, 1991, 92, 99; atty. Tarrytown (N.Y.) Housing Authority. Pres. Hebrew Inst., White Plains; vice chmn. ann. dinner NCCJ. Recipient Pres.'s award Union Orthodox Synagogues, 1982, Owl Club award Temple Univ., 2001; honoree Hebrew Inst., White Plains, 1983. Mem. ABA, N.J. Bar Assn., Fla. Bar Assn., Westchester County Bar Assn. (mem. ethics com. 1995-), White Plains Bar Assn., N.Y. State Trial Lawyers Assn., Criminal Cts. Bar Assn. Westchester County, N.J. Bar Assn. Home: 14 Pinebrook Dr White Plains NY 10605-4713 Office: Greenspan & Greenspan 150 Grand St 6th Fl White Plains NY 10601-4400 Office Phone: 914-946-2500. Business E-Mail: leon@greenspans-law.com.

GREENSPAN, MICHAEL EVAN, lawyer; b. White Plains, NY, Jan. 18, 1967; s. Leon Joseph and Irene (Gordon) G.; m. Diane Gloria Blum, July 2, 1989; children: Daniel, Marc, Julia. BA magna cum laude, Temple U., 1988, JD, 1991. Bar: N.Y. 1992, U.S. Dist. Ct. (so. ea. dists.) N.Y. 1992, U.S. Dist. Ct. (dist Conn.), 1992, U.S. Ct. Appeals (2nd cir.) 1993, U.S. Ct. Appeals (11th cir.) 1996. Assoc. Greenspan, Jaffe & Rosenblatt, White Plains, 1991-92; ptnr. Greenspan & Greenspan, White Plains, 1992—. Mem. com. civil practice laws and rules State Bar N.Y.; Temple U. del. Symposium on the Presidency, Washington, 1987; CLE lectr. Nat. Bus. Inst., 2004-06. Mem. exec. com. Loucks Track & Field Games, White Plains, 1991—. Recipient award for excellence in Trial Advocacy, Barristers Soc., 1990, Love Meml. award, Pa. Trial Lawyers Assn., 1991, James J. Manderino award, Phila. Trial Lawyers Assn., 1991, Lewis F. Powell Jr. medallion, Am. Coll. Trial Lawyers Assn., 1991, Disting. Svc. award, County of Rockland, 2004, Cert. of Appreciation for Extraordinary Svc., NY State Trial Lawyers Assn., 2005. Mem.: White Plains Bar Assn., Westchester County Bar Assn., Assn. Trial Lawyers Am., NY State Trial Lawyers Assn., NY State Bar Assn. (Com. Civil Practice Law & Rules 1998—), Westchester, Rockland, Dutchess, Putnam Track & Field Coaches Assn. (gen. outside counsel 2005—), Westchester Track, Field & Cross-Country Ofcl. Assn., Glenn D. Loucks Mem.l Track & Field Games (exe. com. 1991—). Republican. Jewish. Avocations: officiating high school track and field, race walking, basketball. Office: Greenspan & Greenspan ste 605 150 Grand St White Plains NY 10601-4821 Home: 66 Long Meadow Dr New City NY 10956 Office Phone: 914-946-2500, 800-553-6009. Office Fax: 914-946-1432. E-mail: Mike@greenspans-law.com.

GREENSPAN-MARGOLIS, JUNE E., psychiatrist; b. NYC, June 28, 1934; d. Benjamin Robert and Theresa (Cooperstein) Edelman; divorced; 1 child, Alisa Greenspan; m. Gerald J. Margolis. AB, Bryn Mawr Coll., 1955; MD, Med. Coll. Pa., 1959; grad., Inst Phila Assn Psychoanalysis, Bala Cynwyd, 1975. Intern Albert Einstein Med. Ctr., Phila., 1959-60; pvt. practice medicine specializing in pediatrics Cinnaminson, N.J., 1961-67; psychiat. resident Hahnemann Med. Coll., Phila., 1967-71; practice medicine specializing in adult and child psychiatry, psychoanalysis Jenkintown, Pa., 1971—. Instr. U. Pa. Sch. Medicine, Phila., 1975—77, clin. assoc., 1977—81, clin. asst. prof., 1981—86, clin. assoc. prof., 1986—; tng. and supervisory analyst Psychoanalytic Ctr. Phila., 1986—. Fellow Am. Coll. Psychoanalysts, Am. Psychiat. Assn.; mem. AMA, Am. Psychoanalytic Assn. (cert. adult and child psychoanalysis), Am. Acad. Child Psychiatry, Ctr. for Advanced Psychoanalytic Studies (Princeton). Office: The Pavilion Ste 434 261 Old York Rd Jenkintown PA 19046 Office Phone: 215-887-5355.

GREENSPON, ROBERT ALAN, lawyer; b. Hartford, Conn., Apr. 17, 1947; s. George Arthur and Shirley Jean (Shelton) G.; m. Claire Alice Stone, Aug. 21, 1971; children: Colin Haynes, Alison Shelton. AB, Franklin and Marshall, 1969; JD, Columbia U., 1972. Bar: Conn. 1973, N.Y. 1998, U.S. Dist. Conn. 1973, U.S. Ct. Appeals (2d cir.) 1983. Assoc. Robinson & Cole, Hartford, Conn., 1972-78, ptnr., 1978-81, Stamford, Conn., 1981-86; sr. v.p., gen. counsel Guinness Peat Aviation Corp., Stamford, NYC, 1985-92, Shannon, Ireland, 1985—92; ptnr. Latham & Watkins, NYC, 1992—. Contbr. articles to profl. jours. Mem. ABA (comml. fin. services, aircraft fin.), Conn. Bar Assn., N.Y. State Bar Assn., Internat. Bar Assn., Southwestern Legal Found. (bd. advisors internat. and comparative law ctr.). Home: 49 Old Farm Rd Darien CT 06820-6119 Office: Latham & Watkins 885 3rd Ave New York NY 10022-4834 Home Phone: 203-655-8758; Office Phone: 212-906-1375. Business E-Mail: robert.greenspon@lw.com.

GREENSTEIN, ABRAHAM JACOB, mortgage company executive, accountant; b. Munich, Fed. Republic of Germany, May 5, 1949; arrived in US, 1950; s. Morris and Bella (Yeger) G.; m. Ruth Sanik, June 5, 1974; children: Pinchus, Yisroel, Shlomo. BS in Acctg., Bklyn. Coll., 1972. Sr. auditor State Comptrollers Office, NYC, 1972-75; asst. dir. Office of Spl. Dep. Comptroller, NYC, 1978-82; sr. v.p. fin. N.Y.C. Housing Devel. Corp., 1983-88, exec. v.p., 1988-98. Treas. Housing Assistance Corp., N.Y.C., 1985-98, Residential Mortgage Ins. Co., N.Y.C., 1993-98; exec. v.p., chief oper. officer Housing for N.Y. Corp., N.Y.C., 1986-93, pres., 1993-98; v.p. Greystone & Co., N.Y.C., 1998—. Trustee Congregation Chasdi Gur, Bklyn., 1982-87 Mem. Am. Mgmt. Assn., Govt. Fin. Officers Assn., Council of State Housing Agys., Mortgage Bankers Assn. Jewish. Avocations: swimming, tennis. Office: Greystone & Co 60th Fl 152 W 57th St Fl 60 New York NY 10019-3310 Office Phone: 212-649-9700. Business E-Mail: agreenspein@greyco.com.

GREENSTEIN, GARY, periodontist, dental educator; b. Nyc, Ny, Feb. 2, 1947; s. Sidney and Anne Greenstein; m. Helene Cohen, Nov. 13, 1951; children: Benjamin, Jaclyn, Michele. BA, Queens Coll., New York City, 1964—68; DDS, NYU Coll. of Dentistry, New York City, 1968—72; Periodontal Certification, Eastman Dental Ctr., Rochester, New York, 1978—80; MS, U. of Rochester, Rochester, New York, 1980—81. Periodontal Certification Eastman Dental Ctr., 1980, Board Diplomate Am. Acad. of Periodontology, 1993. Clin. prof., periodontology UMDNJ, Dept. of Periodontology, Newark, 1993—; pvt. practice Dr. Gary Greenstein, Freehold, NJ, 1983—; chief of periodontics Monmouth Med. Ctr., Long Branch, NJ, 1990—97. Cons. US Army Dental Corp, Ft. Gordon, Ga., 1988—; trustee Am. Acad. of Periodontology, Chgo., 1993—99, sci., rsch. and therapy com., 1992—2002. Author: (contributions to periodontal literature) 95 Publications, Jour. of Periodontology, Jour. of Am. Dental Assoc., Compendium of Continuing Ed. in Dentistry, Internat. Jour. of Restorative Dentistry and Periodontics. Maj. US Army, 1972—78, Kans., South Korea, New Jersey. Decorated Cert. of Achievement for Meritorious Svc. US Army, Army Commendation Medal; recipient Gies Award, Am. Acad. of Periodontology, 1997, Fellowship Award, 2000, Hirschfeld Meml. Award, NE Soc. of Periodontists, 2000. Mem.: NJ. Soc. of Periodontists (licentiate), NE Soc. of Periodontists (licentiate), ADA (licentiate), Am. Acad. of Periodontology (licentiate; trustee 1993—99). R-Consevative. Jewish. Achievements include research in Periodontal Therapy; Over 100 Guest Lectures. Avocations: tennis, rafting, mountain biking. Office: Dr Gary Greenstein 900 West Main Street Freehold NJ 07728 Office Phone: 732-780-1450. Personal E-mail: ggperio@aol.com.

GREENSTEIN, JEFFREY IAN, neurologist; b. Durban, South Africa, July 27, 1947; s. Joseph and Miriam (Shamos) G. MD, U. Cape Town, S. Africa, 1971. Diplomate Am. Bd. Neurology and Psychiatry. Asst. to assoc. prof. neurology Temple U. Sch. Med., Phila., 1983-89, prof., 1989—2002, chmn. neurology, 1989—2000; pres. Multiple Sclerosis Inst., 2002—. Chmn. dept. neurology Grad. Hosp., 2002—06; clin. prof. of neurology Drexel U. Sch. Medicine. Pres. Multiple Sclerosis Rsch. Inst., 2004—. Mem. AAAS, Am. Acad. Neurology, N.Y. Acad. Sci., Nat. Multiple Sclerosis Soc. (chmn. profl. adv. com. Phila. 1992-95, bd. of trustees, Del. Valley Chpt. 1996-). Office: Multiple Sclerosis Inst 1740 South St Ste 401 Philadelphia PA 19146-2246 Office Phone: 215-985-2256.

GREENSTEIN, JOEL SANDOR, industrial engineering educator; b. Chgo, May 7, 1952; s. Benjamin and Muriel Greenstein; m. Katherine Marie Lodenkamp, Sept. 1, 1982; children: Claire Elizabeth, Seth Michael, Paul David BS, U. Ill., 1973, PhD, 1979; MS, Stanford U., 1974. Asst. prof. indsl. engrng. and ops. rsch. Va. Poly. Inst. & State U., Blacksburg, 1979-85; assoc. prof. indsl. engrng. Clemson U., SC, 1985—. Contbr. articles in field to profl. jours. Mem. Am. Soc. Engrng. Edn., Assn. for Computing Machinery, Human Factors and Ergonomics Soc., Inst. Indsl. Engr., Usability Profl. Assn. Office: Clemson U Dept Indsl Engring Clemson SC 29634-0920 Office Phone: 864-656-5649. Business E-Mail: iejsg@clemson.edu.

GREENSTEIN, MERLE EDWARD, import/export company executive; b. Portland, Oreg., June 22, 1937; s. Sol and Tillie Germaine (Schnitzer) Greenstein; m. Nasi Jenab; children: Todd Aaron, Boback Emad, Lela Emad. BA, Reed Coll., 1959. Pres. Acme Trading and Supply Co., Portland, 1963—82; chmn. MMI Group, Portland, 1982—91, Internat. Devel. Assocs., Portland, 1991—, Kesef Devel., LLC. Com. mem. ISRI, Washington, 1987—89; dist. export coun. U.S. Dept. Commerce, 1980—; mem. 1st U.S. trade missions to Vietnam, 1996; Ariz. regional export coun. trade mission to Eastern Europe; bd. advisor Ruscan Diamond Internat., Toronto; advisor Sanhe Group, China. Chmn. fin. Portland Opera, 1966; bd. dirs. Met. YMCA, 1964—67; active Internat. Sculpture Invitational Bd.; del. to China State of Oreg. Ofcl. Trade Mission, 1979; chmn. Western Internat. Trade Group, 1981—82; fin. chmn. Anne Frank exhibit, Portland; joint chmn. State of Oreg. Youth Legislature; joint chmn. bldg. campaign Oreg. Mus. Sci. and Industry; treas. ASC; bd. dirs. Waverly Children's Home; property task force com., mem. capital campaign cabinet Oreg. Food Bank; bd. dirs. Metro Family Svc.; mem. Oreg. Mentoring Group; fin. chmn. return of Anne Frank exhibit, 2002; mem. devel. com. Alzheimer's Assn.; mem. scholarship com. Iranian Am. Profl. Assn. Oreg.; mem. Oreg. Uniting Group Discussions; bd. dirs. Oreg. Jewish Cmty. Found.; fin. chmn. Oreg. Holocaust; mem. steering com. Camp Rosenbaum; v.p. Oreg.-Fujian (China) Sister State Assn.; mem. State of Oreg. Legis. Fujian Com.; com. chmn. Oreg. Fujian Joint Econ. Com.; pres. Komak, Non-Profit Charity Corp.; campaign chair United Jewish Appeal; mem. Am. Jewish Com.; bd. dirs. Jewish Welfare Fedn. Named Citizen of the Week, City of Portland, 1953; recipient Pres.'s E for Export, U.S. Dept. Commerce, 1969, Maurice D. Sussman Meml. award, 2007; scholar, U. Chgo. Law Sch., 1959. Mem.: City Club, Multnomah Athletic Club Portland, Rolls Royce Owners Club (London), Shriners, Masons. Avocations: skiing, antique autos, Arabian horses. Personal E-mail: merlenasi@yahoo.com.

GREENSTEIN, RICHARD HENRY, lawyer; b. Newark, June 29, 1946; s. Jacob Harold and Florence G.; m. Irene Beth Polishuk, July 4, 1973; children: Suzanne Beth, Jonathan Henry. AB, Rutgers U., 1968; JD, Boston U., 1971. Bar: N.J. 1971, U.S. Dist. Ct. N.J. 1971, U.S. Supreme Ct. 1985. Law clk. Superior Ct. N.J., Elizabeth, 1971-72; asst. county prosecutor Union County Prosecutor, Elizabeth, 1972-74; assoc. atty. Mandel, Wysoker, Sherman, et al, Perth Amboy, N.J., 1974-77, Fox and Fox, Newark, 1977-83; ptnr. Kein, Pollatschek & Greenstein, Union, N.J., 1983—. Atty. Young Astronauts N.J. Inc., 1989—; mem. ethics com. Supreme Ct. Dist. N.J., 1991-95. Lighting dir. Wash. Sch. PTA Show, Westfield, N.J., 1985-94. Mem. Exchange Club Union (pres.-elect, dir. 1983—). Jewish. Avocations: skiing, hiking, reading. Home: 743 Saint Marks Ave Westfield NJ 07090-2035 Office: Kein Pollatschek & Greenstein 2042 Morris Ave Union NJ 07083-6028 Office Phone: 908-688-4400. E-mail: kdglaw.rhg@verizon.net.

GREENSTEIN, RUTH LOUISE, think-tank executive, lawyer; b. NYC, Mar. 28, 1946; d. Milton and Beatrice (Zutty) G.; m. David Seidman, May 19, 1972. BA, Harvard U., 1966; MA, Yale U., 1968; JD, George Washington U., 1980. Bar: D.C. 1980. Fgn. service info. officer USIA, Washington and Tehran, Iran, 1968-70; adminstrv. asst. Export-Import Bank U.S., Washington, 1971-72; asst. dean Woodrow Wilson Sch. Pub. and Internat. Affairs, Princeton U., 1972-75; budget examiner U.S. Office Mgmt. and Budget, Washington, 1975-79; budget coordinator U.S. Internat. Devel. Coop. Agy., 1979-81; dep. gen. counsel NSF, 1981-84; treas., then v.p. and gen. counsel Genex Corp., Gaithersburg, Md., 1984-90; v.p. fin. and adminstrn., gen. counsel Inst. for Def. Analyses, Alexandria, Va., 1990—. Mem. acad. adv. panel to tech. transfer intelligence com. CIA, 1983-90; mem. def. trade adv. group U.S. Dept. State, 1994-96; mem. com. for protection of human subjects ARC, 1996—; dir. VSA Arts, 1998—2005, PLATO Learning Inc., 2002—. Mem. NAS (panel on future design and implementation of nat. security export controls 1989-91), AAAS (com. on sci. freedom and responsibility 1987-93), D.C. Bar Assn. Home: 2737 Devonshire Pl NW Apt 511 Washington DC 20008-3458 Office: Inst for Def Analyses 4850 Mark Center Dr Alexandria VA 22311-1882 Business E-Mail: rgreenst@ida.org.

GREENSTEIN, STUART MARK, surgical educator; b. Bklyn., Feb. 16, 1955; s. Saul and Anne (Stillman) G.; m. Gayle Suzette Shulman (div. Jan. 1987); 1 child, Samuel; m. Sylvia Redner, July 2, 1989; children: Brian Liedman, Leah Chaya Ruth, Talia Miriam Rachel. BS, CUNY, 1976; MD, Harvard U., 1979. Diplomate Am. Bd. Surgeyy. Intern, instr. surgery NYU Med. Ctr., NYC, 1979-80; resident in surgery, clin. instr. U. Med. and Dentistry N.J., Newark, 1980-84; instr. vascular surgery Hosp. of U. Pa., Phila., 1984-85; clin. asst. instr. SUNY Downstate Med. Ctr., Bklyn., 1985-86; asst. prof. surgery Hahnemann U., Phila., 1986-88, Albert Einstein Coll. Medicine, Yeshiva U., Bronx, N.Y., 1988-93, assoc. prof. surgery, 1993—2002, prof. surgery, 2002—. Mem. staff Montefiore Med. Ctr., Bronx, 1988—. Contbr. articles to med. jours. Salk scholar CUNY, 1975. Fellow ACS (1st prize N.J. chpt. 1982, 2d prize 1983); mem. AAAS, Am. Soc. Transplant Surgeons, Transplantation Soc., N.Y. Acad. Scis. Democrat. Achievements include construction of a competent phonatory neoepiglottis using cervical skin flaps. Office: Montefiore Med Ctr 111 E 210th St Bronx NY 10467-2401 Office Phone: 718-920-8146. Business E-Mail: sgreenst@montefiore.org.

GREENSTONE, MICHAEL, economics professor, researcher; b. Chgo., Dec. 6, 1968; s. J. David and Joan Greenstone; m. Katherine Ozment, July 21, 2000; 1 child, William Pryor. BA, Swarthmore Coll., 1991; PhD, Princeton U., 1998. Robert Wood Johnson scholar U. Calif., Berkeley, 1998—2000; rsch. assoc. Nat. Bur. Econ. Rsch., Cambridge, 2000—; asst. prof. econ. U. Chgo., 2000—03; 3M prof. econ. MIT, Cambridge, Mass., 2003—. Mem. EPA Environ. Econ. Sci. Adv. Bd., Washington, 2003—. Avocations: basketball, hiking, jogging. Office: MIT Dept Econ E52-359 50 Meml Dr Cambridge MA 02142 Office Phone: 617-452-4127. Office Fax: 617-253-1330. E-mail: mgreenst@mit.edu.

GREENSTREET, ROBERT CHARLES, architect, educator; b. London, June 8, 1952; s. Joseph Philip Henry and Joan (Dean) G.; m. Karen Eloise Holland, Sept. 6, 1975. Diploma in architecture, Oxford Brookes U., 1976, PhD in Architecture, 1983. Registered architect, Eng. Vis. asst. prof. Kans. State U., 1978-79; asst. prof. U. Kans., 1979-80; vis. prof. Ball State U., Muncie, 1980-81; prof. U. Wis., 1981—, asst. vice chancellor, 1985-86, chmn. dept. architecture, 1986-90, dean Sch. Architecture and Urban Planning Milw., 1990-2000, dep. chancellor for campus and urban design, 2000—, interim chancellor, 2003—04; dir. planning and design City of Milw., 2004—. Author, co-author 7 books; contbr. more than 150 articles to profl. jours. Fellow Royal Soc. Arts; mem. AIA (assoc.), Royal Inst. Brit. Architects, Wis. Soc. Architects, Chartered Inst. Arbitrators; mem. Am. Arbitration Assn., Assn. Collegiate Schs. of Architecture (pres. 1995-96). Anglican. Office: U Wis Dept Architecture PO Box 413 Milwaukee WI 53201-0413

GREENTHAL, JILL A., investment banker; b. Milw. m. Tom Eisenmann; 2 children. Grad. mem. The Academy, Simmons Coll., 1978; MBA, Harvard Bus. Sch., 1983. Joined Salomon Smith Barney; assoc. Shearson Lehman Hutton (now Lehman Brothers), 1985; head media group Lehman Brothers, 1990—94; mng. dir. Media and Communications Investment Banking Group Donaldson, Lufkin and Jenrette, Boston, 1996; co-head Boston office, mem. exec. bd. investment banking Credit Suisse First Boston; sr. mng. dir. corp. advisory services Blackstone Group, 2003—. Bd. dirs. Martha Stewart Living Omnimedia Inc., NYC, 2006—. Mem. investment com. Noble and Greenough Sch. Office: Blackstone Group 345 Park Ave New York NY 10154

GREENWALD, ALFRED EMANUEL, retired cosmetic surgeon; b. New Brunswick, NJ, Feb. 25, 1920; s. Louis and Ethel (Weiss) G.; m. Leatrice Joy Fleishman, June 15, 1947 (div. June 1995); children: Melvin Alan, Bryna Jane Pomp. Student, George Washington U., 1938-40; BA, NYU, 1942, MS in Chemistry, 1943; MD, N.Y. Med. Coll., 1947, postgrad., 1950-51. Diplomate Am. Bd. Surgery, Am. Bd. Cosmetic Surgery, Nat. Bd. Med. Examiners. Rotating intern Newark Beth Israel Hosp., NJ, 1947-48; surg. intern Flower and Fifth Avenue Hosps., NYC, 1948-49; resident in surgery Hackensack (N.J.) Hosp., 1949-50, Martland Med. Ctr.-Univ. Hosp., Newark, 1951-54; gen. practice medicine Hackensack, 1950-51; pvt. practice surgery, Paramus, N.J., 1954, New Brunswick, N.J., 1957-92; ret., 1992. Examining physician 1 N.Y. State Workers' Compensation Bd., Bklyn., 1994-95; former staff mem. Middlesex Same Day Surg. Ctr., Robert Wood Johnson Univ. Hosp., St. Peter's Univ. Hosp., Meml. Med. Ctr. South Amboy, N.J., Surgicare Ctrl. Jersey. Author: The Aging Face, 1985; contbr. articles to med. jours. Capt. M.C., U.S. Army, 1955-57. Mem. AMA, Am. Assn. Cosmetic Surgeons, Am. Soc. Cosmetic Surgeons, Am. Acad. Cosmetic Surgery, Pan Am. Med. Assn., Internat. Coll. Surgeons, Internat. Soc. Cosmetic, Plastic and Reconstructive Surgery, Internat. Acad. Cosmetic Surgery, French Soc. Esthetic Surgery, Med. Soc. N.J., N.J. Soc. Cosmetic Surgery, Phila. Soc. Facial Plastic Surgeons, Middlesex County Med. Soc., Am. Physicians Fellowship for Israel Med. Assn., Med. Amateur Radio Coun. (founder 1965, treas. 1986-00, conf. chmn. 1984), Princeton Personal Computer Users Group. Jewish. Achievements include pioneer work on high cheek bones, malar augmentation and the lip lift cheilopexy for cheiloptosis. Home: Ten Llewellyn Pl New Brunswick NJ 08901-3027 Office Phone: 732-247-5578. Personal E-mail: alfredgr@aol.com.

GREENWALD, ALICE MARIAN, museum director; b. Oceanside, NY, Jan. 2, 1952; d. Edmund M. G. and Emily Leona (Liebman) Greenwald Meyer; m. David Pearce Ward, Oct. 10, 1976; children: Nathaniel, Leda Ward. BA, Sarah Lawrence Coll., 1973; MA in History of Religions, U. Chgo., 1975. Curatorial asst. Maurice Spertus Mus. of Judaica, Chgo.; asst. curator Hebrew Union Coll. Skirball Mus., LA, 1975—78, curator, 1978—81, acting dir., 1980; exec. dir. Nat. Mus. Am. Jewish History, Phila., 1981-86; prin. Alice M. Greenwald/Mus. Svcs., Washington, 1986—2001; assoc. mus. dir. mus. programs US Holocaust Meml. Mus., Washington, 2001—06; dir. World Trade Ctr. Meml. Mus., 2006—. Cons., tech. advisor Pew Charitable Trusts, Phila., 1987-90; chair, Coun. Am. Jewish Museums, 1984-86. Contbr. articles to profl. jours. Mem., advisor Local Assistance Bd., West Windsor, NJ, 1992. NEA fellow, 1981, Danforth Found. fellow, 1973-75. Democrat. Jewish. Avocations: cooking, travel, poetry.

GREENWALD, ANDREW ERIC, lawyer; b. NYC, May 31, 1942; s. Harold and Lillian G.; m. Paula S., Aug. 20, 1967; children: Brooke Ellen, Karen Michelle. BS, U. Wis., 1964; JD, Georgetown U., Washington, DC, 1967. Bar: DC 1968, Md. 1969, US Ct. Appeals Md. 1969. Lawyer Nat. Labor Rels. Bd., Washington, 1967-68; asst. corp. counsel DC Govt., 1968-69; shareholder Joseph, Greenwald & Laake PA, Greenbelt, Md., 1969—. Past mem. dept. family and cmty. devel. U. Md. Contbr. articles to profl. jours. Active adv. com. Georgetown U. Continuing Legal Edn., 1991, Georgetown U. Law Ctr. Alumni Bd., 1995. Named Top Lawyer, Washingtonian Mag., 2004, Law Dragon, Top 500 Plaintiff's Personal Injury Lawyers; named to, Best Lawyers in Am.; listed in, Md. and DC Super Lawyers. Mem. ATLA (chmn. tort sect. 1985, co-chair birth trauma litigation group 2005, co-chair med. malpractice info. exch. group 2006—, info. exch. group), ABA, Nat. Inst. Trial Advocacy, Am. Bd. Profl. Liability Attys., Am. Bd. Trial Advocates, William B. Bryant Inn, Am. Inns of Ct. Office: Joseph Greenwald & Laake PA 6404 Ivy Ln Ste 400 Greenbelt MD 20770-1407 Office Phone: 301-220-2200. Personal E-mail: aegatty@yahoo.com. Business E-Mail: agreenwald@jgllaw.com.

GREENWALD, ANTHONY GALT, psychology educator; b. NYC, Jan. 30, 1939; BA magna cum laude, Yale U., 1959; MA in Social Psychology, Harvard U., 1961, PhD, 1963. Postdoctoral rsch. fellow Ednl. Testing Svc., Princeton, N.J., 1963-65; from asst. prof. to prof. psychology Ohio State U., Columbus, 1965-86; prof. psychology U. Wash., Seattle, 1986—. Vis. scholar Stanford U., 1978-79, Yale U., 1993. Assoc. editor Jour. Personality and Social Psychology, 1972-76, editor, 1977-79; editl. bd. Psychonomic Sci., 1971-72, Jour. Personality and Social Psychology, 1971-72, Memory & Cognition, 1972—, Psychol. Rev., 1985-89, Jour. Exptl. Psychology: Gen., 1990-95; contbr. articles to Psychol. Found. Attitudes, Psychol. Rev., Jour. Exptl. Psychology, Psychol. Perspectives on the Self, Contemporary Psychology, Jour. Applied Psychology, Memory and Cognition, Jour. Personality and Social Psychology. Fellow Am. Acad. Arts & Scis. Achievements include rsch. on double-blind tests of subliminal self-help audiotapes, differences between backward and simultaneous masking, defining attitude and attitude theories, motivational facets of the self, explorations in social psychology, demonstration of visual subliminal influence, contributions to use of statistical methods, evaluation of problems in student ratings of instructional quality. Office: U Washington PO Box 351525 Seattle WA 98195-1525*

GREENWALD, CAROL SCHIRO, professional services marketing research executive; b. Phila., Mar. 2, 1939; d. Sidney L. and Adele R. (Rosenheim) Schiro; children: David Bruce, William Michael. BA cum laude, Smith Coll., Northampton, Mass., 1961; MA, Hunter Coll., NYC, 1965; PhD in Polit. Sci., CUNY, 1972. Instr. polit. sci. Queen's Coll., CUNY, 1970-73; asst. dir. Evaluation N.Y.C. Adminstrv. Decentralization Project, 1971-73; asst. prof. Richmond Coll., CUNY, 1973-76, Bklyn. Coll., CUNY, 1976-77; research assoc. Bunting Inst., Radcliffe Coll., 1977-79; project dir. Jobs in the 1980s Pub. Agenda Found., NYC, 1979-81; assoc. dir. Grant Thornton acctg. firm, 1984-86; sr. mgr. Seidman and Seidman, 1986-87; market research mgr. KPMG Peat Marwick, 1988-90; cons., 1990-91, 2002—; mktg. dir. Haight, Gardner, Poor & Havens, 1991-92; dir. comm. Richard A. Eisner & Co., LLP, 1993-97; dir. mktg. Hamilton, HMC divsn. Kurt Salmon Assoc., 1997—, Whitman Breed Abbott & Morgan LLP, 1998-2000; cons. MarketForce, a divsn. of Hildebrandt, Internat., 2002; pvt. practice, 2002—. Author: Group Power: Lobbying and Public Policy, 1977; mem. editl. bd. Mktg. Rev., 1997—; contbr. articles on polit. sci. to profl. jours. Lilly Found. fellow Mem. Am. Mktg. Assn. (chair profl. devel. leadership coun. 1995—, mem. edtl. bd. 1996—), Common Cause (chmn. N.Y. 1981-83, nat. dir. 1978-84), Westchester Women in Comm. (treas. 1993-95). Home: 688 Forest Ave Larchmont NY 10538-1535 Office Phone: 914-834-9320. Personal E-mail: greenwaldcarol@hotmail.com.

GREENWALD, DAVID, lawyer; b. NYC, July 31, 1968; BA summa cum laude, Harvard Univ., 1990; JD with high honors, Univ. Chgo., 1993. Bar: NY 1995, US Dist. Ct. (so. and ea. dists.) NY 1995, US Ct. Appeals (2d cir.) 1998, US Ct. of Appeals (4th cir.) 2002, US Ct. Appeals (fed. cir.) 2005, US Supreme Ct. 2005. Law clk., Hon. Richard A. Posner US Ct. of Appeals, 7th Cir.; summer assoc. Cravath Swaine & Moore, NYC, 1992, assoc., 1994—97, 2000—05, ptnr., litig., 2005—; asst. US atty., So. Dist. NY, criminal divsn. US Attorney's Off., 1997—2000. Editor: Univ. Chgo. Law Rev. Mem.: Order of Coif, Phi Beta Kappa. Office: Cravath Swaine & Moore LLP Worldwide Plz 825 Eighth Ave New York NY 10019-7475 Office Phone: 212-474-1922. Office Fax: 212-474-3700. Business E-Mail: dgreenwald@cravath.com.

GREENWALD, JOHN EDWARD, publishing executive, journalist; b. NYC, Oct. 28, 1942; s. Herbert and Carrie (Weisberg) G.; m. Rita Lynn Lipman, May 16, 1987. BA, Syracuse U., 1963. Copy boy N.Y. Post, NYC, 1963-64; assoc. editor Air Force Times, Washington, 1967-70; editor The Times Mag., Washington, 1970-80; editorial dir. Jour. Newspapers, Inc. (Fairfax Jour., Arlington Jour., Alexandria Jour., Prince George's Jour., Prince William Jour., Montgomery Jour.), Springfield, Va., 1980-90; editor Am. Legion Mag., Indpls., 1991-94; asst. mng. editor/Sunday & Spl. Projects The Sun, Lowell, Mass., 1994-98; entertainment columnist Waterbury (Conn.) Republican-Am., 2000—; free-lance writer, 1999—; arts writer Lowell (Mass.) Sun, 2002—. Film reviewer Times Jour. Co., Springfield, Va., 1967-85. Exhibitions include Nude 2002, Lexington (Ky.) Art League, La Boniche, Whistler House Mus. of Art, 2002, 2003, Higher Ground, 2003, Arts League of Lowell, 2005, Prescott St. Gallery, Lowell, Mass., 2005. Coord. Lowell Cultural Roundtable, 1998-; mem. Arts League of Lowell, 2003-; served with U.S. Army, 1964-67. E-mail: johnedit@bigfoot.com.

GREENWALD, JULIE, recording industry executive; b. 1970; 1 child, Tallulah Rose G. BA in polit. sci., Tulane Univ. Personal asst. to pres. Def Jam Records, 1992, head of mktg.; pres. Island Records; exec. v.p. Island Def Jam Records, 2002; pres. Atlantic Records Group, 2004—. Named one of 100 Most Powerful Women in Entertainment, Hollywood Reporter, 2006. Office: Atlantic Records 1290 Ave of the Americas New York NY 10104 Office Phone: 212-707-2000. Office Fax: 212-405-5475.*

GREENWALD, MARTIN, publishing company executive; b. Bronx, NY, Apr. 25, 1942; s. David and Jean (Kaufman) G.; m. Irma Heldman; children: Karen Sue, Craig Mitchell. AB, Lafayette Coll., 1963; MBA, Columbia U., 1965. Mgr. acquisition planning, fin. analyst Macmillan Inc., NYC, 1965-69, bus. mgr., trade div., 1970-72; new bus. devel. analyst Holt div. CBS, NYC, 1969-70; v.p., gen. mgr. Hagstrom Co. Inc., NYC, 1972-76; pres. Paddington Press, NYC, 1976-80; dir. mktg. Facts On File, Inc., 1980-82, v.p. mktg., 1982-88, sr. v.p., 1988-90, pub., exec. v.p., 1990-95; pres. Martin Greenwald Assocs., Inc., NYC, 1995-96; exec. dir. The Pub. Strategists, Bronxville, NY, 1996—; pub. Krugosvet Ency., Moscow, 1996—; pub. mgr. Open Soc. Inst., 1998—. Author: Maps on File, 1981, Historical Maps on File, 1984 V.p. Green Acres Libr. Bd., Hempstead, NY, 1976—80, Green Acres Civic Assn., 1976—89; mem. Nassau County (N.Y.) Rep. Com., 1973—80; bd. dirs. Non-Profit Found. for the Support of Cultural, Ednl. and New Info. Techs.-Russia, 1999—, Internat. Debate Edn. Assn., 2002—, Krugosvet 000, Russia, 2005—. Mem. Assn. Am. Pubs., Canadian Booksellers Assn., Internat. Debate Edn. Assn., N.Y. Road Runners Club. Jewish. Home: 275 Central Park W New York NY 10024-3015 Office: The Publishing Strategists 29 Palmer Pl Leonia NJ 07605 also: Open Soc Inst 400 W 59th St New York NY 10019 Home Phone: 212-877-6834; Office Phone: 212-547-6932. Personal E-mail: mgaig275@yahoo.com. Business E-Mail: mgreenwald@sorosny.org.

GREENWALD, PETER, health facility administrator, director, epidemiologist, researcher; b. Newburgh, NY, Nov. 7, 1936; s. Louis and Pearl (Reingold) G.; m. Harriet Reif, Sept. 6, 1968; children— Rebecca, Laura, Daniel BA, Colgate U., 1957; MD, SUNY Coll. Medicine, 1961; MPH, Harvard U., 1967, DrPH, 1974. Intern Los Angeles County Hosp., 1961-62; resident in internal medicine Boston City Hosp., 1964-66; asst. in medicine Peter Bent Brigham Hosp., 1967-68; mem. epidemiology and disease control study sect. NIH, 1974-78; mem. N.Y. State Gov.'s Breast Task Force, 1976-78; with N.Y. State Dept. Health, Albany, 1968-81, dir., 1968-76, dir. epidemiology, 1976-81; prof. medicine Albany Med. Coll., 1976-81; attending physician Albany Med. Ctr. Hosp., 1968-81; adj. prof. biomed. engring. Rensselaer Poly. Inst., Troy, N.Y., 1976-81; assoc. scientist Sloan-Kettering Inst. for Cancer Research, NYC, 1977-81; dir. div. cancer prevention Nat. Cancer Inst., NIH, Bethesda, Md., 1981-97, 98—. Mem. VA Merit Rev. Bd. Med. Oncology, Washington, 1972-74 Editor-in-chief Jour. Nat. Cancer Inst., NIH, 1981-87; contbr. articles to profl. jours. Rear adm. USPHS, 1962-64, 81—. Recipient Disting. Svc. award N.Y. State Dept. Health, 1975; Redway medal and award for med. writing N.Y. State Jour. Medicine, 1977, N.Y. State Gov.'s Citationfor pub. health achievement, 1981, PHS commendation 1983, 88, Disting. Svc. medal, 1993, Disting. Svc. award, Am. Cancer Soc., 1997, Outstanding Rsch. award Am. Inst. Cancer Rsch., 1997, Pub. Svc. award Cancer Treatment and Rsch. Found., 1997; named to SUNY Honor Roll of Disting. Grads., 1997. Fellow ACP, APHA (epidemiology sect. chmn. 1981), Am. Coll. Preventive Medicine, Am. Soc. Nutritional Scis.; mem. Am. Assn. Cancer Rsch. (DeWitt Goodman lectr. 1998), Am. Soc. Clin. Oncology, Am. Coll. Epidemiology (bd. dirs. 1981-82), Am. Soc. Preventive Oncology (Disting. Achievement award 1998), Internat. Epidemiology Soc., Nat. Acad. Scis. (food and nutrition bd. 1982-88), Am. Cancer Soc. (Cancer Prevention award 2002). Office: NIH/NCI Divsn Cancer Prevention EPN/2040 6130 Exec Blvd Bethesda MD 20892-7309 Home Phone: 301-652-8044; Office Phone: 301-496-6616. Business E-Mail: pg37g@nih.gov.

GREENWALD, ROBERT, public relations executive; b. NYC, Jan. 14, 1927; s. Louis and Rebecca (Shapiro) G.; m. Genevieve Kushnir, Apr. 15, 1957 (div. 1960); m. Dorothy Pearl Brand, Apr. 19, 1963; children: Liza, Mark. BA, NYU, 1949, postgrad., 1951-54; postgrad, Columbia U., 1950, New Sch., 1950-51. Account exec. Ruder & Finn, Inc., NYC, 1954—, sr. assoc., 1955-56, v.p., 1957-65; sr. v.p. Ruder, Finn & Rotman, Inc., NYC, 1965-79, exec. v.p., 1980-83, sr. counsel, 1983-85; vice-chmn. Makovsky & Co. Inc., NYC, 1987—; pvt. quality control cons. NYC, 1994—. Author: (with Dorothy Brand) Learning To Live with The Love of Your Life, 1979. Chmn. pub. relations com. UNICEF, NYC, 1976-82, dir., 1976-82, mem. nat. adv. com., 1983-97, mem. nominating com., 1983-87; bd. dirs. Jewish Family Services, NYC, 1972-75. Served with US Army, 1945-46, ETO. Recipient Silver Anvil award Pub. Relations Soc. Am., 1955, 73, 81; recipient Paul B. Zucker award Ruder & Finn Inc., 1976, 82 Democrat. Jewish. Home: 73 Alexander Ave Montclair NJ 07043 Office Phone: 973-509-3934. Personal E-mail: bobdottl@aol.com.

GREENWALD, SHEILA ELLEN, writer, illustrator; b. NYC, May 26, 1934; d. Julius and Florence (Friedman) Greenwald; m. George E. Green, Feb. 18, 1960; children: Samuel Green, Benjamin Green. BA, Sarah Lawrence Coll., 1956. Author over 24 children's books, including Give Us a Great Big Smile Rosy Cole, 1980, Valentine Rosy, 1984, Rosy Cole's Great American Guilt Club, 1987, Write on Rosy, 1988, Rosy's Romance, 1989, Here's Hermione, 1991, The Mariah Delary Author of the Month Club, 1990, Rosy Cole Discovers America, 1992, My Fabulous NewLife, 1993, Rosy Cole, She Walks in Beauty, 1994, Rosy Cole: She Grows and Graduates, 1997, Stucksville, 2000, Mariah Delany Lending Library Disaster (The Mariah Delany Author of The Month Club 1999), Stucksville, 2001, The Hot Day reissued by Silver Mountain, 2002, Rosy Cole's Worst Ever, Best Yet Tour of New York City, 2003, Rosy Cole's Memoir EXPLOSION, 2006. Mem.: PEN, Authors League. Jewish. Office: Melanie Kroupa Books Ferrar Straus & Geroux 19 Union Sq W New York NY 10003 E-mail: sheilagreenwald@usa.net.

GREENWAY, HUGH DAVIDS SCOTT, journalist; b. Boston, May 8, 1935; s. James Cowen and Helen Livingston (Scott) G.; m. Joy Beverly Brooks, June 11, 1960; children: Julia Livingston, Alice Lauder, Sarah Davids. BA, Yale U., 1958; postgrad., Oxford U., Eng., 1960-62. Corr. Time mag., London, 1962-63, Washington, 1963-64, Boston, 1964-66, Saigon, 1967-68, Bangkok, 1968-70, UN, NYC, 1970-72; corr. Washington Post, Hong Kong, 1973-76, Jerusalem, 1976-78; assoc. editor for nat. and fgn. news Boston Globe, 1978-91, sr. assoc. editor, 1991-93, editl. page editor, 1994-2000, fgn. affairs columnist, 2000—. Corp. mem. Woods Hole (Mass.) Oceanographic Inst. Served with USNR, 1958-60. Nieman fellow Harvard U., 1971-72 Mem.: Internat. Press Inst., Coun. on Fgn. Rels., Am. Soc. Newspaper Editors. Home: 634 Charles River St Needham MA 02492-1031 Office Phone: 781-235-0353. Personal E-mail: greenway@globe.com.

GREENWAY, JOAN M., dean; b. Adelaide, South Australia, Australia; d. John Francis Matthew and Ida Gladys Wilding; m. Elliott D. Full, Feb. 9, 1997; m. Ian MacKinnon Disher, Aug. 30, 1944 (dec. Mar. 16, 1957); children: Carolyn Wilding Whitting, Susan MacIntosh Miller, Jamie Sutherland MacDonald. BA, U. Colo., Boulder, CO, 1968, MA, 1969, PhD, 1970. TV journalist NEWS Ltd., South Australia, Australia, 1957—62, Australian Broadcasting Commn., Australia, 1962—66; asst. prof. Regis Coll., Denver, 1969—71; prof. and chmn. Calif. State U., Pomona, Calif., 1971—76; dean Continuing Edn. Calif. State U., Pomona, Calif., 1976—88. Spl. adv. children Superior Ct. LA County, Los Angeles, Calif., 1993—97. Recipient Disting. Prof. Am., Wash., D.C., 1975. Mem.: Phi Beta Kappa Colo. Chpt.

GREENWELL, RONALD EVERETT, communications executive; b. Louisville, Oct. 28, 1938; s. Woodrow M. and Christine (Comer) Gossett G.; m. Diane J. Greenwell, Mar. 18, 1967; children: Wendy, Robin. With Motorola Inc., Schaumburg, Ill., 1962-94, sr. v.p., gen. mgr. communications internat. group, 1986-94; pres. Motorola Communications Internat. Inc., Schaumburg, Ill., 1986-94, ret., 1994. Bd. dirs. ALTELA, Inc., Albuquerque. Home: 30 Canyon Ridge Dr Sandia Park NM 87047-8506

GREENWOOD, DAVID A., lawyer; b. Salt Lake City, Aug. 9, 1946; BA magna cum laude, U. Utah, 1970; JD, U. Chgo., 1973. Bar: Utah 1973. Shareholder Van Cott, Bagley, Cornwall & McCarthy, Salt Lake City; shareholder, comml. litig. Bendinger Crockett Peterson Greenwood & Casey, Salt Lake City; ptnr., comml. litig. Howrey LLP, Salt Lake City. Fellow Am. Bar Found., Am. Coll. Trial Lawyers (vice chmn. Utah state com.); mem. ABA, Am. Bd. Trial Advocates (assoc., past pres. Utah chapt.), Utah State Bar, Phi Beta Kappa, Phi Kappa Phi. Office: Howrey LLP 170 S Main St Ste 400 Salt Lake City UT 84101 Office Phone: 801-533-8383. Office Fax: 801-531-1486.

GREENWOOD, FRANK, information scientist, educator; b. Rio de Janeiro, Mar. 6, 1924; came to U.S., 1935; s. Heman Charles and Evelyn (Heyns) G.; m. Mary Mallas, Oct. 24, 1972; children: Margaret, Ernest, Nicholas. BA, Bucknell U., Lewisburg, Pa., 1950; MBA, U. So. Calif., LA, 1959; PhD, UCLA, 1963; D (hon.), Commonwealth Open U., 1999. Cert. systems profl., project mgmt. profl. Various positions The Tex. Co., US, Africa and Can., 1950-60; assoc. prof. U. Ga., Athens, 1961-65; chmn. dept. computer sys. Ohio U., Athens, 1966-76; dir. computer ctr. U. Mont., Missoula, 1977-84; prof. mgmt. info. sys. Southea. Mass. U. (now U. Mass.), North Dartmouth, 1985-89, Ctrl. Mich. U., Mt. Pleasant, 1990-93; pres. Greenwood & Assocs., Ltd., Bloomfield Hills, Mich., 1993. Instr. on-line clases Jones Internat. U., Englewood, Colo., Gatlin Ednl. Svcs., Ft. Worth, Tex. Author: Casebook for Management and Business Policy: A Systems Approach, 1968, Managing the Systems Analysis Function, 1968; (with Nicolai Siemens and C.H. Marting Jr.) Operations Research: Planning, Operating and Information Systems, 1973; (with Mary Greenwood) Information Resources in the Office Tomorrow, 1980, Profitable Small Business Computing, 1982, Office Technology: Principles of Automation, 1984, Business Telecommunications: Data Communications in the Information Age, 1988, Introduction to Computer-Integrated Manufacturing, 1990, How to Raise Office Productivity, 1991, Meeting the Challenges of Project Management: A Primer, 1998; columnist: Computerworld mag., 1972-73, The Daily Record, 1982-83, (with Mary Greenwood) Herald News, 1986, The Beacon, 1986, Morning Sun, 1990-93; contbr. monographs, articles to profl. jours. and chpts. to books. Sgt. AUS, 1943-45. UCLA Alumni scholar, 1961; Ford Found. fellow, 1962-63. Mem. Wamsutta Club (New Bedford, Mass.). Greek Orthodox. Avocation: exercise. Home and Office: 7426 Deep Run Apt 1322 Bloomfield Hills MI 48301-3844 Personal E-mail: fgreenw617@aol.com. *Do what you believe you should (and not what others do). Put your trust in your own capacity to provide products/services others need (and don't seek security as a "corporate slave"). Mental and physical health are the key to all else.*

GREENWOOD, JANE, costume designer, educator; b. Liverpool, Eng., Apr. 30, 1934; d. Harold Ralph Pate and Florence Sarah Mary (Humphrey) G.; m. Ben Edwards, children: Sarah, Kate. Attended, Ctrl. Sch. Arts & Crafts, London, Eng. Tchr. Lester Polakov Design Studio, NYC, Julliard Sch., NYC; assoc. prof. design Yale U., New Haven, 1977—. Stage work includes: The Ballad of the Sad Cafe, 1963, Hamlet, 1964, Incident at Vichy, 1964-65, Tartuffe, 1965, Half a Sixpence, 1965-66, A Race of Hairy Men!, 1965, Nathan Weinstein, 1966, Where's Daddy?, 1966, How's the World Treating You?, 1966, More Stately Mansions, 1967-68, The Prime of Miss Jean Brodie, 1968, Seven Descents of Myrtle, 1968, I'm Solomon, 1968, The Wrong Way Light Bulb, 1969, The Penny Wars, 1969, Angela, 1969, Sheep on the Runway, 1970, Othello, 1970, Gandhi, 1970, Hay Fever, 1970, Les Blancs, 1970, Antigone, 1971, Wise Child, 1972, Look Away, 1973, Finishing Touches, 1973, A Moon for the Misbegotten, 1973-74, Cat on a Hot Tin Roof, 1974, 2003-04, Same Time Next Year, 1975-78, A Matter of Gravity, 1976, California Suite, 1976, A Texas Trilogy, 1976, Otherwise Engaged, 1977, Anna Christie, 1977, Vieux Carre, 1977, The Night of the Tribades, 1977, An Almost Perfect Person, 1977, A Touch of the Poet, 1977, Cheaters, 1978, The Kingfisher, 1978, Faith Healer, 1979, Knockout, 1979, Romantic Comedy, 1979, To Grandmother's House We Go, 1981, The Supporting Cast, 1981, The West Side Waltz, 1981-82, Duet for One, 1981, Medea, 1982, The Queen and the Rebels, 1982, Plenty, 1983, Heartbreak House, 1983-84, The Golden Age, 1984, Alone Together, 1984, The Iceman Cometh, 1985, Lillian, 1986, So Long on Lonely Street, 1986, Ah, Wilderness, 1988, Long Day's Journey into Night, 1988, Our Town, 1988, The Secret Rapture, 1989, Lisbon Traviatta, The Circle, 1989, The Tenth Man, 1990, The Big Love, 1991, I Hate Hamlet, 1991, Park Your Car in Harvard Yard, 1991, A Streetcar Named Desire, 1992, The Price, 1992, Lips Together, Teeth Apart, The

Sisters Rosensweig, 1993-94, Abe Lincoln in Illinois, 1993, She Loves Me, 1993, Passion, 1994, The Heiress, 1995, A Month in the Country, 1995, Sylvia, Death Defying Acts, Master Class, 1995, A Delicate Balance, 1996, Once Upon a Mattress, 1996, The Last Night of Ballyhoo, 1997, An American Daughter, 1997, The Little Foxes, 1997, Proposals, 1997, The Scarlet Pimpernel, 1997, The Deep Blue Sea, 1998, Honour, 1998, High Society, 1998, James Joyce's The Dead, 2000, A Moon for the Misbegotten, 2000, The Dinner Party, 2000-01, Major Barbara, 2001, Bea Arthur on Broadway, 2002, Fortune's Fool, 2002, The Retreat from Moscow, 2003-04, The Violet Hour, 2003, The Caretaker, 2003-04, Oldest Living Confederate Widow Tells All, 2003, Who's Afraid of Virginia Woolf?, 2005, On Golden Pond, 2005, Lennon, 2005, Absurb Person Singular, 2005, Heartbreak House, 2006; TV work includes: The House Without a Christmas Tree, 1972, The Easter Promise, 1975, Beyond the Horizon, 1976, Addie and the King of Hearts, 1976, The Royal Romance of Charles and Diana, 1982, The Shady Hill Kidnapping, 1982, The File on Jill Hatch, 1983, Kennedy, 1983, Johnny Bull, 1986, Ike, 1986, Heartbreak House, 1986, Lyndon Johnson, 1987, Dialogue of the Carmelites, 1987, Liberace: Behind the Music, 1988, Our Town, 1989, The Ivory Hunters, 1990, Sensibility and Sense, 1990, Three Hotels, 1991, The End of a Sentence, 1991, A Life in the Theatre, 1993, The Mother, 1994; film work includes: Last Embrace, 1979, Can't Stop the Music, 1980, The Four Seasons, 1981, Arthur, 1981, Wetherby, 1985, Sweet Liberty, 1986, The Squeeze, 1987, Jacknife, Mr. Destiny, 1990, Glengarry Glen Ross, 1992, Oleanna, 1994, Other Voices, Other Rooms, 1995. 14 Tony nominations.*

GREENWOOD, JANET KAE DALY, psychologist, academic administrator, marketing professional; b. Goldsboro, NC, Dec. 9, 1943; d. Fulton Benton and Kelminy Ethel Esther (Ball) Daly; 1 child, Gerald Thompson. AA, Peace Coll., 1963; BS in English and Psychology, East Carolina U., 1965, MEd in Counseling, 1967; postgrad., N.C. State U., 1967-69, U. London, 1969; PhD in Counseling and Higher Ednl. Adminstrn., Fla. State U., 1972. Tchr. English Kinston (N.C.) City Schs., 1965-66, Goldsboro City Schs., 1966-67; counselor and psychometrist primary and secondary schs. County of Wake, NC, 1967-69; coord. Am. Inst. for Fgn. Study, 1969; supr. student tours in Eng., France, Switzerland, Italy, and Capri, 1969; counselor Fla. State U., Tallahassee, 1969-72; asst. dir. counseling Rutgers U., New Brunswick, NJ, 1972-73, cons. to v.p. for student svcs., 1973-74, lectr. in counseling psychology, 1972-74; coord. and assoc. prof. counselor edn. U. Cin., 1974-77, adviser to grad. students, 1974-77, vice provost student affairs, 1977-81; pres. Longwood Coll., Farmville, Va., 1981-87, U. Bridgeport, Conn., 1987-92; cons., ptnr., dir. Heidrick & Struggles, Washington, 1992-2000; v.p. A.T. Kearney, Inc., 2000—04; owner, ptnr. Greenwood & Assocs., Inc., 2004—. Guidance cons. South Plainfield Pub. Schs., 1973-76; adviser Parents without Ptnrs., 1976; bd. dirs. Hydraulic Co.; mem. Gov.'s Partnership To Prevent Substance Abuse in the Workforce, mem. audit com. and cmty. and govt. rels. com. Contbr. articles to profl. jours. Mem. Gov.'s Ad Hoc Edn. Com. on Tchr. Edn. and Counselor Edn., State of Ohio, 1975; mem. state planning commn. Nat. Identification of Women Project; chair Twin Rivers Tenants Rights Assn., 1972-74; bd. dirs. Bridgeport Hosp., Bridgeport Bus. Coun.; mem. adv. com. Bridgeport Pub. Edn. Fund; bd. dirs. Conn. Ballet Theatre, chair South End streeting com; mem. mgmt. adv. com. City of Bridgeport; mem. adv. com. United Way Tri-State; chair South End Partnership Com; mem. The Schiavone Steering Com./Downtown Bridgeport Project, YWCA Bd., Champion/United Way, United Way Community Human Svcs. Planning Coun., Bridgeport Symphony Bd., Bridgeport Opera Bd., Bridgeport Area Coll./Univ. Consortium, Conn. Conf. Ind. Colls., The Newcomen Soc. of U.S., The United Way Ea. Fairfield County; mem. adv. bd. Sacred Heart/St. Anthony Sch., Roosevelt Sch; mem. ct. com. Regional Plan Assn. Fairfield 2000; bd. dirs. Conn. Ballet Theatre; chair The Bridgeport Regional Bus. Coun. Brass Ring Task Force on Leadership; bd. govs. Fairfield County Study; mem. hon. bd. dirs. Conn. Earth Day 20, Inc.; chair L.I. Sound Western Regional Coun.; founding mem. L.I. Sound Assembly; mem. membership com., campus partnership subcom. Drugs Don't Work program, 1989-91. Recipient Spl. award Black Arts Festival, Meritorious Svc. award Am. Assn. State Colls. and Univs. Mem. AAUP, Am. Coll. Pers. Assn. (editor and chair media bd. 1975—), Am. Pers. and Guidance Assn., Cin. Pers. and Guidance Assn., Ohio Psychol. Assn., Cin. Psychol. Assn., Organizational Behavior Assn., Am. Sch. Counselors Assn., Ohio Sch. Counselors Assn., Assn. for Women Faculty, Ohio Counselor Edn. and Supervision Assn., Kappa Delta Pi.

GREENWOOD, JONATHAN RICHARD GUY (JONNY GREENWOOD), musician; b. Oxford, England, Nov. 5, 1972; married. Student in Psychology, Oxford Poly, Eng. Lead guitarist Radiohead, 1992—; composer in residence BBC, 2004—. Musician: (albums) Pablo Honey, 1993, The Bends, 1995, OK Computer, 1997 (Grammy award, 1997), Kid A, 2000 (Grammy award, 2000), Amnesiac, 2001, I Might Be Wrong: Live Recordings, 2001, Hail to the Thief, 2003. Office: Capital Records 1750 North Vine St 10th Fl Hollywood CA 90028

GREENWOOD, M. R. C., biologist, nutrition educator, former academic administrator; b. Gainesville, Fla., Apr. 11, 1943; d. Stanley James and Mary Rita (Schmeltz) Cooke; m. (div. 1968); 1 child, James Robert. AB summa cum laude, Vassar Coll., 1968; PhD, Rockefeller U., 1973; LHD (hon.), Mt. St. Mary Coll., 1989. Rsch. assoc. Inst. of Human Nutrition, Columbia U., NYC, 1974-75, adj. asst. prof., 1975-76, asst. prof., 1976-78; assoc. prof. dept. biology Vassar Coll., Poughkeepsie, NY, 1978-81, prof. biology, 1981-86, dir. animal model, CORE Lab. of Obesity Rsch. Ctr., 1985-89, dir. undergrad. rsch. summer inst., 1986-88, dir. Howard Hughes biol. scis. network program, 1988, chmn. of biology dept., John Guy Vassar prof. natural scis., 1986-89; prof. nutrition and internal medicine, dean grad. studies U. Calif., Davis, 1989-96, chancellor Santa Cruz, 1996—2004; provost, sr. v.p. academic affairs U. Calif. sys., 2004—05; prof. biology U. Calif., Santa Cruz, 2005—; prof. nutrition and internal medicine dept. nutrition U. Calif. Davis, 2005—. Mem. nutrition study sect. NIH, 1983-87; mem. NRC; assoc. dir. for sci. White House Office Sci. and Tech., 1993-95. Editor: Obesity, Vol. 4, 1983; contbr. over 250 articles and abstracts to profl. jours., 1974-89. Recipient Rsch. Career Devel. award NIH, 1978-83; Mellon scholar-in-residence St. Olaf Coll., Northfield, Minn., 1978; NY State Regents fellow, 1968. Mem. AAAS (pres. 1998-99), NRC (policy and global affairs divsn. chair 2004-), Inst. Medicine of Nat. Acad. Scis. (chair food and nutrition bd., diet and health subcom. 1986—), N.Am. Soc. Study of Obesity (pres. 1987-88), Am. Inst. Nutrition (BioServ 1982), Am. Physiol. Soc., The Harvey Soc., Am. Diabetes Assn., Am. Acad. Arts and Scis., Internat. Assn. Study of Obesity (treas. 1991—). Home: 5033 El Cemonte Ave Davis CA 95616 Office: U Calif Davis Meyer Hall Dept Nutrition 1 Shields Rd Davis CA 95616

GREENWOOD, STEPHEN JOHN, environmental engineer; b. Mpls., July 15, 1952; s. John Edward Greenwood and Eileen Remarcke; m. Rosario Sanchez, June 15, 1985; children: Christopher John Greenwood-Sanchez, David Alexander Greenwood-Sanchez, Maria-Luisa Greenwood-Sanchez. BCE, U. Minn., 1975, MSCE, 1982, BME, 1998. Cert. profl. civil engr., Minn. Bd. Architecture, Engring., Land Surveying.; environ. health specialist Minn. Dept. Health. Civil engr. Minn. Dept. Health, St. Paul, 1976—80; prin. engr. Met. Coun., St. Paul, 1983—. Contbr. articles to profl. jours. Engr. Vols. Tech. Assistance, Washington, 1980—2004; mem. Third World Inst., Mpls., 1979—84; ch. musican St. Andrew's and Newman Ctr., St. Paul, 1977—2007. Mem.: Water Environment Fedn. (assoc.; incinerator o&m manual of practice update team, Radebaugh award team 2005—07, Radebaugh Award 2003). Achievements include development of mathematical model for dewatering sewage biosolids using a variable, volume plate and frame press; research in optimizing sewage actived sludge BNR process using a hydraulically controlled SRT, after an evaluation of methods to calculate 'Solids Retention Time'; multiple hearth incinerator and wet scrubber operation; design of new method to accurately determine slag formation temperature of incinerator ash and methods to control incinerator excursion temperatures. Avocations: cross country skiing, music, bicycling, hiking. Home: 1111 Argyle Saint Paul MN 55103 Office: Met Coun 2400 Childs Rd Saint Paul MN 55106 Office Phone: 651-602-8763. Personal E-mail: sjgreenwood@msn.com. Business E-Mail: steve.greenwood@metc.state.mn.us.

GREENWOOD, WILLIAM WARREN, journalist; b. Richmond, Va., Mar. 28, 1942; s. William Rogers and Gloria Vivian (Brown) Warren; m. Marsha Ann Sheppard, Dec. 21, 1968; 1 child, Kelly. Student, Fla. State U., 1960-63; BA, Am. U., 1970. Announcer Sta. WZRO, Jacksonville Beach, Fla., 1956-60; newscaster Sta. WMBR, Jacksonville, Fla., 1960-64, Sta. WPDQ, Jacksonville, 1964-66, Sta. WWDC, Washington, 1966-67; dir. pub. affairs Nat. Ednl. Radio, Washington, 1967-68; news corr. U.P.I., Washington, 1968-70; corr. MBS, Washington, 1970-74, v.p. news, 1974-76; news corr. Sta. WCBS-TV, NYC, 1976-79, ABC News, NYC, 1979, White House corr. Washington, 1980-81, Washington corr., 1981—2006. Guest lectr. NYU, 1975, 76; chmn. Congl. Radio-TV Galleries, Washington, 1975; guest lectr. Am. U., 1967; v.p. Nat. Press Bldg. Corp., 1974, Nat. Press Club, 1974; ABC coverage participant Peabody award, 2002, ABC coverage participant Alfred i. DuPont award, 2002. Recipient award of merit ARC, 1960, 61; Emmy award, 1978, N.Y.C. Firefighters award, 1979, Am. Bankers Assn. award ABC coverage participant, 1981, Edward R. Morrow award 1999, 03, 05; Emmy nomination, 1979. Mem. RTNDA (DC chpt.), Fla. State U. Alumni Assn. (founding v.p. Washington chpt. 1974-75), ARC Lifeguard Alumni Assn. Episcopalian. Home Phone: 202-337-6458.

GREENZANG, KATHERINE, lawyer, insurance company executive; b. 1964; BA, Johns Hopkins U., Balt.; JD, NYU. Bar: NY 1990. Assoc. Dewey Ballantine, NYC, 1990—94; corp. counsel Assurant Inc., NYC, 1994—95, asst. v.p., corp. counsel, 1995—96, v.p., corp. counsel, 1996—2001, sr. v.p., gen. counsel, sec., 2001—. Mem.: ABA, Assn. Corp. Counsel, NY State Bar Assn. Office: Assurant Inc 41st Fl 1 Chase Manhattan Plz New York NY 10005 Office Phone: 212-859-7021. Office Fax: 212-859-7034.*

GREER, ALAN GRAHAM, lawyer; b. El Dorado, Ark., May 31, 1939; s. Arthur W. and Marie (Ross) G.; m. Patricia A. Seitz, Aug. 14, 1981. BS, U.S. Naval Acad., 1961; JD, U. Fla., 1969. Ptnr. Richmnan, Greer Weil Brumbaugh, Miami, Fla., 1969—. Chmn. emeritus WLRN Pub. Radio and TV Sta.; bd. dirs. probono.net Past chmn. Dade County Coun. Arts and Scis.; past mem. Fla. State Task Force on Water Issues, Gov.'s Bus. Adv. Coun. on Edn.; co-chmn. site selection com. Dem. Nat. Com., 1992, also trustee; past bd. dirs. Camillus Ho. With USN, 1961-67. Fellow Internat. Soc. Barristers, Am. Coll. Trial Lawyers (past chmn. professionalism com.); mem. ABA, Fla. Bar Assn. (cert., past chmn. internat. law com.), Fla. Supreme Ct. Hist. Soc. (v.p.). Home: 224 Ridgewood Rd Miami FL 33133-6614 Office: Richman Greer PA Miami Ctr 10th Fl 201 S Biscayne Blvd Miami FL 33131-4332 Office Phone: 305-373-4000. Business E-Mail: agreer@richmangreer.com.

GREER, ALLEN CURTIS, II, lawyer, investment management executive; b. New Rochelle, NY, Dec. 6, 1951; s. Allen Wilkinson and Nancy (Carroll) G.; children: Katharine Burrage, Constance Carroll, Genevieve Forbes. AB, Harvard U., 1972, JD, 1975. Assoc. Cadwalader, Wickersham & Taft, NYC, 1975-79, Palmer & Dodge, Boston, 1979-82; ptnr. Gaston & Snow, Boston and NYC, 1982-91, Rogers & Wells, 1991-97, Cadwalader, Wickersham & Taft, NYC, 1997-99, of counsel, 1999—; with Westbrook Ptnrs., 1999—, RECAP Investments Ltd., Boston, 2004—. Bd. dirs. various pvt. cos. Mem.: Urban Land Inst., Nat. Assn. Real Estate Investment Trusts. Office: RECAP Investments Ltd 222 Berkeley St 22d Fl Boston MA 02116 Address: RECAP Investments Pte Ltd 390 Orchard Rd #09-03/04 Palais Renaissance 238871 Singapore Home Phone: 617-698-7988; Office Phone: 617-646-6114. Business E-Mail: cgreer@recapinvestments.com, cgreer@usrecap.com.

GREER, CARL CRAWFORD, petroleum company executive; b. Pitts., June 12, 1940; s. Joseph Moss and Gene (Crawford) G.; m. Jerrine Ehlers, June 16, 1962 (div.); children: Caryn, Michael, Janet; m. Patricia Taylor, Feb. 4, 1989. BS, Lehigh U., 1962; PhD, Columbia U., 1966; PsyD, Ill. Sch. Profl. Psychology, Chgo., 1993. Lic. clin. psychologist and Jungian analyst. Assoc. in bus. Columbia U., 1964-66, asst. prof. banking and finance, 1966-67; retail mktg. mgr. Martin Oil Service Inc., Alsip, Ill., 1967-68, exec. v.p., 1968, pres., dir., 1968-76, chmn. bd., pres., 1976-85; pres., dir. Gen. Ptnrs. Martin Oil Mktg. Ltd., 1982—, Martin Exploration Mgmt. Co., 1985—. Mem. Beta Theta Pi, Tau Beta Pi, Beta Gamma Sigma, Omicron Delta Kappa. Presbyterian.

GREER, DAVID STEVEN, dean, educator, physician; b. Bklyn., Oct. 12, 1925; s. Jacob and Mary (Zaslawsky) Greer; m. Marion Clarich, June 25, 1950; children: Jeffrey, Linda. BS, U. Notre Dame, 1948; MD, U. Chgo., 1953; MA (hon.), Brown U., 1975; LHD (hon.), Southeastern Mass. U., 1981. Diplomate Am. Bd. Internal Medicine. Intern Yale-New Haven Med. Center, 1953—54; resident in medicine U. Chgo. Clinics, 1954—57; instr. endocrinology and medicine U. Chgo., 1957; practice medicine specializing in internal medicine Fall River, Mass., 1957—74; chief staff dept. medicine Fall River Gen. Hosp., 1959—62; med. dir. Earle E. Hussey Hosp., Fall River, 1962—75; chief staff dept. medicine Truesdale Clinic and Truesdale Hosp., Fall River, 1971—74, pres. med. staff, 1968—70; sr. clin. instr. medicine Tufts U. Coll. Medicine, 1969—71, asst. clin. prof., 1971—78; clin. asso. prof. community health Brown U., 1973—75, dir. family practice residency program, 1975—78, prof. community health, 1975—93, prof. emeritus, 1993—, assoc. dean medicine, 1974—81, dean medicine, 1981—92, dean emeritus, 1992—, chmn. sect. community health, 1978—81. Mem. Gov.'s Task Force on Quality of Care, Medicaid Program, Commonwealth of Mass., 1969—70; del. White House Conf. Aging, 1971, 81; pres. Ind. Living Authority, State of R.I., 1975—81; mem. exec. com. Cancer Control Bd. R.I., 1975—80; mem. R.I. Gov.'s Task Force for Inst. of Mental Health, 1976—81; bd. dirs. Health Planning Coun., Inc., Providence, 1976—78; chmn. com. on aging Jewish Fedn. R.I., 1978—80; chmn. Gov.'s Commn. on Provision of Comprehensive Mental Health Svcs. in R.I., 1980—81; trustee Southeastern Mass. U., 1970—81, chmn., 1973—74, Providence Mayor's Sr. Citizens Task Force, 1975; bd. dirs. Assn. Home Health Agys. R.I., 1975—80; founding dir. Internat. Physicians for Prevention of Nuc. War, Inc., 1980—85; vis. prof. dept. medicine Georgetown U., 1992—93; scholar-in-residence Assn. Am. Med. Colls., 1992—93. Contbr. articles to profl. jours. Named Prof. of the Yr., Brown U., 1992; recipient Outstanding Svc. award, Mass. Easter Seal Soc., 1970, Outstanding Citizens award, Jewish War Vets. Aux., 1973, Disting. Svc. award, U. Chgo. Med. Alumni Assn., Cutting Found. medal, Andover Newton Theol. Sem., 1976, Lifetime Achievement award, Mass. Med. Soc.; fellow in health, Kellogg Found. Internat., 1986—89, vis. fellow, Green Coll. Oxford U., 1985. Master: ACP; mem.: R.I. Med. Soc., Internat. Soc. Rehab. Medicine, Am. Congree Rehab. Medicine, Gerontol. Soc., Inst. Medicine. Jewish. Office: Brown U Box G Providence RI 02912 Office Phone: 401-729-3644. Business E-Mail: David_Greer@brown.edu.

GREER, FRANK ROLAND, pediatrician, neonatologist; b. Gainesville, Fla., Mar. 3, 1946; s. Charles Francis and Elizabeth French Greer; m. Catherine West, June 15, 1946; children: Natalie Greer Nicholson, Jonathan West. BS, Washington & Lee U., 1968; MD, U. Pa., 1972. Pediatircs Am. Bd. of Pediat., Chapel Hill, NC, 1977, Neonatal-Perinatal Medicine Am. Bd. of Pediat., NC, 1981. Resident in pediats. Cin. Children's Hosp., 1972—75, fellow in neonatal-perinatal medicine, 1978—80; prof. of pediat. U. of Wis., Madison, Wis., 1980—. Maj. Med Corps US Army, 1975—78. Office: Dept Pediats Univ Wisconsin 600 Highland Ave Madison WI 53792 Home Phone: 608-233-4686; Office Phone: 608-262-6561. Office Fax: 608-267-6377. E-mail: frgreer@wisc.edu.

GREER, GERMAINE, author; b. Melbourne, Australia, Jan. 29, 1939; d. Eric Reginald and Margaret May Mary (Lafrank) G. BA with honors in English, French Lit., U. Melbourne, 1959; MA with honors in English, U. Sydney, Australia, 1961; PhD (Commonwealth scholar), Newnham Coll. of Cambridge U., Eng., 1967; Doctorate (hon.), U. Griffith, 1996, U. York, Toronto, 1999, Manchester Inst. Tech., 2000; LLD (hon.), Melbourne U., 2003; LittD (hon.), Anglia Polytech. U., 2003. Sr. tutor U. Sydney, 1963-64; lectr. English U. Warwick, Eng., 1967-72; prof. modern letters U. Tulsa, 1980-83; dir. Tulsa Ctr. for Study of Woman's Lit.; prof. English and comparative studies U. Warwick, 1998—2003. Vis. prof. grad. faculty modern letters U. Tulsa, fall 1979; founder-dir. Tulsa Centre for the Study of Women's Lit.; founder, editor Tulsa Studies in Women's Lit., 1981; dir. Stump Cross Books, 1988—; spl. lectr. and unofcl. fellow Newnham Coll., Cambridge, 1989-98; lectr. in N.Am. Am. Program Bur., 1973-78. Author: The Female Eunuch, 1969, The Obstacle Race: The Fortunes of Women Painters and their Work, 1979, Sex and Destiny: The Politics of Human Fertility, 1984, Shakespeare, 1986, The Madwoman's Underclothes, 1986, Daddy, We Hardly Knew You, 1989 (J.R. Ackerly Prize, Premio Internazionale Mondello), The Change: Women, Aging and the Menopause, 1991, Slip-Shod Sibyls: Recognition, Rejection and the Woman Poet, 1995, The Surviving Works of Anne Wharton, 1997; editor: (with Susan Hastings, Jeslyn Medoff, Melinda Sansone) Kissing the Rod: An Anthology of Seventeenth Century Women's Verse, 1988, The Uncollected Verse of Aphra Behn, 1989, The Change: Women, Aging and the Menopause, 1991, Slip-Shod Sibyls: Recognition, Rejection and the Woman Poet, 1995, The Whole Woman, 1999, The Whole Woman, 1999, John Wilmot, Earl of Rochester, 1999 The Boy, 2003; editor 101 Poems by 101 Women, 2001, Poems for Gardeners, 2003; selected journalism published as The Madwoman's Underclothes, 1986, columnist Sunday Times, London, 1971-73, broadcaster/journalist/reviewer various publs. 1972-79. Jr. Govt. scholar, 1952, Diocesan scholar, 1956, Sr. Govt. scholar, 1956, Commonwealth scholar, 1964, Teacher's Coll. Studentship, 1956.

GREER, GORDON BRUCE, retired lawyer, writer; b. Butler, Pa, Feb. 17, 1932; s. Samuel Walker and Winifred (Fletcher) G.; m. Nancy Linda Hannaford, June 14, 1959; children: Gordon Bruce, Alison Clark. BA, Harvard U., 1953, JD cum laude, 1959. Bar: Wis. 1959, Mass. 1961. Assoc. Foley, Sammond & Lardner, Milw., 1959-61; assoc. Bingham Dana LLP, Boston, 1961-67, ptnr., 1967-97, of counsel, 1997—2002; ret., 2002. Lectr. Boston U. Sch. Law, 1998-2002. Author: World in Conflict, 2003, The First Decade, 2004, What Price Security?, 2005, All-Weather Fighters, 2006, The Role of Luck, 2007; editor: Harvard Law Rev. Vols. 71, 72. Maj. USAFR, ret. Mem.: Harvard Club (Boston), Brae Burn Country Club. Republican. Home: 45 Fieldmont Rd Belmont MA 02478-2606

GREER, JEAN REESE, music educator; b. Red Oak, Iowa, Jan. 28, 1949; d. Raymond Leroy and Helen Margaret Reese; m. Gordon Kenneth Greer, Nov. 24, 1973; children: Rebecca Helen, Andrew Gordon, Rachelle Erika. MusB, Simpson Coll., Indianaola, Iowa, 1971; MusM, Ind. U., Bloomington, 1975. Profl. concert/opera singer, Düsseldorf, North Rhein Westphalia, Germany, 1978—85; tvhr. music (voice/piano) Schaumburg Christian Sch. (Bethel Bapt. Ch.), Ill., 1986—89; prof. voice Bob Jones U., Greenville, SC, 1989—, head voice dept. music, 1998—; profl. concert/opera singer Vereinigte Bühnen Krefeld-Mönchengladbach, Krefeld, North Rhein Westphalia, Germany; profl. concert soloist with symphony orchs. Indpls., Des Moines, Greenville, Owensboro, Ind. U., Bob Jones U., and several orchs. and choral organs. in Germany; 25 maj. operatic roles in US and Germany, with Krefeld-Mönchengladbach Opera, Chautauqua Opera Assn., Des Moines Metro Opera, Ind. U. Opera Theater, Bob Jones U. Opera Assn., and Simpson Coll. Dir. children's choir Faith Bapt. Ch., Taylors, SC, 1993—99. Singer (solo/duet recs.): (sacred music) My Savior First of All, 1990, Soldiers of the Cross, 2001; singer: (solo rec.) (classical music) Jean Reese Greer - A Collection, 1997. Recipient various regional and dist. vocal competition awards/honors, Met. Opera Auditions, 1969-1974, semi-finalist, 23d Internat. Music Competition, Munich, Germany, 1974, Performer's Cert., Ind. U. Sch. Music, 1975; grantee vocal music study and audition trip, Martha Baird Rockefeller Found., 1975; Grad. Tchg. assistantship, Ind. U. Sch. Music, 1971-1975. Mem.: Nat. Assn. Tchrs. of Singing, Mu Phi Epsilon, Alpha Chi Omega. Conservative. Baptist. Avocations: reading, swimming, knitting. Home Phone: 864-244-9152; Office Phone: 864-242-5100. Business E-Mail: jgreer@bju.edu.

GREER, JULIANNA PATTERSON, not-for-profit administrator; b. Greenville, Tex., Dec. 5, 1953; d. Malcolm Boyd and Mary Helena Patterson; m. William Nathaniel Greer, Apr. 8, 1978. Student, Inst. Am., Aix-en-Provence, France, 1974—75; BA, Trinity U., San Antonio, 1976; MA, U. North Tex., 1981. V.p. of events Ill. St. Andrew Soc., North Riverside, Ill., 1996—2001; v.p. ops. Frank Lloyd Wright Preservation Trust, Oak Park, Ill., 2001—. Author: (monograph) Beyond the Regulations: Building Superior Facilities for the Aged. Mem.: Phi Beta Kappa. Unitarian Universalist. Avocations: travel, dance. Home: 667 Glen Haven Ln Glen Ellyn IL 60137 Office: Frank Lloyd Wright Preservation Trust 931 Chicago Ave Oak Park IL 60302 Home Phone: 630-214-1185; Office Phone: 708-848-1976. Office Fax: 708-848-1248. Personal E-mail: jpgreer@wowway.com. Business E-Mail: greer@wrightplus.org.

GREER, K. GORDON, banker; b. Tulsa, Oct. 28, 1936; s. H.K. and Afton (Goodman) G.; m. Nancy Lang, Nov. 22, 1958; children— Keith G., Scott A. BS in Banking and Fin., Okla. State U., 1958. Pres. Liberty Nat. Bank, Oklahoma City, 1958-84; CEO The First Nat. Bank and Trust Co., Tulsa, 1984—89; pres. Bank IV, Wichita, Kans., 1989—96; vice chmn. BancFirst Corp., Tulsa, 1996—. With Air Force N.G., 1958-64 Named to Hall of Fame, Bus. Adminstrn. Sch. Okla. State U., 1984 Mem. Am. Bankers Assn., Okla. Bankers Assn. (pres. 1983-84), So. Hills Country. Republican. Methodist. Avocation: golf.

GREER, MARK FRANCIS, information technology executive; b. Washington, Apr. 28, 1954; s. Richard Edwin and Marion Cecilia Greer; m. Donna Therese Weber, June 22, 1985; children: Matthew C., Alexander F., Kathleen M., Andrew W. BS, Duke U., Durham, NC, 1976; MS, Naval Postgrad. Sch., 1991. Liaison officer USN/Def. Intelligence Agy., Ottawa, Ont., Canada, 1984—87; asst. intelligence officer USN/Carrier Group 7, San Diego, 1987—89; project mgr. USN/Atlantic Fleet Hdqs., Norfolk, Va., 1991—93; commanding officer USN/Fleet Intelligence Ctr., Rota, Spain, 1993—96; asst. chief of staff for intelligence USN/Carrier Group 8, Norfolk, 1996—98; dir. info. tech., program mgr. USN/Office of Naval Intelligence, Washington, 1998—2003; dep. chief info. officer Def. Intelligence Agy., Washington, 2003—07; v.p. McNeil Tech., Inc., 2007—. Leader Boy Scouts Am., 1994—. Capt. USN, 1978—2003. Mem.: Naval Intelligence Profls., Armed Forces Comm. Elec. Assn. (v.p. govt. affairs 2001—, Meritorious Svc. in Intelligence award 2003). Office: McNeil Tech 6564 Loisdale Ct Ste 500 Springfield VA 22150 Office Phone: 703-921-1667. Office Fax: 703-921-1610. Business E-Mail: mgreer@mcneiltech.com.

GREER, MELVIN, medical educator; b. NYC, Oct. 14, 1929; s. Aaron and Ceil (Cohen) Jefkel; m. Arline Ebert, Dec. 16, 1951; children: Jonathan, Richard, Alison, David. BA magna cum laude, NYU, 1950, MD, 1954. Intern, resident Bellevue Hosp., NYC, 1954-56; fellow N.Y. Neurol.

Inst., Columbia, 1958-61; prof., chmn. dept. neurology U. Fla. Coll. Medicine, Gainesville, 1963-2000. Cons. NIH, 1971— , Fla. Div. Corrections, 1971—; lectr., cons. Navy Dept.; prof. dept. neurol. dept. psychiatry, dept. pediatrics, U. Fla. Coll. Medicine; endowed professorship neurology U. Fla. Coll. Medicine, Gainesville, 1991—. Author: Mass Spectrometry of Biologically Important Aromatic Acids, 1969, Differential Diagnosis of Neurological Diseases, 1977; also articles.; Editorial bd.: Neurology, Geriatics, 1968—. Served to lt. comdr. USNR, 1956-58. Recipient Medallion award Columbia U., 1968, Hippocratic award U. Fla., 1970, Outstanding Clin. Tchr. award, 1975, 79; NIH grantee, 1962-71 Fellow Am. Acad. Neurology (councillor, sec.-treas. 1977-81, pres.-elect 1983-85, pres. 1985-87), Am. Acad. Pediatrics; mem. Am. Neurol. Assn. (councillor), Soc. Pediatric Research, Am. Pediatric Soc., Phi Beta Kappa, Alpha Omega Alpha. Home: 2058 NW 14th Ave Gainesville FL 32605-5245

GREER, MONTE ARNOLD, endocrinologist, educator; b. Portland, Oreg., Oct. 26, 1922; s. William Wallace and Rose (Rasmussen) G.; m. Peggy Johnson, Dec. 31, 1943; children: Susan Elizabeth, Richard Arnold. Student, Oreg. State U., 1940-43; AB, Stanford U., 1944, MD, 1947. Intern San Francisco Gen. Hosp., 1946—47; rsch. fellow endocrinology New England Med. Ctr., Boston, 1947—49; resident internal medicine Mass. Meml. Hosp., Boston, 1949—50; rsch. assoc. in endocrinology New England Med. Ctr. Hosp., 1950—51; sr. investigator, sr. asst. surgeon USPHS, Nat. Cancer Inst., NIH, Bethesda, Md., 1951—55; chief radioisotope unit D.C. Gen. Hosp., Washington, 1951—55; clin. asst. prof. medicine UCLA, 1955—56; chief radioisotope svc. VA Hosp., Long Beach, Calif., 1955—56; head div. endocrinology Oreg. Health & Sci. U. (formerly U. Oreg. Med. Sch.), Portland, 1956—80, assoc. prof., 1956—62, prof. medicine, 1962—, prof. physiology, 1992—, head divsn. endocrinology, metabolism and clin. nutrition, 1980—84, head sect. endocrinology, 1984—90. Author: (with H. Studer) The Regulation of Thyroid Function in Iodine Deficiency, 1968, (with P. Langer) Antithyroid Drugs and Naturally Occurring Goitrogens, 1977; editor: The Thyroid Gland, 1990, (with D.H. Solomon) The Thyroid, 1974; mem. editorial bd. Endocrinology, 1960-72, Neuroendocrinology, 1965-76, Endocrine Regulations, 1971—; contbr. articles to profl. jours. Mem. Thyroid Task Force NIH Com. for Evaluation of Endocrinology and Metabolic Diseases, 1977-80, Endocrinology Study Sect., NIH, 1977-80. Pharmacol. and Endocrinology fellowship study sect. NIH, 1968-72; recipient Oppenheimer award Endocrine Soc., 1958, Rsch. Career award NIH, 1962-81, Discovery award Med. Rsch. Found. Oreg., 1985, DeMolay Legion of Honor award, 1988. Mem. AAAS, Am. Fedn. for Clin. Rsch. (chmn. Western sect. 1958-59), Western Soc. for Clin. Rsch. (v.p. 1963-64, pres. 1967-68), Endocrine Soc. (mem. council 1965-68, v.p. 1976-77), Am. Thyroid Assn. (v.p., dir. 1974-77, pres. 1980, Disting. Service award 1985), Am. Soc. Clin. Investigation, Soc. Exptl. Biology and Medicine, Western Assn. Physicians (sec.-treas. 1974-77), Assn. Am. Physicians, Internat. Brain Rsch. Orgn., Internat. Soc. Neuroendocrinology, European Thyroid Assn., Japan Endocrine Soc. (hon.), Czechoslovak Endocrine Soc. (hon.), Rotary, Sigma Chi. Office: Oreg Health and Sci Univ Portland OR 97201

GREER, RAYMOND WHITE, lawyer; b. Port Arthur, Tex., July 20, 1954; s. Mervyn Hardy Greer and Eva Swain; m. Pamela V. Brown; children: Emily Ann, Sarah Kelly, Jonathan Collin. BA magna cum laude, Sam Houston State U., Huntsville, Tex., 1977; JD, U. Houston, 1981. Assoc. Hoover, Cox & Shearer, Houston, 1980-83, Hinton & Morris, Houston, 1983-85; pvt. practice Houston, 1985-86; prin. Morris & Greer, PC, Houston, 1986-90, Raymond W. Greer & Assocs., PC, Houston, 1990-98, Rigg & Greer, Houston, 1998—2004, The Greer Law Firm, Houston, 2004—. Mem. dist. 4 grievance com. State Bar Tex., 1999-2005; lectr. in field. Mem. adv. com. Enterprising Girls Scouts Beyond Bars, San Jacinto coun., 1996-98. Recipient Outstanding Alumnus award, Dept. English, Sam Houston U., 1986, Disting. Alumni, Tex. Omicron chpt., Alpha Chi, 1996. Mem.: Ft. Bend County Bar Assn., State Bar Tex., Sam Houston State U. Alumni Assn. (combined charter and membership com. 1995—96, 1st v.p. 1996—97, pres. 1997—98, 2d v.p., chmn. membership com.), Rotary Club Houston (dir. 1999—2001, at large dir. 1998—99, chair Fresh Start com. 1997—98, asst. chair Fresh Start com. 1996—97). Avocation: reading. Office: The Greer Law Firm 13333 Southwest Fwy Ste 100 Sugar Land TX 77478-3545 Office Phone: 281-494-0100.

GREER, ROBERT BRUCE, III, orthopedist, educator; b. Butler, Pa., 1934; BA, Haverford Coll., 1956; MD, Harvard U., 1960. Diplomate Am. Bd. Orthopedic Surgery (bd. dirs. 1985-94, pres. 1990-91). Intern Mich. Med. Ctr., 1960-61, resident in surgery, 1961-62; resident in orthopaedic surgery U. Pitts. Med. Ctr., 1964-67, asst. prof. orthopedic surgery, 1967-71; orthopaedist MS Hershey Med. Ctr., Pa.; prof., chief orthopaedic surgery Pa. State U., 1971-91; ret. Med. dir. Howmedica, Inc., 1997-99. Capt. USAR, 1962-64. Mem. ACS, Am. Acad. Orthopaedic Surgeons, Am. Orthopaedic Assn., Ea. Orthopaedic Assn., Alpha Omega Alpha.

GREER, SUZANNE MICHELLE, music educator; b. Duluth, Minn., May 14, 1968; d. Robert Leonard Moore and Beatrice Mae Sandum; m. David Lee Greer, May 20, 2000. MusB in Piano Performance, St. Olaf Coll., Northfield, Minn., 1990; MusM in Piano Performance, U. Minn., 1994. Cert. music tchr. Music Teachers Nat. Assn., 2001, motorcycle safety instr. Motorcycle Safety Found., 1999. Music dir. Trinity Episc. Ch., Anoka, Minn., 1997—98; piano instr. SG Studio, Minnetonka, Minn., 2002—; depot outreach artist-in-residence Depot Cmty. Outreach Program, Duluth, Minn., 1990—91; motorcycle safety instr. Mpls., 1999—; rider's edge new rider course instr. St. Paul Harley Davidson, 2001—; music instr. North Hennepin C.C., Brooklyn Park, Minn., 1994—2002, Anoka-Ramsey C.C., Coon Rapids, Minn., 2001—02; piano instr. Son-Sheim Music Sch., Anoka, Minn., 1994—2002; piano accompanist Robbinsdale All-District Choir, Robbinsdale, Minn., 2000—02. Liaison for bd. of dirs. Magnum Chorum (St. Olaf Alumni Choir), St. Paul, 1998—2001. Scholar Music scholar, St. Olaf Coll., 1986, U. Minn., 1993, Shar Products scholar, Suzuki Assn. Am., 2002—05. Mem.: Suzuki Assn. for the Ams. (Shar Products Co. Scholarship for Tchr. Tng. 2004, Tchr. Tng. Scholarship 2004), Mpls. Music Tchrs. Forum (pres. 2007—), Suzuki Piano Tchrs. Guild (pres. 2006—07), Music Tchrs. Nat. Assn., West Suburban Music Tchrs. Assn. Republican. Avocations: motorcycling, travel. Personal E-mail: sgstudio@comcast.net.

GREER, WILLIS ROSWELL, JR., finance educator; b. Memphis, Nov. 16, 1938; s. Willis Roswell and Myra Bell (Bridges) G.; m. Melinda S. Scott, June 28, 1963; children: Howard Willis, Catherine Irene Grubbs, Charles Walker. BS, Cornell U., 1961, MBA with distinction, 1966; PhD in Acctg., U. Mich., 1971. Cert. Mgmt. Acct., Cert. Bus. Appraiser. Lectr. acctg. and stats. U. West Indies, Trinidad, 1966-67; teaching asst., Paton fellow U. Mich., 1967-71; asst. prof. acctg. U. Oreg., 1971-75, assoc. prof., 1975-76; vis. prof. acctg. Dartmouth Coll., Amos Tuck Sch., 1976-77, assoc. prof., 1976-82; vis. scholar Manchester (Eng.) Bus. Sch., 1981; prof. acctg. Naval Postgrad. Sch., 1982-88, acad. assoc. fin. mgmt., 1983-84, chmn. dept. adminstrv. scis., 1984-87; prof. acctg. U. Iowa, Iowa City, 1988-96, assoc. dean grad. programs, 1989-92, head dept. acctg., 1992-95; lectr. acctg. and fin. analysis Tohoku U., Japan, 1993-94; dean Coll. Bus. Adminstrn. U. No. Iowa, Cedar Falls, 1996—2001. Cons. U.S. Small Bus. Adminstrn. Minority Bus. Devel. Program, several large firms in various mfg. and svc. industries; presenter numerous seminars and workshops. Co-author: (with Paul Wasserman) Consultants and Consulting Organizations, 1966, (with J. Peter Williamson) Interim Inventory Estimation Error, 1979, (with Shu Liao) Cost Analysis for Dual Source Weapon Procurement, 1983, Cost Analysis for Competitive Major Weapon Systems Procurement: Further Refinement and Extension, 1984; author: A Method for Estimating and Controlling the Cost of Extending Technology, 1988; editor: (with Dan Nussbaum) Cost Analysis and Estimating: Tools and Techniques, 1990; contbr. articles to profl. jours. Treas. Oaknoll Retirement Cmty., 1993—. Mem. Inst. Mgmt. Accts. (dir. Cedar Rapids chpt. 1990—), Am. Acctg. Assn., Decision Scis. Inst., Inst. Bus. Appraisers, Inc. Republican. Achievements include research on conditions under which dual source procurement of major weapon systems is beneficial to goverment; building an accurate model for forecasting research and development costs for specified technology advancement. Home: PO Box 224 Rollins MT 59931-0224

GREETHAM, ELIZABETH M., former health products executive; BSc, U. Edinburgh, MA with honors. Former cons. F. Eberstadt & Co.; former portfolio mgr. Weiss, Peck & Greer; bd. dirs. DrugAbuse Scis., Inc., Los Altos, Calif., 1998—2003, CFO, 1999—2003, CEO, 2000—03; CEO, pres. ACCL Fin. Consultants, 2003—04. Bd. dirs. Guilford Pharms, Sangstat Med. Corp., PathoGenesis Corp., CliniChem Devel. Inc., Stressgen Biotechnologies Corp., 2002—, Ligand Pharmaceuticals Inc., 2007—.

GREEVER, JANET GROFF, history professor; b. Philadelphia, Sept. 12, 1921; m. William St. Clair Greever, Aug. 24, 1951; 1 child. BA, Bryn Mawr Coll., 1942, MA, 1945, Harvard U., 1951, PhD, 1954. Resident head grad. houses Radcliffe Coll., Cambridge, Mass., 1947-48; resident head undergrad. hall Bryn Mawr (Pa.) Coll., 1949-51, instr. history, 1949-50; asst. prof. history Wash. State U., Pullman, 1962-63, U. Idaho, Moscow, 1965-66; ind. rschr., lectr. history Moscow, Idaho, 1954—. Interim lectr. history Whitman Coll., Walla Walla, Wash., 1978; Idaho regional admissions cons. and interviewer Bryn Mawr COll., 1955-81. Author: Jose Ballivian y El Oriente Boliviano, 1987. Bd. dirs. U. Idaho Libr. Assocs., Moscow, 1979-81, pres. 1980-81. Pa. State scholar, 1938-42, History fellow Bryn Mawr (Pa.) Coll., 1944-45, Margaret M. Justin fellow AAUW, Washington, 1948-49; grantee Lucius N. Littauer Found., N.Y.C., 1948-49. Mem. Am. Hist. Assn. (life), Conf. on Latin. Am. History (life), Latin Am. Studies Assn., Soc. for Am. Archaeology (life), Archaeol. Inst. Am. (life), Phi Alpha Theta. Avocations: travel, photography. Home: 315 S Hayes St Moscow ID 83843-3419

GREEVER, JOHN, retired mathematics professor; b. Pulaski, Va., Jan. 30, 1934; s. John Jay Greever and Hulah Lily (Loyd) Bentley; m. Margaret LeSueur Quarles, Aug. 29, 1953; children: Catherine Patricia, Richard George, Cynthia Diane. BS in Math., U. Richmond, 1953; MA in Math., U. Va., 1956, PhD in Math., 1958. Asst. prof. math. Fla. State U., Tallahassee, 1958-61; mem. faculty Harvey Mudd Coll., Claremont, Calif., 1961-95, prof. math., 1970-95, chmn. math. dept., 1972-75, founding dir. math. clinic, 1973-75. Faculty Claremont Grad. Sch., 1962-95; vis. prof. Kyoto (Japan) U. Rsch. Inst. for Math. Sci., 1967-68, U. B.C. Inst. Animal Resource Ecology, Vancouver, 1984-85; rsch. assoc. dept. biology U. Calif., Riverside, 1975-78; vis. rsch. mathematician dept. entomology U. Calif., 1978. Author Theory and Examples of Point Set Topology, 1967; contbr. articles to profl. jours. Master gardner Wash. State U., 2005; mem. pk. bd. San Juan County, 2004. Mem.: Soc. of the Cin., Math. Assn. Am. (sec.-treas. So. Calif. sect. 1973—76, pres. 1981—82), Coun. on Undergrad. Rsch. (councilor 1989—95, vice-chmn. math. and computer scis. sect. 1991—92, chmn. 1992—94), Am. Math. Soc., Pole Pass Power Squadron (comdr. 2001), Orcas Island Garden Club (pres. 2005), Orcas Island Yacht Club (commodore 2002), Sigma Xi, Phi Kappa Sigma, Kappa Mu Epsilon, Pi Mu Epsilon. Avocations: boating, gardening. Home: 260 Grey Havens Loop PO Box 413 Orcas WA 98280-0413 Business E-Mail: greever@hmc.edu.

GREEVER, MARGARET QUARLES, retired mathematics educator; b. Wilkensburg, Pa., Feb. 7, 1931; d. Lawrence Reginald and Ella Mae (LeSueur) Quarles; m. John Greever, Aug. 29, 1953; children: Catherine Patricia, Richard George, Cynthia Diane. Cert. costume design, Richmond Profl. Inst., Va., 1952; student, U. Va., Charlottesville, 1953—56; BA in Math., Calif. State U., LA, 1963; MA in Math., Claremont Grad. Sch., Calif., 1968. Cert. tchr. specializing in Jr. Coll. math., Calif. Tchr. math. Chaffey Unified H.S. Dist., Alta Loma, Calif., 1963—64, L.A. Unified Sch. Dist., 1964—65, Chino (Calif.) Unified Sch. Dist., 1965—81; from asst. prof. to prof. Chaffey Coll., Rancho Cucamonga, 1981—92, chmn. phys. sci. divsn., 1988—92, dean, phys., life, health sci., 1992—96. Mem. AAUW (pres. local chpt. 1998-2000), Orcas Island Garden Club (treas. 1997-2000, pres.-elect 2000, pres. 2001), Orcas Island Yacht Club (corr. sec. 2006), Pi Lambda Theta. Avocations: cooking, sewing, gardening, quilting. E-mail: greever@rockisland.com.

GREGAN, EDMUND ROBERT, landscape architect; b. New Haven, Feb. 4, 1936; s. Edmund Arthur and Elizabeth (Kochiss) G.; m. Janet Lamson Shaw, Aug. 22, 1959; children: Edmund Robert, Darianne Lee, Christyn Elizabeth. BS in Landscape Architecture, R.I. Sch. Design, 1960. Lic. landscape architect, Conn. Landscape architect and site planner Morton S. Fine & Assocs., Hartford, Conn., 1960-62; landscape architect New Haven Redevel. Agy., 1962—66, chief landscape architect, 1966-78; landscape architect, cons., lectr. E. Robert Gregan Landscape Architect, Northford, Conn., 1965—; chief landscape architect New Haven City Plan Dept., 1978-91. Instr. landscape architecture Guilford/Madison (Conn.) Adult Edn. Programs, 1979-88; tchr., critic Yale, R.I. Sch. Design, U. Conn. Conway Sch. Landscape Design, So. Conn. State U.; tchr. environ. design Yale Sch. of Forestry and Environ. Studies Elem. Schs. New Haven, 1992; tchr. Federated Garden Clubs Conn. Sch. Landscape Design, 1979—; lectr. various orgns. and clubs. Contbr. numerous profl. jours. Bd. dirs. North Branford Land Conservation Trust, 1968-72, v.p., 1973—; mem. North Branford Conservation Commn., 1969-73, chmn., 1971-72, assoc. mem., 1973-92; cons. North Branford Ctr. Improvement Com., 1991-95; mem. North Branford-Northford Town Design Dists. Adv. Com., 1995—; bd. dirs. New Haven Urban Resources Initiative, 1991-96, Friends of the Grove St. Cemetery, Inc., 2005—, The Greater New Haven Holocaust Meml., Inc., 2005—; mem. steering com. Long Wharf Nature Preserve, 1995-2000; landscape arch., vice chair spl. events 1995 Spl. Olympics World Games. Recipient Cert. of Achievement award Federated Garden Clubs. Conn., 1981, Bronze medal Federated Garden Clubs Conn., 1991, Cert. of Merit for Excellence in Study of Landscape Architecture, RISD, 1960, Outstanding Urban Forestry Profl. award Urban Forest Coun., 2001, numerous profl. design awards. Fellow Am. Soc. Landscape Architects; mem. Conn. Soc. Landscape Architects (bd. dir. 1981-86, hist. and landscape preservation com. 1987—, George A. Yarwood Cert. Svc. award 1987), Totoket Hist. Soc. (mem. design cons. 1972—), Garden Club New Haven (hon. mem.), Federated Garden Clubs of Conn., Inc. (hon. mem. landscape design critics coun. 1993). Episcopalian. Avocations: design, gardening, photography, travel. Home and Office: 7 Stair Brook Way Northford CT 06472-1495

GREGANTI, MAC ANDREW, physician, educator; b. Cleveland, Miss., Apr. 13, 1947; s. Mack Americo and Grace Margaret (Barbati) G.; m. Susan Taylor, Aug. 8, 1971; children: Paul Andrew, Mack Taylor, Mary Catherine. BS summa cum laude, Millsaps Coll., 1969; MD summa cum laude, U. Miss., 1972. Diplomate Am. Bd. Internal Medicine, Am. Bd. Geriat. medicine. Intern U. Rochester, NY, 1972-73, resident NY, 1973-75; instr. dept. medicine U. Miss. Sch. Medicine, Jackson, 1975-76, asst. prof., 1976-77, U. N.C. Sch. Medicine, Chapel Hill, 1977-83, assoc. prof., 1983-90, prof., 1990—, chief div. gen. medicine, 1986-91, assoc. chair for clin. affairs, 1991-99, acting chmn., 1999-2000, vice-chmn., 2000—. Dir. med./pediatric residency U. N.C. Dept. Medicine, Chapel Hill, 1980-86, dir. medicine residency, 1981-86. Contbr. articles on med. edn. and patient care to profl. jours. Fellow: ACP; mem.: Am. Geriatrics Soc., Alpha Omega Alpha. Roman Catholic. Avocations: computers, tennis, golf, photography. Office: Univ NC Chapel Hill Dept Medicine 125 Macnider Hall Cb 7005 Chapel Hill NC 27599-7005 Office Phone: 919-966-3063. Business E-Mail: gregandr@med.unc.edu.

GREGERSEN, R(OALD) GEORGE, newspaper publishing executive; b. Copenhagen, Mar. 14, 1935; came to U.S., 1948; s. Richard Vilhelm and Eva (Giertsen) G.; m. Gayle Froerer Richards, May 1, 1964 (div. 1978); m. Penney Losse, Dec. 21, 1982; children: Mary Anne Georgia, John Christian. Student, U. Utah, 1953-55. Pres., CEO Mortgage Investment Corp., Salt Lake City, 1955-68; pres., CEO Gregersen & Co., Salt Lake City, 1968-74; pub., CEO The Enterprise (weekly), Salt Lake City, 1974—. Editl. writer The Enterprise, 1974—. Bd. dirs. Utal Mil. & Vets. Affairs com., Salt Lake City, 1982-92. Named Utah Mil. Citizen of Yr., 1986; recipient Assn. U.S. Army Exceptional Svc. award, 1990. Mem. Alta Club (bd. dirs. 1993-96), Rotary. Republican. Episcopalian. Avocation: fly fishing. Office: Enterprise Newspaper Group Inc 136 S Main St Ste 721 Salt Lake City UT 84101-1676 Office Phone: 801-533-0556.

GREGERSON, DANIEL P., retired computer company executive; s. Donald Carl and Sue Gregerson; m. Virginia M. Moore, Apr. 3, 1990; children: Lily Anne, John Luke. BA with honors, U. Calif., Santa Cruz, 1981. Founder, COO Intelligent Technologies, Inc., Palo Alto, Calif., 1982—84; founder, CEO PeerLogic, Inc., San Francisco, 1986—2000. Chmn. Mindfabric, Inc., Saratoga, Calif., 2001—04. Author: Playground of the Fleas. Vol. cons. Hertz Found., Livermore, Calif., 2004—05. Mem.: Commonwealth Club Calif. (assoc.). Achievements include patents in field. Home Phone: 415-785-7774.

GREGERSON, LINDA KAREN, poet, language educator, critic; b. Elgin, Ill., Aug. 5, 1950; d. Olaf Thorbjorn and Karen Mildred Gregerson; m. Steven Mullaney, 1980; children: Emma Mullaney, Megan Mullaney. BA, Oberlin Coll., 1971; MA, Northwestern U., 1972; MFA, U. Iowa, 1977; PhD, Stanford U., 1987. Actress Kraken Theater Co., 1972—75; asst. poetry editor The Atlantic Monthly Press, 1982—86; staff editor Atlantic Monthly, Boston, 1982—87; asst. prof. Dept. English U. Mich., 1987—91, William Wilhartz asst. prof. English, 1991—94, assoc. prof. Dept. English, 1994—2001, prof. Dept. English, 2001—03, Frederick G. L. Huetwell prof., prof. English, 2003—, dir. MFA program in creative writing, 1997—2000. Mem. usage panel Am. Heritage Dictionary, 1987—; vis. asst. prof. creative writing program Dept. English Boston U., 1985—86; instr. lit. MIT, 1985—87; asst. editor Mich. Quarterly Rev., 1987—; editl. cons. Cambridge Univ. Press, 1989—, Harvard Univ. Press, 1989—, Oxford Univ. Press, 1989—, Wesleyan Univ. Press, 1989—, Ind. Univ. Press, 1989—, Bedford Books, 1989—, Univ. Mich. Press, 1989—, Wayne State Univ. Press, 1989—. Author: Fire in the Conservatory, 1982, The Reformation of the Subject: Spenser, Milton, and the English Protestant Epic, 1995, The Woman Who Died in Her Sleep, 1996, Negative Capability: Contemporary American Poetry, 2001, Waterborne, 2002, Magnetic North, 2007. Recipient Levinson Prize award Poetry, 1991, Consuelo Ford award, Poetry Soc. Am., 1992, Isabel MacCaffrey award, Spenser Soc. Am., 1992, Pushcart prize, 1994, 2004, Acad. award in Lit., Am. Acad. Arts and Letters, 2002; fellow, Nat. Endowment Arts, 1985, 1992, Mellon, Nat. Humanities Ctr., 1991—92, Guggenheim, 2000; grantee Arts Found., Mich., 1994; Ingram Merrill grant, 1982—84. Mem.: MLA, Inst. Advanced Study (vis. mem. 1993—94), Milton Soc., Internat. Spenser Soc. (Isabel MacCaffrey award 1992), Renaissance Soc.Am., Shakespeare Assn. Am. Office: U Mich Dept English Lang and Lit 3147 Angell Hall Ann Arbor MI 48109-1045

GREGG, BILLY RAY, seed industry executive, consultant; b. Taylorsville, Miss., Aug. 31, 1930; s. Hinds and Lillie Mae (Moore) G.; m. Mary Frances Barber, Aug. 12, 1950 (div. Jan. 1987); children: Kathryn, Patricia, Lisa; m. Orawan Chonlavorn, Dec. 20, 1988; 1 child, Nathan Paul. AA, Perkinston Jr. Coll., Miss., 1950; BS, Miss. State U., 1954, MS, 1956, PhD, 1968; postgrad., Wash. State U., 1957-63. Asst. prof. Wash. State U., Pullman, 1956-63; mgr. Ala. Crop Improvement Assn., Auburn, Ala., 1964-66; seed technologist Miss. State U., 1966-68; chief party/processing specialist seed improvement project U.S. AID, New Delhi, India, 1968-72, chief party and seed specialist seed project Brasilia, Brazil, 1972-74, chief, seed industry devel. specialist Bangkok, 1977-87, seed industry devel. specialist Cairo, 1987-93; chief party and seed industry specialist IDB and GOB Agiplan Project, Brasilia, 1974-76; seed industry specialist Internat. Plant Breeders, Maringa, Parana, Brazil, 1976, Interam. Agrl. Sci. Inst., Brasilia, 1976-77; seed industry devel. specialist internat. programs Miss. State U., 1993—. Cons./advisor on seed tech. matters, mgmt., quality control and industry devel. nat. govts., pvt. cos., World Bank, Interam. Devel. Bank, FAO, GTZ, U.S. AID in more than 80 countries, 1960-95. Contbr. over 500 articles to profl. jours.; author 2 books. With U.S. Army, 1950-52; ETO. Indian Soc. Seed Technologists fellow, 1987. Mem. Kiwanis Internat. (dir., Kiwanian of the Yr. 1968), Agrl. Sci. Soc. Thailand (hon.), Wash. State Crop Improvement Assn. (hon. life), Phi Kappa Phi, Sigma Xi, Phi Theta Kappa. Buddhist. Avocations: vegetable and flower gardening, writing, travel. Home: PO Box 1756 Starkville MS 39760-1756 Office Phone: 662-323-0035. Personal E-mail: billgregg1@bellsouth.net. E-mail: topgregg@bully.net.

GREGG, CHARLES THORNTON, research and development company executive, molecular biologist, researcher; b. Billings, Mont., July 27, 1927; s. Charles Thornton and Gertrude (Hurst) G.; m. Elizabeth Whitaker, Dec. 20, 1947; children: Paul, Diane, Brian, Elaine. BS in Physics, Oreg. State U., 1952, MS in Organic Chemistry, 1955, PhD in Biochemistry, 1959. Postdoctoral fellow Nat. Cancer Inst., Johns Hopkins Sch. Med., Balt., 1959-63; mem. staff Los Alamos (N.Mex.) Nat. Lab., 1963-85; sr. scientist Mesa Diagnostics, Los Alamos, 1985-86; v.p. rsch. Los Alamos Diagnostics, 1986-90; pres. Innovative Surg. Tech. Inc., 1991—. Pres. Bethco, Inc., 1972—; vis. prof. The Free U., Berlin, 1973-74; cons. internat. tech. div. Los Alamos Nat. Lab., 1985-90. Author: Plague, 1978, The Virus of Love, 1983, Tarawa, 1985; patentee bacterial identification apparatus, surg. knife. Bd. dirs. Friends of Mesa Pub. Libr., Los Alamos, 1981-83, County Libr. Los Alamos, 1983-85, Los Alamos Arts Coun., 1985-87, bd. dir., Lukens Med. Corp., 1996-97. Served in U.S. Navy, 1944-46. Fellow AAAS; mem. Am. Soc. Biochemistry and Molecular Biology, Am. Soc. Microbiology, Sigma Xi, Sigma Pi Sigma, Phi Lambda Upsilon. Democrat. Unitarian Universalist. Avocation: hiking. Office: 190 Central Park Sq Los Alamos NM 87544-4001 Home Phone: 505-662-7429; Office Phone: 505-662-3240. Personal E-mail: cgregg3@yahoo.com. Business E-Mail: president@1stmedmart.com.

GREGG, ELLEN M., lawyer; b. Elkton, Md., July 9, 1961; BA summa cum laude, Campbell U., 1983; JD cum laude, Campbell U. Sch. Law, 1986. Bar: NC 1986, admitted to practice: All NC Fed. Dist. Cts., Ct. Appeals (4th Cir.). Intern Md. State Atty. Office, Cecil County, 1982; clerk to Hon. Gerald Arnold NC Ct. Appeals, 1984, jud. clerk to Hon. John C. Martin, 1986—87; mem. Womble Carlyle Sandridge & Rice, PLLC, Winston-Salem, NC. Membership editor Campbell Law Review; contbr. articles to profl. jours. Mem. jail manual adv. bd. Inst. Govt., Univ. NC. Named Region Champion, Nat. Trial Competition, 1986; recipient Lewis F. Powell Medallion for Excellence in Advocacy, Book Awards in Civil Procedure, Trial Advocacy, Criminal Procedure & Jurisprudence. Mem.: ABA (mem. litig. sect.), Forsyth County Young Lawyers Assn. (mem. litig. sect., mem. career develop. com., mem. trial practice general curriculum com.), NC Bar Assn. (mem. young lawyers divsn., mem. litig. sect.), Forsyth County Bar Assn. (mem. young lawyers sect.), Omicron Delta Kappa, Phi Kappa Phi. Office: Womble Carlyle Sandridge & Rice PLLC

One W 4th St Winston Salem NC 27101 Mailing: Womble Carlyle Sandridge & Rice PLLC PO Box 84 Winston Salem NC 27102 Office Phone: 336-721-3729. Office Fax: 336-733-8384. Business E-Mail: egregg@wcsr.com.

GREGG, JOHN PENNYPACKER, lawyer; b. Phila., May 25, 1947; s. William Pemberton and Sarah E. (High) G. AB, Trinity Coll., 1969; JD, Villanova U., 1974. Bar: Pa. 1974, U.S. Dist. Ct. (ea. dist.) Pa. 1974. Tchr., dir. student activities The Pennington (N.J.) Sch., 1969-71; atty. Pub. Defenders Office, Norristown, Pa., 1974—, High, Swartz, Roberts & Seidel, Norristown, 1975—. Bd. dirs. Rittenhouse Book Distbr. Inc., King of Prussia, Pa. Bd. dirs. PThe Episcopal Acad., Merion, Pa., 1986-89, hila. Toboggan Co., Lansdale, 1987-91, Lower Merion Shared Housing Corp., Ardmore, Pa., 1991-95, Lower Merion Affordable Housing, Bryn Mawr, Pa., 1995—; pres. St. Asaph's Inc., 2006—; ann. giving com. Inglis House, Phila., 1991-92. Recipient Legion of Honor Chapel of the Four Chaplains, Phila., 1980, Harry L. Green Svc. award, 1990, Disting. Svc. award Episcopal Acad., 1990. Mem. Pa. Bar Assn., Montgomery Bar Assn. (com. chmn. 1991-94). Home: 635 Walnut Ln Haverford PA 19041-1225 Office: High Swartz Roberts & Seidel 40 E Airy St Norristown PA 19401-4803 Office Phone: 610-275-0700.

GREGG, JUDD ALAN, senator, former governor; b. Nashua, NH, Feb. 14, 1947; s. Hugh Gregg; m. Kathleen MacLellan, 1973; children— Molly, Sarah, Joshua AB, Columbia U., 1969; JD, Boston U., 1972, LL.M., 1975. Bar: N.H. 1972. Ptnr. Sullivan, Gregg and Horton, Nashua, NH, 1975—80; rep. from 2d N.H. dist. US Ho. of Reps, Washington, 1981-89; gov. State of N.H., Concord, 1989-93; US Senator from NH, 1993—. Mem. NH Exec. Coun., 1979—81; mem. com. health, edn., labor and pensions US Senate, chmn. com. budget, com. appropriations. Pres. Crotched Mountain Rehab. Found. Recipient Visionary award, Gulf Maine Coun., 1992, Robert B. Kerr award, NH Tuberculosis and Health Assn., 1998, Legis. of Yr., Congressional Fire Services Inst., 1999, Chmn.'s award disting. meritorious svc., Atlantic States Marine Fisheries Commn., 2003, Govt. Leadership on Arts award, NH Citizens for the Arts, NH Coun. on Arts, 2003, Public Svc. award, Ctr. Irish Programs Boston Coll., 2003, Disting. Cmty. Health Champion award, Nat. Assn. Cmty. Health Centers, 2004, Leadership award, Friends of Cancer Rsch., Rsch. Am., 2004, Legis. award, Coun. State Adminstr. Vocational Rehab., 2005. Mem. ABA, N.H. BAr Assn., Nashua Bar Assn. Republican. Congregationalist. Office: US Senate 393 Senate Russell Bldg Washington DC 20510-0001 also: District Office 41 Hooksett Rd Manchester NH 03104 Office Phone: 202-224-3324, 603-622-7979. Office Fax: 202-224-4952.*

GREGG, LUCIUS PERRY, JR., aerospace executive; b. Henderson, NC, Jan. 16, 1933; s. Lucius Perry and Rachel (Jackson) G.; m. Doris Marie Jefferson, May 30, 1959 (dec. Nov. 1980); 1 child, Lucius Perry III; m. Beverly E.E. Ward, Jan. 3, 1994. BSEE with distinction, U.S. Naval Acad., 1955; MS in Aero and Astronautics, MIT, 1961; AMP Program, Harvard Bus. Sch., 1975; D of Sci. (hon.), Grinnell Coll., 1973. Pilot, aircraft commdr. mil. air command USAF, 1956-59; project scientist Air Force Office Scientific Rsch., Washington, 1961-65; dir., rsch. coord., assoc. dean sci. Northwestern U., Evanston, Ill., 1965-69; program officer Alfred P. Sloan Found., NYC, 1969-72; pres. First Chgo. U. Finance Corp., Chgo., 1972-79; v.p. First Nat. Bank Chgo., 1972-79; v.p. corp. planning Bristol-Myers Co., NYC, 1979-83; dir. nat. pub. affairs, v.p. gov. rels. Citibank/Citicorp, NYC, 1983-87; v.p. pub. affairs N.Y. Daily News, NYC, 1987-89; v.p. corp. communications Hughes Electronics Corp., LA, 1989—99. Vis. com. on aero and astronautics MIT, Cambridge, 1971-79; vis. com. on physics Harvard U., Cambridge, 1973-79; mem. commn. on human resources Nat. Acad. Sci., Washington, 1973-78; founding trustee Fermi Nat. Accelerator Lab., Batavia, Ill., 1968-72; chmn. White House Fellows selection com. (Midwest), 1977-79; chmn. bd. dirs. Negro Ensemble Co., NYC, 1984-89; bd. dirs. U.S.-South Africa Leadership Exchange Program, Wash., 1975-1982; vice chmn., bd. dirs. Corp. for Pub. Broadcasting, Washington, 1975-81; bd. trustees WNET Pub. TV, NYC, 1981-89; bd. dirs. Chgo. Coun. on Fgn. Rels., Chgo., 1975-79; acad. adv. bd. US Naval Acad., Annapolis, Md., 1971-81; civilian adv. bd. Chief of Naval Personnel, 1975-80; mem. NASA U. Rels., Washington, 1968-72; chmn. bd. visitors Tulane U., New Orleans, 1972-77; intelligence rev. com. Chgo. Police Dept., 1977-79. Maj. USAF, 1965-85. Named Engr. of Yr. Washington Acad. Sci., 1964, One of 10 Outstanding Young Men Chgo. Jr. Assn. Commerce and Industry, 1966. Home and Office: 4143 Via Marina PH18 Marina Del Rey CA 90292 Business E-Mail: lu@lugregg.com.

GREGG, STEPHEN THOMPSON, political scientist, consultant; s. David Almus Gregg II and Virginia Thompson Gregg; m. Karen Hein Gregg; 1 child, John Jefferson. BS in Bus. and Orgnl. Behavior magna cum laude, SUNY, Albany, 1973; MPA, Ind. U., 1996. Relapse Prevention Specialist #438 CENAPS, Inc. - Homewood, IL, 1994, Cognitive-Behavioral Therapist # 10881 NACBT - Weirton, WV, 1996, Extra Class Amateur Radio Operator - N9RKS Fed. Comm. Commn., 2001. Elected selectman, bd. chmn. Town of Holderness, NH, 1985—89; candidate for U.S. Rep., Rep. Primary, Congressional District 2, NH, 1988; counselor S.T. Gregg & Assocs., Indpls., 1992—, pub. affairs, policy, & mgmt. facilitator, 1995—. Disaster radio group ARC, Indpls., 1998—; vol. Am. Radio Emergency Svcs. With US Army, 1965—68, Vietnam. Named to Hon. Order of Ky. Cols., 1981. Mem.: ASPA (assoc.), Am. Radio Relay League (assoc.), Pemigewasset Valley Fish & Game Club (assoc.; v.p., dir. 1986—88), Masons, VFW (life). Moderate. Congregationalist. Avocations: scuba diving, radio communications. Office: ST Gregg & Assocs PO Box 36366 Indianapolis IN 46236-0366

GREGGS, ELANORA, social worker; b. Barnwell County, SC, Nov. 10, 1933; d. Daniel and Georgia (Cobb) Young; children: John, Christopher, Paulette, Doris. BA, Coll. New Rochelle, 1985; MSW, Yeshiva U., 1987. Para-profl. Bd. Edn., Bklyn., 1965—67; salesperson Tira Exclusive, Laurelton, NY, 1982—85, Mary Kay Cosmetics, Stanley Home Products; human svcs. supr. Cath. Charities, Bklyn., 1986—87, social work supr. Jamaica, NY, 1987—95, Jamaica Support Sys., 1995. Tchr. Maranatha Bible Inst., 2001—; cons., spkr. in field. Author: Broken Pieces, 1998. Alumni Coll. New Rochelle, NY, 1985—, Yeshiva U., NYC, 1987—; pub. rels. Lake Arbor Found., Mitchellville, Md., 2000—; vol. in nursing homes, 1996—; active Christian Women of Faith, Mitchellville, Md., 2001—; acting min. Evangel Cathedral, 1995—. Avocations: reading, writing, walking, swimming, gardening.

GREGOIRE, CHRISTINE O., governor, former state attorney general; b. Auburn, Wash., Mar. 24, 1947; m. Michael Gregoire; children: Courtney, Michelle. BA in Speech & Sociology, U. Wash., 1969; JD cum laude, Gonzaga U., 1977, LLD (hon.), 1995. Clerk, typist Wash. State Adult Probation/ Parole Office, Seattle, 1969; caseworker Wash. Dept. Social and Health Scis., Everett, 1974; asst. atty. gen. State of Wash., Spokane, 1977—81, sr. asst. atty. gen., 1981—82, dep. atty. gen. Olympia, 1982—88, atty. gen., 1992—2005, gov., 2005—; dir. Wash. State Dept. Ecology, 1988—92. Chair States/B.C. Oil Spill Task Force, 1989—92, Puget Sound Water Quality Authority, 1990—92, Nat. Com. State Environ. Dirs., 1991—92. Bd. dirs. Wash. State Dept. Ecology, 1988—92. Named Woman of Yr., Am. Legion Aux., 1999; named one of 25 Most Influential Working Mothers, Working Mother mag., 2000; recipient Conservationist of Yr. award, Trout Unlimited/N.W. Steelhead & Salmon Coun., 1994, Gov.'s Child Abuse Prevention award, 1996, Myra Bradwell award, 1997, Wyman award, 1997—98, Bd. of Gov.'s award for professionalism, WSBA, 1997, Kick Butt award, The Tobacco Free Coalition of Pierce County, 1997, Wash. State Hosp. Assn. award, 1997, Citizen Activist award, Gleitsman Found., 1998, Woman of Achievement award, Assn. for Women in Comm. Matrix Table, 1999, Pub. Justice award, WSTLA, 1999, Excellence in Pub. Health award, Wash. State Assn. Local Pub. Health Ofcls., 1999, Women in Govt. award, Good Housekeeping, 1999, Spl. Recognition award, Wash. State Nurses Assn., 2000. Mem.: Nat. Assn. Attys. Gen. (consumer protection and environment com., energy com., children and the law subcom., pres. 1999—2000). Democrat. Office: Office of Gov PO Box 40002 Olympia WA 98504 Office Phone: 360-753-6780. Office Fax: 360-753-4110.*

GREGOIRE, MATHIEU, artist, consultant; s. Armand and Renée Gregoire; m. Amanda Farber; 1 child, Raphael. Student, U. Chgo., 1972—73; BA in Art and Drawing, Portland State U., 1979. Project dir. Stuart Collection, U. Calif., San Diego, 1983—, lectr., 2000—; assoc. prof. U. Nev., Las Vegas, 1999—2000; project dir. U. Calif. San Francisco Mission Bay, San Diego, 2001—. Cons. numerous projects in field; lectr. in field. One-man shows include Boehm Gallery, Palomar Coll., San Marcos, Calif., 1987, Mattress Factory, Pitts., 1988, Dietrich Jenny Gallery, San Diego, 1988, Artpark, Lewiston, NY, 1989, Laguna Mus. at South Coast Plz., Costa Mesa, Calif., 1989, Jan Turner Gallery, LA, 1992, Founder's Gallery, U. Calif., San Diego, 1992, Thomas Babeor Gallery, La Jolla, Calif., 1994, Mus. Contemporary Art San Diego, 1995—, Calif. State U., San Marcos, 1998, Donna Beam Gallery, U. Nev., Las Vegas, 1999, exhibited in group shows at Paris/Green Gallery, La Jolla, 1987, Lannan Mus., Lake Worth, Fla., 1987, Mandeville Gallery, U. Calif., San Diego, 1987, Dietrich Jenny Gallery, 1988, Jan Turner Gallery, LA, 1991, Kohn Turner Gallery, 1994, So. Exposure at Project Artaud, San Francisco, 1994, Mus. Contemporary Art, San Diego, 1997, Madison Art Ctr., Wis., 1997, Donna Beam Gallery, U. Nev., Las Vegas, 1999, Nev. Inst. Contemporary Art, 1999, Littman Gallery, Portland State U., 1999, Flux, San Diego, 2000, 2001, Elizabeth Leach Gallery, Portland, 2000, Southwestern Coll., San Diego, 2005, Represented in permanent collections Calif. Ctr. Arts, Escondido, Waterfront Pk., Portland, Mile High Stadium, Denver. Founding bd. dirs. San Diego Coop. Charter Sch., 1999—2001. Fellow, Nat. Endowment Arts, 1988, 1990; grantee, 1997, Met. Arts Commn., Portland, 1982, Change, Inc., 1988, Louis Comfort Tiffany Found., 1989. Home: 3629 Arnold Ave San Diego CA 92104 Office Phone: 619-220-8850. Business E-Mail: mgregoire@ucsd.edu.

GREGOR, CLUNIE BRYAN, geology educator; b. Edinburgh, Mar. 5, 1929; came to U.S., 1968; s. David Clunie Gregor and Barbara Mary Moller-Beilby; m. Suzanne Assir, Apr. 24, 1955 (div. Apr. 1969); 1 child, Andrew James; m. Anna Bramanti, Apr. 15, 1969 (dec. Oct. 1993); children: Thomas James, Matthew James. BA, Cambridge U., Eng., 1951, MA, 1954; DSc, U. Utrecht, The Netherlands, 1967. Instr. Am. U. Beirut, 1958-64; rsch. asst. Delft (The Netherlands) Inst. Tech., 1964-65, dir. Crystallographic Lab., 1965-67; vis. prof. Case Western Res. U., Cleve., 1968-69; prof. West Ga. Coll., Carrollton, 1969-72, Wright State U., Dayton, Ohio, 1972—. Chmn. USA work group on geochem. cycles, 1972-88, vice chmn. panel on geochem. cycles NAS, 1988-90. Author: (monograph) Geochemical Behaviour of Sodium, 1967, The Evolving Earth, 1997; editor: Chemical Cycles in the Evolution of the Earth, 1988. Grantee, NSF, 1977—82, Sicily, 1978—80. Fellow Geol. Soc. (London); mem. Geol. Soc. Am., Am. Geophys. Union, Geochem. Soc. (sec. 1983-89). Home: 136 W North College St Yellow Springs OH 45387-1563 Office: Wright State U Dept Geol Scis Dayton OH 45435 Office Phone: 937-775-3442 3455, 937-775-3445.

GREGOR, DOROTHY DEBORAH, retired librarian; b. Dobbs Ferry, NY, Aug. 15, 1939; d. Richard Garrett Heckman and Marion Allen (Richmond) Stewart; m. A. James Gregor, June 22, 1963 (div. 1974). BA, Occidental Coll., 1961; MA, U. Hawaii, 1963; MLS, U. Tex., 1968; cert. in Library Mgmt., U. Calif., Berkeley, 1976. Reference libr. U. Calif., San Francisco, 1968-69; dept. libr. Pub. Health Libr. U. Calif., Berkeley, 1969-71, tech. services libr., 1973-76; reference libr. Hamilton Libr., Honolulu, 1971-72; head serials dept. U. Calif., Berkeley, 1976-80, assoc. univ. libr. tech. svcs. dept., 1980-84, univ. libr., 1992-94; chief Shared Cataloging div. Libr. of Congress, Washington, 1984-85; univ. libr. U. Calif.-San Diego, La Jolla, 1985-92, OCLC asst. to pres. for acad. and rsch. libr. rels., 1995—98; docent Asian Art Mus., San Francisco, 1997—, ret. Instr. sch. libr. and info. studies U. Calif., Berkeley, 1975, 76, 83; cons. Nat. Libr. of Medicine, Bethesda, Md., 1985, Ohio Bd. Regents, Columbus, 1987; trustee Online Computer Libr. Ctr., 1988-96; dir. Nat. Coordinating Com. on Japanese Libr. Resources, 1995-98; docent Asian Art Mus., San Francisco, 1997-. Mem.: ALA, Libr. Info. Tech. Assn., Program Com. Ctr. for Rsch. Librs. (bd. chair 1992—93, Hugh Atkinson award 1994). E-mail: dgregor@mcn.org.

GREGOR, TIBOR PHILIP, retired management consultant; b. Levoca, Czechoslovakia, Apr. 25, 1919; arrived in Can., 1951; s. Philip and Emma (Aufricht) Gregor; m. Helen Frances Lorenz, Sept. 15, 1942 (dec. 1989); children: Jan Michael, Charlotte Anne; m. Valma Costa, Dec. 17, 1994 (dec. 2003). Student, U. London, 1938—40. Gen. sales mgr. Eastern Steel Products Ltd., Toronto, Ont., Canada, 1952-57; pres., gen. mgr. Roneo Co. Ltd., Toronto, 1957-63, Roneo, Inc., Phila.; pres. Mcpl. Sand & Gravel Co., Kingston, Ont., Canada, 1964-71; exec. dir. Can. Soft Drink Assn., Toronto, 1972-86; pres. T.P. Gregor Assocs., Toronto, 1986—98, ret., 1998. Mem. Ont. Comml. Registration Appeals Tribunal, 1987—93. Vice chmn. Toronto Centennial Com.; pres. Met. Toronto Assn. Mentally Retarded, 1961—64; past pres. Can. Assn. Mentally Retarded, 1969—71; founder, chmn. Friends Royal Can. Acad. Arts, 1985—89; past chmn. Can. Fund Czech and Slovak Univs. Served as col. Czechoslovak Armoured Brigade, ret., 1945. Decorated Medal of Merit 1st class France; recipient Freedom award, City of Winnipeg, 1970, Centennial medal, Royal Can. Acad., 2000, commendation, City of Toronto. Mem.: Am. Soc. Assn. Execs., Can. Soc. Assn. Execs., Royal Can. Legion, Royal Can. Mil. Inst., Rotary Internat. Found. (trustee 1986—87), Rotary (past gov. dist. 707), Rotary Internat. (dir. and treas. 1980—82), Toronto Lawn Tennis Club. Mem. United Ch. Home and Office: 218 Glen Rd Toronto ON Canada M4W 2X3

GREGORIAN, VARTAN, foundation administrator; b. Tabriz, Iran, Apr. 8, 1934; came to U.S., 1956; s. Samuel B. and Shushanik G. (Mirzaian) G.; m. Clare Russell, Mar. 25, 1960; children: Vahe, Raffi, Dareh. Grad., Coll. Armenian, 1955; BA, Stanford U., 1958, PhD, 1964; degree (hon.), Boston U., 1983, Brown U., 1984, Jewish Theol. Sem., 1984, SUNY, 1985, Johns Hopkins U., 1987, NYU, 1987, U. Pa., 1988, Dartmouth Coll., 1989, Rutgers U., 1989, CUNY, 1990, Tufts U., 1994, Johnson and Wales U., 1999, Julliard Sch., 2000, U. Ill., 2001, Fordham U., 2003, Pa. State U., 2003, San Francisco State U., 2004, Am. U. Beirut, 2004, U. Notre Dame, 2005. From instr. to assoc. prof. history San Francisco State Coll., 1962—68; assoc. prof. UCLA, 1968; from assoc. prof. to prof. U. Tex., 1968—72, dir. spl. programs, 1970—72; Tarzian prof. Armenian and Caucasian history U. Pa., Phila., 1972—80; dean U. Pa. (Faculty Arts and Scis.), Phila., 1974—78, provost, 1978—80; pres. N.Y. Pub. Libr., 1981—89; prof. New Sch. Social Rsch., NYC, 1984—89; prof. History and Near Eastern studies NYU, 1984—89; pres., prof. History Brown U., Providence, 1989—97; pres. Carnegie Corp., NYC, 1997—. Author: The Emergence of Modern Afghanistan, 1880-1946, 1969, The Road to Home: My Life and Times, 2003, Islam: A Mosaic, Not a Monolith, 2003. Bd. dirs. Aaron Diamond Found., 1990-97, Brookings Instns., 1994-97, Inst. for Internat. Edn., 1989-95, Internat. League of Human Rights, 1984-97, Inst. for Advanced Study, 1987—, J. Paul Getty Trust, 1988-2000, Aga Khan U., 1995-2000, Human Rights Watch, 1996—; chmn. bd. visitors Grad. Sch. and Univ. Ctr., CUNY, 1984-90; bd. trustees Mus. Modern Art, 1994—, Providence Jour., 1998-, Cell Therapeutics, Inc., 2001-, Nat. Constn. Ctr., 2002-, Qatar Found., 2003-; bd. mem. Am. Acad. Berlin, 2003-, World Trade Ctr. Meml. Found., 2004-. Decorated Officier de l'Ordre des Arts et Lettres (France), Grand Oficial Ordem Infante D. Henrique Portuguese Govt., 1995; recipient Danforth E.H. Harbison Tchg. award 1969, Cactus Tchg. award 1971, award of distinction Phi Lambda Theta and Phi Delta Kappa, 1980, Silver Cultural medal Italian Ministry Fgn. Affairs, 1977, Gold medal of honor City and Province of Vienna, Austria, 1976, 1st Disting. Humanist award Pa. Humanities Coun., 1983, Nat. Fellowship award Fellowship Commn., Phila., 1984, Gold medal Nat. Inst. Social Scis., 1985, Disting. Svc. to the Arts award Third St. Music Sch. Settlement, 1997, Disting. Svc. to Pub. Edn. award N.Y. Acad. Pub. Edn., 1998, Friends of the Arts award Town Hall, 1998, Nat. Humanities medal, Pres. William J. Clinton, 1998, Eleanor Roosevelt Val-Kill award Eleanor Roosevelt Ctr., 1999; fellow Social Sci. Rsch. Coun., 1960, Ford Found. Fgn. Area Tng., 1960-62, Am. Coun. Learned Socs.-Social Sci. Rsch. Coun., 1965, John Simon Guggenheim Found., 1971-72, Social Sci. Rsch. Coun., 1971-72, Am. Coun. Edn., 1973. Fellow Acad. Arts Scis., Am. Philos. Soc.; mem. Am. Antiquarian Soc., Am. Hist. Assn. (program chmn. 1972), Am. Philos. Soc. (grantee 1965, 66), Internat. Fedn. Libr. Assns. (co-chmn. program com. 1985), Assn. Advancement Slavic Studies (program chmn. Western Slavic Conf. 1967), Mid-East Studies Assn., Coun. Fgn. Rels., Grolier Club, Round Table, Century Club, Econ. Club, Phi Beta Kappa. Office: Carnegie Corp Office of the Pres 437 Madison Ave Fl 27 New York NY 10022-7001 Office Phone: 212-371-3200.*

GREGORIE, CORAZON ARZALEM, operations research specialist; b. Bethesda, Md., Aug. 6, 1947; d. Faustino and Rosalina Arzalem. AA in Bus. Adminstrn., Palm Beach Coll., 1967; postgrad., Fla. Atlantic U., 1967; BA in Bus. Adminstrn., U. Fla., 1969. Mgmt. trainee Burdines Dept. Store, West Palm Beach, Fla., 1969; adminstrv. asst. divsn. econs. Nat. Food Processors Assn., Washington, 1970-71, statis. analyst divsn. econs. and stats., 1972-77, acting dir. divsn. econs. and stats., 1978; asst. editor Airfare Pub. Co., Washington, 1979-81; product specialist Arbitron Co., Beltsville, Md., 1982-83, tng. supr. Laurel, Md., 1984-87, night shift ops. supr. Columbia, Md., 1988—95, survey supr., 1996—. Collective mem., bd. dirs. Glut Food, Mt. Rainier, Md., 1973-78. Force vol. Nat. Park Svc., Washington, 1973-76; coord. College Park Food Coop., Md., 1970-72. Mem. Lotus Ltd. (bd. dirs. 1974—, treas., parts and tech. chmn., membership dir., corr. sec.). Avocations: photography, sports cars. Office: Arbitron Co 9705 Patuxent Woods Dr Columbia MD 21046-1572

GREGORY, BETTINA LOUISE, retired journalist; b. NYC, June 4, 1946; d. George Alexander and V. Elizabeth Friedman; m. John P. Flannery, II, 1981 (div. 2002); 1 child, Diana Elizabeth. Student, Smith Coll., 1964-65; diploma in acting, Webber-Douglas Sch. Dramatic Art, London, 1968; BA in Psychology, Pierce Coll., Athens, Greece, 1972; PsyD, George Washington U., 2002; LittD (hon.), Susquehanna U., 1988, St. Thomas Aquinas U., 1992; LLD (hon.), Wilmington Coll., 1989; D in Journalism (hon.), U. Findlay, 1990; LittD (hon.), Bethany Coll., 2000. Reporter Sta. WVBR-FM, Ithaca, 1972-73, Sta. WCIC-TV, Ithaca, 1972; reporter, anchorwoman Sta. WGBB, Freeport, NY, 1973, Sta. WCBS, NYC; freelance reporter, writer AP, NYC, 1973-74; freelance reporter N.Y. Times, 1973-74; with ABC News, 1974—2001, corr. Washington, 1977-79, White House corr., 1979, sr. gen. assignment corr., 1980, host The American Family, Goodlife TV Network, 2002—; pres. Sunshine State Telephone Co., Miami, Fla., 2004—05, Hollywood Internet Protocols, Inc., 2004—. Elected rep. for corrs. ABC News Women's Adv. Bd.; adj. prof. Robert H. Smith Sch. Bus.; adj. prof. exec. masters in bus. adminstrn. U. Md. Reporter TV spl. Flaws in the Shield, 1989 (1st pl. Headliner award), A&E's Biography of Hillary Rodham Clinton, 1994 (Best Documentary ACE award 1994), Murder Trial O.J. Simpson (Edward R. Murrow award Best News Series 1996), Hannibal Lecter: the Honey in the Lion's Mouth, Am.Journal Psychotherapy, 2002. Recipient 1st Place award Nat. Feature News, Odyssey Inst., NY, 1978, Clarion award Women in Communications, Inc., 1979, hon. mention Nat. Commn. on Working Women, 1979, Media award for Am. Agenda segment on homeless World Hunger Found., 1990, Cable Ace Best Documentary award, 1995, Edward R. Murrow award for coverage of O.J. Simpson Murder trial, 1996, Telly award for Bipolar Teens, 2004; named one of top 10 investigative reporters, TV Guide, 1983. Mem. Radio TV Corrs. Assn., White House Corrs. Assn. Clubs: Newswomen's NY (recipient Front Page award 1976); Nat. Press; Washington Press. Office Phone: 703-283-9088. Personal E-mail: bettinagre@aol.com.

GREGORY, BRENDA KAY, music educator; b. Kingsport, Tenn., Sept. 11, 1957; d. James Edward and Roxie Virginia Dent; m. Philip Ray Gregory, June 25, 1988. B in Music, Mid. Tenn. State U., 1979, MA, 1982. Cert. career tchr. Choral dir., asst. band dir. Shelbyville Ctrl. HS, 1982—84, Oakland HS, Murfreesboro, 1984—2002; choral dir., music dept. chmn. Siegel HS, Murfreesboro, 2002—, fine arts chmn. Conductor: All Mid-State Women's Chorale, 1994. Named Outstanding Tchr. of Arts award, Tenn. Gov.'s Sch. of Arts, 2005, Siegel H.S. Tchr. of Yr., 2007, Rutherford County Sys. Level Tchr. of Yr., 2007; named to Band of Blue Club, Hall of Fame, 1991; grantee, Siegel Found., 2004. Mem.: NEA, Am. Choral Dirs. Assn., Mid. Tenn. Vocal Assn. (exec. com. 1985—87). Democrat. Avocations: reading, singing, theater, yoga, sports. Home: 124 Braley Ct Murfreesboro TN 37129 Office: Siegel High Sch 3300 Siegel Rd Murfreesboro TN 37129 Personal E-mail: choirchick@comcast.net.

GREGORY, CALVIN, real estate investor; b. Bronx, NY, Jan. 11, 1942; s. Jacob and Ruth Gregory; m. Rachel Anna Carver, Feb. 14, 1970 (div. Apr. 1977); children: Debby Lynn, Trixy Sue; m. Carla Deane Deaver, June 30, 1979. AA, L.A. City Coll., 1962; BA, Calif. State U., LA, 1964; MDiv, Fuller Theol. Sem., 1968; M in Religious Edn., Southwestern Sem., Ft. Worth, 1969; PhD in Religion, Universal Life. Ch., Modesto, Calif., 1982; DDiv (hon.), Otay Mesa Coll., 1982. Ordained to ministry Am. Bapt. Conv., 1970; cert. notary pub., real estate lic., casualty lic. Calif. Youth minister First Bapt. Ch., Delano, Calif., 1964—65, 1969—70; youth dir. St. Luke's United Meth. Ch., Highland Park, Calif., 1969—70; tchr. polit. sci. Maranatha High Sch., Rosemead, Calif., 1969—70; aux. chaplain U.S. Air Force 750th Radar Squadron, Edwards AFB, Calif., 1970—72; pastor First Bapt. Ch., Boron, Calif., 1971—72; ins. agt. Prudential Ins. Co., Ventura, Calif., 1972—73, sales mgr., 1973—74; casualty ins. agt. Allstate Ins. Co., Thousand Oaks, Calif., 1974—75; pres. Ins. Agy. Placement Svcs., Thousand Oaks, Calif., 1975—; head youth minister Emanuel Presbyn. Ch., LA, 1973—74; owner, investor real estate, Wales, England, Canada, Australia. Counselor YMCA, Hollywood, Calif., 1964, Soul Clinic-Universal Life Ch. Inc., Modesto, Calif., 1982. Mem.: Life Underwriter Tng. Coun., Apt. Assn. L.A., Kiwanis (club spkr. 1971), X32 Club (Ventura, Calif.), Forensic Club (L.A.). Republican. Office: PO Box 4407 Thousand Oaks CA 91359-1407

GREGORY, CLAIRE DISTELHORST, television producer; b. Chgo., Mar. 6, 1926; d. Robert Henry and Genevieve (McCall) Distelhorst; children: Charles, Martha. Student, Cornell Coll., 1943-46; AB, Ind. U., 1947, MS, 1954. Tchr. pub. schs., Bismarck and Rossville, Ill., 1947-50, Helmsburg, Ind., 1950-51; grad. asst. Audio Visual Ctr. of Ind. U., 1953-55; dir. women's, children's/social svc. programs radio/TV, 1956-59; lectr., 1956-59; exec. dir. Cmty. Svc. Coun., Inc., Bloomington, Ind., 1971-75; asst. supr. instructional TV program devel. Ind. U. Radio and TV Svc., 1975-81, dir. spl. projects, 1982-92; chmn. Bloomington Telecomms. Coun., 1975-80. Writer, prodr: Russian Revolution and Arts, Parts I and II, 1976, Intro. to Immediate Access, 1977-80, Teleconference on Mass Transp., 1976, Transp. Briefing, 1977, videotapes on profl. devel. Internat. Devel. Inst., 1975-80, 16 videotapes on computer instrn., 1978-80, Getting There, 1980, Living Africa, 1979-82, Programming for Microcomputers, 1982, Negotiation, 1984, Ind. Collection, 1987, Joshua's Battle: The Story of Lyles Station, 1988, Charting New Courses teleconferences, 1988;

prodr., videodisc instructional Clarity; prodr., dir., editor videotape SOUTH SHORE LINE: A Good Investment, 1990; prodr., editor Autism: Learning to Live, 1990 (Excellence award Autism Soc. Am. 1991), Autism: Stubborn Love, 1991 (Excellence award Autism Soc. Am. 1992), Autism: Being Friends, 1991; TV advisor Mostly Moliere Troupe, 1981-89; lay reader A Moment of Silence prodn., 1996. Recipient Communication Industry Silver award Assn. Visual Communicators, 1989. Mem. Blue Ridge Assn. (treas. 1978-81), Theta Sigma Phi, Psi Iota Xi.

GREGORY, DAVID STEVEN, physician; s. Wilbur Thomas and Bonnie Bell Gregory; m. Claire Castorina Gregory, Aug. 17, 1991; children: Benjamin Chase, Maxwell Allen, Eliza Rose. MD, Va. Commonwealth U., Richmond, 1994. Diplomate Am. Bd. Family Medicine, 1997. Asst. clin. prof. U. Nebr. Med. Ctr., Omaha, 1997—2001, Uniformed Svcs. U. Health Sci., Bethesda, Md., 1999—2001, U. Va., Charlottesville, 2002—, Va. Commonwealth U., Richmond, 2004—. Maj. USAF, 1990—2001. Fellow: Am. Acad. Family Physicians. Office Phone: 434-947-5210.

GREGORY, DEIRDRE DIANNE, secondary school educator; b. Fairview Park, Ohio, Feb. 12, 1958; d. Richard Whiting and Ruth Elizabeth (Moody) Mason; m. Thomas Bradford Gregory, July 15, 1995. BS, Ashland U., 1981; MS, Ohio State U., 1986; MEd, Ashland U., 1989, U. Dayton, 1993. Cert. tchr., Ohio; cert. vocat. family and consumer sci. sch. guidance counselor and supr.; Praxis III assessor. Tchr. home econs. Mansfield City Schs., Ohio, 1981-93, GRADS coord., 1993-99, guidance counselor, 1999—. Mem. adv. bd. Mansfield (Ohio) City Schs., mentor coord., 2003—; chair Children Family Health Svcs. Consortium, Mansfield, 1996-98; adj. prof. Ashland U., 2003-. Bd. trustees Ashland U. Mem. AAUW (pres. 1997-99), NEA, ACA, Mansfield Sch. Employee Assn. (pres. 1994-95), Am. Assn. Family and Consumer Sci., Order of Eastern Star, Ashland U. Alumni Assn. (pres.), Local Profl. Devel. Com. (co-chair), Local Profl. Devel. Trainer, Ohio Assn. Coll. Admission Counseling, Ohio Sch. Counseler Assn, Ohio Edn. Assn., Kappa Omicron Phi, Phi Delta Kappa (pres. 1994-96, historian 1996-98), Am. Sch. Counselor Assn. Democrat. Presbyterian. Avocations: reading, music, walking, travel. Home: 411 Overlook Rd Mansfield OH 44907-1533 Office: Mansfield Sr H S 124 N Linden Rd Mansfield OH 44906-2621 Office Phone: 419-525-6369 20303. Business E-Mail: DGregory@mansfield.k12.oh.us.

GREGORY, DICK, comedian, volunteer; b. St. Louis, Oct. 12, 1932; m. Lillian Smith, 1959; children: Michele, Lynne, Paula, Pamela, Stephanie, Gregory, Christian, Ayanna, Miss, Yohance. Student, So. Ill. U., 0951—1953, student, 1955—56. Lectr. univs. throughout U.S.; nutritionist world-heavyweight boxing champion Riddick Bowe, 1992. Entertainer, Esquire Club, Chgo., opened night club, Apex, Robbins, Ill., master ceremonies, Roberts Show Club, Chgo., 1959-60, night club appearances, Akron, Milw., Chgo., 1960, San Francisco, Hollywood, numerous other cities, 1961-, comedy act, Playboy Club, Chgo., 1961; TV guest appearances Jack Paar show, others; record albums Dick Gregory: The Light Side-Dark Side; others; Author: The Back of the Bus, 1962, Nigger, 1964, What's Happening, 1965, The Shadow That Scares Me, Write Me In, No More Lies, 1971, Dick Gregory's Political Primer, 1971, Dick Gregory's Natural Diet for Folks Who Eat, Cookin' With Mother Nature, 1973, Dick Gregory's Bible Tales, with Commentary, 1974, Up From Nigger, 1976, (with Mark Lane) Code Name Zorro: The Murder of Martin Luther King, Jr, 1977, Murder in Memphis, 1993, Callus on My Soul, 2002. Peace and Freedom Party presdl. candidate, 1968. Served with AUS, 1953-55. Winner Mo. mile championship, 1951, 52; named Outstanding Athlete So. Ill. U., 1953; recipient Ebony-Topaz Heritage and Freedom award, 1978. Achievements include invention of Dick Gregory's Bahamian Diet Drink. Office: Dick Gregory Hlth Enterprises PO Box 3270 Plymouth MA 02361-3270 Office Phone: 508-746-7427.

GREGORY, DOLA BELL, bishop, customer service administrator; d. Earl James Barnett and Wilda May Claspell-Barnett; 1 child, James DeWayne Gregory. Student, Frontier C.C., 1982—83, Kishwaukee C.C., 1987—88, Inst. Theology, 1995—97; min. lic., Full Gospel Chs. Internat., 1997. Supr. DDT Career Devel. Ctr., Fairfield, Ill., 1981—86; asst. tchr. DeKalb County Spl. Edn., Cortland, Ill., 1986—88; leadership Assembly of God/Full Gospel, Rochelle, Ill., 1988—99; sr. pastor, founder Rock House Ministries I, Rockford, Ill., 1999—, Rock House Ministries II, Demonte, Ind., 2002, Rock House Ministries III, Forest Lake, Minn., 2003; sr., pastor, founder Rock House Ministries IV, Lakeland, Minn., 2005—; customer rels. Credit Union, Rockford, 2001—. Coach Spl. Olympics, Bloomington, Ill., 1981—86; spiritual leader Tres-Dias, Rockford, 1997—98; fundraising chmn. PTA, Fairfield, 1984—86. Author: (audiotape) Spiritual Education, Spiritual Welfare, 2000. Referral sponsor Hope for Women, Rochelle, Ill., 1997—; vol. Rockford Rescue Mission, 1999—. Recipient Eunice Kennedy Spl. Olympics award, 1984. Mem.: Rockhouse Outreach Children Klub (founder, dir. 2005), Women's Aglow Internat. (educator 1993—95), Women in Ministry of Rockford (facilitator 2002—03, 2006). Avocations: reading, motorcycling, singing, sewing, remodeling. Office: Rock House Ministries 1325 7th St Rockford IL 61104 Home Phone: 815-519-0434; Office Phone: 815-962-5067. Business E-Mail: rockhouse1@sbcglobal.net.

GREGORY, FRANK R., history professor; b. Jersey City, Mar. 2, 1944; m. Catherine Gregory, Nov. 25, 1967; children: Denise Wyatt, Nicole. MA, N.E. Mo. State U., Kirksville, 1968. Instr. history Wesley Coll., Dover, Del., 2003—. Mem.: De La Warr History Soc. (advisor 2003—). Home: 113 Hazeltine Rd Dover DE 19904 Office: Wesley Coll 120 N State St Dover DE 19901 Office Phone: 302-736-2523. Business E-Mail: gregorfr@wesley.edu.

GREGORY, FREDERICK DREW, federal agency administrator; b. Washington, Jan. 7, 1941; s. Francis Anderson and Nora Drew Gregory; m. Barbara Ann Archer, June 3, 1964; children: Frederick D. Jr., Heather Lynn Gregory Skeens. BS in Aerospace Engring., USAF Acad., 1964; MS in Info. Systems, George Washington U., 1977; DSc, U. D.C., 1986. Cert. astronaut shuttle comdr., FAA comml. and instrument cert. for singlr- and multi-engine airplanes and helicopters. Commd. 2nd lt. USAF, 1964, advanced through grades to col., 1983, helicopter pilot, 1964-69, fighter pilot, 1969-70; exptl. test pilot NASA and USAF, 1971-78; retired as colonel USAF, 1993; astronaut NASA, Houston, 1978-93, assoc. adminstr., Office of Safety and Mission Assurance Washington, 1992—2001, assoc. adminstr. for space flight, 2001—02, deputy adminstr., COO, 2002—, acting adminstr., 2005. Astronaut pilot, Orbiter Challenger (STS-51B), 1985, spacecraft comdr. aboard Discovery (STS-33), 1989, spacecraft comdr. aboard Atlantis (STS-44), 1991. Bd. dirs. Young Astronaut Coun., Washington, Kaiser Permanente Mid-Atlantic States, Nat. Capital Area coun. Boy Scouts Am., Challenger Ctr. for Space Sci. Edn., Va. Air and Space Ctr.-Hampton Roads History Ctr.; bd. visitors Air Force Inst. Tech., Maxwell AFB, Ala. Decorated Legion of Merit, Air medal (16), Disting. Flying Cross (2), NASA Space Flight medals (3); recipient Def. Meritorious Svc. medal, Meritorious Svc. medal, Air Force Meritorious Svc. medal USAF, Air Force Commendation medal, Def. Superior Svc. medal Dept. Defense, Nat. Intelligence Achievement medal CIA, Black Sci. award, Nat. Tech. Assn., Pres. award Black Enterprise Mag., Disting. Nat. Scientist award, Nat. Soc. Black Engrs., George Washington U. Outstanding Alumni award. Mem. AMVET, Am. Helicopter Soc., Order of Daedalians, The Naval Order, Soc. Experimental Test Pilots, Assn. Space Explorers, Air Force Acad. Assn. of Graduates, Air Force Assn.(Ira Eaker Fellow), Sigma Pi Phi, Nat. Tech. Assn., Tuskegee Airmen. Avocations: audio/video equipment, reading, world travel, specialty cars, hunting, water-skiing.

GREGORY, JAMES ALEXANDER, editor, writer, film producer; b. Marshall, Mich., Apr. 11, 1930; s. Alexander and Chrissoula (Shoupilla) Gregory; life ptnr. Zachariah Brown; children: Ben Tea, Robert Nuñez, Jim Davidson, Daniel G., Chris Montalban. B of English with honors, U. Mich., 1951, MA in English, 1952. Publicist Columbia Pictures, NYC, 1956; press book editor-in-chief RKO Radio Pictures, NYC, 1956—57; editor-in-chief Movieland and TV Time, NYC, 1958—61; West Coast editor, writer Silver Screen, Screenland, Movieland and TV Time, LA, 1960—69; staff reporter Nat. Enquirer, 1974—76, freelance writer, 1976—80; editor, writer Larry Flynt Publ., LA, 1980—83; editor Landscape and Irrigation, Van Nuys, Calif.; sr. editor Arbor Age, 1984—91, ret., 1992. Author: David David David, 1972, The Soul of the Jackson 5, 1973, Donny!, 1973, Donny and the Osmond Family, 1974, The Lucille Ball Story, 1974; co-author: The Wallaces of Alabama with George Wallace, Jr., 1975; author, editor: The Elvis Presley Story, 1960; prodr.: (films) Flaco and the Wizard of Hugs, Lucy Luvs Flaco. Lt. (j.g.) USNR, 1953-55. Democrat.

GREGORY, JAMES FRANCIS, electrical engineer; b. Litsey, Ky., Aug. 18, 1917; s. James Henry Gregory and Minnie Margaret Reed; m. Virginia Thornton Brandenburg, Feb. 9, 1941; children: James Francis, Virginia Thornton, Jane Oliva Gregory Stewart. BSEE, U. Ky., Lexington, 1938. Comml. svc. engr. Ky. Utilities, Norton, 1939; engring. aide TVA, Gilbertsville, Ky., 1940; contract engr. DuPont, Charlestown, Ind., 1941, Pryor, Okla., 1942; design engr. Am. Elevator Co., Louiseville, 1946; plant elec. engr. Colgate Palmolive, Jeffersonville, Ind., 1947—51; plant engr., mgr. GE Co., Louisville and Phila., 1952—79. Treas., commr. City of Hollow Creek, Ky., 1969—79; mem. Common Cause, Louisville, 1970—2007; bd. dirs. Wayside Christian Mission, Louisville, 1970—2007, mem. property com., 1970—2007. Capt. Signal Corp, 1943—46, Pacific. Mem.: AIEE, IEEE (sr.), NSPE. Presbyterian. Home: 2116 Buechel Bank Rd Apt 215 Louisville KY 40218

GREGORY, JIM (JAMES MICHAEL GREGORY), sports association executive, former professional sports team executive; b. Port Colborne, Ont., Can., Nov. 4, 1935; s. Henry Joseph and Catherine Cecilia (Gandour) Gregory; m. Rosalie Donna Bruno, May 1959; children: Andrea, David, Valerie, Maureen. Attended, St. Michael's Coll., Toronto. Head coach Vancouver Canucks, 1967—68; scout Toronto Maple Leafs, 1968—69, gen. mgr., 1969-79; dir. ctrl. scouting NHL, 1979-85, exec. dir. hockey ops., 1986-87, sr. v.p. hockey ops., 1987—. Mem. selection com. Hockey Hall of Fame, 1993—, chmn. selection com., 1998—. Recipient (with team) Meml. Cup, 1961, 1964, 1967. Office: NHL 47th Flr 1251 Ave of the Americas New York NY 10020*

GREGORY, JOHN FORREST, information technology specialist; b. Springfield, Mass., Apr. 3, 1950; s. Howard Burdett and Mary Augustine (Reilly) Gregory. BS of Fgn. Svc., Georgetown U., 1972; MSLS, Simmons Coll., 1974. Libr. Libr. of Congress, Washington, 1974-78, Sino-Soviet Inst., George Washington U., Washington, 1978-80, Heritage Found., Washington, 1981-96; market rsch. and analysis staff U.S. Postal Svcs. Hdqrs., Washington, 1997—2003, market rsch. specialist, 1998—2003, sr. libr., USPS Corp. libr., 2003—06; sr. cons. M Squared Strategies, 2006; prin. cons. The Ambit Group, Reston, Va., 2006—07. Cons., 1997—98. Author: Climber's Guide to Carderock, 1980, Rocksport! Tools, Training and Technique for Climbers, 1989. Democrat. Roman Catholic. Home: 4114 Davis Pl NW Apt 212 Washington DC 20007-3948 Office: The Ambit Group 1895 Preston White Dr Ste 220 Reston VA 20191-5434 Personal E-mail: jgregory@thampbitgroup.com.

GREGORY, JOSEPH M., investment company executive; m. Niki Gregory; 5 children. BA, Hofstra U., 1974. Joined as comml. paper trader Lehman Brothers Holdings Inc., 1974, various mgmt. positions, fixed income div., 1980—91, co-head, fixed income divsn., 1991—96, head, global equities divsn., 1996—2000, chief adminstrv. officer, 2000—02, co-COO, 2002—04, pres., COO, 2004—. Bd. trustees The Millbrook Sch.; bd. dirs. The Posse Found., Inc., Dorothy Rodbell Cohen Found. Office: Lehman Brothers Holdings Inc 745 Seventh Ave New York NY 10019*

GREGORY, KARL DWIGHT, economics professor, consultant; b. Detroit, Mar. 26, 1931; s. Bertram and Sybil Gregory; m. Tenicia Ann Banks, June 7, 1959; children: Karin Diane, Sheila Therese, Kurt David. BA, Wayne State U., 1952, MA, 1957; PhD, U. Mich., 1962. Fiscal economist Office of Mgmt. and Budget, Washington, 1961-64; prof. Wayne State U., Detroit, 1960-61, 64-68, Oakland U., Rochester, Mich., 1968-96, disting. prof. emeritus, 1996—, ret. Chmn. bd. dirs., CEO Greater Detroit Bidco, Inc., 1990—96, Accord, Inc., Detroit, 1969—71; mem. coun. econ. advisors Gov. Engler of Mich., 1992—96, Gov. Granholm of Mich., 2003—; cons. UN Devel. Program, Beijing, 1991; chief organizer, dir. First Ind. Nat. Bank Detroit, 1968—81, interim pres., 1980—81; vis. prof. SUNY, Buffalo, 1975; vis. scholar, mem. exec. staff U.S. Congl. Budget Office, Washington, 1975—76. Author (with others): State of Black Michigan, 1984—87, 1991; contbr. articles to publs. Mem. comty. impact cabinet United Way S.E. Mich., 2006—; mem. Gov.'s Entrepreneurial Commn., Lansing, Mich., 1984—88, Regional Devel. Initiative S.E. Mich. Coun. Govts., 1990—91, Gov.'s Task Force Tourism, Lansing, 1986—89, Detroit Workforce Devel. Bd., 2002—; trustee Episcopal Diocese of Mich., Detroit, 1981—83, 1984—87, 1990—92; mem. Cmty. Impact Cabinet United Way S.E. Mich., 2006—; bd. dirs. Mich. Ctr. High Tech., 1991—95, Detroit Alliance Fair Banking, 1992—, Adult Well-Being Svcs., 1999—. 1st lt. US Army, 1953—56. Recipient Rsch. award, Detroit chpt. NAACP, 1987, Entrepreneurial award, SBA, 1989, Mich. Dept. Commerce, 1992. Mem.: Booker T. Washington Bus. Assn., Nat. Econ. Assn. Avocations: reading, music, photography, computers, travel. Home: 18495 Adrian St Southfield MI 48075-1803 Personal E-mail: gregory_karl@hotmail.com.

GREGORY, LEWIS DEAN, trust company executive; b. Wichita, Kans., May 13, 1953; s. Harry Samuel III and Virginia Dorothy (Womer) G.; m. Laura Lorraine Davis, March 4, 1978; children: Paul Lewis, Erin Elizabeth. BA in Speech Comm., U. Kans., Lawrence, 1975; JD, Washburn U., 1983. Bar: Kans. 1984, U.S. Dist. Ct. Kans. 1984. Cons. Delta Upsilon Frat., Inc., Indpls., 1975-76; mktg. rep. IBM, Kansas City, Mo., 1976-80; assoc. Frazey, Wix & Vetter, Wichita, 1983-84; trust mktg. mgr. Bank IV Wichita, 1984-86; v.p., trust officer, sales mgr. BancOklahoma Trust Co., Tulsa, 1986-88, Boatmen's Trust Co., Kansas City, 1988-97; sr. v.p., dist. trust mgr. Merrill Lynch Trust Co., 1997—. Dir. Am. Heart Assn., Wichita, Kans., 1985—86; pres. YMCA Men's Club, Tulsa, 1987—88; trustee Leukemia Soc., 1992—96, U. Kans. Endowment; del. Rep. Party, Tulsa, 1988. Mem. ABA, Kans. Bar Assn., Johnson County Bar Assn., Kansas City Met. Bar Assn., Estate Planning Soc. (bd. dirs. 1996-98), Kiwanis, Kans. Univ. Alumni Assn. (pres. Greater Kansas City chpt. 1994-96, nat. bd. dirs. 1997-2002), Delta Upsilon (Indpls. dir. 1987-90, dir. Kans. chpt. 1977-90). Republican. Methodist. Avocation: running. Home: 3905 W 125th Ter Leawood KS 66209 Office Phone: 913-906-5301. Personal E-mail: llpegr@aol.com. Business E-Mail: lewis_gregory@ml.com.

GREGORY, LISA, marriage and family therapist; d. Irving and Marilyn Scher; m. Lisa Scher, Nov. 25, 1989. MEd, Manhattanville Coll., Purchase, NY, 1992—94. Aba thereapist HTA NY, Ardsley, 2001—. Office: Lisa Gregory 3 Woodland Ave Port Chester NY 10573

GREGORY, LOUIS P., lawyer, gas industry executive; b. 1955; BA, Stephen F. Austin State U.; JD, Tex. Tech U., 1981. Bar: Tex. 1981. Assoc. Jenkens & Gilchrist, Dallas; prtnr. Gregory, Self & Beuttenmuller, Dallas; from assoc. counsel to sr. v.p., gen. counsel Lomas Financial Corp., Dallas, 1988—96; cons. Siena Holdings, Inc. (formerly Lomas Financial Corp.), 1996—98, Nomas Corp. (formerly Lomas Mortgage), 1996—98; atty. short-term lending & real estate devel. McManemin & Smith, Dallas, 1999—2000; sr. v.p., gen. counsel Atmos Energy, Dallas, 2000—. Mem.: ABA. Office: Atmos Energy PO Box 650205 Dallas TX 75265-0205*

GREGORY, MATTHEW T., attorney general; Former atty. MPLA; atty. gen. Commonwealth of No. Mariana Islands, 2006—. Office: Office of Atty Gen Capitol Hill Caller Box 10007 Saipan MP 96950 Office Phone: 670-664-2341. Office Fax: 670-664-2349.

GREGORY, MEL HYATT, JR., retired insurance company executive; b. Frankfort, Ky., Mar. 28, 1936; s. Mel Hyatt and Audrey (Fraley) G.; m. Joyce Klein, Sept. 9, 1955; children: Susan Gregory Lawson, Scott, Lisbeth Gregory Olesky. BS, Stetson U., 1958. Mgr., agt. Equitable Life Ins. Co., Louisville, 1959-66, agy., mgr. Dayton, Ohio, 1966-70, Atlanta, 1970-73, v.p. Cin., 1974-77, sr. v.p. NYC, 1978-85, pres. so. ops. Atlanta, 1985-90, exec. v.p. NYC, 1990-93; ret., 1993. Bd. dirs. Stetson U. Sch. Bus. Capt. U.S Army, 1958-62. Mem. Gen. Agts. and Mgrs. (pres. 1966-74), Cherokee Country Club. Republican. Home: 4570 Jett Rd NW Atlanta GA 30327-4562 Personal E-mail: mel_gregory@hotmail.com.

GREGORY, NELSON BRUCE, retired motel owner, naval officer; b. Syracuse, NY, Aug. 4, 1933; s. Nelson Bruce and Josephine (Sully) G.; m. Bonnie K. Bannowsky, May 2, 1961 (div. 1970); children: Elizabeth Jo, Jennifer Kay; m. Patricia Ann Greenhalgh, Oct. 15, 1977 (div. 1994); children: Peter Ward, Annette Frances, Michael John, Geoffrey Charles. BS, N.Y. Maritime Coll., 1955; postgrad., USN Pilot Tng., Pensacola, Fla., 1955-57; grad., NATO Weapons Sch., Oberammergau, Fed. Republic of Germany, 1966; diploma, Joint Warfare Sch., Salisbury, Eng., 1967, USN Counter Insurgency, Little Creek, Va., 1968, USAF Space Ops., Montgomery, Ala., 1969. Commd. ens. USN, 1955, advanced through grades to lt. comdr., 1964, operational pilot airborne Early Warning Squadron 2 Patuxent River, Md., 1957-60, flight instr. Airborne Early Warning Tng. Unit, 1960-63, command pilot Air Devel. Squadron 6 McMurdo Sound, Antarctica, 1963-64; airspace control officer NATO, Naples, Italy, 1964-68; chief pilot Naval Support Activity, Danang, Vietnam, 1968-69; space intelligence analyst NORAD, Colorado Springs, Colo., 1969-71; operational pilot Electronic Warfare Squadron 33 USN, Norfolk, Va., 1971-74, ops. officer Nat. Parachute Test Range El Centro, Calif., 1974-75, ret., 1975; owner, gen. mgr. Bonneville Motel, Idaho Falls, Idaho, 1975-99; ret., 1999. Bd. dirs. Am. Travel Inns, 1976-78. Newspaper contbr. Decorated Combat Air medals (3) USN; recipient Vietnamese Gallantry Cross Republic of Vietnam, 1969; Gregory Ridge in Antarctica named for him, 1964. Mem. VFW, Ret. Officers Assn. (life), Am. Legion, Heritage Found., Cato Inst., Elks. Republican. Presbyterian. Avocations: yachting, camping, travel.

GREGORY, PEGGY J., music educator; b. Dallas, Sept. 15, 1935; d. Garnald Morris and Thelma Christean (Turner) Gregory; m. John Curtis Jones, Aug. 24, 1957 (div. June 1980); children: Lewis Gregory, Michael Wayne, Scott Carlton, Cynthia Luanne Jones Pavletic. BS in Home Econs., Baylor U., 1956; MS in Housing and Interior Design, Okla. State U., 1957; student, Rykyu Classical Acad., 1964—68, Hampton Inst., 1968—70. Nat. cert. tchr. music; cert. profl. master. Pvt. practice piano tchr., 1964—2002; founder, dir., tchr. piano, thcr. music theory Music Arts Conservatory, Albuquerque, 1984—2002; ret., 2002. Mem. piano faculty Summer Piano Camp at Mary Hardin-Baylor U., Belton, Tex., summers 1980, 86. Performed two-piano and duet music, 1980-85; performed with ptnr. in master classes for well-known duettists. Choir dir., pianist and organist various chs., Okinawa, 1964-68, Hampton, Va., 1969-72, Las Vegas, Nev., 1972-74; talent judge Miss Teen Pageant, Albuquerque, 1993-96. Mem. Profl. Music Tchrs. N.Mex. (state membership chair 1982-83, pres. 1986-88, adjudicator 1975—, Tchr. of Yr. 1998), Music Tchrs. Nat. Assn., Nat. Guild Piano Tchrs., Tex. Music Tchrs. Assn. Avocations: downhill skiing, hiking, gardening.

GREGORY, ROBERT ERB, surgeon; b. Pitts., Pa., Dec. 31, 1919; s. Floyd Tayman and Nellie Mae Gregory; m. Jean Lindberg, Aug. 30, 1945 (dec. June 24, 2004); children: Kristine G. Hawkins, Robert E. Jr., Karen G. Mullen. BS, U. Pitts., 1941, MD, 1943. Diplomate Am. Bd. Surgery. Resident pathology South Side Hosp., 1946—47; tchg. fellow gen. surgery U. Pitts., 1947—50; various positions including med. explorer Post-at St. Clair Hosp., 1969—72; chmn. dept. surgery South Side Hosp. and St. Clair Hosp. Bd. dirs. South Side Hosp., Pitts., 1974—78; mission surgeon Luth. Ch., Tanzania, 1966, Papua New Guinea, 72. Bd. dirs. South Side Hosp., Pitts. Capt. Med. Corps US Army, 1944—46, ETO. Decorated Bronze Star, Purple Heart. Fellow: ACS (pres. SW Pa. chpt. 1974—75, bd. govs. 1972—78); mem.: Pitts. Surg. Soc. (pres. 1966—67). Home: 8233 E Cortez Dr Scottsdale AZ 85260

GREGORY, ROBIN N., lawyer; b. Syracuse, NY, Feb. 16, 1956; BS magna cum laude, Syracuse U., 1978; JD, Villanova U., 1981. Bar: NY 1982, US Dist. Ct. So. Dist. NY, US Dist. Ct. Ea. Dist. NY. Asst. dist. atty., Kings County, NY, 1981—85; ptnr. Wilson, Elser, Moskowitz, Edelman & Dicker LLP, NYC. Mem.: Am. Bd. Trial Advocates, Assn. of the Bar of the City of NY. Office: Wilson Elser Moskowitz Edleman & Dicker LLP 23rd Fl 150 E 42nd St New York NY 10017-5639 Office Phone: 212-490-3000 ext. 2650. Office Fax: 212-490-3038. Business E-Mail: gregoryr@wemed.com.

GREGORY, ROGER LEE, federal judge; b. Phila., July 17, 1953; s. George Lee and Fannie Mae (Washington) G.; m. Carla Eugenia Lewis, Sept. 6, 1980; children: Adriene Leigh, Rachel Leigh. BA, Va. State U., 1975; JD, U. Mich., 1978. Bar: Mich. 1978, Va. 1980, US Ct. Appeals (6th cir.) 1978, US Ct. Appeals (4th cir.) 1980. Assoc. atty. Butzel, Long, Gust, Klein & Van Zile, Detroit, 1978-80, Hunton & Williams, Richmond, Va., 1980-82; mng. ptnr., chmn. litigation sec. Wilder & Gregory, Richmond, 1982—2001; judge US Ct. Appeals (4th cir.), Richmond, 2001—. Bd. visitors Va. Commonwealth U., Richmond, 1985-;adj. prof. Va. State U., 1981-1985. Bd. dirs. Indsl. Devel. Authority, Richmond, 1984—, Richmond chpt. YMCA, 1989—. Me. Cen. Va. Legal Aid Soc. (exec. com.), Old Dominion Bar Assn. (pres.), Richmond Bar Assn. (bd. dirs.), Metro C. of C. (bd. dirs. 1989—), Alpha Kappa Mu, Alpha Mu Gamma. Baptist. Office: US Ct Appeals 4th Cir 1000 E Main St Rm 212 Richmond VA 23219*

GREGORY, SARA SUSAN (SUDIE), musician, singer, lyricist, poet, recording industry executive, sound recording engineer, archivist; b. DeQueen, Ark., June 24, 1952; d. Eugene Cluran Gregory and Maxine Louise Fulton; m. Steven Eugene Thomas, Nov. 18, 1977 (div. Dec. 1, 1995). Student, East Tex. State U., 1964—66, So. Meth. U., 1967—69, U. Okla., 1971, Southeastern Okla. State U., 1972—75, U. Denver, 1974, Oklahoma City U., 1981, San Francisco State U., 1996, U. North Tex.; Master classes in trumpet, Nat. Trumpet Symposium, North Tex. State U. Auditor, payroll, ins. agt. Okla. Employment Svcs., Oklahoma City, 1975—80; acct. Steven E. Thomas, CPA, Oklahoma City, 1980—82; musician, audio engr., record prodr. World Evangelism Svcs., Oklahoma City, 1983—94; owner Times Two Records and Pub., Oklahoma City and San Francisco, 1986—94, North Beach Rec., San Francisco, 1990—94; receptionist San Francisco Planning and Urban Rsch., 1996—; audio/video engr. Bill Graham Presents, San Francisco, 1996, archivist, 1996; event staff San Francisco Performing Arts Found., 1996—98, Bay Area Music Awards, 1996—98, Black and White Ball, 1996; publicist Daniel Castro Blues Band, 1996—98; prodr. Kimpton Prodns. Live from the Starlight

Room TV show, 1998; hostess Little City & Tavolino Restaurants, 1998; enumerator U.S. Dept. Commerce-Census 2000, 2000; archivist George Tsongas, 2001. Judge No. Calif. Songwriters Assn., San Francisco, 1997; prodr./engr. performance and program com. Upper Grant Ave Fall Art Fair, 2003—. Prodr.: (rec.) Sheer Joy, 1983; prodr., engr., writer, musician: rec. Steve & Sara, 1986, prodr., engr., writer, performer, distbr.: Frontlines, 1988; prodr., engr., writer, performer, distbr.: Songs of the Street, 1992; prodr., engr., writer, performer, distbr.: Streetsinger, 1992, Christmas by the Sea, 1992; author: Collected Lyrics and Poetry, 1999; mem. prodn. crew 150th Anniversary Statehood Celebration, Sacramento, Calif., 1999, audio engr. Trieste Music, North Beach, San Francisco, 2003—, City Lights 50th Anniversary and Landmarking Celebration, 2002, 2003, Tele-Hi Neighborhood Ctr., 2002—, Indonesian Consultate and Telegraph Hill Dwellers Tsunami Relief Benefit, 2005; co-editor: Trieste Music News. Mem. Common Cause, Telegraph Hill Dwellers Assn., San Francisco, 1994—; mem. comm. com. Pioneer Park Project at Coit Tower, San Francisco, 1996—2001, 400 Trees Project Telegraph Hill Dwellers and Friends of the Urban Forest, San Francisco, 1996—98; mem. jazz band S.E. Okla. State U., 1972—75; concert band trumpet soloist Madrigal Singers and Opera Workshop; founder Nat. Campaign for Tolerance, 2005; poll worker presdl. election, 1996, 2000, 2004. Named to, Okla. All Dist. Band, 1965—70, Okla. All-State Band, 1969, 1970; recipient John Philip Sousa award, Broken Bow H.S., 1970, pvt. endowment, Elizabeth Styll Smith, 1983—94. Mem.: LWV, NARAS (staff 1997), Audio Engring. Soc., Music Educators Nat. Conf., Brass Quintet (outstanding brass ensemble 1969—70), Dixieland Combo-SE Okla. Dist. Tchrs., Okla. Music Educator's Conv., Four States Band Masters Conv., 4H Club, Dist. 3 Dem. Club. Democrat. Roman Catholic. Avocations: cooking, sewing, ceramics.

GREGORY, SHAWN ALEN, cardiologist, physician, researcher; b. Gallatin, Tenn., Nov. 4, 1971; s. Gerald Alen and Donna Marjorie Gregory; m. Mary Lucia Partin, Aug. 18, 2001. BS, U. Ala., Tuscaloosa, 1994; MD, U. Va., 1998; MSc in Medicine, Harvard Med. Sch., Boston, 2006. Diplomate Am. Bd. Internal Medicine, in nuc. cardiology Am. Bd. Nuc. Cardiology. Instr. of medicine U. Ala. Sch. of Medicine, Birmingham, Ala., 2001—02; rsch. fellow in medicine Harvard Med. Sch., Boston, 2002—06, scholar in clin. sci., 2004—06, instr., 2006—, attending cardiologist, 2006—; fellow in cardiology Mass. Gen. Hosp., Boston, 2002—06. Physician U. Ala. Hosp., Birmingham, 1998—2002, Mass. Gen. Hosp., Boston, 2002—. Contbr. articles pub. to profl. jour., chapters to books. Grantee Scholars in Clin. Sci. Program, Harvard Med. Sch., 2004-2006; scholar Presdl. scholar, U. Ala., 1990-1994; Nat. Rsch. Svc. awardee, NIH, 2004-2006, Teresa Thomas scholar, U. Va. Sch. of Medicine, 1998, Lawson scholar, 1997. Mem.: Paul Dudley White Soc. of Mass. Gen. Hosp., ACP/Am. Soc. Internal Medicine (assoc.), Am. Coll. Cardiology (assoc.), Phi Beta Kappa, Alpha Omega Alpha, Lambda Chi Alpha. Achievements include research in non-invasive imaging And clin. cardiovascular disease. Avocations: travel, history. Office: Mass Gen Hosp-Yawkey 5800 55 Fruit St Boston MA 02114

GREGORY, STEPHANIE ANN, hematologist, educator; b. Vineland, NJ, June 23, 1940; d. Andonetta Gregory; m. Sheldon Chertow; children: Elizabeth Chertow, Jennifer Chertow, Daniel Chertow, Erica Chertow. BS cum laude, Boston Coll., 1961; MD cum laude, Med. Coll. Pa., 1965. Diplomate in internal medicine and hematology Am. Bd. Internal Medicine. Internal medicine intern Presbyn.-St. Luke's Hosp., Chgo., 1965-66, resident in internal medicine, 1966-68, fellow in hematology, 1969—72; chief resident in internal medicine Presbyn.-St. Lukes Hosp., Chgo., 1968-69; chief spl. morphology lab. sect. hematology Rush-Presbyn.-St. Luke's Med. Ctr., Chgo., 1972-76, dir. sect. hematology divsn. hematology/oncology, 1994—, Elodia Kehm prof. medicine, dir. hematology and stem cell transplantation, 1995—; from asst. prof. medicine to assoc. prof. medicine Rush Med. Coll., Chgo., 1972-86, prof. medicine, 1986—; adminstr., dir. Consultants in Hematology Rush U. Med. Ctr., Chgo., 1985—, sr. attending physician, 1982—, dir. sect. hematology, 2004—. Coord. continuing edn. sect. hematology Rush-Presbyn.-St. Luke's Med. Ctr., Chgo., 1970-76, dir. transfusion therapy svc. sect. hematology, 1972-76, asst. chmn. dept. medicine, 1972-77, clin. dir. Sheridan Rd. Pavilion, 1976-77, acting dir. sect. clin. hematology, 1980-81, assoc. dir. sect. hematology, 1993-94, asst. chair dept. medicine, 1993-94; co-dir. Lymphoma Ctr., Rush Univ Medical Ctr., Chgo., 1992—; mem. UN Security Coun. Commn. Experts, 1994; mem. med. adv. bd. Leukemia Rsch. Found., 1996—, Leukemia/Lymphoma Soc. Am., Lymphoma Rsch. Found.; chair B-cell Edn. Malignancies program, 2005-. Mentor Lean on Me support group for young adults with cancer Rush Univ. Medical Ctr., Chgo., 1992—. Recipient award Am. Women's Med. Assn., 1965, William B. Peck Sci. award for rsch. in hematopoietic stem cell studies Sci. Assembly of Interstate Postgrad. Med. Assn., 1973, Outstanding Alumni award MCP-Hahneman Med. Sch., 1998, Excellence in Medicine award Rush U. Med. Ctr., 2006; grantee Schweppe Found. Rsch., 1969-72, NIH tng. grantee Nat. Heart, Lung and Blood Inst., 1974-79; Schweppe fellow, 1969-72. Fellow ACP (mem. Ill. coun. 1994—, mentor physician mems. for advancement to fellowship designation ann. meeting 1996, Ill. Laureate award 1996); mem. AMA, Internat. Soc. Hematology (Inter-Am. divsn.), Internat. Soc. Exptl. Hematology (charter), Leukemia Soc. Am. (bd. trustees Ill. chpt. 1987—, chmn. patient aid com. Ill. chpt. 1988-90, treas. Ill. chpt. 1992-93, chairperson patient fin. aid com. Ill. chpt. 1992—, v.p. Ill. chpt. 1991-94, mem. med. adv. bd. Ill. chpt. 1996—), Am. Soc. Clin. Oncology, Am. Soc. Hematology (co-editor, 2005-), Cell Proliferation Soc., Ea. Coop. Oncology Group, Inst. Medicine Chgo., Chgo. Soc. Internal Medicine (exec. com. 1992—, sec.-treas. 1992-93, v.p. 1993-94, pres. 1994-95), Aplastic Anemia Found. Am. (hon. bd. trustees 1988—), Mark H. Lepper M.D. Soc. Tchrs. (elected), Alpha Omega Alpha, Sigma Xi. Office: Rush Univ Medical Ctr 1725 W Harrison St Ste 834 Chicago IL 60612-3861 Office Phone: 312-942-5982. Business E-Mail: stephanie_gregory@rush.edu.

GREGORY, THOMAS BRADFORD, mathematics professor; b. Traverse City, Mich., Dec. 13, 1944; s. Philip Henry and Rhoda Winslow (Hathaway) G.; m. Deirdre Dianne Mason, July 15, 1995. *Father, Philip Henry Gregory, received a BS from Bowdoin College in 1926, a Bachelor of Sacred Theology from Yale Divinity School in 1935, and an MA from Oberlin College in 1937. A registered pharmacist, he became a minister, serving Baptist, Congregational and Presbyterian churches in Vermont, Massachusetts, Michigan and Ohio. Mother, Rhoda Winslow Hathaway, a member of the Massachusetts Society of Mayflower Descendants, studied at Massachusetts School of Art. Wife Deirdre Dianne Mason received a BSEd from Ashland College in 1981 and an MEd in 1989. She received an MS from Ohio State University in 1986 and an MEd from the University of Dayton in 1993. She is the former president, Mansfield School Employees Association and is currently guidance counselor, Mansfield City Schools. Dede is the president of the Ashland University Alumni Board of Directors and a member of the Ashland University Board of Trustees.* BA, Oberlin Coll., Ohio, 1967; MA, Yale U., 1969, M of Philosophy, 1975, PhD, 1977. Lectr. Ohio State U., Mansfield, 1977—78, asst. prof. math., 1978—84, assoc. prof. math., 1984—, pres. faculty, 2001—02. Reviewer: Math. Revs., 1984—; contbr. articles to profl. jours. Active Mansfield Symphony Chorus, Ohio, 1977—, Presbytery Youth Ministries Com., New Philadelphia, Ohio, 1980-87, Ohio State U. Cmty. Singers, Mansfield, 1985—; mem. Presbytery Bibl. Authority task force, 1994-95; bd. dirs. Lay Acad. Religion, Wooster Coll., Ohio 1997—; commd. lay min. Presbytery of Muskingum Valley, New Philadelphia, Ohio, 1998—; mem. Presbytery Com. on Ministry, 2004-. Comdr. USNR, 1969-96. Fellow NSF, Washington, 1967; hon. fellow U. Wis., Madison, 1987-88, 92. Fellow Phi Beta Kappa; mem. Am. Math. Soc. (translator 1974-82), Ohio Coun. Tchrs. Math., Am. Soc. Naval Engrs., Res. Officers Assn., Naval Res. Assn., Navy League, Sigma Xi. Avocations: classical piano, singing. Home: 411 Overlook Rd Mansfield OH 44907-1533 Office: Ohio State U 1680 University Dr # O-15 Mansfield OH 44906-1547 Office Phone: 419-755-4247. Business E-Mail: tgregory@math.ohio-state.edu.

GREGORY, TIMOTHY PETER, historian, consultant; b. Newcastle-upon-Tyne, Northumberland, Eng., Aug. 29, 1946; s. Harold Reginald and Dorothy Amelia (LeGallez) Gregory. BA, UCLA, 1968; MLS, U. of Calif., Berkeley, 1974; M of Pub. History and Hist. Preservation, Calif. State U.-Dominguez Hills, Carson, 1991. Registered pub. historian Calif. Coun. for the Promotion of History, cert. archivist Acad. of Cert. Archivists. Tech. svcs. supr. Newport Beach (Calif.) Pub. Libr., 1976—80; libr. svcs. mgr. City of Beverly Hills, Calif., 1980—91; archivist Pasadena (Calif.) Mus. of History, 1991—94; propr. The Bldg. Biographer, Calif., 1992—. Editor: (history book) Altadena: Between Wilderness and City (Commendation, Am. Assn. for State and Local History, 2005). Named Citizen of the Yr., Altadena C. of C. and Civic Assn., 1991. Mem.: Soc. Calif. Archivists (bd. dirs. 2002—03), Am. Assn. for State and Local History, Calif. Coun. for the Promotion of History (assoc.), Soc. of Archtl. Historians, Pasadena Heritage (bd. dirs. 2007—), Altadena Heritage (assoc.; chmn. of the bd. 1985—91), Pasadena Mus. of History (assoc.), Nat. Trust for Hist. Preservation (assoc.), L.A. Conservancy (assoc.), Calif. Preservation Found. (assoc.), Altadena Hist. Soc. (assoc.; vice-president 1995—2006). Democrat. Congregationalist. Avocations: media, travel, photography. Home: 400 East California Blvd #3 Pasadena CA 91106-3763 Office: The Building Biographer 400 E California Blvd 3 Pasadena CA 91106-3763 Home Phone: 626-792-7465; Office Phone: 626-792-7465. Personal E-mail: timgregory@sbcglobal.net.

GREGORY, WILLIAM STANLEY, lawyer; b. Greenwood, Miss., Mar. 12, 1949; s. Carlyle and Charlotte Ruby (Richardson) G.; m. Vicki Sue Lovelady, Aug. 15, 1970. BS in Commerce and Bus. Adminstrn., U. Ala., 1971, MBA, 1973, JD, 1974. Bar: Ala. 1974, U.S. Dist. Ct. (mid. dist.) Ala. 1979, U.S. Ct. Appeals (5th cir.) 1979, U.S. Ct. Appeals (11th cir.) 1980, U.S. Tax Ct. 1979, U.S. Dist. Ct. (no. dist.) Ala. 1991. Assoc. Johnson, Thorington, North, Haskell & Slaughter, Montgomery, Ala., 1974-78; jr. ptnr. Johnson & Thorington, Montgomery, Ala., 1979-90; sr. ptnr. Thorington & Gregory, Montgomery, Ala., 1990-2000; ptnr. Bradley, Arant, Rose & White LLP, Montgomery, Ala., 2000—. Spl. asst. atty. gen. State of Ala., Montgomery, 1978-82, 2004-; mem. taxpayer bill of rights drafting com. tax sect. Ala. State Bar, Montgomery, 1990-91. Pres. Montgomery Symphony Assn., 1980, 92, Highland Ave. Adult & Sr. Citizens Ctr., Montgomery, 1986-04; mem. Montgomery Estate Planning Coun. Capt. USAR, 1971-75. Mem. SAR, Kiwanis (v.p. 1989-90). Presbyterian. Avocation: music. Home: 8218 Wynlakes Blvd Montgomery AL 36117-5101 Office: 401 Adams Ave Ste 780 Montgomery AL 36104 Office Phone: 334-956-7700. E-mail: sgregory@bradleyarant.com.

GREGORY, WILTON D., archbishop; b. Chgo., Dec. 7, 1947; s. Wilton and Ethel Duncan Gregory. Student, Niles Coll., Loyola U., Chgo., St. Mary of Lake Sem., Mundelein, Ill.; PhD in Sacred Liturgy, Pontifical Liturgical Inst., Sant'Anselmo, Rome, 1980. Ordained priest Roman Cath. Ch., 1973; assoc. pastor Our Lady of Perpetual Help Parish, Glenview, Ill.; mem. faculty St. Mary of the Lake Sem.; master of ceremonies to Cardinals Cody and Bernardin; elevated to bishop Roman Cath. Ch., 1983; aux. bishop Archdiocese of Chgo., 1983—94; bishop Diocese of Belleville, 1994—2005; archbishop Archdiocese of Atlanta, 2005—. Avocations: travel, music, racquetball, golf. Office: Archdiocese of Atlanta 680 W Peachtree St NW Atlanta GA 30308 Office Phone: 404-888-7802.

GREGSON, NIGEL CHRISTOPHER, pharmaceutical executive, consultant; b. Hythe, Hampshire, Eng., June 5, 1964; s. Christopher Allen Candy and Susan Mary Gascoigne Storer; m. Trudy Ellen Hauser, Nov. 12, 1988; children: Jordan James, Theo Jacob, Lauren Elise. BA in Bus. Adminstrn. with honors, Loughborough U., Eng., 1986; cert. in Health Econ., U. Aberdeen, 2001. CPA Ill. Sr. auditor KPMG Peat Marwick, London, 1986—89, supervising sr. auditor Phila., 1990—90; operational cons. SmithKline Beecham, Phila., 1990—96, assoc. dir. planning and fin., global mktg., 1996—97, dir. global pricing and econ. analysis, 1998—2000; group dir. global pricing and reimbursement strategy GlaxoSmithKline, Phila., 2001—03; co-founder, prin. PriceSpective LLC, Blue Bell, Pa., 2003—. Author: Pricing Medicines: Theory and Practice, Challenges and Opportunities. Mem.: Internat. Soc. for Pharmacoeconomics and Outcomes Rsch. (assoc.), Inst. Chartered Accountants in Eng. and Wales (assoc.). Home: 1228 Turnbury Ln North Wales PA 19454 Office: PriceSpective LLC 620 Sentry Pkwy Ste 100 Blue Bell PA 19422 Home Phone: 215-661-0686; Office Phone: 610-862-6021. Office Fax: 610-862-6007. Personal E-mail: ngregson@comcast.com. Business E-Mail: ngregson@pricespective.com.

GREHAN, KEVIN J., lawyer; b. Mt. Kisco, NY, Jan. 5, 1956; BA summa cum laude, Fordham Coll., 1978; JD, Columbia Univ., 1981. Bar: NY 1984. Assoc. Cravath Swaine & Moore LLP, NYC, 1981—88, ptnr., corp., 1988—. Trustee Convent of the Sacred Heart. Mem.: ABA, Assn. of Bar of City of NY, NY State Bar Assn. Office: Cravath Swaine & Moore LLP Worldwide Plz 825 Eighth Ave New York NY 10019-7475 Office Phone: 212-474-1490. Office Fax: 212-474-3700. Business E-Mail: krehan@cravath.com.

GREIDER, CAROL WIDNEY, molecular biologist; b. San Diego, Apr. 15, 1961; BA in Biology, U. Calif., Santa Barbara, 1983; PhD in Molecular Biology, U. Calif., Berkeley, 1987. Fellow Cold Spring Harbor Lab., NY, 1988-90, asst. investigator NY, 1990-92, assoc. staff investigator NY, 1992-94, investigator NY, 1994-97; assoc. prof. dept. molecular biology and genetics, Johns Hopkins U. Sch. Medicine, Balt., 1997—99, prof., 1999—2002, acting dir., 2002—03, Daniel Nathans prof. and dir., 2003—; prof., dept. oncology Johns Hopkins U. Sch. Medicine, Balt., 1999—. Organizer Gordon Rsch. Conf. on Nucleic Acids, Providence, 1998, Cold Spring Harbor Lab. Seminar on Telemeres and Telemerase, 1999; mem., site visit com. NIH, 1992, mem. RFA study sect., 98, 93, mem., Ad hoc reviewer, Molecular Cytology Study Sect., 94; mem. Nat. Bioethics Adv. Commn., 1996—2001. Mem. editl. bd. Cancer Cell, 2001-, Molecular Cance Rsch., 2003-;contbr. numerous articles, revs., book chpts. Regents scholar U. Calif., 1981, Pew Biomed. Scis. scholar, 1990-94; recipient Allied Signal Outstanding Project award, 1992, Schering-Plough Sci. Achievement award Am. Soc. for Biochemistry and Molecular Biology, 1997, Ellison Medical Found. Sr. Scholar award, 1998, Gairdner Found. award 1998, Passano Found. award 1999, Rosenstiel award, 1999, Harvey Soc. Lecture, 2000, Lila Gruber Cancer Rsch. award, 2006, Wiley prize, 2006; co-recipient Albert Lasker award Lasker Found., 2006. Fellow AAAS, Am. Acad. Arts and Scis., Am. Acad. Microbiology; mem. NAS (Richard Lounsbery award 2003), Am. Soc. for Cell Biology (coun. mem., 1998-2001, Glenn Found. award, 1995), RNA Soc., Am. Assn. for Cancer Rsch. (Pezcoller award com. mem. 1999, organizer program com. mem. ann. mtg., Phila., 1999, Cornelius Rhoads award 1996), Am. Soc. for Microbiology, Phi Beta Kappa. Office: Johns Hopkins U Sch Med 603 PCTB 725 N Wolfe St Baltimore MD 21205 Office Phone: 410-614-6506. Office Fax: 410-955-0831. Business E-Mail: cgreider@jhmi.edu.

GREIF, JOSEPH, lawyer; b. NYC, June 25, 1943; s. Jacob J. and Dorothy (Harrison) G.; m. Aline Bohm, Jan. 1, 1966; children: Jeffrey, Julie. BBA, U. Pitts., 1964; JD, NYU, 1967. Bar: NY 1967, DC 1968, US Tax Ct. 1986; CPA, Md., DC. Instr. No. Va. CC, Annandale, 1967-68; mgmt. cons. Computer Sci. Corp., Silver Spring, Md., 1967-70; tax mgr. Arthur Andersen & Co., Washington, 1970-75; sr. assoc. Ginsberg, Feldman & Bress, Washington, 1975-77; ptnr. Touche Ross & Co., Washington, 1977-84, McGuffie, Greif, Whitney & Handal, Washington, 1984-90; of counsel McNeily, Rosenfeld & Rubenstein, Washington, 1991-98, Neimark & Nadel, Ft. Lauderdale, Fla., 1998—2001, Washington, 1998—2001, Greif Legal Econ. Svcs., 2002—06; chief legal officer, gen. counsel Mo. State Tchrs. Assn., 2006—. Lectr. George Washington U. Grad. Sch. Bus., Washington, 1993-95. Co-author, editor: Managing Membership Societies, 1979; contbr. articles on taxation, comml. leasing, computer systems contracting, exec. compensation, exec. contracts to profl. jours. Bd. dirs. Nat. Assn. for Mental Health, Washington, 1973-75, Combined Health Appeal, Washington, 1980-81, Assn. Devel. Coun., Washington, 1987-89; task force mem. White House Task Force on Charitable Giving, Washington, 1979-80; vice chair tech., scis. and rsch. com. The Broward Alliance, 2004—, bd. dirs., 2005-06, chair tech., sci. and rsch. com., 2005-06. Mem. AICPA (chmn. fed. tax divsn. task force on exempt orgns. 1983-86), ABA, DC Bar Assn., Am. Soc. Assn. Execs. (mem. govt. affairs and long range planning coms., Outstanding Svc. award, tech. sect. coun. 1996—), DC Inst. CPAs, Greater Washington Soc. Assn. Execs. (tech. task force 1994—), Computer Law Assn., Greater Ft. Lauderdale C. of C. (vice chair tech. com. 2004-05). Avocations: boating, squash. Office Phone: 800-3 9-2053 ext. 1215.

GREIF, ROBERT, mechanical engineering educator; b. NYC, Jan. 17, 1938; s. Harry and Anne (Reiter) G.; m. Joyce Ambrose; children: Jessica, Andrew. BSME, NYU, 1958; SM, Harvard U., 1959, PhD, 1963. Registered profl. engr., Mass. Staff scientist Missile Systems div., Avco Corp., Wilmington, Mass., 1963-65, sr. staff scientist, 1965-67; asst. prof. mech. engring. Tufts U., Medford, Mass., 1967-70, assoc. prof., 1970-78, prof., 1978—, chmn. dept. mech. engring., 1981-89. Cons. Stone & Webster, Boston, 1971-78, U.S. Dept. Transp., Cambridge, Mass., 1977—; vis. scholar Harvard U., Cambridge, 1981; vis. research fellow U. Sussex, Eng., 1974; sr. rsch. assoc. NASA Langley Rsch. Ctr., 1988. Fellow AIAA (assoc.), ASME; mem. AAUP. Office: Tufts U Dept Mech Engring 200 College Ave Anderson Hall Medford MA 02155 Office Phone: 617-627-3238. Business E-Mail: robert.greif@tufts.edu.

GREIFELD, ROBERT, stock exchange executive; b. Queens, New York City, July 18, 1957; m. Julia Greifeld; 3 children. BA Eng., Iona Coll., 1979; MBA, NYU, Stern Sch. of Bus., 1986. Pres., COO Automated Securities Clearance, Inc., 1991—99; v.p. Sunguard Data Sys. Inc. and group CEO, Sunguard Brokerage Sys., 1999—2000; sr. v.p. Sunguard Data Sys., Inc., 2000—02; pres., CEO The Nasdaq Stock Market, Inc., NYC, 2003—. Dir. Knight Trading Group, Inc., 2000—03; vice chmn. Kennedy Ctr. Corp. Fund. Bd.; mem. bd. Partnership for NYC. Chmn. USA Track & Field Found., 2004—. Avocation: running. Office: The Nasdaq Stock Market Inc 1 Liberty Plz #49 New York NY 10006-1404*

GREIG, BRIAN STROTHER, lawyer; b. Austin, Tex., Apr. 10, 1950; s. Ben Wayne Greig and Virginia Ann (Strother) Higgins; m. Jane Ann Sentilles, June 17, 1972; children: Travis Darden, Grace Hanna. BA, Washington and Lee U., 1972; JD, U. Tex., 1975. Bar: Tex. 1975, US Dist. Ct. (ea. dist.) Tex. 1976, US Ct. Appeals (5th cir.) 1976, US Dist. Ct. (so. dist.) Tex. 1977, US Dist. Ct. (we. dist.) Tex. 1980, US Supreme Ct. 1980, US Dist. Ct. (no. dist.) Tex. 1984, US Ct. Appeals (11th cir.) 1984. Law clk. to chief judge US Dist. Ct., Beaumont, Tex., 1975-76; sr. ptnr. Fulbright & Jaworski LLP, Austin, 1976—, mem. policy com., 2004—. Mem. Austin Tomorrow On-Going Goals Assembly Com., 1981; pres. Austin Mgmt. Lawyers Forum, 1987, 93. Editor-in-chief Tex. Assn. Bus. Employment Law Handbook; mem. editl. bd. Tex. Labor Letter, 1994-2001. Pres. Austin Lawyers and Accts. for Arts, 1981; trustee Laguna Gloria Art Mus., Austin, 1983-91, pres., 1989-90, chmn., 1990-91; bd. dirs. Zachary Scott Theater Ctr., Austin, 1981; devel. bd. Inst. Texan Cultures, 1991-98; trustee Westminster Manor Health Facilities Corp. of Travis County, Tex., 1991-96, sec., 1995-96; trustee St. Stephen's Episcopal Sch., 1995-2001. Headliners Found., 2006; pres. Austin Mus. Art, 1991-92, trustee, 1991-93; bd. dirs. Capital of Tex. Pub. Telecomms. Coun., Inc./KLRU-TV, 2001—. Fellow Tex. Bar Found. (life), Am. Coll. Labor and Employment Lawyers; mem. ABA, FBA, Am. Arbitration Assn. (employment adv. coun. 1995—2000), Tex. Bar Assn., Travis County Bar Assn., Tex. Commn. on Human Rights (chmn.'s task force), Tex. Assn. Bus. (bd. dirs. 2000—), Tarry House Club, Headliners Club (trustee 1998—, pres. 2006), Austin Assembly. Roman Catholic. Avocations: hunting, fishing. Office: Fulbright & Jaworski LLP 600 Congress Ave Ste 2400 Austin TX 78701-3271 Office Phone: 512-536-4510. Business E-Mail: bgreig@fulbright.com.

GREIGG, RONALD EDWIN, lawyer; b. Washington, June 29, 1946; s. Edwin E. and Helen Marie (Marcy) G.; m. Patricia Anne Crowe, June 5, 1968; children: Elizabeth, Rebecca. BS in Bus. Adminstrn., Am. U., 1969, MBA in Fin., 1971; JD, Stetson U., 1976. Registered patent atty.; bar: Fla. 1976, D.C. 1978, Va. 1985, U.S. Dist. Ct. (mid. dist.) Fla. 1976, U.S. Dist. Ct. (ea. dist.) Va. 1988, U.S. Ct. Appeals (D.C. cir.) 1979, U.S. Ct. Appeals (fed. cir.) 1982, U.S. Supreme Ct. 1980. Assoc. David E. De Serio, St. Petersburg, Fla., 1977-78, Edwin E. Greigg, Washington, 1979-82, Harris, Barrett & Dew, St. Petersburg, Fla., 1982-84; ptnr. Greigg & Greigg, Arlington, Va., 1984-99; mng. dir. Greigg & Greigg PLLC, Alexandria, 1999—. Author: A Guide to the FTC Franchise Disclosure Rule, 1979, Patent Infringement Damages, 1988. Mem.: D.C. Bar Assn., Fla. Bar Assn., Va. Bar Assn., Inst. of Trademark Attys. (London), Internat. Trademark Assn., Phi Alpha Delta. Republican. Episcopalian. Avocations: sailing, classic cars. Office: Greigg & Greigg PLLC #1 1423 Powhatan St Ste 1 Alexandria VA 22314-1389 Home Phone: 301-229-5591; Office Phone: 703-838-5500. Fax: 703-838-5554. E-mail: rgreigg@greigg.com.

GREILSHEIMER, JAMES GANS, lawyer; b. NYC, Oct. 14, 1937; s. Jerome J. and Lillian (Gans) Greilsheimer; m. Louise B. Steiner, Aug. 11, 1974; children: Lauren, Julie, Michael, Jeremy. AB cum laude, Princeton U., NJ, 1959; LLB, Harvard U., Cambridge, Mass., 1962. Bar: NY 1963, DC 1969. Asst. U.S. atty. So. Dist. NY, 1963-68; litigating asst. corp. counsel City of NY, 1974-77, 1st asst. corp. counsel, 1978-80; ptnr. Blank Rome LLP and predecessor firms, NYC, 1993—. Mediator mediation program US Dist. Ct. (so. dist.) NY, 1993—. Mem., sec. NYC Charter Rev. Commn., 1982-83; pres. NY chpt. Am. Jewish Com., 1981-84; v.p. Jewish Cmty. Rels. Coun. NY, 1981-85, bd. dirs., 1995-2001; bd. dirs. Com. on Decent Unbiased Campaign Tactics, 1983-93, Non-profit Coordinating Com., NY, 1985-2005, Vol. Cons. Group, Inc., 1986—; v.p., bd. dirs. Fund for Pub. Schs., Inc., 1986-91, pres., 1992-2002; mem. Citizens Budget Commn., Inc., 1991-93. Mem.: Assn. Bar of City of NY (mcpl. affairs com. 1979—81, govt. ethics com. 1990—98, com. on condemnation and tax certiorari 1993—95, 2001—04, 2006—), NY County Lawyers Assn. (chmn. fed. cts. com. 1977—80, bd. dirs. 1981—87, spl. com. on condemnation 1990—), NY State Bar Assn. (spl. com. on cts. and cmty. 1975—81). Office: Blank Rome LLP 405 Lexington Ave New York NY 10174-0208 Office Phone: 212-885-5381. Business E-Mail: jgreilsheimer@blankrome.com.

GREINER, HELEN, mechanical engineer; b. London, Dec. 6, 1967; BS in Mech. Engring., MIT, 1989, MS in Computer Sci., 1990. Worked with NASA Jet Propulsion Lab., MIT, Artificial Intelligence Lab.; co-founder IS Robotics (now iRobot Corp.), Burlington, Mass., 1990—, pres., head of rsch.; also chmn. bd. iRobot Corp., Burlington, Mass. Lectr. in field; invited to the World Econ. Forums as a Global Leader of Tomorrow. Named Innovator for the Next Century, Technology Review Mag., (with Colin Angle) Ernst and Young New England Entrepreneurs of Yr., 2003; named one of Top 10 Innovators in the US, Fortune Mag.; recipient DEMO God award, DEMO conf. Achievements include inventor of the ROOMBA robotic vacuum. Avocations: reading, gardening, kayaking, mountain climbing, snowboarding. Office: iRobot Corp 63 South Ave Burlington MA 01803 Office Phone: 781-345-0200. Office Fax: 781-345-0201.

GREINER, KENNETH DONALD, JR., retired management consultant, health facility administrator; b. Cushing, Okla., Aug. 19, 1938; s. Kenneth Donald Greiner and Billie Alene (Williams) Greiner; m. Leitner Louise Jarrell, Sept. 2, 1961; children: Katherine Louise Pierce, Kenneth Donald III, Jennifer Lee Burrell, Cheryl Sue Gumerson. BS in Econs., Okla. State U., 1960; MBA, Harvard U., 1962; BS in Health Care Adminstrn., Okla. Bapt. U., 1977. Adminstrv. asst. Doric Corp., Oklahoma City, 1962-64; asst. to treas. Skelly Oil Co., Tulsa, 1964-66; loan officer AID, Lahore, Karachi, Pakistan, 1966-69; ptnr. Resource Analysis and Mgmt. Group, Oklahoma City, 1969-74; v.p., dir. Texas Internat. Co., Oklahoma City, 1974-76; chmn. Grace Living Ctrs. (formerly Amity Care Corp.), Oklahoma City, 1976—2002; pres. Nursing Home Properties, 2002—; ptnr. Ams. Mgmt. Svcs. LLC, 2003—06. Asst. bankruptcy trustee Four Seasons Nursing Ctrs. Am., 1972—73; bd. dirs. Cmty. bnk Warr Acres, 1972—82, Will Rogers Bank, 1983—94; br. adv. dir. Oklahoma City Nations Bank, 1994—97; bankruptcy trustee Gulf South Corp., 1974, Cleanerator Corp., 1974, Preferred Commodity Options Corp., 1974—75; bd. dirs. Secret Harbour Beach Resort, 2004—07. Treas., bd. dirs. Neighborhood Svcs. Orgn., Oklahoma City Met. Area, 1978—83; chmn. bd. New World Sch., Oklahoma City, 1973—74; mem. Putnam City Sch. Bd., 1988—93, pres., 1992—93; dir. Cowboy Golf, Inc., 1992—2003; trustee Hillcrest Hosp., Oklahoma City, 1989—93; dir. Emergency Med. Svcs. Authority, Oklahoma City, Tulsa, 1998—2001; mem. bd. govs. Okla. State U. Found., 1994—, trustee, 1998—, vice chmn., 2004—05, chmn., 2005—07, Cath. Social Ministries, Archdiocese of Oklahoma City, 1977—86. Mem.: Papal Found. Investment Com., Nat. Assn. Bds. Examiners Nursing Home Adminstrs. (pres. 1994—96), Okla. State Bd. Nursing Homes (bd. dirs. 1988—92), Nursing Home Assn. Okla. (exec. bd. 1988—2003, v.p. 1990—92), Okla. State U. CBA Assocs. (pres. 1993—94), Equestrian Order Holy Seplechre, Ski Island Lake Inc. (pres. 1984—87), Quail Creek Golf and Country Club (v.p., dir. 1998—2001), Bus. Boosters Club (pres. 1985), Harvard Bus. Sch. Alumni Club (pres. Oklahoma City 1970—71), Phi Delta Theta Alumni (pres. Oklahoma City 1969—71). Republican. Roman Catholic. Office: 4350 Will Rogers Pkwy Ste 350 Oklahoma City OK 73108

GREINER, NICOLE K. HUDAK, physical education educator; b. Erie, Pa., May 24, 1976; d. Francis Joseph and Sharon Ann Hudak; m. Nathan Reid Greiner, July 14, 2006. BS, Ohio No. U., Ada, 1998; tchg. cert., Edinboro U., Pa., 1999; MEd, U. Va., Charlottesville, 2004. Cert. Nat. Athletic Trainer. Tchr. elem phys. edn. Fairfax County Pub. Schs., Va., 2006—. Mem. Health and Phys. Edn. Adv. Com., Va.; co-chair after-sch. 6th grade girls program Girl Power!. Mem.: NEA, Fairfax Edn. Assn. Avocations: exercise, reading, dance, travel.

GREINER, STEPHEN W., lawyer; b. NYC, Dec. 14, 1944; BA, Syracuse U., 1965; JD, NYU, 1968. Bar: NY 1969, US Dist. Ct. (so. dist.) NY 1970, US Ct. Appeals (2nd cir.) 1974, US Dist. Ct. (ea. dist.) 1984, US Ct. Appeals (3rd cir.) 1988, US Dist. Ct. (we. dist.) NY 1989, US Ct. Appeals (9th & 11th cir.) 1989, US Supreme Ct. 1989. Law clk. to Judge Frederick van Pelt Bryan US Dist. Ct. (so. dist.) NY, 1968—70; asst. to Independent Counsel Arthur H. Christy; joined Willkie Farr & Gallagher LLP, NYC, 1972, ptnr. Litig. Dept. Contbr. articles to law jours. Mem.: Assn. Bar City NY, Order of Coif. Office: Willkie Farr & Gallagher LLP 787 7th Ave New York NY 10019-6018 Office Phone: 212-728-8224. Office Fax: 212-728-9224. E-mail: sgreiner@willkie.com.*

GREINER, WALTER ALBIN ERHARD, physicist; b. Neuenbau, Germany, Oct. 29, 1935; s. Albin and Elsa (Fischer) G.; m. Barbara Chun; children: Martin, Carsten. MS, U. Darmstadt, Germany, 1959; PhD, U. Freiburg, Germany, 1961; DSci (hon.), U. Witwatersrand, South Africa, 1982, U. Beijing, 1990, U. Tel Aviv, 1991, U. Louis Pasteur, Strasbourg, France, 1991, U. Bucharest, 1992, Kossuth Lajos U., Debrecen, 1997, U. Nantes, 2001, Jilin U., 2001, U. St. Petersburg, 2001, Dubna-Moscow U., 2002, Bogoliabov Inst. Kiev, 2003. Rsch. asst. U. Freiburg, 1961-62; asst. prof. U. Md., 1962-64; prof. theoretical physics U. Frankfurt, Fed. Republic Germany, 1965—; dir. Inst. Theoretical Physics, 1965—2000; founding dir. Frankfurt Inst. for Advanced Studies, 2002—. Guest prof. at numerous univs.; adj. prof. Vanderbilt U.-Oak Ridge Nat. Lab., 1975-2000; hon. prof. U. Beijing, 1990; permanent sci. cons. Gesellschaft fur Schwerionenforschung, Darmstadt. Author: (with others) Nuclear Theory, Nuclear Models Vol. 1, 1970, Excitation Mechanism of Nuclei Vol. 2, 1970, Theory of the Nucleus Vol. 3, 1972, 3d edit., 1987-89, Theoretische Physik Vols. 1-14, 1974-89, translated into English, French, Chinese, Japanese; editor Jour. of Physics, 1975-89, Internat. Jour. Modern Physics, 1990—, Founds. of Physics, 1990—. Named officier dans l'ordre palmes academique, 1999; recipient Max Born prize, Inst. Physics, 1974, Otto Hahn prize, 1982, Alexander von Humboldt medal, 1998, 1st Degree Phys. medal, Czech Phys. Soc., 2006. Mem. European Physics Soc., Am. Physics Soc., Eötvös Lorand Soc. Hungary (hon.), Acad. Sci. Romania (hon.). Office: Frankfurt Inst Advanced Studies Johann Wolfgang Goethe-U Max von Laue Str 1 D60438 Frankfurt Main Germany Office Phone: 49-(0)69-798-47526. Business E-Mail: greiner@fias.uni-frankfurt.de.

GREINKE, EVERETT DONALD, management consultant; b. Elmhurst, Ill., Oct. 31, 1929; s. Herman and Marie Barbara (Kline) G.; m. Clara Joan Plasil, Sept. 29, 1951; children: Donald James, David Carl, Mark Andrew. BS with honors, No. Ill. U., 1951, MS with honors, 1956; postgrad., U. Wis., 1956, George Washington U., 1957. Project officer Bur. Aeronautics USN, Washington, 1956-60, asst. br. head Bur. Aeronautics, 1960-61, tech. advisor Automatic Data Processing Office Chief Naval Ops., 1961-65, asst. dir. command/control Office Chief Naval Ops., 1965-67; sr. staff specialist reconnaissance Office Dir. Def. Research and Engring., Washington, 1967-73, sr. staff specialist tactical command, control and intelligence, 1973-76, asst. dir. combat support, 1976-77, dir. combat support, 1977-80, dir. NATO/Europe affairs, 1980-82; acting dep. undersec. internat. programs and tech. Office UnderSec. Def. Research & Engring., Washington, 1982; scientific advisor to Supreme Comdr. NATO/Supreme Hdqrs. Allied Powers Europe, Casteau, Belgium, 1982-86; dep. undersec. internat. programs and tech. Office Undersec. Def. (Acquisition), Washington, 1986-88; internat. programs cons., 1988-90; v.p. corp. devel. Internat. Partnerships Group (Interpar), 1990-93; v.p. Internat. Planning and Analysis Ctr., 1993-96, Global Mktg. Devel. Solutions, 1996—. Lectr. on armaments cooperation various orgns., 1977—; mem. Army Sci. Bd., 2002—; cons. Def. Sci. Bd., 1988—, U.S. Industry on Internat. Coop. and High Tech. Programs, 1988—. Contbr. articles to profl. jours. Pres. Chapel Sq. Sch. PTA, Annandale, Va., 1966-67, v.p. 1965; pres. W.T. Woodson High Sch. PTA, 1972-73; pres. Hope Luth. Ch. Coun., Annandale, 1970-71, mem. ch. coun., 1987-89, mem. bd. elders, 1974-82, mem. planning com., 1986-87, chmn. bldg. com., 1987-92, trustee, 1993—; com. chmn. Boy Scouts Am., Annandale, 1966-68, chmn. Explorer Post, Annandale, 1972-73, scoutmaster, 1968-78; Santa Claus for local civic orgns., Annandale, 1961-94. Comdr. USNR, 1951-55. Decorated Def. D.S.M. (3), Def. Meritorious Service Medal; Comdr.'s Cross (Austria); recipient Def. Outstanding Pub. Service award, Service plaque W.T. Woodson High Sch. PTA, 1973, Service award Boy Scouts Am., 1975, Disting. Alumni award No. Ill. U., 1987. Mem. Nat. Def. Indsl. Assn. Lutheran. Avocations: gardening, fishing. Home: 8315 Toll House Rd Annandale VA 22003-4630 Office Phone: 703-299-6649. Personal E-mail: greinkee@verizon.net. Business E-Mail: greinkee@gmdsinc.com.

GREITZER, MATT, marketing professional; b. Spencer, NY, 1977; Grad., Bowdoin Coll. Dir. ops. Avenue A/Razorfish, Seattle, 1998—2003, NYC, 2003—04, dir. search engine mktg. for NY, 2005—; founder & pres. Bin 55, LLC, 2004—05. Named one of 40 Under 40, Crain's NY Bus., 2007. Office: Avenue A/Razorfish 19th Fl 1440 Broadway New York NY 10018 Office Phone: 212-789-6600. Office Fax: 212-789-6601.*

GRENDELL, JAMES HENRY, medical educator; b. Cleve., Dec. 7, 1949; married; 3 children. BS in Biology magna cum laude, John Carroll U., 1971; MD cum laude, Ohio State U., 1975. Diplomate Nat. Bd. Med. Examiners, Am. Bd. Internal Medicine with subspecialty in gastroenterology; lic. physician, N.Y. Intern in medicine Beth Israel Hosp., Boston, 1975-76, resident in medicine, 1976-78; fellow in gastroenterology U. Calif., San Francisco, 1978-81, asst. prof. medicine and physiology, 1981-88, assoc. prof., 1989-94; chief gastroenterology sect. San Francisco VA Med. Ctr., 1990-94; prof. medicine Cornell U., NYC, 1994—99; chief divsn. digestive diseases New York Hosp.-Cornell U. Med. Ctr., NYC, 1994-98; chief divsn. gastroenterology, hepatology and nutrition Winthrop U. Hosp., Mineola, NY, 1999—; prof. medicine SUNY, Stony Brook, 2003—. Mem. gastroenterology subsplty. bd. Am. Bd. Internal Medicine, 1995-99; lectr. in field. Editor: Current Diagnosis and Treatment in Gastroenterology, 1996, 2003; assoc. editor Internat. Jour. Pancreatology, 1989—, Pancreas, 1993—; cons. editor Gastroenterology, 1982; ad hoc referee Sci. Jour. of Clin. Investigation, Annals of Internal Medicine, Gastroenterology, Am. Jour. Physiology, Digestive Diseases and Scis., Neuroendocrinology, Western Jour. Medicine, Fedn. Proc., Can. Jour. Physiology and Pharmacology, Endocrinology, Am. Jour. Gastroenterology, Jour. Lab. and Clin. Medicine; contbr. numerous articles and abstracts to profl. jours., chpts. to books. Mem.: ACP (gastroenterology subcom. med. knowledge self-assessment program IX 1989—91), Internat. Assn. of Pancreatology, Western Assn. Physicians, Western Soc. for Clin. Investigation, Am. Pancreatic Assn. (governing coun. 1989—95, pres. 1993—94), Gastroenterology Rsch. Group, Am. Gastroenterol. Assn. (com. on tng. and edn. 1990—94, chmn. tng. subcom. 1991—94, Fall postgrad. course assoc. dir. 1992, co-chair pancreatic disorders sect. 1993—95, chair 1995—97, coun. 1997—2000, governing bd. 1997—2000, course dir. 1998, pub. affairs and advocacy com. 2003—), Am. Fedn. Clin. Rsch., Landacre Soc., Alpha Omega Alpha. Home Phone: 914-288-9678; Office Phone: 516-663-4624. Business E-Mail: jgrendel@winthrop.org.

GRENDLER, PAUL FREDERICK, historian, educator; b. Armstrong, Iowa, May 24, 1936; s. August Paul and Josephine Lucy (Girres) G.; m. Marcella T. McCann, June 16, 1962; children: Peter, Jean. BA, Oberlin Coll., 1959; MA, U. Wis., 1961, PhD, 1964. Lectr. history U. Pitts., 1963-64, U. Toronto, Ont., Canada, 1964—65, asst. prof., 1965—69, assoc. prof., 1969—73, prof., 1973—98; prof. emeritus, 1998. Postdoctoral fellow Inst. Rsch. in Humanities U. Wis., Madison, 1967—68. Author: Critics of the Italian World, 1530-1560, 1969, The Roman Inquisition and the Venetian Press, 1540-1605, 1977 (Marraro prize 1978), rev. Italian transl., 1983, Culture and Censorship in Late Renaissance Italy and France, 1981, Schooling in Renaissance Italy, 1989 (Marraro prize 1989), paperback, 1991, 1995, Italian transl., 1991, Books and Schools in the Italian Renaissance, 1995, The Universities of the Italian Renaissance, 2002 (Marraro prize 2002), paperback edit., 2004, The European Rennissance in Am. Life, 2006, Renaissance Education Between Religion and Politics, 2006; editor: An Italian Renaissance Reader, 1987, 2d edit., 1992, Roman and German Humanism 1450-1550, 1993, Renaissance Quarterly, 2000-03; editor-in-chief: Ency. of Renaissance, 6 vols., 1999, 2d printing, 2000 (Dartmouth medal 2000, Roland H. Bainton prize 2000), Renaissance. An Encyclopedia for Students, 4 vols., 2004; assoc. editor Europe 1450-1789, 6 vols., 2004; mem. editl. bd., exec. com.: Collected Works of Erasmus, from 1976; contbr. articles to profl. jours. Fulbright fellow Italy, 1962-63; Can. Council fellow, 1970-71; Am. Council Learned Socs. fellow, 1971-72; I Tatti fellow Harvard U. Ctr. for Italian Renaissance Studies, Florence, Italy, 1970-72; sr. fellow Soc. for Humanities Cornell U., 1973-74; Guggenheim Meml. fellow, 1978-79; Social Scis. and Humanities Research Council Can. fellow, 1979-80, 85-86; Woodrow Wilson Internat. Ctr. for Scholars fellow, 1982-83; Nat. Humanities Ctr. fellow, 1988-90; grantee NEH, 1989-92; Connaught fellowship, 1998. Mem. Renaissance Soc. Am. (v.p. 1991-92, pres. 1992-94), Am. Hist. Assn., Am. Cath. Hist. Assn. (pres. 1984), Am. Philos. Soc., Soc. Italian Hist. Studies (sr. scholar citation 1998; v.p. 2001-03, pres. 2003-05). Address: 110 Fern Ln Chapel Hill NC 27514-4206 E-mail: pgrendler@cs.com.

GRENELL, JAMES HENRY, retired manufacturing company executive; b. Mpls., Feb. 19, 1924; s. Harrison Morton and Harriet Elizabeth (Kuch) G.; m. Naomi Betty Callerstrom, Sept. 15, 1945; children: Bonita (Mrs. Michael Wolfe), Suzanne Naomi, Andrea Bergine. BBA, U. Minn., 1947; postgrad. Advanced Mgmt. Program, Harvard U., Cambridge, Mass., 1974. With Honeywell Inc., Mpls., 1951-86, accountant, 1951-56, div. controller, 1956-68, group controller, 1968-71, asst. corp. controller, 1971-74, v.p., controller, 1974-82, v.p., staff exec., 1982-86; ret. Instr. Mgmt. Inst. U. Wis.-Madison, 1960-69, Inst. Tech. U. Minn., Mpls., 1963-65; asso. dir. Mgmt. Center U. St. Thomas, 1959-69 Contbr. articles to profl. jours. Bd. dirs. Mpls. Soc. for Blind, 1963-71, pres., 1970-71; bd. dirs. U. Minn. Coll. Bus. Alumni Bd., 1975-82; mem. Acctg. Adv. Coun. U. Minn., 1977-83. Served to 1st lt. 1943-46, European Theatre Operations. Decorated 4 Battle Star US Army. Mem. Fin. Execs. Inst., Alpha Kappa Psi, Harvard Club of Ariz., Ariz. Club. Republican. Home: 10056 E Calle De Cielo Scottsdale AZ 85258-5652 Home (Summer): 1201 Skyview Flagstaff AZ 86004-8718 Personal E-mail: grenellaz@webtv.net.

GRENEVICKI, LANCE FRANCIS, surgeon; b. Plainfield, NJ, May 21, 1967; s. Lawrence Francis and Joann Frances (Bengivenga) Grenevicki; m. Amy Lavonne Bridgers, Apr. 13, 1996; children: Anna Lavonne, Lance Frances Jr. BS, Va. Poly. Inst. and State U., 1989; DDS cum laude, Med. Coll. Va., 1993; MD, U. Mo., Kansas City, 1997. Diplomate Am. Bd. Oral and Maxillofacial Surgery. Intern Truman Med. Ctr., Kansas City, Mo., resident, 1993-99; attending med. staff, chmn. med. records com. Holmes Regional Med. Ctr., Melbourne, Fla., vice chief surgery, chair surg. quality improvement com., 2005—; mem. med. staff, chmn. med. records com. Palm Bay (Fla.) Cmty. Hosp.; courtesy clin. asst. prof. surgery U. Fla.; active med. staff mem. Wuesthoff Hosp., Melbourne, Fla. Mem. adv. coun. Fla. Cancer Control and Rsch., med. quality com., 2006—, bd. quality com., 2006—; bd. dirs. Isaac Walton League of Am., Christiansburg, Va., 1988—89. Named Surg. Resident of Yr., Isaac Walton League Am., 1997; recipient Victim's Advocate award, State Atty.'s Office, 2002. Fellow: ACS, Am. Acad. Cosmetic Surgery, Am. Coll. Oral and Maxillofacial Surgeons, Am. Assn. Oral and Maxillofacial Surgeons (alt. del. Fla.); mem.: ADA, AMA (Brevard County del.), Fla. Soc. Dental Anesthesiology (pres. 2006), Brevard County Med. Soc. (bd. govs.), Brevard County Dental Soc. (adv. com. cancer control and rsch. 2005—, program chair, sec./treas.), So. Med. Assn., Ctrl. Dist. Dental Soc., Fla. Dental Assn., Fla. Med. Assn. (Brevard county del.), Fla. Soc. Oral and Maxillofacial Surgeons (trustee 2001—06, v.p., Young Eagle award 2001), Southeastern Soc. Oral and Maxillofacial Surgeons, Psi Omega, Alpha Omega Alpha, Pi Kappa Alpha. Roman Catholic. Avocations: trap and skeet shooting, hunting, fishing. Office: Inst Facial Surgery 1093 S Wickham Rd Melbourne FL 32904-1652 Home: 2306 N Riverside Dr Indialantic FL 32903-3619 Office Phone: 321-674-3900.

GRENFELL, BRYAN THOMAS, biology professor; PhD. Prof. dept. zoology U. Cambridge, England; alumni prof. biology Pa. State U., Univ. Pk. Acting dir. Ctr. Infectious Disease Dynamics Pa. State U. Contbr. articles to profl. jours.; co-editor: Ecology of Infectious Diseases in Natural Populations, 1995; author: Ecology of Wildlife Host-Parasite Interactions, 1997. Fellow: Am. Acad. Arts & Scis. Office: Dept Biology Pa State U 0208 Mueller Lab University Park PA 16802 E-mail: grenfell@psu.edu.

GRENIER, ADRIAN, actor; b. Bklyn., July 10, 1976; Actor: (films) Arresting Gena, 1997, Hurricane, 1997, Fishes Outta Water, 1998, Celebrity, 1998, The Adventures of Sebastian Cole, 1998, Drive Me Crazy, 1999, Cecil B. DeMented, 2000, Harvard Man, 2001, Artificial Intelligence: AI, 2001, Love In the Time of Money, 2002, Hart's War, 2002, Bringing Rain, 2003, Anything Else, 2003, Tony 'n' Tina's Wedding, 2004, A Perfect Fit, 2005, Across the Hall, 2005, The Devil Wears Prada, 2006; (TV films) Freshening Up, 2002; (TV series) Entourage, 2004—; dir., prodr.: (films) A Shot in the Dark, 2002; composer: (films) Bringing Rain, 2003. Office: c/o Creative Artists Agy 9830 Wilshire Blvd Beverly Hills CA 90212

GRENIER, EDWARD JOSEPH, JR., lawyer; b. NYC, Nov. 26, 1933; s. Edward Joseph and Jane Veronica (Farrell) G.; m. Patricia J. Cederle, June 22, 1957; children: Victoria-Anne, Edward Joseph III, Peter C. BA summa cum laude, Manhattan Coll., NYC, 1954; LLB magna cum laude, Harvard U., 1959. Bar: DC 1959, US Ct. Appeals (DC cir.) 1959, US Ct. Mil. Appeals 1960, US Ct. Appeals (3d cir.) 1966, US Supreme Ct. 1966, US Ct. Appeals (9th cir.) 1973, US Ct. Appeals (10th cir.) 1977, US Ct. Appeals (5th and 11th cirs.) 1982, NY 1983. Law clk. U.S. Ct. Appeals (D.C. cir.), 1959-60; assoc. Covington & Burling, Wahsington, 1960-68; ptnr. Sutherland, Asbill & Brennan, Wahsington, 1968—. Spkr. in field. Contbr. articles in field to legal jours. Chmn. bd. trustees, mem. exec. com. Connelly Sch. Holy Child, Potomac, Md., 1976-85, trustee, 1976-88; bd. dirs. D.C. Recording for the Blind, Washington, 1977-89. 1st lt. USAF, 1954-56. Fellow: Am. Bar Found.; mem.: ABA (chmn. sec. adminstrv. law 1986—87, sec., del. Ho. of Dels. 1991—97), Am. Inns of Ct. (master of bench Prettyman-Leventhal Inn of Ct. 1988—2000, pres. 1991—92, counselor 1997—98), Energy Bar Assn. (bd. dirs. 1986—89, 1995—2001, v.p. 1995—96, pres.-elect 1996—97, pres. 1997—98, del. Ho. of Dels. 1999—2001), D.C. Bar Assn., Fed. Bar Assn., Congl. Country Club, Met. Club. Office: Sutherland Asbill & Brennan LLP 1275 Pennsylvania Ave NW Washington DC 20004-2415 Home Phone: 301-299-4566; Office Phone: 202-383-0138. Business E-Mail: edward.grenier@sablaw.com.

GRENIER, LAURA MARGIOTTA, medical/surgical nurse; b. L'Aquila, Italy, Jan. 18, 1963; arrived in U.S., 1964; d. Guido and Linda (Tedeschi) Margiotta; m. Arthur Jacob Grenier, III, May 3, 1986; children: Danielle Monique, Anthony James, Zachary Jon. Nursing degree, U. Conn., Storrs, 1986; ADN, Greater Hartford C.C., Conn., 1998. Lic. arrhythmia interpretation, cert. health unit coord. Cardiology nurse Hartford (Conn.) Hosp., 1986—. Author: (poetry) Convoluted Dream, 2003 (Pres.'s award, Hon. Mention, 2003), Beyond the Garden Gate, 2006, Desolate Dream, 2006; contbr. poetry to anthologies. Mem. Hilstead Mus., Farmington, Conn., 2001—. Recipient Editor's Choice awards for poetry, 1997, 1998, 2001, Pres.'s award Literacy Excellence for poem "Convoluted" Dream, Illiad Press, 2003, hon. mention for poem "Convoluted" Dream, Summer Competition Illiad Press, 2002. Mem.: Brain Injury Assn. Conn., Am. Brain Tumor Soc., Copper Canyon Press (assoc.), Poetry Soc. Am., Acad. Am. Poets, Quarter Century Club, Hartford Hosp. Qtr. Century Club (assoc.). Roman Catholic. Avocations: poetry, playing piano, going to the beach, travel, tennis. E-mail: bmw6263@aol.com.

GRENQUIST, PETER CARL, publishing executive, consultant; b. East Orange, NJ, Feb. 15, 1931; s. Ernst Alexander and Carmela (Anastasia) G.; m. Barbara Ross Krone, Dec. 20, 1967; children: Carl Robert (dec.), Louisa Beatrice. BA, Dartmouth Coll., 1953; MA, Columbia U., 1957, PhD, 1963. V.p. Am. Assembly Columbia U., 1957-62; dir. Spectrum Books, Prentice-Hall, Inc., 1962-70; v.p. coll. divsn. Prentice-Hall, Inc., 1970-72, pres. Trade Book divsn., 1972-80; CEO Arco Pub., Inc. (subs.), 1981-85; gen. mgr. gen. books divsn. McGraw-Hill Book Co., 1986-89; exec. dir. Assn. Am. Univ. Presses, Inc., NYC, 1990-97; sr. assoc. Moseley Assocs. Inc., 1997—. Served to lt. (j.g.) USNR, 1953-56. Woodrow Wilson fellow, 1956-57. Mem. Devon Yacht Club, Phi Beta Kappa. Office: Moseley Assocs Inc 1202 Lexington Ave # 356 New York NY 10028 Office Phone: 212-988-2834. E-mail: grenquist@aol.com.

GREPPIN, JOHN AIRD COUTTS, philologist, editor, educator; b. Rochester, NY, Apr. 2, 1937; s. Ernest Haquette and Edna Barbara (Kill) G.; m. Mary Elizabeth Cleland Hannan, Sept. 30, 1961; children: Sarah Cleland Coutts, Carl Hannan Haquette. AB in Greek, U. Rochester, NYC, 1961; MA in Classics, U. Wash., 1966; PhD in Indo-European Studies, UCLA, 1972; postdoctoral student, Yerevan State U., USSR, 1974-75. Tchr. Greek, Latin Stowe (Vt.) Prep. Sch., 1961-62; tchr. Woodstock (Vt.) Country Sch., 1962-65, admissions dir., 1968-69; interim asst. prof. U. Fla., Gainesville, 1971-72; tchr. Isidore Newman Sch., New Orleans, 1972-74; from asst. to assoc. to prof. linguistics Cleve. State U., 1975—, dir. program in linguistics, 1979-83, 99—. Vis. prof. linguistics Philipps U., Marburg, Germany, 1993. Author: Initial Vowel and Aspiration in Classical Armenian, 1973, Classical Armenian Nominal Suffixes, 1975, Classical and Middle Armenian Bird Names: A Taxonomic and Mythological Study, 1978, An Etymological Dictionary of the Indo-European Components of Classical Armenian, 1984, Bark Galianosi: The Greek Armenian Dictionary to Galen, 1985, A Handbook of Armenian Dialectology, 1986, An Arabic-Armenian Pharmaceutical Dictionary, 1997, The Diffusion of Greco-Roman Medicine into the Middle East and the Caucasus, 1999; editor: Proc. of 1st Internat. Conf. on Armenian Linguistics, Phila., 1979, (with others) Interrogativity: A Colloquium of the Grammar, Typology and Pragmatics of Questions in Seven Diverse Languages, 1984, When Worlds Collide: The Indo-Europeans and the Pre-Indo-Europeans: The Bellagio Papers, 1990, Studies in Classical Armenian Literature, 1994, Studies in Honor of Jaan Puhvel, Part One: Ancient Languages and Philology, 1997, Part Two: Mythology and Religion, 1997; founding editor Ann. Armenian Linguistics, 1980-2002, Armenian and Anatolian Studies, 1979—, Proc. 4th Internat. Conf. on Armenian Linguistics, 1992, Classical Armenian Literature: Studies in Early Armenian Authors; mng. editor Raft, A Jour. of Armenian Poetry and Criticism, 1987-2000; editor Jour. Soc. Armenian Studies, 2002—; contbr. over 205 articles to Am., European and Soviet jours., over 260 revs. to London Times Lit. Supplement, N.Y. Times Book Rev., Boston Book Rev., others. Recipient Silver medal Congregazione Mekhitarista, Venice, Italy, 1979, Medal of David the Invincible award Armenian Philos. Acad., 2003; fellow Am. Coun. Learned Socs., 1965, NEH, 1978-79, NIH, 1984, Internat. Rsch. and Exchs. Bd., 1974-75, grantee, 1979-81, 84-87, 89, 92, 94, 98; grantee AGBU Manoogian Fund, 1977, 79-06, Gulbenkian Found., 1982, 85, 96, Rockefeller Found., 1987, Am. Coun. Learned Socs., 1987. Mem. Assn. Internat. des Études Arméniennes, Soc. for Study of the Caucasus, Am. Philol. Soc., Soc. Armenian Studies (exec. bd. 1982-86, 02-, sec. 1983-85), Am. Oriental Soc., Soc. Caucasologia Europaea, Cleve. Skating Club. Avocations: piano, chamber music, birdwatching. Home: 3349 Fairmount Blvd Cleveland OH 44118-4262 Office: Cleve State U Dept Linguistics Cleveland OH 44115 Office Phone: 216-687-3967. Business E-Mail: j.greppin@csuohio.edu.

GRESH, PHILIP M., engineering executive; BA in Gen. Arts and Scis., Pa. State U., Univ. Park. Pres. Heuft USA, Downers Grove, Ill.; with Continental Can Co., Inc., Phila., Milw., Conn. and Chgo.; v.p. sales Hi-Cone USA Ill. Tool Works (ITW), Glenview, 1989—90, v.p., gen. mgr. Hi-Cone USA, 1990—94, pres. Hi-Cone Businesses Worldwide, 1994, exec. v.p. Bd. dirs. Ocean Conservancy; mem. fin. com. of bd. dirs. Edward Hosp., Naperville, Ill. Lt. comdr. USN. Office: Ill Tool Works 3600 W Lake Ave Glenview IL 60026-1215 Office Phone: 847-724-7500. Office Fax: 847-657-4572.*

GRESHAM, GEORGE, labor union administrator; b. Richmond, Va., 1955; married; 3 children. BS, Lehman Coll., 1984. MRI technologist Columbia Presbyterian Hosp.; with 1199 Svc. Employees Internat. Union (SEIC), NYC, 1975—, delegate, 1977—88, adminstrv. organizer, 1988—90, v.p., 1990—93, exec. v.p., 1993—2000, sec.-treas., 2000—, incoming pres. Trustee Nat. Benefit Fund of Hosp. and Health Care Employees, 1199 Health Care Employees Pension Fund. Office: 1199 SEIU 310 West 43rd St New York NY 10036 Office Phone: 212-582-1890.*

GRESHAM, KAREN RENEE, elementary school educator, singer; b. Dallas, Jan. 3, 1969; d. Robert James and Beverly Bailey Vinklarek; m. Mark Keith Gresham, Sept. 18, 1993; 1 child, Rachel Bailey. BS in Speech Comm., U.Tex., Austin, 1991. Cert. tchr. Tex., 2001. Tchr. grades pre-K through 6th Brazosport Ind. Sch. Dist., Lake Jackson, Tex., 1999—; profl. singer The Nailers Band, Lake Jackson, Tex., 1998—. Sales/advt. cons. KGNB/KNBT Radio Sta., New Braunfels, Tex., 1991—92; bodily injury claim's adjuster State Farm Ins. Co., Houston, 1992—96. Singer: The Nailers Band. Mem.: Delta Kappa Gamma (licentiate), Alpha Xi Delta (life; songleader 1989—90). Roman Catholic. Avocations: singing, acting. Home: 209 Tearose Ln Lake Jackson TX 77566 Office: Brazosport Independent School District PO Drawer Z Freeport TX 77541 Home Phone: 979-285-2085. Home Fax: 979-285-2082. Personal E-mail: mgresham@houston.rr.com.

GRESHAM, ZANE OLIVER, lawyer; b. Mobile, Ala., Dec. 16, 1948; S. Charles Brandon and Lillian Ann (Oliver) G. BA cum laude, Johns Hopkins U., 1970; JD magna cum laude, Northwestern U., 1973. Bar: Calif. 1973. Assoc. Morrison & Foerster, San Francisco, 1973-79, ptnr., 1980—, co-chair land use and environ. law group, 1987-97, co-chair airports and aviation law group, 1996—; chair Latin Am. Group, 1998—. Dir., v.p. (Latin Am.) Internat. Private Water Assn., 1999—; dir. Fromm Inst., 2000—. Cons. editor: Environ. Compliance and Litigation Strategy. Pres. San Francisco Forward, 1980-85; bd. dirs. Regional Inst. Bay Area, Richmond, Calif., 1989-95, Regional Parks Found., Oakland, Calif., 1992—, pres., 1995; spl. counsel Grace Cathedral, San Francisco, 1991—; dir., exec. v.p. Pan Am. Soc. Calif., 1995-97, pres. 1998-2006; vice chmn. Nat. Youth Sci. Found., 1997—; bd. dir. Found. San Francisco (Calif.) Archl. Heritage, 2004—. Mem. State Bar Calif., Urban Land Inst., Lambda Alpha. Avocations: opera, sketching. Office: Morrison & Foerster 425 Market St Ste 3100 San Francisco CA 94105-2482 Office Phone: 415-268-7145. Business E-Mail: zgresham@mofo.com.

GRESSAK, ANTHONY RAYMOND, JR., sales executive; b. Honolulu, Jan. 22, 1947; s. Anthony Raymond and Anne Tavares (Ferreira) G.; m. Catherine Streb, Apr. 11, 1981; children: Danielle Kirsten, Anthony Raymond III, Christina Michelle. AA, Utah State U., 1967; postgrad., U.S. Army Inf. Officers Candidate Sch., 1968. Restaurant mgr. Ala Moana Hotel, Honolulu, 1970-72; gen. mgr. Fred Harvey, Inc., Ontario, Calif., 1972-73; regional mgr. So. Calif., 1972-73, regional mgr. tollway ops., 1973; divisional mgr. Normandy Lane, 1973; resident mgr. Royal Inns of Am., San Diego, 1974; food and beverage dir. Asso. Inns & Restaurant Co. of Am. (Aircoa), Big Sky, Mont., 1974-75; condominium mgr. Big Sky, 1975; asst. gen. mgr. Naples (Fla.) Bath and Tennis Club, 1975-76; food and beverage dir. Nat. Parks, Grand Canyon, Ariz., 1976-77; gen. mgr. Grand Canyon Nat. Park Lodges, 1977-79; divisional v.p. food services The Broadway, Carter Hawley Hale, Inc., Los Angeles, 1979-82; exec. v.p. Silco Corp., Los Angeles, 1982-84; mktg. mgr. Interstate Restaurant Supply, 1984-85; dir. mktg. and merchandising S.E. Rykoff & Co., Los Angeles, 1986-91; nat. accounts sales mgr. healthcare and hospitality Rykoff-Sexton, Inc., LA, 1991-93; v.p. distbr. sales The Cheesecake Factory Bakery Inc., Calabasas Hills, Calif., 1993—. Mem. edn. culinary steering com. LA Trade Tech. Coll. With U.S. Army, 1967-70. Decorated Silver Star, Bronze Star, Purple Heart; South Vietnamese Cross of Gallantry. Mem.: Internat. Foodservice Mfrs. Assn., Smithsonian Assocs., Nat. Restaurant Assn. (assoc.), Am. Culinary Fedn. (assoc. Presdl. Medallion award 1991), Calif. Restaurant Assn. (assoc.), Internat. Order DeMolay (life; chevalier). Roman Catholic. Home: 20301 Minnehaha St Chatsworth CA 91311-2540 Office: The Cheesecake Factory 26950 Agoura Rd Agoura Hills CA 91301-5335 Home Phone: 818-998-2563; Office Phone: 818-871-3000. Business E-Mail: tgressak@thecheesecakefactory.com. *Common sense isn't so common. Self discipline and respect for yourself will achieve success. Strive for perfection and you will attain it. Never give up. You never get a second chance to make a first impression.*

GRESSMAN, EUGENE, lawyer; b. Lansing, Mich., Apr. 18, 1917; s. William Albert and Bess Beulah (Nagle) G.; m. Nan Alice Kirby, Aug. 6, 1944 (dec. May 2004); children: William, Margot and Nancy (twins), Eric. AB, U. Mich., 1938, JD with distinction, 1940; LLD, Seton Hall U., 1994. Bar: Mich. 1940, U.S. Supreme Ct. 1945, D.C. 1948, Md. 1959. Atty. SEC, Washington, 1940-43; law clk. to Justice Frank Murphy, U.S. Supreme Ct., 1943-48; ptnr. firm Van Arkel, Kaiser, Gressman, Rosenberg & Driesen, Washington, 1948-77, of counsel, 1977-81, Bredhoff & Kaiser, Washington, 1981-84, Brand & Frulla, Washington, 1984—2007. Spl. counsel U.S. Ho. of Reps., 1976-84; William Rand Kenan Jr. prof. law U. N.C., Chapel Hill, 1977-87, prof. emeritus, 1987—; disting. vis. prof. Fordham U. Law Sch., 1982-83, 1987-88; Disting. vis. prof. Seton Hall U. Law Sch., 1987-94; vis. prof. law Ohio State U., 1967, Mich. Law Sch., 1969, George Washington U., 1971-77, Ind. U., 1976, Cath. U. Am., 1977; judge Appeals Tax Ct. Montgomery County, Md., 1959-62; chmn. rules com. U.S. Ct. Appeals for 4th Cir., 1984-89. Author: (with Robert L. Stern and others) Supreme Court Practice, 1950, 9th edit., 2007; (with Charles A. Wright and others) Federal Practice and Procedure: Jurisdiction, vol. 16, 1977; (with David Crump and David Day) Cases and Materials on Constitutional Law, 1989, 4th edit., 2002; contbr. articles to profl. jours. Fellow Am. Acad. Appellate Lawyers (hon.); mem. ABA, Fed. Bar Assn., D.C. Bar, Am. Law Inst. (life), Am. Judicature Soc., Order of the Coif, Order of Barristers, Phi Beta Kappa, Delta Theta Pi (Lifetime Achievement award). Home: 325 Glendale Dr Chapel Hill NC 27514-5915 Office: U NC Sch Law Chapel Hill NC 27599-3380 Home Phone: 919-929-1289; Office Phone: 919-962-3688. Business E-Mail: egressma@email.unc.edu.

GRETZKY, WAYNE DOUGLAS, retired professional hockey player, professional hockey coach; b. Brantford, Ont., Can., Jan. 26, 1961; s. Walter and Phyllis Gretzky; m. Janet Jones, July 16, 1988; children: Paulina, Ty Robert, Trevor Douglas, Tristan Wayne, Emma Marie. Center Peterborough Petes, Jr. Ont. Hockey Assn., 1977—78, Sault Ste. Marie Greyhounds, 1977—78, Indpls. Racers, World Hockey Assn., 1978, Edmonton Oilers, 1979—88, LA Kings, 1988—96, St. Louis Blues, 1996, NY Rangers, 1996—99, ret., 1999; investor Los Arcos Sports LLC / Phoenix Coyotes, 1999—; mng. ptnr., alt. gov. Phoenix Coyotes, 2000—, head coach, 2005—; exec. dir. Can. Nat Team, Olympic Games, Salt Lake City, 2002, Torino, Italy, 2006, Can. Nat Team, World Cup of Hockey, 2004. Named Rookie of Yr., World Hockey Assn., 1978—79, Sportsman of Yr., Sports Illustrated, 1982, Sporting News NHL Player of Yr., 1980—81, 1986—87, Sporting News Man of Yr., 1981, Can. Athlete of Yr., 1985, Dodge Performer of Yr., 1984—85, 1986—87, All-Star Game MVP, 1983, 1989, 1999; named to NHL All-Star Team, 1980—94, 1997—99; recipient Art Ross Meml. Trophy, NHL, 1981—87, 1989—90, 1990—91, 1993—94, Conn Smythe Trophy, 1985, 1988, William Hanley Trophy, 1977—78, Lemms Family award, 1977—78, Hart Meml. Trophy, 1974—80, Lady Byng Meml. Trophy, 1979—80, 1990—91, 1991—92, 1993—94, Lester B. Pearson award, 1982, 1984—85, 1986—87, Emery Edge award, 1983—84, 1984—85, 1986—87, Lester Patrick Trophy, 1993—94. Achievements include being the record holder for points, goals, assists, overtime assists and others; being a member of the Stanley Cup Champion Edmonton Oilers, 1984, 1985, 1987, 1988; being inducted into the Hockey Hall of Fame in 1999. Office: Phoenix Coyotes 5800 W Glenn Dr Ste 350 Glendale AZ 85301-2471

GREUNER, DAVID A., surgeon; b. Harlingen, Tex., June 30, 1976; s. Carl Eugene and Monica Greuner; m. Marlene de Vries. BS, St. Georges U., MD with honors, 1998—2002. Lic. dr. Internat. Coll. Surgeons, 2005. Residency U. Ariz., Phoenix, 2002—05; med. dir. Synapse Biotechnology, NYC, 2004—05; surgeon Atlantic Health, Morristown, NJ, 2005—. Rschr. Weill Cornell Med. Coll., NYC, 2002—04. Mem.: AMA (assoc.), ACS (assoc.), NY Med. Assn. (assoc.), Am. Soc. Laser Medicine & Surgery (assoc.), Am. Acad. Cosmetic Surgery (assoc.). Home Phone: 646-216-8282. Personal E-mail: david.greuner@gmail.com. E-mail: dcg@medesthetik.com.

GREVE, GUY ROBERT, lawyer; b. Bay City, Mich., Oct. 25, 1947; m. Nancy Lisbeth Mueller, Sept. 21, 1991; 1 child, Tyler James. BA, U. Mich., 1970; postgrad., U. Kent, Canterbury, Eng., 1974; JD, Detroit Coll., 1975. Bar: Mich. 1975, U.S. Dist. Ct. (ea. dist.) Mich. 1975. Ptnr. Patterson & Greve, Bay City, 1975-78; asst. atty. City of Bay City, 1975-76, atty., 1976-78; pvt. practice Bay City, 1978—. One-man shows include; co-chair Day in Life of Bay County Photo Project, 2000. Bd. dirs. Am. Cancer Soc., 1975—2001, pres., 1982—83, Muse-Hopper Mobile Mus., Mich., 1980—82; co-chair Delta Coll. Scholarship Fundraiser, 2001; mem. steering com., capital campaign com., bd. dirs. Friends State Theater, 2001—05, vice chair, 2005; bd. dirs. Bay Arts Coun., 1999—, pres., 2007; bd. dirs. Women's Crisis Ctr., Bay City, 1977—79, pres., 2007. Named Disting. Alumnus, Handy HS, 1985; recipient Disting. Svc. award, Bay City Jaycees, 1981. Mem.: ATLA, ABA, Mich. Trial Lawyers Assn., Bay County Bar Assn. (Liberty Bell chmn. 1994—98, bd. dirs. 1994—2000, pres. 1998—99), Mich. Bar Assn. (rep. assembly 1999—2001), Bay Area C. of C., Studio 23 (hon.), U.S. Power Squadron (law officer 2007), Saginaw Bay Yacht Club, U. Mich. Alumni Club (Bay City chpt. pres. 1994—97), Elks Club (lodge # 88), Optimists (pres. Bay City 1979—80, lt. gov. Mich. 1985—86, chmn. new club bldg. 1986—87, chmn. club svcs. 1989—90, founder, chair travel series 1993—, asst. gov. Mich. 1996—97, internat. conv. com. 1997). Home: 2300 Nurmi Dr Bay City MI 48708-6872 Office: PO Box 851 817 Washington Ave Bay City MI 48707 Office Phone: 989-893-9578. Personal E-mail: ggreve@sbcglobal.net.

GREVE, JOHN HENRY, veterinary parasitologist, educator; b. Pitts., Aug. 11, 1934; s. John Welch and Edna Viola (Thuenen) G.; m. Sally Jeanette Doane, June 21, 1956; children— John Haven, Suzanne Carol, Pamela Jean BS, Mich. State U., East Lansing, 1956, D.V.M., 1958, MS, 1959; PhD, Purdue U., West Lafayette, Ind., 1963. Assoc. instr. Mich. State U., East Lansing, 1958-59; instr. Purdue U., West Lafayette, 1959-63; asst. prof. Iowa State U., Ames, 1963-64, assoc. prof., 1964-68, prof. dept. vet. pathology, 1968-99, interim chair dept. vet. pathology, 1992-95, counselor acad. and student affairs, 1991-92. Cons. to dean on alumni affairs Coll. Vet. Medicine; cons. in field. Mem. editl. bd. Lab. Animal Sci., 1971-83, Vet. Rsch. Comm., 1977-84, Vet. Parasitology, 1984-98; contbr. articles to sci. jours., chpts. to books. Dist. chmn. Broken Arrow dist. Boy Scouts Am., Ames, Iowa, 1975-77; devel. bd. Octagon Ctr. for the Arts, Ames, 2004— Named Disting. Tchr. Norden Labs., 1965, 99, Outstanding Tchr. Amoco Oil, Iowa State U., 1972, Faculty Mem. of Yr., Coll. Vet. Medicine, 1999; recipient Faculty Citation Iowa State U. Alumni Assn., 1978. Mem. AVMA (mem. editl. bd. jour. 1975-98, Excellence in Teaching award student chpt. 1990), Iowa Vet. Med. Assn., Am. Soc. Parasitologists, Midwestern Conf. Parasitologists (sec.-treas. 1967-75, presiding officer 1975-76), Am. Assn. Vet. Parasitologists (pres. 1968-70), Helminthological Soc. Washington, World Assn. for Advancement Vet. Parasitology, Am. Assn. Vet. Med. Colls., Izaak Walton League (bd. dirs. Iowa 1968-70), Honor Soc. Cardinal Key, Gamma Sigma Delta, Phi Eta Sigma, Phi Kappa Phi, Phi Zeta. Lodges: Kiwanis (Town and Country-Ames pres. 1967, 2006, Nebr.-Iowa lt. gov. 1972-73). Republican. Avocations: stamp collecting/philately, camping, gardening. Office: Iowa State U Coll Vet Med Found Ames IA 50011-1250 Office Phone: 515-294-0867. Business E-Mail: sdgreve@earthlink.net.

GREVING, ROBERT C., insurance company executive; BS in Math., Quincy U., 1975. Exec. v.p., chief actuary Southwestern Fin. Svcs. Corp., 1990—97; sr. v.p., chief actuary Provident, 1997—2001, sr. v.p. fin., 2001—02; sr. v.p., CFO Unum Group, Chattanooga, 2002—03, exec. v.p., CFO, 2003—. Office: Unum Group 1 Fountain Sq Chattanooga TN 37402*

GREVIOUS, INEZ COBBLE, health facility administrator; m. Robert Allen Grevious, Nov. 9, 2002; children: Shawana Baines, Damon Cobble children: Lacrisia, Lashawna, Melvin Cobble. Cert. clk. typist Lincoln Vocat., Louisville, 1973. Receptionist, cmty. liaison Jefferson County Bd. Edn., Louisville, 1986—93; medicial receptionist U. Physicians Assocs., Louisville, 1999—. Active bearvement ministry Kingdom Land Bapt. Ch., Louisville, 2002—07. Home: 4002 River Park Dr Louisville KY 40211 Office: University Physicians Associates 530 S Jackson St Louisville KY 40203 Home Phone: 502-775-0211; Office Phone: 502-561-8688.

GREVIOUS, MARK ALLEN, plastic surgeon; b. Mpls., Sept. 2, 1967; m. Dolores L. Dixon-Grevious. MD, UMDNJ - N.J. Med. Sch., 1994. Clin. assoc. U. Sch. Hosps., Chgo., 2001—. Home: 849 W Ohio St #1 Chicago IL 60622-6983 Home Phone: 773-324-5474.

GREW, PRISCILLA CROSWELL, academic administrator, geologist, educator; b. Glens Falls, NY, Oct. 26, 1940; d. James Croswell and Evangeline Pearl (Beougher) Perkins; m. Edward Sturgis Grew, June 14, 1975. *Great-grandfather Charles Miller Croswell was governor of Michigan 1876-1880. Great-grandfather Samuel Perkins sailed from Maine around Cape Horn to California in the 1849 Gold Rush. Grandfather James Coffin Perkins (University of California-Berkeley class of 1874) served as a missionary in Kodaikanal, South India for 29 years. Father James Croswell Perkins (Princeton class of 1929) was a Congregational minister and Professor of Religion and Philosophy at Huston-Tillotson College in Austin, Texas. Mother Evangeline Pearl Beougher Perkins attended the Oberlin Conservatory of Music, led church choirs, and taught private piano lessons.* BA magna cum laude, Bryn Mawr Coll., 1962; PhD, U. Calif., Berkeley, 1967. Instr. dept. geology Boston Coll., 1967-68, asst. prof., 1968-72; asst. rsch. geologist UCLA, 1972-77, adj. asst. prof. environ. sci. and engring., 1975-76; dir. Calif. Dept. Conservation, 1977-81; commr. Calif. Pub. Utilities Commn., San Francisco, 1981-86; dir. Minn. Geol. Survey, St. Paul, 1986-93; prof. dept. geology U. Minn., Mpls., 1986-93; vice chancellor for rsch. U. Nebr., Lincoln, 1993-99, prof. dept. geoscis., 1993—, prof. conservation/survey divsn. Inst. Agr., 1993—, dir. U. Nebr. State Mus., 2003—, fellow Ctr. for Great Plains Studies, 2003—; coord. Native Am. Graves Protection and Repatriation Act, 1998—. Vis. asst. prof. geology U. Calif., Davis, 1973-74; chmn. Calif. State Mining and Geology Bd., Sacramento, 1976-77; exec. sec., editor Lake Powell Rsch. Project, 1971-77; cons., vis. staff Los Alamos (N.Mex.) Nat. Lab., 1972-77; com. on minority participation in earth sci. and mineral engring. Dept. Interior, 1972-75; chmn. Calif. Geothermal Resource Task Force, 1977, Calif. Geothermal Resources Bd., 1977-81; earthquake studies adv. panel US Geol. Survey, 1979-83, adv. com., 1982-86; adv. coun. Gas Rsch. Inst., 1982-86, rsch. coord. coun., 1987-98, vice-chmn., 1994-96, chmn., 1996-98, sci. and tech. coun., 1998-2001; bd. on global change rsch. NAS, 1995-99, subcom. on earthquake rsch., 1985-88, bd. on earth scis. and resources, 1986-91, bd. on mineral and energy resources, 1982-88, bd. on internat. sci. orgns., 2006—; mem. Minn. Minerals Coord. Com., 1986-93, US nat. com. for internat. union of geol. scis. (IUGS), 1985-93, US nat. com. for the internat. union of geodesy and geophysics 2001—, chmn., 2003—; mem. US Nat. Com. on Diversitas, 2000—07, vice chmn., 2004—07; adv. bd. Stanford U. Sch. Earth Scis., 1989—, Sec. of Energy Adv. Bd., 1995-97; com. on equal opportunities in sci. and tech. NSF, 1985-86, adv. com. on earth scis., 1987-91, adv. com. on sci. and tech. ctrs. devel., 1987-91, adv. com. on sci. and tech. ctrs., 1996, adv. com. on geoscis., 1994-97; mem. State-Fed. Tech. Partnership Task Force, 1995-99, Fed. Coun. for Continental Sci. Drilling, 1992-98, Gt. Plains Partnership Coun., 1995-99; trustee Am. Geol. Inst. Found., 1988— (Ian Campbell medalist 1999). Contbr. articles to profl. jours. Trustee 1st Plymouth Congl. Ch., Lincoln, 1997—2000; mem. edn. and outreach steering com. Earth-Scope, 2005—, chair edn. and outreach steering com., 2007—; bd. dirs. Abendmusik:Lincoln, 1995—97. Fellow, NSF, 1962—66. Fellow AAAS (chmn. electorate nominating com. sect. E 1980-84, mem.-at-large 1987-91, chmn.-elect 1994, chmn. 1995, coun. del. 1997-98), Geol. Soc. Am. (nominations com. 1974, chmn. com. on geology and pub. policy 1981-84, audit com. 1988-90, chair 1990, com. on coms. 1986-87, 91-92, chmn. com. on coms. 1995, chair Day medal com. 1990, councilor 1987-91), Mineral. Soc. Am. (mem. Roebling medal com. 1999-2003), Geol. Assn. Can., Ctr. Great Plains Studies; mem. Am. Geophys. Union (chmn. com. pub. affairs 1984-89, chair Waldo Smith medal com. 2006-), Soc. Mayflower Descs., Nat. Parks and Conservation Assn. (trustee 1982-86), Nat. Assn. Regulatory Utility Commrs. (com. on gas 1982-86, exec. com. 1984-86, com. on energy conservation 1983-84), Nat. Sci. Collections Alliance (bd. dirs. 2006—), Interstate Oil and Gas Compact Commn. (mem. Petroleum Profls. Task Force, 2001-03), Cosmos Club, Rotary, Country Club of Lincoln, Sigma Xi (pres. U. Minn. chpt. 1990-91). Congregationalist. Office: U Nebr State Mus 307 Morrill Hall Lincoln NE 68588-0338 Office Phone: 402-472-3779. Business E-Mail: pgrew1@unl.edu.

GREW, RAYMOND EDWARD, mechanical engineer; b. Metamora, Ohio, Jan. 11, 1923; s. Edward F. and Coletta (Minck) G.; children: Elizabeth, Mary, Janet, John. BSME, U. Mich., 1948. Registered profl. engr., Calif. Prin. engr. Hoffmann La Roche, Nutley, NJ, 1957—83. Navigator USAF. Mem. English Speaking Union, Pilgrims of U.S., Caterpiller Club. Achievements include patent for chromatographic device.

GREW, ROBERT RALPH, retired lawyer; b. Metamora, Ohio, Mar. 25, 1931; m. Anne Gano Bailey, Aug. 2, 1958. AB in Letters and Law, U. Mich., 1953, JD, 1955. Bar: Mich. 1955, N.Y. 1958. Assoc. Carter, Ledyard & Milburn, NYC, 1957-68, ptnr., 1968-98, of counsel, 1999—2002; ret., 2003—. Mem.: Pilgrims of US, Union Club. Republican. Office: Carter Ledyard & Milburn 2 Wall St New York NY 10005-2001 also: 701 8th St NW Washington DC 20005 Office Phone: 212-238-8803. Personal E-mail: grew@clm.com.

GREWAL, IQBAL S., immunologist, biotechnology company executive; PhD, UCLA, 1993. V.p. preclinical therapeutics Seattle Genetics Inc., Bothell, Wash., 2004—. Office: Seattle Genetics Inc 21823 30th Drive SE Bothell WA 98021 Office Phone: 425-527-4118. Business E-Mail: igrewal@seagen.com.

GREWCOCK, BRUCE E., construction and mining executive; BS, Colo. Sch. Mines, 1976. With Utah Internat., 1976—82; chief engr. Peter Kiewit Sons', Inc., 1982—85; v.p., ops. mgr. Kiewit Mining Group, 1986—91, pres., 1992—95; exec. v.p. Peter Kiewit Sons' Inc., Omaha, 1996—2002, dir., 1997—, pres., COO, 2000—04, pres., CEO, 2004—. Bd. dirs. Kiewit Materials Co., Kinross Gold Corp. Coun. mem. Knights of Ak-Sar-Ben Found., 2002—; bd. dirs. Omaha Cmty. Found., Coll. World Series. Office: Peter Kiewit Sons 1000 Kiewit Plz Omaha NE 68131-3374*

GREY, BRAD, film company executive; b. Bronx, NY, Dec. 29, 1957; m. Jill Grey; children: Sam, Max, Emily. Student, SUNY; BS in Comm. & Bus., U. Buffalo, 1979; LHD (hon.), SUNY, 2003. With Harvey & Corky Productions, Brillstein-Grey Entertainment, Beverly Hills, Calif., 1985—92, ptnr., 1992—96, chmn. CEO, 1996—2005; co-founder (with Jennifer Anniston and Brad Pitt) Plan B Entertainment, 2002; chmn., CEO Paramount Motion Pictures Group, Hollywood, Calif., 2005—. Bd. dirs UCLA Sch. Medicine, Project ALS, KCET LA Pub. TV, Dean's Coun., NYU Tisch Sch. Arts; bd. dirs. Environ. Media Assn., Comic Relief; bd. councilors U. So. Calif. Sch. Cinema. Exec. prodr.: (films) Opportunity Knocks, 1990; exec. prodr.: (films) The Celluloid Closet, 1995, Happy Gilmore, 1996, The Cable Guy, 1996, Bulletproof, 1996, The Replacement Killers, 1998, The Wedding Singer, 1998, Dirty Work, 1998, What Planet Are You From?, 2000, Screwed, 2000, Scary Movie, 2000; prodr. (films) City by the Sea, 2002, View From the Top, 2003, Charlie and the Chocoloate Factory, 2005, The Departed, 2006, Running with Scissors, 2006, prodr., writer The Burning, 1981; exec. prodr.: (TV films) Don't Try This at Home!, 1990, Three Sisters Searching for a Cure, 2004; (TV series) The Boys, 1989, Good Sports, 1991, The Larry Sanders Show, 1992, NewsRadio, 1995, Mr. Show, 1995, The Naked Truth, 1995, The Steve Harvey Show, 1996, The Dana Carvey Show, 1996, Just Shoot Me!, 1997, Alright Already, 1997, C-16: FBI, 1997, Politically Incorrect, 1997—98, 2000—01, Applewood 911, 1998, The Sopranos, 1999— (Golden Globe award for best dramatic series, Emmy award for best dramatic series, 2004), Sammy, 2000, Pasadena, 2001, Real Time with Bill Maher, 2003, My Big Fat Greek Life, 2003, The Lyon's Den, 2003, Cracking Up, 2004, Married to the Kellys, 2003, Jake in Progress, 2005—. Named one of 50 Most Powerful People in Hollywood, Premiere mag., 2005—06; recipient George Foster Peabody award (4 times). Office: Paramount Studios 5555 Melrose Ave West Hollywood CA 90038*

GREY, JERRY, science educator; b. NYC, Oct. 25, 1926; s. Abraham Lewis and Lillian Grey; m. Florence Maier, Feb. 21, 1969; children: Leslie, Jacquelyn(dec.). B of Mech. Engring., Cornell U., 1947, MS, 1949; PhD, Calif. Inst. Tech., 1952. Instr. Cornell U., Ithaca, NY, 1947—49; engine devel. engr. Fairchild Engines, Farmingdale, NY, 1949—50; mem. tech. staff Bell Labs., NYC, 1947; hypersonic aerodynamicist Guggenheim Aero. Lab., Pasadena, Calif., 1950—51; sr. engr. Marquardt Aircraft Co., Van Nuys, Calif., 1950—51; prof. Princeton U., NJ, 1951—; adminstr. tech. activities and pub. policy, dir. sci. and tech. policy AIAA, NYC, 1971—, dir. sci. and tech. policy Reston, Va., 1987—. Pub., editor-at-large Aerospace Am., Reston, 1984—; adj. prof. environ. sci. L.I. U., Southampton, NY, 1978—83; v.p. publs. Am. Inst. Aeronautics and Astronautics, NYC, 1966—71; vice-chmn. space power com. Internat. Astron. Fedn., Paris, 1986—90; v.p. tech. activities Internat. Acad. Astronautics, Paris, 1978—84; pres. Internat. Astronautical Fedn., Paris, 1984—86; mem. sci. adv. coun. NASA Inst. for Advanced Concepts, Atlanta, 1988—; chmn. solar adv. and other panels Office of Tech. Assessment, Washington, 1973—83; dep. sec. gen. UNISPACE-82, United Nations, NYC, 1981—82; dir. Applied Solar Energy Corp., Industry, Calif., 1985—93; vice-chmn. comml. space transp. adv. com. FAA, Washington, 1985—87; chmn. coord. com. on energy Am. Assn. Engring. Socs., NYC, 1976—78; mem. sci. adv. bd. Discover Mag., NYC, 1980—84, George C. Marshall Inst., Washington, 1986—; mem., sec. energy adv. bd. US Dept. Energy, Washington, 1989—92. Author: Race for Electric Power, 1972, Facts of Flight, 1973, Enterprise, 1978, Aeronautics in China, 1981, Beachheads in Space, 1983. Seaman 2d class USN, 1943—46. Recipient Gen.-Interest Mag. award, Aviation/Space Writers Assn., 1985, E.E. Emme Publs. award, Am. Astron. Soc., 1986. Fellow: AIAA (hon.); mem.: Cosmos Club, Key Biscayne Yacht Club. Achievements include patents for Calorimetric Probe. Avocations: tennis, swimming, theater. Office: AIAA 1801 Alexander Bell Dr Ste 500 Reston VA 20191-4344 E-mail: jerryg@aiaa.org.*

GREY, MARGARET, nursing educator; b. Easton, Pa., Sept. 25, 1949; m. Michael Lauterbach. BSN, U. Pitts., 1970; MS in Nursing, Yale U., 1976;

PhD, Columbia U., 1985. Nurse clinician Yale-New Haven Hosp.; asst. clin. prof. Columbia U., NYC; assoc. prof. U. Pa., Phila., dir. primary care grad. program; with Yale U. Sch. Nursing, New Haven, 1993—, founder, doctoral program, 1994, Independence Found. prof. nursing, dir. Ctr. for Self & Family Mgmt., Annie Goodrich prof. nursing, 2005—, assoc. dean, dean, 2005—. Rudin Clin. Nursing Rsch. scholar, Disting. Fellow, NAP-NAP, 1990, Robert Wood Johnson Exec. Nurse Fellowship, 1999-2001; Sch. Nursing Teaching award, UPenn., 1990, Virginia Herderson award for Outstanding Contributions to Nursing Rsch., 1997, Applied Nursing Rsch. award, Coun. Nurse Researchers, ANA, 1998, Disting. Alumni award, U. Pitts. Sch. Nursing, 1999, Achievement in Rsch. award, Natl. Org. Nurse Practitioner Faculties, 2000, Excellence in Nursing Rsch. award, Assn. Faculties of PNP Programs, 2000, Fellow Soc. Behavioral Medicine, Am. Acad. Nursing; mem. ANA (mem. coun. nurse researchers, primary care providers), NAPNAP (membership com.), APHA, Am. Diabetes Assn., Am. Sociol. Assn., Nat. Assn. Pediatric Nurse Assocs. and Practitioners (pres. 1992-93), Inst. Medicine; Sigma Theta Tau. Office: Yale U Sch Nursing PO Box 9740 100 Church St S New Haven CT 06536 Office Phone: 203-785-2393. Office Fax: 203-785-3554. E-mail: margaret.grey@yale.edu.

GREY, ROBERT DEAN, academic administrator, biology educator; b. Liberal, Kans., Sept. 5, 1939; s. McHenry Wesley and Kathryn (Brown) G.; m. Alice Kathleen Archer, June 11, 1961; children: Erin Kathleen, Joel Michael. BA, Phillips U., 1961; PhD, Washington U., 1966. Asst. prof. Washington U., St. Louis, 1966-67; from asst. prof. to full prof. zoology U. Calif., Davis, 1967—, chmn. dept., 1979-83, dean biol. scis., 1985—, interim exec. vice chancellor, 1993-95, provost, exec. vice chancellor, 1995—2001, sr. advisor to chancellor, 2001—02, provost, exec. vice chancellor emeritus, 2002—, exec. asst. to chancellor health affairs Riverside, 2005—07, acting chancellor, 2007—. Author: (with others) A Laboratory Text for Developmental Biology, 1980; contbr. articles to profl. jours. Recipient Disting. Tchg. awrd Acad. Senate U. Calif., Davis, 1977, Magnar Ronning award for tchg. Associated Students U. Calif., Davis, 1978, Disting. Alumnus award Phillips U., 1991. Avocations: music, hiking, gardening. Office: Univ Calif Office of the Chancellor Hinderaker Hall Riverside CA 92521 Business E-Mail: rdgrey@ucdavis.edu.

GREY, ROBERT J., lawyer, electric power industry executive; b. NYC, Sept. 6, 1950; m. Susan Grey; children: Lisa, Laura. BA, Columbia U., 1972; JD, Emory U., 1975; LLM in Taxation, George Washington U., 1979. Bar: Ga. 1975, US Dist. Ct. (no. dist. Ga.) 1975, DC 1976, Md. 1976, NY 1978, Oreg. 1982, US Dist. Ct. (dist. Oreg.) 1984, Wash. 1988, Pa. 1995. Atty., adv., legal asst. EPA, 1975-77; staff counsel NY State Pub. Svc. Commn., 1977-82; assoc. Preston, Gates & Ellis, Seattle, 1982—83, ptnr., 1983-92; gen. counsel LI Lighting Co., 1992—95; v.p., gen. counsel, sec. PPL Corp., Allentown, Pa., 1995—96, sr. v.p., gen. counsel, sec., 1996—. Mem. exec. com. Energy Assn. Pa.; mem. Conf. Bd. Coun. Chief Legal Officers. Bd. dirs., past pres. Jewish Fedn. Lehigh Valley; trustee, chmn. legal com. United Jewish Cmtys. Mem. ABA (coun. group of pub. utility, comm. and transp. law sect.). Office: PPL Co 2 N 9th St Allentown PA 18101-1170 Office Phone: 610-774-5587. E-mail: rjgrey@pplweb.com.*

GREY, ROBERT J., JR., lawyer; b. Richmond, Va., Aug. 5, 1950; BS, Va. Commonwealth U., 1973; JD, Washington & Lee U., 1976. Bar: Va. 1978. Ptnr. Grey & Wesley, 1978—82; asst. prof. Va Commonwealth U., Sch. of Bus., 1979—82; ptnr. Mays & Valentine, 1985—95, LeClair Ryan, Richmond, Va., 1996—2002, Hunton & Williams LLP, 2002—. Chmn., Va. State Alcoholic Beverage Control Bd., 1982-85; pres., Richmond Crusade for Votes, 1988-90; chmn., Youth Matters, 1995-98; co-chmn., MAPS steering com., 1997-2000; chmn., Greater Richmond Partnership, 1999-2000; bd. dir. Margaretten Corp., 1994; bd. dir & mem. ea. reg. adv. bd., Jefferson Nat. Bank, 1995-97; mem. Va. State bd. adv., Wachovia Bank, 1999-2000; bd. dir., Va Biotechnology Rsch. Park Corp., 2000-. Alumni Star award, Va. Commonwealth U. Sch. of Bus.; 1995, Disting. Leader award, Nat. Assn. for Community Leadership, 1997; Flame Bearer award, UNCF, The College Fund, 1998; Hon. mem., Washington and Lee U. Sch. of Law, 1993. Mem. ABA (chair ho. dels., 1998-2000, bd. govs., exec. com., 1998-2000, pres-elect, 2003-04, pres., 2004-05), Grtr. Richmond C. of C. (chair, 1996-97); mem. Va. State Bar (pres., Young Lawyers Conf., 1982-83, chair., Commn. on Women & Minorities in the Profession, 1985-86, chair, Legal Ethics Com., 1986-87); Am. Law Inst.; Nat. Bar Assn. (Wiley A. Branton award 1998, Gertrude E. Rush award 2003); Old Dominion Bar; Richmond Bar Assn.; D.C. Bar; Va. Bar Assn. Office: Hunton & Williams LLP Riverfront Plz E Tower 951 E Byrd St Richmond VA 23219-4074 E-mail: rgrey@hunton.com.*

GREY, RUTHANN E., corporate communications specialist, director; b. Buffalo, May 13, 1945; d. Wilson Campbell and Rosalie (Briggs) Evege; m. Daine A. Grey, Aug. 25, 1990; children: Daine, Jr., Keenan, Nichole. BS, SUNY, Buffalo, 1966, MS, 1970, PhD, 1980; postgrad., Harvard U., 1988. Tchr. Bennett H.S., Buffalo, 1966-69; prof. Erie C.C., Buffalo, 1970-73; adminstr. No. Va. C.C., Annandale, 1975-76, Wayne State U., Detroit, 1978-80; dir. pub. affairs Burroughs Corp., Detroit, 1981-86; exec. asst. to chmn. bd. dirs. The Equitable, NYC, 1986-89; mgr. pub. affairs N.Y. Times, NYC, 1989-90; mgr. divsn. corp. rels. Pub. Svc. Corp. Colo., Denver, 1990-93; v.p. comm. and pub. affairs Hoechst Celanese, Bridgewater, NJ, 1993—; v.p. global media and external rels. Hoechst Marion Roussel, Bridgewater, NJ, 1996—; comm. chief Ednl. Testing Svc., Princeton, NJ; with The Caunos Group, Watchung, NJ, 1998—; dir. global comm. Ethicon, Somerville, NJ. Cons. A+ For Kids, Newark, 1989-90, Rockefeller Found., N.Y.C., 1989-90. Bd. dirs. Citizens Scholarship Found., Minn., 1990-94. Mem. Pub. Rels. Seminar, Arthur Page Soc., The Wisemen, Pub. Rels. Rsch. Found. Avocations: gardening, walking.

GREY, WILMA J., library director; B in Psychology, Howard U.; MLS, Rutgers U., NJ; cert. in Libr. Adminstrs. Devel., U. Md. Cert. pub. mgr. NJ Dept. Pers. and Rutgers U. Supr. brs. Newark Pub. Libr., adminstr. systems, African-Am. and world book collections, asst. dir. cmty. libr. svcs., acting dir., 2004—05, dir., 2005—. Treas. bd. trustees South Orange Pub. Libr. Pres. bd. trustees Newark Literacy Campaign; mem. com. Newark Black Film Festival; bd. dirs. Newark Arts Coun. Named Woman of Yr., Zonta Club Essex County, 2006. Mem.: ALA, NJ Libr. Assn., Rotary Internat., Newark chpt. Office: Newark Pub Libr 5 Washington St Newark NJ 07101 Office Phone: 973-733-7780. Office Fax: 973-733-5919. E-mail: wgrey@npl.org.

GREYSON, CLIFFORD RUSSELL, internist; b. NYC, 1958; AB, Harvard Coll., 1980; MSEE, Stanford U., 1985, MD, 1987. Cert. internal medicine and cardiovascular diseases, critical care medicine. Resident in internal medicine Stanford U. Hosp., 1987-90, fellow in critical care, 1990-91; fellow in cardiovasc. disease U. Calif., San Francisco, 1991-95, faculty cardiology divsn., 1995-99, U. Colo. Health Scis. Ctr., Denver, 1999—. Co-dir. med. intensive care unit San Francisco VA Med. Ctr., 1998-99. Elected to city coun. Town of Woodside, Calif., 1995. Recipient Clinician Scientist award Am. Heart Assn., 1995-96, Clin. Investigator Devel. award NIH, 1996-01, R01 rsch. award NIH, 2003. Fellow Am. Coll. Cardiology; mem. ACP, Western Soc. Clin. Investigation. Office: Denver VA Med Ctr Cardiology 111B 1055 Clermont St Denver CO 80220-3808

GREYSON D'OTAZZO, MEAGHAN REGINA, literary critic; b. Havana, Cuba, Sept. 7, 1942; arrived in US, 1962; d. Miguel Blanco and Virginia Mary de Barzaga-De Herrera; m. Neil Alfred D'Otazzo, Sept. 8, 1958; children: Jesse, Vivian, Patrick, Ann Shirley. B in psychology, U. Ga., 1972, M in hist. and lit., 1973, M in edn., 1976, PhD in hist. and lit., 1984. Tchr. Clark County Dist., Athens, Ga., 1971—75; rschr. Emory U., Psychology Dept., Atlanta, 1975—85; journalist freelance, NYC, 1986—94, Orlando, Fla., 1995; literary critic various newspapers and mags., Los Angeles, Calif., 1995—97, London, 1997—; rschr. US Capitol Hist. Soc., Wash., DC, 2000—02, Smithsonian Inst., Wash., DC, 2003—04, Libr. of Congress, Wash., DC, 2004—. Author: La Musica de Haiti & Others, 1960, Literary Criticism: Conceptual Approach to Theatrical Reviews, 2004; contbr. articles various profl. jours. Poll judge Rep. Party, NYC, 1980—2004; tchr., autistic and deaf children. Mem.: Assn. Am. Writers, Assn. Reviewers and Editors. Republican. Roman Catholic. Avocation: piano. Home: 6150 Forland Garth 204 Columbia MD 21045 Office Phone: 443-319-5871. E-mail: meaghan7@aol.com.

GRIBBIN, DAVID JAMES, IV, (D.J. GRIBBIN), lawyer; b. 1963; m. Mary E. Gribbin. BA, Georgetown U., 1985, JD, 1992. Legis. dir. to US Rep. Larry Combest US Congress, staff mem. House Com. on DC; legis. rep. Nat. Fedn. Ind. Bus., 1989—94; nat. field dir. Christian Coalition, 1994—97; govt. affairs dir. Koch Industries, Inc., 1997—99, pub. sector bus. devel. dir., 1999—2003; chief counsel Fed. Hwy. Adminstrn., US Dept. Transp., 2003—05; divsn. dir. Macquarie Holdings Inc., 2005—07; gen. counsel US Dept. Transp., Washington, 2007—. Office: US Dept Transp 400 7th St SW Rm 10428 Washington DC 20590 Office Phone: 202-366-4702. Office Fax: 202-366-3388.*

GRIBBIN, ROBERT E., III, diplomat; b. Durham, NC, Feb. 5, 1946; m. Connie Chapman; children: Matt, Mark. BA, U. of the South, Sewanee, Tenn., 1968; MA, Sch. Advanced Internat. Studies, Washington, 1973. Vol. Peace Corps., Kenya, 1968-70; econ. and comml. officer Bangui, 1974-76; dep. chief of mission to Rwanda US Dept. State, Kigali, 1979-81, prin. officer US Consulate Mombasa, Kenya, 1981-84, dep. dir. Office of East African and Ctrl. African Affairs, 1985-88, dep. chief of mission to Uganda Kampala, 1988-91, US amb. to Ctrl. African Republic Bangui, 1992—95, US amb. to Rwanda, 1995—99, charge d'affaires to Nigeria Abuja, 2007—; congl. fellow to Rep. Stephen J. Solarz NY, 1984-85; sr. advisor for Africa UN. Recipient Superior Honor awards for combating famine in horn of Africa and for the management of the crisis in Rwanda. Office: US Embassy 8320 Abuja Pl Washington DC 20521-8320*

GRIBBLE, CHARLES EDWARD, editor, language educator; b. Lansing, Mich., Nov. 10, 1936; s. Charles P. and Elizabeth K. Gribble. BA, U. Mich., 1957; AM, Harvard U., 1958, PhD, 1967; postgrad., Moscow State U., 1960-61. Instr., asst. prof. Russian Brandeis U., Waltham, Mass., 1961-68; asst. prof. Slavic langs. Ind. U., Bloomington, 1968-75; assoc. prof. Slavic langs. Ohio State U., Columbus, 1975-89, prof. Slavic lang., 1989—, chairperson of dept., 1990-96. Pres., editor Slavica Pub., Inc., Columbus, 1966-97; vis. assoc. prof. Slavic lang. U. Va., 1977. Author: Russian Root List, 1973, A Short Dictionary of 18th Century Russian, 1976; editor-in-chief Folia Slavica, 1977-88; editor: Studies Presented to Professor Roman Jakobson by His Students, 1968, Medieval Slavic Texts, vol. 1, 1973; contbr. articles to profl. jours. Woodrow Wilson fellow, 1957-58, Am. Coun. Learned Soc. fellow, 1972; Internat. Rsch. and Exch. Bd. grantee, 1960-61, 72, 80, Fulbright grantee, 1987; Marin Drinov award Bulgarian Acad. Scis., 2006. Mem. MLA, Am. Assn. Advancement Slavic Studies, Am. Assn. Tchr. Slavic and Ea. European Lang. (Disting. Contbn. to the Profession award 1992), Linguistic Soc. Am., Linguistic Soc. Europe, Bulgarian Studies Assn. (pres. 2002-03), Phi Beta Kappa. Office: Ohio State Univ Slavic Lang Dept 1775 College Rd #400 Columbus OH 43210-1340 Home Phone: 614-766-9412. Business E-Mail: gribble.3@osu.edu.

GRIBBON, DEBORAH, museum director; b. Washington, June 11, 1948; d. Daniel M. Gribbon and Mary Jane Retzler Gribbon; m. Winston Alt; children: Sarah Alt, Jane Alt. PhD, Harvard U., 1982, MA, 1971; BA, Wellesley Coll., 1970. Tchg. fellow Dept. Fine Arts Harvard U., Cambridge, Mass., 1972—74; curator Isabella Steward Gardner Mus., Boston, 1976—84; asst. dir. curatorial affairs The J. Paul Getty Mus., LA, 1984—87; assoc. dir. curatorial affairs The J. Paul Getty Mus., LA, 1987—91, assoc. dir., chief curator, 1991—98, dep. dir., chief curator, 1998—2000, dir., 2000—04. Instr. Ext. Sch. Harvard U., Cambridge, 1982—84; v.p. J.Paul Getty Trust, LA, 2000—04; bd. dirs. Courtauld Inst. Art, London. Co-author: The J. Paul Getty Museum and Its Collections: A Museum for a New Century, 1997; author (book): Sculpture in the Isabella Stewart Gardner Museum, 1978; contbr. articles to profl. jours. Recipient Plogsterth Prize for Art History, Wellesley Coll., 1970; fellow Theodore Rousseau Fellowship for Mus. Studies, Harvard U., 1982. Mem.: Assn. Art Mus. Dirs., Internat. Women's Forum.

GRICE, NOREEN ALISA-MAY, astronomer, educator; b. Malden, Mass., Mar. 24, 1963; d. Donald James and Edith Elaine Grice; m. Dennis Wade Dawson, Aug. 12, 1988. BA in Astronomy, Boston U., 1985; MS in Astronomy, San Diego State U., 1987; profl. cert. in Mus. Studies, Tufts U., 1997; profl. cert. in Non-Profit Mgmt., Boston Ctr. Adult Edn.; profl. cert. in Assistive Tech., Calif. State U., Northridge. Children's astronomy tchr. Boston U., 1984-85, obs. curator, summer 1984, 85; lab. instr. San Diego State U., 1985-87; sci. instr. Coll. Acad. Stonehill, Easton, Mass., summer 1987; adj. prof. Bentley Coll., Waltham, Mass., 1987-88; edn. cons. Boston Mus. Sci., 1987-88, edn. coord., 1988, planetarium ops. coord.; prof. Northeastern U., Boston, 1998; pres. You Can Do Astronomy, LLC. Sci. advisor Beyond Earth: A Space Adventure (videodisk), Burlington, Mass., 1989—90; developer Nature Co. Astronomy Kit, 1992; host Misson Mars. Author: (book in Braille) Touch the Stars, 1990, 3d edit., 1998, Touch the Universe, 2002, Touch the Sun, 2005, The Little Moon Phase Book, 2005, El Pequeño de las Faces de la Luna, 2005, Touch the Invisible Sky, 2007, Great Events from History: Science and Technology Series, 1991; prodr., writer guided tours for visually and visually imparied Boston Mus. Sci., 1991; columnist: Odyssey mag.; contbr. articles to profl. jours. Recipient Nat. Astronomy Day award, Sky and Telescope mag., Internat. Space Week award, Space Week Hdqs., Klumpke-Roberts award, 2007; grantee, Mass. Charitable Mechanics, 1990, Svc. League, 1988, 1990, 1991, 1994, 1996, 1998, Exxon Corp., 1991, Peabody Found., Inc., 1995, 1996. Mem.: Nat. Fedn. Blind, New Eng. Sci. Writers, Nat. Assn. Sci. Writers, Schwartz Astron. Soc. Pacific (pres. 1986—87, Astron. Dept. award 1986), Internat. Planetarium Soc. (Fellows award), Am. Astron. Soc. (assoc.). Achievements include development of astronomy tactiles. Office: Charles Hayden Planetarium Boston Mus Sci Science Park Boston MA 02114

GRICE, RICHARD W., lawyer; b. Green Bay, Wis., Feb. 12, 1959; BS, Univ. Wis., Madison, 1981; JD, Cornell Univ., 1984. Bar: NY 1984, Ga. 1987. Assoc. Milbank, Tweed, Hadley & McCloy, NYC, 1984—87; ptnr., chmn., leveraged capital group Alston & Bird LLP, Atlanta, 1987—. Sr. editor Cornell Internat. Law Jour. Named Best Lawyers in Am.; named one of Atlanta's Super Lawyers. Mem.: Phi Beta Kappa. Office: Alston & Bird LLP One Atlantic Ctr 1201 W Peachtree St NW Atlanta GA 30309-3424 Office Phone: 404-881-7576. Office Fax: 404-881-7777. Business E-Mail: rgrice@alston.com.

GRIDER, RHONDA PATRIECE, elementary school educator, writer; b. Detroit, Dec. 4, 1968; d. George William and Ida Jane Grider; children from previous marriage: Samuel Henry Scott, David Joseph Henry. BS cum laude, Harris Stow State Coll., Mo., 1988—91; M. U. Mo., 1996. Tchr. Ferguson Florissant Schs., St. Louis, 1989—96; tchr., playwright Hazelwood Schs., 1992—93; tchr. Chgo. Pub. Schs., 1997—2000, Broward County Schs., Ft. Lauderdale, Fla., 2000, DeKalb County Schs., Decatur, Ga., 1996—97, 2000—; asst. prin., educator Archdiocese Atlanta, 2003—04; founder, dir., adminstr. R.S.H Learning Programs, Covington, Ga., 2000—. Instr. Upward Bound Program, St. Louis, 1984—87; life scis. instr. Girls Club of St. Louis, 2005, 06. Author of poems, (handbook) R.S.H. Handbook: Mother and Son, 2004. Foster parent, St. Louis, Atlanta, 1995, 2004; vol. Nat. Jr. Beta, Atlanta, 1996—97, ARC, 2004—; donation collector Diabetes and MS Walkathon. Recipient Forum Honoree, John Ashcroft Leadership Forum, Fitness USA Merit award, All Around Athlete award, Drama Fesitival award Excellence, Archdiocese Tex., 1982, Class Favorite award, 1983, award, Am. Legion; Gus T. Ridgel fellow, U. Mo., 1991. Mem.: ASCD, Soc. Indsl. and Applied Math., St. Pius ProLife Vols., Internat. Soc. Poets, Kappa Delta Pi (pres. 1990—91). Avocations: swimming, aerobics, track, football, golf. Office: R S H Learning Programs PO Box 82605 Conyers GA 30013

GRIDLEY, KELLY ELIZABETH, biotechnologist, researcher; d. Robert Reid Gridley and Martha Elizabeth Greer; 1 child, Ryan. B in Health Sci., U. Fla., Gainesville, 1987, PhD, 1999. Cert. med. technologist Am. Soc. Clin. Pathologists. Rschr. U. Fla., Gainesville; coord. biotechnology lab. tech. program Santa Fe CC, Gainesville, Fla., 2004—. Contbr. articles to profl. jours. Vol. Arbor Ho., Gainesville. Achievements include patents for treatment strategies for neurodegenerative disease involving non-feminizing estrogens. Office: Santa Fe CC 3000 NW 83rd St W-201 Gainesville FL 32606 Home: 2439 NW 47th Ln Gainesville FL 32605 Office Phone: 352-395-5687. Business E-Mail: kelly.gridley@sfcc.edu.

GRIDLEY, MARK CHARLES, psychologist; b. Detroit, Jan. 5, 1947; s. Frederick William and Helen Lucille (Jones) Gridley. BS, Mich. State U., 1969; MS, Case Western Res. U., 1970, PhD, 1977, Psychometrist, research asst. Case Western Res. U. Hosp., 1971-73; saxophonist/flutist free-lance Cleve., 1969—; cons., psychologist Cleve. Bd. Edn., 1977-81; vis. asst. prof. John Carroll U., University Heights, Ohio, 1981-84; prof. psychology Heidelberg Coll., Tiffin, Ohio, 1987—. Author: Jazz Styles: History and Analysis, 1978, 1985, 1988, 1991, 1994, 1997, 2000, 2003, 2005, Concise Guide to Jazz, 1992, 2003, 2006; contbr. articles to profl. jours., chapters to books. Recipient Best Flutist award, Notre Dame Collegiate Jazz Festival, 1968, Disting. Achievement award, Ednl. Press Assn. Am., 1987. Mem.: Soc. Am. Music, Col. Music Soc., Internat. Assn. Jazz Educators. Home: 47 Maple St Tiffin OH 44883-2719

GRIEBENAUW, LIZA-MARIE, secondary school educator; b. Cape Town, South Africa, Oct. 10, 1963; d. Hubert Oswald Beuster and Martha Maria Wilson; 1 child, Liebe. BS, U. Stellenbosch, South Africa, 1984; BA in Recreation and Sports Mgmt. with honors, U. Pretoria, South Africa, 1987; MS, Katholieke Universiteit Leuven, Belgium, 1998; postgrad., U. Va., Charlottesville, 2000—. Instr. phys. tng. South African Police Tng. Coll., Pretoria, 1985—87; tchr. h.s. Pub. Edn., 1987—90; lectr. U. Limpopo, Sovenga, 1990—2000; tchr. Albemarle County Schs., Charlottesville, Va., 2003—05; coord. distance learning Fluvania County H.S., Palmyra, Va., 2006—. Cons. in field, Charlottesville, Va., 2000—. Contbr. chapters to books. Vol. firefighter and EMT Monticello Fire and Rescue, Charlottesville, 2001—05; rep. African continent Internat. Fedn. Adapted Phys. Activity, 1995—2000; instr. various disability activity orgns., Charlottesville, 2000; dir. Camp Holiday Trails, 2003—03. Mem.: Am. Coll. Sports Medicine, Am. Assn. Health, Phys. Edn., Recreation and Dance, Internat. Fedn. Adapted Phys. Activity (bd. mem. 1995—2000), Charlottesville Obesity Task Force. Avocations: travel, piano, guitar, gardening, reading. Home: 4030 Rolling Rd Scottsville VA 24590 Home Phone: 434-245-0140. Personal E-mail: lmgriebenauw@mail.fluco.org.

GRIECO, PAUL ANTHONY, chemistry professor; b. Framingham, Mass., Oct. 27, 1944; married; 4 children. BA, Boston U., 1966; MA, Columbia U., 1967, PhD in Organic Chemistry, 1970. NSF fellow Harvard U., 1970-71; from asst. prof. to prof. chemistry U. Pitts., 1971-80; prof. chemistry Ind. U., Bloomington, 1980-85, Earl Blough prof. chemistry, 1985—, chmn. dept., 1988-97; head of chemistry and biochemistry dept. Mont. State U., 1999—. William P. Timmie lectr. Emory U., 1977; Abbott lectr. Yale U., 1984; H.C. Brown lectr. Purdue U., 1984; Disting. lectr. U. Wyo., 1986; Conv. Intercantonale Romande pour L'Enseignement du Troisième Cycle en Chimie, Switzerland, 1987; Centennial lectr. Abbott Labs., Chgo., 1988; H. Martin Friedman lectr. Rutgers U., 1988; Centennial Anniversary lectr. 1st Internat. Conf. on Organic Chem. Nomenclature, Geneva, 1992. Fellow Alfred P. Sloan Found., 1974-76, Japan Soc. Promising Scientists, 1978-79; recipient Ernest Guenther award, 1982, NIH-Nat. Cancer Inst. Merit award, 1988. Mem. Am. Chem. Soc. (Akron sect. award 1982, Arthur C. Cope Scholar award 1990, award for creative work in synthetic organic chemistry 1991, lectr. French.-Am. socs. meeting in France 1992), Royal Soc. Chemistry, Chem. Soc. Japan, Swiss Chem. Soc. Achievements include rsch. in the devel. of new synthetic methods for constrn. of complex natural products. Office: Mont State U Dept Biochem & Chem 108 Gains Hl Bozeman MT 59717-0001

GRIEFEN, JOHN ADAMS, artist, educator; b. Worcester, Mass., Nov. 24, 1942; s. Robert John and Faith (Adams) G.; 1 child, Katherine Abigail Jacqueline. Student, Chgo. Art Inst., 1964-65, Bennington Coll., 1965-66; BA, Williams Coll., 1966; postgrad., Hunter Coll., 1966-68. Instr. Bennington Coll., 1968-69, Great Neck Adult Edn., NY, 1971-76. One-man shows Kornblee Gallery, 1969, 70, 73, Deitcher O'Reilly Gallery, N.Y.C., shows, William Edward O'Reilly Inc., N.Y.C., Martha Jackson Gallery, N.Y.C., Frank Watters Gallery, Sydney, Australia, 1979, Salander O'Reilly Galleries, N.Y.C., 1981, 82, 84, 85, 91, 93, 99, Harcus-Hrakow Gallery, Boston, Phyllis Kind Galley, Chgo., B.R. Kornblatt Gallery, Balt., Diane Brown Gallery, Washington, 1978, Sunne Savage Gallery, Boston, 1979, Williams Coll. Mus. Art, Williamstown, Mass., 1980, Martin Gerard Gallery, Edmonton, Alta., Can., 1981, Gallery Moos Ltd., Toronto and Calgary, 1981, Edmonton Art Gallery, 1984, Hirondelle Gallery, N.Y.C., 1986, Salander O'Reilly Galleries, L.A., 1991, Edmonton Art Gallery, Alberta, Can., 1993, Swift Current Art Gallery, Sask., 1993, S.C. Schultz Gallery, N.J., 1994; exhibited group shows Indpls. Mus. Art, Phoenix Mus., Sydney Mus., Whitney Mus. Purdue U., N.Y. Mus. Modern Art, Santa Barbara Mus., Boston Mus. Fine Arts; represented in pub. collections Larry Aldrich Mus. Contemporary Art, Allen Art Mus., Arthur A. Anderson Co., Bank of Ill., Calgary (Can.), Boston Mus. Fine Arts, Bklyn. Mus., Carnegie Inst. Mus. Art, Chase Manhattan Bank, Continental Resources Inc., Hines Indsl., Boston, N.Y.C., Washington, Dallas, Hirshhorn Mus. and Sculpture Garden, Washington, Met. Mus. Art, Michner Collections-U. Tex., Musnson-William-Proctor Art Inst., Mus. Modern Art, Newark Mus. Fine Arts, Reader's Digest Assn. Inc., Rose Art Mus., Brandeis U., Rothmans Art Gallery, St. Lawrence U., Sydney Mus., Australia, Whitney Mus., Williams Coll. Art Mus., Worcester Mus. Art, Mass., Met. Mus. Art, N.Y.C., Vassar Coll. Mus. Art, Poughkeepsie, N.Y., Lowcart Gallery, Miami. Recipient Esther Forbes award Bancroft Sch., Worcester, Mass., 1996. Home: 275 Park Ave Apt 6R Brooklyn NY 11205 Office: Salander Oreilly Galleries 22 E 71st St New York NY 10021-4975 Home Phone: 718-858-3281; Office Phone: 718-858-3281. Personal E-mail: jgriefen@aol.com.

GRIEGO, LINDA, entrepreneur; b. Tucumcari, N.Mex., 1949; m. Ronald C. Peterson. BA in History, UCLA, 1975. Pres., CEO Griego Enterprises, Inc., 1985—; restaurant founder, mng. ptnr. Engine Co. No. 28, 1988—; dep. mayor for econ. devel. City of LA, 1991—93, candidate for mayor, 1993; pres., CEO Rebuild LA Inc., 1994—97; pres. Zapgo Entertainment Group LLC, 1997—99; interim pres. & CEO LA Cmty. Devel. Bank, 1999—2000. Mem. Am. Devel. Bank Cmty. Adjustment Com., 1995—2000; sr. fellow UCLA Sch. Pub. Policy, 1998—2000; bd. dirs. Fed. Res. Bank San Francisco, 1998—2003, Granite Construction Inc., 1999—, City Nat. Corp., 2006—, Southwest Water Co., 2001—06, 2006—, CBS Corp., 2007—. Bd. trustees Robert Wood Johnson Found., 1995—2003, 2005—, Cedars Sinai Med. Ctr., 2004—, David & Lucile Packard Found., 2006—.*

GRIEM, HANS RUDOLF, physicist, researcher; b. Kiel, Schleswig-Holstein, Germany, Oct. 7, 1928; came to U.S., 1954; s. Rudolf H. and Paula D. (Schwarz) Griem; m. Irmgard H. Hoehling, May 11, 1957; children: Jens, Torsten, Rowena, Bridget. Abitur, Max-Planck Sch. Kiel, 1949; PhD, U. Kiel, 1954; PhD (hon.), Ruhr U., Bochum, Fed. Republic Germany, 1990. Rsch. asst. U. Md., College Park, 1954-55, asst. prof., 1957-61, assoc. prof., 1961-63, prof., 1963-94; prof. emeritus, sr. rsch. scientist, 1994—; Wissenschaftlicher asst. U. Kiel, 1955-57; dir. Lab. for Plasma Rsch. U. Md., 1980-87. Cons. Naval Rsch. Lab., Washington, 1957-96, Lawrence Livermore (Calif.) Nat. Lab., 1979—. Author: Plasma Spectroscopy, 1964, Spectral Line Broadening by Plasmas, 1974, Principles of Plasma Spectroscopy, 1997; editor: Methods of Experimental Physics, Vol. 9A, 1970; contbr. articles to sci. jours., chpts. to books. NSF sr. postdoctoral fellow, 1963; Guggenheim Found. fellow, 1968; European Space Rsch. Orgn. fellow, 1971; recipient Humboldt prize, 1978, William F. Meggers award Optical Soc. Am., 1987. Fellow Am. Phys. Soc. (councilor 1983-87, J.C. Maxwell prize 1991). Achievements include development of quantitative spectroscopic methods for high temperature plasma diagnostics. Office: Univ of Md Inst Rsch in Electronics and Applied Physics College Park MD 20742-3511 Office Phone: 301-405-4981. Business E-Mail: griem@umd.edu.

GRIEM, JOHN MICHAEL, management consultant; b. San Francisco, Apr. 29, 1945; s. John Drysen and Gwendolyn (Pyeatt) G.; m. Peggy Clarke, Sept. 16, 1967; children: John Michael Jr., Marjorie Lynne. ScBE magna cum laude with high honors, Brown U., 1965, ScME, 1966; MBA, U. Chgo., 1968. Sr. economist USPHS, 1968-70; assoc. to v.p., dir. Cresap, McCormick and Paget, Chgo., 1970-81; mng. ptnr. subs. Cresap, McCormick and Paget do Brasil Servicos Ltda., 1978-81; v.p. A.T. Kearney, Chgo., 1981-95; pres. Kearney, Health Svcs. Cons., Chgo., 1981-87; pres., CEO, Griem & Co., Lake Bluff, Ill., 1995—. Bd. govs. Am. Soc. Sao Paulo, Brazil, 1979-81, John G. Shedd Aquarium, Chgo., 1992-98. Fellow NDEA, 1965-66, Ford Found., 1965, 67-68. Mem.: Mid. Am.-Arab C. of C. (bd. dirs. 1989—91), Inst. Mgmt. Consultants (cert., bd. dirs. 1998—2003, pres. 2000—01), Chgo. Coun. Fgn. Rels., Ill. Curling Assn. (bd. dirs. 2000—, pres. 2002—05), Brown U. Club, Exmoor Country Club, Beta Gamma Sigma, Tau Beta Pi, Sigma Xi. Home and Office: 120 Indian Rd Lake Bluff IL 60044-2714 Office Phone: 847-234-6923. Business E-Mail: m.griem@comcast.net.

GRIEM, KATHERINE LESLIE, radiation oncologist; d. Melvin Luther and Sylvia (Fudzinski) Griem; m. Anthony Gerard Montag; children: Hugh Graham Montag, William Maurice Montag, Caroline Elizabeth Montag. MD, Harvard U., Boston, 1982. Lic. therapeutic radiology Am. Bd. of Radiology. Assoc. prof. Rush U. Med. Ctr., Chgo., 1991—, program dir., 2005—. Mem. Ill. divsn. Am. Cancer Soc., Chgo., 2002; chairperson 57th St. Art Fair, Chgo., 2005—06. Mem.: Am. Soc. for Clin. Oncology, Am. Soc. for Therapeutic Radiology and Oncology. Achievements include research in Breast cancer. Office: Rush Univ Med Ctr 1653 W Congress Pkwy Chicago IL 60612 Office Phone: 312-942-5751.

GRIER, DAVID ALAN, actor; b. Detroit, June 30, 1955; m. Maritza Rivera, 1987 (div.). Grad., U. Mich.; MFA, Yale U., 1981. Actor (Broadway plays) The First (Tony award nomination, Theatre World award), Dreamgirls, A Funny Thing Happened on the Way to the Forum, The Mambo Kings, 2005, The Wiz, 2006; (off-Broadway plays) A Soldier's Play, various other stage credits; (TV series) All is Forgiven, 1986, In Living Color, 1990-94, The Preston Episodes, 1995, "DAG," 2000, Life with Bonnie, 2002-04 Tough Crowd with Colin Quinn, 2002; (TV films) Kingpins, 1987, A Saintly Switch, 1999, The 60s, 1999, Angels in the Infield, 2000, King of Texas, 2002, Rock Stars Do the Dumbest Things, 2003, The Muppets' Wonderful Wizard of Oz, 2005; (films) Streamers, 1983, A Soldier's Story, 1984, Beer, 1985, Ich und Er, 1987, From the Hip, 1987, Amazon Women on the Moon, 1987, I'm Gonna Git You Sucka, 1988, Off Limits, 1988, Almost an Angel, 1990, Loose Cannons, 1990, The Player, 1992, Boomerang, 1992, In the Army Now, 1994, Blankman, 1994, Tales from the Hood, 1995, Jumanji, 1995, Top of the World, 1997, McHale's Navy, 1997, East of A, 1999, Damned If You Do, 1999, (voice) Stuart Little, 1999, The Adventures of Rocky and Bullwinkle, 2000, Tiptoes, 2003, The Woodsman, 2004, Bewitched, 2005, Little Man, 2006; exec. prodr. (TV series) The Preston Episodes, 1995, (TV films) The Davey Gee Show, 2005; prodr. (TV series) Thank God You're Here, 2007.*

GRIER, JAMES EDWARD, hotel executive, lawyer; b. Ottumwa, Iowa, Sept. 7, 1935; s. Edward J. and Corinne (Bailey) G.; m. Virginia Clinker, July 4, 1959; children: Michael, Susan, James, John, Thomas. BSc, U. Iowa, 1956, JD, 1959. Bar: Iowa 1959, Mo. 1959. Mng. ptnr. Hillix, Brewer, Hoffhaus & Grier, Kansas City, Mo., 1964-77, Grier & Swartzman, Kansas City, 1977-89; pres. Doubletree Hotels Corp., Phoenix, 1989-94; chmn. Sonoran Hotel Capital, Inc., Phoenix, 1994-96; mng. ptnr. Copa Investments, 1996—, Gainey Hotel Co., 1996—. Bd. dirs. Iowa Law Sch. Found., Iowa City, St. Joseph Healthcare Ariz., Phoenix, Homeward Bound, Phoenix. Home: 3500 E Lincoln Dr Phoenix AZ 85018-1010 Office: Gainey Hotel Co 7300 E Gainey Suites Dr Ste 169 Scottsdale AZ 85258-2061 Home Phone: 602-840-4979. Business E-Mail: jegrier@gaineysuiteshotel.com.

GRIER, MARK B., diversified financial services company executive; Former exec. Chase Manhattan Corp.; exec. v.p. Prudential Ins., Newark, 1995—2000; dir. Prudential Fin., Inc., Newark, 1999—2001, v.p., 2000, exec. v.p., 2000—02, vice chmn., fin. mgmt., 2002—07, vice chmn., internat. div., 2007—. Office: Prudential Financial Inc 751 Broad St Newark NJ 07102-3777*

GRIERSON, KEVIN WILLIAM, lawyer; b. Ridgewood, NJ, July 27, 1965; s. John William and Sandra Grace Grierson; m. Judith Gail Williams, Aug. 5, 1990; children: Kyle Broaddus, Kendall Noble Minor, Kirk William Troy. BA in Biology, U. Va., Charlottesville, 1987, JD, 1992; MA in Biology, Coll. William and Mary, Williamsburg, Va., 1989. Registered: US Patent and Trademark Office (patent atty.) 1998, bar: U.S. Ct. Appeals (fed. cir.) 2002, U.S. Ct. Appeals (4th cir.) 1994, Va. 1993, U.S. Dist. Ct. (ea. dist.) Va., U.S. Dist. Ct. (we. dist.) Va., U.S. Bankruptcy Ct. (ea. dist.) Va. Law clk. to Justice Henry H. Whiting Supreme Ct. of Va., Winchester, 1992—93; atty. Jones, Blechman, Woltz & Kelly, P.C., Newport News, Va., 1993—99; of counsel Willcox & Savage, P.C., Norfolk, Va., 1999—. Mem. bd. regents Leadership Inst. of the Va. Peninsula, Hampton, 2005—, participant, 2004—05; mem. Ft. Monroe Redevel. Planning Steering Com., Hampton, 2006—; chmn. parish fin. coun. Our Lady of Mt. Carmel Roman Cath. Ch., Newport News, 2005—; pres. Our Lady of Mt. Carmel Home and Sch. Assn., Newport News, 2001—03; bd. dirs. Thomas Nelson C.C. Ednl. Found., Hampton, 2005—. Echols scholar, U. Va., 1983—87. Mem.: Nat. Assn. Patent Practitioners (bd. dirs. 2004—), ABA, Internat. Trademark Assn. (mem. bull. com. 2006—). Roman Catholic. Achievements include development of Excellence in Innovations Award for Tech Nite. Office: Willcox & Savage PC Ste 1800 One Commercial Pl Norfolk VA 23510 Office Phone: 757-628-5603. E-mail: kgrierson@wilsav.com.

GRIERSON, WILLIAM, retired agriculturist; b. Boscombe, Eng., Dec. 15, 1917; arrived in US, 1952; s. Edward James and Winifred (Burridge) Grierson-Jackson; m. Agnes Cray; children: Peter Robert, John Patrick (dec.). BSc in Agr., Ont. Agrl. Coll., Guelph, Can., 1938; PhD, Cornell U., 1951. Asst. prof. U. B.C., Vancouver, Can., 1945-51, U. Fla., Lake Alfred, 1952-60, prof., 1964-82; assoc. dir. Food Industries Rsch. and Engring., Yakima, Wash., 1960-64; prof. emeritus, cons. Winter Haven, Fla., 1983—. Author, editor: (textbook) Fresh Citrus Fruits, 1986; author: (World War II memoir) We Band of Brothers, 1997, also 4 manuals; contbr. over 200 articles to sci. jours. Maj. RCAF, 1940-45. Fla. Citrus Packers grad. fellow, 1992; named Rschr. of Yr. Fla. Fruit and Vegetable Assn., 1972; named to Fla. Citrus Hall of Fame, 1995. Fellow Am. Soc. Hort. Sci. (assoc. editor 1970-74); mem. Fla. State Hort. Soc. (hon. mem., pres. 1981-82, editor 1972-79, Gold medal 1969). Achievements include devel. of designs for citrus degreening rooms now used world wide, of methods for the marketing of Florida lemons; first identification of two physiological diseases of citrus ("zebraskin" and "sloughing"). Home and Office: 18 Golf View Cir NE Winter Haven FL 33881-4302

GRIES, MICHAEL F., diversified financial services company executive; b. Aug. 27, 1954; BS in Acctg. and Fin., Northeastern U., 1975. Ptnr., dir. restructuring and reorgn. Ernst & Young LLP; founder, prin. Conway, Del Genio, Gries, & Co. LLC, NYC, 1998—; chmn., chief restructuring officer Encompass Svcs. Corp., 2002—06; chief restructuring officer OCA, Inc., 2006—, interim CEO, 2006—07. Mem.: Assn. Insolvency Accts., NJ StateSoc. CPA, AICPA. Address: Conway Del Genio Gries & Co LLC Olympic Tower 645 Fifth Ave New York NY 10022 E-mail: mgries@cdqco.com.

GRIESA, THOMAS POOLE, federal judge; b. Kansas City, Mo., Oct. 11, 1930; s. Charles Henry and Stella Lusk (Bedell) G.; m. Christine Pollard Meyer, Jan. 5, 1963. AB cum laude, Harvard U., 1952; LL.B., Stanford U., 1958. Bar: Wash. 1958, N.Y. 1961. Atty. Justice Dept., 1958-60; with firm Symmers, Fish & Warner, NYC, 1960-61, Davis Polk & Wardwell, NYC, 1961-72, partner, 1970-72; judge U.S. Dist. Ct. So. Dist. N.Y., 1972—, chief judge, 1993-2000. Mem.: Stanford Law Rev., 1956-58. Bd. visitors Stanford Law Sch., 1982-84; bd. dirs. Greater N.Y. Coun. Boy Scouts Am. Served to lt. (j.g.) USCG, 1952-54. Mem. Bar Assn. City N.Y., Union Club N.Y.C. Christian Scientist. Office: US Dist Ct US Courthouse 500 Pearl St New York NY 10007-1316 Office Phone: 212-805-0210.

GRIESCHE, ROBERT PRICE, hospital purchasing executive; b. Berkeley, Calif., July 21, 1953; s. Robert Bowen and Lillian (Price) G.; m. Susan Dawn Albers, June 8, 1985 (div. Apr. 1989); 1 child, Sara Christine. AA, Coll. of the Canyons, Valencia, Calif., 1984; BS in Health Care Mgmt., Century U., 2005. Warehouse supr. John Muir Hosp., Walnut Creek, Calif., 1973-82; purchasing mgr. Henry Mayo Newhall Hosp., Valencia, 1982-85; materials mgr. Foothill Presbyn. Hosp., Glendora, Calif., 1985-87; materials mgmt. dir. Huntington Meml. Hosp., Pasadena, Calif., 1987-96; sys. dir. purchasing So. Calif. Healthcare Sys., Pasadena, 1996—2002; materials mgmt. dir. Univ. Med. Ctr. of So. Nev., Las Vegas, 2002—05; med. equipment program planner HDR Architecture, Las Vegas, 2005—. Chmn. Huntington Employee Campaign, 1990-92. V.p. Coll. of Canyons Found., Valencia, 1985-90. Named to Outstanding Young Men of Am., 1988. Mem. Am. Soc. Healthcare Materials Mgmt Republican. Presbyn. Avocations: swimming, gardening, photography. Home: 9621 Kinlock Ct Las Vegas NV 89117 Office: 770 E Warm Springs Rd Las Vegas NV 89119 Office Phone: 702-938-6000.

GRIESE, BRIAN, professional football player; b. Miami, Fla., Mar. 18, 1975; BS in political sci., Univ. Mich. Winner Super Bowl 33; quarter back Denver Broncos, 1998—2002, Miami Dolphins, 2003, Tampa Bay Buccaneers, 2004—06, Chgo. Bears, 2006—. Office: Chicago Bears 1000 Football Dr Lake Forest IL 60045

GRIESS, ROBERT L., JR., mathematics professor; BS, Univ. Chgo., 1961, MS, 1968, PhD, 1971. Grantee Guggenheim Fellowship, 1981—82. Fellow: Am. Acad. Arts & Scis.; mem.: Am. Math. Soc. Office: Dept Math Univ Mich Ann Arbor MI 48109-1109 Office Phone: 734-764-0361. Business E-Mail: rlg@umich.edu.*

GRIEVE, WILLIAM ROY, psychologist, educator, educational administrator, researcher; b. NYC, Mar. 15, 1917; s. Walter Stuart and Grace (Buttendorf) G.; m. Harriet Bush, Mar. 30, 1978; children: Leslie Lynne Grieve Bainbridge, Davelyn Anne Grieve Sandhowe. Student, SUNY, Oswego, 1934—35; BS, NYU, 1937, MA, 1938; EdD, Rutgers U., 1954. Tchr. secondary edn., NYC, 1938—48; rsch. fellow Ohio State U., Columbus, 1942; ind. arts editor High Point Mag. N.Y.C. Bd. Edn., 1984—85, textbook and instrnl. materials com., 1954—65, curriculum specialist Bur. Curriculum Rsch., 1948—50, supr., adminstr. secondary edn., 1950—65; prof. NYU, NYC, 1965—72, ombudsman Sch. Edn., 1969—71, rsch. predictive testing specialist in vocat./tech. edn.; prof. grad. program NYU/U. PR, NYC, 1966—67; ESSA, ESAA, and ESEA evaluation studies in reading, math., ESL and indsl. edn. NY, NJ, Conn., Mass., Md., 1970—83; assoc. dir. evaluation studies divsn. Psychol. Corp., 1972—75; dir. Ednl. Planning and Rsch. Inc., Boston, 1975—83, pres. Glencove and Stuart, Fla., 1983—. Asst. examiner ind. edn., supervision, guidance lics., NYC Bd. Edn., 1950-72; chmn. ind. edn. standing com. Bd. Supts., NYC, 1960-65; adj. prof. psychology L.I. U., Bklyn., 1965-70; adj. prof. edn. NY Inst. Tech., Westbury, 1981-86, SUNY, Westbury, 1986-89; cons. NY C.C. orthotics and prosthetics, 1966, NC State U., 1968, Pub. Edn. Assn./Nat. Alliance Businessmen, NY, 1968-72, Citibank, PR, 1970, Met. Mus. Art (The Art of Black Africa), NYC, 1970, Sta. UFT-TV, NY, 1970; Young and Rubicam, NY, 1974; cons. Cautaulds Internat., Mobile, Ala., 1975, Rheem Mfg., Chgo., 1975, Bankers Trust, NYC, 1975, Republic Steel, Akron and Canton, Ohio, 1977, S.W. Regional Lab., Calif., 1980, N.Y. State Dept. Edn., 1985—, job and task analysis, equal opportunity test devel., alt. edn. programs, coop. edn., work study, career edn., work study, career edn., tng. and devel., 1990—; prof. U. PR, Rio Piedras, 1966-67, rsch. predictive testing specialist, 1970-83. Contbr. articles to profl. jours. Bd. mgrs. Prospect Park YMCA, Bklyn., 1960-65; adviser desegregation measures Boston Pub. Schs., 1976-81. With U.S. Army, 1944-45. Mem.: Am. Psychol. and Guidance Assn., Am. Assn. Tchr. Educators, Am. Vocat. Assn., Am. Vocat. Ednl. Rsch. Assn. (charter), N.Y. Schoolmasters Club, Masons, Kappa Delta Pi, Kappa Phi Kappa, Epsilon Pi Tau, Phi Delta Kappa. Home: 5684 SE Riverboat Dr Stuart FL 34997 Personal E-mail: haribil@aol.com.

GRIFFEL, L. MICHAEL, music educator, researcher; b. NYC, Nov. 12, 1942; s. Joseph and Klara Griffel; m. Margaret Ross, Sept. 15, 1968; 1 child, David S. BA, Yale U., 1963; MS, Juilliard Sch. Music, NYC, 1966; MA, Columbia U., 1968, PhD, 1975. Adj. lectr. music Hunter Coll., CUNY, NYC, 1970—71, instr. music, 1971—75, asst. prof. music, 1975—77, assoc. prof. music, 1978—84, prof. music, 1985—2006, prof. emeritus, 2006—; asst. prof. music Grad. Sch., CUNY, NYC, 1977, assoc. prof. music, 1978—84, prof. music, 1985—2005, prof. emeritus, 2005—; asst. dean arts and scis. Hunter Coll., NYC, 1999—2000, assoc. dean arts and scis., 2000—02, acting assoc. provost, 2002—05. Grad. faculty Mannes Coll. Music, NYC, 1980—99, Juilliard Sch., NYC, 1997—, chair dept. music history, 2005—; artist-tchr. Merrywood Music Sch., Lenox, Mass., 1965—67; editor-in-chief Current Musicology, NYC, 1970—71, co-editor-in-chief, 1971—72. Contbr. chapters to books, articles to profl. jours. Mem.: Schubert Soc. USA (mem. adv. bd. 2003—), Am. Musicol. Soc. (coun. 1969—71), Am. Schubert Inst. (bd. advisors 1995—), Am. Beethoven Soc. (v.p. N.Y. chpt. 1995—2007). Achievements include research in Schubert's symphonies. Home: 3135 Johnson Ave Apt 9E Bronx NY 10463 Office: The Juilliard Sch Box 55 60 Lincoln Center Plz New York NY 10023 Home Phone: 718-543-2017; Office Phone: 212-799-5000 294. Business E-Mail: lgriffel@juilliard.edu.

GRIFFEN, CLYDE CHESTERMAN, retired historian; b. Sioux City, Iowa, July 29, 1929; s. Clyde Rumbaugh and Rosanna Susan (Chesterman) G.; m. Sarah Goldsborough Donoho, Feb. 14, 1959; children: John Winslow, Sarah Bolling, Robert Henry. BA, State U. Iowa, 1952; MA, Columbia U., 1953, PhD, 1960. Lectr. Columbia U., NYC, 1954-57; instr. history Vassar Coll, Poughkeepsie, NY, 1957-61, asst. prof., 1961-67, assoc. prof., 1967-75, Lucy Maynard Salmon prof. Am. history, 1975-92, chmn. dept. history, 1982-85, dir. Am. culture program, 1977-79. Author: (with Sally Griffen) Natives and Newcomers: The Ordering of Opportunity in Mid-Nineteenth-Century Poughkeepsie, 1978; editor: New Perspectives on Poughkeepsie's Past, 1988; co-editor: Meanings for Manhood: Constructions of Masculinity in Victorian America, 1990; co-author: Full Steam Ahead in Poughkeepsie: The Story of Coeducation at Vassar, 1966-1974, 2000; mem. editl. bd. Social Sci. History Assn., 1976-89. NSF grantee, 1973-74; Nat. Humanities Inst. fellow, 1976-77; Fulbright rsch. scholar N.Z., 1984; N.Z. Forst Rsch. fellow, 1996, 98. Home: Collington #5008 10450 Lottsford Rd Mitchellville MD 20721-2734

GRIFFENHAGEN, GEORGE BERNARD, trade association executive; b. Portland, Oreg., June 9, 1924; s. Richard Bernard and Clara (Schoenian) G.; m. Joan Helen Houston, June 21, 1946; children: Gary Bernard, Gordon Wesley, Barbara Clare. BS in Pharmacy, U. So. Calif., 1949, MS, 1950; student, Fresno State Coll., 1946, U. London, 1948. Dir. research Nion Corp., Hollywood, Calif., 1950-52; curator div. med. scis. Smithsonian Instn., Washington, 1952-59; sec. sect. history of pharmacy Am. Pharm. Assn., Washington, 1952-59, pres. local chpt., 1958-59, assoc. exec. dir., 1959-89, hon. pres., 1990-91; trustee Am. Pharm. Assn. Found., Washington, 1989-94; editor Jour. Am. Pharm. Assn., Washington, 1960-76; sec.-gen. 4th Pan Am. Congress Pharmacy and Biochemistry, Washington, 1957; sec. organizing com. 31st Internat. Congress Pharm. Scis., Washington, 1971; sec.-gen. Internat. Congress History of Pharmacy, Washington, 1983, Japan-U.S. Congress of Pharm. Scis., Honolulu, 1987; v.p. Pan Am. Pharm. and Biochem. Fedn., 1963-82, 85-91, Pharmacy World Congress, Washington, 1991. U.S. del. Internat. Pharm. Fedn. Gen. Assemblies, London, 1955, Brussels, 1958, Copenhagen, 1960, Vienna, 1962, Amsterdam, 1964, Hamburg, 1968, Geneva, 1970, Lisbon, 1972, Rome, 1974, Warsaw, 1976, Cannes, 1978; U.S. del. FIP Coun., Bucharest, 1969, Dublin, 1975, Montreal, 1985, Helsinki, 1986, Amsterdam, 1987, Sydney, 1988, Munich, 1989, Istanbul, 1990, Lyon, 1992, Tokyo, 1993, Lisbon, 1994, Jerusalem, 1996, Vancouver, 1997, The Hague, 1998, Barcelona, 1999, Vienna, 2000; congress coord., The Hague, 1977; U.S. del. Pan Am. Fedn. Pharmacy Congress, Mexico City, 1963, Buenos Aires, 1966, Caracas, 1969, Panama, 1972, Guatemala City, 1985, Santo Domingo, 1988, Buenos Aires, 1994, San Jose, Costa Rica, 1997, Rio de Janeiro, 2000; U.S. del. Internat. Congress History of Pharmacy, Budapest, Hungary, 1981, Fedn. Asian Pharm. Assns. Congress, Seoul, Korea, 1982; mem. Nat. Action Com. on Drug Edn., Office of Edn., 1970-71, Va. Gov.'s Coun. on Narcotic and Drug Abuse Control, 1970-72. Editor: Scalpel and Tongs, 1972-73; Contbr. articles to profl. jours. Mem. Fairfax County Rep. Com., Va., 1962-97; adminstrv. asst. to chmn. Va. State Rep. Com., 1969-71; life mem. Rep. Nat. Com., 1979—; founding pres. Nat. Coord. Coun. on Drug Edn., 1968-69. Served with C.E. AUS, World War II, ETO. Recipient Pfizer Merit award U.S. CD Coun., 1964, U. So. Calif. Alumnus award, 1969; Hugo H. Schaefer award Am. Pharm. Assn., 1984; Disting. Svc. award Pharmacy Guild of Australia, 1988, Internat. Pharmacy Jour. Editor's prize, 1989, 95, Remington Honor medal Am. Pharm. Assn., 1991; named to Nat. Philatelic Writers Hall of Fame, 1990. Mem. Am. Inst. History of Pharmacy (pres. 1960-61, Edward Kremers award 1969, sec. 1991-2005), Friends of Hist. Pharmacy (pres. 1957-58), Pharm. Wholesalers Assn. (Distinguished Service award 1971), Am. Topical Assn. (1st v.p. 1972-75, pres. 1976-79, pres. med. subjects unit 1969-72, Distinguished Topical Philatelist award 1970, Myrtle Watt Med. Philately Topicalist award 1980, editor Topical Time 1992—), Am. Philatelic Congress (Jere Hess Barr award 1969), Am. Philatelic Soc. (sec.-treas. Writers Unit 1982—; U.S. commr. to Internat. Exhbn. Thematic Philately, Basel, Switzerland 1983, Luff award 2003), Am. Revenue Assn. (named to Sterling Meml. Roll of Disting. Fiscalists 1979), Council Philatelic Orgns. (treas. 1983-91), Internat. Pharm. Fedn. (hon.), Philatelic Lit. Assn., Academie Internationale d'Histoire de la Pharmacie (treas. 1971-81, 1989-97), Pharm. Soc. Gt. Britain (hon.), Sigma Xi, Rho Chi, Phi Kappa Psi. Home: 2501 Drexel St Vienna VA 22180-6906 Office: Am Pharm Assn 2215 Constitution Ave NW Washington DC 20037-2907 Business E-Mail: ggriffenhagen@aphanet.org.

GRIFFETH, LANDIS KING, nuclear medicine physician; b. Greenville, SC, Aug. 3, 1956; s. Jesse Ellis and Mary Alice (King) G.; m. Terri Blount, Aug. 6, 1978. BA in Chemistry and Zoology summa cum laude, Duke U., 1977, PhD in Pharmacology, 1983, MD, 1984. Diplomate Am. Bd. Nuc. Medicine. Postdoctoral rsch. fellow Duke U. Sch. Pharmacology, Durham, NC, 1983-84; resident in diagnostic radiology Mallinckrodt Inst. of Radiology, Washington U., St. Louis, 1984-86, resident in nuclear medicine, 1986-87, chief resident in nuc. medicine, 1987-88, asst. prof. radiology, 1988-93; dir. nuc. medicine Baylor U. Med. Ctr., Dallas, 1993—; med. dir. North Tex. Clin. P.E.T. Inst., Dallas, 1998—. Dir. nuc. medicine and P.E.T., Am. Radiology Assn., Dallas, 1993—, nat. med. dir., P.E.T., U.S. Oncology, 2000—. Assoc. editor Radiology Jour., 1993-2000; cons. to editor Radiology, 2000-02; contbr. numerous articles to profl. jours; reviewer med. jours; edit. bd. Molecular Imagingand Biology, 2004-. Mem. Univ. Park United Meth. Ch.; bd. dirs. Cavalier Health Found.; mem. devel. coun. Tex. A&M Coll. Vet. Medicine. Mem. Am. Coll. Radiology, Am. Coll. Nuc. Physicians, Soc. Nuc. Medicine, Acad. Molecular Imaging (nat. patient adv. com.), Inst. for Clin. P.E.T., Radiol. Soc. N.Am., Am. Soc. for Law Enforcement Tng., Tex. Med. Assn., Tex. Radiol. Soc., Dallas County Med. Soc., Phi Lambda Upsilon, Alpha Omega Alpha. United Methodist. Methodist. Avocations: target shooting, reading, dogs, travel. Office: Baylor U Med Ctr 3500 Gaston Ave Dallas TX 75246-2096 Office Phone: 214-826-8822. Business E-Mail: lk.griffeth@baylorhealth.edu.

GRIFFEY, KEN, JR., (GEORGE KENNETH GRIFFEY JR.), professional baseball player; b. Donora, Pa., Nov. 21, 1969; s. Ken and Bertie Griffey. Draft pick Seattle Mariners, 1987, outfielder, 1989—2000, Cin. Reds, 2000—. Mem. US Team World Baseball Classic, 2006. Named All-Star Game MVP, 1992, Am. League MVP, 1997, Maj. League Player of Yr., 1997; named to Am. League All-Star Team, Maj. League Baseball, 1990—99, Nat. League All-Star Team, 2000, 2004, 2007, MLB All-Century Team, 1999, All-Time Rawlings Gold Glove Team, 2007; recipient Gold Glove award, 1990—99, Silver Slugger award, 1991, 1993—94, 1996—99, Nat. League Comeback Player of Yr., Maj. League Baseball, 2005. Achievements include led the Am. League in home runs, 1994 (40), 1997 (56), 1998 (56), 1999 (48), runs scored, 1997 (125), and runs batted in, 1997 (147); hit his 500th career home run on June 22, 2004; 6th all-time on career home run list. Office: Cin Reds 100 Main St Cincinnati OH 45202*

GRIFFIN, ANDREW STEVEN, urologist; b. Rocky Mount, SC, Nov. 8, 1956; s. Freddie Morton and Gretchen Jones Griffin; m. Anita Gertrude Paslack, Aug. 4, 1979; children: Andrew, Ashley. BA, Wake Forest U., Winston Salem, NC, 1979; MD, Bowman Gray Sch. Medicine, Winston Salem, 1983. Diplomate Am. Bd. Urology. Urologist Candina Urol. Assocs., Winston Salem, 1988—; pres. med. staff Med. Pk. Hosp., Winston Salem, 1997—98, Forsyth Med. Ctr., Winston Salem, 2005—06. Mem.: NC Med. Soc., Am. Urol. Assn. Avocations: race cars, motorcycling. Office: Candina Urol Assocs 140 Kemel Park Dr Winston Salem NC 27103

GRIFFIN, ANNE, political scientist, educator; d. John Bastin and Elizabeth McCue Griffin; m. Jay Lefer, July 26, 1968; children: David G. Lefer, Theodore B. Lefer. BA, Wellesley Coll., Mass.; MA, NYU, 1973, PhD, 1975. Asst. to dean NYU, 1965—68, asst. prof., politics, 1977—78; asst. prof. to prof., polit. sci. Cooper Union for Advancement of Sci. & Art,

NYC, 1978—; adj. assoc. prof., politics NYU, 1987—89; vis. scholar Ctr. for European Studies, NYU, 2000—. Assoc. Columbia U. Seminar, Am. Studies, NYC, 1978—, Columbia U. Seminar, Hist. and Memory, 2002—; cons. Rsch. & Forecasts, NYC, 1979—81; adv. bd. Women in Sci. Sect., NY Acad. of Sciences, NYC, 1981—2003; mem. Ad Hoc Com. on Animal Rsch., NY Acad. of Sciences, 1982—87; cons. Cornell U, NY Hosp., 1983—87, St. Martin's Press, NYC, 1992—92; adv. bd. Fulbright Found., 2005—. Author: Quebec: The Challenge of Independence, Les Nationalismes au Quebec du XIXe au XXIe siecle; contbr. articles various profl. jours.;, co-editor various profl. pamphlets, author various book reviews; curator (exhibitions) Cooper Union Advancement Sci. and Art, NY, 2005, Arthur A. Houghton Gallery, Cooper Union, NY, 2005; author: (documentary installation) Yeshiva U. Mus., 2006—. Mem., com. chair Cmty. Planning Bd. 8, Manhattan, NYC, 1972—77; v.p. NYU Alumni Assn., NYC, 1999—2001; pres. NYU, Grad. Sch. of Arts & Sci. Alumni Assn., NYC, 1985—87. Grantee, Righteous Persons Found., 2004—05, NY Coun. Humanities, 2005, Belgian Ministry Fgn. Affairs, 2005—06, Laurie Found., 2004—05; Summer Seminar fellow, NEH, 1981, Summer Stipend grant, 1995, 2000, Que. Studies grant, Govt. of Que., 1993-94, 1996-97, Sr. Rsch. fellowship, Fulbright Found., 2001-2002, Fellow, NEH, 2002. Mem.: NY State Polit. Sci. Assn. (Can. polit. chair, dir. 1995—2001), Am. Coun. for Que. Studies, Am. Polit. Sci. Assn., Assn. for Can. Studies in the US (life). Democrat. Office: Cooper Union for the Advancement of Science & Art 51 Astor Pl Rm 113 New York NY 10003 Office Phone: 212-353-4276.

GRIFFIN, ANTHONY, plastic surgeon; b. Kenosha, Wis., Mar. 1, 1960; BA in Biology, Brown U., Providence, RI; MD and MA/MS (honors), Washington U. Med. Sch., St. Louis, 1987. Diplomate Am. Bd. Plastic Surgery. Intern, dept. surgery, Wash. U. Barnes Hosp., St. Louis, 1987—88, jr. asst. resident, dept. surgery, gen. surgery, Wash. U., 1988—90, sr. asst. resident, Dept. surgery, gen. surgery, WASH. U.; asst. resident, dept. surgery, gen. surgery U. Chgo. Pritzker Med. Sch., 1990—91; burn reconstruction fellow U. So. Calif. Med. Sch., Ranchos Los Amigos Med. Ctr., Downey, Calif.; resident, plastic and reconstructive surgery U. So. Calif. Med. Sch., 1991—94, hand fellow, dept. orthopedic surgery, 1994—95; staff mem. Cedars-Sinai Med. Ctr., LA, 1995; faculty mem. UCLA-Charles Drew U., LA, 1998; pvt. practice plastic surgery, med. dir. Beverly Hills Cosmetic Surgery Inst. Inc., Calif.; med. dir. Beverly Hills Robertson Surgery Ctr. Presenter in field. Cons., surgeries featured on Extreme Makeover (ABC), surgeries featured on CNN, Discovery Health Channel, National Geographic, Learning Channel and more, surgeries featured in Time and Essence Mags., regular commentator E!, featured on Access Hollywood; author: Surgery Without Scars" A Worry-Free, Multi-Cultural Guide to Plastic Surgery Today; contbr. scientific articles to several jours. Vol. Operation Smile, 1995—. Recipient NAACP Outstanding Achievement award, Golden Cannula award, Lipoplasty Soc., 1993. Fellow: ACP; mem.: AMA, Am. Soc. Aesthetic Plastic Surgeons, Am. Soc. Plastic Surgeons, Beverly Hills C. of C., LeTip Profl. Soc., Calif. Soc. Plastic Surgeons, Charles Drew Med. Soc., Mound City Med. Forum, St. Louis Met. Med. Soc., Cook County Physicians Assn., Ill. State Med. Assn., Mo. State Med. Assn., L.A. County Med. Assn., Rhinoplasty Soc., Am. Soc. Surgeons, Am. Soc. Plastic and Reconstructive Surgeons, Nat. Med. Assn., Calif. Med. Assn., L.A. Soc. Plastic Surgeons. Achievements include being considered one of the foremost authorities on plastic surgery for African Americans and ethnic skin types; pioneer in scar-free surgery for scar prone minorities; signature procedures (all trademarked): Brazilian Butt Lift, Six-Pack Tummy Tuck, No-Tell Nose Job. Office: Beverly Hills Cosmetic Surgery Inst 8641 Wilshire Blvd Ste 305 Beverly Hills CA 90211 Office Phone: 310-657-8264. Office Fax: 310-657-8268. Business E-Mail: griffinmd@verizon.net.*

GRIFFIN, BETTY LOU, not-for-profit developer, educator; d. Julius Craven and Rachel Idell Best; m. Jack Wayne Griffin, May 28, 1960; children: Cheryle Louann, Melanie Lynn Young, Penelope Griffin-Cashwell. BS in Elem. Edn. magna cum laude, Campbell U., 1967; ME in Adult and Cmty. Coll. Edn., N.C. State U., 1974; ME in Adminstrn. and Supervision, Fayetteville State U., 1995. Tchr. Sampson County Schs., Clinton, NC, 1965-67, Clinton City Schs., 1967-87; founder, exec. dir. U Care Inc., Sampson County Domestic Violence and Sexual Assault Program, Clinton, 1996—2005; CEO, bd. dirs., exec. dir. On Track Youth Svcs., Clinton, 2000—02. Evening bus. math. instr. Sampson CC, 1973—75, instr., 1975—77; notary pub. State of NC, 1995—2005. Author: Poetry Collection, 1997, Rhyme in Time, 1999, The Princess of High Tides, Vol. I, 2006; contbr. poetry to anthologies, articles to publs. Founder, dir. Sampson County Women's Assembly, 1994, 1996, 1998; legis. chmn., monitor chmn. Youth Adv. Coun., Sampson, 1994—98; founder, pres., exec. dir. Sampson County Coun. Women, 1995—. Named N.C. Dem. Women Poet Laureate, 1997, Sampson County Disting. Woman of the Yr., Sampson County Coun. Women, 1998; recipient Carpathian award, N.C. Equity, 1996. Mem.: DAR U. D.C., N.C. Dem. Women (mem. exec. bd. 1995—99, 1st poet laureate 1997—), Sampson County Dem. Women (v.p. 1993, pres. 1994—95, 2d v.p. 1996—97, pres. 1998—99, 2d v.p. 2000—03, v.p. 2006, 1st v.p. 2006—), Order of Eastern Star, Delta Kappa Gamma. Democrat. Methodist. Avocations: reading, creative writing, arts and crafts, hunting, fishing. Home and Office: 2535 Rosebory Hwy Clinton NC 28328

GRIFFIN, CAMPBELL ARTHUR, JR., retired lawyer; b. Joplin, Mo., July 17, 1929; s. Campbell Arthur and Clara M. (Smith) G.; m. Margaret Ann Adams, Oct. 19, 1958; children: Campbell A., Laura Ann. BA, U. Mo., 1951, MA in Acctg., 1952; JD, U. Tex., 1957. Bar: Tex. 1957. Assoc. Vinson & Elkins, LLP, Houston, 1957-67, ptnr., 1968-92, mgmt. com., 1981-90, mng. ptnr. Dallas, 1986-89. Adj. prof. adminstrv. sci. Jones Grad. Sch. Adminstrn., Rice U., 1992-94. Mem. ofcl. bd. Bethany Christian Ch., Houston, 1962-69, chmn. bd. elders, 1968; bd. dirs. Houston Pops Orch., 1982-87; councilman City of Hunters Creek Village, Tex., 1993-95; pres. Windcliff Property Owners Assn., Estes Park, Colo., 1995-96; bd. dirs. Cornell Cos., Inc. (NYSE), 1996-2000; active St. Martin's Episcopal Ch., Houston. Mem. Houston Bar Assn., State Bar Tex. (bus. law sect. chmn. 1974-75), Tex. Bus Law Found. (chmn. 1988-89, dir. 1988-2000), Houston Racquet Club (dir. 1992-94), St. Charles Bay Hunting Club (sr.), Villa d-Este Condominium Owner's Assn. Inc. (dir. 2004—). Personal E-mail: c.griffinjr@sbcglobal.net.

GRIFFIN, CARLETON HADLOCK, accountant, educator; b. Richmond Heights, Mo., Oct. 30, 1928; s. Merle Leroy and Bernice Hilder Edwards (Nelson) G.; m. Mary Lou Goodrich, Dec. 26, 1953; children: Julia, Anne. BBA, U. Mich., 1950, JD, MBA, U. Mich., 1953. Mem. audit and tax staff Touche Ross & Co., Detroit, 1955-59, adminstrv. partner Denver, 1959-71, nat. tax dir. NYC, 1971-72, nat. dir. ops. and adminstrn., 1972-74, chmn. bd., 1974-82, sr. ptnr., 1982-85, regional ptnr., 1983-85; prof. acctg. U. Mich., 1985-95. Dir. Paton Acctg. Ctr., U. Mich., 1997-2001. Contbr. articles to profl. jours. Sr. warden St. Paul's Episcopal Ch., Darien, Conn., 1979-81; trustee Siena Heights Coll., Adrian, Mich., 1988-2000. Served with Fin. Corps AUS, 1953-55. Mem. AICPA, Colo. Soc. CPAs (pres. 1970-71), N.Y. Soc. CPAs, Mich. Soc. CPAs. Republican.

GRIFFIN, CHRISTINE M., commissioner; b. Boston; Grad., Mass. Maritime Acad., Boston Coll. With U.S. Atty.'s Office, Boston, FDA; atty. advisor US Equal Employment Opportunity Commn., 1995—96, commr., 2006—; exec. dir. Disability Law Ctr., Boston, 1996—2005. Interim pres. Mass. Maritime Acad., 1993—94. Former mem. nat. Social Security Adminstrn. Ticket to Work Advisory Panel, Mass. Devel. Disabilities Coun., Mass. Bd. Higher Edn. Served with US Army. Named one of Lawyers of Yr., Lawyers Weekly USA. Office: EEOC 1801 L St NW Washington DC 20507 Office Phone: 202-663-4900.

GRIFFIN, CLEMENT M., information technology executive; b. Vicksburg, Miss., June 22, 1950; s. Howard Clement and Lena Lucille Griffin; m. Hannah Kay Morris, July 26, 1998; m. Sharon G. Walker, Sept. 7, 1987 (div. Jan. 7, 1995); m. Cynthia Ann Kruithof, Mar. 12, 1978 (div. July 12, 1984); children: Leanna Morris, Jessi Lynn, Damien Brent. Tech. degree in computer programming, Midwest Automation Tng., 1968; BS in Computer Sci., Kennesaw State U., 1995; PhD in Computer Sci., Kennedy Western U., 2002. Sr. sys. technician South Ctrl. Bell Tel. & Telegraph, Vicksburg, Miss., 1974—85; integrated sys. specialist AT&T Comm., Huntsville, Ala., 1986—88; tech. trainer, developer AT&T Computer Sys. Tng., Atlanta, 1988—92; tech. support mgr. AT&T Bell Labs, Alpharetta, Ga., 1992—96; data networking tech. cons. AT&T Bus. Comm. Svcs., Memphis, 1996—99; bus. sys. analyst United Am. of Tenn., Memphis, 1999—2000, dir., 2000—01, v.p., 2001—02; sys. analyst, programmer lead Sedgwick Claims Mgmt. Svcs., Memphis, 2002—05; sr. program analyst Hilton Hotels Corp., Memphis, 2005—07; sr. sales sys. analyst FedEx, Memphis, 2007—. Mem.: Golden Key Nat. Honor Soc. (life), Phi Kappa Phi (life). Avocations: music composition, singing, fishing. Office: FedEx Svcs 3650 Hacks Cross Rd Memphis TN 38125 Office Phone: 901-434-4620. Personal E-mail: clement.griffin@earthlink.net. Business E-Mail: clement.griffin@fedex.com.

GRIFFIN, DAVID, photojournalist; married; 1 child. BA in Visual Comm., Ohio Univ.; grad., Stanford Profl. Pub. Program. Part-time photographer Today's Sunbeam, Salem, NJ, 1972; photographer to graphics editor Columbia Daily Tribune, Mo.; asst. dir. photography Miami Herald; art dir. Hartford (Conn) Courant; art dir., Sunday mag. Inquirer Phila. Inquirer; creative dir. US News & World Report; layout editor to assoc. editor layout and design, to design dir., book divsn. Nat. Geographic, Washington, sr. editor, photography and illustration, 2005—. Named Ohio Newspaper Photographer of Yr., 1978; recipient Nat. Mag. award for Photography, Am. Soc. Mag. Editors, 2007. Mem.: Nat. Press Photographers Assn. (Newspaper Mag. Picture Editor of Yr. 1987, 1988, Newspaper Picture Editor of Yr. Spl. Recognition award 1983). Office: Photography & Illustrations Nat Geographic Soc 1145 17th St NW Washington DC 20036-4688 Office Phone: 800-647-5463.*

GRIFFIN, DIANE EDMUND, research physician, virologist, educator; b. Iowa City, Ia., May 12, 1940; d. Rudolph William and Doris Irene (Swanson) Edmund; m. John Wesley Griffin, June 13, 1965; children: Christopher Todd, Erik Edmund. BA, Augustana Coll., Rock Island, Ill., 1962; MD, Stanford U., 1968, PhD, 1970. Diplomate Am. Bd. Internal Medicine, Am. Bd. Infectious Diseases. Resident in medicine Stanford (Calif.) U. Hosp., 1968-70; fellow Johns Hopkins U. Sch. Medicine, Balt., 1970-73, asst. prof., 1973-79, assoc. prof., 1979-86, prof., 1986—; prof., chair molecular microbiol. immunology dept. Johns Hopkins U. Sch. Pub. Health, 1994—. Investigator Howard Hughes Med. Inst., Balt., 1973-79; mem. virology study sect. NIH, 1982-86; mem. adv. com. Nat. Multiple Sclerosis Soc., 1986-92; mem. microbiology and infectious diseases rsch. adv. com. NIH, 1989-92, chair, 1992-94. Author films and tapes; contbr. chpts. to books, articles to profl. jours. Grantee NIH, 1983—, Nat. Multiple Sclerosis Soc., 1986—, WHO, 1993—, Muscular Dystrophy Assn., 1996—. Fellow Infectious Diseases Soc. Am., AAAS; mem. NAS, Am. Soc. for Clin. Investigation, Am. Soc. for Virology (council 1987-89), Interurban Clin. Club, Inst. Medicine, 2004. Democrat. Lutheran. Avocation: gardening. Office: Bloomberg Sch Pub Health Bldg Ste E 5132 615 N Wolfe St Baltimore MD 21205-2103 Office Phone: 410-955-3459. Office Fax: 410-955-0105. E-mail: dgriffin@jhsph.edu.

GRIFFIN, DOMINIC B., III, state agency administrator; s. Dominic B. Griffin Jr. and Margaret Robinson. With Bank of Hawaii, Hawaii, NY and Pacific Islands, Bank of Am., Malaysia and Hawaii; commr. divsn. fin. instns. Hawaii Dept. Commerce and Consumer Affairs, 2003—. Regulatory chmn. governing bd. Conf. State Bank Suprs. Office: Divsn Fin Instns Dept Commerce and Consumer Affairs PO Box 2054 Honolulu HI 96805 Office Phone: 808-586-2820. Office Fax: 808-586-2818. E-mail: dominic.b.griffin@dcca.hawaii.gov.

GRIFFIN, ELAINE B., educator; b. Westfield, NY; m. Ned Griffin; 3 adopted daughters: Vera, Marie, Marjeena. BA in Am. studies, Barnard Coll., 1969; MLS, U. Calif., Berkeley, 1971. Cert. tchr., Ariz. Head tchr. Akhiok Sch., Alaska, Chiniak Sch., Alaska. Recipient Coun. of Chief State Sch. Officers Tchr. of Yr. award, 1995. Office: Chiniak Sch PO Box 5529 Chiniak AK 99615-5529 Personal E-mail: egriffin@kodiak.k12.ak.us.*

GRIFFIN, ELEANOR, publishing executive, editor; BA in Journalism and Political Sci., U. Ind. Merchandising mgr., So. Living So. Progress Corp., 1977—87, promotions mgr. So. Living and So. Accents mags., 1987—91, creative services dir., So. Living, So. Accents and Travel South, 1991—92, editorial coord. So. Living, 1992—93, exec. editor So. Living Birmingham, 1993—2001, custom Publishing editorial dir., 2001—02, corp. mag. develop., editorial dir., v.p. and editor Cottage Living, 2003—. Office: Southern Progress Corp 2100 Lakeshore Dr Birmingham AL 35209-6721

GRIFFIN, GARY ARTHUR, technological products executive; b. Yonkers, NY, Nov. 23, 1937; s. William Edmund and Madeline G.; m. Jacqueline Cahill, June 21, 1958; children: Lynn, Elizabeth, Margaret. Student, Manhattan Coll., Riverdale, NY, 1956-57, Westchester C.C., 1957-62; diploma, LaSalle Extension U., 1968. Engrng. cons. IBM Corp., Yorktown, NY, 1960-61, Perkin Elmer Corp., Norwalk, Conn., 1961-63; product devel. mgr. Technicon Corp., Tarrytown, NY, 1963-69; chmn., pres. Dynacon Rsch. Corp., Rockland, NY, 1969-72; with Nat. Patent Devel. Corp., New Brunswick, NJ, 1973-82; corp. group v.p. new techs., 1977-82; pres. Hydromed Scis. div. NDP Dental Sys., Inc., NDP Epic Sys., Inc., 1978-82; pres., dir. Amalgamated Fin. Svcs., Inc., 1979-82; v.p., dir. NDP Productos Médicos, S.A., 1979-82; pres., dir. Applied Genetics, Inc., 1981-82; dir. FCS Industries, Inc., Flemington, NJ, 1982-98; sr. v.p. NJ, 1982-87; treas., 1984-87; chmn., COO, pres. Circuitech Inc., Eatontown, NJ, 1982-85; dir., 1985-87; chmn., pres., treas. Executrex Internat., Inc., New Brunswick, NJ, 1985—; chmn., CEO Renaissance Resource Group Ltd., New Brunswick, 2002—. Patentee in field. With USNR, 1954-62. Mem. IEEE, Am. Prodn. and Inventory Control Soc., Am. Mgmt. Assn., Am. Assn. Advancement Med. Instrumentation, Am. Entrepreneurs Assn., Internat. Entrepreneurs Assn., Turnaround Mgmt. Assn., Smithsonian Assocs., N.Y. Vet. Police Assn. Republican. Roman Catholic. Office: Executrex 100 Jersey Ave Bldg D-9 New Brunswick NJ 08901-3200 Office Phone: 732-828-4900. E-mail: ggriffin@ren-consultants.net.

GRIFFIN, GLADYS BOGUES, critical care nurse, educator; b. Elizabeth City, NC, July 18, 1937; d. Matthew Boques and Lucy Griffin Boques Eason; m. Oct. 21, 1957 (div.); children: Terry, Lucy, Misty, Derrick. AAS, Nassau CC, NY, 1972. RN, N.C.; cert. ACLS. Nurse Long Beach (N.Y.) Meml. Hosp., 1968-70, staff nurse team leader, 1972-75, head nurse, 1975-76; staff nurse critical care unit Albemarle Hosp., Elizabeth City, 1976-78, staff nurse , then coord. surg. intensive care unit, 1978—; BLS instr., head nurse surg. intensive care, 1981-87. Parish nurse Bethel AME Zion Ch., Elizabeth City, 1993-; pub. spkr. health related topics, Long Beach and Elizabeth City; facilitator cancer support group, N.E. NC. Featurered Life Styles of Elizabeth City. Mem. adv. bd. Nursing Homes. Recipient Glowing Lamp for Nurse award Chi Eta Phi, 2000, NC award outstanding vol. svc. Pasquotank County, 2003, Black Pearls award in arts and sci. Nat. Coun. Negro Women, 2006; named one of Disting. Women NC, 1989. Mem. Am. Assn. Critical Care Nurses, ARC Nurses, Soc. Notary Pub., NAFE, N.Y. Nurses Assn. Democrat. Avocations: reading, bowling, playing guitar, Bingo. Home: 616 Crooked Run Rd Elizabeth City NC 27909-7538

GRIFFIN, HENRY CLAUDE, retired chemistry professor; b. Greenville, SC, Feb. 14, 1937; s. Arthur Gwynn and Christa Lou (Wilson) G.; m. Barbara Jean Pierson, Sept. 3, 1960; children: Gwen Griffin Van Ark, Lyle Griffin Warshauer. BS, Davidson Coll., 1958; PhD, MIT, 1962. Instr. math. New Prep. Sch., Cambridge, Mass., 1960-61; rsch. assoc. Argonne Nat. Lab., Lemont, Ill., 1962-64, guest scientist, 1964-70; asst. prof. chemistry U. Mich., Ann Arbor, 1964-70, assoc. prof., 1970-89, prof., 1989—2005, prof. emeritus, 2005. Vis. scientist Swiss Fed. Reactor Inst., Wurenlingen, 1971-72; vis. rsch. engr. U. Calif., Berkeley, 1978-79; chairperson senate assembly U. Mich., 1993-94; dir. nuc. studies Environ. Rsch. Group, Ann Arbor, 1980-81. Inventor process for separation of Na-22. Mem. AAAS, Am. Chem. Soc. (chairperson steering com. Ctrl. region 1994-95), Am. Phys. Soc. Home: 1410 Harbrooke Ave Ann Arbor MI 48103-3618 Office: Univ Mich Dept Chemistry 930 N University Ave Ann Arbor MI 48109-1055 Home Phone: 734-994-3499; Office Phone: 734-764-1438. Business E-Mail: hcg@umich.edu.

GRIFFIN, J. TIMOTHY, air transportation executive; Grad., Fla. Atlantic U.; M, U. Wash. With Am. Airlines; sr. v.p. schedules and pricing Continental Airlines; sr. v.p. market planning and systems NW Airlines Corp., Minn., 1993—99, exec. v.p. mktg. & distbn., 1999—. Office: NW Airlines Corp 2700 Lone Oak Pky Eagan MN 55121 Office Phone: 612-726-2111.*

GRIFFIN, JAMES ANTHONY, bishop; b. Fairview Park, Ohio, June 13, 1934; s. Thomas Anthony and Margaret Mary (Hanousek) Griffin. BA, Borromeo Coll., 1956; JCL magna cum laude, Pontifical Lateran U., Rome, 1963; JD summa cum laude, Cleve. State U., 1972; DHL (hon.), Ohio Dominican Coll., 1994; DD (hon.), Ohio No. U., 2007. Priest Roman Cath. Ch., 1960. Bishop Roman Cath. Ch., 1979; assoc. pastor St. Jerome Ch., Cleve., 1960—61; sec.-notary Cleve. Diocesan Tribunal, 1963—65; asst. chancellor Diocese of Cleve., 1965—68, vice chancellor, 1968—73, chancellor, 1973—78, vicar gen., 1978—79; pastor St. William Ch., Euclid, Ohio, 1978—79; aux. bishop Diocese of Cleve., vicar of western region Lorain, Ohio, 1979—83; bishop Diocese of Columbus, Ohio, 1983—2004; disting. prof. theology Ohio Dominican U., 2005—07, interim pres., 2007—. Mem clergy rels. bd. Diocese Cleve., 1972—75, mem clergy retirement bd., 1973—78, mem clergy pers. bd., 1979—83; disting. prof. theology Ohio Dominican U., 2005—; Griffin chair in canon law Pontifical Coll. Josephinium, 2005. Author (with A. J. Quinn): (book) Thoughts for Our Times, 1969, Thoughts for Sowing, 1970; author: (with others) Ashes from the Cathedral, 1974, Sackcloth and Ashes, 1976, The Priestly Heart, 1983, Reflections on the Law of Love, 1991, Summary of the New Catholic Catechism, 1994, A Lenten Walk, 1998; author: They Were There, 2004, Easter Joy, 2007. Chmn. bd. govs. N. Am. Coll., Rome, 1984—88; co-chair Columbus Cmty. Rels. Comn., 1992—95; mem Am's Promise, Columbus, 1997—2001, Columbus Coalition Domestic Violence, 2001—04; mem. adv. coun. Cmty. Shelter Bd., 2001—04; mem. adv. team Cmtys. in Sch., 2002—04; chmn. Mayor's Coun Youth, 1986—90; trustee St Mary Sem, 1976—78; bd. dirs., mem pension comt Cath Cemeteries Assn., 1978—83; vice-chancellor Pontifical Col. Josephinum, 1983—2004; treas. Cath. Relief Svc. Bd., 1988—91, pres., 1991—96; bd. dirs. Holy Family Cancer Home, 1973—78, Meals on Wheels, Euclid, 1978—79, Franklin County United Way, 1984—90. Decorated Knight of the Holy Sepulchre; recipient Human Rights award, Anti-Defamation League B'nai B'rith, 1987, Jessing award, Pontifical Coll., 1993, Gov's award, State of Ohio, 1994, Don Bosco medal, 1997, NG Minuteman award, 1999, Cmty. Svc. award, Columbus Urban League, 1999, Bronze Pelican award, Cath. Boy Scouts, 2002, Charity Newsies award, 2002, St. Thomas More award, 2004, Croiser award, Cath. Found. Columbus, 2005. Mem.: Columbus Bar Assn. (chmn. jud. advt. com. 1987—91, Liberty Bell award 1989), Am. Canon Law. Soc. Roman Catholic. Achievements include Griffin chair in canon law established Pontifical College Josephinum 2005.

GRIFFIN, JEAN LATZ, political strategist, writer, publisher; b. Joliet, Ill., Mar. 6, 1943; d. Carl Joseph and Helene Monica (Bradshaw) Latz; m. Dennis Joseph Griffin, Sept. 16, 1967; children: Joseph, Timothy, Peter. BS in Chemistry, Coll. St. Francis, Joliet, 1965; MS in Journalism, U. Wis., 1967. Clin. investigation coord. Baxter Labs., 1967-68; reporter Joliet Herald News, 1968-70, Raleigh (N.C.) Times, 1974-75, Suburban Trib, Hinsdale, Ill., 1976-78, regional edn. reporter, 1978-82; gen. assignment reporter Chgo. Tribune, 1982-84, edn. writer, 1984-88, pub. health writer, 1988-94, govt., politics, and pub. policy reporter, 1994-97, econ. devel. reporter, 1997; strategist The Strategy Group, Chgo., 1998—; owner CyberINK, 1998—. Adj. journalism instr. Roosevelt U., Chgo., 2001—; facilitator U. Phoenix, 2004—. Author: One Spirit, 2006, In The Same Breath, 2006, (DVD) One Spirit, 2007. Bd. dirs. Residents for Emergency Shelter, Chgo., 1978-82, Genesis House, Chgo., 1995-98, vol. cook, 1994-98; devel. com. mem. Hope Now, Inc., 1998-00; membership chair Arlington Hts. C. of C., 2001-02; vol. Taoist Tai Chi instr., 2001-; pres. Taoist Tai Chi Soc.-Midwest, 2005-. Recipient Writing award Am. Dental Assn., 1969, Alumna Profl. Achievement award Coll. St. Francis, Joliet, 1985, First Prize in ednl. writing Edn. Writers Am., 1986, Grand prize, 1988, Benjamin Fine award Nat. Assn. Secondary Sch. Prins., 1988, Edward Scott Beck award for reporting Chgo. Tribune, 1988, Peter Lisagor award for pub. svc. Soc. Profl. Journalists, Chgo. chpt., 1988, Mark of Excellence Chgo. Assn. Black Journalists, 1992, Cushing award for Journalistic Excellence, Chgo. Dental Soc., 1992, Human First award Horizon Cmty. Svcs., Chgo., 1993, Robert F. Kennedy Grand Prize in Journalism, 1994, Editl. Excellence award Ill. Merchandising Coun., 1994; finalist Pulitzer Prize, 1994. Mem. Taoist Tai Chi Soc. USA-Ill. (pres. 2003-05). Office: CyberINK 621 N Belmont Ave Arlington Heights IL 60004 Office Phone: 847-506-4214. Personal E-mail: jlgrif@earthlink.net. *Keep climbing mountains. Invent challenges if you have to. Love all life--amoeba to stars. Dive into the flow of the universe. And wash your dishes when you're done.*

GRIFFIN, JEFFREY FARROW, surgeon; b. Dallas, 1946; MD, Tulane U., 1974. Diplomate Am. Bd. Surgery, Am. Bd. Colon and Rectal Surgery. Intern Ochsner Found. Hosp., New Orleans, 1974-75, resident in gen. surgery, 1975-79; fellow in colon and rectal surgery U. Minn., Mpls., 1979-80; now pvt. practice New Orleans. Mem. staff East Jefferson Gen. Hosp., Metairie, La., So. Bapt. Hosp., La.; clin. asst. prof. medicine Tulane U. Mem. ACS, Am. Soc. Colon and Rectal Surgery. Office: 4429 Clara St Ste 600 New Orleans LA 70115-6951 Mailing: 4224 Houma Blvd Ste 540 Metairie LA 70006

GRIFFIN, JO ANN THOMAS, retired financial planner, tax specialist; b. Dallas, July 20, 1933; d. John Baxton and Joan Marion (Ament) Thomas; m. John Barrett Brown, June 29, 1963 (div. 1972); children: John Barrett Jr., Daniel Thomas; m. Thomas Reese Griffin, Jan. 25, 1976; stepchildren: Gregory Crawford, Kevin Bradley. BA, U. Miss., 1955; BS magna cum laude, Lamar U., Beaumont, Tex., 1964; MEd, U. Del., Newark, 1972. CFP; enrolled agt. U.S. Treasury Dept. Site mgr. Motivational Ctr., Inc., Wilmington, Del., 1976-78; asst. dir. Indochinese social svcs. Assoc. Cath. Charities, New Orleans, 1978-79; dir. continuing edn. St. Mary's Dominican Coll., New Orleans, 1979-80; with fin. mgmt. USDA, New Orleans, 1981; tax auditor IRS, New Orleans, Phila., Del., 1981-86, revenue agt. Wilmington, 1987-92; tax specialist Horty & Horty, CPA's, Wilmington, 1986-87; quality control H&R Block, Wilmington, 1992-94; counselor

Svc. Corps Ret. Execs., Wilmington, 1992—96; dir. Wilmington River-City Com., 1997-2000. Docent Winterthur, New Orleans Mus. Art, Wilmington and New Orleans, 1966—85; sustaining mem., advisor Jr. League, Wilmington, 1989—92, 1998—2000, mem. cmty. adv. bd., 1998—2000; regent Vieux Carre chpt. DAR, New Orleans, 1984; bd. dirs. Neighborhood Watch, New Orleans, 1983—85, Waterfront Coalition, Inc., 1998—2000; sec., mem. exec. bd. Henrietta Johnson Med. Ctr., 1998—2001, mem. adv. coun., 2007—; treas., exec. bd. Civil War Round Table Wilmington, Inc., 1999—2002; bd. dirs. Common Cause Del., 2000—, Del. Medicare and Medicaid Fraud Project, 2000—; CASA vol. Family Ct., State of Del., 2000—01; pres. Wilmington chpt. Nat. Assn. Ret. Fed. Employees, 2001—03; lay reader, mem. outreach com. Episc. Ch. Diocese of Del., Wilmington, 1971—2000. Recipient Grad. Scholarship award AAUW, 1971, Sustained Superior Performance award IRS, New Orleans, 1984, Spl. Achievement awards IRS, Wilmington, 1988, 89, Customer Svc. awards, 1989, 90. Mem. Am. Soc. Women Accts. (sec. 1986-89), Del. Valley Soc. CFPs, Wilmington Tax Group, Estate Planning Coun. Del., Wilmington Women in Bus., Rotary, Blue and Gold Club, Mortar Bd., Phi Kappa Phi, Delta Delta Delta. Democrat. Mem. Soc. Friends. Home: 900 N Broom St Unit 16 Wilmington DE 19806-4546

GRIFFIN, JOHN W., neurologist, medical educator; b. Nebr. BA, Grinnell Coll., 1963; MD, Stanford U., 1968. Cert. Am. Bd. Psychiatry and Neurology. Internship Internal Medicine Stanford U. Hosp., 1968—69, resident, 1969—70; resident Neurology Johns Hopkins Hosp., 1970—73; clin. assoc. Med. Neurology Branch NINDS, NIH, 1973—75; asst. prof. Dept. Neurology Johns Hopkins U., Sch. Medicine, Baltimore, 1975—79, assoc. prof., 1979—86, dir. Peripheral Nerve Labs., 1986—, prof. Dept. Neurology and Neuroscience, 1986—, chair, Neurologist-in-Chief, 1998—, prof. Dept. Pathology, 1999—. Hon. prof. Neurology Hebei Med. Coll., Second Tchg. Hosp., Shijiazhuang, China, 1993; hon. attending physician Hebei Province Min. Health, 1995. Editl. bd. Neurotoxicology, 1982—93, Muscle and Nerve, 1987—91, 1998—2001, Neuromuscular Disorders, 1990—94, editor-in-chief Nature Clin. Practice: Neurology. Recipient Frank R. Ford Tchg. Award, Dept. Neurology, Johns Hopkins U. Sch. Medicine, 1986, Jacob K. Javits Award, Nat. Insts. Neurological Diseases and Stroke, NIH, 1987. Mem.: Inst. Medicine, Soc. Experimental Neuropathlogy, Soc. Neuroscience, Nat. Adv. Neurological Disorders and Stroke (coun. 1999—), Soc. Experimental Neuropathology (pres. 1993—95), Am. Neurological Assn. (pres. elect 2001—03), Am. Acad. Neurology, Alpha Omega Alpha, Phi Beta Kappa. Office: Dept Neurology Johns Hopkins Hosp Meyer Bldg Rm 6-113 600 N Wolfe St Baltimore MD 21287 E-mail: jgriffi@jhmi.edu.

GRIFFIN, JOHNNY LEE, military officer; s. Eula Gines; m. Melissa Copeland, July 2, 1994; children: Jezell Latrice, Jevontez Levell. BA, Touro U. Internat., Cypress, 2004, BS in Human Resource, 2007. Logistic mgmt. officer US Army, Fort Campbell, Ky., 2001—. Logistic mgr. US Army, 1988—. Chief warrant officer US Army, 2001—07, Fort Campbell, Kentucky. Decorated Bronze Star, Army Accomendation(7), AAM(4), Good Conduct Medal(4) US Army. Office: US Army Fort Campbell Fort Campbell KY 42223 Home Phone: 931-217-0059; Office Phone: 931-626-8441. Business E-Mail: johnny.griffin@us.army.mil.

GRIFFIN, KATHY, comedienne, actress; b. Oak Park, Ill., Nov. 4, 1966; d. John and Maggie Griffin; m. Matthew Moline, Feb. 18, 2001 Studied acting, Lee Strasberg Inst. Actress playing Vicki Groener on Suddenly Susan NBC-TV, 1996—. Actor (films) The Unborn, 1991, Shakes the Clown, 1992, It's Pat, 1994, Pulp Fiction, 1994, Courting Courtney, 1995, Four Rooms, 1995, The Cable Guy, 1996, Trojan War, 1997, Can't Stop Dancing, 1999, Dill Scallion, 1999, Muppets From Space, 1999, (voice only) Lion of Oz, 2000, The Intern, 2000, On Edge, 2001, (voice) Dinotopia: Quest for the Ruby Sunstone, 2005, Her Minor Thing, 2005, Bachelor Party Vegas, 2006; (TV movies) The Barefoot Executive, 1995, A Diva's Christmas Carol, 2000; (TV series) Saturday Night Special, 1996, Suddenly Susan, 1996-2000, (voice) Dilbert, 1999-2000; (TV appearances) ER, 1994, Caroline in the City, 1995, Comedy Central, 1995, Mad About You, 1995, Seinfeld, 1996, Partners, 1996, (TV spls.) HBO Comedy Half-Hour: Kathy Griffin, 1996, The VH1 Fashion Awards, 1996; actor, exec. prodr. (TV series) My Life on the D-List, 2005-. Office: United Talent Agy 9560 Wilshire Blvd Ste 500 Beverly Hills CA 90212

GRIFFIN, KEITH BROADWELL, retired economics professor; b. Colon, Panama, Nov. 6, 1938; came to U.S., 1988; s. Marcus Samuel Griffin and Elaine Ann (Broadwell) Fabick; m. Dixie Beth, Apr. 2, 1956; children: Janice, Kimberley. BA, Williams Coll., 1960, DLitt (hon.), 1980; PhB, Oxford U., Eng., 1962, PhD, 1965. Fellow and tutor in econs. Magdalen Coll. Oxford (Eng.) U., 1965-76, fellow Magdalen Coll., 1977-79, pres., 1979-88, hon. fellow, 1988; acting warden, dir. Queen Elizabeth House, Inst. Commonwealth Studies, 1973, 77-78, warden, dir., 1978-79; prof. U. Calif., Riverside, 1988—2004, chmn. dept. econs., 1988-93, Presdl. prof., 1988-90, Disting. prof., 1997—2004. Vis. prof. Inst. Econs. and Planning U. Chile, 1962-63, 64-65; chmn. bd. UN Rsch. Inst. for Social Devel., 1988-95, sr. cons., 1971-72; mem. UN com. for devel. planning, 1987-94; mem. coun. UN Univ., 1986-92, chmn. fin. and budget com., 1988-90; mem. Marshall Aid Commemoration Commn., 1984-88; mem. World Commn. on Culture and Devel., 1994-95; chief ILO Employment Adv. Mission to Ethiopia, 1982; econ. advisor Govt. of Bolivia, 1989-91; pres. Devel. Studies Assn., U.K., 1978-80; chief rural and urban employment policies br. ILO, 1975-76; cons. ILO on rural devel. in Ecuador, 1974; sr. adviser OECD Devel. Centre, Paris, 1986-91; adviser to Inter-Am. Com. for Alliance for Progress on copper expansion programme in Chile, 1968, to FAO/ICO/IBRD World Coffee Study in Guatemala, El Salvador and Colombia, 1967; rsch. advisor Pakistan Inst. Devel. Econs., Karachi, 1965, 70; expert on agrl. planning to Govt. of Algeria, acting chief FAO Mission, Algiers, 1963-64; cons. IBRD on land reform in Morocco, 1973; head UN Devel. Program Poverty Alleviation Mission to Mongolia, 1994; head ILO Social Policy Rev. Mission to Uzbekis, 1995; cons. on econ. reform in Vietnam, UNDP, 1997; head ILO Employment and Social Protection Mission to Kazakstan, 1997; head UNDP mission to Mongolia, 2001, Armenia, 2002; leader UNDP program evaluation team in China, 2004-05. Author: Underdevelopment in Spanish America, 1969, 2d edit., 1971, Spanish edit., 1972, The Green Revolution: An Economic Analysis, 1972, The Political Economy of Agrarian Change, 1974, 2d edit., 1979, Spanish edit., 1982, Hindi edit., 1983, Land Concentration and Rural Poverty, 1976, 2d edit., 1981, Spanish edit., 1983, International Inequality and National Poverty, 1978, Spanish edit., 1984, World Hunger and the World Economy, 1987, Alternative Strategies for Economic Development, 1989, 2d edit., 1999, Chinese edit., 1992, Studies in Globalization and Economic Transitions, 1996, Studies in Development Strategy and Systemic Transformation, 2000; co-author: Comercio Internacional y Politicas de Desarrollo Economico, 1967, Planning Development, 1970, Spanish edit., 1975, The Transition to Egalitarian Development, 1981, Globalization and the Developing World, 1992, Implementing a Human Development Strategy, 1994; editor: Financing Development in Latin America, 1971, Institutional Reform and Economic Development in the Chinese Countryside, 1984, The Economy of Ethiopia, 1992, Poverty and the Transition to a Market Economy in Mongolia, 1995, Social Policy and Economic Transformation in Uzbekistan, 1996, Economic Reform in Vietnam, 1998, Poverty Reduction in Mongolia, 2003; co-editor: Ensayos Sobre Planificacion, 1967, Growth and Inequality in Pakistan, 1972, The Economic Development of Bangladesh, 1974, Human Development and the International Development Strategy for the 1990s, 1990, The Distribution of Income in China, 1993, also numerous articles. Vis. fellow Oxford Ctr. Islamic Studies, 1998. Fellow: AAAS. Avocation: travel. Office: Univ Calif Dept Econs Riverside CA 92521-0001 Home: 24870 SW Mountain Rd West Linn OR 97068 Personal E-mail: keithdixiegriffin@verizon.net.

GRIFFIN, KELLY ANN, public relations executive, consultant; b. Buffalo, May 20, 1964; d. Michael Gerald and Patricia Frances (Lippert) G.; m. Thomas Richard Kleinberger, Oct. 11, 1992. B in Polit. Sci., SUNY, Geneseo, 1986; postgrad., CUNY, Bklyn., 1994—96. Legis. asst. to N.Y. State Assembly Spkrs. Stanley Fink and Mel Miller, Buffalo, 1986-87; acct. exec. Griffin Media Group, NYC, 1987-88, acct. supr., v.p., 1988-90, pres., CEO, 1990-94; pub. rels. cons. NYC, 1994—. Assoc. dir. N.Y. State Funeral Dirs. Assn., N.Y.C., 1992-94, Met. Funeral Dirs. Assn., N.Y.C., 1992-94, County Execs. of Am., N.Y.C. and Washington, 1993-2000; dep. exec. dir. County Execs. Am., 2000—; instr. remedial reading Cornell U. Sch. Industry/Lab. Rels., Buffalo, 1987; v.p. Fairfield Owners Cooperative, Riverdale, 1996-2000. Editor N.Y. State AFL-CIO Unity, 1988-90, County Execs. News, 1993—, N.Y. State Funeral Dirs. Assn./Met. Funeral Dirs. Assn. News, 1992-94, Amalgamated Transit Union News, 1988-90. Cons. Interfaith Assembly on Homelessness, N.Y.C., 1994-97, Voter Assistance Commn., N.Y.C., 1990-92; participant, cons. Erie County Dem. Party, Buffalo, 1985-87; mem. assocs. steering com. Children's Health Fund, N.Y.C., 1991-97; bd. dirs. Kingsbridge Hts. Cmty. Ctr., Bronx, 1999-2005, sec., 2000-01, chair, 2001-04; mem. Parents' Assn., Frances Schervier Home and Hosp. Childcare Ctr., Bronx, 1997-2000, Support Our Schs. Com., Bronx, 1999-2000; class parent Prospect Hill Sch. PTA, Pelham Manor, 2001-05, rec. sec., 2003-04, pres.-elect, 2004-05, pres., 2005-06, v.p. fundraising, 2006—; mem. fundraising com. Transition Learning Ctr., New Rochelle, N.Y.; mem. citizens nominating com. Pelham, N.Y., 2006—. Recipient Acad. award DAR, 1978. Mem. PTA (rep. Pelham coun. 2006—), Pub. Rels. Soc. N.Y.C., The Manor Club (Pelham Manor, N.Y.), N.Y. Athletic Club. Roman Catholic. Avocations: reading, running, yoga, ice skating, tennis. Home: 1061 Hunter Ave Pelham NY 10803-3409 Office: Griffin Media Group Ste 910 1100 H St Washington DC 20005 Office Phone: 800-296-8438. E-mail: kgrif@optonline.net.

GRIFFIN, KENNETH C., investment company executive; b. Boca Raton, Fl. m. Anne Dias. BA in Economics, Harvard U., 1989. With Glenwood Investment Corp.; founder, pres, CEO Citadel Investment Group, 1990—. Bd. trustees Chgo. Museum Contemporary Art, Art Inst. Chgo.; bd. dirs. Chgo. Public Education Fund, 2003—, Chgo. Public Library Found. Named one of Forbes' Richest Americans, 2006; named to Top 200 Collectors, ARTnews mag., 2004, 2006. Avocation: Collector of Imprssionism and Post-Impressionism Art. Office: Citadel Investment Group LLC 131 S Dearborn St Chicago IL 60603 Office Phone: 312-395-2100. Office Fax: 312-368-1348.*

GRIFFIN, LEANN CREASY, science educator; d. Larry E. and Elsie Marie Creasy; m. LaWon Jerome Griffin, Dec. 31, 1999. BS in sci. edn., math. edn., Pensacola Christian Coll., Fla., 1996. Tchr. math, sci., computer Bensalem Bapt. Sch., Pa., 1996—98, Landmark Christian Sch., Fairburn, Ga., 1998—. Cheerleading coach Landmark Christian Sch., Fairburn, 1998—, head dept. sci., 2005—. Mem.: NSTA. Conservative. Baptist. Avocations: hiking, reading. Home Phone: 770-577-7075; Office Phone: 770-306-0647.

GRIFFIN, MARTIN P.A., research scientist; s. Darice Crawford Griffin; m. Joanna Deborah Tober, Sept. 1, 2002; children: Noah Matthew children: Maya Jessamine. BA, Lawrence U., Appleton, Wis., 1997; M of Biology, Boston U., 1999. Rsch. asst. Smithsonian Tropical Rsch. Inst., Balboa, Panama, Panama, 1996—97; fisheries biologist Marine Rsch., Inc., Falmouth, Mass., 1998—2000; marine edn. program mgr. OceanQuest, Inc, Woods Hole, Mass., 1999—2000; fisheries biologist Wis. Dept. Natural Resources, Madison, 2000—01, natural resources rsch. scientist, 2001—07, statewide waterway science, policy leader, 2007—. Editor: Wetland Restoration Handbook for Wisconsin Landowners, 2d edit., 2004 (Nat. Notable Govt. Document Award, 2004), Wisconsin Citizen Lakes Manual, 2005 (Wis. Disting. Document award, 2005); contbr. articles to profl. jours. Asst. soccer coach Madison East HS, Wis., 2006. Mem.: Am. Fisheries Soc. (comm. chmn. 2005—, mem. Wis. chpt., North Ctrl. Divsn. Best Chpt. Newsletter 2005). Office: Wis Dept Natural Resources 101 S Webster St Madison WI 53707 Business E-Mail: martinp.griffin@wisconsin.gov.

GRIFFIN, MICHAEL D., federal agency administrator, aerospace scientist; b. Aberdeen, Md., 1949; BS, Johns Hopkins U., MS in applied physics; MS in aerospace sci., Cath. U.; MS in elec. engring., U. So. Calif.; MS in civil engring., George Washington U.; MBA, Loyola Coll.; PhD in aerospace engring., U. Md. Registered engr., Md., Calif. With Computer Scis. Corp., Jet Propulsion Lab.; dep. for tech. Strategic Defense Initiative Orgn., 1986—91; chief engr., assoc adminstr. for exploration NASA, Washington, DC, 1991—94; sr. v.p. program devel. Space Industries Internat., gen. mgr. Houston; exec. v.p., chief tech. officer Orbital Scis. Corp., Dulles, Va., 1995—2002; pres., COO In-Q-Tel, Arlington, Va., 2002—04; head Space Dept. Applied Physics Lab., Johns Hopkins U., Laurel, Md., 2004—05; adminstr. NASA, 2005—. Adj. prof. U. Md., Johns Hopkins U., George Washington U. Author: (textbook) Space Vehicle Design. Recipient Exceptional Achievement Medal, NASA, Disting. Pub. Svc. Medal, Dept. Defense. Fellow: Am. Astronautical Soc., AIAA (Space Sys. Medal); mem.: NAE, IEEE, Internat. Acad. Astronautics. Avocations: golf, flying, skiing, scuba diving, amateur radio. Office: NASA Two Independence Sq 300 E St NW Rm 9F44 Washington DC 20546*

GRIFFIN, MICHAEL DANIEL, investment counselor; b. New Haven, May 26, 1939; s. Michael F. G. and Mae S. (Griffin); m. Alice N. Griffin, June 15, 1963; children: Michael S., Peter G., Geoffrey S. BA, Yale U., 1960; MBA, Columbia U., 1962. Chartered fin. analyst. With Scudder Stevens & Clark, NYC, 1963-90, gen. ptnr., 1969-85, mng. dir., 1985-90, also dir.; chmn. Chatham Assocs. of N.Y., NYC, 1990—. Bd. govs. Lawrence Hosp., Bronxville, N.Y., 1979— , treas., 1982-88; pres., dir. Bronxville Community Fund, 1975-79; mem. Bd. Zoning Appeals, Bronxville, 1980-87, chmn., 1985-87. Mem. Investment Counsel Assn. Am. (v.p., bd. govs.) Office: Money-Media Inc 1430 Broadway 12th Fl New York NY 10018

GRIFFIN, MICHAEL F., lawyer; b. 1954; AB magna cum laude, Dartmouth Coll., 1976; JD cum laude, NYU, 1980. Bar: NY 1981. Assoc. Townley & Updike, 1980—88, ptnr., 1989—95; ptnr., corp group Dorsey & Whitney LLP, NYC, 1995—2005, and chmn, hedge fund practice group; ptnr., corp., securities group Arnold & Porter LLP, NYC, 2005—. Mem.: ABA, Managed Funds Assn., Futures Industry Assn., Assn. Bar City NY, Order of Coif. Office: Arnold & Porter LLP 399 Park Ave New York NY 10022-4690 Office Phone: 212-715-1136. Office Fax: 212-715-1399. Business E-Mail: Michael.Griffin@aporter.com.

GRIFFIN, PENNI ONCKEN, social worker, educator; b. Cedar Rapids, Iowa, Nov. 11, 1945; d. Edward Charles and Rita Margaret Oncken; m. Walt Griffin, Dec. 6, 1980; children: Rebecca, Kathleen, Shawn, Megan. BA, Coe Coll., 1970; MSW, U. Cin., 1992. LMSW S.C. Lead social worker Iowa Dept. Social Svcs., Cedar Rapids, 1975—79; dir. homemaker svcs. Family Svc. Agy., Cedar Rapids, 1979—80; investigator protective svcs. Iowa Dept. Social Svcs., Waterloo, 1982—89; med. social worker S.C. Dept. Health and Environ. Control, 1992—95; asst. prof. Limestone Coll., Gaffney, SC, 1995—, dir. social work program, 1995—2002, asst. dean, dir. Social Work Program, 2002—06. Founding bd. dir. LinnHaven Home Retarded Adults, Cedar Rapids, 1976—78; mem. adv. bd. Make Today Count, Cedar Rapids, 1976—79, Cherokee County Alcohol and Drug Abuse Commn., Gaffney, SC, 2001—05. Chmn. fin. Linn County Dems., Cedar Rapids, 1979—80, Steve Sovern U.S. Congress, Cedar Rapids, 1980; bd. dirs. Gaffney (S.C.) Little Theatre, 1994—2001. Mem.: NASW, Internat. Assn. Social Workers, Social Work Baccalaureate Program Dirs., Coun. Social Work Edn. Democrat. Avocations: reading, travel. Home: 1008 College Drive Gaffney SC 29340 Office: Limestone College 1115 College Drive Gaffney SC 29340 Office Phone: 864-488-4526. Business E-Mail: pgriffin@limestone.edu.

GRIFFIN, RICHARD ALLEN, federal judge; b. Traverse City, Mich., 1952; m. Christine Griffin; 3 children. BA magna cum laude, We. Mich. U., 1973; JD, U. Mich., 1977. Bar: Mich. 1977. Law clk. to Hon. Ross W. Campbell Mich. Ct. Appeals (23rd cir.), 1975—77; assoc. Williams, Coulter, Cunningham, Davison & Read, 1977—81; ptnr. Coulter, Cunningham, Davison & Read, 1981—85; founder, ptnr. Read & Griffin, Traverse City, Mich., 1985—88; judge Mich. Ct. Appeals, 1989—2005, US Ct. Appeals (6th cir.), 2005—. Chmn. Long Lake Twp. Bldg. Authority, 1987—88. Office: US Ct Appeals 540 Potter Stewart Courthouse 100 E Fifth St Cincinnati OH 45202 Business E-Mail: ca06-griffin_chambers@ca6.uscourts.gov.*

GRIFFIN, RICHARD J., federal agency administrator; b. Chgo., Oct. 9, 1949; m. Mary Jean Lang; three children. B in Econs., Xavier U., 1971; grad., Nat. War Coll., 1983; MBA, Marymount U., 1984, PhD (hon.), 2004. Agt. U.S. Secret Svc., US Dept. Treasury, Chgo., 1971, agt. in charge LA, dep. asst. dir. Office of Investigations, asst. dir. protective ops., dep. dir.; insp. gen. US Dept. Vets. Affairs, Washington, 1997—2005; asst. sec. (diplomatic security) US Dept. State, Washington, 2005—, dir. Office Fgn. Missions, 2005—. Office: US Dept State 2201 C St NW Rm 6316 Washington DC 20520

GRIFFIN, ROBERT H., career military officer; b. Atlanta, Oct. 4, 1947; BS in Mech. Engring., Auburn U., MS in Geotech. Engring.; MBA, Long Island U.; grad., U.S. Army War Coll., Army Command/Gen. Staff Coll. Registered profl. engr., Va. Commd. 2d lt. U.S. Army, advanced through grades to major gen.; served in Dharan, Saudi Arabia; chief of staff US Army CE, Washington, comdr. & divsn. engr. Northwestern divsn. Portland, Oreg., 1997—99, comdr. & divsn. engr. Great Lakes/Ohio River Divsn. Cincinnati, Ohio, 1999—2001, dir. civil works program, 2001—03, dep. chief of engineers, dep. commdg. gen. Washington, 2003—. Chair U.S. section Internat. St. Lawrence River Bd. of Control, 1999—. Decorated Legion of Merit with oak lead cluster, Bronze Star medal, Meritorious Svc. medal with three oak leaf clusters, Army Commendation medal, Army Achievement medal.

GRIFFIN, ROBERT THOMAS, automotive company executive; b. Somerville, Mass., July 3, 1917; s. Michael and Cecelia (Rourke) G.; m. Mary Ellen Mulcahy, Sept. 10, 1960; children: Mary Catherine, Christiane Marie, Justine Dufresne, Joseph Michael. BS, Boston Coll., 1939; MA in Pub. Adminstrn, Boston U., 1954; postgrad., Harvard U. Grad. Sch. Pub. Adminstrn., 1954-55. Regional mgr. War Assets Adminstrn., 1946-49; with GSA, Washington, 1950-56, 58-80, spl. asst. to adminstr., 1961-62, asst. adminstr., 1962-70, asst. commr. property mgmt., 1970-73; spl. asst. to adminstr. for coordination John F. Kennedy Library, 1973-77, acting adminstr., 1977—; dep. adminstr. GSA, 1977-78; sr. advisor Pres.'s Spl. Trade Rep., White House, 1977-78; sr. advisor to Personal Rep. of Pres. to Middle East Negotiations, White House, 1978-80. Staff exec. to pres. Chrysler Corp., 1980—; dir. Van Pool Services, Inc.; mem. Pres.'s Inflation Task Force, 1978-79; conferee White House Conf. Natural Beauty, 1964, Pres.'s Fed. Agy. Task Force on Cost Reduction, 1965; adminstrv. cons. Govt. of Iran, 1956-58; mem. Pres.'s Com. Minority Enterprise. Bd. dirs. Hamlet Citizens Assn., Chevy Chase, Md., 1981—, John F. Kennedy Libr., 1991— (dir. emeritus). Served with USCGR, 1943-46. Mem. Am. Soc. Pub. Adminstrn., DAV Clubs: Washington Athletic, Columbia Country. Office: 1100 Connecticut Ave NW Washington DC 20036-4101

GRIFFIN, RONALD CHARLES, law educator; b. Washington, Aug. 17, 1943; s. Roy John and Gwendolyn (Points) Griffin; m. Vicky Tredway, Nov. 26, 1967; children: David Ronald, Jason Roy, Meg Carrington. BS, Hampton Inst., 1965; JD, Howard U., 1968; LLM, U. Va., 1974. Bar: DC 1970, US Supreme Ct. 1973, Kans. 1986. Asst. corp. counsel Govt. of D.C., 1970; asst. prof. law U. Oreg., 1974-78; assoc. prof. law Washburn U., Topeka, 1978-81, prof. law, 1981—. Vis. prof. U. Notre Dame, 1981—82; vis. scholar Queen's U., Kingston, Ont., Canada, 1988; dir. Coun. Legal Ednl. Opportunity Summer Inst., Gt. Plains Region, 1983; grievance examiner Midwest region EEOC, 1984—85; arbitrator consumer protection complaints NE Kans. Better Bus. Bur., 1989—; commr. Continuing Legal Edn. Commn. Kans., 1989—95; external examiner Sch. Law U. Limerick, Ireland, 2004—05; vis. prof. U. Ghana, Legon, 2006. Contbr. articles to legal jours. Chmn., bd. dirs. Brown Found., 1996—99, Midwest People of Color Legal Scholarship Conf., 2003—05. With JAGC US Army, 1970—74. Named William O. Douglas Outstanding Prof. of Yr., 1985—86, 1994—95; fellow, Parker Sch. Fgn. and Comparative Law, Columbia U., 1981; Rockefeller Found. grantee, Howard U., 1965—68, Kilne Sabbatical Rsch. grantee, Japan, 1985. Mem.: ABA, Ctr. States Law Sch. Assn. (pres.-elect 1987, pres. 1987—88), Kans. Bar, Phi Beta Delta, Phi Kappa Phi. Home: 3448 SW Birchwood Dr Topeka KS 66614-3214 Office: Washburn U Sch Law Topeka KS 66621 Business E-Mail: ronald.griffin@washburn.edu.

GRIFFIN, SYLVIA GAIL, reading specialist; b. Portland, Oreg., Dec. 13, 1935; d. Archie and Marguerite (Johnson) G. AA, Boise Jr. Coll., 1955; BS, Brigham Young U., Provo, Utah, 1957, MEd, 1967. Cert. advanced teaching, Idaho. Classroom tchr. Boise Pub. Sch., Idaho, 1957-59, 61-66, 67-69, reading specialist Idaho, 1969-90, 91-95, 98-2001, inclusion specialist Idaho, 1995-98, early childhood specialist Idaho, 1990-91. Tchr. evening Spanish classes for adults, 1987-88; lectr. in field; mem. cons. pool US Office Juvenile Justice and Delinquency Prevention, 1991—. Author: Procedures Used by First Grade Teachers for Teaching Experience Readiness for Reading Comprehension, The Short Story of Vowels, A Note Worthy Way to Teach Reading, The Little Black Schoolhouse, Hellside Elementary School, Reading, Righting, and Revenge, Memorandum: Murder, Once Upon a Trial; composer: The Second Coming, Progression. Advisor in developing a program for dyslexics Scottish Rite Masons of Idaho, Boise. Mem.: NEA, Acad. Theatrical Arts, Actor's Guild, Idaho Edn. Assn. (pub. rels. dir. 1970—72), Boise Edn. Assn. (pub. rels. dir. 1969—72, bd. dirs. ednl. polit. involvement com. 1983—89), Alpha Delta Kappa. Avocations: music, creative writing. Home: 9948 W Sleepy Hollow Ln Boise ID 83714-3665 Personal E-mail: readwell2@yahoo.com.

GRIFFIN, T. DAVID, family physician, pharmacist; b. Baldwyn, Miss., May 16, 1950; s. George Troy and Jewel Catherine (Towery) G.; m. Ingrid Lavonne Voyles, Dec. 28, 1980; children: Michelle Renee, Jessica Anne. AA, Northeast C.C., Booneville, Miss., 1970; BS in Pharmacy, U. Miss., 1973; DO, U. Health Scis. Kansas City, 1983. Lic. pharmacist, Miss., 1973, Dr. of Pharmacy, Tenn., 1976; MD, Miss., 1984. Cmty. pharmacist Med. Arts Pharmacy, Baldwyn, 1973-79; intern U. Health Scis. Hosp., Kansas City, Mo., 1983-84; staff physician Family Med. Ctr., Vardaman, Miss., 1984-86, Calhoun City, Miss., 1986-90; staff physician, med. dir. Rural Health Clinic, Houston, Miss., 1990—. Vice-chief of staff Trace Regional Hosp., Houston, Miss., 1995—. Active Rep. Com. Miss., 1996—. Fellow Am. Acad. Family Practice; mem. Am. Osteo. Assn., Miss. Osteo. Assn., Psi Sigma Alpha. Methodist. Avocations: civil war studies, hunting, fishing. Home: 115 Highland Rd Houston MS 38851-2424 Office: Houston Rural Health Clinic 105 Hillcrest Dr Houston MS 38851-2404

GRIFFIN, TIM (JOHN TIMOTHY GRIFFIN), former prosecutor; b. Charlotte, NC, 1968; m. Elizabeth Griffin. BA in Economics, Hendrix Coll., Conway, Ark., 1990; JD, Tulane Law Sch., New Orleans, 1994; attended, Oxford U. Bar: Ark., La. Assoc. Jones Walker Waechter Pointevent Carrere & Denegre, New Orleans, 1994—95; assoc. ind. counsel investigating Henry Cisneros US Dept. Justice, 1995—96; sr. counsel Govt. Reform Com., US Ho. of Reps.; dep. rsch. dir. Bush-Cheney Campaign, Rep. Nat. Com., 2000, rsch. dir., 2004; dep. comm. dir. Rep. Nat. Com., 2004; spl. asst. to US atty. (ea. dist) Ark. US Dept. Justice, Little Rock, 2001, spl. asst. to asst. atty. gen. Washington, 2001—02; spl. asst. to Pres. and dep. dir. Office Polit. Affairs The White House, Washington, 2005; interim US atty. (ea. dist) Ark. US Dept. Justice, Little Rock, 2006—07. Officer USAR, maj. JAG, army prosecutor US Army, 2005, Fort Campbell, Ky., Army JAG, 172d Stryker Brigade Combat Team, Brigade Operational Law Team 101st Airborne Divsn. US Army, 2006, Mosul, Iraq. Decorated Combat Action Badge, Army Commendation Medal.*

GRIFFIN, WALTER ROLAND, academic administrator, historian, educator; b. Carbondale, Pa., Nov. 20, 1942; s. Walter Joseph and Maud Loftus (Boland) G.; m. Mary Eleanor Armstrong, Aug. 16, 1961 (div. 1980); children: Rebecca, Kathleen, Shawn; m. Penni Susan Oncken, Dec. 6, 1980; 1 child, Megan. BA, Loyola Coll., Balt., 1963; MA, U. Cin., 1964, PhD, 1988. Lectr. history Xavier U., Cin., 1965—66; asst. prof. history Mt. St. Mary's Coll., Emmitsburg, Md., 1967—68, Upper Iowa U., Fayette, 1966—67, 1968—84, chmn. dept., chmn. divsn. social sci. and bus. adminstrn., 1969—78, assoc. acad. dean, 1977—78, assoc. prof., 1984—89, head coach men's and women's tennis, 1979—88, dir. off-campus programs, 1981—89; assoc. dean Union Inst., Cin., 1989—92; pres. Limestone Coll., Gaffney, SC, 1992—. Contbr. articles to profl. jours. Councilman City of Fayette, 1971-76; chmn. Fayette County (Iowa) Dems., West Union, 1972-77, 79-80; mem. Iowa State Dem. Ctrl. Com., Des Moines, 1974-78; del. Dem. Nat. Conv., N.Y.C., 1976; Dem. candidate for Iowa Sec. of State, 1978; mem. S.C. Higher Edn. Tuition Grants Commn., 1992-95, 99-2000, 2004—; mem. Crustbreakers, 1997—; bd. dirs. Cherokee County Boys and Girls Club, 1993-98; pres. Carolinas-Va. Athletic Conf., 2002-04 Recipient Community Svc. award Fayette Jaycees, 1973, Appreciation award Iowa Democratic Party, 1974, 78, Cert. Appreciation, Iowa N.G., Camp Dodge, 1985; named Coach of Yr. in Men's Tennis, Iowa Intercollegiate Athletic Conf., Waverly, 1985; Taft Teaching fellow U. Cin., 1963-64; Paul Harris fellow 2002. Mem. Phi Alpha Theta, Pi Gamma Mu, Rotary. Avocations: tennis, travel. Home: 1008 College Dr Gaffney SC 29340-3708 Office: Limestone Coll 1115 College Dr Gaffney SC 29340-3778 Home Phone: 864-488-2823; Office Phone: 864-488-4617. E-mail: wgriffin@limestone.edu.

GRIFFIN, WILLIAM MELL, III, lawyer; b. Tallahassee, Feb. 1, 1957; s. William Mell Jr. and June Winona (Cooper) G.; m. Kathryn Elizabeth Lawson, Dec. 11, 1993; children: William Mell IV, George Lawson, James Porter. BA, U. Va., 1979; JD, So. Meth. U., 1982. Bar: Ark. 1982, U.S. Dist. Ct. (ea. and we. dists.) Ark. 1982, U.S. Ct. Appeals (8th cir.) 1983. Assoc. Friday, Eldredge & Clark, Little Rock, 1982-87, ptnr., 1987—. Mem. ABA (torts and ins. practice sect.), Am. Bd. Trial Advocates (advocate), Ark. Bar Assn., Am. Coll. Trial Lawyers (fellow), Pulaski County Bar Assn. (pres. 2006—), William R. Overton Inn of Ct. (pres. 2006—), Ark. Def. Counsel, Def. Rsch. Inst., Fedn. Ins. and Corp. Counsel, Leadership Greater Little Rock, Phi Delta Phi. Avocations: running, hunting. Home: 420 Midland St Little Rock AR 72205-4177

GRIFFIS, KIRBY T., lawyer; b. Bo, Sierra Leone, Dec. 19, 1967; BA summa cum laude, MA summa cum laude, Emory U., 1990; JD, U. Va., 1995. Bar: Va. 1995, DC 1997, US Dist. Ct. (ctrl. dist.), Ill., US Dist. Ct. (we. & ea. dists.), Va., US Ct. of Appeals (4th cir., 7th. cir. & 10th. cir.). Clerk to Judge Glenn Williams US Dist. Ct., Va.; assoc. Spriggs & Hollingsworth, Wash., 1997, ptnr. Contbr. articles to profl. jours. Mem.: ABA (mem. litigation sect. 1995—98), Phi Beta Kappa. Articles editor Va. Law Rev. Office: Spriggs & Hollingsworth Ste 900 1350 I St NW Washington DC 20005 Office Phone: 202-898-5828. Office Fax: 202-682-1639. Business E-Mail: kgriffis@spriggs.com.*

GRIFFITH, ALAN RICHARD, retired banker; b. Mineola, NY, Dec. 17, 1941; s. Charles Ernest and Amalia (Guenther) G.; m. Elizabeth Ferguson, Nov. 28, 1964; children: Timothy, Elizabeth BA, Lafayette Coll., Easton, Pa., 1964; MBA, CUNY, 1971. Asst. credit officer The Bank of N.Y., NYC, 1968-72, asst. v.p., 1972-74, v.p., 1974-82, sr. v.p., 1982-85, exec. v.p., 1985-88, sr. exec. v.p., 1988-90, pres., 1990-94, vice chmn., 1994—2005. Trustee Amyothrophic Lateral Sclerosis Assn., Sherman Oaks, Calif., Chesapeake Bay Found., Annapolis, Md., Chesapeake Bay Maritime Mus., St. Michaels, Md.; chmn. bd. trustees Lafayette Coll Mem. Univ. Club, (N.Y.C.) Address: 300 Piney Point Farm Ln Centreville MD 21617

GRIFFITH, ANDY (ANDREW SAMUEL GRIFFITH), actor; b. Mt. Airy, NC, June 1, 1926; s. Carl Lee and Geneva (Nunn) G.; m. Barbara Edwards, 1949 (div.); children: Sam, Dixie Nan; m. Cindi Knight, Apr. 2, 1983. BA in Music, U. N.C., 1949. Performed for civic clubs, night clubs; TV debut as monologuist: Ed Sullivan show, 1954; Broadway debut as illiterate hillbilly draftee in: No Time for Sergeants, 1955, also in TV prodn., also in motion picture, 1958; motion pictures include A Face in the Crowd, Onionhead, 1958, Second Time Around, Savages, 1974, Adams of Eagle Lake, 1975, The Treasure Chest Murder, 1975, Hearts of the West, 1975, Six Characters in Search of an Author, Hollywood TV Theatre, 1976, The Girl in the Empty Grave, 1977, Rustler's Rhapsody, 1985, Spy Hard, 1996, Daddy and Them, 1999; role: Broadway mus. comedy Destry Rides Again, 1959; rec. What It Was Was Football; TV star: Andy Griffith Show, 1960-68; series Headmaster, 1970-71, The New Andy Griffith Show, 1970, Matlock, 1986-95; TV movies Winter Kill, Abel, Go Ask Alice, Under the Influence, From Here to Eternity, Salvage, 1978, Return to Mayberry, 1986, The Gift of Love, 1994, Gramps, 1995; TV mini series Washington Behind Closed Doors, 1977, Centennial, Murder in Texas (Emmy award), Murder in Coweta County, Fatal Vision, Scattering Dad, 1998; also numerous TV appearances including Hotel; TV spls. include The Andy Griffith-Don Knotts-Jim Nabors Show; exec. producer Mayberry, R.F.D.; appeared in TV commls. for Ritz Crackers and AT&T. Named Outstanding TV Personality of Yr., Advt. Club of Balt., 1968; recipient Tarheel award, 1961, Disting. Salesman award, 1962, Presdl. Medal of Freedom, The White House, 2005. Avocations: swimming, skeet and trap shooting. Office: William Morris Agy care Jerry Katzman 151 S El Camino Dr Beverly Hills CA 90212-2775

GRIFFITH, ARNOLD KOONS, computer consultant; b. Providence, July 1, 1942; s. John Ramsbottom and Barbara Koons G.; m. Patricia Martino, July 10, 1971. BA, Swathmore Coll., Pa., 1964; PhD, MIT, 1970. Divsn. mgr. Info. Internat., Inc., Culver City, Calif., 1971-82; owner A/P Systems, Santa Monica, Calif., 1982—. Contbr. articles to profl. jours. Mem. IEEE, Assn. for Computing Machinery, Jonathan Club, Phi Beta Kappa. Avocations: tennis, music, photography. Home: 802 Washington Ave Santa Monica CA 90403 E-mail: griffitha@acm.org.

GRIFFITH, B(EZALEEL) HEROLD, retired plastic surgeon, retired educator; b. NYC, Aug. 24, 1925; s. Bezaleel Davies and Henrietta (Herold) G.; m. Jeanne B. Lethbridge, 1948; children: Susan, Tristan. BA, Johns Hopkins U., 1992; MD, Yale U., 1948. Cert. Am. Bd. Plastic Surgery, 1959. Asst. in anatomy Yale U., New Haven, 1947—48, asst. in surgery, 1948—49; intern Grace New Haven Cmty. Hosp.-Yale U., 1948-49; resident in surgery VA Hosp., Newington, Conn., 1949-50; asst. resident in surgery 2d (Cornell) Surg. Divsn., Bellevue Hosp., NYC, 1952-53; instr. surgery Cornell U., 1956; resident in plastic surgery VA Hosp., Bronx, 1953-55; resident (sr. registrar) in plastic surgery U. Glasgow, Scotland, 1955; chief resident in plastic surgery N.Y. Hosp. Cornell Med. Ctr., NYC, 1956; rsch. fellow in plastic surgery Cornell U. Med. Coll., 1956-57; pvt. practice specializing in plastic surgery Chgo., 1957-96; attending plastic surgeon Northwestern Meml., Children's Meml., VA Lakeside hosps., Rehab. Inst. Chgo.; instr. surgery Northwestern U., 1957-59, assoc. in surgery, 1959-62, asst. prof. surgery, 1962-67, assoc. prof., 1967-71, prof., 1971-96, prof. emeritus, 1996, chief divsn. plastic surgery, 1970-91; chief plastic surgery Shriners Hosp. for Crippled Children, Chgo., 1994-96; ret., 1996. Chmn. Am. Bd. Plastic Surgery, 1981—82. Mem. editl. bd.: Plastic and Reconstructive Surgery, 1972—78; contbr. articles to profl. jours. Lt. M.C. USNR, 1950—52. Fellow ACS, Am. Assn. Plastic Surgeons, Chgo. Surg. Soc., Royal Soc. Medicine; mem. AAAS, AMA, Am. Bd. Plastic Surgery (dir. 1976-82), Am. Burn Assn., Am. Soc. Plastic and Reconstructive Surgeons (sec. 1972-74), Brit. Assn. Plastic Surgeons (hon.), Plastic Surgery Rsch. Coun. (chmn. 1969), Am. Cleft Palate Assn., N.Y. Acad. Scis., Ill., Chgo. Med. Socs., Midwestern Assn. Plastic Surgeons, Soc. Head and Neck Surgeons, Ill., Yale Soc. Med. History of Chgo., Chgo. Hist. Socs., Civil War Round Table, Evanston Hist. Soc. (trustee 1974-78), Masons, Yale Club (Chgo.), Nathan Smith Clube, Sigma Xi (pres. Northwestern U. 1986-87, 94-95). Achievements include research in transplantation, skin tumors, cleft palate, paraplegia. Home Phone: 847-869-3558.

GRIFFITH, CHARLES T., accountant, consultant; b. Fairmont, W.Va., Aug. 7, 1944; s. James Delligatti and Corinne Brown; m. Tamara S. Griffith, July 12, 2003; children: Tanya B., Lauralea. BS magna cum laude, Salem U., W.Va., 1979. Cert. tax practioner, IRS, 2000. Acct., tax preparer, cons. Log Acctg., Morgantown, W.Va., 1979—. Vol. Hope, Inc., Fairmont, 1995—2001. With US Army, 1965—68. Decorated Army Commendation medal with 1st Oak Leaf Cluster US Army Security Agy.; recipient Gear Up Role Model Recognition award, Fairmont State U., 2005. Mem.: Am. Legion, Elks Lodge #294 (assoc.). Home and Office: Log Accounting 714 Venture Drive #217 Morgantown WV 26508-7306 Home Phone: 304-685-3078. Personal E-mail: ctgriffith50@hotmail.com.

GRIFFITH, CLARK DEXTER, corporate financial executive; b. Suffern, NY, Dec. 21, 1965; s. William Fredrick Jr. and Lillian Griffith. BA in Econs. and Japanese, San Diego State U., 1991; M in Internat. Affairs, Columbia U., NYC, 2000, advanced cert. in East Asian Studies, 2000. Real estate sales agent Elegado Realty & Prudential Calif. Realty, San Diego, 1988-92; coord. import housing projects Sotetsu Real Estate Co., Ltd., Yokohama, Japan, 1991-97; pres. Intradex Corp., Pearl River, NY, 1995-2000; project mgr. pvt. client group Merrill Lynch Internat., 1999; with risk mgmt. GE Capital, 2000—03; v.p. GE Corp. Fin. Svcs., Inc., San Francisco, 2003—05; sr. v.p. GE Comml. Fin., Corp. Lending, Beverly Hills, 2005—. Cons. Kirin Breweries, Inc., Yokohama, 1989, Nichiei Co., Ltd. Yokohama, 1990, Perillo-Griffith Travel Svc., Pearl River, NY, 1984-2000; lectr. Am. Assn. State Colls. and Univs. Japan Studies Inst. Nat. Summer Inst., 1998, 2000. Contbr. articles to profl. jours. Mem. Am. C. of C. in Japan (vice chmn. trade expansion com. 1992-97, chmn. import housing sub-com. 1995-97, bd. govs. appreciation cert., 1997), Japan Studies Assn. (founder, pres. 1989-91), Asia Soc. So. Calif., Japan Am. Soc. So. Calif., Pacific Coun. Internat. Policy, World Affairs Coun., The Family, The Grand Havana Rm. Avocations: scuba diving, golf, skiing, reading, motorcycling, boating. Office: GE Comml Fin 350 S Beverly Dr Ste 200 Beverly Hills CA 90212 Home: 1111 Garfield Ave Venice CA 90291 Office Phone: 310-284-2926. Business E-Mail: clark.griffith@ge.com.

GRIFFITH, DANIEL ALVA, geography educator; b. Pitts., Nov. 15, 1948; s. Donald Sanford and Mary Jane (McClain) G.; m. Diane Elaine Swartz, Jan. 3, 1970; children: Darren Lee, Michele Renee. BS, Indiana U. of Pa., 1970, MA, 1972; MS, Pa. State U., University Park, 1985; PhD, U. Toronto, Ont., Can., 1978; DSc with honors, Indiana U. of Pa., 2006. Instr. Ryerson Polytech. U., Toronto, 1975-78; from asst. prof. to full prof. SUNY, Buffalo, 1978-88; prof. geography Syracuse U., NY, 1988—2003, dir. stats. program, 1991—95, chair, 1995—97; prof. geography U. Miami, Fla., 2003—05; prof. geospatial info. scis. U. Tex., Dallas, 2005—. Adj. prof. Coll. Environ. Sci. and Forestry, 1992-2003; vis. EPA/EMAP rsch. affiliate stats. dept. Oreg. State U., Corvallis, 1990-93; vis. rsch. prof. Erasmus U., Rotterdam, 1992, U. Rome, 1995; dep. dir. NY State program in geographic info. and analysis Syracuse U., 1989-90; ASI dir. NATO Sci. Affairs, Brussels, 1979-82, 85, cons. Peru Minister Edn., 2000-01; Leverhulme vis. prof. Cambridge U., 2004; vis. rschr. Max Planck Inst. Demographic Rsch., Rostock, Germany, 2005, invited lectr. Polish Acad. Scis, Acad. Sinica Taiwan, 2007. Author: Spatial Autocorrelation, 1987, Advanced Spatial Statistics, 1988, Statistical Analysis for Geographers, 1991, Spatial Regression Analysis on the PC, 1993, Multivariate Statistical Analysis for Geographers, 1997, A Casebook for Spatial Statistical Data Analysis, 1999, Spatial Autocorrelation and Spatial Filtering, 2003; contbr. articles to profl. jours. Recipient Award Pa. Geog. Soc., 1999; NSF grantee, 1981, 83-85, 88-90, 92-93, 95-97, 99, 2002, 2004—; Fulbright fellow, 1992-93, 2005—, rsch. fellow ASA/USDA-NASS, 1999, Guggenheim fellow, 2001-02; named to Ashbel Smith Endowed chair U. Tex., Dallas, 2005; fellow U. Miami; sr. specialist Fulbright Found., 2006. Fellow NY Acad. Scis., Spatial Econometrics Assn. (founding fellow); mem. Am. Statis. Assn., Regional Sci. Assn. (pres. 1996-97), Assn. Am. Geographers (chair 1987-88, Nystrom Dissertation award 1980, Pub. Domain Computer Software award 1994, 97), Sigma Xi (Syracuse chpt. pres. 1999-2000). Democrat. Methodist. Avocation: travel. Home: 5804 Bricknell Dr Allen TX 75002-5473 Office: Sch Econ Polit and Policy Scis Univ Texas Richardson TX 75083 Business E-Mail: dagriffith@utdallas.edu.

GRIFFITH, DENNISON W., academic administrator, artist, educator; BFA, Ohio Wesleyan U.; MFA, Ohio State U. Individual artists program coord. Ohio Arts Coun., 1978—83; exec. dir. Ohio Found. Arts; dep. dir. Columbus Mus. Arts, 1988—98; pres. Columbus Coll. Art & Design, 1998—, prof. painting, 1998—. Trustee Ross Art Mus., Delaware, Ohio, 2004—. Mem.: Nat. Assn. Schs. Art and Design (chair ethics com.), Higher Edn. Coun. Columbus (chmn.), Assn. Ind. Coll. Art & Design (exec. com.), Greater Columbus C. of C. (co-chmn. creative svcs. com., bd. mem.). Office: Office of President Columbus College Art & Design 107 N Ninth St Columbus OH 43215 Office Phone: 614-222-3220. Business E-Mail: dgriffith@ccad.edu.*

GRIFFITH, EDWARD, judge; b. Wilkes-Barre, Pa., Feb. 9, 1948; s. Edward Meredith Griffith and Jane (Randall) Griffith Jones; children: Trevor Scribner, Stewart Randall; m. Jessie G. Conyngham, August 6, 2005. BA, Lehigh U., 1970; JD, Dickinson Sch. Law, 1973. Bar: Pa. 1973, U.S. Dist. Ct. (ea. dist.) Pa. 1973, U.S. Ct. Appeal (3rd cir.) 1973, U.S. Supreme Ct. 1978. Ptnr. Duane, Morris LLP, Phila., 1973—2003; judge Ct. of Common Pleas of Chester County, Pa., 2004—. Cons. Pa. State Bd. Law Examiners, Phila, 1974-77. Master John E. Stively Inn of Ct.; mem. Pa. Bar Assn., Chester County Bar Assn. Republican. Presbyterian. Avocations: hunting, fishing, gardening. Office: Chester County Courthouse 2 N High St West Chester PA 19380 E-mail: egriffith@chesco.org.

GRIFFITH, FORREST LEE, III, lawyer; b. Buffalo, Sept. 3, 1947; s. Forrest Lee Jr. and Helen Elizabeth (Lines) G.; children: Amanda, Abigail. BA, Williams Coll., 1969; JD cum laude, Boston U., 1972. Bar: Conn. 1972. Assoc. Day, Berry & Howard, Hartford, Conn., 1972-78, ptnr. Stamford, Conn., 1979—, exec. com., 1989—; ptnr. Day, Barry & Howard LLP, Stamford, Conn. Mem.: Conn. Venture Group., Nat. Assn. Securities Dealers., Panel of Arbitrators, ABA Sect. Corp., Banking & Bus. Law, Internat. Bar Assn. Office: Day Barry & Howard LLP One Canterbury Green Stamford CT 06901 Office Phone: 203-977-7300. Office Fax: 203-977-7301. Business E-Mail: flgriffith@dbh.com.*

GRIFFITH, G. SANDERS, III, lawyer, finance company executive; b. June 27, 1953; BA, LaGrange Coll., 1974; JD, U. Ga. Sch. of Law, 1977. Atty. Davidson & Calhoun, 1978—88; v.p., gen. counsel Synovus Financial Corp., 1988—92, exec. v.p., gen. counsel, sec., 1992—95, sr. exec. v.p., gen. counsel, sec., 1995—, interim lead Fin. Mgmt. Svc. Div., 2005—. Mem. bank counsel section Ga. Bankers Assn., Financial Services Roundtable; dir. Columbus Regional Health Care System; trustee LaGrange Coll.; mem. Governor's Judicial Nominating Commn., Columbus Metropolitan Airport Commn. Mem.: ABA, Am. Soc. of Corp. Secretaries, Am. Corp. Counsel Assn., Am. Bankers Council, Ga. Bar Assn., Columbus Bar Assn. Office: Synovus Financial Corp PO Box 120 Columbus GA 31902

GRIFFITH, H(OWARD) MORGAN, lawyer; b. Phila., Mar. 15, 1958; s. A. Hundley and Charlotte Virginia (Burford) G.; m. Hilary Davis Griffith; 1 child, Davis; 1 stepchild, Abby. BA with honors, Emory and Henry Coll., 1980; JD, Washington and Lee U., 1983. Bar: Va. 1983, U.S. Dist. Ct. Va. 1985. Assoc. Lutins & Shapiro, Roanoke, Va., 1983—84; pvt. practice Salem, Va., 1984—87, 1989—; ptnr. Griffith & Varney, Salem, 1987—89; del. 8th legis. dist. Va. Gen. Assembly, 1994—; house majority leader, 2000—; mem. commerce and labor com.; mem. cts. of justice com.; mem. militia, police and pub. safety com.; mem. rules and joint rules com. Bd. visitors Emory and Henry Coll.; mem. Freedom of Info. Adv. Coun., Joint Legis. Audit and Rev. Commn.; mem. joint subcommittee SW Va. Econ. Devel.; vice-chmn. Joint Commn. Adminstrv. Rules; mem. Blue Ridge Mountains Coun. Boy Scouts Am., advisor, sponsor Legal Explorers Post Salem, 1988—89, chmn. Catawba dist. Blue Ridge Mountains coun., 1984—86, vice chmn., 1987—88, dist. chmn., 1988—91, v.p. rels. and membership, 1991—93; mem. Salem Lions Club, Blue Ridge Mountains Coun.; mem. state ctrl. com. Rep. Party of Va.; chmn. Rep. Party Salem, 1986—88, 1991—94; mem. St. Paul's Episc. Ch., Salem; mem. state bd. dirs. Easter Seals Va.; mem., bd. trustees Jamestown-Yorktown Found.; bd. dirs. Legal Aid Soc. of Roanoke Valley, 1991—92; com. mem. Stonegate Swim Club, Salem, 1984—88, bd. dirs., 1991—. Recipient Dist. Award of Merit, Boy Scouts Am., 1990—91, Silver Beaver award, 1994. Mem. Va. State Bar Assn., Salem/Roanoke County Bar Assn. (pres. 1995-96), State Ctrl. Com. Rep. Party of Va., Lions (bd. dirs. 1988-90). Episcopalian. Avocations: swimming, ornithology, ichthyology. Office: 113 E Main St Salem VA 24153-3804 Office Phone: 540-389-4498. Personal E-mail: hmg1993@aol.com.

GRIFFITH, HUW, advertising executive; With Doyle Dane Bernbach, London, Gold Greenless Trott; worldwide account dir. Batey Ads, 1992—95; joined M&C Saatchi, Singapore, 1995, Malaysia, 2003, CEO N.Am. LA, 2003—. Office: M&C Saatchi 2032 Broadway Santa Monica CA 90404 Office Phone: 310-401-6074. Business E-Mail: hgriffith@mcsaatchi-la.com.*

GRIFFITH, JAMES LEIGH, lawyer; b. Knoxville, Tenn., May 25, 1951; s. James M. and Marguerite B. Griffith; m. Catherine West; children: Catherine Leigh, James Leigh. BA, U. Va., 1973; JD, Vanderbilt U., 1976; LLM, NYU, 1977. Bar: Tenn. 1977, N.Y. 1977, D.C. 1978; CPA, Tenn., Miss. Sr. tax acct. Ernst & Whinney, Nashville, 1977-81; mem. Waller, Lansden, Dortch & Davis LLP, Nashville. Contbr. articles to profl. jours. Past bd. dirs. Grace Eaton Day Home, Nashville, Sneed Forest Homeowners Assn., Franklin, Tenn.; past pres., chmn. bd. Versailes Homeowners Assn., Nashville. Fellow Am. Coll. Tax Counsel, Nashville Bar Assn.; mem. ABA (tax sect., various coms.), Tenn. Bar Assn., D.C. Bar Assn., Tenn. Soc. CPA's (coun. mem.), Am. Tax Policy Inst. (life), Phi Beta Kappa. Achievements include development of New Standard and Poor's and Moody's asset class and first rated security of insurance arbitrage. Office: Waller Lansden Dortch & Davis LLP 511 Union St Ste 2700 Nashville TN 37219-1760 Office Phone: 615-850-8534. Business E-Mail: lgriffith@wallerlaw.com.

GRIFFITH, JAMES W., manufacturing executive; B in Indsl. Engring, MBA, Stanford U. Formerly with Homestake Mining Co., Bunker Hill Co., Martin Marietta; with The Timken Co., Canton, Ohio, 1984—, head rail bus., 1996—98, pres., COO, bd. dirs., 1999—2002, pres., CEO, 2002—. Bd. dirs. Goodrich Corp. Trustee United Way of Ctrl. Stark County. Mem.: Mfrs. Alliance/MAPI (exec. com., trustee). Office: The Timken Co 1835 Dueber Ave SW Canton OH 44706-2798*

GRIFFITH, JAMES WILLIAM, systems engineer, consultant; b. Waco, Tex., Apr. 11, 1922; s. Paul Isaac and Willie Elizabeth (Rawlin) G.; m. Dorothy Louise Cannon., Oct. 17, 1949; children: Pamela D. (Mrs. John Fletcher Freeman), James William. Student, Tex. Tech U., 1940-41, U. Utah, 1943-44; BS, So. Meth. U., 1949, MS, 1956. Dir. engring. grad. div. So. Meth. U., 1960-67, chmn. dept. indsl. engring., 1965-67, prof., chmn. dept. systems engring., 1967-69; ptnr. K-G Assocs., 1970-80; prin. James W. Griffith Inc., Dallas, 1980—. U.S. expert in daylighting Commn. Internat. Eclairage, 1957—; cons. to govt. agys. including HUD, HEW, NAS; tech. cons. Nat. Fenestration Coun., 1984-87, LBL Windows and Daylighting, 1980-85; tech. cons. profl. devel. program AIA, 1982-86, instr., 1982-86, now cons.; mem. AIA Found. Contbr. articles to profl. jours. Served with USAAF, 1942-46. Named to Engrs. of Distinction Engrs. Joint Council, 1970 Fellow Illuminating Engrs. Soc. (nat. pres.); mem. ASHRAE, NSPE, Illuminating Engring. Rsch. Inst., Bldg. Environment and Thermal Envelope Coun., Nat. Fenestration Rating Coun., Bldg. Rsch. Inst. (bd. dirs. 1965-67, 73-75), Tex. Soc. Profl. Engrs., Soc. Mayflower Descs., Sigma Tau, Eta Kappa Nu. Achievements include a patent on the method of and assembly for measuring equiv alent sphere illumination. Home and Office: 31 Brookline Ct The Woodlands TX 77381 Personal E-mail: billgsr@juno.com.

GRIFFITH, JERRY DICE, energy executive, management consultant; b. Sturgis, Mich., Sept. 8, 1933; s. Levi Robert and Vivian Marie (LeVeck) G.; m. Gloria Louise Hessie, June 25, 1965; children: Jennifer Lynn, Bradley Jerome. BS summa cum laude, Mich. State U., 1955, MS, 1957; ME, Calif. Inst. Tech., 1959; PFPA, Princeton U., 1967. Dir. nuclear safety C.E., U.S. Army, Washington, 1967-72; chief research and devel. br. AEC and ERDA, Washington, 1972-76; asst. dir. for reactor safety Dept. Energy, Washington, 1976-79, dir. div. nuclear power devel., 1979-80, dir. office light water reactors, 1980-84, assoc. dept. asst. sec. reactor systems devel. and tech., 1985-94, acting asst. sec. for nuclear energy, 1989, acting prin. dept. asst. sec. for nuclear energy, 1990-92; energy and mgmt. cons. Rockville, Md., 1994—. U.S. rep. to OECD Nuclear Energy Agy., Paris, 1976-86, 89-94. Contbr. articles to profl. jours., 1967—; patentee inherent reactor control concept, small reaction turbine. Served to capt. U.S. Army, 1959-62. Recipient Meritorious Civilian Service award U.S. Army, 1970; Congl. fellow, 1969. Mem. Am. Nuclear Soc. Home: 14711 Bauer Dr Rockville MD 20853-3621 Office Phone: 301-460-1059. E-mail: jerrygriffith@comcast.net.

GRIFFITH, JOHN RANDALL, health facility administrator, educator; b. Balt., Mar. 22, 1934; s. Richard Robinson and Eleanor (Bond) G.; m. Helen Klenner, Sept. 17, 1955; children: Julia, Alison, Richard. BS Indsl. Engring., The Johns Hopkins U., 1955; MBA Hospital Adminstrn., U. Chgo., 1957. From asst. prof. to prof. U. Mich. Sch. Pub. Health Dept. Health Mgmt. Policy, Ann Arbor, 1960—, interim dept. chair, 1987-88, dept. chair, 1988-91, Andrew Pattullo Collegiate prof. Hosp. Adminstrn., 1982—; dir. program, chmn. dept. Bur. Hosp. Adminstrn., Ann Arbor,

Mich., 1970-82. Examiner Baldridge Nat. Quality Award, 1997—98. Author: Quantitative Techniques for Hospital Planning and Control, 1972, Measuring Hospital Performance, 1978, The Well Managed Community Hospital, 1987 (award, 1988), Moral Challenges of Health Care Management, The Well-Managed Health Care Organization, 1995 (award, 1999, 2000), 6th edit., 2006, Designing 21st Century Healthcare: Leadership in Hospitals and Health Systems, 1998; author: (with others) Thinking Forward: Six Strategies for Highly Successful Organizations, 2003. Bd. dirs., pres., Assn. Univ. Programs Health Adminstrn., 1974-75, Pattullo lectr., 1999; bd. dirs. Accredation Commn., 1977-83, Nat. Ctr. Healthcare Leadership, 2002-. Recipient Filerman Prize for Ednl. Leadership, Assn. Univ. Programs in Health Adminstrn., 2002. Fellow Am. Coll. Health Care Execs. (gold medal 1992, James A. Hamilton award), Tau Beta Pi, Omicron Delta Kappa. Home: 333 Rock Creek Ct Ann Arbor MI 48104-1857 Office: U Mich SPH II 109 Observatory St Ann Arbor MI 48109-2029 Home Phone: 734-769-0689; Office Phone: 734-936-1304. Business E-Mail: jrg@umich.edu.

GRIFFITH, JOHN VINCENT, academic official; b. Oneida, NY, Dec. 24, 1947; s. William F. and Dorothy (Roberts) G.; m. Nancy E. Snell, Jan. 25, 1969; children: Matthew, Christopher. BA cum laude, Dickinson Coll., 1969; MDiv magna cum laude, Harvard U., 1972; PhD, Syracuse U., 1980. Dean admissions Davidson Coll., NC, 1979-85, v.p. inst. advancement NC, 1985-89; pres. Lyon Coll., Batesville, Ark., 1989-97, Presbyn. Coll., Clinton, SC, 1998—. Mem. Omicron Delta Kappa, Sigma Alpha Epsilon, Phi Mu Alpha Sinfonia. Office: Presbyn Coll Office of Pres PO Box 975 Clinton SC 29325-0975 Home Phone: 864-938-9340; Office Phone: 864-833-8700.

GRIFFITH, KATHERINE SCOTT, retired communications executive, librarian, reporter; b. Atlanta, Jan. 16, 1942; d. Robert Sherrill and Emily (Reynolds) Howell; m. George Delk, June 1963 (div. Mar. 1968); m. Henry Armand Terjen, Sept. 4, 1970 (div. Nov. 1979); 1 child, Henry Foster Terjen; m. Michael Christopher Healy, May 20, 1995. AB, Sweet Briar Coll., Va., 1964; Masters, Emory U., Atlanta, 1968. Editor South Today, So. Regional Coun., Atlanta, 1969-72; editor Phoenix, Bklyn., 1972-73; dir. comm. N.Y. C. of C. and Industry, NYC, 1978-79; dir. pub. liaison N.Y.C. Dept. Ports and Terminals, 1979-80; sr. pub. affairs officer Citicorp/Citibank, NYC, 1981-83; asst. v.p., pub. rels. mgr. Citicorp Diners Club Media Svcs., NYC, 1983-84; asst. v.p., pub. rels. dir. Citicorp Pub., NYC, 1985-86, asst. v.p. corp. comms., 1986-87; v.p. First Atlanta Corp., Atlanta, 1984; sr. mgr. Can. Imperial Bank of Commerce, NYC, 1987-88, v.p. USA corp. comm., 1989-95; dir. mktg. and comm. Can. Imperial Bank Commerce Wood Gundy, NYC, 1995-97; v.p., dir. corp. comm. Signet Banking Corp., Richmond, Va., 1997; comm. cons. Greenwich, Conn., 1998-99; pub. rels. supr. Ferguson Libr., Stamford, Conn., 1999—2000; dir. comms. and external rels. NY Regional Assn. Grantmakers, 2000—03; libr. Bedford Free Libr., 2003—04; reporter The Chatham County Line, Carrboro, NC, 2006—. Pres. 150 Joralemon Street Corp., Bklyn., 1987-89. Pres. 78th Precinct Cmty. Coun., Bklyn., 1977-78; mem. com. Cmty. Bd. 6, Bklyn., 1978-80; mem. coun. So. Regional Coun., Atlanta, 1984-98; mktg. com. Success by Six, 1999-2000; active Friends of Ferguson Libr., 2000-03, Friend of Pittsboro Meml. Libr., 2005—; founding mem. Chapel Hill Area Compassionate Friends, chpt. leader, 2005-2006, mem. steering com, 2006-. Chatham Coalition, 2006—; mem. Dem. Women of Chatham County, 2006—; sec. Chatham County Dem. Party, 2007—. Mem. LWV, Jr. League, UN Assn., Dem. Club (Fearrington Village), Beta Phi Mu. Democrat. Episcopalian. Home: 342 Fearrington Post Pittsboro NC 27312-2941

GRIFFITH, LAWRENCE STACEY CAMERON, cardiologist, educator; b. Washington, Sept. 16, 1937; s. Ernest Stacey and Margaret Dyckman (Davenport) G.; m. Anne Gorman Young, June 20, 1959; children: Lawrence, John, Melinda, Gordon. BA, Haverford Coll., Pa., 1959; MD with honors, U. Rochester, NY, 1963. Diplomate Am. Bd. Internal Medicine, Am. Bd. Cardiovascular Disease. Intern in medicine and surgery Strong Meml. Hosp., Rochester, NY, 1963—64, asst. resident in surgery, 1964—65, asst. and assoc. resident in medicine, 1967—69; rsch. fellow in cardiology Johns Hopkins U., Balt., 1969—71, asst. prof. medicine Sch. Medicine, 1971—76, asst. prof. radiology, 1974—80, assoc. prof. medicine, 1976—88, prof. medicine, 1988—; med. dir. Johns Hopkins Medicine Internat., 1999—. Cons. VA Coop. Study Surgery for Coronary Artery Disease, Program on Surg. Control of Hyperlipidemias, U. Minn. Contbr. articles to profl. jours. Bd. dirs. Julia Dyckman Andrus Meml., Inc., Yonkers, NY, 1971—, chmn., 1976-2007; bd. dirs. John E. Andrus Meml. Home for Aged, Hastings-on-Hudson, NY, 1974-97; bd. dirs. Surdna Found., NYC, 1976—, v.p., 1988-94; chmn. adv. bd. Balt. Pastoral Counseling Svc., 1971-80. With USPHS, 1965-67. Fellow ACP, Coun. Clin. Cardiology of Am. Heart Assn., Am. Coll. Cardiology; mem. Alpha Omega Alpha. Democrat. Methodist. Home: 802 W Saint Georges Rd Baltimore MD 21210-1409 Office: Johns Hopkins Hosp Halsted 500 600 N Wolfe St Baltimore MD 21287-0005 Office Phone: 410-955-6173.

GRIFFITH, LINDA G. (LINDA GRIFFITH-CIMA), biomedical engineer, chemical engineer, educator; BSChemE, Ga. Inst. Tech., 1982; PhD in Chem. Engring., U. Calif., Berkeley, 1988. Postdoctoral assoc. chem. engring. MIT, 1988—90, asst. prof. chem. engring., 1991—96, assoc. prof. chem. engring., 1996—2002, assoc. prof. chem. and biol. engring., 1998—2002, prof., 2002—03, dir. Biotechnology Process Engring. Ctr., 2003—, prof. mech. and biol. engring., 2003—. Asst. prof. Harvard U.-MIT Divsn. Health Sci. and Tech., 1991—93; H.L. Doherty chair, 1991—93; Karl van Tassel chair, 1993—98; editorial bd. mem. Jour. of Biomaterials Sci. Contbr. articles to profl. jours.; mem. editl. bd.: Jour. Biomaterials Scis. Named one of Brilliant 10, Popular Sci. mag., 2002; recipient Presdl. Young Investigator award, NSF, 1991; fellow Am. Inst. Med. & Biol. Engrs., 1998, Biomaterials Sci. & Engring., Internat. Union of Soc. for Biomaterials Sci. & Engring., 2000; MacArthur fellow, John D. MacArthur and Catherine T. MacArthur Found., 2006. Renowned for human tissue engineering research and development. Office: MIT 77 Mass Ave Room 16-429 Cambridge MA 02139 E-mail: griff@mit.edu.

GRIFFITH, LONZO, JR., technology specialist, educator, farmer; b. Lynnville, Ky., Nov. 20, 1948; s. Elisha Lonzo and Dorthy Lorene G.; m. Diane Louise Tucker, Dec. 21, 1969. BS, Murray State U., 1971, MS, 1980; postgrad., U. Mo., Rolla, 1984-85. Cert. sci., chemistry, physics, math., computer sci. tchr., Fla., sci., math., computer sci. tchr., Ky.' cert. project WILD facilitator, 2000. Assembler, machinist Midland Ross Corp., Paris, Tenn., 1977-80; tchr. Palmersville (Tenn.) H.S., 1980-81; instr. U. Tenn., Martin, 1981-84; tchr. Pahokee (Fla.) H.S., 1985-86, Clewiston (Fla.) H.S., 1986-96, technology specialist, tchr., 1996—. Mem. tech. com. Henry County Bd. Edn., LaBelle, Fla., 1996—; local tech. rep. Fla. Internet Resource Network, Tallahassee, 1996—; cert. facilitor Fla. Wildlife and Game Commn., 2000—. Recipient First Place Ky. award Nat. Corn Growers Assn., 1999, Second Place U.S. award, 1999. Mem.: NEA, Nat. Sci. Tchrs. Assn., Am. Chem. Soc., Fla. Tchg. Profession, Fla. Assn. for Computers in Edn., Henry County Edn. Assn. Democrat. Baptist. Avocations: fishing, carpentry, stamp collecting/philately. Home: 711 Bowden Rd Clewiston FL 33440-5004 Office: Clewiston HS 1501 S Francisco St Clewiston FL 33440-5016 E-mail: mayfield@strato.net.

GRIFFITH, MARY H., bank executive; b. Ky. m. Robert Griffith; 2 children. BA in English, Centre Coll., Danville, Ky. Sr. v.p., dir. pub. rels. First Ky. Nat. Corp.; v.p., dir. corp. comm. Nat. City Corp., Cleve., 1990, sr. v.p. mktg. comm., 1992, vice chmn. Ky., sr. v.p., 2001—. Bd. trustees Centre Coll.; bd. trustees, chair investment com., mem. exec. com. Bellarmine U., Louisville; chmn. bd. dirs. Louisville Free Pub. Libr. Found., Downtown Devel. Corp., Ky. Ctr. for Arts Endowment, Kentuckiana Works; bd. dirs. Shakertown at Pleasant Hill, Ky., Inc., Teach Ky. Recipient Disting. Alumni award Centre Coll., 1991. Office: Nat City Corp 101 S Fifth St Louisville KY 40202 Office Phone: 502-581-6424.*

GRIFFITH, MELANIE, actress; b. NYC, Aug. 9, 1957; d. Tippi Hedren; m. Don Johnson, Jan. 1972 (div. July 1976); m. Steven Bauer May 1982 (div. 1987); 1 child, Alexander; m. Don Johnson, June 26, 1989 (div. Feb. 1996); 1 child, Dakota; m. Antonio Banderas, 1996; 1 child, Stella. Student, Hollywood Profl. Sch., 1981; studied acting with, Stella Adler. Acting debut in Night Moves, 1975, other films include The Drowning Pool, 1975, Smile, 1975, One on One, 1977, Roar, Joyride, 1977, Underground Aces, Body Double, 1984, Fear City, Something Wild, 1986, Cherry 2000, 1988, The Milagro Beanfield War, 1988, Stormy Monday, 1987, Working Girl, 1988 (Acad. Award nominee), In the Spirit, The Grifters, Pacific Heights, 1990, Bonfire of the Vanities, Shining Through, Paradise, 1991, A Stranger Among Us, 1992, Born Yesterday, 1993, Milk Money, 1994, Nobody's Fool, 1994, Two Much, 1996, Mulholland Falls, 1996, Now and Then, 1996, Shadow of Doubt, Another Day in Paradise, Lolita, 1996, Celebrity, 1998, Crazy in Alabama, 1999, Cecil B. DeMented, 2000, Forever Lulu, 2000, Tart, 2001, Stuart Little 2 (voice), 2002, The Night We Called It a Day, 2003, Tempo, 2003, Shade, 2003; TV appearances include (series) Carter Country, (mini-series) Once an Eagle, Buffalo Girls, 1995, (TV movies) She's in the Army Now, 1981, Golden Gate, 1981, Alfred Hitchcock Presents, 1985, Women and Men: Stories of Seduction, 1990, Buffalo Girls, 1995, RKO 281, 1999, Heartless, 2005, (pilots) Golden Gate; (TV series) Twins, 2005-; (Broadway plays) Chicago, 2003. Recipient Golden Globe award, 1989.

GRIFFITH, MELVIN EUGENE, entomologist, public health service officer; b. Lawrence, Kans., Mar. 24, 1912; s. George Thomas and Estella (Shaw) G.; m. Pauline Sophia Bogart, June 23, 1941. AB, U. Kans., 1934, AM, 1935, PhD, 1938; postgrad., U. Mich., summers 1937-40. Instr. zoology N.D. Agrl. Coll., Fargo, 1938—39, asst. prof., 1939—41, assoc. prof., 1941—42; commd. officer USPHS, 1943—71; entomologist malaria control in war areas State Dept. Health, Oklahoma City, 1943—46; assoc. prof. zool. scis. U. Okla., Norman, 1945—52, prof., 1952—56; extended malaria control program, 1946—51; chief malaria advisor ICA, Bangkok, 1951—60; assoc. dir. Malaria Eradication Tng. Ctr., Kingston, Jamaica, 1960; regional malaria advisor SE Asia, AID, New Delhi, 1960—62, Near East and South Asia, AID, 1962—64; dep. chief malaria eradication br. AID, Washington, 1964—67, chief, 1967—71; ret. as capt. USPHS, 1971. Rapporteur founding conf. SE Asia antimalaria coord. bd., Saigon, 1956; cons. Office of Health, AID, Washington, 1971—75; mem. rev. team ind. status assessment of advanced nat. malaria eradication programs WHO, Iran, 1962, Philippines, 73; chmn. first all-Asia malarai eradication conf., Bangkok, 53. Contbr. articles and monographs on entomology, malaria control and pub. health. Recipient citation for disting. svc. U. Kans., 1962. Mem. APHA, Am. Soc. Tropical Medicine and Hygiene, Am. Soc. Limnology and Oceanography, Entomol. Soc. Am., Explorers Club, N.Y. Acad. Scis., Siam Soc., Phi Beta Kappa, Sigma Xi. Address: PO Box 3550 Williamsburg VA 23187-3550 E-mail: melvinegriffith@cs.com.

GRIFFITH, MONICA, psychologist; b. Youngstown, Ohio, Jan. 20, 1979; d. Robert Sferra and Carol Mogulich; m. Monica Sferra, Apr. 21, 2006. B in Arts and Sci., Ohio State U., Columbus, 2001; MEd, Duquesne U., Pitts., 2004. Sch. psychologist Penn Hills Sch. Dist., Pitts., 2004—. Mem.: APA, NASP. Home Phone: 412-823-5623; Office Phone: 412-793-7000.

GRIFFITH, NANCI, singer, songwriter; b. Austin, Tex., 1954; d. Griff and Ruelene G. BA Edn., U. of Tex., Austin. Former kindergarten & 1st grade teacher Austin SD; recording artist, 1978—. Albums include: There's a Light Beyond These Woods, 1978, Poet in My Window, 1982, Once in a Very Blue Moon, 1985, Last of the True Believers, 1986, Lone Star State of Mind, 1987, Little Love Affairs, 1988, One Fair Summer Evening, 1988, Storms, 1989, Late Night Grande Hotel, 1991, The MCA Years - A Retrospective, 1993, Other Voices, Other Rooms, 1993 (Grammy award Best Folk album), The Best of Nanci Griffith, 1993, Flyer, 1994, Country Gold, 1997, Blue Roses From the Moons, 1997, Other Voices, Too, 1998, The Dust Bowl Symphony, 1999, Wings to Fly and a Place to Be, 2000, The Millennium Collection, 2001, Clock Without Hands, 2001, From A Distance: The Very Best Of Nanci Griffith, 2002, Winter Marquee, 2002, Complete MCA Studio Recordings, 2003, Hearts in Mind, 2004, Ruby's Torch, 2006; appeared in Nanci Griffith on Broadway, 1994. Office: care Gold Mountain Entertainment 2 Music Cir S Ste 212 Nashville TN 37203-5708

GRIFFITH, OSBIE HAYES, retired chemistry professor; b. Torrance, Calif., Sept. 14, 1938; s. Osbie and Mary Belle (Neathery) G.; m. Karen Hedberg; 2 sons BA, U. Calif.-Riverside, Riverside, 1960; PhD, Calif. Inst. Tech., 1964; postgrad., Stanford U., 1965. NAS-NRC postdoctoral Stanford (Calif.) U., 1965; asst. prof. chemistry U. Oreg., Eugene, 1966-69, assoc. prof., 1969-72; prof. chem. Inst. Molecular Biology, 1972—2003, prof. emeritus of chemistry, 2003—. Co-editor: Lipid-Protein Interactions, 1982; mem. edtl. bd. Biophysical Jour., 1974-78, Chemistry & Physics of Lipids, 1974-95, Microscopy and Microanalysis, 1995-2002; contbr. articles to profl. jours. Camille and Henry Dreyfus Found. scholar, 1970; Career Devel. award Nat. Cancer Inst., 1972-76; fellow Sloan Found., 1967-69, Guggenheim Found., 1972-76; Faculty Achievement award for Tchg. Excellence, Burlington No. Found., 1987, Dean's Devel. award, 1991, Creativity Ext. NSF, 1992, Outstanding Faculty award U. Oreg. Office of Multicultural Affairs, 2004. Mem. Am. Chem. Soc., Biophys. Soc., Microscopy Soc. Am. Home: 2550 Charnelton St Eugene OR 97405-3216 Office: Univ Oreg Dept Chemistry Eugene OR 97403 Business E-Mail: griffith@uoregon.edu.

GRIFFITH, OWEN WENDELL, biochemistry professor; b. Oakland, Calif., June 19, 1946; s. Charles H. and Gladys C. (Farrar) G. BA, U. Calif., Berkeley, 1968; PhD, Rockefeller U., 1975. Asst. prof. Cornell U. Med. Coll., NYC, 1978-81, assoc. prof., 1981-87, prof., 1987-92; prof., chmn. biochemistry Med. Coll. Wis., Milw., 1992—2001, prof. biochemistry, 2001—, dean sch. biomed. scis., 2007—; sci. founder ArgiNOx Therapeutics, LLC, Milw., 2000—. Mem., chmn. med. biochemistry study sect. NIH, Bethesda, Md., 1988-92; founder ArgiNox Pharm., Inc., Redwood City, Calif., 2000—, bd. dirs. Contbr. more than 160 articles to profl. jours. Grantee NIH. Mem. Am. Chem. Soc., Am. Soc. Biochemistry and Molecular Biology, Am. Soc. Pharmacology and Exptl. Therapeutics. Achievements include more than 40 patents and patent applications in biomedical research. Office: Med Coll Wis Dept Biochemistry 8701 W Watertown Plank Rd Milwaukee WI 53226-3548 Business E-Mail: griffith@mcw.edu.

GRIFFITH, PATRICIA KING, journalist; b. San Francisco, Jan. 20, 1934; d. Earl Beardsley and Frankie Mae (Kelly) King; m. Winthrop Gold Griffith, Oct. 4, 1958 (div. Jan. 1986); children: Kevin Winthrop, Christina Suzanne. BA, Stanford U., 1955. Copy asst., reporter Washington Post, 1956-57, 60-64; reporter San Francisco Examiner, 1957-59; Washington bureau chief Monterey Herald and Toledo Blade, Washington, 1979-81; investigative reporter Monterey (Calif.) Peninsula Herald, 1973-79, city editor, 1981-83, mng. editor, 1983-88; Washington bureau chief, White House corr. Toledo Blade and Pitts. Post-Gazette, Washington, 1988-99. Bd. dirs. Lyceum of Monterey Peninsula, 1977-79, All Sts. Episcopal Day Sch., Carmel, Calif., 1977-79, Monterey Coll. Law, 1978-79; sr. warden St. Dunstan's Episcopal Ch., Carmel Valley, Calif., 1983-84; warden St. Margaret's Episcopal Ch., Belfast, Maine, 2004-05. Recipient Silver Gavel award ABA, 1978. Mem.: Stanford Alumni Assn., Nat. Press Club, Gridiron Club, Stanford Cap and Gown Soc. Home: 103 Dockside Ln Belfast ME 04915

GRIFFITH, ROSITA DENISE, elementary school educator; d. Willie Dwight and Ruby Earl Griffith. BS, Tougaloo Coll., 1985; MS, Iowa State U., 1988. Chemist A.E. Staley Refinery, Decatur, Ill., 1988—90; assoc. food scientist Pepsi Cola, Valhalla, NY, 1991—92; reading asst., datat entry adminstrv. support pers. Simpson County Schs., Mendenhall, Miss., 1993—98; adv. math., chemistry sci. tchr. Piney Woods Sch., Miss., 1999—2005. Author of poems. Recipient Chemist of Yr., Am. Chem. Soc., Washington, 2004. Mem.: Inst. of Food Technologists. Avocations: coin collecting/numismatics, stamp collecting/philately, classical music.

GRIFFITH, ROY LLOYD, design engineer; b. Shrewsbury, Salop, U.K., Feb. 17, 1972; Student, South Cheshire Coll., England, 1988—90, Stockport Coll., 1990—91, Smallpiece Ho. Coll., 1991—93. R&D mgr. Barclay Leisure, Macclesfield, Cheshire, England, 1991—97; tech. mgr. Ultrabronz Am., Richmond, Va., 1997—99; tech. dir. HOTRS, Inc., Kansas City, 1999—2000; design engr. ETS.LLC, Indpls., 2000—. Achievements include patents pending for shoulder tanner evice; flat panel tanning lamp device; variable wattage ballast; rejuvenation LED panel. Home: 1101 Windsor St Indianapolis IN 46201-1165 Personal E-mail: roygrif@hotmail.com.

GRIFFITH, SIMA LYNN, investment banker, consultant; b. NYC, Sept. 7, 1960; d. Morris Benjamin and Mary (Buberoglü) Nahum; m. Clark Calvin Griffith, Sept. 13, 1987. BA in English, Amherst Coll., 1982. Account exec. D.F. King & Co., Inc., NYC, 1982-84, asst. v.p., 1984-86, v.p., 1986-88, Wells & Miller, Mpls., 1988; pres. Griffith, Levi Capital, Inc, Mpls., 1988—96; prin. Aethlon, Capital LLC, Mpls., 1996—, mng. prin. Co-chmn. PRSA, IR seminars, 1987; bd. adv. Pacer, Inc. Bd. dirs. Children's Hosps. and Clinics, 2004—, Mpls. Found.; bd. govs. Children's Theater Co., 1999—2005; bd. adv. PACER; co-chair Women-to-Women. Named Not for Profit Dir. of Yr., Women on Boards, 2005; named one of Twin Cities Women to Watch, The Bus. Jour., 2002, Top Women in Fin., Fin. and Commerce newspaper, 2003; recipient Vision award, Nat. Assn. Women Bus. Owners, 2003. Mem.: Pub. Rels. Soc. Am. (bod. govs., investor rels. sec. 1987—89), Assn. Bus. Communicators (bd. govs. 1987—88). Office: Aethlon Capital LLC 4920 IDS Ctr 80 South 8th St Minneapolis MN 55402-2100 Office Phone: 612-338-0934, 612-338-6065. E-mail: sgriffith@aethlon.com.

GRIFFITH, STEVEN FRANKLIN, SR., lawyer, insurance agent; b. New Orleans, July 14, 1948; s. Hugh Franklin and Rose Marie (Teutone) G.; m. Mary Elizabeth McMillan Frank, Dec. 9, 1972; children: Steven Franklin Jr., Jason Franklin. BBA, Loyola U., New Orleans, 1970, JD, 1972. Bar: La. 1972, U.S. Dist. Ct. (ea. dist.) La. 1975, U.S. Ct. Appeals (5th cir.) 1975, U.S. Supreme Ct. 1976. With Law Offices of Senator George T. Oubre, Norco, La., 1971-75; sole practice Destrehan, La., 1975—. Pres. 29th Jud. Dist. Bar Assn., 1999—2002. Fellow: La. State Bar Found.; mem.: ATLA, ABA, St. Charles Parish Bar Assn. (pres. 1999—2002), Fed. Bar Assn., New Orleans Trial Lawyers Assn., La. Trial Lawyers Assn., La. State Bar Assn. (ho. of dels. 1987—). Democrat. Home: 34 Shadow Ln Destrehan LA 70047-3623 Office: PO Box 999 13358 River Rd Destrehan LA 70047-5000 Office Phone: 985-764-6862. Business E-Mail: griffithlawfirm@aol.com.

GRIFFITH, THOMAS BEALL, federal judge; b. Yokohama, Japan, July 5, 1954; s. Robert Elmon and Jane (Beall) Griffith; m. Susan Ann Stell; children: Chelsea, Megan, Robert, Erin, Victoria, Tanne. BA, Brigham Young U., 1978; JD, U. Va., 1985. Bar: NC 1985, DC 1991. Assoc. Robinson, Bradshaw & Hinson P.A., Charlotte, NC, 1985—89, Wiley, Rein & Fielding LLP, Washington, 1989—93, ptnr., 1993—95, 1999—2000; legal counsel US Senate, Washington, 1995—99; asst. to the pres., gen. counsel Brigham Young U., Provo, Utah, 2000—05; judge US Ct. Appeals (DC cir.), Washington, 2005—. Mem. exec. com. Ctrl. European and Eurasian Law Initiative ABA, 1995—, ex officio council mem., Adminstrv. Law & Regulatory Practice, 1996—99; gen. counsel Adv. Commn. on Electronic Commerce, 1999—2000; mem. Sec. Edn.'s Commn. on Opportunity in Athletics (Title IX Commn.), 2002—03. Office: US Ct Appeals 333 Constitution Ave NW Washington DC 20001*

GRIFFITH, WILLIAM ALEXANDER, former mining company executive; b. Sioux Falls, SD, Mar. 28, 1922; s. James William and Adeline Mae (Reid) G.; m. Gratia Frances Hannan, Jan. 27, 1949; children—Georgeanne Reid, James William, Wade Andrew. BS in Metall. Engring., S.D. Sch. Mines and Tech., 1947; MS in Metallurgy, M.I.T., 1950; Mineral Dressing Engr. (hon.), Mont. Coll. Mineral Sci. and Tech., 1971; D in Bus. Adminstrn. (hon.), S.D. Sch. Mines & Tech., 1986; D in Sci. (hon.), U. Idaho, 1990. With N.J. Zinc Co., 1949-57, chief milling and maintenance Bertha mines divsn., 1956-57; metallurgist Rare Metals Corp. Am., Tuba City, Ariz., 1957-58; dir. rsch. Phelps Dodge Corp., Morenci, Ariz., 1958-68; with Hecla Mining Co., Coeur d'Alene, Idaho, 1968-87, exec. v.p., 1978, pres., chief exec. officer, 1979-86, chmn., chief exec. officer, 1986-87; pres. Granduc Mines Ltd., 1987-88; chmn. Inland N.W. Bancorp., Inc., 1989-96. Bd. dirs. The Coeur d'Alenes Co. With USNR, 1943-46. Mem. AIME (Gaudin award 1977, Richards award 1981, Disting. mem. 1977, Hon. 1987), NAE, Am. Mining Congress (past dir.), Idaho Mining Assn. (past pres.), Idaho Assn. Commerce and Industry (past bd. dirs.), Western Regional Coun. (chmn. 1986-87), Nat. Strategic Materials and Minerals Adv. Com. to Sec. Interior, Silver Inst. (past pres., past chmn.), Nat. Acad. of Engring., Sigma Tau, Theta Tau. Lodges: Rotary. Republican. Home: 846 E Northwood Ct Hayden ID 83835-8546

GRIFFITH, WILLIAM HERBERT, retired psychotherapist, minister; b. Newark, Ohio, May 29, 1930; s. Herbert William and Gladys Winifred Griffith; m. Elsie Mae Collins (div. 1972); children: William Eugene, Deborah Sue; m. Ruby Jane McClain, Apr. 13, 1973. AB, William Jewell Coll., Liberty, Mo., 1959; MDiv, Midwestern Bapt. Theol. Sem., Kansas City, Mo., 1963; MS, Air Command and Staff Coll., Maxwell AFB, Ala., 1973; DMin, So. Bapt. Theol. Sem., Louisville, 1981. Served with USAF, 1948—56; pastor New Liberty Bapt. Ch., Oak Grove, Mo., 1956—60; adminstr. for process engring. Ford Motor Co., Kansas City, 1960—63; chaplain USAF, 1963—77; psychotherapist Vipcare, 1978—86; resident in psychotherapy Va. Inst. Pastoral Care, Richmond, 1981; pvt. practice Richmond, 1986—2001. Bd. dirs. Salvation Army, Valdosta, Ga., 1968—71, Hampton, Va., 1973—77. Maj. USAF, 1948—77. Decorated Meritorious Svc. medal with oak leaf cluster, Air Force Commendation medal with oak leaf cluster. Fellow: Am. Assn. Pastoral Counselors; mem.: Am. Assn. Marriage and Family Therapists (clin. mem.), York Rite Masons, Scholar Shipkey, Phi Alpha Theta, Pi Gamma Mu, Phi Alpha Theta. Democrat. Episcopalian. Avocations: watercolor painting, travel. Home: 1725 Winding Way Richmond VA 23235 Personal E-mail: whgjmg@comcast.net.

GRIFFITH, WILLIAM R., lawyer; AB in Polit. Sci., Brown U., 1970; JD, George Washington U., 1974. Bar: NY 1975. With Certilman Haft Balin Buckley Kremer & Hyman; ptnr. Rivkin Radler Dunne & Bayh, 1988—89, Parker Duryee Rosoff & Haft (combined with Reed Smith in 2002), 1989—2002, Reed Smith LLP, NYC, 2002—, also practice group leader life sciences transactions group. Dir. Nat. Hospice and Palliative Care Orgn.; chmn. bd. Nat. Hospice Found. Office: Reed Smith LLP 599 Lexington Ave 29th Fl New York NY 10022 Office Phone: 212-549-0238, 212-521-5450. Business E-Mail: wgriffith@reedsmith.com.

GRIFFITH, YOLANDA EVETTE, professional basketball player; b. Chgo., Mar. 1, 1970; d. Harvey Griffith; 1 child, Candace. Student, Palm Beach Jr. Coll., Fla. Atlantic U. Player, Germany, 1993—97, Long Beach StingRays, ABL, 1997—98, Sacramento Monarchs, WNBA, 1999—. Mem. USA Basketball Women's Sr. Nat. Team, 1998, 99, 2000, 04. Named Defensive Player of Yr., ABL, 1998, WNBA, 1999, MVP, 1999, Newcomer of Yr., 1999; named to First Team All-ABL, 1998, First Team All-WNBA, 1999, WNBA Western Conf. All-Star Team, 1999—2001, 2003, 2005—07. Achievements include winning a Gold Medal at the 2000 Sydney Olympics. Avocations: softball, music. Office: Sacramento Monarchs One Sports Pkwy Sacramento CA 95834*

GRIFFITHS, BARBARA LORRAINE, psychologist, writer, marriage and family therapist; b. Glendale, Calif., July 15, 1927; d. David William and Mabel Augusta (Gaarder) G.; m. Dale Elmo Rumbaugh, Mar. 28, 1948 (div. 1957); 1 child, David Wynn; m. Knute Flint, Nov. 13, 1964. AA in Journalism, Valley C.C., 1958; BA in Psychology, U. Calif. Riverside, 1972; MS in Rehab. Counseling, Calif. State U., 1976; PhD in Clin. Psychology, Calif. Grad. Inst., 1984. Cert. Diplomate Am. Psychotherapy Assn., 1998, cert. addiction specialist, Marriage and Family Therapist 1979. Alcoholism counselor Kaiser Permanente, LA, 1976-82; pvt. practice Hollywood, L.A., 1979-89, Glendale, Burbank, Calif., 1989-97, LA, 1997—2005. Mem. State of Calif. Med. Diversion Evaluation Com., 1998—2003; screener 6th and 7th Prism awards Entertainment Industry Coun. Film, 2001—02; sci. expert reviewer 6th annual Prism Awards Entertainment Industry Coun., 2002—03; reviewer 6th and 7th Ann. PRISM awards Entertainment Industry Coun. Film, 2002; clinical psychologist Calif. Youth Authority, 2002—03. Editor (child abuse newsletter): Directions, 1976—86; writer, prodr.: (short film) Silver Bullet Kid, 2003; contbr. short stories, feature articles, columns to various mags., newspapers and profl. mags. Mem. Glendale Rotary, 1990-95, Verdugo BPW, 1988-91; Nat. Ski Patrolwoman #122, 1952-56. Recipient Editor's Choice award for poetry, 1997. Mem. APA (assoc.), Los Angeles County Psychol. Assn. Avocations: script writing, tennis, skiing, swimming and water sports, reading. Home and Office: 1565 Virginia Ranch Rd Gardnerville NV 89410

GRIFFITHS, JOSÉ-MARIE, dean, library and information science educator; b. Middlesex County, England; m. Donald W. King; 1 child, Rhiannon Joyce. BSc in Physics with honours, London U., England, 1973, PhD in Info. Sci., 1977. Rsch. fellow Univ. Coll., London U., Teddington, England, 1974-76, lectr. Sch. Libr., Archive and Info. Studies, 1972-79; dir. computing lab. Imperial Cancer Rsch. Fund Labs., London, 1978-79; head edn. and tng. ctr. Marconi Avionics, Hertfordshire, England, 1979-80; v.p., bd. dirs. King Rsch., Inc., Rockville, Md., 1980-89; prof., collaborating scientist in info. sci., dir. U. Tenn. Sch. Info. Scis., Knoxville, Tenn., 1989, dir. Ctr. Info. Studies, 1989, prof., 1989—96, acting vice chancellor computing and telecomms., 1994; prof. Sch. Info., univ. chief info. officer, exec. dir. Info. Tech. Div., founding dir. Collaboratory for Advanced and Academic Tech. U. Mich., Ann Arbor, 1996—2001; Doreen E. Boyce Chair, prof. Sch. Info., dir. Sara Fine Inst. Interpersonal Behavior and Tech., assoc. Learning Rsch. and Devel. Ctr. U. Pitts., 2001—04; dean, prof. Sch. Info. and Libr. Sci., U. NC, Chapel Hill, 2004—. Vis. lectr. dept. libr. and info. studies Queen's U., Belfast, No. Ireland, 1976-77; vis. prof. U. Calif. Sch. Libr. and Info. Studies, U. Calif., Berkeley, 1979-80; cons. dept. librarianship U. Ibadan, Nigeria, 1984; instr. Cath. U. Washington, 1986-89; tech. advisor divsn. gen. infor programme UNESCO, Paris, 1978; mem. US Nat. Commn. on Librs. and Info. Sci., 1996-2002, President's Info. Tech. Adv. Com., 2003-05, US Nat. Sci. Bd., 2006-. Author: (with Donald W. King) Special Libraries and Information Services—Increasing the Information Edge, 1993; editor: Perspectives on Information Management series, 1987-90; mem. editl. bd. Microcomputers for Info. Mgmt., 1984-86; contbr. numerous articles to profl. jours. Recipient rsch. award Spl. Librs. Assn., 1992; rsch. studentship Nat. Phys. Labr., 1972, Brit. Libr., 1974-77; rsch. fellow City U., 1976-78, hon. rsch. fellow Univ. Coll., 1977—, rsch. fellow Royal Soc.-Brit. Libr., 1977-79. Mem. Inst. Info. Scientists (rsch. com. 1976-79), Brit. Computer Soc. (info. retrieval specialist group), Am. Libr. and Info. Sci. Educators (awards com. 1994-96), Am. Soc. for Info. Scis. (chmn. professionalism com. 1987-88, nominations com. 1993—, mem. rsch. com. 1982-86, edn. com. 1983-86, networking com. 1981-87, awards and honors com. 1993—, pres.-elect. 1992, pres. 1993, rep. on Nat. Commn. on Softwre Issues in 80's 1982—, on ALISE-ASIS coop. activities com. 1993-95, rsch. award 1990). Office: Sch Info and Libr Sci U NC at Chapel Hill CB#3360, 100 Manning Hall Chapel Hill NC 27514-3360 Office Phone: 919-962-8363. Office Fax: 919-962-8071. E-mail: jmgriff@unc.edu.*

GRIFFITHS, PETER ROUGHLEY, chemistry professor, consultant; b. Cheam, Surrey, Eng., Jan. 20, 1942; arrived in US, 1967; s. Bertram James and Dorothy Griffiths; m. Marie Frances Burns, Sept. 10, 1971; children: Sian Bethany Griffiths Myers, Megan Claire. BA, Oxford U., Eng., 1964, grad., 1967. Post-doctoral assoc. U. Md., College Park, 1967—69; product specialist Digilab, Inc., Cambridge, Mass., 1969—70; mgr. analytical svcs. Sadtler Rsch. Labs., Phila., 1970—72; from asst. to disting. prof. Ohio U., Athens, 1972—82; prof. U. Calif., Riverside, 1982—89, U. Idaho, Moscow, Idaho, 1989—, dept. chmn., 1989—97, 2001—05. Cons. in field. Author: Fourier Transform Infrared, 1986, 2d edit.; editor: Vibrational Spectroscopy in Difaracentical R&D, 2007; contbr. chapters to books, articles to profl. jours. Recipient Fritz Pregl medal, Austrian Soc. Analystical Chemistry, 1987, award, Spectroscopy Soc. Pitts., 1995, Gerald S. Birth award, Coun. for Near Infrared Spectroscopy, 2004; Rsch. fellow, Alexander von Humboldt Found., 2006—07. Mem.: Soc. for Applied Spectroscopy (hon.; assoc. editor 1995—, pres. 1993—94). Home: 1073 Nearing Rd Moscow ID 83843 Office: Dept Chemistry Univ Idaho Moscow ID 83844-2343

GRIFFITHS, PHILLIP A., mathematician, retired academic administrator; b. Raleigh, NC, Oct. 18, 1938; s. Phillip and Jeanette (Field) G.; m. Ann Lane Crittenden, 1958-67; children: Jan Kirsten, David; m. Marian Folsom Jones, 1968; children: Sarah, Rebecca. BS, Wake Forest U., 1959; PhD, Princeton U., 1962; D (hon.), Angers U., France, 1979; DSc (hon.), Wake Forest U., 1973, U. Peking, China, 1983; DSc (hon.), U. Oslo, 2002. Mem. staff U. Calif., Berkeley, 1964-67; prof. math. Princeton (N.J.) U., 1968-72; prof. Harvard U., Cambridge, Mass., 1972-83, Dwight Parker Robinson prof. math., 1983; provost, James B. Duke prof. math. Duke U., Durham, NC, 1983-91; dir. Inst. for Advanced Study, Princeton, NJ, 1991—2003, prof. math., 2004—; sr. advisor Mellon Fedn., 2001—; Disting. Presdl. fellow for acad. affairs NAS, 2002—. Bd. dirs. Oppenheimer Funds, GSI Lumonics; vis. prof. Princeton U., 1967-68, mem. Inst. Advanced Study, 1968-70; chmn. bd. on math. scis. NRC, 1986-91, chmn. commn. on phys. scis., math. and applications, 1992, chmn. com. on sci., engring. and pub. policy, 1992-99; mem. Nat. Sci. Bd., 1991-96; sec. Internat. Math. Union, 1999— (sec.); chair Sci. Initiative Group, 1999—. Editor Jour. Differential Geometry, 1980-90, Compositio Mathematica, 1980-92, Duke Math. Jour., 1983—, Selecta Mathematica, 1994—, Annals of Math., 1997—, Advances in Function Theory, 2002, Annals of Math. Studies, 2001. Bd. dirs. Rsch. Triangle Inst., 1983-91; trustee Woodward Acad., NC Sch. Sci. and Math. Decorated Nat. Order of Sci. Merit (Brazil); recipient LeRoy P. Steel prize Am. Math. Soc., 1971, Dannie Heineman Preis, Acad. Scis. Gottingen, 1979, Ordem Nat. Mérito Cientifico, Ministry of Sci. and Tech., Brazil, 2002; Miller fellow U. Calif. Berkeley, 1962-64, 1975-76, Guggenheim fellow, 1980-82. Fellow: Accademia Lincei (assoc.; fgn.), Third World Acad. Scis. (assoc.; fgn.); mem.: NAS (disting. sr. pres. fellow internat. rels. 2002—), Coun. on Fgn. Rels., Am. Acad. Arts and Scis., Am. Philos. Soc., N.Y. Yacht Club.

GRIFFITHS, RACHEL, actress; b. Melbourne, Australia, June 4, 1968; d. Anna Griffiths; m. Andrew Taylor, Dec. 31, 2002; children: Banjo Patrick, Adelaide Rose. BEd in Drama and Dance, Victoria Coll. Actor: (films) Muriel's Wedding, 1994 (Best Supporting Actress Australian Film Critics award, Best Supporting Actress Australian Film Inst. award, 1995), Jude, 1996, To Have and To Hold, 1997, My Best Friend's Wedding, 1997, Hilary and Jackie, 1998 (nominee Best Supporting Actress Oscar, 1999), My Son, the Fanatic, 1998, Among Giants, 1998, Amy, 1998, Me Myself I, 1999, Blow, 2001, The Rookie, 2002, The Hard Word, 2002, Ned Kelly, 2003, Angel, 2005, Step Up, 2006; (TV series) Secrets, 1993, Jimeoin, 1994, Six Feet Under, 2001—05 (Best Suppporting Actress Golden Globe award, 2001), Brothers & Sisters, 2006; (TV films) The Feds, 1993, Since You've Been Gone, 1998, Plainsong, 2004.

GRIFFITHS, ROBERT PENNELL, banker; b. Chgo., May 6, 1949; s. George Findley and Marion E. (Winterrowd) G.; m. Susan Hillman, Jan. 31, 1976 (div. 2002); m. Janet Bauer, March, 22, 2003. BA, Amherst Coll., 1972; MS in Mgmt., Northwestern U., 1974. From comml. banking officer to v.p. No. Trust Co., Chgo., 1978—85; sr. v.p. comml. lending Unibanc-Trust Co., Chgo., 1985-88; pres., CEO Old Kent Bank of Naperville, Ill., 1988—90; sr. v.p. Old Kent Bank, Chgo., 1991—92; pres., CEO Uptown Nat. Bank Chgo., 1993—2001; mng. dir. Pvt. Bank and Trust Co., Chgo., 2002—. Mem.: Univ. Club (Chgo.), Onwentsia Club. Home: 2726 Aspen Ct Glenview IL 60026 Office: Pvt Bank and Trust Co 5260 Old Orchard Rd Skokie IL 60077

GRIFFITHS, SYLVIA PRESTON, physician, educator; b. London, Dec. 25, 1924; d. Wheeler Bate and Dorothy (Hartley) Preston; m. Raymond B. Griffiths; 1 dau., Wendy Elizabeth. BA, Hunter Coll., NYC, 1944; MD, Yale U., New Haven, Conn., 1948. Intern Grace-New Haven Cmty. Hosp., 1948-49, resident, 1949-52; fellow in pediatric cardiology Yale U., 1952-54; asst. to prof. clin. pediatrics Columbia U., 1955, prof. clin. pediatrics, 1977-90, prof. emerita, 1990—. Recipient career scientist award Health Research Council, City of NY, 1963-69 Mem. NY Heart Assn. (dir. 1977-83), Am. Acad. Pediatrics, Am. Pediatric Soc., Am. Heart Assn., Am. Coll. Cardiology, Babies Hosp. Alumni Assn. (pres. 1991-92). Office: Columbia Presbyterian Med Ctr 622 W 168th St New York NY 10032-3720

GRIFFITHS, YOLANDA W., occupational therapist, educator; d. Clarence and Violet Chew; m. Calvin E. Griffiths, Mar. 12, 1977; children: Trisha, Megan, Kelly. Degree, U. Puget Sound, Tacoma, Wash., 1976, U. Okla., Norman, Okla., 1994; degree in Occupl. Therapy, Creighton U., Omaha, Nebr., 1999. Registered occupl. therapist Nat. Bd. Occupl. Therapists, 2007, lic. Nebr., 2007. Assoc. prof. Creighton U., Omaha, Albania, 1993—. Fellow: Am. Occupl. Therapy Assn. Home Phone: 402-280-5980; Office Phone: 402-280-5980.

GRIFFY, THOMAS ALAN, physics professor; b. Oklahoma City, Dec. 16, 1936; s. Judson H. and Dicie (Johnston) G.; m. Peggy Lynn Walker, June 6, 1958; children— David, Alan, Marjorie BA, Rice U., 1959, MA, 1960, PhD, 1961. Asst. prof. physics Duke U., Durham, NC, 1961—62; research assoc. High Energy Physics Lab., Stanford U., Calif., 1962-65; assoc. prof. physics U. Tex., Austin, 1965—68, prof., 1968—2004, chmn. dept., 1974—84, assoc. dean grad. sch., 1970—73, 1996—2000, prof. emeritus, 2004—. Contbr. articles to profl. jours. Fellow: Am. Phys. Soc. Methodist. Office: U Tex Dept Physics Austin TX 78712 Home Phone: 512-453-6328; Office Phone: 512-471-1053. E-mail: tgriffy@sbcglobal.net.

GRIFFY, TIMOTHY T., human resources specialist, finance company executive; BA, Rice U., M in Acctg. With Ernst & Young, NYC, 1980—, ptnr., 1992—95, dir. human resources (S.W. area), 1995—98, area mng. ptnr., 1998—2002, global mng. ptnr. people, 2002—. Office: Ernst & Young Internat 5 Times Square New York NY 10036 Office Phone: 212-773-3000. Office Fax: 212-773-6350.

GRIGG, EDDIE GARMAN, minister, educator; b. Shelby, NC, Feb. 20, 1957; s. Gaston Theodore and Sylvia Evlyn (Davis) G.; m. Susan Wanda Ray, May 28, 1977; children: Mark Zolton, Jamie Ray, Steven Russell. BA, Gardner-Webb Coll., 1980; MDiv, Southeastern Bapt. Theol. Sem., 1985; D Ministry, Emmanuel Bapt. U., 1994, DRE, 1995; DD (hon.), New Life U., 1998. Ordained to ministry So. Bapt. Conv., 1976. Pastor Victory Bapt. Ch., Kings Mountain, NC, 1975-79, Christian Freedom Bapt. Ch., Kings Mountain, 1979-81, Sanford Meml. Bapt. Ch., Brodnax, Va., 1981-85, Pleasant Hill Bapt. Ch., Shelby, NC, 1985-89; sr. min. Wilson Grove Bapt. Ch., Charlotte, NC, 1989-93; founder, pastor New Life Bapt. Ch., Charlotte, 1993—2003; founder, pres. New Life Theological Seminary, Charlotte, 1996—; ch. adminstr. Ebenezer Bapt. Ch., 2004—. Mem. First Bapt. Ch., Charlotte. Mem. Nat. Assn. Ch. Bus. Adminstrators, Bapt. Metrolina Ministries Pastor's Conf. (pres. 1995-97), Bapt. Metrolina Ministries Assn. (evangelism com. 1990-93, urban ch. com. 1990-94). Republican. Office: New Life Theol Sem PO Box 790106 Charlotte NC 28206 Office Phone: 704-334-6882. Personal E-mail: eddiegrigg@aol.com.

GRIGG, RICHARD R., energy executive; BS in Mech. Engring., U. Wis., MME. Engr. Lakeside Power Plant Wis. Electric Power Co., 1970, v.p. sys. ops., 1990—92, v.p. customer ops., 1992—94, group exec., v.p. customer ops., customer svcs. and sales and mktg., bd. dirs., 1994—95; pres., COO, bd. dirs. Wis. Energy Corp. (merger of Wis. Electric Power Co. and Wis. Natural Gas), 1995, chief nuc. officer Wis. Electric Power Co., 1996—98, sr. v.p., 2000—02, pres., COO Wis. Electric Power Co. and Wis. Gas Co., 2000, exec. v.p., 2002—04, pres., CEO WE Generation Milw., 2003—04; exec. v.p., COO FirstEnergy Corp., 2004—. Bd. trustees Milw. Boys and Girls Club. Mem.: ASME, Am. Nuc. Soc. Office: FirstEnergy Corp 76 S Main St Akron OH 44308 Office Phone: 800-736-3402.*

GRIGGER, JANE ELIZABETH, earth science educator, photographer; b. Phila., June 7, 1947; d. John Casimer and Rozanne Marie (Peters) G. BS in Geology, Bucknell U., 1969; MEd in Earth Sci. Edn., Temple U., 1971. Tchr. secondary sci. Bensalem Twp. Sch. Dist., Cornwells Heights, Pa., 1970-72, Princeton Regional Schs. (N.J.), 1972-75; tchr. middle sch. earth sci. and phys. sci. Princeton Day Sch., 1975—. Tchr. ptnrs. in edn. geology program Princeton U., 1985, photographer jours. Troop advisor S.E. Pa. coun. Girls Scouts U.S.A., 1969—; photographer Girl Scout Internat. Event, 1975, 76. Mem. Phila. Geol. Soc., Field Conf. Pa. Geologists, N.J. Sci. Tchrs. Assn., Roster Women Geoscis., N.J. Earth Scis. Tchrs. Assn., Nat. Assn. Geology Tchrs., Nat. Sci. Tchrs. Assn., Plainsboro Hist. Soc., Bucknell Alumni Club. Episcopalian. Home: 6413 Ravens Crest Dr Plainsboro NJ 08536-2430 Office: Princeton Day Sch PO Box 75 Princeton NJ 08542-0075 Office Phone: 609-924-6700. Business E-Mail: jgrigger@pds.org.

GRIGGS, GARY BRUCE, oceanographer, geologist, educator, director; b. Pasadena, Calif., Sept. 25, 1943; s. Dean Brayton and Barbara Jayne (Farmer) G.; children: Joel, Amy, Shannon, Cally, Cody. BA in Geology, U. Calif., Santa Barbara, 1965; PhD in Oceanography, Oreg. State U., 1968. Registered geologist, Calif.; cert. engr. geologist, Calif. Rsch. asst., NSF grad. fellow in oceanography Oreg. State U., 1965-68; from asst. prof. to prof. earth scis. U. Calif., Santa Cruz, 1969—; Fulbright fellow Inst. for Ocean & Fishing Rsch., Athens, Greece, 1974-75; oceanographer Joint U.S.A.-N.Z. Rsch. Program, 1980-81; chair earth scis. U. Calif., Santa Cruz, 1981-84, assoc. dean natural scis., 1992-95; dir. Inst. of Marine Scis., 1991—. Vis. prof. Semester at Sea program U. Pitts., 1984-96; guest lectr. World Explorer Cruises, 1987; chair marine coun. U. Calif., 1999—; bd. govs. Consortium for Oceanographic Rsch. and Edn., 1995—. Author: (with others) Geologic Hazards, Resources and Environmental Planning, 1983, Living with the California Coast, 1985, Coastal Protection Structures, 1986, California's Coastal Hazards, 1992, Formation, Evolution and Stability of Coastal Cliffs-Status and Trends, 2004, Living With Changing California Coast, 2005, The Santa Cruz Coast: Then and Now, 2006; mem. editl. bd. Jour. of Coastal Rsch.; contbr. numerous articles to profl. jours. Mem. Am. Geophys. Union, Am. Geol. Inst., Coastal Found. Achievements include research in coastal processes; coastal erosion and protection; coastal engineering and hazards; sediment yield, transport and dispersal; geologic hazards and land use. Office: U Calif Inst Marine Scis Santa Cruz CA 95064 Business E-Mail: griggs@pmc.ucsc.edu.

GRIGGS, JOYCE L., secondary school educator; d. Milo Roger and Mary Louise Hulsebus; m. Thomas J. Griggs, May 26, 1973; children: Brian, Jeffrey. BA, Simpson Coll., 1973; MA, Ariz. State U., 1991. Tchr. Southeast Warren Schs., Liberty Center, Iowa, 1973—75, Marshall U. High Sch., Mpls., 1975—76; sec. Watermation Engring., St. Paul, 1976—79; adminstrv. asst. Neiser, Campara & Horne Law Firm, Phoenix, 1980—84; tchr. Lamson Coll., Glendale, 1984—86; tchr., instructional specialist Ironwood High Sch., 1987—. Author of poems. Grantee, Peoria Ednl. Enrichment. Mem.: ASCD, Phi Kappa Phi. Methodist. Avocations: graphic arts, computers, writing. Office Phone: 623-486-6418. Business E-Mail: jgriggs@peoriaud.k12.az.us.

GRIGGS, JULIE HINDS, foundation administrator; b. Nashville, Mar. 10, 1966; d. James Connelly and Lucy-Fay Morgan Hinds; m. Glynn Jordan Griggs, Dec. 21, 1996. BA in Journalism, Auburn U., Ala., 1988; MEd, Vanderbilt U., Nashville, 2002; PhD student, U. Conn., Storrs, 2003—, MA, 2007. Staff writer Auburn Alumnews, Ala., 1987—88; investgative reporter, rschr. Nashville Bus. Jour., 1988—91; editl. asst. Athlon Sports Comm., Nashville, 1989; staff writer Sourcebook Mag., 1992—92; internat. relief worker various humanitarian orgns., 1992—96; exec. dir., co-founder Providence Internat., 1999—2003; counselor Inst. Family Enrichment, Honolulu, 2000—01, Salvation Army Addiction Treatment Svcs., 2001; exec. dir., co-founder Malama Internat., 2002—; therapist Asylum Family Practice Ctr., Hartford, Conn., 2004—05, Humphrey Ctr. Marital and Family Therapy, U. Conn., Storrs, 2004—06. Presenter in field. Contbr. articles to profl. jours. Mem.: Internat. Family Therapy Assn., Conn. Counseling Assn., Conn. Assn. Marriage and Family Therapy, Am. Assn. Marriage and Family Therapy, Am. Counseling Assn., Nat. Mayflower Soc., Chi Sigma Iota, Phi Eta Sigma, Mensa (life), Internat. Mensa (life). Avocations: genealogy, travel, hiking. Office: Malama Internat PO Box 429 Avon CT 06001

GRIGGS, LEONARD LEROY, JR., air transportation executive, consultant; b. Norfolk, Va., Oct. 13, 1931; s. Leonard LeRoy and Mary (Blair) G.; m. Denise Ziegler, Mar. 18, 1977; children: Margaret Rosalyn, Virginia Lorraine Williams, Julia Blair Havey, Deborah Branham Taylor. BS, US Mil. Acad., 1954; MS in Aero. Engring., Air Force Inst. Tech., 1960; MS in Internat. Affairs, George Wash. U., Washington, DC, 1967; disting. grad., Naval War Coll., 1967, Army War Coll., 1971. Registered profl. engr., Mo. Commd. 2d lt. U.S. Army, 1954; advanced through grades to col. USAF, 1970; served in Vietnam; ret., 1977; dir. Lambert St. Louis Internat. Airport, 1977-87; v.p. Ross & Baruzzini, Inc., 1987-89, Bangert Bros. Constrn. Co., St. Louis and Denver, 1989—; asst. adminstr. for airports FAA, Washington, 1990-93; airport dir. St. Louis Internat. Airport, 1993—2004; aviation cons., 2005—. Adj. prof. St. Louis U.; apptd. to Nat. Civil Aviation Rev. Commn., 1997. Bd. dirs. USO, St. Louis/Lambert, Airports Coun. Internat., 1997-98. Decorated Silver Star, D.F.C. with 4 oak leaf clusters, Bronze Star, Meritorious Svc. medal, Air medal with 22 oak leaf clusters, Purple Heart, Air Force Commendation medal with 2 oak leaf clusters, Army Commendation medal; Medal of Honor; Medal of Gallantry (Vietnam); recipient Aviation Engring. Safety award FAA, 1979. Mem. Airport Operators Coun. Internat., Am. Assn. Airport Execs., Profl. Engring. Soc. St. Louis, Order of Dadelians, St. Louis Air Force Assn., Engr. Club, Mo. Athletic Club, Army Navy Club, Univ. Club, Order DeMolay. Home: 1609 Tradd Ct Chesterfield MO 63017-5627 Office: La Chateau Village 10411 Clayton Rd Ste307 Saint Louis MO 63131 Home Phone: 636-532-4313; Office Phone: 314-692-0044. Personal E-mail: col.griggs@sbcglobal.net.

GRIGGS, LEWIS BROWN, executive producer, speaker, trainer; b. Mpls./St.Paul, Minn., Aug. 16, 1948; s. Charles Edward Bayliss Griggs and Mary Barbara Brown; children: Ashley Copeland, Ian Copeland. BA, Amherst Coll., Amherst, Mass., 1970; MBA, Stanford U. Grad. Sch. of Bus., Stanford, Calif., 1980. Asst. adminstr. office GSA, Washington, 1970—72; sales & mktg. dir. Spellbinder Inc, Concord, Mass., 1972—74; devel. office WGBH / Channel 2 / PBS, Boston, 1974—76, KQED / Channel 9 / PBS, San Francisco, 1976—78; pres. & CEO Griggs Prodn., San Rafael, Calif., 1982—. Bd. dirs. Geog. Expeditions, San Francisco, 1996—. Author: Going International, Valuing Diversity; prodr.: (6-part series of training videos/guides) Human Energy at Work, (3-part series of interactive cd-roms) No Potential Lost, (7-part series of training videos/guides) Going International, Valuing Diversity (Nat. Edn. Film Festival, 1988), (3-part series of training videos/guides) Valuing Relationship (Internat. TV Assn., 1993); cross-cultural diversity speaker/trainer (Valuing Diversity workshops) (Internat. HRD Practitioner Award, 1989, Achieving Performance Excellence Award, 2003). Mem.: Soc. Intercultural Edn. Tng. Rsch., Acad. Mgmt., Am. Soc. for Tng. & Devel., Soc. for Human Resource Mgmt., Diversity Leadership Forum, Assn. for Spirit at Work, Spirit in Bus., World Bus. Acad. Home and Office: Griggs Prodns 220 30th Ave San Francisco CA 94121 Home Phone: 415-750-9040; Office Phone: 415-455-1500, 415-750-5100, 415-750-5145. Office Fax: 415-455-5585. Business E-Mail: lewis@griggs.com.

GRIGGS, NINA M., retired realtor; b. NYC, Sept. 21, 1932; d. John Malcolm Miller and Kathryn Ruth Wilenzick; m. Charles Guy Moseley, Aug. 28, 1954 (dec. Feb. 1970); children: Charles Edward Keeble Moseley, Kathryn Drew Moseley Kristofik; m. Bancroft Gerardi Davis, Dec. 31, 1971 (dec. Dec. 1980); m. Richard Curtis Miles, Feb. 5, 1983 (dec. Sept. 1987); m. Northam Lee Griggs, Feb. 13, 1993 (dec. Mar. 2002). BA, Vassar Coll., 1954; MA, U. Va., 1956; postgrad., Columbia U. Exec. assoc., part-time rsch. assoc., 1961-63; founder, pres. Adventures Abroad, Ltd., 1964-71; also asst. to dir. profl. exams. divn. Psychol. Corp., NYC, 1968-71; program officer Internat. Inst. Ednl. Planning/UNESCO, Paris, 1971-72; program adminstr. French and German lang. tchg. asst. prog. Inst. Internat. Edn., NYC, 1973-85; dir. women's program Internat. Exec. Svc. Corps, 1988-91; real estate associate New England Land Co, Greenwich. Founder, dir. Women's Talent Corps, 1965-67; mem. N.Y. Jr. League; dir. Masters Nursery and Children's Ctr., 1962-81. Author: U.S. Citizenship Today, 1963; editor: (with Kertis, O'Driscoll) English Language and Orientation Programs in the United States, 1978, 80; contbr. articles to profl. jours. Trustee, chmn. nominating com. Dobbs Sch., 1968-71. Mem. Hyannisport Club, N.Y. Jr. League, Harvard Club of N.Y., Delta Delta Delta. Home: 9 Country Rd Westport CT 06880-2524 Personal E-mail: ninagriggs@aol.com.

GRIGORE, ALINA M., anesthesiologist; b. Ploiesti, Romania, Mar. 19, 1965; d. Vasile and Valeria Popa; m. Sorin Grigore, Oct. 3, 1987; 1 child, Audrey Gabrielle. MD, Carol Davila Sch. Medicine, Bucharest, 1989. Diplomate Am. Bd. Anesthesiology. Cardiovasc. anesthesiologist Tex. Heart Inst., Houston, 2000—, dir. cardiovasc. anesthesia echocardiography, 2001—; assoc. prof. anesthesia Baylor Coll. Medicine, Houston, 2005—. Prevention heart disease Am. Heart Assn., Houston, 1998—2006. Recipient Dick Smith award, Duke U.; grantee, Mid-Atlantic afiliates Am. Heart

Assn., 2000. Fellow: Am. Soc. Echocardiography (life). Home: 4422 Betty St Bellaire TX 77401 Office: Tex Heart Inst 6720 Bertner St Rm O-520 Houston TX 77030 Home Phone: 713-592-5918; Office Phone: 832-355-8907. Office Fax: 832-355-6500; Home Fax: 713-660-6864. Personal E-mail: agrigore@pol.net. Business E-Mail: agrigore@heart.thi.tmc.edu.

GRIGORIEV, SERGEI ALEKSANDROVICH, political scientist, researcher; b. Moscow, Feb. 16, 1957; came to U.S., 1991; s. Aleksandr Mironovich Grigoriev and Antonina Nikolayevna Barinova-Sitnikova; m. Valentina M. Maliukovskaya, Nov. 14, 1975 (div. June 1986); 1 child, Helen S. Grigoriev-Pogosyan; m. Elena Borisovna Kostritsyna, June 3, 1989. MA in History, Regional Studies, Langs., Moscow State U., 1979; MPA, Harvard U., Cambridge, Mass., 1993; PhD in Interdisciplinary Studies, Tufts U., Medford, Mass., 1996. Exec. sec. Soviet Chinese Friendship Assn., 1979-84; sr. exec. N.Am. sect. Communist Party Soviet Union, Moscow, 1984-90; asst. press spokesman Office Pres. USSR, Moscow, 1990-91; fellow in residence Princeton U., NJ, 1991-92; fellow Harvard U., Cambridge, Mass., 1992, sr. rsch. assoc., 1992—, exec. dir. Russian fellows program, 1996-99; vis. prof., lectr. Northeastern U., Boston, 1992-96; chief of staff, sr. adviser to Hon. Vladimir Kozhin Head of Office for Gen. Mgmt. and Bus. Adminstrn., 2000—03; v.p., chief of staff Nat. Res. Bank Russia, 2003—04; dep. head Nat. Res. Corp. Russia, 2004—05; v.p. Russia-US Bus. Coun., Moscow, 2005—; dep. dir. gen. Siberian Coal and Energy Co., Moscow, 2007—. Cons. ABC News, NYC, 1991-92; cons., lectr. Leigh Bur., Sommerville, NJ, 1991-94; adviser, cons. to chmn. All-Russian TV and Radio Broadcasting Co., Moscow, 1999-2000; adviser CNN, 2000, Eruasia Group Moscow Trip, 2000. Contbr. articles to newspapers and profl. jours. Cons. Yeltsin for Pres. Campaign, Boston, Moscow, 1996, City Legislature Election, 1998, TV-Ctr., Moscow, 1998; advisor to Hon. Sergei V. Yastrzhembsky, Dep. Premier Moscow City Govt., 1998-99, Hon. Sergei V. Kiriyenko, leader New Force Movement, 1999; cons. Moscow Art Theatre Sch. USA, Cambridge, Mass., 2005—. Mem. Am. Acad. Polit. Sci. Home: 110A Inman St Cambridge MA 02139-1206 also: # 108 Prospect Mira Apt 342 124626 Moscow Russia Office: 7/22 Derbenevskaya nab Ste 20 115114 Moscow Russia Business E-Mail: grigorievsa@msk.suek.ru.

GRIGSBY, SHARLYN ANN, human resources specialist; b. Greevsville, SC, Nov. 6, 1949; d. Defoy and Nannie Ruth Palmer; 1 child, Kenan Dion. BA cum laude, Knoxville Coll., 1971; MA, Trinity Coll., 1975. Personnel mgmt. specialist Dept. of Navy, Wash., DC, 1974—75, US Dept of Treas, Wash., 1975—79; supr. personnel mgmt. specialist US Dept. of Treas., Wash., 1979—80; sr. personnel mgmt. specialist US Dept. of Treas. Office of Sec., Wash., 1981—87, equal employment opportunity comm. dir., 1987—92; dir. of personnel Nat. Labor Relations Bd., Wash., 1992—99; dir. civil svcs. personnel mgmt. US Dept of State, Bur. of Human Resources, Wash., 1999—. Mem.: Internat. Personnel Mgmt. Assn., Alpha Kappa Alpha Sorority, Inc (v.p. Theta Omega Omega Chpt. 1999—2000, pres. Theta Omega Omega Chp. 2001—02, Pres. of Yr. Large Chpt. North Atlantic Region 2002). Democrat. Bapt. Office: US Dept of State 2401 E St NW Washington DC 20522 Office Fax: 202-663-2261. E-mail: sagkdg@aol.com.

GRIJALVA, RAUL, congressman; b. Tucson, Feb. 19, 1948; m. Ramona F. Grijalva; children: Adelita, Raquel, Marisa. BA in Sociology, U. Ariz., 1988. Dir. El Pueblo Neighborhood Ctr.; asst. dean Hispanic student affairs U. Ariz.; mem. Pima County Bd. Suprs., 1989—2003, U.S. Congress from 7th Ariz. dist., 2003—; mem. Edn. and Workforce com., Resources com. and Small Bus. com. U.S. Ho. Reps. Democrat. Roman Catholic. Office: US Ho Reps 1440 Longworth Ho Office Bldg Washington DC 20515-0307*

GRILL, LAWRENCE J., lawyer, accountant, bank executive; b. Chgo., Nov. 5, 1936; s. Samuel S. and Evelyn (Wollack) G.; m. Joan V. Krimston, Dec. 16, 1961; children: Steven Eric, Elizabeth Anne. BS with honors, U. Ill., 1958; postgrad., U. Chgo., 1959—60; LLB, Northwestern U., 1963. CPA Ill.; bar: Ill. 1963, Calif. 1965. Audit and tax mgr. Arthur Anderson & Co., Chgo., 1958-60; with firm Aaron, Aaron, Schimberg & Hess, Chgo., 1963-64, Gendel, Raskoff, Shapiro & Quittner, LA, 1964-66; sec., gen. counsel Traid Corp., LA, 1966-69; v.p., sec., gen. counsel Kaufman & Broad, Inc., LA, 1969-78; pres. Kaufman & Broad Asset Mgmt., dir. subs.; v.p., sec., gen. counsel AM Internat., Inc., Century City, Calif., 1979-82, dir. subs.; sr. v.p., group ops. officer, dir. subs. Wickes Cos., Inc., Santa Monica, Calif., 1982-85; acting CEO, COO, mem. exec. com. Barco of Calif., Gardena, 1985-86; pres. Lawrence J. Grill & Assocs., LA, 1985-94; pres., CEO Pan Am. Bank and United Pan Am. Fin. Corp., San Mateo, Calif., 1994-2000; also bd. dirs. Chmn., pres., CEO Universal Savs. Bank, Orange, Calif., 1988-90; cons. bd. dirs. World Trade Bank, N.A., 1992, Marathon Nat. Bank, 1992-93; spl. advisor to Fed. Home Loan Bank Bd. San Francisco, FDIC for Distressed Savs. Instns., 1986-88; arbitrator Am. Arbitration Assn. Served with AUS, 1958-59. Home: 48437 Vista Palomino La Quinta CA 92253 Office: 1300 S El Camino Real San Mateo CA 94402-2963 Personal E-mail: larg36@yahoo.com.

GRILLER, DAVID, management consultant; b. London, Eng., May 29, 1948; came to Can., 1977; s. Lewis and Renee (Kellinger) G.; m. Alexis Myers, Aug. 22, 1971; children: Hannah, Mark, Nadia. BS, U. Coll. London, 1969, PhD, 1972. Salters Co. fellow, London, 1973; postdoctoral fellow NRC of Can., Ottawa, 1973-75, head organic chemistry, 1977-91; mgmt. cons. Deloitte, Haskins and Sells, London, 1975-77; sr. ptnr. Secor Inc., Ottawa, Ont., Canada; 1991—. Author over 180 sci. papers and books. Recipient CNC-Iupac award Internat. Union Pure and Applied Chemists, 1984, Rutherford medal Royal Soc. Can., 1986, Organic Reaction Mechanisms award Royal Soc. of Chemistry, 1986. Fellow Royal Soc. Can., Can. Inst. Chemistry (Merck Sharp and Dohme award 1985). Avocations: squash, skiing. Office: Groupe Secor 38 McArthur Ave Ste 200 Ottawa ON Canada K1L 6R2 Office Phone: 613-749-8379. E-mail: dgriller@secor.ca.

GRILLER, GORDON MOORE, legal association administrator, consultant; b. Sioux City, Iowa, Feb. 3, 1944; s. Joseph Edward and Arlene (Searles) G. m. Helen Mary Friederichs, aug. 20, 1966; children: Heather, Chad. BA in Political Sci., U. Minn., 1966, MA in Pub. Affairs, 1969. Mgnt. analyst Hennepin County Adminstr., Mpls., 1968-72; asst. court adminstr. Hennepin County Municipal Ct., Mpls., 1972-77, ct. adminstr., 1977-78; judicial dist. adminstr. 2nd Dist. Ct. Minn., St. Paul, 1978-87; ct. adminstr. Superior Ct. Ariz., Phoenix, 1987—2002, Trial Cts. in Maricopa County Ariz., Phoenix, 2002—03; v.p. Justice Practice Group, ACS, Inc. Bd. dirs. Nat. Conf. Metro Cts., 1999—. Vice-chmn. Bloomington Sch. Bd., Minn., 1981-87. Sgt. USAAF, 1968-74 Res. Recipient Warren E. Burger award Inst. Ct. Mgnt.,1988, Leadership Fellows award Bush Leadership Program, 1974. Mem. Nat. Assn. Trial Ct. Adminstrs.(pres. 1983-84), Ariz. Ct. Assn., Nat. Assn Ct. Mgmt. (award of merit), Am. Judicature Soc., (bd. dirs. 1997-2003). Lutheran. Avocations: running, scuba diving, kayaking, hiking. Home: 8507 E San Jacinto Dr Scottsdale AZ 85258-2576 Office: Ste 1750 101 N 1st Ave Phoenix AZ 85003

GRILLO, HENRY R., theater educator, technical director; s. Dominick H. and Margaret A. Grillo; m. Kathryn E. Ganss, Feb. 2, 1953; children: Kristin E., Daniel L. BA, Cornell U., Ithaca, NY, 1975; MFA, Carnegie Mellon U., Pitts., 1981. Dir. tech. tng. NC Sch. Arts, Winston-Salem, 1983—. Pres. NC Scenic Studios, Inc., Winston-Salem, 1983—. Recipient Excellence Tchg. award, U. NC Bd. Govs., 2003—04. Mem.: Am. Inst. Steel Constrn., US Inst. Theatre Tech., Internat. Alliance Theatrical Stage Employees (sec./treas. 1985—2006). Home: 2363 Elizabeth Ave Winston Salem NC 27103-3622 Office: NC School of the Arts 1533 South Main St Winston Salem NC 27127 Home Phone: 336-727-0391; Office Phone: 336-770-3215. E-mail: henrygrillo@ncarts.edu.

GRILLO, HERMES CONRAD, surgeon; b. Boston, Oct. 2, 1923; s. Giacomo and Rose G.; children: Andrea York, Hermes Conrad, Paula, Amy. AB, Brown U., 1943; MD, Harvard U., 1947. Diplomate Am. Bd. Surgery, Am. Bd. Thoracic Surgery (dir. 1979-84). Intern Mass. Gen. Hosp., Boston, 1947-48, resident, 1948-51, 53-55, mem. surg. staff, 1955—, chief gen. thoracic surgery, 1969-94; pvt. practice medicine specializing in thoracic surgery Boston, 1955—. Prof. surgery Harvard U. Med. Sch., 1973—. Author: Surgery of Trachea and Bronchi, 2004; editor 3 books; mem. editl. bd. Jour. Thoracic and Cardiovasc. Surgery, 1975-82; contbr. over 350 sci. articles to profl. jours. Served with USMC, 1951-52; with USN, 1952-53. Decorated Commendation medal with Combat V, Cavaliere dell'Ordine al Merito della Repubblica Italiana, Order Civil Merit (Korea), Korean campaign ribbon with 3 battle stars; Hermes C. Grillo Professorship Thoracic Surgery endowment Harvard Med. Sch., 2002. Mem. ACS, Am. Assn. Thoracic Surgery, Soc. Thoracic Surgeons (pres. 1987-88, Bakken Sci. Achievement award 2002), Am. Surg. Assn., Am. Coll. Chest Physicians (Medallist 1994), Am. Thoracic Soc., Thoracic Surgery Dirs. Assn. (pres. 1983-85), Am. Broncho-Esophagological Assn. (hon.), Belgian Surg. Soc. (hon.), Can. Soc. Cardiovasc. and Thoracic Surgeons (hon.), European Soc. Thoracic Surgeons (hon.), French Surg. Assn. (hon.), Italian Thoracic Surg. Soc. (hon.), Italian Surg. Soc. (hon.), Japanese Assn. for Chest Surgery (hon.), Korean Med. Assn. (hon.), Soc. Thoracic and Cardiovasc. Surgeons Gt. Britain and Ireland (hon.), Assn. Thoracic Surgeons Asia (hon.), Boston Surg. Soc. (pres. 1997, Bigelow medal 2003), Mass. Thoracic Soc. (Chadwick medal 1996), N.E. Surg. Soc. (Nathan Smith award 2000), World Soc. Cardiothoracic Surgery (hon.). Office: Mass Gen Hosp 55 Fruit St/Blake 1570 Boston MA 02114-2620 Office Phone: 617-726-2811. Office Fax: 617-726-7667. Business E-Mail: pguerriero@partners.org.

GRILLO, LEO, actor, photographer; b. Lawrence, Mass., Feb. 6, 1949; s. Leo F. Sr. and Carmela M. (DeLucia) G.; m. Stacy Grillo; children: Erica, Meguire. BS in speech, Emerson Coll., Boston, 1970. Actor, Glendale, Calif., 1965—; pres., founder Dedication and Everlasting Love to Animals Inc., Glendale, 1979—, Living Earth Prodns., 1990—, Horse Rescue Am., 1991—; pres. Leo Grillo Prodns. Inc., 1995, Animals are People, Too, Inc., 2000—, Beach House Prodns., 2002. Author: (with others) Landscam, 1988, Is This the Place?; producer, host Safe House, (TV show) Delta Rescue Story; actor (feature film) The Crap Game, The Rescuer. Mem. Screen Actors' Guild, AFTRA, Actors Equity Assn. Office: DELTA Rescue PO Box 9 Glendale CA 91209-0009

GRILLY, EDWARD ROGERS, physicist; b. Cleve., Dec. 30, 1917; s. Charles B. and Julia (Varady) G.; m. Mary Witholter, Dec. 14, 1942 (dec. 1971); children: David, Janice; m. Juliamarie Andreen Langham, Feb. 1, 1973. BA, Ohio State U., 1940, PhD, 1944. Rsch. scientist Carbide & Carbon Chemicals Corp., Oak Ridge, Tenn., 1944-45; asst. prof. Chemistry U. N.H., Durham, 1946-47; mem. staff U. Calif. Nat. Lab., Los Alamos, N.Mex., 1947-80, cons., 1980—. Contbr. articles to books and profl. jours. Mem. N.Mex. House of Reps., Santa Fe, 1967-70, Los Alamos County Coun., Los Alamos, 1976-78. Mem. Am. Physical Soc., Kiwanis Club, Los Alamos Golf Club (pres. 1974-75). Republican. Avocation: golf. Home: 705 43rd St Los Alamos NM 87544-1807 *The key to my life is discovery. It always amazes me how learning can be so fascinating. Of course, the ultimate is discovery in my own vocation-physics-whether it is of my own doing or learning of a colleague's work. But, I also found that intense involvement in community work can lead to surprising results.*

GRIM, CHARLES W., federal agency administrator; b. Okla. DDS, U. Okla. Coll. Dentistry, 1983; M in Health Services Adminstrn., U. Mich., 1992. Clin. assignment Claremore Svc. unit Indian Health Svc., US Dept. Health & Human Services, Okmulgee, Okla., asst. area dental officer Oklahoma City, area dental officer, 1989—92, dir. divsn. oral health Albuquerque, 1992, acting svc. unit dir., dir. divsn. clin. services and behavioral health, acting exec. officer, assoc. dir. office of health programs Phoenix, 1998—99, acting dir. Oklahoma City, 1999—2000, area dir., 2000—02, interim dir. Rockville, Md., 2002—03, dir., 2003—. Rear adm. Commd. Corps USPHS. Mem.: ADA, Soc. Am. Indian Dentists, Am. Assn. Pub. Health Dentistry, Am. Bd. Dental Pub. Health, Commd. Officers Assn. Office: US Dept Health & Human Services Indian Health Service Reyes Bldg 801 Thompson Ave Rm 440 Rockville MD 20852-1627 E-mail: cgrim@hqe.ihs.gov.*

GRIM, PATRICIA ANN, retired banker; b. Everett, Pa., Sept. 7, 1940; d. Harry Grant and Nellie Elizabeth (Koontz) Foor; m. James Woodrow Grim, Feb. 21, 1970. Student, Am. Inst. Banking, Rolling Meadows, Ill., Bank Adminstrn. Inst., The Bus. Women's Tng. Inst., Penn State Univ. Sec. William H. Snyder, Atty. at Law, Bedford, Pa., 1958-60; sec., loan teller First Nat. Bank of Everett, Pa., 1960-70; teller Orrstown (Pa.) Bank, 1970-81, asst. cashier, asst. sec., 1981-82, v.p., asst. sec., 1982-94; officer, mgr. Mellon Bank, Shippensburg, Pa., 1994-2000; ret., 2000. Recipient Family Tng. Hour Leader of Yr. award Ch. of God State of Pa., Layman of Yr. award, 1979; nat. nominee Layperson of Yr., 1984. Mem. Ch. of God.

GRIM, PATRICK NEAL, philosopher, educator, logician; b. Pasadena, Calif., Oct. 29, 1950; s. Elgas Shull Grim and Dorathy Mae O'Neal; m. L. Theresa Watkins. AB in Philosophy and Anthropology, U. Calif., Santa Cruz, 1971; BPhil, U. St. Andrews, 1975; PhD, Boston U., 1976. Mellon faculty fellow Wash. U., St. Louis, Md., 1977-78; from asst. prof. to prof. SUNY, Stony Brook, 1978-94, prof., 1994—2001, disting. tchg. prof., 2001—. Weinberg Dist. vis. prof. U. Mich., Ann Arbor, 2006. Author: The Incomplete Universe, 1991, The Philosophical Computer, 1998, Questions of Value, 2005; editor: The Philosopher's Annual, Vols. 1-25, 1979-2003, Philosophy of Science and the Occult, 1982, 91; contbr. articles to profl. jours. Fulbright fellow, St. Andrews, Scotland, 1971-72, Mellon Faculty fellow Washington U., St. Louis, 1977-78. Fellow Acad. Tchrs./Scholars; mem. Internat. Assn. Philosophy of Law, Am. Philos. Assn., Cognitive Sci. Soc., Internat. Soc. Artificial Life. Avocations: art, music. Home: Toad Hall 99 Swezey St Patchogue NY 11772 Office: Dept of Philosophy Suny At Stony Brk Stony Brook NY 11794-3750 Office Phone: 631-632-7578. Business E-Mail: pgrim@notes.cc.sunysb.edu.

GRIMALDI, DAVID, financial advisor; b. Manhasset, NY, Mar. 26, 1978; s. Robert Grimaldi and Kathy Blau. BA in Fin. cum laude, Calif. State U., 2003. Fin. advisor Morgan Stanley Wealth Mgmt. Group, NYC. Mem.: Nat. Assn. State Retirement Administrators, Market Technicians Assn. Home Phone: 646-505-9453; Office Phone: 212-883-8533.

GRIMALDI, JAMES V., journalist; Degree in journalism, U. Mo., Columbia U. Grad. Sch. Journalism. With Orange County Register, Calif.; investigative reporter Washington Post, 2000—. Mem. bd. Investigative Reporters & Editors, bd. pres., 2006—. Recipient Pulitzer Prize for investigative reporting, 2006; fellow Knight-Bagehot bus. & econ. fellow. Office: Washington Post Spl Projects Desk 1150 15th St NW Washington DC 20071-0070 Office Phone: 202-334-4459. Office Fax: 202-334-6581. E-mail: grimaldij@washpost.com.

GRIMALDI, NICHOLAS LAWRENCE, fundraising executive; s. Dominick Lawrence and Marian Theresa Grimaldi. Student, Manhattan Coll.; BA summa cum laude, Fordham U. Exec. assoc. Nat. Assn. Regional Ballet, NYC, 1979-87; exec. dir. Nikolais/Louis Found. for Dance, Inc., NYC, 1987-89; dir. devel. Hartley House, NYC, 1989-93, Fountain House, Inc., NYC, 1993—2005, Legal Aid Soc., NYC, 2005—07; asst. v.p. advancement, major gifts Healthcare Chaplaincy Inc., NYC, 2007—. Cons. mgmt. and fund raising; mem. steering com./pastoral coun. Ch. of St. Francis Xavier, N.Y.C., 1993-97. Mem.: Assn. Fundraising Profls., Phi Sigma Tau, Phi Kappa Phi, Alpha Sigma Nu. Office: Legal Aid Society 199 Water St New York NY 10038

GRIMES, DALE MILLS, physics and electrical engineering educator; b. Marshall County, Iowa, Sept. 7, 1926; s. LeRoy and Helen (Mills) G.; m. Janet LaVonne Moore, Mar. 22, 1947; children: Prudence Rae, Craig Alan. BS in Physics, Math. and Chemistry, Iowa State U., Ames, 1950, MS in Physics and Math, 1951; PhD in Elec. Engring, U. Mich., Ann Arbor, 1956. From rsch. assoc. to assoc. prof. elec. engring. U. Mich., 1951-61, prof. elec. engring., 1961-76; chief scientist Conductron Corp., Ann Arbor, 1960-63; prof. elec. engring., chmn. dept. U. Tex., El Paso, 1976-79, pres. grad. faculty, 1978—79; prof. elec. and computer engring. Pa. State U., 1979-91, chmn. dept., 1979-86, prof. emeritus, 1992—. Adj. prof. physics U. Ky., 1996—2000; cons. Environ. Rsch. Inst. Mich., US Dept. Transp., GM Corp., 1968—91; vis. prof. elec. and computer engring. U. Tex.-Austin, 1985—86; chief scientist Crale, Inc., 1985—95. Author: Electromagnetism and Quantum Theory, 1969, Automotive Electronics, 1974, Advanced Electromagnetics: Foundations, Theory, Applications, 1995, Electromagnetic Origin of Quantum Theory and Light, 2002, 2d edit., 2005, Riding Asteroid 869, 2007; contbr. articles to profl. jours. With USNR, 1943—46. Fellow AAAS; mem. IEEE, Am. Phys. Soc., Lexington Acad. Sr. Profls., Torch Club Ctrl. Pa. Achievements include patents in field; research in automotive radar, biconical antennas, quantum theory, electromagnetic radiation. Home: 1325 Megan Dr State College PA 16803 Personal E-mail: dmg6@psu.edu.

GRIMES, DAVID LYNN, communications executive; b. Oklahoma City, June 9, 1947; s. Glenn Ross and Kathleen Sue G.; m. Sandra Kay Belt, Mar. 6, 1970; children: David Edwin, Emily Kathleen. BBA in Mktg., Ctrl. State U., Edmond, Okla., 1978; grad. internat. sr. mgrs. program, Harvard U., 1988. With Southwestern Bell Tel., 1970-83, rates and tariff Oklahoma City, 1975-77, industry mgr., 1977-79, dist. mgr. sales ops. St. Louis, 1979-80, mktg. mgr. Kansas City, Mo., 1980-82, Houston, 1982-83; divsn. mgr. Am. Bell, Houston, 1983-84; br. mgr. nat. accts. AT&T, Houston, 1984-85, v.p. sales Dallas, 1986-98; COO Sharetech, Parsippny, NJ, 1985-86; pres., COO Sykes Enterprises, 1998-2000, pres., CEO, 2000; sr. v.p. Tropic Networks, 2001—04, pres., 2004—06; exec. v.p. Soybaritic, Inc., 2007—. Mem. Nat. Bd. of Visitors Tex. Christian U., 1990-96; mem. adv. coun. Sch. Nat. Sci., U. Tex., Austin, 1988-93; bd. dirs. Tex. Bus. Hall of Fame Found., Dallas, 1988-93. Mem. Dallas C. of C. (mem. exec. com. econ. devel. 1991-93), Harvard Bus. Club Dallas, Univ. Club (Dallas), Avila Country Club, Pinnacle Country Club, Tampa C. of C. (bd. dirs. 2000-01). Republican. Methodist. Avocations: golf, tennis, fishing, hunting. Home: 5510 Merrimac Ave Dallas TX 75206 Office: Tropic Networks Inc 5570 Merrimac Ave Dallas TX 75206 Office Phone: 214-213-6303. Personal E-mail: dlgrimes@sbcglobal.net.

GRIMES, DIANE SPELLMAN, art educator, department chairman, sculptor; b. Phila., Mar. 18, 1960; d. George Walter and Lillian (Hubert) Spellman; m. Kenneth Dion Grimes, Aug. 8, 1981; children: Kenneth Edward, Leanne Elizabeth, Andrew Thomas, Ian Gregory. BS in Art Edn., Moore Coll. Art, Phila., 1983; MA in Art Edn., U. of the Arts, Phila., 1994; postgrad., Pa. Acad. Fine Arts, Phila.; cert. in desktop publ./web design, Moore Coll. Art, 2002; MFA in Advt. Graphic Design, Marywood U., 2005. Cert. tchr. art edn., N.J., Pa. Art dir. Camp Ockonickon YMCA, Medford, NJ, 1993; instr. art St. Mary of the Lakes, Medford, 1993-94; course dir. Pa. Acad. of Fine Arts, 1994-98; instr. art, lectr. fine arts Camden County Coll., Blackwood, NJ, 1994-96; prof. art Burlington County Coll., Pemberton, NJ, 1994-2000; art coord. fine and graphic design programs, assoc. prof. Cumberland County Coll., Pemberton, 2000—05; art chmn. Immaculata U., Immaculata, Pa., 2005—. Instr. Perkins Ctr. for Arts, Moorestown, N.J., 1995-96; cons. and lectr. in field; cons. spl. rsch. SCANS 2000 Project U.S. Dept. Labor and Johns Hopkins U., 1999; started mentorship program Acad. Fine Arts, 2001. Exhibited in group shows at Fleisher Art Meml. Juried Art Show, 1985-86, Pa. Acad. Fine Arts, 1991-93, Am. Art Mus., 1995, Perkins Juried Art Show, 1996, Sculpture Exhbn., Immaculata U., 2007; one-woman show Medford Solo Sculpture Show, 1996, Cumberland (N.J.) County Coll., 1999, Computer Art Show, Princeton, N.J., 1999, Lucas Gallery-Princeton U., 1999, Markiem Art Ctr. Invitational, Haddonfield, N.J., 2003, Gallery 50, Bridgeton, N.J., 2007; designer multi-cultural art program for summer links program Burlington C.C., 1998. Recipient Am. Coll. Sculpture award, 1995, Maxin B. Gottleib Meml. award, 1987, Meyer E. Maurer award, 1986, Dr. Albert N. Lalli Meml. award, 1985, Fellowship Purchase award sculpture Pa. Acad. Fine Arts., 1996, MIO fellow Princeton U., 1999, fellow in computers and art rsch., 1999-2000, PAFA fellow Merion Reproduction Co., 1994; grad. scholar U. of the Arts, 1994; presdl. grantee in computer tech. Burlington County Coll., 1997-98; Mid-career fellow Princeton U., 1999; Profl. Devel. grantee Moore Coll. Art, 200O, Oxford U., Paris, 2006. Mem. Nat. Art Edn. Assn., N.J. Edn. Assn., N.J. Art Edn. Assn. Roman Catholic. Avocations: ice skating, poetry, swimming. Home: 52 Neeta Trl Medford Lakes NJ 08055-1613 Office: Office 323 Loyola Immaculata U 1145 King Rd Immaculata PA 19345 Home Phone: 609-744-6185; Office Phone: 610-647-4400 ext. 3308. Business E-Mail: dgrimes@immaculata.edu.

GRIMES, HOWARD RAY, management consultant; b. Manilla, Iowa, July 24, 1918; s. Ray Herb and Sarah Alice (Saunders) G.; m. Nancy Palmer, Nov. 17, 1993; children from previous marriage: Patricia, Susan, Nancy, Sarah, Laura. Student, U. Wis., Madison, 1939; BA, Grinnell Coll., Iowa, 1940. With Aetna Life & Casualty Co., 1940-82, field supr., regional mgr. Boston, 1950-74, regional dir., v.p. field, 1974-82; mgmt. cons., 1983-95; chmn. Benefit Svcs. Inc., 1968-93. Bd. dirs. Waterville Co. Inc. Served with USAAF, 1942-45. Sports-Illustrated Silver Anniversary All-Am. Mem. Weston Golf Club (Mass.), Bald Peak Colony Club (NH), The Moorings Club (Fla.), Harvard Club (Boston). Home: 1150 Reef Rd Vero Beach FL 32963-2971 Address: PO Box 513 Waterville Valley NH 03215-0513 Personal E-mail: hrgrimes8@aol.com.

GRIMES, JAMES GORDON, geologist; b. Kenosha, Wis., Mar. 18, 1951; s. James Gordon Bennett Jr. and Alyce Louise (Gannaway) G. BS in Earth Sci., U. Wis., Parkside, 1974; MS in Geology, Mich. Tech. U., 1977. Registered profl. geologist, Tenn. Geologist nat. uranium resource evaluation project Union Carbide Corp. Nuclear Div., Oak Ridge, 1977-84; geol. cons. UCC-ND Mercury Task Force, Oak Ridge, 1983; geologist Lockheed Martin Energy Systems Inc., Oak Ridge, 1984-99. Tech. mgr. Y-12 plant Meterol. Info. Support System, 1987-96, ind. cons., Kenosha, 1999—. Mem. Geol. Soc., Air and Waste Mgmt. Assn. E-mail: xjg@worldnet.att.net.

GRIMES, JOHN GRAYSON, federal agency administrator; b. Frederick, Md., Oct. 29, 1935; s. Ira Staley and Wilma Mae (Burrier) G.; m. Sharon Lee Troxell (div. Oct. 1974); children: Tammy Lee Schubel, Terree Ann Long. BS, U. Ariz., 1974; MS, Shippensburg U., 1975. Chief electronic sect. U.S. Army East Coast Telecom Ctr., Ft. Detrick, Md., 1960-64; chief test and evaluation div. U.S. Army Communications-Electronic Agy., Ft. Huachuca, Ariz., 1964-71, dep. dir. communications engring., 1971-73; asst. dep. chief staff for ops. U.S. Army Communications Command, Ft. Huachuca, 1973-81; dep. mgr. Nat. Communications System, Washington, 1981-84; dir. nat. security coun. The White House, Washington, 1984-89; assoc. dir. Def. Communications Agy., Washington, 1989; sr. dir. nat.

security coun. The White House, Washington, 1989-90; dep. asst. sec. for counterintelligence & security countermeasures U.S. Dept. Def., Washington, asst. sec. for networks & info. integration, chief info. officer, 2005—; v.p. for intelligence & info. systems Raytheon Co., Washington. Sgt. USAF, 1956-60. Mem. Armed Forces Communications-Electronics Assn. (bd. dirs. 1986—). Avocations: skiing, sailing, golf, diving. Office: US Dept Def 6000 Def Pentagon Rm 3E172 Washington DC 20301

GRIMES, MARGARET WHITEHURST, artist, educator; b. New Bern, NC, June 5, 1943; d. Alan Pendleton and Margaret (Whitehurst) G. BA, Gov. State U., 1975, MA, 1976; postgrad., Notre Dame U., 1977; MFA, U. Pa., 1980. Prof. painting Western Conn. State U., Danbury, 1980—, asst. chair, 1991-92, coord. MFA program, 2000—. Guest lectr./critic Vt. Coll. Norwich U., Montepelier, 1995-96, Vt. Studio Ctr., Johnson, 1995, Tanglewood Inst., Lenox, Mass., 1997, S.V.A. Conf. on Liberal Arts and Edn. of Artists, 1997, Ctrl. Conn. State U., New Britain, 1997, Weir Farm Nat. Hist. Site, Wilton, Conn., 1998, Gunn Mus., Washington, 2000; vis. artist Am. U., Corciano, Italy, 2001-06, Hendrix Coll., Conway, Ark., 2002, Chautauqua Inst., NY, 2003, 05, 07, Am. U., Washington, 2004; artist-in-residence Weir Farm Trust, 2004; prof. Conn. State U., 1992-. One-woman shows include Green Mountain Gallery, NY, 1979, (biannually) Blue Mountain Gallery, 1980—2007, Fischbach Gallery, 1986, Moravian Coll., Bethlehem, Pa., 1990, Western Conn. State U., 1990, 1998, Ctrl. Conn. State U., 1997, Washington Art Assn., 1990, 2000, Weir Farm Nat. Trust, Wilton, Conn., 2003, 100 Pearl Gallery, Conn., 2003, 3-person show, Provincetown Group Gallery, Mass., 1987, exhibited in group shows at Internat. Women's Art Festival, Walker Art Inst., 1976, Woodmere Mus., Phila., 1977, Provincetown Art Mus., Mass., 1978, Reading Mus., Pa., 1983, Queens Mus., NY, 1983, Rahr-West Mus., Manitowoc, Wis., 1983, Columbus Mus. Art, Ohio, 1987, Katherina Rich Perlow Gallery, 1987, 1988, 1989, 78th Am. ann. show Newport (RI) Mus., 1988, Erector Sq. Gallery, New Haven, 1994, Kline Gallery, Santa Fe, N.Mex., 1994, Creiger-Dane Gallery, Boston, 1995, Park Ave. Atrium, NYC, 1995, Wilmington Ctr. for Contemporary Art, Del., 1996, Conn. State U. biennial, 1987—99, Blue Mountain Gallery, 1996—2007, Davenport Mus., Iowa, 1999—2000, NAS, 2001—02, Nat. Acad. Design, 2004, Salon Show with Henry Matisse, Ober Gallery, Kent, Conn., 2007, Philbrook Mus., Tulsa, Ringling Mus. Art, Sarasota, Fla., Represented in permanent collections Pitts. Plate Glass Co., Conn. Ins. Group, N.Am. Christian Sci. Ch. Ctr., Boston, US Tobacco Co., Bellevue Hosp., NY, Nat. Acad. Sci. Recipient Disting. Lectureship award Henry Barnard Found., 1990, Benjamin Altman prize in painting NAD, 2004; rsch. grantee in painting Conn. State U., 1985. Mem. AAUP (grantee 1986, 90, 91, 93, 95, 99, 2003, 06), Coll. Art Assn. Home: 27 Wykeham Rd Washington CT 06793-1308 Office: Western Conn State U Art Dept 181 White St Danbury CT 06810 Office Phone: 203-837-8402. Business E-Mail: grimesm@wcsu.edu.

GRIMES, R. DALE, lawyer; b. Nashville, Mar. 30, 1953; BA cum laude, U. of the South, 1975; JD, U. Tenn., 1978. Bar: Tenn. 1978. Law clk. to Hon. L. Clure Morton chief judge U.S. Dist. Ct. (mid. dist.) Tenn., 1978-80; mem., litig. practice Bass, Berry & Sims, Nashville, 1980—. Chair fed. civil justice reform act adv. group (mid. dist.) Tenn., 1991-95. Articles editor Tenn. Law Rev., 1977-78. Bd. regents U. of the South, 1989-95, chmn., 1993-95, lectr. exec. seminars, Owen Grad. Sch. Mgmt., Vanderbilt U., pres. bd. trustees, St. Mary's Retreat Conf. Ctr., chair constn. canons com. Episcopal Diocese Tenn. Fellow Nashville Bar Found.; mem. ABA (antitrust law sect., litig. sect., health law sect.), Am. Health Lawyers Assn., Nat. Health Lawyers Assn., Tenn. Bar Assn., Nashville Bar Assn. (co-chair fed. ct. com. 1990, vice chair 1989), Omicron Delta Kappa. Office: Bass Berry & Sims Ste 2700 315 Deaderick St Nashville TN 37238-3001 Office Phone: 615-742-6244. Office Fax: 615-742-2744. Business E-Mail: dgrimes@bassberry.com.

GRIMES, RICHARD ALLEN, banker, educator; b. Toledo, Apr. 24, 1929; s. Robert Howell and Mary Mildred Grimes; m. Helen Ann Schaeffer, Aug. 25, 1951; children: Gregory Allen, Julianne, Frank Edwin, Mary Ann. BS major in Chemistry, U. Ga., 1951; MS in Mgmt., Ga. Inst. Tech., 1959; postgrad., Ga. State U., 1979. Commd. lt. US Army, 1951, advanced through grades to lt. col., ret. 1971; asst. prof. econs. Clayton State Univ., Morrow, Ga., 1971-74; assoc. prof. econs. Ga. Perimeter Coll., Decatur, Ga., 1974—97. Adj. prof. Jacksonville State U., 1959—63, Va. Commonwealth U., 1964—67, Ga. Mil. Coll. , 1979—91, Ctrl. Tex. Coll., 1997—2001, Gordon Coll., 1998—; ednl. cons.; real estate broker, instr. Author: (book) Economics and Finance Study Guide, 2000; reviewer: Economics, 1979—99. Umpire Atlanta Area Football Ofcsl. Assn., treas., 1971—95; evaluator Ga. HS Football Ofcls., 1996—; active Spl. Olympics, Atlanta, 1971—; founding pres. Rex Civic Assn., 1973—2006; sec.-treas. Villages Homeowners Assn.; tax cons., instr. AARP, 2001—; mem. Stockbridge Urban Redevel. Agy., 2005—07; marshall Atlanta LPGA Golf Tournament, 1992—2006. Decorated U.S. Army Soldier's medal for valor Vietnam, Meritorious Svc. medal; named Clayton County Rotarian of the Yr., 1976, Football Ofcl. of the Yr., Atlanta area, 1980; recipient Eagle Scout award, 1944. Mem.: AAUP (pres. Ga. Perimeter Coll.chpt. 1987—97), VFW (life), Cmty. Banking Assn., Mil. Officers Assn. Am. (historian), Nat. Soc. Accts., Ga. Assn. Acctg. Profls. (past pres.), Ga. Assn. Econs. and Fin. (past pres.), Am. Acctg. Assn., So. Econ. Assn., U. Ga. Varsity Letterman, South Metro Atlanta U. Ga. Alumni Club, South Metro. Ga. Tech. Alumni Club (sec., scholarship chmn.), Am. Legion, Chi Psi, Delta Pi Epsilon. Presbyterian. Avocations: football, golf, camping, swimming. Home and Office: Eagles Landing 118 Carron Ln Stockbridge GA 30281-6302 Office Phone: 770-474-2444. Personal E-mail: r_grimes@bellsouth.net.

GRIMES, RUSSELL NEWELL, inorganic chemist, educator; b. Meridian, Miss., Dec. 10, 1935; s. Newell Cleveland and Marion Esther (Zehner) G.; m. Nancy Farrow Hall, Sept. 21, 1962; children— Susan, David BS in Chemistry, Lafayette Coll., 1957; PhD in Chemistry, U. Minn., 1962; postdoctoral, Harvard U., 1962, U. Calif., Riverside, 1962-63. Asst. prof. chemistry U. Va., Charlottesville, 1963-68, assoc. prof. chemistry, 1968-73, prof. chemistry, 1973—2003, chmn. dept. chemistry, 1981-84, prof. emeritus, 2003—. Guest prof. U. Canterbury, N.Z., 1974-75, U. Heidelberg, Fed. Republic of Germany, 1986, 1997-98. Author: Carboranes, 1970; editor: Metal Interactions with Boron Clusters, 1982, Inorganic Syntheses Vol. 29, 1992; contbr. over 240 articles to profl. jours. Grantee Office Naval Rsch., 1965-83, Army Rsch. Office, 1983—, NSF, 1976—; Fulbright sr. rsch. scholar, New Zealand, 1974-75; recipient Alexander von Humboldt Sr. Rsch. prize, 1996. Fellow AAAS; mem. Am. Chem. Soc. (sec.-treas. inorganic divsn. 1981-84, grantee 1965—), Corp. Inorganic Syntheses (pres. 1997-2000), Sigma Xi (President's and Visitors' rsch. prize 1981, 85, 96). Office: U Va Dept Chemistry Mccormick Rd Charlottesville VA 22904-0001 E-mail: rng@virginia.edu.

GRIMES, SALLY, marketing professional; m. Steve Grimes; 2 children. Grad., U. Chgo. Grad. Sch. Bus., 1997. With Kraft Foods, Inc., 1997—, brand mgr. e-commerce, dir. integrated mktg. North Am. grocery sector, 2005—. Named one of Top 40 Under 40, Crain's Chgo. Bus., 2006. Office: Kraft Foods Inc Three Lakes Dr Northfield IL 60093*

GRIMES, STEPHEN HENRY, retired state supreme court justice; b. Peoria, Ill., Nov. 17, 1927; s. Henry Holbrook and June (Kellar) G.; m. Mary Fay Fulghum, Dec. 29, 1951; children: Gay Diane, Mary June, Sue Anne, Sheri Lynn. Student, Fla. So. Coll., 1946—47; BS in Bus. Adminstrn. with honors, U. Fla., 1951, LLB with honors, 1954; LLD (hon.), Stetson U., 1980. Bar: Fla. 1954, U.S. Dist. Ct. (no. and so. dists.) 1954, U.S. Ct. Appeals (5th cir.) 1965, U.S. Supreme Ct. 1972. Since practiced in, Bartow, Fla.; ptnr. Holland and Knight and predecessor firm, Tallahassee, 1954-73, 98—; judge Ct. Appeals 2d Dist. Fla., Lakeland, 1973-87, chief judge, 1978-80; chmn. Conf. Fla. Dist. Cts. Appeals, 1978-80; justice Fla. Supreme Ct., Tallahassee, 1987-97, chief justice, 1994-96; chair Article V Task Force, 1994-96, Supreme Ct. Workload Study Commn., 2000—01. Mem. Fla. Jud. Qualification Commn., 1982-86, vice chmn., 1985-86; chmn. Fla. Jud. Coun., 1989-94. Contbr. articles U. Fla. Law Rev., 1951, 54. Bd. dirs. Bartow Meml. Hosp., 1958-61, Bartow Libr., 1968-78; trustee Polk C.C., Winter Haven, Fla., 1967-70, chmn., 1969-70; bd. govs. Polk Pub. Mus., 1976-97; bd. dirs., chmn. Elder Care. Lt. (j.g.) USN, 1951-53. Fellow Am. Coll. Trial Lawyers; mem. ABA, Fla. Bar Assn. (bd. govs. jr. bar 1956-58, bd. dirs. trial lawyers sect. 1967-69, sec. 1969, vice chmn. appellate rules com. 1976-77, vice chmn. tort litig. rev. commn. 1985-86), 10th Cir. Bar Assn. (pres. 1966), Am. Judicature Soc., Bartow C. of C. (pres. 1964), Rotary (dist. gov. 1960-61). Episcopalian (sr. warden 1964-65, 77). Office: Holland & Knight LLP 315 S Calhoun St Tallahassee FL 32301-1856 Home Phone: 850-668-2098; Office Phone: 830-425-5661. Business E-Mail: steve.grimes@hklaw.com.

GRIMES, STEVEN P., corporate financial executive; m. Sally Grimes; 2 children. With Deloitte & Touche LLP, 1994; prin. fin. officer Inland Western Retail Real Estate Trust, Inc. Named one of Top 40 Under 40, Crain's Chgo. Bus., 2006. Office: Inland Grp Inc 2901 Butterfield Rd Oak Brook IL 60523*

GRIMES, SUZANNE, publishing executive; 2 children. BA in Internat. Mgmt., Georgetown U. With NY Times; advt. dir. Success; with TV Guide, 1990—94, nat. advt. dir., 1994—95, sr. v.p., pub., 1995—97; pub. Women's Sports & Fitness, 1997—2000, Allure, 2000—01; pub., v.p. Glamour Mag., 2001—04; sr. v.p. media group Conde Nast, 2004—07; pres. food & entertaining Reader's Digest Assn., Inc., Pleasantville, NY, 2007—. Office: Reader's Digest Assn Inc Reader's Digest Rd Pleasantville NY 10570

GRIMES, WILLIAM, critic; Book critic NY Times, NYC, restaurant critic. Host Restaurant Times, WQXR. Co-author: The New York Times Guide to New York City Restaurants, 2003. Office: NY Times 229 W 43rd St New York NY 10036 also: WQXR 122 Fifth Ave New York NY 10011 Office Phone: 212-556-7423. Office Fax: 212-556-1516. E-mail: grimes@nytimes.com.

GRIMLEY, JEFFREY MICHAEL, dentist; b. Alton, Ill., Feb. 3, 1957; s. John Richard and Joyce Imogene (Mallin) G.; m. Julie Ellen Gardner, Aug. 2, 1980; children: Joel Michael, Christopher Mark, Benjamin Jeffrey. BS, U. Iowa, 1979, DDS, 1983; cert., Miami Valley Hosp., Dayton, Ohio, 1984. Gen. practice dentistry, Naperville, Ill., 1984—. Mem. ADA, Acad. Gen. Dentistry, Ill. Dental Soc., Chgo. Dental Soc. Methodist. Avocations: sports, photography. Office: Ste 112 1980 Three Farms Ave Naperville IL 60540-5365 Home Phone: 630-416-9583; Office Phone: 630-369-6980. Personal E-mail: grimleydds1@aol.com.

GRIMLEY, ROBERT THOMAS, chemistry professor; b. North Attleboro, Mass., Jan. 3, 1930; s. John Thomas and Ivy (Frost) G.; m. Margaret Rockwood, June 21, 1952 (dec. Feb. 8, 2005); children: Mark, Maureen, Kevin, Terrence, Peter. BS, U. Mass., 1951; PhD, U. Wis., 1958. Rsch. chemist Corning (N.Y.) Glass, Inc., 1957-59; fellow U. Chgo., 1959-61; prof. chemistry Purdue U., West Lafayette, Ind., 1961-94, prof. emeritus, 1995—. Vis. prof. Calif. Inst. Tech., Pasadena, 1992—96; vis. scholar Dartmouth Coll., 2001—. 1st lt. USAF, 1951—53. Mem. Am. Chem. Soc. (chmn. Purdue U. sect.), Am. Phys. Soc., Sigma Xi, Alpha Chi Sigma. Home: PO Box 550 Grantham NH 03753-0550

GRIMM, BEN EMMET, library director, consultant; b. Jersey City, Sept. 27, 1924; s. Benjamin Harrison and Eunice Blanche (Whitenack) G.; m. Jean Kay Bohrer, Aug. 19, 1950 (div. 1982); children: Jeffrey, Kevin, Mark, Wendy; m. Lucy Ann Taylor, Jan. 21, 1989. BA, Washington and Lee U., 1949; MS, Columbia U., 1950. Librarian youth services Detroit Pub. Libr., 1950-52; sr. librarian Fair Lawn (N.J.) Pub. Libr., 1952-54; reference and reading librarian Montclair (N.J.) Pub. Libr., 1955-56; asst. dir. Montclair (N.J.) Pub. Libr., 1956-61; dir. Belleville (N.J.) Pub. Libr., 1961-72, Jersey City Pub. Libr., 1973-85; prin. Grimm/McPherson Assocs., Montclair, N.J., 1988-92; ind. libr. cons., 1992-93. Chmn. Hudson County Audio-Visual Aids Commn., 1975-85; cons. libr. bldgs., svcs. and adminstrn., 1966-93; cons., mem. state aid constrn. adv. bd. N.J. State Libr., 1985-88, chmn. adv. coun. Libr. Svcs. and Constrn. Act, 1979-83. Mng. editor Libr. Trustee Newsletter, 1978-80. Bd. dirs. Orange County (Va.) Hist. Soc., 1994-96, pres., 1995; bd. dirs. Orange County Libr. Found., 1995-98, v.p., 1997-98; bd. dirs. Rapidan Found., 1999—, treas., 2003—; bd. dirs. The Arts Ctr. in Orange, 2002-03. With USAAF, 1942-45. Decorated D.F.C., Air medal with oak leaf clusters. Mem. N.J. Libr. Assn. (pres. 1968-69). Home and Office: PO Box 145 Rapidan VA 22733-0145 Personal E-mail: bgrimm92@yahoo.com. Business E-Mail: b.e.grimm@hotmail.com.

GRIMM, JAMES R. (RONALD), management consultant; b. Monroe, Mich., Nov. 5, 1935; s. Carl S. and Annie B. (Platt) G.; m. Carol Ann Forman, Aug. 24, 1957; children: James R., Phillip H. BS in Bus. Adminstrn, Ariz. State U., 1958. Dir. internal audit Motorola, Inc., Phoenix, 1961-68; bus. and fin. mgr. Europe Motorola Semicondr. Co., Geneva, 1968-70; dir. internat. fin. Fairchild Camera & Instrument Co., Mountain View, Calif., 1970-71; v.p. internat. fin. Computer Scis. Corp., Los Angeles, 1971-74; sr. v.p., chief fin. exec. Pertec Computer Corp., Los Angeles, 1974-80; exec. v.p. fin. and adminstrn. MAPCO, Inc., Tulsa, 1980-84; v.p., chief fin. officer Greyhound Corp., Phoenix, 1984-88; pres. Internat. Bus. Cons., Phoenix, 1988—; sr. v.p., CFO Gulf States Steel Ala., Gadsden, 1998-2000. Bd. dirs. Petro Star Inc., Fairbanks, Alaska, Infinite Tech. Corp., Dallas. Contbr. articles to Inst. Internal Auditors publs., 1964-68. Inducted into Ariz. State U. Hall of Fame, 1982 Mem. Inst. Internal Auditors (founder and 1st pres. Phoenix chpt. 1963), Fin. Exec. Inst., Gadsden Country Club. Home: 527 Mistletoe Holw Gadsden AL 35901-5739 Office Phone: 256-543-0090. Personal E-mail: gjim4al@aol.com.

GRIMM, JOHN LLOYD, marketing professional; b. NYC, Oct. 21, 1945; s. Judson and Nanette Grimm; m. Stephanie L. Cassagne, Dec. 23, 1969; children: Samantha, Jonathan. BBA, Tulane U., 1967, MBA, 1969. Asst. prof. Dillard U., New Orleans, 1969-82; pres. Multi-Quest Internat. Inc., New Orleans, 1966—, Analytical Studies Inc., New Orleans, 1966—, Sybersurveys Inc., New Orleans, 1966—. Author: Interviewer's Handbook & Training Manual, 1970. Chmn. rsch. com. United Way, New Orleans, 1988-89, 94—, mem. mktg. com., 1986-88; mem. mktg. com. YMCA, New Orleans, 1985-98; mem. pub. rels. com. Goodwill Industries, New Orleans, 1986-89. Named Prof. of the Yr., Dillard U., 1981. Mem. Am. Mktg. Assn. (pres. New Orleans chpt. 1985-87, 94-95, treas. 1984-85, sec. 1983-84), Market Rsch. Assn., New Orleans Camellia Club, Baton Rouge Camellia Club, Gainesville Camellia Club, Ft. Walton Beach Camellia Club, So. Calif. Camellia Club. Avocation: growing and showing camellias. Office: Multi-Quest Internat Inc 708 Rosa Ave Metairie LA 70005-2145 Office Phone: 504-835-3507. Business E-Mail: research@multi-questintl.com.

GRIMM, LOUIS JOHN, mathematician, educator; b. St. Louis, Nov. 30, 1933; s. Louis and Florence Agnes (Hammond) G.; m. Barbara Ann Mitko, May 6, 1967; children: Thomas, Mary. BS, St. Louis U., 1954; MS, Ga. Inst. Tech., 1960; PhD, U. Minn., 1965. Chemist USPHS, Savannah, Ga., 1958-61; asst. prof. U. Utah, Salt Lake City, 1965-69; assoc. prof. U. Mo., Rolla, 1969-74, prof., 1974—, chmn. dept. math. and stats., 1981-87, dir. Inst. Applied Math., 1983-87. Vis. asst. prof. U. Minn., Mpls., 1966; vis. prof. U. Nebr., Lincoln, 1978-79, U. So. Calif., L.A., 1987-88; exch. scientist Polish Acad. Scis., Warsaw, 1981. Contbr. articles to profl. jours. With Med. Svc. Corps, AUS, 1956-58. Jefferson Smurfit fellow Univ. Coll. Dublin (Ireland), 1984; NSF rsch. grantee. Mem. AAUP, SAR, Soc. for Indsl. and Applied Math., Polish Math. Soc., Gesellschaft für angewandte Mathematik und Mechanik, Math. Assn. Am. (Disting. Tchg. award 2001), Sigma Xi. Office: U Mo Dept Math & Stats Rolla MO 65409-0001

GRIMM, TERRY M., lawyer; b. Bloomington, Ill., Apr. 3, 1942; BA, Ind. U., 1964, JD cum laude, 1967. Bar: Ill. 1967, US Dist. Ct. (no., ctrl. & so. dists. Calif.), US Dist. Ct. (no. & ctrl. dists. Ill.), US Dist. Ct. (no. dist. Ind.), US Dist. Ct. (so. dist. NY), US Dist. Ct. (dist. Wyo.). Assoc. to ptnr. Winston & Strawn, LLP, Chgo., 1968—, mem. exec. com.; spl. prosecutor DuPage County Prosecutor's Office, Ill., 1975-76. Fellow Am. Coll. Trial Lawyers; mem. Ill. State Bar Assn., Order of the Coif. Office: Winston & Strawn 35 W Wacker Dr Ste 4200 Chicago IL 60601-9703 Office Phone: 312-558-5782. Office Fax: 312-558-5700. E-mail: tgrimm@winston.com.*

GRIMMER, CINDY C., social studies educator; b. Louisville, Ky., Nov. 10, 1974; d. Albert and Beverly Grimmer. BA in Secondary Social Studies Edn., McNeese State U., Lake Charles, La., 1996. Cert. tchr. lifetime La., 2000, Nat. Bd. Profl. Tchg. Standards, 2006. Social studies educator Livingston Parish Pub. Schs., La., 1997—. Parish blackboard monitor Livingston Parish Pub. Schs., 2004—. Sponsor Helping Hands Denham Springs Freshman H.S., La., 2005. Mem.: Lousiana Fedn. Tchrs., Phi Alpha Theta. Baptist. Office: Denham Springs Freshman HS 940 N Range Ave Denham Springs LA 70726 Home Phone: 225-667-0127; Office Phone: 225-665-7890. E-mail: cindy.grimmer@lpsb.org.

GRIMMETTE, MARK, Olympic athlete; b. Ann Arbor, Mich., Jan. 23, 1971; Mem. U.S. Olympic Luge Men's Doubles Team, 1989. Named U.S. Nat. Champion in Doubles, 1996, winner 6 World Cup medals, World Cup champion, 1998, Bell Atlantic Nat. champion Silver medal, 1998; recipient Bronze medal Luge Men's Doubles, Nagano Olympics, Japan, 1998, Bronze medal, Lillehammer Olympics, 1996, All-Japan Championships, Nagano, Silver medal, Luge Challenge Cup, 2000, Bronze medal, World Championship, 2000, 2005. Office: US Luge Assn 35 Church St Lake Placid NY 12946-1805

GRIMSHAW, JAMES ALBERT, JR., retired language educator; b. Kingsville, Tex., Dec. 10, 1940; s. James A. and John Maurine Grimshaw; m. Glenda Darlene Hargett, June 10, 1961; children: Courtney Anne, James A. IV. BA in English, Tex. Tech. U., 1962, MA in English, 1968; PhD in English, La. State U., 1972. Commd. 2d lt. USAF, 1962, advanced through grades to lt. col., ret., 1983; instr. in English USAF Acad., Colorado Springs, 1968-70, asst. prof., 1970-74, assoc. prof., 1974-80, prof., 1980-83; prof. and dept. head Tex. A&M U. (formerly East Tex. State U.), Commerce, 1983-90, prof., 1990—2005, regent's prof., 1995—2005, ret., 2005, prof. emeritus, 2007. Pres. Northeast Tex. Orgn. of Lang. Educators, Commerce, 1984-85, S. Cen. Assn. Depts. English, 1984-85, Tex. Assn. Depts. English, Commerce, 1988-89; chmn. Robert Penn Warren Adv. Group, Bowling Green, Ky., 1990-98; pres. Robert Penn Warren Circle, Durham, N.C., 1991-93. Author: The Flannery O'Connor Companion, 1981, Understanding Robert Penn Warren, 2001; compiler: Robert Penn Warren: A Descriptive Bibliography, 1981; editor: Cleanth Brooks at the United States Air Force Academy, 1980, Robert Penn Warren's A Brother to Dragons: A Discussion, 1983, Time's Glory: Original Essays on Robert Penn Warren, 1986, The Paul Wells Barrus Lectures, 1983-89, 1990, Friends of Their Youth: Cleanth Brooks and Robert Penn Warren, 1993, Cleanth Brooks and Robert Penn Warren: A Literary Correspondence, 1998, (with James A. Perkins) Robert Penn Warren's All the King's Men: Three Stage Rersions, 2000, (with William Bedford Clark) RWP: An Annual of Robert Penn Warren Studies, 2001-05, Dictionary of Literary Biography: Robert Penn Warren Documentary Volume, 2006; gen. editor Sam Rayburn Series on Rural Life, 1997-2005. Mem. vestry Epiphany Episcopal Ch., Commerce, Tex., 1989-91, sr. warden, 95-96. Decorated Bronze Star medal; recipient Disting. Faculty award, Faculty Senate East Tex. State U., Commerce, 1988, 95, East Tex. State U. Honors Prof. of Yr. award, 1993, Tex. Assn. of Coll. Tchrs. Disting. Faculty Tchg. award, 1992-93; named to the Flannery O'Connor Vis. Professorship, Ga. Coll., Milledgeville, 1977, vis. fellow in bibliography, Beinecke Rare Book & Manuscript Libr., Yale U., New Haven, Conn., 1979-80. Mem. Soc. for Study of So. Lit., Robert Penn Warren Cir., Kiwanis. Avocations: swimming, gardening, chess, 5-string banjo. Home: 7400 Crestway Apt 1115 San Antonio TX 78239-3096 Business E-Mail: james_grimshaw@tamu-commerce.edu. E-mail: jgrimshaw@armyresidence.net.

GRIMSLEY, REAGAN LOUIS, archivist, educator; b. Sumrall, Miss., Oct. 10, 1970; s. Willie Louis and Jeanette Grimsley; children: Baylee Quinn, Makenzie Layne. BA in History, U. So. Miss., Hattiesburg, 1992, MA in History, 2000, MLIS in Libr. and Info. Sci., 2000. Spl. collections libr. Pikeville Coll., Ky., 2000—01; asst. prof. Columbus State U., Ga., 2001—. Author: Hattiesburg in Vintage Postcards, 2004, A One Hundred Year History of the First Baptist Church, Sumrall, Mississippi, 2005; editor: Muscogiana: Jour. of Muscogee Geneal. Soc., Provenance: The Jour. Soc. Ga. Archivists, 2006. Recipient Edmund Snyder Grad. fellowship, Stonewall Jackson Ho. and Wash. and Lee U., 1999, Alfred Bell, Jr. fellowship, Forest History Soc., 2000, Faculty Rsch. award, Columbus State U., 2006. Mem.: Soc. Am. Archivists, Soc. Miss. Archivists, Nat. Assn. Grad. and Profl. Students (v.p. 1999—2000), Miss. Hist. Soc., Soc. Ga. Archivists (editor jour. 2006—), Ga. Assn. Historians (archivist 2001—06), Phi Kappa Phi, Phi Alpha Theta (treas. Theta Kappa chpt. 1999—2000). Office: Columbus State Univ 4225 University Ave Columbus GA 31907 Office Phone: 706-568-2247. Business E-Mail: grimsley_reagan@colstate.edu.

GRIMWADE, RICHARD LLEWELLYN, lawyer; b. Chgo., Apr. 26, 1945; s. Eric Illingworth and Pauline J. (Crandall) G.; m. Alexandra M. Galbraith, Feb. 22, 1981; children: Eric Montgomery, Sara Elizabeth. BA, Lawrence U., 1967; JD cum laude, U. Wis., 1971. Bar: Wis. 1971, N.Y. 1972, Ill. 1978, Calif. 1981, U.S. Dist. Ct. (so. and ea. dists.) N.Y., 1972, U.S. Dist. Ct. (no. dist.) Wis., 1971, U.S. Dist. Ct. (no. dist.) Ill., 1978, U.S. Dist. Ct. (ctrl. dist.) Calif., 1981, U.S. Ct. Appeals (2d cir.) 1972, U.S. Ct. Appeals (7th cir.) 1978, U.S. Ct. Appeals (9th cir.) 1981. Atty. Davis Polk, NYC, 1971—76; ptnr. Barton Klugman, LA, 1983—93; pvt. practice LA, 1993—. Mem. U. Wis. Law Rev., 1969-71. Bd. mgrs. Ketchum Downtown YMCA, L.A., 1991-97; trustee Reform L.A. Pub. Schs. (LEARN), 1993-97. Recipient 3 Am. Jurisprudence awards for evidence, legis., and acctg. and law Bancroft-Whitney, 1970. Mem.: State Bar Calif., Toastmasters (Best Performer award 1996, Best Table Topics award 1997, Best Spkr. award 1997), Order of Coif. Avocations: gardening, poetry, running, public speaking, history. Home: 126 S Reeves Dr Beverly Hills CA 90212 Home Phone: 818-634-0034. Personal E-mail: rlgrimwade@yahoo.com.

GRIMWOOD, HELEN PERRY, lawyer; b. Phoenix, Aug. 9, 1953; BSBA magna cum laude, Univ. Ariz., 1973; JD magna cum laude, Ariz. State Univ., 1980. CPA Ariz., 1979. Law clerk Judge L. Ray Haire, Ariz. Ct. of Appeals, 1980—81, Judge William C. Canby Jr., U.S. Ct. of Appeals, Ninth Cir., 1981—82; judge pro tempore Ariz. Superior, Maricopa County, 1993—, Ariz Ct. of Appeals, 1998; ptnr. Grimwald Law Firm PLC, Phoenix. Named a Fellow, Am. Bar Found., 2000; named one of the Valley's Most Influential in Law, Bus. Journal, 2000; recipient Friedman award for excellence in legal edn., Maricopa County Bar Assn., 1995, Justice Gordon award for pro bono svc., 1996, Solin award for outstanding leadership, Ariz. Women Lawyer's Assn. Mem.: Ariz. Women Lawyer's

Assn. (pres. 1996—97), Nat. Conf. of Women's Bar Assn. (dir. 1977—), Maricopa County Bar Assn. (dir. 1992—96, chair, comml. litig. CLE Com. 1993—96), Ariz. State Bar Assn. (mem., bd. gov. 1997—, pres.-elect 2004—05, pres. 2005—06). Office: Grimwood Law Firm PLC Ste A 205 301 E Bethany Home Rd Phoenix AZ 85012-1269*

GRINALDS, JOHN SOUTHY, military officer, retired academic administrator; b. Balt., Jan. 5, 1938; Grad., West Point Mil. Acad., 1959; B in Geography, M in Geography, Oxford U., Eng.; MBA with distinction, Harvard U. Commd. 2d lt. USMC, 1959, advanced through grades to maj. gen.; commdg. gen. Marine Corps Recruit Depot, San Diego, 1989—91; headmaster Woodberry Forest Sch., Woodberry Forest, Va., 1991—97; pres. The Citadel, Charleston, SC, 1997—2005. Decorated Silver Star; recipient Legion d'Honneur, French Pres., Francois Mitterand. Office: The Citadel 171 Moultrie St Charleston SC 29409

GRINBERG, EFRAIM, watch manufacturing company executive; s. Gedalio and Sonia Grinberg; m. Jane Fishman (dec. 2000); children: Marget, Sam. Grad., Brown U., 1980. Joined Movado Group Inc., 1980, v.p. mktg., 1985—86, sr. v.p. mktg., 1986—90, COO, 1990—95, pres., 1990—, CEO, 2001—, also dir., 1988—. Bd. dirs. Lincoln Ctr. for Performing Arts. Mem.: Am. Watch Assn. (bd. dirs.), Jeweler's Security Alliance (bd. dirs.). Office: Movado Group Inc 650 From Rd Paramus NJ 07652 Office Phone: 201-267-8000.

GRINBERG, GEDALIO, watch manufacturing company executive; b. Cuba; arrived in US, 1960; m. Sonia Grinberg; 2 children. Founder Movado Group, Inc., 1961, CEO, 1961—2001, chmn., 1961—. Recipient Lifetime Achievement Award, Jewelry Industry Coun., 2003. Office: Movado Group Inc 650 From Rd Paramus NJ 07652

GRINBERG, NELU, chemist; s. Iosef and Bianca Grinberg; m. Cynthia Coffman; 1 child, Mark. MS, U. Iasi, 1973; PhD in Chemistry, Tech. U. Iasi, Romania, 1982. Sr. rsch. fellow Merck Rsch. Labs, Rahway, NJ, 1987—2003; disting. scientist Boehringer Ingelheim, Ridgefield, Conn., 2003—. Kolthoff fellow, Hebrew U. Jerusalem, 2007. Mem.: Am. Chem. Soc., Conn. Separation Sci. Coun. (pres. 2006—). Home: 274 Aspetuck Ridge Rd New Milford CT 06776 Office: Boehringer Ingelheim Pharm 900 Ridgebury Rd Ridgefield CT 06877-0368 Home Phone: 860-354-3293; Office Phone: 203-791-6339. Personal E-mail: ngrinb3684@aol.com. Business E-Mail: ngrinber@rdg.boehringer-ingelheim.com.

GRINBERG, RAUL, internist; b. Buenos Aires, Aug. 15, 1922; came to U.S., 1958; s. David Grinberg and Ana Tabachicoff; m. Raquel Funes, Feb. 12, 1945 (div. 1962); children: George Anibal, Ricardo Adrian, Diego Xavier. Bachelor's degree, Mariano Moreno, Buenos Aires, 1939; MD, Buenos Aires Med. Sch., 1946. Rsch. assoc. Columbia U., NYC, 1958-62; sr. internist Roswell Pk. Meml. Inst., Buffalo, 1963-64; clin. instr. SUNY, Binghamton, N.Y., 1970-74; pvt. practice Binghamton, 1970—. Vis. prof. Cornell U., Ithaca, N.Y., 1964-66; mem. adv. bd. oncology N.Y. State Med. Soc., Lake Success, 1970-96. Author: (books) Computers and Obesity, 1989, Sexual Education for Doctors, 1998, The Secret Life of a Doctor, 2003; artist (one man shows) include SUNY Art Gallery, Binghamton, 2000, Jewish Cmty. Ctr., 2002, Gallery Unitarian Universalist Ch., Binghamton, NY, 2007. Mem. Roberson Art Mus., Binghamton, 1964-99, H. Johnson Art Mus., Ithaca, 1980-99, Philharmonic Orch., Binghamton, 1964-99; Met. Mus., N.Y.C., 1997-99. Recipient Bronze award Am. Cancer Soc., 1997. Fellow ACP; mem. Endocrine Soc., Am. Assn. for Cancer Rsch, Am. Coll. Forensic Examiners, Inc. Avocations: painting, writing, collecting antiques. Home and Office: Apt 3A Bldg 4 201 Evergreen St Vestal NY 13850

GRINDLAY, JONATHAN ELLIS, astrophysics educator; b. Richmond, Va., Nov. 9, 1944; s. John Happer and Elizabeth (Ellis) G.; m. Sandra Kay Smyrski, Oct. 10, 1970; children: Graham Charles, Kathryn Jane. AB, Dartmouth Coll., 1966; MA, Harvard U., 1969, PhD, 1971. Jr. fellow Harvard U., Cambridge, Mass., 1971-74, asst. prof., 1976-81, prof. astronomy, 1981—2001, Robert Treat Paine prof. astronomy, 2001—, chmn. dept. astronomy, 1985—90, 2001—03; astrophysicist Smithsonian Obs., 1974—76. Cons. MIT Lincoln Lab., Bedford, Mass., 1982—; mem. vis. com. astronomy U. Chgo., 1983, Astrophys. Lab. Saclay, France, 1988—, NASA/Goddard Space Flight Ctr., 1995—96, chmn., 1997; mem. vis. com. dept. physics Columbia U., 1998; mem. vis. com. Naval Rsch. Lab., 1998; mem. vis. com. dept. astronomy and space physics Rice U., 1999; mem. users com. Cerro Tololo Interam. Obs., La Serena, Chile, 1981—84; mem. Aspen Ctr. for Physics, Colo., 1991—2001, trustee, 1989—90; chmn. high energy astrophysics mgmt. ops. group NASA, 1986—88; mem. users com. Compton Gamma Ray Obs., 1992—94; chair users com. NASA High Energy Astrophysics Sci. Archive Ctr., 2000—02; mem. space sci. bd. NAS, 1986—89; mem. com. astronomy and astrophysics NRC, 1992—98, mem. com. on internat. programs, 1996—98, mem. high energy astronomy forum space panel, 1998—99; mem. Space Telescope Inst. Coun., 1993—96, 1989—90, Space Telescope Ind. Sci. Rev. Com., 1996—97; chmn. binary panel Space Telescope Cycle 7 Time Allocation Commn.; chmn. space sci. working group AAU, 1990—92; mem. sci. orgn. com. for numerous internat. mtgs.; mem. NASA Space Sci. Adv. Commn., 2003—05; chmn. Gamma-Ray Large Area Space Telescope Users Group, 2004—, APS Bethe Prize Com., 2005. Contbr. articles to profl. jours. and books. Recipient Bart J. Bok prize dept. astronomy Harvard U., 1976; NSF and NASA rsch. grantee, 1978—; Guggenheim fellow, 1991-93, Sloan fellow, 1981-84. Fellow: AAAS, Am. Astron. Soc. (high energy divsn. nat. sec.-treas. 1982—84, councilor 1989—90, nat. v.p. 1994—97, nat. vice chair 2000—02, nat. chair 2002—04), Am. Phys. Soc. (nat. chair divsn. astrophysics 1998—99, nat. chair Bethe prize com. 2006); mem.: Internat. Astron. Union (pres. commn. 6 1991—94, organizing com. 1997—). Avocations: hiking, mountain climbing, swimming. Home: 195 Lincoln Rd Lincoln MA 01773-4102 Office: Harvard-Smithsonian Ctr Astrophysics 60 Garden St Cambridge MA 02138-1516 Home Phone: 781-259-1147; Office Phone: 617-495-7204. Business E-Mail: jgrindlay@cfa.harvard.edu.

GRINDLEY, BRUCE ALAN, real estate agency executive; b. Woking, England, Mar. 1, 1948; s. Ernest and Ivy (Mummery) G.; children: Andrée, Paul. Brokerage clk. Leslie & Godwin, Lloyds Brokers, London, 1965-67; from enquiry clk. to br. mgr. Abbey Life, London, Croydon, Crawley, England, 1967-86; dir. Sunway Properties, Tenerife, Spain, 1986-94, Tenerife Property Shop, 1994—. Named Best Internat. Residential Estate Agt., 1997—, Best Internat. Estate Agt., 2002—, Best Spanish Estate Agt. London, 2005, Best Spanish Islands Real Estate Agt. Barcelona, 2005; recipient Best Internat. Estate Agt. Gold award, 1996—, Best Spanish Estate Agent Gold award, 1998—99, 1999—2000, 2001—, 2002—, Best Property Website award, 2002—03, Safe Home award, 2000, Best Property Advt., 2001—02, Five Star award Best Property Adv., 2003, Five Star award Best Spl. Estate Agt., 2004. Fellow Life Ins. Assn.; mem. Internat. Real Estate Inst., Nat. Assn. Estate Agts., Liga Internat. de Representacion y Agencia Comml., Coll. Ofcl. Agts. Comml., The Personal Fin. Soc. (life). Office: Tenerife Property Shop SL 117 Puerto Colon Playa de las Americas Adeje Tenerife Spain Office Phone: +34-922-714700. E-mail: info@tenerifepropertyshop.com.

GRINELL, SHEILA, museum director; b. NYC, July 15, 1945; d. Richard N. and Martha (Mimiless) G.; m. Thomas E. Johnson, July 15, 1980; 1 child, Michael; stepchildren: Kathleen, Thomas. BA, Radcliffe Coll., 1966; MA, U. Calif., Berkeley, 1968. Co-dir. exhibits and programs The Exploratorium, San Francisco, 1969-74; promotion dir. Kodansha Internat., Tokyo, 1974-77; traveling exhbn. coord. Assn. Sci. Tech. Ctrs., Washington, 1978-80, exec. dir., 1980-82, project dir. traveling exhbn. Chips and Changes, 1982-84; assoc. dir. N.Y. Hall of Sci., 1984-87; pres., CEO Ariz. Sci. Ctr., Phoenix, 1993—. Cons. Optical Soc. Am., 1987, Nat. Sci. Ctr. Found., 1988, Interactive Video Sci. Consortium, 1988, Assn. Sci. Tech. Ctrs., 1988-89, Found. for Creative Am., 1989-90, Am. Assn. for World Health, 1990, Children's TV Workshop, 1991, Sciencenter, 1991, SciencePort, 1991, The Invention Factory, 1992, N.Y. Bot. Garden, 1992-93. Author: Light, Sight, Sound, Hearing: Exploratorium '74, 1974; editor A Stage for Science, 1979, A New Place for Learning Science: Starting and Running A Science Center, 1992, 2d edit., 2003, (with Mark St. John) Vision to Reality: Critical Dimensions in Science Center Development, Vol. I, 1993, II, 1994. Fulbright teaching asst., 1966; hon. Woodrow Wilson fellow, 1967 Fellow AAAS; mem. Am. Assn. Mus., Phi Beta Kappa.

GRINER, G. CHRISTOPHER, lawyer; BA, Lehigh U., 1971; JD, Rutgers U., 1973. Bar: Pa. 1973, DC 1976. Atty. advisor Office of Gen. Counsel, Dept. of Defense, 1973—77; mng. ptnr. Kaye Scholer LLP, Washington, DC. Mem.: Pa. Bar Assn., DC Bar. Office: Kaye Scholer LLP McPherson Bldg 901 Fifteenth St, NW, Ste 1100 Washington DC 20005 Office Phone: 202-682-3619. E-mail: cgriner@kayescholer.com.

GRINER, PAUL FRANCIS, physician; b. Phila., Jan. 1, 1933; s. John and Josepha (Snyder) G.; m. Miriam Millard; children: Laura, Paul Jr. BA, Harvard U., 1954; MD with honors, U. Rochester, 1959. Diplomate Am. Bd. Internal Medicine, Nat. Bd. Med. Examiners. Intern in medicine Mass. Gen. Hosp., Boston, 1959-60, asst. resident, 1960-61, sr. resident, 1963-64; chief resident in medicine Strong Meml. Hosp., Rochester, NY, 1964-65; fellow in pathology U. Rochester Sch. Medicine & Dentistry, 1956-57, instr. medicine, fellow in hematology, 1964-65, clin. instr., 1965-66, clin. sr. instr., 1966-67, asst. prof. medicine, 1967-69, assoc. prof., 1969-73, Samuel E. Durand prof. medicine, 1973-95, head. gen. medicine unit, 1976-84, acting chmn. dept. medicine, 1977-79, chmn. dept. health svcs., 1985-94; gen. dir. Strong Meml. Hosp., 1984-95; v.p. Assn. Am. Med. Colls., Washington, 1995-2000. Dir. med. edn. Rochester Gen. Hosp., 1965—67, cons., 1969—95, Genesee Hosp., 1969—95, Highland Hosp., 1969—95, Inst. Healthcare Improvement, 2002—; chmn. bd. dirs. Acad. Med. Ctr. Consortium, 1991—92; emeritus prof. medicine U. Rochester Sch. Medicine and Dentistry. Contbr. numerous articles to profl. jours., chpts. to books. Mem. N.Y. Gov.'s Health Care Adv. Bd., 1990-94, Mayoral Commn. on Health and Hosps. Corp. of City of N.Y., 1991-92. Capt. USAF, 1961-63. Decorated Air Force Commendation medal; recipient Doran Stephens prize, U. Rochester, 1959. Master: ACP (chmn. bd. regents 1991—92, pres. 1993—94); mem.: Inst. Medicine Nat. Acad. Scis. (mem. bd. healthcare svcs. 1987—2000), Soc. Med. Adminstrs., So. Gen. Internal Medicine Soc., Assn. Am. Physicians, Am. Clin. and Climatol. Assn., Alpha Omega Alpha. Avocations: skiing, golf, surf fishing, travel.

GRINNAN, KATIE, artist; b. Richmond, Va., 1970; Attended, Studio Arts Ctr. Internat., Florence, Italy, 1991; BFA in Painting, Carnegie Mellon U., 1992; attended, Skowhega Sch. Painting & Sculpture, Skowhegan Maine, 1992; MFA in Sculpture, UCLA, 1999. One-woman shows include Rock Bottom, ACME, L.A., 2001, 2003, Whitney Mus. Am. Art at Altria, 2003, exhibited in group shows at UCLA MFA Thesis Exhbn., New Wight Gallery, LA, 1998, As I love you you become more pretty, 937 Hudson Ave., LA, 2000, Legal Paper Work, Beyond Baroque, LA, 2000, katie grinnan alice konitz christie frields, Guggenheim Gallery, Chapman U., Calif., 2000, Snapshot, UCLA Hammer Mus., 2001, Sharing Sunsets, Mus. Contemporary Art, Tucson, 2001, Bommerang: Collector's Choice, Exit Art, NYC, 2001, Anti-Form, Soc. Contemporary Photog., Kans. City, Mo., 2002, Officina Am., Galeria D'Arte Monderna, Bologna, Italy, 2002, Drive-By, Reynolds Gallery, Richmond, Va., 2002, Strolling Through an Ancient Shrine & Garden, ACME, LA, 2002, Out of the Ground Into the Sky Out of the Sky Into the Ground, Pond, San Francisco, 2002, Wit Form Rainbow (Part I), The Project, LA, 2003, Whitney Biennial, Whitney Mus. Am. Art, NYC, 2004, Material Faith, Kontainer Gallery, LA, 2004, Real World: Dissolving Space of Experience, Modern Art Oxford, England, 2004, Art on Paper, Weatherspoon Art Mus., U. NC, 2004. Mailing: c/o ACME 6150 Wilshire Blvd #1 Los Angeles CA 90048

GRINNELL, ALAN DALE, neuroscientist, educator; b. Mpls., Nov. 11, 1936; s. John Erle and Swanhild Constance (Friswold) Grinnell; m. Verity Rich, Sept. 30, 1962 (div. 1975); m. Feelie Lee Grinnell, Dec. 23, 1996. BA, Harvard U., Cambridge, Mass., 1958, PhD, 1962. Jr. fellow Harvard U., 1959-62; rsch. assoc. biophysics dept. Univ. Coll. London, 1962-64; asst. rsch. zoologist UCLA, 1964-65, from asst. prof. to prof. dept. biology, 1965-78, prof. physiology, 1972—; dir. Jerry Lewis Neuromuscular Research Ctr. UCLA Sch. Medicine, 1978—2003; head Ahmanson Lab. Cellular Neurobiology UCLA Brain Research Inst. 1977—; dir. tng. grant in cellular neurobiology UCLA, 1968—2006, rsch. assoc. Fowler Mus. Cultural History, 1990—, chmn. dept. physiol. sci., 1997—2001. Author: Calcium and Ion Channel Modulation, 1988, Physiology of Excitable Cells, 1983, Regulation of Muscle Contraction, 1981, Introduction to Nervous Systems, 1977, others; contbr. editorial revs. to profl. jours., pub. houses, fed. granting agys. Guggenheim fellow, 1986; recipient Sr. Scientist award Alexander von Humboldt Stiftung, 1975, 79, Jacob Javits award NIH, 1986. Mem. AAAS (mem.-at-large neurosci. steering group 1998-2002), Muscular Dystrophy Assn. (mem. med. adv. com. LA chpt. 1980-92), Soc. for Neurosci. (councilor 1982-86), Am. Physiol. Soc. (mem. neurophysiol. steering com. 1981-84), Soc. Fellow, Phi Beta Kappa, Sigma Xi, others. Avocations: music, anthropology, archaeology, travel. Home: 510 E Rustic Rd Santa Monica CA 90402-1116 Office: UCLA Sch Medicine Dept Physiology Los Angeles CA 90095-0001 Office Phone: 310-825-4468. Business E-Mail: agrinnell@mednet.ucla.edu.

GRINNELL, HELEN DUNN, musicologist, arts administrator; b. NYC, Nov. 22, 1936; d. Kempton and Susan Barret (Gill) Dunn; m. Alexander Grinnell; children: Taylor, James Bodman. Student, New Eng. Conservatory, 1957-60; BMus in Music Theory, San Francisco Conservatory, 1968; MA in Musicology, Am. U., 1982. Dir. Opera and Symphony Previews, San Francisco, 1966-67; arts coord. Del. State Arts Coun., 1977-78; mgr. Performing Arts Libr. Am. U., 1981-84; pres. Music Info. Specialists, 1984—. Cons. Met. Mus. Art, 1996—, China Inst. in Am., 1999, Carnegie Hall, 2000—; vis. com. Mus. Fine Arts, Boston, 2002—; mem. adv. bd. East-West Music Exch. Assn., 2000—. Author: Chinese Musical Iconography: A History of Musical Instruments Depicted in Chinese Art, 1987; program annotator Dumbarton Concert Series, Smithsonian Instn., Kennedy Ctr., Stagebill; editor: Am. Women Composers' Forum, 1986—88; contbr. Orientations, Music in Art, 1995—. Steering com. Friends of Music Smithsonian Instn., 1978—88; pres. Cambridge Music Assn., 2004—; bd. dirs. Nat. Sympony Orch., Washington, 1979—82, Nat. Orchestral Assn., 1993—95, Spring Opera San Francisco, 1967—71, Jr. League of San Francisco, 1967—71, Wilmington Music Sch., 1973—78, Washington Performing Arts Soc., 1980—90, Bargemusic Ltd., NYC, 1992—94, Shelter Island Hist. Soc., 1993—95; bd. overseers New Eng. Conservatory, 1985—90; bd. dirs. New Eng. Conservatory Alumni Coun., 1994—, Cape Cod Chamber Music Festival, 2000—; chair acad. policy com., trustee, adv. bd. San Francisco Conservatory of Music, 1967—71; chair archtl. rev. bd. Village of Dering Harbor, NY, 1991—95. Mem. Am. Musical Instruments Soc., Am. Musicol. Soc., Soc. Ethnomusicology, Cosmopolitan Club.

GRINNELL, JOSEPH FOX, lawyer; b. July 4, 1923; s. Robert L. and Mary King G.; m. Marjorie Volwiler, Aug. 24, 1946; children: Stephen F., Christine K. Burcham, James W. BA, Yale U., 1945; JD, Northwestern U., 1949. Bar: Ill. 1949, U.S. Dist. Ct. (no. dist.) Ill. 1949, Minn. 1954. Assoc. Winston-Strawn, Chgo., 1949-54; sr. v.p. law Investors Diversified Svcs., Mpls., 1954-83; of counsel Pepin Dayton Herman Graham & Getts, Mpls., 1983-87. Bd. dirs. Guthrie Theater, Mpls., 1970-71, Minn. Orch. Assn., Mpls., 1976-78; bd. dirs., chmn. Minn. Pollution Control Agy., Mpls., 1973-81. Served to lt. (j.g.) USN, 1942-46, PTO. Democrat. Presbyterian. Home: 8155 Parkview Ln Bloomington MN 55438 Personal E-mail: jo-margie@comcast.net.

GRINNEY, JAY, health facility company executive; b. Racine, Wis., Mar. 20, 1951; s. Leo Richard and June Louise (Christensen) G.; children: Naomi Hope, Rachel June, Matthew Jay; m. Ellen Heath, May 4, 1988. BA in Psychology, St. Olaf Coll., 1973; Master's in Hosp. Adminstrn., Washington U., St. Louis, 1981; MBA, Washington U., 1981. Adminstrv. resident The Methodist Hosp. System, Houston, 1982-83, asst. v.p., 1982-84, sr. v.p., 1985; CEO, Rosewood Med. Ctr. HCA Healthcare Co., Houston, 1990—92, COO, Houston region, 1992—93, pres., Houston region, 1993—96, pres. Ea. group Nashville, 1996—2004; pres., CEO HealthSouth Corp., Birmingham, 2004—. Treas., bd. dirs. The People's Community Clinic, St. Louis, 1979-81; adj. instr. Washington U., Houston, 1988—. Mem. allocations com. Houston United Way, 1988. Mem. Am. Coll. Healthcare Execs. (mem. regent's adv. coun. 1986—), Am. Hosp. Assn., Tex. Hosp. Assn., Greater Houston Hosp. Coun. (fin. com. 1985). Avocations: weightlifting, running, skiing, horseback riding. Office: HealthSouth Corp One HealthSouth Pkwy Birmingham AL 35243*

GRINOLS, EARL LEROY, III, economist, educator; b. Bemidji, Minn., May 2, 1951; s. Earl Leroy and Betty Annette (Wolfe) G.; m. Anne Dudley Bradstreet, Feb. 2, 1978; children: Kimberly Anne, Lindsay Elizabeth, Daniel Stephen. BS in Econs., BA in Math. summa cum laude, U. Minn., 1973; PhD in Econs., MIT, 1977. Asst. prof. econs. Cornell U., Ithaca, N.Y., 1977-84; assoc. prof. U. Ill., Champaign, 1984-87, prof., 1988—2005; sr. economist Coun. of Econ. Advisers, Washington, 1987-88; disting. prof. Baylor U., 2004—. Cons. Dept. Labor, Washington, 1985-86; vis. prof. U. Chgo., 1991. Author: Uncertainty and the Theory of International Trade, 1987, Microeconomics, 1994, Gambling In America: Costs and Benefits, 2004. Grad. fellow NSF, 1973-76. Mem. Am. Econ. Assn., Econometric Soc. (pres.), Assn. Christian Economists, Royal Econ. Soc., Phi Beta Kappa. Home: 104 Cantor Ct Woodway TX 76712-8818 Office: 357 Hankamer Sch Bus Baylor U One Bear Pl #98003 Waco TX 76798-8003 Office Phone: 254-710-7522.

GRINSPOON, DAVID H., astrobiologist, writer, museum administrator; s. Lester and Betsy Grinspoon; m. Tory Reed, May 1995. PhD, U. Ariz., 1989. Frequent advisor NASA; worked with U. Colo., Southwest Rsch. Inst.; curator, astrobiology Denver Mus. Nature & Science. Mem. sci. team, Mars rover NASA; interdisciplinary scientist, Venus Express Mission European Space Agy. Guest appearances on radio and TV sci. documentaries, writer of popular articles for magazines, writer of Op Ed pieces for newspapers; musician: The Geeks (Semifinalists WBRU (RI) Rock Hunt, 1982), Shagnatty, Hmmbah, Mom's Instant Hot (Westwood Best of Denver 1995 Best World Beat Band), Venus Envy; author: Venus Revealed, 1997 (finalist, LA Times Book Prize, 1998), Lonely Planets: The Natural Philosophy of Alien Life, 2003 (PEN Ctr. USA, Literary award for Rsch. Nonfiction, 2004). Mem.: AAAS, Am. Geophysical Union, Am. Astronomical Soc., Divsn. for Planetary Sciences (Carl Sagan medal for Excellence in Pub. Comm. 2006). Avocations: guitar, percussion, compose songs, singing. Office: Denver Mus Nature & Sci 2001 Colorado Blvd Denver CO 80205 Office Phone: 303-370-6469. Business E-Mail: david.grinspoon@dmns.org. E-mail: david@funkyscience.net.

GRIPE, ALAN GORDON, minister; b. Indpls., Sept. 8, 1920; s. Otto Herman and Bertha (Anderson) G.; m. Elizabeth Howell, Sept. 29, 1951 (div. 1972); children: Stephen, David. BA, Lake Forest Coll., Ill., 1942; BD, Princeton Theol. Sem., 1946; STM, Union Theol. Sem., NYC, 1953. Ordained to ministry, Presbyn. Ch. (U.S.A.), 1946. Asst. prof. Silliman U., Dumaguete City, Philippines, 1946-50; chaplain Davidson Coll., NC, 1951-52; asst. chaplain U.S. Mil. Acad., West Point, 1952-55; pastor First Presbyn. Ch., Westfield, NY, 1955-65; exec. coord. Personnel Svcs., United Presbyn. Ch. USA, 1965-88; interim pastor Genesee Valley Presbytery, Rochester, NY, 1991-99, acting exec. presbyter, 2001—02, ret., 2002; clergy visitor Strong Meml. Hosp., Rochester, NY, 1999—2002. Author: The Interim Pastor's Manual, rev. edit., 1997. Treas. John Milton Soc. for Blind, N.Y.C., 1988-90. Mem. Assn. of Presbyn. Interim Ministry Specialists (coun. mem. 1987-90). Home: 95 Penarrow Rd Rochester NY 14618-1721

GRIPPI, SALVATORE WILLIAM, artist; b. Buffalo, Sept. 30, 1921; s. Leonardo and Josephine (Orlando) G.; m. Rosalind Ratzenberg, Apr. 14, 1945. Student, Mus. Modern Art, NYC, 1944—45, Art Students' League, 1945—48, Atelier 17, 1951—53, Instituto Statale d'Arte, Florence, Italy, 1953—55. Instr. Atelier 17, summer 1953, Cooper Union Art Sch., 1956-59, Sch. Visual Arts, NYC, 1961-62; assoc. prof. art Claremont Grad. Sch., 1962-68, Pomona Coll., 1962-68; prof., founder art dept. Ithaca (NY) Coll., 1968—. Invited participant Ford Found. Conf. Visual Artists, 1961. One-man shows include, NYU, N.Y.C., 1958, Zabriskie Gallery, N.Y.C., 1956, 59, Krasner Gallery, N.Y.C., 1962, 64, 79, 81, Feingarten Galleries, 1967, 70, Everson, Mus., Syracuse, N.Y., 1978, Handwerker Gallery, Ithaca Coll., 1978, group shows include, Met. Mus. Art, N.Y.C., 1952, Schneider Gallery, Rome, 1954, Galleria La Fontanella, Rome, 1955, Whitney Mus. and Smithsonian Inst. Traveling show, 1958-59, Corcoran Gallery Art, Washington, 1959, 63, Whitney Mus., N.Y.C., 1960, Mus. Modern Art, N.Y.C., 1962, 1994-95, Hunter Coll. Leubsdorf Gallery, N.Y.C., 1995; represented in permanent collections, Whitney Mus., Met. Mus. Art, N.Y. Pub. Libr., N.Y.C., Joseph Hirshorn Collection, Washington, Milw.-Downer Coll., Ithaca Coll., St. Lawrence U., Everson Mus., Annex Gallery, Santa Rosa, Calif. Served with USNR, 1942-45. Fulbright grantee, Instituto Statale d'Arte, 1953—55. Mem. Art Students' League (life, treas. 1961-62, bd. control 1961-64), Coll. Art Assn. Home: 9 Orchard Hill Rd Ithaca NY 14850 Office: Ithaca Coll Art Dept Ithaca NY 14850

GRISCHKE, ALAN EDWARD, lawyer; b. Milw., Mar. 2, 1945; s. Rupert Edward and Velma Pearl (Springer) G.; m. Christine A. Bremer, July 4, 1981 (div.). BS, U. Wis., Stevens Point, 1968; postgrad., U. Miami, Fla., 1969; JD, Loyola U., Chgo., 1971. Bar: Ill. 1971, Wis. 1982, U.S. Dist. Ct. (no. dist.) Ill. 1971, U.S. Dist. Ct. (we. and ea. dist.) Wis. 1982, U.S. Ct. Appeals (7th cir.) 1979, U.S. Supreme Ct. 1979; cert. civil trial specialist, Nat. Bd. Trial Attys. 1992. Asst. atty. gen. Ill. Atty. Gens. Office, Chgo., 1971-73; regional counsel Ill. Dept. Mental Health, Chgo., 1973-75, gen. counsel, 1975-80; ptnr. Grischke & Assocs., Ltd., Chgo., 1980-82; assoc. Trembath, Hess, Miller & Seidl, Wausau, Wis., 1982; ptnr. Mallery Law Offices SC, Wausau, Wis., 1983-85; pvt. practice Wausau, Wis., 1985-89; pres. Grischke & Bremer LLSC, Wausau, Wis., 1989—2003, Grischke, Molinaro & Laughlin, LLSC, Wausau, 2003—05, Grischke & Laughlin LLSC, Wausau, 2005—. Adj. prof. John Marshall Law Sch., Chgo., 1975-81; faculty U. Ill., Abraham Lincoln Sch. Medicine, Chgo., 1976-80, Loyola U., Stritch Sch. Medicine, Chgo., 1980-82; chmn. Midwest Consortium Mental Health Attys., 1975-76, Nat. Assn. State Mental Health Attys., 1976-80; bd. dirs. Dept. Natural Resources, Wis., 2003-05. Mem. ABA (sustaining), Am. Trial Lawyers Assn., Wis. State Bar Assn. (bd. profl. responsibility dist. 16 1990-98), Marathon County Bar Assn., Wis. Acad. Trial Lawyers (sustaining, bd. dirs. 1986-88). Home: 3305 Rio Dr Weston WI 54476 Office: PO Box 847 1220 N Sixth St Wausau WI 54402-0847 Office Phone: 715-849-5400. Business E-Mail: alan@glpilaw.com.

GRISCHKOWSKY, DANIEL RICHARD, research scientist, educator; b. St. Helens, Oreg., Apr. 17, 1940; s. Oscar Edward and Christine Hazel (Olsen) G.; m. Frieda Rosa Bachmann; children: Timothy and Stephanie (twins), Daniela BS, Oreg. State U., 1962; AM in Physics, Columbia U., 1965, PhD in Physics, 1968. Postdoctoral studies Columbia U., NYC, 1968-69; mem. rsch. staff IBM Watson Rsch. Ctr., Yorktown Heights, NY, 1969-77; sci. advisor to dir. rsch. div. IBM, Yorktown Heights, 1978; mgr. atomic physics with lasers group IBM Watson Rsch. Ctr., Yorktown Heights, 1979-83, mgr. ultra-fast sci. with lasers group, 1983-93; Regents prof., Bellmon chair optoelectronics Sch. Elec. and Computer Engring. Okla. State U., Stillwater, 1993—. Chmn. Internat. Coun. on Quantum Electronics, 1989-93, Am. Phys. Soc./Optical Soc. Am./IEEE Joint Coun. on Quantum Electronics, 1989-93. Contbr. articles to profl. jours.; patentee in field. Recipient Boris Pregel award N.Y. Acad. of Sci., 1985. Fellow IEEE, Am. Phys. Soc. (chmn. laser sci. topical group 1993-94), Optical Soc. Am. (R.W. Wood prize 1989, William F. Meggers award 2003). Office: Okla State U Sch Elec Computer Engring Stillwater OK 74078-0001 Business E-Mail: grischd@ceat.okstate.edu.

GRISEZ, JAMES LOUIS, physician, plastic surgeon; b. Modesto, Calif., Feb. 25, 1935; s. John Francis and Josephine Marie (Tournahu) G.; m. Diane Madeline Skidmore, Mar. 7, 1989; children: James, Stephen, Suzanne, Kathleen. MD, St. Louis Sch. Medicine, 1960. Diplomate Am. Bd. Plastic and Reconstructive Surgery. Intern D.C. Gen. Hosp., Washington, 1960-61; resident med. ctr. Georgetown U., Washington, 1961-64; resident plastic and reconstructive surgery ctr. St. Francis Meml. Hosp., San Francisco, 1964-66; military surgeon Brook Army Med Ctr., San Antonio, 1966, Second Gen. Hosp., Landstuhl, Germany, 1966-69; pvt. practice Napa, Calif., 1969-82, Salinas, Calif., 1982-90, Kailua-Kona, Hawaii, 1990-93, South Valley Plastic Surgery, Gilroy, Calif., 1993—2002; provl. staff French Hosp. San Luis Obispo, 2002—03; active staff Arroyo Grande Cmty. Hosp., 2003—. Active staff mem. St. Louise Regional Hosp.; chief of staff South Valley Hosp., Hazel Hawkins; chief staff St. Helena Hosp., 1977-78, exec. com. 1973-80; radio talk show host All About Plastic Surgery, sta. KRNY, 1986-88. Contbr. articles to med. jours. Mem. Am. Cancer Soc. (pres. 1988-90), Am. Soc. Plastic Surgeons, Calif. Soc. Plastic and Reconstructive Surgeons, Hawaii Plastic Surgery Soc. Home: 1595 Chesapeake Pl Arroyo Grande CA 93420 Office: 354 South Halyon Rd Ste C Arroyo Grande CA 93420

GRISHAM, JOE WHEELER, cell biologist, educator; b. Smith County, Tenn., Dec. 5, 1931; s. William Wince and Grace (Allen) G.; m. Jean Evelyn Malone, July 2, 1955. BA, Vanderbilt U., 1953, MD, 1957. Intern Washington U.-Barnes Hosp., St. Louis, 1957-58, resident in pathology, 1958-60; mem. faculty Washington U., Med. Sch., 1960-73; prof. pathology and anatomy Washington U. Med. Sch., 1969-73; assoc. pathologist Barnes Hosp., 1969-73; vis. instr. Makerere Med. Coll., Kampala, Uganda, 1961; prof. pathology, chmn. dept. U. N.C. Med. Sch., Chapel Hill, 1973-99; also pathologist-in-chief U. N.C. Hosp., Chapel Hill, 1973-99; Kenan prof. U. N.C. Med. Sch., Chapel Hill, 1992—2003; sr. scientist Nat. Cancer Inst., Bethesda, 2003—. Bd. sci. counsellors Nat. Inst. Environ. Health Scis., 1974-78; mem. sci. advisory panel Chem. Industry Inst. Toxicology, 1977-88, chmn., 1980-88; adv. bd. Given Inst. Pathobiology, 1983-87; mem. pathology study sect. A NIH, 1969-73, chmn. 1970-73, chmn. pathology study sect. B, 1979-83; lectr. in field. Contbr. articles to med. jours. Served to lt. comdr. USNR, 1961-63. Fogarty scholar NCI/NIH, 2000—02; John and Mary R. Markle scholar Acad. Medicine, 1964-69; fellow Life Ins. Med. Rsch. Fund, 1959-61, Nat. Cancer Inst., 1958-59; Brindley prof. U. Tex. Med. Br., 1993; named Disting. Med. Alumnus Vanderbilt U., 1994; named to Order of Long Leaf Pine, State of N.C., 1996. Mem. Am. Assn. Pathologists (pres. 1984-85), Am. Assn. Cancer Research, Fedn. Am. Soc. Exptl. Biology (pres., chmn. bd. 1984-85), Am. Assn. Study Liver Diseases, Am. Soc. Cell Biology, Univ. Assn. Rsch. and Edn. in Pathology (v.p. 1985-86), Tissue Culture Assn., Internat. Acad. Pathology, Cell Kinetics Soc., AMA, AAAS. Home: 1703 Curtis Rd Chapel Hill NC 27514-7614 Office: Lab Expl Carcinogensis CRC NCI NIH Bldg 37 Rm 4146A 37 Convent Dr MSC 4262 Bethesda MD 20892-4262

GRISHAM, JOHN, writer; b. Jonesboro, Ark., Feb. 8, 1955; m. Renee Jones, May 8, 1981; children: Ty, Shea. BS, Miss. State U., 1977; JD, U. Miss., 1981. Bar: Miss. 1981. Practiced law, Southaven, Miss., 1981-91; mem. Miss. Ho. Reps., 1984-90. Author: (novels) A Time to Kill, 1989, The Firm, 1991, The Pelican Brief, 1992, The Client, 1993, The Chamber, 1994, The Rainmaker, 1995, The Runaway Jury, 1996, The Partner, 1997, The Street Lawyer, 1998, The Testament, 1999, The Brethren, 2000, A Painted House, 2001, The Summons, 2002, Skipping Christmas, 2002, The King of Torts, 2003, Bleachers, 2003, The Last Juror, 2004, The Broker, 2005, Playing for Pizza, 2007; (nonfiction) The Innocent Man: Murder and Injustice in a Small Town, 2006; (screenplays) The Gingerbread Man, 1998; actor, dir., prodr. (films) Mickey, 2006; prodr. A Time to Kill, 1996; exec. prodr. (TV movies) The Street Lawyer, 2003 Office: Doubleday Pub 1540 Broadway New York NY 10036-4039 Address: c/o Agent David Gernert 18th Fl 136 E 57th St New York NY 10022*

GRISHAM, LARRY RICHARD, physicist; b. Henderson, Tex., Feb. 2, 1949; s. James Marion and Eva Fay Grisham; m. Jacqueline Lee Criswell, June 24, 1972; children: Austin Nathanial, Rachel Nicole, Hilary Jane. BS in Physics, U. Tex., 1971; PhD in Physics, Oxford U., Eng., 1974. Postdoctoral fellow Plasma Physics Lab. Princeton (NJ) U., 1974—75, staff rsch. physicist, 1975—82, rsch. physicist, 1982—89, prin. rsch. physicist, 1989—, head beam physics, 1988—. Cons. Northrop Corp., L.A., 1985, Phys. Dynamics, La Jolla, Calif., 1986-88, Teledyne Brown Engring., Huntsville, Ala., 1989—; mem. and chmn. various rev. panels U.S. Army Strategic Def. Command, 1986—. Contbr. numerous articles to profl. jours. Mem. NJ Rhodes Scholar Selection Com., 1986—, Dist. 5 Rhodes Scholar Selection Com., 2005—. Recipient Tex. Exes Centennial Honored Alumnus award U. Tex., Austin, 1985, Wolfson Grad. award, 1972, Kaul Found. prize for excellence in plasma physics and tech. devel., 2001; winner Westinghouse Sci. Talent Search, Washington, 1967; Rhodes scholar, 1971; Woodrow Wilson fellow, 1971, invited rsch. fellow Japan Atomic Energy Rsch. Inst., 1996. Methodist. Achievements include research in energy confinement properties of tokamak plasmas as a fuction of major and minor radius; physics and technology of high power neutral beam systems physics of excited nuclear states. Home: 2 Dennick Ct Princeton NJ 08540-2202 Office: Princeton Univ Plasma Physics Lab PO Box 451 Princeton NJ 08543-0451

GRISKEY, RICHARD GEORGE, chemical engineering professor; b. Pitts., Jan. 9, 1931; s. George and Emma (Maskell) G.; m. Pauline Anne Becker, June 11, 1955; children: Paula Louise, David Richard. BChemE, Carnegie-Mellon U., 1951, MChemE, 1955, PhD, 1958. Registered profl. engr., Wis. Sr. engr. E. I. duPont Co., Seaford, Del., 1958-60; asst. prof. U. Cin., 1960-62; assoc. prof. Va. Poly. Inst., 1962-64, prof., 1964-66; prof., head chem. engring. dept. U. Denver, 1966-68; dir. rsch. and found. rsch. prof. Newark Coll. Engring., 1968-71; prof. chem. engring., dean U. Wis., Milw., 1971-82; prof. chem. engring., dean engring. U. Ala., Huntsville, 1982-85; v.p., provost Stevens Inst. Tech., 1985-86, exec. v.p., provost, 1986-88, The Institute prof. chemistry and chem. engring., 1988—. Vis. scientist Polish Acad. Sci.-NAS, 1971; OAS vis. prof. Multi Nat. Food Project, Brazil, 1973; vis. prof. Monash U., Australia, 1974, Algerian Inst. Petroleum, 1975-76; cons. in field. Editor, Marcel Dekker Inc., 1974—; referee, reviewer: Canadian Jour. Chem. Engring., Am. Inst. Chem. Engrs. Jour., Jour. Polymer Sci., Jour. Fluid Mechanics, Jour. Heat Transfer; author: Chemical Engineering for Chemists, 1997; author: Polymer Process Engineering, 1995, Chemical Engineers Portable Handbook, 2000, Transport Phenomena and Unit Operations, 2001, paperback, 2006; contbr. articles to profl. jours. With AUS, 1951-53. Fellow ASME, Am. Inst. Chemists, Am. Inst. Chem. Engrs.; mem. Soc. Rheology, Am. Soc. Engring. Edn., Am. Assn. Higher Edn., Plastics Inst. Am. (bd. dirs. 1986—), Soc. Plastics Engrs., Am. Chem. Soc. (congl. counselor, Exceptional Achievement award 1991), Tau Beta Pi, Sigma Xi, Triangle, Scabbard and Blade. Office: Stevens Inst Tech Dept Chem and Chem Engring Hoboken NJ 07030 Personal E-mail: rgriskey@verizon.net.

GRISMORE, ROGER, physics professor, researcher; b. Ann Arbor, Mich., July 12, 1924; s. Grover Cleveland and May Aileen (White) G.; m. Marilynn Ann McNinch, Sept. 15, 1950; 1 child, Carol Ann. BS, U. Mich., 1947, MS, 1948, PhD, 1957; BS in Computer Sci., Coleman Coll., 1979. From asst. to assoc. physicist Argonne (Ill.) Nat. Lab., 1956-62; assoc. prof. physics Lehigh U., Bethlehem, Pa., 1962-67; specialist in physics Scripps Inst. Oceanography, La Jolla, Calif., 1967-71, 75-78; prof. physics Ind. State U., Terre Haute, 1971-74; from mem. staff to sr. scientist JAYCOR, San Diego, 1979-84; lectr. Calif. Poly. State U., San Luis Obispo, 1984-92, rsch. prof., 1992—, lunar sample investigator, 1994—. Contbr. numerous articles to profl. jours. Served as ensign USNR, 1945-46, PTO. Mem. Am. Phys. Soc., Am. Geophys. Union, N.Y. Acad. Scis., Sigma Xi. Achievements include co-discovery of the radioisotope silver-108m in the general marine environment, and development of the technique of radiosilver dating. Home: 535 Cameo Way Arroyo Grande CA 93420-5574 Office: Calif Poly State U Dept Physics San Luis Obispo CA 93407 Office Phone: 805-756-7556. Personal E-mail: r_grismore@wildblue.net.

GRISSOM, GARTH CLYDE, lawyer, director; b. Syracuse, Kans., Jan. 24, 1930; s. Clyde and Bernice Minnie (Eddy) Grissom; m. Elena Joyce Kerst, Aug. 17, 1958; children: Colin, Grady, Cole, Kent. BS, Kans. State U., 1951; LLB, Harvard U., 1957. Bar: Colo. 1957, U.S. Dist. Ct. (fed. dist.) Colo., 1957, U.S. Ct. Appeals (10th cir.) 1957, U.S. Supreme Ct. 1989. Ptnr., mem., counsel Sherman & Howard, L.L.C., Denver, 1963—. Sec., counsel, trustee Mile High United Way, Denver, 1985-88; trustee Kans. State U. Found., Manhattan, 1962-89; mem. Colo. Gov.'s Commn. on Life and the Law, 1990-99, chmn., 1996-99. Mem. ABA, Colo. Bar Assn., Denver Bar Assn. (pres. 1985-86, award of merit 1994), Rotary (sec. Denver 1983-84, bd. dirs. 1983-86, pres. 1989-90), Pi Kappa Alpha (pres. 1968-70). Office: Sherman & Howard LLC 633 17th St Ste 3000 Denver CO 80202-3665 Office Phone: 303-299-8156. Business E-Mail: ggrissom@sah.com.

GRISWELL, J. BARRY, insurance company executive; b. Ga. Bachelor's, Berry Coll., 1971; master's, Stetson U., 1972. Pres., CEO MetLife Mktg. Corp. (subs. MetLife Ins. Co.); agy. v.p. Principal Fin. Group, Des Moines, 1986-91, sr. v.p. individual ins. dept., 1991-96, exec. v.p., 1996-98, pres., 1998—2000, pres. and CEO, 2000—02, chmn., pres., CEO, 2002—06, chmn., CEO, 2006—. Past chair LIMRA Internat.; past chair bd. trustees Life Underwriting Tng. Coun.; bd. mem. Bus. Roundtable, Am. Coun. Capital Formation; bd. dir. Herman Miller Inc.; trustee S.S. Huebner Found. for Ins. Edn. Dir. Bus. Com. for Arts; trustee United Way Am.; past chmn. United Way Am. Nat. Tocqueville Council; trustee Central Coll., Berry Coll., Ga. Recipient Disting. American award, Horatio Alger Assn., 2003. Fellow: LIMRA Leadership Inst. Office: Principal Fin Group 711 High St Des Moines IA 50392*

GRISWOLD, FRANK TRACY, III, retired bishop; b. Bryn Mawr, Pa., Sept. 18, 1937; s. Frank Tracy Jr. and Louisa Johnson (Whitney) G.; m. Phoebe Wetzel, Nov. 27, 1965; 2 children. AB, Harvard Coll., 1959; student, Gen. Theol. Sem., 1959—60; BA, Oxford U., 1962, MA, 1966. Ordained deacon Episc. Ch., 1962, ordained priest Episc. Ch., 1963. Bishop coadjutor Diocese of Chgo., 1985—87, bishop, 1987—97; presiding bishop Episcopal Church USA, NYC, 1998—2006. Former dep. to Gen. Conv.; former chmn. Pa. Liturgical Commn. Former chair Standing Liturgical Commn., Episcopal Ch. U.S.; former co-chair Anglican-Roman Cath. Dialogue U.S., Anglican-Roman Cath. Internat. Episcopalian. E-mail: pboffice@episcopalchurch.org.

GRISWOLD, TOM, radio personality; b. Cleve., 1953; Grad., Univ. Sch., Chagrin Fall, OH, 1971, Columbia U. Radio host WFBQ-FM, Indpls., 1983—; nat. syndicated radio host Premiere Radio Networks, 1995—. Co-host The Bob & Tom Show, 1983—. Co-recipient Radio Personality of Yr. award, Billboard mag., 1991—98, Marconi Radio award, Nat. Assn. Broadcasters, 1993, 1995, 1997, 1999, Marconi Radio award for Network Syndicated Personality of Yr., 2006. The Sagamore of the Wabash, 1994, Nat. Chmn.'s Citation award, Leukemia Soc. Am., 1996. Office: WFBQ 6161 Fall Creek Rd Indianapolis IN 46220*

GRISWOLD, WILLIAM M., museum director, curator; b. 1960; BA in Art History with honors, Trinity Coll., Conn.; PhD, Courtauld Inst. Art, London. Assoc. curator dept. drawings and prints Met. Mus. Art, NYC; Charles W. Engelhard curator, head dept. drawings & prints Pierpont Morgan Libr., NYC, 1995—2001; assoc. dir. collections J. Paul Getty Mus., LA, 2001—04, acting dir., chief curator, 2004—05; dir., pres. Mpls. Inst. Arts, 2005—. Bd. dir. Am. Friends of Courtauld, Am. Friends of Shanghai Mus., The Courtauld Inst. Art, London. Office: Mpls Inst of Arts 2400 Third Ave S Minneapolis MN 55404 Office Phone: 612-870-3221.

GRITSCH, RUTH CHRISTINE LISA, editor; b. Duisburg, Germany, July 18, 1931; came to the U.S., 1941; d. Carl and Maria Augusta (von Schuman-Janssen) Sandman; m. Eric Walter Gritsch, June 4, 1955 (div. 1993); children: Deborah, Erika. BA, NYU, 1953. Assoc. Inst. for Internat. Edn., NYC, 1953-55; sec. Zeigler Bros., Inc., Gardners, Pa., 1993—2003. Translator: (books) Liberty, Equality, Sisterhood, 1978, Office of the Ministry, 1981, Huldrich Zwingli, 1983, Unity of the Churches, 1984, I Am a Palestinian Christian, 1995, Violence, 1996; co-translator: Luther's Works, Vols. 39, 41, 1966, 67; editor: Roly, 1988; co-editor: The Path of No Return, 2006; translator, editor: Justification of the Ungodly, 1968; editor, co-translator: Thomas Müntzer, A Tragedy of Errors, 1989. Active So. Poverty Law Ctr., Adams Co. Arts Coun. Mem.: LWV (bd. dirs., v.p. 1969—90, 1999—2001), Internat. Platform Assn. Democrat. Lutheran. Avocations: reading, collecting art. Home: 1 West St Gettysburg PA 17325-2130 Home Phone: 717-334-4413.

GRITTER, ELIZABETH, historian, researcher; b. Grand Rapids, Mich., Mar. 26, 1979; d. Robert Dale and Ruth Holstege Gritter. BA in Polit. Sci., Am. U., Washington, 2001; postgrad., U. N.C., 2003—. Promotions intern Keppler Assocs., Inc., Arlington, Va., 1998; intern Rep. John Conyers, Jr., Washington, 1998; curriculum writer Congl. Youth Leadership Coun., Washington, 1999; nat. field program intern Amnesty Internat., Washington, 2000; asst. analyst US Dept. HHS, Washington, 2001—03; rsch. asst. So. oral history program U. NC, Chapel Hill, 2004—06. Cons. Am. U. Scholarship Office, Washington, 2001—; interviewer Julian Bond, Billy E. Barnes Southern Cultures, 2005—06; presenter in field. Mem. Amnesty Internat., 1996—. Recipient Merit award, U.S. HHS, 2001—03; Rsch. grantee, Am. U., 2000, Harry S. Truman scholarship, Truman Found., 2000, Summer Rsch. grantee, Ctr. Study of Am. South, 2004, 2007, Summer fellowship, U. NC, 2004—07, scholarship, Oral Hist. Assn., 2006, Travel grants, Ctr. Study Am. South, 2007, Kennedy Rsch. grant, JFK Libr. & Mus., 2007. Mem.: Urban History Assn., So. Assn. Women Historians, Am. Hist. Assn., Orgn. Am. Historians, So. Hist. Assn., Pi Sigma Alpha, Phi Alpha Theta. Avocations: travel, jogging, reading, classic TV & movies. Office: Dept History U NC CB 3195 Hamilton Hall Chapel Hill NC 27599-3195 Business E-Mail: egritter@email.unc.edu.

GRITTON, EUGENE CHARLES, nuclear engineer, director; b. Santa Monica, Calif., Jan. 13, 1941; s. Everett Mason and Matilda Gritton; m. Gwendolyn O. Gritton; children: Dennis Mason, Kathleen Wanda. BS, UCLA, 1963, MS, 1965, PhD, 1966. Research engr., def. systems analyst RAND, Santa Monica, Calif., 1966-73, project leader advanced undersea tech. program, 1973-76, program dir. marine tech., 1974-76, program dir. applied sci. and tech., 1976-94, head dept. phys. scis., 1975-77, head engring. and applied scis. dept., 1977-86, RAND resident scholar for tech., 1990-93, dep. v.p. Nat. Security Rsch. Divsn., 1986-93, dep. v.p. Rsch. Ops. Group, 1986-90, dir. Acquisition and Tech. Policy Ctr., 1994—2004, acting dir. Nat Security Rsch. divsn., 1997—98, v.p. Nat Security Rsch. divsn., 2004—. Bd. dirs. Nat. Def. Rsch. Inst.; vis. lectr. dept. mech. engring. U. So. Calif., LA, 1967-72; vis. lectr. dept. energy and kinetics UCLA, 1971, 73; mem. Def. Sci. Bd. Study, 1996, 98. Recipient Engring. Alumnus of Yr. award UCLA Sch. Engring. and Applied Sci., 1985-86; AEC fellow, 1963, NSF Coop. Grad. fellow, 1964-66. Mem. Am. Nuclear Soc. (mem. exec. com. aerospace and hydrospace div. 1974-75), AIAA Office: Rand PO Box 2138 1776 Main St Santa Monica CA 90407-2138 Home: 4324 Promenade Way #315 Marina Del Rey CA 90292 Office Phone: 310-393-0411 ext. 6933. Business E-Mail: gene@rand.org.

GRIVER, JEANETTE A., psychologist, consultant; b. NYC, July 2, 1932; d. Lawrence Maurice Rosenthal and Selma Demby-Rosenthal; m. David M Griver, Mar. 15, 1951 (div. Apr. 1991). BA Psychology, UCLA, 1961; MA Psychology Human Factor, U. So. Calif., 1964. V.p. Jan Engring. Electronic Components, Santa Monica, 1955—62; pres. Jan Engring. Human Factors Divsn., Santa Monica, 1962—89; CEO Compsych Sys., Inc., LA, 1969—. Cons. to several orgns., 1962—. Author: Applied Problem Analysis Plus, 1988, Oh No! Not Another Problem, 2000, Curio a Shetland Sheepdog Meets the Crow, 2004, Curio a Shetland Sheepdog and Friends, 2005, Curio a Shetland Sheepdog and Her Pals, 2007; contbr. articles to jours. Mem. Pacific Palisades C. of C., 1990—2003. Mem.: Internat. Assn. Nanotech., Human Factors Soc. (sec. 2003), Lions Club Pacific Palisades (pres. 1990). Avocations: travel, tennis. Office: Compsych Systems Inc PO Box 1568 Pacific Palisades CA 90272 Office Phone: 310-454-6426. E-mail: res04wq4@gte.net.

GRIVNER, CARL J., telecommunications industry executive; BA, Lycoming Coll. Mgmt. positions IBM, Ameritech; pres., CEO Advanced Fibre Comm.; CEO we. hemisphere Cable & Wireless, 1998—99; chmn., CEO Worldport Comm., 1999—2000; exec. v.p. global ops. Global Crossing, 2000—02, COO, 2002—03; CEO XO Communications, Reston, Va., 2003—. Vice-chmn., bd. mem. CompTel. Served USMC, 1975—78. Office: XO Communications 11111 Sunset Hills Rd Reston VA 20190

GRIZZAFFI, KIMBERLY ANNE, secondary school music educator; b. Bronx, NY, Feb. 20, 1978; d. Peter and Loretta Grizzaffi. B, Ithaca Coll., 2000; M, SUNY, 2005. Educator 7th - 8th grade band Sayville Pub. Schs., NY, 2000—. Tchr. summer music program Island Trees, Levittown, NY, 1996—2002; dir. marching band Sayville Mid. Sch., 2000—, dir. jazz band, 2000—07; mem. Stony Brook Wind Ensemble, 2000—07, LI South Shore Jazz Ensemble, 2002—; tchr. Sayville Summer Music Program, 2006—; chair person SCMEA All-County Divsn. II, 2005—06. Dir. Flute Choir, Sayville, 2000—05, Clarinet Choir, 2000—05, Saxophone Quartet, 2000—05, Trumpet Trio, 2003—07, Summer Jazz Band, 2004, L.I. Theater Orch. Mem.: Sayville Tchrs. Assn., NY State Sch. Music Assn., NY State United Tchrs., Suffolk County Music Educators Assn., Music Educators Nat. Conf., Tri-M Music Honor Soc. (hon.). Avocation: bowling. Home: 31 Shepherd Ln Levittown NY 11756 Office: Sayville Mid Sch 291 Johnson Ave Sayville NY 11782 Office Phone: 631-244-6650. Business E-Mail: grizzaffik@sayville.k12.ny.us.

GRIZZARD, GEORGE, actor; b. Roanoke Rapids, NC, Apr. 1, 1928; s. George Cooper and Mary Winifred (Albritton) G. BA, U. N.C., 1949. Appeared at Arena Stage, Washington, 1950, 52-54; Broadway appearances include The Desperate Hours, 1955, The Happiest Millionaire, 1956-57, The Disenchanted, 1958-59 (nominee Tony award), Face of a Hero, 1960, Big Fish, Little Fish, 1961 (nominee Tony award), Mary, Mary, 1962, Who's Afraid of Virginia Woolf?, 1962, The Glass Menagerie, 1965, You Know I Can't Hear You When the Water's Running, 1967, Sweet Potato, 1968, The Gingham Dog, 1969, Inquest, 1970, The Country Girl, 1972, The Creation of the World and Other Business, 1972, Crown Matrimonial, 1973, The Royal Family, 1975, California Suite, 1976, Man and Superman, 1978, A Delicate Balance, 1996 (Best Leading Actor Tony award 1996), Judgement At Nuremberg, 2001, Seascape, 2005; also appeared with Assn. of Producing Artists, N.Y.C., 1961-62, Tyrone Guthrie Theatre, Mpls., 1963-65, Show Boat, Toronto, 1995, London, 1998, Regrets Only, Manhattan Theater Club, 2006; film appearances include From the Terrace, 1960, Advise and Consent, 1961, Warning Shot, 1967, Happy Birthday, Wanda June, 1971, Comes a Horseman, 1978, Firepower, 1979, Seems Like Old Times, 1980, Wrong is Right, 1981, Bachelor Party, 1983, The Wonder Boys, 2000, Small Time Crooks, 2000, Flags of Our Fathers, 2006; TV appearances include Twilight Zone, The Adams Chronicles (nominated Emmy award), 1976, The Oldest Living Graduate (recipient Emmy award 1980), Caroline?, 1988, Simple Justice, 1993, Breaking the Silence, 1993, Queen, 1993, Scarlett, 1994, Suspicion of Innocence, 1997. Named to Theater Hall of Fame. Mem. Kappa Alpha. Office: PO Box 2275 New Preston CT 06777-0275

GRIZZARD-BARHAM, BARBARA LEE, artist; b. Roanoke, Va., Apr. 4, 1935; d. Alton Lee and Mable (Jewell) Grizzard; m. Charles Thomas Barham, Sr., June 25, 1955; children: Charles Thomas, Christopher. BS in Edn., Va. Commonwealth U., 1971, postgrad. Educator Colonial Heights (Va.) Sch. Sys., 1971—88; represented by Agora Gallery, NYC, 1999—2001, 2002, Amsterdam Whitney Gallery, NYC, 2003—05. One-woman shows include Wakefield (Va.) Ctr. for Arts, 1992, 1993, 1994, Petersburg (Va.) Area Art League, 1993, 1995, 2000, Rappahannock Westminster-Canterberry Gallery, Va., 1995, Assn. for Visual Artists Gallery, Chattanooga, Tenn., 1999, Rappahanock Westminster Canterberry Gallery, Va., 1999, Williamsburg Regional Libr./Gallery/Theater Complex, 1999, exhibited in group shows at Richmond (Va.) Jewish Cmty. Ctr., 1991, 1993, Rappahannoc Art League Show, Va., 1995, Assoc. Artists Winston-Salem, N.C., 1991, 1992, 1996, Hoyt Inst. Fine Arts, Pa., 1998, Fredericksburg (Va.) Creative Ctr. Art, 1999, Richmond Shockoe Creative Ctr. Art, 1999, Richmond Women's Caucus for Art, 1999—2000, Shockoe Bottom (Va.) Art Ctr., 1999—2000, Agora Gallery, 1999, 2000, N.Y.C., 2001, 2002, Amsterdam Whitney Gallery, 2003, 2004, Limner Gallery, 2001. Recipient awards for art. Mem. Petersburg Area Art League, Va. Mus. Art, Whitney Mus. Art, Mus. Modern Art. Republican. Episcopal. Avocations: judging and breeding champion American Cocker Spaniels, piano, opera, classical music. Home: 701 Forestview Dr Colonial Heights VA 23834-1116

GRIZZLE, J. DAVID, air transportation executive; m. Anne Grizzle; 3 children. Grad., Harvard U., Cambridge, Mass., Harvard Law Sch. Sr. v.p. corp. devel. Continental Airlines, Inc., sr. v.p. customer experience. Transp. and infrastructure coord. US State Dept. Afghanistan Reconstruction Group. Office: Continental Airlines Inc PO Box 4607 Houston TX 77210 Office Phone: 713-324-5000. Office Fax: 713-324-2637.*

GROAT, CHARLES GEORGE, geologist, former federal agency administrator; b. Westfield, NY, Mar. 25, 1940; married, 1963; 2 children. AB, U. Rochester, 1962; MS, U. Mass., 1967; PhD in Geology, U. Tex., 1970. Rsch. geologist Bur. Econ. Geology, U. Tex., Austin, 1968-71, assoc. dir., 1971-75, assoc. prof. dept. geol. sci., 1971-76, acting dir. Bur. Econ. Geology, 1975-76; assoc. prof. geol. sci., chmn. U. Tex., El Paso, 1976-78;

dir. La. Geol. Survey, 1978-90; exec. dir. Am. Geol. Inst., 1990-92; dir. La. State U. Ctr. Coastal Energy & Environ. Rsch. Lab., Baton Rouge, 1992-95, U. Tex. Ctr. for Environ. Resource Mgmt., El Paso, 1995-98; assoc. v.p. rsch. U. Tex., El Paso, 1998; dir. U.S. Geol. Survey US Dept. Interior, Reston, Va., 1998—2005; dir. Ctr. for Internat. Energy & Environ. Policy U. Tex., Austin, 2005—, chair energy & mineral resources, Dept. Geological Sciences, 2005—. Mem. Geol. Soc. Am., Am. Assn. Petrol Geologists, Am. Geophys. Union, Am. Assn. for Higher Edn. Achievements include research in geology of energy resources, environmental aspects of resource extraction, geomorphology of coastal and arid areas, water resources, science education. Office: U Tex Austin Charles Groat Dept Geological Sciences 1 University Station C1100 Austin TX 78712

GROB, GEORGE FREDERICK, health science association administrator; M in Math., Georgetown U., 1969. Comptr. Office of Asst. Sec. Def.; ops. rsch. analyst Office of Asst. Sec. Navy for Fin. Mgmt.; dir. planning and policy coordination Office of Asst. Sec. Planning and Evaluation, USHHS, 1976-88; chair evaluation and inspection round table PCIE, Washington, 1994—2002; dep. insp. gen. for evaluation and inspections USHHS, Washington, 1988—2002, asst. insp. gen. for evaluation and inspections, 2004—05, dep. insp. gen. mgmt. and policy, 2002—05; exec. dir. Citizens Health Care Working Group, 2005—06; pres. Ctr. for Pub. Program Evaluation, 2006—. Mem. Am. Evaluation Assn. Home: 38386 Millstone Dr Purcellville VA 20132-3739 Office: USHHS 330 Independence Ave SW Washington DC 20301-0001 Office Phone: 540-454-2888. Personal E-mail: georgegrob@cs.com.

GROB, GERALD N., historian, educator; b. NYC, Apr. 25, 1931; s. Sidney and Sylvia G. Grob; m. Lila Kronick, Dec. 25, 1954; children: Bradford S., Evan D., Seth A. BS, CCNY, 1951; MA, Columbia U., 1952; PhD, Northwestern U., 1958; D.Litt. (hon.), Clark U., 2002. From instr. history to prof. Clark U., Worcester, Mass., 1957—69; Henry E. Sigerist prof. of the history of medicine Rutgers U., New Brunswick, NJ, 1969—, chmn. dept., 1969—71, 1973—74, 1981—84. Mem. fellowship adv. com. NEH, 1975—76; chmn. study sect. history of medicine NIH, 1975—77, 1987—89, 1993—98. Author: Ed Jarvis and the Medical World of 19th Century America, 1978, Workers and Utopia, 1961, The State and the Mentally Ill, 1966, Mental Institutions in America, 1973, Mental Ilness and American Society, 1875-1940, 1983, The Inner World of American Psychiatry, 1890-1940, 1985, From Asylum to Community, 1991, The Mad Among Us, 1994, The Deadly Truth: A History of Disease in America, 2002, The Dilemma of Federal Mental Health Policy, 2006; contbr. articles to profl. jours. Elected to inst. medicine NAS. With US Army, 1955—57. Fellow, NEH, 1972—73, 1989—90, Am. Coun. Learned Socs., 1976—77, Guggenheim fellow, 1980—81, Davis Ctr., Princeton U., 1985—86; grantee, NIH, 1960—65, 1967—81, 1984—92. Mem.: Orgn. Am. Historians, Am. Antiquarian Soc., Am. Assn. History of Medicine (coun. mem. 1978—81, v.p. 1994—96, pres. 1996—98, William H. Welch medal 1986, Lifetime Achievement award 2006). Jewish. Home: 821 Starview Way Bridgewater NJ 08807-1824 Office: Rutgers U Inst Health Care Policy 30 College Ave New Brunswick NJ 08901-1293 Home Phone: 908-772-7237; Office Phone: 732-932-8377. Business E-Mail: ggrob@rci.rutgers.edu. *My philosophy of history is essentially a tragic one; a study of the past, if undertaken in as honest and objective a manner as is humanly possible, should render us less certain about our omniscience and ability to control the future.*

GROBAN, MARK D., health care company executive; b. Cin., Nov. 10, 1941; MD, Albany Med. Coll., 1967. Cert. Psychiatry 1976. Joined Mid Atlantic Med. Svcs., Inc., 1990, pres. Alliance Preferred Provide Orgn. Rockville, Md., pres. MAPSI, med. dir. behavioral health and quality improvement, chmn., 1999—. Office: Mid Atlantic Med Svcs Inc 4 Taft Ct Rockville MD 20850

GROBE, CHARLES STEPHEN, lawyer, accountant; b. Columbus, Ohio, May 5, 1935; s. Harry A. and Bertha S. (Swartz) G.; m. Ila Silverman, Aug. 30, 1964; children— Eileen, Kenneth. BS, UCLA, 1957; JD, Stanford U., 1961. Bar: Calif. 1962; CPA, Calif. 1963. Tax acct., Beverly Hills, Calif., 1961—63; tax atty. LA, 1963—. Author: Guide to Investing Pension and Profit-Sharing Trust Funds, 1973, Guardianship, Conservatorship and Trusts on Behalf of Persons Who Are Mentally Retarded— An Assessment of Current Applicable Laws in the State of California, 1974, Using an Individual Retirement Savings Plan and the Related Rollover Provisions of the Pension Reform Act of 1974, 1975, Guide to Setting Up a Group Term Life Insurance Program Under IRC Section 79, 1976, Practical Estate Planning, 1988, Planning for Incapacity, 1989, Planning to Reduce the Generation Skipping Tax, 1989, Estate Planning Considerations for Community Property Interests, 1990, Legal and Tax Problems of Joint Tenancy as a Form of Ownership, 1990, The Tax Economics of Using the Generating Skipping Tax Exemptions, 1992, The Tax Economics of Gifting Property, 1992, Saving Estate Taxes with Life Insurance and a Life Insurance Trust, 1992, Family Wealth Transfer Planning, The Tax Economics of a Qualified Personal Residence Trust, also articles. Capt. US Army, 1957—64. Mem. ABA, State Bar Calif., L.A. County Bar Assn., Beverly Hills Bar Assn., Calif. Soc. CPAs. Office: 12110 Wilshire Blvd Los Angeles CA 90025-1104 Home: 172 S Woodburn Dr Los Angeles CA 90049-3041

GROBE, JIM, college football coach; b. Huntington, WV, Feb. 17, 1952; m. Holly Grobe; children: Matt, Ben. Assoc. sci., Ferrum Coll., 1972; BS in Edn., U. Va., 1975, M Ed in Guidance and Counseling, 1978. Asst. coach Emory & Henry Coll. Wasps, 1978, Marshall U. Thundering Herd, 1979—83, Air Force Acad. Falcons, 1985—94; head football coach Ohio U. Bobcats, 1995—2000, Wake Forest U. Demon Deacons, Winston Salem, NC, 2001—. Recipient Coach of Yr., AP, 2006. Office: Wake Forest U Dept Athletics 499 Deacon Blvd Winston Salem NC 27105*

GROBMAN, ARNOLD BRAMS, retired biology educator, academic administrator; b. Newark, Apr. 28, 1918; s. Samuel H. and Sophia (Brams) G.; m. Hulda Gross, Feb. 20, 1944; children: Marc Ross, Beth. BS, U. Mich., 1939; MS, U. Rochester, 1941, PhD, 1943. Instr. zoology U. Rochester, 1943—44, rsch. assoc. Manhattan project, 1944—46; from asst. prof. to assoc. prof. biology U. Fla., 1946—59; rsch. participant Oak Ridge Inst. Nuc. Studies, 1950, rsch. specialist, med. center study, 1951—52; dir. Fla. State Mus., 1952—59; dir. biol. scis. curriculum study U. Colo., 1959—65, dean Coll. Arts and Scis.; prof. zoology Rutgers U., New Brunswick, NJ, 1965—72, dean, 1966—72; vice chancellor for acad. affairs, prof. biol. scis. U. Ill., Chgo., 1973—74, spl. asst. to pres., 1974—75; chancellor U. Mo.-St. Louis, 1975—85, chancellor emeritus, 1985—, prof. biology, 1975—, rsch. prof., 1986—; adj. curator Fla. Mus. Natural History, 1982—. Vis. lectr. Utah State U., Ind. U./Purdue U., U. So. Ill., Nat. Taiwan Normal U., U. Campinas, Brazil, U. New Delhi, India, U. No. Sumatra, Indonesia, U. Sind, Pakistan, Chulalongkorn U., Bangkok, Thailand, U. Singapore, Sophia U., Japan, Internat. Christian U., Japan, Chiang Mia U., Thailand; cons. to govt., industry, founds. and ednl. instns., 1954—; Mem. divsn. biology and agr. NRC-NAS, 1954-58, com. adult edn., 1956-58; sec. U.S. nat. com. Internat. Union Biol. Scis., 1966-69; chmn. Ednl. Opportunity Ctr. Met. St. Louis, 1976-78; mem. adv. team sci. soc., Thailand, 1971; fgn. observer Treaty Plebiscite, Gov. Panama, 1977-78; mem. Commn. on Adult Learner Author: (with others) Island Life: A Study of the Land Vertebrates of Eastern Lake Michigan, 1948, Our Atomic Heritage, 1951, Genetics Effects of Chronic X-irradiation Exposure in Mice, 1960, BSCS Biology Implementation in the Schools, 1964, The Changing Classroom, 1969, Urban State Universities, 1988; editor: Social Implications of Biological Education, 1970; also articles to profl. jours., encys. and newspapers. Bd. dirs. St. Louis United Way, Laumeier Sculpture Park, Narcotics Svc. Coun., Regional Commerce and Growth Assn., St. Louis Higher Edn. Ctr., St. Louis Pub. Libr.; v.p. St. Louis Conf. Edn., 1980-82; adv. bd. Indian River County Pub. Libr., 1997-2003 Recipient Fred H. Stoye prize Am. Soc. Ichthyologists and Herpetologists, 1941, Cressy Morrison prize N.Y. Acad. Scis., 1943; Macalaster award Nat. Assn. Biology Tchrs., 1966, award of merit Urban League, 1984, Commanders Cross, Order of Merit, Germany, 1985 Mem. Acad. Zoology India (exec. com. 1967-69), Am. Assn. Higher Edn., AAAS (coun. 1961-65), Am. Assn. Museums (mus. tng. com. 1960-63), Am. Assn. State Colls. and Univs. (urban affairs com. 1977-85), Am. Ednl. Rsch. Assn., Am. Inst. Biol. Scis. (exec. com. 1958-61, Disting. Svc. award 1984), Am. Soc. Ichthyologists and Herpetologists (bd. govs. 1952— , pres. 1964), Am. Soc. Naturalists, Am. Soc. Zoologists, Assn. Am. Med. Colls., Assn. Southeastern Biologists, ASCD, Assn. Tropical Biology, Asian Assn. Biol. Edn., Biol. Scis. Curriculum Study (chmn. steering com. 1965-69), Biol. Soc. China, Biol. Soc. Washington, Coun. Fgn. Rels., NEA, Edn. Programs Improvement Corp. (trustee 1970-74), Colo.-Wyo. Acad. Sci., AAUP, Explorers Club, Fla. Acad. Sci., Fla. Found. Future Scientists (chmn. 1957-59), Herpetologists League, Mo. Coun. Pub. Higher Edn. (exec. com. 1977-82, v.p. 1978, pres. 1979), Mo. Bot. Garden, Nat. Coun. Accreditation Tchr. Edn. (chmn. 1970-71), Genetics Soc., Herpetologists League, Philippine Assn. Sci. Tchrs., Nat. Assn. Biology Tchrs. (pres. 1966, editl. bd. 1974-77, dir. 1978-80), Nat. Assn. Rsch. Sci. Tchg., Nat. Assn. State Univs. and Land Grant Colls. (exec. com. 1979-80, coun. acad. affairs 1974-76, chmn. divsn. urban affairs 1978-79), NSTA, Nature Conservancy, Newcomen Soc., N.J. Acad. Scis., Orgn. Tropical Studies, Sci. Soc. Thailand, Soc. Study Amphibians and Reptiles, Soc. Study Evolution, Soc. Systematic Zoology, Soc. Vertebrate Paleontology, Southeastern Museums Conf. (pres. 1955-57), Phi Beta Kappa, Sigma Xi, Phi Kappa Phi, Phi Sigma, Alpha Sigma Lambda, Alpha Epsilon Delta. Home: Oak Hammock 5000 SW 25th Blvd Apt 1115 Gainesville FL 32608 Personal E-mail: agrobman@aol.com.

GROBSCHMIDT, RICHARD A., school system administrator; b. Milw., May 3, 1948; married; 1 child. BS, U. Wis., Oshkosh, 1972; MS, U. Wis., Milw., 1980. Polit. sci. tchr. South Milwaukee H.S., 1972-85; mem. from dist. 21 Wis. State Assembly, Madison, 1984-95; mem. from dist. 7 Wis. Senate, Madison, 1995—2003, chmn. edn. com.; asst. state supt. divsn. for librs., tech. and cmty. learning Dept. Pub. Instrn., State of Wis., Madison, 2003—. Home: 912 Lake Dr South Milwaukee WI 53172-1736 Office: 125 S Webster St PO Box 7841 Madison WI 53707 E-mail: richard.grobschmidt@dpi.state.wi.us.

GROCE, JAMES FREELAN, financial adviser; b. Lubbock, Tex., Nov. 24, 1948; s. Wayne Dee and Betty Jo (Rice) G.; m. Patricia Kay Rogers; 1 child, Jason Eric. BS cum laude, Tex. Tech U., 1971; MS in Personal Fin. Planning, Coll. for Fin. Planning, 2005. Registered profl. engr., Tex. Petroleum engr. Texaco, Inc., Sweetwater, Tex., 1971-74, drilling and prodn. engr. Wichita Falls, Tex., 1974-77, asst. dist. engr. Midland, Tex., 1977-78; sr. prodn. engr. Bass Enterprises Prodn., Midland, 1978-81; petroleum engr. Murphy H. Baxter Co., Midland, 1981-82, Henry Engring., Midland, 1982-87, Fasken Oil and Ranch Interests, Midland, 1987, mgr. engring./ops., 1987-95; 2d v.p. investments, fin. planning specialist Smith Barney, Midland, 1996—. Scoutmaster Boy Scouts Am., Midland, 1980-83, merit badge counselor, 1987; mem. Community Bible Study, Midland, 1987-93. Mem. Soc. Petroleum Engr. (local sect. chmn. 1987, 25 Yr. Mem.), Soc. Petroleum Evaluation Engr. (local sect. chmn. 1996), Fin. Planning Assn., Mensa, Tex. Tech. Ex-Student Assn., Century Club, Tau Beta Pi, Rotary Club of Midland. Presbyterian. Avocations: individual investments, real estate, gardening. Home: 2117 Bradford Ct Midland TX 79705-1726 Office Phone: 432-620-6066. Business E-Mail: james.f.groce@smithbarney.com.

GRODE, SUSAN A., lawyer; BFA, Cornell U., 1964; JD, U. So. Calif., 1977. Bar: Calif. 1977. V.p. Harry N. Abrams, Inc.; ptnr. Kaye, Scholer, Fierman, Hays & Handler, LLP; ptnr., co-chair Entertainment and Media Dept. Katten Muchin Zavis Rosenman, LA. Author: Visual Artist Manual, 1985. Mem.: ABA, Calif. Women's Law Ctr., State Bar Calif., LA County Bar Assn., Beverly Hills Bar Assn., Alpha Alpha Gamma, Phi Kappa Phi. Office: Katten Muchin Zavis Rosenman Ste 2600 2029 Century Park E Los Angeles CA 90067 Office Phone: 310-788-4410. Office Fax: 310-712-8422. E-mail: susan.grode@kmzr.com.

GRODSKY, GEROLD MORTON, biochemistry professor; b. St. Louis, Jan. 18, 1927; s. Louis and Goldie B.; m. Kayla Deane Wolfe, Dec. 6, 1952; children: Andrea, Jamie. BS, U. Ill., 1946, MS, 1947; PhD, U. Calif., Berkeley, 1954; postgrad., Cambridge U., Eng., 1954-55. Prof. biochemistry U. Calif., San Francisco, 1961-92, prof. emeritus (active status), 1992—, cons. to Diabetes Ctr., 1999—. Vis. prof. U. Geneva, 1968—69, U. Paris VII, 1989; Somogyi Meml. lectr., 72; Helen Martin lectr., 76; Herman Rosenthal lectr., 86; cons. in field. Mem. editl. bd. Diabetes, 1965-73, 86-90, Am. Jour. Physiology, 1977-94, Diabetologia, 1990-92, Endocrinology, 1992-96; founding adv. editor: Diabetes Tech. and Therapy, 1998—2006; founding assoc. editor Diabetes Sci. and Tech., 2006—; contbr. chpts. to books; contbr. over 200 articles on diabetes and storage, secretion of insulin to profl. jours. Med. adv. bd. Juvenile Diabetes Found., 1974-77, 80-85; program dir. NIH Diabetic Animal Program, 1978-82, chmn. diabetes rsch. adv. bd. to Sec. Health, 1982-87. Lt. (s.g.) USNR, 1944-54. Recipient David Rumbough Internat. award Juvenile Diabetes Found., 1984, Williams-Levine award, 1990, Merit award NIH, 1987, Juvenile Diabetes Found. annual endowed Grodsky award, 1994—, Western Region Islet Study Group annual Gerold M. Grodsky Disting. Scientist award, 2004—; named Grodsky Lectr. Diabetes Ctr. in his honor U. Calif., San Francisco, 2001; named one of 1000 most cited world scientists. Mem.: Am. Diabetes Assn. (rsch. bd. 1974—77, chmn. rsch. policy com. 1977, bd. dirs. Calif. chpt. 1989—91, nat. grant rev. com. 1992—96), Endocrine Soc., European Diabetes Assn., Am. Fedn. Clin. Rsch., Soc. Exptl. Biology, Am. Soc. Biol. Chemists, Internat. Diabetes Found., Meadowood Club, Harborpoint Club, Calif. Tennis Club. Home: 3969 Washington St San Francisco CA 94118-1613 Office: U Calif Sch Medicine Diabetes Ctr PO Box 0540 San Francisco CA 94143-0001 E-mail: grodoskygm@aol.com.

GRODSKY, JAMIE ANNE, law educator; b. San Francisco; d. Gerold Morton and Kayla Deane (Wolfe) G. BA in Human Biology/Natural Scis. and History with distinction, Stanford U., 1977; MA, U. Calif., Berkeley, 1986; JD, Stanford Law Sch., 1992. Ednl. dir. Oceanic Soc., San Francisco, 1979-81; rsch. asst. Woods Hole (Mass.) Oceanographic Inst., 1983; analyst Office Tech. Assessment U.S. Congress, Washington, 1984-89; counsel Com. Natural Resources, U.S. Ho. of Reps., Washington, 1993—95; counsel to Com. on Judiciary U.S. Senate, Washington, 1995-97; jud. clk. with chief judge U.S. Ct. Appeals (9th cir.), 1997-98; sr. advisor to the gen. counsel U.S. EPA, Washington, 1999—2001; assoc. prof. law U. Minn. Law Sch., Mpls., 2001—05; assoc. prof. Law Sch. George Washington U., Washington, 2005—. Articles editor Stanford Law Rev.; contbr. articles to profl. jours. Trustee Desert Rsch. Inst. Found. Mem.: D.C. Bar Assn., Calif. Bar Assn., Supreme Ct. Bar Assn.

GRODY, DEBORAH, psychologist, director; b. Munich, Mar. 10, 1949; d. Sol and Jenny Chinitz; m. Allan David Grody, June 6, 1970; 1 child, Michael Brandon. BS in Psychology, Queens Coll., 1970, MS and Advanced Cert. in Sch. Psychology, 1972; PhD, Hofstra U., 1982. Lic. psychologist N.Y., cert. sch. psychologist N.Y. Clin. dir., founder Personal Resources, Inc., Employee Assistance Programs, NYC, 1986—; clin. psychologist in pvt. practice NYC, 1983—. Mem.: APA, Am. Psychological Assn., N.Y. State Psychol. Assn. Avocations: gardening, bicycling, writing. Home: 169 E 69th St New York NY 10021 Office: 11 E 68th St New York NY 10021 Office Phone: 212-288-1980. E-mail: grodyd@optonline.net.

GRODY, DONALD, actor, judge, lawyer; b. NYC, Dec. 18, 1927; s. Charles E. and Jeannette (Kessler) G.; m. Judith Anderson Weston, Oct. 21, 1989; children by previous marriage: Dion, Gordon, James, Jeremy. Student, Royal Acad. Dramatic Art, 1949-50; BA cum laude, Hunter Coll., 1951; LLB, N.Y. Law Sch., 1959. Bar: N.Y. State bar 1959. Profl. actor, singer, 1950-58; atty. U.S. Dept. Labor, Washington, 1959-60; labor union atty. NYC, 1960-65; atty.-advisor NLRB, Washington, 1965-67; asst. gen. counsel Retail Clks. Internat. Assn., Washington, 1967-69; gen. counsel dist. 65 Distributive Workers, UAW, NYC, 1970-73; exec. sec. Actors Equity Assn., NYC, 1973-80; asst. exec. dir. NFL Players Assn., Washington, 1980-81, arbitrator, mediator, 1984-93; sole practice law NYC, 1981-89; supervising adminstrv. law judge N.Y.C. Parking Violations Bur., 1989-93. Mem. theatre adv. panel Nat. Endowment for the Arts; mem. exec. bd., dept. profl. employees AFL-CIO; chmn. Equity-League Pension and Welfare Trust Funds, 1973-80 Appeared: (pre-Broadway tour) Yiddle with a Fiddle, 1994-95, Little Shop of Horrors, Tenn. Repertory Theatre, 1995, Sweeney Todd, Pitts. Pub. Playhouse, 1995-96, Let's Do It, Long Wharf Theatre, 1996, Jekyll & Hyde, Broadway, N.Y.C., 1997-98, Gypsy, Paper Mill Playhouse, 1998, Golf With Alan Shepard, Buffalo Studio Arena Theatre, 1998, Guys and Dolls, Dallas Theater Ctr., 2000, Parade (nat. tour), 2000, (returned to theatre) Nat. Co. Guys & Dolls, 1993-94 (nat. tour 2000), (TV show) Law & Order, 1999, 2002, Law & Order: Criminal Intent, 2003, (world premiere) Tooth and Claw, Arden Theatre, Phila., 2004, Caroline or Change, Broadway, NYC, 2004, She Stoops to Conquer, 2005, Irish Repertory Theatre, NYC, Copenhagen, Vt. Stage Co., 2006. Served with AUS, 1945-47. Mem. AFTRA, SAG, Actors Equity Assn., Dramatists Guild. Office Phone: 212-580-3235. Personal E-mail: dongro@verizon.net.

GRODY, WAYNE WILLIAM, physician, educator; b. Syracuse, NY, Feb. 25, 1952; s. Robert Jerome and Florence Beatrice (Kashdan) G.; m. Gaylen Ducker, July 8, 1990. BA, Johns Hopkins U., 1974; MD, Baylor Coll. Medicine, 1977, PhD, 1981. Diplomate Am. Bd. Pathology, Am. Bd. Med. Genetics; lic. physician, Calif. Intern, resident UCLA Sch. Medicine, 1982-85, postdoctoral fellow, 1985-86, asst. prof., 1987-93, dir. DNA Diagnostic Lab., 1987—, assoc. prof., 1993-97, prof. depts. pathology and lab. medicine, pediat., human genetics, 1997—. Panelist Calif. Children's Svcs., 1987—, U.S. FDA, Washington, 1989—; DNA tech. com. Pacific Southwest Regional Genetics Network, Berkeley, Calif.; mem. task force genetic testing, NIH, 1987—; med., tech. cons., writer Warner Bros., NBC, Tri-Star, CBS, Twentieth Century Fox, Universal, others, 1987—; chair, molecular genetics com. Coll. Am. Pathologists, Am. Coll. Med. Genetics, Assn. Molecular Pathology; chmn. genomic medicine adv. com. VA and others. Contbg. editor, film critic: MD Mag., 1981-91; assoc. editor Diagnostic Molecular Pathology, 1993—; contbr. articles to profl. jours., chpts. to books. Recipient best paper award L.A. Soc. Pathology, 1984, Joseph Kleiner Meml. award Am. Soc. Med. Technologists, 1990; Basil O'Connor scholar March of Dimes Birth Defects Found., 1989, Nakamura Lecturship Scripps Clinic, 1996, Moss Lectureship LSU, 1998, Stop Cancer Fdn. Rsch. award, 1998, Hill Lectureship Baylor Coll. Medicine, 2003; named One of Am.'s Top Doctors, 2001—. Mem. AAAS, AMA, Am. Soc. Clin. Pathology, Am. Soc. Human Genetics, Am. Coll. Med. Geneticist (bd. dirs. 2001-), Soc. Inherited Metabolic Disorders, Soc. Pediat. Rsch. Democrat. Jewish. Achievements include application of molecular biology to clinical diagnosis and genetic screening, molecular genetics research and AIDS and cancer research. Office: UCLA Sch Medicine Divsns Med Genetics and Molecular Pathology Los Angeles CA 90095-1732 Home Phone: 310-573-0268; Office Phone: 310-825-5648. Business E-Mail: wgrody@mednet.ucla.edu.

GROEDEL, CARYN G., lawyer; d. Stanley and Elaine Markowitz; m. Howard Groedel, Oct. 12, 1985; children: Hannah, Isabel, Mia. BA, George Washington U., 1979; JD, George Mason U., Arlington, Va., 1985. Bar: Ohio, Md., Pa., DC. Law clk., assoc. Levy, Bivona & Cohen, Washington, 1984—87; assoc. Brault, Graham, Scott & Brault, Rockville, Md., 1987—88, Max & London, Silver Spring, Md., 1988—92; exec. dir. Woman's Law Fund, Inc., Cleve., 1993—95; in-house counsel First Interstate Devel. Co., Cleve., 1993—96; pvt. practice Cleve., 1995—. Vol. atty. A Woman's Pl. Montgomery County, Md., 1988—91; co-chair Access to Legal Svcs. Com. Montgomery County, 1990—92; mem. jud. selections com. Montgomery County Women's Bar Assn., 1990—92; mem. State Md. Coalition for Family Equity in Cts., 1991—92; co-founder Ctr. for Divorcing Families, Montgomery County, 1992; mem. Commn. on Women in the Law Cuyahoga County Bar Assn., 1992—96; mem. Greater Cleve. Cmty. Shares, 1992—95, WomenSpace Roundtable Coalition, 1993—95; presenter in field. Named one of Cleves. Most Interesting People, Cleve. Mag., 2006, Ohio's Top Attys. in Ohio, Ohio Super Lawyer Mag., 2006, 2007. Mem.: Ohio Employment Lawyers Assn., Cleve. Employment Lawyers Assn., Nat. Employment Lawyers Assn., Ohio Acad. Trial Lawyers, Cleve. Employment Lawyers Inn of Ct., Delta Theta Phi. Avocations: tennis, painting, jogging, music. Home: 31000 Woodall Rd Solon OH 44139 Office: Caryn Groedel & Assocs Co LPA 5910 Landerbrook Dr #200 Cleveland OH 44124

GROEN, JEFFREY ALLAN, economist; b. Edina, Minn., July 4, 1973; s. Douglas Dean and Barbara Jean Groen; m. Melissa Lynn Lieske, July 3, 1999; children: Katherine Abigail, Alexander Lawrence. BS in Econ., U. Wis., Madison, 1995; MS in Econ., U. Mich., Ann Arbor, 1999, PhD in Econ., 2002. Fellow Cornell U., Ithaca, NY, 2002—04; rsch. economist Bur. Labor Stats., Washington, 2004—. Contbr. articles to profl. jours. Sch. bd. St. Luke Christian Day Sch., Silver Spring, Md., 2006—07. Recipient John E. Parker Meml. prize in Labor Economics and Human Resources, U. Mich., Dept. Econ., 2002; fellow Regents fellow, U. Mich., 1997—99, U. Mich., Population Studies Ctr., 2001—02. Mem.: Phi Beta Kappa. Office: Bur Labor Stats 2 Massachusetts Ave NE Washington DC 20212 Office Phone: 202-691-7392.

GROENHEIM, HENRI ARNOLD, psychologist, consultant; b. Bklyn., Oct. 18, 1927; s. Herman and Suzanna May (Bierman) G.; m. Gail Thacker, June 29, 1957; children: Lisa Gail, Gary Thomas. BA in Psychology, Pa. State U., 1950; MA in Counseling, George Washington U., 1954; PhD in Counselor Edn., Fla. State U., 1968. Lic. psychologist, Md. Sch. counselor Brookville (Pa.) Jr.-Sr. H.S., 1950-51; dean of boys Derry Twp. Jr.-Sr. H.S., Hershey, Pa., 1951-52; sch. counselor Frederick (Md.) H.S., 1952-54; counselor Nurnberg Am. H.S., Germany, 1954-55; sch. counselor Kenwood Sr. H.S., Balt., 1955-61; coll. counselor U. Minn., 1956; sch. counselor, guidance dept. chair Overlea Sr. H.S., Balt., 1961-66; admissions counselor U. Del., 1966; coll. counselor Catonsville C.C., Balt., 1968-69; assoc. prof. Johns Hopkins U., Balt., 1970-74; prof. psychology Towson U., Balt., 1969-94, prof. emeritus, 1994—. Cons. psychol. testing Disability Determination Svcs., Balt., 1973—, Kennedy Inst., Balt., 1985—86, Balt. City Pub. Schs., 1990—98; sr. counseling profl. mentor dept. counseling George Washington U., 1996—. Contbr. articles to profl. jours.; moderator TV program, 1987. Participant UN Relief and Rehab. Project, Italy, 1946; com. mem. State Dem. Election Com., Balt., 1994; bd. dirs. Cmty. Counseling and Resource Ctr., Cockeysville, Md., 1985—90. Recipient Sparks medal for outstanding scholarship Pa. State U., 1948. Fellow Md. Psychol. Assn. (ins. com.); mem. APA, Balt. Psychol. Assn., Johns Hopkins Club. Avocations: swimming, travel, golf.

GROENING, MATTHEW (ABRAM), writer, cartoonist; b. Portland, Oreg., Feb. 15, 1954; s. Homer Philip and Margaret Ruth (Wiggum) Groening; m. Deborah Lee Caplan (div.); children: Homer, Abe. BA, Evergreen State Coll., 1977. Cartoonist Life in Hell weekly comic strip (syndicated by Acme Features Syndicate), Sheridan, Oreg., 1977—; creator, writer, cartoonist Simpson Shorts, The Tracey Ullman Show, 1987—; creator Akbar and Jeff; pres. Matt Groening Prodns., Inc., LA, 1988—; writer, story, prodr., exec. prodr., creator, developer The Simpsons, 1989—; writer, creator, exec. prodr., developer Futurama, 1999—; founder, pub. Bongo Comic Group, 1993—, Bongo Comics, 1995; exec. prodr. Olive, The Other Reindeer, 1999; writer, exec. prodr. Boo Boo Runs Wild. Author: Work is Hell, Love is Hell, School is Hell, The Big Book of Hell, The Huge Book of Hell, Love is Hell, Akbar & Jeff's Guide to Life, Binky's Guide to Love, The Simpsons: A Complete Guide to Our Favorite Family, The Simpsons Xmas Book, The Simpsons Rainy Day Fun Book, Making Faces With The Simpsons, Bart Simpson's Guide To Life, The Simpsons' Uncensored Family Album, Cartooning With The Simpsons, Simpsons Illustrated mag., Simpsons Comics Simps-O-Rama, Simpson Comics & Stories comic book, Simpsons Comics Extravaganza, Simpsons Comics Spectacular, Bartman: The Best of The Best; creater, developer, exec. prodr. The Simpsons Christmas Special, 1989, writer The Simpsons: Family Therapy, 1989, creater Bart vs the Space Mutants, 1991, original character designer The Simpsons Wrestling, 2001, creative consultant The Simpsons: Hit & Run, 2003, exec. prodr. The Simpsons: Bart's Nightmare, 1993, Bart Wars, the Simpsons Strike Back, 1999, writer, prodr. (films) The Simpsons Movie, 2007, voice of Arturo Olive, the Other Reindeer, 1999, voice of Dill Hair High, 2004, guest appearances The Tracey Ullman Show, 1988, Space Ghost Coast to Coast, 1996, The Big Breakfast, 2000, Great Performances, 2000, (voice) The Simpsons, 2004. Named New Pub. Yr., Diamond Distbn. Gem awards, 1993; recipient The Simpsons, Emmy award for Outstanding Animated Program, 1990, 1991, 1995, 1997, 1998, 2000, 2001, 2003, Futurama, Emmy Award for Outstanding Animated Program, 2002. Achievements include The expression "d'oh!" from The Simpsons was added to the Oxford English Dictionary in 2001. Office: The Simpsons c/o Twentieth Television Matt Groening's Office PO Box 900 Beverly Hills CA 90213 Address: Bongo Comics Group 1999 Avenue of Stars 15th Fl Los Angeles CA 90067 Office Phone: 310-788-1367. Office Fax: 310-788-1200.*

GROETKEN, TROY ALAN, lawyer, pharmacist; b. Sioux City, Iowa, July 26, 1970; s. Alan Leo and Sondra Colleen Groetken; m. Sheryl Lynn Rensink, Apr. 23, 2005; 1 child, Olivia Erin. BS in Pharmacy, Drake U., 1994, JD, 1997; LLM in Intellectual Property Law, John Marshall Law Sch., 1998. Bar: Iowa 1997, Ill. 2000, registered: (patent atty.); pharmacist Iowa, Ill., Mich. Clin. pharmacist Mercy Hosp., Des Moines, 1994—97, St. Francis Hosp., Evanston, Ill., 1997—99; assoc. Price, Henveld, Cooper, Dewitt & Litton, Grand Rapids, 1998—2000; bd. dirs. McAndrews, Held & Malloy, Ltd., Chgo., 2000—. Mem. steering com. Drake U., Des Moines, 2001—; spkr. ann. meeting Am. Pharm. Assn., 2006. Pub., editor: mag. Patent Lawyer Mag., 2004—. Mem.: Iowa Bar Assn., Ill. State Bar Assn., Am. Intellectual Property Law Assn., Assn. Patent Law Firms (treas. 2002—04, pres. 2004—06, Presenter award 2005, 2006), Masons (Master Mason), Scottish Rite, Shriners. Republican. Methodist. Avocations: basketball, antique furniture, investments. Office Phone: 312-775-8259. Business E-Mail: tgroetken@mhmlaw.com.

GROETZINGER, JON, JR., lawyer, pharmaceutical executive, educator; b. NYC, Feb. 12, 1949; s. Jon M. and Elinor Groetzinger; m. Carol Marie O'Connor, Jan. 24, 1981; 3 children. AB magna cum laude, Middlebury Coll., 1971; JD in Internat. Legal Affairs, Cornell U., 1974. Bar: N.H. 1974, N.Y. 1980, Mass. 1980, Fla. 1982, Md. 1985, Ohio 1991, U.S. Supreme Ct. 1980. Assoc. McLane, Graf, Greene, Raulerson and Middleton, P.A., Manchester, NH, 1974-76; pvt. practice NH, Boston, 1977-81; chief internat. counsel Martin Marietta Corp., Bethesda, Md., 1981-88; pres., exec. v.p. Martin Marietta Overseas Corp., Bethesda, 1984-88; sr. v.p., gen. counsel, corp. sec. Am. Greetings Corp., Cleve., 1988—2003; CEO, pres. LifePill, Cleve., 2004—; vis. prof. law Case Western Reserve Sch. Law, Cleve., 2007—. Atty. John A. Gray Law Offices, Boston, 1978-81; chmn. internat. adv. bd. Case Western Res. U. Law Sch., 1995-; bd. mem. Can.-US Law Inst., 1995-. Contbr. articles to profl. pubs. Trustee Middlebury (Vt.) Coll., 1974—76, bd. overseers, 1977—; bd. dirs. Cleve. Coun. on World Affairs, 1992—98, 2000—, vice chmn., 2002—06, chmn. strategic planning com., 2000—02, exec. com., 2000—05, trustee, 1992—96, 1998—2005; bd. dirs. Can.-U.S. Law Inst., 1990—, The Conf. Bds. Coun. Chief Legal Officers, 1996—2003, membership chmn., 1997—98, program chair, 1999—2000, coun. chmn., 2000—02; chmn., pres. Greater Cleve. Gen. Counsel Assn., 2001—04; bd. dirs. Lake Erie Coll., 2002—, vice chmn., 2005—06, chmn. bd., 2006—07. Mem. ABA, N.H. Bar Assn., Fla. Bar Assn., Ohio Bar Assn., Cleve. Bar Assn., Md. Bar Assn., Am. Soc. Corp. Secs. (sec. Ohio chpt. 1995—, v.p. 1996-97, pres. 1997-98, adv. com. 1998-2006), Soc. of Benchers, Phi Beta Kappa. Office: LifePill 37455 Miles Rd Moreland Hills OH 44022 Home Phone: 440-247-8287. Personal E-mail: jgroetzi@yahoo.com.

GROFF, ARTHUR M., controller; b. Easton, Pa., June 24, 1964; s. Arthur M. and Margaret A. (King) Groff; m. Cynthia L. Hutton, Oct. 25, 1997; children: Jacob, Joseph, Ashley, Matthew. BA Bus. Adminstrn., Vt. Coll., 2000; MBA, Norwich U., 2003. Mgr. nat. sales Filtration Engring., Portland, Pa., 1995—2000; contr. Omega Tools Inc., Mt. Bethel, Pa., 2000—04, gen. mgr. fin. and adminstrn., 2004—. Mem. com. Northampton County Rep. Party, Easton, 1988—92. Mem.: Soc. Human Resource Mgmt., Inst. Mgmt. Accts. Roman Catholic. Avocations: fly fishing, travel. Office: Omega Tools Inc 4136 Church St PO Box 217 Portland PA 18351 Home: 512 Stonybrook Rd Nazareth PA 18064 Home Phone: 610-614-0780; Office Phone: 484-245-0552. Personal E-mail: art@groff-family.com. Business E-Mail: groffmba@rcn.com.

GROGAN, DAVID R., work saver company executive; m. Susie Grogan; 2 children. Founder Toter, Inc., 1983—, pres., chmn., CEO Statesville, NC. Office: Toter Inc 841 Meacham Rd Statesville NC 28677-2983

GROGAN, JOHN, writer; b. Detroit, Mich., Mar. 20, 1957; m. Jenny Grogan. BA, Ctrl. Mich. Univ.; MA in Jour., OSU, 1987. Police reporter St. Joseph Herald-Palladium, Mich., 1979; reporter So. Fla. Sentinel; features writer Palm Beach Post; former editor-in-chief Organic Gardening Mag. Author: (novels) Marley & Me: Life and Love with the World's Worst Dog, 2006 (NY Times Best-Seller, Quills award biography/memoir, best Audio Book, The Quills Literacy Found., 2006). Grantee Klippinger Mid-Careers Fell., OSU, 1985, Poynter Inst. Media Studies. Office: c/o Harper Collins 105 E 53rd St New York NY 10022*

GROGAN, VIRGINIA S., lawyer; b. Pasadena, Calif., Nov. 19, 1951; d. Bruce Mason and Helen Maude Gorsuch; m. Aug. 17, 1973 (div. June 1975); m. Allen R. Grogan, Jan. 10, 1982; children: Travis, Tess. BS, Occidental Coll., Eagle Rock, Calif., 1973; JD, U. So. Calif. Bar: Calif. 1979. Assoc. Latham & Watkins, LA, 1979-86, ptnr., 1987-97, chmn. assocs. com., 1995-97, mng. ptnr. Orange County Office Costa Mesa, Calif., 1997—. Mem. exec. roundtable U. Calif., Irvine, 1998—; mem. adv. com. Orange County Performing Arts, Costa Mesa, 1998—, Mem. ABA, Los Angeles County Bar Assn., Orange County Bar Assn. (judiciary com. 1998—), Legion Lex. Avocations: tennis, classical music. Office: Latham & Watkins 650 Town Center Dr Costa Mesa CA 92626-1989

GROGG, JILL ELAINE, library and information scientist; b. 1972; BA in English, minor in Polit. Sci., U. Tenn., 1990—94; MA in English, U. Miss., 1995—98; MS in Info. Sci., U. Tenn., 1999—2001. Proofreader Hazlett, Lewis & Bieter, Chattanooga, 1991—94; young adult mgr. McKay's Used Books, Chattanooga, 1994—95; staff reporter The Enterprise-Tocsin, Indianola, Miss., 1997; rsch. asst. Dept. English U. Miss., 1995—97, grad. instr. Dept. English, 1996—97, 1998; cmty. desk editor The Times Record, Brunswick, Maine, 1998—99; adj. instr. English Pellissippi State Cmty. Coll., Knoxville, Tenn., 1999; grad. tchg. and rsch. asst. Sch. Info. Sci. U. Tenn., 1999—2001, grad. asst. Innovative Tech. Ctr. Office of Rsch. and Tech., 2000—01; asst. prof., instruction services libr. Mitchell Meml. Libr. Miss. State U., 2001—03, asst. prof., serials libr., 2003—04; freelance writer, 2001—04; instr. reference libr., Gorgas Libr. Info. Services U. Ala. Libraries, 2004—05, asst. prof., electronic resources librarian, 2005—; adj. instr. Sch. Libr. and Info. Sci. U. Ala., 2005—. Co-editor The Jefferson City Broadside Soc. U. Ala., 1995—97; bus. mgr. The Yalobusha Rev., U. Miss., 1996, editor, 97; asst. editor Footnotes New Members Roundtable, ALA, 2002—03, editor, 2003—04; editor Instruction Sect. IS Newsletter, Assn. Coll. & Rsch. Libraries; editor Ala. Assn. coll. & Rsch. Libraries Newsletter, 2005—07. Named one of the Movers & Shakers, Libr. Jour., 2007; recipient Gary R. Purcell award of merit, Sch. Info. Sci., U. Tenn., 2001, Chancellor's Citation for Extraordinary Profl. Promis, U. Tenn., 2001. Mem.: Tenn. Libr. Assn., Southeastern Libr. Assn., North Am. Serials Interest Group, Ala. Assn. Coll. & Rsch. Libraries, Ala. Libr. Assn., Assn. Coll. & Rsch. Libraries, ALA, Sigma Tau Delta, Phi Kappa Phi. Office: School Library & Info Sciences 513 Main Library Box 870252 Tuscaloosa AL 35487-0252 E-mail: jill@wedogg.com.

GROH, JENNIFER CALFA, law librarian; b. Patchogue, NY, Mar. 28, 1970; d. Anthony Bernard and Mary (Fogerty) C.; m. William Matthew Groh, May 10, 1997; 1 child, Andrew. BA in Social Sci., St. Joseph's Coll., 1992; MA in Internat. Edn., NYU, 1993; MSLS, Pratt Inst., Bklyn., 1996. Reference page Patchogue-Medford Libr., NY, 1986-93; from libr. asst. to libr. mgr. Morgan & Finnegan, NYC, 1994—. NYU grad. scholar, 1992, Law Libr. Assn. scholar, NY 1995, Am. Assn. Law Librs. scholar, 1996. Mem. ALA, Spl. Librs. Assn., Law Libr. Assn. Greater NY Home: 21 Mohawk Dr North Babylon NY 11703-3303 Office: Morgan & Finnegan 3 World Fin Ctr New York NY 10281-2101 Office Phone: 212-303-2672. Business E-Mail: jgroh@morganfinnegan.com.

GROH, SEBASTIEN STEPHANE, materials scientist, researcher; s. Bernard Francis Groh and Brigitte Mehn. PhD, U. Paris XI, Orsay, France, 2003. Rsch. assoc. Brown U., Providence, 2003—06, CAVS, Mississippi State, Miss., 2006—. Home Phone: 401-419-1947; Office Phone: 401-419-1947. Business E-Mail: groh@cavs.msstate.edu.

GROHL, DAVID ERIC, musician; b. Warren, OH, Jan. 14, 1969; s. James and Virginia Grohl; m. Jennifer Youngblood, 1993 (div. 1997); m. Jordyn Blum, Aug. 2, 2003; 1 child, Violet. Drummer Scream, Nirvana, 1990—94; founder Foo Fighters, 1995, lead vocals, guitar, songwriter, 1995—. With Nirvana (albums) Nevermind, 1991, In Utero, 1993, (songs) Scentless Apprentice (co-writer), 1993; musician: (film soundtrack) Backbeat, 1994; with Foo Fighters (albums) Foo Fighters, 1995, The Colour & the Shape, 1997, There is Nothing Left to Lose, 1999 (Grammy Award, Best Rock Album, 2001), One by One, 2002 (Grammy Award, Best Rock Album, 2004), In Your Honor, 2005, (songs) Big Me, 1996 (MTV Music Video Award for Best Group Video, 1996), Learn to Fly, 1999 (Grammy Award, Best Music Video, Short Form, 2001, named one of VH1: 100 Greatest Videos, 2001), All My Life, 2002 (Grammy Award, Best Hard Rock Performance, 2003); actor: (films) Tenacious D: The Pick of Destiny, 2006. Achievements include Foo Fighters named one of 100 Greatest Rock Artists, VH1, 2000, 100 Sexiest Artists, VH1, 2002, Top Pop Artists of the Past 25 Yrs., 2004. Office Phone: 212-930-4000.*

GROLLI, FRANK THOMAS, retired pharmacist; b. Bklyn., July 25, 1933; s. Frank and Theresa D. G.; m. Maria T. Cerbone, Mar. 30, 1974. BS in Pharmacy, Bklyn. Coll. Pharmacy, 1956. Registered pharmacist Ferro's Pharmacy, Bklyn., 1959-61; mgr., owner Associated Drugs, NYC, 1961-66; mgr., pharmacist Frank's Pharmacy, Staten Island, 1966-76; asst. mgr., pharmacist Savon SuperX, Staten Island, 1976-84, asst. mgr., pharmacy supr., 1984-88, pharmacy coord., 1988-94; n.e. region pharmacy coord. H.S.I., Rutherford, NJ, 1994; pharmacy supr. Revco D.S., Carteret, NJ, 1994-95, ret., 1995. Col. Med. Svc. Corps, 1961-86. Decorated Nat. Def. Svc. medal. Army Reserve Comp. Achievement medal, Meritorous Svc. medal. Mem. APHA, Pharm. Soc. NY, N.Y.C. Pharm. Soc., Italian Pharm. Soc., Res. Officers Assn., Assn. Mil. Surgeons. Avocations: gardening, stamp collecting/philately, fishing, home repairs.

GROLLMAN, JULIUS HARRY, JR., cardiovascular and interventional radiologist; b. LA, Nov. 26, 1934; s. Julius Harry and Alice Carolyn (Greenlee) G.; m. Alexa Jule Silverman, May 20, 1959; children: Carolyn, David, Elizabeth. BA, Occidental Coll., 1956; MD, UCLA, 1960. Diplomate Am. Bd. Radiology. Intern L.A. VA Hosp., 1960-61; resident in radiology UCLA Med. Ctr., 1961-64; chief cardiovascular radiology Walter Reed Gen. Hosp., 1965-67; chief cardiovascular radiology Ctr. Health Svcs. UCLA, 1967-78, clin. prof. radiol. sci., 1978—. Contbr. over 150 articles to profl. jours., 9 chpts. to med. books. Fellow Soc. Cardiac Angiography and Interventions (trustee 1992-95), Am. Coll. Radiology, Coun. Cardiovascular Radiology, Am. Heart Assn., Soc. Cardiovascular and Interventional Radiology; mem. AMA, Am. Roentgen Ray Soc., Radiol. Soc. N.Am., Western Angiographic and Interventional Soc. (pres. 1976-77), N.Am. Soc. for Cardiac Imaging (pres. 1991-92). Republican. Presbyterian. Office: 448 27th St Manhattan Beach CA 90266-2119 Personal E-mail: grollmanj@mac.com.

GROMACKI, SUSAN JEAN, optometrist; b. Greenfield, Mass., Oct. 03; d. George Peter and Jean Klocko Gromacki; m. Scott David Lathrop, June 2, 2001; 1 child, Stephanie Elizabeth; 1 child, Sarah Jean Lathrop. BS, U. Notre Dame, 1989; OD, Ohio State U., 1993, MS in Physiol. Optics, 1993. Lic. optometrist. Resident in hosp.-based optometry U. S. Dept. of Veterans Affairs Med. Ctr., Chillicothe, Ohio, 1993—94; asst. prof. optometry New Eng. Coll. Optometry, Boston, 1994—98; faculty dept. ophthalmology and visual scis. U. Mich., Ann Arbor, 1998—2001; optometrist Hudson Valley Eye Surgeons, Fishkill, NY, 2002—03, Kaiser Permanente, Fairfax, Va., 2004—05, Huron Ophthalmology, 2006—. Speakers' bur. Vistakon (Johnson & Johnson), Jacksonville, Fla., 1995—2003, Sunsoft Contact Lens Co., Albuquerque, 1996—99; adv. bd. Cooper Vision, Rochester, NY, 1996—; examiner Nat. Bd. of Examiners in Optometry, 1998—; speakers' alliance. Alcon, 2004—; speakers' bur. CIBA Vision, 2006—, Bausch & Lomb, 2007—; cons. in field. Contbr. articles to profl. jours. V.p. Mil. Coun. of Cath. Women, West Point, NY, 2002—03; mem. parish coun. Most Holy Trinity Parish, West Point, NY, 2002—03; provider Vision USA, Various, 1994—. Recipient Contact Lens Achievement award, CIBA Vision, 1993, Harold F. Kohn award, Am. Optometric Found., 1993, Allergan Optometry award, Allergan, 1993, Wesley-Jessen award for Excellence, Wesley-Jessen, 1993, Alcon NOVA award, Alcon, 1993, America's Top Optometrists, Consumers' Rsch. Coun. of Am., 2002, 2003, 2004, 2005; Ednl. grant, Vistakon/ Johnson & Johnson, 1992, Optometry Class of 1953 Endowed scholarship, Ohio State U., 1992, U. of Notre Dame scholar, U. of Notre Dame, 1985—89, Bausch & Lomb Contact with the Future Ednl. Travel grant, Bausch & Lomb, 1992. Fellow: Am. Acad. Optometry (nat. comm. com. 2001—); mem.: Va. Optometric Assn., Ohio Optometric Assn., Mass. Soc. Optometrists, Mich. Optometric Assn., NY State Optometric Assn., Am. Optometric Assn., Assn. Contact Lens Educators, Ohio State U. Alumni Assn., U. Notre Dame Alumni Assn. (Boston bd. dirs. 1996—98), Epsilon Psi Epsilon. Roman Catholic. Avocations: physical fitness, golf, tennis, cooking, travel.

GROMADA, THADDEUS V., historian, academic administrator; b. Passaic, NJ, July 30, 1929; s. John W. and Aniela (Pudzisz) Gromada; m. Theresa M. Michalski, Aug. 25, 1951; children: Joseph, John, Ann. BS magna cum laude, Seton Hall U., 1951; MA, Fordham U., 1953, PhD, 1966. From asst. prof. history to prof. European history N.J. City U., 1959-92; v.p., exec. dir. Polish Inst. Arts and Scis., NYC, 1991—. Chmn. Gov.'s Commn. Ea. European History, Trenton, NJ, 1985—89; cons. ethnic heritage Dept. Edn., Washington; cons. NEA, 1975—. Author, editor: book Essays on Poland's Foreign Policy 1918-1939, 1969; co-editor: Polonia Amerykanska, 1988; editor: Jadwiga of Anjou & Rise of East Central Europe, 1991; founder, co-editor: Tatra Eagle, 1947—. Mem. awards com. Korczak Lit. prize, 1980—85; co-organizer Conf. Germany, Poland & Europe, 1992; organizer Conf. Jagiellonian U.and Polish Acad. Arts and Scis., Cracow, Poland, 2000; vice chmn., trustee Kosciusko Found., NYC, 1981—; mem. dialog com. Nat. Polish Am.-Jewish Am. Coun., Washington, 2001—. Sgt. US Army, 1953—55. Decorated Officer's Cross of Merit Pres. Poland, Comdrs. Cross, L'Ordre du Merite Culturel Poland's Min. of Culture and Arts; recipient Haiman medal, Polish Am. Hist. Assn., 1985. Mem.: Polish Am. Hist. Assn. (pres. 1995—96), Am. Hist. Assn., Am. Assn. Advancement Slavic Studies. Roman Catholic. Avocations: classical music, violin, polish highlander folklore, hiking. Home: 2722 Old Oak Walk Johns Island SC 29455-6213 Office: Polish Inst Arts & Scis 208 E 30th St New York NY 10016-8202 E-mail: tgromada@mindspring.com.

GROMEK, JOSEPH R., apparel executive; Sr. mgmt. positions Saks Fifth Ave., Ann Taylor Inc.; pres., CEO Brooks Brothers Inc., 1996—2002; pres., CEO, bd. dir. Warnaco Group Inc., NYC, 2003—. Vice-chmn. Volunteers of Am.; trustee Parsons Sch. Design. Recipient Exec. Leadership award, Fashion Inst. Tech., 2006. Office: Warnaco Group Inc 501 Seventh Ave New York NY 10018*

GRONBECK, BRUCE ELLIOT, communications educator; b. Bertha, Minn., Mar. 9, 1941; s. Edward Leslie and Bernice Cecilia Gronbeck; m. Wendy Lee Gilbert, 1968; children: Christopher E., Jakob A.L.S., Ingrid C. Julyk. BA, Concordia Coll., Moorhead, Minn., 1963, LHD (hon.), 1991; MA, U. Iowa, Iowa City, 1966, PhD, 1970; D in Comms. (hon.), Uppsala U., Sweden, 1997, U. Jyvaskyla, Finland, 2000. Asst. prof. U. Mich., Ann Arbor, Mich., 1967—73; assoc. prof. U. Iowa, Iowa City, 1973—78, prof., 1978—94, A. Craig Baird disting. prof., 1994—. Fulbright sr. specialist U. Jyvaskyla, 2005; lectr. in field. Author: The Articulate Person, 1983, Writing Television Criticism, 1984; editor: Spheres of Argument, 1989, Media, Consciousness, and Culture, 1991, Presidential Campaigns and American Self Images, 1994; author: Communication Criticism: Rhetoric, Social Codes, Cultural Studies, 2001, Persuasion in Society, 2001; editor: Critical Approaches to Television, 2004; author: Principles of Public Speaking, 2007, Principles and Types of Public Speaking, 2007. Dir. pub. rels. United Way Johnson Countrty, Iowa City, 1980—86; mem. ctrl. com. Johnson County Dem., Iowa City, 1976—81, Iowa County Dem., Williamsburg, Iowa, 1996—; commr. youth soccer Iowa City Kickers, Iowa City, 1978—84. Named Outstanding Prof. in Comm., Comm. and Theatre Assn. Minn., 1999, Golden Anniversary Disting. Scholar in Argumentation, Am. Forensic Assn., 1999; recipient Rsch. award, Maharishi U., 1981, Koch prize, Magic Lantern Soc., 2006, Lifetime Achievement award, Pub. Address Conf., 2006; fellow, Ctr. Comm. and Culture, 1978, Fulbright Found., 1992, 2004—, Ctr. Comm. and Culture, 1989; First fellow, U. Colo., Boulder, 2004. Master: Golden Key Internat. Honor Soc. (hon.); fellow: Nat. Comm. Assn. (Mentor award 2002, Disting. Svc. award 1999, Disting. scholar 1998); mem.: Internat. Soc. Study of Argumentation, Ctrl. States Comm. Assn. (life; pres. 1975—76, named Outstanding Young Tchr. 1978), Nat. Comm. Assn. (life; pres. 1993—94), USTA. Democrat. Avocations: tennis, fishing, travel. Home: 3290 275th St Williamsburg IA 52361-8646 Office: Dept Communication Studies Univ Iowa Iowa City IA 52242-1498 Home Phone: 319-828-4033; Office Phone: 319-335-0575. Business E-Mail: bruce-gronbeck@uiowa.edu.

GRONNIER, HENRY MAURICE, violinist, educator; b. Saint Quentin, France, May 7, 1960; arrived in US, 1982, naturalized, 2006; s. Robert Gronnier and Louise Feferman. Grad., Versailles Conservatory, France, 1980; diploma, Univ. Musicale Internationale de Paris, 1982. Concert violinist, 1982—; violinist Rossetti Quartet, 1996—; violin tchr. Colburn Sch., LA, 2001—. Judge Met. Opera, NYC, 1995—, KIME Competition, LA, 2005. Avocations: movies, swimming, chamber music. Home: 3601 Griffith Park Blvd Los Angeles CA 90027 Office Phone: 323-270-9062. Fax: 323-661-6660. E-mail: hg1violin@aol.com.

GRONSTAL, THOMAS B., state agency administrator; b. Carroll, Iowa, June 14, 1951; m. Joan Gronstal; 2 children. Grad., Benedictine Coll., Atchison, Kans., 1973. With Ctrl. Nat. Bank, Des Moines, 1973—75, Iowa Divsn. Banking, 1975—78, supt., 2002—; positions including chmn. Carroll County State Bank, Iowa, 1978—2002. Mem. Iowa Workforce Devel. Regional Adv. Bd., Carroll Area Devel. Corp. Treas. Iowa Bankers Assn., 1987—89, pres., 1990, Carroll C. of C., 1989; mayor City of Carroll, 1994—99; mem. Gov.'s Strategic Planning Coun., 1999—2000, Carroll Area Devel. Corp., 1999—2001. Named to Iowa Vol. Hall of Fame, 1994. Office: Iowa Divsn Banking 200 E Grand Ave Ste 300 Des Moines IA 50309-1827 Office Phone: 515-281-4014. Office Fax: 515-281-4862.*

GROOM, WINSTON FRANCIS, JR., writer; b. Washington, Mar. 23, 1943; s. Winston Francis and Ruth (Knudsen) G.; m. Ruth Noble, Dec. 10, 1969 (div. Mar. 1985); m. Anne-Clinton Bridges, June 6, 1987. AB, U. Ala., 1965. Reporter The Washington Star, 1968-77; author Simon & Schuster, NYC, 1977-81, G.P. Putnams, NYC, Doubleday & Co., NYC, 1984—. Author: Better Times Than These, 1978, As Summer's Die, 1981, Only, 1984, Forest Gump, 1986 (#1 NY Times Bestseller), Gone the Sun, 1988, Gumpisms: The Wit and Wisdom of Forrest Gump, 1994, The Bubba Gump Shrimp Co. Cookbook: Recipes & Reflections from Forrest Gump, 1994, Shrouds of Glory, 1995, Such a Pretty Girl, 1999, The Crimson Tide, 2000, A Storm in Flanders, 2002, 1942: The Year That Tried Men's Souls, 2005, Patriotic Fire, 2006; (co-author) Conversations with the Enemy, 1983 (Pulitzer Prize nomination, 1984). Served to cpt. U.S. Army, 1965-68, Vietnam. Recipient Best Novel award So. Library Assn., 1982, Pulitzer Prize nomination, 1984. Mem. Writers Guild Am. Presbyterian. Office: c/o Theron Raines Raines & Raines Agy 103 Kenyon Rd Medusa NY 12120

GROOMS, BRUCE ESTES, career military officer; b. Cleve. m. Emily Penn; children: Geoff, Jared. BS, U.S. Naval Acad., Annapolis, 1980; M in nat. security & strategic studies, Naval War Coll.; Nat. Security Affairs Fellow, Stanford Univ. Commd. ensign USN, advanced through grades to capt.; exec. officer USS Pasadena (SSN 752); commdg. officer USS Asheville (SSN 758); co. officer U.S. Naval Acad., Annapolis; sr. inspector Atlantic Fleet nuclear propulsion examining bd.; sr. mil. aide to under sec. for policy U.S. Dept. Def., Washington; comdt. of midshipmen U.S. Naval Acad., Annapolis, 2005—. Decorated Def. Superior Svc. medal, Legion of Merit (2 awards), Meritorious Svc. medal; recipient Vice Adm. Stockdale Inspirational Leadership award, 1999. Office: US Naval Academy Commander of Midshipmen 121 Blake Rd Annapolis MD 21402-5000

GROOMS, HENRY RANDALL, retired civil engineer; b. Cleve., Feb. 10, 1944; s. Leonard Day and Lois (Pickell) G.; m. Tonie Marie Joseph; children: Catherine, Zayne, Nina, Ivan, Ian, Athesis, Shaneya, Yaphet, Rahsan, Dax, Jevay, Xava. BSCE, Howard U., 1965; MSCE, Carnegie-Mellon U., 1967, PhD, 1969. Hwy. engr. D.C. Hwy. Dept., Washington, 1965; structural engr. Peter F. Loftus Corp., Pitts., 1966; structural engr., engring. mgr. Rockwell Internat. (now Boeing), Downey, Calif., 1969—2006. Contbr. articles to profl. jours. Scoutmaster Boy Scouts Am., Granada Hills, Calif., 1982-87; basketball coach Valley Conf., Granada

Hills, 1984—; coach Am. Youth Soccer Orgn., Granada Hills, 1985-90, 94—; tutor Watts Friendship Sports League, 1989—; co-founder Project Reach Scholarship Found., 1993. Recipient Alumni Merit award Carnegie-Mellon U., 1985, Lifetime Achievement award Black Engr. of Yr. Awards Conf., 2004, Lifetime Achievement in Industry award Nat. Soc. Black Engrs., 2004; honoree Black History Project Western Res. Hist. Soc., 1989. Fellow Inst. Advancement Engring. (Outstanding Engring. Vol. award, 1999), African Sci. Inst.; mem. ASCE, Tau Beta Pi, Sigma Xi. E-mail: henry.projectreach@gmail.com.

GROOPMAN, JEROME, medical educator; b. Jan. 11, 1952; MD, Columbia Coll. Physicians and Surgeons. Diplomate Am. Bd. Internal Medicine with subspecialties in hematology and med. oncology. Resident in internal medicine Mass. Gen. Hosp., Boston; clin. fellow in medicine Harvard Med. Sch., Boston; fellow divsn. of hematology/oncology U. Calif.; rsch. fellow Boston Children's Hosp.-Sidney Farber Cancer Ctr.; prof. medicine Harvard Med. Sch., Dina and Raphael Recanati chair; chief exptl. medicine, dir. AIDS oncology program, dir. Mapplethorpe Lab. Beth Israel Deaconess Med. Ctr. Contbr. articles; staff writer: New Yorker, 1998—; author: The Measure of Our Days, 1997, Second Opinions, 2000, The Anatomy of Hope, 2003. Recipient Victor Cohn prize, Excellence in Med. Reporting, Coun. for Advancement of Sci. Writing, 2006. Mem.: Inst. of Medicine of NAS. Office: Beth Israel Deaconess Med Ctr Rm 351 4 Blackfan Cir Boston MA 02115 Office Phone: 617-667-0070. Office Fax: 617-975-5244. E-mail: jgroopma@bidmc.harvard.edu.

GROOS, ARTHUR BERNHARD, JR., German studies and music educator; b. Fullerton, Calif., Feb. 5, 1943; s. Arthur Bernhard and Nancy Elizabeth (Stowe) G.; m. Bonnie Cleo Buettner, May 16, 1979; children: Peter, Jan. AB magna cum laude, Princeton U., 1964; MA, Cornell U., Ithaca, NY, 1966; PhD, Cornell U., 1970; postgrad., Freie Universitat Berlin, 1966-67. Asst. prof. UCLA, 1969-73; asst. prof. German lit. Cornell U., 1973-76, assoc. prof., 1976-82, prof., 1982—, dir. medieval studies, 1974-86, chmn. dept. German studies, 1986-91, 96-99, prof. German studies and music, 2003—, Avalon Found. prof. humanities, 2005—. Chmn. German dept. adv. coun. Princeton U., N.J., 1981-85; vis. prof. U. Paderborn, W.Ger., 1982, Freie U. Berlin, 2001-02, U. Amiens, 2004; bd. dirs. Centro Studi Giacomo Puccini (Lucca). Author: Puccini: La Boheme, 1986, Romancing the Grail, 1995; co-author: Medieval Christian Literary Imagery, 1988; editor: Dichtkunst und Lebenkunst, 1981, Magister Regis, 1986, Reading Opera, 1988, Cambridge Opera Jour., 1988-98, Studi pucciniani, 1998—, Perceval/Parzival, 2002, Madama Butterfly: Fonti e documenti, 2005; gen. editor: Cambridge Opera Monographs; co-editor: Kulturen des Manuskriptzeitalters, 2004, Transatlantische Studien. Fulbright fellow Berlin, 1966, Fulbright sr. fellow Munich, 1979, Guggenheim fellow Munich, 1979; recipient ASCAP-Deems Taylor prize, 1993, Humboldt Rsch. prize 1999. Mem. MLA, Internat. Arthurian Soc., Medieval Acad. Am., Wolfram v. Eschenbach Gesellschaft, Internat. Courtly Lit. Soc., Am. Musicol. Soc., Phi Beta Kappa. Home: 492 Valley Rd Brooktondale NY 14817-9701 Office: Cornell U Dept German Studies 185 Goldwin Smith Hall Ithaca NY 14853-3201 Office Phone: 607-255-5265. Business E-Mail: abg3@cornell.edu.

GROPPER, ALLAN LOUIS, judge; BA, Yale U., 1965; JD, Harvard U., 1969. Bar: N.Y. 1969, U.S. Dist. Ct. (so. and ea. dists.) N.Y. 1971, U.S. Ct. Appeals (2d cir.) 1971, U.S. Supreme Ct. 1974. Atty. Civil Appeals Bur., Legal Aid Soc., NYC, 1969-71; assoc. White & Case, NYC, 1972-77, ptnr., 1978-2000; judge US Bankruptcy Ct., NYC, 2000—. Adj. prof. Fordham Law Sch., 2003—. Bd. dirs. Browning Sch., 1990—, pres., 1997-2000; bd. dirs. Legal Aid Soc., 1990-2000, v.p., 1996-2000; bd. dirs. N.Y. Lawyers for Pub. Interest, 1990-2000. Mem. ABA, Assn. of Bar of City of N.Y. (v.p. 1995-96, mem. exec. com. 1991-96, chmn. 1994-95). Office: US Bankruptcy Ct Alexander Hamilton Custom House 1 Bowling Green New York NY 10004 Office Phone: 212-668-5629.

GROSBARD, ULU, film director; b. Antwerp, Belgium, Jan. 9, 1929; came to U.S., 1948; s. Morris and Rose (Tennenbaum) G.; m. Rose Gregorio, Feb. 25, 1965 BA, U. Chgo., 1950, MA, 1952; postgrad., Yale U. Sch. Drama, 1952-53. Dir. plays The Days and Nights of Beebeem, 1962, The Subject Was Roses, 1964 (Tony nomination 1965), A View from the Bridge, 1965 (Obie award 1965), The Investigation, 1966, The Price, 1968, American Buffalo, 1977 (Tony nominations), The Woods, 1980, The Floating Light Bulb, 1981, Weekends Like Other People, 1982, The Wake of Jamie Foster, 1982, The Tenth Man, 1989, Family Week, 2000; (films) The Subject Was Roses, 1968, Who is Harvey Kellerman, 1971, Straight Time, 1978, True Confessions, 1981, Falling in Love, 1984, Georgia, 1994, The Deep End of the Ocean, 1999. Served with U.S. Army, 1953-55 Mem. Dirs. Guild Am., Soc. Dirs. and Choreographers Jewish. Office Phone: 212-586-1616.

GROSCH, LAURA DUDLEY, artist, educator; b. Worcester, Mass., Apr. 1, 1945; d. Daniel Swartwood and Edith Dudley (Taft) G. BA in Art History, Wellesley Coll., 1967; BFA in Painting, U. Pa., 1968. Solo exhbns. include Mint Mus. Art, Charlotte, N.C., 1974, Jerald Melberg Gallery, Charlotte, 1984, 87, Greenville (N.C.) Mus. Art, 1987, Greenville County Mus. Art, 1987, Christa Faut Gallery, Davidson, N.C., 1990, 93, 96, Rock Sch. Arts Found., Valdese, N.C., 2000, Millennium exhbn., Valdese, 2000, others; group exhbns. include Impressions Gallery, Boston, 1973, Rose Mus. Glenbow-Alberta Gallery, Can., 1974, New Orleans Mus. Art, 1975, Bklyn. Mus., 1976, Visual Arts Ctr. Alaska, 1978, Print Club, Phila., 1980, Palazzo Venezia, Rome, 1984, Syracuse U., N.Y., 1987, Wellesley (Mass.) Coll., 1997, Mint Mus. Art, Charlotte, N.C., 2002, Christa Faut Gallery, Cornelius, N.C., 2003, 04, 05, 06, 07, Charlotte Wine and Food, 2004, 250 Years of Art, Winston-Salem, N.C., 2004, Sommerhill Gallery, Chapel Hill, NC, 2006, 07; represented in pub. collections Boston Pub. Libr., Bowdoin Coll., Brunswick, Maine, Brit. Mus., London, Bklyn. Mus., Fla. State U., Manhattan Coll., Mus. Fine Arts, Boston, N.Y. Pub. Libr., Ringling Mus., Sarasota, Fla., Smithsonian Inst., Washington, UCLA, Newark Pub. Libr., Minn. Inst. Arts, Honolulu Acad. Arts, Dayton (Ohio) Art Inst., Carnegie Mellon U., Pitts., Free Libr. Phila., Victoria and Albert Mus., London, many others. Office: PO Box 10 Davidson NC 28036-8006 Home Phone: 704-892-1723; Office Phone: 704-892-1723.

GROSE, CHARLES FREDERICK, pediatrician, epidemiologist; b. Faribault, Minn., Apr. 15, 1942; s. Frederick G. and Marie A. (Swelland) G. BA, Beloit Coll., 1963; MD, U. Chgo., 1967. Bd. cert. in pediatric infectious disease. Resident Albert Einstein Coll. Medicine, Bronx, NY, 1967-68, fellow, 1970—75, U. Calif., San Francisco, 1975-76; asst. prof. Health Sci. Ctr. U. Tex., San Antonio, 1976-84; prof. pediatrics U. Iowa Hosp., Iowa City, 1985—. Cons. NIH, Bethesda, Md., 1988—. Editor Pediat. Infectious Disease Jour., 2003—; mem. editl. bd. Virology Jour.; contbr. articles to profl. and sci. jours. Capt. U.S. Army Med. Corps., Vietnam, 1968-70. Grantee NIH, 1978—. Fellow Infectious Disease Soc. Am., Pediatric Infectious Disease Soc., Am. Acad. Pediatrics, Am. Soc. Virology. Achievements include research on diagnosis and treatment of chickenpox and shingles, and on the etiologic agent which is varicella virus. Office: U Iowa Hosp Pediatrics 200 Hawkins Dr Iowa City IA 52242-1009 Business E-Mail: charles-grose@uiowa.edu.

GROSECLOSE, EVERETT HARRISON, retired editor; b. Childress, Tex., June 25, 1938; s. Everett Jackson and Eula Margaret (Snider) G.; m. Edna Kathryn Hunter, Dec. 24, 1962 (div. 1986); children: Kirsten Lee, Megan Margaret; m. Susan Kahne-Greer, Dec. 22, 1990. BA in Journalism, Tex. Tech. U., Lubbock, 1961. Reporter Wall St. Jour., Dallas and NYC, 1965-70; asst. mng. editor Cleve., 1970-76; dir. pub. affairs Dow Jones & Co., NYC, 1976-80; mng. editor Dow Jones News Services, NYC, 1980-88; exec. editor Dow Jones Profl. Investor Report, NYC, 1988-92; dir. product devel. Dow Jones Info. Services, NYC, 1988-92; dir. internat. mktg., news and database svcs. Telerate, Inc. subs. Dow Jones, NYC, 1992-94; mng. editor Dow Jones Emerging Markets Report, NYC, 1994-97, Servicio Dow Jones Americas, NYC, 1996-97; founder Internet Pub. Group, Inc. (formerly VertiNews.com, Inc.), 1999—2003, Back-Country Angler, 2003—. Served with AUS, 1961-64. Decorated Army Commendation medal. Unitarian Universalist. Home: 57 Goodnight Trl E Santa Fe NM 87506-7925 Office Phone: 505-989-8999. E-mail: egroseclose@gmail.com.

GROSECLOSE, JOANNE STOWERS, special education educator; b. Bland, Va., Dec. 15, 1956; d. Claude Swanson and Josephine (Mustard) Stowers; m. John Vincent Groseclose, June 24, 1979; children: Jouette Nicole, Nicholas Vincent. BS, Radford Coll., 1979; MS, Radford U., 1983. Cert. tchr., Va, exceptional needs specialist, Nat. Bd. Profl. Tchg., 2001. Tchr. kindergarten Bland (Va.) Combined Sch., Bland County Sch. Bd., 1979; tchr. 4th grade Marion (Va.) Intermediate Sch., Smyth County Sch. Bd., 1979-80, tchr. learning disabled 4th, 5th, 6th grades, 1980—. Instr. adult basic edn. Smyth County Schs., Marion, 1989-90. Technician Bland County Rescue Squad, 1975-78; bd. dirs. Am. Cancer Soc., 1985-88, Marion United Way, 1989-91, Smyth County Assn. for Retarded Citizens, 1982-85, Smyth County Cmty. Hosp., 1993-98; sec., vice chair Smith County Cmty. Found., 1998—; vol. Mt. Rogers Smyth House Group Home for Retarded Adults, 1983-85; mem. Hospice of Smyth County; mem. S.W. Va. Reading Coun., 1989-91, 94—, Smyth County Humane Soc.; mem. area Luth. ch. coun., 1996-99. Named Outstanding Young Careerist Marion Bus. and Profl. Women, 1983, Outstand Young Woman of Am., Marion Bus. and Profl. Women, 1981, Radford U. Outstanding Alumi, 1990, Va. Tchr. of Yr. Ency. Britannica/Good Housekeeping/Coun. of Chief State Sch. Officers, 1991. Mem. NEA (del. conv.), Smyth County Edn. Assn. (rep. 1979, 82, 93—, treas. 1981-83, pres. 1985), Smyth County C. of C., Va. Edn. Assn. (del. conv.), Marion Book and Study Club, Phi Kappa Phi, Kappa Delta Pi. Avocations: reading, travel, camping, playing bridge, tennis. Home: 241 Magnolia St Marion VA 24354-4413 Office: Marion Intermediate Sch 820 Stage St Marion VA 24354-4000 Office Phone: 276-783-2609.

GROSECLOSE, LYNN HUNTER, lawyer; b. Marion, Va., Apr. 22, 1943; s. Byron Glen and Wilma Comer G.; m. Sharon L. Pair; children: Seth, Zachery, Meredith. BA, Emory & Henry Coll., 1964; postgrad., Emory U., 1964-65; JD, U. Va., 1970. Bar: Fla. 1971, U.S. Dist. Ct. (mid. dist.) Fla. 1972, U.S. Ct. Appeals (5th cir.) 1980, U.S. Ct. Appeals (11th cir.) 1981, Colo. 1993. Prof. Orlando Jr. Coll., Fla., 1965-67; atty. Langston & Massey, Attys., Lakeland, Fla., 1971-75; ptnr. Sprott & Groseclose, Attys., Lakeland, 1975-80, Jacobs, Valentine, Groseclose, Lakeland, 1980-84, Lane, Trohn, Bradenton, Fla., 1984-96, Brown, Clark, Sarasota, Fla., 1996-99, Thompson, Goodis, Thompson, Groseclose & Richardson, Sarasota, 1999—. Sr., jr. warden St. Davids Episcopal Ch.; pres., bd. dirs. Vols. in Svc. to Elderly, Gulfcoast Legal Svcs., Sarasota Manatee Legal Aid. Mem. Sarasota County Bar Assn., Manatee County Bar Assn., Colo. Bar Assn., Fla. Def. Lawyers Assn., Fedn. Def. and Corp. Counsel, Fla. Bar Found. (legal assistance to poor com. 1997-2002). Democrat. Avocations: history, remodeling, golf. Office: Thompson Goodis Thompson Groseclose & Richardson PO Box 730 Bradenton FL 34206

GROSECLOSE, WANDA WESTMAN, retired elementary school educator; b. Clarks, Nebr., Oct. 5, 1933; m. B. Clark Groseclose; children: D. Kim, Byron C. Jr., Eric P., A. Glenn. B degree, Brigham Young U., 1976; M in Tchg., St. Mary's Coll., Moraga, Calif., 1981. Cert. tchr., Calif. 5th grade tchr. Brentwood (Calif.) Union Sch. Dist., 1977-97; ret. Art tchr., mentor tchr. Contra Costa County Program of Excellence. Author: American Music in Time, 1992, In the Shadow of Our Ancestors, vol. I, vol. II, 2004, The Lees of Southwest Virginia, 2004. Human rels. bd. dirs. City of Livermore, 1968—70. Republican. Mem. Lds Ch. Avocations: painting, sewing, gardening, genealogy. Home: 2763 St Andrews Dr Brentwood CA 94513 Personal E-mail: groscl os@ecis.com.

GROSFELD, JAY LAZAR, surgeon, educator; b. NYC, May 30, 1935; m. Margie Faulkner; children: Lisa, Denise, Janice, Jeffrey, Mark. AB cum laude, NYU, 1957, MD, 1961. Diplomate Am. Bd. Surgery (spl. qualification Pediatric Surgery). Gen. surgery intern Bellevue and Univ Hosps. NYU, NYC, 1961—62; resident in gen. surgery Bellevue and Univ. Hosps. NYU, NYC, 1962—66; resident in pediatric surgery Ohio State U. Coll. Medicine, Children's Hosp., 1968—70; instr. surgery Ohio State U. Coll. Medicine, 1968—70; clin. instr. surgery NYU Sch. Medicine, NYC, 1965—66, asst. prof. surgery and pediatrics, 1970—72; prof., dir. pediatric surgery Ind. U. Sch. Medicine, Indpls., 1972—2005, chmn. dept. surgery, 1985—2003, Lafayette F. Page prof., 1981—2005, Lafayette F. Page prof. emeritus, 2005—; surgeon-in-chief James Whitcomb Riley Hosp. Children, 1972—2005; Lafayette Page prof. surgery, chmn. emeritus Ind. U. Sch. Medicine, Indpls., 2005—. Author: Common Problems in Pediatric Surgery, 1991, Central Surgical Association: The First 50 Years, 1991, Progress in Pediatric Trauma, 1992, Essentials of Pediatric Surgery, 1995, Pediatric Surgery, 6th edit., 2006, The Surgery of Childhood Tumors, 1999, Principles of Pediatric Surgery, 2003; editor-in-chief: Jour. Pediat. Surgery, 1994—; editor: Seminars in Pediat. Surgery; contbr. over 600 papers, reports, book chpts., articles for med. jours. Capt. M.C. US Army, 1966—68. Decorated Commendation medal; named Sagamore of the Wabash, 2002; recipient numerous fellowships, grants, teaching awards. Fellow: ACS (bd. govs. 1985—91), Am. Acad. Pediat. (exec. com. surg. sect. 1989—95, chmn. surg. sect. 1994—95, sec. surg. sect., William E. Ladd medal 2002—), Royal Coll. Physicians and Surgeons Glasgow (hon.), Royal Coll. Surgeons of Eng. (hon.); mem.: AMA, Halsted Soc. (v.p. 1995—96, pres. 1996—97), Accreditation Coun. Grad. Med. Edn. (surg. residency rev. com. 1996—2001, vice chair 2000—01), Am. Bd. Med. Specialities, World Fedn. Assns. Pediat. Surgeons (pres. 1998—2001, v.p.), Am. Bd. Surgery (bd. dirs. 1989—97, vice chair 1995, chmn. 1996—97, chmn.-elect), Am. Pediatric Surg. Assn. Found. (chmn. bd. dirs.), Internat. Soc. Surgery (sec., treas. Internat. Soc. Surgery Found. 2001—), Western Surg. Assn. (pres. 1997—98), Soc. Surg. Oncology, Brit. Assn. Pediat. Surgeons (exec. coun. 1990—93, Denis Browne Gold medal 1998), Ctrl. Surg. Assn. (sec. 1987—, pres.-elect 1988, pres. 1990), Soc. Surgery Alimentary Tract, Am. Trauma Soc., Ind. State Med. Assn., Marion County Med. Soc., Soc. Univ. Surgeons, Am. Surg. Assn. (first v.p. 2005—, pres. 2006—), British Assn. Pediat. Surgeons (hon.), Am. Pediat. Surg. Assn. (pres. 1994—95, bd. govs., pres.-elect), N.Y. Cancer Soc., Assn. Acad. Surgery, Pediat. Surgery Biology Club, Alpha Omega Alpha, Phi Beta Kappa. Office: J W Riley Childrens Hosp 702 Barnhill Dr Rm 2500 Indianapolis IN 46202-5128 Office Phone: 317-274-5716. Business E-Mail: jgrosfel@iupui.edu.

GROSH, WILLIAM W., internist; b. NYC, Aug. 22, 1949; MD, Columbia U. Physicians and Surgeons, 1974. Diplomate Am. Bd. Internal Medicine. Intern Vanderbilt U. Med. Ctr., 1974-75, resident, 1975-77; fellow in oncology Vanderbilt U., Nashville, 1980-83, instr., 1983-84, asst. prof. medicine, 1984-88, Univ. Va., 1988-93, assoc. prof. internal medicine, 1993—. Mem. AMA. Office: U Va Dept Medicine Divsn Hematology/Oncology PO Box 800466 Charlottesville VA 22908-0466 Office Phone: 434-924-1904. Office Fax: 434-243-6086.*

GROSJEAN, SEBASTIEN RENE, professional tennis player; b. Marseille, France, May 29, 1978; m. Marie-Pierre Grosjean, Nov. 16, 1998; children: Lola, Tom. Profl. tennis player ATP Tour, 1996—. Achievements include Finished as the number one ranked jr. in the world in both singles and doubles in 1996; Winner of 3 singles titles: Nottingham, 2000, Paris TMS, 2001, St. Petersburg, 2002; Winner of 4 doubles titles: Casablanca, 2000, Los Angeles, 2002, Marseille, 2003, Indian Wells TMS, 2004. Office: c/o ATP Tour Internat Hdqs 201 ATP Tour Blvd Ponte Vedra Beach FL 32082*

GROSKOPF, AUBREY BUD, broadcast executive, lawyer; b. Milw. s. George Norman and Rose (Becker) G.; 1 child, James E.; m. Mary Jo Gregory. BS, U. Wis., 1952, LLB, 1956. Bar: Wis. 1957. Dir. bus. affairs CBS-TV Network, NYC, 1958-73; exec. v.p. Four Star Internat., LA, 1973-76; pres. Republic Pictures Corp., LA, 1976-87; ind. motion picture and TV prodr. Prodr. motion picture Boys of Paul Street, 1969 (Best Fgn. Film award 1969); writer, prodr., dir. TV spl. and video A Norman Rockwell Christmas, 1994; creator Tales of Edgar Allan Poe, 1998. 1st lt. U.S. Army, 1952-54, Korea; selectman Town of Yarmouth, Cape Cod, 2005—. Decorated Bronze Star. Mem. NATAS, Acad. Motion Picture Arts and Scis.

GROSLAND, EMERY LAYTON, retired banker; b. Holden, Alta., Can., July 19, 1929; s. Arne and Lillie Olivetta (Jacobson) G.; m. Margaret Grace Woodward, Sept. 3, 1952; 1 child, Roberta Jayne Student pub. schs., Holden; student Amos Tuck Sch. Exec Program, Dartmouth Coll., 1980. With The Royal Bank of Can., 1949—, sr. v.p. Toronto, Ont., Canada, 1983—87; ret., 1987. Cons. in field. Avocation: golf.

GROS LOUIS, KENNETH RICHARD RUSSELL, humanities educator; b. Nashua, NH, Dec. 18, 1936; s. Albert W. and Jeannette Evelyn (Richards) Gros L.; m. Dolores K. Winandy, Aug. 28, 1965; children: Amy Katherine, Julie Jeannette. BA, Columbia U., 1959, MA, 1960; PhD (Knapp fellow), U. Wis., 1964. Asst. prof. Ind. U., Bloomington, 1964—67, assoc. prof. English and comparative lit., 1967—73, prof., 1973—, assoc. chmn. comparative lit. dept., 1967—69, assoc. dean arts and scis., 1970—73, chmn. dept. English, 1973—78, dean arts and scis., 1978—80, v.p., 1980—88, chancellor, 1988—2001, v.p. acad. affairs, 1994—2001, trustee prof., 2001—. Bd. dirs. Anthem, Inc.; exec. coun. acad. affairs Nat. Assn. Univ. and Land Grant Colls., 1986-97, bd. dirs. Bd. dirs. Editor Yearbook of Comparative and Gen. Lit., 1968—, Vol. I: Literary Interpretations of Biblical Narratives, 1974, Vol. II, 1982; contbr. articles to profl. jours. Bd. dirs. Assoc. Group, 1983-95, Anthem Blue Cross and Blue Shield, 1995—; mem. Ind. Com. Humanities, chmn., 1980-81; chmn. Com. on Instnl. Coop., 1986-2000; mem. Nat. Commn. on Libr. Preservation and Access, 1986-93; vice chmn., bd. dirs. Ctr. for Rsch. Librs., 1986—, chmn. bd. dirs., 1987-88. Recipient Disting. Teaching award Ind. U., 1970 Mem. MLA, Nat. Coun. Tchrs. English, AAUP, Phi Beta Kappa. Home: 4965 E Heritage Woods Rd Bloomington IN 47401-9313 Office: Ind U Wylie Hall Bloomington IN 47405 E-mail: grosloui@indiana.edu.

GROSMAN, ALAN M., retired lawyer; b. Mar. 13, 1935; s. Charles M. and Grace (Fishman) G.; m. Bette Bloomenthal, Dec. 27, 1967; children, Ellen, Carol. BA, Wesleyan U., 1956; MA, Yale U., 1957; JD, N.Y. Law Sch., 1965. Bar: N.J. 1965, U.S. Dist. Ct. N.J. 1965, U.S. Supreme Ct. 1969. Ptnr. Grosman & Grosman and predecessors, Millburn, NJ, 1965—; asst. prosecutor Essex County, NJ, 1968—69; prosecutor Millburn, 1981—2005, ret., 2005. Mem. family practice com. NJ Supreme Ct., 1984—88, mem. dispute resolution task force, 1987—88, mem. com. on women in the cts., 1991—93; chmn. NJ Trade Coun., 1975—77, dir., 1978—; adj. prof. family law Rutgers U. Sch. Law, 2002—; lectr. in field. Author: New Jersey Family Law, 1999, with annual supplement; reporter: New Haven Jour., 1959—60, Newark Evening News, 1961—62; contbr. articles to profl. jours. Mem. ABA (chmn. alimony, maintenance and support com. family law sect. 1983-87, editor ABA Family Law Quar. 1993—), N.J. State Bar Assn. (exec. editor N.J. Family Lawyer 1980-91, mem. exec. com. family law sect. 1980—, chmn. sect. 1987-88, appellate practice com. 1995—), Am. Acad. Matrimonial Lawyers (pres. N.J. chpt. 1983-85, nat. bd. govs. 1984-88, editor Jour. AAML 1980-90), Essex County Bar Assn. (chmn. family law com. 1970-72), N.Y. Law Sch. Alumni Assn. (bd. dirs. 1988-98), Phi Beta Kappa. E-mail: alan.grosman@verizon.net.

GROS-PIETRO, GIAN MARIA, economics professor; b. Turin, Italy, Feb. 4, 1942; Degree in econs., U. Turin. Tchr. prodn. econs. Sch. Indsl. Adminstrn. U. Turin, 1965-72, prof. indsl. econs., 1974—, full prof. indsl. policy and econs., 1994—2004; head Dept. Econs. and Bus. Luiss U., Rome, 2004—. Rschr. CERIS-Istituto di Ricerca sull'Impresa e lo Sviluppo, Nat. Rsch. Coun., 1965-72, dir., 1977-95; coord. plan for instrumental mechs. Ministry of Industry, Italy, 1977-80; econ. cons. Italian Union Machine Tool Constructors, 1983—; mng. dir. Fincimu, 1983-85; rep. Ministry Public Investment; mem. various sci. couns., sci. com. Nomisma; chmn., CEO IRI, 1997-99; chmn. ENI, 1999-2002, Autostrade, 2002—; bd. dirs. Seat SpA, Fiat SpA, Edison SpA. Author numerous texts in field. Bd. dirs. U. Turin, 1985—96. Mem. Soc. Italiana degli Economisti, Federtrasporto (pres. 2003—). Office: Autostrade Via Bergamini 50 00159 Rome Italy

GROSS, ALLEN JEFFREY, lawyer; b. Wheeling, W.Va., May 2, 1948; s. Arthur and Bertyl (Kahn) G.; m. Carolyn McGuire, May 2, 1982; children: Alexander, Lindsay, Matthew. BS, Ohio State U., 1970; JD, Georgetown U., 1974. Bar: Pa. 1974, U.S. Dist. Ct. (ctrl. and we. dists.) Pa., Calif. 1989, U.S. Dist. Ct. (no., so. and ctrl. dists.) Calif. 1989, U.S. Ct. Appeals (3d and 6th cirs.). Ptnr. Morgan, Lewis & Bockius, Phila., 1974-89, Orrick, Herrington & Sutcliffe, LA, 1989-93; now with Mitchell, Silberberg & Knupp, LA. Mem. Corp. Counsel Inst. adv. bd. Georgetown U. Law Ctr; vice chair Georgetown Corp. Coun. Inst; co-chair Georgetown ELLI, 1993-. Author: Survey of Wrongful Discharge Cases in the United States, 1979, Employee Dismissal Laws, Forms, Procedures, 1986, 2d edit. 1992. Fellow Coll. Labor and Employment Lawyers Inc.; mem. ABA (chair trial advocacy supcom. 1989-93, employee rights and responsibilities com. 1991—, co-chair Nat. Advocacy Inst. 1992, com., Sect. Insts. Spl. Programs sub-com, gov. coun., 1998), L.A. County Bar Assn. Office: Mitchell Silberberg & Knupp 11377 W Olympic Blvd Los Angeles CA 90064-1625

GROSS, AMY, editor-in-chief; Features editor and spl. projects editor Vogue, 1978—88; founding editor Mirabella, 1988—93, editor-in-chief, 1995—97; editl. dir. Elle, NYC, 1993—96; editor-in-chief O, The Oprah Mag., 2000—. Co-author: (books) Women Talk About Breast Surgery: From Diagnosis to Recovery, 1991, Women Talk About Gynecological Surgery: From Diagnosis to Recovery, 1992. Recipient Nat. Mag. award for Leisure Interests journalism, Am. Soc. Mag. Editors, 2007. Office: O The Oprah Mag 1700 Broadway New York NY 10019-6708*

GROSS, BENEDICT H., mathematician; b. South Orange, NJ, June 22, 1950; BA, Harvard U., 1971, PhD, 1978; MSc, Oxford U., 1974. Asst. prof. Princeton U., 1978—82; assoc. prof. Brown U., 1982—85; prof. Harvard U., 1985—98, George Vasmer Leverett prof. math., 1998—, dean undergraduate edn., 2002—03, dean Harvard Coll., 2003—. Selection com. Sloan Postdoctoral Fellowships, 2003—. Author: Arithmetic on Elliptical Curves with Complex Multiplication, 2000; co-author: The Magic of Numbers, 2004. Recipient Cole prize in number theory, AMS, 1987; fellow, Sloan, 1980—83, MacArthur, 1986—91. Mem.: Am. Acad. Arts and Scis., NAS. Office: Harvard U Math Dept 1 Oxford St Cambridge MA 02138-2901 Business E-Mail: gross@math.harvard.edu.

GROSS, BILL, energy executive; BS in Mechanical Engring., California Inst. Tech. Founder, pres. Solar Devices, GNP Loudspeakers, Inc.; co-founder GNP Devel., Inc.; software engr. Lotus Devel. Corp. (acquired GNP Devel. Inc.), 1985—91; founder, pres. Knowledge Adventure, 1991—96; founder, CEO, chmn. Idealab, 1996—, Energy Innovations, Pasadena, Calif., 2000—. Mem. bd. of trustees Art Ctr. Coll. of Design, California Inst. of Tech. Achievements include invention of the Contextual Advertising concept, introduced as paid placement and pay-per-click on GoTo.com and later made popular by Google. Office: Idealab 130 W Union St Pasadena CA 91103 Office Phone: 626-585-6900. Office Fax: 626-535-2701.

GROSS, BRUCE E., construction executive; Sr. v.p., treas., contr. Pacific Greystone; v.p., CFO Lennar Corp., Miami, Fla., 1997—. Office: Lennar Corp 700 NW 107th Ave Ste 400 Miami FL 33172-3154 Office Phone: 305-559-4000. Office Fax: 305-226-4158.*

GROSS, CHARLES GORDON, psychology professor; b. NYC, Feb. 29, 1936; s. Frank and Sara (Gordon) G.; m. Gaby Ellen Peierls, Sept. 23, 1961 (div. Mar. 1985); children: Melanie, Monica (dec.), Derek, Rowena; m. Greta Berman, May 1, 1988. BA, Harvard U., 1957; PhD, Cambridge U., Eng., 1961. From postdoctoral fellow to asst. prof. psychology MIT, 1961-65; vis. lectr., asst. prof., then lectr. Harvard U., 1963-70; prof. psychology Princeton U., 1970—. Vis. prof. U. Calif., Berkeley, 1970-71, MIT, 1975-76, Beijing U., 1986; vis. scientist Tokyo Met. Inst. Neurosci., 1988-89, Nencki Inst. Exptl. Biology, Warsaw, Poland, 1961; Fulbright lectr. Inst. Biophysics, Fed. U. Rio de Janeiro, 1986; U.S. Nat. Program vis. scientist Shanghai Inst. Physiology, 1987; vis. fellow Magdalen Coll., Oxford U., 1990, vis. scholar Wolfson Coll., 1995, McDonneld-Pew vis. fellow Med. Rsch. Coun. Ctr. in Brain and Behaviour, 1995, chair, Psychology Section (J), Am. Assoc. for the Advancement of Science. Author books and papers on brain, visual function and history of science. Grantee NIH, NSF, Spencer Found., Sloan Found., McDonald-Pew Found., Office Naval Rsch. Fellow APA (Disting. Contbn. to Psychology award 2005), AAAS, Soc. Exptl. Psychologists, Brazilian Acad. Sci.(fgn.), Nat. Acad. Sci., am. Acad. Arts and Sci. Home: 45 Woodside Ln Princeton NJ 08540-5417 Office: Princeton Univ Green Hall Princeton NJ 08544 Office Phone: 609-258-4430. Business E-Mail: cggross@princeton.edu.

GROSS, CHARLES ROBERT, county official, former state senator, former bank executive; b. St. Charles, Mo., Aug. 20, 1958; s. Jack Robert and Margaret Ellen (Stumberg) G.; m. Leslie Ann Goralczyk, May 27, 1984; children: Megan Marie, Madelynn Ann. BS in Pub. Adminstrn., U. Mo., 1981, MPA, 1982. Pers. mgr. Army and Air Force Exch. Svc., various cities, 1983-89; pers., safety dir. Ever-Green Lawns Corp., St. Charles, 1989-92; state rep. Mo. Legislature, Jefferson City, 1993—2000; real estate appraiser, 1994—2001; v.p. UMB Bank, 2001—07; state senator Mo. Legislature, Jefferson City, 2001—07; dir. adminstrn. St. Charles County Govt., Mo., 2007—. Pres. St. Charles County Young Reps., 1990-92; active Youth in Need, Bridgeway Counseling. Mem. St. Charles DARE, Kiwanis, Pacaderms, Alpha Kappa Psi (life). Lutheran. Avocations: golf, scuba diving, ice hockey. Home: 3019 Westborough Ct Saint Charles MO 63301-4550 Home Phone: 636-949-7520; Office Phone: 573-751-8635. E-mail: chuckgross58@hotmail.com.

GROSS, CYNTHIA SUE, petrochemicals manufacturing executive; b. Palmyra, Mo., Aug. 14, 1959; d. Floyd Raymond and Carolyn Elizabeth (Howell) Mette; m. Edward Lee Gross, June 8, 1985; 1 child, Ray E.; stepchildren: Troy A., Christina M BS Metall. Engring., U. Mo., Rolla, 1980. Metallurgist Bryon Jackson Pump, Tulsa, 1981—82; metall. engr. Conoco, Inc., Ponca City, Okla., 1982—84, Vista Chem., Houston, 1984—89; staff maintenance engr. Hoechst Celanese, Clear Lake, Tex., 1989—92, sect. leader maintenance engring. Bishop, Tex., 1992—93, sect. leader maintenance, 1993—95; prodn. supt. for polyester Hoechst Celanese, Trevira, Spartanburg, SC, 1995—97; process hazards prevention leader Celanese, Clear Lake, 1997—98, methanol and maintenance mgr., 1999—2000, mgr. tech. and maintenance, 2000—01, dir. corp. reliability, maintenance and engring., 2001—. Spkr. symposium Nat. Petroleum Refiners Assn., San Antonio, 1993, San Antonio, 2000, San Antonio, 02; instr. welding metallurgy San Jacinto Coll., Houston, 1992. Quality mgmt. com. Houston Bus. Roundtable, 1990-92, chmn. Quality Day '91 Mem. NPRA (maintenance com. 2001-05, vice-chair 2005, chmn. 2006), Alpha Chi Sigma Avocations: antiques, piano. Office: Celanese Clear Lake Plant 9502 Bayport Blvd Pasadena TX 77507-1402 Home Phone: 281-486-0103. Business E-Mail: cindy.gross@celanese.com.

GROSS, DAVID F., lawyer; b. NY, 1953; BA cum laude, St. John's Coll., 1974; JD magna cum laude, Harvard U., 1978. Bar: Calif., US Dist. Ct. (no., ea., ctrl. dist.) Calif., US Tax Ct. Ptnr. Graham & James, San Francisco, 1985—89, mng. ptnr., 1989—92, chmn., 1992—93, mng ptnr. Palo Alto, 1994—98; ptnr. DLA Piper, San Francisco. Mem. ABA (mem. sect. of litigation), Bar Assn. San Francisco., Am. Corp. Counsel Assn., San Francisco Barristers Arbitrator, Am. Arbitration Assn. Office: DLA Piper 153 Townsend St Ste 800 San Francisco CA 94107 Office Phone: 415-836-2562. Office Fax: 415-836-2501. E-mail: david.gross@dlapiper.com.

GROSS, DAVID J.F., lawyer; b. St. Paul, 1963; BA, U. Minn., 1985; JD, Harvard U., 1989. Bar: Minn. 1990, admitted to: US Ct. of Appeals, Fed. Cir., US Ct. of Appeals, Eighth Cir., US Dist. Ct., Dist. Minn. Clerk US Ct. of Appeals, First Cir., 1989—90; trail atty. US Dept. Justice, Washington; litigator Covington & Burling, Skadden, Arps, Slate, Meagher & Flom; ptnr. Faegre & Benson LLP, Mpls.; adj. prof., Patent Litig. and Strategy U. Minn. Law Sch. Lectr. U. Minn. Career Guidance Programs. Co-author: The Power Trial Method. Named a Super Lawyer, Minn. Law and Politics; named one of 15 Attorneys of Yr., Minn. Lawyer, Top Ten IP Litigators of Yr., Chambers USA, Litigation's Rising Stars, The Am. Lawyer, 2007. Mem.: U. Minn. Coll. Liberal Arts Alumni Soc. Office: Faegre & Benson LLP 2200 Wells Fargo Ctr 90 S 7th St Minneapolis MN 55402-3901 Office Phone: 612-766-7000. Office Fax: 612-766-1600.*

GROSS, DAVID JONATHAN, physicist; b. Washington, Feb. 19, 1941; s. Bertram M. and Nora (Faine) G.; m. Shulamith Toaff, Mar. 30, 1962; children: Ariela, Elisheva; m. Jacquelyn Savani, Aug. 12, 2001; Miranda Savani (stepdaughter). BSc, Hebrew U., Jerusalem, 1962; PhD, U. Calif., Berkeley, 1966; Doctorate (Docteur Honoris Causa) (hon.), U. Montpellier, 2000, Hebrew U., 2001. Harvard Soc. of Fellows jr. fellow Harvard U., 1966-69; asst. prof. physics Princeton U., 1969-71, assoc. prof., 1971-73, prof., 1973-86, Eugene Higgens prof. physics, 1986—95, Jones prof. physics, 1995—97, Jones prof. physics emeritus, 1997—; dir. U. Calif., Santa Barbara, Inst. for Theoretical Physics, Santa Barbara, Calif., 1997—; prof. U. Calif., Santa Barbara, Calif., 1997—, Gluck prof. theoretical physics, 2001—. Vis. prof. CERN, Geneva, 1968—69, Geneva, 1993, Ecole Normale Superioure, Paris, 1983, Paris, 1988—89, Hebrew U., Jerusalem, 1984, Lawrence Radiation Lab., Berkeley, Calif., 1992; invited lecturer for several universities; chair, evaluation com. Scuola Internazionale Superiore di Studi Avanzati, Italy, 1994—. Assoc. editor Nuclear Physics, 1972—. Dir. Jerusalem Winter Sch., 1999—. Recipient Alfred P. Sloan fellow, 1970-74, MacArthur Prize fellow, 1987, Dirac medal, 1988, Harvey prize, Technion-Israel Inst. Tech., 2000, Oscar Klein medal, Stockholm U., 2000, grande médaille, French Academy Sciences, 2004, Golden Plate award, Acad. Achievement, 2005; co-recipient High Energy and Particle Physics prize, European Physical Soc., 2003, Nobel Prize in Physics, 2004. Fellow AAAS, Am. Phys. Soc. (J. J. Sakurai prize 1986), Am. Acad. Arts and Scis.; mem. Nat. Acad. Scis. Research, numerous publs. in field; discovered asymptotic freedom, 1973; proposal of non-Abelian gauge theories of the strong interactions, 1973, heterotic string theory, 1984; discovery of (with H. David Politzer and Frank Wilczek) the asymptotic freedom in the theory of the strong interaction. Office: Kavli Inst for Theoretical Physics Univ Calif Santa Barbara Kohn Hall 1219 Santa Barbara CA 93106 Office Phone: 805-893-7337. Office Fax: 805-893-2431. Business E-Mail: gross@kitp.ucsb.edu.*

GROSS, DAVID LEE, geologist; b. Springfield, Ill., Nov. 20, 1943; s. Carl David and Shirley Marie (Northcutt) G.; m. Claudia Cole, June 11, 1966; children: Oliver David, Alexander Lee AB, Knox Coll., 1965; MS, U. Ill., 1967, PhD, 1969. Registered profl. geologist, Ill., Calif. Asst. geologist Ill. State Geol. Survey, Champaign, 1969-73, assoc. geologist, 1973-80, geologist, 1980—, coord. environ. geology, 1979-84, head environ. studies, 1984-89, asst. chief, 1991-99, sr. geologist emeritus, 1999—. Exec. dir. Gov.'s Sci. Adv. Com., Chgo., 1989-91; bd. dirs. First State Bank, Beardstown, Ill., chmn. 2001—. Contbr. numerous articles to profl. jours. Bd. govs. Channing-Murray Found., 1973-76, pres., 1976; trustee Unitarian Universalist Ch., Urbana, 1977-80, 99-02, chmn., 1977-79, 99-01; bd. dirs. Vol. Action Ctr., 1981-85, chmn., 1984-85; bd. dirs. United Way Champaign County, 1984-89, exec. com., 1984-85, chmn. United Way Campaign, U. Ill., 1986, chair Youth Vision Coun., 2003-05; bd. dirs. Vol. Ctr., 1994-97; mem. Gov.'s Sci. Adv. Com., 1989-97; vol. summer camp counselor for teenage youth, 1984-05; bd. dirs. Ill. Prairie chpt. ARC, 1997-03. NDEA fellow, 1969 Fellow Geol. Soc. Am., AAAS; mem. Internat. Union Quaternary Rsch., Am. Quaternary Assn., Am. Inst. Profl. Geologists (pres. Ill.-Ind. sect. 1980), Ill. State Acad. Sci., Rotary (pres. Urbana, Ill. chpt. 1986-87), Columbia (Chgo.) Yacht Club, Sigma Xi. Home: 3 Flora Ct Champaign IL 61821-3216 Office: Ill State Geol Survey 615 E Peabody Dr Champaign IL 61820-6918 E-mail: DLGgeology@aol.com. *Strive for reasonable balance among family, volunteer and professional responsibilities. All are essential for a healthy life.*

GROSS, EDWARD, retired sociologist; b. Nagy Genez, Romania; s. Samuel and Dora (Levi) G.; m. Florence Rebecca Goldman, Feb. 18, 1943; children— David P., Deborah L., Teagardin. BA, U. B.C., Can., 1942; MA, U. Toronto, Ont., Can., 1945; PhD, U. Chgo., 1949; JD, U. Wash., 1991. Prof. Wash. State U., Pullman, Wash., 1947-51, 53-60; prof. U. Wash., Seattle, 1951-53, 65-89, prof. emeritus, 1990—; prof. sociology U. Minn., Mpls., 1960-65. Vis. prof. Australian Nat. U., Canberra, 1971, U. Queensland, U. New South Wales, Griffith U., Australia, 1977; invited lectr. Cen. China Poly. Inst., 1987; lectr. arts and sci. honor program U. Wash., 1998—; pres. resident coun. Ida Culver Broadview Ret. Facility, 2005-06. Author: Work and Society, 1958, Univ. Goals and Academic Power, 1968, Changes in Univ. Orgn., 1964-71, The End of a Golden Age: Higher Ed. in a Steady State, 1981, Embarrassment in Everyday Life, 1994; co-author (with A. Etzioni) Orgn. in Soc., 1985; contbg. author: Handbook of Sociology and Encyclopedia of Sociology, 2d edit.; former assoc. editor Social Problems, Symbolic Interaction, Can. Jour. Sociology; contbr. articles to profl. jour. Trustee Temple Beth Am, Seattle, 1993-97. Fulbright scholar Australia, 1977, 87. Mem.: Wash. State Bar Assn., Am. Sociol. Assn. (emeritus), Pacific Sociol. Assn. (pres. 1971, coun. 1983—85). Office: U Wash Dept Sociology Seattle WA 98195-0001

GROSS, GARY NEIL, allergist, physician; b. Fort Lewis, Wash., July 25, 1944; s. Norman Harold and Dorothy Naomi (Bercie) G.; m. Elaina Wee, Mar. 23, 1974; children: Risa, Lara. BA, U. Tex., 1967; MD, Southwestern Med. Sch., Dallas, 1969; MBA, Southern Methodist U., Dallas, 1987. Diplomate Am. Bd. Internal Medicine, Am. Bd. Allergy and Clin. Immunology. Intern U. Utah Med. Ctr. Hosp., Salt Lake City, 1969-70, resident, 1970-71; fellow Nat. Jewish Hosp., Denver, 1971-74; founding physician Dallas Allergy and Asthma Ctr., Tex., 1979—; med. dir. Pharm. Rsch. and Cons., Dallas, 1992—; clin. prof. internal medicine Southwestern Med. Sch., Dallas, 1994—. Contbr. articles to profl. jours. Bd. dirs. Am. Jewish Com., Dallas, 1990-94, Am. Lung Assn., 1978-88, Temple Emanuel Brotherhood, 1978-80. Fellow Am. Coll. Physicians (Disting. Svc. award 2003), Am. Acad. Allergy Asthma and Immunology (chmn. seminars com., 1987-88, chmn. pub. edn. com., 1989-90, Outstanding Vol. Clin. Faculty award 2004); mem. Fedn. Regional State Local Allergy Socs. (gov. reg. 5, 1992-, chmn. 1993-94), Joint Coun. Allergy Clin. Immunology (sec. bd. dirs. 1992-96, exec. v.p. 1998-). Jewish. Avocations: bicycling, skiing, photography. Office: 5499 Glen Lakes Dr Ste 100 Dallas TX 75231-4383 Office Phone: 214-691-1330. Personal E-mail: gary.gross@daac-prc.com.

GROSS, GEOFFREY FRIES, systems architect; b. Cin., Apr. 26, 1950; s. Merrill Jay and Ann Fries Gross; m. Diantha Louise Perry, May 9, 1970 (dec. July 1998); 1 child, Abraham Hart; m. Wendy Robin Levine, Aug. 12, 2000. BA in Math. cum laude, SUNY, Buffalo, 1973, MEd in Math. Instrn., 1976. Acting chmn. math. dept., instr. U. New Eng., Biddeford, Maine, 1979-80; tchr. math. Laconia (N.H.) HS, 1980-81; programmer Franklin, NH, 1982; project leader Mellen Co., Webster, NH, 1983-87; sys. engr. Analysis and Computer Sys. Inc., Burlington, Mass., 1987-90; sys. arch., project mgr. Sys. Resources Corp., Burlington, 1990-95; sr. prin. sys. arch. Raytheon, St. Petersburg, Fla., 1996—2004; day trader, 2004—. Cons. Mus. Fine Arts, Boston, 1995. Mem. Sch. Budget Com., Milford, NH, 1990—91; pres. Congregation Betenu, Amherst, NH, 1991—97; trustee Congregation B'nai Israel, St. Petersburg, 2002—05; bd. dirs. Sun Island Assn., South Pasadena, Fla., 2002—03. Mem.: N.Y. Acad. Scis., Phi Beta Kappa. Jewish. Avocations: American art, presidential campaign materials, chess, photography. Personal E-mail: grossg@tampabay.rr.com.

GROSS, IAN, academic pediatrician, neonatologist; b. Pretoria, Oct. 15, 1943; came to U.S., 1971; s. Kenneth and Gladys Bakst (Cooper) G.; m. Melanie Belman, Dec. 3, 1967; children: David Anthony, Adam Charles. BS, U. Witwatersrand, Johannesburg, Republic of South Africa, 1963, MBBCh, 1967. Diplomate Am. Bd. Pediat., Am. Bd. Neonatal-Perinatal Medicine. Rotating intern Johannesburg Gen. Hosp., 1968; pediatric resident U. Witwatersrand Hosps., Johannesburg, 1970-71, Children's Hosp. Harvard Med. Sch., Boston, 1971-72; postdoctoral fellow in pediat. Harvard Med. Sch., Boston, 1972-73; postdoctoral fellow in pediatrics Yale U., New Haven, 1973-74; asst. prof. Yale U. Sch. Medicine, New Haven, 1974-78, assoc. prof., 1978-85, prof., 1985—. Dir. newborn spl. care unit Yale-New Haven Hosp., 1982—; mem. study sect. NIH, Bethesda, Md., 1981-85; mem. adv. bd. Hood Found., Boston, 1988-94. Editor Pediat. Rsch., 1992-98, Seminars in Perinatology, 1997—; contbr. chpts. to books, numerous articles to profl. jours. Named Most Disting. Med. Grad. U. Witwatersrand, Johannesburg, 1967, Mentor of Yr., Ea. Soc. Pediatric Rsch., 2005; James Hudson Brown fellow, Yale U., 1973; rsch. grantee NIH and Am. Heart Assn. Fellow Am. Acad. Pediat.; mem. Soc. Pediatric Rsch., Am. Physiol. Soc. Avocations: bicycling, photography. Office: Yale Sch Medicine 333 Cedar St New Haven CT 06520-8064 E-mail: ian.gross@yale.edu.

GROSS, IRA KENNETH, lawyer; b. NYC, Nov. 28, 1946; s. Jerome and Hope Esther (Rubenstein) G.; m. Louise A. Gaffney, Dec. 21, 1973; children: Molly E., Katherine G., Anna G., Margaret G. BA magna cum laude, Yale U., 1968, JD, 1974. Bar: NY 1975, Mass. 1977, NY Supreme Ct. 1975, US Dist. Ct. Dist.of Mass. 1977, US Ct. of Appeals (1st cir.) 1980, US Ct. of Appeals (4th cir.) 1988, US Dist. Ct. (so. dist.) NY 1990, US Dist. Ct.(ea. dist.) NY 1993, US Ct. of Appeals (3rd cir.) 1998, US Ct. of Appeals (10th cir.) 1998. Assoc. Rosenman, Colin, Kaye, Petschek, Freund & Emil, NYC, 1974-76, Sullivan & Worcester, Boston, 1976-82, ptnr., 1982—. Instr. Harvard Law Sch., Cambridge, Mass., 1985—; judge moot ct. program Boston Coll. Law Sch., Newton, Mass., 1990—. Recipient Outstanding Achievement award pub. accommodations Wash. Lawyers Com. Civil Rights Under Law, 1991, Mass. Super Lawyer by Boston mag. 2006. Mem. Boston Bar Assn. Office: Sullivan & Worcester 1 PO Sq Boston MA 02109 Office Phone: 617-338-2823. Office Fax: 617-338-2880. E-mail: igross@sandw.com.

GROSS, JAMES HOWARD, lawyer; b. Springfield, Ohio, Sept. 21, 1941; s. Cyril James and Virginia (Stieg) G.; m. Gail Sue Helmick, July 13, 1968; children: Karin G. Cramer, David James. BA, Ohio State U., 1963; LLB, Harvard U., 1966. Bar: Ohio 1966, D.C. 1975. Assoc. Vorys, Sater, Seymour and Pease, Columbus, Ohio, 1966-75, resident ptnr. Washington, 1975-77; ptnr. Vorys, Sater, Seymour and Pease LLP, Columbus, 1975—. White House fellow, spl. asst. to sec. HUD, Washington, 1972-73; city atty. City of Bexley, Ohio, 1985—. Mem. Franklin County Rep. Cen. Com., 1973-75, Bexley City Coun., 1981-85. Lt. comdr. USNR, 1968-74. Mem. ABA, Ohio Bar Assn. (corp. law com.), Columbus Bar Assn., D.C. Bar Assn. Lutheran. Home: 5 Sessions Dr Bexley OH 43209-1440 Office: Vorys Sater Seymour and Pease LLP 52 E Gay St PO Box 1008 Columbus OH 43216-1008 Office Phone: 614-464-6231. Business E-Mail: jhgross@vssp.com.

GROSS, JOHN H., lawyer; b. Cleve., Apr. 2, 1942; BS, U. Pa., 1964; JD, George Washington U., 1967. Bar: N.Y. Asst. U.S. atty. (so. dist.) N.Y., 1969-75, asst. chief criminal divsn., 1974-75; assoc. spl. counsel U.S. Dept. Justice, 1979; ptnr. Anderson, Kill, Olick & Oshinsky, NYC; ptnr., litig. dispute resolution dept. Proskauer Rose LLP. Adj. prof. law N.Y.U., 1983-89. Mem. Assn. of the Bar of the City of N.Y. Office: Proskauer Rose LLP 1585 Broadway Fl 27 New York NY 10036-8299 E-mail: jgross@proskauer.com.

GROSS, JONATHAN LIGHT, computer scientist, mathematician, educator; b. Phila., June 11, 1941; s. Nathan K. and Henrietta E. (Light) G.; m. Susan Fay Kodner, Aug. 29, 1976; children: Aaron, Jessica, Joshua, Rena Lea, Alisa Sharon BS, M.I.T., 1964; MA, Dartmouth Coll., 1966, PhD, 1968. Instr. math. Princeton (N.J.) U., 1968-69; asst. prof. math. stats. Columbia U., NYC, 1969-72, assoc. prof., 1973-78, prof. computer sci., math. and stats., 1978—, vice-chmn. dept. computer sci., 1982-89; dir. edn. Ctr. for Advanced Tech., 1989-93. Cons. Russell Sage Found., Inst. Def. Analyses., AT&T Bell Labs., Alfred P. Sloan Found., IBM, Oak Ridge Nat. Lab.; vis. scientist Carnegie-Mellon U., Pitts., 1984-85. Co-author: Fundamental Programming Concepts, 1972, FORTRAN 77 Programming, 1978, Introduction to Computer Programming, 1979, Pascal Programming, 1982, Measuring Culture, 1985, PASCAL, 1984 FORTRAN 77 Fundamentals and Style, 1985, Topological Graph Theory, 1987, WATFIV-S Fundamental Style, 1986, Graph Theory and Its Applications, 1999; editor: Handbook of Discrete and Combinatorial Mathematics, 2000, Handbook of Graph Theory, 2004; adv. editor: Columbia U. Press, Jour. Graph Theory, Computers and Electronics, CRC Press; contbr. articles to profl. jours. Mem. exec. bd. United Jewish Fedn. of Princeton Mercer-Bucks, 2004—, United Synagogue Mid-Atlantic Region, 2005—. IBM postdoctoral fellow, 1972-73; Sloan fellow in math., 1973-75; rsch. grantee NSF, Office of Naval Rsch., Exxon Found., ARCO Found., Mellon Found., Russell Sage Found., N.Y. State Sci. and Tech. Found., Citicorp. Mem. Am. Math. Soc., Assn. Computing Machinery, Soc. Indsl. and Applied Math. (sec. discrete math. 1994-96), Jewish Ctr. of Princeton (v.p. 1997-99, pres. 2000-02). Jewish. Home: 3 Stuart Ln W Princeton Junction NJ 08550-1844 Office: Columbia U Dept Computer Sci New York NY 10027 *If I ever fail to overstate the case, please call an ambulance.*

GROSS, JOSEPH H., lawyer, educator; b. Tel Aviv, Feb. 28, 1934; s. Woolf and Mali (Timberg) G.; m. Zvia Armon, July 21, 1959; children: Raz, Aeyal, Vardit. LLB, Tel Aviv U., 1955, LLM, 1958; PhD, U. London, 1962. Bar: Israel 1959, N.Y. 1989. Legal advisor Discount Bank Investment Co., Tel Aviv, 1963-76; prof. law Tel Aviv U., 1968—, assoc. dean Law Sch., 1973-78; chmn. law firm Gross, Kleinhandler, Hodak, Halevy, Greenberg & Co., Tel Aviv, 1979—. Vis. scholar Harvard U. Law Sch., Boston, 1977; chmn. com. on mergers Govt. of Israel, 1975—77, com. to reform co. law, 1985—94, chmn. adv. bd. govt. cos., 1986—91, com. to reform tax law, 2002; chmn. Israel Bar Pub. House; bd. dirs. Ta'agidim Ltd., Sano Ltd., Carmel Holdings Co. Ltd.; chmn. transparency internat. Israel br. Bloostein-Genosar Ltd.; ct. appeals on mergers and monopolies, 1995—2000; pub. com. on taxing nonprofit orgns. Israel Income Tax Authority, 1989—90. Author: Israel's Company Law, 1970, Company Promoters, 1972, Securities Law, 1973, Directors in Government Companies, 1977, Tax Planning of Investments, 1984, Corporation Tax, 3 edits., 1987, V.A.T., 1987, Directors and Officers of Corporations, 1989, Director's Manual, 9th edit., 1999; editor: The Director in Practice, 2d edit., 1997, The New Companies Law, 1999, 3d edit., 2003, The New Tax Law, 3th edit., 2003, The Meaning of Control and Its Applications, 2003. Maj. Israeli Army, 1954-57. Mem.: N.Y. Bar Assn., Israel Bar Assn. Home: 10 Berkovitz St 64238 Tel Aviv Israel Office: 1 Azrieli Ctr 67021 Tel Aviv Israel Home Phone: 972 3 6950472; Office Phone: 972 3 6074444. Business E-Mail: joseph@gkh-law.com.

GROSS, KAREN CHARAL, lawyer; b. NYC, Nov. 25, 1940; d. Harry B. and Adele (Hook) Charal; m. Meyer A. Gross, Aug. 16, 1964; children: Dana Leslie, Jennifer P., Pamela A. AB, Barnard Coll., 1962; JD, NYU, 1965. Bar: N.Y. 1965. Atty. Wolder & Gross, NYC, 1965-78, Wolder, Gross & Yavner, NYC, 1978-86; sr. v.p. legal and bus. affairs GoodTimes Entertainment LLC, NYC, 1986—2004; of counsel Schweitzer Cornman Gross & Bondell LLP, NYC, 2005—. Editor NYU Law Rev., 1963-65. Parent liaison Ramaz Sch., N.Y.C., 1980-86; del. Dem. County Com., N.Y.C., 1988—; legal mentor to students Barnard Coll., N.Y.C. John Norton Pomeroy scholar NYU, 1963-65. Mem. Internat. Trademark Assn., Copyright Soc. USA. Avocation: travel. Office: Schweitzer Cornman Gross & Bondell LLP 292 Madison Ave New York NY 10017 Office Phone: 646-424-0770.

GROSS, KENNETH ANDREW, lawyer; b. NYC, Jan. 22, 1951; s. Robert Emanual and Gloria (Polansky) F.; m. Karin Goldsmith, June 29, 1986; 1 child, Jennifer Gail. BS cum laude, U. Bridgeport, Conn., 1972; JD, Emory U. Sch. Law, Atlanta, 1975. Bar: Ga. 1975, DC 1976, US Ct. Appeals (5th cir.) 1975, US Ct. Appeals (DC cir.) 1977, US Ct. Appeals (11th cir.) 1979, US Supreme Ct. 1978, NY 2003. Assoc. Lipshutz, Zusmann & Sikes, Atlanta, 1975-77; atty. Fed. Election Commn., Washington, 1977-78, asst. gen counsel, 1978-79, assoc. gen. counsel, 1980—86; ptnr. political law Skadden, Arps, Slate, Meagher & Flom, Washington, 1986—. Adj. prof. NYU, 2003-06; co-chmn. Practicing Law Inst. annual seminar on "Corporate Political Activities", 2006; served as appointee of former Senator Daniel P. Moynihan on the Fed. Jud. Screening Com. Author: Federal Regulations of Campaign Finance, 1980, Corporate Political Activities--Bureau of National Affairs, 2006; co-author: Ethics Handbook for Entertaining and Lobbying Pub. Officials, BNA's Corporate Political Activities; guest appearances on CNN, Fox News, NPR Radio and other media outlets. Bd. trustee Campaign Fin. Inst.; mem. exec. com., counsel Am. Coun. Young Polit. Leaders. Recipient Highest Ethics award, Coun. on Govt. Ethics Laws, 2006. Mem. ABA (std. com. election law). Home: 10 Eagle Ridge Ct Bethesda MD 20817-3922 Office: Skadden Arps Slate Meagher & Flom LLP 1440 New York Ave NW Ste 900 Washington DC 20005 Office Phone: 202-371-7007. Office Fax: 202-661-7956. Business E-Mail: kgross@skadden.com.

GROSS, LARRY PAUL, communications educator; b. Washington, Nov. 22, 1942; s. Bertram Myron and Nora (Faine) G. BA, Brandeis U., 1964; PhD, Columbia U., 1968; MA (hon.), U. Pa., 1973. Asst. prof. U. Pa., Phila., 1968-73, assoc. prof., 1973-82, prof., 1982—, Sol Worth prof., 1998—, assoc. dean for grad. studies, 1989-93, chair faculty senate, 2000-01, dep. dean, 2001—03; prof., dir. Sch. Comm., U. So. Calif.,

2003—. Author: Contested Closets: The Politics and Ethics of Outing, 1993; editor: Communications Technology and Social Policy, 1973, Between Men-Between Women book series, 1991—, Studying Visual Communication, 1981, Image Ethics, 1988, Studies in Visual Communications, 1977-85, On the Margins of Art Worlds, 1995, The Columbia Reader on Lesbians and Gay Men in Media, Society and Politics, 1999, Up From Invisibility: Lesbians, Gay Men and the Media in America, 2001; author, editor: Image Ethics in the Digital Age, 2003; assoc. editor Internat. Ency. Comm., 1989; contbr. articles to profl. jours. Chair Phila. Lesbian and Gay Task Force, 1981-2000; mem. Pa. Humanities Coun., 1985-90. Guggenheim fellow, 1998-99. Fellow Am. Anthrop. Assn. (co-chmn. rsch. group on homosexuality 1981-84); mem. Internat. Comm. Assn. (chair task force on diversity 1992—, lesbian and gay studies interest group 1993-96), Nat. Comm. Assn., Phi Beta Kappa, Sigma Xi. Home: 329 S Sycamore Los Angeles CA 90036 Office: U So Calif Annenberg Sch Los Angeles CA 90089 Home Phone: 310-306-9376; Office Phone: 213-740-3770. Business E-Mail: lpgross@usc.edu.

GROSS, LAURA ANN, marketing and communications professional, herbalist, acupuncturist; b. Kew Gardens, NY, July 11, 1948; d. Melvin Fredericks and Harriette (Levy) G. BA, Boston U., 1970; MA, Columbia U., 1974; MS, Pacific Coll. Oriental Medicine, 1996. Staff writer Am. Banker, NYC, 1974-82, assoc. editor, 1982-88; dir. fin. svcs., instns., communications Am. Express Travel/Related Svcs. Co., NYC, 1988-89; dir. sales promotion and pub. rels. Am. Express Travelers Cheque Group/Am. Express Travel Svcs., NYC, 1989-92; dir. strategic bus. comm. Am. Express Travel Related Svcs., NYC, 1992-93; pres. Strategic Comm. Cons., NYC, 1993-2000; founder Alternative Ctr. for Natural Healing, 1997—; exec. v.p. mktg. Letsgotrade, Inc., 2000-01; sr. v.p. mktg./ebusiness Muriel Siebert & Co., Inc., 2001—. Spkr. fin. svcs. and Chinese medicine. Author, editor consumer surveys and articles. Recipient editorial awards Pannell Kerr Forster, 1984, N.E. Bus. Press Editors, 1986, N.Y. Bus. Press. Editors, 1987, first Boston U. Coll. of Liberal Arts Young Alumni award, 1985. Avocations: fiction writing, travel, snorkeling.

GROSS, LAWRENCE ALAN, lawyer; b. Phila., Oct. 1, 1952; s. Herbert and Rita Lila (Garelik) G.; m. Lynda Kinsfather, May 27, 1979; 1 child, Alyssa Rachel. AB with highest honor, U. Mich., 1973, AM in Philosophy, 1978, JD magna cum laude, 1979. Bar: Pa. 1979. Assoc. Blank, Rome, Comisky & McCauley, Phila., 1979-86; v.p., gen. counsel Sungard Data Systems Inc., Wayne, Pa., 1986—2006; exec. v.p. legal, interim gen. counsel KLA-Tencor Corp., San Jose, 2006—. Bd. dirs. Sungard Data Sytems Inc. and subs. Mem. ABA, Corp. Counsel Assn., Am. Soc. Corp. Secs., Pa. Bar Assn., Phila. Bar Assn., U. Mich. Alumni Assn. Office: KLA-Tencor Corp 160 Rio Robles San Jose CA 95134*

GROSS, LEE, chef; B in Culinary Arts, Johnson & Wales U., Providence, RI; studied Macrobiotics, Kushi Inst., Becket, Mass., 1999—2001. Rounds cook Domaine Chandon; chef Boston Harbor Hotel, Al Forno Restaurant; head chef The Organic Grill, NYC, 2001; chef de cuisine Chaya, LA, 2005—. Personal chef for Gwyneth Paltrow, 2001—. Named one of LA's Rising Stars, StarChefs.com, 2006. Office: M Cafe de Chaya 7119 Melrose Ave Los Angeles CA 90046 Office Phone: 323-525-0588.*

GROSS, LEONARD, mathematics professor; PhD, U. Chicago, 1958. Prof. Yale U., 1959; rsch. fellow NSF, 1959—60; asst. prof. mathematics Cornell U., 1960—68, prof. mathematics, 1968—. Bd. mem. NSF Inst. for Mathematics & Applications, U. Minnesota; editorial bd. mem. Jour. Functional Analysis, Reviews of Mathematical Physics, Potential Analysis, Soochow Jour. of Mathematics. Recipient Senior Scientist award, Humboldt Found., 1993; grantee Guggenheim Found. fellowship, 1974—75. Fellow: Am. Acad. Arts & Sciences; mem.: Inst. of Mathematics (bd. govs. 1989—91), Am. Mathematical Soc. (co-organizer special session meeting 1998). Office: Cornell U Mathematics Dept 310 Malot Hall Ithaca NY 14853

GROSS, LEROY, retired sugar company executive; b. NYC, Aug. 11, 1926; s. Morris and Sarah (Leichter) G.; m. Betty Koch, Aug. 28, 1949; children: Michael Stephen, Kenneth Richard, Emily Jayne Gross Eider. BS in Acctg., NYU, 1948; postgrad., Fordham U., 1951-53; MBA in Acctg., NYU, 1955. With SuCrest Corp., NYC, 1948-77, internal audit mgr., 1962-65, corp. acctg. mgr., 1965-69, contr., 1969-75, asst. sec., 1971-77; v.p. NYC, 1975-77; v.p., contr. Revere Sugar Corp., 1977-86. Lectr. NYU, 1968-71; cons. in field. With USAAF, 1946-47. Mem. Inst. Internal Auditors, Nat. Assn. Accountants, Fin. Execs. Inst. Home and Office: 118 Winder Rd Yorktown VA 23693-3222 Home Phone: 757-867-6447.

GROSS, LESLIE JAY, lawyer, real estate broker, mortgage company executive; b. Coral Gables, Fla., July 24, 1944; s. Bernard Charles and Lillian (Adler) G.; m. Frances L. Londow, June 16, 1968; children: Jonathan Eric, Jason Marc. BA magna cum laude, Harvard U., 1965, JD, 1968. Bar: Fla. 1971, U.S. Dist. Ct. (so. dist.) Fla. 1971, U.S. Ct. Appeals (5th cir.) 1971, U.S. Tax Ct. 1971, U.S. Supreme Ct. 1971; registered real estate broker, registered mortgage broker. Rsch. aide Fla. 3d Dist. Ct. Appeal, Miami, Fla., 1968-69; prof. social sci. Miami-Dade Community Coll., 1969-70; assoc. Greenberg, Traurig, et al., Miami, 1969-70, Patton, Kanner, et al., Miami, 1970-71, Fromberg, Fromberg, Roth, Miami, 1971-72; ptnr. Fromberg, Fromberg, Gross, et al., Miami, 1973-88; assoc. Thornton, David, Murray, et al., Miami, 1988-94; mortgage lending investment syndication, 1994—; CEO, Comml. Capital Resources, LLC, 2003—. Atty. agt. Atty.'s Title Ins. Fund, First Am. Title, Miami, 1971-94; adj. prof. U. Miami Sch. Law, 1984; lectr. seminar Nat. Aircraft Fin. Assn., 1990. Contbr. articles to profl. jours. Mem. transp. com. Greater Miami C. of C., 1984-85; v.p., pres., bd. dirs. Kendale Homeowners Assn., Miami, 1970-81; vol. Dem. candidates in state and nat. elections, Miami, 1968, 70, 72, 87, 88; mem. Vision Coun. Land Use Task Force, Miami, 1988-89; judge Silver Knight awards Miami Herald, 1987, 92, 93, 94, 95, judge spelling bee, 1987; bd. dirs. Internat. Assn. Fin. Planning, 1983-84; founding mem., bd. dirs. The Actors Playhouse, 1987—, sec., 1990—. Mem. Harvard Law Sch. Assn., Harvard Club of Miami (v.p. 1985-90, pres. 1990-94, dir. 1985-99). Democrat. Jewish. Avocations: gardening, humorous creative writing, photography, aerobics, travel. Home: 10471 SW 126th St Miami FL 33176-4749

GROSS, MARK, lawyer, food products executive; b. 1963; BA, Dartmouth Coll.; JD, U. Pa. Law Sch. Mergers and acquisitions ptnr. Skadden, Arps, Slater, Meagher & Flom, NYC; sr. v.p. C & S Wholesale Grocers, Inc., Keene, NH, 1997—2002, gen. counsel, 1997, CFO, 2001, corp. exec. v.p., 2002, bd. dir., 1997; exec. v.p. GU Markets, 2001—03, pres., 2003; founder Surry Investment Advisors LLC, 2006—. Mem. board of dir. Monadnock Waldorf School; bd. dir. Food Industry Alliance, NY.*

GROSS, MICHAEL LAWRENCE, chemistry professor; b. St. Cloud, Minn., Nov. 6, 1940; s. Ralph J. and Margaret T. (Iten) Gross; m. Kathleen M. Trammer, June 13, 1966 (div. 1981); m. Judith L. Stewart, 1994 (dec. 2003). BA, St. John's U., St. Cloud, 1962; PhD, U. Minn., 1966. Postdoctoral fellow U. Pa., Phila., 1966-67, Purdue U., Lafayette, Ind., 1967-68; asst. prof. chemistry U. Nebr., Lincoln, 1968-72, assoc. prof., 1972-78, prof., 1978-83, 3M alumni prof., 1983-88, C. Petrus Peterson prof., 1988-94; dir. Midwest Ctr. for Mass Spectrometry, Lincoln, 1978-94; prof. chemistry, immunology, and medicine Washington U., St. Louis, 1994—. Mem. metallobiochemistry study sect. NIH, Washington, 1985-88; mem. bd. on chem. scis. and tech. NRC, 1986-91; vis. prof. Internat. Grad. Sch., U. Amsterdam, The Netherlands, 1990, U. Warwick, Eng., 1988. Editor: High Performance Mass Spectrometry, 1978, Biological Mass Spectrometry: A Tutorial, 1991, Biological Mass Spectrometry: Present and Future, 1994, Practical Electrospray Ionization Mass Spectrometry, 2001, Mass Spectrometry Revs., 1982—90, Jour. Am. Soc. Mass Spectrometry, 1990—, Ency. Mass Spectrometry, 2003—; contbr. 460 chpts. to books, numerous articles to profl. jours. Mem. instnl. rev. bd. St. Elizabeth, Lincoln Gen. and Bryan Meml. hosps., 1982-90. Recipient award for disting. tchg. U. Nebr., 1978, Pioneer award Commonwealth of Mass., 1987, Outstanding Mentor award Washington U., 2001, Sommer award U. Nebr., 2004, J.J. Thomson medal, 2006; identified as one of Top 50 Cited Chemists in World, 1984-91. Mem.: Union Concerned Scientists, Am. Soc. Mass Spectrometry, Am. Chem. Soc. (Field and Franklin award 1999, Midwest award 2002, J.J. Thomson medal for disting. contbns. to internat. mass spectrometry 2006), Phi Lambda Upsilon, Sigma Xi. Democrat. Roman Catholic. Home: 6958 Waterman Ave Saint Louis MO 63130-4332 Office: Washington U Dept Chemistry Saint Louis MO 63130 Office Phone: 314-863-2221. E-mail: mgross@wustl.edu.

GROSS, PAMELA H., editor; b. NYC; d. Bernard Walter and Rosemary Gross; m. James Arthur Finkelstein, Feb. 1, 1998; 1 child, Alexander Marks Stein. BA, Sarah Lawrence Coll., NYC; attended, Harvard U., 1982—83. Editor/co-publr. Manhattan File Mag., 1993—98; society editor Talk Mag., NYC, 2000—01; editl. dir. Avenue Mag., 2002—. Chaired Lenox Hill Hosp., NY, 2000, Southampton Hosp., NY, 2002, Parrish Art Mus., Southampton, NY, 2004, Southampton Fresh Air Home, NY, 2005; com. mem. Lenox Hill Neighborhood House, McCarton Ctr. for Autism. Mem.: Doubles, Harvard Club.

GROSS, PATRICIA A., education educator; 1 child, Stephen T. Mounkhall. EdD, Columbia U., NYC, 1991. Cert. tchr. secondary English 7-12 NY State Dept. Edn., 1966, adminstr. NY State Dept. Edn., 1989. Tchr. English, talented and gifted program Sewanhaka Ctrl. HS Dist., Elmont, NY, 1967—87; dist. chair English Bellmore-Merrick Ctrl. HS Dist., NY; assoc. prof. edn. Ursinus Coll., Collegeville, Pa., 1991—2003, U. Scranton, Pa., 2003—. Author: Joint Curriculum Design. Fellow, NDEA, 1966; scholar, NEH, 1985. Office: U Scranton Jefferson Ave Scranton PA 18411 Office Phone: 570-941-6288.

GROSS, PATRICK WALTER, information technology executive; b. Ithaca, NY, May 15, 1944; s. Eric T. B. and Catharine B. (Rohrer) G.; m. Sheila Eve Proby, Apr. 12, 1969; children: Geoffrey Philipp, Stephanie Lovell. Student, Cornell U., 1962-63; B in Engring. Sci., Rensselaer Poly. Inst., 1965; MSE in Applied Math., U. Mich., 1966; MBA, Stanford U., 1968. Cons. info. mgmt. operation Gen. Electric Co., Schnectady, 1965-67; sr. staff mem. Office Sec. Def., Washington, 1968-69, spl. asst., 1969-70; founder, prin. exec. officer, chmn. exec. com. Am. Mgmt. Systems, Inc., Arlington, Va., 1970—2002, also bd. dirs.; chmn. The Lovell Group, 2002—. Also bd. dirs.; chmn. bd. dirs. Medlantic Enterprises, Inc., 1988-94, Baker and Taylor Holdings, Inc., 1994-2003, dir., 1992-2003, Capital One Fin. Corp., 1995-, Mobius Mgmt. & Sys., Inc. Sarnott Corp., several pvt. cos., Computer Network Tech. Corp.; adv. coun. Stanford Grad. Sch. of Bus., 1999-2004, Ctr. for Strategic and Internat. Statis., 1998-2003. Trustee Washington Hosp. Ctr., 1977-87, Georgetown Med. Ctr., 2000—, Sidwell Friends Sch., 1980-88, 92-2000, Wolf Trap Found. Performing Arts, 1997-2002, Com. for Econ. Devel., Georgetown U. Hosp., 2000—, Aspen Inst., 2001—; mem. exec. com., treas. Youth for Understanding, 1984-90, 93—, vice chmn., 1996-2001, Youth for Understanding Found., Germany, 1989-2002; mem. Coun. on Competitiveness, Fed. City Coun., Washington, 1992-; mem. adv. bd. Ctr. Strategic Internat. Studies; adv. coun. Stanford Grad. Sch. Bus.; adv. bd. Stanford Inst. for Econ. Policy Rsch. Mem. Fgn. Policy Assn. (bd. govs., bd. dirs., mem. exec. com. 1977-86, 87—), World Affairs Coun. Washington (bd. dirs., founding vice chmn. 1980-91, chmn. 1991-2002), Coun. Excellence in Govt. (bd. dirs. 1996—, vice chmn. 1999—), Jamestown Found. (bd. dirs. 1997—), Aspen Inst. (bd. dirs. 2001—), Coun. Fgn. Rels., Washington Inst. Fgn. Affairs, Internat. Inst. Strategic Studies (London), World Econ. Forum (Geneva), Econ. Club Washington, Nat. Economists Club, Aspen Inst. Soc. Fellows, Pilgrims of U.S., Smithsonian Luncheon Group, Met. Club Washington, Chevy Chase Club, Univ. Club N.Y.C., Useless Bay Country Club (Wash.), Sigma Xi, Tau Beta Pi. Home: 7401 Glenbrook Rd Bethesda MD 20814-1327 Office: Lovell Group 1725 I St NW Ste 300 Washington DC 20006 Home Phone: 301-951-0173; Office Phone: 703-407-6700. E-mail: pat.gross@thelovellgroup.com.

GROSS, PAUL ALLAN, health products executive; b. Va., VA, Oct. 1, 1937; s. Albert and Cynthia (Saxe) G.; m. Gail Byrd, Nov. 19, 1966; children: Lorri, Garry, Randy. Degree, U. Richmond, 1959; BA, U. Ga., 1961; MHA, Va. Commonwealth U., 1964; cert. in hosp. adminstrn., U. Miami, Jackson Meml. Hosp. Adminstrv. resident in hosp. adminstrn. Tampa Gen. Hosp., Fla., 1964; adminstrv. asst. Dallas County Hosp. Dist., 1964-66, asst. adminstr., 1966-69, sr. asst. adminstr., 1969-70, assoc. adminstr., 1971-72; clin. assoc. prof. hosp. med. care U. Tex. Southwestern Med. Sch., 1964-72, Sch. Allied Health Scis., Dallas, 1964-72; exec. dir. Humana Inc. Suburban Hosp., Louisville, 1972-76; v.p. Fla. region Humana Inc., Miami, 1976-81; sr. v.p. Pacific Region Humana Inc., Newport Beach, Calif., 1981-84, exec. v.p., pres. hosp. div., 1984-92; ret. Humana Inc., 1992; prof., health adminstr. Va. Commonwealth U./Med. Coll. Va., 1992-95, prof. emeritus, 1996—. Nat. cons. emeritus Surgeon Gen. USAF, 1987—; vice chmn. bd. trustees MedEcon, Inc., Louisville, 1993-96, also bd. dirs.; bd. dirs. St. Anthony Pub. Co., Washington, 1993-96; advisor KBL Healthcare Inc., Comprehensive Med. Mgmt., Inc., N.Y.C. 1993-96. Contbr. articles to profl. jours. Mem., chmn. U.S. Selective Svc. System Local Bd. 154, Newport Beach, 1983, Bd. 13, Louisville, 1982-2002; bd. assocs. U. Richmond, Va., 1990-96; bd. dirs. St. Francis High Sch., Louisville, 1989-92; bd. dirs. Louisville Zool. Found., 1989-96, chmn. investment com., 1992; mem. adv. bd. Sch. Nursing, 1992-96, Spalding U., 1997; chmn. devel. bd. Jefferson County C.C., Kentuckiana Edn. and Work Force Com.; bd. dirs U.S. Selective Svc. Bd., 1981-2002, emeritus 2002—; preceptor Fellowship Program-Edn. with Industry, USAF, 1986-92; bd. dirs. Spaulding U., 1996-97, Lake/Sumter County United Way, 2005-, LifeStream Behavioral Ctr., 2004-; bd. mem. chair, Comprehensive Med. Mgmt. Inc, 1993-96; bd. dirs. Med. Coll. Va. Found., chmn. audit and applications com., 1993-2000; pres. bd. dirs. Pelican Cove Two Condo Assn.; bd. dirs. Hospice of Lake and Sumter County, Fla, 2005-, United Way of Lake and Sumter Counties, 2004-05, Lifestream Behavioral Ctr., Leesburg, Fla., 2004-05; CRA adv. bd., mem, chmn. City of Tauares Fla., 2005-. With USNR, 1955—63. Named Outstanding Adminstr., Ctrl Region Humana, 1975, 1976; recipient Humana Club award, Ctrl. Region , Louisville, 1974—76, Presdl. medallion, Va. Commonwealth U., 1995. Fellow Am. Coll. Health Care Execs. (ethics com., chmn. inv. droped sect. 1993—); mem. Tex. Hosp. Assn., Hosp. Coun. So. Calif. (chmn. multi-instnl. corp. liaison com. 1983—), United Hosp. Assn. Calif., Fedn. Am. Healthcare Sys. & Am. Hosp. Assn. (hon. life). Mailing: 1730 Peninsula Dr Tavares FL 32778 E-mail: pagross144@comcast.net.

GROSS, RICHARD A., chemist, educator; PhD in Organic-Polymer Chemistry, Polytechnic Univ., NY, 1986. Postdoctoral fellowship U. Mass., Amherst, 1986—88, asst. prof., dept. chemistry Lowell, 1988—92, assoc. prof., dept. chemistry, 1992—94, prof., dept. chemistry, 1994—98; Herman F. Mark professorship Polytechnic Univ., NY, 1998—, dir., NSF Ctr. for Biocatalysis and Bioprocessing of Macromolecules NY. Contbr. articles to peer-reviewed jours. Recipient Presdl. Green Chemistry Challenge award, US EPA, 2003. Achievements include patents in field; development of a fuel-latent plastic designed for conversion. It can be used like ordinary plastic, for packaging & other purposes, but as waste, can easily be turned into a substitute diesel fuel. Office: Polytechnic Univ Room RH 607 Six Metrotech Center Brooklyn NY 11201 Office Phone: 718-260-3024. Business E-Mail: rgross@poly.edu.*

GROSS, ROBERT ALAN, history professor; b. New Haven, Feb. 17, 1945; s. Samuel and Roslyn (Chadys) G.; m. Ann Leslie Goldman, May 22, 1966; children: Matthew Benjamin, Stephen Alexander, Eleanor Elizabeth. BA, U. Pa., 1966; MA (Woodrow Wilson nat. fellow), Columbia U., 1968, PhD, 1976; MA (hon.), Amherst Coll., 1986. Gen. sec. U.S. Student Press Assn., Washington, 1966-67; asst. editor Newsweek, NYC, 1968-70; NIMH trainee in social history Columbia U., 1970-72; adj. asst. prof. Worcester Poly. Inst., 1973-76; asst. prof. history and Am. studies Amherst Coll., 1976-80, assoc. prof., 1980-86, prof., 1986-88; prof. Am. studies and history, dir. Am. studies Coll. of William and Mary, 1988-98, Forrest D. Murden prof. Am. studies, 1992—2003; James L. and Shirley A. Draper chair of early Am. hist. U. Conn., 2003—. Prof. Am. studies U. Sussex, Brighton, England, 1981-83; vis. prof., dir. studies Ecoles des Hautes Etudes en Sciences Sociales, Paris, 1985; vis. assoc. prof. Brandeis U., 1985; core scholar New England and the Constitution, 1986-88; Am. Studies specialist U.S. Info. Agy., 1991-92; dir. NEH Summer Inst., 1993; Fulbright chair of Am. studies Odense (Denmark) U., 1998-99, Fulbright sr. specialist (Brazil), 2003; book rev. editor William and Mary quar., 1999-2002. Author: The Minutemen and Their World, 1976, 25th Anniversary edit., 2001 (Nat. Hist. Soc. Book award, Bancroft prize), Books and Libraries in Thoreau's Concord, 1988, In Debt to Shays: The Bicentennial of an Agrarian Rebellion, 1993; mem. editl. bd. Jour. Am. History, 1995-98. Bd. dirs. Rare Brook Sch., 2003—. Guggenheim fellow, 1979-80, Charles Warren fellow Harvard U., 1979-80, Amherst Coll. Trustees faculty fellow, 1979-80, Bibliog. Soc. Am. fellow, 1984, Kate and Hall Peterson fellow Am. Antiquarian Soc., 1984, Howard Found. fellow, 1988-89, Old Sturbridge Village Rsch. fellow, 1991, NEH fellow, 1994; residency Rockefeller Found.'s Study and Conf. Ctr., Bellagio, Italy, 1994; named Charles H. Watts Meml. Vis. Prof., Brown U., 2007. Fellow: Soc. Am. Historians; mem.: New Eng. History Tchrs. Assn. (Kidger award 1987), Mass. Hist. Soc., Am. Antiquarian Soc. (chair program in the history of the book in Am. culture 1993—98, coun. 1999—2002, Mellon Disting. scholar in residence 2002—03), Am. Studies Assn. (Mary C. Turple award 2001), Orgn. Am. Historians, Am. Hist. Assn., Colonial Soc. Mass., Grolier Club, Phi Beta Kappa. Democrat. Jewish. Home: 92 Krivanec Rd Willington CT 06279 Office: U Conn 241 Glenbrook Rd Unit 2103 Storrs Mansfield CT 06269-2103 Office Phone: 860-486-6088. Business E-Mail: robert.gross@uconn.edu.

GROSS, RONALD MARTIN, forest products executive, consultant; BA, Ohio State U., 1955; MBA, Harvard U., 1960. With Battelle Meml. Inst., Columbus, Ohio, 1957-58, Champion Internat., 1960-68, Can. Cellulose Co. Ltd., Vancouver, B.C., 1968-78, pres., CEO, dir., 1973-78; pres., COO ITT Rayonier, Inc., Stamford, Conn., 1978-81, pres., CEO, 1981-84, chmn., pres., CEO, 1984-96; chmn., CEO, 1996-98; chmn. emeritus, 1999—. Bd. dirs. Rayonier Inc., 1995-06, Brink's Co., 1998-06, Corn Products Internat. Office: 6 Landmark Sq Ste 400 Stamford CT 06901-2704

GROSS, STANLEY MERHL, chiropractor; b. Breese, Ill., June 27, 1953; s. Walter Frank and Priscilla Dean (Myers) G.; m. Katherine Ferlisi, June 27, 1993; children: Timothy, Carisa, Geno, Zachary. BS in Biomed., Washington U., St. Louis, 1982; PhD, Harvard U., 1983; BS in Biology, Logan Coll., Chesterfield, Mo., 1986, D Chiropractic, 1988. Diplomate Advanced Chiropractic Technique; cert. acupuncture Community Chiropractic Ctr. Pvt. practice, chief staff Community Chiropractic Ctr., O'Fallon, Mo., 1988—; instr., lectr. Logan Coll. Chiropractic, Chesterfield, Mo., 1988—. Author: Bio-Synergistic Integration, 1984, The Physician Within, 1997. Dir. Ankylosing Spondytitis Assn., St. Louis, 1988—; alderman ward II, St. Paul, Mo., 1993—. Recipient Star Scholarship Logan Alumni Assn., Chesterfield, 1987. Mem. Acad. Advancement Sci., Am. Chiropractic Assn., Toastmasters Internat. (Most Able award 1992). Avocations: gardening, swimming, fishing. Office: 305A O Fallon Plz O Fallon MO 63366 Home: 70 Timber Oaks Trl O Fallon MO 63368-8178

GROSS, STEPHEN MARK, pharmacist, dean; b. Bklyn., July 31, 1938; s. Arthur S. and Hazel F. (Marks) Gross; m. Susan S. Farber, Nov. 5, 1961; 1 child, Julie S. BS, Columbia U., 1960, MA, 1969, EdD, 1975. Registered pharmacist N.Y., 1961. Pharmacist/mgr. C.O. Bigelow Chemists Inc., NYC, 1960-65, Bigelow-Americana Chemists Inc., NYC, 1963-65; asst. to dean Coll. Pharm. Scis. Columbia U., NYC, 1965—68, asst. dean, 1968—71, assoc. dean, 1971—72, acting dean, 1972—74, dean, 1974—76; dean grad. studies Arnold & Marie Schwartz Coll. Pharmacy and Health Scis. LI U., 1976—79; dean Sch. Bus. and Pub. Adminstrn., Bklyn. Ctr. LI U., 1983—84; dean grad. studies and rsch. Conolly Coll. LI U., 1979—83, dean Faculties Pharmacy and Health Professions, 1984—88, dean Schwartz Coll. Pharmacy, 1985—, dean Sch. of Health Professions, 1990—2007. Mem. health care quality improvement steering com. Island Profl. Rev. Orgn., 1995—2000; mem. NY State Bd. Pharmacy, 1991—2001, chmn., 1997—98, extended mem., 2001—. Mem. editl. bd. U.S. Pharmacist, 1978—80, Am. Druggist, 1989—92; contbr. articles to profl. publs. Recipient numerous grants instnl. improvement. Mem.: Am. Soc. Health-Sys. Pharmacists, Nat. Cmty. Pharmacists Assn., Pharm. Soc. State N.Y., Am. Assn. Colls. Pharmacy (chmn. sect. continuing edn. 1979—80), Am. Pharm. Assn., Soc. Am. Magicians (v.p. N.Y. Assembly 1981—83, pres. 1983—84). Home: 43 Knott Dr Glen Cove NY 11542-4116 Office: LI U 1 University Plz Brooklyn NY 11201-5301 Office Phone: 718-488-1004. Business E-Mail: stephen.gross@liu.edu.

GROSS, STEVEN ROSS, lawyer; b. NYC, June 15, 1946; s. Alexander and Lola (Mandelbaum) Gross; m. Georgette Francine Kleinhaus, Dec. 14, 1968; children: Amy, Jillian. BA, Columbia U., 1968, MA, 1969; LLB, Cambridge U., 1971; JD, Yale U., 1973. Bar: US dist. Ct. (ea. and so. dists.) NY 1974. Assoc. Debevoise & Plimpton LLP, NYC, 1973-80, ptnr., 1981—, head Bankruptcy and Restructuring Practice Group. Co-author: Collier Business Workout Guide; contbr. Mem.: ABA, Assn. of Bar of City of N.Y. Jewish. Home: 145 E 74th St New York NY 10021-3225 Office: Debevoise & Plimpton 919 3rd Ave 42nd Fl New York NY 10022-3094 Office Phone: 212-909-6586. E-mail: srgross@debevoise.com.

GROSS, THEODORE LAWRENCE, university administrator, author; b. Bklyn., Dec. 4, 1930; s. David and Anna (Weisbrod) G.; m. Selma Bell, Aug. 27, 1955 (dec. 1991); children: Donna, Jonathan; m. Joellen Gross, 2001. BA, U. Maine, 1952; MA, Columbia U., NYC, 1957, PhD, 1960. Prof. English CCNY, 1958—78, chmn. dept., 1970—72, assoc. dean and dean humanities, 1972—78, v.p. instl. advancement, 1976—77; provost Capitol Campus, Pa. State U., Middletown, 1979—83; dean Sch. Letters and Sci. SUNY Coll., Purchase, 1983—88; chmn. SUNY-Purchase Westchester Sch. Partnership, 1984—88; pres. Roosevelt U., Chgo., 1988—2002, chancellor, 2002—03. Vis. prof., Fulbright scholar, Nancy, France, 1964-65, 68-69, Dept. State lectr., Nigeria, Israel, Japan, Austria. Author: Albion W. Tourgée, 1964, Thomas Nelson Page, 1967, Hawthorne, Melville, Crane: A Critical Biography, 1971, The Heroic Ideal in American Literature, 1971, Academic Turmoil: The Reality and Promise of Open Education, 1980, Partners in Education: How Colleges Can Work with Schools to Improve Teaching and Learning, 1988, Roosevelt University: From Vision to Reality, 2002, The Rise of Roosevelt University: Presidential Reflections, 2005; editor: Fiction, 1967, Dark Symphony: Negro Literature in America, 1968, Representative Men, 1969, A Nation of Nations, 1971, The Literature of American Jews, 1973; gen. editor: Studies in Language and Literature, 1974, America in Literature, 1978; contbr. also essays, revs. With AUS, 1952-54. Grantee, Rockefeller Found., 1976-77, Am. Coun. Learned Socs. Mem. MLA, PEN, Nat. Coun. Tchrs. of English (chmn. lit. com.), Century Assn., Univ. Club, Chgo. Club. Home: 1100 N Lake Shore Dr Chicago IL 60611-1070 Office Phone: 312-341-2397. Personal E-mail: ted.gross@gmail.com. Business E-Mail: tgross@rcn.com.

GROSS, WILLIAM H. (BILL GROSS), financial analyst, investment company executive; b. Middletown, Ohio, Apr. 13, 1944; m. Sue Gross; children: Jeff, Jennifer, Nick. BA in Psychology, Duke U., 1966; MBA in Fin., UCLA, 1971. Chartered Fin. Analyst. Investment analyst Pacific Mut. Life Ins. Co., Newport Beach, Calif., 1971-73, sr. analyst, 1973-76, asst. v.p., Fixed Income Securities, 1976-78, 2d v.p., Fixed Income Securities, 1978-80, v.p. Fixed Income Securities, 1980-82; from mng. dir. to chief investment officer Pacific Investment Mgmt. Co. (PIMCO) subs. Pacific Mut. Life Ins. Co., Newport Beach, Calif., 1982—. Regular panelist Wall Street Week with Louis Rukeyser TV program. Author: Everything You've Heard About Investing Is Wrong!, 1997, Bill Gross on Investing, 1998. Served tour of duty USN, Vietnam. Named one of Forbes' Richest Americans, 2006; recipient Fixed Income Mgr. of the Year, Morningstar, 1998, 2000, Disting. Svc. award, Bond Market Assn., 2000. Mem. L.A. Soc. Fin. Analysts. Office: 840 Newport Center Dr Newport Beach CA 92660-6310*

GROSSBERG, GEORGE THOMAS, psychiatrist, educator; b. Hungary, Aug. 20, 1948; came to the U.S., 1957; s. Henry and Barbara (Rothman) G.; m. Darla Jean Brown, June 13, 1976; children: Jonathan, Anna-Leah, Aviva, Aliza Rebecca, Jeremy. BA, Yeshiva U., 1971; MD, St. Louis U., 1975. Diplomate Am. Bd. Psychiatry and Neurology in Psychiatry and Geriatric Psychiatry. Chief resident in psychiatry St. Louis U., 1978-79, instr., 1979-81, asst. prof., 1982-86, assoc. prof., 1986-90, prof., 1990-98, Samuel W. Fordyce prof. and chmn. dept. psychiatry, 1995-98, Samuel w. Fordyce prof., dir. divsn. geriat. psychiatry, 1998—. Cons. on aging U.S. VA Hosps. Assn., Washington, 1990—. Contbr. articles to profl. jours. Adv. bd. St. Louis Alzheimers Assn., 1983-, St. Louis Sr. Olympics, 1998-; bd. dir. St. Louis Jewish Cmty. Ctr., 2000-. Recipient Pub. Svc. award, St. Louis Alzheimers Assn., 1989, Donovan-Sheer award, St. Louis Mental Health Assn., 1999, Fleischman-Hilliard award, Jewish Ctr. for Aged, 2000, Physician of Year award, Mo. Adult Daycare Assn., 2001. Mem. Am. Assn. Geriat. Psychiatry (pres. 1989-90), Am. Psychiat. Assn. (cons. on aging 1990—, Falk fellow 1977-79), Am. Geriat. Soc., Gerontol. Soc. Am., Internat. Psychogeriat. Assn. (treas. 1997—, pres. 2003-05). Avocations: antique collectibles, art, skiing. Office: Saint Louis U Sch Medicine 1438 S Grand Saint Louis MO 63104-1016 Office Phone: 314-977-4850. Business E-Mail: grossbgt@slu.edu.

GROSSBERG, MARC ELIAS, lawyer; b. Houston, Dec. 26, 1940; s. Sylvester and Leah (Hochman) G.; m. Eva M. Wolski, Jan. 3, 1981; 1 child, Nicole; children from previous marriage: Lee Ann Grossberg, Toni Oreck. BS in Polit. Sci., U. Houston, 1961; JD with honors, U. Tex., 1965. Bar: Tex. 1965, Calif. 1966, NY 2006, US Supreme Ct. 1980; bd. cert. fed. income taxation, Tex. Acct. Brochstein Toomim & Co CPAs (now Deloitte Touche), Houston, 1961-62; law clk. hon. Walter Ely US Ct. Appeals (9th cir.), LA, 1965-66; assoc. Fulbright & Jaworski, Houston, 1966-71; ptnr. Schlanger Mills Mayer & Grossberg, LLP, Houston, 1974-99, Thompson & Knight LLP, Houston, 1999—. Pres. Inprint, Inc., 2000—02, chmn. bd. dirs., 2002—04. Articles editor: Tex. Law Rev. Advanceman, speech writer 1968 Hubert Humphrey Presdl. Campaign; pres. Tex. Bill of Rights Found., Houston, 1971-72, Jewish Family Svc., Houston, 1986-87, U. Tex. Law Rev. Assn.; commr. Housing Authority City of Houston, 1974-78. Mem. ABA (tax sect. and litig. sects.), Order of Coif. Democrat. Jewish. Avocations: writing, reading, exercise. Office: Thompson & Knight LLP Ste 3300 333 Clay St Houston TX 77002 Office Phone: 713-928-7571. Business E-Mail: marc.grossberg@tklaw.com.

GROSSBERG, MICHAEL LEE, film critic, writer; b. Houston, Sept. 7, 1952; s. Fred Samuel and Esther R. (Rosenstein) G. BA, U. Tex., 1979, BS in Journalism, 1983. Film, theater critic, reporter Victor Valley Daily News, Victorville, Calif., 1983-85; film, theater critic Columbus (Ohio) Dispatch, 1985-87, theater critic, 1987—. Co-founder Free Press Assn., Mencken awards for outstanding journalism, dir., 1981-94. Contbr. Otis Guernsey/Burns Mantle Theater Yearbook: Best Plays, 1993-02; regional columnist Backstage, 1997—. Recipient First Place, Best Arts Reporting, Ohio SPJ Awards, 2002, 2003, Cleve. Press Club, 2003. Mem. Outer Critics Cir., Am. Theatre Critics Assn. (chmn. awards new plays com. 1993-99, exec. com. 1996-2002, vice chmn. 2001-02), Libertarian Futurist Soc. (chmn. Prometheus award judges com. 1997-, pres. bd. 1999-2002, bd. sec. 2003-). Avocations: reading, travel, meditation, public speaking. Home: 3164 Plymouth Pl Columbus OH 43213-4236 Office: Columbus Dispatch 34 S 3rd St Columbus OH 43215-4241 Office Phone: 614-461-5266. Personal E-mail: mikegrossb@aol.com. Business E-Mail: mgrossberg@dispatch.com.

GROSSER, BERNARD IRVING, psychiatrist, educator; b. Boston, Apr. 19, 1929; s. John and Katherine (Russman) G.; children: Steven, Mark, Minda; m. Karen Grosser. BA, U. Mass., Amherst, 1950; MS, U. Mich., Ann Arbor, 1953; MD, Case Western Res. U., Cleve., 1959. Diplomate Am. Bd. Psychiatry and Neurology. Intern U. Utah, 1959-60, resident in psychiatry, 1960-65; asst. prof. psychiatry U. Utah Sch. Medicine, Salt Lake City, 1967-71, assoc. prof., 1971-75, prof., 1975—, chmn. dept., 1978—2007. Mem. pre-clin. and clin. psychopharm. rev. com. NIMH, Washington, 1974-79, 80-84, mem. internat. sci. adv. bd., 1984-88; mem. merit rev. bd. VA, Washington, 1988-91; sr. sci. advisor Alcohol, Drug Abuse and Mental Health Adminstrn., Washington, 1987-88; ad hoc mem. Mental Health Clin. Rsch. Ctr. rev. com. NIMH, 1997, ad hoc mem. mental health clin. contracts rev. com., 1998, ad hoc mem. spl. emphasis panel, 2000-06; rev. panel R13, 2005, R03, 2006. Contbr. chpts. to books, articles to profl. jours. Capt. USAF, 1965-67. Grantee NIMH, 1959-84, FDA, 1985-88; recipient Exemplary psychiatrist award Nat. Alliance for Mentally Ill, 1997. Fellow Am. Psychiat. Assn. (disting. life); mem. Internat. Soc. Psychoneuroendocrinology (treas. 1974-88), Utah Psychiat. Assn. (pres. 1995-96), Psychiat. Rsch. Soc. (pres. 1986-87), Am. Coll. Neuropsychopharmacology, Soc. Neurosci., NY Acad. Scis., Collegium Internat. Neuro-psychopharmacologicum, Am. Assn. Psychiatry Dept. Chairmen (coun. 1997-2005, sec.-treas. 2005-06). Republican. Jewish. Home: 511 Perrys Hollow Rd Salt Lake City UT 84103-4245 Office: U Utah Sch Medicine Dept Psychiatry 50 N Medical Dr Salt Lake City UT 84132-0001 Office Phone: 801-581-4888. Business E-Mail: bernard.grosser@hsc.utah.edu.

GROSSER, T.J., not-for-profit fundraiser; b. Milw., Oct. 17, 1938; s. Owen Henry and Ethel Clare (Hathazy) G.; m. Mary Janet McClanahan, Apr. 3, 1976; children: Paul Howard, Julie Anne, Philip Owen, Peter John, Elizabeth Michelle. BA, U. Wis., 1958, MA, 1962, EdD, 1971; DD (hon.), Union Theol. Sem., Richmond, Va., 1972. Min. edn. Cross Luth. Ch., Milw., 1957-62; assoc. Christ Luth. Ch., Oshkosh, Wis., 1962-65; preacher/tchr. Trinity Luth. Ch., Santa Barbara, Calif., 1966-71; pres. Amigos de las Ams., Houston, 1972-79, Vols. in Internat. Svc. & Awareness, LA, 1980-84; v.p. Pacific Clinics, Pasadena, Calif., 1985-87; pres., CEO Children's Aid Internat., San Diego, 1987-97, Angelcare, 1998—. Bd. dirs. Am. Devel. Found., Washington, 1981-95; bd. dirs., pres. End Hunger Network, L.A., 1983-87; bd. dirs., v.p. Ind. Charities of Am., San Francisco, pres., 1988—; bd. dirs. Children's Charities Am.; advisor numerous internat. and religious agys. Contbr. 200 articles to profl. jours. Advisor African Refugee Ctr., L.A., 1989—; worker priest Hope Luth. Ch., Hollywood, Calif., 1983—. Named Educator of Yr. Am. Luth. Ch., Mpls., 1966, exec. of Yr. Coun. Internat. Vol. Orgn., Geneva, 1975, 76; recipient Papal medal Pope John Paul II, Rome, 1979. Mem. Fund Raising Execs., Rotary (Paul Harris fellow 1987). Democrat. Avocations: reading, speaking, travel, promoting internat. adoptions. Home: 1146 San Lori Ln El Cajon CA 92019 Office: Anglecare PO Box 600370 San Diego CA 92160-0370 Office Phone: 619-795-6234. E-mail: tjgrosser@angelcare.org.

GROSSETT, DEBORAH LOU, psychologist, consultant; b. Alma, Mich., Feb. 16, 1957; d. Charles M. and Margaret A. (Roethlisberger) Grossett, Charles M. and Margaret A. (Roethlisberger) Grossett. BS, Alma Coll., Mich., 1979; MA, Western Mich. U., Kalamazoo, 1981, PhD, 1984. Lic. psychologist, Tex.; cert. in diagnostic evaluation, Tex.; bd. cert. behavior analyst, Tex. Grad. rsch. and tchg. asst. Western Mich. U., 1979-84; asst. group home supr., cmty. outreach Residential Opportunities, Kalamazoo, 1982-84; psychologist Richmond State Sch., Tex., 1984-87, Shapiro Devel. Ctr., Kankakee, Ill., 1987-88; clin. coord. Monroe Devel. Ctr., Rochester, NY, 1988; chief psychologist Denton State Sch., Tex., 1989-90; dir. psychol./behavioral svcs. Ctr. for the Retarded, Houston, 1990—2002; psychologist Mental Health and Mental Retardation Authority of Harris County, Houston, 2002—, Behavior Treatment and Tng. Ctr., 2005—06; pvt. practice, 2004—. Behavioral cons. Ctr. for Developmentally Disabled Adults, Kalamazoo, 1984, Goodman-Wade Enterprises, Houston, 1987; instr. psychology Houston C.C., 1985-86, U. Houston-Clear Lake, 1987, 92, 95—. Contbr. chpt. to book, articles to profl. jours. Western Mich. U. fellow, 1984. Mem. Am. Psychol. Assn., Am. Assn. on Mental Retardation, Assn. for Behavior Analysis (chair Outreach Bd. 1989-91), Tex. Assn. for Behavior Analysis (bd. dirs. 1989-91, program chair 1996, pres. 1997). Democrat. Presbyterian. Avocations: golf, camping, gardening. Home: 9750 Ravensworth Dr Houston TX 77031-3130 Office: MHMRA Harris County 7011 SW Freeway Houston TX 77074 Office Phone: 713-970-7129. Business E-Mail: deborah.grossett@mhmraharris.org.

GROSSI, JASON, mechanical engineer, consultant; b. Greenville, Miss., 1976; Degree in Mech. Engring., Miss. State U., Starkville, 2000. Registered profl. engr., Miss., 2006. Mech. engr. Cooke, Douglass, Farr and Lemons, Ltd., Jackson, Miss., 2001—. Mem.: ASHRAE (assoc.; pres. 2006—07). Office: Cooke Douglass Farr and Lemons LTD 3780 Interstate 55 North Jackson MS 39211 Home Phone: 601-206-5378; Office Phone: 601-366-3110. Business E-Mail: jgrossi@cdfl.com.

GROSSI, LINDA MARIE, elementary school educator; b. Providence, Jan. 27, 1955; d. Francesco and Helen Marie Grossi; children: Anna Lee Cogean, Karena Lyn Cogean, Joseph William Cogean Jr. BS in Health Sci. and Phys. Edn., RI Coll., Providence, 1995, MEd, 2004. Cert. adapted phys. edn. RI Dept. Edn., nonviolent crisis prevention Crisis Prevention Inst., Inc., teach to change Americorps. Camp dir. Girl Scouts RI, Inc., Providence, 1990—93; health and phys. ed. tchr. Cranston Sch. Dept., RI, 1995—97, Providence Sch. Dept., 1998—; instr. Bristol C.C., Fall River, Mass., 2000—. Leader trainer Girl Scouts RI, Inc., 1994—2002; grad., active mem. Warwick Citizen's Police Acad., RI, 2005—06. Recipient Sr. Departmental award, RI Coll., 1996, Project Sch. Spirit award, Mayor David Ciccilini, City of Providence, 2004, 25 Yrs. Svc. award, Girl Scouts RI, Inc., 1997; grantee Go Girls award, Nat. Assn. for Girls and Women in Sports, 2006. Mem.: AAHPERD, Am. Assn. Health Edn., Nat. Assn. Sports and Phys. Edn., RI Assn. Health, Phys. Edn., Recreation and Dance (treas. 2004—, grantee 2005—06), Warwick Citizen's Police Acad. (v.p. 2005—06), Kappa Delta Pi. Office: Gilbert Stuart Mid Sch 188 Princeton Ave Providence RI 02888 Home Phone: 401-463-6432; Office Phone: 401-456-9340. Office Fax: 401-453-8659. Personal E-mail: physedtchrri@aol.com. Business E-Mail: linda.grossi@ppsd.org.

GROSSMAN, BARBARA, artist, educator; b. NYC, Nov. 10, 1943; d. Emil Carl and Rose (Lehrberger) G.; m. Charles F. Cajori, June 23, 1967; 1 child, Nicole Antonia. BFA, Cooper Union, 1965; postgrad., Academie der Kunst, Munich, 1967-68. Instr. Westover Sch., Middlebury, Conn., 1975, 81, Mattatuck Mus., Waterbury, Conn., 1978-80, Tunxis Community Coll., Farmington, Conn., 1981, Washington (Conn.) Art Assn., 1974-77, 1992, 1996, 2002; resident faculty Chautauqua (N.Y.) Instn., 1987—90, 1992, 1996, 1999, 2001, 2002, 2006, 2007, N.Y. Studio Sch., 1989—90, 1993—94, 1996, 1998, 2001; resident critic Vt. Studio Ctr., Johnson, 1991-94, 95; tchr. MFA program Vt. Coll. Norwich U., Montpelier, Vt., 1991—. Vis. critic summer program Caumsett-Queens Coll., Huntington, N.Y., 1988, Hampshire Coll., Amherst, Mass., 1992, Dartmouth Coll., Hanover, N.H., 1992, 2002; adj. prof. U. Hartford, 1992—; vis. critic, 1986-2005, Sch. of Arch. Yale U., 1986-2005, Bklyn. Coll., 2002, Grad. Sch. Fine Arts U. Pa., 1994-2000; vis. critic Am. U., Washington, 1997, 2003; vis. prof. Knox Coll., Galesburg, Ill., 1999, Brandeis U., 1999, 2004; adj. prof. We. Conn. State U., 1983-94, Lafayette Coll., 2001, We. Conn. State U., 2002, U. Wash., 2002, U. Utah-Salt Lake, 2002, Bklyn. Coll., 2002, Union Coll., 2003, Hollins U. Roanoke, 2003; MFA faculty, Western Carolina U., 2004-06; artist in res./faculty, Hollins U., 2003; master class Nat. Acad. Sch. Fine Arts, 2005, faculty, grad. critic Yale Sch. Art, 2003, 05, Internat. Sch. Printing, Drawing & Sculpture, 2007; juror Masur Mus. Art, Monroe, La., 2005, Mattatuck Mus., Conn., 2006; vis. critic MFA program Boston U., 2005, 07; lectr. in field. One woman shows include Lyman Allyn Mus., New London, 1977, Mattatuck Mus., Waterbury, 1979, Washington Art Assn., Washington Depot, Conn., 1985, Bowery Gallery, N.Y.C., 1973, 77, 81, 85, 88, 92, 95, 98, 2001, 2007, Paessagio Gallery, Hartford, Conn., 1991, Hurlbutt Gallery, Greenwich, Conn., 1994, Pa. Sch. of Art and Design, Lancaster, 1996, Hollins Coll., Roanoke, Va., 1997, Wayne Arts Ctr., Wayne, Pa., 2000, Jaffe Fried & Strays Galleries, 2002, Dartmouth Coll., 2002, Hollins U., Roanoke, Va. 2003, Union Coll., Schenecktady, NY, 2003, New Arts Gallery, Litchfield, Conn., 2004, Washington & Lee U. Dupont Gallery, 2005, Taft Sch., Conn., 2006, Bowery Gallery, N.Y., 2007; exhibited in group shows at Wadsworth Atheneum, 1983, Coll. of William and Mary, 1987, Nat. Acad. Mus., 1986, 90, 92, 94, 97, 98, 99, 2000-04, Guamann Cicchino Gallery, 1990, Bachelier Cardonsky, Kent, Conn. 1990, 92, 96, 2006, N.Y. Studio Sch., 1974, 76, 89, 93, 95, Ind. U., 1987, Margaret Lipworth Fine Art, 1991, Bryn Mawr (Pa.) Coll., 1993, Muscarelle Mus. of Art, Williamsburg, Va., 1994, Munson Gallery, New Haven, Conn., 1995, U. Pa., Phila., 1995, 96, Nat. Acad., N.Y., 1986, 90, 92, 94, 97, 98, 2001, 02, 03, U. Hawaii, Hilo, 1997, Western Carolina U., Cullowhee, 1998, Mangel Gallery, Phila., 1998, Marymount Coll., Tarrytown, N.Y., 1999, 55 Mercer St. Gallery, 2000, Ct. Commn. Arts, 2002, Andrews Gallery, William & Mary Coll., 2002, Wayne Art Ctr., 2002, Wash. Art. Assn., 2003, New Arts Gallery, Litchfield, Conn., 2004, 05, Westport Arts Ctr., Conn., 2005, The Taft Sch., 2006; solo exhbns. include Hollins U., 2003, Atrium Gallery, Union Coll., Schenectady, 2003, New Arts Gallery, Litchfield, Conn., 2004, A Survey, 2004-05: Wright State U., Dayton, Ohio, Lafayette Coll., Easton, Pa., Wash. & Lee Coll., Lexington, Va., N.Y. Studio Sch.; group exhbns. include Wash. Art Assn. Painting on Paper, 2003, Paessagio Gallery, W. Hartford, Conn., Spring Print Exhbn., 2004, Marymount Coll., Tarrytown, N.Y. Women By Women, 2004, Lohin-Geduld, N.Y., Languor, 2004. Participant applied arts adv. com. Tunxis Community Coll., 1979-84, participant art program State of Conn. Evaluation Team, 1984; co-chair exhibition com. Washington Art Assn., 1988—; chair book selection com. Oliver Wolcott Libr., Litchfield, 1984-89; sec., founding mem. Bowery Gallery, 1969—; coun. mem. exhbn. com. Nat. Acad. Mus., 2006-07. Fulbright/Hayes grantee, 1967-68, Conn. Commn. on the Arts grantee, 1978-79, 2002, Ingram Merrill Found. grantee, 1982-83; recipient Grumbacher Art award and Gold medal, 1995, Adolph & Clara Obrie prize Nat. Acad., 2000, Henry Ward Ranger Purchase award Nat. Acad., 2001. Mem. Washington Art Assn. (trustee 1985—), Coll. Art Assn., Nat. Acad. Mus. (award for painting 1995). Mailing: c/o Bowery Gallery 530 West 25th St New York NY 10001 Personal E-mail: barbaragrossman@earthlink.net.

GROSSMAN, BONNIE, art gallery director; m. Sy Grossman. Former kindergarten teacher; founder The Ames Gallery, Berkeley, Calif., 1970—. Lectr. on Am. folk art and outsider art. Exec. prod., co-dir., prod. nine TV programs on Calif. artists; contbr. articles to profl. publs. Avocations: cake sculpture, knitting. Office: The Ames Gallery 2661 Cedar St Berkeley CA 94708 Home Phone: 510-549-1055; Office Phone: 510-845-4949. Office Fax: 510-845-6219. E-mail: amesgal@comcast.net.

GROSSMAN, CAROLYN SYLVIA CORT, retired elementary school educator; b. Cleve., Apr. 26, 1928; d. Louis J. and Esther (Matyas) Cort; m. Melvin J. Grossman, Aug. 7, 1949; children: Richard, Susan, Elaine. BS in Edn., Flora Stone Mather Coll., 1949; MS in Edn., Kent State U., 1974. Tchr. Columbus City Schs., Ohio, 1949—52; tchr. presch. Jewish Cmty. Ctr., Cleve., 1965—68, Carol Nursery, University Heights, Ohio, 1968—70; tchr. Cleveland Heights Schs., Ohio, 1970—93; ret., 1993. Bd. dirs., officer, pres. S. Euclid Lyndhurst (Ohio) LWV, 1957-74; coord. John W. Raper Open Sch., Cleve., 1965-73; bd. dirs. Greater Cleve. Tchr. Ctr., 1974-80; founder, pres., bd. dirs. Heights Parent Ctr., Cleveland Heights, 1975-80, hon. life trustee, 1985; co-chair Hello Israel program Nat. Coun. Jewish Women, Cleve., 1995-00, chair, 2000—. Martha Holden Jennings Found. scholar, 1975; recipient Achievement award City of University Heights, 1992, Arline B. Pritcher award Nat. Coun. Jewish Women-Cleve. Sect., 1998, Irene Zehman award Women's Divsn. Jewish Comty. Fedn. Cleve., 2007; honoree Carolyn Grossman award Heights Parent Ctr., 2003. Mem. Cleve. Heights Tchrs. Union (v.p. 1985-90, Ellen Krebs award 1983), Heights Ret. Tchrs. (founder, officer, bd. dirs. 1993-96). Jewish.

GROSSMAN, CISSY, curator, art historian, appraiser; b. NYC, 1932; BA, Lehman Coll., NYC, 1972; MA in Art History, Hunter Coll., NYC, 1979; PhD in Art History, CUNY, 1998. Asst. curator judaica The Jewish Mus., NYC, 1972-79; lectr. art history Rutgers U., New Brunswick, N.J., 1978-86; lectr. George Washington U., Washington, D.C., 1979; curator Cen. Synagogue, NYC, 1986-98; Judaica appraiser NYC, 1992—. Sr. rschr. Mus. of Jewish Heritage, NYC, 1992—; cons. curator Cong. Emanu-El, NY, 1980-89; cons. in field. Author: A Temple Treasury, 1989, A Jewish Family's Book of Days, 1989; curator, author catalog The Collector's Room: Selections From the Michael and Judy Steinhardt Collection, 1993; curator Fragments of Greatness, Walters Art Gallery, Balt., Americana from The Jewish Mus., NYC. Bd. dirs. Grad. Ctr. for Jewish Art, Jerusalem. Mem. Am. Assn. Mus., Appraisers Assn. Am. E-mail: cissyg@nyc.rr.com.

GROSSMAN, CLAUDIO M., dean, law educator; b. Valparaiso, Chile, Nov. 26, 1947; came to U.S., 1982; s. David and Berta (Guiloff) G.; m. Irene Klinger, Aug. 14, 1971; children: Sandra, Nienke. DSc in Law, U. Amsterdam, The Netherlands, 1980; JD, U. Chile, 1971. Dir., Internat. Legal Studies Prog. Washington Coll. Law, Am. U., 1983—93, acting dean, 1993, dean grad. studies, 1994, dean, 1995—, Prof. Raymond Geraldson Scholar of Internat. and Humanitarian Law., 1985—. Coun. mem. Inter-Am. Inst. Human Rights; Leo Goodwin Disting. Vis. Prof. NOVA Southeastern Sch. Law, 2000; pres. Coll. of Am., 2003. Mem., vice chmn. UN Com., 2004; adv. bd. Latino and Latin Am. Inst. of the Am. Jewish Commn., 2005. Recipient Immigrant Achievement Award, D.C. Chap. Am. Immigration Lawyers Assn. and Internat. Law Soc. of Georgetown U. Law Ctr., 1996, René Cassin award, 1997, Henry LeRoy Jones Award, Washington Foreign Law Soc., 1999, Outstanding Dean of Yr. Award, Nat. Assn. for Pub. Interest Law, 2000, Chapultepec Grand Prize, Inter-Am. Press Assn (IAPA), 2002. Fellow: Am. Bar Found.; mem.: ABA (mem. Task Force on UN 2003—, chair nominating com. 2003—), Assn. Am. Law Schs., Orgn. Am. States (IACHR) (mem. Inter-Am. Commn. on Human Rights 1993—2001, pres. 1996—97, 2001), Inter-Am. Bar Assn. (coun. 1989—, gen. rapporteur 1992). Office: Washington Coll Law Suite 366 4801 Massachusetts Ave NW Washington DC 20016-8001

GROSSMAN, DAN STEVEN, lawyer; b. NYC, Apr. 6, 1953; s. George M. and Jeanne L. (Stickle) G.; m. Patrice Irene Michaelson, June 27, 1976; children: Deborah, Andrea. BA, SUNY, Albany, 1975; JD, Albany Law Sch., 1978; LLM, Georgetown Law Ctr., 1980. Bar: D.C. 1978, N.Y. 1979. Law clk. to judge U.S. Tax Ct., Washington, 1978-80; assoc. Webster and Sheffield, NYC, 1980-84, Finley Kumble Wagner, NYC, 1984-87, Willkie Farr and Gallagher, NYC, 1987-90, ptnr., 1991—. Mem. ABA (tax sect.), N.Y. State Bar Assn. (tax sect.), Assn. of Bar of City of N.Y., D.C. Bar Assn. Office: Willkie Farr and Gallagher 787 7th Ave New York NY 10019-6018 Office Phone: 212-728-8226. Business E-Mail: dgrossman@willkie.com.

GROSSMAN, DANIEL V, investor; b. NY, NY, May 21, 1941; s. Nathan F and Rose G Grossman; m. Martha F Fine, Dec. 10, 1967; children: James B(dec.), Kate H. BA magna cum laude, Harvard Coll., 1958—62; JD cum laude, Harvard Law Sch., 1962—65. Bar: State of NY 1966. Ptnr. Holtzmann, Wise & Shepard, NYC, 1970—80, Werbel, Grossman & McMillin, NYC, 1981—88; chmn. Canfield Technologies, Inc., Sayreville, NJ, 1986—2000; co-founder and exec. v.p. Cytopharm, Inc., Menlo Park, Calif., 1988—; chmn. Tridan Internat., Inc., Danville, Ill., 1989—2000, KW Parts Inc., Pompano Beach, Fla., 1993—, Tech Comm, Inc., Sunrise, Fla., 1997—; founder & chmn. Ind. Precision, Inc., Crawfordsville, Ind., 1998—2000; chmn. Friends Mktg. Inc., Glastonbury, Conn., 2003—. Office: KW Parts Inc 2504 NW 19th St Pompano Beach FL 33069 Home Phone: 561-278-5646; Office Phone: 954-973-8400.

GROSSMAN, EDWARD JEROME, music educator, composer; b. Denver, Feb. 8, 1947; s. Sydney Harold and Adeline Elizabeth (Davis) Grossman. BA with distinction, U. Colo., Boulder, 1969; JD, U. Denver, 1979. Pvt. piano tchr., 1989—. Author: (piano solo) Bangkok Market (selection of Nat. Fedn. Music Clubs Festivals Bull., 2004), 7 other piano solos. Recipient Am. Jurisprudence award, 1968. Mem.: Music Tchrs. Assn. of Calif. (pres. San Fernando East Valley br. 2000—03), Calif. Bar Assn., Colo. Bar Assn, Phi Beta Kappa.

GROSSMAN, ELMER ROY, pediatrician; b. LA, Jan. 30, 1929; s. Harry and Reta (Frankel) G.; m. Rosalind Nagin, June 24, 1951 (div. 1976); children: Deena, Marianna; m. Pamela Canfield Antoncich, July 29, 1976; stepchildren: Camilla Sutter, Michael A. Antoncich. AB, U. Calif.-Berkeley, 1949; MD, U. Calif. Sch. Medicine, San Francisco, 1953. Intern Orange County Gen. Hosp., Orange, Calif., 1953-54; resident U. Calif. Hosps., San Francisco, 1957-59; practice medicine specializing in pediatrics Berkeley Pediatric Med. Group, Calif., 1959-92. Assoc. clin. prof. health and med. scis. U. Calif., Berkeley, 1978-80; clin. prof. pediat. emeritus U. Calif. Sch. Medicine, San Francisco; chmn. dept. pediat. Alta Bates Hosp., Berkeley, 1972-74, chmn. infant care ethics com., 1984-90. Author: Everyday Pediatrics, 1993, Everyday Pediatrics for Parents, 1996; columnist The Everyday Pediatrician; contbr. articles to nat. mags. Mem. Berkeley Schs. Master Plan Com., 1966—68, Berkeley Schs. Child Care Com., 1968—70, Berkeley Cmty. Environ. Adv. Commn., 2000—02, Berkeley Cmty. Health Commn., 2002; pres. Temple Beth El, Berkeley, 1970—72. Served to capt USAF, 1954—56. Fellow Am. Acad. Pediatrics; mem. Alameda-Contra Costa Med. Assn., Physicians for Social Responsibility, Physicians for a Nat. Health Program. Democrat. Jewish. Avocations: wine making, gardening. Home and Office: 899 Euclid Ave Berkeley CA 94708-1305 Office Phone: 510-526-9614. Personal E-mail: elmer@grossmanfamily.com.

GROSSMAN, ESTA S., biology professor; b. NYC, Mar. 1, 1945; d. Max and Anne Katz Shaftel; m. Lawrence Grossman, Dec. 27, 1970; 1 child, Daniel Alan. BA in Biology, Brown U., Providence, RI; MA in Biology, CUNY, NYC; MSW, U. Mich., Ann Arbor. Tchr. biology Hewlett H.S., NY; tchr. sci. Ramona Intermediate Sch., La Verne, Calif.; instr., biology Mt. San Antonio Coll., Walnut, Calif., Washtenaw C.C., Ann Arbor, Mich., co-chmn. dept. biology. Recipient Best Tchr. award, Washtenaw C.C., 1980. Mem.: Mich. Edn. Assn. Office: Washtenaw CC 4800 E Huron River Dr Ann Arbor MI 48104 Office Phone: 734-973-3409.

GROSSMAN, FRANCES KAPLAN, psychologist; b. Newport News, Va., May 28, 1939; d. Rubin H. and Beatrice (Fischlowitz) Kaplan; m. Henry Grossman, July 26, 1970; children: Jennifer, Benjamin. BA, Oberlin Coll., Ohio, 1961; MS, PhD, Yale U., 1965. Diplomate Am. Bd. Profl. Psychology. Asst. prof. Yale U., New Haven, 1965-69, Boston U., 1969-71, assoc. prof. psychology, 1971-82, prof. psychology, 1982—2002, prof. emeritus, 2002—. Author: Brothers and Sisters of Retarded Children, 1971, Pregnancy, Birth and Parenthood, 1980, With the Phoenix Rising, 1999. Trustee Oberlin Coll., 1990-92, pres. Alumni Assn., 1979-80. Recipient Cert. of Appreciation Oberlin Coll. Alumni Assn., 1983. Fellow APA (mem. ethics com. 1994-97); mem. New Eng. Soc. Study Treatment Trauma and Dissociation (bd. dirs. 1995-99), Mass. Psychol. Assn. (chair ethics com. 1989-91, Career Contbn. award 1991), Sigma Xi, Phi Beta Kappa. Jewish. Office: Boston Univ Dept Psychology 64 Cummington St Boston MA 02215-2407 Home Phone: 617-527-6354; Office Phone: 617-332-6505. E-mail: frang@bu.edu.

GROSSMAN, GINGER SCHEFLIN, advocate; b. Bklyn., June 24, 1919; d. Louis Scheflin and Rose Taggert; m. Arthur I. Grossman, Apr. 6, 1941; children: Lynn Grossman Balaban, Boni Grossman Smith. Del. UN Conf. Global Environment, Rio de Janeiro, 1985; mem. adv. bd. South Fla. Food Recovery, 1985—; charter mem. Dade County Women's Coalition for Healthy Planet, 1985; mem. Dade County Commn. on Status of Women, 1983—95, mem. older women's task force, 1990—95; co-founder, v.p. Kids in Dade Soc., 1987—; exec. v.p. Rood Alzheimer's Found., 1989—92; chmn. long-term and managed care task force Alliance for Aging, 1989—93, chmn. advocacy and edn. com., 1990—, bd. dirs., 1999—2002; mem. adv. bd. South Fla. Theater of Deaf, 1991—2004; founder, pres. Aventura-Turnberry chpt. Women's Am. ORT, 1991—95; co-founder, v.p. Youth Cadets of Dade County, 1991—2003; Dem. exec. committeewoman Nassau County, NY, 1971—75, Dade County, Fla., 1981—; founder, pres. William Lehman NE Dade Involved Democrats, 1990—; bd. dirs. Aventure-Turnberry Jewish Ctr., 1991—, Dade County Transit Coalition, 1987—. Named Best Friend, City of North Miami, Fla., 1995, Super Vol., Alliance for Aging, Dade County, Fla., 1999, Woman of Valor, Aventura-Turnberry Jewish Ctr., Fla., 2000; recipient Dr. Jean Jones Purdue award for spl. achievement, Alliance for Aging, 2001. Mem.: Profl. Bus. Women's Assn. Democrat. Personal E-mail: ginart202@aol.com.

GROSSMAN, HERBERT BARTON, urologist, researcher; b. Tampa, Fla., June 25, 1945; s. Benjamin and Pauline (Mattis) G.; m. Amy C. Becker, Aug. 24, 1969; children: Beth, Sara, Rebecca. BA, La Salle Coll., Phila., 1966; MD, Temple U., 1970. Diplomate Am. Bd. Urology. Surg. intern U. Mich. Med. Ctr., Ann Arbor, 1970-71; surg. resident St. Joseph Mercy Hosp., Ann Arbor, 1973-74; urology resident U. Mich. Med. Ctr., Ann Arbor, 1974-77; instr. U. Mich. Med. Sch., Ann Arbor, 1977-78; rsch. and clin. fellow Meml. Sloan-Kettering Cancer Ctr., NYC, 1978-80; asst. prof. U. Mich. Med. Sch., Ann Arbor, 1980-85, assoc. prof., 1985-90, prof., 1990-94; dir., urologic oncology U. Mich. Cancer Ctr., Ann Arbor, 1986-94; prof. U. Tex. M.D. Anderson Cancer Ctr., Houston, 1994—, dep. chair Dept. Urology, 1998—. Cons. Taubman Med. Libr., 1985—94, The Med. Letter, 1991, Jour. Vascular Surgery, 1991; reviewer VA Merit Rev. Bd. for Surgery, 1986, NIH Pathology B Ad Hoc (SI) Study Sect., 1988, NIDDK Ad Hoc Rev. Groups 12 and 13, 1992, Med. Rsch. Coun., UK, 1999, Dutch Cancer Soc., 1999, 2001, NCI Spl. Emphasis Panel, 1999, 2000, 03; spl. reviewer NIH Exptl. Therapeutics Study Sect., 1986, reviewer spl. study sect., 95, reviewer cancer ctr. support grant, 96; reviewer NCI Rev. Group/subcom. 4, 1997; external reviewer Alta. Cancer Bd., 1998; mem. surg. quality control and edn. com SW Oncology Group, 1980—90, GU com., 1980—, organ site chmn. for local bladder cancer, 1991—2000; surg. oncology adv. com. dept. surgery U. Mich. Med. Ctr., Ann Arbor, 1981—82, dept. surgery computer sys. adv. com., 1983—88, cancer ctr. clin. rsch. com., 1987—94, laser safety com., 1987—94, med. sch. admissions com., 1988—94, patient care com., 1989—90, hosps. quality mgmt. com., 1990—94, rsch. coord. sect. urology, 1991, fin. adv. com., adv. promotion com. for primary rsch. staff dept. surgery, 1993—94; med. practice subcom. U. Tex. M.D. Anderson Cancer Ctr., Houston, 1994—, grad. med. edn. com., 1994—2004, surveillance com., 1994—95, dir. clin. rsch., 1994—2004, dep. chmn. dept. urology, 1998—, clin. study sect. rev. grants program, 2002—, vice chmn., 2002—03, chmn., 2003—04; prostate cancer adv. com. Mich. Dept. Pub. Health, 1993—94, clin. rsch. com. mem., 1994—2000, chmn., 1997—2000, dir. bladder cancer multidisciplinary rsch. program, 1999—2004; mem. sci. adv. bd. Anthra Pharms., Inc., 1994—2004, Fujirebio Diagnostics Inc., 1003—; cons. NCI early detection rsch. network, 2002; ad hoc reviewer NCI subcom. E, 2003—04, US Army Med. Rsch. and Materiel Command, 1999; mem. NCI program for assessment of clin. cancer tests strategy group, 2003—, NCI PACCT strategy group, 2004—; molecular biology rev. panel FAMRI, 2001—06, chair therapeutic intervention. Mem. editl. bd. Oncology Reports, 1998—, Jour. Urology, 1999—2007, sect. editor Urologic Oncology, 2000—, Molecular Oncology, 2007—; contbr. articles to profl. jours., chapters to books. Capt. USAF, 1971—73. Recipient 2d prize Ferdinand C. Valentine Urology Essay Contest, 1980, also numerous rsch. grants; named to W.A. "Tex" and Deborah Moncrief, Jr. Disting. Chair in Urology, 1994, Vis. Professorship award in urology, Pfizer/AUA, 2004; Ferdinand C. Valentine fellow N.Y. Acad. Medicine, 1979-80, clin. fellow Am. Cancer Soc., 1979-80. Office: U T MD Anderson Cancer Ctr 1515 Holcombe Blvd # 1373 Houston TX 77030-4009

GROSSMAN, JEREMIAH, information technology executive; Unix adminstr. Amgen Inc., 1998—99; info. security officer to security dir. Yahoo! Inc., 1999—2001; CEO, chief tech. officer WhiteHat Security Inc., Santa Clara, Calif., 2001—. Bd. dir., co-founder, spokesperson Web Application Security Consortium; contbr. mem. Ctr. Internet Security Apache Benchmark Group. Named one of Top 25 Chief Tech. Officers, InfoWorld mag., 2007. Office: WhiteHat Security Inc 3003 Bunker Hill Ln Santa Clara CA 95054 Office Phone: 408-492-1817.

GROSSMAN, JEROME HARVEY, medical association administrator, educator; b. Maplewood, NJ, Sept. 23, 1939; s. Abraham and Sally Grossman; m. Barbara Nan Grossman, June 9, 1968; children: Elizabeth, Katherine, Amelia. BS, MIT, 1961; MD, U. Pa., 1965; DHL (hon.), Lesley Coll., 1996. Fellow Mass. Gen. Hosp., Boston, 1966—69; physician, 1969—79; physician (hon.), 1979—; assoc. dir. computer sci. Mass. Gen. Hosp., Boston, 1969—72, dir. ambulatory care, 1974—79; asst. prof. Harvard Med. Sch., Boston, 1971-72, 74-79; pres. New Eng. Med. Ctr., Boston, 1979—84, chmn., CEO, 1984—95, Health Quality Inc., Boston, 1996—99; chmn. Lion gate Mgmt. Corp., 1999—; prof. Tufts U. Sch. Medicine, Boston, 1979—96; program dir. Commonwealth Fund Acad. Health Ctr. Program, 1982—87; chmn. The Health Inst., 1988—95; scholar in residence Inst. of Medicine, 1996—97; sr. fellow, dir. Harvard/Kennedy Sch. Health Care Delivery Policy Program. Bd. dirs. Stryker Corp., Kalamazoo, Fed. Res. Bank, Boston, chmn., 1992—96; bd. dirs., mem. nat. adv. com. Boston Pub. Libr. Found.; sr. fellow Mossavar-Rahmani Ctr. for Bus. & Govt. Bd. dirs. Boston Pvt. Industry Coun., 1982—96, chmn., 1990—93; trustee Wellesley Coll., 1983—; mem. Bd. Edn., Commonwealth Mass., 1991—96, Jobs Coun., Commonwealth Mass., 1991—96; chair Bd. Transition Sys., Inc., 1985—96. Lt. col. USAF, 1972—74. Recipient Karl Taylor Compton prize, MIT, 1961. Fellow: ACP; mem.: Acad. Med. Ctr. Consortium (chmn. 1992—95), Assn. Am. Med. Colls. (adminstrv. bd. 1986—92, chmn. 1990—91, Disting. Svc. membership), Am. Fedn. Clin. Rsch., Inst. Medicine of NAS, Mill Reef Club, Cosmos Club, Tavern Club, Somerset Club, Country Club. Office: Harvard/Kennedy Sch Health Care Delivery Policy Program Weill Hall 79 John F Kennedy St Cambridge MA 02138 Office Phone: 617-495-7979. Office Fax: 617-547-9696. E-mail: jerome_grossman@ksg.harvard.edu.

GROSSMAN, JEROME KENT, lawyer, accountant; b. St. Louis, Apr. 15, 1953; s. Marvin and Myra Lee (Barnholtz) G.; m. Debbie Ada Kogan, Aug. 7, 1977; children: Hannah Felicia, Marni Celeste. AB cum laude, Georgetown U., 1974, JD, 1977. Bar: Mo. 1977, D.C. 1978, U.S. Ct. Claims 1979, U.S. Tax Ct. 1979, Del. 1980, U.S. Dist. Ct. Del. 1982; CPA, Mo. Acct., controller U.S. Dept. State, Washington, 1974-77; acct. Arthur Andersen & Co., St. Louis, 1977-79; mem. firm Bayard, Handelman and Murdoch, P.A., Wilmington, Del., 1979-88; ptnr. Young Conaway Stargatt & Taylor LLP, Wilmington, 1988—. Co-author: ALI-ABA Course of Study on the Reform Act of 1984, 86. V.p. Jewish Cmty. Ctr., Wilmington, 1986—88, 1989—90, treas., 1989—90; trustee Milton & Hattie Kutz Found., 2001—, Harry Cohen Found., 2002—; bd. dirs. Congregation Beth Shalom, Wilmington, 1985—, pres., 1990—92; treas. Jewish Fedn. Del., 1989—90; pres. Del. Gratz Hebrew H.S., 1997—2000, trustee, 1995—2006, Jewish. Com. of Del. Endowment Fund., 1988—95; co-chmn. Del. State Com. State of Israel Bonds, 1992—95, chmn., 1995—2000; bd. dirs. Del. Symphony Assn., 1998—2004, 2006—, trustee, 1998—2006, vice chmn., 1999—2001; bd. dirs. Jewish Nat. Fund, Del., 2003—, co-pres. Del., 2005—. Fellow: Am. Coll. Tax Counsel; mem.: AICPA (mem. coun. 2000—01), ABA (chmn. inventories subcom. 1982—86, vice chmn. 1986—88, chmn. 1988—90, tax sect., com. on tax acctg.), Del. Soc. CPAs (chmn. tax com. 1980—85, coun. 1985—87, ethics com. 1989—92, coun. 1993—2002, pres. 2000—01), Del. Tax Inst. (planning com. 1985—86, 1994—), Del. Bar Assn. (chair sect. of taxation 1996—97), Alpha Sigma Nu. Democrat. Avocations: choir, opera, bridge. Home: 803 Westover Rd Wilmington DE 19807-2978 Office: Young Conaway Stargatt & Taylor LLP PO Box 391 Wilmington DE 19899-0391 Office Phone: 302-571-6685. Business E-Mail: jgrossman@ycst.com.

GROSSMAN, JONATHAN LEE, sports agent, law educator; b. Bklyn., Dec. 23, 1963; s. Norman and Elizabeth Grossman; m. Evelyn Grossman. BA, U. Miami, Coral Cables, Fla., 1983; MS, St. Thomas U., Miami, 1985; JD, Nova Sch. Law, Ft. Lauderdale, Fla., 1988. Bar: Fla. 2002. Sports agt. Universal Sports Mgmt. Inc., Hollywood, 1989—. Bar exam tutor, Hollywood, 2003—; bar exam preparation instr. St. Thomas Sch. Law, Miami, 2006, Barry Sch. Law, Orlando, 2007—. Contbg. author (book) You Can't Play The Game If You Don't Know The Rules, 1993.

GROSSMAN, JOYCE RENEE, pediatrician, internist; b. Bklyn., Nov. 15, 1951; d. Norman and Sydell (Rashbaum) Katz; m. Arthur Robert Grossman (div.); 1 child, Justin BS, Bklyn. Coll., 1973; MS, Cornell Med. Coll., Ithaca, NY, 1980; MD, Downstate Med. Coll., 1986. Adj. prof. Downstate Med. Ctr., Bklyn., 1994—; attending physician N.Y. Hosp. Network, Bklyn., 1996—97, Beth Israel Med. Ctr., Bklyn., 1997; assoc. med. dir. Cigna of N.Y., NYC, 1998—. Author: (with others) Pediatric Aspects of Tuberculosis & Clinical Handbook, 1995 Fellow: Am. Acad. Physicians, Am. Acad. Pediat. Achievements include patents for gene therapy, antibiotics and chemotherapeutic agents.

GROSSMAN, KATE NADIA, journalist; b. Chgo., Dec. 8, 1969; d. Robert Mayer and Frances Rosenbacher Grossman; m. Peter Fidler, Aug. 29, 1999. BA, Cornell U., 1992; M in Pub. Policy, MS in Journalism, Columbia U., 1997. Prodn. asst. ABC News 20/20, Washington, 1993-94; tchr. Chgo. Pub. Schs., 1994-95; reporter Providence Jour., 1997-99, AP, Chgo., 1999-2000; edn. reporter Chgo. Sun-Times, 2000—. Big sister Big Bros./Big Sisters Met. Chgo., 1999. Recipient 2 first pl. awards R.I. Press Assn., 1997, 1st and 2nd pl. awards R.I. Press Assn., 1998, Journalism award Am. Planning Assn., 2002, award Nat. Edn. Writers Assn., 2002. Mem. Assn. for Women Journalists, Soc. for Profl. Journalists (award 2002). Avocations: bicycling, jogging, hiking, camping, reading. Office: Chicago Sun Times 350 N Orleans St Ste 1270 Chicago IL 60654-2148 Office Fax: 312-321-3084. Business E-Mail: kgrossman@suntimes.com.*

GROSSMAN, LAWRENCE KUGELMASS, former communications and advertising executive; b. NYC, June 21, 1931; s. Nathan F. and Rose (Goldstein) G.; m. Alberta S. Nevler, Mar. 1, 1954; children: Susan Lee, Jennifer Nancy, Caroline Ann. BA, Columbia, 1952; student, Harvard Law Sch., 1953. Editor, promotion exec. Look mag., 1953-56; advt. exec. CBS-TV, 1956-62; v.p. advt. NBC, 1962-66; pres. Lawrence K. Grossman, Inc., NYC, 1966-76, Forum Communications, Inc., 1969-76, PBS, Washington, 1976-84, NBC News, NYC, 1984-88, Brookside Prodns. Ltd., Westport, Conn., 1989—; co-chmn., prin. Digital Promise Project. Vis. lectr. Frank Stanton Chair on 1st Amendement, Kennedy Sch. Govt., Harvard U., 1989—, chair; sr. fellow, vis. scholar Columbia U. Gannett Media Ctr.; trustee Conn. Pub. Broadcasting and various nonprofit health orgns.; bd. dir. Fedn. Am. Scientists. Assoc. editor: A Candid Portrait of the 1964 Presidential Election, 1965; author: The Electronic Republic: Reshaping Democracy in the Information Age, 1996; TV columnist, Columbia Journalism Review; juror, Dupont-Columbia Journalism award. Address: 37 W 12 St New York NY 10011 E-mail: lkgrossm@gmail.com.

GROSSMAN, MARC ISSAIAH, former federal agency administrator; b. LA, Sept. 23, 1951; s. Melvin and Estelle Grossman; m. Mildred Patterson, May 29, 1982; 1 child, Anne. BA, U. Calif., Santa Barbara, 1973; MSc in Internat. Rels., London Sch. Econs./Polit. Sci., 1974. Polit. officer U.S. Embassy, Islamabad, Pakistan, 1977-79; staff asst. Bur. Near Eastern and South Asian Affairs US Dept. State, 1979-80; dep. spl. adviser to Pres. Carter The White House, Washington, 1980; chief profl. staff State Dept. Transition Team, 1980; country officer for Jordan US Dept. State, 1981-83; polit. officer U.S. Mission to NATO, 1983; dep. dir. pvt. office of sec. gen. NATO, 1984-86; exec. asst. to dep. sec. US Dept. State, 1986-89; dep. chief U.S. Mission in Turkey, 1989-92; exec. sec., spl. asst. to sec. US Dept. State, Washington, 1993-94, U.S. amb. to Turkey Ankara, 1995-97, asst. sec. for Europe and Can. affairs Washington, 1997-98, asst. sec. European affairs, 1998-2000, dir. gen. Fgn. Svc., 2000-01, under sec. polit. affairs, 2001—05; vice chmn. The Cohen Group, Washington, 2005—. Mem. Am. Friends of the London Sch. of Econs., Army and Navy Club (Washington). Avocations: reading, travel, sports. Office: The Cohen Group 1200 19th St NW Washington DC 20036

GROSSMAN, MARGARET ROSSO, law educator; b. Alton, Ill., Oct. 17, 1947; d. William H. and Elaine Gorman Rosso; m. Michael Grossman, June 27, 1970; children: Aaron William, Daniel Benjamin. BMus, U. Ill., Urbana, 1969; AM, Stanford U., Palo Alto, Calif., 1970; JD, U. Ill., Urbana, 1979, PhD, 1977. Prof. agrl. law U. Ill., Urbana, 1990—, Bock chair, prof., 2004—. Vis. prof. and sr. rsch. fellow Wageningen U., Netherlands. Recipient Funk Recognition award, Coll. Agr. U. Ill., 1995, Wershow Disting. Lectr. award, U. Fla., 1996; fellow, German Marshall Fund, 1993—94, Fulbright EU Affairs Rsch. Program, 2000—01; Fulbright fellow, Western European Regional Rsch. Program, 1986—87, Fulbright rsch. fellow, Netherlands, 1993—94. Mem.: Ill. State Bar Assn., European Cmty. Studies Assoc., Am. Vet. Med. Law Assoc., Agr., Food, and Human Values Soc. (editl. advisor agrl. and human values 1989), Unione Mondiale degli Agraristi Universitari, Am. Agrl. Law Assn. (pres. 1990—91, Disting. Svc. award 1993, Profl. scholar award 2006), European Coun. Agrl. Law (assoc. Silver medal 1999), Order of the Coif, Phi Kappa Phi, Pi Kappa Lambda, Gamma Sigma Delta. Office: U Ill 333 Mumford Hall 1301 W Gregory Dr Urbana IL 61801 Office Phone: 217-333-1829.

GROSSMAN, MARSHALL BRUCE, lawyer; b. Omaha, Mar. 24, 1939; s. Lee and Elsie (Stalmaster) G.; m. Marlene Belle Delson, Aug. 19, 1962; children: Rodger Seth, Leslie Erin. Student, U. Calif. at Los Angeles, 1957-59; BSL., LL.B., U. So. Calif., 1964. Bar: Calif. 1965. With Alschuler, Grossman, LA, 1965-67, ptnr., 1967—2007, Bingham McCutcheon LLP, LA, 2007—. Lectr. law U. So. Calif., Los Angeles, 1966-69; lectr., author on comml. litigation, 1968—; mem. Calif. Commn. Jud. Performance, 2001—, chmn., 2005—07. Mem. Calif. Coastal Commn., 1981-86; bd. dirs. Bet Tzedek Legal Services, 1986-2006, United Way, 1992-95, Jewish Big Brothers, 1995-, Amer. Jewish Com., 2000-. Mem. ABA, LA Bar Assn., Beverly Hills Bar Assn. (bd. govs. 1971-76), Barristers Bar Assn. (pres. 1972-73), Assn. Bus. Trial Attys. (bd. govs. 1974-75), LA Jewish Fedn. (chmn. commn. on law and legislation 1973-74, chmn. commn. on Soviet Jewry 1981, chmn. cmty. rels. com. 1984-86), Order of Coif, Tau Delta Phi, Phi Alpha Delta. Clubs: Mason. Office: Bingham McCutcheon LLP The Water Garden 1620 26th St Fourth Fl N Tower Santa Monica CA 90404-4060 Office Phone: 310-907-1000.

GROSSMAN, MARY MARGARET, retired elementary school educator; b. East Cleveland, Ohio, Sept. 26, 1946; d. Frank Anthony and Margaret Mary (Buda) G. Student, Kent State U., 1965—67; BS in Elem. Edn. cum laude, Cleve. State U., 1971, postgrad., 1985, Lake Erie Coll., 1974—77, John Carroll U., 1978, postgrad., 1981—83, postgrad., 1985. Cert. elem. sch. tchr. grades 1 to 8 Ohio, cert. data processing Ohio. Tchr. Cleve. Catholic Diocese, 1971-72, Willoughby-Eastlake Sch. Dist., Ohio, 1972—2007; ret., 2007. Participant Nat. Econ. Edn. Conf., Richmond, Va., 1995. Eucharistic min. St. Christine's Ch., Euclid, 1988—, mem. parish pastoral coun., 1995—2000. Recipient Samuel H. Elliott Econ. Leadership award, 1986-87, Consumer Educator award NE Ohio Region, 1986, 1st pl. excellence in tchg. award Tchrs. in Am. Enterprise, 1984-85, 89-90; Martha Holden Jennings scholar, 1984-85. Mem. NEA, Ohio Edn. Assn. (human rels. award 1986-87, cert. merit 1987-88), NE Ohio Edn. Assn. (Positive Tchr. Image award 1988). Roman Catholic. Avocations: racquetball, softball, walking, tennis, bicycling. Home: 944 E 225th St Cleveland OH 44123-3308

GROSSMAN, MICHAEL, economics professor; b. Bklyn., July 12, 1942; s. Norman and Doris (Orent) G.; m. Ilene Joy Gordon, Sept. 11, 1966; children: Sandra Diane, Barri Lynn. BA, Trinity Coll., Hartford, Conn., 1964; PhD, Columbia U., 1970. Asst. prof. Ctr. Health Adminstrn. Studies, Grad. Sch. Bus., U. Chgo., 1969-71; rsch. assoc., co-program dir. health econs. rsch. Nat. Bur. Econ. Rsch., NYC, 1972—; prof. econs. CUNY Grad. Sch., 1974, disting. prof. econs, 1988. Mem. population sci. study sect. Nat. Inst. Child Health and Human Devel., Washington, 2003—; mem. bd. sci. counselors Nat. Ctr. for Health Stats., Hyattsville, Md., 2004—; cons. in field. Author: (Book) The Demand for Health: A Theoretical and Empirical Investigation, 1972 (Nomination for Kulp Award of the American Risk and Insurance Association, 1976); editor: The Economic Analysis of Substance Abuse: An Integration of Econometric and Behavioral Economic Research, 1999, Economic Analysis of Substance Use and Abuse: The Experience of Developed Countries and Lessons for Developing Countries, 2001, Substance Use: Individual Behaviour, Social Interactions, Markets and Politics, 2005; co-editor: Review of Economics of the Household, 2005—; assoc. editor Jour. Health Econs., Amsterdam, Netherlands, 1982—; contbr. articles to profl. jours. Mem. Social Scis., Nursing, Epidemiology and Methods Study sect. Ctr. for Sci. Rev., NIH, Washington, 2000—01. Ford Found. fellow Columbia U. Mem.: APHA, Health Econs. Rsch. Orgn., Population Assn. Am., Internat. Health Econs. Assn., Am. Econ. Assn., Pi Gamma Mu, Phi Beta Kappa. Independent. Jewish. Avocations: tennis, skiing, boating. Home: 115 E 9th St Apt 14C New York NY 10003 Office: Nat Bur Econ Rsch 365 5th Ave 5th Flr New York NY 10016-4309 Office Phone: 212-817-7959. Business E-Mail: mgrossman@gc.cuny.edu.

GROSSMAN, NANCY, artist; b. NYC, 1940; d. Murray and Josephine G. BFA, Pratt Inst., 1962. Mem. jury sculpture N.Y. State Council on Arts, 1973, Prix de Rome fellowships Am. Acad. in Rome, 1974 Exhibited in one-woman shows, Krasner Gallery, N.Y.C., 1964, 65, 65, 67, Cordier & Ekstrom, N.Y.C., 1968, 69, 71, 73, 75, 76, Church Fine Arts Gallery, U. Nev., Reno, 1978, Barbara Gladstone Gallery, N.Y.C., 1980, 82, Heath Gallery, Atlanta, 1981, 86, Terry Dintenfass Gallery, 1984, Exit Art, N.Y.C., 1991, Sculpture Ctr., N.Y.C., 1991, Hillwood Art Mus., Brookville, N.Y., 1991, Exit Art, N.Y.C., 1991, Hillwood Art Mus., Brookville, N.Y., 1991, Sculpture Ctr., N.Y.C., 1991, Artemisia, Chgo., 1992, Beacon St. Gallery, Chgo., 1992, Ark. Art Ctr., Little Rock, 1992, Contemporary Mus., Honolulu, 1992, Binghamton U. Art Gallery, 1992, Hooks-Epstein Galleries, Houston, 1993, 95, LedisFlam, N.Y.C., 1994, Weatherspoon Art Gallery, Greensboro, N.C., 1994, Greenville Cty Museum of Art, 2004; exhibited in numerous group shows, including, Whitney Mus. Am. Art, N.Y.C., 1968, 69, 69, 73, 80, 81, 93, 95, Fogg Art Mus., Cambridge, Mass., 1972, Am. Acad. Arts and Letters/Nat. Inst. Arts and Letters invitational, N.Y.C., 1974, 1987, New Mus. New American Painting exhbn., Hungary, Czechoslovakia, Poland, 1978, Betté Stoler, 1983, Whitney Mus. at Phillip Morris, 1984, Exit Art, N.Y.C., 1991, Michael Rosenfeld Gallery, N.Y.C., 1996, Nat. Acad., N.Y.C., 1996, The Geffen Contemporary, L.A., 1999, Beacon Street Gallery, Chicago, 2001, George Adams Gallery, N.Y.C, 2003, Chelsea Art Museum, N.Y.C., 2004; represented in permanent collections, Whitney Mus. Am. Art, Hirshhorn Mus., Washington, Smithsonian Inst., Dallas Mus. Fine Arts, Balt. Mus., Mus. Boymans Van Beuningen, Rotterdam, Netherlands, U. Calif., Berkeley, Princeton U. Art Mus., N.J., Contemporary Arts Mus., Houston, Met. Mus. Art, N.Y.C., Va. Mus. Fine Arts, Richmond, Weatherspoon Art Gallery, Greensboro, N.C., Contemporary Mus., Honolulu. Recipient Inaugural Contemporary Achievement award Pratt Inst., 1966, award AAAL and Nat. Inst. Arts and Letters, 1974, Hassam, Spreicher, Betts and Symons purchase award Am. Acad. and Inst. Arts and Letters, 1989, Alumni Achievement award Pratt Inst., 1995, Joan Mitchell Found. fellowship, 1996; Ida C. Haskell scholar, 1962; Guggenheim fellow, 1965, fellow for sculpture Nat. Endowment for Arts, 1991; grantee Nat. Endowment for Arts, 1984. Mem. Nat. Acad. Address: 105 Eldridge St New York NY 10002-4405 Office: Michael Rosenfeld Gallery 24 W 57th St New York NY 10019-3918

GROSSMAN, PETER H., plastic surgeon; b. Evanston, Ill., Jan. 21, 1963; m. Rebecca Grossman; 1 child, Alexis. BA in History, Northwestern U., 1984; MD, Chgo. Med. Sch., 1988. Cert. Am. Bd. Plastic Surgery, lic. Calif., Mo., Kans., Ala. Gen. surgery resident Cedars-Sinai Med. Ctr., LA, 1988—92; plastic and reconstructive surgery resident U. Mo., Kans. City, 1992—94; aesthetic and endoscopic surgery fellowship U. Ala., Birmingham, 1994, breast reconstructive surgery fellowship, 1994; surgeon Grossman Med. Group/Burn Care Physicians Med. Group, Sherman Oaks, Calif., 1994—. Assoc. dir. Grossman Burn Ctr., Sherman Oaks, 2000—; expert reviewer Med. Bd. Calif., 2001—; presenter in field. Featured on The Oprah Winfrey Show, ABC's Prime Time Live, The Learning Channel, and Discovery Health Channel; contbr. articles to profl. jours. Surgical mission to Croatia, 1993. Named Hon. Fire Chief, Sherman Oaks, 1998; recipient Mayor's Cert. of Appreciation, City of LA, Physicians' Recognition award, AMA, 2001, 2002, 2003, 2004. Mem.: ACS, Am. Soc. Aesthetic Plastic Surgery, Orange County Health Care Agy.: Emergency Med. Svcs. Agy., Am. Bd. Quality Assurance and Utilization Review Physicians, Assn. for Advanced Wound Care, Calif. Soc. Plastic Surgeons, Lipoplastic Soc., Am. Soc. Plastic and Reconstructive Surgeons, Am. Burn Assn. (chairperson region 9, nat. faculty advanced burn life support program), Am. Assn. Hand Surgery, LA Plastic Surgery Soc., Calif. Med. Assn., LA County Med. Assn. Office: Grossman Med Group Burn Care Physicians Med Group 4910 Van Nuys Blvd Ste 306 Sherman Oaks CA 91403*

GROSSMAN, REX, professional football player; b. Bloomington, Indiana, Aug. 23, 1980; s. Daniel and Maureen Grossman; m. Alison Miska, 2005. Student, U. Fla, 1999—2003. First round draft pick, 2003; quarterback Chgo. Bears, 2003—. Achievements include first freshman ever named MVP Southeast Conf. Championship Game, 2000. Office: Chicago Bears Football Club 1000 Football Dr Lake Forest IL 60045*

GROSSMAN, ROBERT ALLEN, transportation executive; b. Port Jervis, NY, July 24, 1941; s. George and Helen (Garson) G.; m. Joan Ward, June 15, 1962 (div.); children: Jeffrey, Wendy; m. Gloria Schwartz, Nov. 22, 1987. Student, Cornell U., 1959-60, U. Pa., 1960-62. Fin. divsn. North Shore Packing Co., Inc., North Bellmore, NY, 1962-64; mgr. refin. and legal dept. Coburn Corp. Am., Rockville Centre, NY, 1964-67; stockbroker Weis, Volson & Cannon, Inc., NYC, 1967-69, Nadel & Co., NYC, 1969-70; v.p. Emons Industries, Inc., York, Pa., 1971—79, chmn. bd., CEO, 1979—2002; chmn., CEO Emons Transp. Group, 1986—2002; exec. v.p. Genesee & Wyoming Inc., Greenwich, Conn., 2002—06, v.p. govt. affairs Oreg. region, 2007—. Mem. legis. policy com. Am. Assn. Shortline and Regional R.R. Assn., 1998—. Bd. dirs. Better York, Inc., 1996-2003. Mem. Am. Assn. Short Line and Regional R.R.s (dir. 1998—), York Area C. of C. (dir. 1978-83), Pa. Rail Freight (adv. com. 1993-02), Maine Rail Task Force, Keystone State Ra.R. Assn. (pres. 1996-99, exec. com. 1996-02), Nat. Indsl. Transp. League, R.R.s of N.Y. (pres. 2004-06), Oreg. Rail Users League (treas., bd. dirs. 2005—). Office: Genesee & Wyoming Inc 204 North George St Ste 230 York PA 17401

GROSSMAN, ROBERT GEORGE, neurosurgeon, department chairman; b. NYC, Jan. 24, 1933; s. Ferenc and Vivian (Isenberg) Grossman; m. Ellin Friedman, June 26, 1955; children: Amy, Kate, Ruth. BA, Swarthmore Coll., 1953; MD, Columbia U., 1957. Diplomate Am. Bd. Neurosurgery. Intern Strong Meml. Hosp., Rochester, NY, 1957-58; resident Presbyn. Hosp., Columbia U., NYC, 1960-63; acad. practice medicine, specializing in neurol. surgery Houston, 1973—; from instr. to assoc. prof. neurol. surgery U. Tex. S.W. Med. Sch., 1963-68; from assoc. prof. to prof. neurol. surgery Albert Einstein Coll. Medicine, 1969-73; prof., chmn. div. neurol. surgery U. Tex. Med. Br., Galveston, 1973-80; prof., chmn. dept. neurol. surgery Baylor Coll. Medicine, 1980—2005; assoc. dean clin. affairs Baylor Coll. Medicne, 2002—05; dir. Neurol. Inst., chmn. dept. neurosurgery Meth. Hosp., Houston, 2005—. Chmn. neurology B study sect. USPHS, NIH, 1972—74; mem. bd. sci. counsellors Nat. Inst. Neurol. Diseases and Strok, NIH, 1993—96. Author (with W. D. Willis): Medical Neurobiology, 3d edit., 1981; chmn. editl. bd.: Jour. Neurosurgery, 1987. With US Army, 1958—60. Mem.: ACS, Soc. Neurol. Surgeons (pres. 1995), Am. Acad. Neurol. Surgery (v.p.), Am. Bd. Neurol. Surgery (chmn. bd. dirs. 1989—90), Soc. Univ. Surgeons, Am. Assn. Neurol. Surgeons. Home: 2002 Sunset Blvd Houston TX 77005-1651 Office: Tex Med Ctr Scurlock Tower 6560 Fannin St Ste 944 Houston TX 77030-2706 Office Phone: 713-441-3800. Business E-Mail: rgrossman@tmh.tmhs.org.

GROSSMAN, ROBERT LOUIS, lawyer; b. Cleve., Dec. 20, 1954; s. Sidney and Lillian Belle (Davis) G.; m. Rochelle Carol Shear, Nov. 7, 1987; children: Zachary, Jonathan, David, Andrew. BA with honors, Ohio State U., 1975, JD with Honors, 1978, MA with honors, 1979. Bar: Ohio 1978, Fla. 1982, U.S. Ct. Appeals (5th cir.) 1979. Law clk. U.S. Dist. Ct. (so. dist.) Ohio, Columbus, 1977-78; sr. atty. U.S. Govt. EEOC, Houston, 1979-82; shareholder Greenberg, Traurig, P.A., Miami, 1982—. Editor: Florida Corporate Practice, 2d edit., 1991. Chmn. South Dade Jewish Leadership Coun., 1997-99; bd. dirs. Greater Miami Jewish Fedn. South Dade, 1987—, campaign chmn., 1995-97, chmn., 1997-99; bd. dirs. Greater Miami Jewish Fedn., 1995—, mem. exec. com., 1997-99; bd. dirs. Alper Jewish Cmty. Ctr., 1997-00, exec. com., 1998-00; bd. dirs. Children's Bereavement Ctr., 2000—, Orgn. Leadership Advancement Miami, 2001-; chmn. Exec. Inst. OLAM, 2001-; bd. dirs. Beacon Coun., 2000—; chmn. Exec. Inst. for Orgn. for Leadership Advancement in Miami, 2001-03; chmn. Fedn. Agy., Day Sch. and Synagogue Campaign, 2003-; bd. dirs. Temple Beth Am., 2003-05, Project Interchange, 2005-, Jewish Nat. Fund, 2005-, United Jewish Cmtys. Israel Advocacy Com., 2005-. Donald Becker Meml. scholar Ohio State U., 1975, 76, fellow, 1978; Robert Russell fellow Greater Miami Jewish Fedn., 1998; recipient Stanley C. Myers Young Leadership award Greater Miami Jewish Fedn., 1999, Put Something Back Cmty. award, 2003. Mem. ABA (corp. securities sect.), The Fla. Bar, Dade County Bar Assn., Order of Coif. Avocations: sports, reading, travel. Office: Greenberg Traurig 1221 Brickell Ave Miami FL 33131-3224 Home Phone: 305-661-5370; Office Phone: 305-579-0756. Business E-Mail: grossmanb@gtlaw.com.

GROSSMAN, ROBERT MAYER, lawyer; b. Chgo., Oct. 16, 1934; s. Raymond Mandel and Frances Ruth (Krucoff) G.; m. Frances Ann Rosenbacher, Mar. 17, 1963; children— Theodore, Anthony, Kate AB, Dartmouth Coll., 1956; LL.B., Yale U., 1961. Bar: Ill, 1961. Law clk. U.S. Dist. Ct. Judge Hubert L. Will, 1961-63; assoc. Schiff, Hardin, Waite, Dorschel & Britton, 1963-66; exec. dir. Ill. Legis. Commn. Low Income Housing, 1966-67; ptnr. Grossman, Kasakoff, Magid & Silverman, 1968-70; mng. ptnr. Roan & Grossman, Chgo., 1970-83; sr. ptnr. Keck, Mahin & Cate, Chgo., 1983-95, of counsel, 1995-97; counsel to Gardner, Carton & Douglas, Chgo., 1997—2003; of counsel Miller, Shakman and Hamilton, Chgo., 2004—05. Prin. draftsman Ill. Housing Devel. Act, 1967; gen. counsel Dermatology Found., 1979—97; gen. counsel Ill. Housing Devel. Authority, 1967-69, 73-77; adj. prof. Chgo. Theol. Sem., 1996—. Author: Jeshua, Our Brother, 1989, Opening the Door, 1991, Widening the Path, 1997. V.p., bd. dirs. Hyde Park Coop Soc., 1977-81; chmn. by mayoral appointment Hyde Park-Kenwood Conservation Community Coun., 1991—99; bd. dirs. Chgo. Theol. Sem., 1989—2000, life trustee, 2000—; bd. dirs. No. Ill. region NCCJ, 1989—2004; chmn. Coun. for Jewish-Christian Studies Ctr., 1991-99. Lt. (j.g.) USNR, 1956-58 Mem. Chgo. Bar Assn., Law Club, Standard Club. Jewish. Home: 5529 S Kimbark Ave Chicago IL 60637-1618 Personal E-mail: RIGrossman@aol.com.

GROSSMAN, SANFORD JAY, former economics professor, financial consultant; b. Bklyn., July 21, 1953; s. Sloane and Florence G.; m. Naava. BA in Econs. with honors, U. Chgo., 1973, MA in Econs., 1974, PhD in Econs., 1975. Asst. prof. econs. Stanford U., Calif., 1975-77; economist Bd. Govs. Fed. Res., 1977-78; assoc. prof. econs. U. Pa., Phila., 1978-79, prof. econs., 1979-81, U. Chgo., 1981-85; John L. Weinberg prof. econs. Princeton U., NJ, 1985-89; Steinberg trustee prof. fin. U. Pa., Phila., 1989—2000; dir. Wharton Ctr. Quantitative Fin., 1994—2001; chmn., CEO Quantitative Fin. Strategies, Inc., Greenwich, Conn., 2001—. Pub. dir., bd. dirs. Chgo. Bd. Trade, 1992-96. Mem. editl. bd. Finance India, 1994—; mem. adv. bd. Math. Finance, 1994—; contbr. articles to profl. jours. Trustee U. Chgo., 2003—. Recipient Irving Fisher grad. monograph award, award for best article, Graham and Dodd Scroll, Fin. Analyst Jour., 1988, Roger F. Murray 1st Prize award, Q Group, 1988, Math. Fin. Best Paper award, 1993, Profl. Achievement citation, U. Chgo., 2002, 2002, Mathematical Fin. Best Paper award, 1993; fellow, Lilly Found., Guggenheim Meml., Sloan Found., Am. Econometric Soc., 1980, Lilly Found. Fellow AAAS, Econometric Soc., Am. Fin. Assn. (v.p. 1992, pres.-elect 1993, pres. 1994, bd. dirs., fellow 2000); mem. Am. Econ. Assn. (John Bates Clark medal 1987). Office: Quantitative Fin Strategies 10 Glenville St Greenwich CT 06831 Business E-Mail: qfs@qfsfunds.com.

GROSSMAN, STEVEN L., lawyer; b. Chgo., 1957; BA, Stanford U., 1979; JD, U. So. Calif., 1982. Bar: Calif. 1982, US Dist. Ct. (Ctrl. Dist. Calif.) 1982, US Ct. Appeals (9th Cir.) 1982, DC 1992. Corp. and securities ptnr. O'Melveny & Myers LLP, Los Angeles, Calif., co-chair. mergers and acquisitions/private equity practice group. Staff mem. So. Calif. Law Review, 1980—81, mng. editor, 1981—82. Mem.: State Bar Calif. (mem. bus. law sections), ABA. Office: O'Melveny & Myers LLP 1999 Avenue of the Stars 7th Fl Los Angeles CA 90067-6035 Office Phone: 310-246-6727. Office Fax: 310-246-6779. Business E-Mail: slgrossman@omm.com.

GROSSMAN, THEODORE MARTIN, lawyer; b. NYC, Dec. 31, 1949; s. Albert and Sylvia Pia (Greenstein) G.; m. Linda Gail Steinbook, Dec. 5, 1976; children: Andrew Scott, Michael Steven. AB, Cornell U., 1971, JD, 1974. Bar: N.Y. 1975, U.S. Ct. Appeals (D.C. cir.) 1981, U.S. Ct. Appeals (2nd cir.) 1982, U.S. Ct. Appeals (5th cir.) 1984, U.S. Dist. Ct. (no. dist.) Ohio 1986, Ohio 1987, U.S. Dist. Ct. (so. dist.) N.Y. 1988, U.S. Dist. Ct. (ea. dist.) N.Y. 1988, U.S. Ct. Appeals (6th cir.) 1988, U.S. Supreme Ct., 2004. Assoc. Debevoise, Plimpton, Lyons & Gates, NYC, 1974-77, Rosenman Colin Freund Lewis & Cohen, NYC, 1977-80; trial and appellate counsel fed. programs br. of civil div. U.S. Dept. Justice, Washington, 1980-84; assoc. Jones Day, Cleve., 1984-86, ptnr., 1987—. Lectr. on cross-examination, deposition techniques, oral advocacy, trial tactics, and product liability law in ABA presentations and other seminars.; guest lectr. on internat. trade litig. Georgetown U. Law Ctr.; guest lectr. expert witnesses Case U. Law Sch.; counsel on behalf of the Lawyers' Com. for Civil Rights. Editor Cornell U. Law Rev., 1974. Trustee Cleve. Ctr. for Contemporary Art, 1992-96, treas., 1992-94. Named one of Top 10 Litigators, Nat. Law Jour., 2003. Fellow: Am. Coll. Trial Lawyers; mem.: ABA, Am. Law Inst. Home: 2979 Broxton Rd Shaker Heights OH 44120 Office: Jones Day 901 Lakeside Ave E Cleveland OH 44114-1190 Home Phone: 216-751-6486; Office Phone: 216-586-3939, 216-586-7268. E-mail: tgrossman@jonesday.com.

GROSSMAN, WILLIAM, medical researcher, educator; b. NYC, 1940; MD, Yale U., 1965. Intern Peter Bent Brigham Hosp., Boston, 1965-66, resident in medicine, 1968-69, rsch. fellow in cardiology, 1969-71; dir. cardiac catheterization labs. N.C. Meml. Hosp., Chapel Hill, 1971-75, Peter Bent Brigham Hosp., Boston, 1975-81; chief cardiovasc. divsn. Beth Israel Hosp., Boston, 1981-94; tchg. fellow in medicine Harvard U., Boston, 1968-71, assoc. prof., 1975-81, prof., 1981-84, Herman Dana prof. medicine, 1984-94; exec. dir. cardiovasc. rsch. Merck & Co., West Point, Pa., 1994-95, v.p., 1996-97; prof. medicine U. Calif., San Francisco, 1997—, chief cardiology, 1997—. Served as sr. asst. surgeon USPHS, 1966-68. Fellow Am. Coll. Cardiology, Am. Heart Assn., Assn. Am. Physicians, Am. Physiol. Soc., Am. Soc. Clin. Investigation. Office: UCSF Med Ctr Dept Cardiology Box 0124 San Francisco CA 94143-0124

GROSSMANN, EDWARD A., lawyer; b. NYC, Apr. 8, 1948; BA cum laude, Univ. Wis., 1970; JD, Univ. Mich., 1973. Bar: NY 1974, US Dist. Ct. (so. & ea. dist. NY 1974), US Ct. Appeals (2d cir. 1975, 3d cir. 1990, 9th cir. 1991, 5th cir. 1993, 11th cir. 1996). Founding ptnr., litigation, class action Bernstein Litowitz Berger & Grossmann LLP, NYC, 1983—. Mem. com. vis. Univ. Mich. Law Sch.; treas. UJA Fedn. Bergen County NJ. Mem.: Assn. Trial Lawyers Am. (past chmn. Comml. Litigation sect.), ABA (past chmn. Class & Derivitative Action Trials subcom.), NY State Bar Assn. Office: Bernstein Litowitz Berger & Grossmann 1285 Ave of the Americas New York NY 10019 Office Phone: 212-554-1404. Office Fax: 212-554-1444. Business E-Mail: edward@blbglaw.com.

GROSSMANN, IGNACIO EMILIO, chemical engineering educator; b. Mexico City, Nov. 12, 1949; s. Donat and Marie-Louise (Epper) G.; m. Ignacio E. Blanca Espinal, Nov. 26, 1977; children: Claudia, Andrew, Thomas. BSc ChemE, U. Iberoamericana, 1974; MSc ChemE, Imperial Coll., 1975, diploma (hon.), 1975, PhD ChemE, 1977; DTech (hon.), Abo Akademi, 2002. Research and devel. engr. Inst. Mexicano del Petroleo, Mexico City, 1978; asst. prof. chem. engring. Carnegie Mellon U., Pitts., 1979-83, assoc. prof., 1983-86, prof., 1986-90, Rudolph R. and Florence Dean prof. chem. engring., 1990—, head dept. chem. engring., 1994—. Robert W. Vaughan lectr. Calif. Inst. Tech., Pasadena, 1986; Mary Upson vis. prof. engring. Cornell U., Ithaca, N.Y., 1986-87; acad. trustee Computer Aids for Chem. Engring. Edn. (CACHE), Austin, Tex., 1983-2000; mem. governing bd. Coun. for Chem. Rsch. Assoc. editor: AIChE Jour., 2000—, mem. editl. bd.: Computers and Chem. Engring. Jour., 1987—, Jour. Global Optimization, 1991—, Optimization and Engring.; contbr. articles to profl. jours. Recipient Presdl. Young Investigator award NSF, Washington, 1984, Tech. Achievement award HEENAC, 2000. Fellow: AIChE (chmn. computing and sys. tech. divsn. 1992, Computing in Chem. Engring. award 1994, William H. Walker award 1997), Inst. Operation Rsch. and Mgmt. Svc., Am. Chem. Soc.; mem.: NAE, Inst. Ops. Rsch. and Mgmt. Sci. Computing Soc. (award 2003), Mex. Acad. Engring., Sigma Xi. Roman Catholic. Avocation: classical music. Home: 6385 Douglas St Pittsburgh PA 15217-1821 Office: Carnegie Mellon Univ Dept of Chem Engring Pittsburgh PA 15213

GROSSMANN, RONALD STANYER, lawyer; b. Chgo., Nov. 9, 1944; s. Andrew Eugene and Gladys M. Grossmann; m. Jo Ellen Hanson, May 11, 1968; children: Kenneth Frederick, Emilie Beth. BA, Northwestern U., 1966; JD, U. Mich., 1969. Bar: Oreg., 1969. Law clk. Oreg. Supreme Ct., Salem, 1969-70; assoc. Stoel Rives LLP, Portland, Oreg., 1970-76, ptnr., 1976—. Mem.: Am. Coll. Employee Benefits Counsel, Oreg. Bar Assn., ABA. Office: Stoel Rives LLP 900 SW 5th Ave Ste 2600 Portland OR 97204-1268

GROSSO, DOREEN ELLIOTT, management consultant; d. John and Hilda Elliott; m. Joseph Anthony Grosso, May 30, 1971; children: John Cesar, Michael Steven, Joseph Armando. BS, Fordham U., 1971; MBA, Pace U., 1979. V.p. Chem. Bank, NYC, 1981—91; pres. Change Creates Opportunity, Inc., Flushing, NY, 1991—. Dir. ARIL/CrossCurrents, NYC, 1995—2003. Participant, alum Coro-Leadership NY, NYC, 1990—90. Named Woman of Future, NY Women's Agenda, 2001. Mem.: Orgn. and Devel. Network Greater NY, World Future Soc. Roman Catholic. Home Phone: 917-698-6480. Business E-Mail: ccoi@nyc.rr.com.

GROSSO, SUE JANE RIVAS, radiologist; MD, Harvard U., Boston, 1985. Med. dir. breast imaging ctr. Overlook Hosp., Summit, NJ, 2006—. Home Phone: 908-358-3493; Office Phone: 908-277-3335.

GROSVENOR, ALLAN DACE, engineer; b. Toronto, Ontario, Canada, July 9, 1974; s. Greg and Mavis Grosvenor. BS in Mech. Engring., Carleton U., Ottawa, Canada, 1998; MS in Aerospace Engring., Carleton U., 2000. Mgr. Numeca USA, Inc., Phoenix, 2000—04; sr. engr., cfd specialist Ramgen Power Sys., Inc., Bellevue, Wash., 2004—. Contbr. articles to profl. jours. Mem.: ASME. Office: Ramgen Power Sys Inc 11808 Northup Way Ste W 190 Bellevue WA 98005 Office Fax: 425-828-7756. Business E-Mail: allan.grosvenor@ramgen.com.

GROSVENOR, GILBERT MELVILLE, journalist, educator, publishing executive; b. Washington, May 5, 1931; s. Melville Bell and Helen (Rowland) Grosvenor; m. Donna C. Kerkam, June 16, 1961 (div.); children: Gilbert Hovey II, Alexandra Rowland; m. Wiley Jarman, June 1, 1979; 1 child, Graham Dabney. BA, Yale U., 1954; D in Pub. Svc. (hon.), George Washington U., 1983; LHD (hon.), U. Colo., 1983, Curry Coll., 1984; LLD (hon.), Coll. of Wooster, Ohio, 1983; LHD (hon.), Coll. William and Mary, 1987, Miami U., Oxford, Ohio, 1988, Syracuse U., 1989, R.I. Coll., 1991, Old Dominion U., 1993, Longwood Coll., Farmville, Va., 1997, Ind. Univ., 1998, Univ. S.C., 1998, Pa. State Univ., 1999, S.W. Tex. State U., 2002, Appalachian State U., 2004. With Nat. Geog. Soc., 1954—, trustee, 1966—, v.p., 1966—80, assoc. editor, 1967—70, editor, 1970—80, pres., 1980—96, chmn. bd. dirs., 1987—. Bd. dirs. Chevy Chase Bank, FSB, Saul Ctrs., Inc.; former fellow Yale Corp. Former bd. visitors Duke U. Nicholas Sch. Environment and Earth Scis., Coll. William and Mary; former mem. Pres.'s Commn. on Environ. Quality, Washington Cathedral Bldg. Com.; trustee Nat. Wildflower Rsch. Ctr., B.F. Saul Real Estate Trust, Saul Ctrs., Inc.; past vice chmn. Pres.'s Commn. Ams. Outdoors; chmn. emeritus, found. bd. Alexander Graham Bell Assn. for Deaf; bd. dirs. Conservation Fund, Dian Fossey Gorilla Fund Internat. Recipient Editor of Yr. award, Nat. Press Photographers Assn., 1975, Disting. Achievement award, U. So. Calif. Sch. Journalism and Alumni Assn., 1977, Pres. medal, George Washington U., 1993, Golden Plate award, Am. Acad. Achievement, 1996, Presdl. medal of freedom, 2004. Mem.: Assn. Am. Geographers, Chevy Chase (Md.) Club, Cosmos Club, Alibi Club, Alfalfa Club, Newcomen Soc., Explorers Club (citation of merit 1997). Office: Nat Geog Soc 1145 17th St NW Washington DC 20036-4701

GROSZ, BARBARA JEAN, computer science educator; b. Phila., July 21, 1948; d. Joseph Eugene and Judith Phyllis (Zander) Gross. AB in Math., Cornell U., 1969; MA in Computer Sci., U. Calif., Berkeley, 1971, PhD in Computer Sci., 1977. Rsch. mathematician Artificial Intelligence Ctr., SRI Internat., Stanford, Calif., 1973-77, computer scientist, 1981-82, sr. computer scientist, 1981-82, program dir. nat. lang. and representation, 1982-83, sr. staff scientist, 1983-86; co-founder, mem. exec. com., prin. researcher Ctr. for Study of Lang. and Info. Stanford U. and SRI Internat., 1983-86; with divsn. engring. and applied scis. Harvard U., Cambridge, Mass., 1986—, interim assoc. dean for affirmative action, 1993-94, Higgins prof. natural scis., 2001—, dean of sci. Radcliffe Inst. Advanced Study, 2001—, interim dean Radcliffe Inst. for Advanced Study, 2007—. Vis. faculty dept. computer sci. Stanford U., fall 1982, cons. assoc. prof. computer sci. and linguistics, 1984-85, computer sci., 1985-87; vis. scholar dept. computer and info. sci. U. Pa., Jan.-June 1982; conf. chair Internat. Joint Conf. on Artificial Intelligence (IJCAI-91), chair bd. trustees IJCAI Inc., 1989-91, mem. bd. trustees, 1987-97, program com. 1982; Harold Perlman vis. prof. faculty sci. Hebrew U., Jerusalem, 1992; invited spkr. numerous nat. and internat. profl. assns., confs., symposia; reviewer program proposals NSF; participant adv. meetings for rsch. and funding various govtl. agys. Author: (with others) Elements of Discourse Understanding, 1982, Understanding Spoken Language, 1982, Foundations of Cognitive Science, 1988, Intentions in Communications, 1988; editor: (with Sparck Jones, Webber) Readings in Natural Language Processing, 1986; assoc. editor: Ann. Rev. Computer Sci., 1982-1985; editl. bd.: Artificial Intelligence Jour., 1982—, Am. Jour. Computational Linguistics, 1981-83; contbr. articles and papers to profl. jours., workshops and conf. procs. Recipient Disting. Alumna award in computer sci. and engring., U. Calif., Berkeley, 1997, Donald E. Walker Disting. Svc. award, IJCAI, 2001. Fellow Am. Acad. Arts & Sci., Am. Assn. Artificial Intelligence (exec. coun. 1981-84, 86-89, pres.-elect 1991-93, pres. 1993-95, past pres. 1995-97, disting. svc. award, 1999), Assn. Computing Machinery (vice chair 1979-81, chair 1981-83, mem. SIGART), Am. Acad. Arts & Sci.; mem. NRC (computer sci. & telecom. bd. 1994-98), Assn. Computational Linguistics (exec. com. 1986-88), Am. Philos. Soc. Avocations: hiking, wildflower photography, snorkeling. Office: Radcliffe Inst Advanced Study 10 Garden St Cambridge MA 02138*

GROTE, DICK (RICHARD CHARLES), management consultant, educator, writer, radio commentator; b. NYC, Dec. 14, 1941; s. Charles Henry and Muriel (Steele) G.; m. Jacqueline Center, May 11, 1991. BA, Colgate U., 1959; M Liberal Arts, So. Meth. U., 1992. Pers. mgr. GE, Schenectady, 1964—67; mgr. mgmt. devel. United Air Lines, Chgo., 1967-72; mgr. tng. and devel. Frito-Lay, Inc., Dallas, 1972-77; pres. Performance Systems Corp., Dallas, 1977-87; prin. Grote Cons. Corp., Dallas, 1987—. Adj. prof. U. Dallas Grad. Sch. Mgmt., 1977—; commentator NPR, 1993—; reviewer Inst. Mus. Svcs., 1974-77. Author: Positive Discipline, 1985, Discipline Without Punishment, 1995, The Complete Guide to Performance Appraisal, 1996, The Performance Appraisal Q&A Book, 2002, Forced Ranking, 2005; host (film series) Respect and Responsibility; contbr. articles to profl. jours. Trustee, pres. Schaumburg (Ill.) Pub. Libr., 1969-72; bd. dirs. Shakespeare Festival Dallas, 1981-84, Dallas Opera, 1981-88; chmn. So. Meth. U. Conservatory Soc., 1988—; bd. councillors U. Dallas, 1989—. Recipient Torch award ASTD, 1979, Disting. Svc. award Malaysian Soc. for Tng. and Devel., 1984, Bapindo award Govt. of Indonesia, 1984. Republican. Office: Grote Cons Corp 15303 Dallas Pkwy Ste 1310 Addison TX 75001-6725 Office Phone: 972-702-7555. Business E-Mail: dickgrote@groteconsulting.com.

GROTE, JONATHAN, chemist, researcher; b. NJ, Apr. 28, 1957; s. Barbara Grote; m. Elizabeth Werner, May 1992; children: Diana, Timothy. BS in Chemistry, Lebanon Valley Coll., Annville, Pa., 1979; PhD, Ind. U., Bloomington, 1984. Sr. rsch. assoc. Abbott Labs., Abbott Park, Ill., 1989—96, rsch. investigator, 1996—. Contbr. articles to profl. jours. Mem. Libertyville Village Band, Ill., 1998—; cubmaster Pack 194, Libertyville, Ill., 2002—04, commissioner, 2004—05, scoutmaster, 2005—; mem. Libertyville Cmty. Emergency Response Team. Recipient Abbott Diagnostics Divsn. Sci. award, 2002. Mem.: Am. Chem. Soc. (meeting sect. chmn. 1998—99). Achievements include patents for barbiturate assay, tracers, immunogens, antibodies and kit: a fluorescence polarization immunoassay for barbiturates which includes synthetic immunogens and labeled barbiturate compounds; phencyclidine metabolites, assay, tracers, immunogens, antibodies, and reagent kit; propoxyphene assay, tracers, immunogens, antibodies, and kit. Home: 1682 Wilton Libertyville IL 60048 Home Phone: 847-937-2167; Office Phone: 847-937-2167.

GROTEN, BARNET, energy executive; b. Bklyn., Oct. 25, 1933; s. Irving and Pearl G.; m. Iris Diane Brand, Aug. 1955; children: Eric Allen, Kurt David, Jessica Amy. BS, Bklyn. Coll., 1954; PhD, Purdue U., 1961. Joined Exxon Co., various locations, 1961; dir. rsch. and bus. devel. Tex. Eastern Corp., Houston, 1977-87; exec. v.p. Tex. Eastern Devel., Inc., 1980-87; sec. Gulf Univs. Research Consortium, 1980-81; chmn. bd. Gulf Univs. Rsch. Consortium, 1982-83; exec. dir. Energy Ctr. U. Okla., Norman, 1987-91; v.p. Energy Internat., Inc., Bellevue, Wash., 1991-99; pres., CEO Grait Techs., LLC, Bellevue, 1999—, Power Genix Systems, Inc., Bellevue, 2001—03. Contbr. articles to profl. jours. Mem. Gov.'s Energy Adv. Coun.; chmn. Natural Gas Vehicle Task Force. Office: Grait Techs LLC 3810 Agape Ln Austin TX 78735 Home: 3810 Agape Ln Austin TX 78735 Home Phone: 512-351-8569; Office Phone: 512-351-8569, 512-351-8569. E-mail: bgroten@austin.rr.com.

GROTH, ALEXANDER JACOB, political science professor; b. Warsaw, Mar. 7, 1932; came to U.S., 1947; s. Jacob and Maria (Hazenfuss) Goldwasser; m. Marilyn Ann Wineburg, Dec. 15, 1961; children: Stevin James, Warren Adrian. BA magna cum laude, CCNY, 1954; MA, Columbia U., NYC, 1955, PhD, 1960. Instr. polit. sci. Trinity Coll., Hartford, Conn., 1957-58, CUNY, 1960-61; asst. prof. Harpur Coll., Binghamton, NY, 1961-62, U. Calif., Davis, 1962-71, prof., 1971—. Author: Revolution and Elite Access, 1966, Comparative Politics, 1971, Major Ideologies, 1971, 2d rev. edit., 1983, People's Poland, 1972, Progress and Chaos, 1984, Lincoln: Authoritarian Savior, 1995, Democracies Against Hitler, 1999, Holocaust Voices, 2003; co-author: Contemporary Politics: Europe, 1976, Comparative Resource Allocation, 1984, Public Policy Across Nations, 1985; editor: Revolution and Political Change, 1996; mem. editl. bd. Political Crossroads, 1996-, The Jersualem Rev., 2007; contbr. Encyclopedia Americana Annuals, Poland, 1965-2001, The Encyclopedia of Political Revolutions,

1998; contbr. numerous articles to encys., scholarly jours. Recipient Ward medal dept. govt. CCNY, 1954, T. R. Dye award, 2000; grantee Am. Co. Learned Socs. and Social Sci. Research Council, 1965-66; nominee Panunzio award, U. Calif., Davis, 2004, 05. Mem. Western Polit. Sci. Assn., Policy Studies Assn., Far West Slavic Assn., Phi Beta Kappa. Republican. Avocations: baseball, writing, painting, travel, reading. Home: 1848 Rushmore Ln Davis CA 95616-6654 Office: U Calif Dept Polit Sci Davis CA 95616 Office Phone: 530-752-0966. Personal E-mail: marilynag@aol.com.

GROTHENDIECK, ALEXANDRE, retired mathematician; b. Berlin, Mar. 28, 1928; s. Alexander Shapiro and Hanka Grothendieck. Student, Monpellier U., Ecole Normale Supérieur, Paris, 1948-49; PhD, U. Nancy; postgrad., U. San Paulo, 1953-55, U Kans., 1956. With Centre Nat. de la Recherche Scientifique, 1950-53, 56-59; chair Institut des Hautes Etudes Scientifique, 1959-70; vis. prof. Coll. France, 1970-72, Orsay, 1972-73; prof. U. Montpellier, 1973-84; dir. rsch. Centre Nat. de la Recherche Scientifique, 1984-88. Recipient Fields medal, 1966. Achievements include fields of abstract algebra, category theory, algebraic geometry and logic; declined Craford prize, 1988.

GROTJAHN, MARK, painter; b. Pasadena, Calif., 1968; BFA, Univ. Colo., Boulder; MFA, Univ. Calif., Berkeley. Exhibited in group shows at Mus. Contemporary Art, Los Angeles, UCLA Hammer Mus., London Inst. Gallery, 54th Carnegie Internat., Carnegie Mus. Art, Pitts., Pa., 2005, Whitney Biennial, Whitney Mus. Art, NYC, 2006, Mus. Modern Art, NYC, one-man shows include Stephen Friedman Gallery, London, Anton Kern Gallery, NYC, Blum & Poe, Los Angeles, Boom, Chgo., The Saatchi Gallery. Office: UCLA Hammer Gallery 10899 Wilshire Blvd Los Angeles CA 90024

GROTKOWSKI, EDWARD MICHAEL, music educator, director; b. Erie, Pa., June 20, 1954; s. Edward John Grotkowski and Dorothy Patricia Nickerson. BA, Mercyhurst Coll., 1976; MA, Middlebury Coll., 1979; MusM, U. Miami, 1991; postgrad., U. So. Calif., LA, 1992—95. Various tchg. positions, Pa., 1978—90; asst. conductor Greater Miami Youth Symphony, Fla., 1990—91; dir. music West Jefferson H.S., LA, 2000—01, East Jefferson H.S., LA, 2001—. Dir. music St. Philip the Apostle Ch., Pasadena, Calif., 1991—95; music dir. Our Lady of Gulf Ch., Bay St. Louis, Mo., 1996—; adj. prof. Nunez C.C., La., 1998—. Bd. dirs. Philharmonic Youth Orchestra, Erie, Pa., 1985—88. Mem.: Am. Fedn. Tchrs., Am. Guild Organists, Music Educators Nat. Avocations: boating, reading, travel. Home: 6640 Alii Pl Diamondhead MS 39525 Office: East Jefferson HS 400 Phlox Ave Metairie LA 70001

GROTON, JAMES PURNELL, lawyer, arbitrator; b. Newport News, Va., Oct. 29, 1927; s. Lafayette Watson and Mary (Skidmore) Groton; m. Lora Frances Webster, June 13, 1953 (dec. Mar. 1999); m. Eve Oxford, May 6, 2006; children: James Purnell, Hunter W., Molly Groton Urban, Lora Groton Rust. AB cum laude, Princeton U., 1949; LLB, U. Va., 1954. Bar: D.C. 1954, Ga. 1955, U.S. Supreme Ct. 1964. Assoc. Sutherland, Asbill & Brennan, Atlanta, 1954—61, ptnr., 1961—2001. Lectr. to profl. socs. on alternative dispute resolution and constrn. Editor: (articles) Va. Law Rev., 1953—54; contbr. articles to profl. jours. Chmn. Constrn. Industry Dispute Avoidance and Resolution Task Force, 1991—94; bd. dirs. Atlanta Coun. for Internat. Visitors, 1968—75; bd. dirs., treas. N.W. Ga. coun., Girl Scouts U.S., 1973—79; trustee South Kent Sch., Conn., 1973—77, Nat. Assn. Women in Constrn. Edn. Found., 1993—98. Sgt. USMC, 1946—48, capt. USMC, 1950—52. Recipient medal excellence, Engrng. News-Record, 1993. Fellow: Chartered Inst. Arbitrators, Coll. of Comml. Arbitrators, Am. Coll. Constrn. Lawyers (pres. 2000—01); mem.: AIA (hon. Bronze medal 1984), Princeton Alumni Assn. Ga. (v.p. 1964—77), Internat. Inst. Conflict Prevention and Resolution (Alternative Dispute Resolution award 1988, 1994), Ga. Coun. Sch. Bd. Attys. (exec. com. 1971—78), Nat. Assn. Coll. and Univ. Attys., Nat. Sch. Bds. Assn. Coun. of Sch. Attys., Am. Arbitration Assn. (nat. panel constrn. arbitrators 1970—, bd. dirs. 1990—2002, nat. constrn. dispute resolution com. 1992—, internat. panel arbitrators 2001—, Whitney North Seymour medal 1983), Atlanta Bar Assn. (chmn. constrn. sect. 1992—93), State Bar Ga., Nat. Acad. of Constrn., Old War Horse Lawyers Club, Piedmont Driving Club, Peachtree Club, Phi Delta Phi. Democrat. Episcopalian. Office: Suite 2300 999 Peachtree St NE Atlanta GA 30309-3996 Home Phone: 404-815-4865; Office Phone: 404-853-8071. Business E-Mail: jim.groton@sablaw.com.

GROTTEROD, KNUT, retired paper company executive; b. Sarpsborg, Norway, Feb. 12, 1922; emigrated to Can., 1945, naturalized, 1954; s. Klaus and Maria Magdalena (Thoresen) G.; m. Isabel Edwina MacMaster, Feb. 25, 1950; children: Ingrid, Christopher, Karen. Grad., Tech. Coll., Horten, Norway, 1945; BME, McGill U., Can., 1949, postgrad, 1951; DSc (hon.), U. Maine, 1987. Exec. in Residence (hon.), U. N.B., 1989. With Consol. Bathurst Ltd., Que., Canada, 1951-70; v.p. prodn., gen. mgr. N.S. Forest Industries, Port Hawkesbury, Canada, 1970-73; from v.p. mfg. to chmn. Fraser Inc., Edmundston, N.B., Canada, 1973—87; ret., 1987. Chmn. bd. Atlantic Waferboard, Chatam, N.B., 1985-87, Island Paper Mills, Vancouver, B.C., 1985-87, Alta. Newsprint Co. Ltd., Whitecourt, 1988-90, Rsch. and Productivcity Coun., Fredericton, N.B., 1986—, Incutech Brunswick, 1988-94, Potato Devel. and Mktg. Coun., Fredericton, 1989-90. Bd. dirs. Can.-Scandinavian Found., Montreal, 1974-75, v.p., 1975-77, pres., 1978-94; mem. bd. govs. U. N.B. With Norwegian Underground Army, 1941-45. Mem. N.B. Forest Products Assn. (dir. 1983-88, pres. 1985-88), Pulp & Paper Assn. Can., Corp. Profl. Engrs. N.B., Rotary Internat. (dist. gov. 1996-97). Home: 67 Castleton Ct Fredericton NB Canada E3B 6H3 Office: Rsch & Productivity Coun 921 College Hill Rd Fredericton NB Canada E3B 6Z9

GROTZINGER, JOHN PETER, paleontologist, educator; BSc, Hobart Coll., 1979; MSc, U. Mont., 1981; PhD, Va. Poly. Inst. and State U., 1985. Postdoctoral rschr. Columbia U. Lamont-Doherty Geol. Obs., 1985—88; asst. prof. MIT, 1988—91, assoc. prof., 1991—95, prof., 1998—2005, Waldemar Lingren Disting. scholar, 1998—2001, Robert E. Shrock prof. geology, 2001—05; Fletcher Jones prof. geology dept. geol. and planetary scis. Calif. Inst. Tech., Pasadena, 2005—. Mem. geology and long term planning grps. Mars Exploration Rover mission, 2004. Contbr. articles to sci. jours.; co-author: Understanding Earth. Recipient Donath medal, Geol. Soc. Am., 1992, Henno Martin medal, Geol. Soc. Namibia, Jubilee medal, Geol. Soc. South Africa. Mem.: NAS (Charles Doolittle Walcott medal 2007). Office: Calif Inst Tech Dept Geol and Planetary Scis MC 170-25 1200 E California Blvd Pasadena CA 91125 Office Phone: 626-395-6785. E-mail: grotz@gps.caltech.edu.*

GROTZINGER, LAUREL ANN, librarian, educator; b. Truman, Minn., Apr. 15, 1935; d. Edward F. and Marian Gertrude (Greeley) G. BA cum laude, Carleton Coll., 1957; MS, U. Ill., 1958, PhD, 1964. Instr., asst. libr. Ill. State U., 1958-62; asst. prof. Western Mich. U., Kalamazoo, 1964-66, assoc. prof., 1966-68, prof., 1968—, asst. dir. Sch. Librarianship, 1965-72, chief rsch. officer, 1979-86, interim dir. Sch. Libr. and Info. Sci., 1982-86, dean grad. coll., 1979-92, prof. univ. libr., 1993—. Author: The Power and the Dignity, 1966, Perspectives: A Library School's First Quarter Century, 1970, Women's Work: Vision and Changes in Libraianship, 1994; mem. editl. bd. Jour. Edn. for Librarianship, 1973-77, Dictionary Am. Libr. Biography, 1975-77, Mich. Academician, 1990—; contbr. chpts. to books; contbr. articles to profl. jours., books; contbr. book revs. Trustee Kalamazoo Pub. Libr., 1991-93, v.p., 1991-92, pres., 1992-93; pres. Kalamazoo Bach Festival, 1996-97, bd. dirs. 1992-98, exec. com. 1996-98. Recipient Alumna award, U. Ill., Tchg. citation, We. Mich. U. Mem. ALA (sec.-treas. Libr. History Round Table 1973-74, vice chmn., chmn-elect 1983-84, chmn. 1984-85, mem.-at-large 1991-93), Spl. Librs. Assn., Assn. Libr. Info. Sci. Edn., Mich. acad. Sci., Arts and Letters (mem.-at-large, exec. com. 1980-86, pres. 1983-85, exec. com. 1990-94, pres. 1991-93, vice chmn. libr./info. scis. 1996-97, chair 1997-98), Internat. Assn. Torch Clubs (v.p. Kalamazoo chpt. 1992-93, pres. 1993-94, exec. com. 1989-95), Soc. Collegiate Journalists, Goldne Key, Phi Beta Kappa (pres. S.W. Mich. chpt. 1977-78, sec. 1994-97, pres. 1997-99), Beta Phi Mu, Alpha Beta Alpha, Delta Kappa Gamma (pres. Alpha Psi chpt. 1988-92), Phi Kappa Phi. Home: 2729 Mockingbird Dr Kalamazoo MI 49008-1626 Home Phone: 269-381-1865; Office Phone: 269-387-5418. Business E-Mail: laurel.grotzinger@wmich.edu.

GROUDINE, MARK TERRY, oncologist; married. BS in Zoology, U. Wis., 1970; MD, U. Pa., 1975, PhD, 1976. Lic. physician Wash., 1990. Vis. scientist dept. molecular biology Swiss Inst. Exptl. Cancer Rsch., Lausanne, Switzerland, 1972—73; vis. fellow dept. biochem. scis. Princeton U., Princeton, NJ, 1975—76; intern and resident in radiation oncology U. Wash. Sch. Medicine, Seattle, 1976—80, asst. prof. radiation oncology, adj. asst. prof. dept. pathology, 1979—83, assoc. prof. radiation oncology, adj. assoc. prof. pathology, 1983—86, full prof. radiation oncology, adj. full prof. pathology, 1986—; asst. mem. basic scis. divsn. Fred Hutchinson Cancer Rsch. Ctr., 1979—83, assoc. mem. basic scis. divsn., 1983—86, program head molecular medicine program, 1986—95, full mem. basic scis. divsn., 1995—, dep. dir., 1998—. Mem. bd. sci. counselors divsn. cancer treatment Nat. Cancer Inst., 1986—91. Recipient, Allison Eberlein Fund award, 1989; fellow Clin. fellow, Am. Cancer Soc., 1979—80, Leukemia Soc. fellow, 1977—79, Med. Scientist Tng. Program fellow, NIH, 1970—72. Fellow: Am. Acad. Arts & Sciences, AAAS; mem.: Nat. Acad. Sci. and Inst. Medicine (life). Office: Fred Hutchinson Cancer Rsch Ctr 1100 Fairview Ave N A2M-015 PO Box 19024 Seattle WA 98109-1024 Office Phone: 206-667-4497. Office Fax: 206-667-6525. E-mail: markg@fhcrc.org.

GROUF, NICK, information technology, advertising executive; b. NY; BA, Yale U.; MBA, Harvard Bus. Sch. With McKinsey & Co., NYC, Goldman Sachs, NYC; co-founder, chmn. & CEO Firefly Network, Inc., 1995—98; co-founder, dir. Internet Advt. Bur.; co-founder TrustE; venture ptnr. Softbank Tech. Ventures, San Jose, Calif.; co-founder, chmn. & CEO PeoplePC, Inc., 2000—02, Spot Runner, Inc., LA, 2006—. Recipient Norman Holmes Pearson prize, Yale U. Achievements include development of Firefly Passport. Office: Spot Runner 6300 Wilshire Blvd Los Angeles CA 90048 Mailing: Spot Runner Inc PO Box 361253 Los Angeles CA 90036 Office Phone: 310-430-7900. Office Fax: 310-430-7999.*

GROUNDS, VERNON CARL, seminary administrator; b. Jersey City, July 19, 1914; s. John and Bertha Barbara (Heimburg) G.; m. Ann Barton, June 17, 1939; 1 child, Barbara Ann Grounds Owen. BA, Rutgers U., 1937; BD, Faith Theol. Sem., 1940; DD (hon.), Wheaton Coll., 1954; PhD, Drew U., 1960; LHD (hon.), Gordon Coll., 1977. Pastor Paterson (NJ) Gospel Tabernacle, 1935-45; dean, prof. theology Bapt. Bible Sem., Johnson City, 1945-51; dean Denver Conservative Bapt. Sem., 1951-55, pres., 1955-79, chancellor, 1979—. Author: Yes, But How?, Emotional Problems and the Gospel, Evangelicalism and Social Responsibility, The Reason for Our Hope, Revolution and the Christian Faith; contbg. editor Christianity Today, 1980—. Sec. Evang. Theol. Soc., Lynchburg, Va., 1963-76; bd. dirs. Radio Bible Class Ministries. Home: 3455 S Corona St Apt 513 Englewood CO 80113-2878 Office: 6399 S Sante Fe Dr Littleton CO 80120 Office Phone: 303-762-6890.

GROUSBECK, HAROLD IRVING, professional sports team owner, management educator; 1 child, Wycliffe. AB, Amherst Coll., 1956; MBA, Harvard Bus. Sch., 1960; LHD (hon.), Amherst Coll., 2000. Co-founder Continental Cablevision, 1963, pres., 1964—80, chmn. bd., 1980—85; lectr. Harvard U. Grad. Sch. Bus. Adminstrn., 1981—85; vis. lectr. Stanford U., Calif., 1985—86, lectr., 1986—96, consulting prof. mgmt., co-head Ctr. Entrepreneurial Studies, 1996—; mng. ptnr., mem. exec. com. Boston Celtics, 2002—. Bd. dirs. Asurion. Co-author: New Bus. Ventures and the Entrepreneur. Office: Stanford Grad Sch Bus Ctr Entrepreneurial Studies 518 Memorial Way Stanford CA 94305-5015 Office Phone: 650-723-7655. Office Fax: 650-725-7461. E-mail: grous@stanford.edu.*

GROUSBECK, WYCLIFFE, professional sports team owner, venture capitalist; s. H. Irving Grousbeck; m. Corinne Grousbeck. BA in Hist., Princeton U., NJ, 1983; JD, U. Mich.; MBA, Stanford U., Calif. Atty. Brobeck, Phleger & Harrison, 1986—90; founder, pres. MedWise, 1990—95; gen. ptnr. Highland Capital Ptnrs., 1995—2002, venture ptnr., 2002—; mng. ptnr., gov., CEO Boston Celtics, 2002—. Chair planning com. NBA, mem. audit & compensation com., adv./fin. com. Office: Highland Capital Ptnrs 92 Hayden Ave Lexington MA 02421*

GROUT, ROBERT W., lawyer; b. Memphis, Nov. 2, 1944; s. M. Wayne and Evelyn (McClure) G.; m. Marsha Karkula, Aug. 12, 1967; children: Brad, Taylor. BA in Econs., Vanderbilt U., 1966; LLB, U. Va., 1969. Bar: Ga. 1969, Ga. Supreme Ct. 1970, Ga. Ct. of Appeals 1970, U.S. Dist. Ct. (no. dist.) Ga. 1975, U.S. Supreme Ct. 1975. Assoc. Troutman, Sanders, Lockerman & Ashmore, Atlanta, 1969-73; ptnr. Troutman Sanders LLP, Atlanta, 1974-85, sr. ptnr., sect. chief, corp. dept., 1986—2006, mem., exec. com, ptnr. compensation com., opinion com., tech. com. Seminar speaker Atlanta Bar Assn., 1986-99. Bd. dirs. Ashford-Dunwoody YMCA, 1984-93, Met. Atlanta YMCA, 1998-2004, Boy Scouts of Am. Troop, 1986-92; pres. Neighborhood Civic Assn., 1984—2004; mem. fin. com. Cherokee Town & Country Club, 1991—2003, pres. 2003-04. Named a Super Lawyer, Atlanta Mag., 2006; named one of America's Leading Bus. Lawyers, Chambers USA, 2005, Legal Elite, Ga. Trend Mag., 2005. Mem. ABA, State Bar Ga., Atlanta Bar Assn., Dunwoody Rotary Club (dir. 1984-91), Ravinia Club. Avocations: hunting, fishing, computers, photography. Office: Troutman Sanders LLP 600 Peachtree St NE Ste 5200 Atlanta GA 30308-2216 Office Phone: 404-885-3152. Office Fax: 404-962-6789. Business E-Mail: bob.grout@troutmansanders.com.

GROVE, ANDREW STEVEN, electronics executive; b. Budapest, Hungary, Sept. 2, 1936; m. Eva Kaston, 1958; 2 children. BS in Chemical Engrng., CCNY, 1960; PhD, U. Calif., Berkeley, 1963; DSc (hon.), CCNY, 1985; DEng (hon.), Worcester Poly. Inst., 1989; LLD (hon.), Harvard U., 2000. With Fairchild Semiconductor, 1963—67, asst. dir. rsch. & devel., 1967—68; co-founder Intel Corp., Santa Clara, Calif., 1968, v.p., dir. ops., 1968—74, exec. v.p., 1975—76, COO, 1976—87, pres., 1979—97, CEO, 1987—98, chmn. bd., 1997—2005, sr. adviser, 2005—. Mem. bd. dirs. Intel Corp., 1974—; tchr. grad. course in semiconductor device physics U. Calif., Berkeley; lectr. Stanford Grad. Sch. of Bus. Author: Physics and Technology of Semiconductor Devices, 1967, High Output Management, 1983, One on One with Andy Grove, 1987, Only the Paranoid Survive: How To Exploit the Crisis Points That Challenge Every Company and Career, 1996, (autobiography) Swimming Across, 2001; co-author (with Robert A. Burgelman): Strategic Dynamics: Concepts and Cases, 2005, author of articles in Fortune, The Wall Street Journal, and The NY Times, weekly column on mgmt. carried by several newspapers, (column on mgmt.) Working Women. Patient advocate U. Calif., San Francisco, nat. chair of campaign; bd. dir. Prostrate Cancer Found.; active Grove Found. Named Exec. of Yr., U. Ariz., 1993, Citizen of Yr., World Forum Silicon Valley, 1993, Statesman of Yr., Harvard Bus. Sch., 1996, Tech. Leader of Yr., Industry Week, 1997, Man of Yr., Time mag., 1997, CEO of Yr., CEO mag., 1997, Distinguished Exec. of Yr., Acad. Mgmt., 1998, Most Influential Bus. Person in the Last Twenty-Five Yrs., Wharton Sch. Bus., 2004, Nightly Business Report, 2004, in honor of CCNY Grove School of Engrng., 2005; recipient Am. Inst. Chemists medal, 1960, Merit cert., Franklin Inst., 1975, Townsend Harris medal, CCNY, 1980, Hall of Fame award, Information Industries Assn., 1984, Enterprise award, Bus. and Profl. Advt. Assn., 1987, George Washington award, Am. Hungarian Found., 1990, Achievement medal, Am. Electronics Assn., 1993, Heinz Family Tech. Found. award, 1995, John von Neumann medal, Am. Hungarian Assn., 1995, Steinman medal, CCNY, 1995, Internat. Achievement award, World Trade Club, 1997, Cinema Digital Technols. award, Internat. Film Festival, 1997, Cinema Digital Tech. award, Cannes Film Festival, 1997, Disting. Exec. of the Yr., Acad. of Mgmt., 1998, Lifetime Achievement award, Strategic Mgmt. Soc., 2001, Ernest C. Arbuckle award, Stanford U. Grad. Sch. Bus., 2004. Fellow: IEEE (Achievement award 1969, J.J. Ebers award 1974, Engrng. Leadership Recognition award 1987, Computer Entrepreneur award 1997, Medal of Honor award 2000), Am. Acad. Arts and Scis.; mem.: NAE (award 1979). Achievements include patents in field. Office: Intel Corp 2200 Mission College Blvd Santa Clara CA 95052 Office Phone: 408-765-8080. Office Fax: 408-765-9904.

GROVE, BRANDON HAMBRIGHT, JR., diplomat; b. Chgo., Apr. 8, 1929; s. Brandon Hambright and Helen Julia (Gasparska) G.; m. Marie Cheremeteff, 1959 (div. 1983); children: John C., Catherine C.G. Jones, Paul C., Mark C.; m. Mariana Alfaro Moran, 1988 (dec. 2006); 1 step child, Michele Parsons Shotts. AB, Bard Coll., 1950; M.P.A., Princeton U., 1952. Joined U.S. Fgn. Svc., 1959; vice consul Abidjan, Ivory Coast, also Upper Volta, Niger, and Dahomey, 1959-61; staff asst. to undersec. state, 1961-62; spl. asst. to dep. undersec. state for adminstrn., 1962-63; spl. asst. to Am. amb. to India, New Delhi, 1963—65; U.S. liaison officer to city govt. West Berlin Germany, 1965—69; dir. Office Panamanian Affairs, State Dept., 1969-71; mem. Sr. Seminar in Fgn. Policy, 1971-72; dep. dir. State Dept. policy planning staff, Washington; also staff dir. Under Secretaries Com. of NSC, 1972-74; chargé d' affaires, then dep. chief of mission Am. Embassy to German Dem. Republic, Berlin, 1974-76; fgn. svc. sr. insp. Dept. State, 1976-78; dep. asst. sec. state for Inter-Am. affairs, 1978-80; consul gen. Jerusalem, 1980—83; Capstone fellow Nat. Def. U., Fort McNair, Washington, 1984; ambassador to Zaire, Kinshasa, 1984-87; coord. State Dept. Budget Rev., Washington, 1987-88; dir. Fgn. Service Inst., Washington, 1988-92; diplomat-in-residence Georgetown U., Washington, 1992-93; sr. advisor State Dept. Policy Planning Staff, Washington, 1993-94; retired U.S. Fgn. Svc., 1994. Asst. instr. Princeton U., 1953; sr. cons. APCO Assocs., Inc., Washington, 1996-2000, Sol M. Linowitz prof. internat. affairs Hamilton Coll.; pres. Am. Acad. Diplomacy, Washington, 2006-2007, exec. dir. Genocide Prevention Task Force, 2007—. Author: Behind Embassy Walls: The Life and Times of an American Diplomat, 2005; chmn. editl. bd. Fgn. Svc. Jour., 1992-94. Served to lt. USNR, 1954-57. Recipient Pres.'s Meritorious Service award, 1985, 90, 92, John Dewey medal for disting. pub. svc. Bard Coll., 1990. Mem. Am. Acad. Diplomacy, Am. Fgn. Svc. Assn. (achievement award 2000), Washington Inst. Fgn. Affairs, Coun. on Fgn. Rels., Georgetown U. Inst. for Study of Diplomacy (bd. dirs.), Assn. for Diplomatic Studies and Tng. (bd. dirs.), Diplomatic and Consular Officers Ret., Met. Club Washington, Cosmos Club. Home: 2540 Massachusetts Ave NW Washington DC 20008 E-mail: brandongrove@earthlink.net.

GROVE, DAVID D., anthropology professor; PhD Anthropology, UCLA, 1968. Faculty SUNY, Binghamton, Calif. State U., Northridge; prof. U. of IL, Urbana-Champaign, 1970—2001, prof. emeritus, 2001—; prof. U. of FL. Pres., Anthropology div. Am. Anthropology Assoc., 1992—93. Recipient Distinguished Teaching Award, College of Liberal Arts & Sci. Fellow: Am. Acad. Arts & Sci.; mem.: Am. Anthropology Assoc. Office: Dept of Anthropology University of Florida 1112 Turlington Hall PO Box 117305 Gainesville FL 32611

GROVE, DAVID LAVAN, lawyer; b. Johnstown, Pa., Nov. 4, 1937; s. William Morgan and Edith Elizabeth (Boyd) G.; m. Barbara Pearson Fogg, Aug. 26, 1961; children: Jonathan Morgan, Amy Pearson. BA in Polit. Sci. with honors, Dickinson Coll., 1959; LLB, Yale U., 1962. Bar: Pa. 1965, U.S. Dist. Ct. (ea. dist.) Pa. 1966, U.S. Ct. Appeals (3d cir.) 1972, U.S. Supreme Ct. 1976, U.S. Ct. Internat. Trade 1977, U.S. Dist. Ct. (mid. dist.) Pa. 1990. Vol. US Peace Corps, Nigeria, 1962-64, atty-advisor Washington, 1967-69; assoc. Montgomery, McCracken, Walker & Rhoads, LLP, Phila., 1964-67, 69-72; ptnr. Montgomery, McCracken, Walker & Rhoads, 1972—2007, sr. counsel, 2007—. Asst. lectr. law faculty U. Lagos, Nigeria, 1962-64, Office of Peace Corps Gen. Counsel, Washington, 1967-69; adv. fed. law and regulations Peace Corps ofcls.; U.S. del. to Coun. Internat. Secretariat for Vol. Svc., Washington, 1968, Geneva, 1969. Bd. sch. dirs. Wallingford (Pa.)-Swarthmore Sch. Dist., 1975-87, bd. pres., 1977-79, 82-84; active Wallingford-Swarthmore Sch. Authority, 1988-99, pres., 1995-99; bd. dirs. Recs. for Blind and Dyslexic, Phila., 1994-2003; active Corp. Am. Friends Svc. Com., Phila., 2002—, Swarthmore Borough Planning Commn., 2004—; Swarthmore Borough rep. Ctrl. Delaware County Authority, 2004—. Fellow: Am. Coll. Trial Lawyers; mem.: ABA, Phila. Bar Assn., Rolling Green Golf Club (Springfield, Pa.), Theta Chi, Omicron Delta Kappa, Pi Gamma Mu, Delta Phi Alpha. Democrat. Mem. Soc. Of Friends. Avocations: golf, snorkeling, scuba diving. Home: 80 Yale Ave Swarthmore PA 19081-1607 Office: Montgomery McCracken Et Al 123 S Broad St 24th Fl Philadelphia PA 19109 Home Phone: 610-544-8283; Office Phone: 215-772-7234. Personal E-mail: dlgrove@gmail.com. Business E-Mail: dgrove@mmwr.com.

GROVE, JANET E., retail executive; BS in Mktg., Calif. State U., Hayward, 1973. Exec. trainee Macy's West, San Francisco, 1973—74, from asst. buyer to gen. merchandise mgr., 1974—92; from sr. v.p. to exec. v.p. Broadway, Inc., 1992—96; sr. v.p. center core merchandising Federated Merchandising Group, Cin., 1996—97, exec. v.p. ready-to-wear and center core, 1997—98, exec. v.p. center core, cosmetics and home merchandising, 1998, CEO, exec. v.p. center core, cosmetics and home merchandising, 1999—; vice chair Macy's Inc. (formerly Federated Dept. Stores Inc.), Cin., 2003—. Recipient Humanitarian award, Nat. Jewish Med. and Rsch. Ctr., Denver, 2000, HUG award, Intimate Apparel Square Club, 2002. Office: Macy's Inc 7 W Seventh St Cincinnati OH 45202*

GROVE, JEFFREY SCOTT, family practice physician; b. Paxton, Ill., Sept. 21, 1964; s. Ronald Edwin and Delores Ann (Martensen) G.; m. Karen Beth Hanlon, June 17, 1989; children: Garrett Jeffrey, Victoria May. BS in Biology, Fla. So. Coll., 1986; DO, Southeastern Coll. Osteo Med., North Miami Beach, Fla., 1990. Diplomate Am. Bd. Quality Assurance and Utilization Rev. Physicians; bd. cert. family practice and in geriatrics. Intern Suncoast Hosp., Largo, Fla., 1990-91, resident in family practice, 1991-93; pvt. practice SunCoast Family Med. Assocs., Largo, 1993—. Med. dir. Barrington Properties, Largo, 1994-97, Oak Manor Nursing Ctr., Largo, 1993-2000, Drew Village Nursing Ctr., Clearwater, Fla., 1996-99, Highland Pines Nursing Ctr., 1999-2000; rep.-at-large exec. com. Suncoast Hosp., 1995-2000, chief adminstrv. resident, 1992-93, family practice tchg. staff, geriatrics program dir., 1993-96, faculty devel. com., 1994—, legal compliance comm., 1998—; mem. quality assurance/utilization rev. com., 1993—, med. dir. of quality assurance/utilization rev. dept., 1995—06; bd. dirs. Suncoast Cmty. Care PHO, Largo, 1994-98, med. dir., 1998; clin. asst. prof. family medicine Nova Southeastern U. Coll. Osteo. Medicine, North Miami Beach, 1994-2000, clin. assoc. prof., 2000—; clin. instr. Kirksville Coll. Osteo. Medicine, 1993—; trustee SunCoast Hosp. Found., 1996-2002, SunCoast Hosp., 1998—06; regional med. dir. Tampa Bay for Elder Health. Vice-chmn. bd. trustees SCH Found., 1997-98, chmn., 1998-99; trustee St. Paul's Sch., 2003—, chmn. devel. com., 2005—. Named to Outstanding Young Men of Am.; recipient Disting. Trustee award SCH Found., 2000. Mem.: Am. Coll. Family Practitioners (nat. bd. govs.

2004—, Fellows award 2002), Pinellas County Osteo. Med. Soc. (bd. govs. 1995—, treas. 1996—99, pres. 2000—03, Physician of Yr. 2002—03), Fla. Soc. Am. Coll. Osteo. Family Physicians (chmn. membership com. Fla. chpt. 1997—99, trustee 1997—, treas. 1999—2000, v.p. 2000—01, pres. 2001—02, Physician of Yr. 2003—04), Fla. Osteo. Med. Assn. (trustee 2001—, exec. com. 2005—), Am. Osteo. Assn. (mem. coun. continuing med. edn., mem. Bur. of State Govt. Affairs, vice-chmn. coun. on continuing med. edn. 2006—), Nova Southeastern U. Coll. Osteo. Medicine Alumni Assn. (v.p. 2000—01, pres. 2002—03, Disting. Alumni award 2001, Disting. Alumni Achievement award 2003), Scouting Res., Nat. Eagle Scout Assn. (life). Republican. Methodist. Avocations: golf, stamp collecting/philately, travel, skiing. Office: SunCoast Family Med Assocs 12020 Seminole Blvd Largo FL 33778 Home: 53 N Pine Cir Clearwater FL 33756-1453 Office: 120 Medical Blvd Ste 103 Spring Hill FL 34609 Office Phone: 727-588-9572. Personal E-mail: scfma2@earthlink.net.

GROVE, NOEL RANDALL, writer; b. South English, Iowa, Jan. 25, 1938; s. George William and Miriam Helen G.; m. Deanna Sue Goering, Aug. 16, 1958 (div. Feb. 1978); children: Lisa, Amy, Elizabeth; m. Barbara Ann Payne, July 31, 1982; 1 child, Eleni. BA in Eng., McPherson Coll., 1959. Eng., speech tchr. Inman HS, Kans., 1959-61; reporter McPherson Sentinel, Kans., 1961-64; reporter, night editor Hutchinson News, Kans., 1964-66; picture editor Newspaper Enterprise Assn., Cleve., 1966-67, capitol correspondent Washington, 1967-69; writer National Geographic, Washington, 1969-94; freelance writer Middleburg, Va., 1994—. Charter bd. mem. Bicycle Fedn., Washington, 1975—, founding bd. mem. Soc. Environmental Journalists, 1990-93. Author: Wild Lands for Wildlife, 1984, Preserving Eden, 1992, Birds of North America, 1995, Atlas of World History, 1997, Living Planet, 1999, Range of Light, 1999, Earth's Last Great Places, 2003. Democrat. Home: PO Box 1016 Middleburg VA 20118-1016 Personal E-mail: ngrove1253@aol.com.

GROVE, RICHARD CHARLES, retired power tool company executive; b. Bethlehem, Pa., Aug. 13, 1940; s. Dale Addison and Mary Elizabeth G.; m. Cynthia Ann Dimmick, Dec. 7, 1963; 1 child, Jeffrey. BEE, Cornell U., 1962; MBA, U. Pitts., 1967. Mgmt. cons. Touche Ross & Co., Detroit, 1967-72; mgr. bus. planning Amstar Corp., NYC, 1972-75, treas. Spreckels Sugar div. San Francisco, 1975-82, treas. NYC, 1983-84, v.p., controller Stamford, Conn., 1985-88, v.p., chief fin. officer, 1988-89; sr. v.p. Esstar Inc., New Haven, 1989, exec. v.p., dir., 1995; exec. v.p. Milw. Electric Tool Corp., 1990-91, pres., CEO, 1991—2000. Elder Davidson Coll. Presbyn. Ch., 2006; bd. dirs. Carolinas Concert Assn., bd. pres., 2004—06. Served to 1st lt. US Army, 1964—66. Mem.: The Point Lake and Golf Club. Republican. Avocations: golf, reading, travel.

GROVE, TIMOTHY LYNN, geology educator; b. York, Pa., July 15, 1949; s. Arthur Leib and Ruby Janette (Finger) G.; m. Madeline Scadden, June 15, 1971; m. Ann Marie Reilly, June 19, 1979; children: Matthew Brian, Michael Thomas. BA, U. Colo., 1971; AM, Harvard U., 1975, PhD, 1976. Rsch. asst. SUNY, Stony Brook, 1975—79; from asst. prof. to assoc. prof. dept. earth, atmospheric and planet sci. MIT, Cambridge, 1979—91, prof. dept. earth, atmospheric and planet sci., 1991—. Vis. prof. CalTech divsn. geology and tech., Pasadena, 1979; vis. scientist dept. geol. sci. U. Cape Town, 1993—94; rsch. scientist U. Zimbabwe, 1997—2001; vis. prof. divsn. isotope geology and ore deposits Swiss Eidgenossische Tech. Hochschule, Zurich, Switzerland, 2001. Editor Contbns. to Mineralogy and Petrology, 1985—. Fellow: Am. Geophys. Union (Bowen award 1993), Mineralogy Soc. Am.; mem.: Geochem. Soc., Geol. Soc. Am. Home: 87 Menotomy Rd Arlington MA 02476-6111 Office: MIT Earth Atmospheric & Planet Sci 77 Massachusetts Ave # 541220 Cambridge MA 02139-4307 Office Phone: 617-253-2878. Business E-Mail: tlgrove@mit.edu.

GROVER, JAMES ROBB, chemist, editor; b. Klamath Falls, Oreg., Sept. 16, 1928; s. James Richard and Marjorie Alida (van Groos) G.; m. Barbara Jean Ton, Apr. 14, 1957; children: Jonathan Robb, Patricia Jean. BS summa cum laude, valedictorian, U. Wash., Seattle, 1952; PhD, U. Calif., Berkeley, 1958. Rsch. assoc. Brookhaven Nat. Lab., Upton, N.Y., 1957-59, assoc. chemist, 1959-63, chemist, 1963-67, chemist with tenure, 1967-77, sr. chemist, 1978-93, rsch. collaborator, 1993—. Cons. Lawrence Livermore (Calif.) Nat. Lab., 1962; assoc. editor Ann. Rev. of Nuclear Sci., Ann. Revs., Inc., Palo Alto, Calif., 1967-77; vis. prof. Inst. for Molecular Sci., Okazaki, Japan, 1986-87; vis. scientist Max-Planck Inst. für Strömungsforschung, Göttingen, Fed. Republic Germany, 1975-76. Contbr. numerous articles to profl. jours. With USN, 1946-48. Mem. Am. Chem. Soc. (chmn. nuclear chemistry and tech. 1989), Am. Phys. Soc., Triple Nine Soc., Sigma Xi, Phi Beta Kappa, Phi Lambda Upsilon, Zeta Mu Tau, Pi Mu Epsilon. Libertarian. Presbyterian. Achievements include naming of the nuclear yrast levels and discovery of their importance in nuclear reactions; invention of use of short-lived radioactivity in molecular beams; first to successfully use radioactivity for detection in chemically reactive scattering experiments; invention of threshold photoionization method for measuring the dissociation energies of neutral weak complexes in molecular beams. Home and Office: 1536 Pinecrest Ter Ashland OR 97520-3427 E-mail: jrobbgrover@cs.com.

GROVER, MARK DONALD, application developer, computer scientist; b. Augusta, Maine, July 12, 1955; s. Donald William and Aletha D. (Wells) G. BA, U. Fla., 1976; MS, Northwestern U., Evanston, Ill., 1978, PhD, 1982. Cert. EMT and CPR instr. Instr. Northwestern U., Evanston, Ill., 1978—81; mem. tech. staff TRW Def. Sys., Redondo Beach, Calif., Fairfax, Va., 1981—85; sr. computer scientist Advanced Decision Sys., Arlington, Va., 1985—89; prin. software engr. Oberon Software Inc., Cambridge, Mass., 1990—94; sr. software engr. DeLorme Mapping, Yarmouth, Maine, 1995—. Program chmn. Nat. Symbolics User Group Conf., Washington, 1986; mem. computer sci. dept. adv. bd. U. So. Maine; presenter to conferences in field. Contbg. articles to sci. journals. Mem. mcpl. comprehensive plan com. Town of Gray, Maine; exec. dir. Gray Region Citizen Corps, Maine; vol. EMT Gray Fire Rescue, Gray, Maine; trustee First Congl. Ch., Gray, Maine. Named Gray Fire-Rescue Mem. of Yr., 2007. Mem. NRA (life endowment), Phi Beta Kappa, Tau Beta Pi. Avocations: travel, rare books, drama, marksmanship, history. Office: DeLorme Mapping PO Box 298 Yarmouth ME 04096-0298 Office Phone: 207-846-7000. Business E-Mail: mark.grover@delorme.com.

GROVER, NEEL, Internet company executive; BA, U. Calif. Irvine; JD cum laude, U. San Diego. Sr. assoc. Brobeck, Phleger, & Phleger, Jones, Day, Reaves & Pogue; various positions including gen. mgr. ThinkTank Holdings; pres. BuyNetwork, 2003—; pres., COO Buy.com, 2003—. Bd. dirs. TechSpace. Office: Buy dot com 85 Enterprise Ste 100 Aliso Viejo CA 92656 Office Phone: 949-389-2000. Office Fax: 949-389-2800.

GROVER, NORMAN LAMOTTE, theologian, philosopher; b. Topeka, Feb. 9, 1928; s. LaMotte and Virginia Grace (Alspach) G.; m. Anne Stottler, June 24, 1950; children: Jennifer Jean, Peter Neal, Rebecca Louise Grover Verna, Sandra Christine Grover Mason. B. Mech. Engring., Rensselaer Poly. Inst., 1948; B.D., Yale, 1951, S.T.M., 1952, PhD, 1957. Mem. faculty, chaplain Hollins (Va.) Coll., 1954-57, asst. prof. religion, 1956-57; ordained to ministry Presbyn. Ch., 1952; head dept. philosophy and religion Va. Poly. Inst. and State U., 1957-75, prof. philosophy and religion, 1961-83, prof. religion, 1983-91, prof. emeritus, 1991—. Adj. prof. Ctr. for Study Sci. in Soc., 1983-86, guest lectr. computer sci., 2005; mem. supervising com. So. leadership tng. project Fund for Republic, 1955-56; assoc. Danforth Found., 1958—, sr. assoc., 1962—, chmn. Va., N.C. and S.C. conf., 1962; psychotherapeutic counsellor Blacksburg Community Counselling Center, 1962-65 Bd. dirs. YMCA at Va. Tech. (Gold Triangle award 1962); bd. dirs. United Campus Ministries of Blacksburg, 1986-95; mem. Blacksburg Master Chorale and Va. Tech. Concert Choir Concert Tour in Berlin, Poland, Czech Republic, Salzburg, 1992, Germany, Austria, Czech Republic, 1995, England, Scotland, 2003; concert under Robert Shaw, 1998; study trip to Costa Rica, Nicaragua, El Salvador and Guatemala Presbyn. Ch. U.S.A. Presbytery of Peaks Partnership with CEDEPCA, 1989, 91; mem. Habitat for Humanity, New River Valley chpt., Montgomery County Race Rels. Work Group, Ecumenical Alliance of New River Valley; mem. local convening com. Interfaith Social Concerns Network, 1999—; mem. Montgomery County Dem. Com., 2004—; mem. Unified Coalition for Am. Indian Conerns. Danforth Found. grantee, 1967—69. Mem.: AARP (co-chaplain Blacksburg, Va. chpt.), ACLU, NAACP (life; exec. bd. Montgomery, Floyd, Radford br. 1999—, Mountain Climber award 2000, Martin Luther King Jr. Cmty. Svc. award 2006, Kennie B. Hairston Cmty. Svc. award 2006), AAUP (sec.-treas. chpt. 1959—60, v.p. chpt. 1960—61, pres. Va. Poly. Inst. and State U. chpt. 1961—62, sec.-treas. chpt. 1977—80, v.p. chpt. 1980—81, pres. Va. Poly. Inst. and State U. chpt. 1981—82, v.p. chpt. 1992—94), Ctr. for Theology and the Natural Scis., Am. Acad. Religion (chmn. SE region theology/philosophy religion sect. 1983—85, citizen amb. team to Ukraine and Russia 1993, China 1994, Yale U. alumni schs. com. 1997—, Yale Divinity Sch. reunion com. 2006—), So. Soc. Philosophy and Psychology, Va. Philos. Assn. (pres. 1969), People to People Internat. (Am. People amb. del. to India, Nepal and Tibet 1996, China 2000), Wilderness Soc., Smithsonian Assocs., Sierra Club, Bread for the World, Coalition for Justice in Ctrl. Am. (bd. dirs., v.p. 1990—94), Amnesty Internat., So. Poverty Law Ctr. (Wall Tolerance Honoree). Avocations: walking, singing. Home: Warm Hearth Village 1622 Hawthorne Ridge Blacksburg VA 24060-6143 Home Phone: 540-552-3833; Office Phone: 540-552-3833. Business E-Mail: ngrover@warmhearthva.org.

GROVER, ROSALIND REDFERN, oil and gas company executive; b. Midland, Tex., Sept. 5, 1941; d. John Joseph and Rosalind (Kapps) Redfern;m. Arden Roy Grover, Apr. 10, 1982; 1 child, Rosson. BA in Edn. magna cum laude, U. Ariz., 1966, MA in History, 1982; postgrad. in law, So. Meth. U. Libr. Gahr H.S., Cerritos, Calif., 1969; pres. The Redfern Found., Midland, 1982—89; ptnr. Redfern & Grover, Midland, 1986—; pres. Redfern Enterprises Inc., Midland, 1989—. Chmn. bd. dirs. Flag-Redfern Oil Co., Midland. Sec. park and recreation commn. City of Midland, 1969-71, del. Objectives for Convocation, 1980; mem., past pres. women's aux. Midland Cmty. Theatre, 1970; chmn. challenge grant bldg. fund, 1980, chmn. Tex. Yucca Hist. Landmark Renovation Project, 1983, trustee, 1983-88; chmn. publicity com. Midland Jr. League, Midland, Inc., 1972, chmn. edn. com., 1976, corr. sec., 1978; 1st v.p. Midland Symphony Assn., 1975; chmn. Midland Charity Horse Show, 1975-76; mem. Midland Am. Revolution Bicentennial Commn., 1976; trustee Mus. S.W., 1977-80, pres. bd. dirs., 1979-80; co-chmn. Gov. Clements Fin. Com., Midland, 1978; mem. dist. com. State Bd. Law Examiners; mem. bd. visitors Hockaday, 2001-03; trustee Midland Meml. Hosp., 1978-80, Permian Basin Petroleum Mus., Libr. and Hall of Fame, 1989-98, Midland Cmty. Theatre, 2005—. Recipient HamHock award Midland Cmty. Theatre, 1978. Mem. Ind. Petroleum Assn. Am., Tex. Ind. Producers and Royalty Owners Assn., Petroleum Club, Racquet Club (Midland), Horseshoe Bay (Tex.) Country Club, Phi Kappa Phi, Pi Lambda Theta. Republican. Office: 303 W Wall Ste 2102 PO Box 2127 Midland TX 79702-2127 Office Phone: 432-683-9137. E-mail: rozgrover@aol.com.

GROVER, SANJAY, plastic surgeon; b. Calif. married; 1 child. BS, UCLA, 1990; MD, U. Calif., San Diego, 1994. Cert. Med. Bd. Calif., 1995, diplomate Am. Bd. Plastic Surgery, 2002. Surg. intern Stanford U. Med. Ctr., 1994—95, plastic surgery resident, 1997—99, chief resident, 1998—99; surg. resident Stanford Health Svcs., 1995—97; fellow in aesthetic surgery PACES Plastic Surgery, Atlanta, 1999; pvt. practice Newport Beach, Calif., LA. Affiliated Hoag Meml. Hosp. Presbyn., Irvine Multi Specialty Surgery Care Surgery Ctr., Newport Beach Surgery Ctr., Laguna Hills Surgery Ctr. Featured on (TV series) Good Day LA: Style File with Jillian Barbieri, 2002. Fellow: Am. Coll. Surgeons; mem.: AMA (Physician's Recognition award in Continuing Med. Edn. 2004), Orange County Soc. Plastic Surgeons (pres.), Am. Soc. for Laser Medicine & Surgery, Am. Soc. for Aesthetic Plastic Surgery, Am. Soc. Plastic Surgeons. Office: Ctr for Aesthetic Plastic Surgery Ste 507 360 San Miguel Dr Newport Beach CA 92660 also: Ctr for Aesthetic Plastic Surgery Ste 500 9201 Sunset Blvd Los Angeles CA 90069 Office Phone: 949-759-9551, 310-276-4526. E-mail: inquiry@doctorgrover.com.*

GROVER, WILLIAM HERBERT, architect; b. Phila., Feb. 10, 1938; s. William Oliver Grover and Lucy Gertrude (Whetzel) Grover Lott; m. Dora Bradford Apted, Feb. 24, 1962; children: Virginia Lucy, Amy Ellen. Student in mech. engring., Cornell U., 1955-58; B in Profl. Art, Art Ctr. Coll., Pasadena, Calif., 1962; MArch, Yale U., 1969. Registered architect, N.Y., N.H., Conn., Mass. Designer Gen. Motors Corp., Warren, Mich., 1962-65; draftsman MLTW/Moore Turnbull, New Haven, 1969-70; architect, mgr. Charles W. Moore Assocs., Essex, Conn., 1970-75; architect, pres. Moore Grover Harper P.C., Essex, Conn., 1975-84; architect, ptnr. Centerbrook Architects, Essex, Conn., 1984—. Pres. Centerbrook, Architects LLC, Essex, 1984—, bd. dirs.; pres. Mainstream, Inc., 1984—. Prin. works include Jones Lab., 1973 (AIA Honor award 1981), Grace Auditorium, 1986, Neurosci. Ctr., Cold Spring Harbor Lab., 1991, DeKalb Discovery Rsch. Ctr., 1992, Phelps Sci. Bldg., Phillips Exeter Acad., 2003; designer (light fixtures) Slice of Light, 1981 (Progressive Architecture award 1982, 85, Eidolon 1984). Mem. Essex Zoning Commn., 1972-77, Essex Rep. Town Com., 1973-74; bd. dirs. Essex Art Assn., 1989-2000, Community Music Sch., 1991-2003, Essex Land Conservation Trust, 2004—. Recipient Builders' Choice award Nat. Home Builders, 1987, Sportmanship award U.S. Sailing Assn., 1990; named to Domino's Top 30 Architects, 1991, Architectural Digest's Top 100 Architects, 1991. Fellow AIA (Honor award 1981, N.Eng. honor award 1994, 95, Firm award 1998); mem. AIA Conn. Honor awards 1980, 85, 92, 93, 94, 95, 2002), Internat. Etchells Class Assn., Pettipaug Yacht Club (Commodore Essex chpt. 1984-86), Essex Yacht Club. Avocations: yacht racing, jazz musician, watercolor artist, music. Home: 123 Main St Centerbrook CT 06409 Office: Centerbrook Architects PO Box 955 Centerbrook CT 06409-0955

GROVES, BERNICE ANN, retired elementary and secondary school coordinator, educator; b. Bklyn., Feb. 5, 1928; d. Charles and Mary (Silverman) Lichtenstein; m. Stuart Weiss, June 5, 1949 (div. June 1978); children: Joel Weiss, Patricia Weiss Levy; m. Sidney Groves, July 30, 1978 (dec. May 2000). MA, Adelphi U., 1971; MS in Edn., Coll. of New Rochelle, 1975. Cert. adminstr., supr., N.Y. K-6th grade tchr., reading tchr. Ossining (N.Y.) Schs., Byram Hills Schs., Armonk, NY, Bedford (NY) Schs., 1964—84; reading specialist The Hallen Sch., Mamaroneck, NY, 1984-88, coord. testing and curriculum New Rochelle, NY, 1988—2001; ret., 2002. Mgr. nutrition ctr. GNC, Scarsdale, NY, 1981—82; mem. curriculum adv. coun. Lower Westchester BOCES, 1988—2001. Pres. Mineola (N.Y.) Elem. Sch. PTA, 1962-63. Mem. ASCD, Lower Hudson Coun. Adminstrv. Women in Edn., Westchester Reading Coun., Orton Dyslexia Soc., Am. Mensa Ltd. Avocations: tennis, gourmet cooking, nutrition.

GROVES, JOHN TAYLOR, III, chemist, educator; b. New Rochelle, NY, Mar. 27, 1943; s. John Taylor and Frances (Gaylor) G.; m. Karen Joan Morrison, Apr. 15, 1967; children: Jay, Kevin. BS, M.I.T., 1965; PhD, Columbia U., 1969. Asst. prof. U. Mich., Ann Arbor, 1969-76, assoc. prof., 1976-79, prof. organic chemistry, 1979-85; prof. organic and inorganic chemistry Princeton (N.J.) U., 1985—, chmn. dept. chemistry, 1988-93, Hugh Stott Taylor prof. chemistry, 1991—. Morris S. Kharasch Vis. Prof. U. Chgo., 1993; cons. in field; dir. Mich. Center for Catalytic and Surface Scis., Ann Arbor, 1981-85; disting. vis. prof., U. Hong Kong, 2003. Bd. editors: Bioorganic Chemistry, 1984—, Bioorganic and Medicinal Chemistry, 1994—, Bioorganic and Medicinal Chemistry Letters, 1994—; mem. editl. bd.: Reaction Kinetics and Catalysis Letters, 1989—, Jour. of Biol. Inorganic Chemistry, 1995—; contbr. articles to profl. jours.; mem. adv. bd. Inorganic Chemistry, 1995-97. Recipient Phi Lambda Upsilon award for outstanding teaching and leadership, 1978, NSF Extension award, 1990—92. Fellow AAAS, Am. Acad. Arts and Scis.; mem. Am. Chem. Soc. (Arthur C. Cope Scholar award 1991, Alfred Bader award in bio-organic and bioinorganic chemistry 1996), N.Y. Acad. Sci., Sigma Xi. Office: Princeton U Dept Chemistry 203 Hoyt Lab Princeton NJ 08544-0001 Business E-Mail: jtgroves@princeton.edu.

GROVES, MARK, music director; b. Blytheville, Ark., Aug. 14, 1969; s. Jerry Clay and Nancy Carolyn Groves; m. Sarah Standerfer, Mar. 2, 1996; children: Clara Grace, Lily Faith. MusB, Okla. Bapt. U., 1991; MusM, Southwestern Theol. Sem., 1994. Assoc. dir. music Mountain Brook Bapt. Ch., Birmingham, Ala., 1994—96; min. music Indian Springs First Bapt. Ch., Birmingham, 1996—99, First Bapt. Ch., Jonesboro, Ark., 1999—. Contbr. articles to profl. publs. Mem. Camerata Singers, Birmingham, 1996—98; fundraiser City Youth, Jonesboro, 2004; mem. CenturyMen, 1998—2000. Scholar President's scholar, Southwestern Theol. Sem., 1991; B.B. McKinney Royalties scholar, Okla. Bapt. U., 1987—91. Mem.: Am. Guild English Handbell Ringers. Avocations: travel, reading, outdoor activities. Office: First Bapt Ch 701 S Main Jonesboro AR 72401 Office Phone: 870-932-3456. Office Fax: 870-932-3523.

GROVES, ODESSA MARIE, science educator; b. Nashville, July 14, 1937; d. Isaac Herchel and Tennie Eloise (Watkins) Groves. BS, Tenn. State U., Nashville, 1960; MS, Wayne State U., Detroit, 1975; EdD, Calif. U., San Ana, 1992. Dept. head Sanford High Sch., Seal, Ala., 1961—63; officer Detroit Police Dept., 1963—66; edn. officer Detroit Pub. Sch., 1966—97. Author: Toothbrush, Toothpaste & Floss, 2002, French Fry and Ketchup, 2005. Mem.: Sigma Gamma Rho, Phi Delta Kappa, Sigma Gamma Phi (exec. bd. 2002—, pres. ways and means 2002—). Democrat. Meth. Achievements include patents pending for talking toothbrush. Avocations: reading, writing, travel, cooking, painting, music. Home: PO Box 211133 Detroit MI 48221

GROVES, RAY JOHN, accountant; b. Cleve., Sept. 7, 1935; m. Anne Keating, Aug. 18, 1962; children: David, Philip, Matthew. BS summa cum laude, Ohio State U., 1957. CPA, Conn., NY, Ohio. With Ernst & Whinney, Cleve. and NYC, 1957-94, ptnr., 1966-71, nat. ptnr., 1971-77, chmn., chief exec. officer NYC, 1977-89; co-CEO, Ernst & Young, NYC, 1989-91, chmn., CEO, 1991-94; chmn. Legg Mason Merchant Banking, Inc., 1995—2001; sr. officer Marsh, Inc., 2001—. Bd. govs. Am. Stock Exch., 1987-93; bd. dirs. Boston Sci. Corp., Gillette, EDS. Bd. overseers Wharton Sch. U. Pa., 1986-95; vice chmn. bd. trustees Ursuline Coll., Cleve., 1970-86; mng. dir. Met. Opera Assn., 1988—; trustee Pub. Policy Inst. NY State, 1988—, Bus. Coun UN, 1993-99; dir. Ohio State U. Found., 1994—, chmn., 1999-2001. Mem. AICPA (chmn. bd. dirs. 1984-85), Nat. Assn. Securities Dealers (bd. govs. 1981-84), Union Club, Pepper Pike Club, Links Club, Met. Club, Blind Brook Club. Republican. also: 1120 Park Ave Apt 11B New York NY 10128-1242 Office: Marsh Inc 1166 Ave of Americas 44th Flr New York NY 10036-2774 Home Phone: 212-289-6979; Office Phone: 212-345-1823.

GROW, ROBERT THEODORE, economist, trade association executive; b. Newton, Mass., Aug. 14, 1948; s. William and Lempi (Kangas) G.; m. Anita L. Capps, Nov. 20, 1982; 1 child, Margy. BS magna cum laude, U. Mass., Amherst, 1970, MS, 1973. Regional economist Southeastern Va. Planning Dist. Commn., Norfolk, 1973-80; dir. met. coord. Met. Washington Coun. Govts., DC, 1980-85; exec. dir. Washington/Balt. Regional Assn., Washington, 1985—92; dir. govt. rels. The Greater Washington Bd. Trade, 1992—. Exec. dir. Bus. Transp. Action Coalition. Appeared on Comedy Central's Daily Show with Jon Stewart, 1999. Mem. design selection panel Woodrow Wilson Bridge, 1999; bd. mem. Wash. Regional Alcohol Program, Clean Air Ptnrs., No. Va. Transp. Alliance. Fellow: Ford Found. Regionalism and Sustainable Devel. Bd.; mem.: No. Va. Transportation Alliance, Phi Kappa Phi. Avocations: skiing, golf. Home: PO Box 2307 Purcellville VA 20134-2307 Home Phone: 540-338-1790. Business E-Mail: bobgrow@bot.org.

GROWCOCK, TERRY D., manufacturing executive; b. 1945; BS Business Management, U. of St. Francis. Exec. King-Seeley Corp., United Technologies, Universal Nolin, Paragon Electric; v.p., gen. mgr Robertshaw Automotive; exec. v.p., gen. mgr. Manitowoc Ice, 1994—95; pres. Manitowoc Foodservice Group, 1995—98, The Manitowoc Co., Inc., 1998—2002, CEO, 1998—2007, chmn., 2002—. Bd. dir. Harris Corp., 2005—. Office: The Manitowoc Co Inc 2400 S 44th St Manitowoc WI 54221*

GROWICK, PHILIP, advertising executive; children: Matthew, Kevin. Pres. Philip Growick Assocs., NYC, 1975—91; mng. dir. Jerry Fields Assocs., Inc., NYC, 1994—. Author: Hail to the Chief, 1964; editor: Nudeniks, 1964. Avocations: history, politics, scuba diving, ancient Rome.

GRUB, PHILLIP DONALD, business educator; b. Medical Lake, Wash., Aug. 8, 1931; s. Carl Dryer and Barbara Rosalie (Johnson) G. BA in Econs. and Bus. Edn. with honors, Eastern Wash. State U., 1953; MBA (Scottish Rite Found. fellow), George Washington U., 1960, DBA (Am. Security and Trust scholar), 1964; DBus (hon.), U. Internat. Bus. and Econs., Beijing, 1986. Pres. Phillip D. Grub, Inc., Spokane, Wash., 1953-54; pvt. practice, 1956-62; co-owner, co-mgr. 7G Ranch, Medical Lake, 1962-70; assoc. prof., dir. programs in internat. bus. George Washington U., Washington, 1964-70, chmn. dept. bus. adminstrn., 1968-70, prof. bus. adminstrn., 1971-73, Aryamehr prof. multinat. mgmt., 1974-94, Aryamehr prof. emeritus, 1994—, spl. asst. to pres., 1974-80; chmn. Phillip Grub and Assocs., 1994—; disting. internat. exec. in residence Ea. Washington U., Cheney, 1997—2005. Cons. Summa Group, Jakarta, Indonesia, 1991-92; mgmt. cons. to industry and govts.; sr. ptnr. C & P Properties, Medical Lake, Wash., 1988—, Pacific Costal Investments, Medical Lake, Wash., 2001—; mem. Md.-D.C. Export Expansion Coun., 1968-89; vis. prof. internat. bus. adminstrn., acting dir. Ohio World Trade Edn. Ctr., Cleve. State U., 1972-73; dir., chmn. exec. com. Diplomat Nat. Bank, 1978-80; mem. bd. adv. Donaldson, Luftkin & Jenrette, 1980-83; bd. dirs. U.S.-Japan Culture Ctr.; dir. Washington World Trade Inst., 1983-91, pres., 1983-86; dir. U.S. Vietnam Ednl. Found., 1990—; sr. advisor Shanghi Ctr. Internat. Studies, 1987—, Rittenhouse Consulting, Ltd., Shanghai. Author: A Guide to Personnel Development, 1966, A Handbook for Term Papers, Theses and Dissertations, 1967, American-East European Trade: Controversy, Progress, Prospects, 1968; (with Norma M. Loeser) Executive Leadership: The Art of Successfully Managing Resources, 1969, Management U.S.A., 1968; (with Mika S. Kaskimies) International Marketing in Perspective, 1971; (with Ashok Kapoor) The Multinational Enterprise in Transition, 1972, 3d edit., 1986; (with Ghadar and Khambata) Asia Dimensions of International Business, 1982, Foreign Investment Analysis: Cases and Country Studies, 1986, Global Business Management in the 1990's, 1990, Foreign Direct Investment in China, 1991, The Re-Emerging Securities Market in China, 1992, Vietnam, The New Investment Frontier in Southeast Asia, 1992, (with Dara Khambata) The Multinational Enterprise: Strategies for Global Competitiveness, 1993, Global Business Strategies for the Year 2000, 1995; contbr. articles to profl. jours. Bd. dirs. U.S. Forestry, 1987-90; sr. advisor Shanghai Ctr. Internat. Studies, 1987—. With U.S. Army, 1954-56. Named a Univ. Prof. in Peoples Republic of China, 1986. Mem. Acad. Internat. Bus. (pres. 1975-77), Acad. Mgmt.,

Am. Mgmt. Assn., U.S.-Japan Culture Soc. (bd. dirs., exec. sec.), Fellows Acad. Internat. Bus., Masons, Alpha Kappa Psi, Beta Gamma Sigma. Home: 4810 S Saint Andrews Ln Spokane WA 99223-4304 Office: C & P Properties PO Box 220 Medical Lake WA 99022-0220 Office Phone: 509-299-5133. Personal E-mail: phillipg54@aol.com.

GRUBB, DONALD HARTMAN, paper industry company executive; b. West Chester, Pa., Oct. 22, 1924; s. Donald C. and Bessie (Hanthorne) G.; m. Jean Louise Flounders, Sept. 7, 1946; children: Donna Jean (Mrs. Robert Kanich), Deborah Anne (Mrs. James R. Jackson), Donald Philip. BA, U. Pa., 1949; MA, Am. U., 1954; postgrad., NYU, 1963-64. With U.S. Treasury Dept., Washington, 1949-57, recruitment officer, 1951-53, dir. personnel, 1953-57; mgr. personnel Westvaco Corp., NYC, 1957-59, regional adminstrv. mgr. Hoboken, NJ, 1959-61, mgr. sales, 1961-64; asst. to v.p. Huyck Corp., Stamford, Conn., 1964, v.p. adminstrn. and mktg., 1969-70, exec. v.p., 1970-73, pres., dir., chief exec. officer, 1973-81; chmn. BTR Paper Group, 1981-82; pres. Gedon Enterprises, 1982—; v.p., gen. mgr. Formex Co. of Can., Kentville, N.S., 1965-67; also dir.; v.p., gen. mgr. Huyck Formex Co. of U.S., Greeneville, Tenn., 1967-69. Mgr. Grubb Assocs., LLC dba Fasteners Supply of Goldsboro; retired dir. various cos. in U.S. and U.K. Bd. dirs. Blanchard-Fraser Meml. Hosp., Kentville, N.S., Can., 1966-67, Wake County Hosp. System, Raleigh, 1983-87, N.C. State U. Pulp and Paper Found.; mem. N.C. State U. Sch. Engrng. Foun., N.C. State U. Sch. Humanities Found. Served with AUS, 1943-46. Mem. Raleigh C. of C. (dir. 1976-78), Phi Beta Kappa. Presbyterian. Personal E-mail: dongrubb@earthlink.net.

GRUBB, ERICA B., lawyer; b. Sept. 20, 1947; AB cum laude, Radcliffe Coll., 1969; JD cum laude, Harvard U., 1973. Bar: Calif. 1973, Tex. 1979. Trial atty. EEOC, 1973-74; ptnr. Pub. Advocates, Inc., 1974-78; dep. dir. Tex. Legal Svcs. Ctr., 1978-81; mem. Morrison & Foerster, Walnut Creek, Calif.; pvt. practice Berkeley. Adj. prof. U. Tex. Law Sch., 1980-84. Editorial bd. Harvard Civil Rights-Civil Liberties Law Rev., 1972-73. Bd. dirs. Nat. Ctr. Youth Law, 1974-86, dir. Child Nutrition Policy Calif. Food Policy Advocates San Francisco. Mem. Phi Beta Kappa. Office: 52 Uplands Berkeley CA 94705-2815 Office Phone: 510-658-5181. Office Fax: 510-658-5181. Business E-Mail: consulting@rikkigrubb.com.

GRUBB, GARY S., pharmaceutical executive; b. Verona, NJ, Dec. 13, 1952; s. Thomas Christman and Louise Sondermann Grubb; m. Barbara Ward, June 10, 1978; 1 child, Anderson Ward. MD, Case Western Res. U., Cleve., 1979. Diplomate Am Bd. Preventive Medicine. Sr. dir. Wyeth Rsch., Collegeville, Pa., 1995—. Home: 825 Briarwood Rd Newtown Square PA 19073 Office Phone: 484-865-5745. Personal E-mail: garygrubb@aol.com.

GRUBB, ROBERT L., JR., neurosurgeon; b. Charlotte, NC, May 9, 1940; MD, U. N.C., 1965. Intern Barnes Hosp., St. Louis, 1965-66, resident in gen. surgery, 1966-67, resident in neurosurgery, 1969-73; fellow NIH, Bethesda, Md., 1968-69; mem. staff Barnes-Jewish Hosp., St. Louis, St. Louis Children's Hosp.; prof. neurosurgery Washington U., St. Louis. Fellow ACS; mem. Am. Acad. Neurol. Surgery, AANS, CNS, SNS. Office: Washington U Sch Medicine 660 S Euclid Ave Box 8057 Saint Louis MO 63110-1093 Home Phone: 314-965-1330; Office Phone: 314-362-3567. Business E-Mail: grubbr@nsurg.wustl.edu.

GRUBB, WILLIAM FRANCIS XAVIER, consumer products company executive, marketing professional; b. NYC, Aug. 11, 1944; s. William Martin and Eileen F. (Donnelly) G.; m. Eileen B. O'Leary, Apr. 4, 1964; children: Catherine E., William M., Kerri A., Christopher M. BA in Econs., Fordham U., 1966; MBA in Mktg. and Fin., Seton Hall U., 1972. bd. dirs. several privately-held cos. Mktg. and sales exec. Black & Decker, Towson, Md., 1968-79; v.p. mktg. Atari, Sunnyvale, Calif., 1979-81; chmn., pres. New West Mktg., Mountain View, Calif., 1981; pres., chief exec. officer, chmn. Imagic, Los Gatos, Calif., 1981-84; exec. v.p. Dataspeed, 1984-85; pres. Axlon Inc., 1985-86; exec. v.p., gen. mgr. Worlds of Wonder, Inc., Freemont, Calif., 1986-87; pres., chief exec. The Complete PC, San Jose, Calif., 1987-93; CEO, ICTV Inc., Los Gatos, Calif., 1994-96; CEO Millenia Software Inc., Saratoga, Calif., 1996—; pres. Toolz Ltd., Palo Alto, Calif., 1998-99; CEO Grubb Enterprises LLC, Pawleys Island, SC, 1999—. Bd. regents Holy Names Coll. Office: Grubb Enterprises LLC 45 Rookery Trl Pawleys Island SC 29585-5266 Home: 109 Black Duck Rd Pawleys Island SC 29585-5266 Personal E-mail: wfxgrubb@aol.com.

GRUBBA, MATTHEW JOHN, journalist; b. Sydney, Jan. 14, 1983; arrived in US, 1983; s. John and Linda Alese Grubba. BA in Comm. and Rhetoric, U. Pitts., Pa., 2005. Freelance journalist Pitts. Tribune Rev., 2005—06; freelance reporter Metro Networks, Pitts., 2005—06; sports editor Sewickley Herald Coraopolis-Moon Record, Pa., 2006—. Soccer ofcl. US Soccer Fedn., 1997—. Mem.: Mensa. Independent. Avocations: travel, sports, card games, movies, theater. Home: 71 Barry St Pittsburgh PA 15203 Office: Sewickley Herald Coraopolis-Moon Record 533 Beaver St Sewickley PA 15143 Home Phone: 434-238-6431; Office Phone: 412-324-1409. Personal E-mail: abburg13@aol.com. Business E-Mail: m.grubba@gatewaynewspapers.com.

GRUBBE, FREDERICK H., real estate appraisal executive; b. May 14, 1961; BA in Journalism, No. Ill. U., 1984; MBA, Loyola U. Adminstrv. asst. to CEO Coll. Am. Pathologists, 1984—86; exec. asst. to chmn. Regional Transp. Authority Northeastern Ill., 1986—88; spl. asst. to sec. & White House liaison US Dept. Transp., 1987—89; dep. regional polit. dir. Great Lakes region Bush-Quayle Campaign, 1988; with Office Pres-Elect, Office Presdl. Pers., 1988—89; dep. adminstr. Nat. Hwy. Traffic Safety Adminstrn. US Dept. Transp., 1989—93; dep. US Office of Consumer Affair Exec. Office of the Pres., 1989—93; dir. strategic planning and special prog. Million Dollar Round Table, 1993—96; CEO Think First Found.; COO Ed. Resource Group; pres. Join Hands Corp., 2001—07; pres., CEO Nat. Fraternal Congress Am., 2001—07; CEO Appraisal Inst., Ill., 2007—. Office: Appraisal Inst 550 W Van Buren St Ste 1000 Chicago IL 60607*

GRUBBS, ROBERT HOWARD, chemistry professor; b. Calvert City, Ky., Feb. 27, 1942; s. Henry Howard and Faye (Atwood) G.; m. Helen Matilda O'Kane; children: Robert B., Brendan H., Kathleen M. BS, U. Fla., 1963, MS, 1965; PhD, Columbia U., 1968. NIH postdoctoral fellow Stanford U., Calif., 1968-69; asst. prof. Mich. State U., East Lansing, 1969-73, assoc. prof., 1973-78; prof. chemistry Calif. Inst. Tech., Pasadena, 1978—, Victor and Elizabeth Atkins prof., 1989. Contbr. articles to profl. publs.; patentee in field. Recipient award in organic synthesis Bristol Myers Squibb, 2004, Golden Plate award, Acad. Achievement, 2006; co-recipient Nobel Prize in Chemistry, 2005, Paul Karrer Gold medallion, 2005, August-Wilhelm-von-Hofmann-Denkmünze, 2005; fellow Sloan Found., 1974-76, Alexander von Humboldt Found., 1975; Dreyfus Found. scholar, 1975-78. Fellow Am. Acad. Arts and Scis.; mem. AAAS, NAS, Am. Chem. Soc. (Organic Chemistry award 1989, Polymer Chemistry award 1995, Benjamin Franklin medal in chemistry 2000, Herman F. Mark polymer chemistry award 2000, Herbert C. Brown award for creative rsch. in synthetic methods 2001, Arthur C. Cope award, 2002, Richard C. Tolman medal 2003, Tetrahedron prize 2003, Kirkwood medal New Haven sect. 2005). Democrat. Achievements include research in homogeneous or heterogeneous catalysis. Office: Divsn of Chemistry and Chemical Engring Calif Inst Tech Mail Code 164 30 Pasadena CA 91125 Business E-Mail: rhg@caltech.edu.*

GRUBBS, ROBERT W., computer services company executive; Grad., U. Mo. Joined Anixter Internat. Inc., 1978; pres. Anixter U.S.A.; pres., CEO, Anixter Inc. subs. Anixter Internat. Inc., 1994—98; pres., CEO Anixter Internat. Inc., 1998—, bd. dirs., 1997—. Former dir. A. M. Castle & Co., 2000. Office: Anixter Internat Inc 2301 Patriot Blvd Glenview IL 60025-8020*

GRUBE, F. WILLIAM, refining company executive; b. 1947; married BSCE, Rose Humlan Inst., 1970; MBA, Harvard U., 1972. With Rock Island Refining Corp., Indpls., 1972—, v.p. exploration and corp. devel., 1979-83, exec. v.p., 1983—90; pres., CEO, dir. Calumet Specialty Products, Indpls., 1990—. Office: Calumet Specialty Products Ste 200 2780 Waterfront Pky E Dr Indianapolis IN 46214*

GRUBE, KARL BERTRAM, judge; b. Elmhurst, Ill., Jan. 13, 1946; s. Karl Ludwig and Gerturde (Bertram) G.; m. Mary B. Harr, May 4, 1974 (div. Aug. 1991); m. Julia Ross, Dec. 28, 1998. BSBA, Elmhurst Coll., 1967; JD, Stetson U., 1970; M in Judicial Studies, U. Nev., 1992. Asst. pub. defender State of Fla., Clearwater, 1970-73, county ct. judge St. Petersburg, 1977—; pvt. practice Seminole, Fla., 1973-76; city atty. City of Redington Beach, Fla., 1975-76. Asst. dean Fla. Jud. Coll., Tallahassee, 1984-85; faculty mem., course coord., mem. faculty coun. Nat. Jud. Coll., chair faculty coun., 2000—; mem. Nat. Hwy. Traffic Safety Jud. Tng. Implementation Bd.; mem. mediation rev. bd. State of Fla., 2005; assoc. dean Fla. Coll. Advanced Jud. Studies, 2005 Contbr. articles to profl. jours. Dir. Pinellas Comprehensive Addiction Svcs., Clearwater, 1982-88. Jud. fellow U.S. Dept. Transp., 1998, Nat. Hwy. Traffic Safety Adminstn., 1999. Mem. ABA (conf. chmn. divsn. jud. adminstrn. 1992, del. to jud. divsn. coun. 1997—, Dedicated Svc. award 1991, Gov.'s Commendation, N.C. 2000, Nev. 2001), Nat. Jud. Coll. (mem. faculty coun. 1998-2003, chmn. 2001), Nat. Highway Traffic Safety (adminstrn. jud. outreach liaison 2003-), Fla. Bar Assn. (civil rule com.), Colo. Bar Assn., Fla. Conf. County Ct. Judges (pers. com. 1984-85), Rolls Royce Owner's Club (editor 1982-84). Lutheran. Avocations: collecting fountain pens, collecting antique watches, auto restoration. Office: Pinellas County Ct PO Box 10354 Saint Petersburg FL 33733-0354 Office Phone: 727-582-7880.

GRUBER, IRA DEMPSEY, historian, educator; b. Phila., Jan. 6, 1934; married; 3 children. AB, Duke U., 1955, AM, 1959, PhD, 1961. Instr. history Duke U., 1961-62; fellow Inst. Early Am. History and Culture, 1962-65; asst. prof. Occidental Coll., 1965-66; from asst. prof. to assoc. prof., 1966-74; prof. Rice U., Houston, from 1974, now Harris Masterson prof. history, chmn. dept. history, 1983-87. Master Hanszen Coll., Rice U., 1968-73; John F. Morrison prof. U.S. Army Command and Gen. Staff Coll., 1979-80; vis. prof. mil. history U.S. Mil. Acad., 1984-85, 92-93; mem. hist. adv. com. USAF, 1987-91, Dept. Army, 1992-95; trustee Soc. for Mil. History, 1987-95. Author: Lord Howe and Lord George Germain, 1965, The American Revolution as a Conspriacy: The British View, 1969, The Howe Brothers and the American Revolution, 1972, The Education of Sir Henry Clinton, 1990; co-author: Classical Traditions in Early America, 1976, Reconsiderations on the Revolutionary War, 1978, Limits of Loyalty, 1980, Arms and Independence, 1984, Against All Enemies, 1986, America's First Battles, 1986, Warfare in the Western World, 1996; editor: John Peebles American War, 1998; mem. editl. bd. Jour. of Mil. History, 1995—, chair editl. bd., 1999—. Home Phone: 713-668-4062; Office Phone: 713-348-4947. E-mail: gruber@rice.edu.

GRUBER, JOHN BALSBAUGH, physics professor; b. Hershey, Pa., Feb. 10, 1935; s. Irvin John and Erla R. (Balsbaugh) G.; m. Judith Anne Higer, June 20, 1961; children: David Powell, Karen Leigh, Mark Balsbaugh. BS, Haverford Coll., Pa., 1957; PhD, U. Calif., Berkeley, 1961. NATO postdoctoral fellow Inst. Tech. Physics, Tech. U. Darmstadt, Germany, 1961-62, gastdozent, 1961-62; asst. prof. physics UCLA, 1962-66; asso. prof. physics Wash. State U., Pullman, 1966-71, prof. chem. physics, 1971-75; asst. dean Wash. State U. (Grad. Sch.), 1968-70, assoc. dean, 1970-72; prof. physics, dean Coll. Sci. and Math., N.D. State U., Fargo, 1975-80; prof. physics and chemistry, v.p. for acad. affairs Portland (Oreg.) State U., 1980-84; prof. physics San Jose State U., 1984—2005, acad. v.p., 1984-86, v.p. devel., 1986, dir. Inst. for Modern Optics, 1992—2005, chmn. dept. physics, 2001—05; regents prof. rsch. in laser physics U. Tex., San Antonio, 2005—. Vis. prof. Joint Ctr. Grad. Study, Richland, Wash., 1964-66, Ames Lab., Dept. of Energy, Iowa State U., 1976-80; Disting. vis. prof. U.S. Navy Naval Weapons Ctr., China Lake, Calif., 1984-93, Stanford U., 1993-2000; invited lectr., U.S., Can., Europe, 1966—; cons. in laser physics and spectroscopy Aerospace Corp., El Segundo, Calif., 1962-65, Douglas Aircraft and McDonnell Douglas Astronautics Co., Santa Monica, Calif., 1963-69, N.Am. Aviation, Space and Info. Systems, Downey, Calif., 1964-66, Battelle-Northwest, Richland, Wash., 1964-69, Los Alamos (N.Mex.) Sci. Lab., 1969-71, 73-74; mem. task force lunar exploration sci. Apollo, NASA, 1964-69, 71-73; cons. Army Rsch. Lab., Adelphi Ctr., U.S. Army, 1991—, IBM, 1985-90, GTE, 1986-89, Lasergenics, 1986-2005, Night Vision Lab. U.S. Army, Ft. Belvoir, 1993—2005, Deltron, 1990-91, Rey Tech Corp., 1998-2002, Laser Sci. and Tech., 1999—, Bicron Corp., 2000-03, Spectragen Corp., 2000, SAIC, 2002-06, Battelle, 1994-03, 05-, Aculight Corp., 2003-06, Newtec Corp., 2003-04, CACI Techs., 2004; pres. The Gruber Group, 2005-; mem. Rare Earth Rsch. Conf. Com., 1976-83, exec. com., 1977-83, sec. bd. dirs., 1979-84; gen. conf. chmn. XIV Internat. Rare Earth Rsch. Conf., 1979, Novel Laser Sources and Materials, 1992; exec. sec. Internat. Frank H. Spedding Award, 1979, 83, Willig award, 1986, Internat. Spencer prize for outstanding contbrn. to sci., 1987, Pres.'s Scholar, 1994-95, Outstanding Achievement awards U.S. Dept. Def., 1995-96, 98, 01-05, Nom. U.S. Asst. Sec. Def. (Spl. Ops.), 1986-87; chmn. U.S. Navy/ASEE Postdoctoral Selection Bd., 1988-2002, U.S. Nat. Inst. Sci. and Tech. Postdoctoral Selection Bd., 1989-91; mem. rev. panel U.S. Navy/ASEE Grad. Fellowship Program, 1990-02; chmn., mem. NASA/ASEE program rev. bd., 1994-98; chmn. Internat. Conf. on Novel Laser Sources and Applications, San Jose, Calif., 1993, chmn. Battelle U.S. Dept. Def. Scholarship Program, 1994-01; mem. Battelle Sci. Bd. Selection Grad. Scholarship Fellows, 1998-99. Contbr. articles to profl. jours., chpts. to books; holder numerous patents in laser sci. and tech. Trustee Symphony Bd. Fargo-Moorhead Symphony Orch., 1978-80; mem. N.D. State Bd. PTA; chmn. Univ., Coll. and Pub. Sch. Rels. Bd., 1979-80; active Boy Scouts Am.; trustee Pullman Pub. Libr., 1973-75, N.D. Symphony Orchs. Assn., 1978-80; mem. planning commn. City of Pullman, 1972-75; bd. dirs. Westminster Found., 1982-84. Recipient Outstanding Merit and Performance award San Jose State U., 1990, San Jose State Pres.'s Scholar, 1994-95, Dist. Tchr./scholar award, 1996, 97, 99, award in the field of lasers and electro-optics U. Chgo., 1995, Citation for Svc. and Achievement Dept. of Def., 1996, Award for Rsch. into night vision devices U.S. Army, 1997, 2001, 05, Outstanding World Leadership in Sci. award Acad. Scis., Poland, 1998, Outstanding Rsch. award San Jose State U., 2005; grantee AEC-ERDA, 1963-75, NSF, 1966-72, 76-78, 92—, U.S. Army Rsch. Office, Durham, 1979-80, Am. Chem. Soc. Petroleum Rsch. Funds, 1979-80, Dept. Energy, 1979-84, Dept. Def., 1984—, Office Naval Rsch., 1987—2002, Office Naval Tech., 1988-93, Dept. Def., DARPA, 1998-2006; fellow NASA Ames Lab., 1993-95; vis. scholar Stanford U., 1993-2000. Fellow Am. Soc. Engring. Edn. (disting.), Am. Phys. Soc. (chmn. nat. mtg. sessions), Am. Acad. Spectral Scis.; mem. AAAS, IEEE (sec. lasers and electro-optics 1995-96), NSF (reviewer and panel mem. divsn. material sci. 1994—), N.Y. Acad. Scis., N.D. Acad. Sci., Oreg. Acad. Sci., Acad. Scis. of Ukraine, Nat. Acad. Scis. (com. on lasers and electro-optics), Coun. Colls. Arts and Scis., Optical Soc. No. Calif. (v.p. 1992, pres. 1993), Lasers and Electro-optics Soc. (mem. program com. nat. meeting 1995), Internat. Soc. Optical Engrng. (bd. dirs. 1993), Phi Beta Kappa, Sigma Xi, Phi Kappa Phi, Sigma Pi Sigma, Phi Sigma Iota. Office: Univ Tex at San Antonio Dept Physics and Astronomy San Antonio TX 78249-0697 Office Phone: 210-458-5748. Office Fax: 210-458-4919. Personal E-mail: johnbgruber@yahoo.com. Business E-Mail: john.gruber@utsa.edu.

GRUBER, JOHN EDWARD, editor, historian, photographer; b. Chgo., May 18, 1936; s. Edward David and Leah Elizabeth (Diehl) G.; m. Bonnie Jean Barstow, May 12, 1962; children: Richard J., Timothy J. BA in Journalism, U. Wis., 1959, postgrad., 1981-84. Editor, writer U. Wis., Madison, 1960-95; editor Vintage Rails, Waukesha, Wis., 1995-99. Author: Focus on Rails, 1989, (pamphlet) Madison's Pioneer Buildings, 1987; co-author: Caboose, 2001, (posters) Travel by Train, 2002, Railway Photography, 2003, Milwaukee Road's Hiawathas, 2006; acting editor Rail News, 1999; also articles; contbr. photographs to Trains mag., 1960—; contbg. editor: Classic Trains, 2000—; coord. Representatives of Railroad Work 2003-06. Dir. Historic Madison, Inc., 1981-89. Recipient Nat. Award in R.R. History for photography Rwy. and Locomotive Hist. Soc., 1994; James J. Hill Rsch. grant Hill Reference Libr., 1986. Mem. Mid-Continent Railway Hist. Soc. (bd. dirs. 1984-97, pres. 1988-89, sec. 1990-95, v.p. 1995-97, editor Mid-Continent Railway Gazette 1982-99), Ctr. for R.R. Photography and Art (pres. 1997—). Home: 1430 Drake St Madison WI 53711-2211 Office Phone: 608-251-5785. E-mail: jgruber@execpc.com.

GRUBER, JONATHAN H., economist; b. Sept. 30, 1965; m. Andrea Gruber, 1991; children: Sam, Jack, Ava. BS MIT, 1987; PhD, Harvard U., 1992. Asst. prof. economics MIT, Cambridge, Mass., 1992—95, Castle Krob assoc. prof. economics, 1995—97, prof. economics, 1997—. Undergraduate program coordinator MIT Economics Dept., 1994—; faculty rsch. fellow Nat. Bur. Econ. Rsch., 1992—98, dir. Program on Children, 1996—, rsch. assoc., 1998—; academic adv. com. Ctr. Am. Progress, 2004—. Author: Pub. Finance & Pub. Policy, 2005; assoc. editor Jour. Pub. Economics, 1997—2001, co-editor, 2001—, Jour. Health Economics, 1998—2001, assoc. editor, 2001—, adv. bd. Social Sci. Rsch. Network (SSRN) Abstracts in Health Economics, 1998—, SSRN Jour. Unemployment Ins., 2004—, editorial bd. Berkeley Electronic Jours. in Econ. Analysis & Policy, 2001—. Dep. asst. sec. econ. policy US Treasury Dept., 1997—98; mem. Congl. Budget Office long term modeling adv. group, 2000—. Recipient FIRST award, Nat. Inst. Aging, 2003. Mem.: Nat. Acad. Social Ins., Inst. Medicine, Phi Beta Kappa. Office: MIT Dept Economics E52-355 50 Memorial Dr Cambridge MA 02142-1347 Office Phone: 617-253-8892. Office Fax: 617-253-1330. E-mail: gruberj@mit.edu.

GRUBERG, MARTIN, political science professor; b. NYC, Jan. 28, 1935; s. Benjamin and Mollie (Stolnitz) G.; m. Rosaline Kurfirst, Mar. 25, 1967 (dec. 1980); m. Humaira Sayeed, Aug. 15, 1983 (div. 1996); m. Vivian Foss, Feb. 14, 2007. BA, CCNY, 1955; PhD, Columbia U., NYC, 1963. Agt.-adjudicator Passport Agy., Dept. State, NYC, 1960-61; tchr. social studies Pelham (N.Y.) High Sch., 1961-62; instr. polit. sci. CUNY-Hunter Coll., 1961-62; tchr. social studies James Monroe and Seward Park High Schs., NYC, 1962-63; asst. prof. polit. sci. U. Wis., Oshkosh, 1963-66, assoc. prof., 1966-69, prof., chmn. dept., 1969-72, dir. pre-law program, 1966-69, 83—, coord. criminal justice program, 1983-87. Author: Women in American Politics, 1968, A Case Study in U.S. Urban Leadership: The Incumbency of Milwaukee Mayor Henry Maier, 1996, A History of Winnebago County Government, 1998, Introduction to Law, 2003; newspaper column: Women: Our Largest Minority, The Paper for Ctrl. Wiso., 1970-71, Spotlight on Women for Oshkosh Northwestern, 1971-73; Broadcast 16 weeks Civil Rights Revolution, Wis. State FM Network, 1974; editor: Wis. Polit. Scientist, 1986-91; contbr. articles to encys., profl. jours. Pres. Oshkosh Human Rights Coun., 1966-68; v.p. Winnebago chpt. NOW, 1970-71, sec. Oshkosh chpt., 1980-81, pres., 1981-83; pres. Women's Caucus of Midwest Polit. Scientists, 1980-81; pres. Fox Valley ACLU, 1985—. Recipient Am. Legion Aux. Americanism award, 1949, Buckvar award, 1955, Steigman award, 1955; N.Y. State scholar, 1952; Columbia grantee, 1961, 62, Wis. Regents' rsch. grantee, 1964-70, 73-75. Mem. AAUP (state sec. 1975-81, pres.-elect 1981-82, 91-92, pres. 1982-83, 92-93), Am. Polit. Sci. Assn., Midwest Polit. Sci. Assn., Wis. Polit. Sci. Assn. (pres. 1974-75), Law and Soc. Assn., Acad. Criminal Justice Scis., Candlelight Club, Optimists. Home: 2121 Oregon St Oshkosh WI 54902-7058 Office: U Wis Clow Hall Oshkosh WI 54901 Office Phone: 920-424-0146. Business E-Mail: gruberg@uwosh.edu.

GRUBIN, SHARON ELLEN, lawyer, former federal judge; b. Newark, Feb. 9, 1949; d. Harold and Blanche (Dultz) G. AB with honors, Smith Coll., 1970; JD with honors in Legal Writing and Analysis, Boston U., 1973. Bar: N.Y. 1974, U.S. Dist. Ct. (so. and ea. dists.) N.Y. 1974, U.S. Ct. Appeals (2nd cir.) 1974. Litigator White & Case, NYC, 1973-84; judge U.S. Dist. Ct. (so. dist.) N.Y., NYC, 1984-2000; gen. counsel Metroplitan Opera, NYC, 2000—. Chair 2d Cir. Task Force on Gender, Racial and Ethnic Fairness in the Cts.; lectr. NYU Sch. Law, Yale Law Sch., Bklyn. Law Sch., N.Y. Law Sch.; dir., sec., exec. com. Lawyers' Com. on Violence, Inc. Author: (with others) Advocacy-The Art of Pleading a Cause, 1985, Removal, Federal Civil Practice, 1989, and supplement, 1993; spkr. seminars in field. Mem. ABA (chair spl. projects com. 1996-97, nat. conf. fed. trial judges, jud. adminstrn. divsn.), Nat. Assn. Women Judges (chair fed. gender bias com., publicity and pub. affairs com., newsletter com.), Fed. Bar Coun. (trustee, exec. com., chair nominating com. 1994, v.p. 1990-94, award com. 1988-94, com. on 2d cir. cts. 1982-96; long-range planning com. 1992-96), N.Y. State Bar Assn. (exec. com., nominations com., fed. cts. task force, comml. and fed. litig. sect.), N.Y. State Assn. Women Judges (bd. dirs.), Assn. of Bar of City of N.Y. (long-range planning com., chair nominating com. 1995—, chair spl. com. on legal history 1994-96, chair spl. com. on Orison S. Marden Meml. lectrs., chair 1994-96, exec. com. 1990-94, spl. com. on gender bias in fed. cts. 1991-94, coun. on jud. adminstrn. 1986-90, prof. and jud. ethics com. 1986-89, nominating com. 1984-85, 95-96, com. on jud. 1982-83, chair young lawyers com. 1979-81, com. on entertainment law, 2001-), Am. Judicature Soc. (editl. com. 1994-97). Office: Metropolitan Opera Lincoln Ctr New York NY 10023

GRUBISICH, TOM, web editor; b. Peoria, Ill., Dec. 31, 1936; s. Michael Bernard and Mary (Pintar) G.; m. Marilyn J. Burson, Oct. 30, 1965 (div. 1982); children: Emily, Miranda. Graduate, Spalding Inst., Peoria, Ill., 1954; BS, Marquette U., Milw., 1958. Copy boy New Yorker Mag., 1959; reporter Worcester (Mass.) Telegram, 1959-61; copy editor New York Post, 1961-64; reporter New York Herald Tribune, 1964-66; editor, reporter Washington Post, 1966-81; founding editor The Connection Newspapers, Reston, Va., 1981-94; exec. editor Times Community Newspapers, Reston, Va., 1995-96; resident adviser press of Slovak Republic, Bratislava, 1996—97; mng. editor Digital City/America Online, 1997—2001; sr. web editor, external communications World Bank, Washington, DC, 2007—. Author: Reston: First 20 Years, 1985, contbr. Variety, 2003—, Online Journalism Rev., 2005—; op-ed articles in Washington Post and mags. Co-founder Planned Cmty. Archives, George Mason U., 1986, Robert E. Simon Jr. Children's Ctr., 1988, Reston Hist. Trust, 1997; pres. Wash.-Balt. Newspaper Guild, 1976. Recipient Best of Reston award, Reston Interfaith and Greater Reston C. of C.,1992, In My Backyard award Fairfax United Way, 1993; Citation of Merit Fairfax Fedn. Citizens Assn., 1994; Wash. Post fellow Duke U., 1979; 10-yr. honoree The No. Va. Women's Ctr., 1995. Mem. Soc. Profl. Journalists (DC chpt. Dateline award/editing, writing 1987, 91, 93, Disting. Svc. in Local Journalism award 1987), Va. Press Assn. (editl., writing 1st prize 1987), Suburban Newspapers Am. (Cmty. Svc. award 1987, editl. writing 1995), Ctr. for Fgn. Journalists (vol. faculty, 10th anniversary honoree 1995). Roman Catholic. Office: World Bank External Commn 1818 H St NW Washington DC 20433 Office Phone: 202-458-8466. Business E-Mail: tomeditor@msn.com.

GRUBMAN, ALLEN J., lawyer; b. Bklyn., Dec. 30, 1942; m. Deborah Grubman; children: Elizabeth S., Jennifer. BBA, CCNY, 1965; JD, Bklyn. Law Sch., 1967. Bar: N.Y. 1968. Sr. ptnr. Grubman Indursky & Shire P.C., NYC, 1974—. Office: Grubman Indursky & Shire PC 152 W 57th St New York NY 10019-3310

GRUCHACZ, ROBERT S., real estate company officer; b. Bloomfield, NJ, May 15, 1929; s. Stanley A. and Mae (Zalenski) G.; m. LaVerne T. Stein, Mar. 2, 1957; children— Robert S., Thomas A., Christopher J. BS, Seton Hall U., 1950; MBA, NYU, 1971; student, Advanced Mgmt. Program, Harvard U., 1973. C.P.A., N.J. With Arthur Young & Co., C.P.A.'s, 1955-58, Sterling Drug Inc., NYC, 1958-65; controller Nabisco Inc., 1965-72, asst. to pres., 1973-74, 76—, v.p., 1979-84; broker Dunes Mktg. Group and Sea Pines Realty, 1985-2001; exec. v.p. Aurora Products, 1974-76. Served as 1st lt. USAF, 1952-54. Mem. AICPA. Home: 11 Timber Marsh Ln Hilton Head Island SC 29926-2790 Personal E-mail: bobgruchacz@aol.com.

GRUDEN, JON, professional football coach; b. Sandusky, Ohio, Aug. 17, 1963; Student, U. Dayton. Asst. coach U. Tenn., 1986-87, U. Southeast Mo., 1988-89, San Francisco 49ers, 1990, U. Pitts., 1991, Green Bay Packers, 1992-94; offensive coord. Phila. Eagles, 1994-97; head coach Oakland Raiders, 1998—2002, Tampa Bay Buccaneers, 2002—. Office: Tampa Bay Buccaneers One Buccaneer Pl Tampa FL 33607

GRUDZIELANEK, MARK JAMES, professional baseball player; b. Milw., June 30, 1970; Student, Trinidad Jr. Coll., Colo. Selected 11th round free-agt. draft Montreal Expos, 1994, shortstop, 3d baseman, 2d baseman, 1995-99; infielder L.A. Dodgers, 1999—2002, Chgo Cubs, 2003—04, St. Louis Cardinals, 2005. Selected Nat. League All-Star Team, 1996. Recipient Gold Glove award, MLB, 2006.*

GRUEBELE, MARTIN, chemistry and biophysicist professor; b. Stuttgart, Germany, Jan. 10, 1964; arrived in U.S., 1980; s. Helmut and Edith Victoria (Berner) Gruebele; m. Nancy Makri, July 10, 1992; 2 children. BS in Chemistry, U. Calif., Berkeley, 1984, PhD in Chemistry, 1988. Rsch. fellow Calif. Inst. Tech., Pasadena, 1989-92; from asst. prof. to assoc. prof. dept. chemistry U. Ill., Urbana, 1992—99, prof. chemistry and biophysics, 1999—2000, prof. chemistry, physics, and biophysics, 2000—01, Alumni Scholar prof. chemistry, prof. physics, biophysics and computational biology, 2002—05, Lycan prof. chemistry, physics, biophysics and computational biology, 2006—. Baker symposium lectr. Cornell U., 2004. Sr. editor: Jour. Phys. Chemistry, 1998—2005; mem. editl. bd. Jour. Chem. Physics, Chem. Phys. Lett., Ann. Rev. Phys. Chem., Chem. Physics. Recipient New Faculty award, Dreyfus Found., 1992, Nat. Young Investigator award, NSF, 1994, Coblentz award, 2000, Wilhelm Friedrich Bessel prize, Von Humboldt Soc., 2005; fellow, IBM, 1986—87, Dow Chem. Co., 1987—88, David and Lucile Packard Found., 1994; Sloan fellow, 1997, Alfred P. Sloan fellow, 1998, Cottrell scholar, 1995, Camille and Henry Dreyfus scholar, 1998, Univ. scholar, U. Ill., 1998. Fellow: Biophys. Soc., Am. Phys. Soc.; mem.: Am. Chem. Soc., Sigma Xi. Achievements include research in theoretical and experimental studies of novel transiet molecular species; studies in laser-control of chemical reactions and molecular vibrational relaxation; fast time-rsolved protein folding dynamics; laser-assisted scanning tunneling microscopy. Office: U Ill Dept Chemistry Box 5-6 600 S Mathews Ave Urbana IL 61801-3602

GRUEL, STEVEN FRANCIS, lawyer; b. Savannah, Ga., Sept. 24, 1956; s. Virgil Lenard and Nancy Ann (Gruber) G. BA, U. Wis., Eau Claire, 1980; JD, U. Wis., Madison, 1985. Bar: Wis. 1985, US Dist. Ct. (we. dist. Wis.) 1985, US Dist. Ct. (no. dist. Calif.) 1988. Assoc. Lee, Johnson, Kilkelly & Nichol, Madison, 1985-87; trial atty. US Dept. Justice, San Francisco, 1987-88; spl. asst. criminal divsn. US Atty., San Francisco, 1988; asst. US atty. US Atty.'s Office No. Dist. Calif., San Francisco, chief Major Crimes Unit, 2002—05; pvt. practice San Francisco, 2005—. Vol. San Francisco Neighborhood Legal Assistance, 1988—. Recipient Atty. of Yr. award, Calif. Lawyer, 2005. Mem. ABA, Wis. Bar Assn. (active lawyers hotline 1985-87), U. Wis. Alumni Assn., U. Wis.-Eau Claire Alumni Assn. Democrat. Roman Catholic. Avocations: basketball, camping, reading history. Office: 655 Montgomery St Ste 1700 San Francisco CA 94122 Office Phone: 415-989-1253. Office Fax: 415-576-1442. E-mail: attystevengruel@sbcglobal.net.*

GRUEN, ALISON BRETT, dermatologist; b. NYC, Jan. 15, 1974; d. John Fredrick and Judith Smith Gruen; m. Adam Laurence Evans, July 29, 2005. BA in History magna cum laude, Princeton U., 1996; MD, Yale U., 2000. Diplomate Am. Bd. Dermatology, 2004. Resident in dermatology Health Sci. Ctr., Bklyn., 2001—04, chief resident, 2003—04; pvt. practice New York, NY. Recipient Outstanding Physician award, King's County Hosp. Ctr., 2003, Fifteenth Ann. Conrad Stritzler Meml. Resident Competition First Pl. award, Dermatologic Soc. Greater NY, 2004. Mem.: Women's Dermatologic Soc., Am. Acad. Dermatology, Alpha Omega Alpha. Avocations: skiing, fly fishing, cooking. Office: 1020 Park Ave New York NY 10028 also: 35 E 35th St New York NY 10016 Home Phone: 212-987-5548; Office Phone: 212-734-7546, 212-684-5964.

GRUEN, DAVID HENRY, financial analyst; b. Buffalo, Aug. 12, 1929; s. Edward Charles and Florence (Knoche) G.; m. Joan Willard, Jan. 3, 1976; children by previous marriage: David E., Stephen P., Cathryn E., Edward Charles II, William A. BA, Cornell U., 1951, MBA, 1954. C.P.A., N.Y. Sr. accountant Arthur Andersen & Co., NYC, 1954-59; asst. treas. Marine Midland Banks, Inc., 1959-60, asst. v.p., 1960-63, v.p., treas., 1963-69; sr. v.p. Marine Midland Bank-Western, 1969-74; sr. v.p., treas. Marine Midland Banks, Inc., Buffalo, 1974-80; sr. v.p., gen. auditor, 1980-85; cons. Gruen Assocs., Buffalo, 1986—; v.p., chief fin. officer Niagara Envelope Group Inc., Buffalo, 1986-89. Served from 2d lt. to 1st lt. USAF, 1951-53. Mem. Am. Inst. C.P.A.s, Tax Execs. Inst., N.Y. Soc. C.P.A.s, Fin. Execs. Inst. Home: 34 Middlesex Rd Buffalo NY 14216-3616

GRUEN, GERALD ELMER, psychologist, educator; b. Granite City, Ill., July 19, 1937; s. Elmer George and Velma Pearl G.; m. Karol Jane Selvidge, Mar. 20, 1960; children— Tami Jane, Christy Lynn. BA, So. Ill. U., 1959; MA, U. Ill., 1963, PhD, 1964. Postdoctoral fellow Heinz Werner Inst. Devel. Psychology, Clark U. and Worcester (Mass.) State Hosp., 1964-66; asst. prof. dept. psychol. scis. Purdue U., West Lafayette, Ind., 1966-69, assoc. prof., 1969-74, prof., 1974—2005, head dept. psychol. scis., 1987-97, prof. emeritus, 2005—. Author: (with T. Wachs) Early Experience and Human Development; contbr. chpt. to The Structuring of Experience, 1977; contbr. articles to profl. jours. Deacon Calvary Baptist Ch., West Lafayette. Recipient USPHS rsch. awards, 1968-71, Nat. Rsch. Svc. award NIMH, 1976-80, Research award Nat. Insts. Child Health and Human Devel., 1981—; recipient Ind. Psychol. Assn. Gordon Barrows award for disting. career contbns., 2000. Fellow APA, Am. Psychol. Soc. (charter mem.); mem. Midwestern Psychol. Assn., Soc. for Rsch. in Child Devel., Sigma Xi. Home: 3738 Westlake Ct West Lafayette IN 47906 Office: Purdue U Psychology Dept West Lafayette IN 47907 Personal E-mail: jjgruen@insightbb.com. Business E-mail: gruen@psych.purdue.edu.

GRUEN, MARGARET, actress; b. NYC, July 24, 1949; d. Arno G. and Judith (Goldstein) Milenbach. Student, Yale Sch. Drama. Actress. Writer, performer (theatre) Tanya Talks: The Last Jew, 1997, The Young Sophisticate, 1994, What A Wonderful World, 1990, Dracula, 1970; one-woman show: Grenfell's Eccentric Characters; appeared in theatre, TV, and radio prodns., including Uncle Vanya, Garcia Lorca's New York; mem. comedy team The Chamansky Sisters. Mem. Am. Fedn. Television & Radio Artists, Actors Equity Assn., Screen Actors Guild. Office Phone: 917-968-3662. Personal E-mail: gruen_margaret@yahoo.com.

GRUEN, SHIRLEY SCHANEN, artist; b. Port Washington, Wis., Dec. 2, 1923; d. William Frank Schanen and Laura Thien Leffingwell; m. Gerald A. Gruen, Feb. 1, 1947; children: Gerald Jr., Lorelei Hosler, Lorna Nagler. BS in Art Edn., U. Wis., 1945; postgrad., Art Ctr. Sch., LA, 1945—47, Cardinal Stritch U., 1970—90. Instr. portrait and watercolor Milw. Area Tech. Coll., 1972—80; owner Shirley Gruen Art Gallery, Port Washington, 1972—. Bd. mem., curator Port Washington Hist. Soc.; publicity chmn. Eghart House Mus., Port Washington. One-woman shows include West Bend (Wis.) Gallery Fine Arts, 1981, Water Street Gallery, Milw., 1984, exhibitions include New Visions Gallery, Marshfield, Wis., 2002, ICA WE Assn., 2002, Nat. Arts Club, NY, 2006, exhibitions include many others, Represented in permanent collections Ozaukee Bank, Port Washington, Wis., Holiday Inn, Heritage Ins., Sheboygan, Wis., West Pub. Co., St. Paul, Milw. Art Commn., West Bend Fine Arts Gallery, West Bend Mut. Ins. Co., Wausau Hosp. Ctr., Wis., others. Named Citizen of Yr., Port Washington C. of C., 2003; recipient Legis. citation, Wis. Assembly, 2003. Mem.: Wis. Watercolor Soc., Wis. Painters and Sculptors. Democrat. Roman Catholic. Avocations: piano, sailing. Office Phone: 262-284-2273.

GRUENBERG, ELLIOT LEWIS, electronics engineer and company executive; b. NYC, Mar. 16, 1918; s. Lewis and Sadie (Schoenbrun) G.; m. Ruth Frankel, Apr. 19, 1947. BEE, CCNY, 1938. Engr., inspector US Signal Corps Line Inspection, Newark, 1939-43; quality control mgr. Tech. Devices, Roseland, NJ, 1943-48; sr. engr. J.H. Bunnell, Bklyn., 1948-51, Freed Radio, NYC, 1951; sr. engr., mgr. W.L. Maxson, NYC, 1951-58; sr. engring. mgr. Fed. Systems div. IBM, Bethesda, Md., 1958-73; cons. West New York, NJ, 1974-79; chmn. BroadCom, Inc., Secaucus, NJ, 1979-88, also bd. dirs.; chmn., pres. CompFax Corp., West New York, NJ, 1988-92; pres. Digital Compression Tech., L.P., NYC, 1993—. Editor: Handbook of Telemetry and Remote Control, 1967; inventor SYNAPZ Microwave Comm., radar, electronic telecomm., telemetry, BGET Secure Comm., DTIC Digital Transmission Bandwidth Compression, Superresonant Digital Modulation and Filtering; patentee in field; contbr. articles to profl. jours. Fellow Am. Inst. Aeronautics and Astronautics (assoc.); mem. IEEE (sr. life mem. 1940—). Democrat. Mem. Ethical Culture. Avocations: puzzles, astronomy, art collecting, artificial intelligence. Office: Digital Compression Tech LP 6040 Boulevard E Apt 30G West New York NJ 07093-3866 E-mail: elliotlg@aol.com.

GRUENBERG, MARTIN J., federal agency administrator, lawyer; BA, Princeton U., 1975; JD, Case Western Res. Law Sch., Cleve. Past pro. staff mem. Subcommittee Econ. Stabilization House Com. on Banking, Fin. & Urban Affairs, Washington; staff dir. Subcommittee on Intern. Fin. & Monetary Policy Senate Banking Com., Washington, 1987—92; sr. counsel to Senator Paul S. Sarbanes Senate Com. on Banking, Housing & Urban Affairs, Washington, 1995—2005; vice chmn. FDIC, Washington, 2005—. Office: FDIC 550 17th St NW Rm 6000 Washington DC 20429-9990*

GRUENBERGER, PETER, lawyer; b. Czechoslovakia, May 19, 1937; came to US, 1941; s. Leslie and Olga (Zollman) G.; m. Carin Lamm; children: Karen, Richard, Lauren. AB, Columbia U., 1958, LLB, 1961. Bar: NY 1962, US Dist. Ct. (so., ea. and no. dists.) NY 1962, US Ct. Appeals (1st and 2d cirs.) 1963, US Supreme Ct. 1964. Assoc. Hughes, Hubbard & Reed, NYC, 1962-69; ptnr. Weil, Gotshal & Manges, NYC, 1970—, mng. ptnr. Tex. office Houston, 1988-90. Contbr. articles on litigation to profl. jours. Served as 1st lt. US Army, 1961-62. Harlan Fiske Stone scholar, 1959-61. Mem. ABA (chmn. various coms. 1973-75, 79-86, spl. com. on class actions and discovery 1977-86, governing council 1975-78, litigation sect. 1985-87), Assn. of Bar of City of NY (grievance com. 1975-77). Office: Weil Gotshal & Manges 767 5th Ave New York NY 10153-0119 Office Phone: 212-310-8555. Office Fax: 212-310-8007. E-mail: peter.gruenberger@weil.com.

GRUENDER, RAYMOND W., federal judge, former prosecutor; b. St. Louis, July 5, 1963; BA, Washington U., 1984, MBA, JD, Washington U., 1987. Assoc. Lewis, Rice and Fingersh, 1987—90; ptnr. Thompson Coburn LLP, 1994—2000; asst. US atty., (ea. dist.) Mo. US Dept. State, St. Louis, 1990—94, 2000—01, US atty. (ea. dist) Mo, 2001—04; judge US Ct. Appeals, (8th cir.), 2004—. Office: US Courthouse 111 S Tenth St Saint Louis MO 63102*

GRUENWALD, JAMES HOWARD, association executive, consultant; b. Cin., Aug. 30, 1949; s. Howard Francis and Geraldine Emma (Mueller) G. BS, Xavier U., 1971. Cert. profl. in recreation and leisure svc., Ill. Rep. pub. rels. Cath. Youth Orgn., Cin., 1969—72; sales rep. Spade Trucking Co., Cin., 1972—73; field rep. Ohio Dept. Transport, Columbus, 1973—75; editl., sales rep. Cin. Suburban Newspaper, 1977—79; nat. exec. dir. Say Soccer USA, Cin., 1979—93; co-founder, exec. dir. U.S. Indoor Soccer Orgn., 1985—93; bd. dirs. Buckeye Men's Baseball, Cin., 1982—90, chmn., 1982—86, 1989—90; dir. Amateur Athletic Union, Indpls., 1983—85; nat. membership coord. Am. Youth Soccer Orgn., LA, 1993—2001; assoc. customer svc. Sam's Club, Loveland, Ohio, 2001—. Cert. trainer Am. Coaches Effectiveness Program, Champaign, Ill., 1983-92. Editor Touchline jour., 1980-92, Parents Guide to Soccer, 1985-92. Bd. dirs. Mid West Soccer Ofcls. Assn., bd. mem., 2003—05; adv. bd. Ch. Parish, Cin., 1974—76. Recipient cmty. svc. award State of Mich., 1986. Mem. Nat. Coun. Youth Sports Dirs., Nat. Recreation and Parks Assn., Mich. Recreation and Parks Assn. (cmty. svc. award 1986), Soc. for Non Profits. Avocations: hiking, reading, writing, teaching, conducting workshops. Home: 35 Dorsey Dr Hamilton OH 45011-4703 Office Phone: 513-677-8341. Personal E-mail: jimmygee94@fuse.net.

GRUESKIN, WILLIAM STEVEN (BILL GRUSEKIN), editor; b. Sioux City, Iowa, May 28, 1956; s. Harold Ross Grueskin and Charlotte Leiserowitz; children: Julia, Caroline. BA, Stanford U., 1977; MA in Internat. Econ., US Fgn. Policy, Johns Hopkins U., 1981. Mng. editor Dakota Sun, Ft. Yates, N.D., 1977-79; reporter Tampa (Fla.) Tribune, 1981-85; asst. city editor Miami (Fla.) Herald, 1985-89, Broward city editor, 1989-92; Miami city editor, 1992-95; Page One editl. staff The Wall St. Jour., NYC, 1995—98, dep. Page One editor, 1998—2001, dep. mng. editor for news, 2007—; mng. editor The Wall St. Jour. Online, NYC, 2001—07. Office: The Wall St Jour 200 Liberty St New York NY 10281 E-mail: b.grueskin@wsj.com.*

GRUETZMACHER, NANCY LYNN, retired middle schoool educator; b. Elm Grove, Wis., Mar. 1, 1945; d. Warren H. and Genevieve E. Hill; m. James Gruetzmacher, Dec. 21, 1968; 1 child, Beth Geisler. BS in Edn., Whitewater U., Wis., 1967. Tchr. Elmbrook Sch. Dist., Elm Grove, 1967—2006; ret. Named Outstanding Young Educator, Elmbrook Sch. Dist., 1972, Outstanding Educator, 1988. Avocations: reading, bicycling, yoga, organic cooking.

GRUHL, ANDREA MORRIS, librarian; b. Ponca City, Okla., Dec. 9, 1939; d. Luther Oscar and Hazel Evangeline (Anderson) Morris; m. Werner Mann Gruhl, July 10, 1965; children: Sonja Krista, Diana Krista. BA, Wesleyan Coll., Macon, Ga., 1961; MLS, postgrad., U. Md., College Park, 1968, postgrad., 1971—73, Johns Hopkins U., Balt., 1970—71, Oxford U., Eng., 1996. Tchr. Broward County, Fla., U.S. Dept. Def. Montgomery County, Md., 1961—66; libr. Prince Georges County (Md.) Pub. Libr., 1966—68, 1981—83, U. Md., College Park, 1970—72; art. history rschr. Joseph Alsop, Washington, 1972—74; libr. Howard County Pub. Libr., Columbia, Md., 1969—70, 1974—79; European exch. staff Libr. of Congress, Washington, 1982—86; cataloger fed. documents GPO, Washington, 1986—93, supervisory libr., 1993—2001. Women's program adv. com., processing dept. rep. Libr. of Congress, 1983-86, mem. ofcl. Libr. of Congress delegation to Internat. Fedn. Libr. Assn. ann. conf., Munich, 1983, Chgo., 1985; state del. White House Conf. on Librs., 1978, 90. Indexer, editor: Learning Vacations, 3d edit., 1980; editor: Federal Librarian, 1994-99, NCA News & Notes, 2003-04; LCPA Index to Libr. of Congress Info. Bull., 1984. Trustee Howard County CC, 1989-95, Howard County Pub. Libr., Columbia, Md., 1979-87; citizens rep. Howard County, exec. bd. Balt. Regional Planning Coun. Libr. com., 1976-79; Friends of Libr., Howard County, pres., 1976; vol. Nat. Gallery Art Libr., Washington, 1978-80. Mem.: LWV (dir. nat. capital area 2002—06, homeland security com. chmn. 2003—06, co-pres. Howard County 2004—05, dir. civil liberties, Md. 2005—, v.p. nat. capital area 2006—), ALA (councilor 1997—2001, co-chair coun. caucus 2000—01), Govt. Documents Round Table, Fed. and Armed Forces Librs. Round Table (editor 1994—99, IFLA rep. 1996—2006, v.p. 1997—98, pres. 1998—99, chmn. constn. and bylaws com. 2001—06, Disting. Svc. award 2001), Md. Libr. Assn. (pres. trustee divsn. 1982—83), Libr. Congress Am. Fedn. State, County and Mcpl. Employees Union (program chair 1984—86), Libr. Congress Profl. Assn. (coord. ann. staff art shows 1982—83, chair libr. sci. interest group 1985—87), Art Librs. Soc. N.Am. (coord. mems.' publ. exhbn. 1980—82), Internat. Fedn. Libr. Assns. and Instns. (sect. on cataloging, internat. std. bibliog. description/cartographic materials working gro), DC Libr. Assn. (co-chair mgmt. interest group 1996—97, v.p. 2001—02, pres. 2002—03), Oxford U. Soc., Md. Assn. C.C. (bd. dir. 1993—95), UN Assn. Nat. Capital Area Chpt. (Md. tel. chair 1992—94, membership com. 1992—, co-chair endowment com. 2004—), Md. Assn. C.C. Trustees (sec. 1991—92, bd. dir. 1992—93), Women's Nat. Dem. Club, Beta Phi Mu (pres. Washington area chpt. 2005—06). Democrat. Lutheran. Home: 5990 Jacobs Ladder Columbia MD 21045-3817

GRUHL, JAMES, energy scientist, artist; b. Milw., Apr. 9, 1945; s. Alfred and Helen (Vanderveer) G.; m. Nancy Lee Huston, July 4, 1974; children: Amanda Natalie, Steven Christopher. BS, MS, MIT, 1968, PhD, 1973. Lectr. MIT, 1969-83; rsch. scientist MIT Energy Lab., Cambridge, 1973-83, program mgr., 1978-83, rsch. affiliate, 1984; sci. adv. bd. U.S. EPA, 1986-93; energy cons. U.S. Congress, rsch. insts., internat. energy industries, 1973—. Ednl. counselor MIT, 1978—. Recipient Silver Beaver award Boy Scouts Am., 1986, numerous art awards, 1990—; NSF grantee. Mem. IEEE, AAAS, Math. Programming Soc., MIT Alumni Assn. (officer 1978—), Tau Beta Pi, Eta Kappa Nu. Achievements include research in uncertainties and validity of analytic models, validity of government and industry energy policy models, and climate change models. Office: Gruhl Assocs PO Box 36524 Tucson AZ 85740-6524 Personal E-mail: jamesgruhl@gmail.com.

GRUMBACH, MELVIN MALCOLM, pediatrician, educator; b. NYC, Dec. 21, 1925; s. Emanuel and Adele (Weil) G.; m. Madeleine F. Butt, Dec. 1, 1951; children: Ethan Malcolm, Kevin Lawrence, Anthony Havemeyer. Student, Columbia U., 1945, MD, 1948; DM honoris causa (hon.), U. Geneva, 1991; D honoris causa (hon.), U. René Descartes Paris V, 2000. Diplomate Am. Bd. Pediatrics, Am. Bd. Pediatric Endocrinology (com. mem. 1975-79). Resident in pediatrics Babies Hosp., Presbyn. Hosp., Columbia U. Med. Ctr., NYC, 1949-51; trainee Oak Ridge Inst. Nuc. Studies, 1952; postdoctoral fellow, asst. pediatrics Johns Hopkins Sch. Medicine, 1953-55; mem. faculty Columbia U. Coll. Physicians and Surgeons, NYC, 1955-65, from instr. to assoc. prof. pediatrics, 1961-65; from asst. to assoc. attending pediatrician Babies Hosp. and Vanderbilt Clin., Columbia-Presbyn. Med. Ctr., 1955-65, founding head postdoctoral tng. program pediat. endocrinology Pediat. Endocrine Divsn., 1955—65; dir. pediatric svc. U. Calif. Hosps., 1966-86; prof. pediatrics, chmn. dept. U. Calif. Sch. Medicine, San Francisco, 1966-86, first Edward B. Shaw prof. pediatrics, 1983-94, acting dir. Lab. Molecular Endocrinology, 1987-89, Edward B. Shaw prof. emeritus pediatrics (active), 1994—. Vis. prof. Vanderbilt U., 1961, Emory U., 1962, U. Western Ont., 1962, U. NC, 1963, 82, U. Rochester, 1972, UCLA, 1981, U. Tex., Dallas, 1983, Peking Union Med. Coll. and Hosp., 1986, U. Hong Kong, 1986; cons. Letterman Gen. Hosp., 1966-94, Children's Hosp., San Francisco, U.S. Naval Hosp., Oakland, Calif., 1966-94, HEW, NIH, 1961- , Nat. Bd. Med. Examiners, 1964-68; human embryology and devel. study sect. NIH, 1962-66, endocrinology study sect., 1967-71; bd. sci. counselors Nat. Inst. Child Health and Human Devel., 1971-75; gen. clin. rsch. ctrs. com., divsn. rsch. resources NIH, 1976-80, com. for rev. Clin. Ctr., 1984-85, IOM com. study AIDS rsch. program NIH, 1989-91, nat. adv. coun. Nat. Inst. Child Health and Human Devel., 1991-96; sci. adv. com., clin. rsch. adv. com. Nat. Found.-March of Dimes, 1969-94, chmn. clin. rsch. adv. com., 1974-82, Basil O'Connor starter scholar rsch. award comm., 1995-99, grant screening com., 2000-; awards com. Lita Annenberg Hazen Award for Excellence in Clin. Rsch., 1981-86; sci. adv. bd. Scripps Clinic and Rsch. Found., 1977-78, Princesse Marie Christine Found., Brussels, 1981-91, U. Mich. Ctr. for Human Growth and Devel., 1982-89, U. Colo. Health Scis. Barbara Davis Ctr., 1986-93, Rsch. Inst. Hosp. for Sick Children, Toronto, 1984-88, Children's Hosp. LA, 1987-92; sci. and med. adv. bd. Whittier Inst. Diabetes and Endocrinology, 1987-92; adv. bd. Nat. Pituitary Agy., 1965-69; mem. NIH Evaluation of Endocrinology and Metabolic Diseases, 1977-79; Dean's bd. vis. Mt. Sinai Sch. Medicine, NYC, 1986-87; sci. adv. coun. Cin. Children's Hosp. Rsch. Found., 1997-98; pres. bd. trustees Internat. Pediat. Rsch. Found., Inc., 1984-89; sci. coun. Aid Pour la Recherche Medicale a l'enfance, Paris, 1981-89; com. future pub. health Inst. Medicine, 1986-87; del. to Chinese Acad. Med. Scis., 1986; lectr. in field; chmn. various confs. Assoc. editor, mem. editl. bd. Jour. Clin. Endocrinology Metabolism, 1957-70, 2006-; adv. editor Jour. Pediat., 1966-73, mem. editl. bd., 1973-79; assoc. editor Pediat. Rsch., 1970-84, Barnett Pediatrics, 14th-15th edits., Rudolph Pediatrics, 16th-21st edits., Current Topics in Experimental Endocrinology; mem. internat. editl. bd. pediat. and pediatric surgery: Excerpta Medica, 1974-2000; mem. editl. bd. Biology of Reproduction, 1968-70, Endocrinologic Clinica Metabolism, 1981—, Pediat. in Rev., 1982-84, Jour. Endocrinol. Investigation, 1982-90, Endocrine Revs., 1984-88, Jour. Pediat. Endocrinology Metabolism, 1984—, Trends in Endocrinology, 1989—, Monographs on Endocrinology, Springer-Verlag, 1975-90, Clinical Pediat. Endocrinology, 1992—, Jour. Endocrine Genetics, 1999—; contbr. articles to profl. jours. Capt. USAF, 1951—53. Postdoctoral fellow Nat. Found. Infantile Paralysis, 1953-55; recipient Joseph M. Smith prize Columbia U., 1962; Career Scientist award Health Research Coun. City N.Y., 1961-66; Silver medal Bicentennial Columbia Coll. Physicians and Surgeons, 1967, Gold medal, 1988; Clin. Endocrinology Trust medal (U.K.), 1985, Centennial Medallist award Babies Hosp., Columbia-Presbyn. Med. Ctr., 1987, Coll. France medal, 1979, Winthrop award, Am. Fertility Soc., 1981; Sci. Patron, Liggins Inst. Faculty Med. Health Sci., U. Auckland, New Zealand, 2001—. Fellow: AAAS, NY Acad. Scis., Am. Acad. Pediats. (Bordon award 1971, Lifetime Achievement award 1996), Am. Acad. Arts and Scis.; mem.: Lawson Wilkins Pediat. Endocrine Soc. (Inaugural award 2006), NAS Inst. Medicine (mem. nominating com. 2007), Am. Pediat. Soc. (pres.-elect 1988—89, pres. 1989—90, John Howland award 1997), Calif. Acad. Medicine, Western Assn. Physicians, Internat. Neuroendocrinology Soc., Internat. Endocrine Soc. (del. to ctrl. com. 1976—92, exec. com. 1984—92, hon. pres. 2000—04), Endocrine Soc. (coun. 1968—71, pres. elect 1980—81, coun. 1980—83, pres. 1981—82, Robert H. Williams Disting. Leadership award 1980, Fred Conrad Koch award 1992), Teratology Soc., Soc. Pediat. Rsch., Western Soc. Pediat. Rsch. (pres. 1978—79), Lawson Wilkins Pediat. Endocrine Soc. (pres. 1975—76, Judson Van Wyk prize 2006), Harvey Soc., Am. Soc. Human Genetics, Assn. Am. Physicians, Am. Soc. Clin. Investigation, Assn. Med. Sch. Pediat. Dept. Chmn.

(exec. coun. 1967—72, pres. 1973—75, task force on Pediat. Scientist Tng. Program 1984—91, chmn. selection com. 1986—91), Argentine Soc. Endocrinology and Metabolism (hon.), Can. Soc. Endocrinology and Metabolism (hon.), Japanese Soc. Pediat. Endocrinology (hon.), Pacific Coast Fertility Soc. (hon.), Israel Endocrine Soc. (hon.), European Soc. Pediat. Endocrinology (corr.), Soc. Française de Pediatrie (corr.), Inst. Medicine Nat. Acad. Scis. (mem. pub. health com. 1985—87, mem. AIDS rsch. com. 1989—91, chmn. adolescent devel. and biology of puberty 1998—99, mem. com. on understanding the biology of sex and gender differences 2000—01), Johns Hopkins U. Soc. Scholars, U. Club NYC, Alpha Omega Alpha, Sigma Xi. Office: U Calif Sch Medicine Dept Pediatrics S672 San Francisco CA 94143-0434 Office Phone: 415-476-2244. Business E-Mail: grumbach@peds.ucsf.edu.

GRUMMEL, JOHN ARNE, political science professor; s. William John Grummel and Inger Hall; m. Darlene Marie Freitas, May 16, 1992; children: Ashley Haldis, Kristian Johan. MA, San Francisco State U., 1997; MAT, Coll. Notre Dame, Belmont, Calif., 1995; PhD, Kent State U., Ohio, 2001. Asst. prof. W.Va. State U., Institute, 2004—06, U. SC, Spartanburg, 2006—. Contbr. articles to profl. jours. Grantee Instrnl. Devel. grant, W.Va. State U., 2005. Mem.: So. Polit. Sci. Assn., Midwest Polit. Sci. Assn., Am. Polit. Sci. Assn. Home: 2479 Country Club Rd Apt 900G Spartanburg SC 29302

GRUNBERG, NANCY R., lawyer; b. Mankato, Minn., Sept. 26, 1953; BA with distinction, Stanford U., 1975; JD, Columbia U., 1979. Bar: Pa. 1979, DC 1983, Md. 1996. Litigation assoc. Davis Polk & Wardwell, Washington, 1981—88; atty. securities, banking and commercial litigation priv. practice, Washington, 1992—96; lead trial atty., enforcement div. US Securities and Exchange Commn., 1996—99, litigation counsel, office of internat. affairs, 1999—2000, asst. dir., div. of enforcement, 2000—02; ptnr. Venable LLP, Washington, 2002—. Mem.: ABA, Md. Bar Assn., DC Bar Assn. Office: Venable LLP 575 7th St NW Washington DC 20004 Office Phone: 202-344-4730. Office Fax: 202-344-8300. Business E-Mail: nrgrunberg@venable.com.

GRUNBERG, ROBERT LEON WILLY, nephrologist, educator; b. Bucharest, Romania, July 23, 1940; arrived in U.S., 1972, naturalized, 1977; s. William A. and Isabelle L. (Rosen) Grunberg; m. Donna M. Fishman, Oct. 19, 1975; children: Wendie I., Andrea B. MD, U. Orleans-Tours, France, 1969. Diplomate Am. Bd. Internal Medicine, Am. Bd. Nephrology, cert. hypertension specialist in clin. hypertension. Intern, then resident in cardiology Vichy Hosp., France, 1968-72; resident in internal medicine Albert Einstein Med. Ctr., Phila., 1972-74; fellow in nephrology-hypertension Hahnemann Univ. Hosp., Phila., 1974-76, sr. clin. instr. then asst. clin. prof. div. nephrology, 1976; pvt. practice Allentown, Pa., 1976—. Attending physician St. Luke's Hosp., Bethlehem, Pa., Lehigh Valley Ctr. (name now Lehigh Valley Hosp.), Allentown; attending charge divsn. nephrology Easton Hosp., Pa., dir. Renal Dialysis Ctr., 1989; courtesy staff Hahnemann U. Hosp.; chief dialysis Warren Hosp., Phillipsburg, NJ, 1999. Fellow: ACP; mem.: AMA (Physician's Recognition award 1975, 1979, 1982, 1985, 1988—98, 2001), NY Acad. Scis., Nat. Kidney Found., Internat. Soc. Peritoneal Dialysis, Assn. Advancement Med. Instrumentation, Internat. Soc. Nephrology, Internat. Soc. Artificial Organs, Am. Soc. Parenteral and Enteral Nutrition, Internat. Soc. Hypertension, Am. Soc. Artificial Internal Organs, Am. Soc. Nephrology, Pa. Med. Soc. Office: 50 S 18th St Easton PA 18042-3912 also: 401 N 17th St Allentown PA 18104-5034

GRUNBERG, STEVEN MARC, medical educator; b. Paterson, NJ, June 5, 1950; s. Emanuel and Eleanor (Hoffman) G.; m. Kelly Jean McLeod, July 1, 1984; children: Elizabeth, Katherine, Alexandra. BA, Cornell U., 1971, MD, 1975. Diplomate Am. Bd. Internal Medicine. Asst. prof. U. So. Calif., LA, 1981-87, assoc. prof., 1987-93; prof. U. Vt., Burlington, 1993—. Chair initial rev. group subcom. Nat. Cancer Inst., 2002—04. Contbr. articles to profl. jours. Fellow ACP; mem. Am. Soc. Clin. Oncology (procs. editor, 2000—), Am. Assn. Cancer Rsch., No. New England Clin. Oncology Soc. (bd. dirs. 1995—, pres. 2003-04), Multinat. Assn. Supportive Care in Cancer (bd. dirs. 2006—). Office: Fletcher Allen Health Care Divsn Hematology/Oncology 89 Beaumont Ave Given E214-E Burlington VT 05405

GRUNDER, FRED IRWIN, retired industrial hygienist, consultant; b. Detroit, Aug. 17, 1940; s. Fritz and Mary Kathrine (Irwin) G.; m. Barbara Ann Ward, May 7, 1966; children: John Frederick, Robert William. BS in Engr. Physics, U. Mich., 1963, MS in Physics, 1967. Diplomte Am. Bd. Indsl. Hygiene; cert. indsl. hygienist. Rsch. assoc. U. Mich., Ann Arbor, 1960-69; chemist G.D. Clayton & Assocs., Southfield, Mich., 1969-72; lab. dir. Bethlehem Steel Corp., Pa., 1972-85; dir. indsl. hygiene Am. Med. Labs., Fairfax, Va., 1985-92; mgr. lab. accreditation programs Am. Indsl. Hygiene Assn., Fairfax, 1992—2002; indsl. hygiene cons. Fishersville, Va., 2002—07; ret., 2007. Sect. editor: Methods for Biological Monitoring, 1988. Scoutmaster Boy Scouts Am., Bethlehem, 1972-84; pres. U. Mich. Club, Lehigh Valley, 1980-84; mem. toxic planning and oversight panel Chesapeake Rsch. Consortium, Solomons Island, Md., 1990-91, site assessor AIHA Lab., 1992, 2004—; bd. dirs., vice-chair Nat. Coop. Lab. Accreditation, 1997-98, pres., 1998-2000, past pres., 2000-01, evaluation coord., 2004-07; bd. dirs. SAW Habitat for Humanity. Fellow Am. Indsl. Hygiene Assn.; mem. ASTM, Am. Chem. Soc., Am. Acad. Indsl. Hygiene. Democrat. Methodist. Avocations: reading, stamp and coin collecting, gardening. Personal E-mail: fgrunder@mindspring.com.

GRUNDER, HERMANN A., science administrator, director, research scientist; b. Basel, Switzerland; MS in Mech. Engring., KarlsruheU.; PhD in Exptl. Nuc. Physics, U. Basel; doctorate (hon.), U. Frankfurt, 2000. Dep. dir. gen. sci. Lawrence Berkeley Nat. Lab., Calif.; dir. Thomas Jefferson Nat. Accelerator Facility, 1985—2000, Argonne Nat. Lab., 2000—05; ret., 2005. Lab. rep. to lab. ops. bd. Sec. Engery Adv. Bd. (SEAB); chair Nat. Ignition Facility Program Rev.; bd. dirs. vis. com. U. Chgo. Divsn. Physical Scis.; bd. dirs. Ill. Coalition; mem. steering com. U.S. Particle Accelerator Sch.; mem. adv. com. physics Los Alamos AOT Divsn. Named Scientist of Yr., Commonwealth Va., 1998; recipient U.S. Sr. Scientist award, Alexander von Humboldt Found., Germany, 1979, Disting. Assoc. award, U.S. Dept. Energy, 1996, Sec. of Energy Gold award, 2004. Fellow: AAAS, Am. Physical Soc.; mem.: Swiss Physical Soc., European Physical Soc. Home Phone: 630-362-5962. Business E-Mail: grunder@anl.gov.

GRUNDER, STUART EDWIN, social studies educator; s. John and Wanda (Oyer) Grunder; m. Mary Catherine Schoeppner, June 21, 1997. BS in Edn., Bowling Green State U., Ohio, 1989; MEd, Kent State U., Ohio, 1996. Instr. social studies, dept. chair Minerva Local Sch., Ohio, 1993—. Key club advisor Key Club Internat., Ohio. Jennings scholar, Martha Holden Jennings Found., 2003. Mem.: Minerva Local Edn. Assn. (pres. 2004—06). Office: Minerva High School 501 Almeda Ave Minerva OH 44657 Home Phone: 330-862-2626; Office Phone: 330-868-4134. Business E-Mail: segl@minerva.stark.k12.oh.us.

GRUNDFAST, KENNETH MARTIN, otolaryngologist; b. Bklyn., Mar. 12, 1944; s. Theodore Harvey and Anne Gertrude (Goldberg) G.; m. Ruthanne Blatt Grundfast, May 26, 1974; children: Rena Brett, Dara Beth. BA, Johns Hopkins U., 1965; MD, SUNY, Syracuse, 1969. Clin. instr. dept. of community medicine Georgetown U. Sch. of Medicine, Washington, 1972-74, prof. depts. otolaryngology and pediat., 1996-99, interim chmn. dept. otolryngology; resident otolaryngology Boston U. Hosp., 1974-77; fellow in pediatric otolaryngology Childrens Hosp. of Pitts., 1977-78, staff otolaryngologist, 1978-79, asst. prof. of otolaryngology, 1978-79; prof. dept. otolaryngology, 1980-96; chmn. dept. otolaryngology Children's Nat. Med. Ctr., Washington, 1980-94, vice-chmn., 1994-96; prof., chmn. dept. otolaryngology Sch. Medicine Boston U., 1999—; chmn. ethics com. Boston Med. Ctr., 2004—. Lectr. in field. Author: (with others) Ear Infections in Your Child, 1987, Pediatric Otology/Neurotology, 1997; contbr. articles to profl. jours. Lt. comdr. USPHS, 1971-73. Recipient Sylvan Stool Achievement award Sentac, 2000. Fellow ACS, Am. Acad. Pediat.; mem. AMA (Humanitarian award 1973), Soc. Ear, Nose and Throat Advancement in Children (bd. dirs. 1985, v.p. 1988, pres. 1989), Am. Bronchoesophagologic Soc., Soc. U. Otolaryngologists, Am. Neurotology Soc., Trilogical Soc. (hon. mention clin. rsch. thesis), Am. Soc. Pediatric Otolaryngology (pres. 1993-94), Am. Acad. Otolaryngology (v.p. 1994-96, sec.-treas. 2004-, Presdl. Citation award 1996), Nat. Med. Honor Soc., Assn. Acad. Depts. Otolaryngology (pres.-elect). Avocations: swimming, bicycling. Office: Dept Otolaryngology One Boston Med Ctr Pl Boston MA 02118-2393 Office Phone: 617-638-7934. E-mail: kenneth.grundfast@bmc.org.

GRUNDFEST, JOSEPH ALEXANDER, law and business educator; b. NYC, Sept. 8, 1951; s. Michael A. and Esther Grundfest: m. Carol Chia-Ming Hsu, Aug. 6, 1978. Student MSc program in math. economics and econometrics, London Sch. Econometrics, 1971—72; BA, Yale U., 1973; JD, Stanford U., 1978, doctoral studies in Economics, 1975—78. Bar: Calif. 1978, DC 1979, US Supreme Ct. 1987. Economist, cons. Rand Corp., Santa Monica, Calif., 1973-78; rsch. assoc. The Brookings Instn., 1978—79; assoc. Wilmer, Cutler & Pickering, Washington, 1979-84; counsel, sr. economist legal and regulatory matters Coun. Econ. Advisers, Exec. Office of Pres., Washington, 1984-85; commr. SEC, Washington, 1985-90; assoc. prof. law Stanford U. Law Sch., 1990—94, prof., 1994—97, William A. Franke prof. law & bus., 1997—, John M. Olin faculty fellow, 1991—92, Helen L. Crocker faculty scholar, 1996—97, dir. George R. Roberts Program in Law, Bus. and Corporate Governance, 1993—2002, co-dir. Program in Law, Economics and Bus., 2002—, co-dir. Rock Ctr. on Corp. Governance, 2006. Mem. legal adv. com. NY Stock Exch., 1993—96; nat. fellow Hoover Instn. Stanford U., 1992—93; bd. dirs. Oracle Corp., 2001—06. Recipient John Bingham Hurlbut Award for Excellence in Tchg., Stanford Law Sch., 1992, 2001. Fellow Coun. Fgn. Rels.; mem. ABA, Am. Law Inst., Am. Fin. Assn., Am. Economics Assn., Am. Law and Economics Assn. Avocations: swimming, jogging. Office: Stanford Law Sch Crown Quadrangle 559 Nathan Abbott Way Stanford CA 94305-8610 Office Phone: 650-723-0458. Business E-Mail: grundfest@stanford.edu.*

GRUNDHOFER, JERRY A., bank executive; b. Glendale, Calif., 1945; married. BA, Loyola Marymount U., 1967. With Union Bank, 1967-81; pres. Alliance Bank, 1981-83; sr. v.p. So. Calif. corp. banking, sr. v.p. So. Calif. retail banking ops. Wells Fargo Bank, 1983-85, exec. v.p. 440 br. statewidef retail banking sys., 1985-87; vice chmn. Security Pacific Nat. Bank, 1987-90, pres., CEO, 1990-93, Star Banc Corp., Cin., 1993—, chmn.; pres., CEO Star Bank, N.A., 1993—; CEO Firstar Corp., Milw.; pres. US Bancorp (formerly Firstar Corp.), Mpls., 2001—04; CEO US Bancorp, Mpls., 2001—06, chmn., 2002—. Bd. dirs. Arete Assocs., Cin. Equity Fund, L.L.C., Hennegan Co., Visa Internat., Visa U.S.A., Inc., mem. exec. com. Trustee Children's Hosp. Med. Ctr., Health Found. Greater Cin., Cin. Symphony Orch., United Appeal/Cmty. Chest, United Way, U. Cin. Found., Xavier U.; co-chair Fine Arts Fund Campaign, 1995, chmn., 1996; co-chmn. Urban Capital Campaign, 1995, 96; chmn. corp. exec. com. 13th ann. tribute dinner Jewish Inst. Rel. Hebrew Union Coll., 1995; chmn. ann. dinner Nat. Conf. Christians and Jews, 1997; bd. dirs. Nat. Underground Railroad Freedom Ctr. Honoree 15th ann. tribute dinner Jewish Inst. Rel. Hebrew Union Coll., 1997; Named Banker of Yr., Forbes mag., 1998, Am. Banker, 2000 Mem. Am. Bankers Assn. (bd. dirs.), Internat. Fin. Conf. (bd. dirs.), Bankers Roundtable (bd. dirs.), Greater Cin. C. of C. (bd. dirs.), Over-the-Rhine C. of C. (bd. dirs.), Birnan Woods, Cin. Country Club, Comml. Club (mem. exec. com.), Double Eagle Golf Club, Queen City Club. Office: US Bancorp 800 Nicollet Mall Ste 1500 Minneapolis MN 55402-7014*

GRUNDHOFER, JOHN F., bank executive; b. LA, 1939; Student, Loyola U., 1960, U. So. Calif., 1964. Formerly with Wells Fargo & Co., San Francisco, also vice chmn.; now chmn., pres., CEO U.S. Bancorp (formerly First Bank System, Inc.), Mpls., 1990—2001, chmn., 2001—, also dir. Office: Us Bank 800 Nicollet Mall Ste 1500 Minneapolis MN 55402-7014

GRUNDISH, LEE ANNE, small business owner, writer; b. Kalamazoo, Mich., Apr. 13, 1959; d. Allen Grundish and Jeane Gratop. BA in Psychology, U. Toledo, 1984. Bus. owner, pres. Grafix Svcs./Achieve Success!, Toledo, 1989—. Bus. develp. mktg. cons., 1985—89. Lyricist (song) Love Is What We Need; writer: numerous resumes in resume guides including Expert Resumes for Baby-Boomers, Barron's Designing the Perfect Resume, Best Resumes and Letters for Ex-Offenders, others. Parent counselor Family and Child Abuse Prevention Ctr., Toledo, 1984, fund-raising vol., 1998; youth mentor Big Bros. & Big Sisters, Toledo, 1990—91, fundraising vol., 1995—98, Arts Commn. of Greater Toledo, 1998; voters' rights vol. Nat. Voice, Toledo, 2004. Mem.: ASCAP, ACA, Nat. Resume Writers Assn., Nat. Employment Counselors Assn. Democrat. Avocations: poetry, politics. Home: 2242 Portsmouth Ave Toledo OH 43613 Office: 2149 Evergreen Rd Toledo OH 43606 Home Phone: 419-474-3136; Office Phone: 419-534-2709. Business E-Mail: grafixservices@aol.com.

GRUNDSTROM, BRIAN WILBUR, composer; MBA in Arts, SUNY, Binghamton, 1987. Mem.: ASCAP. Home and Office: BrianWilbur Music 1453 S St NW Washington DC 20009 Office Phone: 202-232-3316. Business E-Mail: brian@brianwilbur.com.

GRUNDY, RICHARD DAVID, engineer; b. San Mateo, Calif., Mar. 17, 1937; s. John Richard and Violette Grundy; m. Claudia Copeland, 1977 (div. 1992); m. Jamei C. Haswell, 1997. BSEE, Stanford U., Calif., 1958; MS, U. Calif., 1963, postgrad., 1964, George Washington U., 1965-67, Harvard U., 1980. Exec. sec. Nat. Fuels and Energy Policy Study U.S. Senate, Washington, 1971-76, mem. sr. profl. staff Com. on Environment and Pub. Works, 1967-76, mem. sr. profl. staff Com. on Energy and Natural Resources, 1977-94; pres. Alexandria (Va.) Energy Assoc., Inc., 1995—. Mem. bd. North Coast Region Regional Water Quality Control Bd., EPA, State of Calif., 2001-05; alt. bd. mem. Hearing Bd., S.F. Bay Area Air Quality Mgmt. Dist., EPA, State Calif., 2001—; chmn. protocol com. 2d Internat. Clear Air Congress, Internat. Union Air Prevention Assns., 1970; steering com. Aspen Inst. Energy Forum, 1985-91; observer White Ho. Conf. on Global Climate Change, Washington, 1990, 93-94; mem. U.S. deleg. UN Negotiations on Climate Change, Geneva, 1993, 94; participant UN Conf. on Clean Coal Tech. in Devel. Countries, Beijing, 1991. Author: (with others) Air Pollution and Industry, 1972; co-editor: Consumer Health and Product Hazards, 1974; contbr. numerous articles to profl. jours. Mem. adminstrv. bd. Foundry United Meth. Ch., Washington, 1960-62, 66-70, mem. coun. of mins., 1967-70, chmn. membership commn., 1968-70; mem. nat. planning com. Nat. Youth Govs. Conf., YMCA and Readers Digest Found., Washington, 1975-80; mem. Air Pollution Control Assn., 1967-82; pres. Nat. Capital Orchid Soc., Washington, 1989-90; exec. dir. Ea. Orchid Congress, 1997-00; northcoast regional dir. Steve Westly for Gov., 2005-06. Comdr. USPHS, 1959-67. Recipient Disting. Svc. award U.S. Senate, 1981. Fellow AAAS; mem. IEEE, NSPE, Assn. of Energy Engrs., D.C. Soc. Profl. Engrs. (Young Engr. of the Yr. 1970), Am. Orchid Soc. (conservation com.), U.S. Energy Assn. Methodist. Home and Office: 950 Wikiup Dr Santa Rosa CA 95403-1305 Office Phone: 707-570-2828. Personal E-mail: richardgrundy@att.net, richard.grundy@yahoo.com.

GRUNE, STEVEN BRYAN, publishing executive; s. George G.; m. Nancy Dunn, Apr. 28, 1990. MBA, Rollins Coll. Acct./bus. mgr. McCalls; sales positions Parents Mag., adv. dir., 1994—97, Redbook, 1997—98, assoc. pub., 1998—99; pub. Midwest Living, 1999—2000, Country Living, 2000—, v.p., 2002—; pub. Country Living Gardener, 2000—, v.p., 2002—. Office: Country Living 300 West 57th St New York NY 10019-3788*

GRUNEICH, JEFFREY ALAN, biotechnologist, director; b. Berkeley, Calif., July 27, 1973; s. John A Gruneich and Angie A Holdaway. BS in Chemistry and Math., U. Calif., Berkeley, 1996, MA in Chemistry, 1997; PhD, U. Pa., 2002. Chief bus. officer Infoceutics, Inc., Phila., 2001—; subject matter expert IBM, Phila., 2003—. Chief strategy officer eTechtransfer.com, Phila., 1999—2000. Musician: (performance) Dear Mandy (Conan O'Brien, Best Coll. Band, 1995). Co-pres. U. Pa Biotech Club, Phila., 1999—2000. Recipient Magna cum laude, So. Meth. U., 1996; fellow Grad. Student fellowship, Chemistry, NSF, 1996-2001. Mem.: Am. Soc. of Gene Therapy, Am. Assn. of Pharm. Scientists (assoc.), World Future Soc. (assoc.), Am. Assn. for the Advancement of Sci. (assoc.), Am. Chem. Soc. (assoc.), Phi Beta Kappa. Achievements include patents pending for synthesis and use of reagents for improved DNA lipofection and/or slow release prodrug and drug therapies. Avocations: skiing, weightlifting, travel, guitar, trumpet. Office Phone: 215-738-3852.

GRUNES, ROBERT LEWIS, engineering executive, consultant; b. Bklyn., Aug. 15, 1941; s. Abe and Doris (Dicker) G.; m. Eleonora Grasselli, Oct. 14, 1972; children: Natalie, Daniel, Ian. BS in Engring., Poly. Inst. Bklyn., 1963, MS in Engring., 1965, PhD in Phys. Metallurgy, 1970. Registered profl. engr., N.Y., N.J., Pa. Engr. Pratt & Whitney div. United Aircraft Corp., East Hartford, Conn., 1963; rsch. fellow Poly. Inst. Bklyn., 1963-64, rsch. assoc., 1966-70; rsch. engr. Lewis Rsch. Ctr. NASA, Cleve., 1965; pres. R. L. Grunes & Assocs., Inc., NYC, 1970—. Mem. adj. faculty N.J. Inst. Tech., Newark, 1974-78. Author: Pollution Control Market and Industries, 1971; contbr. articles to profl. jours. 1st lt. CE U.S. Army, 1964-66. Mem. ASME, ASCE, ASTM, Metall. Soc., Soc. Automotive Engrs., Nat. Fire Protection Assn., Am. Boat & Yacht Coun. Office: R L Grunes & Assocs Inc 521 5th Ave New York NY 10175-0003

GRUNEWALD, RAYMOND BERNHARD, lawyer; b. NYC, Feb. 10, 1928; s. Ivan Oscar and Verna Allesandria (Lindgren) G.; m. Irma Geiser; children: Peter Bernhard, Iris Elizabeth. BS, Fordham U., 1949, JD, 1952. Bar: NY 1952, US Ct. Mil. Appeals 1956, US Dist. Ct. (so. and ea. dists.) NY 1957, US Ct. Appeals (2d cir.) 1962, US Supreme Ct. 1963, US Tax Ct. 1970, US Ct. Appeals (fed. cir.) 1986, US Ct. Appeals (3d cir.) 2000. Sole practice law, NYC, 1956-60, 70—; asst. U.S. Atty., chief criminal and civil divsns. Dept. Justice, NYC, 1961-70. Candidate for Nassau County Comptroller, 1985, Nassau County Exec., 1987, Nassau County Ct., 1990, NY Supreme Ct., 1991, 92; dep. chmn. Nassau County Dem. Com., Mineola, NY. Served to Col. JAGC, US Army, 1952-56, Korea, with Res. 1957-83. Decorated Legion of Merit, Meritous Svc. medal, Oak Leaf Cluster, Combat Infantry Badge. Mem. ABA, Nassau County Bar Assn., Fed. Bar Council, Assn. Bar City N.Y., N.Y. County Lawyers Assn. Clubs: Squadron "A". Lutheran. Avocations: politics, reading, art collecting. Home: 1 Hewlett Rd Greenvale NY 11548-1125 Office: 757 3rd Ave Fl 25 New York NY 10017 Personal E-mail: rbg5star@aol.com.

GRUNFELD, A. TOM, history professor; s. Edith Grunfeld; children: Daniel Jason, Ian James. BA, SUNY, Old Westbury, 1972; MA, Sch. Oriental and African Studies, London, 1973; PhD, NYU, 1978. Disting. prof. empire state coll. SUNY, NY, 1978—. Spkr. in field. Author: The Making of Modern Tibet, On Her Own. Journalistic Adventures From San Francisco to the Chinese Revolution, 1917-1927, World Civilizations. Images and Interpretations, The Vietnam War. A History in Documents. Recipient Excellence in Scholarship award; grantee, NEH, 1984, Rsch. Found. CUNY, 1985, Empire State Coll. Found., 1984, 1986, 1988, 2003, 2006, Ford Found., 1993, Fulbright Found. Mem.: Historians Am. Communism (assoc.), Hist. Soc. Twentieth Century China (assoc.), Assn. Asian Studies (assoc.), Am. Hist. Assn. (assoc.). Office: Empire State Coll SUNY 325 Hudson St New York NY 10013 Home Phone: 212-691-4165; Office Phone: 646-230-1248.

GRUNFELD, ERNIE, professional sports team executive, retired professional basketball player; b. Satu-Mare, Romania, Apr. 24, 1955; US, 1964; s. Alex and Livia Grunfeld; m. Nancy Grunfeld; children: Rebecca, Danny. Grad., U. Tenn. Player Milw. Bucks, 1977—79, Kans. City Kings, 1979—82, NY Knicks, 1982—86, asst. coach, 1989—90, dir. adminstrn., 1990—91, gen. mgr., 1991—99, v.p., 1993—96, pres., 1996—99; color radio analyst MSG Radio Network, 1986—89; gen. mgr. Milw. Bucks, 1999—2003; pres. basketball ops. Washington Wizards, 2003—. Developer Doral Arrowwood NY Summer League, Gatorade Knicks Summer Basketball Camps; rep. US Maccabiah Games, Israel; coach US Masters Team, Maccabiah Games, Tel Aviv, 1989; mem. NBA coaches' clinic, Hungary, 1990. Recipient Gold medal Olympics, 1976. Office: Washington Wizards Verizon Ctr 601 F St NW Washington DC 20004*

GRUNNET, MARGARET LOUISE, retired pathologist, educator; b. Mpls., Feb. 20, 1936; d. Leslie Nels and Grace Harriet (Thomson) Grunnet; m. Irving Noel Einhorn, Mar. 10, 1972; stepchildren: Jeffrey Allan, Franne Ruth, Eric Carl, Stanley Glenn. BA summa cum laude, U. Minn., Mpls., 1958; MD, U. Minn., 1962; MS, Ohio State U., 1969. Resident in psychiatry U. Pa. Sch. Medicine, Phila., 1963-64; resident anatomic pathology Presbyn.-U. Pa. Med. Ctr., Phila., 1965-66; fellow neuropathology Phila. Gen. Hosp., 1967, Ohio State U. Hosp., Columbus, 1968-69; instr. Ohio State U., 1969; asst. prof. U. Utah Sch. Medicine, Salt Lake City, 1970-76, assoc. prof., 1976-80; assoc. prof. pathology U. Conn. Sch. Medicine, Farmington, 1980-90, prof., 1990—2006, prof. emeritus, 2006—. Contbr. articles to profl. jours. Mem. Am. Med. Women's Assn., Internat. Soc. Neuropathology, Conn. Soc. Pathologists, World Muscle Soc., Am. Assn. Neuropathologists, Phi Beta Kappa, Alpha Omega Alpha. Mem. Ch. of Christ. Avocations: reading, music, travel. Office: U Conn Health Ctr Dept Pathology Farmington CT 06032 Home: 275 Steele Rd B415 West Hartford CT 06117-2805 Business E-Mail: grunnet@nso1.ucnc.edu.

GRUNSCHLAG, TONI, pianist, researcher; b. Vienna; came to U.S., 1939; d. Morris Grunschlag and Celia Reichmann-Reinharz. Diploma, Vienna Conservatory, Austria, 1938, State Acad.; studies with Robert Casadesus, U.S.A. Formed two-piano recital and touring team with sister Rosi, 1942—; researched, performed and recorded rare pieces for two pianos, internat., 1956-82; instr. Bellas Artes Sch., Mexico City, 1981-83; recorded with VOX, Vienna, 1968, CRI, N.Y.C., 1983, 20th Century Music, 1991. Rec. artist Sonata, 1991, Phantasie, 1991, Coal-Scuttle Blues, 1991—, music by Starer, Martinu and Otto Lüning. Recipient Kreisler prize Vienna State Acad., 1938. Mem. Chamber Music Am. Avocation: collecting antiques. Home: 230 W 107th St New York NY 10025-3038

GRUNSFELD, ERNEST ALTON, III, architect; b. Chgo., June 5, 1929; s. Ernest Alton Jr. and Mary Jane (Loeb) G.; m. Sally Riblett, July 10, 1954 (dec. 1999); children: Marcia Grunsfeld, John Mace; m. Alice B. Kurland, Mar. 4 2006. Student, Inst. Design, Chgo., 1945, Art Inst. Chgo., 1946; BArch, MIT, 1952. Registered architect, Ill., Conn., Ind., Mich., N.C.,

Ohio, Mo., Wis. Ptnr. Yerkes & Grunsfeld, Chgo., 1956-65; owner Grunsfeld & Assocs., Architects, Chgo., 1965-75, sr. ptnr., 1975-84, owner, 1984—2001; prin. Grunsfeld Shafer Architects, LLC, 2001—. Corp. mem. Woodlawn Hosp., Chgo., 1968-70; mem. Highland Park (Ill.) Planning Commn., 1969-75; pres. Grunsfeld Meml. Fund, Chgo., 1970—. Contbr. articles to profl. jours. Bd. dirs. Urban Gateways, Chgo., 1968-89, mem. adv. bd., 1989—; life mem. Field Mus. Natural History, Chgo., 1970—, Chgo. Symphony Orch. Assn., 1975—, governing mem., 1995—; mem. exec. com. Coun. for Arts MIT, Cambridge, 1977-89, bd. dirs., 1977—; hon. life mem. Chgo. Hort. Soc., 1995—, governing mem., 2001—; benefactor, hon. governing mem. Art Inst. Chgo., 1980—. Recipient 1st Honor award Burlington Mills, 1968. Fellow AIA (corp. mem. Chgo. chpt., Honor award 1962, citation of merit 1969); mem. Lake Shore Country Club, Arts Club of Chgo. Office: Grunsfeld Schafer Architects LLC 939 Chicago Ave Evanston IL 60202 Office Phone: 847-424-1800 ext. 1.

GRUNT, JEROME ALVIN, retired pediatric endocrinologist; b. Newark, Apr. 6, 1923; s. Tobias and Rebecca Grunt; m. Hope Howieson, July 29, 1950; children: Rebecca Yord, David Grund, Jonathan Grund, Jennifer Jennison. BS, Rutgers U., 1947, MS, 1948; PhD, U. Kans., 1952; MD, Duke U., 1956. Diplomate Am. Bd. Pediatrics, Am. Bd. Pediatric Endocrinology. Intern in pediatrics Duke U. Med. Ctr., Durham, NC, 1956, resident in pediatrics, 1958—60; fellowship Harvard U. Med. Sch., Boston, 1960-62; assoc. in pediatrics Harvard U. Med. Sch. and Children's Hosp. Med. Ctr., Boston, 1963-64; dir. child gen. clin. research ctr. and pediatric endocrinology div. Yale U. Sch. Med., New Haven, 1964-71, assoc. prof. pediatrics, 1964-71; attending physician Yale-New Haven Hosp., 1964-71, Children's Mercy Hosp., Kansas City, Mo., 1971-97, chief endocrinology sect., 1971-89; prof. pediatrics and physiology U. Mo., Kansas City, 1971-97, assoc. chmn. for research, 1985-97. Mem. senate U. Mo., 1982-87, chmn. faculty council Sch. Medicine, 1986-87; mem. Mo. State Neonatal Metabolic Adv. Bd., Jefferson City, 1976—97. Contbr. articles to profl. jours. Pres. Mo. affiliate Am. Diabetes Assn., Kansas City, 1975-77. Recipient 1st Russell Hayden medal U. Kans. Sch. Medicine, 1952, Symbols of Caregiving award, 1993. Mem. Am. Pediatric Soc., Am. Acad. Pediatrics, Mo. Acad. Pediatrics (exec. bd. 1980—96, sec. treas. 1987-90, v.p. 1990-93, pres. 1993—96), S.W. Pediatric Soc. (pres. 1986-88), Soc. for Pediatric Rsch., Am. Pediatric Soc., Soc. for Pediatric Endocrinology, Endocrine Soc., Phi Beta Kappa. Avocations: reading, travel.

GRUPE, ROBERT CHARLES, corporate communications specialist; b. Alice, Tex., Sept. 3, 1948; m. Dorothy E. Cleveland, Nov. 22, 1975; children: Amber, Robert, Elisabeth, Jonathan. BA, MBA, Calif. Coast U., 1977, PhD, 1992. Announcer Stein Broadcasting Co., Sweetwater, Tex., 1966-68; news announcer Ea. Okla. TV Co., Ada, 1969-72; announcer Anadarko Broadcasting Co., Okla., 1972-74; news dir. Cleveland County Broadcasting Co., Norman, Okla., 1974-75; instr. Elkins Inst., Oklahoma City, 1975-77; mng. editor Okla. World Media, Oklahoma City, 1977-78; pres., owner Quality Prodns. Inc., Oklahoma City, 1978—. Job skills cons. Okla. Pvt. Industry Coun., Oklahoma City, 1989; vol. trainer US Olympic Festival, Oklahoma City, 1989; mem. Total Quality Mgmt. Faculty Okla. State U., 1990-95; TV prodr./host Cox Cable Pub. Programming, Oklahoma City, 1990-96; syndicated radio commentator, 1993-99; talk show host WKY Radio, Oklahoma City, 1999-2000, ind. networking specialist, 2000-06; TV host Pathways to Success, produced for Oklahoma City Ednl. TV Consortium, 2001—. Author: The Miracle of Speech, 1981, The Change, 1993, Creating The Future, 1994, Creating Your Future in Network Marketing, 2002, Building Sand Castles-A Baby Boomer's Journey Through Addictions, 2007; contbr. articles to profl. jours. Vol. media devel. Vol. Action Com. Oklahoma City, 1991. Mem. ASTD (v.p. 1992), Internat. Assn. Bus. Communicators (v.p. 1996-97), Neuro Linguistic Programming Assocs. (v.p. 1991-92), World Assn. of Persons with Disabilities (bd. dirs. 2005-) Avocation: historical research. Office: Quality Prodns Inc 4230 NW 36th St Oklahoma City OK 73112-2910 Office Phone: 800-781-2722. E-mail: dgrupe@drgrupe.com.

GRUPE, SCOTT M., management consultant; BS, U. Minn., Mpls.; M in Project Mgmt., Keller Grad. Sch., Lincolnshire, Ill., MBA. Cert. Project Mgmt. Profl. Project Mgmt. Inst. Program mgr. Motorola, Inc., Libertyville, Ill., 1988—2003; cons. Ind., Mundelein, Ill., 2003—. Mem.: Project Mgmt. Inst., Am. Mensa. Home Phone: 847-502-6966.

GRUPP, EDWARD A., arbitrator, prosecutor; s. Louis and Celia Grupp; m. Anita P. Perlmutter, June 11, 1950; children: Marcia Sue, Lori Ellen, Jerold Scott. Lic.: Ohio (Atty.) 1954, Pa. 1971, NY 1947. Atty. self-employed, NYC, 1947—48, arbitrator Pitts., 1986—; gen. trial atty. NLRB, Cleve., 1948—59, sr. trial atty. Pitts., 1959—62, regional atty., 1962—86. Sgt. US Army, 1942—46. Mem.: FBA (chair 1965—68), PA Bar Assn. (Allegheny County) (chair labor sect. 1960—62). Home: 911 Country Club Dr Pittsburgh PA 15228-2650 Office: Arbitrator 911 Country Club Dr Pittsburgh PA 15228-2650 Home Phone: 412-561-0310; Office Phone: 412-561-0310. Personal E-mail: eagpgh@verizon.net.

GRUSH, JULIUS SIDNEY, lawyer; b. LA, Dec. 4, 1937; children: Robin, Randi, Ronna, Rodney. BS, UCLA, 1960; postgrad., U. Calif., San Francisco, 1960-62; LLB, Southwestern U., 1964. Bar: Calif. 1965. Dep. city atty. City of Los Angeles, 1965-67; sole practice Los Angeles, 1967—. Prof. Bar-Bri Harcourt Brace Pubs. Bar Course, Los Angeles, 1986—. Pres. Lockhurst Booster Club; mem. City of Hope (past pres.). Mem. ABA, Los Angeles Bar Assn., Beverly Hills Bar Assn., Century City Bar Assn., Phi Alpha Delta. Republican. Office: 1900 Avenue of the Stars Fl 25 Los Angeles CA 90067-4301 Office Phone: 310-785-0100. Personal E-mail: juglaws1@yahoo.com.

GRUSHKIN, JAY D., lawyer; b. NYC, 1957; BA magna cum laude, Univ. Pa., 1979; JD, Vanderbilt Univ., 1982. Bar: D.C. 1982, N.Y. 1991. Atty. Milbank Tweed Hadley & McCloy, Washington, Hong Kong, ptnr. in charge Tokyo, ptnr. Global Fin. Group & mem. recruiting com. NYC, 1997—. Adj. prof. Temple Univ. Law Program, Japan; mem. bd. adv. Vanderbilt Jour. Transnational Law. Contbr. articles to profl. jours.; editor (exec.): Vanderbilt Jour. Transnational Law. Mem.: Structured Fin. Inst., ABA, N.Y. State Bar Assn., D.C. Bar, Tokyo Bar Assn. (gaikokuho jimu bengoshi), Order of the Coif. Office: Milbank Tweed Hadley & McCloy 1 Chase Manhattan Plz New York NY 10005-1413 Office Phone: 212-530-5346. Office Fax: 212-530-5219. Business E-Mail: jgrushkin@milbank.com.

GRUSHOW, SANDY, broadcast executive; BA in Comm., UCLA, 1983. Former v.p. creative advtg. 20th Century Fox Film Corp.; sr. v.p. advtg. and promotion Fox Broadcasting Co., 1988—90, exec. v.p. programming and scheduling, 1990—91; exec. v.p. Fox Entertainment Group, 1991—92, pres., 1992—95, Tele-TV Media, 1995—97, Twentieth Century Fox TV, LA, 1997—99; chmn. Fox Entertainment Group, 1999—2004.

GRUSS, MARTIN DAVID, investor; b. NYC, Mar. 1, 1943; s. Joseph Saul and Caroline (Zelaznik) G.; m. Agneta Peterson; m. Audrey Butvay, June 28, 1988; children: Joshua, Amanda. BSE, U. Pa., 1964; LLB, N.Y. U., 1967. Sr. ptnr. Gruss Ptnrs., NYC. Bd. trustee Solomon R Guggenheim Mus., NYC. Mem. N.Y. Bar Assn. Office: Gruss & Co 667 Madison Ave New York NY 10021 Office Phone: 212-688-1500. Office Fax: 212-682-2138.

GRUSS, SHOSHANNA LONSTEIN, apparel designer; b. NYC, May 29, 1975; d. Zach Lonstein and Betty; m. Josh Guss, May 2003; 1 child, Sienna. Degree in Art Hist., UCLA, 1997. Founder Shoshanna clothing line, 1998—, Shoshanna swimwear, 2001—, Shoshanna BabyGirl, 2005—. Style contr. WCBS-TV news. Office: 231 W 39th St Ste 422 New York NY 10018 Office Phone: 212-719-3601. Office Fax: 212-719-0745. Business E-Mail: shoshanna@shoshanna.com.*

GRUTMAN, JEWEL HUMPHREY, lawyer, writer; b. NYC, Mar. 13, 1931; d. Robert and Gladys Humphrey; m. Robert W. Bjork, June 26, 1956 (div. Apr. 22, 1975); 1 child, Bruce Bjork; m. Roy Grutman, Oct. 30, 1975 (wid. 1994); m. Fredrick Yonkman, July 4, 1998. BA magna cum laude, Mt. Holyoke Coll., 1952; LLB, Columbia U., 1955. Bar: N.Y., U.S. Dist. Ct. (So. Dist.) N.Y. 1971, U.S. Dist. Ct. (ea. dist.) N.Y. 1974, U.S. Dist. Ct. Conn. 1984, U.S. Supreme Ct. 1983. Atty. Debevoise & Plimpton, NYC, 1954-60; ptnr. Eaton Van Winkle, NYC, 1976-79, Grutman Greene & Humphrey, NYC, 1979—. Co-author: (with CD-ROM) The Ledgerbook of Thomas Blue Eagle, 1994 (Christopher award 1995, Internat. Reading Assn. award), The Sketchbook of Thomas Blue Eagle, 2001, (CD-ROM) The Journey of Thomas Blue Eagle, 1995 (Best Project award Intermedia, Asia, 1995, Creative NGee ANN Disting. award 1995, EMMA award best visual content 1996); asst. prodr., editor (ednl. film on art) Where Time is a River (1st prize Women's Film Festival); contbr. photograph illustrations: The Reforming Power of the Scriptures, 1996; developer series of designs based on Native Am. art; contbr. articles to mags. and newspapers. Dir. Inwood Ho., N.Y.C., 1970-80; past mem. various coms. Mt. Holyoke Coll.; mem. com. sr. advisors N.Y. Commn. for Internat. Bus. and UN, 1997; past chmn. com. to establish Barbara Black Fellowship at Columbia U. Law Sch.; past pres. 85th St. Playground Assn., N.Y.C.; active supporter The Children's Storefront, Harlem, N.Y.C., N.Y. Jr. League. Mem.: Assn. Bar City N.Y., Coral Ridge Country Club (Ft. Lauderdale, Fla.)., The Stanwich Club (Greenwich, Conn.). Avocations: opera, golf, tennis, poetry. E-mail: bijou203@optonline.net, bijou203@bellsouth.net.

GRUVER, WILLIAM ROLFE (BILL GRUVER), finance educator, retired investment banker; b. Denver, May 31, 1944; s. John and Marion Jean (Plummer) G. AB with distinction, Dartmouth Coll., 1966; MBA, Columbia U., 1968. Ptnr. Goldman, Sachs & Co., NYC, 1972—92; Disting. Exec. in Residence, prof. mgmt. Bucknell U., Lewisburg, Pa., 1993—. Dir. The Street.com., 2003-, Geisinger Found., Danville, Pa., 2005—; mem. adv. bd. Hirtle, Callaghan & Co., West Conshocken, Pa., 1996—, Cornell U. Park Leadership Fellows, Ithaca, N.Y., 2002-05. Vol. Big Bros., Morristown, NJ, 1981—84; mayor Eagles Mere Borough, 1994—2005; dir. Eagles Mere Hist. Village, Inc., 2004—05; trustee Eagles Mere (Pa.) Cmty. Ch., 1993—; chmn. bd. trustees Woodbridge (N.J.) Devel. Ctr., 1982—87; trustee Berea Coll., 1995—, Eagles Mere Found., 1998—; mem. advisor bd. The Lymphoma Found., NYC, 1985—; arbitrator NASD, 1993—. Lt. USN, 1968—72. Mem. Am. Legion. Home Phone: 570-525-3609. Business E-Mail: gruver@bucknell.edu.

GRYSON, JOSEPH ANTHONY, orthodontist; b. Rahway, NJ, Feb. 11, 1932; s. Elmer Joseph Anthony and Joyce Asher (Toms) G.; m. Patricia Ann Huddleston, Nov. 22, 1961; children— Karen Ann, David Joseph. M.Chem. Engring., Cornell U., 1954; D.D.S., U. Calif., San Francisco, 1964. Diplomate: Am. Bd. Orthodontics. Engr. div. refinery tech. service Standard Oil of Calif., Richmond, 1954, 58-60; individual practice dentistry specializing in orthodontics San Rafael, Calif., 1964-96; clin. instr. orthodontics U. Calif., San Francisco, 1965-87, assoc. clin. prof. orthodontics, 1987-99, clin. prof. orthodontics, 1999—. Referee Am. Jour. Orthodontics and Dentofacial Orthopedics. Contbr. articles to profl. jours. Treas., pres., dir. Homeowners Assn., San Rafael, 1970-74. Served as carrier pilot USN, 1954-58. Mem. ADA, Pacific Coast Soc. Orthodontists (dir. 1980-85, pres. 1985-86, award of merit 1992), Am. Assn. Orthodontists (ho. of dels. 1982-87, 94-95, spkr. ho. of dels. 1988-91, James E. Brophy Disting. Svc. award 1996), Calif. Dental Assn. (Disting. Svc. award 1994), E.H. Angle Soc. (sec. No. Calif. component 1992-96). Home: 1060 Lea Dr San Rafael CA 94903-3726 E-mail: jagryson@comcast.net.

GRZYMALA-BUSSE, JERZY WITOLD, engineering educator; b. Warsaw, Apr. 3, 1942; s. Witold Lech and Estera Maria Grzymala-Busse; m. Dobrosława Melania Thomas, Feb. 11, 1967; children: Anna Maria, Witold Jakub, Jan Pawel. MSEE, Tech. U., Poznan, 1964, PhD, 1969; MS in Math., Wroclaw U., 1967; Habilitation in Engring., Tech. U., Warsaw, 1972. Asst. prof. Tech. U. Poznan, Poland, 1970—73, assoc. prof., 1973—80; prof. U. Kans., Lawrence, 1980—. Contbr. (over 200 articles to profl. jours.). Mem.: AAAI, NRC, Assn. Computing Machinery, Internat. Rough Set Soc., Upsilon Pi Epsilon. Avocation: running. Home: 4713 Wimbledon Dr Lawrence KS 66047-9301 Office: U Kans 3014 Eaton Hall Lawrence KS 66045-7621 Office Phone: 785-864-4488. Office Fax: 785-864-3226. Business E-Mail: jerzy@ku.edu.

GSCHNEIDNER, KARL ALBERT, JR., metallurgist, educator, editor, consultant; b. Detroit, Nov. 16, 1930; s. Karl and Eugenie (Zehetmair) Gschneidner; m. Melba E. Pickenpaugh, Nov. 4, 1957; children: Thomas, David, Edward, Kathryn. BS, U. Detroit, 1952; PhD, Iowa State U., 1957. Mem. staff Los Alamos Sci. Lab., 1957-62, sect. chief, 1961-62; vis. asst. prof. U. Ill., Urbana, 1962-63; assoc. prof. materials sci. and engring. Iowa State U., Ames, 1963-67, dir. Rare-earth Info. Ctr., 1966-96, prof., 1967-79, disting. prof., 1979—85, Anson Marston disting. prof., 1986—; vis. prof. U. Calif.-San Diego, La Jolla, 1979-80; cons. Los Alamos Nat. Lab., 1981-86, Teltech, 1987-2000. Author: Rare Earth Alloys, 1961, Scandium, 1975, others; editor: (37 vol. book) Handbook on the Physics and Chemistry of Rare Earths, 1978-2003, Industrial Applications of Rare Earth Elements, 1981; contbr. numerous chpts. in books and articles to profl. publs. Recipient William Hume-Rothery award AIME, Warrendale, Pa., 1978, Burlington No. award for Excellence in Rsch., Iowa State U., 1989, Significant Implication for Energy Related Techs. in Metallurgy and Ceramics award Dept. Energy, 1997; co-recipient Outstanding Sci. Accomplishment in Metallurgy and Ceramics award Dept. Energy, Washington, 1982, Frank H. Spedding award Rare Earth Rsch. Confs., 1991, Russell B. Scott Meml. award Cryogenic Engr. Conf., 1995, David R. Boyland Eminent Faculty award in Rsch. Coll. Engring., Iowa State U., 1997; named Sci. Alumnus of 2000, U. Detroit-Mercy. Fellow Minerals, Metals and Materials Soc., Am. Soc. Materials Internat., Am. Phys. Soc.; mem. AAAS, NAE, Am. Chem. Soc., Am. Crystallographic Assn., Materials Rsch. Soc., Iowa Acad. Sci., Materials Rsch. Soc. India (hon.), Cryogenic Soc. Am., Japan Inst. Metals (hon.). Roman Catholic. Achievements include patents in field. Office: Materials Sci and Engring Iowa State Univ 255 Spedding Hall Ames IA 50011-3020 Office Phone: 515-294-7931. Office Fax: 515-294-9579. E-mail: cagey@ameslab.gov.

GU, BINHE, environmental scientist; b. Qingyuan, Guangdong, China, Mar. 28, 1957; arrived in U.S., 1988; s. Zaizhong Gu and Lianzhen Luo; m. Le Xu; children: Steven B., Diana S. BS in Freshwater Fishery, Guangdong Ocean U., 1981; PhD in Oceanography, U. Alaska, 1993. Post doctoral rsch. assoc. U. Fla., Gainesville, 1993—97; environ. specialist III St. Johns River Water Mgmt. Dist., Palatka, Fla., 1993—97; sr. environ. scientist South Fla. Water Mgmt. Dist., West Palm Beach, 1997—. Guest prof. Guangdong Ocean U., Guangdong, 2004—. Contbr. articles to profl. jours. Mem.: Chinese Assn. Sci., Edn. and Culture South Fla. (bd. dirs. 2002—06), World Aquaculture Soc., Sino-Ecologists Assn. Overseas, Soc. for Wetland Scientists (registered profl. wetland scientist 2001), Ecol. Soc. Am., Am. Soc. Limnology and Oceanography. Home: 3911 Hamilton Key West Palm Beach FL 33411 Office: S Fla Water Mgmt 3301 Gun Club Rd West Palm Beach FL 33406 Home Phone: 561-615-6042; Office Phone: 561-682-2556. Personal E-mail: bengu@netzero.com. E-mail: bgu@sfwmd.gov.

GU, XING, semiconductor engineer, researcher; s. Yuqi Gu and Fuzhen Fu; m. Yikong Yuan; 1 child, Maxwell. B in Engring. (hon.), Zhejiang U., China, 2000; MS (hon.), Va. Commonwealth U., Richmond, 2004, PhD (hon.), 2003—. Semiconductor engr. State Key Lab Silicon Materials, Hangzhou, China, 2000—03. V.p. Chinese Students and Scholars Assn., Richmond, 2004—05. Mem.: Toastmaster Club (Competent Toastmaster 2005). Achievements include research in invent and develop a convenient ZnO substrate preparation technique which produces better results than any CMP provided; growth and fabricate the first prototype AlGaN/GaN/ZnO FET structure; realize the single crystalline ZrO2 as a gate dielectric for AlGaN/GaN MOSFET structure for integration; demonstrate the single-crystalline growth of PZT material using molecular beam epitaxy; realize the single crystalline PZT growth using Molecular Beam Epitaxy for the first time. Home: 520 W Franklin St Apt 412 Richmond VA 23220 Office: Va Commonwealth U 601 W Main St Richmond VA 23284 Personal E-mail: gux@vcu.edu.

GUADAGNINO, FRANK T., lawyer; b. Pitts., Aug. 24, 1956; BS in mktg., Pa. State U., 1978; JD cum laude, U. Pitts., 1983. Bar: Pa. 1983. Assoc. Reed Smith LLP, Pitts., 1983—92, ptnr., 1992—, practice group leader fin. services group, 2002—. Bd. dirs. Downtown Pitts. YMCA, 2002—. Mem.: ABA, Am. Arbitration Assn., Allegheny County Bar Assn. Office: Reed Smith LLP 435 Sixth Ave Pittsburgh PA 15219 Office Phone: 412-288-3236. Office Fax: 412-288-3063. Business E-Mail: fguadagnino@reedsmith.com.

GUAJARDO, ELISA, counselor, educator; b. Roswell, N. Mex., Nov. 13, 1932; d. Alejo Najar and Hortensia (Jiminez) Garcia; m. David Roberto Guajardo, Oct. 15, 1950; 1 child, Elsie Edith. BS, Our Lady of the Lake U., 1962, MEd, 1971; MA, Chapman U., 1977. Cert. tchr., adminstr., counselor, Calif. Elem. tchr. San Antonio (Tex.) Sch. Dist., 1962-63; tchr. social sci. Newport Mesa Sch. Dist., Costa Mesa, Calif., 1963-67, Orange (Calif.) Unified Sch. Dist., 1967-70, project dir., 1970-71, tchr. English, 1972-73, counselor, 1973—. Pres. Bilingual, Bicultural Parent Adv. Bd., Orange, Calif., 1971-72; reader bilingual projects Calif. State Dept. Edn., Orange, 1971-72; vis. lectr. We. Wash. Univ., Bellingham, 1972-73; mem. curriculum and placement couns., Orange Unified Sch. Dist., 1973-78, 95-96. Author: (Able)Adaptations of Bilingual/Bicultural Edn, Fed. Project Proposal. Mem. NEA, AAUW, Calif. Tchrs. Assn., Orange Unified Edn. Assn, Hon., Alpha Chi, Our Lady of Lake U., Tex. chpt. Democrat. Mem. Assemblies of God Church. Avocations: choir and solo singing, piano, marimba, organ. Home: 335 E Jackson Ave Orange CA 92867-5743 Office: Canyon HS 220 S Imperial Hwy Anaheim CA 92807-3945 E-mail: davielisa2@juno.com.

GUAN, SHAN, materials scientist; s. Dayong Guan and Molan Liu; m. Junxian Wu, June 12, 2000; 1 child, Alyssa. BS in Materials Sci. and Engring. with honors, BeiHang U., 1997, MS in Materials Sci., 2000; MEE, U. Minn., Mpls., 2003, PhD, 2004. Rsch. asst. U. Minn., Mpls., 2000—03; sr. scientist Eastman Kodak Co., Dayton, Ohio, 2004—. Contbr. articles to profl. jours. Mem.: Materials Rsch. Soc., Am. Electrochemistry Soc. Achievements include patents in field; patents pending for; research in thin films tech., microelectromechanical sys. (MEMS), ink jet printing tech., electrochem. processing for MEMS, novel microfabrication Techniques. Office: Eastman Kodak 3000 Research Blvd Dayton OH 45420 Office Phone: 937-259-3216. Office Fax: 937-259-3740. Business E-Mail: shan.guan@kodak.com.

GUAN, XIANG, electrical engineer; s. Datian Ye and Zhicheng Guan; m. Yi Shen. BS, Tsinghua U., Beijing, China, 1996; M of Engr., Nat. U. of Singapore, 2000; PhD, Calif. Inst. of Tech., Pasadena, 2005. R&D engr. Agilent Labs., Palo Alto, Calif., 2005—06; sr. microwave and rf engr. SiBEAM Inc., Sunnyvale, Calif., 2006—. Co-recipient Best Paper award, IEEE Jour. of Solid-State Circuits, 2004, Grand Prize, Standford's Innovator Challenge, 2006. Mem.: IEEE. Achievements include one of the key designers who invented the world's first fully-integrated 24-GHz and 77-GHz phased array system in silicon-based technologies. Avocation: ping pong/table tennis. Home: 330 Sierra Vista Ave Apt #33 Mountain View CA 94043 Office: SiBEAM Inc 555 N Mathilda Ave Ste 100 Sunnyvale CA 94085 Home Phone: 408-332-4121; Office Phone: 408-245-3120 ext. 144. Personal E-mail: seanguan@gmail.com. Business E-Mail: xguan@sibeam.com.

GUARASCIO, PHILIP, advertising executive; b. NYC, June 28, 1941; s. Frank and Charlotte (Cohen) G.; m. Ruth Agness Hornick, Sept. 7, 1963, children: Lisa Marie, David Evan BA, Marietta Coll. Sr. v.p., dir. media mgmt. Benton & Bowles, Inc., NYC, bd. dirs.; exec. dir. advt. svcs. Gen. Motors, Detroit, 1985—90, exec. dir. mktg. programs and advt., 1990—91, exec.-in-charge corp. mktg. and advt., 1991—92, gen. mgr. mktg. and advt. N. Am. Ops., 1992—94, v.p./gen. mgr. mktg. and advt. No. Am. Ops., 1994—2000; ind. advisor NFL, 2000—04, lead exec. mktg. and sales, 2004—. Trustee Marietta Coll., Ohio, 1981-83. Served USAR, 1963—70. Mem. Nat. Cable TV Assn., Internat. Radio & TV Found., Am. Assn. Advt. Agys., Radio Advt. Bur., Nissequogue Country Club, St. James, N.Y. Avocations: golfing, tennis.

GUARD, ROGER, information technology executive; s. Alton K. and Edith M. Guard; m. Marcia Jean Hern, June 10, 1995; children: Tricia Lynn Hern, Jeffrey David Hern, Robert Matthew Hern, Charles Timmons, Julia Kay. BS, U. Utah, 1966; MLS, U. Oreg., 1974. Reference libr. Oklahoma City U., 1974—76; co-owner Air Components Mfg., Salt Lake City, 1976—78; mgr. engring. systems NW Alaskan Pipeline Co., Salt Lake City, 1978—82; mgr. quality assurance NW Pipeline Corp., Salt Lake City, 1983—83; cons. Guard Assocs., Salt Lake City, 1984—85; dir. info. services, mktg., and sales MultiVisions Cable TV, Ltd., Anchorage, 1985—86; project analyst, programmer Steiner Corp., Salt Lake City, 1986—88; assoc. dir. So. Ill. U. Sch. Medicine Libr., Springfield, 1988—93; chief info. officer U. Cin. Med. Ctr., 1993—. Mem. com. on telecom. and health care Fed. Comm. Commn., Washington, 1996; bd. mem. Internet Healthcare Coalition, Washington, 1998—2000; chair biomedical libr. and informatics rev. com. Nat. Libr. Medicine, Bethesda, Md., 2003—04. Internet consumer health website, NetWellness.org (Inst. for Sci. Info./Med. Libr. Associations Frank Bradway Rogers Info. Advancement Award, 1997). Mem. class XXIII Leadership Cin., Cin., 1999—2000, co-chair health day, 2001—03; co-chair. health day Regional Youth Leadership, Covington, Ky., 2004—06; vol. Tender Mercies, Cin., 2002—06; co-chair U. Cin. Fine Arts Fund, 2004—06; mem. steering com. Leadership Cin., 2000—03. With US Army, 1968—69. Grantee Funding for NetWellness.org, State of Ohio, 1995—2001, Ohio Tech. Initiative, Ohio Bd. Regents, 1997—98; Med. Informatics fellow, Nat. Libr. Medicine and Marine Biol. Lab., 1993. Mem.: Am. Med. Informatics Assn., Med. Libr. Assn. (chair govt. rels. com. 1995—98, 1995—98), Assn. Am. Med. Colls. (chair elect 2005—06, chair-elect group on info. resources 2005—), Assn. Academic Health Sci. Librs. (pres. 2003—04). Democrat. Unitarian. Achievements include creation and development of NetWellness.org. Avocations: reading, travel, golf. Office: Univ Cin Med Ctr 231 Albert Sabin Way Cincinnati OH 45267-0574 Office Phone: 513-558-5656.

GUARENTE, LEONARD P., medical geneticist, educator; b. Chelsea, Mass., June 6, 1952; s. Leonard and Norma Guarente; m. Barbara Weiffenbach, Sept. 6, 1981 (div. 1985); 1 child, Jeffrey. BS in Biology, MIT, 1974; PhD in Molecular Genetics, Harvard U., 1978. Asst. prof. biology MIT, Cambridge, 1981—85, assoc. prof. biology, 1985—, now Novartis prof. biology. Founder, dir. Elixir Pharm., Cambridge, 2000—. Author: Ageless Quest, 2003; contbr. articles to profl. jours. Recipient Presidential Young Investigator award, NSF, 1984—89. Fellow: Am. Acad.

Arts & Sci.; mem.: Am. Acad. Microbiology. Achievements include patents in field; discovery of gene that regulates aging. Office: MIT Bldg 68-280 77 Massachusetts Ave Cambridge MA 02139 Office Phone: 617-253-6965. Fax: 617-253-8699. E-mail: leng@mit.edu.*

GUARIGILA, DALE A., lawyer; B, U. Kan., 1985; JD, U. Mo., Kansas City, 1985. Bar: Mo. 1985, US Dist. Ct. (ea. and we. dists.) Mo. Ptnr., group dep. Environ. Bryan Cave LLP, St. Louis. Office: Bryan Cave LLP One Metropolitan Sq 211 N Broadway, Ste 3600 Saint Louis MO 63102 Office Phone: 314-259-2606. E-mail: daguariglia@bryancave.com.

GUARINO, ANTHONY MICHAEL, pharmacologist, educator, consultant, counselor; b. Framingham, Mass., Dec. 11, 1934; s. Alfred V. and Nellie L. (Beatrice) G.; m. Aida Iris Gerena, Nov. 9, 1957; children: Theresa, Elizabeth, Barbara, Cathy, Tom, Gregory, Paula, Phil, Richard, Paul. BS in Chemistry, Boston Coll., 1956; MS in Chemistry, U. R.I., 1963, PhD in Pharmacology and Toxicology, 1966; MA in Counseling, Liberty U., Lynchburg, Va., 1993. Lic. profl. counselor. Lt. comdr. USPHS, 1966, advanced through grades to capt., 1979; staff fellow pharmacology-toxicology rsch. assoc. program Nat. Heart Inst., NIH, Bethesda, Md., 1966-68; rsch. pharmacologist NCI Nat. Cancer Inst., NIH, Bethesda, Md., 1968-73, chief lab. toxicology, 1973-80; regulatory pharmacologist Ctr. for Drugs and Biologics-FDA, Md., 1980-84; lab. dir. fishery rsch. br. FDA, Dauphin Island, Ala., 1984-93; marriage and family counselor Cath. Social Svcs., Mobile, Ala., 1993—2006, Castlebrook Counseling Inc., Mobile, Ala., 2006—07, The Carpenter's House, Mobile, 2007—. Adj. prof. U. South Ala. Coll. Medicine, Mobile, 1984—, U. South Ala. Coll. Allied Health Professions, Mobile, 1996-; vice chmn. com. on animals as monitors in environ. hazards NAS. Contbg. author: Handbook of Experimental Pharmacology—Concepts in Biochemical Pharmacology, 1971, Handbook of Experimental Pharmacology, Antineoplastic and Immunosuppressive Agents, 1974, Methods in Cancer Research, 1979, Pesticides and Xenobiotics Metabolism in Aquatic Organisms, 1979, Pesticides and Xenobiotics Metabolism in Aquatic Organisms, 1979, Cisplatin—Current Status and New Developments, 1980, Modern Pharmacology, 1982; contbr. 106 articles to profl. jours. Mem. Am. Soc. Pharmacology and Exptl. Therapeutics, Soc. Toxicology, Am. Chem. Soc., Am. Assn. Christian Counselors. Roman Catholic. Home: 968 Westbury Dr Mobile AL 36609-3332 Office: Carpenter's House PC 601 Bel Air Blvd Ste 409 Mobile AL 36606 Office Phone: 251-476-9994. Business E-Mail: amguarino@earthlink.net.

GUARNIERI, ALBINA, Canadian legislator; b. Faeto, Italy, June 23, 1953; BA, MA, McGill U. Solicitor Gen., Can., 1980; liberal leader1981 election; press sec. Mayor of Toronto, Ont., Can.; M.P. Ho. Commons, 1988—; parliamentary sec. to min. Canadian heritage Govt. of Can., Ottawa, 1993—96, assoc. min. nat. defense, 2003—, min. state (civil preparedness), 2003—, min. VA, 2005—. Office: House of Commons Rm 450 Confederation Bldg Ottawa ON Canada K1A OA6

GUARNIERI, ROBERTA JEAN, elementary school educator, consultant; d. Robert S. Norte and Zenda Giffin Higdon; m. Michael Wayne Guarnieri, May 27, 1967; children: Andrea Nicole Thornton, Aimee Michele. Degree in home econ., Calif. State U., LA, 1968. Cert. tchr. Calif. 7th grade tchr. Our Lady of Guadalupe, LA, 1996—97, 5th grade tchr., 1997—98; 4th-5th grade tchr. Kentwood Elem. Sch., LA, 1998—99, 5th grade tchr., 1999—. Advisor People to People Leadership Program, Spokane, 2003—. Pres. Sandpipers, Hermosa Beach, Calif., 1997—98. Named Eddy Awards Tchr. of Yr., Westchester-Playa del Rey C. of C., 2004; recipient Poetic Achievement award, Creative Communication, 2003—05; Environ. grantee, Playa Vista Found., 1999—2000, Sch. Yard Habitat grantee, Calif. Cmty. Found., 2004—06, Tchr. grantee for Habitat, Rotary Club of Westchester, 2004—05, Colonial Williamsburg scholar, Williamsburg Tchr.'s Inst., 2003. Mem.: NEA, NSTA, Calif. Teachers Assn., Nat. Coun. Tchrs. Math., Delta Zeta (life; rush chmn. 1966—67, Pres.' award 1966). Office: Kentwood Elem Sch 8401 Emerson Ave Los Angeles CA 90045 Home Phone: 310-397-6937; Office Phone: 310-670-8977.

GUASTAFERRO, ANGELO, space science administrator, consultant; b. Hoboken, NJ, June 4, 1932; s. Carlo and Rafaela Nancy (Gioffi) G.; m. Eleanor Lago, Sept. 12, 1954; children: Carl, Mark, John Brian. BS in Mech. Engring, N.J. Inst. Tech., 1954; MBA, Fla. State U., 1963; A.M.P., Harvard U., 1984. With NASA, 1963-85, dep. mgr. Viking project, 1974-76; dir. planetary programs NASA Hdqs., Washington, 1979-81; dep. dir. Ames Research Center, Moffett Field, Calif., 1981-85; v.p., program dir. Lockheed Missiles & Space Co., 1985-96, exec. dir., 1994-96; CEO, chmn. bd. n View Corp., Newport News, Va., 1996; pres., CEO View Corp., Newport News, Va., 1996—98; exec. cons. AG Cons., Williamsburg, Va., 1998—. Bd. trustees Internat. Space U., 1993-96; chmn. bd. dirs. View Corp., 1995-2002; sci. adv. com. NJIT. Chair bd. dirs. Hampton Rds. Tech. Coun. Served with USAF, 1955-58. Recipient Langley Spl. Achievement award NASA, 1974, 77, 78, Outstanding Leadership medal, 1977, Superior Performance award, 1980, Exceptional Service medal, 1981, Presdl. Meritorious rank, 1982; Disting. Alumnus NJIT, 1997. Fellow AIAA (Space Systems medal 1982), Am. Astronautics Soc.; mem. Mars First Landing Soc. (pres. 1978-79), Internat. Astronautics Fedn. (bd. dirs.), Tau Beta Pi (eminent engr. 1989). Roman Catholic. Office: AG Cons 124 Peter Lyall Williamsburg VA 23185-8902 Business E-Mail: gusg@cox.net.

GUAY, ROBERT E., philosopher, educator; b. Hartford, Conn., Oct. 29, 1970; s. Edward and Joye Guay; m. Anna K. Gebbie, July 22, 2000; children: Otto Ryoma, Gustav Xerxes Gebbie. BA, Columbia U., 1992; PhD, U. Chgo., 2000. Vis. asst. prof. Temple U., 2002—05; term asst. prof. philosophy Barnard Coll., NYC, 2005—06; asst. prof. philosophy Binghamton U./SUNY, 2006—. Contbr. articles to profl. jours. Recipient Ky. prize in European philosophy, U. Ky., 2005. Office: Dept Philosophy PO Box 6000 Binghamton NY 13902 Office Phone: 607-777-3983. Office Fax: 607-777-2734. Business E-Mail: rguay@binghamton.edu.

GUBBINS, KEITH EDMUND, chemical engineering educator; b. Southampton, Eng., Jan. 27, 1937; came to U.S., 1962; m. Pauline Margaret Payne, June 28, 1960; children: Nick, Vanessa. B.Sc. in Chemistry, Queen Mary Coll., U. London, 1958; Diploma in Chem. Engring., King's Coll., U. London, 1959, PhD in Chem. Engring., 1962. Vis. lectr. U. London, Eng., 1960-62; postdoctoral fellow U. Fla., Gainesville, 1962-64, asst. prof., 1964-68, assoc. prof., 1968-72, prof., 1972-76; T.R. Briggs prof. engring. Cornell U., Ithaca, NY, 1976-98, T.R. Briggs prof. engring. emeritus, 1998—; dir. Cornell U., Sch. Chem. Engring., Ithaca, NY, 1983-90; W.H. Clark disting. univ. prof. N.C. State U., Raleigh, 1998—; co-dir. N.C. State U., Ctr. for High Performance Simulation, Raleigh, 2004—. Vis. cons. theoretical physics divsn., U.K. Atomic Energy Authority, Harwell, U.K., 1971; vis. prof. dept. physics U. Guelph, 1971-73, 76, U. Kent, Canterbury, Eng., 1975, dept. chemistry U. Oxford, 1979-80, 86-87, Chiba U., Japan, 1999, dept. chem. engring. U. Calif., Berkeley, 1982, Australian Nat. U., Canberra, 1993, Imperial Coll., London, 1970-71, 94, 2002, U. Paris-Sud, 2001-02, dept. chem. engring. U. Wis., 1993, U. Hong Kong, 2007; vis. fellow Fulbright Sr. scholar Australian Nat. U., 1993-94; mem. NAS com. to study formation of Nat. Resource Ctr. for Computing in Chemistry, 1976-77, NRC Assessment Bd. to rev. NIST programs, 1988-91; cons., lectr. in field. Mem. editl. bd. Molecular Physics, 1978-87, 95—, Jour. Chem. Physics, 1995-98, Molecular Simulation, 1986-2006, assoc. editor, 1990-2006; assoc. editor AIChE Jour., 1988-91; editor: Topics in Chem. Engring., Oxford U. Press, 1991—; del. Oxford U. Press, 1991—. Recipient best paper ann. award Can. Soc. Chem. Engring., 1973; named Eppley Found. fellow Imperial Coll. London, 1970-71, Guggenheim fellow, 1986-87, sr. vis. fellow (SERC award) U. Oxford, 1986-87, vis. fellow (SERC award) Imperial Coll., London, 1994; Royal Soc. vis. professorship, Hong Kong, 2007. Mem. NAE, AAAS, AIChE (program com. 1974-81, Alpha Chi Sigma award 1986, William H. Walker award 2000, fellow 2003), Am. Chem. Soc. (Joel Henry Hildebrand award in Theoretical and Exptl. Chemistry of Liquids, 2007), Am. Inst. Physics, Chem. Soc. (London). Home Phone: 919-851-5571. Personal E-mail: kgubbins@aol.com. Business E-Mail: keg@ncsu.edu.

GUBBIOTTI, CHRISTINE M., lawyer; b. Pittston, Pa., Nov. 1, 1968; d. Thomas Joseph and Patricia Ann Gubbiotti; m. Joseph A. O'Boyle, Feb. 1, 2003. BS in Polit. Sci., U. Scranton, Pa., 1990, MA in History, 1990; JD, Dickinson Sch. Law, 1993. Bar: Supreme Ct. Pa. 1993; cert. managed care exec. AHIP. Staff atty. Blue Cross of Northeastern Pa., Wilkes-Barre, 1994—98, corp. counsel, 1998—2000; gen. counsel Geisinger Health Plan, Danville, Pa., 2000—04, v.p., Legal Svcs., 2004—07, Geisinger Quality Options, Inc., Danville, Pa., 2005—07; gen. counsel Mercy Health Ptnrs., Danville, 2007—. Asst. sec. Geisinger Health Plan, 2000—07. Mem. various coms., advisory bds. Am. Health Ins. Plans, Washington, 2000—; bd. dirs. Arthritis Found. of NEPA, Wilkes-Barre, 2000—, Victims Resource Ctr., 2006—. Mem.: Pa. Bar assn. (health, in-house counsel com. 1993—), Am. Health Lawyers Assn., Wilkes-Barre Law Libr. Assn. (health law com. 2000—). Democrat. Roman Catholic. Office: Geisinger Health Plan 100 N Academy Ave Danville PA 17822 Office Phone: 570-340-5078. Office Fax: 570-271-5268. Personal E-mail: cmgubbiotti@hotmail.com.

GUBEN, JAN K., lawyer; b. Balt., Nov. 11, 1942; BA, Tusculum Coll., 1964; LLB, U. Balt., 1967. Bar: Md. 1967, DC, 2001. Ptnr., real estate law Venable LLP (formerly Venable, Baetjer and Howard), Balt., chair. bus. div., 1995—2001. Lectr. real estate Johns Hopkins U., 1986-95, deleg. US Agy. Internat. Devel., 1997. Mem. ABA, Md. State Bar Assn., Bar Assn. Balt. City. Office: Venable LLP 1800 Mercantile Bank & Trust Bldg 2 Hopkins Plz Baltimore MD 21201 Office Phone: 410-244-7624. Office Fax: 410-244-7742. Business E-Mail: jkguben@venable.com.

GUBER, MYLES STUERT, surgeon; b. Denver, July 3, 1956; s. Frank Friday Guber and Celia Elsie Kramish; m. Deborah Ann Bishop, Aug. 25, 1996; children: Michael Albert, Samuel David, Halle Anderson. BS, Northwestern U., 1978, MD, 1980. Diplomate Am. Bd. Surgery, Am. Bd. Thoracic Surgery. Staff cardiac surgeon Porter Meml. Hosp., Denver, 1987—. Fellow: Am. Coll. Surgeons; mem.: Western Thoracic Surg. Assn., County Thoracic Surgeons. Jewish. Avocations: skiing, golf, climbing, basketball. Home: 355 Ash St Denver CO 80222 Office: Colo Cardiovascular Surg Assocs Ste 550 950 E Harvard Ave Denver CO 80210 Office Phone: 303-778-6527. Office Fax: 303-733-1288. E-mail: mgube@aol.com.

GUBER, PETER, executive producer; b. Boston, Mass., Mar. 1, 1942; m. Lynda Gellis. BA, Syracuse U.; SSP, JD, LLM, U. Florence, Italy; postgrad., NYU. Bar: N.Y., Calif., D.C. Exec. asst. Columbia Pictures, studio chief, co-chmn., 1989-94; prin. Peter Guber's Filmworks; co-prin., chmn. bd. Casablanca Record and Filmworks (merger Peter Guber's Filmworks and Casablanca Records), 1976-80; prin. Polygram Pictures, 1980-83, Guber-Peters, 1983-88; co-chmn., mng. dir. Guber-Peters-Barris Entertainment Co, 1988-89, chmn., 1989; chmn., chief exec. officer Sony Pictures Entertainment, 1989-94; chmn., CEO Mandalay, incl. Mandalay Pictures, Mandalay Television, Mandalay Sports Entertainment, Mandalay Media Arts, Mandalay E-Media. Vis. prof., chmn. producer's dept. UCLA Sch. Theatre Arts. Author: Inside the Deep, Above the Title, (with Peter Bart) Shoot Out: Surviving Game and (Mis)Fortune in Hollywood, 2002; prodr.: (films) The Deep, 1977; (with Jon Peters) Vision Quest, 1985, Batman, 1989, Tango & Cash, 1989; (with Peters and Neil Canton) The Witches of Eastwick, 1987, Caddyshack II, 1988; (television) Stand By Your Man, 1981, Brotherhood of Justice, 1986, Bay Coven, 1987, Nightmare at Bitter Creek, 1988, Finish Line, 1989, Autobahn, 2005, The Jacket, 2005; exec. prodr.: Midnight Express, 1978; (with Peters) An American Werewolf in London, 1981, Six Weeks, 1982, Missing, 1982 (Academy award nomination for best picture 1982), Flashdance, 1983, D.C. Cab, 1983, Head Office, 1985, The Legend of Billie Jean, 1985, The Color Purple, 1985 (Academy award nomination for best picture 1985), Youngblood, 1986, Gorillas in the Mist, 1988, Rain Man, 1988 (Academy award for best picture 1988), Missing Link, 1989, The Bonfire of the Vanities, 1990, This Boy's Life, 1993, With Honors, 1994; (with Peters, George Folsey, Jr., and John Landis) Clue, 1985; (with Peters, Mark Damon, John Hyde, and Sydney Kimmel) The Clan of the Cave Bear, 1986; (with Peters, Kathleen Kennedy, Frank Marshall, and Steven Speilberg) Innerspace, 1987; (with Peters and Roger Birnbaum) Who's That Girl?, 1987, (with Peters, Benjamin Melniker, and Michael E. Uslan) Batman Returns, 1992, Galapagos: The Enchanted Voyage, 1999, Alex and Emma, 2003, A Thousand Roads, 2005, Into the Blue, 2005; (television) The Toughest Man in the World, 1984; (with Peters) Television and the Presidency, 1983 (Emmy award nomination 1984), Rude Awakening, 1998; asst. prodr.: High Spirits, 1988. Named Producer of Yr., NATO, 1979; Albert Gallatin fellow NYU.

GUBERMAN, SIDNEY, painter, writer; b. Greenville, SC, Aug. 24, 1936; s. Morris and Louise (Cook) G.; m. Jennifer Glidden, June 5, 1965 (div. 1977); children: Maxwell, Angus; m. Rebecca Wilson, July 31, 1977; children: Elizabeth Tindall, Dore Hopkins Brooks. BA, Princeton U., 1958; MArch, U. Pa., 1967. Asst. prof. Ecole Polytechnique, Lausanne, Switzerland, 1973-75. Vis. artist U. S.C., Columbia, 1991-92, Atlanta Coll. Art, 1989, 91; vis. lectr. Princeton (N.J.) U., 1981; artist invité Federale de Lausanne Ecole des Beaux-Arts, Switzerland, 1971-73; chmn. bd. dirs. New Visions Gallery, Atlanta, 1987-93; bd. dirs. Atlanta Arts Festival, 1986-88. Solo exhbns. include Henri Gallery, Washington, 1970, 73, 75, Galerie R-B, Fribourg, Switzerland, 1975, 79, Image South Gallery, Atlanta, 1976, Harcus/Krakow/Rosen/Sonnabend, Boston, 1976, Fraser's Stable Gallery, Washington, 1978, Heath Gallery, Atlanta, 1979, Leah Levy Gallery, San Francisco, 1979, Diane Brown Gallery, Washington, 1980, Galerie Jonas, Cortaillod, Switzerland, 1980, Barbara Fiedler Gallery, Washington, 1981, Fay Gold Gallery, Atlanta, 1981, 82, 83, 85, Gertrude Herbert Gallery, Augusta, Ga., 1985, Gibbes Art Mus., Charleston, S.C., 1988, Galerie von der Milwe, Aachen, Germany, 1990, Hodges-Taylor, Charlotte, N.C., 1990, Louisa McIntosh Gallery, Atlanta, 1991, Susan Conway Carroll Gallery, Washington, 1991, "New Paintings" Weslyn Coll Gallery, Macon, Ga., 1999, Galerie des Roines, Geneva, 2007; group exhbns. include Prix de peinture, Vevey, Switzerland, 1974, City Gallery Contemporary Art, Raleigh, N.C., 1987, SECCA, Winston-Salem, N.C., 1988, Birmingham (Ala.) Mus. Art, 1988-89; permanent collections include The High Mus., Atlanta, The Hunter Mus., Chattanooga, Tenn., The Nat. Mus. Am. Art, Washington, Princeton (N.J.) U. Mus., Colo. Springs Fine Arts Ctr.; author: Frank Stella: An Illustrated Biography, 1995; curator Frank Stella-Imaginary Landscapes exhbn. The Gibbes Mus., 2001, Charleston, S.C., William Christenberry: Hale County on My Mind, various museums. Individual Artist's grantee NEA, 1980; Guggenheim fellow, 1988-89. Mem. The Ivy Club. Democrat. Avocations: films, tennis, opera. Office: 1174 Zonolite Pl NE # C Atlanta GA 30306-2002 Home: 22 Spring Lake Pl Nw Atlanta GA 30318-1646 Home Phone: 404-875-3438; Office Phone: 404-881-0222. Business E-Mail: st.gubie@mindspring.com.

GUBERT, WALTER ALEXANDER, investment company executive; b. Merano, Italy, June 15, 1947; LLD, U. Florence, Italy, 1970; grad., INSEAD, Fountainbleu, France, 1973. Analyst European chems. J.P. Morgan & Co., Inc., Paris, 1973-77, v.p. treasury mgmt. adv. group London, 1977-81, sr. v.p. capital markets activities U.S. NYC, 1981—87; CEO J.P. Morgan Securities, London, 1987—90; chmn. London Mgmt. Com. J.P. Morgan & Co., Inc., London, 1989—92, co-head Investment Banking Europe, ME & Africa, 1992—95, sr. exec. Europe, ME & Africa, 1995—97, v. chmn., 1998—2000, global head Investment Banking NYC, 1998—2000; vice chmn. J.P. Morgan Chase & Co., NYC, 2001—; chmn. J.P. Morgan Investment Bank, NYC, 2001—04; chmn. Europe, Middle East and Africa J.P. Morgan Chase & Co., 2004—. Office: JP Morgan Chase & Co 270 Park Ave New York NY 10017-2014 also: JP Morgan Chase & Co Investment Bank 10 Aldermanbury London EC2V7RF England Office Phone: 212-270-6000.

GUBLER, DUANE J., virologist, educator, researcher; b. Santa Clara, Utah, June 4, 1939; s. June and Thelma (Whipple) G.; m. Bobbie J. Carroll, Mar. 1, 1958; children: Justin Chase, Stuart Jefferson. BS, Utah State U., 1963; MS, U. Hawaii, 1965; ScD, Johns Hopkins U., 1969; AS, So. Utah State U., 1962, DSc (hon.), 1988. Asst. prof. pathobiology Sch. Hygiene Johns Hopkins U., Balt. and Calcutta, 1969-71; assoc. prof. tropical medicine Sch. Medicine U. Hawaii, Honolulu, 1971-75; head virology dept. Naval Med. Rsch. Unit Number 2, Jakarta, Indonesia, 1975-78; assoc. prof. entomology and microbiology U. Ill., Urbana, 1978-79; rsch. microbiologist divsn. vector-borne viral diseases Ctrs. for Disease Control and Prevention, Fort Collins, Colo., 1980-81, dir. San Juan (P.R.) Labs., 1981-89, dir. divsn. vector-borne infectious diseases Ft. Collins, Colo., 1989—2003; dir. Asia Pacific Inst. Tropical Medicine and Infectious Diseases, U. Hawaii, Honolulu, 2004—; prof., chair, dept. tropical medicine, med. microbiology, and pharm. U. Hawaii Sch. Medicine, 2004—. Cons. NRC, 1972, South Pacific Commn., 1972-76, WHO, Geneva, 1974—, AID, Washington, 1977—, Pan Am. Health Orgn., 1981—, Internat. Devel. Rsch. Ctr., Ottawa, Can., 1977—, Rockefeller Found., NYC, 1987—, US Dept. Defense, 1992-, Nat. Inst. of Allergy and Infectious Diseases, 2002-, numerous nat. ministries of health, 1972—; Bailey K. Ashford meml. lectr. U. P.R. Sch. Medicine, 1999; chmn. bd. coun. Pediat. Dengue Vaccine Initiative, 2002-; mem. sci. adv. bd. Novartis Inst. Tropical Diseases, 2003—, Hawaii BioTech., Inc., 2006-, Environ. Health Inst., Singapore, 2006-; sci. advisor Inviragen Inc., 2006-. Contbr. numerous articles to profl. jours. Lt. USN, 1975—77. Recipient Commendation medal, 1984, Outstanding Svc. medal, 1988, Meritorious Svc. medal, 1991, Outstanding Unit citation, 1995, 98, 2000, Outstanding Alumni award for sci. and rsch. Johns Hopkins U. Sch. Pub. Health, 1997, Chuck Alexander Operational award La. Mosquito Control Assn., 1998, Disting. Svc. award Dept. HHS, 1996, 2000, 01, 03, Charles Shepard award in Sci., Ctr. for Disease Control, 2001; selected as one of 90 Illustrious Alumni in celebration of U. Hawaii's 90th year, 1997, Woodward Lectr. award USN Preventive Medicine Unit, 2000. Fellow Infectious Disease Soc. Am., Am. Assn. for Advancement of Sci., Am. Soc. Tropical Medicine (Charles Franklin Craig lectr. 1988, pres.-elect 1998, pres. 2000), Am. Mosquito Control Assn., Entomol. Soc. Am. (highlights in med. entomology lecture 1979, 95), Soc. Vector Ecologists, Rotary (Rotarian of Yr. San Juan chpt. 1986, Meritorious Svc. award Rotary Found., Evanston, Ill. 1990, Svc. Above Self award Fort Collins Club 1999, Internat. Svc. Above Self award 2000); mem. AAAS. Office: U Hawaii Sch Medicine Kaka'ako Campus BSB 320 651 Ilalo St Honolulu HI 96813 Office Phone: 808-692-1606. Business E-Mail: dgubler@hawaii.edu.

GUBLER, JOHN GRAY, lawyer; b. Las Vegas, June 16, 1942; s. V. Gray and Loreta N. (Newton) G.; m. Mollie Boyle, Jan. 10, 1987; 1 child, J. Gray; children from previous marriage: Laura, Matthew. BA, U. Calif., Berkeley, 1964; JD, U. Utah, 1971; LLM in Taxation, NYU, 1973. Bar: Nev. 1971, U.S. Dist. Ct. Nev. 1973, U.S. Tax Ct. 1974, U.S. Ct. Appeals (9th cir.) 1978. Dep. pub. defender Clark County, Nev., 1973-74; ptnr. Gubler & Gubler, Las Vegas, 1974-88, ptnr. Gubler and Peters, Las Vegas, 1989—; instr. continuing edn. community coll. With U.S. Army, 1966-68. Mem. Clark County Bar Assn., ABA, State Bar of Nev. (disciplinary com. 1979-88), Las Vegas-Paradise Rotary (pres. 1981-82), Knife & Fork Club (pres. 1978-80). Mem. LDS Ch. Office: Gubler & Peters 302 E Carson Ave Ste 601 Las Vegas NV 89101-5989 Home Phone: 702-878-9792; Office Phone: 702-382-4343. Business E-Mail: jgg@gublerlaw.com.

GUBSER, PETER ANTON, political scientist, writer, educator; b. Tulsa, May 9, 1941; s. Eugene Herbert and Mary (Douglass) G.; m. Annie Yeni-Komshian, Aug. 15, 1969; children: Sasha Mary-Helen, Christi Valerie. BA, Yale U., 1964; MA, Am. U. Beirut, 1966; PhD, Oxford U., Eng., 1970. Rsch. fellow U. Manchester, Eng., 1970-72; assoc. rsch. scientist Am. Insts. for Rsch., Washington, 1972-74; asst. rep. Ford Found., Beirut, 1974-77; pres. Am. Near East Refugee Aid, Washington, 1977—2007. Bd. dirs. Internat. Svc. Agys., Washington, Am. Coun. Vol. Internat. Action, Internat. Coll., Beirut, Nat. Coun. on U.S.-Arab Rels., Washington, Found. for Mid. East Peace, Washington, Global Devel. Forum, Amman, Jordan; adj. prof. Georgetown U., Washington, 1990—; lectr. various govt. and non-govt. instns., 1977—. Author: Politics and Change at Karak, Jordan, 1973, Jordan: Crossroads of Middle East Events, 1983, Historical Dictionary of Hashemite Kingdom of Jordan, 1991. Mem. Somerset (Md.) Town Coun., 1994—2004, Montgomery County Adv. Bd., 2004—. Mem.: Washington Inst. Fgn. Affairs, Middle East Studies Assn., Middle East Inst., Am. Polit. Sci. Assn., Cosmos Club, Order of the Hosp. of St. John of Jerusalem. Democrat. Mem. Christian Ch. Avocations: hiking, reading, travel. Office Phone: 202-347-2558.

GUCKENHEIMER, DANIEL PAUL, financial advisor; b. Tel Aviv, Oct. 10, 1943; came to U.S., 1947, naturalized, 1957. s. Ernest and Eva Guckenheimer; m. Helen Sandra Fox, Dec. 21, 1969; children: Debra Ellen, Julie Susan. BBA in Fin., U. Houston, 1970; cert. hosp. adminstrn., Trinity U., San Antonio, 1973. Asst. adminstr. Harris County Hosp. Dist., Houston, 1970-76; pres. Mid Am. Investments, Kansas City, Kans., 1976; exec. dir. Allen County Hosp., Iola, Kans., 1977-78; comml. loan officer Traders Bank, Kansas City, Mo., 1979; v.p., mgr. Traders Ward Pkwy. Bank, 1980; v.p., mgr. installment loans Traders Bank, 1981, v.p., comml. loan officer, 1982; sr. v.p., mgr. comml. loans United Mo. Bank South, 1982-91; sr. v.p., mgr. lending United Mo. Bank, N.A., 1991-93; pres. Guckenheimer Fin. Svcs., 1993—. Bd. dirs. Robert Morris Assocs., 1988-92, Food Distbn., Inc., 1983-88, Crime Stoppers Greater Kansas City, 1989—; clinic adminstr. 190th USAF Clinic, 1977-84. With USAF, 1962-66, maj. Res. ret. Mem. N.G. Assn. Tex., Olympic Soc., Internat. Platform Assn., Assn. Mil. Surgeons U.S., Mil. Officers Assn. Am., Mil. Order World Wars, B'nai Brith (v.p. 1982-83, pres. 1984-85, treas. 1986-95), Amer-Israeli Pub. Affairs Com. Office: 8439 W 113th St Overland Park KS 66210-2437 Office Phone: 913-451-0051.

GUDE, ATISH, telecommunications industry executive; BS, Syracuse Univ.; MBA, Univ. Chgo. Sr. mgr. Deloitte Consulting; v.p. strategic planning Nextel Communications, 2000—05; sr. v.p. corp. strategy Sprint Nextel, Reston, Va., 2005—07, sr. v.p. mobile broadband ops., 2007—. Bd. dir. Virgin Mobile USA. Bd. mem. United eWay. Office: Sprint Nextel 2001 Edmund Halley Dr Reston VA 20191*

GUDE, NANCY CARLSON, lawyer; b. Kane, Pa., Aug. 5, 1948; d. Edward Walter and Theo Alberta (Herzog) Carlson. BA in History, Pa. State U., 1969; MS in Computer Sci., U. Central Fla., 1981; JD, Thomas M. Cooley Law Sch., 2001. Bar: Fla. 2001, U.S. Dist. Ct. (no. and so. dists.) Fla. 2003, U.S. Dist. Ct. (mid. dist.) Fla. 2006. Programmer Group Hospitalization, Inc., Washington, 1969-70; programmer analyst Space Age Computer Sys., Washington, 1970-73, Ky. Fried Chicken, Louisville, 1973-75; sys. analyst Sentinel Comm. Co., Orlando, Fla., 1975-77, programming supr., 1977-78, sys. and programming mgr., 1978-80, asst. dir. data processing, 1980, mgr. staff devel., 1981-82; mgmt. info. svcs. mgr. Sun-Sentinel Co., Ft. Lauderdale, Fla., 1982-83, v.p., dir. info. sys., 1983-94, sys. cons., 1994-98; assoc. atty. Walton Lantaff Schroeder &

Carson, Ft. Lauderdale, 2002—04; office/estate svcs. adminstr. Jo Ann Head Voight, CPA, Ft. Lauderdale, 2007—. Adj. instr. U. Ctrl. Fla., Orlando, 1981—82. Participant Leadership Broward X; chair LBX Art-serve Intervention Group. Recipient Thomas M. Cooley Leadership Achievement award, 2001. Mem.: Broward County Bar Assn., Fed. Bar Assn., The Fla. Bar, Pa. State U. Alumni Assn. (Ft. Lauderdale chpt., treas. 1990—92, v.p. 1992—93, pres. 1993—95). Presbyterian. Home: 9 NE 20 Ave Pompano Beach FL 33060

GUDENBERG, HARRY RICHARD, arbitrator, mediator; b. Frankfurt, Germany, May 20, 1933; m. Sharon Rickey; children— Lori, Bruce. BS, N.Y. U., 1960, MBA, 1964; JD, Seton Hall U., 1970. Bar: N.J. bar 1970, U.S. Supreme Ct 1973. With ITT, NYC, 1970-88, v.p., dir. indsl. and employee relations, employment and labor law, 1978-88; cons. on benefits, compensation and employment law William M. Mercer Inc., NYC, 1988-93. Arbitrator, mediator fact finder, dispute resolution, employment and labor law, panel mem. Am. Arbitration Assn., Fed. Mediation and Conciliation Svc., N.J. State Bd. Mediation, N.J. Pub. Employment Rels. Commn., 1994—, also various pvt. panels. Served with U.S. Army, 1953-55. Mem. ABA, Nat. Acad. Arbitrators, N.J. Bar Assn., Indsl. Res. Rsch. Assn.

GUDENZI-RUESS, IDA CARMEN V., music educator, artist; b. Bronx, NY, Nov. 4, 1926; d. Hamlet G. and Dolores Gudenzi; m. Raymond Edmond Ruess, Aug. 20, 1965; 1 child, Raida. AA, Columbia-Greene C.C., Hudson, NY, 1994; studied drawing and sculpture, Arts Student League, NYC; studied with NYC concert pianist Vladzia Mashke. Montessori tchg. cert. Bergamo, Italy, 1973. Tchr. piano and sculpture, NY. Sculptor (bust) WWII Marine Corps Comdt. Gen. Holland Meade Smith, Hawaii, 1966. Mem.: Phi Theta Kappa. Home: 12 Eldridge Ln Red Hook NY 12571 Home Phone: 845-758-9560; Office Phone: 845-758-9560.

GUDMUNDSSON, FINNBOGI, library administrator; b. Reykjavik, Iceland, Jan. 8, 1924; s. Gudmundur Finnbogason and Laufey Vilhjalmsdottir; m. Kristjana P. Helgadottir, Oct. 1, 1955 (dec.); 1 child, Helga Laufey. Cand. mag., U. Iceland, 1949, Dr. phil., 1961. Assoc. prof. U. Man., Winnipeg, Can., 1951-56; lectr. Icelandic Univs., Oslo and Bergen, 1957-58; tchr. Icelandic Reykjavik Gymnasium, 1958-64; docent U. Iceland, Reykjavik, 1962-64; dir. Nat. Library of Iceland, Reykjavik, 1964-94. Author: Sveinbjörn Egilsson's Translations of Homer, 1960, Stephan G. Stephansson in Retrospect: Seven Essays, 1982, Poets' Letters to Gudmundur Finnbogason, 1987, The Humour of Snorri Sturluson, 1991, Talt og Skrevet, 2002, Nineteen Articles and Speeches, 2003; editor: Arbok Landsbokasafns, 1964-93, Orkneyinga saga, 1965, Andvari, 1968-82, Selected Letters Written to Stephan G. Stephansson I-III, 1971-75; contbr. articles to profl. jours. Mem. Icelandic Studies Soc. (chmn. 1962-64), Icelandic Research Librarians (chmn. 1966-73), Icelandic Patriotic Soc. (pres. 1967-82), Nordinfo (bd. dirs. 1976-79), Icelandic Nat. League (hon.), Icelandic Libr. Assn. (hon.), Rotary (sec. 1983-84). Lutheran.

GUEDRY, JAMES WALTER, lawyer, retired manufacturing executive; b. Morgan City, La., Jan. 7, 1941; s. J. Walter and P. Marie (McNulty) G. AB magna cum laude, Georgetown U., 1962; postgrad., U. Brussels, 1962-63; LL.B., U. Va., 1966. Bar: NY 1967. Assoc. Lord, Day & Lord, NYC, 1966-76; v.p., corp. sec./assoc. gen. counsel Internat. Paper Co., NYC, 1976-2000; retired, 2000. Mem. Assn. Bar City NY Home and Office: 79 Charles St New York NY 10014-2638

GUEDRY, LEO J., agricultural economics educator; b. Baton Rouge, Nov. 2, 1940; s. Leo J. and Beulah LaCour (Monger) G.; m. Nealea Ann Vosbury, Jan. 25, 1964; children: Leigh Ann, Grechen. BS, La. State U., 1962; MS, U. Ill.-Urbana, 1965; PhD, Oreg. State U.-Corvallis, 1970. Asst. prof. agrl. econs. La. State U., 1969-74, assoc. prof., 1974-81, prof. agrl. econs. Baton Rouge, 1981, head dept. agrl. econs., 1981; interim assoc. dean Coll. Agr., 1995-96. Mem. editorial council: So. Jour. Agrl. Econs., 1977-79, editor, 1981. Mem. Am. Agrl. Econs. Assn., Am. Econs. Assn., So. Agrl. Econs. Assn. (recipient, Hon. Lifetime Achievement award, 2003), Western Agrl. Econs. Assn., Internat. Agbus Mgmt. Assn. Office: La State U Dept Agrl Econs & Agribus 101 Agrl Adminstrn Bldg Baton Rouge LA 70803-0001

GUEHENNO, JEAN MARIE, international organization official; b. Paris, Oct. 30, 1949; s. Jean and Annie (Rospabe) G.; m. Mathilde de la Bardonnie, Mar. 26, 1974 (div.); m. Michele Fahy Moss, Apr. 21, 1981; 1 child, Claire Maia. Student, Ecole Normale Superieure, Paris, 1968-72, Ecole Nationale D'Administration, 1974-76, Inst. D'Etudes Politiques, 1972-73. Auditor Cour des Comptes, Paris, 1976-79, referendary counselor, 1978, 1986-87; deputy dir. Policy Planning Staff, Paris, 1979-82; cultural counselor French Embassy, NYC, 1982-86; special advisor to chmn. Banque de l'Union European, Paris, 1987-89; dir. policy planning staff Ministry Fgn. Affairs, 1989—93, amb., Western European Union, 1993—95; mem., Sec. Gen. Advisory Bd. on disarmament UN, NYC, 1999—2000, under sec. gen for peacekeeping ops., 2000—. Chmn. Institut des hautes études de défense nationale, 1998—2000. Contbr. articles to profl. jours. Office: UN S-3727B New York NY 10017 Office Phone: 212-963-8079. E-mail: guehenno@un.org.*

GUENTHER, CHARLES JOHN, librarian, writer; b. St. Louis, Apr. 29, 1920; s. Charles Richard and Hulda Clara G.; m. Esther G. Klund, Apr. 11, 1942; children: Charles John, Cecile Anne, Christine Marie. AA, Harris Tchrs. Coll. (now Harris-Stowe State U.), St. Louis, 1940; postgrad., St. Louis U., 1952—54; BA, Webster Coll. (now Webster U.), St. Louis, 1973, MA, 1974; LHD (hon.), So. Ill. U., Edwardsville, 1979. Editl. asst. St. Louis Star-Times, 1938; with Social Security Commn. Mo., Dept. Labor, U.S. Employment Service, War Dept., C.E., St. Louis, 1941-43; head archives unit USAAF Aero Chart Svc., St. Louis, 1943-45, head rsch. unit, 1945-47; asst. chief, chief of library, translator, historian, geographer, supervisory cartographer, librarian USAF Aero Chart and Info. Center (name changed to DMA Aerospace Center), St. Louis, 1947-57, chief tech. libr., 1957-75. Civilian library specialist Project Crossroads, USAF, 1946; instr. creative writing Peoples Art Center, St. Louis, 1953-56; lectr., poetry workshop leader various U.S. writers confs. Author: Modern Italian Poets, 1961, Paul Valery in English, 1970, (poems) Phrase.Paraphrase, 1970, Voices in the Dark, 1974, Moving the Seasons, 1994; translator: (with others) Selected Poems in Alain Bosquet, 1963, Selected Translations, 1986; contbr. articles to profl. jours.; book reviewer: St. Louis Post-Dispatch, 1953-2003, Globe-Democrat, 1972-82; author numerous poems. Decorated commendatore Ordine al Merito della Repubblica Italiana; recipient Shell Co. Found. grant for book Phrase/Paraphrase, 1970, Witter Bynner grant, 1979; recipient Lit. award Mo. Libr. Assn., 1974, Mo. Writers Guild award, 1987, 94, 96, Mo. and St. Louis Arts awards, 2001. Mem. Poetry Soc. Am. (Midwest regional v.p., James Joyce award 1974), St. Louis Writers Guild (v.p. 1958, pres. 1959, 76-77), St. Louis Poetry Center (chmn. bd. chancellors 1965-72, pres. 1974-76), Mo. Writers Guild (v.p. 1971-73, pres. 1973-74), Spl. Libraries Assn. (pres. Greater St. Louis chpt. 1969-70), Rose Soc. Greater St. Louis; corr. mem. Academie d'Alsace (diplome d'honneur 1957); hon. mem. Les Violetti Picards et Normands, Paris, Academia de Ciencias Humanisticas y Relaciones, Mexico, Academie Chablaisienne, Thonon-les-Bains, France, Biblioteca Partenopea, Naples; asso. mem. Internat. Am. Inst. Home: 9877 Allendale Dr Saint Louis MO 63123-6450 Office Phone: 314-544-0563. *A poet's relation to his time is complex and mutable. A poet's temperament, attitudes, and sense of the function of poetry are all changeable and conflict with each other throughout his life. In a world which tends to be imitative, regimented, and standardized, each poet is his own definition of poet, his own conscience, his own value.*

GUENTHER, JACK DONALD, banker; b. Little Rock, Jan. 21, 1929; s. Gottlob and Josephine Margaret (Presley) G.; m. Margaret Adah Beltz, June 11, 1956; children— Elizabeth, Katherine, John BA, Yale U., 1950; postgrad., King's Coll., Cambridge U., Eng., 1952-53; MA, Harvard U., 1957, PhD, 1959. Various staff positions IMF, Washington, 1960-79; sr. v.p., sr. advisor internat. ops. Citibank, NYC, 1979-95; cons. MBIA, NYC, 1995-98. Served as sgt. U.S. Army, 1953-55 Home: 4101 Albemarle St NW Unit 651 Washington DC 20016

GUENTHER, JACK EGON, lawyer; b. San Antonio, Dec. 14, 1934; m. Valerie Urschel, Feb. 1, 1964; children: Abigail Guenther Kampmann, Jack Egon. BBA, U. Tex.-Austin, 1956; LLB magna cum laude, St. Mary's U., 1959; LLM in Taxation, NYU, 1960. Bar: Tex. 1959; C.P.A., Tex. Practice pub. acctg., San Antonio, 1957-59; pvt. practice, 1960—; assoc. Cox & Smith (and predecessor firm), 1961-65, ptnr., 1965-2001. Chmn. bd. BMW Ctr., Ltd., 1965—, San Antonio Rivergate Toyota, Inc., Nashville, 1983—, Performance Toyota, Memphis, 1984—, Lexus of Nashville, 1989—, Volvo and Porsche Ctr., San Antonio, 1990—, Toyota of Plano, 1990—, Enercorp LLC, 1994—. Bd. dir. Nat. Western Art Found., Nat. Fish and Wildlife, Tex. Pub. Radio Adv. Coun.; trustee V.H. McNutt Meml. Found., Amy Shelton McNutt Charitable Trust, Jack Valerie Guenther Found., Amy McNutt Endowment Fund for Gardens of S.W. Craft Ctr.; adv. dir. Tex. Highway Patrol Mus. Assn. Mem. ABA, Tex. Bar Assn., Tex. Soc. CPA's, Sigma Chi, Phi Delta Phi. Epsicopalian. Office: 153 Treeline Park Ste 300 San Antonio TX 78209-1880 Office Phone: 210-829-1800.

GUENTNER, JAMES FRANCIS, JR., artist, educator; b. Glenshaw, Pa., Feb. 23, 1949; s. James Francis Guentner and Elizabeth McCloskey; m. Linda Louise Kauffman Guentner; 1 stepchild, Ronald Kauffman; m. Cheryl Guentner (div. Apr. 28, 1973); 1 child, Rachel. A. Allegheny C.C., Pa., 1969; BA, Carlow Coll., Pa. Art tchr. Shaler Sch. Dist., Glenshaw, Pa., 1999—; painting instr. North Hills Art Ctr., Pa., 1986—94; truck driver GAGE Co. , Pa., 1979—99, Local 249 Union Hall, Pa., 1976—79; med. equipment installer Robert A. Fulton Co., Pa., 1973—76; substitute art tchr. Shaler Sch. Dist., Glenshaw, Pa., 1972—73. Exhibitions include Borelli-Edwards Gallery, Carnegie Mus. Art. Avocations: guitar, magic, bodybuilding. Home: 220 Lucille St Glenshaw PA 15116

GUEQUIERRE, JOHN PHILLIP, manufacturing executive; b. Milw., Sept. 10, 1946; s. Gerald Herbert and Louise Ann (Fenske) G.; m. Mary Rowlands Speer, Aug. 17, 1968; children: William Edward, Robert John, Elizabeth Louise. BA, U. Wis., 1968; MBA, U. Chgo., 1972. Systems analyst Inland Steel Co., East Chgo., Ind., 1968-72; analyst inventory INRYCO, Milw., 1972-73, supr. material planning, 1973-74, mgr. contract adminstrn., 1974-76; mgr. fin. Inland Steel Devel. Corp., Washington, 1976-78; mgr. fin. analysis Inland Steel Urban Devel. Corp., Chgo., 1978-80; v.p. adminstrn. Scholz Homes Inc., Tol., 1980-83; sr. v.p. adminstrn., dir. Schult Homes Corp., Middlebury, Ind., 1983-92, sr. v.p. ops., dir., 1992-95, pres. manufactured housing group, 1995-99; sr. v.p. mfg. Oakwood Homes, Middlebury, 1999-2000; chmn., CEO Pleasant St. Homes, LLC, 2000—. Chmn. budget subcom. United Way, Elkhart, Ind., 1983-89, bd. dirs. 1989-2000, treas., 1990-92, chmn. 1992; adult leader 4H, Elkhart County, 1983—; bd. dirs. Elkhart Chamber Found., 1993-98; bd. dirs. Ind. Assn. United Ways, 1993-2000, vice chmn., 1995-97, chmn., 1997. Mem.: Beta Gamma Sigma, Phi Kappa Phi, Phi Beta Kappa. Republican. Presbyterian. Office: Pleasant St Homes LLC 51700 Lovejoy Dr Middlebury IN 46540 Business E-Mail: johng@indianabuildingsystems.com.

GUERETTE, SUSAN M., lawyer; b. Fall River, Mass., Jan. 28, 1970; BA, Villanova U., 1991; JD, Georgwtown U., 1995. Bar: Pa., NJ 1995, US Dist. Ct., NJ, US Dist. Ct. (ea. dist.) Pa., US Ct. Appeals (3rd cir.) 1996, US Supreme Ct. 2000. Atty. Rubin Fortunato PC, Paoli, Pa.; spl. counsel Saul Ewing LLP, Wayne, Pa. Court appointed spl. advocate. Mem. Schuylkill Township Zoning Bd. Alternate, Eastern Tech. Coun. — Women's Leadership Networking Bd. Mem.: ABA, Chester County Bar Assn., Pa. Bar Assn. Office: Saul Ewing LLP 1200 Liberty Ridge Dr, Ste 200 Wayne PA 19087-5569 Office Phone: 610-251-5073. Office Fax: 610-722-3267. E-mail: SGuerette@saul.com.*

GUERIN, BILL, professional hockey player; b. Worcester, Mass., Nov. 9, 1970; Right wing NJ Devils, 1991—98, Edmonton Oilers, 1998—2001, Boston Bruins, 2001—02, Dallas Stars, 2002—06, St. Louis Blues, 2006—07, San Jose Sharks, 2007, NY Islanders, 2007—, capt., 2007—. Mem. Team USA, Olympic Games, Nagano, Japan, 1998, Salt Lake City, 2002, Torino, Italy, 06, Team USA, World Cup of Hockey, 1996, 2004. Named to NHL All-Star Team, 2001, 2003, 2004, Second All-Star Team, NHL, 2002. Achievements include being a member of Stanley Cup Champion NJ Devils, 1995; being a member of World Cup Champion Team USA, 1996; being a member of silver medal winning USA Hockey Team, Salt Lake City Olympics, 2002. Office: NY Islanders Nassau Veterans Meml Coliseum 1255 Hempstead Turnpike Uniondale NY 11553*

GUERIN, CHARLES ALLAN, museum director, artist; b. San Francisco, Feb. 27, 1949; s. John Warren and Charlene (Roovaart) G.; m. Katherine Riccio. BFA, No. Ill. U., 1971, MA, 1973, MFA, 1974. Co-dir. Guerin Design Group, Colorado Springs, Colo., 1972-77; dir. exhbns. Colorado Springs Fine Arts Ctr., 1977-80, curator fine arts, 1980-86; dir. U. Wyo. Art Mus., Laramie, 1986—2000. Author catalogues including various Colorado Springs Fine Arts Ctr. catalogues; contbg. author The Encyclopedia of Crafts, 1974; exhbns. include Purdue U. West Lafayette, Ind., 1974, 76, DePauw U., Greencastle, Ind., 1976, Colorado Springs Fine Arts Ctr., 1977, Mus. of Fine Arts, Santa Fe, N.Mex., 1978, Wis. State U., Platteville, 1972, Suburban Fine Arts Ctr., Highland Park, Ill., 1974, Colo. Woodworking Invitational, Silver Plume, 1977, Colo. Craft Invitational, Arvada, 1981, Leslie Levy Gallery, Scottsdale, Ariz., 1983, Robischon Gallery, Denver, 1983, Adams State Coll., Alamosa, Colo., 1984, U. Wyo. Art Mus., 1986—, Elaine Horwitch Gallery, Scottsdale, 1990; represented in permanent collections Lloyds of London, Dallas, Art Inst. Chgo., Marriott Hotel, Albany, N.Y., Ill. State Mus., Springfield, U.S. West Corp., Denver, Thresholds, Chgo., others. Grantee Nat. Endowment for the Arts, Ill. Arts Council, 1973. Mem. Coll. Art Assn. Am., Am. Assn. Mus., Western Mus. Conf. Office: U Wyo Art Mus PO Box 3807 U Laramie WY 82071-3807

GUERIN, D. MICHAEL, lawyer; b. La Crosse, Wis., Dec. 15, 1940; BS, Marquette U., 1970, JD, 1974. Bar: Wis. 1974, U.S. Dist. Ct. Wis.(Ea. and We. dist.) 1974, U.S. Ct. Appeals (7th cir.) 1974, U.S. Supreme Ct. 1995. Spl. agt. Dept. Justice, 1969—71; ptnr. Gimbel, Reilly, Guerin & Brown, Milw., 1971—. Lectr. at law, trial practice Marquette U., 1979—81, adj. prof. evidence, 1975—; bd. dirs., past pres. Marquette U. Law Alumni Assn., 1995—96. Mem. bd. ethics City of Milw., former police officer. Mem.: ABA, Wis. Bar Assn. (pres. 2005—06), Wis. Acad. Trial Lawyers, Assn. Trial Lawyers Am., State Bar Wis. (pres. 2005—06, 2005—06, mem. bd. govs.), Milw. Bar. Assn. (pres. 2000—01), Tau Epsilon Rho, Alpha Sigma Nu. Office: Gimbel Reilly Guerin & Brown Two Plaza East Ste 1170 330 E Kilbourn Ave Milwaukee WI 53202 Office Phone: 414-271-1440. Office Fax: 414-271-7680. E-mail: dmguerin@grgblaw.com.

GUERIN, DEAN PATRICK, metal products executive; b. St. Paul, Feb. 21, 1922; s. Joseph Henry and Della (Booth) G.; m. Jo Alice Maryman, Sept. 3, 1959; children: Dean William, Stephen Patrick, Mark Joseph. BSBA, Boston U., 1949. With Sperry Gyroscope Co., NYC, 1940-42; registered rep. Chas. A. Day & Son, Boston, 1946-49, Dallas Rupe & Son, 1949-51; from exec. v.p. to chmn. bd. dirs. Eppler, Guerin & Turner, Inc., Dallas, 1951-89; CEO, chmn. bd. dirs. Gen. Aluminum Corp., 1990—94; ind. dir. cos., 1994—. Bd. dirs. Components Corp.; chmn. Archaea Solutions, Inc. Past trustee Marine Mil. Acad. With USMCR, 1942-46, PTO. Mem. Dallas Country Club, Dallas Petroleum Club. Republican. Episcopalian. Home: 9016 Broken Arrow Ln Dallas TX 75209-2406 Office Phone: 214-350-0993.

GUERIN, DIDIER, magazine executive; b. Neuilly/Seine, France, Aug. 2, 1950; came to US 1973; s. Jacques Guerin and Jeanine (Vaesken) Florange; m. Margaret Moray, Dec. 31, 1982; 1 son, Didier Guy Jr. BA in Pub. Law, U. Paris, 1973, BA in Comm., 1973; MA in Journalism, Mich. State U., 1975. Editor Soc. Gen. de Presse, Paris, 1976-79; asst. pub. Look mag., NYC, 1979-81; mng. dir. Hachette Comm. Ltd., London, 1982-93; exec. v.p., dir. Hachette Publs., Inc., NYC, 1983-86, Publs. Filipacchi, NYC, 1983-86; pub. ELLE Mag., 1984-85; pres., CEO, dir. Hachette Publs., Inc., NYC, 1987-91; pres., CEO Publs. Filipacchi, NYC, 1987-91, Interdeco Inc., NYC, 1989-91, Hachette-Filipacchi Asia-Pacific, Sydney, 1991-95, Conde Nast Asia-Pacific, Sydney, 1995-2000, Media Convergence Asia-Pacific, Sydney, 2000—. Chmn. The Conde Nast Publs. Pty. Ltd. (VOGUE Australia), Sydney, 1995-2000, The Conde Nast Publs. Pte. Ltd. (VOGUE Singapore), Singapore, 1995-97, The Conde Nast China (VOGUE, GQ Taiwan), Taipei, 1996-2000, Nikkei-Conde Nast (VOGUE Nippon), Tokyo, 1997-2000, Interculture Comm. Ltd., Taipei, 1996-2000; chmn. bd. Toyo Fashion Kaihatsu, Tokyo, 1984-92, Hachette-Consol. Press. (ELLE Australia), Sydney, 1990-95, Hachette Filipacchi Australia, Sydney, 1990-95, Hachette-Interculture, (ELLE Taiwan), Taipei, 1992-95, Hachette Mags. Ltd., Hong Kong, 1993-95, ELLE Mag. Ltd. (ELLE Hong Kong), 1993-95, Hachette Filipacchi-Post, Bangkok (ELLE Thailand), 1994-95, Hachette Filipacchi Japan Ltd., Tokyo (Elle Japan); fgn. trade advisor French Govt., 1988—; mem. bd. dirs. Globecast, Australia, 2007—. Office: Media Convergence Asia-Pacific Knox Manor 17 Knox St Double Bay NSW 2028 Australia Office Phone: 612-9327-8966. E-mail: didier@mediaconv.com.

GUERRA, ALDO BENJAMIN, plastic and cosmetic surgeon; b. Managua, Nicaragua, Dec. 10, 1969; arrived in U.S., 1981; s. Aldo Antonio and Nelly Beatriz Guerra. BS in Biology, U. Calif., San Diego, 1992, MD, 1996. Diplomate Am. Bd. of Plastic Surgery. Chief cosmetic surgeon (face and boby) Aesthetic Surg. Assocs., Metairie, La., 2004—; chief cosmetic surgeon (face and body) McCollough Inst. Appearance and Health, Gulf Shores, Ala., 2004—; dir., chief cosmetic surgery Ab Guerra Plastic Surgery Clinic and Skin Care Ctr., Phoenix. Asst. prof. La. State U., New Orleans, 2002—04. Author: Cosmetic Surgery: A Consumer's Guide to Aesthetic Plastic Surgery, 2004; contbr. articles to profl. jours. Hipanic role model, cmty. outreach Hispanic Med. Assn. of La., Metairie, 2003—05. Named one of Top 100 Hispanic, New Orleans Metro Area, Vocero News Mag., 2004. Mem.: Hispanic Med. Assn. of La. (assoc.). Achievements include first to use new reconstructive techniques in children. Avocations: traveling, sailing. Office: AB Guerra Plastic Surgery Clinic and Skin Care Ctr 6036 N 19th Ave Ste 510 Phoenix AZ 85015 Home: 40402 N Copper Basin Trl Anthem AZ 85086-1836 Home Phone: 504-481-3200; Office Phone: 602-246-3223. Office Fax: 602-249-1282. Personal E-mail: aldissimo1@hotmail.com. E-mail: drguerra@gmail.com.

GUERRA, ALMA DEL ROSARIO, music educator; b. H. Matamoros, Tamaulipas, Mex., Nov. 10, 1953; d. Marin and Eva González de Guerra. Contador Privado, Academia Comercial José Arrese, Mexico, 1972; A Magna Cum Laude in Fine Arts Music (hon.), Tex. Southmost Coll., 1978; BA, Pan Am. U., 1980. Choir dir. Colegio La Salle, H. Matamoros, 1980—81, Secundaria Fed. No. 5, H. Matamoros, 1981—82; music tchr. Colegio Don Bosco, H. Matamoros, 1982—83; piano tchr., prin. Estudio de Música Armonía, H. Matamoros, 1981—2006. Music counselor Guadalupe's Cath. Ch., Valle Hermoso, Tamaulipas, Mexico, 1999—2000; judge practial piano examinations Nat. Guild Piano Tchrs., Austin, Tex., 1999; choir mem. Sacred Heart's Cath. Ch., H. Matamoros, 1999; choir mem., organist San Francisco's Cath. Ch., H. Matamoros, 2000—03. Min. San Francisco de Asís Cath. Ch., 2000—05. Recipient Nat. Honor Roll Guild Tchrs., Nat. Guild Piano Tchrs., 1983-2005; scholar Good Neighbor, Pan Am. U., 1978, 1979, 1980. Mem.: Nat. Guild Piano Tchrs. Roman Catholic. Achievements include enrolling students for Theory and Practical Piano Examinations for associated bd. Royal Schools of Music from London. Avocations: reading, travel, composing music, walking. Personal E-mail: ema_200310@hotmail.com.

GUERRA, LARRY CACAO, engineer, researcher; arrived in US, 2001; s. Francisco and Pacunda Guerra; m. Mercedes Deriquito, Jan. 20, 1990; 1 child, Ruth Isabel; 1 child, Pamela. BSc in Agrl. Engring., U. Philippines Los Banos, 1983; M Engring., Asian Inst. Tech., Klongluang, Thailand, 1986; PhD, Australian Nat. U., Canberra, 1996. Rsch. asst. U. Philippines Los Banos, 1983—84, asst. prof., 1996—2001, divsn. chmn., 2001; rsch. asst. Internat. Rice Rsch. Inst., Los Banos, 1986—91, cons., 1995—96; rschr. Australian Nat. U., 1991—94; postdoctoral rsch. assoc. U. Ga., Griffin, 2001—07; environ. engr. Ga. Dept. Natural Resources, Environ. Protection Divsn., Atlanta, 2007—. Cons. Gaia South, Inc., Makati City, Philippines, 1996—98, Ecosphere Tech. Mgmt., Inc., Los Banos, 1997—98, Internat. Rice Rsch. Inst., Los Banos, 1997, Tetratech EM, Inc., Pasig City, Philippines. Mem. consultation bd. World Jour. Agrl. Scis.; contbr. articles to profl. jours., chpts. to books. Grantee, Philippine Nat. Bank, 1979—83; scholar, Asian Inst. of Tech., 1985—86; Equity and Merit scholar, Australian Agy. for Internat. Devel., 1991—95. Mem.: AAAS, Internat. Consortium Agrl. Sys. Applications, Internat. Soc. Agrometeorology, Soil Sci. Soc. of Am., Crop Sci. Soc. of Am., Am. Soc. Agronomy, Am. Soc. Agrl. and Biol. Engrs., Gamma Sigma Delta (life). Baptist. Office: Ga Dept Natural Resources Environ Protectional Divsn 4220 Internat Pkwy Ste 101 Atlanta GA 30354 Personal E-mail: larryguerra@yahoo.com.

GUERRANT, DAVID EDWARD, retired food company executive; b. Elizaville, Ky., Sept. 27, 1919; s. William Upton and Claire (Jordan) G.; m. Charlotte L. Lander, Feb. 6, 1942; children: Stephen, Jeffrey. BS, Kans. State U., 1941. With Potts-Turnbull Agy., Kansas City, Mo., 1941-48; creative dir. Campbell-Ewald Co., Chgo., 1948-51; with John W. Shaw Advt., Inc., Chgo., 1951-61, pres., 1959-61, MacFarland, Aveyard & Co., Chgo., 1961-64; pres., v.p. mktg. Libby, McNeill & Libby, Chgo., 1964-68, pres., CEO, 1968-73, chmn. bd., 1971-77; chmn., pres., CEO Nestlé Co., Inc., White Plains, NY, 1973-81, Nestlé Enterprises Inc. (holding co. for Nestlé Co. Inc., Libby, McNeill & Libby and Stouffers Inc.), 1977-83; ret., 1983. Mem.: Island Country (Marco Island, Fla.). Presbyterian. Home: 591 Hammock Ct Marco Island FL 34145-5848

GUERRANT, RICHARD LITTLETON, medical educator; b. Roanoke, Va., July 21, 1943; s. Richard Francis and Sara Young (Davis) G.; m. Nancy Brearley, June 5, 1965; children: Jeffrey L., Amy Lee Guerrant Perkins, David I. BS, Davidson Coll., NC, 1964; MD, U. Va., 1968. Intern Harvard Med. Sch./Boston City Hosp., 1968-69, asst. resident, 1969-70; clin. assoc. NIH, Dacca, Bangladesh, 1970-71, NIH/Johns Hopkins U., Balt., 1971-72; chief resident U. Va., Charlottesville, 1972-73, fellow in infectious diseases, 1973-74, from asst. to assoc. prof., 1974-81, prof. internat. medicine, 1981—. Hon. prof. Fed. U. Ceará, Fortaleza, Brazil, 1994; Hunter prof U. Va., 1991—, dir. office internat. health, 1995—; mem. study sect. NIH, Bethesda, Md., 1993-97, VA Merit Rev., Washington, 1984-87; active WHO-Sci. Working Group, Geneva, Switzerland, 1987-89. Contbr. over 400 articles to profl. jours.; editor: At the Edge of Development, 1996, Infections of the GI Tract, 1997, Tropical Infectious Diseases: Principles, Pathogens and Practice, 1999. Chmn. Va. Ptnrs. of the Ams., 1985-87; chmn. U.S.-Japan Cholera Panel, Bethesda, Md., 1991—. Recipient Horsley Meml. Rsch. prize, 1974, Emilio Ribas medal Brazilian Infectious Disease Soc., Bahia, 1997. Fellow ACP, Infectious Diseases Soc. Am. (Smadel medal 1993, Abbott award 1997), Royal Soc. Tropical Medicine and Hygiene; mem. Am. Soc. Tropical Medicine and Hygiene (pres. 1997-98), Am. Soc. Microbiology (chmn. divsn. B 1985), Inst. Medicine, 2004. Avocation: sailing. Home: 2507 Northfield Rd Charlottesville VA 22901-1230 Office: U Va Sch Medicine HSC 485 Charlottesville VA 22908 E-mail: guerrant@virginia.edu.

GUERRERA, LISA E., financial planner; d. James and Vincenza Guerrera. BS, Cornell U., Ithaca, NY, 1986. Adminstrv. asst. Bankers Trust, NYC, 1987—90; mktg. com. specialist Chase Manhattan, NYC, 1990—92; v.p. mktg. and corp. com. SunAm. Asset Mgmt., NYC, 1992—94; account mgr. TIAA-CREF, NYC, 1995—2000; fin. advisor Ameriprise Fin., Mitchel Field, NY, 2002—. Counselor My Sister's Pl., Westchester County, NY, 1997—99; bd. dirs. Daus. of Wisdom, Islip, 2006—. Recipient Chmn.'s award, Am. Express Fin. Advisors, 2004, Excellence award, Life Communicators Assn., 1997; scholar, Am. Agriculturist Found., 1983, 1984. Mem.: The Fin. Planning Assn., Cornell Club. Avocations: travel, yoga, theater, films. Office: Ameriprise Financial 333 Earle Ovington Boulevard Suite 1010 Uniondale NY 11553 Office Phone: 516-228-0100 ext. 212. Office Fax: 516-228-0101. Business E-Mail: lisa.e.guerrera@ampf.com.

GUERRERO, DONNA MARIE, sales executive; b. LA, Apr. 27, 1964; d. Henry Joseph Guerrero and Dolores Catherine Veiga. BA, Whittier Coll., 1985; MPA, Harvard U., 1988. Presdl. intern, pub. rels. mgr. U.S. EEOC, Washington, Houston, 1988—98; profl. sales & leasing cons. Moss Bros. Toyota, Moreno Valley, Calif., 2002—. Bd. mem. Nat. Hispanic Media Coalition, LA, 1994—98. Adv. bd. League of United Latin Am. Citizens, Houston, 1995—97. Recipient Heroes of Reinvention Award, V.P. Al Gore's Nat. Performance Rev., 1994. Roman Catholic. Avocations: christian devotional/spirituality, holistic health, sports memorabilia/collectibles. Home: 11037 Le Grand Ln Moreno Valley CA 92557 Personal E-mail: dguerrero@tmo.blackberry.net.

GUERRERO, LISA (LISA GUERRERO-COLES), former sports reporter; b. Chgo., Apr. 8, 1964; m. Scott Erickson, Feb. 3, 2004. Cheerleader Los Angeles Rams; dir, choreographer Atlanta Falcons Cheerleaders, New England Patriots; reporter Extra, 1994; co-host Sports Geniuses, 2000; reporter The Best Damn Sports Show Period!, FoxSportsNet, 2000—03; sideline reporter Monday Night Football, ABC, 2003—04. Actress: (films) Batman Returns, 1992; Love Potion No. 9, 1992; Fire Down Below, 1997; (TV series) Wild West Showdown, 1994; Sunset Beach, 1998—99. Vol. Salvation Army, Cedar Sinai Med. Ctr. Achievements include appearing in over 200 commercials and the covers of Maxim and FHM.

GUERRERO, REUBEN CASTRO, oncologist, internist; b. Manila, Philippines, Aug. 22, 1935; came to U.S., 1962, naturalized, 1978; s. Jacobo Tolentino and Francisca Claravall (Castro) G.; m. Celina V. Sison, June 18, 1962; children: Chiarina, Leonora, Anthony Paul. AA, U. Philippines, Manila, 1952; MD, U. Philippines, 1957. Intern Philippine Gen. Hosp., Manila, 1956-57; mem. faculty Coll. Medicine, U. Philippines, 1957-62; resident Ch. Home and Hosp., Balt., 1962-64, chief resident, 1965-66; asst. prof. medicine, chief chemotherapy divsn. Philippines and Cancer Inst., 1968-73; med. oncologist, chmn. cancer com., chmn. dept. hematology Straub Clinic & Hosp., Honolulu, 1973—. Clin. assoc. prof. John A. Burns Sch. Medicine, U. Hawaii; chmn. research Philippine Cancer Soc., 1969-73; pres. Hawaii-Pacific div. Am. Cancer Soc., 1989-90; CME coord. Aloha Med. Misson. Contbr. articles to profl. jours. With Philippine Army, Res.,1957-58. Postdoctoral fellow medicine Johns Hopkins Hosp., Balt., 1964-65, postdoctoral fellow med. oncology, 1966-68. Fellow ACP; mem. Am. Soc. Internat. Medicine, Am. Soc. Clin. Oncology, Philippine Soc. Med. Oncology, Honolulu County Med. Soc., Hawaii Med. Assn. (cancer commn.), Philippine Med. Assn. Hawaii (pres. 1998-99), AMA, Am. Geriatric Soc., Aerospace Med. Assn., Honolulu Marathon Assn., Honolulu Club. Republican. Roman Catholic. Home: 2159 Okoa St Honolulu HI 96821-2647 Office: Straub Clinic and Hosp 888 S King St Honolulu HI 96813-3083 Office Phone: 808-522-3808. Personal E-mail: reubenguerrero@aol.com. Business E-Mail: rguerrero@straub.net.

GUERRERO, VLADIMIR ALVINO, professional baseball player; b. Nizao Bani, Dominican Republic, Feb. 9, 1976; Outfielder Montreal Expos, 1996—2004, LA Angels of Anaheim (formerly Anaheim Angels), 2004—. Named Am. League MVP, 2004; named to Nat. League All-Star Team, 1999—2002, Am. League All-Star Team, 2004—07; recipient Silver Slugger award, 1999—2000, 2002, 2004—06. Achievements include leading the Nat. League in hits (206), 2002; led the Am. League in runs (124), 2004; won the 2007 Home Run Derby. Mailing: LA Angels of Anaheim 2000 Gene Autry Way Anaheim CA 92806*

GUERRI, WILLIAM GRANT, lawyer; b. Higbee, Mo., Mar. 30, 1921; s. Grant and Pearl (Zambelli) G.; m. Millicent K. Branding; children: Paula Ann Guerri Baker, Glenda Kay, William Grant. AB, Central Meth. U., 1943; LLB, Columbia, 1946. Bar: NY 1946, Mo. 1947. Ptnr. Thompson Coburn LLP, St. Louis, 1956—. Mem. bd. editors: Columbia Law Rev, 1945-46. Hon. mem. bd. dirs. St. Louis Heart Assn., chmn., 1972-73; bd. dirs. United Way Greater St. Louis, 1976-94; curator Ctrl. Meth. U., 1981-97. Fellow The Fellows of Am. Bar; mem. ABA, Mo. Bar Assn. (trustee 1984-92), Bar Assn. Met. St. Louis, Assn. of Bar of City of N.Y., Am. Law Inst., Am. Judicature Soc., Noonday Club, Round Table Club, Phi Delta Phi. Home: Apt 308 14300 Conway Meadows Ct E Chesterfield MO 63017-9612 Office: Thompson Coburn LLP Ste 3500 1 US Bank Plz Saint Louis MO 63101-1643 Office Phone: 314-552-6000. Business E-Mail: wguerri@thompsoncoburn.com.

GUERTIN, ROBERT POWELL, physics professor, dean; b. Trenton, NJ, July 5, 1939; s. Alfred N. and Rhoda (Thomas) G.; m. Margaret Eipper, Aug. 13, 1966 (div. 1999); children: Lynn Frances, Laura Thomas. BS, Trinity Coll., 1961; MA, Wesleyan U., 1963; PhD, U. Rochester, 1969. Asst. prof. physics Tufts U., Medford, Mass., 1968-75, assoc. prof., 1975-83, prof., 1983—, dean Grad. Sch. Arts and Scis., 1985-96, dean Grad. Sch. Rsch. and Profl. Edn., 1994-96. Bd. govs. Univ. Press New England, Hanover, N.H., 1985-96, chmn., 1986-87, 93-94; vis. scientist Nat. High Magnetic Field Lab., Fla., 1996—. Editor books on crystalline electric fields and anomalous rare earth magnetic effects, 1980, 83, 90, 94; contbr. articles to profl. jours. Mem. Lucretia Crocker adv. council Commonwealth Mass., 1986—; bd. dirs. N.E. Assn. Grad. Schs. NSF and NIH rsch. award, 1972-90. Mem. Am. Phys. Soc. (mem. various coms. 1968—). Unitarian Universalist. Avocations: piano, swimming. Home: Apt 1 345 Commonwealth Ave Boston MA 02115-1928 Home Phone: 617-262-4912; Office Phone: 617-627-3439. E-mail: robert.guertin@tufts.edu.

GUERTIN, TIMOTHY E., medical products executive; BS in Elec. Engring. and Computer Scis., U. Calif., Berkeley. With Varian Med. Systems, Palo Alto, Calif., 1976—, gen. mgr. customer support, 1982—89, gen. mgr., pres. Oncology Systems, 1990—2005, corp. v.p., 1992—99, exec. v.p., 1999—2005, pres., COO, 2005—06, pres., CEO, 2006—. Chmn. bd. dirs., mem. Silicon Valley/No. Calif. Coun. Am. Electronics Assn.; bd. dirs. Diagnostic Imaging sect., chmn. Therapy Systems divsn. Nat. Elec. Mfrs. Assn.; mem. corp. coun. Am. Soc. Therapeutic Radiology and Oncology, Can. Assn. Radiation Oncologists. Office: Varian Med Systems 3100 Hansen Way Palo Alto CA 94304 Office Phone: 650-493-4000. Office Fax: 650-842-5196.*

GUESON, EMERITA TORRES, obstetrician, gynecologist; b. Angeles City, The Philippines, Jan. 4, 1942; came to U.S., 1964; d. Lina (Torres) Gueson. AA, U. Sto. Tomas, Manila, Philippines, 1958, MD, 1963. Resident in ob-gyn. Phila. Gen. Hosp., 1966-71; attending physician Nazareth Hosp., Phila., 1973—, Holy Redeemer Hosp., Meadowbrook, Pa., 1983—. Bd. dirs. Physicians Who Care; lectr. healthcare issues to consumer groups, Phila. Author: Doctors Under Fire, 1989, Scales of Justice: Exploring the Wilderness of Health Care and Society's Moral Conscience, 1992, Do HMO's Cut Costs.and Lives, 1997, Survival Guide for HMO Patients, 1997; pub. ThereseVision Publs.; also med. writer, screenplay writer, line dir., prodr. Hon. co-chair physicians adv. bd. Republican Nat. Com. Fellow ACOG, ACP; mem. AMA, Pa. Med. Soc., Philadelphia County Med. Soc., Pro-Life Ob.-Gynecologists (charter). Avocations: writing, painting, refinishing furniture. Office: 3336 Aldine St Philadelphia PA 19136-3802 E-mail: therese44@aol.com.

GUEST, CHRISTOPHER, actor, director, screenwriter; b. NYC, Feb. 5, 1948; m. Jamie Lee Curtis, Dec. 18, 1984; 2 children. Grad., High Sch. Music and Art, NYC; student, Bard Coll., NYU. Appeared in Broadway plays Room Service (debut) 1970, Moonchildren, 1972; Off-Broadway plays include National Lampoon's Lemmings (also writer), 1973, East Lynne, 1975; actor: (films) The Hospital, 1971, The Hot Rock, 1972, Death Wish, 1974, The Fortune, 1975, La Honte de la Jungle, 1975, Girlfriends, 1978, The Last Word, 1979, The Long Riders, 1980, The Missing Link, 1980, Heartbeeps, 1981, Little Shop of Horrors, 1986, Beyond Therapy, 1987, The Princess Bride, 1987, Sticky Fingers, 1988, A Few Good Men, 1992, Small Soldiers (voice), 1998, Mrs. Henderson Presents, 2005; actor, writer & composer: This is Spinal Tap, 1984; actor, writer, dir., composer: Waiting for Guffman, 1996, Best in Show, 2000, A Mighty Wind, 2003, For Your Consideration, 2006; dir.: The Big Picture, 1989, Edwards & Hunt, 1997, Almost Heroes, 1998; actor: (TV films) It Happened One Christmas, 1977, Haywire, 1980, Million Dollar Infield, 1982, A Piano for Mrs. Cimino, 1982, Close Ties, 1983; dir. (TV films): Attack of the 50 ft. Woman, 1993, D.O.A., 1999; actor, writer & dir.: (TV series) Saturday Night Live with Howard Cosell, 1975, Saturday Night Live, 1984-85, Morton & Hayes, 1991; TV specials: The Lily Tomlin Special (also writer, Emmy award 1976), 1975, Billion Dollar Bubble, 1977, How to Survive the 70's and Maybe Even Bump into Happiness, 1978, Martin Short Concert for the North Americas, 1985, Billy Crystal-Don't Get me Started, 1986; albums: Six albums with National Lampoon, This is Spinal Tap, 1984, Break like the Wind (with Spinal Tap), 1992. Co-recipient Grammy award for Best Song (A Mighty Wind) Written for a Motion Picture, 2004. Office: 190 N Canon DR STE 302 Beverly Hills CA 90210-5314*

GUEST, FLOYD EMORY, JR., lawyer; b. Oglethorpe, Ga., May 5, 1929; s. Floyd Emory and Eula Belle (Jones) G.; m. Mary E. Vick, Oct. 12, 1955 (div. 1959); 1 child, Victoria Elizabeth; m. Martha J. Roy, Oct. 12, 1963; children: Alyson Jane, Emory Roy. AB in Bus. Adminstrn., Duke U., 1952; JD, U. Tex., 1962; MS in Fin. Svcs., Am. Coll., 1980. Bar: Tex. 1962. V.p., controller Cosmopolitan Life, Houston, 1952-59; trust officer Bank of Southwest, 1962-67, Capital Nat. Bank, 1967-69; chmn. Profl. Businessmen Assn. Retirement Plans Co., Houston, 1969—. Pres. Southgate Civic Assn., Houston, 1967, 68. Served to capt. USAFR, 1952-67. Mem. SAR, Tex. Bar Assn., Houston Bar Assn., Houston Estate Planning Coun. Delta Theta Phi Law Frat. (pres. Houston alumni 1964). Lodges: Downtown Optimist (pres. 1982-83), Masons, K.T. Republican. Home: 5826 Doliver Dr Houston TX 77057-2470 Office: Action Advisors Inc 5005 Mitchelldale St Ste 174 Houston TX 77092-7242 Home Phone: 713-952-9479; Office Phone: 713-680-0530. Personal E-mail: floydguest@hotmail.com.

GUEST, RITA CARSON, interior designer; b. Atlanta, Aug. 17, 1950; d. Walter Harold and Doris Rebecca Carson; m. John Franklin Guest Jr., Jan. 20, 1979. B of Visual Arts, Ga. State U., 1973. Registered interior designer Ga., Fla., D.C., Ala. Pres., dir. design Carson Guest, Inc., Atlanta, 1984—. Lectr. in field. Bd. dirs. Mus. of Design, Atlanta, 2002—. Recipient 5 1st place awards Gwinnett Home Show and Interior Design Expo, 1991, Architecture Woodwork Inst. award for Excellence, 2002; named Designer of Yr., Atlanta Decorative Art Ctr., 2006. Fellow: ASID; mem.: Am. Soc. Interior Designers (Ga. chpt. dir. 1984, treas. 1985—86, nominating com. 1987, chmn. interprofl. devel. com. 1988—90, pres.-elect 1991—92, pres. 1992—93, nat. office coun. of pres.'s steering com. 1993—94, nat. dir. for region 14 1995—96, legis. adv. coun. 1997—98, mem. fellows coun. 1997—99, nat. bd. dirs. 2000—02, awards com. 2003, nat. nominating com. 2003, nat. pres. elect 2006—07, pres. 2007—, Comml. Design Project award 1983, Ga. chpt. Presdl. citation 1984, Residential Design award 1987, Ga. chpt. 1st place Office Design award 1987, Comml. Offices 1st place Project award 1989, Profl. Office Design award 1989, 1st place Libr. Design/1st place Comml. Offices award 1991, Pres. citation 1991, Designer of Yr. 1992, 2 Comml. Project awards 1992, 1st place Nat. Project award 1993, 1st place Instnl. Design award 1994, 1st place Healthcare Project award 1995, Ga. chpt. Silver Contract Design award 2000, Bronze Contract Design award 2001, Gold Instl. award 2002, Gold Comml. award 2003, Residential Singular Space Gold award 2004, Custom Furniture Silver and Bronze award 2004, Residential Bronze award 2004, Silver Corp. award 2004, Gold Instl. award 2005, Contract Singular Space Gold award 2005, Residential Bronze award 2005, Gold Corp. award 2006, Contract Singular Space Silver award 2006, Ga. Chpt. Gold award 2007, Ga. Chpt. Silver award 2007, Ga. Chpt. Bronze award 2007), Ga. Alliance Interior Design Profls. (pres. 1991—92, bd. advisors 1993—98), Atlanta C. of C. Presbyterian. Avocation: painting. Office: Carson Guest Inc 1776 Peachtree St NW Ste 120 Atlanta GA 30309 Office Phone: 404-873-3663. Business E-Mail: ritaguest@carsonguest.com.

GUEUDET, EDOUARD PHILIPPE, financial consultant; b. Paris, Jan. 20, 1976; s. Patrick E. Gueudet and Anne I. Coquillon. JD, U. Paris II Panthéon-Assas, 1999; MS, Inst. Supérieur du Commerce de Paris, 2000; LLM in Internat. Legal Studies, Am. U., 2002; MBA, Kogod Sch. Bus., 2006. English U. Pa., 2001. Legal asst. to the sales mgmt. Procar S.A., Paris, 2000, project mgr., 2000—01, Compagnie Financière d'Organisation et de Gestion, Paris, 2002, Gueudet Frères S.A., 2002—05; cons., 2006—07; financier, assoc. Hottinger & Cie, Geneva, 2007—. Founding mem. Union pour un Mouvement Populaire, Paris, 2002. Mem.: French-Am. Found., Am. U. Alumni France (pres. 2004—06, v.p. 2006), Old Fort Bay Club (The Bahamas), The Travellers Paris, Cercle Saint-Germain-des-Près, Cercle France-Amériques, Automobile Club of France. Avocations: genealogy, skiing, golf, running. Office: Hottinger & Cie Place des Bergues 3 Case Postale 1620 CH-1211 Geneva Switzerland Address: 208 E 51st St #222 New York NY 10022 E-mail: egueudet@alum.american.edu.

GUEVARA, AMADO, professional soccer player; b. Tegucigalpa, Honduras, May 2, 1976; married; 1 child. Midfielder CD Motagua, Honduras League, 2003, Major League Soccer, All-Star Team, 2003, 2004, MetroStars, Major League Soccer, East Rutherford, NJ, 2003—. Named Tournament Most Valuable Player, Copa América, 2001, Most Valuable Player, Major League Soccer, All-Star Game, 2004. Led MetroStars in game-winning assists in 2003. Office: MetroStars Meadowlands Sports Complex 50 State Rt 120 East Rutherford NJ 07073

GUGEL, CRAIG THOMAS, advertising executive; b. Detroit, Jan. 18, 1954; s. Paul Walter and Patricia Angela (Sullivan) G. BA, U. Windsor, Ont., Can., 1976. Asst. br. mgr. Mich. Nat. Bank, Livonia, 1975—77; analyst media rsch. Kenyon & Eckhardt, Inc., Birmingham, Mich. and NYC, 1977—81, supr. media rsch. NYC, 1981—82; v.p., asst. dir. media rsch. McCann-Erickson, Inc., NYC, 1982—84; v.p., dir. media rsch. Foote, Cone & Belding, Inc., NYC, 1984—86; sr. v.p., corp. dir. media resources Bozell, Jacobs, Kenyon & Eckhardt, Inc., NYC, 1986—88; sr. v.p., dir. media research Bates Worldwide, Inc., NYC, 1988—91, sr. v.p., exec. dir. media rsch. and tech., 1991—94, sr. v.p., exec. dir. interactive media and rsch., 1994—95, exec. v.p. new media and interactive rsch., 1995—97, exec. v.p., dir. media resources and rsch., 1997; pres., CEO Atlantic Analytics, Ltd. (formerly Manhattan-Pacific Multimedia Inc.), NYC, 1997—; chief rsch. svcs. officer Organic, Inc., NYC, 1997—98; exec. v.p., dir. strategic insights Optimedia Internat., NYC, 2001—03; exec. v.p. worldwide analytics and strategy Interactive Market Sys., Inc., NYC, 2003—06; pres. Telmar Info. Svcs. Corp., NYC, 2007—. Mem.: European Soc. Opinion and Mktg. Rsch., Advt. Rsch. Found. (bd. dirs. 1995—2001, chmn. interactive media com., co-chmn. digital media measurement coun.). Avocations: reading, theater, computers.

GUGEL, MERILYNN SUE, artist; b. Van Wert, Ohio, Nov. 22, 1938; d. Merlin Harvey Smith and Margaret Ann Louise Miller; m. Lorenz Walter Gugel, Dec. 28, 1959 (dec. 1980); children: Scott, Craig, Kristina. Studied with David Humphreys Miller, 1957; student, U. N.Mex., 1965-67, U. Alaska, 1967-71. Tchr. art therapy ARC, El Paso; art tchr. Shiva Paint Co., El Paso, 1972-74, Officers Club, El Paso, Fairbanks, Alaska, 1975-80, Umpqua C.C., 1975—; art tchr. spl. arts, disabilities Umpqua Valley Arts Ctr. One-woman shows include Tolly's Art and Antiques, Oakland, Oreg., Art Mill Gallery, Roseburg, Oreg., Vision Gallery, Sutharlin, Umpqua Valley Art Ctr., Roseburg, 2004, Roseburg Art Ctr., 2004, Bend City Hall, Oreg., 2003, exhibited in group shows at Rickerts Gallery, Newport, Oreg., Fischer Galleries, Washington, Represented in permanent collections Bapt. State Conv. Bldg., Anchorage, Pioneer Hall of Fame, Burrough Pub. Libr., Fairbanks, Alaska, Roseburg Forest Products, Trent Colls., Wash., Oreg., Starfire Lumber, Marsha Leaptrout Collection, Ford Found., others. Charter mem. Nat. Mus. Women in the Arts. Mem. Fairbanks Art Assn. (pres., award), Umpqua Valley Arts Assn. (pres., award), Nat. Soc. Lit. and the Arts, Willamette We. Artists Assn. Republican. Avocations: music, politics. Home: 550 S State St Apt 33 Sutherlin OR 97479 E-mail: lindaf@teleport.com.

GUGGENHEIM, ALAN ANDRE ALBERT PAUL EDOUARD, international consultant; b. Paris, May 12, 1950; arrived in USA, 1982, naturalized, 1991; s. Jacques and Micheline (Raffalovich) Guggenheim; m. Suzanne Marton, Mar. 20, 1974; 1 child, Valerie. BS, U. Paris, 1971; MSCE, Ecole Speciale des Travaux Publics, Paris, 1974; grad., French Command-Gen. Staff Res. Coll., 1981. Asst. prof. math. Nat. Sch. Arts and Architecture, Paris, 1972-75; civil engr. Societe Routiere Colas, Paris, 1976-77, French Antilles, 1977-78; chief exec. officer, exec. dir. C.R.P.G., Pointe A Pitre, Guadeloupe, 1978-81; chief exec. officer, chmn. San Joaquin Software Systems, Inc., Stockton, Calif., 1982-86, CalCar Investment Svcs., Inc., Newbury Park, Calif., 1983—; CEO NagraStar, Englewood, Colo., 2000—07; exec. v.p. Kudelski Group, Switzerland, 2003—07; chmn. Nagr a USA, Inc., 2004—07; pres. CEO Open TV, 2007—. Bd. mem. Sucmanu, Paris, 1976-82, OpenTV, 2007-; bd. organizers Pacific State Bank, Stockton, Calif., 1985-87. Exec. Editor newsletter L'Action Universitaire, 1970-76. Mem. French Res. Policy Rev. Bd., Paris, 1971-77; mem. Ventura County Rep. Cen. Com., Rep. Presdl. Task Force, Rep. Campaign Coun.; mem. bd. Calif. Rep. Assembly; candidate Rep. 37th Assembly Dist., Calif.; mem. cen. com. Calif. Rep. Party, 1992-2001. Maj. French Res., 1981. Recipient Gold Medal Omnium Technique Holding, 1975. Fellow Engr. and Scientist France; mem. AAAS, ADPA, Assn. U.S. Army, Rotary. Republican. Roman Catholic. Avocations: skiing, boating, classical music. Home and Office: Open TV 3047 Three Springs Rd Mount Hamilton CA 95140-9747 Office Phone: 415-962-5110. Personal E-mail: alan.guggenheim@cis-tech.com. Business E-Mail: alan.guggenheim@opentv.com.

GUGGENHEIM, BARBARA SUE, art consultant; b. Phila., Dec. 10, 1946; d. Lester and Sylvia Guggenheim; m. Bertram Harris Fields. BA, Douglass Coll., New Brunswick, NJ, 1968; MA, Columbia U., NYC, 1969; MPhil, PhD, Columbia U., 1976. Instr. art history Bloomfield Coll., NJ, 1969—72, Douglass Coll., New Brunswick, 1972; asst. Sotheby's, 1970—71, head Am. Art, 1974—78; lectr. Whitney Mus. Art, NYC, 1969—86; pres. Art Tours Manhattan, 1976—80, Guggenheim, Asher Assocs., 1981—. Lectr. in field. Author: Decorating on Ebay, 2005, Handkerchiefs: A Collector's Guide I, 2004, Handkerchiefs: A Collector's Guide II, 2005, Your Personal Assistant, 2006; contbr. articles to profl. jours. Grantee, Columbia U., 1972. Mem.: AAUW, Cosmopolitan Club. Avocation: tennis. Office: 139 S Beverly Dr Beverly Hills CA 90212

GUGGENHEIM, DAVIS, film and TV director, producer; b. 1964; s. Charles and Marion Guggenheim; m. Elisabeth Shue, 1994; 3 children. Grad., Brown U., Providence, RI, 1986. Bd. dirs. Creative Commons, San Francisco, 2003—. Assoc. prodr.: (films) Don't Tell Mom the Babysitter's Dead, 1991; dir.: (TV series) Sisters, 1991, Party of Five, 1994, Charlie Grace, 1995, NYPD Blue (3 episodes), 1995—96, Relativity, 1996, ER (1 episode), 1996, C-16: FBI (1 episode), 1997, The Visitor (1 episode), 1997, 24 (2 episodes), 2002, Alias (1 episode), 2002, The Shield (1 episode), 2003, Deadwood (2 episodes), 2004, Numb3rs (1 episode), 2005, 3 lbs. (1 episode), 2006, The Unit (1 episode), 2006, Wanted (1 episode), 2005; (films) Breaking and Entering, 1992, Gossip, 2000; (documentaries) The Art of Norton Simon, 1999; dir., dir.: (documentaries) Teach, 2006; co-prodr.: (films) The Opposite Sex and How to Live with Them, 1993; dir., prodr.: (TV films) The First Yr., 2001; (TV series) Deadwood (12 episodes), 2004; exec. prodr.: (films) Training Day, 2001; prodr., exec. prodr.: (films) An Inconvenient Truth, 2001 (Best Documentary, Nat. Bd. Rev., 2006, Best Nonfiction film, Nat. Soc. Film Critics, 2007). Office: Creative Commons 543 Howard St 5th Fl San Francisco CA 94105-3013*

GUGGENHEIM, FREDERICK GIBSON, psychiatrist, educator; b. Chgo., July 8, 1935; s. Melvin Elias and Marjorie Stone (Gibson) G.; m. Barbary Reed (div. Apr. 1976); m. Olivia Rogers, Nov. 23, 1984; children: Jennifer, Hannah, Russell Alderson, Rhoades Alderson. BA, Yale U., 1957; MD, Columbia U., 1961. Resident in medicine Bellevue Hosp., NYC, 1961-63, Columbia Presbyn. Med. Ctr., NYC, 1963-64; clin. assoc. NIMH, Bethesda, Md., 1964-66; resident in psychiatry Strong Meml. Hosp., Rochester, NY, 1966-69; asst. prof. Harvard Med. Sch., Boston, 1970-79; from asst. in psychiatry to assoc. psychiatrist Mass. Gen. Hosp., Boston, 1969-79; assoc. prof. Southwestern Med. Sch. in Tex., Dallas, 1979-85; Marie Wilson Howells prof. and chair dept. psychiatry U. Ark. for Med. Scis., Little Rock, 1985-2000, prof., 2001—02, prof. and chair emeritus, 2004—; chief psychiat. cons. svc. Univ. Hosp., Little Rock, 2001—02; staff psychiatrist East Bay Mental Health Ctr., Providence, 2002—05; psychiatrist Butler Hosp., 2005—; clin. prof. psychiatry Brown Med. Sch., Providence, 2006—. Mem. nat. adv. com. clin. scholars program Robert Wood Johnson Found., Princeton, N.J., 1988-94; mem. com. on career devel. awards VA, Washington, 1990-95; mem. nat. adv. coun. Substance Abuse and Mental Health Svcs. Adminstrn., 1993-96; chief of staff U. Hosp., 1992-94, sec. med. bd., 1998-2000. Recipient Allison travel fellowship, Yale U., 1956, 1957, Saybrook Fellows prize, 1957, Nancy CA Roeske cert. of recognition for excellence in med. student edn., 2002, Irma Bland MD award for excellence in tchg. residents, 2005, Lifetime Achievement award, Assn. Acad. Psych., 2005. Fellow (Disting. life) Am. Psychiat. Assn., Am. Coll. Psychiatrists, Acad. Psychosomatic Medicine, Assn. Acad. Psychiatry (Disting. life, pres. 1992-93, Life Achievement award 2005); mem. So. Assn. Rsch. in Psychiatry (pres. 1991-92), Am. Assn. Chairmen of Depts. Psychiatry (pres. 1995-96), Ark. Psychiat. Soc. (pres. 1988-89), Cosmos Club of Wash., Alpha Omega Alpha (faculty). Home: 690 Angell St Providence RI 02906-5552 Office: Butler Hosp Partial Hospitalization Program 345 Blackstone Blvd Providence RI 02906 Office Phone: 401-455-6408.

GUGGENHEIM, MARTIN FRANKLIN, lawyer, educator; b. NYC, May 29, 1946; s. Werner and Fanny (Monatt) G.; m. Denise Silverman, May 29, 1969; children: Jamie, Courtney, Lesley. BA, SUNY, Buffalo, 1968; JD, NYU, 1971. Bar: NY 1972, US Dist. Ct. (so. dist. and ea. dist.) NY 1973, US Ct. Appeals (2d cir.) 1974, US Ct. Appeals (3d cir.) 1979, US Ct. Appeals (6th cir.) 1977, US Supreme Ct. 1976. Staff atty. Legal Aid Soc., NYC, 1971-72, dir. spl. litig. unit, juvenile rights divsn., 1972-73; clin. instr. NYU Sch. Law, NYC, 1973-75; staff atty. juvnile rights project ACLU, NYC, 1975-79, acting dir., 1976-77; asst. prof. clin. law NYU, NYC, 1975-77, assoc. prof. clin. law, 1977-79, prof. clin. law, 1980—, Fiorello LaGuardia prof. clin. law, 2005; of counsel Mayerson & Stutman LLP, NYC, 2001—. Exec. dir. Washington Sq. Legal Svcs., Inc., NYC, 1986-2000; pres. Nat. Coalition for Child Protection Reform, 2000—; pres., founding dir. Family Def. Law Project, Inc., NYC, 1992-2000; advisor program for children Edna McConnell Clark Found., 1993-2001; dir. clin. and advocacy programs NYU, 1989-2002; founding dir. Ctr. for Family Representation, NYC, 2002--; cons. juvenile justice stds. project ABA/Inst. Jud. Adminstrn., 1979-81; acting dir. Clin. Advocacy Programs, Sch. of Law NYU, 1988-89. Author: (with Alan Sussman) The Rights of Parents, 1980, Abuse and Neglect Volume, 1982, The Rights of Young People, 2d edit., 1985, (with Anthony G. Amsterdam and Randy Hertz) Trial Manual for Defense Attorneys in Juvenile Court, 1991, (with Alexandra Lowe and Diane Curtis) The Rights of Families, 1996, What's Wrong With Children's Rights, 2005. Dir. William J. Brennan Ctr., NYU, 1995-2000; mem. adv. bd. NYC Adminstrn. Children, 1997—; pres. Nat. Coalition for Child Protection Reform, 2000—. Arthur Garfield Hays Civil Liberties fellow, 1970-71, Criminal Law Edn. and Rsch. fellow, 1969-70; Kathryn A. McDonald award Assn. of the Bar of the City of NY, 2000. Mem. ABA (Livingston Hall award, 2006), Am. Assn. Law Schs., Assn. of Bar of City of NY. Office: NYU Sch Law 5th Fl 245 Sullivan St New York NY 10012 Office Phone: 212-998-6460. Business E-Mail: martin.guggenheim@nyu.edu.

GUGGENHEIMER, HEINRICH WALTER, mathematician, educator; b. Nurnberg, Germany, July 21, 1924; arrived in U.S., 1959; s. Siegfried and Marguerite Erna (Bloch) G.; m. Eva Auguste Horovicz, June 6, 1947; children: S. Michael, Esther H., Tobias I.S., Hanna Y. Diploma in math., Swiss Fed. Inst. Tech., Zurich, 1947, DSc in Math., 1950. Lectr. Hebrew U., Jerusalem, 1954-56; prof. Bar Ilan (Israel) U., 1956-59; assoc. prof. Wash. State U., Pullman, 1959-60, U. Minn., Mpls., 1960-62, prof., 1962-67, Poly U. (formerly Poly. Inst. Bklyn.), 1967—89; prof. emeritus Poly. U. NY (formerly Poly. Inst. Bklyn.), 1989—. Author: Differential Geometry, 2d edit., 1977, Plane Geometry and Its Groups, 1967, Mathematics for Engineering and Science, 1976, Applicable Geometry, 1977, BASIC mathematical Programs for Engineers and Scientists, 1987; (with Eva H. Guggenheimer) Jewish Family Names and Their Origins: An Etymological Dictionary, 1992, German edit., 1996, The Scholar's Haggadah, 1995, Seder Olam: A Translation and Commentary, 1998, The Jerusalem Talmud, bilingual edit., vol. 1, vol. 2, 2000, vol. 3, 2001, vol. 4, 2002, vol. 5, 2003, part III vol. 6, 2004, vol. 7, 2005, vol. 8, 2006, vol. 9, 2007; contbr. articles to profl. jours. With Swiss Army, 1944-54. Mem. Swiss Math. Soc. (life), Math. Assn. Am., Soc. Indsl. Applied Math. Home: PO Box 401 West Hempstead NY 11552-0401

GUGGENHEIMER, TOBIAS IMMANUEL SIMON, architect; b. Basel, Switzerland, Jan. 30, 1953; s. Heinrich Walter and Eva Augusta (Horowicz) G.; m. Lisa Ann Shapiro, June 27, 1976 (div. 1999); children: Anna Bella, Leanora Margaret; m. Yasmin M. DeOcampo, Aug. 11, 2000. BA in Lit., SUNY, Binghamton, 1975; MArch, U. Colo., 1985. Registered architect, N.Y., N.J. Pres. Tobias Guggenheimer Arch., P.C., Dobbs Ferry, N.Y., 1991—. Educator Pratt Inst. Sch. of Architecture, Bklyn., 1987—99; asst. prof. and dir. interior design program Fordham U., Tarrytown, 1999—2003; prof. Parsons Sch. of Design, NYC, 2004—; lectr. in field. Author: A Taliesin Legacy: The Architecture of Frank Lloyd Wright's Apprentices, 1995; contbg. editor: Jour. of Taliesin Fellows, 1996-97; architect: (restorations) Frank Lloyd Wright's Serlin Residence, 1996-97; (projects) Mittman Residence, Spearfish, S.D., 2000; (renovations) Yannuzzi Residence, Tuxedo Park, N.Y., 1997-99, Malek Residence, 1999, Denberg Residence, 2003, Howe Bldg., 2000-02, Holtz-Lamb Residence, 2000, Frank-Mermelstein Residence, 2002, Hunter Residence, 2002, Hanlon Residence, 2002, Shore Residence, 2003, Hellman Residence, 2003, Schmidtberger Residence, 2003, Wells Residence, 2004, Mengel Residence, 2004, Kolleck Residence, 2004, Boukouzis Residence, 2005, Slipp Residence, 2005, Cypers Residence, 2005, Fomenko Residence, 2006, Reede Residence, 2006, others; curator: A Taliesin Legacy: The Independent Work of Frank Lloyd Wright's Apprentices, Pratt Inst. Gallery, 1993, Architectural Competitions in America, 2000. Cons. Village Tuxedo Park, 1999, Frank Lloyd Wright's Reisley Residence, 1999. Mem. AIA, Nat. Coun. Archtl. Registration Bds. Office: Tobias Guggenheimer Arch PC 145 Palisade St Dobbs Ferry NY 10522-1617 Home: 546 Farragut Pkwy Hastings On Hudson NY 10706-3402 Personal E-mail: tobiasarch@aol.com.

GUGGENHIME, RICHARD JOHNSON, lawyer; b. San Francisco, Mar. 6, 1940; s. Richard E. and Charlotte G.; m. Emlen Hall, June 5, 1965 (div.); children: Andrew, Lisa, Molly; m. Judith Perry Swift, Oct. 3, 1992. AB in Polit. Sci. with distinction, Stanford U., 1961; JD, Harvard U., 1964. Bar: Calif. 1965, U.S. Dist. Ct. (no. dist.) Calif. 1965, U.S. Ct. Appeals (9th cir.) 1965. Assoc. Heller, Ehrman, White & McAuliffe, San Francisco, 1965—71, ptnr., 1972—. Spl. asst. to U.S. Senator Hugh Scott, 1964. Mem. San Francisco Bd. Permit Appeals, 1978—86; bd. dirs. Marine World Africa USA, 1980—86; mem. San Francisco Fire Commn., 1986—88, Recreation and Parks Commn., 1989—92, 2003—04; chmn. bd. trustees San Francisco Univ. H.S., 1987—90; trustee St. Ignatius Prep. Sch., 1987—96; mem. San Francisco Airport Commn., 2006—. Mem.: Am. Coll. Probate Counsel, Mayacama Golf Club, Olympic Club (bd. dirs. 1999—2002, pres. 2002), Wine and Food Soc., Bohemian Club. Home: Apt 403 1000 Mason St San Francisco CA 94108 Office: Heller Ehrman LLP 333 Bush St San Francisco CA 94104-2806 Office Phone: 415-772-6374. Business E-Mail: rich.guggenhime@hellerehrman.com.

GUGGENMOS, KARL J., dean; B in Foodservice Mgmt., Johnson & Wales U., MBA; degree, Master Chef Prog., Germany, 1981. Cert. Exec. Chef Am. Culinary Fedn., Cert. Culinary Educator Am. Culinary Fedn. Dir. culinary edn. Johnson & Wales U., Charleston, dean coll. culinary arts Providence, U. dean, 2004—. Lectr., judge World Gourmet Summit, Singapore, 2003—04; mem. bd. edn. Sunrice Acad.; culinary judge Chaine des Rotisseurs Regional, Nat. Young Commis, 1996—; annual disting. chef, lectr. U. Wales, Cardiff, England. Named Chef Instr. of Yr., Johnson & Wales U.; recipient Golden Quill award, Am. Acad. Chefs, 1993, Culinary Traditions award, 2002. Mem.: Am. Culinary Fedn. (Presdl. Medallion). Achievements include bearing the Olympic Torch in the 2002 Salt Lake City Winter Olympics. Avocations: white-water rafting, boating, hunting, martial arts, cars. Office: Johnson & Wales U 8 Abbott Park Pl Providence RI 02903 Office Phone: 401-598-1858. Business E-Mail: karl.guggenmos@jwu.edu.*

GUGINO, CARLA, actress; b. Sarasota, Fla., Aug. 29, 1971; Studied acting, with Gene Bua. Appearances include (TV series) Falcon Crest, 1989-90, Spin City, 1996, Chicago Hope, 1999-2000, Karen Sisco, 2003-04, Threshold, 2005-06, (TV films) Murder Without Motive, 1992, A Private Matter, 1992, Motorcycle Gang, 1994, A Seaspm for Miracles, 1999, Mermaid Chronicles Part 1: She Creature, 2002, (TV miniseries) The Buccaneers, 1995, (films) Troop Beverly Hills, 1989, Welcome Home, 1990, Son-in-Law, 1993, Miami Rhapsody, 1995, Homeward Bound II: Lost in San Francisco, 1996, Michael, 1996, Red Hot, 1996, The War at Home, 1996, Wedding Bell Blues, 1996, Lovelife, 1997, Snake Eyes, 1998, Spy Kids, 2001, Spy Kids 2: Island of Lost Dreams, 2002, The Singing Detective, 2003, Spy Kids 3-D: Game Over, 2003, Life Coach: The Movie, 2005, Sin City, 2005, Even Money, 2006, Night at the Museum, 2006, The Lookout, 2007, Rise: Blood Hunter, 2007; (broadway) After the Fall, 2004, (Theatre World award, 2005), Suddenly Last Summer, 2006. Avocations: yoga, travel. Office: William Morris Agy 151 S El Camino Dr Beverly Hills CA 90212-2704*

GUGLIELMI, RHONDA E., nursing administrator; b. Columbus, Ohio, July 20, 1959; d. Richard Earl Harris and Linda Kay Dillion; m. Richard Lewis Baxter (div.); children: Michael Shane Miller, Eric Robert Miller; m. Gary Robert Guglielmi, Aug. 5, 2000. Lic. nurse, Columbus Pub. Sch. Nursing, 1994. In-home care provider Elder Care, London, Ohio, 1984—91; nursing asst. Arbors, London, 1991—92; charge nurse Sharonview Nursing Rehab., South Vienna, Ohio, 1994; clin. nurse mgr. Arlington Ct. Nursing Rehab., Columbus, 1994—2001. Contbr. short stories to anthologies. Named Ohio Job Tng. Partnership Act Participant of Yr., Madison County Tecumseh Consortium, 1995; recipient Success Is a Journey award, Gov. Voinovich, State of Ohio, 1995, State Hon. award, Gen. Assembly, Ohio Senate, 1995, Award of Excellence, Arlington Ct. Nursing Rehab., 1998. Mem.: Reflex Sympathetic Dystrophy Assn. (co-chairperson 2004—). Avocations: painting, writing, playing piano, violin, mandolin. Home: 1915 N Devon Rd Columbus OH 43212 Personal E-mail: rhondabg2000@yahoo.com.

GUGLIELMINO, LUCY MARGARET MADSEN, education educator, researcher, consultant; b. Charleston, SC, Feb. 20, 1944; d. Robert Allen and Margaret Webb (Rodgers) Madsen; m. Paul Joseph Guglielmino, July 31, 1965; children: Joseph Allen, Margaret Rose. BA in English magna cum laude, Furman U., 1965; MEd in English and Edn., Savannah Grad. Ctr., 1973; EdD in Adult Edn., U. Ga., 1977. Tchr. English various pub. schs., Mass., NJ, SC, Ga., 1965-72; vis. asst. prof. adult and cmty. edn. Fla. Atlantic U., Boca Raton, 1978-87, asst. prof., 1987-88, assoc. prof., 1988-90, prof., 1991—, chmn. dept. ednl. leadership, 1991-94, dir. Melby Cmty. Edn. Ctr., 1994—2000. Cons. AT&T, Motorola, Westvaco, S.E. banks, 1979—; bd. dirs. South Fla. Ctr. for Ednl. Leaders. Author: Adult ESL Instruction: A Sourcebook, 1991, Community Education and Florida's Future: Proceedings of the Commissioner's Summit, 1997; co-author: Administering Programs for Adults, 1997; author: (adult form) Self-Directed Leaning Readiness Scale, 1978, 3 other forms and translations into 17 other langs., 1979—94, Learning Preference Assessment (self-scoring format for business), 1991; editor: Florida GED Teachers' Handbook, 1999, 2001, Florida GED Teachers' Lesson Bank, 2001; co-editor: Internat. Jour. Self-Directed Learning, 2003—; contbr. over 100 articles to profl. jours., chapters to books. Recipient Tchr. of Yr. award Coll. Edn., Fla. Atlantic U., 1990, Outstanding Achievement award 1991, Presdl. Merit award, 1993, Profl. Excellence award, 1998, Malcolm Knowles Meml. award for outstanding lifelong contbn. to rsch. in self directed learning, 2002; named to Fla. Adult and Cmty. Edn. Hall of Fame, Fla. Adminstrs. Adult and Cmty. Edn., 1992; numerous grants, 1979—. Mem. AAUW, Nat. Cmty. Edn. Assn., Am. Assn. for Adult and Continuing Edn., Commn. Profs. Adult Edn. (chmn. self-directed learning task force 1987-88, 90-91), Fla. Adult Edn. Assn. (bd. dirs. 1989-90), Internat. Soc. for Self-Directed Learning (founding co-chair 2006), Phi Kappa Phi, Phi Delta Kappa. Episcopalian. Avocations: reading, swimming, bicycling, flower arranging, gardening, boating. Home: 7339 Reserve Creek Dr Port Saint Lucie FL 34986 Office: Fla Atlantic U CO 113 500 NW California Blvd Port Saint Lucie FL 34986 Office Phone: 772-873-3348. E-mail: lguglie@fau.edu.

GUGLIELMINO, PAUL JOSEPH, educator; b. Bklyn., May 19, 1942; s. Carl and Rose (Loreto) G.; m. Lucy Margaret, July 31, 1965; children: Joseph Allen, Margaret Rose. BA, The Citadel, 1964; MA, U. Ga., 1970, EdD, 1978. Capt. transfer pt. U.S. Army, Ft. Devens, Mass., 1964-66; dir. ctr. for mgmt. Fla. Atlantic U., Boca Raton, 1978-81, adj. prof. mgmt., 1981-86, exec. dir., asst. prof., 1986-94, assoc. prof. mgmt., 1994—. Reviewer: Human Resource Quarterly, 2001, Jour. Managerial Issues, 2002, Human Resource Mgmt. Jour., 2005; patentee in field. Mem. Boca Forum, Boca Raton, 1989-90; del. Fla. Gov.'s Conf. Libr. and Info. Svcs., 1990; mem. Sci. Coun., Centre d'Edudes Populations Pauvrete Politiques Socio-Economiques, Grand Duche Luxembourg, 1990; mem. adv. bd. Selected Ctrs. Excellence, Walt Disney World, Orlando, Fla., 1997. FAU Found. Internat. Rsch. grantee, 1991, FAU Found. Internat. Travel grantee U. Paris, 1999; recipient Fla. Atlantic U. Outstanding Achievement award, 1990, Coleman award rsch. excellence entrepreneurial edn. 38th World Conf. Small Bus. Adminstrn., Las Vegas, 1993, Tchg. Incentive Program award outstanding tchg., 1995, Second Malcolm Knowles Meml. award self-directed learning lifelong contbn. to field, 2002, Tradition of Excellence award Port St. Lucie Campus, 2004; Coll. finalist Excellence Undergrad. Tchg. Award Program, 1996, 97; named U. Disting. Tchr. of Yr. Fla. Atlantic U., 1998. Mem. Acad. Mgmt., Assn. Citadel Men., Acad. Internat. Bus., Phi Beta Lambda, Phi Kappa Phi, Beta Gamma Sigma. Episcopalian. Home: 7339 Reserve Creek Dr Port Saint Lucie FL 34986 Office Phone: 772-429-2425.

GUGLIELMO, EUGENE JOSEPH, computer scientist; b. Bklyn., Nov. 23, 1958; s. Anthony and Carlotta Sylvia (Grossi) G.; m. Nancy Eleanor Booth, Aug. 13, 1983; children: Tiffany, Trevyn, Kyle, Quentyn. BS in Computer Sci., St. John's U., 1979; MS in Computer Sci., Calif. State U., Chico, 1987; PhD in Computer Sci., Naval Postgrad. Sch., 1992. Computer asst. St. John's U., Jamaica, NY, 1977-79; mem. tech. staff Bell Telephone Labs., Whippany, NJ, 1979-80; sys. designer AT&T Comm., Piscataway, NJ, 1980-85; computer scientist Naval Air Warfare Ctr., China Lake, Calif., 1985-94; sr. cons. IBM Cons. Group, Boulder, Colo., 1994; prin. investigator Monterey Bay Aquarium Rsch. Inst., Moss Landing, Calif., 1994-96; prin. cons. BEA Systems, San Jose, Calif., 1996-99; v.p. Media Knowledge Decisions, Inc., San Jose, Calif., 1999; pres. William Enterprises Inc., Carson City, Nev., 1998—; tech. dir. Object Stream, Inc., Pleasanton, Calif., 1999—2001; chief info. officer Silterra Malaysia, Sunnyvale, 2002—. Contbr. articles to profl. jours. Mem.: IEEE, N.Y. Acad. Sci., Assn. Computing Machinery (Info. Retrieval, Artificial Intelligence), IEEE Computer Soc. Roman Catholic. Avocations: model building, baseball, basketball, reading, coaching. Home: 35 Bayview Rd Castroville CA 95012-9725 E-mail: geneg@acm.org.

GUHA, DILIP K., retired urban planner; b. Barisal, Bangladesh, Mar. 1, 1936; s. Dhirendra Mohan and Hiran Bala Guha; m. Pranati Ray; children: Ajanta Kumar, Amrita. BS in Stats., Calcutta U., 1954, MS in Stats., 1956; PhD, Case Western Res. U., Cleve., 1964. Cert. assoc. Actuarial Soc. Am., 1994. Rsch. engr. Port Authority NY & NJ, 1964—89, supr. transp. planner, 1989—2002; ret., 2002. Statistician State Statis. Bur., Calcutta, India, 1957—61. Mem.: Inst. Ops. Rsch. and Mgmt. Sci. Achievements include research in minimization of toll staffing. Home: 10 Van Breemen Ct Upper Montclair NJ 07043 Home Phone: 973-783-5494. Personal E-mail: dilipguha@hotmail.com.

GUHA, SUJATA, education educator; b. Calcutta, West Bengal, India, Dec. 13, 1969; d. Ashoke Kumar and Minu Guha. BS, U. of Dubuque, Iowa, 1994; MS, Purdue U., Ind., 1997, PhD, 2000. Grad. instr. chemistry Purdue U., West Lafayette, Ind., 1994—2000; asst. prof. chemistry Rocky Mountain Coll., Billings, Mont., 2000—03, Tenn. State U., Nashville, 2003—. Author: (book chapter) Stratospheric Bromine Chemistry: Insights from Computational Studies. Presdl. Scholarship, U. of Dubuque, 1991—94. Mem.: Am. Chem. Soc., Am. Assn. for the Advancement of Sci., N.Y. Acad. of Scis., The Math. Assn. Am., Mont. Sci. and Tech. Consortium, NASA-Montana Space Grant Consortium, Phi Lambda Upsilon, Alpha Chi (bd. dirs. 1992—94). Achievements include research in Atmospheric chemistry of novel transient species in the gas phase. Office: Tenn State U 3500 John Merritt Blvd Nashville TN 37209 Home: 5160 Rice Rd Apt 137 Antioch TN 37013 Home Phone: 615-356-7196, 615-367-6286; Office Phone: 615-963-5334. Office Fax: 615-963-5326. Personal E-mail: sujata_guha@yahoo.com. Business E-Mail: sguha@tnstate.edu.

GUHIN, MICHAEL ALAN, ambassador; Grad. summa cum laude, U. So. Calif.; PhD, London Sch. Econs. Sr. advisor White House, Washington, Nat. Security Coun. Staff, US Dept. State, US Nuclear Regulatory Commn., US Arms Control and Disarmament Agency; US fissile material negotiator US Dept. State, 1999—. Author: John Foster Dulles: A Statesman and His Times, 1972; contbr. articles to profl. jours. Office: US Dept State 2201 C St NW Washington DC 20520 Office Phone: 202-647-8321.

GUI, JAMES EDMUND, architect; b. Wooster, Ohio, Aug. 13, 1928; s. Harry Ludwig and Mabel Josephine (Olson) Gui; m. Anne Louise Outram, Oct. 15, 1955; children: Linda Anne, Jeffrey Allen. BArch, Ohio State U., 1954. Assoc. firm Charles F. McKirahan & Assocs., Archs., Ft. Lauderdale, Fla., 1958—63; chief specifications Archs. Collaborative, Cambridge, Mass., 1963—67; propr. James E. Gui, Archtl. and Specifications Cons., Belmont, Mass., 1967—2005, ret., 2005. Prin. works include Archs. Collaborative, Benjamin Thompson & Assocs., Cambridge Seven Assocs., Archtl. Resources Cambridge, Inc., Harvard, MIT, Juilliard Sch. Music, Lincoln Ctr., NYC, U.S. Pavillion Expo 67, Montreal, New Eng. Aquarium, Children's Hosp. Med. Ctr., Harvard U. Law Sch. Complex, Harvard Gutman Libr., Harvard Obs., Kirkland Coll., Berkshire CC, Tufts U. Dental Health Ctr., Independence Nat. Hist. Pk. Visitors Ctr., Navy Pier, Chgo., Wilmington Jewish Cmty. Ctr., Faneuil Hall Marketplace, Boston, Harborplace, Balt., Seaport Market, NYC, Pier 17, Bayside Marketplace, Miami, Century City Market, LA, Harvard Kennedy Sch. Govt., Cambridge, Ordway Music Theater, Mpls., Union Sta. Restoration, Washington, Va. Performing Arts Ctr., Richmond, Va. Recipient Disting Alumnus award, Ohio State U., 2003. Mem.: Constrn. Specifications Inst. Home Phone: 843-785-7641; Office Phone: 843-785-7645. Personal E-mail: jandagui1@aol.com.

GUIDA, WAYNE CHARLES, medical educator, research scientist; b. Tampa, Fla., Mar. 20, 1946; s. Angelo and Violet (Caccamo) G.; m. Natalie Denise Baker, June 5, 1985; children: Marshall Wayne, Mitchell Wayne. BA, U. So. Fla., 1968, PhD, 1976. Postdoctoral fellow Duke U., Durham, NC, 1976; asst., then assoc. prof. Eckerd Coll., St. Petersburg, Fla., 1977-85; sr. rsch. fellow Columbia U., NYC, 1985-86; rsch. scientist Ciba Pharms., Summit, NJ, 1986-90, mgr., 1990-91, dir., 1991-93; exec. dir. Novartis Pharms. Corp. (formerly Ciba Pharms.), 1993—98; CEO, pres. Scrodinger, Inc., NYC, 1999; assoc. then prof. Eckerd Coll., St. Petersburg, 1999—2007; prof. Moffitt Cancer Ctr. and Rsch. Inst., Tampa, Fla., 2001—, U. So. Fla., 2007—. Mem. com. NAS, Washington, 1994-95; mem. adv. bd. biotech. program Cornell U., Ithaca, NY, 1994-97. Contbr. articles to profl. jours.; patentee in field. Grantee Rsch. Corp., 1979-81, NSF, 1980-82, Petroleum Rsch. Fund, 1982-84, NIH/Nat. Cancer Inst., 2003-, 05-, 07-. Mem. Am. Chem. Soc., Phi Kappa Phi, Sigma Xi. Presbyterian. Avocations: golf, fishing, photography, hiking. Office: Moffitt Cancer Ctr and Rsch Inst SRB 24209 12902 Magnolia Dr Tampa FL 33612 Office Phone: 813-745-6047. Business E-Mail: guidawa@moffitt.org.

GUIDER, ELIZABETH GRIER, editor; b. Vicksburg, Miss., Sept. 3, 1951; d. Benjamin Alfred and Mary (Shaw) G.; m. Walter F. Collins, Aug. 7, 1995. BA, NYU, 1969, MA, PhD, 1980. Prof. English lit. NYU, 1974-76; prof. lit. Univ. Studi Sociali, Rome, 1976-81; prof. lit., history Am. Coll. Rome, 1978-82; corr. Variety, London, Rome, 1985-90, internat. editor NYC, 1990-93, mng. editor LA, editor-at-large; editor The Hollywood Reporter, LA, 2007—. Active Women's Health Movement, Rome, 1976-85. Woodrow Wilson fellow, Woodrow Wilson Fellowship Fund, Paris, Rome, 1973. Mem. Women in Radio & TV. Avocations: ballroom dancing, piano, tennis, chess. Office: The Hollywood Reporter 5055 Wilshire Blvd Ste 600 Los Angeles CA 90036*

GUIDO, MICHAEL ANTHONY, evangelist; b. Lorain, Ohio, Jan. 30, 1915; s. Mike and Julia (DePalma) G.; m. Audrey Forehand, Nov. 25, 1943. Student, Moody Bible Inst., Chgo., 1933-35. Ordained to ministry So. Bapt. Conv., 1939. Min. youth and music lst Presbyn. Ch., Sebring, Fla., 1936-38, lst Bapt. Ch., Lake Charles, La., 1939; evangelist Moody Bible Inst., 1940-50; founder, pres., speaker Guido Evangelistic Assn., Metter, Ga., 1950—. Writer, speaker daily telecast A Seed from the Sower, 1972—, daily broadcaster The Sower, A Seed from the Sower, Seeds from the Sower 25, 1957—. Author: (autobiography) Seeds from the Sower, 1990, rev. edit., 1998, Treasury of Illustrations, 1999; editor Sowing and Reaping mag., 1957—; daily newspaper columnist Seeds from the Sower, 1957—. Named Alumnus of Yr., Moody Bible Inst., 1982, Citizen of Yr., Kiwanis Club, Metter, 1982. Baptist. Interstate bridge named in honor of Michael A. Guido, 1998. Home: PO Box 508 Metter GA 30439-0508 Office Phone: 912-685-2222. E-mail: thesower@the-sower.org. *Life to me is loving God and serving Him by finding a need and supplying it, and searching for a lost soul and bringing that one home to God.*

GUIHER, JAMES MORFORD, JR., publisher, writer; b. Clarksburg, W.Va., Feb. 21, 1927; s. James Morford and Ruth Holt (Souders) G.; m. Elizabeth Ewing Hart, Aug. 20, 1954; children: Catharine Brownfield, Deborah Hart. BA, Princeton U., 1951; postgrad., Harvard U., 1951-52, Boston Mus. Sch. Fine Arts, 1953-54. Editor coll. textbooks Prentice-Hall, Inc., Englewood Cliffs, NJ, 1954-66, exec. editor Ednl. Book div., 1966-68, editor-in-chief, 1968-74, v.p., gen. mgr., 1974-76; publishing cons. Author: (play) Aphrodite, 1999. Served with AUS, 1945-47. Home: 4 E 88th St New York NY 10128-0509

GUILD, ALDEN, retired lawyer; b. Boston, July 3, 1929; s. Howard Redwood and Frances Allen (Warren) G.; m. Ruth Ineta Creighton, Sept. 14, 1957; 1 child, Heather Louise. BA, Dartmouth Coll., 1952; JD, U. Chgo., 1957; LLD (hon.), Norwich/Vt. Coll., 1977. Bar: Vt. 1958, U.S. Dist. Ct. Vt. 1958. With law dept. Nat. Life Ins. Co., Montpelier, Vt., 1957-90, asst. v.p., counsel, corp. sec., 1974-83, v.p., gen. counsel, 1983-89, sr. v.p., gen. counsel, 1989-90; ret. McKee, Giuliani & Cleveland, Montpelier, of counsel, 1990-97. Author: Stock-Purchase Agreements, 1960, Professional-Partnership Purchase Agreements, 1961, Business-Partnership Purchase Agreements, 1962; contbr. articles to legal jours. Trustee Norwich U., 1972-96, Vt. Coll., 1967-72, Kimball U. Acad., 1972-74, Wood Art Gallery, 1961-72; mem. Dartmouth Coll. Alumni Council, 1975-78. Served with USAF, 1950-53, Korea. Recipient Disting. Service award Montpelier Jr. C. of C., 1962 Mem. Vt. Bar Assn., Assn. Life Ins. Counsel, Am. Coun. Life Ins., VFW, Am. Legion, Order of Coif, Lake Mansfield Trout Club (Stowe, Vt.), Masons, Elks, Phi Beta Kappa, Theta Chi. Republican. Home: 63 Murray Rd Montpelier VT 05602-8514

GUILD, JEFFREY K., mathematics professor; s. Charles C. and Margaret M. Guild. BA, Flagler Coll., St. Augustine, Fla., 1988; MS, Fla. Atlantic U., Boca Raton, 1999. Cert. tchr. in adolescent & young adulthood math. Nat. Bd. Profl. Tchg. Standards, 2002. Math. tchr., dept. chairperson Boyd H. Anderson HS, Lauderdale Lakes, Fla., 1993—2001; math. tchr. Coll. Acad. Broward CC, Davie, Fla., 2001—05, asst. prof. math., 2005—. Recipient Vocat. Tchr. of Yr., Margate Cmty. Sch., 1994, Tchr. of Yr., Coll. Acad., Broward CC, 2004. D-Liberal. Home Phone: 954-493-9464.

GUILD, NANCY ANN, biology professor; b. Denver, Nov. 13, 1948; d. Chester Philip and Betty Hendrickson Guild; m. Clifford Lee Myers, Nov. 19, 1983; children: Matthew Stevens Myers, Nicholas Clifford Myers. PhD, U. Colo., Boulder, 1986. Tchr. elem. sch. Bergen Pk. Elem. Sch., Evergreen, Colo., 1972—76; lab. coord. III Colo. U., MCD Biology, Boulder, 1987—88, asst. prof., 1988—97, assoc. prof., 1997—2005, prof., 2005—. Chair diversity com. Colo. U., MCD Biology, 1996—. Contbr. chapters to books to profl. jours. Supporter and fund raiser Lymphoma and Leukemia Soc., Denver, 2006—07. Avocations: swimming, hiking, reading. Home: 9135 Hoyt Westminster CO 80021 Office: MCD Biology U Colo Ucb 347 Boulder CO 80309 Home Phone: 303-423-1413; Office Phone: 303-492-5054. Office Fax: 303-492-7744. Personal E-mail: nancy.guild@comcast.net. E-mail: nancy.guild@colorado.edu.

GUILD, RICHARD SAMUEL, trade association management company executive; b. Boston, Nov. 5, 1925; s. Walter Rayford and Anna (Hollander) G.; m. Susan Jane Coughlin, July 3, 1965; children: Laura Ann, Linda Jean. BS, Boston U., 1949. Cert. assn. exec. With Guild Assocs., Inc., Boston, 1949—, mng. dir., 1960-65, pres., 1965—. Owner Copypro, 1975-92; treas. Resource Matching System, Inc., 1982-83; exec. sec. New Eng. Marine Trade Assn., 1963, Liquified Petroleum Gas Assn. New Eng., 1972-1985; mng. dir. Shoe Pattern Mfrs. Assn., 1951-94 , Mass. Automatic Merchandising Coun., 1964-99, Tel. Answering Assn. New Eng., 1983-99; exec. v.p. Am. Boat Builders and Repairers Assn., 1979-90; treas. Wet Ground MICA Assn., 1983-87. With USNR, 1944-45. Mem. Multiple Assn. Mgmt. Inst. (past pres.), Am. Soc. Assn. Execs. (past bd. dirs.), N.Am. Paddlesports Assn. (exec. v.p. 1987-90), Boston Soc. Assn. Execs. (past pres.), Def. Orientation Conf. Assn., Soc. Mgmt. of Profl. Computing (exec. sec. 1985-94), New Eng. Honda Automobile Dealers Assn. (exec. sec. 1985-95), Acura Dealers of N.E. (exec. sec. 1989-93, 96—). Home: 5 Glengarry Rd Winchester MA 01890-2511 Office: 389 Main St Malden MA 02148-5017

GUILFORD, ANDREW JOHN, federal judge; b. Santa Monica, Calif., Nov. 28, 1950; s. Howard Owens and Elsie Jennette (Hargreaves) G.; m. Loreen Mary Gogain, Dec. 22, 1973; children: Colleen Catherine, Amanda Joy. AB summa cum laude, UCLA, 1972, JD, 1975. Bar: Calif. 1975, US Dist. Ct. (ctrl. dist.) Calif. 1976, US Ct. Appeals (9th cir.) 1976, US Supreme Ct. 1979, US Dist. Ct. (so. dist.) Calif. 1981, US Dist. Ct. (no. and ea. dists.) Calif. 1990. Assoc. Sheppard, Mullin, Richter & Hampton, L.A. and Orange County, Calif., 1975-82, ptnr. Orange County, 1983—2006; judge US Dist. Ct. (Ctrl. dist.) Calif., LA, 2006—. Lectr. The Rutter Group, Encino, Calif., 1983—, Continuing Edn. of the Bar, Berkeley, 1978—, Hastings Ctr. for Advocacy, San Francisco, 1988; judge pro tem, arbitrator Calif. Superior Ct., 1983-2006; mem. commn. future legal profession and state bar; mem. adv. task force on multi-juristictional practice, task force on self-represented litigants. Author UCLA Law Review, 1975. Mem. Amicus Publico, Santa Ana, Calif., 1986; bd. dirs. Pub. Law Ctr. Orange County, 1990-2006, pres., 2003-06; bd. dirs. Constl. Rights Found., 1990, Baroque Music Festival, 1992-96, NCCJ, 1995-99, UCLA Law Alumni Assn., 1992-95; subdeacon, warden, del. Episcopal Ch. Recipient resolution of commendation Calif. State Senate and Assembly, Outstanding Svc. award Poverty Law Ctr., 1991, Bernard E. Witkin Amicus Curiae award Calif. Jud. Coun., Jurisprudence award Anti-Defamation League, J. Reuben Clark award, cert. of recognition US Congress, others; co-recipient President's Pro Bono award State Bar; Regents scholar U. Calif., Berkeley, 1968-72; named one of Calif.'s 100 Top Influential Attys., The Daily Jour., Bus. Litig. Trial Lawyer of Yr., Orange County Trial Lawyers Assn. Fellow Am. Coll. Trial Lawyers (named a Best Lawyer in Am.); mem. ABA, FBA (bd. dirs. 2001—), Assn. Bus. Trial Lawyers (founding officer Orange County chpt., pres. 2000-2001), Am. Arbitration Assn. (arbitrator large complex case program 1993-95), Calif. Bar Assn. (pres. 1999-2000, bd. govs. 1996-2000), Orange County Bar Assn. (bd. dirs. 1985-87, officer 1988-90, pres. 1991, chmn. bus. litigation sect. 1983, state bar conv. 1986, 87, law-motion com. 1982, standing com. trial ct. delay reduction 1987-93, Franklin G. West award 2003), 9th Cir. Jud. Conf. (rep. 1990-92, 99—2001), Phi Beta Kappa (sec.-treas. 1978-80, v.p. 1980-84), Pi Gamma Mu, Sigma Pi. Republican. Avocations: theater, photography, sports, gardening, poetry. Office: US Dist Ct 411 W 4th St Rm 10-D Santa Ana CA 92701-4516

GUILLAMA-ALVAREZ, NOEL JESUS, merchant banker, healthcare executive; b. Havana, Cuba, Nov. 30, 1959; arrived in US, 1966, naturalized, 1981; s. Jesus Mario Guillama and Rosa Maria Alvarez Guillama; 1 child, Jahziel Mikhail Guillama. Student, Fla. Internat. U., Miami, Palm Beach C.C., Lake Worth, Fla., 1978—80; BS in Constrn. Mgmt., Allstate Coll., Tampa, Fla., 1983; postgrad., MIT, Cambridge, Mass., 1997—99. Cert. bldg. contractor, Fla.; lic. real estate broker, mortgage broker, gen. ins. agt. Dir. programing Teleprompter Corp., West Palm Beach, Fla., 1976-79; pres., CEO JMG Holdings Inc, Palm Beach, Fla., 1980-90; chmn., CEO Tektonica, Inc., Tequesta, Fla., 1984—; chmn. Medtronics, Inc., Wellington, 1984—; v.p. ops. Quality Care Networks, Boca Raton, Fla., 1990-95; v.p. devel. Medpartners, Inc., Birmingham, Ala., 1995; pres., CEO Met. Health Networks, Boca Raton, 1995-2000; chmn. The Quantum Group, Wellington, Fla., 2000—, TargitInteractive, Portsmouth, NH, 2000—02; dir. Da Vinci Ventures Group, Inc., 2003. Vice-chair Palm Beach County Adv. Bd., West Palm Beach, 1990—92; co-founder, vice-chair Lake Worth Cmty. Devel. Corp., 1990—92; co-founder Project Lake Worth, 1989—92. Writer weekly column Palm Beach Latino Newspaper, 1991-92. Mem. Palm Beach County Edn. Commn., 2007; trustee Palms West Hosp., Loxahatchee, Fla., 2005—; dir., treas. and chmn. fin. and acad. com. Fla. Internat. U., 2004, mem. biomed. engring. adv. bd., 2005, chmn. bus., tech. and edn. advancement bd., 2002—. Western Cmtys., Palm Beach County, 2003—07; mem. Wellington Fla. Edn. Com., 2005—07; committeeman Rep. Exec. Com., Palm Beach County, Fla., 2005—06; bd. dirs. Palm Beach CC Found., Lake Worth, Fla., 2005—, Cultural Trust Palm Beaches, 2006—07. Recipient award Leukemia Soc. Am., 1979, Chin de Plata award Todo Mag., Miami, Fla., 1978. Mem.: Health Info. Mgmt. Soc., Med. Group Mgmt. Assn., Am. Fin. Assn., Am. Coll. Healthcare Execs. (assoc.), Rotary. Republican. Avocations: scuba diving, tennis, golf, fishing. Office Phone: 561-798-9800.

GUILLAUME, RAYMOND KENDRICK, banker; b. June 19, 1943; s. William Raymond and Marguerite (Lyons) G.; m. Ann Greenwell, June 26, 1965; children— Lee Kendrick, Jill Lyons Kissel. BS, Western Ky. U., 1965. Asst. cashier Liberty Nat. Bank, Louisville, 1968, asst. v.p., 1969-70, v.p., 1970-72, sr. v.p., 1973-78, exec. v.p., 1978-92, pres., 1993-95, also bd. dirs.; vice chmn., CEO Bank of Louisville, 1995—2002; pres. Ky. and Louisville metro region Br. Banking & Trust, 2002—04, chmn. Ky. Ops., 2004—, pres. Ky. Ops., 2004, CEO Ky. Ops., 2004—. Chmn., bd. dirs. ARC, Louisville, 1985; treas., bd. dirs. Met. United Way, Louisville, 1984-92, 93—, St. Anthony's Hosp., Louisville, 1985; trustee Christ Ch. United Meth., Louisville, 1984; chmn. Leadership Louisville, 1992-95; chmn. bd. dirs. Metro United Way, Western Ky. Univ. Found., Ky. Ctr. for the Arts Endowment Fund; bd. dirs. Norton Healthcare, The Healing Pl., The Housing Partnership. Mem. Western Ky. U. Nat. Alumni Assn. (pres. 1985), Ky. Bar Assn. (bd. dirs.), Pendennis Club, Louisville Boat Club, Louisville Country Club, Jefferson Club, Kentuckians of N.Y. Home: 415 Rolling Ln Louisville KY 40207-1807 Office: Br Banking & Trust PO Box 1101 Louisville KY 40201-1101 Home Phone: 502-897-9623; Office Phone: 502-562-5802. Business E-Mail: rguillaume@bbandt.com.

GUILLEMIN, ROGER C.L., physiologist; b. Dijon, France, Jan. 11, 1924; arrived in U.S., 1953, naturalized, 1963; BA, U. Dijon, 1941, BSc, 1942; MD, Faculty of Medicine, Lyons, France, 1949; PhD, U. Montreal, 1953; PhD (hon.), U. Rochester, 1976, U. Chgo., 1977, Baylor Coll. Medicine, 1978, U. Ulm, Germany, 1978, U. Dijon, France, 1978, Free U. Brussels, 1979, U. Montreal, 1979, U. Man., Can, 1984, U. Turin, Italy, 1985, Kyung Hee U., Korea, 1986, U. Paris, Paris, 1986, U. Barcelona, Spain, 1988, U. Madrid, 1988, McGill U., Montreal, Can., 1988, U. Claude Bernard, Lyon, France, 1989, Laval U., Quebec, Can., 1990, PhD (hon.), 1996, Sherbrooke U., Quebec, 1997, U. Franche-Comté, France, 1999. Intern, resident, prosecutor of anatomy U. Hosps., Dijon, 1946—47; rsch. asst., assoc. dir., asst. prof. Inst. Exptl. Medicine and Surgery, U. Montreal, 1949—53; asst. prof. physiology Baylor Coll. Medicine, 1953-57, assoc. prof., 1957, prof., dir. labs. neuroendocrinology, 1963-70, adj. prof. physiology, 1970—; assoc. dir. dept. exptl. endocrinology Coll. de France (as joint appt. with Coll. Medicine Baylor U.), Paris, 1960-63; resident fellow, rsch. prof. chmn. labs. neuroendocrinology Salk Inst., La Jolla, Calif., 1970-89, adj. rsch. prof., 1970—, dean, 1972—73, 1976—77, disting. prof., 1989—; disting. scientist Whittier Inst., 1989-97, med. and sci. dir., 1993-94; adj. prof. medicine U. Calif., San Diego, 1994—97. Cons. physiology VA Hosp., Houston, 1954—60, Houston, 1967—70; lectr. exptl. endocrinology dept. biology Rice U., Houston, 1958—60; cons. biochemistry MD Anderson Hosp. and Tumor Inst., Houston, 1967—70; dir. rsch. CNRS, Paris, 1963—68; bd. dirs. Sanofi, 1982—86, Erbamont, Nev., 1986—92, ICN Pharms., 1987—89, 1994—2001, Roussel-UCLAF, Hoechst, 1989—90, SPI Pharm., 1989—95, Whittier Inst. Diabetes Endocrinology, 1989—94, Prizm Pharm., 1992—98, Viratek, 1992—95, Jonas Salk Fedn., 1995—2005, Humetrix, 1999—, Ribapharm, 2001—02. Decorated chevalier Legion d'Honneur France, officer de la Légion d'Honneur French Republic; recipient Gold medal, 1st Internat. Congress Pharmacology, Stockholm, 1961, Saintour award for exptl. endocrinology, Coll. de France, Paris, 1961, Disting. Scientist award, Nat. Diabetes Rsch. Coalition, 1966, U.S. NIH lectureship, Bethesda, Md., 1973, La Madonnina award for medicine, The Carlo Erba Found., 1974, Gairdner Internat. award, 1974, Lasker award, Lasker Found., 1975, Dickson prize in medicine, 1976, Passano award sci., 1976, Schmitt medal neurosci., 1977, Nobel Prize in Medicine, The Nobel Found., 1977, Nat. Medal of Sci., Pres. of the U.S.A., 1977, Barren Gold medal, 1979, Dale medal, Soc. for Endocrinology, UK, 1980, Ellen Browning Scripps Soc. medal, Scripps Meml. Hosps. Found., 1988; scholar, John and Mary R. Markle Found., N.Y., 1952—56. Fellow: AAAS; mem.: NAS, Tex. Med. Ctr. Rsch. Soc. (pres. elect 1959, pres. 1960, hon. 1970), Assn. des Physiologistes, Am. Inst. Biol. Sci., Western Soc. Clin. Rsch., Internat. Soc. Neurosci. (charter), Acad. Royale de Medecine de Belgique, Acad. Sci., Academie Nat. de Medicine, French Acad. Scis., Am. Acad. Arts & Scis., Soc. Neuro-scis., Internat. Soc. Rsch. Biology Reprodn., Internat. Brain Rsch. Orgn., Soc. Exptl. Biology and Medicine, Endocrine Soc. (coun. 1969—73, nominating com. 1974—75, pres. 1986), Assn. Am. Physicians, Am. Physiol. Soc., Soc. Francaise d'Endocrinologie (hon.; pres. 1982—83), Soc. de Biology Paris (hon.), Soc. Can. Biology (hon.), Internat. Soc. for Immunology of Reproduction (hon.), Howard Florey Inst. Exptl. Physiology and Medicine (hon.), Houston Philos. Soc. (hon.), Can. Soc. Endocrinology and Metabolism (hon.), Swedish Soc. Med. Sci. (hon.), Am. Peptide Soc. (hon.), Club of Rome. Office: The Salk Inst 10010 N Torrey Pines Rd La Jolla CA 92037-1099 Address: The Salk Inst PO Box 85800 San Diego CA 92186-5800 Business E-Mail: guillemin@salk.edu.

GUILLEN, MAURO FEDERICO, sociology and management educator; b. Leon, Spain, Sept. 30, 1964; came to U.S., 1987; s. Julian and Maria Flor (Rodriguez) G. BA in Polit. Economy, Oviedo U., Spain, 1987, D Polit. Economy cum laude, 1991; MA, Yale U., 1989, M in Philosophy, 1990; PhD in Sociology, 1992. Instr. Yale U., New Haven, 1989-91, grad. affiliate Calhoun Coll., 1990-92; asst. prof. internat. mgmt. and sociology MIT Sloan Sch. Mgmt., Cambridge, 1992-96; from asst. prof. to prof. mgmt. Wharton Sch. U. Pa., Phila., 1996—; dir. Lauder Inst., 2007—. Rsch. affiliate Ctr. for European Studies, Harvard U., 1992-96; vis. mem. Inst. for Advanced Study, Princeton U., 1998-99. Author: The AIDS Disaster, 1990 (Gustavus Myers award Outstanding Book on Human Rights 1991), La Profesion de Economista, 1989, Models of Management, 1994 (Pres.'s Book award Social Sci. History Assn. 1993), The Limits of Convergence, 2001, The Rise of Spanish Multinationals, 2005, Taylorized Beauty of the Mechanical, 2006. Organizer Grad. Employees and Studen Orgn. at Yale, New Haven, 1991-92. Fulbright fellow Inst. of Internat. Edn., 1989-92, John D. Rockefeller 3d fellow Program on Nonprofit Orgns., Yale U., 1989, Guggenheim fellow, 1998-99. Mem. Am. Sociol. Assn., Internat. Sociol. Assn., Acad. Mgmt., Acad. Internat. Bus. Roman Catholic. Avocations: modernist art, opera, basketball. Office: U Pa Wharton Sch 2016 Steinberg Hall Philadelphia PA 19104-6370 E-mail: guillen@wharton.upenn.edu.

GUILLEN, OZZIE (OSWALDO JOSE BARRIOS GUILLEN), professionall baseball manager; b. Ocumare del Tuy, Miranda, Venezuela, Jan. 20, 1964; m. Ibis Guillen; children: Oswaldo Jr., Oney, Ozney. Player San Diego Padres, 1980-84, Chgo. White Sox, 1984—97, Balt. Orioles, 1998, Atlanta Braves, 1998—2000, Tampa Bay Devil Rays, 2000; third base coach Montreal Expos, 2001—02, Fla. Marlins, 2002—03; mgr. Chgo. White Sox, 2003—. Named Rookie of the Yr. Baseball Writers' Assn. Am., 1985, The Sporting News, 1985; named to Am. League All-Star team, 1988, 90, 91; recipient Gold Glove award, 1990; named Am. League Mgr. Yr., Major League Baseball Writer Assn., 2005 mgr. World Series Champions, 2005, winning AL All-Star Team, 2006. Office: Chgo White Sox Comiskey Park 333 W 35th St Chicago IL 60616-3651

GUILLILAND, MARTHA W., academic administrator; b. Pa. BS in Geology and Math., Catawba Coll., 1966; MS in Geophysics, Rice U., 1968; PhD in environ. engring./sys. ecology, U. Fla., 1973. Rsch. fellow sci. and pub. policy U. Mo., Kan. City, Mo., 1974—77; asst. prof. civil engring. and environment sci. U. Okla., 1975—77; exec. dir. Energy Policy Studies, Inc., El Paso, Tex., 1977—82; assoc. prof. civil engring. U. Nebr., Lincoln, 1988—90, dir. Ctr. Infrastructure Rsch., 1988—99; dean grad. sch. and asst. v.p. rsch. U. Ariz., 1990—93, vice provost academic affairs, 1993—95, academic v.p. info. and human resources, 1995—97, prof. hydrology and water resources, 1995—97; provost Tulane U., New Orleans, 1997—2000; pres. U. Mo., Kans. City, 2000—. Appointee Rsch. and Adv. Panel of Gen. Acctg. Office, Energy Engring. Bd. of Nat. Rsch. Coun., NAS Com. on Strategic Assessment of Dept. of Energy Coal Program, Nat. Inst. Global Change, Pres.'s Coun. of Advisors on Sci. and Tech., 2001. Author: (book) Energy Analysis: A New Public Policy Tool, co-author books; contbr. articles to profl. jours. Recipient Hubert H. Humphrey award, Policy Studies Orgn., 2002, Gov.'s award Excellence Total Quality Efforts, Ariz.; fellow, W.K. Kellogg Found., 1985—88. Office: U Mo 5100 Rockhill Rd Kansas City MO 64110

GUILLORY, BARBARA ANN, elementary school educator; d. Catherine Simon and Leonard Joseph (Stepfather); children: Anastasia Nicole Simon, Christopher Alexander Simon. BS, Xavier U. of La., New Orleans, 1992, MA, 2000, MA, 2002. Cert. elem. tchr., prin., Nat. Bd. Cert. Tchr. Numeracy (math) coach New Orleans Pub. Schs., 2003—05; math tchr. Gwinnett County Schs., Lawrenceville, Ga., 2005—. Ednl. tech. facilitator, New Orleans, 2000—05; curriculum writer (math and sci.) New Orleans Pub. Schs., 2003—05. Mem.: ASCD, Bd. of Profl. Tchg. Stds., Phi Delta Kappan, Delta Sigma Theta. Office: Gwinnett County Schools 3200 Pleasant Hill Rd Duluth GA 30096 Home Phone: 770-717-7484. Personal E-mail: bguillory3@cox.net.

GUILLORY, RICHARD JOHN, retired science educator; b. San Diego, Oct. 3, 1930; s. John Antoine Guillory and Margaret Sophia Zagrapski; m. Stella Jyhlih Jeng, Aug. 24, 1974; children: Cynthia Sherry, Olivia June, Amber Malia. BA, Reed Coll., 1953; PhD, UCLA, 1961; post doctorate, U. Amsterdam, Netherlands, 1963. Assoc. prof. biochemistry Ariz. State U., Tempe, Ariz., 1961—65; assoc. prof. biochemical, molecular biochem. Cornell U., Ithica, NY, 1966—71; prof. biochemistry, biophysics U. Hawaii, Honolulu, 1972—2004, emeritus prof., John A. Burns Sch. Medicine, 2004—. Editor: Journ. Biochemistry and Biophysics, 1975—80; contbr. articles over 100 scientific papers, chapters to books. Organizer scientific meetings Fed. Asian and Oceanic Biochemistry Soc. Sgt. US Army, 1954—55, Taiwan. Fellow: Am. Heart Assn. (established investigator 1966—71); mem.: Am. Soc. Biological Chemistry, British Biochem. Soc., Am. Chem. Soc., Sigma Xi (bd. dirs. 2005—, constituency dir. membership at large). Republican. Roman Catholic. Avocations: golf, historical writing Greco-Roman. Home: 3201 Skye Rd Washougal WA 98671 Personal E-mail: richardg@hawaii.edu.

GUILLOT, CYRIL ETIENNE, international organization administrator; b. Paris, Sept. 24, 1962; s. Jacques Rene and Jacqueline (Lageat) G. Cert., U. de Belgrano, Buenos Aires, 1984, U. de Los Andes, Bogota, Colombia, 1984; BA, Johns Hopkins U., 1984, MA, 1985. Field implementation officer UN Capital Devel. Fund, N'Djamena, Chad, 1987-89; assoc., sr. project mgmt. officer UN Office for Project Svcs., NYC, 1989-93; country officer UN Capital Devel. Fund, NYC, 1993-96, program specialist, 1997—2001, dep. dir. local governance unit, 2002—. Study grantee Orgn. of Am. States, 1984. Mem. Fgn. Policy Assn. Avocation: travel. Office: UN Capital Devel Fund 1 UN Plz # Dc2-2623 New York NY 10017-3515 Home: 14 Springdale Rd New Rochelle NY 10804-4317 Business E-Mail: cyril.guillot@undp.org.

GUILMARTIN, EUGENIA KATHERINE, military officer; d. John Francis Guilmartin and Judith Ellen Meader. BS in Internat. Rels., US Mil. Acad., West Point, NY, 1993; PhD in Polit. Sci., Stanford U., Palo Alto, Calif., 2003. Commd. 2d lt. US Army, advanced through grades to maj., 1993, with Mil. Police, 1993—. Team mem. Coun. Fgn. Rels., 2003.

GUINN, KENNY C. (KENNETH CARROLL GUINN), former governor; b. Garland, Ark., Aug. 24, 1936; m. Dema Guinn, July 7, 1956; children: Jeff, Steve. BA, Calif. State U., Fresno, 1959, MA, 1965; EdD, Utah State U., 1970. Supt. Clark County Sch. Dist., 1969—78; v.p. adminstrn. Nev. Savs. and Loan Assn. (PriMerit Bank), 1978-80; pres., COO Nev. Savs. & Loan Assn. (PriMerit Bank), 1980-85, CEO, 1985-92; pres. Southwest Gas Corp., 1987-88, chmn., CEO, 1988-93; interim pres. U. Nev., Las Vegas, 1994—95; gov. State of Nev., Carson City, 1999—2007. Bd. dirs. MGM Mirage, 2007—. Republican.*

GUINN, STANLEY WILLIS, retired lawyer; b. Detroit, June 9, 1953; s. Willis Hampton and Virginia Mae (Pierson) Guinn; m. Patricia Shirley Newgord, June 13, 1981; children: Terri Lanae, Scott Stanley. BBA with high distinction, U. Mich., 1979, MBA with distinction, 1981; MS in Taxation with distinction, Walsh Coll., 1987; JD cum laude, U. Mich., 1992. CPA Mich., cert. mgmt. acct.; bar: Calif., U.S. Dist. Ct. (so. dist.) Calif., U.S. Tax Ct. Tax mgr. Coopers & Lybrand, Detroit, 1981-87; tax cons. Upjohn Co., Kalamazoo, 1987-89; litig. atty. Brobeck, Phleger & Harrison, 1992-94, Coughlan, Semmer & Lipman, San Diego, 1994-95; consumer fin. atty. Bank Am. NT & SA, San Francisco, 1995-98, GreenPoint Credit, LLC, San Diego, 1998—2005; ret., 2005. With USN, 1974—77. Mem.: Atty.-CPA, Inc., San Diego County Bar, Calif. State Bar Assn., Delta Mu Delta, Beta Alpha Psi, Beta Gamma Sigma, Phi Kappa Phi. Avocations: tennis, racquetball, hiking. Home: 3125 Crystal Ct Escondido CA 92025-7763 Personal E-mail: sguinn1234@cox.net.

GUINN, THEODORE, retired mathematics professor, research scientist; b. Fresno, Calif., Apr. 29, 1924; s. Jesse Braswell and Nancy Guinn; m. Thora M. Guinn, Apr. 10, 1954; 1 child, Nancy Ann. BA in Anthropology, Fresno State Coll., 1951; MA in Math., U. So. Calif., LA, 1953; PhD in Math., UCLA, 1964. Aircraft engr. Douglas Aircraft, Santa Monica, Calif., 1953—64, sr. scientist, 1964—65; asst. rsch. prof. UCLA, 1964—68; asst. prof. math. and engring. Mich. State U., Lansing, 1965—68; prof. math. U. N.Mex., Albuquerque, 1965—82; ret. Pres. Young Dems., LA, 1964—65; founder Calif. Dem. Coun., 1965. With USNR, 1942—45. Avocation: mus. exhibit design.

GUINSBURG, PHILIP FRIED, alcohol and substance abuse counselor; b. NYC, Sept. 13, 1946; s. Theodore and Elena (Fried) G.; m. Debrah Josias Guinsburg, June 15, 1968; children: Mark, Michael. BA, Columbia Coll., 1968; MA, U. ND, Grand Forks, 1970, PhD, 1973. Diplomate Am. Bd. Med. Psychotherapy; lic. alcohol and drug abuse counselor. Clin. dir. Nashville Drug Treatment Ctr., Dede Wallace Ctr., 1973-78; pvt. practice Nashville, 1974—. Asst. clin. prof. psychiatry Vanderbilt U., Nashville, 1987-93; cons. Crisis Intervention Ctr., 1974-99; pres. Dreammakers, Inc., Nashville, 1989-91; cons. Campus For Human Devel. Co-author: Making Love Safe, 2003. Baseball coach Brentwood Civitan Little League, Tenn., 1982-92. Named to Hall of Fame, Howlett Woodmere Alumni Assn., 2006; recipient Voices in Recovery award, Tenn. Assn. Drug and Alcohol Svcs., 2006. Mem. ACA, Am. Group Psychotherapy Assn., Am. Acad. Psychoterhapists (pres.), Assn. for Spiritual, Ethical and Religious Values in Counseling, Nat. Assn. Addiction Counselors (profl. of the yr.), Tenn. Assn. Alcohol and Drug Abuse Counselors (pres., Tenn. Profl. of Yr. 2002, Lifetime Achievement award 2003), Voices in Recovery. Jewish. Avocations: gardening, sports, gourmet foods. Home: 8121 Maryland Ln Brentwood TN 37027-7341 Office: 2313 21st Ave S Nashville TN 37212-4908 Office Phone: 615-386-3333. Personal E-mail: PFG1946@aol.com.

GUINTHER, CHRISTINE LOUISE, special education educator; b. Chgo., Oct. 27, 1949; d. William Joseph and Olga (Sandul) Bacha; m. Paul H. Demper, July 22, 1972 (div. 1987); m. William Robert Guinther, June 25, 1988. BS in Edn., Ill. State U., 1971; MA in Exceptional Child Edn., Ohio State U., 1974. Cert. tchr., Mo. Resource tchr. for learning disabled students Palatine (Ill.) Community Consol. Sch. Dist. #15, 1971-72, Scioto-Darby City Schs., Hilliard, Ohio, 1972-76, Francis Howell Sch. Dist., St. Charles, Mo., 1976—. Mem. NEA (human rels. com. 1987-93, bd. dirs. 1993—), ACLU, ASCD, Nat. Staf devel. Coun., AAUW, Mo. NEA (bd. dirs. 1985-91, human rels. com. 1983—, exec. com. 1993—), Francis Howell Edn. Assn. (pres. 1981-82), NMSA, Delta Kappa Gamma. Methodist. Avocations: walking, music, needlecrafts, reading, Scrabble.

GUION, ROBERT MORGAN, psychologist, educator; b. Indpls., Sept. 14, 1924; s. Leroy Herbert and Carolyn (Morgan) Guion; m. Mary Emily Firestone, June 8, 1947; children: David Michael, Diana Lynn, Keith Douglas, Pamela Sue, Judith Elaine. BA, State U. Iowa, 1948; MS, Purdue U., 1950, PhD, 1952. Vocat. counselor Purdue U., 1948-51, research fellow, 1951-52; mem. faculty Bowling Green (Ohio) State U., 1952—, prof. psychology, 1964—, univ. prof., 1983-85, univ. prof. emeritus, 1985—, chmn. dept., 1966-71. Vis. prof. U. Calif., Berkeley, 1963—64, U. N.Mex., 1965; tech. adviser Dept. Pers. Svcs., State of Hawaii, 1970; vis. rsch. psychologist Ednl. Testing Svc., 1971—72; cons. in field. Author: (book) Personnel Testing, 1965, Assessment, Measurement and Prediction for Personnel Decisions, 1998; editor: Jour. Applied Psychology, 1983—88; co-author (with Scott Highhouse): Essentials of Personnel Assessment and Selection, 2006. With AUS, 1943—46. Recipient Stephen E. Bemis award, Internat. Pers. Mgmt. Assn., 2000. Mem.: APA (pres. divsn. 14 1972—73, pres. divsn. 5 1982—83, James McKeen Cattell award divsn. 14 1965, 1981, Disting. Sci. Contbn. award divsn. 14 1987, Disting. Svc. award divsn. 14 1993, Lifetime Contbn. award divsn. 5 1997), Am. Psychol. Soc. (James McKeen Cattell award 2000). Methodist. Home: 632 Haskins Rd Bowling Green OH 43402-1615 Personal E-mail: rmguion@wcnet.org.

GUISASOLA GAMEZ, ELINA, psychologist; BA summa cum laude, Sacred Heart U., 1982—86; MA, U. PR, 1989, PhD in philosophy, 1993. Pvt. practice, 1989—. Pres. Assn. for World Unity of Women, PR. Mem.: Assn. Psychol. of PR, Am. Psychol. Assn. Office: Metro Office Park Metro Parque 7 Ste 204 Guaynabo PR 00968 Office Phone: 787-793-4307. E-mail: elinaguisasola@hotmail.com.

GUISE, DAVID EARL, architect, educator; b. NYC, Dec. 29, 1931; s. Jack I. and Frances (Haberman) G.; m. Gretchen Grunenfelder, Nov. 21, 1962; children: Gabrielle Ann, John George, Jacqueline Alexis, Ursula Claire. BArch with honors, U. Pa., 1957. Job capt. Kahn & Jacobs, Architects, NYC, 1957-60; designer draftsman E.J. Robin, Architect, NYC, 1961; architect David Guise, Architect, NYC, 1962—; asst. prof. Sch. Architecture, CCNY, 1966-70, assoc. prof., 1970-76, prof., 1976-91; prof. emeritus CCNY, 1991—. Adj. prof. Columbia U., 1983-85, CCNY, 1993—; vis. prof. U. Pa., 1990. Author: Design and Technology in Architecture, 1985, rev. edit., 1991; contbr. articles to profl. jours., Ency. Britannica yearbook; architect numerous comml. and residential bldgs. Mem. nat. panel Am. Arbitration Assn., 1967—; sec. Irvington Planning Bd., N.Y., 1974-88. Mem. Bldg. Rsch. Inst. Home: PO Box 295 Ardsley On Hudson NY 10503

GUISEPI, ROBERT ANTHONY, historian, writer; b. Chgo., Oct. 11, 1946; s. Joseph John Guisepi and Phyllis Eileen Nuzzo; m. Sandra Lynn Paolini, Jan. 28, 1989; children: Cynthia Ann Powell, Robert Anthony Guisepi, JR., Jessica Margaret LeClaire. PhD, Canterbury U., 2006. Prof. U. Calif., Berkeley, 1980—2000; dir. History World Internat., Sacramento, 1991—2006. Author: Ancient Voices, Ancient Times, Modern Times. With USAF, 1961—63, San Antonio, Tex. Recipient Internat. Academic Achievement award, Internat. Ctr. Hist. Studies, 1999; Ancient Lang. Scholar, World Languages Ctr. of London, 2004. Mem.: History Writers of Am. (hon.). Libertarian. Achievements include research in ancient languages. Avocations: chess, reading, writing, ancient languages. Home: 7716 Southbreeze Dr Sacramento CA 95828 Home Phone: 916-612-6837. Personal E-mail: robert@history-world.org.

GUITÉ, J. C. MICHEL, telephone company owner; b. Montreal, Que., Can., Feb. 20, 1945; came to U.S., 1968; s. Jean-Paul Ernest and Mary Alison (Carmichael); m. Eva Maria Balles Guité, 1999; children: Sophie Elizabeth, Diane Rebecca, Jean-Paul, Graham Walker, Wear Gardiner. BA, Dalhousie U., Halifax, Can., 1967; MSc, MIT, 1972; PhD, Stanford U., 1977. V.p. Salomon Bros., NYC, 1985-93; sr. v.p. Dillon Read, NYC, 1993-94; pres., CEO Vt. Tel. Co., Inc., 1994—2001, chmn., owner, 2001—. Bd. dirs. Ctr. for Computer Assisted Rsch. in Humanities, Stanford U., Calif. Democrat. Avocation: mountain climbing. Home: 47 Glenville Rd Greenwich CT 06831-5331 Office: Vt Tel Co 354 River St Springfield VT 05156-2241

GULAN, BONNIE MARION, writer, researcher; b. Kenosha, Wis., Feb. 27, 1922; adopted d. Matthew and Elizabeth Ummy Thomas; m. Edward J. Gulan, Nov. 26, 1949; children: John, Michael, Kathryn. Beauty cons. Globe Dept., Kenosha, Wis., 1950—54; inventor & pitch artist Beauty Blush Cosmetic Line, Waukegan, Ill., 1954—56; creator & founder Felture's Inc., Brookfield, Ill., 1956—59; gen. mgr. & designer Eichling's Flowers Inc., Skokie, Ill., 1960—64; founder, dir. An-Oix-Is In-home Youth Ministry, Winnetka, Ill., 1965—75; founder & ceo The Christmas Tree Story Ho. Mus., Multiple Locations, Ill., 1970—90; author & rschr. Milwaukee, Wis., 1990—98; author Saukville, Wis., 1998—. Founder, pres. World-Wide Women's Inventor's Orgn., Libertyville, Ill., 1961—65; creator, lectr. Miracle Thinking Lecture Series, Mundelein, Ill., 1965—69; spkr. in field. Author: (book) Family Miracles, 1981, Stories From The Christmas Tree Story House, 1981, The Great Bible Dig, 2001, The House of the Seven Cats - An Adventure, 2001, Lost Adventures-House of the 7 Cats, 2001, 7 Cats Promised Land Adventure, 2001, Over the Fence Non-Sense Tales, 2001, Lamp Of Hope, 2001, Back Yard Critter Tales, 2001, A Collection Of Mrs. Claus' Christmas Stories, 2001, The Master Toy Maker, 2001, Adventures Down Nursery Rhyme Lane, 2001, A Collection Of Nodding Off Stories, 2001, Christmas In Our Town, 2002, The Great Journey in Pursuit of Jesus' Way, Truth & Life, 2002; composer: (albums) Sounds of The Christmas Tree Story House, 1975. Founder, pres. & lectr. T.H.E Anti-Drug Youth Program, Winnetka, 1971—75. Home: 1053 South Main Street Saukville WI 53080 Home Phone: 262-268-1224; Office Phone: 262-268-1224. Personal E-mail: bmgulan@aol.com.

GULATI, MARTHA, health facility administrator, cardiologist; b. Lions Head, Ont., Can., May 14, 1969; BS summa cum laude, McMaster U., Hamilton, Can., 1991; MD, U. Toronto, 1995; MS in Health Studies for Clin. Profls., U. Chgo., 2002. Diplomate in internal medicine Am. Bd. Internal Medicine, in cardiology Am. Bd. Internal Medicine. Resident in internal medicine U. Chgo., 1995—98, fellow in cardiology, 1998—2001, clin. assoc. medicine, dept. medicine, divsn. cardiology, 2001—02; asst. prof. medicine and preventative medicine, divsn. cardiology Rush U., Chgo., 2002—05; asst. prof. medicine and preventative medicine, divsn. cardiology, assoc. med. dir. ctr. women's cardiovasc. health Feinberg Sch. Medicine, Northwestern Meml. Hosp., Chgo., 2005—. Named one of Chgo.'s Top 40 under 40 in Bus., Crain's Chgo. Bus., 2005; recipient Girls on the Run Inspiration award, 2005. Mem.: Am. Coll. Cardiology, Am. Heart Assn. (nominated mem. women in cardiology com., coun. clin. cardiology, go red for women com. mem., author current guidelines for heart disease prevention in women). Office: Bluhm Cardiovascular Inst of Northwestern 201 East Huron Ste 10-240 Chicago IL 60611 Office Phone: 312-695-4965, 312-695-0993.

GULAY, ROBERT ROMAN, epidemiologist, educator; BA in Microbiology, Rutgers U., New Brunswick, NJ, 1989; MPH in Infectious Diseases, U. Calif., Berkeley, 1994. Instr. Raritan C.C., Somerville, NJ, 2002—; lectr. Bergen C.C., Paramus, NJ, 2005—; pres., gen. mgr. Ddiscoverygenics, Hamilton, NJ, 2007—. Adj. instr. Fairleigh Dickinson U., Teaneck, NJ, 2005—; adj. asst. prof. County Coll. Morris, Randolph, NJ, 2005—.

GULBIS, NATALIE ANNE, professional golfer, television personality; b. Jan. 7, 1983; d. John and Barbara Gulbis. Student, U. Ariz., Tucson, 1999—2000. Mem. LPGA, 2002—. Mem. US Team Solheim Cup, 2005. Star: (TV series) The Natalie Gulbis Show, 2005—. Founder Natalie Gulbis Found., 2005—. Achievements include winning the 2007 Evian Masters on the LPGA Tour. Mailing: c/o Octagon Giff Breed 7100 Forest Ave Ste 201 Richmond VA 23226 Office Phone: 804-285-4200.*

GULBRANDSEN, PATRICIA HUGHES, physician; b. May 9, 1940; d. Patrick Boland and Anne Hughes; m. Jon Alf Gulbrandsen, Mar. 6, 1972 (dec. Oct. 1984). BA, Cornell U., 1962; MD, U. Pa., 1967; MPH, Johns Hopkins U., 1980. Cert. Am. Bd. Disability Analysts; diplomate Am. Bd. Phys. Medicine and Rehab., Am. Bd. Occupl. Medicine. Rotating intern Chgo. Wesley Meml. Hosp., 1967-68; resident in neurology Pa. Hosp., Phila., 1968-69, Georgetown U. Hosp., Washington, 1972-74; fellow in gynecologic endocrinology Chelsea Hosp. for Women, London, 1969-71; resident in phys. medicine and rehab. Good Samaritan Hosp., Phoenix, 1974-76; commd. maj. U.S. Army, 1979, advanced through grades to lt. col., 1982; with Walter Reed Army Med. Ctr., Washington, 1979-81; occup. medicine officer U.S. Army/Army Environ. Hygiene Agy., Aberdeen Proving Ground, Md., 1981-83; resigned U.S. Army, 1983; med. dir. USN/Naval Surface Warfare Ctr., White Oak, Md., 1984-89, NASA Hdqs., Washington, 1990-93; acting chief med. officer Hdqs. FBI, Washington, 1995; med. officer Orgn. Am. States, Washington, 1999—2001; occupl. health phys., cons. Def. Intelligence Agy., Bolling AFB, Washington, 2001—03; NIOSH occupl. medicine physician Dept. Energy Worker Advocacy Program, 2004; pvt. practice Gulbrandsen Energy Medicine, LLC, 2006—. Occupl. medicine Profl. Occupl. Health Svcs., 1997-98; staff physiatrist, head consultation svc. New Eng. Med. Ctr. Hosps., Boston, 1977-78; instr. neurology and phys. medicine and rehab. Tufts U. Sch. Medicine, Boston, 1977-78; med. cons. Fairfax County (Va.) Health Dept., 1990, Hummer and Assocs., Cleve., 1990-93, Allied Med. Cons., Inc., Washington, 1994-95, AspenMed Svcs., Inc., 1995-96, 01-03, The Westwood Group, 2004, Gulbrandsen Energy Medicine, LLC, 2006—, Occu Save, Inc., Lanham, Md., 1996, staff privileges Drs. Cmty. Hosp., 1996-98, Hummer Whole Health Mgmt., 1998-99. Mem. Am. Coll. Preventive Medicine, Am. Coll. Occupl and Environ. Medicine, Montgomery County Med. Soc., Med. and Chirurg. Faculty Md. Office Phone: 410-795-7309. Personal E-mail: mddocg@yahoo.com.

GULCHER, ROBERT HARRY, aerospace transportation executive; b. Columbus, Ohio, Aug. 26, 1925; s. Alban H. and Beatrice (Plohr) G.; m. Barbara Witherspoon, June, 1949 (div.); 1 child, Robert; m. Anne Cummings, Dec. 14, 1959 (dec.); children: Jeffrey, Donald; m. Suzanne K. Kane, Apr. 12,1969; children: Andrew, Kristin. BS, U.S. Marine Acad., 1945; B.E.E., Ohio State U., 1950. Third asst. engr. Am. Petroleum Transp. Co., NYC, 1945-46; engr. Capital Elevator & Mfg. Co., Columbus, Ohio, 1949-51, Columbus div. N. Am. Aviation, 1951-53, various mgmt. engring. positions, 1953-66; chief engr. Columbus div. Rockwell Internat., 1966-79, v.p. rsch. and engring. N.Am. aircraft ops. El Segundo, Calif., 1979-85, v.p. advanced programs N.Am. aircraft ops., 1985-87, v.p., program mgr. nat. aerospace plane, 1987-90, v.p. hypersonic programs Downey, Calif., 1990-91; retired, 1991; aerospace cons., 1992—. Trustee Little Company of Mary Hosp. Found., 1992—2005, chmn. bd. trustees, 1996-97; trustee coun. LCMH Hosp., 1997—2002, trustee emeritus, 2005; pres. St. Paul Lutheran Ch., 2004-07. Fellow AIAA, IEEE (sr. mem.); mem. Rotary Internat. (dir. cmty. svc. 2006—, Rotarian of Yr. 2006-07). Republican. Lutheran. E-mail: rgulcher@aol.com.

GULDA, EDWARD JAMES, diversified financial services company executive; b. Detroit, Oct. 28, 1945; s. Alfred and Lucy Irene (Ball) G.; m. Nancy Mary Greenlee, Nov. 28, 1964; children: Kimberly Sue Marsh, Nicholas Edward. BS in Aerospace Engring., U. Mich., 1968, MBA, 1979. Systems engr. LTV Aerospace Corp., Sterling Heights, Mich., 1966-72; mgr. systems engring. Ford Motor Co., Dearborn, Mich., 1972-78; mgr., prodn. plan. Rockwell Internat. Corp., Dearborn, Mich., 1978-79, dir. prod. plan. Troy, Mich., 1979-80, dir. mkt. electronics, 1980-81, gen. mgr. auto electronics, 1981-84, v.p. rsch. and engring., 1984-85; pres. ITT Teves Am., Troy, 1985-87; group v.p. engring. ITT Auto, Inc., Troy, 1987-88; pres., chief exec. officer Dayton Walther (Varity) Corp., Dayton, Ohio, 1988-89; pres. Varity Brake Group Kelsey-Hayes Brake Group N.Am., Romulus, Mich., 1989-94; pres. Kelsey-Hayes Co., Romulus, Mich., 1994-95, chief exec. Livonia, Mich., 1995; chmn. and CEO Peregrine Inc., Southfield, Mich., 1996-98; pres. Kinnick Group LLC, 1998—. Mem.: Mensa. Avocations: hunting, golf. Home: 4395 Forest Ave Waterford MI 48328-1110 Home Phone: 248-618-9743; Office Phone: 248-618-9809. Business E-Mail: ejgulda@gulda-associates.com.

GULDEN, SIMON, lawyer, management consultant, consultant; b. Montreal, Que., Can., Jan. 7, 1938; s. David and Zelda (Long) G.; m. Ellen Lee Barbour, June 12, 1977. BA, McGill U., Montreal, 1959; cert., U. Rennes, 1961; LL.L., U. Montreal, 1962; cert., Wharton Sch., 1979; alt. dispute resolution cert., York U., Toronto, 1999. Bar: Que. Ptnr. Genser, Philips, Friedman & Gulden, Montreal, 1963-68; sec., legal counsel Pl. Bonaventure, Inc., 1969-72; legal counsel real estate Steinberg Inc., Montreal, 1972-74; solicitor, prime atty. Bell Can., Montreal, 1975-76; v.p., gen. counsel, sec., dir. Nabisco Ltd, Toronto, 1975-98; pres., dir. Interlude Capital Corp., Markham (Unionville), Ont., 1997—; dir. legal affairs Stream Intelligent Networks Corp., 2000-2001; v.p. corp. and legal affairs Canderel Stoneridge Equity Group, 2001—02. Mem.: ABA, Bar of Que., Inst. Chartered Secs. and Adminstrs. (cert.), Osgoode Law Soc., Lord Reading Law Soc. Que., Can. Bar Assn. Home and Office: 23 Danbury Ct Markham ON Canada L3R 7S1 Home Phone: 905-477-9130; Office Phone: 905-477-9130. E-mail: simongulden@rogers.com.

GULER, OSMAN, education educator, researcher; s. Esref and Zulfiye Guler; m. Colleen Erin Beadling, July 23, 1988; children: Aylin Claire, Timur Daniel. BA, Yale U., Conn., 1978; MS, U. Chgo., 1979, PhD, 1990. Assoc. prof. U. of Md., Balt., 1999—2004, prof., 2004—. Vis. lectr. U. Iowa, 1988—91; vis. scholar Delft (Ariz.) U. Tech., Netherlands, 1991—92; vis. asst. prof. U. Md., Balt., 1992—94, asst. prof., 1994—99. Grantee Several rsch. grants, NSF, 1993—. Mem.: SIAM, Math. Programming Soc. Office: Univ of Md Balt County 1000 Hilltop Cir Baltimore MD 21250 Home Phone: 410-788-7675; Office Phone: 410-455-2421. Office Fax: 410-455-1066. Business E-Mail: guler@math.umbc.edu.

GULICK, JAMES P., bank executive; B in Accountancy, Miami U., Oxford, Ohio. CPA Coopers and Lybrand (now PricewaterhouseCoopers); with corp. treasury dept. Nat. City Corp., Cleve., 1992, mgr. regulatory risk mgmt., enterprise risk mgmt. and svc. quality initiative, gen. auditor, 1995—, sr. v.p. Mem. fin. com. St. John Neumann Parish; bd. dirs., mem. fin. com., treas. West Side Cath. Ctr. Mem.: AICPA, Inst. Internal Auditors, Ohio Soc. CPAs. Office: Nat City Corp Nat City Ctr 1900 E Ninth St Cleveland OH 44114-3484 Office Phone: 216-222-2000.*

GULICK, SIDNEY (DENNY) L., III, mathematics professor, writer; s. Sidney L. Gulick, Jr. and Evelyn Mary Gulick; m. Frances Adelia Frost; children: David William, Barbara Louise, Sharon Marie. BA, Oberlin Coll., Ohio, 1958; MA, Yale U., New Haven, 1960, PhD, 1963. Instr. math. U. Pa., Phila., 1963—65; prof. math. U. Md., College Park, 1965—. Adminstr. dept. math. U. Md. Author: Calculus, Encounters with Chaos. Recipient Kirwan Undergraduate Edn. award, U. Md., 2000. Mem.: Math. Assn. Am., Phi Beta Kappa (treas. chpt. 1990—2007). Home Phone: 301-422-9611; Office Phone: 301-405-5157.

GULICK, WALTER LAWRENCE, psychologist, educator, retired academic administrator; b. Summit, NJ, July 4, 1927; s. Walter Lawrence and Carol (Dewey) G.; m. Winifred Bourn Frazee, Oct. 18, 1952; children: Hans, Tod, Kristina. AB, Hamilton Coll., Clinton, NY, 1952; MA, U. Del., 1955; PhD, Princeton U., 1957; MA (hon.), Dartmouth Coll., 1968; LHD (hon.), St. Lawrence U., 1989. Mem. faculty U. Del., 1957-65, prof. psychology, 1963-65, chmn. dept., 1964-65; prof. psychology Dartmouth Coll., Hanover, NH, 1965-74, chmn. dept., 1970-73, 74-75, Disting. Class of 1925 prof., 1973-75; dean of coll. Hamilton Coll., 1975-79, prof. psychology, 1975-81, William R. Kenan prof., 1979-81; pres. St. Lawrence U., 1981-87, Gulick Assocs., 1987—. Vis. prof. U. Vt., 1977; resident scholar U. Del., 1988-02; cons. Presbyn. Hosp., Phila., 1961-63; editl. cons. Oxford U. Press, 1963—, McGraw-Hill Pub. Co., 1966-67, Harper & Row, 1971-73, Cambridge U. Press, 1979—. Author: Hearing: Physiology and Psychophysics, 1971, Human Stereopsis: Psychophysical Analysis, 1976, Hearing: Physiological Acoustics, Neural Coding and Psychoacoustics, 1989; contbr.: Ency. of Human Behavior, 1994; contbr. articles to profl. jours. Mem. Hanover Sch. Bd., 1972-75, Dresden Bd. Sch. Dirs., 1972-75; mem. grad. coun. Princeton U., 1972-75; mem. adv. coun. Nat. Inst. for Humanities, 1975-; mem. tchg. evaluation project HEW. Served with AUS, 1946-48. Recipient Nat. Svc. award 1955, 81, Dale prize Hamilton Coll., 1952, Alumnni Achievement medal, 1995; Theta Delta Chi fellow U. Del., 1953-55, Psychology scholar Princeton U., 1955-57. Mem. N.Y. Acad. Scis., Ea. Psychol. Assn., Psychonomic Soc., Phi Beta Kappa, Omicron Delta Kappa, Sigma Xi (pres. Dartmouth chpt. 1967-68, Gold Medal Lifetime Achievement award 1995), Psi Chi (pres. U. Del. chpt. 1954-55). Achievements include research in vision and hearing. Home: 347 Greenbriar Ln West Grove PA 19390 Office: Gulick Assocs Inc PO Box 154 Kelton PA 19346 Personal E-mail: w.gulick@comcast.net.

GULINO, FRANK, lawyer, educator; b. Bklyn., Aug. 14, 1954; s. Frank C. and Frances (Cataldo) G.; m. Donna Regina Cramer, June 30, 1984; children: Frank Regis, Mary Elise. BA, NYU, 1976; JD, Fordham U., 1979. Bar: N.Y. 1980, U.S. Dist. Ct. (no., so. ea. and we. dists.) N.Y. 1980, U.S. Tax Ct. 1980, U.S. Ct. Mil. Appeals 1980, U.S. Ct. Appeals (2d cir.) 1980, U.S. Ct. Internat. Trade 1982, U.S. Supreme Ct. 1983, U.S. Ct. Claims 1985, U.S. Ct. Appeals (8th and fed. cirs.) 1985, D.C. 1986, U.S. Dist. Ct. Nebr. 1986, U.S. Dist. Ct. Hawaii 1986, U.S. Ct. Appeals (3d, 5th, 6th, 7th, 9th, 10th and 11th cirs.) 1986, U.S. Ct. Appeals (D.C. cir.) 1988. Law clk. to U.S. magistrate U.S. Dist. Ct. (so. dist.) N.Y., NYC, 1979-80; assoc. Donovan, Leisure, Newton & Irvine, NYC, 1980-83, Carro, Spanbock, Fass, Geller, Kaster & Cuiffo, NYC, 1984-86; dep. gen. counsel N.Y.C. Housing Authority, 1986-88; assoc. Summit Rovins & Feldesman, NYC, 1988; of counsel Stockfield & Fixler, NYC, 1988-89, ptnr., 1989-91, Stockfield, Fixler & Gulino, NYC, 1991-94, Fixler & Gulino, L.L.P., NYC, 1995—98, Fixler & Assocs., LLP, NYC, 1998—2001; counsel Brecher, Fishman, Pasternack, Popish, Heller, Rubin & Reiff, P.C., NYC, 2001—03, ptnr., 2003—. Adj. assoc. prof. Fordham U. Sch. Law, N.Y.C., 1983-88. Author: Judgments in Federal Civil Practice, 1989, supplement, 1993, 97, 2000. Mem. ABA (mem. coun. appellate lawyers), Fed. Bar Coun., N.Y. State Bar Assn. (atty. advisor high sch. mock trial program 1980-87), N.Y. State Trial Lawyers Assn., Assn. Trial Lawyers of Am. Office: 222 Broadway New York NY 10038-2510

GULINO, LAWRENCE CARL, mediator; b. Bklyn., July 22, 1945; s. Joseph and Anna Virga Gulino; m. Annette Marie Spadafina, June 27, 1970; 1 child, Joanne. BA, St. John's U., Bkyln., 1966; MA, Alfred U., NY, 1968. Cert. sch. psychologist NY, 1968, advanced cert. marriage and family counseling Queens Coll., 1982. Sch. psychologist Lockport Schs., NY, 1968—69, Smithtown Schs., NY, 1969—2001; divorce mediator, sole proprietor Divorce Mediation Ctr. Suffolk County, Stony Brook, 1982—97; pvt. practice cons. sch. psychology Stony Brook, 2001—05; divorce mediator, ptnr. NY Divorce Mediation, Stony Brook, 2005—. Com. spl. edn. Smithtown Schs., 1979—89; bd. dirs. NY State Coun. on Divorce Mediation, NYC, 1992—93; lectr. Parent Edn. and Child Evaluation Program, Suffolk County Family Ct., Hauppauge, NY, 1995—99. Mem.: NASP, NY Assn. Sch. Psychology, Assn. Family and Conciliation Cts., Family and Divorce Mediation Coun. Greater NY, NY State Coun. on Divorce Mediation, Suffolk County Psychol. Assn. (life), Smithtown Classroom Tchrs. Assn. (life), Am. Fedn. Tchrs. (life), NY State United Tchrs. (life), Stony Brook Yacht Club. Avocations: boating, exercise. Home: 4 Freshman Ln Stony Brook NY 11790 Office Phone: 631-751-2965. Personal E-mail: lcgmediator@aol.com.

GULKIN, HARRY, arts administrator, film producer; b. Montreal, Que., Can., Nov. 14, 1927; s. Peter Oliver and Raya (Shinderman) G. Portrait photographer, 1942-44; mcht. seaman, trade union organizer, 1944-49; labour journalist, critic, trade union organizer, 1950-56; market researcher, cons., 1956-71; ind. film producer, 1971—; exec. and artistic dir. Saidye Bronfman Ctr., 1983-87; dir. projects Soc. Developpement Entreprises Culturelles, 1987—; producer BAYO, 1985. Challenger Nat. Film Bd., Can., 1979; adv. coun. film dept. Concordia U. Prodr.: Penny and Ann (2d prize Film Festival Internat. Congress Rehab. Centres 1976, award Amtec Media Festival 1977), 1974 (Red Ribbon Am. Film Festival 1977), Lies My Father Told Me (Hollywood Fgn. Critics award as best fgn. film 1975, Grand prize V.I. Internat. Festival 1975, Christopher awards 1975, Assn. Can. TV and Radio Artists award 1976, Canadian Film award 1976, Can. Motion Picture Distbrs. Assn. award 1976, nominated Best Original Screenplay Oscar, 1976), Jacob Two Meets The Hooded Fang, 1976 (Gold medallion spl. jury award Miami Internat. Film Festival 1978, Spl. Jury award 8th Internat. Children's Film Festival, Los Angeles 1979), Two Solitudes, 1977; editor: The Marketer Jour., 1966. Mem. Motion Picture Inst. Can. (pres. 1977), Can. Film Inst. (past pres., chmn.), Assn. Que. Film Producers, Cinematheque Québecoise (v.p. 1995-2000), Am. Mktg. Assn. (past chpt. pres.), Acad. Can. Cinema, Quebec Soc. for Promotion of English Lang. Lit. (mem. adv. coun.). Home: 165 Ch Cote Ste Catherine Apt PH4 Outremont PQ Canada H2V ZA7

GULKO, EDWARD, healthcare executive, consultant; b. Paterson, NJ, Nov. 22, 1950; s. Benjamin and Anita (Yankelevsky) G.; m. Judith Ilene Lee, May 29, 1977. BS in Indsl. Engring., N.J. Inst. Tech., 1972; MBA, Temple U., 1974. Cert. healthcare exec., med. practice exec.; lic. nursing home adminstr. Health program analyst Morrisania Hosp., Bronx, NY, 1974—75; assoc. dir. Mission Health Ctr., San Francisco, 1976; supervising sys. analyst Health and Hosp. Corp., NYC, 1977—78; dep. exec. dir. Greenpoint Hosp., Bklyn., 1978—82; assoc. exec. dir. Woodhull Med. Ctr., Bklyn., 1982—84; adminstr. Montclair Med. Group, NJ, 1984—87; asst. adminstr. Summit Med. Group, NJ, 1987—91; adminstr. Wooster Clinic, Inc., Ohio, 1991—96; COO Grove Hill Med. Ctr., New Britain, Conn., 1996—99; exec. dir. Old Bridge-Sayreville Med. Group, NJ, 1999—2002; adminstr. Digestive Healthcare Ctr. and Ctrl. Jersey Ambulatory Surgery Ctr., Hillsborough, NJ, 2002—04, Englewood Orthop. Assocs., NJ, 2004—. Trustee Society Hill Townhouse Assn., 1986-90, v.p., 1987-88, pres., 1988-89; bd. dirs. Residential Support Svcs., 1993-96, v.p. 1993-96. Lt. cmdr. Med. Svcs. Corps, USNR, 1982—2004. Fellow: Am. Coll. Healthcare Execs., Am. Coll. Med. Practice Execs.; mem.: NJ Med. Group Mgmt. Assn. (exec. bd. 2000—, treas. 2003—04, v.p. 2004—05, pres. 2006—), Am. Acad. Med. Adminstrs. (N.J. state dir. 2000—), Naval Res. Assn. (dist. v.p. 1987—91), Med. Group Mgmt. Assn. (nat. comm. com. 1993—95, jour. editl. bd. 2000—03), Assn. Mil. Surgeons US (exec. com. N.J. chpt. 1985—87, pres. 1988—89). Democrat. Home: 230 Seton Hall Dr Freehold NJ 07728-8878 Office: 401 S Van Brunt St Englewood NJ Office Phone: 201-569-2770. Personal E-mail: edgulko@aol.com.

GULLACE, MARLENE FRANCES, systems engineer, consultant; b. Ft. Belvoir, Va., Jan. 12, 1952; d. Amerigo Francis and Martha Arlene Guy; m. Gerald Lynn Tolley, June 26, 1970 (div. Nov. 1974); 1 child, Gerald Lynn Tolley Jr.; m. Salvatore Gullace, Nov. 19, 1976 (div. Apr. 1991). AA in Pre-Law, Cochise Coll., 1979; BA in Polit. Sci., U. Ariz., 1982; AA in Computer Sci. and Bus., Chaparral Coll., 1985. Realtor, entrepreneur, inventor, Sierra Vista, Ariz., 1977-84; ADP instr. Chaparral Coll., Tucson, 1985; model Barbizon, Tucson, 1986-87; clk. HUD/FHA, Tucson, 1987-88; computer programmer DOD Inspector Gen., Arlington, 1988-89; programmer analyst US Army Corps of Engrs., USAF, Washington, 1989-91, Calibre Sys. Inc., Falls Church, Va., 1991; cons., sys. analyst/programmer EDP, Vienna, Va., 1991-93; info. engr. Ogden/Anteon Corp., Vienna, 1993-96, Orkand Corp., 1996, SRA Internat., Inc., 1997-00, SRA Internat., 2000—01, SAIC, 2002—04, Lockheed Martin, 2004—. Patented toy, registered trademark. Realtor assoc. Cochise County Bd. Realtors, 1977-84. Mem. IEEE, Fed. Women's Program at SBA (sec. 1976). Methodist. Avocations: art, design, crafts, sewing. Home: 7829 Piccadilly Dr Warrenton VA 20186-8623 Personal E-mail: mgullace@aol.com.

GULLAND, EUGENE D., lawyer; b. Endicott, NY, Aug. 27, 1947; s. George Raymond and Virginia (Fisher) G.; m. Kristin Spearing, Aug. 29, 1970; children: Michael Spearing, Molly Spearing, Samuel Spearing. AB, Princeton U., 1969; JD, Yale U., 1972. Bar: D.C., Va., U.S. Supreme Ct., U.S. Ct. Appeals (1st, 2d, 3d, 4th, 6th, 7th, 9th, D.C., Fed. cirs.), U.S. Dist. Ct. D.C., (ea. dist.) Va., Md., Ariz., Ind. Assoc. Covington & Burling, Washington, 1973-80, ptnr., 1980—. Practitioner before London Ct. Internat. Arbitration, Internat. C. of C., ICSID, Am. Arbitration Assn., also other arbitral tribunals; mem. faculty Nat. Inst. for Trial Advocacy, Am. Judicature Soc. Trustee Loudoun Day Sch., Leesburg, Va., 1986-98; vestryman, treas. Our Redeemer Ch., 1987-97; mem. alumni schs. com. Princeton U. Capt. U.S. Army, 1972-73. Woodrow Wilson scholar Princeton U., Princeton U. scholar. Mem. Internat. Arbitration Inst., Nat. Assn. Coll. and Univ. Attys., Am. Judicature Soc., Henlopen Acres Beach Club, Phi Beta Kappa. Home: Little River Farm Aldie VA 20105 Office: Covington & Burling 1201 Pennsylvania Ave NW Washington DC 20004-2401 Home Phone: 703-777-3137; Office Phone: 202-662-5504. Business E-Mail: egulland@cov.com.

GULLEDGE, SANDRA SMITH, publishing executive, film producer; b. Great Lakes, Ill., July 6, 1949; d. Dennis Murrey and Olga (Grosheff) Smith. BS, Northwestern U., 1971; MA, Annenberg Sch Comm., U. So. Calif., 1986. Columnist Camarillo Daily News, Calif., 1971-76; editor Fillmore Herald, Calif., 1976-78; pub. info. officer Oxnard Union High Sch. Dist., Calif., 1980-82, Ventura County Cmty. Coll. Dist., 1982-83; pub. rels. dir. Murphy Orgn., Oxnard, Calif., 1983-84; editor Forum and Solutions GTE, Irving, Tex., 1988-89; mktg. spec. USAA Alliance Svc., San Antonio, 1995-99; pres. Crimson Horse Entertainment & Publ.Co., LLC, 2000—. Business E-Mail: guidepublishing@usa.net.

GULLEY, JOAN LONG, banker; b. Balt., Sept. 10, 1947; d. Thomas F. and Florence (Waldron) Long; m. Philip Gordon Gulley, aug. 2, 1969; 1 child, Colin Jason. BA, U. Rochester, 1969; postgrad., Harvard U., 1985. Analyst U.S. Dept. Commerce, Washington, 1969-70, Fed. Res. Bd., Washington, 1970-74; sr. analyst 5, Washington, 1979-81; asst. v.p. Fed. Res. Bank Boston, 1975-79, v.p., 1981-83; sr. v.p. 5, 1983-86; exec. v.p. The Mass. Co., Boston, 1986-94, pres., CEO, 1994, also bd. dirs.; chmn., CEO PNC Bank New Eng., 1995-97; sr. v.p., mgr. strategic planning PNC Bank Corp., 1997-98, exec. v.p., dep. mgr. consumer bank, 1998—, dep. mgr. regional cmty. bank, 1999—2000; CEO PNC Bus. Banking, 2000—02, PNC Advisors, 2002—; exec. v.p. Retail Bank, 2005—. Chmn. PNC Bank, New Eng., 1997-99. Mem. Allegheny Country Club, Nantucket Golf Club, Duquesne Club, Phi Beta Kappa. Office: PNC Bank Corp 1 PNC Plz 249 5th Ave Pittsburgh PA 15222-2709

GULLEY, WILBUR PAUL, JR., retired savings and loan association executive; b. Little Rock, Aug. 8, 1923; s. Wilbur Paul and JaJa Douglas (Ashburn) Gulley; m. Mary Elizabeth Bragg Hunt, Mar. 13, 1971; children from previous marriage: Wilbur Paul III, William H., James Ransom, Michael Pierce. AB in Bus. Adminstrn., Duke U., 1947. With Gulley Ins. Agy., Little Rock, 1947, ptnr., mng. officer, 1947-58; with Savers Fed. Savs. & Loan Assn., Little Rock, 1947-89, sec., 1948-52, v.p., 1952-58, pres., 1959-83, chmn. bd. dirs., 1983—89, also bd. dirs.; ret., 1989. Bd. dirs. Little Rock br. Fed. Res. Bank St. Louis, 1983—87. Gen. campaign chmn. United Fund, Pulaski County, Ark., 1963—64; v.p. Little Rock Boys Club, 1970—71, pres., 1971—72; commr. Metrocenter Improvement Dist., 1977—81, chmn., 1981; bd. stewards 1st United Meth. Ch. Little Rock, 1960—90, fin. chmn., 1989; trustee Savs. & Loan Found., 1977—81, Hendrix Coll., Conway, 1980—92, Roselawn Meml. Pk., 1975—, v.p. bd. trustees, 1994—; pres. BBB, Ark., 1962; trustee George W. Donaghey Found., 1958—2001, pres., 1969—72, 1981—83, 1995—96; trustee Ark. State U., 1968—73, sec.-treas., 1971—72, chmn., 1972—73. With USNR, 1943—46. Mem.: Ark. Savs. and Loan League, Pulaski County Savs. and Loan League, U.S. League Savs. Instns., Fin. Instns. Retirement Fund, Southwestern Savs. and Loans Conf., Little Rock C. of C., Little Rock Country Club, Phi Beta Kappa, Beta Omega Sigma, Sigma Alpha Epsilon. Home: 3500 Cedar Hill Rd Unit 3 South Little Rock AR 72202-1914 Personal E-mail: wpgulley@aristotle.net.

GULLIFORD, JAMES B., federal agency administrator; b. St. Paul, 1950; m. Yvonne Gulliford; children: Keri, Jason. BS in Forestry Mgmt., Iowa State U., 1973, MS in Forestry Econs. and Mktg., 1975. Asst. dir. ops. coal extraction utilization rsch. ctr. So. Ill. U., 1979—81; dir. Iowa Dept. Soil Conservation, 1982—86; dir. divsn. soil conservation Iowa Dept. Agr. Land Stewardship, 1986—2001; regional adminstr. region 7 EPA, Kansas City, Kans., 2001—06, asst. adminstr. of toxic substances Washington, 2006—. Mem.: Iowa Environ. Coun., Nat. Assn. Conservation Dists., Soil Water Conservation Soc. (pres. 1993—94), Nat. Assn. State Conservation Agys. (pres. 1989), Iowa Assn. Soil Water Conservation Dist. Commrs. (hon.), Gamma Sigma Delta (Alumni Merit award 1990), Xi Sigma Pi (pres. 1974—75). Office: EPA Ariel Rios Bldg 1200 Pennsylvania Ave NW Washington DC 20460

GULLING, MARK V., consumer products company executive; BS in Math. and Econs., Ashland U., 1974; grad. exec. edn. program, Duke U., 1991. Sys. analyst corp. info. sys. divsn. Eastman Kodak Co., 1974, various positions, 1974—85, info. sys. dir. Eastman Savs. and Loan, 1986—89, with Health Group, 1989, reengineering project mgr., 1991—92, info. sys. dir. bus. imaging sys. and office imaging bus., 1993—96, program mgr., corp. enterprise resource planning initiative, 1996—98, asst. CIO, 1998—2000, acting CIO, 2000—01, CIO, v.p. Rochester, NY, 2001—03, dir., global shared services, v.p., 2003—06; pres., global bus. services MeadWestvaco Corp., Glen Allen, Va., 2006—. Recipient CEO Diversity award, 2002. Office: MeadWestvaco Corp 11013 W Broad St Glen Allen VA 23060*

GULLIVER, JOHN STEPHEN, civil engineering educator; b. Torrence, Calif., Sept. 9, 1950; s. Robert David and Jane Elizabeth (Loeffler) G.; m. Karen Lyum, Nov. 27, 1972; children: Djuna, Teigan, Hallon. BSChemE, U. Calif., Santa Barbara, 1974; MSCE, U. Minn., 1977, PhD in Civil Engring., 1980. Registered profl. engr., Minn. Rsch. assoc. U. Minn., Mpls., 1980-81, asst. prof. civil engring., 1981-87, assoc. prof., 1987-96, prof., 1996—, acting head civil engring., 1997-98, head, 1998—2007. Author: Introduction to Chemical Transport in the Environment; editor: Handbook of Hydropower Engineering, 1990, Air-Water Mass Transfer: Selected Papers From the Second Symposium on Gas Transfer at Water Surfaces, 1991; tech. editor Hydro Rev., 1987-2001, Hydro Rev. Worldwide, 1993-2001; contbr. 87 publs. to sci. and engring. jours. Mem ASCE (Rickey medal 1990, 2003), Internat. Assn. for Hydraulic Rsch. (editor Proc. 27th Congress, Vol. D), Internat. Assn. Water, Am. Soc. Engring. Edn., Assn. Environ. Engring. and Sci. Profs., Am. Pub. Works Assn., Minn. Surveyors and Engrs. Soc., N.Am. Lake Mgmt. Soc. Home: 942 Forest Dale Rd Saint Paul MN 55112-2517 Office: U Minn Civil Engring Dept Minneapolis MN 55455 Home Phone: 651-636-8581; Office Phone: 612-625-4080. Business E-Mail: gulli003@umn.edu.

GULOTTA, STEPHEN J., cardiologist; b. Bklyn., Mar. 5, 1933; s. Vito and Dora Gulotta; m. Lee Scaringella Gulotta, June 27, 1954; 1 child, Stephen Gulotta Jr.; children: Ronald, Eric. BS in Chemistry, Bklyn. Coll., 1954; MD, SUNY, Bklyn., 1958. Diplomate Am. Bd. Internal Medicine with subspeciality in cardiovascular diseases. Med. intern Montefiore Hosp., Bronx, NY, 1958—59, resident in medicine, 1959—61; fellow in cardiology N.Y. Hosp. Cornell Med. Ctr., NYC, 1961—62; chief cardiology North Shore Univ. Hosp., Manhasset, NY, 1967—79; dir. catheterization labs. St. Francis Hosp., Roslyn, NY, 1979—2000. Mem. editl. bd. Circulation, Jour. Am. Coll. Cardiology, 1962—, Am. Jour. Cardiology, —; contbr. over 50 articles to profl. jours. Pres. Nassau Heart Assn., 1978—80, Am. Heart Assn., N.Y. Affiliate, 1981—83; bd. dirs. Commn. on Human Rights, Mt. Vernon, NY, 1964—70. Recipient Disting. Svc. award, Am. Heart Assn., 2000. Fellow: Am. heart Assn. Coun. of Clin. Cardiology, Am. Coll. Chest Physicians, Soc. Coronary Angiography and Interventions, Am. Coll. Cardiology, Am. Coll. Physicians. Avocations: skiing, collecting 20th Century American painters. Office Phone: 516-365-5599.

GULYA, AINA JULIANNA, retired medical association administrator; b. Syracuse, NY, Feb. 3, 1953; d. Aladar and Sylvia E. Gulya; m. William R. Wilson, May 21, 1983. AB cum laude, Yale Coll., 1974; MD with distinction in rsch., U. Rochester, 1978. Diplomate Am. Bd. Otolaryngology. Intern, jr. resident in gen. surgery Beth Israel Hosp., Boston, 1978-80; resident in otolaryngology Mass. Eye and Ear Infirmary, Boston, 1980-83; fellow in otology/neurotology Bapt. Hosp. Ear Found., Nashville, 1983-84; asst. prof. surgery George Washington U., Washington, 1984-87, assoc. prof. surgery, 1987-90, clin. prof. surgery, otolaryngology, head and neck surgery, 1998—2005; assoc. prof. otolaryngology and head and neck surgery Georgetown U., Washington, 1990-94, prof., 1994-96; chief clin. trials br. Nat. Inst. on Deafness and other Comm. Disorders, Bethesda, Md., 1996-2000, chief clin. trials epidemiology biostats. sect., 2000—; ret., 2005. Assoc. examiner Am. Bd. Otolaryngology, 1993-97, bd. dirs., 1997-2002, oral exam. leader for otology, 2000-02, chair neurotology sub-specialty cert. com., 2000-02, cons. Nat. Inst. on Deafness and Other Comm. Disorders. Co-author: Anatomy of the Temporal Bone With Surgical Implications, 1986, 95; assoc. editor Am. Jour. Otology, 1989-99; co-editor Surgery of the Ear, 5th edit., 2002. Bd. dirs. Deafness Rsch. Found., 1994—2001. Recipient Libr. award, Rochester Acad. Medicine, 1975, presdl. citation, Am. Otol., Rhinol. and Laryngol. Soc., 1999. Mem.: Am. Acad. Otolaryngology, Head and Neck Surgery (bd. dirs. 1995—97, Honor award 1991, Disting. Svc. award 2001), Am. Neurotology Soc. (coord. for continuing med. edn. 1990—95), Am. Otological Soc. (coun. 1993—, editor-libr. 1995—2000, trustee rsch. fund 1993—2001, pres.-elect 1999—2000, pres. 2000—01). Avocation: water-skiing. Home: 111 Pleasant Grove Rd Locust Grove VA 22508

GULYAS, DIANE H., manufacturing executive; b. Chgo., 1956; BS in Chem. Engring., U. Notre Dame; advanced mgmt. program, Wharton Sch. Bus., 1994. Various sales, mktg., tech. and sys. devel. positions DuPont Polymers Bus. DuPont, Wilmington, Del., 1978, European bus. mgr. for Engring. Polymers Geneva, plant supt. Mechelen, Belgium, site, exec. asst. to chmn. bd. Wilmington, 1993—94, global bus. dir. Nylon Fibers New Bus. Devel. and Global Zytel Engring. Polymers, 1994—97, v.p., gen. mgr. DuPont Advanced Fiber Businesses Richmond, Va., 1997—2003, group v.p. DuPont Electronic and Comm. Techs. Platform Wilmington, Del., 2003—04, chief mktg. and sales officer, 2004—06, group v.p. DuPont performance materials, 2006—. Bd. dirs. Viasystems, St. Louis. Bd. dirs. Ministry of Caring; mem. strategic planning and advocacy com. Del. Nature Soc. Named one of 50 Most Powerful Women in Bus., Fortune mag., 2006. Office: DuPont Bldg 1007 Market St Wilmington DE 19898

GUMBEL, BRYANT CHARLES, broadcaster; b. New Orleans, Sept. 29, 1948; s. Richard Dunbar and Rhea Alice (LeCesne) Gumbel; m. June Carlyn Baranco, Dec. 1, 1973; children: Bradley Christopher, Jillian Beth. BA, Bates Coll., 1970. Writer Black Sports mag., NYC, 1971; editor Black Sports mag, NYC, 1972; sportscaster KNBC-TV, Burbank, Calif., 1972—76, sports dir., 1976—81; sports host NBC Sports, NYC, 1975—82; co-host Today Show NBC, NYC, 1982—97; host, Real Sports with Bryant Gumbel HBO, 1995—; host The Early Show CBS, NYC, 1997—2002. Recipient Emmy award, 1976, 1977, Golden Mike award, LA Press Club, 1978, 1979, Edward R. Murrow award, Overseas Press Club, 1988, Emmy award, Outstanding Sports Journalism, 2006, 2007. Mem.: AFTRA. Office: Home Box Office Inc 100 Ave of the Americas New York NY 10036*

GUMBINER, ANTHONY JOSEPH, investment banker, lawyer; b. Bradford, Eng., Jan. 2, 1945; s. Samuel and Marie (Sweeney) Gumbiner; m. Heather Howie, 1971; 1 child, Charles Maxwell; m. Mylene Monsillon, Feb. 17, 1981; 1 child, Celine Marie. Student Coll. of Law, Brighton Coll., 1962, U. Guildford, Eng., 1965. Sole practice, London, 1965—77; with Hallwood Group Cos. BV, Amsterdam, 1977—; joint mng. dir. Interallianz Hallwood BV, Zurich, Switzerland, 1977—; mng. dir. Hallwood Fin. Corp., 1980—. Chmn., mng. dir. Anglo Met. Holdings Ltd., London, 1979—; chmn., CEO Atlantic Met. Corp., Cherry Hill, NJ, 1983; chmn. First Pa. Mortgage Trust, 1978—; vice chmn., dir. UMET Properties Corp., 1979—; chmn., CEO, pres. Instl. Investors Corp., NYC, 1983—; dir. Saxon Oil Co.; chmn. bd. Stanwick Internat. Corp. NV and predecessors. Mem.: Law Soc. Eng., Lodge Of Light. Jewish. Office: The Hallwood Group Inc 3710 Rawlins Ave Ste 1500 Dallas TX 75219-4236

GUMBINNER, PAUL S., advertising and executive recruitment agency executive; b. NYC, Aug. 30, 1942; s. Paul G. Gumbinner and Ruth (Gumpert) Coben; m. Nancy Levin (div. 1978); children: Elizabeth Susan, Jeffrey Michael; m. Amye Hope Price, Sept. 12, 1982. BS, Temple U., 1964. Asst. account exec. Richard K. Manoff, NYC, 1964-66; account exec. DKG, Inc., NYC, 1966-68; v.p. Kenyon & Eckhardt, NYC, 1969-73; sr. v.p. McCaffrey & McCall, NYC, 1974-77; pres. Anesh, Viseltear, Gumbinner, NYC, 1977-82, The Gumbinner Co., Inc., NYC, 1982—. Contbr. articles to Ad Week, Advt. Age. Pres. Friends Emelin Theatre, Mamaroneck, N.Y., 1976-78; v.p. Larchmont (N.Y.) Pub. Libr., 1975-77; bd. dirs. Urban Glass, Bklyn., 1997—, chmn., 2000-05; bd. dirs. Art Alliance for Contemporary Glass; pres. Southgate Owners Assn., 2000—. Recipient Effie award Am. Mktg. Assn., 1985. Mem. Ad Club N.Y. (guest lectr.). pres. Southgate Owens Assn., 2000-. Democrat. Avocations: photography, glass collecting. Office: The Gumbinner Co Inc 509 Madison Ave Ste 708 New York NY 10022-5501

GUMBRECHT, HANS ULRICH, literary criticism philosophy educator; b. Würzburg, Germany, June 15, 1948; s. Hanns Heinz and Thea (Bender) G.; m. Ulrike Loch, Aug. 30, 1989; children: Marco, Sara, Christopher Vincent, Laura Teresa. PhD, U. Konstanz, 1971; PhD (hon.), U. Montevideo, 1999, U. Montreal, 2004, U. Siegen, Germany, 2007. Asst. prof. U. Konstanz, Germany, 1971-74; prof. Romance philology U. Bochum, Germany, 1975-76, prof. lit. theory, 1976-83; prof. U. Siegen, Germany, 1983-89; Albert Guérard Prof. lit. Stanford (Calif.) U., 1989, chmn. dept. comparative lit., 1990-93, 96-97; prof. attaché U. Montreal, Canada, 1996—. Coll. France, 2003—. Dir. d' études associé Ecole des Hautes Etudes, Paris, 1982—; dir. presdl. lectrs. in Humanities and Arts Stanford U., 1997—2000; vis. prof. Cath. U., Rio de Janeiro, U. of State U., Buenos Aires, Kodai U., Kyoto, numerous other schs.; disting. vis. prof. Commonwealth Ctr. U., Va.; bd. trustees Auto Univ. Volkswagen Corp., Germany, 2004—07, U. Greifswald, Germany, 2005—07; lectr. in field. Author numerous books; contbr. articles to profl. jours. Recipient Cuthbertson award Stanford U., 2000. Mem. MLA, Am. Acad. Arts and Scis., Deutscher Romanistenverband, Wolfram von Eschenbach Assn., Assn. Internat. de Hispanistas. Office: Stanford U Dept Comparative Lit Stanford CA 94305 Business E-Mail: tompkins@stanford.edu.

GUMBS, PAM, pharmacist; d. Sara Yancy and Gayton Yancy Sr.; m. John Gumbs, Apr. 21, 1971. PharmD, U. Calif., San Francisco, 1975, degree in geriatric clinical pharmacy, 1991. Clin. pharmacist Asuereth Med. Svcs., LA, 1990—2006; CEO, clin. affairs Royal Med. Inc, Berkeley, Calif., 1996—. Mem. pharmacy and therapeutics com. Alameda Alliance For Health, Calif., 2004—, rep., 2004—06. Editor: (newsletter) Alameda County Pharmacists Assn. Newsletter, Pills & Potions (Trophy Winner for Commn. Excellence, 1987). Mem.: Am. Pharmacist Assn. (licentiate), Christian Pharmacists Fellowship Internat. (licentiate), Calif. Pharmacists Assn. (licentiate; pres. Alameda county chpt. 2002—03). Office: Royal Medical Inc 2929 Telegraph Ave Berkeley CA 94705 Office Phone: 510-843-3201. Office Fax: 510-843-0308. E-mail: drpam@consultwithdrpam.com.

GUMMARAJU, SRINIVAS CHAKRAVARTHY, oncologist, hematologist; b. Hyderabad, India, July 2, 1967; came to U.S., 1993; s. H.P. Sundar Gummaraju and Subhadra Devi Vemaraju; m. Aruna, Jan. 23, 1997; children: Hala Chakravarthy. MB, BS, Osmania Med. Coll., India, 1989. Diplomate Am. Bd. Internal Medicine, Am. Bd. Hematology and Medical Oncology. Intern Osmania (India) Gen. Hosp., 1990-91; physician Chakravarthy (India) Clinics, 1991-93; resident Cook County Hosp., Chgo., 1993-96; fellow U. Calif., Davis, 1996—99; sr. cons. Apollo Hosps., India, 2000—03; prof. U. Calif., Davis, 2003—. Chmn. Med. Care Rev. bd. Cook County Hosp., Chgo., 1994-96; organizer State Med. Exhbn. Osmania Med. Coll., 1988; chmn. cancer com. Fremont Rideout Health Group, 2004-05; cancer liaison physician ACS, 2003-05. Illustrator: Children's Book of Knowledge, 1986; contbr. poems to mags. Sec. Children's Universe, India, 1986-88; adult educator Govt. Aksharajyoti Movement, India, 1992; representative House Staff Assn. Cook County Hosp., Chgo., 1994-96. Recipient Spl. commendation Govt. India, 1990; named for Quality of Care By a Physician USA Wide Press-Ganey Survey, 2006. Mem. ACP, AMA (Physician Recognition award 1999), Am. Soc. Clin. Oncologists, Indian Med. Assn. (life). Avocations: rare book collecting, travel, languages, golf. Home: 3-4-491/1 Barkatpura Hyderabad 500027 India E-mail: gummaraju02@sify.com.

GUMMEL, HERMANN KARL, retired physicist, lab administrator; b. Hannover, Germany, July 6, 1923; arrived in US, 1953; s. Johannes and Charlotte (Elgeti) G.; m. Erika Ilse Reich, Aug. 31, 1952; children—Monica Ruth, Margaret Grace MS, Syracuse U., 1952, PhD, 1957; diploma in Physics, Philipps U., Marburg-Lahn, 1952. Mem. tech. staff Bell Telephone Labs, Murray Hill, NJ, 1957-62, supr., 1962-67, dept. head, 1967-82, asst. dir., 1982-84; dir. AT&T Bell Labs, Murray Hill, NJ, 1984-86, ret., cons. Contbr. articles to profl. jours.; patentee in field Recipient Phil Kaufman award Electronic Design Automation Co., 1994. Fellow IEEE (David Sarnoff award 1983, Guillemin-Cauer prize paper award Circuits and Systems Soc. 1977, Tech. Achievement award Circuit and Systems Soc. 1990, Golden Jubilee medal 2000, Third Millennium medal 2000); mem. Am. Phys. Soc., Nat. Acad. Engring., Sigma Xi Presbyterian. Home: 123 Valley View Pompton Plains NJ 07444

GUMPERT, CAROLYN L., secondary school educator; d. J. H. and Eva M. Shipman. BS in Edn., U. Cen. Ark., Conway, 1969. Cert. tchr. Mo., Tex. Secondary tchr. Gasconade R-II Schs., Owensville, Mo., 1969—74; adminstrv. sec. U. of Ark., Pine Bluff, 1974—78, Office of Pers. Mgmt., Little Rock, 1978—80, Dept. of the Navy, Virginia Beach, Va., 1982—85, Houston C.C., 1985—88; secondary tchr. Spring Ind. Sch. Dist., Houston, 1988—. Opres. Comty. Teachers' Assn., Owensville, Mo., 1973; pres. Officers' Wives Club, Virginia Beach, Va., 1984; dept. chair Spring Ind. Sch. Dist., Houston, 1990—. Summer missionary Bapt. Student Union, Monticello, Ark., 1968; tchr. Sunday sch. Oak Ridge Bapt. Ch., Houston, 2000—06; voting del. Mo. Teachers' Assn., Owensville, 1972; mem. campus improvement com. Wells Mid. Sch., Houston, 2002. Named Disting. Tchr., Spring Ind. Sch. Tchr., 2002. Mem.: NEA, Tex. State Tchrs. Assn., Parent Tchr. Orgn. Republican. Baptist. Avocations: tole painting, music, theater, reading. Home Phone: 936-441-1618.

GUMPERT, GUNTHER, artist; b. Krefeld, Germany, Apr. 17, 1919; came to U.S., 1967, naturalized, 1971; s. Karl and Erna (Cordes) G.; m. Anita Von Kahler, Nov. 28, 1967. Grad., Human. Gymnasium, Krefeld, 1937, Sch. Fine Arts, Krefeld, 1938, Sch. Fine Arts, Wuppertal, 1939. Numerous one-man shows: Europe and U.S. including: Zurich, 1955, Winterthur, 1959, Paris, 1960, Vienna, 1961, Rome, 1962, N.Y.C., 1963, 96, 98, Chgo., 1963, 64, London, 1963, Pforzheim, 1964, Seattle, 1965, 68, 70, 73, 76, Denver, 1972, Washington, 1966, 68, 69, 72, 75, 79, 82, 85, 87, 88, 90, 93, Cleve., 1971, Santo Domingo, 1978, Wichtrach, Bern, 2004; group shows: Suermondt Mus., Aachen, Ger., 1948, Kaiser-Wilhelm Mus., Krefeld, 1949, 50, 51, Internat. Exhibit Abstract Art, Pistoia, Italy, 1961, Salon Realites Nouvelles, Paris, 1959, 60, 61, Salon De Mai, Paris, 1962, Gruppe Z, Wuppertal, 1960, Internat. Exhbn. Contemporary Art, London, 1964, European Acad. Fine Art, Trier, 2000, Die Grosse Abstraktion, Wichtrach/Bern, 2002; represented in permanent collections, Met. Mus. Art, N.Y.C., Victoria and Albert Mus., London, Albertina, Vienna, The Phillips Collection, Washington, Kaiser-Wilhelm Mus., Krefeld, Museo Nacional de Bellas Artes, Santiago, Chile, Sch. Design, Providence, R.I., Princeton U. Art Mus., Mus. Fine Arts, Dallas, Denver Art Mus., Finch Coll. Mus., N.Y.C., Wesleyan U., Middletown Conn., Ohio U. Mus. Am. Art, Athens, Roosevelt House, New Delhi, India, Museo de Arte Moderno, Santo Domingo, George Washington U., Washington, and others; TV film Gumpert At Work, 1963. Address: 3752 Mckinley St NW Washington DC 20015-2510

GUMPERT, LYNN, gallery director; Student, Sorbonne, Paris, 1971-72; cert. completion first year, Ecole du Louvre, Paris, 1971-72; BA in History of Art with honors, U. Calif., Berkeley, 1974; MA in History of Art, U. Mich., 1977. Curatorial asst. The Jewish Mus., NYC, 1978-80; curator The New Mus. Contemporary Art, NYC, 1980-84, sr. curator, 1984-88; adj. curator Mus. Contemporary Art, LA, 1988-89, We. States Arts Fedn., Santa Fe, 1988-89; coord. Eighth Biennale of Sydney Art Gallery N.S.W., Sydney, Australia, 1989-90; guest curator, adminstrv. dir. Amway (Japan) Ltd. and Setagaya Art Mus., Tokyo, 1989-91, Nat. Mus. Art, Osaka, Japan, 1989-91; cons. curator Gallery at Takashimaya, Inc., NYC, 1992-95; guest curator, U.S. coord. ARC/Musée d'Art Moderne de la Ville de Paris, 1994-95; guest curator Grey Art Gallery, NYU, NYC, 1996-97, dir., 1997—; interim dirl mus. studies program NYU, 1999-2000. Lectr. in field; juror in field; panelist in field; ind. curator/cons., 1988-97; mem. adv. com. Asia Soc. Galleries. Exhbns. include Grey Art Gallery, The New Mus. Contemporary Art, 1980, 81, 82, 84, 86, 89, Pitts. Ctr. Arts, 1983, Mus. Contemporary Art, Chgo., 1988, Galerie Ghislaine Hussenot, Paris, 1992, The Gallery at Takashimaya, N.Y.C., 1994, 95, numerous others; author: Christian Boltanski, 1993, reprint, 1996; editor: The Art of the Everyday: The Quotidian in Postwar French Culture, 1997. Decorated chevalier Order Arts and Letters (France); Univ. fellow U. Mich., 1975. Mem. Internat. Assn. Art Critics, ArtTable (N.Y.). Office: Grey Art Gallery NYU 100 Washington Sq E New York NY 10003-6688 Fax: 212-995-4024. E-mail: greygallery@nyu.edu.

GUMPERTZ, WERNER HERBERT, structural engineering company executive; b. Berlin, Dec. 26, 1917; s. Richard and Olga H. Gumpertz; m. Elizabeth Mildred Lewit, Nov. 25, 1949; children: Richard H., Ruth O. Gumpertz Moses. BCE, Swiss Fed. Inst. Tech., 1939; SBCE, MIT, 1948, SM in Bldg. Engring. and Constrn., 1950, advanced profl. degree in bldg. engring. and constrn., 1954. Registered profl. engr., Mass., Pa., Calif., Colo., Okla., Md., Kans., Tex., Ga., La. Constrn. supr., expeditor, draftsman Homes & Gardens Inc., NYC, 1940; engring. draftsman, surveyor Lockwood Kessler & Bartlett, Bklyn., 1940-41; office engr., estimator, constrn. supr. M. Shapiro & Sons Constrn. Co., NYC and Newport News, Va., 1941-43; engring. asst. to head Kaiser Co. Inc. Shipyard, Vancouver, Wash., 1943; structural engr. U.S. Army C.E., ETO, 1946-47; office and field engr. United Engrs. & Constructors Inc., Phila. and Devon, Conn., 1948-49; prof. civil engring. MIT, Cambridge, Mass., 1949-57; sr. prin. Simpson Gumpertz & Heger Inc., Waltham, Mass., 1956—. Instr. structural engring. Bridgeport Engring. Inst., 1948-49, U. Mass. Extension, 1953-62; cons. bldg. constrn. and material tech., bldg. systems and assemblies of materials; lectr. Harvard Grad. Sch. Design, 1985, 87. Contbr. articles to profl. jours. Mem. Adv. Com. on Pub. Bldg. Constrn., City of Newton, Mass., 1956-68; guidance lectr. Cambridge Pub. Sch. System, 1955-57. Served to cpl. U.S. Army, 1943-46, ETO. Fellow ASCE (nat. com. on stds., sec.-treas., joint com. on profl. conduct Mass. sect.), ASTM Internat (chmn. com. D-8 on roofing, waterproofing and bituminous materials 1981-85, real estate com. 1988-95, Award of Merit 1986, Walter C. Voss award to Engr. for Outstanding Contbn. to Advancement of Bldg. Tech. 1987, William C. Cullen award 2004); mem. Am. Concrete Inst. (com. on residential concrete slabs, cellular concrete com.), U.S. Metric Assn. (cert. advanced metrication specialist), Am. Soc. Engring. Edn. (chmn. archtl. engring. divsn.), Am. Arbitration Assn. (nat. panel arbitrators), Nat. Fire Protection Assn., Midwest Roofing Contractors Assn. (assoc.), Nat. Roofing Contractors Assn. (assoc.), Sigma Xi. Office: Simpson Gumpertz & Heger Inc 41 Seyon St Waltham MA 02453-8335 Home Phone: 617-244-4556. Business E-Mail: whgumpertz@sgh.com.

GUND, AGNES, retired museum administrator; b. Cleve., Ohio; d. George Gund, Jr.; m. Daniel Shapiro, June 13, 1987; children: David, Catherine, Jessica, Anna. BA in art history, Conn. Coll., 1960; MA in art history, Fogg Mus., Harvard U., 1980; LHD (hon.), Case Western Reserve U., 1995, Brown U., 1996. Trustee Mus. Modern Art, NYC, 1976—, v.p., 1988—91, pres., 1991—2002, pres. emerita, 2002—; chair Mayor's Cultural Affairs Adv. Commn., NYC, 2003—. Bd. trustees Wexner Ctr. Found., 1997—; trustee Brown U., Aaran Diamond AIDS Rsch. Ctr., Inst. Advanced Study, Princeton, NJ, J. Paul Getty Trust, Calif.; mem. mus. coun. Cleve. Mus. Art. Named one of Top 200 Collectors, The ARTnews Mag., 2004; named to, 2006; recipient Women in the Arts award, Coll. Art Assn., Art Table award for Disting. Svc. to Arts, 1994, Montblanc de la Culture award, 1997, Nat. Medal Arts, 1997, Arts Edn. award, Am. for the Arts, 1999, Evan Burger Donaldson Achievement award, Miss Porter's Sch., 2003, Centennial Medal, Harvard U. Grad. Sch. Arts and Sciences, 2003. Fellow: Am. Acad. Arts and Sciences; mem.: Studio in a Sch. Assn. (founder, Gov.'s Art award, N.Y. 1988, Dorothy Freeman award, N.Y.C. 1988). Avocation: Collector of Contemporary, African, Chinese Art. Office: care Museum Modern Art 11 W 53rd St New York NY 10019-5401

GUND, ANN, art association administrator; m. Graham Gund. Pres. Friends of Art and Preservation in Embassies. Head, Contemporary Art Com. Mus. Fine Arts, Boston. Trustee Mus. Fine Arts, Boston, Concord Acad., Mass.; bd. chairperson Skowhegan Sch. Painting and Sculpture. Named to Top 200 Collectors, ARTnews Mag., 2006.

GUND, GORDON, venture capitalist, investment company executive; b. Cleve., Oct. 15, 1939; s. George and Jessica (Roesler) G.; m. Llura Liggett; children: Grant Ambler, Gordon Zachary. BA, Harvard U., 1961; DPubSvc (hon.), U. Maryland, 1980; DHL, Whittier Coll., 1993; LLD (hon.), U. Vt., 1994; PhD (hon.), Goteburg U., Sweden, 1997. Chmn., CEO Gund Investment Corp., Princeton, NJ, 1968—. Bd. dirs. Kellogg Co., Corning Inc. Co-founder The Found. Fighting Blindness, 1971; mem. Nat. Adv. Eye Coun., 1980—84, U.S. Olympic Com., 2000—03. Mem.: Phi Beta Kappa (hon.; chair, bd. govs. 1996—99). Office: Gund Investment Corp PO Box 449 14 Nassau St Princeton NJ 08542-4523

GUND, GRAHAM, architectural firm executive; m. Ann Gund. Ed., Kenyon Coll.; post grad. edn., RI Sch. Design; M in Architecture, Harvard U. Graduate Sch. Design, M in Architecture in Urban Design. Founder, pres. GUND Partnership, Boston, 1971—. Design peer Gen. Svcs. Adminstrn., Design Excellence Prog. Trustee Nat. Bldg. Mus., Nat. Trust for Historic Preservation, Boston Mus. Fine Arts; former chmn. Boston Found. for Architecture, Boston Soc. of Architects. Named to Top 200 Collectors, ARTnews Mag., 2006. Office: GUND Partnership 47 Thorndike St Cambridge MA 02141 Office Phone: 617-250-6800. Office Fax: 617-577-9614.

GUNDELFINGER, BENJAMIN FREMONT, military officer; b. Oakland, Calif., Dec. 28, 1917; s. Siegfried and Margaret Hannan Gundelfinger; children: Teruko, Joan, Peter. AB, U. Calif., Berkeley, 1940; MD, U. Calif., San Francisco, 1943; MPH, U. NC, Chapel Hill, 1954. Medical officer US Navy, 1943—74; ret. Contbr. articles to profl. jours. Mem.: An. Soc. Trop. Medicine and Hygiene, Am. Assn. Advancement Sci. Avocations: hiking, woodworking.

GUNDERSEN, WAYNE CAMPBELL, energy executive, consultant; b. Elgin, Ill., May 27, 1936; s. LeRoy Arthur and Jean Ellen (Campbell) Gundersen; m. Gail Andrews, Mar. 21, 1959; children: Thomas Dexter, Lori Ann, Kathy Lee. BS, U. Nebr., 1959, MS, 1961. Advisor fgn. ops. Std. Oil Calif., San Francisco, 1974-76; asst. to v.p. Chevron Overseas Petroleum, San Francisco, 1976-80; dir. oil and gas Kaiser Aluminum & Chem. Corp., Oakland, Calif., 1980-81; v.p., gen. mgr. Kaiser Energy, Inc., Oakland, 1983-85, pres., 1985-87; v.p. Kaiser Aluminum and Chem. Corp., Oakland, 1983-87; pres. Kaiser Aluminum Exploration Co., Oakland, Kaiser Exploration and Mining Co., Oakland, 1985-87; cons. in oil and gas., 1987—; CEO, chmn. bd. dirs. Petroleum Synergy Group, Inc., 1988—. Mem. geology adv. bd. U. Nebr., Lincoln, 1984—87; mgr. Western Geothermal Ptnrs., LLC. Contbr. articles to profl. jours. Pres. Parents Club Foothill Sch., Walnut Creek, Calif., 1978—79. Named Man-of-Yr., New Orleans Jaycees, 1973; Sinclair fellow, 1960—61. Mem.: Am. Assn. Petroleum Geologists. Republican. Methodist. Office: The Petroleum Synergy Group 980 Caughlin Crossing Ste 102 Reno NV 89519-0660 Personal E-mail: renooilman@aol.com.

GUNDERSHEIMER, WERNER LEONARD, library director; b. Frankfurt, Hesse, Germany, Apr. 7, 1937; s. Herman Samuel and Frieda (Siegel) G.; m. Karen Rosenwald, Oct. 16, 1959; children: Joshua, Benjamin. BA, Amherst Coll., 1959, DHL (hon.), 1984; MA, Harvard U., 1960, PhD, 1963; MA (hon.), U. Pa., 1971; DHL (hon.), Williams Coll., 1989, Muhlenberg Coll., 1991, Davidson Coll., 1998, Washington Coll., 2003. Asst. prof. history U. Wis., Madison, 1963-64; jr. fellow Harvard U., Cambridge, Mass., 1962-66; asst. prof. U. Pa., Phila., 1966-68, assoc. prof., 1968-72, prof., 1972-85, chmn. history dept., 1976-78; dir. Folger Shakespeare Library, Washington, 1984—2002, dir. emeritus, 2002—; vis. prof. history Williams Coll., 2003; vis. prof. George Washington U., 2004—. Trustee Rosenbach Mus. and Libr., Phila., 1969-89, The Medici Found., Princeton, N.J., 1984-2005, Brit. Inst. of the U.S., Washington, 1985-90; vis. prof. Tel Aviv (Israel) U., 1982; adj. prof. history Amherst (Mass.) Coll., 1986-02; Phi Beta Kappa vis. scholar, 2004-05. Author: Life and Works of Louis LeRoy, 1966, Ferrara: The Style of a Renaissance Despotism, 1973, Art and Life of the Court of Ercole I d'Este, 1972; editor: The Italian Renaissance, 1965; contbr. articles to profl. jours. Cons. NEH, 1982—; trustee Shakespeare Theatre at the Folger, Washington, 1985-92, PEN/Faulkner Found., 1990-95; v.p. Nat. Humanities Alliance, 1992-95, pres., 1996-00; overseer Hancock Shaker Village, 2004-06, trustee, 2006—; corporator Berkshire Mus., 2005—. Fellow Inst. for Advanced Study, 1970-71, Guggenheim fellow, 1974-75, I Tatti fellow Harvard Ctr. for Renaissance Study, 1974-75. Fellow Am. Acad. Arts & Sci.; mem. Am. Philos. Soc., Am. Hist. Assn., Ind. Rsch. Libr. Assn. (pres. 1994-97), Renaissance Soc. Am., Med. Acad. Am., Century Assn., Grolier Club, Phi Beta Kappa (senator 1994-2000, vis. scholar 2004-05). Democrat. Jewish. Business E-Mail: wgundersheimer@folger.edu.

GUNDERSON, BRENT MERRILL, lawyer; b. Vernal, Utah, Apr. 16, 1960; s. Merrill Ray and Betty Velate (Norton) G.; m. Tamra Jean Gunderson; children: Adam Brent, Jeremy Phillip, Matthew Norton, Hannah, Rachel, Mariah, Kayla, Jacob Elden, Paul, John, Schuyler, Rachael, Austin, Kira. BA, Brigham Young U., Provo, Utah, 1984; JD, Columbia U., NYC, 1987. Bar: Ariz. 1987, US Dist. Ct. Ariz. 1987, US Tax Ct. 1994. Ptnr. Brown & Bain, Phoenix, 1987—96; pvt. practice Gunderson Denton & Profitt, P.C., Mesa, Ariz., 1996—. Pres. Ariz. Mgmt. Soc., Phoenix, 1996-97. Asst. dist. commr. Boy Scouts Am., Mesa, Ariz., 1994-97, scoutmaster troop 611, Mesa, 1991-94, troop 761, Mesa, 1999-2002, mem. varsity scout com., 2002-05, chair, 1997-98; precinct capt. Mesa Rep. Precincts 47 & 17, 1988-94; cubmaster pack 761, Boy Scouts Am., 1998-99; mem. Ariz. Cmty. Found. Breakfast Series com., 2001—04; mem. profl. advisors. com. Leave a Legacy, Ariz. Recipient Mesa Dist. award of Merit, 1997, Scoutmaster award of Merit Boy Scouts Am., 1992, named to Scout Leader Hall of Fame, 1993, Scouting Family Hall of Fame, 1999. Mem. Am. Immigration Lawyers Assn. (v.p. Ariz. chpt. 1992-93, Maricopa County Bar Found. (bd. dirs. 1991-95), East Valley Estate Planning Coun. (bd. dirs. 1997-2001, pres. 1999-2000), Am. Immigration Lawyers Assn., Ariz. Mgmt. Soc. (bd. dirs. 1997—). Avocations: backpacking, fishing, China. Office: Gunderson Denton & Profitt PC 1930 N Arboleda Ste 201 Mesa AZ 85213 Office Phone: 480-655-7440. Business E-Mail: brent@gundersondenton.com.

GUNDERSON, CLARK ALAN, orthopedic surgeon; b. Watertown, SD, Aug. 27, 1948; s. Harvey Alfred and Eugenie (Tulson) G.; m. Robbie Gunderson; children: Ashley, Camille Student, U. Minn., 1966-69; BS, U. S.D., 1971; MD, Baylor Coll. of Medicine, 1973. Diplomate Am. Bd. of Orthopaedic Surgery, 1979. Intern in gen. surgery Charity Hosp., New Orleans, 1973-74, resident in orthopedic surgery, 1974-78; chief of surgery Lake Charles (La.) Meml. Hosp., 1980-83, 90-91, sec., treas. med. staff, 1983-87, pres. med. staff, 1992-93, also trustee, 90-94, chief of surgery, 1998-99; clin. assoc. prof. La. State U. Sch. of Medicine, New Orleans, 1987-90. Bd. dirs. Arthritic Found. La., 1987. Mem. AMA, ACS, Am. Acad. Orthopaedic Surgeons (bd. councilors 2002, com. on state com. 2002), La. Orthopaedic Assn. (pres. 1995-96), Calcasieu Parish Med. Soc., La. State Med. Soc., N.Am. Spine Assn., Mid Am. Orthopaedic Assn., La. Orthopaedic ASsn. (exec. com. 1993—), Lake Charles Country Club (pres. 1987-89), Clin. Orthopedic Rsch. Soc., Sigma Chi. Avocation: golf. Office: 2615 Enterprise Blvd Lake Charles LA 70601-7675

GUNDERSON, GERALD AXEL, economics professor; b. Seattle, May 24, 1940; s. Marian A. and Ethel Ann (Hamon) G.; m. Margaret Jean Overway, Sept. 10, 1965; children: David Eric, Laura Lynn. BA in Econs., U. Wash., 1962, MA in Econs., 1965, PhD in Econs., 1967. Asst. prof. econs. U. Mass., Amherst, 1967-74; vis. assoc. prof. econs. Mt. Holyoke Coll., South Hadley, Mass., 1974-75; spl. lectr. econs. N.C. State U., Raleigh, 1975-78; prof. econs. Trinity Coll., Hartford, Conn., 1978-82, Shelby Cullom Davis prof. Am. bus. and econ. enterprise, 1982—, dir. S.C. Davis Endowment, 1982—. Bd. dirs. exec. com. Yankee Inst. for Pub. Policy Studies; acad. adv. com. Inst. on Research on Econs. of Taxation. Author: A New Economic History of America, 1976, The Wealth Creators: An Entrepenurial History of the United States, 1989; contbg. author: Explorations in Econs. History, 1973— , Jour. Econ. History, 1974, Social Sci. History, 1977, Wall Street Jour.; editor Jour. Pvt. Enterprise. Grantee Freedom Found. at Valley Forge, 1980 Mem. Assn. Pvt. Enterprise Edn. (pres. 1984-85), Econ. History Assn. Home: 6 Andrew Dr Weatogue CT 06089-9725 Office: Trinity Coll 300 Summit St Hartford CT 06106-3100 Office Phone: 860-297-2395. Business E-Mail: gerald.gunderson@trincoll.edu.

GUNDERSON, JUDITH KEEFER, golf association executive; b. Charleroi, Pa., May 25, 1939; d. John R. and Irene G. (Gaskill) Keefer; m. Jerry L. Gunderson, mar. 19, 1971; children: Jamie L., Jeff S.; stepchildren: Todd G. (dec.), Marc W. Student pub. schs., Uniontown, Pa. Bookkeeper Fayette Nat. Bank, 1957-59, gen. leader bookkeeper, 1960-63; head bookkeeper 1st Nat. Bank, Broward, Fla., 1963-64; bookkeeper Ruthenberg Homes, Inc., 1966-69; bookkeeper, asst. sec.-treas. Peninsular Properties, Inc. subs. Investors Diversified, Mpls., 1969-72; conptr., pres. Am. Golf Fla., Inc. (doing bus. as Golf and Tennis World), Deerfield Beach, Fla., 1972-89, stockholder, 1972-92; sales assoc. Realty Brokers Internat., Inc., 1990; sec.-treas. Internat. Golf, Inc., 1974-89, stockholder, 1974-99; dir. Mary Kay Cosmetics, 1993-97; wellness cons. Nikken, Inc., 1997—; assoc. Travel Ptnrs. USA, 2002—06, Elite Getaways, 2007—. Personal E-mail: jkgunde@aol.com.

GUNDERSON, ROBERT VERNON, JR., lawyer; b. Memphis, Dec. 4, 1951; s. Robert V. and Suzanne (McCarthy) G.; m. Anne Durkheimer, May 15, 1982; children: Katherine Paige, Robert Graham. BA with distinction, U. Kans., 1973; MBA, U. Pa., 1974; MA, Stanford U., 1976; JD, U. Chgo., 1979. Bar: Calif. 1979, U.S. Dist. Ct. (no. dist.) Calif. 1979. Assoc. Cooley, Godward, San Francisco, 1979-84, Palo Alto, 1979—84, ptnr. San Francisco, 1984-88, Palo Alto, 1984—88, Brobeck, Phleger & Harrison, 1988-95, mem. exec. com., 1991-95, chmn. bus. and tech. practice, 1992-95; founder, ptnr. Gunderson Dettmer Stough Villeneuve Franklin & Hachigian, Menlo Park, 1995—. Panelist Venture Capital and Pub. Offering Negotiation, San Francisco and N.Y.C., 1981, 83, 85, 92, Practicing Law Inst., N.Y.C. and San Francisco, 1986; moderator, panelist Third Ann. Securities Law Inst., 1985; dir. Vitae Pharms., Ft. Washington, Pa., Theravance, Inc., South San Francisco, Inc.; sec. Dionex Corp., Sunnyvale, Calif., 1983-88, Southwall Techs., Inc., Palo Alto, 1985-88, Conductus, Inc., Sunnyvale, 1992-2001, Remedy Corp., Mountain View, Calif., 1995-97; vis. lectr. U. Santa Clara Law Sch., 1985, 89 Exec. editor U. Chgo. Law Rev., 1978-79; contbr. articles to profl. jours. Mem. ABA (bus. law sect., various coms.), State Bar Calif. (panelist continuing legal edn. 1984), San Francisco Bar Assn., Am. Fin. Assn., Wharton Club (San Francisco Bay area). Avocations: contemporary art, music, travel. Home: 243 Polhemus Ave Atherton CA 94027-5442 Office: Gunderson Dettmer Stough Villeneuve 155 Constitution Dr Menlo Park CA 94025-1106 Home Phone: 650-327-9313; Office Phone: 650-321-2400.

GUNDERSON, STEVEN CRAIG, association executive, former congressman; b. Eau Claire, Wis., May 10, 1951; s. Arthur E. and Adeline C. G. BA, U. Wis., 1973. Mem. Wis. Assembly, 1974-79; legis. dir. to Rep. Toby Roth US Congress, Washington, 1979; mem. 97th-104th Congresses from 3d Wis. dist., Washington, 1981-96; chmn. agrl. subcom. on livestock, dairy and poultry; mem. econ. and ednl. opportunity com.; sr. cons., mng. dir. The Greystone Co., Arlington, Va., 1996—2005; pres., CEO The Coun. on Foundations, Washington, 2005—. Dir. spl. projects Gov. Dreyfus of Wis. campaign, 1978 Mem. Lions (Pleasantville chpt.). Republican. Lutheran. Office: The Coun on Foundations 1828 L St NW Ste 300 Washington DC 20036

GUNDERSON, TED LEE, security consultant; b. Colorado Springs, Colo., Nov. 7, 1928; BBA, U. Nebr. Sales rep. George A. Hormel Co., Austin, Minn., 1950-51; spl. agt. in charge U.S. Dept. Justice FBI, Los Angeles, Dallas, Memphis, Phila., 1951-79; internat. security cons. Ted L. Gunderson & Assocs., Santa Monica, Calif., 1979—; chmn. bd. dirs. HEB Inc., pubs. of Am. Free Press, Washington. Cons. Calif. Narcotic Authority; lectr., cons. on terrorism, cults and related topics. Author: How to Locate Anyone Anywhere, 1989, Be Smart, Be Safe, 1994; appeared on numerous nat. and local TV and radio talk shows; prodr. TV documentary on Satanism. Named Outstanding Law Enforcement Am., AFL CIO Metal Trade Coun., 1977. Mem. Bel Air U.S. Navy League, Internat. Assn. Chiefs of Police, Internat. Footprinters Assn., Philanthropic Found. (Los Angeles chpt.), Royal Soc. Encouragement of Arts, Mfrs. and Commerce, Sigma Alpha Epsilon. Avocations: golf, racquetball. E-mail: tedgunderson@email.com.

GUNDIAN, JULIO CESAR, urologist; b. Havana, Cuba, Aug. 22, 1959; arrived in US, 1961; BS magna cum laude, U. Miami, Fla., 1980; MD, Tulane U., New Orleans, 1984. Intern in gen. surgery Mayo Clnic, Rochester, Minn., 1984—85, resident in urologic surgery, 1985—90; urologic surgeon Winter Park Urology Assocs., Orlando, Fla., 1990—, kidney transplant surgeon, 1990—2001. Chmn. urology dept. Winter Park Hosp., 1996—98. Mem.: Am. Urologic Assn., Pan Am. Med. Assn., Fla. Urologic Soc. Avocations: fishing, reading. Office Phone: 407-897-3499.

GUNEYI, UMIT AHMET, physician, consultant; b. Kirikkale, Turkey, Dec. 22, 1957; arrived in U.S., 1958; s. Selim S. and Muazzez A. Guneyi. BS in Molecular Biology, U. Hawaii, 1981; MD, U. Tech. Santiago, Santo Domingo, Dominican Republic, 1985; MS in Health Svcs. Adminstrn., U. St. Francis, 2003. Cert. terrorism tng. Reno Citizens Police Acad., 2005, Fed. Emergency Mgmt. Agy. cert. Nat. Incident Mgmt. Sys. Dept. Homeland Security, 2006. Surgeon Washoe Med. Ctr., Reno, 1990—91; dep. coroner Washoe County Coroners Office, Reno, 1991; chief instr. med. terminology Truckee Meadows C.C., Reno, 1994—2000; ind. rschr. dept. biomed. engring. U. Nev., Reno, 2000—06; lectr. Associated Counter-Threat Edn. Specialists, Reno, 2003—, cons. bio-terrorism, 2003—; med. dir. Wellness Ctr. at Progreso Latino, Inc., Central Falls, RI, 2006—. Adv. Helping Angels Home Healthcare Svcs., Sparks, Nev., 2002—03; founder, CEO Gulee Enterprises, Reno-Sparks, 1994—98; exec. v.p. med. svcs. Homeland Security Def. Coalition, Rochester, NY; mem. hwy. watch Dept. of Homeland Security, 2006—; mem. nutrition adv. com. U. RI, 2006—; mem. adv. com. RI Dept. Health, 2006—; mem. RI Homeland Security Cmty. Coun. Work Group, 2006—. Active Dept. Homeland Security Hwy. Watch, 2006; mem. Nev. Washoe County Citizen Homeland Security Coun., 2003—, Nev. Washoe County Cmty. Emergency Response Team, 2004—, Truckee Meadows Police Acad. Citizens; lobbyist, co-dir. com. establish state P.A. program Carson City, Nev., 2002—; del. convs. Rep. Party, Nev., 1996, 2000, rep. presdl. task force Washington, 1996—, rep. nat. senatorial com., 1996—. Scholar, Pacific Health Rsch. Inst., 1978. Fellow: Am. Coll. Internat. Physicians; mem.: Am. Fedn. Tchrs., Assn. Former Intelligence Officers, Reno Citizens Inst., Am. Acad. Family Physicians, Am. Coll. Emergency Physicians, Planetary Soc. Republican. Achievements include research in designing artificial pancreas; design of proto-type for artificial pancreas. Avocations: astronomy, parapsychology, coin collecting/numismatics, stamp collecting/philately, antiques. Home: 3025 Socrates Dr Reno NV 89512 Office Phone: 401-728-5920 ext. 320, 775-813-6442. Personal E-mail: uguneyi@sbcglobal.net. Business E-Mail: bguneyi@progresolatino.org.

GUNGER, RICHARD WILLIAM, lawyer; b. Auburn, NY, Aug. 7, 1963; s. William Bruce and Lita Patricia G.; children: William Robinson, James Taber. BA magna cum laude, Alfred U., 1985; JD cum laude, Syracuse U., 1988. Bar: N.Y. 1989, U.S. Dist. Ct. (no. dist.) N.Y. 1991, U.S. Dist. Ct. (we. dist.) N.Y. 1993, U.S. Supreme Ct. 1993. Assoc. Albert D. DiGiacomo, Syracuse, N.Y., 1988-89, Cuddy, Durgala & Timian, Auburn, N.Y., 1989-90; atty. pvt. practice, Auburn, N.Y., 1990—. Bd. dirs. Cayuga Counseling, Auburn. Alan L. Ponyman scholar, 1985. Mem. ABA, N.Y. State Bar Assn. Cayuga County Bar Assn., KC.

GUNN, ALAN, retired law educator; b. Syracuse, NY, Apr. 8, 1940; s. Albert Dale and Helen Sherwood (Whitnall) G.; m. Bertha Ann Buchwald, 1975; 1 child, William BS, Rensselaer Poly. Inst., 1961; JD, Cornell U., 1970. Bar: D.C. 1970. Assoc. Hogan & Hartson, Washington, 1970-72; asst. prof. law Washington U., St. Louis, 1972-75, assoc. prof., 1975-76; assoc. prof. law Cornell U., Ithaca, NY, 1977-79, prof., 1979-84, J. duPratt White prof., 1984-89; prof. law U. Notre Dame, Ind., 1989-96, John N. Matthews prof. Ind., 1996—2005, prof. emeritus Ind., 2005—. Apptd. spl. advocate St. Joseph County Probate Ct., 2001—. Author: (with James R. Repetti) Partnership Income Taxation, 1991, 4th edit., 2005; (with Larry D. Ward) Cases, Text and Problems on Federal Income Taxation, 5th edit., 2002; (with Vincent R. Johnson) Studies in American Tort Law, 1994, 3rd edit., 2005. Methodist. Office: U Notre Dame Law Sch Notre Dame IN 46556

GUNN, ALBERT EDWARD, JR., internist, health facility administrator, lawyer, educator; b. Port Washington, NY, Oct. 31, 1933; s. Albert Edward and Esther Frances (Williams) G.; m. Joan Marie Jacoby, May 18, 1968; children: Albert Edward III, Emily Williams Gunn Hebert, Andrew Robert, Clare Margaret Gunn Berchelmann, Catherine Ann, Philip David. BS, Fordham Coll., 1955, LLB, 1958; MB BCh BAO, Nat. U. Ireland, Galway, 1967. Bar: NY 1958, US Ct. Mil. Appeals 1959, DC 1972, US Supreme Ct. 1972, US Ct. Appeals (DC cir.) 1972; diplomate Am. Bd Internal Medicine, lic. physician Pa., NY, Va., Tex., Eng., Wales. Owner, agt. Albert E. Gunn Ins. Agy., Port Washington, 1953-65; intern Montefiore Hosp., NYC, 1967-68; resident in medicine Roosevelt Hosp., NYC, 1968-70; USPHS trainee in neurology U. Rochester, NY, 1970-72; asst. dir. govtl. rels. AMA, Washington, 1972-74; med. dir. Geriat. Svcs. Suffolk County, Hauppauge, NY, 1974-75, Rehab. Ctr., U. Tex./M.D. Anderson Cancer Ctr., 1975-88, chief rehab. sect., 1988-93, chief geriat. sect., 1993-2000, dep. chmn. dept. internal med. spltys., 1998-2000; prof. mgmt. and policy scis. U. Tex. Houston Sch. Pub. Health, 2001—. Asst. prof. medicine U. Tex. Med. Sch., Houston, 1976-80, assoc. prof., 1980-2000, prof., 2000—, also assoc. dean for admissions, 1979-2006; med. dir. Region IV, Tex. Med. Found., 1986-93; del.-at-large White House conf. on Handicapped Individuals, 1977; pres. Mus. Med. Sci., 1990; cons. CDC, Legal Svcs. Corp., Nat. Libr. Medicine. Co-author: Rehabilitation of the Cancer Patient, 1976, AIDS in Africa, 1988; editor, contbg. author: Cancer Rehabilitation, 1984; mem. editl. bd. Cancer Bull., 1977-90, Gerontology and Geriatrics Edn., 1984-2003, Linacre Quar.; contbr. articles to profl. jours Pres. Cath. Evidence Guild, Fordham, NY, 1953-54; mem. nat. adv. health coun. HEW, 1974-75; mem. adv. com. Nat. Inst. Law Enforcement and Criminal Justice, Law Enforcement Assistance Adminstrn., U.S. Dept. Justice, 1974-76; mem. bd. regents Nat. Libr. Medicine, NIH, 1983-87, chmn., 1986-87, chmn. lit. selection tech. adv. com., 1988-91; bd. dirs. Right to Life Advs., 1977-78, Tex. Med. Ctr. Libr., 1990. With USAF SAC, 1958-61, capt. Res., 1961-75 Mem. Tex. Med. Assn. (trustee ins. trust, chmn. bd. trustees 1997-2000), Harris County Med. Soc. (exec. bd. 1986-90, v.p. 1998), Royal Coll. Physicians London (licentiate), Royal Coll. Surgeons Eng., Houston Acad. Medicine (bd. dirs. 1986-90, pres. 1990), Houston Bar Assn., DC Bar, Cath. Med. Assn. (regional bd. dirs. 1992—, Thomas Linacre award 1997), NRA (life), Res. Officers Assn. (life), Sons of Union Vets. of Civil War, Am. Legion, KC, Army and Navy Club, Cosmos Club, Fellowship Cath. Scholars. Office: U Tex Houston Med Sch 6531 Fannin St Houston TX 77030 Home: 3514 Glen Haven Blvd Houston TX 77025-1306 Office Phone: 713-500-5117.

GUNN, CLARE ALWARD, travel consultant, writer, retired educator; b. Grandville, Mich., Oct. 28, 1916; s. Fred Melvin and Lila Barton (Alward) G.; married; children: Thomas, Bruce, Richard, William. BS, Mich. State U., 1940, MS in Land and Water Conservation, 1952; PhD in Landscape Architecture, U. Mich., 1965. Prof. dept. tourism-recreation devel. Mich. State U., East Lansing, 1945-66; vis. prof. tourism Sch. Travel Industry Mgmt. U. Hawaii, 1966-67; prof. tourism-recreation devel. Tex. A&M U., College Station, 1967-74, prof. dept. recreation, park and tourism scis., 1975-85, prof. emeritus, 1985—. Prof. resources recreation Oreg. State U., summer 1974; prof. Sch. Landscape Arthitecture, U. Guelph, Ont., Can., 1974-75; vis. prof. Clemson U., 1989; cons. state tourism plans N.Y., 1986, Okla., 1987, Wash., 1988, Del., 1990, Ill., 1993; cons. analysis tourism potential Whiteman Park, Perth, Australia, 1989; cons. South African Tourism Bd., 1988, natural resource potential for Tourism in Del., 1991; mem. task force Moorea & Tourism, French Polynesia, 1990, tourism potential Finger Lakes Region, N.Y., 1989-91, resort devel. plan Chun-Cheon Lake Area, Korea, 1991; tourism plan Newfoundland, Labrador, Can., 1994; prepared Agenda Item 13 World Tourism Conf., The Philippines, 1980, major destination zone study for Can., 1982. Author: A Concept for the Design of a Tourism-Recreation Region, 1965, An Annotated Bibliography of Resource Use of the Texas Gulf Coast, 1969, Vacationscape: Designing Tourist Regions, 3d edit., 1997, Chinese edit., 1998, Tourism Planning, 3d edit., 1994, 4th edit., 2002, Western Tourism: Can Paradise Be Reclaimed, 2004, others; contbr. articles to profl. jours. Mem. George Bush Libr. Com., College Station, 1994; chair adv. com.

CVB of Bryan, College Station, 1992-93; mem. sch. bd. Okemos (Mich.) Dist., 1958-64. Recipient Tex. Gov. award, 1984, Disting. Alumni award Landscape Architecture Program, Mich. State U., 1999; named mem. emeritus Internat. Acad. for Study of Tourism, 2001. Fellow Am. Soc. Landscape Architects (Spl. award 1973); mem. Travel and Tourism Rsch. Assn. (bd. dirs., Lifetime Achievement award 2001), Rotary Internat. (chmn. dist. group study exch. com. 1992-93, chair dist. exch. com. 1992-94, Role of Fame award 1990), Gamma Sigma Delta, Epsilon Sigma Phi, Beta Gamma Sigma, Phi Kappa Phi, Sigma Lambda Alpha (Disting. Mem. award 1991). Republican. Methodist. Avocations: photography, travel, sketching. Home: 1602 Glade St College Station TX 77840-4365

GUNN, GILES BUCKINGHAM, language, religios. studies and global and international studies educator; b. Evanston, Ill., Jan. 9, 1938; s. Buckingham Willcox and Janet (Fargo) G.; m. Janet Mears Varner, Dec. 29, 1969 (div. July 1983); 1 child, Adam Buckingham; m. Deborah Rose Sills, July 9, 1983; 1 child, Abigail Rose. BA, Amherst Coll., 1959; student, Episc. Theol. Sch., Cambridge, Mass., 1959-60; MA, U. Chgo., 1963, PhD, 1967. Prof. religion and lit. U. Chgo., 1966-74; prof. religion and Am. studies U. N.C., Chapel Hill, 1974-85; prof. English and Religion U. Fla., 1984-85; prof. English U. Calif., Santa Barbara, 1985—, chmn. English dept., 1993-97, prof. global and internat. studies, 1998—, chmn. global studies, 2001—05, chmn. global and internat. studies, 2005—. Vis. asst. prof. religion Stanford U., Palo Alto, Calif., 1973; Benedict Disting. vis. prof. religion Carleton Coll., Northfield, Minn., 1977; William R. Kenan Disting. vis. prof. humanities Coll. William and Mary, Williamsburg, Va., 1983-84; Humanities Disting. vis. prof. U. Colo., 1989; Eric Yoegelin Disting. prof. Am. Studies, U. Munich, 1994-95; dir. NEH summer sems. for coll. and univ. tchrs., 1979, 81, 85, 94, for sch. tchrs., 1987, 88, 89, 91; cons. Libr. of Am. Author: F.O. Matthiessen, The Critical Achievement, 1975, The Interpretation of Otherness: Literature, Religion and the American Imagination, 1979, The Culture of Criticism and The Criticism of Culture, 1987, Thinking Across the American Grain: Ideology, Intellect, and the New Pragmatism, 1992, Beyond Solidarity: Pragmatism and Difference in a Globalised World, 2001; editor: Literature and Religion, 1971, Henry James, Senior: A Selection of His Writings, 1974, New World Metaphysics: Readings on the Religious Meaning of the American Experience, 1981, The Bible and American Arts and Letters, 1983, Church, State, and American Culture, 1984, Early American Writing, 1994, William James, Pragmatism and Other Writings, 2000, A Historical Guide to Herman Melville, 2005, War Narratives and American Culture, 2005; co-editor: Redrawing the Boundaries: The Transformation of English and American Literary Studies, 1992; contbr. numerous articles to profl. jours. Bd. dirs. Fund for Santa Barbara. Edward John Noble Leadership grantee, 1959-63; Amherst-Doshisha fellow, Kyoto, Japan, 1960-61, Kent fellow, Danforth Found., 1963-65, Guggenheim fellow, 1978-79, Nat. Endowment for Humanities fellow, 1990, U. Calif. Pres.'s Rsch. fellow, 1990; Phi Beta Kappa vis. scholar, 2000-01. Mem. MLA, Am. Acad. Religion (dir. research and pubs. 1974-77), Am. Studies Assn., Soc. Religion, Arts and Contemporary Culture, Soc. Am. Phil., Nat. Critics Book Circle. Democrat. Avocations: walking, motorcycling, travel. Office: U Calif Dept English Santa Barbara CA 93106 Home: 5488 Rincon Beach Park Dr Ventura CA 93001-9749

GUNN, JAMES EDWIN, language educator; b. Kansas City, Mo., July 12, 1923; s. J. Wayne and Elsie M. (Hutchison) G.; m. Jane Frances Anderson, Feb. 6, 1947; children: Christopher Wayne, Kevin Robert. BS, U. Kans., Lawrence, 1947, MA, 1951. Editor Western Printing and Litho, Racine, Wis., 1951-52; asst. dir. Civil Def., Kansas City, Mo., 1953; instr. U. Kans., Lawrence, 1955, mng. editor Alumni Assn., 1956-58, adminstrv. asst. to the chancellor for univ. rels., 1958-70, lectr. English, 1970-74, prof., 1974-93, emeritus prof., 1993—. Cons. Easton Press, Norwalk, Conn., 1985-98; lectr. in field. Author: over 25 books including Station in Space, 1958, The Immortals, 1962, The End of Dreams, 1975, Alternate Worlds: The Illustrated History of Science Fiction (World Sci. Fiction Conv. Spl. award, 1976, Pilgrim award Sci. Fiction Rsch. Assn., 1976), The Listeners, 1972, The Dreamers, 1980, Isaac Asimov: The Foundations of Science Fiction, 1982 (Hugo award World Sci. Fiction Conv., 1983), The Science of Science-Fiction Writing, 2000, The Millennium Blues, 2001, Human Voices, 2002, Gift From The Stars, 2005, numerous plays, screenplays, radio scripts; editor: The Road to Science Fictions, 6 vols., 1977—2002; editor: (with Matthew Candelarie) Speculations on Speculations: Theories of Science Fiction, 2004;: Inside Science Fiction, 2006, 8 other books; contbr. 100 stories to mags.; contbr. articles. Dir. Ctr. for Study Sci. Fiction, Lawrence, 1984—. Lt. (j.g.) USN, 1943-46, PTO. Recipient Eaton award Eaton Conf., 1992, Hugo award, 1983, Grand Master award, Sci. Fiction Writers Am., 2007; Mellon fellow U. Kans., 1981, 84. Mem. Author's Guild, Sci. Fiction and Fantasy Writers Am. (pres. 1971-72; Grand Master award 2007), Sci. Fiction Rsch. Assn. (pres. 1981-82, Pilgrim award 1976). Avocation: bridge. Home: 2215 Orchard Ln Lawrence KS 66049-2707 Office: U Kans English Dept 3116 Wescoe Hall Lawrence KS 66045-7590 Office Phone: 785-864-3380. Business E-Mail: jgunn@ku.edu.

GUNN, JOAN MARIE, health facility administrator; b. Binghamton, NY, Jan. 29, 1943; d. Andrew and Ruth Antoinette (Butler) Jacoby; m. Albert E. Gunn, Jr., May 18, 1968; children: Albert E. III, Emily Williams Gunn Hebert, Andrew R., Clare M. Berchelmann, Catherine A.B., Philip D. Diploma, Binghamton State Hosp., 1966; BS summa cum laude, Tex. Women's U., 1983; MSN, U. Tex., Houston, 1989. RN, NY, Tex., Va. Staff nurse Columbia/Presbyn. Med. Ctr., NYC, 1966-67; head nurse, ICU Montefiore Hosp. and Med. Ctr., NYC, 1967-68; staff nurse Nat. Orthopedic and Rehab. Hosp., Arlington, Va., 1972-73, Woman's Hosp. of Tex., Houston, 1976-80; staff nurse geriatrics St. Anthony's Ctr., Houston, 1985-86; charge nurse gero psychiatry Bellaire Gen. Hosp., Houston, 1986; from head nurse gero psychiat. unit to dir. patient svcs. Harris County Psychiat. Ctr. U. Tex., Houston, 1986—2001, dir. patient svs. Harris County Psychiat. Ctr., 2001—. Mem. NRA, Nat. Soc. Colonial Dames of the XVII Century, Daus. of Union Vets. of Civil War. Roman Catholic. Avocation: reading history. Home: 3514 Glen Haven Blvd Houston TX 77025-1306 Office: U Tex Harris County Psychiat Ctr 2800 S Macgregor Way Houston TX 77021-1032

GUNN, JOSEPH RIDGEWAY, III, consulting economist; b. Ross, Calif., Nov. 28, 1928; s. Joseph Ridgeway, Jr. and Melvine Henrietta (Longley) G.; BS in Bus. Adminstrn., U. Calif., Berkeley, 1954, MA in Econs., 1958; spl. studies Oxford (Eng.) U., 1967; m. Marie Elsie Thurlow, June 16, 1951; children: Dana Carolyn Gunn Winslow, Anita Jayne Gunn Shirley, Janice Marie Gunn Smeallie. Econ. analyst Standard Oil Co., Calif., 1954-61; econ. adv. Ministry Commerce, Govt. Afghanistan, Kabul, sponsored by The Asia Found., 1961-67; econ. cons. UN Econ. Commn. for Asia and the Far East, 1967; cons. economist Nathan Assoc. Inc., Arlington, Va., 1967—95; econ. advisor Ministry of Commerce Govt. Thailand, 1974-76; v.p. Nathan Assocs., Inc., 1978-85, sr. v.p., 1985-95, bd. dirs., 1986—, chmn. bd. dirs. 2001—; officer, treas. Robert R. Nathan Meml. Found., 2003—; advisor Pres. Adv. Coun., Am. U. Afghanistan, 2007—. Mem. Am. Econ. Assn., Asia Soc., Cosmos Club (v.p., 2004-05, pres. 2005—06). Democrat. Episcopalian. Contbr. articles and reports to profl. jours. Office: Nathan Assocs Inc 2101 Wilson Blvd Arlington VA 22201-3062

GUNN, MOREY WALKER, JR., director, musician, educator; b. Orangeburg, SC, June 23, 1939; s. Morey Walker Sr. and Marjorie (Dusek) G.; m. Sheila Dianne Taylor, Nov. 26, 1994; 1 child, Andrew Walker. BA in Music, Furman U., 1961, MA, 1967. Cert. specialist music edn. tchr., S.C. Band dir. Holly Hill (S.C.) H.S., 1961-65, Orangeburg H.S., 1965-71, Greer (S.C.) H.S., 1971-73, Ft. Johnson H.S., Charleston, SC, 1973-77, Berkeley County Schs., Goose Creek, SC, 1978-92; organist St. Andrews United Meth. Ch., 1992—. Mem. Nat. Rep. Senatorial Com. 1978-97; deacon 1st Presbyn, Ch., 1965-71; elder James Island Presbyn. Ch., 1974-76, 78-80, choir dir., organist, 1965-94; organist St. Andrews United Meth. Ch., Orangburg, 1994-2006; music dir., organist Holy Spirit Luth. Ch., Charleston, 2006—; bd. dir. excellence in tchg. award com. Charleston County Youth Symphony, 1975; bd. dir. Charles Towne Landing Band Festival Com., 1988-89; class agt. Furman U., 2003-2004; mem. bd. visitors Meth. Oaks, 2004-. Mem. Am. Guild Organists, Sertoma Club (bd. dir. 1989-90), Kiwanis Club (bd. dir. 1997-2001, sec. 1998-99, pres. 1999-2000, Disting. sec. 1998-99, Disting. pres. 1999-2000, Disting. Kiwanian award 1998-2000), Hibernian Soc., Elks, Orangeburg Music Club, Phi Mu Alpha (hon. life). Avocations: dance, reading, dining out, travel, ping pong/table tennis. Home: 2 Waters Edge Ct Charleston SC 29414

GUNN, TIM (TIMOTHY M. GUNN), apparel executive; b. Washington, July 29, 1953; Assoc. dean. Parsons The New Sch. for Design, NYC, 1989—2000, chair, fashion design dept., 2000—07; chief creative officer Liz Claiborne Inc., 2007—. Mentor, host (TV series) Project Runway, Bravo, 2004—, featured in Time mag., Newsweek, Crain's NY Bus., Martha Stewart Living, Elle Mag., Women's Wear Daily, appearances on CBS, NBC, Metro Channel; author: A Guide to Quality, Taste and Style, 2007. Office: Liz Claiborne Inc 1441 Broadway New York NY 10018*

GUNN, WILL A., foundation administrator, retired military officer, lawyer; b. Ft. Lauderdale, Fla. m. Dawn Gunn; 3 children. BS with military honors, USAF Acad., 1980; JD cum laude, Harvard Univ., 1986; LLM, George Washington Univ., 1994; MS, Indsl. Coll. Armed Forces, 2002; corr., Squadron Officer Sch., 1983, Air Command & Staff Coll., 1993, Air War Coll., 1999. Asst. staff judge adv. USAF, Mather AFB, Calif., 1986—87, area def. counsel, 1988—89, cir. def. counsel Travis AFB, Calif., 1989—90; White House Fellow Exec. Office of the Pres., Washington, 1990—91; trial atty. gen. litigation div., Mil. Pers. Br., Rosslyn, Va., 1991—93; staff judge adv. USAF, Pope AFB, NC, 1996—99, chief cir. def. counsel Randolph AFB, Tex., 1999—2000, exec. officer to Judge Adv. Gen. Washington, 2002—03; chief def. counsel Office of Mil. Commn. for mil tribunals at Guantanamo Bay, Cuba, Washington, 2003—05; CEO Boys & Girls Clubs of Greater Washington, DC, 2005—. 2d lt. USAF, 1980—82, 1st lt., 1982—84, capt., 1984—91, maj., 1991—96, lt. col., 1996—2002, col., 2002—05, ret., 2005—. Decorated Meritorious Svc. medal, four oak leaf clusters USAF, Air Force Commendation medal, one oak leaf cluster; named one of Forty Lawyers Under Forty, Nat. Law Jour.; named to Hall of Fame, Nat. Bar Assn., Mil. Law sect., 2002. Office: BGCGW Ste 600 8380 Colesville Rd Silver Spring MD 20910 Office Phone: 301-562-2000. E-mail: wgunn@bgcgw.org.

GUNNER, MICHAEL RICHARD, real estate manager, hotel executive; b. Fresno, Calif. s. Richard V. and Mimi A. Gunner. BS in Mgmt. Sci. & Engring., Stanford U., Calif., 2003, MS in Engring., Constrn. Engring. & Mgmt., 2004. Project mgr. Gunner Ranch, Santa Barbara, Calif., 2004—. Recipient Robert Byrd scholarship, USA, 1999—2003. Mem.: Inst. for Ops. Rsch. and the Mgmt. Scis., Urban Land Inst., US Chung Do Kwan Assn., Tau Beta Pi. Office: 1482 E Valley Rd 14 Santa Barbara CA 93108

GUNNER, MURRAY, retired religious organization administrator; b. NYC, Mar. 26, 1918; s. Abraham and Sadie (Schnee) G.; m. Pearl O. Katz, June 12, 1949; children: Marilyn Ruth, Janet Marie. BS, CCNY, 1938; MSW, Columbia U., 1946; cert., Hebrew U., 1971. Cert. social worker. Social worker, acting supr. N.Y.C. Dept. Welfare and Camp LaGuardia, 1940-45; adminstrv. asst. Coun. House, St. Louis, 1946-50; program dir. Jewish Community Ctr., Hartford, Conn., 1950-54, exec. dir. Newburgh, NY, 1954-62, Bklyn., 1962-66, Yonkers, NY, 1966-83; cons. Jewish Community Ctr., Jewish Fedn., 1983-89; exec. dir. Jewish Coun. of Yonkers, 1989—2006, exec. dir. emeritus, 2006—. Cons. Hudson River Mus., Elizabeth Seton Coll., 1989-89; co-chmn. commn. of synagogue rels. United Jewish Appeal Fedn., N.Y.C., 1980-81, co-chmn. Jewish Community Ctrs., 1981-82; co-chair adult edn. com. Greystone Jewish Ctr., Yonkers, 1980-82, bd. dirs., 1978-80. Contbr. author to various books. Pres. Yonkers Social Work Orgn., 1973, 1993; Active Charter Revision Commn., Yonkers, 1979, Mayor's Holocaust Commn. Yonkers, 1979, Mayor's Com. on Jewish Affairs, Yonkers, 1990—, Yonkers Crime Commn., 1975, Yonkers Mental Health Coun., 1978—83, Mayor's Cmty. Rels. Com., Yonkers, 1992—, task force City/County Youth Violence; exec. com. Edn. 2000, Yonkers, 1992; cmty. planning coun. Substance Abuse Prevention Com., 1997—; shared decision making commn. Gorton H.S., 1997; exec. com. Yonkers Mayor's Cmty. Rels. Commn., 1997; edn. com. Yonkers City Coun., 1998—; chair Yonkers Flag Day Commn., 1998; mem. Yonkers Family and Cmty. project Columbia U., 1998, NY State Assemblyman Adv. Com., 1997; active Yonker Mayor's Health Comm., 1998—2002; older adults com. Yonkers Mayor Health Commn., 1999; active Older Adult Task Force, Substance Abuse Task Force; apptd. mem. partnership com. Yonkers Bd. Edn., 1999; apptd. bd. dirs. Yonkers Libr. Found., 2001; apptd. by Benedict Found. Elder-Friendly Com., City of Yonkers, 2001; sec. Westchester Jewish Chronicle, 2001—; apptd. Yonkers Libr. Found. Commn., 2001; adv. com. to senator NY State Senate, 1997—; active Mentoring Com. for Youth at Risk, 1993; bd. dirs. Greystone Jewish Ctr., 2000—07, Yonkers United Way, 1981—83, Cmty. Planning Agy., Yonkers, 1992—. Recipient Israel Cummings award Commn. on Synagogue Rels. Fedn., 1963, cert. of merit, 1992, Am. Com. on Italian Migration, 1992, cert. of recognition for outstanding svc. and contbns. Charles Gorton H.S., Yonkers, 1995, Yonkers Martin Luther King Commn. award, 1995, Cmty. Svc. award Mayor of City of Yonkers, 1995, Multi-Cultural Edn. award Yonkers Pub. Schs., 1998, honors for outstanding leadership Westchester County Exec. Dirs., 2001, Outstanding Leadership award S.W. Yonkers Planning Assn., 2001, Outstanding Profl. award Westchester County Execs. of United Jewsih Appeal Fedn., Humanitarian award, C. of C., 2002, Griffon award Untrmeyer Performing Arts Coun., 2002; honored for cmty. svc. Jewish Coun. Yonkers Bd. Dirs., City of Yonkers, County of Westchester, U.S. Congress, Rockland County YM-YWHA, 1998; Murray Gunner Day named in his honor City of Yonkers, 1983, County of Westchester, 1983; named guest of honor Westchester chpt. Am. Heart Assn., 1997., award Cmty. Svc. Rconstructionist Synagogue of scarsdale, N.Y., 2004, Cmty. Svc. award, Jewish Cmty Ctr. on the Hudson, 2004, Outstanding Cmty Svc. award Yonkers Rotary, 2005; proclamation Congresswoman Nita Loway, City Coun. Yonkers, County of Westchester, NY State Assembly, NY State Senate, Outstanding Leadership and Cmty. Svc. for 66 Continuous Yrs. from 1940-2006 NY, 2006; numerous other honors. Mem.: NASW (Gold Care mem., Disting. Svc. award Westchester chpt. 2001, Lifetime Achievement award N.Y. State chpt. 2001), Rotary (chair pub. rels. com. 1988, chair cmty. svcs., bd. dirs. 1993—94, sec. 2006—, presenter invocations, Paul Harris fellow 1994, honored for 34 yrs. of service 2005). Home: 10 Gateway Rd Yonkers NY 10703-1200 Office: Jewish Coun of Yonkers 584 N Broadway Yonkers NY 10701-1731 Office Phone: 914-423-5009. Business E-Mail: m.gunner@jewishcouncil.info. *The struggle for survival we face each day, can be exhillerating or threatening. The manner, in which we handle each challenge, is dependent on the degree of our faith in God, coupled with the strength of belief in ourselves.*

GUNNING, CAROLYN SUE, dean, provost, nursing educator; b. Ft. Smith, Ark., Dec. 16, 1943; d. Laurence George and Flora Irene (Garner) G. BS, Tex. Woman's U., 1965; MS, U. Colo., 1973; PhD, U. Tex., Austin, 1981. RN, Tex. Clinician III Bexar County Hosp., San Antonio, 1968-71; instr. U. Tex. Sch. Nursing, San Antonio, 1973-74, asst. prof., 1974-83, asst. to dean, 1977-79, assoc. prof., asst. dean undergrad. programs, 1983-84, assoc. dean, 1984-88; dean Sch. Nursing Marshall U., Huntington, W.Va., 1988-90; dean Coll. Nursing Tex. Woman's U., Denton, 1991—2003, provost, v.p. academic affairs, 2003—04, 2005—, assoc. v.p. spl. projects, 2004—05. Accreditation site visitor Commn. on Collegiate Nursing Edn. Contbr. articles to profl. jours. Active Leadership San Antonio, 1978-79, Leadership Tex., 1992. Served to capt. Nurse Corps, U.S. Army, 1965-68; to lt. col. Army N.G., 1980-88. Decorated Army Commendation medal. Mem. ANA, Sigma Theta Tau, Kappa Delta Pi, Phi Kappa Phi. Office Phone: 940-898-3301.

GUNNING, FRANCIS PATRICK, lawyer, insurance company executive; b. Scranton, Pa., Dec. 10, 1923; s. Frank Peter and Mary Loretta (Kelly) G.; m. Nancy C. Hill, Aug. 10, 1951; 1 son, Brian F. Student, City Coll. N.Y., 1941-43; LLB, St. John's U., 1950. Bar: N.Y. 1950. Legal editor Prentice Hall Pub. Co., NYC, 1950-51; legal specialist Tchrs. Ins. & Annuity Assn. Am., Coll. Retirement Equities Fund, NYC, 1951-53, asst. counsel, 1953-57, assoc. counsel, 1957-60, counsel, 1960-65, asst. gen. counsel, 1965-67, assoc. gen. counsel, 1967, v.p., assoc. gen. counsel, 1967-73, sr. v.p., gen. counsel, 1973-74, exec. v.p., gen. counsel, 1974-88, ret., 1988. Trustee, mem. exec. and audit coms. Mortgage Growth Investors (now MGI Properties). Contbr. articles on mortgage financing to profl. jours. With USAAF, 1943-46. Mem. ABA, N.Y. State Bar Assn., Am. Land Title Assn., Am. Law Inst., Assn. of Bar of City of N.Y., Assn. Life Ins. Counsel, Nat. Assn. Coll. Univ. Attys., Am. Coll. Real Estate Lawyers. Republican. Roman Catholic. Home and Office: 32 Kewanee Rd New Rochelle NY 10804-1324

GUNNING, ROBERT CLIFFORD, mathematician, educator; b. Longmont, Colo., Nov. 27, 1931; s. Clifford Henry and Inez (Wilhelm) G.; m. Wanda S. Holtzinger, July 9, 1966. AB, U. Colo., 1952, DHL, 2006; MA, Princeton U., 1953, PhD, 1955. NSF fellow U. Chgo., 1955-56; mem. faculty Princeton U., 1956—, prof. math., 1966—, chmn. dept., 1976-79, dean of faculty, 1989-95. Vis. prof. U. São Paulo, Brazil, 1957, U. Munich, 1967, ULCA, 1972, Oxford (Eng.) U., spring 1968, fall, 1980, 88, 95; Sloan fellow, 1958-61; asst. dir. studies, math. St. Catharines Coll., Cambridge (Eng.) U., 1959-60; mem. editl. bd. Princeton (N.J.) U. Press, 1969-73. Author: Lectures on Modular Forms, 1962, (with H. Rossi) Analytic Functions of Several Complex Variables, 1965, Lectures on Riemann Surfaces, Vol. I, 1966, Vol. II, 1967, Vol. III, 1972, Complex Analytic Varieties, Vol. I, 1970, Vol. II, 1974, Generalized Theta Functions, 1976, Uniformization of Complex Manifolds, 1978, Introduction to Holomorphic Functions of Several Variables, 3 vols., 1990; editor: Problems in Analysis, 1970, Theta Functions, 1989, Collected Papers of Salomon Bochner, 4 vols., 1991; contbr. articles to profl. jours. Recipient Pres. Award Disting. Tchg., 2003. Fellow AAAS; mem. Am. Math. Soc., Princeton Club (N.Y.C.), Nassau Club (Princeton), Phi Beta Kappa, Sigma Xi. Episcopalian. Office: Fine Hall Washington Rd Princeton NJ 08544-1000

GUNNING, TOM, art educator; BA, NYU, 1970, MA in Cinema Studies, 1974, PhD, 1986; PhD (hon.), in philosophy, 1998. Prof. dept. art history U. Chgo. Author: D.W. Griffith and the Origins of American Narrative Film: The Early Years, 1991, An Invention of the Devil? Religion and Early Cinema, 1992, The Films of Fritz Lang: Allegories of Vision and Modernity, 2000; contbr. articles to profl. jours. Guggenheim fellow, 1998. Office: Dept Art History U Chgo 5540 S Greenwood Ave Chicago IL 60637-1506 E-mail: tgunning@midway.uchicago.edu.

GUNSAULIS, LINDA C., elementary school educator; b. Elk City, Okla., Feb. 13, 1949; d. Eli and L. Sue Shotwell; m. Darrell F. Gunsaulis, May 28, 1986; children: Todd Atha, Tammy Kelln, Darinda Sellars, Dustin. Student, Sayre Jr. Coll., 1967—68; BS, Southwestern Okla. State U., Weatherford, 1973, MEd, 1979, postgrad., 1987—88, Northwestern Okla. State U., Alva, 1985—87. Nat. bd. cert. tchr. Okla., 2000. Dep. ct. clk. Roger Mills County, Okla., 1974—77; tchr. home econs. Fargo HS, Okla., 1977—80; elem. tchr. Fargo Elem. Sch., 1980—90, Arnett Pub. Sch., 1990—2005; tchr. elem. social studies Okla., 2002; tchr. nat. elem. social studies, 2003; tchr. grade 4 Cornelsen Elem. Sch./Fairview Pub. Schs., 2005—. Lectr. in field; presenter workshops in field; adv. bd. TIME Mag. for Kids, 2004—06. Contbr. articles to profl. jours. Mem. Fairview Centennial Com. Named Tchr. of Today, Masons, 2002; grantee, Okla. Commn. for Tchrs., 1998; scholar, Delta Kappa Gamma, 2000. Mem.: DAR, NEA, Okla. Ctr. for Books, Nat. Bd. Cert. Tchrs., Okla. Edn. Assn., Ellis County Edn. Assn. (pres. 2004—05), N.W. Tech. Consortium, Internat. Reading Assn., Okla. Reading Assn. (v.p. 2001—02, pres. 2003—04, parliamentarian 2004—05), Wheatland Reading Coun., N.W. Reading Coun. (charter mem., 1st v.p., pres.), Nat. Coun. for Social Studies, Okla. Coun. for Social Studies (programs com. mem. winter conf. 2003—04), Order Ea. Star, Delta Kappa Gamma (1st v.p., area dir., 2d v.p., pres.). Democrat. Avocations: gardening, reading, crafts.

GUNSON, DOUGLAS R., lawyer; m. Blythe Gunson; 7 children. Assoc. Moore & Van Allen, NC, 1989—90, Parker, Poe, Adams & Bernstein, NC, 1990—94; corp. counsel SGL Carbon Corp., NC, 1994—2000; gen. mgr. corp. legal affairs Nucor Corp., Charlotte, NC, 2005—. Office: Nucor Corp 2100 Rexford Rd Charlotte NC 28211 Office Phone: 704-972-1832. Office Fax: 704-362-4208. E-mail: dgunson@nucor.com.*

GUNTER, BRADLEY HUNT, capital management executive; b. Norfolk, Va., Dec. 8, 1940; s. J.A. and Virginia (Whalen) G.; m. Susan Mason Hart, Dec. 27, 1962 (div. 1977); children: Bradley Hunt, Valerie Mason; m. Anne Macon, Nov. 7, 1985 (dec. 1994); 1 child, Bradford Macon Gunter; m. Meredith Laura Strohm, Dec. 16, 1994. BA, U. Richmond, 1962; MA, U. Va., 1963, PhD, 1969. Instr. Washington and Lee U., Lexington, Va., 1967-69; asst. prof. Boston Coll., 1969-71; editor Econ. Rev. Fed. Res. Bank, Richmond, Va., 1971—80, corp. sec., 1973—80; pres. Bartleby's Inc., Richmond, 1980-85; dir. found. rels. U. Va., Charlottesville, 1985-86; investment broker Scott and Stringfellow, Richmond, 1987-89; mng. dir. Scott & Stringfellow Capital Mgmt., Richmond, 1989-97, pres., CEO, 1997—2000; pres. Investment Mgmt. of Va., LLC, Richmond and Charlottesville, 2000—. Cons. NEH, Washington, 1975—80. Author: Studies in The Waste Land, 1971, Guide to T.S. Eliot, 1970, Checklist of T.S. Eliot, 1969; contbr. articles to profl. jours. Chmn. fund drive United Way, Richmond, 1980; mem. arts and scis. alumni coun. U. Va., mem. Emeritus Soc., Coll. Found.; pres., bd. dirs. New Va. Rev.; pres. Arts Coun. Richmond; chmn. Hist. Richmond Found.; bd. dirs. Poe Found., Va. Ctr. for the Book; bd. dirs., chmn. U. Va. Cancer Ctr., U. Va. Health Scis. Coun.; mem. regional bd. Sorensen Inst. for Polit. Leadership; chmn. U. Va. Ann. Giving Adv. Bd.; trustee United Way Greater Richmond; vestryman St. Paul's Ch., Richmond, 1975—78; trustee St. Paul's Endowment Fund, Inc.; mem. Va. Coun. Chairs; bd. dirs. St. Christopher's Sch. Found., Richmond, 1981—85, Richmond Ballet, Big Bros. Richmond Inc., Va. Found. for Humanities and Pub. Policy, Scott and Stringfelow Ednl. Found., Elk Hill Farm, Tuesday Evening Concert Series. Mem. Va. Coun. on Econ. Edn. (bd. dirs.), CFA Inst., U. Va. Alumni Assn. (chpt. pres. Richmond 1981), U. Va. Coun. Chairs, Va. Soc. Mayflower Descs. (bd. dirs.), Country Club Va., Colonnade Club, Focus Club, Univ. Club NY, Farmington Country Club, Phi Beta Kappa, Omicron Delta Kappa. Episcopalian. Avocation: walking. Office: Investment Mgmt of Va 310 4th St NE Charlottesville VA 22902-5266 Office Phone: 434-220-0356. Personal E-mail: m1216@comcast.net. Business E-Mail: bgunter@imva.net.

GUNTER, EMILY DIANE, communications executive, marketing professional, educator, real estate developer, writer; b. Atlantic City, Apr. 5, 1948; d. Fay Gaffney and Verlee (Wright) G.; children: Saliha, Kadir,

Amin, Shedia. BA in Math. Stats., Am. U., 1970, postgrad., 1971, San Diego C.C., 1986. Cert. Qualtec Total Quality mgmt. trainer. Traffic engr. C&P Bell, Washington, 1970—71; market analyst Market Towers Inc., Atlantic City, 1978—79; outside plant engr. N.J. Bell, Atlantic City, 1979—81; market analyst Empcor Group, Atlantic City, 1981—83; outside plant engr. Pacific Bell, San Diego, 1983—91, account exec., 1991—93; v.p. Black Am. of Achievement, Inc., San Diego, 1994—95; founder Women's Wholistic Enpowerment Ctr., 1996—97; pres. Gunter Devel. Enterprises, 1987—. Lectr. women and minorities in engring. and math. Princeton (N.J.) U., 1979-81, Atlantic C.C., Atlantic City, 1979-81; customer coord. Pacific Bell-Telsam, San Diego, 1983-85; prof. math. Grossmont Coll., 1992-94, instr. super learning skills seminar, 1992—; motivational spkr. Author: Superlearning 2000: The New Technologies of Self-Empowerment, 1993, Supermath 2000: How to Learn Math Without Fear, 1993, Achieve Goals 2000: A Personal Handbook for the Lifelong Learner, 1995, Living, Learning & Healing Through the Right Use of Your Mind, 1996, SL2000 Learning Made Easy-Everybody Can Learn, 1997, A Rite of Passage to Spiritual Enlightenment-Living with Compassion, 2000, Whole Women-Whole World, 2003, Thirteen Golden Keys to Learning: A Spiritual Journey, 2005. Bd. dirs. Lead, San Diego, Atlantic City Transp. Authority, 1981-82, San Diego Urban Math. Collaborative; trustee Reuben H. Fleet Sci. Found., 1989, San Diego Sci. Found., 1989-97, 1990 class Lead-Leadership Edn. Awareness Devel., San Diego; mem. steering com. United Negro Coll. Fund, San Diego; mem. Atlantic City Urban Area Transp. Commn., 1982-83; mem. Am. Humanics Bd. U. San Deigo, 1991-94; pres. bd. World Beat Cultural Ctr., Balboa Park, Calif., 1992-93; internat. exec. dir. Rites of Passage Youth Empowerment Programs of Am., 1997—; youth advocate, chmn., founder and CEO Rites of Passage Youth Empowerment Found., 1998; chmn. and CEO Heart of Africa Holding Corp., 1998—. Mem. African Am. Womens Conf., Women on Tour (exec. bd. 1992-2003), Coalition Women's Groups (bd. dirs. 1996-97), Sigma Gamma Rho (hon. mem., rites of passage coord. 1996—). Democrat. Avocations: chess, painting, water aerobics, walking, piano. Home: PO Box 72372 Durham NC 27722-2372 also: Gunter Devel Enterprises PO Box 72372 Durham NC 27722-2372 Office Phone: 919-403-8881. Business E-Mail: edgunter@ritesofpassageonline.org.

GUNTER, JAMES HOUSTON, JR., state supreme court justice; b. Atlanta, Tex., Mar. 8, 1943; s. James Houston and Helen Marie (Long) G.; m. Ruth Elma Miller, Jan. 23, 1965 (divl Jan. 1992); children: Christie Gunter Adams, Craig; m. Judee Thompson, May 30, 1992. BBA, Tex. A&M U., 1965; JD, U. Houston, 1972. Bar: Tex. 1972, Ark. 1973, U.S. Dist. Ct. (we. dist.) Ark., U.S. Dist. Ct. (ea. dist.) Tex., U.S. Supreme Ct. Assoc. John Wilson Law Firm, Hope, Ark., 1973-74; ptnr. Wilson & Gunter, Hope, 1974-75, Wilson, Gunter & Walker, Hope, 1975-82; pros. atty. 8th Jud. Dist., Hope, 1976-82, chancery judge, 1982-90, cir. judge, 1990—2004; assoc. justice Ark. State Supreme Ct., Little Rock, 2004—. Asst. scoutmaster Boy Scouts Am., Hope, chair Razorback dist., mem. exec. bd. Cando Area coun.; pres. Ark. Enterprises for the Blind, Little Rock, 1976; bd. dirs. World Svcs. for the Blind, 1976. Mem. ABA, Ark. Bar Assn., Lions (chmn. 1976, dist. gov. Ark. 1975). Avocations: golf, flying, canoeing. Office: Ark Supreme Ct 625 Marshall St Justice Bldg Little Rock AR 72201

GUNTER, JAMES T., research scientist; b. Richmond, Va., Mar. 22, 1962; s. Thomas Jefferson and Joy Ruth Moses Gunter; m. Dolores Kathleen Delaney, Jan. 12, 1962; children: Benjamin Lee, Catherine Ruth, Rebecca Delaney. A in Art and Sci., Allegany Coll., Cumberland, Md., 1986; BS, Va. Tech. U., Blacksburg, 1991; MS, Miss. State U., Starkville, 1994. Cartographic engr. Energy Spatial Analysis Rsch. Lab. Tulane U., New Orleans, 1995—2000; rsch. assoc. I dept. forestry Miss. State U., Starkville, 2000—01; scientist/rschr. II Ctr. for Sci. and Pub. Policy U. Okla., Norman, 2001—04; rsch. scientist Ctr. for Biosecurity Rsch. U. Okla. Health Scis. Ctr., Oklahoma City, 2004—. Participant Cleavland County Livestock Assn., Norman, Okla., 2006—07. Recipient 3rd Pl. Best Paper award, Am. Soc. for Photogrammetry and Remote Sensing, 2001. Home: 8915 Alameda St Norman OK 73026 Office: Center for Biosecurity Research 755 Research Parkway Suite 755 Oklahoma City OK 73104 Home Phone: 405-366-7662; Office Phone: 405-271-3875. Office Fax: 405-271-3865. Personal E-mail: jtgunter@sbcglobal.net. Business E-Mail: jim-gunter@ouhsc.edu.

GUNTER, JOSEPH CLIFFORD, III, lawyer; b. Ft. Worth, Apr. 26, 1943; s. Joseph Cliford Jr. and Helen (Wright) G.; children: Joseph Clifford IV, Grant Norwood. BA, U. Tex., 1965, JD, 1967. Bar: Tex. 1967. Assoc. McDonald Sanders Ginsberg New Kirk Gibson & Webb, Ft. Worth, 1967-68; ptnr. Bracewell & Patterson, Houston, 1968—2005, Bracewell & Guiliani, Houston, 2005—. Adv. Am. Bd. Trial Advocates. Lt. USNR, 1967-73. Fellow Am. Coll. Trial Lawyers, Tex. Bar Found., Houston Bar Found.; mem. ABA, State Bar Tex., State Bar Colo. Episcopalian. Avocations: golf, tennis, skiing, sailing. Office: Bracewell & Giuliani 711 Louisiana St Ste 2300 Houston TX 77002-2781 Home Phone: 713-526-3766; Office Phone: 713-221-1213. Business E-Mail: clifford.gunter@bracewellgiuliani.com.

GUNTER, MICHAEL DONWELL, lawyer; b. Gastonia, NC, Mar. 26, 1947; s. Daniel Cornelius and DeNorma Joyce (Smith) Gunter; m. Barbara Jo Benson, June 19, 1970; children: Kimberly Elizabeth, Daniel Cornelius III. BA in History with honors, Wake Forest U., 1969; JD with honors, U. N.C., 1972; MBA with honors, U. Pa., 1973. Bar: N.C. 1972, U.S. Dist. Ct. (mid. dist.) N.C. 1974, U.S. Tax Ct. 1975, U.S. Supreme Ct. 1979, U.S. Claims Ct. 1982, U.S. Ct. Appeals (DC cir.) 1985, U.S. Ct. Appeals (4th cir.) 1992. Mem. Womble Carlyle Sandridge & Rice PLLC, Winston-Salem, NC, 1974—, chmn. employee benefits practice group, employee benefits counsel. Bd. dirs. Indsl. Belting, Inc. Contbr. articles to benefit jours. Mem. NCAA cert. com. Wake Forest U., former mem. athletic dept. long-range planning com., former pres. Deacon Club, former mem. athletic coun., former mem. alumni coun., mem. bd. visitors; coach youth basketball Winston-Salem YMCA, 1981—90; advisor Winston-Salem United Way Christmas Cheer Toy Shop, 1975; bd. dir. Centenary Meth. Ch., 1980, Goodwill Industries, 1987—; forum chmn. bd., sec. chmn. fin. com., chair CEO search com., mem. cmty. problem solving com. United Way, 1988—99; mem. Leadership Winston-Salem. Named one of Best Employee Benefits Lawyers in Am., Nat. Law Jour., Best Lawyers in Am.; William E. Newcombe scholar, U. Pa., 1972—73. Fellow: Am. Coll. Employee Benefits Counsel (charter); mem.: ABA, Assn. Pvt. Pension and Welfare, ESOP Assn., Profit Sharing Coun. Am., Winston-Salem Estate Planning Coun. (past bd. dirs.), Forsyth County Bar Assn., N.C. Bar Assn. (former chmn. tax sect., mem. continuing legal edn. com., mem. sports and entertainment law com.), So. Pension Conf., Forsyth Country Club (former pres., bd. dirs.), Rotary (former bd. dirs. Reynolda Club), Order of Coif. Democrat. Methodist. Avocations: golf, fishing. Home: 128 Ballyhoo Dr Lewisville NC 27023-9633 Office: Womble Carlyle Sandridge and Rice PLLC One W Fourth St Winston Salem NC 27101 Office Phone: 336-721-3607. Office Fax: 336-733-8392. Business E-Mail: mgunter@wcsr.com.

GUNTER, RUSSELL ALLEN, lawyer; b. Amarillo, Tex., Feb. 21, 1950; s. J.B. and Shirley Ann (Russell) G.; children: Kim, Sarah, Laura, Rachel. BS in Polit. Sci., So. Ark U., 1972; JD, Tex. Tech U., 1975. Bar: Ark., 1975, Tex, 1975, U.S. Dist. Ct. (ea. and we dists.) Ark. 1975, U.S. Dist. Ct. (no. dist.) Tex. 1976, U.S. Ct. Appeals (8th cir.), 1980, U.S. Supreme Ct. 1986. Assoc. Gaines N. Houston, Little Rock, 1975-79, Wallace, Dover & Dixon, P.A., Little Rock, 1979-90, McGlinchey Stafford Lang P.L.L.C., Little Rock, 1990-97; Cross, Gunter, Witherspoon & Galchus P.C., Little Rock, 1997—. Mem. ABA (com. on practice and procedure before NLRB labor sect.), Soc. for Human Resource Mgmt. (cert. sr. profl. in human resources), Ark. Bar Assn., Tex. Bar Assn., Ark. State C. of C. (bd. dirs.). Office: 500 Clinton Ave Ste 200 Little Rock AR 72201-1747 Home Phone: 501-771-0399; Office Phone: 501-371-9999. Business E-Mail: rgunter@cgwg.com.

GUNTER, WILLIAM DAYLE, JR., physicist, consultant; b. Mitchell, SD, Jan. 10, 1932; s. William Dayle and Lamerta Berniece (Hockensmith) G.; m. Shirley Marie Teshera, Oct. 24, 1955; children: Maria Jo, Robert Paul. BS in Physics with distinction, Stanford U., 1957, MS, 1959. Physicist Ames Rsch. Ctr. NASA, Moffett Field, Calif., 1960-81, asst. br. chief electronic optical engring., 1981-85; pvt. practice cons. Photon Applications, San Jose, Calif., 1985-98, Modesto, Calif., 1998-2000; ret. Patentee in field; contbr. articles to profl. jours. With U.S. Army, 1953-55. Recipient Westinghouse Sci. Talent Search award, 1950; Stanford U. scholar, 1950. Mem. IEEE (sr.), Am. Phys. Soc., Optical Soc. Am., Nat. Space Soc., NASA Alumni League. Personal E-mail: billgunter06@comcast.net.

GÜNTER-MCCOY, JANE HUTTON, singer; b. Kingston, NY, Feb. 9, 1938; d. Herman and Elizabeth Mason (Hutton) Günter; m. Seth T. McCoy, Sept. 9, 1978 (dec.). BM, U. Rochester, 1959; MusM, postgrad., Ind. U., 1961—. Prof. voice Mannes Coll. Music, NYC, 1965—76, Lighthouse for the Blind, NYC, 1965—78; pvt. voice instr. NYC, 1965—87. Soloist Robert Shaw Chorale, US, Can., Russia, South Am., 1962—66, Sohola Contorum N.Y., US, Europe, 1970. Singer: (concert) Hansel and Gretel, Wagner Internat. Instn., Les Noces, Met. Opera, numerous performances in recital opera and oratorio. Mem.: Chamber Music Am., Nat. Assn. Tchrs. of Singing. Office: Eastman Sch Music 26 Gibbs St Rochester NY 14604 Office Phone: 585-274-1414. E-mail: realmccoy122@frontiernet.net.

GUNTHER, VIRGINIA F., history educator; b. Bklyn., Feb. 23, 1951; d. Frank and Carmela Giuliano. BA, Fordham U., NYC, 1972; MA, NYU, 1975. Cert. ESL tchr. LI U., NY, 1984. Tchr. Bklyn. Tech. H.S., 1972—75, J.F.K. H.S., Bronx, NY, 1977—80, Briarcliff H.S., NY, 1984—85, Mamaroneck H.S. Continuing Edn., NY, 1985—94, New Rochelle H.S., NY, 1992—. Adj. prof. Manhattanville Coll., NY, 2003. Pres. Jr. League Westchester-On-Sound, Larchmont, NY, 1991—92. Recipient Social Studies Tchr. Yr., Westchester County, 1995, Disting. Social Studies Educator award, NY State Coun. Social Studies, 2006. Mem.: NCSS (Social Studies Tchr. Yr. 1995). Office: New Rochelle High Sch 265 Clove Rd New Rochelle NY 10801

GUNTHER, WILLIAM DAVID, academic administrator, economics professor; b. Balt., Oct. 11, 1940; s. Geneva (Gee) G.; m. Irene Leveja Reineks, Jan. 8, 1966; children: William B., Kristine A., Jennifer R. BS, Kent State U., 1962, MA, 1965; PhD, U. Ky., 1969. Asst. prof. econs. U. Ala., Tuscaloosa, 1968-72, assoc. prof. econs., 1972-76, prof. econs., 1976—98, assoc. dean for rsch., 1988-98; dean sch. bus. U. So. Miss., Hattiesburg, 1998—2003, prof. econs., 1998—. Contbr. articles to profl. jours. Fulbright scholar Fulbright Commn., 1972, Faculty fellow USAF, 1979. Mem. Assn. Coll. Honor Socs. (exec. coun. 1983-2005), Am. Econs. Assn., Omicron Delta Epsilon (sec., treas. 1977-2007). Avocations: boating, coin collecting/numismatics, paper money collecting. Office: U So Miss PO Box 5072 Hattiesburg MS 39406-1000 Business E-Mail: william.gunther@usm.edu.

GUNTHEROTH, WARREN GADEN, pediatrician, educator; b. Hominy, Okla., July 27, 1927; s. Harry William and Callie (Cornett) G.; m. Ethel Haglund, July 3, 1954; children: Kurt, Karl, Sten. MD, Harvard U., 1952. Diplomate: Am. Bd. Pediatrics, Am. Bd. Pediatric Cardiology, Nat. Bd. Med. Examiners. Intern Peter Bent Brigham Hosp., Boston, 1952-53; fellow in cardiology Children's Hosp., Boston, 1953-55, resident in pediatrics, 1955-56; rsch. fellow physiology and biophysics U. Wash. Med. Sch., Seattle, 1957-58, mem. faculty, 1958—, prof. pediatrics, 1969—, head divsn. pediatric cardiology, 1964-91. Author: Pediatric Electrocardiography, 1965, How to Read Pediatric ECGs, 1981, 4th edit., 2006, Crib Death (Sudden Infant Death Syndrome), 1982, 3d edit., 1995, Climbing With Sasha, a Washington Husky, 1995; also more than 300 articles; mem. editl. bd. Am. Heart Jour., 1977-80, Circulation, 1980-83, Am. Jour. Noninvasive Cardiology, 1985-94, Jour. Am. Coll. Cardiology, 1988-94, Am. Jour. Cardiology, Jour. Noninvasive Cardiology, 1996-00; sect. editor Practice of Pediatrics, 1979-87, Pediatric Cardiology, 2004-07. Served with USPHS, 1950-51. Spl. research fellow NIH, 1967. Mem. Soc. Pediatric Rsch., Biomed. Engring. Soc. (charter), Am. Heart Assn. (chmn. N.W. regional med. rsch. adv. com. 1978-80), Cardiovascular System Dynamics Soc. (charter), Am. Coll. Cardiology. Democrat. Home: 13201 42nd Ave NE Seattle WA 98125-4626 Office: U Wash Med Sch Dept Pediatrics PO Box 356320 Seattle WA 98195-6320 Office Phone: 206-543-3186. Business E-Mail: wgg@u.washington.edu. *My career includes medical practice, teaching and research; my hobby is mountain climbing. Both work and hobby benefit from courage. Encouraging students to ask difficult— and even embarrassing— questions, reaching a timely diagnosis, starting treatment in a dangerously ill patient, and raising challenging questions in research that may provoke anger or scorn; all require courage. Silent convictions are not enough.*

GÜNTHER-STIRN, DAGMAR DOROTHEA, retired social sciences educator; b. Tientsin, Hopeh, China, June 8, 1931; arrived in U.S., 1939; d. Wilhelm Otto Carl Franz Günther and Emilie Marcella Stirn. BA, Wellesley Coll., 1953; MIA, Columbia U., 1955, ABD, 1961. Instr. dept. polit. sci. U. Ct., Hartford, 1963—70, Ctrl. Conn. State U., New Britain, 1971; adj. prof. U. Hartford, West Hartford, 1970—83; ret., 1983. Corporator Dana Hall Sch., Wellesley, Mass., 2002—; bd. dirs. J. L. Anthony & Co., 1965—. Trustee Hartford Conservatory Music, 1983—96; from bd. dirs. to pres. Cromwell (Conn.) Hills Condominium Assn., 1996—2004. Scholar, Dept. of State, 1971—73. Mem.: Am. Polit. Sci. Assn., Musical Club Hartford (exec. bd., sec. 2000—04). Republican. United Ch. Of Christ. Avocations: travel, gardening, opera. Home: 23 Cherry Hill Ct Cromwell CT 06416

GUNTON, HOWARD E., insurance company executive; Numerous fin. mgmt. positions Am. Internat. Group Inc.; sr. v.p., CFO AIG Life Cos. (U.S.), Mass. Mutual Life Ins., Springfield, Mass., 1999—. Mem. AICPAs, Del. Soc. CPA's. Office: Mass Mutual Life Ins Co 1295 State St Springfield MA 01111-0002

GUNZBURGER, SUZANNE NATHAN, municipal official, social worker; b. Buffalo, July 12, 1939; d. Lawrence Emil and Ruth Lucille (Wohl) Nathan; m. Gerard Josef Gunzburger, Apr. 10, 1960; children: Ronald Marc, Cynthia Anne, Judith Lynn. BS in Edn., Wayne State U., 1959; MSW, Barry U., 1974. Tchr. pub. schs., Detroit, 1959-63, Trumbull, Conn., 1963-66, North Miami Beach, Fla., 1967-68, Broward County, Fla., 1968-72; pvt. practice clin. social work Hollywood, Fla., 1975—; vice mayor City of Hollywood, 1983-84, 85-87, city commr., 1982-92; commr. Broward County, 1992—, chair, 1994-95, 99-2000. Chmn. Met. Planning Orgn., Broward County, 1984—87, 1989, Statewide Human Rights Adv. Com., 1988—89; pres. Broward County Mental Health Bd., 1984; active Broward County Commn. Status Women, 1978—82, White House Conf. Families, Balt., 1980; del. Broward County League Cities, 1988—92; mem. adv. bd. Broward Homebound, 1991—; mem. Broward Children's Svc. Bd., 1988—92, Broward County Water Adv., 1992—94, 1997—98, Broward County Cmty. Redevel. Agy., 1992—, South Fla. Regional Planning Coun., 1992—94, 1998—99, treas., 1999; vice-chmn. Broward County Planning Coun., 1996—98, chair planning coun., 2000—01, Broward County Cultural Affairs Coun., 1996—; Broward chair Concert Assn. of Fla., Inc., 1996—; mem. Broward Children's Svc. Bd., 1998—; bd. dirs. Environ. Coalition Broward County, 1982—89, 1997—2000, Fla. Assn. of Counties, 1992—, Broward Alliance, 1992—2000, Broward Children's Svcs., 1997, Children's Svcs. Coun., 2001—. Named Broward County Woman of Yr., 1990, Humanitarian of Yr., David Posnack, Jewish Comty. Ctr., 1994, Environmentalist of Yr., Broward County Environ. Coalition, 1994, Polit. Leader of Yr., The Vanguard Chronicle, 1999, Woman of Valor, David Posnack JCC, 2003, First Lady Broward, Broward County Fair, 2004; recipient Woamn of Yr. in Govt. award Women in Comms., 1983, Disting. Achievement award Am. Jewish Congress, 1990, Fla. Philharm. Woman of Style and Substance, 1995, Woman of Distinction award March of Dimes, 1996, Heart award Children's Consortium, 1996, Disting. Alumni award Barry U., 1996, Jesse Portis Helms Dem. of Yr. award Dolphin Dem. Club, 1996, Gracias award Hispanic Unity, 1999, Polit. Alliance of Yr. award Dolphin Dem. Club, 1999, Cmty. Covenant award Broward Outreach Ctr., 2005, Com Leadership award Hispanic Unity, Women of Style and Substance, Social Activist award; inductee Broward County Women's Hall of Fame, 1995, Woman of Distinction award City of Hollywood, 1997, Women's Polit. Caucus, 1997, Encore award Art Serve, 2004; Jewish Mus. Fla., Queen Esther Court Honoree, 2004. Mem. Nat. Assn. Social Workers (diplomate clin. social work), Internat. Acad. Behavioral Med., Counseling and Psychotherapy (diplomate profl. psychotherapy), Am. Acad. Behavioral Med. (clin. mem.), Nat. Coun. Jewish Women (pres. 1980-82, Hannah G. Solomon award 1989), Met. Planning Orgn., Israel Bond Coun., Hollywood C. of C. (leadership devel. 1990—), Kiwanis. Democrat. Avocations: reading, swimming, travel. Office: Office Bd County Commrs Govtl Ctr Rm 412 115 S Andrews Ave Fort Lauderdale FL 33301-1818

GUNZENHAUSER, GERARD RALPH, JR., management consultant, investor; b. Mt. Vernon, NY, Sept. 26, 1936; s. Gerard Ralph and Helen Elizabeth (Carey) G.; m. Alfa Marjorie Vendetti, Sept. 17, 1960; children: Cathy Susan, Michael Gerard, Christopher John, Eric David. BBA, Iona Coll., 1965; postgrad., NYU Sch. Bus. Adminstrn., 1967-68. Asst. mgr. fin. analysis Gen. Foods Corp., White Plains, N.Y., 1962-68; dir. fin. planning and analysis RJR Foods, Inc., Winston-Salem, N.C., 1968-76; area fin. dir. R.J. Reynolds Tobacco Internat., Winston-Salem, 1976-79; comptroller R.J. Reynolds Tobacco. Co., Winston-Salem, 1979-81, v.p., comptroller, 1981-83, v.p. fin., chief fin. officer, 1983-84; sr. v.p., chief fin. officer Del Monte Corp., San Francisco, 1984-85; sr. v.p. fin., controller RJR Nabisco, Inc., Winston-Salem, 1986-87; sr. v.p. fin. R.J. Reynolds Tobacco Co., Winston-Salem, 1987-88, exec. v.p., chief fin. officer, 1988-91, also exec. com., bd. dirs.; pres., chief exec. officer GRG Assocs., Inc., Winston-Salem, 1991—. Mem. local adv. bd. Branch Banking & Trust Co., 1987-99; mem. Consumer Credit Counseling Svc., 1983-84, 87-90; mem. Reynolds Carolina Credit Union Bd., 1973-83. Trustee Winston-Salem Arts Coun., 1987-94; bd. dirs. Winston-Salem Piedmont Triad Symphony, 1986—, Piedmont Opera Theatre, 1989—, Tanglewood Pk. Found., 1991-98; mem. N.C. Gov.'s Bus. Coun. on Arts and Humanities, 1987-91; chmn. fund appeal Bishop McGuinness High Sch., Winston-Salem, 1982-83, mem. bd. edn., 1987-90, chmn. bd., 1988-90; chmn. St. Leo's Parish Coun., Winston-Salem, 1974-77; exec. v.p. Winston-Salem Nat. Little League, 1981-84; chmn. sch. budget task force C. of C., 1976; mem. bd. advisors Catholic Conf. Ctr., 1990-93; exec. com., bd. trustees Forsyth County Park Authority, 1992-99; bd. dirs., vice chmn. Found. Roman Cath. Diocese of Charlottee. Named to Hon. Order Ky. Cols., 1983 Mem. Fin. Execs. Inst. Roman Catholic. Home: 2814 Galsworthy Dr Winston Salem NC 27106-5107 Office: GRG Assocs Inc 110 Oakwood Dr Ste 320 Winston Salem NC 27103

GUO, DONGBAI, application developer; m. Jing Zhang. BS in Mech. Engring., Shanghai JiaoTong U., China, 1994, BS in Computer Sci., 1994; MSc in Engring., Brown U., Providence, RI, 1996, MSc in Computer Sci., 1998, PhD, 2001. Arch. and sr. devel. mgr. OracleUSA Corp., Redwood Shores, Calif., 2000—. Adj. rsch. assoc. Brown U., 2005—. Author: (jour. article) Detection of Cardiac Cycle From Intracoronary Ultrasound, Ultrasound in Medicine and Biology; editor: (hosted application working group) The Digital Imaging and Communications In Medicine. Recipient summa cum laude, Shanghai JiaoTong U., 1994. Mem.: IEEE, Radiology Soc. N.Am. (assoc.), Sigma Xi. Achievements include first to introduce a model driven solution for integrating medical data with a database; development of Oracle interMedia DICOM database; patents pending for methods and apparatus for data conversion; integrating medical images and data in a database management system; research in intravascular ultrasound video segmentation and understanding. Avocations: photography, backpacking, hiking, soccer. Home Phone: 603-440-3339; Office Phone: 603-897-3591.

GUO, MINGRUO, food scientist, educator; s. Wenming Guo and Zhizhen Liu; m. Shengying Qu, Jan. 26, 1986; children: Hongfei, Michael R. PhD, Nat. U. Ireland, 1990. Asst. prof. N.E. Agr. U., Harbin, China, 1990—92; assoc. prof. U. Vt., Burlington, 1997—. Chief scientist Beiya Dairy Co. Inc., Daqing, China, 2003—. Recipient Achievement award, State of China, 1992. Mem.: Am. Soc. Clin. Nutrition, Am. Chem. Soc., Inst. Food Technologists, Am. Dairy Sci. Assn. Achievements include three patents for food technology. Home Phone: 802-863-9505; Office Phone: 802-656-8168. Office Fax: 802-656-0001. E-mail: mguo@zoo.uvm.edu.

GUO, WEI, research scientist; BS in Microbiology, Nankai U., Tianjin, China, 1992; MS in Molecular Bio., Chinese Acad. Scis. Inst. Microbiology, Beijing, China, 1995; PhD in Genetics, U. Tex., Houston, 2002. Rschr. U. Calif., LA, 2003—. Recipient Oncology Scholar-in-Tng. award, AACR-Bristol-Myers Squibb, 2006; Stem Cell fellow, UCLA Inst. For Stem Cell Biology and Medicine, Calif. Inst. For Regenerative Medicine, 2006—, Keystone Symposia scholar, 2001. Mem.: AAAS (assoc.), Am. Assn. for Cancer Rsch. (assoc.). Achievements include research in identification and characterization of a novel human Mix/Bix-like homeobox gene MIXL1 structurally and functionally similar to Xenopus Mix.1; amino terminal tyrosine phosphorylation of human MIXL1; role of the tumor suppressor gene PTEN in hematopoietic stem cells and leukemia. Office: UCLA 650 Charles Young Dr South CHS 23-234 Los Angeles CA 90095 Office Phone: 310-825-5454.

GUO, ZHONGWU, science educator; PhD, Polish Acad. Scis., Warsaw, 1992. Prof. Wayne State U., Detroit, 2005—. Office: Wayne State U 5101 Cass Ave Detroit MI 48202

GUP, BENTON EUGENE, banking educator; married; children: Lincoln, Andrew, Jeremy. BA, U. Cin., 1961, MBA, 1963, PhD, 1966. Economist Fed. Res. Bank of Cleve., 1967-70; prof. fin. U. of Tulsa, 1970-82, prof., chair banking, 1970-82; vis. prof., chair banking U. Va., Charlottesville, 1980-81; prof., chair banking U. Ala., Tuscaloosa, 1983—. Author: Guide to Strategic Planning, 1980, Financial Intermediaries, 2d editl., 1980, Principles of Financial Management, 1983, 2d editl., 1987, Management of Financial Institutions, 1984, The Basics of Investing, 5th edit., 1992; author: (with Charles Meiburg) Cases in Bank Management, 1986; author: Personal Investing: A Complete Handbook, 1987, Commercial Bank Management, 1989, Bank Mergers: Current Issues and Perspectives, 1989, Bank Fraud: Exposing the Hidden Threat to Financial Institutions, 1990; author: (with Donald Fraser and James Kolari) Commercial Banking: The Management of Risk, 1995; author: The Bank Director's Handbook, 1996, Bank Failures in the Major Trading Countries of the World, 1998, International Banking Crises, 1999, The New Financial Architecture, 2000, Megamergers in a Global Economy, 2002, The Future of Banking, 2003, Investing OnLine, 2003, Too Big to Fail: Policies and Practices in Government Bailouts, 2004, The New Basel Capital Accord, 2004, Capital

Markets, Globalization and Economic Development, 2005, Money Laundering, Financing Terrorism, and Suspicious Activity, 2007, Corporate Governance in Banking: A Global Perspective, 2007. With USAF, 1954—58. Mem. Fin. Mgmt. Assn. (chmn. site selection 1975-85), Midwest Fin. Assn. (pres. 1982-83), Am. Fin. Assn., Fin. Execs. Inst., Acad. Fin. Svcs. (v.p., dir. 1988-91). Office: U Ala Dept Fin PO Box 870224 Tuscaloosa AL 35487-0154 Office Phone: 205-348-7842.

GUPCHUP, GIREESH VIJAY, pharmacist, educator; b. Bombay, Dec. 28, 1965; arrived in U.S., 1988; s. Vijay Narhar and Vijaya Gupchup; m. Chatura Chitale-Gupchup, Dec. 27, 1994; children: Samay, Ruhee. BS in Pharmacy, U. Bombay, 1988; MS, U. Toledo, 1990, MS, 1993; PhD, Purdue U., 1996. Lic. pharmacist Maharashtra State Pharmacy Coun., India. Purdue-Merck fellow in pharm. economics, grad. asst. Purdue U., West Lafayette, Ind., 1993—96; chmn. pharmacy adminstrn. grad. program U. N.Mex, Albuquerque, 1996—2000, asst. prof. pharmacy, 1996—2002, assoc. prof. pharmacy, 2002—04; dir. N.Mex Medicaid Retrospective Drug Utilization Rev. Program, Albuquerque, 2000—03; prof., assoc. dean Sch. Pharmacy So. Ill. U., Edwardsville, 2004—. Pharmacoeconomics cons. N.Mex Medicaid Drug Utilization Rev. Program, Albuquerque, 1996—2000. Mem. editl. adv. bd.: Jour. Am. Pharm. Assn., Rsch. in Social and Adminstrv. Pharmacy; contbr. more than 30 article to profl. jours. Recipient Alumni Achiever's award, KMK Coll. of Pharmacy, U. Bombay, 2000; grantee, various state, fed. and industry sources, 1996—2002. Mem.: N.Mex Pharm. Assn. (2d v.p. 2002—03, 1st v.p. 2003—04), Internat. Soc. Pharmacoeconomics and Outcomes Rsch., Am. Pharm. Assn., Kappa Psi, Phi Kappa Phi, Rho Chi. Achievements include development of two instruments to measure health-related quality of life among Native American asthma and diabetes patients. Avocations: golf, swimming. Home: 6 Sharpsburg Ct Edwardsville IL 62025 Home Phone: 618-692-1230. Business E-Mail: ggupchu@siue.edu.

GUPPY, JOHN, professional sports team executive; b. Eng. m. Carla Guppy; 3 children. BSBA, New Hampshire Coll., 1990; M in Sports Mgmt., U. Mass., Amherst, 1992. Player Southampton Football Club, England; with API Soccer (formerly Soccer USA Ptnrs.), 1992—98; grp. dir. Octagon Mktg., Conn.; v.p. mktg. & sales NY/NJ MetroStars (Maj. League Soccer), 2000—02, exec. v.p., 2002—05; pres., CEO Chgo. Fire (Maj. League Soccer), 2005—. Office: Chgo Fire Toyota Pk 7000 S Harlem Ave Bridgeview IL 60455*

GUPTA, ANIL K., philosophy professor; BS, U. London, 1969; MA, U. Pitts., 1973, PhD, 1977. With McGill U., Ill. U. Chgo., Ind. U.; disting. prof. philosophy, prof. history and philosophy of sci., fellow Ctr. for Philosophy Sci. U. Pitts., 2001—. Author: The Logic Common Nouns, 1980, Empiricism and Experience, 2006; co-author (with Nuel Belnap): The Revision Theory of Truth, 1993; contbr. articles to profl. jours. Fellow, Ctr. Advanced Study Behavioral Scis., Stanford, 1998—99, NEH, Am. Coun. Learned Socs. Fellow: Am. Acad. Arts & Sciences. Office: U Pitts Dept Philosophy 1001 Cathedral of Learning Pittsburgh PA 15260 Office Phone: 412-624-5771. E-mail: agupta@pitt.edu.

GUPTA, ANJU, risk management consultant; b. Bangalore, India, Sept. 14, 1971; d. Dharam Singh and Neera Gupta; m. Parag Gupta. PhD, Stanford U., California, USA, 1997. Postdoctoral rsch. scholar Stanford U., Palo Alto, Calif., 1997—98; from sr. engr. to sr. dir. product mgmt. Risk Mgmt. Solutions Inc., Newark, Calif., 1998—2005, sr. dir. product mgmt., 2005—; product mgmt. weather risk Risk Link, 2001—02, 2002—05. Cons. Wharton team on NSF project, Palo Alto, 1996; mem. Curee, LA, 1998; mem. com. earthquake risk financing and transfer Earthquake Engrng. Rsch. Inst., Oakland, Calif., 1999. Contbr. articles to profl. jours. Vol. for adult literacy, Mountain View, Calif., 1998; vol. for childhood literacy New Delhi, 1995—97. Mem.: Earthquake Engrng. Rsch. Inst. Achievements include development of financial risk model for Central America; a standardized national earthquake loss estimation software tool, Hazards US (HAZUS); participation in project dealing with urban search and rescue requirements for responding to catastrophic disasters in the U.S; project to assess annualized losses from earthquakes in the U.S; project to validate and calibrate the HAZUS methodology. Office: Risk Mgmt Solutions Inc 7015 Gateway Blvd Newark CA 94560 Home: 1265 Tainan Pl San Jose CA 95131-2416 Personal E-mail: anjurisk@yahoo.com. E-mail: anju.gupta@rms.com.

GUPTA, ANU, lawyer; d. Puran Chand and Shail Bala Gupta; m. Kaurik Raj, Jan. 2002. BA with honors, Delhi U., 1991, BA, 1993; JD, DePaul U., Chgo., 1996. Bar: Ill. 1997, NY 1997. Assoc. atty. Gurtu & McGoldrick, LLP, NYC, 1997—98; mng. atty. Immigration Desk, Inc., Fremont, Ill., 1998—. Columnist (newspaper) India Post; contbr. articles to mags. and newspapers. Mem.: Am. Immigration Lawyers Assn., Mensa. Achievements include starting an immigration practice that currently has offices in the US, India and Philippines and representations in several other nations. Office: Immigration Desk Inc 40087 Mission Blvd Ste 401 Fremont CA 94539 Office Phone: 800-688-7892. Office Fax: 510-217-6116. Business E-Mail: anu@immigrationdesk.com.

GUPTA, ASHWANI KUMAR, mechanical engineering educator; b. Punjab, India, Oct. 23, 1948; s. Ram Nath and Vidya G. BSc, Panjab U., India, 1966; MSc, Southampton U., Eng., 1970; PhD, Sheffield U., Eng., 1973, DSc, 1986. Chartered engr., fuel technologist, U.K. Rsch. engr. Internat. Combustion Co., Derby, England, 1967-71; rsch. asst. Sheffield U., 1971-73, rsch. fellow, ind. rsch. worker, 1973-76; mem. rsch. staff MIT, Cambridge, 1977-82; prof. dept. mech. engring. U. Md., College Park, 1983—. Mem. sci. adv. bd. State of Md., 1985—. Author: Swirl Flows, 1984, Flowfield Modeling and Diagnostics, 1985, High Temperature Air Combustion: From Energy Conservation to Pollution Reduction, 2003; editor 12 books in Energy and Engineering Science series, 1980—; founding co-editor: Environmental and Energetics series, 1990—; author over 350 tech. papers. Recipient Pres. Kirwan Rsch. award, U. Md., 2003, Rsch. award, U. Md. Coll. Engring., 2006. Fellow AIAA (chmn. propellants and combustion tech. com. 1988-90, chmn. terrestrial energy systems tech. com. 1991-2000, dep. dir. energy 2000—, Energy Sys. award 1990, Propellant and Combustion award 1999), Inst. Energy U.K., ASME (chmn. Fuels and Combustion Tech. divsn. 1998-2000, chmn. computers and info. in engring. divsn. 2002-03, George Westinghouse Gold medal 1998, James Harry Potter Gold medal 2003, Landis medal 2004); mem. Soc. Automotive Engrs., Combustion Inst., Am. Soc. Engring. Edn. Avocations: flying, swimming, squash, photography. Office: U Md Dept Mech Engring College Park MD 20742-0001 Business E-Mail: akgupta@eng.umd.edu.

GUPTA, BARNALI, economics professor; d. Mihir Prakash and Sandhya Gupta; m. Debashis Pal, Dec. 22, 1990; children: Reeti Pal, Rukmini Pal. MA in Econs., U. Delhi, 1986, U. Fla., 1989; PhD in Econs., U. Fla., Gainesville, 1990. Asst. prof. econs. Miami U., Oxford, Ohio, 1993—98, assoc. prof. econs., 1998—2007, prof. econs., 2007—. Contbr. articles to profl. jours. Nat. Merit scholar, U. Delhi Sch. Econs., 1984—86. Mem.: Western Econ. Assn., Am. Econ. Assn., Beta Gamma Sigma. Avocation: travel. Office: Miami Univ High Street Oxford OH 45069 Office Phone: 513-529-2856.

GUPTA, BINA, philosopher, educator; b. Ambala Cantt, Harayana, India, Sept. 30, 1947; d. Dharam Bhushan Bansal and Sarla Agarwal; m. Madan Gupta, Aug. 12, 1970; 1 child, Swati. BA with honors, Shri Shikshayatan Coll., 1966; MA in Philosophy, Ctr. Advanced Study in Philosophy, Visva-Bharati, India, 1968; PhD in Philosophy, So. Ill. U., Carbondale, 1975. Instr. Shri Shikshayatan Coll., India, 1968—70; rsch. assoc. So. Ill. U., Carbondale, 1970—71, tchg. asst., 1971—73; asst. prof. U. Mo., Columbia, 1974—81, assoc. prof., 1981—92, prof. philosophy dept., 1992—2004, Curators' prof. philosophy dept., 2004—, dir. South Asia Lang. and Area Program, 1978—. Presenter in field. Translator: Vedanta Paribhasa; Pancapadikavivarana; contbr. chapters to books, articles to profl. jours. Fellow, NEH, 2006—07. Mem.: Soc. Asian and Comparative Philosophy (pres. 1998—2001), Am. Inst. Indian Studies (assoc.). Home: 2502 Lenox Pl Columbia MO 65203 Office: U Mo Philosophy Dept 418 GCB Columbia MO 65211 Home Phone: 573-445-2178; Office Phone: 573-882-3065. Home Fax: 573-445-2178. Business E-Mail: guptab@missouri.edu.

GUPTA, CHAKSHU, pathologist; BS, U. Delhi, NJ, 1998. Cert. Anatomic and Clinical Pathology Am. Bd. Pathology, Blood Banking and Transfusion Medicine Am. Bd. Pathology. Staff pathologist Heartland Regional Med. Ctr., St. Joseph, Mo., 2005—. Co-med. dir. Pathology & Lab. Recipient Coll. of Am. Pathologists Informatics Award, Coll. of Am. Pathologists Found., Rsch. Awards, SJH, CAP, OHEP Mich., 2000-2004, Listed in Americas Registry of Outstanding Professionals, Americas Registry of Outstanding Professionals, 2005-06, Listed in United Whos Who, United Whos Who. Fellow: Coll. Am. Pathologists; mem.: Mo. Soc. Pathology (v.p. 2006—), Kans. City Soc. Pathologists. Office: Heartland Regional Med Ctr 5325 Faraon St Saint Joseph MO 64506

GUPTA, ERIC K., pharmacist, educator; s. Dalip C. and Carolyn A. Gupta. PharmD, U. of Pacific, Stockton, Calif., 2000. Registered pharmacist Calif., 2000, cert. pharmacotherapy specialist Bd. Pharm. Specialties, 2006. Asst. prof. Western U. Health Scis., Pomona, Calif., 2004—; lipid clinic dir. Orange County Heart Inst. and Rsch. Ctr., Calif., 2004—. Advisor Western U. Am. Pharmacists Assn. Acad. Student Pharmacists, Pomona, 2005—06. Mem.: Kappa Psi (first-vice regent, chaplain, Asklepios Key 1995). Republican. Office: Western U Health Scis 309 E Second St Pomona CA 91776 Office Phone: 909-469-5412.

GUPTA, KRISHNA CHANDRA, mechanical engineering educator; b. 1948; m. Karuna Gupta; 1 child, Anupama. B of Tech. with distinction, Indian Inst. Tech., 1969; MS in Mech. Engring., Case Inst. Tech., 1971; PhD in Mech. Engring., Stanford U., 1974. Grad. asst. Case Inst. Tech., Cleve., 1969-71; rsch. asst. Stanford (Calif.) U., 1971-74; from asst. prof. to prof. emeritus mech. engring. U. Ill., Chgo., 1974—2005, prof. emeritus, 2005—, assoc. dean, 2002—05. Mem. editl. adv. bd. Jour. Applied Mechanisms and Robotics 1993-2000; assoc. editor Mechanism and Machine Theory 1998-2004; contbr. articles to profl. jours. Recipient award of merit Procter & Gamble Co., 1978, South Pointing Chariot award, 1989, AM&R G.N. Sandor award, 1997; grantee in field. Fellow ASME (assoc. editor Jour. Mech. Design 1981-82, mem. editl. adv. bd. Applied Mechanics Rev. 1985-93, chmn. mechanisms com. 1989-90, gen chmn. 1990 design tech. conf., chmn. 1990 mechanisms conf., mem. design divsn. exec. com. 2001-2007, chair design divsn., 2005-06, immediate past chmn., 2006-2007, adv. com. design divsn., 2007—, editor newsletter divsn. design engring., best paper computers in engring. conf. 1991, Henry Hess award 1979, Design Divsn. Mechanisms and Robotics award 2002). Avocations: investments, speed reading. Office: Univ Ill Dept Mech and Indsl Engring MC 251 842 W Taylor St Chicago IL 60607 E-mail: kcgupta@uic.edu.

GUPTA, KULDIP CHAND (KC), retired electrical and computer engineering educator, researcher; b. Risalpur, India, Oct. 6, 1940; arrived in US, 1982; s. Chiranjiva Lal and Gauran (Agarwal) G.; m. Usha Agarwal, Apr. 4, 1971; children: Parul, Sandeep, Anjula. BSc, Punjab U., Chandigarh, India, 1958; BE, Indian Inst. Sci., Bangalore, India, 1961, ME, 1962; PhD, Birla Inst. Tech. Sci., Pilani, India, 1969. Asst. prof. Punjab Engring. Coll., Chandigarh, 1964-65, Birla Inst. Tech. and Sci., Pilani, 1968-69; asst. prof., then prof. Indian Inst. Tech., Kanpur, India, 1969-84; prof. U. Colo., Boulder, 1983—2004. Vis. assoc. prof. U. Waterloo, Ont., 1975-76; vis. prof. Swiss Fed. Tech. Inst., Lausanne, 1976, Zurich, 1979, Tech. I. Denmark, Lynby, 1976-77, U. Kans., Lawrence, 1982-83, Indian Inst. Sci., 1993-94; advisor, cons. UN Devel. Programme, People's Republic of China, 1987, India, 1990, 94-95; cons. UNIDO project, India, 1993, Indian Telephone Industries, 1993-94. Author: CAD of Microwave Circuits, 1981, Chinese transl., 1986, Russian transl., 1987, Microstrip Lines and Slotlines, 1979, 2d edit., 1996, Microwaves, 1979, Spanish transl., 1983; editor, author: Microwave Integrated Circuits, 1974, Microstrip Antenna Design, 1988, Analysis and Design of Planar Microwave Components, 1994; founding editor Internat. Jour. Microwave Millimeter-Wave Computer Aided Engring., 1991—; contbr. articles to profl. jours. and chpts. to books; patentee in field. Bd. dirs. Hindu U. of Am. Fellow IEEE (guest editor spl. issue IEEE Transactions on Microwave Theory and Tech. 1988), Instn. Electronics and Telecommunication Engrs. India (guest editor jour. July 1982) Hindu. *Success in profession should be judged not by how much money one makes, nor by the status one attains; but by the satisfaction we get by being useful to the society.*

GUPTA, MADHU SUDAN, electrical engineering educator; b. Lucknow, India, June 13, 1945; came to U.S., 1966; s. Manohar Lal and Premvati Gupta; m. Vijaya Lakshmi Tayal, July 9, 1970; children: Jay Mohan, Vineet Mohan; m. Manorama Vyas, May 29, 1985. BS, Lucknow U., India, 1963; MS, Allahabad U., India, 1966, Fla. State U., 1967; MA, U. Mich., 1968, PhD, 1972. Registered profl. engr., Ont. Asst. prof. elec. engring. Queen's U., Kingston, Ont., Canada, 1972-73, MIT, Cambridge, 1973-78, assoc. prof. elec. engring., 1978-79, U. Ill., Chgo., 1979-84, prof. elec. engring., 1984-87, dir. grad. studies, 1980-83; vis. prof. elec. and computer engring. U. Calif., Santa Barbara, 1985-86; sr. staff engr. Hughes Aircraft Co., 1987-95; prof. elec. engring., chmn. dept. elec. engring. Fla. State U., Tallahassee, 1995-2000; prof. elec. engring., RF comm. sys. industry chair San Diego State U., 2000—; dir. Comm. Sys. and Signal Processing Inst., 2000—; adj. prof. elec. engring. U. Calif., San Diego, 2002—. Cons. Lincoln Lab. MIT, Lexington, 1976-79, Hughes Research Labs., Malibu, Calif., 1986-87. Editor: Electrical Noise, 1977, Teaching Engineering, 1987, Noise in Circuits and Systems, 1988; editor-in-chief IEEE Microwave and Guided Wave Letters, 1998-2000, IEEE Microwave Mag., 2003-05; contbr. articles to profl. jours. Lilly fellow, 1974-75. Fellow IEEE; mem. IEEE Microwave Soc. (vice chmn. 1984-85, chmn. 1986-87). Achievements include patents in field. Office: San Diego State U Dept Elec Engring 5500 Campanile Dr San Diego CA 92182-1309 Business E-Mail: mgupta@mail.sdsu.edu. *A person's level of maturity is measured by what he wants from other members of the society: something for nothing, equal return for everything, or nothing except the opportunity to put something back in the kitty.*

GUPTA, MAHENDRA R., dean; m. Sunita Gupta; children: Vivek, Sumi. BS in Statistics and Economics, Bombay U., 1978; MS in Indsl. Adminstrn., Carnegie Mellon U., Pitts., 1981; PhD, Stanford U., 1990. Joined Wash. U. Olin Sch. Bus., St. Louis, 1990, Geraldine J. and Robert L. Virgil prof. acctg. and mgmt., 2004—, sr. assoc. dean, dean, 2005—. Avocations: reading, cooking, movies. Office: Wash U Olin Sch Bus Campus Box 1133 One Brookings Dr Saint Louis MO 63130 Office Phone: 314-935-6344. E-mail: guptam@olin.wustl.edu.

GUPTA, MONESHA, pediatrician, educator; arrived in U.S., 1993; d. Surendranath Kedarnath and Vijayalaxmi Gupta; m. Sanjay Malhotra, June 29, 2001. MBBS, Grant Med. Coll., Bombay, 1989. Diplomate in pediatrics and in pediatric cardiology Am. Bd. Pediatrics. Clin. instr. Mich. State U., Flint, 1993—96; pediatric cardiologist NY Presbyn. Hosp., NYC, 1996—99, U. Tex., Houston, 2002—. Cons. pediatric cardiologist U. Minn., Mpls., 2000—02, U. Tex., 2002—; adj. faculty Rockefeller U., NYC, 2001—02. Contbr. articles to profl. jours. Treas. Sci. of Spirituality, Naperville, Ill., 1989. Med. officer Signals Rgt. Indian Army, 1989—90. Fellow: Am. Coll. Cardiology, Am. Acad. Pediat. Avocations: painting, travel, volleyball. Office: Univ Texas Med Sch Houston Divsn Pediat Cardiology 6431 Fannin MSB 3 130B Houston TX 77030 Office Phone: 713-500-5743. Business E-Mail: monesha.gupta@uth.tmc.edu.

GUPTA, MONIKA, nephrologist, researcher; d. Krishna Devi and Vijay Kumar Gupta. MB, BChir, Maulana Azad Med. Coll., New Delhi, 1996. Diplomate Am. Bd. Internal Medicine, Am. Bd. Nephrology. Resident in internal medicine SUNY, Stony Brook, 1998—2001, fellow in nephrology, 2001—03; instr. medicine Med. U. SC, Charleston, 2003—05, asst. prof. medicine, 2005—. Med. dir. Dialysis Clinic Inc., Mount Pleasant, SC, 2003—06, Charleston, SC, 2006—; dir. continuous renal replacement therapies Med. U. SC, Charleston, 2004—. Contbr. articles to profl. jours. Recipient Distinction in Physiology award, Delhi U., 1992, Cert. of Achievement, Kidney and Urology Found. Am., 2003; grantee, Am. Soc. of Nephrology, 1999, Kidney and Urology Found. Am., 2002—03, Dialysis Clinic, Inc, 2006—. Mem.: ACP, SC Med. Assn., Nat. Kidney Found., Internat. Soc. Nephrology, Women in Nephrology, Am. Soc. Nephrology. Office: Med Univ SC CSB 826 96 Jonathan Lucas St Charleston SC 29425 Office Phone: 843-792-4123. Business E-Mail: guptam@musc.edu.

GUPTA, PAUL R., lawyer; b. Cambridge, Eng., Mar. 7, 1950; s. Suraj Gupta and Letty J.R. Paine; m. Mary Lee Gupta, Sept. 30, 1978; children: Adam, Margaret. BA, Yale U., 1971; JD, Harvard U., 1974. Bar: Mass., N.Y. Assoc. Simpson Thacher & Bartlett, NYC, 1974-79, Cravath, Swaine & Moore, NYC, 1980-83; ptnr. Sherin and Lodgen, Boston, 1983-91, Nutter, McClennen & Fish, Boston, 1991-94, Sullivan & Worcester, LLP, Boston, 1995—2002, LeBoeuf, Lamb, Greene & MacRae L.L.P., 2002—04, Mayer, Brown, Rowe & Maw, LLP, NYC, 2004—06, Orrick, Herrington & Sutcliffe, LLP, NYC, 2006—. Frequent lectr. Correspondent European Intellectual Property Review; mem. editl. adv. bd. Elec. Banking Law and Commerce Report, BNA's Computer Tech. Law Report, Electronic Commerce and Law Report, E-Commerce Law and Strategy; contbr. aticles to profl. jours. Mem. ABA (co-chair antitrust subcom., intellectual property litigation com.), Assn. Bar City of NY (computer law com. 1994-96), Phi Beta Kappa. Office: Orrick, Herrington & Sutcliffe LLP 666 Fifth Ave New York NY 10103 Office Phone: 212-506-5145. Business E-Mail: pgupta@orrick.com.

GUPTA, RAJAT KUMAR, retired management consultant, electronics executive; b. Maniktala, Calcutta, India, Dec. 2, 1948; naturalized, 1984; s. Ashwini Kumar and Pran Kumari Gupta; m. Anita Mattoo Gupta; children: Geetanjali, Megha, Aditi, Deepali. B in Mech. Engring., Indian Tech, 1971; MBA, Harvard U., 1973. With NY Office McKinsey & Co., NYC, 1973—81, with Scandinavia Office Copenhagen, 1981—86, with Chgo. Office, 1986—89, prin., 1980—2003, dir., 1984—2003, mng. dir. Chgo. Office, 1989—94, CEO, mng. dir. NYC, 1994—2003, sr. ptnr., 2003—; prof. mgmt. practice Indian School of Business, Hyderabad, India, 2003. Bd. dir. Goldman Sachs Group Inc., 2006—. Adv. bd. Harvard Bus. Sch., Kellogg Bus. Sch.; trustee Rockefeller Found., 2006—; co-chmn. Am. India Found.; bd. mem. Global Fund to Fight AIDS, Tuberculosis & Malaria; mem. Dean's council Harvard Sch. Public Health. Achievements include fluency in English, Hindi & Bengali. Avocations: bridge, classical music. Office: Rockefeller Found 420 Fifth Ave New York NY 10018*

GUPTA, RAJAT KUMAR, lawyer, accountant; b. New Delhi, Apr. 22, 1960; arrived in U.S., 1970; s. Ravindra Kumar and Rama G. BBA, Rutgers U., 1978-82, JD, 1985-88. Bar: NJ and Pa. 1989, US Tax Ct. 1992; lic. CPA; lic. title ins. prodr. NJ Dept. Banking and Ins. Staff acct. Borrelli & Assocs., Highland Park, NJ, 1983-84, S. Kirschenbaum & Co., CPA, East Brunswick, NJ, 1984-85; tax assoc. Coopers & Lybrand, Princeton, NJ, 1988-89; pvt. practice atty. New Brunswick, 1989-98; sr. assoc. Spevack & Cannan, PA, Iselin, NJ, 1998—2000; fin. specialist NJ Supreme Ct. - Office Atty. Ethics, Trenton, 2000—03; pres. OM Title Agy., LLC, Kendall Park, NJ, 2003—. Mentor Rutgers Law Sch., Seton Hall Law Sch., Asian and Pacific Law Students Assn. Prodn. editor Rutgers Computer & Technology Law Jour., 1987-88, Cannonball-One Lap of America, 1988; contbr. articles to profl. jours. Arbitrator Better Bus. Bur., Newark, 1986—87; vol. atty. Rutgers U. Off Campus Housing Ctr., 1996—2000; mem. com. on character N.J. Supreme Ct., 1997—2000. Mem.: AICPA, South Asian Bar Assn., Am. Land Title Assn., NJ State Bar Assn., Asian and Pacific Lawyers Assn. Hindu. Avocations: tennis, travel, photography, art. Office: 18 Michael Ave Kendall Park NJ 08824 Office Phone: 732-297-8865. Personal E-mail: rkgnj@yahoo.com.

GUPTA, RAJENDRA PRASAD, physician; b. Marhura, India, May 19, 1948; naturalized, 1981; s. Ramji Das and Somvati Devi Gupta; m. Vinod K. Gupta, Dec. 14, 1974; children: Vanita, Vikram, Vishal. BSc, Agra U., Mathura, 1964; B Medicine B Surgery, Rajisthan U., Udiapur, India, 1969, MD, 1973; MBA, U. South Fla., 1999. Diplomate Am. Bd. Internal Medicine, Am. Bd. Gastroenterology, Am. Bd. Utilization and Quality Review Physicians. Rotating intern R.N.T. Med. Coll., Udaipur, Ind., 1969-70, resident in internal medicine, 1970-71, casualty med. officer in internal medicine, 1972; med. officer Seema Nursing Home, Udaipur, 1972, cons. physician, 1972-73; resident tng. in internal medicine Nat. Health Svc. Hosps., 1973-75; resident in internal medicine category "C" St. Francis Med. Ctr., Trenton, NJ, 1975-77; fellow in gastroenterology U. Medicine and Dentistry of N.J., Newark, 1977-79; pvt. practice in gastroenterology and internal medicine Trenton, 1979—; practice medicine Hopewell Valley Med. Group PA, Trenton, NJ. Tchr. Ravindra Nath Tagore Med. Coll.; clin. instr. U. Medicine and Dentistry of NJ, 1977-79, Robert Wood Johnson Med. Sch., Piscataway, NJ, 1992-95; clin. sr. instr. Hahneman Med. Coll., Phila., 1981-92; asst. prof. Robert Wood Johnson Med. Sch., Piscataway, 1995—; affiliated Capital Health Sys., Trenton, Robert Wood Johnson at Hamilton Hosp., NJ; chmn. audit com. Mercer Med. Ctr., Trenton, 1982-83, chmn. utilization rev., 1983-88, mem. constitution and bylaws, 1984-88, med. records com., 1983-85, exec. com., 1985-88, chmn. risk mgmt. com., 1987—, chief gastroenterology sect., 1993-95, chmn. com. sect. chiefs, 1995-97, chmn. physician/hosp. orgn. com., 1993-94, steering com., 1994-95, computer com., 1993, co-chmn. joint conf. com., 1995—, strategic planning com., 1995-96, chmn. dept. medicine, 1995-97, search com., med. dir., 1995, pres. med. staff, 1995-96, fin. com., 1995-97; assoc. med. dir. Ctrl. NJ Mercer, Middlesex Preferred Orgn., Prucare, 1985-86; pres. Healthpath Mercer County, Aetna Health Plan Ind. Practice Assocs., Mt. Laurel, NJ, 1992-94; chmn. med. adv. bd. Morris Hall Home for Aged, Lawrenceville, NJ, 1987-90; treas. Physician's Healthcare Plan NJ, Lawrenceville, 1993-95, sec., 1995-96, v.p., 1996-97, fin. com., 1993-97; cons. gastroenterology Bd. Med. Examiners, Trenton, 1990—. Active Am. Cancer Soc. Mercer County chpt., 1990-92; bd. trustees Chapin Sch., Princeton, NJ, 1993-94; mem. Healthcare Adv. Group for Christie Whitman, 1993; chmn. Capital Health Sys. Found., Trenton, NJ, 2003—. Fellow ACP, Internat. Coll. Physicians, Am. Coll. Gastroenterology, Coll. Utilization Rev. Physicians; mem. AMA (category I award cert. 1979—, Physician Outreach award Presentation 1997, 99), Am. Soc. Gastrointestinal Endoscopy, Acad. Medicine NJ, Med. Soc. NJ (trustee 1996—, legis. com. 1992-94, 2d v.p. 2005-06, internat. med. grad. com. 1992-93, pres. coun. 1992-93, vice-chmn. internat medicine grad. com. 1993-94, chmn. reference com. B ho. of dels. 1993, chmn. house of dels. 1994, vice-chmn. coun. on legis. 1994-95, del. organized med. staff sect. 1995—, exec. com. coun. on legis. 1996—, cons. coun. legis. 1996—), NJ Gastrointestinal Soc., Mercer County Med. Soc. (v.p. 1990-91, chmn. numerous coms., pres. 1992-93), Capital Health Found. Republican. Hindu. Avocations: tennis, swimming, skiing. Office: Hopewell Valley Med Group PA 1871 Pennington Rd Trenton NJ 08618-1208 Home Phone: 609-683-5134; Office Phone: 609-882-5317. Personal E-mail: rguptamd@hotmail.com.

GUPTA, RAJESH, engineer, consultant; b. New Delhi, June 10, 1962; s. K.L. and Urmilla Varshney; m. Jaishree Gupta, Mar. 7, 1993; children: Sameer, Salil. BSc in Elec. Engring., Aligarh U., India, 1980—85. Asst engr. Hindustan Aeronautics Ltd., Lucknow, India; sr. systems analyst Emirates Airlines Group, Dubai, United Arab Emirates, 1989—94; cons. Compaq Can. Inc., Toronto, Ont., Canada, 1995—99; prin. cons., pres. E3i Technologies Inc., Mississauga, Ont., Canada, 2000—. Mem.: Metro. Profl. and Exec. Registry (hon.). Home: 3724 Crabtree Crescent Mississauga ON Canada L4T 1S6 Home Phone: 905-677-3243; Office Phone: 905-781-8522. Personal E-mail: rajeshguptaji@msn.com.

GUPTA, RAJIV LOCHAN, chemicals executive; b. Muzzafarnagar, India, Dec. 23, 1945; s. Phool Prakash and Rukmini (Sahai) G.; m. Kamla Varshney, Jan. 24, 1968; children: Amita, Vanita. B of Tech. in Engring. with honors, Indian Inst. Tech., Bombay, 1967; MS in Ops. Rsch., Cornell U., 1969; MBA in Fin., Drexel U., 1971. Mgmt. sci. analyst Scott Paper Co., Phila., 1969-71; treasury mgr. Rohm & Haas Co., Phila., 1971-74, asst. to chief exec. officer, 1974-76, fin. planning mgr., 1976-79, fin. dir. East Croydon, Eng., 1979-81, planning dir. London, 1981-83, dir. gen. adj. Paris, 1983-84; dir. gen. Duolite Internat. SA, Paris, 1984-87; bus. dir. plastics Rohm & Haas Co., London, 1987-89, global bus. dir., 1989-93, v.p. Pacific Region Phila., 1993-96, chmn. comm. electronic materials bus. group, 1996-98, vice-chmn., 1999, chmn., CEO, 1999—. Bd. dirs. Tyco, Vanguard Group; trustee Chem. Heritage Found., Drexel U. Hindu. Avocations: bridge, tennis, golf, travel, reading. Office: Rohm and Haas Co Independence Mall W Philadelphia PA 19105 Office Phone: 215-592-2462.*

GUPTA, RISHAB KUMAR, medical association administrator, educator, researcher; b. Nagina, Utter Pradesh, India, Apr. 18, 1943; came to U.S., 1965; s. Sahu Harbans Lal and Chandravati (Devi) G.; m. Mridula Gupta, May 2, 1972; children: Arvind, Anita. MSc, G.B. Plant U., Pantnagar, India, 1965; MS, PhD, Rutgers U., 1968. Asst. rsch. oncologist UCLA Sch. Medicine, 1972-75, assoc. rsch. oncologist., 1975-79, asst. prof., 1979-81, assoc. prof., 1981-85, prof., 1985-92; v.p., dir immunodiagnosis John Wayne Cancer Inst., Santa Monica, Calif., 1992—. Mem. study sect. NIH, Bethesda, Md., 1989-92; spl. grant reviewer Med. Rsch. Coun. Can., 1991. Editorial bd. Contemporary Oncology, 1991—; Contbr. articles to med. jours. Pres.'s fellow Am. Soc. for Microbiology, 1967; Rsch. grantee Calif. Inst. for Cancer Rsch., UCLA, 1973-75, U. Calif. Cancer Rsch. Com., 1973, 74, 81, Nat. Cancer Inst/NIH, 1981-90. Mem. Am. Assn. for Cancer Rsch., Am. Assn. Immunologists, Am. Soc. for Clin. Oncology, Am. Acad. Microbiology, Am. Soc. Microbiology. Achievements include definition, isolation, and characterization of tumor associated antigens that are immunogenic in cancer host from cultured and biopsy tumor cells; development of monoclonal antibodies to these antigens and untilization of these in immunoassays to detect the antigens in body fluids of cancer patients and determine their clinical significance in terms of immunodiagnosis and immunoprognosis. Home: 7118 Costello Ave Van Nuys CA 91405-3307 Office: John Wayne Cancer Inst 2200 Santa Monica Blvd Santa Monica CA 90404-2302

GUPTA, SANJAY, neurosurgeon, educator, medical correspondent, journalist; Grad., U. Mich.; MD, U. Mich. Med. Ctr. Diplomate Am. Bd. Neurosurgery, cert. Med. Investigator. Neurosurgical tng. U. Mich.; fellow Semmes-Murphy Clinic, Memphis, neurosurgeon; private practice Great Lakes Brain and Spine Inst., Mich., 2000; with Cable News Network, LP, LLLP (CNN), Atlanta, 2001—, chief med. corr., health and med. unit; asst. prof., dept. neurological surgery Emory U. Sch.Medicine, Atlanta; assoc. chief, neurosurgery svc. Grady Meml. Hosp., Atlanta; surgeon Emory U. Hosp., Atlanta, Grady Meml. Hosp., Atlanta. Host (weekend show) House Call with Dr. Sanjay Gupta, CNN, (podcast) Paging Dr. Gupta, CNN.com, New You Resolution, CNN, Fit Nation, CNN, co-host Account Health, Turner Private Networks; contbr.; write a column Time Mag., contbr. with Carol Kinstle and Caleb Hellerman The First Patient: Health and the Presidency (Second Place-News Mag. Program, Nat. Headliner Awards, 2005), med. news corr. Dr. Sanjay Gupta Primetime Special: Killer Flu: A Breath Away, CNN (First Place-Health Reporting, Nat. Headliner awards, 2006), Dr. Sanjay Gupta Primetime Special: Memory, CNN (Second Place-Health Reporting, Nat. Headliner Awards, 2006), Dr. Sanjay Gupta Primetime Special: Anatomy of a Murder, CNN (Third Place-Health Reporting, Nat. Headliner Awards, 2006), Sabrina's Law, CNN (Clarion award, 2006); contbr. articles to Jour. Neurosurgery and Neurosurgical Focus, articles to other profl. jours.; author: Chasing Life, 2007; host (documentaries) Chasing Life, 2007. Mem. Do Something Found., Healing Children Found., Brain Found. Finalist Internat. Health and Med. Media award known as Freddie; named Pop Culture Icon, USA Today, 2003, Journalist of the Yr., Atlanta Press Club, 2004; named one of Sexiest Man Alive, People Mag., 2003; recipient Humanitarian award, Nat. Press Photographers Assn., GOLD award, Nat. Health Care Comm.; White House Fellow (spl. advisor to the First Lady), 1997—98. Mem.: Coun. Fgn. Relations, Congress of Neurological Surgeons, Am. Assn. Neurological Surgeons. Part of the network team covering Sept. 11 attacks and anthrax; Iraq and Kuwait battlefield medicine news (2003) and breaking news about missle attack on mall in Kuwait; reported on the pandemic at the International AIDS conference in Bangkok, Thailand (2004); covered the disaster and aftermath of Sri Lanka Tsunami (2004); (recipient of Emmy award for coverage of Hurricane Katrina, for a segment called "Charity Hospital", about the plight of dozens of doctors, nurses, staff and patients stranded for day at this New Orleans facility (2005). Office: Emory U Sch Medicine Neurological Surgery Faculty Office Bldg #339 80 Jesse Hill Dr SE Atlanta GA 30303 also: Cable News Network PO Box 105366 One CNN Ctr Atlanta GA 30348 Office Phone: 404-778-1398.*

GUPTA, SANJU, education educator, researcher; d. Jagdish Narain and Susheela Gupta. PhD, NC State U., Raleigh, 2002. Vis. scientist U. Akron, Ohio, 2003; pos-doctorate fellow Cambridge U., Cambrisgeshire, 2002—03; post doctorate scientist NC State U., Raleigh, 2003—04; asst. prof. Mo. State U., Springfield, 2004—. Cons. US Photonics, Springfield, Mo., 2006. Panelist NSF, Washington, 2006. Recipient Grad. award, US-NSF; Summer Faculty fellow, Mo. State U. Mem.: Am. Chem. Soc., Coun. for Undergraduates, Optical Soc. of Am., Am. Physics Soc., Materials Rsch. Soc. (assoc.). Achievements include patents for Sulfur-doped Nanocrystalline Carbon Films for Cold Cathode Applications; Thermionic Electron Emitters based on Sulfur Doped Nanocrystalline Diamond; patents pending for Template-free syntheses of nanostructured conducting polymers using electrochemistry for drug delivery; research in -Induced Surface Modifications In Multifunctional Nanostructured Carbons For Space Applications; Microwave Plasma-Assisted Chemical Vapor Deposition Reactor: Instrumentation and Implementation For Carbon-Based Materials; nanodiamond-based biosensing. Home Phone: 573-673-4121, 573-882-0948. Business E-Mail: guptas@missouri.edu.

GUPTA, SHEFALI, internist, nephrologist; m. Aditya Gupta, June 21, 2000. MBBS, Indira Gandhi Med. Coll., Shimla, India, 1999. Diplomate Am. Bd. Internal Medicine, 2005. Ho. staff resident U. Tex. Health Sci. Ctr., Houston, 2002—05, ho. staff fellow, 2005—. Recipient 1st pl. Tex. Chpt./SE Region, ACP, 2005. Mem.: Am. Soc. Nephrology (assoc.), Nat. Kidney Found. (assoc.), Renal Physician Assn. (assoc.). Achievements include research in oncologic nephrology. Office: U Tex Health Sci Ctr 6431 Fannin MSB 4148 Houston TX 77030 Home Phone: 713-790-0603; Office Phone: 713-500-6868. E-mail: shefali.gupta@uth.tmc.edu.

GUPTA, SURAJ NARAYAN, physicist, researcher; b. Haryana, India, Dec. 1, 1924; came to U.S., 1953, naturalized, 1963; s. Lakshmi N. and Devi (Goyal) G.; m. (Letty) J. R. Paine, July 14, 1948; children: Paul, Ranee. MS, St. Stephen's Coll., India, 1946; PhD, U. Cambridge, Eng., 1951. Imperial Chem. Industries fellow U. Manchester, Eng., 1951-53; vis. prof. physics Purdue U., 1953-56; prof. physics Wayne State U., Detroit, 1956-61, disting. prof. physics, 1961-99, disting. prof. emeritus physics, 1999—. Author: Quantum Electrodynamics, 1977. Fellow Am. Phys. Soc., Nat. Acad. Scis. of India. Achievements include research in high energy physics, nuclear physics, relativity and gravitation, quantum theory with negative probability and quantization of the electromagnetic field; flat-space interpretation of Einstein's theory of gravitation and quantization of the gravitational field; regularization and renormalization of elementary particle interactions; phenomena at supercollider energies; development of the theory of bound states in quantum electrodynamics and quantum chromodynamics; mass matrix formulation of quark mixing and CP violation in weak interactions. Office: Wayne State U Dept Physics Detroit MI 48202 Home: 5515 Westwood Ln Bloomfield Hills MI 48301 Business E-Mail: doctorgupta@ameritech.net.

GUPTA, SURENDRA KUMAR, chemicals executive; b. Delhi, India, Apr. 5, 1938; arrived in US, 1963, naturalized, 1971; s. Bishan Chand and Devki Gupta; m. Karen Patricia Clarke, Oct. 12, 1968; children: Jay, Amanda. BSc with honors, Delhi U., 1959, MSc, 1961; MTech, Indian Inst. Tech., Bombay, 1963; PhD, Wayne State U., 1968. Rsch. assoc. Western Mich. U., Kalamazoo, 1968—73; indsl. fellow Starks Assocs., Buffalo, 1973—74; group leader New Eng. Nuc. Co., Boston, 1974—80, Pathfinder Labs., St. Louis, 1981—83; chmn. bd., chemist Am. Radiolabeled Chem., Inc., St. Louis, 1983—; owner Precision Biochem., Inc., Vancouver, BC, Canada, 2003—. Contbr. articles to profl. jours. Mem.: Am. Chem. Soc. (chmn. pub. rels. com. 1970—73). Hindu. Avocations: ping pong/table tennis, stamp collecting/philately, travel. Home: 22 Muirfield Ln Saint Louis MO 63141-7380 Office: Am Radiolabeled Chems Inc 101 ARC Dr Saint Louis MO 63146-3506 Office Phone: 314-991-4545. Business E-Mail: drgupta@arc-inc.com.

GUPTA, V. P., economist, academic administrator; b. Oct. 7, 1950; BSc, U. Rajasthan, Jaipur, India, 1972, MA in Econ., 1974, PhD in Econ., 1983. Assoc. prof. econ. U. Rajasthan, Jaipur, 1989—, head dept. econ., 2001—04, dir. planning commn. chair, 2005—. Mem. tax adv. com. Income Tax Dept., Jaipur, India, 2003—05. Author: Rural Development and Electrification, 1995, Electricity Pricing in India, 1996, Energy Patterns in India, 2002, Federal Finance in India, 2003, Infrastructure and Economic Reforms, 2005, State Finances in India, 2006; contbr. articles to profl. jours.; chief editor: Jour. Develop. and Policy. Recipient Bharat Jyoti award, India Internat. Friendship Soc., New Delhi, 2006. Home: C-357 Pradhan Marg, Malviya Nagar Jaipur, Rajasthan 302017 India Office: Univ Rajasthan Dept Econ Gandhinager Jaipur RA 302004 India Office Phone: 91-141-2700681.

GUPTA, VENU GOPAL, psychology professor; came to U.S., 1966; s. Ram Dass and Ram Piari Aggarwal; m. Sunita Gupta, Nov. 29, 1961; children: Sunil, Sanjiv. BA with 1st class honors, Punjab U., 1953, MA 1st class 1st, 1955, MEd 1st class 1st, 1959; BEd, Delhi U., 1958; PhD, Ga. State U., 1974. Cert. counselor, Pa. Lectr. Colls. Punjab and Kurukshetra U., India, 1955-63; teaching and rsch. fellow U. Alta., Edmonton, Can., 1963-66; asst. prof. psychology U. Wis., Stevens Point, 1966-68; asst. prof. psychology and counseling Ea. Ky. U., 1968-72; teaching and rsch. fellow Ga. State U., 1972-74; prof. psychology Kutztown U. Pa., 1974—. Subject of interviews on radio and TV. Recipient Cert. of merit Dictionary Internat. Biography, 1970. Mem. AAAS, AACD, AAUP, Internat. Coun. Psychologists, Internat. Assn. Applied Psychology, Internat. Assn. for Cross-cultural Psychology, Internat. Coun. on Edn. for Teaching, Am. Psychol. Assn., Am. Ednl. Rsch. Assn., Am. Assn. for Counselor Edn. and Supervision, Am. Mental Health Counselors Assn., Phi Delta Kappa. Avocations: world travel, languages, literature. Home: 744 Highland Ave Kutztown PA 19530-1306 Office: Kutztown U of Pa Dept Psychology Kutztown PA 19530

GUPTA, VIJAY, mathematics professor; b. Dehradun, India, Oct. 9, 1962; s. U. Gupta; m. Shalini Agarwal; children: Arushi, Anshay. MPhil in Math., UOR, Roorkee,India, 1987, PhD, 1990. Asst. prof NSIT, New Delhi, 2000. Office: NSIT Sector 3 Dwarka New Delhi 110075 India

GUPTA, VIJAY KUMAR, retired chemistry professor; b. Ambala Cantt, Haryana, India, Apr. 27, 1941; m. Surjit Mohini Aggarwal, Sept. 5, 1968; children: Sonia, Angela, Ashish. BS in Chemistry with honors, Panjab U., Chandigarh, India, 1961, MS in Chemistry with honors, 1962, PhD in Chemistry, 1969. Asst. prof. chemistry Punjab Engring. Coll., Chandigarh, India, 1962-64, 67-68; postdoctoral rsch. assoc. Wright State U., Dayton, Ohio, 1968-69; rsch. chemist Lawrence Livermore Nat. Lab., Livermore, Calif., summer 1980; adj. faculty mem. Lebanon Correctional Inst., Ohio, fall 1977, 78, summer 1982; fellow Wright Patterson AFB, Dayton, summer 1981, with aero-propulsion lab., 1981-83, with materials lab., 1984, fellow materials lab., 1985, summers 1987, 88, 91, vis. scientist materials lab., 1985-87; adj. faculty mem. Wright State U., 1985; adj. faculty in chemistry Wilberforce U., Ohio, spring/summer 1981, 82, 83, 84, 1983-84, fall 1986-87; prof., chmn. chemistry, researcher Cen. State U., Wilberforce, Ohio, 1969-98, prof. emeritus, 1998—. Cons. E.G.&G. Mound Labs., summer, 1989, 90, 92, 93; researcher in environ. pollution, lubricant devel. and characterization, devel. of radioluminescent light sources, thermodynamics, electrochemistry, chem. kinetics, trace metals analysis, energy conversion and storage, for IBM Corp., Pitts. Plate Glass Fiber Glass Tech. Ctr., NASA, Johnson Johnson Controls Inc., Lawrence Livermore Nat. Lab., Wright Patterson AFB, Universal Energy Systems Inc., AF Office of Sci. Research, San Jose State U., United Tech. Systems Inc., SCEEE, Systran Corp., E.G.&G. Mound Techs., Inc., U. Dayton Rsch. Inst. Contbr. numerous articles to profl. jours. Vol. aux. svcs. Greene Meml. Hosp., 2000—. Recipient Appreciation award Ctrl. State U., 1975-76, Talmadge McKinney award, 1986, Excellence in Rsch. award, 1995, Outstanding Svc. to Cmty. award India Club of Greater Dayton, 1985, Clarence E. Bowman award for Comm. Svcs., 1991, others; Nat. Urban League fellow, IBM Corp. fellow, summer 1973, Pittsburgh Plate Glass Fiberglass Tech. Ctr., summer 1976, Johnson Johnson Control Inc. fellow, 1979, NSF summer fellow, 1979; USAF grantee, 1982-83, NASA grantee, 1976-79, U.S. Army grantee, 1994-98, USN grantee, 1995-96. Mem.: Divine Love Mission, Am. Chem. Soc. (chmn. Dayton sect. 1988, Outstanding Sect. award 1988), India Club (Dayton). Democrat. Hindu. Home: 2308 Weston Dr Fairborn OH 45324-8536

GUPTA, YASH, dean; b. New Delhi; m. Nisha Gupta; children: Ashish, Ashwin. BS in engring., Punjab U., 1973; M in prodn. mgmt., Brunel U., 1974; PhD in mgmt. sci., U. Bradford, 1976. Sr. cons. Coopers and Lybrand, London, 1978—80; asst. prof. Meml. U., Newfoundland, 1980—82; assoc. prof. U. Manitoba, Canada, 1982—88, prof., 1988; Frazier Family prof. and sr. rsch. fellow Telecom. Rsch. Ctr., U. Louisville Sch. Bus., 1988—92; dean, prof. mgmt. U. Colo., Coll. Bus. and Adminstrn., Denver, 1992—99; dean, Kirby L. Cramer endowed chair bus. U. Wash. Bus. Sch., 1999—2004; dean Marshall Sch. Bus., U. So. Calif., 2004—07. Vis. prof. U. Toledo, Ohio, 1985—86; adj. prof. U. Manitoba, Canada, 1991—94; mem. publ. com. Decision Sci. Inst., 1992—95. Mem. editl. bd.: Internat. Jour. Mgmt. and Sys., 1985—88, Technovation: Internat. Jour. Tech. Innovation and Entrepreneurship, Mid-Atlantic Jour. Bus.; area editor Prodn. and Ops. Mgmt. Jour. Mem.: Soc. Orgnl. Behavior, Acad. Mgmt. Achievements include ranked number one prodn. and ops. mgmt. scholar in country in terms of contbns. made to field in Jour. Ops. Mgmt., 1996.*

GUPTA, YOGESH, software company executive; b. India; BEE, Indian Inst. Tech., Madras; M in Computer Sci., U. Wis. With Burroughs Corp.; from sr. mgmt. to sr. v.p., chief tech. officer Computer Assoc. Internat. Inc. (now called CA, Inc.), Islandia, NY, 1989—2006; sr. v.p. bus. develop. CA, Inc., Islandia, NY, 2006—. Spkr. in field. Named one of World's 25 Most Influential Chief Tech. Officers, Infoworld, 2004. Office: Computer Assoc Internat Inc (CA Inc) One Computer Associates Plz Islandia NY 11749

GURA, KATHLEEN MARIE, pediatric pharmacist, educator; b. Worcester, Mass., Aug. 17, 1960; d. Philip J. and Catherine Joyce Kozak; m. Scott Gura, May 5, 1984; children: Alessandra Jeanne, Samantha Anne. BS, Mass. Coll. Pharmacy and Allied Health Scis., 1982; PharmD, Mass. Coll. Pharmacy and Health Scis., 1999. Registered pharmacist Mass. Bd. Pharmacy, 1982, D.C. Bd. Pharmacy, 1983, bd. cert. nutrition support pharmacist Bd. Pharm. Specialties, 1993. Clin. staff pharmacist Children's Hosp. Nat. Med. Ctr., Washington, 1982—84; clin. pharmacy specialist GI/nutrition Children's Hosp. Boston, 1984—. Adj. asst. prof. Mass. Coll. Pharmacy, Boston, 1999—, Northeastern U., Boston, 2002—; preceptor for experiential edn. U. N.C. Coll. Pharmacy, Chapel Hill, 2003—, Wash. State U., 2004—, adj. faculty, preceptor for experiential edn. Sch. Pharmacy, U. Wash., Seattle, 2004—; preceptor U. Conn., 2006—. Author: (textbook) Manual of Pediatric Nutrition, 2000, 2005, Pediatric Nutrition in Your Pocket, 2002, Nutrition in Pediatrics, 4th edit., 2007, Geriatric Nutrition, The Health Professional's Handbook, 3d edit., 2004. Leader Girls Scouts Am., Norfolk, Mass., 1999. Fellow: Am. Soc. Health System Pharmacists (ho. dels. 1996—2003, chair coun. profl. affairs 2000—01); mem.: European Soc. for Clin. Nutrition and Metabolism, Am. Coll. Clin. Pharmacy, Pediatric Pharmacy Advocacy Group (bd. dirs. 2000—04, v.p., finance 2004—05), Am. Soc. for Parenteral and Enteral Nutrition, Mass. Soc. of Health Sys. Pharmacists (pres. 2000—01, bd. dirs. 2005—, Practitioner Excellence award 1994), Rho Chi, Rho Pi Phi (sec. 1980—81, US pharm. conv. ad hoc adv. panel 2007). Avocations: travel, photography. Home: 5 Barnstable Rd Norfolk MA 02056 Office: Children's Hospital Boston 300 Longwood Ave Boston MA 02115 Office Phone: 617-355-2336. Business E-Mail: kathleen.gura@childrens.harvard.edu.

GURA, PHILIP FRANCIS, English and American literature educator; b. Ware, Mass., June 14, 1950; s. Oswald Eugene and Stephanie (Koziara) G.; m. Leslie Ann Cohig, Aug. 4, 1979; children: David Austin, Katherine Blair, Daniel Alden. BA, Harvard Coll., 1972; PhD, Harvard U., 1977. Instr. Am. Lit. Middlebury (Vt.) Coll., 1974-76; asst. prof. U. Colo., Boulder, 1976-80, assoc. prof., 1980-85, prof., 1985-87, U. N.C., Chapel Hill, 1987—98, prof., English, adj. prof. religious studies, 1998—2000, William S. Newman disting. prof. Am. lit. and culture, 2000—. Lectr. in field. Author: The Wisdom of Words, 1981, Critical Essays on American Transcendentalism, 1982, A Glimpse of Sion's Glory, 1984, The Memoirs of Stephen Burroughs, 1988, The Crossroads of American History and Literature, 1996, C.F. Martin and His Guitars, 1796-1873, 2003, Buried from the World: Inside the Massachusetts State Prison, 1829-1831, 2001, Jonathan Edwards: America's Evangelical, 2005, American Transcendentalism: A History, 2007, (with James Bollman) America's Instrument: The Banjo in the Ninteenth Century, 1999; editor Early Am. Lit., 1989-99. Recipient Post-Baccalaureate Disting. Tchg. award, U. N.C., 2004; Peterson fellow Am. Antiquarian Soc., 1989, 1998, 2003, sr. fellow NEH, 1985-86, Charles Warren Ctr. fellow Harvard U., 1980-81. Mem. MLA, Colonial Soc. Mass., Am. Antiquarian Soc. (James Russell Wiggins lectr. 2004, Mellon Dist. scholar 2006—), Inst. Early Am. History and Culture (nat. coun. 1991-94). Office: Wm Newman Disting Prof CB3520 U NC Dept English Chapel Hill NC 27599-3520 Business E-Mail: gura@email.unc.edu.

GURAL, JEFFREY R., real estate company executive; married; 3 children. Ed. in Civil Engring., Rensselaer Poly. Inst. With Morse-Diesel Constrn. Co.; joined Newmark & Co. Real Estate Inc., NYC, 1972—, prin., 1978—, co-pres., 1992—2000, chmn., 2000—. Co-sponsor Chelsea-Elliott "I Have A Dream" Project; bd. dirs. Eldridge St. Synagogue, Jewish Cmty. Ctr. of the Upper West Side, Cooper Union. Mem.: IHAD-NY (chmn.), USO (bd. mem.), 14th St.-Union Sq. Dist. Mgmt. Assn. (bd. dirs.), Dist. Mgmt. Assn. for the Times Sq. Bus. Improvement Dist. (chmn. bd. dirs.), Real Estate Bd. N.Y. (bd. dirs.), UJA-Fedn. (bd. dirs.), The Starlight Found. (pres. N.Y. chpt.), Real Estate Lodge B'nai B'rith (v.p.). Avocation: owner, breeder Standardbred racehorses. Office: Newmark & Co Real Estate Inc 125 Park Ave New York NY 10017 Home Phone: 212-580-7691; Office Phone: 212-372-2400. Office Fax: 212-372-2000. Business E-Mail: jgural@newmarkre.com.*

GURALNICK, SIDNEY AARON, engineering educator; b. Phila., Apr. 25, 1929; s. Philip and Kenia (Dudnik) G.; m. Eleanor Alban, Mar. 10, 1951; children: Sara Dian, Jeremy. BSc, Drexel Inst. Tech., Phila., 1952; MS, Cornell U., 1955, PhD, 1958. Registered profl. engr., Pa.; lic. structural engr., Ill. Instr., then asst. prof. Cornell U., 1952-58, mgr. structural research lab., 1956-58; mem. faculty Ill. Inst. Tech., Chgo., 1958—, prof. civil engring., 1967—, Perlstein disting. prof. engring., now prof. emeritus, 1982—, dir. structural engring. labs., 1968-71, dean Grad. Sch., 1971-75, exec. v.p., provost, 1975-82, trustee, 1976-82, dir. Advanced Bldg. Materials and Sys. Ctr., 1987—. Devel. engr. Portland Cement Assn., Skokie, Ill., 1959-61; participant internat. confs.; cons. to govt. and industry. Author numerous papers in field. Trustee Inst. Gas Tech., 1976-81, Rsch. Inst. of Ill. Inst. Tech., 1976-82; commr.-at-large North Ctrl. Assn. Schs. and Colls., 1985-89, cons., evaluator, 1989-93. With C.E., U.S. Army, 1950-51. McGraw fellow, 1952-53; Faculty Rsch. fellow Ill. Inst. Tech., 1960; European travel grantee, 1961 Fellow: ASCE (Collingwood prize 1961, Lifetime Achievement award Ill. sect. 1997, Civil Engr. of Yr. award Ill. sect. 1998); mem.: Ill. Univs. Transp. Rsch. Consortium (adminstrv. com. 1983—93), Transp. Rsch. Bd., Structural Engrs. Assn. Ill. (bd. dirs., pres.-elect 1989—90, pres. 1990—91, John F. Parmer award 1993), Soc. Exptl. Mechanics, Am. Concrete Inst., Chi Epsilon, Tau Beta Pi, Phi Kappa Phi, Sigma Xi. Office: Ill Inst Tech 3300 S Federal St Chicago IL 60616-3793 Business E-Mail: guralnick@iit.edu.

GURASICH, STEPHEN WILLIAM, JR., advertising executive; b. Long Beach, Calif., Mar. 26, 1948; s. Stephen W. and Joan Marie (Cotter) G.; m. Nancy Ruth Hamlin, June 6, 1970; children: Amy Marie, John Hamlin. BJ, U. Tex., 1971. Co-founder GSD&M's Idea City (formerly GSD&M Advt.), Austin, Tex., 1971, chmn., CEO, 1971—2007, vice chair bd., 2007—. Bd. dirs. Cornerstone Devel., Austin, 1980—, G&S Assn., Inc., 1971—. Served with Tex. N.G., 1970-76. Recipient Addy awards, 1987. Mem. Austin Advt. Club (bd. dirs.), Austin Assn. Advt. Principles (bd. dirs. 1979-80), Am. Assn. Advt. Agys. (mem. client service com. 1986-87). Roman Catholic. Avocations: reading, raquetball, hunting, fishing. Office: GSD&M's Idea City 828 W 6th St Austin TX 78703-5420 Home: 3908 Gyrfalcon Cv Austin TX 78738-6540*

GURDON, JOHN BERTRAND, cell biologist; b. Dippenhall, Hampshire, Eng., Oct. 2, 1933; s. William Nathaniel and Elsie Marjorie (Byass) G.; m. Jean Elizabeth Curtis, June 25, 1965; Elizabeth Aurea, William John. BS in Zoology, Oxford U., 1956, DPhil in Embryology, 1960; DSc (hon.), U. Chgo., 1978; D (hon.), U. Rene Descartes, Paris, 1982; DSc (hon.), Oxford U., 1988, U. Hull, 1998, U. Glasgow, 2000. Beit Meml. fellow dept. zoology Oxford U., 1958—61; Gosney rsch. fellow Calif. Inst.

Tech., 1961—62; rsch. fellow Christ Church, 1963—64; research fellow Oxford U., England, 1961-71; mem. staff Med. Rsch. Coun., Lab. Molecular Biology, Cambridge, England, 1972—83, head cell biology divsn., 1979—83; John Humphrey Plummer prof. cell biology U. Cambridge, 1983—2001; master Magdalene Coll., Cambridge, 1995—2002; Fullerian prof. physiology and comparative anatomy Royal Instn., 1985—; Charles M. and Martha Hitchcock professorship U. Calif., Berkeley, 2005—06; group leader Wellcome CR UK Inst., Cambridge, 2001—. Lectr. dept. zoology Oxford U., 1965-72; vis. rsch. fellow Carnegie Instn., Balt., 1965; fellow Churchill Coll., Cambridge, 1974-94, Eton Coll., Windsor, Eng., 1978-; chmn. Wellcome Trust and Cancer Rsch. Campaign Inst. Cancer and Devel. Biology, Cambridge, 1988-2001; gov. The Wellcome Trust, London, 1995-2000; group leader Wellcome CR UK Inst., Cambridge, 2001-. Author: Control of Gene Expression in Animal Development, 1974; contbr. papers to sci. jours. Hon. fellowhip Christ Church, Oxford, 1985; recipient Albert Brachet prize Belgian Royal Acad., 1968, sci. medal Zoological Soc., 1968, Feldberg Found. award, 1975, Paul Ehrlich prize, Germany, 1977, Nessim Habif prize U. Geneva, 1979, Ciba medal, prize Biochemical Soc., 1980, Comfort Crookshank triennial award for cancer rsch. Middlesex Hosp. Med. Sch., 1983, Prix Charles Leopold Mayer prize, Acad. Scis., France, 1984, William Bate Hardy triennial prize Cambridge Philos. Soc., 1984, Ross Harrison prize Internat. Soc. Devel. Biology, 1985, Emperor Hirohito Internat. Biology prize, Japan, 1987, Wolf prize in medicine, 1989, Jan Waldenstrom medal Swedish Oncology Soc., 1991, Disting. Svc. award, Miami, 1992, Jean Brachet Meml. prize Internat. Soc. Differentiation, 2000, Conklin medal Am. Soc. Devel. Biology, 2001, Pioneer in Stem Cell award Frontiers in Human Embryonic Stem Cell Organizing Com., 2004. Fellow Royal Soc. London (Croonian lectr., John Jaffe prize 1976, Royal medal 1985, Copley medal 2003); mem. Inst. of Medicine, Am. Acad. Arts and Scis. (hon. fgn. mem.), Academie des Sciences, Institut de France (fgn. assoc.), Academia Europaea, Lombardy Acad. Sci. (fgn. mem.), Belgian Royal Acad. Sci., Letters and Fine Arts (fgn. assoc.), Am. Philos. Soc. (fgn. mem.), UGoldsmiths Club London (liveryman 1986). Mem. Ch. Of Eng. Home: Whittlesford Grove Cambridge CB2 4NZ England Office: U Cambridge Dept Zoology Downing St Cambridge CB2 3EJ England Office Phone: 44-1223-334-090. E-mail: jbg1000@cam.ac.uk.

GURE, ANNA VALERIE, retired social worker, consulting psychotherapist; b. Kaunas, Lithuania, Jan. 5, 1921; came to U.S., 1948; d. Salomon and Maria (Kantorovich) Gurvich. BA, CUNY, 1962, MSW, 1965. Cert. social worker, N.Y.; diplomate in clin. social work Am. Bd. Examiners in Clin. Social Work. Psychiat. social worker N.Y. Mental Hygiene Dept., NYC, 1963-64, 66-69; social worker N.Y.C. Housing Authority, NYC, 1965-66; immigration social worker Svc. for Fgn. Born, NYC, 1969-77; psychotherapist, NYC, 1977-86; social worker N.Y.C. Bd. Edn., NYC, 1979-86; cons. Cath. Charities, Bklyn., 1988-89. Mem. Acad. Cert. Social Worker, Delta Phi Alpha. Avocations: painting, classical music, golf, exercise. Home: 95 Christopher St New York NY 10014-6605

GUREVICH, GRIGORY, visual artist, educator, mime; b. St. Petersburg, Russia, Dec. 26, 1937; came to U.S., 1976; s. Abram Grigoryevich Gurevich and Klara Mihailovna (Olshvang) Fleitman; m. Mongita Zalmanovna Freedman, Aug. 8, 1958 (div. Feb. 1967); 1 child, Jelena Gurevich Scherbina; m. Erika Wittmann, Jan. 17, 1987; d. Sept. 6, 2001. 1 child, Alexander. Diploma, Acad. Fine & Indsl. Art, St. Petersburg, 1966. Interior designer Lenprojekt, St. Petersburg, Lenzneeap, 1961-63, 63-65; founder Grigur's Pantomime Theater, St. Petersburg, 1966-69; founder mime sch. St. Petersburg, 1969-75; founder Grigur's Pantomime Theater, NYC, 1977; tchr. visual arts Bergen Sch., Jersey City, 1980-82; instr. sculpture Newark Sch. Fine and Indsl. Art, 1982-96; prof. St. Johns U., Jamaica, NY, 1994-97. Conductor workshops on sculpture U.S., Italy, Denmark; founder Art Workshops Festival, Arts on the Hudson, Jersey City. Exhibited in solo and group exhbns. U.S., Russia, France, Denmark, Germany; bronze sculpture tableau Commuters for Newark Penn Sta., 1985, bronze bust Kazuo Hashimoto, 1996; represented in numerous pvt. collections, Russia, U.S. and Europe, Hermitage Mus., N.Y. Pub. Libr., Libr. Newark Mus., Montclair Mus., Libr. St. Bonaventure U., Yad Vashem Mus., Israel; pub. poetry Reflections, 1992; author: Book of Numbers 1-10, 10-1, 1993 (collections Bklyn. Mus. 1994, Columbia U. Chgo. Libr.); inventor process of wood firing, 1963, manifolding book, 1995; actor: David Letterman Show, 2002, Law and Order, 2003. Founder Arts on the Hudson Sch., Jersey City, N.J., 1998. Recipient Grumbacher award, Marian Reitman award, others. Mem. N.Y. Artists Equity Assn., Am. Artists Profl. League (1st Place Nat. award 1993, 98), Hudson Artists (Artist of Yr. 1995, other awards), Screen Actors Guild. Home: 282 Barrow St Jersey City NJ 07302-3502 E-mail: grigur@netzero.net.

GURFEIN, PETER J., lawyer; b. NYC, Sept. 13, 1948; m. Pamela Hedin, June 23, 1976; children: Diana, William, Eva. BA, NYU, 1969; JD, George Washington U., 1973. Bar: N.Y. 1976, U.S. Supreme Ct. 1976, US. Dist. Ct. (so. and ea. dists.) N.Y. 1976, U.S. Ct. Appeals (2d cir.) 1979, Internat. Ct. Trade 1979, U.S. Ct. Appeals (9th cir.) 1986, Calif. 1986, U.S Dist. Ct. (no., ea., so. and cen. dists.) Calif. 1987, D.C. 1993. Project dir. Commn. on Correctional Facilities and Scs. ABA, Washington, 1973-76; asst. dist. atty., spl. narcotics prosecutor Dist. Atty.'s Office N.Y. County, NYC, 1976-81; assoc. Zalkin, Rodin & Goodman, NYC, 1981-83, Moses & Singer, NYC, 1983-86; ptnr. Morrison & Foerster, San Francisco, 1986-92, Sonnenschein, Nath & Rosenthal, L.A. and San Francisco, 1993-2000, Akin, Gump, Strauss, Hauer & Feld, LLP, LA, 2001—. Editor-in-chief The Calif. Bankruptcy Jour., 1995-2000; contbr. articles to handbooks and profl. jours. Mem. Bar Assn. San Francisco (chmn. bankruptcy and comml. law sect. 1993), L.A. County Bar Assn.; dir. L.A. Bankruptcy Forum, 1995—. Office: Akin Gump Strauss Hauer & Feld LLP Ste 2400 2029 Century Park E Los Angeles CA 90067 Office Phone: 310-229-1000. E-mail: pgurfein@akingump.com.

GURFEIN, RICHARD ALAN, lawyer; b. NYC, Nov. 4, 1946; s. Jack and Ruth (Kronowitz) G.; m. Erica P. Temchin, Oct. 20, 1978; children: Jared L., Amanda, Jessica M., Sarah R. BE, NYU, 1967; JD, Bklyn. Law Sch., 1971. Bar: N.Y. 1972, U.S. Dist. Ct. (so. and ea. dists.) N.Y. 1973, U.S. Supreme Ct. 1976, U.S. Ct. Appeals (2d cir.) 1990. Assoc. Mark B. Wiesen, PC, NYC, 1972-78; ptnr. Wiesen & Gurfein, NYC, 1978-82, Wiesen, Gurfein & Jenkins, NYC, 1982-2001; pres. Trial1.com, Inc., 1997—; prin. Richard A. Gurfein & Assocs., PLLC, 2001—02; founder and ptnr. Gurfein Douglas LLP, 2002—. Moderator, lectr. Nassau Acad. Law, 1984—, N.Y. State Trial Lawyers Inst., 1985—, treas., 1989-91, pres. 1995-96; advocate Nat. Coll. Advocacy, 2004. Recipient Crown of Good Name award, Inst. Jewish Humanities, 1996; Top Legal Rating, Martindale Hubbel. Mem. Assn. Trial Lawyers Am., Am. Assn. for Justice (lectr. 2005-, mem. comm. com. 2006-, mem. exchange adv. com. 2007-), N.Y. State Trial Lawyers Assn. (lectr. continuing legal edn. 1985—, bd. dirs. 1986—, chmn. com. on coms. 1987-88, exec. com. 1987—, dep. treas. 1988-89, treas. 1989-91, sec. 1991-92, v.p. 1992-94, pres. elect 1994-95, pres. 1995-96, past pres. 1996—), N.Y. State Acad. Trial Lawyers (bd. dirs. 2006—), N.Y. County Lawyers Assn., Nassau County Bar Assn. (chmn. com. on med. jurisprudence 1983-86), Million Dollar Advocates Forum, N.Y. State Bar Assn., Bklyn. Bar Assn. Avocations: astronomy, amateur radio, photography, golf, computing. Office: Gurfein Douglas LLP 11 Park Pl Rm 1100 New York NY 10007-2889 Office Phone: 212-406-1600. Personal E-mail: rgurfein@trial1.com.

GURGOVITS, STEPHEN J., financial executive; b. 1944; BA in Econs., Youngstown State U. Teller First Nat. Bank Pa., 1961, pres., 1988; vice chmn. bd. dirs. FNB Corp., Hermitage, Pa., 1998—2004, pres., CEO, 2004—; chmn. Regency Fin. Co. Office: FNB Corp One FNB Blvd Hermitage PA 16148-3301

GURIAN, ELAINE HEUMANN, museum consultant; b. NYC, Sept. 23, 1937; d. Ernst and Hedi Margot (Messer) Heumann; m. Dean W. Anderson; children: Aaron Heumann, Joseph Emanuel, Eve Gurian-Wachhaus. BA in history of art, Brandeis U., 1958; MEd in elementary edn. and art specialist, State Coll. of Boston, 1966. Art tchr. Solomon Schechter Sch., Newton, Mass.; art cons., Summerthing Mayor's Office, Boston, 1969—71; dir. edn. Inst. Contemporary Art, Boston, 1969-72; dir. exhibit ctr. The Children's Mus., Boston, 1972-85, assoc. dir., 1985-87; dep. asst. sec. for Museums Smithsonian Inst., Washington, 1987-90; dep. dir. for pub. program planning Nat. Mus. Am. Indian, Washington, 1990-91; dep. dir. US Holocaust Meml. Mus., Washington, 1991-94; museum cons. The Museum Group, 1994, pres., 2000—05; acting dir. Cranbrook Inst. Sci., Bloomfield Hills, 1998—99; sr. cons., prin. Elaine Heumann Gurian LLC, Arlington, Va., 1994—. Mem. exec. bd. Internat. Coun. on Museums, 1979-86; rep. Mass. Coun. on Arts, Boston, 1972-75; mem. bd. dirs. TyPA Argentina Found. for Arts, 2004-; pres. bd. Am. Poetry Mus., 2004-; mem. editl. bd. Curator; vis. scholar U. Mus., Ann Arbor, Mich., 2006-. Editor: Institutional Trauma, 1995, Civilizing the Museum, 2006; editor Institutional Trauma: The Effect of Major Change on Museum Staff. Recipient Disting. Alumni Award, Brandeis U., 1993, Learning Disabled Achiever Award, The Lab Sch., Washington, 1993; Fulbright grant, Argentina, 2007. Mem.: S.E. Mus. Assn., Internat. Com. for Edn. and Cultural Action (CECA/ICOM) (v.p. 1980—86), Am. Assn. Museums (mem. coun. 1980—82, v.p. 1982—84, treas. 1984—88, mem. coun. 1989—91, Mus. Edn. Award for Excellence 1985, Award for Disting. Svc. to Museums 2004, named to Centennial Honor Roll 2006). Home: 4834 8th St S Arlington VA 22204-1432

GURIAN, MAL, telecommunications executive; b. NYC, Nov. 17, 1926; s. George Joseph and Rose (Graff) G.; m. Gloria Dickler; children: Randy Harlan, Nancy Ellen Newman. Ptnr. Mal Gurian Assocs., NYC, 1946-77; v.p. Radio Telephone Corp., NYC, 1960-83; sr. v.p. Aerotron, Inc., Raleigh, NC, 1965-81; v.p. Oki Advanced Comm., Hackensack, NJ, 1981-84; pres. Oki Telecom, Fairlawn, NJ, 1984-88, Cartell, Inc., Romulus, Mich., 1988, Cellcom Cellular Corp., Fairfield, NJ, 1989-91; CEO Universal Cellular, Inc., Anaheim, Calif., 1992; chmn., CEO Global Link Comm., Inc., Irvine, Calif., 1993—; pres., CEO Authentix Network, Inc., Tucson, 1995-98, 99—, chmn., 1998-2001; pres., CEO SimplySay, LLC, Tucson, 2001—02, Mal Gurian Assocs., Bradenton, Fla., 2002—. Adv. I-Control, Campbell, Calif., 2002-03; bd. adv. pres. Ea. Profl. Photographers Assn., NYC, 1951-53; exec. advisor TRW Wireless Commn., Sunnyvale, Calif., 1994; advisor Sims Comms., Inc., Delray Beach, Fla., 1994-98; arbitrator Am. Arbitration Assn., 1994-2002; bd. electronic comm. Rangestar Internat., San Jose, Calif., 1996-98; bd. advisor Genesis Campus, LP, 2003—; bd. dirs. Airbee Wireless; bd. advisor Mobility Ventures, 2005-. Active Old Tappan (NJ) First Aid Corp., 1966—. Cpl. USMC, 1943-46. Decorated Air medal; recipient Alexander S. Popov Hon. medal, St. Petersburg Electrotech. U., Russia, 1995. Fellow Radio Club Am. (life mem., v.p. 1976-92, exec. v.p. 1993, pres. 1994, pres. emeritus 1995—, Spl. Svcs. award 1986, Sarnoff citation 1988, Fred Link award 1989, inducted into Wireless Hall of Fame, 2003); mem. Am. Assn. Pub. Safety Comm. Officers, Nat. Assn. Bus. and Ednl. Radio (bd. dirs. 1977-84, Chmn.'s award 1986. Home Phone: 941-752-1122; Office Phone: 941-752-1133. Business E-Mail: mgurian@malgurianassoc.com. *Advances in technology is rapidly moving on. Mankind must strive to utilize our developments in a positive vein and promote compatibility amongst each other.*

GURKE, SHARON MCCUE, career officer; b. Apr. 4, 1949; d. James Ambrose and Marion Denise (Coombs) McCue; m. Lee Samuel Gurke, Apr. 16, 1977; children: Marion Dawn, Leigh Elizabeth. BA, Molloy Cath. Coll., 1977. Lic. pilot; first female naval officer selected for aero. engring. tng. Commd. ensign USN, 1970, advanced through grades to capt., 1991; aircraft maintenance duty officer Orgn. Intermediate Maintenance Officer Comdr. Naval Air Force U.S. Pacific Fleet, Naval Air Sta., North Island, San Diego, 1974-77; head quality assurance divsn. Intermediate Maintenance Dept. Supporting Aircraft Naval Air Sta., Miramar, San Diego, 1977-78, avionics divsn. officer, 1978-80; officer in charge Naval Aviation Engring. Svc. Unit Pacific Naval Air Sta., North Island, 1980-82; aircraft Intermediate Maintenance officer Naval Air Sta., Alameda, Calif., 1982-84, Rota, Spain, 1984-86, Naval Air Sys. Command Aviation Maintenance Policy Br., 1986-88; asst. program mgr. NACOLMIS, 1987-88; dir. ops. Naval Aviation Depot, North Island, 1988-90, Dept. of Navy OP-514C, 1990-92; commdg. officer Naval Aviation Depot Co., Pensacola, Fla., 1994-96, chief of naval operation, indsl. facility policy head, 1996-99; mgr. corp. mktg./devel. Newport News Shipbuilding, 1999—. Interviewed by S.D. TV for Success Story. Decorated Legion of Merit (2), Naval Commendation medals (2), Meritorious Svc. medals (3). Mem. Ninety Nines, San Diego Naval Women Officers Network (chmn.), Nat. Capital Coun. Navy League (pres.). Office: 9336 Mt Vernon Cir Alexandria VA 22309-3219 Office Phone: 703-295-2553. E-mail: gurkes@aol.com.

GURLEY, ELISABETH ANNE, art historian, educator, writer; b. Boston, Mar. 5, 1927; d. Harold Coleman and Julia Josephine (Finnin) Ryan; m. Franklin Louis Gurley, June 17, 1950. Student, Boston U., 1947; BSc, Mass. Coll. Art, 1948, BFA (hon.), 1993; postgrad., U. Paris and Ecole du Louvre, 1963—64. Supr. art edn. pub. elem. and high schs., Canton and Stoughton, Mass., 1948-49, pub. elem. and jr. high schs., Dedham, Mass., 1949-51; tchr. Avery Sch., Dedham, 1951-52; teen page editor Detroit News, 1956; juvenile editor Va. Kirkus Lit. Svc., 1957-58. Contbr. articles to profl. jours., newspapers and mags.; subject of articles in Life mag., 1952, La Liberté newspaper, Switzerland, 1988; exhibited in Zagorà, Thessaly, Greece, 1992. Home: 701 Hopeton Rd Wilmington DE 19807

GURM, HITINDER S., cardiologist, educator; m. Roopa Gurm, Jan. 25, 1999. MBBS, Christian Med. Coll., India, 1986—91. Cert. Mrcp Royal Coll. Physicians, 1995. Asst. prof. medicine U. Mich., Ann Arbor, 2005—. Mem.: Soc. Coronary Angiography & Intervention, Am. Heart Assn., Am. Coll. Cardiology. Achievements include patents for devices related to coronary and carotid stenting. Office: Univ Mich TC B1 226 1500 E Medical Center Dr Ann Arbor MI 48109-0311 Office Fax: 734-764-4142. Business E-Mail: hgurm@med.umich.edu.

GURMAN, ANDREW WILLIAM, orthopedist, educator; b. NY, May 20, 1952; m. Nancy Gurman; 2 children. MD, SUNY, Syracuse. Intern, orthop. Montefiore Hosp., Bronx, NY, 1980—81, resident, hand surgery, 1981—85; fellow Hosp. Joint Diseases, 1985—86; hosp. appt. Altoona Hosp., Pa.; practiced Blair Orthop. Associates, Pa., 1986—, pres., CEO Pa.; clin. asst. prof. Pa. State Coll. Medicine. Tchg. faculty mem. Altoona Hosp. Family Practice Residency Program. Mem.: ACS, Am. Soc. for Surgery of the Hand, Am. Acad. Orthop. Surgeons, Blair County Med. Soc. (past pres.), Pa. Med. Soc. (spkr. house delegates 2002—07), AMA (vice-spkr. house delegates 2007—). Address: 3000 Fairway Dr Altoona PA 16602*

GURNETT, DONALD ALFRED, physics professor; b. Cedar Rapids, Iowa, Apr. 11, 1940; s. Alfred Foley and Velma (Trachta) G.; m. Marie Barbara Schmitz, Oct. 10, 1964; children: Suzanne, Christina. BS in Elec. Engring., U. Iowa, Iowa City, 1962, MS in Physics, 1963, PhD in Physics, 1965. Prof. physics and astronomy U. Iowa, Iowa City, 1965-75, 76-79, 80—; rsch. scientist Max-Planck Inst., Garching, Fed. Republic Germany, 1975-76; vis. prof. UCLA, 1979-80; mem. space physics com. Nat. Acad. Sci., Washington, 1975-78, mem. com. on solar terrrestrial research, 1976-79, mem. com. on planetary and lunar exploration, 1982-85. Recipient Alexander von Humboldt Found. award, 1975, Disting. Sci. Achievement award NASA, 1981, Space Act award NASA, 1986, Sci. Achievement medal Gov. of Iowa, 1987, Disting. Iowa Scientist award Iowa Acad. Sci., 1989, Marion L. Huit award U. Iowa, 1990, Iowa Bd. Regents award for faculty excellence, 1994, Alfven medal European Geoscis. Union, 2006. Fellow Am. Geophys. Union (assoc. editor Jour. Geophys. Rsch. 1974-77), Am. Acad. Arts and Sci., Fleming medal 1989, Am. Phys. Soc. (award for excellence in plasma physics 1989); mem. Internat. Union Radio Sci. (Dellinger gold medal 1978), Soaring Soc. Am. (Iowa State gov. 1983-86), Nat. Acad. of Sci. Home: 4664 Canterbury Ct Iowa City IA 52245 Office: U Iowa Dept Physics and Astronomy 715 Van Allen Hall Iowa City IA 52242-1403 Business E-Mail: donald-garnett@uiowa.edu.

GURNEY, ALBERT RAMSDELL, playwright, educator; b. Buffalo, Nov. 1, 1930; s. Albert Ramsdell and Marion (Spaulding) Gurney; m. Mary Forman Goodyear, June 8, 1957; children: George, Amy, Evelyn, Benjamin. BA, Williams Coll., 1952, DDL (hon.), 1984; MFA, Yale U., 1958; LLD (hon.), Buffalo State U., 1992. Mem. faculty MIT, 1960-96, prof. lit., 1970-96. Contbr. works to Best Short Plays, 1955—56, works to Best Short Plays, 1957—58, works to Best Short Plays, 1969, works to Best Short Plays, 1970, works to Best Short Plays, 1992; author: (plays) The Golden Fleece, 1969, Public Affairs, 1970, Scenes from American Life, 1971, Children, 1974, Richary Cory, 1976, The Middle Ages, 1977, The Wayside Motor Inn, 1977, The Golden Age, 1980, The Dining Room, 1981, What I Did Last Summer, 1982, The Perfect Party, 1985, Another Antigone, 1985, Sweet Sue, 1986, The Cocktail Hour, 1988, Love Letters, 1988, The Snow Ball, 1991, The Old Boy, 1991, The Fourth Wall, 1992, Later Life, 1993, A Cheever Evening, 1994, Sylvia, 1994, Overtime, 1995, Let's Do It!, 1996, The Guest Lecturer, 1998, Labor Day, 1998, Far East, 1999, Ancestral Voices, 1999, Human Events, 2000, Buffalo Gal, 2001, The Fourth Wall (revised), 2002, O Jerusalem, 2003, Big Bill, 2003, Strictly Academic, 2003, Mrs. Farnsworth, 2004, Screen Play, 2004, Indian Blood, 2006, Post Mortem, 2006, Crazy Mary, 2007, (teleplays) O Youth and Beauty, 1979, The Hit List, 1988, Love Letters, 1999, (novels) The Gospel According to Joe, 1974, Entertaining Strangers, 1977, The Snow Ball, 1984, (one-act opera) Strawberry Fields, 1999. With USNR, 1952—55. Named to Theatre Hall Fame, 2005; recipient award, N.Y. Drama Desk, 1971, Rockefeller Playwrights, 1977, Playwriting award, Nat. Endowment Arts, 1981—82, Award of Merit, Am. Acad. and Inst. Arts and Letters, 1987, Lucille Lortel award for Body of Work, 1994, William Inge award, 2000. Mem.: Am. Acad. Arts and Letters, Dramatists Guild, Writers Guild, Authors League Am. Home: 40 Wellers Bridge Rd Roxbury CT 06783-1616 Personal E-mail: a.r.gurney@charter.net.

GURNIS, MICHAEL CHRISTOPHER, geological sciences educator; b. Boston, Oct. 22, 1959; s. George Albert and Barbara (Dempsey) G. BS, U. Ariz., 1982; PhD, Australian Nat. U., Canberra, 1987. Rsch. fellow in geophysics Calif. Inst. Tech., Pasadena, 1986-88, assoc. prof. geophysics, 1994-96; asst. prof. geol. scis. U. Mich., Ann Arbor, 1988-93, assoc. prof., 1993—2003; assoc. dir. Seismological Lab. Calif. Inst. Tech., Pasadena, 1995—, prof. geophysics, 1996—; dir. Computational Infrastructure for Geodynamics, 2004—; John and Hazel Smits prof. geophysics Caltech, 2005—. Recipient Presdl. Young Investigator award NSF, 1989, fellowship David and Lucile Packard Found., 1991. Fellow Am. Geophys. Union (Macelwance medal 1993), Geol. Soc. Am. (sr., Donath medal 1993). Achievements include research in the linkage of sedimentary rocks deposited in the interiors of continents to geodynamic processes within the earth; global dynamics, mantle convection, plate tectonics, sea level changes, evolution of mantle and crust; computational and visual fluid mechanics. Office: Calif Inst Tech Seismol Lab-252-21 Pasadena CA 91125-0001

GURSTEL, NORMAN KEITH, lawyer; b. Mpls., Mar. 24, 1939; s. Jules and Etta (Abramowitz) G.; m. Jane Evelyn Golden, Nov. 24, 1984; children: Todd, Dana, Marc. BA, U. Minn., 1960, JD, 1962. Bar: Minn. 1962, U.S. Dist. Ct. Minn. 1963, U.S. Supreme Ct. 1980. Assoc. Robins, Davis & Lyons, Mpls., 1962-67; prin. Gurstel & Gurstel, Mpls., 1967-97; pres. Marc Shawn, Inc., 1997—2003, Q, LLC, 2003—06, Q, Boutique, 2007—. Arbitrator Hennepin County Dist. Ct., 1988-91; parttime referee family ct. Hennepin County Dist.; lectr. U. Minn. Family Law Seminar. Mem. ABA (corp. banking and bus. law and family law sects.), Minn. Bar Assn. (co-chmn. family ct. com. bankruptcy law sect. 1966-67, family law and bankruptcy law), Hennepin County Bar Assn. (chmn. family law com. 1964-65, vice chmn. 1981-91, fee arbitration bd., creditors remedy com.), Fed. Bar Assn., Assn. Trial Lawyers Am., Minn. Trial Lawyers Assn., Am. Acad. Matrimonial Lawyers, Nat. Council Juvenile and Family Ct. Judges, Comml. Law League Am. (recording sec. 1980-81, bd. govs. 1983-89, pres. 1987-88), Comml. Law League Fund for Pub. Edn. (sec. 1981-83, pres. 1989-92, bd. dirs. 1989-94), Phi Delta Phi. Clubs: Oak Ridge Country (Mpls.). Lodges: Shriners, Masons. Jewish. Office Phone: 952-465-0100. E-mail: norman@qfashions.com.

GURTIN, MORTON EDWARD, mathematics professor; b. Jersey City, Mar. 7, 1934; children: Amy Lynn, William Robert. B.M.E., Rensselaer Poly. Inst., 1955; PhD, Brown U., 1961; PhD in Civil Engring. (hon.), U. Rome, 1994. Structures engr. Douglas Aircraft Co., 1955-56, Gen. Electric Co., 1956-59; research asso. Brown U., 1961-62, asst. prof., 1962-64, assoc. prof., 1964-66; prof. math. Carnegie Mellon U., 1966—; alumni prof. math., 1992—. Sr. Fulbright-Hays fellow, Guggenheim fellow U. Pisa, Italy, 1974; lectr., Europe, South Am., Japan, Can; cons. to industry. Author: (with B.D. Coleman, I Herrera, and C. Truesdell) Wave Propagation in Dissipative Media, 1965, An Introduction to Continuum Mechanics, 1981, Thermomechanics of Evolving Phase Boundaries, 1993, Configurational Forces as Basic Concepts of Continuum Physics, 2000; assoc. editor Archive for Rational Mechanics and Analysis, Jour. Elasticity; contbr. articles to profl. jours., including Handbuch der Physik. Recipient Disting. Grad. Sch. Alumnus award Brown U., 1995, Agostinelli prize Acad. dei Lincei, Rome, 2001, Timoshenko medal ASME, 2004. Mem. Soc. Natural Philosophy, Sigma Xi. Office: Dept Math Carnegie-Mellon U Pittsburgh PA 15213

GURUDU, SURYAKANTH R., gastroenterologist, educator; Undergrad., Siddhartha Med. Coll., Vijayawada, India; MD, Robertwood Johnson Med. Sch., New Brunswick, NJ, 2000. Diplomate Am. Bd. Internal Medicine, 2000, Am. Bd. Gastroenterology and Hepatol, 2000. Asst. prof. medicine Mayo Clinic Ariz., Scottsdale, 2003—. Mem.: Am. Coll. Gastroenterology. Office Phone: 480-301-6990. E-mail: suryakanthgurudu@yahoo.com.

GURVICH, VICTOR ALEXANDER, physicist, engineer; b. Moscow, Dec. 24, 1951; s. Alexander and Galina (Shtykanova) G.; m. Irina Makarova, Apr. 29, 1988; children: Marina, Yury. MSME, Moscow Inst. Electronics, 1974; PhD in Med. Engring., Inst. of Med. Devices, Moscow, 1986. Engr. Russian Rsch. Inst. for Light Engring., Moscow, 1974-77; chief lab. x-ray image intensifiers Mosroentgen, Inc., Moscow, 1977-92; gen. mgr. Alvim R&D Ltd. at Shaare Zedec Med. Ctr., Jerusalem, 1993-98, Alvim R&D Ltd., Toronto, 1998—; SQA specialist MDS Sciex, Ont., Canada, 2000—02; med. physicist Windsor Regional Cancer Ctr., Ont., 2003—05, Aurora BayCare Med. Ctr., 2006—. Head project Min. Industry and Trade, Jerusalem, 1995—98; scientific sec. Mosroentgen, Inc., Moscow, 1982—92. Contbr. articles to profl. jours. Inventor State Com. on Discoveries and Inventions Affairs, 1986; silver medalist Exhbn. of Econ. Achievement, USSR, 1985; recipient diploma Internat. Tech. Exhbns. in Plovdiv, Bulgaria, 1985, and Leipzig, Germany, 1987. Mem. Am. Assn.

Physicists in Medicine, Russian Assn. Physicists in Medicine, N.Y. Acad. Scis., Israeli Assn. New Entrepreneurs. Achievements include patents in field. Avocations: tourism, guitar, poetry. Personal E-mail: vigurvich@yahoo.com.

GURWITCH, ARNOLD ANDREW, communications executive; b. Hamburg, Germany, Jan. 29, 1925; came to U.S., 1946; s. Max and Bertha Ida (Schereschevsky) G.; m. Barbara Anne Guthrie, July 21, 1961; children: Laurence Andrew, Sara Anne. Student, U. Basle, Switzerland, 1943-46; LLB, Bklyn. Law Sch., 1955. Bar: N.Y. Resident atty. Leeds Music Corp., NYC, 1956-60; ptnr. Rosen, Seton and Sarbin, NYC, 1960-64; internat. rep. ASCAP, NYC, 1964-74, head fgn. dept., 1974-78, fgn. mgr., 1978-89, dir. internat. rels., 1989-94, cons. internat. rels., 1995-96. Editor: Guide to Jazz, 1956. V.p., bd. dirs. Statesmen of Jazz, Ltd. Mem. N.Y. State Bar Assn., Copyright Soc. U.S.A. Office Phone: 914-834-4625.

GUSEH, JAMES SAWALLA, public administration educator; b. Zenalomai, Liberia, Dec. 5, 1951; s. Abraham Massawalla and Sonie Kennedy; m. Thelma Amy Broderick, Mar. 3, 1984; children: Sawalla J., Sonie K., Nahsan S. BA in Econs., Brandeis U., 1976; MS in Econs., U. Oreg., 1977; JD, Syracuse U., 1980, MPA in Pub. Adminstrn., 1980; PhD in Polit. Economy, U. Tex.-Dallas, Richardson, 1991. Counsellor-at-law, Republic of Liberia. Legal advisor, economist Ministry of Fin. Republic of Liberia, Monrovia, 1980-83, asst. atty. gen. Ministry of Justice, 1983-87; asst. prof. SUNY, Fredonia, 1991-92; asst. prof., dir. Shaw U., Raleigh, NC, 1992-97; assoc. prof. pub. adminstrn. N.C. Ctrl. U., Durham, 1997-2000, asst. interim dir. pub. adminstrn. program, 1999—, assoc. prof., 2000—. Rsch. fellow U. Tex., Dallas, 1990-91; Legal adv. and Economist Ministry fin.Liberia; asst. Minister Justice econ. Affairs-Commercial trans. Ministry Justice. Mem. editl. bd. African Social Sci. Rev., 1998—; contbr. articles to profl. jours. Mem. legis. com. Kannapolis (N.C.) C. of C., 1996-97; proposal reviewer Gov.'s Commn. on Nat. and Com. Svc., Raleigh, 1999. Wien Internat. scholar, 1973-76. Mem. ASPA, Policy Studies Orgn., Liberian Studies Assn. (bd. dirs.), Conf. Minority Pub. Adminstrs., Assn. Third World Studies. Avocations: soccer, basketball, swimming, writing. Office: NC Ctrl U Dept Pub Admins rn Durham NC 27707 Business E-Mail: jguseh@wpo.nccu.edu. E-mail: guseh@juno.com.

GUSEWELLE, CHARLES WESLEY, journalist, writer; b. Kansas City, July 22, 1933; s. Hugh L. and Dorothy (Middleton) G.; m. Katie Jane Ingels, Apr. 17, 1966; children— Anne Elizabeth, Jennifer Sue. BA in English, Westminster Coll., 1955; LHD (hon.), Park Coll., 1990. Reporter Kansas City (Mo.) Star, 1955-66, editorial writer of fgn. affairs, 1966-76, fgn. editor, 1976-79, asso. editor, columnist, 1979—. Author: A Paris Notebook, 1985, An Africa Notebook, 1986, Quick as Shadows Passing, 1988, Far from Any Coast, 1989, A Great Current Running, 1995, The Rufus Chronicle, 1996, A Buick in the Kitchen, 2000, On the Way to Other Country, 2001, Another Cat at the Door, 2004, A Little Christmas Music, 2006; contbr. short stories to Brit., Am. lit. quars.; writer, narrator, host: A Great Current Running, 1995, This Place Called Home (Regional Emmy 1998), Water and Fire: A Story of the Ozarks, 2000, Stories Under the Stone, 2005. 1st lt. AUS, 1956-58. Recipient Aga Khan prize for fiction, 1977, Thorpe Menn Lit. award, 1989; inducted Writers Hall of Fame, 2000, Mo. Press Assn. Newspaper Hall of Fame. Home: 1245 Stratford Rd Kansas City MO 64113-1325 Office: 1729 Grand Ave Kansas City MO 64108-1413 Office Phone: 816-333-0994.

GUSKEY, THOMAS ROBERT, education educator; b. Johnstown, Pa., Feb. 15, 1950; s. Robert C. and Evelyn M. (Yarnick) G. BA, Thiel Coll., 1972; MEd, Boston Coll., 1975; PhD, U. Chgo., 1979. Tchr. St. Andrew's Sch., Erie, Pa., 1972-74; rsch. asst. Boston Coll., Chestnut Hill, Mass., 1974-75; teaching asst. U. Chgo., 1975-78; rsch. cons. Chgo. Bd. Edn., 1975-76, dir. R&D, 1976-78; dir. rsch. Ctr. for Improvement of Teaching, Chgo., 1980-82; asst. prof. edn. U. Ky., Lexington, 1978—81, assoc. prof., 1981—85, prof., 1985—. Chmn. dept. edn. policy studies and evaluation U. Ky., Lexington, 1995-96; vis. prof. various colls. and univs.; cons. edn. systems. Author: Implementing Mastery Learning, 1985, 2d edit., 1997, Improving Student Learning, 1988, High Stakes Performance Assessment, 1994, (with J. Block and S. Everson) School Improvement Programs, 1995, (with M. Huberman) Professional Development in Education, 1995, Communicating Student Learning, 1996, (with J. Block and S. Everson) Comprehensive School Reform: A Program Perspective, 1999, Evaluating Professional Development, 2000, (with J. Bailey) Implementing Student-Led Conferences, 2001, (with Bailey) Developing Grading and Reporting Systems for Student Learning, 2001, How's My Kid Doing? A Parents' Guide to Grades, Marks, and Report Cards, 2002, Benjamin S. Bloom: Portraits of an Educator, 2006; editor Elem. Sch. Jour., 1990—, Focus on Learning, 1996—, Ednl. Measurement: Issues and Practice, 1997—, NASSP Bull., 2005—. Named to Outstanding Young Men of Am., 1981; Ky. Col., 1994; recipient U. Ky. Wethington award, 2004, 05, Disting. Alumnus award Thiel Coll., 2005. Mem. APA, ASCD, Am. Ednl. Rsch. Assn. (Outstanding Contbns. Relating Rsch. to Practice award 2006), Am. Evaluation Assn., Nat. Soc. for Study of Edn., Nat. Staff Devel. Coun. (Article of Yr. award 1996, 99, 2002, Book of Yr. award 1996, 2002, Best Non-Disseration Rsch. Award, 2003), Nat. Coun. on Measurement in Edn., Phi Delta Kappa. Home: 2108 Shelton Rd Lexington KY 40515-1170 Office: U Ky Coll Edn 145 Taylor Edn Bldg Lexington KY 40506-0001 Office Phone: 859-257-8666. Business E-Mail: guskey@uky.edu.

GUSKIN, ALAN E., university president; b. Bklyn., Mar. 22, 1937; s. David N. and Frances (Midler) G.; m. Lois La Shell, 1990; children from previous marriage: Sharon, Andrea. BA with honors, Bklyn. Coll., 1958; PhD, U. Mich., 1968; LHD (hon.), Saybrook Inst., 1989, Antioch U., 1997. Instr., Peace Corps. vol. Chulalongkorn U., Thailand, 1961-64; dir. of selection VISTA, 1964-65; asst. dir. Ctr. for Research on the Utilization of Scientific Knowledge, Inst. for Social Research, 1968-69; lectr. dept. of psychology and residential coll. U. Mich., 1968-71, dir. ednl. change team, Sch. of Edn., 1969-71, assoc. prof. edn., 1971; provost Clark U., Worcester, Mass., 1971-73, acting pres., 1973-74, prof. sociology and edn., 1973-75; chancellor, prof. edn. U. Wis.-Parkside, Kenosha, 1975-85; pres., prof. Antioch Coll. and Antioch U., Yellow Springs, Ohio, 1985-94; chancellor, Disting. univ. prof. Antioch U., 1994-97, disting. prof., 1997—. Author: (with Samuel Guskin) A Social Psychology of Education, 1970; editor New Directions on Teaching and Learning, The Administrator's Role in Effective Teaching, 1981, Notes From A Pragmatic Idealist: Selected Papers of Alan E. Guskin 1985-1997, 1997, (with Barbara Leigh Smith and Mary Marcy) Learning Communities and Fiscal Reality: Optimizing Learning in a Time of Restricted Budgets, 2004; contbr. numerous articles and reports to profl. jours Chmn. bd. Coun. on Adult and Experiential Learning, 1993-95; mem. bd. trustees Wilkes U., 2003-07, Westminister Coll., Salt Lake City, 2003-; mem. nat. adv. com., Ctr. for Accelerated Learning, Regis U., 2000-07; bd. advisors, US Public Svc. Acad., 2006-. Recipient Morris T. Keeton award, Coun. Adult and Experiential Learning, 2001. Business E-Mail: aguskin@antioch.edu.

GUSKOV, SERGEY, security firm executive; b. Moscow, Aug. 31, 1973; BS in Engring. and Econs. with honors, Moscow Aviation Inst., 1995; MBA, U. Pa., 2000. Sr. auditor KPMG, Moscow, 1995—98, Leeds, England, 1998; assoc., mgmt. consulting A.T. Kearney, New York, NY, 2000—01; mgr. bus. analysis Brink's Inc., Darien, Conn., 2001—. Investment banking summer assoc. CIBC World Markets, NYC, 1999. Co-author: (study book) Securities, 1998. Co-founder, v.p. Russian Digital Alliance, Washington, 2001—03.

GUSSOW, SUE FERGUSON, artist, educator; b. Bklyn., Aug. 2, 1935; d. Samuel Nathan and May (Sheinin) Shapiro; m. Donald L. Gerard, Jan. 10, 1999. Student, Bklyn. Mus., 1956-57; Diploma in Fine and Graphic Arts, The Cooper Union, 1956; BS, Columbia U., 1960; MFA, Tulane U., 1964. Prof. The Cooper Union Sch. of Architecture, NYC, 1970—2005, prof. emerita, 2003—. Asst. adj. prof. in painting and drawing NYU, 1973-81; assoc. adj. prof. dept. painting and sculpture, Columbia U., 1977-79; vis. asst. prof. in printmaking Manhattanville Coll., Purchase, N.Y., summer 1971; assoc. prof. printmaking Alfred U., summer 1971, others; vis. prof. The Frick Coll., 2002-2005; Pamela Djerassi Artist-in-Residence, Stanford (Calif.) U., 1982-83; vis. juror Yale U., 1987, 88, Newspapce Gallery, Wilkinson Pl., New Orleans, 1977. Work exhibited in Cooper-Hewitt Mus./Smithsonian Inst., NYC, Dalls Mus. Fine Arts, Seattle Art Mus., New Orleans Mus. Art, New Orleans Jazz Mus., Phila. Free Libr., Mus. Modern Art, NYC, others; one-woman shows include New Orleans Mus. Art, 1966, Loyola Marymount U., LA, 1983, Stanford U. Mus. Gallery, Calif., 1983, Marcelle Fine Arts, Southhampton, NY, 1989, 90, Hall of the Journalists, St. Petersburg, Russia, 1992, Window/Rm., Tokyo, 40-Yr. Retrospective at Houghton Gallery, Cooper Union, 1997, Houghton Gallery, Cooper Union, NY, 1997, others; represented in the pvt. collection of Dore Ashton, Eero Saarinen's C.B.S. Bldg., Van Deren Coke, Morley Safer, George and Mary Schmidt Campbell, others; work featured in 100 New York Painters, 2006. Recipient scholarships Parsons Sch. Design, 1952, Pratt Inst., 1952-53, Bklyn. Mus., 1956-57, Columbia U., 1956-60, Tulane U., 1962-63; fellowships Columbia U., 1961, Tulane U., 1963-64; recipient purchase prizes The St. Paul (Minn.) Art Ctr., 1966, 1965 Artists of La., 1965, Isaac Delgado Mus., New Orleans, 1965, SUNY, Potsdam, 1964, Olivet (Mich.) Coll. Festival of the Arts, 1963-64, others; recipient jurors spl. mention Ark. Art Ctr., Little Rock, 1964, 1st prize Dallas Mus. Fine Art, 1964. Home Phone: 631-267-8016; Office Phone: 212-219-8154.

GUSTAFSON, ALICE FAIRLEIGH, lawyer; b. Houston, Dec. 1, 1946; d. William H. and Mary Davis (McCord) Bell; m. Charles R. Gustafson, May 30, 1971. BA in Econs., Wellesley Coll., Mass., 1968; JD, U. Puget Sound, 1976. Bar: Wash. 1976. Various positions U.S. Dept. HEW, various locations, 1968-75; assoc. Graham & Dunn, Seattle, 1977-83, ptnr., 1983—. Bd. dirs. King County Am. Cancer Soc., Seattle, 1983-85, Women & Bus., Inc., Seattle, 1984-87; mem. nominating com. YWCA Seattle-King County, 1985-88. Mem. ABA, Wash. State Bar Assn. (chair Bench-Bar-Press com. 1988-90), Seattle-King County Bar Assn. (trustee young lawyers divsn. 1980-83, treas. 1985-87), N.W. Comm. Lawyers, Met. Seattle Urban League (bd. dirs. 1991-93). Avocations: sailing, bicycling, skiing. Home: PO Box 2127 Bothell WA 98041-2127

GUSTAFSON, CRAIG THOMAS, theater director, playwright, graphics designer; b. Oak Park, Ill., Aug. 26, 1958; s. Eric O. and Mary Louise (Howlett) G.; m. Marjorie L. Weitzenfeld, July 11, 1998. Student, Second City, Chgo., 1978; AA, Coll. DuPage, 1979. Board operator Wells Fargo Alarm, Elmhurst, Ill., 1978-81; ops. employee Coll. DuPage, Glen Ellyn, 1981—. Prodr., dir. Ad Hoc Theatre Co., Lisle, Ill., 1986-89; dir., writer The Summer Place, Naperville, Ill., 1989-96, Village Theatre Guild, Glen Ellyn; dir., composer, graphic artist Wheaton (Ill.) Drama, Inc., 1990—; artistic dir. Top Banana, Oakbrook Terrace, Ill., 1997-99; v.p., dir., composer, graphic artist First St. Playhouse, Batavia, Ill., 2002-; actor, dir., prodr., composer, choreographer, others, Village Players, Oak Park, Ill., 1995, West Suburban Players, Villa Park, Ill., 1996-98, Music On Stage, Palatine, Ill., 2001, Village Theatre of Palatine, 2002. Actor: The Foreigner, The House of Blue Leaves, Chicago, Bobby Gould in Hell, Rumors, Waiting for Godot, The Fantasticks, Twelfth Night; dir.: Assassins, Luv, Lucky Stiff, Lend Me a Tenor, The Odd Couple, Tartuffe, A Funny Thing Happened on the Way to the Forum, Nunsense, Mingle, Among the Demons; writer, performer (with Joy Kenyon) Tongues and Animal Crackers, Vic Theatre, Chgo., 1992. Named Funniest Person in Chgo., Chgo. Sun-Times, 1981, Best Cmty. Prodn. for "The Nerd," Acad. Theatre Artists and Friends, Chgo., 1996. Mem. Sons of the Desert (vice-shiek 1994-95). Democrat. Avocations: studying history of comedy, irritating conservatives.

GUSTAFSON, DAVID HAROLD, industrial engineering and preventive medicine educator; b. Kane, Pa., Sept. 11, 1940; s. Harold Edward and Olive Albertina (McKalip) G.; m. Rea Corina Anagnos, June 23, 1962; children: Laura Lynn, Michelle Elaine, David Harold BS in Indsl. Engring., U. Mich., 1962, MS in Indsl. Engring, 1963, PhD, 1966. Dir. hosp. div. Community Systems Found., Ann Arbor, Mich., 1961-64; asst. prof. indsl. engring. U. Wis.-Madison, 1966-70, assoc. prof., 1970-74, prof., 1974—, Robert A. Ratner prof. indsl. engring. $D, 2000—, dir., founder Ctr. for Health Systems and Analysis, 1974—, chmn. dept. indsl. engring., 1984-88, adminstrv. com. Grad. Sch., 1995-98, mem. athletic bd., 2000—; sr. analyst Dec. and Designs Inc., McLean, Va., 1974. Dir. rsch. Govt. Health Policy Task Force, State of Wis., 1969-71; prin. cons. Medicaid Mgmt. Study Team, 1977-78; prin. investigator Nursing Home Quality Assurance System, 1979, Computer System for Adolscent Health Promotion, 1983, Computer System to Support Breast Cancer and People with AIDS, 1993; vis. prof. London Sch. Econs., 1983, Harvard U., 1999; developer computer-based support to measure and improve health care quality; chair Fed. Sci. Panel on Interactive Comms. in Health; dir. TECC Ctr. for Excellence in Cancer Comms., 2004, Network for Improvement of Addiction Treatment. Author: Group Techniques, 1975, Health Policy Analysis, 1992, Sustainability, 2005; contbr. articles to profl. jours. Adviser conflict resolution Luth. Ch., 1973-79; active numerous civic orgns. Recipient numerous grants, 1968—, Ragnar Onstad award for cmty. svc., 1990. Fellow Assn. for Health Svcs. Rsch., Inst. for Health Care Improvement (bd. dirs. 1990—), Am. Med. Informatics Assn.; mem. Inst. Indsl. Engring., Ops. Rsch. Soc., Med. Decision Making Avocations: jogging, guitar, water sports, cross country skiing, parenting. Office: U Wis Ctr Health Systems 610 Walnut St Madison WI 53705-2336

GUSTAFSON, DEBORAH ANN, mathematics educator; b. Dec. 9, 1955; BA in Math. and Edn., St. Olaf Coll., Northfield, Minn., 1978; MEd in Math. Edn., U. Minn., Mpls., 1984. Cert. tchr. secondary Ga., tchr. gifted Ga. Tchr. math. Lakeville Mid. Sch., Minn., 1978—79, Prior Lake HS, 1979—84, Etowah HS, Woodstock, Ga., 1984—, dept. head, 2004—, lead tchr. algebra II, 1984—2000, lead tchr. algebra I, 1984—2002, 2004—06. Coach JV math team Etowah HS, 2003—04; advisor Mu Alpha Theta, Woodstock, 2003—04; organizer Am. Math. Competition, Woodstock, 2005—. Contbr. articles to profl. jours. Finalist Educator of Yr., Bell South, 2004; nominee Presdl. award Excellence in Sci. and Math., 1986, 1989, 2007; named Tchr. of Yr. Etowah HS, Cherokee Edn. Assn., 1991, Tchr. of Month, Etowah HS, 1995, 2004, 2006; recipient Outstanding Young Educator award, 1985; scholar, Tandy Tech., 1992. Mem.: NEA, Cherokee Edn. Assn. (rep. Etowah HS chpt. 1984—2004), Ga. Assn. Educators, Nat. Coun. Tchrs. Math. Achievements include development of project work utilizing TI Interactive software. Mailing: 110 Spruce Ct Lake Arrowhead Station 1101 Waleska GA 30183 Business E-Mail: deborah.gustafson@cherokee.k12.ga.us.

GUSTAFSON, JOHN ALFRED, biology professor; b. Boston, Mar. 31, 1925; s. Walter Alfred and Lilly Christine (Anderson) Gustafson; m. Nancy Gay Johnson, June 30, 1951; children: Walter A., Laura E., Paul E.(dec.), Daniel D., Martha E., J. Olaf. AB, Dartmouth, 1948; PhD, Cornell U., 1954. Asst. prof. biology State U. N.Y. Coll., Brockport, 1954-55, asst. prof. biology Cortland, 1955-57, asso. prof. biology, 1957-63, prof. biology, 1963-81, chmn. dept. biol. scis., 1965-77; project dir. NSF Grant for Outdoor Sci. Edn., 1980-82. Participant NSF Inst., 1962; pres. Alliance for Environ. Edn., 1974; mem. Temporary State Commn. on Youth Edn. in Conservation, N.Y., 1969-73; owner, pub. Slingerland-Comstock Co., 1976—. Author: (with B.A. Hall) Laboratory Studies in Botany, 1960; Editor: Nature Study, Jour. Environ. Edn. and Interpretation, 1965-79, Alliance Exchange, 1975-76. Chmn. Town of Homer Zoning Bd., NY, 1959-69, Town of Homer Planning Bd., 1969-75; chmn. Homer Plan Rev. Com., 2001-02, vice chmn. Eastern Susquehanna Water Resources Bd., 1969-76; pres. Highvista Nature Center, Inc., 1973-92; mem. Labrador Hollow Unique Area Adv. Coun., 1978—; chmn. Cortland County Environ. Mgmt. Coun., 1980-82, Cortland County Anderson-Lucey campaign, 1980; mem. bd. edn. Homer Cen. Sch. Dist., 1982-88; treas. Pocono Environ. Edn. Ctr., 1988-91, Lime Hollow Nature Ctr., 1992—; Cortland County rep. to open space com. NY State, Region 7, 1996-2004; bd. dirs. Iroquois Assn., Am. Baptist Chs., 1986-89, 97-2004, moderator, 1987; pres. Cortland County Council of Chs., 1986-89; adminstr. 1st Bapt. Ch., Homer, NY, 1990-94, treas., 1995-99, bd. elders, 2001-02, bd. deacons, 2002-03, dir. visitation, 2003-04; steering com. NY State Grazing Lands Conservation Initiative, 1997—. Served with USMCR, 1943-46, 51-53. Recipient Taft Campus award No. Ill. U., 1989, Griffith-Balcom Leadership award Am. Bapt. Chs., 1998. Fellow AAAS (coun. 1968-73); mem. Am. Nature Study Soc. (pres. 1962-63, treas. 1964-75, 79-97, Disting. Svc. award 1969, John Gustafson award for exemplary svc., 1995), Nature Conservancy (dir., treas., chmn. ctrl. N.Y. chpt., chmn. N.Y. State bd. dirs. 1983-87, vice chmn., ctrl/western N.Y. chpt. 1994-96, Oak Leaf award 1984), Phi Delta Kappa. Republican. Baptist. Home: 5881 Cold Brook Rd Homer NY 13077-9709 *As I think back over my life, I am impressed by the evidence that God, through my commitment to him, has given guidance and direction at those times when crucial decisions were made. So often what seemed at the time to be a relatively insignificant decision turned out to have been a key turning point. It is God's Spirit within me, and his love and concern, that gives meaning to what I do.*

GUSTAFSON, MARDEL EMMA, secondary school educator, writer; b. Waukesha, Wis., June 10, 1922; d. Otto Robert and Emma Bertha (Steffan) Hoppe; m. Wayne Carroll Gustafson, Nov. 1, 1950; children: Faith, Keith, Richard, Wayne, John, Beverly. BS in Edn., U. Wis., Madison, 1946. Sec. Waukesha Motor Co., 1944—45, Wis. Gen. Hosp., Madison, 1945—46; tchr. Hannibal HS, Wis., 1946—49, St. John Pub. Sch., ND, 1949—50. Author: What Is Happening To Our Children? How to Raise Them Right, 1993, Why A Role Mother?, 2001, All My Love, 2001, Don't Do It: Sex: If You Are Not Married, 2007. Mem.: Wis. Alumni Assn., TOPS Club (sec. 1978—83). Lutheran. Avocations: sewing, knitting, crocheting, gardening, walking. Home: W289 S2915 County Rd DT Waukesha WI 53188-9581 Office Phone: 262-968-4565. Personal E-mail: waynemardel@aol.com.

GUSTAFSON, RICHARD ALRICK, retired university president; b. Peekskill, NY, May 15, 1941; s. Richard Alrick Sr. and Faye Alice (Jones) G.; m. Joanne Marie Walters, Sept. 5, 1964; children: Richard III., Peter. AB in Biology and Chemistry, Boston U., 1963, MEd in Sci. Edn., 1964; PhD in Statistics and Measurement, U. Conn., 1970; attended, Harvard Inst. Ednl. Mgmt., 1982; MEd in TESOL, Notre Dame Coll., 1997. Tchr. sci. Newtown (Conn.) Pub. Sch., 1964-65; tchr. chemistry Greenwich (Conn.) Pub. Schs., 1965-68; rsch. specialist Ctr. for Planning and Evaluation, San Jose, Calif., 1970-71; dir. mgmt. svcs. New Eng. Resource Ctr. for Occupl. Edn., Newton, 1971-73; asst. dean career studies Keene (N.H.) State Coll., 1973-78, assoc. dean acad. affairs, 1978-81, v.p. acad. affairs, 1981-87; pres. So. N.H. U. (formerly N.H. Coll.), Manchester, 1987—2003, pres. emeritus, 2003—; interim pres. NH Cmty.-Tech. Coll., Manchester, 2005—06. Bd. dirs. Optima Health, 1997-98. Bd. dirs. Keene Family YMCA, 1975-80, Cheshire Med. Ctr., Keene, 1986-88, Federated Arts., 1989-92, Leadership Manchester., 1989-91, Hillcrest Terr., 1991-93, Elliot Hosp., 1999—, vice chmn., 2005—; bd. dirs. Manchester United Way, 1990-97, chmn., 1993; vice chair N.H. Tuition Savs. Plan Commn., 1997—2003; mem. ops. com. Forum for Higher Edn. in N.H., 2000-03; bd. dirs. N.H. Symphony Orch., 2003-06, AAA No. New Eng., 2000—, Friends of Valley Cemetery, 2003-. Recipient Granite State award, 2000; Augustus Howe Buck scholar Boston U., 1960-62; named Manchester Citizen of Yr., 2003; Fulbright sr. rsch. fellow, Thailand, 1999. Mem. Am. Vocat. Assn. (Svc. award 1980), Nat. Assn. Ind. Colls. and Univs. (bd. dirs. 1991-94), N.H. Coll. and U. Coun. (bd. dirs. 1987-03, chmn. 1995-97), N.H. Postsecondary Edn. Commn. (chmn. 1994-96, bd. dirs. 1987-04), Hellenic-Am. U. (bd. trustees 2004-, vice chair 2004-) Greater Manchester C. of C. (bd. dirs. 1990-97, chmn. 1996), Rotary (bd. dirs. Keene 1985-87). Episcopalian. Avocations: skiing, tennis. Office Phone: 603-645-9688. Business E-Mail: r.gustafson@snhu.edu.

GUSTAFSON, ROBERT ALLEN, pediatric cardiothoracic surgeon; b. Keyser, W.Va., Dec. 6, 1950; s. Oscar Harold and Jacqueline (Simmons) G.; m. Lisa Lynn, Aug. 11, 1973; children: Ashley Lynne, Lindsey Michelle, Jeffrey Andrew. AA, Potomac State Coll., 1970; BA, W.Va. U., 1972, MD, 1976. Diplomate Am. Bd. Surgery, Am. Bd. Thoracic Surgery. Intern in gen. surgery W. Va. U. Med. Ctr., Morgantown, W. Va., 1976, asst. resident in gen. surgery, 1977-80, chief resident in gen. surgery, 1980-81, fellow in thoracic surgery, 1981-83; fellow pediatric cardiothoracic surgery Boston Children' Hosp., Boston, 1983; chief pediatric cardiac surgery W.Va. U., Morgantown, 1984—, asst. prof. surgery, 1984-87, assoc. prof. surgery and pediatrics, 1987-94, prof. surgery and pediatrics, 1994—; surgeon-in-chief W. Va. U. Children's Hosp., Morgantown, 1997—, Children's Hosp. W.Va. U., 1997—. Vis. prof. Allegheny Gen. Hosp., Pitts., 1988, 1995, Johns Hopkins U., 1990. Manuscript reviewer Annals of Thoracic Surgery, 1990—, Jour. of Thoracic and Cardiovascular Surgery, 1995—; contbr. articles to profl. jours. Participating surgeon Internat. Rotary Club Gift of Life Project, N.Y.C., 1985—. Recipient Presdl. award So. Thoracic Surg. Assn., 1988, Alumni Achievement award Potomac State Coll., 1990, Innovation Achievement award W.Va. Univ. Hosp., 1994, High Performance Leadership award, 1998, Miracle Maker award Children's Miracle Network, 1996. Fellow ACS, Am. Acad. Pediatrics; mem. AMA, Am. Assn. Thoracic Surgery, W.Va. Chpt. ACS (state councilor 1990-94, 96-99), W.Va. Med. Assn. (program com. 1991-97), Monongalia County Med. Soc., Southeastern Surg. Congress, Internat. Soc. Pediatric Cardiovascular Surgery, So. Thoracic Surg. Assn., Soc. Thoracic Surgeons, Surg. Sect. Am. Acad. Pediatrics, Lunar Soc. for Congenital Heart Surgery, W.Va. Chpt. Am. Acad. Pediatric, Am. Heart Assn., ARC, Am. Cancer Soc., Habitat for Humanity, Interplast, Inc., Cousteau Soc., Nature Conservancy, W.Va. Audubon Soc., Project Hope, W.Va. Spl. Olympics Inc. Republican. Methodist. Avocations: golf, tennis, travel. Office: W Va U Sch Medicine Dept Surgery PO Box 9238 Morgantown WV 26506-9238 Home: 26 Miramichi Trl Morgantown WV 26508

GUSTAFSON, SALLY ANN, counselor, cosmetologist, educator; b. Olympia, Wash., Sept. 21, 1947; d. Thomas Buchanan and Dorothy May (Long) Ness; m. Douglas Carl Gustafson, Oct. 2, 1967; children: Troy Douglas, Tristan Suzan. Cert. cosmetologist, Mr. Roberts Beauty Coll., Tacoma, Wash., 1966; cert. counselor, Maranatha Inst., Oakley, Calif., 1994. Cosmetology instr. Calif. Beauty Coll., Pleasant Hill, 1969-70; mgr. Jafra Cosmetics, Antioch, Calif., 1970-84; cosmetologist J.C. Penney, Antioch, Calif., 1991—; counselor Pittsburg Christian Assembly, Calif., 1994—. Avocations: arts, crafts, tennis, camping, skiing. Office: Pittsburg Christian Ctr 1210 Stoneman Ave Pittsburg CA 94565-5458 Personal E-mail: sallyagus@yahoo.com.

GUSTAFSON, SETH, lawyer; b. 1970; BA, Pomona Coll., 1993; JD, Univ. Calif., Boalt Hall Sch. Law, 1999. Bar: Calif. 1999, Wash. 2002. Assoc. atty. Buck and Gordon LLP, Seattle. Contbr. articles to numerous profl. jours. Named Wash. Rising Star, SuperLawyer Mag., 2006. Mem.: ABA, King Co. Bar Assn., Wash. State Bar Assn. Office: Buck and Gordon Ste 500 2025 First Ave Seattle WA 98121-3140

GUSTAFSSON, LARS ERIK EINAR, writer, educator; b. Västerås, Sweden, May 17, 1936; came to U.S., 1983; s. Einar H. and Lotten Margaretha (Carlson) G.; m. D. Alexandra Chasnoff, 1982 (div. 2002); children: Benjamin, Karen; m. Angela Bloomquist, 2005. PhD, Uppsala U., Sweden, 1978. Editor-in-chief Bonners Pub. House, Stockholm, 1961-72; rsch. fellow Ctr. Advanced Studies, Bielefeld, Germany, 1980-81; Aby Warburg rsch. prof. Warburg Found. U. Hamburg, Germany, 1997-98, Jammil disting. prof. emeritus, 2006—. Bd. dirs. Svenska Dagbladet Found.; bd. regents Uppsala (Sweden) U., 1994-97; adj. prof. U. Tex., Austin, 1983—; Jamail Disting. prof., 1998—, Michener Regents chair in writing, 2004; fellow Berlin Inst. for Advanced Study, 2004-2005. Author numerous novels and poetry collections. John Simon Guggenheim Meml. fellow of poetry, 1993. Mem. Acad. of Arts (Berlin), Acad. Scis. and Lit. (Mainz, Germany), Royal Swedish Acad. Engring. (Stockholm), Bavarian Acad. Fine Arts (Munich), German Acad. Lang. and Lit. Avocation: painting.

GUSTAFSSON, MARY E., lawyer; b. 1960; m. John Gustafsson; 1 stepchild, Christopher. BA, Boston U., 1981; JD, U. Mich., 1989. Bar: NY 1992. Atty. Hubbard & Reed, NYC, 1989—96; various positions including chief mergers and acquisitions counsel, chief counsel Honeywell Internat. Inc. (formerly AlliedSignal Inc.), 1996—2001; chief corp. counsel Am. Standard Companies Inc., Piscataway, NJ, 2001—03, chief counsel Trane air conditioning systems & svc. unit, 2003—05, sr. v.p., gen. counsel, sec., 2005—. Office: Am Standard Cos Inc One Centennial Ave Piscataway NJ 08855-6820*

GUSTIN, BRENDA SUE, retired art educator, painter; b. Kenosha, Wis., July 22, 1949; d. Ralph Burt and Alene Margaret Robinson; m. John Julius Gustin, Mar. 25, 1972; children: Amy Beth Farr, John Andrew, Daniel Adam. BA, U. Wis. Parkside, Kenosha, 1971. Cert. unltd.life cert. State of Wis. Dept. Pub. Instrn., 1977, art tchr. grades K-8, secondary sch. tchr. grades 7-12. Art tchr. Kenosha Unified Sch. Dist. 1, 1974—2006, coord. art exhibit elem. children, 1991—2006; ret., 2006. Art coord., advertiser Animal Rehab. Kinship, Racine, Wis., 1987—91; coord. art exhibit Anderson Art Ctr., Kenosha, 2004, Bose Elem. Sch. Artist (exhibitions) local restaurants, Kenosha, 1969—71, U. Wis., Racine, Parkside Art Gallery, Kenosha, 1987, 1991, 1997, 1999—2000, 2005, Anderson Art Ctr.; permanent collection, Legacy Mus. and Vets. Ctr., Racine. Recipient Blue Ribbon, Kenosha County Fair, Wilmot, Wis., 1976, Cert. of Appreciation, Kenosha Unified Sch. Dist., 1999. Mem.: Kenosha County Ret. Educators Assn., Wis. Edn. Assn. Coun., Kenosha Edn. Assn., Kenosha Unified Twenty-Five Yr. Club. Independent. Lutheran. Avocations: collecting vintage dog figurines, travel, visiting Southwestern art galleries. Home: 1802 83rd St Kenosha WI 53143-1652

GUSTIN, CARL E., JR., manufacturing executive; Sr. v.p., dir. mktg. svcs. affiliates of Young & Rubicam; pres., gen. mgr. Doyle Dane Bernbach (Midwestern ops.); sr. v.p./ptnr. Doyle Dane Bernbach (regional agency); bus. develop. exec., southeast region Apple Computer, 1988, dir., sales, southern ops., exec. aide to chmn. & CEO, v.p., worldwide comm. and mktg. support; v.p., product and market strategy Digital Equipment Corp., 1994, v.p., computer systems divsn.; v.p. and gen. mgr., digital and applied imaging divsn. Eastman Kodak Co., Rochester, NY, 1994—95, acting pres., gen. mgr., digital and applied imaging divsn., 1995—96, sr. v.p., chief mktg. officer, 1995—. Mem., sr. exec. coun. Eastman Kodak Comp., Rochester, NY, chmn., corp. brand mgmt. coun., chmn., e-business mgmt. coun. Named Corp. Mktg. Exec. of Yr., Delaney Report, 1996, Top 50 marketers, Ad Age, 1996. Office: Eastman Kodak Co 343 State St Rochester NY 14650-0001*

GUSTIN, MARK DOUGLAS, healthcare executive; b. Bklyn. BS in Acctg., N.Y. Inst. Tech., 1969, MBA in Bus. Mgmt., 1973; M Profl. Studies, L.I. U., 1975; residency diploma in hosp. adminstrn., Kings County Hosp. Ctr., 1979; health care fin. mgmt. cert., Molloy Coll., 1993, elder care studies cert., 1994. Cert. Behavioral Healthcare Exec. 1983. Acct. Fass, Tuchler & Muster, NYC, 1969-74; asst. adminstr. Manhattan Kidney Ctr. Nat. Nephrology Found., Inc., NYC, 1974-76; adminstr. Carter Cmty. Health Ctr., Jamaica, NY, 1976-77; resident in hosp. adminstrn. Kings County Hosp. Ctr., N.Y.C. Health and Hosps. Corp., Bklyn., 1978-79, evening dir. (asst. dir.), 1979-80, assoc. dir., 1980-92, sr. assoc. dir., 1992—. Panel mem. surrogate decision making program N.Y. State Commn. on Quality of Care for the Mentally Disabled, 1993—; mem. Nat. Coun. Cmty. Behavioral Healthcare, 1999-2001, bd. dirs. 1999-2001; mem. bd. visitors LI Devel.Disabilities Svcs. Office, 2007-. Vol. Disaster Psychiatry Outreach, PC, 2004—. Fellow Am. Acad. Med. Adminstrs., Am. Coll. Healthcare Execs., Assn. Behavioral Healthcare Mgmt. (pres. N.Y. chpt. 1999-, adv. coun. chair 2000-01, adv. coun. mem. 2003-, Harold Piepenbrink award 2003), Am. Coll. Managed Care Adminstrs.; mem. Mental Health News (adv. coun. mem. 2002-), Mental Health Assn. in N.Y. State (bd. chair 2004-06, Caroline Cash award, 2004). Home: 32 Jasmine Ln Valley Stream NY 11581-2412 Office: Kings County Hosp Ctr 451 Clarkson Ave Brooklyn NY 11203-2097 Office Phone: 718-245-5674.

GUTEK, E(DWARD) PHILIP, plastic and reconstructive surgeon, educator; b. Wadena, Sask., Can., Jan. 1, 1941; came to U.S., 1970; s. Frank and Mary (Leia) G.; m. Donna Elaine Small, Aug. 29, 1975; children: Kristin Leigh, Brian Philip. BA, U. Sask., Can., 1963; MD, U. Sask., Sask., Can., 1967. Diplomate Am. Bd. Plastic Surgery. Intern St. Lukes Hosp., Kansas City, Mo., 1967-68; pvt. practice Wadena, 1968-70; gen. surgery residency St. Luke's Hosp., Kansas City, 1970-74; plastic surgery resident Kansas City Gen. Hosp., 1974-76; plastic surgeon Assoc. Plastic Surgeons, Kansas City, 1977—; assoc. clin. prof. Coll. Medicine U. Mo., Kansas City, 1977—. Mem. faculty plastic surgery dept. Truman Med. Ctr., Kansas City, 1991—. Fellow ACS (Mo. chpt.); mem. AMA, Am. Soc. Plastic and Reconstructive Surgeons, Am. Cleft Palate Soc., Am. Soc. Aesthetic Plastic Surgeons, Can. Soc. Plastic Surgeons, Midwestern Assn. Plastic Surgeons, Mo. State Med. Assn., Kansas City Plastic Surgery Soc., Met. Med. Soc. Greater Kansas City. Roman Catholic. Avocations: skiing, skating, fishing. Office: Associated Plastic Surgeons Town Ctr Bus Pk 11501 Granada Lane Leawood KS 66211 Office Phone: 913-451-3722.*

GUTEKUNST, RICHARD RALPH, retired microbiology professor; b. Allentown, Pa., Jan. 20, 1926; s. George D. and Jennie L. (Alsop) G.; m. Anna Frances Fetterman, Dec. 27, 1946; children: Mary Jane Ellickson, Richard M., Jo Anne Loughery. BS, Phila. Coll. Pharmacy and Sci., 1951; MS, Cornell U., 1957, PhD, 1958. Commd. ensign USN, advanced through grades to comdr., 1968; mem. faculty Hahnemann Med. Coll. and Hosp., Phila., 1968-80, prof. microbiology and immunology, 1974-80; dir. Clin. Micro Lab., 1968-75; dean Coll. Allied Health Professions, 1975-80, Coll. Health Related Professions; prof. dept. med. tech. and microbiology U. Fla., Gainesville, 1980-95; dean emeritus, 1995—. V.p. Lower Gwynedd (Pa.) Twp. Commrs., 1972-80; mem. coun. St. Peter's Luth. Ch., North Wales, Pa., 1972-77, pres., 1974-77; No. Ctrl. Fla. Regional Planning Coun., 1987-92; bd. dirs. Citizens' Crime Commn., Alachua County, 1984-88, vice-chmn., 1986-87; bd. dirs. United Way Alachua County, 1984-90, 98—, pres., 1988; bd. dirs. ARC of Alachua County, 1989-93; pres. Fla. Alliance of 100, Healthcare Manpower, 1988-90; mem. adv. bd. AIDS Inst., UF; mem. com. on pub. health FMA, 1986-95, mem. com. on allied health, 1991-94, mem. task force on nursing shortage, 1990-95; bd. dirs. DAYTOP Fla., 1996-98, chmn. 1998; bd. dirs. Phoenix Ho. of Fla., 1999-2005, chmn. 1999-2005. Served to rank of cmdr. USN, 1943—68. Recipient Lindback award, 1975; Faculty Achievement award Coll. Allied Health Professions; Faculty Achievement award Hahnemann Med. Coll. and Hosp., Phila., 1980, Navy Commendation medal. Fellow Am. Acad. Microbiology, Am. Soc. for Allied Health Professions (pres.-elect 1981-82, pres. 1982-83); mem. Assn. Practitioners Infection Control, Am. Soc. Microbiology, N.Y. Acad. Scis., Masons. Republican. Lutheran. Avocations: sports, softball, basketball. Office: U Health Sci Ctr PO Box 100014 Gainesville FL 32610-0014 Home Phone: 352-372-0331. Personal E-mail: rgutekunst@gator.net.

GUTENTAG, PATRICIA RICHMAND, social worker, family counselor, occupational therapist; b. Newark, Apr. 10, 1954; d. Joseph and Joan (Miller) Leflein; m. Herbert Norman Gutentag; children: Steven, Jesse. BS in Occupational Therapy, Tufts U., 1976; MSW, Boston Coll., 1979. Lic. family and marriage counselor, lic. clin. social worker, N.J.; diplomate Am. Bd. Examiners in Clin. Social Work; registered occupational therapist, N.J. Social worker Jewish Family Svc., Salem, Mass., 1979-82; pvt. practice family and marriage counselor Westfield and Red Bank, N.J., 1982—. Cons. high stress, Westfield and Red Bank, 1982—. Fellow N.J. Soc. for Clin. Social Work; mem. NASW, Am. Occupational Therapists Assn., Registered Occupational Therapists Assn., Soc. for Advancement Family Therapy in N.J., Am. Anorexia-Bulimia Assn., Am. Assn. Marriage and Family Therapy. Avocation: reading. Office: 200 Maple Ave Red Bank NJ 07701-1732

GUTFREUND, JOHN HALLE, investment company executive, consultant; b. NYC, Sept. 14, 1929; s. B. Manuel and Mary (Halle) G.; m. Joyce L. Gutfreund, Apr. 11, 1958 (div. July 18, 1980); children: Nicholas J., Joshua L., Owen David; Susan Kaposta Gutfreund, Feb. 5, 1981; 1 child, John Peter. BA, Oberlin Coll., 1951. Pres. Salomon Bros. Inc., NYC, 1953-91, Gutfreund & Co., Inc., NYC, 1993—2002; sr. advisor C.E. Unterberg, Towbin, NYC, 2002—. Chmn. bd., CEO Salomon Bros., Inc.; co-chmn. Phibro Corp., 1981-83; co-chief exec. officer, 1983-84, CEO, 1984-86, Phibro-Salomon Inc.; dir. AccuWeather, Inc., Nutrition 21, Inc., Evercel, Inc., LCA-Vision, Inc., Maxicare Health Plans, Inc., The Universal Bond Fund., Montefiore Med. Ctr., GVI Security Solutions, Inc.; mem. exec. com. of bd. trustees and fin. Real Estate Coms.; life mem., bd. trustees N.Y. Pub. Libr., Astor, Lenox, Tilden Found.; hon. trustee Oberlin (Ohio) Coll; trustee Aperture Found. Mem. Downtown Lower Manhattan Assn., Bond Club of N.Y. (past pres., mem. bd. govs.). Home: 834 Fifth Ave New York NY 10021 Office: CE Unterberg Towbin 350 Madison Ave New York NY 10017 Home Phone: 212-517-3455; Office Phone: 212-389-8287. E-mail: jgutfreund@unterberg.com.

GUTH, AMBER AZNIV, surgeon, educator; b. Glen Cove, NY, Aug. 14, 1957; BS summa cum laude, Queens Coll., 1979; MD, NYU, 1983. Resident gen. surgery NYU Med. Ctr., NYC, 1983-88, surgeon; attending physician Mt. Sinai Hosp., 1988—91, Tisch Hosp.-NYU, Bellevue Hosp. Assoc. prof. surgery NYU Sch. Medicine. Home: 300 E 33rd St Apt 1M New York NY 10016-9402

GUTH, CARYL JOY, retired anesthesiologist; b. Peoria, Ill., 1935; m. John Falstad, 1968 (dec. 2001). AA, Mars Hill Coll., 1955; BS, Wake Forest U., 1957, MD, 1962. Diplomate Am. Bd. Anesthesiology. Intern U. Kans. Med. Ctr., Kansas City, 1962-63; resident in anesthesiology U. Pa. Hosp., Phila., 1963-65; instr. dept. anesthesiology Wake Forest U. Bapt. Hosp., Winston-Salem, NC, 1965; fellow in anesthesiology Queen Victoria Hosp., Sussex, Eng., 1966; instr. U. Nijmegan, Netherlands, 1966; former chmn. dept anesthesiology Mills-Peninsula Hosps., San Mateo, Calif., ret.; ind. Nikken wellness cons., 1996—; holistic and integrative medicine physician San Mateo, 1998—2003, Advance, NC, 2003—. Mem. bd. sci. and policy advisors Am. Coun. Sci. and Health, 1995—. Bd. visitors Wake Forest U. Bapt. Med. Ctr., Winston-Salem, NC, 2004—. Recipient Crisp-Casey award for best female athlete, Wake Forest U., 1957. Mem. AMA, Am. Soc. Anesthesiology (del. 1976-2000, chair com. on comms. 1987-90, chair com. profl. diversity 1995-97, ann. meeting program organizer 1983-84, 87-88, 94, 97), Calif. Med. Assn. (chair com. splty. socs. 1983-84), Calif. Soc. Anesthesiology (past pres., editor bull. 1976-79, asst. treas. 1979-81, pres.-elect 1981-82, pres. 1982-83, Disting. Svc. award 2006), San Mateo County Med. Assn. (bd. dir. 1984-86, chair med. staff affairs com. 1985-86), Coy C. Carpenter Philanthropic Soc., Wake Forest U. Soc., Pres.'s Club Wake Forest U. (endowed WFU womens golf scholarship 2007—), Wake Forest U. Med. Alumni Assn. (bd. dir. 1999—, sec. 2003-04, pres.-elect 2004-05, pres. 2005-06, dean's leadership coun. 2006—). Achievements include established and endowed chair in holistic and integrative medicine Wake Forest U. Bapt. Med. Ctr., 2002. Home: 105 Willowbrook Pl Advance NC 27006-9480 Office Phone: 336-998-6112. Personal E-mail: cguth@triad.rr.com. Business E-Mail: imhealthy@cheerful.com.

GUTH, SHERMAN LEON (S. LEE), psychologist, educator; b. NYC; s. Arthur and Caroline (Laub) G.; children from previous marriage: Melissa, Victoria; m. Ling Zhao; 1 child, Lillian. BS, Purdue U., 1959; MA, U. Ill., 1961, PhD, 1963. Lectr. dept. psychology Ind. U., Bloomington, 1962-63, instr., 1963-64, asst. prof., 1964-67, assoc. prof., 1967-70, prof., 1970—; dir. research and grad. devel. Sch. Optometry, 1980-88, chmn. dept. visual scis., 1982-85. Vis. assoc. prof. psychology Mich. State U., 1968-69; NIH spl. research fellow in psychology U. Calif., Berkeley, 1971-72; NSF program dir. for sensory physiology and perception, 1977-78 NIH research grantee, 1964—70, NSF research grantee, 1963—86. Fellow Optical Soc. Am. Achievements include being the creator of the ATD model for visual adaption and color perception. Office: Ind U Dept Psychology Bloomington IN 47405 Business E-Mail: guth@indiana.edu.

GUTHART, LEO A., electronics executive; b. NYC, Sept. 26, 1937; s. Harry and Lillian (Singer) G.; m. Laura Carrol, June 16, 1960; children: Rebecca, Margaret. AB, Harvard U., 1958, MBA, 1960, D in Bus. Adminstrn., 1966. Rsch. assoc. Bus. Sch Harvard U., Boston, 1960-62; with Pittway Corp., 1963—, vice chmn. Chgo., 1988—; exec. v.p. Ademco divsn., Syosset, NY, 1963-71, pres., 1971-99; chmn., CEO Pittway Security Group, Syosset, 1999—; exec. v.p. Home and Bldg. Control, Honeywell Internat.; mng. ptnr. Topspin Ptnrs., LP, Roslyn Heights, NY, 2000—. Trustee, Hofstra Univ., Hempstead, N.Y., 1976—, chmn. bd. trustees, 1993-96; bd. dirs. Aptargroup, 1993-, Acorn Fund, 1994-2005, Symbol Technologies, L.I., 2000-04, Venture Fund; chmn. Cylink Corp., Sunnyvale, Calif., 1996-2004; chmn. Alarm Industry Rsch. and Edn. Found., 1997—. Contbr. articles to profl. jours. Fellow Ford Found., 1961; named Baker scholar, Harvard U., 1960. Mem. Harvard Club, Racquet Club, Beta Gamma Sigma (hon.). Avocation: tennis. Office: 3 Expressway Plz Roslyn Heights NY 11577-2045

GUTHEIL, IRENE A., social work educator, researcher; b. St. Louis, June 17, 1944; m. John Gordon Gutheil, June 9, 1968 (dec.); children: David Arthur, Robert Douglas. BA, Brandeis U., 1966; MS, Columbia U., 1968, D Social Welfare, 1988. Lic. social worker, N.Y. Psychiat. social worker Karen Horney Clinic, NYC, 1968-69; social work cons. New Rochelle (N.Y.) Nursing Home, 1973-76, 77-83, Westledge Extended Care Facility, Peekskill, NY, 1973-84; social worker Geriatric Assocs., Montefiore Med. Ctr., Bronx, NY, 1986; from adj. instr. to prof. Fordham U. Grad. Sch. Social Svc., NYC, 1982—2001, Henry C. Ravazzin prof. of gerontology, 2001—; dir. Ravazzin Ctr. Social Work Rsch. in Aging Fordham U., NYC, 1995—. Adj. instr. Mercy Coll., Dobbs Ferry, NY, 1981—83; human svcs. adv. bd, Actors Fund Am., NYC, 1989—92; rsch. adv. bd. Found. for Long Term Care, Albany, NY, 1997—2005; adv. bd. Health Advocates for Older People, NYC, 1998—; bd. dirs. Aging in Am. Cmty. Svcs., Bronx, Andrus on Hudson, Hastings, NY, Elder Craftsmen, NYC; disaster svcs. adv. com. ARC Greater NY, NYC, 2001—02. Contbr. chpts. to books; contbr. articles to profl. jours. Grantee Fordham U., 1991, Grotta Found., 1999, Fan Fox and Leslie R. Samuels Found., 1999, Philanthropic Group, 2000, John A. Hartford Found., 2002, Helen Andrus Benedict Found., 2002, 05, Fan Fox & Leslie R. Samuels Found., 2002, Atlantic Philanthropies, 2004. Fellow Gerontol. Soc. Am. (postdoctoral fellow 1989); mem. NASW, Coun. on Social Work Edn., Am. Soc. on Aging, Assn. for Gerontology in Social Work Edn., State Soc. on Aging NY (exec. bd. 1992-94, 98-99). Office: Fordham U Grad Sch Social Svc Neperan Rd Tarrytown NY 10591 Business E-Mail: gutheil@fordham.edu.

GUTHEINZ, JAMES O'LEARY, military officer, law clerk; b. Wuerzburg, Sept. 24, 1982; s. Joseph Richard Gutheinz Jr. and Lori Ann Gutheinz; m. Stephanie Hamm, Jan. 15, 2005. BA magna cum laude, U. St. Thomas, 2005; grad. US Army Adj. Gen. Officer Basic Course. Law clk. Law Office of Joseph R. Gutheinz, Jr., Houston, 1997—; cadet capt. Army ROTC, Houston, 2001—05; second lt., adj. gen. br. Tex. N.G., Ellington Field, 2003—; with USAR (Mobilized), 2005—. Author: Catholics in American Politics. ROTC scholarship, US Army, 2001 to 2003, Academic scholarship, U. of St. Thomas, 2001 to 2005, scholarship, Tex. N.G., 2003 to 2005. Mem.: ROTC Honor Soc., Aquinias Nat. Honor Soc., Theology Nat. Honor Soc., Social Sci. Nat. Honor Soc., Polit. Sci. Nat. Honor Soc. Roman Catholic. Avocations: running, weightlifting, politics. Home Phone: 281-488-8239; Office Phone: 281-488-1280. E-mail: james.gutheinz@us.army.mil.

GUTHEINZ, JEAN, public relations executive; d. Joseph Richard Gutheinz, Sr. and Rita (O'Leary) Gutheinz; 1 child, Jonathan. BA, San Diego State U., 1994—99. Office mgr., law clk. Law Office Lt. Col. Joseph R. Gutheinz, Sr., San Diego, 1980—97; accounts exec. Unlimited Svcs., Dallas, 1998—2006; pub. rels. officer Law Office Joseph R. Gutheinz, Jr., Houston, 2000—. Dir.: (plays) Stage Performance; actor(stand-up performer): (improv) Situational Comedy; author: (comedy skits) The Funeral. Republican. Roman Catholic. Avocations: reading, writing, acting. Personal E-mail: jeangutheinz@yahoo.com.

GUTHEINZ, JOSEPH RICHARD, JR., criminal justice educator, consultant, lawyer; b. Camp Lejune, NC, Aug. 13, 1955; s. Joseph R., Sr. and Rita C. (O'Leary) Gutheinz; m. Lori Ann Bentley, Jan. 16, 1976; children: Joseph, Christopher, Michael, Jim, Bill, Dave. AS, AA, Monterey Peninsula Coll., Calif., 1975; BA, Calif. State U., Sacramento, 1978, MA, 1979; postgrad., U. Calif., Davis, 1979-80; grad. U.S. Army Mil. Intelligence Officer Basic Course, U.S. Army Tactical Intelligence Sch., 1980; grad., U.S. Army Flight Sch., 1984; MS in Sys. Mgmt., U. So. Calif., 1985; JD, S. Tex. Coll. Law, 1996; grad. Criminal Investigators Basic Course (hon.), Fed. Law Enforcement Tng. Ctrs., 1988; grad. (disting.), Fed. Law Enforcement Tng. Ctrs. Office Inspector Gen., 1989. Bar: Tex. Supreme Ct. 1997, U.S. Dist. Ct. (so. dist.) Tex. 1997, U.S. Armed Forces Ct. Appeals 1998, U.S. Ct. Appeals (5th, 10th, 11th and fed. cirs.) 1998, U.S. Tax Ct. 1998, U.S. Supreme Ct. 2001; lic. FAA comml. pilot, cert. fraud examiner, tchr. aeronautics, mil. sci., bus. and indsl. mgmt., pub. svcs. and adminstrn., sociology and police sci. Calif. Officer U.S. Army, Kitzigen, Fed. Rep. Germany, 1980-82, capt., mil. intelligence officer Stuttgart, Fed. Rep. Germany, 1982-84, capt., aviator Ft. Polk, La., 1984-86; spl. agt. civil aviation security FAA, Oklahoma City, 1986-87; spl. agt. U.S. Dept. Transp., Denver, 1987-90; sr. spl. agt., acting sr. resident agent in charge Office Insp. Gen. NASA, Houston, 1990-2000; pvt. practice atty. Houston, 1997—; mentor, instr. organized crime U. Phoenix, 2002—; instr. criminal justice Alvin C.C., 2004—, mem. paralegal bd. of advisors, 2006—. Police sci. instr. Ctrl. Tex. Coll., Nelligan, 1983; case agt. in charge of investigating space shuttle temperature transducers which grounded Shuttle Fleet, 91; aptd. mem. adv. com. on offenders with med. or mental impairments Tex. Dept. Criminal Justice, 2004—; guest spkr. in field; criminal justice instr.; nine agy. task force leader Omniplan Investigation, 1992—97; lead NASA OIG criminal investigation MIR Space Station Fire and Crash, 1997; lead investigator Jerry Whittredge, The Astronaut Impersonator, 1998; under cover agent Operation Lunar Eclipse, 1998; investigative cons. U.S. Attorney's Office, Little Rock, 2002; affiliated atty. Thomas More Law Ctr., 2005—. Author: Moon Rock Con, 2003, Is it Legal to Privately Own Space ShuttleTiles, 2002, Stealing the Dream, 2002, In Search of the Goodwill Moon Rocks, 2004, There Will Be a Day After Tomorrow, 2004, Building 265, 2005, Marketing an Asteroid Threat, 2005, The Great Astronaut Impersonator, 2005, Cover-up in Space, 2005, Cumbre Vieja: A Terrorist Time Bomb, 2005, Making Safety a Priority: NASA's Path to Mars, 2005, NASA's Plutonium Gamble, 2006, NASA's Fallen Star: The Investigation of Omniplan Corporation, 2006, NASA is for Lovers, Psychos and Homicidal Maniacs, 2007; mil. editor: The Conservative Voice, 2005—; actor: (TV films) Moon for Sale, 2007; contbr. columns in newspapers. Pres. Calif. State U. United Students for Life, 1976—79; chairperson Calif. Rally for Life, 1980; atty./activist against San Jacinto C.C. spl. election to annex parts of Clear Lake Texas, 2003; proponent Calif. Pro-Life Initiative, 1977; rally organizer Morton Downey Dem. Presdl. Campaign rallies, 1979; del. Tex. senatorial resolutions com. Rep. Party, 2000, 2004, del. conv. Tex., 2004; bd. dirs. Sea Isle Property Owners, 2001—02; briefed Pres. Yeltsin's econ. advisors, 1995. Decorated Meritorious Svc. medal US Army, Commendation medal; named Hon. Lt. Gov., Okla., 1987; recipient letter of commendation, FBI Dir. Louis Freeh, 1995, Tex. Spl. Commendation, US Atty. Office So. Dist., 1996, Exceptional Svc. medal, NASA, 2000, Pres.'s Coun. Integrity and Efficiency Career Achievement award, 2000, cert. of appreciation, US Atty. (so. dist.) Tex., 2003, cert. of commendation, U. Phoenix, 2003, writing honorarium, 2004, 2005, 2006, 2007, Excellence in Tchg. cert., Phi Theta Kappa, 2005; Merit scholar, S. Tex. Coll. Law. Mem.: Tex. Pro Bono Coll., Harris County Lawyers assn., Nat. Rep. Lawyers Assn. (mem. spkrs. panel on Calif. recall election), Tex. Criminal Def. Lawyers Assn., Tex. Bar Assn., Cert. Fraud Examiners. Republican. Roman Catholic. Achievements include named world's foremost authority on stolen moon rocks by Irish Mail newspaper, April 22, 2007. Avocations: reading, teaching, public speaking, political activism, helping the poor. Office: 205 Woodcombe Houston TX 77062 Office Phone: 281-488-1280. Personal E-mail: jgutheinz@sbcglobal.net.

GUTHEINZ, MICHAEL JOHN, military officer, lawyer; b. Fort Huachuca, Ariz., Aug. 6, 1980; s. Joseph Richard, Jr. and Lori Ann Gutheinz. BA magnum cum laude, U. St. Thomas, 2003; JD cum laude, South Tex. Coll. Law, 2006. Lic.: Tex. Supreme Ct. (atty.), US Ct. Appeal for Armed Forces, US Ct. Vets. Appeals; US Army Commn. Sec. of Army, 2003. Law clk. Law Office of Joseph Richard Gutheinz, Jr., Houston, 1997—2005, Harris County Civil Atty.'s Office, Houston, 2005; intern Galveston County Dist. Atty's. Office, 2006; Congl. staff mem. for Congresswoman Shelley Sekula Gibbs, 2006—07; atty., capt. US Army's JAG Corps, Ft. Campbell, Ky., 2007—; officer in charge Ft. Campbell Tax Office, 2007—. Vol. Gabriel Project, Houston, 1995—; reading tutor Am. Reads Project, Houston, 2003—. Author: Conditional Suspension of Classification: Improving the Military Administrative Discharge System. Law student mem. Rep. Nat. Lawyers Assn., Houston, 2003—05; mem. Res. Officers Assn., Washington, 2003—05; law student mem. Tex. Criminal Def. Lawyers Assn., Austin, 2003—05. Cadet capt. US Army ROTC, 2001—03, lt. US Army, 2003—05, Houston. Recipient Superior Cadet award, US Army ROTC Command, 2003, Phys. Fitness award, 2003. Mem.: Pi Sigma Alpha, Delta Theta Phi. Roman Catholic. Avocations: politics, running, weightlifting. Office: OSJA 101st Airborne Ft Campbell KY

GUTHERY, JOHN M., lawyer; b. Broken Bow, Nebr., Nov. 22, 1946; s. John M. and Kay G.; m. Diane Messineo, May 26, 1972; 1 child, Lisa. BS, U. Nebr., 1969, JD, 1972. Bar: Nebr. 1972. Pres. Perry, Guthery, Haase & Gessford, P.C., L.L.O., Lincoln, Nebr., 1972—. Bd. govs. Nebr. Wesleyan U. Mem. ATLA, ABA (mem. litigation sect.), Nebr. Bank Attys. Assn. (past pres., 1985-86), Nebr. Assn. Trial Attys., Nebr. State Bar Assn. (pres. 1998-99, mem. Nebr.State Bar Found. mem. ho. dels. 1979-83, 87-95, exec. coun. 1988-94 pres. 1998-99, chair Nebr. bankruptcy sect.), Lincoln

Bar Assn. (trustee 1985-88, pres. 1990-91). Office: Perry Guthery Haase & Gessford PC LLO 233 S 13th St Ste 1400 Lincoln NE 68508-2003 Office Phone: 402-476-9200. Business E-Mail: jguthery@perrylawfirm.com.

GUTHKE, KARL SIEGFRIED, language educator; b. Lingen, Germany, Feb. 17, 1933; arrived in U.S., 1956, naturalized, 1973; s. Karl Hermann and Helene (Beekman) Guthke; m. Dagmar von Nostitz, Apr. 24, 1965; 1 child, Carl Ricklef. MA, U. Tex., 1953; PhD, U. Göttingen, Germany, 1956; MA (hon.), Harvard U., 1968. Faculty U. Calif., Berkeley, 1956-65, prof. German lit., 1962-65, U. Toronto, Ont., Canada, 1965-68, Harvard U., 1968-78, Kuno Francke prof. German art and culture, 1978—. Vis. prof. U. Colo., 1963, U. Mass., 1967; mem., former vis. fellow Sidney Sussex Coll., Cambridge U., Magdalene Coll., Cambridge U.; vis. fellow Nat. Rsch. Ctr., Wolfenbüttel, Inst. Advanced Studies, U. Edinburgh, Humanities Rsch. Ctr., Australian Nat. U., Canberra. Author: Englische Vorromantik und deutscher Sturm und Drang, 1958; author: (with Hans M. Wolff) Das Leid im Werke Gerhart Hauptmanns, 1958; author: Geschichte und Poetik der deutschen Tragikomödie, 1961, Gerhart Hauptmann: Weitbild im Werk, 1961, rev. edit., 1980, Haller und die Literatur, 1962, Der Stand der Lessing-Forschung: Ein Bericht über die Literatur, 1932-1962, 1965, Modern Tragicomedy: An Investigation into the Nature of the Genre, 1966, Wege zur Literatur: Studien zur deutschen Dichtungs-und Geistesgeschichte, 1967, Hallers Literaturkritik, 1970, die Mythologie der entgötterten Welt: Ein literarisches Thema vond der Aufklärung bis zur Gegenwart, 1971, Das deutsche bürgerliche Trauerspiel, 1972, 6th rev. edit., 1994, G.E. Lessing, 3d edit., 1979, Literarisches Leben im 18. Janrhundert in Deutschland und in der Schweiz, 1975, Das Abenteuer der Literatur, 1981, Haller im Halblicht, 1981, Der Mythos der Neuzeit, 1983, Erkundungen, 1983, Das Geheimnis um B. Traven entdeckt, 1984, B. Traven: Biographie eines Rätsels, 1987, The Last Frontier: Imagining Other Worlds, 1990, Letzte Worte, 1990, B. Traven: The Life Behind the Legends, 1991, Last Words, 1992, Trails in No-Man's Land, 1993, Die Entdeckung des Ich, 1993, Schillers Dramen, 1994, 2nd edit., 2005, Ist der Tod eine Frau, 1997, The Gender of Death, 1999, Der Blick in die Fremde, 2000, Goethes Weimar und die grosse Öffnung in die weite Welt, 2001, Epitaph Culture in the West, 2003, Lessings Horizonte, 2003, Die Erfindung der Welt, 2005, Sprechende Steine, 2006, others; translator: Die moderne Tragikomödie: Theorie und Gestalt, 1968; editor: Haller, Die Alpen, 1987; editor: (with Hanser) Gotthold Ephraim Lessing, Werke, 1970—72; co-editor: Joh. H. Füssli, Sämtliche Gedichte, 1973, B. Traven: Briefe aus Mexiko, 1992, Lessing Yearbook, Colloquia Germanica, Twentieth Century Literature, German Quar., Honored in History and Literature: Essays in Honor of Karl S. Guthke, 2000. Fellow: Rsch. Ctr., Wolfenbuttel, Inst. Advanced Studies, Edinburgh, Humanities Rsch. Ctr., Canberra; mem.: Inst. Germanic Studies (London corr. fellow). Office: Harvard U Dept German Cambridge MA 02138

GUTHMAN, JACK, lawyer; b. Cologne, Germany, Apr. 19, 1938; came to U.S., 1939, naturalized, 1945; s. Albert and Selma (Cahn) G.; m. Sandra Polk, Nov. 26, 1967. BA, Northwestern U., 1960; LLB, Yale U., 1963. Bar: Ill. bar 1963. Law clk. to dist. judge U.S. Dist. Ct. No. Ill., 1963-65; since practiced in Chgo.; ptnr. Sidley & Austin, 1970-94, Shefsky & Froelich Ltd., Chgo., 1995—. Mem. City Chgo. Zoning Bd. Appeals, 1970-75, chmn., 1975-87. Democrat. Jewish. Office: Shefsky & Froelich Ltd 111 E Wacker Dr Ste 2800 Chicago IL 60601 Office Phone: 312-836-4034.

GUTHRIDGE, BILL, university basketball coach; b. Parsons, Kans., July 27, 1937; m. Leesie Guthridge; children: Jamie, Stuart, Megan. BS in Math., Kans. State U., 1960, MEd, 1963. Coach Scott City (Kans.) H.S; asst. football coach Kans. State U.; freshman basketball coach, co-asst. varsity coach U. NC, Chapel Hill, from 1973, asst. coach, 1968-97, head coach, 1997—2000. Coach Puerto Rican AAU Summer Leagues; coach Puerto Rican Olympic Team, 1968. Named Coach of Yr., Puerto Rican AAU, Nat. Coach of Yr., Nat. Assn. Basketball Coaches, Sporting News, CBS/Chevrolet, Columbus Touchdown Club, Atlantic Coast Conf., 1998; recipient Naismith award Atlanta Tipoff Club.

GUTHRIE, DIANA FERN, nursing educator; b. NYC, May 7, 1934; d. Floyd George and A. May (Moler) Worthington; m. Richard Alan Guthrie, Aug. 18, 1957; children: Laura, Joyce, Tammy. AA, Graceland Coll., 1953; RN, Independence Sanitarium, Mo., 1956; BS in Nursing, U. Mo., 1957, MS in Pub. Health, 1969; EdS, Wichita State U., Kans., 1982; PhD, Walden U., 1985. Cert. diabetes educator, bd. cert. advanced diabetes mgmt.; RN Mo., Kans., cert. holistic nursing, RN advanced practitioner; lic. profl. counselor Kans., cert. stress mgmt. edn., clin. hypnosis, healing touch, lic. marriage and family therapist. Instr. red cross U.S. Naval Sta., Sangley Point, Philippines, 1961-63; acting head nurse newborn nursery U. Mo., Columbia, 1963-64, birth defect nurse dept. pediat., 1964-65, nursing dir. clin. research ctr., 1965-67, research asst., 1967-73; diabetes nurse specialist Sch. Medicine U. Kans., Wichita, 1973—, asst. then assoc. prof. Sch. Medicine, 1974-85, prof. dept. pediat. and psychiatry Sch. Medicine, 1985-99, prof. emeritus, 2000; prof. dept. nursing Kans. U. Med. Ctr., Wichita, 1985-99, ret., 1999. Nurse cons. diabetes Mo. Regional Med. Program, Columbia, 1970-73; nat. advisor Human Diabetes Ctr. for Excellence, Lexington, Ky., 1982-90, Phoenix, 1983-92, Charlottesville, Ky., 1990-95; adj. prof. Sch. Nursing Wichita State U., 1985—. Author: Nursing Management of Diabetes, 1977, 5th edit., 2002, The Diabetes Source Book, 1990, 5th edit., 2003, Alternative and Complementary Diabetes Case, 2000; contbr. articles to profl. jours. Health adv. bd. Mid-Am. All Indian Ctr., Wichita, 1978-80; bd. dirs. Wichita Urban Indian Health Clinic, 1980-82; bd. trustees Graceland U., Lamoni, Iowa, 1996-2001, bd. trustees emeritus, 2002—. Named Kans. Counselor of Yr., Kans. Counseling Assn., 2006; recipient Disting. Hon. Nursing Alumnus award, Wichita State U. Sch. Nursing/Nursing Alumni Soc., 2007. Fellow: Am. Acad. Nursing; mem.: APHA, ANA, Am. Assn. Med. Psychotherapists (profl. adv. bd. 1985—), Am. Assn. Diabetes Educators (Kans. area Disting. Svc. award 1999), Am. Diabetes Assn. (Kans. area prof. edn. and youth com. 1988—, affiliate bd. dirs. 1979—83, pres. Kans. affiliate 1980—81, 1990—91, Outstanding Educator award 1979, Regional Outstanding Svc. award 1984, South Ctrl. Kans. Counselor of Yr. 2006, Kans. Counselor of Yr. 2006), Sigma Theta Tau (Exemplary Recognition award Epsilon Gamma chpt. 1996). Democrat. Mem. Cmty. Of Christ Ch. Avocations: harp, piano, painting, crafts, reading. Office: 200 S Hillside Wichita KS 67211-2127 Office Phone: 316-687-3100. Business E-Mail: dguthrie@kumc.edu.

GUTHRIE, EDGAR KING, artist; b. Chenoa, Ill., May 12, 1917; s. David McMurtrie and Emily Henrietta (Streid) G.; m. Eva Ross Harvey, Dec. 8, 1945 (dec. Jan. 1978); children: Melody Bliss Johnson, Mark King Guthrie (dec. Nov. 4, 2006). BEd, Ill. State U., 1939; MA, Am. U., 1958; graduate, Command and General Staff Coll., Ft. Leavenworth, Kan., 1967. Artist W.L. Stensgaard Co., Chgo., 1939-40, The Diamond Store, Phoenix, 1941-42; presentation artist CIA, Washington, 1955-72; instr. Columbia Tech. Inst., Arlington, Va., 1966-72; owner, later ptnr. Guthrie Art & Sign Co., Winchester, Va., 1976—; instr. U. Hawaii, Lihue, 1980-81; cartoonist The Kauai Times, Lihue, 1981-90; owner Alo-o-oha-ha-ha Caricatures, Lihue, Honolulu, 1980—. Cons., artist Shenandoah Apple Blossom Festival, Winchester, 1975-78; cartoonist Internat. Salon of Caricature, Montreal, Can., 1976-77; co-chmn. Kauai Soc. of Artists Art Show, Lihue, 1981. One man shows include 50 Yrs. of Painting-A Retrospective, Lihue, 1984; inventor Artists' Kit; Filmic Artist: (documentary film) The River Nile, 1960 (NBC Emmy Award). Bd. dirs. Civil Def., Virginia Hills, 1954; publicity com. Frederick County Taxpayers Assn., Winchester, 1973, Exch. Club, Winchester, 1977. Lt. col. U.S. Army, 1942-54. Decorated Purple Heart, Bronze Star with oak leaf cluster; recipient Spl. Merit award Boy Scouts Am. Aloha Coun., Lihue, 1982. Mem. Mus. of Cartoon Art, U.S. Naval Combat Artist, Daniel Morgan Mus. (contbr. 1976), Nat. Soc. Mural Painters (contbr. 1976), Allied Artists of Am. (contbr. 1977), Pastel Soc. Am. (contbr. 1977-78), Am. Watercolor Soc. (contbr. 1982—), Greek Expeditionary Forces (hon.). Mem. Ch. LDS. Avocations: animation, cinematography, hiking, swimming, genealogy. Home and Office: 2444 Hihiwai St Apt 703 Honolulu HI 96826-5104 Office Phone: 808-955-2644. E-mail: edguthrie@earthlink.net. *Have short term and long term righteous goals. Be able to take risks in those things that most interest you, and gain wisdom from those risks that are least effectual. Instead of merely abandoning a project, try to give it more quality.*

GUTHRIE, FRANK ALBERT, chemistry professor; b. Madison, Ind., Feb. 16, 1927; s. Ned and Gladys (Glick) G.; m. Marcella Glee Farrar, June 12, 1955; children: Mark Alan, Bruce Bradford, Kent Andrew, Lee Farrar. AB, Hanover Coll., 1950; MS, Purdue U., 1952; PhD, Ind. U., 1962. Mem. faculty Rose-Hulman Inst. Tech., Terre Haute, Ind., 1952—, assoc. prof., 1962-67, prof. chemistry, 1967-94, prof. emeritus, 1994—, chmn. dept., 1969-72, chief health professions adviser, 1975-94. Kettering vis. lectr. U. Ill., Urbana, 1961-62; vis. prof. chemistry U.S. Mil. Acad., West Point, N.Y., 1987-88, 93-94, admissions coord., 1989—; vis. prof. chemistry Butler U., spring 2000. Mem. exec. bd. Wabash Valley coun. Boy Scouts Am., 1971-87, scoutmaster, 1979-82, adv. bd., 1988—, v.p. for scouting, 1976; mem. selection chmn. Leadership Terre Haute, 1978-80. Served with AUS, 1945-46 Recipient Vigil Honor Order of Arrow, Boy Scouts Am., 1975, Wood badge, 1976, Dist. award of merit, 1976, Silver Beaver award, 1980. Fellow Ind. Acad. Sci. (treas. 1966-68, pres. 1970, chmn. acad. found. trustees 1986—); mem. Am. Chem. Soc. (sec. 1973-77, editor directory 1965-77, chmn. divsn. analytical chemistry 1979-80; local sect. activities com. 1982-86, nominations and elections com. 1988-94, sec. 1992-94, coun. policy com. 1995, constn. and bylaws com. 1996-2002, membership affairs com., 2003—, chmn. Wabash Valley sect. 1958, counselor 1980—, steering com. for joint ctrl.-Gt. Lakes regional meetings, Indpls., 1978, 91, vis. assoc. com. profl. tng. 1984—, chmn. analytical chemistry exam. inst. std. exam. 1994, Disting. Svc. award 2005), Coblentz Soc., Midwest Univs. Analytical Chemistry Conf., Hanover Coll. Alumni Assn. (pres. 1974, Alumni Achievement award 1977), Masons (32 deg.), Sigma Xi (treas. Wabash Valley chpt. 1994-98), Phi Lambda Upsilon, Phi Gamma Delta, Alpha Chi Sigma (E.E. Dunlap scholarship selection com. 1986—, chmn. 1990—, dir. expansion 1995-99, profl. rep. 1997-2000). Presbyterian. Home: 120 Berkley Dr Terre Haute IN 47803-1708 Office: Rose Hulman Inst Tech 5500 Wabash Ave Terre Haute IN 47803-3999 Personal E-mail: fguthrie@chilitech.com. Business E-Mail: frank.guthrie@rose-hulman.edu.

GUTHRIE, JANET, professional race car driver; b. Iowa City, Mar. 7, 1938; d. William Lain and Jean Ruth Guthrie. BS in Physics, U. Mich., 1960. Comml. pilot and flight instr., 1958-61; research and devel. engr. Republic Aviation Corp., Farmingdale, NY, 1960-67; publs. engr. Sperry Systems, Sperry Corp., Great Neck, NY, 1968-73; racing driver Sports Car Club Am. and Internat. Motor Sports Assn., 1963-86; profl. racing driver U.S. Auto Club and Nat. Assn. for Stock Car Racing, 1976-80; pres. Janet Guthrie Racing Enterprises Inc., 1978—2004; owner Guthrie Racing LLC, 2004—. Highway safety cons. Met. Ins. Co., 1980-87. Author: Janet Guthrie: A Life at Full Throttle, 2005. Named to Women's Sports Hall of Fame, 1980, Internat. Motorsports Hall of Fame, 2006; recipient Curtis Turner award, Nat. Assn. for Stock Car Racing-Charlotte World 600, 1976, First in class award, Sebring 12-hour, 1967, 1970. Mem. Madison Ave. Sports Car Driving and Chowder Soc., Women's Sports Found., Les Dames d'Aspen, Internat. Wine and Food Soc., Road Racing Drivers Club. Achievements include being the first woman to qualify for and race in Daytona 500, 1977, Top Rookie; first woman to qualify for and race in Indpls. 500, 1977, finished 9th, 1978; North Atlantic Road Racing Champion, 1973.

GUTHRIE, JUDITH K., federal judge; b. Chgo., July 13, 1948; d. David Curtis and Kathleen McAfee G.; m. John H. Hannah, Jr., May 9, 1992 (dec. 2003); m. Matthew Watson, May 28, 2006. Student, Ariz. State U., 1966—68; BA, St. Mary's U., 1971; JD cum laude, U. Houston, 1980. Bar: Tex. 1981, U.S. Dist. Ct. (ea. dist.) Tex. 1982, U.S. Ct. Appeals (5th cir.) 1982, U.S. Dist. Ct. (no. dist.) Tex. 1983, U.S. Dist. Ct. (we. dist.) Tex. 1984. Editor Am. Coun. Edn., Washington, 1972-73; exec. asst. Tex. Ho. Reps., Austin, 1973-75; lobbyist Bracewell & Patterson, Austin, 1975-80, assoc. Houston, 1980-81; briefing atty. Tex. Ct. Appeals, Tyler, 1981-82; ptnr. Hannah & Guthrie, Tyler, 1982-86; magistrate judge U.S. Dist. Ct. (ea. dist.) Tex., Tyler, 1986—. Instr. legal asst. program, Tyler Jr. Coll., 1986-87; apptd. Tex. Jud. Coun., 1991-97, gender bias task force, 1991-92; lectr. in field. Contbr. articles to profl. jours. Adv. bd. Main St. Project; legal asst. adv. bd. Tyler Jr. Coll., 1986—2007, chmn. adv. bd., 1996—2007; mem. Citizens Commn. Tex. Jud. Sys., 1992—93; bd. dirs. Habitat for Humanity, 2003—; former Dem. chmn. Smith County; former bd. dirs. Found. Women's Resources, Leadership Am., Leadership Tex. Mem.: ABA (Fed. trial judges legis. com. 1991—93), Smith County Bar Assn. (chmn. law libr. com. 1985—2001), State Bar Tex. (dist. 2A grievance com. 1990—, chmn. 1995—96), 5th Cir. Bar Assn., Fed. Magistrate Judges Assn., Am. Judges Assn. Office: US Dist Ct 300 Fed Bldg & US Ct House 211 W Ferguson St Tyler TX 75702-7212 Office Phone: 903-590-1077.

GUTHRIE, M. PHILIP, corporate financial executive; b. Vicksburg, Miss., Mar. 26, 1945; s. Marion P. Jr. and Aileen (Perry) G.; m. Beverly Alice Blackmon, June 2, 1966; children: Philip Todd, Edward Tait, Stuart Trent. BS, La. Tech U., 1967; MBA, U. Mich., 1968. CPA, La., Tex. Sr. cons. Price Waterhouse & Co., Houston, 1968-72; v.p. fin. and mfg. Vicra div. Baxter Labs., Dallas, 1972-78; v.p. fin., CFO, treas. S.W. Airlines Co., Dallas, 1978-81; exec. v.p., CFO, Braniff Internat., Dallas, 1981-84; pres. Diamond Mgmt. Group, Dallas, 1984-89; mng. dir. Mason Best Co., Dallas, 1989—98; chmn., CEO, Am. Eagle Group, Inc., Dallas, 1992—96; CEO Aircraft Interior Resources Group Inc., 1998—2003, Intech Aerospace Group, LLC, 2004—05, Denham Ptnrs., LLC, 2004—. Bd. dirs. Ariel Holdings, Inc., Bermuda, Mainstream Data, Inc., Salt Lake City, Safeguard Bus. Sys., Ft. Washington, Pa., Internat. Autotech, Dallas, Westmark Sys., Inc., Austin, Tex., Sunrise Pubs., Inc., Bloomington, Ind., Bristol Group (Buenos Aires), Alpargatas (Buenos Aires), Neuro Resource Group, Inc., Dallas, Ariel Holdings, Inc., Bermuda; CEO Neuro Holdings Internat. LLC, 2004-. Assoc. bd. dirs. So. Meth. U. Grad. Sch. Bus., Dallas, 1985—. Mem. AICPA, Fin. Execs. Inst., Nat. Assn. Casualty and Surety Execs., Soc. Internat. Bus. Fellows, Tex. Soc. CPA's, Coun. of Ins. Co. Execs., Phi Kappa Phi, Omicron Delta Kappa, Beta Gamma Sigma, Delta Sigma Pi, Beta Alpha Psi. Office: Three Lincoln Ctr 5430 LBJ Fwy Ste 1480 Dallas TX 75240 E-mail: mphilipguthrie@sbcglobal.net.

GUTHRIE, PHILLIP PATRICK, division production manager; b. Balt, Md, Aug. 19, 1962; s. Dion Francis and Sandra Ann (Fisicaro) G. Bachelor's degree, U. Md., 1984; diploma, Dale Carnegie Mgmt., 1990. Restricted radiotelephone operator permit. Exec. prodr. Sta. WBFF-TV/Fox 45, Balt., 1985-92; sr. prodr., program mgr. Cable 17, Balt., 1992-95; pub. affairs prodr. Sta. WMAR-TV/News channel 2, Balt., 1995; divsn. prodn. mgr. Comcast Creative Group, Balt., 1995—. Sta. WJLA/TV, Washington, 1984; intern, writer Warner Bros. Writing for TV Program, Balt., 1991-93. Writer, prodr., editor, performer: (radio drama) Nothing but Time, 1984 (Grand Prize Audio Entertainment 1984); writer: (screenplay) Prisoner of the Heart, 2000. Nominated Emmy award, 1997, 2001, Cable Ace award, 1998; recipient 5 Telly awards, 1998, 3 Telly awards, 1999, 2 Telly awards, 2000, Telly award, 2001, 02, 05; Cable Advt. Bur. award, 2000, Cable Advt. Bur. award and Best of Show, 2002. Mem. NATAS, Internat. TV Assn. (3d pl. award for orgnl. news 1992, 2d pl. award for orgnl. news 1994, Silver award for pub. svc. announcements 1997), Am. Film Inst., Advt. Assn. Batl. (2 Best in Balt. Addy awards 1999). Avocations: acting, painting, travel. Home: 8113 Glen Arbor Dr Baltimore MD 21237-3372 Office: Comcast Creative Group 160A Golden West Dr ste 190A Hunt Valley MD 21031 Office Phone: 410-568-1113. E-mail: sitcom@comcast.net.

GUTHRIE, RANDOLPH HOBSON, JR., plastic surgeon, consultant; b. NYC, Dec. 8, 1934; s. Randolph Hobson and Mabel Edith (Welton) G.; m. Beatrice Mills Holden, Mar. 20, 1965; children: Randolph Hobson III, Michael Phipps, Philip Holden. AB, Princeton U., 1957; MD, Harvard U., 1961. Intern NY Hosp., NYC, 1961-62, resident, 1962-63, 69-71, chief resident, 1971; resident St. Luke's Hosp., NYC, 1963-66, chief resident, 1966—71; chief plastic & reconstructive surgery svc. Meml. Sloan-Kettering Cancer Ctr., NYC, 1971-77; chief dept. plastic and reconstructive surgery NY Downtown Hosp., NYC, 1979-2000; asst. prof. Cornell U. Med. Coll., 1971-74, assoc. prof., 1974-89, prof., 1989—. Asst. attending surgeon, NY Hosp., 1971-74, assoc. attending surgeon, 1974-89, attending surgeon, 1989—; attending surgeon Sloan-Kettering Cancer Ctr., 1977-93, cons., 1994—. Author: The Truth About Breast Implants, 1994; co-author: Reconstruction and Esthetic Mammoplasty, 1989; contbr. articles to profl. jours., books. Pres. East River Med. Found., NYC, 1970-80, Acacia Found., NYC, 1980-94; alumni dir. St. Paul's Sch., Concord, NH, 1979-83, form agt., 1983-87, term trustee, 1985-89, life trustee, 1989-94; trustee Epsicopal Sch., NYC, 1976-84; bd. dirs. Am.-Italian Found. Cancer Rsch., NYC, 1985-94; bd. dirs., treas. Save Venice, Inc., 1985-89, pres., 1989-97, chmn., 1997—; trustee NY Downtown Hosp., 1985-92, Isabella Stewart Gardner Mus., Boston, 1998-2000. Maj. M.C. AUS, 1966-69. Decorated Cavaliere nell 'Ordine Al Merito della Republica Italiana; rsch. fellow Sloan Kettering Cancer Ctr., 1971-77. Mem. ACS, Plastic Surgery Rsch. Coun., Am. Geriat. Soc., Am. Soc. Plastic and Reconstructive Surgeons, Pan Am. Med. Soc., NY Soc. Plastic and Reconstructive Surgery, NY Med. Soc., Med. Soc. County NY, Herbert Conway Soc., Doubles Club, Century Club, Knickerbocker Club (NYC). Home and Office: 15 E 74th St New York NY 10021-2604 Home Phone: 212-249-0420. E-mail: rhgnyc@aol.com.

GUTHRIE, RICHARD ALAN, physician; b. Pleasant Hill, Ill., Nov. 13, 1935; s. Merle Pruitt and Cleona Marie (Weaver) G.; m. Diana Fern Worthington, Aug. 18, 1957; children: Laura, Joyce, Tamara. AA, Graceland Coll., 1955; MD, U. Mo., 1960. Diplomate Am. Bd. Pediatrics, Am. Bd. Pediatric Endocrinology; cert. Nat. Bd. for Diabetes Educators. Intern US Naval Hosp., Camp Pendleton, Calif., 1960-61, dir. dependent svcs. Sangley Point, Philippines, 1961-63; asst. instr., resident in pediatrics U. Mo., 1963-65, NIH fellow in endocrinology and metabolism, 1965-68, asst. prof., dir. newborn svcs., 1968-71, assoc. prof. pediat., 1971-73; prof., chmn. dept. pediatrics U. Kans. Med. Sch., Wichita, 1973-82; exec. dir. Kans. Regional Diabetes Ctr., Wichita, 1982-84; pres. Mid-Am. Diabetes Assocs., Wichita, 1984—. Dir. Robert L. Jackson Diabetes Treatment, Edn. and Rsch. Ctr., 1985—. Author: Nursing Management in Diabetes Mellitus, 1976, 1997, 2003, The Child with Diabetes, 1970, Physiologic Management of Diabetes in Children, 1986, Diabetes Source Book, 1990, 2003; mem. editl. bd.: Practical Diabetology, 1982—92, Diabetes Self-Management, 1984—97, Diabetes Educator, 1985—89, assoc. editor: Diabetes Spectrum, 2000—05; contbr. articles to profl. jours. Mem. health ministries bd. Reorganized Ch. Jesus Christ Latter-day Saints; mem. adv. bd. Kans. Action for Children, 1978—, Kans. State Diabetes, 1988-93, 95—. With USN, 1960-63. Recipient grants NIH, 1968—, Outstanding Faculty award Wichita State U., 1976, 2000; Disting. alumnus award Graceland Coll., 1984, Humanitarian award Wesley Med. Found., 1997, award for outstanding cmty. svc. Am. Diabetes Assn., 2001; Dr. McIver Furman Disting. lectureship in health scis. Del Mar Coll., Corpus Christi, Tex., 1986. Fellow Am. Acad. Pediatrics, Am. Coll. Endocrinology; mem. AMA, Am. Diabetes Assn. (bd. dirs. 1972-77, Outstanding Contbn. to Camping award 1992, Outstanding award for Reaching People 2003, Outstanding Physician Clinician award 2003), Kans. Diabetes Assn. (pres. 1974, chmn. bd. 1974-77, 85-87), Kans. State Med. Soc., Sedgewick County Med. Soc., Am. Pediat. Soc., Soc. Pediat. Rsch., Wichita Pediat. Soc. (bd. dirs. 1988, pres. 1990-92), Lawson Wilkins Pediat. Endocrinology Soc., Midwest Soc. Pediat. Rsch., Internat. Soc. for Pediat. and Adolescent Diabetes (edn. com. 1995—), Am. Assn. Diabetes Educators (bd. dirs. 1994-97), Am. Assn. Clin. Endocrinology 1992—), Endocrine Soc., Sigma Xi, Alpha Omega Alpha. Office: Mid-Am Diabetes Assocs 200 S Hillside St Wichita KS 67211-2127 Home: 2300 N Tyler Rd Apt 108 Andover KS 67205 Office Phone: 316-687-3100. Personal E-mail: rag33@hotmail.com.

GUTHRIE, ROY A., financial company executive; B Econs., Hanover Coll.; MBA, Drake U. CPA, Tex. Planning analyst consumer fin. operation Assoc. First Capital Corp., Irving, Tex., 1978-88, exec. v.p. subs. Assoc. Ins. Group, 1988-95, exec. v.p. subs. Assoc. Real Estate Fin. Svcs. Co., 1988-95, sr. v.p., comptr., 1988-95, sr. v.p. prin. domestic subs. Assoc. Corp. N.Am., 1988-95, exec. v.p., 1995-96, CFO, sr. exec. v.p., 1996—2001; pres., CEO, CitiCapital Citigroup, Inc., 2001, pres., CEO, CitiFinancial Internat., 2001; exec. v.p., CFO Discover Fin. Services div., Morgan Stanley. Bd. dirs. Dallas Zool. Soc., United Way Met. Dallas. Office: Discover Fin Services 2500 Lake Cook Rd Riverwoods IL 60015*

GUTHRIE, WALLACE NESSLER, JR., naval officer; b. NYC, Feb. 22, 1939; s. Wallace Nessler and Rena Otis (Robertson) G.; m. Virginia Dale Sargeant, June 7, 1961; children: Wallace Edward, Gail Elizabeth, Virginia Lynn. BS, U.S. Naval Acad., Annapolis, Md., 1961; MS, Rollins Coll., 1972, EdS, 1981. Commd. ensign USN, 1961, advanced through ranks to rear adm., 1987; edn. specialist Naval Tng. Systems Ctr., Orlando, Fla., 1967-89; dep. dir. Navy Res., Washington, 1989-92; dir. tng., supt. schs. Am. Forces Info. Svc., 1993-97. Past head Naval Acad. Candidate Selection Com., 9th Congl. Dist., Fla. Sr. officer adv. panel Joint Mil. Intelligence Coll.; bd. dirs., trustee Navy Mut. Aid Assn. Mem. Naval Res. Assn. (life), Res. Officers Assn. (life), Surface Navy Assn. (life), Naval Submarine League, Clan Guthrie (bd. dirs.), Friends of Weedon Island (bd. dirs.). Republican. Avocations: camping, boating, fishing, hiking. Office Phone: 727-522-7978. E-mail: wgguthrie@tampabay.rr.com.

GUTIERREZ, CARL T. C., former governor; b. Agana Heights, Guam, Oct. 15, 1941; s. Tomas Taitano Gutierrez and Rita Benavente Cruz; m. Geraldine Chance Torres, 1963; children: Carla Stahl, Tommy, Hannah. Mem. Senate Guam, beginning 1972, spkr., chmn. of ways and means com., chmn. HUD; vice chmn. rules com., tourism com., transp. com.; gov. Guam, Agana, 1994—2003; dir. GMP Associates. Democrat. Roman Catholic. Mailing: PO Box 404 Hagatna GU 96932-0404*

GUTIERREZ, CARLOS G., chemistry professor; BS, UCLA; PhD in Synthetic Organic Chemistry, U. Calif., Davis, 1975. Prof. chemistry Calif. State U., LA, 1976—. Vis. scholar U. Calif., Berkeley, 1989—91. Recipient Presdl. Award for Excellence in Sci., Math. and Engring. Mentoring, 1996, Lifetime Achievement Award, AAAS, US Professors of Yr. Award for Outstanding Master's Universities and Colleges Prof., Carnegie Found. for Advancement of Tchg. and Coun. for Advancement and Support of Edn., 2005. Office: Calif State U 5151 State University Dr Los Angeles CA 90032 Office Phone: 323-343-2356. Office Fax: 323-343-6411. E-mail: cgutier@calstatela.edu.*

GUTIERREZ, CARLOS MIGUEL, secretary of commerce, former grocery manufacturing company executive; b. Havana, Cuba, Nov. 4, 1953; m. Edilia Gutierrez; children: Carlos, Erika, Karina. Student in Bus. Adminstrn., Monterrey Inst. Tech., Queretaro, Mex. Sales rep., various sales and mktg. positions Kellogg de Mex., Mexico City, 1975—82, gen. mgr., 1984—89; pres., CEO Kellogg Can., 1989-90; supr. L.Am. mktg. svcs. Kellogg Co., Battle Creek, Mich., 1982-83, mgr. internat. mktg. svcs., 1983-84, corp. v.p. product devel., 1990, v.p., 1990-93, exec. v.p., 1994-96, exec. v.p. bus. devel., 1996-98, COO, 1998-99, pres., 1998—2000, CEO, 1999—2004, chmn., 2000—04; sec. US Dept. Commerce, Washington, 2005—. Exec. v.p. sales and mktg. Kellogg USA, Battle Creek, 1990—93, exec. v.p., 1993—94, gen. mgr. cereal divsn., 1993—94; pres. Kellogg Asia-Pacific, 1994—96. Mem.: Grocery Mfrs. Am. (bd. dirs.). Office: US Dept Commerce 1401 Constitution Ave NW Washington DC 20230 Office Phone: 202-482-2000. E-mail: CGutierrez@doc.gov.*

GUTIERREZ, JAY MATTHEW, lawyer; b. June 10, 1951; BS, Georgetown U., 1973; JD, Rutgers U., 1979. Bar: D.C. 1991. Hearing atty. Office Exec. Legal Dir- U.S. Nuc. Regulatory Commn., 1980—83; regional counsel U.S. Nuc. Regulatory Commn.-Region I, 1983—89; counsel Newman & Holtzinger (now Newman Bouknight & Edgar), 1989—94; ptnr., mem. energy practice group Morgan, Lewis & Bockius LLP, 1994—. Author: Fundamentals Nuc. Regulation U.S., 1995. Mem.: ABA. Office: Morgan Lewis & Bockius LLP 1111 Pennsylvania Ave NW Washington DC 20004 Office Phone: 202-739-5466. Office Fax: 202-739-3001. Business E-Mail: jgutierrez@morganlewis.com.

GUTIERREZ, LUIS V., congressman, elementary education educator; b. Chgo., Dec. 10, 1953; m. Soraida Aracho; children: Omaira, Jessica. BA magna cum laude in English, Northeastern Ill. U., 1975. Social worker Ill. Dept. Children and Family Svcs.; adminstrv. asst. Mayor's Subcom. on Infrastructure, 1984-85; alderman for 26th ward Chgo. City Coun., 1986-93, pres. pro tempore, 1992; mem. U.S. Congress from 4th Ill. Dist., 1993—; mem. banking and fin. svcs. com., vet. affair com. Chmn. Housing, Land Acquisition and Disposition com., 1989—93. Democrat. Office: US Ho Reps 2367 Rayburn House Off Bldg Washington DC 20515-1304*

GUTIÉRREZ, NICOLÁS, JR., lawyer; b. May 1, 1964; AB, U. Miami, Coral Gables, Fla., 1985; JD, Georgetown U., Washington, 1988. Bar: Fla. 1989. Assoc. Steel Hector & Davis, LLP, Miami, 1992—94; ptnr. Rafferty, Gutiérrez, Sánchez-Alallí, Stolzenberg & Gelles, PA, Miami, 1998—2003; prin. Borgognoni & Gutiérrez, LLP, Miami, 2003—. Contbr. articles to law jours. Named one of South Fla.'s Top Lawyers, South Fla. Legal Guide, 2006—07; named to Book of Leaders, Miami Today, 2006. Mem.: South Fla. Water Mgmt. Dist. (chmn. governing bd. 1999—), Nat. Assn. Sugar Mill Owners Cuba (pres., dir. 1990—). Office: Borgognoni & Gutiérrez LLP 2665 S Bayshore Dr Ste 701 Miami FL 33133-5401

GUTIERREZ, PHILIP S., federal judge; b. LA, 1959; BA, U. Notre Dame, 1981; JD, UCLA, 1984. Bar: Calif. 1985. Assoc. LaFollette, Johnson, DeHaas, Fesler & Ames, 1986, Kern & Wooley, 1986—88; mng. ptnr. Cotkin & Collins, 1988—97; LA County judge Superior Ct. Calif., 1997—2006; judge US Dist. Ct. (Ctrl. dist.) Calif., 2007—. Office: US Dist Ct 312 N Spring St Los Angeles CA 90012*

GUTIERREZ, SIDNEY M., federal agency administrator; b. Albuquerque, June 27, 1957; BS in Aero. Engring., USAF Acad., 1973; MA in Mgmt., Webster U., 1977. Commd. 2d lt. USAF, advanced through grades to col., test pilot, ret.; dir. satellite ctr. Sandia Nat. Labs., Albuquerque, now dir., sys. assessment and rsch.; ret. space shuttle pilot and comdr. NASA, mem. aerospace safety adv. panel, 2000—03. Chmn. Goodwill Industries of N.Mex., N.Mex. Bd. regents N.Mex. Inst. Mining and Tech. Named one of 50 Most Important Hispanics in Govt., Edn., Hispanic Engineer and Info. Tech. mag., 2005. Office: Sandia Nat Labs PO Box 5800 Albuquerque NM 87185 E-mail: smgutie@sandi.gov.

GUTIERREZ-JONES, CARL SCOTT, English educator; b. Cheverly, Md., Feb. 22, 1960; s. Jose and Joyce (Coleman) G.; m. Leslie Sampson Jones, Aug. 18, 1989; children: Marina, Natalia. BA, Stanford U., 1982; PhD, Cornell U., 1991. Asst. prof. english U. Calif., Santa Barbara, 1990-95, assoc. prof., 1995-2001, full prof., 2001—. Chair English dept., U. Calif. Santa Barbara, July 2000—. Author: (books) Rethinking the Borderlands: Between Chicano Culture and Legal Discourse, 1995, Critical Race Narratives: A Study of Race, Rhetoric and Injury, 2001; editl. bd. (jour.) Aztlan: A Journal of Chicano Studies, 1998—. Mem. leadership coun., So. Poverty Law Ctr., Montgomery, Ala., 1990—, Amnesty Internat., Santa Barbara, 1990—, Nat. Coun. of La Raza, N.Y., 1992—; vol. Head Start, 1990-92. Recipient post-doctoral fellowship, Ford Found., 1993-94, Humanities Faculty fellowship, U. Calif. Regents, 1997-98, Harold J. Plous award, U. Calif. Santa Barbara, 1993, Rockefeller Found. award, 2000—; grantee Calif. State Legislature, 1992—. Mem. Modern Language Assn., Am. Studies Assn., U. Calif. Santa Barbara faculty Assn. (pres. 1999-2001). Democrat. Avocation: rock climbing. Office: U Calif Santa Barbara English Dept 2702 South Hall Santa Barbara CA 93106 Fax: 805-893-4622. E-mail: carlgj@english.ucsb.edu.

GUTKNECHT, GIL (GILBERT WILLIAM GUTKNECHT JR), former congressman, former state legislator; b. Cedar Falls, Iowa, Mar. 20, 1951; s. Gilbert William Sr. and Joan (Kerns) G.; m. Mary Catherine Keefe, June 3, 1972; children: Margaret, Paul, Emily. BA, U. No. Iowa, 1973. Sales rep. J. S. Latta, Cedar Falls, 1973-78, Valley Sch. Supplies, Appleton, Wis., 1978-81; auctioneer Rochester, Minn., 1978-95; mem. Minn. Ho. Reps. from Dist. 30A, Rochester, 1982-95, floor leader, 1990—94; mem. US Congress from 1st Minn. dist., 1995—2007, mem. sci. com., budget com., agriculture com., standards com., human resources com., govt. reform com., 1997—, chmn. dairy nutrition & forestry com. Chair Minn. Presdl. Campaign of Rep. Jack F. Kemp, 1988. Named Guardian of Small Bus., Nat. Fedn. Independence Bus., 2002; recipient Friend of the Farm Bur. award, Minn. Farm Bur. Fedn., 2002, Taxpayers Friend award, Nat. Taxpayers Union, 2003. Republican. Roman Catholic. Avocations: fishing, boating, baseball.*

GUTMAN, HARRY LARGMAN, lawyer, educator; b. Phila., Feb. 23, 1942; s. I. Cyrus and Mildred B. (Largman) Gutman; m. Anne G. Aronsky, Aug. 28, 1971; children: Jonathan, Elizabeth. AB cum laude, Princeton U., 1963; BA, U. Coll., Oxford, Eng., 1965; LLB cum laude, Harvard U., 1965; MA (hon.), U. Pa., 1984. Bar: Mass. 1968, U.S. Tax Ct. 1969, Pa. 1989, DC 1996. Assoc. Hill & Barlow, Boston, 1968-75, ptnr., 1975-77; clin. assoc. Law Sch. Harvard U., Cambridge, Mass., 1971-77; instr. Boston Coll., 1974-77; atty.-advisor Office Tax Legis. Counsel U.S. Dept. Treasury, 1977-78, dep. tax law legis. counsel, 1978-80; assoc. prof. law U. Va., Charlottesville, 1980-84; prof. Law Sch. U. Pa., 1984-89; ptnr. Drinker Biddle & Reath, Phila., 1989-91; chief staff joint com. taxation U.S. Congress, 1991-93; ptnr. King & Spalding, Washington, 1994-99; prin. KPMG LLP, Washington, 1999—. Cons. Office Tax Policy U.S. Dept. Treasury, 1980, Am. Law Inst., 1980—84; reporter Generation-Skipping Tax Project Arden Ho. III Conf.; vis. prof. Law Sch. U. Va., 1985—89, Ill. Inst. Tech., 1986. Author: (book) Transactions Between Partners and Partnerships, 1973, Minimizing Estate Taxes: The Effects of Inter Vivos Giving, 1975; author: (with F. Sander) Tax Aspects of Divorce and Separation, 1985; author: (with D. Lubick) Treaury's New Views on Carryover Basis, 1979, Effective Federal Tax Rates on Transfers of Wealth, 1979; author: (with others) Federal Wealth Transfer Taxes after ERTA, 1983, Reforming Federal Wealth Transfer Taxes after ERTA, 1983, A Comment on the ABA Tax Section Task Force Report on Transfer Tax Restructuring, 1988, Where Does Congress Go From Here? Base Timing and Measurement Issues in the Transfer Tax, 1989. Trustee Washington (D.C.) Nat. Opera. Fellow: Am. Coll. Tax Counsel; mem.: Am. Law Inst., Am. Tax Policy Inst. Office: KPMG LLP 2001 M St NW Washington DC 20036-3310 Home Phone: 202-337-1356; Office Phone: 202-533-3044. Business E-Mail: hgutman@kpmg.com.

GUTMAN, HENRY B., lawyer; b. Phila., Nov. 14, 1950; AB cum laude, U. Pa., 1972; JD cum laude, Harvard U., 1975. Bar: NY 1977, registered: US Dist. Ct. (ea. and so. dists.) NY 1977, US Dist. Ct. (no. dist.) NY 1981, US Ct. Appeals (9th cir.) 1978, US Ct. Appeals (2d and 11th cirs.) 1984, US Ct. Appeals (1st cir.) 1989, US Ct. Appeals (fed. cir.) 1995, US Tax Ct. 1981, US Supreme Ct. 1994. Law clk. to Hon. John F. Dooling Jr., U.S. Dist. Ct., ea. dist. N.Y., 1975—76; ptnr. Simpson Thacher & Bartlett LLP, NYC, chmn. intellectual property group. Mem.: ABA, Am. Coll. Trial Lawyers, Am. Intellectual Property Law Assn., Copyright Soc. Am., Fed. Bar Coun., Assn. Bar City NY. Office: Simpson Thacher & Bartlett LLP 425 Lexington Ave New York NY 10017-3954 Office Phone: 212-455-3180. Office Fax: 212-455-2502. Business E-Mail: hgutman@stblaw.com.

GUTMAN, LUCY TONI, social worker, educator; b. Phila., July 13, 1936; d. Milton R. and Clarissa (Silverman) G.; divorced; children: James, Laurie. BA, Wellesley Coll., Mass., 1958; MSW, Bryn Mawr Coll., Pa., 1963; MA in History, U. Ariz., Tucson, 1978; MEd, Northwestern State U., Natchitoches, La., 1991, MA in English, 1992; postgrad., U. So. Miss., Hattiesburg, 1992—. Cert. sch. social work specialist, Nat. Bd. Cert. Counselor; diplomate in clin. social work; cert. secondary tchr., La.; cert. counselor, La.; cert. Acad. Cert. Social Workers, La. Bd. Cert. Social Workers. Social worker Phila. Gen. Hosp., 1963-65; sr. social worker Irving Schwartz Inst. Children and Youth, 1965-66; sr. psychiat. social worker Child Study Ctr. Phila., 1966-68; chief social worker Framingham (Mass.) Ct. Clinic Juvenile Offenders, 1968-72; dir. clinic, supr. social work Tucson East Cmty. Mental Health Ctr., 1972-74; coord. spl. adoptions program Cath. Social Svcs. So. Ariz., Tucson, 1974-75; social worker Met. Ministry, 1983; supr. social work Leesville (La.) Mental Health Clinic, 1984; sch. social worker Vernon Parish Sch. Bd., Leesville, 1984—2007; ret., 2007. Cons. Nashua Cmty. Coun., NH, 1969-72; adj. instr. English, sociology, Am. and European history Northwestern State U., Ft. Polk, La., 1984-1996; part-time counselor River North Psychol. Svcs., Leesville, 1989-92; presenter in field at confs. Contbr. articles to profl. jours. Nat. Soc. Colonial Dames scholar, 1978-79; fellow Pa. State, 1961-62, NIMH, 1962-63. Mem. NASW (diplomate), La. Hist. Assn., So. Hist. Assn., So. Assn. Women Historians, Gamma Beta Phi, Phi Alpha Theta, Phi Kappa Phi. Home: 2004 Allison St Leesville LA 71446-5104

GUTMAN, RICHARD EDWARD, lawyer; b. New Haven, Apr. 9, 1944; s. Samuel and Marjorie (Leo) G.; m. Jill Leslie Senft, June 8, 1969 (dec.); 1 child, Paul Senft; m. Rosann Seasonwein, Dec. 10, 1987. AB, Harvard U., Cambridge, Mass., 1965; JD, Columbia U., NYC, 1968. Bar: NY 1969, US Ct. Appeals (2d cir.) 1969, US Dist. Ct. (so. and ea. dists.) NY 1975, US Supreme Ct. 1982, Tex. 1991. Counsel Exxon Corp., NYC, 1978-90, Dallas, 1990-91, asst. gen. counsel, 1992-99, Exxon Mobil Corp., Dallas, 1999—. Pres. 570 Park Ave Apts., Inc., NYC, 1984—89, past bd. dirs. Fellow Am. Bar Found. (life); mem. ABA (fed. regulation securities com., vice-chmn. 1995-98), Am. Law Inst., NY State Bar Assn. (exec. com. 1983-86, 1993-2005, securities regulation com. 1980—, chmn. 1993-97, chmn. bus. law sect. 2001-02), Assn. of Bar of City of NY (securities regulation com. 1980-81, 83-86), Dallas Bar Assn., Coll. of the State Bar of Tex., N.A.M. (corp. fin. and mgmt. com.), Harvard Club (NYC, admissions com. 1983-86, chmn. 1985-86, nominating com. 1986-87, bd. dirs. 1988-91, v.p. 1990-91), Harvard Club (Dallas bd. dirs. 1998-2001)

GUTMAN, ROBERT WILLIAM, retired art educator; b. NYC, Sept. 11, 1925; s. Theodore and Elsie G. BA, NYU, 1945, MA, 1948. Instr. New Sch. for Social Research, 1955-57; founder, lectr. Bayreuth Festival Master Classes, 1959-61; lectr. design history art and design div. Fashion Inst. Tech., SUNY, NYC, 1957-66, asst. prof., 1966-71, assoc. prof., 1971-76, prof., 1971-88, dean div. art and design, 1974-79, dean grad. studies, 1979-88, ret., 1988. Vis. prof. Bard Coll., 1991; lectr. PBS Telecast of Bayreuth Festival, 1983, U Melbourne, 2004. Author: Richard Wagner, The Man, His Mind, and His Music, 1968, German transl., 1970, Italian transl., 1983, Mozart, A Cultural Biographgy, 1999; editor: Volsunga Saga (transl. by William Morris), 1961. Bd. dirs. Am. Friends of Internat. Found. Mozarteum, 1991—, The Collegiate Chorale, 1990—. Biography juror Nat. Book Awards, 1973; Guggenheim fellow, 1979 Mem.: Lotos (NYC), Nat. Arts (NYC). Home: 37 W 12th St New York NY 10011-8559

GUTMAN, ROY WILLIAM, reporter; b. NYC, Mar. 5, 1944; s. Ira H. and Linda (Snyder) Gutman; m. Elizabeth Jane Dribben, May 17, 1979; 1 child, Caroline. BA, Haverford Coll., 1966; MS, London Sch. Econs., 1968; DLitt (hon.), Haverford Coll., 1995. Reporter UPI, Frankfurt, Germany, 1968—70; corr. Reuters News Agy., Bonn, Germany, 1971—72, bur. chief Belgrade, Yugoslavia, 1973—75, Dept. State corr. Washington, 1976—80, Capitol Hill bur. chief, 1981; nat. security reporter Newsday, Washington, 1982—89, European bur. chief Bonn, 1990—94, fgn. affairs reporter Washington, 1994—2000; corr. Newsweek, Washington, 2001—. Jennings Randolph sr. fellow U.S. Inst. Peace, 2002—03; adj. prof. Medill Sch. Journalism, 2003. Author: (book) Banana Diplomacy, 1988 (named one of best 200 books of 1988, N.Y. Times, Best Am. Book of the Yr., Times Lit. Supplement, London, 1988), A Witness to Genocide, 1993; co-editor: Crimes of War, 1999; contbr. articles to profl. jours. Named one of best fgn. affairs reporters in Washington, The Washingtonian, 1989; recipient Human Rights in Media award, Internat. League for Human Rights, 1992, Pulitzer Prize for internat. reporting, 1993, George Polk Fgn. Reporting award, 1993, Selden Ring Investigative Reporting award, U. So. Calif., 1993, Nat. Headliner Outstanding News Reporting award, 1993, Heywood Brown award, Newspaper Guild, 1993, Excellence in Series/Investigation award, Deadline Club, 1993, Hal Boyle award, Overseas Press Club, 1993, Exemplary Cmty. Svc. Alumni award, Haverford Coll., 1994. Mem.: Inst. Current World Affairs. Jewish. Avocations: gardening, photography. Office: Newsweek 1750 Pennsylvania Ave NW Washington DC 20006 Home: 31 Westview Rd Northport NY 11768-1040 E-mail: RoyGut@Newsweek.com. *Facts matter. And collecting them requires a readiness to get your fingernails dirty.*

GUTMANN, AMY, academic administrator, political science and philosophy educator; b. Bklyn., Nov. 19, 1949; m. Michael Doyle, 1976; 1 child: Abigail. BA magna cum laude, Harvard-Radcliffe Coll., 1971; MSc in polit. sci., London Sch. Economics, 1972; PhD in polit. sci., Harvard U., 1976. Asst. prof. politics Princeton U., NJ, 1976—81, assoc. prof. politics NJ, 1981—86, prof. politics NJ, 1987—2004, Andrew W. Mellon Professor NJ, 1987—90, dir. grad. studies dept. politics NJ, 1986-88, dir. polit. philosophy program NJ, 1987-89, dir. ethics and pub. affairs program NJ, 1990-95, NJ, 1997—2000, founding dir. U. Ctr. for Human Values NJ, 1990—95, NJ, 1998—2001, dean faculty NJ, 1995-97, academic advisor to pres. NJ, 1997—98, Laurance S. Rockefeller U. Prof. of Politics and the U. Ctr. for Human Values NJ, 1990—2004, provost NJ, 2001—04; pres. U. Pa., Phila., 2004—. Visitor Inst. for Advanced Study, Princeton U., 1981-82; vis. Rockefeller Faculty Fellow, Ctr. for Philosophy and Pub. Policy, U. Md., 1984-85; vis. prof., Kennedy Sch. Govt., Harvard U., 1988-89, adv. coun., 1996-2001; Tanner lectr., Stanford U., 1994-95; academic adv. bd. Inst. Human Sciences, Vienna, 2001-; mem. bd. dirs., exec. com., Centers for Advanced Study in Behavioral Sciences, Stanford U., 1998-, Princeton U. Press, 1996-; secondary faculty appointment Annenberg Sch. for Comm., 2004—; bd. dirs, The Vanguard Group, 2006-. Author: Liberal Equality, 1980, Democratic Education, 1987, 2nd edit., 1999; co-author: (with Dennis Thompson) Democracy & Disagreement, 1996, (with Anthony Appiah) Color Conscious, 1996 (award N.Am. Soc. Social Philosophy), Identity in Democracy, 2003, (with Dennis Thompson) Why Deliberative Democracy? 2004; editor: Democracy and the Welfare State, 1988, Multiculturalism, 1992, Freedom of Association, 1998, U. Ctr. for Human Values Series, Princeton U. Press, 1992-; co-editor: (with Dennis Thompson) Ethics and Politics, 3d edit., 1997; mem. editl bd. Teachers' Coll. Record, 1990-95, Cambridge Studies in Philosophy and Pub. Policy, 1991-, Raritan, 1995-, Jour. Polit. Philosophy, 1995-, Handbook of Polit. Theory, 1999-, Annual Reviews, 2001-05; internat. adv. bd. Ethnicities, 2000-. Trustee Carnegie Corp., 2005—. Fellowship, NEH, 1977, Am. Coun. Learned Societies, 1978-79, U. Hong Kong, 1998-99; Grant, Spencer Found., 1995-98, Sr. Scholar Award, 1999-2003; recipient Gustavus Myers Ctr. for Study of Human Rights in N.Am. Award, 1997, N.Am. Soc. for Social Philosophy Book Award, 1996-97, Ralph J. Bunche Award, Am. Polit. Sci. Assn., 1997, Bertram Mott Award, Am. Assn. Univ. Profs., Rider Coll., 1998, President's Disting. Tchg. Award, 2000, Centennial Medal, Harvard U., 2003, others. Mem. Assn. Practical and Profl. Ethics (exec. com., 1990-), Am. Soc. Political and Legal Philosophy (pres. 2001-04); fellow Am. Academy of Arts and Sciences, Nat. Academy of Edn., Am. Academy Polit. and Social Sci. Office: Univ Pa 100 College Hall Philadelphia PA 19104-6380 Home: President's House Eisenlohr 3812 Walnut St Philadelphia PA 19104 Office Phone: 215-898-7221. Office Fax: 215-898-9659.*

GUTMANN, DAVID LEO, psychology professor; b. NYC, Sept. 17, 1925; s. Isaac and Masha (Agronsky) G.; m. Joanna Redfield, Aug. 18, 1951; children: Stephanie, Ethan. MA, U. Chgo., 1956, PhD, 1958. Lectr. psychology Harvard U., Cambridge, Mass., 1960-62; prof. U. Mich., Ann Arbor, 1962-76, Northwestern U., Chgo., 1976-97, prof. emeritus, 1998—, chief of psychology, 1976-81, dir. older adult program, 1978-95. Vis. emeritus prof. Hebrew U., Jerusalem, 1997. Author: Reclaimed Powers: Toward a New Psychology of Men and Women in Later Life, 1987, Reclaimed Powers: Men and Women in Later Life, 1994, The Human Elder in Nature, Culture, and Society, 1997; co-author: (with Bardwick, Douvan and Horner) Feminine Personality and Conflict, 1979. With U.S. Mcht. Marine, 1943-46. Recipient Career Devel. award, NIMH, 1964—74. Fellow Gerontol. Soc. Am.; mem. Am. Vets. of Israel, Nat. Assn. Scholars. Jewish. Home: 277 W Hill Rd Wallingford VT 05773-9479 Home Phone: 802-446-2923. Personal E-mail: dgutmann2004@yahoo.com.

GUTMANN, RONALD J., retired electrical engineering educator; b. Bklyn., Nov. 16, 1940; s. Ludwig G. and Dorothy (Levy) G.; m. Suzanne French, Aug. 27, 1967; children: David, Jennifer. BSEE, Rensselaer Poly. Inst., 1962, PhD in Electrophysics, 1970; MSEE, NYU, 1964. Mem. tech. staff Bell Telephone Labs., Whippany, NJ, 1962-66; sr. engr. Lockheed Electronics Co., Plainfield, NJ, 1966-67; rsch. asst. Rensselaer Poly. Inst., Troy, NY, 1967-70, asst. prof. elec. engring., 1970-74, assoc. prof., 1974-80, prof., 1980—2006, prof. emeritus, 2006—. Dir. Ctr. for Integrated Electronics, 1989-94; vis. mem. tech. staff Bell Labs., Whippany, 1979; program dir. NSF, Washington, 1981-83; presenter in field; cons. in field; expert witness in field. Author, editor McGraw Hill series on continuing edn. in electonics; co-author: Chemical-Mechanical Planarization of Microelectronic Materials, 1997, Copper-Fundamental Mechanisms for Microelectronic Applications, 2000, Chemical-Mechanical Polishing of Law Dielectric Constant Polymers and Organosilicate Glasses, 2002; contbr. numerous articles to profl. jours. Recipient Disting. Svc. award NSF, 1983; engring. fellow NASA, 1977. Fellow IEEE (chmn. awards com. 1984-85, vice chmn. awards bd. 1987-88, mem. numerous tech. program coms., fellow award for contbns. to microwave semiconductor tech.). Avocations: jogging, tennis, reading. Office: Rensselaer Poly Inst CII 6129 15th St Troy NY 12181 Home Phone: 518-272-6910; Office Phone: 518-276-6794. Business E-Mail: gutmar@rpi.edu.

GUTOWICZ, MATTHEW FRANCIS, JR., radiologist; b. Camden, NJ, Feb. 23, 1945; s. Matthew F. and A. Patricia (Walczak) G.; m. Alice Mary Bell, June 27, 1977; 1 child, Melissa. BA, Temple U., 1968; DO, Phila. Coll. Osteo. Medicine, 1972. Diplomate Am. Bd. Radiology, Am. Bd. Nuclear Medicine. Intern Mercy Hosp., Denver, 1972-73; resident in diagnostic radiology Hosp. of U. Pa., Phila., 1973-76, fellow in nuclear medicine, 1976-77; chief dept. radiology and nuclear medicine Fisher Titus Med. Ctr., Norwalk, Ohio, 1977—; pres. Firelands Radiology, Inc., Norwalk, 1977—. Ptnr. Pacifica Seafood Restaurant, Palm Desert, Calif. Republican. Roman Catholic. Avocations: photography, tennis, scuba diving. Home: 23 Patrician Dr Norwalk OH 44857-2463 Office Phone: 419-668-8101 x 6205. Personal E-mail: matthewg@neo.rr.com.

GUTREUTER, JILL STALLINGS, financial consultant, planner; b. Chgo., Mar. 25, 1937; d. C.G. and Ann (Subject) Stallings; m. Robert L. Gutreuter, June 5, 1971; 1 child, Julia E. BA, U. Ill., 1967; postgrad., Chgo.-Kent, 1968-69, Coll. Fin. Planning, Denver, 1994. Staff dir. ABA, Chgo., 1969-71; trust officer Peoples Trust/Summit Bank, Ft. Wayne, Ind., 1980-87; fin. cons. Merrill Lynch, Ft. Wayne, Ind., 1987—2003; 2d v.p. investments Smith Barney, Ft. Wayne, Ind., 2003—. Fin. planning tchr., continuing edn. divsn. Ind. U.-Purdue U. , Ft. Wayne, 1990—2000. Bd. dirs., mem. fin. com. YWCA, Ft. Wayne, 1997—2003; pres. Art League, Ft. Wayne Mus. Art, 1992—93; trustee Episcopal Diocese of North Ind. Found., South Bend, 1995—2000; bd. dirs. Girl Scouts of the Limberlost, No. Ind., 1997—2000, 2003—. Recipient Women of Achievement award YWCA, Ft. Wayne, 1994. Mem.: Inst. CFPs, Altrusa Internat. (pres. Ft. Wayne chpt. 1992—94), DAR, Rotary Internat. Episcopalian. Avocations: swimming, walking, painting, knitting. Home: 2312 Forest Park Blvd Fort Wayne IN 46805-3619 Office: Smith Barney One Summit Sq 20th Fl Fort Wayne IN 46869-3429

GUTSCH, WILLIAM ANTHONY, JR., astronomer; b. Newark, Jan. 14, 1946; s. William Anthony and Mary (Ellenback) G. BS, St. Peter's Coll., 1967; MS, U. Va., 1973, PhD, 1978; LHD, St. Peter's Coll., 1995. Staff astronomer Rochester Museum and Sci. Ctr., NY, 1973-82; chmn. Am. Mus.-Hayden Planetarium, NYC, 1982-95; ind. cons., writer, prodr. for sci. ctrs., pubs., and TV, computer & multi-media, 1995—; pres., CEO Challenger Ctr. for Space Sci. Edn., Alexandria, Va., 2004—. Cons., lectr. in field; news columnist Rochester Times-Union, 1980-84; sci. reporter Sta.-WOKR-TV, Rochester, N.Y., 1976-82; sci. corr. Sta.-WABC-TV, N.Y.C., 1982-84, sci. editor., 1984-88; on-air meteorologist, spl. sci. corr. ABC Network, 1986-93; sci. columnist Gannett, 1980-90; cons. U. Santiago, Chile, 1982, NASA 2003-; sci. corr. USA Network, 1993—; pres. Great Ideas, 1995-. Author: The Search for Extraterrestrial Life, 1991, 1001 Things Everyone Should Know About the Universe, 1998, (with Isaac Asimov) The Exploding Suns, 1996; author other books, also newspaper articles, TV news and planetarium scripts; writer, contbg. editor New Book of Knowledge, 1992—; writer Discovery Channel, 1994-95. Recipient award of svc. U. Santiago, 1982, City of Buenos Aires, 1983, City of San Juan, 1991, City of Jaharta, Indonesia, 1991; Emmy nominee, 1987. Mem. Am. Astron. Soc., Am. Meteorol. Soc., Am. Assn. Physics Tchrs., Internat. Planetarium Soc. (pres. 1992-94, past pres. 1994-96). Office: Challenger Ctr for Space Sci Edn 1250 N Pitt St Alexandria VA 22314 E-mail: BillGutsch@cs.com.

GUTSCHE, CARL DAVID, chemistry professor; b. LaGrange, Ill., Mar. 21, 1921; s. Frank Carl and Vera (Mutchler) G.; m. Alice Eugenia Carr, June 4, 1944; children: Clara Jean, Betha Lynn, Christopher Glenn. BA, Oberlin Coll., 1943. With Office Sci. Devel., USDA, 1943-44; instr. chemistry Washington U., St. Louis, 1947-48, asst. prof., 1948-51, assoc. prof., 1951-59, prof., 1959-89, prof. emeritus, 1989—, chmn. dept., 1970-76; Robert A. Welch prof. chemistry Tex. Christian U., Ft. Worth, 1989—2002; vis. scholar U. Ariz., Tucson, 2002—. Cons. in field; mem. adv. bd. Petroleum Rsch. Fund., 1971—74; chmn. medicinal chemistry study sect. NIH, 1978—81. Author: The Chemistry of Carbonyl Compounds, 1967, Carbocyclic Ring Expansion Reactions, 1968, Fundamentals of Organic Chemistry, 1975, Calixarenes, 1989, Calixarenes Revisiited, 1998; mem. adv. bd.: Jour. Organic Chemistry, 1979-83; mem. editorial bd.: Organic Preparations and Procedures Internat., 1968—, Jour. Inclusion Phenomena, 1993-2000; contbr. articles to profl. jours. Bd. dirs. St. Louis Conservatory and Schs. for Arts, 1978—82, Ft. Worth Chamber Music Soc., 1999—2002. Recipient Alumni award Washington U., 1977; Guggenheim fellow, 1981. Fellow AAAS; mem. Am. Chem. Soc. (chmn. St. Louis sect. 1959, mem. pub. com. 1974-77, com. on coms. 1977-80, com. on profl. tng. 1980-89, cons. to com. 1990-98, councilor and dir., St. Louis sect. award 1971, Midwest award 1988, Doherty award 1998, Izatt-Christensen award 2002), Chem. Soc. (London), AAUP, Phi Beta Kappa (mem. qualifications com. 1992—2003), Sigma Xi. Home: 7607 S Galileo Ln Tucson AZ 85747 Business E-Mail: d.gutsche@tcu.edu.

GUTSTEIN, CAROL FEINHANDLER, realtor; b. Chgo., Aug. 31, 1941; d. Emanuel Joshua and Rose (Paster) Feinhandler; m. Solomon Gutstein, Sept. 3, 1961; children: Jonathan, David, Daniel, Joshua. BS in Edn., Loyola U., 1962; MA in Spl. Edn., DePaul U., 1969. Cert. comml. investment mem.; grad. residential real estate; cert. comml. real estate. Spl. cons. Mayor's Office of Sr. Citizens and Handicapped, Chgo., 1977-79; realtor C-21 Shoreline, Evanston, Ill., 1982-84, Matanky, Chgo., 1985, Hallmark & Johnston, Chgo., 1986-95, L.H. Properties, Ltd., Lincolnwood, Ill., 1996—. Cons. Nursing Homes, Chgo., 1978—80. Compiler, editor Community Resources for the Disabled Person in the Chicago Metropolitan Area, 1978. Active campaigner Paul Simon for Senate campaign, 1984-85, 89-90; mgr., dir. Aldermanic campaigns, Chgo., 1975, 79, 95; del. 11th Congrl. Dist. Dem. Nat. Conv., 1980; mem. Dist. 1 Chgo. Sch. Coun., 1989-91. Fellowship Northwestern U., 1962. Mem. WCR (bd. dirs. 1997-98), CCIM (bd. dirs. 1997-2006), Camp Ramah (bd. dirs. 1985—), Hadassah (corr. sec. 1998, bd. dirs. 1999—) Democrat. Jewish. Office Phone: 312-659-2936. Personal E-mail: carolfg1@aol.com.

GUTSTEIN, SOLOMON, lawyer; b. Newport, RI, June 18, 1934; s. Morris Aaron and Goldie Leah (Nussbaum) G.; m. Carol Feinhandler, Sept. 3, 1961; children: Jon Eric, David Ethan, Daniel Ari, Joshua Aaron. AB with honors, U. Chgo., 1953, JD, 1956. Bar: Ill. 1956, U.S. Dist. Ct. (no. dist.) Ill. 1957, U.S. Ct. Appeals (7th cir.) 1958, U.S. Ct. Appeals (5th cir.) 1971, U.S. Supreme Ct. 1980; rabbi, 1955. Assoc. Schradzke, Gould & Ratner, Chgo., 1956-60; ptnr. firm Schwartz & Gutstein, Chgo., 1961-65, Gutstein & Cope, Chgo., 1968-72, Gutstein & Schwartz, Chgo., 1980-83, Gutstein & Sherwin, Chgo., 1983-85; ptnr. Arvey, Hodes, Costello & Burman, Chgo., 1991-92, Tenney & Bentley, Chgo., 1992—2000, mem., 2000—. Spl. asst. atty. gen. State of Ill., 1968-69; adj. prof. law John Marshall Law Sch., 1993-96; lectr. bus. law U. Chgo. Grad. Sch. Bus., 1973-82; cons. Ill. Real Property Svc., Bancroft Whitney Co., 1988-89; lectr. in field; real estate broker. Author: Illinois Real Estate, 2 vols., 1983, rev. ann. updates, 1984—95; co-author: Construction Law in Illinois, annually, 1980—84, Judaism in Art (The Windows of Shaare Tivkah), 1995, Illinois Real Estate Practice Guide, 2 edit., 1996, rev. ann. edit., 1997—2002, Illinois Practice Series: Real Estate, 3rd edit., 2006; contbr. chpt. to Commercial Real Estate Transactions, 1962-76, 1962—76; assoc. editor U. Chgo. Law Rev., 1954—56, editl. advisor Basic Real Estate I, also Advanced Real Estate II, 1960—70; author: Analysis of the Book of Psalms, 1962; contbr. articles to profl. publs. Alderman from 40th ward Chgo. City Coun., 1975-79; mem. govt. affairs adv. com. Jewish Fedn., 1984-94. Fuerstenberg scholar U. Chgo., 1950-56; Kosmerl fellow U. Chgo., 1953-56. Mem. Ill. State Bar Assn. (real estate law sect. coun. 2001), Chgo. Bar Assn., Decalogue Soc. Lawyers, B'nai B'rith. Office: Tenney & Bentley LLC 111 W Washington St Ste 1900 Chicago IL 60602-2769 Home Phone: 312-649-1560; Office Phone: 312-407-7800. Business E-Mail: sgutstein@tenbenlaw.com.

GUTTAU, MICHAEL K., state agency administrator, banker; b. Council Bluffs, Iowa, Nov. 8, 1946; s. Detlef Hugo and Ethel Evelyn (Schmidt) G.; m. Judith Ann Frazier, June 28, 1968; children: Heidi Ann, Joshua Michael. BS in Farm Operation, Iowa State U., 1969; postgrad., U. Nebr., Omaha, 1975. Administrv. asst. to dean students, asst. instr. sociology Iowa State U., Ames, 1969; trainee, asst. cashier, cashier Treynor (Iowa) State Bank, 1972-78, pres., chmn., CEO, 1978—. Appt. Iowa Supt. Banking, 1995; bd. dirs. Mercy Midlands Corp., Omaha; advisor N.Y. Fed. Res. Bank, Russian Am. Bankers Forum Acad. for Advanced Studies in Banking and Fin.; presenter Internat. Russian Banking Conf. 1992-93, mem. steering com., 1992-93; mem. U.S. Dept. State-U.S./Slovakian Counterpart Team Agr. Fin. and Credit. Chmn. steering com. Pottawattamie County Riverbend Indsl. Site, Western Iowa Devel. Assn., Mercy Hosp., Council Bluffs, Treynor Cmty. Devel. Com.; bd. dirs. Deaf Missions Worldwide Christian Ministry for Deaf; mem. youth com. Pottawattamie County 4-H; founder, pres., bd. dirs. Treynor Devel. Found. Corp.; deacon, moderator, adult and H.S. Sunday sch. tchr. Zion Congl. Ch., Treynor. With U.S. Army, 1969-72, Vietnam; with Nebr. Army NG, 1972-80. Decorated DFC with oak leaf cluster, Bronze Star, Air medal with V device, 28 Air medals; Recipient Outstanding Citizen award Treynor Town and Country Club, Swords to Plowshares award Bus.-Banks Exch. Newspaper, Moscow, 1992. Mem. Am. Bankers Assn. (chmn. future of cmty. banking study, cmty. bankers adv. bd. and coun., dir. edn. coun., mem. adminstrv. com. govt. rels. com.), Iowa Bankers Assn. (pres.-elect 1994-95, chmn. legis. com., bd. dirs.), S.W. Iowa Bank Adminstrn. Inst. (pres.), Treynor Bus. Assn. (founder, past pres., bd. dirs.), Scabbard and Blade, Gamma Gamma, Theta Delta Chi. Republican. Avocation: aviation.

GUTTENBERG, ALBERT ZISKIND, planning educator; b. Chelsea, Mass., Nov. 6, 1921; s. Harry and Edith (Bernstein) G.; m. Mariella Mascardi, June 29, 1964. AB in Social Rels., Harvard U., 1948; postgrad. in sociology, U. Chgo., 1949-51; postgrad. in city planning, U. Pa., 1958-59. Planning asst. Planning Bd., City of Portland, Maine, 1954-56; planning analyst Planning Commn., City of Phila., 1956-60; chief gen. plans and programming sect. Comprehensive Planning div., 1960-61; sr. planner Nat. Capital Downtown Com., Washington, 1962-63; assoc. prof. urban planning U. Ill., 1964-69, prof. urban and regional planning, 1969-89; chair in urban and regional renewal Dept. Geodesy, Delft U. Tech., The Netherlands, 1977-78. Cons. in field. Author: (with others) Explorations Into Urban Structure, 1964, New Directions in Land use Classification, 1965, (with others) Human Ecology, 1975, The Language of Planning, 1993, The Land Utilization Movement of the 1920s; editor Planning and Public Policy, 1974-89; contbr. articles on land use planning to profl. pubs. Served with U.S. Army, 1942-46. Guggenheim fellow, 1970-71; Brookings Inst. guest scholar, 1970-71; Gelderman Fund grantee Delft U. Tech., 1977; German Marshall Fund Travel grantee, Holland, 1979; recipient Fulbright Travel award Italy, 1986. Mem. Am. Planning Assn., Am. Inst. Cert. Planners (coll. fellows), Soc. Am. City and Regional Planning History, Fulbright Alumni Assn. Home: 711 Hamilton Dr Champaign IL 61820-6811 Office: 111 Temple Hoyne Buell Hall 611 E Lorado Taft Dr Champaign IL 61820-6921

GUTTENPLAN, HAROLD ESAU, retired food company executive; b. Flushing, NY, Oct. 12, 1924; s. Adolph and Mollie (Penner) G.; m. Jeanette Harris, Apr. 17, 1948 (dec. Nov. 28, 2004); children: Bruce David, Mark Stuart. BA, Queens Coll., 1948; MBA, NYU, 1951. Statistician printing ink div. Sun Chem. Corp., 1948-49; cost accountant, chief accountant, asst. treas. DCA Food Industries, Inc., NYC, 1949-66, treas., 1966-96, asst. sec., 1972-73, sec., dir., 1973-96; ret., 1996. Bd. dirs. Nisshin-DCA. Co-chmn. Queens Coll. 50th Alumni Day Reception, 1998; Ccub Scout leader Nassau County Thunderbird coun. Boy Scouts Am., 1955-63; trustee Midway Jewish Ctr., Syosset, NY, 2006-. With USAAF, 1943-45, PTO. Recipient Anti-Defamation League citation award, 1968. Mem. Daus. of Jacob Relatives Assn. (pres. 1976-77), Alpha Phi Omega (pres. 1947-48), B'nai B'rith (pres. Sagamore lodge 1963-64), Am. Assn. Ret. Persons (asst. state coord. Driver Safety Program 1998). Home: 69 Joyce Ln Woodbury NY 11797-2124

GUTTENTAG, CHRISTOPH, dean; BA summa cum laude, U. Calif., Santa Barbara, 1976; MA in Musicology, U. Pa., 1990. Assoc. dean/dir. recruitment planning U. Pa., Phila.; dir. undergraduate admissions Duke U., Durham, NC, 1992—2005, dean undergraduate admissions, 2005—. Office: Duke U Office of Undergrad Admissions Box 90587 Durham NC 27708-0587 Office Phone: 919-684-2898. Office Fax: 919-681-8941.*

GUTTENTAG, LUCAS, advocate, lawyer; b. San Francisco, Mar. 12, 1951; s. Otto Ernst and Erika Guttentag. AB, U. Calif., Berkeley, 1973; JD, Harvard U., 1978. Bar: Calif. 1979, N.Y. 1988, U.S. Supreme Ct. 1982, U.S. Ct. Appeals (2d, 5th, D.C. cirs.) 1989, (9th cirs.) 1980, (6th cirs.) 1988, (4th cirs.) 1990, U.S. Dist. Ct. Calif. (ctrl. dist.) 1979, (no. dist.) 1990, (ea. dist.) 1992, N.Y. (so. dist., ea. dist., we. dist,) 1988. Law clk. to judge William Wayne Justice U.S. Dist. Ct. (ea. dist.) Tex., Tyler, 1978-79; staff atty. Ctr. for Law in the Pub. Interest, LA, 1979-83; clin. prof. Columbia U. Sch. Law, NYC, 1983-88; dir. immigrants rights project ACLU Nat. Hqrs., NYC and San Francisco, 1987—. Adj. prof. Columbia U. Law Sch., 1989-98, U. Calif. at Berkeley Law Sch., 1997-, Stanford Law Sch., 2004. Co-author: Rights of Aliens and Refugees, 1990; contbr. books and TV shows, profl. law jours. Recipient Wasserman Excellence in Litigation award Am. Immigration Lawyers Assn., 1990, 91, 97, 2002, King Contbn. to Immigration Law award Nat. Immigration Project of NLG, 1991. Mem. ABA (co-chair labor law sect., immigration law com. 1991-94, coordinating com. immigration law 1995-98. Office: ACLU Immigrants' Rights Project 39 Drumm St San Francisco CA 94111 Business E-Mail: lguttentag@aclu.org.

GUTTERIDGE, THOMAS G., academic administrator, consultant, arbitrator; b. Flint, Mich., Oct. 31, 1942; s. George Ernest and Mary Ruth (Stewart) G.; m. Judith Kay Grubbs Gutteridge, Aug. 28, 1965; children: Theresa, Debbie, Cindy. BS in Industrial Engring., Gen. Motors Inst., 1965; MS in Ind. Admin., Purdue U., 1966, PhD, 1971. Teaching asst. Purdue U., Lafayette, Ind., 1967-70; asst., assoc. prof. SUNY, Buffalo, 1970—83; dean, full prof. So. Ill. U., Carbondale, 1983—92; dean, disting. prof. U. Conn., Storrs, 1992—2002, emeritus dean, disting. prof., 2002—03; dean, prof. mgmt. Coll. Bus. Adminstrn. U. Toledo, 2003—. Safety engr. Buick Motors, Flint, Mich., 1964-65; corp. recruiter Industrial Nucleonics, Columbus, Ohio, 1966-67; labor arbitrator Am. Arbitration Assn., Fed. Mediation and Conciliation Svc., 1972—; mem. Conn. State Bd. Labor Rels., 1995-98. Co-author: Organizational Career Development: Benchmarks for Building a World-Class Workforce, Organizational Career Development: State of the Practice; contbr. numerous articles to profl. jours. Recipient Career Devel. awards Am. Soc. for Tng. and Devel., 1983. Mem. Acad. of Mgmt. Human Resource Planning Soc., Golden Key Honor Soc., Beta Gamma Sigma. Democrat. Avocation: sports. Home: 523 Forest Lake Holland OH 43528 Office: U Toledo Coll Bus Adminstrn Mail Stop # 103 2801 W Bancroft St Toledo OH 43606 Office Phone: 419-530-4612. E-mail: thomas.gutteridge@utoledo.edu.

GUTTMACHER, ALAN EDWARD, physician, medical educator; b. Balt., Nov. 24, 1949; s. Manfred Shanfarber G. and Carola (Blitzman) Eisenberg; m. Diane Highum, 1978 (div. 1988); m. Brigid Mary Coles, Sept. 22, 1990. BA, Harvard U., 1972, MD, 1981. Diplomat Am. Bd. Med. Genetics. Spl. intern Children's Hosp., Boston, 1981-82, pediats. resident, 1982-85, fellow genetics, 1985-87; asst. prof. U. Vt., Burlington, 1987-90, assoc. prof., 1990—; sr. clin. adv. to dir. Nat. Human Genome Rsch. Inst. (NHGRI), 1999—2002, dep. dir., 2002—, dir. Office of Policy, Commn. & Ed. Dir. Vt. Regional Genetics Ctr., Burlington, Vt. Human Genetics Initiative; pres. bd. Alan Guttmacher Inst., NYC, 1998—. Co-editor: Genomic Medicine, 2003; contbr. articles to profl. jours., chpt. to book. Bd. dirs. Planned Parenthood Fedn. Am., NYC, 1995—; pres. bd. dirs. Planned Parenthood No. New Eng., Williston, Vt., 1992-94; mem. med. adv. bd. HHT Found. Internat., 1993—; mem. exec. com. Vt. chpt. March of Dimes, 1987-91; pediatrician Vt. Spl. Olympics, 1990-93. Farley fellow Children's Hosp., Boston, 1985-86; named Vol. of Yr. Vt. chpt. March of Dimes, 1989, HHT Found. Internat., 1996. Fellow Am. Acad. Pediats., Am. Coll. Med. Genetics; mem. Am. Pub. Health Assn., Am. Soc. Human Genetics, Vt. Med. Soc., Inst. Medicine, Nat. Academies, Hidden Hill Rd. Assn. (pres. 1993), Alpha Omega Alpha. Office: Nat Human Genome Rsch Inst NIH Bldg 31 Rm 4B09 9000 Rockville Pike MSC 2152 Bethesda MD 20892-2152 Office Phone: 301-402-0911. Office Fax: 301-402-2218. E-mail: guttmach@mail.nih.gov.

GUTTMAN, EGON, law educator; b. Niewruppin, Netherlands, Jan. 27, 1927; came to US, 1958, naturalized, 1968; s. Isaac and Blima (Liss) G.; m. Inge Weinberg, June 12, 1966; children: Geoffrey David, Leonard Jay. Student, U. Cambridge, 1945-48; LLB, U. London, London, England, 1950, LLM, 1952; post grad., Northwestern U. Sch. Law, Evanston, Ill., 1958-59. Barrister: Eng. 1952. Sole practice, England, 1952-53; faculty Univ. Coll. and U. Khartoum Sudan, 1953-58; legal advisor to chief justice, 1953-58; founder, editor Sudan Law Jour. & Reports, Sudan, 1956-57; researcher, lectr. Rutgers U. Sch. Law, Newark, 1959-60; asst. prof. U. Alta., Edmonton, Canada, 1960-62; prof. Howard U. Law Sch., Washington, 1962-68, vis. adj. prof., 1968-96; adj. prof. law Washington Coll. Law, Am. U., Wash., 1964-68, Levitt Meml. Trust scholar-prof. Wash., 1968—, dir. JD-MBA joint degree program Wash., 1990-2000; lectr. Practicing Law Inst., 1964—. Adj. prof. law Georgetown U. Law Ctr., 1972-74, Johns Hopkins U., Balt., 1973-81; vis. prof. Faculty of Law, U. Cambridge, Wolfson Coll., Eng., 1984, U. Haifa, Israel, 2000; atty.-fellow SEC, 1976-79; cons. to various U.S. agys. and spl. commns.; US rep. to UNCITRAL working groups; mem. various ALI-ABA working groups on the revision of the uniform comml. code; mem. Sec. of State's Adv. Com. on Pvt. Internat. Law; arbitrator NY Stock Exch. and NASD, 1997—. Author: Crime, Cause and Treatment, 1956; author: (with A. Smith) Cases and Materials on Domestic Rels., 1962; author: Modern Securities Transfers, 3d edit., 2002, 4th edit., 2007; author: (with R.G. Vaughn) Cases and Materials on Policy and the Legal Environment, 1973, rev., 1978, 3d edit., 1980; author: Problems and Materials on Sales Under the Uniform Comm. Code and the Convention on Internat. Sale of Goods, Comm. Transactions, vol. 2, 1990; author: (with F. Miller) supplement, 1996—98; author: (with L.F. Del Duca) Secured Transactions Under the Uniform Comm. Code, Comm. Transactions, vol. 1, 1992; author: supplement, 1997, Problems and Materials on Negotiable Instruments Under the Uniform Comm. Code and the UN Conv. on Internat. Bills of Exch. and Internat. Promissory Notes, Comm. Transactions, vol. 3, 1993, supplement, 1995; author: (with R.B. Lubic) Secured Transactions-A Simplified Guide, 1996; author: Securities Laws in the United States-A Primer for Fgn. Lawyers, 1996—99; author: (with L.F. Del Duca, F.H. Miller, P. Winship, W.H. Henning) Secured Transactions Under the Uniform Comm. Code and Internat. Commerce, 2002; author: (with L.F. Del Duca, F.H. Miller, P. Winship) Sales Under the Uniform Commercial Code and the UN Convention on International Sale of Goods, 2005; contbg. author: United States Laws of Trade and Investment, 2001; contbr. numerous articles, revs., briefs to profl. lit. Howard U. rep. Fund for Edn. in World Order, 1966-68; trustee Silver Spring Jewish Ctr., Md., 1976-79; mem. exec. com. Sha'are Tzedek Hosp., Washington, 1971-72, 97—. Leverhulme scholar, 1948-51; U. London studentship, 1951-52; Ford Found. grad. fellow, 1958-59, NYU summer workshop fellow, 1960, 61, 64; Levitt Meml. Trust scholar-professor 1982—; recipient Outstanding Svc. award Student Bar Assn., Am. U., 1970, Law Rev. Outstanding Svc. award, 1981, Washington Coll. of Law Outstanding Contbn. to Acad. Program Devel. award, 1981. Mem. Am. Law Inst., ABA, Fed. Bar Assn. Assn. Trial Lawyers Am., Brit. Inst. Internat. and Comparative Law, Soc. Legal Scholars (Eng.), Hon. Soc. Middle Temple, Hardwick Soc. of Inns of Ct., Sudan Philos. Soc., Assn. Can. Law Tchrs., Am. Soc. Internat. Law, Can. Assn. Comparative Law, B'nai Brith, Argo Lodge, Phi Alpha Delta (John Sherman Myers award 1972). Home: 14801 Pennfield Cir Silver Spring MD 20906-1580 Office: Am U Washington Coll Law 4801 Massachusetts Ave NW Washington DC 20016-8196 Office Phone: 202-274-4213. Office Fax: 202-274-4130. Business E-Mail: guttman@wcl.american.edu.

GUTTMAN, HELENE NATHAN, biomedical consultant, transpersonal counselor; b. NYC, July 21, 1930; d. Arthur and Mollie (Bergovoy) Nathan. BA, Bklyn. Coll., 1951; AM, Harvard U., 1956; MA, Columbia U., 1958; PhD, Rutgers U., 1960. Registered and cert. profl. past-life regression therapist; bd. cert. nutrition specialist; bd. cert. and registered hypnotherapist; registered and cert. transpersonal counselor; cert. and registered neurolinguistic therapist. Rsch. technician Pub. Health Rsch. Inst., NYC, 1951-52; control bacteriologist Burroughs-Wellcome, Inc., Tuckahoe, NY, 1952-53; vol. rschr. Haskins Labs., NYC, 1952-53, rsch. asst., 1953-56, rsch. assoc., 1956-60, staff microbiologist, 1960-64; lectr. dept. biology Queens Coll., NYC, 1956-57; rsch. collaborator Brookhaven Nat. Labs., Upton, L.I., NY, 1958; guest investigator Botanisches Institut der Technisches Hochschule, Darmstadt, Germany, 1960; rsch. assoc. dept. biol. scis. Goucher Coll., Towson, Md., 1960-62; vis. asst. rsch. prof. dept. medicine Med. Coll. Va., Richmond, 1960-62; asst. prof., then assoc. prof. dept. biology NYU, 1962-67; from assoc. prof. to prof. dept. biol. scis. U. Ill.-Chgo., 1967-75, prof., 1969-75; prof. dept. microbiology U. Ill. Med. Sch., 1969-75; assoc. dir. for rsch. Urban Systems Lab. U. Ill., 1975; expert Office of Dir. Nat. Heart, Lung and Blood Inst., NIH, Bethesda, Md., 1975-77, coord. rsch. resources Office Program Planning and Evaluation, 1977-79; dep. dir. Sci. Adv. Bd., Office of Adminstr., EPA, 1979-80; program coord., post-harvest tech., food safety and human nutrition, sci. and edn. adminstrn. USDA, 1980-83, assoc. dir. Beltsville (Md.) Human Nutrition Rsch. Ctr., Agrl. Rsch. Svc., 1983-89; pres. HNG Assocs., 1983—; nat. animal care coord. Nat. Program Staff Agr. Rsch. Svc./USDA, Beltsville, 1989-95. Bd. advisors The Monroe Inst., 1993—. Sr. author: Experiments in Cellular Biodynamics, 1972; co-editor (procs.) First Joint USA-USSR Joint Symposium on Blood Transfusion, Moscow, 1976, DHEW Publ. No. (NIH) 78-1246, 1978; editl. bd. Jour. Protozoology, 1972-75, Jour. Am. Med. Women's Assn., 1978-81, Methods in Cell Sci., 1994-2004; sr. editor: Science and Animals: Addressing Contemporary Issues, 1989; editor: Guidelines for Well-being of Rodents in Research, 1990, Rodents and Rabbits: Current Research Issues, 1994; (with others) Rodents and Rabbits: Addressing Current Issues, 1994; contbr. articles to profl. jours. Edn. com. Ill. Commn. on Status Women, 1974-75; cons. EPA, sci. adv. bd., 1974-79; bd. dirs. Du Page County Comprehensive Health Care Agy., 1974-75. Andelot fellow Harvard U., 1956, Rutgers U. scholar, 1960; recipient Thomas Jefferson Murray prize Theobald Smith Soc., 1959; Spl. award for work in Germany Deutscher Forschungs Gemeinschaft, 1960; Fellow Dazian Found., 1956; rsch. grantee. Fellow: AAAS, N.Y. Acad. Scis., Am. Acad. Microbiology, Am. Inst. Chemists (chmn. com.); mem.: Univ. and Coll. Women Ill. (past v.p.), Fed. Orgn. Profl. Women (past chmn. task force, past pres.), Assn. Women in Sci., Soc. Protozoology (past mem. exec. com., past com. chmn.), Am. Soc. Clin. Nutrition, Am. Soc. Cell Biology (past com. chmn.), Am. Soc. Microbiologists, Neuroscis. Soc., Am. Soc. Biol. Chemistry and Molecular Biology, Tissue Culture Assn. (com. chmn. Nat. Capital Area br. 1988—90), Soc. Sci. Exploration, Soc. for In Vitro Biology (chmn. constn. and bylaws com. 1994—2002, Disting. Svc. award 1995, 1999), Assn. for Transpersonal Psychology (profl. mem.), Soc. Am. Bacteriologists (pres.'s fellow), Internat. Assn. Regression Therapies (life profl.), Am. Running and Fitness Assn. (bd. dirs., mem. editl. bd., mem. bd. advisors 1993—95), Sigma Xi, Sigma Delta Epsilon (past coord. regional ctrs.). Home and Office: 5607 Mclean Dr Bethesda MD 20814-1021 *Personal philosophy: If it's worth having, it's worth fighting for.*

GUTWIRTH, MARCEL MARC, literature educator; b. Antwerp, Belgium, Apr. 11, 1923; s. Jacob Nahum and Frieda (Willner) G.; m. Madelyn Katz, June 20, 1948; children: Eve, Sarah, Nathanael. Student, NYU, 1941—42; AB, Columbia U., NYC, 1947, MA, 1948, PhD, 1950. Mem. faculty Haverford (Pa.) Coll., 1948-87, William R. Kenan, Jr. prof. French lit., 1977-82, John Whitehead prof., 1983-87; Disting. Prof. Grad. Ctr. CUNY, 1987-94, exec. officer PhD program in French, 1987-93. Vis. prof. Johns Hopkins U., 1967, Queens Coll., 1968, Bryn Mawr Coll., 1969, 76; Andrew Mellon vis. prof. humanities Tulane U., 1980; lectr. Folger Inst., 1985. Author: Molière ou l'Invention comique, 1966, Jean Racine: Un Itinéraire poétique, 1970, Stendhal, 1971, Michel de Montaigne ou le Pari d'exemplarité, 1977, Un merveilleux sans éclat: La Fontaine ou la poésie exilée, 1987, Laughing Matter, 1993, Madame de Sévigné-Classique à son insu, 2004. Bd. dirs. Childbirth Edn. Assn. Greater Phila., 1961-64. With AUS, 1943-46, ETO. Fulbright postdoctoral fellow Paris, 1953-54, Am. Coun. Learned Socs. fellow, 1964-65, Guggenheim fellow, 1971-72, 85, Nat. Humanities Ctr. fellow, 1985-86. Mem. ACLU, MLA (mem. editl. bd. publs. 1973-76), Am. Assn. Tchrs. of French. Jewish. Home: 3300 Darby Rd # 2221 Haverford PA 19041-1098

GUTZWILLER, MARTIN CHARLES, theoretical physicist, research scientist; b. Basel, Switzerland, Oct. 12, 1925; 1951, naturalized, 1971; 2 children. BS, Swiss Fed. Inst. Tech., Zurich, 1947, MS, 1950; PhD in Physics, U. Kans., 1953; DSc honoris causa, U. Lausanne, Switzerland, 1995, U. Freiburg, Germany, 2000, Nat. Chiao-Tung U., Hsinchu, Taiwan, 2006. Physicist Brown, Boveri & Co., Baden, Switzerland, 1950-51; with exploration and production divsn. Shell Devel. Co., Tex., 1953-60; with rsch. divsn. Internat. Bus. Machines, Zurich, 1960-63; IBM Corp., NYC, 1963-70, rsch. sci., physicist Yorktown Heights, NY, 1970-93, rsch. sci. emeritus, 1993—. Adj. prof. Columbia U., 1963-83, Yale U., 1993-. Recipient Max-Planck medal, German Phys. Soc., 2003. Fellow Am. Phys. Soc. (Dannie N. Heineman prize for math. physics 1993), Am. Acad. Arts and Sci.; mem. NAS. Achievements include research in propagation of waves, electron correlation in metals, quantum and classical mechanics, especially the chaotic phenomenon, celestial mechanics. Office: 370 Riverside Dr 14B New York NY 10025 E-mail: moongutz@aol.com.

GUY, ARTHUR WILLIAM, electrical engineering educator, researcher; b. Helena, Mont., Dec. 10, 1928; s. Arthur Jack and Evelyn (Hebb) G.; m. Vivian Ruth Walker, June 12, 1952; children: William, Sandra, Fred, Arla. BSEE, U. Wash., 1955, MSEE, 1957, PhDEE, 1966. Rsch. asst. elec. engring. dept. U. Wash., Seattle, 1956-57; rsch. engr. Boeing Airplane Co., Seattle, 1957-63; cons. engr. rehab. medicine U. Wash., Seattle, 1963-65, rsch. engr. elec. engring. dept., 1964-66, prof. elec. engring. dept., rehab. medicine, 1966-83, prof., dir. bioelectromagnetics rsch. lab. Ctr. for Bioengineering, 1983-91, prof. emeritus, 1991—. Cons. Bioelectromagnetics Cons., Seattle, 1991-2000; telecomms. facilities adv. com. Seattle City Coun., 1991-92; Sci. Adv. Group on Wireless Tech., 1993-95; active Wireless Tech. Rsch., LLC, 1993-97. Contbr. articles to profl. jours. Mem. Electromagnetic Field Task Force State Dept. Health, Olympia, Wash., 1991-92. Sgt. USAF, 1947-52. Recipient Achievement award, Westinghouse Co., 1954, spl. award for the decade internat., Power Inst. for Med. and Biol. Rsch., 1980. Fellow AAAS, IEEE (life, vice chair SCC 28 stds. bd. 1989-94, mem. COMAR 1974-89, 92-98, chair COMAR 1987-89); mem. Nat. Coun. on Radiation Protection and Measurements (hon.), Bioelectromagnetic Soc. (charter mem., pres. 1984, d'Arsenval award 1987). Methodist. Home and Office: 18122 60th Pl NE Kenmore WA 98028-8901 Home Phone: 425-486-6439. Personal E-mail: gbemc@comcast.net.

GUY, ELEANOR BRYENTON, retired writer; b. Pitts., Sept. 6, 1930; d. Lloyd Charles and Verda Eleanor (Hooper) Bryenton; m. Daniel Sowers Guy, Dec. 22, 1962; children: Stanley, Sharon. BA, Ohio Wesleyan U., 1953. Program dir. Lakewood Br. Cleve. Met. YWCA, Lakewood, Ohio, 1953-56, ctr. dir., 1956-57; residence dir., mem. faculty St. Luke's Hosp. Sch. Nursing, Shaker Heights, Ohio, 1957-59; pers. asst., counselor Acacia Mutual Life Ins. Co., Washington, 1959-62; admissions counselor Ohio No. U., Ada, 1963-64; freelance writer, photographer Kenton (Ohio) Times, 1984-88, Ada Herald, 1988-96; coord. external affairs, editor the Writ, Pettit Coll. of Law, Ohio No. U., 1995-96, ret., 1996. Sec. bd. trustees, chmn. pub. rels. com. Ada Pub. Libr., 1982—86; mem. pub. rels. com., bd. dirs. Hardin County Alcohol and Drug Abuse Ctr., Kenton, 1989—92; chmn. publicity Town and Gown Planning Com., Ada, 1988; tchr., mem. co-chair edn. com., mem. missions com., mem., sec. adminstrv. coun., mem. centennial com., publicist United Meth. Ch., 1985—2003, lay dist. del. to West Ohio Ann. conf., 1998—2004, 2006—. Mem. AAUW (pres. local br. 1978-80), Ohio No. U. Women (parliamentarian, pub. rels. chair Christmas Arts Festival 1990-96), P.E.O. (v.p. 1994-96, sec. 1998-99), Twice Ten Art Club (pres. 1984-85, 90-91, 97-98, sec. 1988-89, 99-01, mem. v.p. 2000-05), United Meth. Women (dist. spiritual growth coord. 2000-03, chmn. publicity and pub. rels. 2006). Methodist. Avocations: photography, travel, music.

GUY, MARY ELLEN JOHNSTON, political science professor; b. Carlinville, Ill., Dec. 2, 1947; d. Charles Oren and Marilyn Elinor (Denby) Johnston; divorced. BA cum laude, Jacksonville U., 1969; M of Rehab. Counseling, U. Fla., 1970; MA in Psychology, U. SC, 1976, PhD in Polit. Sci., 1981. Rehab. counselor Ga. Dept. Human Resources, Augusta, 1970-73; psychologist SC State Hosp., Columbia, 1973-80, quality assurance coord., 1980-82; prof. polit. sci. and pub. affairs U. Ala., Birmingham, 1982-97; Collins prof. pub. adminstrn. Fla. State U., 1997—. Adv. bd. Cooper Green Hosp., Birmingham, 1991-97. Editor: Women and Men of the States, 1992, Review of Public Personnel Administration, 2001-06; author: Ethical Decision Making, 1990, From Organizational Decline, 1989, Professionals in Organizations, 1985. Mem. ASPA (Disting. Rsch. award 1992, Outstanding Paper award 1992, coun. mem. 1987-90, pres. 1997-98), So. Polit. Sci. Assn. (pres. 2001-02), Am. Polit. Sci. Assn., Women's Caucus in Polit. Sci./South (pres. 1990-92). Unitarian Universalist. Avocations: golf, dog breeding. Office: Fla State U Askew Sch Pub Adminstrn & Policy Tallahassee FL 32306-2250 Business E-Mail: mary.guy@fsu.edu.

GUY, RALPH B., JR., federal judge; b. Detroit, Aug. 30, 1929; s. Ralph B. and Shirley (Skladd) G. AB, U. Mich., 1951, JD, 1953. Bar: Mich. 1953. Sole practice, Dearborn, Mich., 1954—55; asst. corp. counsel City of Dearborn, 1955—58, corp. counsel, 1958—69; chief asst. US Atty.'s Office (ea. dist.), Detroit and Mich., 1968—70, U.S. Atty., 1970—76; judge US Dist. Ct. (ea. dist.) Mich., Ann Arbor, 1976—85, US Ct. Appeals (6th cir.), Ann Arbor, 1985—94, sr. judge, 1994—. Treas. Detroit-Wayne County Bldg. Authority, 1966—73; chmn. sch. study com. Dearborn Bd. Edn., 1973; mem. Fed. Exec. Bd., 1970—, bd. dirs., 1971—73. Recipient Civic Achievement award, Dearborn Rotary, 1971, Distinguished Alumni award, U. Mich., 1972. Mem.: FBA (pres. 1974—75), ABA (state chmn. sect. local govt. 1965—70), Cin. Bar Assn., Out-County Suprs. Assn. (pres. 1965), Mich. Municipal League, Mich. Assn. Municipal Attys. (pres. 1962—64), Nat. Inst. Municipal Law Officers (chmn. Mich. chpt. 1964—69), Am. Judicature Soc., Dearborn Bar Assn. (pres. 1959—60), Detroit Bar Assn., State Bar Mich. (commr. 1975—), U. Mich. Alumni Club (local pres. Dearborn 1961—62), Rotary (local pres. 1973—74), Lambda Chi Alpha, Phi Alpha Delta. Office: US Ct Appeals 200 E Liberty St Rm 226 Ann Arbor MI 48104 also: Potter Stewart US Courthouse 100 E 5th St Cincinnati OH 45202-3988*

GUY, SALLIE T., artist; b. NYC, Dec. 17, 1928; d. Julius Paul Turner and Bessie Alice Cohen; m. John K. Mount, Dec. 24, 1949 (dec.); children: Deborah Akins, Daniel, Laurel, Paul; m. Carroll W. Guy, Dec. 1, 1966; stepchildren: Patricia Funk, Peggy Panter. BA with high honors in History, U. Rochester, 1950. Juried mem. Ky. Dept. Art, Frankfort, 1984; bd. mem. Midwest Weavers Assn., 1981—86; mem. stds. com. Ky. Guild Artists and Craftsmen, Berea, 1982—83, Berea, 1987—90; chair new bylaws com. Complex Weavers, 1994—95. Author, instr.: instrnl. video Tips, Tricks & Problem Solvers for the Handweaver, 1989, Warping and Loom Preparation, 1997; contbr. articles to profl. jours. Pres. LWV, Murray, 1980, Friends of Oakhurst, Murray State U., 1995, Murray Civic Music Assn., 1996—97; elder, trustee First Presbyn. Ch., Murray; staff, mem. evaluation com. Synod of the Covenant; chair divsn. presbytery resourcing Synod of Living Waters, 1988—90, chair comm. com., 1996—2000; moderator Presbytery Western Ky., 1980—81. Mem.: Murray Art Guild (treas. 2002—04, Artist of Yr. 2004), Handweavers Guild Am. (state rep. Ky. 1978—81, bd. dirs. 1981—89, sec. 1983—85, third v.p. 1985—86, first v.p. 1986—88). Democrat. Presbyterian. Avocations: watercolor, knitting, photography. Home: 424 Moser Ln Murray KY 42071-5029 E-mail: kenlake2@aol.com.

GUY, STEPHEN OTTO, agronomist, educator; s. Harold Paul and Sarah Katherine Guy; m. Carolyn Grace Burns, Dec. 28, 1995; children: Jeremy Otto, Lauren Kay, Kristin Mae. BS, Colo. State Univ, Ft. Collins, 1973; MS, Colo. State U., Ft. Collins, 1975; PhD, U. Wis., Madison, 1988. Project mgr. Landis Internat., Valdosta, Ga., 1988—90; prof. agronomy, ext. educator U. Idaho, Moscow, 1990—. Contbr. chapters to books. Coun. Emmanual Luth., Moscow, Idaho, 2003—06. Mem.: Western Soc. Crop Sci. (pres. 2006—), Am. Soc. Agronomy, Autosports NW (instr. novice racers 2004—). Democrat. Luthern. Avocations: autocross, car racing, skiing, gardening, travel. Office: Univ Idaho Department of Plant Soil and Ent Sci Moscow ID 83844-2339 Home Phone: 208-882-3178; Office Phone: 208-885-6744. Office Fax: 208-885-7760. Business E-Mail: sguy@uidaho.edu.

GUYAUX, JOSEPH C., corporate financial executive; BS, Brown Univ., 1972; MBA, Univ. Pitts., 1984. CEO Regional Cmty. Bank; mgmt. positions PNC Bank, 1972—, pres., 2002—, head of consumer banking, 2005—. Mem. bd. dir. Duquesne Light Holdings, Inc., Private Export Funding Corp.; chmn. Consumer Bankers Assn., 2005—. Trustee Carnegie Mus. Pitts. Office: PNC One PNC Plz 249 5th Ave Pittsburgh PA 15222-2707*

GUYER, CHARLES GRAYSON, II, psychologist; b. High Point, NC, May 22, 1949; s. Charles Grayson Sr. and Mildred Louise (Wrokman) G.; m. E.R. Ward, June 24, 1986; children: Charles Grayson III, Jarvis Griffith. BA, Appalachian State U., 1972, MA, 1974; EdD, Coll. William & Mary, 1978. Bd. cert. in counseling psychology and family psychology Am. Bd. Profl. Psychology. Resident No. Wyo. Mental Health, Buffalo, 1978-80; pvt. practice High Point, N.C., 1980-83, Greensboro, NC, 1988—98; chief sch. psychologist Perquimans County Schs., Hertford, NC, 1998—2002; pvt. practice Jacksonville, NC, 2002—. Pres. Am. Bd. Family Psychology, 1992-94, bd. dirs., 1991-96, 2000-03, sec. family bd., 2000-03, Am. Bd. Counseling Psychology, 1991-93. Contbr. chapters to books, articles to profl. jours. Lt. USN, 1983—88. Recipient Irving I. Sector award, Am. Soc. Clin. Hypnosis, 1997. Fellow APA, Am. Soc. Clin. Hypnosis (chmn. ethics com. 1993-97), Acad. Family Psychology (pres. 1995-96), Am. Acad. Counseling Psychology (found. sec. 1991-94, pres. 1995-96), Am. Acad. Counseling Psychology (bd. dirs. 1991-93, founding pres. 1993-95), Soc. Clin. Exptl. Hypnosis; mem. Am. Group Psychotherapy Assn., Va. Acad. Clin. Psychologists, Va. Psychol. Assn., NC Soc. Clin. Hypnosis, NC Psychol. Assn., Guilford County Psychol. Assn. (treas. 1997-98). Methodist. Avocations: running, reading. Home: 103 Tryon Ct Jacksonville NC 28546 Office: 217 Station St Jacksonville NC 28546 Home Phone: 910-353-2922; Office Phone: 910-353-1461. Personal E-mail: drguyerii@yahoo.com.

GUYMON, GARY LEROY, civil engineering educator; b. Farmington, N.Mex., Nov. 5, 1935; s. Leland W. and Grace E. (Cumming) G.; m. Lucinda A. Kemmis, June 11, 1988; children by previous marriage: Gary Jr., Richard, Marisa, Michael. BS, U. Calif., Davis, 1966, MS, 1967, PhD, 1970. Asst. civil engr. Calif. Dept. Water Resources, LA, 1955-66; asst. rsch. engr. U. Calif., Davis, 1969-71; assoc. prof. U. Alaska, Fairbanks, 1971-74; prof. U. Calif., Irvine, 1974-94, chmn. dept. civil engring., 1984-88, prof. emeritus, 1994—. Mem. coordinating bd. U. Calif. Water Resources Ctr., Berkeley, 1985-89; del. Univs. Coun. on Water Resources, Carbondale, Ill., 1980-94. Author: Unsaturated Zone Hydrology, 1994; contbr. numerous articles to profl. jours.; assoc. editor Advances in Water Resources, Southampton, U.K., 1981-89. Fellow ASCE; mem. Am. Geophys. Union, U.S. Com. on Large Dams, Phi Beta Kappa, Tau Beta Pi, Chi Epsilon. Independent. Avocations: woodworking, physical fitness. Office Phone: 760-635-0233. Business E-Mail: gguymon@att.net.

GUYNES, DEMI See MOORE, DEMI

GUYNN, JACK (GEORGE C. GUYNN), retired bank executive; b. Staunton, Va., 1942; BS in Indsl. Engring., Va. Polytech. Inst. and State U., 1964; MS in Indsl. Mgmt., Ga. Inst. Tech., 1969; Grad., Harvard Bus. Sch.for Mgmt. Devel., 1974. Joined Fed. Res. Bank Atlanta, 1964, first v.p., COO, 1984—96, pres., CEO, 1996—2006. Advisory bd. Va. Tech.; bd. councilors Carter Ctr.; bd. trustees Furman U., Oglethorpe U.; bd. dirs. Midtown Alliance, Atlanta, Cmty. Found.; bd. trustees Ga. Tech. Found.; mem. exec. bd. Atlanta Area Coun. Boy Scouts Am. Mem.: Atlanta Rotary Club.

GUYNN, ROBERT WILLIAM, psychiatrist, educator; b. Streator, Ill., Oct. 27, 1942; s. William Digby and Helen Louise (Dancey) G. BA, Mich. State U., 1963; MD, Johns Hopkins U., 1967. Diplomate Am. Bd. Psychiatry and Neurology. Clin. fellow Nat. Inst. of Mental Health, Washington, 1970-73; asst. prof. Dept. of Psychiatry and Behaviorial Scis. U. Tex., Houston, 1973-76, assoc. prof., 1976-83, vice-chmn., prof. psychiatry, 1983-87, interim chmn., 1987-89, chmn., 1989—. Dir. U. Tex. Mental Scis. Inst., 1987—; exec. dir. Harris County Psychiat. Ctr., 1988—; sr. oral examiner Am. Bd. Psychiatry and Neurology, 1994—2003, mem. written exam com., 1998—; editl. bd. Acad. Psychiatry, 2006—. Contbr. articles to profl. jours. and book chpts.; mem. editl. bd. Internat. Rev. Psychiatry, 1988-93, editor-in-chief, 1989-93. Bd. dirs. Vols. of Am., Houston, 1982—88; with Passages, 1991—94; mem. adv. bd. The Gathering Place, The Club House, 2004—. Surgeon USPHS, 1970—73. Recipient Psychiat. Excellence award, Tex. Soc. Psychiat. Physicians, 2000. Fellow Am. Psychiat. Assn. (disting.), Am. Coll. Psychiatrists; mem. Am. Soc. Biol. Chemistry, Tex. Rsch. Soc. on Alcoholism (pres. 1985-87), Tex. Soc. of Am. Assn. Psychiat. Adminstrs. (treas. 1990-91, pres. 1992-93), Biochem. Soc., Rsch. Soc. on Alcoholism, Houston Psychiat. Soc. (v.p. 1989-90, pres. 1991-92), Harris County Med. Soc. (bd. ethics 1989-92), Tex. Dept. Mental Health and Mental Retardation (med. adv. com. 1997—2003), Mental Health and Mental Retardation Auth. (adv. bd. 1992—). Avocations: printmaking, painting. Office: U Tex Health Sci Ctr PO Box 20708 Houston TX 77225-0708 Office Phone: 713-500-2554. Business E-Mail: robert.w.guynn@uth.tmc.edu.

GUYON, JOHN CARL, retired university administrator; b. Washington, Pa., Oct. 16, 1931; s. Carl Alexander and Sara Myrle (Bumgarner) G.; m. Elizabeth Joyce Smith, Nov. 12, 1955; children— Cynthia Joan, John Carl, II. BA, Washington and Jefferson Coll., 1953; MS, Toledo U., 1958; PhD, Purdue U., 1961. Mem. faculty U. Mo., 1961—71, prof. chemistry, chmn. dept., 1970—71, Memphis State U., 1971—74; dean Coll. Sci., So. Ill. U., Carbondale, 1974—75, Coll. Sci., So. Ill. U. (Grad. Sch.), assoc. v.p. research, 1976—80, v.p. acad. affairs and research, 1980; pres. So. Ill. U., 1987—95, chancellor, 1996—97; ret., 1997—. Author: Aanlytical Chemistry, 1965, Qualitative Analysis, 1966, Solution Equilbria, 1969; also articles, abstracts.; Gen. editor: Instrumental Methods of Analysis. With AUS, 1954—56. Eli Lilly Co. fellow, 1959-61; Owens Ill. Co. fellow, 1958; Jesse W. Lazear scholar, 1953 Mem. Am. Chem. Soc., AAAS, Phi Beta Kappa, Sigma Xi, Phi, Lambda Upsilon.

GUYTON, SAMUEL PERCY, retired lawyer; b. Jackson, Miss., Mar. 20, 1937; s. Earl Ellington and Eulalia (Reynolds) G.; m. Jean Preston, Oct. 11, 1959; children: Tamara Reynolds, William Preston, David Sage. BA, Miss. State U., 1959; LLB, U. Va., 1965. Bar: Colo. 1965, U.S. Dist. Ct. Colo. 1965, U.S. Tax Ct. 1977, U.S. Ct. Appeals (10th cir.) 1965, U.S. Ct. Appeals (5th cir.) 1981. Ptnr. Holland & Hart, Denver, 1965-92, ret., 1992. Mem. faculty Am. Law Inst. ABA, 1976-88, bd. dirs. Royal St. Corp., Royal St. Utah Inc., Deer Valley Ski Resort. Co-author: Cattle Owners Tax Manual, 1984, Supplement to Federal Taxation of Agriculture, 1983, Colorado Estate Planning Desk Book, 1984, 90; author: (chpt.) Success Briefs For Lawyers, 2000; contbr. articles to profl. jours., mags.; bd. advs. Agrl. Law Jour., 1978-82; mem. editl. bd. Jour. Agrl. Tax and Law, 1983-92. Sec., trustee Colo. Hist. Found., 1971-92, pres., 1983-87; trustee Music Assn. Aspen and Aspen Music Festival, 1980-88; precinct com. chmn. Dem. Party, 1968-70; mem. Gov.'s Mansion preservation com., 1989-92; bd. advisors Coll. Arts and Scis., Miss. State U., 1996-98; mem. com. govt. and legal affairs Hampshire Coll., 1996-2000; chmn. com. on legis. Woodmen of the World, 1972-2000. Fellow Am. Coll. Tax Counsel (bd. regents 1985-92, chmn., pres. 1989-91), Am. Tax Policy Inst. (trustee 1989-92, v.p. 1989-92); mem. ABA (sect. taxation 1967-92, chmn. sect.'s com. on agr. 1980-82), Colo. Bar Assn. (tax coun. 1983-86, sec. 1983, chmn. 1985-86), Colo. Bar Found. (life), Greater Denver Tax Csls. Assn. (chmn. 1978), Law Club Denver, Little River Lectures Assn. (bd. dirs., v.p. 1985-96, pres. 1996-2000), Am. Alpine Club (life), Colo. Mountain Club (life, joint devel. com.), Eleanore Mullen Weckbaugh Found. (trustee 1983-95), William P. Guyton Found. (co-trustee), Humphreys Found. (pres., v.p., treas. 1995-2006, dir.), Colo. Trail Found. (trustee 1987-99), Colo. Mountain Club Found. (dir., v.p. 1999-2006), Colo. Hist. Soc. (bd. dirs., chmn. nominating com. 1997-2001, co-chair dirs. coun.), Holland & Hart Found. (bd. dirs., pres. 1998-2004). Mem. Unity Ch. Home and Office: 12345 W 19th Pl Lakewood CO 80215-2516 Personal E-mail: jsguyton@msn.com. *To live fully and consciously in the present is both challenge and reward.*

GUZICK, DAVID S., dean, educator; b. 1952; MD, NYU, 1979, PhD. Resident in ob-gyn. John Hopkins Hosp., 1979—83; fellow in reproductive endocrinology U. Tex. Southwestern Med. Sch., 1983—85; dir. divsn. reproductive endocrinology Magee Women's Hosp., U. Pitts.; assoc. prof. U. Pitts., 1986—94, prof., 1994—95; chief svc. ob-gyn. Strong Meml. Hosp., Rochester, NY; Henry A. Thiede prof. and chair ob-gyn. U. Rochester Sch. Medicine and Dentistry, 1995—2002, dean and prof. ob-gyn., 2002—. Named one of America's Best 400 Doctors for Women, Good Housekeeping mag. Mem.: Soc. Assisted Reproductive Tech., Soc. Reproductive Endocrinologists, Am. Soc. Reproductive Medicine, The Endocrine Soc., Am. Bd. Obstetrics and Gynecology, Coun. Chairs of Obstetrics and Gynecology, Soc. Gynecologic Investigation, Am. Gynecologic and Obstetric Soc., Soc. Scholars. Office: Univ Rochester Sch Medicine and Dentistry 601 Elmwood Ave PO Box 706 Rochester NY 14642 Office Phone: 585-275-0017. Business E-Mail: david_guzick@urmc.rochester.edu.

GUZMAN, KATHLEEN MCFADDEN, antiques appraiser, auctioneer; b. NYC, Dec. 31, 1955; d. Walter Michael and Mary Ann (Plummer) McFadden; m. Wilfredo Guzman, Sept. 3, 1977; 1 child, Caitlin. A degree, Finch Coll., 1975; BA, Manhattanville Coll., 1977; MA in Art History, Queens Coll., 1979; exec. program (hon.), Columbia U., 1989. Auctioneer Plaza Art Galleries, NYC, 1979-80; dir. Art Deco Christie's, NYC, 1981-84, mgr., 1984-90; pres. Christie's East, NYC, 1990—2000; ind. appraiser, 2000—. Lectr. in field; regular featured appraiser PBS' Antiques Roadshow. Bd. mem. Heaven on Earth, Dixon Pl.; auctioneer Make-a-Wish, Juvenile Diabetes, Am. Craft Mus. Avocation: restoring old homes. Office: 200 E End Ave New York NY 10128

GUZMAN, MARTHA PATRICIA, science educator; b. Mexicali, Mexico, Apr. 24, 1978; arrived in U.S., 1989; d. Jose Alfredo and Andrea Concepcion Guzman. BA, Columbia Union Coll., 2002, BS in Phys. Edn., 2003. Spanish tchr. John Nevins Andrews Sch., Takoma Park, Md., 2001—03, Sligo Adventist Sch., Takoma Park, 2001—03; sci. tchr. YSA Montgomery Coll., Takoma Park, 2003—04, Spencerville Adventist Acad., Silver Spring, Md., 2003—. Mem. acad. evaluation team Columbia (Md.) Union Office of Edn., 2006. Mem.: NSTA. Seventh-Day Adventist. Office: Spencerville Adventist Acad 15930 Good Hope Rd Silver Spring MD 20905

GUZY, CAROL, photojournalist; b. Bethleham, PA, Mar. 7, 1956; ADN, Northampton County Area C.C., Pa., 1978; AAS in Photography, Art Inst. Ft. Lauderdale, 1980. Staff photographer The Miami Herald, 1980-88, The Washington Post, 1988—. Named Newspaper Photographer of Yr., Nat. Press Photographer Assn., 1989, 1992, 1996, Photographer of Yr., White House News Photographers Assn., 1991, 1993, 1994, 1995, 1996, 1997, 1997, 1998, 2000; recipient Best Portfolio Award, Atlanta Seminar Photojournalism, 1982, 1985, 1990, Robert F. Kennedy award, 1984, Excellence Citation, Overseas Press Club, 1986, Leica Excellence medal, 1994, Pulitzer Prize in spot news photography, 1986, 1995, Pulitzer Prize in feature photography, 2000. Office: The Washington Post 1150 15th St NW Washington DC 20071-0002 Office Phone: 202-334-6000.

GUZZI, ANTHONY J., construction executive; BS, USMA, West Point, 1986; MBA, Harvard Univ., 1993. With Carrier Corp., 1997—2001, pres. No. Am. parts, svc., distbn., 2001—04; pres., COO EMCOR Group Inc., Norwalk, Conn., 2004—. Served to capt. light infantry, Ranger qualified US Army, 1986—91. Office: EMCOR Group Inc 301 Merritt 7 Norwalk CT 06851*

GUZZO, JESSICA ANN, music educator; b. Pittsfield, Mass., Sept. 10, 1979; d. Joseph Olin and Donna Linda Guzzo. BS in Music Edn., Coll. St. Rose, Albany, 2001. Music dir. Lisbon Ctrl. Sch., 2001—03, Springfield Ctr. Sch., Springfield, 2004—05; performing arts tchr. BArt Charter Sch, Adams, Mass., 2005—06, dir. musicals and plays, 2001—06; music dir., vocal Pittsfield Pub. Sch., 2006—. Condr. Seaway Valley Sr. High Chorus, Ogdensburg, NY, 2003. Carol choir dir. First United Meth. Ch., 2004—. Recipient Employee of Month, Lisbon Sch., 2002. Mem.: Shakespeare and Co., Berkshire Boch Soc., Town Players Pittsfield. Office: Taconic High Sch 96 Valentine Rd Pittsfield MA 01201 Office Phone: 413-448-9634. Business E-Mail: jguzzo@pittsfield.net.

GUÐMUNDSDÓTTIR, BJÖRK See BJÖRK

GWADOSKY, DAN A., former state official, federal agency administrator; b. Fairfield, Maine, Feb. 16, 1954; m. Cheryl Norton; children: Joshua, Jessica. BS in Mgmt., Thomas Coll., LHD (hon.). Mem. Maine Ho. Reps., Augusta, 1978-96, asst. majority floor leader, house majority leader, 1988-94, spkr., 1994-96; sec. of state State of Maine, Augusta, 1997—2004; dir. Bur. Alcoholic Beverages and Lottery Ops., 2005—. Adminstr. Atrium Hotels Corp., 1985—. Mem. adv. bd. Kennebec Valley Vocat. Tech. Coll., State YMCA; bd. trustees Thomas Coll.; bd. dirs. State Leaders Found.; mem. exec. com. Coun. of State Govts.; co-chair Fairfield Cmty. Fest; co-chair bldg. com. Lawrence Pub. Libr.; active Lawrence HS Alumni Assn., Booster Club; coach boys and girls baseball, soccer, and basketball teams. Democrat. Office: Bur Alcoholic Beverages and Lottery Ops 4216 King St Alexandria VA 22302 Office Phone: 703-578-4200. Office Fax: 703-820-3551.

GWALTNEY, CORBIN, publishing executive, editor; b. Balt., Apr. 16, 1922; s. Howell Corbin and Margaret (Bell) G.; m. Doris Jean Kell, July 13, 1946 (dec.); children: Margaret Kell, Jean Corbin, Thomas Stewart; m. Jean Caryl Wyckoff, June 20, 1973 (dec.); m. Pamela I. Stokes, Sept. 11, 2003. BA, Johns Hopkins U., 1943; LHD (hon.), L.I. U., 1970; DHL (hon.), Johns Hopkins U., 1998. Instr., English Johns Hopkins U., 1946; with indsl. relations dept. Western Electric Co. and Locke div. Gen. Electric Co., 1946-49; editor Johns Hopkins Mag., 1949-59; editor, exec. dir., chmn. Editorial Projects for Edn., Inc., Balt. and Washington, 1959-78; exec. editor Chronicle Higher Edn., Washington, 1966-2000, chmn., 2000—; exec. editor Chronicle of Philanthropy, 1988—2000, chmn., 2000—. Served with AUS, 1943-45. Recipient Robert Sibley award Am. Alumni Council, 1951, 56, 59, Disting. Service to Higher Edn. awards Columbia U. Alumni Fedn., 1964, Disting. Service to Higher Edn. awards Am. Coll. Public Relations Assn., 1971; George Polk award for edn. reporting, 1979 Home: 5104 Brookview Dr Bethesda MD 20816-1602 also: 4755 Bayfields Rd Harwood MD 20776-9576 Office: Chronicle Higher Edn 1255 23rd St NW Ste 700 Washington DC 20037-1146 Business E-Mail: corbin@chronicle.com.

GWATHMEY, CHARLES, architect; b. Charlotte, NC, June 19, 1938; s. Robert and Rosalie Dean (Hook) G.; m. Bette-Ann Damson, Dec. 15, 1974. Student, U. Pa., Phila., 1956-59; M.Arch., Yale U., New Haven, Conn., 1962. Ptnr. firm Gwathmey-Siegel & Assocs. Architects, NYC, 1968—. Vis. prof. archtl. design Pratt Inst., Yale U., Princeton U., Harvard U., Columbia U., Cooper Union, UCLA; William A. Bernoudy resident architecture, Am. Acad., 2005. Pres. bd. trustees Inst. Architecture and Urban Studies, NYC, 1978. Recipient Arnold Brunner prize AAAL, 1970; William Wirt Winchester traveling fellow, 1962-63; Fulbright grantee France, 1962-63; recipient AIA Nat. Honor awards for Straus residence, Purchase, NY, 1969, Whig Hall, Princeton U., 1976, Dormitory, Dining and Student Union SUNY, Purchase 1976, Taft Residence, Cin., 1984, Westover Sch., Middlebury, Conn., 1988, AIA NY awards for Sch. Agr. Cornell U., 1991, Guggenheim Mus., NYC, 1995, Yale Alumni Arts award for outstanding achievement, 1985, Lifetime Achievement medal in visual arts Guild Hall Acad., 1988, Lifetime Achievement award NY State Soc. Archs., 1990. Fellow AIA (firm award 1982, Medal of honor 1983); mem. Am. Acad. Arts and Letters. Office: Gwathmey Siegel & Associates Architects 475 10th Ave 3d Fl New York NY 10018-1198 Business E-Mail: c.gwathmey@gwathmey-siegel.com.

GWATHMEY, GAINES, lawyer; b. Glen Cove, NY, Dec. 26, 1946; s. Gaines and Rachel (Parker) G.; m. Rose H. Harvey, May 16, 1987. AB, Harvard Coll., 1969; JD, Georgetown U., 1973. Bar: N.Y. 1974, D.C. 1975, N.J. 1985, U.S. Dist. Ct. (so., ea. and no. dists.) N.Y., U.S. Dist. Ct. N.J., U.S. Dist. Ct. D.C., U.S. Ct. Appeals (2d and 9th cirs.). Assoc. Poletti Freidin Prashker Feldman & Gartner, NYC, 1973-77; asst. U.S. atty. So. Dist. N.Y., NYC, 1977-79, chief environ. protection unit, 1979-82; assoc. Beveridge & Diamond, NYC, 1983-85, ptnr., 1985-89; ptnr., Environmental Dept. Paul Weiss Rifkind Wharton & Garrison, NYC, 1989—. Recipient Spl. Commendation U.S. Dept. Justice, N.Y.C., 1982. Mem. Fed. Bar

Coun., N.J. Bar Assn., D.C. Bar Assn., Bar Assn. City N.Y. Office: Paul Weiss Rifkind Wharton & Garrison 1785 Ave of Americas New York NY 10019 Office Phone: 212-373-3351. Fax: 212-373-2104. E-mail: ggwathmey@paulweiss.com.

GWATHMEY, JOE NEIL, JR., retired broadcast executive; b. Brownwood, Tex., Jan. 4, 1941; s. Joe Neil and Grace Christine (Henry) G.; m. Linda Sue Sams, Aug. 22, 1965; children: Sara Lynn, David Alan. BA, Howard Payne Coll., 1963; postgrad., U. Denver, 1963-64, George Washington U., 1964-65. Sta. mgr. Sta. KUT-FM, Austin, 1965-71; various mgmt. positions Nat. Pub. Radio, Washington, 1971-83, v.p., 1983-88; pres. Tex. Pub. Radio, San Antonio, 1988—2006; ret., 2006. Review panel chair United Way Bexar County, San Antonio, 1994-97; mem. adv. coun. Coll. Fine Arts U. Tex., Austin, 1990-93; trustee Tex. Student Publs., Austin, 1995-98, World Affairs Coun., San Antonio, 1999—; mem. bd. advisors N.Y. Festivals, 1986—2006. Recipient Edward R. Murrow award Corp. Pub. Broadcasting, 1988. Mem. Rotary. Democrat. Protestant. Avocations: singing, acting, public speaking, reading. Home: 2926 Meadow Cir San Antonio TX 78231-1720

GWIN, JOHN MICHAEL, retired economics professor, management consultant; b. Montgomery, Ala., June 21, 1949; s. Emmett Brindley Jr. and Irma Rebecca (Watkins) G.; m. Pamela Jane Blair, Sept. 7, 1970 (dec. Dec. 1998); children: Colin Blair, Connor Brindley BSBA in Fin. and Acctg., Auburn U., Ala., 1971; MBA, U. Ga., 1973; PhD in Mktg., Psychology, U. NC, 1979; MS in Counseling, with honors, U. S. Ala., Mobile, 2004. Fiscal officer U. Ga., Athens, 1971—73; mgr. ops. Bedsole & Gwin Inc., Fairhope, Ala., 1973—75; instr. Faulkner Coll., Bay Minette, Ala., 1975—76; rsch. asst. U. N.C., Chapel Hill, 1976—78, vis. lectr., 1978—79; asst. prof. Ind. U., Bloomington, 1979—81, U. Va., Charlottesville, 1981—83, assoc. prof. bus., 1983—2000, area coord. mktg., 1990—93, dir. Ctr. for Entrepreneurial Studies, 1992—96, prof. emeritus, 2000—. Fulbright prof. Trinity Coll., Dublin, Ireland, 1986-87, vis. prof., 1993; exec. educator numerous US firms, 1981—; cons. numerous internat. and U.S. firms, 1983—; invited lectr. Sorbonne, U. Paris, Alsace Inst., Strasbourg, France, IESA, Caracas, Venezuela, 1987; mng. ptnr. Conversations Group LLC, 2002—; vis. prof. mktg. U. Mobile, Ala., 2005-07, vis. prof. mktg. and global studies, 2007-. Managing bd. Marietta Johnson Sch., 2000—01; capital campaign com. Battleship Ala., 2001; vol. ARC; lay reader St. James Parish. Recipient Sesquicentennial Rsch. Assoc., U. Va., 1986—87, 1993—94. Fellow: Am. Mktg. Assn. (conf. coord. Ctrl. Va. chpt. 1986, chair collegiate conf. 1984, coun. mem. 1982—84); mem.: APA, ACA, European Personal Construct Assn., Am. Soc. Bus. and Behavioral Studies, N. Am. Personal Construct Assn., Chi Sigma Iota, Kappa Delta Pi, Phi Kappa Phi, Beta Gamma Sigma. Episcopalian. Inventor LaMaze Timer and audio text. Home: 8 Rolling Oaks Dr Fairhope AL 36532-3060 Office Phone: 251-689-6812. Business E-Mail: johngwin@conversationsgroup.com.

GWINN, MARY ANN, editor; d. Lawrence Baird and Frances Evelyn (Jones) Gwinn; m. Richard A. King, June 3, 1973 (div. Jan. 1981); m. Stephen E. Dunnington, June 10, 1990. BA in Psychology, Hendrix Coll., 1973; MEd in Spl. Edn., Ga. State U., 1975; MA in Journalism, U. Mo., 1979. Tchrs. aide DeKalb County Schs., Decatur, Ga., 1973—74, tchr., 1975—78; reporter Columbia (Mo.) Daily Tribune, 1979—83, Seattle Times, 1983—, internat. trade and workplace reporter, 1992—96, asst. city editor, 1996—98, book editor, 1998—. Instr. ext. divsn. U. Wash., Seattle, 1990; instr. journalism Seattle U., 1994. Bd. dir. Nat. Book Critics Cir. Recipient Edn. Reporting award, Charles Stewart Mott Found., 1980, Enterprising reporting award, C.B. Blethen Family, 1989, Pulitzer Prize for Nat. Reporting, 1990. Mem.: Newspaper Guild. Avocations: writing, gardening, reading, camping. Office: Seattle Times PO Box 70 Seattle WA 98111-0070

GWINN, MARY DOLORES, organization administrator, writer, lecturer; b. Oakland, Calif., Sept. 16, 1946; d. Epifanio and Carolina (Lopez) Cruz; m. James Monroe Gwinn, Oct. 23, 1965; 1 child, Larry Allen. Student, Monterey Peninsula Jr. Coll., 1965. Retail store mgr. Consumer's Distbg. divsn. May Co., Hayward, Calif., 1973-78; mktg. rep. Dale Carnegie Courses, San Jose, Calif., 1978-79; founder, pres. Strategic Integrations, Ariz.'s Innovative Bus. Devel. Ctr., Scottsdale, 1985—, Gwinn Genius Inst., Scottsdale, 1998—. Spkr. St. John's Coll. U. Cambridge, England, 1992, INC. Mag., U.S.A., 1996, Clemson Univ., 1996, Antelope Valley Coll., Lancaster, Calif., 1998; founder, pres. Internat. Inst. for Conceptual Edn., Scottsdale, 1993—; chairperson Keble Coll., Oxford (Eng.) U., 1997; spkr. Willard Internat. Hotel, Washington, 2000. Founder new fields of study Genestics and NeuroBus.; profiled the Thought Process of Genius; conceived Whole Brain Business Theory, 1985; author: Genius Leadership Secrets from the Past for the 21st Century, 1995; writer bus. column Gwinn on Bus., IMAGE Networker, Pa., 1996; contbr. articles to profl. jours. Chairperson Keble Coll., Oxford (Eng.) U. Republican. Avocations: reading, imagination games. Home and Office: 5836 E Angela Dr Scottsdale AZ 85254-6410

GWIRE, WILLIAM, lawyer; b. Hof, Germany, Nov. 27, 1946; BA, Boise State U., 1971; JD with high honors, Golden Gate U., 1974. Bar: Calif. 1974, US Dist. Ct. (no. dist. Calif.) 1974, US Dist. Ct. (so. dist. Calif.) 1984. Served in air rescue and recovery USAF, 1966—70. Named a Super Lawyer, No. Calif. Super Lawyers, 2005, 2006; named one of Top 100 Attys., Worth mag., 2005, 2006. Mem.: Assn. Profl. Responsibility Attys., Internat. Bar Assn., San Francisco Trial Lawyers Assn., ABA (mem. litig. sect.), State Bar Calif. (arbitrator, fee disputes 1991—), Bar Assn. San Francisco (arbitrator, fee disputes 1991—, mem. litig. sect.). Office: Gwire Law Offices Ste 1100 235 Pine St San Francisco CA 94104 Office Phone: 415-296-8880. Office Fax: 415-296-8029. E-mail: gwire@gwirelaw.com.*

GWOZDZ, KIM ELIZABETH, interior designer, furniture designer; b. Spokane, Wash., June 10, 1958; d. Myron Marcus and Marilyn Kay (Alsterlund) Westerkamp; children: Ryan Marcus, Lauren Taylor. Student, U. Florence, Italy, 1979; BFA in Graphic Design, Illustration and Art History, U. Ariz., 1980. Interior designer Pat Bacon & Assocs., 1983-88; prin. interior designer Kim E. Gwozdz/Provenance, Phoenix, 1988—. Prin., designer Marcus Taylor Furniture. Contbr. articles to profl. jours. Mem. Mt. Cavalry Luth. Ch., Phoenix, 1981-96, trustee, 1993-96; mem. Christ Luth. Ch., Phoenix, 1996-2002; Jr. League of Phoenix, 1989—, HIV/AIDS com., 1994-2000; mem. Orpheum Theater com., 1989-94, vice chmn., 1990-91, chmn., 1992-2002, Gift Mart com. Design Decorations, 1991-92, chmn., 1991, exec. com. Orpheum Theatre Found., 1989-91, bd. dirs., 1992—; active annual gala com. Am. Cancer Soc., 1993-94, 94-95, 95-96, 97-98, 98—, March of Dimes Gourmet Gala, 1991, 93, 95, 97; design affiliate Nat. Trust for Hist. Preservation, 1986—. Recipient 1st place award Ann. Wool Rug Design Competition, Edward Fields, Inc., 1989, 2d place award, 1990, 3d place award, 1991; Internat. Illumination design awards, 1998, Cutler award, 1998, Lumen award, 1998. Mem. Am. Soc. Interior Designers (assoc. Ariz. North chpt., significant interiors survery com. 1975-91, chmn. 1990-91, Phoenix Home and Garden com. 1989-90, Herberger Theatre com. 1989-91, awards com. 1989, 91, chmn. 1990, competitions com. 1991, 96, chmn. 1989-90, Rosson House Christmas chmn. 1986-91, hist. preservation chmn. 1988-91, directory chmn. Designers Market 1991, project designer, 1996, 97, mem. nominating com. 1991-92, 98, mktg. com. 1995, 3d place award Ariz. Norh 1987, 96, 2d place award 1987, 88, 92, 95, 1st place award Nat. 1989, 94, 95, 97). Republican. Lutheran. Avocations: art, gardening, cooking. Home: 4820 E Merrell St Phoenix AZ 85018 Office: 2415 E Camelback Rd Ste 700 Phoenix AZ 85016-4245 Home Phone: 602-944-8663; Office Phone: 602-912-8552.

GWYNN, ANTHONY KEITH (TONY GWYNN), former professional baseball player; b. LA, May 9, 1960; m. Alicia Gwynn; children: Anthony, Anisha Nicole. Student, San Diego State U. Player minor league teams, Walla Walla and Amarillo, Hawaii, 1981—82; outfielder San Diego Padres, 1982—2001; ret.; baseball coach San Diego State, 2002; now baseball analyst ESPN. Baseball analyst TBS Network, 2007—. Named MVP, N.W. League, 1981; named to All-Star Team, 1984—87, 1989—96, Silver Slugger Team, Sporting News Nat. League, 1984, All-Star Team, 1984, World Sports Humanitarian Hall of Fame, 1999, MLB All Century Team, 2000, Nat. Baseball Hall of Fame, 2007; recipient Batting Title award, Nat. League, 1984, 1987, 1988, 1989, 1995, Gold Glove award, 1986—87, 1989—91, Silver Slugger Team, Sporting News Nat. League, 1986—87, 1989—91, All-Star Team, 1986—87, 1986—87, 1989, 1994, Branch Rickey award, 1995, Roberto Clemente Man of the Yr. award, 1999, Lou Gehrig Meml. award, 1999. Achievements include being drafted by both MLB San Diego Padres and NBA LA Clippers. Mailing: care ESPN Baseball 935 Middle St Bristol CT 06010*

GYEMANT, ROBERT ERNEST, diversified financial services company executive, merchant banker; b. Managua, Nicaragua, Jan. 17, 1944; arrived in U.S., 1949, naturalized, 1954; s. Emery Gyemanat and Magda (Von Rechnitz) Gyemant; m. Sally Bartch Libhart, Oct. 17, 1992; children: Emily Bartch, Amanda Nancy, Katherine Libhart;children from previous marriage: Robert Ernest Jr., Anne Elizabeth. AB magna cum laude, UCLA, 1965; JD, U. Calif., Berkeley, 1968. CPA Calif.; bar: Calif. 1969, NY 1981. Tax acct. Ernst & Ernst, CPAs, Oakland, Calif., 1966—68; assoc. atty. Orrick, Herrington, Rowley & Sutcliffe, San Francisco, 1968—69; ptnr. Skornia, Rosenblum & Gyemant, San Francisco, 1969—74, Robert Ernest Gyemant PC, San Francisco, 1975; exec. v.p. fin. Topps & Trowsers, San Francisco, 1977—79; cons., pvt. investor ComDial Corp., San Francisco, 1979; co-founder Com Vu Corp., NYC, 1979—83, San Francisco, 1993—97; prin. Knapp, Petersen & Clarke, P.C., Glendale, Calif., 1997—99, Hill, Farrer & Burrill, LLP, LA, 1999—2000; mng. dir. Trinity River Capital Ventures, LLC; CEO Trio Industries Holdings, LLC. Instr. U. Calif., Berkeley, 1968; gen. coun., sec. Advanced Micro Devices, Inc., Sunnyvale, Calif., 1972—74. Editor: Calif. Law Rev., 1967—68; contbr. articles to profl. jours. Hon. vice consul Republic of Costa Rica, 1981—; trustee French-Am. Bilingual Sch., San Francisco, 1978—82; mem., ptnr. Calif. Council Criminal Justice Jud. Process Task Force, 1971—73; mem. Calif. State Rep. Ctrl. Com. Mem.: AICPA, ABA, Calif. Trial Lawyers Assn., Assn. Def. Counsel, Calif. CPA Soc. (mem. accounting prins. com. 1969), State Bar Calif. (cert. specialist criminal law 1988—93, com. on unauthorized practice law 1974—76, spl. com. on juvenile justice 1974, commr. San Francisco County juvenile justice comm. 1976—), San Francisco Bar Assn. (co-chmn. sect. on juvenile justice 1971), San Francisco Downtown Assn., Racquet and Tennis Club, N.Y. Athletic Club (N.Y.C.), Brook Haven Country Club. E-mail: rgyemant@trioindustries.net.

GYENES, GÁBOR, physician, educator; b. Budapest, Dec. 14, 1959; s. George and Marianne (Ferenczi) G.; m. Erika Müllner, July 13, 1991; children: Balázs, Dóra. MD, Semmelweis U. Med. Sch., Budapest, Hungary, 1984; postgrad., Karolinska Inst., Stockholm, 1994-97. Asst. prof. 3rd Dept Med. Semmelweis Med. U., 1984-98; clin. fellow adult cardiology U. Toronto, Ont., Can., 1998-2001; asst. prof. divsn. cardiology U. Alta., Edmonton, Canada, 2001—07, assoc. prof., 2007—. Author: Pharmindex Kompendium, 1995, Hypertension: Data and Facts, 1997, Handbook of Coronary Angiography and Angioplasty, 2001; editor: Cardiology, 2000; co-author, editor: 25 Landmark Trials in Cardiology, 2006. Recipient Eminent Young Scientist award Internat. Rsch. Promotion Coun., 2000. Mem. Hungarian Soc. of Cardiology, Hungarian Soc. Internal Medicine, Can. Cardiovascular Soc. Avocations: rock and classical music, tennis, soccer. Office: U Alta Walter Mackenzie Health Ctr 2C2 Edmonton AB Canada T6G 2B7 Office Phone: 780-407-7929. Personal E-mail: gyenesgabor@hotmail.com. Business E-Mail: ggyenes@cha.ab.cA.

GYENES, SCOTT MATTHEW, history professor; b. Elizabeth, NJ, July 15, 1971; BA in History, York Coll. Pa., York, 1993; MA in History, We. Mich. U., Kalamazoo, 1996. Adj. prof. York Coll. Pa., 1997—; history instr. York Country Day Sch., Pa., 2001—. Bd. dir. East Berlin Libr., Pa., 1996—98. Mem.: Nat. Coun. Social Studies, Am. Hist. Assn., World History Assn., York Coll. Alumni Assn. (bd. dirs. 1998—2003). Home: 1065 Sequoia St York PA 17404 Office: York Country Day Sch 1071 Regents' Glenn Blvd York PA 17403 Office Phone: 717-815-6736. Business E-Mail: sgyenes@ycp.edu.

GYFTOPOULOS, ELIAS PANAYIOTIS, mechanical and nuclear engineering educator; b. Athens, Greece, July 4, 1927; came to U.S., 1953, naturalized, 1963; s. Panayiotis Elias and Despina (Louvaris) G.; m. Artemis S. Scalleri, Sept. 3, 1962; children: Vasso, Maro, Rena. Diploma in Mech. and Elec. Engring., Tech. U. Athens, 1953; Sc.D. in Elec. Engring., M.I.T., 1958; Dr. (hon.), Tech. U. Athens, Greece, 1992, Tech. U. Nova Scotia, Halifax, Canada, 1997, Dalhousie U. Poly., Halifax, Can., 1997, U. Patras, Greece, 2001. Registered profl. engr., Mass. Instr. MIT, Cambridge, 1955-58, asst. prof., 1958-61, assoc. prof., 1961—65, prof., 1965—70, Ford prof. engring., 1970-96; chmn. Nat. Energy Council Greece, 1975-78. Bd. dirs. Thermo Electron Corp., Waltham, Mass., Thermo Retec Corp., Waltham, ThermoLase Corp., San Diego, ThermoCardio Systems, Woburn, Mass., Thermo Spectra Corp., Waltham, Trex Med. Corp., Dunbury, Conn., others; cons. in field. Author: Thermionic Energy Conversion, vol. 1, 1973, vol. 2, 1979, Fuel Effectiveness in Industry, 1974; editor-in-chief 17 Energy Conservation Manuals, 1982, Thermodynamics: Foundations and Applications, 1991, 2d edit., 2005. Trustee Anatolia Coll., Salonika, Greece, 1971-2001; vice chmn. bd. trustees, 1988-2001. With Greek Navy, 1948-51. Fellow: AAAS, ASME (James Harry Potter Gold medal 1995, Robert Henry Thurston award 2002, Edward Obert award 2001), NAE, Acad. Athens, Am. Acad. Arts and Scis., Am. Nuc. Soc. (bd. dirs. 1966—69); mem.: Philol. Soc. Parnassos. Greek Orthodox. Office: MIT Dept Nuclear Sci and Engring Rm 24-111 77 Mass Ave Cambridge MA 02139-4307 Home Phone: 781-259-9748; Office Phone: 617-253-3804. E-mail: epgyft@aol.com.

GYLES, ROBERT, mathematics professor; b. Aiken, SC, Aug. 18, 1945; s. Nossie Gyles Dillard; 1 child, Taisha Elaine. BS, S.C. State U., 1967; MA, NYU, 1975, PhD, 1988. Dir. math. Cmty. Sch. Dist., N.Y.C. Dept. Edn., 1983—91, dir. curriculum and profl. devel., 1991—95, dep. supt., 1996—2003; prof. math. Hunter Coll., CUNY, 2003—. Cons. math. edn. Create-A-Vision, Forest City, Calif., 1995—; mem. math. stds. adv. panel N.Y. State Edn. Dept., Albany, 2004—; mem. math. adv. com. N.Y. City Dept. Edn., 2004—. Co-author: Math Central, 1998, Breakaway Math, 2004. With US Army, 1969—71. Decorated Commendation medal. Mem.: Nat. Coun. Tchrs. Math., Alpha Phi Alpha, Phi Delta Kappa. Avocations: jogging, spinning. Home: 301 Cathedral Pky Apt 11G New York NY 10026 Office: Hunter Coll CUNY 695 Park Ave New York NY 10021

GYLL, JOHN SÖREN, marketing executive; b. Skorped, Västernorrland, Sweden, Dec. 26, 1940; s. Josef and Gertrud G.; m. Lilly Margareta Hellman, 1974; 3 children. Higher cert. exam. and univ. degrees; D in Tech. (hon.), Linköping U., 2004. Mktg. mgr., v.p. Rank-Xerox AB, 1963-77; pres. Uddeholm-Sweden, 1977-79, exec. v.p., 1979-81; pres., CEO, Uddelholm-AB, 1981-84; CEO, Procordia AB, Stockholm, 1984-92; pres., CEO, AB Volvo, Göteborg, Sweden, 1992-97. Bd. dirs. SCA AB, Skanska AB, SKF AB. Mem.: Royal Swedish Acad. Engring. Scis. Avocations: hunting, golf, skiing. Office: Strand Promenaden 3 SE-131 50 Saltsjö-Duvnäs Sweden

GYLLENHAAL, ANDERS, editor; b. Cleve., Oct. 4, 1951; m. Beverly Mills Gyllenhaal; children: Grey, Sam. B in journalism, George Washington U. Reporter The Daily News Record, Harrisonburg, Va., The Press, Atlantic City, The Miami Herald, 1979—89, editor Ft. Lauderdale bur., 1989—91; metro editor News & Observer, Raleigh, NC, 1991—95, mng. editor, 1995—97, exec. editor, sr. v.p., 1997—2001; sr. v.p., editor Star Tribune, Mpls., 2002—07; exec. editor The Miami Herald, 2007—. Mem. Pulitzer Prize Bd., 2001—. Mem.: Am. Soc. Newspaper Editors. Office: The Miami Herald One Herald Plz Miami FL 33132 Office Phone: 205-376-3790. E-mail: agyllenhaal@miamiherald.com.*

GYLLENHAAL, JAKE, actor; b. LA, Dec. 19, 1980; s. Stephen Gyllenhaal and Naomi Foner. Attended, Columbia U. Actor: (films) City Slickers, 1991, A Dangerous Woman, 1993, Josh and S.A.M., 1993, Homegrown, 1998, October Sky, 1999, Donnie Darko, 2001, Bubble Boy, 2001, Lovely and Amazing, 2001, The Good Girl, 2002, Moonlight Mile, 2002, Highway, 2002, The Day After Tomorrow, 2004, Proof, 2005, Jarhead, 2005, Brokeback Mountain, 2005 (Best Supporting Actor, Nat. Bd. Review, 2005, Actor in a Supporting Role, British Acad. Film and TV Arts, 2006, Best Performance, MTV Movie awards, 2006), Zodiac, 2007; (plays) This is Our Youth (London Evening Standard Theatre award Oustanding Newcomer, 2002). Named one of 50 Most Powerful People in Hollywood, Premiere mag., 2006; recipient Best Supporting Actor award, Nat. Bd. Rev., 2005. Office: Creative Artists Agy 9830 Wilshire Blvd Beverly Hills CA 90212-1825*

GYLLENHAAL, MAGGIE, actress; b. NYC, Nov. 16, 1977; d. Stephen Gyllenhaal and Naomi Foner; 1 child, Ramona. BA in English, Columbia U., 1999. Actor: (TV series) Shake Rattle and Roll: An American Love Story, 1999; (TV films) Shattered Mind, 1996, The Patron Saint of Liars, 1998, Resurrection, 1999, Strip Search, 2004; (films) Waterland, 1992, A Dangerous Woman, 1993, Homegrown, 1998, The Photographer, 2000, Cecil B. Demented, 2000, Pornographer: A Love Story, 2000, Donnie Darko, 2001, Riding in Cars with Boys, 2001, Secretary, 2002, 40 Days and 40 Nights, 2002, Adaptation, 2002, Confessions of a Dangerous Mind, 2002, Casa de los babys, 2003, Mona Lisa Smile, 2003, Criminal, 2004, Happy Endings, 2005, The Great New Wonderful, 2005, Trust the Man, 2005, Sherrybaby, 2006 (Best Actress award, Stockholm Internat. Film Festival, 2006), Paris, je t'aime, 2006, World Trade Center, 2006, Stranger Than Fiction, 2006, (voice) Monster House, 2006, High Falls, 2007. Office: Creative Artists Agy 9830 Wilshire Blvd Beverly Hills CA 90212*

GYLSETH, DORIS HANSON (DORIS LILLIAN GYLSETH), retired librarian; b. Helena, Mont., May 26, 1934; d. Richard E. and Lillie (Paula) Hanson; m. Arlie Albeck, Dec. 26, 1955 (div. Apr. 1964); m. Hermann M. Gylseth, Apr. 29, 1983 (dec. Aug. 1985). BS Edn., We. Mont. Coll. Edn., 1958; MLS, U. Wash., 1961. Tchr. Helena Sch. Dist., 1955—56, Dillon Elem. Sch., Mont., 1957—59, Eltopia Unified Sch. Dist., Wash., 1959—60; sch. libr. Shoreline Sch. Dist., Seattle, 1960—64, Dept. Def., Chateauroux, France, Hanau, Germany, Tachikawa, Japan, 1964—68, Long Beach Unified Sch. Dist., Calif., 1968—70; br. libr. Long Beach Pub. Libr., 1970—74, coord. children's svcs., 1974—85; libr. Long Beach Unified Sch. Dist., 1986—94; realtor Century 21, All Pacific, 1994—96. Bd. dirs. Children's Svcs. divsn. Calif. Libr. Assn., 1985, Lit. Guild Orange County; co-chmn. Long Beach Authors Festival, 1978—86; mem. planning coun. Third Pacific Rim Conf. on Children's Lit. UCLA, 1986. Mem.: So. Calif. Coun. on Lit. for Children and Young People (bd. dirs. 1974—88, pres. 1982—84), Men of Mystery, Friends Long Beach Pub. Libr. (bd. dirs.), Lit. Guild Orange County, Helen Fuller Cultural Carousel (bd. dirs. 1985—99), Snowboarders Ski Club, Over-the-Hill Gang, Zonta (pres. 1978—80). Avocations: cats, travel. Home: 19191 Harvard Ave Unit 159D Irvine CA 92612 Personal E-mail: dgylseth@msn.com.

GYOHTEN, TOYOO, economist; b. Yokohama, Japan, 1931; married; 2 children. BA in Econs., U. Tokyo, 1955; postgrad., Princeton U., U.S.A., 1956-58. With Ministry Fin., Tokyo, 1955-89, Japan Desk, Internat. Monetary Fund, Washington, 1964-66; spl. asst. to pres. Asian Devel. Bank, Manila, Philippines, 1966-69; dir. gen. Internat. Fin. Bur., Ministry of Fin., Tokyo, 1984-86; vice min. fin. for internat. affairs Ministry of Fin., Tokyo, 1986-89; with The Bank of Tokyo, Ltd. (merged with Mitsubishi Bank Ltd.), Tokyo, 1991—; chmn. bd. dirs. The Bank of Tokyo, Ltd., Tokyo, 1992-96; sr. advisor The Bank of Tokyo-Mitsubishi, Ltd., 1996—; spl. advisor to Prime Minister of Japan, 1998. Pres. Inst. for Internat. Monetary Affairs, 1995—; chmn. working party III OECD, Paris, 1988-90; vis. prof. Harvard U., 1990, Princeton U., 1990-91, U. St. Gallen, Switzerland, 1991; trustee Princeton in Asia, N.J.; mem. adv. panel East African Devel. Bank, Uganda, Asia Pacific Adv. Comm., N.Y. Stock Exch.; mem. exec. com. Trilateral Comm., N.Y., Paris, Tokyo; mem. internat. coun. The Asia Soc., N.Y., Group of Thirty, Washington. Co-author (with Paul Volcker): Changing Fortunes, 1992. Office: The Bank of Tokyo-Mitsubishi Ltd Inst Internat Monetary Aff 1-3-2 Nihombashi-Hongokucho Tokyo 103-0021 Japan

GYSBERS, NORMAN CHARLES, counselor, educator; b. Waupun, Wis., Sept. 29, 1932; s. George S. and Mabel (Landaal) Gysbers; m. Mary Lou Ziegler, June 23, 1954 (dec. July 1997); children: David(dec.), Debra, Daniel; m. Barbara K. Townsend, May 12, 2001. AB, Hope Coll., 1954; MA, U. Mich., 1959, PhD, 1963. Tchr. Elem. and Jr. H.S., Muskegon Heights, Mich., 1954-56; lectr. edn. U. Mich., 1962-63; prof. counseling psychology U. Mo., Columbia, 1963—, now prof. with distinction. Cons. U.S. Office Edn.; mem. nat. adv. coms. ERIC Clearinghouses in Career Edn. and Counseling and Pers. Svcs.; rsch. and devel. com. for CEEB, Am. Insts. for Rsch. Project on Career Decision Making, Comprehensive Career Edn. Model, TV Career Awareness Project KCET-TV, L.A.; dir. 10 nat. rsch. projects and state projects in career devel.-guidance; Francqui prof. Universite Libre de Bruxelles. Editor: Vocat. Guidance Quar. 1962-70; (with L. Sunny Hansen) spl. issue Personnel and Guidance Jour., May 1975, Jour. Career Devel., 1979-, (with E. Moore and W. Miller) Developing Careers in the Elementary School, 1973, (with E. Moore and H. Drier) Career Guidance: Practices and Perspectives, 1973; author: (with E. Moore) Improving Guidance Programs, 1981, Designing Careers, 1984, (with E. Moore) Career Counseling, 1987, (with P. Henderson) Developing and Managing Your School Guidance Program, 1988, 4th edit., 2006, (with C. McDaniels) Counseling for Career Development, 1992, (with P. Henderson) Guidance Programs that Work, 1997, (with M. Heppner and J. Johnston) Career Counseling, 1998, 2d edit., 2003 (translated into Italian, Japanese, Korean and Chinese), (with P. Henderson) Leading and Managing Your School Guidance Program Staff, 1998, (with P. Henderson) Implementing Comprehensive School Guidance Programs, 2002; contbr. articles to profl. jours. and chpts. to textbooks. Elder Presbyn. Ch. Served with arty. U.S. Army, 1956-58. Recipient Am. Spirit award, USAF, 1987, Pillar of Excellence Ten Yr. award, Coll. Edn. U. Mo., 2003, Excellence in Tchg. award, Gov., 2004; William T. Kemper Excellence in Tchg. fellow, U. Mo., 2002. Mem.: ACA (pres. 1977—78, disting. profl. svc. award 1983), Internat. Assn. Ednl. and Vocat. Guidance, Mo. Guidance Assn. (outstanding svc. award 1978), Am. Vocat. Assn. (v.p. 1979—82, merit award guidance divsn. 1978), Am. Sch. Counselor Assn. (post-secondary sch. counselor of yr. 2001, Mary Geheke Lifetime Achievement award 2004), Assn. for Counselor Edn. and Supervision, Nat. Career Devel. Assn. (pres. 1972—73, nat. merit award 1981, Eminent Career award 1989). Home: 4 Bingham Rd Columbia MO 65203 Office: U Mo 201 G Student Success Ctr Columbia MO 65211-6060 Office Phone: 573-882-6386. E-mail: gysbersn@missouri.edu.

HA, ANDREW KWANGHO, education educator; b. Korea, Nov. 14, 1949; s. Hyunku and Soonnam (Kim) H.; m. Kathy Lim; children: Susan, Steve, Joanna, Toby. BA, Chosun U., Kwangju, Korea, 1965; MA, Glassboro State Coll., NJ, 1967; EdD, Seton Hall U., 1988. Cert. elem. and secondary English and social studies tchr., guidance counselor, prin., supr., NJ. Tchr. Mantua Twp. Pub. Schs., NJ, Greenwich Twp. Pub. Schs., Gibbstown, NJ; instr. ESL tchg. Passaic County CC, Paterson, NJ; adj. prof. English tchg. Glassboro State Coll., NJ; tchr. reading and English lang. arts methods SUNY Potsdam, 1991—. Invited spkr. Oxford Round Table Oxford U., England, 2007. Author: The Key to Reading Comprehension, 1994, Get'em to Plunge into the Sea of English, 1995, Get'em to Swim in the Sea of English, 1996, Get'em to Rise in the Sea of English, 1997, Dr. Ha's English Grammar, 1998, English Composition with Great Names in History, 2001, English Grammar in Living Context, 2007. Elected into the Internat. Ctr. Ednl. Achievement, 1997. Mem. NEA, ASCD, NJ Edn. Assn., Am. Fedn. Tchrs., Am. Ednl. Rsch. Assn., United Univ. Profession, Nat. Coun. Tchrs. English, Internat. Reading Assn., Tchrs. English to Speakers of Other Langs, Phi Delta Kappa, Kappa Delta Pi, Home: PO Box 873 Potsdam NY 13676-0873 Office Phone: 315-267-2124. Business E-Mail: haak@potsdam.edu.

HA, CHANG SIK, polymer science educator; b. Pusan, Jan. 30, 1956; s. Won Do and Bong Soon (Eh) H.; m. Sun Ja Han, Jan. 13, 1983; children: Ji Won, Ji Hyun, Jae Hun. BS, Pusan Nat. U., 1978; MS, Korea Adv. Inst. Sci. & Tech., Seoul, 1980, PhD, 1987. Engr. Lucky Chem. Co. Ltd., Pusan, 1982; from instr. to asst. prof. Pusan Nat. U., 1982-89, faculty advisor univ. English newspaper, 1987, assoc. prof., 1989-94, chmn. dept., 1992-94, prof., 1994—, assoc. dean of planning, 2000-01. Vis. scholar U. Cin., 1988-89, Stanford U., 1997-98, SUNY-Buffalo, 2004; mem. editl. adv. bd. Materials Sci. Found. (Trans Tech. Publs. Switzerland). Author: Polymer Chemistry, 1990, Polymer Processing, 1991, Polymer Engineering, I, 1995, II, 1997; editor: Polymer: Structure and Properties, 1988; mem. editl. bd. Material Sci. Found., 1998—; editor Macromolecular Rsch.; contbr. numerous articles to sci. jours. on polymer blends and composites, periodic mesoporous organosilicas, or organic electroluminescent devices. Recipient Best Paper of Yr. award, Korean Fed. Sci. Tech. Soc., 2003, Scientists of Month award, Ministry Sci. and Tech., Korea, 2006. Fellow Korean Acad. Sci. Tech.; mem. Nat. Acad. Engring. Korea, Am. Chem. Soc., Am. Phys. Soc., N.Y. Acad. Scis., Polymer Soc. Korea (Polymer Sci. award 1995), Soc. Polymer Sci. Japan, Korean Inst. Rubber Industries (Best Paper of Yr. award 1989). Roman Catholic. Avocations: classical music, climbing. Office: Pusan Nat Univ Dept Polymer Sci & Engring Busan 609-735 Republic of Korea Home Phone: +82-51-507-7065; Office Phone: 82-51-510-2407. Office Fax: 82-51-514-4331. Personal E-mail: csha@pusan.ac.kr. Business E-Mail: csha@pnu.edu.

HA, CHONG WAN, information technology executive; b. Chin-ju, Kyung-Nam, South Korea, Oct. 25, 1938; came to U.S., 1963; s. Kyung-sik and Kyung-Nam (Park) H.; m. Karen Hye-Ja Han, Aug. 19, 1968; children: Jean Frances, Julie Ann. BA in Econs., UCLA, 1970; MA in Mgmt., Claremont U., Calif., 1985. Sr. systems analyst Atlantic Richfield Co., Los Angeles, 1972-78; asst. v.p. 1st Interstate Services Co., Los Angeles, 1978-85; v.p. Ticor Title Ins. Co., Los Angeles, 1985-91; assoc. dir. MCA/Universal Studios, 1991; dir. State of Calif. Stephen P. Teale Data Ctr., Sacramento, 1991-97; v.p. LCS, Inc., Sacramento, 1997-99; pres., chief tech. officer Ha Technologies, Burbank, Calif., 1999-2000; chief tech. officer enterprise tech. svcs. 21st Century Ins. Group, Woodland Hills, Calif., 2000—. Exec. com. Calif. Forum on Info. Tech.; adv. bd. Govt. Tech. Conf., 1994. Res. police officer Monterey Park (Calif.) Police Dept., 1981-82; bd. dirs. Asian Pacific Alumni Assn., UCLA, 1988, Asian Pacific Am. Legal Found., L.A., 1988, Korean Youth Ctr.; mem. alumni coun. Claremont Grad. Sch., 1993. Recipient Peter Drucker Ctr. Alumni award, 1994, Calif. State Atty. Gen. award, 1994, Carnegie Mellon U. and AMS Achievement award in mng. info. tech., 1995. Mem.: Soc. Info. Mgmt., UCLA Chancellors Cir. Avocations: golf, classical music, reading. Office Phone: 818-715-6537. Personal E-mail: chong.ha@21st.com.

HA, KIET TUAN, hospital administrator; b. Saigon, Vietnam, Mar. 18, 1963; arrived in U.S., 1982; s. Duc Van Ha and Lac Chau; children: Kelsey Diemmi, Kian Viet Long. BS in Biology, San Jose State U., 1991; MBA, U. Phoenix, 2000. Dir. physician svcs. Regional Med. San Jose, Calif., 2000—02; dir. bus. devel. O'Connor Hosp., San Jose, 2002—. Bd. dirs. Kelley Pk. Cmty., San Jose, Calif., Asian Am. Cmty. Involvement, San Jose, Calif. Recipient Achievement award, Premier Care IPA, 2004. Office: OConnor Hosp 2105 Forest Ave San Jose CA 95128 Office Phone: 408-947-2906. Office Fax: 408-995-0117. Personal E-mail: kietha@dochs.org.

HAACK, JOEL K., mathematics professor, academic administrator; b. Iowa City, Iowa, Aug. 26, 1954; s. Robert J. and Jeanne K. Haack; m. Linda L. Lawton, May 20, 1973. BA in Math. Scis., U. Iowa, 1974, MS in Math., 1975, MS in Stats., 1978, PhD in Math., 1979. Prof. math. U. No. Iowa, Cedar Falls, 1991—, head dept. math., 1991—2000, dean Coll. Natural Scis., 2005—. Mem.: Rotary Club of Cedar Falls (pres. 1998—99, Paul Harris fellow 2000). Office: U No Iowa College Natural Scis Cedar Falls IA 50614-0181 Home Phone: 319-266-7862; Office Phone: 319-273-2585. Business E-Mail: joel.haack@uni.edu.

HAACK, RICHARD WILSON, retired police officer; b. Chgo., July 7, 1935; s. Arthur Frank and Mildred Ann (Meyer) Haack; m. Ruth Marie Tietz, May 27, 1972; children: Laura Marie, Karl Richard. Grad., Sheriff's Police Acad., Cook County (Ill.), 1967; AS, Triton Coll., 1973; cert., Chgo. Police Acad., 1974; BA, Lewis U., 1975; MA, Northeastern Ill. U., 1979; BS in Bus. Adminstrn., Elmhurst Coll., 1982. Shipping clk. Am. Furniture Mart, Chgo., 1955-60; quality control insp. Nat. Can Co., Chgo., 1961-67; police officer Northlake (Ill.) Police Dept., 1967-92, watch comdr. patrol divsn., 1978-85, dept. chief of police, 1986-87, in-svc. tng. coord., 1991-92; ret., 1992. Realtor Internat. Realty World-Norton & Assocs., 1984—87. Author: Ency. Am. Judiciary; contbr. articles to profl. jours. Mem. Bill Bruce fundraising com. Aid Assn. Luths., Christ Evang. Luth. Ch., Northlake, 1981—82; mem. Gala Varsity Show, 1982, chmn. evang. bd., 1981—85; dir., emcee German-Am. Police Assn., 1980—2001; emcee Oktoberfest, 1980—99, chmn. entertainment, 1984—2001, assoc. membership chmn., 2001—06; coach baseball team Northlake Little League, 1985; trustee Northlake Police Pension Fund, 1997—; active March of Dimes-Mothers March, 1997—99; dir. emcee Greeter Immanuel Luth. Ch., 2003—05; ch. rep. Internat. Luth. Laymen's League, 1984—, pub. rels. dir., usher, 1973—85; choir Apostles Luth. Ch., 1985—87; membership chmn. Redeemer Luth. Ch. Men's Club, 1995—99; chmn. program com. Greater Immanuel Luth. Ch., 2003—06. With USMC, 1952—55, with USMCR, 1955—60, Korea. Recipient John Edgar Hoover Meml. Gold medal, 1987, numerous letters of commendation, competitive shooting awards. Mem.: NRA, Realtors Polit. Action Com. Ill. (inner cir. 1984—87), Internat. Platform Assn., Leyden Real Estate Bd. (inner cir. 1984—87), N.W. Real Estate Bd., Am. Polit. Sci. Assn., Emerald Soc. Ill. Irish/Am. Police Assn., Ill. Juvenile Officers Assn., Internat. Juvenile Officers Assn., Combined Counties Police Assn., Nat. Police Officers Assn., St. Jude Police League, Internat. Assn. Chiefs Police, German/Am. Police Assn. (life; bd. dirs.), Internat. Assn. Police (life), Fraternal Order Police (life; sec.-treas. Perri-Nagle Meml. Lodge 18 1977—85), Ill. Police Assn. (life), Korean War Vets.-Navy League, Northeastern Ill. U. Alumni Assn. (bd. dirs. 1980—86), Internat. Police Assn. (life), Ret. and Disabled Polic Am., Kaire Ind. Distbr., Sharkhunters, Die Hard Cub Fans, Moose, Am. Legion Post 888, Schwaben Verein. Republican. Home: 244 E Palmer Ave Northlake IL 60164-1735 Office: 55 E North Ave Northlake IL 60164-1735 Office Phone: 708-562-0634. Personal E-mail: haackpack@comcast.net.

HAACKE, HANS CHRISTOPH CARL, artist, educator; b. Cologne, Germany, Aug. 12, 1936; s. Carl and Antonie Haacke; m. Linda Snyder, 1965; 2 sons. MFA, State Acad., Kassel, 1960; DFA (hon.), Oberlin Coll., 1991; D (hon.), Bauhaus U., Weimar, Germany, 1998. Asst. prof. Cooper Union for Advancement of Sci. and Art, NYC, 1971—75, assoc. prof., 1975-79, prof., 1979—2002, prof. emeritus, 2002—. Guest prof. Hochschule für Bildende Künste, Hamburg, 1973, 94, Gesamthochschule, Essen, 1979. One-man shows include Galerie Schmela, Düsseldorf, 1965, Howard Wise Gallery, NYC, 1966, 68, 69, Galerie Paul Maenz, Cologne, 1971, 74, 81, Museum Haus Lange, Krefeld, 1972, John Weber Gallery, NYC, 1973, 75, 77, 79, 81, 83, 85, 88, 90, 92, 94, Kunstverein Frankfurt, 1976, Galerie Durand-Dessert, Paris, 1977, 78, Mus. of Modern Art, Oxford, 1978, Stedelijk Van Abbemuseum, Eindhoven, 1979, Renaissance Soc., Chgo., 1979, Galerie France Morin, Montreal, Que., Can., 1983, Tate Gallery, London, 1984, Neue Gesellschaft für Bildende Kunst, Berlin, 1984, Kunsthalle, Berne, 1985, Le Consortium, Dijon, France, 1986, The New Mus. Contemporary Art, NYC, 1986, Victoria Miro Gallery, London, 1987, Centre Georges Pompidou, Paris, 1989, Biennale Venice, Italy, 1993, Fundació Antoni Tàpies, Barcelona, 1995, Mus. Boijmans Van Beuningen, Rotterdam, 1996, German Parliament Bldg., commn. permanent installation, Berlin, opened 2000, Portikus, Frankfurt, 2000, Serpentine Gallery, London, 2001, Generali Found., Vienna, 2001, Paula Cooper Gallery, NY, 2005, Acad. Künste, Berlin, 2006, Deichtorhallen, Hamburg, 2006; group exhbns. Stedelijk Mus., Amsterdam, 1962, 65, 82, Mus. Modern Art, NYC, 1968, 70, 88, 99, Tokyo Biennale, 1970, Jewish Mus., NYC, 1970, 94, Documenta Kassel, 1972, 82, 87, 97, Biennale Venice, 1976, 78, Mus. van Hedendaagse Kunst, Ghent, Belgium, 1980, Hirshhorn Mus., Washington, 1984, Palais des Beaux-Arts, Brussels, 1984, Sydney (Australia) Biennale, 1984, 90, Sao Paulo (Brazil) Biennale, 1985, Nationalgalerie, Berlin, 1984, Centre Georges Pompidou, 1987, 89, 90, 92, 96, 2000, 07, Musée d'Art Moderne de la Ville de Paris, 1981, 89, LA Cty. Mus., 1987, 2001, 04, Whitney Mus., NY, 1989, 1999, 2000, 06, State Russian Mus., St. Petersburg, 1990, Irish Mus. Modern Art, Dublin, 1992, Musée d'art contemporain, Montreal, 1992, 2003, Bundeskunsthalle, Bonn, Germany, 1992, Kunsthalle Basel, Basel, Switzerland, 1994, 2004, Mus. Contemporary Art, LA, 1995, 2004, Mus. Contemporary Art, Tokyo, 1995; Stage set: Ernst Jünger, Volksbühne, Berlin, 1994, Skulptur Projekte Münster, Germany, 1997, Deutschlandbilder, Gropius-Bau, Berlin, 1997, Berlin-Moskau, Gropius-Bau, Berlin, 2003-04, Johannesburg Biennale, 1997, Mus. Hamburger Bahnhof, Berlin, 1999, Museu Serralves, Porto, Portugal, 1999, 2004, Mus. Contemporary Art, Barcelona, 2000, 04, Tate Modern London, 2000, 05, Generali Found., Vienna, 2001, 05, Nat. Portrait Gallery, London, 2000, Hayward Gallery, London, 2000, Haus der Kunst, Munich, 2000, 05, ZKM, Karlsruhe, Germany, 2002, Moscow-Berlin, Hist. Mus., Moscow, 2004, Nat. Mus. Art, Osaka, Japan, 2004, Mus. Kunst Palast, Düsseldorf, 2006; author: (with Edward F. Fry) Werkmonographie, 1972, (with others) Framing and Being Framed, 1975, Nach allen Regeln der Kunst, 1984, (with others) Unfinished Business, 1987, Artfairismes, 1989, (with others) Bodenlos, 1993, Mia san mia, 2001, (with Pierre Bourdieu) Libre-Echange, 1994, Obra Social, 1995, AnsichtsSachen/ViewingMatters, 1999, (with others) Hans Haacke, 2004, Hans Haacke-For Real: Works 1959-2006, 2006; contbr. articles to profl. jours. Recipient Golden Lion Venice Biennale, Peter Weiss prize, Bochum, 2004. Office: The Cooper Union Cooper Square New York NY 10003

HAAG, EVERETT KEITH, architect; b. Cuyahoga Falls, Ohio, Jan. 27, 1928; s. Arnold and Lois (Martz) H.; m. Eleanor Jean Baker, Nov. 1, 1961; children— Kurt, Paula, Pamela. BS in Architecture, Kent State U., 1951; B.Arch., Western Res. U., 1953. Founder, prin. firm Keith Haag & Assos. (architects), Cuyahoga Falls, 1955-72; founder, pres. Keith Haag Assos. Inc. (architecture-engring.-planning), Cuyahoga Falls, 1972-81; archtl. and planning cons. Cuyahoga Falls, 1981—. Instr. Kent State U., 1952-54 Pres. Tri-County Planning Commn., 1960-61; chmn. Urban Renewal Review Commn., Cuyahoga Falls, 1971— , Regional Planning Group, Northampton Twp., 1970—; mem. Akron Regional Devel. Bd.; bd. dirs. Goodwill Industries, chmn. strategic planning com., 1988—, Akron, Stan Hywet Hall Found., Inc. (pres. 1991-92); chmn. Historic Bldgs. Com., 1988—; mem. alumni bd. Kent State U., 1970-72, co-developer Polymer Housing system, 1989. Recipient 46 archtl. design awards. Fellow AIA (past pres. Akron chpt., nat. com. on office practice); mem. Architects Soc. Ohio (exec. com., sec. 1975-76, v.p. 1977-78, pres. 1979, Gold medal 1986), Northampton C. of C. (pres. 1972), Summit County Hist. Soc. (dir. 1974—) Clubs: President's (Kent State U.), Hilltoppers (Akron U.). Home: 1007 W Steels Corners Rd Cuyahoga Falls OH 44223-3111 Office: PO Box 1147 Cuyahoga Falls OH 44223-0147

HAAG, JOYCE P., lawyer, imaging company executive; BA in Math., Mt. Holyoke Coll., South Hadley, Mass.; JD cum laude, Cornell Law Sch., Ithaca, NY. Assoc. Boylan, Brown, Code, Fowler, Vigdor & Wilson, LLP, Rochester, NY; lawyer Eastman Kodak Co., Rochester, 1981—91, asst. sec., 1991—95, corp. sec., 1995—2003, asst. gen. counsel, 2001—03, dir. mktg., antitrust, trademark and litig., 2003—04, gen. counsel Europe, Africa and Mid. East region, 2004—05, sr. v.p., gen. counsel, 2005—. Bd. trustees Monroe County Bar Assn., 1984—85; dir. Via Health, Inc., 1995—97, Fleet Bank, NA, 1996—98; mem. gen. counsel com. Nat. Ctr. State Cts.; sec. Am. Soc. Corp. Secs. Bd. govs. Genesee Hosp., 1988—96; chair Genesee Hosp. Found., 1988—96; bd. trustees Margaret Woodbury Strong Mus., 1996—98; mem. Pres.'s Coun. Cornell Women; bd. trustees Susan B. Anthony House, Inc. Mem.: Assn. Corp. Counsel, Assn. Gen. Counsel. Office: Eastman Kodak Co 343 State St Rochester NY 14650 Office Phone: 585-724-4000.*

HAAGEN, PAUL HESS, law educator; b. Lancaster, Pa., June 19, 1950; s. Conrad Hess and Marian Helen (Nelson) H.; m. Lucy Emerson Weinstein, Aug. 25, 1973; children: Jonathan Conrad, Christopher Edwin. BA magna cum laude (hon.), Haverford Coll., 1972; BA in Modern Hist., Oxford U., 1974; MA, PhD in Hist., Princeton U., 1976-86; JD, Yale U., 1982. Law clk. U.S. Ct. Appeals (3d cir.), Phila., 1982-83; assoc. Dechert Price & Rhoads, Phila., 1983-85; asst. prof. Duke U. Law Sch., Durham, N.C., 1985-88, assoc. prof., 1988-91, prof., 1991—, sr. assoc. dean, 1991-93; prof. of Law Duke U Law Sch., Durham, NC. Mem. Rhodes Scholarship Selection Com., R.I., 1980-81, NC, 1989, Alaska Law Review, moderator Am. Assembly, Conf. on Bicentennial of Constitution, Chapel Hill, NC, 1989, Future of Intercollegiate Athletics, 1999, panelist NC.Am. Soc. Legal History, Chgo., 1990, dir. Moot Ct., spkr. in field. Author: Neither a Borrower Nor a Lender Be, contbr. artical to profl. jour. Rhodes scholar Oxford U., 1972, Princeton fellow Princeton U., 1974, Kent fellow, 1975, Whiting fellow, 1978, Dept. Prize (religion). Mem. ABA, Pa. Bar Assn., Ad Hoc 1st Year & Upperclass Curriculum Review Com., 1992-93, Duke U Sch. of Law (admissions com. 1985-86, 1988-89, 1991-93, 1998-99, chair admissions com. 1999-2000, chair clerkship com. 1986-88, 1995-96, dean search com. 1987-88), Phi Beta Kappa. Mem. Yale Law and Policy Review (editor in chief 1980-81, Yale jour. of world pub. order, articles editor 1981-82, assco. editor 1979-1981). Office: Duke U Sch of Law PO Box 90360 Durham NC 27708 Office Phone: 919-613-7088, 919-613-7088. Office Fax: 919-613-7231. Business E-Mail: haagen@law.duke.edu.

HAALAND, GORDON ARTHUR, retired academic administrator; b. Bklyn., Apr. 19, 1940; s. Ole E. and Ellen R. (Hansen) H.; m. Carol E. Anderson, Jan. 19, 1963; children: Lynn, Paul. AB, Wheaton Coll., Ill., 1962; PhD, SUNY, Buffalo, 1966. Instr. SUNY, Buffalo, summer, 1965; asst. to assoc. prof. psychology U. N.H., Durham, 1965-74, prof., 1974-83, chmn. dept. psychology, 1970-74, v.p. for acad. affairs Coll. Arts and Scis., 1979-83, interim pres. of univ., 1983-84, pres., 1984-90; dean Coll. Arts and Scis., prof. psychology U. Maine, Orono, 1975-79; pres. Gettysburg (Pa.) Coll., 1990—2004. Vis. prof. U. Bergen, Norway, 1972-73; mem. New Eng. Land-Grant Univs., chmn. 1985-86; v.p. N.H. Coll. and Univ. Coun., 1985-87; bd. dirs. New Eng. Bd. Higher Edn., 1986—, chmn., 1988-90; bd. dirs. Eisenhower World Affairs Inst.; chmn. N.H. Postsecondary Edn. Commn., 1986-88; dir. Maine Coun. Econ. Edn., 1975-79; evaluator NSF CAUSE Project, U. Maine, 1980-83; bd. dirs. First N.H. Banks, Inc., 1987—, mem. First NH Investment Svcs., 1987—; corporator Bangor (Maine) Savs. Bank, 1975-79. Contbr. articles, papers to profl. publs. and confs. procs. Incorporator N.H. Charitable Fund, 1985-88, Trust for N.H. Lands, 1986—; bd. dirs. Ctr. for N.H.'s Future, 1980—, N.H. Coun. World Affairs, 1986-89; mem. Gov.'s Commn. on N.H. in 21st Century, 1989—; trustee Theater-by-the-Sea, Portsmouth, N.H., 1980-83, N.H. Higher Edn. Assistance Found., 1986—; co-dir. series pub. workshops Dickey-Lincoln and Passamaquoddy Hydroelectric Projects; chair Coun. Higher Edn. Accreditation, dir., 1997-2002. Norwegian Rsch. Coun. fellow, 1972-73; grantee NSF, NIMH, HEW, 1966-75. Mem. AAAS, AAUP, NCAA (pres. commn. 1996-2000), Council of Colls. of Arts and Scis. (bd. dirs. 1977-79), Nat. Assn. State Univs. and Land-Grant Colls. (commn. on arts and scis. 1978-81, chair exec. com. council on acad. affairs 1983, internat. affairs com. 1985-87, exec. com. 1986—, chair commn. edn. for teaching professions 1987-88), Nat. Assn., Ind. Colls. and Univs. (bd. dirs. 1993—), Am. Psychol. Assn. (div. 8 and 26, coun. of reps. N.H., Vt., Maine and R.I. 1968-71, com. on structure and function of coun. 1968-71), Eastern Psychol. Assn., N.H. Psychol. Assn. (program dir. 1971), Eisenhower World Affairs Inst. (bd. dirs. 1991—), Soc. Exptl. Social Psychology, Phi Kappa Phi, Sigma Xi.

HAAN, PHILIP C., air transportation executive; married; 2 children. BA in Biology and Chemistry, Calvin Coll., Grand Rapids, Mich.; MS in Indsl. Adminstrn., Purdue U., West Lafayette, Ind. Various positions Ford Motor Co., Am. Airlines; with NW Airlines Corp., 1991-95, v.p. revenue mgmt., v.p. inventory sales and systems, v.p. pricing and area mktg., sr. v.p., internat., 1995-99, exec. v.p. internat., sales and info. svcs., 1999—2004, exec. v.p. internat., alliances and info. tech., chmn. NW Cargo, 2004—. Co-chair alliance steering com. KLM Royal Dutch Airlines; pres. Narita Radisson Hotel. Mem. internat. adv. bd. U. Minn. Carlson Sch. Mgmt. Office: NW Airlines Corp 2700 Lone Oak Pky Eagan MN 55121 Office Phone: 612-726-2111.*

HAAS, AARON C., sales executive; s. Richard E. Haas and Carolyn M. Holder. BA in Psychology, U. Akron, Ohio, 1998; MBA, Carnegie Mellon U., Pitts., Pa., 2005. Cardiovas. sales specialist Abbott Labs., Abbott Park, Ill., 2002—. Capt. US Army, 1998—2002, with USAR, 2002—. Decorated Commendation medal US Army, Achievement medal. Independent. Home Phone: 304-723-3539; Office Phone: 412-607-6469.

HAAS, BRIAN D., surgeon; b. Oct. 18, 1960; BA, Harvard U., Cambridge, Mass., 1982; MD, Columbia U., NY, 1986. Staff surgeon Nat. Naval Med. Ctr., Bethesda, Md., 1990—95; pvt. practice Orlando, Fla., 1996—. Dir. oculoplastic surgery Nat. Naval Med. Ctr., Bethesda, 1990—91; clin. assoc. prof. U. South Fla., 1996—2006; chmn. dept. ophthalmology Orlando Regional Med. Ctr., 1999—. Recipient Surgical Tchg. award, U. So. Fla., 1999, Disting. Physician award, Fla. Med. Assn., 2006. Fellow: AAO (Achievement award 2006), ACS; mem.: Ctrl. Fla. Soc. Ophthalmology (pres. 1999—2000). Office: 16 W Columbia St Orlando FL 34747

HAAS, CHARLIE, screenwriter; b. Bklyn., Oct. 22, 1952; s. Philip and Eunice (Dillon) H.; m. Barbara K. Moran, Dec. 21, 1981. BA, U. Calif., Santa Cruz, 1984. Editorial dir. Warner Bros. Records, Burbank, Calif., 1974-76; contbg. editor New West Mag., Beverly Hills, Calif., 1976-80; freelance writer LA, 1976-80, Oakland, Calif., 1980—. Co-author: (movies) Over the Edge, 1979, Tex, 1982, Gremlins 2, 1990, Matinee, 1993, Runaway Daughters, 1994; contbr. articles to mags. Mem. Friends of Oakland Parks & Recreation, Friends of Oakland Pub. Libr. Avocations: fountain pens, mountain bikes.

HAAS, DANIEL LOUIS, structural engineer; b. Bloomington, Ill., Sept. 6, 1949; s. Louis Francis and Dorothy Jean Haas; m. Joyce Lowe; children: David, Virgina. BSCE, Univ. Ill., Urbana, Ill., 1971. cert. structural, Ill., profl., Ill., Ga., Mo., Okla., Tenn., Kans., SD.; registered NCEES. Structual engr. Campbell & Wieland, St. Louis, 1972—74, Lemessurier Sci., St. Louis, 1974—76, Bendy Engring., St. Louis, 1976—82, Gillum Assoc., St. Louis, 1976, EDM Corp., St. Louis, 1983—89; sr. structual engr. Penta Engring., St. Louis, 1989—. Named Engr. of Yr., EDM Corp., 1987; recipient Michael Von-Siebach award, Penta Engring., 2004. Christian. Achievements include design of St. Louis Union Station; Dragon Cement Thomasion Maine; TWA Dome. Home: 14 Seabiscuit Dr Saint Charles MO 63301 Office: Penta Engring Co 1807 270 Dr Ste 500 Saint Louis MO 63146

HAAS, EDWARD LEE, management consultant; b. Camden, NJ, Nov. 9, 1935; s. Edward David and Mildred Haas; m. Maryann Lind, Dec. 27, 1958; children: John Eric, Gretchen Haas Theodore. BA, LaSalle U., Phila., 1958. Cryptanalyst Nat. Security Agy., Ft. Meade, Md., 1958—59; mgr. sys. devel. RCA Corp., Cherry Hill, NJ, 1966—71; mgr. computer tech. svcs. Gencorp, Akron, Ohio, 1971—74; sr. mgr. computer applications R & D Ernst & Young LLP, Cleve., 1974—75, dir. nat. software products, 1976—77, chief info. officer, nat. dir. software products, 1977—80, nat. ptnr., 1978—82, cons. ptnr. Phila., NYC, L.A., 1983—95; ind. mgmt. cons. L.A., 1996—98; v.p. info. tech. Sunbeam Corp., Boca Raton, Fla., 1998—99; ind. mgmt. cons. NYC, 2000—. 1st lt. arty. US Army, 1958—59. Mem.: Tournament Players Club (Sawgrass), Plantation Country Club. Republican. Roman Catholic. Office Phone: 904-285-5735.

HAAS, FREDERICK CARL, retired paper company executive, retired chemicals executive; b. Buffalo, Feb. 16, 1936; s. Karl A. and Marie S. (Shilling) H.; m. Dorothy A. Wittlief, Aug. 31, 1957; children— Kenneth Karl, Lawrence Frederick, Sandra Dorothy. BS in Chem. Engring, Purdue U., 1957; MS in Nuclear Engring, Rensselaer Poly. Inst., Troy, NY, 1959, PhD in Chem. Engring, 1960; grad., Advanced Mgmt. Program, Harvard U., 1978. Registered profl. engr., N.Y. Research engr. Cornell Aero. Lab., 1960-63; with Westvaco Corp., 1963-98, corp. research dir., then v.p., 1978-81, sr. v.p. ops. NYC, 1982—. Asst. prof. Potomac State Coll., 1966; mem. curriculum com., research com. U. Maine; chmn. research adv. com. Inst. Paper Chemistry; mem. president's key exec. com. Rensselaer Poly. Inst. Author papers in field. Bd. dirs. Syracuse Pulp and Paper Found. AEC fellow, 1957, Tappi fellow, 1994; recipient Disting. Engring. Alumnus award Purdue U., 1993, Outstanding Chem. Engring. award, 1993. Mem. Am. Mgmt. Assn. (research and devel. council), Am. Inst. Chem. Engrs., Am. Chem. Soc., TAPPI, Nat. Soc. Profl. Engrs., Indsl. Research Inst., Dirs. Indsl. Research, Can. Pulp and Paper Assn., Tri-State Shetland Sheep Dog Club, Sigma Xi. Methodist.

HAAS, GERHARD JULIUS, microbiologist, educator; b. Munich; arrived in U.S., 1943; s. Alfred and Elsa Haas; m. Rita Zondek; children: David J., Andrea C. BA, Cambridge U., Eng., 1939, MA, 1943; PhD, U. Pa., Phila., 1952. Sr. chemist Hoffman LaRoche, Nutley, NJ, 1943—50; dir. rsch. Rheingold Brewery, Bklyn., 1952—60; chief chemist Desitin Co., Providence, 1960—61; prin. scientist Gen. Foods, Tarrytown, NY, 1961—87; rsch. assoc. NY Bot. Garden, Bronx, 1987—92; rsch. prof. Fairleigh Dickinson U., Teaneck, NJ, 1992—. Contbr. articles to profl. publs., chpts. to books. Vice chmn. Bd. Health, Woodcliff Lake, NJ. Recipient, U. Pa., awards, Gen. Foods Corp., 1973, 1984, Indsl. Scientist award, Inst. Food Technologists, 1995. Fellow: AAAS, Soc. Indsl. Microbiology; mem.: Inst. Food Tech., Am. Soc. Microbiology, Am. Chem. Soc. Achievements include patents in field. Avocations: bridge, swimming, gardening. Office: Fairleigh Dickinson U Sch Natural Sciences 1000 River Rd Teaneck NJ 07666

HAAS, HOWARD GREEN, retired bedding manufacturing company executive; b. Chgo., Apr. 14, 1924; s. Adolph and Marie (Green) H.; m. Carolyn Werbner, June 4, 1949; children: Jody, Jonathan Student, U. Chgo., 1942; BBA, U. Mich., 1948. Promotion dir. Esquire, Inc., Chgo., 1949—50; advt. mgr. Mitchell Mfg. Co., Chgo., 1950—52, v.p. advt., 1952—56, v.p. sales, 1956—58; sales mgr. Sealy, Inc., Chgo., 1959—60, v.p. mktg., 1960—65, exec. v.p., 1965—67, pres., treas., 1967—86, 1987. Bd. dirs. Brogden Tool & Die Co., Aurora Custom Machinery, Inc.; adj. prof. strategic mgmt. U. Chgo. Grad. Sch. Bus., 1989— Author: The Leader Within, 1993 Past mem. nominating com. Glencoe Sch. Bd.; mem. print and drawing com. Art Inst. Chgo.; past chmn. parent's com. Washington U., St. Louis; past bd. dirs. Jewish Children's Bur.; mem. vis. com. Oriental Inst., U. Chgo.; past pres. Orch. of Ill. (Chgo. Philharm). 1st lt. USAAF, 1943-45, ETO Decorated Air medal with 3 oak leaf clusters; recipient Brotherhood award NCCJ, 1970, Human Rels. award Am. Jewish Com., 1977 Mem. Nat. Assn. Bedding Mfrs. (past vice chmn., trustee), Birchwood Tennis Club (Highland Park, Ill.), Masons Jewish. Personal E-mail: hghhaas@aol.com.

HAAS, JAMES WAYNE, accountant; b. Merrill, Wis., Sept. 27, 1944; s. Frank Joseph and Verna Antoinette (Beilke) H.; m. Patrice Marie Will, June 2, 1973 (div. Sept. 1997); children: Christopher Jon, Scott James; m. Patricia Burbach Stach, Oct. 3, 2004. A in Acctg., N. Cen. Tech. Coll., 1968; BA, Am. Coll., 1989. Cert. tax profl., accredited tax preparer; lic. ins. agt. Minn., Wis. Contr., asst. treas. House of Merrill, Inc., Merrill, 1968-72; controller Semling Menke Co., Inc., Merrill, 1968-72; treas., dir. North Star Comms., Ltd., Gleason, Wis., 1971-72; pres., dir. Profl. Acctg. Systems, Inc., La Crosse, Wis., 1975-88; pres. Haas Enterprises, Inc., 1971-82; pres., treas. Adventure Capital, Ltd., 1971—; treas., prodn. mgr., dir. Modu-Line Windows, Wausau, Wis., 1977—78; ptnr. 1st St. Investments, Black River Falls, Wis., 2006, Brunner, Robinson & Haas, LLC, Black River Falls, 2006—. Treas. Sys. Mgmt., Inc., St. Paul, 1983—84, Gateway Acctg. Svcs., Inc., Ft. Myers, Fla., 1982—83; v.p., treas., ops. mgr. Acctg. Bookkeeping Co., Inc., Wauwatosa, Wis., 1975—76; v.p. Marathon Mining & Mfg. Corp., Wausau, Wis., 1976, pres., 1977—78; mng. ptnr. Haas Properties, Mosinee, Wis., 1979—83; owner Midwest Investments, Winona, Minn., 1980—; pres., dir. Acctg. Bookkeeping Cons., Ltd., 1987—88; owner Jim Haas Assocs., 1988—; pres. Jim Haas Assocs., LLC, Winona, 1999—; chmn., sec., dir. Consol. Bus. Svcs., Inc., La Crosse, Wis., 1984—; treas. Am. Bending Supply, Inc., Galesville, Wis., 1992—94; owner Tri-State Markers, La Crosse, 1995—; chmn., sec., treas., dir. Ferrous, Inc., Winona, 1995—2006, Mid-Am. Heat Treat, Inc., Winona, 1998—2006, Mid Am. Core and Mold, Inc., Winona, 2000—06; sec. Goodview Clin., Ltd., 1998—; treas. M2 Comms., Ltd., Reno, 1998—; pres. The Watch Dog Group, Ltd., Shakopee, Minn., 2001—; chmn. The Aichalden Group, Ltd., La Crosse, Wis., 2002—. Mem. Adminstrv. Mgmt. Soc., Inst. Internat. Auditors, Nat. Notary Assn., Inst. Record Mgrs. and Adminstrs., Am. Soc. Notaries, Nat. Assn. Accts., Am. Inst. Profl. Numismatists (charter mem.), Am. Acctg. Assn., Nat. Soc. Pub. Accts., Nat. Soc. Tax Profls., Nat. Assn. Life Underwriters, Internat. Cmty. Corrections Assn., Am. Assn. Altruistic CPAs and Fin. Planners, Am. Soc. Tax Profls., Am. Soc. Metallurgists, Inst. Mgmt. Cons., Cath. Order of Foresters, KC, Kiwanis (New Club Bldg. award), Optimists, Winona Lions. Home: 1339 Lauderdale Pl Onalaska WI 54650-3277 Office: 611 Broadway Cashton WI 54619 also: 201 E 3rd St Winona MN 55987 also: 312 W Main St Arcadia WI 54612 Office Phone: 608-784-5507. E-mail: jhaas@fflax.net.

HAAS, JOHN C., architect; b. Columbus, Ohio, Nov. 3, 1934; s. John Clyde and Margaret (Merideth) H.; m. Jean Ann Scigliano, June 12, 1958 (dec. Apr. 1986); m. Joyce Conklin, May 9, 1987; children: Jeffrey, Joel, John, Paige. BArch, Pa. State U., 1958. Registered architect Pa., Ohio, NJ, NY, Del., W.Va., Md., Va., Mass., Fla., NC. Archtl. draftsman Arthur E. Tennyson, Pitts., 1959-62; archtl. designer Diehl and Stein Architects, Princeton, NJ, 1962—63; staff architect Hankin and Hyres, Trenton, NJ, 1963—67; architect Mahony and Zvosec, Princeton, NJ, 1967-71; dir. archtl. planning dept. Gen. Housing Industries, State College, Pa., 1971-72; founder, prin. Haas Bldg Solutions, State College, Pa., 1972—. Sec., treas. Pa. Archs. Licensure Bd., 1998—2002, v.p., 2002—03; mem. adv. bd. dirs. PNC Bank of Ctrl. Pa., 1998—2005; pres. Pa. Architects Licensure Bd., 2004, 05. Prin. works include Nittany Apt. Housing, The Meadows Clinic, Fraser St. Parking Garage, BCH Office Bldg., Geisinger Med. Clinic, The Bryce Jordan Convocation Ctr., Pa. State U. (all State Coll.), Beaver Stadium Expansion, Pa. State U., Recreation Ctr., Lycoming Coll., Williamsport, Pa. Campaign cabinet Centre County United Way, 1994-96, bd. dirs. 1998—; county chmn. United Way Campaign, 1997; bd. dirs. Chamber of Bus. and Ind. of Centre County, 1996-2003. Capt. US Army, 1958-59. Mem. AIA (pres. mid. Pa. chpt. 1986-87), Nat. Coun. Archtl. Registration Bds., Pa. Soc. Architects (pres. 1993), State College Area C. of C. (pres. 1990-91, bd. dirs. 1984-92), Rotary (pres. 1988-89, bd. dirs.). Republican. Presbyterian. Home: 14 High Meadow Ln State College PA 16803-1853 Office: Haas Bldg Solutions 1301 N Atherton St State College PA 16803-2932 Office Phone: 814-238-1551. Business E-Mail: jhaas@haasbuildingsolutions.com.

HAAS, JOSEPH MARSHALL, retired petroleum consultant; b. Alexandria, La., June 21, 1927; s. Samuel and Lulu Susan (Haupt) H.; m. Mary Louise Nance, June 4, 1949 (dec. Jan. 1950); 1 child, Samuel Douglas; m. Marion Barker, Apr. 9, 1954; children: Joseph Marshall, Suzanne M., Thomas B., Katherine L. B of Mech. Engring., Ga. Inst. Tech., 1949. With Gen. Am. Oil Co., Dallas, 1949-78, asst. v.p. prodn. and engring., 1957—60, v.p. engring., 1960—78; bd. dirs. Gen. Am. Ore Co., 1978—83. Pres., bd. dirs. Conejo Investments Inc., 1994—; mgr. Tiger Bend LLC, 2005—. With USNR, 1945-46. Mem. Am. Inst. Mining and Metall. Engrs., Masons (32 degree, Shriner), Dallas Petroleum Club, Tau Beta Pi, Sigma Chi, Pi Tau Sigma. Methodist. Home: 1119 Challenger St Austin TX 78734-3801 Office: 1123 Challenger St Austin TX 78734-3801

HAAS, MARK, pathologist; b. NYC, Jan. 30, 1955; s. Alvin and Ruth (Heller) H. BA, Duke U., 1977, PhD, MD, 1982. Diplomate Am. Bd. Pathology. Assoc. rschr. dept. physiology Duke U., Durham, N.C., 1983; resident dept. pathology Yale-New Haven Hosp., 1983-85; postdoctoral fellow dept. physiology Sch. Medicine Yale U., New Haven, 1985-86; asst. prof. pathology Yale U., New Haven, 1986-89, U. Chgo., 1989-93, assoc. prof., 1993—99, dir. renal pathology, 1994—99; assoc. prof., dir. electron microscopy lab. Johns Hopkins U., Balt., 1999—, dir. renal pathology, 2004—, prof., 2004—. Reviewer: Am. Jour. Physiology, 1984—, mem. editl. bd., 1993-99; reviewer: Jour. Membrane Biology, 1985—, Jour. Biol. Chemistry, 1987—, Jour. Clin. Investigation, 1990—, Sci., 1991—, Jour. Am. Soc. Nephrology, 1995—, Am. Jour. Pathology, 1998-, Am. Jour. Transplantation, 2006-; mem. editl. bd. Am. Jour. Kidney Diseases, 1999-2001, Kidney Internat., 2002-; contbr. articles to profl. jours, chpts. to med. books. Recipient Established Investigator award, Am. Heart Assn., 1992-97; rsch. grantee NIH, Am. Heart Assn., Cystic Fibrosis Found.; fellow John A. Hartford Found., 1986-89. Mem. Am. Soc. for Investigative Pathology, U.S. and Canadian Acad. Pathology, Am. Soc. Nephrology, Renal Pathology Soc. (concillor 2003-06, v.p. 2007), Alpha Omega Alpha (v.p., organizer symposium 1981-82). Office: 600 N Wolfe St Pathology 712 Baltimore MD 21287 Business E-Mail: mhaas@jhmi.edu.

HAAS, MARK RICHARD, management consultant researcher; b. Dallas, Apr. 12, 1954; s. Richard Harry and Betty (Vadner) H.; m. Phyllis Marcia Levinson, May 10, 1980; children: Danielle, Ethan. BA, Colgate U., 1976; MA in City and Regional Planning, Harvard U., 1979. Cert. mgmt. cons., Inst. Mgmt. Cons., Wash., 1996, 2006; lic. commercial airplane pilot Fed. Aviation Adminstrn. Asst. to chief Nat. Park Service, Washington, 1976-77; intern Nat. Capital Planning Commn., Washington, 1977; asst. bus. mgr. Mass. Port Authority, Boston, 1978; teaching asst. Harvard U., Cambridge, Mass., 1978, teaching fellow, 1979; research assoc. Lewin and Assocs., Washington, 1979-83, sr. assoc., 1983-86, prin., 1986—87; project mgr. ICF Resources Inc., Fairfax, Va., 1987—94; pres. Rsch. Organization Mgmt. Inc., Bethesda, Md., 1994—; mng. ptnr. Interscope Consulting, Bethesda, Md., 2005—. Speaker in field. Contbr. Vol. tutor DC Pub. Schs., 1987—88; mem. Nat. Commn. on Tech. Edn. Standards; mem. advisory com. Montgomery County Commn. on Gifted and Talented Children; bd. examiners US Senate Productivity award, Md. State Quality award, lead examiner, 1997—2003. Mem.: Inst. Mgmt. Cons. (chpt. pres. 2000—03, ethics com. chmn. 2003—05, nat. dir. 2003—06, chmn. nat. bd. 2006—), Soc. Petroleum Engrs. (nat. tech. com. 1985—87, chmn. 1987, pres. 1988, dir. 1989—91, career guidance com. 1990—92, Outstanding Svc. award 1988), Internat. Assn. Energy Economists, Am. Assn. Engring. Soc. (edn. com. 1993—96, rsch. and devel. policy task force), Kennedy Sch. Alumni Assn. (bd. mem. 2005—). Democrat. Jewish. Avocations: golf, reading, writing, woodworking. Office Phone: 301-320-5889. Business E-Mail: mhaas@rominc.com.

HAAS, PAUL RAYMOND, petroleum company executive; b. Kingston, NY, Mar. 10, 1915; s. Frederick J. and Amanda (Lange) H.; m. Mary F. Diedrick, Aug. 30, 1936; children: Rheta Marie, Raymond Paul, Rene Marie. AB, Rider Coll., 1934, LL.D., 1976. C.P.A., Tex. Acct. Arthur Andersen & Co. (C.P.A.s), NYC and Houston, 1934-41; with La Gloria Oil & Gas Co., Corpus Christi, Tex., 1941-59, v.p., treas., dir., 1947-59; adminstrv. v.p. Tex. Eastern Transmission Corp., Houston, 1958-59; pres., chmn. bd. Prado Oil & Gas Co., 1959-66, Wiltex Corp., 1950-65, Garland Co., 1956-65, Citronelle Oil & Gas Co., 1967-69, Corpus Christi Oil and Gas Co., 1968-90, Corpus Christi Leaseholds Inc., 1990—, Corpus Christi Exploration Co., 1976-90; ltd. partner Salomon Bros., 1973-81. Ind. oil and gas operator, 1959—. Trustee Corpus Christi Ind. Sch. Dist., 1951-58, pres., 1956-58; mem. Tex. Bd. Edn., 1962-72, vice chmn., 1970-72; mem. Gov.'s Com. Edn., 1966-69; Trustee Paul and Mary Haas Found., 1954—, Robert T. Wilson Found., 1954-72, Rider Coll., 1959-67, Moody Found., 1966-73, Found. Center, 1970-75, Council on Founds., 1970-76, Commn. on Philanthropy and Pub. Needs, 1973-75, Univ. Cancer Found. M.D. Anderson Hosp. and Tumor Inst., 1975—. Presbyn. (elder). Home: 4500 Ocean Dr Apt 9A Corpus Christi TX 78412-2572 Office: Corpus Christi Holding Co PO Box 779 Corpus Christi TX 78403-0779

HAAS, RAYMOND P., lawyer; b. Corpus Christi, Tex., Dec. 9, 1942; BA cum laude, Yale U., 1964, LLB, 1967. Bar: Calif. 1967. Law clk. to Hon. Roger J. Traynor Supreme Ct. of Calif., 1967-68; atty. Howard, Rice, Nemerovski, Canady, Falk & Rabkin, San Francisco. Trustee San Francisco U. High Sch., 1973-78, 85-88, chmn., 1973-76, treas., 1986-88; trustee Pacific Presbyn. Med. Ctr., 1979-91, vice chmn. 1986-91. Mem. ABA (forum com. on franchising, antitrust law sect., bus. law sect., internat. law sect., patent, copyright and trademarks sect., sci. and tech. sect.), State Bar Calif., Bar Assn. San Francisco (computer law sect.), Licensing Execs. Soc., Computer Law Assn., Order of Coif. Office: Howard Rice Nemerovski Canady Falk & Rabkin 3 Embarcadero Ctr Ste 7 San Francisco CA 94111-4074 Office Phone: 415-399-3090.

HAAS, RICHARD ALLEN, physician; b. Boston, Nov. 14, 1951; s. Felix and Violet (Bushwick) H.; m. Ann Linda Mitchell, Mar. 29, 1980; children: Derek Adam, Brian Mitchell, Andrea Violet. BS in Chemistry, MIT, 1973; MD, U. Calif., San Francisco, 1977. Cert. in endocrinology, diabetes, metabolism, and internal medicine Am. Bd. Internal. Medicine. Resident in internal medicine Mt. Sinai Hosp., NYC, 1977-80; fellow in endocrinology Columbia Presbyn. Hosp., NYC, 1980-82; pvt. practice Worcester, Mass., 1982—. Asst. prof. medicine U. Mass. Med. Sch. Contbg. author to profl. jours. Fellow Am. Coll. Endocrinology; mem. Am. Diabetes Assn., Phi Beta Kappa, Alpha Omega Alpha. Home: 1 Broushane Cir Shrewsbury MA 01545-2050 Office: 200 Lincoln St Worcester MA 01605-2528 Office Phone: 508-755-1222.

HAAS, RICHARD JOHN, artist; b. Spring Green, Wis., Aug. 29, 1936; s. Joseph Francis and Marie H.; m. Cynthia Dickman, Sept. 1963 (div. 1971); m. Katherine Sokolnikoff, May 12, 1981; 1 child, Gregory Alexander. BS in Art Edn., U. Wis., Milw., 1959; MFA, U. Minn., 1964. Instr. U. Minn., Mpls., 1963-64; asst. prof. art Mich. State U., East Lansing, 1964-68; instr. printmaking Bennington (Vt.) Coll., 1968-78; mem. fine arts faculty Sch. Visual Arts, 1977-81; dir. Abbey Mural Fund Nat. Acad. Fine Arts and Mus., NY, 2000—. Instr. fresco Skowhegan Sch. Painting and Sculpture, 1984. Author: The City is My Canvas, 1981, An Architecture of Illusion, 1981, Catalogue Raisonné The Prints of Richard Haas, 1970-2004, 2005; one-man shows include Rhona Hoffman Gallery, Chgo., 1983, 90, Art and Architecture Gallery, U. Tenn., 1984, St. Louis Art Mus., 1984, Aspen Art Mus., 1985, Williams Coll. Mus. of Art, Williamstown, Mass., 1987, Brooke Alexander, 1985-89, Sam Houston State U., Huntsville, Tex., 1992, Miramar Gallery, Sarasota, Fla., 1992, Condeso/Lawler Gallery, N.Y., 1982, U. Wis., Milw., 1992, Marsha Orr Contemporary Fine Arts Gallery, Tallahasse, 1996, Huntington (W.Va.) Mus. Art, 1997, Century Assn., N.Y.C., 1997, Art on Main Street, Yonkers, N.Y., 1997, 98, Southern Alleghenies Mus., Pa., 1999, Prinkworks, Chgo., 2000, Michael Ingbar Gallery, NYC, 2002, David Findlay Jr, NYC, 2004, Nashville Pub. Libr., 2005, Kunsthandel Elisabeth Michitsch, Vienna, Austria, 2005, David Findlay Jr. Fine Art, 2006, Boston Coll. Architecture, 2006; Gerald Peters Gallery, Dallas, 2007, group exhibitions include Am. Acad. Arts & Letters, Tuscon Mus. Art; over 125 nat. and internat. mural commns., 1973—. Trustee Hudson River Mus., 1989-04, 2006—, NY State Preservation League, 1983-88; bd. govs. Skowhegan Sch. Painting and Sculpture, 1982—; bd. dirs. Pub. Art Fund, 1981-88; v.p. Archtl. League of NY, 1978-81; mem. NYC Art Commn.; v.p. Nat. Acad. Arts Mus. and Sch. Fine Arts, 2000-; pres. Abbey Mural Fund, Nat. Acad., 2000-. active duty US Army, 1959, 1st lt. USAR, 1959-66. Fellow Nat. Endowment Arts, 1978, Guggenheim Found., 1983-84, MacDowell Fellowship, 2003; recipient medal of honor AIA, 1977, award Mcpl. Art Soc., 1977, Doris Freedman award N.Y.C., 1989, Disting. Alumnus award U. Wis., Milw., 1991, Individual Artist award, Westchester Arts Coun., 2003; honoree Yonkers Friends of Arts Pub. Art, 2003, Jimmy Ernst award of art, Am. Acad. Arts & Letters, 2005. Mem. Century Assn., Racquet Ball on Park Hill. Office: 361 W 36th St 5A New York NY 10018-6408

HAAS, ROBERT DOUGLAS, apparel executive; b. San Francisco, Apr. 3, 1942; s. Walter A. Haas Jr. and Evelyn (Danzig) Haas; m. Colleen Gershon, Jan. 27, 1974; 1 child, Elise Kimberly. BA, U. Calif., Berkeley, 1964; MBA, Harvard U., 1968. With Peace Corps, Ivory Coast, 1964-66; fellow White House, Washington, 1968-69; assoc. McKinsey & Co., 1969-72; with Levi Strauss & Co., San Francisco, 1973—, sr. v.p. corp. planning and policy, 1978-80, pres. new bus. group, 1980, pres. operating groups, 1980-81, exec. v.p., COO, 1981-84, pres., CEO, 1984-89, CEO, 1989—99, chmn. bd. dir., 1989—. Pres. Levi Strauss Found.; mem. Global leadership team. Hon. dir. San Francisco AIDS Found.; trustee Ford Found.; bd. dirs. Bay Area Coun.; past bd. dirs. Am. Apparel Assn. Fellow White House fellow, 1968—69. Mem.: Meyer Freidman Inst. (bd. dirs.), Calif. Bus. Roundtable, Trilateral Commn., Coun. Fgn. Rels., Conf. Bd., Bay Area Com., Brookings Inst. (trustee), Phi Beta Kappa. Office: Levi Strauss & Co 1155 Battery St San Francisco CA 94111-1256*

HAAS, ROBERT JOHN, aerospace engineer; b. Dayton, Ohio, Apr. 14, 1930; s. Robert J. Haas and Harriett (Longstreth) Bevan; m. Florence A. Eldred, June 6, 1952 (div. June 1984); adopted children: Jeffrey (dec.), Lisa Haas Cappuccio; m. Gayle F. Byrne, Dec. 14, 1984; stepchildren: Patrick Barton, Marissa Barton; children: Amber Haas, Robert J. Haas III. Student, U.S. Mil. Acad., 1948-51; BS in Petroleum Engring., U. Tulsa, 1954. Petroleum engr. Skelly Oil Co., Tulsa, 1953-54; propulsion engr., supr. Marquardt, Van Nuys, Calif., 1957-64, mgr. rocket programs, 1964-69, dir. test and facilities, 1969-72, gen. mgr. environ. systems, 1972-75; plant gen. mgr. Williams Internat., Ogden, Utah, 1975-79, sr. v.p. engring. Walled Lake, Mich., 1979-86, sr. v.p. product planning and mktg., 1986-90; sr. advisor, cons. Las Vegas, Nev., 1990—; CEO Haas Enterprises, Consulting Firm, Las Vegas, 1992—. Cons. Marquardt, Van Nuys, 1961-75; bd. dirs. Verile Corp. Author: Approach to Aerospace Plane Propulsion, 1960. Lectr. and advisor Weber State Coll., U. Utah and various high schs. and clubs., 1975-79; pres. Marquardt Mgmt. Club, 1971. 1st lt. USAF, 1954-56. Mem. AIAA, Navy League (lifetime). Republican. Roman Catholic. Achievements include contribution to devel. and prodn. of world's smallest turbofan for cruise missiles; discoveries in the field of integrated propulsion modules for missiles, economical methods of testing ramjets, turbines and rocket engines. Home and Office: Haas Enterprises PO Box 33126 Las Vegas NV 89133-3126

HAAS, ROBERT LANCE, surgeon, consultant; b. NYC, Oct. 7, 1933; s. Kalman and Ruth Haas; m. Lois Feldman, Apr. 14, 1957; children: Kara, Robyn, Bradley, Felice. BS in Biology, Ohio State U., 1953; DDS, Columbia U., 1957; cert. in Surgery, NYU, 1959; MPH, Columbia U., 1973. Diplomate Am. Bd. Oral & Maxillofacial Surgery. Intern in maxillofacial surgery Harlem Hosp., NYC, 1958; resident in maxillofacial surgery Grasslands Hosp., Valhalla, NY, 1960; assoc. prof. NJ Coll. Medicine and Dentistry, 1971; pvt. practice; assoc. attending maxillofacial surgeon N.Y. Med. Coll.-Grassland Hosp., Valhalla, Bronx (N.Y.)-Lebanon Med. Ctr., Fordham-Misericordia Med. Ctr., The Bronx; attending maxillofacial surgeon Royal Hosp., The Bronx; attending surgeon, chief maxillofacial surgery & dentistry Newark Beth Israel Med. Ctr., dir. out-patient dept. Adj. prof. Columbia U. Coll. Physicians and Surgeons, 1973; lectr. U. South Fla., 1977; chmn. Heritage Eagle Bd. Co. Contbr. articles to profl. jours. Adminstrv. judge City of Tampa; co-chmn. New Tampa Emergency Prepared Com. Fellow Am. Coll. Oral and Maxillofacial Surgeons, Am. Acad. Cosmetic Surgeons, Internat. Soc. Oral and Maxillofacial Surgeons, Am. Dental Soc. Anesthesiology, Internat. Assn. Study Pain, Am. Pain Soc., Internat. Rehab. Med. Assn.; mem. APHA, state and local affiliates of ADA, Internat. Assn. Maxillofacial Surgery, Hillsborough County Hosp. Authority, Am. Assn. Oral and Maxillofacial Surgeons, Nat. Ctr. Health Edn. (charter assoc.), N.Y. Acad. Scis., Alpha Omega. Home: 8248 S Winnipeg Cir Aurora CO 80016-7160 Office Phone: 303-927-7397. Personal E-mail: bobloishaas@comcast.net.

HAAS, SALLY MARIE, mathematician, educator; b. Lufkin, Tex., May 22, 1963; d. Richard Eugene and Sara Nelson Haas. BS in Applied Math. Scis., Tex. A&M U., College Station, 1985; MS in Math. Secondary Tchg., Stephen F. Austin U., Nacogdoches, TX, 1990; PhD, Tex. A&M U., College Station, 1998. Tchr. h.s. math. Lufkin ISD, 1987—94, math. facilitator grades 7 - 12, 1992—94; instr. math. Blinn Coll., Brenham, Tex., 1994—96, Angelina Coll., Lufkin, 1996—. Mem.: Assn. Math. Tchr. Educators, Nat. Coun. Tchrs. Math., Tex. Cmty. Coll. Tchrs. Assn., Angelina Bicycle Club, Century Club, Lufkin H.S. Alumni (life), Alumni and Friends-Angelina Coll. (life). Avocations: bicycling, camping, water sports, racquetball. Home: 505 Willow Bend Dr Lufkin TX 75901 Office: Angelina Coll South First St Lufkin TX 75902 Home Phone: 936-632-4061; Office Phone: 936-633-5361. Business E-Mail: shaas@angelina.edu.

HAAS, SHEILA JEAN, secondary school educator; b. Rock Island, Ill., Sept. 26, 1947; d. Marcel Henry and Ida Germaine Vroman, Catherine Honora Vroman (Stepmother); m. David Joseph Haas, May 10, 1996; children: Laura, Joshua, Elena. BA, Bradley U., Peoria, Ill., 1971; MA, North Cen. Coll., 1998; postgrad., No. Ill., DeKalb, 2000. Cert. tchr., adminstr. Ill. English aide North Jr. High, Crystal Lake, Ill., 1987—88; substitute tchr. Sch. Dist. 155, Crystal Lake, 1989—90; social sci. tchr. South HS, Crystal Lake, 1990, Cen. HS, Crystal Lake, 1991—96, Prairie Ridge HS, Crystal Lake, 1997—, social sci. dept. chair, 2000—. Curriculum facilitation staff Sch. Dist. 155, Crystal Lake, 2002—, AP adv. com., 2004—06. Active Dem. Party, Lake Zurich, Ill., 2004—06. Mem.: NEA, AP Audit Com. (mastery mgr. for curriculum alignment facilitation, chair book selection), Time Mgmt. Com., Ill. Coun. for Social Sci., Nat. Coun. for Social Sci. Democrat. Jewish. Avocations: travel, cooking, classical music, art, reading. Home: 206 Parkview Dr Wauconda IL 60084 Office: Prairie Ridge High Sch 6000 Dvorak Dr Crystal Lake IL 60012

HAAS, STEVEN B., orthopedist, surgeon, educator; BA, U. Rochester, 1981, MD, MPH, U. Rochester, 1985. Lic. NY, Board Certified Orthopaedic Surgery. Resident Hosp. Spl. Surgery, fellow, knee svc., assoc. attending orthopaedic surgeon, chief of knee svc.; assoc. attending orthopaedic surgeon NY-Presbyn. Hosp., NYC. Assoc. prof. clin. orthopaedic surgery Weill Med. Coll., Cornell U.; speaks nationally and internationally on knee and hip topics. Contbr. articles to med. jours.; featured as a developer & expert on Minimally Invasive Total Knee Replacement on WNBC News, New York 1 television station, Runner Magazine, New York Daily News and the Cleveland Clinic Newsletter, appeared on WABC News as an expert on Gender knee replacement. Recipient Lewis Clark Wagner Award, 1989. Mem.: Phi Beta Kappa, Alpha Omega Alpha. Achievements include development of a ground breaking surgical technique and instrumentation for performing Minimally Invasive Knee Replacement; holds two US patents for orthopedic devices which was co-developed with Hospital for Special Surgery. Office: Hosp for Spl Surgery 535 E 70th St New York NY 10021 Office Phone: 212-606-1852. Office Fax: 212-288-1572.*

HAAS, SUZANNE ALBERTA, elementary and secondary school educator; b. Perrysburg, Ohio, Nov. 29, 1934; d. Albert Joseph and Mary Elizabeth (Gurtzweiler) Haas; m. Robert Chester Kemp (dec.). BA, Xavier U., 1961; MS, Eastern Mich. U., 1975; attended, Mary Manse Coll., 1956—64, Toledo U., 1963, George Peabody U., 1964—65, St. Louis U., 1967, Bemidui U., 1979. With Religious Sisters of Mercy, Cin., 1952—68; tchr. St. Catherine Cath. Sch., Toledo, 1956—57, 1961—62, St. Peter Cath. Sch., Upper Sandusky, Ohio, 1957—58, St. Anne Cath. Sch., Fremont, Ohio, 1958—59, St. Rita Cath. Sch., Cin., 1959—61, St. Vincent de Paul Sch., Toledo, 1962—63, St. Mary Cath. Sch., Vermilion, Ohio, 1963—64, St. Polycarp Cath. Sch., Pleasure Ridge, Ky., 1964—65, Mother of Mercy Acad., Louisville, 1965—66, Mercy HS, Louisville, 1966—68, Rosarian Acad., W. Palm Beach, Fla., 1968—69, Howell Watkins Jr., Sr. High, Palm Beach Gardens, Fla., 1969—71, Brighton Jr. High, Brighton, Mich., 1972—76, St. Mary Mission Sch., Red Lake, Minn., 1977—82, Groveland NY State Prison, Attica, NY, 1989—92, Attica NY State Prison, Attica, 1993—95, Wyo. NY State Prison, Attica, 1995—. Sunday sch. tchr. Parochial Sch., Fort Knox Mil. Base, Fort Knox, Ky., 1966, St. John Fischer, W. Palm Beach, 1969. Author (poetry): Treasured Poems of America, 1993—2004, Poetic Voices of America, 1993—2004, Irish Wolfhound Quarterly, 2005. Recipient Honorary Boy Scout award, Boy Scouts of Am., 1999; grantee, NSF, 1964—65. Mem.: Profl. Educator Fedn., Nat. Arbor Day Found., N.Am. Butterfly Assn., Nat. Audubon Soc. Republican. Roman Catholic. Avocations: showing Irish Wolfhounds, birdwatching, writing, gardening, butterfly watching. Home Phone: 585-591-8379.

HAAS, THOMAS JOSEPH, academic administrator, chemistry educator; b. SI, NY, Mar. 5, 1951; s. Joseph Walter and JoAnne (Pawloski) H.; m. Marcia Jane Knapp, Jan. 12, 1974; children: Eric, Gregory, Sarah. BS with honors, USCG Acad., New London, Conn., 1973; MS in Chemistry, U. Mich., 1976, MS in Environ. Health Sci., 1977; MS in Human Rsch. Mgmt., Rensselaer Poly. Inst., 1981; PhD, U. Conn., 1987; MLE, Harvard U., 1999. Cert. indsl. hygienist. Commd. ensign USCG, 1973, advanced through grades to capt., 1996; ops. officer USCG Cutter Acacia, Port Huron, Mich., 1973-75; mem. staff USCG Hdqrs., Washington, 1977-80, br. chief, 1980-81; advanced from asst. prof. to prof. USCG Acad., New London, 1981-96, from section chief to assoc. dean acads., 1981—; v.p. acad. and student affairs William Penn Coll., Oskaloosa, Iowa, 1996-98; dean, supervisory prof. USCG Acad., New London, Conn., 1998—2003; pres. SUNY, Cobleskill, 2003—06, Grand Valley State U., Allendale, Mich., 2006—. Disting. vis. faculty U. Mich., Ann Arbor, 1980; mem. group experts UN, Geneva, 1980; mem. Chem. Transport Adv. Com., Washington, 1977-81, 87-92; data mgr. USCG Valdez (Alaska) Oil Spill, 1989; vis. faculty fellow Yale U., 1991-92. Editor: Descriptions of Selected Hazardous Materials, 1991; contbr. articles to profl. jours. Chair Ledyard (Conn.) Congregation Ch. Session, 1983-90, deacon, 1985; chair Scholarship Com., Ledyard, 1987-90; pres. Parsonage Hill Homeowners Assn., Ledyard, 1987-91. Yale fellow, 1991-92, Am. Coun. on Edn. fellow, 1992-93. Mem. Am. Chem. Soc., Am. Conf. Govtl. Indsl. Hygienists, USCG Officers Assn., N.Y. Acad. Scis., USCG Acad. Officers Club. Republican. Achievements include research on investigation of synthetic materials. Office: Grand Valley State U Office of Pres 22 Zumberge Library Allendale MI 49401-9401 Office Phone: 616-331-2100. E-mail: president@gvsu.edu.

HAAS, TOMMY (THOMAS MARIO HAAS), professional tennis player; b. Hamburg, Germany, Apr. 3, 1978; s. Peter and Brigette Haas. Profl. tennis player ATP Tour, 1996—. Achievements include Winner singles titles: Memphis, 1999, Adelaide, 2001, LI, 2001, Stuttgart TMS, 2001, Vienna, 2001, Houston, 2004, LA, 2004, Delray Beach Internat. Championships, 2006; winner Regions Morgan Keegan Championships, 2006, 2007, Countrywide Classic, LA, 2006. Office: c/o Bollettieri Tennis Acad 5500 34th St W Bradenton FL 34210*

HAAS, WILLIAM PAUL, humanities educator, retired academic administrator; b. Newark, May 31, 1927; s. Joseph J. and Elizabeth (Ryan) H. AB, Providence Coll., 1948; STL, Pontifical Inst., Washington, 1954; PhD, U. Fribourg, Switzerland, 1962; DBA (hon.), Bryant Coll., Providence, 1966; LLD, U. R.I., 1967, Brown U., 1969; DD, Conn. Wesleyan U., 1969; DHL, R.I. Coll., 1970, Salve Regina Coll., 1971. Ordained priest Roman Cath. Ch., 1953, laicized, 1973; prof. theology and philosophy Emmanuel Coll., Boston, 1954-60; prof. philosophy Providence Coll., 1962-63, 71-72, pres., 1965-71; asso. prof. U. Notre Dame, 1963-65; on leave as post-doctoral research asso. Boston U., 1972-73; vice chancellor for acad. affairs Mass. State Coll. System, 1973-79; pres. North Adams State Coll., Mass., 1979-83; prof. humanities Bryant Coll., Smithfield, R.I., 1983-96. Inaugurated spl. program religious studies Purdue U., 1963-65; vis. prof. contemporary theology Wabash Coll., Crawfordsville, Ind., 1964-65; vis. distinguished prof. U. R.I., 1971-72; Mem. R.I. Council Arts, 1967-70, R.I. Adv. Council State Tech. Services Act, 1965, 1967-71; mem. commn. learning Assn. Am. Colls., 1966-69; adv. council extension and continuing edn. Dept. Health, Edn. and Welfare, 1966-70; mem. commn. humanities in schs. Nat. Found. on Arts and the Humanities, 1967-71; chmn. R.I. Higher Edn. Council, 1969-71 Author: The Conception of Law and the Unity of Peirce's Philosophy, 1964, The Contemporary Arts, 1965; Contbr. articles to profl. jours. Bd. dirs. R.I. Philharmonic Orch., 1965-68, R.I. Found. Repertory Theatre, 1966-71, R.I. Urban Coalition, 1969-71, Packard Manse (center ecumenical studies), Boston, 1965-67; trustee John F. Kennedy Meml. Fund R.I., 1966-71, New Eng. Colls. Fund, 1970-71, Rocky Hill Sch., 1971-73, Bryant Coll., 1971-79; bd. dirs. United Fund R.I., 1967-71, Howard Found., Brown U., 1969-73; chmn. R.I. com. Rhodes Scholarship Trust, 1969, mem., 1970; bd. dirs. Humanities Forum of R.I., 1989—; mem. R.I. Com. for the Humanities, 1991-98. Mem. Am. Soc. Aesthetics, Nat. Cath. Edn. Assn. (exec. com. coll. and univ. dept. 1970-73) Home: 2 Vanderbilt Ave Newport RI 02840-4342

HAASE, ASHLEY THOMSON, microbiology professor, researcher; b. Chgo., Dec. 8, 1939; s. Milton Conrad and Mary Elizabeth Minter (Thomson) H.; m. Ann DeLong, 1962; children: Elizabeth, Stephanie, Harris. BA, Lawrence Coll., 1961; MD, Columbia U., 1965. Intern Johns Hopkins Hosp., Balt., 1965—67; clin. assoc. Nat. Inst. Allergy and Infectious Disease, Bethesda, Md., 1967—70; vis. scientist Nat. Inst. Med. Rsch., London, 1970—71; chief infectious disease sect. VA Med. Ctr., San Francisco, 1971—84, med. investigator, 1978—83; prof. microbiology U. Minn., Mpls., 1984—99, head dept., 1984—, Regents' prof., 1999—. Mem. fellowship screening com. Am. Cancer Soc., San Francisco, 1978-81; mem. UNESCO Internat. Cell Rsch. Orgn., India, 1978; mem. nat. adv. coun. Nat. Inst. Allergy and Infectious Diseases, 1986-91, mem. task force on microbiology and infectious diseases, 1991, Method to Extend Rsch. in Time investigator, 1989—, chair AIDS rsch. adv. com., 1993-96, chmn. vaccine subcom.; Javits neurosci. investigator Nat. Inst. Neurol. and Communicative Disorders and Stroke, 1988-95; chmn. panel on AIDS, 1988-95, U.S.-Japan Coop. Med. Sci. Program, 1988-95, chair US Delegation, 2005-; mem. OAR AIDS Rsch. Evaluation Working Group, 1995-96; mem. adv. com. for career awards in biomed. scis. Burroughs-Wellcome Fund, 1995-2000; trustee Lawrence U., 1997-2000; adv. coun. NIH Office AIDS Rsch., 2002—05, Inst. Medicine, 2003—. Editor: Microbial Pathogenesis, 1988-94; contbr. articles on AIDS pathogenesis and other topics in neurovirology to profl. jours. Recipient Lucia R. Briggs Disting. Achievement award Lawrence Coll., 1990. Mem. AAAS (coun. del. sect.on med. scis. 2006—), Am. Soc. Microbiology, Assn. Am. Physicians, Am. Soc. Clin. Investigation, Am. Soc. Virology, Assn. Med. Schs. Microbiology Chmn., Infectious Diseases Soc. Am., Nat. Multiple Sclerosis Soc. (adv. com. 1978-84), Am. Assn. Immunologists, Phi Beta Kappa, Alpha Omega Alpha Democrat. Home: 14 Buffalo Rd Saint Paul MN 55127-2136 Office: U Minn Dept Microbiology 420 Delaware St SE Minneapolis MN 55455-0374 Business E-Mail: haase001@umn.edu.

HAASS, RICHARD NATHAN, federal official; b. Bklyn., July 28, 1951; s. Irving B. and Marcella Haass BA, Oberlin Coll., Ohio, 1973; MA in Philosophy, Oxford U., Eng., 1975, PhD, 1982. Legis. asst. U.S. Sen. Claiborne Pell, Washington, 1975; research assoc. Internat. Inst. for Strategic Studies, London, 1977-79; spl. asst. to undersec. def. U.S. Dept. Def., Washington, 1979-80; dir. office regional security affairs U.S. Dept. State, Washington, 1981-82, dep. for policy bur. European and Can. affairs, 1982-85, spl. Cyprus coordinator, 1983-85; lectr. pub. policy John F. Kennedy Sch. govt. Harvard U., Cambridge, Mass., 1985-89; spl. asst. to pres. Nat. Security Affairs, 1989-93; sr. dir. near east and south Asia Nat. Security Coun., 1989-93; sr. assoc. Carnegie Endowment for Internat. Peace, Washington, 1993-94; dir. nat. security programs, sr. fellow Coun. on Fgn. Rels., Washington, 1994-96; v.p., dir. fgn. policy programs Brookings Instn., 1996—2001; dir. policy planning U.S. Dept. State, 2001—03; pres. Coun. on Fgn. Rels., NYC, 2003—. Author: Congressional Power: Implications for American Security Policy, 1979, Beyond the INF Treaty: Arms, Arms Control and the Atlantic Alliance, 1988, Conflicts Unending: The United States and Regional Disputes, 1990, The Power to Persuade, 1994, Intervention: The Use of American Military Force in The Post-Cold War World, 1994, The Reluctant Sheriff: The United State after the Cold War, 1997, The Bureaucratic Entrepreneur, 1999, The Opportunity: America's Moment to Alter History's Course, 2005; editor: Superpower Arms Control: Setting the Record Straight, 1987, Economic Sanctions and American Diplomacy, 1998, Transatlantic Tensions, 1999, Honey and Vinegar: Incentives, Sanctions, and Foreign Policy, 2000. Recipient Superior Honor award Dept. State, 1982, Presdl. Citizens medal, 1991, Disting. Honor award Dept. State, 2003; Rhodes scholar Oxford U., 1973. Mem. Internat. Inst. for Strategic Studies, Coun. on Fgn. Rels., Trilateral Commn. Office: Coun on Fgn Rels 58 E 68th St New York NY 10021 E-mail: president@cfr.org.

HAAYEN, RICHARD JAN, academic administrator, insurance company executive; b. Bklyn., June 30, 1924; s. Cornelius Marius and Cornelia Florence (Muskus) H.; m. Marilyn Jean Messner, Aug. 30, 1946; children— Richard Jan, Peter Wyckoff, James Carell. BS, Ohio State U., 1948; D in Pub. Svc. (hon.), Nat. Coll. Edn., Evanston, Ill. With Allstate Ins. Co., 1950—, v.p. underwriting, 1969-75, exec. v.p. Northbrook, Ill., 1975-80, pres., 1980-86, chmn., chief exec. officer, 1986-89; exec.-in-residence So. Meth. U., Dallas, 1989—. Bd. dirs. Guaranty Fed. Savs. Bank, Dallas. Bd. dirs. Communities-in-Schs., Dallas. Mem. Am. Arbitration Assn. (arbitrator), Phi Delta Theta. Republican. Home: 9 Glenshire Ct Dallas TX 75225-2040 Office: 7557 Rambler Rd Ste 1424 Dallas TX 75231-2390

HABACHY, SUZAN SALWA SABA, economist, not-for-profit developer; b. Cairo, July 15, 1933; came to the U.S., 1952; d. Saba and Gameela (Gindy) H. BA, Bryn Mawr Coll., Pa., 1954; MA, Harvard U., Cambridge, Mass., 1956. Teaching fellow Ohio U., Athens, 1957-58; economist Mobil Oil Co., NYC, 1959-64; reporter, editor Petroleum Intelligence Weekly, NYC, 1964-65, McGraw Hill News Bur., London, England, 1965-68; program officer UN, NYC, 1969-75, section chief, 1975-88; focal point for women UN Office of Pers., NYC, 1988-93; exec. dir. The Trickle Up Program, NYC, 1994-2001. Avocations: theater, travel, reading. Home: 1056 5th Ave New York NY 10028-0112

HABAL, NIZAR, oncologist, surgeon, educator; b. New York, Nov. 1, 1965; s. Saleh and Munawar Habal; m. Razan Istwany, Jan. 8, 1998; children: Yasmine, Kamal. BA, Cornell U., Coll. Arts Sciences, Ithaca, NY, 1983—87; MS, Columbia U., Sch. Human Nutrition, NY, 1987—88; MD, NY Med. Coll., Valhalla, 1989—93. Cert. Am. Bd. Surgery, 1999. Attending surgeon Pitt County Meml. Hosp., Greenville, NC, 2000—; adj. prof. dept. clin. nutrition NY Inst. Tech., Westbury, 1988; coord. AIDS edn. program dept. health NY Med. Coll., Westchester County, Valhalla; resident surgeon The NY Hosp., Cornell Med. Ctr., New York, 1993—98; sr. clin. fellow John Wayne Cancer Inst., Santa Monica, Calif., 1998—2000. Cons. Physicians East Breast Cancer Ctr., Greenville, NC, 2002—. Author: (rsch.) Annals Of Surgical Oncology, Seminars In Oncology, Anticancer Research, Journal Of Surgical Oncology. Recipient, Alpha Omega Alpha Honor Med. Soc., 1991; fellow Fellow, Am. Bd. of Surgery, 2003; scholar, NY Med. Coll. Bd. Of Trustees, 1990-1993. Fellow: ACS; mem.: Am. Bd. Surgery, Am. Soc. Gen. Surgeons, N.C. Med. Soc. (county del. 2002—02), Am. Soc. Breast Surgeons, Am. Soc. Clin. Oncology, Soc. Surg. Oncology. R-Liberal. Muslim. Home: 2308 Crooked Creek Road Greenville NC 27858 Office: Carolina Breast and Oncologic Surgery 2245-H Stantonsburg Rd Greenville NC 27834 Office Phone: 252-413-0036. Business E-Mail: nh.cbos@earthlink.net.

HABASH, KHALIL M., computer engineer, educator; s. Musa and Hilda Habash. Student, Wright State U., Dayton, Ohio, 1994—. Asst. prof Wilberforce U., Ohio, 1998—. Office: Wilberforce Univ PO Box 1001 Wilberforce OH 45384 Office Phone: 937-708-5666. Business E-Mail: khabash@wilberforce.edu.

HABASHI, FATHI, retired metallurgy professor, consultant; b. Al Minia, Egypt, Oct. 9, 1928; s. Habashi Khalil and Martha Boulos; m. Nadia Edward-Boulos, May 25, 1982; m. Eleonore Johanna Lechner, May 0, 1958 (div.); children: Hani Fathi, Hatem Fathi. BSc, U. Cairo, 1949; Docktor der technischenwissenschaft, Technische Hochschhule, Vienna, 1959; postgrad. (hon.), St. Petersburg Mining U., Russia, 1993. Chem. engr. Fertilizer Factory, Suez, Egypt, 1949—52, Misr Cotton Mills, Mahalla Al Kobra, Egypt, 1952—53; chief chemist Municipality of Alexandria, Egypt, 1953—56; postdoctoral fellow dept. chemistry U. Vienna, 1959—60; post-doctoral fellow Mines Br., Mines and Tech. Surveys, Ottawa, Canada, 1960—62; editor Chem. Abstracts Svc., Columbus, 1962—63; assoc. prof. Mont. Sch. Mines, Butte, 1964—67; sr. rsch. engr. Anaconda Co., Tucson, 1967—70. Pres. Métallurgie Extractive Québec, Quebec City, Canada, 1973—. Editor, author: four volume work Handbook of Extractive Metallurgy. Fellow: Can. Inst. Mining, Metallurgy, and Petroleum (Silver medal 1999). Home: 800 rue Alain # 504 Quebec City PQ Canada G1X 4E7 Office: Laval University Pavillion Pouliot University City Quebec City PQ Canada G1K 7P4 Home Phone: +(418) 651 5774; Office Phone: +(418) 656 7269. Office Fax: +(418) 656 5343; Home Fax: +(418) 656 5343. Personal E-mail: fdathi.habashi@arul.ulaval.ca. E-mail: fathi.habashi@arul.ulaval.ca.

HABECK, CHRISTIAN GEORG, medical educator; s. Horst Karlheinz and Rita Elisabeth Habeck. MS; PhD, U. Sussex, Brighton, UK, 1998. Fellow Neurosci. Inst., La Jolla, Calif.; asst. prof. Columbia U., New York, NY, 2000—. Mem.: Soc. Neurosci. Achievements include research in multivariate analysis of neuroimaging data for the the early detection of Alzheimer's disease. Office Phone: 212-305-0945.

HABECK, JAMES ROY, judge; b. Berlin, Wis., Aug. 11, 1954; s. Roy J. and Phyllis J. (Hazelwood) H.; m. Penny Ann Gillman. BS, U. Wis., Stevens Point, 1976; JD, Marquette U., 1979. Bar. Wis. 1979, U.S. Dist. Ct. (ea. and we. dists.) Wis. 1979, U.S. Supreme Ct. 1990. Atty. Rutgers Law Office, Sheboygan Falls, Wis., 1979-80; pvt. practice Shawano, Wis., 1980—2002; judge Shawano County Courthouse, Shawano, Wis., 2002—. Family ct. commr. Shawano, Menominee County, 1983-2002; corp. counsel Shawano County, 1984-87, 90, 93; legal counsel Wis. Towns Assn., Shawano, 1987-2002. Pres. Big Brothers/Big Sisters, Shawano, 1984-88; v.p. Rep. Ctrl. Com., Shawano County, 1993-99, chmn. 1999-2002; atty. St. James Lutheran Ch., Shawano, 1983-2001. Named Friend of 4-H Shawano County 4-H, 1990. Mem.: Wis. Family Ct. Commrs. Assn. (sec.-treas, pres. 1992—96, bd. dirs. 1998—2002), Shawano County Bar Assn. (sec-treas, pres. 1987—93), Wild Turkey Fedn., White Tails Unltd., Shawano Area C. of C. (bd. dirs. 2000—03), Rotary (bd. dirs. 2001—03, sec. 2003—04, pres.-elect 2004—05, pres. 2005), Shawano County Agrl. Soc. Lutheran. Avocation: scoring high school basketball games. Office Phone: 715-526-9352. E-mail: jrhabeck2002@yahoo.com.

HABECKER, EUGENE BRUBAKER, academic administrator; b. Hershey, Pa., June 17, 1946; s. Walter Eugene and Frances (Miller) H.; m. Marylou Napolitano, July 27, 1968; children: David, Matthew, Marybeth. AB, Taylor U., 1968; MA, Ball State U., 1969; JD, Temple U., 1974; PhD, U. Mich., 1981. Bar: Pa. 1974. Asst. dean Ea. Univ., St. Davids, Pa., 1970-74; dean students, asst. prof. polit. sci. George Fox U., Newberg, Oreg., 1974-78; exec. v.p. Huntington (Ind.) Coll., 1979-81, pres., 1981-91; pres, CEO Am. Bible Soc., NYC, 1991—2005; pres. Taylor U., 2005—. Evaluation cons. North Ctrl. Assn., Chgo., 1982-91; dir. Christian Colls. and Univs., Washington, 1982-88; bd. dirs. Christianity Today Internat., United Bible Socs. internat. exec. com., 1992-2001, LeTourneau U.; pres. Taylor U., 2005. Author: Affirmative Action in Independent College, 1977, The Other Side of Leadership, 1987, Leading With a Follower's Heart, 1990, Rediscovering the Soul of Leadership, 1996; contbr. articles to profl. jours. Recipient Christian Mgmt. award Christian Mgmt. Assn., 1989. Mem. Nat. Assn. Intercollegiate Athletes (coun. of pres.' 1985-90), Nat. Assn. Evangs. (bd. dirs. 1985-90), Christian Mgmt. Assn. Republican. Presbyterian.

HABEIN, HAROLD CLINTON, retired surgeon; b. Mpls., Aug. 18, 1923; s. Harold Clinton Habein and Margaret Elizabeth Schmitt; m. Jeanne Elizabeth MacGillivray, Nov. 12, 1955; children: Peter Franklin, Jared William, Christopher James. AB, Dartmouth Coll., 1945; MD, U. Minn., 1946, MS in Surgery, 1954. Diplomate Am. Bd. Surgery, Am. Bd. Thoracic Surgery. Intern Mary Hitchcock Hosp., Hanover, NH, 1949—50; fellow in gen. surgery Mayo Clinic, Rochester, Minn., 1951—54, fellow in thoracic surgery, 1956—58; surgeon USAF, Wiesbaden, Germany, 1954—56; pvt. practice Billings, Mont., 1958—88. Capt. USAF, 1954—56. Recipient Hwy. Traffic Safety award, Mont. Safety Found., 1975. Fellow: ACS (chmn. Mont. com. on trauma 1969—77, gov.-at-large for Mont. 1980—86); mem.: AMA, Mont. Med. Assn., Southwestern Surg. Congress, Western Surg. Assn., Mayo Alumni Assn. Home: 2525 Raymond Pl Billings MT 59102 Personal E-mail: h.habein@bresnan.net.

HABEL, CHRISTOPHER S., lawyer; b. Cin., Oct. 14, 1969; BS in Civil and Environ. Engring., U. Cin., 1992; JD, Ohio State U., 1995. Bar: Ohio 1995, US Dist. Ct. (no. dist.) Ohio 1999, US Dist. Ct. (so. dist.) Ohio 1999, US Ct. of Appeals (6th cir.). Ptnr. Frost Brown Todd LLC, Cin. Bd. dirs., pres. Valley View Found.; mem. Hamilton County Earthworks Appeals Bd.; mem. steering com. Met. Sewer Dist., Cin. Named Leading Lawyer in Environ. Law, Chambers USA, 2006; named one of Best Lawyers in Am., 2005, 2006, Ohio's Rising Stars, Super Lawyers, 2005, 2006. Mem.: ABA, Cin. Acad. Leadership for Lawyers, Cin. Bar Assn. (chair environ. law com. 2004—05), Ohio State Bar Assn. (mem. environ. law com.), Chi Epsilon. Office: Frost Brown Todd LLC 2200 PNC Ctr 201 E Fifth St Cincinnati OH 45202-4182 Office Phone: 513-651-6993. Office Fax: 513-651-6981. E-mail: chabel@fbtlaw.com.

HABEN, MARY KAY, candy company executive; b. Chgo., Apr. 12, 1956; d. Mitchell and Helen (Wrobleuski) Kretch; m. Edward Raymond Haben, Dec. 18, 1982; 1 child, Michael William. BSBA, U. Ill., 1977; MBA, U. Mich., 1979. Mktg. rsch asst. Kraft Foods Inc., Glenview, Ill., 1979-80, assoc. br. mgr., 1980-82, br. mgr., 1982-84, category mgr., 1984-88, exec. v.p., pres. Kraft Cheese divsn., 1998—2000, group v.p., pres. Kraft Cheese Mex. & Puerto Rico, 2000—01, group v.p., pres. cheese, enhancers & meals, 2001—04, sr. v.p. global convenience meals grocery & snacks sector, 2004—06; group v.p., mng. dir N. Am. The William Wrigley Jr. Co., Chgo., 2007—. Bd. dirs. Liz Claiborne, Inc., 2004—. Named one of 100 Best and Brighest Women in Advtg. Advertising Age Mag., 1988, 100 Best Mgrs. in the U.S. Bus. Month Mag., 1989, 40 Women Under AO Savvy Mag., 40 Under 40 to Watch Crain's Chgo. Bus., 1990. Avocations: sports, reading, travel. Office: The William Wrigley Jr & Co 410 N Michigan Ave Chicago IL 60611*

HABER, ANN, biology professor, physiologist; d. Lewis and Lois Haber. BS, Purdue U., West Lafayette, Ind., 1983; MS, U. Ariz., Tucson, 1989. Cert. med. technologist ASCP, 1984. Biology faculty Pima County CC, Tucson, 2001—; exercise physiologist, cardiac rehab. Triad Hospitals, Tucson, 1991—. Mem.: AEA, NEA. Office Phone: 520-206-6088.

HABER, FREDERIC, lawyer; b. NYC, June 20, 1958; s. Alan Walter and Carol Haber; m. Jill Anne Jacobs, Oct. 9, 1988. AB, AM, Harvard U., 1979, JD, 1983. Bar: N.Y. 1984, Conn. 1985, Mass. 1997, U.S. Dist. Ct. (so. and ea. dists.) N.Y. 1984. Assoc. Weil, Gotshal & Manges, NYC, 1983-90; of counsel, 1991-93; sr. atty. R.H. Macy & Co., Inc., 1993-95; gen. counsel, corp. sect. Copyright Clearance Ctr., Inc., Danvers, Mass., 1995—. Mem. ABA, Am. Corp. Coun. Assn., N.Y. State Bar Assn. Office: Copyright Clearence Ctr Inc 222 Rosewood Dr Danvers MA 01923-4510 Office Phone: 978-750-8400. E-mail: fhaber@copyright.com.

HABER, GEOFFREY JOHN, rabbi; s. Serge and Elinor Ruth Haber; m. Jill Milessa Lewis, Aug. 21, 1983; children: Ariella Michal, Noam Daniel, Leora Deena. BA, Columbia U., NYC, 1981, Jewish Theol. Sem., 1981, MA, 1985, degree in Rabbinical Studies, 1986; D in Ministry, Hebrew Union College, NYC, 2006. Rav HaMakhshir Jewish Theol. Sem., NY, 2002. Dir. program Am. Jerusalem Acad., Highland Park, NJ, 1986—89; asst. rabbi Highland Pk. Conservative Temple and Ctr., Highland Park, 1986—89; rabbi Congregation Shaare Tikvah, Chgo., 1989—92, Beth Tzedec Congregation, Calgary, Alt., Canada, 1992—96, Temple Emanu-El, Closter, NJ, 1996—. Bd. mem. World Coun. Conservative/Masorti Synagogues, NYC; mem. rabbinic cabinet Nat. United Jewish Cmtys., NYC, 2001—, United Jewish Fedn. No. NJ, River Edge, NJ, 1998—; instr. Florence Melton adult sch. Hebrew U., New Milford, NJ, 2000—. Author: (book) Make for Me a Sanctuary: The Windows of Temple Emanu-El, Zeman Simhateinu: The Time of our Joy-A Bar/Bat Mitzvah Handbook; author: (transslator, transliterator) Call the Sabbath a Delight; prodr.: (cd) Call the Sabbath a Delight; (TV series) (Solomon Schechter Worship and Ritual award, 2006), TLC: Torah Learning Center (Nat. and Regional Gold Solomon Schechter awards, 1997). Bd. mem. Jewish Com. Scouting, Calgary, Alt., Canada, 1992—96; mem. regional bd. Coun. Christians and Jews, Calgary, 1992—96; commr. Ethics Commn., Highland Park, 1987—89; mem. coun. Cmty. Rels. Interfaith Clergy Coun., Englewood, 1996—2001; mem. substance abuse task force Jewish Family Svc., New Brunswick, NJ, 1988—89; mem. ritual com. assn. developmentally disabled United Jewish Appeal, River Edge, 1998—2006. Recipient award, Youth Achievement Internat., 1981, Dr. Bernard Samson and Mrs. Sara Bluma Samson Levinthal Meml. award, Jewish Theol. Sem., 1981, Sarah Barcon Scoffin Meml. award, 1985, Sarah and Morris Rosenberg Philosophy prize, 1986; grantee, Synagogue Leadership Initiative, 2006. Mem.: Rabbinical Assembly (mem. nominations com. 1997—2005), Nat. Assn. Jewish Chaplains, No. Valley Clergy Assn. (sec. 2001—03), NJ Region Rabbinical Assembly (trustee 1999—2007, v.p. 2003—07), North Jersey Bd. Rabbis (trustee 1997—2003, pres. 2003—07), Am. Assn. Pastoral Counselors (licentiate), NJ Coalition Inclusive Ministries, World Coun. Conservative/Masorti Synagogues (bd. mem. 2005—07). Independent. Jewish. Achievements include formed Tizmoret Emanu-El ensemble; first to created partnership with Florence Melton adult school of Hebrew University; created handicap-accessible congregation; research in field school of Jewish studies. Avocations: camping, hockey, reading, winter sports, Tae Kwon Do. Home Phone: 201-750-7583; Office Phone: 201-750-9997.

HABER, IRA JOEL, artist, educator; b. NYC, Feb. 24, 1947; s. Oscar and Rosalind (Tilzer) H. Student public schs. Instr. art SUNY, Stony Brook, 1981—, U. Calif.-San Diego, 1982, 84, Ohio State U., Columbus, 1984, United Fedn. Tchrs. Retiree Program, 2005—. One-man shows include Fischbach Gallery, N.Y.C., 1971, 72, 74, Kent (Ohio) State U., 1977, Pam Adler Gallery, N.Y.C., 1978, 80, 82, Rutgers U., 1980, SUNY, Stony Brook, 1981, Phila. Art Alliance, 1984, J.N. Herlin Inc., N.Y.C., 1984, 86, 55 Mercer St. Gallery, N.Y.C., 1991; group shows include Mus. Modern Art, N.Y.C., 1970, Whitney Mus., N.Y.C., 1971, 73, Public Sch. One, L.I., N.Y., 1976, Albright-Knox Gallery, Buffalo, 1979, Ohio State U., 1984; represented in permanent collections NYU, Guggenheim Mus., N.Y.C., Hirshhorn Mus., Washington, Allen Meml. Art Mus., Oberlin (Ohio) Coll., Albright-Knox Gallery, Buffalo. NEA fellow, 1974, 77, 84; grantee Creative Artists Pub. Svc., 1974, 77, Ariana Found., 1982, Pollock-Krasner Found., 1986-87, 2001, Adolph and Esther Gottlieb Found., 2004. Address: 311 85th St Brooklyn NY 11209 E-mail: irajoelirajoel@yahoo.com.

HABER, JONATHAN H., lawyer; b. LA, Mar. 10, 1953; s. George Martin and Leah (Levy) H.; m. Bonnie Levin, Mar. 28, 1982; 1 child, Erin Nicole Levin. BA, UCLA, 1976; JD, U. San Francisco, 1981. Bar: Calif. 1982, U.S. Dist. Ct. (no. dist.) Calif. 1983. Assoc. Lossing & Elston, San Francisco, 1983-86, McGlynn, McLorg & McDowell, San Francisco; counsel & comm. dir., Agriculture, Nutrition, & Forestry Com. US Senate,

1989—92; CEO ATLA, 2005—. Cons. local, state, nat. polit. campaigns. Cons. Congressman Ted Weiss, Washington, 1979; mem. nat. advance com. Kennedy for pres., Washington, 1980; dep. campaign mgr. Brown for U.S. Senate, Los Angeles, 1982. Democrat. Jewish. Avocations: woodwork, backpacking, photography. Office: ATLA 1050 31st St Washington DC 20007

HABER, MARGARET WILSON, informatics specialist, director; b. Rockledge, Fla., May 21, 1962; d. Davis Eldon and Shirley Nelson Wilson; m. Francis Colin Haber, 1987 (dec. 1990); m. Allan Williams Cameron, 2006. BA in Arabic Langs. and Mid. East History, U. Md., College Park, 1985. RN Md., cert. oncology nurse. Tchg. fellow history U. Md., College Park, 1986—89, staff nurse transplant surgery Balt., 1996; staff nurse oncology ICU Georgetown U. Hosp., Washington, 1996—99; clin. informatics specialist KEVRIC Co., Silver Spring, Md., 1999—2001; med. informatics specialist Nat. Cancer Inst., Rockville, Md., 2001—, co-dir. Enterprise Vocabulary Svcs. Nat. Cancer Inst. liaison Clin. Data Interchange Std. Consortium, Austin, Tex., 2003—, Systematized Nomenclature of Medicine, Northfield, Ill., 2003—; presenter in field. Contbr. articles to profl. jours. Recipient Fulbright Scholarship study grant, 1984. Mem.: Oncology Nursing Soc., Health Level Seven, Am. Med. Informatics Assn. (mem. systematized momenclature of medicine internat. standards bd.), Cosmos Club (assoc.). Office: Nat Cancer Inst Ste 300A Rm 3111 6116 Executive Blvd Rockville MD 20852

HABER, PIERRE-CLAUDE, psychologist; b. Landau, Germany, June 8, 1931; s. Kurt S. and Hedwig (Kuhn) H.; came to U.S., 1943, naturalized, 1949; BA, Bklyn. Coll., 1952; MA, Duke U., 1953; PhD, U. Paris, 1956; Counselor, dir. adult edn. Central Sch. Dist. 2, Yorktown Heights, N.Y., 1956-59; psychologist Manpower Devel. Program, Bklyn., 1959-65; asst. prof. Queens Coll., 1965-70; exec. sec., exec. dir. Psychology Soc., N.Y.C., 1970—; cons. forensic psychologist N.Y. State, 1978—; assoc. prof. Jersey City State Coll., 1967-80; organizer of biennial overseas study and visitation trips. Bd. advisors Nat. Reference Inst. Mem. APA, Am., N.Y. State personnel and guidance assns., Psychology Soc., N.Y. Assn. Public Sch. Adult Educators (v.p. 1957-59), Pi Delta Phi. Republican. Jewish. Author: The Social and Political Attitudes of Andre Gide, 2000; contbr. to Compton's Ency., also articles to profl. jours.

HABER, RALPH NORMAN, psychology consultant, researcher, educator; b. Lansing, Mich., May 15, 1932; s. William and Fannie (Gallas) Haber; m. Ruth Lea Boss, 1961 (div. 1974); children: Sabrina Beth, Rebecca Ann; m. Lyn R. Roland, 1974. BA, U. Mich., 1953; MA, Wesleyan U., Middletown, Conn., 1954; PhD, Stanford U., 1957; Postdoctoral fellow, Med. Research Council, Applied Psychology Unit, Cambridge, Eng., 1970-71. Rsch. assoc. Inst. for Comm. Rsch., Stanford, 1957-58; instr. psychology San Francisco State Coll., Calif., 1957-58; asst. prof. psychology Yale, 1958-64; assoc. prof. psychology U. Rochester, NY, 1964-67, prof. psychology NY, 1967-70, prof. psychology and visual sci. NY, 1970-79, chmn. dept. psychology NY, 1967-70, mem. faculty senate NY, 1968-70, sec., mem. steering com. NY, 1969-70; prof. psychology U. Ill., Chgo., 1979-91, rsch. prof., 1991-94, rsch. prof. emeritus, 1994—; ptnr. Human Factors Cons., Swall Meadows, Calif., 1988—; rsch. assoc. psychology U. Calif., Santa Cruz, 1990. Chmn., divisional maj. III Yale, 1959—64; vis. asst. prof. New Sch. Social Rsch., 1963; rsch. cons. VA, 1967—71; adv. editor exptl. psychology Holt, Rinehart & Winston Book Pubs., 1969—77; vis. scientist Med. Rsch. Coun. Applied Psychology Unit, Cambridge, England, 1970—71; ptnr. Human Factors Cons., Highland Park, Ill., 1979—94; vis. prof. Air Force Human Resources Lab., Williams AFB, Ariz., 1981—83; adj. prof. U. Calif., Riverside, 1997—99. Author (with Hershenson): The Psychology of Visual Perception, 1973, 2d edit., 1980; author: (with Fried) An Introduction to Psychology, 1975; author: (with others) Discovering Psychology, 1977; editor: Current Research on Motivation, 1966, Contemporary Theory and Research on Visual Perception, 1968, Information Processing Approaches to Visual Perception, 1969; contbr. articles to profl. jours. Commr. Wheeler Crest Fire Prevention Dist., Swall Meadows, Calif., 1995—2000; founder, 1st pres., bd. dirs. Eastern Sierra Conservancy, 2000—02; bd. dirs. Andrea Lawrence Inst. Mountains and Rivers, 2005—; committeeman 18th ward Birghton Dem. Com., NY, 1967—70; founding mem., trustee Admission Prep. Program, Rochester, 1968—70. Recipient Outstanding Achievement award, U. Mich., 1977; grantee, NSF, NIH, Nat. Inst. Edn., Air Force Office Sci. Rsch., Dept. Army; Behavioral Sci. fellow, Ford Found., 1953—54. Fellow: AAAS, APA, Am. Psychol. Soc.; mem.: Internat. Assn. Identification, Human Factors and Ergonomics Soc., Optical Soc. Am., Brit. Psychol. Assn., Psychonomics Soc., Am. Contract Bridge League (dir. Bishop unit 517 1996—), Sigma Xi, Pi Lambda Pi. Office Phone: 760-387-2458. Business E-Mail: ralph@humanfactorsconsultants.com.

HABER, SCOTT R., lawyer; BA, Cornell U., 1980, MBA, 1983, JD magna cum laude, 1984. Bar: Calif. 1984. Law clk. Hon. Richard J. Cardamone, US Ct. of Appeals, Second Cir., 1984; joined Latham & Watkins, 1985—, now ptnr. San Francisco. Editor: Cornell Law Rev., 1984. Mem.: ABA, Calif. Bar Assn., Order of Coif. Office: Latham & Watkins Ste 2000 505 Montgomery St San Francisco CA 94111-2562 Business E-Mail: scott.haber@lw.com.

HABERMAN, CHARLES MORRIS, mechanical engineer, educator; b. Bakersfield, Calif., Dec. 10, 1927; s. Carl Morris and Rose Marie (Braun) H. BS, UCLA, 1951; MS in Mech. Engring., U. So. Calif., 1954, MS in Aeronautical Engring., 1960. Lead, sr. and group engr. Northrop Aircraft, Hawthorne, Calif., 1951-59, cons., 1959-61; asst. prof. to prof. mech. engring. Calif. State U., LA, 1959-91. Cons. Royal McBee Corp., 1960-61. Author: Engineering Systems Analysis, 1965, Use of Computers for Engineering Applications, 1966, Vibration Analysis, 1968, Basic Aerodynamics, 1971. Served with AUS, 1946-47. Mem. Am. Soc. Engring. Edn. Democrat. Roman Catholic.

HABERMAN, CLYDE, columnist; married; 3 children. BA, CCNY, 1966. Reporter NY Post; joined NY Times, 1977, editor, Week in Review sect., City Hall bur. chief, metro staff reporter, mem. fgn. staff, 1982, bur. chief Tokyo, 1983—88, bur. chief Rome, 1988—91, bur. chief Jerusalem, 1991—95, NYC columnist, met. desk, 1995—. Office: NY Times 229 West 43rd St New York NY 10036 Office Phone: 212-556-1533. Office Fax: 212-556-3690.

HABERMAN, F. WILLIAM, lawyer; b. Princeton, NJ, Apr. 20, 1940; s. Frederick William and Louise (Power) H.; m. Carmen Marie Duffy, June 15, 1963; children: Frederick, Sarah. BA, U. Wis., 1962; LLB, Harvard Law Sch., 1965. Bar: Wis. 1965, Fla. 1993, U.S. Dist. Ct. (ea. dist.) Wis. 1966, U.S. Dist. Ct. (we. dist.) Wis. 1967. Ptnr. Michael, Best & Friedrich, Milw., 1965—. Bd. dirs. U. Wis. Milw. Found., 2003—. Co-author: Marital Property Law in Wisconsin, 1986. Trustee Pub. Policy Forum, Milw., 1998—; bd. dirs. Ctrl. YMCA, Milw., 1988-93, Richard and Ethel Herzfeld Found., Milw., 1985—, Wis. affiliate Am. Heart Assn., 1993-97; mem. Greater Milw. Com., 2000—; mem. adv. bd. Milw. Fair Housing Coun., 1989-90; mem. deferred giving adv. bd. Milw. Sch. Engring., 1989-93; bd. dirs. Milw. Children's Hosp. Found., 1994-98, Milw. Repertory Theater, 1997-2002. Fellow Am. Coll. Trust & Estate Counsel; mem. ABA, Wis. Bar Assn., Phi Beta Kappa. Home: 2727 E Shorewood Blvd Milwaukee WI 53211-2459 Office: Michael Best & Friedrich 100 E Wisconsin Ave Ste 3300 Milwaukee WI 53202-4108 Office Phone: 414-271-6560.

HABERMAN, JEREMY, music venue executive; b. 1972; Pres. Haberman Productions Inc., Ferndale, Mich.; co-founder The Magic Bag, The Bosco. Named one of 40 Under 40, Crain's Detroit Bus., 2006. Office: The Magic Bag 22920 Woodward Ave Ferndale MI 48220

HABERMAN, SETH, advertising executive; b. NYC, Jan. 13, 1950; BA in Physics and Computer Sci., Columbia U., 1981. Founder, CEO Montage Grp, Visible World, 1999—. Spkr. in field The MIT Forum, the RVC Tech. Conf., the ANA's Advt. Mgmt. Com. Named one of 100 People to Know in Media, Media Mag., 2004; recipient Acad. Award for tech. achievement, 1987, Emmy Award, 1993. Office: Visible World 527 W 34th St Fl 6 New York NY 10001 Office Phone: 212-739-1900. Office Fax: 212-739-1999.*

HABERMAN, SHELBY JOEL, statistician, educator; b. Cin., May 4, 1947; s. Jack Leon and Miriam Leah (Langberg) H.; m. Elinor Penny Levine, Feb. 18, 1979 (dec. 1996); children: Shoshanah, Chasiah, Sarah, Milcah, Boaz, Devorah. AB, Princeton U., 1968; PhD, U. Chgo., 1970. Asst. prof. to prof. U. Chgo., 1970-82; prof. Hebrew U., Jerusalem, 1982-84; prof. stats. Northwestern U., Evanston, Ill., 1984—2002, chmn. dept., 1986-88; dir. statis. and psychometric theory and practice Ednl. Testing Svc., Princeton, NJ, 2002—. Author: Analysis of Frequency Data, 1974, Analysis of Qualitative Data, Vol. I, 1978, Vol. II, 1979, Advanced Statistics, Vol. I, 1996; contbr. articles to profl. jours. Guggenheim fellow, 1977-78. Fellow AAAS, Inst. Math. Stats., Am. Statis. Assn. Home: 414 S 4th St Highland Park NJ 08904- Office: Ednl Testing Svc Rosedale Rd 08541 Princeton NJ 08541-0001 Home Phone: 732-339-9699; Office Phone: 609-734-5787. Business E-Mail: SHaberman@ets.org.

HABERMANN, HELEN MARGARET, botanist, educator; b. Bklyn., Sept. 13, 1927; AB, SUNY, Albany, 1949; MS, U. Conn., 1951; PhD, U. Minn., 1956. Asst. botanist U. Conn., Storrs, 1949-51; asst. U. Minn., Mpls., 1951-53, asst. plant physiologist, 1953-55, head residence counselor, 1955-56; rsch. assoc. U. Chgo., 1956-57; rsch. fellow Hopkins Marine Sta. Stanford (Calif.) U., 1957-58; from asst. prof. to prof. biol. scis. Goucher Coll., Towson, 1958—82, chmn. dept. biology, 1963-66, 68, 78-79, Lilian Welsh prof. biol. scis., 1982-92; prof. emeritus, 1992—. Co-author Biology: A Full Spectrum, 1973, Mainstreams of Biology, 1977. NIH spl. rsch. fellow Rsch. Inst. Advanced Study, Balt., 1966-67. Fellow AAAS; mem. Phytochem. Soc. N.Am. (sec. 1987-93), Am. Soc. Plant Physiologists, Am. Soc. Hort. Sci., Soc. Devel. Biology, Am. Soc. Photobiology, Am. Inst. Biol. Scis., Scandinavian Soc. Plant Physiology, Internat. Soc. Plant Molecular Biology, Japanese Soc. Plant Physiology, Soc. Exptl. Biology and Medicine, Am. Camellia Soc., Pioneer Camellia Soc. (pres. 1994-95, sec. 2000-01), Am. Hort. Soc., Sigma Xi. Personal E-mail: hhabermann@wans.net.

HABERMANN, JAMES HERBERT, retired pathologist; b. Cassville, Wis., June 18, 1926; s. Matthew Herbert and Clara Cordelia (Reilly) H.; m. Helen Audrey Howe, June 14, 1952; children: Thomas, Patrick, Michael, Jane, Mary Ann. MD, Marquette U., Milw., 1952. Diplomate in anat. and clin. pathology Am. Bd. Pathology. Family practice physician, Mt. Calvary, Wis., 1953-60; resident in pathology Denver Gen. Hosp., 1960-64; dir. labs. Mercy Hosp. and Luth. Hosp. (merged into Trinity Hosp.), Ft. Dodge, Iowa, 1964-77; staff pathologist Freeman Hosp., Joplin, Mo., 1977-80, St. John's Med. Ctr., Joplin, 1980-91; ret. Pres. bd. dirs. Trinity Regional Hosp., Ft. Dodge, 1973-77; chief of staff St. John's Med. Ctr., Joplin, 1984-85. 1st lt. U.S. Army, 1944-47, Germany. Fellow Am. Soc. Clin. Pathologists, Coll. Am. Pathologists. Roman Catholic. Avocation: woodworking. Home: 2111 E 36th St Joplin MO 64804-4232 Personal E-mail: JHHabermann@webtv.net.

HABERMANN, TED RICHARD, lawyer; b. Waupaca, Wis., Nov. 1, 1957; s. Richard Dale and Laura Aleen (Defrates) H. BS, U. Wis., 1980; JD, Valparaiso U., 1983. Bar: Ind. 1983, Tenn. 1989, U.S. Dist. Ct. (no and so. dists.) Ind. 1983, U.S. Dist. Ct. (mid. dist.) Tenn. 1990, U.S. Tax Ct. 1984, U.S. Supreme Ct., 1989. Mng. atty. Davisson & Davisson, P.C., Anderson, Ind., 1984-89; corp. counsel Spectra Distbn./Sound Stage Cos., Nashville, 1989-91; gen. counsel, sec. Servpro Industries, Inc., Gallatin, Tenn., 1991-98; asst. gen. counsel, asst. sec. Shoney's LLC, Nashville, 1998-2000; gen. counsel, sec. Servpro Industries, Inc., Gallatin, Tenn., 2000—02; v.p., gen. counsel, sec. Shoney's, Inc., Nashville, 2002—. Contbr. Valparaiso U. Law Rev. Mem. ABA, Ind. Bar Assn. (mem. forum on franchising), Tenn. Bar Assn., Jaycees (v.p. 1987), Exchange Club (dir. 1987), Sigma Phi Epsilon, Delta Theta Phi. Republican. Methodist. Home: 4724 Aaron Dr Antioch TN 37013-4218 Office: Shoney's LLC 1717 Elm Hill Pike Nashville TN 37210 E-mail: tedhabermann@msn.com, ted_habermann@shoneys.com.

HABERMEHL, LAWRENCE LEROY, philosophy educator; b. Joplin, Mo., June 13, 1937; s. Roland William and Ruth Esther (Kelly) H.; m. Kathryn J. Barnes, June 8, 1958 (div. 1974); children: Elizabeth Anne, R. William, Edward Hale; m. Sue Ellen Lovejoy, Sept. 16, 1989 (div. 1996). AB, Phillips U., 1959; BD, Union Theol. Sem., 1961; PhD, Boston U., 1967. House mgr. Boston Seaman's Friend Soc., 1963-65; teaching fellow Boston U., 1965-66; asst. prof. philosophy Am. Internat. Coll., Springfield, Mass., 1966-73, assoc. prof., 1973—2001, prof., 2001—. Author: The Counterfeit Wisdom of Shallow Minds: A Critique of Some Leading Offenders of the 1980s, 1994; author/editor: Morality in the Modern World, 1976. Mem. AAUP, SAR, Am. Philos. Assn., Metaphys. Soc. Am., Common Cause, Amnesty Internat., Assn. Informal Logic and Critical Thinking. Unitarian-Universalist. Home: 1235 Enfield St Enfield CT 06082 Office: Am Internat Coll Dept Philosophy 1000 State St Springfield MA 01109 Office Phone: 413-205-3327. E-mail: LawLH@aol.com.

HABGOOD, ANTHONY JOHN, wholesale distribution executive; b. Woodbastwick, Eng., Nov. 8, 1946; s. John Michael and Diana Margaret (Dalby) H.; m. Nancy Ray Atkinson, June 29, 1974; children: Elizabeth Ann, John Alan, George Michael. BA in Econs., Gonville and Caius Coll., Cambridge U., 1968; MA, Cambridge U., 1972; MS in Indsl. Adminstrn., Carnegie-Mellon U., 1970. From staff to v.p. and dir. Boston Cons. Group Inc., 1970-86, exec. com., 1983-86; CEO Tootal, PLC, London, 1991, Bunzl, PLC, London, 1991-96, chmn., 1996—, Whitbread, PLC, 2005—; dir. SVG Capital, PLC, London, 1995—; chmn. Molnlycke Health Care Ltd., London, 2006—07. W.L. Mellon fellow, 1968-70. Mem.: Royal Norfolk and Suffolk Yacht. Anglican. Office: 110 Park St London W1K 6NX England

HABIB, IBRAHIM WAHBY, computer engineer, educator; b. Cairo, Aug. 16, 1959; arrived in U.S., 1988; s. Wahby Mohamed Habib and Salwa Kamel Essawy. BSEE, Ain Shams U., Cairo, 1981; MSEE, Poly. U. N.Y., 1984; PhD in Elec. Engring., CUNY, 1991. Cons., NJ, 1998—, NY, 1998—; assoc. prof. CUNY, 1998, prof., 2004—. Part-time tech. cons. AT&T, 1997—2000, Telecordia, 2000—01; spkr. at several Am. and European univs. Guest editor IEEE JSAC, IEEE Comms. Mag., John Wiley Jour. on Wireless Networks; contbr. over 100 articles to profl. publs. Mem. IEEE (sr., reviewer 1991—, editor 1993-97, mem. tech. program com. numerous internat. confs.). Office: CUNY Elec Engring Dept 137 St and Convent Ave New York NY 10031 Office Phone: 212-650-7184. Personal E-mail: ibrahimhabib@hotmail.com.

HABIB, SHAHID, medical association administrator; b. Lahore, Punjab, Pakistan, Nov. 2, 1963; s. Habibullah Khawaja and Sarfraz Habib; m. Huma Sheikh, Apr. 16, 1993; children: Sana Shahid, Namrah Shahid, Mohammad Ibrahim Shahid. MBBS, Quaid-e-Azam med. Coll., Bahawalpur, Pakistan, 1987. Fellow Coll. of Physician and Surgeon Pakistan, 1994, mem. Royal Coll. of Physicians, 1999, cert. Am. Bd. Internal Medicine, 2004. Registrar Fed. Postgraduate Med. Inst., Sheikh Zayad Hosp., Lahore, Punjab, Pakistan, 1990—93; sr. registrar Mayo Hosp., Lahore, Punjab, Pakistan, 1993—94; cons. physician Ministry of Health, Abha, Assir, Saudi Arabia, 1994—96; staff physician Chase Farm Hosp., London, 1997—99; resident internal medicine U. Pitts., 2003—04, fellow in hepatology, 2003—04; med. dir. Iowa Health, Des Moines, 2005—. Cons. hepatologist/transplant hepatologist Iowa Health, 2005—. Grantee, Shadyside Found., 2003. Mem.: Am. Soc. Transplantation, Am. Assn. Study Liver Disease. Islam. Achievements include research in Liver Transplantation. Avocations: travel, swimming. Office: Iowa Health 1215 Pleasant St Des Moines IA 50309 Home Phone: 515-225-6678; Office Phone: 515-241-4044. Office Fax: 515-241-4100. Business E-Mail: habibs2@ihs.org.

HABICHT, CHRISTIAN HERBERT, history professor; b. Dortmund, Germany, Feb. 23, 1926; came to U.S., 1972; s. Hermann Christian and Emile Julie (Diefenbach) H.; m. Freia Renate Wilkowski, Aug. 15, 1952; children: Susanne, Christoph, Nikolaus. Dr.Phil., U. Hamburg, 1952, Habil, 1957. Asst. to assoc. prof. U. Hamburg, 1952-61; prof. ancient history U. Marburg/Lahn, 1961-65; prof. U. Heidelberg, 1965-73, dean, 1966-67; prof. Inst. Advanced Study, Princeton, N.J., 1973-98; vis. prof. Princeton U., 1973-80. Author books; contbr. articles to profl. jours. Mem. British Acad., Am. Philos. Soc., Acad. Heidelberg, Acad. Athens, German Archeol. Inst., Austrian Archeol. Inst., Am. Inst. Archeology, Assn. Ancient Historians (Reuchlin-Price award 1991, Moe-Price award 1996, Criticos-Price award 1998). Office: Inst Advanced Study Sch Hist Studies Princeton NJ 08540 Business E-Mail: habicht@ias.edu.

HABICHT, FRANK HENRY, retired manufacturing executive; b. Chgo., Sept. 4, 1920; s. Geroge Jr. and Gertrude A. (Tronc) H.; m. Jeanne Ellen Patrick, Mar. 9, 1943; children: Pamela, Patricia, Frank Henry II. BSME, Purdue U., 1942; postgrad., Cornell U., Ithaca, NY, 1942, Am. U., Washington, DC, 1944. From sales engr. to pres. Marshall & Huschart Machinery Co., Chgo., 1946-70; vice chmn. Cone-Blanchard Machine Co., Windsor, Vt. and Aldridge, England, 1971-74; chmn. bd., pres. United Tech. Corp., Chgo., 1970-81; pres. Steego Tech. Corp., West Palm Beach, 1981-86; chmn., pres. Corp. Assocs., Inc., 1986-97, ret., 1997. Tech. cons. US Dept. Def., Washington, 1963-64; pres. UNISIG Corp., 1980-86, King & Gavaris Cons. Engrs. Inc., 1980-84; US projects mgr. Boehringer GmbH, Germany, 1989-95; 1997; lectr. in field; bd. dirs. Am. SIP Corp., Botemp Corp., Switzerland. Author: Modern Machine Tools, 1964; contbr. articles to profl. jours. Mem. def. indsl. plant equipment com. Dept. Def. Lt. comdr.USN, 1942-45. Mem. ASME, Am. Machine Tool Distbrs. Assn. (dir., past pres.), Fabricating Mfrs. Assn. (dir., past pres.), Assn. of RAF Warbirds, Conf. Bd. (exec. coun.), Order Knights St. John of Jerusalem, Oakbrook Polo Club, Palm Beach Club, Beach Club, Palm Beach Yacht Club, Governor's Club, Soc 4 Arts (Palm Beach), Navy League (bd. dirs.), Masons. Episcopalian. Avocations: hunting, fishing, tennis.

HABICHT, JEAN PIERRE, public health educator; b. Geneva, Dec. 15, 1934; arrived in US, 1962; s. Max H. and Elizabeth (Peterson) Herzog; m. Pat Hinxman, Jan. 3, 1959 (div. Oct. 1990); children: Heidi, Christopher, Oliver; m. Gretel H. Pelto, June 13, 1997. MD, U. Zurich, Switzerland, 1964; MPH, Harvard U., 1968; PhD, MIT, 1969. Cert. in clin. nutrition Am. Bd. Nutrition. Biochem. rsch. asst. Merck, Sharpe, and Dohme, Rahway, NJ, 1958; pediat. intern Children's Hosp. Med. Ctr., Boston, 1965—66; med. officer WHO, Guatemala, 1969—74; prof. maternal and child health U. San Carlos, Guatemala, 1972—74; spl. asst. Nat. Ctr. Health Stats., Washington, 1974—77; James Jamison prof. Cornell U., Ithaca, NY, 1977—2005, grad. prof. nutritional epidemiology, 2005—. Cons. pub. health issues nat. and internat. govt., profl. agy., 1975—; mem. expert com. nutrition WHO, Geneva, 1975—, mem. com. epidemiology and disease prevention, 1986—89, chmn. expert com. phys. status, 1991—93; chmn. expert com. optimal duration exclusive breast feeding, 2001; mem. tech. adv. com. Child and Adolescent Health and Devel., 2001—05; mem. epidemiology and disease control study sect. NIH, Washington, 1980—83; mem. joint nutrition monitoring and evaluation com. HHS-USDA, 1982—86; mem. adv. group coordinating subcom. nutrition UN, 1983—89, chmn., 1986—87; mem. food and nutrition bd. NAS, Washington, 1981—84, mem. com. internat. nutrition, 1975—79, mem. com. uses dietary reference intakes Inst. Medicine, 1997—2000. Contbr. articles to profl. jours., chapters to books. Fellow: Soc. Internat. Nutrition Rsch. (pres. 2002—04, Kellogg prize 1994), Am. Soc. Nutrition (Atwater Meml. lectr. 1998, Conrad A. Elvehjem award 1999, McCollum Internat. lectureship 2006—07), Am. Coll. Epidemiology; mem.: APHA, Internat. Soc. Environ. Epidemiology, Internat. Soc. Rsch. Human Milk and Lactation (exec. com. 1995—96), Internat. Epidemiol. Assn., Soc. Epidemiologic Rsch., Am. Soc. Clin. Nutrition, Delta Omega, Gamma Sigma Delta, Sigma Xi. Office: Cornell U Divsn Nutritional Sci Savage Hall Ithaca NY 14853 Office Phone: 607-255-4419.

HABUSH, ROBERT LEE, lawyer; b. Milw., Mar. 22, 1936; s. Jesse James and Beatrice (Liebenberg) Habush; m. Miriam Lee Friedman, Aug. 25, 1957; children: Sherri Ellen, William Scott, Jodi Lynn. BBA, U. Wis., 1959, JD, 1961. Bar: Wis. 1961, U.S. Dist. Ct. (ea. and we. dists.) Wis. 1961, U.S. Ct. Appeals (7th cir.) 1965, U.S. Supreme Ct. 1986. Pres. Habush, Habush & Rottier, S.C., Milw., 1961—. Advisor restatement of torts products liability 3rd and gen. principles Am. Law Inst.; lectr. U. Wis. Law Sch., Marquette U. Law Sch., Wis., State Bar Wis., others. Author: The Art of Advocacy: Cross Examination of Non Medical Experts, 1981; contbr. articles to profl. jours. Benefactor scholarships, funds chairs, and founds. Capt. US Army, 1959—75. Named one of Top Ten Litigators in U.S., Nat. Law Jour., 2001, Ten Wis. Leaders in the Law, Wis. Law Jour., 2003; recipient Evan P. Helfaer Donor award, Nat. Assn. Fundraising Execs., 2000, Cmty. Svc. Human Rels. award, Milw. chpt. AJC, 2004, UW Law Sch. Disting. Svc award, 2003. Mem.: ABA, ATLA (bd. govs. 1969—70, 1983—86, pres. 1986—87, former ATLA-PAC trustee and chmn. pub. affairs com., Harry Philo award 1999, Leonard Ring Champion of Justice award 2002, Robert L. Habush ATLA Endowment re-named in his honor), Wis. Bar Found., Trial Lawyers Pub. Justice, Inner Cir. Advs., Wis. Acad. Trial Lawyers (pres. 1968—69, 1971—72, named Robert L. Habush Trial Lawyer of the Yr. award in his honor 2000), Wis. Bar Assn., Am. Soc. Writers Legal Subjects, Am. Bd. Trial Advs., Nat. Bd. Trial Advs., Nat. Coll. Advocacy, Internat. Soc. Barristers, Internat. Acad. Trial Lawyers (bd. dirs. 1983—87, 1991—92), Roscoe Pound Found. Office: Habush Habush & Rottier 777 E Wisconsin Ave Ste 2300 Milwaukee WI 53202-5381 Office Phone: 414-271-0400. Business E-Mail: rhabush@habush.com.

HAC, ANNA BARBARA, computer scientist, educator; b. Warsaw, Aug. 1, 1954; arrived in U.S., 1983; d. Aleksander and Barbara (Galecka) Hac. MS, Warsaw U. Tech., 1977, PhD, 1982. Rsch. asst. Warsaw U. Tech., 1977-83; postdoctoral fellow U. Calif., Berkeley, 1983-84; asst. prof. Johns Hopkins U., Balt., 1984-87; mem. tech. staff AT&T Bell Labs., Naperville, Ill., 1987-91; assoc. prof. U. Hawaii, Honolulu, 1991-97, prof., 1997—. Author: Multimedia Applications Support for Wireless ATM Networks, 2000, Mobile Telecommunications Protocols for Data Networks, 2002, Wireless Sensor Network Designs, 2003; mem. editl. adv. bd. Internat. Jour. Network Mgmt., 1996—, mem. editl. bd. IEEE Transactions Multimedia, 1999—. Mem.: IEEE (sr.). Achievements include design of algorithms to improve performance of distributed systems; reliable software architecture for switching systems. Avocation: travel. Office: U Hawaii Dept Elec Engineering 2540 Dole St Honolulu HI 96822-2303 Personal E-mail: anna.hac@gmail.com. Business E-Mail: hac@spectra.eng.hawaii.edu.

HACCOUN, DAVID, electrical engineering educator; b. Bizerte, Tunisia, July 4, 1937; arrived in Can. 1957; s. Charles and Emma (Melloul) H.; m. Lyson Tobaly, Dec. 26, 1971; children: Nathalie, Laurent. B.Sc. Engring. Physics, U. Montreal, 1965; SM, MIT, 1966; PhD, McGill U., 1974. Registered profl. engr., Que. Comms. City of Montreal, 1965; rsch. asst. MIT, Cambridge, 1965-66; prof. Ecole Polytech. U., Montreal, 1966—. Vis. rsch. prof. Concordia U., Montreal, 1984-85, U. Lund, Sweden, 1989-90, Ecole Technologie Superieure, Montreal, 1996-97; project leader Can. Inst. for Telecom. Rsch. under Nat. Ctrs. Excellence of Govt. Can., 1990-2003; vis. rsch. fellow Advanced Study Inst., U. BC, Vancouver, 1992; vis. rschr. INRIA, Paris, 1992, 1998-99; co-founder, pres. Can. Soc. Info. Theory, 1986-87; vis. rsch. prof. Higher Sch. Tech., Montreal, 1999, U. Victoria, B.C., Can., 1999; mem. exec. com. Telecom. Engring. Mgmt. Inst. Can., 1997—; cons. in field. Co-author: Digital Communications by Satellite, 1981, translated in Japanese, 1984, in Chinese, 1989, The Communications Handbook, 1997, 2001, The Encyclopedia of Telecommunications, 2002; contbr. articles to profl. jours. Mem. exec. com. Can. Jewish Congress, 1996—; bd. dirs. Comm. Rsch. Ctr., Ottawa, 1999—. Commonwealth fellow London, 1965; Grass fellow MIT, 1966, MIT scholar, 1965-66; Hydro-Que. fellow, Montreal, 1969-72. Fellow IEEE (life, co-gen. chair. vehicular technology Montreal conf., 2006), Engring. Inst. Can.; mem. AAAS, Order of Engrs. of Que., NY Acad. Scis., Sigma Xi. Avocations: photography, swimming, skiing. Office: Ecole Polytechnique PO Box 6079 Sta Centre Ville Montreal PQ Canada H3C 3A7 Business E-Mail: david.haccoun@polymtl.ca.

HACHEY, THOMAS EUGENE, British and Irish history educator; b. Lewiston, Maine, June 8, 1938; s. Leo Joseph and Margaret Mary (Johnson) H.; m. Jane Beverly Whitman, June 9, 1962. BA, St. Francis Coll., 1960; MA, Niagara U., 1961; PhD, St. John's U., 1965. Asst. prof. history Marquette U., Milw., 1964-69, assoc. prof., 1969-77, prof., 1977—, chmn. dept. history, 1979-93, dean Coll. Arts and Scis., 1993-2000; exec. dir. Irish programs, endowed chair dept. history Boston Coll., 2000—. Vis. prof. history Sch. Irish Studies, Dublin, 1977-78; cons. investments in Ireland Frost & Sullivan, N.Y.C., 1978-82; pres. Am. Conf. Irish Studies, 1983-85; dir. Bradley Inst. for Democracy and Pub. Values, 1988-99. Author: Problem of Partition: Peril to World Peace, 1972, Britain and Irish Separatism, 1977; co-author: The Irish Experience, 1988, expanded edit., 1996, Perspectives of Irish Nationalism, 1988; editor: Voices of Revolution, 1972, Confidential Despatches, 1975; contbr. articles profl. jours. and newspapers. Danforth assoc., 1979-85. Fellow Anglo-Am. Assocs. Roman Catholic. Home: 20 Deerpath Rd Dedham MA 02026 Office: Boston Coll Connolly House 300 Hammond St Chestnut Hill MA 02467-3930 Home Phone: 781-461-6166; Office Phone: 617-552-4847. Business E-Mail: thomas.hachey@bc.edu.

HACHTEN, RICHARD ARTHUR, II, healthcare system executive; b. LA, Mar. 24, 1945; s. Richard A. and Dorothy Margaret (Shipley) H.; m. Jeanine Hachten, Dec. 12, 1970; children: Kristianne, Karin. BS in Econs., U. Calif., Santa Barbara, 1967; MBA, UCLA, 1969. Mgmt. intern TRW Systems Group, Redondo Beach, Calif., 1969-72; adminstrv. asst. Meth. Hosp., Arcadia, Calif., 1972-73, asst. adminstr., 1973-74, assoc. adminstr., 1974-76, v.p. adminstrn., 1976-80; exec. v.p., adminstr., 1980-81; pres., adminstr., 1981-84; CEO Tri-City Hosp. Dist., Oceanside, 1984-91; pres. Bergan Mercy Health Sys., Omaha, 1991-95, Algent Health, Omaha, 1996—. Instr. health care mgmt. Pasadena (Calif.) City Coll. Bd. dirs., pres. Hospice of Pasadena, Inc.; bd. dirs. ARC, Arcadia, Mercy Housing Midwest, Omaha, Metropolitan Cmty. Coll. Found.; bd. governing mems. Omaha Symphony. Fellow Am. Coll. Healthcare Execs.; mem. Hosp. Coun. San Diego and Imperial Counties (chmn., bd. dirs.), Nebr. Hosp. Assn. (chmn. bd. dirs., chmn. dist. 1), Calif. Assn. Hosps. and Health Sys. (bd. dirs.), Am. Hosp. Assn. (policy bd. mem.), Rotary, Beta Gamma Sigma. Republican. Methodist. Office: Alegent Health Ste 200 1010 N 96th St Omaha NE 68114-2595 Home: 1910 S 183rd Cir Omaha NE 68130-2769 Home Phone: 402-393-6988; Office Phone: 402-343-4420. Business E-Mail: rhachten@alegent.org.

HACK, GARY ARTHUR, dean; b. Abernethy, Sask., Can., Apr. 8, 1942; came to U.S., 1964; s. Arthur and Marie (Banerd) H.; m. Lynda Lloy Lewis, 1964 (dec.); children: Andrew Arthur, Carolyn Sarah; m. Lynne Beyer Sagalyn, 2002. BArch, U. Manitoba, 1964; MArch, U. Ill., 1966, M in Urban Planning, 1967; PhD, MIT, 1976; LLD (hon.), Dalhousie U., 2006. Project mgr. Gruen Assocs., NYC, 1967-69; asst. prof. MIT, Cambridge, 1970-75; dir. gen. Min. of State for Urban Affairs, Ottawa, 1975-79; prof. MIT, Cambridge, 1979-96, dir. urban planning dept., 1982—86; prin. Carr Lynch Hack & Sandell, Cambridge, 1986-94; dean, Paley prof. U. Pa., Phila., 1996—. Chief planner West Side Waterfront, N.Y.C., 1986-91, Prudential Ctr. Redevel., Boston, 1988-91; Nell-Norris fellow in arch., U. Melbourne; visiting prof., Tsinghua U., Beijing. Co-author: Site Planning, 3d edit., 1984, Global City Regions, 2000, Global Urban Design, 2006. Bd. dirs. William Penn Found., 2004—. Mem. Am. Inst. Cert. Planners. Avocations: travel, architectural photography, collecting yi cheng teapots. Office: U Pa 101 Meyerson Hall 210 S 34th St Philadelphia PA 19104 Business E-Mail: gahack@design.upenn.edu.

HACK, RANDOLPH C., advocate, educator, counselor; b. NYC, Feb. 14, 1947; s. Sidney and Eleanor (Bermak) Hack. BA, U. Hawaii, Honolulu, 1980. Per diem tchr. Hawaii Dept. Edn., Honolulu, 1984—92; dir. consumer adv. United Self-Help, Honolulu, 1989—95; program dir. United Self Help, Honolulu, 1992—95, exec. dir., 1995—99; consumer advisor Adult Mental Health Divsn., Honolulu, 1999—, acting dir. consumer affairs, 2003. Counselor Army Cmty. Svc., Schofield Barracks, Hawaii, 1987—92; mem. Statewide Ind. Living Coun., 1999—2005; participant White House Conf. Mental Health, 1999; fed. grant application reviewer, 96, 98, 2005—06. Chair pro tem, vice-chmn. State Coun. Mental Health, 2004—07; active Diamond Head Svc. Area Bd. Mental Health & Substance Abuse, Honolulu, 1989—92; consumer rep. western states decision support group Western Interstate Commn. Higher Edn., 2006—07; precinct chmn. Dem.Party of Hawaii, Honolulu, 2000—06; bd. dirs. Mental Health Assn. Hawaii, 1984—86, Waikiki Health Ctr., 1999—, Mental Health Kokua, 1990—2004. Recipient Cmty. Svc. award, Mental Health Assn., 1991, Senator Daniel K. Inouye award, Hawaii Psychol. Assn., 1998, City Coun. commendation, Waikiki Friendly Neighbors Program, 1998, commendation, NAMI Oahu, 2006. Mem.: Nat. Alliance on Mental Illness (bd. dirs. Hawaii 1997—2005, bd. dirs. Oahu 1997—, state rep., nat. consumer coun. 1998—2004, alt. rep. 2004—05, v.p. 2004—). Avocations: swimming, fundraising. Office: Adult Mental Health Divsn 1250 Punchbowl St Honolulu HI 96813 Office Phone: 808-586-4688, 808-306-8041. Personal E-mail: randolphhack@earthlink.net. Business E-Mail: randolph.hack@doh.hawaii.gov.

HACKAM, REUBEN, electrical engineering educator; b. Baghdad, Iraq, Feb. 18, 1936; arrived in Can., 1978; s. Yechiel and Rachel (Cohen) H.; m. Estelle Malkinson, June 7, 1964; children: Judy, David, Abby, Dan. BSc, Israel Inst. Tech., Haifa, 1960; PhD, U. Liverpool, Eng., 1964, DEng, 1988. Sr. engr. GE, Stafford, Eng., 1964-69; lectr. elec. engring. U. Sheffield, Eng., 1969-73, sr. lectr., 1973-74, reader, 1974-78; prof. U. Windsor, Ont., 1978—2001, prof. emeritus, 2001—, chmn. dept., 1981-82, 84-86. Vis. staff dept. math. Staffordshire Poly., Stafford, 1964-69, Sheffield Poly, 1970-78, Hong Kong Poly. U., 1990-91; cons. Brit. Rail, Derby, Eng., 1975-78, English Electric Co., Stafford, 1975-77, Windsor Star, 1981-91, Corp. City of Windsor, 1983-92, Green Shield Prepaid Svcs., Inc., 1982—, County of Essex Libr., 1986—, Can. Salt Co., 1988—, Windsor Real Estate Bd., 1996-2004; vis. prof. Kumamoto U., Japan, 1998-99. Contbr. articles to profl. jours. Cons. Windsor Bd. Edn., 1988, Essex Bd. Edn., Windsor, 1989-94. Fellow: IEEE (bd. dirs. conf. on elec. insulation and dielectric phenomena 1985—91, gaseous dielectrics tech. com. 1985—, mem. tech. program com.IEEE-CEIDP 1986—97, asst. editor Digest IEEE Transactions on Dielectrics and Elec. Insulat 1990—99, mem. editl. bd. IEEE Insulation Mag. 1990—2001, permanent sci. com. int. synomps. on discharges and elec. insulat 1991—2001, sec. 1992—93, fellows award com. 1993—96, vice chmn. conf. on elec. insulation and dielectric phenomena 1994—95, chmn. 1996—97, various working groups 1997—, assoc. editor 1999—2001, editor-in-chief 2002—, program com. publicity and pub. chmn., fellows award com. 2005—, mem. editl. bd. Transactions on Dielectrics and Electrical Insultation, Third Millennium medal 2000, Eric O. Forster Disting. award 2000, Innuishi Meml. lecture award 1998); mem.: IEEE Dielectrics and Elec. Insulation Soc. (nominating and adv. coms. 1988—91, pub. com. 1988—96, chmn. publ. com. 1990—91, edn. com. 1990—95, asst. treas. 1991, treas. 1993—94, v.p. adminstrn. 1995—96, pres., meetings and svcs. com. 1997—98, chair 1999—2000, treas., pub. com. 1999—2001). Jewish. Office: U Windsor 401 Sunset Ave Windsor ON Canada N9B 3P4 Office Phone: 519-253-3000. Business E-Mail: hackam@uwindsor.ca.

HACKBARTH, DONALD A., JR., medical educator, orthopedist; b. Milw., June 14, 1952; s. Donald A., Sr. and Opal A. Hackbarth; m. Sandra J. Vrzal-McCann, July 25, 1981; children: Julie C., Paul D. MD, Med. Coll. Wis., Milw., 1977. Diplomate Nat. Bd. Med. Examiners, 1978, Am. Bd. Orthop. Surgery, 1984. Resident orthop. surgery Med. Coll. Wis. Affiliated Hosps., Milw., 1977—82; instr. orthop. surgery Med. Coll. Wis., 1982—83, asst. prof. orthop. surgery and orthop. oncology, 1986—93, assoc. prof. orthop. surgery and musculoskeletal oncology, 2000—; orthop. surgeon Burlington Clinic, S.C., Wis., 1983—85; fellow orthop. oncology Dept Orthop. U. Fla., Gainesville, 1985—86; ptnr. Assn. Orthop. Surgeons, Ltd., 1993—2000. Bd. dir. Musculoskeletal Transplant Found., Edison, NJ, chmn. bd. trustees, 1990—94, vice-chair bd. dir., 2007—; chief orthop. surgery St. Luke's Med. Ctr., Milw., 1998—2000. Congregation v.p. Christ the Life Luth. Ch., Waukesha, Wis., 1998—2000, congregation pres., 2000—01; bd. dir. Luth. HS Assn. Greater Milw., 1990—96, Harwood Pl. divsn. Luth. Living Svcs., Wauwatosa, Wis., 2005. Named one of Best Doctors in Am., 2005—06; recipient Cum Deo award, Luth. HS Assn. Greater Milw., 2000, Health Care Hero award, Small Bus. Times, 2005. Fellow: ACS, Am. Acad. Orthop. Surgeons; mem.: Wis. Orthop. Soc. (sec.-treas. 2001—05, pres. 1998—2000). Lutheran. Avocations: travel, hiking, flying. Office: Med College Wis Orthop Surgery 9200 W Wis Ave Milwaukee WI 53226 Home Phone: 262-792-1337; Office Phone: 414-805-7424. Office Fax: 414-805-7499.

HACKBARTH, STEVEN LYLE, writer, educator, audio-visual specialist; b. St. Cloud, Minn., July 7, 1945; s. Randall Clifford Hackbarth and Viola Maxine Geisinger; m. Teresa Fatima Palacios, Nov. 15, 1996; m. Joyce Marie Brown, Sept. 11, 1965 (div.); children: Valerie Lynn Lires, Grace Maria, Andrew Joseph. BA in Psychology, Calif. State U., Sacramento, 1967; MA in Psychology, Calif. State U., 1968; PhD, UCLA, 1976; MS in Edn., U. So. Calif., LA, 1984; MA, NYU, 1995. Cert. tchr. NY, 1995, instr. Calif., 1990. Mem. profl. staff SW Regional Lab. R & D, LA, 1969—71; tchg. asst., rsch. assoc. U. Calif., LA, 1971—76; dir. office student svcs., adj. asst. prof. U. So. Calif., LA, 1977—91; cons. UN Children's Fund, NYC, 1993—96; computer specialist tchr. City of NY, NYC, 1994—. Author: The Educational Technology Handbook: A Comprehensive Guide: Process and Products for Learning; cons. editor: Tech Trends: For Leaders in Education and Training, 2000—, contbg. editor: Educational Technology: The Magazine for Managers of Change in Education, 1996—; contbr. chapters to books, articles to profl. jours. Tennis and softball coach, 1970; scout leader, 1978—79; fund raiser Fresh Air Fund, 2004—07; chair fin. com. Good Shepherd United Meth. Ch., Astoria, NY, 2004—06. Recipient Disting. Svc. Most Outstanding Grad. award, Doctoral Alumni Assn., UCLA, 1976; Academic scholar, NYU, 1993—95. Mem.: Far Western Philosophy Edn. Soc. (pres. 1990—91), Assn. for Ednl. Comm. and Tech. (life; membership com., cons. editor 2000—, Ann. Achievement award 2001), Phi Delta Kappa (life Most Outstanding New Member award 1991), Tau Kappa Epsilon (v.p., chaplain 1966—68, Top TKE Alumnus 1968). Democrat. Lutheran. Achievements include research on changes in computer literacy as a function of race and gender; design of The Computer Literacy Assessment Tool; development of rational for discipline-based inquiry learning; documenting of current practice in math and science education; articulating in Lancet strategies for reaching currently unreached populations with health and education services. Avocations: photography, tennis, chess, astronomy, computers. Office: The Lillie Devereux Blake School 45 East 81st St New York NY 10028 Home Phone: 718-626-0919. Personal E-mail: hackbarths@aol.com.

HACKEL, EMANUEL, science educator; b. Bklyn., June 17, 1925; s. Henry N. and Esther (Herbstman) H.; m. Elisabeth Mackie, June 24, 1950 (dec. Apr. 1978); children: Lisa M., Meredith Anne, Janet M.; m. Rachel A. Fisher, Oct. 18, 1981; stepchildren: Daniel E., Tabitha A., and Jessica K. Harrison. Student, N.Y. U., 1941—42; BS, U. Mich., 1948, MS, 1949; PhD, Mich. State U., 1953. Fisheries biologist Mich. Dept. Conservation, 1949; mem. faculty Mich. State U., East Lansing, 1949—, prof. natural sci., 1962-74, chmn. dept. natural sci., 1963-74, prof. medicine, 1974-95, prof. emeritus, 1995—, prof. zoology, 1974-95, prof. emeritus, 1995—. Asst. dean coll. 1958-63; rsch. fellow Galton Lab., U. Coll., London, 1970-71, 77-78; vis. investigator blood group rsch. unit Lister Inst., London, 1956-57; cons. Mpls. War Meml. Blood Bank, 1983-95. Author: Guide to Laboratory Studies in Biological Science, 1951, Studies in Natural Science, 1953, Natural Science, 1955, Vols. 1, 2, 3, 1952-63. Editor: The Search for Explanation-Studies in Natural Science, Vols. 1, 2, 3, 1967-68, Laboratory Manual for Natural Science, Vol. 1, 2, 3, 1967-68, Human Genetics, 1974, Theoretical Aspects of HLA, 1982, Bone Marrow Transplantation, 1983, HLA Techniques for Blood Bankers, 1984, Human Genetics 1984: A Look at the Last Ten Years and the Next Ten, Transfusion Management of Some Common Heritable Blood Disorders, 1992, Advances in Transplantation, 1993, HLA Typing Section, Clinical Laboratory Medicine, 1994, Human Genetics '94: A Revolution in Full Swing, 1994; contbr. articles on genetics, human blood group immunology and chem. nature of blood group antigens, human biochem. genetics, tissue typing, human histocompatability antigens to sci. jours. Served to lt. (j.g.) USNR, 1943-47; now lt. comdr. USNR Ret. Recipient Cooley Meml. award Am. Assn. Blood Banks, 1969, Elliott Meml. award Am. Assn. Blood Banks, 1987, alumni disting. faculty award Coll. Natural Sci. Mich. State U., 1995. Mem. Assn. Gen. and Liberal Studies (sec.-treas. 1962-65), AAUP, AAAS, Genetics Soc. Am., Am. Soc. Human Genetics, Am. Assn. Blood Banks (dir. 1983-84, chmn. sci. sect. 1983-84), Mich. Assn. Blood Banks (v.p. 1970, pres. 1975-77), Am. Inst. Biol. Sci., Biometric Soc., Transplantation Soc. Mich. (dir. 1975-84), Am. Assn. for Clin. Histocompatability Testing, N.Y. Acad. Scis., Sigma Xi, Phi Kappa Phi. Home: 244 Oakland Dr East Lansing MI 48823-4747

HACKEL-SIMS, STELLA BLOOMBERG, lawyer, former government official; b. Burlington, Vt., Dec. 27, 1926; d. Hyman and Esther (Pocher) Bloomberg; m. Donald Herman Hackel, Aug. 14, 1949; children: Susan Jane, Cynthia Anne; m. Arthur Sims, Aug. 28, 1980. Student, U. Vt., 1943-45; JD cum laude, Boston U., 1948. Bar: Vt. 1948, Mass. 1948, D.C. 1979, Va. 1982. Individual practice law, Burlington, 1948-49, Rutland, Vt., 1949-59, 73—; city prosecutor City of Rutland, 1957-63; commr. Vt. Dept. Employment Security, 1963-73; treas. State of Vt., 1975-77; dir. U.S. Mint, Dept. Treasury, Washington, 1977-81. Chmn. Vt. Municipal Bond Bank, 1975-77 Mem. Vt. Adv. Com. on Mental Retardation, Interdept. Council on Aging, Commn. on Status Women, Human Resource Inter-Agency Com., Emergency Resource Priorities Bd., Info. Planning Council, Legis. Council Equal Opportunity Com., Vt. Indsl. Devel. Authority, Vt. Housing Fin. Agy., Vt. Claims Commn., Vt. Tchrs. Retirement Fund. Bd., Vt. Home Mortgage Guaranty Bd.; chmn. Vt. State Employees Retirement Fund; ex-officio mem. Nat. Manpower Adv. Com., 1971-72, Fed. Adv. Council on Unemployment Ins., 1971-72; Pres. Rutland Girl Scouts Leaders Assn., 1949-50, Rutland League Women Voters, 1951-52, Rutland Council Jewish Women, 1955-56; chmn. womens div. Rutland Community Chest Dr., 1952, Rutland County-Vt. Assn. for Blind, 1953-56; pres. Rutland County Democratic Women's Assn., 1956-63; treas. Rutland City Dem. Com., 1957-63; former rep. office women's activities Dem. Nat. Com., Regional Council I., Women's CD Councils; mem. Vt. bd. Girl Scouts USA; chmn. Arlington County Tenant-Landlord Commn., Va., 1986—; mem. citizen police review bd. City of Naples, Fla., 2006—. Mem.: LWV, AAUW (pres. Rutland County br. 1961—62), Interstate Conf. Employment Security Agys. (v.p. region I 1966—68, legis. com. 1969, sr. v.p. 1970—71, pres. 1971—72), Am. Soc. Pub. Adminstrn., Vt. Coun. Social Agys., Bus. and Profl. Women's Club, Rutland County Bar Assn. (pres. 1973), Vt. Bar Assn., Emblem (dir. 1960-63), Woodmont Country; Internat. (Washington), Moorings Country Club (Naples, Fla.) (bd. dirs. 2003—), Emblem Club (dir. 1960—63), Delta Phi Epsilon. Personal E-mail: stellahs@earthlink.net.

HACKENSON, ELIZABETH, information technology and telecommunications industry executive; BS, NY State U. IT mgmt. positions EDS, Computech, TRW, Grumman and Sperry; with UUNET, Concert Communication, MCI Inc., Ashburn, Va., 1997—2006, exec. v.p., chief info. officer, 2004—06; chief info. officer Lucent Technolgies, Murray Hill, NJ, 2006; head, info. systems & info. tech. Alcatel Lucent, 2006—. Bd. dir. Serena Software, Inc., San Mateo, Calif., 2006—. Named one of Top 200 female executives, Washington Post, 2004, Premier 100 IT Leaders, Computerworld, 2006. Office: Lucent Technolgies 600 Mountain Ave New Providence NJ 07974 Fax: 601-460-8269.*

HACKER, EILEEN DANAHER, nursing educator, researcher; PhD, U. Ill., Chgo., 2001. RN Ill., 1983, cert. advanced oncology nurse, Oncology Nursing Certification Corp., 1996, advanced practice nurse, Ill., 2001. Practitioner, tchr. Rush-Presbyterian-St. Luke's Med. Ctr., Chgo., 1985—87; educator, clin. nurse mgr. U. Chgo. Hosps., 1987—89; clin. nurse specialist Ingalls Meml. Hosp., Harvey, Ill., 1989—2001; asst. prof. U. Ill., Chgo., 2001—. Contbr. articles to profl. jours. Scholar, Am. Cancer Soc., 1999—2001, Oncology Nursing Soc., 1999—2000. Mem.: Midwest Nursing Rsch. Soc. (Harriett H. Werley New Investigator award 2006), Am. Coll. Sports Medicine, Oncology Nursing Soc. (sci. reveiw com.), Sigma Theta Tau. Home: 15241 Brassie Dr Orland Park IL 60462 Office: Univ Ill Chgo 845 S Damen Ave M/C 802 Rm 720 Chicago IL 60612 Home Phone: 708-403-7545; Office Phone: 312-996-7924. Office Fax: 312=996-4979. Business E-Mail: ehacker@uic.edu.

HACKERMAN, WILLARD J., construction executive; m. Lillian Patz Hackerman. BS in Civil Engring., Johns Hopkins U., Balt., 1938, degree (hon.), 1990. Timekeeper Whiting-Turner Contracting Co., Balt., 1938, pres., 1955—, CEO, chmn. Trustee emeritus Johns Hopkins U. Recipient Disting. Alumni award, Johns Hopkins U., 2001, Phoenix award, Achievement Initiative for Md.'s Minority Students Excellence Awards, 2007. Office: Whiting-Turner Contracting Co 300 E Joppa Rd Baltimore MD 21286 Office Phone: 410-821-1100. Office Fax: 410-337-5770.*

HACKERT, MARVIN LEROY, chemistry professor, biophysical researcher; b. Pella, Iowa, Sept. 23, 1944; s. Henry and Johanna Mae (Vanden Berg) H.; children: Christopher Lee, Brian Mitchell. BA, Central Coll., Pella, 1966; PhD, Iowa State U., 1970. Fellow Purdue U., West Lafayette, Ind., 1970-74; asst. prof. U. Tex., Austin, 1974-80, assoc. prof., 1980-86, prof. Dept. Chemistry and Biochemistry, 1986—, grad. advisor, 1991-95, dept. chair, 1995-2000, assoc. dean Grad. Sch., 2005—, dir., Biochemical Inst., 1995—. Chair U.S. Nat. Com. Crystallography, 2000-03. Author: chemistry study guide, 1982, 87, 93, 97, 2000; contbr. articles to profl. jours. State sci. contest dir. Univ. Interscholastic League, 1984-96. Mem. AAAS, Am. Chem. Soc., Am. Crystallographic Assn. (chair BIOMAC SIG, 1991-92, v.p. 2007). Avocations: photography, computer graphics, woodworking. Office: U Tex Dept Chemistry & Biochemistry 1 University Station A5300 Austin TX 78712-0165 Office Phone: 512-471-1105. E-mail: m.hackert@mail.utexas.edu.

HACKETT, CAROL ANN HEDDEN, physician; b. Valdese, NC, Dec. 18, 1939; d. Thomas Barnett and Zada Loray (Pope) Hedden; m. John Peter Hackett, July 27, 1968; children: John Hedden, Elizabeth Bentley, Susanne Rochet. BA, Duke U., 1961; MD, U. N.C., 1966. Intern Georgetown U. Hosp., Washington, 1966—67, resident, 1967—69; clinic physician DePaul Hosp., Norfolk, Va., 1969—71; chief spl. health svcs. Arlington County Dept. Human Resources, Va., 1971—72; gen. med. officer USPHS Hosp., Balt., 1974—75; pvt. practice family medicine Seattle, 1975—. Mem. staff, chmn. dept. family practice Overlake Hosp. Med. Ctr., 1985-86; clin. asst. prof. Sch. Medicine U. Wash. Bd. dirs. Mercer Island (Wash.) Presch. Assn., 1977-78; coord. 13th and 20th Ann. Inter-profl. Women's Dinner, 1978, 86; trustee Northwest Chamber Orch., 1984-85. Fellow Am. Acad. Family Practice; mem. King County Acad. Family Practice (trustee 1993-96, pres.-elect 1997-98, pres. 1998-99), King County Med. Soc. (chmn. com. TV violence), Wash. Acad. Family Practice, Wash. State Med. Assn., DAR, Bellevue C. of C., N.W. Women Physicians (v.p. 1978), Seattle Symphony League, Eastside Women Physicians (founder, pres.), Seattle Yacht Club, Sigma Kappa. Episcopalian. Home: PO Box 3098 Bellevue WA 98009-3098 Office: 1380 112th NE Ste 100 Bellevue WA 98004 Office Phone: 425-454-8191. Home Fax: 425-462-5313.

HACKETT, EARL RANDOLPH, neurologist; b. Moulmein, Burma, Feb. 16, 1932; s. Paul Richmond and Martha Jane (Lewis) H.; m. Shirley Jane Kanehl, May 25, 1953; children: Nancy, Raymond, Susan, Lynn, Laurie, Richard, Alicia. BS, Drury Coll., Springfield, Mo., 1953; MD, Western Res. U., 1957. Diplomate Am. Bd. Psychiatry and Neurology, Am. Bd. Electrodiagnostic Medicine. Intern, then resident in neurology Charity Hosp., New Orleans, 1957-62; resident in internal medicine VA Hosp., New Orleans, 1958-59; mem. faculty La. State U. Med. Sch., New Orleans, 1962—, prof. neurology, 1973-88, head dept., 1977-88; clin. prof. neurology U. Mo., Columbia, 1988—. Mem. med. adv. bd. Myasthenia Gravis Found. Fellow Am. Acad. Neurology; mem. Am. Assn. Electrodiagnostic Medicine, Soc. Clin. Neurologists, Mo. Med. Assn., Greene County Med. Soc., AOA. Methodist. Home: 2517 S Brentwood Blvd Springfield MO 65804-3201 Office: 1965 S Fremont Ave Ste 2800 Springfield MO 65804-2258

HACKETT, GEORGE, editor; BA in Lit., Yale U.; MA in Journalism, U. Calif. Berkeley. With Newsweek, 1980—, editorial asst., 1980—81, reporting intern, 1981, 1982, editor Cyberscope sect., 1994—, editor Focus on Technology sect., 1995—, with nat. affairs sect., tech. editor, 1995—97, editor Periscope, Perspectives, My Turn sects., sr. editor sci. and tech., dept. chief, 1997—. Office: Newsweek 251 West 57th St New York NY 10019-1894 Office Phone: 212-445-4000.

HACKETT, JAMES P., manufacturing executive; b. Columbus, Ohio, Apr. 22, 1955; BA, U. Mich., 1977. With Proctor and Gamble Co., 1977-81; joined Steelcase Inc., Grand Rapids, Mich., 1981—, sr. v.p. sales and mktg., 1990—93, pres. Turnstone, 1993, exec. v.p. Steelcase Ventures, 1994; exec. v.p., CEO Steelcase N. Am., 1994, pres., CEO, 1994, Steelcase Inc., 1994—. Bd. dir. Northwestern Mutual Life, Fifth Third Bancorp. Mem., past pres. bd. overseers Inst. Design, Ill. Inst. Tech. Office: Steelcase Inc 901 44th St SE Grand Rapids MI 49508*

HACKETT, JAMES T., oil industry executive; m. Maureen Hackett; 4 children. BS, U. Ill., 1974; MBA, Harvard U., 1979. With NGC Corp., Burlington Resources, Amoco Oil Co.; exec. v.p. Pan Energy Corp., 1996—97; pres. energy svcs. divsn. Duke Energy Corp., 1997—98; pres., CEO Seagull Energy Corp., 1998—99, chmn., pres., CEO, 1999; pres., CEO Ocean Energy Inc., 1999—2000, chmn., pres., CEO, 2000—03; pres., COO Devon Energy Corp., 2003; pres., CEO Anadarko Petroleum Corp., The Woodlands, Tex., 2003—05, chmn., pres., CEO, 2006—. Mem. exec. com., past. chmn. Domestic Petroleum Council; mem. exec. com. Am. Petroleum Inst.; bd. dirs. Temple-Inland Corp., Fluor Corp., Fed. Res. Bank, Dallas. Bd. mem. (past chmn.) Houston Grand Opera; bd. mem. Baylor Coll. Med., Nat. Humanities Ctr. Mem.: Soc. Petroleum Engineers, Bus. Roundtable. Office: Anadarko Petroleum Corp 1201 Lake Robbins Dr The Woodlands TX 77380-1046*

HACKETT, JOHN BYRON, advertising executive, lawyer; b. NYC, Dec. 28, 1933; s. John Joseph and Cecelia Elizabeth (Meehan) H.; m. Patricia P. Briordy, May 23, 1964 (div. 1980); children: Kimberly, John; m. Kathryn Meyer, Mar. 28, 1982. BBA, Iona Coll., 1956; JD, St. Johns U., 1960. Bar: N.Y. 1961. Sales adminstr. NBC, NYC, 1962-65; with J. Walter Thompson Co., NYC, 1965-85, v.p. legal dept., 1971-76, sr. v.p. adminstrn., 1976-80, sr. v.p., gen. mgr. entertainment div., 1980-83, sr. v.p., dir. spot broadcasting U.S.A., 1983-85; pvt. legal practice, 1985—. Home and Office: 1 Toms Point Ln Apt 10B Port Washington NY 11050-2120

HACKETT, JOHN PETER, dermatologist; b. NYC, Feb. 10, 1942; s. John Thomas and Helen (Donohue) H.; m. Carol A. Hedden, July 27, 1968; children: John, Elizabeth, Susanne. AB, Holy Cross Coll., 1963; MD, Georgetown U., 1967. Diplomate Am. Bd. Internal Medicine, Am. Bd. Dermatology. Intern Georgetown U. Hosp., 1967-68, resident, 1968-69; fellow Johns Hopkins Hosp., 1972-75, chief resident, 1975; practice medicine specializing in dermatology Seattle, 1975—. Chmn. bd. dirs. NW Dental Ins. Co., 1989-92; clin. asst. prof. dermatology U. Wash., 1976-88, clin. assoc. prof., 1988—; active staff Swedish Hosp., Providence Hosp.; cons. Wash. State Dept. Labor and Industries, 1992—; pres. Psoriasis Treatment Ctr., Inc., 1978-80; cons. physician Children's Orthopedic Hosp. Contbr. articles to profl. jours. Bd. dirs. Mercer Island Boys and Girls Club, 1976-81, Seattle Ctr. for Blind, 1979-80, N.W. Chamber Orch., 1983-86. Served to lt. condr. USNR, 1969-71. Mem. Am. Acad. Dermatology, Seattle Dermatol. Soc. (pres. 1981-82), Soc. Investigative Dermatology, Am. Contact Dermatitis Soc., Wash. State Med. Soc., King County Med. Soc. (chmn. media rels. com. 1977-80, grievance com. 1991—), Wash. Physicians Ins. Exch. (chmn. actuarial subcom. 1983-85, chmn. subscribers adv. com. 1986-90, audit com. 1988-92, fin. com. 1990-92), Seattle Yacht Club, Marine Corps Meml. Office: 1605 116th Ave NE Ste1 02 Bellevue WA 98004-4601 Office Phone: 425-456-0709. Fax: 425 462 5313.

HACKETT, JOHN THOMAS, retired economist and financial executive; b. Ft. Wayne, Ind., Oct. 10, 1932; s. Harry H. and Ruth (Greer) H.; m. Ann E. Thompson, July 24, 1954; children: Jane, David, Sarah, Peter. BS, Ind. U., 1954, MBA, 1958; PhD, Ohio State U., 1961. Instr. Ohio State U., 1958-61; asst. v.p., economist Fed. Res. Bank, Cleve., 1961-64; dir. planning Cummins Engine Co., Columbus, Ind., 1964-66, v.p. finance, 1966-71, exec. v.p., 1971-88, also dir.; v.p. fin. and adminstrn. Ind. U., Bloomington, 1988-91; mng. gen. ptnr. CID Equity Ptnrs., L.P., Indpls., 1991—2002, ret., 2002. Former chmn. bd. dirs. Wabash Nat. Corp.; bd. dirs. Intertnhen Arts Acad., Mich. Land Use Inst. 1st lt. AUS, 1954-56. Mem.: Ind. Acad., Beta Gamma Sigma. Home: PO Box 466 Keene NH 03431 also: PO Box 100 Glen Arbor MI 49736

HACKETT, KEVIN R., real estate company executive, lawyer; b. Atlantic City, Apr. 16, 1949; BA summa cum laude, Boston Coll., 1971; JD, Harvard U., 1974. Bar: N.Y. 1975. Ptnr. Shearman & Sterling, NYC; pres., CEO The Rockefeller Group Devel. Corp., 2004—06. Fellow: Am. Coll. Real Estate Lawyers; mem.: Phi Beta Kappa. Office: Rockefeller Grp Dev Corp 1221 Ave of the Am 29th Fl New York NY 10020 Home Phone: 212-369-7160; Office Phone: 212-282-2260. Business E-Mail: khackett@rockgrp.com.

HACKETT, LARRY, editor; Nat. reporter, entertainment reporter, features editor NY Daily News; sr. editor People mag., 1998—2001, asst. mng. editor, 2001—03, exec. editor, 2003—04, dep. mng. editor, 2004—06, mng. editor, 2006—. Office: People Rockefeller Ctr 1271 Ave of the Americas New York NY 10020*

HACKETT, MARY J., lawyer; b. Pitts., Sept. 8, 1962; m. Arlie R. Nogay; children: Walter, Robert. BA in economics & politics, Mt. Holyoke Coll., 1984; JD with honors, U. Pitts., 1987. Bar: Pa. 1987, US. Dist. Ct. We. Dist. Pa., US Ct. Appeals 3rd Cir., US Ct. Appeals 4th Cir., US Ct. Appeals 6th Cir., US Ct. Appeals 8th Cir. Law clk. to Judge Donald E. Ziegler US Dist. Ct. We. Dist. Pa., 1989—90; chief counsel-litig. PNC Fin. Services Group Inc., 1998—2001; assoc. Reed Smith LLP, Pitts., 1987—89, 1990—96, ptnr., 1996—98, 2001—, practice group leader fin. services litig. group, 2003—. Mem.: ABA, Allegheny County Bar Assn., Pa. Bar Assn. Office: Reed Smith LLP 435 Sixth Ave Pittsburgh PA 15219 Office Phone: 412-288-3250. Office Fax: 412-288-3063. Business E-Mail: mhackett@reedsmith.com.

HACKETT, ROBERT JOHN, lawyer; b. NYC, Feb. 6, 1943; s. John P. and Marie S. (Starace) Hackett; m. Anita Carlile, Apr. 19, 1969; children: Robert John Hackett Jr., John Peter, Kathryn Marie. AB, Rutgers U., 1964; JD, Duke U., 1967. Bar: NY 1967, Ariz. 1972. Assoc. Milbank, Tweed, Hadley, McCloy, NYC, 1967—71; ptnr. Evans, Kitchel & Jenckes, Phoenix, 1971—89; dir. Fennemore Craig, Phoenix, 1989—2004, course dir. seminar on mergers and acquisitions, 1996, 1999; mem. Jennings, Strouss & Salmon, P.L.C., Phoenix, 2004—. Mem. editl. bd. Duke Law Jour., 1966—67. Former bd. dirs. Xavier Coll. Prep., mem. steering com. for Fine Arts Ctr. capital campaign. Mem.: ABA (com. on fed. securities regulation), Maricopa County Bar Assn., State Bar Ariz. (past chmn. securities regulation sect.), Assn. Corp. Growth (past bd. dirs., past pres. Ariz. chpt.), Phoenix Duke U. Law Alumni Club (past pres.), Pi Sigma Alpha. Republican. Roman Catholic. Home Phone: 602-254-8038. Business E-Mail: rhackett@jsslaw.com.

HACKETT, ROGER FLEMING, historian, educator; b. Kobe, Japan, Oct. 23, 1922; s. Harold Wallace and Anna Luena (Powell) H.; m. Caroline Betty Gray, Aug. 24, 1946; children: Anne Marilyn, David Gray, Brian Vance. BA, Carleton Coll., 1947; MA, Harvard U., 1949, PhD, 1955. Prof. history Northwestern U., Evanston, Ill., 1953-61; prof. history U. Mich., Ann Arbor, 1961-93, prof. emeritus, 1993—, chmn. dept., 1975-77; dir. Ctr. for Japanese Studies, 1968-71, 78, 79. Cons. Office of Edn., HEW; mem. sub-com., joint com. Social Sci. Rsch. Coun. Author: Yamagata Aritomo in the Rise of Modern Japan 1838-1922, 1971; Editor: Jour. Asian Studies, 1959-62; contbr. articles and chpts to profl. jours. and books. Served with USMC, 1942-46. Social Sci. Rsch. Coun. fellow; Japan Found. fellow; Fulbright-Hays fellow; fellow St. Antony's Coll. Oxford U. Mem. Japan Soc., Assn. Asian Studies (exec. com., bd. dirs. 1966-69), Internat. House of Japan, Ann Arbor Racquet Club, Phi Beta Kappa. Home: 2122 Dorset Rd Ann Arbor MI 48104-2604 Office: U Mich Dept History Ann Arbor MI 48109 Business E-Mail: fhackett@umich.edu.

HACKETT, STANLEY HAILEY, lawyer; b. Houston, May 31, 1945; s. Harley Benjamin and Rebecca Easterling (Willis) H.; m. Ann Elaine Aiken, May 29, 1971; children: Elizabeth Ann, Rebecca Aiken. BS in Banking Fin., U. S.C., 1967, JD magna cum laude, 1970; LLM, Harvard U., 1971. Bar: S.C. 1970, D.C. 1975, Ga. 1975. Atty, Office of Chief Counsel IRS, Washington, 1971—72; atty. Office Chief Counsel IRS, Washington, 1971-72, spl. asst. to chief counsel, 1972-73; legis. asst. to Sen. Strom Thurmond U.S. Senate, Washington, 1973-74; assoc. Henkel & Lamon, P.C., Atlanta, 1974-81; ptnr. Henkel, Hackett, Edge & Fleming, Atlanta, 1981-85; ptnr., tax dept. Troutman Sanders LLP, Atlanta, 1985—. Bd. dirs. Small Bus. Coun. Am., Washington, 1978—; mem. liaison com. S.E. region IRS, 1985—. Contbr. articles on taxation to profl. jours. Mem. Lawyers for Reagan/Bush, 1984; trustee Ga. Fed. Tax Conf.; advisor Ga. State Law Sch. Tax Clinic. Named a Super Lawyer, Atlanta Mag., 2004, 2006, Legal Elite in taxes, estates, and trusts, Ga. Trend Mag., 2004, 2005, 2006; recipient Super Lawyer, Atlanta Mag., 2005. Fellow Am. Coll. Tax Counsel; mem. ABA (tax sect.), Ga. Bar Assn. (chmn. tax sect. 1985-86), Phi Delta Theta. Republican. Episcopalian. Office: Troutman Sanders LLP 600 Peachtree St NE Atlanta GA 30308-2216 Office Phone: 404-885-3154. Office Fax: 404-962-6579. Business E-Mail: stanley.hackett@troutmansanders.com.

HACKETT, STEPHANIE R., educational association administrator; d. John C. and Julia R. Hackett. BS in Health Info. Mgmt., U. Pitts., 2000, MS in Health and Rehab Sci., 2004, postgrad. in Rehab. Sci., 2004—. Registered health info. adminstr. Am. Health Info. Mgmt. Assn., 2000. Bus. sys. analyst ii U. Pitts. Med. Ctr. Health Sys., Magee Women's Hosp., Pitts., 2001—03; grad. student asst. and clin. edn. coord. U. Pitts., 2003—07; project mgr. U. Pitts. Med. Ctr. Health Plan, 2007—. Contbr. articles to profl. jours. Mem. Health Careers Futures, Pitts., 2007. Fellow, Jewish Healthcare Found., 2006; scholar, Healthcare Info. Mgmt. and Systems Soc., 2006—. Mem.: Healthcare Info. Mgmt. and Sys. Soc., Student Adv. Bd. (bus. mgr. 2007). Home: 506 Meridan St Pittsburgh PA 15211 Home Phone: 412-480-7801. Personal E-mail: stephanie_hackett@hotmail.com. Business E-Mail: hackettsr@upmc.com.

HACKETT, WESLEY PHELPS, JR., lawyer; b. Detroit, Jan. 3, 1939; s. Wesley P. and Helen (Decker) H.; children: Kelly D. Hackett Pell, Robin C. Hackett Story. BA, Mich. State U., 1960; JD, Wayne State U., 1968. Bar: Mich. 1968, U.S. Dist. Ct. (we. dist.) Mich. 1971, U.S. Ct. Appeals (6th cir.) 1972, U.S. Dist. Ct. (ea. dist.) Mich. 1972, U.S. Supreme Ct. 1972, U.S. Ct. Mil. Appeals 1991. Law clk. Mich. Supreme Ct., Lansing, 1968-70; ptnr. Brown & Hackett, Lansing, 1971-73; pvt. practice Lansing, 1973-84; ptnr. Starr, Bissell & Hackett, Lansing, 1984-87; pvt. practice East Lansing, Mich., 1987-98, Saranac, Mich., 1998—. Adj. prof. Thomas M. Cooley Law Sch., Lansing, 1973—; instr. Lansing C.C., 1981-99. Author: Evidence: A Trial Manual for Michigan Lawyers, 1981, Hackett's Evidence: Michigan and Federal, 2d edit., 1995, Michigan Lawyers Manual Part L, 1994, revised, 2002; co-author: Hiring Legal Staff, 1990. Mem. City of East Lansing Planning Commn., 1969-72; mem. Village of Saranac Planning Commn., 2000—; bd. dirs. St. Vincent Home for Children, Lansing, 1974-82; vestry St. John's Episcopal Ch., Ionia, Mich., 2004-, sr. warden, 2004-. 1st lt. USAF, 1961-65. Fellow Coll. Law Practice Mgmt.; mem. State Bar Mich. (chair legal econs. sect. 1990-91). Home Phone: 616-642-9094; Office Phone: 616-642-6074.

HACKFORD, TAYLOR, film director; b. Santa Barbara, Calif., Dec. 31, 1944; s. Joseph and Mary (Taylor) H.; m. Helen Mirren, Dec. 31, 1997. BA, U. So. Calif., 1968. Vol. Peace Corps, Bolivia, 1968-69; dir., prodr., reporter, writer Sta.-KCET, Community TV of So. Calif., Los Angeles, 1970-77; dir., prodr., writer Hackford Littman Films, Los Angeles, 1977-79; dir. United Artists Films, Los Angeles, 1979-80, Paramount Pictures, Los Angeles, 1981-82; prodr., dir. Columbia Pictures, Los Angeles, 1983—. Exec. prodr.: (films) Rooftops, 1989, The Long Walk Home, 1990, Sweet Talker, 1991, Queens Logic, 1991, Defenseless, 1991, Mortal Thoughts, 1991; exec. prodr., dir. (films) The Devil's Advocate, 1998; prodr., dir.: (films) Against All Odds, 1984, White Nights, 1985, Everyone's All American, 1988, Bound by Honor (Blood In, Blood Out), 1993, Dolores Claiborne, 1995, When We Were Kings, 1996, Greenwich Mean Time, 1999, Proof of Life, 2000; prodr.: (films) La Bamba, 1987, G:MT Greenwich Mean Time, 1999; dir. (films) Teenage Father, 1978 (Oscar 1979), The Idolmaker, 1980, An Officer and A Gentleman, 1982, Chuck Berry Hail! Hail! Rock and Roll, 1987; prodr., dir., writer, (films) Ray, 2004; exec. prodr. (TV films): Genius: A Night for Ray Charles, 2004; prodr. (TV series): E-Ring, 2005-, (soundtracks) Bound by Honor, 1993, Ray, 2004, More Music from Ray, 2005. Recipient Silver Reel award San Francisco Film Festival, 1972, Emmy award Acad. TV Arts and Scis., 1974, Emmy award Acad. TV Arts and Scis., 1977, Acad. award Acad. Motion Picture Arts and Scis., 1979, Grammy award for Best Compilation Soundtrack Album for Ray, 2006, 2006 Robert B. Alrich Avc. award, Directors Guild of Am. Mem. Dir.'s Guild Am., Writers Guild Am. Office: Creative Artists Agency 9830 Wilshire Blvd Beverly Hills CA 90212-1825*

HACKL, DONALD JOHN, architect; b. Chgo., May 11, 1934; s. John Frank and Frieda Marie Hackl; m. Bernadine Marie Becker, Sept. 29, 1962; children: Jeffrey Scott, Craig Michael, Cristina Lynn. BArch., U. Ill., 1957, MS in Architecture, 1958. With Loebl Schlossman & Hackl Architects, Chgo., 1963—, assoc., 1967-74, exec. v.p., dir., 1974, pres., dir., 1975—. Prof. architecture Internat. Acad. Architecture, Sofia, Bulgaria; mem. Nat. Coun. Archtl. Registration Bds., 1980—; bd. dirs. Chgo. Bldg. Congress, 1983-94, v.p., 1985-94; design juries include: Reynolds Metals, Western Mont. Regional Design, Am. Inst. Steel Constrn., Precast Concrete Inst., Okla. Soc. Architects, UIA Gold Medal (6), UIA Celebration of Cities (2), Seoul, Korea, 2004, Sewaen Dist. 4 Internat. Design Competition, 2004; chmn. Ariz. Soc. Architects, Midwest Design Conf., 1983; design critic dept. arch. U. Ill., 1975-76, 81; vis. critic sch. architecture U. Notre Dame, 1977-78, 80, 82; adj. prof. Kent Coll. Law, Ill. Inst. Tech., 1983—; adj. faculty Shenzhen U., China, 1998-; guest lectr. Tongi U., Shanghai, 2004; cons. Pub. Svcs. Adminstrn., Washington, 1974-76; cons. in field. Prin. works include Water Tower Place, Chgo., 1976, King Faisel Specialist Hosp. and Rsch. Ctr., Riyadh, Saudi Arabia, 1978, Household Internat. Hdqrs., Prospect Heights, Ill., 1978, Shriners Hosp. for Children, Chgo., 1979, Square D Co. Hdqrs., Palatine, Ill., 1979, West Suburban Hosp., Oak Park, Ill., 1981, Allstate Pla. West, Northbrook, Ill., 1990, Sears Roebuck & Co. stores of future concept, 1985-89, Ford City Shopping Ctr. Redevel., Chgo., 1989, Commerce Clearing House, Riverwoods, Ill., 1986, Physicians' Pavilion Greater Balt. Med. Ctr., 1987, Two Prudential Plaza, Chgo., 1990, City Place with Omni Hotel, Chgo., 1990, 350 N. LaSalle, Chgo., 1990, Infinitec, Assistive Tech. Application Ctr. for United Cerebral Palsy Assn., Chgo., 1992, Shenzhen AVIC Plaza Bldg., Shenzhen, China, 1993, Ill. State U. Biol. and Chemistry Scis. Lab. Bldg., Normal, 1995, Old Orchard Shopping Ctr. Redevel., Skokie, Ill., 1994, Sun Comml. City, Changchun, China, 1993, Shekou Harbor Bldg., Shenzhen, 1995, East Shanghai Film and TV Ctr., 1995, Luo-Hu Comml. Ctr., Shenzhen, 1994, Shenzhen Internat. Exch. Plz., 1996, Jin Hui Plz., Shanghai, 1996, Shenzhen Cultural Ctr., 1997, Changchun Sun Housing Estates, China, 1999, Hdqrs. for Almacenes Paris LTDA, Santiago, Chile, 1999, John H. Stroger, Jr. Hosp. of Cook Cty., 2002, Grand Pier Ctr., Chgo., 2004 Computer/Engring. Bldg. U. Ill., 1999—, Bank of Mauritius, Port Louis, 2006, Olympic Swimming Facility-Design Study, Tianjin, China, 2006, North Ctrl. Coll. Performing Arts Ctr., 2006, Riva de Lago: Lake of the Ozarks, 2007. Mem. Met. Am. Cancer Crusade, 1973; life trustee West Suburban Hosp., 1983—, mem. exec. com., 1986-87; vice chmn. North Ctrl. Coll., 1990-2005, life trustee, 2006—; mem. Pres.'s Coun. U. Ill. Found.; mem. curricula adv. com. Dept. Architecture, U. Ill.; bd. dirs. World Trade Ctr., Chgo., 1995—; dir. Chgo. Loop Alliance, 2006, Resurrection Healthcare Found., 2007. With Ill. Air Nat. Guard, 1957—63. Fellow AIA (treas. Chgo. chpt. 1977-78, exec. com. 1978-81, v.p. 1981, pres. 1981, bd. dirs. Chgo. AIA Found. 1981-83, nat. v.p. 1985, 1st v.p. 1986, nat. pres. 1987, chmn. design com. 1985, exec. com. 1985-87, bd. dirs. 1981-87, documents com. 1974-79, chmn. 1980, exec. com. AIA Svc. Corp. 1983-84, chmn. internat. com. 1987-91, exec. com. 2006, sec. exec. com. AIA Coll. Fellows 2006), Nat. Coun. Archtl. Registration Bds., Royal Archtl. Inst. Can. (hon.), Colegios Architectos Mexicanos (hon.), Internat. Acad. Architecture (hon., prof.), Korean Inst. Archs. (hon.); mem. Internat. Union Archs. (bd. dirs., del. 1987—, 1st v.p. 1990-93, coun. 1993-96, v.p. region III 1996-99, treas. 2000—), Union Bulgarian Archs. (hon.), Soc. Cuban Archs., Japan Inst. Archs. (hon.), Colegio Arquitectos Cochabamba (Bolivia), Colegios Arquitectos Espana (hon.), Instituto do Arquiteclos do Brazil (hon.), Tavern Clubs, Carlton Club, Econ. Club, Lake Zurich Club. Office: Loebl Schlossman and Hackl Inc 233 N Michigan Ave ste 3000 Chicago IL 60601-5708 Office Phone: 312-565-4500. Business E-Mail: dhackl@lshchicago.com.

HACKLEMAN, KELLY KER, music educator; b. Indpls., Mar. 16, 1959; d. Charles Arthur Ker and Ann Hall; m. Martin Hackleman, June 23, 2001; children: Michael Steele DeVuyst, Daniel Vigeant DeVuyst. MusB, U. Cin., 1982; MusM, New Eng. Conservatory, Boston, 1985; D of Musical Arts, U. Memphis, 1993. Faculty music Rhodes Coll., Memphis, 1987—92; pianist Memphis Symphony Orch., 1987—92; keyboard extra Montreal Symphony Orch., 1993—2000; faculty music Frederick C.C., Md., 2000—02, Shepherd Coll., Shepherdstown, W.Va., 2000—02, George Mason U., Fairfax, Va., 2002—; organist Kirkwood Presbyn. Ch., Springfield, Va., 2005—; pianist Alexandria Symphony Orch., Va. Artistic dir. Concerts from Kirkwood, Springfield, Va., 2006—. Composer: (anthem/hymn) In This House. Recipient 4th prize, Nat. Masters Piano Competition, 1987, 2d prize, Internat. Beethoven Sonata Competition, 1990. Mem.: Am. Guild Organists, Springfield Music Club. Avocations: scuba diving, skiing, bicycling, photography. Home: 5950 Oakland Park Dr Burke VA 22015 Office: George Mason University 4400 University Dr MSN 3E3 Fairfax VA 22030 Home Phone: 703-249-0015; Office Phone: 703-993-1380. Personal E-mail: kkerhack@gmu.edu.

HACKLEMAN, PHYLLIS ANN, artist, genealogist; b. Columbus, Ohio, Dec. 12, 1943; d. John Tapley Clem and Della Florence Fogle; m. B. Keith Hackleman, Feb. 26, 1966; children: Brian Keith, Brady Keith. Exec. sec. Western So. life, Athens, Ohio, 1964—65, Abex Corp., Athens, 1965—67, Beechnut Foods, Rochester, 1968—69; legal sec. Frank Ferris Sr. Atty., Rochester, 1969—70; photo retoucher A and R Color Lab, Rochester, 1972; owner Hackleman Assocs., Inc., Rochester, 1989—99; author, photographer, Rochester, 1980—. Author: (book) Reunion Planner, 1993; co-author: Hackleman's in America, 1998. Vol. Assn. For Blind, Rochester, 1975, Boy Scouts Am., Rochester, 1976—86. Recipient Silver Beaver award, Boy Scouts Am., 1984, Dist. Merit award, Black and White Photographer Yr., Kodak Camera Club, Rochester. Mem.: Arena Art Group (mem. chair 2006—, mem.-at-large 2003—06).

HACKLEY, CAROL ANN, public relations educator, consultant; b. Sacramento, Mar. 20, 1940; d. Charles Peter and Alice Marian (Schmidt) Cusick; m. William E. Hall, Sept. 1, 1966 (dec. Aug. 1991); children: Kevin Dennis Hall, Kimberlee Marian Hall Floyd; m. T. Cole Hackley, Apr. 10, 1993. BA, Calif. State U., Sacramento, 1961; MA, Ohio State U., 1984, PhD, 1985. Pub. rels. dir., tchr. Lincoln Unified Schs., Stockton, Calif., 1961-63; advt. promotion copy writer, columnist Hawaii Newspaper Agy., Legis. Bur., Honolulu Star-Bull., 1964; instr. U. Nebr., Lincoln, 1964-66, Ohio State U., Columbus, 1972-80, 82-85; exec. dir. Jour. Assn. Ohio Schs., Columbus, 1974-80, 82-85; asst. prof. U. Hawaii, Manoa, 1980—82; prof. pub. rels. comm. dept. U. Pacific, Stockton, 1985—, chair comm. dept., 1992-94, intern coord., 1985—2006, experiential edn. dir. comm. dept., 2006—; pub. rels. cons. Hackley Ent. Inc., 1995—; owner, pub. rels. and sr. cons. Pacific Pub. Rels., 1999—. Pub. rels. cons. Hall & Hall Prescriptive Pub. Rels., Stockton, 1987—91; prof.-in-residence Edelman Pub. Rels. Worldwide, Syndey, London, San Francisco, 1990—92; dir. mktg. and univ. rels. U. of Pacific, Stockton, San Francisco, Sacramento, 1997—98; adj. prof. Benerd Sch. Edn., 2006—. Co-author: Wordsmithing: The Art and Craft of Writing for Public Relations, 2006. Chmn. bd. dirs. Mountain Valley Multiple Sclerosis, Stockton, 1989—91; pub. rels. dir., sec. Battleship Iowa Mus. Meml. Found., 2006—07. Fellow: Coll. Fellows, Pub. Rels. Soc. Am. (v.p. Oakland/East Bay chpt. 1994, educators sect., internat. sect., mem. internat. pub. rels. exec. com. 1995, del. nat. assembly 1995—97, pres.-elect 1997, pres. 1998, del. nat. assembly 2001—03, ethics officer 2001—03, del. nat. assembly 2006, Nat. Paul M. Lund Pub. Svc. award 2006); mem.: Assn. Edn. Journalism and Mass Comm., Internat. Comm. Assn., Stockton C. of C. (edn. task force 1996—99), Navy League US (life; pres. Stockton coun. 1997—98, chair nat. pub. affairs com. 1997—99, nat. dir. 1997—, mem. steering com. spl. adv. pub. rels. 2003—04, mem. Puerto Vallarta coun., pres. amb. to Mex. 2003—05, nat. v.p. pub. rels. 2004—05, Pacific Ctrl. region v.p. PR 2005—06, pres. Stockton coun. 2006—, mem. internat. com. 2006—, nat. v.p. pub. rels. 2001—02, Nat. Pres. award 2004). Avocations: singing, cooking, travel. Home: 2618 Sheridan Way Stockton CA 95207-3246 Office: Univ of the Pacific 3601 Pacific Ave Stockton CA 95211-0197 Home Phone: 209-478-3470; Office Phone: 209-946-3046. Personal E-mail: tchackley@yahoo.com.

HACKMAN, ANNA, pharmacist; b. Marshfield, Wis., Jan. 11, 1958; d. Jack and JoAnne Wirtz Hackman; m. David Ross Morris, Mar. 24, 2001; 1 child, Harli Ann Morris. PhD in Pharmacy, U. Minn., Mpls., 2003. Lic. pharmacist Minn., 2003, Wis., 2004. Staff pharmacist VA Med. Ctr., Mpls., 2003—. Medication reconciliation pilot Va. Med. Ctr., 2006—07. Contbr. articles to profl. jours. Avocations: sailing, motorcycling. Office: Va Med Ctr One Veterans Dr Minneapolis MN 55417 Business E-Mail: anna.hackman@med.va.gov.

HACKMAN, GENE (EUGENE ALDEN HACKMAN), actor; b. San Bernardino, Calif., Jan. 30, 1930; s. Eugene Ezra H.; m. Faye Maltese, Jan. 1, 1956 (div. 1986) children: Christopher, Elizabeth, Leslie; m. Betsy Arakawa, 1991. Appeared in stage prodns. The Natural Look, Death and the Maiden, others; film roles include Mad Dog Coll, 1961, Lilith, 1964, Hawaii, 1966, First to Fight, 1967, A Covenant With Death, 1967, Bonnie and Clyde, 1967, First to Fight, 1967, The Split, 1968, Riot, 1969, The Gypsy Moths, 1969, Downhill Racer, 1969, I Never Sang for My Father, 1969, Marooned, 1970, Doctor's Wives, 1971, The Hunting Party, 1971, The French Connection 1971 (Acad.award for Best Actor, Golden Globe award, Brit. Acad. award, N.Y. Film Critics award), Cisco Pike, 1971, Prime Cut, 1972, The Poseidon Adventure (Brit. Acad. award), 1972, Scarecrow, 1973 (Cannes Film Festival award), The Conversation, 1974, Zandy's Bride, 1974, Young Frankenstein, 1974, The French Connection II, 1975, Bite the Bullet, 1975, Night Moves, 1975, Lucky Lady, 1975, A Bridge Too Far, 1977, The Domino Principle, 1977, March or Die, 1977, Superman, 1978, Superman II, 1980, All Night Long, 1981, Reds, 1981, Two of a Kind (voice only), 1983, Under Fire, 1983, Uncommon Valor, 1983, Misunderstood, 1984, Eureka, 1984, Target, 1985, Twice in a Lifetime, 1985, Power, 1986, Superman IV: The Quest for Peace, 1987, No Way Out, 1987, Another Woman, 1988, Bat*21, 1988, Split Decisions, 1988, Mississippi Burning, 1988 (Best Actor award Nat. Soc. Film Critics, Acad. Award nomination), Full Moon in Blue Water, 1988, The Package, 1989, Postcards From The Edge, 1989, Class Action, 1989, Loose Cannons, 1990, Narrow Margin, 1990, Company Business, 1991, Unforgiven, 1992 (Acad. award for Best Supporting Actor, Golden Globes, N.Y., L.A., Boston Film Critics, Nat. Soc.Film Critics awards), The Firm, 1993, Geronimo: An American Legend, 1993, Wyatt Earp, 1994, The Quick and the Dead, 1995, Crimson Tide, 1995, Get Shorty, 1995, Extreme Measures, 1996, The Chamber, 1996, The Birdcage, 1996, The Magic Hour, 1997, Absolute Power, 1997, Enemy of the State, 1998, Antz (voice only), 1998,

Twilight, 1998, The Replacements, 2000, The Mexican, 2001, Heartbreakers, 2001, Heist, 2001, The Royal Tenenbaums, 2001 (Golden Globe/Best Actor in a Comedy 2001, Chgo. Film Critics award for best actor 2002, Nat. Soc. Film Critics award 2002, AFI award 2002), Behind Enemy Lines, 2001, Runaway Jury, 2003, Welcome to Mooseport, 2004; acted, exec. prodr. Under Suspicion, 1999; (TV films) Ride with Terror, 1963, Shadow on the Land, 1968, My Father and My Mother, 1968.; (TV appearances-)The United States Steel Hour, 1959, 60, 62, The Defenders, 1961, 63, Look up and Live, 1963, Naked City, 1963, The DuPont Show of the Week, 1963, East Side/West Side, 1963, The Trials of O'Brien, 1966, The F.B.I., 1967, The Invaders, 1967, The Iron Horse, 1967, I Spy, 1968; Author (with Daniel F. Lenihan) Wake of the Perdido Star, 2000, Justice for None, 2004. Hon. chmn. Permanent Charities Com. of the Entertainment Industries. USMC, 1946—49. Named Star of Year, Nat. Assn. Theatre Owners, 1974 Office: care Fred Spector 9830 Wilshire Blvd Beverly Hills CA 90212-1804

HACKMAN, MARVIN LAWRENCE, lawyer; b. Jasper, Ind., Jan. 29, 1934; s. Theodore Peter and Sarah Rose (Bellner) H.; m. Jane Marie Sermersheim, Aug. 23, 1958; children: Stephen J., Anne M., Michael A., Daniel T. AB summa cum laude, St. Joseph Coll., 1956; JD magna cum laude, Ind. U., 1959. Bar: Ind. 1959, U.S. Dist. Ct. (so. dist.) Ind. 1959, U.S. Ct. Appeals (7th cir.) 1960. Law clk. to chief judge U.S. Dist. Ct., Indpls., 1959-61; mem. Hackman Hulett & Cracraft LLP, Indpls., 1961—. Mem. ABA, Ind. State Bar Assn., Indpls. Bar Assn., Phi Delta Phi, Order of Coif. Home: 4021 Royal Pine Blvd Indianapolis IN 46250-2272 Office: 111 Monument Cir Ste 3500 Indianapolis IN 46204 Home Phone: 317-849-5634; Office Phone: 317-636-5401. Business E-Mail: mhackman@hhclaw.com.

HACKMAN, VICKI LOU, physician; b. Lancaster, Pa., Nov. 11, 1952; d. Harry Eugene and Marian Ruth (Miller) Hackman; m. James Roger Begley, June 3, 1989 (dec.). BS cum laude, Lebanon Valley Coll., 1974; MD, Med. Coll. of Pa., 1978. Resident St. Margaret Meml. Hosp., Pitts., 1978—81; family practitioner Norlanco Med. Assoc., Elizabethtown, Pa., 1981-84; physician KRON Med. Corp., Chapel Hill, NC, 1984—88; hosp. based family practice Mary Breckenridge Hosp., Hyden, Ky., 1988—90; pvt. family practice Medway (Maine) Family Practice, 1990—94; physician Intermountain Health Care, South Jordan, Utah, 1995—99, Berea (Ky.) Primary Care, 1999—. Active staff Millinocket (Maine) Regional Hosp., 1990—94, Cottonwood Hosp., Salt Lake City, 1995—99, Berea Hosp., 1999—; cons. Elizabethtown (Pa.) Hosp. and Rehab. Ctr., 1982—84. Mem.: Am. Acad. Family Practice. Republican. Methodist. Avocations: horses, farming. Home: 1080 College Hill Rd Waco KY 40385-9735 Office Phone: 859-985-1415. E-mail: vichac@msn.com.

HACKNEY, HUGH EDWARD, lawyer; b. McGregor, Tex., July 17, 1944; BA, So. Meth. U., 1966, JD, 1970. Bar: Tex. 1970. Ptnr. Fulbright & Jaworski, LLP, Dallas, 1970-97, Locke Liddell & Sapp LLP, Dallas, 1997—2005; shareholder Greenberg Traurig, LLP, Dallas, 2005—. Fellow: Coll. of Labor and Employment Lawyers; mem. ABA, London Ct. Internat. Arbitration, Chartered Inst. Arbitrators (London), State Bar Tex., Dallas Bar Assn., Houston Bar Assn., Phi Alpha Delta, Soc. Internat. Bus. Fellows, Internat. Bar Assn. Business E-Mail: hackneyh@gtlaw.com.

HACKNEY, JACK DEAN, physician; b. Marion, Ill., Oct. 11, 1924; s. William F. and Betty (Monical) H.; m. Dorothy Anne Stublefield, Sept. 8, 1946; children: Richard W., Robert J. Student, So. Ill. Univ., 1941-43, Yale U., 1943; MD, St. Louis U. Sch. Medicine, 1948. Diplomate Am. Bd. Internal Medicine, Acad. Toxicol. Scis. Resident in internal medicine VA Hosp., St. Louis, 1949-51, White Meml. Hosp., LA, 1953-54; rsch. assoc. Loma Linda U., LA, 1954-57, asst. to assoc. prof., 1957-69; prof. medicine U. So. Calif., LA, 1969-94, prof. emeritus, 1994—; dir. pulmonary lab. Rancho Los Amigos Med. Ctr., Downey, Calif., 1969-92, chief environ. health, 1970-94, emeritus, 1994—. Mem. EPA Sci. Adv. Bd., Washington, 1984-86; cons., 1986-92. Editor/author: Inhalation Toxicology of Air Pollution, 1993; contbg. author: Bronchial Asthma: Mechanics and Therapeutics, 1985, 93; contbr. articles to profl. jours. Mem. air quality adv. com. Dept. Health Svcs., State of Calif., 1974-94, med. adv. panel South Coast Air Quality Mgmt. Dist., 1985-92. 1st lt. AMC, 1951-53, Korea. Recipient Calif. medal Am. Lung Assn. Calif., 1992. Fellow Am. Coll. Chest Physicians, Am. Coll. Toxicology; mem. Am. Physiol. Soc., Am. Thoracic Soc., Alpha Omega Alpha, Sigma Xi. Achievements include development of indirect method for measuring respiratory ventilation; extraction of gases from blood for Gas Chromatographic analysis; control of exposure facilities and methods to study human inhalation toxicology and use of these facilities to demonstrate ozone toxicity, adaptation to ozone, and determine exposure responses to many inhaled gas and particle pollutants. Home: 5181 Duenas Laguna Hills CA 92637-1878 Office: Environmental Health Svc RLAMC 7601 Imperial Hwy # 51 Downey CA 90242-3456

HACKNEY, JAMES ACRA, III, industrial engineer, consultant, retired manufacturing executive; b. Washington, NC, Sept. 27, 1939; s. James Acra Jr. and Margaret Dunston (Hodges) H.; m. Constance Garrenton, June 5, 1961; children: Kenneth Ross, Jane H. Kemsley. BSME, N.C. State U., 1961, BS in Indsl. Engring, 1962. Registered profl. engr., N.C. With Hackney Industries, Inc., Washington, NC, 1961—95, chief engr., 1961—63, asst. gen. mgr., 1963—65, exec. v.p., gen. mgr., 1965—70, pres., CEO, 1970—90; chmn. bd. dirs. Hackney & Sons, Inc., Washington, 1990—95; mng. dir. Hackney Group, Washington, 1995—. Bd. dirs. Sprint Mid-Atlantic Telecom, Wake Forest, N.C., 1987-97, Bank of Am., North Coast region, N.C., chmn., 1995—; mem. adv. coun. Sch. Engring., East Carolina U., 2004—; mem. adv. coun. Sch. Mech. and Aerospace Engring., N.C. State U., 2002—. Chmn. Blackbeard dist. Boy Scouts Am., 1970-74, pres. East Carolina coun., 1976-77, mem. nat. exec. bd., 1987—, pres. S.E. region, 1987-89; chmn. bd. trustees Beaufort County Hosp., 1975-77; trustee N.C. State U., Raleigh, 1979-87, chmn. bd. trustees, 1985-87; mem. Interam. Scout Com., World Orgn. Scout Movement, 1984-88; lay Eucharistic min. Zion Episcopal Ch., Washington, N.C., 2002—; gen. campaign chmn. Beaufort County United Way, 1998-2000. Recipient Disting. Service award Washington Jaycees, 1970; Silver Beaver award Boy Scouts Am., 1975, Silver Antelope award, 1982, Disting. Eagle Scout award, 1980, Silver Buffalo award, 1992; Youth of the Ams. award World Orgn. Scout Movement, 1990, John Southam Journalism award Sail Am., 1997; named N.C. Small Businessman of Yr., SBA, 1971, Young Engr. of Yr., NSPE, 1971. Fellow NSPE; mem. Inst. Indsl. Engrs. (chpt. pres. 1967-68), Profl. Engrs. N.C. (pres. Ea. Carolina chpt. 1971-72, state sec. 2000-01, state treas. 2001-02, pres.-elect 2002-03, pres. 2003-04, Outstanding Young Engr. 1970-71), N.C. Engring. Found. (bd. dirs. 1977-79, N.C. Citizens for Bus. and Industry (bd. dirs. 1979-86), Washington C. of C. (pres. 1972-74, Outstanding Cmty. Svc. award 2000), N.C. State U. Alumni Assn. (bd. dirs. 1976-80, Outstanding Young Alumnus 1975, Disting. Engring. Alumnus 1984, Watauga Medal 1997), Rotary (pres. 1978-79), Pamlico Plantation Yacht Club (commodore 1993).

HACKNEY, MARCELLA WICHSER, biology professor; b. New Orleans, La., Sept. 29, 1947; d. Celeste George Wichser and Lucille Eileen Leach; m. William Philip Hackney, Dec. 28, 1968; children: Amy Hackney Blackwell, Philip, Madeleine, Ryan. BS in Sci. Edn., U. New Orleans, 1968; MNS in Natural Scis., La. State U., Baton Rouge, 1984; PhD in Curriculum Instrn., La. State U., 1999. Type A 049885 gen. sci., biology, chemistry, academically gifted La. Tchr. biology and chemistry Dominican H.S., New Orleans, 1969—70; tchr. life sci. Istroma Mid. Magnet, Baton Rouge, 1985—86; tchr. biology Scotlandville Magnet H.S. and H.S. for Engring., Baton Rouge, 1986—2000; asst. prof. biology Baton Rouge C. C., 2000—. Presenter in field. Co-author: The Power of Analogy: Teaching Biology with Relevant Classroom-Tested Activities, 2002; contbr. articles to profl. jours. Mem., docent, sec., pres. Patrons of La. State U. Mus. Natural Sci., Baton Rouge, 1983—90. Recipient Tchg. Excellence award, NISOD, 2003, LCTCS, 2003. Mem.: Nat. Assn. Biology Tchrs. (presenter, Outstanding Biology Tchr. 1990), Phi Kappa Phi. Avocations: travel, reading, gardening. Office: Baton Rouge C C 5310 Florida Blvd Baton Rouge LA 70806

HACKNEY, (FRANCIS) SHELDON, history professor, former academic administrator; b. Birmingham, Ala., Dec. 5, 1933; s. Cecil Fain and Elizabeth (Morris) H.; m. Lucy Judkins Durr, June 15, 1957; children: Virginia Foster, Sheldon Fain, Elizabeth Morris. BA, Vanderbilt U.; MA, Yale U., 1955, Ph.D, 1963; LLD (hon.), U. Pa., 1966. Asst. prof. history Princeton U., NJ, 1965—69, assoc. prof. NJ, 1969—72, prof., provost NJ, 1972—75; pres. Tulane U., New Orleans, 1975—80; prof. history U. Pa., Phila., 1981—, pres., 1981-93, pres. emeritus, 1993—, Boies prof. history, 2004—; chmn. NEH, Washington, 1993-97. Bd. dirs. Nat. Trust for the Humanities, Am. Forum Global Edn., Nat. Video Resources. Author: Populism to Progressivism in Alabama, 1969, One America Indivisible, 1997. Bd. dirs., chmn. Rosenback Mus. and Libr.; vestry Christ Ch., Phila. With USNR, 1956-61. Recipient Charles S. Sydnor award So. Hist. Assn., 1970; Bevridge prize Am. Hist. Assn., 1970. Mem. Am. Philos. Soc., Am. Hist. Assn., So. Hist. Assn., Orgn. Am. Historians. Office: U Pa 215D College Hall Philadelphia PA 19104 Business E-Mail: shackney@history.upenn.edu.*

HACKNEY, VIRGINIA HOWITZ, lawyer; b. Phila., Jan. 11, 1945; d. Charles Rawlings and Edith Wrenn (Pope) Howitz; m. Barry Albert Hackney, Feb. 15, 1969; children: Ashby Rawlings, Roby Howison, Trevor Pope. BA in Econs., Hollins Coll., 1967; JD, U. Richmond, 1970. Bar: Va. 1970. Assoc. Hunton & Williams, Richmond, Va., 1970-77, ptnr., capital fin., real estate, 1977—, also dep. gen. counsel. Pres. Am. Acad. Hosp. Attys. Chgo., 1992-93. Mem. agy. evaluation com. United Way of Greater Richmond, 1981-86; sustainer Jr. League of Richmond; mem. and fellow Am. Health Lawyers Assn. (pres. 1992-93, bd. dirs. 1988-94). Recipient Women of Achievement award, Met. Richmond Women's Bar Assn., 1998, Distinction award Va. Women Attys. Assn., 2006; named Outstanding Woman in Field of Law, YWCA, Richmond, 1981. Fellow Am. Health Lawyers Assn. (past pres.); mem. ABA (forum com. health law 1982—), Va. State Bar (long range planning com. 1985-90, chmn. standing com. lawyer discipline 1986-90, exec. com. 1988-90, Bar Coun. mem. 1984-90), Va. Bar Assn. Avocations: book tapes, reading, boating, jogging/walking. Office: Hunton & Williams Riverfront Plz East Tower 951 E Byrd St Richmond VA 23219-4074 Office Phone: 804-788-8263. Office Fax: 804-788-8218. Business E-Mail: vhackney@hunton.com.

HADAS, ELIZABETH CHAMBERLAYNE, editor; b. Washington, May 12, 1946; d. Moses and Elizabeth (Chamberlayne) H.; m. Jeremy W. Heist, Jan. 25, 1970 (div. 1976); m. Peter Eller, Mar. 21, 1984 (div. 1998). AB, Radcliffe Coll., 1967; postgrad., Rutgers U., 1967—68; MA, Washington U., St. Louis, 1971. Editor U. N.Mex. Press, Albuquerque, 1971—85, dir., 1985—2000, spl. acquisitions editor, 2000—06. Bd. dirs. N.Mex. Humanities Coun., 2001—07. Mem. Assn. Am. Univ. Presses (pres. 1992-93). Democrat. Home: 2900 10th St NW Albuquerque NM 87107-1111 E-mail: ehadas@unm.edu.

HADAS, RACHEL, poet, educator; b. NYC, Nov. 8, 1948; d. Moses and Elizabeth (Chamberlayne) H.; m. Stavros Kondilis, Nov. 7, 1970 (div. 1978); m. George Edwards, July 22, 1978; 1 child, Jonathan. BA in Classics, Radcliffe Coll., 1969; MA, Johns Hopkins, 1977; PhD, Princeton U., 1982. From adj. to assoc. prof. Rutgers U., Newark, 1981-92, prof., 1992—, Bd. Govs. Prof., 2002—; adj. prof. Columbia U., NYC, 1992-93. Vis. prof. Hellenic studies program Princeton U., 1995. Author: (poetry) Slow Transparency, 1983, A Son From Sleep, 1987, Pass It On, 1989, Living in Time, 1990, Mirrors of Astonishment, 1992, Other Worlds Than This, 1994, The Empty Bed, 1995, The Double Legacy, 1995, Halfway Down the Hall: New and Selected Poems, 1998, Indelible, 2001, Laws, 2004, The River of Forgetfulness, 2006, (criticism) Merrill, Cavafy. Poems and Dreams, 2001. Recipient award Am. Acad. Inst. Arts and Letters, 1990; Guggenheim fellow in poetry, 1988-89. Fellow Am. Acad. Arts and Scis.; mem. MLA, Poets, Essayists and Novelists. Democrat. Avocation: reading. Home: 838 W End Ave Apt 3A New York NY 10025-5365 Office Phone: 973-353-5279 ext. 520. Business E-Mail: rhadas@rutgers.edu.

HADDA, JANET RUTH, language educator, lay psychoanalyst; b. Bradford, Eng., Dec. 23, 1945; arrived in US, 1948; d. George Manfred and Annemarie (Kohn) H.; m. Allan Joshua Tobin, Mar. 22, 1981; stepchildren: David, Adam. BS in Edn., U. Vt., 1966; MA, Cornell U., 1969; PhD, Columbia U., 1975. Rsch. psychoanalyst So. Calif. Psychoanalytic Inst., LA, 1988—, tng. and supervising analyst, 1995—, Inst. Contemporary Psychoanalysis, 1993—; prof. Yiddish emerita UCLA, 2004—. Author: Yankev Glatshteyn, 1980, Passionate Women, Passive Men: Suicide in Yiddish Literature, 1988, Isaac Bashevis Singer: A Life, 1997, with New Introduction, 2003; contbr. articles to profl. jours. Mem. MLA, Assn. Jewish Studies, Am. Psychoanalytic Assn., Inst. Contemporary Psychoanalysis, New Ctr. Psychoanalysis, Phi Beta Kappa.

HADDAD, EDMONDE ALEX, public affairs executive; b. LA, July 25, 1931; s. Alexander Saleeba and Madeline Angela (Zail) H.; m. Harriet Ann Lenhart; children: Mark Edmonde, Brent Michael, John Alex. AA, Los Angeles City Coll., 1956; BA, U. Southern Calif., 1958; MA, Columbia U., 1961. Staff writer Sta. WCBS, NYC, 1959-61; news commentator, editor Sta. KPOL AM-FM, LA, 1961-67, dir., pub. affairs, 1967-73; exec. dir. L.A. World Affairs Coun., 1973-84, pres., 1984-88; dep. asst. sec. of state for pub. diplomacy Dept. State, Washington, 1987-88. Steering com., moderator Conf. environ., LA, 1989-90; pres. Nat. Coun. World Affairs Orgns., 1981-83; pres. Radio and TV News Assn. So. Calif., 1965-66; sr. fellow Ctr. Internat. Rels., U. Calif.; apptd. by Gov. Gray Davis to Gov.'s Blue Ribbon Adv. Panel on Hate Groups, 1999—. Author: Look to the Rainbow, 1997; contbg. author: How Peace Came to the World, 1985; founder, pub. World Affairs Jour. Quar., 1981; chair editl. bd. The Episcopal News, 2002-. Apptd. hon. canon Episcopal Cathedral St. Paul, LA, 2004. Recipient Am. Polit. Sci. Assn. award for Disting. Reporting of Pub. Affairs, 1967. Democrat. Avocations: poetry, reading, travel. Personal E-mail: edmondeh@aol.com.

HADDAD, ERNEST MUDARRI, lawyer; b. Boston, Oct. 30, 1938; s. Abraham and Elaine (Mudarri) H.; children: Barton Edward, Scott Cochrane and Mark Mudarri. BA, Trinity Coll., Hartford, Conn., 1960; LLB, Boston U., 1964. Bar: Mass. 1964, U.S. Dist. Ct. Mass. 1966, U.S. Supreme Ct. 1981. Asst. dean sch. law Boston U., 1966-71; asst. sec., gen. counsel Commonwealth of Mass. Exec. Office Human Svcs., Boston, 1971-76; gen. counsel Blue Cross and Blue Shield Mass. Inc., Boston, 1976-80; sec., gen. counsel The Mass. Gen. Hosp., Boston, 1981—2002, Ptnrs. HealthCare Sys., Inc., Boston, 1995—2002; assoc. dean, prof. law Boston U. Sch. Law, 2002—. Bd. dirs. Internat. Inst. Boston, chmn. nominating and governance com., 2003—, mem. exec com., 2003—. Program chmn., mem. exec. com. Boston Study Group, 1979—; bd. dirs. New Eng. Legal Found., 2001—. Recipient Trinity Coll. Alumni medal for Excellence, 1990. Mem. ABA, Am. Soc. Law, Medicine and Ethics, Boston Bar Assn. (mem. coun. 1998-02, exec. com. 1999-02, fin. com. 1999-02, treas. 2001-02, audit com. 2003—, chmn. 2005—), Boston Bar Found. (trustee 1998-04, nominating com. 1999-2004, chmn. audit com. 2005-), Boston U. Law Sch. Alumni Assn. (pres. 1998-99), Discovering Justice (bd. visitors 2004-). Office: 765 Commonwealth Ave Boston MA 02215 Home: 620 Lewis Wharf Boston MA 02110 Home Phone: 617-645-5220, 617-314-3520; Office Phone: 617-353-3105. Business E-Mail: ehaddad@bu.edu.

HADDAD, FRANCOIS, cardiologist, researcher; s. Fouad Haddad and Denise Maziade. MD, Montreal U., 1998. Lic. Med. Bd. Internal Medicine, 2003, Med. Bd. Cardiology, 2004. Intern Sacre Couer Hosp., 1998—99; resident Montreal U. Med. Ctr.; cardiovasc. fellow Montreal Heart Inst., 2004—05, chief fellow in cardiology, 2003—04; advanced fellow heart failure & heart transplantation Stanford U., Palo Alto, Calif., 2005—06, advanced fellow heart failure & pulmonary hypertension, 2006—07. Contbr. articles to profl. jours. Supporter Wild Life funds, San Francisco, 2002—07. Recipient Young Investigator award, U. Montreal, 2002, Montreal Heart Inst., 2005; grantee Rsch. grant, Quebec Cardiology Assn., 2005—07. Fellow: Royal Coll. Physicians and Surgeons Can. (assoc.); mem.: Am. Heart assn., Am. Coll. Cardiology, Pulmonary Hypertension Soc. (assoc.). Achievements include research in heart failure, heart transplantation and pulmonary hypertension; comparative linguistics. Avocations: history, hiking, classical music, linguistics. Office: Stanford Univ 300 Pasteur Dr Palo Alto CA 94305 Office Phone: 650-723-4000. Business E-Mail: fhaddad@stanford.edu.

HADDAD, FREDDIE DUKE, JR., resource development professional; b. Charleston, W.Va., Oct. 18, 1952; s. Freddie Duke Haddad Sr. and Betty Jane (Perry) Campbell; m. Cynthia Ann LaMaster, July 17, 1976; children: Freddie Duke III, Shannon Lynn. BS, W.Va. U., 1974; MPA, Marshall U., 1976; EdD, W.Va. U., 1986. Grad. asst. W.Va. Grad. Coll., Charleston, 1974-75; assoc. dir. devel. U. Louisville, Ky., 1976—77; dir. alumni affairs Fla. Internat. U., Miami, 1977-79; dir. alumni/devel. U. Charleston, W.Va., 1979-81; pvt. practice bus. cons. Charleston, 1981-82; dir. alumni/devel. Butler U., Indpls., 1982-89; dir. devel. St. Vincent Hosp. Found., Indpls., 1989-98, v.p. devel., exec. dir., 1998—2005; exec. dir. St. Vincent Mercy Hosp. Found., Elwood, Ind., 1995-99; sr. assoc. Demont & Assocs., Inc., Portland, Maine, 2005—06; v.p. for devel. The Children's Med. Ctr. Dayton, Ohio, 2007—. Adj. prof. Nova U., Ft. Lauderdale, Fla., 1978-79; cons. in field. Contbr. articles to profl. jours. Mem. parish coun. St. George Orthodox Ch., Indpls., 1990-93; mem. com. Hall of Fame awards com. ARC, Indpls., 1991—; sec., v.p. Lawrence Twp. Babe Ruth League, Indpls., 1991-93; bd. dirs. Lawrence Twp. Edn. Found., Indpls., 1994-98, pres., 1999; mem. deve. com. Archochion Orthodox Christian Archdiocese N.Am. Recipient Disting. Alumnus award Marshall U. Grad. Coll., 2002, Hon. Sec. of State award State of Ind., 2002, Outstanding Fundraising Exec. award Ind. AFP, 2003; named Ky. Col., Gov. Ky., Frankfort, 1976, Outstanding Young Men of Am., 1986, Outstanding West Virginian, Gov. W.Va., Charleston, 1994, Sagamore of Wabash, Gov. Ind., 1996. Mem.: Assn. Healthcare Philanthropy (Jour. award 1993), Assn. Fundraising Profls. (cert. fund raising exec., bd. dirs. 1990—95, v.p., pres.-elect Ind. chpt. 1992—94, Red Cross Hall of Fame com. 1992—, pres. 1995, nat. AFP edn. curriculum com. 1996, Pres.'s award 1993), Ascension Health Nat. Coun. Philanthropy (1st v.p. 1998—99, pres. 1999—2000, bd. dirs. 2001—), W.Va. U. Alumni Assn. (mountaineer amb. 1991—), N.E. Indpls. Kiwanis (pres. 2006). Avocations: reading, writing, race walking, golf. Office: Childrens Med Ctr Dayton One Childrens Plaza Dayton OH 45404-1815 Office Phone: 937-641-5960. Personal E-mail: fdhaddad1@aol.com. Business E-Mail: haddadd@childrensdayton.org.

HADDAD, HESKEL MARSHALL, ophthalmologist, educator; b. Baghdad, Iraq, Sept. 26, 1930; came to US, 1953, naturalized, 1962; s. Moshe M. and Masuda (Cohen) H.; m. Doris I. Fatzer, July 4, 1963; children: Ava Masuda Geffen, Andreas Moshe, Michael Albert. Student, Royal Coll. Medicine, Baghdad, 1945—50; MD, Hebrew U., Jerusalem, 1953. Diplomate Am. Bd. Pediatrics, Am. Bd. Ophthalmology; ordained rabbi, 1997. Intern Donolo Hosp., Jaffo-Tel Aviv, Israel, 1950-51; rotating intern Hadassah U. Hosp., Jerusalem, 1951-53; pediatric resident Children's Med. Center, Boston, 1953-56; fellow in pediatric endocrinology Johns Hopkins Hosp., Balt., 1956-58; fellow in clin. endocrine br. Nat. Inst. Arthritis and Metabolic Diseases, NIH, Bethesda, Md., 1958-59, pediatrician sect. clin. endocrinology, 1959-60; asst. prof. pediatrics sch. medicine Howard U., Washington, 1959-60; resident, asst. dept. ophthalmology sch. medicine Washington U., St. Louis, 1960-64; leave of absence, 1962-63; fellow pediatric ophthalmology Inst. Visual Sci., San Francisco, 1962; research fellow Hôpital des Quinze-Vingts, Laboratoire de Physiologie de Vision, Ecole des Hautes Etudes, Paris, 1962-63; ophthalmologist Hôpital Beni Messous, Algiers, Algeria, 1964; asst. attending ophthalmic surgeon, also asst. prof. ophthalmology Mt. Sinai Hosp. and Sch. Medicine, NYC, 1964-67; dir. dept. ophthalmology Beth Israel Med. Center, NYC; also assoc. prof. ophthalmology Mt. Sinai Sch. Medicine, 1967-71; clin. prof. ophthalmology NY Med. Coll., 1971—. Author: Endocrine Exophthalmos, 1973, Metabolic Eye Diseases, 1974, Metabolic-Peditric Eye Diseases, 1979, Metabolic Ophthalmology: Diagnostic Techniques Vols. I and II, 1985, Jews of Arab and Islamic Countries: History, Problems and Solutions, 1984, (autobiography) Flight from Babylon, 1986, Born in Baghdad, 2005; editor-in-chief: Metabolic Ophthalmology, 1976-79, Metabolic and Ophthalmology, 1976-79, Metabolic and Pediatric Ophthalmology, 1979-82, Metabolic, Pediatric and Systemic Ophthalmology, 1982—; contbr. articles to profl. jours.; holder 7 US patents. Pres. Am. Com. for Rescue and Resettlement of Iraqui Jews, World Orgn. Jews from Arab Countries, Parents' Assn. of Sch. of Performing Arts, 1980-83. Fellow ACS, Am. Inst. Chemists; mem. Am. Endocrine Soc., Am. Fedn. Clin. Research, Assn. Research Ophthalmology and Vision, AMA, NY County Med. Soc., AAAS, Am. Acad. Ophthalmology, NY Acad. Medicine, NY Acad. Scis., NY Soc. Clin. Ophthalmology, Soc. Eye Surgeons, Société Française d' Ophthalmologie, German Ophthal. Soc., Internat. Soc. Metabolic Eye Disease (founder, sec.-treas. 1973—), World Soc. on Systemic Ophthalmology (founder, sec.-treas. 1982, chmn.), NY County Med. Soc. (chmn. com. fgn. med. grads. 1985-90, del. NY State Med. Soc. 1985-86, chmn. rev. commn. 2005—). Achievements include patents in field. Office: 1125 Park Ave New York NY 10128-1243 Office Phone: 212-427-1246. Personal E-mail: optoedcorp@aol.com. *The Commandment of "loving one's neighbor" should read "Thou shalt love for thy neighbor as for thy self." Whereas we cannot always control the emotion of love, we are consciously able to stop doing unto others what we do not like for ourselves.*

HADDAD, JAMES HENRY, chemical engineer, consultant; b. Willimantic, Conn., Jan. 30, 1923; s. William Addy and Nellie (Birbarie) H.; m. Isabel Serrano, Feb. 3, 1962; children: Frederick William, Francis Xavier. BS in Engring., Yale U., 1944. Chem. engr. Conn. Hard Rubber Co., New Haven, 1943-44; engr. rsch. dept. Mobil Rsch. Devel. Corp., Paulsboro, N.J., 1944-52, engr. engring. dept. NYC, 1952-70, sr. engring. cons. Princeton, N.J., 1971-89; ind. cons. worldwide Catalytic Processing/Solids Sys., Princeton Junction, N.J., 1989—. Contbr. articles to profl. publs.; patentee in field, petroleum refining and shale retorting sys. Budget com., trustee Princeton Area Communities United Way, 1977-90. Mem. Am. Chem. Soc., Am. Inst. Chem. Engrs., Alpha Chi Sigma. Avocation: swimming. Home and Office: 120 Tunicflower Ln Princeton Junction NJ 08550-1645 Home Phone: 609-918-1535; Office Phone: 609-918-1535. Fax: 609-918-1536.

HADDAD, JAMIL RAOUF, retired physician; b. Mosul, Iraq, Aug. 18, 1923; came to U.S., 1952, naturalized, 1965; s. Raouf Sulaiman and Fadhila (Shaya) Haddad; m. Mary Lou Scorsone, Aug. 1, 1959 (dec. 2001); children: Ralph J.(dec.) , John L., James M. M.B., Ch.B., Iraqi Royal Coll. Medicine, Baghdad, Iraq, 1946. Med. officer Khanaqin (Iraq) Hosp., 1946-52; asst. resident pathology Crawford W. Long Meml. Hosp., Atlanta, 1953-54; resident Bellevue Hosp., NYC, 1954-56; practice medicine specializing in pathology NYC, 1963—, Passaic, NJ, 1981—; chmn. dept. anatomic and clin. pathology St. Clare's Hosp. and Health Center, NYC, 1971-81; dir. pathology and clin. lab. Gen. Hosp. Ctr. at Passaic, 1981—2003; ret. Assoc. Sloan-Kettering Inst. for Cancer Rsch., NYC, 1960—66; asst. prof. pathology NYU Coll. Medicine, 1959—65, asst. clin. prof. pathology, 1965—67, assoc. clin. prof. pathology, 1967—70, clin. prof. pathology, 1970—85; asst. prof. exptl. cell biology Mt. Sinai Grad Sch. Biol. Scis., NYC, 1966—70, lectr., 1971—83, adj. asst. prof., 1983—88. Mem. Coll. Am. Pathologists, Am. Soc. Clin. Pathologists, AMA, N.Y. Pathol. Soc., N.Y. State, New York County med. socs. Home: 420 E 23rd St Apt MC New York NY 10010-5043 Office Phone: 212-982-0655.

HADDAD, MARK E., lawyer; BA magna cum laude, Boston Coll., 1980, JD cum laude, 1983. Bar: Mass. 1983, Supreme Judicial Ct. Mass., US Dist. Ct. (Mass.), US Ct. Appeals (1st & 4th cir.). Adminstrv. ptnr. & mem. mgmt. com. Kirkpatrick & Lockhart Nicholson Graham LLP, Boston. Mem.: ABA (Forum on Constrn. Industry), Mass. Bar Assn., Boston Bar Assn. (Constrn. & Real Estate Com.). Office: Kirkpatrick & Lockhart Nicholson Graham LLP 75 State St Boston MA 02109-1814 Office Phone: 617-261-3116. Office Fax: 617-261-3175. Business E-Mail: mhaddad@klng.com.

HADDAD, NADIM FAWZI, engineer, researcher; b. Ramleh, Palestine, Nov. 2, 1943; s. Fawzi Salim and Margaret Haddad; m. Selma (Sally) Siemer Burkhart, Apr. 4, 1971; children: Randa Margaret Downs, Michael Nadim. BA in Physics and Math., Kans. Wesleyan U., Salina, 1965; MSEE, Mich. State U., East Lansing, 1966. Sr. tech. staff IBM Corp., Manassas, Va., 1967—94, Loral Corp., Manassas, 1994—97, Lockheed Martin, Manassas, 1997—2000; engring. fellow BAE Sys., Manassas, 2000—. Contbr. 90 articles to profl. jours. Active Holy Transfiguration Melkite Cath. Ch., McLean, Va. Named one of Outstanding Young Men of Am., 1972; recipient Def. Cert. of Recognition award, US Dept. Def., 2006. Mem.: IEEE. Independent. Melkite Greek Catholic. Achievements include development of 8 genertions of radiation hardened electronic tech. for space applications; 20 inventions in hardened microelectronics. Avocation: music. Home: 2704 Berryland Dr Oakton VA 22124 Office: BAE Sys 9300 Wellington Rd Manassas VA 20110 Home Phone: 703-620-5182; Office Phone: 703-367-5251. Business E-Mail: nadim.haddad@baesystems.com.

HADDAD, RAMSI, medical geneticist, educator; m. Catherine Elizabeth Le Feuvre, Sept. 27, 1997; children: John Ramsi, Thomas Samir. BS with honors, McMaster U., Hamilton, Ontario, Can., 1990; PhD, SUNY, Buffalo, 1999. Rsch. scientist Van Andel Inst., Grand Rapids, Mich., 2001—03; rsch. assoc., perinatology rsch. br. Nat. Inst. Child Health and Devel., Detroit, 2003—06; asst. prof. Wayne State U. Sch. Medicine, Detroit, 2006—. Dir., lab. translational oncogenomics Karmanos Cancer Inst., Detroit, 2006—. Mem.: Am. Assn. Cancer Rsch. Home: 4352 Showdown Ave Ontario Windsor Canada N9G 3C2 Office: Karmanos Cancer Inst 4100 John R St Detroit MI 48201 Home Phone: 519-250-8576; Office Phone: 313-576-8857.

HADDADY, SHIRIN, medical educator; b. Tehran, Iran, June 14, 1967; d. Nayereh Pezeshk and Hamid Haddady; m. Farshid Alizadeh-Shabdiz, June 17, 1993; children: Pardis Alizadeh-Shabdiz, Sarah Alizadeh-Shabdiz, Jasmin Alizadeh-Shabdiz. MD, Tehran U., 1992. Resident Tehran U., Georgetown U., Washington, 1999—2002; fellow U. Mass., Worcester, 2002—05, instr., 2005—. Rsch. asst. Walter Reed Army Med. Ctr., Wash. Hosp. Ctr., Washington, 1998—99; rschr. U. Mass., 2002—. Contbr. articles to profl. jours. Recipient Appreciation for Quality of Patient Care, 1994, Best Poster Presentation, 2001, 2002. Mem.: AMA, Internat. Soc. Clin. Densitometry, Am. Assn. Clin. Endocrinologists, Am. Soc. Reproductive Medicine, Endocrine Soc. Avocations: travel, cooking. Home Phone: 508-358-1013; Office Phone: 508-856-1128.

HADDAWAY, JAMES DAVID, retired insurance company official; b. Louisville, July 25, 1933; s. Charles Montgomery Jr. and Viola (Sands) H.; m. Myrna Lou (Harris), June 5, 1954 (dec. Sept. 1999); children: Peggy Ann, Robert Marshall, Susan Gayle; m. Janie Louise (Young), Mar. 25, 2000. BS in Commerce, U. Louisville, 1960; MBA, Xavier U., Cinn., 1973. Cert. adminstrv. mgr., purchasing mgr., sr. profl. human resources. Ins. cons. Met. Life Ins., Louisville, 1955—59; supt. Byck Bros. and Co., Louisville, 1959—61; purchasing mgr. Liberty Nat. Bank, Louisville, 1961—63; v.p., mgr. gen. svcs. adminstrn. Citizens Fidelity Bank, Louisville, 1963—79; asst. v.p., mgr. human resources Ky. Farm Bur. Ins. Co., Louisville, 1979—95; ret., 1995. Founder, chmn. emeritus Kentuckiana Expn. Bus. and Industry, 1973-85; mem. First Bapt. Ch., Hillsboro, Tex; Rep. party Hill county precinct chmn., Hillsboro, Tex., 2006-07. Served in the 11th Airbourne Divsn., U.S. Army, 1953-55. Named Boss of Yr., Louisville Chpt. Nat. Sec. Assn., 1978, 79. Mem.: Internat. Caravaning Assn., North Tex. Airstream Cmty. (chmn. pub. rels. com. 2006—07, bd. mem. 2006—07), Nat. Assn. Purchasing Mgmt. (dir. nat. affairs 1970—71), Louisville Soc. Advancement Mgmt. (pres. 1993—94, dir. 1994—95, charter), Ky. C. of C. (chmn. banking and ins. health and welfare sub-com. project 21 1988), Nat. Assn. Ind. Insurers (pers. com. 1987—95), Soc. Human Resource Mgmt. (chmn. conf. com. region nine 1984, dist. dir., western Ky. 1984, v.p. region nine 1985—86, Ky. coun. chmn. 1986), Conf. Casualty Ins. Co. (chmn. nat. pers. conf. com. 1983), Louisville Soc. Human Resource Mgmt. (pres. 1983—84, chmn. reorgn. com. 1992, Profl. Excellence award 1993), Purchasing Mgmt. Assn. Louisville (pres. 1969—70), Adminstrv. Mgmt. Soc. (pres., Louisville 1975—76, bd. dir. 1976—92, nat. dir. 1979—81, charter mem. found.), Am. Assn. Individual Investors (life), Bass Anglers Sportsman Soc. (life), Land Yacht Port O'Call Airstream Pk. (co-chmn. computer club 1998, chmn. 1999), Nat. Eagle Scout Assn. (life), Wally Byam Caravan Club Internat. (life; pres., Ky. unit 1993, chmn. long range planning com. 1994, second v.p. region five 1996—97, first v.p. region five 1998—99, pres. region five 2000—01, internat. second v.p. 2002—03, internat. first v.p. 2003—04, internat. pres. 2004—05, chair internat. nominating com. 2005—06, chmn. Nat. Merit award com. 2006), Univ. Club Louisville (charter), Good Sam Recreational Vehicle Club (life), Shriners, Am. Legion, Masons, Order Ky. Col. Home: 200 Walnut Hill Ave # 90 Hillsboro TX 76645

HADDEN, ARTHUR ROBY, lawyer, retired judge; b. San Antonio, Feb. 13, 1929; s. Will Alexander and Kathleen (Westerman) H.; m. Marellyn Frances Denton, June 23, 1956; children: Neilson, Lynne, Wesley, Arthur. BBA, U. Tex., 1952, LLB, 1957. Bar: Tex. 1957, U.S. Dist. Ct. (ea. dist.) Tex. 1959, U.S. Ct. Appeals (5th cir.) 1961, U.S. Supreme Ct. 1970, U.S. Dist. Ct. (no. dist.) Tex. 1975. Lawyer Ramey, Brelsford, Hull and Flock, Tyler, Tex., 1957-70; U.S. atty. Ea. Dist. Tex., Tyler, 1970-77; lawyer, sole practice Law Offices Roby Hadden, Tyler, 1977-94; justice 12th Ct. Appeals, Tex., 1995-2000; assigned justice Tex. Ct. Appeals, Tex., 2001—04; ret., 2004. Mem. Fed. State Law Enforcement Commn. Tex., Austin, 1976-77. Mem. Human Subjects Investigation Commn. U. Tex. Hosp., Tyler, 1980-90, Mayor's Anti-Crime Task Force, Criminal Justice Div., Tyler, 1986-88. Capt. USAF, 1952-54. Fellow Tex. Bar Found.; mem. Smith County Bar Assn., Nat. Assn. Former U.S. Attys., Coll. of State Bar of Tex., Downtown Rotary Tyler, Rotary Internat. Republican. Home and Office: 3335 Heines Dr Tyler TX 75701-9034

HADDEN, JOHN WINTHROP, immunopharmacology educator; b. Berkeley, Calif., Oct. 23, 1939; s. David Rodney Hadden; m. Elba Mas, July 31, 1964; children: John W. II, Paul J. BA, Yale U., 1961; MD, Columbia U., 1965. Asst. prof. pathology U. Minn., Mpls., 1972-73; assoc. prof. Cornell Grad. Sch., NYC, 1973-82; assoc. mem., dir. lab. immunopharmacology Sloan-Kettering Meml. Cancer Inst., NYC, 1973-82; prof. medicine, dir. div. immunopharmacology U. South Fla., Tampa, 1982-99; founder, chief sci. officer IRX Therapeutics, NYC, 1999—. Cons. in field.; vis. prof. U. South Fla. Med. Coll., Nat. Cancer Inst., Mex. Assoc. editor Internat. Jour. Immunopharmacology, 1978-86, editor, 1986-99; editor 12 textbooks; contbr. chpts. to books, more than 300 articles to profl. jours. Mem. Am. Assn. Immunologists, Am. Soc. Pharm. & Exptl. Therapy, Internat. Soc. Immunopharmacology (v.p. 1982-85, pres. 1985-88, publ. officer 1988-99, treas. 1999-2002), Tampa Yale Club (v.p. 1986-91) Achievements include patents for 10 methods of imparting immunomodulating activity. Home: 428 Harbor Rd Cold Spring Harbor NY 11724-2108 Office: Immuno-Rx Inc 140 W 57th St Ste 9C New York NY 10019-3326 Office Phone: 212-582-1199. E-mail: jwhadden@optonline.net.

HADDOCK, FRED(ERICK) T(HEODORE), JR., retired astronomer; b. Independence, Mo., May 31, 1919; s. Fred Theodore Sr. and Helen (Sea) H.; m. Margaret Pratt, June 24, 1941 (div. Sept. 1976); children: Thomas Frederick, Richard Marshall; m. Deborah J. Fredericks, Dec. 7, 2003. SB, MIT, Cambridge, 1941; MS, U. Md., 1950; DSc (hon.), Rhodes Coll., Memphis, 1965, Ripon Coll., Wis., 1966. Physicist U.S. Naval Rsch. Lab., Washington, 1941-56; assoc. prof. elec. engring. and astronomy U. Mich., Ann Arbor, 1956-59, prof. elec. engring., 1959-67, prof. astronomy, 1959-88, emeritus prof., 1988—. Lectr. radio astronomy Jodrell Bank U. Manchester, Eng., 1962; vis. assoc. radio astronomy Calif. Inst. Tech., 1966; vis. lectr. Raman Inst., Bangalore, India, 1978; sr. cons. Nat. Radio Astron. Obs., W.Va., 1960-61; founder, dir. U. Mich. Radio Astron. Obs., 1961-84. Contbr. chpts. to books, articles to profl. jours. and publs. Mem. Union Radio Sci. Internat., nat. chmn. commn. on radio astronomy, 1954-57; trustee Associated Univs., Inc., 1964-68; prin. investigator, five Orbiting Geophys. Observatories, 1960-74, and Interplanetary Probe 9, 1964-77; co-investigator on Voyager planetary probes, 1970-86, NASA, Washington; mem. astronomy adv. panel NSF, Washington, 1957-60, 63-66. With USN, 1944-45. Fellow IEEE (life), Am. Astron. Soc. (v.p. 1961-63); mem. Internat. Astron. Union (commn. on radio astronomy 1948—), NAS (adv. panel astronomy facilities 1962-64), AIA (hon. mem. Huron Valley chpt. 1980—), Sigma Xi (past pres. U. Mich. chpt. 1956—). Achievements include design and development of first submarine periscope radar antenna, 1943-44; early discoveries in microwave astronomy, gaseous nebulae in 1953 and early space detection of kilometer waves from galaxy and the sun, 1962. Home: 3935 Holden Dr Ann Arbor MI 48103-9415 Office: U Mich Astronomy Dept Ann Arbor MI 48109 Office Phone: 734-662-7245. Business E-Mail: fhaddock@umich.edu.

HADDOCK, JORGE, industrial engineering educator, consultant; b. Caguas, PR, Aug. 15, 1955; s. Jorge and Francisca (Acevedo) H.; m. Maria A. Valentin, June 7, 1980; children: M. Angelique, D. Alexander. BSCE, U. P.R., 1978; MS in Mgmt. Engring., Rensselaer Poly. Inst., 1979; PhD in Indsl. Engring., Purdue U., 1981. Instr. engring. U. P.R., Mayaguez, 1978-81, asst. prof. Rio Piedras, 1981-83, Clemson (S.C.) U., 1984-86; asst. prof. indsl. engring. and ops. rsch. Rensselaer Poly. Inst., Troy, N.Y., 1986-90, assoc. prof., 1990—. Cons. Sistema, Inc., San Juan, P.R., 1980, Mgmt. and Janitorial Svcs., San Juan, 1982-83, Computer Data Svcs., San Juan, 1982, Baxter-Travenol Labs., Maricao, P.R., 1982, Citibank, N.A., San Juan, 1982, Michelin Tires, Greenville, S.C., 1986, Globe Internat., Buffalo, 1988, Jiffy Lube, Albany, N.Y., 1990, Bendix, Green Island, N.Y., 1990, also others; participant numerous workshops, confs. and meetings. Author: User-Oriented Operations Research Methodologies, 1987, (with S. Bohl) Instructor's Manual for Engineering Economy, 1989; mem. editorial bd. Internat. Jour. Computer Simulation; contbr. articles to profl. jours., chpts. to books. Bd. dirs. Hispanic Outreach Svcs., Albany, 1990-92. Recipient numerous grants. Mem. Inst. Indsl. Engrs. (sr., pres. Capital-Berkshire chpt. 1989-90, bd. dirs. 1990—, Outstanding Young Indsl. Engr. award 1990), Ops. Rsch. Soc. Am., Inst. Mgmt. Scis. (assoc.), Soc. Computer Simulation, Nat. Acad. Engring. Mex. (corr.), KC (3 degree, chancellor Clemson 1985-86), Tau Beta Pi (charter sec.-treas. Piedmont chpt. 1985-86). Avocation: basketball. Office: Dept Decision Scis-Engring Syst Rensselaer Poly Instit Troy NY 12180

HADDOCK, RAYMOND EARL, retired career officer; b. Oklahoma City, Sept. 26, 1936; s.Clyde William and Ida Belle (Lemmon) H.; m. Brunhilde Ernestine Becker, Oct. 21, 1960; children: Ralph William, Ronald Raymond, Karen Elizabeth Haddock Fralen. BS in Chemistry, W. Tex. State U., Canyon, 1958; MS in Pub. Adminstrn., Shippensburg Coll., Pa., 1977; grad., US Army War Coll., Carlisle Barracks, Pa., 1977. Commd. 2d lt. US Army, advanced through grades to maj. Gen., capt. and maj. advisor to Vietnam forces, 1966—67, bn. comdr. Pershing Missile Bn., 56th F.A., 1973-75, pers. staff officer (G-1) 8th Inf. Div. Germany, 1975-76, dir. internat. programs Tng. and Doctrine Command Fort Monroe, Va., 1977-80, comdr. 9th Div. Arty. Fort Lewis, Wash., 1980-83, chief of staff Tng. Ctr. Fort Dix, NJ, 1983-84, comdg. gen. Pershing Missile Command 56th F.A. Germany, 1984-87; comdr., dir. US mil. forces US Command, Berlin, 1988-90; comdg. gen. US Army Security Assistance Command, Alexandria, Va., 1990-92; v.p. ITT Def. Internat., McLean, Va., 1993—2003, ret., 2003. Participant fall of Berlin wall, reunification of Germany and US-Soviet nuclear forces treaty, 1987. Decorated D.S.M. with two oak leaf clusters; Fed. Order of Merit, Berlin; Order of Merit (Fed. Republic Germany); Gold Nat. Def. medal (France). Avocations: sailing, fishing, jogging, hunting, genealogy.

HADDOCK, ROBERT LYNN, information services entrepreneur, writer; b. Vallejo, Calif., May 12, 1945; s. Orville Walter and Lee Ellen (Alexander) H. BA, Union Coll., 1967; postgrad., NYU, 1977-81. Editor So. Pub. Assn., Nashville, 1969-74, controller, 1974-75; mktg. analyst Bus. Publs. div. Prentice-Hall, Englewood Cliffs, N.J., 1975-78, bus. mgr., 1978-81, Ziff-Davis Pub. Co., NYC, 1981-82, dir. bus. devel., 1982-83; pres. Personal Access, Inc., NYC, 1983-84; v.p., dir. product devel. Citicorp Global Report, NYC, 1984-86, v.p., dir. mktg., 1986-88; v.p., dir. product devel. Citibank, N.A., NYC, 1989-90; v.p., dir. product devel. and mktg. Enhanced Telephone Svcs., Inc., NYC, 1990-91; pres. M-Power Corp., NYC, 1991-98, Global Strategy Ptnrs., NYC, 1998—2004. Author: The Broken Web, 1973, How to Stop Smoking, 1974; inventor database accessing system, 1983, enhanced telephone, 1989, digital screen phone, 1993. Mem. IEEE, Am. Assn. Artificial Intelligence, Software and Info. Industry Assn., Mensa. Business E-Mail: rhaddock@globalstrategypartners.com.

HADDON, HAROLD ALAN, lawyer; b. Flint, Mich., Dec. 2, 1940; s. Russell Daniel and Virginia Sibyl (Johnston) H.; m. Beverly Jean Reading, July 2, 1966. AB, Albion Coll., 1962; A.M., U. Mich., 1963; JD, Duke U., 1966. Bar: Colo. 1966, U.S. Dist. Ct. Colo. 1966, U.S. Ct. Appeals (10th cir.) 1966, U.S. Supreme Ct. 1977; cert. trial counsel U.S. Cts. Martial. Asso. firm Davis, Graham & Stubbs, Denver, 1966-70; chief trial dep. Colo. Pub. Defender, 1970-73; ptnr. Haddon, Morgan & Foreman, Denver, 1975—. Adj. prof. law in criminal trial advocacy U. Denver Sch. Law, 1972-73; spl. prosecutor Colo. State Grand Jury, 1976-78 Editor-in-chief Duke Law Jour., 1965-66. Sec. Nat. Multiple Sclerosis Soc., 1970-76; mem. Colo. U.S. Jud. Selection Com., 1977, 93; campaign mgr. U.S. Sen. Gary W. Hart, 1974-80; fin. chmn. Colo. Gov. Richard D. Lamm, 1978; nat. polit. coordinator Hart for Pres. campaign, 1987. Lt. comdr. USNR, 1968—. Fellow Am. Coll. Trial Lawyers, 1988; mem. Am., Colo., Denver bar assns., Nat. Assn. Criminal Def. Lawyers, Order of Coif, Phi Beta Kappa, ABA (commn. on complex fed. criminal cases, 1981-82, criminal justice standards com., 1991-92, 2002-). Democrat. Office: Haddon Morgan Mueller Jordan Mackey & Foreman PC 150 E 10th Ave Denver CO 80203

HADDON, JAMES FRANCIS, banker; b. Columbia, SC, Aug. 12, 1954; s. Wallace James and Ida Beatrice (Bassette) H.; m. Sezelle Antoiniette Gereau. BA, Wesleyan U., 1976; MBA, Stanford U., 1980. Bank mgmt. trainee Mellon Bank, Pitts., 1976-78; assoc. Blyth Eastman Paine Webber Inc., NYC, 1980-83; v.p. Paine Webber Inc., NYC, 1983-93; mng. dir. pub. fin. Smith Barney, Inc., NYC, 1993—. Mem. Sponsors for Ednl. Opportunities, N.Y.C., 1982—; trustee Wesleyan U., 1994-97. Mem. Nat. Assn. State Treas., Nat. Assn. of Securities Profls. (treas. 1993-97, sec. 1997—, Skull and Serpent Soc., Wesleyan Black Alumni Assn (steering com. 1984-86). Clubs: N.Y. Athletic. Office: Smith Barney Inc 390 Greenwich St New York NY 10013-2375

HADDY, FRANCIS JOHN, internist, educator; b. Walters, Minn., Sept. 6, 1922; s. Thomas J. and Frances (Shaheen) H.; m. Theresa Eileen Brey, Sept. 21, 1946; children: Richard, Carol, Alice. Student, Luther Coll., Decorah, Iowa, 1940-42; BS, U. Minn., 1943, M.B., 1946, MD, 1947, MS in Physiology, 1949, PhD in Physiology (Am. Heart Assn. fellow), 1953. Diplomate: Am. Bd. Internal Medicine. Intern Mpls. Gen. Hosp., 1946—47; fellow internal medicine Mayo Found., 1949—51; asst. prof. physiology and medicine Northwestern U. Med. Sch., 1953—61; clin. investigator VA Rsch. Hosp., Chgo., 1957—59; prof. physiology, chmn. dept., assoc. prof. medicine U. Okla. Med. Center, 1961—66; prof. physiology, chmn. dept. Mich. State U., East Lansing, 1966—76; prof. physiology Uniformed Svcs. U., Bethesda, Md., 1976—99, chmn. dept. physiology, 1976—87; mem. Mayo grad. faculty dept. physiology and biomed. engring. Mayo Clinic Coll. Medicine, Rochester, Minn., 2003—. Mem. cardiovasc. study sect. NIH, 1963-69; tng. com. Nat. Heart and Lung Inst., NIH, 1970-73; mem. atherosclerosis and hypertension adv. com. Nat. Heart, Lung and Blood Inst., NIH, 1983-86; rsch. com. Am. Heart Assn., 1974-80; mem. life scis. adv. com. NASA, 1986-92, chmn., 1988-92, mem. aerospace med. adv. com. 1988-93, mem. NASA-NIH adv. com., 1993-95; sr. scientist NASA/Johnson Space Ctr. SC med. scis. divsn., Houston, 1989-90; cons., peer rev. adminstr. for cardiopulmonary, integrative physiology, and clin. areas NASA, 1995—. Mem. editl. bd. Am. Jour. Physiology, 1963-69, 80-86, Jour. Applied Physiology, 1963-69, Procs. Soc. Exptl. Biology and Medicine, 1969-72, Circulation Rsch., 1975-81, Microvascular Rsch., 1978-81, Hypertension, 1978-81, Jour. Am. Coll. Nutrition, 1993-99. Recipient Med. Sci. Achievement award Am. Heart Assn., 1987, Scientist Emeritus awrd Soc. Exptl. Biology and Medicine, 1996-97, Disting. Alumnus award Mayo Found., 2003, Disting. Svc. award Luther Coll., 2004. Fellow Am. Coll. Nutrition (coord. hypertension and cardiovasc. diseases 1992-98, bd. dirs. 1993-97, publs. com. 1994-99, ann. award 1986); mem. Am. Physiol. Soc. (steering com. circulation group 1972-75, chmnm. com. on coms. 1974-77, coun. 1976-79, pres. 1981, fin. com. 1983-89, chmn. fin. com. 1985-89, select com. on animal care 1988-91, chmn. long range planning com. 1990-93, hon. com. 1993-95, chmn. 1995, Carl J. Wiggers award 1966), Am. Soc. Clin. Investigation, Fedn. Am. Socs. Exptl. Biology (bd. dirs. 1980-83, treas. 1990-92, rep. to Am. Assn. Accreditation Lab. Animal Care trustees 1993-96, exec. com. 1995-96), Internat. Union Physiol. Scis. (US nat. com. 1976-79, 81-84), Nat. Hypertension Assn. (trustee 1979—, v.p. 2003—), NAS (basic biomed. scis. panel, com. on nat. needs for biomed. and behavioral rsch. pers. Inst. Medicine 1983-86), Assn. Chairmen Depts. Physiology (chmn. animal welfare com. 1986-87), Aerospace Med. Assn. (publ. com. 1994-95), Am. Soc. for Gravitational and Space Biology (awards com. 1994-99), Montgomery County Art Assn. (pres. 1997-98), Mayo Found. (Disting. Alumnus award, 2003). Achievements include left heart catherization, small vein and artery catherization, mechanisms of pulmonary edema, fluid flux across the capillary membrane, local regulation of blood flow, ionic action on blood vessels, and low renin hypertension. Home: 211 2nd St NW Apt 1607 Rochester MN 55901-2896 Business E-Mail: tbhaddy@aol.com.

HADDY, THERESA BREY, pediatrician, educator, hematologist, oncologist; b. Wabasso, Minn., Feb. 27, 1924; d. Francis William and Elizabeth Katherine (Daub) Brey; m. Francis John Haddy, Sept. 21, 1946; children: Richard Ian, Carol Haddy Froelich, Alice Haddy Hellen. BS, U. Minn., 1944, MB, 1946, MD, 1948. Diplomate in pediatrics and in pediatric hematology/oncology Am. Bd. Pediatrics. Intern Mpls. Gen. Hosp., 1947—48; resident in pediat. U. Minn., Mpls., 1950—52; fellow in hematology U. Okla., 1962—64; practice medicine, specializing in gen. pediatr. Des Plaines, Ill., 1954—61; asst. prof., dir. pediat. hematology oncology U. Okla., Oklahoma City, 1961—66; chief child health Mich. Dept. Pub. Health, Lansing, 1966—69; assoc. prof., dir. pediat. hematology oncology Mich. State U., East Lansing, 1969—76; expert in blood diseases NIH, Bethesda, Md., 1977—79; assoc. prof. , dir. pediat. hematology oncology Howard U., Washington, 1979—87, prof., 1987—89, prof. emeritus, 1989—. Guest rschr. pediat. oncology br. NIH, NCI, Bethesda, 1989-2001; mem. acad. adv. staff Children's Nat. Med. Ctr., Washington, 2000—. Author: Country Doctor and City Doctor: Father and Daughter, 2006; contbr. over 100 articles to profl. jours. Mem. Am. Soc. Hematology, Am. Soc. Pediat. Hematology/Oncology (publs. com. 2002-04), Nat. Hypertension Assn. (adv. bd. 2002—), Am. Soc. Clin. Oncology, NIH Alumni Assn. Episcopalian. Personal E-mail: tbhaddy@aol.com.

HADEN, CLOVIS ROLAND, retired academic administrator, engineering educator; b. Houston, Apr. 10, 1940; s. Clovis Newton and Mary Aline (Baker) H.; m. Joyce Elaine Weathers, Aug. 8, 1956; children: Cathy, Kimberly, Clay. Student, Navarro Coll., Corsicana, Tex., 1958—59; BSEE, U. Tex., Arlington, 1961; MSEE, Calif. Inst. Tech., Pasadena, 1962; PhD, U. Tex., 1965. Lic. profl. engr., Tex., Okla. Asst. prof. U. Okla., 1965—68; dir. Sch. Elec. Engring. and Computing Scis., 1972—78; assoc. prof. Tex. A&M U., College Station, 1968—71, prof., 1971—72, dir. Inst. Solid State Electronics, 1969—72; dean Coll. Engring and Applied Scis. Ariz. State U., Tempe, 1978—87, dean Coll. Engring. and Applied Scis., 1989—91, v.p. for acad. affairs, 1987—88, provost west campus Phoenix, 1988—89, mem., pres. Rsch. Park bd. Tempe, 1983—91; bd. dirs. Ariz. Transp. Rsch. Ctr., 1980—91; vice chancellor for acad. affairs La. State U., Baton Rouge, 1991—93; vice chancellor/dean engring., dir. engring. experiment sta. Tex. A&M U., 1993—2002. Mem. Ariz. Gov.'s Commn. on Sci. and Tech., 1980-82, chmn. transp. subcom., 1981-83, mem. adv. coun. for engring., 1979-91; mem. Ariz. Gov.'s High Tech. Coun., 1990-91; mem. Tex. Gov.'s Coun. Sci. & Tech., 1997-2002; chair strategic planning La. Ednl. Quality Support Fund, 1991-93; mem. Nat. Engring. Dean's Exec. Bd., 1984-87, 95-2000; mem. adv. group Coun. on Competitiveness, 1994-95; chmn. bd. Ariz. R&D Co., 1983-90; mem. adv. bd. A.T. Kearney, 1986-90; mem. Tex. Bd. Profl. Engrs., 2002-06. Exec. editor: Electric Power Sys. Rsch. Jour., 1978—. Bd. mgrs. Tempe YMCA, 1982-84; mem. Ariz. Econ. Devel. Bd., 1982-85; bds. dirs. Harrington Arthritis Rsch. Ctr., 1983-87, Inter-tel, Inc., 1983-05, Square D. Co., 1985-91, E-Sys., 1994-95, WAVO Corp., 1990-99, Crosstex Energy, 2002-06, Res. Valley Partnership, 2004—. Recipient George Washington Honor medal Freedoms Found., 1989, Disting. Alumnus award U. Tex., Arlington, 1995, Econ. Devel. award Phoenix area, 1985; Bur. Engring. rsch. fellow, 1964. Fellow IEEE (Oklahoma City Engr. of Yr. award 1977), Am. Soc. Engring. Edn. (chair pub. policy com. 1997-99, Marlowe award 1998, Lamme award 2007); mem. NSPE, Ariz. Soc. Profl. Engrs. (Engr. of Yr. award 1983), Ariz. Assn. Indsl. Devel., Coun. Tex. Engring. Deans (chmn. 1995-98), Tex. Soc. Profl. Engrs. (bd. dirs. 1995-98), Soc. Mfg. Engrs., Sons of Republic of Tex., Golden Key, Sigma Xi, Phi Kappa Phi, Eta Kappa Nu, Tau Beta Pi. Republican. Mem. Ch. of Christ. Personal E-mail: r-haden@tamu.edu.

HADEN-PINNERI, KATHRYN, pathologist; b. Harrisonburg, Va. m. Jason Pinneri. BS, La. Tech U., Ruston, 1986—89; MD, U. Tex., Dallas, 1993—97. Diplomate Am. Bd. Pathology, 2006. Asst. chief med. examiner Office of Chief Med. Examiner, Fairfax, Va., 2003—05; asst. med.

examiner Harris County Med. Examiners Office, Houston, 2005—. Mem.: Nat. Assn. Med. Examiners, Am. Acad. Forensic Scis. Office: Harris County Medical Examiners Office 1885 Old Spanish Trl Houston TX 77054

HADGES, THOMAS RICHARD, media consultant; b. Brockton, Mass., Mar. 13, 1948; s. Samuel Charles and Ethel Toli (Prifti) H.; m. Beth Evelyn Rastad, Oct. 22, 1988. BA in Biology magna cum laude, Tufts U., Medford, Mass., 1969; student, Harvard Sch. Dental Med., Cambridge, Mass., 1969—71. Announcer Sta. WOKW, Brockton, 1965-67, Sta. WTBS-FM, MIT, Cambridge, 1966-68; announcer, program dir. Sta. WTUR, Medford, Mass., 1967-69; announcer Concert Network, Sta. WBCN-FM, Boston, 1968-78, program dir., 1977-78, Sta. WCOZ-FM, Blair Broadcasting, Boston, 1978-80, Sta. KLOS-FM, ABC, LA, 1980-85; sr. programming advisor Pollack Media Group, Pacific Palisades, Calif., 1985-89, pres., 1989—, Pollack/Hadges Enterprises, Pacific Palisades, 1985-89. Coordinating prodr. live AID concerts Worldwide Radio, 1985, prodr. live 8 concerts, 2005, exec. prodr. live earth concerts, 07. Named Program Dir. of Yr., LA Times, 1981. Mem. Phi Beta Kappa. Avocations: jogging, electronics. Office: Pollack Media Group 860 Via De La Paz Ste D2 Pacific Palisades CA 90272-3663

HADJIANGELIS, NICOS PAVLOS, medical educator, consultant; b. Nicosia, Cyprus, Aug. 21, 1970; s. Pavlos Hadjiangelis and Litsa Hadjiangeli. Diploma in medicine, Nat. Kapodistrian U. of Athens, Greece, 1995; MBA, Columbia U., NYC, 2007. Diplomate Am. Bd. Internal Medicine, 2001, Am. Bd. Pulmonary Disease, 2003, Am. Bd. Critical Care Medicine, 2004. Intern in internal medicine Mt. Sinai Sch. Medicine at Englewood Hosp., NJ, 1998—99, resident in internal medicine, 1999—2001; fellow in pulmonary and critical care medicine NYU Sch. Medicine, NYC, 2001—04, med. instr., 2004—; med. cons. Odyssey Ho. Inc, NYC, 2004—. Chief med. resident Englewood Hosp., 2000—01; tchg. asst. medicine Mt. Sinai Sch. Medicine, Englewood, 2000—01. Recipient Outstanding Intern award, Englewood Hosp., 1999, Outstanding Student Tchg. award, 2000, Resident Leadership award, 2001, Gerald Weissman MD award for excellence in rsch., NYU Sch. Medicine, 2004; Travel Award grantee, Am. Thoracic Soc., 2004. Mem.: Hellenic Med. Soc. Greek Orthodox. Achievements include research in how the integrin avb6 knock-out mouse is protected from radiation induced pulmonary fibrosis; cryptic miliary tuberculosis with a prodrome resembling pancreatitis; propylthiouracil-related diffuse alveolar hemorrhage with negative serologies; membrane diffusion in diseases of pulmonary vasculature. Avocations: chess, weightlifting, swimming. Office: NYU Sch Medicine 462 1st Ave NB 7N New York NY 10016 Home Phone: 347-886-3308; Office Phone: 212-263-8423. Personal E-mail: nhadji@hotmail.com.

HADJILIADIS, DENIS, physician; arrived in US, 2005, permanent resident, 2007; s. Nick and Marietta Hadjiliadis; m. Tara Morrison, Apr. 8, 2000; 1 child, Caitlin S. MD, U. Toronto, Can., 1995; MHS, Duke U., 2001; PhD, U. Ioannina, Greece, 2004. Diplomate Am. Bd. Internal Medicine, Greek Ministry Health, Royal Coll. Physicians Can. Instr. U. Toronto, 2001—03, asst. prof. medicine, 2003—05, site edn. dir. Sunnybrook Hosp., med. dir. B4 med. team, 2003—05; asst. prof. medicine, assoc. med. dir. lung transplantation U. Pa., Phila., 2005—. Recipient McCabe award, U. Pa., 2006; Summer Student grantee, Ont. Lung Assn., 2003. Fellow: Royal Coll. Physicians and Surgeons Can., Am. Coll. Chest Physicians; mem.: Internat. Soc. Heart and Lung Transplantation, Am. Soc. Transplantation, Am. Thoracic Soc. Office: U Pa 835 W Gates Bldg 3400 Spruce St Philadelphia PA 19104 Home Phone: 856-489-3639; Office Phone: 215-615-0869. Office Fax: 215-662-3226. Business E-Mail: denis.hadjiliadis@uphs.upenn.edu.

HADL, JOHN, marketing executive; b. 1970; JD, NYU. Corp. lawyer Simpson Thatcher & Bartlett; exec. v.p., corp. devel. and strategy position Creative RX; chief strategy officer, co-founder Enverta; mng. dir. Quigley-Simpson Interactive; founder, CEO Brand in Hand. Adv. US Venture Partners; chief mobile strategy adv. Procter & Gamble. Spkr. in field. Named a Marketer of the Next Generation, BrandWeek, 2007; named one of 40 Under 40, Advt. Age, 2007.*

HADLEY, CHARLINE A., protective services official; b. Coffeyville, Kans., Aug. 8, 1947; d. Charles Wesley and Geraldine Virginia (Bates) Clithero; children: Melissa Reneé (Hadley) Dos Santos, Kimberly Dawn (Hadley) Mominah, George Edward. AA, Tulsa CC, 2002. Cert. notary pub. Sec. State Okla. Purchasing agt. Wagone County Okla., Wagoner, Okla., 1982—84; regional fin. officer Okla. Dept. of N.E. Dist. Corrections, 1996—2002, adminstv. programs office, 2002—. Fin. com. So. States Correctional Assn., 1994—. Treas. St. James Espic. Ch., Wagoner, 1985—92. Recipient Employee of Yr., Okla. Dept. Corrections, 1986, 1990, 1991, 2000, 2001. Mem.: Coun. for Exceptional Children, Okla. Edn. Assn., Nat. Edn. Assn., Okla. Corrections Assn., Am. Corrections Assn., So. States Corrections Assn. Democrat. Episcopalian. Avocations: reading, travel. Office: Okla Dept Corrections NE Dist Cmty Corrections 70015 Azalea Pack Dr Wagoner OK 74467

HADLEY, JOHN LIVINGSTON, V, management executive, writer; b. Nashville, Apr. 8, 1928; s. John Livingston Hadley IV and Eugenia Margaret Johnston-Hadley; m. Mary Lou Burt, Aug. 26, 1950; children: Pamela Diane, John Livingston, Burt Alexander. Student, Peabody Coll., 1946—47; BS in Indsl. Mgmt., U. Tenn., 1951. Messenger Western Union, Pryor, Okla., 1943—45; projectionist Pryor Theater, 1944—45; supr., foreman E.I. DuPont Co., Seaford, Del., 1952—53, supr. tech. lab. Kinston, NC, 1953—60, shift supr. mfg. Old Hickory, Tenn., 1960—78, supr. power engring., 1978—88; dir. Miss Rodeo Am. Pageant, Tenn., 1985—91; pres., corp. agt. Miss Rodeo Tenn. Pageant Inc., 1991—; amb./del. Miss Rodeo Am. Pageant, Pueblo, Colo., 1985—. Author: Trail Legacy, 1998, Alien Trail, 1999, Jonas One Horse Trail, 2000, The Two Horse Trail, 2001, Vicks Gold, 2002, Black Mountain Lair, 2003, Trouble in High Town, 2004, Ambush on the Rio Grande, 2006, Rattlesnake Smith, 2007. Mem.: NRA (benefactor), Gallatin Gun Club (past pres.). Republican. Avocations: reading, genealogy, hunting, rodeo, target shooting. Home and Office: Miss Rodeo Tenn Pageant Inc PO Box 53 Madison TN 37116 Office Phone: 615-868-4782.

HADLEY, KATHERINE G. (KIT), library director; Staff atty. So. Minn. Regional Legal Svcs. and the Legis. Advocacy Project, 1980—89; dep. commr., dir. intergovernmental rels. Minn. Fin. Housing Agy., commr., 1994—2002; dir. Mpls. Pub. Libr., 2003—. Mem. adv. bd. Met. Libr. Svc. Agy. Mem.: Minn. Libr. Assn. (Pres.'s award 2006). Office: Mpls Pub Libr 300 Nicollet Mall Minneapolis MN 55401 Office Phone: 612-630-6200. E-mail: kghadley@mplib.org.

HADLEY, LEILA ELIOTT-BURTON (MRS. HENRY LUCE III), writer; b. NYC, Sept. 22, 1925; d. Frank Vincent and Beatrice Boswell Eliott Burton; m. Arthur T. Hadley, II, Mar. 2, 1944 (div. Aug. 1946); 1 child, Arthur T. III; m. Yvor H. Smitter, Jan. 24, 1953 (div. Oct. 1969); children: Victoria C. Van D. Smitter Barlow, Matthew Smitter Burton Eliott, Caroline Allison F.S. Nicholson; m. William C. Musham, May 1976 (div. July 1979); m. Henry Luce III, Jan. 1990 (dec. Sept. 8, 2005). MD, St. Timothy's Sch., 1943; LLD (hon.), Mount St. Mary's Coll., Newburgh, NY, 2006. Author: Give Me the World, 1958, reprinted, 1999, Give Me the World, 2003, How to Travel with Children in Europe, 1963, Manners for Children, 1967, Fielding's Guide to Traveling with Children in Europe, 1972, rev., 1974, 1984, Traveling with Children in the U.S.A., 1974, Tibet-20 Years After the Chinese Takeover, 1979; author: (with Theodore B. Van Itallie) The Best Spas: Where to Go for Weight Loss, Fitness Programs and Pure Pleasure in the U.S. and Around the World, 1988, rev., 1989; author: A Journey with Elsa Cloud, 1997, paperback edit. with afterword, 2003, Give Me the World, 1999, A Garden by the Sea, 2005; assoc. editor Diplomat mag., N.Y.C., 1964—65, Saturday Evening Post, 1965—67, contbg. editor ICON: World Monuments Mag.; contbg. editor: Tricycle, the Buddhist Rev., 1991—; editl. cons. TWYCH, N.Y.C., 1985—87, book reviewer Palm Beach Life, Fla., 1967—72, consulting editor Tricyle, The Buddhist Rev., 1991—, garden columnist Fishers Island Gazette; contbr. articles to various newspapers, mags. Bd. dirs. Wings World Quest, Inc., 1992, Tibet House, 1995, Fishers Island Conservancy, 1995, Donald & Shelley Rubin Cultural Trust, 2001. Recipient Norman Vincent Peale award, 2002. Fellow Royal Can. Geog. Soc. (hon.); mem. Acad. Am. Poets, Soc. Woman Geographers, Authors Guild, Nat. Writers Union, Nat. Press Club, PEN, Explorers Club, Central Park Conservancy, Ocean Conservancy, N.Y. Acad. Medicine (guest bd.), The Kitchen Ctr. Haleakala, Inc., Nat. Arts Club, Lansdowne Club (Eng.). Office Phone: 212-759-8640. E-mail: leilahadleyluce1@aol.com.

HADLEY, MARLIN LEROY, financial planner, consultant; b. Mankato, Kans., Jan. 5, 1931; s. Charles LeRoy and Lillian Fern (Dunn) H.; m. Clarissa Jane Payne, Sept. 17, 1949; children: Michael LeRoy, Steven Lee. BS, U. Denver, 1953; postgrad., Harvard U., 1966. Pres. Jewel Home Shopping Service div. Jewel Cos., Inc., Barrington, Ill., 1953-72; pres., chief exec. officer, dir. Beeline Fashions, Inc., Bensenville, Ill., 1972-82; chmn. bd. HAS Originals, Blairstown, NJ, 1984—; fin., bus. cons. Pres., dir. Beeline Real Estate Corp., Act II Jewelry, Inc., Home Galleries, Inc.; dir. Goulder Co., Inc., Climax Spltys., Inc. Mem.: Economics (Chgo.). Home and Office: 7062 W Arlington Dr Lakewood CO 80123

HADLEY, RALPH VINCENT, III, lawyer; b. Jacksonville, Fla., Aug. 20, 1942; s. Ralph V. and Clare (Cason) H.; m. Carol Fox Hadley, Sept. 18, 1993; children: Graham Kimball, Christopher Bedell, Blair Vincent. BS, U. Fla., 1965, JD, 1968. Bar: Fla. 1968, Calif. 1972. Assoc. Kurz, Toole, Taylor & Moseley, Jacksonville, 1968-69; asst. atty. gen. State of Fla., Orlando, 1972-73; ptnr. Davids, Henson & Hadley, Winter Garden, Fla., 1973-80; sr. ptnr. Hadley & Asma, Winter Garden, 1980-89, Parker, Johnson, Owen, McGuire, Michaud, & Hadley, Orlando, 1989-91, Owen & Hadley, Orlando, 1991-94, Hadley, Gardner & Ornstein, P.A., Winter Park, Fla., 1994-95, Swann, Hadley & Alvarez, P.A., Winter Park, 1995—96; with Swann & Hadley, 1996—. Vice chmn. bd. dirs. Tucker State Bank, Winter Garden, 1981-88; vice chmn. bd. dirs., sec. Tucker Holding Co., Jacksonville, 1984-88; bd. dirs. BankFIRST. Bd. dirs. Orange County Dem. Exec. Com., Orlando, 1974-81, Spouse Abuse, Inc., Orlando, 1975-81. Lt. comdr. USN, 1969-72, Vietnam. Recipient Navy Achievement medal, Award of Merit, Orange County Legal Aid Soc., 1987, Disting. Svc. award Judge J.C. Jake Stone Legal Aid Soc., 1989, Pres. Pro Bono Svc. award Fla. Bar, 1992. Mem. ABA, Fla. Bar Assn., Calif. Bar Assn., Orange County Bar Assn. (legis. chmn. 1979, 82), Am. Inn of Ct. (master), Winter Park C. of C. (bd. dirs. 1979-80), West Orange C. of C. (bd. dirs. 1979-82), Rotary. Presbyterian. Office: Ste 350 1031 W Morse Blvd Winter Park FL 32789-3715 Home Phone: 407-862-2324; Office Phone: 407-647-2777. Business E-Mail: rhadley@swannhadley.com.

HADLEY, ROBERT JAMES, lawyer; b. Wilmington, Ohio, Oct. 27, 1938; s. Robert Edwin and Ethel Edith (Slade) H.; m. Judith Ellen Gilbert, Aug. 11, 1962; children: Scott, Laura, Stephen. BA in History cum laude, Ohio State U., 1960; LLB, Harvard U., 1963. Bar: Ohio 1963. Assoc. Smith & Schnacke, Dayton, 1963-69, ptnr., 1970-89, Thompson Hine LLP, Dayton, 1989—2003. Pres. Man-to-Man Assocs., 1978-84, Dayton Habitat for Humanity, 1988; v.p. COPE Halfway House, Dayton, 1982-85; dir., sec. Friendship Village of Dayton, 1985-2006; loaned exec. United Way, 1980-82, cabinet 2001-02; active Kettering Civic Band, 1968—; bd. dirs. Parish Resource Ctr., 1995-2005, pres., 1999-2000; bd. dirs. South Cmty. YMCA, 1996-98, Greater Dayton Youth for Christ, 1980-86; bd. dirs., sec. Ministry of Money, 1992—. Named Kettering Man of the Yr., 1986; Rotary Found. grantee, Israel, 1974. Mem. Dayton Bar Assn., Dayton Racquet Club, Rotary (pres. Kettering 1986-87, dist. gov., group rep. Dist. 6670 1989-90, dist. gov. 1993-94), Phi Beta Kappa. Methodist. Avocations: music, travel, sports. Home: 4848 Glenmina Dr Dayton OH 45440-2002 Personal E-mail: rjh4848@earthlink.net.

HADLEY, STANTON THOMAS, manufacturing executive, director, lawyer; b. Beloit, Kans., July 3, 1936; s. Robert Campbell and Helen (Schroeder) H.; m. Charlotte June Holmes, June 9, 1962; children: Gayle Elizabeth, Robert Edward, Stanton Thomas, Steven Holmes. BS in Metall. Engring., Colo. Sch. Mines, 1958; LLB, U. Colo., 1962. Bar: Colo. 1962, U.S. Dist. Ct. 1962, U.S. Patent Office 1963. Metallurgist ASARCO, Leadville, Colo., 1957; tng. engr. Allis-Chalmers Co., West Allis, Wis., 1958—61; adminstrv. engr. Ball Corp., Boulder, Colo., 1961—62, atty., 1962—65; patent counsel Scott Paper Co., Phila., 1965—71, USG Corp., Chgo., 1971—76, gen. mgr. metals div., 1976—79, group v.p. indsl. group, 1979—84, sr. v.p. adminstrn., sec., 1984, sec., 1984—87, sr. v.p. staff services, 1987—89; pres. Ansco Photo-Optical Products Corp., Chgo., 1989—93, Visador Co., Marion, Va., 1994—98. Bd. dirs. Masonite Corp., WJE Assocs. Inc., USG Found. Bd. dirs. Ill. Safety Council, North Suburban YMCA, Northbrook Symphony Orch.; former mem. founders' council Field Mus.; mem. Chgo. United, Chgo. Assn. Commerce and Industry. Served with U.S. Army, 1959. Mem. Am. Soc. Metals, Licensing Execs. Soc., Assn. Corp. Patent Counsel. Clubs: Union League, Sunset Ridge Country, Executives. Republican. Home: 555 Valley Way Northfield IL 60093-1067 Office: STH Cons 555 Valley Way Northfield IL 60093-1067

HADLEY, STEPHEN JOHN, national security advisor; b. Toledo, Feb. 13, 1947; m. Ann Simon; 2 children. BA, Cornell U., 1969; JD, Yale U., 1972. Analyst for the comptr. US Dept. Def., Washington, 1972—74; mem. NSC, Washington, 1974—77; assoc. Shea & Gardner, Washington, 1977—81, ptnr., 1981—89, 1993—2001; asst. sec., internat. security policy US Dept. Def., Washington, 1989—93; prin. The Scowcroft Group, Inc.; asst. to the Pres. & dep. asst. for nat. security affairs. NSC, Washington, 2001—05, asst. to the Pres. for nat. security affairs, 2005—. Counsel Presdl. Spl. Review Bd. on Arms Sales to Iran, 1986—87; former mem. Def. Policy Bd., Nat. Security Advisory Panel to the Dir. of Ctrl. Intelligence. Office: National Security Coun 1600 Pennsylvania Ave NW Washington DC 20500*

HADLEY, WILLIAM MELVIN, retired dean; b. San Antonio, June 4, 1942; s. Arthur Roosevelt and Audrey Merle (Barrett) H.; m. Dorothy J. Hadley, Jan. 21, 1967 (div. July 1989); children: Heather Marie, William Arthur; m. Jane F. Walsh, Oct. 13, 1990. BS in Pharmacy, Purdue U., West Lafayette, Ind., 1967, MS in Pharmacology, 1971, PhD in Toxicology, 1972. Teaching and grad. asst. Purdue U., West Lafayette, 1967-72; asst. prof. U. N.Mex., Albuquerque, 1972-76, assoc. prof., 1976-82, prof., 1982—2002, asst. dean Coll. Pharmacy, 1984-86, acting dean Coll. Pharmacy, 1985, dean Coll. Pharmacy, 1986—2002; prof. and dean emeritus Coll. Pharmacy, 2002—. Vis. scientist Lovelace Inhalation Toxicology Inst., Albuquerque, 1981, adj. scientist, 1991-2002, sr. scientist, 2002—; adv. bd. Waste Edn. Rsch. Consortium, Las Cruces, N.Mex., 1989-2003; dirs. adv. com. Nat. Ctr. for Eviron. Health, CDC, 2002-04, mem. NIH Proposal Rev. Panels, Bethesda, Md., 1983-84; mem. Gov.'s PCB Expert Adv. Panel, Santa Fe, 1985-86; sci. adv. bd. Carlsbad Environ. Monitoring Ctr., 1992-97; sci. adv. com. S.W. Regional Spaceport, Las Cruces, 1992-94; bd. dirs. Ctr. Excellence Hazardous Materials Mgmt., Carlsbad, N.Mex., 2005—; cons. in field. Steering com. United Fund, U.N.Mex., 1987, key person, 1988—97. NIH grantee, 1974-80, 83-87; Bowl of Hygeia, N.Mex. Pharm. Assn., 1998. Mem. AAAS, Am. Pharm. Assn., Am. Assn. Colls. of Pharmacy, Soc. Toxicology (pres. Rocky Mt. chpt. 1990-91), Western Pharmacology Soc. Republican. Achievements include research in biotransformation of xenobiotics with emphasis on nasal tissue; effects of heavy metals on biotransformation with emphasis on cadmium; toxic effects of xenobiotics on the immune system. Office Phone: 623-465-1813. Personal E-mail: wmhadley@aol.com.

HADLOW, VIVIAN JEAN, elementary school educator; b. Scottdale, Pa., June 5, 1934; d. Harry and Martha Pearl (Dailey) Wigley; m. Clarence Eugene Hadlow, Dec. 5, 1953 (dec.); children: Martin Lee, Patrick Donn, John Michael. B in Elem. Edn., Cleve. State U., 1972; M in Adminstrv. Supervision, Baldwin Wallace Coll., Berea, Ohio, 1984. Cert. tchr. Ohio, 1972. Tchr. Avon Local Schs., Ohio, 1965—92, prin., 1988—89; tchr. Pearl River County Schs., Carriere, Miss., 1998—2005; ret. Chairperson Task Force to Update Curriculum, Avon, 1979—80; substitute tchr. Sulphur Springs Pub. Schs. Recipient Martha Holden Jennings Scholar Plate, Martha Holden Jennings Found., Cleve., 1987—88. Republican. Methodist. Achievements include incorporating DARE program into Avon East Elementary School. Avocation: antiques. Home: 201 Marianne Cir Sulphur Springs TX 75482

HADYK-WEPF, SONIA MARGARET, artist, real estate manager; b. May 30, 1931; d. Albert and Margaret Wepf; m. Walter Hadyk, Feb. 14, 1957 (div.June 1976); 1 child, W. Gordon Hadyk. BS in Art Edn., Pratt Inst., 1954. Tchr. art Midland Park (N.J.) Jr. H.S., 1954-55, Lyncourt (N.Y.) Pub. Sch., 1969-70; staff artist Norcross Greeting Cards, NYC, 1955-56, Spencer Advt. Art, Union City, N.J., 1956-58, L.W. Peckham Advt., Syracuse, N.Y., 1958-59; freelance artist Syracuse, 1959-74; mgr. jewelry dept. Naum's, DeWitt, N.Y., 1974-75; owner Hadyk House of Gem Design, Syracuse, 1974—; mgr. Walter Hadyk Rental Homes, Syracuse, 1993—. Guest lectr. Carrier Women's Club, Syracuse, 1972, Nat. League Pen Women, Syracuse, 1972; juror Arts and Crafts Festival, Camillus (N.Y.) Hist. Soc., 1973. Designer, craftsman (cultured pearl necklace) Golden Claws, 1971, (bracelet) Bubbles, 1971, (ring) Elipses, 1983; designer, goldsmith numerous pieces including All Done With Mirrors, 1980 (Judges prize for Most Creative); designer, platinumsmith (earrings) Snowflake, 1982 (1st Runner-up). Recipient numerous awards Diamond Info. Ctr., N.Y.C., 1973, DeBeers Mines, N.Y.C., 1977, 1st prize award Jewelers' Circular Keystone, Radnor, Pa., 1979; finalist in color catalog of winning designs "Colored Gemstone Design award 2000,"; sponsored by Signity N.Y. Ltd., Stuller, Jewelers of Am., Nat. Jeweler Mag.; numerous others. Mem. Real Estate Investors Ctrl. N.Y., Gem and Mineral Soc. Syracuse Inc. Unitarian-universalist. Avocations: gem carving, gardening. Office: 102 Dewey Ave Fayetteville NY 13066-1607

HAEBICH, ARTHUR T., retired thoracic surgeon; b. Chgo., Apr. 7, 1925; s. Arthur C and Nellie M Haebich; m. Patricia B. Brewer, Aug. 8, 1981; m. Hubertine E. Van Der Heyden, June 5, 1954 (dec. Feb. 1980); 1 child, Christian. MD, Northwestern Univ., Chgo., 1948. Diplomate Am. Bd. Surgery, 1959, Am. Bd. Thoracic Surgeo, 1961. Intern Ill. Masonic Hosp., Chgo., 1948, resident in surgery, 1949—54; resident in thoracic surgery Emory U. Hosp., Atlanta, 1954—56; pres. med. staff Ill. Masonic Med. Ctr., Chgo., 1970—72, 1980—82, mem. bd. trustees, 1983—2000. Fellow: ACS; mem.: AMA, Ill. Thoracic Surg. Soc. (pres.), Chgo. Med. Soc. (Irving Pk. br. pres. 1964—65, councilor 1965—75), Ill. Med. Soc., Masons, Pleides Lodge #478, St John's Conclave, Red Cross of Constantine (hon.). Episcopalian. Home: 1540 Primrose Ln Glenview IL 60026 Home Phone: 847-729-1127. Personal E-mail: haebich@comcast.net.

HAECK, JAMES F., manufacturing executive; m. Carolyn Haeck; 1 child, Jessica. BA in Economics, U. Pitts. Joined The LTV Corp., 1968, v.p., gen. mgr. Tubular Prods. Co., 1991—93, v.p., gen. mgr. Cleveland Works, 1993—94, sr. v.p. flat rolled opers., 1994, sr. v.p. comml., 1995—98, exec. v.p. Cleve., 1998—2001; v.p. sales mktg. Universal Steel Co. Bd. dirs. Bayou Steel Corp., 2004—. Office: Universal Steel 6600 Grant Ave Cleveland OH 44105

HAEFELE, EDWIN THEODORE, political theorist, consultant; b. Burnt Prairie, Ill., Oct. 5, 1925; s. Monroe Edwin and Lola Amanda (Coles) H.; m. Ruth Anne Woods, Dec. 23, 1948; children: Ann Katherine, Douglas Monroe, John Joseph. Student, Mich. State U., 1943, Ill. Wesleyan U., 1946-48, U. Chgo., 1948-50. Staff asst. Pub. Adminstrn. Clearing House, Chgo., 1951-54; asst. dir. Transp. Center, Northwestern U., 1954-62; mem. sr. staff Brookings Instn., Washington, 1962-67; mem. sr. research staff Resources for Future, Inc., Washington, 1967-73; prof. polit. sci. U. Pa., Phila., 1973-82, prof. emeritus, 1982-84, 88—, prof., chmn. dept. polit. sci., 1985-88; exec. v.p. Consortium of Govtl. Counselors Inc., 1989-96. Author: Government Controls on Transport, 1965, Representative Government and Environmental Management, 1973, What Constitutes the American Republic?, 1993; editor: Transport and National Goals, 1967, The Governance of Common Property Resources, 1974 Served with AUS, 1943-46. Decorated Purple Heart, Presdl. Unit citation. Republican. Congregationalist. Home: 1215 Box Butte Ave Alliance NE 69301-2522

HAEFNER, DON PAUL, retired psychology educator; b. Albany, NY, Mar. 7, 1928; s. Carl William and Mary Theresa (Diamond) H.; m. Allegra Ouida Turner, June 11, 1951 (dec. Oct. 1981); children: Carol, Ann, Thomas; m. Cynthia Jean Stewart, May 29, 1982. AB in psychology, Clark U., 1951; PhD, U. Rochester, 1956. Chief soc. psychologist Vets. Adminstrn. Ctr., Bath, NY, 1956—57; rsch. soc. psychologist VA Hosp., Brockton, Mass., 1957—60, U.S. Pub. Health Svc., Washington, 1960—62; rsch. assoc., lectr. to prof. U. Mich. Sch. Pub. Health, Ann Arbor, 1962—93, asst. dean, 1968—84, prof. emeritus, 1993—. Vis. instr. U. Rochester, N.Y., 1956-57; lectr. psychology Boston U., 1958-60; reviewer profl. jours., 1975-94; cons. to health orgns., 1975-85. Contbr. articles to profl. jours. Fellow APHA, Soc. Pub. Health Edn.; mem. APA, Sigma Xi, Delta Omega. Unitarian Universalist. Avocations: travel, photography, choral singing. Home: 2250 Pine Grove Ct Ann Arbor MI 48103-2338 E-mail: dhaefner@umich.edu.

HAEGELE, PATRICIA, publishing executive; b. Wheeling, W.Va., Dec. 19, 1950; d. Thomas J. and Marcella (Kissell) Cook. Student, W. Liberty Coll., 1970-71, Brevard Community Bus. Coll., 1973-74, Rollins Coll., 1974-76. Retail advt. rep. Coca Today/Gannett Co., Cocoa, Fla., 1973-76, Tampa Tribune Co., Tampa, Fla., 1976-79; corp. advt. rep. Washington Post Co. Inc., Washington, 1979-82; corp. advt. mgr. USA Today/Gannett Co. Inc., NYC, 1982-84, div. sales mgr., 1984-85, v.p., eastern sales mgr., 1985, v.p., advt. dir., 1985-86; v.p., advertising dir. USA Weekend, NYC, 1986-88, pub., 1988; sr. v.p. advt. USA Today, NYC, 1988—91; pub. Travel Holiday mag. (Gannett Co.), 1991—94; pres. gen. mgr. Newspaper Nat. Network, 1994—97; sr. v.p., pub. Good Housekeeping, 1997—. Selected to YWCA's Acad. of Women Achievers, 1988; profiled On The Rise column Fortune mag., Aug., 1988. Mem. Am. Newspapers Pubs. Assn., Internat. Newspaper Advt. Mktg. Assn., Am. Mktg. Assn. Republican. Roman Catholic. Avocations: running, biking, body tng. Office: Good Housekeeping 250 West 55th St New York NY 10019*

HAEGER, JOHN DENIS, academic administrator; BA, M, D, Loyola U., Chgo. Prof., history dept. Ctrl. Mich. U., chair, history dept., interim dean, coll. grad. studies, assoc. dean, coll. grad. studies, dean, coll. arts & sci., dir., grad. student affairs; provost, v.p. Towson U.; provost, academic student affairs divsn. Northern Ariz. U., pres., 2001—. Chair, coun. of presidents Big Sky Conf.; mem. Ariz. Bd. Edn., P-20 Coun.; mem., bd.

dirs. Transitional Genomics Rsch. Inst.; commr. Western Insterstate Commn. Higher Edn. Contbr. articles to jours. Former chair United Way, Northern Ariz. bd. Office: No AZ U S San Francisco St Flagstaff AZ 86011*

HAEMMERICH, DIETER, biomedical engineer; PhD, U. Wis., 2001. Scientist U. Wis., Madison, 2001—04; asst. prof. dept. pediatric cardiology Med. U. SC, Charleston, 2004—; pres. Med. Engring. Innovations LLC, Madison, 2005—. Cons. Bard Electrophysiology, Lowell, Mass., 2000—01, Richmar, Inc., Inola, Okla., 2002—03, Biosense-Webster, Diamond Bar, Calif., 2003—04; adj. prof. bioengring. Clemson U., 2004—. Contbr. chapters to books. Mem.: IEEE (assoc.). Achievements include invention of multiple probe radiofrequency ablation; radiofrequency assisted resection device. Office: MUSC 165 Ashley Ave PO Box 250915 Charleston SC 29425 Office Phone: 843-792-1396. Personal E-mail: haemmeri@hotmail.com.

HAENDIGES, ANNE R., marriage and family therapist; d. James A. and Anne P. Bohan; m. Roger H. Haendiges, Nov. 25, 2000; m. Donald J. Rudolph (dec.); children: Anne O'Donnell, Donald J. Rudolph, Lisa A. Haig. RN, NYU, 1957; BSN, Columbia U., 1960; MSc, Russell Sage Coll., 1975; PhD, Walton U., Coral Gables, Fla., 1977. RN N.Y.; cert. sex therapist, sex educator, sexual diplomat Am. Bd. Sexuality. Nurse Bellevue Hosp., NYC, 1957—59; tchg. nurse Albany Manpower Tng. Program, 1963—69; asst. prof. SUNY, Albany, 1969—80; instr. Albany Med. Sch., 1970—75; pvt. practice as sex therapist Clifton Park, NY, 1970—2000. Sec. faculty SUNY, Albany; lectr. on human sexuality. Recipient fed. grant, Russell Sage Coll., 1969; scholar, Tchrs. Coll., Columbia U., 1958. Fellow: Am. Assn. Sex Counselors, Educators, and Therapists (cert.); mem.: N.Y. Nurses Assn. (mem. adv. bd.). Republican. Roman Catholic. Avocations: golf, swimming, walking. Home: 1011 Park Ave N Winter Park FL 32789 Office Phone: 407-622-7648. Personal E-mail: ahaendiges@cfl.rr.com, adlrud@aol.com.

HAENICKE, DIETHER HANS, academic administrator emeritus, educator; b. Hagen, Germany, May 19, 1935; came to U.S., 1963, naturalized, 1972; s. Erwin Otto and Helene (Wildfang) H.; m. Carol Ann Colditz, Sept. 29, 1962; children: Jennifer Ruth, Kurt Robert. Student, U. Gottingen, 1955-56, U. Marburg, 1957-59; PhD magna cum laude in German Lit. and Philology, U. Munich, 1962; DHL (hon.), Cen. Mich. U., 1986; DHL, We. Mich. U., 1998. Asst. prof. Wayne State U., Detroit, 1963-68, assoc. prof., 1968-72, prof. German, 1972-78, resident dir. Jr. Year in Freiburg (Ger.), 1965-66, 69-70, dir. Jr. Year Abroad programs, 1970-75, chmn. dept. Romance and Germanic langs. and lits., 1971-72, assoc. dean Coll. Liberal Arts, 1972-75, provost, 1975-77, v.p., provost, 1977-78; dean Coll. Humanities Ohio State U., 1978-82, v.p. acad. affairs, provost, 1982-85; pres. Western Mich. U., Kalamazoo, 1985-98, interim pres., 2006. Asst. prof. Colby Coll. Summer Sch. of Langs., 1964-65; lectr. Internationale Ferienkurse, U. Freiburg, summers 1961, 66, 67 Author: (with Horst S. Daemmrich) The Challenge of German Literature, 1971, Untersuchungen zum Versepos des 20. Jahrhunderts, 1962; editor: Liebesgeschichte der schonen Magelone, 1969, Der blonde Eckbert und andere Novellen, 1969, Franz Sternbalds Wanderungen, 1970, Wednesdays with Diether, 2003, University Governance and Humanistic Scholarship (Festschrift), 2002; contbr. articles to acad. and lit. jours. Mem. Mich. State Atty. Discipline Bd. Fulbright scholar, 1963-65 Mem. MLA, AAUP, Am. Assn. Tchrs. of German, Mich. Acad. Arts and Scis., Mich. Coun. for Arts and Cultural Affairs, Phi Beta Kappa. Office: Western Mich U Office of Pres Kalamazoo MI 49008-5202 Home Phone: 269-353-0942; Office Phone: 269-387-2351. Business E-Mail: diether.haenicke@wmich.edu.

HAENSLY, PATRICIA ANASTACIA, psychology professor; b. Kronenwetter, Wis., Dec. 4, 1928; d. Paul Frank and Valeria (Woyak) Banach; m. William E. Haensly, 1954; children: Paul, Robert, Thomas, James, John, David, Mary, Katherine. BS, Lawrence U., Appleton, Wis., 1950; MS in Genetics, Iowa State U., Ames, 1953; PhD in Ednl. & Devel. Psychology, Tex. A&M U., College Station, 1982. Histo technique specialist dept. vet. pathology Iowa State U., Ames, 1958-63; asst. prof. dept. ednl. psychology Tex. A&M U., College Station, 1982-97; instr. Blinn Jr. Coll., College Station; prin. Investigator Project Mustard Seed, U.S.D.O.E. Javits Grant, 1993-96; assoc. dir. programs Inst. for Gifted and Talented Tex. A&M U., College Station, dir. summer presch. program Minds Alive, 1987-95. Mem. adj. faculty psychology Western Wash. U., Bellingham, 1996—2006. Contbg. editor Roeper Rev., 1996—; mem. editl. bd. Gifted Child Quar., 1996—, Gifted Child Today, 1997-2006; guest editor: (spl. issues) Gifted Teachers/Teachers of Gifted Learners, Parenting the Gifted; contbr. articles to profl. jours., chpts. to books. Alt. US del. World Coun. Gifted and Talented Children, 1997-99, 2001-02, del., 1999-2001; del. People to People amb. program Pacific N.W. Initiative to the People's Rep. of China., 1998. Recipient Outstanding Woman award AAUW, 1980, Govt. Rsch. Javits grante, 1993-96 Mem. Tex. Assn. for Gifted and Talented (1st v.p. 1988, 89, editor news mag. 1988, 89), Nat. Assn. Gifted Children (co-chmn. rsch. and evaluation com. 1985-87, John Curtis Gowan Rsch. award 1981, program chair Conceptual Found. divsn. 1997-99, chair 2000-01), World Coun. for Gifted and Talented Children, Inc., Soc. for Rsch. in Child Devel., Coun. for Exceptional Children, Assn. for Childhood Edn. Internat., Am. Creativity Assn. (charter), Am. Psychol. Soc., Phi Kappa Phi. Home: Eagle's Trace 102 Pecan Grove Apt 216 Houston TX 77077 Personal E-mail: patricia1015@earthlink.net.

HAERI, NILOOFAR M., linguist, educator; d. Jamaleddin Mazandarani Haeri and Behjat Sadat Altoma; m. Thomas Philip Porteous, June 19, 2004; 1 child, Daniel Haeri Porteous. PhD in Liguistics, U. Pa., Phila., 1979—91. Prof. Johns Hopkins U., Balt., 1990—. Fellow Radcliffe Inst. for Advanced Study, Harvard U., 1999—2000. Office: Johns Hopkins Univ 3400 N Charles St Baltimore MD 21218 Home Phone: 410-366-7383. Office Fax: 410-516-6080; Home Fax: 410-516-6080. Business E-Mail: haeri@jhu.edu.

HAERING, EDWIN RAYMOND, chemical engineering educator, consultant; b. Columbus, Ohio, Dec. 8, 1932; s. Edwin Jacob and Mary Mildred (Kunst) H.; m. Suzanne Rowe, June 9, 1956; children: Cynthia, David Arthur, Elizabeth. BChemE, MS, Ohio State U., 1956, PhD, 1966. Mem. faculty Ohio State U., Columbus, 1959-91, assoc. prof., 1973-82, prof. chem. engring., 1982-91, prof. emeritus, 1991—, vice chmn. dept., 1974-76, chmn. dept., 1977-78. Cons. in field. Author: Laboratory Manual for Unit Operations Laboratory, 1980; contbr. articles to profl. jours. Disaster svcs. vol. ARC, 1997—2005. Lt. (j.g.) USNR, 1956—59. NROTC scholar, 1951-56, Dow Chem. Co. scholar, 1956; Koppers tchg. fellow, 1962. Mem. AIChE (treas. Cen. Ohio sect. 1974-79), Am. Chem. Soc., Port Clinton Power Squadron (exec. com. 2003), Ohio State U. Faculty Club (pres. 1988-89), Sandusky Yacht Club, Lake Erie South Shore Hunter Sailing Assn. (treas. 1997-99), Sigma Xi, Tau Beta Pi. Avocations: golf, gardening, sailing. Home: 701 Stoutenberg Dr Lakeside Marblehead OH 43440-2049 Office: Ohio State U Dept Chem Engring 701 Stoutenberg Dr Lakeside Marblehead OH 43440-2049

HAERING, MARGARET ELAINE, lawyer; b. Columbus, Ohio, Mar. 3, 1947; d. Robert Lee and Mary E. (Brewer) Haering. BA, Douglass Coll., 1969; JD, George Washington U., 1975. Accredited investment fiduciary auditor: Ctr. Fiduciary Studies at U. Pitts. Joseph M. Katz Grad. Sch. Bus. Editor, atty. Bur. Nat. Affairs, Washington, 1975—78; ptnr. Cole, Raywid & Braverman, Washington, 1978; mng. dir. Ind. Fiduciary Advs., LLC, Woodbridge, Conn., 2006—. Named one of Top 100 Attys., Worth mag., 2005. Mem.: ABA. Office: Ind Fiduciary Advs LLC 1 Bradley Rd Ste 902 Woodbridge CT 06525 Office Phone: 203-389-1417. Office Fax: 800-784-1290. E-mail: peggy@indfa.com.*

HAERLE, PAUL RAYMOND, judge; b. Portland, Oreg., Jan. 10, 1932; s. George William and Grace (Soden) H.; m. Susan Ann Wagner, May 30, 1953 (div. Apr. 1973); children: Karen A. Haerle D'Or, David A.; m. Michele A. Monson, June 1, 1991. AB, Yale U., 1953; JD, U. Mich., 1956. Bar: Calif. 1956, U.S. Supreme Ct. 1962. Assoc. Thelen, Marrin, Johnson & Bridges, San Francisco, 1956-64, ptnr., 1965-67, 69-94, mng. ptnr., 1990-93; appointments sec. Office of Gov., State of Calif., Sacramento, 1967-69; assoc. justice Calif. Ct. Appeal (1st dist.), San Francisco, 1994—. Lawyer rep. 9th Cir. Jud. Conf., 1985-88. Editor-in-chief Mich. Law Rev., 1955-56 Presdl. elector, 1972; del. Rep. Nat. Conv., 1972; vice chmn. Calif. Rep. Com., 1973-75, chmn., 1975-77; mem. Rep. Nat. Com., 1975-77; chair applicants evaluation and nominating com. 2003-; trustee World Affairs Coun. No. Calif., 1997-2003; mem. adv. com. on internat. law U.S. Dept. State, 2002-06; regional panelist, White House Fellowship Program, 2003-. Fellow Am. Coll. Trial Lawyers; mem. Yale Club of San Francisco, Order of Coif. Avocations: tennis, travel, hiking. Office: Calif Ct Appeal 350 McAllister St San Francisco CA 94102-3600

HAESKE, RON A., financial analyst, singer; s. L. Henry and Emily Haeske; m. Judith D. Bender. EdB, U. Mich., Ann Arbor, 1975; MusM, Berean Bible Coll., Springfield, Mo., 1984. Bus. analyst Consumers Power Co., Saginaw, Mich., 1979—. Author: (novels) Devine Appointment; composer: New Testament of the Bible in Song; composer, singer, musician: 40 CDs. Music min. First Assembly of God, Saginaw, 1982—. Home Phone: 989-791-5974.

HAESSLE, JEAN-MARIE GEORGES, artist; b. Buhl/Haut/Rhin, France, Sept. 12, 1939; came to U.S., 1967; s. Georges and Marguerite H. Student, Ecole Nationale des Beaux Arts, Paris, France, 1965-67, Ecole de la Grande Chaumiere, Paris, 1966-67. Painter, Paris, 1965-67, NYC, 1967—. One man shows include Panoras Gallery, N.Y.C., 1968, West Broadway Gallery, N.Y.C., 1973, Atlantic Gallery, Washington, 1979, Nat. Acad. Sci., Washington, 1979, RR Gallery, N.Y.C., 1980, Gabrielle Bryers Gallery, N.Y.C., 1981, Kerr Gallery, N.Y.C., 1984-85, Little John-Smith Gallery, N.Y.C., 1986, Lucien Durand Galerie, Paris, 1987-91; exhibited in groups shows U.S. and abroad including Salon de la Jeune Peinture, Musee d'Art Moderne, Paris, 1968, Palace of Fine Arts, Mexico City, 1972, Aldrich Mus. Contemporary Art, Ridgefield, Conn., 1978; represented in permanent collections U.S. and abroad including So. Ill. U., Edwardsville, Bank of N.Y., N.Y.C., Atlantic-Richfield, Los Angeles, Am. Express, Fla., IBM, Los Angeles, Exxon, Fla., Chase Manhattan Bank, Los Angeles, Citibank, Los Angeles, Owen Corning Fiberglass, Toledo; works reviewed in profl. and popular publs. Roman Catholic. Home: 106112 Spring St New York NY 10012 Office Phone: 212-226-0618. Personal E-mail: jmhaessle@netscape.net.

HAEUSER, MICHAEL JOHN, library administrator; b. LaCrosse, Wis., July 5, 1943; s. Loyal Eldon and Kamilla (Brenengen) H.; m. Linda Kay Johnsrud, Aug. 31, 1968 (div. 1981); 1 child, Britton; m. Irene Jeanette Morris, June 20, 1987. BS in History, U. Wis., 1970, MA in History, 1972, MLS, 1973, cert., 1986. Readers svcs. libr. Knox Coll., Galesburg, Ill., 1973-74, head readers svcs., 1974-76; head libr. Linfield Coll., McMinnville, Oreg., 1976-81; dir. learning resources, head libr. Gustavus Adolphus Coll., St. Peter, Minn., 1981-97, coll. archivist, 1997—. Co-instr. Mil. History WWII, 1979; presenter in field. Author: With Grace, Elegance and Flair: The First 25 Years of Library Associates, 2002; cons. to editor books for coll. librs., Choice mag.; contbr. articles to profl. jours. Chmn. Core Curriculum Rev. Task Force, Linfield Coll., 1977-7; mem. coll. libr. com. Nat. Commn. Preservation and Access, 1989, team Bibliographic Instrn., 1982—; bd. dirs. Minn. Humanities Commn., 1990-97. With U.S. Army, 1963-66. NEH fellow, 1978; grantee, 1980, 83; grantee: Japan Found., 1978, U.S. Office Edn., 1979, 80, Murdock Trust, 1979, Hearst Found., 1980, Collins Found., 1980, Nat. Archives and Records Svc., 1983, Presser Found., 1983; recipient John Cotton Dana Libr. pub. rels. award 1983, 94. Mem. ALA (selected vol. pres.' program Chgo. chpt. 1985, sec. coll. libr. sect. 1990, Outstanding Pub. Rels. 1983), Assn. Coll. And Rsch. Librs., Assn. Coll. and Resource Librs. (nat. adv. coun. libr. sect. 1985), Am. Hist. Assn., Minn. Libr. Assn. (pres. 1988-90), Minn. Assn. Libr. Friends (bd. dirs. 1990), Minn. Humanities Commn. (bd. dirs. 1991-97). Lutheran. Avocations: skiing, outdoor work, reading, travel, association activities. Office: Gustavus Adolphus Coll Folke Bernadotte Meml Libr 800 W College Ave Saint Peter MN 56082-1485 Office Phone: 507-933-7572. Business E-Mail: haeuser@gac.edu.

HAFEMEISTER, BEVERLY RAE, consumer products company executive; b. Detroit, Mar. 25, 1937; d. Raymond H. Hafemeister and Eleanor Ann Hofmann Hafemeister. BS in Art Edn., U. Wis., 1958. Art tchr. Howell Pub. Sch., Mich., 1958—60, Detroit Pub. Sch., 1960—67; co-owner Bill Kuehn Shade Co., Ann Arbor, Mich., 1980—84; owner Vintage Valances, Mich., 1984—87, Cin., 1987—. Works at re-creating accurate historic draperies for museums and old homes nationwide, 1984—. Contbr. articles to profl. jours.

HAFEMEISTER, DAVID WALTER, physicist; b. Chgo., July 1, 1934; s. Lester David and Alma Doris (Schmidt) H.; m. Gina Rohlander, June 10, 1961; children: Andrew, Jason, Heidi. MS in Physics, U. Ill., 1959, PhD in Physics, 1964. Asst. prof. physics Carnegie-Mellon U., Pitts., 1966-69; prof. physics Calif. Poly. State U., San Luis Obispo, 1969-2000; study dir. on arms control on beyond START NAS, Washington, 2000—02; chair external rev. com. Los Alamos Nonproliferation Divsn., 2003—06; sci. fellow Ctr. Internat. Security and Cooperation Stanford U., 2005—06. Sci. advisor Sen. John Glenn U.S. Senate, Washington, 1975-77; spl. asst. to Under Sec. State Benson and Nye U.S. State Dept., Washington, 1977-79; vis. scientist U. Groningen, The Netherlands, 1971, 80, Program Sci. Tech. in Internat. Security, MIT, Cambridge, 1983-84, Ctr. for Bldg. Scis. Lawrence Berkeley (Calif.) Lab., 1985-86, Office Strategic Nuc. Policy U.S. Dept. State, 1987, Ctr. Internat. Security and Arms Control Stanford U., 1988; program on nuc. policy alternatives Princeton U., 1989; profl. staff Senate Fgn. Rels. Com., 1990-92; staff Senate Gov. Affairs Com., 1992-93, Sch. Pub. Affairs, U. Md., 1996; Foster fellow Office of Strategic Negotiations, U.S. Arms Control and Disarmament Agy., 1997-98. Author: Physics of Societal Issues, 2007; co-author: Physics of Modern Architecture, 1983; co-editor: Energy Sources: Conservation and Renewables, 1985, Arms Control Verification, 1986, Nuclear Arms Technologies in the 1990s, 1988, Physics and Nuclear Arms Today, 1990, Global Warning: Physics and Facts, 1991, Biological Effects of Low-Frequency Electromagnetic Fields, 1998. Fellow Am. Phys. Soc. (chmn. forum on physics and soc. 1985-86, chair panel on pub. affairs 1996, Leo Szilard award for Physics in the Pub. Interest 1996); mem. AAAS (congl. fellow 1975-76, arms control fellow 1987), Fedn. Am. Scientists, Arms Control Assn., Am. Inst. Physics (co-editor books). Home: 553 Serrano Dr San Luis Obispo CA 93405 Business E-Mail: dhafemei@calpoly.edu.

HAFER, BARBARA, state official; b. LA, Aug. 1, 1943; m. Jack Pidgeon; 4 children , John, Kelly, Bethany, Regan. BS, Duquesne U., Pitts., 1969; postgrad., U. Pitts., U. London. Founder, exec. dir. Allegheny County Ctr. for Victims of Violent Crime, 1973—79; account exec. Sautel Agency, 1979—82; employee relations mgr. South Hills Health System, 1982—83; auditor gen. State of Pa., Harrisburg, 1989-96, state treas., 1997—. Commr. Allegheny County bd. commissioners, 1984—89; mem. Del. River Port Authority, 1989—, Pa Partnership for Econ. Edn., 1997—, Pa. Pub. School Employees Retirement System Bd., 1996—. Office: State of Pennsylvania Treasury Dept 129 Finance Building Harrisburg PA 17120-0018 E-mail: barbarahafer@patreasury.org.

HAFER, JOSEPH PAGE, lawyer; b. Harrisburg, Pa., June 28, 1941; s. George Horace and Betty (Page) H.; m. Margaret B. Cady; children: Bradford G., Susan P., David E. AB, Lafayette Coll., 1963; JD with distinction, U. Mich., 1966. Bar: Pa. 1966, U.S. Dist. Ct. (mid. dist.) Pa. 1966, U.S. Supreme Ct. 1969, U.S. Ct. Appeals (3d cir.) 1976. Assoc. Metzger, Hafer, Keefer, Thomas & Wood, Harrisburg, 1966-77; mng. ptnr. Thomas, Thomas & Hafer, Harrisburg, 1977—. Adj. prof. law Dickinson Law Sch., Carlisle, Pa. Pres. Cumberland Valley Sch. Bd., Mechanicsburg, Pa., 1976-85; pres. Hampden Twp. Rep. Assn., Camp Hill, Pa. Fellow Am. Coll. Trial Lawyers; mem. The Fedn. of Def. and Corp. Counsel, Pa. Bar Assn., Assn. Trial Lawyers Am., Pa. Trial Lawyers Assn., Dauphin County Bar Assn. (ct. rels. com.). Methodist. Home: 1530 Waterford Camp Hill PA 17011-9000 Office: Thomas Thomas & Hafer PO Box 999 Harrisburg PA 17108-0999 Business E-Mail: jhafer@tthlaw.com.

HAFETS, RICHARD JAY, lawyer; b. NYC, Apr. 23, 1951; s. Meyer Hafets and Marilyn (Glanzrock) Bell; m. Claire Margolis, June 18, 1972; children: Brooke, Amy. BS in Bus. summa cum laude, Am. U., Washington, 1973, JD magna cum laude, 1976. Bar: Md. 1976, U. S. Dist. Ct. Md. 1976, U.S. Ct. Appeals (4th cir.) 1976, U.S. Supreme Ct. 1981, D.C. 1997, U.S. Dist. Ct. (D.C.) 1997. Assoc. Piper & Marbury, Balt., 1976-84, ptnr., 1984—, chmn. labor and employment practice, 1990—, chmn. hiring and assoc. coms., 1988-91. Labor atty. Balt. Symphony Orch., 1986-93; bd. dirs., gen. counsel Am. Cancer Soc., Balt., 1983-89; bd. dirs. Md. Ballet, Balt., 1978-80. Mem. ABA, Md. Bar Assn., Balt. City Bar Assn., Order of Coif. Avocations: horses, skiing. Home: 7346 Narrow Wind Way Columbia MD 21046-1262 Office: DLA Piper Rudnick Gray Cary LLP 6225 Smith Ave Baltimore MD 21209-3600 Office Phone: 410-580-4168. Business E-Mail: richard.hafets@dlapiper.com.

HAFEY, JOSEPH MICHAEL, health association executive; b. Annapolis, Md., June 25, 1943; s. Edward Earl Joseph and Verna (Hedlund) H.; m. Mary Kay Miller, Dec. 30, 1978; children: Erin Catherine, Ryan Michael. BA, Whittier Coll., 1965; MPA, UCLA, 1967. Sr. asst. health officer HHS, Washington, 1967-69; dir. govt. relations Alliance for Regional Community Health, St. Louis, 1969-71; exec. dir. Contra Costa Comprehensive Health Assn., Richmond, Calif., 1971-74, Bay Area Comprehensive Health Planning Coun., San Francisco, 1974-76, Western Ctr. for Health Planning, San Francisco, 1976-86, Western Consortium for Pub. Health, Berkeley, 1980-95; pres., CEO Pub. Health Inst. (formerly Calif. Pub. Health Found.), 1985—. Chmn. Contra Costa Pub. Health Adv. Body, Martinez, Calif., 1987-93; founder Calif. Coalition for Future of Pub. Health, Sacramento, 1988—; co-founder Calif. Healthy Cities Program, Berkeley, 1987—. Chmn. United Way Com. for the Uninsured, San Francisco, 1985-93; bd. dirs. Eugene O'Neill Found., 1980-89. With USPHS, 1967-69. Recipient fellowship WHO, Geneva, 1987. Mem. Am. Pub. Health Assn. (governing coun. 1984-87), Am. Health Planning Assn. bd. dirs., chmn. annual meeting 1982). Avocations: jogging, tennis, skiing, collecting political campaign buttons. Home: 1749 Toyon Rd Lafayette CA 94549-2111 Office: Pub Health Inst 555 12th St Oakland CA Office Phone: 510-285-5531. Business E-Mail: joehafey@phi.org.

HAFEZ, MAHMOUD A., orthopedic surgeon; MB BCh, MSc, Cairo U. Med. Sch., Egypt, 1985. Fellow Royal Coll. of Surgeons of Edinburgh, 1997. Fellow, scientist Inst. for Computer Assisted Orthopedic Surgery, The Western Pa. Hosp., Pitts., 2004—; v.p. Soc. Computer Assisted Orthopaedic Surgery, Cairo, 2005—. Regional v.p. and uk del. Am. Fracture Assn., Chgo., 2001—03. Author (poet): (poetry, medical bioengineering writing) Insall-Scott, JBJS Br, F (Japanese-SICOT, BOA, Pfizer, AFA, ESPRC). Recipient Meyerding Essay award, Am. Fracture Assn., 1999, Travel Fellowship award, Brit. Orthop. Assn., 2004, Academic award, Pfizer, 2004, Japanese-SICOT award, Japanese Orthop. Assn. and Soc. Internat. de Chirurgie Orthopedique et de Traumatologie, 2005; grantee Rsch. grant, Engring. and Phys. Sci. Rsch. Coun., 2001. Fellow: Royal Coll. Surgeons of Edinburgh; mem.: Internat. Soc. for Computer Assisted Orthopedic Surgery, Orthopedic Rsch. Soc. (assoc.), Brit. Orthopedic Assn. (assoc. BOA travel fellowship award 2004). Achievements include patents pending for Computer assisted templating in knee surgery; research in Orthopedic Surgery; design of Computer assisted orthopaedic surgery tools. Home Phone: 412-897-3440. Office Fax: 412-605-6376.

HAFFER, EDWARD ANTHONY, lawyer; b. Paterson, NJ, Oct. 25, 1944; s. Edward and Helen Haffer; m. Marilyn L. Butler; children: Gretchen A., Nicholas A. BA with Distinction, U. Va., 1966; JD Cum Laude, Boston Coll., 1972. Bar: U.S. Supreme Ct. 1976, U.S. Ct. Appeals (1st cir.) 1972, U.S. Ct. Appeals (Fed. Circuit) 2004, (NH) 1972, (MA) 1972. Asst. atty. gen. NH Atty. Gen. Office, Concord, NH, 1972—87; ptnr. Sheehan Phinney Bass & Green, Manchester, NH, 1978—. Fellow NH Bar Found.; founding dir. NH Chpt. Sierra Club. Lt. US Army, 1966—69. Mem.: ABA, Am. Intellectual Property Law Assn., Order of Coif. Achievements include appeals court decisions establishing expert standards in complex patent cases; establishing new cause of action for malicious defense of civil proceedings. Office: Sheehan Phinney Bass & Green PA 1000 Elm St PO Box 3701 Manchester NH 03105-3701 Office Phone: 603-627-8115. Business E-Mail: ehaffer@sheehan.com.

HAFFNER, ALDEN NORMAN, academic administrator; b. Bklyn., Oct. 3, 1928; s. Irving and Irene (Gutfleisch) H. AB, Bklyn. Coll., 1948; OD, Pa. Coll. Optometry, 1952; MPA, NYU, 1960, PhD, 1964; DOS (hon.), Mass. Coll. Optometry, 1960; ScD (hon.), Pa. Coll. Optometry, 1973. Exec. dir. Optometric Center of N.Y., NYC, 1957—; acting chief adminstrv. officer State Coll. Optometry, SUNY, NYC, 1970-71, dean, 1971-76, pres., 1976-78; assoc. chancellor for health scis. SUNY, Albany, 1978-82, vice chancellor for research, grad. studies and profl. programs, 1982-87, pres. coll. optometry, 1987—. Pub. svc. prof. health poligy Rockefeller Coll., SUNY-Albany, 1986; chmn. N.Y. State Com. on Health Personnel and Productivity, 1990—; cons. in field. Contbr. articles in field to profl. jours. Mem. adv. com. Commn. for Blind and Visually Handicapped, State Dept. Social Services, 1966-70; mem. bd. nat. study commn. on optometry Nat. Commn. on Accrediting, 1968-70; mem. health manpower planning com. Comprehensive Health Planning Agy., N.Y.C., 1969-73; project dir. Fed. Program of Identification, Counseling, Guidance and Recruitment of Minority Students in Profession of Optometry, 1968-74; mem. Mayor's Com. for Study of Aging, N.Y.C., 1958; chmn. bd. trustees Manhattan Health Plan, Inc., 1976-81. Served to 1st lt. M.C. U.S. Army, 1953-55. Recipient Albert Fitch Meml. award, 1962; Prof. Frederick A. Woll Meml. award, 1961; Distinguished Achievement award Alumni Assn., N.Y. U. Grad. Sch. Pub. Health Adminstrn., 1974 Fellow Am. Pub. Health Assn., AAAS, Am. Sch. Health Assn., Am., N.Y. Acad. Optometry; mem. N.Y. Acad. Scis., Group Health Assn. Am., Am. Pub. Welfare Assn., Am. Soc. Pub. Adminstrn., Nat. Rehab. Assn., Illuminating Engring. Soc., Am. Optometric Assn., N.Y. State Optometric Assn., Gerontol. Soc., Am. Assn. Univ. Adminstrs., Pub. Health Assn. City of N.Y. (dir. 1967—), Nat. Assn. Land Grant Colls. and State Univs. (com. health affairs 1981), Community Family Planning Coun., Am. Coun. on Edn., Assn. Cad. Health Ctrs., Hermann Biggs Soc., Beta Sigma Kappa (Gold Medal award 1974), Home: 201 E 36th St New York NY 10016-3668 Office: SUNY Coll Optometry 33 W 42nd St New York NY 10036-8003

HAFFNER, CHARLES CHRISTIAN, III, retired printing company executive; b. Chgo., May 27, 1928; s. Charles Christian and Clarissa (Donnelley) Haffner; m. Anne P. Clark, June 19, 1970. BA, Yale U., 1950.

With R.R. Donnelley & Sons Co., Chgo., 1951—62, treas., 1962-68, v.p., treas., 1968-83, vice-chmn., treas., 1983-84, vice-chmn., 1984-90; ret., 1990. Chmn. Morton Arboretum, 1975—2001, Sprague Found., 1996—2000, Newberry Libr., 1986—2000, trustee; life trustee Sprague Found.; bd. govs. Nature Conservancy, 1973—84, chmn. Ill. chpt., 1984—87, life trustee, 1987—; mem. Chgo. Plan Commn., 1986—91; trustee Art Inst., Chgo., Latin Sch., Chgo., 1974—84, Ill. Cancer Coun., 1984—92, Chgo. City Day Sch., Lincoln Pk. Zool. Soc., Brooks Sch., 1987—95. 1st lt. USAF, 1952—54. Mem.: Casino Club, Caxton Club, Racquet Club, Commonwealth Club, Comml. Club, Chgo. Club. Home: 1530 N State Pkwy Chicago IL 60610-1610 Office: 35 E Wacker Dr Ste 1078 Chicago IL 60601-2398

HAFFNER, DAVID S., manufacturing executive; BS, U. Missouri-Columbia, 1974, MBA, 1980. Joined Leggett & Platt, Inc., Carthage, Mo., 1983, exec. v.p., 1995—2002, bd. dir., 1995—, COO, 1999—2002, pres., COO, 2002—06, pres., CEO, 2006—. Bd. dirs. Bemis Co. Inc., 2004—. Office: Leggett & Platt Inc PO Box 757 1 Leggett Rd Carthage MO 64836-9649*

HAFFNER, F. KINSEY, lawyer; b. San Francisco, Feb. 20, 1948; BA with distinction, Stanford U., 1971, JD, 1974. Bar: Calif. 1974, DC. Ptnr. Pillsbury, Madison & Sutro, San Jose & Palo Alto, Calif., 1980—2000; sr. v.p. & gen. counsel Converge Inc., 2001; ptnr. Pillsbury Winthrop LLP, NYC & Palo Alto, Calif., 2002—05; ptnr., co-chmn. Global Sourcing practice Pillsbury Winthrop Shaw Pittman, NYC & Palo Alto, Calif., 2005—. Office: Pillsbury Winthrop Shaw Pittman 1540 Broadway New York NY 10036 also: Pillsbury Winthrop Shaw Pittman 2475 Hanover St Palo Alto CA 94304-1114 Office Phone: 212-858-1747. Office Fax: 212-858-1500. Business E-Mail: kinsey.haffner@pillsburylaw.com.

HAFFNER, MARLENE ELISABETH, internist, public health administrator; b. Cumberland, Md., Mar. 22, 1941; Student, Western Res. U., 1958—61; MD, George Washington U., 1965; MPH, John Hopkins U., 1991. Intern Geroge Washington U., Washington, 1965-66; fellow in dematology Columbia-Presbyn. Med. Ctr., NYC, 1966-67; resident in internal medicine St. Luke's Hosp., NYC, 1967-69; fellow in hematology Albert Einstein Coll. Medicine, Bronx, 1969-71; vis. asst. attending Bronx Mcpl. Hosp. Ctr. (N.Y.), 1969-71; clin. assoc. in family, cmty. and emergency medicine U. N.Mex. Sch. Medicine, Albuquerque, 1974-83; asst. clin. prof. medicine Albert Einstein Coll. Medicine, Bronx, 1971-73; clin. assoc. dept. med., 1974-83; acting clin. dir. Gallup Indian Med. Ctr. (N.Mex.), 1973-74; chief adult outpatient dept., 1971-74; chief dept. internal medicine, 1971-74; dir. Navajo Area Indian Health Svc. Indian Health Svc., Window Rock, Ariz., 1974-81; assoc. dir. for health affairs Bur. Med. Devices, FDA, Rockville, 1981-82; dir. Office Health Affairs Ctr. for Devices and Radiol. Health, 1982-87; dir. office of orphan products devel. FDA, 1987—; adj. prof. preventive medicine/biometrics. Clin. prof. dept. medicine Uniformed Svcs. U. Health Scis., Bethesda, Md., 2003—. Advanced through grades to rear admiral; U.S. Pub. Health Svc. Fellow: Royal Coll. Physicians (London), Am. Coll. Physicians. Office: Orphan Products Devel FDA HF 35 5600 Fishers Ln Rockville MD 20857-1750 Home Phone: 301-984-5729; Office Phone: 301-827-3666. Business E-Mail: marlene.haffner@fda.hhs.gov.

HAFFORD, FAYE O'LEARY, writer; b. St. John Plantation, Maine, Apr. 27, 1925; d. Lee and Clara Mills O'Leary; m. Joseph Lee Hafford, Nov. 5, 1949 (dec. 1993); children: Michael Lee, Randi Lou. Student, Colby Coll., 1942—44; BS in Edn., U. Maine, 1965. Cert. elem. sch. tchr. Maine. Tchr. towns of Allagash, Limestone, Brunswick, Ft. Kent, Maine, 1951—76; ret. Author: 16 booklets on folklore of St. John Valley, 1986—. Contbr. curriculum guide Town of Brunswick; organizer, pres., vol. librarian Allagash Pub. Libr., 1998. Named Woman of Yr., Ft. Kent Bus. and Profl. Women's Club; named to Sr. Spotlight, Srs. Club, Ft. Kent; recipient County All Star award, Aroostook County, Presque Isle, Maine, 2000, Calendar award, Maine Ctr. for Women, 2000, Meritorious award, Nat. Coun. Geographic Edn., 1970, commendations for work on Allagash waterway, Gov. Maine, commendation, Maine Legis., Ken York award for work on Allagash Wilderness Waterway, Cmty. Involvement award, Kraft and New Eng. Patriots. Mem.: NEA, Aroostook Ret. Tchrs. Assn., Maine Ret. Tchrs. Assn., AARP. Republican. Congregationalist. Avocations: knitting, crocheting, fishing, camping, reading. Home and Office: Allagash Pub Libr 894 Allagash Rd Saint Francis ME 04774 Office Phone: 207-398-4454.

HAFKENSCHIEL, JOSEPH HENRY, JR., cardiologist, educator; b. Youngstown, Ohio, Apr. 2, 1916; s. Joseph Henry and Anna Marie (Conroy) H.; m. Lucinda Buchanan Thomas, July 18, 1942 (dec. 1983); children: Joseph Henry III, Benjamin A. Thomas, Mark Conroy, John Proctor; m. Carol MacDonald Smith Rush, Jan. 25, 1985 (div. April 4, 2007). AB, Swarthmore Coll., 1937; MD, Johns Hopkins U., 1941. Diplomate Am. Bd. Internal Medicine. Intern U. Pa. Hosp., Phila., 1941-42; instr. pharmacology U. Pa. Sch. Medicine, 1946-47; resident U. Pa. Hosp., 1948-49, fellow in cardiology, 1949; instr. medicine U. Pa. Sch. Medicine, 1949-51; cardiovasc. disease physician, pvt. practice, 1949-65; assoc. medicine U. Pa. Sch. Medicine, 1951-66; med. dir. West Coast Office Sandoz Pharm., San Francisco, 1965-67; clin. instr. medicine Stanford U., 1966-69, staff physician Cowell Student Health Svcs., 1967-69; cardiovasc. disease physician, pvt. practice Palo Alto, 1969-78; asst. to assoc. prof. Stanford U., 1969-84, emeritus clin. assoc. prof. medicine, 1984—. Staff physician Extended Care Svc. VA Med. Ctr., Palo Alto, 1978-84. Contbr. articles to profl. jours. Pres. Peninsula Meml. and Funeral Soc., Palo Alto, 1984. Maj. M.C., USAAF, 1942-46. Fellow ACP, Coll. Physicians Phila., Am. Heart Assn., Am. Physiol. Soc.; mem. Air Force Assn., Am. Irish Hist. Soc., San Francisco Golf Club, Ballybunion Golf (Ireland) Club, Am. Legion (post comdr. 1960-62), Sigma Xi. Republican. Roman Catholic. Avocations: world travel, golf, gardening, art history. Home: Apt 11H 501 Portolla Rd Portola Valley CA 94028-8226

HAFLEY, DAVID ALLEN, military officer; b. Jefferson City, Mo., July 13, 1948; s. Calvin Edward Hafley and Violet Mae Nicholes; m. Evelyn Sue Rhodes, Feb. 28, 1986; children: Danny Ray Maasen, Kurt Allen, Kimberly Ann, Brian Andrew Maasen, Kady Jo, Davey Allen. Student, Coastline CC, Calif., 2007—. US property and fiscal office divsn. sgt. maj., safety non-commisioned officer in charge Mo. Army N.G., Jefferson City, 2001—. Decorated Nat. Defence Svc. medal Mo. Army N.G., Army Good Conduct medal, Mo. State Emergency Duty Ribbon, Army Res. Component Acheivement medal, Armed Forces Res. medal, Humanitarian Svc. medal, Army Commendation medal, Mo. State Long Svc. Ribbon, Non-commissioned Officer Profl. Devel. Ribbon US Army, Army Svc. Ribbon. Home: 304 Chris Dr Jefferson City MO 65101 Office: US Property and Fiscal Office 4101 Military Cir Jefferson City MO 65101-1200 Home Phone: 573-556-8700; Office Phone: 573-638-9577. Office Fax: 573-638-9833. Personal E-mail: dhafley8700@aol.com. Business E-Mail: david.allen.hafley@us.army.mil.

HAFNER, JOSEPH A., JR., food products executive; b. San Bernadino, Calif., Oct. 9, 1944; s. Joseph Albert and Mary Florence (McGowan) H.; m. Merrill Hafner; children: John Michael, Daniel Stephen, Caroline Elizabeth. AB cum laude, Dartmouth Coll., 1966; MBA with high distinction, Amos Tuck Sch. Bus. Adminstrn., 1967. C.P.A. Intern Latin Am. Cornell U.-Ford Found., Lima, Peru, 1967-69; sr. cons. Arthur Andersen & Co., Houston, 1969-71; controller C/A div. Riviana Internat., Inc., Guatemala City, Guatemala, 1972-73, treas., v.p. fin. Houston, 1973-77; v.p. Riviana Foods Inc., Houston, 1977-81, pres., chief operating officer, 1981-84, pres., chief exec. officer, 1984—2005, dir., 1985—, chmn., 2005—. Recipient C.P.A. Gold medal Ark. State Bd. Pub. Accountancy, 1969 Mem. AICPA, Coun. on Fgn. Rels. Office: Riviana Foods Inc 2777 Allen Pky Houston TX 77019-2141 Office Phone: 713-529-3251.

HAFNER, KATIE, reporter; b. 1957; m. Matthew Lyon (dec. 2002); 1 child, Zoe. BA in German Lit., Univ. Calif., San Diego; MS in Journalism, Columbia Univ. Tech. writer, 1983—; reporter Computerworld; contributing editor Newsweek mag.; reporter Business Week.; now tech. reporter NY Times, San Francisco. Teaching fellow Univ. Calif. Grad. Sch. Journalism, Berkeley. Co-author (with John Markoff): Cyberpunk: Outlaws and Hackers on the Computer Frontier, 1991; co-author: (with Matthew Lyon) Where Wizards Stay Up Late: The Origins of the Internet, 1996; author: The House at the Bridge: A Story of Modern Germany, 1995, The Well: The Story of Love, Death & Real Life in the Seminal Online Community, 2001. Office: Tech Reporter NY Times 201 Spear St San Francisco CA 94105

HAFNER, TRAVIS LEE, professional baseball player; b. Jamestown, ND, June 3, 1977; Attended, Cowley County CC, Kans. Infielder, designated hitter Cleve. Indians, 2002—. Achievements include being one of two players to hit 5 grandslams in one season (2006). Office: Cleveland Indians Jacobs Field 2401 Ontario St Cleveland OH 44115-4003*

HAFT, GAIL KLEIN, pediatrician; b. NYC, Mar. 5, 1938; d. Herbert and Pearl (Mittleman) Klein; m. Jacob I. Haft, Mar. 27, 1964; children: Bethanne, Ian. AB in Chemistry, Vassar Coll., 1959; MD, U. Rochester, 1963. Diplomate Nat. Bd. Med. Examiners, Am. Bd. Pediatrics. Intern Albert Einstein Coll. Medicine, NYC, 1963-64, resident, 1964-65, Mt. Sinai Hosp., NYC, 1967-68; pediatrician Dept. Health, Staten Island, NY, 1965-67, Head Start, Englewood, NY, 1969-71, Dept. Health, Hackensack, NJ, 1970-71; utilization rev. physician Hosp. Corp., NYC, 1973-76; pediatrician Westchester County Health Dept., NY, 1974-76; sch. physician Bd. Edn., Yonkers, NY, 1974-76; bus. mgr. Heartronics, Newark, 1980-94; chief med. officer Bergen County Spl. Svcs., Paramus, NJ, 1984—; physician Tenafly (N.J.) Sch. Bd. Edn., 1990-94. Mem. Tenafly Bd. Edn., 1983-89, pres., 1986-88.

HAFTER, JEROME CHARLES, lawyer; b. Orlando, Fla., May 16, 1945; s. Jerome Sidney and Mary Margaret (Fugler) H.; m. Jo Cille Dawkins, July 18, 1976; 1 child, Jerome Bryan. BA summa cum laude, Rice U., 1967; BA with first class honours, Oxford U., 1969, MA, 1976; JD, Yale U., 1972. Bar: Miss. 1974, U.S. Ct. Appeals (5th cir.) 1974, U.S. Dist. Ct. (no. and so. dists.) Miss. 1974. Law clk. to presiding judge U.S. Ct. Appeals (5th cir.), Jackson, Miss., 1972—73; assoc. Lake, Tindall, Hunger & Thackston (now Lake Tindall LLP), Greenville, Miss., 1973—76, ptnr., 1976—2001, Phelps Dunbar LLP, Jackson, 2001—. Chmn. Miss. Bd. Bar Admissions, Jackson, 1979-2002; sec., treas. Hafter Realty Inc., Greenville, 1969-92, pres., 1992—; mem. gov.'s constn. commn., Jackson, 1985-87; sec., gen. counsel Delta and Pine Land Co., Scott, Miss., 1993— Author: Family History of Peter Quin, 1964, 2d. rev. edit., 1970. Pres. Downtown Improvement Assn. Greenville, 1980—, Common Cause/Miss., 1976—78; mem. Greenville City Election Commn., 1978—, Greenville Mcpl. Sch. Bd., 1988—, pres., 1995—96, 1999—2000, 2002—03, 2006—07; chmn. com. on tax Miss. Econ. Coun., Jackson, 1985, 1987, 1996—98; pres. Greenville Area C. of C., 1992; v.p. I-69 Mid-Continent Hwy. Coalition, 1992—. Marshall scholar, 1967-69; Leadership Miss. Program fellow, 1976-77; Best Lawyers in Am., 2001-07. Fellow: Miss. Bar Found.; mem.: ABA (young lawyer divsn. 1980—82, law sch. accreditation com. 1998—2002, coun. sect. legal edn. and admissions to bar 2000—06, chmn. bar admissions com. sect. on legal edn. and admission to bar 2006—07, vice chmn. com. on issues affecting legal profession), Miss. Bankruptcy Conf. (chmn. com. on bankruptcy rules 1988), Am. Law Inst., Am. Judicature Soc., Nat. Conf. Bar Examiners (MBE com. 1986—88, trustee 1989—2000, chmn. 1998—99, chmn. tech. com. 2000—), Fed. Bar Assn. (v.p. no. Miss. 1977—78, 1981—82), Miss. Bar Assn. (bd. dirs. young lawyers divsn. 1976—79, chmn. sect. corp. fin. bus. law 1989—90, pres. fellows young lawyers divsn. 2000—01), Washington County Hist. Soc. (pres. 1981), Greenville C. of C. (bd. dirs. 1976—79, pres. 1992—93), Kiwanis (Greenville pres. 1978—79, lt. gov. 1982—83), Oxford & Cambridge Golfing Soc. (Rye, Eng.), Annandale Golf Club (Madison, Miss.), Huntercombe Golf Club (Nuffield, Eng.), Greenville Golf and Country Club (v.p. 1977—79), Vincents Club (Oxford, Eng.), Phi Beta Kappa. Episcopalian. Home: 315 Wetherbee St Greenville MS 38701 Office: Phelps Dunbar LLP PO Box 23066 111 E Capitol Ste 600 Jackson MS 39201 Office Phone: 601-360-9347. Personal E-mail: hafter@tecinfo.net. Business E-Mail: hafterj@phelps.com.

HAGA, ENOCH JOHN, computer educator, writer, editor; b. LA, Apr. 25, 1931; s. Enoch and Esther Bonser (Higginson) H.; m. Elna Jo Wright, Aug. 22, 1957 (dec. Aug. 22, 2004). AA, Grant Tech. Coll., 1950; AB, Sacramento State Coll., 1955, MA, 1958; PhD, Calif. Inst. Integral Studies, 1972. Tchr. bus. Calif. Med. Facility, Vacaville, 1956-60; asst. prof. bus. Stanislaus State Coll., Turlock, Calif., 1960-61; engring. writer, publs. engr. Hughes Aircraft Co., Fullerton, Calif., 1961-62, Lockheed Missiles & Space Co., Sunnyvale, Calif., 1962, Gen. Precision, Inc., Glendale, Calif., 1962-63; sr. adminstrv. analyst Holmes & Narver, Inc., LA, 1963-64; tchr., chmn. dept. bus. and math. Pleasanton Unified Dist., Calif., 1964-92, coord. computer svcs., adminstrn., instrn., 1984-85. Vis. asst. prof. bus. Sacramento State Coll., 1967-69; instr. bus. and computer sci. Chabot Coll., Hayward, Calif., 1970-89; instr. bus. and philosophy Ohlone Coll., Fremont, Calif., 1972; prof., v.p., mem. bd. govs. Calif. Inst. Asian Studies, 1972-75; pres., prof. Pacific Inst. East-West Studies, San Francisco, 1975-76, also mem. bd. govs.; dir. Cert. Couns., Livermore, Calif., 1975-80; mem., chmn. negotiating team Amador Vly. Secondary Educators Assn., Pleasanton, 1976-77, pres. 1984-85. Coordinating editor: Total Systems, 1962; editor: Automation Educator, 1965-67, Automated Educational Systems, 1967, Data Processing in Biomedicine and Medicine, 1973; contbg. editor: Jour. Bus. Edn., 1961-69, Data Processing mag., 1967-70; contbr.: Carlos Rivera: The Prime Puzzles & Problems Connection, 1992—, The On-Line Encyclopedia of Integer Sequences, 1992—; author, compiler: Understanding Automation, 1965; author: Simplified Computer Arithmetic, Simplified Computer Logic, Simplified Computer Input, Simplified Computer Flowcharting, 1971-72, Before the Apple Drops, 15 Essays on Dinosaur Education, 2007, Exploring Prime Numbers on Your PC and the Internet, 2007, Write and Publish Your Family History on Your PC, 2007, TAROsolution: A Complete Guide to Interpreting Tarot, 1994, The 2000-Year History of the Haga-Helgoy and Krick-Keller Families, Ancestors and Descendants, 1994; editor Data Processor, 1960-62, Automedica, 1970-76, FBE Bull., 1967-68. With USNR, 1947—49, with USNR, 1953—57, with USAF, 1949—52. Mem. Internat. Assn. Computer Info. Sys. (co-founder 1960), Sacramento Statis. Assn. Avocations: genealogy, prime numbers, mathematical sequences. Mailing: PO Box 489 Folsom CA 95763-0489 Personal E-mail: Enokh@comcast.net.

HAGA, KAZUNORI, medical researcher; MD, Hokkiado U., Japan, 1994, PhD, 2002. Attending urologist Hokkaido U., Sapporo, 1994—2005; rsch. assoc. UCLA, 2005—. Achievements include research in gene therapy.

HAGAN, JOHN CHARLES, III, ophthalmologist; b. Mexico, Mo., Oct. 7, 1943; s. John Charles Hagan II and Cleta L. (Book) Neely; m. Rebecca Jane Chapman, July 15, 1967; children: Carol Ann, Catherine Elizabeth. BA, U. Mo., 1965; MD, Loyola U., Chgo., 1969. Diplomate Am. Bd. Ophthalmology. Intern Med. Coll. Wis., Milw., 1969-70; resident in ophthalmology Emory U., Atlanta, 1972-75; practice medicine, Kansas City, Mo., 1975—. Cons. Am. Running and Phys. Fitness Assn., Washington, 1973—. Editor: Mo. Medicine: The Jour. of the Mo. State Med. Assn.; contbr. over 120 articles to profl. jours Capt. M.C., USAF, 1970-72. Fellow ACS; mem. AMA, Am. Soc. Cataract and Refractive Surgery, Mo. Soc. Eye Physicians and Surgeons (pres. 1998), Kansas City Soc. Ophthalmology. Office: Discover Vision Ctrs 9401 N Oak Trafficway Kansas City MO 64155 Office Phone: 816-478-1230.

HAGAN, JOSEPH HENRY, educational consultant; b. Providence, Mar. 2, 1935; s. Joseph Henry and Claire Veronica (Gorman) H.; m. Patrice O'Malley; 1 child, Kevin O'Malley. AB, Providence Coll.; EdM, Boston U.; D. Min., EdD, Grad. Theol. Found.; DCL (hon.), Salve Regina Coll., 1968; DPA (hon.), Mt. St. Joseph Coll., 1976; MBA (hon.), Bryant Coll., 1992; LLD (hon.), Boston U., 1993; DPS (hon.), Providence Coll., 1996; EdD (hon.), Assumption Coll., 1998, Rivier Coll., 1998; LHD (hon.), John Cabot U., 2004. Tchr. Providence Public Schs., 1958-61; legis. asst. U.S. Ho. of Reps., 1961-64; staff asst. Pres.'s Com. on Juvenile Delinquency, 1964-65; spl. asst. OEO, 1965-68; dir. planning, devel. and fed. relations Bryant Coll., Smithfield, RI, 1968-70, v.p. for public affairs, 1970-73, lectr. public adminstrn., adj. prof. social scis.; asst. to chmn. Nat. Endowment for Humanities, Washington, 1973-78; pres., lectr. politics Assumption Coll., Worcester, Mass., 1978-98, pres. emeritus, 1998—; pres. Roger Williams U., Bristol, RI, 1999—2001. Chmn. bd. trustees John Cabot U., Rome; mem. Nat. Coun. on the Humanities, 1992-00; trustee Cardinal Tardini Charitable Trust; chmn. budget com. Little Compton, R.I., 1999-01, chmn. zoning bd., 2001-04, town moderator, 2004-06; mem. bd. overseers Boston U.; mem. R.I. Bd. Govs. of Higher Edn. Decorated knight of honor and devotion in Obedience of Malta, knight Grand Cross, St. Gregory the Great, comdr. Palmes Academiques (France), knight Grand Cross of Justice of the Sacred Mil. Constantinian Order St. George, knight comdr. Order of Saints Maurice and Lazarus, knight grand cross of the Holy Sepulchre, comdr. Order of Merit, Knights of Malta, Gentleman-in-Waiting to the Pope. Mem. Am. Antiquarian Soc., N.Am. Assn. Constantinian Order (pres.), Am. Assn. Malta (bd. councillors), Univ. Club (Providence), Circulo della Caccia (Rome), KC, Univ. Club (Washington). Roman Catholic. Personal E-mail: jhagan67@cox.net.

HAGAN, KATE (KATHRYN T. HAGAN), library director, editor; b. 1958; BSJ, Ohio U., 1980. Editor Ohio Lawyer, Columbus; asst. dir. pub. rels., ctrl. Ohio chapter Am. Heart Assn.; asst. exec. dir. Ohio State Bar Assn., 1995—2000; exec. v.p. Comml. Law League Am.; dir. section family law ABA, 2003—05; dir. fund devel. Radiological Soc. N. Am., 2005—07; exec. dir. Am. Assn. Law Libraries, Chgo., 2007—. Office: Am Assn Law Libraries 53 W Jackson Blvd Ste 940 Chicago IL 60604 E-mail: aallhq@aall.org.

HAGAN, KEVIN F., plastic surgeon, educator; BA, Johns Hopkins U., Balt., 1971, MD, 1974. Cert. Am. Bd. Surgery, 1980, Am. Bd. Plastic Surgery, 1983, of added qualifications in surgery of the hand 1993, lic. Tenn., 1982. Intern surgery Med. Coll. Va., Richmond, 1974—75, resident surgery, 1975—79; fellow microsurgery Dr. Harry Buncke, San Francisco, 1980; resident plastic surgery U. Calif., San Francisco, 1980—82; assoc. prof. plastic surgery Vanderbilt-Ingram Cancer Ctr., Nashville. Named Golf Digest 2006 Top 250 Golfer Doctors in Am. Office: Vanderbilt U Med Ctr Dept Plastic Surgery D-4207 Med Ctr N Nashville TN 37232-2345 Office Phone: 615-322-2350. Office Fax: 615-936-0167. E-mail: kevin.hagan@vanderbilt.edu.*

HAGAN, MARY ANN, lawyer; b. Phila., Feb. 18, 1935; d. Harry A. and Marie (Farrell) H. BA, Immaculata Coll., Pa., 1956; MA in History, U. Pa., 1958; LLB, Temple U., 1963. Bar: Pa. 1964, U.S. Dist. Ct. Pa. 1972, U.S. Ct. Appeals (3d cir.) 1980, U.S. Tax Ct. 1965, U.S. Ct. Appeals for Federal Cir., 1996. Historian U.S. Dept. Interior, Phila., 1958-60; atty. Urban Renewal Adminstrn., Phila., 1963-65; trial atty. IRS, Office of Chief Counsel, Washington & Phila., 1965-73; supervisory trial atty. U.S. Equal Employment Opportunity Commn., Phila., 1973-77; pvt. practice Phila., 1978—. Arbitrator U.S. Dist. Ct., Phila., 1975—, mem. employment panel, 1989—, fed. mediator, 1991—; lectr., Phila. Bar Edn. Ctr., 1997. Author: Working With the Federal Sector Equal Employment Opportunity Regulations, 29 CFR 1614, 1997. Mem. Nat. Employment Lawyers Assn., Phila. Bar Assn. Office: 1700 Sansom St 4th Fl Philadelphia PA 19103

HAGAN, THOMAS M., electric power industry executive; m. Marilyn Hagan. Grad., U. Tex., Austin. Staff mem. Tex. Lt. Gov. William P. Hobby; legis. dir. to adminstrv. asst. US Senator Lloyd Bentsen; state and fed. lobbyist Ctrl. and South West Corp., 1980, asst. to v.p. govtl. affairs, 1981—88, v.p. govtl. affairs, 1988—92, v.p. govtl. rels., 1992—93, v.p. govtl. rels., office of chmn., 1993—96, sr. v.p. external affairs, 1996—2000; sr. v.p. govtl. affairs Am. Electric Power Svc. Corp., Columbus, Ohio, 2000—02, exec. v.p. shared svcs., 2002, exec. v.p. AEP Utilities-West. Capt. USMC, Vietnam. Office: Am Electric Power Svc Corp 1 Riverside Plaza Columbus OH 43215-2373 Office Phone: 614-716-1000.*

HAGANS, VALERIE MAE GEE, special education educator; b. San Antonio, Mar. 23, 1966; d. George Francis and Mae (Smith) Gee; m. Danny Franklin Hagans, June 24, 1989. Bachelors in Early Childhood Edn., Meth. Coll., 1988; MA in Edn.-Spl. Edn., Fayetteville State U., 1993. Cert. tchr., N.C.; nat. bd. cert. tchr. Spl. educator Cumberland County Pub. Schs., Fayetteville, N.C., 1989—. Mem. Alpha Delta Kappa (Gamma Sigma chpt.), Coun. for Exceptional Children, Omicron Delta Kappa. Methodist. Home: 171 Water Ridge Ln Stedman NC 28391 Office: Warrenwood Elem Sch 4618 Rosehill Rd Fayetteville NC 28311 Office Phone: 910-488-6609. E-mail: valeriehagans@ccs.k12.nc.us.

HAGAR, RICHARD JOSEPH, music educator, musician; b. Brockton, Mass., July 15, 1954; s. Preston Irving and Marie Mahoney Hagar; m. Charlene Ann Peterson, Aug. 2, 1986. B in Music and Music Edn., Hartt Coll. of Music, 1976. Cert. tchr. music K-12 Mass., Conn., N.Y. Tchr. string instruments, orch. and chorus dir. Delaware Acad., Delhi, NY, 1976—78; tchr. string instruments, orch. dir. Bedford (Mass.) Pub. Schs., 1978—88, Westborough (Mass.) Pub. Schs., 1988—. Named Mass. Orch. Dir. of Yr., 2000; recipient Lowell Mason award for outstanding contbns. to music edn., 1999. Mem.: Mass. Music Educators' Assn. (treas. Northea. Dist. 1982—86, all-state conf. exec. bd. 1993—98, 2002—, membership coord. Northea. Dist. 1980—93, all-state orch. mgr. 1998—2000), Westborough Tchrs. Assn., Mass. Tchrs. Assn., Am. String Teachers Assn. with Nat. Sch. Orch. Assn. (pres. Mass. chpt. 1982—86, exec. bd. Mass. chpt. 1990—), Music Educators' Nat. Conf. Home: 20 Greybert Ln Worcester MA 01602 Personal E-mail: rchag@aol.com.

HAGAR, SAMMY, musician, vocalist, composer; b. Oct. 13, 1947; m. Kari Karte, Nov. 29, 1995; 2 children; 2 children from previous marriage. Vocalist, guitarist Montrose, 1974-75, Van Halen, 1986-96, 2003—, Sammy & the Waboritas; solo career, 1975—; founder Cabo Wabo Cantina, Mexico. Solo albums include Nine on a Ten Scale, 1976, Sammy Hagar Two, 1977, All Night Long, 1978, Street Machine, Danger Zone, 1979, Centre Hole, 1980, Standing Hampton, 1981, Red Alert! Dial Nine, 1982, Three Lock Box, 1983, VOA, 1984, I Never Said Goodbye, 1987, Very Live in Concert, 1989, Red Hot, 1992, Marching to Mars, 1997, Red Voodoo, 1999, Ten 13, 2000, Not 4 Sale, 2002, Live: Hallelujah, 2003, Livin' It Up!, 2006; singles include Your Love Is Driving Me Crazy, 1982, I Can't Drive 55, 1984, Never Say Goodbye, 1986; albums with Montrose include Montrose, 1973, Paper Money, 1974; albums with Van Halen include 5150, 1986, OU812, 1988, For Unlawful Carnal Knowledge, 1991 (Favorite Hard Rock album, Am. Music Awards, 1992, Best Hard Rock performance, Grammy Awards, 1992), Van Halen Live: Right Here, Right Now, 1993, Balance, 1995, Best of Both Worlds, 2004. Named to Rock & Roll Hall of Fame, with Van Halen, 2007. Office: c/o FWO Inc 1724 Marin Ave Berkeley CA 94707 E-mail: info@redrocker.com.*

HAGARTY, MARK, lawyer; b. Hartford, Conn., June 26, 1954; s. Thomas Joseph and Frances E. (Martel) H.; m. Molly Lou Drown, Sept. 9, 1989; children: Maclean Joseph, Murphy Thomas. BA, Coll. Holy Cross, Worcester, Mass., 1976; JD Summa Cum Laude (hon.), Harvard U., 1979. Bar: Calif. 1979, US Dist. Ct. (so. dist.) Calif. 1979, US Dist. Ct. (ctrl. dist.) Calif. 1980. Assoc. Luce Forward, Hamilton & Scripps, San Diego, 1979-85, ptnr., 1985, Luce Forward, San Diego. Author: Practice Guide Landlord/Tenant , Rutter Grp., 1989, update 1990-95, Getting Results in Landlord/Tenant Litigation, Rutter Grp., 1985. Mem. Friendly Sons of St. Patrick. Mem. ABA, San Diego County Bar Assn., Am. Inns of Ct. (barriste), Assn. Bus. Trial Lawyers, Barristers Club, San Diego, Phi Beta Kappa. Office: Luce Forward 600 W Broadway Ste 2200 San Diego CA 92101-3391 Office Phone: 619-236-1414. Office Fax: 619-744-5393. Business E-Mail: mhagarty@luce.com.

HAGBERG, CARL THOMAS, financial executive; b. SI, NY, Dec. 19, 1942; s. Charles W. and Dorothy (Van Hoesen) H.; m. Patricia Rasile, Sept. 21, 1972; children: Karl, Peder, Erik. BA, NYU, 1971; MS, Columbia U., 1983. V.p. Mfrs. Hanover Trust Co., NYC, 1972-83, sr. v.p., 1984-92; chmn., CEO Carl T. Hagberg and Assocs., Investor Rels., Jackson, NJ, 1992—. Bd. dirs., chmn. audit com. Mfrs. Hanover Trust Co. of Calif., San Francisco, 1984-92; dir. Minerva Fund, Inc., 1994-98, Roundtable Ensemble, 1999-2003; pub. Shareholder Svc. Optimizer. Mem. adv. bd. Fountain Gallery, 2006—. Mem. Am. Arbitration Assn., Soc. Corp. Secs. and Governance Officers (nat. treas. 1991-97, NY chpt. pres. 1991-92), Nat. Assn. Securities Dealers (bd. arbitration), Nat. Investor Rels. Inst., Shareholders Svcs. Assn., Soc. Corp. Compliance and Ethics, Tiro A. Segno NY, Pamet Harbor Yacht and Tennis Club. Home and Office: 6 S Lakeview Dr Jackson NJ 08527-2703 Personal E-mail: cthagberg@aol.com.

HAGBERG, CHRIS ERIC, lawyer; b. Steubenville, Ohio, Dec. 19, 1949; s. Rudolf Eric and Sara (Smith) H.; m. Viola Louise Wilgus, Feb. 19, 1978. BS, Duke U., 1975; JD, U. Tulsa, 1978; postgrad., Nat. Law Ctr., George Washington U. Bar: Okla. 1978, Va. 1979, U.S. Ct. Appeals (4th cir.) Calif. 1986. Law clk. to presiding justice U.S. Dist. Ct. (no. dist.) Okla.; asst. counsel ADP Selection Office Dept. Navy, Navy Regional Contracting Ctr., Washington; counsel Naval Supply Ctr., Pearl Harbor, Hawaii; Pacific area counsel Naval Supply Sys. Command, Dept. Navy, Makakilo, Hawaii; assoc. counsel Navy Supply Sys. Command, Washington; atty. Pettit & Martin, LA, 1985-87, Seyfarth, Shaw, Fairweather and Geraldson, Washington, 1988-91, U.S. Coast Guard HQ, Washington, 1992-93, USN, 1993-95, Dept. Navy OGC/NSWC Carderock, West Bethesda, Md., 1995—. Contbr. articles to legal jours. Lt. USN, 1970-74. Recipient David I. Milsten award, 1978, 7 Am. Jurisprudence awards, 1976-78, First prize Dept. Navy Legal Writing Contest, 1981. Mem. ABA, FBA, Nat. Contract Mgmt. Assn., Order of Coif. Presbyterian.

HAGBERG, VIOLA WILGUS, lawyer; b. July 3, 1952; d. William E. and Jean Shelton (Barlow) Wilgus; m. Chris Eric Hagberg, Feb. 19, 1978. BA, Furman U., Greenville, SC, 1974; JD, U. SC, Columbia, 1978, U. Tulsa, 1978; diploma (hon.), DOD Army Logistics Sch., Ft. Lee, Va., 1981—82. Bar: Okla. 78, US Ct. Appeals (4th cir.) 79. With Lawyers Com. for Civil Rights, Washington, 1979; pub. utility specialist Fed. Energy Regulatory Commn., Washington, 1979—80; contract specialist US Army, C.E., Ft. Shafter, Hawaii, 1980—81; contract officer/supervisory contract specialist Tripler Army Med. Ctr., Hawaii, 1981—83; supervisory procurement analyst and chief policy Procurement divsn. USCG, Washington, 1983; contracts officer and chief Avionics Engring. Contracting Br., 1984; procurement analyst office of sec. Dept. Transp., 1984—85; contracting officer Naval Regional Contracting Ctr., Long Beach, Calif., 1985—87; chief acquisition rev. and policy Hdqrs. Def. Mapping Agy., Washington, 1987—92, dir. acquisitions Fairfax, Va., 1992—93, dir. acquisition policy, 1994—96; dir. acquisition policy, tech. and legis. programs Nat. Mapping and Imagery Agy., 1996—97, dep. assoc. and sr. counsel for adminstrv. law and litigation; dir. acquisition policy, tech. and legis. programs Office Gen. Counsel, Nat. Geospatial Intelligence Agy., Bethesda. Mem.: ABA (law student divsn. liaison 1977—78), Okla. Bar Assn., Va. State Bar Assn., Nat. Contract Mgmt. Assn., Kappa Delta Epsilon, Phi Alpha Delta. Office: Nat Geospatial Intelligence Agy Office Gen Counsel 4600 Sangamore (MS-D-10) Bethesda MD 20816

HAGE, LILLIAN C., religious organization administrator, director, dean; d. McKinley H. and Doris L. Trent; m. Arthur D. Hage, Oct. 28, 1978; children: Mary, John, Grace, Hannah, Charity. Masters, Marshall U., Huntington, W.Va., 1978; Doctorate, Truth and Liberty Bible Coll., Hurricane, W.Va., 2004. Teen dir. Hurricane Bible Coll., 1977—; prin. Truth and Liberty Ch. Sch., Hurricane, 1979—; dir. program activities Camp Grace, Milton, W.Va., 1994—; academic dean Truth and Liberty Bible Coll., Hurricane, 1996—; asst. to CEO Faith Mission, Hurricane, 2001—. Mem., leader Hurricane Bible Ch., 1977—. Avocation: water color. Office: Hurricane Bible Ch PO Box 151 Hurricane WV 25526 Personal E-mail: lilie1954@yahoo.com.

HAGE, SHARON, chef; b. Detroit, Mich. Grad., Culinary Inst. Am., 1984. Cook Arizona 206, NYC; chef Sam's Cafe, NYC; exec. chef Harvey Hotels, Dallas, Neiman Marcus, Dallas, Hotel St. Germain, Dallas; owner, exec. chef York St., Dallas, 2001—. Named one of Dallas' Rising Stars, StarChefs.com, 2007. Office: York St 6047 Lewis St Dallas TX 75206-0968 Office Phone: 214-826-0968.*

HAGEDORN, ALAN PATRICK, social studies educator; b. Beech Grove, Ind., Mar. 16, 1972; s. Paul Edward and Patricia Ann Hagedorn; m. Sherry Deanna Engle, July 22, 1995; 1 child, Isaac; 1 child, Sophia. BS in History and Social Studies Edn., Ball State U., Muncie, Ind., 1995; MS in Edn., Ind. Wesleyan U., Marion, 2000. Tchr. Ctr. Grove Cmty. Sch. Corp., Greenwood, Ind., 1995—. Cons. Ind. Dept. Edn., Indpls., 2002—05, Ind. U., Bloomington, 2003—06. Sec. Ctr. Grove Trails Com., Johnson County, Ind. Mem.: Nat. Coun. Soc. Studies, Ind. Assn. Historians, History Educators Network Ind. (founding bd. mem. 2005—07), Ind. Coun. for History Edn. (bd. mem. 2004—07), Geography Educators Network Ind. (bd. mem. 2005—07), Ind. Coun. for the Social Studies (bd. mem., pres. 2005—07). Avocations: cartooning, writing, welding. Home: 6818 Travis Rd Greenwood IN 46143

HAGEDORN, HILDI, psychologist, researcher; PhD, U. Md., Balt., 2000. Lic. clinical psychologist State Bd. Psychology, Minn., 2001. Staff psychologist Mpls. VA Med. Ctr., Mpls., 2000—; asst. prof. U. Minn., 2004—. Exec. com. mem. VA Quality Enhancement Rsch. Initiative, 2001—. Contbr. articles to profl. jours., chapters to books. Grantee, VA Health Svcs. R & D, 2006—. Office: Minneapolis VA Medical Center One Veterans Drive Minneapolis MN 55417 Office Phone: 612-467-3875. Business E-Mail: hildi.hagedorn@va.gov.

HAGEDORN, JAMES, landscape company executive; Grad. AMP program, Harvard Bus. Sch. Sr. mgmt. roles Miracle-Gro; with The Scotts Co., 1995—, pres. N.Am. ops., pres., COO, 2000—03, chmn., CEO, 2003—. Exec. v.p. Scotts' U.S. Bus. Groups. Officer USAF. Office: c/o Scotts Co 14111 Scottslawn Rd Marysville OH 43041*

HAGEL, CHUCK (CHARLES TIMOTHY HAGEL), senator; b. North Platte, Nebr., Oct. 4, 1946; s. Charles Dean and Betty (Dunn) Hagel; m. Lilibet Ziller, 1985; children: Allyn, Ziller. Student, Brown Inst. Radio & TV, Minn., 1966; BA, U. Nebr., 1971. Adminstrv. asst. to Rep. John Y. McCollister US Congress, 1971—77; vice chmn. Reagan-Bush Presdl. Inaugural Com., 1981; adminstr. US Vets. Adminstrn., 1981-82; co-founder, dir., & pres. Collins, Hagel and Clarke, Inc., 1982—85; co-founder, dir., & exec. v.p. Vanguard Cellular Systems, 1985—87; founding chmn. Comm. Corp. Internat. Ltd.; pres., CEO World USO, 1987-90; pres. McCarthy & Co. Investment Banking Firm, 1991-96; US Senator from Nebr., 1997—. Select com. intelligence US Senate, Congressional-Exec. Commn. China, com. rules and adminstrn., fgn. relations, com. banking, housing and urban affairs; mem. Bus.-Govt. Relations Coun., Washington, Coun. Excellence in Govt., Coun. Fgn. Relations. Bd. trustees Am. Red Cross (Heartland Chpt.), Bellevue U., Nebr., Constl. Heritage Inst., Eisenhower World Affairs Inst., Free Enterprise Coun., Fund for Democracy and Develop., German-Am. Bus. Assn., Hastings Coll., Nebr., Manville Personal Injury Settlement Trust, Nat. D-Day Mus., Nat. Fedn. Independent Bus. Found.; adv. bd. Friends of Vietnam Veterans' Meml.; chmn. bd. dirs. Am. Info. Systems, Inc., No Greater Love; bd. dirs. Eureka Bank, San Francisco, MTT Corp., Hungary, Omaha C. of C., Arlington Nat. Cemetery Hist. Soc.; chmn. Agent Orange Settlement Fund Payment Program, Vietnam Veterans' Meml. Tenth Anniversary; chmn. Great Plains Chpt. Paralyzed Veterans of Am.; v.p. Desert Storm Homecoming Found.; bd. govs. United Svc. Orgn. World. Served to sergeant 2nd bn., 47th inf., ninth inf. divsn. US Army, 1967—68, South Vietnam. Decorated Combat Infantryman Badge, Purple Heart with Oak Leaf Cluster, Vietnamese Cross of Gallantry; recipient Legis. of Yr., Vietnam Veterans Assn. Am., 2000, George W. Norris Disting. Lectr. award, U. Nebr., Kearney, 2002, Edmund S. Muskie Disting. Public Svc. award, Ctr. Nat. Policy, 2004, Disting. Internat. Leadership award, Atlantic Coun., 2004. Mem.: Internat. Republican Inst., Disabled Am. Veterans, Veterans of Fgn. Wars, Am. Legion. Republican. Episcopalian. Office: US Senate 248 Russell Office Bldg Washington DC 20510-0001 also: District Office 294 Federal Bldg 100 Centennial Mall North Lincoln NE 68508 Office Phone: 202-224-4224, 402-476-1400. Office Fax: 202-224-5213, 402-476-0605.*

HAGEL, JOHN, III, management consultant; b. Berlin, NH, Sept. 14, 1950; s. John Jr. and Evelyn Gertrude (Parent) H. BA, Wesleyan U., 1972; PhB, Oxford U., 1974; MBA, JD, Harvard U., 1978. Bar: Mass. 1978. Cons. Boston Cons. Group, 1978-80; pres. Sequoia Group, Larkspur, Calif., 1980-82; v.p. Atari, Inc., Sunnyvale, Calif., 1982-83, sr. v.p., 1983-84; sr. engagement mgr. McKinsey and Co., NYC, 1984-87, prin. San Francisco, 1987-2000; chief strategy officer 12 Entrepreneuring, Inc., San Francisco, 2000—02; pres. Bus. Performance Network, Burlingame, 2002—. Author: Alternative Energy Strategies, 1976, Assessing The Criminal, 1977, Net Gain: Expanding Markets Through Virtual Communities, 1997, Net Worth: Shaping Markets When Customers Make the Rules, 1999, Out of the Box: Strategies for Achieving Profits Today and Growth Tomorrow through Web Services, 2002, The Only Sustainable Edge: Why Business Strategy Depends on Productive Friction and Dynamic Specialization, 2005; contbr. articles to profl. jours. Keasbey Found. fellow, 1972-74; Forum fellow World Econ. Forum, 1999-. Mem. ABA, Mass. Bar Assn. Episcopalian. E-mail: jh@johnhagel.com.

HAGEL, LAWRENCE B., federal judge; b. Washington, Ind. 3 children. BS, U.S. Naval Acad., 1969; JD, Univ. Pacific, 1976; LLM with highest honors, George Washington Univ., 1983. Counsel Paralyzed Vets. Am., Washington, 1990—2003; judge US Ct. Appeals Vets. Claims, Washington, 2004—. Mem. Adminstrv. Conf. U.S., 1995, rules adv. com., U.S. Ct. Appeals Vets. Claims, 1992—2003, exec. bd., Vets. Pro Bono Consortium, steering com. D.C. Bar, 1999—2003. Lt. col. (ret.) USMC, infantry, Vietnam, Judge Advocate. Decorated Combat Action Ribbon, Meritorious Svc. Medal (3 awards), Joint Svc. Commendation Medal, Army Commendation Medal. Mem.: Fed. Bar Assn. (chmn., Vets. Law com. 1994—95). Office: US Ct Appeals Vets Claims Ste 900 625 Indiana Ave NW Washington DC 20004-2950

HAGEL, RAYMOND CHARLES, publishing company executive, educator; b. Jersey City, Sept. 5, 1916; s. Morris and Theresa (Feigenbaum) H.; m. Ruth Block, May 30, 1941; children: Keith W., Wendy A.; m. Alma Triner, Dec. 24, 2002. BS cum laude, NYU, 1937. Promotion mgr. McGraw-Hill Pub. Co., 1937-38, 41-42, 45-46; with bus. dept. N.Y. World-Telegram, 1939-40; with Asso. Mag. Contbrs., Inc., 1947-48; pres. Smith, Hagel & Knudsen, Inc., NYC, 1948-59, P.F. Collier & Son Corp., NYC, 1959-60, chmn. bd., 1961-65; exec. v.p. Crowell-Collier Pub. Co. (name changed to Crowell Collier and Macmillan, Inc. 1965, Macmillan Inc., 1973), 1959-60, pres., 1960-76, chief exec. officer, 1963-80, chmn. bd., 1964-80, also bd. dirs. David L. Tandy exec.-in-resident, vis. prof. M.J. Neeley Sch. Bus., Tex. Christian U., 1980-81, mem. adv. bd. dept. journalism, 1981—; prof. mgmt. Barney Sch. Bus. and Public Adminstrn., U. Hartford, 1981-90, chmn. dept. mgmt., 1983-84; mem. Rockefeller Center adv. bd. Chem. Bank, N.Y.C.; mem. Council Internat. Exec. Service Corps.; disting. adj. prof. Coll. Bus. and Pub. Adminstrn., NYU, 1972-79, mem. dean's adv. council, 1973 Trustee, Coll. of New Rochelle, 1970-76, 77-80. Served with USNR, 1942-45. Recipient John T. Madden Meml. medal NYU, 1972; Disting. Service award in investment edn. Investment Edn. Inst. of Nat. Assocs. Investment Clubs, 1973; Madden asso., Gallatin asso. NYU Mem. Fgn. Policy Assn., Am. Assn. Higher Edn., Dirs. Table, Assn. Am. Pubs., Alpha Delta Sigma, Beta Gamma Sigma, Beta Alpha Psi, Econ. Club, Metro. Club, Pub.'s Lunch Club. E-mail: rhagel@sbcglobal.net.

HAGEL, WILLIAM CARL, metallurgical consultant; b. Pitts., Apr. 5, 1927; s. William and Mabel Florence (Geary) H.; m. Mary Ellen Roosa; children: Lisa Christine, Karen Andrea, Juliana Margaret. B in Metall. Engring., Cornell U., 1951; MS, PhD in Metallurgy, Carnegie-Mellon U., 1954. Metallurgist GE Co. Rsch. Lab., Schenectady, NY, 1954-66; prof., chmn. metallurgy dept. U. Denver, Colo., 1966-70; mgr. materials devel. GE Aircraft Engines, Evendale, Ohio, 1970-72; mgr. advanced materials Kelsey-Hayes R & D, Ann Arbor, Mich., 1972-73; mgr. R&D Climax Molybdenum Co., Ann Arbor, 1973—84; pres. Arbormet Ltd., Ann Arbor, 1984—. Disting. vis. prof. Minas Inst. Tech., Minas Gerais, Brazil, 1969. Co-editor: The Superalloys, 1972, Superalloys II, 1987; contbr. articles to profl. jours.; patentee in field. Chair adv. bd. Northside Cmty. Ch., Ann Arbor, 1993-94. With USN, 1945-46. Fellow Am. Soc. for Metals, Am. Inst. for Chemists; mem. Am. Inst. Mining and Metall. Engrs., Am. Ceramic Soc., Electrochem. Soc., N.Y. Acad. Sci., Sigma Xi, Phi Kappa Phi. Avocations: archaeology, numismatics. Home: 929 Greenhills Dr Ann Arbor MI 48105-2721 Office Phone: 734-668-8069.

HAGELSTEIN, ROBERT PHILIP, publisher; b. NYC, Dec. 15, 1942; s. H. Robert and E. Ann Hagelstein; m. Ann G. Linguvic, Apr. 26, 1970; children: Christopher R., Jonathan W. BA in English Lit., L.I. U., 1964. Prodn. mgr. Johnson Reprint Corp., NYC, 1965-68, editor-in-chief, 1968-70; v.p. Greenwood Press, Inc., Westport, Conn., 1970-73; pres. Greenwood Pub. Group, 1973-99; pub. and electronic pub. cons., 1999—; pub. Reclamation Press, 2005—; exec. dir. Confrontation Press, 2004—. Bd. dirs. Aldwych Press, London. Author: New York to Boston: Travels in the 1840's, 2005; contbr. articles to profl. jours.; (CD's) Smile, A Collection of Piano Favorites, 2007, Sentimental Mood, 2007. Mem.: U.S. Power Squadron, South Norwalk Boat Club, North Palm Beach Yacht Club.

HAGEMAN, DALE, alternative staffing company executive; CPA, Okla., Nebr.; lic. ins. agt., 3d party adminstr. CFO, Price Edwards & Co., comml. real estate mgmt.-brokerage co., Oklahome City, 1982—92; pres., CEO, Accord Human Resources, Inc., Oklahome City, 1992—. Former chmn. bd. dirs. Oklahoma City Health Care Coalition. Mem. AICPA, Nat. Assn. for Alternative Staffing (bd. dirs. 1994—, pres. 1997-98, past pres. 1998—, nat. affairs chmn. 1998—), Okla. Soc. CPA's, Oklahoma City Human Resource Soc., Oklahoma City C. of C. (health ins. com.). Office: Accord Human Resources Inc 210 Park Ave Ste 1200 Oklahoma City OK 73102-5603

HAGEMAN, RICHARD PHILIP, JR., educational administrator; b. Derby, Conn., Dec. 21, 1941; s. Richard Philip and Jane Elizabeth (Serafinowicz) H.; m. Patricia Steele; children: Margaret Anne, Sheila Marie. BS, Cen. Conn. State U., 1964; MS, U. Bridgeport, 1968, profl. diploma, 1972. Cert. counselor Nat. Bd. Cert. Counselors; cert. tchr., Conn. Tchr. Stony Brook Sch. Stratford (Conn.) Bd. Edn., 1964—69, elem. sch. guidance counselor, 1969—81, secondary sch. guidance counselor, 1981—83; asst. prin. Stratford Acad., 1983—90; prin. Whitney Sch., 1990—95, Ctr. Sch., 1995—99; ret., 1999; univ. supr. Sacred Heart U., Fairfield, Conn. Lectr. edn. Fairfield U. Grad. Sch. Edn., 1971-93; head counselor Stratford Continuing Edn. Program, 1983-91, program facilitator, 1999—; chief examiner Gen. Ednl. Devel., 1986-91; assessor, trainer Beginning Educator Support and Tng. program Conn. State Dept. of Edn.; mem. adv. bd. counselor edn. Fairfield (Conn.) U., 1970-74; co-chmn. Stratford Juvenile Deliquency Prevention Team, 1979-81; pres. Stratford Elem. Prin. Assn., 1991-92; chief reader Conn. Adminstrs. Test, 1999—. Mem. Youth Adv. Bd. Stratford, 1981-85, chairperson, 1984-85; radio announcer Sta. WMNR, Monroe, Conn., 1982—. Mem. ACA, ASCD, NEA (life), Stratford Edn. Assn. (pres. 1978-79), New Eng. Assn. Specialists Group Work (pres. 1982-83, v.p. 1999-2003), Phi Delta Kappa. Roman Catholic. Democrat. Personal E-mail: hagemanrandp@msn.com.

HAGEMANN, ROBERT A., health care company executive; Sr. fin. positions Ernst & Young, Crompton & Knowles, Inc., Prime Hospitality, Inc.; from mem. staff to v.p., CFO Quest Diagnostics, Teterboro, NJ, 1992—98, v.p. to sr. v.p., CFO, 1998—. Office: Quest Diagnostics One Malcolm Ave Teterboro NJ 07608*

HAGEN, BARBARA C., music educator; b. Beaumont, Tex., June 3, 1952; d. Bobbie Carlyle and Doris Mae (Lindberg) Mabry; m. Keith Thomas Hagen, Dec. 21, 1973; children: Holly Hagen Buche, Heidi Noel. BS in Music Theory, Lamar U., 1974. Piano accompianist First Bapt. Ch. Youth Choir, Beaumont, Tex., 1972—73; viola player Symphony of S.E. Tex., 1972—74; viola player, music arranger various ch. activities, 1972—98, San Antonio, 1972—98; viola player profl. string quartet for weddings, Beaumont, 1990—98; tchr. piano & strings Hagen's Happy Notes, 1972—. Judge piano competition World Piano Pedagogy Conf., Atlanta, 2006. Recipient Nat. award Gladys Robinson Youse Composition Contest, Nat. Fedn. Music Clubs, 1995. Mem.: DAR, ASCAP, Tex. Music Tchrs. Assn., Music Tchrs.' Nat. Assn., Nat. Fedn. Music Clubs, Beaumont Music Tchrs. Assn. (pres. 1996—98), Kingwood/Humble Music Tchrs. Assn. (sec. 1999—2004), Wednesday Morning Music Club, Delta Omicron, Delta Omega, Delta Delta Delta (music chmn. 1987—88). Avocations: composing music, piano, viola, drawing, reading. Home: 2331 Crimson Valley Ct Kingwood TX 77345-2101 E-mail: barbarachagen@yahoo.com.

HAGEN, GLENN W., lawyer; BS in Chemistry, U. Ala., 1970; JD, Valparaiso U., 1973. Bar: Mich. 1973, U.S. Dist. Ct. (we. dist.) Mich. 1974, Colo. 1981, U.S. Dist. Ct. Colo. 1982. With Peters, Seyburn & Hagen, Kalamazoo, 1973-76; dep. city atty. City of Battle Creek, Mich., 1976-79; staff and regulatory counsel CF&I Steel Corp., Pueblo, Colo., 1979-81; gen. counsel Commonwealth Investment Properties Corp., Littleton, Colo., 1981-82; assoc. Berkowitz & Brady, Denver, 1982-83, Zarlengo, Mott, Zarlengo & Winbourn, Denver, 1983-87; pvt. practice Glenn W. Hagen, P.C., Denver, 1987—. Lectr. in field. Referee property tax appeals Douglas and Jefferson Counties; del. Colo. Rep. Com., 1986, 1990—2006; chmn. 18th Jud. Dist., 1999—; bd. dirs. Douglas County Cmty. Found., 2005—; small bus. cons. South Met. Denver C. of C., 1994—2000. Mem.: ABA (young lawyers exec. coun. 1978—81, chmn. small bus. enterprises 1986, regional dir. constabars 1992—94, nat. editors conf. 1995, mem. constrn. forum 1996—), Highlands Ranch C. of C. (founder, bd. dirs., chmn. 2006—07), Colo. Lawyers for Arts, Am. Arbitration Assn., Douglas-Elbert County Bar Assn., Denver Bar Assn, Colo. Bar Assn. (chmn. long range planning com. 1983—86, gen. practice exec. coun. 1985, bus. law sect. 1986—91, mem. exec. bd. chmn. budget com. 1987—89, mem. svcs. com. 1987—89, alt. dispute resolutions com. 1990—94, chmn.small firm section 1991—96, law office mgmt. com. 1995—99, constrn. law sect. 1996—, chmn. 2001—03), Mich. Bar Assn. (young lawyers exec. coun. 1978—80). Office: Highlands Ranch Bus Pk Ste 108 8925 S Ridgeline Blvd Highlands Ranch CO 80129-2354 Office Phone: 303-683-1163. Personal E-mail: hagenlaw4biz@msn.com.

HAGEN, JODY LYNN, neuropsychologist, educator; b. Lincoln, Jan. 3, 1971; d. Mark Walter Krueger and Jaque Lee Frayer; m. Richard C. Hagen, June 15, 2001. Bachelor, Mo. State U., Springfield, 1996; Master, Appalachian State U., Boone, NC, 1998; PhD, U. Mont., Missoula, 2003. Lic. Clin. Psychologist Ark. Psychology Bd. & Mo. State Com. on Psychology, 2004, cert. Health Svc. Provider in Psychology Nat. Register, 2005. Adj. rsch. prof. U. Ark., Little Rock, 2003—; neuropsychologist Living Well, PLLC, Little Rock, 2004—. Contbr. articles articles to mags. Mem.: Am. Assn. Christian Counselors, Ark. Psychology Assn. (profl. devel. com.), Internat. Neuropsychological Soc., Nat. Acad. Neuropsychology. Conservative. Avocations: camping, hiking, scuba diving, travel. Office: Living Well PLLC 1225 Breckenridge Dr Ste 204 Little Rock AR 72205 Office Phone: 501-255-1574. Office Fax: 501-255-1446.

HAGEN, JOHN WILLIAM, psychology professor; b. Mpls., May 11, 1940; s. Wayne Sigvart and Elfie Marie (Erickson) H.; adopted children—Darus Gene, Lonny John, Frederick F. BA, U. Minn., 1962; PhD, Stanford U., 1965. Asst. prof. psychology U. Mich., Ann Arbor, 1965-69, assoc. prof., 1969-73, prof., 1973—, chmn. developmental program, 1971-83, dir. Ctr. Human Growth and Devel., 1982-93. Mem. Mich. Gov.'s Spl. Commn. on Age of Majority, 1970-71; dir. Reading and Learning Skills Ctr., 1985—1996; exec. officer Soc. for Rsch. in Child Devel., 1989—; adv. coun. Mich. Dept. Edn., 1972-74; chmn. Univ. Com. on Internat. Year of Child, 1979-80; rsch. rev. com. Nat. Inst. Child Health and Human Devel., 1980—. Co-author: Perspectives on the Development of Memory and Cognition, 1977; cons. editor Merrill Palmer Quar, 1968-80, Child Devel, 1972—; contbr. articles to profl. jours. Bd. dirs. Guild House Campus Ministry, Ann Arbor, 1972-83; bd. dirs. Humane Soc. Huron Valley, 1991-2000; profl. adv. bd. Nat. Assn. Learning Disabilities, 2001-. Recipient Standard Oil Found. award, 1967; USPHS trainee, 1963-65; Woodrow Wilson fellow, 1962-63; James Neubacher Award, 1997. Fellow Am. Psychol. Assn., Internat. Acad. for Rsch. in Learning Disabilities (exec. com. 2001-), Am. Psychol. Soc.; mem. Am. Edn. Rsch. Assn., Midwestern Psychol. Assn., Soc. Research in Child Devel. (chmn. program com. 1981-83), Internat. Soc. Study of Behavioral Devel., Phi Beta Kappa. Clubs: Univ. (Ann Arbor), Alumni (Ann Arbor). Unitarian Universalist. Home: 3421 Burbank Dr Ann Arbor MI 48105-1518 Office: Soc Rsch in Child Devel 3131 S State St #302 Ann Arbor MI 48108 Office Phone: 734-998-6565. Business E-Mail: jwhagen@umich.edu.

HAGEN, MICHAEL DALE, family physician educator; b. St. Louis, Nov. 11, 1949; s. Hubert Dale and Gwendel (Carden) Hagen; m. Barbara Carroll Keifer, Aug. 21, 1971; children: Laura Carrol, Sandra Ann. BS in Biology, Denison U., 1971; MD cum laude, U. Mo., Columbia, 1975. Cert. family practice bd. Pvt. practice Family Medicine Assocs., Aurora, Mo.,

1978—81; asst. prof. dept. family practice U. Ky., Lexington, 1981—87, assoc. prof. dept. family practice, 1987—92, prof. dept. family practice, 1993—, interim chmn. dept. family practice, 1992—93, assoc. chmn. dept. family practice, 1993—97, project dir., computer-based assessment, 1996—; assoc. dir. assessment methods Am. Bd. Family Practice, 2003—. Fellow clin. decision making New Eng. Med. Ctr., Boston, 1987—89; at-large dir. Am. Bd. Family Practice, Lexington, 1991—96, pres., 1995—96; residency rev. com. family practice Accreditation Coun. for Grad. Med. Edn., Chgo., 1994—97. Author: Saunders Review Family Practice, 1992, 1997, 2002; contbr. articles to profl. jours. Mem.: AMA, Omicron Delta Kappa, Soc. for Med. Decision Making, Am. Acad. Family Physicians (clin. policies task force 1994—95), Phi Kappa Phi, Alpha Omega Alpha. Presbyterian. Avocations: amateur radio, gardening. Home: 2012 Blairmore Rd Lexington KY 40502-2435 Office: Am Bd Family Medicine 2224 Young Dr Lexington KY 40505-4219 Office Phone: 859-268-8440. Business E-Mail: mhagen@assesstech.com. E-mail: hagenmd@prodigy.net.

HAGEN, NICHOLAS STEWART, medical educator, consultant; b. Plentywood, Mont., Aug. 6, 1942; s. William Joseph and June Janette (Reuter) H.; m. Mary Louise Edvalson, July 26, 1969; children: Brian Geoffrey, Lisa Louise, Eric Christopher, Aaron Daniel, David Michael. BS in Chemistry, Ariz. State U., 1964; MBA in Internat. Bus., George Washington U., 1969; MD, U. Ariz., 1974. Lic. physician Ariz., Utah, Idaho.; diplomate Nat. Bd. Med. Examiners. Intern., resident Good Samaritan Hosp., Phoenix, 1974-75; pvt. practice Roy, Utah, 1975-77; dir. clin. rsch. Abbott Labs., North Chicago, Ill., 1977-84; v.p. med. affairs Rorer Group, Inc., Ft. Washington, Pa., 1984-88; clin. prof. Ariz. State U., Tempe, 1988-90. Pres. Southwestern Clin. Rsch., Tempe, 1987—, Travel Profl. Internat., Tempe, 1989-98; mem. Ariz. Bd. Med. Student Loans, 1998-2002. Author: Valproic Acid: A Review of Pharmacologic Properties and Clinical Use in Pharmacologic and Biochemical Properties of Drug Substances, 1979; contbr. articles to med. jours.; patentee in field. Bishop Ch. Jesus Christ of Latter-day Saints, Gurnee, Ill., 1981-84; various positions with local couns. Boy Scouts Am., 1988—; active Rep. campaigns, Mesa, Ariz., 1988—; 2d vice chmn. Maricopa County Rep. Assembly, 1997-99; dist. republican chmn., 1996-98; mem. governing bd. East Valley Inst. Tech., 1998-2003. Lt. comdr. USCG, 1965-69. Joan Mueller-Etter scholar Ariz. State U., 1960, Phelps-Dodge scholar Ariz. State U., 1961; NASA fellow Brigham Young U., 1964. Mem. Am. Coll. Sports Medicine, Eagle Forum, Nat. Right-to-Life Assn., Utah Hist. Soc., Nat. Geneal. Soc., Bucks County Geneal. Soc., Sons of Norway, Soc. Descendants Emigrants from Numedal, Hallingdal and Hedmark, Norway, Blue Key, Archons, Kappa Sigma (treas. Greater Phoenix alumni chpt. 1999—), Beta Beta Beta, Alpha Epsilon Delta, Phi Eta Sigma, Sophos. Republican. Mem. Lds Ch. Avocations: genealogy, swimming, stamp collecting/philately, medieval history, art collecting. Office: 9802 E Irwin Ave Mesa AZ 85209

HAGEN, PAUL BEO, pharmacologist; b. Sydney, Feb. 15, 1920; emigrated to Can., 1959, naturalized, 1965; s. Conrad and Mary (McFadzean) von H.; m. Jean Himms, Sept. 29, 1956; children— Anna, Nina. M.B., BS, U. Sydney, 1945. Intern, resident New South Wales Dept. Health, Sydney, 1945-48; lectr. physiology U. Sydney, 1948-50; sr. lectr. physiology U. Queensland, 1950-52; research fellow Oxford U., 1952-54; asst. prof. pharmacology Yale U., 1954-56, Harvard U., 1956-59; head biochemistry dept. U. Man., 1959-64, Queens U., 1964-67; dir. NRC, Ottawa, Ont., 1967-68; dean grad. studies U. Ottawa, 1968-83, chmn. pharmacology dept., 1983-86. Mem. med. bd. Muscular Dystrophy Assn. Can., 1961-87, chmn., 1976-87, nat. pres., 1980-83; vice chmn. Med. Research Council, 1967; trustee Can. Inst. Particle Physics, 1971-79 Mem. Editorial bd. Biochem. Pharmacology, 1961-66, Jour. Pharmacology and Exptl. Therapeutics, 1960-64, Can. Jour. Biochemistry, 1963-67; contbr. to books and periodicals on physiol., biochem. and pharm. subjects. Chmn. Ont. Bd. Libr. Coordination, 1971-73; trustee Ottawa Gen. Hosp., 1984-94. Recipient Lederle Faculty award Yale U., 1956, Centennial medal Govt. of Can., 1967; Jubilee medal, 1977; C.J. Martin fellow Oxford U., 1952; J.H. Brown fellow Yale U., 1954; Fulbright fellow, 1954 Fellow Chem. Inst. Can. (v.p., pres. biochem. div. 1962-64); mem. Brit. Pharm. Soc., Am. Soc. Pharmacology. Home: 507-420 MacKay St Ottawa ON K1M 2C4 Canada

HAGEN, THOMAS BAILEY, business owner, former state official, retired insurance company executive; b. Buffalo, Sept. 19, 1935; s. Walter B. and Isabella S. (Bailey) H.; m. Susan R. Hirt, May 31, 1958; children: Jonathan, Sarah. Student, Pa. State U., Erie, 1953—55; BS in Commerce, Ohio State U., 1957; DPubSvc (hon.), Edinboro U. Pa., 1996. With Erie (Pa.) Ins. Group, 1953—, exec. v.p., 1976-82, pres., 1982-90, chmn., CEO, 1990-93, spl. asst. to chmn., 1993-95, chmn., 2007—; sec. of commerce Commonwealth of Pa., 1995-96, sec. cmty. and econ. devel., 1996-97; chmn. bd. dirs. Custom Engring. Co., 1997—; chmn. Team Pa. Found., 1997-2001, also bd. dirs.; chmn., bd. dirs. GPU, Inc., 1988—95, 1997—2001, Venango Machine Co., 1999—, Lamjen, Inc., 2000—, Custom Group Industries, Ltd., 2000—. Bd. dirs. Pa. Housing Fin. Agy., 1995-, Bliley Techs., Inc., Case Mgmt. Support Svcs., Inc., Erie, Erie Indemnity Co., Erie Ins. Group, 1979-98, 2007-, chmn., 2007-; chmn. Pa. Indsl. Devel. Authority, 1995-97, Pa. Econ. Devel. Fin. Authority, 1995-97, Pa. Ben Franklin/IRC Partnership, 1995-97. Bd. dirs. Erie Philharmonic, pres., 1970-71; bd. dirs. Erie Coun. Navy League U.S., 1977-86; pres. Erie Tomorrow Corp., 1979-86; vice-chmn., bd. dirs. Bayfront East Side Taskforce, Erie, 1978-96; bd. dirs. Erie Conf. on Cmty. Devel., 1985-93, hon. dir., 1993-2003; bd. dirs. Pa. Chamber Bus. and Industry, Harrisburg, 1986-95, 99—, first vice chair, 2007—; bd. dirs. Pa. Econ. Devel. Partnership, 1987-94, Pa. for Effective Govt., 1987-95, Athenaeum Phila., 1995-; chmn. Team Pa. Found., 1997-2000. Capt. USNR ret. Alumni fellow Pa. State U., 1988; recipient Ins. Mentor award U. Ala., 1976, Golden Baton award Erie Philharmonic, 1974, Disting. Pennsylvanian award Gannon U., 1987, Phila. C. of C., 1980, Outstanding Community Service award Multiple Sclerosis Soc., 1980, Alumni Citizenship award Ohio State U., 1981, Man of the Yr. award Erie and Chautauqua Mag., 1986, Preservationist of Yr. award (now Otto Haas award) Pa. Hist. and Mus. Commn., 1987, Honor award Pa. Soc. Architects, 1993. Mem. Internat. Ins. Soc. (bd. dirs. 1978-92, hon. counselor award 1998), Ins. Fedn. Pa. (bd. dirs. 1970-91, chmn. 1984-86), Ins. Inst. Am. (inst. for property and liability underwriters, trustee 1987-93), Griffith Found. (v.p. 1985-92, trustee 1985-95, trustee emeritus 1995—), The Pa. Soc. (pres. 1995-97, bd. dirs. 1990—), 10,000 Friends Pa., Pa. Heritage Soc. Office: 100 State St Ste 440 Erie PA 16507-1456 Home Phone: 814-838-1893; Office Phone: 814-459-7405.

HAGEN, WENDY W., public relations executive; Grad., Georgetown U. Exec. v.p./chief mktg. officer Arnold Worldwide; now ptnr. Porter Novelli, Washington. Mem. bd. trustees The Robert Wood Johnson Found., Princeton, NJ, 2001—. Office: Porter Novelli 1909 K St NW Washington DC 20006 Office Phone: 202-973-5800. Office Fax: 202-973-5858.

HAGENBECK, FRANKLIN LEE, academic administrator, career military officer; b. Rabat, Morocco, Nov. 25, 1949; m. Judy Vaughn; children: Kelly, Leeann. BS, U.S. Mil. Acad., 1971; MS, Fla. State U., 1978; MA, L.I. U., 1979. Advanced through grades to lt. gen., 2003; brigade comdr. 3rd Tng. Brigade, Ft. Leonard Wood, Mo., 1993—95; chief of staff to 10th Mountain Divsn. US Army, Ft. Drum, 1995—97, dir., officer pers. mgmt. directorate Washington, 1997—98, asst. divsn. comdr. ops. 101st Airborne Divsn. Ft. Campbell, Ky., 1998—99; dep. dir. global/multilateral issue/internat. American affs., J-5 Joint Staff, US Dept. Def., Washington, 1999—2000, dep. dir. ops., J33, 2000—01; commdg. gen. 10th Mountain Divsn. US Army, Ft. Drum, NY, 2001—03; commdg. gen., coalition task force-mountain Operation Anaconda, Afghanistan, 2001—02; dep. chief of staff for personnel US Army, Washington, 2003—06; supt. US Mil. Acad., West Point, NY, 2006—. Decorated Disting. Svc. medal, Def. Superior Svc. medal with one oak-leaf cluster, Legion of Merit with 4 oak-leaf clusters, Bronze Star with one oak-leaf cluster, Meritorious Svc. medal with two oak-leaf clusters, Army Commendation medal, Army Achievement medal. Mem.: Assn. of U.S. Army, Am. Legion. Office: US Mil Acad 646 Swift Rd West Point NY 10996 Home Phone: 315-775-1140.*

HAGENBUCH, JOHN JACOB, investor; b. Park Forest, Ill., May 31, 1951; s. David Brown and Jean Iline (Reeves) H.; m. Kimberly A. Steel, Aug. 20, 2000; children: Henry, Hunter, Hilary, Sydney, John. AB magna cum laude, Princeton U., 1974; MBA, Stanford U., 1978. Assoc. Salomon Bros., NYC, 1978-80, v.p. San Francisco, 1980-85; gen. ptnr. Hellman & Friedman, 1985-93; chmn. M&H Realty Ptnrs., L.P., 1993—. Chmn. Onconome, Inc., 2005—. Mem. Burlingame Country Club, Pacific-Union Club, Calif. Tennis Club, Villa Taverna Club, Bohemian Club, Valley Club. Office: M&H Realty Ptnrs 425 California St San Francisco CA 94104

HAGENBUCH, RODNEY DALE, financial consultant; b. Saxville, Wis. s. Herbert Jenkin and Minnie Leona (Hayward) Hagenbuch; children: Kris, Beth, Patricia; m. LaVerne Julia Scoonover, Sept. 1, 1956. BS, Mich. State U., East Lansing, 1980. Cert. fin. mgr. Designer Olds div. Gen. Motors, Lansing, Mich., 1960-66; instl. account exec. Merrill Lynch, 1966-75, instl. mgr., 1975-80, sales mgr. Columbus, Ohio, 1980-82, sr. resident v.p. Tacoma, 1982-93, LA, 1993-98; prin. Quantum Group, 1999—; portfolio analyst Affinity Investment Advisors, 2001—05, COO, 2006—. Prin. Securities Expert Witness Network, 1999—2006, Quantum Leap Inst., 1999, Quantum Leap Securities, 2001—06, 2006; mem. adv. bd. U. Wash. Sch. Bus., Tacoma, 1998—2002; bd. dirs. Employers Group, chmn., 2006; mng. dir. Arque Capital, 2005—. Author (with Richard J. Capalbo): Investment Survival: How to Use Investment Research to Create Winning Portfolios, 2002; author: Becoming a Life Advisor (The Ultimate Customer Service Model), 2005. Mem. adv. bd. Charles Wright, 1989—93; mem. econ. devel. bd. City of Tacoma, 1986—93, chmn., 1987—88; pres. Downtown Tacoma Assn., 1986; chmn. Corp. Coun. for the Arts, 1986, United Way, LA, 1993—2000; pres. Tacoma Symphony, 1988; chmn. human resource commn. Meridian Twp., 1972—74; mem. Meridian Planning Commn., Mich., 1964—70, Meridian Police and Fire Commn., Mich., 1964—70; pres. adv. bd. U. Wash., Tacoma, chmn., 1992; mem. State Wash. Arts Stblzn. Bd.; sec. bd. dirs. Tacoma Art Mus., 1992; legis. chmn. N.W. Securities Industry Assn.; campaign chmn. Pierce County United Way, 1991—92; non-resident dir. Tacoma Art Mus., 1994—2003, Tacoma Urban League, 1983—93; exec. com. fraternity of friends LA Music Ctr.; hon. mem. bd. govs. Streetlights LA, 1998—; vice chair Ingham County Housing Commn., 1978—80; bd. dirs. LA Acad. Fin., 1993—98, United Cerebral Palsy, LA, 1994—; bd. dirs., chmn. LA Red Cross, 2002—05; bd. dirs. Forward Wash., New LA Mktg. Plan, 1995—97; bd. dirs., mem. dist. 2 com. NASD, 1996—99; bd. govs. LA Children's Hosp. Rsch. Inst., 1994—99, mem. fin. com., 1999—2003; bd. govs. LA Town Hall, 1996, mem. fin. com., 1999—2002; bd. govs. LA Employers Group, chmn., 2006—; bd. dirs. LA Ctr. for Nonprofit Mgmt. Recipient Outstanding Citizen award Mcpl. League Pierce County, 1988, VIP award U. Wash., Tacoma, 2005; named Nat. Vol. of Yr., Urban League Western Divsn., 1987, The Rod Hagenbuch award U. Wash., Tacoma, 2005 Mem.: Tacoma C. of C., Calif. Club, Tacoma Club (bd. dirs. 1984—93, pres. 1993). Avocations: running, skiing. Home: 16826 Monte Hermoso Dr Pacific Palisades CA 90272-1910 Office Phone: 310-488-6047. Personal E-mail: rdhagen@earthlink.net.

HAGENDORN, WILLIAM HULL, lawyer; b. Bklyn., Sept. 1, 1925; s. William V. and Florence (Hull) H.; m. Patricia Yarvote, Apr. 6, 1974; children: Katherine Florence, Patricia Ann. AB, Princeton U., 1944; JD, Harvard U., 1949; LLM, NYU, 1952. Bar: NY 1949. Practiced in, NYC, 1949—2002; assoc. firm Debevoise, Plimpton & McLean, NYC, 1953-61, Carter, Ledyard & Milburn, NYC, 1961-65; gen. counsel Am. Express Co., 1965-72, Wells Fargo & Co., 1965-68, Equitable Securities, Morton & Co., NYC, 1966-72; sr. atty. Shearman & Sterling, NYC, 1973-91; ptnr. Burlingham Underwood, NYC, 1991—2002; pvt. practice Bronxville, NY, 2002—. Adviser to com. uniform consumer credit code Nat. Conf. Uniform State Laws, 1966-68; adj. prof. Rutgers Law Sch., Newark, 1991, 93; arbitrator NY Stock Exch., NASD, 1991-. Served with inf. AUS, 1944-46. Mem.: Assn. Bar City NY, NY State Bar Assn. (exec. com. internat. law sect. 1990—, chmn. com. admiralty law, 1990-93 1998—2000, com. banking law 2003—), Univ. Club (NYC). Home and Office: 25 Parkview Ave Apt 3A Bronxville NY 10708-2936 Office Phone: 914-337-5861. E-mail: whagendorn@aol.com.

HAGENLOCKER, EDWARD E., retired automobile company executive; b. 1939; married. BS, MS, Ohio State U., 1962, PhD, 1964; MBA, Mich. State U., 1982. With Ford Motor Co., 1964-98, chief engr., 1973—77, gen. mgr., 1978—80, dir., v.p. ops. Brazil, 1984-85, dir., pres., 1985-86, v.p., gen. mgr. truck ops. Dearborn, Mich., 1986-92, exec. v.p. N.Am. automotive ops., 1992-94, pres. Ford automotive ops., 1994-96, vice chmn., 1996-98.

HAGENSTEIN, WILLIAM DAVID, forester, consultant; b. Seattle, Mar. 8, 1915; s. Charles William and Janet (Finigan) H.; m. Ruth Helen Johnson, Sept. 2, 1940 (dec. 1979); m. Jean Kraemer Edson, June 16, 1980 (dec. 2000). BS in Forestry, U. Wash., Seattle, 1938; MForestry, Duke U., Durham, NC, 1941. Registered profl. engr., Wash., Oreg. Field aid in entomology U.S. Dept. Agr., Hat Creek, Calif., 1938; logging supt. and engr. Eagle Logging Co., Sedro-Woolley, Wash., 1939; tech. foreman U.S. Forest Svc., North Bend, Wash., 1940; forester West Coast Lumbermen's Assn., Seattle and Portland, Oreg., 1941-43, 45-49; sr. forester FEA, South and Central Pacific Theaters of War and Costa Rica, 1943-45; mgr. Indsl. Forestry Assn., Portland, 1949-80, exec. v.p., 1956-80, hon. dir., 1980-87; pres. W.D. Hagenstein and Assocs., Inc., Portland, 1980—. H.R. MacMillan lectr. forestry U. B.C., 1952, 77; Benson Meml. lectr. U. Mo., 1966; S.J. Hall lectr. indsl. forestry U. Calif. at Berkeley, 1973; cons. forest engr. USN, Philippines, 1952, Coop. Housing Found., Belize, 1986; mem. U.S. Forest Products Trade Mission, Japan, 1968; del. VII World Forestry Congress, Argentina, 1972, VIII Congress, Indonesia, 1978; mem. U.S. Forestry Study Team, West Germany, 1974; mem. sec. Interior's Oreg. and Calif. Multiple Use Adv. Bd., 1975-76; trustee Wash. State Forestry Conf., 1948-92, Keep Oreg. Green Assn., 1957—, v.p., 1970-71, pres., 1972-73; adv. trustee Keep Wash. Green Assn., 1957-95; co-founder World Forestry Ctr., dir., 1965-89, v.p., 1965-79, hon. dir. for life, 1990. Author: (with Wackerman and Michell) Harvesting Timber Crops, 1966; Assoc. editor: Jour. Forestry, 1946-53; columnist Wood Rev., 1978-82; contbr. numerous articles to profl. jours. Trustee Oreg. Mus. Sci. and Industry, 1968-73. Served with USNR, 1933-37. Recipient Hon. Alumnus award U. Wash. Foresters Alumni Assn., 1965, Dist. Svc. award, 2003, Forest Mgmt. award Nat. Forest Products Assn., 1968, Western Forestry award Western Forestry and Conservation Assn., 1972, 79, Gifford Pinchot medal for 50 yrs. Outstanding Svc., Soc. Am. Foresters, 1987, Charles W. Ralston award Duke Sch. Forestry, 1988, Lifetime Achievement award Oreg. Soc. Am. Foresters, 1995; honored as only surviving co-founder World Forestry Ctr., 2000, Centennial Resource Stewardship award, US Forest Svc., 2005; named Lumberman of Yr. Portland Wholesale Lumber Assn., 2005. Fellow Soc. Am. Foresters (mem. coun. 1958-63, pres. 1966-69, Golden Membership award 1989); mem. Am. Forestry Assn. (life, hon. v.p. 1966-69, 74-92, William B. Greeley Forestry award 1990), Commonwealth Forestry Assn. (life), Internat. Soc. Tropical Foresters, Portland C. of C. (forestry com. 1949-79, chmn. 1960-62), Nat. Forest Products Assn. (forestry adv. com. 1949-80, chmn. 1972-74, 78-80), West Coast Lumbermen's Assn. (v.p. 1969-79), Forest History Soc. (bd. dirs. 2001-04), David Douglas Soc. Western N. Am., Lang Syne Soc., Hoo Hoo Club, Xi Sigma Pi (outstanding alumnus Alpha chpt. 1973). Republican. Office: 921 SW Washington St Ste 803 Portland OR 97205-2826 Home: 2545 SW Terwilligen Blvd Portland OR 97201

HAGER, ELIZABETH SEARS, state legislator, social services administrator; b. Washington, Oct. 31, 1944; d. Hess Thatcher and Elizabeth Grace (Harper) Sears; m. Dennis Sterling Hager, Sept. 3, 1966; children: Annie Elizabeth, Lucie Caroline. BA, Wellesley Coll., 1966; MPA, U. N.H., 1979. Prin. Philbrook Ctr., Concord, NH, 1970-71; rep. N.H. Gen. Ct., Concord, 1973-76, 85-94, 1996—; del. N.H. Constitutional Conv., Concord, 1974, 84; campaign coord. Anderson for Pres. Rep. Primary, NH, 1980; mem. Concord City Coun., 1982-90; mayor City of Concord, 1988-90; exec. dir. United Way of Merrimack County, Concord, 1996—. Bd. dirs. Lincoln Fin. Variable Funds, TD Banknorth, NH. Pres. Greater Concord United Way, 1980-81; campaign chair United Way of Merrimack County, Concord, 1986. Republican. Episcopalian. Office: 46 N Main St Concord NH 03301-4913 Home: 5 Pleasant View Ave Concord NH 03301-2555

HAGER, GEORGE V., JR., health services executive; BA in Econs., Dickinson Coll., 1978; MBA, Rutgers U. CPA. Ptnr. in charge of health care practice KPMG Peat Marwick LLP, Phila., 1979-92; v.p., CFO Genesis Health Ventures, Inc., Kennett Square, Pa., 1992-94, sr. v.p., CFO, 1994-99, exec. v.p., CFO, 1999—2003; chmn, CEO Genesis HealthCare Corp., Kennett Square, Pa., 2003—07; CEO Genesis HealthCare, Kennett Sq, Pa., 2007—. Recipient Cain Bros. award Cain Bros. & Modern Healthcare Mag., 1996. Mem. AICPA, PICPA. Office: Genesis HealthCare 101 E State St Kennett Square PA 19348*

HAGER, GORDON DOUGLAS, scientist, engineering educator; b. Tacoma, Wash., Jan. 18, 1943; s. Herbert Gordon Hager and Virginia Anita Johnson; m. Frankie Orlean Creamer, 1980 (div.); children: Kerie Buckley, Kevin Douglas, Bruce Gordon, Matthew James; m. Barbara Ann Stewart, Oct. 14, 1989. Student, Peninsula Jr. Coll., Port Angeles, Wash., 1965—66; BA in Chemistry magna cum laude, Western Wash. State U., 1968; PhD in Chem. Physics, Wash. State U., 1973. Staff scientist Bell Aerospace Co., Niagara Falls, NY, 1974—78, Rocketdyne, Canoga Park, Calif., 1978—82; tech. advisor gas phase and chem. laser br. Air Force Rsch. Lab., Kirtland AFB, N.Mex., 1982—2004; prof. mech. engring. U. N.Mex., Albuquerque, 2005—. Adj. prof. physics U. N.Mex., Albuquerque, 1992—. Contbr. articles to profl. jours. With USCG, 1960—65. Recipient Quarterly award sr. scientist and engr., AF Rsch. Lab., 1998, Giller award, 2000, Spl. Act/Svc. award, 2001, Outstanding Civilian Career Svc. award, 2005, Disting. Alumni award, Wash. State U. Coll. Scis., 2002, Grad. Alumni Achievement award, Wash. State U. Grad. Sch., 2002; fellow, AF Rsch. Lab., 2002; NRC postdoctoral fellow, Air Force Weapons Lab., Albuquerque, 1973—74. Mem.: IEEE, Optical Soc. Am. Democrat. Achievements include patents for repetitively pulsed photolytic iodine laser by gain switching with a pulsed magnetic field; subsonic rep-pulsed chemical oxygen iodine laser using gain switching with a pulsed magnetic field; supersonic oxygen iodine laser; subsonic rep-pulsed chemical oxygen iodine laser using CW intactivity magneto-optic q-switch; magnetically switched chemical oxygen iodine laser; diode pumped TM: YAG four-micron laser system; supersonic all gas-phase iodine laser. Avocations: fishing, blues guitar, rockhounding, racquetball, travel. Office: AF Rsch Lab/EL Kirtland AFB Albuquerque NM 87117-0001 E-mail: drydoc@cableone.net.

HAGER, JOHN HENRY, political organization, former federal agency administrator, former lieutenant governor; b. Durham, NC, Aug. 28, 1936; m. Margaret Dickinson Chase, Feb. 27, 1971; children: John Virgil, Henry Chase. BSME, Purdue U., 1958; MBA, Harvard U., 1960; degree (hon.), Averett Coll., 1999, Mary Washington Coll., 1999, U. No. Va., 1999. Various positions Am. Tobacco Co., 1961—74; lt. gov. State of Va., Richmond, 1998—2002, asst. to the Gov. for Commonwealth Preparedness, 2002—04; asst. sec. for spl. edn. & rehabilitation svc. US Dept. Edn., Washington, 2004—07; chmn. Va. Rep. Party, Richmond, 2007—. Chmn. Disability Commn.; co-chmn. com. on Ednl. Infrastructure; chmn. Faith Based Cmty. Svcs. Task Force; vice-chmn. Gov.'s Commn. on Transp. Policy; bd. dir., vice-chair Aerospace State Assn.; trustee, v.p. Jamestown Yorktown Found.; hon. chmn. Greater Richmond Conv. Ctr.; dir., pres. Sorensen Inst. Polit. Leadership; dir. Ctr. for Politics, Port Jamestown 2001; past dir. Partnership for Urban Va., past dir. Va. State C of C; trustee, exec. com., fin. com. Va. Mus. Fine Arts; 1st v.p., dir. Va. Pub. Safety Found., Inc.; past pres., trustee, exec. com. Children's Hosp.; Met. Richmond Conv. and Vis. Bur. (past chmn., dir., founding dir.); Va. Health Care Found. (past chmn., dir., exec. com.); 7th Dist. Rep. Party (past vice chmn. 3rd district, exec. com. mem. past precinct, ward and campaign chmn.); Rep. Party of Va. and del./alt. to 4 natl. convs. (past treas., past exec. com. mem., state ctrl. com. mem.); ruling elder 1st Presbyn. Ch., Richmond; mem. drug task force Va. State Crime Commn. 2nd lt. U.S. Army, 1960-61, capt. USAR. 2nd lt. US Army. Named one of Outstanding Young Men of Am., 1976, Man of Yr., Tobacco Internat. Mag., 1990; recipient Alumni Citizenship award Purdue U., 1987, Svc. award Richmond Rep. Com., 1992, Disting. Alumni award Durham Acad., 1992, Good Govt. award Richmond First Club, 1996, Tourism Leadership award Met. Richmond Convention and Visitors Bur., 1997, Lettie Pate Whitehead Evans award Westminster-Canterbury, 1997, Citizenship award Va. Coun. Indians, 1998, Heritage award, Radford U., 2000, Vol. Fundraiser of Yr. award ARC, 2004, Humanitarian award Nat. Conf. Cmty. and Justice, 2002. Mem. Am. Legion, Va. C. of C. (dir.), Nat. Assn. Lt. Govs. (mem. exec. com., So. sector chmn.), So. Growth Policies Bd., Adv. Bd. Tobacco History Corp., Jamestown, Youth Forum Found., Richmond Rep. Party Com., Richmond German, Richmond Hundred (past pres., dir.), City of Richmond Electoral Bd. (past chmn.) Pub. Affairs Group (past chmn.), Forum Club (past pres.), Commonwealth Club (past dir.), Custis Fishing and Hunting Club (past dir.), Country Club Va. (past pres. and CEO, past dir.). Republican. Office: Va Rep Party 115 E Grace St Richmond VA 23219 E-mail: johnhager1@comcast.net.*

HAGER, MICHAEL W., museum director; m. Denise LeAnn Rikansrud; children: Amy, Brian. BA in Biology, Grinnell Coll.; PhD in Geology, U. Wyo. Asst. prof. geology Augustana Coll., 1973-78; dir. Mus. of the Rockies, Mont., 1978-89, Va. Mus. Natural History, Va., 1989-91; exec. dir. San Diego Natural History Mus., Calif., 1991—. Mus. cons. Exec. prodr. film Baja California, 2000. Bd. dirs. com. Balboa Pk., Cultural Partnership, Immigration Mus. New Ams. Mem. Assn. Sci. Mus. Dirs. (past pres.). Office: San Diego Natural History Mus PO Box 121390 San Diego CA 92112-1390 Office Phone: 619-255-0216, 619-255-0216. Business E-Mail: mhager@sdnhm.org.

HAGER, ROBERT WORTH, retired aerospace executive; b. Longview, Wash., June 20, 1928; s. Josiah Denver and Merle (Worth) H.; m. Margaret Goodnough, Aug. 25, 1950; children: Stephen M., Sandra Hager Dahl, Shane D. BS in Civil Engring, U. Wash., 1949, MS in Civil Engring, 1950; DSc (hon.), U. Ala., 1995. Rsch. fellow U. Wash., 1949-50; rsch. engr. U.S. Navy Civil Engring. Lab., Port Hueneme, Calif., 1950-53; mem. staff Sandia Corp., Albuquerque, 1953-55; with Boeing Co., Seattle, 1955-93, Minuteman program mgr., 1973-78, v.p., gen. mgr. ballistic missile and space div., 1978-80, v.p. engring., 1980-84, v.p. space sta. Huntsville, Ala., 1984-89, v.p., gen. mgr. Huntsville div. Boeing Aerospace and Electronics, 1989-91, v.p., gen. mgr. Missiles and Space Div. Boeing Def. and Space Group, 1991-93. Past chmn. bd. Univ. Space Rsch. Assn.; past chmn. Bus. Coun. Ala.; co-chair Lower Hood Canal Watershed Com.; dir. emeritus

Pacific N.W. Salmon Ctr.; sec. United Meth. Found. of the N.W.; bd. dir. Hood Canal Salmon Enhancement Group. Fellow AIAA, Am. Astron. Soc. Methodist. Home: 51 E Sunset Beach Dr Belfair WA 98528-9534

HAGER, SUSAN KULKA, public relations executive; b. Washington, Oct. 19, 1944; d. Joseph A. and Mary Margaret (Berry) Kulka; m. C. Eric Hager, Nov. 3, 1967; 1 child, Elizabeth Hager Finley. BA in Sociology, Brescia U., 1966. VISTA vol., vol. leader Office Econ. Opportunity, White Mountain, Alaska, 1966—67; VISTA and Peace Corps recruiter, cons. Gale Assocs., Washington, 1968; program asst. Office Econ. Opportunity, Washington, 1969—70, program analyst, 1970—71; program dir. Nat. Ctr. for Voluntary Action, Washington, 1971—73; chair, CEO Hager Sharp, Inc., Washington, 1973—. Founder, first pres. Nat. Assn. Women Bus. Owners, Washington, 1974; chmn. U.S. Dept. Small Bus. Adv. Coun., Washington, 1980—82; pres. Nat. Small Bus. United, Washington, 1992. Editor: (monthly column) Washington Bus. Jour., 1995—97. Bd. dirs. Greater Washington Bd. Trade, Washington, 1990—, Lab Sch. Washington, 1991—95, pres. bd. dirs., 1996—2003. Named Bus. Woman of the Yr., Nat. Assn. Women Bus. Owners, Washington, 1985, Small Bus. of the Yr., D.C. C. of C., Washington, 1995, Bus. Woman of the Yr., United Cerebral Palsy, Washington, 1998; named one of 25 Heroines and Heroes Whose Actions Over the Last Quarter Century Have Given Women in the Workplace a Better Shot, Working Women mag., 2001; named to, Pub. Rels. Soc. Am.'s Nat. Capital Chpt. Hall of Fame, 2005; recipient Washingtonian of Yr. award, Washington Bus. Jour., 2004, Woman of Yr. award, Washington Women in Pub. Rels., 2004. Mem.: Leadership Washington (bd. dirs. 1987—88), Cosmos Club. Office: Hager Sharp Inc 1090 Vermont Ave NW Washington DC 20005

HAGERMAN, DOUGLAS M., consumer products company executive, lawyer; b. South Bend, Ind., Dec. 1960; m. Jane Elizabeth Tadych; children: Caroline, Nora. BA summa cum laude, Drake U., Des Moines, Iowa, 1983; JD cum laude, Harvard U., 1986. CPA; bar: 1986. Assoc. Foley & Lardner LLP, Milw., 1986—95, ptnr., 1995—98, Chgo., 1998—2004; sr. v.p., gen. counsel, sec. Rockwell Automation Inc., Milw., 2004—. Office: Rockwell Automation Inc 1201 S 2Nd St Milwaukee WI 53204-2498 E-mail: dmhagerman@ra.rockwell.com.*

HAGERMAN, JOHN DAVID, lawyer, investment advisor; b. Houston, Aug. 1, 1941; s. David Angle and Noima L. (Clay) H.; m. Linda J. Lambright, June 25, 1975; children: Clayton Robert, Holly Elizabeth. BBA, So. Meth. U., 1963; JD, U. Tex., Austin, 1966. Bar: Tex. 1966, U.S. Ct. Appeals (5th cir.) 1967, U.S. Supreme Ct. 1969; cert. civil trial law, 1980-95; real estate broker Tex. Pres., owner Hagerman & Sereau, Inc., The Woodlands, Tex., 1966—. Condr. bank creditor rights seminars; mem. adv. bd. Amegy Bank. Contbr. articles to profl. jours. Res. dep. sheriff Montgomery County, Tex.; former bd. dirs. 100 club of Montgomery County Fair Assn., 1978—, Montgomery County Hosp. Dist. Found., Seven Coves Homeowners Assn. Mem.: ABA, Houston Philosophy Soc., Comml. Real Estate Assn. Montgomery County, Tex. Assn. Bank Counsel, Tex. Assn. Civil Trial Specialists, Houston Outdoor Advt. Assn., Houston Bar Assn., Tex. Bar Assn., River Oaks Country Club, Briar Club, Woodlands Country Club, Petroleum Club (Houston), Woodlands Rotary Club, Beta Theta Pi. Republican. Avocations: golf, tennis, jogging, shooting. Office: Hagerman & Seureau Inc 24800 I-45 Ste 100 The Woodlands TX 77386-1987 Office Phone: 281-367-8800.

HAGERMAN, MICHAEL CHARLES, lawyer, arbitrator, mediator; b. Webster City, Iowa, Aug. 20, 1951; s. Charles Arnold and Jill Hamilton (Son de Regger) H.; m. Birgit A. Hagerman; children: Kelly, Douglas, Alexander, Christine, Jacqueline. BA with honors, U. Iowa, 1973; MBA, U. Utah, 1978; JD, Drake U., 1981; Grad., U.S. Army Command/Gen. Staff, Coll., Ft. Leavenworth, Kans., 1988. Bar: Iowa 1981, Mass. 1995. Clk. Iowa Resources, Legal Aid of Polk County, and State of Iowa, Des Moines, 1978-81; contract atty. Fisher Controls Internat., Inc., Marshalltown, Iowa, 1981-84; contracts mgr. Emerson & Cuming, Inc., Canton, Mass., 1984-85; contract atty. GTE Govt. Sys., Taunton, Mass., 1986-90; v.p., gen. counsel, sec. ISI Sys., Inc., Andover, Mass., 1990-94; legal counsel Swan Tech. Inc., Marlboro, Mass., 1994—95; pvt. practice Franklin, Mass., 1995—2004; counsel Fleet Boston Fin., 1998—2004; asst. gen. counsel Bank of Am., 2004—06, v.p., sourcing mgr., 2006—. Contbr. articles to profl. jours. Capt. U.S. Army, 1973-78, Germany; lt. col. U.S. Army Res. ret. Mem. Sigma Chi (chpt. Balfour award 1973), Phi Alpha Delta (chpt. pres. 1980-81). Avocations: writing, travel, horseback riding. Home Phone: 704-843-1546. Business E-Mail: mchagermanesq@msn.com.

HAGERTY, ROBERT E., academic administrator; b. Detroit, Mar. 16, 1937; s. Arthur E. and Paula (Buntrock) H.; m. Barbara Ann Anderson, Aug. 16, 1959; children: Scott Robertson, Mark David. AB, Western Mich. U., 1959; MA, Wayne State U., 1961, EdD, 1971. Tchr. Hazel Park (Mich.) Cmty. Schs., 1959-68, bldg. adminstr., 1968-74, dir. spl. edn., 1974-79, dir. evaluation and pupil svcs., 1979-83; supt. Kokomo (Ind.) N.W. Sch. Corp., 1983-85, Ionia (Mich.) Pub. Schs., 1985-93; head, dept. of ednl. leadership Grand Valley State U., Grand Rapids, Mich., 1993—2003, dean, sch. of edn., 1999—2003; pres. William Tyndale Coll., Farmington Hills, Mich., 2004—. Author: Making Special Education Work, 1978, The Crisis of Confidence in American Education, 1994. Bd. dirs. Royal Oak (Mich.) YMCA, 1976-83, Met. YMCA, Ionia, 1989-93, Boys and Girls Clubs of Oakland, Hazel Park, 1974-83; chair High Hopes Com., Ionia, 1985-87; exec. bd. Hazel Park Youth Protection Com., 1959-83, Hazel Park Youth Aid Found., 1961-83. Recipient Disting. Svc. award Bd. Edn. Ionia, 1993, Disting. Award of Honor, Outstanding Man of Yr., Hazel Park Jaycees, 1970. Mem. Mich. Assn. Profs. of Edn. (past pres., Disting. Leadership award 1993), Am. Assn. Sch. Adminstrs. (Supt. of the Yr. 1989, 90), Nat. Sch. Pub. Rels. Assn. (Award of Honor 1987, Disting. Achievement award 1989), Ionia C. of C. (bd. dirs. 1985-93, exec. bd. 1987-92). Home: 6530 Balsam Dr # D Hudsonville MI 49426-9267 Office: William Tyndale College PO Box 2297 Farmington Hills MI 48333-2297

HAGGAR, J. M., III, retail executive; s. Isabell Salloum and J.M. Haggar. With Haggar Corp., Dallas, 1969—, dir., 1983—, CEO, 1990—, pres., 1990—94, chmn. bd., 1994—. Office: 11511 Luna RD Dallas TX 75234-6022

HAGGARD, GERALDINE LANGFORD, primary school, adult education educator, consultant, writer; b. Wellington, Tex., Dec. 12, 1929; d. Frank and Zelma Dell (Edmondson) Langford; children: Colby, Sarah, Mary. MEd, Tex. Women's U., 1973, EdD, 1980; Cert. in Reading Recovery, Ohio State U., 1989. Elem. sch. tchr. Denton County (Tex.) Schs., 1949-62, Plano (Tex.) Ind. Sch. Dist., 1963-69, reading tchr., reading dir., 1999-2001. Vis. prof. Tex. Woman's U.; cons. for sch. dists. Editor and author lang. arts texts; contbr. articles to profl. jours.; author: Teaching and Assessing Reading Comprehension Grade 3, 2003, Grade 4, 2004, Grade 5, 2005, Grades K-2, 2007, Plans for Grief Support Programs. Sunday Sch. tchr. Prairie Creek Baptist Ch., Plano, 1994—; vol. facilitator Journey of Hope program for grief counseling. Named Hero Plano ISD centennial celebration, 1998, Dreamers, Doers and Unsung Hero Real Estate Found., 2006; recipient Outstanding Edn. Vol. of Yr. award, 2006. Mem. N.Am. Coun. Reading Recovery (bd. mem. 1995-99), Internat. Reading Assn., Tex. State Coun. Reading, Tex. Assn. Improvement of Reading, Coalition Reading English Suprs. Tex. (sec. 1994-97), Tex. Ret. Tchrs. Assn. (Plano chpt.), Alpha Delta Kappa, Delta Kappa Gamma, Phi Delta Kappa. Home: 2017 Meadowcreek Dr Plano TX 75074-4663 Personal E-mail: ghaggard@verizon.net.

HAGGARD, JOAN CLAIRE, church musician, piano instructor, accompanist, adjudicator; b. Ann Arbor, Mich., July 7, 1932; d. Clifford Buell and Bertha (Woodhurst) Wightman; m. Harold Wallace Haggard, June 30, 1956; children: Alan C., Stephen T., John A., Marian E. BA, Carleton Coll., 1954; postgrad., Ecole des Beaux Arts, Fontainebleau, France, 1954, U. Mich., 1954—55; A., Am. Guild Organists, 1980. Cert. pvt. piano tchr. Organist, choir dir. St. Paul's Episc. Ch., Riverside, Ill., 1955-59; dir. of music St. Andrew's Episc. Ch., Livonia, Mich., 1960-72; organist Christ Episc. Ch., Dearborn, Mich., 1973-83; dir. of music St. Philip's Episc. Ch., Rochester, Mich., 1983-92; organist, music coord. 1st United Meth. Ch., Farmington, Mich., 1992-2000. Pvt. piano tchr., Livonia, 1960—; piano instr. Southfield (Mich.) Sr. Adult Ctr., 1992-99; accompanist Creative and Performing Arts High Sch., Livonia, 1987-90; accompanist many solo instrumental and vocal performances, 1959—; student performance on piano and voice adjudicator Nat. Fedn. Music, Mich. State Band and Orch. Assn. Editor Livonia Youth Symphony Soc. newsletter, 1972-77; contbr. articles to profl. jours. Pres. Livonia Youth Symphony Soc., 1973-76; program dir. Episcopal Diocese Mich. Jr. Choir Camp, 1981-84, 87-89; coord. daily worship Triennial Conv. Episcopal Ch., Detroit, 1988. Mem. Am. Guild Organists (dean Detroit chpt. 1976-79, gen. chmn. nat. conv. 1986, councillor Region V 1986-92), Nat. Guild Piano Tchrs. (judge piano auditions 1987—), Music Tchrs. Nat. Assn., Assn. Anglican Musicians, Hymn Soc. in the U.S. and Can., Assn. Diocesan Liturgy and Music Commns., Music Commn. Episcopal Diocese Mich. (chmn. 1980-81), Mich. Fedn. Music Clubs (pres. eastern dist. 1998-2000), Mich. Music Tchrs. Assn. (local assn. chmn. 1996-2005, student performance on piano and voice adjudicator), The Tuesday Musicale Detroit (pres. 2005—), Piano Tchrs. Forum (Livonia area, pres. 1995-97, Tchr. of Yr. 2002), SAI Friend of Arts, PEO. Avocations: birdwatching, nature, reading. Home: 33974 Hampshire St Livonia MI 48154-2722

HAGGARD, MERLE RONALD, songwriter, recording artist; b. Bakersfield, Calif., Apr. 6, 1937; s. James Frances and Flossie Mae (Harp) H.; m. Leona Hobbs, 1957 (div.); children: Dana, Marty, Kelli, Noel; m. Bonnie Owens, 1965 (div.); m. Leona Williams, 1978 (div.); m. Debbie Haggard. Grad. high sch. Rec. artist Capitol Records, 1963-76, Tally Records, 1977—, MCA Records, 1977-81, CBS Records, 1981-89, Curb Records, 1990—; pres. Shade Tree Music Pub. Co., 1970—, Hag Prodns. Inc., 1973—. Appeared in: TV spls. The Waltons; writer, composer: TV mus. scores including Movin' On; albums include Strangers, 1965, Just Between the Two of Us, 1966, Best of Merle Haggard, 1968, Okie from Muskogee, 1969, Same Train, a Different Time, 1970, Land of Many Churches, 1972, I Love Dixie Blues, 1974, Serving 190 Proof, 1979, Rainbow Stew-Live at Anaheim Stadium, 1980, (with Willie Nelson) Pancho and Lefty, 1983, Amber Waves of Grain, 1985, Big City, 1985, Merle Haggard: His Best, 1985, A Friend in California, 1986, Out Among the Stars, 1986, Songwriter, 1986, Back to the Barrooms/The Way I Am, 1987, (with Nelson) Seashores of Old Mexico, 1987, (with Nelson and George Jones) Walking the Line, 1987, Chill Factor, 1988, Merle Haggard's Greatest Hits, 1988, Live at Billy Bob's Texas, 1999, Ultimate Collection, 2000, If I Could Only Fly, 2000, Cabin in the Hills, 2001, Two Old Friends, 2001, Like Never Before, 2003, I Wish I Was Santa Claus, 2004, Chicago Wind, 2005, Tough Country Heroes, 2006, (with Nelson and Ray Price) Last of the Breed, 2007; author: Sing Me Back Home, 1981, Down Every Road, 1996, 1996, 1996. Inducted into Country Music Hall of Fame, 1994; recipient 18 awards Acad. Country and Western Music, 56 Achievement awards Broadcast Music Inc., 7 awards Shade Tree Music Pub., 7 gold album awards, 1 platinum album award, 4 awards Music City News; named Songwriter of Yr., Nashville Songwriters Assn. 1970, 81, also 5 outstanding writer achievement awards; Grammy award for Best Male Country Vocal Performance, 1984, Country Collaboration with Vocals, 1998. Mem. Country Music Assn. (6 awards), Am. Fedn. TV and Rec. Artists, Screen Actors Guild, Am. Fedn. Musicians. Address: PO Box 536 Palo Cedro CA 96073-0536 also: Capitol 3322 W End Ave Nashville TN 37203-1031 also: 11031 S Bannock St Phoenix AZ 85044-1535 E-mail: merle@merlehaggard.com.*

HAGGARD, WILLIAM ANDREW, lawyer; b. Miami, Feb. 20, 1942; s. Curtis Andrew and Marjorie (Tumlin) H.; m. Carole Ann Erali; children: Michael Andrew, Rebecca M. BA, Fla. State U., 1964; JD, Mercer U., 1967. Bar: Fla. 1967, U.S. Dist. Ct. (5th cir.) 1972, U.S. Supreme Ct. 1972, U.S. Ct. Appeals 1981. Clk. Fla. State Atty.'s Office, 1967; asst. state atty. Eleventh Jud. Cir., 1967-68; chief prosecutor, mil. judge, trial counsel USAF; sr. ptnr. The Haggard Law Firm P.A. Instr. CLE Fla. Bar, 1977-82; vis. lectr. U. Fla. Law Sch., 1977-82; mem. com. Orange Bowl. Commr. Fla. Commn. on Ethics, 1990-91; mem. Mercer U. Alumni Bd.; bd. dirs. Fla. State U. Found.; chmn. Fla. State U. Coll. Arts and Scis. Leadership Counsel; Gov. Crist appointee Fla. State Bd. Trustees. Fellow Internat. Acad. Trial Lawyers (state chair); mem. ATLA, ABA, Am. Bd. Trial Advocates, Dade County Bar Assn., Orange Bowl Com., Acad. Fla. Trial Lawyers (bd. dirs. 1995-96), Internat. Soc. Barristers, Million Dollars Advocates Club, Phi Delta Phi, Sigma Chi. Office: 330 Alhambra Cir Coral Gables FL 33134-5004 Business E-Mail: wah@haggardparks.com.

HAGGARD, WILLIAM HENRY, meteorologist; b. Woodbridge, Conn., Nov. 20, 1920; s. Howard Wilcox and Josephine Cecelia (Foley) H.; m. Blanche Woolard, Mar. 21, 1944 (div. May 1967); children: William Henry Jr., Robert H.; m. Martina Wadewitz, Oct. 1, 1967. BS in Physics, Yale U., 1942; cert. in profl. meteorology, MIT, 1942; MS in Meteorology, U. Chgo., 1946; postgrad., Fla. State U., 1958-59. Instr. meteorology N.C. State U., Raleigh, 1946-47; rsch. meteorologist U.S. Weather Bur., 1947-48; forecaster USWB Nat. Airport, 1949-50; instr. U.S. AID, Washington, 1950-51; staff weather rsch. project U.S. Navy, Norfolk, Va., 1951-54; chief adv. svcs. br. U.S. Weather Bur., Washington, 1954-59, asst. chief Office of Plans, 1960-61; dep. dir. Nat. Weather Records Ctr., Asheville, NC, 1961; dir. Nat. Climatic Ctr., Asheville, 1963-75; pres. Climatol. Cons. Corp., Asheville, 1976-97, v.p., 1998; cons., 1999—. Weather com. US Power Squadron, Raleigh, NC, 1988—98. Contbr. articles to tech. jours., 1947-99. Bd. dirs. ARC, Asheville, 1965-70, United Way, Asheville, 1964-70. Capt. USN, 1942-45, with Res. 1951-54. Recipient Tech. Adminstr. award NOAA, Washington, 1970, Am. Meteor. Soc. award outstanding Contbrns. to Applid Meteorology, 2001. Fellow Am. Meteorol. Soc. (cert. cons. meteorologist, bd. dirs. pvt. sector meteorology sect. 1989-92, mem. cert. cons. meteorologist bd. 1983-88), Nat. Coun. Indsl. Meteorologists (pres. 1988-89, bd. dirs. 1987-90, 94-96, 99-2001, sec., treas. 1994-2002). Republican. Presbyterian. Avocations: sailing, photography. Office: William H Haggard CCM LLC 150 Shope Creek Rd Asheville NC 28805-9795 Home Phone: 828-298-7264; Office Phone: 828-298-4237. Personal E-mail: cccavl@bellsouth.net.

HAGGERSON, NELSON LIONEL, JR., education educator; b. Silver City, N.Mex., June 11, 1927; s. Nelson L. and Gladys Lenore (Jackson) H.; m. B. Kate Baldwin, June 1, 1949 (dec. 2001); children: Patrick, Frederick, Teresa, Rebecca, Lionel, Mary; m. Catherine Rumsey, Dec. 1, 2001. BA, Vanderbilt U., 1949; MS, Western N.Mex. U., 1952; PhD, Claremont Grad. U., 1960. Cert. secondary tchr.; cert. adminstr. Dir. Exptl. Sch. Webster Coll., Webster Groves, Mo.; asst. prof. edn. Western N.Mex. U., Silver City; prin. Cobre High Sch., Bayard, N.Mex.; prof. edn. Ariz. State U., Tempe, 1961—63, 1964—89, prof. emeritus edn., 1989—. Vis. prof. U. W.I., St. Augustine, Trinidad and Tobago, 1993-99, U. Pitts., 1982, 91, 92, R.I. Coll., 1991, Western N.Mex. U., 1988, 97, 98, 99, 2000, 01. Author: Secondary Education Today, 1967, To Dance With Joy, 1971, Naturalistic Research Paradigms: Theory and Practice, 1983, Informing Educational Policy and Practice Through Interpretive Inquiry, 1992, From Geronimo's Lookout, Growing Up and Living in the Southwest: An Autobiography, 1993, 2d edit., 2005, Oh Yes I Can!, A Biography of Arlena Seneca, 1994, A Celebration: The Life of Father Ramon Estivill, Renaissance Man of God, 1999, Expanding Curriculum Research and Understanding, 2000, Stories of the Academy: Learning From the Good Mother, 2002, The Mission of the Scholar: Research and Practice, A Tribute to Nelson Haggerson, 2002, also 12 book chpts.; guest editor: Education in Asia, Silver Ann Edit., World Coun. Curriculum and Instrn., Winter, 1995; contbr. over 50 articles to profl. jours. With USN, 1945-46. Fulbright fellow, 1986; recipient Award in Curriculum, MacDonald, 1986; named Outstanding Researcher, Coll. Edn., 1987, Outstanding Tchr., 1988; rsch. grantee Deakin U., Victoria, Australia, 1988, The Mission of the Scholar, Rsch. and Practice: A Tribute to Nelson Haggerson, 2002; inductee N.Mex. Mil. Inst. Hall of Fame, 2004. Mem. AERA, ASCD, Profs. Curriculum, Soc. for Study of Curriculum History, World Coun. for Curriculum and Instrn. (program chmn. 1989), Order Internat. Fellowship, Phi Delta Kappa, Phi Kappa Phi, Kappa Delta Pi. Home: PO Box 24177 Tempe AZ 85285-4177 Business E-Mail: haggerson@asu.edu.

HAGGERTY, GRETCHEN R., metal products executive; BS in Acctg., Case Western Res. U., Cleve.; JD, Duquesne U., Pitts. CPA. Mgmt. trainee tax divsn. US Steel Group, Pitts., 1976—77, tax asst., 1977—80, leasing analyst, 1980—82, sr. fin. analyst, 1982—84, corp. fin. mgr., 1984—85, dir. plant and gen. acctg. USS Chems. Divsn., 1985—86, gen. tax atty., 1986—87, dir. taxes, 1987—88, asst. treas. corp. fin. Pitts., 1988—89, asst. comptr. corp. acctg., 1989—91, v.p. acctg. and fin., 1998—2002, sr. v.p., contr., 2002, sr. v.p., treas., 2002—03, treas., 2003—04, exec. v.p., CFO Pitts., 2003—; v.p., treas. USX Corp., Pitts., 1991—98. Chmn. US Steel and Carnegie Pension Fund; mem. exec. com. Pa. Bus. Roundtable; bd. dir. Highmark Inc. Bd. mem. Civic Light Opera, United Way Allegheny County. Mem.: Allegheny County Bar Assn. Office: US Steel 600 Grant St Pittsburgh PA 15219-2800 Office Phone: 412-433-4961.*

HAGGERTY, JAMES JOSEPH, lawyer; b. Scranton, Pa., June 12, 1936; s. James J. Haggerty and Margaret W. Cummings; m. Cecelia Ellen Lynett; children: Jean Margaret McGrath, Mauri Elizabeth Collins, James Joseph Jr., Matthew Edward, Cecelia Ellen, Daniel Patrick, Kathleen Mary Janes. BA in Econs., Holy Cross Coll., Worcester, Mass., 1957; JD, Georgetown U., 1960; LLD (hon.), U. Scranton, 1987; LHD (hon.), Villanova U., 1995. Bar: Pa. 1961, Ct. Common Pleas Lackawanna County 1961, U.S. Dist. Ct. (mid. dist.) Pa. 1961, U.S. Ct. Appeals (3d cir.) 1962, U.S. Ct. Claims 1985. Assoc. Farrell Butler Kearney & Parker, Scranton, 1961-62; law clk. to Hon. William J. Nealon U.S. Dist. Ct. (mid. dist.), Scranton, 1963-64; ptnr. Casey Haggerty and McDonnell, Scranton, 1965-70, Haggerty McDonnell O'Brien, Scranton, 1970-87; former sec. of commonwealth State of Pa., Harrisburg, 1987-89; gen. counsel to gov. Commonwealth of Pa., Harrisburg, 1989-93; ptnr. Haggerty, McDonnell & O'Brien, Scranton, 1993—. Apptd. by U.S. Dist. Ct. trustee in bankruptcy of Blue Coal Corp., 1976-86; mem. hearing com. 3.03 Disciplinary Bd. Pa. Supreme Ct.; permanent mem. Jud. Conf. U.S. 3d Jud. Cir.; mem. Fed. Jud. Screening Com., 1996-2001; chmn. bd. dirs. Shamrock Comm. Corp.; past bd. dirs. Specialty Plastics Products Inc.; past. bd. dirs., solicitor 1st Nat. Community Bank Dunmore. Trustee U. Scranton, 1979—86, chmn. bd., 1982—86, mem.Pres.'s Cir., mem. Pres.'s Club; chmn. Real Bob Casey Com., 1985—86; trustee Scranton Prep. Sch., 1995—2000, chmn. bd., 1999—2000; former bd. dirs. Lackawanna United Way, former chmn. profl. and geog. divsn.; bd. dirs. assocs. Scranton Area Found. With US Army, with Pa. N.G. Mem. ABA, ATLA, Am. Bankers Assn., Pa. Bar Assn. (Spl. Achievement award 1988-89), Pa. Trial Lawyers Assn., Pa. Bankers Assn., Lackawanna Bar Assn. (past pres., bd. dirs.), Greater Scranton C. of C. (bd. dirs., former v.p.), Holy Cross Coll. Alumni Assn. N.E. Pa. (past pres., Outstanding Alumnus award 1982), Scranton Prep. Sch. Alumni Assn. (past mem. bd. govs., T. Donald Reinfret S.J. award Outstanding Alumnus of Yr. 1985), Friendly Sons of St. Patrick Lackawanna County (mem. exec. com., past pres.), Country Club Scranton (bd. dirs.). Roman Catholic. Office: Haggerty McDonnell & O'Brien 203 Franklin Ave Ste 1 Scranton PA 18503-1989 Home Phone: 570-344-5794; Office Phone: 570-344-9845. Business E-Mail: hmolaw@epix.net.

HAGGERTY, LUANE RUTH DAVIS, theater director, educator, actress; b. Binghamton, NY, Sept. 10, 1960; d. Paul Joseph and Ruth Hardin (Wheeler) D., m. Jonathan Allen Fluck, (div. Dec. 1994); m. Peter Lester Haggerty, Sept. 21, 2002. BS, Hunter Coll., 1983; MA, Goddard Coll., 1992; stage interpretation in ASL cert., The Juilliard Sch., 1994; PhD, Antioch U., 2006. Performer Broadway, regional, stock prodns.; dir., choreographer showcase, cruise lines, children's shows, 1986—2006; adminstr. Maverick Theatre, NYC, 1986-88; artistic dir. Interborough Repertory Theatre, NYC, 1986—; writer self help, plays, 1990—; pub. edn. specialist Dept. Mental Retardation Devel. Disabilities, NYC, 1990-95; program coord. for deaf svcs. St. Vincent's Hosp., NYC, 1997-98; prof. Nt. Tech. Inst. for the Deaf Rochester (N.Y.) Inst. Tech., 1998—. Am. Sign Lang. interpreter; creator Del-Sign acting technique, Interborough Repertory Theatre, N.Y.C., 1992—; coord. theater program Roberts Wesleyan Coll., 2005*2007; spkr. in field; presenter Nat. Inst. Trial Lawyers. Author: (self-help) Taking Stage, 1995; (musical) Women of the American Revolution, 1991, The World in Her Hands: The Story of Helen Keller, 1993; author, prodr.: (musical) The Little Matchgirl, 1995; author, dir. Eye Music, 2000, Lute Song, 2001, Walls, 2002, Windows Of The Soul (nominee Pulitzer prize, 2007). Recipient Women of Achievement award Gov. Pataki's Women Run N.Y.C., 1998. Mem. AFTRA, DAR, Actor's Equity Assn., Soc. Stage Dir. and Choreogrphers, League of Prof. Theatre Women, Registry of Interpreters of the Deaf, Deaf Entertainment Guild. Episcopalian. Avocations: running, bicycling. Home: 25 Mayapple Ln West Henrietta NY 14586-9518 Office: Interborough Theatre 154 Christopher St Ste 3B New York NY 10014-2840

HAGGERTY, MARY ANN, medical educator; b. Jersey City, Mar. 19, 1948; d. Cornelius Joseph and Catherine Teresa (Mulroy) H.; m. Thomas Gerard Curran, Aug. 7, 1976; children: Catherine, Margaret. BS, Chestnut Hill Coll., 1970; AM, Dartmouth Coll., 1972; MD, U. Medicine & Dentistry N.J., 1979. Tchr. St. Peter's Prep. Sch., Jersey City, 1972-75; sr. pub. health physician N.J. State Dept. Health, Trenton, 1982-83; dir. med. clinic U. Medicine & Dentistry N.J.-Univ. Hosp., Newark, 1983-85; dir. intro. clin. svcs. U. Medicine & Dentistry N.J.-N.J. Med. Sch., Newark, 1985-91, assoc. prof. clin. medicine, 1990—; dir. primary care medicine Newark-Beth Israel Med. Ctr., 1991—2000, interim dir. medicine, 1997-98. Bd. dirs. St. Barnabas Provider Partnership. Mem. AMA, Am. Coll. Physicians, Am. Geriatrics Soc., Am. Med. Women's Assn., Med. Soc. N.J., Essex County Med. Soc. Avocation: walking. Office: 2115 Millburn Ave Maplewood NJ 07040 Office Phone: 973-275-1322. Personal E-mail: mahaggerty@comcast.net.

HAGGERTY, ROBERT JOHNS, pediatrician, educator; b. Saranac Lake, NY, Oct. 20, 1925; s. Gordon Abbott and Nina (Johns) H.; m. Muriel Ethel Protzmann, Oct. 29, 1949; children: Robert, Janet, Richard, John. AB, Cornell U., 1946, MD, 1949; AM (hon.), Harvard U., 1975; DSc (hon.), Ind. U., 1990. Diplomate Am. Bd. Pediat. Intern Strong Meml. Hosp., Rochester, NY, 1949-51; from resident to chief resident pediat. Children's Hosp. Med. Ctr., Boston, 1953-55; med. dir. family health care program, asst. prof. pediat. Harvard Med. Sch., 1953-64; prof. pediat., chmn. dept. U. Rochester Sch. Medicine, 1964-75; Roger I. Lee prof. health svcs., chmn. dept. health svcs. Harvard Sch. Pub. Health, 1975-78; prof. pediat. Harvard Med. Sch., Boston, 1975-78, clin. prof., 1978-80; pres. William T. Grant Found., NYC, 1980-92; clin. prof. pediat. Cornell U. Med. Sch., NYC, 1980-92; prof. pediat. emeritus U. Rochester Sch. Medicine, 1992—; exec. dir. Internat. Pediatric Assoc., 1993-98. Dir. gen. pediat. acad. devel. program Robert Wood Johnson Found., 1978-88; mem. health svcs. rsch. sect. USPHS, 1964-70, 82-84, chmn., 1968-70, 82-84;

mem. N.Y. State Health Planning Adv. Coun., Carnegie Coun. on Children, 1972-77; chmn. panel health scis. rsch., com. on nat. needs for biomed. and behavioral rsch. per. NRC, 1975-78; mem. bd. U.S. Com. on UNICEF, 1981-87; mem. Gov.'s Coun. on Grad. Med. Edn., N.Y. State, 1989-93. Editor: (with M. Green) Ambulatory Pediatrics, 1968, 5th edit., 1999, (with J. Lucey) Pediatrics, 1973-80, Pediatrics in Rev., 1978-2004, Bull. N.Y. Acad. Medicine, 1992-99; assoc. editor New Eng. Jour. Medicine, 1959-64; contbr. articles to med. jours. Mem. vis. com. Grad. Sch. Edn., Harvard U., 1982-88; bd. dirs. Grantmakers in Health, 1985-89; bd. overseers, social scis. dept., Tufts U., 1990-94; bd. visitors U. Okla. Sch. Pub. Health, 1991-94. Capt. USAF, 1951-53. Recipient Martha M. Eliot award Am. Pub. Health Assn., 1976, Disting. Alumni award Cornell U. Med. Coll., 1987, 6 awards various pediatric socs., 1989, Primary Care Achievement award PEW Found. Health Professions Commn., 1994; Markle scholar in acad. medicine, Markle Found., N.Y.C., 1962-67; fellow Ctr. for Advanced Study Behavioral Scis., Stanford, Calif., 1974-75 Mem.: Alliance for Health Care for All (trustee 1991—94), Am. Health Fedn. (trustee 1989—92), NY Acad. Medicine (trustee, sec. 1989—92), Inst. of Medicine (coun. 1974—77, chmn. com. on prevention of mental illness 1992—93, chmn. steering com. nat. study quality assurance programs 1975—76, Gustave Lienhard award 1989), Soc. Pediat. Rsch. (v.p. 1970—71), Internat. Epidemiol. Assn., Assn. Am. Med. Colls., Ambulatory Pediat. Assn. (chmn. 1963—64, George Armstrong award 1969), Am. Pediat. Soc. (Joseph St. Geme award 1989, John Howland award 1998, E.H. Christopherson award for internat. child health 2001, Alfred I. Du Pont award 2004), Am. Acad. Pediat. (v.p., pres. 1983—85, Grulee award 1981, Dale Richmond award 1981, Aldrich award 1986, Job Smith award 1987, Abraham Jacobi award 1996, E.H. Christopherson award for internat. child health 2001, Lifetime Edn. award 2002), Am. Assn. Poison Control Ctrs. (pres. 1962—64), Assn. Med. Sch. Pediat. Dept. Chairmen (pres. 1969—70), Royal Coll. Pediats. and Child Health (hon.), Harvard Club N.Y.C., Alpha Omega Alpha, Phi Beta Kappa. Personal E-mail: robert_haggerty@urmc.rochester.edu.

HAGGETT, ROSEMARY ROMANOWSKI, academic administrator; BA in Biology, U. Bridgeport, 1974; PhD in Physiology, U. Va., 1979. Postdoctoral fellow Northwestern U., Evanston, Ill., 1979-82; asst. prof. biology Loyola U. Chgo., 1982-87; from program dir. to divsn. dir. animals and nutrition USDA, 1988-94, dep. assoc. adminstr., 1988-94; prof. animal and vet. sci. W.Va. U., Morgantown, 1994—, dean Coll. Agr., Forestry and Consumer Scis., 1994-99, assoc. provost acad. programs, 1999—2003; dir. divsn. undergrad. edn. NSF, 2003—; acting dep. asst. dir. EHR, 2005—. Office: EHR NSF Ste 805 4201 Wilson Blvd Arlington VA 22230 Office Phone: 703-292-8600. Business E-Mail: rhaggett@nsf.gov.

HAGGIS, ARTHUR GEORGE, JR., retired military officer, educator, publisher; b. Youngstown, Ohio, June 3, 1924; s. Arthur George Sr. and Mary Mildred (Campbell) H.; m. Lewanna Evalyn Strom, Apr. 7, 1944; children: Lynda Lee, Arthur George III, Richard Charles, Douglas Hood, Pamela Sue. BS in Edn., Wayne State U., 1957, MEd, 1959, EdD, 1961. Enlisted pvt. U.S. Army, 1943, advanced through enlisted grades to staff sgt., commd. 2d. lt., field artillery/Battle of the Bulge, 1945, advanced through ranks to Brig. Gen., 1964; bn. survey officer field artillery U.S. Army ETO, 1943-46; S-2 475th Field Artillery Battalion and asst. indsl. engr. U.S. Steel Corp., McDonald, Ohio, 1946-51; post dep. comdr., adj. 2d Armored Div. Trains, Bad Kreuznach, Fed. Republic Germany, 1951-54; spl. mil. asst. to Sec. of Army, Chief of Info. U.S. Army, Ft. Wayne, Mich., Detroit Arsenal, Mich. Mil. Dist.; with ordnance tank automotive command Washington and Detroit; mem. gen. staff U.S. Army, Washington, 1954-64; pres., CEO Haggis Assocs. Inc., Washington and Hollywood, D.C. and Fla., 1964-71, Atlantis Pvt. Schs., Inc., Hollywood, 1971—; chmn., CEO The Atlantis-Lewart Group, Inc., Hollywood, 1987—. Pres., CEO Ednl. Cons., Washington and Hollywood, 1966—, Atlantis Pub. Co., Hollywood, 1978—, Atlantis Rsch. Insts., Inc., Hollywood, 1981—, Perfect Body Products, Inc., Hollywood, 1981—; apptd. gubernatorial mem. State of Fla. Bd. Correctional Edn., Correctional Edn. Sch. Authority, term ending 1994; aide-de-camp to Gen. of Army Omar N. Bradley, 1955; negotiator Dept. Def. Armed Forces res. Ann. Unit Tng. Clause, UAW-CIO/GM contract, 1956; comdr. Army Task Force Ground Zero, Operation Plumbbob, atmospheric nuclear exlposion experiment, Frenchman Flat, Nev., 1957; liaison Sec. of Army, 1st U.S. Satellite Explorer I, 1957-58; comdr. U.S. Joint Task Force Mackinac, Mackinac Bridge Dedication Ceremony Mich., 1958; originator Dept. Def. Nat. Com. for Employer Support of Guard and Res., 1955-58; developer Dept. Def. Armed Forces Week, 1955-61. Co-editor, Small Business Library, The Government Market, 1966, Selling to the U.S. Government and its Contractors, vol. I, 1966, Bids, Proposals, Contracts and Contract Administration, vol. II, 1966, Texts of Small Business Enterprise Institute, vol. III, 1966, Bids, Proposals and Contracts for Small Business Enterprise Course Handbook, vol. IV, 1966; author: Educational Evaluation Program: Predicting College Success, 1967; author: (with others) Edu-Care, the New School Concept, 1991, also supporting texts, Atlantis Beginning Language and Number Development Program, Books 1 and 2, 1981, Atlantis Basic Spelling Series, Books A-H, 1981-85, Atlantis Computer Series, Books I-VII, 1982-87, Atlantis Health Series, 1981-87. Sustaining mem. Freedoms Found. at Valley Forge, 1985—, Mus. of Art, 1986—, Opera Soc.; founder Performing Arts Ctr. Pacers, 1985; mem. Opera Guild, Inc., 1986—; pres. Wayne State U. Alumni Club Washington D.C., 1963-69; trustee Philharmonic Orchestra Fla., 1987—; mem. Rep. Presdl. Task Force, 1983—, Rep. Senatorial Inner Circle, Rep. Pres.' Club, 1984—, Mayor's Prayer Breakfast Com., Ft. Lauderdale, 1988—; mem. adv. coun. Broward Community Found., 1987—; sec. of def. appointee nat. com. for employer support of the guard and res. Dept. Def. Decorated Bronze Star, Purple Heart; recipient award City of St. Ignace, 1958, Nat. USO award 1959, citation City of Detroit, 1959, Exceptional Svc. Nat. award Assn. U.S. Army, 1990; decorated Nat. Soc. of SAR, 1985; U.S. Army doctoral scholar Wayne State U., 1960-61; grantee Detroit Edison Co., 1964-65, Litton Industries, 1965-66. Mem. Assn. U.S. Army (state pres., regional v.p. 1984-87, sustaining mem. Landpower Edn. Fund Inc. 1984, chmn. Fla. state exec. coun. 1985-87, bd. dirs. Fla. Gulf Stream chpt. 1984—, nat. adv. bd. dirs. 1990-96), Navy League (bd. dirs. Ft. Lauderdale coun. 1988—), USO (pres. greater Ft. Lauderdale Inc. coun. 1988—, Freedoms Found. at Valley Forge George Washington medal 1991), Nat. Assn. Atomic Vets., Mil. Order of Purple Heart (life), Ret. Officers Assn., Mil. Order of World Wars, Am. Legion, VFW, Disabled Am. Vets., Nat. Sojourners Inc., Nat. Order Battlefield Commns., Nat. Eagle Scout Assn., Vets. of Battle of the Bulge, Greater Ft. Lauderdale C. of C. (founding trustee 1989—), Air Force Assn. (citation 1961), Clan Campbell Soc. of Fla., Inc., Scots-Am. Soc. of Brevard, Army and Navy (Washington), Patrick AFB Officers, K.T., Masons. Republican. Lutheran. Avocations: woodworking, bridge, sailing, water sports. Office: 11911 Snapdragon Rd Tampa FL 33635-6232

HAGGIS, MARY RIPLEY, nurse, genealogist; b. Ellsworth, Ohio, July 13, 1934; d. Sehon Miller and Hazel Emma (Hoyle) Ripley; m. William Campbell Haggis, Aug. 7, 1955; children: Cheryl Rene, William Campbell II. Grad., Salem City Hosp. Sch. Nursing, Ohio, 1955. RN Ohio. RN, surgical nurse operating room Mercy Hosp., Springfield, Ohio, 1955—57; RN gen. duty Good Samaritan Hosp., Zanesville, Ohio, 1959—60; RN gen. duty and intensive care unit Ohio Valley Hosp., Steubenville, Ohio, 1968—72; RN Family Practice Office of Dr. Paul W. McFadden, Dover, Ohio, 1979—99. Leader Steubenville Brownies, 1968, Jr. Girl Scouts, Steubenville, 1969, Cub Scouts, Steubenville, 1970—71; sec. Dover Band Boosters, Ohio, 1976—78; pres. Arts Coun. Tuscarawas, Dover, Ohio, 1979—84; stats. sec. Ctrl. Conf. Ohio United Luth. Ch. Women, Columbus, Ohio, 1961; tchr. Grace Luth. Ch., 1984—97, deacon, 1990—98; bd. mem. Young Women's Christian Assn., Steubenville, 1966—67, Personal and Family Counseling, Dover, 1974—75. Recipient Surg. Nurse award, Salem City Hosp. Sch. Nursing, 1955, Founder's Day award, Grace Luth. Ch., 1997. Mem.: DAR, Settlers and Builders of Ohio, Ohio Ea. Star, Pioneer Families of Trumbull County, Pioneer Families of Mahoning County, Soc. Civil War Families, First Families of Ohio, South Ctrl. Pa. Geneal. Soc., Tuscarawas County Geneal. Soc., New Eng. Hist. and Geneaology Soc., Order St. Luke the Physician, Trumbull County Geneal. Soc., Mahoning County Geneal. Soc., Ohio Geneal. Soc. Republican. Lutheran. Avocations: genealogy, travel, bible study. Home: 827 E 4th St Dover OH 44622-1319 Personal E-mail: mbhaggis@tusco.net.

HAGGIS, PAUL EDWARD, scriptwriter, television producer, television director; b. London, Ont., Can., Mar. 10, 1953; came to U.S., 1979; s. Edward H. and Mary Yvonne (Metcalf) H.; m. Diane Christine Gettas, Apr. 9, 1977-94; children: Alissa Sullivan, Lauren Kilvington, Katy Elizabeth; m. Deborah Rennard, Jun. 21, 1997; 1 child. Writer: (TV series) One Day at a Time, 1975, The Love Boat, 1977, Diff'rent Strokes, 1978, The Facts of Life, 1979, (also prodr. 1984-86), The Tracey Ullman Show, 1987, Thirtysomething, 1987 (Emmy award for Outstanding Drama Series, 1988), Walker, Texas Ranger, 1993 (also creator), (TV films) The Return of the Shaggy Dog, 1987, (films) The Last Kiss, 2006, Flags of Our Fathers, 2006, Casino Royale, 2006; writer, dir.: (films) Red Hot, 1993; writer, exec. prodr.: (TV films) Due South, 1994, (TV series) Michael Hayes, 1997; writer, prodr.: (films) Million Dollar Baby, 2004; writer, exec. prodr., dir.: (TV series) EZ Streets, 1996-97, Family Law, 1999, (TV films) Ghost of a Chance, 1998; writer, prodr., dir.: (films) Crash, 2004 (Best Writer, Broadcast Film Critics Assn., 2006, Original Screenplay, British Acad. Film and TV Arts, 2006, Best First Feature, Independent Spirit award, 2006, Motion Picture of Yr. and Original Screenplay, Acad. Motion Picture Arts & Sciences, 2006) Trustee Found. for Religious Freedom; mem. adv. bd. Mus. Broadcasting; co-founder Artists for Peace and Justice, bd. dirs. Hollywood Edn. Lteracy Project, For the Arts for Every Child, Environmental Media Assn.; founding mem. Earth Comm. Office; mem. adv. bd. Ctr. Advancement Non-Violence; mem. Pres. Coun. Defenders of Wildlife.*

HAGGLUND, CLARANCE EDWARD, lawyer, publishing executive; b. Omaha, Feb. 17, 1927; s. Clarance Andrew and Esther May (Kelle) H.; m. Dorothy Souser, Mar. 27, 1953 (div. Aug. 1972); children: Laura, Bret, Katherine; m. Merle Patricia Hagglund, Oct. 28, 1972. BA, U. S.D., 1949; JD, William Mitchell Coll. Law, 1953. Bar: Minn. 1955, U.S. Ct. Appeals (8th cir.) 1974, U.S. Supreme Ct. 1963; diplomate Am. Bd. Profl. Liability Attys. Ptnr. Hagglund & Johnson and predecessor firms, Mpls., 1973—; mem. Hagglund, Weimer and Speidel, PA; publ., pres. Common Law Publishing Inc., Golden Valley, Minn., 1991—; mem. Blackwell Igbanogo Attys., Mpls., 2004; with Hagglund Law Offices, 2004—. Pres. Internat. Control Sys., Inc., Mpls., 1979—, Hill River Corp., Mpls., 1976—; gen. counsel Minn. Assn. Profl. Ins. Agts., Inc., Mpls., 1965-86; CFO, Pro-Trac, software for profl. liability ins. industry. Contbr. articles to profl. jours. Served to lt. comdr. USNR, 1945-46, 50-69. Fellow Internat. Soc. Barristers; mem. Lawyers Pilots Bar Assn., U.S. Maritime Law Assn. (proctor), Acad. Cert. Trial Lawyers Minn. (dean 1983-85), Nat. Bd. Trial Advocacy (cert. in civil trial law, bd. dirs.), Douglas Amdahl Inns of Ct. (pres.), Ill. Athletic Club (Chgo.), Edina Country Club (Minn.), Calhoun Beach Club (Mpls.). Roman Catholic. Avocation: flying. Home and Office: Common Law Publishing Inc 3168 Dean Ct Minneapolis MN 55416-4386 Office Phone: 612-926-0210. Personal E-mail: chagglund@comcast.net.

HAGIN, JOSEPH WHITEHOUSE, II, federal official; b. Lexington, Ky., Jan. 6, 1956; s. Joseph Whitehouse and Hannah (Hargett) H. BA, Kenyon Coll., 1979. Personal asst. to v.p. U.S. The White House, Washington, 1981-83, asst. to v.p. for legis. affairs, 1983-85; dir. pub. affairs Federated Dept. Stores, Cin., 1985-87; asst. v.p. pub. affairs Chiquita Brands Internat. Inc., 1988, v.p. corp. affairs Cin., 1991—2000; dep. asst. to pres. of U.S. for appointments and scheduling The White House, Washington, 1989—91; dep. campaign mgr. Bush-Cheney presdl. campaign, 2000; asst. to the Pres. & dep. chief of staff for ops. The White House, 2000—. Govt. affairs com. Cin. C. of C., 1985-88; bd. dirs. Clean Cin., 1986-88, Hamilton County Rep. Fin. Com., 1986—. Mem. Camargo Club, Bankers Club (Cin.). Episcopalian. Office: The White House 1600 Pennsylvania Ave NW W Wing 1st Fl Washington DC 20500

HAGIN, T. RICHARD, lawyer; b. Thomasville, Ga., Sept. 13, 1941; s. Wesley R. and Elizabeth (Skinner) H.; m. Deborah Hayes, June 19, 1981; children: Jennifer Bridges, Lori Bridges; children from previous marriage: John Wesley Hagin, Grace Elizabeth Hagin. AA, North Fla. C.C., Madison, 1961; student, Fla. State U., 1961-62; JD, Stetson U., 1964. Fla. 1964, Oreg. 1992, U.S. Dist. Ct. (mid. dist.) Fla. 1965, U.S. Ct. Appeals (5th cir.) 1965, U.S. Ct. Appeals (11th cir.) 1981, U.S. Ct. Mil. Appeals 1991, U.S. Supreme Ct. 1971. Atty. Law Offices of David A. Davis, Bushnell, Fla., 1964; ptnr. Davis and Hagin, Bushnell, 1965; atty. in pvt. practice Bushnell, 1966-67; ptnr. Hagin, Hughes, Rardon & Rodriguez, Bushnell, 1989-1996, Getzen and Hagin, Bushnell, 1967-71; pres. Getzen & Hagin, P.A., Bushnell, 1971—. Local counsel CSX R.R., Bushnell, 1967-87; gen. coun. Fla. Nat. Bank at Bushnell, 1970-1987, gen. counsel Sumter County Zoning Commn., 1970-1976, Bushnell; gen. counsel Lake Panasoffkee Water Authority, 1967-87, Sumter County Hosp. Authority, Bushnell, 1969-85, Fla. Nat. Bank, Bushnell, 1970-87, Tax Collector of Sumter County, Bushnell, 1976-95, Sumter County Indsl. Authority, Bushnell, 1979-89; city atty. City of Webster, Fla., 1966-87, City of Coleman, Fla., 1969-73; county atty. Sumter County, Fla., 1969-76; pres. Lake-Sumter Bar Assn., Leesburg, Fla., 1969-70, Fla. County and City Prosecutors Assn., Bushnell, 1969-72, Tri-County Bar Assn., Inverness, Fla. 1973-74, sec. 1971-73; mem. Fla. traffic ct. rev. com., Fla. Supreme Ct., Tallahassee, 1971-72, Nat. Assn. County Civil Attys., bd. dirs., Chgo., 1973-75; chmn. Sumter County subdivision adv. com., Bushnell, 1973-76; forfeiture atty. Sumter County Sheriff Dept., Bushnell, 1983-89. Mem. City Coun., Bushnell, 1967-69; pros. atty. Sumter County, 1969-73; chmn. Withlacochee Regional Planning Coun., Ocala, Fla., 1973-75; chmn. 5th Jud. Cir. Grievance Com., 1973-76. Mem. ABA, Assn. Trial Lawyers Am., Fla. Bar, Oreg. Bar Assn., Acad. Fla. Trial Lawyers. Democrat. Office: Getzen and Hagin PO Box 248 Bushnell FL 33513-0019 Office Phone: 352-603-0874.

HAGNER, JOHN D., lawyer; b. Apr. 12, 1945; BSME, U. Cin., 1968; JD, Georgetown U. Law Ctr., 1973. Bar: DC 1973, Md. 1973. Founder David, hagner, Kuney & Davidson, Washington, 1977—98; mem. Womble Carlyle Sandridge & Rice, PLLC, Washington. Notary pub., Washington, 1973—93, Washington, 1994—, Md., 2000—; pro bono atty. Army Retirement Residence Found., Potomac, 1984—; dir., pro bono atty. St. Mark Elderly Housing Corp., 1987—; dir., treas., pro bono atty. George Washington Boyhood Home Found., 1991—97; adj. prof. law, fin. of real & personal property Georgetown U. Law Ctr., 1995—; lectr. in field. Bd. editors Georgetown Law Jour., 1971—73; contbr. articles to profl. jours. Lt., sanitary engr. (bio-medical lab. design & construction) US Pub. Health Svc., NIH, Bethesda, Md. Named 2000 Assoc. Mem. of Yr., Mortgage Bankers Assn. of Metropolitan Washington. Mem.: Am. Coll. of Real Estate Lawyers, DC Bar Assn. (mem., Capital Markets & Edn. & Practice Technology Committees), ABA. Office: Womble Carlyle Sandridge & Rice PLLC 1401 Eye St NW 7th Fl Washington DC 20005 Office Phone: 202-857-4404. Office Fax: 202-261-0004. Business E-Mail: jhagner@wcsr.com.

HAGOOD, RICHARD A., academic administrator, educator; b. Ontario, Oreg. m. Junella Hagood; children: Heidi, Holly, Lincoln. BA in History, Northwest Nazarene U.; MA, U. Oreg.; PhD in Educational Policy Studies, U. Ill. With Wash. State U., 1983—93, assoc. provost office of exec. v.p. and provost Pullman, 1990—93; pres. N.W. Nazarene U., 1993—. Spkr. in field. Mem. bd. dirs. Nampa Sch. Dist., US/Can. Coun. of Edn., Ch. Nazarene; mem. gen. bd. Ch. Nazarene, 1997—2001; mem. bd. dirs. Boise Airport Comm., Great Northwest Athletic Conf., United Way; chmn. bd. dirs. Mercy Med. Ctr. Office: NW Nazarene U 623 Holly St Nampa ID 83686*

HAGOORT, THOMAS HENRY, retired lawyer; b. Paterson, NJ, May 30, 1932; s. Nicholas Hugh and Rae (Sytsma) H.; m. Lois Ann Bennett, Sept. 6, 1954; children: Nancy Hagoort Treuhold, Susan Hagoort Bick. AB cum laude, Harvard U., 1954, LLB magna cum laude, 1957. Bar: N.Y. 1959. Assoc. firm Cleary, Gottlieb, Steen & Hamilton, NYC, 1957-67, ptnr., 1968-90; gen. counsel Albany Internat. Corp., 1991—2002, sr. v.p., 2002—05. Note editor: Harvard Law Rev., 1956—57. Pres. Mountainside Hosp., Montclair, N.J., 1983-85, chmn. bd. trustees, 1985-88; pres. Internat. Baccalaureate of N.Am., N.Y.C., 1980-91, Montclair Bd. Edn. 1966-70; mem., Coun. of Found. Internat. Baccalaureate Orgn., Geneva, 1982-96, pres. and chair exec. com., 1990-96. Mem.: ABA, N.Y. State Bar Assn., Sea Pines Country Club, S.C. Yacht Club, Harvard Club of N.J. (pres. 1977—78). Democrat. Home: PO Box 3229 Hilton Head Island SC 29928-0229

HAGSTROM, JACK WALTER CARL KLING, retired pathology educator; b. Rockford, Ill., Dec. 2, 1933; s. Walter Carl Paul Hagstrom and Loretta Christine (Kling) Pearson; life ptnr. Thomas J. Fleming. AB, Amherst Coll., 1955; MD, Cornell U., 1959. Instr. dept. pathology Cornell U. Med. Coll., NYC, 1962-65, asst. prof., 1965-68; assoc. prof. Case We. Res. U., Cleve., 1968-70, Columbia U., NYC, 1970-75, prof. pathology, 1975-91, prof. emeritus, 1991—. Attending pathologist Univ. Hosp., Cleve., 1968—70, Presbyn. Hosp., NYC, 1981—91; dir. dept. pathology Harlem Hosp., NYC, 1981—91; hon. curator modern poetry Amherst Coll. Libr., Amherst, Mass., 1981—. Author: Thom Gunn: A Bibliography, 1979, Dana Gioia: A Descriptive Bibliography with Critical Essays, 2002; contbr. articles to profl. jours. Mem. corporator Holden Arboretum, Mentor, Ohio; chmn. Friends of Amherst Coll. Libr., 1973—90. Fellow: Am. Coll. Cardiology; mem.: Pvt. Librs. Assn., Acad. Am. Poets, Printing History Soc., Bibliog. Soc. London, Bibliograph. Soc. U. Va., Bibliograph. Soc. Am., Kiambu Club, Northport Yacht Club, Durban Club, Jockey Club, Club Odd Vols., Grolier Club, Pratts Club, Travellers' Club, Garrick Club. Episcopalian. Home: PO Box 105 Seven Ponds Towd Rd Water Mill NY 11976

HAGUE, WILLIAM EDWARD, writer; b. Duquesne, Pa., Feb. 2, 1919; s. William Edward and Edith (Osburn) H.; m. Margaret Cleland Anderson, July 22, 1950 (div.). AB, Princeton U., 1940; postgrad., U. Pitts. Sch. Law, 1940-41. Assoc. editor Tide mag., 1947-49; promotion dir. Living for Young Homemakers mag., 1949-50, copy editor, 1951-54, mng. editor, 1954-61; editor Living's Guide to Home Planning mag., 1958-61; with Conde Nast Publs., NYC; sr. editor House & Garden, 1961; editor-in-chief House & Garden Guides, 1962-72; asst. account exec. Fitzgerald Advt. Agy., New Orleans, 1950-51. Author: How to Decorate With Color, 1964, What You Should Know About Furniture, 1965, Planning Your Vacation Home, 1968, Plan Your Baths for Beauty and Efficiency, 1969, Plan The Kitchen That Suits You, 1969, Making The Most of The One-Room Apartment, 1969, Your Vacation House, How To Plan It, 1972, Doubleday's Complete Basic Book of Home Decorating, 1976, Know Your America, California, 1978, Remodel, Don't Move, 1981, The New Complete Basic Book of Home Decorating, 1983; editor: Country Kitchens and Baths, 1987; contbg. editor: Reader's Digest's Household Hints, 1987, Tumbleweed, A Book of Poems, 2006. Lt. USNR, 1942—46. Recipient Dorothy Dawe award for disting. journalistic coverage in home furnishings field, 1969 Mem.: Princeton Triangle Club. Home: 49 E 73rd St Apt 5F New York NY 10021-3560

HAGY, JAMES C., lawyer; b. Cleve., 1955; BA, Case Western Reserve U., 1975, JD, 1978. Bar: Ohio 1978, Ill. 1988. Ptnr., co-chair, real estate practice worldwide Jones Day, Chgo., 1992—2006; mng. dir. Rooftops Group LLC, Glenview, Ill., 2007—. Faculty mem. CoreNet Learning (formerly Inst. of Corp. Real Estate); adj. prof. Case Western Res. U. Sch. Law, Real Estate Ctr. John Marshall Law Sch. Editor: Law Rev., 1978; founding mem. (editorial bd.) Journ of Corp. Real Estate, Henry Stewart Publications, London; author: numerous articles in profl. publications. Named one of World's Leading Real Estate Lawyers, Euromoney mag. Mem.: Am. Coll. Real Estate Lawyers, Phi Beta Kappa, Order of Coif. Mailing: PO Box 716 Glenview IL 60025-0716 Office Phone: 312-269-4152. Business E-Mail: jchagy@jonesday.com, rooftopsgroup@comcast.net.

HAH, SANG SOO, biomedical researcher; m. Jee Young Hong; 1 child, Matthew S. PhD, Seoul Nat. U., Republic of Korea, 2001. Postdoctoral rschr. Columbia U., NYC, 2001—03; mem. postdoctoral rsch. staff Lawrence Livermore Nat. Lab., Calif., 2004—. Recipient Best Poster award, Bioscis. Directorate, Lawrence Livermore Nat. Lab., 2006, Best Abstract award, 2005; grantee, Dept. Energy/Lawrence Livermore Nat. Lab., 2005. Mem.: Environ. Mutagen Soc. (assoc.), Am. Chem. Soc. (assoc.), Am. Assn. Cancer Rsch. (assoc.). Office: Lawrence Livermore Nat Lab 7000 East Ave L-441 Livermore CA 94550 Home Phone: 925-551-0103; Office Phone: 925-423-1469. E-mail: hah2@llnl.gov.

HAHN, ARTHUR W., lawyer; b. Chgo., July 30, 1944; s. Bernard and Ruth (Fireman) H.; m. Kathy Miller, June 20, 1969; children: Noah, Samuel. Student, London Sch. Econs., 1964—65; BA, Miami U., Oxford, Ohio, 1966; JD, Northwestern U., 1969. Law clk. to presiding judge U.S. Dist. Ct. Ill., Chgo., 1969—71; assoc., then ptnr. Pope, Ballard, Shepard & Fowle, Chgo., 1971—79; ptnr. Katten, Muchin, Zavis, Pearl & Galler, Chgo., 1979—80; dir. Mercantile House Holdings, Chgo., 1980—84; pres., CEO N.Am. Futures divsn., Chgo., 1980—84; ptnr. Katten Muchin Zavis Rosenman, Chgo., 1984—. Faculty chmn. Ill. Inst. Tech. Chgo. Kent Coll. Law Grad. Sch. Fin. Svcs. Law, 1987-99; mem. Ill. Task Force on Fin. Svcs., Springfield, 1987, Mem. chmn. subcom. on internat. bankruptcy of CFTC. Editl. bd. mem. Capitol Markets Law Jour.; contbr. articles on corp. and commodities law to profl. jours. Mem. Dem. Senatorial Campaign Com., Washington, 1988—. Mem. ABA (vice chair fin. products and svcs. com.), Chgo. Bar Assn. (founding chmn. commodities law com.), Futures Industry Assn. (bd. dirs. 1983-84), Inst. Fin. Mkts. (exec. com., trustee 1989—, chmn. internat. divsn.), Econ. Club, Std. Club, Legal Club, Wigmore Club. Office: Katten Muchin Rosenman LLC 525 W Monroe St Ste 1600 Chicago IL 60661-3693 Office Fax: 312-577-8892. Business E-Mail: arthur.hahn@kattenlaw.com.

HAHN, DOWON, pharmaceutical researcher, educator; b. Hoo-Chang, Korea, Nov. 20, 1931; came to U.S., 1955; s. Sung-Bum Hahn and Wan-Ok Cho; m. Myung Yun Kim, Aug. 31, 1963; children: Charles, Helen, Anna. BS in Agrl. Mechanics, Mich. State U., 1960, MS in Animal Breeding, 1963; PhD in Endocrinology, U. Mo., 1967. Assoc. scientist Ortho Pharm. Corp., Raritan, N.J., 1968-69, scientist, 1969-70, sr. scientist, 1970-72, group leader, 1973-74, sect. head, 1975-82, asst. dir., 1982-87, dir., 1987-92; Disting. rsch. fellow R.W. Johnson Pharm. Rsch. Inst., Raritan, NJ, 1993—2002; ret., 2002; cons. in field, 2002—. Adj. prof. dept. animal sci. Rutgers U., New Brunswick, N.J., 1982—, dept. ob/gyn. Ea. Va. Med. Sch., Norfolk, 1967—; postdoctoral fellow Worcester Found., 1967-68. Recipient grant Danforth Found., 1958, fellowship Ford Found., 1967, Phillips B. Hoffman Rsch. Scientist award Johnson and Johnson, 1973, 85, Johnson medal Johnson and Johnson, 1990. Achievements include discovery of and development of new progestin Norgastimate, the component of birth control pill Ortho-Tri-Cyclin. Home and Office: 9109 Down Crest Way Windermere FL 34786 E-mail: dowon@bellsouth.net.

HAHN, ELLIOTT JULIUS, lawyer; b. San Francisco, Dec. 9, 1949; s. Leo Wolf and Sherry Marion (Portnoy) H.; m. Toby Rose Mallen; children: Kara Rebecca, Brittany Atira Mallen, Michael Mallen, Adam Mallen. BA cum laude, U. Pa., 1971, JD, 1974; LLM, Columbia U., 1980. Bar: N.J. 1974, Calif. 1976, D.C. 1978, U.S. Dist. Ct. N.J. 1974, U.S. Dist. Ct. (cen. dist.) Calif. 1976, U.S. Supreme Ct. 1980. Assoc. von Malitz, Derenberg, Kunin & Janssen, NYC, 1974-75; law clk. L.A. County Superior Ct., 1975-76; atty. Atlantic Richfield Co., LA, 1976-79; prof. Summer in Tokyo program Santa Clara Law Sch., 1981-83; assoc. prof. law Calif. Western Sch. Law, San Diego, 1980-85; atty. Morgan, Lewis & Bockius, LA, 1985-87; assoc. Whitman & Ransom, LA, 1987-88, ptnr., 1989-93, Sonnenschein Nath & Rosenthal, LA, 1993-97, Hahn & Bolson, LLP, 1997—. Vis. scholar Nihon U., Tokyo, 1982; vis. lectr. Internat. Christian U., Tokyo, 1982; adj. prof. law Southwestern U. Sch. Law, 1986-93, Pepperdine U. law Sch., 1986-93, U. So. Calif. Law Sch., 1997-98; lectr. U. Calif., Davis, Law Sch. Orientation in U.S.A. Law Program, 1994-97. Author: Japanese Business Law and the Legal System, 1984; contbr. chpt. on Japan to The World Legal Ency.; internat. law editor Calif. Bus. Law Reporter. Vice-chmn. San Diego Internat. Affairs Bd., 1981-85; bd. dirs. San Diego-Yokohama Sister City Soc., 1983-85, L.A.-Nagoya Sister City Soc., 1986-1996; mem. master planning com. City of Rancho Palos Verdes, Calif., 1989-91; advisor, exec. com. Calif. Internat. Law Sect., 1990-91, 95, appointee exec. com., 1991-94, vice-chmn., 1992-93, chair, 1993-94; appointee, trustee Palos Verdes Libr. Dist., 1993-94; bd. dirs. Internat. Student Ctr. UCLA, 1996-2004, pres., 2000-01. Fellow Ctr. Internat. Legal Studies; mem. ABA, State Bar Calif., LA County Bar Assn. (bd. dirs. internat. sect., exec. com. Internat. Legal Sec. 1987—, sec. 1995-96, 2d v.p. 1996-97, 1st v.p. 1997-98, chmn. 1998-99, appointee Pacific rim com. 1990-98, chmn. 1991-92, 95-98, trustee 1997-98), Assn. Asian Studies, U. Pa. Alumni Club (pres. San Diego chpt. 1982, pres. coun. Phila. 1983), Anti Defamation League, Japanese-Am. Soc. (book rev. editor Seattle 1983-85). Jewish. Office: Hahn & Bolson LLP 1000 Wilshire Blvd # 1600 Los Angeles CA 90017-2457 Home Phone: 310-377-4940; Office Phone: 213-630-2620. Business E-Mail: ehahn@hahnbolsonllp.com.

HAHN, ERWIN LOUIS, physicist, researcher; b. Sharon, Pa., June 9, 1921; s. Israel and Mary Hahn; m. Marian Ethel Failing, Apr. 8, 1944 (dec. Sept. 1978); children: David L., Deborah A., Katherine L.; m. Natalie Woodford Hodgson, Apr. 12, 1980. BS, Juniata Coll., 1943, D.Sc., 1966; MS, U. Ill., 1947, PhD, 1949; D.Sc., Purdue U., 1975, U. Stuttgart, Germany, 2001; DrRerNat, U. Stuttgart, 2001; DSc in Physics, U. Warwick, Eng., 2007. Asst. Purdue U., 1943-44; research assoc. U. Ill., 1950; NRC fellow Stanford, 1950-51, instr., 1951-52; research physicist Watson IBM Lab., NYC, 1952-55; assoc. Columbia U., 1952-55; faculty U. Calif., Berkeley, 1955—, prof. physics, 1961—, assoc. prof., then prof. Miller Inst. for Basic Rsch., 1958-59, 66-67, 85-86. Eastman vis. prof. Balliol Coll., Oxford, Eng., 1988-89; cons. Office Naval Rsch., Stanford, 1950-52, AEC, 1955—; spl. cons. USN, 1959; adv. panel mem. Nat. Bur. Stds., Radio Stds. div., 1961-64; mem. NAS/NRC com. on basic rsch.; advisor to U.S. Army Rsch. Office, 1967-69; faculty rsch. lectr. U. Calif., Berkeley, 1979. Author: (with T.P. Das) Nuclear Quadrupole Resonance Spectroscopy, 1958. Served with USNR, 1944-46. Fellow Guggenheim Found., 1961-62, 69-70, NSF, 1961-62; recipient prize Internat. Soc. Magnetic Resonance, 1971, Humboldt Found. award, 1977, 94, Alumni Achievement award Juniata Coll., 1986, citation U. Calif., Berkeley, 1991, Russell Varian prize Varian Corp., 2004; Wolf prize in physics, Wolf Found., Israel, 1984; named to Calif. Inventor Hall of Fame, 1984; vis. fellow Brasenose Coll., Oxford U., 1969-70, life hon. fellow, 1984—. Fellow AAAS, Internat. Soc. Electron Paramagnetic Resonance, Am. Phys. Soc. (past mem. exec. com. div. solid state physics, Oliver E. Buckley prize 1971), Soc. Magnetic Resonance in Medicine (hon.), Royal Soc. U.K. (London fgn. mem.); mem. NAS (co-recipient Comstock prize in electricity, magnetism and radiation 1993), French Acad. Sci. (fgn.), Acad. Arts and Scis., Slovenian Acad. Scis. and Arts (fgn.), Berkeley Fellows. Home: 69 Stevenson Ave Berkeley CA 94708-1732 Office: U Calif Dept Physics 257 Birge Berkeley CA 94720-0001

HAHN, FRANK HORACE, economics professor; b. Berlin, Apr. 26, 1925; s. Arnold and Maria (Katz) H.; m. Dorothy Salter, 1946. BSc in Econs., London, 1945, PhD, 1951; MA, Cambridge U., Eng., 1960; D in Social Scis. (hon.), Birmingham U., Eng., 1981; DLitt (hon.), U. East Anglia, Norwich, 1984; Doctor honoris causa, U. Strasbourg, 1984; DSc in Econs. (hon.), London, 1985; D (hon.), U. York, 1991; LittD (hon.), U. Leicester, 1993; PhD (hon.), U. Athens, 1993; doctor honoris causa, De L'Univ. Paris X, Nanterre, 1999. Lectr., reader math. econs. Birmingham U., 1948-60; lectr. econs. Cambridge U., 1960-66; prof. econs. London Sch. Econs., 1967-72, prof., 1972-92, prof. emeritus, 1992; prof. ordinario U. Siena, 1989—2000; hon. fellow London Sch. Econs., 1989; fellow Churchill Coll., Cambridge, 1960—; emeritus U. Siena, 2000—. Co-author (with Kenneth J. Arrow): General Competitive Analysis, 1971; author: The Share of Wages in the National Income, 1972, Money and Inflation, 1982, Equilibrium and Macroeconomics, 1984, Money, Growth and Stability, 1985; co-author (with Robert Solow): A Critical Essay on Modern Macroeconomic Theory, 1995; editor: The Economics of Missing Markets, Information, and Games, 1989; co-editor (with Ben Friedman): Handbook of Monetary Economics, 1990; co-editor: (with Fabio Petri) General Equilibrium: Problems and Prospects, 2003; mng. editor Rev. Econ. Studies, 1965—68, assoc. editor Jour. Econ. Theory, 1971—76. Recipient Palacky gold medal Czechoslovak Acad. Scis., 1991. Fellow Brit. Acad., Econometric Soc. (pres. 1968-69), NAS (fgn. assoc. 1988), Am. Acad. Arts and Scis. (hon.), Am. Econ. Assn. (hon.), Royal Econ. Soc. (pres. 1986-89), Brit. Assn. Advancement Sci. (pres. sect. F 1990), Italian Assn. History Polit. Economy (hon.).

HAHN, FREDERIC LOUIS, lawyer; b. Chgo., Apr. 28, 1941; s. Max and Margery Ruth (Goodman) H.; m. Susan Firestone, Mar. 26, 1967; 1 child, Frederic Firestone. AB with highest distinction, Cornell U., 1962, MBA with highest distinction, 1963; JD magna cum laude, Harvard U., 1966. Bar: Ill. 1966; CPA, Ill. Assoc. Hopkins & Sutter, Chgo., 1966-72, ptnr., 1973-94, Mayer, Brown & Platt (now Mayer, Brown, Rowe & Maw), Chgo., 1994—. Bd. dirs. Lyric Opera of Chgo., 1988—. Recipient Gold medal (CPA exam) State of Ill., 1963. Mem. Phi Beta Kappa. Home: 1377 Scott Ave Winnetka IL 60093-1444 Office: Mayer Brown Rowe & Maw 71 South Wacker Dr Chicago IL 60606-4637 E-mail: fhahn@mayerbrownrowe.com.

HAHN, GEORGE LEROY, agricultural engineer, biometeorologist; b. Muncie, Kans., Nov. 12, 1934; s. Vernon Leslie and Marguerite Alberta (Breeden) H.; m. Clovice Elaine Christensen, Dec. 3, 1955; children—Valerie, Cecile, Steven, Melanie. BS, U. Mo., Columbia, 1957, PhD, 1971; MS, U. Calif., Davis, 1961. Agrl. engr., project leader and tech. advisor Agrl. Rsch. Svc., US Dept. Agr., Columbia, Mo., 1957, Davis, Calif., 1958-61, Columbia, 1961-78, Clay Center, Nebr., 1978—. Contbr. articles to profl. jours. and books on impact of climatic and other environ. factors on livestock prodn., efficiency, and well-being, evaluation of methods of reducing impact and techniques for measuring dynamic responses and characterizing stress in meat animals. Recipient award Am. Soc. Agrl. Engrs.-Metal Bldgs. Mfrs. Assn., 1976 Fellow Am. Soc. Agrl. Engrs. (dir. prof. coun. 1991-93); mem. Am. Meteorol. Soc. (award for outstanding achievement in bioclimatology 1976), Internat. Soc. Biometeorology (treas. 1999-06), Am. Soc. Animal Sci. Office: US Meat Animal Rsch Ctr PO Box 166 Clay Center NE 68933-0166 Office Phone: 402-762-4271. Business E-Mail: leroy.hahn@ars.usda.gov.

HAHN, GEORGE THOMAS, materials engineering educator, researcher; b. Vienna, July 28, 1930; came to U.S., 1938; s. Rudolph and Stella (Honig) H.; m. Charlotte Minovitz, June 10, 1956; children: Claudia Abbott, Elizabeth. BSME, NYU, 1952; MS in Metall. Engring., Columbia U., 1956; ScD in Metall. Engring., MIT, 1959. Rsch. engr. Westinghouse Rsch. Labs., Pitts., 1952; cons. Mfg. Labs., Cambridge, Mass., 1956-60; rsch. assoc. metal sci. sect. Battelle Meml. Inst., Columbus, Ohio, 1960-66, mgr. metal sci. sect., 1966-79; prof. materials sci. and engring. Vanderbilt U., Nashville, 1979-98, prof. materials sci. and engring. emeritus, 1998—, chmn. dept. materials sci. and engring., 1988-93; co-dir. Ctr. Materials Tribology, Nashville, 1987-96; pres. Mechanics & Materials Techs. Inc., Nashville, 1988—. Co-editor: Fracture, 1959, Fast Fracture and Crack Arrest, 1977, Crack Arrest Methods, 1980; co-author: Structural Shear Joints, 2005; contbr. numerous articles to profl. jours. Capt. USAF, 1953-57. Fellow Am. Soc. Metals (Campbell Meml. Lectr. 1981), Metall. Soc., Am. Soc. Lubrication Engrs. Avocation: painting. Office: Vanderbilt U Dept Mech Engring Box 1592 Sta B Nashville TN 37235 E-mail: hahngt@vuse.vanderbilt.edu.

HAHN, JOHN WILLIAM, retired insurance company executive; b. NYC, July 12, 1940; s. Ferdinand J. and Evelyn H. H. (Hauser) Hahn; m. L. Dale Mazza, 1963; children: Nancy, John. BA, Queen's Coll., 1962; postgrad., Harvard U., Cambridge, Mass., 1973-74. With Atlantic Mut. Cos., NYC, 1963—2002, v.p., adminstrv. svcs., 1963—2002, sr. v.p., adminstrv. svcs. Roanoke, Va., 1978-85, exec. v.p., adminstrn. Madison, NJ, 1985—2002; exec. cons., 2002—. Mem. exec. com., bd. dirs. Ins. Value Added Network Svc., Conn., 1985—92; mem. std. com. Agy. Co. Orgn. R & D; spl. advisor Artbase, NYC, 2003—; bd. dirs. Sun Trust Bank, Luxury Market Coun. Exec. v.p. Mil. Family Support Ctr., Inc., 2005—. With USMC, 1959—66. Mem.: Alliance Productive Tech. (chmn. bd. dirs. 1997—98), Mil. Family Support Ctr., Inc. (exec. v.p.), AGENA Corp. (chmn. bd. dirs. 1993—95), Marines Meml. Assn., Waters Edge Country Club, Piedmont Club, Hidden Valley Country Club (Va.), Roanoke Country Club, Harvard Club (NYC). Home: 85 Loving Cir Penhook VA 24137-5225 Office Phone: 540-576-1984. Personal E-mail: pmd261@aol.com.

HAHN, LORNA, political organization executive, author; b. Phila., June 16; d. Charles William and Belle Herman; m. Walter F. Hahn; 1 child, Randolph P. BA, Temple U.; MA, U. Pa., PhD in Internat. Rels., 1962. Instr. Temple U., Phila.; researcher Spl. Ops. & Rsch. Office, Washington; rsch. coord. Hist. Evaluation & Rsch. Orgn., Washington; dir. Masters program Am. U., Washington; exec. dir. Assn. Third World Affairs, Washington, 1968—. V.p. Internat. Fedn. for Protection of Religious, Linguistic & Ethnic Minorities, Washington, 1987—; pub. Third World Forum, 1976—; advisor Save Cambodia, Inc.,Washington, 1980—; lectr. Cath. U., Washington, 1965-66, Howard U., Washington, 1971-73, 82-83. Author: North Africa: Nationalism to Nationhood, 1960, Undergrounds in Insurgency, Revolutionary and Resistance Warfare, 1964, Morocco: Old Land, New Nation, 1966, An Historical Dictionary of Libya, 1981; author numerous monographs, articles and reviews; frequent guest on talk shows. Advisor Dem. candidates. Recipient Scholarship medal Phi Gamma Mu. Mem. Dems. 2000. Mem. Unitarian Ch. First woman to lecture at U.S. Nat. War Coll. and other mil. staff colls. Office: Assn Third World Affairs 1629 K St NW Washington DC 20006-1602

HAHN, MARC B., physician, dean; b. Providence, 1958; m. Robin Hahn; 2 children. BS in Biology, Syracuse U.; DO, Des Moines U., 1984. Intern Walter Reed Army Med. Ctr., Washington, 1984-85, resident in anesthesiology, 1985-87; fellow in pain mgmt. Nat. Inst. Health, Bethesda, Md., 1987-88; prof. dept. anesthesiology & dir. pain medicine fellowship program Pa. State U. Coll. Medicine, Hershey, 1995—2001, chief pain medicine and palliative care divsn., Milton S. Hershey Med. Ctr.; Robert Wood Johnson Health Policy fellow Inst. Medicine Nat. Acad. Sciences, Washington, 1998—99; dean Texas Coll. of Osteopathic Med. U. North Tex. Health Sci. Ctr., 2001—, prof. surgery and pathology/anatomy. Lectr. in fields of anesthesiology, pain medicine, med. edn. and health policy; oral examiner and question writer Am. Bd. Anesthesiology, 1993—. Reviewer Anesthesia and Analgesia Jour., Jour. of Gastroenterology, Am. Jour. Physical Medicine and Rehabilitaion; author: (textbook) Regional Anesthesia: An Atlas of Anatomy and Technique. Served to maj. US Army. Mem.: Pa. Soc. Anesthesiologists (bd. dirs.), Internat. Assn. Study of Pain, Am. Acad. Pain Medicine (pres. 2002—03, bd. dirs., chmn. membership com., chmn. clin. practice com.), Am. Soc. Anesthesiologists (perioperative pain guidelines com., govt. affairs com., economics com.), Am. Pain Soc., Am. Osteo. Assn., AMA. Office: Tex Coll of Osteopathic Med 3500 Camp Bowie Blvd Fort Worth TX 76107-2699

HAHN, MARY DOWNING, writer; b. Washington, Dec. 9, 1937; d. Kenneth Ernest and Anna Elisabeth (Sherwood) Downing; m. William Edward Hahn, Oct. 7, 1961 (div. 1977); children: Katherine Sherwood, Margaret Elizabeth; m. Norman Pearce Jacob, Apr. 24, 1982. BA in Fine Arts and English, U. Md., 1960, MA in English, 1969. Asst. libr. children's sect. Prince George's County (Md.) Meml. Libr. System, 1975-91; instr. English U. Md., College Park, 1970-74; free-lance illustrator PBS/WETA, Arlington, Va., 1973-75. Author: The Sara Summer, 1979, The Time of the Witch, 1982, Daphne's Book, 1983 (William Allen White Children's Choice award 1985-86), The Jellyfish Season, 1985, Wait Till Helen Comes: A Ghost Story, 1980 (11 Children's Choice awards); Tallahassee Higgins, 1987, Following the Mystery Man, 1988, December Stillness, 1988 (Book award Child Study Assn. 1989, Calif. Young Readers' medal 1990-91), The Doll in the Garden, 1989 (Md. Children's Book award 1990-91, 7 Children's Choice awards), The Dead Man in Indian Creek, 1990 (4 Children's Choice awards), The Spanish Kidnapping Disaster, 1991, Stepping on the Cracks, 1991 (Scott O'Dell Hist. Fiction award 1992, ALA notable 1991, Joan G. Sugarman award, Hedda Seisler Mason award, Children's Choice awards), The Wind Blows Backward, 1993 (ALA Best Books for Young Adults), Time for Andrew, 1994 (7 Children's Choice awards), Look for Me by Moonlight, 1995 (Yalsa Quick Picks for Reluctant Readers), The Gentleman Outlaw and Me-Eli, 1996, Following My Own Footsteps, 1996, As Ever, Gordy, 1998, Anna All Year Round, 1999, Promises to the Dead, 2000, Anna on the Farm, 2001, Hear the Wind Blow, 2003, The Old Willis Place, 2004, Janey and the Famous Author, 2005 Recipient Scott O'Dell award for hist. fiction, 1992, author's award Md. Libr. Assn., 1997. Mem. Soc. Children's Book Writers, Washington Children's Book Guild. Personal E-mail: mdh12937@aol.com.

HAHN, ROBERT ALAN, philosophy educator; b. NYC, Aug. 25, 1952; s. Stanley Lawrence and Shirley Laura (Wishner) Hahn; m. Amy Lynn Knoblock; children: Zoë Shirley, Chava Sara. BA summa cum laude, Union Coll., 1973; MA in Philosophy, Yale U., 1975, MPhil, 1975, PhD, 1976. Postdoctoral rsch. fellow U. Calif., Berkeley, 1976; lectr. philosophy Yale U., New Haven, 1977; asst. prof. philosophy U. Tex., Arlington, 1977—78; asst. prof. philosophy and history of ideas Brandeis U., Waltham, Mass., 1978—81; asst. prof. Harvard U., Cambridge, Mass., 1979—81; from asst. prof. philosophy to assoc. prof. philosophy So. Ill. U., Carbondale, 1982—, prof. philosophy, 2002—. Vis. prof. Am. Coll. Greece, 1980. Author: Kant's 'Newtonian Revolution' in Philosophy, 1988, Self-Identity and Moral Decisions, 1989, 2nd edit., 1991, Formal Deductive Logic, 1993, 7th edit., 2003, Conduct and Contraints: Testing the Limits of the 'Harm Principle', 1994, 6th edit., 2001, Anaximander and the Architects: The Contribution of Egyptian and Greek Architectural Technologies to the Origins of Greek Philosophy, 2001, Anaximander in Context: New Studies on the Origins of Greek Philosophy, 2003; contbr. articles to profl. jours. including Phronesis, Jour. History of Philosophy, Apeiron, Southwest Jour. Philosophy, Philos. Rsch. Archives, Jour. Chinese Philosophy. Fellow, Yale U., 1974—76; Regents scholar, N.Y. State, Archibald scholar, 1972—73. Mem.: Am. Philol. Assn., Ill. Philos. Soc., N. Am. Kant Soc., Soc. Ancient Greek Philosophy, Archeol. Inst. Am., Am. Philos. Assn., Nat. Classics Honor Soc. (hon.), Phi Beta Kappa. Avocation: semi-profl. tennis player. Office: So Ill U Dept Philosophy Carbondale IL 62901-4505 Business E-Mail: rhahn@jinx.umsl.edu.

HAHN, ROBERT J., lawyer; BA, St. John's U., 1979, JD, 1984. Bar: NY 1985, NC 1995. Ptnr. Hunton & Williams LLP, Charlotte, NC, 2006—. Mem.: ABA. Office: Hunton & Williams LLP Bank of America Plaza Ste 3500 - 101 S Tryon St Charlotte NC 28280 Office Phone: 704-378-4764. Business E-Mail: rhahn@hunton.com.

HAHN, STEVEN, history professor, writer; b. NYC, July 18, 1951; BA, U. Rochester, 1973; MA in History, Yale U., 1975, MPhil. in History, 1976, PhD in History, 1979. Lecturer Yale College, 1976, 1979; assist. prof. history U. Del., 1979—81, U. Calif., San Diego, 1981—83, assoc. prof. history, 1983—87, prof. history, 1987—98, Northwestern U., 1998—2003; Roy F. and Jeannette P. Nichols prof. history U. Pa., 2003—. Author: The Roots of Southern Populism: Yeoman Farmers and the Transformation of the Georgia Upcountry, 1850-1890, 1983 (Frederick Jackson Turner award best first book in American History, 1984, Allan Nevins prize outstanding doctoral diss. in Am. History, 1980), Nation Under Our Feet: Black Political Struggles in the Rural South From Slavery to the Great Migration, 2003 (Pulitzer Prize for History, 2004, Bancroft prize in Am. History, 2004, Merle Curti award best book in Social History, 2004, Lincoln prize finalist, 2004, Mark Lynton History prize finalist, 2004); co-editor: The Countryside in the Age of Capitalist Transformation: Essays in the Social History of Rural America, 1985, Freedom: A Documentary History of Emancipation, Land and Labor in 1865, 2004; contbr. scholarly articles to Am. Hist. Review, Past and Present, Journ. So. Hist. Recipient E. Harold Hugo Meml. Book prize, 1973, ABC Clio Am.: History and Life award, Org. Am. Hist., 1991; fellow, Guggenheim Found., 1989, Am. Coun. Learned Societies and Ctr. Advanced Studies Behavioral Sci., Stanford, 1987, Soc. Am. Historians, 1993. Office: U Pa 218 College Hall Philadelphia PA 19104-6379

HAHNEMANN, MARCUS, professional soccer player; b. Seattle, Wash., June 15, 1972; m. Amanda Hahnemann; 2 children. Attended, Seattle Pacific Univ. Goalkeeper Seattle Sounders, 1994—96, Colorado Rapids, 1997—99, Fulham FC, England, 1999—2001, Rochdale FC, England, 2001—02, Reading FC, England, 2002—. 6 caps U.S. Nat. Soccer team, 1994—; mem. U.S. World Cup team, 2006. Named Div. II All-American, 1991—93. Mailing: US Soccer Fedn 1801 S Prairie Ave Chicago IL 60616

HAHTO, SAMI K., physicist; b. Vaasa, Finland, Jan. 19, 1975; s. Kalle J. and Maria-Liisa Hahto; m. Sari T. Luodes; children: Sofia children: Juho. PhD, U. Jyvaskyla, Finland, 2003. Ion source technician U. of Jyvaskyla (Finland), 1998—2000; vis. rschr. Lawrence Berkeley Nat. Lab., 2001—03; post doc rschr. Lawrence Berkeley Lab, 2003—05; sr. physicist SemEquip, Inc., N. Billerica, Mass., 2006—. Ion source tech. cons. AIMA Inc., Nice, France (incl. Monaco), 2004—06. Recipient Tech. Transfer award, Lawrence Berkeley Nat. Lab., 2005; fellow Full Scholarship for sci. rsch., Finnish Acad. of Sci. and Letters, 2001—04; grantee Full grant for Post Doctoral rsch. abroad, Acad. of Finland, 2005. Achievements include research in Fast pulsing methods for ion source and neutron generator applications; short pulse neutron generator for cargo screening applications; development of cluster ion sources and extraction systems for ion beam implantation. Home: 17 Autumn Glen Nashua NH 03062 Home Phone: 510-717-6958. Personal E-mail: shahto@semequip.com, hahtos@comcast.net.

HAIDER, STEVEN JOHN, economics professor; BA, Washington U., St. Louis, 1993—93; PhD, U. Mich., Ann Arbor, 1998. Economist RAND Corp., Santa Monica, Calif., 1998—2002; prof. Mich. State U., East Lansing, 2002—. Office: Michigan State U 110 Marshal-Adams Hall East Lansing MI 48824 Office Phone: 517-355-1860.

HAIDOSTIAN, ALICE BERBERIAN, concert pianist, volunteer, not-for-profit fundraiser; b. Highland Park, Mich., Sept. 21, 1925; d. Harry M. and Siroun Vartabedian Berberian; m. Berj H. Haidostian, Oct. 1, 1949; children: Cynthia Esther Haidostian Wilbanks, Christine Rebecca Haidostian Garry, Dicran Berj. MusB, U. Mich., 1946, MusM, 1949. Pvt. piano tchr., 1946-48; tchr. music Detroit Pub. Sch., 1953; dir. vocal trio The Haidostians, 1959—71; dir. youth choral group Cultural Soc. Armenians from Istanbul, 1965—72. Chmn. adv. coun. Armenian Studies Program, U. Mich., 1984-99. Initiator (Operas) Anoush, Mich. Opera Theatre, 1981—82, 2001—02, Transparent Anatomical Manikin exhibit, Detroit Sci. Ctr., 1976. Initiated Centennial Celebration U. Mich. Sch. Music, Detroit, 1980; mem. Armenian Gen. Benevolent Union Alex Manoogian Sch., 1981—91, Detroit chpt. core group com., 1992—; chmn. Marie Manoogian group Armenian Gen. Benevolent Union Alex Manoogian Sch, 1993—; active Detroit Women's Symphony Orch, Mich. Opera; bd. trustees Mich. Opera Theatre, 1982—; active Oakway Symphony Orch.; mem. Save Orch. Hall women's divsn.Project HOPE, 1964—, pres., 1995—96, Detroit Armenian Women's Club, 1957—; active women's chpt. Armenian Gen. Benevolent Union, Detroit, 1944—93; bd. dirs. Childhelp USA Greater Detroit Aux., 1998—; active Detroit Sci. Ctr., 1976—, bd. trustees, 1999—; organist, choir dir. Armenian Congl. Ch., Detroit, 1946—48; mem. Chancel Choir Westminster Ch. Detroit, 1965—80; bd. dirs. Detroit Symphony Orch., 1986—88. Recipient Spirit of Detroit award, 1980, Heart of Gold award United Found. City Detroit, 1981, Nat. Svc. citation U. Mich. Alumnae Coun., 1980, Disting. Alumni Svc. award U. Mich., 1981, Leadership plaque Detroit Symphony Orch., 1988, Magic Flute award Internat. Found. Mozarteum, Salzburg, Austria, 1989, Lifetime Achievement award Outstanding Woman Mich. Project HOPE, 1998, Cmty. Svc. award Wayne County Med. Soc. Alliance, 2000; named Armenian Mother of Yr., Internat. Inst. Detroit, 1981. Mem. AAUW, Detroit Assn. Univ. Mich. Women (pres. 1969-71), Mich. Fedn. Music Clubs, Mich. State Med. Soc. Alliance, Wayne County Med. Soc. Aux. (pres. 1975-76), Pro Mozart Soc. Greater Detroit (pres. 1982-02, pres. emeritus 2002-, Cert. Appreciation 2002), Pro Musica Detroit (sec. 1969-90, 1st v.p. 1990—), Tuesday Musicale Detroit (pres. 1970-72), Univ. Mich. Alumni Assn. (chmn. alumnae coun. 1977-79), Univ. Mich. Sch. Music Alumni Soc., Women's Assn. Detroit Symphony Orch. (pres. 1986-88, vol. coun. Detroit Symphony Orch.), U. Mich. Alumni Assn. (bd. dirs.), U. Mich. Emeritus Club (pres. 1997-98). Avocation: piano. Home: 6838 Valley Spring Dr Bloomfield Hills MI 48301-2845

HAIG, ALEXANDER MEIGS, JR., former secretary of state, retired military officer; b. Phila., Dec. 2, 1924; s. Alexander Meigs and Regina Anne (Murphy) H.; m. Patricia Antoinette Fox, May 24, 1950; children: Alexander P., Brian F., Barbara E. Student, U. Notre Dame, 1943; BS, U.S. Mil. Acad., 1947; MA, Georgetown U., 1961; grad., Naval War Coll., 1960, Army War Coll., 1966; grad. hon. law degree, Niagara U.; LL.D. (hon.), U. Utah. Commd. 2d lt. U.S. Army, 1947, advanced through grades to gen., 1973, staff officer Office Chief of Staff for Ops., 1962-64, mil. asst. to sec. of army, 1964, dep. spl. asst. to sec. and dep. sec. of def., 1964-65, bn. and brigade comdr. 1st Inf. Div. Vietnam, 1966-67; regtl. comdr., dep. comdt. U.S. Mil. Acad., 1967-69; mil. asst. to asst. to Pres. for Nat. Security Affairs, Washington, 1969-70; dep. asst. to pres. NSC, Washington, 1970-73; vice chief of staff U.S. Army, Washington, 1973; chief of staff White House, 1973-74; comdr.-in-chief U.S. European Command, 1974-79; supreme allied comdr. Europe SHAPE, 1974-79; ret., 1979; pres., chief oper. officer, dir. United Techs. Corp., Hartford, Conn., 1979-81; sec. state Washington, 1981-82. Chmn., pres. Worldwide Assocs., Inc., 1984, pres., 1984—; bd. dirs. Compuserv Interactive Svcs., Inc., Inc., Interneuron Pharms., Inc., MGM Mirage, Inc., Metro-Goldwyn-Mayer Inc., 506

Internat., Inc. Author: Caveat: Realism, Reagan and Foreign Policy, 1984, Inner Circles: How America Changed the World, A Memoir, 1992; TV host (weekly program) World Bus. Rev. Decorated D.S.C., Silver Star with oak leaf cluster, Legion of Merit with 2 oak leaf clusters, D.F.C. with 2 oak leaf clusters, Bronze Star with oak leaf cluster, Air medal with 23 oak leaf clusters, Army Commendation medal, Purple Heart U.S.; Nat. Order 5th Class; Gallantry Cross with palm; Civil Actions Honor medal 1st Class; grand officer Nat. Order of Vietnam, Republic of Vietnam; medal of King Abdel-Aziz Saudi Arabia; grand cross Order of Merit Fed. Republic Germany; recipient Disting. Svc. medal Dept. of Def.; Disting. Svc. medal U.S. Army; Man of Yr. award Air Force Assn.; James Forrestal Meml. award, Disting. Grad. award Assn. Grads. West Point. Mem. Soc. of 1st Divsn. Office: Worldwide Assocs Inc 4301 Fairfax Dr Ste 300 Arlington VA 22203-1633 E-mail: ahaig@aol.com.

HAIG, FRANK RAWLE, physics professor, priest; b. Phila., Sept. 11, 1928; s. Alexander M. and Regina A. (Murphy) H. AB, Woodstock Coll., Md., 1952, S.T.L., 1960; Ph.L., Bellarmine Coll., Plattsburgh, NY, 1953; PhD, Catholic U., 1959; LHD honoris causa, SUNY, 1987. Ordained priest Roman Cath. Ch. 1960. Joined S.J., 1946; postdoctoral fellow U. Rochester, NY, 1962-63; asst. prof. Wheeling Coll., W.Va., 1963-66, pres. W.Va., 1966-72; asst. and assoc. prof. Loyola Coll., Balt., 1972-81; pres. Le Moyne Coll., Syracuse, NY, 1981-87; prof. physics Loyola Coll., Balt., 1987-2000, emeritus prof., 2000—. V.p. Md. Sci. Ctr. Adv. Bd., 2006, bd. chmn., 2007—, bd. trustees, 2007—. Editor Jour. Md. Assn. Higher Edn., 1979-81; contbr. articles on nuclear physics, bibl. theology and internat. politics to profl. publs. Pres., Wheeling C. of C., 1969-71; pres. Syracuse Opera Co., 1983-85, chmn. bd., 1985-87; gen. campaign chmn. United Way Onondaga County, Syracuse, 1985-86; trustee Md. Sci. Ctr., 2007—; pres. bd. advisors Md. Sci. Ctr., 2007—. Recipient Mayor's Achievement award Mayor of Syracuse, 1983; Harry J. Carman award Middle States Council for Social Studies, 1985; NSF fellow, 1962-63 Mem.: KC, AAUP (v.p. Md. Conf. 1990—92, 1995, pres. 1995—98, 2005—), Charles Carroll House of Annapolis (chmn. bd. 2001—04), Washington Acad. Scis. (pres. 1993—94, treas. 1999—2005, bd. mem.-at-large 2005—), Am. Phys. Soc., Am. Assn. Physics Tchrs. (pres. Chesapeake sect. 1976—77, 1990—92), Alpha Sigma Mu (bd. dirs. 2006—). Republican. Roman Catholic. Office: Loyola Coll Dept Physics 4501 N Charles St Baltimore MD 21210-2699 Office Phone: 410-617-2574.

HAIG, ROBERT LEIGHTON, lawyer; b. Plainfield, NJ, July 30, 1947; s. Richard Randall and Edith (Remington) Haig. AB, Yale U., 1967; JD, Harvard U., 1970. Bar: N.Y. 1971, U.S. Dist. Ct. (so. and ea. dists.) N.Y., U.S. Ct. Appeals (2d cir.). Assoc. Kelley Drye & Warren, NYC, 1970-79, ptnr., 1980—. Mem. bd. advisors Law Dept. Mgmt. Advisor, 1995—. Co-author: Preparing for and Trying the Civil Lawsuit, 1987, 1991, 1994, 1997, 2000, Federal Civil Practice, 1989, 1993, 1997, 2000, Federal Litigation Guide, 1992, 1993, 1994, Corporate Counsel's Guide, 1996, 1997, Products Liability in New York, 1997, 2002; mem. bd. editors Fed. Litigation Guide Reporter, 1989—, In-House Law Practice Management, 1997—, editor-in-chief Comml. Litigation in N.Y. State Cts., 1995, Bus. and Comml. Litigation in Fed. Cts., 1998, Successful Partnering Between Inside and Outside Counsel, 2000; contbr. chpts. in books, articles to profl. jours. Co-chair Comml. Cts. Task Force, 1995—; mem. legis. com. Com. for Modern Cts., NYC, 1986—, bd. dirs., exec. com., 2001—; mem. Am. Law Inst., 1998—; mem. exec. coun. N.Y. State Conf. Bar Leaders, 1988—90, dept. disciplinary com. appellate divsn., 2003—, hearing panel chair, 1999—2001, policy com. mem., 2003—; mem. N.Y. State Jud. Salary Comm., 1997—, policy com., 2003—, Nat. Ctr. State Ct. Lawyers Com., 2002—. Recipient Excellence in CLE award, Assn. CLE Adminstrn., 1991. Fellow: N.Y. Bar Found. (life; v.p. 2002—03, pres. 2003—, bd. dirs.), Am. Bar Found. (life); mem.: ABA (del. 1991—, standing com. on jud. selection, tenure and compensation 1995—96, bus. cts. com. 1996—, chair subcom. on rels between inside and outside counsel 1997—, spl. advisor standing com. fed. judiciary 2002), N.Y. State Bar Assn. (lectr. 1985—, chmn. com. on fed. cts. 1986—88, chmn. comml. and fed. litig. sect. 1988—90, del. 1988—, exec. com. 1991—94, steering com. on commerce and industry 1997—, chair com. on multi-disciplinary practice and legal profession 1998—99, 1st Ann. award for Disting. Pub. Svc. Comml. and Fed. Litig. Sect. 1995), N.Y. County Lawyers Assn. (chmn. com. on supreme ct. 1984—86, lectr. 1984—, v.p. 1986—92, exec. com. 1986—95, chmn. fin. com. 1988—90, pres. 1992—94, pres. Found. 1992—94, dir.), Assn. of Bar of City of N.Y. (jud. com. 1985—88, chmn. 1989—92, coun. on jud. adminstrn. 1989—92, chmn. 1996—99). Office: Kelley Drye & Warren LLP 101 Park Ave Fl 30 New York NY 10178-0062 E-mail: rhaig@kelleydrye.com.

HAIG, SUSAN, conductor; BA in Music Theory and Composition, Princeton U.; DMA in Orchestral Conducting, MM in Orchestral Conducting, MM in Piano, State U. N.Y., Stony Brook; PhD in Humanities (hon.), U. Windsor, 1998. Coaching/conducting fellow Juilliard Am. Opera Centre, 1981—83; assistant conductor Minnesota Opera, 1983—84, New York City Opera, 1984—86, Santa Fe Opera, 1986; resident coach and conducting assistant Canadian Opera Co., 1986—88; resident staff conductor Calgary Philharmonic Orch., 1988—91; artistic dir. and principal conductor Windsor Symphony Orch., 1991—2001; music dir. S.D. Symphony Orch., 2001—02; assoc. conductor Fla. Orch., Tampa, 2003—. Recipient Heinz Unger Conducting award, 1992, Mayor's award for excellence in the performing arts, 1999. Mailing: c/o Michael Gerard Mgmt Group 192 Catherine St E PO Box 22 Callander ON P0H 1H0 Canada

HAIGH, JENNIFER, writer; b. Barnesboro, Pa., Oct. 1968; B, Dickinson Coll.; MFA in Fiction Writing, Iowa Writers' Workshop. Lectr. creative writing Boston U. Author: Mrs. Kimble, 2003 (PEN/Hemingway award for outstanding first fiction), Baker Towers, 2005, (short stories) Good Housekeeping, Hartford Courant, Alaska Quarterly Rev., Va. Quarterly Rev., others. Fulbright Scholar, James A. Michener Fellowship, 2002. Mailing: c/o Wm Morrow Publishers HarperCollins Inc 10 E 53rd St New York NY 10022

HAIGHT, CHARLES SHERMAN, JR., federal judge; b. NYC, Sept. 23, 1930; s. Charles Sherman and Margaret (Edwards) H.; m. Mary Jane Peightal, June 30, 1953; children: Nina E., Susan P. BA, Yale U., 1952, LL.B., 1955. Bar: N.Y. State 1955. Trial atty., admiralty and shipping dept. Dept. Justice, Washington, 1955-57; assoc. firm Haight, Gardner, Poor & Havens, NYC, 1957-68, ptnr., 1968-76; judge U.S. Dist. Ct. (So. Dist. NY), 1976—95, sr. judge, 1995—. Bd. dirs. Kennedy Child Study Ctr.; adv. trustee Am.-Scandinavian Found., chmn., 1970-76; bd. mgrs. Havens Fund. Mem. Maritime Law Assn., U.S., N.Y. State Bar Assn., Bar Assn. City N.Y., Fed. Bar Council. Episcopalian. Office: US Dist Ct US Courthouse 500 Pearl St New York NY 10007-1316

HAIGHT, DAVID HULEN, ophthalmologist; b. Highland Park, Ill., Mar. 30, 1954; s. Thomas Hulen and Virginia Ellen (Olsson) H. AB in Biochemistry magna cum laude, Brown U., 1976; MD, Johns Hopkins U., 1980. Diplomate Am. Bd. Ophthalmology. Resident ophthalmology Manhattan Eye, Ear and Throat Hosp., NYC, 1981-84, fellow in cornea dept., 1984-85, resident instr., ophthalmology, 1985-87, residency coord., 1989-91, chief Contact Lens Clinic I, 1986—, chief coord. investigator, 1991—, with laser rsch. study, 1991—. Quality assurance com. Manhattan Eye, Ear and Throat Hosp., N.Y.C., 1987—, chmn. ophthalmology credentials com. 1993—; surgeon dir. Manhattan Eye, Ear and Throat Hosp., 1997—, dir. refractive surgery, 1997—; mem. adv. bd. N.Y. Eye Bank for Sight Restoration, N.Y.C., 1992—; sec. med. adv. bd. N.Y. Eye Bank for Sight Restoration, 1995-97; skills transfer adv. com. Am. Acad. Ophthalmology, San Francisco, 1992-96; lectr. ophthalmology Columbia U., N.Y.C., 1997—; clin. asst. prof. ophthalmology N.Y. Weill-Cornell Med. Coll., N.Y.C., clin. prof. ophthalmology NYU Sch. Medicine. Contbg. author: Corneal Surgery, 1986, 4th edit., 2007, Color Atlas of Ophthalmology, 1999. Fellow Am. Acad. Ophthalmology (honor award 1993); mem. Med. Soc. of State of N.Y., N.Y. State Ophthalmologic Soc., Internat. Soc. Refractive Surgery, Contact Lens Assn. of Ophthalmologists, Am. Soc. Cataract and Refractive Surgery, Phi Beta Kappa, Sigma Xi (assoc.). Avocations: photography, golf, travel, aviation, birding. Office: 155 E 72nd St New York NY 10021-4371 Office Phone: 212-772-9474. E-mail: dhaight@laserlasik.com.

HAIGHT, JAMES THERON, lawyer; b. Racine, Wis., Dec. 10, 1924; s. Walter Lyman and Geraldine (Foley) H.; m. Patricia Aloe, Apr. 26, 1952; children: Alberta, Barbara, Catherine, Dorothy, Elaine. Student, U. Nebr., 1943—44, U. Bordeaux, France, 1947; diplome d'Etudes, U. Paris, 1948; BA, U. Wis., 1950, LLB, 1951. Bar: D.C. 1952, U.S. Supreme Ct. 1955, Calif. 1968. Atty. Covington & Burling, Washington, 1951-56, Goodyear Tire & Rubber Co., Goodyear Internat. Corp., Akron, Ohio, 1956-61; gen. counsel, sec. George J. Meyer Mfg. Co., Milw., 1961-66; sr. v.p., sec., chief corp. counsel Thrifty Corp., LA, 1966-92, spl. counsel, 1992-96. Fellow: Am. Bar Found. (life); mem.: ABA (chmn. internat. law sect. 1974—75), Am. Soc. Corp. Secs., Pasadena Bar Assn., Calif. Bar Assn., Order of Coif. Home and Office: 1390 Ridge Way Pasadena CA 91106-4514

HAIGHT, WARREN GAZZAM, investor; b. Seattle, Sept. 7, 1929; s. Gilbert Pierce and Ruth (Gazzam) H.; m. Suzanne H., Sept. 1, 1951; children— Paula Lea, Ian Pierce; m. Ottina Mehau, June 25, 1985 AB in Econs, Stanford U., 1951. Asst. Treas. Hawaiian Pineapple Co., Honolulu, 1955-64; v.p., treas. Oceanic Properties, Inc., Honolulu, 1964-67, pres., dir., 1967-85, chmn., 1983-85; pres. Hawaii, Castle & Cooke Inc., 1983-85, Warren G. Haight & Assocs., 1985—; chmn. Molokai Ranch, Ltd., 1996—2002, Pacific Is. Resources, LLC, 2000—03. Bd. dirs. Round Hill Enterprises, Inc., Las Positas Land Co., Inc., Baldwin Pacific Properties, Inc., Hawaii Project Mgmt., Inc., Transamerica Realty Advisors, Inc., Queen Emma Corp., Queens Devel. Corp., Dole Corp., Standard Fruit and Steamship Co., Inc., Bumble Bee Seafoods, Inc. Mem. Transit Coalition, Honolulu, Gov.'s Com. on Econ. Futures; pres., bd. dirs. Land Use Rsch. Found. of Hawaii, Pacific Found. for Cancer Rsch., Hawaii Nature Ctr.; mem. policy adv. bd. for elderly affairs State of Hawaii; bd. dirs. Downtown Improvement Assn., Oahu Devel. Conf., Hawaii Island Econ. Devel. Bd., Econ. Devel. Corp. Honolulu, Intellect, Inc., Hawaii Resort Developers Conf., Homeless Solutions, Inc., Mutual Housing of Hawaii, Mediation Ctr. of the Pacific. Mem. Housing Coalition, Calif. Coastal Coun., Outrigger Canoe Club, Plaza Club, Pacific Club, Mid Pacific Country Club. Home: 319 Lala Pl Kailua HI 96734-3224 Office: 220 S King St Ste 1170 Honolulu HI 96813-4542 Personal E-mail: haighthawaii@aol.com.

HAIL, KAREN L., bank executive; b. 1954; 4 adopted children. Founding exec. officer MidSouth Bancorp, 1984—, bd. dirs., 1988—, sr. exec. v.p., COO; CFO, dir. MidSouth Bank (subsidiary of MidSouth Bancorp). Mem. technology com. Independent Community Bankers of Am. Named one of 25 Women to Watch, US Banker, 2005, 2006. Office: Midsouth Bancorp 102 Versailles Blvd Lafayette LA 70501*

HAILE, ALLEN CLEVELAND, academic administrator; b. Forbes Rd., Pa., Aug. 26, 1930; s. Wesley Matthew and Mary Olivia (Hall) H.; m. Barbara Honey, Dec. 30, 1975; children: Mark, Brice, Scott, Marybeth, Jonathan, Courtney. AB, U. Nebr., Omaha, 1959; MS, U. So. Calif., 1966, MPA, PhD, U. So. Calif., 1971. Commd. 2d lt. USAF, 1953, advanced through grades to lt. col., retired, 1973; v.p. urban affairs Pepperdine U., LA, 1969-73; sr. rschr. Dept. Info. Scis. Rand Corp., Santa Monica, Calif., 1972-73; regional rep. Pacific Basin U.S. Sec. Commerce, LA, 1977-81; dept. mgr. human resources devel. Bechtel Civil, Inc., Jubail City, 1981-85, mgr. bus. devel. for bldgs. and infrastructure ops., 1985-87, mgr. mktg., 1987-89, mgr. infrastructure devel. Pacific Rim countries, 1991—; dean Coll. of Bus. Calif. Poly State U., San Luis Obispo, 1993-94, dir. cmty. and govt. rels., 1994—. Adj. prof. Golden Gate Univ., 1992. V.p., bd. dirs. San Luis Obispo ARC, C. of C.; pres. Filipino Am C. of C., 1991; bd. dirs. United Way, San Luis Obispo, Econ. Forecast Project, San Luis Obispo, Larkin St. Youth Ctr., San Francisco Edn. Fund, Ct. Appointed Spl. Advocates for Children, Western Govtl. Rsch. Assn., pres. 1989; pres. San Francisco Social Svcs. Commn. 1989, San Francisco Planning and Urban Rsch. Assn., 1992. Decorated DFC and seven air medals. Mem. Am. Soc. Pub. Adminstrn. (bd. trustees found., chmn. constitution revision com. 1988, 89). Home: 1022 Islay St San Luis Obispo CA 93401-4026 Office: Calif Poly State U Cmty and Govt Rels San Luis Obispo CA 93407

HAILE, H. G., German language and literature educator; b. Brownwood, Tex., July 31, 1931; s. Frank and Nell (Goodson) H.; m. Mary Elizabeth Huff, Sept. 1, 1952; children: Jonathan, Christian, Constance Haile Hunsaker. BA, U. Ark., 1952, MA, 1954; student, U. Cologne, Germany, 1955-56; PhD, U. Ill., 1957. Instr. U. Pa., 1956-57; asst. prof., then asso. prof. U. Houston, 1957-63; mem. faculty U. Ill., Urbana, 1963—, prof. German, 1965—, head dept., 1964-73; asso. mem. U. Ill. (Center for Advanced Study), 1969—. Vis. prof. U. Mich., U. Ga. Author: Das Faustbuch nach der Wolfenbuttler Handschrift, 1963, 95, The History of Doctor Johann Faustus, 1965, 1996, Artist in Chrysalis: A Biographical Study of Goethe in Italy, 1973, Invitation to Goethe's Faust, 1978, Luther: An Experiment in Biography, 1983, We Are All Sonsabitches Now, 2000; contbr. numerous articles to profl. and popular jours. Fulbright fellow, 1955; fellow Am. Coun. Learned Socs., 1961-62. Office: U Ill 707 S Mathews 3072 Foreign Languages Urbana IL 61801 Home Phone: 217-649-1255. Personal E-mail: harryhaile@lettersfromthedustbowl.com. E-mail: harryhaile@aol.com. *A child of the Dust Bowl who became a foreign language teacher, I was skeptical about America. I have learned to accept skepticism as the American trait which protects us from correctness, collectivism and coercion.*

HAILE, L. JOHN, JR., journalist, publishing executive; b. Cleveland, Tenn., Mar. 20, 1945; m. Gwen Marie, 1965; children: Philip Alan, John Christopher. BA, Vanderbilt U., Nashville, 1967; MS in Journalism, Boston U., 1969. Polit. reporter The Nashville Tennessean, 1966-79; dep. mng. editor The Orlando Sentinel, Fla., 1979-81, assoc. editor Fla., 1981-85, editor Fla., 1985—2000; founding ptnr., prin. Inside Out Media Ptnrs., 2000—. Juror Pulitzer Prize Com., 1992—93; former chair New Directions for News; sr. fellow The Media Ctr. at the Am. Press Inst., 2002—; cons. Tribune Co., 2001—, Media Gen., 2003, CCN, Trinidad, 2003, Denver Newspaper Agy., 2005. Bd. dirs. Mt. Evans Hospice. Nat. Endowment Humanities Profl. Journalism fellow, 1975-76 Home Phone: 303-489-2430; Office Phone: 303-679-3262. E-mail: johnhaile@aol.com.

HAILE, LISA A., lawyer; BA in Biology, Rollins Coll., 1982; PhD in Microbiology & Immunology, Georgetown U. Sch. Medicine, 1987; JD, Calif. Western Sch. Law, 1991. Bar: Calif. 1992, cert.: US Patent and Trademark Office. Postdoctoral fellow La Jolla Cancer Rsch. Found., NIH, 1987—89; ptnr. Gray, Cary, Ware, & Freidenrich, 1999—2004; ptnr., co-chmn. Life Sciences practice group DLA Piper, San Diego, 2005—. Adj. prof. patent law Calif. Western Sch. Law; bd. mem. BIOCOM Sci. and Tech. Com., 2004. Bd. mem. Am. Liver Found., Athena. Named one of Top 45 Attorneys Under 45, The Am. Lawyers, 2003. Mem.: ABA, Licensing Exec. Soc., Am. Intellectual Property Law Assn., Calif. Bar Assn., San Diego Bar Assn., San Diego Intellectual Property Law Assn. (pres. 1997—99), Ass. for Women in Sci. Office: DLA Piper 4365 Executive Dr San Diego CA 92121 Office Phone: 858-677-1456. Office Fax: 858-677-1401. Business E-Mail: lisa.haile@dlapiper.com.

HAILEY, GARY D., lawyer; b. Joplin, Mo., May 30, 1952; BA cum laude, Rice U., 1974; JD cum laude, Harvard U., 1977. Bar: Tex. 1978, DC 1996. Staff atty. & program advisor, bureau of consumer protection Federal Trade Commn., 1977—85, atty. advisor to Mary L. Azcuenaga, 1985—91; v.p. & gen. counsel, regulatory affairs Nat. Media Corp., 1992—95; assoc. Venable LLP, Washington, 1996—2000, ptnr., advertising, trade regulation, 2000—. Mem.: ABA, DC Bar Assn. Office: Venable LLP 575 7th St NW Washington DC 20004 Office Phone: 202-344-4997. Office Fax: 202-344-8300. Business E-Mail: gdhailey@venable.com.

HAILPARN, DIANA FINNEGAN, psychotherapist, writer; b. Newark, Jan. 25, 1949; d. Thomas Patrick Finnegan and Aurora Floyd Durden; m. Michael Hailparn, May 10, 1973. BA, William Paterson U., 1971; MA, Fairleigh Dickinson U., 1973; MS, Columbia U., 1975. LCSW, diplomate Clin. Social Work Assn. Psychotherapist Clifton Mental Health Clinic, NJ, 1975—79, Diana Assoc., Mahwah, NJ, 1979—. Cons. in field, 1979—. Author: Fear No More: A Psychotherapist's Guide to Overcoming Anxiety and Panic, 2000; contbr. articles to profl. pubs. Mem.: NASW (licentiate), Columbia U. Sch. Social Work Alumni Assn. Avocations: travel, art, fine dining, design, writing. Home: 19 North Bayard Ln Mahwah NJ 07430 Office: Diana Assoc 19 N Bayard Ln Mahwah NJ 07430-2236 Office Phone: 201-934-6295. Personal E-mail: leaurore@yahoo.com.

HAILS, ROBERT EMMET, retired aerospace engineer, manufacturing executive, retired military officer; b. Miami, Fla., Jan. 20, 1923; s. Daniel Troy and Jean (Burke) H.; m. Ethel Fitzgerald Gayle, Mar. 2, 1957; children: Robert Emmet Jr., Merrily Hails Joiner, Florence T. Hails Patton, Laura Hails Smith. BS in Aero. Engring., Auburn U., 1947; MS in Indsl. Engring., Columbia U., 1950; postgrad., C&CS Air U., 1955; postgrad. AMP, Harvard U. Sch. Bus., 1965. Enlisted USAAF, 1942, commd. 2d lt., 1944, advanced through grades to lt. gen., 1974, combat pilot Pacific Theater, 1944-45; assigned to SAC, 1947-48; inspector gen. Hdqrs. USAF, 1950-53; program devel. officer Marcel Dassault Mystere IV Jet Aircraft, French Air Force Am. embassy, Paris, 1953-55; air staff project officer F-104/F-105 aircraft HQ USAF, 1956-60; comdr. procurement dist. USAF, San Francisco, 1960-62; mil. asst. for weapons systems acquisition Office Sec. AF, 1962-66; system program dir. Joint USAF/USN A-7D Aircraft Engring., Devel., Test & Prodn., AF Systems Commd., 1966-68; dep. chief staff maintenance engring. Air Force Logistics Command, 1968-71; comdr. Def. Pers. Support Ctr. Def. Log. Agy., Phila., 1971-72; comdr. Air Logistics Ctr. USAF, Warner Robins AFB, Ga., 1972-74; vice comdr. Tactical Air Command Langley AFB, Va., 1974-75; dep. chief staff systems and logistics Hdqrs. USAF, Washington, 1975-77; ret. USAF, Washington, 1977; mgmt. cons. Atlanta, 1978-80; sr. v.p. internat. ops. LTV Corp., Dallas, 1980-84; pres. Hails Assoc. Inc., Macon, Ga., 1984—2006; ret., 2006. Mem. sci. bd. Loral Corp., Yonkers, NY, 1992-96. Regional exec. Boy Scouts Am.; mem. Auburn U. Alumni Engring. Coun., 1982—; bd. advisors Wesleyan Coll., 1985-90; mem. Found. Bd., Macon State Coll., 1998-2001. Decorated DSM with 2 oak leaf clusters, legion of Merit with 2 oak leaf clusters, Air medal with 2 oak leaf clusters; Order of Nat. Security (Korea); recipient Engring. Achievement award Auburn U., 1998; inducted into State of Ala. Engring. Hall of Fame, 2001, State of Ga. Aviation Hall of Fame, 2001. Mem. AIAA, Air Force Assn., Daedalians, Auburn U. SPADES, Army-Navy Country Club (Arlington, Va.), Idle Hour Golf and Country Club, Omicron Delta Kappa, Sigma Alpha Epsion. Roman Catholic. Achievements include introduction of first heads-up-display (HUD) in a US military aircraft. Home: 101 Wolf Creek Dr N Macon GA 31210 Office Phone: 478-474-5588. E-mail: bobehails@cox.net.

HAIMAN, FRANKLYN SAUL, writer, communications educator; b. Cleve., June 23, 1921; s. Alfred Wilfred and Stella (Weiss) H.; m. Louise Goble, June 11, 1955; children— Mark David, Eric Saul. BA, Case Western Res. U., Cleve., 1942; MA, Northwestern U., Evanston, Ill., 1946, PhD, 1948. Mem. faculty Northwestern U., Evanston, Ill., 1948—, chmn. dept. communication studies, 1964-75, prof. communication studies, 1970-88, John Evans prof. communication studies, 1988-91, John Evans prof. emeritus, 1991—. Adj. prof. U. San Francisco, 1992—. Author: Group Leadership and Democratic Action, 1951, Freedom of Speech: Issues and Cases, 1965, Freedom of Speech, 1976, Speech and Law in a Free Society, 1981, "Speech Acts" and the First Amendment, 1993, Freedom, Democracy, and Responsibility: The Selected Works of Franklyn S. Haiman, 2000, Religious Expression and the American Constitution, 2003; co-author: The Dynamics of Discussion, 1960, 2d edit., 1980; editor: (book series) To Protect These Rights, 1976-77; contbr. articles to profl. jours. Pres. ACLU of Ill., 1964-75, nat. bd. dirs., 1965-96, nat. corp. sec., 1976-82, nat. v.p., 1987-96, vice chair nat. adv. coun., 1996—. With USAAF, 1942-45. Mem. ACLU, Nat. Comm. Assn., Am. Psychol. Assn., AAUP, Phi Beta Kappa. Home: 5283 Broadway Ter Apt 4-b Oakland CA 94618-1491

HAIMAN, IRWIN SANFORD, lawyer; b. Cleve., Mar. 19, 1916; s. Alfred W. and Stella H. (Weiss) H.; m. Jeanne D. Jaffee, Mar. 8, 1942; children: Karen H. Schenkel, Susan L. Bensoussan. BA, Western Res. U., 1937; LL.B., Cleve. Marshall Law Sch., 1941; JD, Cleve. State U., 1969. Bar: Ohio 1941, U.S. Ct. Appeals (6th cir.) 1961, U.S. Supreme Ct. 1961. Asst. to pres. Tremco Mfg. Co., Cleve., 1936-42; house counsel William Edwards Co., Cleve., 1947-48; pvt. practice Cleve., 1948-68; ptnr. firm Garber, Simon, Haiman, Gutfeld, Friedman & Jacobs, 1968-80; ptnr. McCarthy, Lebit, Crystal & Haiman, 1981—. Lectr. in speech Western Res. U., 1948-70; dir. Washington Fed. Savs. and Loan Assn.; asst. law dir., prosecutor City of Lyndhurst, Ohio, 1965-79, law dir., 1979-84. Trustee Montefiore Home, Cleve., 1974-88 (life trustee 1988—)—, East End Neighborhood House, 1962-68; councilman City of South Euclid, 1948-54, pres., 1952-54; pres. Young People's Congregation, Fairmount Temple, 1951-52; sec., trustee Surburban Temple, 1962-65, trustee, 1983— , pres., 1984-87; chmn. speakers div., bd. dirs. Cleve. chpt. ARC, 1959-62; chmn. speaker and film div. Cleve. United Appeal, 1961-62; chmn. speakers div. Jewish Welfare Fund Cleve., 1973-79. Served as 1st lt. AUS, 1943-47. Mem. Ohio, Cleve. bar assns., Assn. Trial Lawyers Am., Zeta Beta Tau. Clubs: Oakwood Country, Lake Forest Country (pres. 1971-72, 75-79). Home: 20201 N Park Blvd Cleveland OH 44118-5000 Office Phone: 216-696-1422.

HAIMAN, ROBERT JAMES, editor, journalist, educator, media consultant, expert witness, critic; b. Norwich, Conn., May 6, 1936; s. Albert and Letta (Cone) H.; m. Elizabeth Royce Greenlaw, Sept. 26, 1964 (div. Aug. 1996); 1 child, Robert Greenlaw. Student, U. Conn., 1953-55; BS, U. Fla., 1957. Reporter St. Petersburg (Fla.) Times, 1958-60, copy editor, 1962-63, nat. editor, 1964-66, mng. editor, 1966-76, exec. editor, 1976-83; pres., mng. dir. Poynter Inst. Media Studies, 1983-96, pres. emeritus and disting. editor in residence, 1997—. Bd. dir. Times Pub. Co., St. Petersburg; trustee Fla. InterAm. Scholarship Found.; mem. minority mgmt. task force Inst. Journalism Edn. Mem. pres. round table Eckerd Coll.; trustee Poynter Inst. Media Studies, St. Petersburg; mem. Pulitzer Prize jury, 1977, 90, 91, 96, 97; internat. adv. bd. Inst. Advancement Journalism, Johannesburg, South Africa; mem. nat. adv. bd. Inst. for Journalists and Pub. Policy Gordon Pub. Policy Ctr. Brandeis U.; expert witness. Mem. bd. advisors U. Fla. Coll. Journalism and Comms.; elder Presbyn. Ch.; trustee Bayfront City Found.; sr. fellow Freedom Forum, Washington, 1998—; mem. Pres.'s coun. U. Fla., U. South Fla., chmn. campus adv. bd., 1989—91; mem. adv. bd. U. Fla. Internat. Ctr.; mem. journalism adv. bd. Knight Found., Inst. Current World Affairs, Hanover, NH, Tampa Bay Com. Coun. on Fgn. Rels. With USMC, 1961. Named Disting. Alumnus, U. Fla., 1988. Mem. AP Mng. Editors Assn. (pres. 1982), Am. Soc. Newspaper Editors (dir. 1992-98), Internat. Press Inst. (Vienna), World Editors Forum (Paris), Interam. Press

Assn. Miami, St. Petersburg Yacht Club, Dragon Club, Quarterback Club, Golden Triangle Club, Soc. Profl. Journalists. Independent. Home: 5155 Isla Key Blvd S Apt 103 Saint Petersburg FL 33715-1687 Office: 801 3rd St S Saint Petersburg FL 33701-4920

HAIMAN, ZOLTAN, astronomer, educator; b. Budapest, Hungary, May 8, 1971; BS in Physics, MIT, 1993, BSEE, 1993; MA in Astronomy, Harvard U., 1994, PhD in Astronomy, 1998. Tchg. fellow MIT, 1993—95, Harvard U., 1993—95; rsch. fellow Harvard-Smithsonian Ctr. Astrophysics, 1995—98; rsch. assoc. astrophysics theory grp. Fermi Nat. Accelerator Lab., 1998—99; Hubble fellow astrophysics Princeton U., NJ, 1999—2002; asst. prof. astronomy Columbia U., NYC, 2003—. Mem. Sci. Working Grp. for Next Generation Space Telescope, 1996—97; organizer KIAS World Cup Cosmology Workshop, Republic of Korea, 2001; co-investigator DUO, 2003. Contbr. numerous articles to profl. jours. including Astrophysy. Jour., Physics Rev., Astronomy Jour. Named one of Brilliant 10, Popular Sci. mag., 2002; recipient Isaac Newton Studentship, Cambridge U., 1994—95; grantee Merit fellowship, Harvard U., 1997—98. Mem.: Am. Astron. Soc., Hungarian Astron. Assn. Office: Columbia U Astronomy Dept Mailcode 5246 550 W 120th St New York NY 10027 Office Phone: 212-854-6822. Office Fax: 212-854-8121. E-mail: zoltan@astro.columbia.edu.*

HAIMES, BURTON KENNETH, lawyer; b. NYC, May 22, 1943; s. David and Mildred Florence (Hirscher) H.; m. Elaine Susan Knopping, June 17, 1967; children: Matthew Collins, Spencer Wyatt, Meredith Brooke; m. Monique N.A. Rigon, Nov. 21, 1982; children: Charlotte Elizabeth, Trevor Henry. BA cum laude, Yale U., 1965; LLB, U. Pa., 1968; LLM in Taxation, NYU, 1979. Bar: NY 1968, Tex. 1982. Law clk. to judge U.S. Ct. Appeals (3rd cir.), Wilmington, Del., 1968-69; assoc. Coudert Bros., London, 1969-70; ptnr. Gottesman & Ptnrs., London, 1970-72; assoc. Fried Frank Harris Shriver & Jacobson, NYC, 1972-77; ptnr. Stanley Cohen P.C., NYC, 1977-82; mng. ptnr. Boyle, Vogeler & Haimes, NYC, 1982—; ptnr., bus. dept. Thelen Reid & Priest LLP. Adj. prof. law U. Notre Dame- London Branch, 1969—71. Nat. pres. Am. Youth Soccer Orgn., Hawthorne, Calif., 1985—89, chmn. bd.; bd. dir. US Soccer Hall of Fame; chmn. Action Against Hunger-USA; bd. dir. Yale Alumni Fund, New Haven, 1988—. Fellow: ABA; mem.: State Bar Tex., NY State Bar Assn. Democrat. Jewish. Fluent in French. Office: Thelen Reid & Priest LLP 875 Third Ave New York NY 10022-6225 Office Phone: 212-603-2060. Office Fax: 212-603-2001. Business E-Mail: bhaimes@thelenreid.com.

HAIMM, NEIL KEITH, lawyer; b. Bklyn., Sept. 1, 1955; s. Sydney and Martha (Zimmer) H.; m. Laura Bell, June 29, 1980; children: Caroline Ashley, Ethan Harrison. BA, U. Pa., 1977; JD, NYU, 1980, LLM in Taxation, 1985. Bar: N.J. 1980, N.Y. 1981, Pa. 1984. Assoc. Bondy & Schloss, NYC, 1980-83, Cohen, Shapiro, Polisher, Shiekman and Cohen, Phila., 1983-88, ptnr., 1988—95, Drinker Biddle & Reath LLP, Phila., 1995—2004, mng. ptnr., 2004—. Bd. dirs., mem. exec. com. Anti-Defemation League, Phila., 1987-94; bd. dirs. Golden Slipper Uptown Home, 1988-2006. Democrat. Jewish. Avocations: reading, running. Office: Drinker Biddle & Reath LLP One Logan Sq 18th & Cherry Sts Philadelphia PA 19103-6996 Office Fax: 215-988-2757. Business E-Mail: neil.haimm@dbr.com.

HAIMS, BRUCE DAVID, lawyer; b. NYC, Nov. 25, 1940; s. Samuel Harold and Judith (Feller) H.; m. Judith Jackson; children: Carolyn, Daniel, Nolan. BS in Econs., U. Pa., 1962; LLB magna cum laude, Harvard U., 1965; LLM in Taxation, NYU, 1972. Bar: Conn. 1965, NY 1968, US Ct. Appeals (2nd cir.) 1968, US Tax Ct. 1972. Assoc. Debevoise & Plimpton, LLP, NYC, 1967-72, ptnr., 1973—, head Tax Dept., 1994—2004. Bd. dirs. The Jeffrey Co., Axe Houghton Found., Brookfield Craft Ctr. Capt. US Army, 1965—67. Named one of Top 100 Attys., Worth mag., 2006. Mem. NY State Bar Assn., Assn. of Bar of City of NY (mem. com. on taxation, 1983-86, Internat. Fiscal Assn., NYC Tax Club, Beta Gamma Sigma. Office: Debevoise & Plimpton 919 3rd Ave Fl 2 New York NY 10022-3904 Office Phone: 212-909-6441. Office Fax: 212-521-7441. E-mail: bdhaims@debevoise.com.*

HAIN, PAMELA CHASE, historian, writer; b. Washington, Sept. 14, 1936; d. Richard and Judith Wragg Chase; m. Peter M. Hain, Nov. 23, 1963; children: Michael Chase, Christel Elizabeth. AA, Pine Manor Jr. Coll., Wellesley, Mass., 1956; BA, Syracuse U., NY, 1958; MA in Slavic Langs. and Lit. Russian Inst., Columbia U., NYC, 1962. Intelligence analyst CIA, Washington, 1963—68, photographic technician, 1975—78; libr. Town Vienna, Va., 1988—89; real estate agt. Mr. Real Estate, Vienna, 1982—89. Author: (biography) A Confederate Chronicle: The Life of a Civil War Survivor, 2005. Sec. Boardwalk Property Owners Assn., Moneta, Va., 2006—. Mem.: SC. Hist. Soc., Writers' Guild, Va. Writers Assn., Ga. Hist. Soc., Morgans Men Assn., Roanoke Civil War Round Table. Avocations: swimming, guitar, singing. Personal E-mail: pwchasehain@hotmail.com.

HAINER, EUGENE, state librarian; Grad., U. Colo., Boulder; MLS, U. Tex., Austin. Tchr.; music instr.; libr. media specialist Poudre Sch. Dist., Fort Collins, Colo.; sch. libr. cons. Colo. State Libr., Denver, head libr. devel., 2000—05, state libr., 2005—. Office: Colorado State Library State Office Bldg Rm 309 201 E Colfax Ave Denver CO 80203-1799 Office Phone: 303-866-6733. Business E-Mail: hainerg@cde.state.co.us.*

HAINES, CLIFFORD E., lawyer; b. Phila., Sept. 29, 1944; BA, Muskingum Coll., 1966; JD cum laude, Ohio State U., 1971. Bar: Pa. 1971, US Supreme Ct. 1977, US Dist. Ct., Eastern Dist. Pa. 1981. Asst. dist. atty. City of Phila., 1971—80; shareholder Litvin, Blumberg, Matusow & Young, 1980—2004; pres. Haines and Assoc., 2004—. Faculty mem. Acad. Advocacy, 1979—94, dir., 1995—; faculty mem. Nat. Inst. Trial Advocacy, 1979—, Pa. Def. Inst. Trial Advocacy Tng. Program, 1989—, Phila. Dist. Atty. Tng. Program, 1992, 93, Trial Advocacy Tng. Program for City Solicitors, 1993; lectr. in law Temple U. Sch. Law, 1984—; program planner and faculty mem. Bar Assn. Trial Advocacy Tng. Program, 1988—; mem. Fourth Nat. Inst. Patent Trial Advocacy, Washington; chmn. bd. Pennsylvanians for Modern Cts., 2001—. Editor: Tips from the Trenches, Lit. Section, ABA. Bd. dirs. PILCOP, 1998—; mem. Phila. Vol. Lawyers for Arts Leadership Coun., 2002. With US Army, 1966—68. Named to Top 100 Pa. Super Lawyers, Phila. Mag., 2004, 2005; recipient Equal Justice award, Cmty. Legal Svcs., Inc. Phila., 1999, Award for Excellence in Tchg. Trial Advocacy, Roscoe Pound Found., 2000. Fellow: Am. Coll. Trial Lawyers, Pa. Bar Found. (life); mem.: Internat. Acad. Trial Lawyers (fellow 2002), Pa. Futures Commn., Phila. Trial Lawyers Assn. (bd. dirs. 1989—99), Assn. Trial Lawyers Am., Pa. Bar Assn. (co-chair task force legal svcs. to poor part II 1998—99, mem. bd. govs. 2002—05, chair 2006, Pres. award 1999), ABA (del. House Del. 1998—2000), Phila. Bar Assn. (mem. medico/legal com. 1982—, chair profl. responsibility com. 1986—87, chair state civil judicial procedures com. 1987—88, mem. prof. guidance com. 1987—, bd. gov. 1989—91, bd. mem. campaign for qualified judges 1990, chair bd. gov. 1991, chair lawyer info. referral svc. 1991, chair evidence code task force 1992—97, mem. Hamilton Cir. 1992—, co-chair by-laws com. 1993, vice-chancellor 1995, chancellor-elect 1996, chancellor 1997, Advocates award Com. Legal Rights Lesbians and Gay Men 1998), Vol. Phila. V.I.P., Tau Epsilon Rho. Achievements include apptd. by Gov. Edward G. Rendell and approved by State Senate to sit on Pa. Coun. Arts, 2004. Office: Haines & Assoc PC 1700 Market St Ste 2710 Philadelphia PA 19103 Home Phone: 215-978-0830; Office Phone: 215-246-2200. Business E-Mail: chaines@haines-law.com.

HAINES, CORRIE GERALD, history professor; s. Jack and Gladys Haines; m. Roberta Elizabeth Medlock, 1976; children: Cushmeer, Cishma, Caliph. BA in African-Am. Studies, Howard U., Washington, 1975, MA in African History, 1977; PhD in African History, U. London, 1981. Polit. cons. US Race Rels. and South African Affairs, Washington, 1981—84; prof. Howard U., Washington, 1984—85; with St. Antony's coll. Oxford U., England, 1985—86; prof. U. DC, Washington, 1988, Morgan State U., Balt., 1994—97, Prince George's C.C., Largo, Md., 1994—; polit. analyst Fund for America's Future, Washington, 1986—88; human resource devel. specialist US Agy. Internat. Devel. Africa Bur., Washington, 1989—93. Contbr. articles to profl. jours. Vol. AfriCare, Washington, 2006. Mem.: Am. Hist. Assn., Orgn. Am. Historians, C.C. Humanities Assn. Avocations: reading, chess. Home: 13103 Bridge View Ct Upper Marlboro MD 20772 Office: Prince Georges Community College 301 Largo Rd Largo MD 20774-2199 Home Phone: 301-627-7129; Office Phone: 301-322-0535.

HAINES, DANIEL WEBSTER, engineering consultant, engineering educator; b. Nashville, Nov. 8, 1937; s. I. Snowden and Elsie (Davis) Haines; m. Brynne Levinson, Nov. 9, 1962; children: Gordon, Laurel. BS, Rutgers U., 1959; MS, Lehigh U., 1961; ScD in Engring., Columbia U., 1968. Registered profl. engr., N.Y., S.C. Rsch. asst. Lehigh U., 1959—61; vol. Peace Corps, Ibadan, Nigeria, 1961—63; trainee NASA, 1964—66; prof. engring. U. SC, Columbia, 1969—77; product engring. mgr. Ciba-Geigy Corp., Ardsley, NY, 1977—81; prin. Midlantic Testing and Cons., White Plains, NY, 1982—87; prof. Manhattan Coll., Riverdale, NY, 1983—2006, chair mech. engring. dept., 1995—99. Vis. lectr. Yale U., 1975—76; vis. assoc. prof. Stevens Inst., Hoboken, NJ, 1975—76; cons. Institut National de la Recherche Agronomique, Nancy, France, 1999—. Editor (in chief): CAS Jour., 1989—95; mem. editl. adv. bd. CAS Jour., 1999—2003; contbr. articles to profl. jours. Clk., Coun. of Proprs., Western Divsn. of NJ. Fellow, Sloan Found., Princeton U., 1968—69; grantee, NSF, 1969—77. Mem.: ASME, ASCE, Catgut Acoustical Soc. (trustee 1981—99, treas. 1982—90). Home: 142 Greenridge Ave White Plains NY 10605-3109

HAINES, DAVID HARRY, consulting executive; b. Kane, Pa., Nov. 23, 1949; s. Joseph Harry Haines and Loma Ruth Housely; m. Rashelle Harrison, May 26, 1990; children: Steffanie, Amber, Jamie. Attended, Ecole Internat., Geneva, 1964—65; BA in Journalism/Econs., U. Fla., 1972; MA in Internat. Econs., Am. U., 1974; attended, Georgetown U. Law Sch., 1976—80; grad. Exec. Mgmt. Program, Columbia U. Sch. Bus., NY, 1980; grad. Negotiation Inst., Harvard U., 1996. Dir. western region New York Times Co., NYC, Wash. (DC), San Francisco, 1975—80; nat. acct. mgr. Control Data/Source Telecomms. Corp., McLean, Va., 1980-83; dir. internat. mktg. and sales Context Mgmt. Sys., LA, 1983-85; mng. dir. McGraw-Hill DRI, San Francisco, 1985-89, Maxwell/Macmillan, San Francisco, 1989-93; dir. bus. devel. Arthur Andersen LLP/Andersen Consulting, San Francisco, 1993-99; v.p. bus. devel. and strategy Cotelligent Inc., San Francisco, 1999—2004, sr. v.p. 360 powered Bus. Intelligence, 2001—03; sr. v.p. Daticon Inc. & Electronic Evidence Discovery, San Francisco, 2004—06; exec. v.p. strategy devel. The Superior Group, NYC, 2005—. Vice chmn., bd. dirs. APEX Computing, San Francisco, 1984—; dir., bd. dirs. Beverly Hills Releasing/Sunset Studios, LA, 1985—. Author: Warp Speed Marketing, 1998, Controlling the Cost of Electronic Discovery; contbr. articles to profl. jours. Recipient Entrepreneur of Yr. award, Venture Club, San Francisco, 1997; Athletic, Academic scholar, Kiwanis Club Internat., NYC, 1967—71. Fellow Sales and Mktg. Executives; mem. ABA (sec. intellectual property and litig. sect.), Nat. Assn. Computer Cons., Info. Tech. Assn. Am., Pub. Rels. Soc. Am., Am. Soc. Info. Scientists, St. Vincent de Paul Soc. (bd. dirs. 1998—). Avocations: snow and water skiing, scuba diving, mountain biking, music. Office Phone: 415-630-0016. E-mail: hainesdr@comcast.net.

HAINES, HARRY ALLEN, federal judge; b. Mont., 1939; BA, St. Olaf Coll., 1961; JD, U. Mont. Law Sch., 1964; LLM Taxation, NYU Law Sch., 1966. Bar: Mont. 1964, US Dist. Ct. Mont. 1964. Ptnr. Worden, Thane & Haines, 1966—2003; adj. prof. law U. Mont., 1967—91; judge US Tax Ct., Washington, 2003—. Office: US Tax Ct 400 Second St NW Washington DC 20217 Office Phone: 202-521-0699.

HAINES, JOHN MEADE, poet, translator, writer; b. 1924; Homesteader in Alaska, 1947-69; poet-in-residence U. Alaska, Anchorage, 1972-73; vis. prof. English U. Wash., Seattle, 1974; vis. lectr. U. Mont., Missoula, 1974-75; Guggenheim fellowship, 1984-85; disting. vis. lectr. U. Calif., Santa Cruz, 1986; writer-in-residence Montalvo Ctr. for the Arts, 1987-88, Djerassi Found., 1988; vis. prof. Ohio U., Athens, 1989-90. Vis. writer George Washington U., 1991-92; Elliston fellow in poetry U. Cin., 1992; chmn. creative arts Austin Peay State U., Clarksville, Tenn., 1993—; vis. lectr. Ann. Summer Wordsworth Conf., Grasmere, Eng., 1996; writer-in-residence Bellagio Ctr., Italy, 2000; poet-in-residence Bucknell U., 2001; guest poet Internat. Shakespeare Conf, Vladimir U., Russia, 2002; reader Libr. of Congress, 2005. Translator: El Amor Ascendia, 1967; author: Winter News: Poems, 1966, Suite for the Pied Piper, 1967, The Legend of Paper Plates, 1970, The Mirror, 1971, The Stone Harp, 1971, Twenty Poems, 1971, Leaves and Ashes: Poems, 1974, In Five Years Time, 1976; The Sun on Your Shoulder, 1976, Cicada, 1977, In a Dusty Light, 1977, Living Off the Country: Essays on Poetry and Place, 1981, Of Traps and Snares, 1981, Other Days, 1982, News from the Glacier: Selected Poems 1982, Forest Without Leaves, 1984, Stories We Listened To, 1986, The Stars, The Snow, The Fire, 1989, Meditation On a Skull Carved in Crystal, 1989, New Poems, 1980-88, 1990 (Western States Art Fedn. award, Lenore Marshall/Nation award, Poets prize 1990), (poetry) Rain Country , 1990, The Owl in the Mask of the Dreamer, Collected Poems, 1993, A Guide to the Four-Chambered Heart, 1996, At the End of this Summer, 1948-54, 1997, (essay) Fables and Distances, New and Selected Essays, 1996, For the Century's End, Poems 1990-1999, 2001, Of Your Passage, O Summer, Uncollected Poems from the 1960s, 2004, Wartime, A Late Memoir, 2004. Recipient Acad. award in Lit. Am. Acad. of Arts and Letters, 1995; 63d fellow Acad. Am. Poets, 1997; named Alaska Poet Laureate, 1969-73; Gugggenheim fellow, 1965-66, NEA fellow, 1967-68; Amy Lowell traveling scholar, 1976-77; No. Momentum scholar U. Alaska, 2003. Home: 717 Longstaff Missoula MT 59801-3605 Office Phone: 907-474-6612. Business E-Mail: ffjmh@uaf.edu.

HAINES, KATHLEEN ANN, pediatrician, educator; b. NYC, July 28, 1949; d. George Raymond and Gertrude Ann (Driscoll) H.; m. Emil Claus Gotschlich, May 24, 1975; 1 child, Emily Claire. BA, CUNY, 1971; MD, Albert Einstein Coll. Medicine, 1975. Diplomate Am. Bd. Pediatrics, Am. Bd. Allergy and Immunology. Intern, resident NY Hosp./Cornell U., NYC, 1975-77, fellow in allergy/immunology, 1977-80; from instr. in pediatrics to assoc. prof. Sch. Medicine NYU, NYC, 1980—91, assoc. prof. clin. pediatrics and medicine Sch. Medicine, 1991—2005, adj. assoc. prof. Sch. Medicine, 2005—; dir. pediat. rheumatology Hosp. Joint Diseases/NYU Med. Ctr., 1994—2002; dir. clin. immunology lab. Hosp. Joint Diseases, 1995—2002; sect. chief pediat. immunology Hackensack U. Med. Ctr., NJ, 2002—; assoc. prof. pediat. U. Medicine and Dentistry NJ/NJ Med. Sch., 2005—. Mem. rsch. coun. NY Heart Assn., 1988-90; program com. Am. Coll. Rheumatology, 2000-03, vis. prof., 2001. Contbr. articles to profl. jours., chpts. to books in field. Med. and Scientific Com. N.Y.C. chpt. Arthritis Found., 1993-99. Grantee, N.Y. Arthritis Found., 1990, 1996, NIH, 1993—98. Fellow Am. Acad. Allergy and Immunology, Am. Acad. Pediatrics (mem. exec. com. rheumotology sect., 2003—); mem. Am. Fedn. Med. Rsch., Allergy, Asthma and Immunology Soc. of Greater N.Y. (sec. 1995-97, pres.-elect 1997-98, pres. 1998-99), Harvey Soc., Soc. Pediatric Rsch., Clin. Immunology Soc. Office: Hackensack U Med Ctr 30 Prospect Ave Hackensack NJ 07601 Home Phone: 212-722-6380; Office Phone: 201-996-5306. Business E-Mail: khaines@humed.com.

HAINES, KENNETH H., sports television broadcasting and marketing executive; b. Spokane, Sept. 5, 1942; s. Kenneth A. and Helen Elizabeth (Evans) H.; m. Stephanie Marie Phelps, Nov. 23, 1981; 1 child, Avery Jordan. BA, Dakota Wesleyan U., 1964; MA, U. Wyo.; MS, Troy State U., 1970; CAGS, Va. Tech., 1976. News dir. KORN TV, Mitchell, SD, 1962-64; sta. mgr. KUWR Radio, Laramie, Wyo., 1965-67; gen. mgr. KLME Radio, Laramie, 1967-68; instr. flight ops. U.S. Army, Ft. Rucker, Ala., 1968-70; from dir. radio, tv, film to dir. pub. affairs, univ. rels. Va. Tech., Blacksburg, 1970-81; from exec. v.p., COO to pres., CEO, Raycom Sports, Charlotte, NC, 1981—2002, pres., CEO, 2002—. Bd. dirs. Charlotte Sports Commn., ACC Properties; trustee Dakota Wesleyan U.; exec. dir. Continental Tire Bowl, 2002—. Bd. dirs. Sunshine Football Classic, 1989—, Charlotte Basketball Challenge, 1987—; tournament dir. LPGA Golf, 1997—; exec. dir. Continental Tire Bowl. Named Reporter of Yr., UPI, 1967, Opperman Disting. Lectr., Dakota Wesleyan U., 1998, Outstanding TV Sports Exec., All-Am. Football Found., 1999, Outstanding Bowl Dir., Football Found., 2004, Alumnus of Yr., Dakota Wesleyan U., 2005; recipient golden award Coun. Support Higher Edn., 1978. Mem. Am. Assn. Agr. Writers, Am. Coll. Pub. Rels. Assn. (exceptional achievement award 1974), Va. Press Assn., Coun. for Advancement and Support of Edn. (pres. univ. faculty club 1980-82), Nat. Acad. TV Arts and Scis. (judge), Charlotte C. of C. (bd. dirs.), Phi Kappa Delta, Pi Delta Epsilon, Omicron Delta Kappa. Avocations: sports, photography, television, travel, reading. Home: 1909 Carmel Rd Charlotte NC 28226-5021 Office: Raycom Sports 2815 Coliseum Centre Dr Ste 200 Charlotte NC 28217-1378 Office Phone: 704-378-4426. E-mail: khaines@aol.com, ken9542@aol.com.

HAINES, MARTHA MAHAN, lawyer; b. Detroit, Feb. 4, 1952; d. Albert F. and Martha M. (Sager) Mahan; divorced; children: Ella Catherine, Emily Martha. Student, U. Utah, 1970-72; BA magna cum laude, Wayne State U., 1974; JD, U. Mich., 1977. Bar: Ill. 1978, U.S. Dist. Ct. (no. dist.) Ill. 1982. Assoc. Chapman and Cutler, Chgo., 1978-82, jr. ptnr., 1982-86; of counsel Altheimer & Gray, Chgo., 1986-90, ptnr., 1990-97, Barnes & Thornburg, Chgo., 1997-99; chief Office Mcpl. Securities, SEC, Washington, 1999—; asst. dir. divsn. mkt. regulation SEC, 2000—. Office: Office Mpcl Securities SEC 100 F St NE Washington DC 20549-1001 Office Phone: 202-551-5681. Business E-Mail: hainesm@sec.gov.

HAINES, RICHARD FOSTER, retired psychologist; b. Seattle, May 19, 1937; s. Donald Hutchinson and Claudia May (Bennett) H.; m. Carol Taylor, June 17, 1961; children: Cynthia Lynn, Laura Anne. Student, U. Wash., 1955-57; BA, Pacific Luth. Coll., Tacoma, 1960; MA, Mich. State U., 1962, PhD, 1964. Predoctoral rsch. fellow NIH, 1964; Nat. Acad. Sci. postdoctoral resident rsch. assoc. Ames Rsch. Ctr./NASA, Moffett Field, Calif., 1964-67, rsch. scientist, 1967-86, chief of space human factors office, 1987-88, rsch. scientist Rsch. Inst. Advanced Computer Sci., 1988-90; assoc. prof. dept. psychology San Jose State U., 1988-89; computer scientist RECOM Techs., Inc., Moffett Field, Calif., 1993-2000, Raytheon Corp., 2000—01; ret., 2001. Rsch. cons. to NASA Foothill Coll.; cons. Stanford U. Sch. medicine, 1966-67, TRW-Systems Group, 1969-70; mem. adv. com. on vision NRC; founding mem. advanced tech. applications com. Calif. Coun. AIA and NASA, 1975-80; mem. adv. bd. Space Scis. Ctr.-Foothill Coll., 1976-78; bd. advisors Fund for UFO Rsch., Washington; chmn. bd. Novosibirsk Christian Pub.-Calif., 1993—; chief scientist Nat. Aviation Reporting Ctr. on Anomalous Phenomena, 2001—. Author: UFO Phenomena and the Behavioral Scientist, 1979, Observing UFOs, 1980, Melbourne Episode: Case Study of a Missing Pilot, 1987, Advanced Aerial Devices Reported During the Korean War, 1990, Night Flying, 1992, Project Delta, 1994, Close Encounters of the Fifth Kind, 1999, Aviation Safety in America - A Previously Neglected Factor, 2000; mem. editl. and sci. bd. Jour. UFO Studies, Internat. UFO Reporter, Cuadernos de Ufologica; contbr. articles to profl. jours. Mem. Palo Alto (Calif.) Mayor's Com. on Youth Activities, 1967; chmn. adv. coun. Christian Cmty. Progress Corp., Menlo Park, Calif.; v.p., dir. Ctr. Counseling for Drug Abuse, Menlo Park; bd. dirs., chmn. sci. adv. team Threshold Found.; founding co-dir. Joint Am.-Soviet Aerial Anomaly Fedn., 1991—97. Named Alumnus of Yr., Pacific Luth. U., 1972 Fellow Aerospace Med. Assn. (assoc.); mem. Optical Soc. Am., Soc. for Sci. Exploration, Sigma Xi. Achievements include patents for device of advanced detection of glaucoma, optical projector of vision performance data for design engineers, visual simulator optical alignment device, grooming aid for use by astronauts in space.

HAINES, STEPHEN JOHN, neurosurgeon; b. Burlington, Vt., Sept. 4, 1949; s. Gerald Leon and Frances Mary (Whitcomb) H.; m. Jennifer Lea Plombon; children: Christopher, Jeremy. AB, Dartmouth Coll., 1971; MD, U. Vt., 1975. Diplomate Am. Bd. Neurol. Surgery; diplomate Nat. Bd. Med. Examiners. Intern U. Minn., Mpls., 1975—76; resident neurol. surgery U. Pitts., 1976—81; from asst. prof. to prof. U. Minn., Mpls., 1982—93, prof. neurosurgery, otolaryngology and pediatr., 1993—97, head divsn. pediat. neurosurgery, 1985—97, chmn. and head dept. neurosurgery, 2003—; prof. neurosurg., Lyle A. French chair, head dept. neurosurg. U. Minn. Med. Sch., 2003—; prof. neurol. surgery, otolaryngology and pediats., chmn. dept. neurol. surgery Med. U. S.C., 1997—2003. Adv. panel FDA Neurologic Devices, 2002—05, chair, 2005; mem. Com. Postmarket Surveillance Pediat Med. Devices, Inst. Medicine, 2004—05. Contbr. articles to profl. jours. Fellow ACS; mem. AMA, Am. Assn. Neurol. Surgeons (Van Wagenen fellow 1981), Congress Neurol. Surgeons (pres. 1996), Soc. Clin. Trials, Neurosurg. Soc. Am., Am. Acad. Neurol. Surgery, Soc. Neurol. Surgeons. Office: Dept Neurosurgery MMC 96 420 Delaware St SE Minneapolis MN 55455 Office Phone: 612-626-5767. Business E-Mail: shaines@umn.edu, headneurosurg@umn.edu.

HAINES, TERRY L., lawyer, consultant; b. Washington, Pa., Oct. 2, 1957; s. John A. and Ann C. Haines. BA, Oberlin Coll., Ohio, 1979; JD, Vt. Law Sch. Ind. Instn., South Royalton, 1982. Bar: Pa. 1983, U.S. Dist. Ct. (we. dist.) Pa. 1983. Legis. asst. com. on judiciary Pa. Assembly, Harrisburg, 1983; sr. staff atty. FCC, Washington, 1983-87; rep. counsel com. on energy and commerce U.S. Ho. of Reps., Washington, 1987-91; chief of staff FCC, Washington, 1991-93; divsn. gen. counsel TCI East, Inc., Bethesda, Md., 1993-94; COO, gen. counsel Boland & Madigan, Inc., Washington, 1995—2001; chief counsel, staff dir. U.S. Ho. of Reps. Com. on Fin. Svcs., Washington, 2001—03; ptnr. Alexander Strategy Group, Washington, 2003—06; shareholder, dir. govt. rels. Buchanan Ingersoll & Rooney, Washington, 2006—. Avocations: golf, history. Office: Buchanan Ingersoll & Rooney PC 1700 K St NW Ste 300 Washington DC 20006 Office Phone: 202-452-5489. Business E-Mail: terry.haines@bipc.com.

HAINES, TERRY L., plastics company executive; b. Aug. 5, 1946; Gen. mgr. Canada A. Schulman Inc., v.p. No. Am. sales Akron, Ohio, 1989—90, COO, 1990—91, pres., CEO, 1991—2006, chmn., pres., CEO, 2006—. Bd. dir. FirstMerit Corp., Ameron Internat. Corp. Office: A Schulman Inc 3550 W Market St Akron OH 44333*

HAINES, THOMAS DAVID, JR., lawyer; b. Dallas, Oct. 30, 1956; s. Thomas David Sr. and Carol V. (Mullins) H.; m. Nanette Cluck, Mar. 1, 1986; children: Bennett Ann, Maison Cluck. BS in Polit. Sci., Okla. State U., 1979; JD, U. Okla., Norman, 1982. Bar: Okla. 1982, N.Mex. 1983, US Ct. Appeals (10th cir.) 1983, US Dist. Ct. N.Mex. 1983. Assoc. Hinkle, Cox, Eaton, Coffield & Hensley, Roswell, N.Mex., 1982-87, ptnr., 1988—. Contbg. editor N.Mex. Tort and Worker's Compensation Reporter, 1987-90, Employment Law Deskbook for New Mexico Employers, 1997, 99.

Coach Roswell Youth Soccer Assn., 1995—98, 2001; youth sponsor First United Meth. Ch., Roswell, 1986—88, chmn. stewardship com., 1990—91, chmn. adminstrv. coun., 1998—99, trustee, 1996—98. Mem. State Bar Assn. N.Mex. (com. on continuing legal edn., young lawyers divsn. 1989-2002, mem. med.-legal rev. commn. 1988-2004, sec. 2003, treas. 2004, membership benefits com. 2006—), Chaves County Bar Assn.(pres., 2006-07), N.Mex. Def. Lawyer's Assn., N.Mex. Trial Lawyer's Assn., Kiwanis (Roswell club, Outstanding Club Sec. award 1993-95, pres. 1998-99), named one Outstanding Young Men in Am. 1990, George L. Reese Am. Inn of Ct. (barrister), Phi Delta Phi, Phi Kappa Phi. Republican. Avocations: golf, basketball, music, politics. Office: Hinkle Hensley Shanor & Martin LLP 400 N Pennsylvania Ave Ste 700 Roswell NM 88201-4777 Office Phone: 505-622-6510. Business E-Mail: thaines@hinklelawfirm.com.

HAINES, THOMAS HENRY, biochemist, educator, researcher; b. NYC, Aug. 9, 1933; s. Charles and Elizabeth Cubbon Haines; m. Mary Manning Cleveland, Aug. 6, 1986; m. Adrian Sheila Rappaport, Nov. 26, 1960 (dec. May 5, 1985); 1 child, Avril Danica. BS, CUNY, 1957; PhD, Rutgers U., 1965; MS, CUNY, 1999. Rsch. biochemist Boyce Thompson Inst. for Plant Rsch., Yonkers, NY, 1959—62; asst./assoc. prof. chemistry CUNY, NYC, 1964—72, prof. chemistry and biochemistry doctoral program, 1972—2006; acting dean, founder Sophie Davis Biomed. Program CUNY Med. Sch., NYC, 1971—73, dir. biochemistry, 1973—2004; vis. prof. Rockefeller U., NYC, 2007—. Vis. assoc. prof. U. Calif., Berkeley, 1970—71, vis. rsch. scientist, 1993—94; chair symposium on lipids Internat. Union Pure and Applied Biochemistry, Riga, Latvia, 1970; vis. scholar Nat. Ctr. for Sci. Rsch., Gif-sur-Yvette, France (incl. Monaco), 1970—71; vis. prof. U. Minn., Mpls., 1978—79, Beijing Med. Sch., 1986—87; vis. scientist Mitsubishi-Kasai Inst. for the Life Scis., Machida, Tokyo, Japan, 1986—87; mem., exec. com. Levich Inst. for Hydrodynamics, NYC, 1991—2001; ad hoc mem. biochemistry and cell biology study sect. Nat. Inst. Alcoholism and Alcohol Abuse, Washington, 1992—95; cons. Liposome Tech. Inc., Menlo Park, Calif., 1993—95, Sequus, Inc., Menlo Park, 1995—2000; chair rev. com. evaluate brain sci. rsch. Fla. Atlantic U., 2003—05. Co-founder Partnership for Responsible Drug Info., NYC, 1993—2002, Voluntary Com. Lawyers, NYC, 1994—2002. Grantee, NIH, 1972—78, NSF. Mem.: AAAS (life), Assn. Grad. and Med. Schs. Biochemistry Chairs, N.Y. Acad. Scis. (life; chair biophysics sect. 1991—94), City Coll. Sci. Alumni Assn. (pres. 1993—). Achievements include design of model for why animals need cholesterol; research in lipid structure and function; the role of cardiolipin in ATP synthesis; the role of polyunsaturated fatty acid in signaling. Avocations: gardening, politics, travel. Home: 14 West 68 St New York NY 10023 Office: Rockefeller U 1230 York Ave Box 187 New York NY 10021 Home Phone: 212-873-2982. E-mail: thaines@rockefeller.edu.

HAINES, WALTER WELLS, retired economics professor; b. Stamford, Conn., Dec. 1, 1918; s. Thomas Kelly Peterson and Carrie Hooker (Williams) H.; m. Hazel Ellen Maxwell, Jan. 1, 1945 (div.); children: Jennifer Jean, Deborah Lee, Pamela Ann, Christopher Alan, Liseli Ellen, Timothy Maxwell; m. Mary Lou Peck, Nov. 30, 1991. BA, U. Pa., 1940, MA, 1941, Harvard U., 1942, PhD (Lehman nat. fellow), 1943. Instr. econs. Kenyon Coll., 1946-47; mem. faculty NYU, 1947—, prof. econs., 1960-89, emeritus prof. of econs., 1989—, chmn. dept. Univ. Coll., 1956-68, dir. undergrad. studies, 1983-89; adminstr. Friends Hosp., Tiriki, Kenya, 1969-70. Fulbright prof. econs. U. Peshawar, Pakistan, 1962-63; Fulbright prof. environ. conservation Middle East Tech. U., Ankara, Turkey, 1973-74; lectr. Siena Coll., 1989-92 Author: Money, Prices and Policy, 1961; contbr. articles to profl. jours. Lehman Nat. fellow Harvard U., 1941-43. Fellow Internat. Inst. for Social Econs.; mem. AAAS, World Future Soc., Fulbright Alumni Assn., Am. Econ. Assn., Fellowship of Reconciliation, Assn. for Social Econs., Soc. for Advancement of Socio-Econs., Internat. Soc. Ecol. Econs., Amnesty Internat., World Federalists, Parliamentarians for Global Action, Internat. Physicians for the Prevention of Nuc. War, Nat. Wildlife Fedn. Wilderness Soc., Citizens for Global Solutions, Union of Concerned Scientists, Carter Ctr., Albert Einstein Inst., UN Assn. U.S., Habitat for Humanity, Natural Resources Def. Coun., Phi Beta Kappa. Mem. Religious Soc. of Friends. Home: 196 Vosburgh Rd Averill Park NY 12018-5710 Personal E-mail: hainesww@earthlink.net. E-mail: peckm@sage.edu. *The wellspring of my life is a belief that there is something of God in every person. From this universality of the divine spark emerge many principles of faith; the brotherhood of man, the importance of the golden rule, the primacy of love. These in turn call for social action to promote civil rights, nondiscrimination, peace, cooperation, democracy, world equality, the preservation of a quality environment, and conservation of resources for future generations. I have no illusion that this belief has brought me "success", but it has contributed much to the richness of life.*

HAINES, WILLIAM JOSEPH, retired pharmaceutical executive; b. Crawfordsville, Ind., Sept. 26, 1919; s. Burt and Lala R. (Luster) Haines; m. Wilma M. Hester, June 6, 1993; 2 children , Paula Sue Haines Curtis-Burn, Eric J. AB summa cum laude, Wabash Coll., 1940, DSc (hon.), 1970; PhD, U. Ill., 1943; grad. exec. program in bus. adminstrn., Columbia Bus. Sch., 1965. Rsch. biochemist Upjohn Co., Kalamazoo, 1943-50, head dept. endocrinology rsch., 1950-54; tech. dir. Armour Labs., Kankakee, Ill., 1954-58; v.p. dir. rsch. Ortho Pharm. Corp., Raritan, NJ, 1958-65, exec. v.p., 1965-67; vice chmn. Johnson & Johnson Internat., 1967-69; dir., mem. exec. com. Johnson & Johnson, New Brunswick, NJ, 1969-79, v.p. corp. office sci. and tech., 1979-82; pres. Bucks-Tech Assocs., Inc. (cons. in mgmt., sci. and tech.), Doylestown, Pa., 1982—. Chmn. sci. adv. com. Alliance Internat. Health Care Trust, 1983-87; former dir. Quidel Corp., La Jolla, Calif.; invited lectr. Laurentian Hormone Conf., 1952, Gordon Rsch. Conf., 1952. Contbr. numerous sci. articles to profl. jours., including pioneer paper on human requirement for essential amino acids, 1942. One of initial investigators to identify essential amino acids for human nutrition; patentee biosynthesis of adrenal cortex hormones, paper chromatography and automatic partition column chromatography of steroids. Trustee Wabash Coll., 1972-93, trustee emeritus, 1993—; trustee Hood Coll., 1975-87, vice chmn. bd., 1982-87, trustee emeritus, 1989—; Joslin Diabetes Found. Inc., Boston, 1974-79; elder Thompson Meml. Presbyn. Ch., New Hope, Pa. Recipient William E. Upjohn prize and medal, 1952, Alumni Merit award Nat. Assn. Wabash Men, 1973. Fellow AAAS, Am. Inst. Chemists; mem. Am. Chem. Soc. (med. cheistry div.), N.Y. Acad. Scis., Endocrine Soc., Am. Soc. Biol. Chemists, Soc. Chem. Industry (former chmn. Am. sect.), Pharm. Mfrs. Assn. (former chmn. R&D sec.), Assn. Rsch. Dirs., Indsl. Rsch. Inst., (dir. emeritus), N.J. Acad. Scis., Soc. Exptl. Biology and Medicine, Pacific Coast Fertility Soc., Am. Fertility Soc., Internat. Soc. Rsch. in Biology Reproduction (charter), Am. Inst. Mgmt. (exec. council), Am. Mgmt. Assn., Am. Found. Pharm. Edn. (Century Club), Ind. Covered Bridge Soc., Sons of Ind. (N.Y.C. chpt.), Chemists Club (N.Y.C.), Masons, Elks, Kiwanis (emeritus), Lake Naomi Club, Phi Beta Kappa, Phi Lambda Upsilon, Phi Kappa Phi, Sigma Xi, Alpha Chi Sigma. Republican. Home: 5 Bedford Dr Doylestown PA 18901-9463 Office: Johnson & Johnson 1 Johnson And Johnson Plz New Brunswick NJ 08933-0002

HAINING, JEANE, psychologist; b. Camden, NJ, May 2, 1952; d. Lester Edward and Adina (Rahn) H. BA in Psychology, Calif. State U., 1975; MA in Sch. Psychology, Pepperdine U., 1979; MS in Recreation Therapy, Calif. State U., 1982; PhD in Psychology, Calif. Sch. Profl. Psychology, 1985. Lic. clin. psychologist 1987, lic. ednl. psychologist 1982. Crisis counselor Calif. State U., Northridge, 1973-74; recreation therapist fieldwork Camarillo (Calif.) State Hosp.-Adolescent/Children's Units, 1974; Intern recreation therapist UCLA Neuropsychiatric Inst., LA, 1975-76; substitute tchr./recreation therapist New Horizons Sch. for Mentally Retarded, Sepulveda, Calif., 1976-79; sch. psychologist Rialto (Calif.) Unified Sch. Dist., 1979-82; clin. psychologist field work San Joaquin County Dept. Mental Health, Stockton, Calif., 1982-83; intern clinical psychologist Fuller Theol. Sem. Psychology Ctr., Pasadena, Calif., 1984-85; clin. psychologist U.S. Dept. Justice, Terminal Island, Calif., 1985-86; cmty. mental health psychologist L.A. County Dept. Mental Health, 1987-89; clin. psychologist Calif. Dept. Corrections, Parole Outpatient Clinic, LA, 1990—, Mary Magdeline Project, Commerce, Calif., 1992-2000. Adv. bd. Camarillo (Calif.) State Hosp., 1994-97, vice-chmn. adv. bd., 1996-97; examiner Lic. Ednl. Psychologist Oral Examinations, Calif. Bd. Behavioral Sci. Examinations, Sacramento, 1985. Recipient award Outstanding Achievement Western Psychology Conf., Calif., 1974. Mem. APA, Forensic Mental Health Assn. (con. planning com. 1993). Democrat. Lutheran. Avocations: rock climbing, skiing, skating, tennis, piano.

HAINLINE, BRIAN, neurologist; b. Detroit, Dec. 23, 1955; s. Forrest Arthur Jr. and Nora Marie (Schrot) H.; m. Pascale Clauzet, Dec. 22, 1979; children: Clotilde, Arthur, Juliette. BA, U. Notre Dame, 1978; MD, U. Chgo., 1982. Intern U. Chgo. Hosps. and Clinics, 1982-83; resident in neurology N.Y. Hosp., NYC, 1983-86; attending neurologist North Shore U. Hosp., Manhasset, NY, 1986-91, program dir., acting co-chmn. dept. neurology, 1990-91; dir. sports and clin. neurology Hosp. for Joint Diseases, NYC, 1991-97, vice chmn. dept. neurology, 1994-97, co-dir. The Pain Ctr., 1996-97; chief neurology and integrative pain medicine ProHealth Care Assocs., NYC, 1997—. Instr. neurology Cornell U. Med. Coll., N.Y.C., 1986-87, asst. prof. neurology, 1987-91, NYU Sch. Medicine, 1991-95, clin. assoc. prof. of neurology, 1995; med. rev. officer U.S. Tennis Assn., N.Y.C., 1991-96; chief med. officer U.S. Open Tennis Championships, Flushing Meadows, N.Y., 1992—, bd. dirs., 2007—; chair med. commn. Internat. Tennis Fedn., London, 1993—; mem. sports medicine com. U.S. Olympic Com., 1997-2000; bd. dirs. US Tennis Assn. Author: USTA Drug Education Handbook, 1992, Back Pain Understood: A Cutting-Edge Approach to Healing Your Back, 2007; co-author: Drugs and the Athlete, 1989; co-editor: Neurological Complications of Pregnancy, 1994. 2d edit., 2002; contbr. articles to profl. jours. and chpts. to books. Recipient Ednl. Merit award, Internat. Tennis Hall of Fame, 2001. Mem. Am. Acad. Neurology, Physicians for Social Responsibility, Am. Coll. Sports Medicine. Avocations: tennis, piano, writing. Home: 122 Grosvenor St Flushing NY 11363-1007 Office: ProHealth Care Assocs 2800 Marcus Ave New Hyde Park NY 11042-1052 Office Phone: 516-622-6088. Business E-Mail: bhainline@prohealthcare.com.

HAINSWORTH, MELODY MAY, library and information scientist, researcher; b. Vancouver, BC, Can., May 13, 1946; m. Robert John Hainsworth, Jan. 6, 1968; children: Kaleeg William, Shane Alan. BA with honors, Simon Fraser U., 1968; MLS, Dalhousie U., 1976; PhD, Fla. State U., 1992. Libr. Dept. Edn. of Tanzania, Mbeya, 1969—72, Dept. of Edn. of Zambia, Mwinilunga, 1972—74; law libr., deptl. libr. Dept. of Atty. Gen. of N.S., Halifax, 1975—77; regional libr. Provincial Ct. Librs. Dept. of Atty. Gen. of Alta., Calgary, 1977—80, So. Alta. Law Soc. libr., 1980—89; dir. librs. Keiser Coll., Tallahassee, 1992—93; v.p. info. resources and svcs. Internat. Coll., Naples, Fla., 1993—2005; with HMSMG Mgmt. Group, Coquitlam, B.C., Canada, 2005—; census mgr. Stats. Can., 2005—06; instn. officer Pvt. Career Tng. Inst. Agy., 2006—. Census mgr. Stats. Can., 2005—; adj. instr. Sch. Libr. and Info. Studies Fla. State U., Tallahassee, 1990-91, libr. cons., 2004—; spkr. in field; co-founder Naples Free-Net, pres. 1993—; co-founder World Class Acad., rschr. law and info. sci.; mem. faculty Practising Law Inst.; active Women's Polit. Caucus; evaluator SACS/COC, 1999—; mem. external rev. panel ALA/COA, 1999—; spkr. Practising Law Inst.; institution officer Pvt. Career Tchg. Inst. Agy. Contbr. articles to profl. jours. Co-chair adv. com. edn. and tech. com. Fla. State Bd. Ind. Colls. and Univs., 1993-2001; founding mem. Pub. Access to Law of Fla., 1990—; mem. exec. bd. Calgary Legal Guidance, 1985-89, vice chmn., 1988-89, hon. life mem.; tech. grant com. Collier County Edn. Found., 1994-96, sec./webmaster World Class Collier, supt. search com., 1998; chair edn. com. East Naples Civic Assn., 1998; bd. dirs. Seacrest Country Day Sch., 1996-2002; mgr. local census office Statistics Can. Census, 2006. Student Leader Bursaries Simon Fraser U. scholar, 1966-68; H.W. Wilson scholar Dalhousie U., 1974; recipient Woman of Distinction award AAUW, 1999, Women of Distinction, Tempo Internat., Naples, 2005, Woman of Style, 2005. Mem. Spl. Librs. Assn (pres. 1994-95), Assn. Online Profls., Fla. State Ct. and County Librs. Assn., Tallahassee Law Librs. Assn., Fla. Libr. Assn., Assn. Libr. and Info. Sci. Edn., Alta. Legal Archives Soc. (hon. life), Collier County Bar Assn., Women's Polit. Caucus (webmaster 1999—), Tempo Internat. (bd. dirs., Named Woman of Distinction 2005), Naples Press Club (bd. dirs.), Women in Bus. Vancouver Avocations: squash, hiking, travel. Home: 472 Alouette Dr Coquitlam BC Canada V3C 4Y8

HAIR, ROBERT EUGENE, editor, writer, historian; b. Winamac, Ind., Apr. 11, 1921; s. Charles Franklin and Lucy Agnes (Zellers) H.; m. Marian Martha Emerson, Dec. 11, 1949; children: Donald Edward, Martha Anne. AB, DePauw U., Greencastle, Ind., 1942; postgrad., U. Mich., Ann Arbor, 1943-44, 53-56. Newspaper writer and editor; editor Mich. Dept. Health, Lansing, 1956-60; asst. editor Encyclopedia Britannica, Chgo., 1960-64; exec. editor Battelle Rsch. Outlook, Columbus, 1964-69; editor Cordis Corp., Miami, 1969-80. Author: (books) Sturgis, Michigan: Its Story to 1930, 1992, Sturgis, Michigan: 1930-1945, 1996, Sturgis and Its Industrial Growth, 1998, Klinger Lake.Its Origins and Growth, 2001; contbr. articles to profl. jours. Pres. Civic Auditorium Bd., Sturgis, 1994, St. Joseph County Hist. Soc., Centreville, Mich., 1995; v.p. Sturgis Hist. Soc., Mich., 1996, Centennial Celebration Com., Sturgis, 1996. Recipient Award of Merit Hist. Soc. of Mich., 1996, 2001. Mem. Am. Med. Writers Assn., Soc. Profl. Journalists, Masonic Blue Lodge, Sturgis Exchg. Club (pres. 1951-52), Lambda Chi Alpha. Republican. Presbyterian. Avocations: preserving history, stamp collecting/philately, music, photography, collecting antiques. Home: 428 Mortimer St Sturgis MI 49091-2228

HAIR, WILLIAM BATES, III, librarian, dean; b. Gastonia, NC, Mar. 16, 1952; s. William Bates and Lou (Holland) Hair; m. Mary Elizabeth Timanus, Dec. 9, 1972; children: Melissa Bain, Laura Elizabeth, Megan Holland. BS, U. Tenn, 1976; MDiv, Mid-Am. Bapt. Theol. Sem., 1980; MLS, Vanderbilt U., 1982. Sales rep. Groves Thread Co., Gastonia, NC, 1972—73; youth min. Lexa Bept. Ch., Ark., 1977—78; libr. asst. Mid-Am. Bapt. Theol. Sem., Memphis, 1978—80, cataloger and tech. svcs. head, 1980—82, dir. libr., 1982—88, Golden Gate Bapt. Theol. Seminary, Mill Valley, Calif., 1988—94; faculty mem. Baylor U., Waco, Tex., 1994—, assoc. prof., assoc. dean, dir. Univ. Librs., interim dean librs. Trustee Memphis and Shelby County Pub. Libr. and Info. Ctr., 1983, v.p., 85, pres., 1986—87. Mem.: ALA, Calif. Library Assn., Southeastern Library Assn., Tenn. Library Assn., Tenn. Theol. Library Assn. (v.p. 1985), Am. Theol. Library Assn., Kappa Sigma, Beta Phi Mu. Republican. Home: 316 Tree Grove Cir Waco TX 76712-6474 Office: Baylor U One Bear Pl #97143 Waco TX 76798 Office Phone: 254-710-3591. Office Fax: 254-741-9855. Business E-Mail: bill_hair@baylor.edu.*

HAIRFIELD-MARRS, JUDY L., elementary school educator; b. Fredericksburg, Va., Oct. 1, 1956; d. Claude Elton and Clara Maonis Hairfield; m. Bradley Dean Marrs, Mar. 11, 2000; 1 child, Cameron Tyler Marrs. BA, Mary Washington Coll., Fredericksburg, Va., 1977, MA in Liberal Studies, 1994; PhD, LaCrosse U., Fredericksburg, Va. Cert. tchr. Va. Tchr. English, reading specialist, athletic dir. Spotsylvania City Schs., Va., 1977—. Adj. asst. prof. Germanna CC, Fiburg, Va., 2000—. Author: (novels) When the Dancing Ends, 1997, (story) New Beginnings, 1981. Sec. Parish Coun., Fredericksburg, 1992—. Mem.: Nat. Tchrs. English, Ladies Philoptochos Soc. Greek Othodox. Avocations: writing, dance, sports, travel.

HAIRSTON, NELSON GEORGE, JR., ecologist, educator; b. Asheville, NC, Sept. 26, 1949; s. Nelson George and Martha Turner (Patton) H.; m. Deborah Susan (Whitaker)Hairston, Nov. 30, 1974; 1 child, Peter Whitaker Hairston. BS, U. Mich., 1971; PhD, U. Wash., 1977. Asst. prof. U. RI, Kingston, 1977-81, assoc. prof., 1981-85, Cornell U., Ithaca, NY, 1985-87, prof., 1988—, Frank H.T. Rhodes prof. environ. sci., 1996—, chmn. dept. ecology and evolutionary biology, 2001—05, sr. assoc. dean Coll. Arts and Scis., 2006—. Vis. disting. ecologist U. Mich. Biol. Sta., Pelston, 1984; vis. eminent ecologist Mich. State U. Biol. Sta., Hickory Corners, 1989; cons. Westinghouse Savannah River Co., 1990-95, NSF Program in Population Biology and Physiol. Ecology, 1985-87, Swedish Nat. Rsch Coun., 1991, 99, U. Stockholm, 1996, Max Planck Inst. for Limnology, 1997, U. Uppsala, 1998, Stony Brook U., 2005, U. Amsterdam, 2006, Internat. Ecology Inst., Oldendorf, Germany, 2003-06; vis. scientist Archbold Biological Station, 1992, Max-Planck-Inst. Limnology, 1998; guest prof. Swiss Fed. Inst. Tech., 2007. Mem. editl. bd. Limnology and Oceanography, 1986-89, 2003-04, Ecology/Ecol. Monographs, 1989-92, 94-96; contbr. more than 85 articles and papers to sci. jours. NSF grantee, 1980, 83, 86, 88-89, 89-90, 91-92, 92-93, 95, 97, 99, 2000; EPA grantee, 1997, 2001; Andrew Mellon Found. grantee, 1997,2003. Mem. Ecol. Soc. Am. (coun. reps. 1990-93, chair awards com. 1992-95, governing bd. 1996-99, 2001-2004), Internat. Assn. Theoretical and Applied Limnology (nat. rep. 1992-95, 2002-07). Avocations: gardening, skiing, reading. Home: 6125 Perry City Rd Trumansburg NY 14886-9011 Office: Cornell U Dept Ecology and Evolutionary Biology Ithaca NY 14853 Office Phone: 607-254-4231. Business E-Mail: ngh1@cornell.edu.

HAIRSTON, WALTER ALBERT, school system administrator; b. Winston-Salem, NC, Sept. 14, 1928; s. Harvey and Ethel (Marshall) H.; m. Genell Rosella Bright, Mar. 10, 1951 (div. Sept. 12, 1972); m. Jeanette Olivia, Jan. 2, 1979; children: Jacqueline, Walter, Denice, Roslyn, Michael, Linda, Brenda, Telly. BS, Morgan State U., 1959; MEd, Loyola Coll., 1970; graduate, Command and Gen. Staff Coll., 1974, Nat. Def. U., 1979. Commd. U.S. Army, 1955, advanced through grades to col., 1979, ret., 1988; commandant 2071st U.S. Army Sch., 1979; mem. functional area assessment team Transp. Corps, U.S. Army, Fort Eustis, Va., 1984; chief evaluator and dir. Command Gen. Staff Coll., 1979-81; from tchr. to prin. Balt. City Dept. Edn., 1960—. Col. U.S. Army, 1948-85. Mem. Masons, Kappa Alpha Psi, Kappa Delta Pi. Democrat. Presbyterian. Avocations: golf, fishing, boating, woodwork. Home: 14300 Robcaste Rd Phoenix MD 21131-1426 Fax: 410-527-0021. Personal E-mail: walthairst@aol.com.

HAISCH, BERNARD MICHAEL, astronomer, researcher; b. Stuttgart-Bad Canstatt, Federal Republic of Germany, Aug. 23, 1949; s. Friedrich Wilhelm and Gertrud Paula (Dammbacher) H.; m. Pamela S. Eakins, July 29, 1977 (div. 1986); children: Katherine Stuart, Christopher Taylor; m. Marsha A. Sims, Aug. 23, 1986. Student, St. Meinrad Coll., Ind., 1967-68; BS in Astrophysics, Ind. U., 1971; PhD in Astronomy, U. Wis., 1975. Rsch. assoc. Joint Inst. Lab. Astrophysics, U. Colo., 1975-77, 78-79; vis. scientist space rsch. lab. U. Utrecht, The Netherlands, 1977-78; rsch. scientist Lockheed Rsch. Lab., Palo Alto, Calif., 1979-83, staff scientist, 1983-99; dep. dir. Ctr. for EUV Astrophysics U. Calif., Berkeley, 1992-94; dir. Calif. Inst. Physics and Astrophysics, 1999—2002; chief sci. officer Many One Networks, Scotts Valley, Calif., 2004—; pres. Digital Universe Found., Scotts Valley, Calif. Guest investigator Internat. Ultraviolet Explorer, Einstein Obs., Exosat, ROSAT Obs., EUVE Obs., Astro-D (ASCA), X-Ray Timing Explorer, 1980—; vis. fellow Max Planck Inst. Extraterr. Physik, Garching, Germany, 1991-94. Author: The God Theory, 2006; editor-in-chief Jour. Sci. Exploration, 1988-99, Solar and Stellar Flares, 1989; sci. editor The Astrophys. Jour., 1993-2003; monograph The Many Faces of the Sun, 1999; mem. editl. bd. Solar Physics, 1992-95, Speculations in Sci. and Tech., 1995-99; contbr. articles to profl. jours. Fellow AIAA (assoc.), Royal Astron. Soc.; mem. Internat. Astron. Union, Am. Astron. Soc., European Astron. Soc., Sigma Xi, Phi Beta Kappa, Phi Kappa Phi. Avocations: skiing, song writing. Business E-Mail: haisch@calphysics.org.

HAIT, GERSHON, pediatric cardiologist; b. May 10, 1927; came to U.S., 1952, naturalized, 1965; s. Nahum and Leah H.; m. Doris J. Coburn, Mar. 20, 1957; children: Jonathan, Yael. MD, U. Lausanne, Switzerland, 1952. Intern Michael Reese Hosp., Chgo., 1952-53; resident Cook County Hosp., Chgo., 1961-62, fellow in pediatric cardiology, 1954-56, 59-60; instr. pediatrics, NIH fellow in pediatric cardiology Albert Einstein Coll. Medicine, Bronx, NY, 1962-64, dir. pediatric cardiology, 1966-85, prof. pediatrics, 1979—2005, prof. emeritus, 2005—. Mem. staff Bronx Mcpl. Hosp. Center, Montefiore; cardiac cons. to depts. of health of Bronx, SI, and Rockland counties. Contbr. articles to profl. jours. Served to lt. M.C. Israeli Army, 1956-59. Grantee NIH; Grantee Am. Heart Assn.; Grantee others. Mem. Am. Physiology Soc., Soc. for Pediatric Research, Am. Acad. Pediatrics, Am. Fedn. Clin. Research, Am. Heart Assn., Am. Coll. Cardiology, Sleep Rsch. Soc., Am. Acad. Sleep Medicine. Jewish. Home: 14 Withington Rd Scarsdale NY 10583-3306 Office: Childrens Hosp Montefiore 3415 Bainbridge Ave Bronx NY 10467 Personal E-mail: gershonhait@aol.com.

HAIT, PATRICK DAVID, elementary school music educator; b. West Islip, NY, Nov. 21, 1979; s. David Hait and Mary Coonerty; m. Melissa Lanfrit, Feb. 18, 2006. BA in Music Performance, SUNY, Stony Brook, NY, 2002; MS in Edn. Music, CUNY, 2006. Lic. 100 ton masters inland USCG, 1999, cert. tchr. NY State, 2004. Tchr. band A.T. Morrow Elem. Sch., Ctrl. Islip, NY, 2004—. Mem.: NY State Sch. Music Assn., Suffolk County Music Educators Assn., Golden Key. Democrat. Home Phone: 631-274-1897; Office Phone: 631-348-5037. Personal E-mail: patrickhait@hotmail.com. Business E-Mail: phait@centralislip.k12.ny.us.

HAIT, WILLIAM NEIL, oncologist, educator; b. Newark, Mar. 23, 1949; BA, U. Pa., 1971; MD cum laude, PhD, Med. Coll Pa., 1978. Diplomate Am. Bd. Internal Medicine, Am. Bd. Med. Oncology. Intern, internal medicine Yale U. Sch. Medicine, New Haven, 1978-79, resident in internal medicine, 1979—82, chief resident in internal medicine, 1981-82, fellow med. oncology, 1982-83, from instr. to to assoc. prof. internal medicine, 1983-92, from asst. prof. to assoc. prof. pharmacology, 1986-92; prof. medicine and pharmacology Robert Wood Johnson Med. Sch., Piscataway, NJ, 1993—2007; sr. v.p., worldwide head for hematology oncology rsch. develop Johnson & Johnson, 2007—. Acting chief med. oncology Yale U. Sch. Medicine, New Haven, 1986-88, dir. breast cancer unit, co-dir. lung cancer unit, 1987-92, chief sect. med. oncology, 1988-92; assoc. dir. Yale U. Comprehensive Cancer Ctr., 1986-92; acting chief med. oncology West Haven (Conn.) VA Hosp., 1991-92; adj. prof. pharmacy Rutgers U., Piscataway, 1993-; founding dir. The Cancer Inst. N.J., New Brunswick, 1993-2007; co-dir. N.J. Comprehensive Breast Care Ctr., 1994—; chief med. oncology U. Medicine Dentistry NJ Robert Wood Johnson Med. Sch., New Brunswick, 1994-2007, assoc. dean for oncology programs, 1994-2007; med. adv. bd. N.J. Breast Coalition, 1993—; lectr. in field. Mem. editl. bd. Oncology Rsch., Hem/Onc Annals, Abstracts in Oncology, Clin. Cancer Rsch.; patentee method of sensitizing multidrug resistant cells to antitumor agents, synthesis of inhibitors of calmodulin-mediated enzymes inclding KS-501, KS-502 and their enantiomers; co-inventor potent and selective inhibitors of protein kinase C; contbr. articles to profl. jours. Carden fellow, 1982; recipient Excellence in the Field Psychiatry award Sandoz Pharm. Co., 1977, Burroughs-Wellcome Clin. Pharmacology award, 1987, Disting. Svc. award Am. Fedn. for Clin. Rsch., 1991. Fellow Acad. Medicine N.J.; mem. AAAS, Am. Fedn. for Clin. Rsch. (nat.

councilor at large 1985-87, chmn. oncology sect. nat. meeting 1985-86, 90, rep. coun. acad. societies 1987-88, co-chmn. pub. policy com. 1988-89, chmn. pub. policy com. 1989—), Am. Cancer Soc. (chemotherapy and hematology com., sci. rev. group 1989—, bd. dirs. N.J. chpt. 1994—), Am. Assn. Cancer Rsch. (membership com. 1990-, pres.-elect 2006-2007, pres. 2007-), Am. Soc. Clin. Oncology (program com., spl awards com. 1994—), Am. Assn. Cancer Rsch.-Am. Assn. Cancer Inst., Am. Soc. for Clin. Investigation; Alpha Omega Alpha Home: 48 Roper Rd Princeton NJ 08540-4070*

HAITH, DOUGLAS A., engineering educator, researcher; b. Cooperstown, NY, Apr. 13, 1942; s. Clinton Dirstein Haith and Blanche Irene Fassett; m. Ellen Ralston Douglass, May 13, 1967; children: Robert Arthur, Benjamin Fassett. BS, MIT, Cambridge, Mass., 1964; MS, MIT, Cambridge, Mass, 1966; PhD, Cornell U., Ithaca, NY, 1971. Hydraulic engr. Charles A. Maguire & Assocs., Boston, 1966—67; project engr. Quirk, Lawler and Matusky Engrs., NYC, 1967—68; asst. prof. Cornell U., Ithaca, 1971—77; sr. engr. Quirk, Lawler and Matusky Engrs., Tappan, NY, 1973—74; assoc. prof. Cornell U., 1977—83, prof. biol. and environ. engring., 1983—. Dir. Am. Water Resources Assn., Middleburg, Va., 1993—95. Author: (book) Water Resource Systems Planning and Analysis, 1981, Environmental Systems Optimization, 1982, Simulation of Pollution by Soil Erosion and Soil Nutrient Loss, 1984. Organist and choir dir. Ch. of Epiphany, Trumansburg, NY, 1980—97, St. James A.M.E. Zion Ch., Ithaca, 1997—99. Recipient Walter L. Huber Civil Engring. Rsch. prize, ASCE, 1981, Wesley W. Horner Environ. Engring. award, 1988, Spl. Svc. award, NY State Assn. of Conservation Districts, 1990, Outstanding Engring. Faculty award, Cornell Soc. of Engrs., 1998, Chancellor's Excellence in Tchg. award, SUNY, 1998, Edgerton Career Tchg. award, Cornell Coll. of Agr. and Life Scis., 2002. Mem.: Am. Water Resources Assn. (dir. 1993—95). Avocations: sailing, rowing, fishing, bicycling, music. Office: Cornell U Riley Robb Hall Ithaca NY 14853 Home Phone: 607-387-5381; Office Phone: 607-255-2802. Office Fax: 607-255-4080. E-mail: dah13@cornell.edu.

HAITINK, BERNARD J. H., conductor; b. Amsterdam, Mar. 4, 1929. MusD (hon.), U. Oxford, 1988, U. Leeds, 1988, Royal Coll. Music. Condr., Netherlands Radio Philharmonic Orch., 1955-61; guest condr. Concertgebouw Orch., Amsterdam, then joint condr., 1956-64, chief condr., music dir., 1964-88; prin. condr. London Philharm. Orch., 1967-79; guest condr. Glyndebourne Festival Opera, 1972-77, music dir. Glyndebourne, 1978-88; music dir. Royal Opera House, Covent Garden, London, 1988-2002; pres. London Philharm. Orch., 1990—; music dir. European Union Youth Orch., 1994-1999; condr. emeritus Boston Symphony; prin. condr. Chgo. Symphony, 2006—. Recordings include Don Giovanni, Cosa fan Tutte, Figro, Der Rosenkavalier, The Magic Flute, Daphne, Tannhauser, The Ring, Peter Grimes, Fidelio; recorded with Philips, Decca and EMI. Decorated Order Oranje Nassau; chevalier Ordre des Arts et des Lettres; Hon. knight Brit. Empire, 1977; officer Order of Crown (Belgium); recipient Bruckner medal of honor Bruckner Soc., 1970, Gold medal Royal Philharm. Soc., 1991, Erasmus prize The Netherlands, 1991. Mem. Royal Acad. Music (London) (hon.), Royal Coll. Music (hon.), Internat. Gustav Mahler Soc. (hon.; gold medal 1970). Office: Askonas Holt Ltd c/o Tiggy Sawbridge Lincoln House 300 High Holborn London WC1V 7JH England Office Phone: 20 7400-1700. Office Fax: 20 7400 1799.*

HAIZLIP, VIOLA, medical/surgical nurse; b. Albany, NY, Mar. 16, 1969; d. William and Viola Augusta Haizlip; life ptnr. Sean Glaze, Nov. 28, 2004; 1 stepchild, Devon Glaze. BSN, Coll. New Rochelle, 1991; postgrad., HSI Sch. Intuitive Abilities, 2004—. RN NY. Nurse St. Peter's Hosp., Albany, NY, 1990—2000, N.E. Nursing, Glenmont, NY, 1992—2003; nurse care mgr. Value Options, Troy, NY, 2003—05; pub., owner Vix Pub. Co.; coord. inpatient care Capital Dist. Physicians Healthplan, 2005—. Author: (children's book) Kitty of My Heart, 2004. Active Helping Healing Program, Schenectady, NY, 2004. Recipient award, Nat. Libr. Poetry, 1999, 2001, 2002. Home: 1115 6th Ave Watervliet NY 12189 Office: Vix Pub Co PO Box 692 Glenmont NY 12077 Office Phone: 518-253-9341. Business E-Mail: vixpub@yahoo.com.

HAJDU, MICHAEL A., cardiologist; b. Washington, Mar. 4, 1955; s. Stephen Hajdu and Margaret Patricia Hajdu. BA, Knox Coll., 1978; PhD, U. Nebr., 1988; MD, U. Iowa, 1997. Resident Fletcher Allen Health Care, U. Vt., Burlington, 1997—2000, cardiology fellow, 2000—02; cardiologist Cardiology Cons., Kans. City. Named a Kans. City Super Doctor, Kans. City mag., 2007. Avocations: fishing, bicycling. Office: Cardiovasc Cons 330 Arkansas Ste 202 Lawrence KS 66044*

HAJEK, FRANCIS PAUL, lawyer; b. Hobart, Tasmania, Australia, Oct. 21, 1958; came to U.S., 1966; s. Frank Joseph and Kathleen Beatrice (Blake) H. BA, Yale U., 1980; JD, U. Richmond, 1984. Bar: Va. 1984, U.S. Dist. Ct. (ea. dist.) Va. 1984, U.S. Ct. Appeals (4th cir.) 1986. Law clk. to presiding magistrate U.S. Dist Ct., Norfolk, Va., 1984-85; assoc. Seawell, Dalton, Hughes & Timms, Norfolk, 1985-87, Weinberg & Stein, Norfolk, 1987-89, I'Anson-Hoffman Am. Inn of Ct., 1991-97; ptnr. Hajek, Shapiro, Cooper & Lewis, P.C., Virginia Beach, Va., 1989—. Legal counsel United Transp. Union, 1999-2004. Mem. ABA, ATLA, Am. Rail Labor Acad. (bd. dirs. 2003-2004), Va. Bar Assn., Norfolk-Portsmouth Bar Assn. (chmn. exec. com. young lawyer's sect. 1990-91). Roman Catholic. Avocations: squash, tennis. Office: Hajek Shapiro et al 1294 Diamond Springs Rd Virginia Beach VA 23455 Home: 1836 Green Hill Rd Virginia Beach VA 23454-1115 Home Phone: 757-496-8875; Office Phone: 757-460-7776. E-mail: fhajek@hsinjurylaw.com.

HAJEK, OTOMAR, mathematician, educator; b. Beograd, Serbia, Dec. 22, 1930; arrived in U.S., 1966, naturalized, 1974; s. Frantisek Josef and Ruzena (Houdekova) Hajek; m. Olga Barbara Nemcova, Feb. 12, 1955; 1 child, Michael. Diploma in math., Caroline U., Prague, Czech. Rep., 1953, candidate sci., 1963; RNDr, Caroline U., Prague, Czech Rep., 1966. Asst. prof. Czech Inst. Tech., Prague, 1953-56, sr. asst. prof., 1956-60; sci. officer Research Inst. Computing Machinery, Prague, 1960-65; sr. sci. officer Caroline U., Prague, 1965-66; assoc. prof. Case Western Res. U., Cleve., 1966-69, prof. math., 1969—, prof. sys. engring., 1988-96, prof. emeritus, 1996—. Author: (book) Dynamical Systems in the Plane, 1968, Pursuit Games, 1975, Control Systems in the Plane, 1991; co-author: Local Semi-Dynamical Systems, 1969; co-editor: Global Differentiable Dynamics, 1970. Recipient von Humboldt award, 1975; Deutsche Forschungsgemeinschaft fellow, Bonn, 1979, 1990, Fulbright fellow, 1990. Mem.: Union Czech Math. and Physicists, Fulbright Assn., von Humboldt Assn., Czechoslovak Soc. Arts and Scis., Am. Math. Soc. Lutheran. Home: 11330 Savannah Dr Fredericksburg VA 22407-9109 Personal E-mail: ohajek@comcast.net.

HAJEK, ROBERT J., SR., lawyer, real estate broker; b. May 17, 1943; s. James J. Sr. and Rita C. (Kalka) H.; m. Maris Ann Enright, June 19, 1965 (div. Oct. 1991); children: Maris Ann, Robert J., David H., Mandie J. BA, Loras Coll., 1965; JD, U. Ill., 1968; post doctoral studies, Nat. Lewis U., Evanston, Ill., 1985—87. Bar: Ill. 1968, U.S. Tax Ct. 1970, U.S. Dist. Ct. (no. dist.) Ill. 1971, U.S. Ct. Appeals (7th cir.) 1972, U.S. Supreme Ct. 1972; lic. real estate broker, Ill., Nat. Assn. Securities Dealers; registered U.S. Commodities Futures Trading Commn. Ptnr. Hajek & Hajek, Berwyn, Ill., 1968-76; pres., bd. chmn. Hajek, Hajek, Koykar & Heying, Ltd., Westchester, Ill., 1976-85; pres., CEO Land of Lincoln Real Estate, Ltd., Glendale Heights, Ill., 1985-89, also bd. dirs.; ptnr., owner Camelot Manor Nursing Home, Streator, Ill., 1978—, Ottawa (Ill.) Care Ctr., 1981—2005, Glenwood House Nursing Home, Streator, 1988—, Sullivan House Nursing Home, Ottawa, 1991—, Law Ctr. Bldg., Westchester, 1976-91; pres., CEO, chmn. bd. Rock River Computer Resources, LLC, 2005—; mng. gen. ptnr. H.S. Enterprises, 2006—. Exec. v.p., gen. counsel Ottawa Long Term Care, Inc.; owner Garfield Ridge Real Estate, Chgo., 1973—78, Centre Realty, Westchester, 1976—85; ptnr. Westbrook Commodities, Chgo., 1983—2005; v.p., bd. mem., gen. counsel DeHart Gas and Oil Devel., Ltd., 1970—73; prin. Northeastern Okla. Oil and Gas Prodn. Venture, Tulsa, 1982—92; exec. v.p., gen. counsel Garrett Plante Corp., 1978—2004. Sr. boys' basketball coach Roselle Recreation Assn., Ill., 1981—83. Mem. ABA, Ill. Bar Assn., Nat. Assn. Realtors, Ill. Assn. Realtors, N.W. Suburban Bd. Realtors, Ill. Health Care Assn., Amateur Radio Club, No. Ill. DX Assn., Phi Alpha Delta. Republican. Episcopalian. Home Phone: 815-732-4520; Office Phone: 815-732-4520. Personal E-mail: k9ltn@yahoo.com. Business E-Mail: rjhajeksr@rreinc.net.

HAJ-HARIRI, HOSSEIN, engineering educator, department chairman; b. Tehran, Iran, Apr. 8, 1962; s. Mehdi Amir Houshang and Farzaneh Haj-Hariri; m. Sarah Williams Haj-Hariri, Aug. 12, 2000; children: Mitra Minter, Dara Davisson. SB, MIT, Cambridge, 1983, SM, 1984, PhD, 1987. Prof. mech. and aerospace engring. U. Va., Charlottesville, 1988—, chair, dept. mech. and aerospace engring., 2005—. Mem.: Am. Phys. Soc. Office: Univ Va Dept Mech and Aerospace Engring 122 Engineer's Way PO Box 400746 Charlottesville VA 22904-4746 Office Phone: 434-924-7422. Business E-Mail: haj-hariri@virginia.edu.

HAJJ-ALI, RULA ADEL, rheumatologist, researcher; d. A. Hajj-Ali and S. Badran; m. Jihad Kaouk, Sept. 1, 1994; children: Sahar Kaouk, Reem Kaouk, Reda Kaouk; m. Jihad Kaouk. BS, Am. U. Beirut, Beirut Lebanon, 1989, MD, 1993. Diplomate Am. Bd. Medicine, 2002, in rheumatology Am. Bd. Medicine, 2003. Resident in internal medicine Am. U. Beirut, 1993—95, fellow in rheumatology, 1996—98, chief resident in internal medicine, 1998—99; fellow clin. rheumatology Cleve. Clinic Found., 1999—2002, assoc. staff rheumatology, 2003—. Mem. Ctr. Vasculitis Care and Rsch. Cleve. Clinic Found., 2002—. Recipient Best Graduating Fellow award, Cleve. Soc. Rheumatology, 2001; grantee, Vasculitis Found., 2005. Mem.: Am. Coll. Medicine, Am. Coll. Rheumatology. Achievements include research in central nervous system vasculitis. Avocations: bicycling, travel. Office: Cleveland Clinic Foundation 9500 Euclid Ave A50 Cleveland OH 44195 Home Phone: 440-498-8641. Office Fax: 216-445-9643. Business E-Mail: hajjalr@ccf.org.

HAJJAR, KATHERINE AMBERSON, physician, pediatrician; b. Rochester, NY, Oct. 29, 1952; d. James Burns Amberson and Shirley Elizabeth (Huber) Kuntz; m. David Phillip Hajjar, May 26, 1984; children: Esther Katherine, Amanda Elizabeth. AB, Smith Coll., 1974; MD, Johns Hopkins U., 1978. Diplomate Am. Bd. Pediatrics, Am. Bd. Pediatric Hematology-Oncology. Resident pediatrics Children's Hosp. Pitts., 1978-81, chief resident pediatrics, 1981-82; fellow pediatric hematology-oncology Johns Hopkins U., Balt., 1982-84; asst. prof. Cornell U. Med. Coll., NYC, 1984-89, assoc. prof., 1989-94; Stravros S. Niarchos prof. pediatrics, Brine Family prof. cell and develop. biology Cornell U. Med. Ctr., NYC, 1992-94. Mem. thrombosis study sect. Am. Heart Assn., Dallas, 1990-92; mem. rev. com. NIH, Bethesda, Md., 1992—. Contbr. articles to profl. jours. Recipient Rsch. Career Devel. award NIH, 1989, Irvine S. Page award Am. Heart Assn., 1991; named Established Investigator Am. Heart Assn., 1989-94; scholar Syntex Corp., 1989-92. Fellow Am. Acad. Pediatrics; mem. Soc. for Pediatric Rsch., Am. Soc. Hematology, Am. Soc. Biochemistry and Molecular Biology, Am. Soc. Clin. Investigation, Am. Soc. Cell Biology. Achievements include research on endothelial cell biology, thrombosis and fibrinolysis, annexins. Office: Weill Cornell U Med Coll PO Box 45 New York NY 10021-0030

HAKA, CLIFFORD HUGHEY, library director; b. Chgo., Sept. 14, 1949; s. Leo Walter and Cliffern Grace (Hughey) H.; m. Susan Frances Verschage, June 26, 1971; 1 child: Abigail Susan. BA in History, Western Ill. U., 1971; MA in Am. History, Sangamon State U., 1976; MA in Libr. Sci., U. Ill., 1977; MA in Bus. Adminstrn., U. Kans., 1981. Hist. rsch. editor Ill. State Hist. Libr., Springfield, 1971-73, field svc. rep., 1973-76; asst. curator Kans. collection U. Kans., Lawrence, 1977-78, circulation libr., 1978-82; info. libr. Mich. State U., East Lansing, 1982-85, head info. reference, 1985-87, head access svcs., 1987-91, asst. dir. adminstrn. svcs., 1991—97, dir. librs., 1997—. Cons. Fla. Atlantic U., Boca Raton, 1988, Loyola U., Chgo., 1988, U. Glasgow, 1989, U. New Haven, 1990; mem. Libr. Mich. Bd. Trustees, 2002—, vice chair, 2003—04, chair, 2004—. Contbr. articles to profl. jours. 2nd lt. USNG, 1971-76. Fellow Spl. Libr. Assn., 1976. Mem.: ALA, Mich. Libr. Assn., Ctr. Rsch. Librs., Assn. Rsch. Librs. Democrat. Avocation: golf. Home: 1028 Cresenwood Rd East Lansing MI 48823-4120 Office: Mich State U Main Libr East Lansing MI 48824-1048 Office Phone: 517-355-2314. E-mail: hakac@msu.edu.*

HAKALA, KAREN LOUISE, retired real estate specialist; b. Lansing, Mich., Dec. 8, 1941; d. Herod Maxson and Flora Belle (Barton) Mitchell; m. Paul Kenneth Hakala, June 24, 1959 (div. Nov. 1972); children: Chris, Craig. BS, No. Mich. U., Marquette, 1986. Real estate specialist Cleve.-Cliffs Iron Co., Ishpeming, Mich., 1967-99; ret., 1999. Mediator Cmty. Resolution Resource Ctr., 2002—. Mem. devel. com. Planned Parenthood No. Mich., Marquette, 1996—99; bd. dirs. Marquette Symphony Orch., 1998—2000, treas., 1999—2000; planning commn. City of Negaunee, Mich., 2001—, sec., 2001—02, 2005—; trustee Negaunee Area Cmty. Fund, 2006—07. Mem.: LWV (bd. dirs. Marquette County 2002—06), AAUW (pub. policy rep. Marquette County chpt. 1995—99, pres. 1999—2001), Ret. Sr. Vol. Program.

HAKALA, REINO WILLIAM, mathematician, educator; b. Albany, NY, 1923; m. Eunice Irma Kazanowski, 1950; children: Jonathan, Lisamaria, Christina. AB, Columbia U., NYC, 1946, MA, 1947; PhD, Syracuse U., NY, 1965. Chemistry instr. Associated Coll. of Upper NY, Plattsburgh, 1947—48; atomic energy commn. fellow and grad. asst. Syracuse U., 1948—53; adj. prof. chemistry Pa. State U., State College, 1953; assoc. prof. chemistry Fairfield (Conn.) U., 1954—57; asst. prof. chemistry Earlham Coll., Richmond, Ind., 1957—59, Howard U., Washington, 1959—63; NSF sci. faculty fellow Syracuse U., 1963—64; prof. chemistry and math. Mich. Tech. U., 1964—67; chmn. depts. math. and physics Oklahoma City U., 1967—72, pres. faculty senate, 1972; prof. of math. Wash. Tech. Inst., 1972—73; dean of the sch. of sci. and tech. Lake Superior State Coll., Sault Ste Marie, Mich., 1973—77, asst. to v.p. for acad. affairs, 1977, prof. of math., 1978—80, pres. faculty senate, 1978; dean Coll. Arts and Sci. Governors State U., University Park, Ill., 1980—81, spl. asst. to provost, 1982, interim chair divsn. sci., 1983, prof. math., 1984—. Cons. Nat. Bur. Standards, 1962—63. Contbr. articles to profl. jours. Fellow, Washington (D.C.) Acad. of Scis., 1961, Am. Inst. of Chemists, 1969, fellowships and grants, Atomic Energy Commn., NSF, NATO, Petroleum Rsch. Fund. Mem.: IEEE (mem. tech. com. pattern recognition), Soc. Indsl. and Applied Math., Internat. Assn. Pattern Recognition, Am. Math. Soc., Math. Assn. Am. Home: 2945 Chayes Pk Dr Homewood IL 60430 Office: Governors State University 1 University Pkwy University Park IL 60466 Home Phone: 708-957-4338; Office Phone: 708-534-4527. Office Fax: 708-534-1641. Business E-Mail: r-hakala@govst.edu.

HAKALA, THOMAS JOHN, private banker, financial planner, accountant; b. Bayonne, NJ, July 6, 1948; s. John R. and Anna J. (Vida) H.; m. Marilynn Freund, Aug. 15, 1976; children: Lauren V., John C. AB in History, Georgetown U., 1970; JD, St. John's U., 1975; postgrad., NYU, 1975-80. Bar: N.J. 1975, N.Y. 1976; CPA, Tex. Supr. Weeden & Co., NYC, 1970-73; mgr. Coopers & Lybrand, NYC, 1975-87; sr. mgr. KPMG Peat Marwick, NYC, 1987-89, ptnr., 1989-99; exec. dir. fin. planning and wealth mgmt. UBS Warburg, NYC, 1999-2001; dir. UBS Trust Co., NYC, 1999-2001; mng. dir. fin. planning and wealth mgmt. Wilmington Trust, NYC, 2001—. Bd. advisers Jour. Taxation of Estates and Trusts, N.Y.C., 1990-92. Contbr. articles to profl. jours. Mem. Estate Planning Coun. NYC, bd. dirs., 2004-07. Mem. AICPA, Finnish Am. Lawyers Assn., Ocean Beach and Yacht Club, Normandy Beach Club, Univ. Club, Phi Delta Phi. Republican. Roman Catholic. Avocations: reading, history, photography, walking on beaches, swimming. Office: Wilmington Trust FSB 520 Madison Ave New York NY 10022 Home Phone: 732-549-0680; Office Phone: 212-415-0544. E-mail: thakala@wilmingtontrust.com.

HAKAN, KAYA, oncologist, hematologist; b. Samsun, Turkey, June 2, 1968; s. Altan and Asuman Kuyu; married, Apr. 8, 1993; 1 child, Erin Asena Kaya. MD, Ankara U., Ankara, 1993. Diplomate Am. Bd. Internal Medicine, 1997, Am. Bd. Internal Medicine-Med. Oncology, 2005. Intern U. Okla. Health Scis. Ctr., 1997; fellow hematology and oncology, stemcell transplant Wake Forest U., 2000; mem. clin. faculty U. Wash. Sch. Medicine, Spokane, 2002—; med. oncologist, hematologist Cancer Care NW, Spokane, 2004—. Med. dir. Inland NW Autologous Stem Cell Transplant Program, Spokane, Wash., 2005—. Contbr. articles to profl. publs. Mem.: AMA, Am. Soc. Hematology, Am. Soc. Clin. Oncology, Assembly Turkish Am. Assns. (v.p. 2005—, Outstanding Achievement in Arts and Scis. award 2004). Avocation: Tae Kwon Do. Office: Cancer Care NW 601 S Sherman St Spokane WA 99202 Office Phone: 509-228-1000. Office Fax: 509-228-1184.

HAKANSSON, NILS HEMMING, economist, educator; b. Marby, Sweden, June 2, 1937; came to U.S., 1956; s. Nils and Anna (Nilsson) H.; m. Joyce Beth Kates, Aug. 28, 1960; children— Carolyn Ann, Nils Alexander BS with honors, U. Oreg., 1958; MBA, UCLA, 1960, PhD, 1966; D. of Econs. (hon.), Stockholm Sch. Econs., 1984. C.P.A., Calif. Staff acct., cons. Arthur Young & Co., LA, 1960-63; asst. prof. UCLA, 1966-67, Yale U., New Haven, 1967-69; assoc. prof. U. Calif.-Berkeley, 1969-71, prof., 1971-77, Sylvan C. Coleman prof. fin. and acctg., 1977—2003, chmn. fin., 1976-79, 1997—2000. Cons. Rand Corp., Santa Monica, Calif., 1965-71, Bell Labs., Murray Hill, NJ, 1974, 79-81; chmn. bd. dirs. Anna och Nils Hakanssons Stiftelse; bd. dirs. Excelsior and Laudus Mut. Funds. Editorial cons. Acctg. Rev., 1977-80; cons. editor Jour. Acctg. and Econs., 1978-81; contbr. articles to profl. jours. Served with Royal Swedish Corps Engrs., 1956. Recipient Graham and Dodd award Fin. Analysts Fedn., 1976, 82; Ford Found. fellow UCLA, 1963-66; Hoover fellow U. New South Wales, 1975 Fellow Acctg. Rschrs. Internat. Assn.; mem. AICPA (hon. mem.), Fin. Economists Roundtable, Am. Fin. Assn., Western Fin. Assn. (pres. 1983-84), Am. Acctg. Assn., Soc. for Promotion Fin. Studies (founding). Office: U Calif Sch Bus Berkeley CA 94720-1900 Business E-Mail: hakansso@haas-berkeley.edu.

HAKE, RALPH F., former appliance manufacturing executive; b. Cin., Jan. 25, 1949; m. Robin Hake; 1 child, Mark. BBA, U. Cin., 1971; MBA, U. Chgo., 1975. V.p. adminstrn.l. Mead Corp., Escababa, Mich., 1980-84, dir. corp. devel. Dayton, Ohio, 1984-87; various fin. and ops. positions including corp. v.p., contr. Whirlpool Corp., Benton Harbor, Mich., from 1987, pres. Bauknecht appliance group, exec. v.p. N.Am. appliance group, sr. exec. v.p. ops., until 1997, sr. exec. v.p., CFO, 1997-1999; exec. v.p., CFO Fluor Corp., Aliso Viejo, Calif., 1999—2001; chmn., CEO Maytag Corp., 2001—06. Bd. dirs. ITT Industries, 2002—. Served in U.S. Army, 1971-73. Mem. NAM (bd. dirs.). Avocations: woodworking, reading.

HAKEEM, MUHAMMAD ABDUL, artist, educator; b. NYC, Oct. 15, 1945; s. Cheveland and Ruby (Rountrea) Marshall; m. Sarah Sockarso, Feb. 9, 2003. Student of sculpture and painting, Pratt Inst., Pietrasanta, Italy, 1972; BFA, Pratt Inst., 1974; MA, Tchr. Coll., 1976; MEd, Columbia U., 1980. Artist NY Daily News, NYC, 1976-78; asst. technician Bklyn. Mus., 1980-81, instr. African Art, 1981; tchr. Holy Rosary Sch., Bklyn., 1982-89; arts and crafts specialist Fresh Air Fund Camp, Fishkill, NY, summer 1983, Camp Merrimac, Contoo Cook, NH, summers 1986-88; tchr. art Mid. Sch. 319, Bronx, NY, 1997-98, Denver Sch. Dist., 2000—; dealer Dan Gallery, 2005. Adj. prof. Naropa Inst., Boulder, Colo.; part-time tchr. Boulder and Denver Pub. Schs., 2000—; workshop facilitator, lectr. Islamic culture and faith Arapahoe Ridge H.S., 2001—. One-man shows include Christ Hosp. Primary Care Ctr., Jersey City, 1997; exhibited in group shows at Bklyn. Mus., 1973, Lynn Kottler Galleries, 1974, Hansen Galleries, 1974, Galleries Internat., 1975, Cmty. Gallery, 1977, Waverly Gallery, Inc., 1977, Allan S. Park Gallery, 1978, Greenwich Bar and Restaurant, 1979, Macy Gallery, 1980, West Side Story, 1981, Lynn Kittler Galleries, 1981, World Trade Expo-Keane Mason Gallery, 1981, Tabor Gallery, 1982, Gallery II, St. George, Utah, 1984, Beaulahland, 1986, Morin-Miller Galleries, 1987, 89, Ednl. Alliance, 1988, Steamboat Springs (Colo.) Art Coun./Eleanor Bliss Ctr. for the Arts of the Depot (hon. mention), 1992, Boulder Art Ctr., 1993, Louisville (Colo.) Arts Ctr., 1993, Emmanuel Gallery-U. Colo., Denver, 1994, Cross Gallery, Boulder, 1995, Cross Gallery, Denver, 1995, Bklyn. Children's Mus., 1996, The Christ Hosp. Primary Care Ctr., 1997, Boulder Mus. Contemporary Art, 2000, Sovereign Gallery, Boulder, 2003, Mia Trattoria Restaurant, 2003, Dan Gallery, Denver, 2005, others; works represented at Kearon-Hempenstall Gallery, Jersey City; multimedia exhbn. at Colo. History Mus., 1996. Art tchr. Lower East Side Cmty Sch., NYC, 1976-77, Urban League, Bklyn., 1969; counselor Office of Cath. Edn., Bklyn., 1987-88; mem. customer panel Regional Transp. Divsn. Winner Cheekwood Nat. Contemporary Painting Competition, Cheekwood Mus. Art, Tenn., 1993. Mem. Kappa Delta Pi (Kappa chpt.). Office Phone: 720-423-3231. Personal E-mail: vanburen318@yahoo.com.

HAKEL, MILTON DANIEL, JR., psychologist, educator, writer, consultant; b. Hutchinson, Minn., Aug. 1, 1941; s. Milton Daniel and Emily Ann (Kovar) H.; m. Lee Ellen Pervier, Sept. 1, 1962; children: Lane, Jennifer BA, U. Minn., 1963, PhD, 1966. Diplomate in Indsl. and Orgnl. Psychology Am. Bd. Profl. Psychology. Prof. psychology Ohio State U., Columbus, 1968-85, U. Houston, 1985-91, chmn. dept., 1987-91; pres. Orgnl. Rsch. and Devel., 1977—2006; ptnr. Applied Rsch. Group, 1984-87; Ohio Bd. Regents eminent scholar, prof. Bowling Green State U., 1991—. Trustee Am. Bd. Profl. Psychology, 1987-90; mem. US nat. com. Internat. Union Psychol. Sci., 1997-01, mem. com. on assessment and tchr. quality NRC, 1999-00, mem. bd. testing and assessment, 1999-05, evaluate advanced tchr. cert., Ohio Bd. Regents, 2005—; chair com. higher learning accountability and productivity, 2005—. Co-author (sr.): Making It Happen: Doing Research with Implementation in Mind, 1982; author: Beyond Multiple Choice: Evaluating Alternatives to Traditional Testing, 1998; editor Current Directions in Psychol. Sci., 1998-99, Personnel Psychology, 1973-84, pub., 1984-2004; co-editor: Applying the Science of Learning to University Teaching and Beyond, 2002; contbr. 40 articles to profl. jours. Chair Human Capital Initiative Coordinating Com., 1991-99, co-chair Applying Sci. Learning to U. Edu. conf. steering com. Recipient James McKeen Cattell award, 1965; Fulbright-Hays Sr. scholar, 1978; NSF grantee, 1966-73; Disting. Svc. Contbrs. award, 1995. Fellow Assn. for. Psychol. Sci. (founding bd. dirs., co-chair Lifelong Learning at Work and at Home 2006—), Soc. Indsl. and Orgnl. Psychology (pres. 1984), Am. Assn. Adv. Sci., Internat. Assn. Applied Psychology (bd. dirs. 2004-), Summit Conf.; mem. Ohio Bd. Regents Com. Higher Learning Accountability and Productivity (chair 2006). Presbyterian. Home: 1435 Cedar Ln Bowling Green OH 43402-1476 Office: Bowling Green State U Dept Psychology Bowling Green OH 43403-0001 Office Phone: 419-372-8144. Business E-Mail: mhakel@bgsu.edu.

HAKES, JAY EDWARD, library director, former federal agency administrator; b. Gallipolis, Ohio; m. Anita Zervigon. Grad., Wheaton Coll., 1966; M, Duke U., 1968, PhD, 1970. Tchr. polit. sci. U. New Orleans, 1970-77; with AID, Dept. of Interior, Exec. Office of Pres., 1977-80; state energy dir. Fla. Gov. and U.S. Senator Bob Graham, 1980-93; adminstr. Energy Info. Adminstrn., U.S. Dept. Energy, Washington, 1993-2000; dir. Jimmy Carter Presdl. Libr. and Mus., Atlanta, 2000—. Office: Jimmy Carter Presdl Libr and Mus 441 Freedom Pky NE Atlanta GA 30307-1498 Office Phone: 404-865-7100. E-mail: jay.hakes@nara.gov.*

HAKIM, BESIM SELIM, architecture and urban design educator, researcher, consultant, urban planner; b. Paris, July 31, 1938; came to U.S., 1978; s. Selim D. and Meliha M. (Yamulki) H.; children: Omar, Lena, Sara, Malak. BArch, Liverpool U., Eng., 1962; MArch in Urban Design, Harvard U., 1971. Registered architect, Ariz. Asst. prof. Tech. U. of Nova Scotia, Halifax, Can., 1967-74, assoc. prof., 1974-80, adj. rsch. prof., 1980-83; adj. assoc. prof. U. N.Mex., Albuquerque, 1982-83; assoc. prof. King Fahd U. of Petroleum and Minerals, Dhahran, Saudi Arabia, 1984-85; assoc. prof. Coll. of Architecture and Planning King Faisal U., Dammam, Saudi Arabia, 1985-93. Ind. scholar, 1994—; vis. prof. McGill U., Montreal, 1974, Tech. Inst. Architecture and Urbanism, Tunis, Tunisia, 1975, King Saud U., Riyadh, Saudi Arabia, 1982, 87, 89, 92, MIT, 1977; vis. scholar MIT, 1981, Cornell U., 1995; architect, engr. King Khaled Internat. Airport, Riyadh, Saudi Arabia, 1983-84; cons. in field; lectr. in field. Prin. works include urban design downtown Halifax, N.S., Coors Corridor Study, Albuquerque, Hist. Old Town, Albuquerque, revitalization of Old Muharraq, Bahrain, 11 custom-built houses, 8-story office bldg., hosp. renovations/additions, apt. bldgs. and a religious facility, U.S., Can., Mid-East; author: Arabic-Islamic Cities: Building and Planning Principles, 1986, 2d edit., 1988, Japanese edit., 1990, Farsi edit., 2002; contbr. articles to profl. jours. Recipient citation for rsch. Progressive Architecture, 1987, Edn. Honors award AIA, 1990, Initiative for Architectural Rsch., 2002. Fellow Am. Inst. Cert. Planners; mem. AIA, Am. Planning Assn., Middle East Studies Assn. N.Am. E-mail: arcan@sprynet.com.

HAKIM-ELAHI, ENAYAT, obstetrician, gynecologist, educator; b. Teheran, Iran, Nov. 23, 1934; came to U.S., 1959, naturalized, 1973; s. Mohamed-Ali and Masoomeh Rahimi; MD, Med. Sch., Teheran, 1959; lic. physician, Maine, Conn., Vt., N.Y., N.H., Calif.; diplomate Am. Bd. Ob-Gyn. m. Renate Emsters, Nov. 15, 1967; 1 child, Cristina. Intern, Queens Hosp. Ctr., N.Y.C., 1960, resident in internal medicine, 1961, resident in ob-gyn, 1961-64, resident in radiotherapy of gynecologic cancer, Am. Cancer Soc. fellow Queens divsn., 1965; resident in gynecology Cancer Rsch. Inst., Columbia-Presbyn. Med. Ctr., N.Y.C., 1964-65; practice medicine specializing in ob-gyn, N.Y.C., 1968—; mem. staff N.Y. Hosp., N.Y.C.; med. dir. Margaret Sanger Ctr., N.Y.C., 1973—, Planned Parenthood of N.Y.C., 1977-96, v.p. for med. and clin. affairs, 1996—; LaGuardia Hosp., Forest Hills, 1993-95; asst. prof. ob-gyn Cornell U. Med. Coll., N.Y.C., 1973—, assoc. prof., 1995—; dir. dept. of ob-gyn LaGuardia Hosp., 1990-95, med. dir., 1993-95; dir. dept of ob-gyn Harlem Hosp. Ctr., 1995-97; med. dir., dir. Ob-Gyn. Choices Med. Ctr. Served with U.S. Army, 1965-67. Fellow ACS, Am. Coll. Ob-Gyn., Internat. Coll. Surgeons, Am. Fertility Soc.; mem. APHA, Am. Soc. Gynecol. Laparoscopists, Am. Soc. Colposcopy and Cervical Neoplasia, Am. Coll. Physician Execs., Assn. of Reproductive Health Profls., Royal Soc. Medicine (London), World Med. Assn., N.Y. State Med. Soc., Queens Gynecol. Soc. Contbr. articles to profl. jours.

HAKIMOGLU, AYHAN, electronics executive; b. Erbaa, Turkey, Aug. 19, 1928; came to U.S., 1955; s. Mekki and Mediha H.; children by previous marriage: Zeynep B., Incigul R. O'Brien, Deborah A. Cueto, Leyla P.; m. Rachida Elmir, July 12, 1997; 1 child, Ayhan, Jr. BSEE, Robert Coll., Istanbul, 1949; MSEE, U. Cin., 1950. Founder, pres., chmn. bd. Dynaplex Corp., Princeton, NJ, 1962-67; gen. mgr. Teledyne Telemetry Co., Los Angeles, 1966-67; founder, chmn. bd., pres. Aydin Corp., Horsham, Pa., 1967-96. Cons. Aydin Corp., Plymouth Meeting, Pa.; investor. Served to lt. Turkish Army, 1951-52. Named Turkish Am. of Yr. Assembly Turkish Am. Assn., 1985; recipient Outstanding Pub. Svc. award, Assembly Turkish Am. Assns., 1988, 89, Disting. Alumni award U. Cin., 1991. Muslim.

HAKKI, AYESHA, editor-in-chief; BA in Journalism & Mass Media, Rutgers U. Asst. editor Men's Club mag., Pakistan; editor NJ Goodlife/Home Design mag., Ladies Home Journal, NYC, photo editor, special interest pub.; art dir. Jupiter Comm., NYC, Compaq Computer Corp., Houston; founder Alias Art, NYC; now editor & publisher Bibi Mag., Hoboken, NJ. Recipient Achievement award, Asia Houston Network, Bronze medal, Art Dirs. Club, Golden Web award, 2003. Office: Bibi Mag 66 Willow Ave Hoboken NJ 07030

HAKKINEN, RAIMO JAAKKO, aerospace scientist; b. Helsinki, Feb. 26, 1926; came to U.S., 1949, naturalized, 1960; s. Jalmari and Lyyli (Mattila) H.; m. Pirkko Loyttyniemi, July 16, 1949 (dec. Jan. 2004); children: Bert, Mark Diploma in Aero. Engring., Helsinki U. Tech., 1948, DSc (hon.) in Tech., 1998; MS, Calif. Inst. Tech., 1950, PhD cum laude, 1954. Head tech. office Finnish Aero. Assn., Helsinki, 1948; instr. engring. Tampere Tech. Coll., Finland, 1949; design engr., aircraft div. Valmet Corp., Tampere, 1949; research asst. Calif. Inst. Tech., 1950-53; mem. research staff MIT, 1953-56; aerodynamics engr. Western div. McDonnell Douglas Astronautics Co., Santa Monica, Calif., 1956-64, chief scientist phys. scis. dept., 1964-70; chief scientist flight scis. McDonnell Douglas Research Labs., St. Louis, 1970-82, dir. research, flight scis., 1982-90; prof. mech. engring., dir. fluid mechanics lab. Washington U., St. Louis, 1991—. Lectr. engring. UCLA, 1957-59; vis. assoc. prof. aeros. and astronautics MIT, 1963-64; cons., 1990—. Contbr. articles to profl. jours. Served with Finnish Air Force, 1944 Fellow AIAA (mem. fluid dynamics com. 1969-71, honors and awards com. 1975-83, tech. activities com. 1975-78, dir. at large 1977-70); mem. Am. Phys. Soc., Engring. Soc. in Finland, Calif. Inst. Tech. Alumni Assn., Sigma Xi. Home: 5 Old Colony Ln Saint Louis MO 63131-1509 Office: Washington U Campus Box 1185 1 Brookings Dr Saint Louis MO 63130-4899 Office Phone: 314-935-4084. Personal E-mail: rjhakkinen@att.net.

HAKOSHIMA, SHIN-ICHI, publishing executive; b. Dec. 9, 1937; Grad., Kyushu U., 1962. With Asahi Shimbun, 1962—, assoc. editor econ. news dept., 1979-84, econ. editor, Nagoya Head Office, 1985-86, econ. editor Tokyo Head Office, 1987-89, dep. mng. editor Nagoya Head Office, 1990-91, mng. editor Seibu Head Office, 1991, mng. editor Tokyo Head Office, 1992-93, mng dir., adminstrn., 1996-97, mng. dir., CEO, 1998, sr. mng. dir., COO, 1998, pres., CEO, 1999—2005, non-exec. advisor, 2005—. Chmn. Japan Newspaper Publishers & Editors Assn., 2003—05. Office: The Asahi Shimbun Co 5-3-2 Tsukiji Chuo-ku Tokyo 104-11 Japan

HALABE, UDAYA BHATTA, civil engineering educator, researcher; b. Kathmandu, Nepal, Nov. 19, 1961; arrived in US, 1985, naturalized; s. Gangadhar Bhatta and Shailaja Bhatta H.; m. Anjali Marathe; children: Esha Bhatta H., Shivali Bhatta H. BE in Civil Engring., U. Roorkee, India, 1984; M in Tech. (Civil Engring.), Indian Inst. Tech., Kanpur, India, 1985; MS in Civil Engring., MIT, 1988, MS in Mgmt., 1990, PhD in Civil Engring., 1990. Registered profl. engr., W. Va. Asst. prof. W.Va. U., Morgantown, 1990-96, assoc. prof., 1996-2001, prof., 2001—. Contbr. numerous articles to profl. jours. and conf. proceedings, over 90 sci. papers, over 35 rsch. reports. Mem. ASCE, Am. Concrete Inst., Am. Soc. for Nondestructive Testing. Hindu. Avocations: walking, reading, tennis, swimming. Home: 1504 Foxtrot Dr Morgantown WV 26508-9175 Office: W Va U PO Box 6103 Engring Sci Bldg Rm #645 Morgantown WV 26506-6103 Office Phone: 304-293-3031. Business E-Mail: uhalabe@alum.mit.edu.

HALABY, NOELLE M., lawyer; BA, UCLA, 1993; JD, Southwestern Univ., 1996. Bar: Calif., US Dist. Ct. (ctrl. dist.) Calif., US Ct. Appeals (9th cir.), cert.: family law specialist, Calif. Ptnr. Moore, Halaby & Associates, Pasadena, Calif.; assoc. Lisa Helfend Meyer & Associates, Century City, Calif.; prin., family law private practice Glendale, Calif., 2003—. Family Law Judge Pro Tem LA Superior Ct., mediator, Family Law dept. Named a Rising Star, So. Calif. Super Lawyers, 2006. Mem.: State Bar Calif., LA County Bar Assn., Beverly Hills Bar Assn., Century City Bar Assn., Calif. Assn. Family Law Specialists, Woman Lawyers LA, Am. Bus. Women Assn. Office: Noelle M Halaby Ste 200 130 N Brand Blvd Glendale CA 91203 Office Phone: 818-502-3939. Office Fax: 818-502-3999. Business E-Mail: noelle@noellehalaby.com.

HALABY, SAMIA ASAAD, painter, educator, writer; b. Jerusalem, Palestine, Dec. 12, 1936; d. Asaad Saba and Foutounie Assad (Atallah) H. BS in Design, U. Cin., 1959; MA in Painting, Mich. State U., 1960; MFA in Painting, Ind. U., 1963. Teaching asst. Ind. U., Bloomington, 1962-63, assoc. prof., 1969-72; instr. U. Hawaii, Honolulu, 1963-64, vis. lectr., summer 1966; asst. prof. Kansas City (Mo.) Art Inst., 1964-66, U. Mich., 1967-69; vis. lectr. art Yale U., 1972-73, assoc. prof., 1973-76, adj. assoc. prof., 1976-82. Lectr. in field; vis. prof. U. Hawaii, Honolulu, 1985-86, U. South Fla., 1990; adj. instr. Cooper Union, 1989-92; artist-in-residence Tamarind Lithography Workshop, Albuquerque, 1972; presenter 4th Internat. Symposium on Electronic Art, Mpls., 1993, 7th symposium, Rotterdam, 1996. One-artist shows include Gima Gallery, Honolulu, 1964, The Gallery, Bloomington, 1970, Phyllis Kind Gallery, Chgo., 1971, Yale Sch. Art Gallery, 1972, Spectrum Gallery, N.Y.C., 1973, Marilyn Pearl Gallery, N.Y.C., 1978, 22 Wooster Gallery, 1982, 83, Tossan-Tossan Gallery, N.Y.C., 1983, 88, Housatonic Mus., Bridgeport, 1983, Galaria de arte Palace, Granada, Spain, 1986, Gallery II U. Mich., Kalamazoo, 1989, 911 Gallery, Indpls., 1993, Darat Al-Funun, Amman, Jordan, 1995, Galerie Atassi, Damascus, Syria, 1997, Galerie Le Porte, Halab, Syria, 1997, Agial Gallery, Beirut, 1999, 2004, SKOTO Gallery, N.Y.C., 2000, Sakakini Art Ctr., Ramallah, Palestine, 2000, Artim Gallery, Strasbourg, France, 2001, Kahaf Gallery, Internat. Ctr. Bethlehem, 2004, Agial Gallery, Beirut, 2004; group shows include Solomon R. Guggenheim Mus., N.Y.C., 1975, Susan Caldwell Gallery, N.Y.C., 1977, Iraqi Cultural Ctr., London, 1979, Kunsternes Hus, Oslo, Norway, 1981, U. Art Mus., N.Mex., 1985, Hudson Ctr. Gallery, N.Y.C., 1985, Tercera Bienal de la Habana, Cuba, 1989, Prix Ars Electronica, Linz, Austria, 1990, Art and Algorithm, Mpls. Coll. Art, 1991, Hilo Internat. Exhbn. of Works on Paper, U. Hawaii, 1990, Digitized and Manipulated, Sangre De Cristo Arts Ctr., Pueblo, Colo., 1991, opening exhbn. Darat Al Funun of Shoman Found., Amman, Jordan, 1993, Fourth Internat. Symposium Electronic Art, Mpls., 1993, Arab Women, Nat. Mus. Women in the Arts, Washington, 1994, World Artist at the Millennium, Elizabeth Found., UN Lobby, 1999, Bradley U., Ill., 2001, Musee du Chateau DuFresne, Montreal, 2001, 13th Afro-Asian L.Am. exhbn. Tokyo Met. Mus. 2002, Williamsburg Bridges Palestine, WAH Ctr., Bklyn., Sta. Mus., Houston, 2003, 05, Chikyudo Gallery, Tokyo, 2004, 4 Walls Gallery, Amman, Jordan, 2005, The Bridge GAllery, N.Y., 2006; performance art (computer abstractions) Bklyn. Mus., 1994, Poetry Project, N.Y.C., 1995, Lebanese Am. U., Beirut, 1995, HERE, N.Y.C., 1996; represented in permanent collections Solomon R. Guggenheim Mus., Inst. Du Monde Arab, Paris, Indpls. Mus. Art, Art Inst. Chgo., Nelson Rockhill Gallery Art, Kansas City, Ind. U. Mus., Mich. State U. Mus., Ft. Wayne (Ind.) Mus. Art, Detroit Inst. Art, Cleve. Mus. Art, Cin. Art Mus., Nat. Gallery Jordan, Amman, Yale U. Gallery, Tamarind Inst. Collection, Albuquerque, Alternative Mus., N.Y., Honolulu Acad. Arts, Ind. U. Mus., Bloomington, Mead Art Mus., Amherst, Conn., Palm Springs (Calif.) Desert Mus., Yale U. Gallery, New Haven, The Jane Voorhees Zimmerli Art Museum, New Brunswick, N.J., corp. collections, U.S. Steel, ATT Longlines, First Nat. Chgo, Kemper Ins. Chgo., S.E. Banking Corp. Fla., Witko Chem. Corp., Standard Oil Ohio, IBM, Arab Bank; author: Liberation Art of Palestine, 2003; contbr. articles to profl. jours.; subject of book Samia A. Halaby, 2007. Subject of Profl. Publs.; Kansas City Coun. for Faculty Devel. traveling fellow, 1965; Creative Artists Pub. Svc. Program grantee, 1978-79, UN grant UNDP cons., 1999. Studio: PO Box 965 New York NY 10013-0861 Personal E-mail: sahalaby@yahoo.com.

HALADA, RICHARD STEPHEN, physics educator; b. NY, Aug. 5, 1954; m. Barbara Kemp, June 7, 1980; children: Elizabeth, John. BS in Physics, SUNY, Stony Brook, 1976; MS in Geology and Geophysics, U. Hawaii-Manoa, Honolulu, 1978. Cert. secondary tchr. in math. and physics. Sr. geophysicist Mobil Oil, Dallas, 1978-81, Hunt Energy, Dallas, 1981-84, Arco Oil and Gas, Midland, Tex., 1984-86; tchr. Dallas Ind. Sch. Dist., 1986-88; sci. asst. Weckerling Sci. Labs., Dallas, 1988-89; tchr. Richardson (Tex.) Ind. Sch. Dist., 1989-96, Garland (Tex.) Ind. Sch. Dist., 1996—. Coach/sponsor Jr. Engring. Tech. Soc., Richardson and Garland, 1993-97, Odyssey of the Mind, Richardson, 1992-94; mem. textbook selection com. Richardson Ind. Sch. Dist., 1993, Garland Ind. Sch. Dist., 1997. Contbr. articles to The Physics Tchr. Mem. Am. Assn. Petroleum Geologists, Am. Geophys. Union, Soc. Physics Students, Mensa. Avocations: reading, camping.

HALAGAO, AVELINO GARABILES, lawyer; b. Santa Lucia, Ilocos Sur, The Philippines, Nov. 4, 1938; came to U.S., 1972; s. Manuel Habon and Marciana Garabiles H.; m. Concepcion Lorenzana Jimeno, aug. 1, 1962; children: Jesus Michael, Arleen Bernadette, Avelino Jr., Anna Maria, Amanda Marie. LLB, San Beda Coll. Law, Manila, 1962; M in Comparative Law, George Washington U., 1986. Bar: Va. 1987, D.C. 1992, The Philippines 1963. Ptnr. Bello, Halagao & Pimentel, Manila, 1963-65; atty. Commn. on Elections, Manila, 1965-70; judge Republic of The Philippines, Manila, 1970-72; trust officer Nat. Bank Washington, 1973-87; assoc. Coates & Davenport, McLean, Va., 1987-88; mng. ptnr. Avelino G. Halagao & Assocs., Tysons Corner, Va., 1989—. Pres., chmn. bd. dirs. Manuel H. Halagao & Sons Transp. Co., Manila, 1968-72; chmn. bd. dirs. QX, Inc., Washington, 1995-97. Mem. Philippine-Am. Bar Assn. (founder, treas. 1976-78, pres. 1984-85, Leadership and Disting. Membership award 1990), Ilocano Soc. Am. (co-founder, pres. 1983-84). Roman Catholic. Avocations: basketball, golf, fishing, dance, singing. Office: Avelino G Halagao Associates 3311 Cullers Ct Woodbridge VA 22192-1086

HALAMA, NIELS, physician, researcher; b. Göttingen, Germany, Aug. 6, 1977; s. Klaus and Erika Halama; m. Silke Grauling-Halama. Gen. qualification for univ. entrance, Goethe Gymnasium, Bensheim, 1997; MD, U. Heidelberg, Germany, 2005. Vis. med. student Tex. Heart Inst., Houston, 2002; final yr. trainee Med. U. of Ohio, Toledo, 2005; resident internal medicine Nat. Ctr. for Tumor Diseases, Heidelberg, Germany, 2006—. Editor: Medicle, 2004—, author poetry. Group leader YMCA, Bickenbach, Germany, 1995—2001. Scholar, Studienstiftung des deutschen Volkes, 1980. Achievements include research in Characterization of a novel genetic syndrom with abdominal benign tumors; Characterization of candidate genes for diabetic nephropathy; development of Bioinformatical software for the analysis of gene-structure. Avocations: canoeing, piano, guitar. Home: Im Schecken 33 Hessen Seeheim-Jugenheim 64342 Germany Home Phone: 49-6257-690493; Office Phone: 49-06221-5638397. Personal E-mail: nhalama@gmx.net.

HALAMKA, JOHN D., emergency physician, information technology executive; b. Des Moines, May 1962; BS in Med. Microbiology (with distinction), Stanford U., 1984, BA in Pub. Policy (with distinction), 1984; student in Bioengineering, U. Calif. Berkeley, 1986—89; MD, U. Calif., San Francisco, 1993; MS in Med. Informatics, Harvard/MIT Health Sci. and Tech., 1997. Lic. Calif., 1994, Mass., 1996, Bd. Cert. Emergency Medicine, 1997. Intern, emergency medicine Harbor-UCLA, 1993—94, resident, emergency medicine, 1994—96; Douglas P. Porter Informatics Fellow, Ctr. for Clin. Computing Harvard Med. Sch., Boston, 1996—97; CEO Ibis Rsch. Labs, Calif., 1981—92; assoc. in medicine, attending physician, divsn. Emergency Med. Beth Israel Deaconess Med. Ctr., Boston, 1996—, chief info. officer; exec. dir. Ctr. for Quality and Value CareGroup Health Sys., Boston, 1997—99, chief info. officer, 1998—; co-founder & chmn. New England Health Electronic Data Interchange Network, 1999—; instr. in Med. Harvard Med. Sch., Boston, 1996—99, asst. prof. of Med., 2000—, assoc. dean for ednl. tech., 2000—, chief info. officer, Ctr. for. Clin. Computing, Harvard Med. Sch., Boston, Harvard Clin. Rsch. Inst., 2001—. Mem., rsch. com. Stanford U., 1980—84; mem. Ctr. for Disease Control and Prevention Nat. Working Group on the Electronic Emergency Dept. Record, 1996; advisor, Tri-State Tech. Adv. Group on Clin. Data Security and Confidentiality Robert Wood Johnson Found., 1997, advisor, Five State Project on Healthcare Security, 2000; co-chair Med. Intranet Forum, 1998—2000; cons. Nat. Libr. Medicine Informatics Tng. Grant Study Sect., 2001; mem., clin. data working group Mass. Health Data Consortium, 1997, mem., CIO Forum, 1998—; mem. Mass. Adminstrv. Task Force, 2000; mem., caregroup emergency medicine computing group Beth Israel Deaconess Med. Ctr., 1996—97, co-chair, emergency dept. quality improvement task force, 1997—98; co-chair, physician computer com. Harbor-UCLA Med. Ctr., 1993—96, mem., adult emergency dept. coun., 1993—94; adj. faculty Ctr. for Clin. Computing, Harvard Med. Sch.; tech. cons. for several start-up companies; bd. dir. Epocrates, San Mateo, Calif., 2005—. Author of three books on tech. related issues; columnist Infoworld, tech. editor Computer Language Mag., 1984—87. Recipient Phi Beta Kappa, 1983, Sigma Pi Alpha, 1984, commendation for svc., LA County Bd. of Supervisors, 1996, Martin J. Epstein award, Am. Med. Informatics Assn., 1997, Best Presentation award, Nat. Libr. Medicine, 1997, numerous tech. innovation awards, PC Week, Info. Week, Ernst and Young. Mem.: Am. Med. Informatics Assn., Soc. for Acad. Emergency Med., Am. Coll. of Emergency Physicians. Office: Harvard Med Sch CareGroup Health 6th fl 1135 Tremont St Boston MA 02120 also: Harvard Med Sch Gordon Hall 25 Shattuck St Boston MA 02115

HALAS, CYNTHIA ANN, business information specialist; b. Norristown, Pa., July 24, 1961; d. George and Maria (Mitrik) H. Student, Temple U., 1979-80; AS in Bus. Adminstrn., Montgomery County Coll., Blue Bell, Pa., 1993; student, Springhouse Computer Sch., Exton, Pa., 1994-95. Columnist, corr. The Recorder, Conshohocken, Pa., 1980-81; claims supr. Liberty Mut. Ins. Co., Blue Bell, 1980-84; claims svc. rep. Met. Property & Liability Ins. Co., Wayne, Pa., 1984-87; model Frank James Assocs., Phila., 1986-87; auditor/tng. coord. Coresource, Inc., Wayne, 1987-94; sys. support analyst Del. Valley Fin. Svcs., Inc., Berwyn, Pa., 1994-95; sys. support coord. Aetna Inc., Blue Bell, Pa., 1995—2007, BWD Agy., Blue Bell, 2007—. Active Nat. Arbor Day Found. Mem. NAFE, U.S. Fencing Assn. Byzantine Catholic. Avocations: golf, fencing, horseback riding, needlepoint, travel. Office: BWD Agy 980 Harvest Dr Ste 205 Blue Bell PA 19422-1959

HALAS, PAUL ANTHONY, JR., business appraisal and valuation specialist, consultant; b. Chgo., June 27, 1933; s. Paul Aloysius and Elonia Bernidene (Zelinski) H.; m. Shirley Donna Willis, Aug. 17, 1957 (dec.); children: Julie, Vickie, Jon, Carl, Jim; m. Nina Romanenko, Feb. 19, 2000. Student, Columbia Sch. Broadcasting, 1951-53, Northwestern U., 1957-59; MBA, Brunswick U., Laurel, Md., 1983. Cert. mgmt. cons., N.Y. Rep. Solar Chgo. divsn. USI's, 1957-60; rep. J. W. Bolton, Inc., Lawrence, Mass., 1960-62; gen. sales mgr. Schimanek, Internat., Chgo., 1962-63; v.p. mktg. Products Engring. Co., Tinley Park, Ill., 1963-68; gen. sales mgr. Vacudyne Corp., Chicago Heights, Ill., 1968-70; mktg. mgr. Fastron Co., Franklin Park, Ill., 1970-72, Scandura, Inc., Charlotte, NC, 1972-78; mgmt. cons. Halas & Assocs., Charlotte, 1978-85, valuation specialist, 1985—. Contbr. numerous articles on bus. valuation and appraisal. Recipient Printed award Grain Age Mag., 1976. Mem. BBB, ASME (coord. ANSI A90 com. 1974-77), Nat. Ctr. for Employee Ownership, Inst. Bus. Appraisers, Inst. Mgmt. Cons., Charlotte C. of C. Green Party. Roman Catholic. Avocations: music, photography, travel. Office: Halas & Assocs 425 Roselawn Pl Charlotte NC 28211-4162 Office Phone: 704-364-4440. E-mail: hbvs@halas.com.

HALASKA, TERRELL L., federal agency administrator; BA, U. Calif. San Diego; MA, Monterey Inst. Press sec. to Congressman Scott Klug; dir. Washington Office for State of Wis., Office of Gov. Tommy Thompson, Wis.; dep. chief of staff US Dept. Health & Human Svcs., Washington; spl. asst. to Pres. for domestic policy The White House, Washington, 2003—05; asst. sec. edn. for legislation & congl. affairs US Dept. Edn., Washington, 2005—. Office: US Dept Edn 400 Maryland Ave SW Rm 6W315 Washington DC 20202-1510 Office Phone: 202-401-0020. Office Fax: 202-401-1438.*

HALASYAMANI, P. SHIV, inorganic chemist, researcher; b. Calicut, India, Mar. 6, 1970; came to U.S., 1971; s. Paramasiva and Premalatha (Nagarajan) H. BS in Chemistry with honors, U. Chgo., 1992; PhD in Inorganic Chemistry, Northwestern U., 1996. Postdoctoral assoc. U. Oxford, U.K., 1997-98, jr. rsch. fellow Christ Church, 1998—. Recipient Young Scientist award Internat. Union Crystallography, 1995.

HALASZ, STEPHEN JOSEPH, retired electro-optical systems engineer; b. Eger-Csehi, Hungary; s. Sandor and Ilona (Huszák) H.; children: Stephen S., Christopher L. Jacqueline R. BS, Columbia U., 1955. Project engr. GE Co., Utica, NY, 1956—58; sr. physicist Avion divsn. ACF Industries, Paramus, NJ, 1958—65; head IR and Display Lab. Aerojet Gen., 1965—72; sr. specialist Xerox Electro-Optical, Pasadena, Calif., 1972—75, Ford Aeronutronic, Newport Beach, Calif., 1975—83; chief scientist Hughes Aircraft, El Segundo, Calif., 1983—92. Contbg. author: (handbook) IR Handbook, 1969. With U.S. Army, 1945. Achievements include numerous designs and research projects including optical guidance for satellite interception; IR moving target tracker; handheld thermal imager; scanned matrix for IR pattern recognition; high speed target acquisition with fused sensors; others; patentee in field.

HALBACH, EDWARD CHRISTIAN, JR., law educator; b. Clinton, Iowa, Nov. 8, 1931; s. Edward Christian and Lewella (Sullivan) H.; m. Janet Elizabeth Bridges, July 25, 1953; children: Kristin Lynn, Edward Christian III, Kathleen Ann, Thomas Elliot, Elaine Diane. BA, U. Iowa, 1953, JD, 1958; LLM, Harvard U., 1959; LLD, U. Redlands, 1973. Assoc. prof. Sch. Law, U. Calif., Berkeley, 1959-62, prof., 1963—, dean, 1966-75. Co-author: Materials on Decedents' Estates and Trusts, 1965, 73, 81, 87, 93, 2000, 06, Materials on Future Interests, 1977, Death, Taxes and Family Property, 1977, California Will Drafting, 1965, 77, 92; author: Use of Trusts in Estate Planning, 1975, 81, 84, 86, 91, Fundamentals of Estate Planning, 1983, 86, 87, 89, 91, 93, 95, Summary of the Law of Trusts, 1990, 1998, 2004, 07, Principles and Techniques of Estate Planning, 1995; reporter Uniform Probate Code, 1969, Restatement 3d Trusts Prudent Investor Rule, 1992, Restatement of Law of Trusts, vols. 1 and 2, 2003, vol. 3, 2007; also articles. 1st lt. USAF, 1954-56. Mem. ABA (chmn. various coms. sect. individual rights and responsibilities and sect. real property probate and trust law, dir. probate and trust divsn., sect. chmn.), Iowa Bar Assn., Am. Law Inst. (reporter Restatement 3d Trusts, advisor Restatement 2d, 3d Property), Am. Acad. Polit. and Social Scis., Am. Bar Found., Am.

Coll. Trust and Estate Counsel, Am. Coll. Tax Counsel, Internat. Acad. Estate and Trust Law (v.p., exec. com., pres.). Home: 679 San Luis Rd Berkeley CA 94707-1725 Office: U Calif Sch Law Boalt Hall Berkeley CA 94720

HALBERG, CHARLES JOHN AUGUST, JR., mathematics professor; b. Pasadena, Calif., Sept. 24, 1921; s. Charles John August and Anne Louise (Hansen) Halberg; m. Ariel Arfon Oliver, Nov. 1, 1941 (div. July 1969); children: Ariel Walters, Charles Thomas, Niels Frederick; m. Barbro Linnea Samuelsson, Aug. 18, 1970 (dec. Jan. 1978); 1 stepchild, Ulf Erik Hjelm; m. Betty Reese Zimprich, July 27, 1985. BA summa cum laude, Pomona Coll., Claremont, Calif., 1949; MA (William Lincoln Honnold fellow), UCLA, 1953, PhD, 1955. Instr. math. Pomona Coll., Claremont, Calif., 1949-50; assoc. math. UCLA, 1954-55; instr. math. U. Calif.-Riverside, 1955-56, asst. prof. math., 1956-61, assoc. prof. math., 1961-68, prof. math., 1968—, vice chancellor student affairs, 1964-65. Dir. Scandinavian Study Ctr. Lund U., Sweden, 1976—78; docent U. Goteborg, Sweden, 1969—70; bd. dirs. Fulbright Commn. Ednl. Exch. between U.S. and Sweden, 1976—79. Author (with John F. Devlin): Elementary Functions, 1967; author: (with Angus E. Taylor) Calculus with Analytic Geometry, 1969; author: Aftermath, 1996. With USAAF, 1945—46. NSF fellow, U. Copenhagen, 1961—62. Mem.: Swedish Math. Soc., Am. Math. Soc., Math. Assn. Am. (chmn. So. Calif. sect. 1964—65, gov. 1968), Phi Beta Kappa, Sigma Xi. Home: 2855 Carlsbad Blvd S 225 Carlsbad CA 92008 Personal E-mail: chalberg@roadrunner.com.

HALBERSTADTER, DAVID, lawyer; b. Elizabeth, NJ, Sept. 1, 1957; BA, Cornell U., 1979; JD magna cum laude, Georgetown U., 1982. Bar: Calif. 1982. Ptnr., co-chair entertainment and media practice Katten Muchin Rosenman LLP, L.A. Mem.: ABA, LA County Bar Assn., LA Copyright Soc. Office: Katten Muchin Rosenman LLP 2029 Century Park E STe 2600 Los Angeles CA 90067 Office Phone: 310-788-4408. Office Fax: 310-712-8481. E-mail: david.halberstadter@cattenlaw.com.

HALBERSTAM, HEINI, mathematics professor; b. Most, Czechoslovakia, Sept. 11, 1926; came to Eng., 1939, naturalized, 1998. s. Michael and Judith (Honig) H.; m. Heather M. Peacock, Mar. 11, 1950 (dec. 1971); children: Naomi Deborah, Judith Marion, Lucy Rebecca, Michael Welsford; m. Doreen Bramley, Sept. 28, 1972. BS with honours, Univ. Coll., London U., 1946, MS, 1948, PhD, 1952. Lectr. math. U. Exeter, 1949-57; reader Royal Holloway Coll., London U., 1957-62; Erasmus Smith prof. Trinity Coll., Dublin, Ireland, 1962-64; prof. Nottingham U., England, 1964-80; prof. math. U. Ill., Urbana-Champaign, 1980-96, prof. emeritus, 1996—. Vis. lectr. Brown U., 1955-56; vis. prof. U. Mich., 1966, U. Tel Aviv, 1973, U. Paris-South, 1972 Co-author: Sequences, 1966, 2d edit., 1983, Sieve Methods, 1975; co-editor math. papers of, W.R. Hamilton, H. Davenport; contbr. articles to profl. jours. Mem. London Math. Soc. (v.p. 1962-63, 74-77), Am. Math Soc. Business E-Mail: heini@math.uiuc.edu.

HALBERSTAM, MALVINA, lawyer, educator; b. Kempno, Poland, May 2, 1937; came to U.S., 1947; d. Marcus and Pearl (Halberstam) H.; m. Wolf Z. Guggenheim (dec. 2002); children: Arye, Achiezer. BA cum laude, Bklyn. Coll., 1957; JD, Columbia U., 1961, MIA, 1964. Bar: N.Y. 1962, U.S. Dist. Ct. (so. dist.) N.Y. 1963, U.S. Ct. Appeals (2d cir.) 1965, U.S. Supreme Ct. 1966, Calif. 1968. Law clk. Judge Edmund L. Palmieri Fed. Dist. Ct. (so. dist.) N.Y., 1961-62; rsch. assoc. Columbia Project on Internat. Procedure, 1962-63; asst. dist. atty. N.Y. County, 1963-67; with Rifkind & Sterling, LA, 1967-68; sr. atty. Nat. Legal Program on Health Problems of the Poor, LA, 1969-70; prof. Sch. Law Loyola U., LA, 1970-76; prof. Benjamin N. Cardozo Sch. Law Yeshiva U., NYC, 1976—. Vis. prof. Gould Law Ctr., U. So. Calif., L.A., 1972-73, U. Va. Sch. Law, 1975-76, U. Tex. Sch. Law, summer 1974, Hebrew U., Jerusalem, 1984-85; counselor on internat. law U.S. State Dept. Office of Legal Adviser, 1985-86; cons., 1986-92. Author (with De Feis): Women's Legal Rights: International Agreements An Alternative to ERA?, 1987; articles and rev. editor Columbia Law Rev., 1960—61, reporter Am. Law Inst. Model Penal Code Commentaries, 1977—81, mem. editl. bd. Jour. Nat. Security Law and Policy, 2005—; contbr. articles, commentary, book revs. to profl. jours. Mem. Bklyn. Coll. Alumni Adv. Bd. on Women's Career Devel. and Leadership Program.; adv. com. to standing com. on law and nat. security, ABA; study group on shape Arab-Israeli settlement, humanitarian, and demographic issues Coun. on Fgn. Rels. Kent scholar (2x); Stone scholar; recipient Jane Marks Murphy prize. Mem.: Am. Assn. Law Schs. (chair sect. internat. law 2002—03, co-vice chmn. sect. nat. security law 2003—04, co-chmn. elect nat. security law sect. 2004—05, mem. exec. com. 2005—), Am. Assn. Jewish Lawyers and Jurists (bd. govs.), Internat. Law Assn. (Am. br. exec. com., human rights com.), Assn. Bar City of N.Y. (coun. on internat. affairs 1998—2004), Am. Soc. Internat. Law, Am. Law Inst. (life), Columbia Law Sch. Alumni Assn., Phi Beta Kappa. Home: 160 Riverside Dr New York NY 10024-2106 Office: Benjamin N Cardozo Sch Law Yeshiva U 55 Fifth Ave New York NY 10003-4391 Office Phone: 212-790-0394. E-mail: halbrstm@yu.edu.

HALBERT, GARY L., lawyer; b. 1956; BS, US Air Force Acad.; JD, U. Tex., Austin. Bar: Tex. 1986, DC 2006. Dir. exec. issues Headquarters US Air Force, staff judge advocate, legal counsel to comdr. 3rd Air Force Mildenhall Royal Air Force Base, England, exec. asst. to air force judge advocate gen., sr. atty. and legal counsel to comdr. of Barksdale Air Force Base, chief counsel info. and privacy law Pentagon, chief counsel adminstrv. law; gen. counsel Nat. Transp. Safety Bd., Washington, 2006—. Office: Office of Gen Counsel Nat Transportation Safety Bd 490 L'Enfant Pl E SW Rm 6401 Washington DC 20594 Office Phone: 202-314-6080. Office Fax: 202-314-6090.

HALBREICH, KATHY, museum director; b. NYC, Apr. 24, 1949; d. Irwin and Betty Ann (Stoll) H.; m. John Kohring; 1 child, Henry. BA, Bennington Coll., 1971; postgrad., Skowhegan Sch. Painting and Sculpture, Maine, 1965, Am. U., Mexico City, 1966. Adminstr. spl. programs Bennington (Vt.) Coll., 1975-766; dir. teaching seminar Assn. Collegiate Schs. Architecture, Washington, 1977; v.p. programs, trustee Artist Found., Boston, 1979-84; dir. com. on visual arts Hayden Gellery, List Visual Arts Ctr., MIT, Cambridge, Mass., 1976-86; ind. curatorial cons., 1986-88; curator contemporary art Mus. Fine Arts, Boston, 1988-90; dir. Walker Art Ctr., Mpls., 1991—. Cons. St. Louis Art Mus., Artists Space, N.Y.C., Capp St. Project, San Francisco, Mus. Modern Art, N.Y.C., Seattle Arts Commn., Southeastern Ctr. for Contemporary Art, Louis Comfort Tiffany Found., Beacon Cos., Frito-Lay Inc., New Eng. Gen. Svcs. Adminstrn. Art-in-Architecture Program, Nat. Endowment for Arts, VA Art-in-Architecture Program; trustee MA Coun. on the arts and Humanities; advisor Pub. Art Policy Project and Publ., Nat. Endowment for Arts, 1987; mem. nat. com. P!ub. Art in Am. Conf., Phila., 1987. Trustee Twin Cities Pub. TV, 1992. Mem. Assn. Art Mus. Dirs., Andy Warhol Found. for Visual Arts Inc. (bd. dirs. 1992), Mpls. Club. Named to Centennial Honor Roll, Am. Assn. Museums, 2006. Office: Walker Art Ctr 1750 Hennepin Ave Minneapolis MN 55403-1138

HALBREICH, URIEL MORAV, psychiatrist, educator; b. Jerusalem, Nov. 23, 1943; arrived in U.S., 1978, naturalized, 1982; s. Mordechai and Zipora (Tennenbaum) H.; m. Judith Thadine, 1987; children: Jasmine, Bethany. MD, Hebrew U., 1969. Diplomate Tel Aviv U. Psychiatry and Psychotherapy. Intern gen. medicine Hadassah U. Hosp., Jerusalem, 1968; comdr., vice-chief med. officer Israeli Navy, 1970—72, chief psychiatrist, 1977—78; resident, 2d then 1st asst. Hadassah Hosp. Hebrew U., Jerusalem, 1972—78; temp. chief physician Hadassah U. Hosp., Jerusalem, 1978; asst. prof., rsch. psychiatrist Columbia U., NYC, 1978—80; assoc. prof., dir. divsn. biol. psychiatry Albert Einstein Coll. Medicine, NYC, 1982—85; prof. psychiatry, dir. biobehavioral rsch. SUNY, Buffalo, 1985—, prof. ob-gyn., 1988—; pres., CEO Incline Read. Vis. prof. Harvard U., 1996-98, exec. cons. dept. psychiatry, 1998-2001; chmn. 1st Internat. Congress on Hormones, Brain and Neuropsychopharmacology, 1993, chmn. sect. on interdisciplinary collaboration World Psychiat. Assn., 1997—, others; chmn. 2d Congress on Hormones, Brain and Neuropsychopharmacology, 2000; chmn. bd. dirs. Internat. Inst. Edn. in Mental Health and Psychopharmacology, 1997-2006; cons. in field. Editor: Transient Psychosis, 1983, Resistance to Treatment with Antidepressant Drugs, 1986, Hormones and Depression, 1987, Multiple Sclerosis: A Neuropsychiatric Disorder, 1992, Psychopharmacology of Women, 1996, Psychiatric Issues in Women, 1996, Training in Psychiatry and Psychopharmacology, 1998, Psychopharmacology of Mood Anxiety and Cognition, 2000, Psychiatry and the Law in Eastern Europe, 2000, Womens Mental Health, 2002; contbr. articles to profl. jours., chpts. to books. Recipient Ben Gurion award Gen. Fedn. Labor, 1976, Yair Gon award Hebrew U. Hadassah Med. Sch., 1978, Nat. Rsch. Svc. award NIH, 1978, Svc. award Internat. Soc. Psychoneuroendocrinology, 2003; grantee NIMH, 1982—. Fellow: Am. Coll. Psychiatrists, Am. Psychiat. Assn. (disting.), Coll. Internat. Neuropsychopharmacology (co-chmn. edn. com. 1994—96), Am. Coll. Neuropsychopharmacology (chmn. rules and constitution com. 1996), Am. Psychopathology Assn.; mem.: Hormones, Brain and Neuropsychopharmacology (pres.), Endocine Soc., Assn. Med. Psychiatry (chmn. edn. com. 1992—96, councilor 1992—96), Soc. Biol. Psychiatry (chmn. program com. 1992—93), Am. Coll. Psychiatrists, Internat. Assn. Women's Mental Health (pres. 2001—04), Internat. Soc. Psychol. Neurol. Endocrinology (chmn. 21st congress 1990, pres. 1999—2002). Jewish. Office: SUNY Sch Med & Biomed Hayes C Ste 1 3435 Main St Bldg 5 Buffalo NY 14214-3016 Office Phone: 716-829-3808. Business E-Mail: urielh@buffalo.edu.

HALDANE, F(REDERICK) DUNCAN M(ICHAEL), physics educator; b. London, Sept. 14, 1951; came to U.S., 1981; BA, Cambridge U., Eng., 1973, PhD in Physics, 1978. Physicist Inst. Laue-Langevin, Grenoble, France, 1977-81; asst. prof. physics U. So. Calif., LA, 1981-85; mem. tech. staff AT&T Bell Labs., Murray Hill, N.J., 1985-87; prof. physics U. Calif., San Diego, 1987-90, Princeton (N.J.) U., 1990—, Eugene Higgins Prof., 1999—. Trustee Aspen (Colo.) Ctr. for Physics, 1985-90, mem. adv. bd., 1990-1999. Contbr. articles to profl. jours. Alfred P. Sloan Found. fellow, 1984-88. Fellow AAAS, Am. Phys. Soc. (Oliver E. Buckley Condensed Matter Physics prize 1993), Am. Acad. Arts and Scis., Royal Soc. London, Inst. Physics, Eng. Achievements include research in theoretical condensed matter physics; contributions to the understanding of quantum magnetism and the fractional quantum Hall effect. Office: Princeton U Dept of Physics 327 Jadwin Hall Princeton NJ 08544-0708 Office Fax: 609-258-1006.

HALDEMAN, ED (CHARLES EDGAR HALDEMAN JR.), investment company executive; b. Phila., Oct. 29, 1948; s. Charles E. and Betty Jane (Adams) H.; m. Barbara Chow, June 10, 1974; children: Matthew Adams, Charlotte Elisse, Catherine Jane. AB, Dartmouth Coll., 1970; MBA, JD, Harvard U., 1974. Bar: Pa. 1974; cert. fin. analyst. Ptnr., dir. Cooke & Bieler, Inc., Phila., 1974—99; pres., COO United Asset Mgmt., 1999—2000; CEO Delaware Investments, 2000—02; sr. mng. dir., co-head investment divsn. Putnam, LLC (Putnam Investments), 2002—03, pres., CEO, 2003—. Bd. govs. Investment Counsel Assn. Am., N.Y.C., 1983-91, pres., 1989-90, chmn. bd., 1990-91. Trustee Abington (Pa.) Meml. Hosp., 1977—, vice chmn., 1983-89, chmn. bd., 1989-92; trustee Abington Meml. Healthcare Corp., 1983-92. Mem. Pa. Bar Assn., Fin. Analyst Fedn., Union League Club, Racquet Club (Phila.), Huntingdon Valley (Pa.) Country Club, Merion Cricket Club. Republican. Presbyterian. Avocations: squash, tennis, paddle tennis. Office: Putnam LLC 1 Post Office Sq Boston MA 02109

HALDEMAN, JOE WILLIAM, writer; b. Okla. City, June 9, 1943; s. Jack Carroll and Lorena (Spivey) H.; m. Mary Gay Potter, Aug. 21, 1965. BS in Physics and Astronomy, U. Md., 1967; MFA in Writing, U. Iowa, 1975. Assoc. prof. writing program MIT, 1983—. Author: War Year, 1972, The Forever War, 1975, Mindbridge, 1976, Planet of Judgment, 1977, All My Sins Remembered, 1977, Infinite Dreams, 1978, World Without End, 1979, Worlds, 1971, (with Jack C. Haldeman II) There Is No Darkness, 1983, Worlds Apart, 1993, Dealing in Futures, 1985, Tool of the Trade, 1987, Buying Time, 1989, The Hemingway Hoax, 1990, Worlds Enough and Time, 1993, 1968, 1995, None So Blind, 1996, Saul's Death and Other Poems, 1997, Forever Peace, 1997, Forever Free, 1999, The Coming, 2000, Guardian, 2002, Camouflage, 2004, Old Twentieth, 2005, War Stories, 2005; editor: (with Martin H. Greenburg and Charles Waugh) Body Armor: 2000, 1986, Supertanks, 11987, Spacefighters, 1988; editor: Cosmic Laughter, 1974, Study War No More, 1977, Nebula Awards 17, 1983. Served with U.S. Army, 1967-69. Decorated Purple Heart; recipient Hugo award World Sci. Fiction Soc., 1976, 77, 91, 95, 98, Nebula award Sci. Fictions Writers Am., 1975, 91, 93, 98, 2001, Rhysling award Sci. Fiction Poetry Assn., 1984, 91, 2001, World Fantasy award, 1993, John W. Campbell award Sci. Fiction Rsch. Assn., 1998, James Tiptree award, 2004. Mem. Sci. Fiction Writers Am. (treas. 1970-73, chmn. grievance com. 1977-79, pres. 1992-94), Authors Guild, Writers Guild, Poets and Writers, Inc., Nat. Space Inst. E-mail: haldeman@mit.edu.

HALE, ALLAN L., lawyer; b. Mar. 14, 1957; s. Lemont Allen and Norma Stratton Hale; m. Gwen Marie Swenson, Jan. 10, 1982; children: Lindsay Augusta, Ingrid Swenson, Ilsa Aryia. BA, Harvard U., Cambridge, Mass., 1979; JD, U. Denver, 1985—85. Bar: Colo. 1985, US Dist. Ct. Colo. 1985, US Ct. Appeals (10th cir.) Colo. 1985, US Supreme Ct. 2002. Assoc. atty. Davis Graham & Stubbs, Denver, 1985—91, ptnr. atty., 1991—93; founder, mng. ptnr., shareholder atty. Hale Pratt Midgley Laitos Green & Hackstaff, PC, Denver, 1993—97; founder, mng. ptnr., ptnr. Hale Friesen LLP, Denver, 1998—. Staff asst. US Senator Gary Hart, Washington, 1979—81, dir., western slope office, Grand Junction, Colo., 1981—82; faculty Nat. Inst. for Trial Advocacy, 1996—. Alumni coun. U. Denver Coll. Law, 1994—2000; law rev. adv. bd. U. Denver, 1995—2007; co-founder Colo. Girls Soccer Acad., 2001—07, bd. dirs., 2001—07; pres. exec. coun. St. Philip Luth. Ch., 2001—03. Mem.: Colo. Bar Assn. (law office mgmt. com. 1994—), Denver Bar Assn. (alt. dispute resolution com. 1994—, Richard M. Davis award 1996), Ct. Apptd. Spl. Advocates Jefferson and Gilpin Counties (bd. dirs. 2002—06). Republican. Lutheran. Office: Hale Friesen LLP 1430 Wynkoop St Ste 300 Denver CO 80202 Office Phone: 720-904-6001. Office Fax: 720-904-6006. E-mail: ahale@halefriesen.com.

HALE, C. ROBERT, III, (BOB), real estate company executive; b. Tex. m. Susie Hale. BBA in Internat. Bus., U. Tex., JD. Dir. govtl. affairs Tex. Assn. Realtors, Austin, Tex.; from legal and legis. counsel to exec. v.p., gen. counsel Houston Assn. Realtors, 1973—88, exec. v.p., 1988—, gen. counsel, 1988—89, pres., 1989—. Spkr. in field. Named one of 10 People to Watch, Inman News, 1998, 100 Most Influential Real Estate People, 2005—06, Real Estate's 25 Most Influential Thought Leaders, Realtor Mag., 2006; recipient Tom D. Morton Meml. award, Tex. Assn. Realtors Convention, 1997. Mem.: Houston Soc. Assn. Execs. (pres. 1993), Tex. Soc. Assn. Execs. (pres. 1993, chmn. 1997—98). Office: Houston Association Realtors 3693 SW Freeway Houston TX 77027 Office Phone: 713-629-1900. Office Fax: 713-961-4869.*

HALE, DANNY LYMAN, insurance company executive; b. Ft. Lauderdale, Fla., Mar. 23, 1944; s. Thomas Hatten and Marion June (Frizzell) Hale; m. Reda Fay Kofahl, June 10, 1966; 1 child, Matthew Bryan. BA in Econs., Yale U., 1966. Cons. in fin. planning GE, Fairfield, Conn., 1977-78, mgr. fin. strategy devel. Louisville, 1978-79, mgr. fin. ops., 1979-80; mgr. divsn. fin. ops. GE Credit Corp., Stamford, Conn., 1980-82, v.p., dept. gen. mgr., 1982-84; mng. dir., mgr. bus. devel. Kidder Peabody Group, NYC, 1987-88; pres. Chase Comml. Corp., Chase Manhattan Bank, Paramus, NJ, 1988-91; exec. v.p. U.S.F. & G. Corp., Balt., 1991, exec. v.p., CFO, 1993-98, Promus Hotel Corp., Memphis, 1999; v.p., CFO Allstate Ins. Co., Northbrook, Ill., 2003—. With US Army, 1967—69. Republican. Congregationalist. Office: Allstate Ins Co 2775 Sanders Rd F8 Northbrook IL 60062*

HALE, DAVID FREDRICK, biotechnology executive; b. Gadsden, Ala., Jan. 8, 1949; s. Millard and Mildred Earline (McElroy) Hale; m. Linda Carol Sadorski, Mar. 14, 1975; children: Shane Michael, Tara Renee, Erin Nicole, David Garrett. BA, Jacksonville State U. Dir. mktg. Ortho Pharm. Corp. divsn. Johnson & Johnson, Raritan, NJ, 1978—80; v.p. mktg. BBL Microbiology Sys. divsn. Becton Dickinson & Co., Cockeysville, Md., 1980—81, v.p., gen. mgr. BBL Microbiology Sys. divsn., 1981—82; sr. v.p. mktg. and bus. devel. Hybritech, Inc., San Diego, 1982, pres., 1983—86, CEO, 1986—87; pres., CEO, dir. Gensia Sicor, Inc., San Diego, 1987—97; pres., CEO Women First HealthCare, Inc., 1998—2000; pres., CEO, dir. CancerVax Corp., Carlsbad, Calif., 2000—06; chmn. Hale BioPharms Ventures LLC, 2006—. Chmn. bd. Santarus, Inc., Somaxon Pharms., SkinMedica, Metabasis Therapeutics; bd. dirs. Verus Pharms., BIO, Children's Hosp., San Diego Econ. Devel. Corp., BIOCOM San Diego, Calif. HealthCare Inst.; co-founder, chmn. Connect. Mem.: Chief Exec.'s Orgn., World Pres.'s Orgn. Republican. Episcopalian. Home: PO Box 8925 17079 Circa del Sur Rancho Santa Fe CA 92067 Office: 1042 B W El Camino Rd Ste480 Encinitas CA 92024 Office Phone: 858-756-2480.

HALE, DAVID M., ambassador; Grad., Georgetown U. Joined Fgn. Svc., 1984; with US Dept. State, 1984—, dir. office Israel and Palestinian affairs, exec. asst. to Sec. of State, US amb. to Hashemite Kingdom of Jordan Amman, 2005—; dep. chief of mission US Embassy Beirut, Lebanon. Office: US Dept State 6050 Amman Pl Washington DC 20521-6050

HALE, EARL F., JR., lawyer; b. Ranger, Tex., Aug. 17, 1945; AB cum laude, Stanford U., 1967; JD cum laude, Columbia U., 1970. Bar: Tex. 1970, NY 1980. Ptnr. Carrington, Coleman, Sloman & Blumenthal, LLP, Dallas; atty. sole practice, Dallas. Named one of Best Lawyers in Dallas, D Mag., 2005; recipient Disting. Faculty award, Tex. Ctr. Legal Ethics and Professionalism. Fellow: Dallas Bar Found., Tex. Bar Found. (life); mem.: Am. Health Lawyers Assn., Assn. Conflict Resolution, Assn. Atty.-Mediators, Dallas Bar Assn., ABA. Office: 4144 North Central Expy Ste 225 Dallas TX 75204 Office Phone: 214-515-0199. Office Fax: 214-515-0192.*

HALE, JAMES THOMAS, retail executive, lawyer; b. Mpls., May 14, 1940; s. Thomas Taylor and Alice Louise (Mc Connon) H.; m. Sharon Sue Johnson, Aug. 27, 1960; children: David Scott, Eric James, Kristin Lynn. BA, Dartmouth Coll., 1962; LLB, U. Minn., 1965. Bar: Minn. Law clk. Chief Justice Earl Warren, U.S. Supreme Ct., 1965-66; assoc. firm Faegre & Benson, Mpls., 1966-73, ptnr., 1973-79; v.p., dir. corp. growth Gen. Mills, Inc., 1979-80, v.p. fin. and control consumer non-foods, 1981; sr. v.p., gen. counsel, corp. sec. Dayton-Hudson Corp., Mpls., 1981-2000; exec. v.p., gen. counsel, corp. sec. Target Corp., 2000—04, cons., 2004—. Adj. prof. U. Minn., 1967-73; bd. dirs. Tennant Co., 2001- Mem. exec. com. Fund Legal Aid Soc., others. Mem. Order of Coif, Phi Beta Kappa. Office: Target Corp 1000 Nicollet Mall Minneapolis MN 55403-2467*

HALE, JANET S., accounting firm executive, former federal agency administrator; b. Buffalo, Apr. 2, 1949; d. Herman Haltom and Rachel (Townes) H. BS, Miami U., Oxford, Ohio, 1971; M.P.A., Harvard U., 1980. Adminstrv. asst. to Rep. Tom Gallagher US Congress, Washington, 1974-76; research asst. House Republican Com., Washington, 1976-77; spl. asst. to Senator Edward Brooke US Senator, Boston, 1977-79; spl. asst. to sec., dir. exec. secretariat US Dept. Housing & Urban Devel., Washington, 1981-82, dep. asst. sec. for policy, fin. mgmt. & adminstrn., 1982-86, acting asst. sec., 1985—86; asst. sec. for budget & programs US Dept. Transp., Washington, 1986—89; assoc. dir. for economics & govt., Office Mgmt & Budget Exec. Office of the Pres., Washington, 1989—93; exec. v.p. U. Penn, Phila., 1993—94; v.p., lobbyist US Telephone Assn., 1995—98; policy dir. Elizabeth Dole for President Campaign, 1998—99; assoc. adminstr. for fin. US Ho. Reps., Washington, 1999—2000; sr. adv. to sec. US Dept. Health & Human Services, Washington, 2001—02, asst. sec. budget, tech., & fin., CFO, 2002—03; under sec. for mgmt. US Dept. Homeland Security, Washington, 2003—06; dir. pub.-sector bus. transformation Deloitte & Touche LLP, Washington, 2006—. Bd. dirs. Big Sisters Boston, 1978-80 Avocation: tennis. Office: Deloitte & Touche LLP 555 12th St NW Ste 500 Washington DC 20004*

HALE, JEFFREY L., economics educator; b. Richmond Heights, Ohio, Dec. 1, 1962; s. George R. and Elaine C. Hale; m. Machelle Capaldi, Oct. 14, 2006. AA, Lakeland C.C., Mentor, Ohio, 1984; BS in Secondary Edn., Kent State U., Ohio, 1987; MEd in Curriculum and Instrn., Ashland U., Ohio, 2004. Substitute tchr. secondary edn. various schs., Mentor, Ohio, 1988—2000; owner Hales Woodcrafting, 1990—; tchr. Mentor H.S., 2000—. Bd. mem. Cardinal Cmty. Credit Union, Mentor. Child sponsorship Compassion Internat., Colorado Springs, 2000—06; elder Pilgrim Luth. Brethren Ch., Mentor, 2001—06. Mem.: NEA (assoc.; del. 2004), Nat. Coun. Social Studies (assoc.), Ohio Edn. Assn. (assoc.; state rep. 2002—06), North East Ohio Edn. Assn. (assoc.; dist. rep. 2002—06), Mentor Tchrs. Assn. (assoc.; rep. 2002—06). Lutheran. Avocations: baseball, history, travel, coin collecting/numismatics. Office: Mentor High School 6477 Center Street Mentor OH 44060 Home Phone: 440-953-2384; Office Phone: 440-974-5300.

HALE, JERRY B., information technology executive; b. July 1951; B in Math., Berea Coll., Ky.; addition studies, E. Tenn. State and U. Tenn. Dir., global bus. sys. Eastman Chemical Co., Kingsport, Tenn., v.p., e-info. svc. & chief info. officer, 2002—. Office: Eastman Chem 100 North Eastman Rd PO Box 511 Kingsport TN 37662-5075

HALE, JOE (JOSEPH RICE), church organization executive; b. Texarkana, Tex., Mar. 25, 1935; s. Alfred Clay and Bess (Akin) Hale; m. Mary Richey, June 2, 1964; 1 child, Jeffrey Glen. BA, Asbury Coll., Wilmore, Ky., 1957; BD, So. Methodist U., 1960; DD, Asbury Theol. Sem., 1978, Asbury Coll., 2005; LHD (hon.), Fla. So. Coll., 1994; LHD (hon.), Fla. So. U., 1994. Ordained to ministry Meth. Ch., 1958. Pastor Meth. Ch., Sunset, Tex., 1958-60; evangelist, 1960-66; assoc. dir. dept. evangelism Bd. Evangelism, Meth. Ch., 1966-68, dir. ecumenical evangelism, 1968-74; dir. evangelization devel. Bd. Discipleship, United Meth. Ch., 1975; gen. sec. World Meth. coun., 1976—2001, gen. sec. emeritus, 2001. Exec. com. Key 73, 1970-73; sec. working group evangelism Nat. Coun. Chs., 1972; exec. com. Evangelization Forum, 1973-75; pres. Comm. Found., Inc., 1974-75; world amb. Internat. Prayer Fellowship, 1974; registrar World Meth. Evangelism Convocation, Jerusalem, 1974; mem. Conf. Secs. Christian World Communions, 1976-2001, chmn., 1983-86; gen. sec. World Meth. Coun., 1976-2001, with world confs. in Hawaii, 1981, Nairobi, 1986, Singapore, 1991, Rio de Janeiro, 1996, Brighton, Eng., 2001. Author: Design for Evangelism, 1970, Christ Matters!, 1971, God's Moment, 1972; contbr. articles to profl. jours.; prodr.: The Spirit is Moving, 1980 (video prodn.) Decorated Great Cross of Merit, Equestrian Order of the Holy Sepulchre in Jerusalem; recipient Key to City of Daytona Beach Fla., 1963-64, Asbury Coll. Alumni award, 1977, Disting. Svc. award Christian Meth. Episcopal Ch., 1994, Svc. award Gen. Commn. on Archives and History United Meth. Ch., 2002, Philip award Nat. Assn. United Meth.

Evangelists, 1998; named Ky. col., 1977, Ecumenical Svc. award Gen. Commn. on Christian Unity United Meth. Ch., 2000, World Meth. Peace award World Meth. Coun., 2001; named Disting. Evangelist, United Meth. Ch., 2001, Disting. Alumnus, Perkins Sch. Theology So. Meth. U., 2002. Methodist. Home and Office: 34 Forest Park Dr Waynesville NC 28785 Office Phone: 828-926-0144.

HALE, JUDSON DRAKE, SR., publishing executive, editor, writer; b. Boston, Mar. 16, 1933; s. Roger Drake and Marian (Sagendorph) H.; m. Sara Huberlie, Sept. 6, 1958; children: Judson Drake, Daniel, Christopher. BA, Dartmouth Coll., 1958; D of Journalism (hon.), New Eng. Coll., 1984; LittD (hon.), Franklin Pierce Coll., 1987; LHD (hon.), Keene State Coll., 1989. Asst. editor Yankee, Inc., Dublin, NH, 1958-61, assoc. editor, 1961-63, mng. editor, 1963-69; editor-in-chief Yankee Mag., Old Farmers Almanac; sr. v.p. Yankee Pub. Inc., Dublin, 1969—, sr. v.p., chmn., 2003—. Editor, v.p. Old Farmers Almanac. Author: Inside New England, 1982, The Education of a Yankee, 1987, Discovering Our Faraway Brother, 2007; editor: That New England, 1968; editor The Best of Yankee mag., 1985, The Best of the Old Farmer's Almanac, 1991, The Old Farmer's Almanac Book of Everyday Advice. Trustee Shevan Arts Ctr. Served with AUS, 1955-57. Mem.: Mass. Hist. Soc., Cheshire County Dartmouth Alumni Club, Phi Kappa Psi. Democrat. Episcopalian. Home: 47 Valley Rd Dublin NH 03444 Office: Yankee Pub Inc Main St Dublin NH 03444-0520 Home Phone: 603-563-8433; Office Phone: 603-563-8118 x104. Business E-Mail: judh@yankeepub.com.

HALE, LOIS J., retired mathematics educator; b. Oakland, Calif., Mar. 17, 1942; d. Edward Everett and Frances Elizabeth Hale. Student, U. Calif., Berkeley, 1959—63; BA, Calif. State U., Hayward, 1964; MA, U. San Francisco, 1978. Tchg. credential secondary, elem., adminstrv. svcs., math. Tchr. Chatom Union Sch. Dist., Turlock, Calif., 1966—67, Ballico-Cressey Sch. Dist., Calif., 1967—2004; ret. Mem.: Stanislau Math. Coun. (mem. exec. bd., sec. 2003—05), Calif. Math. Coun. (sec. 2000—02, 2006—08, pres.-elect 2002—04, pres. 2004—06, George Polya award 2000). Avocations: needlecrafts, golf, spectator sports, gardening. Home: 3105 Liquid Amber Dr Denair CA 95316 Personal E-mail: loishale@aol.com.

HALE, MARGARET SMITH, insurance company executive, educator; b. Browning, Mont., May 10, 1945; d. Stephen Howard and Evelyn Sarah (Beer) Smith; m. Lawrence L. Hale, Apr. 25, 1970 (div. Jan. 1984); children: Katherine Moore, Laura Ellen. BSBA, Boston U., 1967; AS in Risk Mgmt., Ins. Inst. Am., 1986. Underwriter Chubb & Son, Inc., NYC, 1967-70, br. mgr., asst. v.p. Boston, 1970-80; asst. v.p., account exec. Marsh & McLennan Inc., Boston, 1980-84; sr. v.p. Frank B. Hall, Boston, 1984-87; resident v.p. Warwick Ins. Co., Needham, Mass., 1987-90; pres. Smith & Hale Assocs., Inc., South Orleans, Mass., 1990—. Lectr. Risk and Ins. Mgrs. Soc., Boston, 1975—85; mem. fin. divsn. Babson Coll., Wellesley, Mass., 1987—. Bd. dirs. Lupus Erythematosus Assn., Boston, 1975-78, Parker Hill Med. Ctr., Boston, 1978-80; tchr. Congl. Ch. Sch., Needham, Mass., 1982—; chmn. ins. adv. com. Town of Needham, 1982-95; pres. Interfaith Coun. for the Homeless, 1999—. Mem. Ins. Mgrs. Assn. (treas. Boston 1971-80), Ins. Library Assn. (dir. 1980-82). Office: Smith & Hale Assocs PO Box 136 South Orleans MA 02662-0136 Home Phone: 860-267-1463; Office Phone: 508-237-3723. Personal E-mail: smithhale@bigplanet.com.

HALE, MARIE STONER, performing company executive; b. Greenwood, Miss. Student in Piano, U. Miss., Hattiesburg; studied with Richard Ellis, Christine du Boulay, Jo-Anna Kneeland, David Howard. Tchr. Ellis/du Boulay Sch., Chgo., Jo-Anna Kneeland Imperial Studios, Palm Beach County, Fla.; co-founder Ballet Arts Found., West Palm Beach, Fla., 1973-86; founder, artistic dir. Ballet Fla., West Palm Beach, 1986—. Office: Ballet Florida 500 Fern St West Palm Beach FL 33401-5726*

HALE, MARTHA LARSEN, dean, library and information science educator; b. Pitts., Nov. 30, 1942; d. Olaf and Corinne (Carlson) Larson; m. Frank A. Hale, Dec. 26, 1964 (div. 1976); children: Matthew, Jennifer. BA, U. NH, 1965; MLS, Syracuse U., 1977; PhD, U. So. Calif., 1983. Dean Sch. Libr. and Info. Mgmt., Emporia State U., Kans., 1987—94, founder, dir., prof. Inst. of Continuous Edn. Kans., 2001—03; dean, prof. Sch. Libr. and Info. Sci., Cath. U. Am., Washington, 2003—. Vis. scholar Sch. Libr., Archival and Info. Studies, U. BC, Vancouver, 1998; vis. faculty mem. Sch. Libr. and Info. Sci., U. Wash., Seattle, 1999. Named to Mid-Am. Edn. Hall of Fame, 1997. Democrat. Presbyterian. Office: Cath U Am Sch Libr and Info Sci Cardinal Station Washington DC 20064 Office Phone: 202-319-5085. E-mail: halem@cua.edu.*

HALE, NANCY ANNETTE BILLS, kindergarten educator; b. Paris, Tex., Sept. 6, 1959; d. William Richard and Ruby Lee (Davidson) Bills; children: Christopher Wayne Hale, Jacob C. Gomez. BA in Elem. Edn., U. Tex., San Antonio, 1986, MEd in Early Childhood Edn., 1995. Cert. elem. tchr., reading specialist, early childhood specialist, kindergarten team leader, Tex. Presch. tchr. Adventure Presch., San Antonio, 1986-87; 1st grade tchr. Bob Hope Elem. Sch. S.W. Ind. Sch. Dist., San Antonio, 1987-89, 1st grade tchr. Hidden Cove Elem. Sch., 1989-91, kindergarten tchr. Hidden Cove Elem. Sch., 1991—. Mem. Districtwide Improvement Coun. S.W. Ind. Sch. Dist., 1990-91, instnl. coord., 1992-93, site-based mgmt. com., 1992-93, social studies instrnl. coord., 1992-93, dist. curriculum design com., 1996-98, campus improvement com., 1996-97, kindergarten team leader, 1996-2002, dist. curriculum designer, 1996-2001, mentor tchr., 1996, campus improvement com., 1996-2005. Mem. NEA, ASCD, Am. Fedn. Tchrs., Nat. Assn. for Edn. of Young Children, Tex. Tchrs. Assn., Kindergarten Tchrs. Tex. Avocations: reading, camping, travel, Arts and Crafts, gardening. Office Phone: 210-623-6220. Personal E-mail: nbillshale@yahoo.com.

HALE, NATHAN CABOT, sculptor, artist, poet; b. LA, July 5, 1925; s. Nathan Cabot Hale, Virginia Markoe Ferris; m. Alison Elizabeth Boothby, Dec. 27, 1964; children: Terri Dean, Lisa Jenny Rose. BS, Empire State Coll., 1973; PhD, The Union Inst., Cin., 1976. Instr. sculpture Pratt Inst., Bklyn., 1960; instr. anatomy and the elements of drawing Art Students League of N.Y., 1975—86; instr. sculpture Nat. Acad. Schulpture, NYC, 1985. Dir. The Ages of Man Found., 1968—; lectr. in field; cons. in field; instr. drawing and anatomy Art Student's League, 1985—90; sr. editor Art World, 1985—89. Author: Creating Welded Sculpture, 1968, 1994, The Embrace of Life, 1969, Abstraction in Art and Nature, 1972, 1993, The Birth of a Family, 1979, The Spirit of Man, 1981, (book of poetry) Fox Tails, 1993, (book of fables) The Elephant's Peaceable Kingdom, On the Perception of Human Form in Sculpture, 2000; contbr. numerous articles to profl. jours.; one-man shows include Felix Landau Gallery, L.A., 1957, Washington Irving Gallery, N.Y., 1960, Feingarten Gallery, Chgo., 1961, N.Y., 1961, Midtown Galleries, 1964, Hazelton Art League, Pa., 1966, Mus. of Ft. Wayne, Ind., 1966, Queens Coll., N.Y., 1966, NYU, 1967, Franklin and Marshall Coll., 1967, Midtown Galleries, N.Y., 1968, Quinata Gallery, Nantucket, 1968, Midtown Galleries, N.Y., 1973, exhibited in group shows at L.A. County Mus., Colo. Springs Fine Art Ctr., Norfolk Mus., Lehigh Univ., Philbrook Art Ctr., Ball State Univ., Hunterdon Art Ctr., Albright-Knox Art Gallery, Herron Mus. of Art, Davenport Mcpl. Art Gallery, Corcoran Gallery, Wayne State U., Pace Coll., Audubon Artists, Nat. Acad. Design, Columbus Gallery of Fine Art, Stamford Mus., Joslyn Mus., Springfield Mus. of Fine Art, Heckscher Mus., The Gallery of Modern Art; author: (novels) The Van Zanzibar Testaments. Dir. Ages of Man Found., 1969—. With USMC, 1941—42, with U.S. Merchant Marine, 1944—45. Recipient Purchase award in sculpture, L.A. County Mus., 1955, Silver medal, Audubon Soc. Sculpture, 1972. Fellow: Nat. Sculpture Soc.; mem.: Nat. Acad. Design (Gold medal in sculpture 1990), Century Assn. Avocations: sailing, fly fishing. Mailing: 57 Sheffield Rd Amenia NY 12501

HALE, NATHAN KELLY, music educator, artist; b. Fairfax, Okla., Oct. 13, 1942; s. Roy Willis and Veda Belle Hale; m. Natalie Cecile Schuppert, May 6, 1972; children: Jonathan Franklin, Rebecca Rose Elizabeth. MusB in Edn., U. Okla., Norman, 1964; MusM, U. Tex., Austin, 1973, D of Musical Arts, 1973. Asst. condr. Santa Fe Opera, 1963—65; tchr. vocal music Chatham Borough Pub. Schs., NJ, 1965—67; head music staff Christian Arts Inc., South Orange, 1967—68; prof. opera U. Cin., 1976—; instr. U. Tex., Austin, 1973—75; condr. Austin Civic Ballet, 1973—75; min. music Calvary Episcopal Ch., Cin., 1979—98; artist-in-residence Bay View Music Festival, Mich., 1979—; dir. music Ascension & Holy Trinity Episcopal Ch., Cin., 1999. Pianist Art of Song - Duo with soprano Blythe Walker, Cin., 1977—2006; accompanist vocal tour Caribbean islands US Info. Svcs., Washington, 1992; vocal coach master class Opera Australia, Sydney, 2000; vocal recital accompanist Save Children Benefit Concert, Wellington, New Zealand, 2000. Composer: (choral music) An American Hymn Requiem, The Young Dead Soldiers, (church music) Descants for Days, (choral) A Child's Prayer, (violin solo with piano) Passacaglia; composer: (organist) (cd recording) Hymns from Bay View; composer: (organist/arranger) (cd recording with frederick chao) The Sacred Cello; musician (organist): (cd recording of christmas improvisations) Bells & Whistles from Bay View. Bd. mem. MacDowell Soc., Cin., 1997—99. Democrat. Episcopalian. Avocations: gardening, yoga instructor. Office: University of Cincinnati College-Conservatory of Music Cincinnati OH 45221-0003 Home: 14 Stacia St Los Gatos CA 95030-6207 Home Phone: 513-541-2549; Office Phone: 513-556-9518. Personal E-mail: halenk@aol.com. E-mail: halenk@ucmail.uc.edu.

HALE, RICHARD LEE, magazine editor; b. Formoso, Kans., Jan. 3, 1930; s. Glenn Becton and Ruby Tiarena (Johnson) H.; m. Nancy June Craig, Feb. 22, 1953; children— Steven Craig, Kristin Lee Hale Shurtz, Michael John, Sarah Johanna Hale Wilcher. BS in Journalism, U. Kans., 1952. Editor Bird City (Kans.) Times, 1955-58; editor, pub. St. Francis Herald, Kans., 1958-74; editor Golf Course Mgmt., Lawrence, Kans., 1974-76, PGA Mag., Palm Beach Gardens, Fla., 1976-80; dir. comm. GCSAA, Lawrence, 1980-82; editor Dental Econs., Penn Well Pub. Co., Tulsa, 1982-97, pub., 1989-97. Editor: (ann.) PGA Book of Golf, 1977-80; cons. editor Odontos Pub. Co., 1997-2002. Chmn. local com. Boy Scouts Am., St. Francis, 1970-74; trustee Trinity United Meth. Ch., Palm Beach Gardens, 1979-80, Am. Fund for Dental Health, 1989—. Spl. agt. CIC, U.S. Army, 1952-54. St. Francis Herald named Best Weekly Newspaper Kans. Press Assn., 1962. Mem. Am. Assn. Dental Editors, Am. Fund for Dental Health (trustee, advisor 1989-93), Kans. Press Assn. (bd. dirs. 1973-74), Golf Writers Assn. Am., Riverside Country Club (St. Francis; pres. 1971), Rotary (pres. local chpt. 1970), Alvamar Country Club (pres. 2003-04). Democrat. Mem. United Ch. Of Christ. Avocations: golf, travel, nature walks. Home: 5000 W 18th St Lawrence KS 66047 Personal E-mail: dhale1@juno.com.

HALE, ROBERT FARGO, federal association executive; b. Jan. 21, 1947; s. William David and Elizabeth (Wells) H.; m. Susan Kohn, June 23, 1973; children: Scott, Michael. BS with hons., Stanford U., 1968, MS, 1969; MBA, George Washington U., 1976. Cert. Def. Fin. Mgr., Am. Soc. Mil. Comptrollers. Analyst, study dir. Ctr. for Naval Analysis, Washington, 1972-75; analyst Congl. Budget Office, Washington, 1975-78, dep. asst. dir., 1978-81, asst. dir. def. issues, 1981-94; asst. sec. fin. mgmt. USAF, Washington, 1994-2001; program dir., sr. fellow LMI Gov't Cons., Washington, 2001—05; exec. dir. Am. Soc. Mil. Comptrollers, Alexandria, Va., 2005—. Nat. pres. and v.p. Am. Soc. Mil. Comptrollers; mem. bus. bd. Sec. Def.; mem. task force on Future of Military Health. Lt. USNR, 1969—76. Fellow: Nat. Acad. Pub. Adminstrn.; mem.: Nat. Contract Mgmt. Assn., Am. Soc. Mil. Comptrollers, Assn. Govt. Accts. Jewish. Home: 3357 Taleen Ct Annandale VA 22003-1161 Office: Am Soc Mil Comptrollers 415 N Alfred St Alexandria VA 22314 Business E-Mail: hale@asmconline.org.

HALE, ROGER LOUCKS, manufacturing executive, director; b. Plainfield, NJ, Dec. 13, 1934; s. Lloyd and Elizabeth (Adams) H.; m. Sandra Johnston, June 10, 1961 (div.); children: Jocelyn, Leslie, Nina, Deirdre; m. Eleanor L. Hall, Nov. 24, 1989. BA, Brown U., 1956; MBA, Harvard U., 1961. With Tennant Co., Mpls., 1961-99, pres., CEO, 1975-98, chmn., CEO, 1998-99, chmn., 1999, bd. dirs., VisionShare, Inc., 2001—, chmn., 2005—. Bd. dirs. Walker Art Ctr., 1970-2005, pres., 1975-77, 2002-05, chmn. 2005—; bd. dirs. Ploughshares Fund, 1996—, chmn, 2005—; bd. dirs. Winning Workplaces, 1999-; bd. dirs., chmn. Pub. Radio Internat., 1990, 2003; chmn. Minn. Bus. Partnership, 1993-95; chmn. Gov.'s Workforce Devel. Coun., 1999-2004. Named Exec. of Yr., Corp. Report mag., 1988, One of Minn.'s 5 Outstanding Corp. Dirs., Twin Cities Bus. Monthly, 1996; recipient Mpls. Spl. Recognition award for Svc. to City of Mpls., 1993; named to Vol. Hall of Fame, Mpls.-St. Paul Mag., 2005. Office: Union Plz 333 Washington Ave N Ste 313 Minneapolis MN 55401-1364

HALE, THOMAS MORGAN, professional services executive; b. Syracuse, NY, Nov. 29, 1936; s. Thomas Morgan and Ruth Ingrid (Stangeland) H.; m. Marilyn Johnson, June 12, 1959 (div. Aug. 1980), m. Linda Diana Pappas, Feb. 12, 1981; Children: Rodney, Kenneth, Timothy, Marilee. BS, Fla. State U., 1959; MA, U. Houston, 1967; DPA, George Mason U., 1990; diploma, Nat. War Coll., DC, 1980. Commd. ensign USN, 1959, advanced through the grades to capt., 1983; served on destroyers, ops. officer USS Sampson, 1963-65; assoc. prof. naval sci. Tex. A&M U., 1965-67; chief staff officer, comdr. Destroyer Squadron Five, 1967-71; with Bur. of Naval Personnel, 1971-74; comdg. officer USS Paul, 1974-76; staff, chief naval ops., chmn. Joint Chiefs of Staff, 1976-83; ret. USN, 1983; sr. mgr. RCI, Vienna, Va., 1983-87, v.p., 1987-96, divsn. gen. mgr., 1992-96, sr. v.p., 1996—2005; ret., 2005. Qualified expert witness Federal Dist. Ct. System. Contbr to profl. jours. Recipient Legion of Merit award Sec. of the U.S. Navy, 1983. Mem. U.S. Naval Inst. (life), Assn. Career Mgmt. Firms N. Am. (bd. dirs. 1998-2003), The Retired Officer's Assn. (life), The Tower Club (life), Army Navy Country Club. Methodist. Home: 3783 Center Way Fairfax VA 22033-2602 Personal E-mail: thomash463@aol.com.

HALE, VICTORIA G., chemist, pharmaceutical executive; m. Ahvie Herskowitz. BS, Univ. Md., 1983; PhD pharmaceutical chemistry, Univ. Calif., San Francisco, 1990. Sr. reviewer U.S. FDA, 1990—94; scientist Genentech Inc., 1994—97; co-founder, chief sci. officer Axiom Biomedical Inc., 1999—2000; founder, chmn., CEO Inst. for OneWorld Health, San Francisco, 2000—. Adj. assoc. prof. biopharmaceutical sciences Univ. Calif., San Francisco, 2002—; mem. indsl. adv. bd. Calif. Quantitative BioMedical Rsch. Group; adv. WHO; expert reviewer NIH. Named one of Most Outstanding Social Entrepreneurs, Schwab Found. Switzerland, 2004; recipient Exec. of the Yr., Esquire mag., 2005, Innovation award for social & econ. innovation, The Economist mag., 2005, Skoll award for social entrepreneurship, Skoll Found., 2005; fellow, Ashoka Innovators for the Public, 2006; MacArthur Fellow, John D. and Catherine T. MacArthur Found., 2006. Office: Inst for OneWorld Health Ste 500 50 California St San Francisco CA 94111

HALE, WESLEY RAYMOND, research associate, chemical engineer, polymer scientist; b. Roanoke, Va., Apr. 20, 1969; s. John Raymond and Bettie Jane Hale; m. Michaela Christina Hale; children: Sarah, Joshua, Ethan. BS in Chem. Engring. (with honors), Va. Tech., 1993; PhD in Chem. Engring. (with honors), U. Tex., Austin, 1998. Rschr. in polyrotaxanes Va. Tech., 1992—93; grad. internship Acadia Polymers, 1993; grad. rsch., tchg. asst. U. Tex., Austin, 1993—98; advanced rsch. scientist Eastman Chem. Co., Kingsport, Tenn., 1998—2000, sr. rsch. scientist, 2000—02, prin. rsch. scientist, 2002—05, rsch. assoc., 2006—. Reviewer Macromolecules, Polymer Engring. and Sci., Jour. Polymer Sci.; contbr. 11 refereed publs. and 3 conf. publs., over 45 tech. papers in field. Active mem. Meals on Wheels, 1994—. Recipient Rhone-Poulenc/Allied Signal Study Abroad Scholarship, 1992, Outstanding Jr. award, DOW Chem. Co., 1992, Rsch. Scholarship, NSF, 1993, Larry Holmes/SPE Endowed Presdl. Scholarship, 1997, Best Conf. Presentation award, INTC-India, 2001. Mem.: Soc. Plastics Engrs., Am. Chem. Soc., Omega Chi Epsilon Chem. Engring. Soc., Tau Beta Pi Engring. Honor Soc., Zeta Beta Tau Fraternity (chpt. advisor 1995—96, 1999—2002, Founding Father, Va. Tech. chpt. 1991—93). Achievements include over 30 patents in field; technical expertise in condensation polymer synthesis, barrier and diffusion kinetics, theoretical modeling, material optics, polymer and blend thermodynamics; technical expertise in optical physics and liquid crystal display technology; research in reactive compatibilization of polybutylene terephtalate/ABS blends by methyl methacrylate, glycidyl methacrylate, ethyl acrylate terpolymers. Avocations: photography, genealogy, gardening.

HALE, WILLIAM BRYAN, JR., newspaper editor; b. Stephenville, Tex., Apr. 26, 1933; s. William Bryan and Gladys (Tittle) H.; divorced; children: Shandra Hale Ferguson, Tamara Hale Cameron, Nicholas, Sabrina Hale Park. Student, UCLA, 1953-54. Police beat/courts reporter Santa Monica (Calif.) Outlook, 1953-58; gen. reporter Ontario (Calif.) Daily Report, 1958-59; criminal court writer L.A. City News Service, 1959-60; gen. reporter L.A. Times, 1960-61; reporter Houston Chronicle, 1961-62; news editor Somerset (Pa.) American, 1962-63; night editor Elmira (N.Y.) Star-Gazette, 1963-64; copy editor, investigative reporter Milw. Jour., 1964-70; Tucson corr. Time mag./Time-Life Books, 1970-71; night city editor Tucson Citizen, 1970-71; nat. desk copy editor Los Angeles Times, 1971-90; sr. lectr. U. So. Calif., 1974-88; pres. Nat. Copy Editors Sch., Thousand Oaks, Calif., 1984-90; founder and dir. Australian Sub-Editors Sch., Sydney, Australia, 1989-94. Cpl. USMC, 1951-53. Avocations: horseback riding, hiking. Home: PO Box 35128 Tucson AZ 85740-5128

HALES, ALFRED WASHINGTON, mathematics professor, consultant; b. Pasadena, Calif., Nov. 30, 1938; s. Raleigh Stanton and Gwendolen (Washington) H.; m. Virginia Dart Greene, July 7, 1962; children— Andrew Stanton, Lisa Ruth, Katherine Washington BS, Calif. Inst. Tech., 1960, PhD, 1962. NSF postdoctoral fellow Cambridge U., Eng., 1962-63; Benjamin Peirce instr. Harvard U., 1963-66; faculty mem. UCLA, 1966-92, prof. math., 1973-92, prof. emeritus, 1992—; dir. IDA Ctr. Comm. Rsch., 1992—2003. Cons. Jet Propulsion Lab., La Canada, Calif., 1966-70, Inst. for Def. Analyses, Princeton, N.J. and LaJolla, Calif., 1964-65, 76, 79-92; vis. lectr. U. Wash., Seattle, 1970-71; vis. mem. U. Warwick Math. Inst., Coventry, Eng., 1977-78, Math. Sci. Rsch. Inst., Berkeley, 1986-87. Co-author: Shift Register Sequences, 1967, 82; contbr. articles to profl. jours. Bd. trustees Math. Sci. Rsch. Inst., Berkeley, 1995—99. Mem. Am. Math. Soc., Math. Assn. Am., Soc. Indsl. and Applied Math. (Polya prize in combinatorics 1972), Pasadena Badminton Club, Sigma Xi. Office: Ctr for Comm Rsch 4320 Westerra Ct San Diego CA 92121-1969 Home Phone: 858-454-8126; Office Phone: 858-622-5423. Business E-Mail: hales@ccrwest.org.

HALES, DANIEL B., lawyer; b. Oak Park, Ill., Sept. 29, 1941; s. Burton W. and Marion (Jones) Hales; m. Deborah J. Dorr, June 4, 1966 (dec. Nov. 2002); children: Daniel R. J., Marion P., George B. BA in Econs., U. Mich., 1963; JD, Northwestern U., 1966. Bar: Ill. 1966, U.S. Dist. Ct. (no. dist.) Ill. 1967, U.S. Ct. Appeals (7th cir.) 1968, U.S. Supreme Ct. 1977. Gen. counsel Philadelphia Soc., Chgo. Dir. Chgo. Crime Commn.; pres., dir. Ams. for Effective Law Enforcement, Inc., Chgo.; chmn. Ill. Lawyers for Reagan and Bush, 1980; gen. counsel New Trier Rep. Orgn.; mem. bd. govs., v.p., treas. United Rep. Fund Ill. Mem.: Chgo. Bar Assn. (mem. trust law com. 1975—), Commonwealth Club, Law Club, Federalist Soc. (advisor). Office: 711 Oak St # 102 Winnetka IL 60093 Home Phone: 847-446-6474; Office Phone: 847-446-6474.

HALES, RALEIGH STANTON, JR., retired mathematics professor, academic administrator; b. Pasadena, Calif., Mar. 16, 1942; s. Raleigh Stanton and Gwendolen (Washington) Hales; m. Diane Cecilia Moore, July 8, 1967; children: Karen Gwen, Christopher Stanton. BA, Pomona Coll., 1964; MA, Harvard U., 1965, PhD, 1970. Tchg. fellow Harvard U., Cambridge, Mass., 1965—67; instr. math. Pomona Coll., Claremont, Calif., 1967—70, asst. prof., 1970—74, assoc. prof., 1974—85, prof., 1985—90, assoc. dean. coll., 1973—90; pres. Claremont Computations, 1983—90; prof. math. scis., v.p. acad. affairs Coll. Wooster, Ohio, 1990, pres., 1995—2007, pres. emeritus, 2007—; sr. cons. Academic Search, Inc., 2007—. Cons. Calif. Divsn. Savs. and Loan, 1968—70; Econs. Rsch. Assocs., LA, 1969, Devel. Econs., LA, 1971, Fed. Home Loan Bank Bd., Washington, 1971—72. Author: computer software; contbr. articles to profl. jours.; patentee calculator. Trustee Polytech. Sch., Pasadena, Calif., 1973—79, Foothill Country Day Sch., Claremont, 1985—90, chmn., 1989—90; coun. Internat. Badminton Fedn., 1989—99; bd. dirs. U.S. Badminton Assn., 1967—73, 1978—89, pres., 1985—88; mem. exec. bd. U.S. Olympic Com., 1989—90. Named Wig Disting. prof., Pomona Coll., 1971. Mem.: Wooster Country Club, Math. Assn. Am., Am. Math. Soc., Univ. Club N.Y., Pasadena Badminton Club (pres. 1978—85). Republican. Episcopalian. Home: 1573 Willoughby Dr Wooster OH 44691 Office Phone: 330-264-0972. E-mail: shales@wooster.edu.

HALES, ROBERT ERNEST, psychiatrist, educator; s. Herbert and Matilda Hales; m. Dianne Plucinnik, Dec. 24, 1977; 1 child, Julia. MD, George Wash. U., Washington, 1977. Diplomate Am. Bd. Psychiatry and Neurology, 1983. Chair,dept. psychiatry Calif. Pacific Med. Ctr., San Francisco, 1990—95; Joe P. Tupin prof., chair dept. psychiatry U. Calif.,Sch. Medicine, Sacramento, 1995—. Dep. editor: Jour. Neuropsychiatry and Clinical Neurosci., editor in chief: Am. Psychiat. Pub., Inc., 2001—. Mem. Am. Psychiat. Pub., Arlington, Va., 2001—07. Named Educator of Yr., Assn. Acad. Psychiatry, 2006. Fellow: Am. Psychiat. Assn. (chair sci. program com. 1984—88). Office: Univ Calif Davis 2230 Stockton Blvd Sacramento CA 95817 Home Phone: 415-383-0803; Office Phone: 916-734-2960. Office Fax: 916-734-3384. Business E-Mail: rehales@ucdavis.edu.

HALEY, DAVID ALAN, healthcare executive; b. St. Louis, Aug. 29, 1943; s. John David and Helen Ermyl (Richardson) H.; children: Trisha Lynn, Jason Alan, Eric Nathan. BA, So. Ill. U., Edwardsville, 1966; MPH magna cum laude, UCLA, 1971. Adminstrv. asst. Kaiser Found. Hosp., Panorama City, Calif., 1971; assoc. adminstr. Our Lady of Lourdes Hosp., Pasco, Wash., 1971-74, Garfield Hosp., Monterey Park, Calif., 1974-75; assoc. exec. dir. Gen. Hosp., Ft. Walton Beach, Fla., 1976-79; v.p. ops. Our Lady of the Lake Regional Med. Ctr., Baton Rouge, 1979-88; pres. Phoenix Connection, Baton Rouge, 1988-89; CEO Gibson Gen. Hosp., Princeton, Ind., 1989-93; pres., CEO Four States Physicians Assn., Joplin, Mo., 1993-94; exec. dir. MedQuest Health Resources, Inc., 1995-96; pres., CEO The Haley Group, Frankfort, Ill., 1996—2004; CEO St. Anthony's Hospice, Henderson, Ky., 2004—06; v.p., COO Ctr. for Hospice and Palliative Care, South Bend, Ind., 2006—. Mem. Four Rivers Comprehensive Health Planning Agy., Richland, Wash., 1972-74; treas. S.E. Wash. State Hosp. Coun., Pasco, 1973, v.p. 1974; corp. mem. Mid La. Health Systems Agy., Baton Rouge, 1979-82; gubernatorial appointee La. Statewide Health Coord. Coun., Baton Rouge, 1984; gubernatorial appointee, Healthcare Facility Adminstrn. Bd., Indpls., 1991-93; sec.-treas. S.W. Ind.

Hosp. Coun., Evansville, 1992-93. Served with USNR, 1967-69. USPHS fellow, 1969-71. Fellow Am. Coll. Healthcare Execs.; mem. Healthcare Fin. Mgmt. Assn., La. Hosp. Assn. (council on planning, 1984-87), Ind. Hosp. Assn. (mem. coun. pub. rels. 1992-93), Vis. Nurse Assn. Southwestern Ind. (bd. dirs. 1992-93), La. Assn. Bus. and Industry (health care council 1987); Kiwanis, Rotary. Republican. Home and Office: The Haley Group 3628 Raleigh Ct Mishawaka IN 46545 Business E-Mail: dhaley@haleygroup.com.

HALEY, GEORGE, Romance languages educator; b. Lorain, Ohio, Oct. 19, 1929; s. George and Mary (Haley). AB, Oberlin Coll., 1948; MA, Brown U., 1951, PhD (Pres.'s fellow), 1956. Prof. U. Chgo., 1968—, chmn. dept. Romance langs., 1970-74. Author: Vicente Espinel and Marcos de Obregón, 1959, The Narrator in Don Quixote, 1965, Diario de un Estudiante de Salamanca, 1977, El Quijote de Cervantes, 1984, Vicente Espinel y Marcos de Obregon: Biografia, Autobiografia y Novela, 1994, Indagaciones, 2005; mem. editl. bd. Modern Philology, 1967-95, Canente, 2004— Guggenheim fellow, 1962-63 Mem. Hispanic Soc. Am., MLA, Phi Beta Kappa. Home: 901 S Plymouth Ct Chicago IL 60605-2059 Office: 1050 E 59th St Chicago IL 60637-1559

HALEY, GEORGE BROCK, JR., retired lawyer; b. Atlanta, Feb. 9, 1926; s. George Brock and Naomi Esther (Alverson) H.; m. Marjorie Elizabeth Griffiths, June 24, 1950; children: Susan Haley Brumfield, Katherine Haley Herman, George Brock III, Victor Pearse. AB, Harvard U., 1948, LLB, 1951. Bar: Ga. 1951, D.C. 1976. Assoc. Kilpatrick & Cody (name changed to Kilpatrick Stockton), Atlanta, 1951-60, ptnr., 1960-93, of counsel, 1994—; ret. Mem. Ga. Gov.'s Jud. Process Rev. Commn., Atlanta, 1988-89; trustee Frances Wood Wilson Found. Staff sgt. AUS, 1944-46, MTO. Mem. ABA, State Bar Ga., Atlanta Bar Assn., Atlanta Lawyers Club, Capital City Club. Methodist. Avocations: boating, travel. Office Phone: 404-815-6370. E-mail: ghaley@kilpatrickstockton.com.

HALEY, GEORGE PATRICK, lawyer; b. Bad Axe, Mich., Sept. 23, 1948; s. Glen Kirk and Bernice (Cooper) H.; m. Theresa L. Thomas, Dec. 24, 1975. BS, U. Mich., 1970; MS, U. Calif., Berkeley, 1971; JD, Harvard U., 1974. Bar: Calif. 1974, U.S. Dist. Ct. (no. dist.) Calif. 1974, U.S. Dist. Ct. (ea. dist.) Calif. 1980. Assoc. Pillsbury Winthrop Shaw Pittman LLP, San Francisco, 1974-81, ptnr., 1982—. Prof. U. Shanghai, Shanghai-San Francisco Sister City Program, 1986-1989. Author numerous articles on uniform comml. code, project fin. Dir. Calif. Shakespeare Festival, Berkeley, 1986-93; dir. Nat. Writing Project, 1996—. Mem. ABA (chmn. com. 1976-93), Am. Coll. Comml. Fin. Lawyers, State Bar Calif. (chmn. fin. instns. com. 1980, comml. code com. 1988). Republican. Methodist. Avocations: tai chi chuan, golf, cooking. Home: 1825 Marin Ave Berkeley CA 94707-2414 Office Phone: 415-983-1272. Business E-Mail: george.haley@pillsburylaw.com.

HALEY, GEORGE THOMAS, marketing educator; b. San Antonio, Tex., Feb. 15, 1952; s. James Bennett and Helen Basila Haley; m. Usha Venkatesan, July 12, 1984. BA, U. Tex., 1972, BBA, 1977, PhD, 1989. Asst. prof. Forham U., NYC, 1989—93; vis. prof. Itesm, Monterrey, Mexico, 1993—94; vis. fellow Nat. U. of Singapore, Singapore, 1994—96; sr. lectr. Queensland U. Tech., Brisbane, Australia, 1996—97; assoc. prof. DePaul U., Chgo., 1997—98; prof. U. New Haven, New Haven, 1998—, dir. Ctr. for Internat. Industry Competitiveness. Author: New Asian Emperors: The Overseas Chinese, Their Strategies and Competitive Advantages, 1998, The Chinese Tao of Business: The Logic of Successful Business Strategy, 2004; contbr. articles various profl. jours.; editor Am. Bus. Rev., mem. editl. bd. Indsl. Mktg. Mgmt., Jour. Bus. and Indsl. Mktg., Internat. Mktg. Rev., Mktg. Intelligence and Planning, Jour. Asia Entrepreneurship and Sustainability. Numerous monetary grants, 1991—93. Mem.: Acad. Internat. Business, Am. Mktg. Assn. Avocations: travel, reading, golf, hiking, swimming. Office: U New Haven Sch of Bus 300 Boston Post Rd West Haven CT 06516 Office Phone: 203-931-6004. Office Fax: 212-208-2468. E-mail: gthaley@sbcglobal.net.

HALEY, JACKIE EARLE, actor, film director; b. Northridge, Calif., July 14, 1961; s. Evan Earle Haley; m. Sherry Haley (div.); m. Amelia Cruz, 2004; children from previous marriage: Christopher, Olivia. Actor: (films) The Day of the Locust, 1975, The Bad News Bears, 1976, The Bad News Bears in Breaking Training, 1977, Damnation Alley, 1977, The Bad News Bears Go to Japan, 1978, Breaking Away, 1979, Losin' It, 1983, The Zoo Gang, 1985, Dollman, 1991, Nemesis, 1993, Maniac Cop 3: Badge of Silence, 1993, Prophet of Evil: The Ervil LeBaron Story, 1993, Little Children, 2006 (Best Supporting Actor, NY Film Critics Circle award, 2006), All the King's Men, 2006; (TV films) Every Stray Dog and Kid, 1981, Miss Lonelyhearts, 1983, (TV appearances) Wait Till Your Father Gets Home, 1972, The Outside Man, 1972, The Partridge Family, 1973, Marcus Welby M.D., 1973, (voice only) Valley of the Dinosaurs, 1974, Planet of the Apes, 1974, Shazam!, 1974, The Waltons, 1975, The Love Boat, 1979, Insight, 1980, Whiz Kids, 1983, MacGyver, 1985, Murder, She Wrote, 1986, Get a Life, 1991, Renegade, 1992, (voice): (TV series, TV appearances) Gravedale High, 1990; performer: (Broadway plays) Slab Boys; writer: TV series Twilight Zone.*

HALEY, JAMES F., JR., lawyer; b. Boston, 1945; BS in chemistry, U. Notre Dame, 1967; MA in chemistry, Brandeis U., 1969, PhD in organic chemistry, 1975; JD magna cum laude, Suffolk U., 1975. Bar: Mass. 1975, NY 1977, U.S. Patent & Trademark Office, US Dist. Ct. So. & Ea. N.Y., US Ct. Appeals 7th & Fed. cir. Ptnr. Fish & Neave, NYC, 1983—2004; ptnr. Fish & Neave IP group & co-head corp. intellectual property practice group Ropes & Gray, NYC, 2005—. Mem. law review Suffolk U., 1973—75. Co-author: (book) From Clones to Claims: European and US Case Law on the Patentability of Biotech. Inventions, 2002. Served to lt. comdr. USN, 1969—71. Named one of Top 10 Patent Lawyers Worldwide, PLC Global Counsel, 2002. Mem.: Fed. Cir. Bar Assn., Internat. Patent and Trademark Assn., NY Intellectual Property Law Assn., Am. Intellectual Property Law Assn. (past chmn., internat. subcom. biotech. com.). Office: Fish & Neave IP Group Ropes & Gray 1251 Ave of the Americas New York NY 10020-1104 Office Phone: 212-596-9034. Office Fax: 212-596-9090. Business E-Mail: james.haley@ropesgray.com.

HALEY, JOHN CHARLES, retired bank executive; b. Akron, Ohio, July 24, 1929; s. Arthur and Katherine (Moore) H.; m. Rheba Hopkins, June 11, 1951; children: Alyson, Susan, John, Thomas. AB, Miami U., Oxford, Ohio, 1950; MS, Columbia Grad. Sch. Bus., 1951; LL.D. (hon.), Pace U., 1984. With Chase Manhattan Bank, NYC, 1953—, asst. treas., 1959-62, asst. v.p., 1962-64, v.p., 1964-70; exec. v.p. Chase Manhattan Corp. 1975-84; dep. chmn. Kissinger Assocs., 1984-85; chmn., chief exec. officer Bus. Internat. Inc., NYC, 1986-87. Group pres. Orion Banking Group, London, 1970-73, dir. Armco Corp., chmn., bd. 1995-96. Trustee Siemens Found.; chmn. emeritus bd. trustees Pace U. Served with AUS, 1951-53. Mem. Beta Theta Pi. Home and Office: 8 Deer Run Path Rutland VT 05701-9654

HALEY, JOHNETTA RANDOLPH, music educator; b. Alton, Ill., Mar. 19; d. John A. and Willye E. (Smith) Randolph; children from previous marriage: Karen, Michael. MusB in Edn., Lincoln U., 1945; MusM, So. Ill. U., 1972. Cert. cons. 1995. Vocal and gen. music tchr. Lincoln H.S., East St. Louis, Ill., 1945-48; vocal music tchr., choral dir. Turner Sch., Kirkwood, Mo., 1950-55; vocal and gen. music tchr. Nipher Jr. H.S., Kirkwood, 1955-71; prof. music Sch. Fine Arts So. Ill. U., Edwardsville, 1972—, dir. East St. Louis Campus, 1982—. Adjudicator music festivals; area music cons. Ill. Office Edn., 1977-78; program specialist St. Louis Human Devel. Corp., 1968. Interim exec. dir. St. Louis Coun. Black People, summer, 1970; bd. dirs. YWCA, 1975-80, Artist Presentation Soc., St. Louis, 1975, United Negro Coll. Fund, 1976-78; bd. curators Lincoln U., Jefferson City, Mo., 1974-82, pres., 1978-82; chairperson Ill. Com. on Black Concerns in Higher Edn.; mem. Nat. Ministry on Urban Edn. Luth. Ch.-Mo. Synod, 1975-80; bd. dirs. Coun. Luth. Chs. Stillman Coll.; pres. congregation St. Phillips Luth. Ch.; bd. dirs. Girls, Inc.; mem. Ill. Aux. Bd., United Way; v.p. East St. Louis Cmty. Fund, Inc.; trustee emeritus Stillman Coll., Ala., 2005. Recipient Cotillion de Leon award for Outstanding Cmty. Svc., 1977, Disting. Alumnae award Lincoln U., 1977, Disting. Svc. award United Negro Coll. Fund, 1979; SCLC, 1981; recipient Cmty. Svc. award St. Louis Drifters, 1979, Disting. Svc. to Arts award Sigma Gamma Rho, Nat. Negro Musicians award, 1981, Sci. Awareness award, 1984-85, Tri Del Federated award, 1985, Martin Luther King Drum Maj. award, 1985, Bus. and Profl. Women's Club award, 1985-86, Fred L. McDowell award, 1986, Vol. of Yr. award Inroads Inc., 1986, Woman of Achievement in Edn. award Elks, 1987, Woman of Achievement award Suburban Newspaper of Greater St. Louis and Sta. KMOX-Radio, 1988, Love award Greeley Cmty. Ctr., Sammy Davies Jr. award in Edn., 1990, Yes I Can award in Edn., 1990, Merit award Urban League, 1994, Legacy award Nat. Coun. Negro Women, 1995, Diversity award Mo. ARC, 2001, St. Louis Coun. of Govts. Outstanding Achievement award, 2006, St. Louis' Argus Disting. Citizen award, 2006, Lifetime Achievement award East West Coun. Govs., 2006; named Disting. Citizen St. Louis Argus Newspaper, 1970, Dutchess of Paducah, 1973; Johnetta Haley Scholars Acad. minority scholarship named in her honor So. Ill. U. Mem. AAUP, Music Educators Nat. Conf., Nat. Choral Dirs. Assn., Nat. Assn. Negro Musicians, Coll. Music Soc., Coun. Luth. Chs., Ill. Music. Educators, Jack and Jill, Inc., Women of Achievement in Edn., Friends of St. Louis Art Mus., The Links, Inc. (nat. parliamentarian, chair constnl. and by-laws com.), Las Amigas Social Club, Alpha Kappa Alpha (internat. parliamentarian, dir. 17th ctrl. region 1970-74, Golden Soror award 1995, Grad Svcs. award 2001), Mu Phi Epsilon, Pi Kappa Lambda. Lutheran.

HALEY, PAUL RICHARD, lawyer, state legislator; b. Boston, June 9, 1953; s. Robert Edward and Mary Louise (Hogan) H.; m. Jacqueline Suzanne Holmes, Oct. 11, 1986. BA in Econs., Harvard U., 1976; JD, Suffolk U., 1986. Bar: Mass., 1986; U.S. Dist. Ct. Mass., 1987; U.S. Supreme Ct., 1993. Asst. dist. atty. Norfolk County, Dedham, Mass., 1986-90; mem. Mass. Ho. of Reps., Boston, 1990—. Overseer South Shore Hosp., Weymouth, Mass. Comdr. USNR, 1977—. Mem. Mass. Bar Assn., Norfolk County Bar Assn., VFW, Elks. Democrat. Roman Catholic. Avocations: flying, athletics. Office: Mass Ho of Reps State House Rm 243 Boston MA 02133

HALEY, ROGER KENDALL, librarian; b. Boston, Oct. 29, 1938; s. John F. and Rose (Walker) Haley; m. Mary Hannon; 1 child, Michael J. AB, Georgetown U., 1960; M.L.S., U. Md., 1976. Reference asst. U.S. Senate Library, Washington, 1964-71, asst. librarian, 1971-73, librarian, 1973-97. Mem. Spl. Librs. Assn. (John Cotton Dana award 1993, Hall of Fame award, 2001). Office: 1243 Independence Ave SE Washington DC 20003-1445

HALEY, ROSLYN TREZEVANT, educational program director; b. Washington, July 23, 1955; d. Morti Trezevant and Sara Roslyn Kebe; m. Darrell D. Haley, July 30, 1988; children: Jessica, Darrell Jr., Donald, Anthony, Krystal. BA in History, SC State U., 1976; MPA, Calif. State U., LA, 1983; EdD, UCLA, 1999. Cert. tchr. Calif., adminstr. Calif. Admissions evaluator UCLA, 1979-81, counselor Sch. Pub. Health, 1981-83, head counselor dept. theater, 1983-93; dir. student, counseling, and recruitment svcs. UCLA Sch. Theater, Film and TV, 1993—2005; faculty chair gen. studies Univ. Coll., 2005—. Adult edn. tchr. LA Unified Sch. Dist., 1984-93; assoc. prof., faculty area chair. U. Phoenix, Costa Mesa, Calif., 1996—; bd. dirs. Palmdale HS, Calif., Visual and Performing Arts Acad., 1999; co-founder, adminstr. Jesus is Lord Christian Ch.; state coord. Calif. March for Jesus, 2005. Author of poetry. March organizer March for Jesus, LA, 1994, Antelope Valley, 1995-02; adminstr. Command Ctr., Convoy of Hope, Palmdale, 1998; sch. site coun. Palmtree Elem. Sch., Palmdale, 1998-99; recruiter Boy Scouts Am. Western LA Coun. Bd., 1998-99; campaign chair Antelope Valley YMCA, 2001; adminstr. Jesus is Lord Christian Ch.; state coord. March of Jesus, Calif. Recipient Outstanding Svc. award March for Jesus, LA, 1994, Outstanding Svc. award First Missionary Bapt. Ch., Littlerock, Calif., 1997, Outstanding Svc. award Jesus Day, Antelope Valley. Mem. Am. Assn. Ednl. Rsch. Avocations: reading, swimming, horseback riding, bicycling. Home: 37518 Larchwood Dr Palmdale CA 93550-6037 Office: UCLA Sch TFT 405 Hilgard Ave Los Angeles CA 90095-9000 Office Phone: 661-274-0889. Personal E-mail: drrozhaley@msn.com.

HALEY, ROY W., finance company executive; b. 1947; BS, MIT, 1969. With Arthur Andersen & Co., Houston, 1969-71, 73-88, ptnr., 1980—88; with Ruhmann Mfg. Co., Schulenburg, Tex., 1971-73; pres. Am. Gen. Fin. Inc. (formerly Credithrift Fin. Inc.), 1989-91; also exec. v.p. adminstrn. Am. Gen. Corp., Houston; CEO Am. Gen. Fin. Inc., Evansville, Ind., 1989-91; pres. Am. Gen. Corp., Houston, 1991-93; CEO Wesco Distbn., Pitts., 1994—; chmn., CEO Wesco Internat. Inc., Pitts., 1998—. Chmn. Fed. Res. Bank of Cleve. (Pitts. Branch); dir. United Stationers Inc., Cambrex Corp. Office: Wesco Internat Inc Suite 700 225 W Station Square Dr Pittsburgh PA 15219*

HALEY, VINCENT PETER, retired lawyer; b. Phila., Oct. 6, 1931; s. Vincent Paul and Madeline R. (McCrystal) H.; m. Mary Ann Harron, Apr. 14, 1956; children: Paul V., Kevin G., Maureen T., Patricia Ann M., Kathleen A., Brian M., Regina E., Christopher P., Megan A. BS, Villanova U., 1953, JD cum laude, 1959. Bar: Pa. 1960, Fla. 1979. Acct. Arthur Young & Co., CPAs, Phila., 1955-56; assoc. Schnader, Harrison, Segal & Lewis, Phila., 1959-67, ptnr., 1968-99, mem. exec. com., 1985-88, 89-94, sr. counsel, 2000—03; ret. Mem. bd. consultors Law Sch. Villanova U., 1985—2005; lectr. in field. Sec. Mercy Health Sys., Conshohocken, Pa., 1969—; mem. Archdiocese of Phila. Bd. Edn., 1973-79, pres., 1977-79; mem., bd. dirs. Police Athletic League of Phila., 1994-2001. With USNR, 1953-55. Mem. Pa. Bar Assn. (chmn. corp., banking and bus. law sect. 1979-81), Villanova U. Law Alumni Assn. (pres. 1962-63), Huntingdon Valley Country Club, Roosevelt Racquet Club (Huntingdon Valley, Pa., bd. dirs. 1969-80, 91-94, 97-2000, treas. 1972-80), Order of Coif (chpt. v.p. 1962-63). Home: 1375 Harper's Ln Huntingdon Valley PA 19006-6713 Office: Schnader Harrison Segal et al 1600 Market St Ste 3600 Philadelphia PA 19103-7287 Personal E-mail: vphaley@comcast.net.

HALFACRE, ROBERT GORDON, ombudsman, landscape architect, horticulturist, educator; b. Newberry, SC, June 22, 1941; s. Edwin Harvey and Lela (Ruff) H.; m. Carolyn F. Halfacre, Jan. 24, 1963 (div. Jan., 1980); children: Angela, Robert. BS, Clemson U., 1963, MS, 1965; PhD in Horticulture, Va. Poly. Inst., 1968; MLA, N.C. State U., 1973. Registered landscape architect, S.C. Asst. prof. N.C. State U., Raleigh, 1968-71, assoc. prof., 1971-74; assoc. prof. horticulture Clemson (S.C.) U., 1974-79, prof., 1979-90, Alumni disting. prof., 1990—2006, univ. ombudsman, 1998—. Landscape architect Landscape Archtl. Svcs., Clemson, 1977—; mem. Planning Commn. City of Clemson, 1990-93; pres. faculty senate, Clemson U., 1989-90, bd. visitors, 1992-94, chmn. grievance bd., 1996-98. Author: Carolina Landscape Plants, 1971, Keep 'em Growing, 1972, Fundamentals of Horticulture, 1975, Horticulture, 1979, Plant Science, 1987, Landscape Plants of the Southeast, 5th edit., 1989. Dir. Horticulture Gardens, Clemson U., 1974-77; pres. bd. dirs. Daniel H.S. P.T.A., Clemson, 1985-86; chmn. United Way Campaign, Clemson U., 1996-97. Recipient Silver Seal award Nat. Coun. State Garden Clubs, 1984, Helen S. Hull award, 1979, Sigma Xi Rsch. award, 1968, Outstanding Tchr. award N.C. State U., 1970, Outstanding Faculty award AAUP, 1997, award for Faculty Excellence, Clemson U. Bd. Trustees, 1997. Mem.: Internat. Ombudsman Assn. (bd. dirs. 2005—07), Univ. and Coll. Ombuds Assn. (bd. dirs. 2004—05), Am. Soc. Hort. Sci. (Julian C. Miller rsch. award 1968, L.M. Ware Outstanding Tchr. award So. region 1982), Am. Soc. Landscape Archs., Nat. Ombudsman Assn. Republican. Lutheran. Avocations: water-skiing, writing, tennis, travel. Office: Clemson U 101 Clemson House 248 Palmetto Blvd Clemson SC 29631-5107 Home Phone: 864-985-1123; Office Phone: 864-656-4353. Office Fax: 864-656-4373. Business E-Mail: ombudsman@clemson.edu.

HALFEN, DAVID, retired publishing executive; b. Newark, July 23, 1924; s. Abraham and Rachael (Sudit) Halfen; m. Geneviève Alberte Martin, Jan. 15, 1948; children: Daniel William(dec.) , Alexandre Anthony. Student, U. Pitts., 1944—45, Seoul U., 1945—46, Columbia U., 1946; BS with high honors, U. Wis., 1948; Diploma in French Civilization with high honors, U. Paris, 1949, PhD with highest honors, 1954. From asst. to chief cost acct. Atlas Constructors, Morocco, 1952-54; from asst. editor to editor-in-chief Hart Pub. Co., NYC, 1954-56, 58-62; fgn. affairs editor Scholastic mag., NYC, 1956-58; from field editor to v.p., gen. mgr. Coll. divsn. Scott, Foresman and Co., Glenview, Ill., 1962-78, v.p., gen. mgr. Lifelong Learning divsn., 1978-87, ret., 1987. Chmn. adv. com. USN Courses at Sea Program, 1987-92; sr. assoc. Middlesex Rsch. Ctr., Bethesda, Md., 1991-93; vol. exec. Internat. Exec. Svc. Corps, Zimbabwe, 1993, cons., 1994-96. Author: La Plume: Revue Symboliste 1889-1899, 1954. With AUS, 1942-46, PTO.

HALFERTY, JAMES BURKHARDT, lawyer; b. Lancaster, Wis., Oct. 9, 1930; s. Clay E. and Leone F. (Burkhardt) H.; m. Jo Anne M. Bullock, Sept. 14, 1964; children: Matthew C., Susan E., Laura E. BA, U. Wis., 1952, LLB, 1956. Bar: Wis. 1956, U.S. Dist. Ct. (we. dist.) Wis. 1956. Assoc. I.E. Rasmus, Chippewa Falls, Wis., 1956-61; sole practice Lancaster, Wis., 1961—; dist. atty. Grant County (Wis.), 1962-72; city atty. City of Lancaster, 1975-80, 87-90; instr. criminal evidence and procedure U. Wis.-Platteville, 1968-87. Bd. dirs. Lancaster Meml. Hosp., 1975-86. Mem. Wis. State Bar, Grant County Bar. Republican. Club: Masons. Home: 6883 Badger Rd Lancaster WI 53813-9558 Office: 108 S Madison St Lancaster WI 53813-1761 E-mail: halfertylaw@chorus.net.

HALICZER, JAMES SOLOMON, lawyer; b. Ft. Myers, Fla., Oct. 27, 1952; s. Julian and Margaret (Shepard) H.; m. Paula Fleming, Oct. 3, 1987. BA in English Lit., U. So. Fla., 1976, MA in Polit. Sci., 1978; JD, Stetson U., 1981. Bar: Fla. 1982. Assoc. Conrad, Scherer & James, Ft. Lauderdale, Fla., 1982-86, ptnr., 1988-92; assoc. Bernard & Mauro, Ft. Lauderdale, Fla., 1985-86; shareholder Cooney, Haliczer, Mattson, Lane, Blackburn, Pettis & Richards, Ft. Lauderdale, Fla., 1992-96, Haliczer, Pettis & White, P.A., Ft. Lauderdale, Fla., 1996—2002, Haliczer Pettis, P.A., Ft. Lauderdale, Fla., 2002—. Mem. ABA, Fla. Bar Assn., Broward County Bar Assn., Assn. Trial Lawyers Am., Def. Rsch. Inst., Am. Acad. Healthcare Attys., Phi Kappa Phi, Pi Sigma Alpha, Omicron Delta Kappa. Democrat. Methodist. Avocations: reading, jogging. Office: 1 Financial Plaza 7th Fl 100 SE 3rd Ave Fort Lauderdale FL 33394 Office Phone: 954-523-9922.

HALIL, SUSAN TERRELL, dental hygienist; b. Bessemer, Ala., June 23, 1949; d. Jack Ingram Terrell and Betty May Hardiment; m. Donald William Halil, Sr., Sept. 29, 1972; children: Donald William, Douglas Winston, Melissa Marie. AS, Pensacola Jr. Coll., 1969. Registered dental hygienist Fla. Bd. Dentistry. Dental hygienist Dr. Maxwell de la Rua, Pensacola, Fla., 1969—70, Dr. Reuben Groom, Jacksonville, Fla., 1970—72, Dr. A.J. Bauknecht, Jacksonville, 1972—86; new patient orientation/dental hygienist Dr. Bruce Kanehl, Jacksonville, 1986—87; periodontal dental hygienist Dr. Lamar Pearson, Jacksonville, 1987—89; ins. assoc. Capital Ins. Agy., Jacksonville, 1989—91; dental hygienist Dr. Eric Townsend, Ponte Vedra, Fla., 1991—2001, new patient coord., dental hygienist, 2003—, Dr. Joseph Barton, Jacksonville, 2001—02. Presenter in field. Newsletter editor: Pres. San Jose Cath. Women's Guild, Jacksonville, 1983—84, San Jose Cath. Parish Coun., Jacksonville, 2003—04; catechist, 2004—07; lector, 1983—. Recipient Svc. award, N.E. Dist. Dental Hygienists' Soc., 1971, 1980. Mem.: N.E. Fla. Dental Hygiene Assn. (first v.p. 1972—73, pres. 1973—74, newsletter editor 1973—74, 1980—81, Achievement award 1995), Fla. Dental Hygiene Assn. (N.E. Fla. rep. coun. on govtl. affairs 1991—97, N.E. Fla. del. 1992—97, v.p. 1994—95, pres. elect 1995—96, pres. 1996—97, immediate past pres. 1997—98, mem. nominating com. 1997—, Disting. Svc. award 2002, Component Outstanding Mem. award 2002, 2004), Am. Dental Hygienists' Assn. (alt. del. 1970—71, nat. del. 1971—73, 1994—97, chairperson nat. del. 1996—97, liaison Inst. for Oral Health 1998—99). Republican. Avocations: gardening, walking, bicycling, dance, yoga. Home: 7104 St Augustine Rd Jacksonville FL 32217 Home Phone: 904-733-0046; Office Phone: 904-285-7711. Personal E-mail: shalil@bellsouth.net.

HALILI, ANTONIO MARQUEZ, facilities maintenance mechanic; b. Caloocan City, Philippines, Jan. 9, 1951; s. Pedro Nosa Halili and Virginia Ileto Marquez; m. Brenda gotay Ferrer, Jan. 22, 1992; children: Jocelyn Jimeno, Anthony Bonifacio, Mark Solomon, Sara Virginia, Celina Marie. Diploma, Nat. Tech. Sch., LA, 1983—85; attended, El Camino C.C., Torrance, Calif., 1986—88. Seafarer AB/QM prodn. elect. tech., merchant marine, Long Beach, Calif., 1971—76; seafarer Domain of Neptunes Rex, 1974. Biographer Cry of the Dying Medicine Man. Vice-chair Asian Pacific Islanders Employee Resource Group/Am. Airlines, 2003; participant, Saving Babies Lives March of Dimes, LA, 2001—02; relief crew chief and leadman Go for Broke Found.; advocate WW II Filipino Vets.; participant Walk America March of Dimes, 2004; participant Nat. WWII Meml., Washington, 2003—04; lifetime charter mem. WWII Vets. Mem.: Nat. Mgmt. Assn., United Tondo Assn. (assoc.; adviser 2004—05), Knights of Columbus. Achievements include invention of a liquid hose clean up attachment. Home: 1318 E 55th St Long Beach CA 90805 Personal E-mail: tbhalili@hotmail.com.

HALITSKY, STEVE, data analyst, statistician, researcher; b. Vinnitsa, Ukraine, Aug. 31, 1943; s. Konstantyn and Olga Halitsky; m. Roxanne Bedzyk, July 8, 1975; children: Andrei, Edward. MS in Applied Stats. and Computers, Cybernetics Inst., Kyiv, Ukraine. C++ cert. Brainbench, 2002. Rschr. Cybernetics Inst., Kyiv, 1972—80; sr. scientist Database Rsch. Inst., Kyiv, 1982—91; translator Bible Socs. Printing Ho., Stockholm and Pasadena, Calif., 1990—93; rschr. Isomedix, Inc., Libertyville, Ill., 1997—98; data analyst SPR, Inc., Oak Brook, Ill., 1998—99, WorldCom, Oak Brook, 2000—01; pres., CEO, co-founder Theta Criteria, Inc., Skokie, Ill., 2003—. Co-organizer internat. confs. Ukraine's Univs. Open Sys., Applied Math., Economy and Bus. Translator: The Practical Guide to Splines, 1985; contbr. articles to profl. jours. Humanitarian aid organizer Former GULAG Prisoners Fellowship, Kyiv, 1991—98; organizer Studies Anti-Nazi Resistance and Holocaust in Proximity to Hitler's Werewolf HQ, Podolia, Ukraine, 2001—; translator, humanitarian Humanitarian Missions, Kyiv, 1988—91; co-founder Ukraine's Bible Soc. Mem.: Internat. Linear Algebra Soc. (ILAS) (assoc.), Soc. Indsl. Applied Math. (SIAM). Independent. Jewish. Achievements include development, formalization and verification of new and highly efficient methods of analysis of multidimensional stochastic dynamic systems; established human rights watch for PhysTech Scientists. Avocations: jazz and classical music, herbal properties and remedies, humanitarian aid, history, reading. Business E-Mail: shalitsky@thetacriteria.com.

HALIW, JEROME MICHAEL, civil engineer; s. Harry Jerome and Lillian Haliw; m. Kari Lynn Gagnon, May 20, 1989. BS, Colo. Sch. of Mines, 1991. Design engr. Isbill Associates, Inc., Aurora, Colo., 1992—97;

project design engr. Raytheon Infrastructure, Inc., Englewood, Colo., 1997—2000; project mgr. Wash. Infrastructure Services, Inc., Littleton, Colo., 2000—02; chief discipline engr. Wash. Infrastructure Svcs., Inc., Denver, 2002—; airport design mgr. Washington Group Internat., Inc., Denver, 2002—06; sr. aviation engr. Reynolds, Smnith and Hills, Inc., Englewood, Colo., 2006—. Mem.: ASME, Am. Soc. Civil Engrs., Colo. Sch. of Mines Alumni Assn., Order of the Engr. Office: 5600 S Quebec St Ste 340C Greenwood Village CO 80111 Office Phone: 303-409-9700. Office Fax: 303-409-9701. Business E-Mail: jerry.haliw@rsandh.com.

HALKETT, ALAN NEILSON, lawyer; b. Chungking, China, Oct. 5, 1931; came to U.S., 1940; s. James and Evelyn Alexandrina (Neilson) H.; m. Mary Lou Hickey, July 30, 1955; children: Kent, James, Kate BS, UCLA, 1953, LL.B., 1961. Bar: Calif. 1962. Mem. firm Latham & Watkins, LA, 1961-95, mem. exec. com., 1968-72, chmn. litigation dept., 1980-86, chmn. succession com., 1986-87. State chmn. Am. Coll., Calif., 1992-94; designee CPR panel Disting. Neutrals, 1994—. Served to lt. USN, 1954-58 Fellow Am. Coll. Trial Lawyers; mem. Calif. Bar Assn., Nat. Arbitration Forum, Chancery Club, UCLA Law Alumni Assn. (pres. 1968), Order of Coif, Palos Verdes Country Club (Palos Verdes Estates, Calif.). Republican. Avocations: golf, old cars. Office: Latham & Watkins 633 W 5th St Ste 4000 Los Angeles CA 90071-2005 Personal E-mail: halkett6@aol.com.

HALKIN, HUBERT, mathematics professor, researcher; b. Liege, Belgium, June 5, 1936; came to U.S., 1960; s. Leon E. and Denise H.; m. Carolyn Mulliken, June 22, 1964 (div. 1971); children: Christopher, Sherrill-Anne; m. Katherine Hodges, Dec. 24, 1988 (div. 2001); m. Kathy Ziegler, Oct. 10, 2004. Ingenieur, U. Liège, 1960; PhD, Stanford U., 1963. Tech. staff Bell Telephone Labs., Whippany, NJ, 1963-65; assoc. prof. math. dept. U. Calif., San Diego, 1965-69, prof., 1969—, dept. chmn. San Diego, 1981-87; chief scientist Chrometics Co., 2002—; resident scientist, 2003—. Editor Jour. Optimization Theory and Applications, 1968—, Revue Française d'Automatique de Recherche Operationnelle, 1973—. Guggenheim fellow, 1971-72. Mem.: Idyllwild, Club Aroma, Sierra Club. Office: U Calif San Diego Dept Math La Jolla CA 92093 Business E-Mail: hhalkin@ucsd.edu.

HALL, ADAM STUART, lawyer; b. Atlanta, June 19, 1971; s. Andrew Clifford Hall and Patricia Ann Bursten. BA with honors, U. Fla., 1993, JD with honors, 1996. Bar: Fla. 1997, U.S. Dist. Ct. (so. dist.) Fla. 1997, U.S. Dist. Ct. (mid. dist.) Fla. 1998. Intern Supreme Ct. Fla., Tallahassee, 1995; assoc. Andrew Hall & Assocs., P.A., Miami, Fla., 1997-98, Hall, David and Joseph, P.A., Miami, 1998—2005; ptnr. Hall, Lamb and Hill, P.A., Miami, 2005—. Chmn. unsecured creditor's com. Inre Telephone Co. Ctrl. Fla., Inc., Orlando, 1998-99. Mem. U. Fla. Coll. Law Alumni Coun., Gainesville, 1997—; mem. young leadership coun. United Way of Dade County, Miami, 1997—. Mem. ABA, ATLA, Acad. Fla. Trial Lawyers, Dade County Bar Assn. Avocations: scuba diving, skiing, football. Office: Hall David and Joseph PA 1428 Brickell Ave Penthouse Miami FL 33131

HALL, ADRIENNE A., international marketing communications executive; b. LA; d. Arthur E. and Adelina P. Kosches; m. Maurice Hall; children: Adam, Todd, Victoria, Stefanie; adopted children: Joe Hibbitt, Kim Hibbitt, Joe Kwan, Georgina Kwan, Carlos Moreno, Miriam Moreno. BA, UCLA. Founding ptnr. Hall & Levine Advt., LA, 1970-80; vice chmn. bd. Eisaman, Johns & Laws Advt. Inc., L.A., Houston, Chgo., NYC, 1980-94; pres., CEO The Hall Group, Beverly Hills, Calif., 1994—. Co-founder, chair, bd. dirs. Women, Inc.; chair bd. dirs. Women's Pres. Orgn., 1999—, co-chair, State Econ. Network, 2000—; chmn. Eric Bovy Inc., 1986-89, Hall Partnership, Venture Capital; bd. dirs. Calif. Mfrs. Assn., Calif. Life Corp., Inc.; mem. adv. bd. Global Asset Mgmt., The Edison Co., Sempra Energy, The Gas Co., Nestle, Merrill Lynch. Trustee UCLA; bd. regents Loyola-Marymount U., 1990—, Natl. Bus. Counc., Wash. D.C.; mem. The Founders of Music Ctr., Save the Children, Vietnam and Haiti.; mem., chair women's leadership bd. Kennedy Sch. Govt., Harvard U.; commr. L.A. County Arts Commn.; commr. Calif. Gov.'s Commn. on Econ. Devel., task force Rebuild L.A.; chair Leading Women Entrepreneurs of the World; bd. dirs. United Way, ARC, Exec. Svc. Corps, The Com. of 200, Shelter Partnership; trustee Nat. Health Found., Women's Enterprise Devel. Corp.; gov. Town Hall; mem. adv. coun. Girls' Clubs Am.; mem. adv. bd. Girl Scouts U.S., Asian Pacific Women's Adv. Bd., Coalition of 100 Black Women, Nat. Network of Hispanic Women, Women of Color, Women in Bus., Downtown Women's Ctr. and residence, Leadership Am., Washington, L.A., Food Bank; mem. exec. bd. Greater L.A. Partnership for Homeless, Recipient Nat. Headliner award Women in Comm., 1982, Profl. Achievement award UCLA Alumni, 1979, Award for Cmty. Svc., 1994, Asian Pacific Network Woman Warrior award, 1994, Woman of the Yr. award Am. Advt. Fedn., 1973, Ad Person of West award Mktg. and Media Decisions, 1982, Bus. Woman of Yr. award Boy Scouts Am., 1983, Women Helping Women award Soroptimists Internat., 1984, 1st ann. portfolio award for exec. women, 1985, Communicator of Yr. award Ad Women, 1986, Leader award YWCA, 1986, L.A. Women's Found. Mentor award, 1997, Leading Women Entrepreneurs of World award, 2003; named Bus. Leader of Yr., L.A. Bus. Coun., 1999, NAW Legal Defense/Edn. Fund. award, 2001, Cosmo award, Women's Leadership Exch., 2006; named NAWBO Hall of Fame, 2002, Hall of Fame Enterprising Women Mag., NY, 2004; Adrienne Hall Women's Mentorship Fund established in her honor, The Adrienne Hall Scholars, The Adrienne Hall annual lecture, Kennedy Sch. Govt., Harvard U., 2005. Mem. Internat. Women's Forum (Woman Who Made a Difference award 1987), Am. Assn. Advt. Agys. (bd. dirs. 1980, chmn. bd. govs. western region), Western States Advt. Agys. Assn. (pres. 1975), Hollywood Radio and TV Soc. (dir.), Nat. Advt. Rev. Bd., Overseas Edn. Fund, Com. 200 (western chmn.), Women in Communications, Orgn. Women Execs., Calif. Women's Forum (founder, chmn. The Trusteeship), Rotary (L.A. 5 chpt.), Internat. Bus. Fellows (mem. adv. bd.), Women's Econ. Alliance, Nat. Assn. Women Bus. Owners (adv. bd.), L.A. Area C. of C. (chmn., alumni dir.). Clubs: Calif. Yacht; Stock Exchange, Los Angeles Advt. (pres.) (Los Angeles). Lodges: Rotary. Achievements include having the Harvard University and Kennedy School of Government establish the Adrienne Hall Women's Mentorship Fund in perpetuity in her honor in 2006; founding the first advertising agency in the nation headed by women. Personal E-mail: aahall@earthlink.net.

HALL, AMY MATTHEWS, science educator; b. Shreveport, La., Dec. 7, 1941; d. James William and Annie Ruth (Brown) Matthews; m. Jon H. Hall, June 19, 1962; children: Jon William, Elizabeth Anne May. BS in Edn., Centenary Coll., 1967. Fifth grade tchr. Caddo Parish Schools, Shreveport, La., 1968—71; sci. tchr. Agnew Town and Country Sch., Shreveport, 1971—72, Southfield Sch., Shreveport, 1972—86, Caddo Mid. Magnet, Shreveport, 1986—. Mem. exec. bd. Caddo Fed. Tchrs. and Support Pers. Author: (books of poetry) Coll. Anthology of Poetry, 1960, rev. sci. curriculm, rev. Caddo Parish Discipline policy. Named Master Tchr., So. Assn. Ind. Sch., 1985. Mem.: Caddo Fedn. Tchrs. (exec. bd.), La. Mid. Sch. Assn., Nat. Biology Tchr. Assn., Paw Prints Club. Republican. Meth. Avocations: antiques, gemology, needlecrafts. Home: 9815 E Trails End Shreveport LA 71118 Office: Caddo Mid Magnet Sch 7635 Cornelius Lane Shreveport LA 71106

HALL, ANDREW CLIFFORD, lawyer; b. Warsaw, Sept. 16, 1944; arrived in U.S., 1949, naturalized, 1954; s. Edmund and Maria (Hahn) Hall; m. Gail Meyers, 1993; children: Michael Ian, Adam Stuart, Hilary Meyers Azrael, Katie Meyers. BA, U. Fla., 1965, JD with high honors, 1968. Bar: Fla. 1968, U.S. Dist. Ct. (so. dist.) Fla. 1968, U.S. Dist. Ct. (no. dist.) a. 1971, U.S. Ct. Appeals (5th cir.) 1971, Ga. 1973, U.S. Supreme Ct. 1974, U.S. Ct. Appeals (D.C. cir.) 1974, U.S. Ct. Appeals (11th cir.) 1981. Law clk. to judge U.S. Dist. Ct.; assoc. Haas, Holland, Levison, Gilbert, Atlanta, 1970—72, Frates, Floyd, Pearson, Stewart, Miami, 1972—75; ptnr. Storace, Hall & Hauser, Miami, 1975—79, Hall & Hauser, Miami, 1979—82, Hall, Lamb and Hall, P.A., 1982—. Instr. bus. law U. Fla. Mem. Coun. of 100 Fla. Internat. U.; trustee U. Fla. Coll. of Law Found.; bd. dirs. Greater Miami Jewish Fedn.; chmn. bd. trustees, bd. dirs. Ctrl. Agy. Jewish Edn., Ash Ha Torah. Mem.: ATLA, ABA, Acad. Fla. Trial Lawyers (diplomate), U. Fla. Coll. Law Alumni (mem. coun.), Am. Judicature Soc., Fla. State Bar Assn., Hebrew Immigrant Aid Assn. (nat. bd. dirs.), Order of Coif, Phi Alpha Delta, Phi Kappa Phi. Democrat. Jewish. Home: 3515 Bayshore Villas Dr Miami FL 33133 Office: Hall Lamb and Hall PA Att/Karen Fernandez 1428 Brickell Ave Ph Miami FL 33131-3411

HALL, ANTHONY ELMITT, agriculturist, physiologist; b. Tickhill, Yorkshire, Eng., May 6, 1940; came to U.S., 1964; s. Elmitt and Mary Lisca (Schofield) H.; m. Bretta Reed, June 20, 1965; children: Kerry, Gina. Student, Harper Adams Agrl. Coll., Eng., 1958-60; student in agrl. engring., Essex Inst. Agrl. Engring., Eng., 1960-61; BS in Irrigation Sci., U. Calif., Davis, 1966, PhD in Plant Physiology, 1970. Farmer Dyon House, Austerfield, England, 1955-58; extension officer Ministry of Agr., Tanzania, 1961-63; research asst. U. Calif., Davis, 1964-70, asst. research scientist, 1971; research fellow Carnegie Inst., Stanford, Calif., 1970; prof. U. Calif., Riverside, 1971—2003, chmn. dept botany and plant scis., 1994—97, prof. emeritus, 2003. Adv. UN; cons. in field. Author: Crop Responses to Environment, 2001, Sahelian Droughts: A Partial Agronomic Solution, 2007; editor: Agriculture in Semi-Arid Environments, 1979, Stable Isotopes and Plant Carbon-Water Relations, 1993; contbr. articles to profl. jours. Recipient BIFAD chair's award for scientific excellence, 2000, USDA Sec.'s Honor award plant breeding rsch., 2001. Fellow: Crop Sci. Soc. Am., Am. Soc. Agronomy; mem.: Phi Kappa Phi, Phi Beta Kappa, Gamma Sigma Delta (Disting. Achievement in Agr. award of merit 1999), Alpha Zeta. Achievements include design (with others) of a steady state porometer for measuring stomatal conductance; research on the physiology and breeding of heat and chilling tolerant, pest resistant and drought adapted cowpea cultivars including developing cowpea varieties CB27 and Ein El Gazal; patents in field, no6,501,006 B1, 2002. Mailing: 2922 Lindsay Lane Quincy CA 95971 Home Phone: 530-283-3052; Office Phone: 951-236-1580. Business E-Mail: anthony.hall@ucr.edu.

HALL, ARTHUR RAYMOND, JR., retired minister; b. Danville, Ill., Apr. 16, 1922; s. Arthur Raymond and Hetta Ada (Wheeler) H.; m. Lou Ann Benson, Mar. 16, 1946; children: Janet Marie Hall Graff, Laura Ann Hall Scott Abell, Nancy Marion Hall Berens. AB, U. Ill., 1946, MA, 1948; MDiv cum laude, Union Theol. Sem., NYC, 1951; DD, Hanover Coll., 1961. Ordained to ministry Presbyn. Ch., 1951. Staff asst. McKinley Meml. Ch. and Found., Champaign, Ill., 1946-48; student asst. First Presbyn Ch., NYC, 1948-50; pastor First Presbyn. Ch., Monmouth, Ill., 1951-58, Ctrl. Presbyn. Ch., Louisville, 1958-67, Bradley Hills Presbyn. Ch., Bethesda, Md., 1967-89. Pres. bd. Christian edn. United Presbyn. Ch., 1968-73; sec., bd. dirs. Louisville Presbyn. Sem., 1962-70; chmn. renewal and extension of ministry (United Presbyn. Gen. Assembly), 1965-68; mem. joint com. on Presbyn. Reunion, 1969-83; moderator Synod of Piedmont, 1974-75; trustee U.P. Ch., 1974-83; bd. dirs. U.P. Found., 1974-83; del. Uniting Assembly of World Alliance of Ref. Chs., Nairobi, Kenya, 1970; mem. com. on theol. edn. Presbyn. Ch., U.S.A., 1987, assoc. dir. 1988-90. Contbr. articles to periodicals. Pres. Citizens Met. Planning Coun., Louisville, 1962; chmn. Mayor's Adv. Com. for Cmty. Devel., 1963-67; v.p. Louisville YMCA Downtown Bd., 1963; bd. dirs. Louisville Health and Welfare Coun., 1963-67, Greater Washington Coun. Chs., Johnson C. Smith Theol. Sem., Atlanta, 1973-2000, trustee emeritus, 2000—, Interdenominational Theol. Ctr., Atlanta, 1974-99, trustee emeritus; trustee Centre Coll. Ky., 1959-73, Union Theol. Sem., N.Y.C., 1975-84; trustee Travelers Aid Soc., Louisville, 1959-67, v.p., 1961-67. Lt. (j.g.) USNR, 1943-46. Mem. Am. Guild Organists, Washington Interchurch Club, Rotary, Beta Theta Pi, Phi Delta Phi. Democrat. Home: 580 Russell Ave Gaithersburg MD 20877-2868 Personal E-mail: a3a4hallbenson@starpower.net.

HALL, BEVERLY BARTON, librarian; b. Cin., July 15, 1918; d. Clarence Earl Barton and Maude Ethel Wedmore; m. Randolph Van Lew Hall, Apr. 26, 1947; children: Barton M., Martha H. Kern, Patricia H. Pellerin. BA, Middlebury Coll., 1940; BS, Columbia U., 1941; MS, So. Conn. State Coll., 1975. Cert. tchr./libr. grades K-12, Conn. Libr. Wellesley (Mass.) Coll., 1941-42, Great Neck (N.Y.) Pub. Libr., 1942-44, Yale U. Sch. Law, New Haven, 1944-50, Amity Regional H.S., Woodbridge, Conn., 1967-80. Author: Secret of the Lion's Head, 1995; also short stories. Founder, bd. dirs. Orange (Conn.) Pub. Libr., 1956-63; founder, head libr. St. John's Ch. Libr., Naples, Fla., 1993—; active Collier County Geneal. Soc., Collier County Hist. Soc., Collier County Friends of the Libr. Mem. Ch. and Synagoge Libr. Assn. (sec. 1999-2000). Republican. Episcopalian. Avocations: reading, water aerobics, counted cross-stitch, crocheting, music. Home: Apt 107 49 High Point Circle South Naples FL 34103

HALL, BEVERLY L., school system administrator; b. Montego Bay, Jamaica; m. Luis Hall, Dec. 22, 1973; 1 child, Jason. BA in English, Bklyn. Coll., 1970, MA in Guidance and counseling, 1973; PhD in Adminstrn., Fordham U., 1990. English tchr. Jr. H.S. 265, Bklyn., 1970—76; asst. prin. Satellite West Jr. H.S., Bklyn., 1977—83; prin. Pub. Sch. 282, Bklyn., 1983—87, Jr. H.S. 113, Bklyn., 1987—92; supt. Cmty. Sch. Dist. 27, Queens, NY, 1992—94; dep. schs. chancellor for instrn. N.Y.C. Pub. Schs., 1994—95; supt. Newark City Schs., 1995—99, Atlanta Pub. Schs., 1999—. Office: Atlanta Pub Schs 130 Trinity Ave SW Atlanta GA 30303 Office Phone: 404-802-2820.

HALL, BLAINE HILL, retired librarian; b. Wellsville, Utah, Dec. 12, 1932; s. James Owen and Agnes Effie (Hill) H.; m. Carol Stokes, 1959; children: Suzanne, Cheryl, Derek. BS, Brigham Young U., 1960, MA, 1965, MLS, 1971. Instr. English, Brigham Young U., Provo, Utah, 1963—72, humanities libr., 1972—96. Book reviewer Am. Reference Book Ann., l984-2000. Author: Collection Assessment Manual, 1985, Saul Bellow Bibliography, 1987, Jerzy Kosinski Bibliography, 1991, Jewish American Fiction Writers Bibliography, 1991, Conversations with Grace Paley, 1997; editor: Utah Libraries, 1972-77 (periodical award ALA 1977); contbr. articles to profl. jours. Bd. dirs. Orem (Utah) Pub. Libr., 1977-84; mem. Orem Media Rev. Commn., 1984-86; chmn. Utah Adv. Commn. on Librs., 1983-91. With U.S. Army, 1953-54, Korea. Mem. ALA (coun. 1988-92), Utah Libr. Assn. (pres. 1980-81, Disting. Svc. award 1989), Mountain Plains Libr. Assn. (bd. dirs. 1978-83, editor newsletter 1978-83, pres. 1994-96, grantee 1979, 80, Disting. Svc. award 1991), Phi Kappa Phi. Mem. Lds Ch. Avocations: writing, photography, carpentry, reading. Home: 230 E 1910 S Orem UT 84058-8161 Personal E-mail: blainehall@comcast.net.

HALL, BREDA FAYE KIMBROUGH INMAN, counselor, educator; d. Byron C. and Vera J. Kimbrough; m. Charles Roland Inman (dec.); m. James Webster Hall (div.); 1 child, Rachel Lauren Hall Clark. BS, U. Ala., Birmingham, 1984; MA, U. N.D., Grand Forks, 1987. Nat. cert. counselor Nat. Bd. for Cert. Counselors, Inc., lic. profl. counselor N.Mex. Counseling and Therapy Practice Bd., clin. mental health counselor N.Mex. Grad. asst. learning svcs. U. N.D., Grand Forks, 1985—86, practicum counseling ctr., 1986; counseling intern St. Luke's Hosp. Chaplaincy and Radiation Oncology, Fargo, ND, 1986—87; counselor, instr., dir. student svcs. U. N.Mex., Los Alamos, 1987—90, practicum instr. human svcs. Valencia, 1990—91, counselor/sr. counselor with grief intervention program Office Med. Investigator Albuquerque; therapist Gulf Coast Mental Health, Gulfport, Miss., 1994—97. Divsn. health svcs. rsch. mem., mental health profl., vol. The ARC; spkr. in field; developed grief ctr. for children; vol., mental health profl. Ctr. for Hope & Healing. Author: A Manual for the American Voter, Personality Development from the Biblical Perspective. Vol. paraprofessional Rape Crises Ctr., Birmingham; vol. Civitan's Spl. Olympic's, Los Alamos; vol. paraprofessional McDonough Ho., Birmingham. Recipient Psychology Rsch. award, U. Ala., Birmingham, 1984. Mem.: Ala. Counseling Assn., Am. Counseling Assn. (assoc.). Achievements include research in severity of illness and emotional relationships with patients in tri-state area of ND, SD, MN (UND); development of interactive grief support groups between parents and teenagers suffering loss of child (or sibling) between ages of 0-18; research in difference between cognitive and emotional intake of information in recruiting Apheresis Donors. Avocations: reading, movies, gardening, skiing, waterskiing. Home and Office: PO Box 1643 Brandon MS 39043-1643 Office Phone: 601-951-1583, 601-898-4947. Personal E-mail: bredaihall@yahoo.com. Business E-Mail: bhall@mc.edu.

HALL, BRIAN KEITH, biology professor, writer; b. Port Kembla, N.S.W., Australia, Oct. 28, 1941; s. Harry J. and Doris (Garrad) Hall; m. June Denise Priestley, May 21, 1966; children: Derek Andrew, Imogen Elizabeth. BSc, U. New Eng., Australia, 1963, BSc with honors, 1965; PhD, U. New Eng., 1968, DSc, 1978. Teaching fellow U. New Eng., Armidale, 1965-68; asst. prof. biology Dalhousie U., Halifax, N.S., Canada, 1968-72, assoc. prof., 1972-75, prof., 1975—, chmn. dept. biology, 1978-85, Killam rsch. prof., 1990-95, faculty sci., Killam prof. biology, 1996-2001, George S. Campbell prof. of biology, 2001—, univ. rsch. prof., 2002—; Killam rsch. fellow, 2003. Vis. prof. U. Guelph, 1975, U. Queensland, Australia, 1981, Southampton U., England, 1982; mem. adv. com. on life scis. Natural Scis. and Engring. Rsch. Coun. Can., 1985; Turner-Newall lectr. U. Manchester, England, 1985; Frontiers in Biology lectr. Tex. A&M U., 1992; Von Hofsten lectr. Uppsala U., Sweden, 1993; Plenary lectr. Internat. Congress Vert. Morphol., 1994; Fry lectr. Can. Soc. Zoologists, 1994; Sarnat lectr. UCLA, 1994; Miller vis. res. prof. U. Calif., Berkeley, 1997; Landsdowne vis. prof. U. Victoria, 1998; Glaser Disting. vis. prof. Fla. Internat. U., 2000; Rayne mem. vis. prof. U. Western Australia, 1993, 2006. Author: (book) Developmental and Cellular Skeletal Biology, 1978; author: (with N. MacLean) Cell Commitment and Differentiation, 1987; author: The Neural Crest, 1988, Evolutionary Developmental Biology, 1992, Evolutionary Developmental Biology, 2d edit., 1998, The Neural Crest in Development and Evolution, 1999; editor: Cartilage, 3 vols., 1983; author: Bones and Cartilage, 2005;; editor: Bone, A Treatise, 9 vols., 1990—94; editor: (with S. Newman) (book) Cartilage: Molecular Aspects, 1991; editor: (with J Hanken) The Vertebrate Skull, 3 vols., 1993, Homology: The Hierarchical Basis of Comparative Biology, 1994; editor: (with M. H. Wake) The Origin and Evolution of Larval Forms, 1999; editor: (with W. Olson) Keywords and Concepts in Evolutionary Development Biology, 2003; editor: (with W. R. Pearson and G. Muller) Environment, Development and Evolution, 2003; editor: (with B. Hallgrimsson) Variation, 2005; editor: Fins and Limbs: Development, Evolution and Transformation, 2006. Recipient Young Scientist of Yr. medal, Atlantic Provinces Interuniv. Com. in Scis., 1974, Fry medal, Can. Soc. Zoologists, 1994, Craniofacial Biology Rsch. award, 1996, Alexander Kowalvsky medal, 2001, award of excellence in rsch., Govt. of Can., 2002, Killam prize, Govt. Can., 2003—05; fellow, Nuffield Found., 1982, Warwick James, London U., 1989, Ctr. Human Biology, U. Western Australia, 1993—; Killam Rsch. fellow, Govt. Can., 2005—. Fellow: Royal Soc. Can.; mem.: Am. Acad. Arts and Sci. (hon. fgn.). Home: 15/6770 Jubilee Rd Halifax NS Canada B3H 2H8 Office Phone: 902-494-3522. Business E-Mail: bkh@dal.ca.

HALL, BRUCE A., music educator; b. Detroit, Dec. 11, 1948; s. Henry Yelland Hall and Muriel Eileen Hall (nee McMillan); m. Sunny Joy Langton, May 29, 1982; children: Jason Matthew, Corey Lynn, Kirby Anne, Kristin Leigh. MusB, U. Mich., 1972, MusM, 1973. Instr. Va. Poly. Inst. and State U., Blacksburg, 1973—77; asst. prof. Auburn U., Ala., 1986—89; sr. lectr. Northwestern U., Evanston, Ill., 1989—. Dir. Voices of the Acad., Lake Zurich, Ill., 2003—. Internat. operatic baritone: Lyric Opera of Chicago, Cologne Opera, Wuppertal Opera, Stuttgart Opera, Netherlands Opera, Seattle Opera, Cleve. Opera, Mich. Opera Theater, Chicago Opera Theater, Detroit Symphony, Rotterdam Symphony, Seattle Symphony, Honolulu Symphony, Sudwestfunk Orch., Westdeutsher Rundfunk Orch. Grantee Alumnae grantee, Northwestern U., 1994, 1995. Mem.: Am. Choral Dirs. Assn. Avocations: sailing, travel, skating, sports. Office: Northwestern University School of Music 711 Elgin Rd Evanston IL 60208-1200 Home Phone: 847-550-1242; Office Phone: 847-491-7545. Office Fax: 847-491-5260. Business E-Mail: bruce@northwestern.edu.

HALL, BRYAN H., lawyer; Grad., U. Wis., 1985; JD, Ind. U., 1987. Assoc. Morgan Lewis & Bockius, NYC, Fried, Frank, Harris, Shriver & Jacobsen, NYC, 1997—99, spl. counsel corp. dept., 1999—2000, ptnr., 2000—04; gen. counsel, sec. Virgin Media Inc. (formerly NTL Inc.), NYC, 2004—. Office: Virgin Media Inc 909 Third Ave Ste 2863 New York NY 10022*

HALL, CARL WILLIAM, agricultural and mechanical engineer; b. Tiffin, Ohio, Nov. 16, 1924; s. Lester and Irene H.; m. Mildred Evelyn Wagner, Sept. 5, 1949; 1 dau., Claudia Elizabeth. BS, B. in Agrl. Engring. summa cum laude, Ohio State U., 1948; M.M.E., U. Del., 1950; PhD, Mich. State U., 1952. Registered profl. engr., Mich., Ohio. Instr. U. Del., 1948-50, asst. prof., 1950-51, Mich. State U., 1951-53, assoc. prof., 1953-55, prof., 1955-70, chmn. dept. agrl. engring., 1964-70; dean, dir. research (Coll. Engring.); prof. mech. engring. Wash. State U., Pullman, 1970-82, pres. WSU Rsch. Found., 1973-82; dep. asst. dir. Directorate for Engring. NSF, 1982-90; ret., 1990. With ESCOE, Inc., Washington, 1979; dist. vis. prof. Ohio State U., 1991; del. to USSR, 58, 87; mem. Wash. State mission to Libya, 1977; mem. engring. edn. del. to People's Republic of China, 1978, Indonesia, 1978, 93, 94; co-chmn. NRC-India Nat. Sci. Acad. Workshop, New Delhi, 1979; with ACA, Inc., 1956—70, pres., 1962—70; chmn. Nat. Dairy and Food Engring. Conf., 1953—66; mem. postgrad. edn. select com. USN, Monterey, Calif., 1975; rsch. fellow Japan Soc. Promotion Sci., 1991; cons. in field. Author: Drying Farm Crops, 1957, Agricultural Engineering Index 1907-60, 1961-70, 71-80, 81-90, (with others) Drying of Milk and Milk Products, 1966, 71, Agricultural Mechanization for Developing Countries, 1973; co-editor: Agricultural Engineers Handbook, 1960, Processing Equipment for Agricultural Products, 1963, 2d edit., 1979, Spanish edit., 1968, Milk Pasteurization, 1968, Ency. of Food Engineering, 1971, 86, Drying Cereal Grains, 1974, 2d edit., 1991, Dairy Technology and Engineering, 1976, Errors in Experimentation, 1977, Dictionary of Drying, 1979, Drying and Storage of Agricultural Products, 1980, Biomass as an Alternative Fuel, 1981, Dictionary of Energy, 1983, Food and Energy, 1984, Food and Natural Resources, 1988, Biomass Handbook, 1989; (with others) Drying and Storage of Grains, 1992, Literature of Agricultural Engineering, 1992, The Age of Synthesis, 1995, Laws and Models, 1999, Biographical Dictionary of People in Engineering Literature, 2007; editor, emeritus: Drying Technology: Taylor & Francis, Inc.; contbr. articles to profl. jours., chpts. to books. Staff sgt. infantry US Army, 1943—46, ETO. Decorated Bronze Star and CIB; named Engr. of Yr., DC Coun. Engrs. and Archs., 1999; recipient Disting. Faculty award, Mich. State U., 1963, Centennial Achievement award, Ohio State U., 1970, Massey-Ferguson Edn. medal, 1976, Max Eyth medal, Germany, 1979, Medal du Merite, France, 1979, Silver medal, Paris, 1980, Cyrus Hall McCormick medal, 1984, Disting. Svc. award and medal, NSF, 1988, Excellence in Drying award, IDS, 1990, Food Engring. award and medal, 1993, Disting. Alumni award, Ohio State U., 1983, 2003, Mich. State U., 2004, Internat. Peace prize, United Collateral Conv., 2005, Mech. Engring. Disting. Career award, U. Del., 2006. Fellow: Am. Soc. Agr. and Biol.

Engrs. (life; pres. 1974—75), ASME (life; v.p. rsch. 1993—95), AAAS (life), Internat. Commn. Agrl. Engrs. (v.p. 1965—74), Accreditation Bd. Engring. and Tech., Am. Inst. Med. and Biol. Engring.; mem.: VFW, NAE, Inst. Biol. Engring., Inst. Food Tech., Am. Soc. Engring. Edn. (life), Engrs. Coun. for Profl. Devel. (exec. com., bd. dirs., sec. 1973—74, chmn. EAC-ABET engring. accreditation commn. 1979—80), Va. Soc. Profl. Engrs. (pres. No. Va. chpt. 1987—88), Wash. Soc. Profl. Engrs. (nat. dir. 1975—79), Am. Inst. Biol. Scis., Nat. Inf. Assn., Combat Infantrymens Assn. (life), Philos. Soc. Washington (life), 99th Inf. Divsn. Assn., Univ. Club Wash., Phi Lambda Tau, Gamma Sigma Delta, Phi Kappa Phi, Sigma Xi, Tau Beta Pi (life). Achievements include rsch. in energy, drying, food engring., properties of materials and biomass. Office: Engring Info Svcs 2454 N Rockingham St Arlington VA 22207-1033 Office Phone: 703-534-8321.

HALL, CAROL K., chemical engineering educator, researcher; b. Bklyn., Apr. 23, 1946; d. Harris J. and Celia (Reitman) Klein; m. Thomas Maxwell Hall; children: Katherine, Adam, Norah. BA, Cornell U., 1967; MA, SUNY, Stony Brook, 1969, PhD, 1972. Postdoctoral rsch. assoc. Cornell U., Ithaca, NY, 1973-76; mem. tech. staff Bell Labs., Murray Hill, NJ, 1976-77; asst. prof. Princeton U., NJ, 1977-85; assoc. prof. N.C. State U., Raleigh, 1985-87, prof., 1987-98, Alcoa prof., 1998—. Contbr. more than 125 articles to profl. jours. Recipient Outstanding Rsch. award N.C. State U. Alumni Assn., 1992, Disting. Grad. Prof. award, 1998, Disting. Engring. Rsch. award N.C. U. Alcoa Found., 1994. Mem. NAE, AIChE, Am. Chem. Soc., Biophys. Soc., Assn. for Women in Sci. (pres. local chpt. 1993-94). Achievements include research in application of statistical thermodynamics and computer simulation to problems in chemical engineering and chemistry. Home: 10716 Dunhill Ter Raleigh NC 27615-1439 Office: NC State U PO Box 7905 Raleigh NC 27695-0001

HALL, CHARLES M., manufacturing executive; B in Bus., Western Mich. U., Kalamazoo; M in Bus. Mgmt., Ctrl. Mich. U., Mt. Pleasant. Machinist Chrysler Corp., 1971; mgr. Sterling Electronics and Optical Mfg. plant Gen. Dynamics (acquired Chrysler Def. in 1982), 1983, plant mgr. arsenal tank plant Warren, Mich., 1986, mgr. Army Tank Plant Lima, Ohio, v.p. mfg. Land Systems, 1990, various prodn. and mfg. mgmt. positions, v.p. prodn. and delivery Land Systems, 1997—99, pres. Land Systems, 1999—2005, exec. v.p. combat systems, 2005—. Office: Gen Dynamics 2941 Fairview Park Dr Ste 100 Falls Church VA 22042-4513 Office Phone: 703-876-3000. Office Fax: 703-876-3125.*

HALL, CHARLES WASHINGTON, lawyer; b. Dallas, June 30, 1930; s. Albert Brown and Eleanor Pauline (Hopkins) H.; m. Mary Louise Watkins, Aug. 3, 1957; children: Kathryn Louise, Allison Ash (dec.), Charles Washington III. BA, U. of South, 1951; JD, So. Meth. U., 1954, LLM in Taxation, 1959. Bar: Tex. 1954. Ptnr. Storey, Armstrong & Steger, Dallas, 1954-57; sr. ptnr. Fulbright & Jaworski, Houston, 1957—. Mem. adv. com. on tax litigation Dept. Justice, 1979-80; dir. Friedman Ind., Inc., Tex. Med. Ctr., Inc. Houston; mem. Commr. Internal Revenue Adv. Group, 1990-91; mem. adv. coun. U.S. Claims Ct., 1988-2006. Pres., trustee Sarah Campbell Blaffer Found., Houston; dir. Goodwill Industry, Houston, 1977-84; trustee Inst. Religion, Houston, 1990-2000, Killson Found., Houston, M.D. Anderson Found., Houston, Allbritton Found., Houston, Allbritton Art Inst., Houston, John S. Dunn Rsch. Found., Houston, Houston Child Guidance Ctr., 1974-86, The Howell Family Found., Houston; trustee, treas. Ctr Am. Internat. Law, 1973-2005 (formerly Southwestern Legal Found.), Dallas, 1973-2006; S.W. Rsch. Inst., San Antonio, 1974-2005; gov. Houston Forum, 1992-95. Recipient Disting. Alumni award, So. Meth. U., 1989. Fellow Am. Bar Found.; mem. ABA (chmn. sect. taxation 1987-88, ho. dels. 1991-95, nat. conf. lawyers and CPAs chmn. 1988-2000), Houston Bar Assn., Dallas Bar Assn., State Bar Tex. (chmn. sect. taxation 1970-71, Lifetime Achievement in Taxation award 2006), Internat. Bar Assn., Am. Coll. Tax Counsel (regent 1982-91), Am. Law Inst., River Oaks Country Club, Met. Club (Washington), Old Baldy Club (Saratoga, Wyo.), Riverhill Country Club (Kerrville, Tex.). Episcopalian. Office: Fulbright & Jaworski LLP 1301 Mckinney St Ste 5100 Houston TX 77010-3031

HALL, CHARLES WORTH LEO, college administrator; b. Louisville, Ky., Dec. 18, 1946; s. Worth Leroy and Gertrude Omega (Greenwell) H.; m. Judelyn Lumbab Montebon, Jan. 26, 1990; children: Evelyn, Nghia, Hanh, Wanda, Charlotte, Shenandoah, Michelle, Annamarie, Andre, Angelyn, Bernadette; m. Lenie Dumagat Cabalfin, May 17, 1995; children: Ariel, Allexus, Alexander, Andrew, Aetari. AA, Hartnell Coll., 1975; BS, U. So. Miss., 1976; MEd, U. Louisville, 1978; EdS, U. So. Miss., 1982; DD, 1983; PhD, U. San Carlos, 1994. Cert. tchr., Tenn., Ind., Calif.; lic. profl. counselor Miss., La., Tex., Tenn.; registered profl. cons., Mo.; ordained to ministry Ch. Modern Apostles, 1983. Commd. capt. U.S. Army, 1963, tchr. Montrey, Calif., 1972-73, advanced through grades to maj., 1988, career counselor Jackson, Miss., 1976-77; fin. aid counselor Ind. State U., New Albany, 1978; admissions officer Ind. Vocat. Tech. Coll., Sellersburg, 1979-81, asst. dir. student svcs., 1979-81; profl. devel. coord. U. So. Miss., Hattiesburg, 1981-83, asst. registrar, 1981-83; v.p. student affairs Excel Bus. Coll., Madisonville, Tenn., 1984; military personnel officer Camp Shelby, Miss., 1984-86; tng. adminstr. USDA, New Orleans, 1986-92; dir., dean Internat. Bus. Coll., Agana, Guam, 1992—93; prof. social sci., psychology U. San Carlos, 1994—95; vis. prof. bus. De La Salle U., Manila, 1995—96; prof. social sciences U. Mindanao, 1996; ret., 1996. Pres. Personnel Svc. Orgn., Jackson, Miss., 1977-78; dir. Marquis Adv. Bd., Hattiesburg, Miss., 1978-82; chmn. Franklin Battlefield Restoration, Tenn., 1983-92; exec. dir. New Horizons Devel. Co., Louisville, 1988—; lectr. in field. Author: Professional Development, 1981, Needs Assessment for Professional Development, 1982, Professional Development Procedural Guide, 1982, Professional Development Bibliography, 1982, A Sagittarian's Quest, 2004, History of the 27th Miss. Infantry, 2005, History of the 46th N.C. Infantry, 2006, History of the 2nd Ky. Infantry, 2006, The Life and Times of Confederate General Samuel Cooper, 2007. Dist. sec. Transatlantic coun. Boy Scouts Am., Heidelberg West Germany, 1964-68, dist. commr. Pine Burr coun., Hattiesburg, 1968-83, field commr. Monterey Bay coun., Salinas, Calif., 1972-73; del. coun. assembly Boy Scouts Philippines, Cebu, 2000, exec. mem., coun. bd., Davao, 2001-03; senator U. So. Miss. Student Govt. Assn., Hattiesburg, 1974-75; pres. U. So. Miss. Young Dems., Hattiesburg, 1975-76; SMF social case worker ARC, Hattiesburg, 1975-76; active Foster Parent Plan; assoc. pastor youth Ctrl. Christian Ch., Hattiesburg, 2004—, elder, 2004-05; youth bd. dirs. Regional Youth Commn., Little Rock, Ark, 2005-06. Major USAR, 1963-90, major AGC USAR, 1963-2006. Decorated Army Commendation medal, Army Achievement medal, Army Reserve Achievement medal, Vietnam Cross Gallantry with bronze palm; recipient Commissioner's Key award Boy Scouts Am.; Walden U. fellow, 1982-84, Acad. Mgmt. fellow Pa. State U., Vanderbilt U. fellow, 1984-86. Mem. KC (treas. 4th patriotic degree 1975-76), VFW (surgeon 1991-92), NRA, Philippine-Am. Guardian Assn., Internat. Scout Assn., Am. Assn. Counselor Devel., Career Coll. Assn., Am. Soc. Pers. Adminstrs., So. Coll. Pers. Assn., Miss. Assn. Registrars and Admissions, Nat. Career Devel. Assn., Internat. Assn. Profl. Cons., Am. Soc. Notaries, Ind. Personnel and Guidance Assn. (pres. 1979-80), Order Battle Flag, Am. Assn. Philippines, Children Internat., Confederate Alliance, Friends Confederate Soc., Mensa, Career Coll. Assn., Nat. Bus. End. Assn., Am. Legion, Vets. Vietnam War, Order Vietnam Republic of Cross of Gallantry, Mil. Order World Wars, Reserve Officers Assn., Adjutant Gen. Regimental Assn., Order So. Cross, Hon. Order Ky. Cols., Hub City Kiwanis Club (bd. dirs. 1982-83), Nat. Eagle Scout Assn., North Am. Hunting Club, Omicron Delta Kappa, Phi Kappa Phi, Alpha Phi Omega (pres. 1976-77, Disting. Svc. key), Phi Gamma Mu (v.p. 1975-76), Phi Delta Kappa, Phi Tau Chi, Psi Chi, Delta Tau Kappa, Epsilon Delta Chi. Mem. Disciple Of Christ. Avocations internat. youth work, internat. Boy Scout Movement. Office Phone: 601-988-4857. Personal E-mail: charleswlhall@yahoo.com. E-mail: chall.chaplainmsg@hotmail.com, colegewarcsa@yahoo.com.

HALL, CHARLOTTE HAUCH, editor; b. Washington, Sept. 30, 1945; d. Charles Christian and Ruthadele Bertha (LaTourrette) H.; m. Robert Lindsay Hall, June 8, 1968; 1 child, Benjamin H. BA, Kalamazoo Co., 1966; MA, U. Chgo., 1967. Reporter, news editor Ridgewood (NJ) Newspapers, 1971-74; copy editor, news editor The Record, Hackensack, NJ, 1975-76; asst. mng. editor Boston Herald Am., 1977-78; dep. met. editor Washington Star, 1979-80; copy chief, met. editor, Nassau editor Newsday, Melville, NY, 1981—86, Washington news editor, 1986—88, asst. mng. editor for Long Island, 1988-94; mktg. dir. Newsday, Inc., Melville, NY, 1994-96, mng. editor, 1997-99, v.p., mng. editor, 1999—2003, v.p. planning, 2003—04; v.p., editor Orlando Sentinel, Fla., 2004—. Trustee Kalamazoo Coll. Recipient Robert G. McGruder Awards for Diversity Leadership award, Am. Soc. Newspaper Editors, 2003. Mem. Am. Soc. Newspaper Editors (bd. dirs., treas. designate 2004-05, treas. 2005-06, sec. 2006-07, v.p. 2007-08), Newspaper Assn. Am., Phi Beta Kappa. Office: Orlando Sentinel 633 N Orange Ave Orlando FL 32801-1349 Office Phone: 407-420-5195. E-mail: editor@orlandosentinel.com.*

HALL, CHRISTOPHER GEORGE LONGDEN, academic administrator; b. Coventry, Eng., June 7, 1956; came to U.S., 1980; s. Alfred Frederick and Margaret Anne (Robinson) H.; m. Avril Jacqueline Wardell, July 3l, l982. MA, Oxford U., 1977, DPhil, 1980; MS in Bus., Columbia U., 1983. Asst. to chmn. Gold Fields Am. Corp., NYC, 1980-83; pres. Hall Mgmt. Assocs., San Francisco, 1983-87, Congden and Carpenter Co., Seekonk, Mass., 1987-88; mng. dir. Petralex Stainless Ltd., Malvern, Pa., 1985-86; v.p. planning Levinson Steel Co., Pitts., 1988-89; v.p. mktg. Thypin Steel Co., NYC, 1989-95; ptnr. Stafford Bus. Advisors, Portland, Maine, 1995—2007; pres. Am. U. in Kosovo, 2007—. Internat. commercial arbitrator Am. Arbitration Assn., 1991-2005. Author: Britain, America and Arms Control, 1921-1937, 1987, Steel Phoenix, The Fall and Rise of the American Steel Industry, 1996, Ports and Railroads of the Atlantic Northeast, 1999. Councilman City of Oxford (Eng.), 1979-81; mem. Dem. Nat. Com., 1996-97; chmn. Maine Dem. Com., 1997-99; pres. Genesis Cmty. Loan Fund; bd. dirs. Maine Coun. Chs; mem. Maine Ho. of Reps., 2000-02; mem. Maine Senate, 2002-04, chair utilities and energy com. Mem. United Oxford and Cambridge Univs. Club (London). Episcopalian. Avocations: travel, cricket, naval history.

HALL, CHRISTOPHER S., retail executive; Mem. audit staff Arthur Anderson, LLP; v.p. acctg. Ralph's Grocery Co., 1995—98, sr. v.p. fin., 1998—99; exec. v.p., CFO Golden State Foods Corp., 1999—2000; sr. v.p., chief acctg. officer Rite Aid Corp., Camp Hill, Pa., 2000, sr. v.p. fin. and acctg., 2000—01, exec. v.p. fin. and acctg., 2001—02, exec. v.p., CFO, 2002—04, sr. v.p. real estate & planning, 2004—. Office: Rite Aid Corp 30 Hunter Ln Camp Hill PA 17011 Office Phone: 717-761-2633.*

HALL, CURTIS E., lawyer; b. 1956; BA, U. Va., 1978; JD, Yale U., 1981. Bar: NY 1981, DC 1984, Mich. 1989. Asst. dist. atty. Manhattan, NYC; asst. US atty. Washington; atty. Miller, Canfield, Paddock & Stone, Kalamazoo, ptnr., 1992—94; gen. counsel Stryker Corp., Kalamazoo, 1994—, v.p., 2004—. Office: Stryker Corp 2725 Fairfield Rd Kalamazoo MI 49002*

HALL, CYNTHIA HOLCOMB, federal judge; b. LA, Feb. 19, 1929; d. Harold Romeyn and Mildred Gould Holcomb; m. John Harris Hall, June 6, 1970 (dec. Oct. 1980). AB, Stanford U., 1951, JD, 1954; LLM, NYU, 1960. Bar: Ariz. 1954, Calif. 1956. Law clk. to judge US Ct. Appeals (9th cir.), 1954—55; trial atty. tax divsn. Dept. Justice, 1960—64; atty.-adviser Office Tax Legis. Counsel, Treasury Dept., 1964—66; mem. firm Brawerman & Holcomb, Beverly Hills, Calif., 1966—72; judge US Tax Ct., Washington, 1972—81, US Dist. Ct. for Ctrl. Dist. Calif., LA, 1981—84, US Ct. Appeals (9th cir.), Pasadena, Calif., 1984—97, sr. judge, 1997—. Lt. (j.g.) USNR, 1951—53. Office: US Ct Appeals 9th Cir 125 S Grand Ave Pasadena CA 91105-1621*

HALL, DAVID, newspaper editor; b. Lebanon, Tenn., Mar. 7, 1943; s. Hal Turner Hall and Mildred (Durham) Hall Carson; m. Suzanne Lovell, Sept. 5, 1964; children: Carson, Matthew, Amanda. BS, U. Tenn., 1965, MA in Econs., 1966; postgrad., Northwestern U., 1995. Fin. news reporter, asst. fin. editor, Middle East corr., chief editorial writer, asst. mng. editor Chgo. Daily News, 1966-78; asst. mng. editor Chgo. Sun-Times, 1978; mng. editor St. Paul Pioneer Press, 1978-82; exec. editor St. Paul Pioneer Press and Dispatch, 1982-84; editor, v.p. The Denver Post, 1984-86, editor, sr. v.p., 1986-88; editor, v.p. The Record, Hackensack, N.J., 1988-92; editor The Plain Dealer, Cleve., 1992-99. Bd. dirs. Coun. on World Affairs. With U.S. Army, 1967-69, Vietnam. Recipient Disting. Alumni award Castle Heights Mil. Acad., Lebanon, 1984. Mem. Am. Soc. Newspaper Editors, Cleve. Com. on Fgn. Rels., Soc. Profl. Journalists, Scarabbean Soc.,Phi Gamma Delta. Presbyterian. Home: 426 Anderson St Greencastle IN 46135-1727

HALL, DAVID, law educator, dean, department chairman; b. Savannah, May 26, 1950; s. Levi and Ethel Hall; m. Marilyn Braithwaite-Hall; children: Sakile, Kiamsha, Rahsaan. BS in Polit. Sci., Kans. State U., 1972; MA in Human Rels., U. Okla., 1975, postgrad., 1975—78, JD, 1978; LLM, Harvard U., 1985, Doctor Juridical Scis., 1988. Bar: Ill. 1978, Mass. 1978, Okla. 1978. Profl. basketball player Spaidero Pallacanestro, Inc., Udine, Italy, 1972—74; grad. asst. human rels. dept. U. Okla., Norman, 1974—75, assoc. prof. law Sch. Law, 1983—85; lawyer Chgo. regional office Fed. Trade Commn., 1978—80; asst. prof. law Sch. Law U. Miss., 1980—83; prof. law Northeastern U., Boston, 1985—, assoc. dean academic affairs Sch. Law, 1988—92, dean Sch. Law, 1993—98, provost, 1998—2002. Instr. ethnic studies dept. and law ctr. U. Okla., Norman, 1975—79; Robert D. Klien U. lectr. Northeastern U.; co-chair legal edn. forum Law Sch. Harvard U., Cambridge, Mass., 1984—85, co-coord. Nat. Symposium on the Constitution and Race, 1987; coord. law student outreach program Barron Assessment Ctr., Boston. Contbr. articles to profl. jours. Mem. bd. Mass. Civil Liberties Union, 1987—88, Inst. Affirmative action, Boston, TransAfrica Forum Scholars Adv. Coun., Washington, commn. on equal justice Mass. Legal Assistance Corp., 1995—, Nat. Consumer Law Ctr., 1993—; pres. African Cultural Soc. St. Paul A.M.E. Ch., Cambridge, Mass.; bd. dirs. Gang Peace Inc., 1995—. Named Professor of the Yr., NAACP, Outstanding Dean of Yr., Nat. Assn. Pub. Interset Lawyers, 1997; named to Savannah Athletic Hall of Fame; recipient African Am. 1st Oratory Competition, Black Rose award, Sigma Gamma Rho, Humanitarian award, Nat. Conf. Cmty. and Justice. Fellow: Am. Sociol. Assn.; mem.: ABA (standing com. lawyers' pub. svc. responsibility 1995—), Nat. Black Wholistic Soc. (pres. 1993, mem. bd. 1984—), Black Faculty and Staff Orgn., Nat. Conf. Black Lawyers (pres. Mass. chpt. 1986—), Okla. Bar Assn. (Outstanding Sr. award), Mass. Bar Assn. (mem. bd. minorities in the profession 1995—96), Boston Bar Assn., Assn. Law Sch. (diversity in legal edn. 1995—96), Order of the Coif. Office: 400 Huntington Ave Boston MA 02115 Office Phone: 617-373-3668. Business E-Mail: d.hall@neu.edu.

HALL, DAVID, principal; b. Kans. s. Wardell and Earlene Hall; m. Arlene Hall. A in Gen. Studies, Kansas City Kans. C.C., 1982; BS in Music Edn., Fla. A & M U., Tallahassee, 1985; M in Music Edn., Fla. State U., Tallahassee, 1989. Cert. ednl. leadership Nova Southeastern U., Fla., 1997. Dir. bands Nova Mid. Sch. Broward County Sch. Bd., Ft. Lauderdale, 1989—93, dir. bands Boyd Anderson H.S., 1993—98, asst. prin. Dillard H.S., 1998—2002, prin. Pky. Mid. Sch. of the Arts, 2002—. Trustee First Bapt. Ch. Piney Grove, Oakland Park, Fla., 1998—2007, mem. music com. Named High Performing Prin., Fla. Dept. Edn., 2006. Mem.: ASCD, Broward Mid. Sch. Prins. Exec. Bd., Broward Prins. and Asst. Prins. Assn., Fla. Assn. Sch. Adminstrs., Phi Beta Kappa, Kappa Kappa Psi, Phi Mu Alpha, Omega Psi Phi. Home: 7506 NW 115 Terrace Parkland FL 33076 Office: School Board of Broward County Florida 600 SE 3rd Ave Fort Lauderdale FL 33301

HALL, DAVID MCKENZIE, business and management educator; b. Gary, Ind., June 21, 1928; s. Alfred McKenzie and Grace Elizabeth (Crimiel) H.; m. Jaqueline Virginia Branch, Apr. 30, 1960; children: Glen D., Gary D. BA, Howard U., 1951; MS, N.C. Agrl. Tech. State U., 1966; PhD, Kennedy Western U., 2002. Enlisted USAF, 1951; advanced through grades to brig. gen.; chief social actions Hdqrs. Mil. Airlift Command, Scott AFB, Il., 1972-1974; dep. base comdr. 375th Air Base Group, Scott AFB, 1974-75, base comdr., 1975-76; dir. data processing Air Force Logistics Command, Wright-Patterson AFB, Ohio, 1976-77, comptr., 1977-83; ret. USAF, 1983; dir. data processing Delco-Remy div. GM, Anderson, Ind., 1983-85; regional mgr. Electronic Data Systems, Anderson, 1985-88, Saginaw, Mich., 1988-93; prof. mgmt. and mktg. Northwood Univ., Midland, Mich., 1993-97; exec. in residence Saginaw Valley State U., University Center, Mich., 1997—. Brig. gen. USAF, 1951—83. Recipient Hon. Citizenship East St. Louis, Ill., 1975, Key to City Gary Ind., 1981, spirit of Saginaw award, 1999, Sagimore of the Wabash, 1999. Mem. NAACP, Saginaw Cmty. Found., Cmty. Affairs Com., Prince Hall Masons, Kappa Alpha Psi. Methodist. Avocations: reading, woodworking. Home: 49 W Hannum Blvd Saginaw MI 48602-1938 Office: Saginaw Valley State U Curtiss Hall 7400 Bay Rd University Center MI 48710 Business E-Mail: dhall@svsu.edu.

HALL, DEANGELO, professional football player; b. Chesapeake, Va., Nov. 19, 1983; Student in Sec. Edn., Va. Tech., 2004. Cornerback Atlanta Falcons, 2004—. Vol. Atlanta Coaches Acad., 2004. Named to All-Am. Team, NCAA, 2002, NFC Pro Bowl Team, 2007. Office: Atlanta Falcons 4400 Falcon Pkwy Flowery Branch GA 30542*

HALL, DON ALAN, editor, writer; b. Indpls., Aug. 7, 1938; s. Oscar B. and Ruth Ann (Leak) H.; m. Roberta Louise Bash, Apr. 30, 1960; children: Alice Leigh, Nancy Elizabeth. BA, Ind. U., 1960, MA, 1968. News editor Rock Springs (Wyo.) Daily Rocket-Miner, 1960-63; mag. editor, picture editor Waukegan (Ill.) News-Sun, 1964-66; reporter, copy editor Salem (Oreg.) Capital Jour., 1966-70; freelance journalist Victoria, B.C., Canada, 1970-74; copy editor, sci. writer, music reviewer Corvallis (Oreg.) Gazette-Times, 1974-78, copy desk chief, 1978-82, news editor, 1983-84, author weekly opinion column, 1985-87; author weekly nature column for Oreg. newspapers, 1976-85; instr. dept. journalism Oreg. State U., 1984-87. Author: On Top Of Oregon, 1975, Bird in the Bush, 1986; editor Mammoth Trumpet, Center for the Study of the First Americans, 1991-2001. Recipient Westinghouse-AAAS sci. writing award, 1977 Home and Office: 620 NW Witham Dr Corvallis OR 97330-6535

HALL, DONALD, poet; b. New Haven, Sept. 20, 1928; s. Donald Andrew and Lucy (Wells) H.; children: Andrew, Philippa; m. Jane Kenyon, Apr. 17, 1972 (dec. Apr. 22, 1995). BA, Harvard U., 1951; B. Litt. (Henry fellow), Oxford U., 1953; postgrad., Stanford U., 1953-54; LHD (hon.), Plymouth State Coll; DLitt (hon.), Presbyn. Coll., Colby-Sawyer Coll., Daniel Webster Coll., Franklin Pierce Coll., New Eng. Coll., Bates Coll., U. N.H., U. Mich. Creative writing fellow Stanford U., 1953; jr. fellow Soc. Fellows, Harvard U., 1954-57; asst. prof. U. Mich., Ann Arbor, 1957-61, assoc. prof., 1961-66, prof., 1966-77; poetry editor Paris Review, 1953-61; mem. poetry bd. Wesleyan U. Press, 1958-64; cons. Harper & Row, 1964-81; poet laureate Library of Congress, Washington, 2006—. Judge Bollingen Prize for Poetry, 1958, 59, Lamont Poetry Competition, 1967-69, Nat. Book Awards, 1968, 92, Edgar Allen Poe and Copernicus awards Acad. Am. Poets, 1975, Nat. Poetry Series, 1979, 93. Author: (poetry) Exiles and Marriages, 1955, The Dark Houses, 1958, A Roof of Tiger Lilies, 1963, The Alligator Bride, 1969, The Yellow Room, 1971, The Town of Hill, 1975, A Blue Wing Tilts at the Edge of the Sea, 1975, Kicking the Leaves, 1978, The Toy Bone, 1979, The Happy Man, 1986, The One Day, 1988, Old and New Poems, 1990, The Museum of Clear Ideas, 1993 (National Book award nominee, 1993) The Old Life, 1996, Without, 1998, The Painted Bed, 2002; (essays) Goatfoot, Milktongue, Twinbird, 1978, To Keep Moving, 1980, The Weather for Poetry, 1982, Fathers Playing Catch with Sons: Essays on Sport, 1985, Seasons at Eagle Pond, 1987, Poetry and Ambition, 1988, Here at Eagle Pond, 1988, Life Work, 1993, Death to the Death of Poetry, 1994, Principal Products of Portugal, 1995, Breakfast Served Any Time All Day, 2003, White Apples and the Taste of Stone: Selected Poems 1946-2006, 2006; (juvenile) Andrew the Lion Farmer, 1959, Riddle Rat, 1977, Ox Cart Man, 1979, The Man Who Lived Alone, 1985, The Farm Summer, 1992, 94, Lucy's Christmas, 1994, I Am the Dog, I Am the Cat, 1994, Lucy's Summer, 1995; (short stories) The Ideal Bakery, 1987, When Wellard Met Babe Ruth, 1996, Old Home Day, 1996, Willow Temple, 2003; (play) The Bone Ring, 1987, (memoirs) String Too Short to be Saved, 1961, 79, Remembering Poets, 1978, Their Ancient Glittering Eyes, 1992, (biography) Henry Moore, 1966, Dock Ellis in the Country of Baseball, 1976, (with David Finn) As the Eye Moves, 1970, limericks The Gentleman's Alphabet Book, 1972, Writing Well, 1973, 3d edit., 1979, 4th edit., 1982, 5th edit., 1985, 6th edit., 1988, , 7th edit., 1991, The One Day, 1988 (Nat. Book Critics award); editor: Harvard Adv. Anthology, 1950, (with L. Simpson and R. Pack) The New Poets of England and America, 1957, (with R. Pack) New Poets of England and America, Second Selection, 1962, A Poetry Sampler, 1962, Contemporary American Poetry, 1962, 2d edit., 1971, (with W. Taylor) Poetry in English, 1963, 2d edit., 1970, (with S. Spender) A Concise Ency. of English and American Poets and Poetry, 1963, 2d edit., 1970, Faber Book of Modern Verse, 1966, The Modern Stylists, 1968, A Choice of Whitman's Verse, 1968, Man and Boy, 1968; Anthology American Poetry, 1969, Pleasures of Poetry, 1971, (with D. Emblen) A Writer's Reader, 1976, 2d edit., 1979, 3d edit., 1982, 85, 4th and 5th edit., 1988, To Read Literature, 1981, rev., 1992, To Read Poetry, 1982, Oxford Book American Literary Anecdotes, 1981, Claims for Poetry, 1982, To Read Fiction, 1987, Oxford Book of Children's Verse in America, 1985, (with Pat Corrington Wykes) Anecdotes of Modern Art, 1990; (memoir) The Best Day The Worst Day: Life with Jane Kenyon, 2005. Deacon South Danbury Ch. Recipient Lloyd McKim Garrison prize for poetry Harvard, 1951, John Osborne Sergeant prize for Latin translation Harvard, 1951, Newdigate prize for poetry Oxford U., 1952, Lamont Poetry Selection Acad. Am. Poets, 1955, Edna St. Vincent Millay Meml. award Poetry Soc. Am., 1955, Longview Found. award, 1960, Sarah Joseph Hale award, 1983, Lenore Marshall award, 1987, Lenore Marshall The Nation award, 1991, Robert Frost Silver medal Poetry Soc. Am., 1991, New Eng. Booksellers Assn. award, 1993, Ruth Lilly prize, 1994; Guggenheim fellow, 1963, 72. Mem. PEN, Authors Guild, Am. Acad. Arts and Letters.

HALL, DONALD JOYCE, SR., greeting card company executive; b. Kansas City, Mo., July 9, 1928; s. Joyce Clyde and Elizabeth Ann (Dilday) H.; m. Adele Coryell, Nov. 28, 1953; children: Donald Joyce, Margaret Elizabeth, David Earl. AB, Dartmouth, 1950; LL.D., William Jewell Coll., Denver U., 1977. With Hallmark Cards, Inc., Kansas City, Mo., 1953—, adminstrv. v.p., 1958-66, pres., chief exec. officer, 1966-83, chief exec. officer, 1983-86, chmn. bd. only, 1983—. Dir. United Telecommunications, Inc., Dayton-Hudson Corp., William E. Coutts Co., Ltd.; past dir. Fed. Res. Bank Kansas City, Mut. Benefit Life Ins. Co., Business Men's Assurance Co., Commerce Bank Kansas City, 1st Nat. Bank Lawrence. Pres. Civic Council Greater Kansas City; past chmn. bd. Kansas City Assn. Trusts and

Founds.; Bd. dirs. Am. Royal Assn., Friends of Art, Eisenhower Found.; bd. dirs. Kansas City Minority Suppliers Devel. Council, Kans. City Minority Suppliers Devel. Council,Kansas City Symphony; past pres. Pembroke Country Day Sch., Civic Council of Greater Kansas City; trustee, past chmn. exec. com. Midwest Research Inst.; trustee Nelson-Atkins Museum of Art. Served to 1st lt. AUS, 1950-53. Recipient Eisenhower Medallion award, 1973; Parsons Sch. Design award, 1977; 3d Ann. Civic Service award Hebrew Acad. Kansas City, 1976; Chancellor's medal U. Mo., Kansas City, 1977; Disting. Service citation U. Kans., 1980; named one of Forbes' Richest Americans, 2006 Mem. Kansas City C. of C. (named Mr. Kansas City 1972, dir.), AIA (hon.) Office: Hallmark Cards Inc Office Chmn Bd 2501 Mcgee St Kansas City MO 64108-2600

HALL, DONALD JOYCE, JR., consumer products company executive; b. Nov. 6, 1955; m. Jill Hall; 2 children. BA in Econs. and Lit., Claremont Coll.; MBA, U. Kans. With Hallmark Cards, Inc., Kansas City, Mo., 1975—, various pos., including dir. splty. store devel., gen. mgr. Keepsake Ornaments, v.p.-creative, v.p. product devel., 1997—99, exec. v.p. strategy and devel., 1999—2002, pres., CEO, 2002—. Bd. dirs. Greater Kansas City Cmty. Found., Civic Coun. Greater Kansas City; chmn. bd. dirs. Heart of Am. United Way; bd. dirs. Midwest Rsch. Inst.; trustee Sci. City at Union Sta.

HALL, ELEANOR WILLIAMS, public relations executive; b. Boston, 1923; d. James Murray and Julia Eleanor (Williams) Hall. AB cum laude, Radcliffe Coll., 1945. Exec. sec. Am. Express Co., NYC, 1950—62, adminstrv. asst. corp. mktg., 1963—65, mgr. corp. mktg., 1965—69, mgr. corp. pub. rels., 1969—71; mgr. mktg. svcs. Am. Express Bank Ltd., NYC, 1971—72, asst. treas. advt. and pub. rels., 1972—76, asst. v.p. advt. and pub. rels., 1976—82; pres. Eleanor Hall Assocs., 1982—90. Mem.: Harvard-Radcliffe Club. Address: 342 102d Ave SE Ste 218 Bellevue WA 98004-6165

HALL, FRANKLIN PERKINS, lawyer, bank executive, state official; b. Amelia, Va., Dec. 12, 1938; s. Perkins Lee and Lois E. Hall; m. Phoebe Ann Poulterer, July 26, 1969; children: Kimberly Ann, Franklin P. Jr. BS, Lynchburg Coll., 1961; MBA, Am. U., 1964, JD, 1966. Bar: Va. 1966. Aide to U.S. Senate, Washington, 1964; asst. sec. Dept. HUD, Washington, 1968-69; sr. ptnr. Hall & Hall, Richmond, 1969—. Chmn. bd. Cardinal Savs. and Loan Assn., Richmond, Va., 1979-84; chmn. bd. Commonwealth Bank, Richmond, 1984—; spl. counsel Va. Gen. Assembly, Richmond, 1970-75. Del. Va. House of Dels.; active Va. Gen. Assemly, 1976—; chmn. bd. Cen. Richmond Assn., 1974-75; pres. Richmond Jaycees, 1972-73; dem. minority leader Va. Ho. Dels., 2001 Recipient Disting. Svc. award Richmond Jaycees, 1972, Award Va. Jaycees, 1974, Disting. Citizen award Nat. Mcpl. League, 1976; named Outstanding Young Man of Va. award, 1973. Mem. Va. Trial Lawyers Assn. (bd. govs. 1982-84), Richmond Bar Assn. (exec. com. 1973-76), Soc. Advancement Mgmt., Newcomen Soc. Democrat. Presbyterian. Office: Hall & Hall 1401 Huguenot Rd Ste 100 Midlothian VA 23113-2662

HALL, GARY, JR., Olympic athlete; b. Cin., Sept. 26, 1974; Recipient Gold medal 100 medly relay, Gold medal 100 free relay, Silver medal 50-meter freestyle and Silver 100-meter freestyle Atlanta Olympics, 1996; Gold medal 50-meter freestyle, Gold medal 100 medley relay, Silver medal 100 freestyle relay and Bronze medal 100-meter freestyle Sydney Olympics, 2000, Gold medal, 50-meter freestyle, Athens Olympics, 2004, Bronze medal, 4x100 relay, Athens Olympics, 2004; set Am. record for 50-meter freestyle. Office: USA Swimming 1 Olympic Plz Colorado Springs CO 80909-5746

HALL, GENE E., education educator; b. Rutland, Vt; BS, Castleton State Coll.; MS, PhD, Syracuse U. Faculty mem., project dir. nat. R&D Ctr. for Tchr. Edn. U. Tex., Austin, Tex., 1968—86; prof. ednl. leadership U. Fla., 1986—88; dean Coll. Edn. U. NC, 1988—93; prof. ednl. leadership U. No. Colo., Colo., 1993—98; dean Coll. Edn. U. Nev., Las Vegas, 1999—2004, prof., 2004—. Bd. mem. WestEd Regional Edn. Lab. Author (with S.M. Hord): Implementing Change: Patterns, Principles and Potholes, 2d edit., 2006; contbr. articles to profl. jours. Office: Univ Nev Las Vegas 4505 Maryland Pkwy Las Vegas NV 89154 Office Phone: 702-895-3441. Business E-Mail: gene.hall@unlv.edu.

HALL, GREGORY, composer, engineer; b. San Francisco, Oct. 9, 1959; s. John Wallace and Tove Karen Hall; life ptnr. Karen Jane Norteman. BA, U. Calif., Santa Barbara, 1982; diploma, Curtis Inst. Music, Phila., 1986; MEng, U. Maine, Orono, 1996. V.p. Maine Composers Forum, Portland, Maine, 1994—2004, pres., 2004—. Tech. support engr. Boeing, Bangor, Maine, 1997—2004. Composer (commissioned works): Arkadia, 2001, Hardanger Trio, 2001, Asa Adams-We Found You, 2002, Brass Quintet, 2007, Sax Quartet, 2008. Recipient Maine Composer of Yr. award, Gamper Contemporary Music Festival, 1997. Mem.: Am. Composers Alliance, Soc. Electro-Acoustic Music in US, Am. Music Ctr., Am. Composers Forum. Achievements include development of 21st Century Baroque, a MAX programming language algorithm. Avocations: hiking, yoga, art.

HALL, GWENDOLYN MIDLO, historian, educator; b. New Orleans; d. Herman Lazard and Ethel Samuelson Midlo; m. Harry Haywood, Apr. 10, 1956; children: Leonid Avram Yuspeh, Haywood, Rebecca. Student, Newcomb Coll., New Orleans, 1947—49; BA, U. of the Ams., Mexico City, 1962, MA, 1963; PhD, U. Mich., Ann Arbor, 1970. Instr. history Elizabeth City State Coll., NC, 1965; prof. history Rutgers U., New Brunswick, NJ, 1971—. Internat. adv. bd. mem. Harriet Tubman Resource Inst. on the African Diaspora York U., Toronto, Canada; sr. rsch. fellow Tulane U., 2007; cons. and interviewee numerous documentary films; reviewer scholarly content and significance of manuscripts for numerous univ. presses; lectr. in field. Author: Slavery and African Ethnicities in the Americas: Restoring the Links, 2005, paperback edit., 2007, Social Control in Slave Plantation Societies: A Comparison of St. Domingue and Cuba, 1971, paperback edit., 1996, African's in Colonial Louisana: The Development of Afro-Creole Culture in the Eighteenth Century, 1992, paperback edit., 1995; editor: Love, War, and the 96th Engineers (colored): The New Guinea Diaries of Captain Hyman Samuelson During World War II, 1995, paperback edit., 2000, Databases for the Study of Afro-Louisiana History and Genealogy, 2000; mem. editl. bd.: The So. Quarterly; contbr. chapters to books, articles to profl. jours. Named Humanist of Yr., La. Endowment for the Humanities, 1994, Knight of the Order of Arts and Letters, Ministry Culture France, 1997; recipient Willie Lee Rose prize, So. Assn. for Women Historians, 1993, John Hope Franklin prize, Am. Studies Assn., 1993, Theodore Saloutos Meml. Book award in Am. immigration history, Immigration History Soc., 1993, Erniminie Wheeler Voegelin prize, Am. Soc. for Ethnohistory, 1993, Cert. Commendation, Am. Assn. for State and Local History, 1993, Outstanding Book award, Gustavus Myers Ctr. for the Study of Human Rights in the US, 1993, George W. Lucas Cmty. Svc. award, NAACP New Orleans chpt., 1997, Merit award, Am. Assn. for State and Local History, 2001; fellow, NEH, 2006. Mem.: Orgn. Am. Historians (Disting. Svc. award 2004, Elliott Rudwick award 1993), Am. Hist. Assn. Achievements include established the Ethel and Herman Midlo endowed chair and research center at University of New Orleans. Avocations: music, forestry, architecture, environment. Home: 1300 Dante St New Orleans LA 70118 Office: PO Box 28 New Orleans LA 70118 Office Phone: 504-710-3757. E-mail: ghall1929@aol.com.

HALL, H. DALE, federal agency administrator; b. Harlan, Ky. m. Sarah Hall; children: Erin, Adam, Emily. BS in biology and chemistry, Cumberland Coll., Williamsburg, Ky.; M in fisheries sci., La. State U. Mgr. catfish farms Eden Fisheries and Farm, Inc., Miss.; joined US Fish & Wildlife Svc., US Dept. Interior, 1978, named sr. staff biologist Tex., 1982, promoted to field supr. Houston, dep. asst. dir. fisheries Washington, 1987, asst. regional dir. ecol. services Pacific region Portland, Oreg., 1991, dep. regional dir. S.E. region Atlanta, 1997, regional dir. S.W. region Albuquerque, 2001—05, dir., 2005—. Served USAF, 1968—72. Recipient Meritorious Svc. award, US Fish & Wildlife Svc., 1996. Office: US Fish & Wildlife Svc 1849 C St NW Washington DC 20242

HALL, HANSEL CRIMIEL, communications executive; b. Gary, Ind., Mar. 12, 1929; s. Alfred McKenzie and Grace Elizabeth (Crimiel) Hall. BS, Ind. U., 1953; LLB, Blackstone Sch. Law, 1982. Officer IRS, 1959-64; gasoline svc. sta. operator, then realtor Chgo., 1964-69; program specialist HUD, Chgo., 1969-73; dir. equal opportunity St. Paul, 1973-75; dir. fair housing Indpls., from 1975; human resource officer U.S. Fish and Wildlife Svc., Twin Cities, Minn. Cons. in civil rights; pres. bd. dirs. Riverview Towers Cooperative Assn., Inc., 1984-87; pres., CEO Crimiel Comms., Inc., 1988-; pres. West Bank Cmty. Coalition, Inc., 2002-03; CFO, treas. Korean War Vets. Edn. Grant Corp., 1996-2001; del. U.S. parliamentarian to Russia and Czechoslovakia, 1992, to Cuba, 1999; bd. dirs. Nat. Korean War Vets. Assn., 1992. With USAF, 1951-53, Korea. Recipient Amb. for Peace cert. Korean Vets. Assn., 1991, Korean Svc. medal Rep. of Korea, 1991. Mem. Res. Officers Assn. (life), Am. Inst. Parliamentarians, Nat. Assn. Parliamentarians, Minn. State Assn. Parliamentarians (pres. 1997-99), Toastmasters DTM, Ind. U. Alumni Assn., Omega Psi Phi, Phi Alpha Delta. Personal E-mail: crimielhh@hotmail.com.

HALL, HENRY KINGSTON, JR., chemistry professor; b. NYC, Dec. 7, 1924; s. Henry Kingston and Agnes (Furrer) H.; m. Alene Winifred Brown, Mar. 9, 1951; children: Joan, Douglas, Lillian. BS, Poly. Inst. Bklyn., 1944; MS, Pa. State U., 1946; PhD, U. Ill., 1949. Sr. research chemist textile fibers dept. E.I. DuPont de Nemours & Co., Inc., Wilmington, Del., 1952-65, group leader central research dept., 1965-69; prof. chemistry U. Ariz., Tucson, 1969-96, chmn. dept., 1970-73, emeritus prof., 1996—. Cons. Eastman Kodak Co., Rochester, Ticona Corp., Summit, N.J.; vis. prof. Imperial Coll., London, 1976, Max Planck Inst. for Polymer Rsch., Mainz, Federal Republic of Germany, Jan.-June, 1988; sr. vis. fellow Japan Soc. for Promotion Sci., summer 1981 Contbr. articles profl. jours. Recipient Japan Award for Disting. Svc. in Advancement of Polymer Sci., Soc. Polymer Sci., 1996. Mem. Am. Chem. Soc. (PMSE divsn. award for industry-univ. coop. 1997, Award for Polymer Chemistry 1996, H.F. Mark award 2000). Achievements include research in mechanisms of organic reactions and synthesis of new high polymers. Office: U Ariz Dept Chem PO Box 210041 Tucson AZ 85721-0041 Office Phone: 520-621-6325. Business E-Mail: hkh@u.arizona.edu.

HALL, HENRY LYON, JR., lawyer; b. Boston, July 23, 1931; s. Henry Lyon and Edith Page (Blanchard) H.; m. Jean Elizabeth Haring, Sept. 13, 1958; children: Henry Lyon, George B. AB, U. Mass., 1953; JD, George Washington U., 1962. Bar: Va. 1963, Mass. 1963. Assoc. Ropes & Gray LLP, Boston, 1963—73, ptnr., 1973—97, of counsel, 1998—. Lectr., panelist seminars Mem. Mass. Gov.'s Commn. Sch. Dist. Orgn., 1971-73; mem. sch. com. Minuteman Reg. Vocat. Sch. Dist., 1971-83, chmn. 1971-75; mem. permanent audit com. town of Belmont, Mass., 1979—, chmn. 1982-92; chmn. by law rev. com. 1979-83, bylaw rev. com., 1983-91; town moderator, Belmont, 1991—; corporator, trustee Belmont Savs. Bank. Served in U.S. Army, 1953-56. Mem. ABA, Mass. Bar Assn., Mass. Moderators Assn. (bd. dirs. 1995—, 1st v.p. 1997-98, pres. 1998-99), Nat. Assn. Bond Lawyers, Va. State Bar, Boston Bar Assn., Mass. Taxpayers Found., Govt. Fin. Officers Assn., Mass. Charitable Soc., Mass. Mcpl. Assn., Order of Coif, Phi Delta Phi. Home: 22 Randolph St Belmont MA 02478-3540 Office: Ropes & Gray LLP One International Place Boston MA 02110-2624 Office Phone: 617-951-7000. Business E-Mail: hhall@ropesgray.com, henry.hall@ropesgray.com.

HALL, H(ERBERT) GLEN, lawyer; b. Tarrytown, NY, Apr. 28, 1933; s. Herbert Van Auken and Elizabeth Eleanor (Glenn) H.; m. Jane Lottridge, Dec. 27, 1956 (dec. Dec. 1991). Regent's diploma, Washington Irving H.S., Tarrytown, NY, 1951; BA, Principia Coll., 1955; JD, Albany Law Sch., 1958. Bar: NY 1964, Pa. 1991, US Dist. Ct. (so. dist.) NY 1973, US Ct. Appeals (2d cir.) 1966, US Supreme Ct. 1968. Ptnr. Hall & Hall, Tarrytown, NY, 1965-74, Brown & Hall, Pleasantville, NY, 1974-83, Hall & Murdock, Briarcliff Manor, NY, 1983-88; pvt. practice Briarcliff Manor, 1988—2000; ptnr. Daly, Lavery & Hall, Ossining, 2000—06; pvt. practice Ossining, 2006—. Dep. town atty., Greenburgh, NY, 1969-73; mem. adv. bd. Pace U. Sch. Law, 1975-79; trustee 9th Jud. Dist. Supreme Ct. Libr., White Plains, NY, 1989—, chair, 1991-93. Mem. editl. bd. NY State Bar Jour., contbr. articles, 1983-93. Pres. Exch. Club of the Tarrytowns, 1977, 87, NY Dist. Exch. Club, 1989-90, Hist. Soc. for the Tarrytowns, 1973-75, 03-04; mem. adv. bd. Salvation Army, Westchester County, 1975—, chmn., 2003-06; pres. Briarcliff Woods Condominium Assocs., Ossining, NY, 1987, 90; mem. 9th Jud. Dist. Grievance Com., 1995-03. Fellow NY Bar Found., Am. Bar Found.; mem. SAR, Am. Soc. Writers on Legal Subjects, Tarrytown Bar Assn. (pres. 1972-74), Ossining Bar Assn. (pres. 2005—07), Westchester County Bar Assn. (pres. 1983-85, editor-in-chief Westchester Bar Jour. 1976-78), Exch. Club (pres. White Plains 1997-98), NY State Bar Assn. (v.p. 9th jud. dist. 1998-2000). Christian Scientist. Avocations: pen and ink with watercolors, photography. Home: 81 Briarcliff Dr S Ossining NY 10562-2301 Office: 500 Exec Blvd Ste 303 Ossining NY 10562-4933 Office Phone: 914-762-1790.

HALL, HOUGHTON ALEXANDER, electrical engineer, municipal official; b. Kingston, Jamaica, W.I., Aug. 17, 1936; arrived in U.S., 1985; s. James Alexander and Clarice Viola Hall; m. Grace Yvonne Anglin, Feb. 22, 1964; children: Andrew Geoffery, Christine Elizabeth. BS, U. W.I., Kingston, 1958, diploma in chem. tech., 1959, diploma in mgmt., 1977. Registered profl. engr., Fla.; chartered engr. Great Britain. Elec. engr. Jamaica Pub. Svc. Co., Kingston, 1960—84; dir. R&D Ministry of Sci., Tech. and the Environ., Kingston, 1984—85; elec. engr. electric dept. City of Tallahassee, 1985—90, mgr. substation engring. electric dept., 1990—. Fellow Fla. Engring. Soc.; mem. IEEE (sr.), NSPE, Inst. Elec. Engrs., Tallahassee Sci. Soc. (charter pres. 1989-97, pres. 2000—04), Fla. Acad. Scis. (chmn. engring. sect. 1994-97, 2000—, pres. 1997-99). Baptist. Avocations: electronics, scientific pursuits. Home: 4335 Sherborne Rd Tallahassee FL 32303-7607 Office: City of Tallahassee 2602 Jackson Bluff Rd Tallahassee FL 32304-4408 Office Phone: 850-891-5038. Business E-Mail: halla@talgov.com.

HALL, HOWARD HARRY, lawyer; b. Syracuse, NY, Jan. 9, 1933; s. Harold Gibner and Mildred E. (Way) H. AB, Syracuse U., 1953, JD, 1959. Bar: NY 1960, Calif. 1978, US Dist. Ct. (we., no. and so. dists.) NY 1960, US Dist. Ct. (cen. and so. dists.) Calif., 1978, US Ct. Appeals (2d cir.) 1960, US Ct. Appeals (9th cir.) 1978, US Supreme Ct. 1963. Assoc. Hiscock, Cowie, Bruce, Lee and Mawhinney, Syracuse, N.Y., 1959-61; pvt. practice Syracuse, N.Y., 1961-74, Long Beach, Calif., 1978-82, Paramount, Calif., 1982—. Commr. of edn. Syracuse, N.Y., 1968-72. Capt. USMC, 1953-56. Mem. State Bar of Calif., Calif. Trial Lawyers Assn., Bar Register of Preeminent Lawyers. Office: 15559 Paramount Blvd Paramount CA 90723-4330 Office Phone: 562-634-1625. Business E-Mail: info@howard.hallattorney.com.

HALL, HOWARD PICKERING, engineering and mathematics educator; b. Boston, July 8, 1915; s. George Henry and Elizabeth Isabel (McCallum) H.; m. Ellen Marguerite Ide, June 25, 1945 (dec. 1984); children: Charlotte McCallum, Stephanie Wilson, Lindsey Louise, Gretchen Elizabeth. AB, Harvard U., 1936, MS, 1937, DSc, 1951. Registered structural engr., Ill., 1953. Instr., civil engring. Brown U., Providence, 1937—38; structural analyst Mark Linenthal, Engr., Boston, 1938—39; instr., asst. prof., assoc. prof. civil engring. Northwestern U., Evanston, Ill., 1939—56; design engr, field engr. Porter, Urquart, Skidmore, Owings, Merrill, Casablanca, Morocco, 1951—53; dean, sch. engring., acad. v.p. Robert Coll., Istanbul, Turkey, 1956—68; dir. studies, acting headmaster St. Stephen's Sch., Rome, 1968—72; prof. math. Iranzamin Internat., Tehran, 1973—80; math. tchr. Vienna Internat. Sch., 1980—83, Copenhagen Internat. Sch., 1983—86. Cons. S.J. Buchanan, Bryan, Tex., Eng., 1955. Contbr. articles to profl. jours. Served to pvt. to capt. U.S. Army, 1942-46, ETO. Recipient Clemens Herschel award, Boston Soc. Civil Engrs. Mem. Sigma Xi. Home: 2425 SW 6th Ave Apt 252 Portland OR 97201-4916

HALL, JAMES BRYAN, gynecologist, oncologist; b. Dayton, Ohio, Nov. 24, 1946; s. Mitchell Z. and Moyne L. H.; m. Edith Miller, Mar. 22, 1975; children: James B. Jr., William B. AB, Taylor U., 1969; MD, Med. U. S.C., 1974. Diplomate Am. Bd. Ob-Gyn., Oncology. Rotating intern Miami Valley Hosp., Dayton, 1974-75; resident in ob-gyn. Wright State U.-Miami Valley Hosp., 1975-78, chief resident in ob-gyn., 1977-78; fellow in gynecologic oncology, asst. in gynecology Mass. Gen. Hosp., Boston, 1978-80; pvt. practice Charlotte, N.C., 1988-95. Instr. ob-gyn. Harvard U., Boston, 1978-80; dir. gynecologic oncology, dept. ob-gyn. Carolinas Med. Ctr., 1980—, dir. gynecology, Blumenthal Cancer Ctr., coord. med. student clerkship, 1982-87, acting dir. dept. ob-gyn., 1987-88, assoc. prof., 1986-88; asst. prof. U. N.C., Chapel Hill, 1980-86, assoc. prof., 1986-88, clin. prof., 1995—; spkr. at profl. confs. Contbr. numerous articles to med. jours. Fellow ACS, Am. Coll. Ob-Gyn.; mem. Am. Soc. Clin. Oncology, Soc.Gynecologic Oncology , Charlotte Gynecol. and Obstetrical Soc. (sec.-treas. 1984-86, v.p. 1986-87, pres. 1987-88, treas. 1998-2000), Am. Cancer Soc. (bd. dirs. Mecklenburg County chpt., chmn. profl. edn. com., exec. com.), AMA, N.C. Med. Soc., Assn. Profs. of Gynecologists and Obstetricians (pres.), James H. Nelson Jr. Oncology Soc. (pres.). Republican. Evang. nondenominational. Avocations: tennis, gourmet cooking. Office: Cancer Ctr Carolinas Med Ctr 1000 Blythe Blvd Charlotte NC 28203-5812 Office Phone: 704-355-2884.

HALL, JAMES CURTIS, business professor; b. Galax, Va., Feb. 12, 1926; s. Alonzo A. and Clara (Crissman) H.; m. Mary Anne Jones, Mar. 13, 1954; children: Michael Crissman, Suzanne King; m. Barbara P. Stamps, May 10, 1985. Student, U. N.C., 1943-44; AB, Duke, 1947; MS, Va. Poly. Inst. and State U., 1952; EdD, Columbia, 1956. Tchr. Galax H.S., 1947-50; instr. Va. Poly. Inst. and State U., 1951-54, Montclair State Coll., 1955; research asst. Columbia, 1955-56; asst. prof. Va. Poly. Inst. and State U., 1956-57; prof. Auburn U., 1957-62; dean Sch. of Bus., Va. Commonwealth U., 1962-88, Univ. prof., 1988-96, prof. emeritus, 1996—. Cons. to So. sch. systems; nat. lectr. econ. edn.; pres. Investment Enterprises, Inc.; dir. Richmond Investment Properties; chmn. adv. coun., divsn. adult and continuing edn., Bluefield Coll., 1998-99. Author: (with E.M. Robinson) College Business Organization and Management, 1964, (with others) General Business for Everyday Living, 3d edit, 1966, 4th edit., 1972, Business and You, 5th edit, 1979. Trustee Nat. Coun. on Econ. Edn., 1972-85, 93-94, mem. bd. founders, 1994—. Recipient John Robert Gregg award McGraw-Hill Co., 1983. Mem. Va. Council Econ. Edn. (exec. com. 1969—, pres. 1971-88, vice chmn. 1988-92, chmn. policies commn. for bus. and econ. edn. 1971-73), Nat. Bus. Edn. Assn. (pres. 1970-71), So. Bus. Edn. Assn. (pres. 1967), So. Bus. Adminstrn. Assn. (v.p. 1987-88), Adminstrv. Mgmt. Soc. (pres. Richmond chpt. 1969-70), Phi Beta Kappa, Phi Kappa Phi, Beta Gamma Sigma, Beta Alpha Psi, Delta Pi Epsilon. Home: 741 Farnham Dr Richmond VA 23236-4108 Personal E-mail: jcurtishall@comcast.net. *Since I can remember, my desire has been to learn something new or to have some new experience every day that I live. I have tried always to treat every other person just as I would want to be treated under the same circumstance. I ask nothing of any person except that he tell the truth and that he treat every other human being with respect.*

HALL, JAMES EVAN, lawyer; m. Anne Stewart Impink; 2 daughters. B, U. Tenn., 1967. Counsel U.S. Senate Subcommittee on Intergovernmental Rels.; staff U.S. Senator Al Gore, Sr.; pvt. practice Chattanooga; mem. cabinet staff Tenn. Gov. Ned McWherter; dir. Tenn. State Planning Office; chief of staff U.S. Senator Harlan Mathews; mem. Nat. Transp. Safety Bd., Washington, 1993—2001, vice-chmn., 1994, chmn., 1994—2001; mng. ptnr. Hall & Assoc. LLC, 2001—. Mem. aviation inst. adv. bd. George Washington U.; com. on combating terrorism Nat. Acad. Engring. Officer US Army, 1967—73, Vietnam. Decorated Bronze Star.

HALL, JAMES FREDERICK, retired college president; b. Detroit, Dec. 30, 1921; s. Cortez Rogers and Bertha Wilhelmina H.; m. Betty Louise Stark, Sept. 17, 1949; children— Kristine Martha, Jay Charles. Student, U. Mich., 1939-41; BA, Wayne State U., 1947, MEd, 1948; Ed.D., Tchrs. Coll., Columbia U., 1954. Instr. Highland Park Jr. Coll., 1948-49; adminstrv. asst., instr. N.Y.C. Community Coll., 1950-51; dir. student personnel services, dept. head Orange County Community Coll., Middletown, NY, 1952-55; dean collegiate tech. div., exec. asst. to pres. Ferris State U., Big Rapids, Mich., 1955—57; founding pres. Dutchess Community Coll., Poughkeepsie, NY, 1957—72; pres. Cape Cod Community Coll., 1972-87; pres. emeritus, 1987. Trustee, Mass. rep., Gov.'s appointment New Eng. Bd. Higher Edn., 1975-87; chmn. Pres.'s Council of Regional Community Colls. in Mass., 1976-78; mem. Mass. Postsecondary Edn. Commn., 1978-85; trustee Middle States Assn. Schs. and Colls., 1966-72; mem. mgmt. team Labor Negotiations for Regional Bd. Community Colls., 1978; bd. incorporators Bass River Savs. Bank, 1979-85 Bd. dirs. Cape Code Conservatory, West Barnstable, Mass., 1973-87, Cape Cool YMCA, 1991—, YMCA, 1991-2001; trustee Cape Cod Hosp., Hyannis, Mass., 1978-87; mem. Mass. Health Facilities Appeal Bd., 1988-91; mem. Gov. Oversight Com., Town of Yarmouth, Mass., 1992—; mem. Town of Yarmouth Appeals Bd., 1992-93; apptd. Town of Yarmouth alt. rep. to Steam Ship Authority, 1997-98, 99-2003; trustee Hist. Soc. Old Yarmouth, 1994—. Lt. (j.g.) USNR, 1942-46. Named The James F. Hall Legacy Soc. in his honor, bd. trustees, Dutchess Cmty. Coll., 2004. Mem. New Eng. Assn. Schs. and Colls. (accreditation teams 1975-77), Southeastern Assn. Cooperation in Higher Edn. in Mass. (dir. 1972-79, pres. 1976, treas. 1978), Mass. Adminstrs. in Community Colls. (pres. 1974-75), Associated Colls of Mid-Hudson Area (chmn. bd. trustees 1963-64, 72, trustee 1963-72), Internat. Edn. Consortium (chmn. Coll. Consortium Internat. Studies, bd. dirs. 1985-87), Dutchess County Hist. Soc., South Yarmouth Lawn and Tennis Club (bd. dirs. 1991-93). Home: 29 Liverpool Dr Yarmouth Port MA 02675-1526

HALL, JAMES H(ERRICK), JR., philosophy educator, writer; b. Houston, Oct. 20, 1933; s. James Herrick and Loula Ben (Vining) H.; m. Bonlyn Goodwin, 1957 (div. 1977); children: Christopher Vining, Jonathan Goodwin; m. Myfanwy Seaver Monroe, 1977; 1 child, Charles Trevor. AB, Johns Hopkins U., 1955; BD, Southeastern Sem., Wake Forest, NC, 1958, ThM, 1960; PhD, U. N.C., Chapel Hill, 1964. Instr. philosophy U. N.C., Chapel Hill, 1960-62; asst. prof. Furman U., Greenville, SC, 1963-65; assoc. prof. U. Richmond, Va., 1965-74, chmn. dept. philosophy, 1965—89, 1999—2004, prof., 1974—2005, The Thomas chair, 1982—2005, Thomas prof. emeritus, 2005—, guest dir., 1999—2001. Author: Knowledge Belief and Transcendence, 1975, Logic Problems, 1991; (with others) Biblical and Secular Ethics, 1988, Philosophy of Religion, 2003, Practically Profound, 2005, Tools of Thinking, 2005. Mem. vestry St. Paul's Episcopal Ch., Richmond, 1988-91, 2004—, sr. warden, 2007—; profl. ch. musician, Chapel Hill, Raleigh, Balt., Washington, Richmond. Rsch. grantee Duke Found., Durham, 1964, Mednick Trust, 1973-74; named Disting. Educator, U. Richmond, 2001, Outstanding Prof., 2005; Coun. for Philosophic Studies fellow, Grand Rapids, 1973, U.

Warwick fellow, Coventry, U.K., 1989-90, Kenan fellow U. NC, 1960-61. Mem. AAUP (chpt. pres. 1991-92), ACLU, Am. Philos. Assn., Soc. for Philosophy of Religion, So. Soc. for Philosophy and Psychology, Omicron Delta Kappa. Democrat. Episcopalian. Avocations: choral music, computers, travel. Home: 209 Wood Rd Richmond VA 23229-7538 Office: U Richmond Dept Philosophy North Ct Richmond VA 23173 Business E-Mail: jhall@richmond.edu.

HALL, JAMES STANLEY, jazz guitarist, composer; b. Buffalo, Dec. 4, 1930; s. Harold S. and Louella (Cowles) H.; m. Jane Susan Yuckman, Sept. 9, 1965; 1 dau., Debra Jean. MusB, Cleve. Inst. Music, 1955; PhD in Music (hon.), Berklee Sch. Music, Boston, 1995. Author: Exploring Jazz Guitar; joined Chico Hamilton, 1955; mem. Jimmy Giuffre Trio, 1957, tour US and Europe with Jazz at Philharmonic, 1958, 59, Europe and S.A. with Ella Fitzgerald, 1959, 60; featured by Sonny Rollins, 1961-62; formed quartet with Art Farmer, 1962-64; leader own trio and quartet, 1962—; performed at White House, 1969; albums include Jazz Guitar, 1957, Undercurrent, All Across the City, Dedications & Inspirations, Diaglogues, Textures, 1997. By Arrangement, 1998, Jim Hall and Pat Metheny, 1999, Grand Slam, 2000, Jim Hall and Basses, 2001, Magic Meeting, 2004, Free Association: Duet with Jim Hall and Geoff Keezer, 2005; motion picture appearance in Jazz on a Summer's Day, 1958; appearance on Ralph Gleason's TV Show, 1962-63, BBC, 1964, Jim Hall Invitational Concert, 1990, Tonite show, 1992; tour Europe, 1967, 69, 79-82, 86-87, 89—, Japan, 1970, 76, 79, 87, 90—; (documentary film) A Life in Progress. Recipient award Downbeat Critics Poll, 1963-65, 74, 76-80, 82-88, 89-90, 91-93, award Downbeat Readers' Poll, 1965-66, 2001, award Playboy Mag. All-Star Poll for Guitar, 1968-71, Jazzpar prize, Denmark, 1998, Disting. Alumni award Cleve. Inst. Music, Jazz Master Nat. Endowment award NEA, 2004; named Best Performer Jazz Mag., 1965-66, 99, 2006, Best Composer-Arranger, Jazz Critics Cir. NY, 1997, Choc D'Annee Jazzman of Yr., 2005, 06, Best Jazz Guitarist, Jazz Critics Cir. NY, 2006; winner Jazz Times poll as Best Guitar, 1991. Mem. BMI, Chevalier de l'Ordre des Arts et Letters. Personal E-mail: amsala@aol.com.

HALL, JAMES WILLIAM, university chancellor; b. Chester, Pa., Oct. 14, 1937; s. James William and Margaret (Crothers) H.; children: Laura, Janet, Carol. MusB, Bucknell U., Lewisburg, Pa., 1959; M of Sacred Music, Union Theol. Sem., NYC, 1961; MA, U. Pa., Phila., 1964, PhD, 1967; DHL (hon.), Thomas Edison State Coll. NJ, 1992, U. Sys. NH, 1994, DePaul U., Chgo., 1996, SUNY, 2006. Instr. Cedar Crest Coll., Allentown, Pa., 1961-66; vis. asst. prof. SUNY, Albany, 1966-71, asst. acad. personnel, sys. adminstrn., 1966-68; assoc. univ. dean univ.-wide activities, 1968-70; asst. vice chancellor policy and planning, 1970-71; pres. Empire State Coll. SUNY, Saratoga Springs, 1971-97, pres. emeritus, 2006—; interim pres. SUNY Coll., Old Westbury, NY, 1981-82; vice-chancellor for ednl. tech. SUNY System, 1993-95; chancellor Antioch U., Yellow Springs, Ohio, 1998—2002, chancellor emeritus, disting. prof., 2002—. Editor: Am. Problem Series, Forging the American Character, 1971, (with B. Kevles) In Opposition to Core Curriculum: Alternative Models for Undergraduate Education, 1982, Access Through Innovation: New Colleges for New Students, 1991; contbr. articles to profl. jours. Trustee Monmouth Coll., NJ, 1981-93, U.S. Open U., 1999-02, Fielding Inst., Santa Barbara, Calif., 1990-99, chair 1995-97; bd. dirs. Saratoga Hosp., 1990-93, Nat. Commn. on Coop. Edn., 1999-02; bd. overseers Nelson A. Rockefeller Inst. Govt., SUNY, 1983-95. Danforth fellow, 1959-67 Mem. Am. Studies Assn., Soc. Values in Higher Edn., Am. Assn. Higher Edn., Assn. Am. Colls. (bd. dirs. 1986-89), Coun. for Adult and Experiential Learning (bd. dirs., chmn. 1987-88). E-mail: jhall@antioch.edu.

HALL, JAY, social psychologist; b. Houston, Oct. 18, 1932; s. Ernest James and Jamie (Clark) H.; m. Missy Hall; children: Kelly, Allison, Jeffrey. BA in Psychology, U. Tex., 1959, MA in Psychology, 1961, PhD in Psychology, 1963. Lectr. dept. psychology U. Tex., Austin, 1961-63, dir. S.W. Ctr. for Law and Behavioral Scis., 1964-66, assoc. prof. Grad. Sch. Bus., 1966-69; assoc. dir. Nat. Parole Insts., Austin, 1963-64; founder, chmn. bd. Telemetrics Internat., The Woodlands, Tex., 1969-93; CEO, chmn. Leadership Systems Internat., The Woodlands, Tex., 1996—. Author: Ponderables: Essays on Managerial Choice-Past and Future, 1982, The Competence Connection: A Blueprint for Excellence, 1988, Models for Management: The Structure of Competence, 1988, The Executive Trap, 1992, Why Some Leaders are Better than Others, 1995, Benchmarks: For a Thoughtful Journey, 2000; co-author: GolfThink: Train Your Mind to Train Your Body, 2004; contbr. numerous articles and psychol. tests to profl. publs. Trustee The Woodlands Med. Ctr., 1980-91, Community Life Found., 1985-88, The John Cooper Sch., The Woodlands, 1986-91; dir. Interfaith, The Woodlands, 1980-88. 1st lt. U.S. Army, 1955-58. Mem. Am. Psychol. Assn., AAAS, N.Y. Acad. Sci., Sigma Xi. Episcopalian. Achievements include invention of swangletrainer for golf; Halford Grip sports/grip prosthesis; creator NASA moon survival task. Avocation: golf. E-mail: drjayhall@houston.rr.com.

HALL, JEFFREY CONNOR, biology educator, behavioral genetics researcher; b. Bklyn., May 3, 1945; AB, Amherst Coll., 1967; MS, U. Wash., 1969, PhD in Genetics, 1971. Fellow behavioral genetics Calif. Inst. Tech., 1971-73; asst. prof. biology Brandeis U., Waltham, Wash., 1974-79, assoc. prof., 1979—. Mem.: NAS. Office: Brandeis Univ Biology Dept Bassine 119 Mailstop 008 415 South St Waltham MA 02454-9110 Office Phone: 781-736-3170. E-mail: hall@brandeis.edu.

HALL, JEROME WILLIAM, research engineering educator; b. Brunswick, Ga., Dec. 1, 1943; s. William L. and Frances K. H.; m. Loretta E. Hood, Aug. 28, 1965; children: Jennifer, Bridget, Bernadette. BS in Physics, Harvey Mudd Coll., Claremont, Calif., 1965; MS in Engring., U. Wash., 1968, PhDCE, 1969. Registered profl. engr., D.C., N.Mex., Va. Asst. prof. civil engring. U. Md., College Park, 1970-73, assoc. prof., 1973-77, U. N.Mex., Albuquerque, 1977-80, prof., 1980—, dir. bur. engring. research, 1981-88, asst. dean engring., 1985-88, chmn. dept. of civil engring., 1990-97. Cons. in field. Co-author: Fundamentals of Traffic Engineering, 2007; contbr. articles to profl. jours. Recipient Teetor award Soc. Automotive Engrs., 1975; Pub. Partnership award Alliance Transp. Rsch., 1997.; ITE Western District, Lifetime Achievement Award, 2006. Fellow Inst. Transp. Engrs. (pres. N.Mex. sect. 1985, pres. western dist. 1989, internat. bd. dir. 1993-95); mem. Transp. Rsch. Bd. (chmn. com. 1986-92, chmn. group coun. 1992-95, panel chmn. 1990-03), Am. Soc. Engring. Edn., Am. Rd. and Transp. Builders Assn. (pres. rsch. and edn. divsn. 2002-03, bd. dirs. 2003-05), Nat. Assn. County Engrs. Republican. Roman Catholic. Office: Dept Civil Engring MSC01 1070 UNM Albuquerque NM 87131 Office Phone: 505-277-1418. Business E-Mail: jerome@unm.edu.

HALL, JOAN LORD, literature and language educator; d. John Lord and Mary Urmson Leay; m. Clifton Dale Hall, Dec. 21, 1977 (dec. 2001); 1 child, Alison Jane. BA Honors, U. Coll. London, 1968; M Lit., Girton Coll. Cambridge, Eng., 1971. Lectr. English Lang. and Lit. U. Lancaster, Lancashire, England, 1971—78; lectr. English U. Colo., Boulder, 1979—2000, instr. writing and rhetoric, 1986—. Author: Four Guides to Shakespeare (Henry V, Othello, Antony and Cleopatra, The Winter's Tale, The Dynamics of Role-Playing in Jacobean Tragedy. Mem.: MLA (chair Shakespeare panel Rocky Mountain chpt. 2004). Home: 3958 Bosque Court Boulder CO 80301 Office: Program of Writing and Rhetoric University of Colorado Boulder CO 80304 Office Phone: 303-492-8188. Personal E-mail: hallj123@juno.com.

HALL, JOHN E., medical educator; PhD in Physiology, Mich. State U., 1974. Postdoctoral fellow U. Miss. Med. Ctr., Jackson, Miss., 1974—76, faculty, 1976—82, prof. dept. physiology and biophysics, 1982—, chair dept. physiology and biophysics, 1989—, dir. Ctr. of Excellence in Cardiovascular-Renal Rsch., Guyton prof. Burroughs Wellcome Fund vis. prof. in basic med. scis. Co-author (with Arthur Guyton): Medical Physiology; chief editor Hypertension Physiology: Regulatory, Integrative and Comparative Physiology, author/editor 13 books, mem. editl. bds. several internat. jours.; contbr. over 450 articles to profl. jours. Recipient Merck Sharp and Dohme Internat. Rsch. award, Internat. Soc. Hypertension, Spl. Rsch. Achievement award, Am. Heart Assn.-Miss., NIH Career Devel. award, A.P. Barnard and Billy S. Guyton Disting. Professorships award, U. Miss., Novartis award, AHA; grantee Nat. Heart, Lung and Blood Inst. grantee, 1975—. Fellow: Am. Physiol. Soc. (mem. coun. 1991, mem. strategic planning com. 1992—2000, chair SAC 1997—2000, pres., mem. long range planning com., numerous others, chair, treas. and councillor water and electrolyte homeostasis sect., mem. renal sect., mem. cardiovascular sect., Ernest Starling Lectureship); mem.: Inter-Am. Soc. Hypertension (pres.), Am. Soc. Hypertension (exec. com., Richard Bright award, Marion Young Scholar award), Am. Heart Assn. (past chmn. coun. for high blood pressure rsch., chmn. com. of sci. couns., bd. dirs., Harry Goldblatt award, Lewis Dahl award). Achievements include research in in cardiovascular and renal physiology, mechanisms of hypertension, the renin-angiotensin system, obesity and insulin resistance; also in modeling and computer simulation of the cardiovascular-renal systems. Office: Univ Miss Med Ctr Dept Physiology/Biophysics 2500 N State St Jackson MS 39216-4505

HALL, JOHN FRY, retired psychologist; b. Phila., Apr. 24, 1919; s. Harry R. and Alta (Herner) H.; m. Jean Midlam, May 14, 1943; 1 son, John. BS, Ohio U., 1946; MA, Ohio State U., 1947, PhD, 1949. Mem. faculty Pa. State U., University Park, 1949—, prof. psychology, 1958—; prof. emeritus, 1985—; Program dir. psychobiology NSF, Washington, 1966-67. Vis. prof. U. Va., 1952, U. Wis., 1954, U. Calif. at Berkeley, 1962, U. Hawaii, 1968, Fla. State U., 1975-76 Author: Psychology of Motivation, 1961, Psychology of Learning, 1966, Readings in the Psychology of Learning, 1967, Verbal Learning and Retention, 1971, Classical Conditioning and Instrumental Learning, 1976, An Invitation to Learning and Memory, 1982, Learning and Memory, 1989; contbr. articles to profl. jours. Mem. AAAS, APA, Psychonomics Soc.

HALL, JOHN HERBERT, lawyer; b. Orange, NJ, Dec. 5, 1942; s. Embert Brown Hall and Elizabeth (Sullivan) Carnahan; m. Suzanne Steeger, Aug. 21, 1965 (div. Apr. 1988); children: Christopher Evan, Jeremy Randall; m. Lisa Gersh, June 19, 1988 (div. Dec. 2005); children: Samantha, Madeleine; m. Anne Lawrence Gilchrist, Jan. 12, 2007. BA, Wesleyan U., 1965; MBA, NYU, 1966; JD, Columbia U., 1969. Bar: N.Y. 1970, U.S. Dist. Ct. (so. dist.) N.Y. 1972, (ea. dist.) N.Y. 1981, U.S. Ct. Appeals (2d cir.) 1974, (10th cir.) 1977, (5th cir.) 1980, (11th cir.) 1981, (4th cir.) 1989, (D.C. cir.) 1982, U.S. Supreme Ct. 1981. Assoc. Debevoise, Plimpton, Lyons & Gates, NYC, 1969-72, 73-78, Cmty. Law Offices, NYC, 1972-73; ptnr. Debevoise & Plimpton, NYC, 1979—, chair litig. dept., 1993—2002, mem. mgmt. com., 2003—06. Co-author: Takeovers-Attack and Survival, 1987, 2d edit., 1993; author: Global Counsel-Dispute Resolution Handbook, 2004-2005, 2005 Bd. dirs. Legal Aid Soc. NY, 1980-88, Vols. Legal Svcs., 1990-96, Nat. Ctr. Law and Econ. Justice, 2006—. Named a Leading Litigator, Yearbook, 2005. Mem. N.Y. Bar Found. (fellow bd. dirs.), ABA (criminal, bus. law, litig. sects.), N.Y. Lawyers for Pub. Interest (bd. dirs. 1987-00), Am. Judicature Soc., Supreme Ct. Hist. Soc., Assn. of Bar of City of N.Y. (fed. cts. com. 1981-84), Prep for Prep Inc. (dir. 1984—, v.p., sec.), U.S. Cycling Fedn., Nat. Legal Aid/Defenders Assn., Law Soc. Eng. and Wales, Global Counsel 3000. Avocations: bicycle racing, tennis. Office: Debevoise & Plimpton 919 3rd Ave 43rd Floor New York NY 10022-6225 Home: 1220 Park Ave Apt 14C New York NY 10128 Office Phone: 212-909-6591. Business E-Mail: Jhhall@debevoise.com.

HALL, JOHN HOPKINS, retired lawyer; b. Dallas, May 10, 1925; s. Albert Brown and Eleanor Pauline (Hopkins) H.; m. Marion Martin, Nov. 23, 1957; children: Ellen Martin, John Hopkins II. Student, U. Tex., 1942, U. of South, Sewanee, Tenn., 1942-43; LL.B., So. Meth. U., 1949. Bar: Tex. 1949. Ptnr. Strasburger & Price, Dallas, 1957-93, ret., 1993. With US Army, 1943—45. Fellow Tex. Bar Found., Am. Bar Found., Internat. Acad. Trial Lawyers, Am. Coll. Trial Lawyers; mem. Tex. Bar Assn., Tex. Assn. Def. Counsel, Internat. Assn. Def. Counsel. Episcopalian.

HALL, JOHN J., congressman, musician; b. Balt., July 23, 1948; s. James A. and Marie W. Hall; m. Pamela Melanie Bingham; 1 child, Sofi. Attended, Notre Dame U., 1964—65, Loyola Coll., Balt., 1965—66. Musician, composer, activist; founding mem. rock band Orleans, 1972—77; co-founder Musicians United for Safe Energy; mem. Ulster County Legis., NY, 1990—91; mem., pres. Saugerties Bd. Edn., NY, 1996—98; mem. US Congress from 19th NY dist., 2007—, mem. transp. & infrastructure com., vets. affairs com., congressional progressive caucus, vice chair subcommittee on aviation, mem. select com. on energy independence and global warming. Profl. musician, Washington, NYC; founding mem. Orleans band, 1972—77, John Hall Band. Composer (and performer): numerous songs, record albums, and music for Broadway & off-Broadway musicals, worked closely with Janis Joplin, Seals & Crofts, Bonnie Raitt; performer: (songs) Still the One, Dance With Me, (albums) Rock Me on the Water, 2005, and others. Mem.: A.F. of M., AFTRA. Democrat. Roman Catholic. Avocations: french horn, guitar, bass and drums. Office: US House Reps 1217 Longworth House Office Bldg Washington DC 20515 also: Putnam County Office Bldg 3rd Fl 40 Gleneida Ave Carmel NY 10512 Office Phone: 202-225-5441. Office Fax: 202-225-3289.*

HALL, JOHN LEWIS, physicist, researcher; b. Denver, Aug. 21, 1934; s. John Ernest and Elizabeth Rae (Long) H.; m. Marilyn Charlene Robinson, Mar. 1, 1958; children: Thomas Charles, Carolyn Gay, Jonathan Lawrence. BS in Physics, Carnegie Mellon U., Pitts., 1956, MS in Physics, 1958, PhD in Physics, 1961; PhD (hon.), U. Paris XIII, 1989; DSc (hon.), Carnegie Mellon U., Pitts., 2006. Postdoctoral rsch. assoc. Nat. Bur. Standards, Washington, 1961-62, physicist Boulder, Colo., 1962-75, sr. scientist, 1975—2004, sr. fellow, emeritus, 2005—. Lectr. U. Colo., Boulder, 1977-; cons. Los Alamos Sci. Labs., 1963-65; cons. numerous firms in laser industry, 1974—. Contbr. articles to profl. jours.; patentee in laser tech.; editor: Laser Spectroscopy 3, 1977. Recipient IR-100 award IR Mag., 1975, 77, Nat. Bur. Stds. Stratton award, 1971, E.U. Condon award, 1979, Gold medal Dept. Commerce, 1969, 74, 2002, Presdl. Meritorious Exec. award, 1980, 2002, Meritorious Alumnus award Carnegie Mellon U., 1985, Humboldt Sr. Scientist award Munich, 1989, A.V. Astin award NIST, 2000, Rabi award IEEE, 2004, Golden Plate award, Acad. Achievement, 2006; co-recipient Nobel Prize for Physics, 2005; named Knight French Legion Honor, 2004; Sherman Fairchild Disting. scholar Calif. Tech., 1992. Fellow Optical Soc. Am. (bd. dirs. 1980-82, Charles H. Townes award 1984, Frederic Ives medal 1991, Max Born award 2002), Am. Phys. Soc. (Davisson-Germer award 1988, Arthur L. Schawlow prize 1993); mem. NAS. Office: U Colo JILA Boulder CO 80309-0440 Office Phone: 303-492-7843. Business E-Mail: jhall@jila.colorado.edu.

HALL, JOHN RAYMOND, JR., fire protection executive; b. Washington, Feb. 25, 1948; s. John Raymond and Elizabeth Florence (Lord) H.; m. Jean Baird Horky, Dec. 2, 1972. BA cum laude, Brown U., 1967; PhD, U. Pa., 1972. Rsch. analyst Resource Mgmt. Corp., Bethesda, Md., 1972-73; sr. rsch. assoc. Urban Inst., Washington, 1973-79; ops. rsch. analyst U.S. Fire Adminstrn., within Fed. Emergency Mgmt. Agy., Washington, 1979-82, Ctr. for Fire Rsch., within Nat. Bur. of Stds, Gaithersburg, Md., 1982-84; asst. v.p. fire analysis and rsch. Nat. Fire Protection Assn., Quincy, Mass., 1984—. V.p. mem. activities Inst. of Mgmt. Scis., Providence, 1983-86, sec. 1979-83, mem. at-large of coun., 1977-79, chmn. orgn. and bylaws com., 1979-94, pres. Washington chpt. 1978-79, v.p. for membership coll. on pub. programs and processes, 1982-85; trustee Washington Ops. Rsch./Mgmt. Sci. Coun., 1980-81, 83-84. Author: (with others) Procedures for Improving the Measurement of Local Fire Protection Effectiveness, 1976, How Effective Are Your Community Services?, 1977, 92, The SFPE Handbook of Fire Protection Engineering, 1988, 95, 2002, Fire Protection Handbook, 1986, 97; editor TIMS Chpts. Newsletter, 1976-79; columnist Mgmt. Sci. Update, 1980-81; columnist/editor Applications Rev., 1976-88; contbr. articles to profl. jours. Chmn. Fire Protection Commn., Norwood, Mass., 1986—, Fire Safety Inst., 2004—. Recipient (4) Cert. of Outstanding Performance Fed. Emergency Mgmt. Agy., 1981-83, Cert. of Spl. Achievement, 1982, Cert. of Recognition Nat. Bur. of Stds., 1983-84, Leadership Giving award United Way of Neponset Valley, 1991. Fellow: Inst. Ops. Rsch. and Mgmt. Sci. (mem. fin. com. 1997—99, past pres.); mem.: ASTM (E5 exec. com. 1996—2003, 4th vice chair 1998—2003, chair E5.31 2006—, Wayne P. Ellis award 2004), AAAS, Nat. Fire Protection Assn. (exec. sec. rsch. sect. 1990—2005), Internat. Standardization Orgn. (chair fire risk assessment), Inst. Mgmt. Scis., Soc. for Risk Analysis, Ops. Rsch. Soc. Am. (tech. sects. com. 1972—76), Internat. Assn. for Fire Safety Sci. (program com. 1991—2004, newsletter editor 1994—2004, exec. com. 1994—2004, chmn. arrangements com. 2000—02), Sigma Xi, Phi Beta Kappa. Democrat. Achievements include rsch. on the modeling and conceptual framework innovations in fire risk analysis in the USA. Home: 10 Alden Dr Norwood MA 02062-5326 Office: Nat Fire Protection Assn 1 Batterymarch Park Quincy MA 02169-7471

HALL, JOHN WESLEY, JR., lawyer; b. Watertown, NY, Jan. 28, 1948; s. John Wesley and Mary Louise Hall; m. Alison Hall; children: Justin William, Mark Daniel, Juliana Gebb. BA, Hendrix Coll., 1970; JD, U. Ark., 1973. Bar: Ark. 1973, US Dist. Ct. (ea. and we. dists. Ark.) 1973, US Ct. Appeals (8th cir.) 1973, DC 1975, US Ct. Appeals (5th cir.) 1976, US Supreme Ct. 1976, US Ct. Fed. Claims, 1984, Tenn. 1988, US Ct. Appeals (fed. cir.) 1988, US Ct. Appeals (6th cir.) 1991, Nev. 1993, US Ct. Appeals (9th cir.) 1995, NY 1996, US Dist. Ct. (so. dist. NY), 1999, US Ct. Appeals (2nd cir.) 1999, US Dist. Ct. (dist. Nev.) 2000, US Dist. Ct. (ea. dist.) Tex. 2004, US Dist. Ct. (mid. dist.) Tenn. 2005. Law clk. Ark. Supreme Ct., Little Rock, 1974; dep. pros. atty. Office Pros. Atty., Little Rock, 1973-79, head career criminal divsn., 1978-79; pvt. practice atty., 1974—. Instr. trial advocacy Ark. Pros. Attys. Assn., 1977-79; adj. prof. Sch. Law, Grad. Sch. Criminal Justice, U. Ark., Little Rock, 1985-88, 91; mem. Ark. adv. com. US Commn. Civil Rights, 2003-04; war crimes trial Spl. Ct. Sierra Leone, 2004-06; speaker to lawyer and police groups. Author: Search and Seizure, 3rd edit., 2000, Professional Responsibility in Criminal Defense Practice, 3rd edit. 2005, Trial Handbook for Arkansas Lawyers, 5th edit., 2007; editor, author: Arkansas Prosecutor's Trial Manual, 1976-77, Arkansas Extradition Manual, 1978; editor: (with B. Scheck and P. Neufield) DNA: Understanding, Controlling, and Depleting the New Evidence of the 90's, 1990; contbr. articles to law jours. Recipient Robert C. Heeney Meml. award, 2002. Fellow Am. Bd. Criminal Lawyers; mem. NACDL (life, bd. dirs. 1989-95, 97-2003, officer 2003-, mem. ethics adv. com. 1990-2005, lawyer's assistance strike force 1994-97, exec. com. 2000-01, 03-, Robert C. Heeney Meml. award 2002), Ark. Bar Assn. (ho. dels. 1976-79), Ark. Assn. Criminal Def. Lawyers (pres. 1987-89, Champion of Justice award 2003), NY State Assn. Criminal Def. Lawyers, First Amendment Lawyers Assn., Internat. Criminal Bar, Internat. Criminal Def. Attys. Assn. Episcopalian. Office: John Wesley Hall Jr PC 1311 Broadway Little Rock AR 72202-4843 Office Phone: 501-371-9131.

HALL, JO(SEPHINE) MARIAN, editor; b. Aberdeen, SD, July 12, 1921; d. Charles Martin Sykes and Deddie Mae (Keiser) Gruett; m. Winston Hall, Dec. 4, 1940 (dec.); children: Wendy Diane, Willis Edward. Student, U. Colo., 1958, U. S.D., 1976. With advt. dept. Mobridge Reminder, SD, 1955-61, columnist, 1956-61; with advt. dept., columnist Mobridge Tribune, 1961-67, 93—, news editor, photographer, 1968-81, editor people page, 1981—. Airway observer US Weather Bur., Mobridge, 1939—84; sec. bd. dirs. Klein Mus., Mobridge, 1976—82; chpt. pres. Am. Field Svc., 1972—82; vol. Mobridge Regional Hosp., 1990—; grand marshall Sitting Bull Parade and Rodeo, Morbridge, 2003; organist, dir. choir, sr. warden vestry St. James Episcopal Ch., Mobrdige; mem. SD Episcopal Diocesan Coun., 1993—99. Named SD State Homefront Hero of WWII, 2002; recipient numerous state and nat. awards feature stories, news stories, columns, obituaries, photography, spl. sects. headlines, 1959—, Hebert Bayard Swope award, 1978, 1st pl. award for newspaper editing, Nat. Fedn. Press Women, 1979, 1st pl. award for spl. edit., 1982, Honor 50 Yrs. as Journalist, Mobridge Tribune, 2006, Golden Quill award, SD Press Women, 1988. Democrat. Avocations: water aerobics, swimming, reading, cooking, gardening. Home: 910 3rd Ave W Mobridge SD 57601-1605 Office Phone: 605-845-3646. Personal E-mail: hallenterprises@westriv.com.

HALL, JOYE, elementary school educator; b. Union, SC, Dec. 19, 1963; d. Don and Joyce Brock; m. Michael Hall, Mar. 9, 1985; children: Anna, Christian, Alicia, Erica. BS, Lander U., Greenwood, SC, 1984—86; M in Elem. Edn., Clemson U., SC, 1988—90. Cert. tchr. Nat. Bd. Profl. Tchg. Standards, 2002. Sci. & math tchr. Whitmire HS, SC, 1987—88; 2d grade tchr. Pk. St. Sch., Whitmire, 1988—94, Whitmire Cmty. Sch., 1994—. Recipient Tchr. of Yr. award, Pk. St. Sch., 1994. Mem.: Reading Coun. Avocations: gardening, reading, walking, crafts. Office: Whitmire Cmty Sch 2597 Hwy 66 Whitmire SC 29178 Home Phone: 803-694-2624.

HALL, KATHY, health facility administrator; b. Covington, Ky., Feb. 15, 1953; d. Joseph B. and Mary Louise (Weindel) Dusing; m. Harold G. Hall, Oct. 6, 1973; children: Becky, Amy, Sarah. AA, Eastern Ky. U., 1973, BS in Nursing, 1978; MS in Nursing, Bellarmine U., 1999. Med.-surg. staff nurse Good Samaritan Hosp., Lexington, Ky., 1973; infection control nurse Pattie A. Clay Hosp., Richmond, Ky., 1975-93, orientation instr., 1978-82, quality assurance dir., 1982-93; nurse epidemiologist U. Ky. Chandler Med. Ctr., Lexington, 1993—99; edn. dir. Shriners Hosp. for Children, Lexington, 1999—2002; dir. continuing edn. and devel. Coll. Health Sci. Ea. Ky. U. Mem.: NNSDO, KNA, ANA, Ctrl. KY Staff Devel. Group, Sigma Theta Tau. Office: CHS Continuing Edn and Devel 202 Perkins Bldg Ea Ky U 521 Lancaster Ave Richmond KY 40475-3102 Office Phone: 859-622-1826. Business E-Mail: Kathy.Hall@eku.edu.

HALL, KENNETH RICHARD, chemical engineering professor, consultant; b. Tulsa, Okla., Nov. 5, 1939; s. Snipes Webster and Selina Rose (Scarpin) H.; m. Janet Beulah Blood, June, 1964 (div. 1975); children: Tara Marie, Deirdre Rene; m. Frieda Maria Karner, Mar. 12, 1976; children: Kent Max, Keith Anton, Krysta Maria. BS ChemE, U. Tulsa, 1962; MS, U. Calif., Berkeley, 1964; PhD, U. Okla., 1967. Registered engr., Tex. Asst. prof. U. Va., Charlottesville, 1967-70, 71-74; asst. to pres. ChemShare Corp., Norman, Okla., 1970; sr. rsch. engr. AMOCO, Tulsa, 1970-71; vis. prof. U. Louvain, Belgium, 1971-72; assoc. prof. Tex. A&M U., College Station, 1974-78, prof., 1978—, dir. Thermodynamics Rsch. Ctr., 1979-85, 97-2000, asst. dir. Tex. Engring. Experiment Sta., 1985-88, assoc. dean engring., 1987—94, 2002—03, from assoc. dir. to dep. dir., 1988—94, 2002—03, assoc. dep. chancellor for engring., 1990—94, 2002—03, interim head petroleum engring., 1991, interim head chem. engring., 1994; dir. CTS divsn. NSF, Va., 1994-96; GPSA prof. Tex. A&M U., College Station, 1997-2000, Jack E. and Frances Brown chair, 2001—, head dept. chem. engring., 2002—06. Cons. OPC Engring., Houston, 1980-85, Quantum Tech., Houston, 1981-85; cons. Precision Measurement Inc., Duncanville, Tex., 1981-90; bd. dirs. Lorax Corp., Syn Fuels. U.S. editor

Flow Measurement and Instrumentation; contbr. articles to profl. jours. Recipient numerous grants for research. Mem.: Am. Inst. Chem. Engrs. (chmn. ctrl. Va. chpt. 1969, chmn. cyrogenics 1977—79, exec. position II South Tex. sect. 1991—92, bd. dirs. fuels and petrochems. divsn. 1992—94), Am. Chem. Soc. Avocations: sports, reading. Home: 1401 Millcreek Ct College Station TX 77845-8352 Office: Tex A&M U Dept Chem Engring College Station TX 77843 Home Phone: 979-696-3579; Office Phone: 979-845-3357.

HALL, LARRY DEAN, utilities executive, lawyer; b. Hastings, Nebr., Nov. 8, 1942; s. Willis E. and Stella W. (Eckoff) H.; m. Jeffe D. Bryant, July 5, 1985; children: Scott, Jeff, Mike, Bryan. BA in Bus., U. Nebr., Kearney; JD, U. Nebr. Bar: Nebr. 1967, Colo. 1981. Ptnr. Wright, Simmons, Hancock & Hall, Scottsbluff, Nebr., 1967-71; atty., asst. treas. KN Energy Inc., Hastings, 1971-73, dir. regulatory affairs, 1973-76, v.p. law divsn. Lakewood, Colo., 1976-82, sr. v.p., 1982-85, exec. v.p., 1985-88, pres., COO, 1988-94, pres., CEO, 1994—99, also bd. dirs., 1988-94, chmn., CEO, pres., 1996-99; mng. dir. CPS Investments, 1999—. Bd. dirs. Colo. Assn. Commerce and Industry, Gas Rsch. Inst., Colo. Alliance for Bus., MLA, Magnum Techs., Riverview Tech. Corp.; chmn. Natural Gas Coun., 1998, Ingaa, 1998. Bd. dirs. Boy Scouts Am., St. Mary's Hosp. Found., Western Slope Hospice; active Canyon View Vineyard Ch. Mem. ABA, Colo. Assn. Commerce and Industry (bd. dirs.), Interstate Natural Gas Assn. Am. (chmn. 1997), RTC (bd. dirs.), Nebr. Bar Assn., Colo. Bar Assn., Midwest Gas Assn. (chmn.). Avocations: skiing, golf, photography. Home: 329 Red Ridge Ct Grand Junction CO 81503 Office: CPS Investments LLC 1400 16th St Ste 400 Denver CO 80202

HALL, LEE, artist, educator, writer; b. Lexington, NC, Dec. 15, 1934; d. Robert Lee and Florence (Fitzgerald) H. BFA, U. N.C., 1955; MA, N.Y. U., 1959, PhD, 1965; postgrad., Warburg Inst. U. London, 1965; DFA (hon.), U. N.C.-Greensboro, 1976. Asst. prof. N.Y. State U. Coll., Potsdam, 1958-60; assoc. prof., chmn. art dept. Keuka Coll., 1960-62; assoc. prof. art Winthrop Coll., 1962-65; asst. prof., chmn. art dept. Drew U., Madison, NJ, 1965-67, assoc. prof., chmn. art dept., 1967-70, prof., chmn. art dept., 1970-74; dean visual arts State U. N.Y. Coll. at Purchase, 1974-75; pres. R.I. Sch. Design, Providence, 1975-83; sr. v.p., dir. div. arts and communications Acad. for Ednl. Devel., NYC, 1984-92. Dir. rsch. on Pres. Kennedy's image in recent art, John F. Kennedy Meml. Library; panelist NEH, 1972-80. Exhibited in group shows in London, N.Y.C., Winston-Salem, Eugene, Oreg., others; author: Wallace Herndon Smith: Paintings, 1987, Ale Ajay, 1989, Betty Parsons: Artist, Dealer, Collector, 1991; Common Threads: A Parade of American Clothing, 1992; Elaine and Bill (de Kooning), 1993, Olmsted's America, 1994, Athena: A Biography, 1994; contbr. articles to profl. jours. Recipient research grant Am. Philos. Soc., 1965, 68; Childe Hassam Purchase award Am. Acad. Arts and Letters, 1977; RISD Athena medal, 1983 Home: 14 Silverwood Ter South Hadley MA 01075-1237 Personal E-mail: tobybrowndog@comcast.com.

HALL, LISA GERSH, broadcast executive, lawyer; m. John Hall; 2 children. JD, Rutgers U., 1983. Atty. Debevoise & Plimpton, LLP; founding ptnr. Friedman, Kaplan & Seiler, LLP, NYC; co-founder Oxygen Media, Inc., NYC, 1998—, chief adminstrv. officer and gen. counsel, 1998—99, COO, 1999—, pres., 2004—. Office: Oxygen Media Inc 7th Fl 75 9th Ave New York NY 10011

HALL, LOIS BREMER, secondary school educator, volunteer; b. Oak Park, Ill., July 27, 1923; d. Frederick Statler and Mabel (Forbes) Bremer; m. Bruce Hall, Sept. 9, 1955 (dec. Mar. 1981); children: Donald, Richard, Barbara. B in Music Edn., U. Mich., 1946. Cert. elem., secondary tchr. Mich., Ky.; ordained elder Presbyn. Ch. Tchr. handbell ringing Elm St. Recreation Ctr., Atlantic Recreation Ctr. Handbell ringer AARP, Osprey Village and Quality Health, Bapt. Hosp., 1st Presbyn. Ch. Fernandina Beach; dir. Amelia Handbell Choir; singer Amelia Island Chorale, Meml. United Meth. Ch., Amelia Plantation Chapel, Amelia Bapt. Ch., St. Peter's Episcopal Ch., tenor Amelia Island Cmty. Corale. Mem. com. Peck Ctr.; founding mem., vol. coord. CROP Walk, 1989—99; vol. Michah's Place (abused women refuge); player Praise Band, 2000—04; vol. Abused Women Shelter, 2003—04; mem. New Horizon Band, 2004; vol. advocate Abused Women's Shelter, 2004—06; mem. exec. bd. Meml. United Meth. Ch.; vol. Church World Svc., Fernandina Beach, Synod of South Atlantic Coun., 1989; mem. Presbytery of St. Augustine Coun., 1984—97, music coord. of handbell and choral workshops, 1990—98; mem. hunger com. Presbyn. Gen. Assembly, 1992—96; vol.-in-mission New Hope Meth. Presbyn. Ch., N. Pole, Alaska, 1991—94, 1996; bass, clarinet Ch. Choirs; mem. Meth Ch. Handbell Choir, 2002—06; dir., pres. Ch. Handbell Choir, 2004; dir. Presbyterian Ch. Handbell Choir, 2004—06; bd. dirs. Amelia Arts Acad., 1994—2003, Ann. Fernandina Beach Talent Show, 2001—02. Recipient award for cultural enrichment, City of Fernandina Beach, 2001. Mem.: AARP (bd. dirs.), Woman's Club Fernandina Beach (pres. 1983—84, 1991—92, Outstanding New Mem. 1980—81, Cmty. Svc. award 1987—88), Rose Garden Club (treas. 1998—2002), Alpha Omicron Pi, Delta Omicron. Republican. Home: 607 Goldenrod Way Saint Marys GA 31558

HALL, MARCIA JOY, non-profit organization administrator; b. Long Beach, Calif., June 24, 1947; d. Royal Waltz and Norine (Parker) Stanton; m. Stephen Christopher Hall, Mar. 29, 1968; children: Geoffrey Michael, Christopher Stanton. AA, Foothill Coll., 1967; student, U. Oreg., 1967-68; BA, U. Washington, Seattle, 1969. Cert. contracts count presenter 2005. Instr. aide Glen Yermo Sch., Mission Viejo, Calif., 1979—80; market rsch. interviewer Rsch. Data, Framingham, Mass., 1982—83; instr. adult edn. Community Sch. Use Program, Milford, Mass., 1982—83; coord. career info. ctr. Milford High Sch., 1983—86; dir. corp. rels. Sch. Vols. for Milford, Inc., 1985—86; coord. N.E. area YWCA of Annapolis and Anne Arundel County, Severna Park, Md., 1987—89; exec. dir. West Anne Arundel County C. of C., Odenton, Md., 1989—2001, also exec. dir. Found., Inc., 1999—2001; coord. bus. and entrepreneurship continuing profl. edn. and outreach Anne Arundel C.C., Arundel Mills, Md., 2001—03, lead instr. nonprofit leadership devel., 2003—; pres., CEO, cert. contracts ct. presenter Marcia Hall & Assocs., LLC, Severna Park, Md., 2003—; founder Reputation Counts, Severna Park, Md., 0200—. V.p. Corridor Transp. Corp., 1997-99; bd. dirs. Entrepreneur's Exch.; founder Reputation Counts; presenter in field. Author: Navigating Newbie-ism: 12 Simple Ways to Thrive in Your First Job and Career, The College Student's Guide, 2007. Pres. PTO, Mission Viejo, 1979-80, Milford, 1981-84; consumer assistance vol., Calif. Pub. Interest Rsch. Group, 1977-78; chmn. grant com. 21st Century Edn. Found., Ann Arundel Pub. Schs., Leadership Anne Arundel. Mem.: Nat. Speakers Assn., Md. Assn. C. of C. Execs. (pres. 1999—2000), Toastmasters (treas. 1988—, pres. 1989—). Avocations: piano, music composition, bridge, reading. Home: 507 Devonshire Ln Severna Park MD 21146-1017 Office Phone: 410-987-0857. E-mail: marcia@reputationcounts.com.

HALL, MICHAEL C., actor; b. Raleigh, NC, Feb. 1, 1971; m. Amy Spanger. Grad., Earlham Coll., 1993; MFA, NYU. Actor: (TV series) Six Feet Under, 2001—05, Dexter, 2006—07; (films) Showboy, 2002, Paycheck, 2003, Bereft, 2004; (plays) Macbeth, Cymbeline, Timon of Athens, Henry V at the Public, The English Teachers, Corpus Christi, Skylight, Cabaret, R Shomon, 2004, Mr. Marmalade, 2005; TV appearances includ The Tonight Show with Jay Leno, 2003. Office: c/o Don Buchwald & Assocs 10 E 44th St New York NY 10017

HALL, MICHAEL HOWARD, thoracic surgeon; b. Albany, Ga., July 6, 1946; MD, U. Ky. Coll. Medicine, 1972. Cert. Am. Coll. Surgeons, Am. Coll. Cardiology, Am. Coll. Chest Physicians, Soc. Thoracic Surgeons, Soc. Critical Care Medicine. Intern, gen. surgery NYU Med. Ctr., 1972—73, resident, thoracic & cardiovascular surgery, 1973—77, fellow, 1977—79; hosp. appointment North Shore U. Hosp., Manhasset, NY, 1979—, chief, divsn. cardiovascular surgery, dept. cardiovascular and thoracic surgery; assoc. prof. clin. surgery Cornell U. Med. Coll. Office: North Shore U Hosp 300 Community Dr Manhasset NY 11030*

HALL, MILES LEWIS, JR., lawyer; b. Ft. Lauderdale, Fla., Aug. 14, 1924; s. Miles Lewis and Mary Frances (Dawson) H.; m. Muriel M. Fisher, Nov. 4, 1950; children: Miles Lewis III, Don Thomas. AB, Princeton U., NJ, 1947; JD, Harvard U., Cambridge, Mass., 1950. Bar: Fla. 1951, US Supreme Ct., 1972, US Ct. Appeals (11th cir.), US Dist. Ct. (so. and mid. dist.) Fla. Since practiced in, Miami; ptnr. Hall & Hedrick, Miami, 1953—. Dir. Gen. Portland, Inc., 1974-81. Author: Election of Remedies, Vol. VIII, Fla. Law and Practice, 1958. Pres. Orange Bowl Com., 1964-65, dir., 1950—, sec., treas. 1984-86; vice-chmn., dir. Dade County ARC, Fla., 1961-62, chmn., 1963-64, dir., 1967-73; nat. fund cons. ARC, 1963, 66-68, trustee, 1985—; pres. Ransom Sch. Parents Assn., 1966; chmn. South Fla. Gov.'s Scholarship Ball, 1966; mem. exec. bd. South Fla. council Boy Scouts Am., 1966-67; citizens bd. U. Miami, 1961-66; mem. Fla. Council of 100, 1961-97, vice chmn., 1961-62; mem. Coral Gables Biltmore Devel. Com., Fla., 1972-73; mem. bd. visitors Coll. Law, Fla. State U., 1974-77; bd. dirs. Coral Gables War Meml. Youth Ctr. Assn. Inc., 1967—, pres., 1969-72; bd. dirs. Salvation Army, Miami, 1968-83, Fla. Citizens Against Crime 1984-89; bd. dirs. Bok Tower Gardens Found. Inc., 1987—, sec., 1991—; trustee St. Thomas U., 1990-96, vice chmn., 1993-96; trustee Fla. Supreme Ct. Hist. Soc., 1988—, v.p., 1991-92, pres., 1993-95. 2d lt. USAAF, 1943-45. Fellow Am. Bar Found. (life), Fla. Bar Found. (life); mem. ABA (Fla. co-chmn. membership com. sect. corp. banking and bus. law 1968-72), Dade County Bar Assn. (dir. 1964-65, pres. 1967-68), Fla. Bar Assn., Am. Judicature Soc., Miami-Dade County C. of C. (v.p. 1962-64, dir. 1966-68), Harvard Law Sch. Assn. Fla. (dir. 1964-66), Cottage Club, The Miami Club (v.p., dir. 1989-91, pres. 1990-91), Princeton Club So. Fla. (past pres.), Miami Found. for Cancer Rsch., Inc. (pres. 1998—), Alpha Tau Omega. Methodist.

HALL, MILTON REESE, retired oil company executive, accountant, controller; b. Vicksburg, Miss., July 5, 1932; s. Alvin Howard and Adelle Vera (McKay) H.; m. Margaret Louise Bailey, Feb. 17, 1957; children: Mark Russell, Stacy Elaine. BS in Acctg., Miss. So. U., 1953; MBA in Acctg., U. Miss., 1956; postgrad., La. State U., 1958-62. CPA, Miss. Trainee, div. contr. Kaiser Aluminum & Chem. Co., various locations, 1956-66; analyst Tex. Instruments, Inc., Dallas, 1966-67; contr., v.p. Koch Industries, Inc., Wichita, Kans., 1967-92; retired, 1993. With U.S. Army, 1953-55. Republican. Baptist. Avocations: music, skiing.

HALL, MONTY, television producer, actor; b. Winnipeg, Man., Can., Aug. 25, 1921; came to U.S., 1955; s. Maurice Harvey and Rose (Rusen) Halparin; m. Marilyn Doreen Plottel, Sept. 28, 1947; children: Joanna, Richard David, Sharon Fay. BS, U. Man., 1945, LLD (hon.), 1987; D Human Scis. (hon.), Hanneman U., 1988; PhD (hon.), Haifa U., 1989. TV personality, emcee, NYC and Hollywood, Calif., 1955—. Lectr. in field. Actor, U. Man., Canadian Army shows; emcee: NBC-Radio, Monitor on NBC-TV, Keep Talking, Byline: Monty Hall, Video Village on CBS-TV, ABC-TV; host Let's Make a Deal, 1964-86, Split Second, 1986-87; Author: Emcee: Monty Hall, 1974; producer (TV show) Your First Impression; guest appearances numerous TV series: starring role (stage prodn.) High Button Shoes, 1978. Bd. dirs. numerous charitable orgns.; bd. govs. Cedars-Sinai Med. Ctr.; active numerous orgns. on behalf of Israel; hon. mayor, Hollywood, 1973-79. Decorated officer Order of Can., Order of Manitoba; recipient star on Hollywood's Walk of Fame, 1973, on Palm Springs Walk of Fame, 1996, on Can. Walk of Fame, 2002; Internat. Humanitarian award Variety Clubs, 1983, over 500 other awards, including Monty Hall floor at U. Calif./L.A. Hosp., Johns Hopkins U., Balt., Mt. Sinai Hosp., Toronto, Hahneman Hosp., Phila. Mem. AFTRA, Screen Actors Guild, Variety Clubs (internat. pres. 1975-77, internat. chmn. 1981—). Clubs: Hillcrest Country. Avocations: golf, tennis. Office Phone: 323-874-3000. Business E-Mail: kelekis@aol.com. *The longer I live, the more I am obsessed with man's inhumanity directed against his fellow man. Is there a basic flaw in man's makeup which prevents the good from overtaking and defeating the evil? I have spent my adult life dedicated to helping children around the world, the diseased, handicapped and underprivileged. The rewards tangible and intangible have shaped my life, have given me an inner peace with myself, and yet a frustration at what could be and is not. The same holds for nation against nation. What could be—and is not. Is this the order of things past and things to come? I pray with all my heart that the teachings of peace shall prevail.*

HALL, PAMELA S., environmental services administrator; b. Hartford, Conn., Sept. 4, 1944; d. LeRoy Warren and Frances May (Murray) Sheely; m. Stuart R. Hall, July 21, 1967 (dec.). BA in Zoology, U. Conn., 1966; MS in Zoology, U. NH, 1969, BSBA summa cum laude, 1982; postgrad., Tufts U., Medford, Mass., 1986-90. Curatorial asst. U. Conn., Storrs, 1966; rsch. asst. Field Mus. Natural History, Chgo., 1966-67; tchg. asst. U. NH, Durham, 1967-70; program mgr. Normandeau Assocs. Inc., Portsmouth, NH, 1971-79, marine lab. dir., 1979-81, programs and ops. mgr. Bedford, NH, 1981-83, v.p., 1983-85, sr. v.p., 1986-87, pres., 1987—. Mem. Conservation Com., Portsmouth, 1977-90, Wells, Estuarine Rsch. Res. Rev.Commn., 1986-88, Great Bay Estuarine Rsch. Res. Tech. Working Group, NH, 1987-89; trustee Trust for NH Lands, 1990-93; trustee NH chpt. Nature Conservancy, 1991—, chair 1995-99, chair emeritus, 1999, trustee, 2000—, incorporator NH Charitable Fund, 1991-99; bd. advisors Vivamos Mejor, USA, 1990-2006; bd. dirs. Environ. Bus. Coun. New England, 1995—, treas. 1997—; bd. emeritus Phiaizy Swamp Ecosystems Inst., 1997—; commr. NH Land and Heritage Commn., 1998-99; bd. advisers NH Corp. Wetlands Restoration Partnership, 2003—; bd. dirs. Seacoast Sci. Ctr., Rye, NH, 2004—, vice chair, 2006-07. Recipient Environ. Leadership award Environ. Bus. Coun. New Eng., 1998; Graham Found. fellow, 1966; NDEA fellow, 1970-71. Mem. Nature Conservancy, Soc. of the Protection NH Forests, Nat. Audubon Soc., Audubon Soc. NH, Am. Mgmt. Assn., Phi Sigma, Sigma Xi. Office: Normandeau Assocs Inc 25 Nashua Rd Bedford NH 03110-5500 Office Phone: 603-472-5191. Personal E-mail: phall@normandeau.com.

HALL, PEGGY CRAFT, poet, retired secondary school educator; b. Jenkins, Ky., Mar. 8, 1942; d. Ulysses Simpson Fitzhugh and Bernice Spradling Craft; m. Richard Dale Hall (div. 1969); 1 child, Derron Keith. BA with high distinction, U. Ky., Lexington, 1963; MA, Barry U., Miami Shores, Fla., 1968; postgrad., U. South Fla., Tampa. English tchr. Fayette County Pub. Schs., Lexington, Ky., 1963—64, Dade County Pub. Schs., Miami, Fla., 1964—94; poet Miami, 1994—. Curriculum writer Dade County Pub. Schs., 1991—94; adj. instr. English Fla. Atlantic U., Boca Raton, 1981; music cons., pianist Abaco Cultural Soc., Green Turtle Cay, Bahamas, 1986—; poetry judge New River Poets/WITA, Fla. and Ill., 2005—06. Author: Curriculum Guides for the Gifted, 1985, (poetry) In Case of Bears, 2006; contbr. poems, articles and revs. to jours. Co-sponsor human rels. com. Norland Sr. HS, Miami, 1972—73; chair marriage and divorce task force NOW, Miami, 1973; founding dir., music cons., resident editor Crystal Parrot Players, 1996—; editor bull. South Miami Music Club, 1994—97. Mem.: Women in the Arts, Pa. Poetry Soc., Phi Kappa Phi, Phi Beta Kappa. Democrat. Avocations: piano, travel, theater, reading. Personal E-mail: rileyhall33@bellsouth.net.

HALL, PENELOPE COKER, editor, writer; b. Charlotte, NC, Mar. 19, 1932; d. James Lide and Elizabeth (Boatwright) Coker; m. William Parmenter Wilson, Sept. 6, 1964 (div. 1971); 1 child, Eliza Wilson Ingle; m. Mortimer Waddhams Hall, Dec. 8, 1972; stepchildren: Dorothy, Margaret, Mary Howland, Matthew. Student, Sarah Lawrence Coll., Bronxville, NY, 1954; DHL (hon.), Coker Coll., Hartsville, SC, 2006. Sr. editor, biographer Cleveland Amory's Celebrity Register, NYC; prodr., commentator Wrap-Up with Mike Wallace, NYC; co-prodr., interviewer for series of hr. long spls. NBC-TV, NYC; co-host 10 Around Town Channel 10 TV, Phila.; co-host The New Yorkers Channel 5 TV, NYC, 1968-70; reporter, Sunday anchor 10 O'Clock News, Channel 5, NYC, 1970-73; host cable cooking show Millbrook, NY, 1976; editor-at-large, columnist Dutchess Mag., 1993—2002; CEO Alpacalypse Hall LLC, 2005—. Contbr. numerous articles to profl. jours.; author: Fancy and the Cement Patch, 1966, The Wish Bottle, 1967, Riding High, 1990. Bd. trustees Spoleto Festival, Charleston, SC, 1997-2006, Coker Coll., Hartsville, SC, 2000— Mem. Authors League, Nat. Trust for Hist. Preservation Nat. Trust Coun., Sandanona Beagles, Millbrook Hounds, Century Assn., Millbrook Golf and Tennis Club (bd. dirs. 1989-93), Cosmopolitan Club. Democrat. Episcopalian. Avocations: painting, horseback riding, boating. Home: PO Box 516 Millbrook NY 12545-0516

HALL, PETER FRANCIS, retired physiologist; b. Sydney, Dec. 12, 1924; s. William and Ruby Alice (Price) H.; m. Helen Ruth Godfrey, Nov. 10, 1968; children: Philip Charles, Warwick David. MB, BS, U. Sydney, 1947, MD, 1956; PhD, U. Utah, 1962. Sr. med. officer Royal Prince Alfred Hosp., Sydney, 1947—50; registrar Guys Hosp., 1954—59; NIH fellow U. Utah, 1959—62; asst. prof. dept. physiology U. Pitts., 1962—64; prof. biochemistry Melbourne U., 1964—71; prof., chmn. dept. physiology U. Calif.-Irvine, 1971—78; prin. scientist Worcester Found. Exptl. Biology, Shrewsbury, Mass., 1978—86; chmn. endocrinology U. New South Wales and Prince Henry/Prince of Wales Hosps., Sydney, 1986—2007; ret., 2007. Hon. med. officer Sydney Hosp., 1954—59; pvt. practice medicolegal medicine, 1998—2007. Author: Gynaecomastia, 1959, Function of the Endocrine Glands, 1959; contbr. articles to profl. jours. Recipient Merck prize for chemistry, 1959. Fellow Royal Australian Coll. Physicians, Royal Coll. Physicians (London); mem. Am. Physiol. Soc., Am. Soc. Cell Biology, Am. Soc. Biol. Chemistry, Endocrine Soc. Mem. Ch. Of Eng. Home: 81 Ocean St Woollahra NSW 2025 Australia

HALL, SIR PETER GEOFFREY, urban and regional planning educator; b. London, Mar. 19, 1932; came to U.S., 1980; s. Arthur Vickers and Bertha (Keefe) H.; m. Carla Maria Wartenberg, Sept. 7, 1962 (div. 1967); m. Magda Mroz, Feb. 13, 1967. BA in Geography, Cambridge U., Eng., 1953, PhD, 1959; DDS (hon.), Birmingham U., Eng., 1991; PhD (hon.), Lund U., Sweden, 1992; DLitt (hon.), Sheffield U., 1995, Newcastle U., 1995; DEng (hon.), Tech. U. Nova Scotia, Can., 1996; ArtsD (hon.), Oxford Brookes U., 1997; LLD (hon.), Reading U., 1999; DSc (hon.), U. West Eng., 2000; DSc, U. Loughborough, 2005; D Laws, U. Manchester, 2001; DLitt (hon.), Herriot Watt U., 2002, Guildhall U., London, 2002; DSS (hon.), Queen Mary, U. London, 2004; DTech (hon.), U. Greenwich, 2004; DSc (hon.), Loughborough U., 2005. Lectr. Birkbeck Coll., U. London, 1957-65; reader London Sch. Econs., 1966-67; prof. U. Reading, Eng., 1968-89, chmn., 1971-77, dean faculty urban and regional studies, 1975-78, bd. mgmt., 1983-86, prof. emeritus, 1989—; prof. dept. city and regional planning U. Calif., Berkeley, 1980-92, assoc. dir. Inst. Urban and Regional Devel., 1980-88, dir., 1989-92, prof. emeritus, 1993—. Prof. planning Bartlett Sch. Planning Univ. Coll. London, London, 1992—, dir. sch. pub. policy, 1996—97; spl. advisor Dept. of Environment, London, 1991—94; mem. Urban Task Force, 1998—99; dir. Inst. of Cmty. Studies, 2001—04; chair Reblackpool, 2004—. Author: The World Cities, 1966, 3d edit., 1984, Europe 2000, 1977 (Bentinck prize 1979), Great Planning Disasters, 1980, The Inner City in Context, 1981, Silicon Landscapes, 1985, Can Rail Save the City?, 1985, High-Tech America, 1986, Western Sunrise, 1987, Cities of Tomorrow (Balzar prize 2005), 1988, London 2001, 1989, Cities and Civilization, 1998; co-author: The Rise of the Gunbelt, 1991, Technopoles of the World, 1994, Sociable Cities, 1998, Cities in Civilization, 1998, Urban Future 21, 2000, Working Capital, 2002, The Polycentric Metropolis, 2006, London Voices London Lives, 2007. Advisor Social Dem. party, 1983-85; active S.E. Econ. Planning Coun., 1966-79, Social Sci. Rsch. Coun., 1974-79. Recipient Belzan Internat. prize, 2005. Fellow Brit. Acad., Royal Geog. Soc. (Gill Meml. prize 1968, Founder's medal 1991), St. Catharine's Coll. (hon.); mem. Royal Town Planning Inst. (hon., Gold medal 2003), Am. Planning Assn., Athenaeum Club, Brit. Acad. Avocations: reading, travel. Office: U Coll London Bartlett Sch Planning 22 Gordon St London WC1 H0QB England Home Phone: 020 8997 3717; Office Phone: +020 88 10 8723. Business E-Mail: p.hall@ucl.ac.uk.

HALL, PETER MICHAEL, physics professor, electronics engineer; b. Belmont, NY, July 31, 1934; s. Harris Tremaine and Dorothy Lou (Harris) H.; m. Betty Jane Bressell, Dec. 21, 1956; children: Michael, Ann, Sarah, Philip. BA, Hobart Coll., 1954; MS, Iowa State U., 1956, PhD, 1959. Registered profl. engr., N.C. Mem. tech. staff AT&T Bell Labs., Murray Hill, NJ, 1959-64, fellow Allentown, Pa., 1964-90; Disting. prof. physics Johnson C. Smith U., Charlotte, NC, 1990—2001. Co-author: Thin Film Technology, 1968; contbr. articles to profl. jours., chpt. to book; patentee on fabrication of circuit packages. Recipient award for best paper Electronic Components Conf., 1984. Fellow IEEE (components, hybrids and mfg. tech. group, best paper award 1988); mem. ASME (editor 1989-95), Am. Phys. Soc., Am. Assn. Physics Tchrs., Phi Beta Kappa, Sigma Xi. Democrat. Episcopalian. Avocation: sailing. Home: 140 Lakeside Dr Middletown DE 19709-1372

HALL, PETER W., federal judge, former prosecutor; b. Hartford, Conn., Nov. 9, 1948; BA, U. N.C., 1971, MA, 1974; JD, Cornell U., 1977. Law clk. to Hon. Albert W. Coffrin, 1977—78; asst. US atty, Dist. Vt. US Dept. Justice, 1978—82, 1st asst. US atty., Dist. Vt, 1982—86; ptnr. Reiber, Kenlan, Schwiebert, Hall and Facey, Rutland, Vt., 1986—2001; US atty. ea. dist. US Dept. Justice, Vt., 2001—04; judge US Ct. Appeals (2nd cir.), 2004—. Office: US Ct Appeals 40 Foley Sq New York NY 10007*

HALL, RALPH MOODY, congressman; b. Fate, Tex., May 3, 1923; s. Hugh O. and Maude Hall; m. Mary Ellen Murphy, Nov. 14, 1944; children: Hampton, Brett, Blakeley; grandchildren: 5. Student, Tex. Christian U., Ft. Worth, 1943, U. Tex., Austin, 1946—47; LLB, So. Meth. U., Dallas, 1951. Bar: Tex. 1951. County judge Rockwall County, Tex., 1950-62; mem. Tex. State Senate, 1962-72, pres. pro tempore, 1968—69; pres., CEO Tex. Aluminum Corp., 1967—68; gen. counsel Tex. Extrusion Co., Inc.; organizer, chmn. bd. Lakeside Nat. Bank of Rockwall; chmn. bd. dirs. Bank of Crowley, Lakeside News, Inc., Linrock Inc.; pres. North and East Trading Co., Crowley Holding Co.; mem. US Congress from 4th Tex. dist., 1981—. Mem. sci. com. US Congress, mem. energy and commerce com., chmn. energy and air quality subcommittee. Lt. (sr. grade) aircraft carrier pilot USN, 1942—45. Mem. Am. Legion, VFW, Rotary (past pres.). Republican. Methodist. Office: US Ho Reps 2405 Rayburn Ho Office Bldg Washington DC 20515-4304 Office Phone: 202-225-6673.*

HALL, RANDY JARVIS, lawyer; b. Ft. Worth, Feb. 24, 1951; s. Benton Garrett Jr. and Janine Hall; m. Gloria Pine, July 18, 1981; children: Randy Jarvis Jr., Matthew Brian. BBA, Tex. Tech U., 1973, JD, 1976. Bar: Tex. 1976, cert.: Nat. Bd. Trial Advocacy (civil trial advocate), Tex. Bd. Legal Specialization (personal injury trial law specialist), Tex. Bd. Legal Specialization (civil trial law specialist), Tex. Bd. Legal Specialization (civil appellate law specialist). Chmn. litig. sect. Decker, Jones, McMackin, McClane, Hall & Bates, Ft. Worth, 1991—. Named a Super Lawyer, Tex. Monthly Mag., 2003—07; named Top Atty., Ft. Worth Mag., 2002—07, Atty. of Excellence, Ft. Worth Bus. Press, 2003—06. Fellow: Tex. Bar Found. (life), Tex. Bar Coll. (life); mem.: Am. Bd. Trial Advocates (advocate), Def. Rsch. Inst., Tex. Assn. Def. Counsel. Republican. Avocations: golf, fine dining, travel. Home: 6712 Morning Dew Dr Fort Worth TX 76132-1155 Office: Decker Jones McMackin McClane Hall 801 Cherry St Ste 2000 Fort Worth TX 76102 Office Phone: 817-336-2400. Personal E-mail: bigr817@charter.net. Business E-Mail: rhall@deckerjones.com.

HALL, RICHARD, lawyer; b. Melbourne, Australia, June 23, 1962; B.Comm. with honors, Univ. Melbourne, Australia, 1984; LLB with honors, Univ. Melbourne, 1986; LLM, Harvard Univ., 1988. Bar: Victoria, Australia 1987, NY 1989. Assoc. Cravath Swaine & Moore LLP, NYC, 1988—96, ptnr., corp., 1996—. Mem.: ABA. Office: Cravath Swaine & Moore LLP Worldwide Plz 825 Eighth Ave New York NY 10019-7475 Office Phone: 212-474-1293. Office Fax: 212-474-3700. Business E-Mail: rhall@cravath.com.

HALL, RICHARD CLYDE, JR., retired religious educational administrator; b. Florence, Ala., Apr. 13, 1931; s. Richard Clyde Sr. and Annie Hazel (Darrah) H.; m. Mildred Marie Denham, May 19, 1957; children: Richard Denham, Darralyn Marie, Kevin Clyde, Edward Earnest. AA, U. Fla., 1950, BA, 1953; MRE, Southwestern Bapt. Theol. Sem., 1958, DRE, 1966, EdD, 1975, MA, 1984. Ordained to gospel ministry So. Bapt. Conv., 1955. Youth dir. 1st Bapt. Ch., Miami, Fla., 1953; ednl. sec., youth dir. Ave. J Bapt. Ch., Ft. Worth, 1953-54; dir. Bapt. Student Union Fla. Bapt. Conv., Jacksonville, 1954-57; min. edn. Eastover Bapt. Ch., Ft. Worth, 1957-61; minister edn. 1st Bapt. Ch., Elizabethton, Tenn., 1961-63, Gambrell Street Bapt. Ch., Ft. Worth, 1963-65; assoc. ch. tng. dept. Bapt. Gen. Conv. Tex., Dallas, 1965-72, sec. ch. tng. dept., 1972-73; mgmt. cons. Pro., Inc., San Diego, 1973-74; cons. adult work ch. tng. dept. Bapt. Sunday Sch. Bd., Nashville, 1974-75, cons. gen. adminstrn. ch. tng. dept., 1975-76, mgr. youth sect. discipleship tng. dept., 1976-2000—. Teaching fellow religious psychology and drama Southwestern Bapt. Theol. Sem., Ft. Worth, 1960-61; del. Bapt. World Alliance, Tokyo, 1970; instr. youth edn. Sem. Extension, 1981—; discipleship workshop leader, family group leader Bapt. Youth World Conf., Buenas Aires, 1984; conf. leader, coord. numerous youth confs. Queensland, Australia, New South Wales, Australia, Auckland, New Zealand, Gaza City, Gaza, 1997-98, Victoria, Australia, Windhoek, Namibia, Gaza City, Gaza; conf. leader Caribbean Bapt. Fellowship, Montego Bay, Jamaica, 1986; sem. leader Bapt. Youth World Conf., Glasgow, Scotland, 1988, chaplain, Harare, Zimbabwe, 1993; del. Lausanne II-World Congress on Evangelism, Manila, Philippines, 1989; teaching fellow religious psychology and drama Southwestern Bapt. Theol. Sem., Ft. Worth, 1960-61; guest lectr. Southwestern Bapt. Theol. Sem., New Orleans Bapt. Theol. Sem., So. Bapt. Theol. Sem., Midwestern Bapt. Theol. Sem., Southeastern Bapt. Theol. Sem. and Golden Gate Bapt. Theol. Sem., 1985—; adj. prof. New Orleans Bapt. Theol. Sem., Golden Gate Bapt. Theol. Sem. and Midwestern Bapt. Theol. Sem., 1985—; instr. Okla. Bapt. U., 1991—. Author: Source, 1967-70, Church Training, 1970—; (cassette and workbook) The Work of the Associational Age Group Leader, 1980; (filmstrip) DiscipleLife: Training Youth in Discipleship, 1981, DiscipleLife, 1984; compiler: Youth Leadership Training Pak, 1982, DiscipleHelps: A Daily Quiet Time Guide and Journal, 1985; (with Joe Ford) DiscipleYouth I Kit, 1982, DiscipleYouth I Notebook, 1982, DiscipleYouth II Kit, 1985, DiscipleYouth II Notebook, 1985, DiscipleYouth Library, 1992, (with Dean Finley) The Notebook: A Disciple Youth Experience, 1996; (with Wesley Black) DiscipleNow Manual; (with Valerie Hardy) Mission Trip Administrative Manual. Trauma Center Plus, Handbook for Youth Discipleship, Basic Church Stuff: A Guide for Assimulating New Youth Church Members, Compiler. Recipient Career of Excellence award LifeWay Christian Resources, 1998. Mem. ASTD, Internat. Religious Edn. Assn., So. Bapt. Religious Edn. Assn. (sec.-treas. 1982-83), Ea. Bapt. Religious Edn. Assn. (sec.-treas. 1975-79, pres. 1980), Southwestern Bapt. Religious Edn. Assn., Adult Edn. Assn.

HALL, RICHARD MURRAY, JR., finance executive, consultant; b. St. Joseph, Mo., Jan. 1, 1947; s. Richard Murray and Alice Elaine (Huff) H.; m. Joyce Ann Stearns, Mar. 28, 1971 (div. Nov. 1983). BBA in Econs., Wichita State U., Kans., 1969, MS in Fin., 1972; Grad. Degree in Banking, So. Meth. U., Dallas, 1975. Asst. v.p. Fourth Nat. Bank & Trust, Wichita, Kans., 1969-75; v.p. Citizens Frost Bank, San Antonio, 1975-77, United Bank Denver, 1977-84; pres. Am. Nat. Bank/United Bank-City Ctr., Aurora, Colo., 1984-86; sr. v.p. Corp. Fin. Asocs., Denver, 1987-89; dir. Colo. Nat. Leasing, Inc., Denver, 1989-95, pres., 1989-95, chmn. bd. dirs., 1993-95; v.p. and mgr. comml. banking divsn. Colo. Nat. Bank, Denver, 1992-94; pres., chmn. bd. dirs. Colo. Bus. Leasing, Inc., Denver, 1995—2001; pres. Alliance Capital Resources, Inc., 2000—; regional pres. Cache Bank & Trust, Denver, 2003—06; market pres. FirsTier Bank, 2007—; pres. Identity Rehab. Corp., Denver, 2006—07. Bd. dirs. Am. Heart Assn. Colo., 1980—, pres., 1987-88, emeritus, 1998-; dir. Craig Hosp., 2004-, treas., 2006-; mem. Leadership Denver Assn., 1981, dir., 1990-95, pres. 1994-95; chmn. ArtReach, Inc., Denver, 1988, 89; bd. dirs. Colo. Spl. Olympics, 1994—, vice chmn., 1997, 99, chmn., 2000, dir. emeritus, 2001; bd. dirs. Health Agys. of Colo., 1997—, chmn., 1998-2000; nat. dir. Cmty. Health Charities, 2005—. Mem. Denver Athletic Club, Meridian Golf Club. Republican. Avocations: golf, skiing, writing. Office: FirsTier Bank 1225 17th St Ste 150 Denver CO 80202 Office Phone: 303-464-6642.

HALL, ROBERT ALAN, construction company executive; b. Montgomery, Ala., Oct. 30, 1958; s. Mack Luverne and Miriam (Johnston) H. BS in Commerce and Bus. Adminstrn. with honors, U. Ala., 1981. CPA, Ala., cert. internal auditor. Sr. acct. Jackson and Thornton, CPAs, Montgomery, 1981—83; sr. auditor Vulcan Materials Co., Birmingham, Ala., 1983—86, supr. internal audit, 1986—87; mgr., fin. and adminstrn. Saudi Arabian Vulcan Ltd., Jubail, Saudi Arabia, 1987—90; spl. assignments analyst Vulcan Materials Co., 1990—91; contr., treas., asst. sec. Bill Harbert Internat. Constrn. Inc., Birmingham, Ala., 1991—95, v.p., CFO, 1995—2000; sr. v.p., CFO, sec. B.L. Harbert Internat., LLC, 2000—. Presdl. appointee White House Conf. on Small Bus., 1995; mem. Pres.'s Bus. Adv. Coun., Washington, 1995-2001; mem. profl. adv. bd. Sch. Accountancy/U. Ala., 1991—. Charter mem. Rep. Presdl. Task Force, Washington, 1984-86; presdl. appointee White House Conf. Small Bus., 1995. Recipient Presdl. Achievement award Pres. Ronald Reagan, 1983, Cert. of Appreciation, Gov. of Ala., 1988, Sch. of Accountancy U. Ala. Career Achievement award, 2003; named hon. citizen City of L.A., 1984, hon. asst. atty. gen. State of Ala., 1984, hon. gov. of Tex., 1995, hon. lt. gov. of Ala., 1998. hon. col. State of Ala., 2001; named one of Outstanding Young Men of Am., 1986. Mem. AICPA, Ala. Soc. CPAs, Am. Businessmen's Assn. Saudi Arabia (bd. dirs. 1988-90), U. Ala. Sr. Execs. Club., Coll. Commerce, Hon. Order Ky. Cols. Baptist. Home: 416 Old Brook Cir Birmingham AL 35242-2658 Address: PO Box 531390 Birmingham AL 35253-1390 Office Phone: 205-802-2826. Business E-Mail: ahall@bharbert.com.

HALL, ROBERT EMMETT, JR., investment banker, realtor; b. Sioux City, Iowa, Apr. 28, 1936; s. Robert Emmett and Alvina (Faden) H.; m. De Phan. BA, U. S.D., 1958, MA, 1959; MBA, U. Santa Clara, 1976; grad., Am. Inst. Banking, Realtors Inst. Grad. asst. U. S.D., Vermillion, 1958-59; mgr. ins. dept., asst. mgr. installment loan dept. Northwestern Nat. Bank Sioux Falls, S.D., 1959-61, asst. cashier S.D., 1961-65; asst. mgr. Crocker Nat. Bank, San Francisco, 1965-67, loan officer, 1967-69, asst. v.p., asst. mgr. San Mateo (Calif.) br., 1969-72; v.p., western regional mgr. Internat. Investments & Realty, Inc., Washington, 1972—; owner Hall Enterprises Co., San Jose, Calif., 1976—; pres. Alamaden Oaks Realtors, Inc., 1976—. Instr. West Valley Coll., Saratoga, Calif., 1972-82, Grad. Sch. Bus., U. Santa Clara (Calif.), 1981-82, Evergreen Valley Coll., San Jose, Calif. Treas. Minnehaha Leukemia Soc., 1963, Lake County Heart Fund Assn., 1962, Minnehaha Young Rep. Club, 1963. Mem. Am. Inst. Banking, Calif. Assn. Realtors (vice chmn.), Alamaden Country Club, Elks, Rotary (past pres.), KC, Beta Theta Pi. Home: 6951 Castlerock Dr San Jose CA 95120-4705 Office: Hall Enterprises 100A Crown Blvd San Jose CA 95120-2903 E-mail: rehall5257@aol.com.

HALL, ROBERT ERNEST, economics professor; b. Palo Alto, Calif., Aug. 13, 1943; s. Victor Ernest and Frances Marie (Gould) H.; m. Susan E. Woodward; children: Christopher, Anne, Jonathan, Andrew. BA in Econs., U. Calif.-Berkeley, 1964; PhD in Econs., MIT, 1967. Asst. prof., acting assoc. prof. U. Calif., Berkeley, 1967-70; from assoc. prof. to prof. MIT, Cambridge, 1970-78; prof., sr. fellow Stanford U., Calif., 1978—, Robert and Carole McNeil joint prof. and sr. fellow, 1998. Dir. econ. fluctuation program Nat. Bur. Econ. Research, Cambridge, 1978—; adv. com. Congl. Budget Office, Washington, 1993—. Author: Macroeconomics, 1985, 7th rev. edit., 2006, Booms and Recessions in a Noisy Economy, 1990, The Rational Consumer: Theory and Evidence, 1990, Flat Tax, 1995, Economics, 1997, 4th rev. edit., 2007, Digital Dealing, 2001; editor: Inflation, 1983. NSF fellow, 1964, Ford Found. faculty rsch. fellow, 1969. Fellow: Soc. Labor Economists, Am. Acad. Arts and Scis., Econometric Soc.; mem.: NAS, Am. Statis Assn., Am. Econs. Assn. (Ely lectr. 2001, v.p. 2005). Democrat. Office: Stanford U Hoover Instn Stanford CA 94305 Office Phone: 650-723-2215. Business E-Mail: rehall@stanford.edu.

HALL, ROBERT JOSEPH, internist, educator; b. Buffalo, June 4, 1926; s. Joseph M. and Florence C. (Kirst) H.; m. Dorothy Nowak, Aug. 28, 1948; children: Thomas R., Kathleen A. Hall Noble, Mary J. Hall Stuart, Michael F., Steven E. Student, Canisius Coll., Buffalo, 1943-45; MD, U. Buffalo, 1948. Diplomate Am. Bd. Internal Medicine, Sub Bd. Cardiovascular Disease (mem. cardiovascular disease sect. 1969-75). Intern Mercy Hosp., Buffalo, 1948-49; commd. 1st lt. M.C. U.S. Army, 1948, advanced through grades to col., 1966; resident in internal medicine Walter Reed Gen. Hosp., Washington, 1949-52, resident in cardiovascular diseases, 1956-57; asst. cardiovascular research Walter Reed Army Inst. Research, 1957-58; service in Korea and Japan, 1952-55; chief cardiology service Brooke Gen. Hosp., Ft. Sam Houston, Tex., 1961-66, Walter Reed Gen. Hosp., 1966-69; ret., 1969; clin. assoc. prof. medicine Georgetown U. Med. Sch., 1967-69; clin. prof. medicine Baylor U. Coll. Medicine, Houston, 1969—, prof. emeritus, 2004—; clin. prof. medicine U. Tex. Med. Sch., Houston, 1977—; med. dir. Tex. Heart Inst., Houston, 1969-93, chmn. exec. com. profl. staff, 1969-93; dir. div. cardiology St. Luke's Episcopal Hosp., Houston, 1969-95, assoc. chief med. service, 1970-83; dir. edn., cardiology Tex. Heart Inst. Tex. Heart Inst. and St. Luke's Episcopal Hosp., 1992—2002, dir. emeritus, 2002—. Cons. Tex. Children's, VA, Brooke Gen. hosps., M.D. Anderson Hosp. and Tumor Inst.; mem. cardiovascular study sect. NIH, 1958-61; mem. phys. evaluation team Gemini project NASA, 1958-61; mem. nat. adv. heart counseil Dept. Def., 1966-69; adv. council Mended Hearts, 1970-78 Contbr. numerous articles med. jours. Mem. President's Adv. Panel Heart Disease. Decorated Legion of Merit; recipient Disting. Alumnus award Canisius Coll., 1995. Fellow A.C.P., Am. Coll. Cardiology (gov. 1968-71-74, chmn. bd. govs. and trustee 1973-74); mem. Am. Heart Assn. (fellow council clin. cardiology; pres. Houston chpt. 1974-75, advisor corp. cabinet 1980-86), Assn. Mil. Surgeons U.S., Assn. Advancement Med. Instrumentation, Pan Am. Med. Assn. (chmn. sect. cardiovascular diseases 1978-81), Assn. Univ. Cardiologists, Tex. Med. Assn., Tex. Cardiology Club, Harris County Med. Soc., Houston Cardiology Soc. (chmn. 1976-77), Houston Soc. Internal Medicine, Alpha Omega Alpha, 1948—. Home: 5504 Sturbridge Dr Houston TX 77056-1623 Office: 6624 Fannin St Ste 2480 Houston TX 77030-2309 Business E-Mail: rjhall@wt.net.

HALL, ROBERT L., curator, educator; s. Sanford and Sadie Mae Hall. BS in Art, Fisk U., Nashville, 1968—72; MA in Music Edn., George Wash. U., DC, 1974—75. Curator art collection U. Galleries, Fisk U., 1973—; head edn. Anacostia Cmty. Mus., Smithsonian Instn., DC, 1984—. Mem. nat. programs rev. panelist Inst. Mus. & Libr. Svcs., DC, 2005—; nat. juror for pres. com. on arts and humanities White Ho., DC, 2005; advisor DC Humanities Coun., 2005; nat. advisor Lemelson Ctr. for Study Invention & Innovation, Smithsonian Instn., DC, 2006—. Author: (children's genealogy activity book) Precious Memories: Family History Research for Intermediate-level Students; curator (exhibitions) On Their Own: Selected Works by Self-taught Artists, New Visions: Emerging Trends in African American Art, In the Arms of the Elders, Gathered Visions: Selected Works by African American Women Artists. Mem.: Commonwealth Assn. Mus., African-Am. Museums Assn., Am. Assn. Mus.

HALL, ROBERT STEVENS, dentist; b. Hartford, Conn., Apr. 19, 1938; s. Llewellyn and Caroline (Doane) Hall; m. Marcia Smith, June 29, 1963; children: Gretchen Ashley, Robert Stevens Jr., Sabra Lee. AB, Middlebury Coll., 1960; DDS, U. Pa., 1964. Pvt. practice dentist, Hartford, 1966—73, Farmington, Conn., 1973—. Instr. U. Conn. Sch. Dental Medicine, 1973—85, 2000—. Capt. US Army, 1964—66. Recipient Order of St. John, 2007. Master: Acad. Gen. Dentistry; fellow: Am. Coll. Dentists; mem.: Hartford Dental Soc. (dentist peer rev./patient rels. 1980—), Order St. John. Avocations: travel, sports, photography. Home: 53 Sunset Farm Rd West Hartford CT 06107-1332 Office: 291 Farmington Ave Farmington CT 06032 Office Phone: 860-677-8666.

HALL, ROBERT T., pediatrician, medical educator, researcher; b. Lincoln, Nebr., Oct. 26, 1939; s. Ted G. and Margaret M. Hall; m. Janice E. Bottom, June 18, 1961; children: Kathryn L Elvestrom, Carolyn S Hullings, Amy A Archer. BS in Medicine, U. Nebr., Omaha, 1962, MD, 1964. Cert. pediatrician, neonatologist Am Bd. of Pediat., NC, 1967. Rotating intern Kansas City Gen. Hosp., 1964—65; pediat. resident Children's Mercy Hosp., Kansas City, 1965—69; fellow neonatal biology U. Wash., Seattle, 1969—70; neonatologist Childrens Mercy Hosp., Kansas City, Mo., 1970—2006, chief neonatology, 1971—97. Prof. pediat. U. Mo. KC Sch. Medicine, 1975—; presenter and cons. in field. Contbr. articles to profl. jours. Ctrl. governing bd. Childrens Mercy Hosp., Kansas City, 1980—86; program dir. Neonatal/Perinatal Sect. Am Acad Pediat, Chgo, 1976—80. Capt. USAF, 1967—69, Scott AFB. Mem.: Kans. City Met. Med. Soc., Acad. Pediat. Soc., Am Acad. Pediats. Episcopalian. Achievements include research in clinical research in nutrition, pulmonary disease, infections and jaundice in newborn infants. Avocations: hiking, golf. Office: Childrens Mercy Hosp 2401 Gillham Rd Kansas City MO 65614 Home Phone: 316-634-0440.

HALL, ROBERT TURNBULL, III, lawyer; b. Norfolk, Va., Aug. 25, 1945; s. Robert Turnbull and Mary Evelyn H.; m. Colleen Coffee, Aug. 17, 1968; children— Meghan, Robert. B.S., Washington and Lee U., 1967; J.D., Georgetown U., 1971. Bar: U.S. Dist. Ct. D.C. 1971, D.C. Ct. Appeals 1971, U.S. Ct. Appeals (D.C. cir.) 1972, U.S. Ct. Appeals (5th cir.) 1972, U.S. Supreme Ct. 1975, U.S. Ct. Appeals (11th cir.) 1981, U.S. Ct. Appeals (9th cir.) 1982, U.S. Ct. Appeals (8th cir.) 1983. Assoc. Thelen, Reid & Priest, N.Y.C., 1971-77, ptnr., 1978—. Mem. ABA, D.C. Bar Assn., Fed. Energy Bar Assn. Home: 162 Mercer St Princeton NJ 08540-6827 Business E-Mail: rhall@thelenreid.com.

HALL, ROBERT WILLIAM, philosophy religious studies educator; b. Arlington, Mass., Apr. 6, 1928; s. Samuel Harry and Agness (Babikian) H.; m. Mary Alice Starritt, Oct. 25, 1958; children— Christopher Allen, Jonathan Brooks, Pamela Leigh, Timothy Randall, Jennifer Lane, Nicholas Ramsay. AB, Harvard, 1949, MA, 1951, PhD, 1953. Vis. asst. prof. philosophy Vanderbilt U., 1955-57; asst. prof. philosophy and religion U. Vt., Burlington, 1957-63, assoc. prof., 1963-67, prof., 1967—, Marsh prof. intellectual and moral philosophy, 1985—2002, chmn. dept., 1963-72, prof. emeritus, 2002—. Author: Plato and the Individual, 1963, Studies in Religious Philosophy, 1969, Plato, 1981; editor: APEIRON, 1966-87. Served with CIC AUS, 1953-55. Shedd fellow in religion in higher edn., 1968-69 Mem. Am. Philos. Assn., Soc. Ancient Greek Philosophy (sec.-treas. 1963-72), Am. Soc. Aesthetics, Phi Beta Kappa. Home: 165 N Prospect St Burlington VT 05401-1607 Office: 70 S Williams St Burlington VT 05401-3404

HALL, ROGER LEE, musicologist, educator, composer; b. Glen Ridge, NJ, Nov. 13, 1942; Cert., Trinity Coll., London, 1967; BA, Rutgers U., 1970; MA, SUNY, 1972. Music cons. Nat. Geographic Soc., Washington, 1972; lectr. various colls., mus., 1974—; researcher, writer various jours., mags., 1975—; instr. Stonehill Coll., North Easton, Mass., 1979-82, Brookline (Mass.) Adult and Community Edn. Program, 1983-96; composer ASCAP, NYC, 1985—; cable TV producer Pinetree Prodns., Stoughton, Mass., 1987—. Cons. Paul Revere House, Boston, 1981, The Shaker Seminar, Pittsfield, Mass., 1984-87. *An American music specialist with over 25 years of experience. Music consultant for recordings, seminars and workshops. Coordinator for two festivals dealing with early American music. Music historian for the oldest choral society in America and chairman of its Bicentennial Committee. Teacher and lecturer on classical and popular music topics. Local music history project for use in public schools and by residents. Founder of Pine Tree Productions, an audio and video music service. Award-winning compositions. Arrangements and editions of Shaker folk music included on several recordings. Producer of cable television and radio programs, including a series on American songs. President, Society for Earlier American Music (S.E.A.M.)* Editor: (music collection) The Happy Journey, 1982, Love is Little, 1992, Joy of Angels, 1995; composer: Piano Variations, 1984, Peace - A Patriotic Ode, 1989, A Little Theatre Music, 1990, Three Shaker Poems, 1996; feature writer: The World of Shaker, 1985—96; prodr., host Continental Cablevision, Stoughton, Mass., 1986; author: (pamphlet) Singing Stoughton, 1985, (booklets) Story of Simple Gifts, 2006, Music in Stoughton, 1989, The Stoughton Songster, 1991, A Guide to Film Music, 1997, 2d edit., 2002, A Guide to Shaker Music, 1997, 6th edit., 2006, New England Songster, 1997, A Guide to George Gershwin, 1998, 2d edit., 2004, Remembering Radio, 1998, 2nd edit., 2005, A Guide to Christmas Music in America, 1999, 2d edit., 2003; radio tributes Sta. WBET-AM, 1985—93, Sta. WGBH-FM, 1981—98. Chmn. bd. Stoughton Arts Coun., 1980-84; mem. Town Hall Centennial Com., Stoughton, 1981. Served with U.S. Army, 1960-63. SUNY assistantship, 1971-72; Title IV fellow Case Western Res. U., 1972-74; Mass. Arts Lottery grantee, 1985-90. Mem.: Tune Lovers Soc. (pres. 2001—), Soc. For Am. Music, Old Stoughton Mus. Soc. (v.p. 1978—86), Shaker Study Group (pres. 1987—89). Lutheran. Avocations: collecting autographs, poetry, photography. Home and Office: 235 Prospect St Stoughton MA 02072-4163 Personal E-mail: tunemaker3@aol.com.

HALL, ROGER V., cardiac surgeon; b. Mar. 11, 1940; MD, U. Utah, Salt Lake City, 1967. Chief cardiac surgery Rogue Valley Med. Ctr., 1987—. Mem.: Soc. Thoracic Surgeons, Am. Bd. Thoracic Surgery, Am. Coll. Surgeons, Am. Bd. Surgery. Office: Cardiovascular and Thoracic Clinic 2954 Siskiyou Blvd Medford OR 97504-8161

HALL, SHARON GAY, retired language educator, artist; b. Centralia, Ill., Oct. 2, 1942; d. Leon Lucene and Olyve Elizabeth Hall. BS, So. Ill. U., 1966, MS, 1984; postgrad., Ea. Ill. U., 1985—90. Cert. secondary tchr. Ill. English tchr. Webber Twp. H.S., Bluford, Ill., 1966—67, Mt. Vernon (Ill.) H.S., 1967—99, ret., 1999. Artist-in-residence Cedarhurst Art Guild, Cedarhurst Mus., 1974—. Treas. bd. dirs. Bus. and Profl. Women's Club, Mt. Vernon, 1966—76; mem. Jefferson County Hist. Soc., 2000—. Recipient Recognition award, Cedarhurst Mus., 2000. Mem.: NEA, AAUW, Ill. Edn. Assn., Mt. Vernon Edn. Assn. (sec., treas., bd. dirs. 1967—99), Phi Delta Kappa, Phi Theta Kappa, Alpha Delta Kappa. Republican. Avocations: raising exotic animals, handspinner, weaver, fiber artist, seamstress. Home: 11384 E Idlewood Rd Mount Vernon IL 62864

HALL, STEPHEN CHARLES, lawyer; b. Carmel, Calif., Sept. 14, 1948; s. Melvin Wiley and Dorothy Louise (Hoyt) H.; m. Kristi Lee Roberts, Feb. 23, 1983; children: Spencer Stephen Rodrigo, Rachel Genevieve Cristina, Trevor Charles. AB, Dickinson Coll., 1971; JD, Vt. Law Sch., 1977. Bar: Pa. 1978, Va. 1979, U.S. Dist. Ct. (ea. dist.) Va. 1982, U.S. Dist. Ct. (we. dist.) Va. 1990, U.S. Ct. Appeals (4th cir.) 1982. Title atty. Chgo. Title Inst. Co., Richmond, Va., 1978-79; assoc. Edward E. Willey Jr., P.C., Richmond, 1979-82; ptnr. Willey & Hall, P.C., Richmond, 1983-88; assoc. Hazel & Thomas, P.C., Richmond, 1988-90, ptnr., 1990-94, Keith & Hall, Richmond, 1994—2003, Hairfield Morton PLC, Richmond, 2004—. Contbr. articles to profl. jours. Past chmn. bd. trustees St. Michael's Episcopal Sch. Mem. Richmond Bar Assn. (past chmn. publs. com.), Chesterfield County Bar Assn. (past pres. 2003—), Bon Air Bus. and Profl. Assn. (past pres.), Salisbury Country Club. Episcopalian. Avocations: golf, photography. Office: Hairfield Morton PLC 2800 Buford Rd Ste 201 Richmond VA 23235 Office Phone: 804-320-6600. Business E-Mail: shall@hmalaw.com.

HALL, SUSAN LAUREL, artist, educator, writer; b. Point Reyes Station, Calif., Mar. 19, 1943; d. Earl Morris and Avis Mary (Brown) H. BFA, Calif. Coll. Arts and Crafts, Oakland, 1965; MA, U. Calif., Berkeley, 1967. Mem. faculty Sarah Lawrence Coll., Bronxville, NY, 1972—75, Sch. Visual Arts, NYC, 1981—92, Skowhegan Sch. of Painting and Sculpture, Maine, 1981, U. Colo., Boulder, 1981, Art Inst. Chgo., 1981, U. Tex., Austin, 1993, San Antonio, 1995, San Francisco Art Inst., 1996. One-woman shows include San Francisco Mus. Art, 1967, Quay Gallery, San Francisco, 1969, Phillis Kind Gallery, Chgo., 1971, Henderson Mus. U. Colo., Boulder, 1973, Paule Anglim Gallery, San Francisco, 1975—83, Nancy Hoffman Gallery, N.Y.C., 1975, U. R.I. Gallery, Kingston, 1976, Harcus Krakow Rosen Sonnabend Gallery, Boston, 1976, Hal Bromm and Getler-Pall Galleries, N.Y.C., 1978, Helene Shlien Gallery, Boston, 1978, Hamilton Gallery, N.Y.C., 1978—79, 1981, 1983, Ovsey Gallery, L.A., 1981—82, 1984, 1987, 1989, 1991, Ted Greenwald Gallery, N.Y.C., 1986, Trabia Macafee Gallery, 1988—89, Wyckoff Gallery, Aspen, Colo., 1990—92, Milagros Contemporary Art, San Antonio, 1995, Brendan Walter Gallery, L.A., 1995, U. Tex., San Antonio, 1996, Jan Holloway Gallery, San Francisco, 1997, Phillis Kind Gallery, Chgo., 1998, San Francisco Mus. Art Gallery, 1998, Gail Harvey Gallery, L.A., 1999, 2001, Frank Lloyd Wright Civic Ctr., San Rafael, 1999, Jernigan Wicker Gallery, San Francisco, 1999, Bolinas (Calif.) Mus., 2002, Tobys Gallery, Point Reyes Sta., Calif., 2005, Whitney Mus., NYC, Erickson Fine Arts Gallery, 2007, Toby's Gallery, Pt. Reyes Sta., Calif., 2007, exhibited in group shows at Whitney Mus. Am. Art, San Francisco Mus., 98 Greene St. Loft, N.Y.C., Oakland Mus., Balt. Mus., Inst. Contemporary Art, Phila., Hudson River Mus., Bklyn. Mus., Nat. Mus. Women in the Arts, Mus. Fine Arts, Boston, Aldrich Mus. Contemporary Art, G.W. Einstein Gallery, Blum Helman Downtown, Leo Castelli Gallery Uptown, Graham Modern, N.Y.C., Kunstmus., Luzern, Switzerland, Landesmus., Bonn, Ranches and Rolling Hills, Nicasio, Calif., 2001, 2002, 2003, 2004, 2005—06, Represented in permanent collections pub. collections Whitney Mus., San Francisco Mus., Bklyn. Mus., Carnegie Inst., St. Louis Mus., Nat. Mus. Women in the Arts, others; author: Painting Point Reyes, Susan Hall, 2003, Home Before Dark Color Plates of Painting, 2005. Nat. Endowment Arts fellow, 1979-87, Adolph Gottleib Found. fellow, 1995; grantee: Pollack Krasner Found., N.Y. State Coun. on Arts; recipient Marin Arts Coun. Bd. Dirs. award, 1999.

HALL, TAFFEY RENA, archivist; d. Phillip Michael and Mildred Louise Hall. BA in History magna cum laude, Tenn. Welseyan Coll., Athens, 2001; MA in History, Mid. Tenn. State U., Murfreesboro, 2005. Cert. archivist Acad. Cert. Archivists, 2005. Lifestyles reporter Daily Post Athenian, Athens, 1999—2000; archivist So. Bapt. Hist. Libr. and Archives, Nashville, 2003—. Governing bd. So. Archivists Conf., 2005—. Editor: Bapt.

Echoes, 2005—. Mentor Christian Women's Job corps, Nashville, 2006—. Recipient Ann Vaught Daughtry award, Tenn. Wesleyan Coll., 1998—99, Isobel Griscom English award, 1998, Religious Studies award, 1998. Mem.: Soc. Am. Archivists, Bapt. History and Heritage Soc., Assn. Librs. and Archivists (chair comm. com. 2006—), Soc. Tenn. Archivists (v.p. 2005—06, pres. 2006—). Southern Baptist. Avocation: piano. Office: So Baptist Hist Libr and Archives 901 Commerce St # 400 Nashville TN 37203

HALL, TERESA RUTH, publishing executive; b. Sunnyvale, Calif., May 8, 1969; d. Brent Peter and Maria Lucia Delia Yolanda Fabbi; m. James Joseph Hall, May 16, 1994; children: Cameron James, Mackenzie Victoria. BS in Secondary Edn. with distinction, U. Nev., Reno, 1995. Math. instr. Truckee Meadows C.C., Reno, 1996—97; math. lectr. U. Nev., Reno, 1997—98; math. instr. Edgewood Coll., Madison, 1998; edn. program specialist Wis. Dept. Pub. Instrn., Madison, 2000—02; devel. mgr. CTB/McGraw-Hill, Monterey, Calif., 2002—. Active mem. Country View Elem. Parent Tchr. Assn., Verona, Wis., 2002—; treas. Ridge Oak Dr. Homeowners Assn., Madison, 2001—02; mem. Hawthorne Elem. Parent Tchr. Assn., Madison, 1999—2002. Recipient Team Mem. award, CTB/McGraw-Hill, 2003. Mem.: Nat. Orgn. Female Execs. Avocations: gardening, reading, Latin ballroom dancing, travel. Home Phone: 608-848-4774.

HALL, TERRY, accountant; b. Champaign, Ill., Dec. 10, 1949; d. Albert L. and Catherine A. (Comstock) Hall; m. Thomas F. Johnston, Sept. 27, 1971 (div. Jan. 1979); 1 child, Daniel K. Johnston. BA, Barat Coll., Lake Forest, Ill., 1984. CPA Ill. Acct. Terry Hall, CPA, PC, Gurnee, Ill., 1985—. Bd. dirs. Lake Forest Profl. Women's Round Table, Ill. Bd. dirs. YWCA Lake County, Waukegan, Ill., 1987-89, Women in Dir.'s Chair, Chgo., 1989-96, Stage Two Theater Co., 1991-2003, Sch. Dist. 50, Ill., 2007—; found. bd., Ctr. for Women, 2006-; alumni coun. Lake Forest Acad., 1986-98; mem. Dist. 50 Ill. (Woodland) Sch. Bd., 2007—. Mem. AICPA, ABA (assoc.), Nat. Assn. Tax Preparers, Nat. Soc. Tax Profls., Ill. Soc. CPAs (mem. faculty, mem. state litigation com. 1988-95), Wis. Inst. CPAs (state litigation com. 1989-92), Chgo. Soc. Women CPAs, Lake County Estate Planning Coun., CPAs for the Pub. Interest (Outstanding Vol. 1991). Avocation: travel. Office: 5250 Grand Ave Ste 14 Gurnee IL 60031 Office Phone: 847-623-3025.

HALL, THOMAS J., lawyer; b. Elizabeth, NJ, July 25, 1955; BA, Rutgers U., 1977; JD, Fordham U., 1980. Bar: NY 1980, US Dist. Ct. NJ 1980, US Dist. Ct. (so. dist.) NY 1981, US Dist. Ct. (ea. dist.) NY 1981, US Dist. Ct. (no. dist.) NY 1995, US Ct. Appeals (3rd cir.) 1980, US Ct. Appeals (2d cir.) 1989, US Ct. Appeals (4th cir.) 1999, US Supreme Ct. 2002. Ptnr., Litig. Chadbourne & Parke LLP, NYC. Mediator, Comml. Divsn. NY Supreme Ct., 1997—. Mng. editor Fordham Law Rev., 1979—80; editor: The Banking Law Jour., 1999—; contbr. articles to profl. jour. Mem.: Fed. Bar Coun., ABA (comml. & banking litig. com., internat. litig. com.), NY Bar Assn. Office: Chadbourne & Parke LLP 30 Rockefeller Plaza New York NY 10112 Office Phone: 212-408-5487. Office Fax: 212-541-5369. Business E-Mail: thall@chadbourne.com.

HALL, TOM T., retired country singer, songwriter; b. Olive Hill, Ky., May 25, 1936; s. Virgil Hall; m. Dixie Dean. Student, Roanoke Coll. Founder pub. co. Hallnote Music. With group Tom Hall and the Kentucky Travelers, disc jockey, Sta. WMOR, Morehead, Ky., songwriter with, Newkeys Music, Inc., rec. artist with Mercury Records until 1977, with RCA, Mercury, Polygram records, 1977-2003; performed with band, The Storytellers, Carnegie Hall, N.Y.C., 1973; performed at Smithsonian Instn., 1979, White House, 1980; albums include Magnificent Music Machine, Natural Dreams, 1984, Homecoming, I Witness Life, The Storyteller, Songs of Fox Hollow, Country Classics, Ol' T's in Town, Places I've Done Time, Everything From Jesus to Jack Daniels, many others; songs include Harper Valley P.T.A.; author: Songwriter's Handbook, Laughing Man of Woodmont Coves, Acts of Life, Christmas and the Old House, The Storyteller's Nashville, What a Book! Served in U.S. Army, 1957-61.

HALL, TONY P., former ambassador, retired congressman; b. Dayton, Ohio, Jan. 16, 1942; m. Janet Dick, 1973; 2 children. Student, Ohio State U.; AB, Denison U., 1964; LLD (hon.), Asbury Coll., Eastern Coll. Vol. Peace Corps, Thailand, 1966-67; mem. Ohio Ho. of Reps., 1969-72, Ohio Senate, 1973-78, U.S. Congress from 3d Ohio dist., Washington, 1979—2002; mem. rules com., ranking minority mem. subcom. tech. and the house; amb. U.N. Agencies for Food & Agr., 2002—06. Founder, steering com. Congl. Friends of Human Rights Monitors; bd. mgrs. Air Force Mus. Found.; trustee Holiday Aid; adv. com. Emergency Resource Bank; chmn. Dem. Caucus Task Force on Hunger; founder Congrl. Hunger Ctr. Recipient Disting. Svc. Against Hunger award Bread for the World, 1984, 87, Tree of Life award Jewish Nat. Fund, 1986, Golden Apple award Nat. Assn. Nutrition and Aging Svcs. Programs, 1986, Freedom award Asian Pacific Am. C. of C., 1986, Presdl. End Hunger award, 1988, Silver Anniversary award NCAA, 1989, Silver World Food Day medal Food and Agriculture Orgn. of UN, Ptnrs. award Oxfam Am., 1992; nominated for Nobel Peace prize, 1998, 99, 2001. Mem. Nat. Assn. Women, Infants & Children (Leadership award 1991). Democrat.

HALL, TRISH, editor; married; 1 child. BA, U. Calif., Berkley, 1972. Reporter Wall St. Jour., 1981—87; reporter, editor NY Times, 1987—2002, Escapes sect. editor, 2002—03, Money & Bus. sect. editor, 2003—04, Real Estate editor, 2004—, editor House & Home, Dining sects., 2006—. Contbr. (articles) NY Times, Wall St. Jour., Martha Stewart Living, Gourmet; co-author: A Little Work: Behind the Doors of a Park Avenue Plastic Surgeon, 2004. Office: NY Times Real Estate 229 W 43rd St New York NY 10036 Office Phone: 212-556-1346. E-mail: trish@nytimes.com.

HALL, WAYNE MICHAEL, management consultant; b. Fairbury, Nebr., Nov. 11, 1946; s. Frank Ehman and Bonnie Jean Hall; m. Sandra Kay Overby, Jan. 1, 1999; children: Jennifer E. Austin, Christopher M. BS, U. Nebr., 1969; MS, Kans. State U., 1977; M. Mil. Arts and Sci., U.S. Army Command and Gen. Staff Coll., 1985; EdD, George Washington U., 1985. Commd. 2d lt. U.S. Army, 1969, advanced through grades to brig. gen., 1997, G-2 intelligence officer 82d Airborn Divsn. Ft. Bragg, NC, 1987—89, comdr. 313d Mil. Intelligence Bn., 1989—91, comdr. 501st Mil. Intelligence Bn. Republic of Korea, 1994—96; J2 intelligence officer U. S. Forces Korea, Republic of Korea, 1996—98; dir. intelligence XXI study U.S. Army, Washington, 1998; dir. knowledge adv. Oak Ridge (Tenn.) BWXT, 1999—2001; ret. U.S. Army, 1999; cons. Hall & Assocs., Inc., Suffolk, Va., 2001—02; sr. exec. v.p., Homeland Security & Future Conflict MZM Inc., Washington, 2002—05; pres., CEO, Hall Cons. Svcs., Inc., 2005—. Author: Stray Voltage: War in the Information Age, 2003; contbr. articles to profl. jours. Republican. Home: 5225 Regatta Pointe Rd Suffolk VA 23435 Office Phone: 757-638-4806. E-mail: waynemichaelhall@msn.com.

HALL, WILBUR DALLAS, JR., medical educator; b. Calhoun, Ga., June 22, 1938; m. Marguerite Holt, July 4, 1992; children: Ashley, Brent, Marianne, Tommy. MD, Emory U., 1963. Diplomate Am. Bd. Internal Medicine and Nephrology. Chief med. resident Grady Meml. Hosp., 1966; prof. medicine, dir. div. hypertension Emory U., Atlanta, 1976-97, prof. emeritus, 1997—, program dir. Gen. Clin. Rsch. Ctr., 1988-97. Author 3 books; contbr. 75 chpts. to books, over 100 articles to profl. jours. Master ACP; mem. Ga. Heart Assn. (pres. 1984-85). Home: 1100 Parker Pl NE Atlanta GA 30324-5402

HALL, WILLIAM DARLINGTON, lawyer; b. Elkins, W.Va., Jan. 12, 1914; s. Nathan I. and Grace (Darlington) H.; m. Louise Brown, Aug. 3, 1949; children: Carolyn L., Dorothy K., Beverly G. BEE, W.Va. U., 1934, MEE, 1935, EE, 1940; JD, George Washington U., 1946. Bar: DC 1945, D.C. 1945. Engr. GE, Lynn, Mass., 1936-39; radio engr., patent adviser Signal Corps U.S. Army, Washington, 1939-47, chief patent sect., 1946-47; practiced in Washington, 1947-74; ptnr. Hall, Myers and Rose, 1974-89; of counsel Shlesinger & Myers, Bethesda, Md., 1989, Myers, Rose & Liniak, Bethesda, 1990-92, Myers, Liniak and Berenato, Bethesda, 1992-98, Hall, Priddy, Myers and Vande Sande, Potomac, Md., 1998—. Mem. Army-Navy Patent Adv. Bd., 1946-47 Home: 10850 Stanmore Dr Potomac MD 20854-1522 Office: Hall Priddy & Myers 10220 River Rd Potomac MD 20854-4916

HALL, WILLIAM JOEL, retired civil engineer, educator; b. Berkeley, Calif., Apr. 13, 1926; s. Eugene Raymond and Mary (Harkey) H.; m. Elaine Frances Thalman, Dec. 18, 1948; children: Martha Jane, James Frederick, Carolyn Marie. Student, U. Calif., Berkeley, 1943-44, Kings Point, 1944-45; BSCE, U. Kans., Lawrence, 1948; MS, U. Ill., Urbana, 1951, PhD, 1954. Teaching asst. U. Kans., 1947-48; engr. Sohio Pipe Line Co., 1948-49; mem. faculty U. Ill., Urbana, 1954—93, prof. civil engring., 1959-93, head dept. civil engring., 1984-91; prof. emeritus, 1993—. Cons. in structural dynamics, seismic, materials to govts. and industrial orgns. Author books, articles, revs., book chpts. Recipient A. Epstein Meml. award, U. Ill., 1958, Halliburton Engring. Edn. Leadership award, 1980, Disting. Engring. Svc. award, U. Kans., 1985; Univ. scholar, U. Ill., 1986—89. Fellow AAAS; mem. NAE, ASCE (hon., pres. Ctrl. Ill. sect. 1967-68, chmn. structural divsn. exec. com. 1973-77, chmn. tech. coun. on lifeline earthquake engring. exec. com. 1982-85, Kans. sect. award 1948, Walter L. Huber award 1963, Howard award 1984, Newmark medal 1984, C. Martin Duke award 1990, Norman medal 1992), Am. Concrete Inst., Am. Welding Soc. (Adams Meml. membership award 1967), Earthquake Engring. Rsch. Inst. (Housner medal 1998), Seismol. Soc. Am., Structural Engrs. Assn. Ill. (John Parmer award 1990), Sigma Xi, Tau Beta Pi (Daniel C. Drucker eminent faculty award 1993), Sigma Tau, Chi Epsilon (nat. honor mem. 1998), Phi Kappa Phi. Office: U Ill Civil Engring 3103 Newmark Lab 205 N Mathews Ave Urbana IL 61801-2350 Home: 101 W Windsor Rd #4308 Urbana IL 61802-6661 Office Phone: 217-333-3927. Personal E-mail: wj-efhall@insightbb.com. Business E-Mail: w-hall3@uiuc.edu.

HALL, WILLIAM STERLING, psychology educator; b. Lonoke County, Ark., July 6, 1934; s. Joseph William and Mattie (Brock) H. AB, Roosevelt U., 1957; PhD, U. Chgo., 1968. Instr., asst. prof. ednl. psychology NYU, NYC, 1966-68; assoc. rsch. psychologist Ednl. Testing Svc., Princeton, N.J., 1968-70; asst. prof. psychology Princeton U., 1970-73; assoc. prof. Vassar Coll., Poughkeepsie, N.Y., 1973-74, Rockefeller U., NYC, 1974-78; prof. psychology and ednl. psychology U. Ill., Urbana-Chamaign, 1978-81, co-dir. Ctr. for Study Reading, 1978-81; prof. psychology U. Md., College Park, 1981—2007, chmn. dept., 1993—2006. Mem. study sect. NIMH, 1977-81; mem. grad. evaluation panel NRC; Henry B. Luce vis. prof. psychology Williams Coll., 1985; chair Coun. of Grad. Depts. Psychology, 2000. Bd. dirs. Lazurus awards com. NRMA, N.Y.C., 1975-82, Nat. Coll. Adv. Svc., N.Y.C., 1982—2002. Recipient AERA award, 1982; grantee Carnegie Corp., 1975, 77, Ford Found., 1975. Fellow APA, N.Y. Acad. Scis., Am. Psychol. Soc.; mem. AAAS (sci. fellows selection com.), Soc. for Rsch. in Child Devel., Cosmos Club, Sigma Xi, Alpha Phi Alpha. Home: 1140 23d St NW Washington DC 20037-1437 Office: U Md Dept Psychology College Park MD 20742-0001

HALL, ZACH WINTER, former health science association administrator; b. Atlanta, Sept. 15, 1937; s. Dixon Winter and Marjorie Elizabeth (Owens) H.; m. Anne Browning, June 1958 (div. Aug. 1960); m. Marion Nestle, Dec. 1973 (div. June 1985); m. Julie Ann Giacobassi, Nov. 9, 1987. BA, Yale U., 1958; PhD, Harvard U., 1966. Asst. prof., then assoc. prof. Harvard Med. Sch., Boston, 1968-76; prof. U. Calif., San Francisco, 1976-94; dir. Nat. Inst. Neurol. Disorders and Stroke, Bethesda, Md., 1994-97; assoc. dean for rsch. U. Calif., San Francisco, 1997-98, vice chancellor rsch., 1998-2000, exec. vice chancellor, 2000—01; pres., CEO EnVivo Pharms., Inc., 2001—02; sr. assoc. dean for rsch. Keck Sch. Medicine, U. So. Calif., 2002—05; pres. Calif. Inst. Regenerative Medicine, 2005—07. Med. Adv. Bd., Chevy Chase, Md., 1995-99, Howard Hughes Med. Inst.; Alexander Forbes lectr. Grass Found., 1994; David Nachmanson lectr. Weizmann Inst., Rehovath, Israel, 1996; adv. coun. RIKEN Inst., Tokyo, 2001-. Author, editor: Molecular Neurobiology, 1992; editor jour. Neuron, 1988-94. Recipient Purkynje medal for sci. achievement, Czech Acad. Sci., 2003. Fellow AAAS; mem. Am. Acad. Arts and Scis., Inst. Medicine. Office Phone: 415-396-9105.

HALLA, BRIAN L., electronics executive; b. Springfield, Ill., 1946; BSEE, U. Nebr., 1969. Applications engr. Control Data Corp., 1969—74; dir. mktg. Intel Corp., 1974—78; exec. v.p. LSI Logic, 1988—96; chmn. bd., pres., CEO Nat. Semiconductor Corp., Santa Clara, Calif., 1996—2006, chmn., CEO, 2006—. Bd. dir. Cisco Systems Inc., 2007—, Semiconductor Ind. Assn. Mem.: N.Y. Stock Exch. (adv. com.), Foveon Inc. (bd. dirs.), Tech. Network (bd. dirs.), Silicon Valley Mfg. Group, Semi-Conductor Indsl. Assn. (bd. dirs.,). Office: Nat Semiconductor Corp 2900 Semiconductor Dr Santa Clara CA 95051-0695*

HALLADAY, LAURIE ANN, public relations consultant, food products executive; b. Monroe, Mich., Aug. 18, 1945; d. Alvin John and Florence (Lowrey) Kohler; m. Edward L. Howell, Aug. 27, 1966; m. 2d Fredric R. Halladay, May 24, 1980. BJ, U. Mo., 1967. Reporter, staff writer Copley Newspapers, LA, 1967-69; account exec. Furman Assocs., LA, 1969-71, v.p., 1971-74; account supr. Bob Thomas & Assocs., LA, 1974-76, v.p., 1976-78; v.p., sr. ptnr. Fleishman-Hillard, Inc., St. Louis, 1980-84; owner, operator McDonald's, Portland, Oreg., 1984-87, McDonald's McStop of Mid.-Mo., Kingdom City, 1988-92. Chmn. press ops. for Budweiser/G.I. Joe's Portland 200 Indy Car Race, 1984-87; mem. advt., promotions com. Hollywood Boosters, 1986. Bd. dirs. Waterman Place Assn., St. Louis, 1983; mem. pub. rels. com. Winston Churchill Meml., Fulton, 1988-92. Recipient Merit award Calif. Press Women, 1969, Lulu award Los Angeles Women's Ad Club, 1976, McDonald's Outstanding Store award, 1985, 86, 89, 90, 91. Mem. PRSA (Prism award 1977), Soc. Am. travel Writers (assoc. 1981-84), Women in Comm. (dir. St. Louis 1980-82), Nat. Tour Assn., Mo. Travel Coun., Delta Delta Delta (alumna adviser 1989, 90, v.p. Delta Xi House Corp. 1991, collegiate dist. officer 1991, 94, regional program chmn. 1994, program resource team pub. rels. specialist 1995-96, nat. chmn. pub. rels. 1996, cons. pub. rels. chpt. 1998-2000). Address: 1602 Alabama Dr 304 Winter Park FL 32789 Personal E-mail: halladayl@yahoo.com.

HALLADAY, ROY (HARRY LEROY HALLADAY), professional baseball player; b. Denver, May 14, 1977; Pitcher Toronto Blue Jays, 1998—. Named to All Star Game, 2002, 2003; recipient Cy Young award, Am. League, 2003. Achievements include led Am. League wins in 2003. Office: 1 Blue Jays Way Ste 3200 Toronto ON Canada M5V 1J1*

HALLAKE, MARCELLO, lawyer; b. Rio de Janeiro, Jan. 28, 1970; s. Ignacio Hallake and Esther Evelyne Levy; m. Flavia Nucci Dezotti, Jan. 12, 2001; children: Nathan, Carolina. BA, Facultes Universitaires Saint-Louis, Brussels, 1990; JD, Louvain U., Belgium, 1993; LLM, Georgetown U., 1994; M in Pub. and Internat. Affairs, Louvain U., 1994. Ptnr. Coudert Bros., NYC, 2004—05, Thompson & Knight LLP, 2005—. Pres., dir. Geneva Initiative N.Am., NYC, 2004, CDI Internat., 2005; dir. Brazil Found., 2001. Dir. Meretz USA, 2007—; mem. Coun. Americas, US-Mex. C. of C.; bd. trustees Inter-Am.Culture and Devel. Found., 2007—. Mem.: ABA, Brazilian Inst. Bus. Law, Inst. Brasileiro Direito Empresarial (bd. advisors 2006—), NYC Bar Assn. (chair com. inter-Am. affairs 2004—), Brazilian-Am. C. of C., Cyrus R. Vance Ctr. Internat. Justice Initiatives (bd. advisors 2005—), Internat. Bar Assn. Office: Thompson & Knight LLP 919 Third Ave New York NY 10022 Home Phone: 212-327-3485; Office Phone: 212-751-3070. Office Fax: 214-999-1544. E-mail: marcello.hallake@tklaw.com.

HALLAM, BEVERLY (BEVERLY LINNEY), artist; b. Lynn, Mass., Nov. 22, 1923; d. Edwin Francis and Alice (Linney) Hallam Murphy. BS in Edn, Mass. Coll. Art, 1945; postgrad., Cranbrook Acad. Art, Mich., 1948; MFA, Syracuse U., 1953. Chmn. dept. art Lasell Jr. Coll., Auburndale, Mass., 1945-49; assoc. prof. Mass. Coll. Art, 1949-62. Bd. dirs. Barn Gallery Assocs., Inc., Ogunquit, Maine. One-person shows include Joe and Emily Lowe Art Center, Syracuse U., 1953, DeCordova Mus., Lincoln, Mass., 1954, Shore Galleries, Boston, 1959, 62, 68, 73, 74, Witte Meml. Mus., San Antonio, 1968, U. Maine, 1969, Lamont Gallery, Exeter, N.H., 1969, Addison Gallery, Andover, Mass., 1971, Fitchburg Art Mus., 1972, Fairweather Hardin Gallery, Chgo., 1972, Hobe Sound (Fla.) Galleries, 1973, Inst. Contemporary Art, Boston, 1977, PS Galleries, Maine, 1981, Payson-Weisberg Gallery, N.Y.C., 1984, Farnsworth Mus., Rockland, Maine, 1984, 98, Midtown Galleries, N.Y.C., 1988, Francesca Anderson Gallery, Boston, 1988, Hobe Sound Galleries North, Portland, Maine, 1988, Evansville (Ind.) Mus. Arts and Sci., 1990, Sheldon Swope Mus., Terre Haute, Ind., 1990, Art Mus. S.E. Tex., Beaumont, 1990, Bergen Mus. Art and Sci., Paramus, N.J., 1990, Polk Mus. Art, Lakeland, Fla., 1991, Farnsworth Art Mus., 1998, Ogunquit Art Assn., 1999, Mass. Coll. Art, Boston, 2000, U. New England, 2000, Berkshire C.C., Pittsfield, Mass., 2003, River Tree Ctr. for the Arts, Kennebunk, Maine, 2003, George Marshall Store Gallery, York, Maine, 2005; two-person show, Inst. Contemporary Art, Boston, 1956, numerous group shows including Barn Gallery, 1954-2005, Busch-Reisinger Mus., Harvard U., 1956, 59, 60, Portland Mus., 1959, 84, 92, 93, 97, 2004, Mus. Fine Arts, Boston, 1960, Inst. Contemporary Art, Boston, 1960, 63, 68, 77, Pace Gallery, Boston, 1962, DeCordova Mus., 1963, 64, 68, 69, 70, 71, 75, Ward-Nasse Gallery, N.Y.C., 1971-72, Ogunquit (Maine) Mus. Am. Art, 1964, 70, 71, 78, 80, 84, 89, 91-93, 95, 98, 00, 03, River Tree Ctr. Arts, 2004, R.I. Arts Festival, 1966, Smithsonian Instn., Washington, 1966, Am. Water Color Soc. Traveling Exhbn., 1967, Watercolor U.S.A., Springfield, Mo., 1968, Maine State Mus., 1976, 04, Maine Coast Artists, 1974, 75, 77, 83, 89, 92, 93, Joan Whitney Payson Gallery of Art, Maine, 1980, Farnsworth Art Mus., 1982, 87, 92, 95, 96, Bowdoin Coll. Mus. Art, 1984, 92, Midtown Payson Galleries, N.Y.C., 1985, 87, 90, 92, Expo '92, Seville, Spain, Barbara Scott Gallery, Bay Harbor Island, Fla., 1993, Fitchburg (Mass.) Art Mus., 1994, Monmouth (N.J.) Mus., 1995, Evansville Mus. Arts and Sci., 1996, U. New England, 2000, 05, Francesca Anderson Fine Art, Lexington, Mass., 2002, Addison Gallery Am. Art, Andover, Mass., 2003, River Tree Ctr. for Arts, Kennebunk, Maine, 2004, 06, Ctr. Maine Contemporary Art, Rockland, 2006, Greenhut Galleries, Portland, 2006, Coolidge Ctr. Arts, Portsmouth, NH, 2007; represented in permanent collections Rose Art Mus. Brandeis U., Fogg Art Mus., Cambridge, Mass.; Corcoran Gallery Am. Art, Washington, Witte Meml. Mus., San Antonio, DeCordova Mus., Lincoln, Addison Gallery, Andover, Bowdoin Coll. Mus. Art, Fitchburg Art Mus., Ogunquit Mus. Am. Art, Portland Mus., Colby Coll., U. Maine, Currier Gallery Art, Manchester N.H., Farnsworth Library and Art Mus., Rockland, Maine, U. N.H. Art Galleries, Durham, Everson Mus., Syracuse, First Nat. Bank, Boston, Ernst and Ernst, Chgo., Carnegie Corp., N.Y., Nat. Mus. Women in the Arts, Washington, Gouws Capital Mgmt., Inc., Portland, Maine, Marion Koogler Art Mus., San Antonio, Tex., others, also, pvt. collections, U.S. Can., Paris, Switzerland; Publ. Beverly Hallam, Paintings, Drawings and Monotypes, 1956-71, 1971; subject of book and video Beverly Hallam: The Flower Paintings, 1990, Beverly Hallam: An Odyssey in Art, 1998, (by Carl Little) One Hundred Works From the 20th Century at Colby College Museum of Art, 1996, Maine In America, Farnsworth Art Mus., 2000, On Paper: Masterworks From The Addison Collection, 2003, others. Recipient Pearl Safir award Silvermine Guild Artists, New Canaan, Conn., 1955, Painting prize Boston Arts Festival, 1957, Blanche E. Colman Found. award, 1960, Hatfield awards Boston Soc. Watercolor Painters, 1960, 64, 1st prize Edwin Webster award, 1962, Am. Artist Achievement award, 1993, Disting. Alumna award Mass. Coll. Art, 2000, Maine Coll. Art award for Visual Artist Achievement, 2001. Mem. Ogunquit Art Assn. (past pres.), Archives Am. Art. Avocations: photography, digital abstractions. Home: 30 Surf Point Rd York ME 03909-5053

HALLARD, WAYNE BRUCE, retired economist; b. Plainfield, NJ, Dec. 28, 1951; s. Donald Jay and Patricia (Adelmann) H.; m. Grace Elizabeth Farrell, Apr. 29, 1972 (div. 1979); 1 child, Travis; m. Deborah Jane Russo, Aug. 16, 1987. Student, Brown U., 1970—71; AA in Bus., Union Coll., 1977; BS in Econs., Fairleigh Dickinson U., 1980, MBA in Econs., 1984; postgrad., N.Y.U., 1984—87. Store mgr. Wine Art of NJ, Watchung, 1972; mgr. Verizon, Newark, 1972—2003; ret., 2003. Cons. NJ Coun. Savs. Instns., West Orange, 1987-95, F.A. Russo Assocs., Scotch Plains, NJ, 1989—; ea. conf. organizing com., session chmn. Ctr. Rsch. in Regulatied Industries, 1986-2003. Trustee, treas. Lehmen Found., Newark, 1979-84; bd. dirs., treas. Vol. Ctr. of Greater Essex County, 1990-97; mem. Mental Health Assn., East Orange, 1979-80, Newark Mus., 1987—; trustee, past sec., treas. Newark Jaycees Internat. Senators Scholarship Found., 1986-99; umpire Scotch Plains-Fanwood Youth Baseball Assn., 1982—; trustee, past pres. Brotherhood Temple Sharey Tefilo Israel, South Orange, N.J., 1980—; trustee Fairleigh Dickinson U., 2003-2005. With USAFR, 1971-80. Named one of Outstanding Young Men of Am., 1981, 1983, 1985—86, 1988; recipient Cert. of Appreciation, Cts. and Corrections Assn. NJ, 1982. Mem. ACLU, Am. Econ. Assn., Greater Newark C. of C. (bd. dirs. 1980-82), Telephone Pioneers Am., Fairleigh Dickinson U. Alumni Assn. (bd. govs. 1997—, v.p. 1999-2001, pres.-elect 2001-2003, pres. 2003-2005), Am. Dog Show Judges, Ea. Stewards Assn. (treas. 2004—), Am. Sealyham Terrier Club (past bd. dirs.), Garden State All Terrier Club (past treas., past corr. sec.), Mastiff Club Am., Aircraft Owners and Pilots Assn., Stewards Club Am., ARZA, Jewish Chatauqua Soc., Confrerie de la Chaine des Rotisseurs, Soc. Mondialie du Vin, Delta Mu Delta. Democrat. Jewish. Avocations: cooking, reading. Home: 518 Jerusalem Rd Scotch Plains NJ 07076-2011 Personal E-mail: wayne.b.hallard@verizon.net.

HALLAUER, ARNEL ROY, geneticist; b. Netawaka, Kans., May 4, 1932; s. Roy Virgil and Mabel Fern (Bohnenkemper) H.; m. Janet Yvonne Goodmanson, Aug. 29, 1964; children: Elizabeth, Paul BS, Kans. State U., 1954; MS, Iowa State U., 1958, PhD, 1960. Rsch. agronomist USDA, Ames, Iowa, 1958-60, geneticist Raleigh, NC, 1961-62, rsch. geneticist Ames, 1963-89; prof. Iowa State U., 1990—2002, C.F. Curtiss Disting. prof. agr. emeritus, 2003—. Author: (with J.B. Miranda) Quantitative Genetics in Maize Breeding, 1981, 2d edit., 1988; editor: Specialty Corns, 1994, 1st edit., 2000. 2d lt. US Army, 1954-56. Recipient Applied Rsch. and Ext. award 1981, Henry A. Wallace award for disting.svc. to agr., 1992, Disting. Alumni Achievement citation, 1996, Iowa State U., Genetics and Plant Breeding award Nat. Coun. Plant Breeding, 1984, Gov.'s Sci. medal State of Iowa, 1990, Burlington No. Career Rsch. Achievement award Iowa State Found., 1991, Centennial medal Phi Kappa Phi, 1997, Verdent Plant Genetics award Verdent Ptnrs., Chgo., 2001; named to USDA/Agrl. Rsch. Sci. Hall of Fame, 1992; named one of 150 Visionaries Iowa State U., 2007; honored Inter-Am. Inst. Coop. Agr. significant contbns. to agr., Washington, 2003, Arnel R. Hallauer Internat. Symposium plant breeding, Mexico City, 2003; USDA grantee, 1982, 85, 87, 90. Fellow Am. Soc. Agronomy (Agronomic Achievement award for crops 1989, Agronomic Rsch. award 1992), Crop Sci. Soc. (Dekalb Pfizer Crop Sci. award 1981, Pres.'s award 2002), Iowa Acad. Sci. (disting. fellow 1985); mem. NAS,

Nat. Agri-Mktg. Assn. (nat. award for excellence in rsch. 1993), Am. Genetic Assn., Am. Statis. Assn., Kans. State U. Alumni Assn. (alumni fellow 1997), Iowa State Alumni Assn. (faculty citation 1987, Disting. Achievement Citation 1995), Gamma Sigma Delta (Disting. Svc. to Agr. award 1990, Rsch. Award of Merit 1999). Republican. Lutheran. Home: 516 Luther Dr Ames IA 50010-4735 Office: Iowa State U 1505 Dept Agronomy Ames IA 50010 Office Phone: 515-294-7823. Business E-Mail: hallauer@iastate.edu.

HALL-BARRON, DEBORAH, lawyer; b. Oakland, Calif., Oct. 7, 1949; d. John Standish Hall and Mary (Swinson) H.; m. Eric Levin Meadow, Feb. 1973 (div. June 1982); 1 child, Jesse Standish Meadow Hall; m. Richie Barron, 1997. Paralegal cert., Sonoma State U., Rohnert Park, Calif., 1984; JD, John F. Kennedy U., Walnut Creek, Calif., 1990. Bar: Calif. 1991. Paralegal Law Offices Marc Libarle/Quentin Kopp, Cotati, Calif., 1983-84, MacGregor & Buckley, Larkspur, Calif., 1984-86, Law Offices Melvin Belli, San Francisco, 1987-88, Steinhart & Falconer, San Francisco, 1988; mgr. Computerized Litigation Assocs., San Francisco, 1986; law clk. Morton & Lacy, San Francisco, 1989-91, assoc., 1991-96; atty. Law Offices of Charlotte Venner, San Francisco, 1996-97, Plastiras & Terrizzi, San Francisco, San Rafael, Calif., 1998, Bishop, Barry, Howe, Haney & Ryder, San Francisco, 1998-99, McLemore, Collins and Toschi, Oakland, Calif., 1999-2000, Nevin Levy, LLP, Walnut Creek, 2000—01, Curtis & Arata, Modesto, Calif., 2001—03, Parker Sommers, Sacramento, 2003—05, Law Offices of Deborah Barron, Sacramento, 2005—. Mediator El Dorado County Superior Ct., 1995—. Atty. Vol. Legal Svcs., San Francisco, 1991-96; judge San Francisco Youth Ct., 1995-97; com. chmn. Point Richmond (Calif.) coun., 1994-96. Recipient Whiley Manuel Pro Bono award State Bar Calif., 1993. Mem. Nat. Assn. Ins. Women, Def. Rsch. Inst., Bar Assn. San Francisco (del. 4th world conf. on women 1995, chair product liability com.), Sacramento Bar Assn., Internat. Com. Lawyers for Tibet (litigation com. 1991-97, co-chair women's com.), Ins. Claims Assn. (chmn. membership com. 1994-96), Hon. Order of Blue Goose Internat., Queen's Bench (chmn. employment com. 1994-97, bd. dirs. 1996—, newsletter editor and webmaster 1999), BASF intellectual property/entertainment law), Sacramento Blues Soc. (pres. 2004). Democrat. Avocations: human rights advocate, boating. Home: 2411 Tuscano Ct Rancho Cordova CA 95670-3836 Office Phone: 916-486-1712. Business E-Mail: deborah.barron@lawbarron.com.

HALLBERG, BUDD JAYE, management consulting firm executive; b. Ottumwa, Iowa, Oct. 2, 1942; s. Melvin Kenneth and Janet Berina (Dowden) H.; m. Diana May Pierce, Dec. 30, 1962. BA, MA, Goddard Coll., Plainfield, Vt., 1980; BS, SUNY, 1981; diploma, Command & Gen. Staff Coll., 1981; cert., Wharton Sch., 1984, Yale U., New Haven, Conn., 1996, Harvard U., Cambridge, Mass., 2006. Account exec. Francis I. duPont & Co., Moline, Ill., 1966-69, sales mgr. NYC, 1969-70, br. mgr. Toledo, 1970-71; v.p. Dominick & Dominick, Inc., NYC, 1971-72, Hornblower & Weeks, Inc., NYC, 1972-74; mem. N.Y. Mercantile Exchange, NYC, 1974-76; dir. U.S. Commodity Future Trading Commn., Washington, 1976-83; v.p. Heinold Commodities, Inc., NYC, 1983-85; pres. SCAN Mgmt. Inc., Gettysburg, Pa., 1985—. Prof. bus. & fin. Grad. Sch. of Bus. Mt. St. Mary's Univ., Emmitsburg, Md., 2000—. Contbr. articles to profl. jours. Fund raiser Rep. party Old Greenwich, Conn., 1974, Gettysburg, Pa., 1995, St. Saviours Episc. Ch., Old Greenwich, 1975, Prince of Peace Episc. Ch., Gettysburg, 1985—. Lt. col. USAR, ret. Mem.: Swedish Colonial Soc., St. Nicholas Soc. of N.Y., Soc. of Colonial Wars, Friends of The Holland Soc. of N.Y., Sons of Union Vets of Civil War, The William Soc., Pa. Soc. Sons of the Revolution, Colonial Soc. Pa., Rotary, Franklin Inn Club (Phila.), Racquet Club Phila., Army and Navy Club Washington, Scottish Rite, York Rite, Masons (32 deg.). Avocations: tennis, golf. Home: 320 Spangler School Rd Gettysburg PA 17325-8639 Office: SCAN Mgmt Inc 320 Spangler Sch Rd Gettysburg PA 17325

HALLECK, CHARLES WHITE, lawyer, photographer, former judge; b. Rensselaer, Ind., July 6, 1929; s. Charles Abraham and Blanche (White) H.; m. Carolyn L. Wood, Dec. 23, 1950 (div. Oct. 1968); children: Holly Louise, Charles White, Todd Alexander, Heather Leigh, Heidi Lynne, William Hemsley, Hope Leslie; m. Jeanne Wahl, May 16, 1970. AB, Williams Coll., 1951; JD, George Washington U., 1957; LL.D. (hon.), St. Joseph's Coll., 1971; AA in Photography, Foothill Coll., Los Altos Hills, Calif., 1996. Asst. U.S. atty. for D.C., 1957-59; assoc. Hogan and Hartson, Washington, 1959-65; judge Superior Ct. D.C., 1965-77; mem. firm Lamb, Halleck & Keats, Washington, 1977-80; sole practice, 1980-86; photojournalist, 1986-99; fine art photographer, 1999—. Served with USNR, 1951-55; to lt. Res. (ret.). Mem. Beta Theta Pi, Phi Delta Phi.

HALLEN, BARRY, philosopher, educator; b. Chgo., Apr. 5, 1941; s. George and Betty Hallen; m. Carla De Benedetti, Apr. 30, 1986; m. Patricia Slattery, Aug. 5, 1966 (div. Nov. 26, 1974). BA in Philosophy, Carleton Coll., 1963; MA in Philosophy, Boston U., 1968, PhD in Philosophy, 1970. Lectr. in philosophy U. Lagos, Lagos, Nigeria, 1970—75; from lectr. to reader in philosophy U. Ife, Ile-Ife, Nigeria, 1975—83, reader in philosophy, 1983—88; project dir. UNESCO, Milan, 1989—98; vis. prof. philosophy Morehouse Coll., Atlanta, 1997—2000, prof. philosophy, 2000—, chmn. dept. philosophy and religion, 2001—. Rschr. W.E.B. DuBois Inst. Harvard U., Cambridge, Mass., 1995—. Co-author: Knowledge, Belief & Witchcraft, 1997; author: The Good, The Bad & the Beautiful, 2000, A Short History of African Philosophy, 2002, African Philosophy: The Analytic Approach, 2006. Borden Parker Bowne fellow, Boston U., 1968—69, Fulbright rsch. grantee, 2003. Mem.: Internat. Soc. African Philosophy and Studies (pres. 2004—06), Soc. African Philosophy in N.Am. (gen. sec. 1998—2006). Avocations: sailing, bicycling, writing detective stories. Office: Morehouse College 830 Westview Drive SW Atlanta GA 30314 Office Phone: 404-215-2607. Business E-Mail: bhallen@morehouse.edu.

HALLENBECK, RACHEL KIRSTEN, music educator, director; b. Jackson, Calif., Nov. 1, 1965; d. Ronald K. and Martha Lou Grabke; m. Jeffrey B. Hallenbeck; children: Kirsten Elizabeth, Brianna Ruth. BSc in Music Edn., Ea. Nazarene Coll., 1989, MEd in Elem. Edn., 1999, MEd in Adminstrn., 2000. Music specialist Braintree Pub. Schs., 1989—2000, dir. music, 2000—. Soloist Boylston Congl. Ch., Boston, 1990—, Town of Braintree, 1990—; accompanist Quincy Pub. Schs., 1998—, vocal dir. performing arts workshops, 2004—; condr. Braintree Choral Soc., 2001—02; musical dir. Harmony Youth Chorus and No Place for Hate Project, 2004—05. Singer: Boston (Mass.) Symphony Orch., 1989—; dir.: Quincy (Mass.) Dinner Theater, 1990—93; singer: (albums) The Boston (Mass.) Pops Orch., The Boston (Mass.) Symphony Orch.; music dir.: Needham Cmty. Theater, 2006—07. Republican. Avocations: singing, choreography, piano. Office: Braintree Public Schools 128 Town St Braintree MA 02184

HALLENBERG, ROBERT LEWIS, lawyer; b. Oct. 21, 1948; s. Daniel Ward and Anna Mae (Lewis) H.; m. Susan Annette Shaffer, Nov. 29, 1980; children: Shea F., Jonathan E.R., Robert Lewis Jr. BA, U. Ky., 1970, JD, 1973; LLM in Taxation, U. Miami, Fla., 1974. Bar: U. Ky. 1970, U.S. Dist. Ct. (we. dist.) Ky. 1975, U.S. Tax Ct. 1986. Ptnr. Woodward, Hobson & Fulton, Louisville, 1974—. Adj. prof. U. Louisville Sch. Law, 1974-80. Pres. Louisville Estate Planning Coun., 1979—80; bd. dirs. Louisville Theatrical Assocs., 1980—90, v.p., sec., 1985—90; bd. dirs. Goodwill Industries Ky., 1987—93, sec., 1988—91; bd. dirs. Louisville Estate Planning Forum, 1986—93, sec., 1992—93; bd. dirs. Estate Planning Coun. of Louisville, 1989—95, pres., 1993—94. Named one of Best Lawyers in Am. (trusts and estates). Fellow Am. Coll. Trust and Estate Counsel, Best Lawyers in Am. (trusts and estates); mem. Ky. Bar Assn. (sec. tax com. 1984-85), Owl Creek Country Club (bd. dirs. 1988-91, pres. 1989-90, treas. 1990-91). Republican. Episcopalian. Office: Woodward Hobson & Fulton 2500 Nat City Tower Louisville KY 40202 Office Phone: 502-581-8013. Business E-Mail: bhallenberg@WHF-law.com.

HALLER, ARCHIBALD ORBEN, sociologist, educator; b. San Diego, Jan. 15, 1926; s. Archie O. and Eleanor (Brizzee) Haller; m. Hazel Laura Zimmermann, Feb. 15, 1947 (dec. 1985); children: Elizabeth Ann, Stephanie Lynn Bylin, William John; m. Maria Camila Omegna Rocha, Apr. 12, 1986 (div. 1987); m. Maria Cristina Del Peloso, Sept. 16, 1989; stepchildren: Graziella, Camila. BA magna cum laude, Hamline U., 1950; MA, U. Minn., 1951; PhD, U. Wis., 1954; D of Social Scis. (hon.), Ohio State U., Columbus, 2007. Assoc. prof., then prof. sociology Mich. State U., East Lansing, 1956—65; postdoctoral rschr. U. Wis., Madison, 1954—56, vis. prof., 1964, prof. sociology and rural sociology, 1965—94, emeritus prof., 1994—, affiliated faculty Indsl. Rels. Rsch. Inst., 1975—94, faculty in Latin Am., Caribbean and Iberian studies, 1965—94, affiliated faculty Inst. Environ. Studies, Conservation Biology and Sustainable Devel., 1990—94, ind. rsch., writing, lectr., 2002—. Fulbright prof. sociology Rural U. of Brazil, 1962, U. Sao Paulo, 1974, 83, 1987—90; vis. prof. sociology Brigham Young U., Provo, Utah, 1973; Fulbright travel grantee Univ. Sao Paulo, Brasilia, Pernambuco, Paraiba and Ceara, Brazil, 1979; cons. on Amazonian rsch. Govt. of Brazil, 1979, 1991—95; vis. fellow Australian Nat. U., 1981; disting. vis. prof. rural sociology Ohio State U., 1982—83; cons. UNESCO, 1989, Fed. U. Pernambuco, 1994, Fed. Rural U. Amazonia, 1997—98, Ind. U., Bangladesh, 1998; cons. nat. social change Pres. of Brazil, 1994—96; cons. on Amazonian rsch. Govt. of Brazil, 1997; vis. prof. doctoral program in sociology and polit sci. Fed. U. Minas Gerais, Brazil, 1998, Brazil, 2000—02; organizer symposia on Brazil. Author: The Occupl. Aspiration Scale: Theory, Structure and Correlates, 1963, 71, The Socioeconomic Macroregions of Brazil-1970, 1983; co-editor (with R.M. Hauser et al) Social Structure and Behavior: Essays in Honor of William Hamilton Sewell, 1982; editor spl. issues Luso-Brazilian Rev.; author rsch. monographs and tech. articles; contbr. articles to profl. jour. Mem. Mich. Com. on Mental Health Policies, 1961-62; Nat. Exec. Res., 1959-66; mem. sociology fellowship panel Coun. on Internat. Exch. Scholars, 1977-81, chmn., 1981. Active duty aviation electronics USNR, 1943—46, mem. Nat. Def. Exec. Res., 1959—65. Decorated grand officer Order of Merit of Labor (Brazil); univ. fellow U. Wis., 1953-1954; recipient John Luddy Phalen award in Latin Am. Studies U. Wis., 2000, Rsch. award Brazilian Sociol. Soc., 2005; fellow Nat. Rsch. Coun. Brazil, 2000-02; Ann. Haller Disting. Lecture Series named in his honor U. Wis., 2000—; festschrift in his honor The Shape of Social Inequality, 2005. Fellow: AAAS, Am. Sociol. Assn.; mem.: Rural Sociol. Soc. (pres. 1970—71, AAAS rep. 1973—86, Disting. Rural Sociologist 1990), Sociol. Rsch. Assn., Internat. Sociol. Assn., Internat. Rural Sociol. Assn., Brazil Com. U. Ariz., Univ. Club, Gamma Sigma Delta, Sigma Xi, Phi Beta Kappa. Achievements include contbr. to theory of societal stratification, to processes of status allocation, to the demographic structure of societal inequality, to identifying the socioeconomic develop. regions of Brazil, and to the measurement of internat. devel. Home and Office: 12928 Salt Cedar Dr Oro Valley AZ 85755 Office Phone: 520-297-2912. Personal E-mail: haller@ssc.wisc.edu.

HALLER, CALVIN JOHN, banker; b. Buffalo, July 9, 1925; s. John Martin and Emelia (George) H.; m. Yvette Ann Hogrewe, June 12, 1948; children: Cary John, Darlene Ann Haller Kalfahs. BS in Bus. Adminstrn. with distinction, U. Buffalo, 1949; DHL (hon.), Keuka Coll., 2005. With Buffalo Savs. Bank (now Goldome), from 1949, now ret. pres. Western N.Y. Bd. dirs. Niagra Luth. Health Sys. Bd. dirs. Children's Found., Erie County, Buffalo Fedn. of Neighborhood Ctrs.; trustee, past pres. Met. YMCA Buffalo and Erie County; chmn. bd. trustees YMCA Greater Buffalo; trustee emeritus, past chmn. bd. Keuka Coll. Lt. (j.g.) USNR, 1943-46. Mem. N.Y. Soc. Security Analysts, Newcomen Soc. N.Am., Nat. Assn. Bus. Economists, U. Buffalo Alumni Assn., Beta Gamma Sigma. Clubs: Mason. Clubs (Buffalo), Country (Buffalo), Bond (Buffalo), Buffalo (Buffalo), Equality (Buffalo). Lutheran. Home: 235 Westfall Dr Tonawanda NY 14150-7136 Personal E-mail: calvette@localnet.com.

HALLER, CHARLES EDWARD, engineer, consultant; b. Fairfield, Conn., Sept. 5, 1924; s. William Charles and Gertrude Ida Mae (Belinski) H.; m. Eleanor Margret Hoffman, Oct. 11, 1950 (dec. 2003); children: Carolyn, Debra Lynn, Mark, Charles. Student, Yale U., 1943-44; BEE, Rensselaer Poly. Inst., 1947. Project engr. Western Union Telco., NYC, 1948-56; assoc. lab. dir. ITT Labs., Nutley, N.J., 1956-62; v.p., dir. ops. ITT Worldcom, NYC, 1962-67; pres. ITT Def. Communications, Nutley, N.J., 1967-74; mng. dir. I.O. ITT Telecom N.Am., Nutley, N.J., 1974-83; group gen. mgr., pres. ITT Asia Pacific, NYC, 1983-87; cons. Internat. Enterprises, Kinnelon, N.J., 1987—. Author: Communications Switching Systems, 1964. With USN, 1943-46. Fellow IEEE (life). Republican. Avocations: politics, bowling, golf, reading, travel. Home and Office: 2 Summit Ter N Kinnelon NJ 07405-2436

HALLER, EUGENE ERNEST, materials scientist, educator; b. Basel, Switzerland, Jan. 5, 1943; s. Eugene and Maria Anne Haller; m. Marianne Elisabeth Schlittler, May 26, 1973; children: Nicole Marianne, Isabelle Cathrine. Diploma in Physics, U. Basel, 1967, PhD in Physics, 1970. Postdoctoral asst. Lawrence Berkeley (Calif.) Nat. Lab., 1971—73, from staff scientist to sr. staff scientist, 1973—80, faculty sr. scientist, 1980—; assoc. prof. U. Calif., Berkeley, 1980-82, prof. materials sci., 1982—. Co-chmn. Materials Rsch. Soc. Symposia, Boston, 1982, 89, Internat. Conf. on Shallow Levels in Semiconductors, Berkeley, 1984, 94; chair 20th Internat. Conf. on Defects in Semicondrs., 1999; adv. com. Paul Drude Inst., Berlin, 2001—; rev. com. instrument div. Brookhaven Nat. Lab., Upton, N.Y., 1987-93; mem. Japanese tech. panel on sensors NSF-Nat. Acad. Sci., Washington, 1988; vis. prof. Max-Planck-Inst. for Solid State Rsch., Stuttgart, 1986, Imperial Coll. Sci., Tech. and Medicine, London, 1991, German Aerospace Assn., Berlin, 1996; disting. prof. Keio u., Tokyo, 2004. Mem. editl. bd. Jour. Phys. and Chem. Solids, 1993—, Material Sci. Founds., 1998—; contbr. articles to profl. jours. U.S. Sr. scientist award Alexander von Humboldt Soc., Germany, 1986, Max-Planck Rsch. award, 1994; rsch. fellow Miller Inst. Basic Rsch., Berkeley, 1990, 2001. Fellow AAAS, Am. Phys. Soc. (James C. McGroddy prize in new materials 1999); mem. Materials Rsch. Soc. (David Turnbull Lectureship award 2005), Swiss Phys. Soc., Sigma Xi. Achievements include patents in surface passivation of semiconductors, synthesis of crystalline carbon nitride potentially a superhard material, and far infrared germanium laser. Office: U Calif Berkeley 328 Hearst Mining Meml Bldg Berkeley CA 94720-1760 Office Fax: 510-486-5530. Business E-Mail: eehaller@lbl.gov.

HALLER, HEINZ, chemicals executive; MBA, IMD, Lausanne Switzerland; cert. adv. exec. prog., UCLA. Sales & mktg. positions Dow Chem. Co., Switzerland, 1980—94; mng. dir. Plüss-Staufer AG, 1994—99; CEO Red Bull Sauber AG, Sauber Petronas Engring. AG, 1999—2002; mng. dir. Allianz Capital GmbH, 2002—05; sr. v.p. strategic develop. & new ventures, mem. office of chief exec. Dow Chem. Co., Midland, Mich., 2005—. Office: Dow Chem Co 2030 Dow Ctr Midland MI 48674*

HALLER, JORDAN D., cardiovascular surgeon; b. Pitts., Sept. 5, 1932; s. Max Leopold and Pearl H.; children: Matthew, Nina, Andrew. BS, U. Pitts., 1953; MD, Ind. U., Indpls., 1957. Diplomate Am. Bd. Surgery, Am. Bd. Thoracic and Cardiovascular Surgery, Am. Bd. of Thoracic Sugery. Intern Ind. U. Med. Ctr., Indpls., 1957-58; resident Bronx Mcpl. Hosp. Ctr., NY, 1958-63; fellow in cardiovascular surgery St. Luke's Hosp., Tex. Children's Hosp., 1970; clin. investigator in cardiopulmonary surgery VA Hosp., Pitts., 1963-66; dir. thoracic and cardiovascular surgery Maimonides Med. Ctr., Bklyn., 1966-71; pvt. practice cardiovascular-thoracic surgery LA, 1972-84; founder, dir. Laser Inst. Shadyside Hosp., Pitts., 1984-85; med. dir. C.R. Bard, Inc., Billerica, Mass., 1985—91; lectr. biomedical tech. Columbia U., NYC, 1992—2000; v.p. med. and regulatory affairs, for excimer laser photorefractive keratectomy and LASIK Visx Inc., Sunnyvale, Calif., 1994—96; founder, pres., CEO Lajor BioMedical Tech. Inc., Pitts., 1999—. Asst. instr. surgery, Albert Einstein Coll. Medicine, 1962-63; instr. surgery, U. Pitts., 1963-66; dir. dept. thoracic and cardiovascular surg., residency tng. program, Maimonides Med. Ctr., 1966-71; asst. prof. cardiovascular-thoracic surgery, SUNY, Bklyn., 1966-71; guest prof. cardiovascular-thoracic surgery, Italian Hosp. Buenos Aires, 1977-81; sr. instr. advanced trauma course, Northridge Found. Hosp., 1979-83; sr. lectr. in engring., Carnegie-Mellon U., Pitts., 1985-86; sr. instr. advanced trauma course Am. Coll. of Surgeons; cons. cardiovascular thoracic medicine and surgery, 1991-; vol. faculty, med. ethics, U. Pitts. Sch. Medicine, 2003. Patentee, heart valves, vascular clamps, chest drainage devices, bioactive peptides; contbr. articles to med. publs. Fellow ACS, Am. Soc. Laser Medicine and Surgery; mem. Denton Cooley Cardiovascular Soc., N.Y. Soc. Thoracic Surgery, Soc. Clin. Vascular Surgery, Soc. Thoracic Surgeons, Western Thoracic Surg. Assn., AAAS, Am. Heart Assn., Am. Soc. Artificial Internal Organs, Assn. for Advancement of Med. Instrumentation, Internat. Soc. Artificial Organs, N.Y. Acad. Scis., Laser Inst. of Am. Avocations: music, theater, literature.

HALLETT, CHARLES ARTHUR, JR., language educator, humanities educator; b. New Haven, July 19, 1935; s. Charles Arthur and Bridie D. Hallett; m. Elaine Stewartson, Nov. 7, 1958. BA, The New Sch., 1961; MA, Columbia U., NYC, 1963; DFA, Yale U., New Haven, Conn., 1967. Mem. faculty Fordham U., Bronx, NY, 1967—, assoc. prof. English, 1971-81, prof., 1981—. Asst. project dir. NEH Shakespeare Summerfest, N.Y.C., 1981; vis. prof. U. Warwick, Eng., 1978, Loyola U., New Orleans, 1994, Dartmouth Coll., 2001-. Author: Middleton's Cynics, 1975, The Revenger's Madness, 1981, Analyzing Shakespeare's Action, 1991, (play) Aaron Burr, (monograph) Poetry and Reality: The Zetema and Its Significance for Poetics, 1977; contbr. to Ency. Americana; contbr. articles to profl. jours including Studies in Philology, Jour. English and German Philology, Shakespeare Quar., Shakespeare Bulletin. Fellow Lawrence Langner Theatre Guild Found., 1965-66; Am. Coun. Learned Socs. grantee, 1981. Home: 116 E 91st St Apt 5 New York NY 10128-1667 Office: English Dept Fordham U Bronx NY 10458

HALLETT, JUDITH PELLER, classical studies educator; b. Chgo., Apr. 4, 1944; d. Leonard and Celia (Stern) Peller; m. Mark Hallett, June 26, 1966; children: Nicholas, Victoria. BA, Wellesley Coll., Mass., 1966; MA, Harvard U., Cambridge, Mass., 1967; PhD, Harvard U., 1971. Lectr. classics Clark U., Worcester, Mass., 1972-74; asst. prof. classical studies Boston U., 1974-82; Blegen vis. rsch. scholar Vassar Coll., Poughkeepsie, NY, 1980; Mellon vis. asst. prof. Brandeis U., Waltham, Mass., 1982-83; assoc. prof. classics U. Md., College Park, 1983-92, prof. classics, 1993—, acting equity adminstr. Coll. Arts & Humanities, 1988-89, chair classics, 1996—2004. Asst. to assoc. editor The Classical World, 1980—; founder, mem. steering com. Women's Classical Caucus, 1972—. Author: Fathers and Daughters in Roman Society, 1984; co-editor: The Personal Voice in Classical Scholarship and Roman Sexualities, 1997; contbr. more than 50 articles to scholarly jours. Mem. Md. Humanities Coun., 2001—; bd. trustees Balt. Hebrew U., 2002—. Fellow, NEH; grantee. Mem. AAUP (pres. chpt. 1994—), Am. Philol. Assn. (dir. 1997-99), Assn. Ancient Historians, Classical Assn. Atlantic States (2d v.p. 1997-98, pres. 1999-2000), Md. Humanities Coun., Phi Beta Kappa (pres. U. Md. College Park chpt. 1996-98). Democrat. Jewish. Home: 5147 Westbard Ave Bethesda MD 20816-1413 Office: Dept Classics U Md College Park MD 20742-0001 Office Phone: 301-405-2024. Business E-Mail: jeph@umd.edu.

HALLETT, MARK, neurologist, educator, medical researcher, director; b. Phila., Oct. 22, 1943; s. Joseph Woodrow and Estelle (Barg) H.; m. Judith E. Peller, June 26, 1966; children: Nicholas L., Victoria C. BA magna cum laude, Harvard U., 1965, MD cum laude, 1969. Diplomate Am. Bd. Psychiatry and Neurology. Resident in neurology Mass. Gen. Hosp., Boston, 1972-75; Moseley fellow Harvard U., London, 1975-76, lectr., assoc. prof. neurology Boston, 1976-84; head clin. neurophy. lab. Brigham and Women's Hosp., Boston, 1976-84; clin. dir. Nat. Inst. Neurol. Disorders and Stroke NIH, Bethesda, Md., 1984-2000, chief human motor control sect. NINDS, 1984—. Author: (with others) Entrapment Neuropathies, 1990, 3d edit., 1998; editor: (with M.F. Brin and J. Jankovic) Scientific and Therapeutic Aspects of Botulinum Toxin, 2002, (with S. Chokroverty) Magnetic Stimulation in Clinical Neurophysiology, 2d edit., 2005, (with others) Psychogenic Movement Disorders. Neurology and Neuropsychiatry, 2006; editor-in-chief: Clinical Neurophysiology, 2000—; assoc. editor Brain, 2006—; contbr. numerous articles to profl. jours. Bd. dirs. Easter Seals Rsch. Found., Chgo., 1985-87; mem. med. adv. bd. Nat. Parkinson Found., Miami, 1985—, Dystonia Med. Rsch. Found., Chgo., 1989-93, 2000-03, Benign Essential Blepharospasm Rsch. Found., Beaumont, 1990—, Myoclonus Rsch. Found., Fort Lee, N.J., 1989-2003. Recipient Physician Rschr. of Yr. award, Physicians Profl. Adv. Com. to Surgeon Gen. of Pub. Health Svc., 1999, Adrian lecture, Internat. Fedn. Clin. Neurophysiology, 1999, Geoffrey Parr Meml. lecture, British Soc. Clin. Neurophysiology, 2004. Mem. Am. Assn. Electrodiagnostic Medicine (pres. 1991-92, Disting. Rschr. Award 2002), Am. Acad. Neurology (v.p. 2001-05, Movement Disorders Rsch. award 2005), Am. Neurol. Assn., Am. Clin. Neurophysiology Soc. (Pierre Gloor award 2004), Soc. for Neurosci., Movement Disorder Soc. (pres. 1999-2000, C. David Marsden lecture 2006), Phi Beta Kappa, Alpha Omega Alpha. Democrat. Jewish. Home: 5147 Westbard Ave Bethesda MD 20816-1413 Office: NINDS NIH Msc 1428 Bldg 10 Rm 5n226 10 Center Dr Bethesda MD 20892-1428 Home Phone: 301-229-2706; Office Phone: 301-496-9526. Business E-Mail: hallettm@ninds.nih.gov.

HALLEY, DIANE ESTHER, artist; b. Jasper, Ind., May 14, 1939; d. John and Esther Margaret (Kruse) Darden; m. Norman B. Halley, May 21, 1966; 1 child, William Tull. BS in Elem. Edn., Ind. State U., Terre Haute, 1961. Tchr. 4th grade, New Albany, Ind., 1961, Seymour, Ind., 1962-64, Westminster, Colo., 1964-68; portrait artist Arvada, Colo., 1979—. Juror fall exhbn. Colo. Watercolor Soc., 2002. Paintings included in books, Colo., 1990—, Denver Art Mus., Best of Watercolor-Painting Textures, 1997, Splash Six-The Magic of Texture, 2000; one-woman shows include Denver Nat. Bank, 1983, Foothills Art Ctr., Golden, Colo., 1984, Nat. Ctr. Atmospheric Rsch., Boulder, Colo., 1991, Colo. Christian U., 2000, exhibitions include Lincoln Ctr., Ft. Collins, Colo., 2003, Challenge of Champions, Watercolor Art Soc. Houston, 2003, 53rd Nat. Exhbn. of Contemporary Realism in Art, Acad. Artists Assn., 2003, Artists Who Happen to be Women, Tex. A&M U., 2004, Watercolor Mo. Nat., Winston Churchill Meml. Libr., 2004 (Bd. Dirs. award, 2004), Great 8 Exhbn., Kans. Watercolor Soc., Wichita Art Mus., 2004, 2006, 50th Anniversary Mem. Exhbn., Colo. Watercolor Soc., 2004, Small Works Exhbn., Attleboro Art Mus., 2005, Brand Libr. and Art Ctr., 2006, Karpeles Libr. Mus., 2006, Ports of Call Gallery, 2006, Western Fedn. Watercolors Socs., Arvada Ctr. for the Arts, 2007. Pres. Clear Creek Valley Med. Aux., Lakewood, Colo., 1973—74, 1991—92. Recipient Founder's award, Colo. Watercolor Soc., 1992, Pres.'s award, 1994, Best in Show award, Colo. Watercolor Soc. 50th Ann. Exbn., 2004, Grumbacher award, Pikes Peak Watercolor Soc., 1995, Cash award, Lakewood Arts Coun., 2001, Award of Distinction, Mo. Nat. Watercolor Exhbn., 2003, Westminster Cmty. Artist Series award, 2003. Mem.: Mo. Watercolor Soc. (signature mem.), Kans. Watercolor Soc. (signature mem., Am. artist cash award 1999), Rocky Mountain Nat. Watermedia Soc. (signature mem.), Nat. Watercolor Soc. (signature mem., Del Mar Coll. award 1981), Nat. Assn. Women Artists (signature mem., Cecil Shapiro Meml. award 1998), Catherine Lorillard Wolf Art Club (signature mem., Adriana Zahn award 1985, Cynthia Goodgal award 1986). Avocations: Bible study, bridge, gardening. Home: 6631 Osceola Ct Arvada CO 80003-6426

HALLEY, JAMES WOODS, physics professor; b. Chgo., Nov. 16, 1938; m. Merile Hobbs (dec. 2001); 2 children. BS, MIT, 1961; PhD, U. Calif., Berkeley, 1965. NSF predoctoral fellow U. Calif., Berkeley, 1963-65; NSF postdoctoral fellow Faculte des Scis., Orsay, France, 1965-66; asst. prof. U. Calif., Berkeley, 1966-68; assoc. prof. U. Minn., Mpls., 1968-77, prof. physics, 1977—, fellow Supercomputing Inst., grad. faculty materials sci., 1989—. Vis. prof. Oxford U., 1973, Harwell AERE, 1973, U. Oreg., 1975, Yale U., 1976, Brookhaven N.L., 1976, 79, Harvard U., 1979, Mich. State U., 1980, Argonne, 1981—, Inst. Theoretical Physics, Santa Barbara, Calif., 1983, Santa Barbara, 97, Santa Barbara, 98, U. Calif., Santa Barbara, 1984, Berkeley, 93, IBM Almaden Rsch. Ctr., 1987, Australian Nat. U., 1988; cons. 3M, 1985—89, UNESCO, 1986, GM Corp., 1989—90, Ednl. Testing Svc., 1989, mem. GRE bd. examiners, 1991—96; cons. Nat. Renewable Energy Lab., 1992—97; physics bd. dirs. US Com. Sci. Coop. with Vietnam, 1985—. Author: Physics of Human Motion, 1981, Statistical Mechanics, 2006; editor: 7 books; contbr. articles to profl. jours. Recipient George Taylor Tchg. award, 1979, McMillan professorship, 1979; grantee, NSF, 1972—79, 1995—, Rsch. Corp., 1970—72, Corrosion Ctr., 1980—92, Ednl. Devel. Program, 1973, 1979, 3M, 1982, 2002—05, IBM Advanced Edn. Project, 1985, Dept. Edn., 1986, IBM, 1988—90, Electric Power Rsch. Inst., 1988—90, Dept. Energy, 1990—, Sumitomo Metal Industries, 1992—93, NASA, 1992—95; Bush fellow, 1983—84. Fellow: Am. Phys. Soc.; mem.: AAAS, Materials Rsch. Soc., Am. Chem. Soc. Achievements include research in theory of disorder in condensed matter; statistics and dynamics of polymers; physics of the fluid-solid interface; high temperature superconductivity; condensate fraction in bose superfluids. Office: Univ Minn Sch Physics and Astronomy Minneapolis MN 55455 Office Phone: 612-624-0395. E-mail: woods@woods1.spa.umn.edu.

HALLEY, JANET E., law educator; BA in English Lit. summa cum laude, Princeton U., 1974; PhD in English Lit., UCLA, 1980; JD, Yale U., 1988. Mem. English faculty Hamilton Coll., Clinton, NY, 1980—85; law clk. to Chief Judge Gilbert Merritt US Ct. Appeals 6th Cir., 1988—89; assoc. Skadden, Arps, Slate, Meagher & Flom, Boston, 1989—91; assoc. prof. Stanford Law Sch., 1991—95, prof., 1995—2000; prof. law Harvard Law Sch., Cambridge, Mass., 2000—. Vis. prof. law Harvard Law Sch., 1999. Author: Don't: A Reader's Guide to the Military Anti-Gay Policy, 1999. Named Robert E. Paradise Faculty Scholar for Excellence in Teaching and Rsch., Stanford Law Sch., 1996. Office: Harvard Law Sch 1563 Massachusetts Ave Cambridge MA 02138 Office Phone: 617-496-0182. Office Fax: 617-496-4947.

HALLGREN, RICHARD EDWIN, meteorologist; b. Kersey, Pa., Mar. 15, 1932; s. Edwin Leonard and Edith Marie Hallgren; m. Maxine Hope Anderson, Apr. 17, 1954; children: Scott, Douglas, Lynette. BS, Pa. State U., 1953, PhD, 1960; DSc (hon.), SUNY, 1989. Sys. engr. IBM Corp., 1960-64; sci. adv. to asst. sec. of commerce, 1964-66; dir. world weather sys. ESSA, Rockville, Md., 1966-69, asst. adminstrn., 1969-70; asst. adminstr. NOAA, Rockville, 1970-71, assoc. adminstr. environ. monitoring and prediction, 1971-73, asst. adminstr. for ocean and atmospheric scis., 1977-79; dep. dir. Nat. Weather Svc., Silver Spring, Md., 1973-77, dir., 1979-88; exec. dir. Am. Meteorol. Soc., 1988-99, exec. dir. emeritus, 1999—. Permanent U.S. rep. World Meteorol. Orgn., 1980—88. Contbr. articles to sci. jours. With USAF, 1954—56. Named Meritorious Sr. Exec., 1980, Disting. Sr. Exec., 1986; recipient Arthur S. Flemming award, U.S. C. of C., 1968, Gold medal, Dept. Commerce, 1969, Internat. Meteorol. Orgn. prize, Wold Meteorol. Orgn., 1990, Spl. Achievement award, NOAA, 2001, Charles L. Hosler medal, 2002; Alumni fellow, Pa. State U. Fellow: AAAS, Am. Meteorol. Soc. (hon.; pres., Cleveland Abbe award 2003, C.F. Brooks award 1986); mem.: Am. Geogphys. Union, Oceanog. Soc. Lutheran. Home: 11428 Cedar Ridge Dr Potomac MD 20854-3761 Office: Am Meteorol Svc 1120 G St NW Ste 800 Washington DC 20005-6115 Office Phone: 202-737-9006 ext. 413. Business E-Mail: hallgren@ametsoc.org.

HALLIBURTON, LLOYD, retired Romance philology educator; b. Shreveport, La., July 31, 1934; s. Ralph Eloe and Mary Katherine (Smith) H.; m. Donna Lee Cavanagh, May 27, 1965 (div. Sept. 1976); children: Richard Lloyd, William Cavanagh de Tuite, Cristopher Lee, Manon Lee; m. María F. Sánchez, Jan. 6, 1993; children: Carlos David, Lawden Nerea. AB, Centenary Coll., 1955; MA, La. State U., 1961, PhD, 1970; C en F y L, U. de Valladolid, Spain, 1965; LittD (hon.), London Inst. for Applied Rsch., 1993. Instr. Spanish U. Notre Dame, Ind., 1962-63; asst. prof. Spanish Centenary Coll., Shreveport, 1963-66, Va. Mil. Inst., Lexington, 1966-69, assoc. prof. Spanish, 1970-80, asst. commandant, 1971-74; asst. prof. fgn. langs. La. Tech. U., Ruston, 1981-84, assoc. prof., 1984-91, prof., 1991—2007, dir. grad. program in romance langs., 1992-95; ret., 2007. Vis. lectr. Romance langs. U. N.C., 1970; adj. prof. Spanish U. Va., Charlottesville, 1978—80; vis. prof. English Ga. Mil. Coll., Barksdale AFB, La., 1980—81, Grambling State U., 1986, 2001—05, U. Autónoma de Coahuila, Centro de Idiomas, Mexico, 2002; cons. USAF, U.S. Dept. Justice, Mosher Steel Co., Studebaker Internat., Irrigation Internat. de Mex., others; rsch. bd. advisors Am. Biog. Inst. Author: Colombia en la Poesía, 1967, Hendaye, 1990, Saddle Soldiers: General William Stokes and the 4th South Carolina Cavalry, 1993, The Cemaco Seed, 1996, García Lorca and Other Things Spanish: Critical Essays, 2002, John William Corrington: Reflections, 2003, The Duende: A Novel, 2005, The Duende: A Play, 2007; contbr. articles to profl. jours., US, Colombia, Spain, Hungary and Germany. Mem. State Dem. Com., Lincoln Parish, La., 1984-94. Capt. U.S. Army, 1955-57. NDEA fellow, 1959-62; Fulbright fellow, 1965; NEH fellow, 1971; postdoctoral fellow La. State U., 1992; grantee VMI Found., La. Tech. U., 1967-92, La Tech summer rsch. grantee, Spain, 1998, 2001, 04, 05. Mem. Coun. for Devel. of Spanish in La., Phi Kappa Phi, Phi Sigma Iota, Sigma Tau Delta, Sigma Delta Pi, Alpha Chi, Omicron Delta Kappa. Roman Catholic. Avocations: gardening, hunting, fishing.

HALLIDAY, IAN, astronomer; b. Lloydminster, Sask., Can., Nov. 10, 1928; s. Clarence Peter and Edith Victoria (Phillips) H.; m. Norma Lillian Mobley, July 7, 1951; children— John Douglas, Janet Elizabeth. BA, U. Toronto, 1949, MA, 1950, PhD, 1954. Sr. sci. officer Dominion Obs., Dept. Energy, Mines and Resources, Ottawa, 1952-70; sr. research officer Herzberg Inst. Astrophysics, Nat. Research Council Can., Ottawa, 1970-90, guest worker, 1990-96. Author research papers in field; editor: Jour. Royal Astron. Soc. Can, 1970-75; co-editor: Solid Particles in the Solar System, 1980. Recipient Polish Medal of Merit, 1976, Queen's Silver Jubilee medal, 1977. Fellow Royal Soc. Can.; mem. Internat. Astron. Union (pres. commn. 22 1976-79), Royal Astron. Soc. Can. (pres. 1980-82, hon. pres. 1989-93), Can. Astron. Soc., Am. Astron. Soc., Meteoritical Soc., Planetary Soc., Internat. Halley Watch (chmn. steering group 1985-90). Home: 825 Killeen Ave Ottawa ON Canada K2A 2X8

HALLIDAY, JOHN MEECH, investment company executive; b. St. Louis, Oct. 16, 1936; s. William Norman and Vivian Viola (Meech) Halliday; children: Richard M., Elizabeth. BS, US Naval Acad., 1958; MBA, Harvard U., 1964. Dir. budgeting and planning Automatic Tape Control, Bloomington, Ill., 1964-66; dir. planning Ralston-Purina, St. Louis, 1966-67, v.p. subsidiary, 1967-68, dir. internat. banking, 1967-68; v.p. Servicetime Corp., St. Louis, 1968-70; assoc. R.W. Halliday Assocs., Boise, Idaho, 1970-87. V.p. Sawtooth Comm. Corp., Boise, 1970-73, Comdr. Corp., 1979-81; pres., CEO, bd. dirs. May Lundy Mine, San Francisco, 1979-2005, H.W.L. Inc., San Francisco, 1985-93; pres. Halliday Labs., Inc., 1980-91; exec. v.p., bd. dirs. Franchise Fin. Corp. Am., Phoenix, 1980-85; bd. dirs., v.p. Harvard Bus. Sch. Assn. No. Calif., 1980-87; pres., CEO, bd. dirs. Cycletrol Diversified Industries, Inc., 1992—; guest lectr. U. Calif. Berkeley, 1991-2000, Calif. Bus.-Higher Edn. Forum, 1995-98; sponsor Halliday lectr. in astronomy, U. Calif. Santa Cruz, 2000—. Pres. Big Bros. San Francisco, 1978-81; trustee, pres. U. Calif.-Santa Cruz Found., 1988—, mem. Pres.Circle, US Naval Acad., Annapolis, 1997—; mem. ad hoc com. on corrections Calif. State Senate, 1995-96; fellow bd. visitors and fellows viticulture and enology U. Calif., Davis, 1999—; sponsor undergrad. rsch. symposium U. Calif. Santa Cruz, 2002—; bd. dirs., charter dir. circle Seymour Marine Discovery Ctr., 2002—. Mem. Restaurant Assn. (v.p. 1969-70), Olympic Club (San Francisco). Republican. Baptist. Office: 55 New Montgomery St Ste 317 San Francisco CA 94105-3426 Home: Apt 4 190 Miller Ave Mill Valley CA 94941-2779 Office Phone: 415-957-1221. Personal E-mail: jhalli8835@aol.com.

HALLIDAY, JOSEPH WILLIAM, lawyer; b. NYC, Aug. 9, 1938; s. Joseph John and Marie (Marro) H.; m. Vivian Ross Talbird, July 10, 1960; children: Katherine Ann Langan, Mary Allison Shaw. AB egregia cum laude, Fordham U., 1960, LLB cum laude, 1963. Bar: NY 1964, DC 1965. Assoc. White & Case, NYC, 1965-72, ptnr., 1972-85, Skadden, Arps, Slate, Meagher & Flom, LLP, NYC, 1985—2003, of counsel, 2004—, founder, banking and institutional investing group. Mem. Tribar Legal Opinion Com., lectr. Ctr. for Internat. Banking Studies, U. Va., Banking Law Inst., Inst. Internat. Rsch., Law and Bus., Euromoney, Practicing Law Inst., Law and Business, ABA, NY State Bar Assn. Prog. Editor-in-chief Fordham Law Rev., 1962-63; contbr. author, The Banking Jour. Served to 1st lt. US Army, 1963—65. Mem. ABA, NY State Bar Assn.(banking law com.), Assn. of Bar of City of NY, NY County Lawyers Assn., Larchmont Yacht Club (commodore 1985-86). Independent. Roman Catholic. Avocations: yachting, skiing, golf. Office: Skadden Arps Slate Meagher & Flom LLP 4 Times Sq New York NY 10036 Office Phone: 212-735-3260. Office Fax: 917-777-3260. Business E-Mail: jhallida@skadden.com.

HALLIDAY, WILLIAM ROSS, retired physician, speleologist, writer; b. Atlanta, May 9, 1926; s. William Ross and Jane (Wakefield) H.; m. Eleanore Hartvedt, July 2, 1951 (dec. 1983); children: Marcia Lynn, Patricia Anne, William Ross III; m. Louise Baird Kinnard, May 7, 1988. BA, Swarthmore Coll., 1946; MD, George Washington U., 1948. Diplomate Am. Bd. Vocat. Experts. Intern Huntington Meml. Hosp., Pasadena, Calif., 1948-49; resident King County Hosp., Seattle, Denver Children's Hosp., L.D.S. Hosp., Salt Lake City, 1950-57; pvt. practice Seattle, 1957-65; with Wash. State Dept. Labor and Industries, Olympia, 1965-76; med. dir. Wash. State Div. Vocat. Rehab., 1976-82; staff physican N.W. Occupational Health Ctr., Seattle, 1983-84; med. dir. N.W. Vocat. Rehab. Group, Seattle, 1984, Comprehensive Med. Rehab. Ctr., Brentwood, Tenn., 1984-87. Dep. coroner King County, Wash., 1964—66. Author: Adventure Is Underground, 1959, Depths of the Earth, 1966, 76, American Caves and Caving, 1974, 82, Floyd Collins of Sand Cave, 1998; co-author: (with Robert Nymeyer) Carlsbad Cavern: The Early Years, 1991; editor Jour. Spelean History, 1968-73, Hawaiian Volcanoes, 2005; contbr. articles to profl. jours. Cons. Egyptian Environ. Affairs Agency; mem. North Cascades Conservation Coun., v.p., 1962—63; pres. Internat. Speleological Found., 1981—87, Internat. Union Speleol. Com. on Volcanic Caves, 1992—98, hon. pres., 1998—; asst. dir. Internat. Glaciospeleological Survey, 1972—76; mem. Gov.'s North Cascades Study Com., 1967—76; chmn. Hawaii Speleol. Survey, 1989—97; dir. We. Speleol. Survey, 1957—83, dir. rsch., 1983—96. Served to lt. USNR, 1949—50, served to lt. comdr USNR, 1955—57. Recipient medal Geol. Soc. China; named Alumnus of Yr., George Sch., 1992. Fellow Am. Coll. Chest Physicians, Nat. Speleological Soc. (hon. mem. 1965, bd. govs. 1950-2001), Explorers Club; mem. AMA, Nat. Trust (Scotland), Geol. Soc. Am. (geol. and health divsn.), Mars Soc., Seattle Tennis Club, Internat. Union Conservation Nature World Com. on Protected Areas.

HALLIGAN, JAMES EDMUND, academic administrator, chemical engineer; b. Moorland, Iowa, June 23, 1936; s. Raymond Anthony and Margaret Ann Halligan; m. Ann Elizabeth Sorenson, June 29, 1957; children: Michael, Patrick, Christopher. MS in Chem. Engring, Iowa State U., 1962, MS, 1965, PhD, 1968. Registered profl. engr., Okla. Process engr. Humble Oil Co., 1962-64; mem. faculty Tex. Tech U., 1968-77; dean engring. U. Mo., Rolla, 1977-79, U. Ark., Fayetteville, 1979-82, vice chancellor for acad. affairs, 1982-83, interim chancellor, 1983-84; pres. N.Mex. State U., Las Cruces, 1984-94, Okla. State U., Stillwater, 1994—2003, pres. emeritus, 2003—. Mem. Gov. Tex. Energy Adv. Council, 1972-74; prof. achievement citation engr. Iowa State U. Coll. Engring., 1984. Served with USAF, 1954-58. Recipient Disting. Teaching award Tex. Tech U., 1972, Disting. Research award, 1975, 76; Disting. Teaching award U. Mo., Rolla, 1978, Disting. Achievement citation Iowa State U. Alumni Assn., 1996. Mem. AIChE, Rotary, Tau Beta Pi, Phi Kappa Phi, Pi Mu Epsilon. Roman Catholic. Office: Okla State U 470 SU Stillwater OK 74078-1010

HALLILA, BRUCE ALLAN, welding engineer; b. Washington, Nov. 2, 1950; s. Esko Ensio and Gertrude Naomi (Tilley) H.; m. Pamela Joan Guerin, Dec. 18, 1982; children: Gregory Michael Decedue, April Patrice, Andrew Allan, Joshua Scott. BSME, BS in Welding Engring., LeTourneau U., 1974. Welding engr. Chgo. Bridge & Iron Co., Houston, 1975-77, Avondale Shipyards, Inc., New Orleans, 1977-80, asst. shipbuilding supt., 1980-82; steel supt. Halter Marine, Inc., New Orleans, 1982; welding supt. Bell Halter, Inc., New Orleans, 1982-84; sr. welding engr. Avondale Industries, Inc., New Orleans, 1984-86, chief welding engr., 1986-97; asst. plant sup. Pellerin Milnor Corp., Kenner, La., 1997—. Vice chmn. welding com. Ogden Corp., N.Y.C., 1984-86; welding cons. Gas Tech. Cons., Inc., Metairie, La., 1990—; CWI test proctor Am. Welding Soc., Miami, 1979-97; welding industry cons. State of La VoTech Welding Coun., Metairie, 1982—; panel mem. welding R & D, Maritime Adminstrn.; adv. bd. La. Tech. Coll.-Jefferson Campus, 2002-. Mem. com. troop 33 Boy Scouts Am., 1991-97. Recipient Gov.'s award State of La., Baton Rouge, 1982. Mem. Am. Welding Soc. (dist. 9 dir. 1994-97, D3 com., 1997, CWI test supr. 1997—, chmn. sect. cert. 1997—, judge regional sci. and engring. fair 1997—, chmn. student scholarship award 1997—, Proposer award 1982, Dist. Meritorious award 1987, 92, named Disting. Mem. 1989, Sect. Educator award 2000, Silver mem. 2000), Am. Bur. Shipping (spl. com. on materials and welding 1997), Delta Sigma Psi. Republican. Avocations: woodworking, welding, photography. Home: 8725 Carriage Rd River Ridge LA 70123-3605 Office: Pellerin Milnor Corp PO Box 400 Kenner LA 70063-0400 E-mail: bahallila@aol.com.

HALLIN, DANIEL CLARK, communications educator; b. Palo Alto, Calif., June 11, 1953; BA in Polit. Sci. with honors, U. Calif., Berkeley, 1973, MA in Polit. Sci., 1974, PhD in Polit. Sci., 1980. Fellow Freedom Forum Media Studies Ctr., Columbia U., NYC, 1991-92; prof. dept. comm., adj. prof. polit. sci. U. Calif., San Diego, 1980—, chairperson, 1994-97. Assoc. Ctr. for War, Peace and News Media; presenter, keynote spkr. various ednl. symposia and confs., most recently at U. Stockholm, 2005, U. Goteborg, 2005, Copenhagen Bus. Sch., 2005, U. Milan, 2005, ITESM, Monterrey, Mex., 2004; Merkator prof. Inst. Medienwissenschaft U. Dusseldorf, 2000. Author: The "Uncensored War": The Media and Vietnam, 1989, The Presidency, The Press and the People, 1992, We Keep America on Top of the World: Television Journalism and the Public Sphere, 1994, Comparing Media Systems: Three Models of Media and Politics, 2004; contbr. chpt. to: Critical Theory and Public Life, 1985, Political Communication: Approaches, Studies, Assessments, 1987, Reading the News, 1986, Watching Television, 1986, Is the Cold War Over? Images of the USA and the USSR in Soviet and American Media, 1991, Comparatively Speaking, 1992, Viewing War: How the Media Handled the Persian Gulf, 1994; co-contbr. chpt. to: Taken by Storm: The Media, Public Opinion and U.S. Foreign Policy in the Gulf War, 1994, Mass Media and Society, 2005, Dewesternizing Media Studies, 2000, Tabloid Tales, 2000,Bourdieu and the Journalistic Field, 2004; mem. editl. bd. Polit. Comm.; contbr. articles and revs. to profl. publs. Pres. Binat. Assn. Schs. of Comm. of the Californias, 1997-99; bd. dirs. Internat. Comm. Assn. Recipient 1st prize media studies project essay contest Woodrow Wilson Internat. Ctr. for Scholars, 1990, Goldsmith Book award Harvard U, 2005. Mem. Am. Polit. Sci. Assn., L.Am. Studies Assn., Internat. Comm. Assn., Nat. Comm. Assn. (Diamond Anniversary Book award 2005). Home: 3315 31st St San Diego CA 92104-4619 Office: Univ Calif San Diego Dept Comm 0503 La Jolla CA 92093 E-mail: dhallin@weber.ucsd.edu.

HALLINAN, JOSEPH THOMAS, journalist; b. Barberton, Ohio, Sept. 3, 1960; s. Neil Patrick and Judith Ann (Tonovitz) H.; m. Pamela L. Taylor, Sept. 10, 2000; children: Jack, Katherine, Anne. BS magna cum laude, Boston U., 1984. Reporter The Indpls. Star, 1984-91; nat. corr. Newhouse News Svc., Washington, 1991-99; reporter Chgo. Tribune, 1999-2000; staff reporter The Wall St. Jour., 2000—07. Vis. prof. Vanderbilt U., 2006. Author: Going Up The River: Travels in a Prison Nation, 2001. Recipient Pulitzer prize for investigative reporting, 1991; named Disting. Alumni, Boston U., 1992; Nieman fellow Harvard U., 1997-98. Roman Catholic. Avocations: fishing, travel. Home: 3750 Lake Shore Dr Chicago IL 60613

HALLINAN, MAUREEN THERESA, sociologist, educator; BA, Marymount Coll., 1961; MS, U. Notre Dame, 1968; PhD, U. Chgo., 1972. Prof. U. Wis., Madison, 1980-84; with U. Notre Dame, Ind., 1984—, William P. and Hazel B. White prof. arts and letters dept. sociology, dir. Ctr. Rsch. Ednl. Opportunity. Author: The Structure of Positive Sentiment, 1974; editor: Sociology of Edn., 1981—86, The Social Context of Instruction: Group Organization and Group Processes, 1983, The Social Organization of Schools: New Conceptualizations of the Learning Process, 1987, Change in Societal Institutions, 1990, Restructuring Schools: Promising Practices and Policies, 1995, Handbook of the Sociology of Education, 2000, Handbook of the Sociology of Education, Chinese edit., 2004, Handbook of the Sociology of Education, paperback edit., 2006; co-editor: Stability and Change in American Education: Structure, Process and Outcomes, 2003, School Sector and Student Outcomes, 2006; assoc. editor: Social Forces, 1977—80, Sociology of Edn., 1979—81, 1991—2001; contbr. articles to profl. jours. Mem.: Nat. Acad. Edn. (v.p. fellows 2001—05), Sociol. Rsch. Assn. (sec.-treas. 1999—2000, pres. 2000—01), Am. Sociol. Assn. (session organizer 1980, 1984, sec.-treas. 1988—90, session organizer 1989, chmn. sociology edn. sect. 1991—92, chmn. 1991—92, session organizer 1992, pres. 1995—96, session organizer 1996—2001, Willard Waller award 2004), Phi Beta Kappa. Office: U Notre Dame Dept Sociology Notre Dame IN 46556 Business E-Mail: pauley.1@nd.edu.

HALLISSEY, MICHAEL, retired management consultant; b. Southampton, England, Mar. 6, 1943; s. John Francis and Mary (Kendall) H. Grad., Magdalen Coll., Oxford U., Eng., 1964. Chartered acct., Eng. With Price Waterhouse, 1964-98, asst. mgr. Melbourne, Australia, 1968, Milan, 1969, ptnr. London, 1974-98, head practice devel., 1979-81, head strategic planning, 1981-82, head corp. fin. svcs., 1983-88; dir. strategy Price Waterhouse Europe, 1988-98, PricewaterhouseCoopers (formerly Price Waterhouse), 1998—2003; vis. fellow Imperial Coll. Sci. and Tech., London, 1998—2003; ret., 2003. Contbr. articles to profl. publs. Fellow Royal Soc. of Arts; mem. Inst. Chartered Accts. Eng. and Wales. Mem. Ch. of Eng. Avocations: politics, sailing, music, opera. Home: 66 Waterside Point Anhalt Rd London SW11 4PD England

HALLMAN, CECILIA ANN, real estate consultant; d. James Cecil and Lillie Mae Hallman. Certificate in dentistry, Midland Tech. Coll., Columbia, SC, 1972; student, U. S.C., Aiken, 1993; MBA in Essentials 1 Cert., Tulane U., 2004; Art certificate, Oxford U., 2005. Lic. real estate S.C., Ark. Property mgr. Wyatt Devel. Co., Inc., Aiken, 1987—89, The Keenan Co., Columbia, 1989—90; co-owner, mgr. Aiken Indsl. Supply, Inc., 1990—92; office adminstr. Dr. Rocky L. Napier, Aiken, 1992—96; dir. of mem. svcs. Wyatt Devel./Sage Valley Golf Club, Aiken, SC, 1996—2002; dir. mem. svcs. Stephens Inc./The Alotian Club, Little Rock, 2002—04. Author, pub.: The Memphis Kingmaker, 2006. Vol. Am. Cancer Soc., Aiken, 1990—92. Mem.: Woodside Plantation Country Club (assoc.), Green Boundary Club (assoc.), Rotary. Home and Office: 223 Forest Pines Rd Aiken SC 29803 Home Phone: 803-644-4244. Office Fax: 803-642-8023. Personal E-mail: irgllc@gforcecable.com.

HALLMAN, GARY L., photographer, educator; b. St. Paul, Aug. 7, 1940; s. Jack J. and Helen A. Hallman; 1 child, Peter J. BA, U. Minn., 1966, MFA, 1971. Mem. faculty dept. studio arts U. Minn., Mpls., 1970—, assoc. prof. photography, 1976—. Vis. adj. prof. R.I. Sch. Design, 1977-78; vis. exchange prof. U. N.Mex., 1984-85; vis. assoc. prof. The Colo. Coll., Colorado Springs, 1990; mem. visual arts adv. bd. Minn. State Arts Coun., 1973-76; bd. dirs. Minn. Artists Exhbn. Program, 1989-91. Exhbns. include Internat. Mus. Photography, George Eastman House, 1974, Light Gallery, N.Y.C., 1975, Balt. Mus., 1975, Mus. Modern Art, N.Y.C., 1978, Mpls. Inst. Arts, 1996, B. Gray Gallery East Carolina U., Greenville, N.C., 1997, Nat. Mus. of Am., Washington, 1984, Frederick R. Weisman Art Mus., Mpls., 1998; Mississippi/Neva curator The State Russian Mus., St. Petersburg, 1998; Barg Gallery/Teheran Mus. Contemporary Art, 2001, Risk/Revisit: The Photography of Gary Hallman, PARTs Gallery, Mpls., 2002, McKnight Found. Open Spaces Project, 2002; co-curator Persian Silver, Tehran Mus. Contemporary Art, 2004, (solo) Mus. of Non-Conformist Art, St. Petersburg, Russa, 2005; represented in permanent collections Mus. Modern Art, N.Y.C., Internat. Mus. Photography, Rochester, N.Y., Nat. Gallery Can., Fogg Art Mus., Harvard U., Princeton U. Art Mus., Nat. Mus. Am. Art, Smithsonian Instn., Washington., Mus. Non-conformist Art, St. Petersburg, 2005, Gallery 13, Mpls., 2005. Served with USN, 1958-61. Nat. Endowment Arts fellow, 1975-76; Bush Found. fellow, 1976-77; McKnight Found. fellow, 1982, 90, Artist Assistance fellowship grant, 1996. Mem. Soc. Photog. Edn., Coll. Art Assn. Am. Office: U Minn Dept Studio Arts Minneapolis MN 55455 Office Phone: 612-625-8096. Business E-Mail: hallm001@umn.edu.

HALLMAN, LINDA D., medical association administrator; b. Wash., DC; BA in Music Edn., Indiana U.; MS in Orgnl. Mgmt., George Wash. U. COO Am. Coll. Heathcare Adminstrs., Alexandria, Va.; dir. profl. svcs. Am. Coll. Healthcare Adminstrs., 1989—94, dir. member svcs., 1989—94; pres. Am. Hort. Soc., Alexandria, Va., 1997—2002; exec. dir. Am. Med. Women's Assn., Alexandria, Va., 2002—. Mem.: Assn. Fundraising Professionals, Am. Soc. Assn. Executives.

HALLMAN, MAX O., humanities professor, philosophy professor, director; b. Graniteville, SC, Feb. 21, 1952; s. Oneal and Naomi (Screws) Hallman; m. Gail Ann Davis Marconi, June 15, 1972 (div. July 21, 1975); m. Bobbie Ann Redd, June 28, 1978 (div. Oct. 7, 1998); children: Hannah, Dylan, Aliena Kyzer; m. Cheryl Louise Botts, July 11, 2007. BA, U. SC, Columbia, 1974, MA, 1976; PhD, Tulane U., New Orleans, 1985. Instr. philosophy Loyola U., New Orleans, 1983—85; prof. philosophy and humanities Merced Coll., Calif., 1986—, dir. honors program, 1987—, chair humanities divsn., 2006—. Contbr. articles to profl. jours. Recipient Advisor Continued Excellence award, Phi Theta Kappa, 1997, 1999.

Mem.: Am. Philos. Assn. D-Liberal. Avocations: record collecting, travel, poetry. Home: 2927 Santa Cruz Ave Merced CA 95340 Office: Merced Coll 3600 M St Merced CA 95348 Home Phone: 209-726-5156; Office Phone: 209-384-6327. Business E-Mail: hallman.m@mccd.edu.

HALLMAN, PATRICIA L., musician, educator; d. Robert A. and Theda E. Laubach; m. Donald L. Hallman, June 3, 1967; children: Jonathan A., Katherine E. BS in Music Edn., Susquehanna U., Selinsgrove, Pa., 1966. Cert. tchr. Pa. Jr. HS music tchr. Quakertown Cmty. Sch. Dist., Pa., 1966—69; elem. music specialist Upper Merion Area Sch. Dist., King of Prussia, Pa., 1968—2006. Musician, substitute musician Trinity Luth. Ch., Ft. Washington, Pa., 1965—; dir. children's summer history camp Hope Lodge State Hist. Site, Ft. Washington, 1986—96; accompanist Philomusica Chorale of Delaware Valley, Phila., 1984—. Transcriber, writer, arranger (musical for children) The Bubble Gum Mayor, 1994. Sunday sch. tchr., choir mem.; bd. dirs., sec. Laubach Family Assn. Named Friend of Libr., Upper Merion Twp. Libr., 2004; named to Wall of Fame, Upper Merion Area Sch. Dist., 1995. Mem.: NEA, Upper Merion Area Edn. Assn., Pa. State Edn. Assn., Pa. Music Educators' Assn., Music Educators' Nat. Conf., Sigma Alpha Iota. Lutheran. Avocations: reading, travel. Home: 609 Hartranft Ave Fort Washington PA 19034 Office: Caley Elem Sch 725 Caley Rd King Of Prussia PA 19406 Home Phone: 215-643-2111. Business E-Mail: phallman@umasd.org.

HALLMARK, DONALD PARKER, museum director, educator; b. McPherson, Kans., Feb. 16, 1945; s. Daniel Clell and Esther Ione (Hart) H.; m. Linda Lorraine Lego, June 10, 1967; m. Monica Lynn, Amy Kristen. BFA, U. Ill., 1967; MA, U. Iowa, 1970; PhD, St. Louis U., 1980. From asst. prof. to prof. Greenville (Ill.) Coll., 1970-81, chmn. art dept., 1976-81; dir. Richard W. Bock Sculpture Collection, Greenville, 1975-81, Frank Lloyd Wright's Dana-Thomas House Hist. Site, Springfield, Ill., 1981—. Founding bd. mem. Frank Lloyd Wright Bldg Conservancy, Chgo., 1988-96; adj. prof. Sangamon State U., Springfield, 1986-90; lectr. FLW Bldg. Conservancy, Hollyhock House, L.A., The Gamble House, Pasadena, Calif., The High Mus., Atlanta, Decorative Arts Soc. SAH, Chgo., Indpls. Pub. Libr., The Natural Pattern of Structure Herberger Lectrs., Ariz. State U., Tempe, Art Inst. Chgo., FLW Bldg. Conservancy, Unity Temple, Oak Park, Ill., FLW Home and Studio Lectrs., Oak Park Pub. Libr., Mus. of Our Nat. Heritage, Lexington, Mass., The Chgo. Arch. Found., Santa Fe Bldg., Chgo., Nat. Bldg. Mus., Washington, Ctrl. Ill. AIA, Decatur. Author: (booklet) The Dana-Thomas House: Its History, Acquisition and Preservation, 1992, (catalogue) Paul Ashbrook, 1990, (illustrated book) Springfield's Lawrence School Memorial Library, 1993, The Natural Pattern of Structure, 1995; TV interview appearances Bob Vila's Guide to Historic Homes, The Dana-Thomas House, 1996, interview Frank Lloyd Wright and the Prairie School, Films for Humanities and Scis., 1999, Home and Garden TV, 2000; editor newsletter Guidelines for the Conservation of Frank Lloyd Wright Decorative Arts, 1996. Cons., sponsor Ill. Govt. Intern Program, Springfield, 1985—; libr. cons., vol. Michael Victor II Libr. Springfield Art Assn., 1988-93. Faculty grantee Shell Found., 1975; Grad. fellow St. Louis U., 1976. Mem.: Nat. Trust for Historic Preservation, The Frank Lloyd Wright Bldg. Conservancy. Presbyterian. Avocations: slide library collecting, antiques, travel, gardening. Home: 605 W Sheridan Rd Petersburg IL 62675-1359 Office: Ill Hist Preservation Agy 301 E Lawrence Ave Springfield IL 62703-2232 Office Phone: 217-782-6776.

HALLO, WILLIAM WOLFGANG, literature and language professor, writer; b. Kassel, Germany, Mar. 9, 1928; came to U.S., 1940, naturalized, 1946; s. Rudolf and Gertrude (Rubensohn) H.; m. Edith Sylvia Pinto, June 22, 1952 (dec. Oct. 10, 1994); children: Ralph Ethan, Jacqueline Louise; m. Nanette Stahl, Oct. 18, 1998. BA magna cum laude, Harvard U., 1950; candidatus Litterarum Semiticarum, U. Leiden, Netherlands, 1951; MA, U. Chgo., 1953, PhD, 1955; MA (hon.), Yale U., 1965; DHL (hon.), Hebrew Union Coll.-Jewish Inst. Religion, 1986. Rsch. asst. U. Chgo. Oriental Inst., 1954—56; from instr. to asst. prof. Bible and Semitic langs. Hebrew Union Coll.-Jewish Inst. Religion, Cin., 1956-62; asst. prof. Assyriology Yale U., 1962—65, prof. Assyriology, 1965-75, William M. Laffan prof. Assyriology and Babylonian lit., 1976—2002, prof. emeritus, 2002—; curator Babylonian collection, 1963-2001; master Morse Coll., 1982-87; chmn. dept. Near Eastern langs. and civilizations, 1975-82, 85-89. Chmn. Univ. (now adv.) com. on Judaic Studies, 1979-84, acting chmn., 1998; vis. prof. Mid. Eastern civilization Columbia U., 1970-71, 80, Jewish Theol. Sem., 1981, 82-83, 2002; Franz Rosenzweig guest prof. U. Kassel, Germany, 1991. Author: Early Mesopotamian Royal Titles, 1957, Sumerian Archival Texts, 1973, The Book of the People, 1991, Origins: The Ancient Near Eastern Background of Some Modern Western Institutions, 1996; (with J.J.A. van Dijk) The Exaltation of Inanna, 1968; (with W.K. Simpson) The Ancient Near East: A History, 1971, 2d edit., 1998; (with Briggs Buchanan) Early Near Eastern Seals in the Yale Babylonian Collection, 1981; co-author: The Torah: A Modern Commentary, 1981, 2d edit., 2005, Heritage: Civilization and the Jews, 2 vols., 1984, The Tablets of Ebla, 1984; editor: Essays in Memory of E.A. Speiser, 1968; (with Carl D. Evans and John B. White) Scripture in Context: Essays on the Comparative Method, 1980; (with James C. Moyer and Leo G. Perdue) Scripture in Context II: More Essays on the Comparative Method, 1983; (with Bruce W. Jones and Gerald L. Mattingly) The Bible in Light of Cuneiform Literature: Scripture in Context III, 1990; (with K. Lawson Younger Jr. and Bernard F. Batto) The Biblical Canon in Comparative Perspective: Scripture in Context IV, 1991; (with K. Lawson Younger Jr.) The Context of Scripture, vol. I: Canonical Compositions from the Biblical World, 1997, Vol. II Monumental Inscriptions from the Biblical World, 2000, Vol. III Archival Documents from the Biblical World, 2002; (with Irene J. Winter) Seals and Seal Impressions, 2001; translator: The Star of Redemption, 1971; contbr. articles and book revs. to profl. jours.; mem. editl. bd. Yale Near Eastern Researches, 1967—2002; editor, 1970-2002; mem. editl. bd. Moment Mag., Bible Rev., Archaeology Odyssey, 1980-2003, Bibl. Archaeology Rev., 2004—. Mem. commn. Jewish edn. Union Am. Hebrew Congregations, 1967-71; co-founder, dir., mem. exec. com. Assn. Jewish Studies, 1970-71, v.p., 1972-74. Fulbright scholar, 1950-51; fellow Guggenheim, 1965-66, Inst. Advanced Studies, Hebrew U., Jerusalem, 1978-79, Nat. Humanities Inst., 1987-88, Shelby Cullom Davis Ctr. for Hist. Studies, Princeton U., 1996-97; honored by an anniversary volume: The Tablet and the Scroll: Near Eastern Studies in Honor of William W. Hallo, 1993. Mem. Am. Oriental Soc. (assoc. editor, 1965-71, chmn. Ancient Near East sect. 1971-78, v.p. 1987-88, pres. 1988-89), World Union Jewish Studies, Fulbright Assn. (v.p. Conn. chpt. 2002-), Harvard Club (So. Conn.), Yale Club (N.Y.C.), Phi Beta Kappa. Home: 245 Blake Rd Hamden CT 06517-3324 Office: Yale Babylonian Collection PO Box 208240 New Haven CT 06520-8240 E-mail: william.hallo@yale.edu.

HALLOCK, ROBERT BRUCE, physics professor; b. Washington, Dec. 9, 1943; s. Robert Frederick and Dorothy Hallock; m. Norma Hallock, June 19, 1965; children: Robert William, Kevin Frederick. BS, U. Mass., 1965; MS, Stanford U., 1967, PhD, 1969, postdoctoral, 1969-70. Asst. prof. U. Mass., Amherst, 1970-74, assoc. prof., 1974-79, prof., 1979—2001, disting. prof., 2001—, dir. lab. low temp. physics, 1978—, head dept. physics and astronomy, 1985-93, interim dean Coll. Natural Scis. and Math., 2000—01. Vis. assoc. prof. Brown U., Providence, 1975, Cornell U., Ithaca, NY, 1977—78; co-chair Gordon Rsch. Conf. on Quantum Fluids and Solids, 1982; adj. prof. dept. polymer sci. and engring. U. Mass., 1985—; mem. 5 colls. Radio Astronomy Policy Bd., 1985—87; mem. Rsch. Corp. Grants Adv. Bd., 1989—96; mem. fundamental physics discipline working group NASA, 1997—2001; chair Quantum Fluids and Solids Internat. Conf., 1998—2000; sec. commn. 5 Internat. Union Pure and Applied Physics, 2005—; bd. dirs. Rsch. Corp. Author, editor: Superfluid Helium, 1983; contbr. articles to profl. jours. Leader Cub Scout Am., Hadley, Mass., 1975—80. Named Disting. Tchr. of Yr., U. Mass., 1998; fellow, 1974, 1993; Woodrow Wilson Found. fellow, 1965, Air Force Office Sci. Rsch.-NRC fellow, 1969, A. P. Sloan Found. Rsch. fellow, 1972—76, J. S. Guggenheim Meml. fellow, 1992—93. Fellow: Am. Phys. Soc. (mem. exec. oun. New Eng. sect. 1986—89); mem.: Sigma Xi, Phi Beta Kappa. Avocation: photography. Office: U Mass/Hasbrouck Lab Dept Physics Amherst MA 01003 Office Phone: 413-545-3529. E-mail: hallock@physics.umass.edu.

HALLORAN, DANIEL JAMES, lawyer; b. NYC, Mar. 16, 1971; s. Daniel James and Ellen Judith Halloran; m. Cynthia Massimo, Sept. 26, 2003. BA cum laude in Anthropology and History, CUNY, 1997; JD, St. John's U., Jamaica, NY, 2000; LLM, SUNY, Buffalo, 2001; D of Jurisprudence Arts, Belford U., 2005. Bar: US Ct. Appeals (2d cir.) 2005, US Dist. Ct. (no., ea., so. and we. dists.) NY 2003. Judicial intern clerk NYS Supreme Ct., Kew Gardens, NY, 1999—2000; legal asst., criminal ct. grand jury bur. Bronx County Dist. Attys. Office, Bronx, NY, 1999—2000; spl. asst. dist. atty. intern Queens County Dist. Attys. Office, Kew Gardens, NY, 2000; spl. asst. dist. atty. Erie County Dist. Atty., Buffalo, 2000—01; trial counsel, appellate Atty. Palmieri & Castiglione, LLP, Mineola, NY, 2001—. Of counsel Patrolman's Benevolent Assn. - NYC Police Dept., 2003—. Contbr. articles to profl. jours. Assoc. advisor Boy Scouts Am.-Order of the Arrow, Queens, NY, 1993—2004. Mem.: ABA, ATLA (assoc.), Federalist Soc., Queens County Bar Assn., Nassau County Bar Assn., Internat. Bar Assn., NYC Criminal Bar Assn., NYS Acad. Trial Lawyers, NYS Defenders Assn., Assn. Trial Lawyers Am., NYS Trial Lawyers Assn., Nat. Assn. Criminal Defence Lawyers, NYS Bar Assn., Assn. Fed. Criminal Defence Attys., Fed. Bar Assn., Nat. Eagle Scout Assn., Assn. Endowment, Nat. Rifle Assn., Am. Archaeological Assn., Nat. Anthropological Assn. Libertarian. Avocation: camping. Office: Palmieri & Castiglione LLP 250 Mineola Blvd Mineola NY 11501 Home Phone: 718-886-9733; Office Phone: 516-248-9595. Office Fax: 516-248-7897; Home Fax: 484-348-0139. Personal E-mail: omisson@nysbar.com. Business E-Mail: dhalloran@pcllp.com.

HALLORAN, JEAN M., human resources specialist; b. NY; B in History, Princeton U.; MBA, Harvard U. Various positions in human resources, mfg., and strategic planning med. products group Hewlett-Packard, 1980—93, personnel mgr. measurement sys. orgn., 1993—97, dir. corp. edn. and devel., 1997—99; sr. v.p. human resources Agilent Technologies, Palo Alto, Calif., 1999—. Office: Agilent Technologies Inc 395 Page Mill Rd Palo Alto CA 94306 Office Phone: 650-752-5633. Office Fax: 650-752-5633.*

HALLORAN, JOHN ALAN, information technology executive; b. Pasadena, Calif., Jan. 11, 1954; s. Raymond Leroy Heacock and Katherine Davis; m. Patricia Valles Halloran, Dec. 18, 1998. BA in Mid. Ea. & Religious Studies cum laude, U. Calif., Santa Barbara, 1975. Clk. Probation Dept., LA, 1975—76; planner jobs program Cmty. Devel. Dept., LA, 1976—79; cons. cities of Burbank, Santa Monica and non-profit agys., 1979—82; microcomputer specialist various temp assignments, LA, 1982—85; tech. writer Travelers Health Network, LA, 1985—89; editor Logogram Pub., LA, 1984—; pres. Halloran Software, LA, 1985—. Author: (software) Astrology for Windows, 1994, AstrolDeluxe Report Writer, 1997; editor: (book) Sumerian Lexicon, 2006. Charter mem. Calif. Mus. Ancient Art. Mem.: Jack Sprat Gourmet Club, Mensa. Democrat. Office: Halloran Software PO Box 75713 Los Angeles CA 90075 Office Phone: 818-901-1221.

HALLORAN, MICHAEL JAMES, lawyer; b. Berkeley, Calif., May 20, 1941; s. James Joseph and Fern (Ogden) H.; m. Virginia Smedberg, Sept. 6, 1964; children: Pamela, Peter, Shelley. BS, U. Calif., Berkeley, 1962, LLB, 1965. Bar: Calif. 1966, D.C. 1979, Wyo. 1996. Assoc. Keatinge & Sterling, L.A., 1965-67, Pillsbury, Madison & Sutro (now Pillsbury Winthrop Shaw Pittman LLP), San Francisco, 1967-72, ptnr., 1973—90, 1997—2006, mng. ptnr. Washington, 1979-82, sr. ptnr. corp. & securities practice San Francisco, 1997—2006; exec. v.p., gen. counsel BankAm. Corp. and Bank of Am., San Francisco, 1990-96; counselor to the chmn. and dep. chief of staff SEC, Washington, 2006—. Mem. legal adv. com. N.Y. Stock Exch., 1993-96; bd. overseers Inst. Civil Justice, 1994-98. Author, editor: Venture Capital and Public Offering Negotiation, 1982-; mem. editl. adv. bd. M&A Lawyer and the Bur. Nat. Affairs Corp. Accountability Report, 2002-; mem. bd. adv. Stanford Jour. of Law, Bus. & Fin. Mem. corp. governance, shareholder rights and securities transactions com. Calif. Senate Commn., 1986-98; bd. dirs. Am. Conservatory Theater, 1994-2000; trustee, past bd. pres. Boalt Sch. Law, Univ. Calif. Berkeley. Named one of Top Lawyers in Silicon Valley, San Jose Mag., 2001, 2002, 2004. Mem. ABA (chmn. state regulation of securities com. 1981-84, mem. com. of sect. of bus. law 1986-90, chmn. banking law com. 1992-96, mem. corp. laws com. 1997—2006), Bar Assn. San Francisco (bd. dirs. 1993-96). Avocations: skiing, golf, fishing, hiking. Office: US SEC 100 F St NE Washington DC 20549 Office Phone: 202-551-2133. Office Fax: 202-772-9200. E-mail: halloran@sec.com.

HALLORAN, PHILIP FRANCIS, nephrologist, immunologist; b. Hamilton, Ohio, June 14, 1944; MD, Univ. Toronto, 1968; PhD, Univ. London, Eng., 1978. Asst. prof. Univ. Toronto, 1975—80, assoc. prof., 1980—86, prof., 1986—87; dir., renal transplantation Toronto Gen. and Mount Sinai Hosp., 1975—87; staff phys. Tri-Hosp. Nephrology Svc., 1975—87; med. dir., HOPE program Univ. Alberta Hosp., 1987—99, dir., tissue typing lab., 1987—99, med. dir., transplantation programs, 1987—99; dir., divsn. nephrology, immunology Univ. Alberta, 1987—2003, prof., med. microbiology, immunology, 1987—, prof., dept. medicine, 1987—, Muttart chair, clin. molecular immunology & autoimmunity, 1993—; dir. Alberta Transplant Inst., 2002—. Vis. prof., immunology Hammersmith Hosp., Imperial Coll. Sch. Medicine, London, 2002. Named Officer of the Order of Can., 2005; named one of Top 100 Physicians of Century in Alberta, 2005; recipient Medical award, Kidney Found. Can., 1991, Commemorative Medal, 1993, Medal of Excellence in Rsch., 2000, Disting. Scientist award, Can. Soc. Clin. Investigation, 2006. Fellow: Royal Coll. Phys.and Surgeons of Can. (Medal in Medicine 1985); mem.: AAAS, Internat. Soc. Nephrology, Fedn. Am. Soc. Experimental Biology, Can. Inst. Academic Medicine, Can. Transplantation Soc. (pres. 1988—89, Lifetime Achievement award 2005), Can. Soc. Nephrology, Can. Soc. Immunology, Can. Med. Assn., Brit. Transplantation Soc., Brit. Soc. Immunology, Am. Soc. Transplant Surgeons, Am. Soc. Transplantation (Roche Ernest Hodge Disting. Achievement award 2007), Am. Soc. Clin. Investigation, Am. Assn. Immunologists, Alta. Med. Assn. Office: Nephrology & Transplantation Immunology Univ Alberta 250 Heritage Medical Research Centre Edmonton AB T6G 2S2 Canada Office Phone: 780-407-8880. Business E-Mail: phil.halloran@ualberta.ca.*

HALLORAN, RICHARD COLBY, writer, reporter, communications executive, editor; b. Washington, Mar. 2, 1930; s. Paul James and Catherine (Lenihan) H.; m. Carol Prins, June 21, 1958; children: Christopher Paul, Laura Colby, Catherine Anne; m. Fumiko Mori, Nov. 11, 1978. AB with distinction, Dartmouth Coll., 1951; MA, U. Mich., 1957. Staff writer, then asst. fgn. editor Business Week mag., 1957-61; Tokyo bur. chief McGraw-Hill World News, 1962-64; Asia specialist Washington Post, 1965-66, bur. chief Northeast Asia Tokyo, 1966-68, Washington corr., 1968-69; corr. N.Y. Times, Washington, 1969-72, Tokyo bur. chief, 1972-76, investigative reporter Washington Bur., 1976-78, energy corr., 1978-79, def. corr., 1979-84, mil. corr., 1985—90; dir. comm. and journalism East-West Ctr., Honolulu, 1990-94; ind. writer Honolulu, 1994—2000; editl. dir. Honolulu Star-Bull., 2001—02; columnist The Rising East, 2002—. Adj. fellow Pacific Forum-Ctr. Strategic and Internat. Studies; vis. instr. Asia Pacific Ctr. for Security Studies. Author: Japan: Images and Realities, 1969, Conflict and Compromise: The Dynamics of American Foreign Policy, 1973, To Arm a Nation: Rebuilding America's Endangered Defenses, 1986, Serving America: Prospects for the Volunteer Force, 1988, Sparky: A Portrait of Senator Spark M. Matsunaga of Hawaii, 2002, My Name is Shinseki and I am a Soldier: Brief Biography of Gen. Eric K. Shinseki, U.S. Army. Mem. Honolulu Com. Fgn. Rels., Pacific and Asian Affairs Coun., Japan-Am. Soc. Hawaii. 1st lt. U.S. Army, 1952-55. Recipient citation for interpretation fgn. affairs Overseas Press Club, 1969, George Polk award for nat. reporting L.I. U., 1982, Gerald R. Ford prize for disting. reporting on nat. def. Gerald R. Ford Found., 1988, Outstanding Civilian Svc. medal U.S. Army, 1989, Japan's Order Sacred Treasure, Gold Rays with Rosette, 1998, Lifetime Achievement award Pacific and Asian Affairs Coun., 2000, Fellow of Pacific, Hawaii Pacific U., 2003; Ford Found. fellow Columbia U., 1964-65, Woodrow Wilson nat. fellow Furman U., S.C., Luther Coll., Iowa, Union Coll., N.Y., U. Redlands, Calif., Linfield Coll., Oreg., Goucher Coll., Md., Ohio Wesleyan U., McMurry U., Tex., Trinity Coll., Vt., St. Mary's Coll., Calif., Wabash Coll., Ind., Elon U., N.C. Mem. 100th Infantry Bn. Vet. Assn. (hon.), Fgn. Corrs. Club Japan. Roman Catholic. Home: 1065 Kaoopulu Pl Honolulu HI 96825-1364 Office Phone: 808-395-0511. Personal E-mail: oranhall@hawaii.rr.com.

HALLQUIST, JOHN O., engineering company executive; BS in Indsl. Engring. magna cum laude, Western Mich. U., 1970; MS in Engring. Mechanics, Mich. Technol. U., 1972, PhD in Mech. Engring. and Engring. Mechanics, 1974. With weapons lab. Lawrence Livermore Nat. Lab.; founder, pres. Livermore Software Tech. Corp., Calif., 1987. Recipient Dept. Energy award for Significant Contbns. to Nuc. Weapons Prog., 1986, Applied Mechanics Divsn. award, ASME, 2003. Mem.: NAE. Office: Livermore Software Tech Corp 7374 Las Positas Rd Livermore CA 94551 Business E-Mail: john@lstc.com.

HALL-STOODLEY, LUANNE, science educator, researcher; m. Paul Stoodley, Aug. 27, 1983; children: Victoria Marie Stoodley, Emily Michelle Stoodley. PhD, Mont. State U., Bozeman, 1995. Adj. faculty WWAMI Med. Scis. Mont. State U., Bozeman, 1995, asst. rsch. prof. dept. microbiology, 2000—03, asst. rsch. prof. vet. molecular biology; lectr. immunology dept. biol. scis. U. Exeter, Devon, England, 1997—99; asst. prof. Ctr. for Genomic Scis., Allegheny-Singer Rsch. Inst., Pitts., 2004—; asst. prof. microbiology and immunology Drexel U. Coll. Medicine, Phila., 2005—. Cons., prin. investigator LigoCyte Pharmaceuticals, Inc., Bozeman, 2002—03. Recipient Sir Henry Wellcome award for Innovative Rsch., Wellcome Trust, 1997—98. Mem.: Am. Assn. Microbiology. Achievements include research in mycobacteria biofilms; discovery of biofilms on human pediatric middle ear mucosa associated with chronic otitis media; patents pending for Biofim EPS Enhancer. Avocations: cross country skiing, cooking, gardening, archaeology, canoeing. Office: Allegheny-Singer Research Institute 320 East North Ave Pittsburgh PA 15212-4772 Office Phone: 412-359-5016.

HALLSTRAND, SARAH LAYMON, denomination executive; b. Nashville, Oct. 25, 1944; d. Charles Martin and Lillian Christina (Stenberg) Laymon; m. John Peter Hallstrand, July 6, 1974; 1 child, Lillian Johanna. BA cum laude, Fla. So. Coll., 1966; ThM, Boston U., 1971; D of Ministry, McCormick Theol. Sem., 1985; grad., Coll. for Fin. Planning, Denver, 1990. Ordained Am. Baptist Ch., 1976; cert. ret. counselor, fin. counselor; CFP. Dir. Christian edn. Trinity United Meth. Ch., Bradenton, Fla., 1968-70, Univ. United Meth. Ch., Syracuse, N.Y., 1971-73; assoc. min. First Bapt. Ch., Syracuse, 1973-78; pastor Oneida (N.Y.) Bapt. Ch., 1978-80; midwest rep. Mins. and Missionaries Benefit Bd., Am. Bapt. Chs., Oak Park, Ill., 1981—2002; pastor First United Meth. Ch., Tellico Plains, Tenn., 2002—03; cons. MMBB, 2002—04; interim exec. min. ABCCONN, 2004; exec. min. ABC of Greater Indpls., 2005—. Leader ret. planning seminars Am. Bapt. Assembly, Green Lake, Wis., 1985-02, AutumnQuest Ret. Sems., Midwest Ministry Devel. Svc., 1994—, chair, 1993-96; mem. rep. Midwest Ministerial Leadership Commn., Valley Forge, Pa., 1985-02; adj. prof., pastoral care McCormick Theol. Sem., Chgo., 1986-01; adj. prof. retirement planning Divinity Sch., Rochester, NY, 1994; vis. scholar Am. Bapt. Bd. Ednl. Ministries, Valley Forge, 1986-87; program com. and women in ministry rep. Roger Williams Fellowship, 1988-95; nat. continuing edn. team Am. Bapt. Chs., Valley Forge, Pa., 1991-98; strategic planning com. Celebration of a New Bapt. Covenant, 2006—, conf. leader for women's spiritual renewal weekends; spkr. in field. Contbg. author: Songs of Miriam: A Women's Book of Devotions, 1994; contbr. articles to profl. jours. including The Inclusive Pulpit Jour. Mem. Fin. Planning Assn., Alpha Gamma Delta. Democrat. Home and Office: 126 Santee Way Loudon TN 37774 Personal E-mail: sh4406@hotmail.com. *The church has not been called to be successful as measured by the world's standards. It has always been and will always be that the true goal of the church is faithfulness as measured by the liberating and transforming gospel of Jesus Christ.*

HALLSTROM, LASSE, film director; b. Stockholm, June 2, 1946; m. Lena Olin, Mar. 18, 1994; 1 child, Tora; m. Malou Hallstrom (div.); 1 child, Johan. Dir. feature films, including A Lover and His Lass, 1975, Abba: The Movie, 1977, Father to Be, 1979, The Rooster, 1981, Happy We, 1983, My Life as a Dog, 1985, Children of Bullerby Village, 1987, Once Around, 1991, What's Eating Gilbert Grape, 1993, Something To Talk About, 1995, The Cider House Rules, 1999, Chocolat, 2000, The Shipping News, 2001, An Unfinished Life, 2005, Casanova, 2005, The Hoax, 2006. Office: ICM 8942 Wilshire Blvd Beverly Hills CA 90211-1934 also: Francis & Assocs 501 S Beverly Dr 3d Fl Beverly Hills CA 90211*

HALLUIN, ALBERT PRICE, lawyer; b. Nov. 8, 1939; children: Russell, Marcus. BA, La. State U., 1964; JD, U. Balt., 1969. Bar: US Patent and Trademark Office, 1969, Md. 1970, NY 1985, Calif. 1991, US Supreme Ct. 1976, US Ct. Appeals (fed. cir.) 1982); instrument-rated pilot. Assoc. Jones, Tullar & Cooper, Arlington, Va., 1969-71; sr. patent atty. CPC Internat. Inc., Englewood Cliffs, NJ, 1971-76; counsel Exxon Rsch. & Engring. Co., Florham Park, NJ, 1976-83; v.p., chief intellectual property counsel Cetus Corp., Emeryville, Calif., 1983-90; ptnr. Fleisler, Dubb, Meyer & Lovejoy, San Francisco, 1990-92, Limbach & Limbach, San Francisco, 1992-94, Pennie & Edmonds, Menlo Park, Calif., 1994-97, Howrey LLP, Menlo Park, 1997—2004; pres., CEO, chmn. Halzyme Tech., Inc., 1995—. Wilson Sonsini Goodrich & Rosati, Palo Alto, Calif., 2004—. Contbr. articles to legal jours. Pres. Belle Roche Homeowners Assn., Redwood City, Calif., 1995-2004. Named One of Top 20 Intellectual Property Lawyers, Calif. Lawyer's Mag., 1993, One of 10 Attys. named to IP Law and Bus. Patent Prosecution Hall of Fame; inducted into U. Balt. Sch. Law's Hall of Fame, 2006; recepient Govenor's citation, Md. Mem. ABA, Am. Intellectual Property Law Assn. (chmn. chem. practice com. 1981-83, sec. 1984-85, bd. dirs. 1984-89, founding chmn. biotech. com. 1990-92), Licensing Exec. Soc., Assn. Corp. Patent Counsel, Bar Assn. San Francisco, San Francisco Patent Assn. Republican. Episcopalian. Achievements include patents in field; first to recognize the patent potential for the Nobel prize-winning polymerase chain reaction process. Avocations: flying, music, songwriting. Office: WIlson Sonsini Goodrich & Rosati 650 Page Mill Rd Palo Alto CA 94304-1050 Office Phone: 650-565-3585. Fax: 650-493-6811. E-mail: ahalluin@wsgr.com.

HALM, NANCYE STUDD, retired academic administrator; b. Jamestown, NY, Mar. 26, 1932; d. Thomas Howerton and Margaret Hazel (LeRoy) Neathery; m. David Philip Mack, Aug. 25, 1951 (div. 1972); children: Margaret, Jennifer, Geoffrey, Peter; m. Loris L. Studd, July 6, 1974 (dec. 1987); m. James Richard Halm, Aug. 30, 1991 (dec. 2005). BS in Edn., SUNY, Fredonia, 1954, postgrad., 1954—68, St. Bonaventure U., 1970, postgrad., 1981, Wesley Theol. Seminary, 2005—. Tchr. Morning Sun (Iowa) Consolidated Schs., 1956-57, Panama (N.Y.) Cen. Schs., 1958-65, Jamestown (N.Y.) Pub. Schs., 1967-69, Olean (N.Y.) Pub. Schs., 1969-72, Jamestown Pub. Schs., 1972-73; pers. mgr. F.W. Woolworth Co., Lakewood, N.Y., 1972-79; dir. Nat. Conf. Christians & Jews, Jamestown, 1979-86; counselor N.Y. State Div. for Youth, Jamestown, 1979-89; exec. rep. Am. Bapt. Found., Valley Forge, Pa., 1989-94; adminstr. New Castle Christian Acad., 1996—2002; ret., 2002. Pastor West Pitts. United Meth. Ch., 2003—04, Ellington United Meth. Ch., 2004—, Conewango Valley United Meth. Ch., 2007—. V.p. Chautauqua County Am. Bapt. Women, 1981—90; pres. Falconer Bapt. Women, 1986—90; love gift chmn. Pitts. Bapt. Assn., 1990—91; trustee, chair endowment fund Chautauqua Bapt. Union at Chautauqua Inst., 1982—; pres. ch. coun. Wesley United Meth. Ch., 2001—03; mem. nat. bd. dirs. Am. Bapt. Chs. U.S.A., Valley Forge, Pa., 1988—89. Recipient Cert. of Merit, Cassadaga Job Corp, 1984. Mem. Rebekah. Democrat. Avocations: reading, crafts, quilting. Home: 60 Morgan St Falconer NY 14733

HALMI, ROBERT, SR., film, television producer; b. Budapest, Hungary, Jan. 22, 1924; s. Bela and Sarah (Deri) H.; m. Esther Szirmay, Sept. 9, 1980; children: Kevin Gorman, Kim Gorman, Robert, Bill. Grad., U. Budapest, 1946. Mag. photographer, 1946-52; photographer Life mag., 1952-62; documentary producer, 1962-75; chmn. Hallmark Entertainment. Producer over 200 TV movies, miniseries and theatrical features including Nurse, 1980, Wilson's Reward, 1980, Nairobi Affair, 1984, Grand Larceny, 1987, Mayflower Madam, 1987, Pack of Lies, 1987, Best Friends, 1987, Cheetah, 1989, Ivory Hunters, 1990, Call of the Wild, 1993, The Yearling, 1994, Promise Kept: The Oksana Baiul Story, 1994, Getting Out, 1994, The Sunshine Boys, 1995, Kidnapped, 1995, Bye Bye Birdie, 1995, Gulliver's Travells, 1996, Captain Courageous, 1996, 20,000 Leagues Under the Sea, 1997, Moby Dick, 1998, Merlin, 1998, Crime & Punishment, 1998, Rear Window, 1998, Land of Oz, 1999, Don Quixote, 1999, Cleopatra, 1999, Arabian Nights, 1999, Alice in Wonderland, 1999, Noah's Ark, 1999, Mr. & Mrs. Bridge, Gypsy, 1993, The Incident in a Small Town, 1994, Lily in Love, Barnum, Prince Charming, 2001; exec. prodr.: Mother Teresa: In the Name of God's Poor, 1997, Mike Bassett: England Manager, 2001; exec. prodr.(TV): Izzy and Moe, 1985, Cook & Peary: The Race to the Pole, 1983, Spearfield's Daughter, 1986, Spies, Lies & Naked Thighs, 1988, The Josephine Baker Story, 1991, Mrs. Lambert Remembers Love, 1991, An American Story, 1992, Family Torn Apart, 1993, Scarlett, 1994, White Dwarf, 1995, Robinson Crusoe, 1996, Jakes Women, 1996, London Suite, 1996, Mary & Tim, 1996, In Cold Blood, 1996, For Love Alone: The Ivana Trump Story, 1996, Bridge of Time, 1997, Tidal Wave: No Escape, 1997, The Odyssey, 1997, Forbidden Territory: Stanley's Search for Livingstone, 1997, A Christmas Memory, 1997, The Long Way Home, 1998, Moby Dick, 1998, Merlin, 1998, Only Love, 1998, Animal Farm, 1999, Magical Legend of the Leprechauns, 1999, A Christmas Carol, 1999, The 10th Kingdom, 2000, Arabian Nights, 2000, Jason and the Argonauts, 2000, Voyage of the Unicorn, 2001, The Lost Empire, 2001, Infinite Worlds of H.G. WElls, 2001, Snow White, 2001, Stranded, 2002, King of Texas, 2002, Dinotopia, 2002, Mr. St. Nick, 2002, The Snow Queen, 2002, Dreamkeeper, 2003, Prince Charming, 2003, The Lion in Winter, 2004; author: Into Your Hands Are They Delivered, Animals of Africa, Animals of North America, Sports Cars of the World, How To Photograph Women, Zoos of the World, Recipient 15 Emmy awards, Peabody award, Christopher award, Genesis award, CINE Golden Eagle award, numerous Houston Film Festival awards. Address: Hallmark Entertainment 21st Fl 1325 Avenue of the Americas New York NY 10019-6026

HALMRAST, LYNN JAMES, psychologist; b. Wahpeton, ND, Oct. 27, 1949; s. Gerhard Elmer and Lilly Halmrast; m. Rae Mathews, Oct. 12, 1984; children: Nathan, Meghan, Timothy, Patrick, Julia. MS, Moorhead State U., Minn., 1974, specialty degree psychology, 1986, PhD Clin. Psychology, 1987. Lic. psychologist, marriage and family therapist, profl. clin. counselor; cert. sch. psychologist. Psychologist Crookston Regional Interdist. Coun. Exceptional Children, Minn., 1974—76, Ind. Sch. Dist. #152, Moorhead, 1976—2007; coord. psychol. svcs. Edn. Coop., St. Cloud, Minn., 1980—81; pvt. practice psychology Moorhead, 1981—. Psychologist, therapist Solutions Behavioral Health, 2003—, Triumph Luth. Ch., Moorhead; pres. Red River Coun. Family Rels.; class sec. Men's Bible Study Fellowship, Fargo, ND. Mem. Minn. Coun. Exceptional Children (pres. 1987-88, bd. govs. rep. 1988-91), Am. Assn. Marriage and Family Therapy (clin.). crew member Hjemkomst Viking Ship Hjemkomst Heritage Ctr., Moorhead, 1980-82. Home Phone: 218-233-7896; Office Phone: 218-284-5472, 218-287-4338. Business E-Mail: lhalmrast@cableone.net.

HALPER, EMANUEL B(ARRY), lawyer, real estate developer, consultant, writer; b. Bronx, NY, June 24, 1933; s. Nathan N. and Molly (Rabinowitz) H.; m. Ilona Rubinstein, Mar. 5, 1961; children: Eve Brook, Dan Reed. AB, CCNY, 1954; JD, Columbia U., 1957. Bar: NY 1958; real estate broker, NY. House counsel Howard Stores Corp., Bklyn., 1960; ptnr. Zissu, Halper & Martin, NYC, 1965—87, of counsel, 1987—97; ptnr. Can. Pacific Realty Co., Fairfield, NJ, 1970—; v.p. devel. Chase Enterprises, Hartford, Conn., 1987-89; pres. Texam. Horizon Ventures, 1989-93, Am. Devel. and Cons. Corp., Greenvale, NY, 1989—. Adj. prof. real estate NYU, 1973-83; spl. prof. law Hofstra U., 1998-2006, disting. scholar in residence, vis. prof. law, 2007—. Author: Wonderful World of Real Estate, 1975 (republished as Conversations in Real Estate, 1990), Shopping Center and Store Leases, 1979, Ground Leases and Land Acqusition Contracts, 1988; columnist NY Law Jour., 1982-1992; contbg. editor Real Estate Review, 1973-99; chmn. editl. policy com. Internat. Property Investment Jour., 1982-87. With USAR, 1957-63. Recipient Disting. Teaching award NYU, 1978, Dean's award Hofstra U. Law Sch., 1987. Mem. ABA (chmn. comml. leasing com. 1986-93, chmn. comml. and indsl. leasing group 1993-94, mem. supervisory coun. of real property, probate and trust law sect. 1994-2000, mem. standing com. on CLE, 1994-96, mem. standing com. pubs. 1997-98, mem. standing com. on diversity 1999—, chmn. standing com. cmty. outreach 2004-, Gavel award 1977, Partnership award, 2006, Spirit of Excellence award 2005), World Assn. Lawyers (chmn. internat. real estate com. 1982-90), Internat. Inst. for Real Estate Studies (chmn. bd. 1980-87), Am. Coll. Real Estate Lawyers. Jewish. Avocations: writing, painting, gardening, yoga, running. Office: PO Box 261 Greenvale NY 11548-0261 Office Phone: 516-625-8300. Personal E-mail: e1h@aol.com. Business E-Mail: emanuel.halper@hofstra.edu.

HALPER, THOMAS, political science professor; b. Bklyn., Dec. 1, 1942; s. Albert and Pauline (Friedman) H.; m. Marilyn S. Snyder, Jan. 14, 1979; 1 dau., Pauline. AB, St. Lawrence U., 1963; MA, Vanderbilt U., 1967, PhD, 1970. Instr. Tulane U., 1967-68; asst. prof. polit. sci. Coe Coll., 1968-74, Baruch Coll., 1974-76, prof., chmn. dept., 1976—. Author: Foreign Policy Crises, 1971, Power, Politics and American Democracy, 1981, The Misfortunes of Others, 1989, Positive Rights in a Republic of Talk, 2003; contbr. articles to profl. jours. Home: 75 Livingston St Brooklyn NY 11201-5054 Office: Baruch Coll Dept Polit Sci 1 Bernard Baruch Way New York NY 10010-5518 Office Phone: 646-312-4413. Business E-Mail: thomas_halper@baruch.cuny.edu.

HALPERIN, BERTRAND ISRAEL, physics professor; b. Bklyn., Dec. 6, 1941; s. Morris and Eva (Teplitsky) H.; m. Helena Stacy French, Sept. 23, 1962; children: Jeffery Arnold, Julia Stacy. AB, Harvard U., 1961; A.M., U. Calif., 1963, PhD, 1965; vis. grad. student, Princeton U., 1964-65. NSF postdoctoral fellow U. Paris, 1965-66; mem. tech. staff Bell Labs., Murray Hill, NJ, 1966-76; lectr. Harvard U., 1969-70, prof. physics, 1976—, chmn. dept. physics, 1988-91, Hollis prof. math. and natural philosophy, 1992—; sci. dir. Ctr. for Imaging and Mesoscale Structures, 1994—2004. Cons. Lucent Technologies, Schlumberger-Doll Rsch. Labs. Assoc. editor: Revs. Modern Physics, 1973-80. Recipient Wolf prize in physics, Wolf Found., Israel, 2003. Fellow Am. Phys. Soc. (Oliver Buckley prize 1982, Lars Onsager prize 2001), Am. Acad. Arts and Scis.; mem. NAS, Am. Philos. Soc. Achievements include rsch. in solid state theory, statis. physics. Office: Harvard U Dept Physics Cambridge MA 02138

HALPERIN, DANIEL I., law educator; b. Bklyn., Jan. 2, 1937; BBA, City Coll. of NY, 1957; JD, Harvard U., 1961. Bar: NY 1962, Pa. 1977, DC 1984. Dep. tax legis. counsel US Dept. Treasury, 1969—70, tax legis. counsel, 1977—78, dep. asst. sec., 1978—80; prof. law U. Pa., 1970—77, Georgetown U., 1981—96; Stanley S. Surrey Prof. Law Harvard Law Sch., Cambridge, Mass., 1996—. Vis. prof. law Harvard Law Sch., 1993. Office: Harvard Law Sch 1563 Massachusetts Ave Cambridge MA 02138 Office Phone: 617-496-5505. Office Fax: 617-496-4880. Business E-Mail: halperin@law.harvard.edu.

HALPERIN, DAVID RICHARD, lawyer; b. Bklyn., June 12, 1944; s. David and Mareva (Vinade) Halperin. BA, Columbia U., 1965; MAT, Harvard U., 1966, JD, 1974. Bar: N.Y. 1975. Spl. asst. to Henry Kissinger, asst. to Pres. for Nat. Security Affairs, Washington, 1970-71; assoc. Davis Polk & Wardwell, NYC, 1974-76, Coudert Bros., Hong Kong, 1976—83, ptnr., 1983—2006, Orrick, Herrington & Sutcliffe, 2006—. Mem. adv. bd. Olympus Capital Ltd., Overlook Investments Ltd.; mem. takeovers and mergers panel Hong Kong Securities and Futures Commn., 1999—2001; mem. disciplinary com. Share Registrars, 2003—; bd. dirs. Altfield Enterprises, Ltd., Staunton Capital, Ltd., Blue Pool Capital Ltd. Contbr. articles to profl. jours. Served to lt. comdr. USNR, 1965—71, served as aide to dep. comdr. USN, 1968—70, Vietnam, spl. asst., chied of naval ops. USN, 1970—71. Decorated Bronze Star with combat V. Mem.: ABA, Coun. Fgn. Rels., Assn. Bar City of N.Y., Internat. Bar Assn., RBSC Polo Club (Bangkok), Hong Kong Club, Royal Hong Kong Yacht Club, Univ. Club (Washington), Harvard Club N.Y.C., Racquet and Tennis Club, Knickerbocker Club. Home: 47 Conduit Rd Apt 1A Hong Kong China also: Baan Piyasathorn 5 Soi Suan Plu, S Sathorn Bangkok Thailand Office: Orrick Coudert Gloucs Tower 15 Queens Rd Ctrl 39th Fl Hong Kong China Office Phone: (852) 2218-9100.

HALPERIN, ERROL R., lawyer; b. Jan. 3, 1941; BS, De Paul U., 1964, JD, 1967; LLM in Taxation, NYU, 1968. Bar: Ill. 1968; U.S. Tax Ct. 1972. Asst. branch chief, legis. and regulations divsn. IRS, 1968-72; legis. atty., joint com. on taxation U.S. Congress, 1977-79; sr. ptnr., Corp. & Securities practices, mem. exec. com. DLA Piper Rudnick Gray Cary, Chgo. Mem.: Nat. Assn. Real Estate Investment Trusts, Nat. Assn. Bond Lawyers, Ill. State Bar Assn., Chgo. Bar Assn. Office: DLA Piper Rudnick Gray Cary Suite 1900 203 N La Salle St Chicago IL 60601-1293 Office Phone: 312-368-4033. Office Fax: 312-236-7516. Business E-Mail: errol.halperin@dlapiper.com.

HALPERIN, GEORGE BENNETT, education educator, retired military officer; b. NYC, Aug. 7, 1926; s. George and Muryal (Lesser) H.; m. Ellen Elizabeth Barber, Dec. 18, 1957 (div. 1988); children: Gail Susan, Thomas Allyn; m. Kathleen Bourdon, Aug. 22, 2000. BS, U.S. Naval Acad., 1950; MBA, Stanford U., 1958; postgrad., Naval War Coll., Newport, RI, 1965—66; MA in History, U. Vt., 1976; MEd, Harvard U., 1979; postgrad., Oxford U., 1987—88, St. Catherine's Coll., 1987—88. Commd. ensign U.S. Navy, 1950, advanced through grades to comdr., 1965; dir. systems and standards div. Naval Supply Ctr., Oakland, Calif., 1963-65; freight terminal officer Naval Support Activity, Danang, Vietnam, 1966-67; supply officer Naval Air Sta., Barbers Point, Hawaii, 1967-70; ret., 1970; tchr. history Stowe (Vt.) High Sch., 1972-80, asst. prin., 1975-76; tchr. John F. Kennedy Sch., Berlin, 1980-86. Chmn. Lamoille South Dist. Profl. Growth Com., 1977—78. Decorated Navy Commendation medal. Mem. U.S. Naval Acad. Alumni Assn., Army-Navy Country Club, Oxford Soc., Harvard Club Home: # 79 Apple Blossom Dr West Lebanon NH 03784

HALPERIN, JEROME ARTHUR, retired pharmaceutical executive; b. Paterson, NJ, Feb. 21, 1937; s. Harry Nathan and Frieda (Niestat) Halperin; m. Barbara Anne Hott, Sept. 1, 1963; children: Alicia Jennifer Odom, Rachel Elizabeth Halperin Montgomery. BS, Rutgers U., 1958; MPH, Johns Hopkins U., 1962; MS, MIT, 1974; DSc (hon.), Mercer U., 1993, Mass. Coll. Pharmacy, 1995, Phila. Coll. Pharmacy and Sci., 1996; DHL (hon.), Western U. Health Scis., 2000. Commd. officer USPHS, 1958, advanced through grades to rear admiral, 1983; staff pharmacist USPHS Hosps., Dept. HEW, Albuquerque and NYC, 1958-61; radiol. health specialist Calif. Health Dept., Berkeley, 1962-65; agreement states coord. Bur. Radiol. Health, Rockville, Md., 1965-66; dir. indsl. radiation and air hygiene Kans. Dept. Health, Topeka, 1966-68; regional rep. Bur. Radiol. Health, Chgo., 1968-71; dir. Northeastern Radiol. Health Lab., FDA, HEW, Winchester, Mass., 1971-73; dep. assoc. dir. new drug evaluation Bur. Drugs, FDA, HEW, Rockville, 1974-77, dep. dir., 1977-82; acting dir. Office of Drugs Nat. Ctr. Drugs and Biologics FDA, Rockville, 1982-83; v.p. tech. CIBA Consumer Pharms., Edison, NJ, 1983-89; exec. dir. U.S. Pharmacopeial Conv., Inc., Rockville, 1989-95, exec. v.p., CEO, 1995-2000; pres., CEO Food & Drug Law Inst., Washington, 2000—06; ret., 2006. Chmn. Conf. Pharmacy 21st Century Va., 1984; cons. WHO, 1979—2000; trustee Davis and Elkins Coll., 2003—. Contbr. articles to profl. jours. Mem. Bd. Health, Hoffman Estates, Ill., 1971; bd. dirs. Perspective Woods Citizen Assn., Olney, Md., 1977—80. Named Alumnus of Yr., Rutgers U. Coll. of Pharmacy, 1981, Disting. Person of Yr., Pharmaceutical Planning Svc., Inc., 1998; recipient Outstanding Svc. award, Federally Employed Women's Assn., 1983, Disting. Career award, Drug Info. Assn., 2001, Career Achievement award, Profl. Fraternities Assn., 2001, Disting. Alumni award, FDA, 2002. Fellow: APHA, AAAS, Am. Pharm. Assn. (Remington Honor medal 2001), Am. Assn. Pharm. Scientists; mem.: Food & Drug Adminstrn. Alumni Assn. (treasurer 2004—), Internat. Pharm. Fedn. (expert mem. bd. pharm. scis.). Jewish. Personal E-mail: jeromehalperin@comcast.net.

HALPERIN, JOHN JACOB, neurology educator, researcher; b. Montreal, Que., Can., Jan. 25, 1950; came to U.S., 1967; s. David M. and Maizie Halperin; m. Toula Jaravinos, June 15, 1975; 1 child, Daniel Mark SB Physics, MIT, 1971; MD, Harvard U., 1975. Diplomate Am. Bd. Internal Medicine, Am. Bd. Psychiatry and Neurology, Am. Bd. Electrodiagnostic Medicine added qualifications clin. neurophysiology. Intern, resident in medicine U. Chgo., 1975—77; resident neurology Mass. Gen. Hosp., Boston, 1977—80, fellow, 1980—83; asst. prof. SUNY, Stony Brook, 1983—89, assoc. prof., vice chmn. dept., 1989—91, acting chmn. dept., 1990—91; chmn. dept. North Shore U. Hosp., Manhasset, NY, 1992—2004; med. dir. Atlantic Neurosci. Inst., Summit, NJ, 2004—; chmn. neurosci. Overlook Hosp., Summit, acting chmn. dept. medicine, 2006—07. Assoc. prof. Cornell U. Med. Coll., 1992-93, prof. 1993-96; prof. NYU Sch. Medicine, 1996— Contbr. numerous articles to med. jours., chpts. to books Fellow Am. Acad. Neurology, Am. Assn. for Electrodiagnostic Medicine (edn. com. 1989-93, examiner 1991—, tng. com. 1995-97); mem. Soc. for Neuroscis., Am. Acad. Clin. Neurophysiology (exec. coun. 1993-96), Am. Neurol. Assn Achievements include research on electrodiagnosis, nervous system Lyme disease. Office: Overlook Hosp Dept Neurscience 99 Beauvoir Ave Summit NJ 07902 Office Phone: 908-522-3501.

HALPERIN, JOHN WILLIAM, English literature educator; b. Chgo., Sept. 15, 1941; s. S. William and Elaine P. H. AB, Bowdoin Coll., 1963; MA, U. N.H., 1966, Johns Hopkins U., 1968, PhD, 1969. Asst. prof. English SUNY, Stony Brook, 1969-72, dir. summer session, 1969-72, asst. to acad. v.p., 1971-72; assoc. prof. English U. So. Calif., 1972-77, prof., 1977-83, dir. grad. studies in English, 1973-75; Centennial prof. English Vanderbilt U., Nashville, 1983—. Fellow Wolfson Coll., Oxford U., 1976; vis. prof. U. Sheffield, Eng., 1979-80. Author: The Language of Meditation, 1973, Egoism and Self-Discovery in the Victorian Novel, 1974, (with Janet Kunert) Plots and Characters in the Fiction of Jane Austen, The Brontes and George Eliot, 1976, Trollope and Politics, 1977, Gissing: A Life in Books, 1982, C.P. Snow: An Oral Biography, 1983, The Life of Jane Austen, 1984, reprint, 1996, Jane Austen's Lovers and Other Essays, 1988, Novelists in Their Youth, 1990, Eminent Georgians, 1995, reprinted, 1998; editor: Henry James, The Golden Bowl, 1972, The Theory of the Novel, 1974, Jane Austen: Bicentenary Essays, 1975, George Gissing, Denzil Quarrier, 1979, Anthony Trollope, Lord Palmerston, 1981, Anthony Trollope, Sir Harry Hotspur of Humblethwaite, 1981, Trollope Centenary Essays, 1982, Anthony Trollope, Dr. Wortle's School, 1984, George Meredith, The Ordeal of Richard Feverel, 1984, George Gissing, The Emancipated, 1985, George Gissing, Will Warburton, 1985, Anthony Trollope, The Belton Estate, 1986, Anthony Trollope, The American Senator, 1986, George Gissing, In The Year of Jubilee, 1987, Proust, 1988, Gissing, New Grub Street, 1992, Anthony Trollope, The Vicar of Bullhampton, 1997; contbr. articles and essays to profl. jours. With U.S. Army, 1963-69. NDEA fellow, 1966-69, Rockefeller Found. fellow, 1976, Am. Philos. Soc. fellow, 1978, Guggenheim fellow, 1978-79, 85-86, Am. Coun. Learned Socs. fellow, 1981. Fellow Royal Soc. Lit.; mem. MLA, PEN. Office: Vanderbilt U Dept English Nashville TN 37235

HALPERIN, JONATHAN L., medical school administrator; b. Boston, Jan. 29, 1949; s. Meyer H. and Libby (Shoer) H.; m. Michelle Copeland, June 21, 1970; children: Robert, Libby. AB, Columbia U., 1971; MD, Boston U., 1975. Diplomate Bd. Cardiovascular Disease. Teaching fellow medicine Boston U. Sch. Medicine, 1976-78, teaching asst. medicine, 1978-80; asst. prof. medicine Mt. Sinai Sch. Medicine, NYC, 1980-85, assoc. prof. clin. medicine, 1985-88, assoc. prof. medicine, 1986—. Assoc. attending physician cardiology Mt. Sinai Hosp., N.Y.C., 1983—; dir. clin. svcs. Mt. Sinai Med. Ctr., N.Y.C., 1983—; cardiology liaison div. cardiothoracic surgery Mt. Sinai Med. Ctr., N.Y.C., 1980-85; staff physician Lynn (Mass.) Hosp., 1978-80. Office: Mt Sinai Med Ctr PO Box 1030 New York NY 10029-0310

HALPERIN, MARK EVAN, editor; b. Cambridge, Mass., Jan. 11, 1965; s. Morton H Halperin and Ina Young. AB, Harvard U., 1987—87. Desk asst. ABC News, NYC, 1988, with investigative unit, World News Tonight, 1988—92, prodr. spl. events unit, 1994—97, polit. dir., 1997—2007; founder, editor The Note ABCnews.com, NYC; editor-at-large, sr. polit. analyst TIME mag., 2007—. Co-author (with John F. Harris): The Way to Win: Clinton, Bush, Rove, and How to Take the White House in 2008, 2006. Office: TIME mag 1271 Ave Americas New York NY 10020 also: ABC News 47 West 66th St New York NY 10023*

HALPERIN, MORTON H., political scientist; b. Bklyn., June 13, 1938; s. Harry and Lillian (Neubert) H.; m. Ina Elaine Weinstein, June 19, 1960 (div. Dec. 1979); children: David, Mark, Gary; m. Carol Pitchersky, Sept. 29, 1991 (dec. Oct. 2004); m. Diane Orentlicher, Nov. 12, 2005. AB, Columbia U., 1958; MA, Yale U., 1959, PhD, 1961. Rsch. assoc. Harvard U., 1960-66, asst. prof., 1963-66; dep. asst. sec. U.S. Dept. Def., Washington, 1966-69; sr. staff mem. NSC, Washington, 1969; sr. fellow Brookings Instn., Washington, 1969-73; rsch. project dir. Twentieth Century Fund, Washington, 1974-75; dir. Ctr. Nat. Security Studies, Washington, 1975-92; dir. Washington office ACLU, 1985-92; sr. assoc. Carnegie Endowment for Internat. Peace, 1992-94; Barer Prof. Internat. Rels. The George Washington U., Washington, 1992-94; spl. asst. to pres., sr. dir. for democracy NSC, Washington, 1994-96; sr. fellow Coun. Fgn. Rels., Washington, 1996-98; sr. v.p. Twentieth Century Fund/Century Found., Washington, 1997-98; dir. policy planning staff Dept. of State, 1998-2001; sr. fellow Coun. Fgn. Rels., Washington, 2001—03; dir. Washington office Open Soc. Inst., 2002—04; sr. v.p. Ctr. for Am. Progress, 2003—05, sr. fellow, 2006—. Dir. US Advocacy Open Soc. Instn., 2005—. Author: Limited War in the Nuclear Age, 1963, Contemporary Military Strategy, 1967, Bureaucratic Politics and Foreign Policy, 1974, 2d edit., 2006, Nuclear Fallacy, 1987, Self-Determination in a New World Order, 1992, The Democracy Advantage, 2005. Recipient Meritorious Civilian Svc. award U.S. Dept. Def., 1969; recipient Hugh M. Hefner 1st Amendment Playboy Found., 1981, W. Lucius Cross medal Yale Grad. Sch. Alumni Assn., 1983, John Jay award Columbia Coll., 1986; MacArthur Found. fellow, 1981-85. Mem. ACLU, Coun. Fgn. Rels., Internat. Inst. Strategic Studies. Democrat. Jewish. Home: 3710 McKinley St NW Washington DC 20015 Home Phone: 202-588-5444; Office Phone: 202-721-5602. Personal E-mail: mortonhalperin@yahoo.com. Business E-Mail: mhalperin@osi-dc.org.

HALPERIN, RICHARD E., lawyer, finance company executive; b. NYC, Dec. 7, 1954; s. Alvin M. and Anne (Beecher) H.; m. Lucy Landesman, Oct. 5, 1980. BS cum laude, Boston U., 1976; JD, New Eng. Sch. of Law, 1979. Bar: N.Y. 1980. Adminstrv. asst. to atty. gen. N.Y. State Exec. Bur., 1979-84; pres. R.O.P. Aviation, Teterboro, N.J., 1984-99; exec. v.p., spl. counsel to the chmn. Revlon Group Inc., NYC, 1985-99, MacAndrews & Forbes Group, Inc., NYC, 1984-99; founder, CEO Velocity Group LLC, NYC, 1999-2000; pres. Quellos Group LLC, NYC. Pres. Revlon Found., 1985-99, MacAndrews & Forbes Found., N.Y.C., 1984-99; prin. Quadra Fin. Group. Address: Quellos Group LLC 667 Madison Ave Fl 25 New York NY 10021-8029 Office Phone: 212-609-4100. E-mail: rhalperin@quellos.com.

HALPERIN, RICHARD GEORGE, information technology executive; b. Chgo., Apr. 5, 1948; s. Robert Charles and Phyllis Dorothy (Jewel) H.; m. Carolyn A'Della Bacino, Oct. 5, 1974; children: Nicole, Heidi, Erik. BSBA, Northwestern U., 1970. Mktg. mgr. IBM, Des Plaines, Ill., 1970-79; nat. sales mgr. Kast Metals, Shreveport, La., 1979-83; area dir. Wang Labs., Rolling Meadows, Ill., 1983-85; v.p. sales and svcs. System Software Assoc., Chgo., 1985-89; sr. v.p. Software Group XL Datacomp, Hinsdale, Ill., 1989-91; pres. Ex, Inc., Chgo., 1991-92; pres., CEO JBA Internat., Inc., Birmingham, Eng., 1992-98; CEO Coherent Networks Internat., 1998—99. Bd. dirs. Genesis, Glenview, Ill., Advanced Graphical Applications, Schaumburg, Am. Indian Svcs., Phoenix, Alliance, Anderson Cons., Chgo., Made 2 Manage, Indpls.; partnership CADDO Petroleum, Shreveport, La., 1981-86, BLM, Shreveport, 1981—. Named Top Dist. Mgr., Wang, Chgo., and Rome, 1984. Mem. Internat. Soc. Philos. Enquiry, Data Processing Mgrs. Assn., Info. Tech. Assn. Am., Northwestern Club of Chgo., Delta Upsilon, N Club Mens. Address: 641 Golf Rd Crystal Lake IL 60014-5650 Home Phone: 815-459-2959; Office Phone: 815-459-0366.

HALPERIN, ROBERT MILTON, retired electrical machinery company executive; b. Chgo., June 1, 1928; s. Herman and Edna Pearl (Rosenberg) H.; m. Ruth Levison, June 19, 1955; children: Mark, Margaret, Philip. Ph.B., U. Chgo., 1949; B.Mech. Engring., Cornell U., 1949; MBA, Harvard U., 1952. Locomotive prodn. engr. Electro-Motive divsn. Gen. Motors Corp., La Grange, Ill., 1949—50; trust rep. Bank of Am., San Francisco, 1954—56; adminstr. Dumont Corp., San Rafael, Calif., 1956—57; with Raychem Corp., 1957—94, pres., 1982—90, vice chmn. bd. dir. Menlo Park, Calif., 1990—94; chmn. bd. dir. Avis Tech., 1994—2004, Vitira Tech., Inc., 1994—2004; ret., 2004. Life trustee U. Chgo.; bd. dir. Harvard Bus. Sch. Pub. Co., Stanford U. Hosp. and Clinics; vice-chair, bd. dir. Stanford U. Hosp. and Clinics. Lt. USAF, 1952-53. Mem. Harvard Club of N.Y.C. Office: 2121 Sand Hill Rd Menlo Park CA 94025 E-mail: rmhalperin@sbcglobal.com.

HALPERIN, SAMUEL, education and training policy analyst; b. Chgo., May 10, 1930; married; 2 children. Student (scholar), Ill. Inst. Tech., 1948-49; AB, A.M. (scholar 1950-52), Washington U., St. Louis, 1952, PhD in Polit. Sci. (fellow 1954-56), 1956; postgrad., Columbia U., 1953-54. Asst. prof. polit. sci. Wayne State U., 1956-60; Am. Polit. Sci. Assn. congl. fellow Com. on Edn. and Labor, U.S. Ho. of Reps., 1960-61; legis. asst. to Hon. Cleveland M. Bailey and Adam C. Powell, 1960-61; cons. to subcom. on edn. and Senator Wayne Morse, Com. on Labor and Public Welfare, U.S. Senate, 1961, subcom. on reorgn., research and internat. orgns., 1970-73; specialist, dir. legis. services br. U.S. Office Edn., Washington, 1961-64; asst. U.S. commr. edn. for legis. and dir. office legis. and congl. relations, 1964-66; dep. asst. sec. for legis. HEW, Washington, 1966-69; founder, dir. Ednl. Staff Seminar, Washington, 1969-73; dir. Inst. for Ednl. Leadership, George Washington U., 1973-81, pres., 1981, sr. fellow, 1981-86; fellow Jerusalem Ctr. Pub. Affairs, 1981-84; coordinator Relief Activities in South Lebanon, Am. Jewish Joint Distbn. Com., 1982; founder, dir. Am. Youth Policy Forum, Washington, 1993—. Professorial lectr. Am. U., 1962-63; adj. prof. Tchrs. Coll. Columbia U., 1966-68; lectr. in edn. policy Duke U. Inst. Policy Scis. and Public Affairs, 1974-75; mem. vis. com. Harvard Grad. Sch. Edn., 1973-79; mem. Urban Edn. Task Force, Nat. Urban Coalition; mem. profl. rev. panels; cons. speaker, guest lectr. in field; mem. nat. adv. bd. U.S. Peace Corps, Exec. High Sch. Internships Am., Nat. Sch. Vol. Program, HEW Steering Com. on Life-Long Learning, Nat. Student Ednl. Fund, Am. Council Edn.'s Nat. Identification Program for Advancement Women in Higher Edn. Adminstrn., United Student Aid Funds; mem. Sec. of Navy's Adv. Bd. on Edn. and Tng.; mem. adv. panel on human resources research Rand Corp. Author: The Political World of American Zionism, 1961, 2d edit., 1985, A University in the Web of Politics, 1960, Essays on Federal Education Policy, 1975, A Guide for the Powerless, 1981, 2d edit. 2000, Any Home a Campus: Open University of Israel, 1984, The forgotten Half Revisited, 1998; co-editor, contbg. author: Perspectives on Federal Educational Policy, 1976, Federalism at the Crossroads, Improving Educational Policymaking, 1976, Shaping the Future of American Youth, 2003, Whatever It Takes: How 12 Communities Are Reconnecting Out-of-School Youth, 2006; contbr. numerous articles, revs. to profl. publs.; cons. Change mag.; mem. nat. adv. bd. Crossreference, Jour. Multi-Cultural Edn. Mem. nat. adv. bd. Am. Jewish Com.; founder, sec. DC Youth Svc. Corps.; nat. adv. coun. sch.-to-work, DC Commn. on Nat. Svc.; exec. bd. Coalition for Nat. And Cmty. Svc.; mem. coun. DC Pvt. Industry; bd. dirs. Learning Matters: mem. Merrow Report on PBS, Ctr. for Youth as Resources, Assocs. for Renewal in Edn., Coun. for Advancement of Adult Lit., Nat. Commn. Adult Lit., Alliance for Excellent Edn.; adv. bd. Gelman Libr., George Washington U.; Maj. ROTC, 1948-52. Recipient Superior Svc. award HEW, 1964, 67, Disting. Svc. award, 1968; award of merit Nat. Assn. Pub. Sch. Adult Edn.; Disting. Svc. awards Nat. Assn. State Bds. Edn., 1977, Nat. Assn. of Svc. and Conservation Corps., 1990, 97, Jobs for the Future, 1994, Pres.'s medal George Washington U., 1994, Harry S. Truman award Am. Assn. C.C., 1995, Lewis Hine award Nat. Child Labor Com., 1999; AFL-CIO rsch. grantee, 1959-60, Wayne State U. faculty rsch. grantee, 1958-59; Rockefeller Found. fellow, Bellagio, 1981, 92. Mem. Phi Beta Kappa, Pi Sigma Alpha (pres.) Home: 3041 Normanstone Ter NW Washington DC 20008-2731 Office: Am Youth Policy Forum 1836 Jefferson Pl NW Washington DC 20036-2505 Home Phone: 202-965-4831; Office Phone: 202-775-9731. Office Fax: 202-775-9733. Personal E-mail: shalperin18@comcast.net. Business E-mail: shalperin@aypf.org.

HALPERN, ABRAHAM LEON, psychiatrist; b. Warsaw, Feb. 2, 1925; came to U.S., 1957, naturalized, 1962; s. Rubin M. and Helen (Perelman) H.; m. Marilyn Lois Benjamin; children: Howard, Lon, Marnen, Heather Halpern Schneid, Mark, Emily Halpern Lewis, John. MD, U. Toronto, Ont., Can., 1952. Diplomate Am. Bd. Psychiatry and Neurology with cert. in forensic psychiatry, Am. Bd. Forensic Psychiatry; cert. mental hosp. adminstr.; cert. correctional health profl. Intern Toronto Western Hosp., 1952-53; resident Warren (Pa.) State Hosp., 1957-60, Ea. Pa. Psychiat. Inst., Phila., 1959; assoc. research scientist Mental Health Research Unit, Syracuse, NY, 1961-62; commr. mental health Onondaga County, 1962-67; practice medicine specializing in psychiatry Mamaroneck, NY, 1967—; dir. psychiatry United Hosp. Med. Ctr., Port Chester, 1967-91; attending psychiatrist Beth Israel Hosp., NYC, 1968-73, Westchester County Med. Ctr., 1971—; cons. forensic psychiatry High Point Hosp., Port Chester, 1969-93; cons. St. Vincent's Hosp., Harrison, NY, 1973-93; clin. assoc. prof. psychiatry N.Y. Med. Coll., Valhalla, NY, 1973-80, clin. prof. psychiatry, 1980-94, prof. emeritus of psychiatry, 1994—; cons. Rye (N.Y.) Hosp. Ctr., 1994—; attending psychiatrist Kirby Forensic Psychiat. Ctr., Ward's Island, NY, 1994-95; attending psychiatrist dept. alcohol/substance abuse treatment Yonkers (N.Y.) Gen. Hosp., 1995-96; clin. dir. mental health svcs. Dept. Correctional Program, Westchester County, NY, 1996; staff psychiatrist Bedford Hills Correctional Facility, NY, 2003—05. Clin. asst. prof. SUNY, Syracuse, 1964-67; asst. clin. prof. Mt. Sinai Sch. Medicine, 1970-74; clin. prof. forensic psychiatry, NY Sch. Psychiatry, 1979-82; med. adv. com. Vis. Nurse Assn., Syracuse, 1962-67; mem. NY State Mental Hygiene Med. Rev. Bd., 1982-86; bd. govs. High Point Hosp., 1989-92. Assoc. editor Bull. Am. Acad. Psychiatry and the Law, 1982-88, Jour. Am. Acad. Psychiatry and the Law, 2002-05; mem. editorial bd. Psychiat. Jour. of U. Ottawa, 1979-91; mem. exec. editorial com. Psychiat. Quar., 1982-90, assoc. editor, 1990—. Chmn. Syracuse chpt. Com. to Abolish Capital Punishment, 1962-65; mem. profl. adv. com. N.Y. State Assn. for Mental Health, 1964-67; mem. N.Y. State Law Revision Adv. Com. on the Insanity Def., 1979-80; mem. Westchester County Community Mental Health Bd., 1976-78, chmn., 1977-78; mem. Westchester County Hosp. Bd., 1992—; bd. visitors Harlem Valley Psychiat. Center, 1978-82; mem. N.Y. State Correction Med. Rev. Bd., 1980-87, N.Y. State Mental Hygiene Med. Rev. Bd., 1982-85; bd. dirs. Westchester Council on Alcoholism, 1980-85. Served to surgeon lt. comdr. Royal Can. Navy, 1942-45, 53-57. Recipient Citizenship award, NY State Bar Assn., 1966, Liberty Bell award, Onondaga County Bar Assn., 1966, Falun Dafa Appreciation award, 2000. Fellow ACP (William C. Menninger Meml. award for Disting. Contbns. to the Sci. of Mental Health, 2004), Royal Coll. Psychiatrists (hon.), Am. Acad. Forensic Scis., Am. Coll. Psychiatrists, Am. Psychiat. Assn. (com. psychiatry and law 1973-75, com. on abuse and misuse psychiatry and psychiatrists 1993-2003, com. on jud. action, 2006—, Human Rights award 2000), Am. Assn. Psychoanalytic Physicians (dir. 1978-84, Sigmund Freud award 2002) Can. Acad. Psychiatry and Law (Bruno Cormier award 2006) Am. Pub. Health Assn., Academia, Medicinae and Psychiatriae Found. (charter); mem. AMA, N.Y. State Med. Soc. (com. on mental health, com. bioethical issues, com. on child abuse and domestic violence, Pres.'s Citizenship award, 2003), Internat. Assn. Forensic Psychotherapy, Soc. Correctional Physicians, Pan Am. Med. Assn. (mem. council sect. on psychiatry 1983-85), Westchester County Med. Soc., Westchester Psychiat. Soc. (pres. 1973-74), Soc. Med. Jurisprudence (trustee 1980-85, 99-), Internat. Acad. Law and Mental Health (pres. 1983-87), Am. Acad. Psychoanalysis (sci. assoc. 1987), Am. Acad. Psychiatry and Law (councilor 1978-81, pres. elect 1981-82, pres. 1982-83, Golden Apple award 1987), Accreditation Coun. on Fellowships in Forensic Psychiatry (pres. 1990-93), Internat. Coun. on Prison Med. Svcs. (v.p. 1991-). Home and Office: 720 The Pky Mamaroneck NY 10543-4227 Office Phone: 914-698-2136. Personal E-mail: ahalpernmd@verizon.net.

HALPERN, ALVIN MICHAEL, retired physicist, educator, consultant; s. Bernard and Gilda (Reiss) H.; m. Mariarosa Roffi, Dec. 2, 1966; children: Kenneth, Marc. AB, Columbia U., 1959, MA, 1961, PhD, 1965. Instr. Pratt Inst., NYC, 1964-65; instr. physics Bklyn. Coll., 1965-66, asst. prof., 1966-69, assoc. prof., 1970-74, prof., 1975—, chmn. dept., 1980-90; exec. dir. Applied Scis. Inst., 1990-93; univ. dir. rsch. devel., v.p. rsch. found. CUNY, 1993-97, univ. dean rsch., interim pres. rsch. found., 1997-2000; retired. Contbr. articles to profl. jours. Recipient awards CUNY, 1976, 78, 80, 81, 84; Pfister fellow Columbia U., 1961-64, NSF predoctoral fellow Columbia U., 1959-61; NSF grantee, 1970, 72, 73, 78-80, 79-80, 80-82 Mem. AAAS, AAUP, Am. Phys. Soc., N.Y. Acad. Scis. Personal E-mail: alvin_halpern@yahoo.com.

HALPERN, BARRY DAVID, lawyer; b. Champaign, Ill., Feb. 25, 1949; s. I. L. and Trula M. Halpern; m. Cynthia Ann Zedler, Aug. 4, 1972; children: Amanda M., Trevor H. BA, U. Kans., 1971, JD, 1973. Bar: Kans. 1973, U.S. Dist. Ct. Kans. 1973, Fla. 1975, U.S. Supreme Ct. 1976, Ariz. 1978, U.S. Dist. Ct. Ariz. 1978, Colo. 1991. Ptnr. Snell & Wilmer, Phoenix, 1978—. Faculty Ariz. State U., 2002—03. Mem. Gov.'s Task Force Edn. Reform, 1991; judge pro tem Maricopa County Superior Ct.; bd. dirs. Crisis Nursery, Phoenix, 1987, Friends of Foster Children, Phoenix, 1987, Phoenix Symphony, Greater Phoenix Econ. Coun., 2003—, Combined Orgn. Met. Phoenix Arts and Scis., 1994—98, pres., 1996—97, mem. exec. com., 1998—2002. Mem.: ABA, Maricopa County Bar Assn. (chmn. med.-legal com. 1995—96), State Bar Colo., State Bar Kans., State Bar Fla., State Bar Ariz., Phoenix C. of C. (health care coun. 1993—96). Office: Snell & Wilmer 1 Arizona Ctr Phoenix AZ 85004-2202 Home Phone: 602-943-3384; Office Phone: 602-382-6345. Business E-Mail: bhalpern@swlaw.com.

HALPERN, BRUCE PETER, academic administrator, researcher, educator; b. Newark, Aug. 18, 1933; s. Leo and Thelma (Rubin) H.; m. Pauline Touber Anklowitz, June 9, 1956; children: Michael Touber, Stacey Rachael. AB, Rutgers U., 1955; M.Sc., Brown U., 1957, PhD, 1959. Asst. prof. physiology SUNY Upstate Med. U., Syracuse, NY, 1961-66; assoc. prof. psychology, neurobiology and behavior Cornell U., Ithaca, NY, 1966-73, prof., 1973-95, chmn. dept. psychology, 1974-90, 91-96, Susan Linn Sage prof. psychology, 1995—, prof. neurobiology and behavior, 1974—. Mem. Adv. Panel Sensory Physiology and Perception NSF, 1976-79; mem. adv. com. Nat. Inst. Neurol. and Communicative Disorders and Stroke, NIH, 1978-79, 85-87, Internat. Commn. on Olfaction and Taste, Union of Physiol. Scis., 1986-94; Fogarty sr. internat. fellow, vis. prof. oral physiology Osaka U., 1982-83; chmn. Gordon Conf. on Chem. Senses: Taste and Smell, 1987-90; PHS-NIMH postdoctoral fellow physiology, rsch. assoc., lect. psychology Cornell U., Ithaca, N.Y., 1959-61; vis. scientist Monell Chem. Senses Ctr., 1996-97. Exec. editor Chem. Senses, 1984-88; contbr. articles to profl. jours. NIMH grantee, 1958-62; NIH grantee, 1963-72; NSF grantee, 1972-90. Mem. Am. Physiol. Soc., Assn. Chemoreception Scis. (pres. 1982-83). Office: Cornell U Dept Psychology Dept Neurobiology/Behavior Uris Hall Ithaca NY 14853-7601 Home Phone: 607-257-0245; Office Phone: 607-255-6433. Business E-Mail: bph1@cornell.edu. *For those with power: As one's ability to influence or control the actions of others increases, one must become increasingly unwilling to use that ability. For scholars: Any generally accepted scientific idea is an ideal area for creative research, since the idea is almost certainly incorrect.*

HALPERN, DIANE F., psychology educator, professional association executive; b. Phila. BA in psychology, U. Penn., 1969; MA in psychology, Temple U., 1973, U. Cin., 1977, PhD in psychology, 1979; PhD (hon.), St. Mary's Coll., LA, 2004. Tchg. assistantship U. Cin., 1977—78, cons. behavioral scis. lab., 1978—79; lectr., dept. psychology U. Calif., Riverside, 1979—81; asst. prof. dept. psychology Calif. State U., San Bernardino, 1981—84, assoc. prof. dept. psychology, 1984—86, prof. dept. psychology, 1986—2001, chair, dept. psychology, 1996—99; dir. Berger Inst. for Work, Family, and Children Claremont McKenna Coll., 2001—, prof. psychology, 2001—, chair psychology dept., 2005—. Named Scholar-in-Residence, Rockefeller Found., 1995; recipient Prof. Yr. award, C. of C., 1986, Silver Medal, Coun. Advancement and Support Edn. (CASE), 1986, Ednl. Equity award, Assn. Black Faculty and Staff, 1987, Outstanding Alumni award, U. Cin., 1988, Birkett Williams Meml. Lecture award, Ouachita Baptist U., 1992, Fulbright Scholar award, 1994, Arthur Moorefield Meml. award, 1997, Disting. Vis. Scholar award, James Madison U., 1998, Wang Family Excellence award, 1999—2000, Disting. Alumni award, U. Cin. McMicken Coll. Arts & Scis., 2003. Fellow: Western Psychological Assn. (pres. 1999—2000, Outstanding Tchg. award 2002), Am. Psychological Soc. (charter mem.); mem.: APA (pres. 2004, named G. Stanley Hall Lecture 1991, Disting. Career Contbns. to Edn. and Training 1996—97, Eminent Women in Psychology 1998, Am. Psychological Found. award for disting. tchg. 1998—99, fellow divsn. 1, 2, 3, 35 1989), Psychonomic Soc., Am. Assn. Higher Edn. Office: Berger Inst Work, Family, and Children Claremont McKenna Coll Dept Psychology 850 Columbia Ave Claremont CA 91711: APA Pres's Office 750 First St NE Washington DC 20002-4242 Office Phone: 202-336-6074. Office Fax: 909-607-9647, 909-607-9672, 202-336-6157. Business E-Mail: diane.halpern@claremontmckenna.edu.

HALPERN, ERIC FRANKLIN, university publishing director; b. Portsmouth, NH, Feb. 28, 1952; s. Stephen and Irene Sally (Needle) H.; m. Frances Jane Weatherburn; children: Helen Augusta, Ian Henry. BA, U. Calif., Santa Cruz, 1974, Oxford U., 1977; MA, Stanford U., 1980. Asst. editor acquisitions Cornell Univ. Press., Ithaca, NY, 1981-84; editor humanities Johns Hopkins Univ. Press., Balt., 1984-90, editor-in-chief, 1990-96; dir. Univ. Pa. Press, Phila., 1996—. Trustee Fairmount Park Art Assn. Mem. Assn. Am. Univ. Presses. Office: Univ Pa Press 3905 Spruce Philadelphia PA 19104-4112 E-mail: ehalpern@pobox.upenn.edu.

HALPERN, JACK, chemist, educator; b. Poland, Jan. 19, 1925; came to U.S., 1962, naturalized; s. Philip and Anna (Sass) H.; m. Helen Peritz, June 30, 1949; children: Janice Henry, Nina Phyllis. BS, McGill U., 1946, PhD, 1949, DSc (hon.), 1997, U. B.C., 1986. NRC postdoc. overseas fellow U. Manchester, England, 1949-50; instr. chemistry U. B.C., 1950, prof., 1961-62; Nuffield Found. traveling fellow Cambridge (Eng.) U., 1959-60; prof. chemistry U. Chgo., 1962-71, Louis Block prof. chemistry, 1971-83, Louis Block Disting. Svc. prof., 1983—. Vis. prof. U. Minn., 1962, Harvard, 1966-67, Calif. Inst. Tech., 1968-69, Princeton U., 1970-71, Max. Planck Institut, Mulheim, Fed. Republic Germany, 1983—, U. Copenhagen, 1978; Sherman Fairchild Disting. scholar Calif. Inst. Tech., 1979; guest scholar Kyoto U., 1981; Firth vis. prof. U. Sheffield, 1982, Phi Beta Kappa vis. scholar, 1990; R.B. Woodward vis. prof. Harvard U., 1991; numerous guest lectureships; cons. editor Macmillan Co., 1963-65, Oxford U. Press; cons. Am. Oil Co., Monsanto Co., Argonne Nat. Lab., IBM, Air Products Co., Enimont, Rohm and Haas; mem. adv. panel on chemistry NSF, 1967-70; mem. adv. bd. Am. Chem. Soc. Petroleum Rsch. Fund, 1972-74, Trans Atlantic Sci. and Humanities Program, 2001--; mem. medicinal chemistry sect. NIH, 1975-78, chmn., 1976-78; mem. chemistry adv. coun. Princeton U., 1982—; mem. univ. adv. com. Ency. Brit., 1985—; mem. chemistry vis. com. Calif. Inst. Tech., 1991—; chmn. German-Am. Acad. Coun., 1993-96, chmn. bd. trustees, 1996—. Assoc. editor: Inorganica Chimica Acta, Jour. Am. Chem. Soc.; co-editor: Collected Accounts of Transition Metal Chemistry, vol. 1, 1973, vol. 2, 1977; assoc. editor Procs. NAS; mem. editl. adv. bd. Oxford Univ. Press, Internat. Series Monographs on Chemistry; mem. editl. bd. Jour. Organometallic Chemistry, Accounts Chem. Rsch., Catalysis Revs., Jour. Catalysis, Jour. Molecular Catalysis, Jour. Coord. Chemistry, Gazzetta Chimica Italiana, Organometallics, Catalysis Letters, Kinetics and Catalysis Letters; contbr. articles to Ency. Britannica, rsch. jours. Trustee Gordon Rsch. Confs., 1968-70; bd. govs. David and Arthur Smart Mus., U. Chgo., 1988—; bd. dirs. Ct. Theatre. Recipient Young Author's prize Electrochem. Soc., 1953, award in catalysis Noble Metals Chem. Soc., London, 1976, Humboldt award, 1977, Richard Kokes award Johns Hopkins U., 1978, Willard Gibbs medal, 1986, Bailar medal U. Ill., 1986, Wilhelm von Hoffman medal German Chem. Soc., 1988, Chem. Pioneer's award Am. Inst. Chemists, 1991, Paracelsus prize Swiss Chem. Soc., 1992, Basolo Medal, Northwestern U., 1993, Robert A. Welch award, 1994, Henry J. Albert award Internat. Precious Metals Inst., 1995, award in Organometallic Chem. Am. Chem. Soc., 1995, Order of Merit Federal Republic of Germany, 1996. Fellow AAAS, Royal Soc. London, Royal Soc. Can., Am. Acad. Arts and Scis., Chem. Inst. Can., Royal Soc. Chemistry London (hon.), N.Y. Acad. Scis., Japan Soc. for Promotion Sci.; mem. NAS (fgn. assoc. 1984-85, mem. coun. 1990—, chmn. chemistry sect. 1991-93, v.p. 1993—, assoc. editor Proceedings NAS), Am. Chem. Soc. (editl. bd. Advances in Chemistry series 1963-65, 78-81, chmn. inorganic chemistry 1985, award in inorganic chemistry 1968, award for disting. svc. in advancement of inorganic chemistry 1985, award in organometallic chemistry 1995), Max Planck Soc. (sci. mem. 1983—), Art Inst. Chgo., Renaissance Soc. (bd. dirs.), New Swiss Chem. Soc. (Paracelsus prize 1992), Am. Friends of the Royal Soc. (bd. dirs.), Sigma Xi. Home: 5801 S Dorchester Ave Apt 4A Chicago IL 60637 Office: U Chgo Dept Chemistry Chicago IL 60637 Office Phone: 773-702-7095. Business E-Mail: jhjh@uchicago.edu.

HALPERN, JAMES BLADEN, lawyer; b. Buffalo, Apr. 20, 1936; s. Philip and Goldene P. (Friedman) H.; m. Jessie Malkoff, July 6, 1958 (div.); 1 child, Jennifer; m. Niesa N. Brateman, Aug. 26, 1979; 1 child, Sheri. BA, Harvard U., 1958, JD, 1961. Bar: D.C. 1970. Atty. corp. fin. div. SEC, Washington, 1961—64; chief counsel-instns., instl. investor study, 1969—70; assoc. firm Proskauer Rose Goetz & Mendelsohn, NYC, 1964—69; assoc. Arent Fox LLP, Washington, 1971—73, ptnr., 1974—2003. Mem. Am. Law Inst. Democrat. Jewish.

HALPERN, JAMES S., federal judge; b. NYC, Oct. 16, 1945; s. William and Marion (Kohn) H.; m. Nancy A. Nord, Mar. 8, 1984; children: W. Dyer, Hilary A. BS cum laude, U. Pa., 1967, JD, 1972; LLM in Taxation, NYU, 1975. Bar: N.Y. 1973, D.C. 1983. Assoc. Mudge, Rose, Guthrie & Alexander, NYC, 1972—74; asst. prof. law Washington and Lee U., Va., 1975—76, St. John's U., 1976-78; vis. prof. law sch. NYU, 1978-79; assoc. Roberts & Holland, NYC, 1979-80; prin. tech. adv., asst. commr., assoc. chief counsel IRS, 1980-83; ptnr. Baker & Hostetler, Washington, 1983-90; judge US Tax Ct., Washington, 1990—. Adj. prof. law George Washington U., 1984—. Col. USAR. Mem. ABA (tax sect.). Office: US Tax Ct 400 2nd St NW Washington DC 20217-0002*

HALPERN, JOSEPH ALAN, physician; b. Bklyn., Feb. 28, 1952; s. Lester A. and Adele Janet (Tax) H.; m. Cynthia Gould, Sept. 1, 1979; 1 child, Elyza. AB, Bard Coll., Annandale on Hudson, NY, 1974; MD, N.Y. Med. Coll., Valhalla, 1978. Diplomate ABEM, ABIM. Resident family practice SUNY, Buffalo, 1978-79; resident in medicine Norwalk (Conn.) Hosp., 1979-81, chief resident medicine, 1981-82; emergency physician Kent and Queen Anne Hosp., Chestertown, Md., 1982-83, North Arundel Hosp., Glen Burnie, Md., 1983-85; attending emergency physician Johns Hopkins Hosp., Balt., 1986-87; emergency physician Anne Arundel Med. Ctr., Annapolis, Md., 1987—, assoc. chief emergency medicine, 1994—99. Attending physician Bayview Med. Ctr., Balt., 1992-94. Fellow Am. Coll. Emergency Physicians; mem. ACP, Med. Chi. Md. Avocations: sailing, bicycling. Office: Anne Arundel Med Ctr 2001 Medical Pkwy Annapolis MD 21401 Office Phone: 443-481-1293. E-mail: jhalp228@aol.com.

HALPERN, MARTIN BRENT, physics professor; b. Newark, Aug. 26, 1939; s. Melvin M. and Blanche B. (Friedman) H.; m. Penelope J. Dutton, June 2, 1988; 1 child, Tamar Lillian. BSc, U. Ariz., 1960; PhD, Harvard U., 1964. Postdoctoral fellow CERN, Geneva, 1964—65, U. Calif., Berkeley, 1965—66, prof. physics, 1967—; postdoctoral fellow Inst. Advanced Study, Princeton, NJ, 1966—67. Office: U Calif 366 Le Conte Hall Berkeley CA 94720-7303

HALPERN, MERRIL MARK, retired investment banker; b. Bayonne, NJ, May 4, 1934; s. Samuel and Belle (Schwartz) H.; m. Phyllis Goldstein, June 14, 1960 (div.); children: Belle Linda, Jennifer, Samuel, Isaac; m. Dolores M. Eckersley, Aug. 28, 1991. BS, Rutgers U., 1956; MBA, Harvard U., 1962. With Ernst & Ernst, NYC, 1956-60, sr. acct., 1958-60; with McDonnell & Co., Inc., 1962-68, v.p., 1967-68; ptnr., dir. corp. fin. H. Hentz & Co., NYC, 1969-70; prin. Merril M. Halpern & Co., NYC, 1970-73; pres. Charterhouse Group, Inc., NYC, 1973-84, chmn. bd., 1984—2006, emeritus chmn., 2007—. Trustee Nat. Humanities Ctr., 2000—, Continuum Health Ptnrs., 2001—. With US Army, 1957—58. Office: Charterhouse Group Inc 535 Madison Ave New York NY 10022-4212

HALPERN, PAUL G., retired history professor; b. NYC, Jan. 27, 1937; s. Harry and Teresa (Ritter) H. BA with honors, U. Va., 1958; MA, Harvard U., 1961, PhD, 1966. Instr. Fla. State U., Tallahassee, 1965-66, asst. prof., 1966-70, assoc. prof., 1970-74, prof. dept. history, 1974—2005; emeritus prof., 2005—. Vis. prof. strategy dept. Naval War Coll., Newport, R.I., 1986-87. Author: The Mediterranean Naval Situation, 1908-14, 1971, The Naval War in the Mediterranean, 1914-18 1987, A Naval History of World War I, 1994, Anton Haus: Österreich-Ungarns Grossadmiral, 1998, The Battle of the Otranto Straits, 2004; editor: The Keyes Papers, 3 vols., 1972-81, The Royal Navy in the Mediterranean, 1915-1918, 1987. Mem. Naval Aviation Mus. Found., Pensacola, Fla., Naval War Coll. Found., Newport, R.I. 1st lt. U.S. Army, 1958-60. Fellow Woodrow Wilson Nat. Fellowship Found., 1958. Fellow Royal Hist. Soc.; mem. Am. Hist. Assn., The Navy Records Soc. (coun. 1968-72, 82-86), Naval Rev., U.S. Naval Inst., Royal United Svcs. Inst. Def. Studies, Friends of Imperial War Mus., Friends of Nat. Maritime Mus., Naval Hist. Found., Soc. for Mil. History, Phi Beta Kappa, Phi Eta Sigma. Avocations: model ship collecting, book collecting, model soldier collection. Home: 3103 Brandemere Dr Tallahassee FL 32312

HALPERN, PHILIP MORGAN, lawyer; b. Derby, Conn., Apr. 17, 1956; s. Edwin Vincent and Carol Veronica (Gallagher) H.; m. Carolyn G. McElwreath, Mar. 11, 1989. BS magna cum laude, Fordham U., 1977; JD, Pace U., 1980. Bar: N.Y. 1981, U.S. Dist. Ct. (so. and ea. dists.) N.Y. 1981, U.S. Ct. Appeals (2d cir.) 1982, U.S. Tax Ct. 1984, U.S. Supreme Ct. 1985, U.S. Dist. Ct. Conn. 1989, Conn. 1989, U.S. Ct. Appeals (3d cir.) 1991; cert. trial adv. Nat. Bd. Trial Advocacy, 2002. Law clk. to sr. judge U.S. Dist. Ct. (so. dist.) N.Y., NYC, 1980-82; assoc. litigation dept. Kimmelman, Sexter & Sobel, NYC, 1982-83; ptnr. Collier, Halpern, Newberg, Nolletti & Bock, NYC, 1983—; mng. ptnr. Collier, Haplern, Newberg, Nolletti & Bock LLP, White Plains, NY, 1996—. Arbitrator Civil Ct. City N.Y. and Am. Arbitration Assn., 1987-96; adv. coun. Bd. of Judges, So. Dist. of N.Y., 1995-2000; mediator U.S. Dist. (so. dist.) N.Y., 1998—, mem. office ct. adminstrn. adv. com. on civil practice, 1999—; mem. bd. vis. Pace U. Sch. Law, 2006-. Author: Age Discrimination in Employment Act: Employers Can Enforce Releases Too!, 1992, Fair Value Proceedings: Fixing Fair Value in New York, 1996; author, editor: Civil Pretrial Proceedings in New York, 2 vols., 1999, updated annually through 2004, Court of Appeals Sharply Dimishes the Substantive Due Process Rights of Property Owners In New York, 2006, Unlocking a Valuable Tool: Summary Judgment Hearings on Issues of Fact, 2006. Chmn. Young Reps., Tuckahoe, N.Y., 1975-77; chmn. taxi commn. Village of Mamaroneck, N.Y., 1986-87, mem. planning bd., 1987-89. Fellow Am. Bar Found. (life); mem. N.Y. State Bar Assn. (com. on lawyer competency, com. on fed. judiciary), Assn. of Bar of City of N.Y., ATLA, N.Y. Trial Lawyers Assn., N.Y. County Lawyers Assn., Fed. Bar Coun., Profl. Golfers Assn. (adv. coun. metro. sect. 1992—), Westchester Country Club. Roman Catholic. Office: Collier Halpern Newberg Nolletti & Bock LLP One N Lexington Ave White Plains NY 10601 also: 99 Park Ave New York NY 10016-1601 Office Phone: 914-684-6800 x120. Business E-Mail: phalpern@chnnb.com.

HALPERN, RALPH LAWRENCE, lawyer; b. Buffalo, May 12, 1929; s. Julius and Mary C. (Kaminker) H.; m. Harriet Chasin, June 29, 1958; children: Eric B., Steven R., Julie B. LLB cum laude, U. Buffalo, 1953; BA in Math., SUNY, Buffalo, 2006. Bar: NY 1953. Teaching assoc. Northwestern U. Law Sch., 1953-54; assoc. firm Jaeckle, Fleischmann, Kelly, Swart & Augspurger, Buffalo, 1957-58; asso. firm Raichle, Banning, Weiss & Halpern (and predecessors), 1958-59, ptnr., 1959-86, Jaeckle Fleischmann & Mugel LLP, Buffalo, 1986—. Pres. Buffalo Coun. World Affairs, 1972-74, Temple Beth Zion, Buffalo, 1981-83, Bur. Jewish Edn., 2000-02; chmn. Buffalo chpt. Am. Jewish Com., 1975-77; bd. govs. United Jewish Fedn., Buffalo, 1972-78, 91-97, 1999-2004, 06—, v.p., 1992-95; dir. Landmark Soc. Niagara Frontier, 2006—. Served to capt. JAGC U.S. Army, 1954-57. Recipient Cmty. Svc. award, Am. Jewish Com., Buffalo, 2005. Mem. ABA (ho. dels. 1989-95, 97-99), N.Y. State Bar Assn. (chmn. com. profl. ethics 1971-76, chmn. com. jud. election monitoring 1983-86, chmn. spl. com. to consider adoption of ABA model rules of profl. conduct 1983-85, sec. internat. law and practice sect. 1992-93, vice chmn. 1993-95), Erie County Bar Assn., Am. Judicature Soc., Am. Law Inst. Home: 88 Middlesex Rd Buffalo NY 14216-3618 Office: Jaeckle Fleischmann & Mugel LLP 12 Fountain Plz Ste 800 Buffalo NY 14202-2292 Home Phone: 716-877-2039; Office Phone: 716-843-3846. Personal E-mail: rlhalpern@adelphia.net. Business E-Mail: rhalpern@jaeckle.com.

HALPERN, RICHARD I., lawyer; b. Pitts., June 10, 1949; BA with distinction, Stanford U., 1971; MBA, U. Pa., 1973; JD, NYU, 1976. Bar: Pa. 1976. Ptnr. Marcus & Shapira, LLC, Pitts. Mem. ABA. Office: Marcus & Shapira LLC 35th Fl One Oxford Ctr Pittsburgh PA 15219 E-mail: halpern@marcus-shapira.com.

HALPERSON, MICHAEL ALLEN, publishing executive; b. Boston, Sept. 11, 1946; s. Bertram David and Rose (Doolan) H. AB, Union Coll., 1968; MA in Teaching, U. Mass., 1970. Asst. to group v.p. Plymouth Rubber Co., Inc., Canton, Mass., 1972-73, corp. dir. pers. and indsl. rels., 1973-79, mgr. mktg., cons. products, 1979-81, dir. sales and mktg., 1981-85, v.p., 1985-92; v.p., gen. mgr. Plymouth Office Products a Hon Industries Co., Pawtucket, R.I., 1992-93; exec. v.p., COO Kryptonite Corp., Canton, Mass., 1994-95; exec. v.p. Dome Pub. Co. Inc., Warwick, R.I., 1995—, Data Binding, Inc., Warwick, R.I., 1995—; v.p. Parkway Realty, Inc., Warwick, R.I., 1995—, Dome Industries, Inc., Warwick, R.I., 1995—. Bd. dirs., v.p. Cape Cod Sea Camps, Inc., Capt. Del Assocs., Inc., Brewster, Mass.; treas. Camp Wono, Inc., Brewster, Mass. Bd. dirs. Canton Assn. Industries, Inc., 1977-92, Neponset Valley Nursing Assn., Inc., 1979-97, Southwood Cmty. Hosp., Norfolk, Mass., 1983-92, Neponset Valley Hospice, 1993-97, Norfolk-Bristol Homemakers Svc., Inc.; bd. dirs. Neponset Valley Health Sys., Inc., Norwood, Mass., 1985-92, chmn., 1990-92; bd. dirs. Norwood Hosp., Inc., 1983-92, chmn., 1988-90; bd. overseers Boston Ballet, 1992-93, Boston Symphony Orch., 1995—; trustee Boston Ballet Ctr. for Dance Edn., 1993-96, Boston Ballet, 1996-2002, sec. 1999-2000, Grant W. Koch Scholarship Trust, 1981—; mem. bd. visitors New Eng. Conservatory of Music, 2003—; mem. Mass. Cultural Facilities Fund Adv. Com., 2007—. With USAF, 1970-72. Mem. Bus. Products Industry Assn., (bd. dirs. 1996-99), Office Products Mfrs. Assn. (bd. dirs. 1985-92, 2000—05, pres. 1989, chmn. 1990); St. Botolph Club, Boston, Williams Club, N.Y.C. Avocations: reading, swimming. Home: 78 Cannon Forge Dr Foxboro MA 02035-5217 Office: Dome Pub Co Inc PO Box 1220 Ten New England Way Warwick RI 02887-1220 Office Phone: 401-738-7900.

HALPERT, DAVID H., lawyer; b. Detroit, May 18, 1946; BS magna cum laude, U. Mich., 1967; MS, Stanford U., 1968; JD cum laude, Harvard U., 1971; LLM, Boston U., 1976. Bar: Mass. 1971, DC 1974. Mem. Mintz, Levin, Cohn, Ferris, Glovsky and Popeo P.C., Boston. Adj. faculty Boston U Law Sch.; spkr. in field. Contbr. articles to profl. jour. Mem. ABA, DC Bar Assn., Boston Bar Assn., Mass. Bar Assn., Phi Beta Kappa. Office: Mintz Levin Cohn Ferris Glovsky and Popeo PC 1 Financial Ctr Fl 39 Boston MA 02111-2657 Office Phone: 617-542-6000, 617-348-1650. Office Fax: 617-542-2241. Business E-Mail: dhhalpert@mintz.com.

HALPIN, ANNA MARIE, retired architect; b. Murphysboro, Ill., July 24, 1923; d. John William and Anna Christina (Weilmuenster) Halpin. BS in Architecture, U. Ill., 1948. Designer, project arch. various firms, San Francisco, Rome, NYC, 1948-67; editorial dir. Sweet's div. McGraw-Hill, Inc., NYC, 1967-88; freelance cons., 1988-98; ret., 1998. Rep. to constrn. industries coordination com. Am. Nat. Metric Coun., 1974—80. Mem.: AIA (treas., bd. dirs. N.Y. chpt. 1974—78, coll. fellows 1976, nat. bd. dirs. 1977—79, nat. v.p., dir. Found. 1980, Richard Upjohn fellow 1991), Alliance Women Architecture, Constrn. Specifications Inst., Women's Equity Action League (pres. N.Y. 1976—77). Home: Apt 401 1404 NW 122nd St Oklahoma City OK 73114-8052

HALPIN, DANIEL WILLIAM, engineering educator, consultant; b. Covington, Ky., Sept. 29, 1938; s. Jordan W. and Gladys E. (Moore) H.; m. Maria Kirchner, Feb. 8, 1963; 1 child, Rainer. BS, U.S. Mil. Acad., 1961; MSCE, U. Ill., 1969, PhD, 1973. Research analyst Constrn. Engring. Research Lab., Champaign, Ill., 1970-72; faculty U. Ill., Urbana, 1972-73; mem. faculty Ga. Inst. Tech., Atlanta, 1973-85, prof., 1981-85; A.J. Clark prof., dir. Constrn. Engring. and Mgmt. U. Md., 1985-87; dir. divsn. Constrn. Engring. and Mgmt. Purdue U., West Lafayette, Ind., 1987—2006, interim head Sch. Civil Engring., 2000—01, Bowen engring head of constrn. engring. and mgmt., 2006—06, Bowen engring. head emeritus, 2006—. Cons. constrn. mgmt.; vis. assoc. prof. U. Sydney, Australia, 1981; vis. prof. Swiss Fed. Inst. Tech., 1985, U. Karlsruhe, Germany, 1998; vis. scholar Tech. U., Munich, 1979; vis. lectr. Ctr. Cybernetics in Constrn., Bucharest, Romania, 1973; cons. office tech. assessment U.S. Congress, 1986-87; mem. JTEC Team to evaluate constrn. tech., Japan, 1990; juror emeritus Constrn. Innovation Forum, 1994. Author: Design of Construction and Process Operations, 1976, Construction Management, 1980, 3d edit., 2005, Planung und Kontrolle von Bauproduktionsprozessen, 1979, Constructo - A Heuristic Game for Construction Management, 1973, Financial and Cost Control Concepts for Construction Management, 1985, Planning and Analysis of Construction Operations, 1992. Served with C.E., U.S. Army, 1961-67. Decorated Bronze Star; recipient Lifetime Achievement award INFORMS Constrn. sect., Coll. Simulation, 2004; grantee NSF, Dept. Energy, NIOSH. Mem. ASCE (hon.; past sect. pres. 1981-82, chmn. constrn. rsch. coun. 1985-86, Walter L. Huber prize 1979, Peurifoy Constrn. Rsch. award 1992, named disting. mem., 2006), Am. Soc. Engring. Edn., Nat. Acad. Constrn. (elected 2003), Constrn. Industry Inst. (rsch. com. 1996-2005, Carroll H. Dunn award 2006), Constrn. Innovation Forum (juror emeritus), Sigma Xi. Methodist. Business E-Mail: halpin@purdue.edu.

HALPRIN, ALBERT, lawyer; b. NYC, Oct. 18, 1947; m. Janice Obuchowski, Jan. 8, 1983 BA, Western Wash. State Coll., 1971; JD, Harvard U., 1974. Sr. atty.-adviser CAB, 1978-80; sr. FCC, Washington, 1980-81, chief policy and program planning div., 1981-83; ptnr. Kestenbaum & Halprin, Washington, 1983-84; pres. Albert P. Halprin Assocs., Inc., Washington, 1984; former chief Common Carrier Bur., FCC, Washington; now ptnr. Halprin, Mendelsohn & Goodman, Washington; ptnr. Halprin, Temple, Goodman, & Maher, Wash., DC. Office: Halprin Temple Goodman & Maher 555 12th St NW Ste 950 N Washington DC 20004

HALPRIN, ANNA SCHUMAN (MRS. LAWRENCE HALPRIN), dancer; b. Wilmette, Ill., July 13, 1920; d. Isadore and Ida (Schiff) Schuman; m. Lawrence Halprin, Sept. 19, 1940; children: Daria, Rana. Student, Bennington Summer Sch. Dance, 1938-39; BS in Dance, U. Wis., 1943; PhD in Human Services (hon.), Sierra U., Riverside, Calif., 1987; PhD (hon.), U. Wis., 1994, Santa Clara U., Calif.; student, Calif. Arts Coll., Calif., 2003; PhD (hon.), Art Inst. of San Francisco, Calif., 2003. Presenter opening invocation State of the World Forum by spl. invitation from Mikhail S. Gorbachev. Author: Moving Toward Life, Five Decades of Transformative Dance, Dance as a Healing Art, A Teachers' Guide and Support Manual for People with Cancer; dancer: at Kennedy Ctr., Washington, Yerba Buena Ctr. for Arts, San Francisco, Joyce Theatre, NYC, 2001—, d'Autumne Festival Paris, Pompidou Theatre, 2004, Cowell Theatre, Returning Home (1st prize Film Dance Festival N.Y.C., 2004), (film) Moving with the Earth Body, Learning Lessons in Life, Loss & Liberation, 2003, Intensive Care, Reflections on Death and Dying, 2003, Jewish Cmty. Ctr. Kinball Theatre, 2006, San Francisco, Jewish Cmty. Ctr., 2006, others Bd. dirs. East West Holistic Healing Inst.; mem. Gov.'s Coun. on Phys. Fitness and Wellness. Recipient award Am. Dance Guild, 1980, Guggenheim award, 1970-71, Woman of Wisdom award Bay Area Profl. Women's Network, Tchr. of Yr. award Calif. Tchrs. Assn., 1988, Lifetime Achievement award in visual and performing arts San Francisco Bay Guardian newspaper, 1990, Women of Achievement, Vision and Excellence award, 1992, Balasaraswati/Joy Ann Dewey Bieneke chair for disting. tchg. Am. Dance Festival, 1996, Lifetime Achievement in Modern Dance award Am. Dance Festival, 1997, Lifetime Achievement award Calif. Arts Coun., 2000, Breast Cancer Watch, 2001, Dance Mag. N.Y.C. award, 2004; Person of Yr. in field of Dance award Ballet-ranz, Berlin; named to Isadora Duncan Hall of Fame, Bay Area Dance Coalition, 1986; Nat. Endowment Arts Choreographers grantee, 1976, NEA choreography grantee, 1977, San Francisco Found. grantee, 1981, Calif. Arts. Coun. grantee, 1990—; inductee Marin Women's Hall of Fame, 1998, lifetime achievement award Marin Arts Coun., Sustained Achieve. award Am. Theatre Edn. Assn., 2005, award Healing Arts Network, 2006. Fellow Am. Expressive Therapy Assn.; mem. Assn. Am. Dance, Conscientious Artists Am., San Francisco C. of C. Home and Office: 15 Ravine Way Kentfield CA 94904-2713 Home Phone: 415-461-5362; Office Phone: 415-461-5362. Personal E-mail: anna@annahalprin.org. *Today I am deeply involved in making a contribution as an artist to world peace. I'm interested in the development of public workshops and dance rituals to create harmony and understanding in social and healing interactions in communities. The Planetary takes place around the world and this year 2007 is its 27th anniversary.*

HALPRIN, LAWRENCE, landscape architect, urban planner; b. Bklyn., July 1, 1916; s. Samuel W. and Rose (Luria) H.; m. Ann Schuman, Sept. 19, 1940; children: Daria, Rana. BS in Plant Scis, Cornell U., 1939; MS in Plant Scis, U. Wis., 1941; B.Landscape Architecture, Harvard U., 1942. Sr. assoc. Thomas D. Church & Assos., San Francisco, 1946-49; prin. Lawrence Halprin & Assos., San Francisco, 1949-76; co-founder Round House, San Francisco, 1976-78; founder Lawrence Halprin Studios, 1978—; lectr. U. Calif.-Berkeley, 1960-65, Regents prof., 1982-83. Dir., Halprin Summer Workshop, 1966, 1968; prin. works include Ghirardelli Sq., San Francisco, Sea Ranch, Calif., Nicolett Mall, Mpls., Old Orchard Shopping Center, Skokie, Ill., Lovejoy Fountain, Pettigrove Park, Forecourt Fountain, Portland, Oreg., Market St. reconstrn, San Francisco, Seattle Freeway Park, Rochester Manhattan Park, Franklin Delano Roosevelt Meml, Washington, Levi Park and Plaza, San Francisco, Haas Promenade, Jerusalem, Bunker Hill Stairs, Central Library, Hope St. and Olympic Park, Los Angeles; author: Cities, 1963; rev. edit., 1972, Freeways, 1966, New York, New York, 1968, The RSVP Cycles, 1970, Lawrence Halprin Notebooks, 1959-71, 1972; co-author: The Freeway in the City, 1968, Taking Part: A Workshop Approach to Collective Creativity, 1974, The Sketch Books of Lawrence Halprin, 1981; filmmaker: Le Pink Grapefruit, Franklin Delano Roosevelt Memorial, How Sweet It Is!, Designing Environments for Everyone. Panelist White House Conf. Natural Beauty, 1965; mem. bd. urban cons. Bur. Pub. Roads, 1966-67; design cons. Calif. Div. Hwys., 1963-65; landscape architect, urban cons. San Francisco Bay Area Rapid Transit Dist., 1963-66; mem. Gov.'s Conf. Calif. Beauty, 1966, Nat. Council Arts, 1966— , Adv. Council, Historic Preservation, 1967—; bd. dirs., San Francisco Dancers Workshop Co., 1950—. Served to lt. (j.g.) USN, 1943-46. Named One of Leaders of Tomorrow, Time mag. 1953, recipient awards including Allied Professions Gold medal AIA 1964, Thomas Jefferson award in architecture 1979, Richard J. Neutra award for Excellence, 1986, National Medal of Arts, 2002, Friedrich Ludwig von Sckell Golden Ring, 2002, Michaelangelo award, 2005; honored Changing Places Exhbn., San Francisco Mus. Modern Art, 1986. Fellow Am. Soc. Landscape Architects (Design medal 2003); mem. Am. Acad. Arts and Scis., Sierra Club. Democrat. Jewish.

HALPRIN, RICK (RICHARD ALLAN HALPRIN), lawyer; b. Chgo., Feb. 28, 1940; s. David Harold and Mary (Stepansky) H.; m. Dale Lawrence, Mar. 17, 1967 (div. June 1970); 1 child, Eden; m. Robyn Douglass. BA, Roosevelt U., 1964; JD, Massey Coll., 1968. Bar: Mass. 1970, Ill. 1970, U.S. Dist. Ct. (no. dist.) Ill. 1970. Pvt. practice. Capt. USMCR, 1970-72. Mem. Nat. Assn. Criminal Defense Lawyers (advisor), Ill. Bar Assn. (criminal justice com.), Chgo. Bar Assn. Office: 542 S Dearborn St Ste 750 Chicago IL 60605-1525*

HALSBAND, FRANCES, architect; b. NYC, Oct. 30, 1943; d. Samuel and Ruth H.; m. Robert Michael Kliment, May 1, 1971; 1 child, Alexander H. BA, Swarthmore Coll., 1965; MArch, Columbia U., 1968. Registered architect, N.Y., N.J., Mass., Conn., Ohio, Va., N.H., Pa., D.C., N.C., Ill., Miss., La., Fla.; cert. Nat. Coun. Archtl. Reg. Bds. Arch. Mitchell/Giurgola Archs., NYC, 1968-72; ptnr. R.M. Kliment & Frances Halsband Archs., NYC, 1972—. Vis. critic archtl. design Columbia U., 1975-78, 87, N.C. State U., 1978, Rice U., 1979, U. Va., 1980, Harvard U., 1981, U. Pa., 1981, U. Calif., Berkeley, 1997; dean Sch. Architecture, Pratt Inst., 1991-94; Freidman prof. U. Calif., Berkeley, 1997; Emens Disting. prof. Ball State U., 1998; Kea prof. U. Md., 2000; mem. N.Y.C. Landmarks Preservation Commn., 1984-87; lectr. U. So. Calif., U. Va., Temple U., Washington U., Tulane U., Harvard U., U. Oreg., U. Washington. Projects include: computer Sci. Bldg., Columbia U. (AIA Nat. Honor award 1987), Gilmer Hall addition U. Va., Town Hall, Salisbury Conn., Computer Sci. Bldg., Princeton U. (AIA Nat. Honor award 1994), Case Western Res. Adelbert Hall restoration (AIA Nat. Honor award 1994), Alvin Ailey Am. Dance Theater Found., N.Y.C., hdqs. Marsh & McLennan Co., Ind. Bank Hdqs., Bklyn. Coll. Master Plan, Entrance Pavillion L.I. Rail Rd. Penn Sta. (AIA Nat. award), U.S. Courthouse and Post Office, Bklyn., Yale Div. Sch., Dartmouth Roth Ctr. for Jewish Life, U.S. Courthouse, Gulfport, Miss.; works exhibited in Cooper-Hewitt Mus., Bklyn. Mus., Nat. Acad. Design, Deutsches Architekturmuseum, Frankfourt; author: Annotated Bibliography of Technical Resources for Small Museums, 1983. Trustee Nat. Inst. Archtl. Edn., 1988-93; mem. archtl. rev. panel Fed. Res. Sys., 1993—; mem. U.S. Dept. State Office Fgn. Bldgs. Ops. Archtl. Adv. Bd., 1998—; U.S. Gen. Svcs. Adminstrn. Nat. Register Peer Profls., 1998—. Fellow AIA (exec. bd. N.Y.C. chpt. 1979, pres. N.Y.C. chpt. 1991-92), Century Assn.; mem. Archtl. League N.Y. (exec. bd. 1975—, v.p. arch. 1981-85, pres. 1985-89), Assn. Collegiate Schs. Architecture (N.E. regional dir. 1993-95). Office: RM Kliment & Frances Halsband 255 W 26th St New York NY 10001-8001

HALSE, FRANK ADAMS, JR., retired minister; b. Troy, NY, May 3, 1927; s. Frank Adams and Anna Evelyn Halse; m. Joyce Holcomb Halse, June 7, 1952; children: Laurie Halse Anderson, Lisa Halse Stevens. AB in Psychology and Religion, Boston U., 1955, MA in Sacred Theology, Psychology and Religion, 1958; MA in Family Studies, Syracuse U., 1972, postgrad., 1972—75. Pastor United Meth. Ch., Parish, NY, 1955—62, exec. dir. Wesley Found. Potsdam, NY, 1962—65, pastor Pulaski, NY, 1965—66, chaplain Syracuse (N.Y.) U., 1966—75; exec. dir. County North Counseling Ctr., Syracuse, 1976—78, N.W. Counseling Ctr., Syracuse, 1978—80; pastor United Meth. Ch., Navarino, NY, 1981—83, Cazenovia, NY, 1984—86; ret., 1990. Travelling elder United Meth. Ch.; cons., lectr. in field; specialist adolescent suicide. Author: (newspaper column) Family Talk, 1976—80, (book of poetry) Sidewalks of Fog, 1962, Poems of the Spirit, 1970, A Portable Ark, 1978, The Wreckage of Christianity, 2001, The Lord's Prayer, 2002, The Sadducean Rag and Other Critical Poems, 2004; editor: Stepparents: Living, Loving and Learning, 1977. Del. Dem. Nat. Conv., Miami, Fla., 1972. Cpl. U.S. Army Air Corps, 1945—49, ETO. Mem.: Am. Assn. Marriage and Family Therapists (clin.), Acad. Am. Poets, Poetry Soc. Am. Avocations: poetry, gardening. Home: 15 Kimberley Ln Ap A2D Mexico NY 13114 Personal E-mail: fhalse@twcny.rr.com.

HALSEY, ASHLEY, III, newspaper editor; b. Phila., Aug. 4, 1952; s. Ashley Jr. and Margaret (Woods) H.; children: Graham Ketchum Halsey, Ellery Ketchum Halsey. BA, Temple U., 1974. Reporter Germantown Courier, Phila., 1972, sports editor, 1973, mng. editor, 1975-77; reporter Phila. Bull., 1977-79, Phila. Inquirer, 1980-81, nat. corr., 1982-85, asst. nat. editor, 1985-86, dep. nat. editor, 1986-88, dep. fgn. editor, 1989-91, nat. editor, 1991-96, travel editor, 1996-97; asst. city editor Washington Post, 1997-98, dep. Md. editor, 1999, Md. editor, 1999—2005, assoc. metro editor, 2005—. Avocations: sailing, running, bicycling. Office: The Washington Post 1150 15th St NW Washington DC 20071-0002 Office Phone: 202-334-6000. Business E-Mail: halseya@washingtonpost.com.

HALSEY, DOUGLAS MARTIN, lawyer; b. Warwick, RI, 1953; s. Donald Post Jr. and Marita H.; m. Amy Klinow, Sept. 5, 1976; children: Mark, Meredith. BA, Columbia U., 1976; JD cum laude, U. Miami, 1979. Bar: Fla. 1979, U.S. Ct. Appeals (11th cir., 5th cir.), U.S. Dist. Ct. (so. dist., mid. dist.) Fla. Assoc. Paul & Thomson, Miami, Fla., 1979-85; ptnr. Thomson, Bohrer, Werth & Razook, Miami, 1985-88, Douglas M. Halsey, P.A., Miami, 1989-97, Halsey & Burns, P.A., Miami, 1997-2000, White & Case LLP, Miami, 2000—. Rsch. editor U. Miami Law Review, 1978-79. Mem. Alexis de Tocqueville Soc., United Way of Miami-Dade County, 1995—; chmn.Children's Home Soc. Fla., 2000-2002; chmn. Foster Care Rev., Inc., Miami, Fla., 1998-2000. Mem. Fla. Bar (chmn. environ. and land use law sect. 1993-94, President's Pro Bono Svc. award 1991). Office: Wachovia Fin Ctr 200 S Biscayne Blvd Ste 4900 Miami FL 33131-2352 Office Phone: 305-371-2700. E-mail: dhalsey@whitecase.com.

HALSEY, JAMES ALBERT, entertainer, theater producer; b. Independence, Kans., Oct. 7, 1930; s. Harry Edward and Carrie Lee (Messick) H.; m. Minisa Crumbo; children: Sherman Brooks, Gina, Cris, Woody. Student, Independence Community Coll., 1948-50, U. Kans.; doctorate of Fine Arts honoris causa, Baker Univ., 1992. Pres. Thunderbird Artists, Inc., Independence, from 1950, Jim Halsey Co., Inc., Tulsa, from 1952, Norwood Advt. Agy., James Halsey Property Mgmt. Co., Tulsa Proud Country Entertainment, Stas. KTOW/KGOW, J.H. Radio Mgmt., Cyclone Records, Tulsa Records, J.H. Lighting and Sound Co., Singin' T Prodns.; v.p. Gen. Artists Corp., Beverly Hills, Calif., 1966; chmn., chief exec. officer Century City Artists Corp., Tulsa, Nashville; personal mgr. various entertainment personalities; pres. Internat. Fedn. Festival Orgns.; mgr. Oakridge Boys, 1975. Internat. jurist Golden Orpheus Festival, Bulgaria, 1981-82, 84, 88, 94; ptnr. Billboard Song Contest; cons. William Morris Agy., 1990-95; producer shows for auditoriums, fairs, rodeos, TV, internat. music fests also others in U.S. and internationally including Tulsa Internat. Music Festival, 1977-80, Neewollah Internat. Music Festival, 1981-83; gen. ptnr. Parker Ranch, Tulsa; bd. dirs. Merc. Bank and Trust, Tulsa, Citizens Nat. Bank, Independence, Farmers & Mchts. Bank, Mound City, Kans., Nashville Symphony; chmn. mus. bus. dept. Okla. City U., 1994—; lectr., speaker colls., univs., 1992—. Trustee Philbrook Art Ctr., Tulsa; bd. dirs. Thomas Gilcrease Mus. Assn., Tulsa Philharm. Assn., Roy Clark Celebrity Golf Classic, UNICEF, Nashville Symphony, Nat. Music Coun. Served with U.S. Army, 1954-56. Recipient Disting. Service award U.S. Jr. C. of C., 1959, Ambassador of Country Music award SESAC Corp., 1978, citation Cashbox Mag., 1980, citation Golden Orpheus Festival, 1982, Hubert Long award Wembley Festival, Eng., 1982, commendation Los Angeles Mayor Tom Bradley, Gov.'s medal Kans. Commn., 1986, Frederic Chopin medal Polish Artist Bur., 1987, Lifetime Achievement award Internat. Buyers Assn., 1997, Okla. Govs. award for excellence art and edn., 1998, Cherokee medal of honor Cherokee Hist. Soc., 1999; named Disting. Kansan Topeka Capital Jour.; inductee Okla. Music Hall of Fame, 2000. Mem. Country Music Assn. (bd. dirs. 1963-64, 70-71, v.p. 1979-80, Founding Pres.'s award 1985), Acad. Country Music (bd. dirs. 1969-70, 73-74, v.p. 1975-76, 78-79, 79-80, 88-89, Jim Reeves Meml. award 1977), Internat. Fedn. Festival Orgns. (Am. pres., Oscar Midem award 1982). Home: 720 N 136 Rd Mounds OK 74047-5275 Office Phone: 918-827-6529. E-mail: jim@jimhalsey.com.

HALSEY, JEAN MICHELE, nursing educator; b. St. Louis, Oct. 16, 1949; d. Martha Idabelle Halsey and George Orlander Johnson; 1 child, Rene' Erle Jordan. Diploma, St. Louis Mcpl. Sch. of Nursing, 1972. RN Mo., 1972, Wyo., Calif., 1979, Fla., Okla., 1982, Wash., 2004. Staff nurse St. Louis City Hosp., 1972—75, St. Louis U. Hosp., 1975—78; travel nurse Comprehensive Nursing Svcs., St. Louis, 1979; staff nurse Cedar Sinai Med. Ctr., LA, 1979—82; critical care instr. Los Altos Hosp., Long Beach, Calif., 1981—82; staff nurse City of Faith, Tulsa, Okla., 1982—83, St. Mary's Hosp., West Palm Beach, Fla., 1983—85, PRN Nursing Agy., Clearwater, Fla., 1985—. Vol. nurse educator Am. Heart Assn., West Palm Beach, Fla., 1982—85. Prayer ptnr. City of Faith, Tulsa, Okla., 1982—83. Republican. Achievements include research in the effects of intravenous inderal on the outcome of post myocardial infarction patient; the effects of streptokinase, urokinase and tissue plasminogen activator on myocardial infarction patients; the effects of intravenous nitroglycerine, intravenous amiodarone, intravenous dopamine, intravenous dobutrex, and intravenous nitroprusside on the outcomes of cardiogenic shock patients; the use of angioplasty on post myocardial infarction patients; the use of various types of Swan Ganz catheters in the treatment of myocardial infarction patients. Avocations: domestic and European travel, gardening, reading, gourmet cooking. Home: 731 Park Pl West Palm Beach FL 33401 Office: PRN Nursing Agy Ste 102 13575 58th St N Clearwater FL 33760 Home Phone: 561-385-7198; Office Phone: 727-443-4443. Office Fax: 727-538-4258. Personal E-mail: jhals3@aol.com.

HALSEY, MARTHA TALIAFERRO, Spanish language educator; b. Richmond, Va., May 5, 1932; d. James Dillard and Martha (Taliaferro) H. AB, Goucher Coll., 1954; MA, U. Iowa, 1956; PhD, Ohio State U., 1964. Asst. prof. Spanish Pa. State U., University Park, 1064—1970, assoc. prof., 1970—79, prof., 1979—95, prof. emeritus, 1995—. Vis. Olive B. O'Connor prof. lit. Colgate U., Hamilton, NY, 1983. Author: Antonio Buero Vallejo, 1973, Dictatorship to Democracy: the Recent Plays of Buero Vallejo (La Fundación to Música cercana), 1994; editor: Madrugada, 1969, Hoy es fiesta, 1978, Los inocentes de la Moncloa, 1980, El engaño, Caballos desbocaos, 1981, (with Phyllis Zatlin) The Contemporary Spanish Theater: A Collection of Critical Essays, 1988, Entre actos: Diálogos sobre teatro español entre siglos, 1999, Estreno, 1992-98; gen. editor Estreno Contemporary Spanish Plays, 1992-98, Estreno Studies in Contemporary Spanish Theater, 1998—; mem. editl. bd. Modern Internat. Drama, 1968-75, Ky. Romance Quar., 1970-76, Annals Contemporary Spanish Lit., 1991—, Tesserae: Jour. Iberian and Latin Am. Studies, 1997—; contbr. articles to profl. jours. Grantee Am. Philos. Soc., 1970, 78, Inst. for Arts and Humanistic Studies, 1977, Program Cultural Coop. Between Spanish Ministry Culture and U.S. Univs., 1992, 94-95. Fellow Hispanic Soc. Am. (hon.); mem. MLA, N.E. MLA, Am. Assn. Tchrs. Spanish and Portuguese, Fellowship of Reconciliation, War Resisters League, Phi Beta Kappa, Phi

Sigma Iota, Sigma Delta Pi. Democrat. Episcopalian. Home: 500 E Marylyn Ave Apt I-140 State College PA 16801-5248 Office: Pa State U Dept Spanish University Park PA 16802

HALSTEAD, REBECCA S., career military officer; b. Willseyville, NY; d. Richard and Betty Jeanne Halstead. Grad., U.S. Military Acad., 1981; M in Military Art and Sci., Command and Gen. Staff Coll.; M in Nat. Resource Strategy, Nat. Def. U. Advanced through ranks to gen. US Army; platoon leader 69th Ordnance Co., 559th Artillery Group, Vicenza, Italy, ops. officer, exec. officer; comdr. Hdqs. Co., 63rd Ordnance Co.; materiel officer 80th Ordnance Battalion, Fort Lewis, Wash.; exec. officer battalion and support ops. 101st Airborne Divsn., Fort Campbell, Ky.; comdr. 325th Forward Support Battalion, 25th Infantry divisn., Shofield Barracks, Hawaii, 10th Mountain Divsn Support Command, Fort Drum, NY; exec. asst. to combatant comdr. U.S. So. Command, Miami; dep. commdg. gen. 21st Theater Support Command, Kaiserslautern; comdr./comdt. Army Ordnance Ctr. and Schools Aberdeen Proving Ground, Md., 2006—. Decorated Def. Superior Svc. Medal, Legion of Merit, Meritorious Svc. Medal with five oak leaf clusters, Army Commendation Medal with oak leaf cluster, Army Achievement Medal, Air Assault Badge, Army Staff Badge. Achievements include becoming first female West Point graduate to achieve the rank of general. Office: US Army Aberdeen Proving Ground 2201 Aberdeen Blvd Aberdeen Proving Ground MD 21005-5001

HALSTED, MARGO, music educator, carillonneur; b. Bakersfield, Calif., Apr. 24, 1938; d. Anthony Charles and Rose Louise Armbruster; m. A. Stevens Halsted, Sept. 12, 1959 (div. 1987); children: Suzanne, Christopher; m. Peter LeSourd, July 21, 2002. BA, Stanford U., Calif., 1960, MA, 1965, U. Calif., Riverside, 1975; diploma, Netherlands Carillon Sch., 1981. Cert. tchr. Calif. Assoc. carillonneur Stanford (Calif.) U., 1967—77; lectr. U. Calif., Riverside, 1977—87; from asst. prof. to assoc. prof. emeritus U. Mich., Ann Arbor, 1987—2003, assoc. prof. and carillonneur emeritus, 2003—. Vis. carillonneur Mich. State U., 1996—98; cons. in field. Musician: various recitals internationally. Recipient Berkeley medal, U. Calif., 1959, Bell and Citation awards, World Carillon Fedn., 1986, 2003. Mem.: Guild of Carillonneurs in N.Am. (sec., com. chmn., del., Extraordinary Svc. cert. 1997), American Guild Organists, Coll. Music Soc. Achievements include discovery of 2 historic carillon manuscripts in Belgium. Avocations: skiing, languages, hiking. Home: 330 Cordova St # 324 Pasadena CA 91101-3602

HALSTON, DANIEL WILLIAM, lawyer; b. Mineola, NY, Sept. 19, 1960; s. James Matthew and Mary Rita (Magner) H.; m. Liliane Regina Wong, Sept. 27, 1986. BA with honors, Vassar Coll., 1982; JD cum laude, Boston U., 1986. Bar: Mass. 1986, U.S. Dist. Ct. Mass. 1987, U.S. Ct. Appeals (1st cir.) 1987. Law clk. Judge William G. Young, U.S. Dist. Ct. Mass., Boston, 1986-87; assoc. Hale & Dorr, Boston, 1987—91; asst. atty. gen. Office of Mass. Atty. Gen., 1991-94; assoc. Hale & Dorr, Boston, 1994—98, ptnr., 1998—2004; ptnr., Securities dept. & Litigation dept., chmn. Hiring com. Wilmer Cutler Pickering Hale & Dorr, Boston, 2004—. Instr. Boston U. Sch. Law, 1989-90. Contbr. articles to profl. jours. Dir. Mass. Appleseed Ctr. for Law & Justice. Edward G. Hennessey scholar Boston U., 1983-86; named a Mass. Super Lawyer, Boston Mag., 2004-06; named one of Leading Lawyers in Litigation, Chambers USA, 2005, 06. Mem. ABA, Supreme Jud. Ct. Hist. Soc., Mass. Bar Assn., Boston Bar Assn. Democrat. Roman Catholic. Avocations: reading, golf, basketball, travel. Office: Wilmer Cutler Pickering Hale & Dorr 60 State St Boston MA 02109-1816 Office Phone: 617-526-6654. Office Fax: 617-526-5000. Business E-Mail: daniel.halston@wilmerhale.com.

HALSTRÖM, FREDERIC NORMAN, lawyer; b. Boston, Feb. 26, 1944; s. Reginald F. and Margaret M. (Graham) H.; divorced, 1989, m. Lena Strelnikova, 2001; children: Ingrid Alexandra, Reginald Frederic II, Mikhail Strelnikova. Student, Northeastern U., 1961-63, USAF Acad., 1963-65; AB, Georgetown U., 1967; JD, Boston Coll., 1970. Bar: Mass. 1970, U.S. Dist. Ct. Mass., 1971, U.S. Dist. Ct. R.I. 1981, U.S. Tax Ct., 1981, U.S. Ct. Appeals (1st cir.) 1971, U.S. Ct. Appeals (11th cir.) 1991. Assoc. Schneider and Reilly, P.C., Boston, 1970-73; ptnr. Parker, Coulter, Daley and White, Boston, 1973-78; prin. Halström Law Office, Boston, 1978—. Spl. prosecutor Dist. Atty., Norfolk County, 1969-70; spl. asst. city solicitor City of Quincy, 1980. Editor Mass. Law Quar., 1972; contbr. articles to profl. jours. Fellow Boston Coll. Law Sch., v.p. 1988-91, pres. 1991—, benefactor Frederic N. Halström Nat. Moot Ct. Team. Mem. ABA (chmn. products liability com. gen. practice sect. 1980-85, award of achievement young lawyers divsn. 1978, vice chmn. taxation on ins. cos. sect. 1986-88), Assn. Trial Lawyers Am. (gov. 1981-84, 87—), state del. 1976-78, 86-87, chair various coms.), Mass. Acad. Trial Attys. (co-chmn. tort law sect. 1980—, bd. of govs. 1976—, sec. 1987-88, pres.-elect 1995-96, pres. 1996-97), Mass. Bar Assn. (pres. young lawyers divsn. 1977-78, bd. dels. 1978-80), Middlesex County Bar Assn., Mass. Trial Lawyers Assn. (mem/ Bd. of Govs., 2001—), Trial Lawyers Pub. Justice (sustaining founder, v.p. 1989—), Thomas F. Lambert Jr. Endowed Chair Trust), Algonquin Club. Home: 483 River Rd Carlisle MA 01741-1873 Office: 132 Boylston St Boston MA 02116-4616 Home Phone: 979-369-0673; Office Phone: 800-442-9855. Fax: 617-426-4791. E-mail: FHalstrom@aol.com.

HALTER, BILL (WILLIAM A. HALTER), lieutenant governor; b. Little Rock, Nov. 30, 1960; m. Shanti Patching, Jan. 28, 2006. AB, Stanford U., 1983; MPhil in Economics, Oxford U., 1986. Mgmt. cons. McKinsey and Co.; economist Econ. Com., US Congress; chief economist US Senate Fin. Com.; sr. adv. Office Mgmt. & Budget, Exec. Office of Pres., 1993—99; dep. commr. Social Security Adminstrn., 1999—2001, acting commr.; lt. gov. State of Ark., Little Rock, 2007—. Bd. dirs. Akamal Technologies, 2001—07, webMethods, Xenogen, InterMune, Threshold Pharmaceuticals. Trustee emeritus Stanford U., chair, Academic Policy Com., mem., Humanities and Sciences Coun.; mem., Adv. Coun. Stanford U. Libraries. Mem.: Phi Beta Kappa. Democrat. Office: Office Lt Gov 270 State Capitol Little Rock AR 72201 Office Phone: 501-376-2727.*

HALTER, HENRY JAMES, JR., (DIAMOND JIM HALTER), retail executive; b. Fernandina, Fla., Feb. 28, 1947; s. Henry James and Grace (Bealey) H.; m. Wanda O'Quinn, Mar. 15, 1970; children: Jennifer, John, Elizabeth, Amelia. BS in Mgmt., Valdosta State Coll., 1970. Residential mem. Am. Inst. Real Estate Appraisers, 1974, sr. real property appraiser Soc. Real Estate Appraisers, 1974, diamond cert. Gemological Inst. Am. Sales mgr. Southwestern Co., Nashville, 1969; collection mgr. Fla. Title & Mortgage Co., Jacksonville, 1970-72; appraiser Richard Hamilton & Assocs., Jacksonville Beach, 1972-74; exec. v.p. Developers Investors Svc. Corp., Jacksonville, 1975-78; pres. A-Coin and Stamp Gallery, Inc., Jacksonville, 1978-81; ptnr. Jacksonville Precious Metals, 1981, Sidetrack Video Arcade Chain, Ga., 1982-84; pres. Diamond House Corp., Valdosta, Ga., 1985—, J-Mart Jewelry Outlets, Inc., Tifton, Ga., 1988-91, chmn. bd., 1990-91; pres. K&H Ltd., Valdosta, 1992-94; exec. dir. Soc. for Legalization of Drugs, Valdosta, 1994-97; pres. VHS Band Boosters, 2002—03. Sr. appraiser Collectors Road Show, 2006—; bus. cons., 1996—. Author: May I Help You, 1988, LIZ, Inc., 1998; co-author Olympic Awareness award for 1996 Olympic Games, 1994—95, voice of Ernie Beaver for nationally syndicated TV cartoon Coots and Critter, 1996. Mem. exec. bd. Alapaha coun. Boy Scouts Am., 1982—; youth spkr. Atlanta Com. Olympic Games, selected local hero torch bearer Olympic Games, Atlanta, 1996; mem. Ga. Small Bus. Task Force; pres. Valdosta H.S. Band Boosters Inc., 2002—03; co-founder Boy Scouts Am. Olympic Expo, 2000—; mem. Lowndes County Rep. Exec. Com., 2000—; bd. dir. Park Ave. United Meth. Ch., Valdosta, 1986—88; charter dir. Redirecting Attitudes of Persons; mem. Alumni Bd. Valdosta State U. Recipient Addy award, 1980, 83, God and Svc. nat. award Meth. Ch. and BSA, Cmty. Hero Torch Bearer, Coca Cola Olympic Torch Relay, 1996, Evangelism award King Solomon Missionary Bapt. Ch., 2000; named Adm. in Ga. Navy, 1983, Outstanding Ga. Citizen, 1990. Mem. Nat. Speakers Assn., Toastmasters, Sertoma, Vigil Honor, Order of the Arrow, Rotary, Sigma Iota (pres. charter), Am. Numismatic Assn. (life), Fla. United Numismatists, Alpha Phi Omega. Avocations: motivational speaking, antique paper money, Georgia history. Home and Office: 208 Breckenridge Dr Valdosta GA 31605-6402 Office Phone: 229-241-8286. Personal E-mail: jim_halter@hotmail.com.

HALTER, JON CHARLES, retired magazine editor, writer; b. Hamilton, Ohio, Nov. 24, 1941; s. Sam Lesher and Helen Louise (Olds) H.; m. Corina Garcia, Feb. 14, 1968; children: Jon Julian, Helen Margaret. BA, Syracuse U., 1964, MA, 1966. Vol. U.S. Peace Corps, Venezuela, 1966-68; asst. editor Nat. Petroleum News mag. McGraw-Hill Inc., NYC, 1968-72; editor, writer Boys' Life mag. Boy Scouts Am., North Brunswick, NJ, 1972-79, Irving, Tex., 1979-90, exec. editor Scouting Mag., 1990-94; editor Scouting Mag., Irving, Tex., 1994—2007, Exploring Mag., Irving, Tex., 1994—98. Author: Bill Bradley: One to Remember, 1974, Reggie Jackson: All-Star in Right, 1975, Top Secret Projects of World War II, 1978, Their Backs to the Wall: Famous Last Stands, 1980 Mem. Soc. Profl. Journalists, Authors Guild. Democrat. Presbyterian. Avocations: reading, model building, walking. Home: 505 E Huitt Ln Euless TX 76040-5532 Personal E-mail: jchalter@yahoo.com.

HALTIWANGER, ROBERT SIDNEY, JR., book publishing executive; b. Winston-Salem, NC, Mar. 15, 1923; s. Robert Sidney and Janie Love (Couch) H.; m. Marguarite C. LaBelle, Aug. 23, 1994. AB, Harvard U., 1947. Coll. field rep. Prentice-Hall Inc., Atlanta, 1947—56, Southeast regional mgr., 1956-65, dir. Two Year div. Englewood Cliffs, NJ, 1965-71; v.p. sales Prentice-Hall Inc, Englewood Cliffs, NJ, 1971-80, exec. v.p. coll. div., 1980-85, pres. sales and mktg. coll. div., 1985—. Cons. Simon & Shuster, 1988-89. Served to 1st lt. USAF, 1943-46, PTO. Recipient Chmn. award Gulf and Western, 1985, Frank Enenbach award Prentice-Hall Coll. Div., 1987. Mem. Am. Assn. Pubs. (liason com. 1975-82), Harvard Club (N.Y.C. chpt.), Knickerbocker Club. Democrat. Presbyterian. Home: 1 Horizon Rd Fort Lee NJ 07024-6502 Office: Prentice Hall Inc Englewood Cliffs NJ 07632 E-mail: bobhalti@aol.com.

HALTOM, B(ILLY) REID, lawyer; b. Artesia, N. Mex., Sept. 9, 1945; s. Felix Tucker and Shirley Mae (Lucado) H.; m. Elizabeth Ann Berger, Dec. 25, 1964; 1 child, Robb Reid. BA in Philosophy, U. N.Mex, Albuquerque, 1969; JD, Tex. Tech U., Lubbock, 1972. Bar: N.Mex. 1973, US Dist. Ct. N.Mex. 1977, US Ct. Appeals (10th cir.) 1980, US Ct. Claims 1980, US Supreme Ct. 1992, US Dist. Ct. Ariz. 1992. Ptnr. Nordhaus, Haltom, Taylor, Taradash & Bladh, Albuquerque, 1980—2003; cons. econ. devel. Native Am. Projects, 2005—. Fellow N.Mex. State BAr Assn., Albuquerque Bar Assn., Albuquerque Lawyers Club. Avocations: snow and water skiing, tennis, cooking. Home: 570 Black Bear Rd NE Albuquerque NM 87122 Home Phone: 505-856-6891; Office Phone: 505-235-5043. Business E-Mail: bhaltom@comcast.net.

HALTOM, WILLIAM H., lawyer; b. Memphis, June 10, 1952; BA, U. Tenn., 1975, JD, 1978. Bar: Tenn. 1978, U.S. Supreme Ct. 1982. Ptnr. Thomason, Hendrix, Harvey, Johnson & Mitchell PLLC, Memphis. Former editor-in-chief of barrister, assoc. editor: Tenn. Bar Jour., humor columnist:. Fellow: Tenn. Bar Found., Am. Bar Found.; mem.: ABA (chmn. bd. editors ABA Jour.), Tenn. Bar Assn. (pres.-elect 2004, pres. 2005), Memphis Bar Assn. (pres.), Phi Delta Phi, Omicron Delta Kappa. Office: Thomason Hendrix Harvey Johnson & Mitchell PLLC 29th Fl One Commerce Sq 40 S Main St Memphis TN 38103 Office Phone: 901-577-6128. E-mail: haltom@thomasonlaw.com.*

HALVARSSON, MISHA, business development strategist, entrepreneur; d. Carl Maurice and Ruth Halvarsson; m. Dillon E. Jackson, Aug. 19, 1989; children: David Jackson, Anne Jackson-Kelly. Prin., sr. designer Halvarsson Design Co., Lincoln City, Oreg., 1968—75; co-founder, sr. designer IceFire Glassworks, Ltd., McMinnville, Oreg., 1975—79; gen. contractor, sr. designer HDA, Inc., Woodinville, Wash., 1979—83; ptnr., sr. designer Chrysalis Studios, Inc., Redmond, Wash., 1981—83; pres. TOPAC, Inc., Woodinville, 1983—86; founder, mng. dir. SouthAsia Resources, Inc., Seattle, 1987—; co-founder, v.p. iCopyright, Inc., Renton, Wash., 1998—2001; founder, mng. mem. Ddm2, Llc., Seattle, 1998—; Seattle assoc. Names at Work, NYC, 2005—. Founding mem. steering com. Pacific N.W. Region Environ. Coun., Seattle, 1993; mem. U.S.-Asia environ. partnership tech. cooperation working group USAID, Washington, 1993—94; founder, chmn. Applied Environ. Techs., Seattle, 1993—; conf. coord. Internat. Erosion Control Assn. 27th Ann. Conf. and Trade Expn., Seattle, 1996; co-chair internet devel. com. N.W. Capital Network, Seattle, 1997—98; founding bd. dirs., past pres. N.W. chpt. Forum Women Entrepreneurs, Seattle, 1999—2004; pres. Ctr. Entrepreneurial Women, Seattle, 2002—. Contbg. writer: Washington CEO Mag.; exhibitions include Etched and Blown Glass. Invited participant and panel mem. White Ho. Regional Roundtable Confs. Environ. Techs., Washington; chmn. Citizen's Against Noise, McMinnville, 1976—79; mem. citizen adv. com. State of Oreg. Land, Conservation, and Devel., McMinnville, 1976—79; chair revitalization com. City of Duvall, Wash., 1980—81. Recipient Trailblazer award, Nat. Forum Women Execs. and Entrepreneurs, 1999. Mem.: Systers, Indo-Am. C. of C. (Bombay), Am. Water Works Assn., Nat. Environ. Law Ctr., Software Info. Industry Assn. (former mem. intellectual property and trade policy com.), Am. Bankruptcy Inst. (assoc.; mem. internat. com.), Nat. Mus. Women Arts, Nat. Trust Hist. Preservation. Avocations: sailing, raising/training Golden Retrievers, writing. Office: Ddm2 Llc 117 E Louisa St Ste 113 Seattle WA 98102 Office Phone: 206-323-1820. Business E-Mail: mh@esgus.com.

HALVER, JOHN EMIL, nutritional biochemist; b. Woodinville, Wash., Apr. 21, 1922; s. John Emil and Helen Henrietta (Hansen) Halver; m. Jane Loren, July 21, 1944; children: John Emil, Nancylee Halver Hadley, Janet Ann Halver Fix, Peter Loren, Deborah Kay Halver Hanson. BS, Wash. State U., 1944, MS in Organic Chemistry, 1948; PhD in Med. Biochemistry, U. Wash., 1953. Plant chemist Assoc. Frozen Foods, Kent, Wash., 1946-47; asst. chemist Purdue U., 1948—49; instr. U. Wash., Seattle, 1949—50, affiliate prof., 1960—75; prof. U. Wash. Sch. Fisheries, 1978—92; prof. emeritus U. Wash., 1992—. Condr. research on vitamin and amino acid requirements for fish; identified aflatoxin B1 as specific carcinogen for rainbow trout hematoma; identified vitamin C2 for fish; dir. Western Fish Nutrition Lab. U.S. Fish and Wildlife Service, Dept. Interior, Cook, Wash., 1950—75, sr. scientist, nutrition, Seattle, 1975—78; cons. FAO, UNDP, Internat. Union Nutrition Scientists, Nat. Fish Research Inst., Hungary, World Bank, Euroconsult, UNDP, IDRC; affiliate prof. prof. U. Oreg. Med. Sch., 1965—69; vis. prof. Marine Sci. Inst. U. Tex., Port Aransas; pres. Fisheries Devel. Technology, Inc., 1980—90, Halver Corp., 1978—. Lay leader Meth. Ch., 1965—70. Capt. US Army, World War II, col. USAR. Decorated Purple Heart, Bronze Star with oak leaf cluster, Meritorious Service Conduct medal. Fellow: Am. Inst. Nutrition, Am. Inst. Fishery Research Biologists; mem.: NAS, Hungarian Acad. Sci., World Aquaculture Soc., Am. Fishery Soc., Am. Chem. Soc., Am. Sci. Affiliation, Soc. Exptl. Biol. Medicine, Rotary, Alpha Chi Sigma, Pi Mu Epsilon, Phi Lambda Upsilon. Achievements include founder JE Halver Fellowship at University of Washington; founder JE Halver Lecture at Washington State University. Home: 16502 41st Ave NE Seattle WA 98155-5610 Office: U Wash Box 355100 Sch Fisheries and Aquatic Scis Seattle WA 98195-5100 Office Phone: 206-543-9619. Business E-Mail: halver@u.washington.edu.

HALVERSTADT, DONALD BRUCE, urologist, educator; b. Cleveland, July 6, 1934; s. Lauren Oscar and Lillian Frances (Jones) H.; m. Margaret Ann (Marcy), Aug. 4, 1956; children: Donna, Jeffrey, and Amy. BA magna cum laude (hon.), Princeton U., 1956; MD cum laude (hon.), Harvard U., 1960. diplomate Am. Bd. Urology. Intern, then resident in surgery Mass. Gen. Hosp., Boston, 1960—62, resident in urology, 1964—67; pvt. practice medicine specializing in urology Okla City, 1967; chief pediatric urology svc. Okla. Children's Meml. Hosp., Okla. City, 1967; clin. prof. urology and pediat. U. Okla. Med. Sch., 1970; chief staff Okla. Children's Meml. Hosp., Okla. City, 1974—79; interim provost U. Okla. for Health Sci., Okla. City, 1979—80; CEO State of Okla. Tchg. Hosp., 1980—83; spl. asst. to pres. for Hosp. affairs Okla. U., 1980—84; vice chair dept. urology U. Okla. Med. Sch., 1982; bd. dir. State of Okla. Tchg. Hosp.; CEO State Regents for Higher Edn., 1988—93. Mem. U. Okla. Bd. Regents, 1993-2000, (chmn. 1999); founder, vice chmn., dir. Lincoln Nat. Bank, Oklahoma City, 1984-2003; bd. dir. BancFirst of Okla., 2004-. vice chair bd. gov. Okla. Med. Ctr. Hosp. Sys., 1998—; bd. dir. Triad Hosp., Inc., chair compliance com., 2000—, nominating com. Contbr. articles to med. journals. Vice chair bd. gov. Univ. Health Ptnrs.; pres., chmn. bd. Okla. Ind. Phys. Svc. Corp., 1986-96; trustee Columbia Presbyn. Hosp., 1990-96, chmn., 1995-96; bd. dir. Nat. Assn. Basketball Coaches FDTN; athletic dir. adv. coun. U. Okla., 2003. Fellow ACS; mem. AMA (Physicians Recognition Award 1969, 72, 79, 82, 85, 91, 94, 96, 99, 2002), Am. Urol. Assn., Am. Acad. Pediat., Soc. Pediat. Urology, Am. Soc. Nephrology, Soc. Univ. Urologists, So. Med. Assn., Okla. Med. Assn., Okla. County Med. Soc., Okla. State Regents for Higher Edn., Am. Coll. Physician Exec., Assn. Governing Bd. Coll. and Univ. (bd. dir., sec. 1996-97, treas. 1997-98). Presbyterian. Office: 711 Stanton L Young Blvd #707 Oklahoma City OK 73104-5023 Home: 2932 Lamp Post Ln Oklahoma City OK 73120-6105 Business E-Mail: donald-halverstadt@ouhsc.edu.

HALVERSTADT, ROBERT DALE, mechanical engineer, metal products executive; b. Warren, Ohio, Jan. 25, 1920; s. Roscoe B. and Dorothy (Grubbs) Halverstadt; m. Maryella Green, Dec. 31, 1941; children: Marta Jean Halverstadt Carmen, Linda Anne Halverstadt Orelup, Sally Jo Halverstadt Ham. BS in Mech. Engring., Case Inst. Tech. (now Case Western U.), Cleve., 1951. Registered prof. engr., NY, Ohio. Journeyman machinist Republic Steel Corp., Cleve., 1939-51; design engr. GE, Evendale, Ohio, 1951-53; supr. Metalworking Lab., 1953-58; corp. cons. NYC, 1958—59; mgr. Thomson Engring. Lab., Lynn, Mass., 1959—63; gen. mgr. ops. engring. Continental Can Co., NYC, 1963—64; group v.p. Booz, Allen & Hamilton Inc., NYC, 1964-73; CEO Foster D. Snell Inc. subs., NYC, 1964-73; pres. Design and Devel., Inc. subs., NYC, 1966-73; mng. officer BA&H Environ. Resources Group (ERG), 1970—73; v.p. tech. Singer Co., NYC, 1973-74; pres. Spl. Metals Corp. subs. Allegheny Ludlum Industries, Inc., New Hartford, NY, 1974-82, Materials Tech. Group, New Hartford, 1980—85; mng. dir. Allegheny Ludlum Industries Ltd., New Hartford; sr. staff v.p. Allegheny Internat., New Hartford, 1983-85; pres. AIMe Assocs., New Canaan, Conn., 1985—. Co-chmn. Titanium Metals Corp. Am., 1980—83; dir. Oneida Nat. Bank, 1979—82, Carus Corp., 1980—, Centrex Lab., 1975—80; mem. adv. bd. Flexmedics, Inc., 1982—92; chmn. bd. Spl. Metals Corp., 1987—2000, chmn. bd. emeritus, 2000—01. Mem. editl. bd.: Internat. Jour. Turbo and Jet Engine Tech. Pres. industry, labor and edn. coun. Mohawk Valley, Inc., 1975—80. Lt (j.g.) USCGR, 1942—45. Recipient Jubilee of Victory medal, Govt. France, 1996, Cert. Recognition, Govt. France & Normandy, 2001. Fellow: Am. Soc. Metals (past treas., bd. dirs., Disting. Life mem. 2002); mem.: ASME, Univ. Club (NYC), Woodway Country Club, Theta Tau, Tau Beta Pi, Sigma Xi. Mem. United Ch. Of Christ. Achievements include patents in field. Office Phone: 917-816-6468. Home Fax: 203-544-9237.

HALVORSEN, CLAY A., lawyer, construction executive; BA in Econs., Calif. State U., 1982; JD, U. Southern Calif., 1985. Bar: Calif. Atty. Gibson, Dunn & Crutcher, 1985—95, ptnr., 1995—97; v.p., gen. counsel, sec. Standard Pacific Corp., Costa Mesa, Calif., 1998—2001, sr. v.p., gen. counsel, sec., 2001—04, exec. v.p., gen. counsel, sec., 2004—. Mem.: Calif. State Bar Assn. Office: Standard Pacific Corp 15326 Alton Pkwy Irvine CA 92618-2338*

HALVORSEN, PER-KRISTIAN, software company executive, former educator, researcher; Received edn., U. Olso, MIT; PhD in Theoretical Linguistics, U. Tex. Austin. Post-grad. work MIT; prof. U. Tex., Austin; cons. prof. Stanford U., U. Oslo; prin., Ctr. for Study of Lang. and Info. Stanford U.; founding dir., prin. scientist , Info. Sciences and Technologies Lab Xerox, Palo Alto Rsch. Ctr. (PARC), 1983—2000; v.p., dir., Solutions and Services Technology Ctr. in HP Labs Hewlett-Packard (HP), 2000—05; acting chief tech. officer Intuit, Inc., Calif., 2006, chief tech. officer Calif., 2006—. Bd. dir. Autodesk, Inc., 2000—, Symantec Corp., Finn, FinnTech. Contbr. articles to scientific jours. Mem. adv. bd. Cyber Coll., U. Ark. Little Rock. Mem.: NAS (mem. com. on internet navigation anf the Domain Name System). Achievements include patents in field. Office: Intuit Inc 2632 Marin Way Mountain View CA 94043*

HALVORSON, GEORGE CHARLES, healthcare insurance company executive; b. Fargo, ND, Jan. 28, 1947; s. George Charles and Barbara Theone (Johnson) H.; m. Mary Elizabeth Probst, June 27, 1986; children: Jonathan Dale, Seth Gregory, George Charles IV, Michael Thomas. BA, Concordia Coll., Moorhead, Minn., 1968. Cert. health cons., 1981. Successively mgr. market rsch., mgr. corp. planning, dir. planning and budget, v.p. planning and budget, sr. v.p. Blue Cross & Blue Shield, St. Paul, 1968-76; exec. dir. HMO Minn., St. Paul, 1976-83; pres. Sr. Health Plan, St. Paul, 1983-86, Health Accord, Inc., Mpls., 1983-86, Group Health, Inc., Mpls., 1986—2002; chmn., CEO Kaiser Permanente, 2002—. Ops. dir. HMO/Jamaica, Kingston, 1985-86; cons. AIG/Am. Internat. Health, Washington, 1987-88; lectr. in field. Author: How to Cut Your Company's Health Care Costs, 1987; contbr. articles to profl. jours. Chmn. Boy Scout Food Drive, St. Paul, 1988; fund raiser United Way, Mpls., 1987-88. Recipient Internship award Wall St. Jour. Newspaper Fund, 1968. Mem. Nat. Coop. Bus. Assn. (bd. dirs.), Minn. Bus. Partnership (bd. dirs.), Group Health Assn. Am., Minn. Council HMO's (bd. dirs.), Decathlon Club (Bloomington, Minn.), Mpls. Club. Avocations: writing, hunting, chess. Address: Kaiser Permanente Oakland 1 Kaiser Plaza Oakland CA 94612 Office Phone: 510-271-5910.

HALVORSON, NEWMAN THORBUS, JR., lawyer; b. Detroit, Dec. 17, 1936; s. Newman Thorbus and Virginia Westbrook (Markle) H.; m. Sally Clark Stone, May 3, 1969; children: Christina English, Charles Burgess Westbrook. AB, Princeton U., 1958; LLB, Harvard U., 1961. Bar: Ohio 1962, D.C. 1963, U.S. Supreme Ct. 1965. Assoc. Covington & Burling, Washington, 1962-70; asst. U.S. atty. Office of U.S. Atty., Washington, 1983-85; assoc. ind. counsel (spl. prosecutor under Ethics in Govt. Act), 1987-90; ptnr. Covington & Burling, Washington, 1970—83, 1985—2002, sr. counsel, 2002—05; ret. ptnr., 2005—. Editor, Harvard Law Rev., 1960-61; author: Intermediate Sanctions Regs: Many Questions Remain, Tax Notes, 1998. Sr. warden, jr. warden, vestryman Christ Ch. Georgetown, Washington, 1983-86, 89-92, chmn. fin. com., 1992-96; bd. dirs. Lupus Found. D.C., 1974-85; mem., bd. dirs. Eugene and Agnes E. Meyer Found., Washington, 1976-91, chmn., 1989-90, asst. sec./treas., 1990—; trustee Hist. Soc. Washington, 1995—2004, 06—, chmn. investment com., 1999—2004, chmn. audit comm., 2001—04, vice chmn., 2003-04, gen. counsel, 2006—; bd. dirs. Coun. for Ct. Excellence, Washington; trustee Potomac Sch., McLean, Va., 1980-86, chmn., 1981-83; mem. Com. of 100 on Federal City, 1970—, trustee, treas., 1975-79; trustee, mem. exec. com. Greater Washington Rsch. Ctr., 1997-2001; trustee Cleveland Park Hist. Soc., 1997—, pres. 2002-03; dir. Rosedale Conservancy, 2002-03; bd. govs. Coord. Coun. Internat. Univs, 2001—; mem. devel. com. Washington

Nat. Cathedral, 2003-. With USMCR, 1961-67. Mem. ABA, D.C. Bar, Met. Club (Washington), Chevy Chase (Md.) Club. Republican. Episcopalian. Home: 3500 Lowell St NW Washington DC 20016-5025 Office: Covington & Burling 1201 Pennsylvania Ave NW Washington DC 20004-2401

HALWIG, J. MICHAEL, allergist; b. Denver, Apr. 15, 1954; s. John Philip and Hilda (Fuggis) H.; m. Nancy Diane Graupman, June 14, 1975; children: Courtney Elizabeth, J. Christopher. BA, Johns Hopkins U., 1975; MD, Northwestern U., Chgo., 1980. Diplomate Am. Bd. Allergy and Immunology, Am. Bd. Internal Medicine. Intern in internal medicine Northwestern U. Meml. Hosps., Chgo., 1980-81, resident in internal medicine, 1981-83; allergy fellowship Northwestern U. Med. Sch., Chgo., 1983-85; practice medicine specializing in allergy, asthma, immunology Atlanta, 1985—. Instr. Northwestern U. Med. Sch., Chgo., 1984-85, admissions amb., 1989—; clin. asst. prof. Emory U. Sch. Medicine, 1989—. Bd. dirs. Am. Lung Assn. Ga., 1996-2001. Fellow Am. Coll. Allergy, Asthma and Immunology (allergy practice and practice guidelines com. 1992—), Am. Acad. Allergy, Asthma and Immunology (Managed Care Key Contact Network 1996—); mem. AMA, Asthma and Allergy Found. of Am. (nat. chpt. bd. dirs., chpt. rels. and devel. com. 1997-99, mktg. and fundraising com. 1997-99, Ga. chpt. founder, bd. dirs., med. dir. 1995-99, chmn. med. adv. com. 1995-99), Joint Coun. on Allergy and Immunology, Med. Assn. Ga. (rep. Coun. on Legis. 1989-95), Allergy, Asthma and Immunology Soc. Ga. (pres. 1993-95, v.p. 1991-93, program chmn. 1991-93, co-chmn. third party payors com. 1992—, rep. Ga. medicare carrier adv. com. 1993—), So. Med. Assn., Cobb County Med. Assn., Cobb Area Pediat. Soc., Wellstar Health Care Sys. (pediat. asthma task force 1996-2001, asthma/COPD task force 1998-2001), Ga. Partnership for Caring, Phoenix Soc. (bd. dirs., 2007-08). Presbyterian. Avocations: running, jazz, golf. Office: 1620 Mulkey Rd Ste 100 Austell GA 30106-8116 Home Phone: 404-351-7418; Office Phone: 770-948-3774. Business E-Mail: mhalwig@atlantaallergy.com.

HAM, SOMMY L., publisher, writer; b. Houston, Sept. 12, 1953; 5. Robert Steele Jr. and Nellie (McGuinness) Gray; child by previous marriage: Laura Ann; m. Robert E. Ham Jr., Feb. 14, 1986 (div. June 1996); children: Mark, Katie, Jeffrey. AA with honors, Houston CC, 1994; student, U. Houston, 1994-95; BS cum laude in Profl. Writing and Tech. Comm., U. Houston, Downtown, 2007. V.p. adminstrn. Cordovan Corp. Pubs., Houston, 1975-82; advt. rep. Golfer Mags., Inc., Houston, 1983-88, gen. mgr., 1996-97, pub., 1997—2001; editor Tomball-Magnolia Tribune, Magnolia, Tex., 2001—03; pres. Sommy's Ink Profl. Comms., 2003—. Editor: Houston Sports Car News, 2004—06. Mem. city coun., Magnolia, 2003—05. Houston C.C. scholar, 1993, Alice B. Rogers scholar Advt. Fedn. Houston, 1995-96 Mem. Women in Comms., Exec. Women's Golf Assn., Romance Writers Am. (conf. co-chair N.W. chpt. 1995, treas.), Phi Theta Kappa, Sigma Tau Delta. Avocation: journalism.

HAMADA, DUANE TAKUMI, architect; b. Honolulu, Aug. 12, 1954; s. Robert Kensaku and Jean Hakue (Masutani) H.; m. Martha S.P. Lee, Dec. 22, 1991; children; Erin, Robyn, David. BFA in Environ. Design, U. Hawaii, 1977, BArch, 1979. Registered architect, Hawaii, Guam, Florida, Puerto Rico, Saipan. Intern Edward Sullam, FAIA & Assocs., Honolulu, 1979-80; assoc. Design Ptnrs., Inc., Honolulu, 1980-86; prin. AM Ptnrs., Inc., Honolulu, 1986-98, Design Ptnrs. Inc., Honolulu, 1998—. Chmn. 31st Ann. Cherry Blossom Festival Fashion Show, Honolulu, 1982, 32d Ann. Cherry Blossom Festival Cooking Show, 1983, mem. steering com., 1982, 83. Recipient Gold Key award for Excellence in Interior Design Am. Hotel and Motel Assn., 1990, Renaissance '90 Merit award Nat. Assn. Home Builder's Remodeler Coun., Merit award Honolulu mag., 1990, Cert. of Appreciation PACDIV USN, 1992, Gold Nugget award of Merit, 1997, Design Excellence Concept Design award USAF Hawaii, 2003, Pub. Govt. New Project award NAIOP, 2005 Mem. AIA (jury student awards 1997, 98, jury profl. awards 1999), Constrn. Specifications Inst., Nat. Coun. Archtl. Registration Bds., Colegio de Arcquitectos de P.R Avocations: astronomy, music. Office: Design Ptnrs Inc 1580 Makaloa St Ste 1100 Honolulu HI 96814-3240 Home Phone: 808-988-1753. E-mail: dhamada@hawaii.rr.com.

HAMADA, RICK, electronics executive; BS in Fin., San Diego State U. Various positions including tech. specialist Hamilton/Avnet Electronics, 1983—94; v.p. mktg. Hall-Mark Computer Products (now Avnet Hall-Mark), 1994—97; exec. v.p. Avnet Computer (now Avnet Enterprise Solutions), 1998—99; corp. v.p. Avnet, Inc., 1999, sr. v.p., 2002—, COO; pres. Avnet Hall-Mark N.Am., 2000—02, Avnet Computer Mktg. (now Avnet Tech. Solutions), 2002. Named one of Top 25 Most Influential Execs. in Computer Industry, Computer Reseller News mag., 2002. Office: Avnet Inc 2211 S 47th St Phoenix AZ 85034-6403 Office Phone: 480-643-2000.*

HAMADA, ROBERT S(EIJI), dean, educator, economist, entrepreneur; b. San Francisco, Aug. 17, 1937; s. Horace T. and Maki G. Hamada; m. Danielle Hamada; children: Matthew, Janet. BE, Yale U., New Haven, Conn., 1959; SM, MIT, Cambridge, 1961, PhD, 1969. Economist Sun Oil Co., Phila., 1961—63; instr. U. Chgo., 1966—68, asst. prof. fin., 1968—71, assoc. prof., 1971—77, prof., 1977—89, Edward Eagle Brown prof., 1989—93, Edward Eagle Brown Disting. Svc. prof., 1993—2003, Edward Eagle Brown Disting. Svc. prof. emeritus, 2003—, dir. Ctr. for Rsch. in Security Prices, 1980—85, dir. Ctr. Internat. Bus. Edn. and Rsch., 1992—94, dep. dean for faculty Grad Sch. Bus., 1985—90, dean, 1993—2001; CEO, dir. Merchants' Exchange, 2001—02. Vis. prof. London Bus. Sch., 1973, 79-80, UCLA, 1971, U. Wash., Seattle, 1971-72, U. B.C., Vancouver, Can., 1976; bd. dirs. A.M. Castle & Co., Fleming Cos., Inc., No. Trust Corp., Fed. Signal Corp.; pub. dir. Chgo. Bd. Trade, 1989-2000; cons. in field. Past assoc. editor Jour. Fin., Jour. Fin. and Quantitative Analysis, Jour. Applied Corp. Fin.; cons. editor Scott, Foresman & Co. fin. series; contbr. articles to profl. jours. Bd. dirs. numerous non-profit orgns., including Hyde Park Neighborhood Club, Chgo., Harper Ct. Found., Chgo., Hyde Park Co-op, U. Chgo. Lab. Schs., Window to the World, Inc. (WTTW-TV), Terra Found. for the Arts. Named to 8 Outstanding Bus. Sch. Profs., fortune Mag., 1982; recipient 1st Outstanding Tchr. award, Grad. Sch. Bus., U. Chgo., 1970, McKinsey Tchg. prize, 1981; Sloan Found. fellow, 1959—61, Ford Found. fellow, 1963—65, Standard Oil Found. fellow, 1965—66, MIT scholar, 1959—61, Yale scholar, 1955—59. Mem. Am. Fin. Assn. (bd. dirs. 1982-85), Econometric Soc., Nat. Bur. Econ. Rsch. (bd. dirs., mem. investment and exec. coms.), Am. Econ. Assn. (investment com.), Inst. Mgmt. Scis. (investment com.), Tau Beta Pi. Office: U Chgo Grad Sch Bus 5807 S Woodlawn Ave Chicago IL 60637-1511 Office Phone: 773-834-1369. Business E-Mail: robert.hamada@gsb.uchicago.edu.

HAMAI, JAMES YUTAKA, manufacturing executive; b. Oct. 14, 1926; s. Seizo and May (Sata) H.; m. Dorothy K. Fukuda, Sept. 10. 1954; children: Wendy A. BS cum laude, U. So. Calif., 1952; MS, 1955; postgrad. bus. mgmt. program ind. exec., UCLA, 1962—64. Lectr. chem. engring. dept. U. So. Calif., LA, 1961—64; process engr., sr. process engr. Fluor Corp., LA, 1954—64; sr. project mgr. ctrl. rsch. dept. Monsanto Co., St. Louis, 1964—67, mgr. rsch., devel. and engring. graphic sys. dept., 1967—68; mgr. comml. devel. New Enterprise Divsn., 1968—69; exec. v.p., dir. Concrete Cutting Industries, Inc., LA, 1969—72; pres., dir. Concrete Cutting Internat. Inc., LA, 1972—78, chmn. bd., 1978—; pres., CEO, dir. Techno Enterprises U.S.A., Ltd., LA, 2000—04. Cons. Fluor Corp., Los Angeles, 1970-74; dir. Intech Systems Co., Ltd., Tokyo, Cutting Industries Co., Ltd., Tokyo; internat. bus. cons. Served with AUS, 1946-48. Mem. AIChE, Am. Mgmt. Assn., Tau Beta Pi, Phi Lambda Upsilon. Club: Rotary (gov. dist. 1982-83). Home: 6600 Via La Paloma Rancho Palos Verdes CA 90275-6449 Office: PO Box 700 Wilmington CA 90748-0700

HAMAMOTO, PATRICIA, school system administrator, educator; b. Honolulu, Sept. 30, 1944; BA in History, Calif. State Coll., Long Beach, 1967, profl. tchg. diploma, 1967; education administrator's cert., U. Hawaii M, 1985. Social studies tchr. Fountain Valley H.S., Calif., 1967—72; social studies tchr., dept. chair Iiima Intermediate Sch., Ewa Beach, Hawaii, 1976—81; tchg. grad. asst. geography dept. U. Hawaii at Manoa, 1981—83; tchr. guidance/math. Pearl City H.S., Hawaii, 1985; vice prin. Maui H.S., Kahlui, Hawaii, 1983—85, Nanakul H.S. and Intermediate Sch, Nanakuli, Hawaii, 1985—87; prin. Pearl City Highlands Elem. Sch, Hawaii, 1987—89; contract adminstrn. specialist II Office Personnel Svcs., Honolulu, 1989—91; prin. Likelike Elem., 1991—92, Pres. William McKinley H.S., Honolulu, 1992—99; dep. supt. Hawaii Dept. Edn., Honolulu, 1999—2001, interim supt., 2001; supt. of edn. Hawaii Dept Edn., Honolulu, 2001—. Co-chairperson Tchr. Edn. Coordinating Com., Venture Edn. Forum; mem. adv. coun. Univ. Hawaii Coll. Edn. Mem.: ASCD, Am. Assn. Sch. Adminstr., Assn. for Supervision and Curriculum Develop., Pacific Resources for Edn. and Learning, Coun. of Chief State Sch. Officers, Nat. Assn. Secondary Sch. Prins. Avocations: golf, reading, travel, walking. Home: 1767 Puowaina Dr Honolulu HI 96813 Office: Hawaii Dept Edn PO Box 2360 Honolulu HI 96804-2360 Home Phone: 808-536-0296; Office Phone: 808-586-3310. E-mail: patricia_hamamoto@notes.k12.hi.us.*

HAMAN, RAYMOND WILLIAM, retired lawyer; b. St. Maries, Idaho, Jan. 22, 1927; s. William and Eva Kate (Colliver) H.; m. Phyllis Maxine Garrett, June 24, 1948; children: Lorinda Ann, Bradley Lawrence (dec.). Student, Whitman Coll., 1947-49; JD, Washington and Lee U., 1952. Bar: Wash., 1952, U.S. Dist. Ct. (we. dist.) Wash. 1952, U.S. Ct. Appeals (9th cir.), U.S. Supreme Ct. Assoc. Evans, McLaren, Lane, Powell & Beeks, Seattle, 1952-59, ptnr., 1959-66, Lane Powell, Seattle, 1966-89, 1989-91, of counsel, 1991-2001; ret. Legal counsel Gov. Daniel J. Evans, Olympia, Wash., 1965, 67; mem. statute Law Com., 1966-95, chmn. 1988-95. Trustee, past pres. Lighthouse for the Blind, Inc., Seattle, 1964—; mem. vestry St. Augustine's Episcopal Ch., 1999—2002; bd. dirs. Mercer Island (Wash.) Sch. Dist., 1967—72, Island County (Wash.) United Way, 1993—, pres., 1997—98. With USMC, 1945—46, PTO. Mem.: Wash. Bar Assn., Order of the Coif. Republican. Episcopalian. Home: PO Box 926 Langley WA 98260-0926 Office: Lane Powell PC 1420 5th Ave Ste 4100 Seattle WA 98101-2338

HAMANN, DERYL FREDERICK, lawyer, bank executive; b. Lehigh, Iowa, Dec. 8, 1932; s. Frederick Carl Hamann and Ada Ellen (Hollingsworth) Hamann Geis; m. Carrie Svea Rosen, Aug. 23, 1954 (dec. 1985); children: Karl E., Daniel A., Esther Hamann Brabec, Julie Hamann Hodgson; m. Eleanor Ramona Nelson Curtis, June 20, 1987. AA, Ft. Dodge Jr. Coll., Iowa, 1953; BS in Law, U. Nebr., 1956, JD cum laude, 1958. Bar: Nebr. 1958, U.S. Dist. Ct. Nebr. 1958, U.S. Ct. Appeals (8th cir.) 1958. Law clk. U.S. Dist. Ct. for Nebr., Lincoln, 1958-59; ptnr. Baird, Holm, McEachen, Pedersen, Hamann & Strasheim, Omaha, 1959—2003, sr. counsel, 2003—. Chmn. adv. com. Supreme Ct. Nebr., Omaha, 1986-95; chmn. bd. Great Western Bancorporation, Inc. Past pres. Omaha Estate Planning Coun. Mem. Nebr. Bar Found. (pres. 1981-86), Nebr. Assn. Bank Attys. (pres. 1985-86). Republican. Lutheran. Avocations: boating, reading. Office: Baird Holm McEachen Pedersen Hamann & Strasheim 1500 Woodmen Tower Omaha NE 68102 Business E-Mail: dhamann@bairdholm.com.

HAMAS, ROBERT STEVEN, plastic surgeon; b. Cleve., Mar. 9, 1946; s. Steve and Matilda (Girman) H.; children: Wendy, Kevin, Reagan. BA, Coll. Wooster, Ohio, 1967; MD, Ohio State U., 1971. Diplomate Am. Bd. Plastic Surgery. Surg. intern Mt. Carmel Hosp., Columbus, Ohio, 1971-72; gen. surgery resident U. Tex. Med. Br., Galveston, 1972-73; hand surgery fellow U. N.Mex., Albuquerque, 1974, Grace Hosp., Detroit, 1974-75; resident in plastic surgery U. Pitts., 1977-79; pvt. practice Dallas, 1979—. Faculty U. Tex. Southwestern Med. Ctr., Dallas, 1995-2005; instr. endoscopic surgery courses (various), 1993—. Contbr. articles to profl. jours.; prodr./writer: Endoscopic Plastic Surgery (videotape), 1995, 97. Bd. dirs. Life Anew Adoption Agy., Paris, Tex., 1987-92. Maj. USAF, 1975-77. Mem. Am. Soc. Plastic Surgery, Am. Assn. Accreditation Ambulatory Surgery Facilities (newsletter editor 1995-97), Dallas Soc. Plastic Surgery (pres. 1989-91, sec.-treas. 1986-89), Am. Soc. Aesthetic Plastic Surgery. Avocation: travel. Office: 8345 Walnut Hill Ln Ste 120 Dallas TX 75231-4214 Office Phone: 214-363-1073.

HAMBIDGE, DOUGLAS WALTER, archbishop; b. London, Mar. 6, 1927; emigrated to Can., 1956; s. Douglas and Florence (Driscoll) H.; m. Denise Colvill Lown, June 9, 1956; children: Caryl Denise, Stephen Douglas, Graham Andrew. Assoc. London Coll. Divinity, London U., 1953, BD, 1958, DD, 1969. Ordained deacon Church of England, 1953, priest, 1954, consecrated bishop, 1969; asst. curate St. Mark's Ch., Dalston, London, 1953-55, priest-in-charge, 1955-56; incumbent All Saints Ch., Cassiar, B.C., Canada, 1956-58; rector St. James Parish, Smithers, B.C., 1958-64, North Peace Parish, Ft. St. John, B.C., 1964-69; canon St. Andrew's Cathedral, 1965; lord bishop of Caledonia, 1969-80, New Westminster, BC, 1980-81; metropolitan BC and Yukon, 1981—93; prin. St. Mark's Theol. Coll., Dar es Salaam, Tanzania, 1993-95; asst. bishop Diocese of Dar es Salaam, Dar es Salaam, 1993-95. Mem. Anglican Consultative Coun., 1985-93; chancellor Vancouver Sch. Theology, 1999. Anglican.

HAMBLEN, LAPSLEY WALKER, JR., retired judge; b. Chattanooga, Dec. 25, 1926; s. Lapsley Walker Sr. and Libby (Shipley) H.; m. Claudia Royster Terrell, Mar. 20, 1971; children by previous marriage: Lapsley Walker III, Allen M., William Shipley. BA, U. Va., 1949, LLB, 1953. Bar: W.Va. 1954, Ohio 1955, Va. 1957. Trial atty. IRS, Atlanta, 1955; atty. advisor U.S. Tax Ct., 1956; ptnr. Caskie Frost Hobbs & Hamblen and predecessor firms, Lynchburg, Va., 1957-82; dep. asst. atty. gen. tax divsn. U.S. Dept. Justice, 1982; judge U.S. Tax Ct., Washington, 1982-92, chief judge, 1992-94, 94-96, sr. judge, 1996-2000, ret., 2000. Former trustee So. Fed. Tax Inst.; former co-dir. ann. conf. on fed. taxation U. Va. With USN, 1945—46. Fellow: Am. Bar Found., Am. Coll. Trust and Estate Counsel, Am. Coll. Tax Counsel; mem.: Raven Soc., Phi Alpha Delta, Omicron Delta Kappa, Order of the Coif. Presbyterian.

HAMBLETON, GEORGE BLOW ELLIOTT, retired management consultant; b. Balt., Dec. 20, 1929; s. John Adams Hambleton and Margaret (Elliott) Carey; m. Janet Findlay MacLaren, Mar. 17, 1962 (dec. 1991); children: Anne Carey, Charles MacLaren, James Elliott; m. Diana Lea Walker, June 29, 1998. AB, Princeton U., 1952; cert. program for mgmt. devel., Harvard U., 1964. Various positions with Latin Am. divsn. Pan Am, 1955—62, asst. divsn. svc. mgr. Miami, Fla., 1963—64, dir. USSR Moscow, 1966—70, dir. internat. affairs Washington, 1971—76, dir. comml. sales NYC, 1977—80; v.p. mktg. N.Y. Airways, NYC, 1976—77; exec. dir., vice chmn. Project Orbis, Inc., NYC, 1980—83; pres. Andrews MacLaren, Inc., NYC, 1983—86; dep. asst. sec., dep. dir. gen. U.S. and fgn. comml. svc. Dept. Commerce, Washington, 1986—88; sr. v.p. Mgmt. Internat. Inc., Westport, Conn., 1988—2001; ret., 2001. Bd. dirs. Flight Found., Inc., Washington, Andrews MacLaren Ltd., Northants, Eng. Dir. Fgn. Policy Discussion Group, Washington, 1975-96; mem. NJ Conservation Found.; mem. adv. com. East-West Trade US Dept. Commerce, Conn., 1973-79, mem. dist. export coun., 1989-93; bd. dirs. River Blindness Found., Houston, 1990-95, Coll. of Atlantic, Bar Harbor, Maine, 1996—, Pan Am. Hist. Found., 1998-, Am.-Russian Cultural Coop. Found., Washington, 2005-, Summer Residents Assn., Mt. Desert, Maine, 1999-. 1st lt. US Army, Korea, 1952-55. Mem. Upper Raritan Watershed Assn., Brook Club (NY), Met. Club (Washington), Md. Club (Balt.), Princeton Club (NY), Essex Hunt Club (Far Hills, NJ), Union Club (NY), Harvard Bus. Sch. Club (Washington, v.p. 1973-76), Wings Club (NY), Morristown (NJ) Club. Republican. Episcopalian. Avocations: flying, fishing, skiing, running, hunting. Home: 280 Pleasant Valley Rd Mendham NJ 07945-2920 E-mail: georgehambleton@gmail.com.

HAMBLEY, DOUGLAS FREDERICK, geological and environmental engineer; b. Toronto, Ont., Can., Jan. 14, 1950; s. Fredrick Armstrong and Gwendolyn Shannon (Plant) H.; m. Sherrie Kate Barham Hambley, May 24, 1992 (div. June 2000)); m. Paulette Julia Dyon, May 7, 2004. BS in Mining Engring., Queen's U., 1972; MBA, Lewis U., Romeoville, Ill., 1986; PhD in Earth Scis., U. Waterloo, Ont., Can., 1991. Registered profl. engr., Can., Ill., Va., Pa., Md., Wis., profl. geologist, Pa., Wis., Ill., Ind. Jr. engr. Iron Ore Co. of Can., Schefferville, Que., 1972-73; mining engr. trainee Falconbridge Nickel Mines, Ltd., Ont., Canada, 1974-75; mining engr. Harrison Bradford & Assocs., Ltd., St. Catharines, Ont., 1975-76; project engr. Denison Mines, Ltd., Elliot Lake, Ont., 1977-80; sr. mining engr. Engrs. Internat., Inc., Westmont, Ill., 1980-84; mining engr. Argonne Nat. Lab., Ill., 1984-88, civil/geol. engr. Ill., 1990-91; rsch. asst. U. Waterloo, Ontario, 1988; sr. cons. Dunn Geosci. Corp., West Chicago, Ill., 1989; mgr., geo-environtl. group Nova, Environtl. Svcs., Des Plaines, 1991; project mgr. Graef, Anhalt, Schloemer and Assocs., Inc., Chgo., 1992-2000; sr. cons. Practical Environ. Cons., Inc., Schaumburg, Ill., 2000—05; pvt. practice, 2000, 2005—07; assoc. Agapito Assocs., Inc., Lombard, Ill., 2007—. Contbr. articles to profl. jours. Recipient Cert. of Appreciation, Office of Geologic Repositories, 1987, Ill. Dept. Profl. Regulation, 2000. Mem. Soc. Mining, Metallurgy and Exploration (chmn. Chgo. sect. 1987-88), Assn. Engring. Geologists (treas. NC sect. 1987-88), Can. Inst. Mining and Metallurgy, Assn. Groundwater Scientists and Engrs. (Brownfields task force, 2003-05), Soc. Am. Mil. Engrs. (treas. Chgo. post 1996-97, 3rd v.p. 1998, 2d v.p. 1999, pres. 2000), Ill. Cornish Soc. (co-pres. 2005—), Rotary. Avocations: travel, cello, guitar, music. Home: 1404 Childs St Wheaton IL 60187-4602 Office: Agapito Assocs Inc 2 E 22nd St Ste 307 Lombard IL 60148 Office Phone: 630-792-1520. Personal E-mail: dfhambley@comcast.net.

HAMBLIN, TERRY ROBERT, JR., historian, educator; b. Groton, Conn., Jan. 19, 1971; s. Terry Robert Hamblin, Sr. and Roberta Vivian Zelinski; m. Jennifer Anne Blume, Aug. 26, 2000. BA, Stony Brook U., NY, 1995, MA, 1996; PhD, Stony Brook U., 2006. Assoc. prof. Coll. Tech. SUNY, Delhi, NY, 2004—. County com. mem. Otsego County Dem. Com., Cooperstown, NY. Recipient Faculty of Semester award, Morrisville State Coll., 2004. Mem.: Soc. Historians Am. Fgn. Rels., Orgn. Am. Historians, Am. Hist. Assn., Phi Alpha Theta, Pi Sigma Alpha. D-Liberal. Methodist. Avocations: golf, baseball. Home Phone: 607-369-5428; Office Phone: 607-746-4454. Business E-Mail: hamblitr@delhi.edu.

HAMBRECHT, WILLIAM R., investment banking firm executive; b. 1935; married; 5 children. Student, Princeton U. Broker Francis I. DuPont & Co., San Francisco; co-founder Hambrecht & Quist, San Francisco, 1968, mng. ptnr., 1968-97, past pres., CEO, chmn. bd. dirs., ret., 1997; founder, chmn. W.R. Hambrecht & Co., San Francisco, 1998—, CEO, 1998—99, co-CEO, 1999—. Bd. dirs. People Express, Inc., Internet Travel Network, Adobe Sys. Inc., Calyx and Corolla, LXR Biotech. Inc. Bd. dirs. pub. radio and TV sta. KQED Inc., San Francisco; trustee Am. Univ. Beirut; mem., adv. investment com., Bd. Regents, Univ. Calif. Fellow: Am. Acad. Arts & Sciences. Office: WR Hambrecht & Co PO Box 677 Berwyn PA 19312-0677 also: WR Hembrecht & Co 555 Lancaster Ave Ste 200 Berwyn PA 19312

HAMBRICK, ERNESTINE, retired colon and rectal surgeon; b. Griffin, Ga., Mar. 31, 1941; d. Jack Daniel Hambrick and Nanni (Harper) Hambrick Rubens. BS, U. Md., 1963; MD, U. Ill., 1967. Diplomate Am. Bd. Colon and Rectal Surgery, Am. Bd. Surgery. Intern in surgery Cook County Hosp., Chgo., 1967-68, resident in gen. surgery, 1968-72, fellow colon and rectal surgery, 1972-73, attending surgeon, 1973-74, part-time attending surgeon, 1974-80; pvt. practice colon and rectal surgery Chgo., 1974-97; pres. med. staff Michael Reese Hosp., Chgo., 1990-92, chief surgery, 1993-95; founder, chmn. STOP Colon/Rectal Cancer Found., 1997—. Mem. Nat. Colorectal Cancer Round Table, 1997—, mem. steering com., 2000—. Contbr. articles to profl. jours. Trustee Rsch. and Edn. Found. Michael Reese Med. Staff, Chgo., 1994—98, treas., 1994—98. Fellow: ACS, Am. Coll. Gastroenterology, Am. Soc. Colon and Rectal Surgeons (v.p. 1992—93, trustee Rsch. Found. 1992—98). Avocations: travel, photography, scuba diving, flying, writing. Office: PMB 133 47 W Division St Chicago IL 60610 Personal E-mail: ehcrsone@aol.com.

HAMBRICK, GEORGE WALTER, JR., dermatologist, educator; b. Charlottesville, Va., Dec. 4, 1922; s. George W. and Sallie Anna (McCallum) H BS, Concord Coll., 1944; MD, U. Va., 1946. Intern Hosp. U. Iowa, 1946—47; asst. resident dermatology U. Va. Hosp., 1947—48; resident Columbia-Presbyn. Hosp., NYC, 1950—51; fellow dermatology Duke U., Durham, NC, 1951—52, assoc. dermatology, 1953; instr. Columbia U., NYC, 1953—55, assoc., 1955—57, asst. prof., 1957—62; assoc. prof. U. Pa., 1962—66, Johns Hopkins U., Balt., 1966—69, prof., 1969—76; dir. dermatology Johns Hopkins Med. Inst. Johns Hopkins U., 1967—76; prof. U. Cin., 1976-81, dir. dermatology, 1976-81; prof. Cornell U. Coll. Medicine, NYC, 1981—96; chief dermatology N.Y. Hosp., 1981—96, prof emeritus, 1996—; sr. lectr. Columbia U., 2001—. Capt. AUS USMC, 1948—50. Fellow ACP; mem. AMA (del. 1981-90), Soc. Investigative Dermatology (pres. 1971-72, hon. mem.), Dermatology Found. (trustee, pres. 1974), Assn. Profs. Dermatology, Am. Dermatol. Assn. (hon.), Am. Acad. Dermatology (hon. dir. 1978), Am. Skin Assn. (pres. 1988-93, 2000-), Alpha Omega Alpha. Office: Am Skin Assn 346 Park Ave S New York NY 10010 Office Phone: 212-889-4858.

HAMBRICK, JAMES L., chemicals executive; BS in Chem. Engring., Tex. A&M U. Mgmt. & mktg. positions Lubrizol Corp., Wickliffe, Ohio, 1978—98, global mgr. engine oil additives, 1998—2000, v.p. Asia-Pacific, 2000—03, pres., 2003—04, chmn., pres., CEO, 2004—. Bd. mem. Hospice of Western Reserve, Univ. Health Sys., Greater Cleve. Partnership, NE Ohio Council Higher Edn. Mem.: Am. Chemistry Council (bd. mem.), Am. Inst. Chem. Engineers. Office: Lubrizol Corp 29400 Lakeland Blvd Wickliffe OH 44092*

HAMBRUSCH, SUSANNE, computer engineering educator; MS in Computer Sci., Tech. Univ. of Vienna, 1977; PhD in Computer Sci., Penn. St. Univ., 1982. Prof., Dept. Computer Sci. Purdue Univ., Ind., Ind. Contbr. articles to numerous profl. jours. Fellow: IEEE (mem. tech. com. parallel processing). Achievements include Outstanding Engring. Alum award, UPenn, 2003; TechPoint Mira Edn. award, 2004. Office: Purdue Univ Computer Sci Dept 250 N Univ St West Lafayette IN 47907-2066 Office Phone: 765-494-1831. Office Fax: 765-494-0739. E-mail: seh@cs.purdue.edu.

HAMBURG, CHARLES BRUCE, lawyer; b. Bklyn., June 30, 1939; s. Albert and Goldie (Blume) Hamburg; m. Stephanie Barbara Steingesser, June 23, 1962; children: Jeanne M., Louise E. B in Chem. Engring., Poly. Inst. Bklyn., 1960; JD, George Washington U., 1964. Bar: NY 1964. Patent examiner U.S. Patent Office, 1960-63; patent atty. Celanese Corp. Am., NYC, 1963-65, Burns, Lobato & Zelnick, NYC, 1965-67, Nolte & Nolte,

NYC, 1967-75; prin. C. Bruce Hamburg, NYC, 1976-79; ptnr. Jordan & Hamburg, L.L.P., NYC, 1979—. U.S. corr. Patents and Licensing, Japan, 1986—. Author: Patent Fraud and Inequitable Conduct, 1972, 78, Patent Law Handbook, 1983-84, 84-85, 85-86, Doctrine of Equivalents in U.S. (in Japanese), 1995, 2d edit. (in Korean), 1998; monthly columnist Patent and Trademark Rev., 1976-85; U.S. corr. Patents and Licensing, 1989—; contbr. chpts. to books. Mem.: ABA, Internat. Fedn. Intellectual Property Attys., Licensing Execs. Soc., Internat. Assn. Protection Intellectual Property, NY Intellectual Property Law Assn., Am. Intellectual Property Law Assn., Masons. Office: 122 E 42nd St New York NY 10168-0002 Office Phone: 212-986-2340. Business E-Mail: jandh@ipattorneys.com.

HAMBURG, DAVID A., psychiatrist, foundation administrator; b. Evansville, Ind., 1925; MD, Ind. U., 1947, D.Sc. (hon.), 1976, Rush U., 1977, Mt. Sinai Sch. Medicine, 1980, U. Rochester, 1981, U. Ill., Chgo., 1984, Albert Einstein Sch. Medicine, 1985, U. Pitts., U. So. Calif., Hahnemann U., 1986; LHD (hon.), Ramapo Coll., 1991, Duke U., 1993, So. Indiana U., 2000. Diplomate Am. Bd. Psychiatry and Neurology. Intern Michael Reese Hosp., Chgo., 1947-48, resident in psychiatry, 1949-50, Yale U.-New Haven Hosp., 1948-49; staff psychiatrist Brooke Army Hosp., San Antonio, 1950-52; practice medicine specializing in psychiatry, 1950-75; research psychiatrist Walter Reed Army Inst. Research, Washington, 1952-53; assoc. dir. Psychosomatic and Psychiat. Inst., Michael Reese Hosp., Chgo., 1954-56; fellow Center for Advanced Study in Behavioral Scis., Palo Alto, Calif., 1957-58, 67-68; chief Adult Psychiat. Br. NIMH, Bethesda, Md., 1958-61; prof., chmn. dept. psychiatry Stanford U. Med. Sch., 1961-72, Reed-Hodgson prof. human biology, 1972-76; Sherman Fairchild Disting. scholar Calif. Inst. Tech., Pasadena, 1974-75; pres. Inst. Medicine Nat. Acad. Scis., Washington, 1975-80; dir. div. health policy research and edn., John D. MacArthur prof. health policy and mgmt. Harvard U., Cambridge, Mass., 1980-82; pres. Carnegie Corp., NYC, 1983-97, pres. emeritus, 1997—; dist. scholar Weill Cornell Med. Coll., 2004—. Adv. com. med. rsch. WHO, 1975-86; mem. exec. panel adv. com. Chief of Naval Ops, 1984-92; chmn. sci. adv. bd. NIMH, 1986-87; sec. Energy Adv. Bd., 1990-94; mem. Ctr. for Naval Analysis, 1990-93. Author: No More Killing Fields: Preventing Deadly Conflict, 2002, Learning to Live Together: Preventing Hatred and Violence in Child and Adolescent Development, 2003. Bd. dirs. Rockefeller U., 1979—, Mt. Sinai Med. Ctr., N.Y.C., 1984—; trustee Stanford U., 1988-94, Internat. Devel. Rsch. Ctr., Ottawa, Ont., Can., 1990-94, Am. Mus. Natural History, N.Y.C., 1990—; co-chmn. Carnegie Commn. on Preventing Deadly Conflict, 1994-99; mem. Pres.'s Com. of Advisors on Sci. and Tech., 1994-2001; dep. chmn. Fed. Res. Bank N.Y., Def. Policy Bd., U.S. Dept. Def., 1994-95; chmn. to sec. gen. prevention genocide United Nations Adv. Com., 2006-. Recipient numerous awards including: Pres.'s medal Michael Reese Med. Ctr., 1974, Peace award Cranbrook Found., 2003; A.C.P. award, 1977; MIT Bicentennial medal, 1976, Presdl. Medal of Freedom, 1996; Disting. Presdl. fellow for internat. activities Nat. Acads., 2002. Mem. Am. Psychiat. Assn. (Vestermark award 1977, Disting. Svc. award 1991, Pres.'s medal Bank St. Coll. 1994, Charter medallion Radcliffe Coll. 1994), Nat. Acad. Scis. (com. on internat. security and arms control 1981-86, Pub. Welfare medal 1998, Fgn. Policy Assocs. medal 2004), AAAS (pres. 1984-85, chmn. bd. 1985-86), Assn. Rsch. Nervous and Mental Disease (pres. 1967-68), Am. Philos. Soc., Am. Acad. Arts and Scis., Phi Beta Kappa, Alpha Omega Alpha. Office: Weill Cornell Med Coll Dept Psych 525 E 68th St Box 171 New York NY 10065 Business E-Mail: dab2013@med.cornell.edu.

HAMBURG, MARC D., investment company executive; V.p., CFO Berkshire Hathaway Inc., Omaha. Office: Berkshire Hathaway Inc 1440 Kiewit Plz Omaha NE 68131 Office Phone: 402-346-1400.*

HAMBURG, MARGARET ANN (PEGGY HAMBURG), public health administrator; b. Chgo., July 12, 1955; d. David Alan and Beatrix Ann (Mc Cleary) H.; m. Peter Fitzhugh Brown, May 23, 1992; children: Rachel Ann Hamburg Brown, Evan David Addison Brown. BA magna cum laude, Harvard/Radcliffe Coll., 1978; MD, Harvard, 1983. Diplomate Am. Bd. Internal Medicine, Nat. Bd. Med. Examiners. Intern, resident in internal medicine The N.Y. Hosp., Cornell Med. Coll., NYC, 1983-86; spl. asst. to the dir., office of disease prevention and health promotion, office of the asst. sec. for health U.S. Dept. Health and Human Svcs., Washington, 1986-88; spl. asst. to the dir. Nat. Inst. Allergy and Infectious Diseases, NIH, Bethesda, Md., 1988-89, asst. dir., 1989-90; deputy commr. Family Health Svcs., N.Y.C. Dept. Health, NYC, 1990-91; commr. of health N.Y.C. Dept. Health, NYC, 1991-97; asst. sec. planning and evaluation U.S. Dept. HHS, Washington, 1997—2001; v.p. biological programs Nuclear Threat Initiative, Washington, 2001—. Guest investigator The Rockefeller U., N.Y.C., 1985-86; clin. instr. dept. medicine Georgetown U. Sch. Medicine, Washington, 1986-90; asst. prof. clin. pub. health Columbia U. Sch. Pub. Health, N.Y.C., 1991-97; adj. asst. prof. medicine Cornell U. Med. Coll., N.Y.C., 1991-97; scholar Pub. Health Leadership Inst. Ctr. for Disease Control U. Calif., 1992; bd. dirs. N.Y.C. Health Systems Agy., Med. and Health Rsch. Assn., Health Hosps. Corp, Nat. Coun. on Women's Health, Primary Care Devel. Corp.; steering com. women and aids NIH, 1991; bd. govs. Greater N.Y. Hosp. Assn., 1991-97; mem. bd. sci. advisors. Nat. Pub. Radio, 1992-97; com. mem. on substance abuse mental health issues in aides rsch., 1993; advisory bd. mem. Medunsa Trust, Inc., Med. U. So. Africa, 1993-97; mem. defense sci. bd. task force on Gulf War Syndrome U.S. Dept. Defense, 1993—; bd. mem. sci. counselors Nat. Ctr. Infectious Diseases, U.S. Ctrs. for Disease, 1994-97. Editorial bd. mem. Jour. N.Y. Acad. Sci., 1992-97, The Bull. of N.Y. Acad. Medicine, 1992-97, Current Reviews in Pub. Health, 1993-97; contbr. to numerous profl. jours. Vol. attending physician The Washington Free Clinic, Washington, 1988-90; coun. fgn. rels. bd. overseers Harvard U., 1999—; trustee Rockefeller Found. Recipient commendation Pub. Health Svc., 1988, 90, Spl. Recognition award Pub. Health Svc., 1990, cert. of Honor The Women's Club of N.Y., 1993, N.Y. Rotary Club award, 1993, Robert F. Wagner Pub. Svc. award NYU, 1993. Fellow AAAS (med. scis. section com. 1989—), ACP; mem. APHA, Am. Med. Women's Assn., Nat. Acad. Scis., Coun. on Fgn. Rels., Health Care Exec. Forum, N.Y. Acad. Medicine, Pub. Health Assn. N.Y.C., Inst. Med. (coun. mem. 2006-), Soc. Social Biology, Women in Health Mgmt., Med. Office: Nuclear Threat Initiative 1747 Pennsylvania Ave NW 7th Fl Washington DC 20006

HAMBURGER, PHILIP ANDREW, law educator; b. 1957; BA in History summa cum laude, Princeton U., 1979; JD, Yale U., 1982. Bar: Pa. 1982. Assoc. Schnader, Harrison, Segal & Lewis, Phila., 1982—85; assoc. prof. U. Conn. Sch. Law, 1985—88, prof., 1988—92; prof. law & legal history George Washington U. Nat. Law Ctr., 1992—95, Oswald Symister Colclough rsch. prof. law, 1995—2000; John P. Wilson prof. law U. Chgo. Law Sch., 2000—, also Herbert and Marjorie Fried rsch. scholar, dir. legal history program. Vis. assoc. prof. U. Va. Law Sch., 1986; vis. prof. George Washington U. Nat. Law Ctr., 1991—92, U. Chgo. Law Sch., 2000; Jack N. Pritzker disting. vis. prof. law Northwestern U. Sch. Law, 1999. Author: Separation of Church and State, 2002. Mem.: Am. Soc. Legal History (program com. chair 1993—94, mem. nominating com. 1998—2001, bd. dirs. 2004—, Sutherland Prize 1991, 1995), Am. Assn. Law Schools (chair provisional sect. on scholarship 1995). Office: U Chgo Law Sch 1111 E 60th St Chicago IL 60637 Office Phone: 773-834-4162. E-mail: philip_hamburger@law.uchicago.edu.

HAMBURGER, ROBERT N., pediatrician, educator, consultant; b. NYC, Jan. 26, 1923; s. Samuel B. and Harriet (Newfield) H.; m. Sonia Gross, Nov. 9, 1943; children: Hilary, Debre (dec.), Lisa. BA, U. NC, 1947; MD, Yale U., 1951. Diplomate Am. Bd. Pediatrics, Am. Bd. Allergy and Immunology. Instr., asst. clin. prof. sch. medicine Yale U., New Haven, 1951-60; assoc. prof. biology U. Calif. San Diego, La Jolla, 1960-64, assoc. prof. pediatrics, 1964-67, prof., 1967-90, prof. emeritus, 1990—, asst. dean sch. medicine, 1964-70, lab. dir., 1970-98, head fellows tng. program allergy and immunology divsn., 1970-90; pres., CEO RNA and Co., Inc., 1997—. Chmn., bd. dirs. BioVigilant Sys., Inc., 2002-; cons. various cos., Calif., Sweden, Switzerland, 1986—. Author 1 book; contbr. articles to profl. jours. Vol. physician, educator Children of the Californias, Calif. and Baja California, Mex., 1993—, Baker Sch. Free Clinic, 1999—. 1st lt. Air Corps, U.S. Army, 1943-45, PTO. Decorated Air medal with oak leaf clusters, Purple Heart; grantee NIH and USPHS, 1960-64, 64-84; Fulbright fellow, 1980, Disting. fellow Am. Coll. Allergy, Asthma, Immunology, 1986. Mem. U. Calif. San Diego Emeriti Assn. (pres. 1992-94). Achievements include patentee for allergy peptides, allergen detector, Pathogen Detector System and Methods. Avocations: flying, skiing, writing. Office: U Calif San Diego Revelle Coll Sch Medicine La Jolla CA 92093-0950 Office Phone: 858-534-7555. E-mail: rhamburger@ucsd.edu.

HAMBY, GENE MALCOLM, JR., lawyer; b. Florence, Ala., Mar. 23, 1943; s. Gene Malcolm Sr. and Katherine (Koonce) H.; m. Judy Priscilla Brown, Apr. 10, 1971; children: Mark Clifton, Anne Tyler. BS with honors, U. North Ala., 1965; JD, U. Ala., Tuscaloosa, 1968. Bar: Ala. 1968, U.S. Dist. Ct. (no. dist.) Ala. 1972, U.S. Ct. Appeals (11th cir.) 1981. Assoc. Heflin & Rosser, Attys., Tuscambia, Ala., 1968-70; ptnr. Pitts & Hamby, Sheffield, Ala., 1970-80; pvt. practice Sheffield, 1981-84; ptnr. Hamby & Baker, Attys., Sheffield, 1984-87, Jones, Hamby & Baker, Attys., Sheffield, 1987-89; pvt. practice, Sheffield, 1989—. Bd. dirs. Shoals Indsl. Devel. Authority, Sheffield, Law Sch. Found., U. Ala. Sch. Law, 1985—; past dist. v.p. U. Ala. Alumni, Tuscaloosa; past pres. U. North Ala. Alumni, Florence, Colbert County United Way, Sheffield; chmn. Sheffield Indsl. Devel. Bd., Sheffield, Sheffield Edn. Found.; past bd. dirs. United Cerebral Palsy NW Ala., Sheffield, Shoals Indsl. Devel. Authority. With USAR, 1968-74. Recipient Kiwanis Citizen of Yr. award City of Sheffield, 1991, 2001. Mem. ATLA, ABA, Colbert County Bar Assn (past pres.), Ala. State Bar Assn., Ala. Trial Lawyers Assn. (past mem. exec. com.), Sheffield Bus. and Profl. Assn. (pres. 1999-2001), Kiwanis Club (past pres. Sheffield chpt.), Colbert County C. of C. (past pres.), Shoals Dem. Club (past pres.), Phi Kappa Phi Democrat. Avocation: indian artifacts. Home: PO Box 328 Sheffield AL 35660-0328 Office: 406 N Nashville Ave Sheffield AL 35660-2938 Office Phone: 205-381-7673. Personal E-mail: ham015@aol.com.

HAMBY, KRISTIE LYNNE, director; b. Wilkesboro, Nc, Dec. 19, 1971; d. Danny Lee and Judith Redmond Hamby. MusB in Edn., Appalachian State U., Boone, NC, 1995. Dir. bands anson county sch. Anson H.S. Band, Wadesboro, NC, 1995—. 911 communicator Anson County Govt., Wadesboro, NC, 2000—. Recipient Dir. of Honors Band, Wingate U., 1999. Mem.: NC Music Educators Assn. (licentiate). R-Liberal. Meth. Avocations: travel, music, theater. Office: Anson H S Hwy 74 West Wadesboro NC 28170 Home Phone: 704-694-2420; Office Phone: 704-694-7445. Business E-Mail: kristieb28@hotmail.com.

HAMDAN, LAWRENCE ANISE, investment banker, lawyer; b. South Orange, NJ, Aug. 31, 1961; s. Ali A. and Dorothea E. (Nevola) H. AB magna cum laude, Princeton U., 1983; MBA with high distinction, Harvard U., 1989, JD magna cum laude, 1989. Bar: N.Y. 1990. Rsch. analyst Brown Bros. Harriman & Co., NYC, 1983-84; pres. FLYERS Svcs. Inc., Cambridge, Mass., 1985-89; assoc. Credit Suisse First Boston (formerly First Boston Corp.), NYC, 1989—98, mng. dir., vice chmn. global mergers & acquisitions, 1998—. Author: F.L.Y.E.R.S., 1985, Youth Trends, 1987. Baker scholar Harvard Bus. Sch., 1989. Mem. Phi Beta Kappa. Roman Catholic. Office: Credit Suisse First Boston Park Avenue Plz New York NY 10055-0002

HAMDI, HAMID S., neurologist, neurorehabilitation specialist, consultant, researcher; b. Karachi, Sind, Pakistan, May 5, 1959; s. Mohammad Abul Aas, Habiba Bano Aas; m. Imrana Y. Hamdi, Mar. 26, 1959; children: Mia, Samiha. MBBS, Dow Medical College, Karachi, Pakistan, 1978—84. Medical Officer Civil Hospital and Dow Medical College, Karachi, Sind, Pakistan, 1986—88, Saudi Ministry of Health, Riyadh, Saudi Arabia, 1988—93; Resident Lincoln Medical Center, Bronx, NY, 1993—94; Resident in Neurology Nassau County Medical Center, East Meadow, NY, 1994—97; Fellow in Neurorehabilitation Hospital for Joint Diseases, New York, NY, 1997—99; clin. asst. prof. neurology Ind. U., 2003—. Cheif Resident in Neurology Nassau County Medical Center, East Meadow, NY, 1996—97; Faculty Member New York University School of Medicine, New York, NY, 1999—99; Visiting Lecturer Purdue University, West Lafayette, IN, 2000—01; clin. asst. prof. Ind. U. Sch. of Medicine, Ind.; Principal Investigator-KEEPER trial Heartland Neurology Associates, Lafayette, IN, 2000—01, Principal Investigator-Betaserone trial, 2000—01. Author: (Reveiw article) Neurocysticercosis- a reveiw., 1997; editor: (Periodical) NCMC Proceedings, 1996. Speaker National MS Soceity Indiana Chapter, West Lafayette, IN, 2000—00, Renssalaer, IN, 2001—01, Stroke Support Group, Lafayette, IN, 2001—01. Mem.: AMA, Am. Acad. Neurology, Am. Soc. Neurorehab. Home: 3137 Covington street West Lafayette IN 47906 Office: Heartland Neurology Assocs 1345 Unity Pl #365 Lafayette IN 47905 Office Phone: 765-446-5300.

HAMDY, RONALD CHARLES, geriatrician; b. Alexandria, Egypt, July 31, 1946; came to U.S., 1985; s. Charles and Mary Hamdy; m. Eleanor Gertrude Hamdy, Aug. 19, 1977; children: Conrad, Gerard, Ronan. MB, ChB with honours, U. Alexandria, 1968, DM, 1971. Rotating intern U. Alexandria, 1968-69; resident in internal medicine Al-Gomhouriya Gen. Hosp., Alexandria, 1969-70; resident registrar internal medicine U. Alexandria Main Tchg. Hosp., 1970-72; sr. ho. officer geriatric and internal medicine Farnborough (Eng.) Hosp., Kent, 1972-73; registrar in geriatric medicine Bromley (Eng.) Group of Hosps., Kent, 1974; sr. registrar in geriatric medicine King's Coll. Group Hosps., London, 1975-77; consulting physician St. John's Hosp. Richmond (Eng.), Twickenham & Roehampton Health Authority, 1977-85, chmn. dept. clin. gerontology, ethics rsch. com., 1981-85; prof. internal medicine, Cecile Cox Quillen prof. geriatric medicine, head divsn. gerontology East Tenn. State U., Mountain Home, 1985—. Cecile Cox Quillen prof. geriatric medicine, head divsn. gerontology, 1990—, dir. osteoporosis ctr., 1997—; chief geriat. VA Med. Ctr., Mountain Home, 1985-88, assoc. chief of staff geriatric and extended care, 1988—2004. Hon. sr. lectr. geriatric medicine St. George's Hosp. Med. Sch., U. London, 1981-85; planning team for elderly Wandsworth Health Care, 1982-85; med. dist. initiated peer rev. orgn. VA Hosps., Dist. 8, 1986-89; vis. prof. Health Care for Elderly, U. London, 1991-93; Burroughs Wellcome vis. prof. geriatric medicine Royal Soc. Medicine, 1994-95; co-chmn. pharmacy and therapeutics com. VA Med. Ctr., Johnson City, Tenn., chmn. adverse drug reaction com.; chmn. program com. Coll. Medicine Continuing Med. Edn., East Tenn. State U.; mem. Gov.'s task force on Alzheimer's Disease, Tenn., task force on edn., prevention and detection of osteoporosis; mem. advisor to pub. guardian 1st Tenn. Devel. Dist.; adv. bd. Colonial Hill Health Care Ctr., Johnson City, Golden J-55, Johnson City Med. Ctr. Hosp., Inc.; sr. health adv. com. 1st Tenn. Regional Health Office; adj. clin. prof. divsn. clin. nutrition and psychiatry East Tenn. State U. Author: Diuretic Therapy in the Older Patient, 1978, Paget's Disease in Bone, Assessment and Management, 1981, Geriatric Medicine: A Problem Oriented Approach, 1984; editor: (with J. Turnbull, M. Lancaster, L. Norman) Alzheimer's Disease: A Handbook for Caregivers, 1990, 3d edit., 1998; mem. editl. adv. bd. Revs. Clin. Gerontology, South Med. Jour., Geriatria; reviewer for med. jours.; contbr. chpts. to books, articles to profl. jours. Fellow ACP (com. geriat. 1987-90, chmn. com. geriat. MKSAP IX 1991-94), Royal Coll. Physicians, Royal Soc. Medicine; mem. Internat. Soc. Clin. Densitometry, Am. Geriat. Soc. (membership com., reviewer jour., ann. meeting planning com. 1993), Gerontol. Soc. Am., Royal Coll. Surgeons, So. Med. Assn. (vice-chmn. coun. 1995-96, chmn. coun. 1996-97, v.p. 1997-98, pres.-elect 1998-99, pres. 1999-2000, editor geriatric medicine sect. Dial-Access program, from assoc. councilor to councilor state Tenn., chmn. adv. com. sci. activities, reviewer jour., assoc. editor So. Med. Jour. 1995-2000, editor 2000—), So. Assn. Geriatric Medicine (pres. 1990-92), So. Assn. for Primary Care (editor clin. revs.), Tenn. Med. Assn. (reviewer jour.), Tenn. Geriat. Soc. (founding), Brit. Med. Assn., Brit. Geriat. Soc., Bone and Mineral Soc., Alzheimer's Assn. (pres. bd. dirs. N.E. Tenn. chpt. 1990-91). Office: Ea Tenn State U Coll Medicine PO Box 70429 Johnson City TN 37614-1704 Home Phone: 423-737-8368; Office Phone: 423-439-8830. Business E-Mail: hamdy@etsu.edu.

HAMECS, FRANCELLA CHESLOCK, elementary and secondary school educator; b. Hazleton, Pa., Mar. 7, 1947; d. Richard Mark and Helen (Zanfofski) Cheslock; m. Robert Thomas Hamecs; children: Bryan Robert, Daniel Raphael. BS, Pa. State U., State College, 1969; MA, Fairleigh Dickinson U., Teaneck, NJ, 1978. Tchr. Warminster Schs., Pa., 1969—70, Wayne Bd. Edn., NJ, 1970—. Counselor London Police, 1986—88; chmn. Focus Orgn., London, 1986—88. Leader Team Tobago, West Indies, 2004—06; mem. advance coun. com. WEA, 2004—. Named Outstanding Tchr. of Yr., Pa. State U., 2006, A+ Tchr., NJ Edn. Assn. Rev.; recipient Gov.'s award, State of NJ, 2002, Honor award, USMC, 2003, Congl. award, US Ho. of Reps., 2007. Mem.: NEA, Nat. English Coun., Wayne Edn. Assn. (rep. 2001—06), Pa. State Alumni Assn. Business E-Mail: fhamecs@wayneschools.com.

HAMED, MARTHA ELLEN, retired small business owner; b. Washington, Jan. 14, 1950; d. Rockford Norris and Dorothy Hope Hamed. AA, George Washington U., 1985, BA in Psychology and Sociology, 1989; MS in Adminstrn., Ctrl. Mich. U., 1999. Command fed. women's program mgr. U.S. Atlantic Fleet, Norfolk, Va., 1978-79; fed. women's program mgr. Naval Ordnance Sta., Indian Head, Md., 1979-80; pers. mgr., Equal Employment Opportunity course dir. Naval Civilian Pers. Command, Arlington, Va., 1980-83; dep. Equal Employment Opportunity officer, site mgr. Ship R&D Ctr., Bethesda, Md., 1983-85, Naval Surface Weapons Ctr., Silver Spring, Md., 1985; command fed. women's program mgr. Naval Sea Sys. Command, Washington, 1985-87, mgr. command tng. programs, 19987-88, asst. dir. awards and performance appraisal programs, 1988-89; asst. mgmt. analysis Office of Insp. Gen., 1989-92; project mgr. Office of Under Sec. of Def., 1992—98; ret. fed. govt., 2005; owner Spiral Path - Women's Empowerment Cir. Chief interagy. bus. integration divsn. Def. Human Resource Office Under Sec. Def., 1998—2005. Comnr Anne Arundel County Women's Commn., 1990—92. Named to Oustanding Young Women Am, US Jaycees, 1983; recipient V P Hammer Award Bus Processing Re-Eng, 1995, Commendation Award, VA Vets Benefits Admin, 1996, Award and Medal, Pres's Comn Y2K, 2000, Commendation Award Y2K Transition, Secy Def, 2000. Mem.: AAUW, NOW (life), Fed. Exec. Inst. Alumni Assn., Nat Assn. Ret. Fedn. Employees, Federally Employed Women. Democrat. Avocations: natural history, cats, salt-water fishing. Office Phone: 252-489-9202.

HAMEKA, HENDRIK FREDERIK, chemistry professor; b. Rotterdam, Netherlands, May 25, 1931; arrived in US, 1960, naturalized, 1963; s. Dirk C. and Johanna (Mannebeck) Hameka; m. Charlotte C. Proacci, Aug. 3, 1972. Doctorandus, U. Leiden, Netherlands, 1953, DSc cum laude, 1956; MA (hon.), U. Pa., Phila., 1971. Rsch. assoc. U. Rome, 1956—57; fellow Carnegie Inst. Tech., 1957—58; rsch. physicist N. V. Philips Lamps, Eindhoven, Netherlands, 1958—60; asst. prof. chemistry Johns Hopkins U., Balt., 1960—62; assoc. prof. chemistry U. Pa., Phila., 1962—67, prof. chemistry, 1967—. Disting. vis. rsch. prof. USAF Acad., 1986—87. Author: Advanced Quantum Chemistry, 1965, Introductory Quantum Theory, 1967, Physical Chemistry, 1977, Chemistry, Fundamentals and Applications, 2002, Quantum Mechanics, A Conceptual Approach, 2004; contbr. articles to profl. jours. Recipient Alexander von Humboldt prize, 1981; Alfred P. Sloan Rsch. fellow, 1963—67. Achievements include research on theory of molecular structure and optical and magnetic properties of molecules; calculations of spin-orbit and spin-spin coupling; research on theory of resonance optical rotation, spectral predictions. Home: 1503 Argyle Rd Berwyn PA 19312-1905 Office: U Pa Dept Chemistry Philadelphia PA 19104 Office Phone: 215-898-8303. Business E-Mail: hameka@sas.upenn.edu.

HAMEL, DANA BERTRAND, academic administrator; b. Rumford, Maine, Aug. 9, 1923; s. Donat H. and Louise (Kenison) H.; m. Shirley Elmeree Smith Knavel, Dec. 19, 1945; children— Dana Randolph, Michelle, April. AB, Ashland Coll., Ohio, 1951; MA, Ohio State U., 1952; EdD, U Cin., 1962; AA in Humanities (hon.), Southside Va. C.C., 2004; AA in Humane Letters (hon.), Va. Western C.C., 2005. Master watchmaker Thomas J. Apryle & Sons, Johnstown, Pa., 1946; owner Hamels, Jewelers, Conemaugh, Pa., 1946-48; mem. mgmt. dept. Gen. Motors Inst., Flint, Mich., 1955-57; dean adminstrv. affairs Ohio Coll. Applied Sci. and Ohio Mechanics Inst., Cin., 1957-63, acting pres., 1961-62, exec. v.p., dean of faculties, 1962-63; dir. Roanoke Tech. Inst., 1963-64; exec. dir. Va. Dept. Tech. Edn., Richmond, 1964-66; founding chancellor Va. Community Coll. System, Richmond, 1966-79, cons., 1979-80; cons. to pres., dir. spl. acad. programs Va. State U., Petersburg, 1980-961980—; exec. dir. Va. Ctr. Pub./Pvt. Initiatives; pres. Hamel & Assocs., Richmond, 1996—. Coord. for offices of Va. Sec. of Edn. and Dept. of Edn. for WorkForce 2000, V-Quest Programs, 1992-96; co-chair Metro Richmond 2000; acting dir. Adminstrv. Affairs, CEBAF. Founder, Gov.'s liaison SURA/Continuous Electron Beam Accelerator Facility, 1983—; trustee, v.p. 1983-99, Southeastern Univs. Rsch. Assn., Inc., 1981—; mem. Va. Adv. Coun. Vocat. Edn.; bd. dirs. Richmond Eye and Ear Hosp. Authority, 1989—, Ctr. Excellence, Inc., Richmond Cmty. HS, 1981—; chmn. bd. Va. Edn. Rsch. 1981-85, Network for Supercomputers, 1986—; sr. cons. 1986-93, So. Growth Policies Bd. Tech. Coun., 1987-95; Va. coord. Vamanuf Networking, 1990—; exec. dir. Mfg. Networking and Indsl. Modernization Project, 1992—; interim exec. dir. Va. Alliance Mfg. Competitiveness, 1993—; interim dir. Sch. to Work Program, 1994-95. Wth USAAF, 1942-45. Scribes acad. scholar, Ashland Coll. Mem. So. Assn. Schs. and Colls. (former pres.), Am. Assn. Jr. Colls. (commn. on legis.), Nat. Coun. State Dirs. (former chmn.), Am. Soc. Engring. Edn., Am. Psychology and Guidance Assn., Nat. Assn. for Gifted Children, Am. Coll. Pers. Assn., Cin. Guidance and Pers. Assn., Va. League Nursing (pres. 1987), Forum Club, Masons, Kiwanians, Phi Delta Kappa, Psi Chi, Iota Lambda Sigma. Home and Office: Hamel & Assocs 300 Coalport Rd Richmond VA 23229-7019

HAMEL, DOUGLAS E., lawyer; b. Anchorage, Feb. 21, 1951; BA, U. Va., 1972, JD, 1976. Bar: Tex. 1976. Ptnr., co-head Employment Litig. and Labor Sect. Vinson & Elkins LLP, Houston. Chmn. Civil Svc. Commn. City of Houston, 1984-87. Office: Vinson & Elkins First City Tower 1001 Fannin St Ste 2300 Houston TX 77002-6760 Office Phone: 713-758-2036. E-mail: dhamel@velaw.com.

HAMEL, LORIE ANN, psychologist; b. Greenville, SC, Oct. 23, 1957; d. Francis Joseph and Jessie Pearl (Spoone) Boniface; m. Adrian Paul Cooper, Aug. 7, 1977 (dec. July 1990); children: Paul, Philip, Andrew; m. Loren B. Hamel, Oct. 21, 1995; stepchildren: Chad, Matthew, Jason, Angela BS Elem. Edn., So. Adventist U., Collegedale, Tenn., 1979; MA Cmty. Counseling, Andrews U., Berrien Springs, Mich., 1994; PhD Counseling Psychology, Andrews U., 1997; DMin Formational Counseling, Ashland Theol. Sem., Ohio, 2006. Missionary Ctrl. African Union, Bujumbura, Burundi, 1979—82, Adventist U. Ctrl. Africa, Gisenyi, Rwanda, 1982—90; psychologist U. Med. Specialties, Berrien Springs, Mich., 1994—. Cons., psychologist Adventist Frontier Missions, 1994—2005.

Recipient Sirrine scholarship, Greenville, 1975, Steele scholarship, Berrien Springs, 1992, 94, Weniger scholarship, 1994 Mem. APA, Am. Acad. Experts in Traumatic Stress, Internat. Soc. Traumatic Stress Studies, Phi Kappa Phi Seventh-day Adventist. Avocations: travel, birdwatching, skiing. Office: Univ Med Ctr Berrien Springs MI 49103

HAMEL, LOUIS REGINALD, retired systems analyst; b. Lowell, Mass., July 23, 1945; s. Wilfred John and Angelina Lucienne (Paradis) H.; m. Roi Anne Roberts, Mar. 24, 1967 (dec.); 1 child, Felicia Antoinette; m. Anne Louise Staup, July 2, 1972 (div.); children: Shawna Michelle, Louis Reginald III. AA, Kellogg C.C., 1978. Cert. worker's compensation profl.; cert. notary pub., Minn.; cert. personal care asst., Minn. Retail mgr. Marshall Dept. Stores, Beverly, Mass., 1972-73; tech. svc. rep. Monarch Marking Systems, Framingham, Mass., 1973—74; employment specialist Dept. Labor, Battle Creek, Mich., 1977-78; v.p. corp. Keith Polygraph Cons. and Investigative Svc., Inc., Battle Creek, 1978-79; indsl. engr., engine components divsn. Eaton Corp., Battle Creek, 1979-82; tooling and process engr. Kelley Tech. Svcs., Battle Creek, 1983-84, Clark Equipment Inc., 1983-84; tooling and mfg. engr., mfg. mgr. Trans Guard Industries Inc., Angola, Ind., 1983-85; facilitator employee involvement, safety dir. Wohlert Corp., Lansing, Mich., 1985—2004, workers compensation adminstr., tng. dir., 1985—2004, system analysis cons., 1975—; gen. mgr. Teddy Bear Mgmt. LLP, Anoka, Minn., 2005—07; ret., 2007. Cons. in field. Mem. Calhoun County Com. on Employment of Handicapped, Battle Creek, Mich., 1977-78; mem. Capital Area Labor Mgmt. Com., 1986-91. With USN, 1963-71, Vietnam. Recipient Svcs. to Handicapped award Internat. Assn. Pers. in Employment Security, Mich. chpt. 1978. Mem. VFW, Nat. Geog. Soc., Mich. Assn. Concerned Vets. (dir. 1974-79), Nat. Assn. Concerned Vets. Democrat. Roman Catholic. Personal E-mail: hamellm@prodigy.net. *Personal philosophy: A warm handshake, with a smile, will give more people a lift than all the elevators in the world.*

HAMEL, MARK EDWIN, lawyer; b. Ontonagon, Mich., Apr. 9, 1953; s. Peter C. and Marian E. (Peterson) H.; m. Pamela Kay Jenkins, May 31, 1975; children: Nathan, Gregory. BA, Carroll Coll., 1975; JD, Harvard U., 1978. Bar: Minn. 1979, U.S. Dist. Ct. Minn. 1979. Law clk. to presiding justice Minn. Supreme Ct., St. Paul, 1978-79; assoc. Dorsey & Whitney LLP, Mpls., 1979-85, ptnr., 1985—, chmn., real estate and land use practice group. Chmn. bd. dirs. Accessible Space, Inc., bd. dirs. Downtown Coun., Mpls., Minn. Mem. Minn. Bar Assn. (cert. real property law specialist), Hennepin County Bar Assn (real property sect.), Mpls. Lifetime Athletic Club. Presbyterian. Office: Dorsey & Whitney LLP Ste 1500 50 S 6th St Minneapolis MN 55402-1498 Office Phone: 612-340-8716. Office Fax: 612-340-2868. Business E-Mail: hamel.mark@dorsey.com.

HAMEL, MICHAEL A., career officer; BS in Aero. Engring., USAF Acad., 1972; MBA, Calif. State U., Dominguez Hills, 1974; grad., Squadron Officer Sch., 1975, Air Command and Staff Coll., 1980. Commd. 2d lt. USAF, 1972, advanced through grades to Lt. Gen.; devel. planner Space and Missile Sys. Orgn., L.A. AFB, 1972-75; missile analyst fgn. tech. divsn. Lowry AFB, Colo., 1975-77; mission dir. Aerospace Data Facility, Buckley Air N.G. Base, Colo., 1975—79; air staff tng. officer Hdqs. USAf, Washington, 1979-80; project mgr., manned spaceflight engr. Office of Sec. of Air Force for Spl. Projects, L.A. AFB, 1980-86; staff exec. officer Hdqs. USAF, Washington, 1986-90; chief plans divsn. Hdqs. Air Force Space Command, Peterson AFB, Colo., 1991-94; comdr. 750th Space Group, Onizuka Air Sta., Calif., 1994-95; vice comdr. 21st Space Wing, Peterson AFB, 1995-96; mil. adviser to v.p. The White House, Washington, 1996-98; vice comdr. Space and Missile Sys. Ctr., L.A. AFB, 1998-99, comdr., 2005—; dir. requirements Air force Space Command HQ, Peterson AFB, Colo., 1999—; dir. space ops. and intergration HQ USAF, Pentagon, 2000—02; comdr. 14th AF Vanderberg AFB, Calif., 2002—05. Decorated Def. Superior Svc. medal, Disting. Svc. medal, Legion of Merit, Meritorious Svc. medal with 3 oak leaf clusters. Office: Space & Missile Ctr 2420 Vela Way Ste 1 Bldg 6 El Segundo CA 90245 Business E-Mail: michael.hamel@losangeles.af.mil.

HAMEL, RODOLPHE, retired lawyer, pharmaceutical executive; b. Lewiston, Maine, June 3, 1929; s. Rodolphe and Alvina Melanie (Bilodeau) H.; m. Marilyn Vivian Johnsen, June 10, 1957; children: Matthew Edward, Anne Melanie. BA, Yale U., 1950; LLB, Harvard U., 1953. Bar: Maine 1953, D.C. 1953, N.Y. 1957. Assoc. firm Shearman & Sterling, NYC, 1956-66; v.p., corp. sec., gen. counsel Macmillan Inc., NYC, 1972-73; internat. counsel Bristol-Myers Squibb Co. (formerly Bristol-Myers Co.), NYC, 1966-72, 73, v.p., counsel internat. divsn., 1974-81, assoc. gen. counsel, 1978-89, v.p., 1983-92, gen. counsel, 1989-94, sr. v.p., 1992-94; ret., 1995; cons., 1995—2005. 1st lt. AUS, 1953-56. Mem. ABA, N.Y. State Bar Assn., Assn. of Bar of City of N.Y., Yale Club. E-mail: rod173hamel@aol.com.

HAMEL, WILLIAM JOHN, church administrator, minister; b. Marquette, Mich., July 30, 1947; s. John Peter and Jayne B. (Berklund) H.; m. Karen Margaret Holleen, Aug. 10, 1968; children: Krista Joy, Kari Elise. BS, Wheaton Coll., 1969; MDiv, Trinity Evang. Div. Sch., Deerfield, Ill., 1972; DD, Trinity Internat. U., 1998; DCM, Trinity Western U., 1998. Ordained minister Evang. Free Ch. Am., 1978. Pastor West Bloomington (Minn.) Evang. Free Ch., 1972-86; dist. supt. Midwest Dist. Evang. Free Ch. Am., Kearney, Nebr., 1986-90; exec. v.p. Evang. Free Ch. Am., Mpls., 1990-97, pres., 1997—. Mem. Evangelist Free Ch. Am. Office: Evang Free Ch Am 901 E 78th St Minneapolis MN 55420-1334 Office Phone: 952-854-1300. Business E-Mail: president@efca.org.

HAMELIN, MARCEL, historian, educator; b. Saint-Narcisse, Que., Can., Sept. 18, 1937; m. Judy Purcell, Aug. 18, 1962; children— Danielle, Christine, Marc. Doctorat es Lettres, Universite Laval, Can. Faculty U. Ottawa, Ont., Canada, prof. history, 1966—2003, chmn. dept. history, 1968-70, vice dean sch. grad. studies, 1972-74, dean faculty of arts, 1974-90, rector, vice chancellor, 1990—2001, rector emeritus, 2001—; exec. dir. Interamerican Orgn. Higher Edn., 2002—. Chmn. Can.-Africa Cmty. Health Alliance, 2002—. Author: History of the Province of Quebec. Mem. Canadian Hist. Assn., Assn. Canadienne-francaise pour l'avancement des Scis. (pres. 1976-77), Royal Soc. Can. (Chevalier, Légion d'honneur). Business E-Mail: mhamelin@uottawa.ca.

HAMELS, COLE (COLBERT MICHAEL HAMELS), professional baseball player; b. San Diego, Dec. 27, 1983; m. Heidi Strobel, Dec. 31, 2006. Draft pick Phila. Phillies, 2002, pitcher, 2006—. Named to Nat. League All-Star Team, Maj. League Baseball, 2007. Mailing: Phila Phillies Citizens Bank Park One Citizens Bank Way Philadelphia PA 19148*

HAMENT, ANDREW STANTON, lawyer; b. Salina, Kans., Jan. 4, 1955; s. Carrol and Barbara June Hament; m. Priscila Morgan Fenton, May 5, 1990; children: Blake Fenton, Caroline Adams. BA in Humanistic Studies, John Hopkins U., Balt., 1977; JD, U. Balt., 1981. Bar: Fla. 1981. Assoc. Muller & Mintz, PA, Miami, Fla., 1981—87; sr. counsel labor law Harris Corp., Melbourne, Fla., 1987—90, European counsel Brussells, Belgium, 1990—93, sr. counsel aerospace Palm Bay, Fla., 1993—95; ptnr. Holland & Knight, LLP, Melbourne, 1995—2003, Gray Robinson, PA, Melbourne, 2003—06, Ford & Harrison, LLP, Melbourne, 2006—. Contbr. articles to profl. jours. Mem. human resource mgmt. S.Brevard Soc., Melbourne, 1995; bd. mem. ARC Brevard, Melbourne, 2000; mem. US Mid. Dist. Advisory Com., 2002—; bd. mem. United Way Brevard, Melbourne, 2005, Holy Trinity Academy, Melbourne, 2005. Recipient Atty. of Yr. award, Harris Corp., 1990. Mem.: Inns Ct. (barrister), Acad. Fla. Mgmt. Attys. (charter mem.). Republican. Achievements include successfully argued Bruer vs. Jim's Concrete of Brevard actions under Fair Labor Standards Act before the US Supreme Court, 2003. Office: Ford & Harrison LLP 1901 S Harbor City Blvd Melbourne FL 32901 Office Phone: 321-724-5633.

HAMERLY, MICHAEL T., librarian, historian; b. Seattle, Sept. 23, 1940; s. James Charles Riley and Harriet Elinor (Jackson) H.; m. Carmen Victoria Flores Rosero, Jan. 19, 1963; 1 child, Michael Charles. BA, U. Wash., 1963, MA, 1965, M in Librarianship, 1979; PhD, U. Fla., 1970. From instr. to asst. prof. U. No. Colo., Greeley, 1970-74; dir. Archivo Arzobispal, Ecuador, 1975-78; rschr. Dept. Historia Maritima, Armada del Ecuador, 1975-77; vis. sr. lectr. dept. Spanish and Latin Am. studies Hebrew U., Jerusalem, 1981; cataloguer Pre-Columbian studies Dumbarton Oaks Rsch. Library and Collections, 1983-84; bibliographer/cataloguer Latin Am. Bibliographic Found., Redlands, Calif., 1985—88; catalog librarian, assoc. prof. Pacific collection Micronesian Area Rsch. Ctr., U. Guam, Mangilao, 1988-91; collection devel. lib., assoc. prof. to prof. Robert F. Kennedy Meml. Lib. U. Guam, 1991-98, chmn. press coun., 1990-97, prof., curriculum resources ctr. coord., 1997; spl. project/catalogue libr. John Carter Brown Libr., Providence, 1998—. Andean area editor The Americas; a quar. rev. of Inter-Am. Cultural history, 1974-88; assoc. editor Revista del Archivo Historico del Guayas, 1975-90; contbg. editor Handbook of Latin Am. Studies, 1971-2006; editor Ecuadorian Studies/Estudios Ecuatorianos, 2000—; contbr. articles to profl. jours. NDEA, Title VI, Doherty and Fulbright-Hays grantee, fellow; Am. Coun. Learned Socs. and Social Sci. Rsch. Coun. grantee. Mem. Latin-Am. Studies Assn., Conf. on Latin-Am. History, Centro de Investigaciones Historicas de Guayaquil, Acad. Arquidiocesana de Historia Eclesiastica, Asian-Pacific Am. Librs. Assn., Assn. Historiadores Ecuatorianos, Acad. Nat. Historia, Fulbright Assn., Guam Libr. Assn., Pacific Islands Assn. Librs. and Archives, Beta Phi Mu. Home: 158 Medway St Providence RI 02906 Office: John Carter Brown Libr PO Box 1894 Providence RI 02912-1894 Office Phone: 401-863-3923. Office Fax: 401-863-3477. Business E-Mail: Michael_Hamerly@brown.edu.

HAMERMESH, DANIEL SELIM, economics professor; b. Cambridge, Mass., Oct. 20, 1943; s. Morton and Madeline (Goldberg) H.; m. Frances Witty, Dec. 18, 1966; children: David J., Matthew A. AB, U. Chgo., 1965; PhD, Yale U., 1969. Asst. prof. Princeton (N.J.) U., 1969-73; assoc. prof. Mich. State U., East Lansing, 1973-76, prof., 1976-93, chmn. dept., 1984-88; Edward Everett Hale centennial prof. econs. U. Tex., Austin, 1993—. Rsch. dir. ASPER-U.S. Dept. Labor, Washington, 1974-75, rsch. assoc. Nat. Bur. Econ. Rsch., 1979-; vis. prof. Harvard U., Cambridge, Mass., 1981, Latrobe U., Melbourne, Australia, 1987, Gadjah Mada U., Indonesia, 1990, Australian Nat. U., 1991, Rijksuniversiteit Limburg, The Netherlands, 1992, New Econ. Sch., Moscow, 1993, Hebrew U., Jerusalem, 1995, Erasmus U., The Netherlands, 1997, U. Bristol, Eng., 2000, U. Aberdeen, Scotland, 2002, McMaster U., 2003, U. Mich., 2004; mem. econ. adv. panel NSF, 1995-97; program dir. Inst. for Study of Labor, Bonn, Germany; chmn. sci. adv. bd. German Inst. Econ. Rsch., 2003-. Mem. bd. editors Am. Econ. Rev., 1990-94; co-editor Econ. Letters, 1994-98, Labour Econs., 1996-00, Jour. Population Econs., 2001-03, Ind. and Labor Rels. Rev., 2004—. Pres. Congregation Kehillat Israel, Lansing, 1988-90. Recipient Best Article award Western Econ. Assn., 1987, Parents' Assn. Centennial Teaching fellow U. Tex., 1995-96; NSF rsch. grantee, 1980-82, 84-86, 86-91, 95—2003. Fellow Econometric Soc., Soc. Labor Economists (pres. 2000-01); mem. Am. Econ. Assn., Midwest Econ. Assn. (pres. 1988-89). Jewish. Avocations: running, classical music. Office: U Tex Dept Econs Austin TX 78712 Home Phone: 512-206-0908; Office Phone: 512-475-8526. Business E-Mail: hamermes@eco.utexas.edu.

HAMEROW, THEODORE STEPHEN, historian, educator; b. Warsaw, Aug. 24, 1920; arrived in U.S.A., 1930, naturalized, 1930; s. Haim Schneyer and Bella (Rubinlicht) H.; m. Margarete Lotter, Aug. 16, 1954 (div. Dec. 27, 1996); children: Judith Margarete, Helena Francisca; m. Diane Franzen, Oct. 4, 1997. BA, CUNY, 1942; MA, Columbia U., 1947; PhD, Yale U., 1951. Instr. Wellesley Coll., 1950-51, U. Md., 1951-52; instr., asst. prof., then asso. prof. U. Ill, 1952-58; mem. faculty U. Wis., 1958-91, prof. history, 1961-91, G. P. Gooch prof. history, 1978-91, chmn. dept. history, 1973-76. Cons. editor Dorsey Press, 1961-71; mem. coun. Internat. Exch. Scholars, 1983-85, Nat. Coun. on Humanities, 1992-2000. Author: Restoration, Revolution, Reaction, 1958, Otto von Bismarck: A Historical Assessment, 1962, The Social Foundations of German Unification 1858-1871, 2 vols, 1969-72, The Birth of a New Europe: State and Society in the Nineteenth Century, 1983, Reflections on History and Historians, 1987, From the Finland Station: The Graying of Revolution in the Twentieth Century, 1990, On the Road to the Wolf's Lair: German Resistance to Hitler, 1997, Remembering a Vanished World: A Jewish Childhood in Interwar Poland, 2001; co-author: History of the World, 1960, A History of the Western World, 1969; editor: Otto von Bismarck, Reflections and Reminiscences, 1962, The Age of Bismarck, 1973; editorial bd.: Jour. Modern History, 1967-70, Central European History, 1968-72, Revs. in European History, 1974-78. Served with inf. AUS, 1943—46. Mem. Am. Hist. Assn., Conf. Group Central European History (sec.-treas. 1960-62, chmn. 1976), Wis. Assn. of Scholars (pres. 1989-91). Home: 885 Terry Pl Madison WI 53711-1956 Office: U Wisc Dept History Madison WI 53711 Business E-Mail: dkhamerow@facstaff.wisc.edu.

HAMERS, ROBERT J., chemistry educator, researcher; BS, U. Wis., Madison, 1980; PhD, Cornell U., 1985. Prof. chemistry U. Wis., Madison, Evan P. Helfaer chair, 1996—, Irving Shain chair, 2004—, dept. chair chemistry, 2007—. Recipient IBM Corp. Outstanding Innovation award for Scientific Accomplishments with Scanning Tunneling Spectroscopy, 1987, IBM Rsch. Divsn. award for STM Studies of Surface Reactions on Semiconductors, 1989, Camille and Henry Dreyfus New Faculty award, 1990-1995, Vilas Associates award, 1998, IBM Corp. Faculty award, 2002, Arthur W. Adamson award for Disting. Svc. in the Advancement of Surface Chemistry, Am. Chem. Soc., 2005; NSF Presdl. Faculty fellow, 1992-97, John Simon Guggenheim Found. fellow, 2000, S.C. Johnson Co. Disting. fellow, 2000-03. Fellow: AAAS, Am. Vacuum Soc. (Peter Mark Meml. award 1993). Office: U Wisconsin 3345a Chemistry 1101 University Ave Madison WI 53706-1322 Home Phone: 608-829-3744; Office Phone: 608-262-6371. Fax: 608-262-0453. Business E-Mail: rjhamers@wisc.edu.

HAMES, MICHAEL J., electronics executive; BSEE, U. Notre Dame, Ind. With Tex. Instruments Inc., 1980—, v.p. worldwide DSP bus., 1982, DSP mktg. mgr., US DSP product mgr., sr. v.p., mgr. application specific products Dallas. Mem.: IEEE. Office: Tex Instruments Inc PO Box 660199 Dallas TX 75266-0199 Office Phone: 972-995-2011. Office Fax: 972-995-4360.*

HAMES, WILLIAM LESTER, lawyer; b. Pasco, Wash., June 21, 1947; s. Arlie Franklin and Nina Lee (Ryals) H.; m. Pamella Kay Rust, June 3, 1967; children: Robert Alan, Michael Jonathan. BS in Psychology, U. Wash., 1974; JD, Willamette U., 1981. Bar: Wash. 1981, U.S. Dist. Ct. (ea. dist.) Wash. 1982, U.S. Ct. Appeals (9th cir.) 1985, U.S. Dist. Ct. (we. dist.) Wash. 1985. Counselor Wash. Juvenile Ct., Walla Walla, 1974—76; reactor operator control rm. United Nuc. Inc., Richland, Wash., 1976—77; assoc. Sonderman, Egan & Hames, Kennewick, Wash., 1981—84, Timmons & Hames, Kennewick, 1984—86, Sonderman, Timmons & Hames, Kennewick, 1987—88; ptnr. Hames, Anderson & Whitlow, Kennewick, 1988—. Mem. Wash. State Bar Assn. (chair creditor debtor sect.), Benton-Franklin County Bar Assn., Bankruptcy Bar Assn. (bd. dirs.), Rotary. Democrat. Methodist. Home: 410 W 21st St Kennewick WA 99337 Office: Hames Anderson & Whitlow PO Box 5498 Kennewick WA 99336-0498 E-mail: billh@hawlaw.com.

HAMID, BASEM, neurologist, consultant; s. Hamid and Jalbout; children: Yussra, Bushra, Noor. BS in Biology, Damascus U. Sch. Medicine, MD, 1995. Intern Mount Sinai Sch. Medicine, Elmhurst Hosp., 1996—97; resident W.Va. U. Hosps. and Clinics, 1997—2002; fellowship U. Iowa, Iowa City, 2002—03, asst. prof., 2003—06, MD Anderson Cancer Ctr., Houston, 2006—. Recipient Above and Beyond award, U. Iowa, 2006. Achievements include research in pain medicine. Office: MD Anderson Cancer Ctr 1515 Holcombe Blvd unit 409 Houston TX 77030

HAMID, MICHAEL, electrical engineering educator, consultant; b. Dannaba, Tulkarm, Jordan, June 7, 1934; arrived in Can., 1958; m. Khetam Dahlah; Sept. 1, 1973; children: Rumsey, Sammy, Nady, Reema. BEE, McGill U., 1960, MEE, 1962; PhDEE, U. Toronto, 1966. Registered profl. engr., Ont., Man. Asst., assoc., full prof. U. Man., Winnipeg, Canada, 1965; dean scholar's affairs Universite Internacional, Ann Arbor, Mich., 1972—75; chmn. grad. studies elec. engring dept. U. Man., 1983—88; prof. elec. engring. U. South Ala., Mobile, 1990—, acting chair, 1999—. Mem. Can. Del. to Internat. Union of Radio Sci., 1965; pres., bd. dirs., treas. Internat. Microwave Power inst., 1969-73; adj. prof. Agrl. Engring., U. Man., 1970-77; vis. prof. U. Ctrl. Fla., Orlando, 1987-89; W.W. Clyde chair dept. elec. engring. U. Utah, 1987; mem. Man. Rsch. Coun., Prov. of Man., 1971-75; gen. chmn. Microwave Power Symposium, Monterey, Calif., 1971; vis. prof. Defence Rsch. Establishment, Dept. Nat. Defence Can., Ottawa, 1972; cons. Defence Rsch. Bd. Can., 1971-73; chmn. Internat. Conf. Biol. Effects of Microwaves and Ultrasound, U. Man., 1969; session arganizer and chmn., invited speaker, Internat. Union Radio Sci. Gen. Assembly, Commn. VI., Warsaw, Poland, 1972; invited speaker Microwave State-of-the-Art Internat., IEEE Microwave Theory and Techniques Symposium, Chgo., 1972;; mem. Man. Rsch. Counc. and chmn. of Elec. and Electronics Products Rsch. Com., 1971-75, Nat. Rsch. Coun. Can. Assoc. Com. on Bird Hazards to Aircraft, 1972-77, Policy Com. and Grants Selection com., Transp. Inst., U. Man., 1972-78; session organizer, invited speaker, Internat. URSI-IEEE-Antennas and Propagation Symposium, U. Colo., 1973; chmn. IEEE edn. activities bd., 1972; invited speaker Brazilian Soc. for Advancement Sci., 25th meeting, Sao Paulo, 1973; invited speaker, mem. Internat. Organizing Com., Colloquium on Microwave Communication, Hungarian Acad. Sci., 1970—; invited speaker NATO Adv. Group for Aerospace R&D E.M. Wave Propagation Panel, The Netherlands, 1974; adj. prof. Naval Postgrad. Sch., Monterey Calif., 1979-81; invited speaker Internat. Conf. on Communications Cirs. and Systems, India, 1981; invited speaker and mem. tech. program com., Internat. Symposium on Microwaves and Communication, Kharagpur, India, 1981; chmn. libr. and fin. coms., U. Man. Transport Inst., 1982-84; mem. Radar Subcom. of Radarsat, Can. Adv. Com. on Remote Sensing, Ottawa, 1983-88; mem. Grad. Studies Awards Com, U. Man., 1984-88; session chmn. URSI/IEEE-Antennas and Propagation Soc. Internat. Symposium, U. B.C., Vancouver, 1985; me. Antenna Tech. and Applied Electromagnetics Conf. Program Com., U. Man., 1986—; expert witness Andrew Antennas vs. Gabriel Electronics, patent infringement litigation, Portland, Maine, 1984-86; expert witness radio interference litigation WKRG, Inc. vs. State of Ala., 1990-91; invited speaker, 78th meeting of N.D. Acad. Sci., U. N.D., Grand Forks, 1986; vis. prof. U. Cen. Fla., dept. elect. engring., 1987—; gen. chmn. Symposium on Electromagnetic Detection of Latent Objects, 1989; me. Internat. Adv. and Tech. Program Com., Internat. Symposium on Recent Advances in Microwave Tech., Beijing, 1989, Reno, 1991, New Delhi, 1993. Author or co-author over 310 tech. articles, 7 monographs and book chpts., over 190 conf. papers, 26 rsch. reports, 25 patents; assoc. editor Jour. Microwave Power, 1969-77; mem. editorial bd. Microwave Jour., Jour. Microwave Power, IEEE Transactions on Microwave Theory and Techniques, 1969—. Fellow IEE, IEEE (life, award for contbns. to electromagnetic scattering and diffraction, devel. dielectric-loaded waveguides, resonators and antennas, life 2000—), Internat. Microwave Power Inst., Electromagnetics Acad. (invited mem.), U. South Ala. Alumni Assn. (Outstanding Scholar award 1998), Am. Assn. Engring Soc., Phi Eta Sigma, Tau Beta Pi, Phi Kappa Phi (scholar 1998). Office: U South Ala Dept Elec Engring Mobile AL 36688-0001 Office Phone: 251-460-7512. Business E-Mail: mhamid@usouthal.edu.

HAMIL, BURNETTE WOLF, science educator; d. Jessie Lang and Stella Wolf; m. James G. Hamil; 1 child, Olivia Hamil Penrod. BS in Edn., Miss. Coll.; MS in Curriculum and Instrn., U. So. Miss., Hattiesburg, PhD, 1994. Cert. secondary sci. tchr. Miss. Dept. Edn., 1970. Tchr. sci. Hawkins Mid. Sch., Forest, Miss., 1970—92; assoc. prof. Miss. State U., 1996—. Sci. program improvement reviewer NSTA, Arlington, Va., 2005—06; reviewer Nat. Coun. for Accreditation of Tech. Edn. Author: (grant) Preparing Teachers to Deliver Technology-Rich, Problem-Based Learning Experiences. Del. NSTA, Arlington, 2001—04. Named to Wall of Fame, Hawkins Mid. Sch., 2005, Oxford Round Table, Oxford U., England. Mem.: Miss. Sci. Tchrs. Assn. (pres. 2003—04, Outstanding Coll. Sci. Tchr. 2002), Mind, Brain and Edn. Soc., Phi Kappa Phi, Phi Delta Kappa (Outstanding Rsch. award 2002). Methodist. Achievements include research in problem solving perception in education. Home Phone: 601-625-8004; Office Phone: 662-325-7109.

HAMILL, DOROTHY STUART, professional ice skater; b. Chgo., July 26, 1957; d. Chalmers C. and Carolyn C. (Clough) H.; m. Dean Paul Martin, Jan. 8, 1982, (div. June 1984); m. Kenneth Forsythe, Mar. 5, 1987 (div. 1995); 1 child, Alexandra. Student, Colo. Acad., Greenwich High Sch. Co-owner, pres. The Ice Capades, 1993-95. With Winter Tour World Figure Skating Champions, 1997. Profl. skater: Ice Capades, 1977—; former tour co. Dorothy Hamill on Ice, 1985—; author: Dorothy Hamill On or Off the Ice; actor: (TV films) The Christmas Angel: A Story on Ice, 1998, (films) Blades of Glory, 2007. Mem. Pres.'s Council Phys. Fitness. Achievements include being an Olympic Gold medalist, 1976; world figure skating champion, 1976; U.S. figure skating champion; Emmy award Romeo and Juliet on Ice, 1984. Address: Beachport Entertainment Corp 12725 Ventura Blvd Studio City CA 91604-2437

HAMILL, MARSHALL BOWES, medical educator; b. Boston, Nov. 9, 1951; s. John Marshall Hamill and Joan Bowes; m. Cathy Ann McGonigle, Aug. 2, 1975; children: Scott Bowes, Eric Barnes. MD, Baylor Coll. Medicine, Houston, 1979. Diplomate Am. Bd. Ophthalmology. Resident in ophthalmology Baylor Coll. Medicine, 1980—83, fellow in ocular infectious and inflammatory diseases, 1983—84, assoc. prof., 1985—; fellow in corneal and anterior segment surgery Johns Hopkins, Wilmer Inst., Balt., 1984—85. Home: 3833 Southwestern Houston TX 77005 Office: Dept Ophthalmology Baylor Coll 6565 Fannin Ste NC-205 Houston TX 77030 Office Phone: 713-798-4299. Business E-Mail: mhamill@bcm.edu.

HAMILL, PETE (WILLIAM PETE HAMILL), newspaper columnist, author, editor; b. Bklyn., June 24, 1935; s. William and Anne (Devlin) H.; m. Ramona Negron, Feb. 3, 1962 (div. 1970); children— Adriene, Deirdre; m. Fukiko Aoki, May 23, 1987. Student, Pratt Inst., 1952, Mexico City Coll., 1956-57. Comml. artist, 1957-60; reporter N.Y. Post, later columnist, 1960-74; columnist N.Y. Daily News, 1975-79, 82-84; contbg. editor Saturday Evening Post, 1963-64; contbr. Village Voice, New York Mag., NYC, 1974—; editor Mexico City News, 1986-87; columnist Esquire, 1989-91, N.Y. Post, 1988-93, N.Y. Newsday, 1994—; editor-in-chief N.Y. Daily News, 1997. Disting. writer in residence NYU, 2005—. Author: (novels) A Killing for Christ, 1968, The Gift, 1973, Flesh and Blood, 1977, Loving Women, 1990, Snow in August, 1997, Forever, 2003, North River, 2007;(non-fiction) Irrational Ravings, 1972, A Drinking Life: A Memoir, 1994, Tools as Art, 1995, Piecework, 1996, News is a Verb, 1998, Why Sinatra Matters, 1998, Diego Rivera, 1999, Downtown: My Manhattan, 2004; (short stories) The Invisible City: A New York Sketchbook, 1980, Tokyo Sketches, 1993; contbr. articles to numerous mags. Trustee Mus.

City N.Y.; coun. mem. Writers Guild Am. Past. Served with USN, 1952-54. Recipient Meyer Berger award Columbia Sch. Journalism, 1962, award Newspaper Reporters Assn., 1962, 25 Yr. Achievement award Soc. of Silurians, 1989, Peter Kihss award, Silurians, 1992. Mem. PEN, Nat. Assn. Hispanic Journalists, Silurians. Democrat.

HAMILTON, ALLEN PHILIP, financial advisor; b. Albany, Calif. s. Allen Philip Sr. and Barbara Louise (Martin) H.; m. Mary Williams, July 18, 1981 (div. Mar. 1987). AA, Contra Costa State Coll.; postgrad., San Jose State U.; AB, NW Mo. State U.; BA in Bus. Mgmt., St. Mary's U., Moraga, Calif., 1989. CFP. Fin. advisor Consol. Investment Svcs., Kansas City, Mo., 1968—70; pres., CEO Balanced Mgmt. Assn., Mission, Kans., 1969—72, Advanced Svc. Assn., Overland Park, Kans., 1971—78; divisional mgr. Waddell & Reed, Inc., Kansas City, 1978—81; sr. v.p., regional dir. WZW Fin. Svcs., Kansas City, 1981—86; exec. v.p. Skaife & Co., Orinda, Calif., 1986—88; v.p., mktg. dir. Consol. Securities Corp., Walnut Creek, Calif., 1988; sr. dir. and cert. trainer Club Am., Inc., LA, 1990—; fin. planner, prin. Hamilton Fin. Adv., Am. Investment Svcs., Pleasant Hill., Calif., 1989—; silver mktg. distbr., corp. trainer, Can. mktg. distbr. and trainer Nikken, Inc. Internat., 1991—; sales mgr., ind. distributor, sales trainer Alpine Industries, 1992—; prin. advisor Environ. Solutions Internat.; exec. dir., CEO Environ. Air Quality and Health Found. (Environ. Solutions Internat.), 1998—; sales, mktg. dir. Exthel Wireless Comm. Inc., 1998—99; trainer, presdl. dir. Builders Referral Inc., Orange County, Calif., 1998—2005; CEO Stage Coach Line Inc., Huntington Beach, Calif., 1999—2005, Fin. Enhancement Svcs. Inc., Newport Beach, Calif., 2000—05; mgr. bus. devel. Mortgage Profl. Group Indymac Bank, Irvine, Calif., 2005—. Sr. dir. Club Am., L.A., 1990-92; presdl. dir. FundAmerica, Irvine, Calif., 1988—; bus. devel. mgr. Indymac Bank, 2005—; spkr. in field. Author: (with others) The Financial Planner A New Profession, 1986. Asst. dist. commr. Boy Scouts Am., Kansas City, Kans., 1970—79, nat. Eagle Scout Assn. com., 2003—; corp. dir. United Campaign, Overland Park, Kans., 1965—73; active TV show Kidney Found., Kansas City, Mo., 1969—70; sr. arbitrator San Francisco Bay Area Better Bus. Bur., 1986—. Lt. US Army, 1963—65. Recipient Citation Nat. Campaign Re-election 1992, 1992m Senatorial Comm. Rep. Senatorial Inner Circle, 1991. Mem. Inst. Cert. Fin. Planners, Internat. Assn. for Fin. Planning (v.p., bd. dirs. 1982-87, practitioner div.), Registry of Fin. Planning Practitioners, Mt. Diablo Distbrs. Assn., Nat. Eagle Scout Assn. Com. Republican. Avocations: cars, outdoors, tennis, travel, boating. Office: Mortgage Profl Group Indymac Bank 82125 Travolta Ave Indio CA 92201 Home Phone: 760-393-8657; Office Phone: 949-887-5330. Personal E-mail: aphamilton_2000@yahoo.com, aphamilton007@hotmail.com.

HAMILTON, ANTHONY, singer; b. Charlotte, NC; m. Tarsha McMillian. Barber; signed to Uptown Records, NYC, 1993—95, various music labels, 1996—2003, So So Def Records, 2003—. Singer: (albums) XTC, 1996, Comin' from Where I'm From, 2003, Soulife, 2005, Ain't Nobody Worryin', 2005; background vocals (songs) Po' Folks, 2002 (nominated for Grammy award for Best Rap/Sung Collaboration, 2003). Recipient J Cool Like That award, Black Entertainment TV (BET), 2006. Office: Zomba Label Group 3923 7th St S Arlington VA 22204 Office Phone: 703-979-5483.

HAMILTON, BEVERLY LANNQUIST, investment executive; b. Roxbury, Mass., Oct. 19, 1946; d. Arthur and Nancy Lannquist. BA cum laude, U. Mich., 1968; postgrad., NYU, 1969-70. V.p. Auerbach, Pollak & Richardson, NYC, 1972-75, Morgan Stanley & Co., NYC, 1975-80, United Techs., Hartford, Conn., 1980-87; dep. comptr. City of N.Y., 1987-91; pres., ret. ARCO Investment Mgmt Co, LA, 1991-2000. Bd. dirs. Oppenheimer Funds, Am. Fund's Emerging Markets Growth Fund; trustee The Calif. Endowment, Monterey Inst. Internat. Studies, Cmty. Hosp. Monterey, Middlebury Coll.; investment coms. U. Mich. Trustee Hartford Coll. for Women, 1981-87, Stanford Univ. Mgmt. Co., 1991-99; bd. dirs. Inst. for Living, 1983-87. Mem. NCCJ (bd. dirs. 1987-91). Address: 5485 Quail Meadows Dr Carmel CA 93923-7971

HAMILTON, BRONWYN ELIZABETH, radiologist; b. Winchester, Mass., May 3, 1969; d. Dean Elwyn and Glenys Audrey Hamilton. BS Biochem., Atlantic Union Coll., So. Lancaster, Mass., 1992, BA in French, 1992; MD, Loma Linda U., Calif., 1996. Asst. prof. U. Utah, Salt Lake City, 2004—06, Oreg. Health & Scis. U., Portland, 2006—. Clin. dir. mri Oreg. Health & Scis. U., Portland, U. Utah. Contbr. articles to profl. jours. Recipient Chemistry award, Atlantic Union Coll., 1992, Biology award, 1990; fellow, U. Utah, Salt Lake City, 2001—03; scholar, Atlantic Union Coll., 1989—92. Fellow: Am. Soc. Neuroradiology; mem.: Am. Soc. Head & Neck Radiology, Am. Roentgen Ray Soc. (assoc.), Radiol. Soc. N.Am. (assoc.). Avocation: aviation. Office: Oregon Health & Scis U 3181 SW Sam Jackson Park Rd Portland OR 97239 Home Phone: 503-342-6212; Office Phone: 503-494-7576. Office Fax: 503-494-7129.

HAMILTON, CARL HULET, retired academic administrator; b. Morris, Okla., Sept. 30, 1934; s. Alva H. and Olah E. (Pryor) H.; m. Gloria Joyce Gore, Sept. 3, 1954; children: Ray, Carla Jo, Deanna Jean. ThB, Southwestern Coll., 1956; BA, Oklahoma City U., 1957; MA, U. Tulsa, 1962; PhD, U. Ark., 1968. English tchr. Southwestern Coll., Oklahoma City, 1957-60; editor Oral Roberts Evangelistic Assn., Tulsa, 1960-62; English tchr., editor Oral Roberts U., Tulsa, 1966-68; acad. dean, 1968-75; provost Oral Roberts U., Tulsa, 1975-84; adminstr. World Evangelism, San Diego, 1984-86; chief of staff Feed the Children, Oklahoma City, 1986-88; provost, chief acad. officer Oral Roberts U., 1989-98; ret., 2001. Min. adminstrn. First United Meth. Ch., 1999-2001, pastor Ketchum United Meth. Ch., 2006-07. Republican. Methodist. Avocations: fishing, water sports, motorcycling. Home: PO Box 488 Disney OK 74340-0488 Office Phone: 918-782-9037. E-mail: piscatore@brightok.net.

HAMILTON, CARLOS ROBERT, JR., endocrinologist, consultant, academic administrator; b. Houston, June 12, 1939; s. Carlos Robert and Berta (Denman) H.; m. Carolyn Burton, Aug. 12, 1961; children: Carlos R. III, Patricia Frances. BA, U. Tex., 1961; MS, MD with honors, Baylor Coll. Medicine, 1966. Diplomate Am. Bd. Internal Medicine, Am. Bd. Endocrinology and Metabolic Diseases. Intern in internal medicine Johns Hopkins Hosp., Balt., 1966-67, asst. resident in internal medicine, 1967-69, chief resident in medicine, 1970-71; clin. and rsch. fellow Harvard Med. Sch./Mass. Gen. Hosp., Boston, 1969-70; asst. prof. medicine Johns Hopkins U. and Hosp., Balt., 1971-72; staff endocrinologist Wilford Hall USAF Med. Ctr., San Antonio, 1972-74; clin. prof. medicine Baylor Coll. Medicine, Houston, 1974—; clin. prof. medicine Med. Sch. U. Tex., Houston, 1999-2000, prof. internal medicine, 2000—, exec. v.p. for external affairs Health Sci. Ctr., 2002—. Cons. endocrinology and internal medicine Med. Clinic of Houston, L.L.P., 1974—2000; med. advisor employee benefit com. Southwestern Bell Tel. Co., 1975—93; attending physician in endocrinology Ben Taub Gen. Hosp./Baylor Coll. Medicine, 1980—; attending physician, mem. active staff The Meth. Hosp./Meml.-Hermann Hosp., Houston, 1974—; mem. active staff St. Luke's Episcopal Hosp., 2000—, Meml. Hermann Hosp., 2000—; practicing physicians adv. coun. U.S. Dept. HHS, 2003—07; mem. health, sci. and rsch. com. World Anti-Doping Agy., Montreal, 2003—07. Contbr. articles to profl. jours. Dist. and coun. chair, area pres., regional bd. dirs., v.p. Boy Scouts Am., Houston, Atlanta, Irving, Tex., 1980—; bd. regents Tex. Woman's U., 1999-2001; chair, bd.dirs. Mus. Health and Med. Sci., Houston, 2006—. Recipient Dist. award of merit, Silver Beaver award, Silver Antelope award, Disting. Eagle Scout award, Silver Buffalo award Boy Scouts Am., 1982-99. Fellow ACP (bd. dirs. Tex. chpt., Mead-Johnson Residency scholar 1970, bd. dirs. Tex. Acad. Internal Medicine and ACP-ASIM health and pub. policy com., Tex. Laureate award 2003), Am. Coll. Endocrinology (trustee 1999-2000, sec.-treas. 2001-02, chancellor 2005-06, pres. 2007—); mem. SAR (bd. dirs. Paul Carrington chpt. 1992—, pres. 1993), Am. Soc. Internal Medicine (bd. dirs. polit. action com. 1995-98, Key Congl. Contact of Yr. 1996), Am. Assn. Clin. Endocrinologists (bd. dirs. 1995—, chair legis. and regulatory com. 1998-2000, sec. exec. com. 2000-01, treas. 2001-02, v.p. 2002-2003, pres.-elect 2003-04, pres. 2004-05), Tex. Med. Assn. (exec. com. polit. action com. 1989-01, chair 1995, 96), Harris County Med. Soc. (bd. dirs. 1992-99, pres.-elect 1998, pres. 1999), Kiwanis (bd. dirs. Houston chpt. 1986-95, pres. 1995), Alpha Omega Alpha, Sigma Xi. Office: U Tex Health Sci Ctr 7000 Fannin Rm 1535 Houston TX 77030 Home Phone: 713-960-1707; Office Phone: 713-500-3825. Business E-Mail: carlos.r.hamilton@uth.tmc.edu.

HAMILTON, CHARLES EDWARD, information technology consultant, military officer; b. El Paso, Tex., May 19, 1980; s. Charles Edward and Stephanie Jo Hamilton, Lawrence Edward Hudson (Stepfather) and Patricia Kay Hamilton (Stepmother). CSSAMO technician US Army, 1998—2003, sr. CSSAMO technician, sr. webmaster Kuwait, 2003, Baghdad, Iraq, 2003; mgr. network ops. ctr. Internet Connection, Easton, Md., 2004; dir. info. tech. Dyer & Assoc. PC, Kensington, Md., 2005—. Sgt. US Army, 1998—2004. Decorated Army Svc. Medal US Army, Non-Commissioned Officer Profl. Devel. Medal, Overseas Svc. Medal, Army Commendation Medal, Joint Svc. Commendation Medal, Joint Svc. Achievement Medal, Army Achievement Medal, Global War on Terrorism Svc. Medal, Nat. Def. Medal with Bronze Star, Army Good Conduct Medal, Global War on Terrorism Expeditionary Medal, Iraq Campaign Medal. Libertarian. Avocations: photography, martial arts, marksmanship, archery, exercise. Home Phone: 410-829-6529; Office Phone: 301-654-6200. Personal E-mail: musashi@nefaria.com.

HAMILTON, CLYDE HENRY, federal judge; b. Edgefield, SC, Feb. 8, 1934; s. Clyde H. and Edwina (Odom) Hamilton; children: John C., James W. BS, Wofford Coll., 1956; JD with honors, George Washington U., 1961. Bar: SC 1961. Reference asst. US Senate Libr., Washington, 1958—61; assoc. J.R. Folk, Edgefield, 1961—63; assoc., gen. ptnr. Butler, Means, Evins & Browne, Spartanburg, SC, 1963—81; judge US Dist. Ct. SC, Columbia, 1981—91, US Ct. Appeals (4th cir.), Richmond, Va., 1991—99, sr. judge, 1999—. Gen. counsel Synalloy Corp., Spartanburg, 1969—80. Mem. editl. staff: Cumulative Index of Congl. Com. Hearings, 1935—58, bd. editors: George Washington Law Rev., 1959—60. Pres. Spartanburg County Arts Coun., 1971—73, Spartanburg Day Sch., 1972—74, sustaining trustee, 1975—81; past mem. steering com. undergrad. merit fellowship program and estate planning coun. Converse Coll., Spartanburg; trustee Spartanburg Meth. Coll., 1979—84; bd. commrs. on grievances and discipline SC Supreme Ct., 1980—81; del. Spartanburg County, 4th Congl. Dist. and SC Rep. Convs., 1976, 1980; active, past chmn. fin. com. and adminstrv. bd. Trinity United Meth. Ch., Spartanburg, trustee, 1980—83. Capt. USAR, 1956—62. Recipient Alumni Disting. Svc. award, Wofford Coll., 1991, The Order of The Palmetto, Gov. Beasley, SC, 1999. Mem.: SC Bar Assn., Piedmont Club (bd. govs. 1979—81). Office: US Ct Appeals 4th Cir 1901 Main St Columbia SC 29201-2443 Office Phone: 803-765-5461.*

HAMILTON, DAGMAR STRANDBERG, lawyer, retired educator; b. Phila., Jan. 10, 1932; d. Eric Wilhelm and Anna Elizabeth (Sjöström) Strandberg; m. Robert W. Hamilton, June 26, 1953; children: Eric Clark, Robert Andrew Hale, Meredith Hope. AB, Swarthmore Coll., 1953; JD, U. Chgo. Law Sch., 1956, Am. U., 1961. Bar: Tex. 1972. Atty. civil rights divsn. U.S. Dept Justice, Washington, 1965-66; asst. instr. govt. U. Tex., Austin, 1966-71; lectr. Law Sch. U. Ariz., Tucson, 1971-72; editor, rschr. Assoc. William O. Douglas U.S. Supreme Ct., Washington, 1962-73, 75-76; editor, rschr. Douglas autobiography Random House Co., 1972-73; staff counsel Judiciary Com. U.S. Ho. of Reps., 1973-74; asst. prof. L.B. Johnson Sch. Pub. Affairs U. Tex., Austin, 1974-77, assoc. prof., 1977—83, assoc. dean, 1983—87, prof., 1983—2006, prof. emeritus, 2007—. Interdisciplinary prof. U. Tex. Law Sch., 1983—; vis. prof. Washington U. Law Sch., St. Louis, 1982, U. Maine, Portland, 1992; Godfrey Disting. vis. prof. U. Maine Law Sch., 2002; vis. fellow U. London, QMW Sch. Law, 1987—88; vis. prof. U. Maine, Portland, 2002; vis. fellow U. Oxford Inst. European & Comparative Law, 1998. Contbr. to various publs. Mem. Tex. State Bar Assn., Am. Law Inst., Assn. Pub. Policy Analysis and Mgmt., Swarthmore Coll. Alumni Coun. (rep.), Kappa Beta Phi (hon.), Phi Kappa Phi (hon.). Democrat. Mem. Soc. Of Friends. Personal E-mail: dagmar.hamilton@mail.utexas.edu.

HAMILTON, DAVID ARNOLD, retired librarian; b. Grand Rapids, Mich., Aug. 16, 1927; s. Ralph Samuel Hamilton and Margit Agnes Cherny; m. Christine Mary Pearson, Sept. 20, 1956; children: Eric Beth Hamilton Barrett, Mark David. BS in Edn., No. Ill. U., 1960, MS in Edn., 1964. Tchr. English, French Waterman (Ill.) Pub. HS, 1960—62; libr. Simmons Jr. HS, Aurora, Ill., 1962—64; periodical libr. No. Ill. U., DeKalb, 1964—70, cataloging libr., 1970—89, reference libr., 1989—92; dir. Maple Park (Ill.) Pub. Libr., 1990—94; ret., 1994. Archivist advisor George Williams Coll., Williams Bay, Wis., 1999—2004. Co-author: Ballet Plot Index, 1987, Opera Plot Index, 1990. With US Army, 1950—52. Home: 1227 Gifford St Dekalb IL 60115-4644

HAMILTON, DAVID EUGENE, minister, educator; b. Pyeng Yang, Korea, Jan. 21, 1929; m. Marilyn Long Hamilton; children: Beth Jean Hamilton Stanton, Rebecca Sue Hamilton Vierling, Sarah Ruth Hamilton Goeglein, Jill Linette Hamilton Martin. AB in Theology, Gordon Coll., Wenham, Mass., 1950; MDiv, Gordon Div. Sch., Wenham, Mass., 1953; ThM, Columbia Theol. Seminary, Decatur, Ga., 1960, Fuller Theol. Seminary, 1983. Ordained to ministry Presbyn. Ch. of U.S., 1954. Asst. to pastor McIlwain Presbyn. Ch., Pensacola, Fla., 1954-55; founding pastor Fairfield Presbyn. Ch., Pensacola, 1956-60; pastor El Presbiterio del Pacifico ch., Teloloapan, Mexico, 1961-66, Northside Presbyn. Ch., Burlington, N.C., 1972-76; moderator Pacific Presbytery of the PCA; dir. Bible Inst., Telolapan; missionary Mexico; dean of students, dir. field edn. Westminster Theol. Seminary, Escondido, Calif., 1984-87; min. to srs. Ind. Presbyn. Ch., Memphis, 1987-96; dir. evangelistic mins. Grace Evangelical Ch., Germantown, Tenn., 1997—. Involved numerous ch. and missionary endeavors, including coord. ch. planting team in Quito, Ecuador, 1977-81, dir. Cosecha dept., Radio Sta. HCJB, establisher Family Counseling ministry, leader weekly Bible studies; organizer Gideon camp to distribute Bibles in Acapulco; interim pastor Covenant Presbyn. Ch., Bakersfield, Calif., 1982, others. Avocations: reading, classical music, all sports. Personal E-mail: davidmarilyn16@comcast.net.

HAMILTON, DAVID LEE, sports association administrator, retired environmental company executive; b. Pitts., Mar. 26, 1937; s. James Arthur and Margaret (Kennett) H.; m. Molly Anne Wolford, June 27, 1959; children: David Scott, Bryan Lee, Timothy Drew. BSChemE, Bucknell U., 1957; MBA, U. Pitts., 1965. Various positions Exxon Co., USA, 1957-79; exec. asst. to pres. Exxon Corp., NYC, 1979—80, v.p. supply and transp. Exxon Internat. Co., 1980—82, sr. v.p. Exxon Internat. Co., 1982—83, dep. mgr. dept. petroleum products, 1983—85; v.p. Esso Europe, London, 1985-86; v.p. mktg. Exxon Co., Internat., Florham Park, NJ, 1986-88; exec. v.p. OHM Corp., Findlay, Ohio, 1989-92; exec. dir., COO U.S. Tennis Assn., 2003—. Trustee Bucknell U., Lewisburg, Pa., 1984—, chair long-range planning com., 1997—2001, chair Presdl. Search com., 1999, chmn. bd. trustees, 2001—03; pres. Dallas Tennis Assn., 1994—97; treas. Tex. sect. USTA, 1997—99, pres., 1999—2000, chair comm. mktg. coun., 1999—2002, chmn. strategic planning com., 2003, chair blue ribbon commn., 2002; bd. dirs. The Std. Steamship P&I Club, Bermuda, 1982—85, Concord Resource Group, Lawrenceville, NJ, 1989—91. Mem.: Canyon Creek Country Club (Dallas), TBarM Racquet Club (Dallas), Omicron Delta Kappa, Beta Gamma Sigma, Sigma Chi (Significant Sig award 1985). Avocations: tennis, travel, reading. Home: 12115 Elysian Ct Dallas TX 75230-2221 Office Phone: 914-696-7026. E-mail: kelcarchas@aol.com.

HAMILTON, DAVID MIKE, publishing executive; b. Little Rock, 1951; s. Ralph F. and Mickey G. Hamilton; m. Carol N. McKenna, Oct. 25, 1975; children: Elisabeth M., Caroline E. BA, Pitzer Coll., 1973; MLS, UCLA, 1976. Cert. tchr. libr. sci. Calif. Editor Sullivan Assocs., Palo Alto, Calif., 1973-75; curator Henry E. Huntington Library, San Marino, Calif., 1976-80; mgr. prodn., mktg. William Kaufmann Pubs., Los Altos, Calif., 1980-84; pres. Live Oak Press, LLC, Palo Alto, 1984—. Cons., editor, gen. ptnr. Sensitive Expressions Pub. Co., Palo Alto, 1985—98; consulting dir. AAAI Press, 1994—; mng. editor, pub. AI Mag. Author: To the Yukon with Jack London, 1980, The Tools of My Trade, 1986; co-author: Book Club of California Quarterly, 1985, Research Guide to Biography and Criticism, 1986, Making A Digital Book, 1994; contbg. editor, webmaster: AAAI world-wide web site, 1995—; contbr. articles to jours. Trustee Jack London Ednl. Found., San Francisco; bd. dirs. ISYS Forum, Palo Alto, 1987—96; pres. site coun., mem. supt.'s adv. com. Palo Alto Unified Sch. Dist.; bd. dirs. Trinity Parish, Menlo Park, 1985—87, sec. vestry, 1986; mem. parent's coun. Wellesley Coll., 1997—2004. Mem.: ALA, Assn. Computing Machinery (chmn. pub. com. 1984), Soc. Scholarly Pubs. (mem. program com. 1999), Soc. Tech. Comm. (judge 1984), Bookbuilders West (mem. bookshow com. 1983), Author's Guild, Am. Assn. Artificial Intelligence (bd. dirs., dir. publ.), Med. and Ednl. Publs., Coun. Scholarly, Save the Redwoods League (life), Book Club Calif., Commonwealth Club, Sierra Club (life). Democrat. Episcopalian. Avocations: backpacking, camping, hiking, book collecting. Office: The Live Oak Press LLC PO Box 60036 Palo Alto CA 94306-0036

HAMILTON, DOROTHY CANN, academic administrator; BA, U. Newcastle-upon-Tyne, Eng.; MBA, NYU. Founder French Culinary Inst., NYC, 1984—; chair woman Am. Inst. Wine and Food, chair woman emerita. Mem. adv. bd. US Dept. Edn.; chmn. bd. trustees James Beard Found. Host (TV series) Chef's Story. Bd. mem. Abraham House, Calhourn Sch., NYC, HELP USA, NYC; lectr. Mahidol U. Peace Corps, Bangkok, 1972—74. Recipient Nat. Order of Merit award, French Govt., 2001, Agrl. Merit Knighthood, Silver Spoon award, Food Arts mag., Outstanding Am. Educator award, Madrid Fusion, Knighthood, Assn. Internat. de Maîtres Conseil dans la Gastronomie Française, Diplôme d'Honneur, Vatel Club des Etats-Unis, Dame de l'Anée, Culinary Acad. France, 2006, Award of Excellence for Vocat. Cooking Sch., Internat. Assn. Culinary Professionals, 2006. Mem.: Internat. Assn. Women Chefs and Restaurateurs (mem. adv. bd.), Nat. Assn. Tng. Tech. Schools (mem. adv. bd.). Office: French Culinary Inst 462 Broadway New York NY 10013-2618*

HAMILTON, DOUGLAS WARREN, real estate executive; b. Sacramento, Calif., Feb. 21, 1947; s. Albert James and Maxene Ruth (Gergens) H.; m. Sara Binder, Jan. 19, 1992; children: Ethan A.S.W., Antonia K.R.R. BA in Math., U. Nebr., 1972; MBA, U. Pa., 1977. Asst. v.p. DLJ, NYC, 1977-79; mng. dir. Merrill Lynch & Co., NYC, 1979-93; CEO, chmn. Barker & Little, Inc., Rapid City, SD, 1993—. With USMC, 1966-69. Office: 818 Saint Joseph St PO Box 2800 Rapid City SD 57709-2800 Personal E-mail: dwhrc@aol.com.

HAMILTON, ELIZABETH ANN, elementary school educator; life ptnr. Degree, U. North Tex., Dallas, 1971, U. Tex., 1981. Tchr. kindergarten Richardson Ind. Sch. Dist., Tex., 1981—84; tchr. reading, edn. leader Hutto Elem. Sch., 1984—95; tchr. Nadine Johnson Elem. Sch., 1995—. Mem. leadership team Hutto Primary Sch., 1994—2005, Nadine Johnson Elem. Sch., 2006—; presenter in field. Mem.: Assn. Tchrs. Pub. Educators, Internat. Reading Assn. (assoc.). Avocation: reading. Office: Nadine Johnson Elem Sch Hutto Ind Sch Dist 955 Carl Stern Blvd Hutto TX 78634

HAMILTON, FRANK STRAWN, musician, composer, educator; b. NYC, Aug. 3, 1934; s. Frank Strawn and Gladys (Bley) Hamilton; m. Sheila Lofton, Nov. 7, 1957 (div. Nov. 1971); children: Cameron Auguste (dec. 1998), Evan Baird, Liam Christopher (dec. Oct. 2001), Heather Alexa; m. Deeanne Lee Walter, May 5, 1972 (div. Oct. 1980); m. Mary Doyle, Jan. 15, 1983. Student, Los Angeles City Coll., 1952-53, Chgo. Mus. Coll., 1959-62, L.A. Valley Coll., 1963-64. Organizer, head teaching staff, v.p., co-founder Old Town Sch. Folk Music, Chgo., 1957-62; ho. musician Gate of Horn, Chgo., 1959-61; mem. The Weavers, 1962-63. Founder The Hot Club of Atlanta, 1995. Appeared Asheville (N.C.) Folk Festival, 1953, Newport Folk Festival, 1959; motion picture appearance in Subterraneans, 1958; rec. artist Folkways, Vanguard records, Long Lonesome Home, ITR records; devel. method annotation folk guitar and 5 string banjo; film score: A Time Out of War, 1952; TV score: Survival; folk singer with wife Mary, The Hamiltons. Mem. ACLU, Fellowship Reconciliation, UN Assn., Dramatist Guild, Chgo. Hist. Soc. (hon.). Home: 852 Cinderella Ct Decatur GA 30033-5812 Personal E-mail: songlines@comcast.net, songlines2@hotmail.com.

HAMILTON, GEORGE HENRY, JR., geologist, consultant; b. Gary, Ind., Apr. 7, 1939; s. George Henry and Tina Lauree (Magee) H. BS in Geology, George Washington U., 1968. Dir., Andean Found., Washington, 1970-72; mem. profl. staff Gen. Electric Co., Washington, 1972-73; pres. Solar Energy Co., Washington, 1973-77; prin. devel. mgr. Pullman Corp., Houston, 1977-78; gen. mgr. no. hemisphere ops. Solar Energy Co., Washington; cons. in energy policy devel. and advanced energy systems, 1978—2003; cons. geologist Hamilton Exploration, Virginia Beach, Va., 2003—. Contbr. articles to profl. jours. Served with U.S. Army, 1962-65. Mem. Am. Assn. Petroleum Geologists, Am. Geol. Soc., AAAS Clubs: Nat. Aviation (Washington). Patentee solar energy heating module, power generating array. Home: PO Box 5381 Virginia Beach VA 23471-0381 Office Phone: 757-363-8093.

HAMILTON, HARRY LEMUEL, JR., academic administrator, science educator; b. Charleston, SC, May 26, 1938; s. Harry Lemuel and Velma Fern (Bell) H.; m. LaVerne McDaniel, June 26, 1965 (div. 1978); children: David M., Lisa L; m. Mary MacIntyre, May 10, 1997. BA in Physics, Beloit Coll., 1960; MS in Meteorology, U. Wis., 1962, PhD in Meteorology, 1965. Asst. prof. atmospheric sci. SUNY, Albany, 1965-71, assoc. prof., 1971-90, dir. ednl. opportunity program, 1968-71, chairperson atmospheric sci., 1976-83, dean undergrad. studies, assoc. v.p. acad. affairs, 1983-88; rsch. scientist GE, Schenectady, NY, 1973-75; sr. v.p., provost Chapman U., Orange, Calif., 1990-2000, prof. atmospheric sci., 2000—05, interim provost, exec. v.p., 2005—. Trustee Beloit (Wis.) Coll., 1972—, Newport Beach Pub. Libr., 2001—, pres., 2003--; bd. dirs. Albany Med. Ctr., 1988-90, Mohawk Hudson Cmty. Found., 1988-90; pres. Empire State Inst. for Performing Arts, Albany, 1986-90; bd. dirs. world affairs coun. Orange County, 1995-2003; treas. Arts Orange County, 1995-2000; bd. dirs. Discovery Sci. Ctr., 1998-2004. Mem. Am. Meteorol. Soc., Am. Assn. for Higher Edn. Office: Chapman U 1 University Dr Orange CA 92866-1005 Home Phone: 949-760-1918; Office Phone: 714-997-6826. Business E-Mail: hamilton@chapman.edu.

HAMILTON, JACKSON DOUGLAS, lawyer; b. Cleve., Feb. 5, 1949; m. Margaret Lawrence Williams, Dec. 19, 1971; children: Jackson Douglas Jr., William Schuyler Lawrence. BA, Colgate U., 1971; JD, U. Pa., 1974. Bar: Calif. 1974, U.S. Dist. Ct. (cen. dist.) Calif. 1974, U.S. Tax Ct. 1978, U.S. Ct. Claims 1984, U.S. Ct. Appeals (6th and 11th cirs.) 1988, N.C. 1991, U.S. Supreme Ct. 1991, US Ct. Appeals (4th cir.), 2004. Ptnr.

Kadison, Pfaelzer, Woodard, Quinn & Rossi, LA, 1986-87, Spensley, Horn, Jubas & Lubitz, LA, 1987-91, Roberts & Stevens, Asheville, N.C., 1991—. Adj. prof. law U. San Diego, 1981, Golden Gate U., San Francisco, 1981-85, U. N.C., Asheville, 1994; cons. Calif. Continuing Edn. Bar, 1983-84, select com. on sports Calif. Senate, 1983-85. Editor Entertainment Law Reporter, 1979—; contbr. articles to profl. jours. Mem. ABA (tax sect., internat. law sect.), N.C. Bar Assn. (tax. sect. coun., vice chmn.). Republican. Episcopalian. Office: Roberts & Stevens BB & T Bldg Asheville NC 28802 Office Phone: 828-252-6600.

HAMILTON, JACQUELINE, arts consultant; b. Tulsa, Mar. 28, 1942; d. James Merton and Nina Faye (Andrews) H.; m. Richard Sanford Piper, Jan. 2, 1968 (div. June 1976). BA, Tex. Christian U., 1965; grad., Stockholm U., 1967; postgrad., Harvard U., 1972—73, Tufts U., 1971, Rice U., 1982—83, Houston CC, 1986—87. Art cons. for corps., pvt. collectors and mus., Houston, 1979—. Expert witness in lawsuits regarding art. Contbr. articles to profl. publs. Bd. dirs. Opera in the Heights. Mem.: AIA (affiliate), Internat. Assn. Profl. Art Advisors, Rice Design Alliance, Assn. Corp. Art Curators, Assn. Fund Raising Professionals, French-Am. C. of C., Norwegian-am. C. of C., Swedish-Am. C. of C., Swedish Club, L'Alliance Francaise, The Forum Club, The Houstonian Club. Presbyterian. Office: PO Box 1483 Houston TX 77251-1483 Home Phone: 713-974-3011.

HAMILTON, JEAN, financial services executive, e-commerce and software executive; BS in Comms., U. Ill.; MBA in Fin. and Acctg., U. Chgo. Sr. v.p., head N.E. banking First Nat. Bank Chgo. (now J.P. Morgan Chase); pres. Prudential Capital Group, Prudential Asset Sales and Syndicates, 1988—95, Prudential Diversified Group, 1995—98; exec. v.p. Prudential Fin., Newark, 1998—2002; CEO Prudential Instl. Prudential Ins. Co. Am., 1998—2002; CEO Broadstairs Capital, 2002—, Xonos.com, Inc., 2006—; mem. Brock Capital Group, LLC, 2005—. Bd. dirs. Renaissance Re Holdings, Ltd., First Eagle Funds, First Eagle Variable Funds, Prudential Investment & Mgmt. Svcs., Prudential P&C Holdings, Pruco Life, Prudential Bank & Trust Co., Prudential Savs. Bank. Bd. dirs. The Prudential Found., The Ind. Coll. Fund NJ, Rewards Plus, The Women's Econ. Roundtable, Standing Tall, Glass Roots, Nat. Urban League, Women's Forum NY, Women's Forum Edn. Fund, Grad. Sch. Bus., U. Chgo., Four Nations; mem. adv. bd. Hudson Opera House. Named one of Bus. Ins. Top 100 Women in Ins., Risk Mgmt. and Employee Benefits; named to Who's Who in NJ Bus. Leader List, NJ Star Ledger's 10 Most Powerful Women in Bus. List, Women Bus. Leaders list, Bus. News, NJ. Mem.: Com. of 200, Internat. Women's Forum, Cosmopolitan Club, Econ. Club NY. Office Phone: 212-354-2418.

HAMILTON, JEAN CONSTANCE, judge; b. St. Louis, Nov. 12, 1945; AB, Wellesley Coll., 1968; JD, Washington U., St. Louis, 1971; LLM, Yale U., 1982. Atty. Dept. of Justice, Washington, 1971-73, asst. U.S. atty. St. Louis, 1973-78; atty. Southwestern Bell Telephone Co., St. Louis, 1978—81; judge 22d Jud. Circuit State of Mo., St. Louis, 1982-88; judge Mo. Ct. Appeals (ea. dist.), 1988-90, U.S. Dist. Ct. (ea. dist.) Mo., 1990—, chief judge, 1995—2002. Office: US Courthouse 111 S 10th St Saint Louis MO 63102

HAMILTON, JERALD, musician; b. Wichita, Kans., Mar. 19, 1927; s. Robert James and Lillie May (Rishel) H.; m. Phyllis Jean Searle, Sept. 8, 1954; children: Barbara Helen, Elizabeth Sarah, Catharine Sandra. MusB, U. Kans., Lawrence, 1948, MusM, 1950; postgrad., Royal Sch. Ch. Music, Croydon, Eng., summer 1955, Union Theol. Sem. Sch. Sacred Music, NYC, summer 1960; studies with, Laurel Everette Anderson, Andre Marchal, Catharine Crozier, Gustav Leonhardt. From instr. to asst. prof. organ and theory Washburn U., Topeka, 1949-59; dir. Washburn Singers and Choir, 1955-59; asst. prof. organ, dir. univ. singers and chorus Ohio U., Athens, 1959-60; asst. prof. organ and ch. music U. Tex., Austin, 1960-63; lectr. ch. music Episcopal Theol. Sem. S.W., Austin, 1961-63; mem. faculty U. Ill., Urbana-Champaign, 1963-88, prof. music, 1967-88, prof. emeritus, 1988—; organist, choirmaster Grace Cathedral, Topeka, 1949—59, St. David's Ch., Austin, 1960—63, St. John the Divine, Champaign, 1963—88, St. John's Cathedral, Albuquerque, 1988-93, organist-choirmaster emeritus, 1994—. Mem., chmn. commn. ch. music Episc. Diocese Kans., 1951-59; mem. bishop's commn. ch. music Episc. Diocese of Springfield, 1978-80, 82-88; concert organist, 1955-96. Author (with Marilou Kratzenstein) Four Centuries of Organ Music, Detroit Studies in Music Bibliography No. 51, 1984. Fulbright scholar, 1954-55. Mem. Assn. Anglican Musicians, Omicron Delta Kappa, Pi Kappa Lambda, Phi Mu Alpha. Episcopalian. Home: PO Box 3837 Edgewood NM 87015-3837

HAMILTON, JOAN NICE, editor-in-chief; b. Chgo., 1948; d. William and Dorothy Nice. Grad., Pomona Coll., 1970. Former editor High Country News; editor Climbing Mag.; editor-in-chief Sierra Mag., San Francisco. Contbr. articles to Audubon, Defenders, Nat. Wildlife Mags. Office: Sierra Mag 85 2nd St San Francisco CA 94105-3459

HAMILTON, JOHN MCFARLAND, plastic surgeon, real estate developer; b. Lebanon, Tenn., July 5, 1925; s. Courtnay Cowper and Sarah Louise (Williamson) H.; m. Imogene Nicholson, Dec. 19, 1951; children: Susan Richards Hamilton Churuti, John McFarland Jr., Courtnay C., Scott Deering. BS, Tulane U., 1946; MD, La. State U., 1949. Diplomate Am. Bd. Plastic Surgery. Inter, resident in gen. surgery George Washington U. Hosp., Washington, 1949-51; resident in gen. and plastic surgery Baylor Med. Sch., Houston, 1953-56, instr. plastic surgery, 1956-57; pvt. practice, St. Petersburg, Fla., 1957—2001. Dir. cleft palate team All Children's Hosp., St. Petersburg, 1957-77; chief staff Children's Hosp., St. Petersburg, 1962-63, Bayfront Med. Ctr., St. Petersburg, 1982-83; lectr. med. jurisprudence Stetson U. Law Coll., St. Petersburg, 1974-80; vice chmn. Bayfront Life Svcs., St. Petersburg, 1985-86, Fla. Med. Polit. Action Com., Tallahassee, 1982-83; real estate developer various profl. bldgs. Assoc. editor Fla. Med. Jour., 1969-79; contbr. articles to med. jours., including Plastic and Reconstructive Surgery, Fla. Med. Jour., So. Med. Jour., Aesthetic Surgery Jour., Tech. Forum. Founder, treas. Pinellas County Polit. Action Com., St. Petersburg, 1963—; bd. dirs. Fla. Orch., Tampa, 1998-2004; vol. St. Petersburg Clinic, 2003-. Lt. USN, 1943-46; capt. USAF, 1950-53, Korea. Recipient A.J. Gorday award Bayfront Med. Ctr., 1986, Fund Raiser of Yr. award for Fla. West Coast Nat. Soc. Fund Raising Execs., 1987, Golden Baton award Fla. Orch., 1998. Fellow ACS; mem. AMA, Southeastern Soc. Plastic and Reconstructive Surgeons (editor Bull. 1964-68, pres. 1976), Fla. Med. Assn. (del. 1970-78), Fla. Soc. Plastic Surgeons (founding, pres. 1967-68), Pinellas County Med. Soc. (pres. 1975-76, Achievement award 1978, Svc. awards 1988, 2001). Republican. Methodist. Avocations: photography, clarinet, poetry. Home: 2302 Parkshore Plz 300 Beach Drive NE Saint Petersburg FL 33701 Office: St Petersburg Free Clinic 863 3d Ave N Saint Petersburg FL 33701

HAMILTON, JOSEPH HANTS, JR., physicist, researcher; b. Ferriday, La., Aug. 14, 1932; s. Joseph Hants and Letha (Gibson) H.; m. Jannelle Jauree Landrum, Aug. 5, 1960; children: Melissa Claire, Christopher Landrum. BS, Miss. Coll., Clinton, 1954; MS, Ind. U., Bloomington, 1956, PhD, 1958; DSc (hon.), Miss. Coll., Clinton, 1982; PhD (hon.), Nat. U. Frankfurt, Germany, 1992, U. Bucharest, Romania, 1999, U. St. Petersburg, Russia, 2001, Joint Inst. for Nuc. Rsch., 2004, Ravi Shankar Shukla U., India, 2006, Berea Coll., Ky., 2007. Mem. faculty Vanderbilt U., Nashville, 1958—, prof. physics, 1966—, Landon C. Garland prof. physics, 1981-92, Landon C. Garland disting. prof. physics, 1992—, chmn. dept., 1979-85; adj. prof. Tsinghua U., China, 1986—. Hon. adv. prof. Fudan U., People's Republic of China, 1988—; NSF postdoctoral fellow U. Uppsala, Sweden, 1958-59; rsch. fellow Inst. Nuclear Studies, Amsterdam, 1962; vis. prof. U. Frankfurt, 1979-80, 90, 98, U. Louis Pasteur, Strasbourg, France, 1991; mem. adv. panel Nat. Heavy Ion Labs., 1971-73; mem. nat. policy bd. Holifield Heavy Ion Facility, 1974-84; organizer, chmn. exec. com., prin. investigator Univ. Isotope Separator, Oak Ridge, 1970-95; organizer Univ. Radioactive Ion Beam Consortium, 1996; cons. Oak Ridge Nat. Lab., 1972—; mem. coun. Oak Ridge Assoc. Univs., 1974-80, bd. dirs., 1995-97; organizer, dir. Joint Inst. for Heavy Ion Rsch., Oak Ridge, 1980—; mem. Oak Ridge Health Agreement Steering Panel for State of Tenn., 1993-00; sci. and tech. advisor coun. for State of Tenn., 1994-01; chmn. Internat. Conf. Internal Conversion Processes, 1965, Internat. Conf. Radioactivity in Nuclear Spectroscopy, 1969, Internat. Conf. Future Directions in Studies Nuclei far from Stability, 1979, Internat. Conf. Dirs. Nuclear Structure Rsch., 1984; co-chmn. Internat. Workshop Physics with a Recoil Mass Spectrometer, 1986; chmn. Internat. Symposium on Reflections and Directions in Low Energy Heavy Ion Physics, 1991, Internat. Conf. on Fission and Properties of Neutron Rich Nuclei, 1997, Internat. Symposium Perspectives in Nuclear Physics, 1998; co-chair Second Internat. Conf. on Fission and Properties of Neutron Rich Nuclei, 1999; chair third Internat. Conf., on fission and properties neutron rich nuclei, 2002; co-chair fourth Internat. Conf. on Fission and Properties of Neutron Rich Nuclei, 2007; dir. Vanderbilt Summer Sci. Collaborative for High Sch. Students and Tchrs., 1991-2004; vis. disting. lab. fellow Oak Ridge Nat. Lab., 2000—. Co-author: Science: Faith and Learning, 1972, ORAU from the Beginning, 1980, Graphical Representation of K-shell and Total Internal Conversion Coefficients from Z=30-104, 1984, Modern Atomic and Nuclear Physics, 1996; co-author, editor: Internal Conversion Processes, 1966, Radioactivity in Nuclear Spectroscopy, 1972, Reactions Between Complex Nuclei, 1974, Future Directions in Studies of Nuclear Far from Stability, 1980, Microscopic Models in Nuclear Structure Physics, 1989, Reflections and Directions in Low Energy Heavy Ion Physics, 1993, Structure of the Vacuum and Elementary Matter, 1997, Fission and Properties of Neutron Rich Nuclei, 1998, Perspectives in Nuclear Physics, 1999, Fission and Properties of Neutron Rich Nuclei, 2000; Third Internat. Conf. Fission and properties of Neutron Rich Nuclei, 2003. assoc. editor Jour. Physics G: Nuc. Physics, 1984-87; internat. advisor nuc. physics World Sci. Pub. Corp., 1986-91, Jour. Modern Physics Letters A, 1986-91; mem. editl. bd. Progress in Particle and Nuc. Physics, 1993-98; contbr. articles to profl. jours., chpts. in books. Mem. Mayor Nashville Citizens Adv. Com. Housing, 1970-74; bd. dirs. Vineyard Conf. Center, Louisville, 1972-77, Danforth assoc., 1965-86, So. Bapt. Conv. Hist. Commn., 1983-91. Recipient Harvie Branscomb Disting. Prof. award Vanderbilt U., 1983-84, Humbolt prize W. Germany, 1979, Order Golden Arrow Outstanding Alumni award Miss. Coll., 1985, Sutherland prize for rsch., 1988, Guy and Rebecca Forman award for outstanding physics tchg., 1990, Thomas Jefferson award for svc. in univ. couns., 1995, Jeffrey Nordhaus award for excellence in undergrad. tchg., 1996, Outstanding Sci. Tchr. award, Tenn., 1998, First Outstanding Svc. award Oak Ridge Associated U., 2000, D. Ilkovic Gold medal Slovak Acad. Sci., 2002; Internat. Sci. and Tech. Cooperation award, Peoples Republic China 2002, GN. Flerov Prize Russia 2003; named State of Tenn. Outstanding Prof. of Yr. Coun. Advancement and Support Edn., 1991; grantee NSF, 1959-76, ERDA-Dept. Energy, 1975—. Fellow AAAS (Internat. Cooperation award 1996), Am. Phys. Soc. (vice chmn. Southeastern sect. 1972-73, chmn. 1973-74, mem. coun. 1994-2004, Jesse Beams Gold medal for rsch. 1975, George Peagram Gold medal tchg. 1988, Francis Slack gold medal for Svc. 2000); mem. Am. Assn. Physics Tchrs., Am. Inst. Physics (governing bd. 2004-07), Sigma Xi (chpt. pres. 1970). Home: 305 Mountainside Dr Nashville TN 37215-4324 Office Phone: 615-322-2456. Business E-Mail: j.h.hamilton@vanderbilt.edu.

HAMILTON, LAIRD JOHN, professional surfer; b. San Francisco, Mar. 2, 1964; s. Bill and Joann Hamilton; m. Gabrielle Reece, Nov. 30, 1997; 1 child, Reece Viola. Featured on the cover of numerous magazines including Sports Illustrated, People, Life, GQ, L"Uomo Vogue (Italy), High Wind (Japan), Surf (Germany) and Paris Match (France); host The Extremists Outdoor Life Network, 1996—97, host, Fox Sports Net Planet Extreme Championships, 2000. Film appearances include: The Endless Summer 2, 1994; Waterworld, 1995; Die Another Day, 1995; Step into Liquid, 2003; exec. prodr.: (films) Riding Giants, 2004. Recipient Breakout Performance of Yr., Surfer Poll awards, 2000, Rider of Yr. award, France, 2000, ESPN's, Action Sports & Music award for Feat of Yr., 2001. Achievements include invention of the foilboard surfboard which incorporates hydrofoil technology; popularized the tow-in surfing technique.

HAMILTON, LAURELL K., writer; b. Heber Springs, Ark., 1963; Author: Guilty Pleasures, 1993, The Laughing Corpse, 1994, Circus of the Damned, 1995, The Lunatic Cafe, 1996, Bloody Bones, 1996, The Killing Dance, 1997, Burnt Offerings, 1998, Blue Moon, 1998, Obsidian Butterfly, 2000, A Kiss of Shadows, 2001, Narcissus in Chains, 2002, A Caress of Twilight, 2003, Seduced By Moonlight, 2004, Incubus Dreams, 2004 (Publishers Weekly Bestseller), The Harlequin, 2007. Office: c/o Author Mail Berkley Pub Penguin Group 375 Hudson New York NY 10014*

HAMILTON, LAWRENCE STANLEY, environmental consultant; b. Toronto, Ont., Can., June 5, 1925; s. Stanley Samuel Hamilton and Gretta Pearl Walker; m. Helen Margaret Halliday, Sept. 13, 1947 (div. May 6, 1980); children: L. Blair, Bruce H., Anne K. Johnson, Lynne M. Silverberg; m. Linda Eleanor Schenck, July 12, 1980. BSc in Forestry, U. Toronto, 1948; MS, Coll. Forestry, Syracuse, NY, 1951; PhD, U. Mich., Ann Arbor, 1963. Zone forester lands and forests, Galt, Ont., 1948—51; ext. forester Cornell U., Ithaca, NY, 1951—54, prof., 1954—80, prof. emeritus, 1980; rsch. fellow East West Ctr., Honolulu, 1980—91, sr. fellow, 1991—93; cons., ptnr. Islands and Highlands, Charlotte, Vt., 1993—. Vis. prof. U. Queensland, Brisbane, Australia, 1969—70; adj. prof. U. Hawaii, Honolulu, 1980—93; vice chair mountains World Commn. on Protected Areas, Gland, Switzerland, 1992—2004, sr. advisor, 2004—; trustee Vt. Nature Conservancy, Montpelier, 1996—. Editor: Mountain Protected Areas Update, 1992—, Religion, Ethics and Biodiversity, 1993; co-editor: Tropical Montage Cloud Forests, 1995; contbr. articles to profl. jours. Tree warden Town of Charlotte, 1995—, fence viewer, 2006—. Leading naval airman Royal Navy Fleet Air Arm, 1943—45. Recipient Vis. Prof. award, Fulbright-Hays Fellowship Found. Waikatao New Zealand, 1978, King Albert L. Gold medal, King Albert Found., 2004, Disting. Scientist award, U. Hawaii, 2004; NSF postdoctoral fellow, U. Calif., 1965. Mem.: Soc. Am. Foresters (sect. chair 1956—58). Avocations: hiking, nature study, tennis, music. Home: 342 Bittersweet Ln Charlotte VT 05445

HAMILTON, LEE HERBERT, educational association administrator, retired congressman; b. Daytona Beach, Fla., Apr. 20, 1931; m. Nancy Ann Nelson, Aug. 21, 1954; children: Tracy Lynn, Deborah Lee, Douglas Nelson. AB, DePauw U., 1952, degree (hon.); scholar, Goethe U., Germany, 1952-53; JD, Ind. U., 1956; degree (hon.), Hanover Coll., Detroit Coll. Law, Ball State U., US Ind., Wabash Coll., Union Coll., Ind. U., Am. Univ., Marian Coll., Suffolk U. Mem. US Congress from 9th Dist. Ind., Washington, 1965-99; ranking minority mem. House com. internat. rels.; former chmn. select. com. to investigate covert arms transactions with Iran; mem. joint econ. com., former chmn. fgn. affairs com., former co chair Joint com. Orgn. Congress; former chmn. Ho. intelligence com., former chmn. Ho. com. investigate Oct. surprise; dir. Woodrow Wilson Ctr. Internat. Scholars Smithsonian Instn., Washington, 1999—. Vice chmn., The Nat. Commn. on Terrorist Attacks Upon the U.S. (The 9-11 Commn.), 2002-04, co-chair Iraq Study Group, 2006 Co-author (with Thomas H. Kean): Without Precedent: The Inside Story of the 9/11 Commission, 2006. Fellow: Am. Acad. Arts & Sciences. Democrat. Office: Woodrow Wilson Ctr Internat Scholars One Woodrow Wilson Plz 1300 Pennsylvania Ave NW Washington DC 20004-3027

HAMILTON, LEONARD DERWENT, physician, molecular biologist; b. Manchester, Eng., May 7, 1921; came to U.S., 1949, naturalized, 1964; s. Jacob and Sara (Sandelson) H.; m. Ann Twynam Blake, July 20, 1945; children: Jane Derwent, Stephen David, Robin Michael. BA, Balliol Coll., Oxford U., Eng., 1943, BM, 1945, MA, 1946, DM, 1951; MA, Trinity Coll., Cambridge U., Eng., 1948, PhD, 1952. Diplomate Am. Bd. Pathology. USPHS rsch. fellow U. Utah, 1949-50; staff Sloan-Kettering Inst., NYC, 1950-79, head isotope studies sect., 1957-64, assoc. scientist, 1965-79; staff Meml. Hosp., NYC, 1950-65; faculty Sloan-Kettering div. Grad. Sch. Med. Scis. Cornell U., 1956-64; sr. scientist, head divsn. microbiology Med. Research Ctr. Brookhaven Nat. Lab., Upton, NY, 1964-76; head biomed. and environ. assessment divsn. Office. Environ. Policy Analysis, 1973-94. Attending physician Hosp. Med. Rsch. Ctr., 1964-85; dir. WHO Collaborating Ctr. for Assessment of Health and Environ. Effects of Energy Systems, 1983-97, WHO focal point on health and environ. effects of energy systems, 1983—, mem. WHO expert adv. panel on environ. hazards, 1983-98; prof. medicine Health Sci. Ctr., SUNY, Stony Brook, 1968—; adj. prof. biometry and epidemiology Med. U. S.C., Charleston, 1996—; cons. HEW, Ctr. Disease Control, Nat. Inst. Occupational Safety and Health, epidemiology study of Portsmouth Naval Shipyard, 1978-88; vis. fellow St. Catherine's Coll., Oxford U., 1972-73; internat. panel experts on fossil fuel UN Environment Programme, 1978, panel on nuclear energy, 1978-79, panel on renewable sources and comparative assessment of different sources, 1980; com. mem. Nat. Acad. Sci.-NRC, Washington, 1975-80; mem. NYC Mayor's Tech. Adv. Com. on Radiation, 1963-77, NYC Commr. of Health Tech. Adv. Com. on Radiation, 1978—; energy panel WHO Commn. on Health and Environment, 1990-91; mem. Internat. Expert Group 3, Comparative Environ. and Health Effects of Different Energy Systems for Electricity Generation, 1990-91; sr. expert Symposium on Electricity and the Environ., Helsinki, Finland, 1991. Editor: Gerrard Winstanley, Selections from His Works, 1944; Physical Factors and Modification of Radiation Injury, 1964; The Health and Environmental Effects of Electricity Generation-a Preliminary Report, 1974. Recipient Fed. Lab. Consortium award, 1990; Am. Cancer Soc. scholar, 1953-58; Commonwealth Fund grantee, 1955-62. Mem. AMA, Am. Assn. Cancer Rsch., Am. Soc. Clin. Investigation, Am. Soc. for Investigative Pathology, Soc. for Risk Analysis, Harvey Soc., Cosmos Club (Washington). Office: Brookhaven Nat Lab Upton NY 11973 Office Phone: 631-344-2004. Business E-Mail: vanslyke@bnl.gov.

HAMILTON, LINDA, actress; b. Salisbury, MD, Sept. 26, 1956; m. Peter Horton, 1979 (div. 1980); m. Bruce Abbott Dec. 19, 1982 (div. 1989); 1 child, Dalton Abbott; m. James Cameron, July 26, 1997 (div. 1999); 1 child, Josephine Archer. Appeared in plays Looice, 1975, Richard III, 1977, The Night of the Iguana, 2006; films include T.A.G.: The Assassination Game, 1982, Children of the Corn, 1984, The Stone Boy, 1984, The Terminator, 1984, Black Moon Rising, 1986, King Kong Lives!, 1986, Mr. Destiny, 1990, Terminator 2: Judgment Day, 1991, Silent Fall, 1994, The Shadow Conspiracy, 1996, Dante's Peak, 1997, The Secret Life of Girls, 1999, Skeletons in the Closet, 2001, Wholey Moses, 2003, Jonah, 2004, Smile, 2005, Missing in America, 2005, The Kid and I, 2005; TV series include The Secrets of Midland Heights, 1980-81, King's Crossing, 1982, Beauty and the Beast, 1987-89 (Golden Globe award nomination 1988, 89), (voice) Hercules, 1998, Thief, 2005-; TV movies include Reunion, 1980, Rape and Marriage - The Rideout Case, 1980, Country Gold, 1982, Secrets of a Mother and Daughter, 1983, Secret Weapons, 1985, Club Med, 1986, Go Toward the Light, 1988, The Way to Dusty Death, 1995, A Mother's Prayer, 1995, On The Line, 1998, Point Last Seen, 1998, Resuers: Stories of Courage - Two Couples, 1998, The Color of Courage, 1999, (voice) Batman Beyond: The Movie, 1999, Sex and Mrs. X, 2000, Bailey's Mistake, 2001, Silent Night, 2002. Office: United Talent Agency 5th Floor 9560 Wilshire Blvd Fl 5 Beverly Hills CA 90212-2400

HAMILTON, LYMAN CRITCHFIELD, JR., telecommunications industry executive; b. LA, Aug. 29, 1926; s. Lyman Critchfield and Edna Lorraine (Gluck) H.; m. Mary W. Shepard, June 25, 1949 (div. 1984); children: William, Richard, Douglas, David; m. Beverly C. Lannquist, Nov. 17, 1984. Student, U. Redlands, Calif., 1944-45; BA, Principia Coll., Elsah, Ill., 1947; MPA, Harvard U., Cambridge, Mass., 1949; LLD (hon.), Waynesburg Coll., Pa., 1979. Budget examiner U.S. Bur. of Budget, Washington, 1950-56; asst. adminstr. U.S. Civil Adminstrn. of Ryukyu Islands, Okinawa, Japan, 1956-60; investment officer World Bank & IFC, Washington, 1960-62; with Internat. Telephone & Telegraph Corp., NYC, 1962-79, treas., 1967-76, v.p., 1968-73, sr. v.p., 1973-74, exec. v.p., 1974-77, pres., 1977-79, chief oper. officer, 1977, chief exec., 1978-79; chmn., pres. Tamco Enterprises, Inc., NYC, 1980-89; chmn., pres., chief exec. officer Imperial Corp. of Am., 1989-90; pres., chief exec. officer Alpine Polyvision, Inc., 1991-93, chmn., 1993. Vis. com. Gerald R. Ford Sch. Pub. Policy U. Mich.; adv. com. Monterey Inst. Internat. Studies, Calif.; trustee Monterey Symphony, Monterey History and Art Assn., York Sch. Lt. (j.g.) USNR, 1944—46. Mem. LA Country Club, Farmington Woods Country Club, Univ. Club, Old Capital Club (Monterey). Republican. also: 5485 Quail Meadows Dr Carmel CA 93923

HAMILTON, MARK R., academic administrator; m. Patty Hamilton; 4 children. BS, US Mil. Acad., 1967; MA in English Lit., Fla. State U., 1973; grad., Armed Forces Staff Coll., US Army War Coll. Comdr. Divsn. Artillery, Fort Richardson, 1988-90; chief staff Alaskan Command, Elmendorf AFB, 1992-93; dep. dir. force structure, resource and analysis Joint Staff, Washington, 1995-97; head recruiting US Army, Fort Knox, Ky., 1997-98; pres. U. Alaska, Fairbanks, 1998—. Mem. Denali Commn.; chair, bd. dirs. Alaska Aerospace Devel. Corp.; mem., bd. dirs. Alaska Air Group, Inc.; chair Alaska Distance Edn. Technology Consortium; co-chair Alaska State Com. on Rsch. Mem., bd. dirs. Alaska SeaLife Ctr.; mem. Morris Thompson Cultural Ctr. Bd. Decorated DSM US Army, Joint Disting. Svc. medal; named Person of Wk., Peter Jennings, ABC News; named one of 25 Most Powerful Alaskans for past 5 yrs., Alaskan Jour. Commerce. Office: U Alaska PO Box 755000 Fairbanks AK 99775-5000 Office Phone: 907-450-8000.

HAMILTON, PAMELA JANE, psychologist, special education educator; d. Harry Joseph and Darlene Lillian (Mortenson) Anderson; m. John Robert Hamilton, Dec. 22, 1973 (dec. July 6, 2006); children: Ian, Sean. BA in Psychology and Elem. Edn., U. Wash., Seattle, 1972, MEd in Spl. Edn., 1990; post-master's cert. in sch. psychology, Seattle U., 2005. Gen. edn. tchr. Granite Falls Sch. Dist., Wash., 1972—76, spl. edn. tchr., 1990—2004, sch. psychologist, 2005—; substitute tchr. Quillayute Valley Sch. Dist., Forks, Wash., 1984—89; spl. edn. tchr. St. Christopher Acad., Kent, Wash., 1990—92, Highline Sch. Dist., Seattle, 1992—98. Mem. Cmty. Coalition, Granite Falls, 2004—; worship leader For His Glory Reigns Ministries, Granite Falls, 2004—, bd. dirs., 2005—, area rep., 2005—. Mem.: Wash. State Assn. Sch. Psychologists, Nat. Assn. Sch. Psychologists. Home: PO Box 387 Granite Falls WA 98252 Office: Granite Falls Sch Dist Monte Cristo Elem/Mt Way Elem 702 N Granite Ave Granite Falls WA 98252

HAMILTON, PARKER, library director; m. J. Mauri Hamilton. BA, MLS, U. Ill., Urbana. Libr. Champaign Pub. Libr., Ill., Evanston Twp. HS; part time libr. I, Long Branch libr. Montgomery County Pub. Librs., Rockville, Md., br. mgr. Long Branch and Davis librs., pub. svc. adminstr. human resources, 1993—2001, acting dir., 2005, dir., 2005—; asst. chief adminstrv. officer Montgomery County, 2001—05. Office: Montgomery County Pub Librs 21 Maryland Ave Ste 310 Rockville MD 20850 Office Phone: 240-777-0002. Office Fax: 240-777-0014.*

HAMILTON, PAT R., retired lawyer, state representative; b. Feb. 14, 1923; LLB, W.Va. U., 1949. With FBI, 1949-54; sr. ptnr. Hamilton, Burgess, Young & Pollard, Oak Hill, W.Va., 1954—90, 1997—2002, ret., 2002; mem. W.Va. Senate, 1972-80, W.Va. Ho. of Dels., 1982-86. Address: 10 Arbuckle Rd Oak Hill WV 25901-3109

HAMILTON, PATRICIA ROSE, art dealer; b. Phila., Oct. 21, 1948; d. William Alexis and Lillian Marie (Sloan) Hamilton. BA, Temple U., Phila., 1970; MA, Rutgers U., New Brunswick, NJ, 1971. Sec. to curator Whitney Mus., NYC, 1971-73; sr. editor Art in Am., 1973; curator exhbns. Crispo Gallery, 1974-75; dir. Hamilton Gallery, 1976-84; artist's agt., 1984—2002; art dealer, 2002—. Democrat. Avocations: tennis, swimming, cooking. Home and Office: 6753 Milner Rd Los Angeles CA 90068-3214 Home Phone: 323-512-4737; Office Phone: 323-512-4737. Personal E-mail: hamiltonpatricia@sbcglobal.net.

HAMILTON, PETER BANNERMAN, manufacturing executive, lawyer; b. Phila., Oct. 22, 1946; s. William George Jr. and Elizabeth Jane (McCullough) H.; m. Elizabeth Anne Arthur, May 8, 1982; children—Peter Bannerman, Jr., Brian Arthur. AB, Princeton U., 1968; JD, Yale U., 1971. Bar: D.C. 1972, Pa. 1972, Ind. 1985. Mem. staff Office Asst. Sec. Def. for Systems Analysis and Office Gen. Counsel, Dept. Def., Washington, 1971-74; mem. firm Williams & Connolly, Washington, 1974-77; gen. counsel Dept. Air Force, Washington, 1977-78; dep. gen. counsel HEW, Washington, 1979, exec. asst. to sec., 1979; spl. asst. to Sec. and Dep. Sec. Def., Washington, 1979-80; ptnr. Califano, Ross & Heineman, Washington, 1980-82; v.p., gen. counsel, sec. Cummins Inc., 1983-86, v.p. law and treasury, 1987-88, v.p., CFO, 1988-95; sr. v.p., CFO, Brunswick Corp., Lake Forest, Ill., 1996-98, exec. v.p., CFO, 1998-99; vice chmn., pres. Brunswick Bowling and Billiards, 2000—04; vice chmn., pres Life Fitness, 2005, Brunswick Boat Group, 2006. Bd. dirs. Spectra Energy Corp. Articles editor: Yale Law Jour, 1970-71. Served to lt. USN, 1971-74. Home: 970 E Deerpath Lake Forest IL 60045-2212

HAMILTON, REBECCA L., state librarian; BA in Psychology, La. State U., MLIS. Dir. St. Mary Parish Libr. of La.; assoc. state libr. State Libr. of La., state libr., commr., 2005—. Mem.: Chief Officers of State Libr. Agencies, Libr. Adminstrn. and Mgmt. Assn., Pub. Libr. Assn., La. Libr. Assn., ALA. Office: State Library of La 701 N 4th St Baton Rouge LA 70802 Office Phone: 225-342-4923. Office Fax: 225-219-4804. Business E-Mail: rhamilto@state.lib.la.us.*

HAMILTON, RICHARD ALFRED, academic administrator, marketing executive; b. Pitts., Dec. 22, 1941; s. Robert Curtis and Dorothy Katherine (Sexauer) Hamilton. BA, Otterbein Coll., 1965; MBA, Bowling Green State U., 1968; D in Bus. Adminstrn., Kent State U., 1973. Prodn, rate analyst dept. indsl. engring. RCA, Findlay, Ohio, 1966—67; computer sys. analyst dept. market rsch. Marathon Oil Co., Findlay, 1967—68; tchg. fellow Coll. Bus. Adminstrn. Kent State U., 1968—71; assoc. profl. direct mktg. U. Mo., Kansas City, 1971—, dir. dept mktg., 2005—06; pres. Mission Woods Cons., Inc., 1977—2006. Cons. U.S. Senate Permanent Subcom. on Investigation, 1973—74, Midwest Rsch. Inst. and Office of Tech. Assessment of U.S. Congress, 1974—75; spkr. to profl. orgns. Author (with David R. Bywaters): How to Conduct Association Surveys, 1976; author: Tourism U.S.A.-Marketing Tourism, Vol. 3, 1978, Quantitative Direct Response Market Segmentation, 1989, Readings and Cases in Direct Marketing, NTC Business Books, Helzberg Diamonds-A Retailer's Use of Direct Marketing to Generate Store Traffic, 1995; contbr. articles to profl. jours. Recipient Cray Faculty award, U. Mo., 1987, Robert B. Clarke Outstanding Direct Mktg. Educator award, Direct Mktg. Ednl. Found., 1994, Disting. Rsch. in Mktg. award, Allied Acads., 2001; Univ. fellow, 1968—71, dissertation fellow, Marathon Oil Co., 1972, grant, UNKC, 1982. Mem.: Direct Mktg. Assn., Am. Mktg. Assn., Beta Gamma Sigma. Methodist. Home: 5306 Mission Woods Rd Shawnee Mission KS 66205-2008 Office: U Mo Bloch Sch Adminstrn Kansas City MO 64110 Home Phone: 913-362-7637; Office Phone: 816-235-2313. E-mail: hamiltonr@umkc.edu.

HAMILTON, RICHARD CLAY, professional basketball player; b. Coatesville, Pa., Feb. 14, 1978; Student, U. Conn. Profl. basketball player Washington Wizards, 1999—2002, Detroit Pistons, 2002—. Named one of Top Good Guys in Sports, Sporting News, 2004; named to USA Basketball Sr. Men's Nat. Team, 1999, Ea. Conf. All-Star Team, NBA, 2007. Achievements include winning the NBA Championship, 2004. Office: Detroit Pistons 4 Championship Dr Auburn Hills MI 48326*

HAMILTON, RITA, library director; BA in Libr. Sci., Western Mich. U., Kalamazoo, 1975; MLS, U. Ariz., Tucson, 1986. Libr. tech. asst. reference dept. Tucson Pub. Libr., 1979—84, adminstrv. asst., 1984—88, prin. cataloger tech. svcs. dept., 1988—89, cataloging mgr. tech. svcs. dept., 1989—91; tech. svcs. mgr. Pub. Libr. Nashville and Davidson County, 1991—95, asst. dir., 1995—2000; pub. svcs. adminstr. Phoenix Pub. Libr., 2000—02; dir. Scottsdale Pub. Libr., Ariz., 2002—. Contbr. articles to profl. publs. Recipient Scottsdale City Mgr.'s Award of Excellence, 2006, Honor award, ALA/Internat. Interior Design Assn., 2006. Mem.: ALA, Ariz. State Libr. Assn. (pres. pub. libr. divsn. 2001—02, mem. libr. automation roundtable 1988—91), Maricopa County Libr. Coun. (v.p./pres.-elect 2003—04, pres. 2004—05), Urban Librs. Coun. (mem. forecasting strategy group 2003—, chair Highsmith/Urban Librs. Coun. award jury 2006—07), Pub. Libr. Assn. (chair cataloging needs of pub. libr. 1994—96, mem. evaluating electronic info. com. 1998—2002, mem. Charlie Robinson award jury 2001—02, mem. 1004 nat. conf. prog. com. 2002—04, mem. Highsmith award jury 2003, bd. dirs. 2003—06, mem. Highsmith award jury 2004, mem. 2006 nat. conf. prog. com. 2004—06), AMIGOS (bd. dirs. 2005—, mem. budget and fin. com. 2005—, sec. 2006—). Office: Scottsdale Pub Libr Sys 3839 N Drinkwater Blvd Scottsdale AZ 85251-4452 Office Phone: 480-312-7049. Office Fax: 480-312-7993. E-mail: rhamilton@scottsdaleaz.gov.

HAMILTON, ROBERT OTTE, lawyer; b. Marysville, Ohio, July 27, 1927; s. George Robinson and Annette (Otte) H.; m. Phyllis Eileen Clark, Dec. 16, 1962; children: Nathan Clark, Scott Robert. AB, Miami U., Oxford, Ohio, 1950; JD, U. Mich., 1953. Bar: Ohio 1953, U.S. Supreme Ct. 1960. Sole practice, Marysville, 1953—; pros. atty. Union County, Ohio, 1957-65; city atty. City of Marysville, 1956-81. Mem. Union, Morrow and Del. Mental Health Bd.,d 1957-72; pres. Marysville Jaycees, 1954; mem. Union County Rep. Exec. Com., 1955-65, sec., 1955-60. Served with USN, 1945-46, to lt. (j.g.) USNR, 1946-66. Mem. ABA, Ohio State Bar Assn. (chmn. jr. bar sect. 1961, ho. of dels. 1976-86, exec. com. 1983-86), Ohio State Bar Found. (pres. 1996), Union County Bar Assn. (pres. 1960), Ohio Acad. Trial Lawyers, Masons. Home: 432 W 6th St Marysville OH 43040-1464 Office: 116 S Court St Marysville OH 43040-1545 Office Phone: 937-642-5877.

HAMILTON, ROBERT WOODRUFF, retired legal association administrator, educator; b. Syracuse, NY, Mar. 4, 1931; s. Walton Hale and Irene (Till) H.; m. Dagmar S. Strandberg, June 2, 1953; children: Eric Clark, Robert Andrew, Meredith Hope. BA, Swarthmore Coll., 1952; JD, U. Chgo., 1955. Bar: D.C. 1956, U.S. Ct. Appeals (D.C. cir.) 1960, U.S. Supreme Ct. 1965. Law clk. to justice Tom Clark US Supreme Ct., Washington, 1955-56; assoc. Gardner, Morrison & Rogers, Washington, 1956-64; assoc. prof. law U. Tex., Austin, 1964-67, prof., 1967—2004, prof. emeritus, 2004—, Minerva House Drysdale Regents chair in law. Rsch. dir. U.S. Admin. Conf., Washington, 1972-73; vis. prof. U. Pa., U. Minn., Washington U., St. Louis, others; Godfrey Disting. prof. law U. Maine Law Sch., 1992, 2003; mem. rev. panel on new drugs HEW, Washington, 1974-77. Author: Texas Practice, vols. 19 and 20, 1973, Cases on Corporations, 1975; author: (with Jonathan Macey) 9th rev. edit., 2005; author: Cases on Contracts, 1984, 2d rev. edit., 1992, Nutshell on Corporations, 1980, 5th rev. edit., 2000, Cases on Corporate Finance, 1984, 2d rev. edit., 1989, Fundamentals of Modern Business, 1990, Money Management for Lawyers and Clients, 1993, Business Organizations: Unincorporated Businesses and Closely Held Corporations, 1996, Business Basics for Law Students, 2d edit., 1998; author: (with Richard Booth) 3d edit., 2002. Chmn. bd. dirs. U. Tex. Coop., 1989-01, U. Coop. Soc., Austin, 1989-02; elected mem. Westlake Hills (Tex.) City Coun., 1969-72; chmn. zoning commn. Westlake Hills, 1983-87. Rsch. grantee U. Tex., 1970, 84, 92, 97. Mem. ABA (reporter), Am. Law Inst., Tex. Bar Assn. (partnership com., corp. laws com.), Tex. Bus. Law Found., Order of Coif. Democrat.

HAMILTON, ROGER PAUL, JR., lawyer; b. St. Martinville, La., Sept. 16, 1976; s. Roger Paul Hamilton, Sr. and Carmen Ann Savoy Hamilton; 1 child, Regan Paige. BA, Nicholls State U., 1994—98; JD, La. State U. Paul M. Hebert Law Ctr., 1998—2001. Bar: La. 2002. Rsch. asst. La. State U. Paul M. Hebert Law Ctr., Baton Rouge, 1999—2000; law clk. La. Dist. Atty. Assn., Baton Rouge, 2000—01, La. Legislative Bur., Baton Rouge, 2001; jud. law clk. 16th Jud. Ct., Hon. Paul J. deMahy, St. Martinville, La., 2001—02; asst. dist. atty. 16th Jud. Dist., New Iberia, La., 2002—. Presenter Iberia Parish Sheriff Office Tng. Ctr. Juvenile Acad., New Iberia, 2004—04. Editor: (newsletter) The Civilian. V.p. Chez Hope; committeeman Rep. State Ctrl. Com., La., 2003—04; mem. Diocese of Lafayette Diocesan Pastoral Coun., Lafayette; bd. mem. Iberia Comprehensive Cmty. Health Ctr., New Iberia, 2003—04; bd. mem. region 5 La. Dist. Atty. Assn. ADA Sect., Baton Rouge, 2004—. Recipient Outstanding African Am. Alumni Award, Nicholls State U., 2004, Another Success Story, 2004. Mem.: ABA, La. State Bar Assn., La. Hist. Assn., Inn on the Teche, Phi Alpha Delta. Roman Catholic. Avocations: golf, card collecting, baseball. Office: 16th Jud Dist Attorney Office 300 Iberia St Ste 200 New Iberia LA 70563 Home Phone: 337-364-6085; Office Phone: 337-369-4420. Office Fax: 337-364-5302; Home Fax: 337-364-5302. Personal E-mail: paulhouse@prodigy.net. Business E-Mail: rhamilton@16jda.com.

HAMILTON, RONALD RAY, minister; b. Evansville, Ind., May 6, 1932; s. Floyd Ray Hamilton and Ruby Dixon (Chism) Hahn; m. Norma Jean Robertson, Mar. 25, 1956; children: Ronnetta Jean, Andrea, Robert Rae. BA, U. Evansville, 1955; BD, Garrett Theol. Sem., 1958, MDiv, 1972; PhD, Oxford Grad. Sch., Eng., Dayton, Tenn., 1989. Ordained elder United Meth. Ch. Minister Scobey (Mont.) Meth. Ch., 1958-61, St. Andrew Meth. Ch., Littleton, Colo., 1961-67; sr. minister First Meth. Ch., Grand Junction, Colo., 1967-75, Christ United Meth. Ch., Salt Lake City, 1975-80, Littleton United Meth., 1980-86, U. Park United Meth., Denver, 1986-91, First United Meth. Ch., Sun City, Ariz., 1992-98; chaplain Sun Health Corp., Sun City, 1998—. Author: The Way to Success, 1972, The Greatest Prayer, 1983, A Chosen People, 1986; editor jour., 1978. Recipient Spl. award Mental Health Assn., Mesa County, Colo., 1974, Goodwill Rehab. Inc., 1975. Mem. Lions Club, Rotary Club, Civitan (chaplain 1964-67). Republican. Avocations: acting, directing, travel, chess. Home: 20846 N 107th Dr Sun City AZ 85373-2388 Office: Boswell Meml Hosp 10401 W Thunderbird Blvd Sun City AZ 85351

HAMILTON, SAMUEL C., not-for-profit fundraiser; Grad., Clark Coll., 1965. Regional dir. Aetna Life and Casualty Co.; deputy dir. Hartford Econ. Develop. Com., exec. dir. Sr. grand vice polemarch; grand polemarch Kappa Alpha Psi, 2003—. Named one of 100 Most Influential Black Americans, Ebony mag., 2004, 2005, 2006; recipient Cmty. Svc. award, United Way Capital Area, 2001. Office: Kappa Alpha Psi 2322-24 N Broad St Philadelphia PA 19132-4590 Office Phone: 215-228-7184. Office Fax: 215-228-7181.

HAMILTON, STEPHEN DAVID DERWENT, lawyer; b. NYC, Oct. 26, 1952; s. L.D. and Ann T. Hamilton; m. Ona Petra Murdoch, Dec. 1, 1984; 3 children. AB magna cum laude, Princeton U., 1973; JD magna cum laude, Harvard U., 1976. Bar: N.Y. 1977, Pa. 1989. Law clk. to Judge J. Edward Lumbard U.S. Ct. Appeals (2d crct.), NYC, 1976-77; assoc. Paul, Weiss, Rifkind, Wharton & Garrison, NYC, 1977-88, Drinker Biddle & Reath, Phila., 1988-90, ptnr., bus., fin. dept., 1991—, and head, tax practice group. Editor Harvard Law Rev., 1974-76; contbr. articles on fed. income taxation to profl. jours. Mem. ABA (taxation sect., mem. partnerships and LLCs com.), Phila. Bar Assn. (chmn. fed. tax com. 1992-95), Am. Coll. Tax Counsel, Phi Beta Kappa. Office: Drinker Biddle & Reath LLP One Logan Sq 18th & Cherry Sts Philadelphia PA 19103-6996 Office Phone: 215-988-1990. Office Fax: 267-402-4631. Business E-Mail: stephen.hamilton@dbr.com.

HAMILTON, THOMAS MICHAEL, marketing executive; b. Bronxville, NY, Jan. 8, 1947; s. Harold Thomas and Mary Theresa (Byrne) H.; m. Kathryn Borys, May 24, 1984. BS, SUNY, Buffalo. Sales mgr. Herk, Inc., NYC, 1971-73; account exec. William Esty Co., Inc., NYC, 1973-77, account supr., 1977-80, v.p., assoc. dir. sales promotion, 1980-83, sr. v.p., dir. sales promotion, 1983-88; pres. Hamilton Promotions, Inc., Katonah, NY, 1988-89; v.p. mktg. Harrington, Righter & Parsons Inc., NYC, 1989-94; prin. Hamilton Integrated Mktg. Solutions LLC, Katonah, NY, 1994—. Fundraiser United Way of Greater N.Y., 1976-84; council mem. HIP Consumer Council, N.Y.C., 1985; mem. North East Katonah (N.Y.) Community League, 1987—. Served to 1st lt. USAF, 1968-71. Mem. Mktg. Communications Execs. Internat. (bd. dirs. 1983-86), Promotion Mktg. Assn. Am. (bd. dirs. 1986-93, exec. com. 1987-93, vice-chmn. 1989-90, chmn.-elect 1990-91, chmn. bd. 1991-92, chmn. emeritus 1993-94). Avocations: golf, travel.

HAMILTON, TYLER, professional cyclist, Olympic athlete; b. Mar. 1, 1971; Profl. Cyclist, 1995—, U.S. Postal Service, 1998—2001, CSC-Tiscali Team, 2001—03, Phonak Team, 2004. Mem. U.S. Olympic Cycling Team, Sydney, 2000, Athens, 04. The Tyler Hamilton Foundation, 2003—. Recipient Coeur de Lion awards, 16 Tour de France, 2003. Achievements include finished 1st, Liege-Bastogne-Liege, 2003; won Tour of Romandie, 2003. Office: c/o USOC 1 Olympic Plaza Colorado Springs CO 80909

HAMILTON, VIRGINIA VAN DER VEER, historian, educator; b. Kansas City, Mo., Sept. 7, 1921; d. McClellan and Dorothy (Rainold) Van der Veer; m. Lowell S. Hamilton, Aug. 4, 1946; children: Carol, David. AB, Birmingham Coll., Ala., 1941, MA (Ford Found. Fund Adult Edn. fellow), 1961; PhD, U. Ala., 1968, LittD, 1992. Staff writer AP, Washington, 1942—46, Birmingham News, 1948—50; asst. prof. history U. Montevallo, Ala., 1951—55; asst. prof., asst. to pres. pub. rels. Birmingham-So. Coll., 1955—65; lectr. in history U. Ala., Birmingham, 1965—68, asst. prof., 1968—71, assoc. prof., 1971—75, prof., 1975—87, prof. emerita, 1987—. Author: Hugo Black: The Alabama Years, 1972, Alabama: A History, 1977, The Story of Alabama, 1980, Your Alabama, 1980, Seeing Historic Alabama, 1982, rev. edit., 1996, Lister Hill: Statesman from the South, 1987, Looking For Clark Gable and Other 20th Century Pursuits, 1996; editor: Hugo Black and the Bill of Rights, 1978. Faculty Rsch. grantee U. Ala. at Tuscaloosa, 1969, U. Ala. at Birmingham, 1973-74, 74-75. Mem. So., Am. hist. assns., Orgn. Am. Historians, Soc. Am. Historians, Ala. Assn. Historians, Ala. Hist. Soc.

HAMILTON, WARREN BELL, geologist, geophysicist, educator, researcher; b. LA, May 13, 1925; s. Errett Campbell and Erva Laura (Bell) Hamilton; m. Alicita Victoria Koenig, Dec. 23, 1947; children: Lawrence C., Kathryn E., James D. BA, UCLA, 1945, PhD, 1951; MS, U. So. Calif., 1949. Asst. prof. U. Okla., Norman, 1951-52; from geologist to sr. scientist U.S. Geol. Survey, Denver, 1952-95, Pecora fellow emeritus, 1995-96; Disting. sr. scientist Colo. Sch. Mines, Golden, 1996—. Sr. exch. scientist Acad. Scis., USSR, 1967; vis. prof. Scripps Inst. Oceanography, San Diego, 1968, 79, Calif. Inst. Tech., Pasadena, 1973, Yale U., New Haven, 1980, U. Amsterdam, 1981; mem. plate tectonics del. to China and Tibet, 79; disting. lectr. Am. Assn. Petroleum Geologists, 1983—84; nominator MacArthur Found., 1984—85; vis. scholar We. Mich. U., 1984; Wilbert disting. lectr. La. State U., 1985, adj. prof., 2000—02; regents lectr. U. Calif., Santa Barbara, 1986, San Diego, 90, UCLA, 1988; Hooker disting. lectr. McMaster U., 1990; Ketin lectr. Istanbul (Turkey) Tech. U., 1998; adj. prof. U. Wyo., 2000—; Allday lectr. U. Tex., Austin, 2002; Disting. Alumni lectr. UCLA, 2004. Author: Tectonics of the Indonesian Region, 1979, others, monographs; contbr. articles to profl. jours.; assoc. editor: Geology, 1973—82, Jour. Geophys. Rsch., 1974—76. With USN, 1943—46. Recipient Disting. Svc. award, U.S. Dept. Interior, 1981. Fellow: Geol. Assn. Can., Geol. Soc. Am. (chmn. Cordilleran sect. 1987—88, councilor 1995—98, Penrose medal 1989, Structural Geology and Tectonics Career Achievement award 2007), Geol. Soc. London (hon.); mem.: NAS, Am. Geophys. Union, Colo. Sci. Soc. (hon.). Office: Colo Sch of Mines Dept of Geophysics Golden CO 80401 Business E-Mail: whamilto@mines.edu.

HAMILTON, WILLIAM BERRY, JR., retired transportation executive; b. Birmingham, Ala., Apr. 4, 1929; s. William Berry and Nettie (Whatley) H.; m. Jean Lucile Patteson, Feb. 1, 1951; children: Jean Lucile, Ann Elizabeth, William Berry III. BA, Vanderbilt U., 1951. Accountant Hiwassee Constructors, Chattanooga, 1952; cert. pub. acct. O.E. Johnson & Assocs., Chattanooga, 1952-54; controller, gen. mgr. Spl. Products Co., Inc., Chattanooga, 1954-59; v.p., controller Ryder Truck Lines, Inc., Jacksonville, Fla., 1959-65; v.p. finance Chgo. Rawhide Mfg. Co., 1965-67; v.p., controller-treas. Sea-Land Service Inc., Elizabeth, NJ, 1967-69, exec. v.p. adminstrn., dir., 1969-75; v.p., treas., asst. sec. McLean Industries, Inc., Elizabeth, 1968-74; pres. Monterey Transp. Co., Inc. (subs. R.J. Reynolds Industries, Inc.), Winston-Salem, NC, 1975-77; pres., dir. Security-First Corp., Jacksonville, Fla., 1977-82; chmn. bd., pres. St. John's Marine Fin. Co. Inc., 1979-95; chmn., chief exec. officer Port of Monmouth Devel. Corp., 1983-87; dir., mem. exec. com. J.J. Henry Co., Inc., NYC, 1981-85; ret. Chmn. bd. Henry Laurel Co. Inc., 1983-87; dir. Henry Properties Ltd., L.I. Devel. Co. Ltd.; instr. acctg. U. Chattanooga, 1953-54 Served with USAF, 1951-52. Recipient Guest Lectr. award U. Fla., 1965 Mem. Am. Bur. Shipping, Soc. Naval Architects and Marine Engrs., Am. Inst. C.P.A.s, Financial Execs. Inst., Am. Trucking Assn. (nat. bd. dirs., chmn. methods and procedures nat. accounting and finance council, 1959-65), Nat. Def. Transp. Assn., Nat. Assn. Accountants (named most valuable mem. Jacksonville 1959-60, chpt. v.p., bd. dirs. 1960-63), Tenn. Soc. C.P.A.s, Am. Accounting Assn., Nat. Officer Mgmt. Assn., Am. Mgmt. Assn., U.S. Power Squadron, USCG Aux., Propeller Club of U.S., Navy League, Phi Delta Theta, Pi Delta Epsilon. Episcopalian (vestryman). Clubs: Fla. Yacht, River (Jacksonville); Ponte Vedra, Sawgrass (Ponte Vedra Beach, Fla.); Sea Bright (N.J.) Beach; N.Y. Yacht, World Trade Center, Vanderbilt Alumni, Whitehall (N.Y.C.); Twin-City (Winston-Salem); Cat Cay (Bahamas). Lodge: Kiwanis. Home: 695B Ponte Vedra Blvd # 103 Ponte Vedra Beach FL 32082-2783 E-mail: bhamijr@bellsouth.net.

HAMILTON, WILLIAM F., lawyer; s. Donald Harris and Shirley Lennon Hamilton; m. Cynthia Louise Tejcek, May 16, 2003; children: Eric Michael, Kristopher Patrick, Michelle Francis. BA with honors, Lehigh U., 1970; MA, Washington U., 1975; JD with honors, U. Fla., 1983. Bar: Fla. 1983, US Dist. Ct. (so. dist.) Fla. 1983, US Dist. Ct. (mid. dist.) Fla. 1987, US Ct. Appeals (11th cir.) 1984, US Ct. Appeals (9th cir.) 1997, US Supreme Ct. 2004. Assoc. Holland & Knight LLP, Tampa, 1983—89, Miami, 1983—89, ptnr. Tampa, 1989—. Presenter and spkr. in field; mem. nat. panel arbitrators and mediators Am. Arbitration Assn.; mem. Assn. Conflict Resolution. Editor: So. Dist. Digest, 1984—85; co-author: Florida Manual of Trademark Examining Procedure, 1986; contbr. articles to to profl jours. Pres. Performing Arts Cmty. and Edn. Inc., Miami, 1984—89, dir., 1984—89. Master: Am. Inns Ct. Tampa Bay Chpt.; fellow: Fla. Bar Found.; mem.: ABA (mem. intellectual property, lit., and antitrust sections, mem. standing com. tech. and info. svcs.), Assn. Conflict Resolution, Am. Arbitration Assn. (mem. nat. panel arbitrators & mediators), Hillsborough County Bar Assn., Intellectual Property Soc. (bd. dirs. U. Fla. Holland Law Ctr.), Internat. Trademark Assn. (mem. pub. info. com. brand names edn. found.), Dade County Bar Assn., Fla. Bar Corp. (mem. banking and bus. section, mem. commerical litig. com., patent, trademark & copyright com.). Home: 15233 Merlington Pl Lithia FL 33547 Office: Holland & Knight LLP 100 N Tampa St Ste 4100 Tampa FL 33602 Office Phone: 813-227-6480. Office Fax: 813-229-0134. Business E-Mail: william.hamilton@hklaw.com.

HAMILTON JACKSON, MARILYN J., dancer, educator, choreographer; d. Albert Arthur Jr. and Gwendolyn Aenid Atkinson; m. Kenneth D. Hamilton (div.); 1 child, Kalik Damione Hamilton. BA, CUNY, 1973; MA, Columbia U., 1984. Dance tchr. ElmCor Youth and Adult Activities, Inc., East Elmhurst, NY, 1975—76; dance dir. Langston Hughes Libr., Corona, NY, 1976—82; tchr. Harbor Sch. (now Tito Puente Performing Acad.), NYC, 1977—, asst. dir., 1982—83; owner, dir. Encore! Dance Sch., Corona, 1982—92. Mentor Joyce Theater Dance Edn. Program, NYC, 1998—; mem. Sammy Davis Jr. Internat. Tour, 1968—69. Dancer Alvin Ailey II Dance Co., 1972, (Broadway plays) Raisin, 1973—76, Seesaw, 1973, Images Performing Ensemble, 1980—82; TV appearances: Hollywood Palace; Jerry Lewis Telethon. Named Tchr. of Yr., Harbor Sch. Performing Arts, 1998—99; recipient cmty. svc. award, ElmCor Youth and Adult Activities, Inc., 1987, cert. of appreciation, Langston Hughes Cmty. Libr., 1992, proclamation, Office of Mayor Dinkins, NYC, 1992, Recognition and Appreciation cert., Assn. Black Educators, 2002, Excellence in Tchg. award, Union Settlement Assn., 2004; Am. history fellow, NY State Dept. Edn., 2001—02. Avocations: reading, Scrabble, travel, crocheting. Office: Tito Puente Performing Acad 240 E 109th St New York NY 10029

HAMILTON-KEMP, THOMAS ROGERS, organic chemist, educator; b. Lebanon, Ky., May 13, 1942; s. Thomas Rogers and Catherine Rose (Hamilton) K.; m. Lois Ann Groce, Sept. 13, 1980. *Revolutionary War participant Thomas Hamilton and his wife Ann Hodgkin (maternal ancestors) were among the first Catholic settlers in Kentucky (Washington County) in 1798. Prior to migration, the Hamilton family lived among the Catholic colonists in Southern Maryland (Charles County) for more than 100 years following departure from Scotland in the late 17th century.* AA, St. Catharine Coll., 1962; BA, U. Ky., 1964, PhD in Chemistry, 1970. Asst. prof. natural products chemistry U. Ky., Lexington, 1970-75, assoc. prof., 1975-85, prof., 1985—2005, prof. emeritus, 2005—. Contbr. articles to profl. jours. Mem. SAR, Am. Chem. Soc., Am. Soc. Hort. Sci., Sigma Xi, Gamma Sigma Delta Democrat. Roman Catholic. Home: 2025 Williamsburg Rd Lexington KY 40504-3015 Office: U Ky Agrl Sci Ctr N Rm N308 Lexington KY 40546-0001 E-mail: tkemp@uky.edu.

HAMIT, FRANCIS GRANGER, novelist, playwright; b. NYC, Oct. 6, 1944; s. Harold Francis and Ethel Cordelia (Granger) H.; m. Doris Elaine Pratt Kaesser, May 31, 1974 (div. Mar. 1978). B of Gen. Studies, U. Iowa, 1972, MFA in English, 1976. Freelance writer, Iowa City, Chgo., L.A., 1975—; area capt. RRS Security, Ill., 1977; assoc. editor Video Action Mag., Chgo., 1982; v.p. sales and mktg. EPIC Pvt. Security, West Covina, Calif., 1989-90; prin., owner Francis Hamit Electronic Publishing, 2004—. Author: Virtual Reality and the Exploration of Cyberspace, 1993, Sunday in the Park with George, 2005, The Shenandoah Spy, 2006; author: (dir.)

Marlowe: An Elizabethan Tragedy, 1988; author: (plays) Memorial Day, 2005; contbg. editor: Security Technology and Design Mag., 1993—2000, Advanced Imaging Mag., 1994—2001, contbg. writer: 15th edit. Ency. Britannica, 1981—82. With U.S. Army, 1967-71, Vietnam, Germany. Mem.: Assn. Former Intelligence Officers, Nat. Mil. Intelligence Assn. Democrat. Buddhist.

HAMLEN, KEVIN WILLIAM, computer scientist, educator; b. Buffalo, June 2, 1976; s. William Arthur and Susan Margaret Hamlen; m. Rebecca Anne Geiger, July 1, 2006. BS, Carnegie Mellon U., Pitts., 1998; MS, Cornell U., Ithaca, NY, 2002, PhD, 2006. Rschr. Cornell U., Computer Sci. Dept., 1998—2006; asst. prof. computer sci. U. Tex., Dallas, 2006—. Tech. cons. Microsoft Rsch., Redmond, Wash., 2001—01. Leader Bible study, pianist Cornell Grad. Christian Fellowship, Ithaca, 1998—2006. Fellow, Lockheed Martin, 1998—99; scholar, Carnegie Mellon U., 1994—98. Mem.: Phi Beta Kappa, Phi Kappa Phi. Evangelical. Achievements include invention of certified program-rewriting as a means of enforcing computer security.

HAMLETT, CURT, music educator, director; b. Henderson, Tenn., July 23, 1949; s. Lee Martin; m. Janet Susan Trevathan, Mar. 22, 1975; children: Jennifer, Chris. BS in Music Edn., U. Tenn., Martin, 1971; student, Westminster Choir Coll., Princeton, NJ, 1970, student, 1972; MusM in Conducting, U. So. Miss., Hattiesburg, 1981, PhD in Music Edn., 1983. Choral dir. Haywood County HS, Brownsville, Tenn., 1971—80; grad. tchg. asst. U. So. Miss., Hattiesburg, 1980—83; choral dir., instr. voice Laredo CC, Laredo, 1983—85; dir. choral activities Howard Payne U., Brownwood, Tex., 1985—88; prof. music, dir. choral activities La. Coll., Pineville, 1988—. Min. music 1st United Meth. Ch., Pineville, La., 1990—93, dir. music ministries, 1999—, min. music Alexandria, La., 1998—99. Mem.: Internat. Fedn. Choral Music, Am. Choral Dirs. Assn. (state chair choral music in ch. stds. and repertoire 1990—2007). Republican. Methodist. Home: 125 Spring Creek Dr Pineville LA 71360 Office: Louisiana Coll College Station Box 604 Pineville LA 71359 Home Phone: 318-640-2910; Office Phone: 318-487-7450. Office Fax: 318-487-7336. Business E-Mail: hamlett@lacollege.edu.

HAMLIN, DAN WILLIAM, accountant, management consultant; b. Macon, Ga., Oct. 4, 1947; s. Dan William Hamlin and Lillian (Beasley) Moran; m. Sally Johns, June 20, 1970; 1 child, Gwendolyn Breese. AA, Indian River Community Coll., Ft. Pierce, Fla., 1967; BA, U. South Fla., 1969; MS, Johns Hopkins U., 1976. Cert. govt. fin. mgr. Pers. specialist City of Tampa, Fla., 1967-69; mgr. cost analysis U. South Fla., Tampa, 1969-72; asst. contr. Johns Hopkins U., Balt., 1972-76; exec. dir. fin. ops. U. So. Calif., LA, 1976-81; sr. mgr. KPMG Peat Marwick, Washington, 1981—83, ptnr., 1984—86, nat. practice dir., ptnr., 1987—2000; sr. v.p. N.Am., sales pub. sector KPMG Cons., 2000—04; v.p. edn. Bearing Point, Inc., 2004—05; pres. Higher Edn. Profl. Svcs., LLC, 2005—. Bd dirs. Milletec, Inc., chmn. strategic planning com.; spkr. in field. Contbr. articles to profl. jours. Mem. Indian Bluff Island Civic Assn., Palm Harbor, 1984-95. Mem. Soc. Rsch. Adminstrs., Nat. Assn. Coll. and Univ. Bus. Officers, Coalition Higher Edn. Assistance Orgns., Skull and Dagger, Kappa Sigma, Iron Horse Golf and Country Club. Republican. Episcopalian. Personal E-mail: breeses@earthlink.net.

HAMLIN, DON AUER, retired military officer, financial health care executive; b. Klamath Falls, Oreg., Oct. 6, 1934; s. Don Fessler and Margaret May (Auer) H.; m. Karen Ruth Wagner; children by previous marriage: Michael, Kathryn, Stephen, Mary, Mark, John, Matthew. BBA, Loyola U. of South, New Orleans, 1955; grad., USAF Command and Staff Coll., 1967; MS in Bus. Adminstrn., George Washington U., 1968. Commd: 2d lt. U.S. Army, 1955, advanced through grades to lt. col., 1975, served with inf., ordnance, M.P. various locations, 1955-64, inf. comdr. and staff officer Alaska, Hawaii, Vietnam, 1964-68, cost analyst and dep. agy. comdr. Pentagon Gen. Staff Washington, 1968-72, inf. adviser Vietnam, 1972, comptr. Ft. Sam Houston, Tex., 1972-75, ret., 1975; comptr. Severance & Assocs., San Antonio, 1975-81; sec.-treas., dir. Severance Reference Lab., Inc., San Antonio, 1981-82; co-founder, pres. Engring. Cybernetics, Inc., San Antonio, 1982-85; dir. fin. Whittaker Health Svcs., Austin, Tex., 1985-86; v.p. fin. Metlife Healthcare Network, 1986-88, Harris Meth. Health Plan, Ft. Worth, 1989-91, sr. v.p., CEO; pres. Harris Meth. Health Ins. Co., Ft. Worth, 1991-94; CEO Heritage Southwest Med. Group, Irving, Tex., 1994-96. Treas. San Vincente Artists, Silver City, N.Mex., 1996—2000; trustee, bd. chmn. Gila Regional Med. Ctr., Grant County, N.Mex., 1998—; bd. dirs. Mimbres Region Arts Coun., Silver City, N.Mex., 1997—99, Copper Crest Country Club, 1999—2002, pvt. investor, 1983—; dir. Data Terminal Corp., San Antonio, 1981; pres. Balance Point Youth Ranch, San Antonio, 1980—81; bd. dirs. Wichita Falls Symphony Orch., 2007—. Pres. St. Pius X Bd. Edn., San Antonio, 1979; mem. Wichita County Heritage Soc., Kemp Ctr. for Arts, Wichita Falls, Wichita Falls, Mus. Arts. Decorated Legion of Merit with oak leaf cluster, Bronze Star with oak leaf cluster, Air medal with oak leaf cluster, Purple Heart with oak leaf cluster, 1955-75. Mem. San Antonio Med. Mgrs. Assn. (pres. 1982-84), Silver City C. of C. (named with spouse Silver City/Grant County Citizens of Yr. 2004). Home and Office: 2013 Hampstead Ln Wichita Falls TX 76308 Personal E-mail: donhamlin@sbcglobal.net.

HAMLIN, GEORGE L., writer; b. Des Moines, Aug. 25, 1939; s. George L Hamlin and Marian E Haven; m. Betsy A. Hamlin, June 9, 1962. BS, Iowa State U., 1961. Tech. writer Naval Ordnance Lab., White Oak, Md., 1962—69, sr. tech. writer, 1969—74, Naval Surface Weapons Ctr., White Oak, 1974—88, Naval Surface Warfare Ctr., White Oak, 1988—94, Advanced Tech. and Rsch., Burtonsville, Md., 1995—2001. Mem. stds. com. Soc Technical Comm., Washington, 1969—70; corp. planning group dir. Navy Labs., Washington, 1976—84; tech. manual stds. Naval Sea Sys. Command, Washington, 1982—89; mg.r White Oak Lab. Employees Assn., 1988—93. Co-author: (book) Packard: A History of the Motor Car and the Company, 1978 (Best History Book, 1979), Complete Handbook of Automobile Hobbies, 1981; editor (sr ed): The Packard Cormorant, 1975—; contbr. articles to profl jours. Police commr. Riverdale Police Dept., 1972—73; town councilman Riverdale Town Coun., Md., 1971—73; bd. dirs. Am.'s Packard Mus., Dayton, Ohio, 1996—97; trustee Packard Found., Detroit, 1998—2006. With US Army, 1963. Recipient Excellence in Newspaper Writing Award, William Randolph Hearst Found, 1960. Mem.: Profl Car Soc (founder, chpts chmn 1985—, Appreciation Award 1999), Soc Automotive Historians, Theodore Roosevelt High Sch Found, Studebaker Drivers Club (regional mgr 1966—), Antique Automobile Club Am, Packard Automobile Classics Inc (trustee, v.p. internat. 1991—, Weiss Trophy 1999). Avocations: automobile restoration, Pepsi collectibles. Office: PO Box 123 Fulton MD 20759-0123 Personal E-mail: geohamlin@isualum.com.

HAMLIN, HARRY ROBINSON, actor; b. Pasadena, Calif., Oct. 30, 1951; s. Chauncey Jerome and Bernice (Robinson) H.; c. 1 son, Dimitri Alexander (with Ursula Andress); m. Laura Johnson, 1985-89; m. Nicollette Sheridan, 1991-93; m. Lisa Rinna, Mar. 29, 1997; c. Delilah Belle and Amelia Gray BA, Yale U.; postgrad., Am. Conservatory Theatre, San Francisco. Performances include: (films) Movie Movie, 1979, Clash of The Titans, 1981, King of the Mountain, 1981, Making Love, 1982, Blue Skies Again, 1983, Maxie, 1985, Dinner At Eight, 1990, The Celluloid Closet, 1995, Badge of Betrayal, 1996; (TV mini-series) Studs Lonigan, Master of the Game, 1984, Space, 1985, Favorite Son, 1988, Night Sins, 1997, Strange Hearts, 2001, Perfume, 2001, Shoot or Be Shot, 2002, Strang Wilderness, 2007; (TV films) Laguna Heat, 1987, Deceptions, 1990, Deadly Intentions.Again?, 1991, Deliver Them From Evil: The Taking of Alta View, 1991, Save Me, 1992, Under Investigation, 1993, Poisoned by Love: The Kern County Murders, 1993, In the Best of Families: Marriage, Pride and Madness, 1994, Tom Clancy's Op Center, 1995, Her Deadly Rival, 1995, One Clean Move, 1996, Badge of Betrayal, 1996, Allie & Me, 1997, Night Sins, 1997, Stranger in Town, 1998, Frogs for Snakes, 1998, The Hunted, 1998, Like Father, Like Santa, 1998, Quarantine, 1999, Silent Predators, 1999; (TV series) L.A. Law, 1986-91, Movie Stars, 1999, Veronica Mars, 2004-06, Dancing with the Stars, 2006; (Broadway debut) Awake and Sing!, 1984, Chicago, 2007. ITT Fulbright grantee, 1977; Named Sexiest Man Alive People mag., 1987. Office: care Larry Taub Gersh Agency Inc 232 N Canon Dr Beverly Hills CA 90210-5302*

HAMLIN, ROBERT HENRY, public health service officer, educator, management consultant; b. Cambridge, Mass., Apr. 2, 1923; s. Howard E. and Margaret E. (Henry) H.; m. Beate Kraschewski, Dec. 16, 1960; 1 son, Andrew Werner. AB summa cum laude, Ohio State U., 1944; BSM., Northwestern Med. Sch., 1945, B.M., 1946, MD with honors, 1947; M.P.H. magna cum laude, Harvard, 1952, JD, 1953. Diplomate: Am. Bd. Preventive Medicine. Intern Johns Hopkins Hosp., Balt., 1946-47; cons. Mass. commn. reporting, preparing and promulgating legislation on pub. and mental health and pub. welfare, 1950-53; 1st asst. to commnr. pub. health Mass., 1952-53; asst. prof. legal medicine Harvard Law Sch., 1952-57; lectr. pub. health law and adminstrn. Harvard Sch. Pub. Health, 1952-57, asso. prof. pub. health adminstrn., 1959-62, Roger Irving Lee prof. pub. health, 1962-65, chmn. dept. pub. health practice, 1963-65; v.p. Booz, Allen and Hamilton (mgmt. cons.), 1965-67; ind. mgmt. cons., 1968; chmn. bd. MACRO Systems, Inc. (mgmt. cons.), Washington, 1969-80; clin. prof. dept. comprehensive medicine Coll. Medicine, U. South Fla., 1980-83; acting dir., prof. pub. health program Coll. Pub. Health, U. South Fla., 1983; pres. United Health Techs., Inc. (mgmt. cons.), 1981—. Adj. prof. health adminstrn. Columbia U. Sch. Public Health and Adminstrv. Medicine, 1972-80; cons. Rockefeller Found., 1959-61; staff dir. spcl. commn. Harvard health services, 1953-54; mem. U.S. Commn. for UNESCO, 1958-60; dir. pub. health, Brookline, Mass., 1953-57; cons. Hoover Commn. II, 1954-55; asst. to sec. health, edn. and welfare, 1957-59; vis. lectr. pub. health adminstrn. and law Harvard, 1957-59 Contbr. articles profl. publs. U.S. del. 10th session gen. conf. UNESCO, Paris, 1958, pub. health adminstrn. cons. to pvt. orgns., state and local govts. Served as apprentice seaman USN, 1943-46; lt. (j.g.) M.C. USNR, 1947-49. Fellow Am. Pub. Health Assn.; mem. Mass. Med. Soc., Phi Beta Kappa, Phi Eta Sigma, Alpha Epsilon Delta, Alpha Omega Alpha, Delta Omega. Office: United Health Techs 13300 Indian Rocks Rd-1904 Largo FL 33774-2010 Office Phone: 727-596-8178. Fax: 727-595-5581.

HAMLIN, SONYA B., communications specialist; b. NYC; d. Julius and Sarah (Saltzman) Borenstein; m. Bruce Hamlin (dec. 1977); children: Ross, Mark (dec. 1992), David. BS, MA, NYU; HLD (hon.), Notre Dame Coll., 1970. Host arts program Sta. WHDH-TV, Boston, 1963-65; host, prodr., writer (syndicated PBS program) Meet the Arts Sta. WGBH-TV, Boston, 1965-68; cultural reporter Sta. WBZ-TV, Boston, 1968-71, TV host, producer The Sonya Hamlin Show, 1970-75; host, producer Sunday Open House program Sta. WCVB-TV, Boston, 1976—81; host, producer, writer Speak Up and Listen program Lifetime Cable Network, NYC, 1982-84; pres. Sonya Hamlin Communications, Boston and NYC, 1977—, Different Drummer Prodns., NYC, 1982-86. Pvt. comm. cons., U.S., Can., and Europe, 1977—; adj. lectr. Harvard Grad. Sch., Edn., Cambridge, Mass., 1974-76, Harvard Law Sch., 1977-81, Kennedy Sch. Govt., Harvard U., 1978-79; adj. asst. prof. Boston U. Med. Sch., 1977-80; mem. faculty Nat. Inst. Trial Advocacy, South Bend, Ind., 1977—, U.S. Dept. Justice, Washington, 1979-87, ABA, Chgo., 1979—; chmn. Law/Video Co., N.Y.C. and Waltham, Mass., 1987-92; comm. cons., weekly and weekend performer Today in NY (NBC), 1995-98; daily panelist O.J. Today (Fox), 1995-96. Author: What Makes Juries Listen, 1982, How to Talk So People Listen, 1988, What Makes Juries Listen Today, 1998, How to Talk So People Listen: Connecting in Today's Workplace, 2006, Now What Makes Juries Listen, 2007; prodr., dir., writer (films) China" Different Path, 1979 (Emmy nominee), Paul Revere: What Makes a Hero, 1976, others; contbr. articles to numerous profl. jours. Mem. Gov. Commn. Status Women, Mass., 1973-83; campaign co-chair Mass. ERA Campaign, 1975-76; cons. Gov. Michael Dukakis, 1978, Dem. Nat. Party, Washington, 1979; bd. dirs. mem. Nat. Vol. Action com. United Way, Washington, 1986-91; bd. dirs. Taubman Ctr. Kennedy Sch. Harvard U., 1989-95; mem. adv. bd. Martha Graham Dance Co., 1997—; bd. overseers Shakespeare & Co., 2003—; mem. Women's Leadership Bd., Kennedy Sch. Govt., Harvard U., 1999-2002. Recipient Best Program award for Meet the Arts Internat. Ednl. TV Assn., Tokyo, 1969, Ohio State Cultural Reporting award, 1970; named Outstanding Broadcaster New Eng. Broadcasters, Boston, 1973; Sonya Hamlin Day named in her honor Mayor of Boston, 1974.; archive of her works established Boston U. Library, 1983. Mem.: NATAS (two Emmy nominations), Internat. Women's Forum, Am. Fedn. TV and Radio Artists. Avocations: skiing, tennis, piano, dance, museums. Home Phone: 212-333-3252. Business E-Mail: sonyaham@aol.com.

HAMLISCH, MARVIN, composer, conductor, musician, entertainer; b. NYC, June 2, 1944; s. Max and Lilly (Schachter) Hamlisch; m. Terre Blair, 1989. Grad., Juilliard Sch. Music, 1951—64; BA, Queens Coll., 1967. Prin. Pops condr. Pitts. Symphony, 1994—, Balt. Symphony Orch., 1996—2000, Nat. Symphony Orch., Washington, 2000—. Rehearsal pianist Broadway shows including Funny Girl, Fade Out-Fade In, (TV series) Bell Telephone Hour, early 1960's; composer: (films) The Swimmer, 1968, Take the Money and Run, 1969, Bananas, 1971, Save the Tiger, 1973, Kotch, 1971, The Way We Were, 1974 (Academy Award for best original dramatic score and best title song, 1974), The Sting, 1974 (Academy Award for arranging and playing, 1974), Same Time Next Year, 1979, Ice Castles, 1979, Chapter Two, 1979, Starting Over, 1979, Ordinary People, 1980, Three Men and a Baby, 1987, Sophie's Choice, 1982, Frankie and Johnny, 1991, Switched at Birth, 1991, Seasons of the Heart, 1994, Open Season, 1996, The Mirror Has Two Faces, 1996, (popular songs include) Sunshine, Lollipops and Rainbows, 1960, Nobody Does It Better, 1977, (Broadway Musicals) Minnie's Boys, 1970, Seesaw, 1973, A Chorus Line, 1975 (Pulitzer Prize, Tony award for best musical score, 1976), They're Playing Our Song, 1979, Jean, 1983, Smile, 1986, The Goodbye Girl, 1993, Sweet Smell of Success, 2002, Imaginary Friends, 2002, theme song for Good Morning America, 1975, symphonic work in one movement "Anatomy of Peace" (performed by Dallas Symphony Orch., London Symphony Orch., Symphony for UN at Carnegie Hall), 1991; composer: (lyrics by Alan and Marilyn Bergman) One Song (internat. debut at Barcelona Olympics), 1992; author: The Way I Was, 1992; musical dir. Barbra Streisand: The Concert (Emmy awards for outstanding music direction & achievement in music and lyrics, 1994), Am. Film Inst.'s 100 Years.100 Movies, 1999 (Emmy award for outstanding music and lyrics, 1999), Timeless: Live in Concert, 2001 (Emmy award for outstanding music direction, 2001). Recipient three Oscar awards, four Grammy awards, four Emmy awards, a Tony award and three Golden Globe awards. Office: Nat Symphony Orch 2700 F St NW Washington DC 20566 also: Pitts Symphony Heinz Hall 600 Penn Ave Pittsburgh PA 15222-3259*

HAMM, DAVID BERNARD, lawyer; b. Bklyn., Oct. 6, 1948; s. Isidore I. and Sarah (Lamm) H.; m. Margaret Weiss, June 20, 1971; children: Jennifer A. Maltz, Michael S. BA cum laude, CUNY, Bklyn., 1971; JD magna cum laude, N.Y. Law Sch., 1977. Bar: N.Y. 1978, U.S. Dist. Ct. (no. dist.) N.Y. 1978, U.S. Dist. Ct. (so. and ea. dists.) N.Y. 1979, U.S. Supreme Ct. 1981, U.S. Ct. Appeals (2d cir.) 1982, (3d cir.) 1988. Law clk. to presiding judges N.Y. State Ct. Appeals, Albany, 1977-79; assoc. Herzfeld & Rubin P.C., NYC, 1979-85, mem., 1986—. Mem. Commn. Legis. and Civic Action Agudath Israel of Am., N.Y.C., 1979—. Recipient Cmty. Svc. award Agudath Israel of Am., 1986. Mem. ABA, N.Y. State Bar Assn. (com. civil practice law and rules), N.Y. County Lawyers Assn., Jewish Lawyers Guild, N.Y. Law Sch. Alumni Assn. (Prof. Vincent LoLordo award 1977). Democrat. Home: 2015 E 22nd St Brooklyn NY 11229-3615 Office: Herzfeld & Rubin PC 40 Wall St 53d Fl New York NY 10005-2301 Home Phone: 718-336-7083; Office Phone: 212-471-8542. Office Fax: 212-344-3333. Business E-Mail: dhamm@herzfeld-rubin.com.

HAMM, MIA (MARIEL MARGARET HAMM), retired professional soccer player; b. Selma, Ala., Mar. 17, 1972; m. Christian Corry, 1994 (div. 2001); m. Nomar Garciaparra, Nov. 22, 2003; 2 children. BS in Polit. Sci., U. NC, 1994. Forward U.S. Women's Nat. Soccer Team, 1987—2004; profl. soccer player Washington Freedom, 2001—03. Mem. US Women's Soccer Team, Athens Olympic Games, 2004. Author: Go for the Goal: A Champions Guide to Winning in Soccer and Life, 1999. Founder Mia Found., 1999. Named US Soccer Female Athlete of Yr., 1994—98, MVP, US Women's Cup, 1995, Best Female Athlete of Yr., ESPY, 1998, 2000, Women's World Player of Yr., FIFA, 2001, 2002; named to Pele's 100 greatest living soccer players list, U.S. Nat. Soccer Hall of Fame, 2007; recipient Soccer Player of Yr. Award, ESPY, 2000, 2001, Best Female Soccer Player, 2004. Achievements include being a member of U. NC NCAA National Championship teams, 1989-93; having number retired, U. NC, 1994; being a member of US Women's Soccer Gold Medal Team, Atlanta Olympics, 1996, Athens Olympic games, 2004; being a member of US Women's Soccer World Cup Championship Team, 1999; being a member of US Women's Soccer Silver Medal Team, Sydney Olympics, 2000; being the all-time leading international goal scorer for men and women. Office: US Soccer Fedn US Soccer House 1801 S Prairie Ave Chicago IL 60616-1319

HAMM, PAUL, Olympic athlete; b. Washburn, Wis., Sept. 24, 1984; s. Sandy and Cecily Hamm. Student, Ohio State U. Mem. U.S. Sr. Nat. Gymnastics team, 2000—, U.S. Gymnastics Team, Sydney Olympics, 2000, U.S. Gymnastics Team, Athens Olympics, 2004. Named Gymnast of the Year, Internat. Gymnastics Federation, 2003. With twin brother Morgan, became first set of twins ever to compete in same Olympic games gymnastics competition, Sydney, 2000; First U.S. male in history to win a World All-Around championship, 2003; Silver medal U.S. Team, World Championships, 2001, 2003, two Gold medals all-around & floor exercise, World Championships, 2003, 1st prize pommel horse, vault, U.S. Nat. Championships, 2002, 1st prize all-around competition, U.S. Nat. Championships, 2002, 2003, 2004, Silver medal, U.S. Gymnastics Team, Men's High Bar, Athens Olympics, 2004, Gold medal, All-around, Athens Olympic games, 2004. Address: 2747 Marblevista Blvd Columbus OH 43204

HAMMAD, ALAM E., international business consultant, educator; b. Cairo, 1943; 1 child, Adam. BA in Commerce, Cairo Poly. Inst., 1965; MS in Mktg., La. State U., 1971; D of Bus. Adminstrn., George Washington U., 1977. Advisor Min. State & Gov. of Dhofar, Oman, 1977-79; advisor Min. Petroleum and Minerals, Oman, 1979; advisor to min., head planning Min. Agr. and Fisheries, Oman, 1979-83; chmn. MicroAge Computers Corp., Va., 1984-86; prof., lectr. George Washington U., Washington, 1984-88; internat. cons., 1984—; pres., founder Pizza Club, Inc., Va., 1987-97; class A contractor, 1987—. Mem. found. com. Sultan Qaboos U., 1981-86; pres. Info. Security Found., 1991-93; vis. prof. George Washington U., 1988-90; chmn. found. com. Oman Nat. Fisheries Co., 1980-81, Oman Bank Agr. and Fishing, 1981-82; bd. dirs. Oman Sun Farms Co., 1979, Oman Devel. Bank, 1979-83; founder Am. Global Pub., 1992—; pub. policy expert Heritage Found., 1996—; writer Okaz Saudi Newspaper, 1996-97, Gulf News, 1992-93; sr. assoc. Ctr. Strategic and Internat. Studies, 1997-2001; gov. conf. asst., 1998-2001; advisor GLG Policy and Econ. Coun., 2005. Author: Development of Agriculture and Fisheries in Oman, 1981, Agriculture, Animal Wealth, Water Resources and Fisheries of Oman, 1987, Islamic Banking: Theory and Practice, 1989, Encyclopedia of Computer Terms, English-Arabic, 1994, Dictionary of Computer Terms, English-Arabic, 1994; editor Newsweek in Arabic, 2000, Encyclopedia of Computer and Internet Terms, English-Arabic, 2007; contbr. articles to profl. jours., radio, TV shows. Chmn. pub. affairs, exec. vice chmn., 1st vice chmn. Alexandria Rep. City Com.; pres. Nat. Arab-Am. Rep. Coun., 1994; mem. George Washington Dist. Com., Boy Scouts Am.; trustee George Mason U., 1994-98, vice rector, 1996-98; commr. Alexandria Indsl. Devel. Authority, 1996-98; mem. Nat. Policy Coun., Heritage Found., No. Va. Rep. Bus. Forum, Com. for a Safe Va., Campaign for Honest Change, Empower Am., Bachelor 95 & Master Commr. Sci. 97 U. Scouting; chmn. advancement Rep. Party Va., 1994-96; mem. Rep. Presdl. Task Force; nat. advisor New Majority Coun., 1997; mem. Alexandria Citizen Police Acad., 1997, pres. Alexandria Citizen's Police Acad. Assn., 1998, Comm. VA Coun., 2000; maj. gen. mil. Aide-de-Camp to Va. Gov., 2001; vol. Bush-Cheney Transp. Com., 2001, Presdl. Inaugural Com., 2001; grad. FBI Citizens Acad., 2002; mem. Rep. Nat. Com., Nat. Rep. Senatorial Com., 2002; sec., bd. dirs. Alexandria Police Found., 2002-. Decorated Order of Sultan Qaboos (Oman); recipient Alexandria Chief of Police award, 2000, Outstanding Cmty. Svc. award Am. Indian Exch., 1994, Recognition honor Immigrant Ams.-Orgn. Chinese Am., 1996, Scroll of Achievements George Mason U., 1998, Outstanding Svc. award, 1998, Outstanding Svc. award VA Prof. Occupl. Reg. Bd., 1999, Appreciation cert. VA DPOR, 2001, Patrick Henry award, 2001. Mem. Am. Coun. Trustees and Alumni, Beta Gamma Sigma. Home: 819 S Fairfax St Alexandria VA 22314-4311 Personal E-mail: alamehammad@aol.com.

HAMMAM, M. SHAWKY, electrical engineer, educator; b. Aug. 5, 1919; BSc, U. London, Eng., 1943, PhD, 1946. Registered profl. engr., N.Y. Sr. lectr. Alexandria U., Egypt, 1948-55; assoc. prof. Ein Shamus U., Egypt, 1955-63; vis assoc. prof. U. Kans., 1963-64; prof. Clarkson U., Potsdam, N.Y., 1964—. Niagara Mowhawk Power prof. Clarkson U., 1965. Fellow IEEE; mem. Inst. Elec. Engrs. (U.K.), Inst. Physics. E-mail: dmshammam@aol.com.

HAMMANN, GREGG C., fitness equipment executive; b. Ft. Madison, Iowa, Mar. 3, 1963; s. Clifford Carl and Nancy Ann (Schruers) H.; m. Carol Craddock, June 20, 1987;children: Derek Henry, Grant Campbell. BBA, U. Iowa, 1985; MBA, U. Wis., 1997. Sales rep., unit mgr., then oral care brand project mgr. Procter & Gamble, Cin., 1985-91; dir. trade mktg. Rayovac Corp., Madison, 1991-92, pres., gen. mgr. of Can. Toronto, Ont., Can., 1992-94; v.p. mktg. and strategic planning, Famous Footwear, Madison, 1994-96; dir. strategic issues The Coca-Cola Co., Atlanta, 1996, v.p. fountain products divsn., 1997, v.p. nat. chain accounts, 1999; group v.p. bus. devel. McLeodUSA, 2000; sr. v.p., chief customer officer Levi Strauss & Co., 2001—03; pres, CEO The Nautilus Group Inc., 2003—. Active Big Bros./Big Sisters, 1995—, Give Kids the World, 1997—; bd. dirs. Edn. Found., Chgo., 1997—. Avocations: hiking, biking, tennis, golf, running.

HAMMAR, LESTER EVERETT, retired manufacturing executive; b. Tillamook, Oreg., Dec. 15, 1927; s. Leo E. and Harriet L. (Parsons) H.; m. Margrit Steigl, May 9, 1964; children: Lawrence, Thomas, Stephanie. BS, Oreg. State U., 1950; MBA, Washington U., 1964. With Montsanto Co., 1952-69; controller Monsanto-Europe, 1966-69; v.p., controller Smith Kline & French Labs., Phila., 1969-72, Abbott Labs., North Chgo., Ill., 1972-88; ret., 1988. Bd. trustees Asia House Investments; project mgr. Exec. Svc. Corp. Chgo. Mem. audit com. City of Lake Forest; ruling elder, clk. of session 1st Presbyn. Ch. of Lake Forest; bd. dirs. Haven, Clara Abbott Fund; bd. dirs. Teton County Housing Authority; dir., treas. Lake Forest/Lake Bluff Sr. Citizens Found. 1st lt. F.A., AUS, 1951-52. Mem. Fin Execs. Inst., Am. Mgmt. Assn. (former chmn. fin. coun., bd. mem.), 100 Club of Lake Country Club. Home: 634 Academy Woods Dr Lake Forest IL 60045 Personal E-mail: leshammar@aol.com.

HAMMAR, SHERREL LEYTON, medical educator; b. Caldwell, Idaho, May 21, 1931; m. Shirley; children: Kathryn M., David Jefferson. BA, Coll. Idaho, 1953; MD, U. Wash., 1957. Intern Mpls. Gen. Hosp., 1957-58; resident U. Wash., Seattle, 1958-60; instr. dept. pediat. U. Wash. Sch. Medicine, Seattle, 1962-64, asst. prof. dept. pediat., 1964-69, assoc. prof. dept. pediat., 1969-71, U. Hawaii, Honolulu, 1971-73; prof. U. Hawaii Sch. Medicine, Honolulu, 1973—2001; interim dean John A. Burns Sch. Medicine U. Hawaii, Honolulu, 1996-99, emeritus prof., 2001—. Chief adolscent clinic U. Wash., 1964-65, acting dir. clin. tng. unit devel. & mental health ctr., 1964, asst., 1965-71, acting dir. clin. tng. unit child devel. and mental retardation ctr., 1970-71; dir. ambulatory pediatric svcs., chief adolescent medicine Kauikeolani Children's Hosp., Honolulu, 1971-72, dir. med. svcs. and tng., 1972-73, chief pediat., 1973—, dir. pediatric med. edn., 1979—; chmn. dept. pediat. U. Hawaii, 1973-97, residency program dir., 1973-97; cons. in field. Contbr. articles to profl. jours. Fellow U. Wash., 1960-62. Fellow APHA, Am. Acad. Pediat. (com. youth 1967-73, 75-81, sect. adolescent health, exec. coun. 1978-80, com. early childhood, adoption and dependent care 1990-92, task force on AIDS 1990-92); mem. AMA (med. sch. sect.), Western Soc. Pediatric Rsch., Hawaii Med. Assn. (pres. 2003-04), Ambulatory Pediatric Assn., Seattle Pediatric Soc., Honolulu County Med. Soc., Alpha Omega Alpha. Personal E-mail: lerram@aol.com.

HAMMEL, IRIANA SIMONA, geriatrician; b. Bucharest, Romania, Jan. 27, 1973; arrived in U.S., 1999; d. Alexandru and Liliana Carmen Curtifan; m. Jeffrey Lee Hammel, Aug. 21, 2004; 1 child, Alexandra Lynn; m. Gabriel Gavrilescu (div.). MD, Carol Davila U., Bucharest, 1997. Bd. cert. internal medicine Am. Bd. Internal Medicine, bd. cert. geriatrics Am. Bd. Internal Medicine. Internal medicine resident Westlake Hosp., Melrose Park, Ill., 1999—2002; geriatrics fellow Loyola U., Chgo., 2002—03; geriatrician, primary care physician Great Lakes Med. Clinics and Hillsdale Comty. Health Ctr. and Hillsdale Comty. Med. Care Facility and Litchfield Nursing Home, Hillsdale, Mich., 2003—06; clin. asst. prof. Mich. State U., 2005—; geriatrician, clin. asst. prof. Synergy Med. Edn. Alliance, Saginaw, Mich., 2006—. Med. dir. Litchfield Nursing Home, Mich., 2005—06, Hillsdale County Home Care Agy., 2005—06. Cons. physician St. Anthony's Free Clinic, Hillsdale, 2006. Mem.: AMA (Physician's Recognition award 2002, 2005), ACP, Mich. State Med. Soc., Am. Geriatrics Soc. Avocations: crafts, reading, travel, swimming. Office: Synergy Med Edn Alliance 1000 Houghton Ave Saginaw MI 48602 Personal E-mail: irianahammel@yahoo.com.

HAMMER, ALFRED EMIL, artist, educator; b. New Haven, Jan. 11, 1925; s. Forrester L. and Eugenie (Bauer-Enquist) H.; m. Marian Valle, Aug. 14, 1948; children: Alfred Emil, Paul Forrester, Eric Valdemar, Eugenie Bauer; m. Jeanne Baker, Dec. 18, 1966; children: Stephen Drake, Rosamond Swan. BFA, R.I. Sch. Design, 1950, Yale U., 1951, MFA, 1952. From instr. to assoc. prof. painting and drawing R.I. Sch. Design, Providence, 1952-69, chmn. grad. studies, 1958-60, dean students, 1960-61; dean Cleve. Inst. Art, 1969-74; dir., prof. Sch. Art, U. Man., Winnipeg, Can., 1974-82; dir. Pacific N.W. Coll. Art, Portland, Oreg., 1982-83; prof. Hartford Art Sch., U. Hartford, Conn., 1983-88, dean Conn., 1983-86; freelance artist, 1988—. Exhibited in group shows R.I. Ann. (1st prize award 1952), Providence Art Club Ann. (1st prize award 1953, 54, 55, 57), Newport Ann. (1st prize 1959), Boston Arts Festival, 1958, Shippee Gallery, N.Y.C., 1985, Joseloft Gallery U. Hartford, 1992, Conn. Watercolor Soc. (prize 1992, 97), New Britain Mus. Am. Art (1st prize for watercolor 1988); one-man shows include U. Maine, 1954, U. Man., 1980, Thomas Gallery, 1980, Melnyschenko Gallery, Winnipeg, 1981, Movie House Studio Gallery, Millerton, N.Y., 1992; represented in collections Agnes Gund, Jr. C. of C., Nat. Mus. Israel, R.I. Sch. Design Mus., Portland Art Mus., Conn. Bank and Trust Co., N.E. Savs., Hartford, Corp. Hdqrs. Otis Elevator Corp., Farmington, Conn., Bank of New Eng., Boston, Shawmut Bank, Hartford, Aenta Ins., Hartford, Govt. of Man., Gov.'s Coll. of Conn. Artists; represented in book Prize Winning Artists, 1960. Mem. Conn. Watercolor Soc., Lyme Art Assn. Home: 55 Bolton St Hartford CT 06114 E-mail: alfredhammer@sbcglobal.net.

HAMMER, BONNIE, broadcast executive; m. Dale Huesner. BA in Edn., Boston U., MA in Media and New Tech. With WGBH, Boston; dir. devel. Dave Bell Associates, LA; programming exec. Lifetime Television Network; v.p. current programs USA Networks, NYC; sr. v.p. Sci-Fi programming and USA org. productions NBC Universal, 1998—99; exec. v.p., gen. mgr. Sci-Fi Channel (subsidiary of USA Networks), 1999, pres. Universal City, Calif., 2001; pres. USA Network, Sci-Fi Channel NBC Universal, 2004—. Named one of 100 Most Powerful Women in Entertainment, Hollywood Reporter, 2006; recipient Lillian Gish award, Women in Film. Office: Sci-Fi Channel c/o Vivendi Universal 100 Universal City Plaza Universal City CA 91608-1002*

HAMMER, CHARLES F., retired chemistry professor; b. Fremont, Ohio, July 22, 1933; m. Lois Reel, 1957; 1 child, Laurence N. BA, Bowling Green State U., Ohio, 1955; PhD in Organic Chemistry, U. Minn., Mpls., 1959. NIHPD fellow NMR and x-ray crystallography of steroids Brandeis U., 1961—63; from asst. prof. to assoc. prof. Georgetown U., 1963—82, prof. chemistry, 1982-95, emeritus prof., 1995—. Vis. prof. dept. hydrocarbon Chem. Sch. Eng. Kyoto Nat. U., Japan, 1971-72; vis. scholar dept. chem. U. Calif., Berkeley, 1978, Nat. Inst. Diabetes, Digestive & Kidney Disease NIH, 1986, Inst. Chemistry, Ljubjana, Slovenia, 1993, Nanjing U., 1994; pres. governing coun. Acad. Tech. and the Classics Charter Sch. 7-12, Santa Fe County, 2000—; bd. dirs. Hoya N.Mex. Schs. Chemobile, Santa Fe, N.Mex. Founder ATC Found., 2002, bd. dirs., 2004—; bd. mem. Santa Fe CC Training Ctr. Corp., 2005—. Recipient Alan Berman Rsch. Publication award NRL, 1987. Mem. AAAS, Am. Chem. Soc. (ChemTec Writing Team 1970-72, Am. Chem. Soc. award for creative invention 1990), Am. Soc. Mass Spectrometry, Soc. Appl. Spectros, Am. Soc. Testing & Materials, Sigma Xi. Achievements include research in chemistry and mechanisms of nitrogen heterocyclics and steroids; bromination-dehydrobromination reactions; structure elucidation of natural products by instrumental methods; complete structure by 2D-nuclear magnetic resonance; isotope ratio kinetics by mass spectrometry; computer software applications to spectrometric analysis; synthesis of plant growth hormones and antitumor agents. Office: Hoya/NMex Schs Chemobile 2017 Calle Lejano Santa Fe NM 87501-8747 Business E-Mail: cfhammer@cybermesa.com.

HAMMER, DAVID LINDLEY, lawyer, writer, investor; b. Newton, Iowa, June 6, 1929; s. Neal Paul and Agnes Marilyn (Reece) H.; m. Audrey Lowe, June 20, 1953; children: Julie, Lisa, David. BA, Grinnell Coll., 1951; JD, U. Iowa, 1956. Bar: Iowa 1956, U.S. Dist. Ct. (no. dist.) Iowa 1959, U.S. Dist. Ct. (so. dist.) Iowa 1969, U.S. Ct. Appeals (8th cir.) 1996, U.S. Supreme Ct. 1977. Ptnr. Hammer Simon & Jensen, Dubuque, Iowa, Galena, Ill.; mem. grievance commn. Iowa Supreme Ct., 1973—85, mem. adv. rules com., 1986—92. Author: Poems from the Ledge, 1980, The Game is Afoot, 1983, For the Sake of the Game, 1986, To Play the Game, 1986, The 22nd Man, 1989, The Quest, 1993, My Dear Watson, 1994, The Before Breakfast Pipe, 1995, A Dangerous Game, 1997, The Vital Essence, 1999, A Talent for Murder, 2000, Yonder in the Gaslight, 2000, Straight Up with a Twist, 2001, A Deep Game, 2001, The Game is Underfoot, 2002, You Heard What Jesse Said, 2003, O College Fairest of Our Dreams, 2004, A Distinct Touch Watson, 2004, Heaven Will Protect the Working Girl, 2005, Cases of Identity, 2006. Bd. dirs. Linwood Cemetery Assn., 1973—, pres., 1983-84; bd. dirs. Dubuque Mus. Art, 1998-2001, hon. dir., 2001—; bd. dirs., past pres. Finley Hosp., hon. dir.; bd. dirs. Finley Found., 1988-95; past campaign chmn., past pres. United Way; past bd. dirs. Carnegie Stout Pub. Libr. With U.S. Army, 1951-53. Named to, Finley Hosp. Hall of Fame, 2004. Fellow Am. Coll. Trial Lawyers; mem. ABA, Young Lawyers Iowa (past pres.), Iowa Def. Counsel Assn. (pres. 1991-92, del. to Def. Rsch. Inst. 1992-93), Assn. Def. Trial Attys. (exec. coun. 1983-86, past chmn. Iowa chpt.), Iowa State Bar Assn. (past chmn. continuing legal edn. com.), Iowa Acad. Trial Lawyers, Dubuque County Bar Assn. (past pres.), Baker St. Irregulars. Republican. Congregationalist. Mailing: PO Box 1808 Dubuque IA 52004-1808 Office Phone: 563-583-4010.

HAMMER, DEBORAH MARIE, librarian, paralegal; b. Bronx, NY, Nov. 16, 1947; d. Ben and Helen (Lorenz) Halprin; m. Mark Stewart Hammer, May 30, 1976; 1 child, Joshua Robert. BA, CCNY, 1968; MLS, Rutgers U., 1969. Cert. libr. NY. Gen. asst. info. tel. ref. divsn. Queens Borough Pub. Libr., Jamaica, NY, 1969-71, gen. asst. popular libr., 1972-80, asst. div. head history, travel & biography, 1972-81, divsn. head history, travel & biography, 1981-92, div. mgr. social scis., 1992-98; fee conciliation coord., computer systems mgr. Nassau County Bar Assn., Mineola, NY, 1999—. Democrat. Avocations: reading, cooking, handcrafts, camping. Office: 15th and West Sts Mineola NY 11501 E-mail: halimer@juno.com.

HAMMER, JACOB MYER, physicist, consultant; b. NYC, Sept. 14, 1927; s. Joseph Israel Hammer and Miriam Silverman; m. Rose Kizner (div. 1975); children: Daniel, Jonathan, Miriam; m. Katrina Schuyler, July 10, 1982; 1 stepson, David Reisberg. BS in Engring. Physics, NYU, 1950, PhD in Physics, 1956; MS in Physics, U. Ill., 1951. Mem. tech. staff Bell Telephone Labs., Murray Hill, NJ, 1956-59, RCA Labs., Princeton, NJ, 1959-68, David Sarnoff Rsch. Ctr., Princeton, 1970-87, photonics cons., 1987—. Sr. visitor Cavendish Lab., Cambridge U., 1968-69. Co-author: Integrated Optics, 1975, Fiber & Integrated Optics, 1979; co-editor: Surface Emitting Semiconductor Lasers and Arrays, 1993; contbr. numerous articles to profl. jours.; patentee in field. With AUS, 1946-47. Fellow IEEE (life, assoc. editor Jour. Quantum Electronics, 1987-90); mem. Am. Phs. Soc., Optical Soc. Am. Office: 42 City Gate Ln Annapolis MD 21401-2736 Office Phone: 410-280-0351. E-mail: jakehammer@ieee.org.

HAMMER, JANE AMELIA ROSS, advocate; b. Charlotte, NC, Apr. 9, 1916; d. Otho Bescent and Lucy (Harris) Ross; m. Philip Gibbon Hammer, Aug. 27, 1937; children: Philip Jr., Thomas Ross, Michael Levering. AB, U. N.C., Chapel Hill, 1936; MA, U. N.C., 1937; postgrad., Radcliffe Coll., New Eng. Conservatory, Cambridge, Mass., 1938-39. Charter mem. N.C. Symphony, 1933-36; mem. faculty philosophy Spelman Coll., Atlanta, 1946-58. Bd dirs., PiPa Tag, Inc., Tarpon Springs, Fla., 1995—. Violinist Symphony String Quartet, N.C., 1933-36, Atlanta Symphony, 1947-52, Friday Morning Music Club Orch., Washington, 1975-82; author: Protector: A Life History of Richard Cromwell, 1997; editor: Logic for Living, Lectures of H.H. Williams, 1951; editor, pub.: Origin of Belief (H.H. Williams), 1972; contbr. articles to profl. jours. Dir. tng. programs Overseas Edn. Fund U.S. LWV, Washington, 1962-63, mem. registration and voting projects staff Edn. Fund LWV, 1964-65, dir. Inner City Project in 10 U.S. cities, 1965-67, mem. spl. projects com., 1970-75, advisor natural resources com. LWV of Fla., Palm Harbor, 1990-92, bd. dirs. LWV Atlanta and State of Ga., 1942-61, pres. LWV of North Pinellas County, Fla., 1989-90; appointed pub. rep. mem. com. for feasibility study of health of residents of Pinellas County, U.S. Dept. Energy and Fla. Dept. Health and Rehab. Svcs., 1991-94; co-chmn. OASIS Coalition for Integration of Pub. Schs., Atlanta, 1960-61; mem. bd. overseers Dag Hammerskjold Coll., Columbia, Md., 1968-71; pres. FMMC Music Club Inc., Washington, 1973-76, trustee found., Washington Internat. Competition, 1968-71; treas. H.W. Philos. Soc., Washington and Fla., 1975—; mem. Pres. Clinton's Nat. Steering Com., 1995-2000; mem. Nat. Women's Dem. Club; chmn.'s cir. Dem. Nat. Com., 2007. Recipient Good Housekeeping Mag. award for Citizenship in Action, OASIS, 1962, named 500 Environ. Achiever, Friends of UN Environ. Programme, 1987; fellow Kenan, Univ. N.C., 1937. Mem. Friday Morning Music Club (Washington), The Social List (Washington), Jefferson Soc. (leadership cir. 1996-2000), Cromwell Assn., Clan Ross Assn., Chi Omega. Presbyterian. Avocations: gardening, research, writing. Home: 10450 Lottsford Rd 4107 Mitchellville MD 20721-2734

HAMMER, JOYCE MAE, retired gifted and talented educator; b. Milw., May 21, 1933; d. George and Sara (Arne) Leviton; children: Deborah, Lori. BS, U. Ill., 1954; MA, Northwestern U., 1958, postgrad., 1974-78, Nat. Coll. Edn., Evanston, Ill., 1986-89, Aurora U., 1990—92, postgrad., 1995. Tchr. math. Fairview South Sch., Skokie, Ill., 1957-65, Arie Crown Sch., 1967-72, Fairview South Sch., Skokie, 1972-77, elem. tchr. gifted math. edn., coord. gifted edn., designer sch. gifted program, 1978—2007; ret., 2007. Tchr. Fairview South Sch., 2007—. Recipient Those Who Excel award; grantee. Mem. Nat. Coun. Tchrs. Math., Ill. Assn. Gifted Children, Phi Delta Kappa.

HAMMER, LINDA See LINDROTH, LINDA

HAMMER, SCOTT M., medical researcher, educator; BA, Columbia Coll., 1968; MD, Columbia U. Coll. Physicians & Surgeons, 1972. Resident internal medicine Stanford U., Presbyn. Hosp., chief med. resident; fellow infectious disease Mass. Gen. Hosp.; mem. faculty Deaconess Hosp., 1982, dir. Rsch. Virology Lab.; mem. faculty Harvard Med. Sch., 1982, assoc. prof. medicine; mem. faculty to Harold C. Neu prof. medicine, chief divsn. infectious diseases Columbia U. Coll. Physicians & Surgeons, NYC, 1999—; mem. faculty to prof. pub. health dept. epidemiology Columbia U. Mailman Sch. Pub. Health, NYC, 1999—. Adv. Swiss HIV Cohort Study, French Nat. Rsch. Agy. AIDS, HIV Netherlands-Australia-Thailand Rsch. Collaborative; investigator HIV Vaccine Trials Network, chair phase I/II com.; mem. exec. com. Adult AIDS Clin. Trials Grp. Contbr. articles to profl. jours.; editor-in-chief: WHO Antiretroviral Guidelines for Resource Ltd. Settings. Mem.: Internat. AIDS Soc. (mem. governing coun.). Office: Columbia U Dept Medicine Divsn Infectious Diseases 630 W 168th St Box 82 New York NY 10032 E-mail: smh48@columbia.edu.

HAMMER, TERENCE MICHAEL, physician; b. Chgo., May 7, 1946; s. Albert S. and Minnetta Elizabeth (Nichols) H.; 1 child, Kathryn Gyo Hammer. BS, U. Ill., 1968; MD, Stanford U., 1973. Diplomate Am. Bd. Family Practice. Intern L.A. County-U. So. Calif. Med. Ctr., 1973—74; med. dir. Long Beach Health Dept. Drug Program, Calif., 1974—75; resident family medicine Contra Costa Med. Svcs., Martinez, Calif., 1975—77; pvt. practice family medicine Redondo Beach Med. Group, Calif., 1977—81, Family Practice Assocs., Torrance, Calif., 1981—96, Med. Inst. Little Co. of Mary Hosp., Torrance, 1996—. Bd. dirs., treas. Med. Inst. of Little Co. of Mary Hosp.; lectr. in field. Bd. trustees Peninsula Edn. Found., Palos Verdes, Calif., 1991-99; bd. examiners Malcolm Baldridge Nat. Quality Awards, 1999, 2001. Named Calif. Rep. of Yr., 2001; named one of America's Top Family Drs., Consumers Rsch. Coun. Am., 2002. Mem. Am. Coll. Physician Execs., Premier Health Med. Group (pres. 1991—), South Bay Ind. Physicians Med. Group (pres. emeritus). Lutheran. Avocations: fishing, art, swimming, writing. Office: Med Inst Little Co Mary Hosp 20911 Earl St Ste 440 Torrance CA 90503-4355 Office Phone: 310-542-0455. Personal E-mail: hefish1@aol.com.

HAMMER, WADE BURKE, retired oral and maxillofacial surgeon, educator; b. Lakeland, Fla., Apr. 21, 1932; s. Orval Seown and Lilly Pearl (Wade) H.; m. Betty Dean Webb, June 22, 1956; children: Robert Burke Hammer, Joanna Wade Hammer Dykes. AA, U. Fla., 1956; D.D.S., Emory U., 1960. Diplomate Am. Bd. Oral and Maxillofacial Surgery; Merchant Marine Master. Pvt. practice dentistry, Orange Park, Fla., 1960-61; resident in oral and maxillofacial surgery U. Pa. Grad. Sch. Medicine, Phila., 1961-62, Grady Meml. Hosp., Atlanta and Emory U., 1962-65; practice dentistry specializing in oral and maxillofacial surgery Atlanta, 1965-68; mem. staff Med. Coll. of Ga. Hosp., Augusta; asst. prof. oral and maxillofacial surgery Med. Coll. Ga., Augusta, 1968-71, assoc. prof., 1971-75, prof., 1975-93, prof. emeritus oral and maxillofacial surgery, 1993. Staff VA Hosp. Complex, Augusta, 1969-99; cons. Ft. Gordon Army Med. Ctr., 1970-93, Univ. Hosp., Augusta, 1968-93. Contbr. articles to profl. jours. Chmn. exec. com. Gen. Faculty Orgn. Med. Coll. Ga., 1988; mem. USCG Auxiliary. With USN, 1950-54, col. USAR, 1976-92, ret. Decorated Legion of Merit, Meritorious Svc. medal, Army Commendation medals (5), Knight Comdr. and Lt. Grand Prior US, Hospitaler Order St. John of Jerusalem, Knight Sovereign Mil. Order of the Temple of Jerusalem. Fellow Am. Assn. Oral and Maxillofacial Surgeons (life), Am. Coll. Dentists, Am. Soc. Dental Anesthesiology; mem. ADA (life), Internat. Assn. Dental Rsch., Ga. Dental Assn., Ea. Dist. Dental Assn., Am. Assn. Dental Schs., Augusta Dental Soc., Ga. Soc. Oral and Maxillofacial Surgeons, Southeastern Soc. Oral and Maxillofacial Surgeons (pres. 1984-85), Res. Officers Assn. (Nat. Dental Surgeon 1990-92, Dept. of Ga. Pres. 1998-99, nat. counsilman, 2003-06), Interallied Confedn. of Res. Officers (US. del. 1992—), Assn. Mil. Surgeons (life), USCG Aux., Exptl. Aircraft Assn., Am. Legion, VFW, U.S. Army Order Mil. Med. Merit, U.S. Sailing Assn., Boat-U.S., Mil. Officers Assn. Am., Sigma Xi, Omicron Kappa Upsilon (pres. Supreme chpt. 1980-81). Methodist. Personal E-mail: wbhammer@aol.com.

HAMMER, (STANLEY KIRK BURRELL), musician; b. Oakland, Calif., 1962; m. Stephanie Burrell; children: Akeiba Monique, Jamaris, Sarah, Stanley, Jeremiah, Samuel. Albums include: Feel My Power, 1987, Let's Get Started, 1988, Please Hammer Don't Hurt'Em, 1990, Too Legit to Quit, 1991, The Funky Headhunter, 1994, Inside Out, 1995, Greatest Hits, 1996, Family Affair, 1998, Active Duty, 2001, Look 3X, 2006; single rec.: U Can't Touch This, 1991; film appearances include: One Tough Bastard, 1995, Cheyenne, 1996, Reggie's Prayer, 1996, The Right Connections, 1997, Deadly Rhapsody, 2001; TV Series: The Adventures of Hammerman 1991-92 (voice), Story of a People, 1993, Dance Fever, 2003; composer (films) Please Hammer, Don't Hurt 'Em: The Movie, 1990. Ordained minister, 2004. Recipient 3 Grammy awards, 1990, People's Choice music award, 1991, Am. Music award rap favorite album, rap favorite artist, 1990, 91, soul, rhythm and blues favorite album, 1991, soul, rhythm and blues favorite single, 1991.

HAMMERGREN, JOHN H., health products executive; BBA, U. Minn.; MBA, Xavier U. With Baxter Healthcare Corp./Am. Hosp. Corp. and Lyphomed Inc., 1981-91; pres. med./surgical divsn. Kendall Healthcare Products Co., Mansfield, Mass., 1991-96; corp. exec. v.p., pres., CEO supply mgmt. bus. McKesson HBOC, Inc., 1996-99; group pres. McKesson Health Systems, 1997—99; chief exec. officer supply chain mgmt. McKesson Corp. (formerly McKesson HBOC, Inc.), 1997—99, dir., 1999—, co-pres, co- CEO, 1999—2001, pres., CEO, 2001—, chmn. bd., 2002—. Dir. Nadro, S.A. de C.V., Mexico, Verispan LLC; bd. trustee Healthcare Leadership Coun. Recipient Cap Gemini Ernst & Young Leadership award for Global Integration, 2004, Warren Bennis award for Leadership, 2004. Office: McKesson Corp One Post St San Francisco CA 94104*

HAMMERLE, FREDRIC JOSEPH, metal products executive; b. Newark, Jan. 2, 1944; s. Fredric Frank and Catherine G. (Wankmuller) H.; m. Nancy Elizabeth Looby, June 16, 1979; children: Oliver, Dora. BA, Rutgers U., 1966, MBA, 1967. Prodn. mgr. Engelhard Corp., Plainville, Mass., 1967-72, group v.p., 1978-86; v.p. mfg. Franklin Mint Corp., Franklin Center, Pa., 1972-78; exec. v.p., COO, sr. group exec. Cookson Precious Metals, Providence, 1986—2003; pres., CEO Precision Engineered Products, Inc., Attleboro, Mass., 2003—. Bd. dirs., treas. Internat. Precious Metals Inst. Referee Amateur Hockey Assn. U.S., 1980—; bd. dirs., sec. Sturdy Meml. Hosp., 1989—. Sgt. USMCR, 1966-72. Mem.: Silver Users Assn. (bd. dirs. 1985—, pres.), Gold Filled Assn. (bd. dirs. 1980—, sec., pres.), Mfg. Jewelers Silversmiths of Am. (bd. dirs. 1983—, pres.), Bass Anglers Sportsman Soc. (Montgomery, Ala.), Jewelry Info. Ctr., 24 Karat Club N.Y., Boston Jewelers Club (bd. dirs. 1995—, pres. 2001—). Roman Catholic. Avocations: ice hockey, restoring autos, fishing. Office: Precision Engineered Products Inc 110 Frank Mossberg Dr Attleboro MA 02703 E-mail: fhammerle@pep-corp.com.

HAMMERMAN, HERBERT, retired economist; b. NYC, Apr. 20, 1917; s. Nathan and Fannie Miller Hammerman; m. Constance Gay Morenus, Sept. 3, 1955; children: Joseph Richard, Daniel Aaron. BS, CCNY, NYC, 1938; M in Social Scis., New Sch. for Social Rsch., NYC, 1942. Analyst War Prodn. Bd., Washington, 1942—43; analyst, sect. chief War Labor Bd., Washington, 1943—45, Wage Stabilization Bd., Washington, 1945—47; contract negotiator Comm. Workers Union, Atlanta, 1948; asst. rsch. dir. United Rubber Workers Union, Akron, Ohio, 1947—49; rsch. analyst Textile Workers Union, NYC, 1949—50; rsch. dir. Ins. Agts. Union, Washington, 1950—56; rsch. and analysis staff US Dept. Labor, Washington, 1956—66; chief reports divsn. US EEO Commn., Washington, 1966—81; ret., 1981. Expert witness NAACP, Washington, 1986—94. Author: A Decade of New Opportunity: Affirmative Action in the 1970s, 1984; contbr. articles to profl. jours. V.p. US Govt. Employees Union, Dept. Labor, Washington, 1958—64; active Arlington Fair Housing Commn., Va., 1988—89. Avocation: acting. Home: 3440 S Jefferson St #833 Falls Church VA 22041 Personal E-mail: herbert2@verizon.net.

HAMMERMAN, MARC RANDALL, nephrologist, educator; b. St. Louis, Sept. 29, 1947; s. Elmer and Lillian Hammerman; m. Nancy Tutt, Aug. 9, 1974; children: Seth, Megan. AB, Washington U., St. Louis, 1969, MD, 1972. Intern Barnes Hosp., St. Louis, 1972-73, resident, 1973-74, Mass. Gen. Hosp., Boston, 1976-77; instr. Washington U., St. Louis, 1977-78, asst. prof., 1979-84, assoc. prof., 1984-89, prof., 1989—, dir. renal div. Sch. Medicine, 1991—. Mem. study sect. NIH, 1990-95; investigator Am. Heart Assn., 1984. Contbr. over 100 sci. articles, revs. to profl. publs., chpts. to books. Lt. comdr. USPHS, 1974-76. NIH grantee, 1980—. Mem. Am. Fedn. for Clin. Rsch., Am. Soc. Clin. Investigation, Assn. Am. Physicians. Office: Washington U Sch Medicine Renal Div Box 8126 660 S Euclid Ave Saint Louis MO 63110-1010 E-mail: mhammerm@im.wustl.edu.

HAMMERSCHMIDT, JOHN PAUL, retired congressman, lumber company executive; b. Harrison, Ark., May 4, 1922; s. Arthur Paul and Junie (Taylor) H.; m. Virginia Sharp, deceased; 1 child, John Arthur. Student, The Citadel, U. Ark., Okla. State U.; BS in Bus. Mgmt., Canbourne U., London, MA in Philosophy magna cum laude; PhD in Internat. Studies, Wallingham U., London. Ordained elder, deacon. Chmn. bd. Hammerschmidt Lumber Co., Harrison, 1946-84; mem. 90th-102d Congresses from 3d Ark. Dist., 1967-93. Mem. Pub. Works and Transp. Com., 1967-93, ranking mem., 1987-93; mem. V.A. Com., 1967-93, ranking mem., 1973-86; bd. dirs. 1st Fed. Bank of Ark.; sr. chmn. bd. 1st Fed. Bankshares of Ark.; bd. dirs. Dillard's Dept. Store, Southwestern Energy Co.; chmn. emeritus N.W. Ark. Coun.; nat. committeeman Ark. Citizen of Yr. Com.; mem. Presdl. Commn. on Aviation Security and Terrorism; mem. Pres.'s task force on Vets. Health Care; mem. Claude and Mildred Pepper Found., 1989-90 (PVA Speedy award), bd. Met. Washington Airports Authority; past chmn. bd., trustee Ark. State U., U. of the Ozarks; committeeman Nat. Rep. Party, 2002, Chmn. Ark. Republican Com., 1964-66; mem. Rep. Nat. Finance Com., 1960-64, nat. Rep. committeeman from, Ark., 1976-80; mem. Harrison City Coun., 1948, 60, 62. Served as pilot USAAF, World War II, CBI.

Decorated Air medal with 4 oak leaf clusters, D.F.C. with 3 oak leaf clusters, 3 Battle Stars, The China War Meml. medal, Meritorious Svc. award VFW Congl. award, Silver Helmet award, Nat. Order Trenchrats Legis. Svc. award, Award for Life Svc. to Vets.; named. Ark. Citizen of Yr., 1991, Ark. Aerospace Found. Hall of Fame, 1991. Mem. Ark. Lumber Dealers Assn. (past pres.), Midwest Lumbermens Assn. (past pres.), Harrison C. of C. (named Man of Yr. 1965), Am. Legion, Masons (33 degree-Grand Cross), Scottish Rite, Shriners, Jesters, Elks, Rotary (past pres. Harrison). Republican. Presbyterian. Office Phone: 870-391-3325. Personal E-mail: jph@northark.edu.

HAMMES, C. LESLIE GREENE, musician, educator; b. Vallejo, Calif., May 24, 1947; d. Ronald and Paula Frances Greene; m. Richard K. Hammes, Sept. 3, 1988. MusB, U. Dayton, Ohio, 1969; performance diploma, Royal Schs. Music, London, 1978; MEd, Harvard U., Cambridge, Mass., 1989. Pvt. piano tchr., 1965—80; commd. ens. USN, 1980, advanced through grades to lt. comdr., ret.; founder, piano instr. Ocala Piano Conservatory, Fla., 2000—. Pianist Ctrl. Fla. Symphony, Ocala, 1998—2002. Mem. adv. bd. dirs. Ctrl. Fla. Symphony, 1999—2004; pres. Ctrl. Fla. Philharm., Ocala, 2003—04; mem. adv. bd. pub. rels., publicity chmn. Marion Chamber Music, Ocala, 2005—; mem. Ocala Royal Dames Cancer Rsch., Ocala, 2006—. Mem.: Fla. Music Tchrs. Assn. (adjudicator 2003—), Ocala C. of C., Music Tchrs. Nat. Assn., Nat. Fedn. Musicians, Nat. Guild Piano Tchrs., Mensa, Nat. Fedn. Music Clubs (adjudicator 2003—). Democrat. Jewish. Avocation: flying. Home: 2052 NW 50th Cir Ocala FL 34482 Office: Ocala Piano Conservatory 108 N Magnolia Ste 103 Ocala FL 34475

HAMMES, GORDON G., chemistry professor; b. Fond du Lac, Wis., Aug. 10, 1934; s. Jacob and Betty (Sadoff) H.; m. Judith Ellen Frank, June 14, 1959; children: Laura Anne, Stephen R., Sharon Lyn. AB, Princeton, 1956; PhD, U. Wis., 1959. NSF postdoctoral fellow Max Planck Inst. fur physikalische Chemie, Göttingen, Germany, 1959-60; from instr. to assoc. prof. Mass. Inst. Tech., Cambridge, 1960-65; prof. Cornell U., Ithaca, NY, 1965-88, chmn. dept. chemistry, 1970-75, Horace White prof. chemistry and biochemistry, 1975-88, dir. biotech. program, 1983-88; prof. U. Calif., Santa Barbara, 1988-91, vice chancellor, 1988-91; prof. Duke U., Durham, NC, 1991—; vice chancellor Duke U. Med. Ctr., Durham, NC, 1991-98; univ. disting. svc. prof. biochemistry Duke U., Durham, NC, 1996—. Mem. physiol. chemistry sect., phys. biochemistry study sect., Tng. grant com. NIH; bd. counselors Nat. Cancer Inst., 1976-80; mem. adv. coun. chemistry dept., Princeton, 1970-75, Poly. Inst. N.Y., 1977-78, Boston U., 1977-92; mem. NRC, U.S. nat. com. for biochemistry, 1989-95. Author: Principles of Chemical Kinetics, 1978, Enzyme Catalysis and Regulation, 1982; author: (with I. Amdur) Chemical Kinetics: Principles and Selected Topics, 1966, Thermodynamics and Kinetics for the Biological Sciences, 2000, Spectroscopy for the Biological Sciences, 2005; author: Physical Chemsitry for the Biological Sciences, 2007; editor: Biochemistry, 1992—2003, Physical Chemistry for the Biological Sciences, 2007; contbr. articles to profl. jours. NSF sr. postdoctoral fellow, 1968-69; NIH Fogarty scholar, 1975-76 Mem. NAS, Am. Acad. Arts and Scis., Am. Chem. Soc. (award biol. chemistry 1967, editl. bd. jours., exec. com. div. phys. chemistry 1976-79, exec. com. div. biol. chemistry 1977-88, com. profl. tng. 1985-92, task force on biotech. 1989-90), Am. Soc. Biochemistry and Molecular Biology (coun., editl. bd. jour. pres., William C. Rose award 2002), Phi Beta Kappa, Sigma Xi, Phi Lambda Upsilon. Home: 11 Staley Pl Durham NC 27705-2421 Office Phone: 919-684-8848. Business E-Mail: hamme001@mc.duke.edu.

HAMMESFAHR, ROBERT WINTER, lawyer; b. Pittsfield, Mass., May 17, 1954; s. Frederick W. and Patricia Lue (Winter) H.; m. Susan Shaw; 1 child, Scott Gardner. BA, Colgate U., 1975; JD, Northwestern U., Chgo., 1978. Bar: Ill. 1978, U.S. Dist. Ct. (no. dist.) Ill. 1978, N.Y. 1991, U.S. Supreme Ct. 1989. Mem. Cozen O'Connorr, Chgo., 2001—06; global head reinsurance claims P&C Swiss Reinsurance Group, Zurich, 2006—. Author (with others): Punitive Damages: A Guide to the Insurability of Punitive Damages in the United States and Its Territories, 1988, Punitive Damages: A State-By-State Guide to Law and Practice, 1991, eth edit., (pocket parts 1993, 96, Japanese edits., 1995, 2001 to 2006), 2006, Reinsurance Claims, 2004, The Law of Reinsurance Claims, 1994, supplement, 1997; editor, author (with others): @Risk-Internet and E-commerce Insurance and Reinsurance, 2000, 2.0 version, 2002; contbr. articles to profl. jours. Mem.: ABA. Avocations: skiing, reading. Office: Swiss Reinsurance Co Mytheguai 50/60 8022 Zurich Switzerland Office Phone: 011 41 43 285 4361. Personal E-mail: robert_hammesfahr@ameritech.net. Business E-Mail: robert_hammesfahr@suisse.com.

HAMMES-SCHIFFER, SHARON, chemist, educator; b. Ithaca, NY, May 27, 1966; d. Gordon G. and Judith (Frank) Hammes; m. Peter Ernest Schiffer, Apr. 1, 1990; children: Zachary J. Schiffer, Benjamin G. Schiffer. BA, Princeton U., NJ, 1988; PhD, Stanford U., Calif., 1993. Mem. tech. staff AT&T Bell Labs., Murray Hill, NJ, 1993—95; Clare Boothe Luce asst. prof. chemistry and biochemistry U. Notre Dame, Ind., 1995—2000; Shaffer assoc. prof. chemistry Pa. State U., University Park, 2000—03, prof. chemistry, 2003—06, Eberly prof. biotechnology, 2006—. Charter mem. study sect. NIH, 2002—06; adv. bd. Theoretical Chemistry Accts., 2002—, Accts. Chem. Rsch., 2006—. Sr. editor: Jour. Phys. Chemistry, 2001—; contbr. articles to profl. jours. Recipient Career award, NSF, 1996, Camille Dreyfus Tchr.-Scholar award, 1999, Agnes Fay Morgan Rsch. award, Iota Sigma Pi, 2005, medal, Internat. Acad. Quantum Molecular Sci., 2005; NSF Grad. fellow, 1988—91, Alfred P. Sloan Rsch. fellow, 1998. Mem.: Am. Chem. Soc. (chair theoretical subdivision 2005). Office: Pa State U 104 Chemistry Bldg University Park PA 16802 Business E-Mail: shs@chem.psu.edu.

HAMMETT, BETH A., language educator; d. Tommy and Pat LaMascus; m. Mike Hammett, July 27, 1988; children: Terra M. Martinez, Zach M children: Melea A., Trey T Tackett. MS, U. Houston, 2004. Cert. tchr. Tex., 1999. Asst. prof. English Coll. of Mainland, Texas City, Tex., 2004—. Cons. Effective Tchg. Solutions, Houston, 2005—. Author: (novel) Natalie: Diary of a Senior Year, 2005, (textbook) Developmental Writing Workshop, 2006. Core mem. Achieving the Dream, Texas City, 2006—. Named Tex. State Mid. Sch. Tchr. of Yr.; recipient Channel 2 Sunshine award, Secondary Tchr. of Yr., Dickinson Ind. Sch. Dist.; Tex. President's Rsch. and Travel grantee, Tex. Coun. Tchrs. English Lang. Arts, 2006. Fellow: Nat. Writing Project (life; co-dir. 2005—06). Office: Coll of Mainland 1200 Amburn Rd Texas City TX 77591 Home Phone: 281-534-0887; Office Phone: 409-938-1211. Business E-Mail: bhammett@com.edu.

HAMMETT, KIRK LEE, musician; b. El Sobrante, Calif., Nov. 18, 1962; m. Rebecca Hammett, Dec. 3, 1987 (div.); m. Lani Hammett, Jan. 31, 1998. Band mem. Exodus, 1981—83; band mem., guitarist Metallica, 1983—. Albums include Kill 'em All, 1983, Ride the Lightning, 1984, Master of Puppets, 1986, ...And Justice for All, 1988, Metallica, 1991, Live Sh*t: Binge and Purge, 1993, Kill 'Em All, 1995, Load, 1996, Reload, 1997, Garage Inc., 1998 (Grammy award), S & M, 1999, St. Anger, 2003 (Grammy award best metal performance, 2003); played on compilation albums including Metal Massacre, 1982, The Good, The Bad and The Live, 1990, Rubaiyant: Elektra's 30th Anniversary, 1990, For Those About To Rock: Moscow, 1992, Woodstock '94, 1994, Spawn: The Album, 1997, Woodstock '99, 2000, WCW: Mayhem The Music, 1999, M:I-2, 2000, NASCAR: Full Throttle, 2001, Swizz Beatz Presents G.H.E.T.T.O. Stories, 2002, Biker Boyz Soundtrack, 2003, We're A Happy Family: Tribute to the Ramones, 2003, I've Always Been Crazy: Tribute to Waylon Jennings, 2003. Recipient Grammy award for Best Metal Performance for One, 1989, Grammy award for Best Metal Performance for Stone Cold Crazy, 1990, Grammy award for Best Metal Performance for Better Than You, 1998, Grammy award for Best Hard Rock Performance for Whiskey in the Jar, 1999, Grammy award for Best Rock Instrumental Peformance for The Call of Ktulu, 2000. Office: Elektra Entertainment Group 75 Rockefeller Plaza New York NY 10019-7284

HAMMON, BECKY (REBECCA LYNN HAMMON), professional basketball player; b. Mar. 11, 1977; d. Martin and Bev Hammon. Grad., Colo. State U., Ft. Collins, 1999. Guard NY Liberty, 1999—2006, San Antonio Silver Stars, 2007—; guard (off-season) Nat. Women's Basketball League Tenn. Fury, 2002—03, Nat. Women's Basketball League Colo. Chill, 2004—06, Rivas Futura, Spain, 2007. Named a Peak Performer, WNBA, 2007; named MVP, Nat. Women's Basketball League, 2006; named to Ea. Conf. All-Star Team, WNBA, 2003, 2005, Western Conf. All-Star Team, 2007, All-WNBA Second Team, 2005, 2006. Achievements include winning the 2005 National Women's Basketball League Championship as a member of the Chill. Avocations: hunting, fishing, water sports, softball, movies. Mailing: San Antonio Silver Stars One AT&T Ctr San Antonio TX 78219*

HAMMON, JOHN WILLIAM, JR., medical educator, thoracic surgeon; b. Springfield, Mo., Mar. 9, 1942; m. Mary Lisa Hammon; children: Ian, Dudley, Daniel. BA, Drury Coll., 1964; MD, Tulane U., 1968. Diplomate Am. Bd. Surgery, 1978, Am. Bd. Thoracic Surgery, 1997. Intern Duke U. Med. Ctr., Durham, NC, 1968—69, resident, 1969—70, resident, gen./thoracic surgery, 1972—77, tchg. scholar cardiac surgery, 1977—78; asst. prof. surgery Vanderbilt U., Nashville, 1978—83, assoc. prof. surgery, 1983—89, prof. dept. cardiac and thoracic surgery, 1989—91; chief cardiac and thoracic surgery VA Hosp., Nashville, 1987—91; Howard Holt Bradshaw prof., chmn. Bowman Gray Sch. Medicine, Winston-Salem, NC, 1991—95; prof. surgery Sch. Medicine Wake Forest U., Winston-Salem, NC, 1995—. Prin. investigator NIH Grants, 1979—2007. Mem. editl. bd. Jour. Surg. Rsch., 1986—91, Cardiac Chronicle, 1986—91, Annals of Thoracic Surgery, 1991—2002, Jour. Cardiac Surgery, 1993—, Jour. Thoracic and Cardiovascular Surgery, 2006—. Lt. comdr US Naval Hosp., 1970—77. Recipient Disting. Alumni award, Drury Coll., 1989, 2001; scholar, NIH, 1974. Mem.: ACS (gov. 2002, membership com. 2002—04), N.C. Surg. Assn. (pres. 2006—07), Winston-Salem Surg. Assn. (pres. 1999—2000), So. Thoracic Surg. Assn. (v.p. 1999—2000, pres. 2007—, pres.'s award for best sci. paper 1985), Am. Assn. Thoracic Surgery (residents com. 1999—2003, membership com. 2002—05, sci. and govt. affairs com. 2007—), Omicron Delta Kappa. Avocations: golf, fishing. Office: Dept Cardiothoracic Surgery Medical Ctr Blvd Winston Salem NC 27157-1096 Office Phone: 336-716-6002. Office Fax: 336-716-3348. Business E-Mail: jhammon@wfubmc.edu.

HAMMOND, ALLEN LEE, editor, consultant, former broadcaster, nonprofit policy research center executive; b. West Chicago, Ill., Sept. 6, 1943; s. R. Philip and Amy Louise (Farmer) H.; m. Alice Reed Rajchman, May 17, 1969; children— Ross Alan, Lily Alice BS, Stanford U., 1966; A.M., Harvard U., 1967, PhD, 1970. Research news editor Science mag., Washington, 1970-79; founder, editor-in-chief Science 80-86 mag., Washington, 1979-86; editor, report on sci. CBS radio, Washington, 1982-86; editor Issues in Sci. and Tech. mag., Washington, 1984-86; founder Information Please Environmental Almanac, 1994; pres. Allen L. Hammond & Assocs., Inc., 1986—; editor Sci. Impact Letter, 1987-89, World Resources series, World Resources Inst., Washington, 1990—; chief info. officer, sr. scientist, v.p., spl. projects and innovation programs and spl. fellows World Resources Inst., Washington, dir., digital dividends project. Lectr. in field; cons. White House Sci. Office, several US Fed. Agencies, UN, and several private founds. Author: (with others) Energy and the Future, 1973, Solar Energy in America, 1978 (NASW award 1978), Resource Flows: The Material Basis of Industrial Economies, 1997, Which World?:Scenarios for the 21st Century, 1998, Critical Consumption Trends and Implications: Degrading Earth's Ecosystems, 1999, What Works: Serving the Poor, Profitably, 2002; editor: A Passion to Know: 20 Profiles in Science, 1984; contbr. articles to profl. jours. Recipient Nat. Mag. award Columbia Sch. Journalism, 1982, 83, 86; NSF fellow Fellow AAAS; mem. Am. Soc. Mag. Editors, Phi Beta Kappa, Tau Beta Pi, Sigma Xi (bd. dirs. 1987-90). Democrat. Unitarian Universalist. Avocations: skiing; sailing. Office: World Resources Inst 10 G St NE Ste 800 Washington DC 20002 Office Phone: 202-729-7777. Business E-Mail: allen@wri.org.

HAMMOND, ANN P., retired elementary. high school and college educator, poet; b. Worthing, Great Britian, June 11, 1936; arrived in U.S., 1964; d. Sydney Martyn Hammond and Elizabeth Mathewson. BS, Adelphi U., Garden City, NY, 1973, MA, 1974. Cert. permanent tchr. NY, 1974. Dir. phys. edn. Pipers Corner Sch., High Wycombe, England, 1958—60, Arundel Sch., Harare, Zimbabwe, 1960—64, East Woods Sch., Oyster Bay, NY, 1964—74; health educator East Hampton Sch. Dist., East Hampton, NY, 1974—96. Pres. Assn. of Women in Phys. Edn., NY, 1976—80; cons. Bklyn. Coll., NYC, 1973—74, Adephi, NY, 1974. Author: Ann Hammond: Selected Poems, 2006; contbr. poems to lit. publs. and anthologies. Avocations: writing, sailing, swimming, golf, reading. Personal E-mail: annhammonda@excite.com.

HAMMOND, BENJAMIN FRANKLIN, microbiologist, educator; b. Austin, Tex., Feb. 28, 1934; s. Virgil Thomas and Helen Marguerite (Smith) H. BA, U. Kans., 1954; D.D.S., Meharry Med. Coll., 1958; PhD, U. Pa., 1962. Mem. faculty U. Pa. Sch. Dental Medicine, Phila., 1958—, prof. microbiology, 1970—, chmn. dept., 1972-85; Pres.'s lectr. U. Pa., 1981, assoc. dean acad. affairs, 1984, dir. periodontal microbiology lab., 1985—; prof. of medicine, dir. oral microbiology testing svc. lab. Med. Coll. Pa., 1995—; rsch. prof. periodontology Temple U., Phila., 1998—. Mem. oral biology and medicine study sect. NIH, 1972-75, 95-99; mem. Nat. Adv. Dental Rsch. Coun., 1975—; Ralph Metcalf disting. vis. prof. Marquette U., 1986; disting. lectr. U. Paul Sabatier, Toulouse, France, 1991. Trustee Atwater Kent Mus., 1999—, Arthur Ross Gallery, 2001, Brandywine (Pa.) Conservancy, 2004—; bd. dirs. Am. Poetry Soc., 2001, FIRE. Recipient USPHS Research Career Devel. award, 1965, Lindback award U. Pa., 1969; Silver medal City of Paris, 1978; NIH grantee, 1981—. Mem. Am. Soc. Microbiology, Internat. Assn. Dental Rsch. (E.H. Hatton award 1959), Am. Assn. Dental Rsch.(pres. 1978-79), Coll. Physicians of Phila., Phila. Mus. Art (trustee), The Phila. Club. Home: 560 N 23d St Philadelphia PA 19130-3132 Office Phone: 215-707-5857. Business E-Mail: bhammond@dental.temple.edu.

HAMMOND, BRUCE RAY, academic administrator, consultant; s. Donald Wheeler and Cecilia Margaret Hammond; m. June Hammond, June 17, 1989; children: John Ray, Vanessa Louise. BS, SUNY, Fredonia, 1963; MS, Canisius Coll., Buffalo, 1967; MA, SUNY, Buffalo, 1969, PhD, 1972. Assoc. prof. Canisius Coll., Buffalo, 1966—84; pres. Am. Mgmt. Cons., St. Augustine, Fla., 1984—90; sr. cons. Achieve Global, Tampa, Fla., 1990—2003; assoc. v.p., academic affairs Saint Leo U., Fla., 2003—. Cons. Prudential, London, 1994—96, Time Warner Cable, Cin., 1996—2000, Brit. Telecom, London, 2000—02. Author: Winning the Job Interview Game, 1990; contbr. articles to profl. jours., chapters to books. Project mgr. Fla. Dept. Labor, Tallahassee, 1984—85; pres. Big Brothers/Big Sisters, St. John's County, Fla., 1986—88; task force leader Greater Dade City Chamber, Dade City, Fla., 2004. Sgt. USAR, 1956—64. Mem.: APA, Southern Speech Comm. Assn., Am. Arbitration Assn. (panel mem. 1985). Office: Saint Leo Univ SR 54 Saint Leo FL 33574

HAMMOND, CALEB DEAN, III, publishing executive; b. Orange, NJ, May 11, 1947; s. Caleb Dean Jr. and Patricia Treacy (Ehrgott) H.; m. Stephanie Hoagland, Aug. 9, 1969 (div. Jan. 1978); 1 child, Joshua Dean; m. Kathleen Theresa Doorish, July 8, 1978 (div. Nov. 1998); children: Connor Dean, Kathleen Treacy. BSBA, Susquehanna U., 1970; postgrad., Stetson U. Sch. Law, 1970-72. Pres. Chainwheel Dr., Clearwater, Fla., 1972—99; chmn. Hammond, Inc., Maplewood, NJ, 1999—; CEO Neighborhood Energy, LLC, Maplewood, NJ, 2002—. Mem. Assn. Am. Pubs.

HAMMOND, CELESTE M., law educator; BS cum laude, Loyola U.; JD, U. Chgo. Practicing atty., Chgo.; mem. faculty to prof., dir. real estate law prog. John Marshall Law Sch., Chgo., 1976—. Contbr. articles to profl. jours., chapters to books. Mem.: Chgo. Bar Assn. (chair real property law com. 2002), ABA, Chgo. Real Estate Exec. Women, Lambda Alpha Internat. Land Econs. Soc., Am. Coll. Real Estate Lawyers. Office: Ctr Real Estate John Marshall Law Sch 315 S Plymouth Ct Chicago IL 60604 Office Phone: 312-987-2366. E-mail: 7hammond@jmls.edu.*

HAMMOND, CHARLES BESSELLIEU, obstetrician, gynecologist, educator; b. Ft. Leavenworth, Kans., July 24, 1936; s. Claude G. and Alice (Sims) H.; m. Peggy A. Hammond, June 21, 1958; children: Sharon L., Charles B. BS, The Citadel, 1957; MD, Duke U., 1961. Diplomate Am. Bd. Ob-Gyn. Intern in surgery Duke U., 1961-62, resident in ob-gyn, 1962-63, 66-69, fellow in reproductive endocrinology, 1963-64, asst. prof. dept. ob-gyn, 1969-73, asso. prof., 1973-78, prof., 1978-81, E.C. Hamblen prof., 1981—, chmn., 1980—2002. Contbr. in field. Served with USPHS, 1964-66. Fellow Royal Coll. Ob-gyn. (ad eundeum), Soc. Ob-gyn. Can. (hon.); mem. AMA, Am. Fertility Soc. (pres. 1985), ACOG (chmn. dist. IV 1997-2000, pres. 2002), Am. Assn. Ob-Gyn. Found. (pres. 1996-2002), Assn. Profs. Obstetrics and Gynecology, Am. Gynecol. and Obstet. Soc. (pres. 1993-94), Soc. Gynecol. Investigation, Am. Gynecol. Soc., Am. Assn. Obstet. and Gynecology, N.C. Med. Soc., N.C. Soc. Obstetricians and Gynecologists (pres. 1985), Am. Gynecol. Club (pres. 1994), Inst. of Medicine. Presbyterian. Home: 2827 McDowell Rd Durham NC 27705-5604 Office: Duke U Med Ctr PO Box 3853 Durham NC 27710 Office Phone: 919-684-3008. Business E-Mail: hammo005@mc.duke.edu.

HAMMOND, DARRELL, actor; b. Melbourne, FL, Oct. 8, 1960; m. Elizabeth Hammond, May 9, 1990; 1 child. Grad., U. Fla. Actor: (TV series) Saturday Night Live, 1995—; (films) Celtic Pride, 1996, Blues Brothers 2000, 1998, King and I (voice), 1999, The Devil and Daniel Webster, 2001, Agent Cody Banks, 2003, Scary Movie 3, 2003, New York Minute, 2004, Kiss Me Again, 2005, Puff, Puff, Pass, 2006, Ira and Abby, 2006, Epic Movie, 2007. Office: c/o NBC 30 Rockefeller Plaza Studio 8h New York NY 10112*

HAMMOND, DAVID ALAN, stage director, educator; b. NYC, June 3, 1948; s. Jack and Elizabeth Alida (Furno) H. BA magna cum laude, Harvard U., 1970; MFA, Carnegie-Mellon U., 1972. Mem. faculty Juilliard Theatre Ctr., NYC, 1972-74; asst. conservatory dir. Am. Conservatory Theatre, San Francisco, 1974-81, assoc. stage dir., 1974-78; dir. Summer Tng. Congress, 1976-80, resident stage dir., 1979-81. Adj. assoc. prof. acting and directing Yale Sch. Drama, New Haven, 1981—85; adj. prof. dept. dramatic art U. NC, Chapel Hill, 1985—88, prof., 1988—2007; prof. theatre studies Guilford Coll., Greensboro, NC, 2007—; artistic dir. PlayMakers Repertory Co., Chapel Hill, 1985—92, 1999—2006, artistic dir. emeritus, 2006—, assoc. producing dir., 1992—99; guest artist Pacific Conservatory Performing Arts, 1976, U. Wash., 1977, SUNY, Purchase, 1979, Am. Repertory Theatre Inst. for Advanced Theatre Tng. at Harvard U., 2006—, Tisch Sch. Arts/NYU, NYC, 1999—; guest dir. Aspen (Colo.) Music Festival, 1974—75, San Francisco Opera, 1978, Carmel (Calif.) Bach Festival, 1979—80, Sherwood Shakespeare Festival, Oxnard, Calif., 1981, Roundabout Theatre, NYC, 1983, Valley Shakespeare Festival, Saratoga, Calif., 1984, 86, 88, Shakespeare Festival of Dallas, 1990, Teatro Alianza, Montevideo, 1992, 94, 97, Inst. Teatral El Galpon, Montevideo, 1995, Opera Co. NC, 1998, 99; resident dir. Yale Repertory Theatre, New Haven, 1981—85; Arts Am. cultural specialist U.S. Info. Svc., 1992, 94; guest prof. Escuela Mcpl. de Arte Dramatico, 2003, Escuela de Expression Teatral Anglo-o.m.b.u., 2003, El Univ. del Plata, Montevideo, 2003. Recipient Drama-Logue Critics award, LA, 1980, 81, Florencio award, Montevideo, 1992. Mem. Soc. Stage Dirs. and Choreographers, Actors' Equity, Am. Guild Mus. Artists, Dramatists' Guild, Nat. Theater Conf., Assn. for Theatre in Higher Edn. Office: Guilford Coll Dept Theatre Studies Founders B13 5460 W Friendly Ave Greensboro NC 27410 Office Phone: 336-316-2477. Business E-Mail: hammondda@guilford.edu.

HAMMOND, ELEA ANNE, special education educator; b. Nashville, July 15, 1957; m. Kevin Neil Hammond, Aug. 2, 1977; children: Benjamin Neil, Laura Anne, Emily Elisabeth. EdB, Harding U., Searcy, Ark., 1978; EdM, Ga. State U., Atlanta, 2002. Cert. early childhood edn. Ga., 2006, interrelated spl. edn. Ga., 2006, mental retardation Ga., 2006, mid. grades Ga., 2006. Kindergarten tchr. Greater Atlanta Christian Schs., Norcross, Ga., 1986—88; elem. tchr. Cobb County Schs., Marietta, Ga., 1988—2000, tchr. elem. children with severe and profound intellectual disabilities, 2000—. Hosp./homebound tchr. Cobb County Schs., Marietta, 2000—. Tchr. Ch. of Christ, Marietta, 1986—2004, small group leader, 1992—2004, missionary, 2000—04; mentor Grace Pointe Cmty. Ch., Marietta, 2004—06. Scholar, Harding U., 1975—78. Republican. Avocations: travel, reading, shopping, playing cards, gardening. Office: Dowell Elementary School 2121 W Sandtown Rd Marietta GA 30064 Home Phone: 770-337-9577; Office Phone: 770-337-9577. Business E-Mail: elea.hammond@cobbk12.org.

HAMMOND, GLENN BARRY, SR., judge, electrical engineer; b. Roanoke, Va., Sept. 3, 1947; s. Howard Reichard and Billie (Cromer) Hammond; m. Elizabeth Wickham, Aug. 4, 2001; 1 stepchild, T. Rigsby Wickham; 1 child from previous marriage, Glenn Barry. BA, Va. Mil. Inst., 1969; MBA, So. Ill. U., 1974; JD, U. Richmond, 1978; BSEE, Nova Coll., 1995. Bar: Va. 1979, U.S. Dist. Ct. (we. dist.) Va. 1979, U.S. Ct. Appeals (4th cir.) 1981, U.S. Ct. Mil. Appeals 1989, Air Force Ct. Mil. Rev. 1989, U.S. Supreme Ct., 1992. Assoc. Wilson, Hawthorne & Vogel, Roanoke, 1978-79; pvt. practice Roanoke, 1979—80, 1986—2004; atty., advisor to chief adminstrv. law judge Social Security Adminstrn., HHS, Roanoke, 1980-86; ptnr. Wooten & Hart P.C., 1995-98; pres. R.F. Cons., Inc., Roanoke, Va., 1998—2004; fed. adminstrv. law judge Office Of Hearings and Appeals, Social Security Adminstrn., 2004—. Pres., bd. dirs. LCH Broadcasting Group, Inc. Roanoke. Editor: Psychiatry in Military Law, 1988. Sr. vice-comdr. Mil. Order World Wars, Roanoke, 1981. Col. JAGC, USAF, 1969-75, Res. 1975—. Mem. Air Commando Assn. (life), DAV (life), VFW (life), AFA (life), Nat. Mil. Intelligence Assn. (life), Armed Forces Comms. Electronics Assn., Nat. Orgn. Social Security Claimants Reps., Masons. Personal E-mail: bluetig@earthlink.net.

HAMMOND, GRAEME LORD, surgeon, educator; b. NYC, Jan. 30, 1933; married; 2 children. BS, Denison U., Granville, Ohio, 1958; MD, McGill U., Montreal, Can., 1962. Diplomate Am. Bd. Surgery, Am. Bd. Thoracic Surgery; lic. surgeon, N.Y., Mass., Conn. Intern in surgery Royal Victoria Hosp., Montreal, 1962-63; resident in surgery Mass. Gen. Hosp., Boston, 1963-65, 66-68, clin. rsch. fellow in surgery, 1965-66; from asst. prof. to assoc. prof. surgery Yale U. Sch. Medicine, New Haven, 1969—79, prof., 1979—; attending surgeon Yale-New Haven Hosp., 1969—, prin. investigator lung transplant program, 1988—. Vis. rsch. scientist dept. biochemistry Hormone Rsch. Lab., U. Calif., San Francisco, 1981-82; mem. examining bd. Nat. Bd. Med. Examiners, 1987-90. Mem. editorial bd. Thoracic and Cardiovascular Surgery, 4th edit., 1982, 5th edit., 1990, 6th edit., 1996. With U.S. Army, 1953-55. Fellow USPHS, 1965-66. Mem. Am. Surg. Assn., Soc. Univ. Surgeons, Am. Assn. Thoracic Surgery, Am. Coll. Surgeons, Am. Heart Assn. (fellow coun. cardiovascular surgery, established investigator 1972-76), Am. Soc. for Biochemistry and Molecular Biology, New England Surg. Soc., Internat. Soc. Cardiovascular Surgery, Internat. Soc. Heart Rsch., Assn. Acad. Surgery, Soc. Thoracic Surgeons, Internat. Soc. for Heart and Lung Transplantation, The Transplantation Soc., The European Assn. for Cardio-Thoracic Surgery, Soc. Vascular Surgery. Home Phone: 203-248-9229; Office Phone: 203-785-2699. Business E-Mail: graeme.hammond@yale.edu.

HAMMOND, HARMONY, artist, educator; b. Chgo., Feb. 8, 1944; d. William Joseph and Harmony R. (Jensen) H.; m. Stephen Clover, May 1963 (div. 1970); 1 child, Tanya Hammond. BA, U. Minn., 1967. Prof. art dept. U. Ariz., Tucson, 1988—2005. Vis. artist Phila. Coll. Art, Rutgers U., Art Inst. Chgo., U. N.Mex., Tyler Sch. Fine Art, Santa Fe Art Inst., Anderson Ranch, Vt. Studio Ctr.; co-founder Heresies Mag., A.I.R. Gallery. Author: Wrappings: Essays on Feminism, Art and the Martial Arts, 1984, Lesbian Art in America: A Contemporary History, 2000; one-woman shows include A.I.R. Gallery, N.Y.C., 1973, 1982, 1984, Lerner-Heller Gallery, 1982, Matrix Gallery, Wadsworth Atheneum, Hartford, Conn., 1984, Luise Ross Gallery, N.Y.C., 1984, Bernice Steinbaum Gallery, N.Y.C., 1986, Trabia-MacAffe Gallery, N.Y.C., 1987, Etherton-Stern Gallery, Tucson, 1987, 1994, Linda Durham Gallery, Galisteo, N.Mex., 1988, Tucson Mus. Art, 1993, Linda Durham Gallery, Santa Fe, 1998, Site Santa Fe, 2002, Mus. Contemporary Art, Tucson, 2002, Dwight Hackett Projects, Santa Fe, 2004, Ctr. Contemporary Arts, Santa Fe, 2005, others, Represented in permanent collections Dwight Hackett Projects. Recipient award, Nat. Endowment of Arts-Sculpture, 1979, Nat. Endowment for Arts-Graphics, 1983; grantee, Pollock-Krasner Found., 1989, Guggenheim Found., 1991, Rockefeller Found. Bellagio, 1994, Adolph and Ester Gottlieb Found., 1995, Joan Mitchell Found., 1998, Andrea Frank Found., 2000; CAPS grantee, NY State Coun. of Arts-Sculpture, 1982. Mem. Coll. Art Assn. Avocation: Aikido.

HAMMOND, HAROLD LOGAN, oral and maxillofacial pathologist, retired educator; b. Hillsboro, Ill., Mar. 18, 1934; s. Harold Thomas and Lillian (Carlson) H.; m. Sharon Bunton, Aug. 1, 1954 (dec. 1974); 1 child, Connie; m. Pat J. Palmer, June 3, 1986. Student Millikin U., 1953-57, Roosevelt U., Chgo., 1957-58; DDS, Loyola U., Chgo., 1962; MS, U. Chgo., 1967. Diplomate Am. Bd. Oral and Maxillofacial Pathology. Intern, U. Chgo. Hosps., Chgo., 1962-63, resident, 1963-66, chief resident in oral pathology, 1966-67; asst. prof. oral pathology U. Iowa, Iowa City, 1967-72, assoc. prof., 1972-80, assoc. prof., dir. surg. oral pathology, 1980-83, prof., dir., 1983-2004, prof. emeritus oral pathology, radiology and medicine, 2004-, dir. emeritus, Surg. Oral Pathology Lab., 2004-; cons. pathologist Hosp. Gen. de Managua, Nicaragua, 1970-90, VA Hosp., Iowa City, 1977-2004. Cons. editor: Revista de la Assn. Nicaragua, 1970-71, Revista de la Federacion Odontologica de Centroamerica y Panama, 1971-77. Contbr. articles to profl. jours. Mosby Pub. Co. scholar, 1962. Fellow AAAS, AAUP, Am. Acad. Oral and Maxillofacial Pathology; mem. Am. Men and Women of Sci., NY Acad. Scis., Internat. Assn. Oral Pathologists, Internat. Assn. Dental Rsch., N.Am. Soc. Head and Neck Pathologists, Am. Dental Assn., Am. Assn. Dental Rsch. Avocations: collecting antique clocks, collecting gambling paraphernalia, collecting toys. Home: 1732 Brown Deer Rd Coralville IA 52241-1157 Office: U Iowa Dental Sci Bldg Iowa City IA 52242-1001

HAMMOND, HERBERT J., lawyer, arbitrator, mediator; b. Santa Fe, May 19, 1951; m. Myra Hammond; children: Ariel, Jay. BS magna cum laude, U. N.Mex., 1973; JD, NYU, 1976. Bar: Tex. 1977, U.S. Patent and Trademark Office 1977. Sr. ptnr. Thompson & Knight, Dallas, 1994—. Contbr. articles to profl. jours. Mem. State Bar Tex. (vice-chmn. com. on computerization of the profession 1989-92, chair computer sect. 1994-95, newsletter editor computer sect.), Am. Intellectual Property Law Assn., Dallas Bar Assn. (chmn. intellectual property sect. 1998), Phi Beta Kappa, Phi Kappa Phi, Kappa Mu Epsilon. Office: Thompson & Knight 1700 Pacific Ave Ste 3300 Dallas TX 75201-4693 Office Phone: 214-969-1607. Business E-Mail: herbert.hammond@tklaw.com.

HAMMOND, HOWARD DAVID, retired botanist, editor; b. Phila., Feb. 10, 1924; s. Clarence Elwood Jr. and Myrtle Iva (Sprowles) H.; m. Sarah Lichtenberg, Apr. 30, 1955; 1 child, Julia Ethel. BS, Rutgers U., 1945, MS, 1947; PhD, U. Pa., 1952. Asst. prof. U. Del., Newark, 1957-58, Howard U., Washington, 1958-68; from asst. prof. to assoc. prof. SUNY, Brockport, 1968-83; assoc. editor N.Y. Bot. Garden, Bronx, 1984-92. Co-editor: Floristic Inventory Tropical Countries, 1989, Southwestern Rare and Endangered Plants: Proceedings of the Second Conference/USDA Forest Service, 1996; regional reviewer for Flora of North America, 1997—. Vol. Deaver Herbarium, No. Ariz. U., 1993—; pub. art adv. com. City of Flagstaff, 1996-2002; adj. curator botany Mus. No. Ariz., 1998-2002 Mem. Am. Inst. Biol. Scis., Bot. Soc. Am., Torrey Bot. Soc.(editor 1976-82, 87-92, pres. 1992), Sigma Xi. Home: 4025 Lake Mary Rd Apt 33 Flagstaff AZ 86001-8608

HAMMOND, J. D., retired academic administrator; b. Maitland, Mo., Nov. 14, 1933; s. William Byron and Lillian Irene (Goodpasture) H.; m. Marian Jane Idle, Aug. 20, 1960; children: Nancy Lee, Michael James. AB, N.W. Mo. State U., 1955; PhD, U. Pa., 1961. Asst. prof. econs. Ohio State U., Columbus, 1959-64, assoc. prof. bus. adminstrn., 1964-69, prof. ins., 1969-82, William Elliot prof. ins., 1982-86, William Elliot endowed chairholder, 1986-99; dean Smeal Coll. Bus. Adminstrn. Pa. State U., University Park, 1989-99. Pres. Risk Theory Seminar, 1973-74; bd. dirs. Atlantic Mut. Ins. Co.; disinterested trustee Scudder Kemper Investments, 1985-2001, Scudder Variable Life Fund, 1985-2000; chmn. workforce diversity task force Am. Assembly Collegiate Schs. of Bus., 1993. Chair campaign Pa. chpt. United Way, 1998. Office: Smeal Coll Bus Admnistrn Pa State U 361 Business Admin Bldg University Park PA 16802-3008 Business E-Mail: jdh9@psu.edu.

HAMMOND, JOHN, professional sports team executive; m. Marsha Hammond; 1 child, Lauryn Shay. B, Greenville Coll., Ill. Coach U. Nebr., Lincoln, 1979—81, Houston Baptist U., 1981—83, S.W. Mo. State U., 1983—89; asst. coach, scout Minn. Timberwolves, 1989—90; asst. coach LA Clippers, 1990—93, 2000—01; scouting dir. Detroit Pistons, 1994—99, asst. coach, 1997—99, dir. player pers., 2001—02, v.p. basketball ops., 2002—. Office: Detroit Pistons 5 Championship Dr Auburn Hills MI 48326*

HAMMOND, LARRY AUSTIN, lawyer; b. Wichita, Kans., Sept. 17, 1945; BA, U. Tex., 1967, JD, 1970. Bar: Calif. 1971, Ariz. 1975. Law clk. to Hon. Carl McGowan U.S. Ct. Appeals (D.C. cir.), Washington, 1970-71; law clk. to Hon. Hugo L. Black U.S. Supreme Ct., Washington, 1971, law clk. to Hon. Lewis F. Powell Jr., 1971-73; asst. spl. prosecutor Watergate spl. prosecution force U.S. Justice Dept., Washington, 1973-74, dep. asst. atty. gen. office legal counsel, 1977-80; mem. Osborn Maledon P.A., Phoenix, 1995—. Adj. prof. law Ariz. State U., 1977, 85—, U. Ariz., 1983, U. N.Mex., 1983. Editor-in-chief Tex. Law Rev., 1969-70. Mem. ABA, Am. Judicature Soc. (pres. 2003-05), Order of Coif. Office: Osborn Maledon PO Box 36379 Phoenix AZ 85067-6379 Office Phone: 602-640-9361. Business E-Mail: lhammond@omlaw.com.

HAMMOND, LOU RENA CHARLOTTE, public relations executive; b. Muenster, Tex. d. Louis Martin and Regina L. (Schoech) Wolf; m. Christopher Weymouth Hammond, Sept. 6, 1964; 1 child, Stephen. BA, U. Houston, 1962. Rep. pub. rels. Pan Am. Airways, NYC, 1968-76, mgr. pub. rels., 1977-79, dir. pub. rels., 1980-81, dir. pub. affairs, 1981; pres., ptnr. Taylor and Hammond, NYC, 1981-84; prin., pres. Lou Hammond and Assocs., NYC, 1984—. Editor: (calendar) Avenue mag., 1976-79. Recipient Matrix award in pub. rels., 1992, Winthrop W. Grice award Hotel Sales and Mktg. Assoc. Internat., 1992, Inside PR Mag.'s All-Star award, 1992, Circle of Excellence award Public Relations, Internat. Furnishings and Design Assn (IFDA). Mem. Soc. Am. Travel Writers, Fashion Group, Les Dmes de Escoffier (bd. dirs., v.p.), Women's Forum, Spolero USA (v.p. bd.), Charlston Food and Wine Festival, Doubles Club. Avocations: bridge, tennis, 18th century antiques. Office: Lou Hammond & Assocs Inc 39 E 51st St New York NY 10022-5916 Office Phone: 212-308-8880. Personal E-mail: louh@lhammond.com.

HAMMOND, MARIAN CORLEENE, retired literature educator; b. Ramage, W.Va., Dec. 8, 1919; s. Booker Shumate and Sadie Mearl Workman; m. John Elam Moore, July 7, 1942 (annulled Oct. 1945); m. Joseph Hammond, Nov. 17, 1945 (dec. Apr. 1998); children: Terry Colette Humphrey, Lisa Suzanne. AB in English, Berea Coll., 1941; EdM, Mills Coll., 1955; postgrad., Stanford U., 1958—76; adminstrv. credential, Calif. State U., Hayward, 1974; MA in drama, San Francisco State U., 1976. Cert. prin. Calif. Tchr. English and drama Scott H.S., Madison, W.Va., 1941—42; children's libr. N.Y. Pub. Libr., NYC, 1941; sci. tchr. Eccles (W.Va.) Jr. H.S., 1942—43; statistician, speech writer Del Monte Corp., San Francisco, 1946—53; tchr. English and drama San Lorenzo (Calif.) H.S., 1955—57; tchr. drama San Francisco State U., 1958—62; tchr. drama, speech and English Chabot Coll., Hayward, Calif., 1962—70; prin., tchr. grades 7-12 Fremont (Calif.) Unified Sch. Dist., 1968—85; tchr. English, speech and tech. writing Heald Inst. Tech., Hayward, 1992—93; tchr. speech and English Western Career Coll., San Leandro, Calif., 2000—01; ret. Contbr. articles to mags. Active Liberty Counsel, Orlando, Fla., 1999—2005, Am. Ctr. for Law and Justice, Atlanta, 1999—2005, Parents TV Coun., LA, 2000—05. Mem.: AFTRA, Actors Equity, Hayward Arts Coun., Castro Valley Mineral and Gem Soc. (life; dealer), Alpha Psi Omega (chmn. casting com. Berea Coll. chpt.), Pi Gamma Mu, Tau Kappa Alpha. Republican. Baptist. Avocations: bead stringing and design, writing. Home: 27937 El Portal Dr Hayward CA 94542 Office Phone: 510-886-5095.

HAMMOND, MARK, state official; b. Lancaster, SC, Nov. 29, 1963; m. Ginny Hammond; children: Matthew, Ross, Grace. BA in Polit. Sci., Newberry Coll., 1986; MEd, Clemson U., 1988. Criminal investigator 7th Cir. Solicitor's Office, 1990—96; clk. of ct. County of Spartanburg, 1996—2002; sec. state State of SC, 2002—. Mem. St. Paul United Meth. Ch., Spartanburg. Henry Toll fellow, 2007. Republican. Office: Office Sec of State Edgar Brown Bldg 1205 Pendleton St Ste 525 Columbia SC 29211 Office Phone: 803-734-2170. Office Fax: 803-734-1661.

HAMMOND, MARK L., biology professor, academic administrator; PhD, U. SC., Columbia. Dean, coll. of arts and scis. Campbell U., Buies Creek, NC, 2001—. Achievements include patents for high speed DNA sequencing; high speed DNA fragment sizing and sorting. Office: Campbell Univ PO Box 1135 Buies Creek NC 27506 Home Phone: 910-555-1212; Office Phone: 910-893-1200.

HAMMOND, MICHELLE, middle school educator; 2 children. BA in English, Hobart and William Smith Coll., NY, 1987; M equivalency in Reading, Salisbury Univ., 2003. Tchr. Stephen Decatur Mid Sch, Berlin, Md., 2003—. Named Md. Tchr. of Yr., 2007. Mem.: Md. State Tchrs. Assn. Office: Stephen Decatur Middle Sch 9815 Seahawk Rd Berlin MD 21811 E-mail: diverdown36@excite.com.*

HAMMOND, NORMAN DAVID CURLE, archaeology educator, researcher; b. Brighton, Eng., July 10, 1944; BA, U. Cambridge, Eng., 1966, Diploma in Classical Archaeology, 1967, MA, 1970, PhD, 1972, ScD, 1987, DSc (hon.), 1999. Rsch. faculty Cambridge U., Eng., 1967-75; faculty Bradford U., Eng., 1975-77; vis. prof. Rutgers U., 1977-78, faculty, 1978-88, assoc. prof., 1978-84, prof., 1984-88; member staff Peabody Mus., Harvard U., 1988—, Willey lectr., 2000; prof. archaeology Boston U., 1988—, chmn., 2005—. Vis. prof. U. Calif., Berkeley, 1977, Jilin U., China, 1981, Calif. Acad. Sci., 1984-85, U. Paris, 1987, Acad. Scis., USSR, 1991, U. Bonn, 1994; vis. faculty U. Cambridge, 1981-82, 91, 96-97, 2004, U. Oxford, 1989, 2004; archaeology corr. The Times, London (Press award, Brit. Archaeol. Awards 1994, 98), 1967—; field work in North Africa, Afghanistan, Greece, Guatemala, Belize, Ecuador, Spain; disting. lectr. Montana State U., 1996, Bushnell lectr. Cambridge U., 1997, Stone lectr. AIA, 1998, 2004, Brush lectr. AIA, 2001, Armand Brunswick disting. lectr. Met. Mus. Art, 2001. Author: (with F.R. Allchin) The Archaeology of Afghanistan, 1977, (with G.R. Willey) Maya Archaeology and Ethnohistory, 1979, Ancient Maya Civilization, 1982, 5th edit., 1994, various foreign edits., Cuello: An Early Maya Community in Belize, 1991, The Maya, 2000; numerous monographs on excavations in No. Belize, 1973, 75, 76, Lubaantun, 1975, Nohmul, 1985; gen. editor: Procs., 44th Internat. Congress of Americanists, 1982-84. Dumbarton Oaks fellow, 1988; Rockefeller Found. scholar, 1997. Fellow Soc. Antiquaries London (medallist 2001), Brit. Acad. (Reckitt lectr. 2006) Office: Boston Univ Dept Archaeology 675 Commonwealth Ave Boston MA 02215-1406 Home Phone: 617-739-9077; Office Phone: 617-358-1651.

HAMMOND, PAUL YOUNG, political science professor; b. Salt Lake City, Feb. 24, 1929; s. James Thaddeus and Hortense Clair (Young) H.; m. Merylyn Felt Simmons, Aug. 29, 1950; children: Paul Brett, Wendy Simmons, Robyn Simmons, Spencer Blair, Clifford Simmons. BA, U. Utah, 1949; MA, Harvard U., 1951, PhD, 1953; postgrad. Fulbright scholar, London Sch. Econs., 1952-53. Instr. govt. Harvard U., Cambridge, Mass., 1953—55; lectr. Columbia U., NYC, 1956—57; asst. prof. polit. sci. Yale U., New Haven, 1957—62; rsch. assoc. Washington Ctr. Fgn. Policy Rsch. Johns Hopkins U., 1962—64; mem. rsch. staff Rand Corp., Santa Monica, Calif., 1964—76, head social sci. dept., 1973—76; vis. rsch. polit. scientist U. Calif., Berkeley, 1971—72; Edward R. Weidlein prof. environ. and pub. policy studies U. Pitts., 1976—83, disting. svc. prof. pub. and internat. affairs, 1983—2004, disting. svc. prof. emeritus, 2004—; dir. Ridgway Ctr. of Internat. Security Studies, 1988—91, Energy and Environ. Center, 1979—81; Fulbright rsch. prof. Inst. of S.E. Asian Studies, Singapore, 1993—94. Lectr. U. Tex., U. So. Calif., U. Calif., Santa Barbara and L.A.; mem. aux. faculty U. Utah, 2004—; cons. in field. Author/co-author: Organizing for Defense: The Adminstration of the American Military Establishment, 1961, The Cold War Years: American Foreign Policy Since 1945, 1969, Cold War and Detente: The American Foreign Policy Process Since 1945, 1975, NATO Strategic Planning: Preparations That Do No Harm, 1988, Fulfilling the Promise of the Goldwater-Nichols Act: Operational Planning and Command, 1989, NATO: The Infrastructure of Reassurance, 1989, What Future For the U.S. Military Presence in Europe, 1990, LBJ and the Presidential Management of Foreign Relations, 1992, Towards a Workable European Architecture: Political-Military Problems in the New Europe, 1994, Doing Without America?, 1996, On Taking Peacekeeping Seriously, 1997, Culture Versus Civilization: A Critique of Huntington, 1997; co-author: The American Civil-Military Decisions, 1963, Information System Applications for a High Level Staff, 1972, Social Choice and Soviet Strategic Decision Making, 1977, Regional Energy Policy Alternatives, 1977, Administration of Security Assistance: Systems and Process, 1978, Individual Energy Conservation Behaviors, 1980, The Reluctant Supplier, 1983, Alternative Organizational Structures for NATO, 1992; co-editor: Political Dynamics in the Middle East, 1971. Forrestal fellow in naval history, 1955, Stimson Fund fellow Yale U., 1959, Rockefeller fellow in internat. studies, 1963-64; Fulbright scholar London Sch. Econs., 1952-53. Mem. Am. Polit. Sci. Assn., Internat. Studies Assn. Mem. Lds Ch. Personal E-mail: pyhpyh70@yahoo.com.

HAMMOND, R. PHILIP, chemical engineer; b. Creston, Iowa, May 28, 1916; s. Robert Hugh and Helen Hammond; m. Amy L. Farmer, Feb. 28, 1941 (div. 1969); children: Allen L., David M., Jean Phyllis, Stanley W.; m. Vivienne Fox, 1972. BSChemE, U. So. Calif., 1938; PhD in Phys. and Inorganic Chemistry, U. Chgo., 1947. Registered profl. engr., Ill., Calif. Chief chemist Lindsay Chem. Co., West Chicago, Ill., 1938-46; group leader Los Alamos (N.Mex.) Sci. Lab., 1947-62, assoc. divsn. leader reactor devel. divsn., 1960-62; dir. nuc. desalination program Oak Ridge Nat. Lab., 1962-73; adj. prof. UCLA, 1972—80; head energy group R & D Assos. Corp., Santa Monica, Calif., 1973-83; desalination cons., 1987—; leader advanced sea water evaporator design Met. Water Dist. of So. Calif., LA, 1989-98. Contbr. to encyclopedias, articles to profl. jours. Mem. U.S. del. Conf. on Peaceful Uses Atomic Energy, Geneva, Switzerland, 1955, 65, 71, IAEA Panel on Desalination, Vienna, Austria, 1964, 65, 66, 71; mem. U.S. team to USSR on desalination, 1964. Naval Rsch. fellow, U. Chgo. Mem. Am. Nuc. Soc. (charter), Am. Chem. Soc., Am. Inst. Chem. Engrs., Sigma Xi, Phi Kappa Phi, Phi Lambda Upsilon. Achievements include patents for improved safety for high speed rail transport, for devices for preventing collisions at sea and for storing nuclear waste; origination of advanced concepts in sea water evaporator construction, and efficient coupling to nuclear energy sources; design (with others) of advanced reactor containment system capable of withstanding melt-down accidents with zero leakage, and of automotive engine using liquid air and liquid natural gas as fuel. Home and Office: PO Box 3971 Laguna Hills CA 92654-3971 Personal E-mail: hammondp@comline.com. *With our achievements in desalination, efficient agriculture, and nuclear power, it is now clear that the food producing ability of the earth is not limited by technology. But our political and social institutions have not kept up. Over a billion people live in hopeless poverty, and without hope, terrorism is an easy choice. Yet small investments by the rich countries in energy supply and clean water will create self-supporting communities with purchasing power. The war on terror is really a war on poverty.*

HAMMOND, RAYMOND WILLIAM, pharmacotherapy specialist; b. Port Arthur, Tex., May 16, 1944; s. Woodrow Wilson and Anna Mary (Brockman) H.; m. Sandra Louise Borel, Feb. 1, 1964; children: Cynthia Lynn, Jeffrey Carl. BS in Pharmacy, U. Houston, 1973; PharmD, U. Tenn. Ctr. Health Scis., 1981. Lic. pharmacist, Tex.; cert. pharmacotherapy specialist. Staff pharmacist USPHS Hosp., SI, NY, 1974-75; dep. chief pharmacist Med. Ctr. Fed. Prisoners, Springfield, Mo., 1975-77, USPHS Outpatient Clinic, Savannah, Ga., 1977-78, chief pharmacist, 1978-79, USPHS Outpatient Clinic, Port Arthur, Tex., 1981; pharmacist USPHS Indian Hosp., Whiteriver, Ariz., 1981-83; asst. chief inpatient clin. pharmacy services W.W. Hastings Indian Hosp., Tahlequah, Okla., 1983-91; chief customer svc. and quality assurance br. divsn. Supply Mgmt. Indian Health Svc., Albuquerque, 1991-94; asst. prof. pharmacy, experiential programs coord. Coll. Pharmacy, U. N.Mex., dir. drug utilization rev. program, 1994-97; clin. pharmacy corrd. Sierra Med. Ctr., El Paso, Tex., 1997-98; clin. assoc. prof. pharmacy coop. pharmacy program U. Tex., Austin and El Paso, 1998-99; assoc. dean practice programs Coll. Pharmacy U. Houston, 1999—. Clin. resource speaker SW Okla. State U. Sch. Pharmacy, 1984-91; adj. asst. prof. Northeastern State U. Coll. of Optometry, Tahlequah, Okla., 1986-90; adj. assoc. prof., 1991; mem. Pharmacotherapy Splty. Coun., 1994-2000; mem. adv. bd. Cherokee County Elder Care. Contbr. chpt. to book and articles to profl. jours. Mem. instl. rev. bd. NE State U., Tahlequah, 1985-91; bd. dir. Cherokee County Hospice Assn., 1986-87. Capt. USPHS, 1974-94. Fellow Am. Coll. of Clin. Pharmacists; mem. Am. Soc. Health Systems Pharmacists, Tex. Soc. Health-Sys. Pharmacists, N.Mex. Soc. Hosp. Pharmacists (pres. 1997), Commd. Officers Assn. USPHS, Mensa, Rho Chi. Democrat. Roman Catholic. Avocations: photography, backpacking, computer science, fishing, beer and winemaking. Home: 3015 Marble Falls Dr Pearland TX 77584-7067 Office Phone: 713-795-8337. E-mail: rayhammond@uh.edu.

HAMMOND, ROBIE LEE, health science association administrator; d. Robert Lee Higginbotham and Claudia Elizabeth Elrod; widowed; children: Robby Lee, Gary Joe, Debra Lynn H. Olson. AA, Draughans Bus. Coll., Greenville, SC, 1946. Cert. med. staff coord. Nat. Assn. of Med. Staff Svcs. Svc. rep. Bell Tel. & Telegraph Co., Greenville, SC, 1946—52, Chesapeake & Potomac Tel. Co., Norfolk, Va., 1953; sec. Portsmouth Psychiat. Ctr., Va., 1976—81; med. libr. Portsmouth Gen. Hosp., Va., 1981—82, med. staff coord., 1983—98; exec. dir. Portsmouth Acad. of Medicine, Va., 1998—, exec. dir. med. found., 1998—. Mem. citizens adv. com. Educare for Seniors, Portsmouth. Mem.: Portsmouth Consortium of Founds., Va. Conf. of Med. Execs. Avocations: golf, gardening, reading, creative writing, decorating. Office Phone: 757-398-4100. Business E-Mail: bobbie_hammond@bshsi.com.

HAMMOND, ROY JOSEPH, reinsurance company executive; b. St. Louis, Jan. 9, 1929; s. Edward Herman and Alvera Ann (Herzog) H.; m. Donna LaSalle Perkins, Apr. 12, 1951 (div. July 2001); children— Douglas Edward, Donald Erwin, Laura Ann Hammond Budniakiewicz; m. Gloria June Kirkpatrick, Dec. 19, 2001. BS, Northwestern U., Evanston, Ill., 1954; JD, DePaul U., Chgo., 1959. Bar: Ill. bar 1959. With Am. Mut. Reins. Co., Chgo., 1963-91, v.p., then sr. v.p., gen. counsel and sec., 1967-76, pres., chief exec. officer, bd. dirs., 1976-91; pres., chief exec. officer Whitehall Cons., Ltd., Camden, NC, 1991—; pres. Wheeling Mcpl. Park Dist., Ill., 1963-65. Past mem. Reins. Assn. Am., bd. dirs., 1976—86. Served with U.S. Army, 1946-48. Mem. ABA, Ill. State Bar Assn., Internat. Assn. Def. Counsel, Fedn. Ins. and Corp. Counsel, Chgo. Casualty Adjusters Assn. (pres. 1972-73), Chgo. Yacht Club. Republican. Lutheran. Home and Office: Whitehall Shores 201 Azalea Dr Camden NC 27921-6991

HAMMOND, TRACY ANNE, computer scientist, educator; b. Syracuse, NY, Aug. 21, 1976; d. John Finley Zeigler and Janice Dale Hammond, Raghavan Parthasarthy (Stepfather). BS in Applied Math., Columbia U., NYC, 1997, BA in Math., 1997, BS in Computer Sci., 2000, BA in Anthropology, 2001; Fin. Tech. Option, MIT, Cambridge, Mass., 2003, PhD in Computer Sci., 2007. Telecom analyst Goldman Sachs, NYC, 1996—2000; instr. Columbia U., NYC, 1999—2006; rsch. asst. MIT, 2000—06; asst. prof. Tex. A&M U., College Station, 2006—. Contbr. articles to profl. publs. Clare Booth Luce fellow, 2000, New Faculty fellow, Frontiers in Edn., 2002. Mem.: IEEE. Achievements include design of LADDER sketch language. Home: 1211 Winding Rd College Station TX 77840 Office: Texas A&M U Dept Computer Sci Box 3112 College Station TX 77843 Office Phone: 979-862-4284. Business E-Mail: hammond@cs.tamu.edu.

HAMMOND, WILLIAM MICHAEL, historian, educator; b. Pasadena, Calif., Jan. 1, 1943; s. Paul Chester Hammond and Mary Ethel Champieux; m. Lillamaud Munsell Leike, Apr. 28, 1973; children: Michael Anthony, Elizabeth Anne. STB, Cath. U. Am., 1967, MA, 1968, PhD, 1973. Sr. lectr. U. Md., College Park, 1991—; chief gen. histories br. U.S. Army Ctr. Mil. History, Washington, 2001—. Author: The Unknown Serviceman of the Vietnam Era, 1985, The U.S. Army in Vietnam: Public Affairs: The Military and the Media, 1962 - 1968, 1988 (Notable Govt. Docs., ALA, 1989), Public Affairs: The Military and the Media, 1968-1973, 1996, Black Soldier, White Army: The 24th Infantry in Korea, 1996, Reporting Vietnam, Military and Media at War, 1998 (Richard W. Leopold award, Orgn. Am. Historians, 2000). Editor, web master, bd. dirs. Strathmore - Bel Pre Civic Assn., Silver Spring, Md., 1986—. Rsch. fellow, Joan Shorenstein Ctr. for the Press and Pub. Policy, Harvard U., 1999. Fellow: Interuniv. Seminar on Armed Forces and Soc.; mem.: Orgn. Am. Historians

(Disting. Lectr. 2002—), Soc. Mil. History. Roman Catholic. Avocations: photography, watercolor painting, travel. Home: 2604 Bainbridge Ln Silver Spring MD 20906 Office: US Army Ctr Mil History Fort Lesley J McNair Washington DC 20319-5058

HAMMONDS, BRUCE L., bank executive; m. Sandy Hammonds; 2 children. Grad., U. Balt. Branch mgr. Pacific Finance Co.; joined Md. Nat. Bank, Balt., 1978; with Md. Bank N.A. (now MBNA Am. Bank N.A.), 1982, dir., 1986; COO MBNA Corp., Wilmington, Del., 1991—2002, pres., CEO, 2003—05; chmn, CEO MBNA Am. Bank N.A., 2002—05; pres. Bank Am. Cards Services, Charlotte, NC, 2006—. Bd. dirs. Del. State C. of C., Del. Housing Ptnrship., Del. Bus. Roundtable, Fin. Svcs. Roundtable; trustee Goldey-Beacom Coll.; mem. vis. com. Coll. of Bus. and Econs., U. Del. Office: Bank of America 100 N Tryon St Charlotte NC 28255*

HAMMONS, BRIAN KENT, lawyer; b. Wurzburg, Germany, Mar. 6, 1958; arrived in U.S., 1958; s. R. Dwain and Donna G. (Carender) H.; m. Kimberly M. Pflumm, July 26, 1980; children: April Michelle, David Dwain, Adam Carender. BS summa cum laude, Mo. State U., Springfield, 1980; JD cum laude, So. Meth. U., Dallas, 1985. Bar: Mo. 1985. Exec., treas., v.p. Hammons Products Co., Stockton, Mo., 1980-86, exec. v.p., sec., 1987-96, pres., COO, CEO, 1997—; assoc. Stinson, Mag & Fizzell, Kansas City, Mo., 1986-87. Bd. govs. Mo. State U., 2006—. Mem. Stockton Airport Bd., 1987—89, Stockton City Coun., 1989—91, Ozark Empire Fair Bd., 2004—; pres. Stockton Cmty. Found., 2002—, Stockton Cmty. Devel. Bd., 2003—; former cub scout leader Boy Scouts Am.; former soccer coach; mem. Leadership Mo., 1990; Sunday sch. and Bible study tchr.; chair United Meth. Mo. Conf. Fin. and Adminstrn., 2004—. Mem.: Mo. Chamber Commerce and Industry (bd. dirs. 2003—), Springfield Area C. of C. (bd. dirs. 2003—05), Mo. Bar Assn., Young Presidents Orgn., Lions (pres. 1990—91), Masons (sec. 1980—81), Phi Delta Phi. Republican. Methodist. Avocations: running, flying, tennis, golf, hunting. Office: Hammons Products Co 105 Hammons Dr PO Box 140 Stockton MO 65785

HAMNER, LANCE DALTON, prosecutor; b. Fukuoka, Japan, Sept. 18, 1955; parents Am. citizens; s. Louie D. and Mary Louise (Sloan) H.; m. Karla Jean Cleverly, Sept. 22, 1980; children: Lance Dalton Jr., Nicholas James, Louie Alexander, Samuel Sean, Victoria Jean. BS summa cum laude, Weber State Coll., 1984; JD magna cum laude, Ind. U., 1987. Bar: Ind., US Dist. Ct. (no., so. dist.) Ind. 1988. Atty. Barnes & Thornburg, Indpls., 1988-89; dep. prosecuting atty. Marion County Prosecutor's Office, Indpls., 1989-90; pros. atty. Johnson County, Franklin, Ind., 1991—. Legal corr. WGGR Radio News, Indpls., 1995; adj. prof. law Sch. Law Ind. U., Indpls., 1995—96, Bloomington, 1996—98; frequent spkr. on legal topics including search and seizure and interrogation law; lectr. Ind. Continuing Legal Edn. Forum, Indpls., 1992; mem. faculty Newly-Elected Pros. Sch. Ind. Pros. Attys. Coun., 1999; mem. faculty Indpls. Police Acad., 1999, Ind. Police Corps, 2000—05. Author: Indiana Search & Seizure Courtroom Manual, 2001, 2002, 2004; editor: Ind. Law Jour., 1987. Scoutmaster Boy Scouts Am., Franklin, Ind., 1999-2003. Mem. Nat. Dist. Attys. Assn., Assn. Govt. Attys. in Capital Litigation, Ind. Prosecuting Atty.'s Coun., Nat. Eagle Scout Assn., Order of the Coif. Republican. Mem. Lds Ch. Avocations: fitness, writing. Office: Prosecutor's Office Courthouse Annex N 80 S Jackson St Franklin IN 46131-2353 Office Phone: 317-736-3750. Personal E-mail: lhamner@aol.com.

HAMNER, REGINALD TURNER, lawyer; b. Tuscaloosa, Ala., June 4, 1939; s. Raiford Samuel and Ellie Wells (Turner) Hamner; m. Anne Ellen Young, Nov. 8, 1969; children: Patrick Turner, William Christian. BS, U. Ala., 1961, JD, 1965. Bar: Ala. 1965, U.S. Dist. Ct. (mid. dist.) Ala. 1966, U.S. Ct. Appeals (5th cir.) 1966, U.S. Ct. Mil. Appeals 1968, U.S. Supreme Ct. 1968, U.S. Ct. Appeals (11th and 5th cirs.) 1981. Law clk. Supreme Ct. Ala., Montgomery, 1965; dir. legal-legis. affairs Med. Assn., State of Ala., 1968-69; sec., exec. dir. Ala. State Bar, Montgomery, 1969-94; ct. project coord. U.S. Dist. Ct. (Mid. Dist.) Ala., Montgomery, 1995—2006. Bd. dirs. S.E. br. YMCA, Montgomery, 1978—81; former legal counsel govtl. adv. panels investigating Ala. Prison Sys.; vice chmn. State Child Welfare Com.; bd. dirs. Attys. Ins. Mut. Ala., Inc.; sec., treas. Ala. Law Found., 1987—93; chmn. Ala. Rhodes Scholarship Com., 1989—94; bd.dirs. Ala. Humanities Found., 2004—. With JAG USAF, 1965—68, col. USAFR. Named Disting. alumnus, U Ala., 2004. Fellow: Am. Bar Found. (life; state chmn. 1994—95); mem.: ABA (mem. ho. dels. 1972—76, 1985—89, 1993, 1996—), Jud. Conf. U.S. Ct. Appeals (11th cir. 1981—96), Ala. Law Inst. (coun.), Ala. Coun. Assn. Execs. (pres. 1984), Am. Soc. Assn. Execs. (commr. certification com. 1978—79), Nat. Assn. Bar Execs. (pres. 1978—79), Am. Judicature Soc., U. Ala. Nat. Alumni Assn. (pres. 1989—90), Montgomery Country Club, Delta Tau Delta, Phi Alpha Delta, Alpha Epsilon Delta, Omicron Delta Kappa. Episcopalian. Home: 7518 Wynford Cir Montgomery AL 36117-7498 Office: US Courthouse One Church St Ste Rm 400 FMJ Montgomery AL 36104 Office Phone: 334-324-4372.

HAMNER, ROME, social services administrator; b. 1974; Grants mgr. Our Family Services, Inc. Co-founder Odaiko Sonora. Vol. grant reviewer Tucson Pima Arts Coun. Named one of 40 Under 40, Tucson Bus. Edge, 2006. Mem.: Arizona Commn. on Arts Roster of Artists, Southern Ariz. Alliance of Nonprofits, Japan Am. Soc. of Tucson (bd. dir.), OTO Dance Studios. Avocation: Taiko drumming. Office: c/o Tucson Pima Arts Council 10 E Broadway 106 Tucson AZ 85701

HAMNER, W. EASLEY, architect; b. Altavista, Va., Sept. 22, 1937; s. Robert Wilbourne and Isabelle (Easley) H.; m. Suzanne Leath, June 18, 1961; children: Janine, Michael. Diploma, Ecole de Beaux Arts, Fontainebleau, France, 1959; BArch, N.C. State U., 1960; MArch, Harvard U., 1967. Registered arch. Mass., La., Nev. Assoc. Thompson B. Burk, New Orleans, 1961-66; prin. The Stubbins Assocs., Cambridge, Mass., 1967—2003; founder Boston Internat. Design Collaborative, LLC, 2003—. Architect Citicorp Ctr., 1970-77; bd. dirs. Hyman/Stubbins, Inc.; internat. design juror Jin Mao Bldg., Shanghai, Beijing Olympics, Beihei (China) Beach Resort, Beijing MXD Complex. Prin. works include Citicorp Ctr., NYC (11 awards), Riverpark, Norwalk, Conn. (award), The MITRE Corp. (award), O'Neill Fed. Bldg., Boston, Bristol-Myers Rsch. Labs, Wallingford, Conn. (award), Suffolk County Jail, Boston (2 awards), Suffolk County House of Corrections, Boston (award), Anhui Internat. Trade Ctr., Hefei, China, Venetian Hotel/Casino, Las Vegas (5 awards), Shezhen City (China) Plz. Bd. dirs. Cambridge Cmty. Svcs., 1981—, pres., 1982-99, Ellery Sq. Owners Assn., 1983-85; chmn. bd. trustees Pro Arte Chamber Orch., 1993-2004; bd. dirs. Cambridge Cmty. Found., 1993-98; elected mem. Harvard Grad. Sch. Design Alumni Coun., chmn. com. of five, 1983-84. Lt. U.S. Army Intelligence, 1960. Fellow AIA; mem. Boston Soc. Arch., Nat. Assn. Indsl. and Office Properties (mem. nat. mixed-use forum 1997-2002), Urban Land Inst. (vice-chair coun.), Harvard U. Alumni Assn. (dir. 1984-88), Cambridge Club (pres. 1988-89), Boston Harbor Yacht Club. Democrat. Office: Bldg C 3 Ellery St Cambridge MA 02138 Home Phone: 617-354-8055; Office Phone: 617-354-8055. E-mail: wehamner@earthlink.net.

HAMOUI, OMAR, advertising executive; BS Computer Sci., UCLA; stud. MBA, Wharton Sch. With FotoChatter; founder, CEO AdMob, 2006—. Spkr. in field. Named one of 40 Under 40, Advt. Age, 2007. Office: AdMob US Hdqs 60 E 3rd Ave San Mateo CA 94401 Office Phone: 650-931-3940. E-mail: omar@admob.com.

HAMOY, CAROL, artist; b. NYC, May 22, 1934; d. Morris David and Selma (Essex) Cohen. Student, Newark Sch. Fine Art, 1952-54, Art Students League, NYC, various yrs. Lectr., spkr. in field. Solo exhibitions include USMA/West Point, NY, 1978, Katonah (NY) Gallery, 1983, Lower Manhattan Cultural Coun., NYC, 1986, May Mus./Lawrence, NY Ceres, NYC, 1992, MTA-Arts for Transit, NYC, 1993, Robert Kahn Gallery, Houston, 1993, Temple Judea Mus., Elkins Park, Pa., 1993, Univ. Art Ctr., Shreveport, La., 1994, Ceres, NYC, 1995, 98-99, 2001, Goldman Art Gallery, Rockville, Md., 1996, Nat. Mus. Am. Jewish History, Phila., 1996, Broadway Windows, NYC, 1997, Ellis Island Immigration Mus., NYC, 1997, Mizel Mus., Denver, 1997, Breman Heritage Mus., Atlanta, 1998, Eldridge St. Project, NYC, 1998, Inter-Am. Gallery, Miami, Fla., 1998, Skirball Mus., Cincinnati, 1999, Franklin Marshall Coll., Lancaster Pa., 1999, Margolis Gallery, Houston, 1999, Lower East Side Tenement Mus., NY, 2000, The Neuberger Mus., Purchase, NY, 2000, Ceres, NYC, 2001, Dacotah Prarie Mus., Aberdeen, S.D., 2002, Azarian/McCullough Gallery, Sparkill, NY, 2002, Futernick Gallery, Miami, 2003, Longyear Mus., Hamilton, NY, 2005, Hebrew Union Coll. Mus., NYC, 2005—, Mizel Mus., Denver, 2005—, Kansas City Jewish Mus., Overland Pk., Kans., 2006, Catherine Murphy Gallery, St. Paul, Minn., 2007, Fine Arts Gallery, Valhalla, NY; exhibited in group shows at Pelham (NY) Art Ctr., 1988, U. Ky., Lexington, 1989, HUC, NYC, 1989, Kentuck Mus., Northport, Ala., 1989, Clough Hansen Gallery, Memphis, 1989, JRC Gallery, Evanston, Ill., 1992, Soho 20, NYC, 1993, Charach-Epstein Mus., West Bloomfield, Mich., 1994, 97, Nat. Jewish Mus., Washington, 1995, Fine Arts Rosen Mus., Boca Raton, Fla., 1995, Right Brain Gallery, Atlanta, 1999, Miss. Univ. for Women, 1999, Skirball Mus., Cin., 1999, Neuberger Mus., Purchase, NY, 2000, Ellipse Arts Ctr., Arlington, Va., 2000, Contemporary Crafts, Pitts., 2000, Ceres, 2000, The Joseph Gallery Mus, NYC, 2000-01, Moving On/Frauen Mus., Bonn, Germany, John Jay Coll., 2001—, Joseph Gallery, NY, 2000-01, Frauen Mus., Bonn, Germany, 2001-02, Detritus Show John Jay College, NY, 2001-02, Judaica Mus., Riverdale, NY, 2001-02, Kommunale Galerie Wilmersdorf, Berlin, 2001-02, Ctr. for Visual Art & Culture, Stamford, Conn., 2002, Am. Craft Mus., NY, 2002-03, Joseph Gallery, NYC, HUC Mus., NYC, 2003—, 2005-06, Jewish Mus. Md., Balt., 2004, Alper Art Gallery, Miami, Fla., 2004, Wain Ling Art Ctr., Haverford, Pa., 2005, Futernick Art Gallery, Miami, 2005, Rutgers U., Camden, N.J., 2005, Gotthelf Gallery, La Jolla, Calif., 2006, others; permanent collections include Elizabeth A. Sackler Women Artists Archives, Brooklyn Mus., NY, Mabel Smith Douglass Libr. Art Collection, New Brunswick, NJ, Rutgers U. Librs. Women Artist Archives, New Brunswick, Coll. St. Catherine, St. Paul, Minn., Nat. Mus. Women in the Arts, Nat. Jewish Mus., Washington, Frauen Mus., Bonn, Duke U., Durham, NC, Ringling Sch. Art, Sarasota, Fla., others. Nominee, Joan Mitchell Found., 2000; grantee Va. Ctr. for Creative Arts, Sweet Briar, Va., 1980, Artists' Space, NYC, 1981, Hillwood Art Mus., NY State Coun. for Creative Arts, 1992, MTA-Arts for Transit, NYC, 1993, Lucius N. Littauer Found. Bessemere Trust Co. N.A., 1997, Meml. Found./Jewish Culture Artists' Fellowship, Inc. of NYC, 1999, Pollock-Krasner Found., 2005. Studio: 340 E 66th St New York NY 10065

HAMPL, PATRICIA, writer, educator; b. St. Paul, Minn., Mar. 12, 1946; d. Stanislaus Rudolph Hampl and Mary Teresa Marum; m. Terrence J. Williams, Sept. 10, 1988. BA, U. Minn., Mpls., 1968; MFA, U. Iowa, Iowa City, 1970; LHD (hon.), Coll. St. Catherine, St. Paul, 1993, Luther Coll., Decorh, IA, 1994, U. St. Thomas, St. Paul, 1996. Editor Minn. Monthly, St. Paul, 1972—75; freelance writer, tchr., 1975—82; English prof. U. Minn., Mpls., 1982—97, Regents prof., McKnight Disting. prof., 1997—. Permanent faculty Prague summer program, Western Mich. U., in Prague, 1992—. Author: A Romantic Education, 1981, Resort & Other Poems, 1983, reprint, 2001, Spillville, 1987, Virgin Time, 1992, I Could Tell You Stories, 1999, Afterword, 1999. Recipient Guggenheim award, 1988; Mac Arthur fellow, John D. & Catherine C. Mac Arthur Found., 1990, Fulbright fellow, 1995. Fellow: Am. Acad. Arts & Scis.; mem.: The Loft Lit. Ctr., PEN. Office: English Lang and Lit Univ Minn--210M LindH 207 Church St S E Minneapolis MN 55455 Office Phone: 651-625-3546. Personal E-mail: hampl@umn.edu.*

HAMPLE, JUDY G., academic administrator; BA in Speech Comm. and Secondary Edn./French, David Lipscomb U.; MA and PhD in Comm., Ohio State U. Univ. fellow, asst. dir. intercollegiate debate Ohio State U.; faculty dept. speech comm. U. Ill., Champaign-Urbana; divsn. dir. dept. comm. arts and scis. Western Ill. U., assoc. dean for budget and pers. Coll. Arts and Scis.; dean Coll. Liberal Arts and Scis. Emporia State U., 1983—86; dean Coll. Arts and Scis. Ind. State U., 1986—93; sr. v.p. acad. affairs U. Toledo, 1993; vice chancellor planning, budget and policy analysis, vice chancellor and chancellor bd. regents State Univ. Sys. Fla., 1998—2001; chancellor Pa. State Sys. of Higher Edn., Harrisburg, 2001—. Cons.-evaluator North Cen. Accreditation Assn.; pub. cons.-evaluator ABA. Co-editor: Teaching in the Middle Ages, 3 vols.; editor: Studies in Medieval and Renaissance Teaching; contbr. articles to profl. jours. Office: Pa State Sys of Higher Edn Dixon Univ Ctr 2986 N 2d St Harrisburg PA 17110 Office Phone: 717-720-4010.*

HAMPSON, THOMAS MEREDITH, lawyer; b. Ann Arbor, Mich., Feb. 18, 1929; s. Harold Snover and Louise Susan (Goetchius) H.; m. Margaret H. Clark, Nov. 24, 1951 (div. Dec. 1969); children: Melissa Clark, Douglas Meredith; m. Zena Collier, Dec. 30, 1969. BA, Harvard U., 1951, LLB with distinction, 1955. Bar: N.Y. 1955, U.S. Dist. Ct. (we. dist.) N.Y. 1955, U.S. Supreme Ct. 1964. Assoc. Harris, Beach, Wilcox, Rubin & Levey, Rochester, NY, 1955-62; ptnr. Harris Beach, LLP, Rochester, 1962—. Vis. instr. Cornell Law Sch., Ithaca, N.Y., 1969-75. Radio broadcaster The Jazz Scene, 1960-80, Jazz Notes, 1979-81, Mostly Jazz, 1985-; newspaper columnist, 1985-88. Chmn. Monroe County Fair Campaign Practices Com., Rochester, 1977-91; trustee Rochester Pub. Libr., 1976-98; dir. Cornell Lab. Ornithology, Ithaca, N.Y., 1984-90, Hawk Mountain Sanctuary Assn., 1990-98, Rundel Libr. Found., 1995—; bd. dirs. N.Y. State Civil Liberties Union, N.Y.C., 1963-69; commr. Rochester Civil Svc. Commn., 1997—, chmn. 2000—. 1st lt. USAF, 1951-53. Recipient Civil Liberties award N.Y. Civil Liberties Union, Genesee Valley chpt., 1987, Harold Hacker Lifetime Libr. Achievement award, 2006. Mem. ABA, N.Y. State Bar Assn., Monroe County Bar Assn., City Club (pres. 1965-66), Philosophers' Club (pres. 1985-88). Democrat. Unitarian Universalist. Avocations: birding, jazz. Home: 83 Berkeley St Rochester NY 14607-2207 Office: Harris Beach LLP 99 Garnsey Rd Pittsford NY 14534 Office Phone: 585-419-8941. E-mail: thampson@frontiernet.net.

HAMPTON, BENJAMIN BERTRAM, brokerage house executive; b. NYC, Aug. 3, 1925; s. max and Pauline (Weinberger) H.; m. Elizabeth Golub-Cohen, Oct. 16, 1975; 1 child by previous marriage, Roger Neil; stepchildren: Laurence, James, Lisa. B Aero. Engring., NYU, 1947; cert. in mech. engring., Pa. State Coll., 1945; MBA, Harvard U., Cambridge, Mass., 1949. Sales mgr. Carew Products, Inc., NYC, 1949-51; project mgr. Emerson Radio & TV Corp., 1951-52; div. mgr. Paragon Oil Co., Mineola, NY, 1952-55; mgmt. cons. E.N. Kagan & co., NYC, 1955-60; exec. asst. to pres. mktg. sect. Fed. Pacific Electric co., Newark, 1960-62; asst. to pres. Seagrave Corp., NYC, 1962-63; v.p. Swingline Inc., Long Island City, N.Y., 1963-68, exec. v.p., 1968-71, bd. dirs., 1970-71; exec. v.p., bd. dirs. Poloron Products Inc., New Rochelle, N.Y., 1971-73, pres., CEO, bd. dirs., 1973-74; exec. v.p., bd. dirs. West Chem. Products, Inc., Long Island City, 1975-78; prin. Hampton Assocs., 1979-82; v.p. Merrill Lynch Pierce Fenner & Smith, Great Neck, NY, 1982—2007; ret., 2007. Co-chmn. N.Y. State fin. com. J.F. Kennedy presdl. campaign, 1960. With AUS, 1944-46. Mem. Harvard Club, Pi Lambda Phi. Home: Apt B 6224 Island Bend Boca Raton FL 33496 Office Phone: 800-536-2988. Personal E-mail: bhampton08@comcast.net.

HAMPTON, CAROL MCDONALD, priest, educator, historian; b. Oklahoma City, Sept. 18, 1935; d. Denzil Vincent and Mildred Juanita (Cussen) McDonald; m. James Wilburn Hampton, Feb. 22, 1958; children: Jaime, Clayton, Diana, Neal. BA, U. Okla., 1957, MA, 1973, PhD, 1984; cert. individual theol. study, Episcopal Theol. Sem. of S.W., 1998; MDiv summa cum laude, Phillips Theol. Sem., 1999. Ordained to Episcopal Transitional Diaconate, 1999, ordained priest, 1999. Tchg. asst. U. Okla., Norman, 1976—81; instr. U. Sci. and Arts Okla., Chickasha, 1981—84; coord. Consortium for Grad. Opportunities for Am. Indians U. Calif., Berkeley, 1985—86; trustee Ctr. of Am. Indian, Oklahoma City, 1981. Vice chmn. Nat. Com. on Indian Work, Episc. Ch., 1986; field officer Native Am. Ministry of Episc. Ch. (Nat.), 1986-94, sec., co-chmn., advising elder, prin. elder coun., 1994-96; field officer for Congl. Ministries of Episc. Ch. (Nat.), 1994-97; mem. nat. coun. Chs. Racial Justice Working Group, 1990-97, co-convenor, 1991-93, convenor, 1993-95; officer Multicultural Ministries of Episc. Ch. (Nat.), 1994-97; (hon.) canon of St. Paul's Cath., Oklahoma City, 2001—. Mem. editl. bd.: First Peoples Theology Jour.; contbr. articles to profl. jours. Trustee Western History Collections, U. Okla., Okla. Found. for the Humanities, 1983-86; mem. bd. regents U. Sci. and Arts Okla., 1989-95; bd. dirs. Okla. State Regents for Higher Edn., mem. adv. com. on social justice; mem. World Coun. of Chs. Program to Combat Racism, Geneva, 1985-91; bd. dirs. Caddo Tribal Coun., Okla., 1976-82; accredited observer Anglican Consultative Coun. UN 4th World Conf. on Women, 1995; v.p. Nat. Conf. Cmty. Justice, 1999-2002; bd. dirs. Ctrl. Okla. Human Rights Alliance, 1999—; dir. Planned Parenthood of Ctr. Okla. Bd., 2002—; mem. Okla. Coun. Indian Ministry, 1998—, co-chair, 2006—. Recipient Okla. State Human Rights award, 1987; Francis C. Allen fellow Ctr. for the History of Am. Indian, 1983. Mem.: Okla. Coun. Indian Ministy (co-chair 2006—), Okla. Conf. Chs. (bd. dirs. 2000—), Indigenous Theol. Tng. Inst. (bd. dirs. 2000—), Jr. League (Oklahoma City), Am. Assn. Indian Historians (founding mem. 1981—), Okla. Hist. Soc., Am. Hist. Assn., Orgn. Am. Historians, Western Social Sci. Assn., Western History Assn. Democrat. Episcopalian. Avocation: travel. Home: 1414 N Hudson Ave Oklahoma City OK 73103-3721 Office Phone: 405-235-3436. E-mail: cjchampton@sbcglobal.net, champton@stpaulsokc.org.

HAMPTON, JAMES WILBURN, hematologist, oncologist; b. Durant, Okla., Sept. 15, 1931; s. Hollis Eugene and Ouida (Mackey) Hampton; m. Carol McDonald, Feb. 22, 1958; children: Jaime, Clay, Diana, Neal. BA, U. Oklahoma, 1952, MD, 1956. Int. U. Okla. Hosps., 1956-57, res.; instr. to prof. U. Okla., Oklahoma City, 1959-77; clin. prof. med., 1977—. Mem. admissions bd., 1965—; bd. dirs., 1995—2006; head hematology/oncology, 1972—77; head hematology, mem. Okla. Med. Rsch. Found., Oklahoma City, 1972—77; dir. cancer prog. and med. oncology Bapt. Med. Ctr., 1977—85; med. dir. Cancer Ctr. S.W., 1985—94, Troy and dollie Smith Cancer Ctr., 1994—; mem. Internat. Com. Thrombosis and Hemostasis; cons. NIH, Biomed. and Nat. Cancer Inst., Karolinska Inst., Stockhom; vis. scientist Career Devel. Award, 1966—67; vis. prof. U. NC, Chapel Hill, 1966; founder Stewart Wolf Soc., 1967, pres., 1990—92; founder Robert Montgomery Bird Soc., 1973, pres., 1996—98. Contbr. articles to profl. jours. Chmn. Network Cancer Prevention and Control Rsch. Am. Indians/Alaska Natives Nat. Cancer Inst.; mem. Interncultural Cancer Coun., 1996—, chair-elect, 2000—01, chair, 2001—02; initiator Hospice Oklahoma County, 1990—; bd. dirs. Am. Cancer Soc., mem. at large, nat. bd. dirs., 1990—96; mem. com. task force Cancer Socio-Economically Disadvantaged, 1990—2002; chmn. Okla. divsn. svc. and rehab. com., collaborating ptnr. Pres. Bush Dialogue on Cancer, 1999—; chmn. Okla. Pain Initiative, 1996; mem. adv. com. Office Minority Health NIH, 1996—99; co-chmn. Save St. Paul's Episcopal Cathedral Com., 1983; chmn. bishop's Okla. com. Indian work, mem. province VII Indian com., alt. del. Diocesan Conv. Okla., 1991—95, 2000—05; mem. coun. combating racism Epis. Ch. Am., 1995—97, del. to elect bishop to Okla., 2007, del. to Diocesan Conv., 2007. Named Physician of the Yr., U. Okla. Alumni Assocs., 1998; recipient Humanitarian award, ACS, 1999, honor by Lakota Tribe at Mayo Clinic, 1999, Leap of Faith award, Intercultural Cancer Coun., 2006; Career Devel. grantee, NIH, 1966—76. Fellow: ACP; mem.: AMA (mem. minority affairs consortium, mem. steering com. 1997—2000), Intercultural Cancer Coun. (chairperson 2003), Am. Psychosomatic Soc., So. Soc. Clin. Investigation, Am. Soc. Clin. Oncology, Am. Soc. Hematology, Assn. Am. Pathologists, Am. Phyhsiol. Soc., Assn. Am. Indian Physicians (pres. 1978—79, 1988—89, Indian Physician of the Yr. award 1987), Internat. Soc. Thrombosis and Hemostasis, Oklahoma County Med. Soc. (editor bull. 1981—, bd. dirs. 1982—85, 1989—91), Ctrl. Soc. Clin. Rsch. (assoc. editor Jour. Lab. and Clin. Med. 1975—76), Am. Fedn. Clin. Rsch. (pres. midwest sect. 1970—71), English Speaking Union, Blue Cord Club, Oklahoma City Golf and Country Club, Chaine des Rotisseurs. Home: 1414 N Hudson Ave Oklahoma City OK 73103-3721 Office: Cancer Care Assocs Lake Hefner Campus 11100 Hefner Pointe Dr Oklahoma City OK 73120-5049 Office Phone: 405-749-0415. Business E-Mail: james.hampton@cancercareokla.com.

HAMPTON, JOHN LEWIS, retired newspaper editor; b. Verda, Ky., Jan. 13, 1935; s. John Lewis and Ruby Lillian (Slagle) H.; m. Lillian Valls; children from previous marriage: Rachel, Jessica Hampton Fazio, Jonathan Hugh. AB in Journalism (Outstanding Journalism Grad. award 1959), U. Ky., 1959; MA in Communications and Journalism (grad. fellow 1960), Stanford U., 1960. Staff writer AP, Lexington, Ky., 1960-61; bur. chief Louisville (Ky.) Courier-Jour., 1961-67; staff writer Nat. Observer, Washington, 1967-71, sr. editor, then asst. mng. editor, 1971-77; mem. editorial bd. Miami (Fla.) Herald, 1977, editor, 1978-99; Clendinen prof. journalism U. South Fla., Tampa, 2005—. Served with AUS, 1953-56. Named to Hall Disting. Alumni U. Ky., Ky. Journalism Hall of Fame, 2000; recipient Pulitzer prize in editorial writing, 1983 Mem. Am. Soc. Newspaper Editors, Inter Am. Press Assn. (bd. dirs. 1987-99), Fla. Soc. Newspaper Editors. Office: Miami Herald 1 Herald Plz Miami FL 33132-1693 Personal E-mail: jhampton@miamiherald.com.

HAMPTON, LEROY, retired chemical company executive; b. Ingalls, Ark., Apr. 20, 1927; s. Ed Levi and Kitty Annie (Larry) H.; m. Anne Neris Herndon, July 11, 1954; children: Mary Louise, Gloria, Stanley Lamar, Cedric Leroy, Candice La Neris. BS, U. Colo., 1950; MS, Denver U., 1960. Registered pharmacist, Colo., Mich. Registered pharmacist Rocky Mountain Drug Co., Denver, 1950-53; scientist-chemist Dow Chem. Co., Golden, Colo., 1953-58, profl. scientist-chemist in charge, 1958-61, devel. chemist, 1961-63, devel. leader, 1963-67, recruiting supr. Midland, Mich., 1967-68; recruiting mgr. N.E. Region, 1968-70, mgr. minority employee relations, 1970-75; dir. Dow Chem. Employees Credit Union, 1975-95, pres., 1979, 85, v.p., 1991, pres., chmn., 1992; mgr. issue analysis Dow Chem. Co., 1976-80, rsch. assoc., 1981-86. Owner, operator hardware store, Denver, 1965-67; mem. cmty. adv. panel Do Chem. Co., Mich. Ops. V.p. Midland Bd. Edn., 1981—82, sec., 1979—80; dir.affirmative action Saginaw Valley State U., Univ. Ctr., Mich., 1987—90; v.p. Midland Assn. Retarded Citizens, 1985—86, treas., 1986—87; mem. Midland/Dow Cmty. Adv. Panel, 2001—05; deacon Meml. Presbyn. Ch., Midland, 1985—87, 1995—97; bd. dirs. ARC, Midland, 1974—76; mem. Midland Bd. Edn., 1978—82; bd. dirs. Midland Assn. Retarded Citizens, 1982—88. Mem. Am. Chem. Soc., Am. Pharm. Assn., Mich. Pharmacists Assn., LWV of the Midland Ams., Kiwanis (pres. Midland club 1976-77), Alpha Phi Alpha. Democrat. Presbyterian. Home: 2206 Burlington Dr Midland MI 48642-3895

HAMPTON, LORI BETH, psychologist; b. Corbin, Ky., Apr. 30, 1980; d. John Rex and Karen Sue Hampton. BS magna cum laude, Ea. Ky. U., 2002, Specialist in Psychology, 2005. Sch. psychologist Whitley County Bd. Edn., Williamsburg, Ky., 2004—. Mem.: NASP, Ky. Assn. Sch. Psychologists, Phi Kappa Pi.

HAMPTON, MARK GARRISON, architect; b. Tampa, Fla., July 17, 1923; s. Ham Stonewall and Laura (Bingenheimer) H. BS, B.Arch., Ga. Inst. Tech., 1949. Owner Mark Hampton, Architect, Tampa, 1952-65, Miami, Fla., 1974—; partner Herbert H. Johnson Assocs., Miami, 1966-73. Prin. works include Chemistry and Life Sci. bldgs, U. So. Fla., Tampa, 1961, First Fed. Office Bldg, Sarasota, 1973. Bd. dirs. Lannan Found., Palm Beach, Fla., 1972-88; pres. Tampa Art Inst., 1958, 64. Served with inf. AUS, 1943-46. Decorated Bronze Star, Purple Heart; recipient award Homes for Better Living competition, 1957, 62; Nat. Design award Horizon Home program, 1963 Fellow AIA (juror Nat. Honor awards 1963, 64, medal of honor for design Fla. Central chpt. 1974, award of honor for design 1987, test of time award 1987). Episcopalian. Office: Mark Hampton Architect FAIA 3900 Loquat Ave Miami FL 33133-5622 Office Phone: 305-443-6946. E-mail: archmark@mac.com.

HAMPTON, PHILIP MICHAEL, consulting engineering company executive; b. Asheville, NC, Sept. 5, 1932; s. Boyd Walker and Helen Reba (Smith) H.; m. Wilma Christine Gross, July 7, 1951; children: Philip Michael, Deborah Lynn, Gregg Ashley. AB in Geology, Berea Coll., Ky., 1954. Draftsman-designer Johnson & Anderson, Inc., Pontiac, Mich., 1955-57, designer, also project mgr., 1957-59, dir. bus. devel., 1962-76, v.p., 1966-74, exec. v.p., 1974-76; v.p. Spalding G. DeDecker & Assos., Inc., Madison Heights, Mich., 1976-84; founder, pres. Hampton Engrng. Assocs., Inc., 1985—; pres. HMA Consultants Inc., 1977—, Geo Internat., Inc., 1978—. V.p. JAVLEN Internat., 1971-73, Micuda-Hampton Assocs., Inc., 1985-86; co-founder, owner My World Shops and Hampton Galleries, Ltd., 1976-90; co-owner Hampton-Tyedten Galleries Ltd., 1979-81; mem. public adv. panel GSA, 1977-78; chmn. task force of com. fed. procurement of architect/engr. svcs. ABA, 1977-79. Editor: Total Scope, 1963-71. Pres. Waterford Bd. Edn., 1969-71; mem. state resolution com. Democratic Conv., 1972; exec. com. Oakland County Dem. Com., 1973-74; precinct del., 1972-76, 80—; trustee Environ. Research Assocs., sec.-treas., 1969-71, pres., 1971-73; chmn. Waterford Cable Communications Commn., 1981-88; mem. Cultural Council Pontiac, 1987-90; bd. dirs. Oakland C. of C., 1972-74, Readings for the Blind, Inc., 2002-; chmn. utilities com. Oakland Bus. Roundtable, 1993—; vice chmn. Pontiac Urban League, 1996—. Named to Honorable Order Ky. Colonels. Fellow Am. Cons. Engrs. Coun. (internat. engrng. com. 1971-76, vice chmn. pub. rels. com. 1970-72, chmn. publs. com. 1972-74, chmn. ABA model procurement code com. 1977-79, nat. dir. 1986-89, mem. com. fellows 1988—, Pres. award 1990); mem. ASCE, AAAS, Nat. Water Well Assn. (chmn. tech. div. 1969-71), Cons. Engrs. Coun. Mich. (awards com. 1970-74), Am. Arbitration Assn. (comml. panel 1977—), Pontiac C. of C. (co-founder 1989), Oakland Bus. Roundtable (charter). Clubs: Pontiac Exchange, Pontiac-Detroit Lions Quarterback Club (co-founder, Am. Coun. Engrng. Cons. Vernon B. Spalding Leadership award 2007). Presbyterian. Home and Office: 2440 Ostrum St Waterford MI 48328-1829 Office: 35 W Huron St Ste 801 Pontiac MI 48342-2128 Office Phone: 248-332-4332. Personal E-mail: heainc35@aol.com. *My first employment, at age 13, was as a janitor at a small southern college. The superintendent of facilities taught me to pay attention to detail. He advised, "clean under the stairwells and the entrance will take care of itself." I understood his meaning and adopted the philosophy as my own in many areas of my life and career.*

HAMPTON, PHILLIP JEWEL, artist, educator; b. Kansas City, Mo., Apr. 23, 1922; s. Cordell Bernard Daniels and Goldie Kelley Powell; m. Dorothy Louise Smith, Sept. 28, 1946 (dec. Oct. 1986); children: Harry James, Robert Keith. Student, Drake U., 1947—48; BFA, Kans. City U., Kan. City Art Inst., 1951; MFA, Kans. City Art Inst., 1952. Dir. art program Savannah State Coll., Ga., 1952-69; prof. art So. Ill. U., Edwardsville, Ill., 1969-92, emeritus prof. fine arts, 1992—; artist, spl. projects Hampton Studio, Edwardsville, Ill., 1992—. Dir. day camp City of Kansas City Recreation, 1952; art cons. US GSA, East St. Louis, Ill., 1995-98; curator 2 spl. exhbns. St. Louis Artists' Guild, 1998—; judge Watercolor Mo. Nat., Winston Churchill Meml., Fulton, Mo., 2001; lectr. St. Louis Ar Mus., 2001. Author: (catalogs) 3d World Drawings, 1979, Schemata of Ethnic Minority Artists, 1980; artist book/promotional materials Symphony Kids, KFUO-99FM, 1996; exhibited in one-man shows at So. Ill. U., Edwardsville Gallery, 2000, (retrospective) Sheldon Galleries, St. Louis, 2005, Ethical Soc. St. Louis Gallery, 2006; represented in permanent collection at St. Louis Art Mus. Mem. adv. bd. West Broad YMCA, Savannah, 1966-69; bd. dir. United Fund, Edwardsville, 1971-74; mem. Citizens Adv. Coun. Dist. 7, Edwardsville, 1973-75. Recipient Gov.'s award for best-in-show Ill. State Fair Profl. Art Exhbn., 1990 (Salute to Black Men award, Omicron Eta Omega chpt. 2001), Oustanding Achievement in Fine Arts award Nat. Alliance African Am. Art Support Groups Conf., 2005, others Mem. St. Louis Art Mus., Art St. Louis, St. Louis Artists' Guild. Presbyterian. Avocations: reading, writing, chess, market studies. Home: 832 Holyoake Rd Edwardsville IL 62025-2315

HAMPTON, SHELLEY LYNN, hearing impaired educator; b. Muskegon, Mich., Nov. 27, 1951; d. Donald Henry and Ruth Marie (Heinanen) Tamblyn; m. John Pershing Hampton Jr., Aug. 10, 1985; 1 child, Sarah Elizabeth. BA, Mich. State U., 1973, MA, 1978. Cert. tchr., Wash., Mich., N.Y. Tchr. presch. thru 3d grade N.Y. State Sch. for Deaf, Rome, 1973-78; cons. Ingham Intermediate Sch. Dist., Lansing, Mich., 1978-81; hearing impaired coord. Shoreline Sch. Dist., Seattle, 1981—. N.W. rep. Bur. of Edn. Handicapped, N.Y.C., 1978; N.Y. del. Humanities in Edn., 1977; adv. bd. State Libr. for the Blind, Lansing, 1980-81; adj. prof. Mich. State U., 1979-81, Seattle Pacific U., 1984-86; participant World Cong. Edn. and Tech., Vancouver, B.C., 1986; computer resource technician Spl. Programs, 1988-92, collegial team leader, 1992-95; rep. Site-Based Mgmt. Coun., Seattle, 1992-95. Writer: Social/Emotional Aspects of Deafness, 1983-84. Del. N.Y. State Assn. for Edn. of Deaf, N.Y.C., 1974-78; N.Y. del. Humanities in Edn., 1977; mem. bd. Plymouth Congl. Ch., Seattle, 1983-87; coord., Kids on the Block puppet troupe, 1999-2003. Recipient Gov.'s Plaque of Commendable Svc., State of Mich., 1981; grantee State of Wash., 1979, 82, Very Spl. Arts Festival, 1979-81; recipient Outstanding Svc. award Mich. Sch. for the Blind, 1980. Mem. NEA, Wash. State Edn. Assn., Shoreline Edn. Assn., Alexander Graham Bell Assn., Regional Hearing Impaired Coop. for Edn., Internat. Orgn. Educators of the Hearing Impaired, Auditory-Verbal Internat., U.S. Pub. Sch. Caucus, Conf. Edn1. Adminstrs. Serving the Deaf. Home: 14723 62nd Dr SE Everett WA 98208-9383 Office: Shoreline Hearing Program 16516 10th Ave NE Seattle WA 98155-5904 Business E-Mail: shelley.hampton@shorelineschools.org.

HAMPTON, THOMAS E., state agency administrator; BS in Acctg., NC Ctrl. U.; MBA, St. John's U., NY. CPA, cert. fin. examiner. With Cigna Worldwide, NYC; supr. gen. acctg. Am. Internat. Group; with DC Dept. Ins., Securities and Banking, 1988—, dep. commr., acting commr., 2005—06, commr., 2006—. Office: DC Dept Ins Securities and Banking Ste 701 810 1st St NE Washington DC 20002 Office Phone: 202-727-8000. Office Fax: 202-535-1196. E-mail: disb@dc.gov.

HAMPTON, VERNE CHURCHILL, II, lawyer; b. Pontiac, Mich., Jan. 5, 1934; s. Verne Churchill and Mildred (Peck) H.; m. Stephanie Hall, Oct. 5, 1973; children: J. Howard, Timothy H., Julia C. Thibodeau. BA, Mich. State U., 1955; LLB, U. Va., 1958. Bar: Mich. 1958. Since practiced in, Detroit; ptnr. firm Dickinson Wright, 1967—. Bd. dirs., sec. Carhartt, Inc., R & R Radio Corp. Former mem. Mich. Rep. Fin. Com.; bd. dirs. Detroit Bus./Edn. Alliance; corp. mem. Boys' Clubs Met. Detroit. Mem. ABA, State Bar Mich. (chmn. bus. law sect. 1980-84), Detroit Athletic Club, Country Club Detroit, Yondotega Club, Moorings Club (Fla.), Sigma Alpha Epsilon, Phi Alpha Delta. Republican. Episcopalian. Home: 360 Provencal Rd Grosse Pointe Farms MI 48236-2959 Office: Dickinson Wright PLLC 500 Woodward Ave Ste 4000 Detroit MI 48226-3416 Business E-Mail: vhampton@dickinsonwright.com.

HAMRAH, PEDRAM, ophthalmologist, scientist; b. Datteln, Germany, Sept. 16, 1971; m. Satgin Hamrah. BS in Software Engrng., U. Cologne, Germany, 1992, MD, 1999. Tchg. asst. dept. anatomy U. Cologne, Germany, 1993—95, rsch. asst. dept. ophthalmology, 1996—98, rsch. asst. dept. internal medicine, divsn. oncology, 1996—98; rsch. assoc., dept. cell and neurobiology Doheny Eye Inst., U. So. Calif., 1999; postdoctoral fellow dept. ophthalmology Schepens Eye Rsch. Inst., Harvard Med. Sch., Boston, 1999—2001; med. resident dept. internal medicine Good Samaritan Hosp., Cin., 2001—02; vis. scientist dept. ophthalmology Harvard Med. Sch., 2002; postdoc. fellow dept. ophthalmology and visual scis. U. Louisville, 2002—, resident dept. ophthalmology, 2003—06, chief resident dept. ophthalmology, 2005—06; fellow cornea and refractive surgery svc. Mass Eye and Ear Infirmary, Harvard Med. Sch., Boston, 2006—. Mem. internal commn. com. Schepens Eye Rsch. Inst., Harvard Med. Sch., 2001; mem. members-in-training com. Assn. Rsch. in Vision and Ophthalmology, Bethesda, Md., 2003—; presenter in field; organizer clinician-sci. forum Assn. Rsch. vision and Ophthalmology, 2005—. Contbr. chapters to books, articles to profl. jours. including Nature Medicine, Jour. Exptl. Medicine, Am. Jour. Pathology; ad hoc reviewer:; editl. bd. mem. Graefe's Archives of Clinical & Experimental Ophthalmology, asst. editor Ocular Immunology and Inflammation. Recipient Young Investigator award, 2000, 2001, 2002, Travel award, Nat. Eye Inst., 2001, Young Pathologist fellowship, 2003, Conf. Travel award, 2003, Cornea Rsch. award, 2003, Rsch. award, Assn. U. Profs. Ophthalmology/Rsch. to Prevent Blindness, 2004. Mem.: Am. Soc. Cataract and Refractive Surgeons (Excellence in Rsch. Recipient award 2005), Am. Acad. Ophthalmology, Am. Soc. Investigative Pathology, Fedn. Clin. Immunology Soc., Tearfilm and Ocular Surface Soc. (chair, assoc. adv. bd.), Ocular Microbiology and Immunology Group, Assn. Rsch. in Vision. Achievements include discovery of MHC class II-negative population of resident corneal langerhans cell-type dendritic cells in the corneal epithelium; identification of novel resident dendritic cells in the corneal stroma; vascular endothelial growth factor receptor (VEGFR)-3 and VEGF-C on dendritic cells in the cornea; research in draining lymph nodes of corneal transplant hosts exhibit evidence for donor major histocompatibility complex (MHC) class II-positive dendritic cells derived from MHC class II-negative grafts; VEGFR-3 mediates induction of corneal alloimmunity; first to breaking of two dogmas in corneal immunology: namely that immune privilege of the cornea is dependant on the absence of bone marrow-derived cells, and that the cornea does not have any BM derived cell. Office: Harvard Med Sch Mass Eye and Ear Infirmary 243 Charles St Boston MA 02114 Office Phone: 617-888-3363. Business E-Mail: pedram_hamrah@meei.harvard.edu.

HAMRE, JOHN J., think-tank executive, former federal agency administrator; b. Watertown, SD, July 3, 1950; s. Melvin Sanders and Ruth Lucile (Larson) H.; m. Julia Pfanstiehl, Sept. 4, 1976. BA summa cum laude, Augustana Coll., Sioux Falls, SD, 1972; MA with highest distinction, Sch. of Internt. Studies, Washington, 1976; PhD, Johns Hopkins U., 1978. Dep. asst. dir. Congl. Budget Office, Washington, 1978-84; profl. staff Senate Armed Svcs. Com., Washington, 1984-94; comtroller, CFO, U.S. Dept. Def., Washington, 1993-97, dep. sec., 1997-00; pres., CEO Ctr. for Strategic & Internat. Studies, Washington, 2000—. Bd. dirs. MITRE Corp., 2000—, ITT Industries, 2000—, Sci. Applications Internat. Corp., 2005—. Office: Ctr for Strategic & Internat Studies 1800 K St NW Washington DC 20006 E-mail: jhamre@csis.org.

HAN, BERNARD L., communications executive; BS, Cornell U., 1986, M in Engrng., 1987, MBA, 1988. Various positions Am. Airlines, Northwest Airlines; v.p. fin. planning and analysis Am. West Airlines, 1996—98, sr. v.p. planning, 1998—2000, sr. v.p. mktg. and planning, 2000—01, exec. v.p., CFO, 2001—02, Northwest Airlines, Eagan, Minn., 2002—05, EchoStar Communications Corp., Englewood, Colo., 2006—. Office: EchoStar Communications Corp 9601 S Meridian Blvd Englewood CO 80112*

HAN, CHIEN-PAI, statistics educator; b. Hunan, China, Dec. 17, 1936; came to U.S., 1960; s. Chung-Shih and Pei-Wen Han; M. Maria Han, Aug. 28, 1965; children: Richard, Julie. BA, Nat. Taiwan U., Taipei, 1958; MA, U. Minn., 1962; PhD, Harvard U., 1967. Asst. prof. stats. Iowa State U., Ames, 1967-69, assoc. prof., 1970-75, prof., 1975-82; prof. math. U. Tex.-Arlington, 1982—. Statis. cons. Mus. N.Mex., Santa Fe, 1965; vis. asst. prof. Harvard U., Cambridge, Mass., 1970 Author: (with T.A. Bancroft) Statistical Theory and Inference in Research, 1981; mem. editl. bd. Comms. in Stats. Theory and Methods, 1975-92, Jour. Statis. Rsch., 1994; assoc. editor Comms. in Stats., 1993—; co-editor Jour. Probability and Statis. Sci., 2004—, Jour. Applied Probability and Stats., 2006—. Fellow Am. Statis. Assn. (pres. Iowa chpt. 1971-72); mem. Internat. Statis Inst. (elected), Inst. Math. Stats., Internat. Assn. Survey Statisticians, Internat. Chinese Statis. Assn. (bd. dirs. 1987-92, pres. 2000), Sigma Xi, Mu Sigma Rho. Office: U Tex Dept Math PO Box 19408 Arlington TX 76019-0408

HAN, DENNIS PAUL, physician; b. Crown Point, Ind., Sept. 10, 1963; s. Daniel and Grace Han; m. Amy Wong Han, July 16, 1994; children: Nicola Grace, Casey Daniel. MD, U. Chgo., 1989. Diplomate Am. Bd. Otolaryngology, 1995. Ptnr. CarePointe Ear, Nose and Throat, Inc., Merrillville, Ind., 1994—. Clin. instr. Ind. U. Sch. Medicine, NW, Gary, Ind.; pres. Asian Am. Med. Soc., Merrillville, Ind., Albania, 1999—2000. Fellow, Am. Acad. Otolaryngology/Head and Neck Surgery, 1995, Am. Coll. Surgeons, 1996. Home: 1008 Killarney Dr Dyer IN 46311 Office: CarePointe Ear Nose and Throat Inc 99 E 86th Ave Merrillville IN 46410 Home Phone: 219-865-1818; Office Phone: 219-738-2617.

HAN, HEE-WON, professional golfer; b. Seoul, South Korea, June 10, 1978; m. Hyuk Son. Attended, Rukoku U. Winner Wendy's Championship for Children at Tartan Fields, 2003, Sybase Big Apple, 2003, Safeway Classic, 2004. 48 victories as amateur; mem. Nat. Conf. Team, 1992—97; silver medallist Hiroshima Asia Games, 1994. Recipient Louise Suggs Rolex Rookie of Yr., 2001. Avocation: quilting. Office: c/o LPGA 100 International Golf Dr Daytona Beach FL 32124-1092

HAN, JIAHUAI, medical researcher; BS in Biochemistry, Beijing U., 1982, MS in Protein Biochemistry, 1988; PhD in Molecular Biology, U. Brussels, 1990. Rsch. fellow Dept. Internal Medicine and Howard Hughes Med. Inst., U. Tex. Southwestern Med. Ctr., Dallas, 1987—92; rsch. assoc. Dept. Immunology, The Scripps Rsch. Inst., La Jolla, Calif., 1992—93, sr. rsch. assoc., 1993—96, asst. mem. to prof., 1996—. Contbr. articles to profl. jours. Recipient Established Investigator award, Am. Heart Assn., 1995. Office: Scripps Rsch Inst IMM-9 10550 N Torrey Pines Rd La Jolla CA 92037-1000

HAN, JIAPING, research scientist; BS in Material Sci. and Engrng. with honors, Zhejiang U., Hangzhou. China, 1991; MS in Elec. Materials, Huazhong U. Sci. Tech., Wuhan. China, 1994; PhD, U. Aveiro, Portugal, 2001. Rsch. fellow City U. Hong Kong, 2002—03; rsch. scientist Mont. State U., Bozeman, 2003—. Contbr. articles to profl. jours. Post-Doctoral fellow, Portugal Nat. Found. Sci. and Tech., 2001, 2002. Mem.: Am. Ceramic Soc., Materials Rsch. Soc. Office: Montana State Univ Physics Dept Bozeman MT 59717 Office Phone: 406-994-6150. Office Fax: 406-994-4452. Business E-Mail: jiaping.han@gmail.com.

HAN, JONGWOO, political science professor; s. Yong Kyu Han and Sung Ja Cho; m. Kyunghee Lee, Mar. 25, 1989; children: Hyemin, Jeongyoon. PhD, Syracuse U., NY, 1997. Sr. assoc. Ctr. Info. Tech. and Policy, Syracuse, 1998—2007; adj. prof. Syracuse U., 1998—. Project asst. dir. (exch. program with North Korean U.) Syracuse U., 2002—; dir. Maxwell Sch. Citizenship and Pub. Affairs, Syracuse, 2000—. First lt. Korean Air Force Acad., 1988—91. Grantee, Lockheed Martin Corp., 2000—06, Korean Tobacco & Ginsaeng Corp., 2002, Korea Found., 2003—, Henry Luce Found., 2003—, Ford Found., 2003—04, Dept. Unification, Korea, 2005—, Beautiful Found., 2006, United Bd. Christian Higher Edn. in Asia, 2007—; scholar, Seoul Met. Govt., Korea, 2000; Tchg. Asst. scholar, Syracuse U., 1991—95, Postdoctoral Rsch. fellow, 1997—98. Independent. Avocations: travel, golf. Office: Syracuse Univ 410 Crouse-Hinds Hall Syracuse NY 13244 Home Phone: 315-637-9836; Office Phone: 315-443-5856. Business E-Mail: jonghan@maxwell.syr.edu.

HAN, MOO-YOUNG, physicist, educator; b. Seoul, Korea, Nov. 30, 1934; came to U.S., 1954; s. Sunghoon and Kiejer (Kim) H.; m. Changki Hong, Aug. 29, 1959; children: Grace, Chris, Tony. BS, Carroll Coll., Waukesha, Wis., 1957; PhD, U. Rochester, 1964. Research assoc. Syracuse U., 1964-65; asst. prof. U. Pitts., 1965-67; asst. prof. physics Duke U., Durham, NC, 1967-71, assoc. prof., 1971-77, prof., 1977—. Vis. prof. Kyoto U., 1974, Korea Advanced Inst. of Sci., 1982 Author: The Secret Life of Quanta, 1990, The Probable Universe, 1992, Quarks and Gluons, 1999, A Story of Light, 2005, Quantum Field Theory of Quarks and Leptons, 2005; editor-in-chief Korean Am. Sci. and Tech. News, 1995—. Recipient Outstanding Prof. award Duke U., 1971, Disting. Tchg. award Duke U., 1972, Disting. Fgn. Scholar award Kyoto U., 1974, Global Korea award Mich. State U., 1998. Mem. Soc. Korean-Am. Scholars, Golden Key (hon.). Home: 615 Duluth St Durham NC 27705-1824 E-mail: myhan@phy.duke.edu.

HAN, NONG, artist, sculptor, painter; b. Seoul, Oct. 10, 1930; arrived in U.S.A., 1952, naturalized, 1958. Commr. Asian Art Commn. Asian Art Mus. San Francisco, The Avery Brundage Collection, city and county of San Francisco, 1981—84. One-man exhbns. paintings and or sculpture include Ft. Lauderdale, Fla. Mus. Arts, Santa Barbara,Calif. Mus. Art, Crocker Art Mus., Sacramento, 1965, Ga. Mus. Art, Athens, 1967, El Paso, Tex. Mus. Art, 1967, Nat. Mus. History, Taiwan, 1971, Nihonbashi Gallery, Tokyo, Japan, 1971, Shinsegye Gallery, Seoul, Korea, 1975, Nat. Mus. Modern Art, Seoul, 1975, San Francisco Zool. Garden, 1975, Tongin Art Gallery, Seoul, 1978, Consulate Gen. Republic of Korea, L.A., 1982, Choon Chu Gallery, Seoul, 1982, Mee Gallery, Seoul, 1984, 86, Leema Art Mus., Seoul, 1985, Tong A Dept. Store, Taegu, Korea, 1986, Tongso Gallery, Masan, Korea, 1986, Han Kwang Art Mus., Pusan, Korea, 1986, Union de Arte, Barcelona, Spain, 1987, Acad. de Belles Arts, Sabadell, Spain, 1987, Nong Hyup Art Mus., Ft. Lee, N.J., 1995, The Info. Ctr. Korean Embassy, Washington, 1997; Gallery Art Exchange, N.Y.C., 1998, Korean Cultural Ctr., Annandale, Va., 1999, Paeksang Meml. Hall The Korea Times, Seoul, 2000, The Korea Central Daily, Vienna, Va., 2001, YTN, 24 hour news channel Seoul, Korea, 2004, KM Art Ctr., Sandy Spring, Md., 2005, Visitor's Ctr. Mormon Ch., Kensington, Md., 2005, Seoul Gallery, Korea, 2006; numerous group exhibits including most recently Taipei Gallery Taiwanese Cultural Ctr., N.Y.C., 1998, Fisher Gallery U. So. Calif., L.A., 1998, Japanese Am. Nat. Mus., L.A., 1998, Bedford Gallery, Dean Lesker Regl. Ctr. for the Arts, Walnut Creek, 1998, The Kaohsing Museum of Fine Art, 1998, Taipei Mus. of Fine Arts, 1998, Marugame Genichiro Inokuma Mus. of Contemporary Art, Japan, 1999, Fukuoka Asian Art Mus., Fukuoka City, 1999, Akita Senshu Mus. Art, Akita City, 1999; represented in numerous permanent collections including, Santa Barbara Mus. Art, Anchorage Alaska Hist. and Fine Art Mus., Museo de Arte, Lima, Peru, Govt. Peru, Nat. Mus. History, Govt. of Republic of China, Oakland, Calif. Art Mus., Ga. Mus. Art, Athens, Korean Embassy, Lima, Peru, Nat. Mus. of Modern Art, Nat. Mus. Korea, Govt. of Republic of Korea, Seoul, Nat. Gallery of Modern Art, New Delhi, India, Asian Art Mus. San Francisco, Govt. of People's Republic China, Beijing and Shanghai, Palacio de la Zarzuela, Madrid, Palacio de la Moncloa, Madrid, The Korean Embassy, Madrid, Mus. Art de Sabadell, Spain, Mus. Nat. des Beaux-Arts, Monte Carlo, Monaco, The Philatelic Mus. Palais des Nations, Geneva, Korean Embassy, Wash., Nat. Mus., Manila, Philippines, Daesung Group, Seoul, Hyndai Group, Seoul, YTN, Seoul, others; author: Nong Questions, 1982. Chmn. San Francisco, Seoul Sister City Com., city and county San Francisco, 1981-84. Served in U.S. Army, 1956-59; USAF, 1959-60. Recipient numerous awards including citations from Republic of Korea; Cert. Disting. Achievement, State of Calif., 1982, Proclamation City and County of San Francisco, 1982; Nong Stamp issued in his honor UNISEF, 1996. Home: 114 Kirtley Rd Leon VA 22725 *Beauty and ugliness, good and bad, right and wrong. Which test should I choose to measure these? Then, how long can I rely on the test I choose?.*

HAN, OKSOO, musician, educator; b. Seoul, Korea, June 18, 1938; d. Kyung-Seok H. and Young-Hwan Kim; m. Won-Hoon Park, Sept. 25, 1971; children: Suzanne, Thomas. BA, Ewha Women's U., Seoul, Korea, 1960; MA, Cin. Conservatory Music, 1962; DMA, William Penn Coll., 1983. Artist Eric Semon Mgmt., NYC, 1965-72; prof. LI U., 1966-75, Kyunghee U., Seoul, Korea, 1976-78, Dankook U., Seoul, Korea, 1983—; dir. Korean chpt. World Piano Competition, Cin., 1987—; chmn. Han Romanson Internat. Piano Competition, Seoul, 1994—. Jury Tchaikovsky, Prokofiev, Cin. Internat. Competitions, others, 1987—. Musician (soloist): Carnegie Recital Hall, 1964, European Debut Recitals, 1964; musician: (recording) My Favorite Chopin, 1991, Beethoven Piano Concerto No. 5, 2003; author: Chopin Etudes, 1983, Chopin Preludes, 1984, Rachmaninoff Etudes-Tableaux, 2000. Recipient Cultural Merit citation Korean Govt., 1967; named Musician of Yr., Seoul, 1982. Mem. Am. Music Scholarship Assn. (bd. dirs. 1987—, adv. bd. 2007—), Gawon Internat. Music Soc. (chair 1994-). Home: 17-29 Kookee-Dong Chongroku Seoul 110-011 Republic of Korea Office: Dankook U San 8 Hannam-Dong Seoul 140-210 Republic of Korea Office Phone: +82-2-379-5698. Personal E-mail: hanoksoo1@yahoo.com.

HAN, QINGYOU, research scientist, metallurgist; b. Wuhan, Hubei, China; s. Han and Wang; m. Lu Shao; children: Lucy Yiou, Hannah Yifei. BS, Wuhan Inst. Tech., China, 1982; MS, U. Sci. & Tech., Beijing, 1985; PhD, Oxford U., England, 1991—94. Rsch. fellow Oxford U., 1994—97; rsch. scientist Oak Ridge Nat. Lab., Tenn., 1997—. Program mgr. Oak Ridge Nat. Lab., 2003—05. Contbr. articles to profl. jours. Rsch. grant, US Dept. Energy, 2003—. Mem.: Minerals, Metals & Materials Soc. (symposium chair 1999—), TMS. Achievements include patents for materials processing. Home: 9005 Roemeadow Ln Knoxville TN 37922 Office: Oak Ridge Nat Lab Bldg 4508 MS 6083 Oak Ridge TN 37831

HAN, RUNLIN, biochemist, researcher; b. Huhhot, Neimongol, China, Aug. 10, 1966; arrived in U.S., 2002; s. Gaohuai Han and Erhua Zhang; m. Zhihong Zhao, Oct. 15, 1992; 1 child, Zhengyang. BSc, Jilin Agrl. U., China, 1987; MS, Hebei Agrl. U., China, 1990; PhD, Chinese Acad. of Sci., Beijing, China, 2001. Postdoctoral rsch. assoc. U. Toledo, 2002—03; chief engr. Fangzhou Sino-USA Biopaharmaceutical Co., Suzhou, Jiangsu, China, 2003—04; rsch. assoc. W.Va. U., Morgantown, W.Va., 2004—. Contbr. scientific papers pub. to profl. jour. Recipient Outstanding Dissertation, Inst. of Process Engrng., Chinese Acad. of Sciences, 2001. U.S.

Taxpayers. Christian. Avocations: travel, music. Office: W Va U 1 Med Ctr Dr Morgantown WV 26506 Home Phone: 304-293-3318; Office Phone: 304-293-2474. Personal E-mail: runlinhan@yahoo.com.

HANAHAN, DOUGLAS, biochemist, educator; s. Donald J. and Lillian Marie H. BS in Physics, MIT, 1976, MA, 1976; MA in Biophysics, Harvard Univ., 1983, PhD, 1983. Sr. staff scientist Cold Spring Harbor Lab., 1983—88; assoc. prof., biochemistry, biophysics, Hormone Rsch. Inst. Univ. Calif., San Francisco, 1988—93, prof., 1993—; and Am. Cancer Soc. rsch. prof., 2001—. Fellow: Am. Acad. Arts & Scis. Office: Dept Biochemistry UCSF PO Box 0534 San Francisco CA 94143-0534 Office Phone: 415-476-9209, 415-476-4661. Business E-Mail: dh@biochem.ucsf.edu.*

HANAHAN, JAMES LAKE, retired insurance executive; b. Burlington, Iowa, Aug. 27, 1932; s. Thomas J. and Clarice P. (Lorey) Hanahan; m. Marilyn R. Lowe, Dec. 27, 1952; children: Bridget Sue Bahlke, Erin Hoff-Hanahan. BS, Drake U., DesMoines, 1955; postgrad., George Williams Coll., Stevens Point, Wis., 1955—56. Phys dir. Monmouth (Ill.) YMCA, 1955-56; cmty. rels. staff Caterpillar Tractor Co., Peoria, Ill., 1956-57; rep. Conn. Gen. Life Ins. Co., Des Moines, 1957-59, asst. mgr., 1959-63, mgr. group ins. ops. Tampa, Fla., 1963-80; pres., chief exec. officer WHP, First In Employee Benefits Inc., 1980-91, J&H Cons. Group Inc., 1980-91; v.p. AON Cons., 1991-2000; ret., 2000. Instr. C.P.C.U. courses; seminar leader C.L.U. workshop; cons. ins. seminar Fla. State U.; guest instr. U. South Fla., Hillsborough County Schs. Great Am. Teach-In. Bd. dirs. West Coast Employee Benefit Coun., Tampa Sports Found., Jr. Achievement, Tampa Bay Acad.; chmn. joint bd. trustees Town and Country Hosp. and Meml. Hosp, Tampa; past pres. Pinellas Emergency Mental Health Svcs.; mem. Hillsborough County Health Coun. Recipient Double D award, Drake U., PEMHS Cmty. Svc. award. Mem. Sales Mktg. Execs. Tampa (past pres., Exec. of Yr. 1982), Nat. Risk Mgmt. Soc., Greater Tampa C. of C., Mineret Soc. Tampa U., Tampa Sports and Recreation Coun. (bd. dirs.), Self Ins. Assn. Am., Pinellas Econ. Devel. Coun. (chmn.), Health Ins. Inst. Am., Profl. Benefit Adminstrs. Assn., Com. of 100, Nat. D Club (Drake U.; dir.), Timber Greens Country Club, Pres.'s Assn., Phi Sigma. Democrat. Roman Catholic. Home: 6659 Garden Palm Ct New Port Richey FL 34655-5117 Office Phone: 813-636-3046. Personal E-mail: hanahanjim@aol.com.

HANAKI, NOBUYUKI, economics professor; s. Shigeru and Matsuko Hanaki; m. Nina Ota, Jan. 11, 1999; children: Erina, Masaharu. BA in Internat. Politics, U. Tsukuba, Japan, 1997; MA in Econs., Columbia U., NYC, 1999, PhD in Econs., 2003. Rsch. fellow Earth Inst., Columbia U., NYC, 2003—05; asst. prof. internat. polit. economy U. Tsukuba, Ibaraki, Japan, 2005—. Contbr. articles to profl. jours. Grantee, Nomura Found., 2005, Japan Bank Fund, 2005, Japan Security Fund, 2006. Mem.: Ea. Econ. Assn., Soc. Computational Econ., Am. Econ. Assn. Achievements include research in interacting agent based model and related fields. Office: Univ Tsukuba Dept Internat Political Economy 1-1-1 Tennodai Ibaraki Tsukuba 305-8573 Japan Office Phone: +81-29-853-7432. Office Fax: +81-29-853-7440. Business E-Mail: hanaki@dpipe.tsukuba.ac.jp.

HANAMEY, ROSEMARY T., nursing educator; b. Detroit, May 16, 1937; d. Albert Edward and Catherine Margaret (Shaheen) Hanamey. BSN, Mercy Coll., Detroit, 1959; MS, Boston Coll., 1963; postgrad., U. Mich., 1982. RN Mich., 1959. Staff nurse Mt. Carmel Mercy Hosp., Detroit, 1959—60, Mass. Gen. Hosp., Boston, 1960—63; instr. nursing Mercy Coll., Detroit, 1963—65, asst. prof., 1967—69; asst. exec. sec. Mich. Nurses Assn., Lansing, 1965—67; exec. sec. Mich. Conf. AAUP, Detroit, 1969—70; instr. nursing Madonna Coll., Livonia, Mich., 1972—76; asst. prof. nursing Ea. Mich. U., Ypsilanti, 1976—80; vol. parish nurse St. Joseph Cath. Ch., Dexter, Mich., 1997—. Mem. careers com. Mich. League Nursing, Detroit, 1977—97; cons. Detroit Practical Nurse Ctr., 1980—85; mem. parish nurse partnership St. Joseph Mercy Health Sys., Ann Arbor, Mich., 1997—. Author: (videotape) Intravenous Therapy: Monitoring and Problem Solving, 1977 (2nd place, 1978), Intravenous Therapy: Basic Concepts, 1977 (3rd place, 1978). Precinct del. Dem. Party, Detroit, 1966—69. Grantee, USPHS, 1961—62; scholar, Marygrove Coll., Detroit, 1955—56. Mem.: AAUP, Cath. Med. Assn. Avocations: swimming, walking. Home: 8074 Huron St Unit 1 Dexter MI 48130-1053 Office Phone: 734-426-8483.

HANAN, PATRICK DEWES, foreign language professional, educator; b. New Zealand, Jan. 4, 1927; s. Frederick Arthur and Ida Helen (Dewes) H.; m. Anneliese Drube, July 1951; 1 son, Rupert Guy. BA, Auckland U., 1948, MA, 1949; BA, U. London, 1953, PhD, 1960; DLitt (hon.), Aukland U., 2006. Lectr. Sch. Oriental and African Studies, 1954-63; assoc. prof., then prof. Stanford U., 1963-68; Victor S. Thomas prof. Chinese lit. Harvard U., Cambridge, Mass., 1968—98, prof. emeritus, 1998—. Dir. Harvard-Yenching Inst., 1987-95. Author: The Chinese Short Story, 1973, The Chinese Vernacular Story, 1981, The Invention of Li Yu, 1988, Chinese Fiction, 2004; transl.: The Carnal Prayer Mat, 1990, Silent Operas, 1990, A Tower for the Summer Heat, 1995, The Sea of Regret, 1995, The Money Demon, 1999, Falling in Love, 2006. Named Officer of New Zealand Order of Merit. Fellow Am. Council Learned Socs., Guggenheim Found.; Mem. Am. Acad. Arts and Scis. Office: 2 Divinity Ave Cambridge MA 02138-2020

HANAU, KENNETH JOHN, III, venture capitalist; b. Ridgewood, NJ, Apr. 30, 1965; s. Kenneth John Jr. and Carol Lee (Rossner) H.; m. M. Ranson Smith, June 4, 1994; children: Lindsay Lee, Hollin Ranson, Kenneth John IV. BA magna cum laude, Amherst Coll, 1988; MBA, Harvard U., 1993. CPA, Vt. Assoc. Coopers & Lybrand, Boston, 1989-90; asst. to pres. K&H Corrugated Case Corp., Walden, NY, 1990-91; assoc. Morgan Stanley & Co., Inc., NYC, 1993-94; mng. dir. Weiss, Peck & Greer, Private Equity Ptnrs., LLC, NYC, 1994—2002, Halyard Capital, NYC, 2002—. Bd. dirs. K&H Corrugated Case Corp., Walden, NY, Shelter Distbn., Inc., Indpls., Richelieu Foods, Inc., Crofton, Md., Color Assocs., Inc., St. Louis, Lionheart Newspaper Inc., Ft. Worth, Regent Comm., Inc., Covington, Ky., Village Voice Media, LLC, NYC, Tama Broadcasting, Tampa, Fla. Mem.: Young Pres. Orgn., Links Club, Fishers Island Club, Hay Harbor Club, Madison Beach Club, Harvard Club (N.Y.C.), Siwanoy Country Club. Avocations: reading, music, golf. Home: 12 Ridge Rd Bronxville NY 10708-1618 Office: Halyard Capital 600 5th Ave 17th Flr New York NY 10020 Office Phone: 212-554-2132. E-mail: khanau@halyard.com.

HANAUER, JOE FRANKLIN, real estate company officer; b. Stuttgart, Fed. Republic Germany, July 8, 1937; came to U.S., 1938; s. Otto and Betty (Zurndorfer) H.; m. Jane Boyle, Oct. 20, 1972; children: Jill, Jason, Elizabeth. BS, Roosevelt U., 1963. Pres. Thorsen Realty, Oak Brook, Ill., 1974-80; sr. v.p. Coldwell Banker, Newport Beach, Calif., 1980-83, pres., 1984, chmn. bd., CEO, 1984-88; prin. Combined Investments LP, Laguna Beach, Calif., 1989—; chmn. bd. dirs. Grubb & Ellis Co., San Francisco, 1993-97. Bd. dirs. MAF Bancorp, Chgo.; chmn. bd. Move, Inc., Calamos Mutual Funds; chmn. policy adv. bd. Joint Ctr. for Housing Studies Harvard U., 1995-96. Bd. dirs. Chgo. Chamber Orch., 1976—; trustee Roosevelt U. Home: 105 S La Sensa Dr Laguna Beach CA 92651 Office: Combined Investments LP 1200 S Coast Hwy Ste 204 Laguna Beach CA 92651-2146

HANAWALT, PHILIP COURTLAND, biology professor, researcher; b. Akron, Ohio, Aug. 25, 1931; s. Joseph Donald and Lenore (Smith) H.; m. Joanna Thomas, Nov. 2, 1957 (div. Oct. 1977); children: David, Steven; m. Graciela Spivak, Sept. 10, 1978; children: Alex, Lisa. Student, Deep Springs Coll., 1949-50; BA, Oberlin Coll., 1954, ScD (hon.), 1997; MS, Yale U., 1955, PhD, 1959; doctorate honoris causa, U. Bio Bio, Concepcion, Chile, 2006. Postdoctoral fellow U. Copenhagen, Denmark, 1958-60, Calif. Inst. Tech., Pasadena, 1960-61; rsch. biophysicist, lectr. Stanford U., Calif., 1961-65, assoc. prof., 1965-70, prof., 1970—, Howard H. and Jessie T. Watkins univ. prof., 1997—, chmn. dept. biol. scis., 1982-89; faculty dept. dermatology Stanford Med. Sch., 1979—. Mem. physiol. chemistry study sect. NIH, Bethesda, Md., 1966—70, mem. chem. pathology study sect., 1981—84; mem. sci. adv. com. Am. Cancer Soc., NYC, 1972—76, Coun. for Extramural Grants, 1998—2001; chmn. 2d ad hoc senate com. on professoriate Stanford U., 1988—90; mem. NSF fellowship rev. panel, 1985; mem. carcinogen identification com. Calif. EPA, 1995—98; mem. toxicology adv. com. Burroughs-Welcome Fund, 1995—2001, chmn., 1997—2000; mem. sci. adv. bd. Fogarty Internat. Ctr., NIH, 1995—99; chmn. Gordon Conf. on Mutagenesis, 1996, Gordon Conf. on Mammalian DNA Repair, 1999; mem. bd. on radiation effects rschr. NAS Commn. on Life Scis., 1996—98; trustee Oberlin Coll., 1998—2007; lectr. Curie Inst., Paris, 2003; keynote lectr. for conf. on DNA repair & mutagenesis Am. Soc. Microbiology, 2004; pres., chair organizing com. 9th Internat. Conf. on Environ. Mutagens, San Francisco, 2005. Author: Molecular Photobiology, 1969; author, editor: DNA Repair: Techniques, 1981, 83, 88, Molecular Basis of Life, 1968, Chemical Basis of Life, 1973, Molecules to Living Cells, 1980; mng. editor DNA Repair Jour., 1982-93; sr. editor Jour. Cancer Rsch., 2003—; assoc. editor Jour. DNA Repair, Molecular Carcinogenesis, Environ. Health Perspectives, Biotechniques; bd. rev. editors Sci.; mem. editl. bd. Procs. of NAS, 2003—; contbr. more than 400 articles to profl. jours. Recipient Outstanding Investigator award Nat. Cancer Inst., 1987-2001, Excellence in Tchg. award No. Calif. Phi Beta Kappa, 1991, Environ. Mutagen Soc. Ann. Rsch. award, 1992, Peter and Helen Bing award for Disting. Tchg., 1992, Am. Soc. for Photobiology Rsch. award, 1996, Internat. Mutation Rsch. award, 1997, Ellison Found. Sr. scholar award, 2001—, John B. Little award in radiation scis. Harvard Sch. Pub. Health, 2002; Hans Falk lectr. Nat. Inst. Environ. Health Scis., 1990, Severo Ochoa Meml. Hons. lectr. NYU, 1996, IBM-Princess Takamatsu lectr. Japan, 1999, Sonnebonn lectr. Ind. U., 2002; Fogarty sr. rsch. fellow, 1993. Fellow: AAAS, Am. Acad. Microbiology; mem.: NAS, European Molecular Biology Orgn. (fgn. assoc.), Radiation Rsch. Soc., Environ. Mutagen Soc. (pres. 1993—94, Student Mentoring award 2001), Am. Soc. Biochemistry and Molecular Biology, German DNA Repair Network (hon.), Biophys. Soc. (exec. bd. 1969—71), Genetics Soc., Am. Soc. for Photobiology, Am. Assn. Cancer Rsch. (bd. dirs. 1994—97). Achievements include co-discovery of DNA excision-repair and transcription-coupled DNA repair; research on the role of DNA changes in human genetic disease and aging. Office: Stanford U Dept Biol Scis Herrin Biology Labs 371 Serra Mall Stanford CA 94305-5020 Office Phone: 650-723-2424. Business E-Mail: hanawalt@stanford.edu.

HANAWAY, CATHERINE LUCILLE, prosecutor; b. Schuyler, Nebr., Nov. 8, 1963; m. Christopher; children: Lucy, Jack. BA, Creighton U., 1987; JD, The Catholic U. of Am., 1990. Owner, atty. Hanamore Solutions, LLC; atty. Peper, Martin, St. Louis, 1990—93; campaign mgr. Bredemeier for Atty. Gen., 1996; dist. dir. Senator Kit Bond, 1993—96, 1996—98; polit. advisor Missourians for Kit Bond, 1998; mem. Mo. State Ho. of Reps., 1998—2004, spkr., 2002—04; exec. dir. Mo. Bush/Cheney, 2002; US atty. (ea. dist.) Mo. US Dept. Justice, St. Louis, 2005—. Mem. Housing Adv. Bd.; bd. dirs. Hope House, Foster and Adoptive Care Coalition. Mem.: Mo. Bar Assn., St. Louis Junior League, St. Louis Jaycees (past pres.). Republican. Roman Catholic. Office: US Attys Office 111 S 10th St 20th Fl Saint Louis MO 63102 Office Phone: 314-539-2200.*

HANBALI, FADI, neurosurgeon, educator; b. Beirut, July 12, 1967; s. Samir Hanbali and Dunia Ghossayni; m. Rana N Kronfol. BS, Am. U. Beirut, Lebanon, 1988; MD, Am. U., Beirut, 1992. Resident neurol. surgery Beirut Med. Ctr. Am. U., 1992—98; fellow complex spine surgery Cleve. Clinic Found., 1998—99; fellow neurosurgery and oncology MD Anderson Cancer Ctr., Houston, 1999—2001; asst. prof. neurosurgery and orthop. surgery U. Tex. Med. Br., Galveston, 2001—06; asst. prof. neurosurgery Tex. Tech. U. HSC, El Paso, 2006—. Contbr. articles to profl. jours., chapters to books. Mem.: AMA, Am. Coll. Surgeons, World Assn. of Lebanese Neurosurgeons, Singleton Surg. Soc., Congress of Neurol. Surgeons. Office: Tex Tech U HSC 4800 Alberta Ave El Paso TX 79905 Home: 5871 Via Cuesta Dr El Paso TX 79912 Home Phone: 915-581-9292; Office Phone: 915-545-6676. Business E-Mail: fadi.hanbali@ttuhsc.edu.

HANBURY, GEORGE LAFAYETTE, II, academic administrator; b. Norfolk, Va., Sept. 20, 1943; s. Emmette Cecil and Ada Christine (Nelligar) H.; m. Jana Hanbury; 1 stepchild, Jia; children from previous marriage: George Lafayette III, Melissa Lee. BS in Pub. Adminstrn, Va. Poly. Inst., 1965; MPA, Old Dominion U., 1977; postgrad., Sr. Exec. Inst. Govt., U. Va., 1985; PhD, Fla. Atlantic U., 2001. Asst. to city mgr., Norfolk, 1967-70; asst. city mgr. Virginia Beach, Va., 1970-74; city mgr., 1974-82, Portsmouth, Va., 1982-90, Ft. Lauderdale, Fla., 1990-98; exec. v.p. Nova Southeastern U., Ft. Lauderdale, 1998—. Mem. Internat. City Mgmt. Assn., Am. Soc. Pub. Adminstrs., Pi Alpha Alpha. Home: The Four Seasons 333 Sunset Dr Apt 807 Fort Lauderdale FL 33301-2655 Office: Nova Southeastern Univ 3301 College Ave Fort Lauderdale FL 33314-7796 Office Phone: 954-262-7555. Business E-Mail: hanbury@nova.edu.

HANCE, JAMES HENRY, JR., former bank executive; b. St. Joseph, Mo., Sept. 16, 1944; s. James Henry Sr. and Kathryn (Lichty) H.; m. Beverly Vaughan Smith, May 20, 1960; children: Samantha, Lindsay, Meredith, Blair. BA in Econs., Westminster Coll., 1966; MBA in Fin., Washington U., 1968. CPA. Ptnr. Price Waterhouse, Phila. and Charlotte, NC, 1968-85; chmn. bd. Consolidated Coin Caterers Corp., Charlotte, 1985-86; exec. v.p., chief acctg. officer NCNB Corp., Charlotte, 1987-88; CFO Bank Am. (formerly NationalBank), Charlotte, 1988—2004; co-vice chmn. Bank Am., Chalotte, NC, 1988—2004; sr. adv. The Carlyle Group, NYC, 2005—. Bd. dirs. Nationsbank, Tenn., D.C., Md., Charlotte. Bd. dirs. Microelectronics Ctr., NC, Rsch. Triangle Pk., 1988; trustee Presbyn. Hosp. and Presbyn. Hosp. Health Svcs. Corp., Charlotte, 1989, Charlotte Country Day Sch., 1990; mem. acctg. and fin. commn. Bank Adminstrn. Inst., Rolling Meadows, Ill., 1989. Fellow Soc. Internat. Bus. Fellows. Republican. Presbyterian. Office: The Carlyle Group 520 Madison Ave New York NY 10022*

HANCE, KENT RONALD, academic administrator, former congressman; b. Dimmitt, Tex., Nov. 14, 1942; m. Susie Hance; 5 children. BA, Tex. Tech U., 1965; LLB, U. Tex., 1968. Bar: Tex. 1968. Prof. bus. law Tex. Tech U., 1968—73; mem. Tex. State Senate, 1974—78, US Congress from 19th Tex. dist., 1979—85, Texas Railroad Commn., 1987—90; ptnr. Hance Scarborough Wright, Austin, Dallas; chancellor Tex. Tech U. Sys., Lubbock, 2006—. Office: Office of Chancellor 124 Administration Bldg Mailstop 42013 Lubbock TX 79409 Office Phone: 806-742-0012. Office Fax: 806-742-8050. E-mail: Chancellor@ttu.edu.*

HANCOCK, ARTEMUS WARD, SR., music educator; b. Taylor, Tex., Aug. 31, 1937; s. Wellington and Bennie Louise Hancock; m. Mertha Marie Wiltz, July 13, 1995; children from previous marriage: Lisa Denise Barnes, Artemus Ward Jr. BA in Music, Huston-Tillotsom U., 1959; MusMEd, U. North Tex., 1969. Cert. mid-mgmt. adminstrn. Lamar U., Tex. Band dir. Fred Douglas Jr. & Sr. HS, Sherman, Tex., 1959—69; asst. band dir. Lincoln HS, Port Arthur, Tex., 1970—79, 1984—94, band. dir., 1994—2002; band dir. Stephen F. Austin Sch., Port Arthur, 1980—84, Meml. HS, Port Arthur, 2002—. Orch. musician Port Arthur Little Theater, 1985—95; chmn. adv. bd. Port Arthur Ind. Sch. Dist., 1985—. Chmn. bd. deacons Rock Island Ch., 2002—. Recipient 35-yr. Pin, Port Arthur Sch. Dist., 2004. Mem.: Tex. Music Educators Assn., Tex. Band Dirs. Assn., Port Arthur Tchrs. Assn., Tex. State Tchrs. Assn., Music Educators Nat. Conf., NEA, Nat. Assn. Amateur Radio, Phi Delta Kappa, Omega Psi Phi (state rep. 1975—90). Democrat. Baptist. Avocations: computers, chess, music, fishing, hunting. E-mail: artemushancock@sbcglobal.net.

HANCOCK, CAROLE PATRICIA, academic administrator; b. Taylor, Tex., Dec. 4, 1939; d. Wellington Lorenzo and Bennie Louise Hancock. BS, Lincoln U., Jefferson City, Mo., 1960; MA in Tchg., Webster U., St. Louis, 1971. Cert. edn. adminstrn. specialist U. Mo. Tchr. St. Louis Pub. Schs., 1963—96, dept. head, coach, 1975—96, adminstr., 1996—2002; dir. City Divsn. Recreation, St. Louis, 1964—75; counselor, athletic coord. Upward Bound, Webster U., 1976—79; drug edn. specialist St. Louis CC at Forest Park, 1989—95, coach, adj. faculty, 1994—97; ofcl. Nat. Fedn. HS Ofcls., St. Louis, 1987—, Tex. Assn. Sports Ofcls., Wichita Falls, 2002—. Advisor, reviewer Health Edn. Curriculum, St. Louis, 1996—99; mem. Harvard Prins. Ctr., 1997—2002; facilitator Leadership Acad., Jefferson City, Mo., 1998—2002; edn. amb. People to People Internat., Kansas City, Mo., 2000—; adj. faculty St. Charles County CC, 2001. Vol. Am. Stroke Assn., St. Louis, 2001—04; mem., participant Susan G. Komen Found., Wichita Falls, Tex., 2002—; active Ptnrs. in Edn. Wichita Falls Ind. Sch. Dist., 2000—; active Nat. Com. to Conserve Social Security, Washington, 2004—. Named Coach of Yr., Inner City Athletic Assn., 1981, 1982, 1987, Wall of Tolerance honoree, So. Poverty Law Ctr., 2004; named to U. Mo. St. Louis African-Am. Student Honor Roll, 1995, 1996, St. Louis Am. Salutes Century's Best in St. Louis Sports, 2000, Nations Bank/Southwestern Bell Leadership Acad. for Character Edn. Class of 2000; recipient Humanitarian award, St. Louis Am., 1996; scholar, Mo. Leadership Acad., 1998, 1999. Mem.: ASCD, AARP, Mo. State HS Athletic Assn., Nat. Assn. Sports Ofcls., Nat. Health and Wellness Club, Am. Fitness Assn., Delta Sigma Theta. Democrat. Baptist. Avocations: walking, jogging, weightlifting, reading, singing. Home: 1420 N Rosewood Ave Wichita Falls TX 76301-1413

HANCOCK, CHARLES R., education educator; BA in Edn., La. State U., MA in Secondary Edn.; attended, Fondation Franco-Américaine, Paris; PhD, Ohio State U. Assoc. supt. divsn. secondary, vocation, adult and community edn. Balt. City Pub. Schs.; coord. of foreign lang. Montgomery County Pub. Schs., 1984-85; prof. edn., assoc. dean Coll. Edn. Ohio State Univ., 1986—. Pres. Am. Coun. Tchg. Fgn. Lang., 1984-85, Md. Fgn. Lang. Assn., 1990-91, Ohio Fgn. Lang. Assn., 1990-91. Recipient Anthony Papalia award for Excellence in Tchr. Edn., 1992, Florence Steiner award for Leadership in Foreign Lang., 1980. Office Phone: 614-292-7231.

HANCOCK, ELLEN MARIE, communications executive; b. NYC, Apr. 15, 1943; d. Peter Joseph and Helen Gertrude (Houlihan) Mooney; m. W. Jason Hancock, Sept. 17, 1971. BA, Coll. New Rochelle, 1965; MA, Fordham U., 1966. With IBM, 1966—, programmer Armonk, NY, 1966-81, dir. communications programming sect., communication products div. Raleigh, NC, 1981-83, v.p. communications programming sect., communication products div., 1983-84, asst. group exec. systems devel. info. systems and storage group Armonk, NY, 1985, v.p. telecommunication systems communication prodn. div., 1985-86, pres. communications products div., 1986-88, v.p., gen. mgr. communication system Somers, NY, 1988-91, v.p., gen. mgr. networking systems Staines, England, 1991-92, sr. v.p., 1992—95; exec. v.p., COO Nat. Semiconductor Corp., 1995—96; exec. v.p. R&D, chief tech. officer Apple Computer. Inc., Cupertino, Calif., 1996-97; pres. Exodus Comm., Inc., 1998—2000, CEO, 1998—2001, chmn., 2000—01; co-founder, pres., COO, CFO, sec., bd. dir. Acquicor Tech. Inc., Irvine, Calif., 2005—. Bd. dirs. Aetna, Inc., Colgate-Palmolive, Watchguard Technologies, Inc., Electronic Data Systems Corp., Inst. for Advanced Catholic Studies Trustee Marist Coll., Poughkeepsie, Santa Clara Univ. Council on Fgn. Rels., Pacific Council of Internat. Policy Roman Catholic. Office: Acquicor Tech Inc 4910 Birch St Ste 102 Newport Beach CA 92660

HANCOCK, GERRE EDWARD, musician, educator; b. Lubbock, Tex., Feb. 21, 1934; s. Ervin Edward and Flake (Steger) H.; m. Judith Duffield Eckerman, July 22, 1961; children: Deborah, Lisa. MusB, U. Tex., 1955; diploma, U. Sorbonne, Paris, 1956; M in Sacred Music, Union Theol. Sem., NYC, 1961; MusD, Nashotah House Episcopal Sem., 1986, U. South, 1999; DD, Gen. Theol. Sem., 2004. Asst. organist St. Bartholomew's Ch., NYC, 1960-62; organist, choirmaster Christ Ch. Cathedral, Cin., 1962-71; mem. artist faculty Coll.-Conservatory Music, U. Cin., 1964-71; organist, master choristers St. Thomas Ch., NYC, 1971—2004; faculty Juilliard Sch., NYC, 1971—2004, Inst. Sacred Music, Yale U., New Haven, 1974—2002, Eastman Sch. Music, U. Rochester, NY, 1995—2000, Sch. of Music, U. Tex. Austin, 2004—. Concert organist McFarlane Mgmt., Cleve., 1964—; condr. choral festivals, U.S. and Europe, 1964—; clinician organ and choral workshops, Australia, Korea, and Republic of South Africa, 1964—. Author: Organ Improvisations, 1976, Improvising: How to Master the Art, 1994; composer: (cantata) Plum Line and City, 1967, (choral works) Missa Resurrectionis, 1979; performer concerts throughout U.S., Can., Europe, South Africa, Australia, Japan. Served with U.S. Army, 1956-58. Recipient The Cross of St. Augustine, Archbiship Canterbury, 2004. Fellow Royal Sch. Ch. Music, Am. Guild Organists (past mem. coun.), Royal Coll. Organists (hon.); mem. Assn. Anglican Musicians (founder, past pres.), Phi Mu Alpha Sinfonia (past pres.), Pi Kappa Lambda. Clubs: St. Wilfrid (N.Y.C.) (pres. 1973-74). Independent. Episcopalian. Avocation: tennis. Office: U Tex Austin Sch Music 1 Univ Sta E 3100 Austin TX 78712-0435 Home Phone: 512-371-3631.

HANCOCK, HERBERT JEFFREY (HERBIE HANCOCK), composer, pianist, publisher; b. Chgo., Apr. 12, 1940; s. Wayman Edward and Winnie (Griffin) Hancock; m. Gudrun Meixner, Aug. 31, 1968. Student, Grinnell Coll., Iowa, 1956-60, Roosevelt U., Chgo., 1960, Manhattan Sch. Music, 1962, New Sch. Social Research, 1967. Owner-pub. Hancock Music Co., 1962—; founder Hancock and Joe Prodns., 1989—; pres. Harlem Jazz Music Center, Inc. Performer: Chgo. Symphony Orch., 1982, Coleman Hawkins, 1960, Donald Byrd, 1960—63, Miles Davis Quintet, 1963—68; recorded with Chick Corea, scored (films) Blow Up, 1966, The Spook Who Sat By the Door, 1973, Death Wish, 1974, A Soldier's Story, 1984, Jo Jo Dancer, Your Life is Calling, 1986, Action Jackson, Colors, 1988, Harlem Nights, 1989, Livin' Large, 1991, scored and appeared 'Round Midnight, 1986 (Academy award best original score, 1986), albums Takin' Off, 1963, Succotash, Speak Like a Child, 1968, Fat Albert Rotunda, 1969, Mwandishi, 1971, Crossings, Sextant, 1972, Headhunters, 1973, Thrust, The Best of Herbie Hancock, 1974, Man-Child, 1975, The Quintet, V.S.O.P., 1977, Sunlight, 1978, An Evening with Herbie Hancock and Chick Corea in Concert, Feets Don't Fail Me Now, 1979, Monster, Greatest Hits, 1980, Lite Me Up, 1982, Future Shock, 1983, (with Foday Musa Suso albums) Village Life, 1985, (with Dexter Gordon albums) The Other Side of 'Round Midnight, 1987, Perfect Machine, 1988, Jamming, 1992, Cantaloupe Island, Tribute to Miles, 1994, Dis Is Da Drum, 1995, The New Standard, 1996, 1 + 1, 1997, Gershwin's World, 1998 (3 Grammy awards), (albums) Future 2 Future, 2001. Named top jazz artist Black Music mag., 1974; recipient citation of achievement Broadcast Music, Inc., 1963, Jay award Jazz mag., 1964, critics poll for talent deserving wider recognition Down Beat mag., 1967, 1st place piano category, 1968, 1969, 1970, composer award, 1971, All-Star Band New Artist award Record World, 1968, Grammy award for best rhythm and blues instrumental performance, 1983, 1984, Grammy award for best jazz instrumental composition (co-composer), 1987, Grammy award best jazz instrumental performance,

1995. Mem.: Nat. Acad. TV Arts and Scis., Nat. Acad. Rec. Arts and Scis., Broadcast Music, Jazz Musicians Assn., Pioneer (Grinnell Coll.). Address: Hancock Music # 1600 1880 Century Park E Ste 1600 Los Angeles CA 90067-1661

HANCOCK, JOHN WALKER, III, banker; b. Long Beach, Calif., Mar. 8, 1937; s. John Walker and Bernice H.; m. Elizabeth Hoien, June 20, 1959; children: Suzanne, Donna, Randy, David. BA in Econs, Stanford U., 1958, MBA, 1960. With Security Pacific Nat. Bank, LA, 1960-92, v.p., 1968-77, sr. v.p., 1977-84, exec. v.p., 1984-92; pres. Bancap Investment Group, Long Beach, Calif., 1992—. Bd. dirs. Harbor Bank; chmn. Meml. Med. Ctr.; pres. Port of Long Beach. Bd. dirs. Long Beach Symphony, Meml. Hosp., Long Beach City Coll. Found. Mem. Stanford U. Alumni Assn., Calif. Club (L.A.), Va. Country Club, Balboa Bay Club, Pacific Club, Bohemian Club, Thunderbird Country Club. Republican. Home: 258 Roycroft Ave Long Beach CA 90803-1717 Office: Bancap Investment Group 192 Marina Dr Long Beach CA 90803-4613

HANCOCK, PATRICIA ANN, artist; b. Columbia, SC, Apr. 1, 1956; d. William Edwards and Joan Marie (Moore) H. Student, Queens Coll., 1973-75; BFA, U. Ga., 1979; postgrad., Va. Commonwealth U., 1980-81. Art tchr. Thornwell Sch., Clinton, S.C., 1979-80. Author, illustrator: Rupert, The Fantastic Flamingo, 1989; exhibitions include C&S Bank Show, 1991-92, Florence Mus., 1998, Chapel Hill Mus., 1999. Mem. DAR, Nat. Soc., Jr. League (sustaining). Presbyterian. Avocations: sewing, jogging.

HANCOCK, S. LEE, lawyer, business executive; b. Knoxville, Tenn., Aug. 11, 1955; s. Melton Donald and Alma Helen (McDaniel) Hancock; m. Kathleen Ann Koll, July 26, 1986. BS summa cum laude, Southwest Mo. State U., 1975; JD cum laude, So. Meth. U., 1979. CPA Mo.; bar: Mo. 1979, U.S. Dist. Ct. (we. dist.) Mo. 1979, U.S. Tax Ct. 1982, U.S. Ct. Claims Calif. 1983, Calif. 1988, U.S. Supreme Ct. 1992. Assoc. Blackwell, Sanders, Matheny, Weary & Lombardi, Kansas City, Mo., 1979-83, ptnr., 1984-88, Allen, Matkins, Leck, Gamble & Mallory, Newport Beach, Calif., 1988—99; chmn., CEO Go2, Newport Beach, 1998—2006; CEO Go2 Directory Systems, Newport Beach, 1998—. Bd. dirs. Calif./Orange County Venture Forum, Orange County Cmty. Found., sec., 1994—95, pres., 1995—97; mem. Young Pres. Orgn., 2000—. Mem.: ABA, Lawyers Assn. Kansas City (pres. young lawyers sect. 1986—87, bd. dirs. 1986—87), Orange County Bar Assn., Mo. Bar Assn., Calif. Bar Assn., Young Execs. Am. (bd. dirs. Orange County chpt. 1992—96, pres. Orange County chpt. 1994—95), Order of Coif. Republican. Avocations: flying, sailing, skiing, photography. Home: 4 Hampshire Ct Newport Beach CA 92660-4933 Office: Go2 18400 Von Karman Ave Ste 610 Irvine CA 92612-1514

HANCOCK, TIMOTHY DANIEL, architect, musician; b. Columbus, Ohio, Dec. 6, 1980; s. Timothy Coleman and Sherrie Lynn Hancock. BA in Architecture, Drury U., Springfield, Mo., 2004. Organist Grace United Meth. Ch., Springfield, 1999—, St. Agnes Cathedral, Springfield, 2001—04; intern arch. Butler, Rosenbury & Ptnrs., Springfield, 2004—. Historian First United Meth. Ch., Springfield, 2002—, sec. bd. trustees, 2005—; bd. dirs. Preservation Springfield, 2005—06. Mem.: Organ Hist. Soc., Am. Guild Organists (dean Springfield chpt. 2004—), Mo. Preservation, Ptnrs. Sacred Places. Home: 897 S Weller Ave Springfield MO 65802 Office: Butler Rosenbury & Ptnrs 319 N Main St Ste 200 Springfield MO 65806

HANCOCK, WILLIAM FRANK, JR., management consultant; b. Richmond, Va., Jan. 4, 1942; s. William Frank and Gladys Elizabeth (George) H.; m. Donna G. Hosmer, May 18, 1968; children: Peter James, Jeffrey William, Jennifer Beth. BBA, U. Iowa, 1964; MBA, U. Pa., 1966; postgrad., Capella U. CPA, CLU, CPCU, CMA, CDP. Exec. asst. to exec. v.p. John Hancock Mutual Life Ins. Co., Boston, 1966-69; mgmt. cons. Keane Assocs., Boston, 1969-74, regional mgr., 1974-75; v.p., gen. mgr. comml. sys. SofTech, Inc., Waltham, Mass., 1975-79; dir. internat. sales and field ops. Nixdorf Computer Co., Burlington, Mass., 1979-80; mgr. mktg. Digital Equipment Corp., 1980-84, electronic commerce mgr., 1984-97; mgmt. cons. electronic commerce Grant Thornton LLP, 1997—98; mgmt. cons., nat. electronic commerce practice Ernst & Young, LLP, 1998—2000; prin. IBM, 2000—02; mng. dir. 3 Rivers Assocs., Sherborn, Mass., 2002—. Adj. prof. acctg. and fin. Grad. Sch. Bus., Northeastern U., Boston, 1966—, sr. instr. acctg. Grad. Sch. Bus. Babson Coll., Wellesley, Mass, 1985—; assoc. dean Sch. Mgmt., Cambridge Coll., 2002—. Treas. Pilgrim Ch.; trustee Sherborn Libr.; chmn. Sherborn coun. Boy Scouts Am. With U.S. Army, 1967-72. Recipient Outstanding Teacher of Yr. Awd., Northeastern Univ., 1989. Mem. AICPA, Data Processing Mgmt., Nat. Assn. Accts., Assn. Computing Machinery, Boston C. of C., Exec. Club Boston, Wharton Alumni Club, U. Iowa Alumni Assn. Congregationalist. Home and Office: 3 Rivers Assocs 24 Dexter Dr Sherborn MA 01770-1124 Home Phone: 508-653-2576; Office Phone: 617-413-6117. Personal E-mail: william.hancock@comcast.net.

HANCOX, DAVID R(OBERT), audit administrator, educator; b. Albany, NY, Aug. 1, 1951; s. Robert F. and Elaine C. (Morgart) H.; m. Judith A. Gaylord, Jan. 17, 1975; children: Robert, Bradford, Ryan D. AS, Hudson Valley Community Coll., 1973; BBA, Siena Coll., 1975. Cert. internal auditor; cert. govt. fin. mgr. State auditor N.Y. State Comptr., Albany, 1974—; lectr. Albany Bus. Coll., 1982-83, Schenectady (N.Y.) Community Coll., 1988, Siena Coll., Loudonville, NY, 1991—, Sage Coll., Albany, 1992-97; dir. state audits N.Y. State Comptr., 1989—. Co-author: State and Local Government, Program Control and Audit: Handbook for Managers and Auditors, 1997, Small Government Finance Library: Accounting, Reporting, Auditing, 1999, Government Performance Audit in Action, 2001, 2d edit., 2004. Chair adminstrn. com., v.p. parish coun. St. James Ch., 1994-98, pres. parish coun., 1998-99; cluster leader Albany Diocese, 1995-96; bd. dirs. Homeless and Travelers Aid Soc., 1999. Mem. Assn. Govt. Accts. (pres. NY Capital chpt. 1986-87, bd. dirs. 1987-89, Arlington, Va. regional v.p. 1990—, Gold award 1991, Educator of Yr. 2005, Nat. Pres.'s award 2007), Inst. Internal Auditors (Albany chpt. bd. govs. 1988-90, 93-96, pres. 1996-97). Roman Catholic. Avocations: reading, computers, exercising. Office: N Y State Comptr 110 State St Albany NY 12236-0001 Home: 57 Maxwell St Albany NY 12208-1638 E-mail: dhancox@nycap.rr.com, dhancox@osc.state.ny.us.

HAND, ANN SPARENBERG, marketing executive; b. Muncie, Ind., 1969; Grad., DePauw U., 1990. Worked for Mobil Oil, Phila., McDonald's Corp., Chgo.; joined British Petroleum (BP) Amoco, 1997; sr. v.p. global retail mktg. BP, sr. v.p. global mktg. & innovation, 2007—. Named one of 40 Under 40, Advt. Age, 2007. Office: BP Chgo Offices 28100 Torch Pkwy Warrenville IL 60555 Office Phone: 630-836-5000.

HAND, HERBERT HENSLEY, finance educator, writer, entrepreneur; b. Hamilton, Ohio, July 11, 1931; s. Herbert Lawrence and Berta Elizabeth (Hensley) H.; m. Katharine Harris Gucker, July 26, 1952; children: Stephen Harris, Herbert Gucker. BS, Ind. U., 1953; MSEE, ABT, MIT, 1955; MBA, U. Miami, 1966; PhD, Pa. State U., 1969. V.p. Hand Oil Co., 1955—65; instr. Pa. State U., 1968—69; asst. and assoc. prof. Ind. U., Bloomington, 1969—73, assoc. prof., 1973—76; disting. prof. entrepreneurship U. S.C. Coll. Bus. Adminstrn., Columbia, 1976—95. State dir. Small Bus. Devel. Ctr. S.C., 1968-69; exec. v.p. Carter-Miot Engring. Co., Columbia, S.C., 1981, also bd. dirs.; pres. Carolina Consultants, 1973-84; chmn., CEO, pres. Phronesis, Inc., 1985-92, Alternative Control Sys. Corp., 1993-99; cons. to numerous cos., 1973—. Author: (with H.P. Sims, Jr.) Managerial Decision Making in the Business Firm-A Systems Approach, 1972, The Profit Center Simulation, 1975; (with A.T. Hollingsworth) A Guide to Small Business Management, 1979, Practical Readings in Small Business, 1979; contbr. over 90 research articles and papers in field to profl. jours.; mem. editorial bd. Bus. Horizons, 1971-73, Acad. of Mgmt. Review, 1975-79; holder numerous U.S. and fgn. patents in field of biotech. Served to 1st lt. USAF, 1953-55, col. USMC, 1976-78. Recipient Western Electric award for most innovative bus. course, 1971, 23 other teaching awards; Small Bus. Inst. Regional award SBA, 1976, 80, 81, Small Bus. Inst. Nat. award, 1980; Office Naval Research grantee, 1976, 77, 78. Mem. Acad. Mgmt., So. Mgmt. Assn., Am. Inst. Decision Scis., Internat. Coun. for Small Bus., Rotary, Beta Gamma Sigma. Presbyterian. Personal E-mail: hekat@msn.com.

HAND, JOHN OLIVER, museum curator; b. NYC, Aug. 17, 1941; s. John Osborn and LaBelle (Bridges) H. BA, Denison U., Granville, Ohio, 1963; MA, U. Chgo., 1967; M.F.A. (Samuel Kress Found. fellow 1969-72), Princeton U., 1971, PhD (Belgian Am. Found. fellow 1972-73), 1978. With edn. dept. Nat. Gallery Art, Washington, 1965-69, curator No. Renaissance painting, 1973—. Preceptor Princeton U., 1971 Author papers in field. Office: Nat Gallery Art Washington DC 20565-0001 Address: 2000B S Club Dr Landover MD 20785 Office Phone: 202-842-6145. Business E-Mail: j-hand@nga.gov.

HAND, LINDA MARIE, mathematics professor; b. Kansas City, Mo., Jan. 18, 1959; d. Jim E. and Mary E. Hand; m. David Scott Royer, May 23, 1996; children: Andrew P. Noel, Valerie C. Royer. AS in Engring., Longview C.C., Lee's Summit, Mo., 1979; BS in Applied Math., U. Mo., Rolla, 1982; MS in Applied Math., Cen. Mo. State U., Warrensburg, 1984; EdD in Coll. Tchg., Okla. State U., 1991. Prof. Mo. So. State U., Joplin, 1988—, asst. dir. honors program, 2007—. Recipient Outstanding Faculty award, Mo. So. State U., 2000, Gov.'s award, Gov. Bob Holden, State of Mo., 2004. Mem.: Math. Assn. of Am. Office: Mo So State U 3950 E Newman Rd Joplin MO 64801

HAND, LLOYD N., lawyer; BA, U. Tex., 1952, LLB, JD, U. Tex., 1957. Bar: Tex. 1957, DC 1970, US Supreme Ct. Asst. to Majority Leader Lyndon Johnson US Senate, Washington, 1957—61; US Chief of Protocol, with rank of amb. The White House, Washington, 1965—66; ptnr. Allbritton McGee & Hand, Washington; sr. v.p. & asst. to bd. chmn. TRW; sr. ptnr. Verner Liipfert Bernhard McPherson & Hand, Washington, 1984—2002; sr. ptnr., Energy, Federal Affairs & Legis. practices DLA Piper Rudnick Gray & Cary, Washington, 2002—07; sr. counsel King & Spaulding LLP, Washington, 2007—. Vice chmn. Washington Roundtable, Ctr. for Strategic & Internat. Studies; mem. Exec. Council on Diplomacy; mem. bd. dir., treas. Blair House; mem. Council of Am. Ambassadors. Officer USN, 1951—55, Korean War. Mem.: Coun. on Fgn. Rels., ABA, DC Bar Assn., Tex. Bar Assn., Phi Alpha Delta. Office: King & Spaulding LLP 1700 Pennsylvania Ave NW Ste 200 Washington DC 20007 E-mail: lhand@kslaw.com.*

HAND, MARYANNE KELLY, artist, educator; b. Augusta, Ga., Apr. 15, 1955; d. Issac Marvin and Dorothy Whaley Kelly; children: Jill Estes Tatum, Micah Kelly. AA in Graphic Design/Visual Comm., Art Inst. Atlanta, 1974; postgrad., Ga. So. U., Statesboro, Ga. State U., Atlanta. Tchr. Episcopal Day Sch., Augusta, 1984—91; tchr. art Augusta State U., 1993—2000; pvt. tchr. sales and design Transatlantic Antiques, Augusta, 2002—; freelance artist. Exhibitions include Phipps Plz., Atlanta, The Historic Cotton Exch., Augusta Mus. History, Ga. Welcome Ctr., Augusta Mayor's Office, Barnes and Noble, Augusta, Sacred Heart Cultural Ctr., Hawg Wild and Big Iron Saloon, Snug, Vallarte Restaurant, Augusta, Villa, Southern Design Trans Atlantic Antiques, Atlanta, Cottage Collection, The Blue Door, Pastel, Eclectics of the South, Debris, Atlanta, Represented in permanent collections Augusta Mus. History, coverpiece, SASS mag. Named to Nat. Archives Women Artists; recipient Hon. Mention, Manhattan Arts. Mem.: S. Ea. Pastel Soc. Avocations: interior decorating, painting, dance, woodcarving.

HAND, PETER JAMES, neurobiologist, educator; b. Oak Park, Ill., Jan. 5, 1937; s. James Harold and Edna Mae (Watson) H.; m. Mary Minnis, Sept. 16, 1958; children: Katherine Patricia, Carol Jane, Margaret Anne, Robin Lynn, Stephen Douglas, Peter James; m. Carol Louise Corson, Oct. 23, 1976; m. Christine L. Arnold, Sept. 19, 1986. VMD, U. Pa., 1961, PhD, 1964. Mem. faculty U. Pa., Phila., 1964—, prof. anatomy, 1979-99, head dept. anatomy, 1980-87, 91-97, emeritus prof., 1999—. Mem. NIH rev. com. Regional Primate Ctrs., 1985-89; mem. nominating com. Lifu Acad. award in Chinese Medicine; adj. faculty Indian River C.C., 2003-; COO Hand Wine Cons., Inc. Contbr. articles to profl. jours. Pres. coun. USO, Cape May, NJ, 1972—73, nat. del.; wine columnist Hometown News, 2005—; mem. ch. coun. Jupiter First Ch., 2002—05; trustee Mid-Atlantic Ctr. for Arts, Cape May, NJ, 1973—74; bd. dirs. Cape May Taxpayers Assn., 1972—74, University City Hist. Soc., Phila., 1978—80; v.p. bd. dirs. Arbors Village Assn., 2002—03, chmn. environ. com., 2003—04. NIH grantee, 1970-82, 86-92, 95—2003. Mem. Am. Assn. Anatomists, Am. Assn. Vet. Anatomists, Soc. Neurosci. (pres. Phila. chpt. 1984-85), Internat. Brain Rsch. Orgn., World Assn. Vet. Anatomists, Internat. Assn. for Study of Pain, Am. Coll. Acupuncture (pres. 1997-98), Internat. Coll. Acupuncture and Electro-Therapeutics, Sigma Xi, Alpha Psi (trustee 1965-87). Republican. E-mail: handpain@comcast.net.

HAND, ROGER, physician, educator; b. Bklyn., Sept. 25, 1938; s. Morton and Angela (Belvedere) H.; m. Susan Hand; children: Christopher, Jessica. BS, NYU, 1959, MD, 1962. Intern, then resident in internal medicine NYU Med. Ctr., 1962-68; postdoctoral fellow, asst. prof. Rockefeller U., NYC, 1968-73; clin. asst. prof. medicine Cornell U. Med. Coll., NYC, 1970-73; asst. prof., then assoc. prof. medicine McGill U., Montreal, Que., Canada, 1973-80; prof. medicine, dir. McGill Cancer Ctr., 1980-84; sr. physician Royal Victoria Hosp., Montreal, 1980-84; chmn. internal medicine Ill. Masonic Ctr., Chgo., 1984-88; prof. medicine U. Ill., Chgo., 1984—, chief sect. gen. internal medicine, 1988-95, prof. health policy and adminstrn. Sch. Pub. Health, 1995—2002. Prin. clin. coord. Ill. Found. Quality Health Care, Chgo., 1996-00; physician advisor OLR Med. Ctr., Chgo., 2000-01, ret., 2001-. Contbr. articles to profl. jours. Brig. gen. USAR, 1963-71, 85-03, ret.; diaster relief-search-and-rescue pilot auxs. USCG, USAF; vol. disaster relief programs ARC, FEMA. Decorated Air medal, Meritorious Svc. medal, Army Commendation medal, Legion of Merit; med. rsch. grantee. Fellow ACP, Royal Coll. Physicians and Surgeons, Am. Coll. Med. Quality; mem. Am. Soc. Clin. Investigation, Am. Soc. Biol. Chemists, Am. Assn. Cancer Research, Am. Soc. Clin. Oncology, Infectious Disease Soc., Can. Soc. Clin. Investigation, Cen. Soc. Clin. Rsch., Am. Cancer Soc.(bd. dirs. Ill. div.), Am. Health Quality Assn. Office Phone: 847-926-8229. E-mail: buckgeneral@ameritech.net.

HANDAL, KENNETH V., computer software company executive, lawyer; b. NYC, Feb. 7, 1949; m. Mary Francina Golden; children: Brianne, Kolbe. AB, Georgetown U., 1970; JD, U. Chgo., 1973. Bar: N.Y. 1974, D.C. 1975. Law clk. to Hon. Robert A. Ainsworth Jr. US Ct. Appeals (5th Cir.), New Orleans, 1973-74; asst. U.S. atty. criminal divsn. (so. dist.) NY US Dept. Justice, 1977-82; ptnr. Arnold & Porter LLP, NYC, 1988—96; assoc. gen. counsel Altria Group, 1996—2004; exec. v.p. global risk and compliance, corp. sec. CA, Inc., Islandia, NY, 2004—. Frequent lectr. at continuing legal edn. confs. Mng. editor U. Chgo. Law Rev., 1972-73. Mem. adv. bd. Hosp. for Spl. Surgery, Corp. Counsel mag.; bd. dirs. Nat. Ctr. for Missing and Exploited Children. Office: CA Inc One CA Plaza Islandia NY 11749

HANDEL, DAVID JONATHAN, health facility administrator; b. NYC, Jan. 2, 1946; s. Milton M. and Ruth (Stamer) H.; m. Julia Elizabeth Noll, June 26, 1971; chldren: Daniel, Jennifer. BS, Cornell U., 1966; MBA, U. Chgo., 1968. Assoc. planning coordinator for health scis. Northwestern U., Chgo., 1970-73, adminstr. Northwestern U. Med. Clinics and Med. Assocs., 1973-76; dir. planning and implementation Mid-Ohio Health Planning Fedn., Columbus, Ohio, 1976-79; assoc. hosp. adminstr. Vanderbilt U. Hosps., Nashville, 1979-82, assoc. dir. ops., 1982-85; dir. Ind. U. Hosps., Indpls., 1985-96; exec. v.p., COO Clarian Health Ptnrs., Inc., Indpls., 1997—2004; dir. MHA program Ind. U., 2004—. V.p. United Hosp. Svcs., Indpls., 1986-88, pres., 1989-90, Bedford Reg. Med. Ctr., 1997-2004, La Porte Regional Health Sys., Inc., 1998-2004; chmn. Rehab. Hosp. Ind., 2002—; with Goshen Health Sys., 2000-2004; bd. dirs. Ruth Lilly Health Edn. Ctr., Indpls. Contbr. articles to profl. jours. Sr. asst. health svcs. officer USPHS, 1968-70. Fellow Am. Coll. Health Care Execs.; mem. Ind. Hosp. Assn. (bd. dirs. 1994-97). Office: Ind U BS4085 801 W Michigan St Indianapolis IN 46202 Business E-Mail: dhandel@iupui.edu.

HANDEL, KAREN, state official; b. Washington, Apr. 18, 1962; m. Steve Handel, 1992. Clk. typist Am. Assn. Retired Persons; exec. asst. to v.p. govt. affairs Hallmark Co.; mgr. internat. comm. CIBA Vision; mgr. govt. and cmty. rels. KPMG; dep. chief of staff Staff of US V.P. Dan Quayle and Marilyn Quayle; pres., CEO North Fulton C. of C.; mem. transition team State of Ga., dep. chief of staff to Gov.; chmn. Fulton County, Ga., 2003—06; sec. state State of Ga., Atlanta, 2007—. Named a Ga. Diva, B2B Mag.; named one of 100 Most Influential Polit. Leaders in Ga., Ga. Trend, Ga.'s Most Influential Polit. Leaders, James Mag., Most Influential Atlantans, Atlanta Bus. Chronicle. Republican. Office: Office Sec State 214 State Capitol Atlanta GA 30334 E-mail: karenhandel@chairmanhandel.com.*

HANDEL, MORTON EMANUEL, film company executive, management consultant; b. NYC, Apr. 12, 1935; s. Benjamin and Mollie (Heller) H.; m. Irma Ruby, Aug. 5, 1956; children: Mark, Gary, Karen. BA, U. Pa., 1956; postgrad., NYU, 1957-59; DHum (hon.), U. Hartford, 2002. V.p. Dale Plastic Playing Card Corp., NYC, 1955-57; gen. mgr. Handel Nets & Fabrics Corp., NYC, 1957-62; pres. A.M. Industries, Inc., Farmingdale, NY, 1962-68, Allan Marine, Inc., Deer Park, NY, 1969-71; chmn. bd. Marlow Yacht Corp., Deer Park, 1969-71; v.p. fin., sec.-treas. Aurora Products Corp. (subs. Nabisco Inc.), 1971-73, sr. v.p., CFO, 1973—74; v.p. fin., CFO Coleco Industries Inc., 1974—78, sr. v.p., CFO, 1978—82, exec. v.p. fin. and adminstrn., 1982-83, exec. v.p. corp. com., 1983-85, exec. v.p. corp. devel., 1985-88, chmn., dir., CEO, 1988—90; pres., dir. Morton Handel Co., Inc., Boca Raton, Fla., 1990—. Pres. and dir. Ranger Industries, Inc., Bloomfield, Conn., 1997-2001; chmn. bd. dirs. Marvel Entertainment, Inc., NYC, 1997—; bd. dirs. Linens 'N Things, Clifton, NJ, 2000-06, Trump Entertainment Resorts, 2005—. Pres. Rochdale Village Civic Assn., 1964-65; pres. bd. dirs. Hartford Symphony Orch., 1976—; bd. dirs. Jewish Children's Svc. Corp., 1976-78; corporator St. Francis Hosp., 1982—; bd. dirs. One Thousand Corp., 1983-95, Greater Hartford Arts Coun., Inc., 1987-89, Hebrew Home for the Aged, 1989—2004; regent U. Hartford, 1990—; vice chmn. bd. regents U. Hartford, 1992-2000; trustee, vice chmn. Hartt Sch. Music, 1991—; bd. dirs. Jewish Fedn. of Greater Hartford, 1996-2000, Hartford Dispensary Inc., 1996-2002; bd. overseers Bushnell Ctr. for Performing Arts, 2002—; trustee Jewish Cmty. Found., 2005-. Mem. Am. Mgmt. Assn., Fin. Execs. Inst., Alpha Epsilon Pi. Office: Morton Handel Co Inc 3475 Windsor Pl Boca Raton FL 33496 Office Phone: 561-995-8586. Personal E-mail: morthandel@aol.com.

HANDEL, NEAL, plastic surgeon, researcher; b. LA, Sept. 2, 1947; s. Max and Ruth H. BA, Columbia U., 1969; MD, Yale U., 1973. Diplomate Am. Bd. Plastic Surgery. Resident UCLA, 1975-76, Tulane U., New Orleans, 1976-78, U. Colo., Denver, 1978—; plastic and reconstructive surgeon The Breast Ctr., Van Nuys, Calif., 1982—99, assoc. med. dir., 1982—99; plastic surgeon Aesthetic Surgical Ptnrs., Santa Barbara, 1999—. Mem. adv. bd. Ctr. for Devel. Biology Calif. State U., Northridge, 1985—. Featured on Body Work series, Plastic Surgery Beverly Hills, The Learning Channel, 2005; contbr. articles to profl. jours. Rsch. grantee Am. Soc. Aesthetic Plastic Surgery, 1991. Fellow ACS; diplomat, Am. Bd. Plastic Surgery; mem. Am. Soc. Plastic and Reconstructive Surgery, Calif. Soc. Plastic and Reconstructive Surgeons, Am. Soc. Plastic Surgeons, Am. Soc. Aesthetic Plastic Surgery, Am. Assn. Plastic Surgeons. Office: Aesthetic Surgical Ptnrs 427 W Pueblo St Ste C Santa Barbara CA 93105 Office Phone: 805-682-7222.*

HANDEL, PETER H., physics professor; b. Hermannstadt, Siebenbuergen, Transylvania, Oct. 16, 1937; came to U.S., 1969; s. Peter and Anna (Broneske) H.; children: Susanne C., Christine D., Peter F. MS in Physics, U. Bucharest, Romania, 1959; PhD in Physics, U. Bucharest, 1965. Scientist Hydrotechnic Rsch. Inst., Bucharest, 1959; rsch. scientist Physics Inst. of Romanian Acad., Bucharest, 1960-66, Physics Inst. Max von Laue-Paul Langevin, Munich, Fed. Republic Germany, 1967-69; assoc. prof. physics dept. U. Mo., St. Louis, 1969-72, prof. physics, 1972—. Cons. Emerson Electric Co., St. Louis, 1975-81; sr. scientist, cons. McDonnell Douglas Rsch. Labs., St. Louis, 1982-83; 20 prestigious vis. prof. appointments, various univs. in Europe, Australia, Japan, and U.S., 1970—; mem. internat. program com. of conf. series on noise in phys. systems and head conf. series on quantum 1/f noise. Contbr. over 200 articles to profl. jours. Grantee NSF, 1971-77, 90—; rsch. grantee Air Force Office of Sci. Rsch., 1984—, Office of Naval Rsch, Army Rsch. Office, 1978-82, 90—, Ultra-low Phase Noise Multidisciplinary Univ. Rsch. Initiative, 2001—. Achievements include creation of quantum 1/f noise theory; research in phase noise; polarization catastrophe theory of cloud electrification; M.S.T. theory of ball lighteningidentified origin of excess heat in electrolysis; patents in field. Office: U Mo Dept Physics 8001 Natural Bridge Rd Saint Louis MO 63121-4901 Office Phone: 314-516-5021. Business E-Mail: handel@umsl.edu.

HANDEL, RICHARD CRAIG, lawyer; b. Hamilton, Ohio, Aug. 11, 1945; s. Alexander F. and Marguerite (Wilks) H.; m. Katharine Jean Carter, Jan. 10, 1970. AB, U. Mich., 1967; MA, Mich. State U., 1968; JD summa cum laude, Ohio State U., 1974; LLM in Taxation, NYU, 1978. Bar: Ohio 1974, S.C. 1983, U.S. Dist. Ct. (so. dist.) Ohio 1975, U.S. Dist. Ct. S.C. 1979, U.S. Tax Ct. 1977, U.S. Ct. Appeals (4th cir.) 1979, U.S. Supreme Ct. 1979; cert. tax specialist. Assoc. Smith & Schnacke, Dayton, Ohio, 1974—77; asst. prof. U. S.C. Sch. Law, Columbia, 1978—83; ptnr. Nexsen, Pruet, Jacobs & Pollard, Columbia, 1983—87, Moore & Van Allen, Columbia, 1987—88, Nexsen Pruet Jacobs & Pollard, Columbia, 1988—89; chief tax policy and appeals S.C. Tax Commn., Columbia, 1989—95; chief coun. Policy S.C. Dept. Revenue, Columbia, 1995—2003, sr. adminstr., gen. counsel, 2003—06, sr. adminstr., gen. counsel policy, 2006—. Adj. prof. U. S.C. Sch. Law, 1990—2001. Contbr. articles to legal jours. Bd. dirs. Friends of Richland County Pub. Libr., 1993-99. With U.S. Army, 1969-70, Vietnam. Recipient Outstanding Law Prof. award, 1980—81; Gerald L. Wallace scholar, 1977—78. Mem.: ABA (vice-chmn. com. tax procedures 1993—94, chmn. membership state and local taxes com. 1997—2007, sec. 2003—05, vice chair state and local taxes com. 2005—, com. stds. tax practice), Order of Coif., S.C. Bar Assn. Office: SC Dept Revenue PO Box 12265 301 Gervais St Columbia SC 29211 Home Phone: 803-254-0439; Office Phone: 803-898-5132. Personal E-mail: rickch@aol.com. Business E-Mail: handelr@sctax.org.

HANDEL, WILLIAM WOLF, radio personality; b. Brazil, 1951; m. Marjorie Handel; children: Pamela, Barbara. BA, Calif. State U. Northridge; JD, Whittier Coll. Law. Dir. Ctr. Surrogate Parenting, Inc., Encino, Calif., 1980—; morning talk show host KFI-AM 640, LA, 1989—.

Adj. prof. Whittier Coll., Sch. Law. Host (radio shows) Handel on the Law, 1989—, Handel Yourself in the Morning, 1993—. Recipient Major Market Personality of Yr., NAB Marconi Radio Awards, 2005. Office: KFI-AM Ste 550 3400 W Olive Ave Burbank CA 91505-5544 also: Ctr for Surrogate Parenting Ste 675 15821 Ventura Blvd Encino CA 91436 Office Phone: 818-559-2252. Fax: 818-729-2514. E-mail: bill@kfi640.com.

HANDELMAN, ALBERT G., lawyer; b. River Edge, NJ, Oct. 5, 1953; BS cum laude in Econs., U. Pa. Wharton Sch., 1975; JD, U. So. Calif., 1978. Bar: Calif. 1978, US Dist. Ct. (ctrl. and no. dists. Calif.) 1979, US Dist. Ct. (ea. dist. Calif.) 1989, cert.: State Bar Calif. Bd. Legal Specialization (estate planning, trust and probate law). Pvt. practice atty., Santa Rosa, Calif. Officer, dir. Redwood Empire Estate Planning Coun., 1992—96, pres., 1994—95; mem., founder Calif. Trust and Estate Counselors, LLP. Contbg. author, cons.: Calif. Wills and Trusts, 1991—; editor: Calif. Trusts and Estates Quarterly, 2001—04. Mem. profls. adv. grp. Cmty. Found. Sonoma County, 1995—, chmn., 1997—2001, bd. dirs., 2004—, chmn. bd. dirs., 2006—. Named one of Top 100 Attys., Worth mag., 2006. Fellow: Am. Coll. Trust and Estate Counsel; mem.: State Bar Calif. (mem. exec. com. Trusts and Estates Sect. 1998—2004), Sonoma County Bar Assn. Office: 420 Aviation Blvd Ste 203 Santa Rosa CA 95403 Office Phone: 707-521-2800. Office Fax: 707-521-2803. E-mail: aghlaw@sonic.net.*

HANDELSMAN, JO, plant pathologist, educator; BS in agronomy, Cornell Univ., Ithaca, NY; PhD in molecular biology, U. Wis.-Madison. Asst. prof. to prof. U. Wis.-Madison, 1985—, dir. Inst. Pest & Pathogen Mgmt., 1997—99, Clark Lectr. Soil Biology, 2002—. Co-author: Biology Brought to Life, 1997. Grantee professorship, Howard Hughes Med. Inst., 2002—. Achievements include establishing Women in Sci. & Engring. Leadership Inst. Office: Dept Plant Pathology U Wisconsin-Madison 1630 Linden Dr Madison WI 53706 Office Phone: 608-263-8783. Office Fax: 608-265-5289.

HANDELSMAN, JOHN ELLIS, pediatric orthopedist, surgeon; b. Johannesburg, Dec. 14, 1930; arrived in U.S., 1977; s. Maurice Handelsman and Rose Betty Braude; m. Barbara Jan Ebenstein, June 24, 1979; children: Sarah Rose, Leanne Beth, Risa Carlyn. MBBChir, Witmatersrand U., 1953; CM in Orthopedics, Liverpool U., Eng., 1963; MD, SUNY, 1977; MA (hon.), Brown U., 1982. Diplomate Am. Bd. Orthop. Surgery, 1978. Intern Gen. Hosp. and Baragwanath Hosp., Johannesburg, 1954—56; resident gen. surgery War Meml. Hosp., High Wycombe, 1957—58, Whipps Cross and St. James Hosps., London, 1957—58; resident orthopedic Nuffield Orthopedic Ctr. and Radcliffe Infirmary, Oxford, England, 1959—61, Royal Victoria Hosp., Montreal, Canada, 1961—62, St. Bartholomew's Hosp., Rochester, England, 1962; fellow Liverpool (Eng.) U. and Walton Hosp., 1963; orthop. surgeon Baragwanath Hosp., Johannesburg, 1964—65; sr. prin. orthop. surgeon Johannesburg Gen. Hosp., 1966—67; chief pediat. orthopedics U. Hosp., Stony Brook, NY, 1977—81; dir. pediat. orthopedics Nassau County Med. Ctr., East Meadow, NY, 1977—81, R.I. Hosp., Providence, 1981—86; chief pediat. orthopedics Schneider Children's Hosp., New Hyde Park, NY, 1986—2002, attending orthopedics and pediatrics, 2002—. Contbr. articles to profl. jours. Fellow: Royal Coll. Surgeons (Eng.); mem.: Pediatric Orthop. Soc. N.Am. (emeritus), Am. Orthop. Assn. (sr.; mem. com. 1985—), Am. Acad. Orthop. Surgeons (mem. com. 1978—). Achievements include research in a neuromuscular cause for club foot; the use of the small A.O. external fixator in osteotomies of the femur, tibia and humerus. Avocations: swimming, bicycling, music, reading, woodworking. Office: Pediatric Orthop Surgery Hillside Med Assocs 915 Hillside Ave New Hyde Park NY 11040 Office Phone: 516-488-5885. Office Fax: 516-328-9355. Personal E-mail: jhandelsman@verizon.net.

HANDELSMAN, LAWRENCE MARC, lawyer; b. NYC, Jan. 17, 1945; s. David and Ruth (Litner) H.; m. Sara Pruzan, June 10, 1967; children: Sharon, Carolyn. BBA, CCNY, 1965; JD, NYU, 1968. Bar: N.Y. 1968, U.S. Ct. Mil. Appeals 1969, U.S. Dist. Ct. (so. and ea. dists.) N.Y. 1973, U.S. Ct. Appeals (2d cir.) 1973, Fla. 1978. Assoc. Stroock & Stroock & Lavan, NYC, 1973-78, ptnr., 1979—. Served to capt. JAGC US Army, 1969—73. Fellow Am. Coll. Bankruptcy; mem. ABA (bus. bankruptcy com. 1969—), Assn. of Bar of City of NY (bankruptcy com. 1974-77, 1985—). Home: 22 Scarsdale Farm Rd Scarsdale NY 10583-1919 Office: Stroock & Stroock & Lavan 180 Maiden Ln Fl 36 New York NY 10038-4937 Office Phone: 212-806-5426.

HANDELSMAN, WALT, cartoonist; married; 2 children. Grad., U. Cin. Cartoonist Scranton (Pa.) Times, 1985—89, New Orleans Times-Picayune, 1989—2001, Newsday, Melville, NY, 2001—. Recipient Nat. Headliner award for Editl. Cartoons, 1989, 1993, Soc. Profl. Journalists award, 1992, Robert F. Kennedy Journalism award, 1996, Pulitzer Prize for Editl. Cartooning, 1997, 2007, Scripps Howard Nat. Journalism award, 2003. Office: Newsday 235 Pinelawn Rd Melville NY 11747*

HANDFORD, H. ALLEN, retired psychiatrist, medical educator; b. Des Moines, July 1, 1930; s. Harvey Eugene and Lenore (Allen) Handford; m. Sandra Lee Betz, Sept. 3, 1955 (div.); children: Lee Allen, Christiana Lenore, Jennifer Miriam, Alice Faith; m. Laura Jane Diller, May 2, 1972 (div.). AB, Harvard U., 1953; MD, State U. Iowa, 1957. Intern Broadlawns, Des Moines, 1957-58; fellow in psychiatry Pa. Hosp. Inst., 1958-60; fellow child psychiatry St. Christopher's Hosp., Phila., 1960-62; pvt. practice Villanova, Pa., 1962—78; dir. rsch. unit autistic children Eastern State Sch. and Hosp., Phila., 1962-73; dir. children's unit Haverford State Hosp., Pa., 1973-74; dir. children and youth programs mental Pa. Dept. Pub. Welfare, 1976-79; clin. asst. prof. psychiatry and human behavior Jefferson Med. Coll., Phila., 1974-78; assoc. prof. psychiatry Coll. Medicine, Pa. State U., Hershey, 1978—2000, co-founder, past dir. divsn. child psychiatry residency tng.; ret., 2000. Dir. psychiatry/psychology Univ. Hosp. Rehab. Ctr., 1979—84; dir. psychosocial program Hemophilia Ctr. Ctrl. Pa., 1979—96; past mem. mental health com. Nat. Hemophilia Found. Contbr. articles to profl. jours. Bd. dirs. Dauphin County Mental Health/Mental Retardation. Mem.: AMA, Coll. Physicians Phila., Ctrl. Pa. Regional Coun. Child Psychiatry (founder), Pa. Psychiat. Soc., Pa. Med. Soc., Am. Acad. Child and Adolescent Psychiatry, Am. Psychiat. Assn. Achievements include research in childhood autism; psychosocial aspects of hemophilia; childhood depression; child and parent reaction to Three Mile Island nuclear accident; sleep disorders of childhood; eating disorders of childhood. Personal E-mail: hhandford@aol.com.

HANDLER, ARTHUR M., lawyer; b. NYC, Feb. 16, 1937; BS, Queens Coll., 1957; LLB, Columbia U., 1960. Bar: N.Y. 1960, U.S. Dist. Ct. (ea. dist.) N.Y. 1960, U.S. Dist. Ct. (so. dist.) N.Y. 1963, U.S. Tax Ct. 1971, U.S. Ct. Appeals (2d cir.) 1971, U.S. Supreme Ct. 1965. Staff counsel SEC, Washington, 1960-61; law clk. to Judge Richard H. Levet, U.S. Dist. Ct. for So. Dist.N.Y., NYC, 1961-62; asst. U.S. atty. So. Dist. N.Y., NYC, 1962-65; assoc. Proskauer, Rose, Goetz & Mendelsohn, NYC, 1965-67, Golenbock and Barell, NYC, 1967-70, ptnr., 1970-89, Whitman & Ransom, NYC, 1990-93, Burns Handler & Burns, NYC, 1993-99, Handler & Goodman, NYC, 1999—. Arbitrator NASD and Am. Stock Exchange, NYC, 1986—. Vol. atty. Lawyer's Com. for Civil Rights under Law, Jackson, Miss., 1966. Mem. ABA, N.Y. State Bar Assn., Bar Assn. of City of N.Y., Fed. Bar Council, Am. Arbitration Assn. (arbitrator 1969—). Nat. Assn. Securities Dealers, University Club, Lords Valley Country Club (Hawley, Pa.) (bd. govs. 1977-80). Avocations: golf, skiing, theater, travel. Office: Handler & Goodman LLP 805 3d Ave New York NY 10022 Home Phone: 212-534-8125; Office Phone: 646-282-1900. Business E-Mail: amhandler@handlergoodman.com.

HANDLER, CAROLE ENID, lawyer, city planner; b. NYC, Dec. 23, 1945; d. Milton and Marion Winter (Kahn) Handler; m. Peter U. Schoenbach, May 30, 1965 (div. Sept. 1979); children: Alisa, Ilana. AB, Radcliffe Coll., 1957; MS, U. Pa., 1963, JD, 1975. Bar: Pa. 1975; Calif. 1987; U.S. Dist Ct. Ea. Pa. 1976, N.J. 1979, Ctrl. Calif. 1987, So. Calif. 1990, So. N.Y. 1990, No. Calif. 1991, Ea. Calif. 1993, Mid. & So. Fla. 1994; U.S. Ct. Appeals 3d cir. 1976, 9th cir. 1988, 2d cir. 1989, 11th cir. 1992; Pa. Supreme Ct.; U.S. Supreme Ct. Planner Boston Redevel. Authority, 1959-61; head gen. plans sect. Phila. City Planning Commn., 1963-66; ednl. facilities planning cons. Phila. Sch. Dist., 1966-67, coordinator and dir. policy planning, 1967-69; instr. U. Sao Paulo, Rio de Janeiro, 1970-71, Cath. U., Rio de Janeiro, 1970-71; law clk. to Hon. Edmund B. Spaeth Jr. Pa. Superior Ct., Phila., 1975-76; assoc. Goodman & Ewing, Phila., 1976-78, Schnader, Harrison, Segal & Lewis, Phila., 1978—; sr. v.p., gen. counsel MGM/UA Distbn. Co., Los Angeles, 1985-87; ptnr. Le Boeuf, Lamb, Leiby & MacRae, LA, 1987-89, Proskauer Rose Goetz & Mendelsohn, LA, Alschuler Grossman Pines, LA, Kaye Scholer Fierman Hays & Handler, LA, 1997—2000, O'Donnell & Shaeffer, LA, 2000—04, Thelen Reid & Priest, LA, 2004—05, Foley & Lardner, LLP, Century City, Calif., 2005—. Adj. prof. Univ. So. Calif. Bd. dirs. St. Peter's Sch.; former bd. dirs. Soc. Hill Synagogue, LA Chamber Orch., 1990—, Public Counsel 1999-; exec. bd. Am. Jewish Congress 2004-; mem Bet Tzedek Legal Svcs. Named one of Top 50 Women Litigators in Calif., Daily Journal Extra, 2002—04. Mem. Phila. Vol. Lawyers for the Arts (v.p.), ABA, Fed. Bar Assn., Pa. Bar Assn., N.Y. Bar Assn., Beverly Hills Bar Assn., L.A. County Bar Assn. (chair antitrust sect. 1992-93), Assn. Bus. Trial Lawyers, Copyright Soc., Calif. Women's Law Ctr. Jewish. Office: Foley & Lardner LLP Ste 3500 2029 Century Park East Los Angeles CA 90067-3021 Office Phone: 310-975-7860. Business E-Mail: chandler@foley.com.

HANDLER, DANIEL (LEMONY SNICKET), writer; b. San Francisco, Feb. 28, 1970; s. Louis and Sandra Handler; m. Lisa Brown, 1998; 1 child. BA in English and Am. Studies, Wesleyan U., 1992. Author: The Basic Eight, 1999, Watch Your Mouth, 2000, (short story collections) Adverbs, 2006; author: (under pen name Lemony Snicket) The Bad Beginning, 1999, The Reptile Room, 1999, The Wide Window, 2000, The Miserable Mill, 2000, The Austere Academy, 2000, The Ersatz Elevator, 2001, The Vile Village, 2001, The Hostile Hospital, 2001, The Carnivorous Carnival, 2002, The Slippery Slope, 2003, The Grim Grotto, 2004, The Penultimate Peril, 2005 (Quill award for Children's Chapter/Middle Grade Book, 2006), The End, 2006, Lemony Snicket: The Unauthorized Biography, 2002, The Beatrice Letters, 2006; writer (films) Kill the Poor, 2003, Lemony Snicket's A Series of Unfortunate Events, 2004, actor, writer Rick, 2003, accordionist (albums) 69 Love Songs, with Magnetic Fields, 1999, Hyacinths & Thistles, with The 6th's, 2000, Kecam, with Speed Dial, 2000. Bd. advisors LitPAC, San Francisco. Recipient prize, Acad. Am. Poets, 1990; Olin fellow, 1992. Office: c/o HarperCollins Childrens Books 1350 Avenue of the Americas New York NY 10019 Business E-Mail: lsnicket@harpercollins.com.

HANDLER, EVELYN, former academic administrator; b. Budapest, Hungary, May 5, 1933; U.S. citizen; m. 1965; two children. BA, Hunter Coll., 1954; MSc, NYU, 1962, PhD in Biology, 1963; LHD (hon.), Rivier Coll., 1982, U. Pitts., 1987, Hunter Coll., 1988. Rsch. assoc. Sloan-Kettering Inst., 1958-60, Merck Inst. Therapeutic Rsch., 1958-60; lectr. Hunter Coll., 1962-64, from asst. to prof. biol. sci., 1965-80, dean sci. and math., 1977-80; pres. U. N.H., 1980-83, Brandeis U., 1983-91; exec. dir. Calif. Acad. Scis., San Francisco, 1994-98; pres. Merrimack Consultants LLC, Bow, NH, 1999—2004. Vis. scientist Karolinska Inst., 1971-72; evaluator Com. Higher Edn., Middle States Assn., 1972—; vice chmn. univ. faculty senate CUNY, 1974-76; generalist, mem. Am. Coun. Pharm. Edn., 1978-83; bd. dirs. New Eng. Life Ins. Co., Student Loan Corp. Trustee Bay Area Biosci. Ctr., 1995—, Mills Coll., 1995—. Sr. fellow Carnegie Found. Advanced Tchg., 1990-92; scholar in residence Harvard U., 1991-92, assoc. in edn. 1992-93; rsch. grantee NIH, 1964-69, 73-76, NSF, 1965-67, 70-72, CUNY, 1972-74. Fellow AAAS, N.Y. Acad. Sci.; mem. Internat. Soc. Hematology, Harvey Soc. Office: Student Loan Corporation Board of Directors 750 Washington Blvd Stamford CT 06901

HANDLER, HAROLD ROBERT, lawyer; b. Jersey City, Aug. 24, 1935; s. Morris Sidney and Fan (Krieger) Handler; m. Lynne Tishman Handler; children from previous marriage: Maren, Jeremy, Jolyon. BS, Lehigh U., 1957; LLM, Columbia U., 1961. Bar: N.Y. 1961, U.S. Tax Ct. 1963, U.S. Ct. Appeals (2d cir.) 1980. Atty., advisor U.S. Tax Ct., Washington, 1961-63; assoc. Simpson Thacher & Bartlett, NYC, 1963-69, ptnr., 1970-97, of counsel, 1998—. Adj. assoc. prof. law NYU, 1978-80. Chmn. fin. com., citizens adv. com. Met. Transp. Authority, NYC, 1975—79; trustee Citizens Budget Commn.; pres., chmn. exec. com. Jewish Cmty. Ctr. in Manhattan, NYC, 1992—2001; trustee Jewish Communal Fund, 1997—, pres., 2005—. Fellow Am. Coll. Tax Counsel; mem. ABA, N.Y. State Bar Assn. (chmn. subcom. tax sect. 1979-83, mem. exec. com. tax sect. 1990—, officer 1996-2000, chair 1999-20000), Assn. of Bar of City of N.Y. (chmn. tax com. 1983-86, mem. tax coun. 1990-98), Am. Law Inst., Inst. Fed. Taxation (panelist), Inst. Securities Regulation (panelist).

HANDLER, JANET BOUGASH, elementary school educator; b. July 9, 1940; BS in Edn., Fairleigh Dickinson U., Teaneck, NJ, 1962; MS in Edn., CUNY: Lehman Coll., Bronx, NY, 1968. Cert. tchr. NY, 1962. Tchr. NYC Bd. Edn., 1962—. Mem.: Art Students League (life merit scholar 1996—97), Audubon Artists (dir. sculpture 2004—, Cleo Hartwig award 2005). Home: 408 W 57th St New York NY 10019

HANDLER, JEROME SIDNEY, anthropology educator; b. NYC, Sept. 3, 1933; s. Sam and Sara (Wieder) H.; children: Joshua Martin, Lisa Frances. BA, UCLA, 1956, MA, 1959; PhD, Brandeis U., 1965. From asst. prof. to prof. anthropology So. Ill. U., Carbondale, 1964-93, prof. Black Am. studies, 1993-95, prof. emeritus, 1995—. Olive B. O'Connor vis. prof. Am. instns. Colgate U., Hamilton, N.Y., 1971-72; hon. rsch. asst. Univ. Coll., London, 1966-67; staff archaeologist New World Archaeol. Found., Chiapas, Mex., 1957; cons. AID, fall, 1964, Peace Corps, summer 1969; cons. Libr. of Congress, 1998, 99, 2000, 01, panelist NEH, 1977-79, 82, NSF, 2004; mem. adv. com. African Burial Ground, N.Y.C., GSA, 1991-93. Author: A Guide to Source Materials for the Study of Barbados History, 1627-1834, 1971, The Unappropriated People: Freedmen in the Slave Society of Barbados, 1974, Supplement to A Guide to Source Materials for the Study of Barbados History, 1991; co-author: Plantation Slavery in Barbados: An Archaeological and Historical Investigation, 1978, Searching for a Slave Cemetery in Barbados: A Bioarcheological and Ethnohistorical Investigation, 1989 Vis. rsch. fellow U. W.I., Jamaica, 1969-70, Barbados, 1983; rsch. assoc. Rsch. Inst. for Study of Man, N.Y.C., 1978-79; vis. scholar Ctr. for Afro-Am. Studies, UCLA, 1980, dept. Afro-Am. Studies, Harvard U., summer 1992; Rsch. grantee NSF, 1966-67, 71-73, Wenner-Gren Found. Anthrop. Rsch., 1971-72, 87, Rsch. Inst. Study Man, 1962, 70, NIH, 1965, Am. Philos. Soc., 1968, Nat. Geographic Soc., 1987, NEH Inst. for Coll. Tchrs., 1997-98; NEH fellow, 1969-70, 75-76, 79; Travel grant Am. Coun. Learned Socs., 1977, grantee Social Sci. Rsch. Coun. and Am. Coun. Learned Socs. Joint Com. on Latin Am. Studies, 1983; Nat. Humanities Ctr. fellow, 1982-83, John Carter Brown Libr. fellow, 1985, 88, 2002, 06, 07, DuBois Inst. Afro-Am. Rsch. fellow Harvard, 1989-90; fellow Va. Found. Humanities, 1995-99, sr. fellow, 2002; Va. Found. sr. fellow, 2002—; fellow Libr. Co. Phila., 2002; Sch. Am. Rsch. fellow, Santa Fe, summer 2004. Fellow Am. Anthrop. Assn. (rep. to Am. Coun. Learned Socs. 1985-90); mem. Caribbean Studies Assn. (past mem. exec. council) Home: 120 Blithe Ct Charlottesville VA 22901 Office: Va Found Humanities 145 Ednam Dr Charlottesville VA 22903-4629 Office Phone: 434-924-3296.

HANDLER, JOEL F., law educator; b. 1932; AB, Princeton U., 1954; JD, Harvard U., 1957. Asst. prof. Vanderbilt U., 1961-62, U. Ill., 1962-64; prof. U. Wis., 1965-80, George A. Wiley prof., 1980-82; vilas rsch. prof., 1982-85; vis. prof. UCLA, 1984-85, prof., 1985—. Vis. prof. Stanford, 1969-70. Fellow John Simon Guggenheim, 1974-75, German Marshall Fund, 1978. Mem. Law and Soc. Assn., Nat. Res. Coun. Status of Black Am; fellow, Am. Acad. of Arts and Sci. Office: UCLA Law Sch 405 Hilgard Ave Los Angeles CA 90095-9000

HANDLER, RICHARD B., investment company executive; BA, Univ. Rochester, 1983; MBA, Stanford Univ., 1987. Exec. v.p. high yield dept. Jefferies Group Inc., NYC, 1990—93, mng. dir. high yield dept., 1993—2000, bd. dir., 1998—, co-pres., COO, 2000, CEO, 2001—02, chmn., CEO, 2002—. Mem. adv. bd. Wayland Fund Cargill Fin. Services Corp. Office: Jefferies Group Inc 12th Fl 520 Madison Ave New York NY 10022*

HANDLEY, GERALD MATTHEW, lawyer, educator; b. Phila., Dec. 7, 1942; s. John F. and Helen E. (Gerdelman) H.; m. Sandra I. Martin, June 13, 1970; children: Christopher, Elizabeth. BS, La Salle Coll., Phila., 1965; JD, U. Mo., Kansas City, 1972. Bar: Mo. 1972, U.S. Dist. Ct. (we. dist.) Mo. 1972, U.S.Supreme Ct., 1976, U.S. Ct. Appeals (8th and 10th cirs.) 1980, U.S Dist. Ct. Kans. 1998. Asst. pub. defender Office Pub. Defender, Kansas City, Mo., 1972—73, 1st asst. pub. defender, 1973—75, interim pub. defender, 1975—76; ptnr. Speck & Handley, Kansas City, 1980—90; pvt. practice Law Offices of G. Handley, Kansas City, 1991—92, 1993—. Lectr. Rockhurst Coll., Kansas City, 1976-78; instr. U. Mo. Sch. Law. Contbr. chpts. to law books. Pres., Home Owners Assn., Kansas City, 1980. Served with U.S. Army, 1966-67, Vietnam. Named Best of the Bar, Kansas City Bus. Jour., 2000—06, Top 100 Super Lawyers, Kans. and Mo., 2005, 2006. Fellow Am. Bd. Criminal Lawyers; mem. ABA, NACDL, Fed. Bar Assn., Mo. Bar Assn., (Lon Hocker Trial Lawyer award 1977), Mo. Assn. Criminal Def. Lawyers (pres. 1980, hon. bd. dirs.), U.S. Supreme Ct. Bar Assn., 8th Cir. Bar Assn., Kansas City Met. Bar Assn. Roman Catholic. Avocations: golf, gardening. Office: 1100 Main St Ste 2800 Kansas City MO 64105 Home Phone: 816-361-9207; Office Phone: 816-471-7145. Personal E-mail: ghandley@swbell.net.

HANDLEY, LEON HUNTER, lawyer; b. Lakeland, Fla., Sept. 9, 1927; s. Driskle Hubert and Mamie (Denmark) H.; m. Mary Virginia Wolfe, May 2, 1953; children: Leon Hunter, Mary Ellen, Laura Catherine, Leann Virginia. BSBA with honors, U. Fla., Gainesville, 1949, JD, 1951. Bar: Fla. 1951, US Dist. Ct. (so. dist.) Fla. 1952, US Dist. Ct. (mid. dist.) Fla. 1962, US Supreme Ct. 1956, US Ct. Appeals (5th cir.) 1960, US Ct. Appeals (11th cir.) 1981. Pres. Gurney & Handley, Orlando, Fla., 1951—2005; ptnr. Rumberger, Kirk & Caldwell, P.A., Orlando, 2005—. Bd. dirs. Orlando/Tampa Cracker Groves, Inc., Orlando, 1964—; v.p., bd. dirs. So. Indsl. Savs. Bank, Orlando, Claude H. Wolfe, Inc., Orlando, 1969—; pres., chmn. bd. dirs. Mine & Mill Supply Co., Lakeland, 1966—; gen. counsel, life dir., past pres. Cen. Fla. Fair; chmn. bd. trustees Sta. WMFE-TV. Pres. Chesley Magruder Charitable Trust; elder Presbyn. Ch.; trustee Lake Highland Prep. Sch., Orlando. Warrant officer US Maritime Svc., 1945-46, ETO; sgt. US Army, 1946-48, Korea; capt. USAFR, 1949-59. Named one of Best Lawyers in Am.; named to U. Fla. Hall of Fame. Fellow Am. Coll. Trial Lawyers; mem. ABA, Am. Bd. Trial Advocates (Fla. Trial Lawyer of Yr. 1966, advocate), Orange County Bar Assn. (past pres.), Fla. Bar Assn. (past pres. sta. jr. bar sect., bd. govs. 1959-60), Fedn. Ins. and Corp. Counsel, Internat. Assn. Def. Counsel, Assn. Def. Trial Attys., Trial Attys. Am., Am. Judicature Soc., Pres.'s Coun. (founder U. Fla. chpt.), Citrus Club, Orlando Country Club, Univ. Club, Masons (grand orator Fla. 1982, 86), K.T., Shriners, Scottish Rite (33d degree, insp. gen. hon. 1979), Rotary (pres. Orlando chpt. 1984, Paul Harris fellow), Travelers' Century Club, Fla. Blue Key (pres. 1951), Phi Delta Phi, Alpha Tau Omega (pres. U. Fla. chpt. 1951), Phi Kappa Phi, Alpha Kappa Psi, Beta Gamma Sigma. Republican. Avocations: jogging, handball. Office: Rumberger Kirk & Caldwell PA PO Box 1873 Orlando FL 32801 Home: 70 W Lucerne Cir Apt 1715 Orlando FL 32801 Office Phone: 407-872-7300 ext. 2159. Office Fax: 407-841-2133. Business E-Mail: lhandley@rumberger.com.

HANDLEY, LOUISE PATRICIA, artist; b. Portland, Oreg., Apr. 9, 1938; d. Willard Alan and Dorothy Davis Johnson; m. Richard Dale Handley, June 7, 1957; children: Beth, Richard Jr., Jennifer, Michael. Studied, Lewis & Clark Coll., Portland, Oreg., 1957. Tchr. decorative painting Handleycrafts, Bandon, Oreg., 1973—86. Author: Fabric Silhouettes-Quilted Treasures from the Family Album, 2006. Mem.: Designing Women, Nat. Soc. Decorative Painters (cert.). Democrat. Achievements include development of snapshot silhouette technique. Home: 640 8th St SW Bandon OR 97411 Personal E-mail: louiseh@mycomspan.com.

HANDLEY, SIOBHAN A., lawyer; BA cum laude, Coll. of Holy Cross, 1990; JD, NYU, 1994. Bar: NY, US Dist. Ct., NY (Ea. & So. Dist.). Assoc. Orrick, Herrington & Sutcliffe LLP, NYC, ptnr., product liability litigation, 2003—. Mem.: NY State Bar Assn. Office: Orrick, Herrington & Sutcliffe LLP 666 Fifth Ave New York NY 10103-0001 Office Phone: 212-506-5000. Office Fax: 212-506-5151. Business E-Mail: shandley@orrick.com.

HANDLY, KEVIN JOHN, lawyer, educator; b. Madison, Wis., Nov. 5, 1952; s. Arthur Moore and Anne Frenette Handly; m. Piney M. Kesting, July 19, 1984; children: Theodore Arthur, Zoë Alexandra. BS in Fgn. Svc., Georgetown U., 1975, JD, 1979. Bar: N.Y. 1980, Mass. 1988. Asst. dist. atty. Kings County, Bklyn., 1979—82; sr. atty. Fed. Res. Bd., Washington, 1982—87; ptnr. Goodwin Procter & Hoar, Boston, 1987—95, Peabody & Brown, Boston, 1995—2001; dir. Goulston & Storrs, P.C., Boston, 2001—05; dir., shareholder Gallagher, Callahan & Gartrell, P.C., Boston, 2005—. Lectr. law Boston U. Law Sch., 2001—. Mem.: ABA (bus. law sect.), Boston Bar Assn., N.Y. Bar Assn. (bus. law sect.). Avocations: running, mountain scrambling, skiing, sailing. Home: 26 Arborway Jamaica Plain MA 02130 Office: Gallagher Callahan & Gartrell PC 112 South St Boston MA 02111 Office Phone: 617-426-5349. Business E-Mail: handly@gcglaw.com.

HANDS, ERIC WILLIAM, civil engineer, researcher; b. Oakland, Calif., Sept. 27, 1943; s. Richard Ford Hands and Esther Mae (Larson) Hazelet; m. Monica Louise Ulery, 1968 (div. 1973); 1 child, Lars Michael; m. Sherrill Ann Gardner, 1977 (div. 1986); 1 child, Lief Forrest. Student, U. Calif., Davis, 1975-80, U. Wash., Seattle, 1981-82, 84, Griffin Bus. Coll., Sealttle, 1983; BS, Regents Coll., SUNY (now Excelsior Coll.), Albany, 1984; student, West Coast U., Lompoc, Calif., 1988. Engr.-in-tng., Calif., 1985, EPA universal type, Rule 608, 2001; lic. med. provider 2004; cert. advanced marine firefighter 2002, lic. Mcht. Marine officer, 2004, cert. marine radio operator 2005. Engring. technician, software developer Naval Undersea Warfare Engring. Sta., Keyport, Wash., 1980-81; engr., carpenter, marine electrician, mariner, sales profl. various orgns., 1984—; real estate/ins. sales staff Channel Islands Real Estate/Met. Ins., Port Hueneme, Camarillo, Calif., 1985; civil engr. Martin, Northart & Spencer, Santa Barbara, Calif., 1985-86, Dept. Pub. Works, County of Santa Barbara, Santa Barbara, Calif., 1986-87; owner, tech. cons. Winters Soldiers Cons., Seattle, 2001—; vendor Eagle-1 Mfg. Cons./logistics support Operation Enduring Freedom, 2001—05, Operation Iraqi Freedom, 2003—05. Author, editor: Energy and Resources, 1976. Sr. team leader, sustaining mem. Rep. Nat. Com., 2000—; contbg. mem. Dem. Nat. Com., 1993; hon. mem. Rep. Nat. Com., 1992; sr. team leader Nat. Rep. Congl. Com., 2001, sr. del., mem. bus. adv. coun., 2002—03; active Citizens Against Govt. Waste; founding mem. Rep. Leadership Found.; platinum mem. Rep. Presdl. Task Force; active New Rep. Majority Fund, Svc. Support Enduring Freedom, 2001—02, Logistics Support Iraqi Freedom, 2003—04; mem. John

McCain Presdl. Exploratory Com., 2007. Nominee 2000 Outstanding Scientists of 21st Century, 2002; named Rep. of Yr., Nat. Rep. Congl. Com., 2006; named one of 2000 Outstanding Scientists of 20th Century, 2001; recipient Cert. of Appreciation, Nuc. and Plasma Sci. Soc., 2000, Congl. Order of Merit, Nat. Rep. Congl. Com., 2006, 2007. Mem.: NSPE, ASCE, IEEE, Internat. Brotherhood Elec. Workers, Sailors Union of the Pacific, NY Acad. Sci., Wash. Soc. Profl. Engrs. (rec. sec. Seattle chpt. 1998—2001), United Brotherhood Carpenters and Joiners (Shipwrights and Joiners), Internat. Orgn. Masters, Mates and Pilots, Am. Legion. Office Phone: 310-961-7221. Personal E-mail: eds2@seanet.com.

HANDS, TERENCE DAVID (TERRY), theater and opera director; b. Jan. 9, 1941; s. Joseph Ronald and Luise Berthe (Kohler) H.; m. Josephine Barstow, 1964 (div. 1967); m. Ludmila Mikaël, 1974 (div. 1980); 1 child; ptnr. Julia Lintott, 1988-1996; 2 children; m. Emma Lucia, 2002. BA in English Lang. and Lit. with honors, Birmingham U., Eng., 1962, DLitt (hon.), 1988; diploma with honors, Royal Acad. Dramatic Art, 1964; DLitt (hon.), Middlesex U., 1997, Liverpool U., 2006. Founder, artistic dir. Liverpool (Eng.) Everyman Theatre, 1964-66; artistic dir. RSC Theatre-ground, 1966-67; from assoc. dir. to artistic dir. Royal Shakespeare Co., England, 1967-91, dir. emeritus, 1991—. Cons. Comedie Francaise, 1975-80, Clwyd Theatr Cymru, dir., 1997— contbr. to Theatre 72, Playback pubs.; translator of plays; v.p. Llangollen Internat. Gsteddfod. Dir.: (plays) Hamlet, 1994, Merry Wives of Windsor, 1995, The Pretenders, 1996, The Royal Hunt of The Sun, 1996, The Importance of Being Ernest, 1997, A Christmas Carol, 1997, Equus, 1997, The Journey of Mary Kelly, 1998, The Seagull, 1998, The Norman Conquests, 1998, Macbeth, 1999, 12th Night, 1999, Under Milk Wood, 1999, Macbeth (Broadway), 2000, Private Lives, 2001, King Lear, 2001, Bedrom Farce, 2001, The Rabbit, 2001, Rosencrantz and Guildenstern Are Dead, 2002, Betrayal, 2002, Romeo and Juliet, 2002, The Four Seasons, 2002, Blithe Spirit, 2003, Crucible, 2003, Pleasure and Repentance, 2003, One Flew Over the Cuckoo's Nest, 2004, Brassed Off, 2004, Troilus & Cressida, 2005, Night Must Fall, 2005, A Chorus of Disapproval, 2006, Hamlet, 2006, Chicago, 2006, Memory, 2006, Arcadia, 2007. Decorated chevalier des Arts et des Lettres; recipient Pragnell Shakespeare award 1991. Fellow Shakespeare Inst. (hon.), Royal Welsh Coll. Music and Drama, North East Wales Inst.; v.p. Llangollen Internat., Gisteddfod; joint pres. Arvon Found. Office: Clwyd Theatr Cymru Mold Flintshire North Wales CH7 1YA England

HANDSCHU, BARBARA ELLEN, lawyer; b. Buffalo, June 28, 1942; d. Joseph and Rose H. BA, NYU, 1963; JD, U. Mich., 1966. Bar: N.Y. 1967, U.S. Dist. Ct. (ea., so. and we. dists.) N.Y., U.S. Supreme Ct. Hearing examiner Erie County Family Ct., Buffalo, 1981-82; lectr. SUNY, Buffalo, 1983; pvt. practice Buffalo; spl. counsel Mayerson Stutman, NYC. Contbr. articles to legal publs. Mem. Buffalo Housing Ct. Adv. Bd., 1981-84; pres., bd. dirs. Neighborhood Legal Svcs., Buffalo, 1981-85. Recipient proclamation Buffalo City Coun., 1983, Women Helping Women award NOW, Buffalo, 1986. Fellow Internat. Acad. Matrimonial Lawyers; mem. ABA (co-chmn. custody com. 1987—), NY State Bar Assn. (chair family law sect. 1990-92), Am. Acad. Matrimonial Attys. (pres. 2004-05, v.p. 1997-2003, pres. NY chpt. 1995-97, bd. mgr. NY State chpt. 1986—, editor-in-chief jour. 1995-97), Phi Beta Kappa. Democrat. Jewish. Office Phone: 716-885-8005. E-mail: bhandschu@mayersonstutman.com.

HANDSCHUMACHER, ROBERT EDMUND, biochemistry professor; b. Abington, Pa., Oct. 16, 1927; m. Joan A. Goddard; children: Kurt, Mark. BSChemE, Drexel Inst., 1949; MS in Biochemistry, U. Wis., 1951, PhD in Biochemistry, 1953. Postdoctoral fellow Lister Inst., 1953-54; postdoctoral fellow pharm. Yale U. Sch. Medicine, New Haven, 1955-56, asst. prof. pharm., 1956-60, assoc. prof. pharm., 1960-64, dir. div. biol. scis., 1969-72, chmn. dept. pharm., 1974-77, prof. pharm., 1964-95, prof. emeritus, 1996—. Chmn. Eleanor Roosevelt Internat. Fellowship Com., 1966-73, Am. Cancer Soc. Coun. Rsch. Grants, 1977-78, sci. rev. com. Ludwig Cancer Unit, Brussels, 1980-84, health and med. care com. Conn. Acad. Sci., 1984—; sec., treas. Am. Assn. Cancer Rsch., Phila., 1982-88; rsch. prof. Am. Cancer Soc., 1977-95; Philips Meml. lectr. Meml. Sloan-Kettering, N.Y.C., 1985; chmn. exp. therap. adv. bd. B-W Fund, 1990-93; coun. mem. Nat. Inst. Environ. Health Scis., 1987-91. Author 250 articles, book chpts., etc. Sci. dir. Anna Fuller Fund, Yale U. Sch. Medicine, 1973-88; chmn. Samuel Roberts Noble Found. Adv. Bd., Okla., 1982-90; mem. bd. govs. Yale U. Press, New Haven, 1989-93; bd. dirs., v.p. Lutherans in Mission, 1999—. Fellow AAAS; mem. Conn. Acad. Sci. & Engring. (charter). Democrat. Lutheran. Achievements include development of new cancer treatments involving Asparaginase, 5-Fluorouracil; initial purification of the Lymphokine IL-1; discovery of receptor for the transplantation drug Cyclosporin.

HANDY, BEVERLY C., medical educator; d. Sylvia J. Turman; m. Dexter R. Handy, May 28, 1981. BS in Behavioral Scis., USAF Acad., Colo. Springs, 1980; MS in Indsl. Psychology, St. Mary's U., San Antonio, 1987; MD, U. Tex., Houston, 1992. Lic. dr. Tex. State Bd. Med. Examiners, 1993, anatomic & clinical pathology Am. Bd. Pathology, 1997, chemical pathology Am. Bd. Pathology, 1999. Pathology resident U. Tex. Health Sci. Ctr., 1992—96; chemichal pathology fellow in lab. medicine U. Tex. M.D. Anderson Cancer Ctr., Houston, 1998—99, instr., 1999—2002, asst. prof., 2002—. Co-chair Orgn. Minority Employees U. Tex. M.D. Anderson Cancer Ctr., 2005—. Alt. voting mem., instl. rev. com. Wilford Hall Usaf Med. Ctr., San Antonio, 1984—85; exec. com. mem. Tuskegee Airmen Inc., San Antonio, 1984—85. Decorated Marksmanship Ribbon USAF, Commendation medal; recipient Lackland Air Force Pacesetter award, USAF Lackland AFB, 1980, MVP Varsity Rifle Team, USAF Acad., 1980, Jr. Officer of Quarter award, USAF Occupl. Measurement Ctr., 1983, Jr. Officer of Quarter, USAF 3507th Airman Classification Squadron, 1985, Paul E. Strandjord Young Investigator award, Acad. Clin. Lab. Physicians & Scientists, 1999. Mem.: Am. Assn. Clin. Chemistry (bd. dirs. 2005—), Clin. Ligand Assay Soc., Alpha Omega Alpha. Achievements include being one of the first class of women to graguate from the USAF Academy; Finisher - Boston Marathon, 2004, 2005. Office: MD Anderson Cancer Center 1515 Holcombe Houston TX 77030 Personal E-mail: drhandy@aol.com. Business E-Mail: bhandy@mdanderson.org.

HANDY, EDWARD OTIS, JR., retired diversified financial services company executive; b. Akron, Ohio, Jan. 9, 1929; s. Edward Otis and Alice (Saalfield) H.; m. Susan Eastabrooks, May 12, 1951; children: Susan Littlefield, John E., Edward O. III, Seth H. AB, Harvard U., Cambridge, Mass., 1951, LLB, 1956. Bar: RI 1956, U.S. Dist. Ct. RI 1956. Assoc. Edwards & Angell, Providence, 1956-59; staff atty. Textron Inc., Providence, 1960-74, asst. gen. counsel, 1974-76, v.p. employee benefits, 1976-87, v.p., sec., 1987-91; ret., 1991. Bd. dirs. ERISA Industries Com., 1982-91, vice chmn., 1990-91; pres., bd. dirs. Providence Athenaeum, 1972-78; trustee various orgns. Capt. USMC, 1951-53, Korea. Mem. Providence Art Club, Hyannisport Club. Republican. Unitarian Universalist.

HANDY, JOHN W., shipping company executive, retired military officer; b. Raleigh, NC, Apr. 29, 1944; BS in History, Meth. Coll., 1966; Diploma, Squadron Officer Sch., 1972, Air Command and Staff Coll., 1979; MS in Systems Mgmt., U. So. Calif., 1979; Diploma, Air War Coll., 1982, Nat. War Coll., 1984; postgrad., Harvard U., 1993. Commd. 2d lt. USAF, 1967, advanced through ranks to gen., 2000; various assignments to dir. of programs and evaluations Hdqtrs. USAF, Washington, 1995-97; comdr. 21st Air Force, McGuire AFB, N.J., 1997-98; dep. chief of staff for installations and logistics Hdqtrs. USAF/The Pentagon, Washington, 1998-2000; vice chief of staff USAF/The Pentagon, Washington, 2000—01; comdr. U.S. Transp. Command, Scott AFB, Ill., 2001—05; exec. v.p. Horizon Lines, LLC, Charlotte, NC, 2005—. Bd. dir. Alien Tech., 2006—, American Roll-On Roll-off Carrier, Am. Auto Logistics; bd. trustee Methodist Coll., Fayetteville, NC, St. Louis Sci. Ctr. Decorated Def. Disting. Svc. medal, Disting. Svc. medal, Legion of Merit with oak leaf cluster, Meritorious Svc. medal with three oak leaf clusters, Air medal with oak leaf cluster, Antarctica Svc. medal, Vietnam Svc. medal with three svc. stars, Republic of Vietnam Gallery Cross with Palm, Order of Sword, 2005, others. Office: Horizon Lines Inc 4064 Colony Rd Ste 200 Charlotte NC 28211

HANDY, MARY THOMAS, retired elementary school educator; b. Marion, Md., Apr. 9, 1936; d. Monroe Henry Thomas and Agnes Elizabeth Mack; m. William Thomas Handy, Dec. 23, 1961 (div. Feb. 1972); children: Andrew Eltonio Thomas, William Thomas Jr. BS, Bowie State U., 1958; MEd, U. Va., 1971; Advanced Grad. Specialist, U. Md., 1988. Tchr. elem. sch. Withams Elem. Sch., Va., 1963—64, North Accomack Elem. Sch., Mappsville, Va., 1964—70, Prince St Elem Sch, Saisbury, Md., 1970—85; tchr. mid. sch. Wicomico Mid. Sch., Salisbury, 1985—98; ret., 1998. Counselor dormitory U. Va., Charlottesville, 1971—. Mem. prin. adv. bd. Carter G. Woodson Mid. Sch., Crisfield, 2003—; adv. bd. Somerset County Pub. Charter Sch.; discipline com. Somerset County Bd. Edn.; v.p. Somerset Advocates for Edn., 2005—; with Somerset County Bd. Elections, 2007; bd. dirs. United Cmty. Ministries. Recipient Cert. of Appreciation, Wicomico County Bd. Edn., Salisbury, Md., 1995, McCready Found., Inc. Jr. Aux. Bd., Crisfield, Md., 2000, Letter of Appreciation dedication, Wicomico County Bd. Edn., Salisbury, 1998, Ret. Tchr. award, Crisfield-Woodson Alumni Assn., 1999, Top Vol. award, 2004. Mem.: AARP, NAACP (life; sec. edn. com. 2001, bd. dirs. Somerset County chpt., by-laws com., strategy team), Somerset Advs. for Edn. (v.p. 2005, sec. 2006), Wicomico County Ret. Tchr.'s Assn. (Top Vol. award 2004), Md. Ret. Tchr.'s Assn., Crisfield-Woodson Alumni Assn. (sec. Ea. Shore chpt. 1997—2007), Bowie Alumni Assn. (life), Somerset County Democratic Club. Avocations: bicycling, exercising, walking, singing, travel. Home: 28152 Holland Crossing Rd Marion Station MD 21838

HANDY, RICHARD LINCOLN, civil engineer, educator; b. Chariton, Iowa, Feb. 12, 1929; s. Walter Newton and Florence Elizabeth (Shoemaker) H.; married, Apr. 18, 1964 (div. 1980); 1 child, Beth Susan.; m. Kathryn Etona Claussen, Feb. 13, 1982. BS in Geology, Iowa State U., 1951, MS, 1953, PhD in Soil Engring. and Geology, 1956. Asst. prof. civil engring. Iowa State U., Ames, 1956-59, assoc. prof., 1959-63, prof., 1963-87, disting. prof., 1987-91, disting. prof. emeritus, 1991—; prof.-in-charge Spangler Geotech. Lab., 1963-91; cons. in soil engring., soil and rock testing, landslide stabilization; v.p. research W.N. Handy Co., 1958-91, chmn. bd., 1986-90; pres. Handy Geotech. Instruments, Inc., 1980-93, 1999—, chmn. bd. dirs., 1993—; mem., chmn. bd. dirs. Geopier Found. Co., L.C., 1993-95. Author: The Day the House Fell, 1995; co-author: (with M.G. Spangler) Soil Engineering 3rd edit., 1972, 4th edit. 1983, Geotechnical Engineering, 5th edit., 2007; contbr. articles to profl. jours. Recipient faculty citation Iowa State U., 1976; named Anson Marston Disting. Prof. Engring., Iowa State U., 1987. Fellow AAAS, Geol. Soc. Am., Iowa Acad. Sci.; mem. ASCE (Thomas A. Middlebrooks award 1986), Soil Sci. Soc. Am., Internat. Soc. Soil Mech. and Found. Engrs. Achievements include patents for soils and rock testing instruments. Home and Office: 1502 270th St Madrid IA 50156-7522 Home Phone: 515-795-3355; Office Phone: 515-795-3355. Business E-Mail: rlhandy@iowatelecom.net.

HANDY, ROLLO LEROY, philosopher, researcher; b. Kenyon, Minn., Feb. 20, 1927; s. John R. and Alice (Kispert) H.; m. Toni Scheiner, Sept. 17, 1950 (dec. July 1997); children: Jonathan, Ellen, Benjamin. BA, Carleton Coll., Northfield, Minn., 1950; MA, Sarah Lawrence Coll., 1951; postgrad., U. Minn., 1951-52; PhD, U. Buffalo, 1954. Mem. faculty U. S.D., 1954-60, prof. philosophy, head dept., 1959-60; assoc. prof. Union Coll., Schenectady, NY, 1960-61; mem. faculty SUNY, Buffalo, 1961-76, prof. philosophy, 1964-76, chmn. dept., 1961-67, chmn. divsn. philosophy and social scis., 1965-67, provost faculty ednl. studies, 1967-76; pres. Behavioral Rsch. Coun., Great Barrington, Mass., 1976-84, Am. Inst. Econ. Rsch., Great Barrington, Mass., 1977-91, pres. emeritus, 1991—; ret. Author: Methodology of the Behavioral Sciences, 1964, Value Theory and the Behavioral Sciences, 1969, The Measurement of Values, 1970, (with Paul Kurtz) A Current Appraisal of the Behavioral Sciences, 1964; (with E.C. Harwood) rev. edit., 1973, (with E.C. Harwood) Useful Procedures of Inquiry, 1973; co-editor: Philosophical Perspectives on Punishment, 1968, The Behavioral Sciences, 1968, The Idea of God, 1968. With USNR, 1945-46. Mem. AAUP (chpt. pres. 1964-65), Am. Anthrop. Assn., Am. Philos. Assn. E-mail: rhandy4728@aol.com.

HANDY, VIRGINIA MAE, writer; b. Benton Harbor, Mich., July 21, 1935; d. C. Russell and Mary Charlotte Edwards Handy. AA, Benton Harbor Jr. Coll., 1954; BA cum laude, Western Mich. U., 1956. Cert. libr. Mich. Bd. Librs. Cataloger Detroit Pub. Libr., 1956—62, Lakehead U. Libr., Thunder Bay, Ont., Canada, 1964—67, Sodus Twp. Libr., Sodus, Mich., 1968—72; med. records abstractor Mercy-Meml. Med. Ctr., Benton Harbor and St. Joseph, Mich., 1972—91; Log Cabin Day coord., editor Log Cabin Soc. Mich., Sodus, 1987—; fiber arts instr. Salvation Army Ctr. for the Arts, Benton Harbor, 1997—2005. Spinning and weaving demonstrator, 1975—; profl. cons. for log cabins Mich. Humanities Coun., East Lansing, 2002—; columnist Mich. Mag., 1992—. Photographs in: Life's Canvas, Internat. Soc. Photographers, 2000, Best Photos of 2000, 2001, Best Photos of 2003; author: The Palmer Park Log Cabin: A Souvenir History, 2001, Flax Craft, a Collection of Newsletters, 1993-1999, 2002, rev. edit., 2006, From the Little Log Cabin in the Lane, 2004, The Log Cabins of Michigan, a Pictorial Survey, 2007; editor: Log Cabin News, the Quar. Newsletter of the Log Cabin Soc. Mich., 1989—, The Memoirs of John Handy, Sodus Farmer, 2005; contbr. articles to jours. in field. Founder Log Cabin Day in Mich., 1987; leader 4-H, 1975—85; mem. Blossomland Arts and Cultural Coun., St. Joseph, Mich., 1993—94; organizer Detroit 300 Event and Log Cabin Day, 2001; lobbyist for Log Cabin Day bill Mich. Legis., Lansing, 1988—89. Recipient Award of Merit for founding Log Cabin Soc. Mich., Hist. Soc. Mich., 1991, 1st place for linen curtain, Fiberfest, 1992, Silverbowl award for outstanding achievement, Internat. Soc. of Photographers, 2004, Eagle award, Mich. Mag. TV, 2006; Artist-in-Residence grantee, Arts Coun. of Greater Kalamazoo, 2003. Mem.: Mich. League of Handweavers, Mich. Festivals and Events Assn., Mich. Centennial Farm Assn., Pioneer Am. Soc., Log Cabin Soc. Mich. (co-founder 1988, sec.-treas. 1988—, 10th Log Cabin Day plaque 1996), Mich. Archival Assn., Hist. Soc. Mich., Mich. Barn Preservation Network. Achievements include gave the Dr. Frank Bicknell lecture to the Grosse Pointe Historical Society for February, 1999; gave a paper "From the Michigan Frontier to the City Beautiful" to the Pioneer America Society in Richmond, Va., 2000. Avocations: photography, piano, genealogy, restoring old garden and farm buildings, book collecting. Home: 3503 Rock Edwards Dr Sodus MI 49126-8700 Office Phone: 269-925-3836. Business E-Mail: logcabincrafts@qtm.net.

HANDZEL, STEVEN JEFFREY, accountant; b. Phila., Nov. 9, 1954; s. Joseph Leo and Dori Lou (Kistler) H.; m. Beth Ann Barrick, Apr. 20, 1985; children: Samantha Nicole, Patrick Ryan, Daniel Joseph. BBA, Coll. William and Mary, Williamsburg, Va., 1976; MBA, West Chester U., Pa., 1991. CPA Pa. Staff auditor Peat, Marwick, Mitchell & Co., Phila., 1976-79, supr. sr., 1979-80; mgr. fin. reporting U.S. Cold Storage, Inc., Phila., 1980-83, treas. fed. credit union, 1982-83; audit mgr. Barbacane, Thornton & Co., Wilmington, Del., 1983-86; audit supr. Chester County, West Chester, Pa., 1986-88, acctg. mgr., 1988-92; pvt. practice Steven J. Handzel, CPA, West Chester, Pa., 1993—; CFO Graphic Arts Sales Found., Inc., 1997—. Bd. dirs., treas. J.L. Handzel Marine Engring. Svcs., Inc., Pa.; exec. dir. Safe Harbor Greater West Chester, Inc., 2000-01, W.C. Atkinson Meml. Cmty. Svc. Ctr., Inc., 2002-04 Rep. committeeman Chester County, 1977-94; mem. coun. West Chester Borough, 1980-88, v.p. couns., 1980-81; mem. sch. bd. West Chester Area Sch. Dist., 1989-93, 95-99, pres. 1997-98; treas. West Chester Recreation Commn., 1987-88, Chester County Assn. Boroughs, 1983, sec., 1984, v.p., 1985, pres., 1986-87; mem. Chester County Intermediate Unit Sch. Bd., 1991-93, 95-99, v.p., 1997-98, pres. 1999; pres. West Chester Jaycees, 1990-91, dist. dir. Pa. Jaycees, 1991-92, regional dir., 1992-93, state v.p., 1993-94, state treas., 1994, Eyreman award, 1990, Statesman award, 1991. Mem. AICPA, Pa. Inst. CPAs (local gov. auditing and acctg. com., non-profit orgns. com. 1994-96), Govt. Fin. Officers Assn. (spl. rev. com. 1990-99), Lions. Avocations: skiing, sailing, gardening. Home: 302 N High St West Chester PA 19380-2614 Office: PO Box 3492 West Chester PA 19381-3492

HANDZLIK, JAN LAWRENCE, lawyer; b. NYC, Sept. 21, 1945; s. Felix Munso and Anna Jean Handzlik; m. Jennifer Maria Handzlik; children: Grant, Craig, Anna, Jacob, Magritte. BA, U. So. Calif., 1967; JD, UCLA, 1970. Bar: Calif. 1971, US Dist. Ct. (ctrl. dist.) Calif. 1971, US Ct. Appeals (9th cir.) 1971, US Supreme Ct. 1975, US Dist. Ct. (no. dist.) Calif. 1979, US Tax Ct. 1979, US Dist. Ct. (ea. dist.) Calif. 1981, US Dist. Ct. (so. dist.) Calif. 1982, US Ct. Internat. Trade 1984, US Ct. Appeals (2d cir.) 1984, US Ct. Appeals (11th cir.) 2007. Law clk. to Hon. Francis C. Whelan, US Dist. Ct. (ctrl. dist.) Calif., LA, 1970-71; asst. US atty. fraud and spl. prosecutions section criminal divsn. US Dept. Justice, LA, 1971-76; assoc. Greenberg & Glusker, LA, 1976-78; ptnr., prin. Stilz, Boyd, Levine & Handzlik, P.C., LA, 1978-84; prin. Jan Lawrence Handzlik, P.C., LA, 1984-91; ptnr. Kirkland & Ellis, LLP, LA, 1991—2004, Howrey LLP, LA, 2004—. Counsel to Ind. Christopher Commn. Investigation regarding racism and brutality LA Police Dept., 1991; dep. gen. counsel to Ind. Webster Commn. Investigation LA Police Dept. response to urban disorders, 1992; mem. adv. com. Office LA County Dist. Atty., 1994—96; mem. standing com. on atty. discipline US Dist. Ct. (ctrl. dist.) Calif., 1997—2001; dep. gen. counsel Rampart ind. rev. panel investigation police corruption LA Police Commn., 2000; mem. blue ribbon rev. panel for investigation handling of Rampart corruption incident L.A. Police Dept., 2003—06. Mem. editl. adv. bd. DOJ Alert, 1994—95. Bd. dirs. Friends Child Advs., LA, 1987—91, Inner City Law Ctr., LA, 1995—2002. Fellow: Am. Bar Found.; mem.: FBA, ABA (mem. criminal justice sect. 1990—, chair west coast white collar crime com. 1996—98, vice chmn. nat. com. white collar crime 1998—2000, chair nat. com. white collar crime 2000—02, mem. criminal justice sect. governing coun. 2002—05, mem. task force on implementation of Sarbanes-Oxley Act 2002—, mem. task force on implementation of Sarbanes-Oxley Act of 2002 2002—, chair criminal justice sect. working group on atty.-client privilege 2003—04, mem. anti-terrorism and money laundering working group 2003—04, mem. pres.'s task force on atty.-client privilege 2004—, mem. criminal justice standards com. 2006—), 2d Cir. Fed. Bar Coun., Internat. Bar Assn., Supreme Ct. Hist. Soc., LA County Bar Assn. (coms. on fed. cts. 1988—2001, chair criminal practice subcom. 1989—90, fed. appts. evaluation 1989—93, white collar crime com. 1991—97, exec. com. criminal justice sect. 1997—2002, fed. cts. coord. com. 2001—), State Bar Calif. (sects. on criminal law and litigation), The Calif. Club, Chancery Club. Office: Howrey LLP Ste 1100 550 S Hope St Los Angeles CA 90071-2636 Home Phone: 310-546-3050; Office Phone: 213-892-1802. Office Fax: 213-402-8721. Business E-Mail: handzlikj@howrey.com.

HANEMAN, VINCENT SIERING, JR., consulting engineer, educator, dean; b. Orange, NJ, Feb. 19, 1924; s. Vincent Siering and Helen (Harris) H.; m. Adelaide Russell, Oct. 3, 1961 (dec.); children: Vincent Siering III, Charles Frederick, Rosalyn Tullos, Kaye Kavísic; m. Barbara Gilliam, June 1, 2002. S.B., MIT, 1947; MS in Aero. Engring, U. Mich., 1950, PhD, 1956. Registered profl. engr., Ohio, Okla., Tex., Ala., Alaska. Asst. head flight research Project Meteor, Mass. Inst. Tech., 1947-49; project head automatic wind tunnel data reduction U. Mich., 1949-51; project officer analogue computer research Wright Air Devel. Center, Ohio, 1951-52; assoc. prof., asst. dept. head aero. engring. Air Force Inst. Tech., Wright Patterson AFB, Ohio, 1955-59; chief spl. projects div. guidance and control directorate Air Force Ballistic Missile Div., 1959-60; pres., sr. asso. Haneman Assos., Richardson, Tex., 1960-66, Stillwater, Okla., 1967-72, Auburn, Ala., 1972-73; chmn. bd. Haneman Assos., Inc., Richardson, Stillwater and Auburn, 1961-73, exec. v.p. Stillwater, 1966-67; prof. mech. engring., dir. engring. research, asso. dean Coll. Engring., Okla. State U., 1966-72; prof. aeros. engring., dean Sch. Engring., Auburn U., 1972-80; prof. mech. engring., dean sch. engring. U. Alaska, Fairbanks, 1980-91, prof. emeritus, dean emeritus sch. engring., 1991—. Cons. flight simulator project U. Mich., 1952-55, Gen. Electric Co., Gen. Dynamics, Space Tech. Labs., Chance Vought Corp., Ling Temco-Vought, Nat. Acad. Scis., Union Carbide, Auburn U., State of Ark., U. Tex. Pan-Am., Brownsville, others. Contbr. articles on instrumentation, control and guidance, aircraft performance, engring. edn. to tech. jours. Mem. Army Sci. Adv. Panel, 1967-77; chmn. night low level com. Project Master, Point of Contact Airmobile. Served to 1st lt. USAAF, 1943-45, MTO; to maj. USAF, 1951-60; to maj. gen. Res., moblzn. asst. to dep. chief staff for research and devel. Decorated D.S.M., Legion of Merit with oak leaf cluster, D.F.C. with oak leaf cluster, Air medal with 7 oak leaf clusters, Air Force Commendation medal. Assoc. fellow Am. Inst. Aeros. and Astronautics; fellow Am. Soc. Engring. Edn. (past sec. mech. and aero. divs., past nat. chmn. aero. div., past mem. gen. council, past mem. exec. com., past chmn. engring. research council, past 1st v.p., chmn. dean's inst. 1978, chmn. planning factors com. Engring. Coll. Council 1976-80, pres. 1980-81), Am. Astronautical Soc. (sr.), Am. Helicopter Soc., IEEE, Nat. Soc. Profl. Engrs. (ethics com. 1974-75, nat. chmn. Engring. Week 1977, 78, chmn. cost of engring. edn. com., nat. dir. 1979-80), Ala. Soc. Profl. Engrs. (state chmn. Engring. Week 1973-76), Alaska Soc. Profl. Engrs. (pres. 1985-86, pres. Fairbanks chpt. 1982-83, gov. 1974—, exec. com. Sustaining U. Program com.), Nat. Conf. Advancement Research (ad hoc mem. exec. com. 1977-79), Sigma Xi, Tau Beta Pi, Sigma Tau, Phi Kappa Phi, Pi Epsilon Gamma, Sigma Nu. Address: 1906 Leonard St #4 Columbus GA 31906

HANER, MATTHEW S., mathematics professor, statistician; s. Kathryn Carroll. PhD in Math. Sci., Binghamton U., NYC, 2002. Asst. prof. Mansfield U., Pa., 2002—. Dir. applied stats. program Mansfield U., 2002—04. Contbr. articles to profl. jours. Mem.: Mathamatical Assn. Am. Office: Mansfield Univ 215 Elliott Hall Mansfield PA 16933 Office Phone: 570-662-4707. E-mail: mhaner@mansfield.edu.

HANES, FRANK BORDEN, writer, former business executive, farmer; b. Winston-Salem, NC, Jan. 21, 1920; s. Robert March and Mildred (Borden) H.; m. Barbara Mildred Lasater, Dec. 3, 1942 (dec. Feb. 1990); children: Frank Borden, Nancy Hanes White, Robin March; m. Jane Craig, July 3, 1991. BA, U. N.C., 1942, DHL (hon.), 2005, St. Andrew's Presbyn. Coll., 1992. Columnist, feature writer, reporter, copy editor Winston-Salem Jour. and Sentinel, 1946—49; vice chmn., dir. Mchts. Devel. Co., shopping center, Winston-Salem, 1956—64. Dir. Chatham Mfg. Co., Elkin, N.C., Hanes Cos., Winston-Salem. Author: Abel Anders, 1951, The Bat Brothers, 1953, The Fleet Rabble, 1961, Journey's Journal, 1958, Jackknife John, 1964, The Seeds of Ares, 1977, The Garden of Nonentities, 1983. Chmn. com. for endowed professorships U. N.C., 1965-67; chmn. Friends of U. N.C. Libr., 1966-68, Old Salem, Inc., 1968-70, Summit Sch., 1959-62; pres. Winston-Salem Operetta Assn., 1949-50, Winston-Salem Arts Coun., 1955-56, N.C. Lit. and Hist. Assn., 1973-74; mem. bd. visitors U. N.C., 1980-86; chmn. Arts and Sci. Found., 1976-90; vice chmn., trustee John Motley Morehead Found.; chmn. John W. and Anna Hodgin Hanes Found.; bd. govs. U. N.C. Press; mem. bd. N.C. Soc.; bd. dirs. N.C. Children's

Home Soc., N.C. Zool. Soc. With USNR, 1942-45 Recipient Roanoke Chowan award for poetry N.C. Lit. and Hist. Assn., 1953, award Winston-Salem Arts Coun., 1957, Cum Laude Soc. award Woodberry Forest Sch., 1961, Sir Walter Raleigh award for fiction, 1961, Disting. Alumnus award U. N.C., 1975, Disting. Svc. medal U. N.C., Alumni Assn., 1978, Ragan award for contbns. to fine arts, 1985, William R. Davie award U. N.C. Bd. Trustees, 1989, Fortner award for contbns. to writers and cmty. St. Andrew's Presbyn. Coll., 1995, Frederic W. Marshall disting. svc. award, 2002, N.C. Soc. award for contbns. to N.C. culture, 2002, N.C. award pub. svc., 2003. Mem. PEN, NC Writers Conf. (chmn. 1951-52), NC Quarter Horse Assn. (pres. 1963-64), Order of Gimghoul (pres. 1940-42), Order of Minotaur (pres. 1940-41), Rotary (pres. Winston-Salem chpt. 1961), Old Town Club (Winston-Salem), Rancheros Visitadores (Santa Barbara, Calif.), Roaring Gap Club (pres. NC 1976-78), Rainbow Springs Club (Macon County, NC), Sigma Alpha Epsilon. Home: 1057 W Kent Rd Winston Salem NC 27104-1131

HANES, JOHN WARD, civil engineer, sculptor, rancher, director; b. San Francisco, June 5, 1936; s. Ward Herbert and Ruth Florence (Jacks) H.; m. Virginia Rae Meadows, Nov. 27, 1957 (div. Feb. 1966); children: Derek S., Kim R., Mark A.; m. Meda Lee Walter, June 29, 1968; 1 child, Ward W BS in Engring., U. Calif., Davis, 1979. Registered civil engr., Calif. From engr. technician to civil engr. Soil Conservation Svc. USDA, Berkeley, Calif., 1960—79, civil engr. Soil Conservation Svc. Davis, 1979—83, 1983—90; sculptor, consulting civil engr. Boonville, Calif., 1990—; CEO Hanes Ranch, Inc., Boonville, 1999—. Pres. Santa Rosa (Calif.) Ski Club, 1971 Mem. Gualala Arts Ctr., Mendocino Arts Ctr., Nat. Sculpture Soc Avocations: multi media art, hunting, fishing. Home: Box 510 29000 Mountain View Rd Boonville CA 95415

HANES, RALPH PHILIP, JR., retired textiles executive, horse breeder; b. Winston-Salem, NC, Feb. 25, 1926; s. Ralph Phillip and Dewitt H (Chathan); m. Joan Audrey Humpstone, Jan. 14, 1950 (dec. Jan. 1983); m. Mary Charlotte Metz, Dec. 23, 1984. Grad., Woodberry Forest Sch., 1944; student, U. NC, 1944-46; BA, Yale U., New Haven, Conn., 1949; LHD (hon.), St. Andrews Coll., Laurinburg, NC, 1981; DFA (hon.), NC Sch. of Arts, Winston-Salem, 1987; HHD (hon.), Wake Forest U., Winston-Salem, 1990. With Hanes Cos., Inc. (formerly Hanes Dye and Finishing Co.), Winston-Salem, NC, 1950-93; pres. Hanes Dye and Finishing Co., 1965-68, chmn. bd., 1968-88, chmn. emeritus, 1988-93; chmn. bd. Ampersand, Inc., 1976-85. Mem. coun. of sr. fellows Salzburg Seminars in Am. Studies. Author: How to Get Anyone to Do Anything, 2006; cons. editor: Performing Arts Rev., 1981—85, Jour. Arts Mgmt. and Law, 1981—86, mem. editl. adv. bd.: Art Economist, 1982—86. Mem. (appt. by Pres. L. B. Johnson) Nat. Coun. Arts, 1965—70; mem. Moravian Music Found., 1963—65; founder/mem. bd. visitors NC Sch. Arts, 1985—, trustee exec. com., 1966—78; bd. visitors Barter Theatre State Theatre of Va., 1967—75; assoc. fellow Jonathan Edward Coll., Yale U., 1971—74; mem. Spoleto Festival, 1979—86, Nat. Mus. Am. Art, Renwick Gallery, 1976—89, Alliance for Arts Edn., 1976—79; mem. exec. com. Nat. Coun. for Arts and Edn., 1976—79; mem. adv. coun. for arts Fed Res. Bank of Richmond, 1977—78; mem. Bus. Com. for Ars Arena Stage, Washington, 1980—86; mem. Gov.'s Coun. Bus., Arts and Humanities, 1977—85; mem. fine arts com. Fed. Res. Bank of Washington, 1979—81; mem. adv. bd. Pauline Koner Dance Consort, 1977—80; mem. Arts Resources Corp., 1981—83; chmn. Am. Art Forum, 1986—87, bd. dirs., 1986—90, Arena Stage, 1990—92; com. mem. State of NC award, 1993; mem. Yr. of Mountains Commn., NC, 1995—96; corp. mem. Woods Hole Oceanog. Inst., 1994—98; mem. coun. advisors Blue Ridge Pky., 1998—; exec. com. Ambs. for the Arts, NEA, 1999—; mem. Art Based Elem. Schs., 2000; founder/commr. Winston-Salem Commn. Cultural Affairs, 2001—; co-chair Artsignite Fest., 2002; initiator New River Blue Way, N.C., Va., W.Va., 2002; mem. adv. bd. Blue Ridge Rural Land Trust, 2003—; craft adv. com. Mint Mus., Charlotte, 2004—; mem. Winston-Salem Commr. Cultural Affairs, 2001—; mem. coun. of advisors Blue Ridge Pkwy, 2002—; initiator New River VA Blueway, 2002, H. John Heinz III Ctr. for Sci., Econs. and the Environment, 2004—; arts cons. Govt. of Austria, 1978; bd. dirs. Nat. Coun. Friends of Kennedy Ctr., 1975—80; mem. founding com. Agri-Rsch. Extension Network of N. Am., 1995—97; chmn. cabinet Spl. Olympics World Games, 1999; bd. dirs. (appt. by Pres. J.F. Kennedy) Nat. Cultural Ctr. for Performing Arts, 1962—65; bd. dirs. Am. Symphony Orch. League, 1958—61; trustee Salem Coll., 1961—64; bd. dirs. Jargon Soc. Inc., 1968—69, pres., 1968—75; founder NC State Arts Coun., chmn., 1964—66; founder/bd. dirs. Ams. for the Arts (formerly Am Coun. Arts), 1960—69; pres. Ams. for the Arts, 1964—66, vice chmn., 1967—69; mem. nat. adv. com. Brevard Sch. Music, 1969—74, Am. Crafts Coun., 1970—72, Appalachian Trail Conf., 1973—76; chmn. com. on music Yale U. Coun., 1970—73; bd. dirs. Nat. Audubon Soc., 1972—78, John. W. and Anna H. Hanes Found., 1974—, So. Appalachian Highlands Conservancy, 1974—78, Old Salem Inc., 1974—77, Isaak Walton League Am., 1974—78, Nature Conservancy, 1975—79; bd. dirs. (apptd. by Pres. Gerald Ford) Kennedy Ctr. for the Performing Arts, 1975—80; bd. dirs. Salzburg Seminar of Am. Studies, 1978—82, Am. Land Trust, 1976—93, Arts Internat., 1981—85; adv. com. Am. Farmland Trust, 1983—97; mem. internat. coun. NYC Ballet, 1984—86; trustee emeritus Kennedy Ctr. for the Arts, Washington, 1999—; bd. govs. Nat. Com. for the New River, N.C., Va., W. Va., 1999—2001; commissioner of cultural affairs Nat. Com. for the New River, N.C., Va., W. Va., 2001—; mem. internat. coun. Mus. Modern Art, 1978—83. Named Young Man of Yr., Winston-Salem Jaycees, 1958, NC Jaycees, 1958, Hon. Comdr., USS NC, 1998; recipient Chmn.'s award, NEA, 1966, 2005, Gov.'s award for preservation of natural area, 1969, pub. svc. award, State of NC, 1976, Morrison award for the Arts, 1977, Swan award, Tenn., 1970, award, NC Soc. of NYC, 1979, Cmty. Svc. award, Winston-Salem Urban League, 1979, Conservation award, Isaac Walton League Am., 1982, award for disting. svc. to arts, Nat. Gov.'s Assn., 1982, NC Gov.'s award in fine arts, 1982, awards, Winston-Salem chpt. NAACP, 1983, Nat. Medal of Arts Amb. for the Arts presented by Pres. George Bush, 1991, award, Piedmont Opera Theatre, 1992, tribute, Nat. Arts Club, NYC, 1995, Southeastern Ctr. for Contemporary Arts Leadership award, 1998, Young Leadership award, Winston-Salem Arts Coun., 2000, Charlotte & Philip Hanes Art Gallery award, Wake Forest U., 2001, Excellence award, Downtown Winston-Salem, 2003, award, Phil and Charlotte Hanes Student Commons Bldg., NCSA, 2003, Winston-Salem Found., 2003, Founder award, Nat. Assn. of State Arts Agencies, 2005, Disting. Svc. to the Arts award, NEA, 2005, Entrepreneurial Am. Leadership award, Ptnrs. for Livable Places, 2007. Mem.: Assn. Fundraising Profls., Am. Assn. Fund Raising Profls. (Lifetime Achievement award 2005, 2002), Nat. Assn. of State Arts Agencies (Nat. Endorsement for the Arts Chmns. award 2005, Founder award 2005), Piedmont Triad Entrepeneurs Network, Piedmont Triad Partnership Bd., Century Assn. (NYC), Walpole Soc., Wilderness Soc., Royal Soc. Arts, Ut Prosim Soc., Pa. Acad. Fine Arts, N.Am. Mycological Assn., Nat. Wildlife Fedn., East African Wildlife Soc., Appalachian Consortium, World Bus. Coun., Trout Unltd., S.E. Coun. on Founds., Peale for Visual Arts (Phila.), Appalachian Trail Conf., Am. League Anglers, Potomac Appalachian Mountain Club, Isaac Walton League, Currituck, Bohemian Club, Cane River Club, Twin City Club, Piedmont Club, Met. Club (Washington), Lotos Club (NYC), Yale Club (NYC). Home and Office: PO Box 1704 Winston Salem NC 27102-1704 Office Phone: 336-761-0570.

HANESIAN, DERAN, chemical engineer, educator, environmental scientist, consultant; b. Niagara Falls, Sept. 26, 1927; s. Vahan and Anna (Kabasakallian) H.; m. Eva Hanesian. BChE, Cornell U., Ithaca, NY, 1952, PhD, 1961. Registered profl. engr., N.Y., N.J. Prodn. engr. E.I. duPont de Nemours, Niagara Falls, 1952—57, rsch. engr. Deepwater, NJ, 1960—63, E.I. duPont, 1964—66; prof. and master tchr. Otto H. York dept. chem. engring. N.J. Inst. Tech., 1963—, chmn. Otto H. York dept. chem. engring., 1975—88. Rsch. engr. Exxon, Florham Park, N.J., 1967-70; tchr. Celanese, 1977, 80, Algerian Petroleum Inst., 1978; vis. prof. U. Edinburgh, 1981, Yerevan Poly. Inst., Armenia, USSR, 1982, 83; acting dep. dir., vis. prof. Ctr. for Plastics Recycling Rsch., Rutgers U., Piscataway, N.J., 1989-93. Served with U.S. Army, 1945-46. Recipient Robert Van Houten award N.J. Inst. Tech., 1977, 2001, Outstanding Profl. Devel. by Tenured Faculty Mem. award, 1994, Excellence in Tchg. (lower divsn. undergrad.) award, 1998, 2004, Engring. Excellence in Tchg. award Newark Coll., 2004, Bd. Overseers Pub. and Inst. Svc. award, 1999, Newark Coll. Engring. Innovation in Engring. award, 2000, Newark Coll. Engring. Excellence in Tchg. award, 2004, Saul K. Fenster Innovation in Edn. award Newark Coll. Engring., 2006; grantee NSF, 1967, 72, 91, German Acad. Exch. Svc., 1982, Fulbright grantee Yerevan Poly. Inst., 1982. Fellow: AIChE (emeritus), Am. Chem. Soc., Am. Soc. Engring. Edn. (life), Mid-Atlantic AT& T Found. (award 1986, Centennial cert. award 1993, John Fluke award 1994, Mid Atlantic Disting. Tchg. award 1997, Mid Atlantic Outstanding Campus Rep. award 1999, Zone 1 Outstanding Campus Rep. award 1999, Mid Atlantic Outstanding Campus Rep. award 2001, Outstanding US Campus Rep. award 2001, Chester F. Carlson award 2003); mem.: AAUP, Armenian Students Assn. Am. (Prof. Dicran H. Kabakjian award 1998), Sigma Xi, Alpha Chi Sigma, Omega Chi Epsilon, Omicron Delta Kappa, Tau Beta Pi, Order of Engrs., Fulbright Assn. Armenian Apostolic. Office: NJ Inst Tech 323 Dr ML King Blvd Newark NJ 07102 Home: 6 Edgemont Rd Montclair NJ 07042-2305 Office Phone: 973-596-3597. Business E-Mail: hanesian@njit.edu.

HANEY, J. TERRENCE, retired insurance consultant; b. Omaha, Nov. 26, 1933; s. James Cletus and Claire (Wilson) H.; m. Joanne M. Beach, Feb. 12, 1966 (div. Nov. 1971); children: Terrence L., Kim Marie, Robert R., J. Stephen, Patrick M., Amy Liz; m. Judy Lynch, May 27, 1989. Student, Creighton U., Omaha, 1952; BS, U. Nebr., Omaha, 1991, MA, 1998. CLU. Salesman, unit mgr., div. mgr., dir. mass mktg. R.D. Marcotte & Assocs., Omaha, 1958-64; exec. v.p., gen. mgr. Ins. Cons., Inc., Omaha, 1964-85, pres., CEO, 1985-99. Former pres. St. Margaret Mary Bd. Edn.; former chmn. bd. dir. Roncalli High Sch.; former bd. dir. Creighton Prep H.S.; bd. dirs., mem. fin. com. Omaha Cmty. Found.; bd. dir., chmn. Cmty. Found; trustee U. Nebr. Found. Named to Order of the Tower, U. Nebr. at Omaha, 2003; recipient Herber Locke Disting. Svc. award, 2005. Mem. Soc. CLUs (past pres. Omaha chpt.), Edward and Maria Lucretia Creighton Soc. (chmn.), Creighton U. Alumni Assn. (past pres. Omaha chpt.), Golden Key, Toastmasters (past pres.), Internat. Order Rocky Mountain Goats. Republican. Roman Catholic. Avocations: bicycling, physical fitness. Home: 407 N Elmwood Rd Omaha NE 68132-2602 Office: 235 Kiewit Plz Omaha NE 68131-3376

HANEY, ROBERT LOCKE, retired insurance company executive; b. Morgantown, W.Va., June 14, 1928; s. John Ward and Katherine Eugenia (Locke) H. BA, U. Calif., Berkeley, 1949. Sr. engr. Pacific Telephone Co., San Francisco, 1952-58; mgmt. analyst Lockheed Missiles & Space Co., Sunnyvale, Calif., 1958-64; sr. cons. John Diebold, NYC, 1964-65; sr. indsl. economist Mgmt. & Econs. Research, Inc., Palo Alto, Calif., 1965-67; prin. economist Midwest Research Inst., Kansas City, Mo., 1967-69; dir. mktg. coordination Transam. Corp., San Francisco, 1969-73; staff exec. Transam. Ins. Corp., LA, 1974-82; 2d v.p. Transam. Life Cos., LA, 1982-93; ret., 1993. Cons. in field. Co-author: Creating the Human Environment, 1970. Lt. (j.g.) USN, 1949-52. Mem. Scabbard & Blade. Republican. Episcopalian. Avocations: photography, gardening, bicycling. Home: The Ariz Sr Acad Village 7709 S Vivaldi Ct Tucson AZ 85747 Office Phone: 520-647-3737. Personal E-mail: Bhan83@cs.com.

HANFORD, AGNES RUTLEDGE, retired investment advisor; d. Warren Day and Agnes Beatrice (Kane) H. Grad., Convent of Sacred Heart Prep. Sch., NYC; BA in English, French, Newton Coll., 1950. Asst. clk. rules com U.S. Ho. of Reps., Washington, 1953-56; account exec. W.E. Hutton & Co., NYC, 1956-74; fin. cons. Thomson McKinnon Securities, NYC, 1974-80, Tampa, Fla., 1980-89; fin. adviser Prudential Securities, Inc., Tampa, 1989-94; ret., 1994. Mem. Hillsborough County Rep. Exec. Com., Tampa, 1980-93, Women's Econ. Coun., NY, 1979-80, Tampa Mus. Art, 1980—, Tampa Bay History Ctr., 1995—, Henry B. Plant Mus., Tampa; bd. mem. Friends of Plant Park, 1995—, bd. dirs., 1997—; mem. adv. coun. U. South Fla. Contemporary Art Mus., 1996—. Mem. Women's Nat. Rep. Club (mem. bd. govs. 1970-75, v.p. 1975-76), Soc. of Descendants of Signers of Constitution (hon. mem.), Tampa Yacht and Country Club, Lawrence Beach Club. Roman Catholic. Home: 4141 Bayshore Bivd No 301 Tampa FL 33611-1803

HANFORD, GEORGE HYDE, retired educational association administrator; b. Cambridge, Mass., July 29, 1920; s. Alfred Chester and Ruth Hyde H.; m. Elaine Halstead, Sept. 15, 1942 (dec.); children: Anne Catherine, Mary Lee Hanford Wile; m. Yvonne Wharton, June 15, 2006. BA, Harvard U., 1941, MBA, 1943; L.L.D. (hon.), W.Va. Wesleyan Coll.; EdD (hon.), Thomas Edison State Coll. Asst. dean Harvard Grad. Sch. Bus. Adminstrn., 1946-48; treas., bus. mgr., tchr., coach N. Shore Country Day Sch., Winnetka, Ill., 1948-55; treas., then v.p., exec. v.p. Coll. Entrance Exam. Bd., NYC, 1955-79, pres., 1979-86, pres. emeritus, 1987—. Author: Life with the SAT, 1991, A Tale of Three Cities in One, 1996, For the Entertainment of Strangers, 1997. Former trustee Nat. Scholarship Svc. and Fund Negro Students, Dwight Sch., Ednl. Testing Svc., Am. Coun. on Edn., Ea. Ednl. Consortium, United Bd. Coll. Devel., Thomas A. Edison State Coll., N.J. Inst. Collegiate Tchg. and Learning, Nat. Coun. for Excellence in Critical Thinking; bd. overseers Mt. Auburn Hosp. With USNR, 1943-46. Recipient disting. or spl. svc. awards Am. Sch. Counselors Assn., Nat. Assn. Coll. Admissions Counselors, Nat. Assn. Secondary Sch. Prins., Nat. Assn. Student Fin. Aid Adminstrs., Johnson C. Smith Univ.; named to Harvard Varsity Club Hall of Fame, 1997. Mem. Exec. Svc. Corps of New Eng., Hawaiian Mission Children's Soc., Cambridge Hist. Soc. (pres. 1995-97), Canterbury Soc. (symposiarch 1993-2004, symposiarch emeritus, 2004-), Belmont Hill Club, Cambridge Boat Club. Episcopalian. Personal E-mail: symposiarch@comcast.net.

HANFT, JAMES, lawyer; b. Huntington, NY, May 21, 1967; BSEE, Clarkson U., 1989. Bar: NY 1994, US. Dist. Ct. (so. dist.) 1994, US. Dist. Ct. (so. dist.) 1994, US. Ct. Appeals (Fed. Cir.) 1999, US. Ct. Appeals (1st. Cir.) 2004. Engr. IBM, Fishkill, NY, 1989—90. Mem.: ABA. Office: Darby & Darby 7 World Trade Ctr 250 Greenwich St New York NY 10007 Office Phone: 212-527-7616.

HANFT, NOAH JONATHAN, lawyer; b. NYC, Jan. 12, 1953; s. Edwin and Gladys (Potash) H.; m. Dora Barlaz Hanft, May 31, 2004; children: Alexandra Julia, Elizabeth Anna, Genevieve Suzanne. BA in Govt. and Pub. Adminstrn., Am. U., 1973; JD, Bklyn. Law Sch., 1976; LLM in Trade Regulations, NYU, 1982. Sr. trial atty. Legal Aid Soc., NYC, 1977-81; assoc. Ladas & Parry, NYC, 1982-84; sr. atty. Mastercard Internat., NYC, 1984-87, v.p., counsel, 1987-90; sr. v.p., asst. gen. counsel AT&T Universal Card Svcs. Corp., Jacksonville, Fla., 1990—93; from sr. v.p., asst. gen counsel Mastercard Internat., Purchase, NY, 1993—2001, gen. counsel, corp. sec., 2001—. Instr. Cordoza Inst. of Trial Advocacy, N.Y.C., 1982—. Mem, Legal Aid Society (bd. dir.) Office: Mastercard Internat 2000 Purchase St Purchase NY 10577*

HANFT, RUTH S. SAMUELS, economist, consultant; b. NYC, July 12, 1929; d. Max Joseph and Ethel (Schechter) Samuels; m. Herbert Hanft, June 17, 1951; children: Marjorie Jane, Jonathan Mark. BS, Cornell U., 1949; MA, Hunter Coll., 1963; PhD, George Washington U., 1989; ScD (hon.), U. Osteo. Med & Health Scis., 1993. Cons. Urban Med. Econs. Project, Hunter Coll., N.Y.C. and D.C. Dept. Health, 1962—63; health economist Office of Rsch. and Stats., Social Security Adminstrn., Washington, 1964—66; chief grants mgmt. health div. Office Econ. Opportunity, Washington, 1966—68; sr. health analyst Office of Asst. Sec. Planning and Evaluation HEW, Washington, 1968—71, spl. asst., asst. sec. health, 1971—72, dep. asst. sec. for health policy, rsch. and stats. Office of Asst. Sec. for Health, 1977—79, dep. asst. sec. for health rsch., stats. and tech., 1979—81; health care cons., 1981—88; cons., prof. dept. health svcs. mgmt. and policy George Washington U., Washington, 1988—91, prof., 1991—95; cons., 1995—. Vis. prof. Dartmouth Med. Sch., 1976—; sr. rsch. assoc. Inst. Medicine NAS, Washington, 1972—76; adj. Ctr. for Bioethics, U. Va., 1999—; adj. prof. James Madison U., 2004—. Contbr. articles to profl. jours. Mem. Med. Assistance Svc. Bd. Commonwealth Va., 1984—89; trustee Meharry Med. Coll., 1989—94; mem. adv. bd. Inst. on Innovation in Health and Human Svcs., James Madison U., 2004—; bd. dirs. N.W. Va. Health Sys., 2003—. Fellow: Acad. Health Svcs. Rsch., Hastings Ctr., Nat. Acad. of Social Ins. (charter mem.); mem.: NAS, Inst. Medicine, Cosmos Club. Jewish. Home: 3340 Brookside Dr Charlottesville VA 22901-9566 Personal E-mail: hrhanft@earthlink.net.

HANGEN, TERRA, librarian, writer; d. Dwight and Annetta Werner Pelkin, Barbara Pelkin (Stepmother); m. Will Hangen, Nov. 20, 1971; children: Colt, Lane. BA, Beloit Coll., 1967; MLS, U. Wis., 1968; Govt., Art History, Robert Kolej, Istanbul Turkey. Maps cataloger U. Calif., Santa Cruz, 1981—. Contbg. editor: (mag.) Gaited Horse, Hobby Farms; contbg. author: Rainy Day Book, columnist:; contbr. numerous mags. Personal E-mail: thekilns@excite.com.

HANGLEY, WILLIAM THOMAS, lawyer; b. Long Beach, NY, Mar. 11, 1941; s. Charles Augustus and Faustine Charmillot H.; m. Mary Dupree Hangley, July 24, 1965; children: Michele Dupree, William Thomas, Katherine Charmillot. BS in Music, SUNY, Fredonia, 1963; LLB cum laude, U. Pa., 1966. Bar: Pa. 1966, US Ct. Appeals (3d cir.) 1966, US Dist. Ct. (ea. dist.) Pa. 1966. Assoc. Schnader, Harrison, Segal & Lewis, Phila., 1966-69; mem., CEO, Hangley Connolly Epstein Chicco Foxman & Ewing, Phila, 1969-94; CEO Hangley Aronchick Segal & Pudlin, 1994—; Judge protem Phila. Ct. of Common Pleas, 1991—; mem. adv. bd. Pub. Interest Law Ctr. Phila. Contbr. articles to profl. publs. Bd. dirs. Ams. for Dem. Action, 1972-81. Fellow Am. Coll. Trial Lawyers (chmn. com. fed. rules of evidence, 2001-02, mem. Pa. state com. 1999—, comms. com. 2002—), Am. Bar Found.; mem. ABA (co-chmn. litigation sect. com. on fed. procedure 1990-95—, co-chair task force on merit selection of judges 1995-97, mem. task force on discovery 1997-98, task force on judiciary 1998—), Pa. Bar Assn. (ho. of dels. 1989-92), Am. Law Inst., Phila. Bar Assn., Legal Club (v.p. 2001—), Jr. Legal Club, Order of Coif, U. Pa. Inns of Ct. (master of bench). Roman Catholic. Office: Hangley Aronchick Segal & Pudlin 1 Logan Sq Fl 27 Philadelphia PA 19103-6995 E-mail: whangley@hangley.com.

HANI, ANTOINE GEORGE, psychiatrist, psychoanalyst; b. Beirut, May 1, 1925; came to U.S., 1953; s. George Antoine Hani and Marie Haddad; m. Virginia Helen Ahlstrom; children: George, Valerie; m. Théa Jeitani Hani, Oct. 6, 1984; 1 child, Stéphanie. MD, St. Joseph U., Beirut, 1953. Bd. cert. Adult Psychoanalysis and Child and Adolescent Psychoanalysis. Pvt. practice, Chevy Chase, Md., 1958—; supervising and tng. analyst Washington Psychanalytic Inst., 1981—, dir., 1996-99. Tchg. analyst Washington Psychanalytic Inst., 1969, supervising and tng. analyst, 1981—, dir., 1996—99; clin. prof. psychiatry and behavorial scis. George Washington U., 2002—; tchg. and supervising psychoanalyst IPA Eastern European Psychoanalytic Inst. Contbr. articles to profl. jours. Cross fertilizing rels. Fedn. European Psychoanalysts, Fedn. Latin Am. Psychoanalysts. Recipient cert. of honor, Washington Psychoanalytic Soc., Inst. and Found., 2002. Fellow: Am. Coll. Psychoanalysts (honor 1999), APA (disting. life, honor 1973); mem.: Washington Psychoanalytic Soc. (pres. 1987—89, honor and recognition for disting. career in psychoanalysis), Am. Psychoanalytic Assn. (fellow bd. on profl. stds. 1993—99), Internat. Psychoanalytic Assn. (mem. new groups com. 1995—, chmn. com. to develop psychoanalysis in Mid. East 1995—), Cosmos Club. Roman Catholic. Home: 8501 Thornden Ter Bethesda MD 20817 Office: 5480 Wisconsin Ave # 1619 Chevy Chase MD 20815 E-mail: antoinehani@aol.com.

HANIGAN, LAWRENCE, retired rail transportation executive; b. Notre-Dame-de, Stanbridge, Can., Apr. 3, 1925; s. John Henry and Alice (Lareau) H.; m. Anita Martin, July 20, 1946; children: Carmen, Doris, Guy, Patricia, Michael. Sales mgr. Boisse Lumber Co., Montreal, 1950-52; regional mgr. Cooper-Widman Ltd., Montreal, 1952-70; mem. City of Montreal Exec. Com., 1970-78; chmn. Montreal Urban Community Exec. Com., 1972-78; chmn., gen. mgr. Montreal Urban Community Transit Commn., 1974-85; chmn. VIA Rail Canada Inc., 1985-93. Home: 358 du Baron St Saint-Sauveur PQ Canada J0R IR4

HANIN, ISRAEL, pharmacologist, educator; b. Shanghai, Mar. 29, 1937; s. Arie and Rebecca (Lubarsky) Hanin; m. Leda Toni, June 12, 1960; children: Adam, Dahlia. BS, UCLA, 1962, MS, 1965, PhD in Pharmacology, 1968. Vis. scientist dept. toxicology Karolinska Inst., Stockholm, 1968; staff pharmacologist Lab. Preclin. Pharmacology, NIMH, Washington, 1969-73; from asst. prof. to assoc. prof. psychiatry and pharmacology U. Pitts. Sch. Medicine, 1973-81, prof., 1981-86; prof., chmn. dept. pharmacology and exptl. therapeutics Loyola U. Chgo. Stritch Sch. Medicine, Maywood, Ill., 1986—2003, dir. Inst. Neurosci. and Aging, 1986—2000, dir. MD/PhD program, 1992—2003, prof. emeritus, 2004—; pres. IQL Initiatives, Inc., 2002—04. Rsch. grant rev. com. NIMH, 1979—82, Nat. Inst. Aging, 1987—92, NIH Res., 1991—95; pharmacology test com. Nat. Bd. Med. Examiners, 1987—90; sci. adv. bd. Interneuron Pharms., Inc., Lexington, Mass., 1991—2000; cons. UCB Pharm., Brussels, 1981—98; Alzheimer's disease rsch. fund panel Ill. Dept. Pub. Health, 1995—2000; AMVETS rsch. initiative com. Hines VA Hosp., 1996—2003. Editor 20 books; contbr. articles to profl. jours. Served to 2d lt. Armored Corps, Israeli Army, 1955-58 NIMH, NIH, Nat. Inst. Aging grantee, 1965—2003. Mem.: Assn. Med. Sch. Pharmacology Chairs (treas. 1998—2002, pres. 2002—04), Am. Coll. Neuropsychopharmacology, Am. Soc. Pharmacology and Exptl. Therapeutics (co-founder Great Lakes chpt. 1987, pres. 1990—92), Am. Chem. Soc., Neurosci. Soc. (pres. Pitts. chpt. 1982—83, pres. Chgo. chpt. 1990—91). Address: Loyola U Chgo Stritch Sch Medicine Pharmacol Rm 3621 Bldg 102 Maywood IL 60153 Home Phone: 520-393-7793. E-mail: ihanin@lumc.edu.

HANISCH, TOULA, legal assistant; d. William and Jane Polychrone; m. Bernard Hanisch; children: Arthur, William. BA, Hunters Coll., NYC, 1964; cert. in legal asst., Adelphi U., Garden City, NY, 1981. Legal asst. Office of Atty. Gen., NYC, 1982—. Instr. St. John's U., Queens, NY, 1990—. Office: Atty General's Office 120 Broadway New York NY 10271 Office Phone: 212-416-8416. Business E-Mail: toula.hanisch@oag.state.ny.us.

HANKENSON, E(DWARD) CRAIG, JR., performing arts executive; b. Mankato, Minn., Apr. 12, 1935; s. Edward Craig and Ethel Irene (Favre) H.; m. Francis Joyce Hall, Mar. 23, 1957 (div. 1978); 1 child, Meridith Joyce.; m. Catherine Ann Donaldson, 1981; 1 child, Jennifer Leigh. MusB, Eastman Sch. Music, 1957, MusM, 1959. Head voice and opera dept. Auburn U., Ala., 1959-62; bus. mgr. Chautauqua Opera Assn., NY, 1958-61, stage mgr., 1957-59, stage dir., 1962; mgmt. intern San Francisco Opera Co., 1962-65; assoc. dir. Brevard Mus. Center, NC, 1965-68; gen. mgr. Saratoga Performing Arts Ctr., NY, 1968-75, dir., 1975—78; exec. dir. Wolf Trap Found. Performing Arts, Vienna, Va., 1978-81; pres. Producers,

Inc., 1980; dir., chmn. dept. arts mgmt. and events U. South Fla., Tampa, 1983-86; pres. KiddyCart Inc., 1987—, Producers, Inc., 1981—; chmn. bd. PICASTAR, 1985—. Dir. Rochester Comty. Opera, N.Y., 1957-59; mem. Title III adv. coun. N.Y. Dept. Edn., 1969-75, N.Y. Gov.'s Commn. on Arts in Edn., 1978; cons. N.Y. Coun. on Arts; coun. bd. Rensselaer Poly. Inst.; cons. theater constrn. and mgmt. Concord Pavillion, Calif., Blossom Music Ctr., Cleve., Art Park, Buffalo, Mud Island, Memphis, Tampa Bay Performing Arts Ctr., Tampa, Robin Hood Dell, Phila.; ops. cons. Worcester Ctr. Performing Arts, 2005—. Prodr.: (TV spls.) Snow White, PBS, 1973, Al Hirt and Pete Fountain Together, PBS, 1979, Great Jazz Pianists, PBS, 1979-81, Brigadoon, Majestic Theatre, N.Y.C., 1980-81, Lionel Hampton's Return to the Paradise, PBS, 1988, Thames Live Cinema, Radio City Music Hall, 1988; nat. tour of Show Boat, 1980, Kiss Me Kate and Taming of the Shrew, Washington Internat. Jazz Festival, 1980, nat. tour Pete Fountain, Jerry Mulligan and Al Hirt, 1982, 83, Tom Paxton, Dab O' Dixie, 1987, translator: Haydn's Lo Speziale, 1958, Smetana's Bartered Bride, 1964; creator Ticket Reservation Systems, 1968, prodr. of Glenn Miller, Artie Shaw, Woodie Herman, Helen O'Connell, Warren Covington, Don Cornell, Pied Pipers BigBand Nat. Tour Show, 1993; prodr.: (tours) Midnight in the Garden of Good and Evil, 1999, Last Swing of the Century, 1999, Irish Christmas, 1999. Bd. dirs. Capitol Area Resident Opera Co., 1969-71; mem. alumni adv. bd. Eastman Sch. Music, 1974-78; mem. com. performing arts Leukemia Soc. Am., Inc.; mem. spl. adv. com. on spl. projects and presenting orgns. Nat. Endowment for the Arts, 1979-80; elder, mem. ruling session Temple Ter. Presbyn. Ch., 1990—, chmn. rsch. and planning, 1992—; bd. dirs., sec. Ter. Landings Assn.; youth group leader H.S., 1996—, Terrace Presbyn. Ch., 1996—; small group leader, Montreat, NC, Youth Conf., 2000, 01, leader 12-step program, 2001; pres. Univ. Cmty. Civic Assn., 1997—; mem. adv. bd. Tampa Habitat for Humanity, 2000—, mem. com., 2001; bd. dirs. Parents Coun. Hollins U., 2001-, vice chmn., 2003—; co-chair Hollins U. Parents Coun., 2003-04, chair, 2004—. Recipient citation Ctrl. Theaters, Moscow, 1973. Mem. Internat. Assn. Concert and Festival Mgrs. (dir.), Performing Arts Assn. N.Y. (pres. 1972-78), Orgn. Summer Festival Mgrs. (moderator 1971-79 , dir), N.Y. Fedn. Music Clubs (dir.), Saratoga Springs C. of C. (dir. 1969-72, chmn. promotion com. 1970-72), Council of Pres.'s, Albany League Arts, Saratoga Springs PTA (pres. 1972-73), Temple Terrace C. of C. (spl. events com., bd. dirs., bd. dirs. Farmer's Market), Univ. Cmty. Civic Assn. (pres.), Pleasant Terr. Civic Assn. (pres. 2004—), Rotary (chair programming com., bd. dirs. 2003—, bd. dirs. Temple Terr. chpt. 2003—), Hollins U. Parents' Coun. Bd., Temple Terrace Police (adv. coun., 2000—) Achievements include conceiving process of computerized event tickets and consulted for Ticketron ticket system. Office: Producers Inc 11806 N 56th St Ste B Tampa FL 33617-1652 Office Phone: 813-988-8333. Personal E-mail: craighank@verizon.net. Business E-Mail: craigh@producersinc.com.

HANKET, MARK JOHN, lawyer; b. Jan. 28, 1943; s. Laddie W. and Florence J. (Kubat) H.; m. Carole A. Dalpiaz, Sept. 14, 1968; children: Gregory, Jennifer, Sarah. AB magna cum laude, John Carroll U., 1965; JD cum laude, Ohio State U., 1968; MBA, Xavier U., 1977. Bar: Ohio 1968, Mich. 1993. Atty. Chemed Corp., Cin., 1973-77, asst. sec., 1977-82, sec., 1982-84, v.p., sec., 1984-86; v.p., gen counsel DuBois Chems. Divsn., 1986-87; v.p., sec. gen. counsel DuBois Chems., Inc., 1987-91; sec. gen. counsel Diversey Corp., 1991-94, v.p., sec. gen. counsel, 1994-96; v.p. law and people excellence, sec. Americlean Sys., Inc., 1996-99; asst. gen. counsel Diversey Lever, Inc., 1999—2002; sr. counsel JohnsonDiversey, Inc., Southfield, Mich., 2002—06; pvt. practice, 2006—. Capt. US Army, 1968—73. Decorated Meritorious Svc. medal, Army Commendation medal with oak leaf cluster. Mem. ABA, Mich. Bar Assn., Am. Corp. Counsel Assn., Ohio Bar Assn. Office Phone: 248-514-0353. Personal E-mail: mjhanket@aol.com.

HANKIN, JOSEPH NATHAN, college president; b. NYC, Apr. 6, 1940; s. Harry and Beatrice H.; m. Carole G. Hankin, Aug. 20, 1960; children—Marc, Laura, Brian. BA in Social Scis. (N.Y. State Regents scholar), CCNY, 1961; MA in History, Columbia U., 1962, Ed.D. in Adminstrn. Higher Edn. (Kellogg fellow), 1967; postgrad. seminar, Harvard U. Grad. Sch. Bus., 1979; Litt.D. (hon.), Mercy Coll., 1979; DHL (hon.), Coll. New Rochelle, 1996; D Pedagogy (hon.), Manhattan Coll., 2000; DHL (hon.), Lehman Coll., 2002. Cert. large complex case arbitrator Am. Arbitration Assn. N.Y. State Regents coll. teaching fellow, 1961-63; fellow dept. history CCNY, 1962-63, lectr., 1963-65; lectr. history Bklyn. Coll. CUNY, summer 1963, lectr. history Queens Coll., summer 1964; course asst. dept. higher and adult edn. Tchrs. Coll., Columbia U., spring 1965, occasional lectr., 1965—, adj. prof. higher and adult edn., 1976—; dir. evening div. and summer session Harford Jr. Coll., Bel Air, Md., 1965-66, dean continuing edn. and summer session, 1966-67, pres., 1967-71, Westchester C.C., Valhalla, NY, 1971—. Mem. vis. team Md. State Bd. Cmty. Colls., Annapolis, 1976; bd. dirs. Mut. Funds Trust, 1988—; mem. task force on study higher edn. in D.C., 1966-67; spkr., panelist and cons. in field; condr. workshops and seminars. Contbr. articles and revs. to profl. publs. and newspapers. Mem. adv. com. Columbia U. Tchrs. Coll. C.C. Ctr., 1970—; bd. dirs., mem. exec. com. Westchester C.C. Found., 1971—; mem. Tri-State Coll. Consortium (now Eastern Ednl. Consortium), 1975—, pres., 1977-89, fin. com., 1982-87; mem. adv. com. SUNY Ednl. Opportunity Ctr., 1975—; mem. Coun. for Arts in Westchester, N.Y., 1971—, mem. coll. adv. com., 1971, mem. arts action plan for Westchester com., 1974-75, mem. Friends of Arts, 1976—, mem. benefit com., 1983-86, trustee, 1983-85; mem. Westchester Rockland Newspapers Lend-A-Hand Adv. Bd., 1974-90; mem. Friends Harrison Pub. Libr., 1980—, Friends Neuberger Mus., 1979—; bd. advisors Hudson River Mus., 1985—; mem. adv. bd. Westchester County Hist. Soc., 1981-84; trustee Westchester Econ. Understanding Found., 1979, Hartford Family Found., 1984—. Recipient Disting. Service award Bel Air (Md.) Jaycees, 1968, Brotherhood award Westchester region NCCJ, 1975, Arabic Soc. plaque, 1977, Plaque Pres. Ea. Ednl. Consortium, 1978, Championship of Youth award Youth Services div. B'nai B'rith, 1978, Community Svc. award Soc. Italian-Am. Orgns., 1986, plaque Alpha Beta Gamma and Drucker Mgmt. Soc., 1983, plaque Italian Club, 1984, plaque French Club, 1977, Honor award AIA, 1983, Cert. Vol. Services United Way Westchester, 1986, Cert. Appreciation Westchester 2000, 1988; Kellog fellow in C.C. adminstrn. Columbia U., 1965. Mem. Am. Assn. Jr. Colls. (v.p. 1971-74, bd. dirs. 1971-74, pres.'s acad. 1976—, various coms., Cert. Recognition 1981), Am. Assn. Higher Edn. (charter, life), Assn. Pres.'s Public C.C.s (legis. com. 1974-76, 86—, exec. com., mem.-at-large 1987-88), Faculty Student Assn. Westchester C.C. (dir. 1971—), Coll. Consortium for Internat. Studies (exec. com. 1974-88, sec.-treas. 1984-88, mem. ad hoc com. on by-laws 1983), Middle States Assn. Colls. and Schs. (ad hoc com. centennial celebration 1985—, pres. 1999) N.Y. State Assn. Jr. Colls., Young Presidents Orgn. (pres.'s forum 1979-90, founding dir. 1979-80, 84-85, day chairperson 1977-89), CEO Orgn., World Pres. Orgn., Westchester County C. of C. (bd. dirs. 1981-85, chmn. 1988, reaccreditation task force com. on staff 1982-83, chmn. nomination com. 1983-85), Phi Delta Kappa, Alpha Beta Gamma (hon.), Phi Theta Kappa. Home: 4 Merion Dr Purchase NY 10577-1302 Office: Westchester Community Coll 75 Grasslands Rd Valhalla NY 10595-1636 Office Phone: 914-606-6707. Business E-Mail: joseph.hankin@sunywcc.edu. *In order to succeed, to do the best we can at whatever level on whatever path we choose, we do not need brilliance, nor money, nor luck, nor successful parents, nor benign climate, nor even perfect health. We do need belief and hope, imagination and inventiveness, foresight, preparation, and also motivation and perseverance, as well as hard work.*

HANKINS, ANTHONY P., chemicals executive; Various mgmt. positions in plastics, fibers and polyurethanes ICI, 1980—98; v.p. Asia Pacific for Polyurethanes bus. Huntsman Corp., 1998—2000, v.p. Ams. for Polyurethanes bus., 2000—01, global v.p. rigids divsn. Polyurethanes bus., 2002—03, pres. performance products, 2003—04, divsn. pres. polyurethanes, 2004—. Office: Hunstman Corp 500 Huntsman Way Salt Lake City UT 84108 Office Phone: 801-584-5700.*

HANKINS, IRVIN W., III, lawyer; b. Charlotte, NC, Sept. 1, 1946; AB, U. N.C., 1968, JD with honors, 1975. Bar: N.C. 1975, US Dist. Ct. (NC), US Ct. Appeals (4th cir.), US Supreme Ct. Ptnr., litig. & gen. counsel Parker Poe Adams & Bernstein LLP, Charlotte, NC, mng. ptnr., 1987—2002. Adminstrv. editor N.C. Law Rev., 1974-75. Trustee Queens Univ., Charlotte; past gen. counsel Charlotte C. of C. Lt. USN, 1968—72. Mem. NC State Bar Coun. (pres.-elect, mem. exec. com.), NC Assn. Def. Attys., Order of the Coif, U. NC Law Alumni Assn. (past pres.). Office: Parker Poe Adams & Bernstein LLP Ste 3000 3 Wachovia Ctr 401 S Tryon St Charlotte NC 28202-1935 Office Phone: 704-335-9016. Office Fax: 704-335-9667. Business E-Mail: iwhankins@parkerpoe.com.

HANKINSON, DEBORAH G., former state supreme court justice; BS with distinction, Purdue U.; MS, U. Tex., Dallas; JD, So. Meth. U. Bar: Tex., U.S. Ct. Appeals (5th cir.) 1995; cert. civil appellate law Tex. Bd. Legal Specialization. Spl. edn. tchr. Plano (Tex.) Ind. Sch. Dist.; assoc. Thompson and Knight, Dallas, 1983-95; judge U.S. Ct. Appeals (5th cir.), Dallas, 1996, Tex. Supreme Ct., Dallas, 1997—2003. Liaison Gender Bias Reform Implementation Com., family law sect. Dallas Bar. Editor-in-chief Southwestern Law Jour. Fellow Tex. Bar Found., Dallas Bar Found. Mem. ABA (litigation sect., com. appellate practice, judicial sect.), State Bar Tex. (judicial, litigation, appellate sects.), Dallas Bar Assn. (apellate law sect.), 5th Cir. Bar Assn., Coll. of State Bar Tex., Order of the Coif. Home: Apt 2F 3510 Turtle Creek Blvd Dallas TX 75219-5543

HANKINSON, RISDON WILLIAM, retired chemical engineer; b. St. Joseph, Mo., Dec. 11, 1938; s. William Augusta and Rose Mary (Thompson) H.; m. Lyla Pollard, June 4, 1960; children: Kenneth, Michelle, Michael, Mark, Douglass. BS, U. Mo., Rolla, 1960, MS, 1962, degree in Chem. Engring., 1982; PhD, Iowa State U., 1972. Registered engr., Okla. Instr. chem. engring. U. Mo., Rolla, 1960-62, Iowa State U., 1964-67; engr. Phillips Petroleum Co., Bartlesville, Okla., 1967-69, group leader, 1969-70, cons., 1970-78, prin. thermodynamics, 1978-80, prin. process engr., 1980-82, sr. staff assoc., 1982-85, mgr. engring. scis. br. tech. sys. devel., 1985, mgr. tech. sys. br. engring. and svcs., 1985-87, div. mgr. client applications and tech. svcs., 1991-92, mgr. arch. and new tech. corp. info. tech., 1992-93, sr. scientist R&D, 1993-96, mgr. advanced modeling techs., corp. engring., 1996-99, ret., 1999. Mgr. comml. sys. Phillips 66 Natural Gas Co., 1987-91; adj. prof. math. Okla. State U., 1967-75, Bartlesville Wesleyan Coll., 1969-71. Contbr. articles to profl. jours. V.p. Tech. Careers Adv. Com., 1972-73, pres., 1973-74; v.p. Vol. Okla. Overseas Mission Bd., 1970-71; cub scout leader Boy Scouts Am.; tchr. religious edn., minister of Eucharist, lector Roman Cath. Ch., 1976—; chmn. bd. dirs. Alcohol and Drug Ctr. Inc., 1984-87, bd. dirs., 1987—89; mem. fin. coun. St. John Cath. Chs., 1998-2006, RCIA instr., coord., 1993-, instr. adult religious edn., 2000-, pres. parish coun., 2002-. 1st lt. AUS, 1962-63, hon. discharge, capt. AUS 1969. Recipient Outstanding Alumnus Achievement award Iowa State U., 1971; named Outstanding Young Engr. in Okla., 1970, Outstanding Engr. in Okla., 1984, Hanlon award Gas Processors Assn., 1996; Am. Oil fellow Iowa State U. Fellow Am. Inst. Chem. Engrs. (dir. past pres. Bartlesville sect., Achievement award 1990); mem. Okla. Soc. Profl. Engrs. (v.p. membership 1988-89, exec. v.p. 1989-90), Am. Petroleum Inst. (chmn. phys. properties com. static measurement 1979-82, founder, co-chmn. electronic flow measurement com. 1989-91), Hilcrest Country Club, Elks, KC (grand knight, coun. 1987-89, state ch. activities dir. 1989-91, faithful navigator 4th degree 1991-93, dir. state program 1993-95), Kiwanis (pres. Bartllesville Downtown GP 2006). Home: 701 Sooner Park Dr Bartlesville OK 74006-8954 Personal E-mail: rwhankin@swbell.net.

HANKS, ALAN R., retired chemistry professor; b. Balt., Nov. 30, 1939; s. Raymond Hanks and Lillian (Simon) Miller; m. Beverly Jean Henson, Jan. 17, 1961; children: Craig, Denise, Leta. BS in Physics, West Tex. State U., 1962; MS in Biophys. Chemistry, N. Mex. Highlands U., 1964; PhD in Biophysics, Pa. State U., 1967. Nuclear med. sci. officer Armed Forces Inst. Pathology, Washington, 1967-69; from asst. to prof. biochemistry, biophysics Tex. A&M U., Coll. Sta., Tex., 1969-82; state chemist, seed commnr., prof. Purdue U., West Lafayette, Ind., 1982—2005, prof. emeritus, 2005. Corr. mem., liaison Collaborative Internat. Pesticide Analytical Coun., 1988—2006; mem. FAO panel on pesticides UN, 1991—2006, mem. WHO panel on pesticides, 2001—06. Contbr. articles to profl. jours. Recipient World Food Day Bronze medal, FAO, 2006, Commrs. Citation Honor award, FDA, 2007. Fellow Assn. Ofcl. Analytical Chemists (chmn. methods bd. 1986-89, bd. dirs. 1990-96, sec.-treas. 1992-93, pres.-elect 1993-94, pres. 1994-95, chmn. liaison com. 1997-2001); mem. Assn. Am. Feed Control Ofcls. (chmn. minerals com. 1985-96, pres. 1999-2000, lab. methods and svc. com. 1988-93, bd. dirs. 1996-2001, codex observer mem. to codex com. on methods of analysis and sampling 2000-2005), Assn. Am. Plant Food Control Ofcls. (chmn. Magruder check sample com. 1988-90, bd. dirs. 1989-94, chmn. environ. affairs com. 1990-99, pres.-elect 1991-92, pres. 1992-93). Avocations: fishing, gardening, sports, travel. Personal E-mail: abhanks@netscape.com.

HANKS, EUGENE RALPH, real estate developer, rancher, forester, retired military officer, investor; b. Corning, Calif., Dec. 11, 1918; s. Eugene and Lorena B. Hanks; m. Frances Elliot Herrick, Mar. 4, 1945; children: Herrick, Russell, Stephen, Nina. Student, Calif. Poly. Coll., 1939—41, U. So. Calif., 1949—50, Am. U., 1958—59; grad., Command and Staff Coll., Norfolk, Va., 1960. With Naval Aviation Flight Tng.,V-5 Program USN, 1941-42, commd. ensign, 1942, advanced through ranks to capt., 1963; carrier fighter pilot, Am. Ace, six victories, 1942-45; team leader Two WWII Combat Tours; test pilot Naval Air Test Ctr., 1945—48; mem. Navy Flight Exhbn. Team Blue Angels, 1950; commdg. officer 3 jet fighter squadrons including VF-142 Navy's 1st Mach II fighter squadron, Miramar, Calif., 1952-61; tng. sr. squadron fighter pilots for Vietnam; 1st ops. officer Super Carrier U.S.S. Constellation, 1961-62; dir. ops. Naval Air Missile Test Ctr., 1963—66; test dir. Joint Task Force Two, Albuquerque, 1966-69; ret., 1969. Owner, mgr. developer Christmas Tree Canyon, Cebolla Springs and Mountain River subdivsns., Mora, N.Mex., 1967—; owner Hanks Family, LLC. Decorated Navy Cross, DFC with star (2), Air medal (7), Legion of merit; named Citizen of Yr., Citizen's Com. for Right to Bear Arms, 1987, 93—. Mem.: NRA, Mus. Flight, Am. Forestry Assn., Naval Aviation Assn., Am. Air Mus. Gt. Britian, Am. Air Mus., Mora C. of C., Combat Pilots Assn., Ret. Officers Assn., Am. Fighter Aces Assn., Blue Angels Assn., Am. Aviation Mus., Naval Aviation Mus. Found., 1940 Coll. Crops Club (pres.), Oxford Club (chmns. cir.), Dun and Bradstreet's Million Dollar Club, Am. Legion, Legion of Valor. Republican. Home and Office: Christmas Tree Canyon Box 239 Mora NM 87732-0239 Office Phone: 505-387-5126. Business E-Mail: rhanks@nnmt.net.

HANKS, GEORGE CAROL, JR., state judge; b. Breaux Bridge, La., Sept. 25, 1964; s. George Carol and Quenola Reese Hanks; m. Stacey L. Hanks, Apr. 29, 1995. JD, Harvard U., 1989; BA summa cum laude, La. State U., 1986. Bar: Tex. 1989, U. S. Dist. Ct. (so. dist.) Tex. 1992, U.S. Ct. Appeals (5th cir.) 1993, U.S. Dist. Ct. Ariz. 1994, U.S. Supreme Ct. 2003, U.S. Ct. Internat. Trade 2003, D.C. 2003. Jud. law clk., Houston, 1989-91; assoc. atty. Fulbright & Jaworski, Houston, 1991-96; shareholder Wickliff & Hall PC, Houston, 1996-2001; judge 157th Dist. Ct., State of Tex., 2001—02; justice Tex. Ct. Appeals (1st cir.), Houston, 2003—. Panel chmn. grievance com., spl. disciplinary counsel State Bar Tex., Houston, 1993—99. Contbr. articles to profl. jours. Bd. dirs. Big Bros. and Big Sisters, Houston, 1995—97, Houston chpt. ARC, 2001—. Fellow Houston Bar Assn.; mem. Fed. Bar Assn., Nat. Bar Assn., Am. Judges Assn., Houston Bar Assn. Avocations: aviation, scuba diving. Home: 12035 Circle Dr E Houston TX 77071 Office: 1037 San Jacinto Fl 10 Houston TX 77002 Home Phone: 713-270-7716; Office Phone: 713-655-2708. Personal E-mail: georgehanks@sbcglobal.net. Business E-Mail: george.hanks@1stcoa.courts.state.tx.us.

HANKS, JAMES JUDGE, JR., lawyer; b. Washington, Jan. 31, 1943; s. James Judge and Dorothy (Teeple) H. AB, Princeton U., 1964; LLB, U. Md., 1967; LLM, Harvard U., 1969. Bar: Md. 1967. Law clk. to judge U.S. Ct. Appeals (D.C. cir.), 1967—68; assoc. Weinberg and Green Law Firm, Balt., 1969—74; ptnr. Weinberg and Green, Balt., 1975—93, Ballard Spahr Andrews & Ingersoll, LLP, Balt., 1993—2003, Venable, LLP, Baltimore, 2003—. Vis. prof. law Cornell U. Law Sch., Ithaca, NY, 1993, adj. prof. law, 1994—; vis. sr. lectr. Cornell U. Bus. Sch., 1999—; adj. prof. law Northwestern U. Law Sch., 1997, 2000—; lectr. various profl. orgns. and law schs.; Commerzbank vis. prof. law Bucerius Law Sch., 2003, 05. Author: Maryland Corporation Law; co-author: Legal Capital, 3d edit.; contbr. articles to profl. jours. Fellow Am. Bar Found.; mem. ABA, Am. Law Inst., Md. State Bar Assn. (chmn. bus. law sect. 1982-83), Md. Club. Democrat. Episcopalian. Home: 1159 Riverside Ave Baltimore MD 21230-4119 Office: Venable LLP Two Hopkins Plz Ste 1800 Baltimore MD 21201 Office Phone: 410-244-7500. Business E-Mail: jhanks@venable.com.

HANKS, RICHARD, information company executive; b. Ipswich, Suffolk, Eng., June 4, 1964; BA in Indsl. Economics, Nottingham U., Eng., 1985. Chartered Acct. Sr. fin. positions Pearson PLC, SmithKline Beecham PLC; divisional fin. dir. corp. and media info. div. Reuters; CFO Factiva, 1999—2006; COO enterprise media group Dow Jones & Co., Inc., 2006—. Office: Factiva PO Box 300 Princeton NJ 08543-0300 Business E-Mail: richard.hanks@dowjones.com.

HANKS, RICHARD ALAN, archivist; b. Beardstown, Ill., Aug. 4, 1951; s. Hardin E. and Martha Louise Hanks; m. Robin Sue Dilday, Aug. 12, 1972; children: Rachel Christine, Rylan Taylor. BA in Comm., U. Calif., Riverside, 1980—82, MA in History, 1996—98, PhD in Native Am. History, 2004—06. Archivist Riverside Local History Resource Ctr., 1998—99, project mgr., 1999—2000; assoc. archivist A.K. Smiley Pub. Libr. Lincoln Meml. Shrine, Redlands, Calif., 2000—. Adv. com. mem. Ctr. Calif. Native Nations U. Calif., 2006—. Prodr.: (Exhibition) We Cannot Escape History, The Lives of Abraham Lincoln and Robert Watchorn; contr.: to periodicals including Blue and Gray Magazine, to profl. jours. including Southern California Quarterly, The Lincoln Herald. Spkr. LIFE Soc., Riverside, 2002—02, San Bernardino County General. Soc., Calif., 2001, 28th Ann. Conf. Am. Indian Edn., San Diego, 2005. Recipient Chancellor's award, U. Calif., 1982; Libr. & Svcs. Tech. Act grant, Calif. State Libr., 1999. Mem.: Soc. Am. Archivists (assoc.), Soc. Calif. Archivists (assoc.; spkr.), Abraham Lincoln Assn. (assoc.; mem. 1993). Avocations: reading, genealogy. Office: AK Smiley Pub Libr 125 W Vine St Redlands CA 92373 Personal E-mail: rhanks3@aol.com. Business E-Mail: rhanks@akspl.org.

HANKS, ROBIN, rehabilitation nurse; b. 1968; PhD from Dept. Psych., Wayne State U., 1996. Postdoctoral fellow U. Washington Sch. of Medicine; project dir. Southeastern Mich. Traumatic Brain Injury System; dir., Tng. predoctoral and postdoctoral tng. prog., Clinical Psych.; assoc. prof., Phys. Medicine and Rehab. Wayne State U. Sch. of Medicine; adj. prof., Psych. Wayne State U. Sch. of Sci.; chief of Rehab Psych. & Neuropsychology Rehab. Inst. Mich., 1999—. Named one of 40 Under 40, Crain's Detroit Bus., 2006. Office: Rehabilitation Institute of Michigan 261 Mack Ave Detroit MI 48201 Office Phone: 313-745-1203.

HANKS, STEPHEN GRANT, construction executive, lawyer; b. Rexburg, Idaho, June 7, 1950; s. Grant E. and Elaine (Stephens) H.; m. Debra Joan Dyrr, Aug. 6, 1975; children: Adrianne, Brandon, Tiffany, Lindsey. BS, Brigham Young U., 1974; MBA, U. Utah, 1975; JD, U. Idaho, 1978. Bar: Idaho 1978, U.S. Dist. Ct. Idaho 1978. Corp. atty. Morrison-Knudsen Co., Inc., Boise, Idaho, 1978-82, asst. gen. counsel, 1982-85, Morrison Knudsen Corp., Boise, 1985-86, assoc. gen. counsel, 1986-90, sec., assoc. gen. counsel, 1990—91, v.p., corp. sec., gen. counsel, 1991—92, sr. v.p., gen. counsel, 1992—95, exec. v.p., chief legal officer, 1995—2000; pres. Washington Group Internat. (formerly Morrison Knudsen Corp.), Boise, Idaho, 2000—01, pres., CEO, bd. dir., 2001—. Bd. dir. Danny Thompson Memorial Leukemia Found., Inc., U. Idaho President's Spl. Adv. Group; bd. dir., pres. Boise Pub. Schs. Edu. Found., Discovery Ctr. Idaho, Ore-Idaho Coun. of Boy Scouts of Am., St. Alphonsus Reg. Med. Ctr. Found.; adv. bd. U. Idaho Coll. Bus. and Econs., U. Idaho Found.; chmn. Character and Fitness Com. of Idaho State Bar. Mem. ABA, AICPA, Idaho Soc. CPAs. Home: 3130 Terra Dr Boise ID 83709-3860 Office: Washington Group International PO Box 73 720 Park Blvd Boise ID 83729-0073*

HANKS, TOM, actor, film producer, film director; b. Concord, Calif., July 9, 1956; m. Samantha Lewes, Jan. 24, 1978 (div. Mar. 19, 1987); children: Colin, Elizabeth; m. Rita Wilson, Apr. 30, 1988; children: Chester Marlon, Truman Theodore. Student, Calif. State U., Sacramento. Actor: (films) He Knows You're Alone, 1980, Splash, 1984, Bachelor Party, 1984, Volunteers, 1985, The Man with One Red Shoe, 1985, The Money Pit, 1986, Nothing in Common, 1986, Every Time We Say Goodbye, 1986, Dragnet, 1987, Big, 1988, Punchline, 1988, Turner and Hooch, 1989, The 'Burbs, 1989, Joe Versus the Volcano, 1990, The Bonfire of the Vanities, 1990, Radio Flyer, 1992, A League of Their Own, 1992, Sleepless in Seattle, 1993, Philadelphia, 1993 (Golden Globe for Best Actor - Drama 1994, Academy Award for Best Actor 1994), Forrest Gump, 1994 (Academy Award for Best Actor 1995), Apollo 13, 1995, Celluloid Closet, 1995, Toy Story (voice), 1995, Saving Private Ryan, 1998 (nominated Acad. awards), You've Got Mail, 1998, Toy Story 2 (voice), 1999, The Green Mile, 1999, Cast Away, 2000 (also prodr.) (Golden Globe for Best Actor 2001), Road to Perdition, 2002, Catch Me If You Can, 2002, The Ladykillers, 2004, The Terminal, 2004, The Polar Express, 2004 (also exec. prodr.), Da Vinci Code, 2006; actor, dir., writer (films) That Thing You Do!, 1996; prodr. (films) My Big Fat Greek Wedding, 2002, Connie and Carla, 2004, Neil Young: Heart of Gold, 2006, The Ant Bully, 2006; actor (TV movies) Mazes and Monsters, 1982, I Am Your Child, 1997; exec. prodr. We Stand Alone Together, 2001; actor (TV series) Bosom Buddies, 1980-82; exec. prodr. West Point, 2000, My Big Fat Greek Life, 2003; dir., prodr., writer (mini-series) From the Earth to the Moon, 1998 (Emmy award for best mini-series, 1999), Band of Brothers, 2001 (Emmy awards for best directing and best mini-series, 2002). Recipient Louella O. Parsons Awd., Hollywood Women's Press Club, 1994, Golden Globe award, 1995, People's Choice award, 1995, 99, Disting. Pub. Svc. award, USN, 1999, Life Achievement award, Am. Film Inst., 2002; named Man of the Yr., Harvard's Hasty Pudding Theater Club, 1995; named one of 50 Most Powerful People in Hollywood Premiere mag., 2004-06, 100 Most Powerful Celebrities, Forbes.com, 2007; inducted as an honorary mem., US Army Ranger Hall of Fame, 2006. Mem. Actors' Equity Assn., Screen Actors Guild, AFTRA., Am. Acad. Motion Picture Arts & Sciences (v.p., 2007-), Internat. Thespian Soc. Office: Creative Artists Agy c/o Richard Lovett 9830 Wilshire Blvd Beverly Hills CA 90212-1804*

HANLEY, ALLISON ANNE, federal agency administrator; b. Glenridge, NJ, Oct. 31, 1964; d. Michael Joseph Hanley and Carole Helen Matosin. AA in Bus., Abraham Baldwin U., 1984; BSc in Edn., Western Ill. U., 1989; MA, Seton Hall U., 2000. Mil. police sgt. U.S. Army, 1990—96;

canine enforcement officer U.S. Customs, Newark, 1997—2001, supr. canine officer Washington, 2001—02; program mgr. Anti-Terrorism Divsn. Customs and Border Protection Dept. Homeland Security, Washington, 2002—05, program mgr. Anti-Terrorism Divsn. Customs and Border Protection, 2005—. Nat. recruiter U.S. Customs, Newark, 1998—2001, Washington, 1998—2001; nat. K-9 evaluator Customs and Border Protection, mem. def. tactics and baton. Sgt. US Army, 1991—96, discharged US Army, 1996. Decorated NATO medal U.S. Army, Expeditionary award. Mem.: Women in Fed. Law Enforcement, Nat. Women's History Mus., Seton Hall U. Hon. Soc. Republican. Roman Cath. Avocations: sports, reading, fishing. Office: Dept Homeland Security Customs and Border Protection 1300 Penn Ave Office Tng and Devel Washington DC 20229

HANLEY, FRED WILLIAM, librarian, educator; b. Booneville, Miss., May 13, 1939; s. John Martin and Ethel May (Robertson) H.; m. Bethany Nell Holt, June 21, 1971; children: Seth Patrick, Cassandra May. BS, Lambuth Coll., Jackson, Tenn., 1961; MDiv, Meth. Theol. Sch., Delaware, Ohio, 1964; MA in History, Ariz. State U., 1966, MA in Counseling, 1968. Cert. secondary tchr., Ariz. Assoc. pastor Prospect Street Meth. Ch., Marion, Ohio, 1961-64; tchr. history Phoenix Union High Sch. Dist., 1965-74, curriculum coord., 1974-78, chmn. English dept., 1978-89, varsity cross country coach, 1977—80, chmn. libr. dept., 1989—, chmn. tech. com., 1991—, varsity golf coach, 1980-89, 99—, varsity tennis coach, 2001—. Editor Ariz. Health Svcs. jour., 1965. Bd. dirs. Wesley Found., Tempe, Ariz., 1964-69; vol. Am. Cancer Soc., Phoenix, 1985-91; chmn. Phoenix Symphony Guild Symphonette Orch., 1993—; mem. exec. com. Phoenix Symphony Guild Orchestral Tng. Program, 1994—; libr. Phoenix Symphony Guild, 1998—. Recipient Tchr. of Yr. award West HS, Phoenix, 1969, Metro Region Coach of the Yr., 2001-02, 06-07, Disting. Alumnae award Lambuth Coll., 1979. Mem. ALA, NEA, Ariz. Edn. Assn., Ariz. Libr. Assn., N. Cen. Assn. of Sec. Schs. Accreditation Team for Ariz., Nat. Coun. Tchrs. English., Phi Alpha Theta. Democrat. Avocations: marathon running, golf, hiking. Home: 10411 W Flower St Avondale AZ 85323-4403 Office: Alhambra High Sch 3839 W Camelback Rd Phoenix AZ 85019-2598 Business E-Mail: fhanley@phxhs.k12.az.us.

HANLEY, HENRY GORMAN, cardiologist; b. Providence, Feb. 11, 1941; s. James Lawrence and Mary Rose (Gorman) Hanley; m. Linda Ellis, June 20, 1970 (div. Jan. 1989); children: Tara, April; m. Kathy Davis, Nov. 18, 1989; children: Eric, Alan. AB, Harvard U., 1962; MD, Yale U., 1966. Diplomate Am. Bd. Internal Medicine, Am. Bd. Cardiovascular Diseases, Am. Bd. Interventional Cardiology. Asst. prof. Baylor Coll. Medicine, Houston, 1971-76, asst. prof. dept. cell biophysics, 1974-76; assoc. prof. medicine U. Ky. Coll. Medicine, Lexington, 1976-80; prof., chief sect. cardiology La. State U. Med. Ctr., Shreveport, 1980—2002; cardiologist Freedman Meml. Cardiology LLC, Alexandria, La., 2002—. Contbr. articles to profl. jours. Fellow: Am. Coll. Cardiology (mem. exec. coun. La. chpt. 1997—98, gov. La. chpt. 2000—03); mem.: Am. Heart Assn. (pres. La. chpt. 1988—90). Roman Catholic. Avocations: golf, travel. Office: Freedman Meml Cardiology LLC Doctors Bldg Ste 112 3311 Prescott Rd Alexandria LA 71301 Home: 6400 Genevieve Alexandria LA 71303 Home Phone: 318-442-1739; Office Phone: 318-767-0960. E-mail: hghanley@aol.com.

HANLEY, KATHERINE KEITH, state official; b. Columbia, Mo., Mar. 5, 1943; d. Everett E. and Anna Catherine (Blanchard) Keith; m. Edward John Hanley, Aug. 6, 1966; children: Cecelia Anne, Patrick Keith. BA in French Civilization, BSin Secondary Edn., U. Mo., 1965; MA in Tchg., Harvard U., 1966. Tchr., guidance counselor City of Falls (Va.) Church Pub. Schs., 1966-78; owner, operator Manor Home Ctr., Mt. Lake Park, Md., 1976-79; counselor U. Mo.; mem., Providence Dist. rep. Fairfax County Bd. Supervisors, Fairfax, Va., 1986-95, chmn., 1995—2006; sec. commonwealth Commonwealth of Va., Richmond, 2006—. Chmn. human svcs. subcom., chmn. info. tech. subcom., chmn. audit com. Fairfax County Bd. Suprs.; pres.-elect Va. Mcpl. League; mem. exec. com. Transp. Coordinating Coun.; mem., past chmn. No. Va. Transp. Commn.; mem. No. Va. planning Dist. Commn., 1987—, chmn. legis. com.; bd. dirs., mem. transp. planning bd., mem. bd. vision planning steering com., past mem. met. devel. policy com. Met. Washington Coun. Govts.; mem. regional mobility panel Washington Met. Area Transit Authority; mem. adv. bd. Va. Inst. of Govt. Mem. exec. com. Greater Washington Initiative; mem. State Supt.'s Cmty. Adv. Com., Dulles Airport Regional Econ. Study Commn., Dulles Corridor Rail Study Policy Com.; mem. Commn. on State and Local Govt. Responsibility and Taxing Authority, mem. subcom. on devolution; past bd. dirs. Urban Partnership; past trustee Fairfax Hosp. Sys.; past mem. Commn. to Study Efficiency in Use of Pub. Edn. Funds, Task Force on Tchg. as a Profession, Fairfax County Child Care Adv. Coun., Citizens' Com. on Changing Enrollment in Secondary Schs., Fairfax County Cmty. Action Adv. Bd., other civic orgns.; past vice chmn. Fairfax County Supt.'s Cmty. Adv. Coun.; past pres. Holmes Run Woods and Crossing Civic Assn. Named Pub. Servant of Yr., Greater Merrifield Bus. Assn., 1992; award recipient Mental Health Assn. No. Va., 1995. Mem. Va. Assn. Counties (immediate past pres.), Phi Beta Kappa. Democrat. Office: Office Sec of Commonwealth PO Box 2454 Richmond VA 23218 Office Phone: 804-786-2441. Office Fax: 804-371-0017.*

HANLEY, KEVIN LANCE, maintenance company executive; b. Oil City, Pa., Nov. 25, 1961; s. Harold Edward and Helen Louise (Banta) H.; m. Patricia Yolanda DeLeon, Sept. 29, 1984 (div. Feb. 2001); children: Jennifer Jessica, Kevin Lance Jr; m. Carolyn Jean Rydman, May. 18, 2002; 1 adopted child, Jessica Joy Rydman Grad. high sch., Titusville, Pa.; diploma, McDonald's Regional Hdqs., LA, 1986. Maintenance supr. Paschen Mgmt. Corp. McDonald's, Camarillo, Calif., 1980-86, asst. mgr., 1986-88, 95, maintenance cons., 1988-89; apartment mgr. Bartlein & Co., Ventura, Calif., 1990-97; mgr. phys. plant Westmont Coll., Santa Barbara, Calif., 1988—2004; gen. cons. "R" Cleaning Maintenance, Santa Paula, Calif., 1989—91; owner Custodial-Plus Svcs., Montecito, Calif., 1996—. Veteran Operation Iraqi Freedom, 2004. Sec.-treas. Ch. of God of Prophecy, Carpinteria, Calif., 1987—95, 1997—2000, asst. pastor, 1988—95. 1st class petty officer USNR, 1994—. Decorated Achievement medal USN, USMC, Global War on Terrorism Expeditionary medal, Nat. Def. medal. Republican. Avocations: backpacking, bowling, camping. Office: Custodial Plus Svcs PO Box 5304 Montecito CA 93150 Office Phone: 805-455-0310. Business E-Mail: khanley@custodialplus.com.

HANLEY, MARK YOUNG, historian, educator, researcher; b. Pueblo, Colo., Oct. 18, 1953; s. Harold Gordon Hanley and Winifred Haskell Snyder; m. Janet Susan McCormick, Aug. 7, 1976; children: Matthew Mark, Kelly Suzanne. BA, Western State Coll., 1976; MA, U. Ill., 1984; PhD, Purdue U., 1989. Vis. asst. prof. history Ind. U.-Purdue U., Indpls., 1991—91; asst. prof. history N.E. Mo. State U., Kirksville, 1991—96; assoc. prof. history Truman State U., Kirksville, Mo., 1997—2004, prof. history, 2004—. Chmn. editl. bd. Truman State U. Press, Kirksville, 2000—03. Author: (book) Beyond a Christian Commonwealth: The Protestant Quarrel with the American Republic, 1830-1860; co-editor: Encyclopedia Modern Christian Politics, 2006; chair, mem. editl. bd.: Truman State U. Press; contbr. Grantee, Pew Charitable Trust and Nat. Assn. for the Study Am. Evangelicals, 1997. Mem.: Nat. Assn. for the Study Am. Evangelicals, Soc. for Historians the Early Am. Republic, Am. Soc. Ch. History, Rotary Internat. Avocations: antiques, skiing. Home: 22535 Harrison Trail Kirksville MO 63501 Office Phone: 660-785-4098. E-mail: ss04@truman.edu.

HANLEY, ROBERTA LYNN, alternative education coordinator, educator; b. Gary, Ind., May 4, 1953; BA, Purdue U., 1975; MS, Ind. U., Gary, 1982. Substitute tchr. Hobart (Ind.) High Sch., 1974-77, social studies tchr., 1977—, sophmore gifted/talented tchr., future problem solving coach, 1985-89, 90-91, coord./tchr. Challenge Program, Alternative Edn. Program, 1991-94; coord. Hobart (Ind.) Challenge Sch., 1994—. Faculty advisor Hobart Jr. High Sch. yearbook, 1978-80, 81-84. Choir libr. Hobart Presbyn. Ch., 1980-93, Sunday sch. sec., 1987-93, ch. historian, 1988-93. Recipient Tchr. of Yr. award Hobart Rotary Club, 1988, Tchr. of Yr. award Inland Steel-Ryerson Found., 1992. Mem. Nat. Coun. Social Studies, Ind. Coun. Social Studies. Office: Sch City Hobart 32 E 7th St Hobart IN 46342-5154

HANLEY, THOMAS PATRICK, obstetrician, gynecologist; b. St. Louis, Apr. 16, 1951; s. Thomas P. and Virginia Barbara (Lydon) H.; m. Patricia Ann McHargue, Dec. 27, 1975; children: Colleen, Thomas III, Timothy, Matthew. BA, St. Louis U., 1973, MD, 1977. Diplomate Am. Bd. Ob-gyn. Intern St. Louis U., 1977-78, resident, 1978-81; practice medicine specializing in ob-gyn St. Louis, 1981—; pres. med. staff St. Mary's Health Ctr., 1993; mem. staff Mo. Bapt. Hosp., St. Joseph's Hosp., Kirkwood, Mo.; clin. prof. St. Louis U. Med. Sch., 1983—. Mem. AMA (Physicians Recognition award 1981—), Am. Coll. Ob-Gyn. (Physicians Excellence award 1986—), Mo. State Med. Soc., St. Louis Gynecol. Soc. (pres. 1989-90), St. Louis Met. Med. Soc. Independent. Roman Catholic. Avocation: golf. Office: 3555 Sunset Office Dr 107 Saint Louis MO 63127 Office Phone: 314-238-9000.

HANLEY, THOMAS RICHARD, engineering educator; s. Thomas Jesse and Dorothy Louise (Hay) H.; m. Norma Kathryn Decker, Dec. 27, 1979; children: Thomas Jeffrey, Alan Michael, Andrew Richard, Caitlin Marisa. BSChemE, Va. Poly. Inst., 1967; MSChemE, Va. Poly. Inst. & State U., 1971, PhDChemE, 1972; MBA in Mgmt., Wright State U., 1975. Registered profl. engr., Ky. Devel. engr. AF Materials Lab., Wright Patterson AFB, Ohio, 1972-75; asst. prof. Tulane U., New Orleans, 1975-79; assoc. prof. Rose-Hulman Inst. Tech., 1979-83; prof., dept. head La. Tech. U., Ruston, 1983-85; prof., chmn. dept. Fla. State U., Fla. A&M U., Tallahassee, 1985-91; dean Speed Sci. Sch. U. Louisville, 1991—2003; provost Auburn (Ala.) U., 2003—05, v.p., 2005—06, prof., 2006—. Divsn. advisor NSF, Washington, 1987-93; presenter at numerous nat. and internat. profl. confs. Contbr. articles to profl. jours. Bd. dirs. Plasticolors, Ashtabula, Ohio, AAES, Washington, 2007-. Capt. USAF, 1972—75. Recipient award Soc. Am. Mil. Engrs., 1966, 67, Acad. award Am. Legion, 1967, Ralph R. Teetor Ednl. award SAE, 1989, Outstanding Engr. in Edn. award Ky. Soc. Profl. Engrs., 1994; grantee NSF, Nat. Renewable Energy Lab., GE, Colgate-Palmolive, United Catalysts, IKA Works, Swan Biomass, Toro, Olin, Stone and Webster. Fellow AIChE (profl. devel. recognition cert. 1980, student chpt. advisor award 1979, bd. dirs., NYC 2006-); mem. Am. Soc. Engring. Edn., Nat. Assn. Basketball Coaches, Sigma Xi, Phi Kappa Phi, Tau Beta Pi, Phi Lambda Upsilon, Omega Chi Epsilon. Office: Auburn U Dept Chem Engring Auburn AL 36849 Home Phone: 502-228-0161; Office Phone: 334-844-7773. Business E-Mail: hanley@auburn.edu.

HANLIN, SHAWN, academic administrator; Grad., Santa Barbara City Coll., 1987. Cert. Exec. Chef Am. Culinary Fedn. Apprenticeship The Greenbrier, White Sulphur Springs, W.Va.; dir. dining services, exec. chef Holladay Park Plaza; regional corp. chef Pacific Retirement Services, Portland, Oreg.; exec. dir. Oreg. Coast Culinary Inst., Coos Bay, Oreg., 2007—. Mem.: Am Culinary Fedn. (western regional certification coord. 2005—, Western Regional Chef of Yr. 2006). Office: Oreg Coast Culinary Inst 1988 Newmark Coos Bay OR 97420 Office Phone: 541-888-1546.*

HANLON, BARBARA JEAN, family and consumer sciences educator; b. Johnstown, Pa., July 17, 1953; d. Bernard Charles and Jean Rigo; m. Robert S. Hanlon, Aug. 20, 1988; children: Jennifer, Gina Kessler, Charles. BS in Home Econs. Edn., Ind. U. Pa., 1974; MEd in Secondary Edn., West Chester U., 1981. Tchr. home econs. edn. Phoenixville Area Sch. Dist., Pa., 1978—89; instr. early childhood Chester County Intermediate Unit, 1989—2005, cooperative edn. coord., 2005—. Advisor Family Career & Cmty. Leaders Am., 1989—2006, Key Club advisor, 2005—; mem. Future Dirs. Family & Consumer Scis. Task Force, Pa. Dept. Edn., Harrisburg, 2003—. Pres. bd. dirs. Phoenixville Area Children's Learning Ctr., 2000—06, Phoenixville Area Violence Prevention Network. Mem.: NEA, Pa. State Edn. Assn., Pa. Early Childhood Educators Assn., Nat. Child Care Assn., Assn.Career and Tech. Edn., Chester County Assn. Family and Consumer Scis., Pa. Assn. Family and Consumer Scis., Am. Assn. Family and Consumer Scis., Pa. Assn. Coop. Edn., Nat. Assn. Edn. Young Children, Kappa Omicron Nu. United Methodist. Avocations: reading, sewing, camping, swimming. Office: Ctr Arts & Tech Pickering Campus 1580 Charlestown Rd Phoenixville PA 19460 Office Phone: 610-933-8877. E-mail: barbha@cciu.org.

HANLON, FRANCIS X., lawyer; b. Aug. 27, 1941; BA, Dartmouth Coll., 1964; LLB, Univ. N.C., 1967. Bar: Mass. 1967. Assoc. Ropes & Gray, Boston, 1967—76, ptnr. corp. dept., 1976—, head real estate practice group. Order of the Coif Office: Ropes & Gray 1 Internat Pl Boston MA 02110-2624 Home Phone: 617-661-0220; Office Phone: 617-951-7232. Office Fax: 617-951-7050. Business E-Mail: francis.hanlon@ropesgray.com.

HANLON, GLEN, professional hockey coach; Goaltender Vancouver Canucks, 1978—82, St. Louis Blues, 1982—83, NY Rangers, 1983—86, Detroit Red Wings, 1986—91; asst. coach Vancouver Canucks, 1992—99; head coach Portland Pirates, 1999—2002; asst. coach Washington Capitals, 2002—03, head coach, 2003—. Office: Washington Capitals 401 9th St NW Ste 750 Washington DC 20004

HANLON, JAMES ALLISON, confectionery company executive; b. Oak Park, Ill., Nov. 27, 1937; s. James Graves and Frances (Allison) H.; m. June Weiland, May 30, 1959; children: Perian, Loretta, Jill, James. BA, U. Notre Dame, 1959; postgrad., U. London, 1979, U. Pa., 1980. Mgr. accounts Needham Harper Steers Advt., Chgo., 1959-67; mgr. mktg. L.S. Heath & Co., Inc., Robinson, Ill., 1967-70; v.p. mktg. Peter Paul Cadbury, Naugatuck, Conn., 1970-79, pres., chief exec. officer, 1983-86; pres. Cadbury Can., Toronto, Ont., 1979-83, also bd. dirs.; pres., chief exec. officer Leaf N.Am., Bannockburn, Ill., 1988-95; chmn., CEO, pres. Harmony Foods, Santa Cruz, Calif., 1996—2004. Nat. trustee Boy's Clubs of Am. With USMCR, 1956-59. Named Mktg. Warrior of Yr., AMR, Inc., 1979, Most Motivated Exec., 1992; recipient Kettle award Confectionary Industry, 1992, Lifetime Achievement award Nat. Confectionary Assn., 2002. Mem. Pasadera Country Club. Roman Catholic. Home: 403 Estancia Ct Monterey CA 93940 Home Phone: 831-656-9961. *Life unfolds itself at it's own pace.Any grand plans should be tempered by the unaticipated events.*

HANLON, MICHAEL GREGORY, lawyer; b. Palo Alto, Calif., May 7, 1953; s. Paul David and Carol Claire (Crowley) H. BA, U. Oreg., 1975; JD, Lewis & Clark Coll., Portland, 1979. Bar: Oreg. 1979, U.S. Dist Ct. Oreg. 1979, U.S. Ct. Appeals (9th cir.) 1979, U.S. Supreme Ct. 1995. Assoc. Law Offices Henry A. Carey, Portland, 1979, 81-83; asst. atty. gen. Antitrust div. State of Oreg. Dept. Justice, Salem, 1980; pvt. practice Portland, 1983—. Mem. ABA, Oreg. State Bar Assn. (chair antitrust sect. 1999-2000, chair fed. practice and procedure com. 2004), Multnomah County Bar Assn. (mem. MBA legis. com., chair professionalism com. 2000-01, Award of Merit 2001), U.S. Dist. Ct. (Oreg.) Hist. Soc., Univ. Club, Multnomah Athletic Club, Columbia-Edgewater Country Club. Democrat. Roman Catholic. Office Phone: 503-228-9787. Business E-Mail: mgh@hanlonlaw.com.

HANLON, STEPHEN F., lawyer; b. St. Louis, Dec. 1, 1941; BS in English and History, St. Louis U., 1963; JD, U. Mo. Sch. Law, 1966. Bar: Mo. 1966, Fla. 1976, DC 2003. Ptnr. pro bono Holland & Knight LLP, Washington. Past pres. Fla. Legal Svcs., Inc. Named Boss of Yr., Tampa Legal Secretaries Assn.; recipient Nelson Poynter award, ACLU Fla., 1996, Steven M. Goldstein Criminal Justice award, Fla. Assn. of Criminal Lawyers, 2000, Equal Justice award, So. Ctr. for Human Rights, 2001, Award for Human Rights Advocacy, Tampa Urban League, Award for Betterment of Race Rels., Office of Cmty. Rels. for the City of Tampa, Achievement award for Meritorious Svc. in the Field of Edn., Fla. Edn. Assn./United, "Keep the Dream Alive" award, Dr. Martin Luther King Commemorative Com. in Hillsborough County. Mem.: Fla. Bar Found. (dir. 1995—96), ABA (chair exec. coun. individual rights and responsibilities sect., mem. commn. on legal problems of the elderly 1991—93, past mem. coordinating group on bioethics and the law), DC Bar, Mo. Bar, Fla. Bar (chmn. pub. interest law sect. 1992—93). Office: Holland & Knight LLP 2099 Pennsylvania Ave NW Ste 100 Washington DC 20006 Office Phone: 202-828-1871. Business E-Mail: shanlon@hklaw.com.

HANLON, WILLIAM R., lawyer; BA, Coll. William and Mary, 1975; BA in Jurisprudence with honors, St. John's Coll., Oxford Univ., 1977; JD cum laude, Univ. Pa., 1979. Bar: DC 1981. Law clerk, Hon. Arlin M. Adams US Ct. Appeals (3rd cir.), 1979—80; adminstrv. ptnr., mem. exec. com. Shea & Gardner (merged with Goodwin Procter, 2004); ptnr., co-leader, litig. dept., mem. exec. com. Goodwin Procter LLP, Washington, 2004—. Assoc. editor Univ. Pa. Law Rev. Office: Goodwin Procter LLP 901 New York Ave NW Washington DC 20001 Office Phone: 202-346-4239. Office Fax: 203-346-4444. Business E-Mail: whanlon@goodwinprocter.com.

HANMER, STEPHEN READ, JR., retired federal official; b. Denver, Aug. 15, 1933; s. Stephen Read and Mary Virginia (Marchant) H.; m. Lois Eileen Boteler, June 25, 1955; children: Susan Eileen Hanmer Alexander, Stephen Read III, Sara Lynn. BS in Phys., Va. Mil. Inst., Lexington, 1955; MS in Aerospace Engring., MSME, U. So. Calif., 1964. Commd. 2d lt. U.S. Army, 1956, major, 1965, lt. col., 1968, comdg. 6th bn., 32d Artillery Vietnam, 1968, col., 1975, retired, 1977; assoc. prof. dept. mechanics U.S. Mil. Acad., 1964-67; def. plans div. staff mem. U.S. Mission to NATO, Brussels, 1978-81; dir. theater nuclear force policy Office of Sec., Dept. Def., Washington, 1981-84; prin. dep. asst. sec. Internat. Security Policy Dept. Def., Washington, 1984-85; amb., dep. head U.S. del. Strategic Arms Reduction Talks, 1985-87, amb., chief U.S. del., 1988-89; dep. dir. ACDA, 1989-93; asst. to pres. Kaman Scis. Corp., Alexandria, Va., 1993-98; ret., 1998. Mary Moody Northen chair dept. internat. studies Va. Mil. Inst., 2002. Decorated Legion of Merit, Bronze Star; recipient Meritorious Civilian Svc. medal U.S. Dept. Def., 1981, Sec. of Def. medal, 1987, Sr. Exec. Svc. Disting. Exec. award, 1988, Sec. State Superior Honor award, 1993, Disting. Honor award ACDA, 1993. Mem. St. Andrews Soc. Washington (sec. 1995-96, v.p. 1997, 2004, pres. 2006), Sertoma Club (bd. dirs. 1977), Am. Def. Preparedness Assn. Republican. Episcopalian.

HANN, LUCY E., radiologist, educator; b. 1946; MD, Harvard Med. Sch., 1971. Cert. diagnostic radiology 1977. Resident U. Pa. Hosp., Mass. Gen. Hosp.; radiologist, dir. ultrasound Meml. Sloan-Kettering Cancer Ctr., NYC; prof. radiology Weill Med. Coll., Cornell U. Office: Meml Sloan-Kettering Cancer Ctr 1275 York Ave Rm C278 New York NY 10021

HANN, ROY WILLIAM, JR., civil engineer, educator; b. Oklahoma City, Mar. 21, 1934; s. Roy W. and Irene (Billups) H.; m. Ann Mullman, Dec. 27, 1960 (div. Apr. 1983); children: Kimberly Anne, Sharon Irene, Roy Lee, Karen Bea; m. Martha D'Anne Metting, June 23, 1984; children: Tyson Orion, Heather Eileen. BS, U. Okla., 1956, MCE, 1957, PhD, 1963. Registered profl. engr., Okla., Tex., bd. cert. gen. environ. engr.; lic. real estate broker, Tex. lic. comml. pilot. Engr. C.H. Guernsey and Assos., Oklahoma City, 1959-60; asst. prof. civil engring U. S.C., Columbia, 1962-64; asst. prof. civil engring. dept. environ. engring. div. Tex. A&M U., College Station, 1965-67, assoc. prof., 1967-71, prof., rsch. engr., 1971—, head environ. engring. div., 1970-75, 81-86, dir. sea grant program, 1976-77; dir. Inst. for Oil Spill Tech. Tex. Engring. Experiment Sta., 1991—. Pres. Civil Engring. Systems, Inc., Internat. Spill Tech. Corp., Hann Investments; owner, operator Spring Valley Ranches; cons. in field. Author: Fundamental Aspects of Water Quality Management, 1972; contbr. articles to profl. jours. With USPHS, 1957—59; mem. Bryan-College Station Apt. Assn., pres., 1975—76, dir., 1977—84. Recipient Palladium medal Nat. Audubon Soc. and Am. Assn. Engring. Socs., 1983. Fellow: ASCE (life Paper award 1970—72), Am. Water Works Assn. (Outstanding Paper award 1969), Tex. Soc. Profl. Engrs. (Named Outstanding Young Engr. Brazos chpt. 1969), Am. Acad. Environ. Engring., U. Okla. Alumni Assn. (life), Tau Beta Pi (life), Omicron Delta Kappa (life), Chi Epsilon (life), Sigma Chi (life), Sigma Xi (life). Achievements include research in computer methods, oil pollution control and water supply, water pollution. Home: 1300 Walton Dr College Station TX 77840-2529 Office: Tex A&M Univ Dept Civil Engring College Station TX 77843-3136 Office Phone: 979-845-3012. Business E-Mail: r-hann@civil.tamu.edu.

HANNA, ANNE MARIE, artist; b. Bloomington, Ind., Mar. 16, 1938; d. August de Belmont Hollingshead and Carol Evaleen Dempsey; m. Gary E. Hanna, June 10, 1961; children: Haldee Calore, Mark H., Scot E. Student, Cen. Sch. Art, London, 1958—59; BA, BS, Ind. U., 1961. Mgr. art dept. Curry's Coll. Bookstore, Ind. U., Bloomington, Ind., 1961—65; nursery sch. tchr. Powder Mill Village, Beltsville, Md., 1965—67; art tchr. Prince Georges County Schs., Laurel, Md., 1973—89; dir. Savage Mill Galleries Savage Mill Corp., Savage, Md., 1989—96; artist Mid-Atlantic region, 1980—. Pres. Laurel Art Guild, 1973—74; lectr. art film series South Coastal Lab., Bethany Beach, Del., 2003—; grad. sculpture instr. Ind. U., 1960; chair vol. program JHES/Prince Georges County Schs., 1972—86; docent Rehobeth Art League, 1998—. Represented in permanent collections Am. Founders of Scouting, portaits, Boy Scouts Am., Qoro LLC, Internat. Art Expo NY Javits Ctr., 2004. U.S. rep. Citizen Amb. Program to China, 1993; ofcl. portrait artist Nat. Capital Area Coun. Boy Scouts Am., Washington, 1984—2000; leader Girl Scouts Am., Prince Georges County, Md., 1968—76, Boy Scouts Am., Washington, 1974—94, leader Sea Scout, 1986—94, dist. tng. chair Patuxent dist., 1984—89, woodbadge instr., 1984—94. Named one of Top 10 Artists to Track, Del. Beach Life Mag., 2006; recipient Best in Show award, Rehobeth Art League, 2002, 2004, Zwanfendael Art Gallery, Nat. Landscape Show, 2003, Silver Beaver award, Boy Scouts Am., 1986, Sea Badge award, 1992, Best in Show award, Rehoboth Art League, 2002, 2004, 2005, Best in Show, Bethany Beach Watercolor, 2006; Individual Artist Opportunity grantee, Del. State Arts Divsn. Mem.: Gallery One Co-Op, Del. Watercolor Soc. (Biggs Mus. award 2005, Best in Show 2006), Nat. League Am. Pen Women, Nat. Portrait Soc., Potomac Valley Watercolorists, Balt. Watercolor Soc. (life), DAR (historian Laurel chpt. 1981—95). Home: 143 Riverview Dr Dagsboro DE 19939 Personal E-mail: artfoxag@msn.com.

HANNA, COLIN ARTHUR, management consultant, political organization worker, consultant; b. Abington, Pa., Dec. 3, 1946; s. Arthur and Jean Victoria (McClure) H.; m. Anne Price Hemphill, Dec. 28, 1967; children: Jean Price, Colin Alexander. AB, U. Pa., 1968. With CBS, Inc., 1969-76; account exec. CBS Radio Spot Sales, NYC, 1969-70, 71-72, sales mgr. Phila., 1974-76; mgr. creative svcs. CBS-Viacom Group, NYC, 1970-71; acct. exec. WCAU Radio, Phila., 1972-74; dir. sales devel. WCAU-TV, Phila., 1976; pres. Hanna & Wile Advt., Wayne, Pa., 1976-77, Tri-State Trade Exch., Inc., West Chester, Pa., 1978-80, Hanna Enterprises Ltd., 1980—. Prin. Whittlesey and Assocs., West Chester, 1980-85; pres. The Cheshire Group, West Chester, 1985-91, The Bank Execs. Network, Inc.,

1988-90, PC Helper, 1991-95. Vestryman Ch. of Good Samaritan, Paoli, Pa.; mem. bd. overseers Sch. Arts and Scis. U. Pa.; elected mem. Chester County Rep. Com.; county commr. Chester County, 1995-2003, chmn. bd. commrs., 1998, 99, 2001, 03; bd. mem. Delaware Valley Regional Planning Commn., 1996—, chmn., 1996-97, 98—; apptd. co-chmn. Pa. Census 2000 advisory panel; apptd. mem. Human Resources Investment Coun., Sound Land Use Adv. Panel; pres. Let Freedom Ring, Inc., 2004—. With USNR, 1968-69. Mem. Shakespeare Soc. Phila., Coll. Alumni Soc. U. Pa. (pres.), Gen. Alumni Soc. U. Pa. (v.p.), Alumni Assn. U. Pa. (pres.), County Commrs. Assn. Pa., Mensa, Racquet (Phila.), Radley Run Country (West Chester), Tred Avon Yacht (Oxford, Md.). Republican. Episcopalian. Home and Office: 603 Fairway Dr West Chester PA 19382-2013 Office Phone: 610-793-1800. E-mail: colin@hanna.net.

HANNA, DUKE ELLSWORTH, retired neurological surgeon; b. Indpls., July 24, 1923; s. Duke Ellsworth and Alice Roosevelt (Morehouse) H.; m. Eleanor Jane Myron, Mar. 10, 1945; children: Anita, Cheryl, Robert. BS, Ind. U., 1944, MD, 1946. Diplomate Am. Bd. Neurol. Surgery. Resident neurol. surgery U. Chgo., 1951-54, instr. neurol. surgery, 1954-55; asst. clin. prof. neurol. surgery UCLA, 1972-83, assoc. clin. prof. neurosurgery, 1983—2004. Chief neurol. surgery St. John's Hosp., Santa Monica, Calif., 1976-79, Santa Monica, UCLA Med. Ctr., 1965-75. Author: Illustrative Cranial Neuroradiology, 1967; contbr. articles to profl. jours. Coroner Jay County Ind., Redkey, 1950-51. Lt. (j.g.) USN, 1946-48. Mem. AMA, Calif. Med. Assn., Am. Soc. of Neuroimaging, Congress of Neurol. Surgery, Calif. Assn. Neurol. Surgery, Am. Assn. Neurol. Surgery. Republican. Avocations: aviation, photography. Personal E-mail: dukehanna@cs.com.

HANNA, FRANK JOSEPH, JR., credit company executive; b. Apr. 20, 1939; s. Frank Joseph and Josephine (Nahoom) Hanna; m. Vail Deadwyler, Sept. 15, 1960; children: Frank, Lisa, David; m. Courtney Hollis, Feb. 26, 2005. BBA, U. Ga., 1961. Credit mgr. Sears, Roebuck & Co., Atlanta, 1961—63, GM, Atlanta, 1963—65; gen. mgr. Rollins Acceptance Corp., Atlanta, 1965—81; with Credit Claims & Collections, 1981—90, First Fin. Mgmt. Corp., 1990—93, Worldwide, Inc., Atlanta, 1993—. Real estate investor, 1968. Office: 245 Perimeter Center Pky Ste 300 Atlanta GA 30346

HANNA, GEORGE VERNER, III, lawyer; b. Shelby, NC, Mar. 2, 1943; s. George and Mildred Mae (McSwain) H.; m. Linda Faye Tyndall, May 4, 1982 (div.); children: George Verner IV, Mark W., Elizabeth P.; m. Deborah Henson Hannon, Apr. 14, 1984. AB, U. N.C., 1965, JD, 1968. Bar: N.C. 1968, U.S. Dist. Ct. (we. dist.) N.C. 1969, U.S. Dist. Ct. (ea. dist.) N.C. 1972, U.S. Dist. Ct. (mid. dist.) 1974, U.S. Ct. Appeals (4th cir.) 1976, U.S. Supreme Ct. 1976; cert. mediator N.C. Dispute Resolution Commn. Law clk. N.C. Supreme Ct., Raleigh, 1968-69; assoc. Moore & Van Allen, PLLC, Charlotte, NC, 1969-73, ptnr., 1974—. Arbitrator Am. Arbitration Assn. Past vice-chair bd. mgrs. Harris YMCA, Charlotte; past chmn. bd. mgrs. McCrorey YMCA, Charlotte; past pres., bd. dirs. So. Piedmont Legal Svcs., Charlotte, Children's Law Ctr., Charlotte. Fellow: Am. Bar Found.; mem.: ABA, Mecklenburg Bar Found. (past pres.), Mecklenburg County Bar (past pres.), N.C. Bar Assn. (past bd. govs.), Quail Hollow Club. Methodist. Home: 244 Hempstead Pl Charlotte NC 28207-1922 Office: Moore & Van Allen PLLC Bank of Am Corp Ctr 100 N Tryon St Ste 4700 Charlotte NC 28202-4003 Home Phone: 704-377-0618; Office Phone: 704-331-1030. Fax: 704-378-2030. E-mail: georgehanna@mvalaw.com.

HANNA, HAROLD B., retired lawyer; b. Wenatchee, Wash., Feb. 14, 1921; s. John W. and Maude E. (Pepper) Hanna; m. Grace C. Parker (div.); children: Deborah Carlin, Maxwell H.; m. Franc D. Fraley; stepchildren: Burt Fraley, Pat Fraley. Student, Wenatchee Jr. Coll.; LLB, Valparaiso U., Ind. Bar: Wash. Atty. Wash. State-Chelan County, 1950—2001; ret., 2001. Legal counsel to Gov. Dixy Lee Ray State of Wash., Olympia, 1955—69; dist. ct. judge Douglas County, East Wenatchee, Wash., 1973—77. State rep. and senator Oheland and Douglas County, Wenatchee, Wash., 1981—99. Sgt. US Army, 1942—46, ETO. Decorated Bronze Star US Army. Mem.: Wash. State Bar Assn., Eagles Lodge, Elks Lodge. Democrat. Avocations: fishing, golf, gardening. Home: 1930 Valley View Blvd East Wenatchee WA 98802

HANNA, HARRY MITCHELL, lawyer; b. Portland, Oreg., Jan. 13, 1936; s. Joseph John and Amelia Cecelia (Rask) H.; m. Patricia Ann Shelly, Feb. 4, 1967; 1 child, Harry M. Jr. BS, U. Oreg., 1958; JD, Lewis and Clark Coll., 1966. Bar: Oreg. 1966, Wash. 2005, U.S. Tax Ct. 1967, U.S. Dist. Ct. Oreg. 1970, U.S. Ct. Appeals (9th cir.) 1973, U.S. Ct. Claims 1973, U.S. Supreme Ct. 1971. Airport mgr. Port of Portland, 1964-66; mng. ptnr. Hanna & Purcella, Portland, 1966-80, Niehaus, Hanna, Murphy, Green, Holloway & Connolly, Portland, 1980-88; shareholder, v.p. Hanna Strader, P.C., Portland, 1988—2004; spl. counsel Sussman Shank LLP, Portland, 2004—. Judge pro-tempore U.S. Dist. Ct. Oreg., 1973-78; adj. prof. N.W. Sch. Law, Lewis and Clark Coll., Portland, 1976-77. Trustee Emanuel Med. Ctr. Found., 1989-94; pres. Ctrl. Cath. H.S. Bd., 1992-95; vice chair Life Flight Devel. Bd., 1994-97, chair, 1997—. Mem. ABA, Fed. Bar Assn., Oreg. State Bar Assn., Wash. State Bar Assn., Multnomah Bar Assn., Rotary (pres. East Portland club 1989-90). Avocations: tennis, hunting, fishing, coaching youth athletics. Office: SussmanShank LLP 1000 SW Broadway Ste 1400 Portland OR 97205 Office Phone: 503-227-1111. Business E-Mail: harry@sussmanshank.com.

HANNA, JACK BUSHNELL, zoo director; b. Knoxville, Tenn., Jan. 2, 1947; s. Edwin Ross and Caroline (Bushnell) H.; m. Suzanne (Egli) Hanna, Dec. 20, 1968; children: Kathaleen, Suzanne, Julie. BA, Muskingum Coll., New Concord, Ohio, 1969; postgrad., U. Tenn.; DSc (hon.), Otterbein Coll., 1983, Capital U., 1985, Muskingum Coll. Head curator Knoxville Zool. Park, 1970-72; dir. Central Fla. Zool. Park, Sanford, Fla., 1973-75; v.p., asso. producer Stan Brock Wilderness Adventure Movie Co., 1975-78; exec. dir. Columbus Zool. Park, Ohio, 1978-92, dir. emeritus Ohio, 1992—. Speaker, cons. in field. Assoc. prodr. documentary The Forgotten Wilderness, 1975; co-host (TV series) Hanna's Ark, 1981, host Jack Hanna's Animal Adventures, 1993-; regular guest Good Morning Am., 1983-, The Late Show with David Letterman, 1985-, Larry King Live, 1988-; wildlife corr., FOX News, 1998-; author: Monkeys on the Interstate, 1989, Let's Go to the Petting Zoo with Jungle Jack, 1992, Jack Hanna's Pocketful of Bugs, 1996, Jungle Jack Hanna's Safari Adventure, 1996, Jack Hanna's Ultimate Guide to Pets, 1996, What Zookeepers Do, 1998, Wild About Babies: What Animals Teach Us About Parenting, 2004; co-author: The Lion's Share, 1992. Trustee Muskingum Coll., 1985—95, Ohio Leukemia Assn., 1980-81, Kiski Prep. Sch., Saltsburg, Pa., 1982-90; bd. dirs., The Dian Fossey Gorilla Fund; nat. spokesprson, A Spl. Wish Found., Columbus, Ohio. Recipient Disting. Alumni award Muskingum Coll., 1980, Citizen of Yr. award Columbus K.C., 1980; named Outstanding Citizen Columbus Jaycees, 1979, 80; recipient Disting. Service award, 1980, Local Ronald McDonald House award for community svc. to youth, 1992, Ohio Marketer of Yr. award Columbus Sales Execs., 1993 Fellow Internat. Wildlife Fedn.; mem. Am. Zool. Assn., Appalachian Zool. Soc. (dir.), Columbus Zool. Assn. (dir.) Presbyterian. Avocations: hiking, listening to country music. Office: Columbus Zoological Park 9990 Riverside Dr Powell OH 43065-9606 Mailing: PO Box 1450 Powell OH 43065 Office Phone: 614-645-3480. E-mail: info@jackhanna.com.*

HANNA, JULIET MARIE, lawyer; b. Englewood, Colo., May 28, 1970; d. Bruce Edward and Kanchana Kosiyasthit Hanna; m. Michael James Reilly, Sept. 18, 1999. BA in Linguistics and Anthropology, UCLA, 1992; JD, Columbia U., 1998. Bar: Colo. 1998, U.S. Dist. Ct. Colo. 1998. Assoc. Gibson Dunn & Crutcher, LLP, Denver, 1998—2003, 2005—; atty. Greenberg Traurig, LLP, Denver, 2004—05. Author: (screenplay) Off Center, 2001 (film festival finalist, 2002); contbr. articles to profl. jours. Vol. Denver Pub. Schs., 1998—. Fulbright scholar, Inst. Internat. Edn., Cologne, Germany, 1993—94, European law fellow, Columbia U., 1996—97. Mem.: ABA, Denver Bar Assn., Colo. Bar Assn., Internat. Bar Assn. Avocations: reading, writing, skiing, scuba diving, travel. Office: Gibson Dunn & Crutcher LLP 1801 Calif St Ste 4200 Denver CO 80202 Home Phone: 303-399-1188. Business E-Mail: hannaj@gtlaw.com, jhanna@gibsondunn.com.

HANNA, KATHRYN LURA, university administrator; b. Fairmont, Minn., Jan. 23, 1947; d. Russell George and Dorothy Jane (Buchner) Hanna; m. Jeffrey R. Hoelmer, June 10, 1968 (div. Dec. 1980). BA, Hamline U., 1969; MA, Mankato State U., 1971; PhD, U. Minn., 1999. Instr. biology U. Minn., Waseca, 1971-77, asst. prof., 1977-86, assoc. prof., 1986—, dir. arts & scis., 1990, vice chancellor acad. affairs, 1990-93, asst. dean Coll. Biol. Scis. St. Paul, 1993—99, assoc. dean Coll. Biol. Scis., 2000—01, dir. biology colloquium program, 2001—. V.p. membership Grad. Women in Sci., Mpls., 1993-97; mem. Commn. on Women, U. Minn., Mpls., 1988-97. Author: The New Bio Book, 1984; co-author: The Bio Book Too, 1984. Bd. dirs. Mpls. Coll. of Art and Design Assocs., 1991—, Minn. Acad. Sci., 2001–. Recipient Svc. award Sigma Delta Epsilon, 1989; named Outstanding Educator Adminstr. South Cen. Edn. Assn., 1991. Mem. AAAS, Assn. for Study of Higher Edn. Office: U Minn Coll Biol Scis 123 Synder Hall 1475 Gortner Ave Saint Paul MN 55108-6172 Home: 1816 Commerce Blvd Mound MN 55364-1127

HANNA, MARSHA L., artistic director; b. Tiffin, Ohio, Nov. 27, 1951; d. Willis Leondadis and Frances Lucille (Neeley) H. BS, Bowling Green State U., 1980. Drama specialist City of Dayton, Ohio, 1975-80; gen. mgr. Illumination Theatre, 1978-85; product analyst Lexis/Nexis, 1980—86; instr. Sinclair C.C., 1986—; freelance stage dir., 1986—; resident dir. Human Race Theatre Co., 1986—, artistic dir., 1990—. Dir.: Equus, 1981, Beyond Therapy, 1983, The Diviners, 1984, Amadeus, 1985,Getting Out, 1987, Orphans, 1988, Fool for Love, 1989, A Shayna Maidel, 1990, A Christmas Carol, 1991, Closer Than Ever, 1993, The Good Times Are Killing Me, 1994, Cloud Nine, 1995, Three Tall Women, 1996, The Cherry Orchard, 1996, Quilters, 1997, Taking Sides, Stonewall Jackson's House, 1998, On Golden Pond, 1999, Three Days of Rain, 1999, Art, 2000, Resident Alien, 2001, I Hate Hamlet, 2002, The Dazzle, 2003, Odd Couple, 2004, Every Good Boy Deserves Favour (with Dayton Philharmonic), Johnny Appleseed, Copenhagen, 2005, The Elephant Man, Moonlight and Magnolias, 2006. Office: The Human Race Theatre Co 126 N Main St Ste 300 Dayton OH 45402-1766 E-mail: Marsha@humanracetheatre.org.

HANNA, MICHAEL GEORGE, JR., immunologist, pharmaceutical executive; b. Cleve., July 7, 1936; s. Michael George and Camella (Karem) Hanna; m. Barbara Ann Pearson, Sept. 6, 1958; children: Michael George, Christina Louise, Suzanne Kathleen. BS in Biology, Baldwin-Wallace Coll., 1958; MS in Biology, Notre Dame U., 1960; PhD, U. Tenn., 1964; DSc (hon.), Baldwin-Wallace Coll., 2000. Rsch. biologist biology div. Oak Ridge Nat. Lab., 1964-68, dir. immunology carcinogenesis group, 1968-75; dir. cancer biology, head host tumor interaction sect. cancer biology program Nat. Cancer Inst. Frederick (Md.) Cancer Rsch. Facility, 1975-79, dir., 1979-82, Litton Inst. Applied Biotech., Rockville, Md., 1982-85; sr. v.p., COO Biotech. Rsch. Inst., Rockville, Md., 1985-94; pres., CEO PerImmune, Inc., Rockville, Md., 1994-98; founder, chmn., pres., chief sci. officer Intracel, Frederick, 1998—2002, chmn. emeritus, chief sci. officer, 2002—07; founder, chmn., CEO Vaccinogen Inc., 2007—. Cons. NASA Lunar Receiver Lab., 1968—70; chmn. tech. adv. com. biotech. U.S. Dept. Commerce, 1985—90; mem. working group biotech. U.S. Dept. Def., 1985—90; mem. bd. overseers Ctr. Advanced Rsch. Biotech., 1984—88; commencement spkr. Baldwin-Wallace Coll., 2000. Gen. editor: Contemporary Topics in Immunobiology, 1971—85, Vaccine Rsch., 1991—96, mem. editl. bd.: Immunopharmacology, 1978—2003, Cancer Rsch., 1978—92, Jour. Biol. Response Modifiers, 1982—2002, Cancer Metastasis, 1984—; contbr. articles of 300 to profl. jours. Chmn. local emergency planning com. homeland security Frederick County, 2002—04; trustee Baldwin-Wallace Coll., 1998—. Recipient Charles Thornton award, Litton Industries, 1984, Ohio Found. Ind. Colls. Career Excellence award, 2005. Mem.: Internat. Soc. Immunopharmacology (coun. 1991—), Am. Assn. Immunologists, Am. Assn. Cancer Rsch., Soc. Exptl. Pathology. Achievements include patents in field; development and registration for TICE-BCG treatment of bladder cancer; development of technology platform for Oncovax autologous tumor cell vaccine for treatment of stage II colon cancer. E-mail: mghannajr@gmail.com.

HANNA, NESSIM, marketing educator; b. Assiut, Egypt, Apr. 30, 1938; came to U.S., 1961, naturalized, 1973; s. Yanni and Lulu Shehata (Oweda) H.; m. Dana Lascu, Aug. 28, 1987 (div. 1988); m. Margaret Ann Curzan, 1996. BS in Commerce, Cairo U., 1958; MS in Mktg., U. Ill., 1964, PhD in Mktg, 1969. Asst. prof., chmn. dept. mktg. W.Va. Inst. Tech., Montgomery, 1968-69; asso. prof. bus. adminstrn. Mid. Tenn. State U., Murfreesboro, 1969-70; prof. mktg. No. Ill. U., De Kalb, 1970—98; mktg. cons. Arab Rsch. and Adminstrn. Ctr., 1975-77, Investments Cons. Internat., 1974-77; with Roosevelt U., Schaumburg, Ill., 2001—. Vis. prof. mktg. U. Petroleum and Minirals, Dharan, Saudi Arabia, 1980-81, Norwegian Sch. Mgmt., Oslo, 1988; chmn. dept. mktg., dir. research inst. King Saud U., Kassim, Saudi Arabia, 1983-84; vis. scholar Hong Kong Bapt. U., fall 1991. Author: Marketing Opportunities in Egypt: A Business Guide, 1977, Principles of Marketing, 1985, Pricing Policies and Procedures, 1995, Winning Strategies, 1991, Consumer Behavior: An Applied Approach, 2001, 2d edit., 2005; contbr. articles to profl. jours. Named Outstanding Citizen Citizenship Council Met. Chgo., 1974 Mem. Southwestern Social Sci. Assn., Am. Mktg. Assn., Midwest Bus. Adminstrn. Assn., Assn. Egyptian-Am. Scholars (treas.), Acad. Mktg. Sci., Am. Inst. Decision Scis., Phi Beta Lambda, Beta Gamma Sigma, Phi Kappa Phi, Alpha Mu Alpha. Republican. Christian Orthodox. Avocation: overseas travel. Home: Ste 2219 1900 Lincoln Vill Cr Larkspur CA 94939 Home Phone: 415-785-7937. Personal E-mail: nessimh@aol.com.

HANNA, NOREEN ANELDA, adult education educator, consultant; b. Napa, Calif., Nov. 28, 1939; d. Thomas James and Eileen Anelda (Jordan) H.; m. Leon O'bine Gotcher, Aug. 14, 1971 (div. Nov. 1980); children: John Allen, Tamara Kay. BA, San Francisco State U., 1963; postgrad., Sonoma State U., 1974-81, Ctr. for Leadership Devel., 1982-83; MA, U. San Francisco, 1989. Cert. gen. elem., specialist in reading, gen. adminstrv. svcs. Classroom tchr. Ullom Elem. Sch., Las Vegas, Nev., 1963, J. L. Shearer Elem. Sch., Napa, 1963-78, reading resource tchr., 1978-80; asst. prin. Napa Valley Adult Sch., Napa, 1980-81, acting prin., 1981-82; prin. El Centro Elem. Sch., Napa, 1982-83; adminstr. J.T.P.A./Gain Programs, Napa, 1983-90; prin. Napa Valley Adult Sch., Napa, 1983-99, ret., 1999; inst., curriculum for adult learners U.C. Berkley, 2001—. Commn. mem. Calif. Post Secondary Edn., 1987-89; adv. bd. dir. Ctr. for Adult Edn., San Francisco State U., 1988-95, Immigration Reform & Control Act, Sacramento, 1989-92; presenter, cons. in field. Exec. bd. dir. Leadership Napa Valley, 1985-93; sec. Leadership Napa Valley Found., 1988-99. State Edn. scholar Calif. PTA, 1976, Grad. Edn. scholar Delta Kappa Gamma, Napa, 1977; recipient Cmty. Leadership award Napa Valley Unified Sch. Dist., 1988, George C. Mann Discing. Svc. award Calif. Coun. for Adult Edn., 1994; named Outstanding Adult Edn. Adminstr., Calif. Adult Edn. Adminstrs. Assn., 1998. Mem. ASCD, Am. Assn. Adult and Continuing Edn., Assn. Calif. Sch. Adminstrs. (chair to state adult edn. com. 1988-1991, 93—95, state rep. assembly del. 1989-92, state adult edn. com. chairperson 1989-92, Adult Edn. Adminstr. of Yr. award 1992), Calif. Coun. Adult Edn. (North Coast chpt. bd. dir. 1988-99), Napa C. of C. (bd. dir. 1985-88, edn./bus. com. 1985-99, others), Correctional Educators Assn., Soroptimist Internat. of Napa, Napa Valley Historical Soc. (pres. 1999-01), Napa Valley Geneological and Bio. Soc. (chart. mem.), Phi Delta Kappa, Delta Kappa Gamma. Democrat. Roman Catholic. Avocations: needlepoint, reading, sailing, swimming, hot air ballooning. Home Phone: 707-252-4317; Office Phone: 707-315-1599. Personal E-mail: napalady1139@sbcglobal.net.

HANNA, TERRY ROSS, lawyer, small business owner; b. Wadsworth, Ohio, May 17, 1947; s. Harry Ross and Geraldine (Frensley) H.; m. Max Anna Hindes, Jan. 20, 1968; children: Travis, Taylor, Molly. BBA, U. Okla., 1968, JD, 1972; LLM, NYU, 1973; MA in Bibl Studies, Dallas Theol. Sem., 1988. Bar: Okla. 1972, U.S. Tax Ct. 1974, U.S. Ct. Appeals (10th cir.) 1979, U.S. Supreme Ct. 1989; CPA, Okla. Mem. McAfee & Taft, Oklahoma City, 1972-80; pres. P 356 Inc., Oklahoma City, 1980—; of counsel Crowe & Dunlevy, Oklahoma City, 1987—. Owner Mo Jo Video, 1995—; spl. lectr. Oklahoma City U. Sch. Law, 1974-75. Editor Okla. U. Law Rev., 1970-72. Mem. internat. com. Boy Scouts Am., 1988—; dir. U.S. Found. for Internat. Scouting, Irving, 1989—. Baden-Powell fellow World Scout Found., 1988—; recipient Silver Beaver award Boy Scouts Am., 1988. Mem.: Sports Lawyers Assn., Okla. Bar Assn. (pres. taxation sect. 1978—79), Order of Arrow (lodge advisor 1989—2003), Phi Delta Phi (magister 1972), Kappa Sigma (chpt. advisor 1974—75). Republican. Mem. Christian Ch. Avocations: coach, patch collector, fishing, golf, computers. Home: 2600 W Coffee Creek Rd Edmond OK 73003-3326 Office: Crowe & Dunlevy 1800 Mid America Towers Oklahoma City OK 73102 E-mail: HANNAT@crowedunlevy.com, terryhanna@aol.com.

HANNA, WILLIAM BROOKS, publishing executive, literary agent; b. Montreal, Can., Feb. 22, 1936; s. George Spencer and Phyllis Edith (Brooks) H.; children: Catherine Frances, Philip Spencer; m. Frances Ann Gerhardt, Nov. 20, 1982. Grad., Upper Can. Coll., 1954; BA in Modern History, U. Toronto, 1958. Successively coll. sales mgr., sch. sales mgr., editor-in-chief Collier-Macmillan-Can., Ltd., 1958-65; pres. Pergamon of Can., Ltd., also dep. chmn. bd. Toronto, 1967-68; exec. v.p., dir. Pergamon Press, Inc., 1966-68; v.p., dir. Burns & MacEachern, Ltd., Toronto, 1968-70; pres., dir. GLC Pubs., Toronto, 1970-75; pres., chief exec. officer, dir. Holt Rinehart & Winston of Can., Ltd., Toronto, 1975-78; pub. joint UNICEF/Red Cross Com. for 1979 Internat. Yr. of Child, 1978-79; v.p. Gen. Pub. Co. Ltd., Toronto, 1979—84, Stoddart Pub. Co. Ltd., Toronto, 1984—2000, Acacia House Pub. Svcs. Ltd., 2001—. Chmn. convocation Trinity Coll., U. Toronto, 1994-96, trustee 1996-2002; chmn. export com. Can. Book Publ. Coun., 1993-95. Recipient Arbor award, U. Toronto, 1998. Mem. Assn. Can. Pubs. (rep. to 25th Congress of Internat. Assn. Publs., dir. CANCOPY 1997-98, co-chmn. copyright com. 1998-2000), Faculty Club U. Toronto, Royal Can. Mil. Inst. Home and Office: 62 Chestut Ave Brantford ON Canada N3T 4C2 Business E-Mail: bhanna.acacia@rogers.com.

HANNA, WILLIAM JOHNSON, electrical engineering educator; b. Longmont, Colo., Feb. 7, 1922; s. William Grant and Anna Christina (Johnson) H.; m. Katherine Fagan, Apr. 25, 1944 (dec. 1993); children: Daniel August, Paul William; m. Helen Yeager McCarty, Sept. 19, 1996. BSEE, U. Colo., 1943, MS, 1948, D in Elec. Engring., 1951. Registered profl. engr., Colo., Kans. Mem. faculty U. Colo., 1946-91, prof. elec. engring., 1962-91, prof. emeritus, 1991—; ret., 1991. Cons. in field; mem. Colo. Bd. Engring. Examiners, 1973-85; with Ponderosa Assocs., Lafayette, Colo. Author articles, reports. Served to 1st lt. AUS, 1943-46. Recipient Faculty Recognition award Students Assn. U. Colo., 1956, 61, Alfred J. Ryan award, 1978, Archimedes award Calif. Soc. Profl. Engrs., 1978, Outstanding Engring. Alumnus award U. Colo., 1983, Faculty Service award, 1983; named Colo. Engr. of Yr. Profl. Engrs. Colo., 1968; named to Hon. Order of Ky. Cols. Mem. IEEE, Am. Soc. Engring. Edn., Nat. Soc. Profl. Engrs. (pres. Colo. 1967-68), Nat. Coun. Engring. Examiners (pres. 1977-78, Disting. Svc. award with spl. commendation 1990), AIEE (chmn. Denver 1961-62) Clubs: Masons. Republican. Presbyterian. Home and Office: 27 Silver Spruce Nederland Star Rt Boulder CO 80302-9604 Office Phone: 307-666-8112. *Honors and awards I have received are but a reflection of the character of my friends and associates. To them and my family go the accolades.*

HANNAFORD, PETER DOR, public relations executive, writer; b. Glendale, Calif., Sept. 21, 1932; s. Donald R. and Elinor (Nielsen) H.; m. Irene Dorothy Harville, Aug. 14, 1954; children: Richard H., Donald R. II. AB, U. Calif., 1954. Acct. exec. Helen A. Kennedy Advt., 1957; v.p. Kennedy-Hannaford, Inc., San Francisco and Oakland, Calif., 1957-62, pres., 1962-67, Pettler & Hannaford, Inc., Oakland, Calif., 1967-69; v.p. Wilton, Coombs & Colnett, Inc., 1969-72; pres. Hannaford & Assoc., Oakland, Calif., 1973; asst. to Gov. of Calif., Calif.; dir. pub. affairs Gov. Office, Calif., 1974; chmn. bd. Hannaford Co., Inc. (formerly Deaver & Hannaford, Inc.), 1975-95; pub. Ferndale Enterprise, Calif., 1996-98; pres. Hannaford Enterprises Inc., 1998—; sr. counselor APCO Worldwide, 2001—. Vice chmn. Calif. Gov. Consumer Fraud Task Force, 1972—73; bd. dirs. Eberle Comms. Group Inc. Author: The Reagans: A Political Portrait, 1983, Talking Back to the Media, 1986 (Japanese edit. 1990); co-author: Remembering Reagan, 1994, Recollections of Reagan, 1997, My Heart Goes Home: A Hudson Valley Memoir, 1997, The Quotable Ronald Reagan, 1998, The Essential George Washington, 1999, The Quotable Calvin Coolidge, 2000, Ronald Reagan and His Ranch, 2002. Mem. Alameda County Rep. Ctrl. Com., Rep. State Ctrl. Com. Calif., 1968-74, Commonwealth Fund's Commn. on Elderly People Living Alone, 1986-91; Rep. nominee for U.S. Congress, 1972; governing bd. Tahoe Regional Planning Agy., 1973-74; trustee White House Preservation Fund, 1981-89, pub. rels. adv. com. USIA, 1981-92; adv. com. Mt. Vernon 1991-96; fin. adv. commn. City of Eureka, Calif., 2007—. 1st lt. Signal Corps, U.S. Army, 1954-56. Shapiro fellow, George Washington U. Sch. Media and pub. affairs, 2002. Mem.: Author's Guild, Bohemian Club, Cosmos Club, Theta Xi. Presbyterian. Office: 3555 J St Eureka CA 95503 Personal E-mail: hannafordwashdc@aol.com.

HANNAH, DARYL, actress; b. Chgo., Dec. 3, 1960; d. Don and Sue Hannah. BA, U. So. Calif.; student, Goodman Theater Co., Chgo. Ind. actress, 1978—. Films include The Fury, 1978, The Final Terror, 1981, Hard Country, 1981, Summer Lovers, 1982, Blade Runner, 1982, Reckless, 1984, Splash, 1984, The Pope of Greenwich Village, 1984, The Clan of the Cave Bear, 1986, Legal Eagles, 1986, Roxanne, 1987, Wall Street, 1988, High Spirits, 1988, Steel Magnolias, 1989, Crimes and Misdemeanors, 1989, Crazy People, 1990, At Play in the Fields of the Lord, 1991, Memoirs of an Invisible Man, 1992, Grumpy Old Men, 1993, The Little Rascals, 1994, A Hundred and One Nights, 1995, The Tie that Binds, 1995, Grumpier Old Men, 1995, Two Much, 1996, The Last Days of Frankie the Fly, 1996, the Real Blonde, 1997, Gun, 1997, The Gingerbread Man, 1998, Hi-Life, 1998, Tripwire, 1999, Wild Flowers, 1999, Hearts and Bones, 1999, Speedway Junky, 1999, My Favorite Martian, 1999, Enemy of My Enemy, 1999, Dancing at the Blue Iquand, 2000, Diplomatic Siege, 1999, Cord, 2000, Cowboy Up, 2001, Jackpot, 2001, A Walk to Remember, 2002, Run for the Money, 2002, Bank, 2002, Northfork, 2003, The Job, 2003, The Big Empty, 2003, Casa de los babys, 2003, Kill Bill: Volume 1, 2003, Kill Bill: Volume 2, 2004, Silver City, 2004, Careful What You Wish For, 2004, Lucky 13, 2005; (TV films) Paper Dolls, 1982, Attack of the 50 Foot Woman, 1993, The Last Don, 1997, The Last Don II, 1998, Rescuers: Stories of Courage: Two Families, 1998, Addams Family Reunion (voice), 1998, Rear Window, 1998, Hard Target, 2000, Jack and the Beanstalk: The Real Story, 2001; prodr, dir.(feature films), Strip Notes, 2001; (short films) The Last Supper (Jury award for Best Short, Berlin Internat. Film Festival, 1994), 1994. Office: c/o UTA 9560 Wilshire Blvd #500 Beverly Hills CA 90212

HANNAH, DAVID H., metal products executive; BSBA, U. So. Calif. CPA. Mgr. audit divsn. Ernst & Whinney, LA, 1973-81; CFO Reliance Steel & Aluminum, LA, 1981-87, v.p., 1987-92, dir., exec. v.p., CFO, 1992-95, pres., 1995—2002, CEO, 1999—. Office: Reliance Steel & Aluminum Ste 5100 350 S Grand Ave Los Angeles CA 90071 Office Phone: 213-687-7700. Office Fax: 213-687-8792.*

HANNAH, JAMES, state supreme court justice; b. Dec. 26, 1944; BSBA in Acctg., U. Ark., JD. Pvt. practice Lightle, Tedder, Hannah & Beebe; city atty. City of Searcy, Ark., 1969—78; juvenile judge White County, 1976—78; chancery,probate judge 17th Jud. Dist., 1979—99; assoc. justice Supreme Ct. Ark., 2001—04, chief justice, 2004—. Faculty adv. Nat. Jud. Coll. Former chmn. of bd. of adv. Wilbur Mills Alcoholism Treatment Ctr. Mem.: Ark. Bar Assn., Ark. Jud. Coun., Ark. Bd. of Pardons and Paroles (sec. 1972—79), White County Bar Assn. (former pres., treas., sec.), Am. Judges Assn. Office: Ark Supreme Ct Justice Bldg Rm 230 625 Marshall St Little Rock AR 72201 Business E-Mail: jim.hannah@arkansas.gov.*

HANNAH, JOHN P., federal official; b. Jan. 5, 1962; m. Laura Hannah. BA, Duke U., 1984; JD, Yale U. Bar: 2000. Dep. dir. Wash. Inst. for Near Ea. Policy, Washington; aide Office of Arms Control and Internat. Security US Dept State, Washington; dep. nat. security advisor to v.p. The White House, Washington, 2001—05, asst. to v.p. for nat. security affairs, 2005—. Office: The White House 1600 Pennsylvania Ave Washington DC 20500

HANNAH, JUDY CHALLENGER, private education tutor; b. Balt., Oct. 8, 1948; d. John Thomas and Doris Rose (Etherington) Diehl; m. Brian Challenger, Apr. 15, 1968 (div. Dec. 1994); children: John Joseph, Jennifer Elizabeth; m. W. P. Hannah, Oct. 6, 2001. AA, Arlington Bible Coll., 1985; BS, Liberty U., Lynchburg, Va., 1991; M in Edn., Mt. St. Mary's Coll., 1996; Diploma, Inst. of Children's Lit., 1997; postgrad., Regent U., Va., 2005—. Cert. elem. tchr. Md., 1996. Tchr., K-4 Mill Valley Sch., Owing Mills, Md., 1984—85, Arlington Bapt. Sch., Balt., 1985—86, Mill Valley Sch., 1986—87; bookkeeper, sec. Challenger Engr., Inc., Finksburg, 1987—92; dir. B/A child care ABC Care Inc., 1992—95; tchr. internship Thurmont Elem. Sch., Md., 1995—96; tutor/office mgr. Learning Resources, Westminster, Md., 1996—97; pvt. tutor, owner A Lesson Learned, Inc., Union Bridge, Md., 1997—. Mem. delegation People to People Amb. Programs, China, 2001, Global Peace Mission, People to People Internat., Egypt, 2003. Vol. Crisis Hotline, Balt., 1972, leader/tchr. Pioneer Girls Internat., Arlington Bapt. Ch., 1975-78. Recipient Plato award, Internat. Biog. Ctr. Eng., 2006, Tchg. award, St. Catherine's, Oxford U., Eng., 2006. Mem. Md. Emmaus, Internat. Dyslexia Assn., Smithsonian Inst., Vol. in Missions, Pi Lamba Theta, People To People Internat. Republican. Avocations: writing, hiking. Home: 48 Bucher John Rd Union Bridge MD 21791-9527 Personal E-mail: judyhannah@verizon.net.

HANNAH, LAWRENCE BURLISON, lawyer; b. Urbana, Ill., Aug. 5, 1943; s. Lawrence Hugh and Margaret Alene (Burlison) H.; 1 child, Scott David. BA, Dartmouth Coll., 1965; JD cum laude, U. Pa., 1968. Bar: Wash. 1971, U.S. Dist. Ct. (we. dist.) Wash. 1971, Ct. of Appeals (9th cir.) 1971, U.S. Supreme Ct. 1990. Analyst U.S. Central Intelligence Agency, Langley, Va., 1969-71; ptnr. Perkins Coie, Bellevue, Wash., 1971—. Contbr. articles to profl. jours. Mem. King County Personnel Bd., Wash., 1984-90; mem. fin. com. Mcpl. Gov. Candidates, King County, 1972—. 1st lt. USAF, 1968-69. Mem. ABA, Wash. State Bar Assn., Seattle-King County Bar Assn. Methodist. Avocations: jogging, boating, tennis. Home: 1611 103rd Ave SE Bellevue WA 98004-7002 Office: 10885 NE 4th St Ste 700 Bellevue WA 98004 Home Phone: 425-455-4632; Office Phone: 425-635-1401. Business E-Mail: hannl@perkinscoie.com.

HANNAH, WAYNE ROBERTSON, JR., lawyer; b. Freeport, Ill., Aug. 18, 1931; s. Wayne Robertson and Edith (Biene) H.; m. Patricia Anne Matthews, June 1, 1957; children— Tamara Lee, Wendy, Wayne Robertson III BA, Ill. Coll., 1953; JD, NYU, 1957. Bar: Ill. 1957, U.S. Dist. Ct. (no. dist.) Ill., U.S. Supreme Ct. Ptnr. Sonnenschein, Nath & Rosenthal, Chgo., 1965—. Dir. Checker Motors Corp., N.Y.C. and Kalamazoo, 1982-86; lectr. Ill. Inst. Continuing Edn. Sec. 7th cir. Root-Tilden Scholarship Program NYU, 1967-94; chmn. Root-Tilden-Kern scholarship com., 1981-86, trustee law ctr., 1985—; pres. bd. Firman Cmty. Svcs, Chgo., 1972-75; trustee, pres., chmn. bd. Chgo. City Ballet, 1982-86. 2d lt. USMC, 1951-54. Fulbright scholar, 1953—54, Root-Tilden scholar, NYU, 1954—57. Mem. ABA (real estate com.), Chgo. Bar Assn. (chmn. condominium subcom. real estate com. 1977-78, sec., dir. condominium assn. 1991—), Ill. Bar Assn. (real estate com.), Econ. Club (Chgo.), Skokie Country Club (Glencoe, Ill.). Presbyterian. Avocations: tennis, golf. Office: Sonnenschein Nath and Rosenthal 233 S Wacker Dr Ste 8000 Chicago IL 60606-6491 Home Phone: 847-446-7409; Office Phone: 312-876-8045. Business E-Mail: whannah@sonnenschein.com.

HANNAMAN, ALBERTA ANNA, artist; b. Passaic, NJ, Dec. 11, 1932; d. Henry George and Alice Edith Hannaman. Student, Newark Sch. Fine & Indsl. Art, 1950-53. Offset stripper Screenline Photo, NYC, 1956-84, Verilen Graphics, NYC, 1984-87; offset stripper inhouse printing dept. DDB Needham Worldwide, NYC, 1987-88, Screen Images, NYC, 1988-91. Poet, artist: Prince of Flowers, 1987; contbr. articles to poetry anthologies; exhibited in group shows at Del Bello Gallery, Toronto, Ont., Can., 1988-91, The Miniature Painters, Sculptors and Gravers Soc., Washington, 1990, 91, 98-2006, Long Beach Island Art Gallery, Surf City, NJ, 1990, 91, 98, 2003-06.

HANNAY, WILLIAM MOUAT, III, lawyer; b. Kansas City, Mo., Dec. 3, 1944; s. William Mouat and Gladys (Capron) H.; m. Donna Jean Harkins, Sept. 30, 1978; children: Capron Grace, Blaike Ann, William Mouat IV. BA, Yale U., New Haven, Conn., 1966; JD, Georgetown U., Washington, DC, 1973. Bar: Mo. 1973, DC 1974, NY 1975, Ill. 1980. Law clk. to Judge Myron Bright US Ct. Appeals, 8th Cir., St. Louis, 1973-74; law clk. to Justice Tom Clark US Supreme Ct., Washington, 1974-75; assoc. Weil Gotshal & Manges, NYC, 1975-77; asst. dist. atty. NY County Dist. Atty.'s Office, NYC, 1977-79; ptnr. Schiff Hardin LLP, Chgo., 1979. Adj. prof. IIT/Chgo.-Kent Law Sch., 1983—. Author: International Trade: Avoiding Criminal Risks, 1994, Designing an Effective Antitrust Compliance Program, rev. 2006, Tying Arrangements, rev. 2006, International Antitrust Enforcement, rev. 2006; contbr. articles to profl. jours. Chmn. bd. dirs. Gilbert and Sullivan Soc. Chgo., 1984-87, Served with US Army, 1967-68, Vietnam. Mem. ABA (chmn. sect. internat. law and practice 1998-99, chmn. Africa law initiative coun. 2000-02, mem. ho. of dels. 2001-06), Chgo Bar Assn. (chmn. antitrust com. 1986-87), Yale Club (pres. 1987-89), Chgo. Yacht Club, Union League Club (Chgo.), Am. Law Inst. Democrat. Episcopalian. Home: 591 Plum Tree Rd Barrington IL 60010-2329 Office: Schiff Hardin LLP 7200 Sears Tower Chicago IL 60606 Home Phone: 847-381-8464; Office Phone: 312-258-5617. Business E-Mail: whannay@schiffhardin.com.

HANNEMAN, LEROY C., JR., real estate executive; married; 2 children. BS in Constrn. Engring., Ariz. State U. Estimator Del Webb Corp., Sun City, 1972, v.p. housing, 1984, exec. v.p., 1996, pres., COO, Phoenix, 1998—2001, CEO, 1999—2001; co-founder, CEO Element Homes, 2003—. Office: Element Homes One Gateway 426 N 44th St Ste 204 Phoenix AZ 85008

HANNEMAN, RODNEY ELTON, metallurgical engineer; b. Spokane, Wash., Mar. 14, 1936; s. Christie Luther and Viva Helen (Sugrue) H.; married; 3 children. BS in Phys. Metallurgy, Wash. State U., Pullman, 1959; MS in Metallurgy, MIT, Cambridge, 1961, PhD, 1964; grad., GE Mgmt. Devel. Inst., 1979. With GE Co., Schenectady, 1963-81, mgr. materials characterization lab., 1977-80, mgr. materials programs, 1980-81; v.p. research, devel. and energy resources Reynolds Metals Co., Richmond, Va., 1981-85, v.p. quality assurance and tech. op., 1985-98; dir. Face Internat., 1988—2002; chmn. Aluminum Assn. Tech. Comm., 1989—97; pres. Mgmt. and Tech. Consultants, Richmond, Va., 1998—2002. Mem. vis. com. dept. materials sci. and engring. MIT, 1975—80, mem. adv. bd. Materials Processing Ctr, 1980—97; mem. adv. bd. U. Va., 1982—87, chmn. indsl. adv. bd. grad. engring. program, 1983—86; chmn. rsch. coordinating coun. Gas Rsch. Inst., 1985—87, adv. coun., 1988—2001; bd. dirs. Materials Properties Coun., 1982—90; mem. adv. com. Va. Ctr. for Innovative Tech., 1999—2002; adv. bd. Commonwealth Grad. Engring., Richmond, 1996—2006. Exec. v.p. found. bd. Sci. Mus. Va., 1989—; v.p. Civic Assn., 1990-92. Recipient Alumni Achievement award Wash. State U., 1978; Joint Engring. Coun. award, 1984 Mem. AIME, MAPI, SAE, Am. Soc. Metals (Geisler award 1971, Engring. Materials Achievement award 1973), Am. Chem. Soc. (Chem. Innovator award 1970, Edison medallion 1979), Indsl. Rsch. Inst., Sigma Xi. Achievements include patents in field.

HANNEMANN, MUFI, mayor; b. Honolulu, July 16, 1954; s. Gustav and Faiaso Hannemann; m. Gail Hannemann. BA with honors, Harvard Univ.; graduate degree, Victoria Univ., New Zealand. Former v.p. C. Brewer Hawaiian Juices, C. Brewer & Co.; former staff asst. V.P. George H.W. Bush; chmn. City Coun., Honolulu, 1995—2000; mayor City of Honolulu, Hawaii, 2005—. Mem. President's Council on 21st Century Workforce, 2004, U.S. Secy. Labor Adv. Comm. on Apprenticeship, 2005; former dir. Hawaii Dept. Bus., Econ. Develop. & Tourism, Hawaii Off. Internat. Relations. Office: Office of the Mayor 530 S King St Honolulu HI 96813 E-mail: mayor@honolulu.gov.*

HANNERS, G(ARY) DALE, retired psychological mental health professional; b. Leachville, Ark., Sept. 16, 1942; BS, Memphis State U., 1966; MS, Ark. State U., 1968; PhD, U. Memphis, 1995. Lic. psychol. examiner, Ark.; cert. sch. psychologist. Tchr. Memphis Pub. Schs., 1964-65; with personnel dept. Sears, Roebuck and Co., Memphis, 1965-66; supr. client svcs. Abilities Unltd., Jonesboro, 1966-70; rehab. counselor State of Ark., Jonesboro, 1970-74, psychol. examiner, 1979—; psychologist, human resources cons., 1994—. Pvt. practice cons. human svcs., Ark., 1970-79; cons. Little People Am., Calif. Mem. APA (assoc.), Ark. Psychol. Assn., Ark. Sch. Psychol. Assn., Civitan (sec.-treas. Jonesboro chpt. 1967-70). Republican. Baptist. Avocations: music, reading, farming, landscaping. Home: 2113 Club Cv Jonesboro AR 72401-6100 E-mail: d0916@webtv.net.

HANNES, MARTIN ROY, telecommunications company executive; b. Sydney, NSW, Australia, Mar. 10, 1950; s. Jack Dieter and Morna Jean (Houghton) H.; m. Diana Elizabeth Sutton, Jan. 21, 1989; children: William, Amelia. B in Engring., Sydney U., 1973; MBA, Harvard U., 1978. Exec. v.p. Baia Corp., Jackson, Mich., 1979-86; mng. dir. Hanimex Corp., Sydney, 1984-86; CEO Palcolor Ltd., Sydney, 1985-86, 91-93; sr. v.p. Continental Cablevision Asia Pacific, 1996-99; mng. dir. USWest Asia Pacific, 1999—. Dir. Singapore Cablevision Ltd., Trans Nat. Investments Ltd., Hong Kong, Hanset Pty. Ltd., Road Runner Internat. Fellow Australian Inst. Dirs., Australian Inst. Mgmt.; mem. Inst. Engrs. Australia, Australian Inst. Mgmt., Harvard Club (Boston), Royal Prince Alfred Club (Newport, Australia), Yacht Club. Avocations: skiing, yachting, tennis, golf. Home: 4520 Foxhall Crescent Washington DC 20007 Office: 13241 Woodland Park Dr Round Hill VA 20141 E-mail: mhannes@attglobal.net.

HANNIG, GARY L., state representative; b. Litchfield, Ill., July 22, 1952; m. Elizabeth Hannig. BS, U. Ill., Champaign, 1974. CPA. Mem. Ill. Ho. of Reps., 1978—, asst. majority leader, 1997—2005, dep. majority leader, 2005—. Mem. Holy Family Cath. Ch. Mem.: NRA, Wolfpack Antique Car Club, Macoupin County Hist. Soc., K. of C., Benld Croation Lodge. Democrat. Office: 300 Capitol Bldg Springfield IL 62706 Address: 218 S Macoupin St PO Box 8 Gillespie IL 62033

HANNIGAN, ALYSON, actress; b. Washington, Mar. 24, 1974; m. Alexis Denisof, Oct. 11, 2003. Actor: (films) My Stepmother Is an Alien, 1988, Dead Man on Campus, 1998, American Pie, 1999, Boys and Girls, 2000, American Pie 2, 2001, Beyond the City Limits, 2001, American Wedding, 2003, Date Movie, 2006; (TV films) Switched at Birth, 1991, The Stranger Beside Me, 1995, A Case for Life, 1996, For My Daughter's Honor, 1996, Hayley Wagner, Star, 1999; (TV series) Free Spirit, 1989—90, Buffy the Vampire Slayer, 1997—2003, How I Met Your Mother, 2005—; guest star Picket Fences, 1992, Roseanne, 1988, Touched by an Angel, 1994, The Torkelsons, 1991. Office: c/o Innovative Artists 1505 10th St Santa Monica CA 90401

HANNIGAN, ROBYN E., science educator, researcher; BS, Coll. NJ, 1988; MS in Geology, SUNY, Buffalo, 1994; MS in Geochemisty, Univ. Rochester, 1995, PhD in Earth and Environ. Sciences, 1997. Chemist NJ Dept. Health, 1988—89; head tchg. asst., dept. geological sciences SUNY, Buffalo, 1989—92, rsch. asst., dept. geological sciences, 1992—93; rsch. asst., dept. earth and environ. sci. Univ. Rochester, 1995—97; asst. prof. chemistry, dept. chemistry & physics Ark. State Univ., 2000—03, dir., McNair Scholars Program, 2003—05, assoc. prof. chemistry, 2003—, Judd Hill Chair, dir. grad. program Environ. Sciences, 2005—; chief scientific officer Hyphenated Solutions, 2005—. Adj. faculty, dept. liberal arts Rochester Inst. Tech., 1995—97; adj. asst. prof. chemistry, dept. chemistry Old Dominion Univ., 2000—03; Also Leopold Leadership Program fellow, 2001—; chair Consortium of Universities for the Advancement of Hydrologic Sciences, Edn. and Outreach, 2002—; mem. NAS Bd. on Earth Sciences and Resources, 2003—, NSF DBI REU Leadership Coun., 2003—, NSF, REU Biol. Sciences Leadership Coun., 2004—; US Delegate Internat. Geologic Congress, 2003; mem. environ. geology adv. bd. Am. Geological Inst., 2003—; dir. Rsch. Internships in Sci. of the Environment, 2003—; adj. assoc. prof. physiology and biophysics U. Ark. Med. Sch., 2006—; adj. grad. faculty, dept. civil engring. Univ. Memphis, 2006—; spkr. in field. Contbr. articles to profl. jours. Recipient Awardee, Jonesboro C. of C. Women in Bus., 2006, award for Encouraging Disadvantaged Students into Careers in Chemical Sciences, Am. Chem. Soc., 2007; Ford Found. Minority Dissertation Fellow, 1995—97. Mem.: European Virtual Inst. for Speciation Analysis, European Assn. of Geochemistry, Soc. for Environ. Toxicology and Chemistry, Am. Chem. Soc.- Geochemistry Divsn., Geochemical Soc., Geological Soc. Am.- Hydrogeology Divsn., Am. Geophysical Union- Biogeosciences Sect., AAAS (geochemical soc. rep. 2001—05), Faculty of 1000 Biology-Marine and Freshwater Ecology, Phi Kappa Phi. Achievements include patents in field; patents pending in field. Office: Ark State Univ PO Box 847 Environmental Science ABI 207 State University AR 72467 Office Phone: 870-680-4360, 870-972-2007. Office Fax: 870-680-4347. Business E-Mail: hannigan@astate.edu.*

HANNING, GARY WILLIAM, utilities executive, consultant, water transportation executive; b. Sherman, Tex., Aug. 30, 1942; s. William Homer and Mary Maxine (Harshbarger) H.; m. Robin Dale Smith, June 8, 1974 (div. 2005); children: Tony William, TJ, Lorissa Diane. BS, Rollins Coll., 1974; MBA, Stetson U., 1976. Mgr., co-owner Hanning Water Systems, Denison, Tex., 1963-66; engring. technician Gen. Dynamics, Ft. Worth, 1966-67; engr. supr. Bendix Field, Pasadena, Calif., 1967-70; engr. Philco-Ford Corp., Cape Kennedy, Fla., 1970-73, Jet Propulsion Lab., Pasadena, 1973-74; sect. mgr. Planning Rsch. Corp., Kennedy Space Ctr., 1974-77; pres. S.S.S. Water Systems, Inc., Denison, 1978-83, Texoma Svcs. Corp., Pottsboro, Tex., 1980-99, Tanglewood Water Co., 1994-99; exec. Tecon Water Cos. Inc., 1999—2004. Bd. dirs. Boy Scouts Am., Circle Ten, Dallas; entrepreneur Bells Discount Supply, Tex., 1983-87; adv. bd. Expresiv Techs., Austin, 2000-03. Contbr. articles to profl. jours. Mem. City Coun., Pottsboro, Tex., 1992-98. With USN, 1960-63. Mem. State Bar Tex. (grievance com. 2000-02), Tanglewood Golf Assn. (sec.-treas. 1992-96), Am. Legion, C. of C. Mem. Ch. of Christ. Avocations: inventing, camping, reading, golf, boating, hunting. Home and Office: 27 Ellen Dr Pottsboro TX 75076-3305

HANNON, BRUCE MICHAEL, engineering educator; b. Champaign, Ill., Aug. 14, 1934; s. Walter Leo and Kathleen Rose (Phalen) H.; m. Patricia Claire Coffey, Aug. 11, 1956; children: Claire, Laura, Brian. BSCE, U. Ill., 1956, MS in Engring. Mechanics, 1966, PhD in Engring. Mechanics, 1970. Engr. with chem. industry, 1957-66; instr. U. Ill., Urbana, 1966-71, assoc. prof. energy rsch., 1974-83, prof. regional sci., 1983—, Jubilee prof. liberal arts and scis., 1991—. Vis. prof. Nat. Ctr. for Supercomputing Applications; cons. NSF, NAS, NAE, chem. industry, various fed. energy agys; patentee in field. Contbr. articles to profl. jours. 1st lt. C.E. AUS, 1956-57. Named Engring. Tchr. of Yr., U. Ill., 1970, Man of Yr., Sierra Club, 1971; recipient 1st prize Mitchell Award Club of Rome, 1975. Home: 1208 W Union St Champaign IL 61821-3229 Office: U Ill 220 Daven Hall Urbana IL 61801 Office Phone: 217-333-0348. Business E-Mail: bhannon@uiuc.edu.

HANNON, GERARD V., lawyer; b. London, Oct. 9, 1951; s. Charles Stephen and Mary (McHugh) Hannon; m. Anne Theresa Murtagh, July 30, 1988; children: Charles Patrick, Martin James, Erin Mary. BA magna cum laude, Queen's Coll., NYC, 1974; JD cum laude, Fordham U., 1977. Bar: NY 1978, US Dist. Ct. (ea. dist.) NY 1978, US Dist. Ct. (so. dist.) NY 1978, US Supreme Ct. 1987. Assoc. Milbank Tweed Hadley & McCloy, NYC, 1977—82, Parker Chapin EW, NYC, 1982—84; ptnr. Coudert Bros. LLP, NYC, 1984—2005, Baker & McKenzie LLP, NYC, 2005—. Adj. prof. Columbia U. Grad. Sch. Bus., NYC, 1989; mem. adv. bd. Fordham U. Sch. Law, NYC, First Am. Title Ins. Co. N.Y., NYC. Mem. adv. bd. St. Anglia Merci Sch., NYC. Mem.: ABA, Assn. Bar City N.Y., N.Y. State Bar Assn., Japan Soc., Cornell Club N.Y., Phi Beta Kappa. Avocations: tennis, travel. Office: Baker & McKenzie LLP 1114 Avenue of Americas New York NY 10036 Office Phone: 212-626-4700. Office Fax: 212-310-1625. Business E-Mail: gerard.v.hannon@bakernet.com.

HANNON, GREGORY J., biology professor, researcher; BA in Biochemistry, Case Western Reserve U., PhD, 1992. Prof. Watson Sch. Biol. Sciences, Cold Spring Harbor Lab., Cold Spring Harbor, NY; investigator Howard Hughes Inst., 2005—. Contbr. articles to profl. jours. Recipient Am. Assn. for Cancer Rsch. award for Outstanding Achievement in Cancer Rsch., 2005, US Army Breast Cancer Rsch. Program Innovator award, NAS award in Molecular Biology, 2007; Pew Scholar in Biomedical Sciences, 1997. Office: Watson Sch Biol Sciences Cold Spring Harbor Lab 1 Bungtown Rd Cold Spring Harbor NY 11724 Office Phone: 516-367-8455. Office Fax: 516-367-8874. Business E-Mail: hannon@cshl.edu.*

HANNON, PATRICIA ANN, library director; b. Passaic, NJ, Jan. 1, 1947; d. L. Robert and Frances Laurent Hannon. BA in Math., Caldwell Coll., 1968; MLS, L.I. U., 1972. Libr. Hackensack Pub. Libr., NJ, 1968-75; dir. Wood-Ridge Pub. Libr., NJ, 1975-81, Wanaque Pub. Libr., NJ, 1983-84, Oakland Pub. Libr., NJ, 1984-88, Emerson Pub. Libr., NJ, 1988—2005, W. Milford Twp. Libr., NJ, 2005—. Pres. St. Joseph's Parish Coun., E. Rutherford, NJ, 1979, Regency Pk. Condominium Assn., Ramsey, NJ, 1990-91. Named Outstanding Young Women of Am., 1977. Mem.: Highlands Regional Libr. Coop. (pres. 1999—2001), Bergen County Libr. Coop. Sys. (pres. 1988, 1997), NJ Libr. Assn. (pres. 2003—04), Emerson C. of C. (sec. 1992—94, 1997—2002), Beta Phi Mu. Avocations: guitar, needlepoint houses. Office: Director W Milford Township Libr West Milford NJ 07480 Office Phone: 973-728-2824. Business E-Mail: hannon@wmtl.org.

HANNON, TIMOTHY PATRICK, lawyer, judge, educator; b. Culver City, Calif., Nov. 29, 1948; s. Justin Aloysius and Ann Elizabeth (Ford) Hannon; m. Patricia Ann Hanson, May 1, 1976; children: Sean Patrick, James Patrick. Student, U. Vienna, 1968-69, Naval War Coll., 1988; BA, U. Santa Clara, 1970, JD cum laude, 1974; cert. phase I, Air Command Staff and Coll., 2004; student in Law, U. London, 2004—. Bar: Calif. 1974, U.S. Dist. Ct. (no. dist.) Calif. 1974, U.S. Dist. Ct. (so. dist.) Calif. 1978, U.S. Ct. Appeals (9th cir.) 1978, U.S. Ct. Appeals Armed Forces 1979, DC 1981, U.S. Tax Ct. 1983, U.S. Ct. Claims 1983, cert.: Uniform Code Mil. Justice (trail and def. lawyer); pilot with tailwheel endorsement FAA. Assoc. N. Perry Moerdyke, Jr., Palo Alto, Calif., 1975-81; ptnr. Moerdyke & Hannon, Palo Alto, 1982-84, Attwood, Hurst, Knox & Anderson, 1984-86; pvt. practice Campbell, Calif., 1986-97; U.S. Adminstrv. law judge Social Security Adminstrn., 1997—. Instr. U. Calif., Santa Cruz, 1982—83, San Jose State U., 1985—89, De Anza Jr. Coll., Cupertino, Calif., 1987—97; lectr. Lincoln Law Sch., San Jose, Calif., 1988—97; arbitrator Santa Clara County Superior Ct., Santa Clara Mcpl. Ct.; sr. mil. mem. Interant. Mil. Edn. Tng., Uganda, 1995; judge pro temp Santa Clara County Mcpl. Ct.; commr. Navy & Marine Corps Ct. Criminal Appeals, 2001—02, mil. appellate judge, 2006—07; lectr. in field. Chmn. Menlo Park Housing Commn., 1979—81; allocations com. vol. United Way Clara County, 1987—90; mem. San Jose Vets. Meml. Com., 1993—99, treas., 1996—99; elected as force judge advocate Operation Bright Star, 2003. With Calif. N.G. US Army, 1970—76, capt. USNR, 1979—, adm. Tex. Navy, 1998, appellate mil. judge Navy and Marine Corps Ct. Criminal Appeals, 2006—07. Mem.: Sana Clara County Bar Assn. (mem. exec. com.), U. Santa Clara Law Alumni Assn. (bd. dirs. 1980—81, sec. 1981—83, v.p. 1983—85, pres. 1985—87), Santa Clara U. Nat. Alumni, Kiwanis. Roman Catholic. Avocation: flying. Home: 806 Buckwood Ct San Jose CA 95120-3306 Office: Social Security Adminstrn 280 S 1st St # 300 San Jose CA 95113-3002 Office Phone: 408-275-1690.

HANNOOSH, MICHELE ANN, language educator; b. Ft. Wayne, Ind., Apr. 4, 1954; d. Mitchell M. and Eleanor B. (Kfoury) Hannoosh; m. Richard C. Janko, May 26, 1984. BA, Wellesley Coll., Mass., 1976; MA, Stanford U., Calif., 1978, PhD, 1982. Fellow Columbia U., NYC, 1982—85; asst. prof. French and comparative lit. U. Calif., Davis, 1987—91, assoc. prof. French and comparative lit., 1991—94; prof. French U. Coll. London, 1995—98; lectr. French, fellow U. Cambridge St. Catharine's Coll., 1998—2000; reader French lit. and art U. Cambridge, 2000—02; prof. French U. Mich., Ann Arbor, 2003—. Chair dept. romance langs. and lit. U. Mich., Ann Arbor, 2007—. Author: (books) Parody and Decadence Laforgue's Moralities Legendaries, 1989, Baudelaire and Caricature: From The Comic To An Art Of Modernity, 1992, Painting and the Journal of Eugene Delacroix, 1995, Eugene Delacroix: Nouvelles Lettres, 2000. Recipient Ind. Scholars award, Nat. Endowment For Humanities, 1986; fellow, John Simon Guggenheim, 1998; grantee, Nat. Endowment For Humanities, 1993—97. Mem.: MLA, Coll. Art Assn., Soc. Etudes Romantiques, Soc. French Studies, Internat. Assn. Word and Image Studies (sec. 2002—). Office: Univ Mich Dept Langs and Lits 812 E Washington Ann Arbor MI 48109-1275

HANOWSKI, RICHARD JOSEPH, transportation engineer, director; b. Saskatoon, Saskatchewan, Canada, Mar. 20, 1965; s. Edward and Mary (Graff) Hanowski; m. Julie Cook, Dec. 10, 1994; children: Jack children: Kalina, Anna. BA, U. Sask., Can., 1988; MS, U. Idaho, Moscow, 1993; PhD in Indsl. and Sys. Engring., Va. Tech., Blacksburg, 2000, Rsch. scientist Battelle Meml. Inst., Seattle, 1993—96, Va. Tech. Transp. Inst., Blacksburg, Va., 1996—2005; dir. ctr. truck and bus safety Va. Tech Transp. Inst., 2005—. Cons., Blacksburg, Va., 1999—; expert witness. Recipient William G. Reese award, U. Idaho, 1992, First pl. Outstanding

Rsch. Phys. Scis. and Engring., Va. Tech, 1997, 2000. Mem.: Soc. Automotive Engrs. (Oral Presentation award 2004, 2006), Intelligent Transportation Soc. Am. (chmn. safety and human factors com. 2000—02), Human Factors and Ergonomics Soc. Achievements include prinicipal investigator for the largest (to date) commercial vehicle naturalistic data collection study conducted by the US Dept. of Transportation. Office: Va Tech Transportation Inst 3500 Transportation Rsch Plz Blacksburg VA 24061 Home Phone: 540-951-1210; Office Phone: 540-231-1513. Business E-Mail: hanowski@vtti.vt.edu.

HANRAHAN, LAWRENCE MARTIN, healthcare consultant; b. Cin., Mar. 9, 1961; adopted s. Robert Donald and Mary Francis (Doran) Hanrahan, s. Barry Wright and Kathryn Regina Kinkaid; m. Madeleine Carol Routon. AB in Chemistry, Miami U., 1983; MD, U. Cin. Coll. Medicine, 1988; MBA, U. Tex. Grad. Sch. Bus., 1992. Founder, owner Landscaping group, Cin., 1975—85; chief ultrasound tech., instr., rsch. assoc. Good Samaritan Hosp. Peripheral Vascular Lab., Cin., 1983—84; instr., technologist Clin. Vascular Lab. Christ Hosp., Cin., 1986; tech. cons., instr. Biosound, Inc., Indpls., 1983—89; surg. rsch. fellow divsn. surgery Boston U. Sch. Medicine; instr. peripheral vascular technologist Seton Med. Ctr., Austin, 1991; summer assoc. health care ops. Deloitte & Touche, Houston, 1991, cons. health care ops., 1991—92, sr. cons., 1992—94, mgr. health care ops., 1994—; sr. assoc. healthcare provider cons. William M. Mercer, Inc., Houston, 1995—97; co-founder Hanrahan Williams LLC, Houston, 1997—2000; dir. Genesis Healthcare Internat., Inc., Houston, 2000—01; co-founder, chmn. Interna Quality Healthcare, Profl. Connection, L.P., Houston, 2001—04; sr. mgr. Capgemini US LLC, 2004—05, Accenture, 2005—. Founder, chmn., pres. CORE Med. Techs., Inc., Houston, 1992—; sr. mgr., treas. Miami Med. Edn. and Devel., Miami U., 1975-79; com. mem. Disting. Lecture Series, U. Tex. Sch. Bus., Austin, 1990-91; founding pres. Tex. Bus. Hall of Fame Found. Scholarship Alumni Assn., 1992-93; bd. dirs., exec. com., 1992-93; mem. adv. bd. Healthcorp MBA, Owen Sch., Vanderbilt U., 2005-06; lectr. healthcare adminstrn. program U. Houston, 2002—. Contbr. articles to profl. jours. Finalist ACS resident competition, 1990, San Diego State U. Entrepreneurship competition; winner New Eng. Surg. Soc. resident competition, 1990; Tex. Bus. Hall of Fame Found. scholar, 1991, Abell-Hanger Endowed presdl. scholar, 1991, Accenture HLS Innovation award, 2006. Mem. AMA, Soc. for Vascular Tech., Mass. Med. Soc., Harris County Med. Soc., Med. Student Surg. Soc., Tex. Med. Assn. (chair com. on physician access 1999-2006, alt. del. 2003-06, del. 2006-, cons. coun. on med. edn. 2006—), Harris County Med. Soc., Beta Theta Pi. Achievements include patents in field. Avocation: jazz music. Office: Ste 2000 2929 Allen Pkwy Houston TX 77019-7107 Office Phone: 713-837-1311, 281-610-6258. Business E-Mail: lawrence.m.hanrahan@accenture.com.

HANRAHAN, PATRICK M., computer scientist; PhD, U. Wis., 1986. Canon USA prof. dept. computer scientist Stanford (Calif.) U. Fellow Am. Acad. Arts & Scis.; mem. NAE. Office: Stanford U Rm 3B Gates Computer Sci Bldf 370 Stanford CA 94305-4070*

HANRAHAN, PAUL THADDEUS, utilities executive; b. Phila., Nov. 10, 1957; s. Paul and Mary (Walsh) H.; m. Rodanthe Nichols, July 30, 1988; two children. BS in Mech. Engring., U.S. Naval Acad., 1979; MBA, Harvard Bus. Sch., 1986. Submarine officer USS Parche, San Francisco, 1979-84; project dir. AES Corp., Washington, 1986-89, pres., CEO, 2002—; mng. dir. AES Transpower, London, 1990-93; pres., CEO AES China, Hong Kong, 1993—2002. Office: AES Corporation 11th Fl 4300 Wilson Blvd Arlington VA 22203

HANRAHAN, ROBERT JOSEPH, chemist, educator; b. Chgo., Jan. 7, 1932; s. James Richard and Lucille Florence (Granger) H.; m. Mary Ellen Hogan, Oct. 28, 1957; children: Ann Marie, Sheila Frances, Robert Joseph, Margaret Evyleen. BS, Loyola U., Chgo., 1953; PhD, U. Wis., Madison, 1957. Research chemist Pure Oil Co., Crystal Lake, Ill., 1953; teaching asst., research asst. Monsanto research fellow U. Wis., Madison, 1953-57; NSF postdoctoral fellow Leeds (Eng.) U., 1957-58; asst. prof. phys. chemistry U. Fla., 1958-64, assoc. prof., 1964-71, prof., 1971—2004, chmn. phys. chemistry div., 1977-86, prof. emeritus, 2004—. Vis. sci. Hahn-Meitner Inst. Nuclear Research, Berlin, 1976; cons. in field. Patentee in field; contbr. articles to profl. jours. AEC rsch. grantee, 1963-74; ERDA grantee, 1975-77; Dept. Energy grantee, 1977-88, 2001-06; Dreyfus Found. grantee, 1983. Mem. Am. Chem. Soc., Am. Phys. Soc., Radiation Research Soc., AAAS, Am. Soc. Mass Spectrometry, Inter-Am. Photochem. Soc. Democrat. Roman Catholic. Achievements include rsch. in chem. effects of nuclear radiation and on solar energy systems. Home: 3730 NW 16th Pl Gainesville FL 32605-4848 Office: U Fla Dept Chemistry Gainesville FL 32611 Office Phone: 352-392-1442. Business E-Mail: hanrahan@chem.ufl.edu.

HANRATH, LINDA CAROL, librarian, archivist; b. Chgo., Aug. 22, 1949; d. John Stanley and Victoria (Fraint) Grzesiakowski; m. Richard Alan Hanrath, Nov. 1, 1980; 1 child, Emily BA History, Rosary Coll., 1971, MLS, 1974. Tchr. social studies Notre Dame HS, Chgo., 1971—75; outreach libr. Indian Trails Pub. Libr., Wheeling, Ill., 1975—76, Arlington Heights Meml. Libr., Ill., 1976—78; corp. libr. William Wrigley Jr. Co., Chgo., 1978—. Mem. Spl. Librs. Assn. (chmn. libr. jobline com. 1981-83, 86-87, food agrl. and nutrition divsn. 1988-89, sec. Ill. chpt. 1984-86, pres.-elect 1993-94, pres. Ill. chpt. 1994-95, conf. bd. info. svcs. adv. coun. 1990—, winner Outstanding Achievement award 1997), Assn. Records Mgrs. and Adminstrs., Soc. Am. Archivists, Midwest Archives Conf., Beta Phi Mu Avocations: needlecrafts, skiing, reading, gourmet cooking, tap dancing. Home: 715 E Devon Ave Roselle IL 60172-1461 Office: William Wrigley Jr Co 410 N Michigan Ave Chicago IL 60611-4213 E-mail: lhanrath@wrigley.com.

HANSBURY, STEPHAN CHARLES, judge; b. Mt. Holly, NJ, Nov. 3, 1946; s. Charles Clark and Kathryn Irene (Meyer) H.; m. Sharon Buckley; children: Elizabeth Kathryn, Jillian Judith, Stephanie Clark. BA, Allegheny Coll., 1968; MBA, Fairleigh Dickinson U., 1973; JD, Seton Hall U., 1977; cert. civil trial atty., Supreme Ct. N.J., 1989. Bar: N.J. 1977, U.S. Dist. Ct. (no. dist.) N.J. 1977, U.S. Supreme Ct. 1982. Dir. spl. programs Bloomfield (N.J.) Coll., 1968-71; dir. fin. aid Monmouth Coll., West Long Branch, NJ, 1971-72; asst. adminstr. Morris View, Morris Plains, NJ, 1972-78; assoc. Hansbury, Martin & Knapp, Morris Plains, 1978-87, pres., 1987-92; ptnr. Kummer Knox, Naughton & Hansbury, Parsippany, NJ, 1992-99, pres., 1996-97; ptnr. Cooper, Rose & English, LLP, 2000-2001; judge Superior Ct. of N.J., 2001—, presiding judge Family Part, 2005—. Complimentary disputes resolution com. NJ Supreme Ct., 2002—; gen. counsel Cheshire Home, Florham Park, NJ, 1978-2000, Ciba-Geigy Corp., Summit, NJ, 1980-92 Legis. aide Assemblyman Arthur Albohn, Morristown, NJ, 1980-83; active Morris County Bd. Social Svcs., 1989-96, chmn. 1992-94; bd. dirs. Colonial Symphony, 2000-04. Mem. ABA, NJ Bar Assn., Morris County Bar Assn. (trustee 1987-90), Morris County Bar Assn. (professionalism com. 2003-), Rotary (pres. 1998-99), Morristown Club, Mendham Golf and Tennis Club, Worrall F. Mountain Inn of Ct. (master) Republican. Episcopalian. Avocations: tennis, golf, reading. Office: Courthouse PO Box 910 Morristown NJ 07963-0910 Office Phone: 973-656-4039.

HANSCH, CORWIN HERMAN, chemistry professor; b. Kenmare, ND, Oct. 6, 1918; s. Herman William and Rachel (Corwine) H.; m. Gloria J. Tomasulo, Jan. 8, 1944; children: Clifford, Carol. BS, U. Ill., 1940; PhD, NYU, 1944; degree (hon.), U. Torino, 2004. Research chemist Manhattan project E.I. du Pont de Nemours & Co., Inc., 1944-45, research chemist, 1945-46; prof. chemistry Pomona Coll., 1946—88. Spl. research relationship chem. structure and drug action. Guggenheim fellow Fed. Inst. Tech., Zurich, Switzerland, 1952-53, Pomona Coll., 1966-67, Petroleum Rsch. Fund fellow U. Munich, 1959-60; recipient medal Italian Soc. Pharm. Sci., 1967, Coll. Chemistry Teaching award Mfg. Chemists Assn., 1969, Rsch. Achievement award Am. Pharm. Assn., 1969, E.A. Smissman award Medicinal Chemistry Am. Chem. Soc., 1975, Undergrad. Rsch. award, 1986, Tolman award Los Angeles sect., 1976, award for computers in chem. and pharm. rsch. ACS, 1999, Pratesi Medal, Soc. Chem. Italiana, 2003; named hon. prof. Beijing Med. U., 1990. Fellow Royal Soc. Chemistry (London, hon.); mem. L'Istituto Lombardo Accademiadi Scienze E Letters (Milan, hon.), L'Istituto Lombardo (hon.), Italian Soc. Pharm. Sci. (hon.). Home: 4070 Olive Knoll Pl Claremont CA 91711-1411 Office Phone: 909-621-8445.

HANSCHEN, PETER WALTER, lawyer; b. San Francisco, July 7, 1945; s. Walter A. and Dorothy E. (Watkins) H.; m. Brenda C. Hanschen, Feb. 7, 1987. BA, San Francisco State U., 1967; JD, U. Calif.-Berkeley, 1971. Bar: Calif. 1972, U.S. Supreme Ct. 1985, U.S. Ct. Appeals D.C. Cir. 1975. Assoc. Lawler, Felix & Hall, LA, 1971-73; atty. Pacific Gas Transmission Co., San Francisco, 1973-76, Pacific Gas & Elec. Co., San Francisco, 1976-79; gen. counsel Pacific Gas Transmission, San Francisco, 1979-83; asst. gen. counsel Pacific Gas & Elec. Co., San Francisco, 1983-88; ptnr. Graham & James, San Francisco, 1988-99, Morrison & Foerster, San Francisco, 1999—. Arbitrator Am. Arbitration Assn. Mem. ABA, Internat. Bar Assn., Fed. Energy Bar Assn., Counsel of Calif. Pub. Utilities. Avocations: golf, gardening, sports. Office: Morrison & Foerster LLP Ste 450 101 Ygnacio Valley Rd PO Box 8130 Walnut Creek CA 94563-8130 Office Phone: 925-295-3450. Personal E-mail: phanschen@mofo.com.

HANSEL, JAMES GORDON, retired engineer, educator; b. NYC, Oct. 17, 1937; s. Gordon Franklin and Edith (Bradshaw) H.; m. Sarah Elizabeth Martin, Dec. 27, 1964 (dec. Mar. 2003); 1 child, Claire E.; m. Joan Nancy Lasko, Jan. 3, 2004. BS in Engring. with high honors, Stevens Inst. Tech., 1959, MSME, 1960, ScD, 1964. Mem. rsch. faculty Princeton U., Guggenheim Labs., NJ, 1964-69; rsch. engr. Exxon Rsch., Linden, NJ, 1969-72; mgr. new catalyst devel. Engelhard Corp., Menlo Park, NJ, 1972-81; sr. engring. assoc. Air Products and Chems., Inc., Allentown, Pa., 1981—2007; ret., 2007. Adj. assoc. prof. Columbia U., NYC, 1976-80; vis. lectr. mech. engring. Stevens Inst. Tech. Hoboken, NJ, 1970-76; cons. on engring. safety to major corps., 1987—; adj. prof. chem./mech. engring. Pa. State U., State Coll., 1992-2000. Author: Theory of Experiments, 1967; contbg. author Book of Knowledge ency., 1979, Encyclopedia of Chemical Technology, 1994; contbr. articles to profl. jours. Bd. dirs. Am. on Wheels Mus., 1998—; indsl. and profl. adv. coun. Pa. State U., Coll. of Engring., 1998—. Mem. AIChE (tech. com. on reactive chems.), Internat. Stds. Orgn. (tech. com. on hydrogen vehicles), NY Acad. Sci., Sigma Xi, Tau Beta Pi. Achievements include patents for on applications of oxygen; development of Three Way Conversion catalyst and automotive engine control system used in over 900 million automobiles worldwide; first to apply hydrogen industry safety practices to hydrogen powered vehicles. Home: 5227 Carriage Path Schnecksville PA 18078 Personal E-mail: dochansel@ptd.net.

HANSEL, WILLIAM, biology professor; b. Vale Summit, Md., Sept. 16, 1918; s. John W. and Helen M. (Sperlein) H.; m. Milbrey Downey, Aug. 16, 1942; children: Barbara, Kay. MS, Cornell U., 1947, PhD, 1949. Asst. prof. Cornell U., Ithaca, N.Y., 1949-52, assoc. prof., 1952-61, prof., 1961-90, Liberty Hyde Bailey prof., 1983-90, chmn. physiology dept., 1978-83; Gordon D. Cain prof. La. State U., Baton Rouge, 1990—. Scientific adv. Merck, Sharp and Dohme, Rahway, 1980-85, Smith, Kline, Beecham, Westchester, Pa., 1986-91. Author: Genetic Engineering of Animals, 1990, Nutrition and Reproduction, 1998; contbr. over 300 articles to profl. jours. Maj. U.S. Army, 1941-46, ETO. Recipient 13 nat. or internat. rsch. and svc. awards including first Pharmacia and Upjohn Internat. award for life time rsch. in ruminant reproduction, 1998. Fellow AAAS; mem. Soc. Study Reprodn. (pres. 1976), Am. Physiol. Soc., Endocrine Soc., Soc. Exptl. Biology and Medicine (treas. 1975), Gamma Sigma Delta, Sigma Xi, Phi Kappa Phi. Achievements include isolation and identification of cusative agent of bovine x-disease; development of successful technique for estrous cycle regulation in cattle; pioneered development of assays for hormones in blood of animals; discovery of control mechanisms for corpus luteum function in cattle; demonstrated the relationships between nutrition and reproduction in cattle; development of successful targeted treatment for human prostate, breast, ovarian and testes cell tumors and metastases grown in test mice. Office: Pennington Biomed Rsch Ctr 6400 Perkins Rd # B1047 Baton Rouge LA 70808-4124 Home Phone: 225-767-1372; Office Phone: 225-763-3198. Business E-Mail: hanselw@pbrc.edu.

HANSELL, DEAN, lawyer; b. Bridgeport, Conn., Mar. 24, 1952; BA, Denison U., 1974; JD, Northwestern U., 1977. Bar: Ill. 1977, US Dist. Ct. (no. dist.) Ill. 1977, US Ct. Appeals (7th cir.) 1978, US Ct. Appeals (DC cir.) 1978, US Ct. Appeals (9th cir.) 1979, Calif. 1980, US Dist. Ct. (ctrl. dist.) Calif. 1981, US Dist. Ct. (so. dist.) Calif. 1989, US Supreme Ct. 1998, US Ct. Appeals (8th cir.) 2001. Asst. atty. gen. for environ. control State of Ill., Chgo., 1977-80; atty. FTC, LA, 1980-83; assoc. Donovan Leisure Newton & Irvine, LA, 1984-86; ptnr. LeBoeuf, Lamb, Greene & MacRae, LA, 1986—2001, co-mng. ptnr. LA office, 2001—. Mem. Ill. Solar Resources Adv. Panel, 1978—80; adj. assoc. prof. Southwestern Univ. Sch. Law, LA, 1982—86; judge pro tem LA County Mcpl. Ct., 1987—97, LA County Superior Ct., 1989—2005; mem. adv. bd. Fayette Haywood Legal Svcs., Tenn., 1979—83, Nat. Inst. Citizen Edn. in Law, 1989—94, Asian Pacific Am. Legal Ctr., 1996—. Mem. editl. bd.: Los Angeles Lawyer Mag., 1995—2005, Internat. Reins. Dispute Reporter, 1996—2001; contbr. articles to profl. jours. V.p., commr. LA Bd. Police Commrs., 1997—2001, v.p., 2001; commr. LA Bd. Info. Tech., 2001—, v.p., 2003—04, pres., 2004—; trustee Denison U., 2006—; mem. adv. bd. UCLA Sch. Pub. Health; bd. dirs. Jewish Fedn. Coun. Met. LA Region, 1984—87, Project LEAP, Legal Elections All Precincts, Chgo., 1976—80, Martin Luther King Jr. Ctr. Nonviolence, LA, 1991—95, LA Pub. Libr. Found., 1997—2005. Mem.: ABA, Calif. Bar Assn., LA County Bar Assn. (mem. exec. com. antitrust sect. 1982—92, chair 1989—90), Phi Beta Kappa, Omicron Delta Kappa. Office: LeBoeuf Lamb Greene & MacRae 725 S Figueroa St Ste 3100 Los Angeles CA 90017-5404 Home Phone: 323-931-4883; Office Phone: 213-955-7331. Office Fax: 213-955-7399. Business E-Mail: dhansell@llgm.com.

HANSELL, EDGAR FRANK, lawyer; b. Leon, Iowa, Oct. 12, 1937; s. Edgar Noble and Celestia Delphine (Skinner) H.; m. Phyllis Wray Silvey, June 24, 1961; children: John Joseph, Jordan Burke. AA, Graceland Coll., 1957; BBA, U. Iowa, 1959, JD, 1961. Bar: Iowa 1961. Assoc. Nyemaster, Goode, West, Hansell & O'Brien, P.C., Des Moines, 1964-68, ptnr., shareholder, 1968—. Bd. dirs. The Vernon Co., Des Moines Internat. Airport, vice chair; mem. adv. com. to bd. dirs. The Lauridson Group, Inc.; adj. prof. law Drake U., Des Moines, 1990—95. Mem. editorial adv. bd. Jour. Corp. Law, 1985—. Bd. dirs. Des Moines Child Guidance Ctr., 1972-78, 81-87, pres., 1977-78; trustee Iowa Law Sch. Found., 1975-90, pres., 1983-87; bd. dirs. Iowa Natural Heritage Found., 1988-93, Iowa Sports Found., 1986-97; bd. dirs. Iowa State Bar Found., 1991-2000, pres., 1996-98. With USAF, 1961-64. Mem. ABA, Iowa Bar Assn. (pres. young lawyers sect. 1971-72, bd. govs. 1971-72, 85-87, mem. grievance commn. 1973-78, Merit award young lawyers sect. 1977, 98, chmn. corp. and bus. law com. 1979-85, pres. 1989-90), Polk County Bar Assn., Des Moines Club (pres. 1979-80). Home: 139-37th Des Moines IA 50312-4303 Office: Nyemaster Goode West Hansell & O'Brien PC 700 Walnut St Ste 1600 Des Moines IA 50309-3800 Office Phone: 515-283-3150. Business E-Mail: efh@nyemaster.com.

HANSELL, JOHN ROYER, retired pathologist; b. Phila., June 30, 1931; s. Henry Lewis and Elizabeth (Campbell) H. AB, U. Pa., Phila., 1953; MD, Jefferson Med. Coll., 1957. Diplomate Am. Bd. Pathology, Am. Bd. Nuclear Medicine (chmn. 1988-89). Intern Germantown Hosp., Phila., 1957-58, resident, pathologist, 1956-61, Bryn Mawr Hosp., Pa., 1961-62; pathology fellow New Eng. Deaconess Hosp., Boston, 1962-63; resident Mayo Clinic, Rochester, Minn., 1966-67; chief nuclear medicine VA Med Ctr., Phila., 1967-93. Contbr. chpts. to books and articles to profl. jours. Comdr. USPHS, 1963-66. Fellow Soc. Nuclear Medicine, Coll. Am. Pathologists. Republican. Avocations: antiques, gardening.

HANSELL, PHYLLIS SHANLEY, nursing educator, administrator, researcher, consultant; b. NYC, Jan. 3, 1947; s. Peter James and Jewell Mae (Altis) S.; m. Robert Lewis Hansell, June 16, 1984; children: Benjamin, Christopher. BS, Fairleigh Dickinson U., 1972; MEd, Columbia U., 1975, EdD, 1981. RN. Staff nurse Mountainside Hosp., Montclair, NJ, 1967-69; head nurse NY Med. Coll., NYC, 1970-72, clin. instr., 1972-75; instr. Seton Hall U., South Orange, NJ, 1975-77, asst. prof., 1977-79, prof. nursing, 1986-94, 96—, dir. nursing rsch., 1986-94, dept. chair, 1996-99, acting dean, 1999-2000, dean Coll. Nursing, 2000—, dean, prof. Coll. Nursing, 2000; dir. nursing rsch. Meml. Sloan-Kettering, NYC, 1984-86. Chair NJ Assn. of Baccalaureate and Higher Degree Programs in Nursing; commr. Nat. Commn. for VA Nursing, 2002—04; mem. adv. coun. Future of Nursing in NJ, 2002—04. Contbr. articles to profl. jours., chpt. to book. Bd. dirs. Jr. League, Montclair, 1992-94, chair grants and corp. devel., chair Newark Teen Arts Festival, Montclair and Newark, 1994-95. Recipient Gov.'s merit award Gov. NJ, 1994. Fellow: Am. Acad. Nursing; mem.: ANA (chair rsch., Gov.'s award 1994), NJ State Nurses Assn. (mem. coun., Rsch. award 1994), Am. Acad. Practice (Disting. Practitioner 2000), Sigma Theta Tau (v.p. Gamma Nu chpt. 1994—96, Rsch. award 1983). Avocations: opera, ballet, skiing, tennis, golf. Office: Seton Hall U 400 S Orange Ave South Orange NJ 07079-2697

HANSELL, RICHARD STANLEY, obstetrician, gynecologist, educator; b. Indpls., Nov. 18, 1950; s. Robert Mathey and Jewell (Martin) H.; m. Cathy C., Oct. 7, 1995; children: Elizabeth, Victoria. BA, DePauw U., 1972; MD, Ind. U., 1976. Cert. Am. Bd. Obstetrics and Gynecology. Practice medicine specializing in ob-gyn. Cedarwood Med. Ctr., St. Joseph, Mich., 1980-86; asst. prof. ob-gyn. Ind. U., Indpls., 1986-93, assoc. prof., 1993—2002, prof., 2002—. Instr. Western Mich. U., Kalamazoo, 1980-86; med. bd. Planned Parenthood, Benton Harbor, Mich., 1980-86; med. dir. Planned Parenthood of Ctrl. Ind., 1991-95; examiner Am. Bd. Ob-gyn., 1994—. Mem. AMA, Am. Coll. Ob-gyn., Assn. of Profs. of Gynecology and Obstetrics, Ind. State Med. Soc., Ctrl. Assn. Ob-gyn., Indpls. Med. Soc. Presbyterian. Avocations: golf, fishing. Office: Ind U Med Sch Dept Ob-Gyn 1001 W 10th St Indianapolis IN 46202-2859 Home Phone: 317-823-4235; Office Phone: 317-630-6594. Business E-Mail: rhansell@iupui.edu.

HANSELL, SAUL HENRY, reporter; b. NYC, Jan. 11, 1962; s. Sanford and Elizabeth (Rose) H. BA, Columbia U., 1984. Reporter Bank Letter, NYC, 1984-86; mng. editor Bank Letter, 1986-87; mng. editor Wall St. Letter Instl. Investor, NYC, 1987; writer Instl. Investor mag., NYC, 1987-92; bus. news, new tech. reporter N.Y. Times, 1992—. Recipient Morton Frank award for best bus. and/or econ. reporting from abroad Overseas Press Club, 1989, First Place award for in depth feature New Eng. chapt. Am. Soc. Bus. Press Editors. Office: NY Times 229 W 43rd St New York NY 10036-3959

HANSELMAN, RICHARD WILSON, entrepreneur; b. Cin., Oct. 8, 1927; s. Wendell Forest and Helen E. (Beiderwelle) H.; m. Beverly Baker White, Oct. 16, 1954; children: Charles Fielding, II, Jane White. BA in Econs, Dartmouth Coll., 1949. V.p. merchandising RCA Sales Corp., Indpls., 1964-66, v.p. product planning, 1966-69, v.p. product mgmt., 1969-70; pres. luggage divsn. Samsonite Corp., Denver, 1970-73, pres. luggage group, 1973-74, exec. v.p. ops., 1974-75, pres., 1975-77; sr. v.p. Beatrice Foods Co., Chgo., 1976-77, exec. v.p., 1977-80; pres., COO, dir. Genesco Inc., Nashville, 1980-86, CEO, 1981-86, pvt. investor, corp. dir., 1986—. Lead dir. Forward Air; dir. Healthnet of Calif. Hon. trustee Com. for Econ. Devel. Served with U.S. Army, 1950-52. Mem. Belle Meade Country Club, Union League, Phi Kappa Psi. Office: 104 Westhampton Pl Nashville TN 37205 Office Phone: 615-662-1911.

HANSEN, ALEXANDER E., advertising agency executive; BA, Williams Coll.; MDiv, Princeton Theol. Seminary; studied, Cal State LA bus. program. CPA Lic., Calif. Fin. exec. with DS Waters of Am. LP, Groupe Danone, J. Walter Thompson; pres., CEO Bravant LLC, LA; fin. leadership (CFO) ptnr. Tatum CFO Ptnrs., LLP, LA; CFO Adchek, Ventura, Calif. Mem.: Calif. Soc. CPA, AICPA. Office: Tatum CFO Ptnrs LLP 11755 Wilshire Blvd Ste 1100 Los Angeles CA 90025 also: Adchek 2225 Sperry Ave Ste 2000 Ventura CA 93003

HANSEN, ANDREW MARIUS, retired library director; b. Storm Lake, Iowa, Mar. 25, 1929; s. Andrew Marius and Margaret Mary (Van Wagenen) H.; m. Rina M. Rennie Smith, Feb. 24, 1967; 1 child, Neil S. BA, U. Omaha, 1951; postgrad., U. Md., 1955; MA, U. Minn., 1962; postgrad, U. Iowa, 1968-71. Librarian Bismarck (N.D.) Public Library, 1957-63, Sioux City (Iowa) Public Library, 1963-67; instr. Sch. of Library Sci., U. Iowa, Iowa City, 1967-71; exec. sec. ALA, Chgo., 1971-80, exec. dir. reference and adult services div., 1980-94; reference librarian Wilmette Pub. Libr., 1996—. Vis. asst. prof. Ind. State U., Terre Haute, 1966; adj. faculty Dominican U., River Forest, Ill., 2001. Pres. Friends of Wilmette Pub. Libr., 1984-85; mem. Village of Wilmette Transp. Commn., 1995—2003; bd. dirs. United Way of Wilmette, 2004-05. Served with USAF, 1951-55. Mem. ALA (Mudge-Bowker award 1993), N.D. Libr. Assn. (pres. 1958-59, sec.-treas. 1962-63), Iowa Libr. Assn. (pres. 1967-68), Coalition Adult Edn. Orgns. (bd. dirs. 1972-93), Ch. and Synagogue Libr. Assn. (treas. Northeastern Ill. chpt. 1985-91), Chgo. Libr. Club (sec. 1983-84), Rotary. Presbyterian. Home: 314 Skokie Blvd Wilmette IL 60091-3002 E-mail: andrewmhansen@comcast.net.

HANSEN, ANNE KATHERINE, poet; b. Coulter, Iowa, Oct. 29, 1928; d. Carl Christian and Else Katherine (Paulsen) H. BA, Chapman U., 1958; MA, U. Redlands, 1971. Life credential, Calif. Elem. tchr. Bloomington (Calif.) Schs., 1958-60, San Bernarndino (Calif.) Unified Sch. Dist., 1960-87; ret., 1987. Pub.: book of poetry Listen To My Heart, 1999; contbr. poetry to anthologies. Recipient Golden Poet award World of Poetry, 1988, 89, 90, 91, 92, Poet of Merit award Internat. Soc. Poets, plaque, 1993, 94, 96, medallion, 1996. Home: 1371 Parkside Dr Apt 230 San Bernardino CA 92404-5356

HANSEN, B. J. (BOBBY J. HANSEN), management consultant, real estate investor and developer; b. Newton, Kans., Jan. 30, 1926; s. Clarence Nielsen and Blanche Eleanore (Andrews) H.; m. Helen Hansen; children: Cherokee E. Stock, Jody K. Abbott, Christopher Nielsen (dec.), Mimi E. Heldreth, Nicole M. Nickols. BS, U. So. Calif., 1949; MA Pub. Adminstrn., Am. U., 1966. Cert. sailbd. instr. U.S. Sailing Assn., Internat. Yachting Fellowship Rotarians, dingy sailboat sailor Brit. Royal Yachting Assn., internat. open water diver Brit. Sub-Aqua Club, Profl. Assn. Diving Instrs. Pres. Trak-Life Inc., Portland, Oreg., 1957-59; staff specialist Lockheed Missile & Space Co., Sunnyvale, Calif., 1959-61; program mgr. Ops. Research Inc., Silver Spring, Md., 1961-62; exec. v.p. Computer Dynamics Corp., Silver Spring, 1961-65; sr. v.p., cons. for U.S. Dept. Def. in Vietnam, John I. Thompson & Co., Washington, 1965-68; pres. Decision Research Corp., Washington, 1968-70; chmn., mem. Commn. on Changein-Govt., county exec. Prince William County, Manassas, Va., 1970-71; county adminstr. Wythe County, Wytheville, Va., 1971-73; city mgr. Marion, Va., 1973-77; mgr. Williams Crane & Rigging Inc., Wytheville, 1977-80; prin. adminstr. and investors coordinator Royal Commn. Jubail (Saudi Arabia)-Yanbu, 1980-83; div. mgr. Al-Rushaid Investment Co., Dammam, Saudi Arabia, 1983-85; investor Hansen Assocs., Wytheville, 1985—. Owner Surfun Co., InTech Internat. & Tax Shak; adj. faculty professorial lectr. Wytheville Community Coll., Am. U., New River Community Coll., Golden Gate U., Jubail, Saudi Arabia; guest lectr. fgn. affairs dept. Bluefield State U.; mem. adv. bd. ADP, No. Va. Community Coll.; boat safety coord. Southwest Va., Dept. Game and Inland Fisheries. Author: Practical Program Evaluation and Review Technique, 1962 (Nat. Lit. award); guest editor Government Exec. Mag.; former columnist Southwest Va. Enterprise, columnist Smith County News; patentee in field. Mem., former chmn. small bus. adminstrn. coun. Met. Washington SBA, tech. adv. com. Claytor Lake, Va.; bd. dirs. No. Va. Police Acad.; founder, chmn. Master Swimming, Kingdom of Saudi Arabia; founder Va. Master Swimming Assn., 1st pres., 1979-80; mem. Spencer London UK Master Swim Team, Nat. Sr. Broadsailing Coun.; former pres. Va. Mt. Rogers affiliate Nat. Alliance for Mentally Ill, 1990-91; mem. Am. Businessmen's Alliance, Kingdom of Saudi Arabia; mem. Consumer Adv. Coun. SW Va., Mental Health Inst. Ensign USNR, 1943-47, lt., 1951-53, Korea, capt. USN, 1966-67, Vietnam. Mem. SAG, VFW (life), SAR, DAV (life), Fedn. Internat. des Professions Immobilieres, Internat. Platform Assn., Am. Inst. Mgmt., Am. Mgmt. Assn., Nat. Assn. Real Estate Appraisers (sr.), Coll. Real Estate Appraisers, Armed Forces Mgmt. Assn. (past v.p.), Def. Orientation Conf. Assn., Navy League Malibu Calif. (pres.), United Inventors and Scientists, Associated Gen. Contractors, Am. Waterworks Assn., Internat. City Mgrs. Assn., English Speaking Union, Nat. Assn. County Adminstrs., Am. Soc. Pub. Adminstrs., Nat. Security Indsl. Assn., Am. Arbitration Assn. (nat. panel arbitrators), Internat. Soc. Poets, Naval Res. Officer's Assn., Am. Legion (life, China Post 1), Nat. Space Club, US Sailing Assn., US Windsurfing Assn., US Waterpolo Assn. (player), Brit. Amateur Swimming Assn., Danish Brotherhood in Am., Evergreen Country Club (Haymarket, Va.), Evansham Swim & Racquet Club (Wythe County), Va. Masters Assn. (pres. 1976-77), Chantilly Country Club (Va.), Beverly Hills Country Club, Rotary (former chmn. sr. olympics), Moose, Confederate Air Force of Am. (col.), Nat. Aviation Club, Beta Gamma Sigma (Beta U. So. Calif. chpt.), Kappa Mu Epsilon (math. hon.), Sigma Nu, Phi Sigma Epsilon. Holder 2 Relay World Records. British Nat. Championship Amateur Swimming, Assn., 1992. Home and Office: 1145 Barry Ave # 211 Brentwood CA 90049 Personal E-mail: surfunning@aol.com.

HANSEN, BARBARA CALEEN, physiologist, science educator; b. Boston, Nov. 24, 1941; d. Reynold L. and Dorothy (Richardson) Caleen; m. Kenneth Dale Hansen, Oct. 8, 1976; 1 child, David Scott. BS, UCLA, 1964, MS, 1965; PhD, U. Wash., 1971. Asst. prof. then assoc. prof. U. Wash., Seattle, 1971—76; prof., assoc. dean U. Mich., Ann Arbor, 1977—82; assoc. v.p. acad. affairs and research, dean grad. sch. So. Ill. U., Carbondale, 1982—85; v.p. for grad. studies and research U. Md., Balt. and Balt. County, 1985—90, prof. physiology, dir. obesity and diabetes rsch. ctr., 1990—. Mem. adv. com. to dir. NIH, Washington, 1979—83; mem. joint health policy com. Assn. Am. U., Washington, 1982—86, Nat. Assn. State U. and Land-Grant Colls., Washington, 1982—86, Am. Coun. on Edn., Washington, 1982—86; mem. nutrition study sect. NIH, 1979—83; mem. program com. Inst. Medicine-NAS, Washington, 1982—84; mem. Armed Forces Epidemiology Bd., 1991—95; mem. bd. sci. counselors NIEHS, 1992—94, NIH, 1992—94, mem. nat. toxicology bd., 1992—94, NIEHS, 1992—94; mem. search com. Office of Rsch. Integrity, NIH, 1992—93. Author: The Commonsense Guide to Weight Loss for People with Diabetes, 1998, The Metabolic Syndrome X, 1999; co-editor: Controversies in Obesity, 1983, editor chpts. on physiology; contbr. articles to profl. jours.; co-editor: Insulin Resistance and Insulin Resistance Syndrome, 2002. Mem. adv. com. Am. Bur. Med. Advancement China, NYC, 1982—85; mem. adv. bd. African-Am. Inst., 1987—91; mem. adv. com. Robert Wood Johnson Found., Princeton, NJ, 1982—91. Fellow Nueroscis. fellow, U. Pa., 1966—68. Mem.: Internat. Assn. Study of Obesity (pres. 1986—90), Nat. Assn. State U. and Land Grant Colls. (chmn. coun. on rsch. policy and grad. edn. 1986—87), N.Am. Assn. Study of Obesity (pres. 1984—85, 1986—), Am. Soc. for Clin. Nutrition (pres.-elect 1994—95, pres. 1995—96, v.p.), Am. Soc. for Nutritional Scis., Inst. Medicine of NAS, Am. Physiol. Soc., Phi Beta Kappa (Arthur Patch McKinley scholar 1964). Republican. Presbyterian. Achievements include discovery of of periodic (10-14 min.) cycling pattern of pancreas insulin secretion; identification of the pattern of progressive defects in insulin secretion and insulin action preceeding overt clinical type 2 diabetes mellitus; showed prevention of obesity prevents most type 2 diabetes. Office: U Md-Balt Sch Medicine Obesity-Diabetes Rsch Ctr 10 S Pine St MSTF 600 Baltimore MD 21201-1116

HANSEN, BECK See BECK

HANSEN, CARL R., management consultant; b. Chgo., May 2, 1926; s. Carl M. and Anna C. (Roge) Hansen; m. Christia Marie Loeser, Dec. 31, 1952; 1 child, Lothar. MBA, U. Chgo., 1954. Dir. mkt. rsch. Kitchens of Sara Lee, Deerfield, Ill., Earle Ludgin & Co., Chgo.; svc. v.p. Mkt. Rsch. Corp. Am., 1956—67; pres. Chgo. Assoc., Inc., 1967—. Chmn. Ill. adv. coun. SBA, 1973—74; exec. com. Ill. Gov.'s Adv. Coun., 1969—72; resident officer U.S. High Commn., Germany, 1949—52; chmn. Viking Ship Restoration Com.; mem. Cook County Bd. Commrs., 1970, 1974—, chmn. legis. com., adminstrn. com.; active Am. Scandinavian Found.; vice chmn. Rep. Ctrl. Com. Cook County; chmn. Cook County Young Reps., 1957—58, 12th Congl. Dist. Rep. Orgn., 1971—74, 1978—82, Suburban Rep. Orgn., 1974—78, 1982—86; del. Rep. Nat. Conv., 1968, 1984, 1992; chmn. Legis. Dist. Ill., 1964—; del. Rep. State Conv., 1962—96; committeeman Elk Grove Twp. Rep., 1962—2002; pres. John Ericsson Rep. League of Ill., 1975—76; Rep. presdl. elector State of Ill., 1972; bd. dir. Nat. Assn. Counties. 1st lt. US Army, 1948, maj. USAR. Mem.: VFW, Planning Forum, Nat. Assn. Counties, Am. Statis. Assn., Am. Mktg. Assn., Swedish Am. Hist. Soc., Dania Soc., Chgo. Hist. Soc., Lions, Am. Legion, Res. Officers Assn., Shriners, Masons, Sons of Norway. Home: 110 S Edward St Mount Prospect IL 60056-3414 Office: 118 N Clark St Chicago IL 60602-1304

HANSEN, CAROL LOUISE, literature and language professor; b. San Jose, Calif., July 17, 1938; d. Hans Eskelsen and Thelma Josephine (Brooks) Hansen; m. Merrill Chris Davis, July 17, 1975 (div.). BA in English, San Jose State U., 1960; MA in English Lit., U. Calif., Berkeley, 1968; PhD in English Lit., Ariz. State U., 1975. Asst. prof. English City Coll. San Francisco, Calif., 1985—, Coll. San Mateo, Calif., 1987—, De Anza Coll., 1998-99; lectr. expository writing U. San Francisco, 2001; prof., dean of journalism Olivet U., San Francisco, 2005—. Writing coord. Calif. State U., Monterey Bay, 1996; mem. rsch. com. Conf. on Coll. Composition and comm., 2001; presenter in field. Author: Woman as Individual in English Renaissance Drama, 1993, 2d edit., 1995, 3d edit., 2000, The Life and Death of Asham: Leonard and Virginia Woolf's Haunted House, 2000, Beyond Evil: Cathy and Cal in East of Eden, 2002; contbr. articles to profl. jours. Active Grace Cathedral, San Francisco. Fellow NDEA. Mem.: MLA (chair exec. com. discussion group on two-yr. colls. 1999), Virginia Woolf Soc. Episcopalian. Office: City Coll San Francisco 50 Phelan Ave San Francisco CA 94112-1821 Personal E-mail: carhansen@sbcglobal.net.

HANSEN, CHARLES, lawyer; b. Jersey City, May 23, 1926; s. Charles Henry and Katherine (Bensch) H.; m. Carolyn P. Smith, Sept. 26, 1953; children: Mark, Melissa. BS, U. Mich., 1946; JD, Mich. Law Sch., 1950. Bar: N.Y. 1951, Wis. 1961, Mo. 1980. Engr. Westinghouse Electric Co., 1946; assoc. Mudge, Stern, Williams & Tucker, 1950-53; chief labor counsel, div. counsel Sylvania Electric Products, 1953-61; sec., gen. counsel Trane Co., La Crosse, Wis., 1961-69, exec. v.p., 1968-73; pres. Cutler-Hammer World Trade, Inc., 1973-77; v.p. Cutler-Hammer, Inc., 1973-77, exec. v.p., 1977-79; sr. v.p. law Emerson Electric Co., 1979-84, sr. v.p., sec., gen. counsel, 1984-89; ptnr. Bryan Cave, 1989-95, of counsel, 1995—. Adj. prof. Sch. Law St. Louis U., 1987—99. Served to lt. (j.g.) USNR, 1943-46. Mem. ABA, Wis., Mo. bar assns., Am. Law Inst., Order of Coif, Tau Beta Pi. Home: 8 Wydown Ter Saint Louis MO 63105-2217 Office: 211 N Broadway 1 Metropolitan Sq Ste 3600 Saint Louis MO 63102-2750 Office Phone: 314-259-2676. Personal E-mail: hansenc1h@aol.com. Business E-Mail: chansen@bryancave.com.

HANSEN, CHARLES MARTIN, III, lobbyist; s. Charles Martin Hansen, Jr. and Sheila Anne Madigan; m. Anjali Hansen; children: Charles Martin Hansen, IV, Katarina Genevieve, Alexander Keegan. BA, Vanderbilt U., 1985; MPA, U. Tex., 1995. Legislative staff Office of U.S. Senator Lloyd Bentsen, Washington, 1985—89; assoc. dir. State of Tex. Washington Office, 1991; dir. congl. liaison U.S. Internat. Trade Commn., Washington, 1992—94; mng. ptnr. Podesta Assoc., Washington, 1994—2001; pres. Hansen Govt. Rels., Washington, 2001—. Contbr. articles to profl. jours. D-Liberal. Roman Catholic. Office: Hansen Govt Rels 2600 Virginia Ave NW Ste 505 Washington DC 20037 Office Phone: 202-333-2524. E-mail: hansen@hansen-gr.com.

HANSEN, CHARLES MORTON, editor, retired military officer; b. Huntington Park, Calif., Sept. 27, 1933; s. Andrew Hansen and Lena S. Andrew. BA in History, UCLA, 1955; MA in History, San Francisco State U., 1985. Commd. 2d lt. U.S. Army, 1955, platoon leader Republic of Korea, 1957-59, co-comdr., 1962—63, sr. adv. Vietnam, 1965-66, bn. comdr. Republic of Korea, 1969-70, advanced through grades to col., 1977, ret., 1982; contbg. editor Am. Genealogist, 1988—; editor The Genealogist, 1996—. Contbr. articles to profl. jours. Decorated Legion of Merit, Bronze Star, Combat Infantry Badge, Cross of Gallantry Republic of Vietnam; recipient Coddington award for Merit, New Eng. Hist. Geneal. Soc., 1995. Fellow: Am. Soc. Genealogists; mem.: Soc. Heraldica Scandinavia (Denmark), Heraldry Soc. (London), Soc. Genealogists (London), Ninth Infantry Rgt. Assn., Harbor Point Racquet Club. Methodist. Avocation: tennis. Home: 25 Rodeo Ave Apt 22 Sausalito CA 94965-1783

HANSEN, CHRISTIAN ANDREAS, JR., plastics and chemical company executive; b. New Braunsfels, Tex., Sept. 12, 1926; s. Christian Andreas and Velma Arbeda (Ivy) Hansen; m. Emily Dann. BS, Rice U., 1948. Dir. mfg. chem. div. G.A.F. Corp., NYC, 1969—71; chmn. bd., CEO, pres., founder Hanlin Group, Inc., Linden Chlorine Products, Inc., 1971—93, LCP/Nat. Plastics, Inc., 1977—93; retired, 1993. With Exxon 21 years, last position gen. mgr., Linden, N.J.; founder, chmn., CEO, pres. Pathways, Inc., 1994-98, Hansen Plastics, Inc., 1994-98; co-founder Ultrapure Products, Inc., 2000-; real estate agt. Weichert Realtors, N.J. Pub.: God's Bible and Jesus' Papers, 1994; patentee in field. Councilman City of Baytown, Tex., 1961—63; pres. Union County United Fund, NJ, 1967—69; chmn. Chem. Industry Coun., Trenton, NJ, 1977—82; mem. Gov.'s Commn. on Hazardous Waste Disposal; leader Boy Scouts, Sea Scouts; mem. Eastern Union County C. of C., v.p., 1968—69. Lt. USNR, 1943—46. Named Man of Yr., Union County United Fund, 1970. Mem.: Chlorine Inst. (past. pres., past bd. dirs.), Am. Inst. Chem. Engrs. Home and Office: 1 Scenic Dr Highlands NJ 07732-1329 E-mail: edam75@comcast.net.

HANSEN, CHRISTOPHER AGNEW, lawyer; b. Yakima, Wash., Dec. 10, 1934; s. Raymond Walter and Christine F.M. (Agnew) H.; m. Sandra Ridgely Pindell, Aug. 4, 1959; Anne Ridgely, Christopher Agnew Jr., Eric Bruce. BS, Cornell U., 1957; JD, U. Md., 1963. Bar: Md. 1963, U.S. Supreme Ct. 1973, U.S. Ct. Appeals (4th cir.) D.C. 1978. Law clk. Cir. Ct. for Balt. County, Towson, Md., 1960-63; assoc. Piper & Marbury, Balt., 1963-74; of counsel Casey, Scott, Canfield & Heggestad PC, Washington, 1982-93; ptnr. Constable, Alexander & Skeen, Towson, 1984-86, Parks, Hansen & Ditch, Towson, 1986-94; of counsel Heggestad & Weiss, PC, Washington, 1993—2001; pvt. practice Towson, 1974-83, 95—. With U.S. Army, 1957-60. Mem. ABA, D.C. Bar, Md. State Bar Assn., Bar Assn. Balt. County, Balt. City Bar Assn., Phi Alpha Delta. Episcopalian. Home: 15152 Players Way Glenwood MD 21738-9658

HANSEN, CLAIRE V., financial executive; b. Thornton, Iowa, June 3, 1925; s. Charles F. and Grace B. (Miller) H.; m. Renee C. Hansen, Aug. 17, 1946; children: Charles James, Christopher David, Peter Chrissis. BSc, U. Notre Dame, 1947; MBA, Harvard U., 1948. Chartered fin. analyst. With Salk, Ward & Salk, Inc.; v.p. Salk Inst. Agency, 1954-59; with Duff, Anderson & Clark, Chgo., 1959-67, v.p., dir., 1967-71; dir. Duff and Phelps, Inc., 1972-88; exec. v.p. Duff & Phelps, 1973-75, pres., chief exec. officer, 1975-84, chmn. and CEO, 1984—87; chmn. bd. dir. Duff & Phelps Utilities Income, Inc., Chgo., 1987—2001, CEO, 2000—01; chmn. bd. dir. DNP Select Income Fund, Inc., 2002—05. Bd. dir. Chgo. Lung Assn., 1962-80, pres. 1973-75; bd. dir. Am. Lung Assn., 1971-83, Ctr. Religion and Psychotherapy in Chgo., 1979-83; trustee Glenwood Sch., 1974-95, chmn., 1983-87; bd. dirs. Auditorium Theatre Coun., 1983-88, treas., 1987-88; bd. dir. Schwab Rehab. Hosp., 1978-82, pres., 1980-82; bd. dir. Pelican Bay Found. Inc., 1993-99, treas., 1993-96, pres., 1996-97. Mem. Inst. Chartered Fin. Analysts, Univ. Club, Chgo. (Ill.) Club, Olympia Fields Country Club, Club Pelican Bay, Hole-in-the-Wall Golf Club. Republican. Episcopalian. Home: 5601 Turtle Bay Dr Apt 2001 Naples FL 34108-2703 Office: 5601 Turtle Bay Dr # 2001-02 Naples FL 34108 Personal E-mail: verdelle@msn.com.

HANSEN, CURTIS LEROY, federal judge; b. 1933; BS, U. Iowa, 1956; JD, U. N.Mex., 1961. Bar: N.Mex. Law clk. to Hon. Irwin S. Moise N.Mex. Supreme Ct., 1961-62; ptnr. Snead & Hansen, Albuquerque, 1962-64, Civerolo, Hansen & Wolf, P.A., 1964—92; dist. judge U.S. Dist. Ct., N.Mex., 1992—2003, sr. dist. judge N.Mex., 2003—. Mem. State Bar N.Mex., Albuquerque Bar Assn., Am. Coll. Trial Lawyers, Am. Bd. Trial Advocates, Albuquerque Country Club. Mailing: PO Box 669 Albuquerque NM 87103 Office: US Courthouse 421 Gold Ave SW 5th Fl Albuquerque NM 87102

HANSEN, DAVID RASMUSSEN, federal judge; b. Exira, Iowa, 1938; BA, N.W. Mo. State U., 1960; JD, George Washington U., 1963. Asst. clk. to minority House Appropriations Com. Ho. of Reps., 1960—61; adminstrv. aide 7th Dist. Iowa, 1962—63; law clerk, assoc. atty. Jones, Cambridge & Carl, Atlantic, Iowa, 1963—64; capt., judge advocate General's Corps US Army, 1964—68; pvt. practice Barker, Hansen & McNeal, Iowa Falls, Iowa, 1968—76; ptnr. Win-Gin Farms, Iowa Falls, 1971—; judge Police Ct., Iowa, 1969—73, 2d Jud. Dist. Ct., Iowa, 1976—86, US Dist. Ct. (no. dist.), Cedar Rapids, Iowa, 1986—91, US Ct. Appeals (8th cir.), Cedar Rapids, 1991—2002, chief judge, 2002—03, sr. judge, 2003—. Chmn. Hardin County Rep. Central Com., 1975—76; mem. Jud. Conf. of US, 2002—03, US Jud. Panel on Multidistrict Litig., 2004—. Mem.: Dean Mason Ladd Inn of Ct., Iowa State Bar Assn. Office: US Courthouse Rm 304 101 1st St SE Cedar Rapids IA 52401-1202*

HANSEN, ELAINE TUTTLE, academic administrator; m. Stanley Hansen; children: Emma, Isla. AB with greatest distinction cum laude, Mt. Holyoke Coll., 1969; MA, U. Minn., 1972; PhD, U. Wash., 1975. Asst. editor Mid. English dictionary U. Mich., 1975-77, assoc. rsch. editor, 1977—78; asst. prof. dept. English Hamilton Coll., NY, 1978—80, Haverford Coll., Pa., 1980—86, assoc. prof., 1986—90, chair, 1989—92, prof., 1991—2002, provost, 1995—2002; pres. Bates Coll., Lewiston, Maine, 2002—. Lectr. in field. Author: The Solomon Complex: Reading Wisdom in Old English Poetry, 1988, Chaucer and the Fictions of Gender, 1992, Mother Without Child: Contemporary Fiction and the Crisis of Motherhood, 1997; mem. editl. bd. Coll. Lit.; reader manuscripts for jours. and univ. presses; contbr. articles to profl. jours., also revs. and papers. NEH Summer stipendee, 1981; Mellon grantee for faculty devel. in humanities, 1983-84, Whitehead grantee for faculty in the humanities, 1987-88; Am. Coun. Learned Socs. fellow, 1993-94. Mem. MLA (mem. Chaucer divsn. exec. com. 1995-99, divsn. rep. to del. assembly 1996-99, com. on acad. freedom and profl. rights and responsibilities 1997-2000), Am. Coun. Learned Socs. (prescreener Cen. Fellowship Program), Medieval Acad., New Chaucer Soc., Nat. Women's Studies Assn., Soc. for Feminist Medieval Scholarship (pres. 1993-95). Office: Bates College Office of the Pres Lane Hall Rm 204 Lewiston ME 04240 Office Phone: 207-786-6100. E-mail: president@bates.edu.*

HANSEN, ERIK FREDERICK, lawyer; b. Wadena, Minn., Oct. 12, 1974; BA with honors, U. Minn., Morris, 1997; JD, U. Minn., Mpls., 2000. Bar: Minn. 2000, US Dist Ct. (dist. Minn.) 2000, US Ct. Appeals (8th cir.). Assoc. Hellmuth & Johnson, P.L.L.C., Eden Prairie, Minn. Named a Rising Star, Minn. Super Lawyers mag., 2006; named an Up and Coming Atty., 2006. Mem.: Minn. State Bar Assn. (chair membership com. 2004—06, mem. publs. com.). Office: Hellmuth & Johnson PLLC 10400 Viking Dr Ste 500 Eden Prairie MN 55344 Office Phone: 952-941-4005. E-mail: ehansen@hjlawfirm.com.*

HANSEN, GRANT LEWIS, retired air transportation executive; b. Bancroft, Idaho, Nov. 5, 1921; s. Paul Ezra and Leona Sarah (Lewis) H.; m. Iris Rose Heyden, Apr. 21, 1945; children: Alan Lee, Brian Craig, Carol Margaret, David James, Ellen Diane. BS in Elec. Engring., Ill. Inst. Tech., 1948; postgrad. engring. and mgmt., UCLA, Calif. Inst. Tech.; D.Sc., Nat. U., 1978. With Douglas Aircraft Co., 1948-60; v.p., program dir. for Centaur (Convair div.), 1960-65; v.p. launch vehicle programs Convair div. Gen. Dynamics Corp., 1965-69, v.p., gen. mgr., 1973-78; asst. sec. air force for research and devel., 1969-73; v.p. Gen. Dynamics Corp., San Diego, 1974-78; exec. v.p. System Devel. Corp., Santa Monica, Calif., 1978-86; also pres. SDC Systems Group, 1978-84. U.S. del. NATO (Adv. Group for Aerospace Research and Devel.), 1969-73; U.S. mem. sci. com. for nat. reps. SHAPE Tech. Center, The Hague, Netherlands, 1969-73; mem. research and tech. adv. council NASA, 1971-73; mem. sci. adv. bd. Dept. Air Force, 1976-86. Served with USNR, World War II Decorated Purple Heart; recipient Pub. Service award NASA, 1966, Disting. Pub. Service award NASA, 1975, Alumni Recognition award Ill. Inst. Tech., 1967, USAF Exceptional Civilian Service medal, 1973, 83; inducted Ill. Inst. Tech. Hall of Fame, 1984. Fellow AIAA (nat. pres. 1975), Am. Astronautical Soc., AAAS, Internat. Acad. Astronautics; mem. IEEE (sr.), German Soc. Air and Space Travel (corr.), Nat. Acad. Engring., NRC, Eta Kappa Nu, Tau Beta Pi. Home: 10737 Fuerte Dr La Mesa CA 91941-5740 *I've given my whole self to each challenge I've accepted, believing that what's best for my future is an honest day's effort today. I have great faith in my God and my country.*

HANSEN, H. JACK, management consultant; b. Chgo., Mar. 28, 1922; s. Herbert Christian John and Laura Elizabeth (Osterman) Hansen; m. Joan Dorothy Norum, Nov. 28, 1980; children: Marilyn Joan, Gail Jean(dec.) , Mark John, Jacquelyn Lee. BSME, Ill. Inst. Tech., 1944. Cert. mgmt. cons. Mech. and indsl. engr. Harper Wyman Co., Chgo., 1944-51; chief indsl. engr. Shakeproof divsn. Ill. Tool Works, Des Plaines, 1951-53; cons., prin. A.T. Kearney & Co., Chgo. and NYC, 1953-71; pres. H.J. Hansen Co., Elburn, Ill., 1971—2000. Acting mfg. engring. mgr. European Ops., Hobart Corp., 1974—78; owner, mgmt. cons. Hansen Mgmt. Search Co., Mt. Prospect, Ill., 1980—93; active turnaround cons., 1992—2000; apptd. by Kane County States Atty. Second Chance Panel, 2001—; apptd. to Kane County Chronicle's Readers adv. bd., 2002—04. Mem. Planning Commn. Village of Elburn, 1995—97, trustee, 1997—2001, chmn. Pers. Commn., mem. Fin. Commn., mem. Pub. Works Commn.; pres. Men's Club, 1987—90, Good Shepherd Luth. Ch., Des Plaines, Ill., 1988—90; active mem. mcpl. legis. com. DuKane Valley Coun., 1997—2001; bd. dirs. Elburn and Countryside Cmty. Ctr., 2006—. With US Army, 1945—46. Named to Tilden Tech. Alumni Assn. Hall of Fame, 2000. Mem. Inst. Mgmt. Cons. (founding), Methods-Time Measurement Assn. (bd. dirs. 1964-70, pres. 1967-68), Am. Arbitartion Assn., Soc. Advancement Mgmt. (past bd. dirs.), coun. for Internat. Progress in Mgmt. (past bd. dirs.), Found. Internat. Progress in Mgmt. (past bd. dirs.), Econ. Devel. Com. (tech. com., membership com.), Elburn C. of C. Achievements include research in shingles prevention. Office: H J Hansen Co 317 Prairie Valley St Elburn IL 60119-8977

HANSEN, H. REESE, law educator, former dean; b. Logan, Utah, Apr. 8, 1942; s. Howard F. and Loila Gayle (Reese) H.; m. Kathryn Traveller, June 8, 1962; children: Brian T., Mark T., Dale T., Curtis T. BS, Utah State U., 1964; JD, U. Utah, 1972. Bar: Utah, 1974. Atty. Strong, Poelman & Fox, Salt Lake City, 1972-74; from asst. prof. to assoc. prof. Brigham Young U., Provo, Utah, 1974-79, prof. law, 1979—, from asst. dean to assoc. dean, 1974-89, dean, 1989—2004. Commr. ex officio Utah State Bar, Salt Lake City, 1989-2004; commr. Nat. Conf. Commrs. on Uniform State Laws, 1988-95. Co-author: Idaho Probate System, 1977, Utah Probate System, 2nd edit., 2005, Cases and Text on Laws of Trusts, 7th edit., 2001; editor: Manual for Justices of Peace--Utah, 1978; contbr. articles to profl. jours. Mem. Lds Ch. Office: Brigham Young U 536 JRCB Provo UT 84602-1029 Home Phone: 801-375-1795; Office Phone: 801-422-3616.

HANSEN, HAROLD B., JR., assistant principal; b. Sewickley, Pa., July 3, 1955; s. Harold B. and Mary Clara (Van derVort) Hansen; m. Patty Jo Gabhart, Sept. 19, 1976; children: Jeremiah James, Joshua Andrew, Esther Beth, Christopher Seth. BA in Elem. Edn., Purdue U., 1980; MA in Sch. Adminstrn., Western N.Mex. U., 1987. Cert. secondary lang. arts and spl. edn. tchr., TESOL tchr., instrnl. leader, sch. adminstr., elem. tchr., coach N.Mex. Resource rm. tchr. Flossmoor/Homewood Pub. Schs., Ill., 1981, Newcomb HS, N.Mex., 1981—82; tchr. self-contained spl. edn. Chester Pub. Schs., Mont., 1982—84; adminstr., prin., tchr. Bennett Bapt. Ch. Sch., Colo., 1984; propr., tutor Hemispheric Learning Tutorial Svcs., 1982—; tchr. resource room, coach cross county, wrestling, track and field Gallup-McKinley County Pub. Schs., Tohatchi/Navajo Reserv., N.Mex., 1985—90, elem. tchr. phys. edn. and health, at-risk tchr. Tohatchi Elem. Sch. Tohatchi, 1990—98, 5th grade track & field head coach, 1991—98, 5th grade boys' and girls' basketball asst. coach, 1995—98; prin. Smith Lake Elem. Sch., Gallup-McKinley County Pub. Schs., 1998—2003; tchr. Mission Ave. Elem. Sch., Albuquerque Pub. Schs., 2003—06; asst. prin. Painted Sky Elem. Sch., Albuquerque Pub. Schs., 2006—07; asst prin. Barcelona Elem. Sch. & Mid. Sch. Acad., Albuquerque Pub. Schs., Albuquerque, 2007—. Mem. various sch. coms. Gallup-McKinley County Pub. Schs., 1990—98, 2001—03; seminar leader on hemispherecity; dep. registration officer McKinley County, N.Mex., 1986—98; profl. devel. dossier, external reviewer VisionLink, Inc., 2005—, Teach N.Mex., 2005—, N.Mex. Pub. Edn. Dept., 2005—, U. N.Mex. Past pres. Village of Hope, substance abuse tng. ctr.; co-founder, past bd. dirs. Christian Home Educators Assn.; past dir. Approved Workmen Are Not Ashamed; past coord. Jump Rope for Heart, Am. Heart Assn.; past mem. Coun. for

Curricular Excellence, McKinley County; pst TESOL rep. for Western N.Mex. U.'s Gallup Grad. Ctr.'s Advd. Coun., 1997—99. Named one of Outstanding Young Men of Am., 1987. Home: 631 Sienna St NW Albuquerque NM 87120-5921 Office Phone: 505-877-0400 ext. 34002. Personal E-mail: hbchansen@yahoo.com. Business E-Mail: hansen_ch@aps.edu.

HANSEN, HERBERT W., management consultant; b. June 16, 1935; s. Olive Anita (Read) French; m. Susan Lockwood Develin; children: Mary, Kathryn. AB, Dartmouth Coll., 1957; MBA, U. New Haven, 1973. Gen. mgr. clay pipe divsn. Interpace Corp., LA, 1974-75, v.p., gen. mgr. structural products divsn. Seattle, 1975-77, pres. retail dinnerware and tile divsn., 1977-79, pres., gen. mgr. Tuttle & Bailey divsn. New Britain, Conn., 1979-81; pres. Greater Hartford C. of C., Conn., 1981-86, Hartford Mgmt. Group, Inc., 1986-90; chmn. Hi-Speed Machine Products, 1990; pres. No. R.I. C. of C., Lincoln, 1991-92, Hansen Assocs., 1992—; tax advisor H & R Block, 1998—. Bd. dirs. Downtown Coun., Hartford, 1981-87, Hartford Area Pvt. Industry Coun., 1981-87, BBB, 1981-85, World Trade Ctr. of Conn., 1987-90; pres. Greater Hartford Corp., 1981-84; treas. Greater Hartford Arts Coun., 1981-87, exec. com., 1986, arts coun. dir., 1987-88; corporator Wadsworth Atheneum, 1985-91, Hartford Hosp., 1982-81, Mt. Sinai Hosp., 1981-90; overseer Dartmouth Hitchcock Med. Ctr., 1993—; chmn. Hartford Sem., 1987-90, trustee, 1990-92, pres. coun., 1992—; sec. bd. visitors Mortensen Libr.; dir. Riverfront Recapture, 1981-91; chmn. Episc. Charities Found., Hartford, 1985-87, dir., 1987-88; pres. Episc. Bishop's Fund, 1983-91; mem. Fellow-Am. Leadership Forum, audit com. Op. Fuel, 1986-88. Lt. comdr. USN, 1957-68. Episcopalian. Home: Box 917 13 Fernwood Ln Grantham NH 03753 Office: Hansen Assoc PO Box 917 Grantham NH 03753-0917 Home Phone: 603-863-1542; Office Phone: 866-238-7976. Personal E-mail: hhansen@adelphia.net.

HANSEN, JACK WINSOR, musician, educator; b. Seward County, Nebr., Dec. 5, 1927; s. Grant Elbert Hansen and Ruby Gertrude Winsor. MusB, Roosevelt U., 1950, MusM cum laude, 1952; studied with, Rudolph Ganz and Mollie Margolies; pvt. studies with Marguerite Long, Paris; pvt. studies with Maurice Dumesnil, pvt. studies with Sir William Walton. Mem. piano faculty Chgo. Mus. Coll., 1952—54; tchr. piano Sherwood Sch. Music, Chgo., 1954—56; instr. piano and composition N.D. State Coll., Minot, 1956—57; concert pianist various U.S. cities, 1957—87. Author: The Sibyl Sanderson Story - Requiem for a Diva, 2005; musician: NBC Artist Showcase Symphony, WGN Symphony, CBS Beethoven Bicentennial celebration with Chgo. Chamber Orch., numerous radio shows throughout U.S.; musician: (soloist) Am. premiere of Haydn G Major Concerto, 1955, world premiere of Markaitis Concerto for piano and woodwinds, 1966, Can. premiere of Haydn G Major Concerto, 1968, Am. TV premiere of Beethoven post. Rondo for piano and orch., 1970; contbr. articles to profl. publs. Recipient Richard Strauss award, 1949, Midwest Young Artists award, Soc. Am. Musicians, 1949, Allied Arts award, 1956—57. Mem.: N.W. Ind. Music Tchr.'s Assn., South Suburban Music Tchr.'s Assn., Chgo. Area Music Tchr.'s Assn., Nat. Music Tchr.'s Assn., Massenet Soc. (former bd. dirs.). Avocations: writing, poetry, collecting antiques, Egyptology. Home: 6346 Hohman Ave Hammond IN 46324

HANSEN, JACOB BERNARD, military officer; b. Milw., Oct. 20, 1959; s. Jacob and Nancy Ann Hansen; m. Jennifer Leigh Word; children: Erin Marie, Erica Leigh, Brianna Rose, Mitchell Carey. BS in Bus. Adminstrn., U. Wis., La Crosse, 1983; MS in Material Acquisition Mgmt., Naval Postgraduate Sch., Monterey, Calif., 1992; MS in Strategic Studies, US Army War Coll., Carlisle, P., 2004. Platoon leader 76th Heavy Equipment Maintenance Co., Ft. Knox, Ky., 1983—84; aide de camp 2d ROTC Region Hdqs., Ft. Knox, 1984—86; co. cmdr. 25th Inf. Divsn., Schofield, Hawaii, 1987—89, discom adj., 1989—90; contracting officer Def. Intelligence Agy., Missile and Space Intelligence Ctr., Huntsville, Ala., 1992—96; assignment officer US Army Pers. Command, Alexandria, Va., 1996—98; dep. comdr. Def. Contract Mgmt. Agy., Balt., 1998—2000, comdr. St. Petersburg, Fla., 2001—03, Baghdad, 2005—06; faculty instr. US Army War Coll., Carlisle, Pa., 2004—05; dir. combat support ctr. Defence Contract Mgmt. Agy., Alexandria, 2006—. Fed. coordinating com. chmn. Combined Fed. Campaign, St. Petersburg, 2002—03. Col. Army Acquisition Corps US Army, 2006—07, Springfield, Va. Decorated Meritorious Svc. medal US Army, Def. Meritorious Svc. medal, Bronze Star. Mem.: Army Acquisition Corps. Avocations: golf, cooking, travel, billiards. Home: 7402 Arundel Pl Springfield VA 22153 Office: Defense Contract Mgmt Agy 6350 Walker Ln Ste 300 Alexandria VA 22310-3241 Personal E-mail: jacob.hansen@us.army.mil. Business E-Mail: jacob.hansen@dcma.mil.

HANSEN, JAMES ALLEN, state agency administrator; b. West Point, Nebr., Jan. 10, 1939; s. Walter J. and Dorothy (Kay) H.; m. Janice A. Wenke, June 27, 1964 (div. 1975); m. Rebecca A. Bayer, Nov. 28, 1975. BA, Wayne State Coll., 1965. Pres. Farmers State Bank, Lexington, Nebr., 1972-80, No. Bank, Omaha, 1980-86, 1st Nat. Bank, Fremont, Nebr., 1986-87; regional v.p. Am. First Co., Omaha, 1987-90; mng. agt. FDIC/RTC, Burnsville, Minn., 1990; dir. Nebr. Dept. Banking & Fin., Lincoln, 1991-98; chmn., CEO Centennial Bank, Omaha, 1999—. Chmn. Conf. State Bank Suprs., Washington, 1992-97, vice-chmn. adv. bd., 2002—. Group study exch. team to Australia, Rotary Internat., 1970. 1st lt. U.S. Army N.G., 1960-66. Home: 18109 Mayberry St Omaha NE 68022 Office: Centennial Bank 9003 S 145th St Omaha NE 68138-3636

HANSEN, JAMES E., physicist, meteorologist, federal agency administrator; b. Mar. 29, 1941; BA in Physics and Math. with highest distinction, U. Iowa, 1963, MS in Astronomy, 1965; postgrad., U. Kyoto and Tokyo U., 1965-66; PhD in Physics, U. Iowa, 1967. NAS-NRC resident rsch. assoc. Goddard Inst. for Space Studies, NYC, 1967-69, mem. staff, space scientist, mgr. planetary and climate programs, 1972-81; NSF postdoctoral fellow Leiden Observatory, Netherlands, 1969; rsch. assoc. Columbia U., 1969-72; dir. NASA Goddard Inst. for Space Studies, NYC, 1981—. Adj. assoc. prof. dept. geol. scis. Columbia U., 1978-85, adj. prof., earth and environmental sciences, 1985—; co-prin. investigator AEROPOL (airbourne terrestrial infrared polarimeter) Project, 1971-74; co-investigator Voyager Photopolarimeter Experiment, 1972-85; prin. investigator Pioneer Venus Orbiter Cloud-Photopolarimeter Experiment, 1974-78, co-investigator, 1978-1994; prin. investigator Galileo (Jupiter Orbiter) Photopolarimeter Radiometer Experiment, 1977-2000, Earth Observing System Interdisciplinary Investigation: Interannual Variability of Earth's Carbon, Energy and Water Cycles, 1989-2000. Author: Spaceflight Revolution: NASA Langley Rsch. Ctr. from Sputnik to Apollo, 1995, Engineer in Charge: A History of the Langley Aeronautical Lab., The Bird Is on the Wing: Aerodynamics & the Progress of the Am. Airplane, 2003, First Man: The Life of Neil A. Armstrong, 2005; co-author: Radiation in the Atmosphere, 1978, Carbon Dioxide Review, 1982, others; contbr. articles to profl. publications. Recipient Goddard Spl. Achievement award (Pioneer, Venus), 1977, NASA Group Achievement award, 1982 (Voyager, Photopolarimeter), 1993 (Galileo, Polarmeter/Radiometer), NASA Exceptional Svc. medal (Radiative Transfer), 1984, Nat. Wildlife Federation Conservation Achievement award, 1989, NASA Presdl. Rank award of Meritorious Executive, 1990, 1997, U. Iowa Alumni Achievement award, 1991, John Heinz Environment award, 2001, Duke of Edinburgh Conservation medal, World Wildlife Fund, 2006, Leo Szilard Lectureship award, Am. Phys. Soc., 2007; nominee Rave award in Science, WIRED, 2005; named U. Iowa Alumni Fellow, 2000; named one of 100 Most Influential People, Time Mag., 2006; named a Dan David Prize Laureate, 2007. Fellow: Am. Geophys. Union (Roger Revelle Medal 2002); mem.: NAS. Achievements include research in radiative transfer in planetary atmospheres, interpretation of remote sounding of planetary atmospheres, the properties of the clouds of Venus leading to their identification as sulfuric acid; development of simplified climate models and 3-D global climate models, climate mechanisms such as the role of clouds in climate, current climate trends from observational data and projections of man's impact on climate. Known for his testimony on climate change to congressional committees in the 1980s that helped raise awareness to the global warming issue. Office: NASA Goddard Inst Space Studies 2880 Broadway New York NY 10025 Address: Columbia U 750 Armstrong Hall 2880 Broadway New York NY 10025 Office Phone: 212-678-5500, 212-678-5500. Business E-Mail: jhansen@giss.nasa.gov.*

HANSEN, JAMES EDWARD, medical educator, researcher; b. Green Bay, Wis., Sept. 4, 1926; s. James Christian and Helen Dorothy (Terp) H.; m. Beverly May Kapke, June 5, 1948; children: Barbara Parry, Patricia Begley, Linda DeGroot, James H. Student, St. Norbert's Coll., 1942-43, U. Wis., 1943-44, Marquette U., 1944-45; MD, Johns Hopkins U., 1945-49. Diplomate Am. Bd. Internal Medicine. Intern, then resident Letterman Army Med. Ctr., San Francisco, 1949-53; commd. 1st lt. U.S. Army, 1949, advanced through grades to col. Kans., Colo., London, Japan, France, and Jordan, 1975, physician Kans., Colo., London, 1950-62; chief physiology div. U.S. Army Med. Rsch. and Nutrition Lab., Denver, 1962-65; sci. dir. U.S. Army Rsch. Inst. Environ. Medicine, Natick, Mass., 1965-71; chief clin. investigation svcs. Tripler Army Med. Ctr., Honolulu, 1971-75; assoc. prof. dept. medicine UCLA, Torrance, 1976-78, prof. dept. medicine, 1978-86, emeritus prof. dept. medicine, 1986—. Instr., asst. prof. U. Colo., 1961-65; liaison mem. applied physiology study sect. NIH, 1965-71; cons. environ. medicine U.S. Army Surgeon Gen., Washington, 1965-73; lectr. environ. medicine Johns Hopkins U., Balt., 1966-71; clin. prof. physiology U. Hawaii, 1972-75; mem. bd. dirs. Cardiopulmonary Dynamics, Atlanta. Co-author: Principles of Exercise Testing and Interpretation, 1986, 4th rev. edit., 2005; contbr. numerous articles to profl. jours. Chmn. congregation St. Matthew's Luth. Ch., Aurora, Colo., 1962-64, Gloria Dei Luth. Ch., Pearl City, Hawaii, 1972-74; sch. supt. Luth. Ch., Natick, 1967-69; elder, mission com. chmn. St. Peter's By the Sea Presbyn. Ch., Rancho Palos Verdes, Calif., 1992-95; mem. bd. dirs. Vol. Am., LA, 2005-. Pulmonary fellow Fitzsimons Army Med. Ctr., 1960, UCLA Ctr. Health Scis., 1975-76; recipient Sustaining Membership award Assn. Mil. Surgeons, 1970, Calif. medal Am. Lung Assn., 1996; named Layperson of Yr., South Coast Interfaith Coun., 2004. Fellow ACP, Am. Coll. Chest Physicians; mem. Am. Physiol. Soc., Am. Thoracic Soc. (sci. adv. bd. 1983-00), Calif. Thoracic Soc. (pulmonary chmn. 1980-83, physiology com), Internat. Soc. Exercise Intolerance Rsch. and Edn. (founding mem. 2005-, advisor bd. dirs. 2005-). Avocations: piano, tennis. Home: 1692 Morse Dr San Pedro CA 90732-4336 Office: Harbor-UCLA Med Ctr PO Box 405 1000 W Carson St Torrance CA 90502-2004 Office Phone: 310-222-3803. Personal E-mail: jimandbev@cox.net. Business E-Mail: jhansen@labiomed.org.

HANSEN, JAMES LEE, sculptor; b. Tacoma, June 13, 1925; s. Hildreth Justine and Mary Elizabeth Hansen; m. Annabelle Hair, Aug. 31, 1946 (dec. Sept. 1993); children: Valinda Jean, Yauna Marie; m. Jane Lucas, May 13, 1994. Grad., Portland Art Mus. Sch. Faculty Oreg. State U., Corvallis, 1957-58, U. Calif., Berkeley, 1958, Portland (Oreg) State U., 1964-90. One-man shows include Fountain Gallery, Portland, 1966, 69, 77-81, U. Oreg. Art Mus., Eugene, 1970, Seligman (Seders Gallery), Seattle, 1970, Portland Art Mus., 1971, Cheney Cowles Meml. Mus., Spokane, Wash., 1972, Polly Freidlander Gallery, Seattle, 1973, 75-76, Smithsonian Instn., Washington, 1974, Hodges/Banks Gallery (now Linda Hodges Gallery), Seattle, 1983, Abanté Gallery, Portland, 1986, 88, 92, Maryhill Mus. of Art, Goldendale, Wash., 1997-98, Bryan Ohno Gallery, Seattle, 1997, 99, 2002, 04, Mus. Northwest Art, La Conner, Wash., 1999; exhibited in group shows at N.W. Ann. Painters and Sculptors, Seattle, 1952-73, Oreg. Ann. Painters and Sculptors, Portland Art Mus., 1952-75, Whitney Mus. Am. Art, NYC, 1953, Santa Barbara (Calif.) Mus. Art, 1959-60, Denver Art Mus., 1960, San Francisco Art Mus., 1960, Smithsonian Instn., Washington, 1974, Wash. State U., Pullman, 1975, Benton County Hist. Mus., 1998; represented in permanent collections Graphic Arts Ctr., State Capitol, Olympia, Wash., U. Oreg., Eugene, Salem (Oreg.) Civic Ctr., Clark Coll., Vancouver, Wash., Portland Art Mus., Transit Mall, Portland, Seattle Art Mus., Gresham Town Fair (Oreg.), Oreg. Health Scis. U., Portland, Vancouver Sculpture Park, others; represented by Hansen Studio, Battle Ground, Wash., Peter Bartlow Gallery, Chgo. Address: 28219 NE 63rd Ave Battle Ground WA 98604-7107 Office Phone: 360-687-4627. Business E-Mail: info@jamesleehansen.com.

HANSEN, JO-IDA CHARLOTTE, psychology professor, researcher; b. Washington, Oct. 2, 1947; d. Gordon Henry and Charlotte Lorraine (Helgeson) H.; m. John Paul Campbell. BA, U. Minn., 1969, MA, 1971, PhD, 1974. Asst. prof. psychology U. Minn., Mpls., 1974-78, assoc. prof., 1978-84, prof., 1984—, dir. Ctr. for Interest Measurement Rsch., 1974—, dir. counseling psychology program, 1987—, dir. Vocat. Assessment Clinic, 1997—, prof. human resources and indsl. rels., 1997—, assoc. dean for grad. studies Coll. Liberal Arts, 2005—. Author: User's Guide for the SII, 1984, 2d edit., 1992, Manual for the SII, 1985 2d edit. 1994; editor: Measurement and Evaluation in Counseling and Development, 1993-2000; editor Jour. Counseling Psychology, 1999-2005; contbr. over 150 articles to profl. jours., chpts. to books. Recipient early career award U. Minn., 1982, E.K. Strong, Jr. gold medal, 1984. Fellow APA (coun. reps. 1990-93, 97-99, pres. divsn. counseling psychology 1993-94, chmn. joint com. testing practices 1989-93, com. to revise APA/Am. Ednl. Rsch. Assn. nat. coun. measurement evalation testing stds. 1993-99, exam. com. Assn. State Provincial Psychology Bds. 1996-99, bd. sci. affairs, 2003-05, chair coun. of editors 2003-04; Leona Tyler award for rsch. and profl. svc. 1996); mem. ACA (extended rsch. award 1990, disting. rsch. award 1996), Assn. for Measurement and Evaluation (pres. 1988-89, Exemplary Practice award 1987, 90). Avocations: golf, theater, music, water and downhill skiing, spectator sports. Office: U Minn Dept Psychology Ctr Interest Measurement 75 E River Rd Minneapolis MN 55455-0280 Office Phone: 612-626-9062. Business E-Mail: hanse004@umn.edu.

HANSEN, JOSEPH T., labor union administrator; Organizer, rep., pacific regional dir. United Food & Comml. Workers Internat. Union, dir. food processing, packing and mfg., sec.-treas., 1997—2004, internat. pres., 2004—. Mem. com. on immigrant workers AFL-CIO; pres.-elect Union Network Internat. Office: UFCW Internat Union 1775 K St NW Washington DC 20006 Office Phone: 202-223-3111.*

HANSEN, KAREN THORNLEY, accountant; b. Chgo., June 1, 1945; BA, Marycrest Coll., Davenport, Iowa, 1967. CPA, N.Y.; cert. med. technologist. Med. staff tech. Mercy Hosp., Davenport, Iowa, 1967-68, St. Joseph Hosp., Chgo., 1968, Spl. Hematology, Wilford Hall, USAF Hosp., Lackland AFB, Tex., 1973-78; staff acct. Lewittes & Co., Poughkeepsie, N.Y., 1980-81; sr. acct. Urbach, Kahn & Werlin, Poughkeepsie, 1981-82; ptnr. Hansen & Dunn, CPA's, Poughkeepsie, 1982-94, Hansen & Arnold, Poughkeepsie, 1995-2000, Sedore & Co., CPA, 2001—. Bd. dirs., sec. United Way Dutchess County, Poughkeepsie, 1988—94; mem. Jr. League Poughkeepsie, 1979—; mem. membership com. and econ. devel. com. Poughkeepsie Partnership, Inc.; trustee St. Martin de Porres Ch.; bd. dirs. YMCA Dutchess County, Girl Scouts U.S.A., 1983—87, Mid-Hudson Civic Ctr., Inc., 1993—95, Civic Properties, Inc., 1992—, Poughkeepsie Inst., 1999—2006, Am. Heart Assn. Dutchess and Ulster Counties, 2001—, Dutchess County Econ. Devel. Corp., 2007. Mem. AICPA, N.Y. State Soc. CPAs, Greater Poughkeepsie Area C. of C. (bd. dirs. 1986—, 1st vice chair 1996, chair, 1997, sec. exec. com. 1991, Amrita Club (bd. dirs. 1982-92, pres. 1990), Poughkeepsie Tennis Club. Republican. Roman Catholic. Office: 2678 South Rd Poughkeepsie NY 12601-5254

HANSEN, KENNETH, lawyer; b. Columbus, Ohio, Jan. 27, 1951; AB cum laude, Harvard Coll., 1974; MA, Yale U., 1976; MPA, Harvard U., 1979; JD cum laude, U. Pa., 1983. Bar: Mass. 1984, DC 2002. Counsel, sr. comml. counsel, asst. gen. counsel, assoc. gen. counsel Overseas Pvt. Investment Corp., Washington, 1986—95; counsel Baker & Botts, 1995; gen. counsel Export-Import Bank, Washington, 1995—99; ptnr., Fin. Chadbourne & Parke, LLP, Washington, 1999—, hiring ptnr. Washington Office. Adj. prof. Georgetown U., 1991—, Boston U., 1992—99, George Washington U., 1992—94, Tufts U., 1993; professorial lectr. John Hopkins U., 2000—. Contbr. articles to profl. jour.; spkr. in field. Mem.: Washington Fgn. Law Soc. (pres. 2004—), Am. Soc. Internat. Law, ABA. Office: Chadbourne & Parke LLP 1200 New Hampshire Ave NW Washington DC 20036-6802 Office Phone: 202-974-5600. Office Fax: 202-974-5602. Business E-Mail: khansen@chadbourne.com.

HANSEN, KENNETH D., lawyer, ophthalmologist; b. Seattle, Mar. 26, 1947; s. George R. and Elaine D. (Jacobsen) H.; m. Barbara Caleen, Oct. 8, 1976; 1 son, David Scott. BS in Psychology, U. Wash., 1969, JD, 1972, MD with honors, 1976. Bar: Wash. 1972, Mich. 1977, Ill. 1984, D.C. 1986, U.S. Supreme Ct. 1981; diplomate Am. Bd. Ophthalmology. Legal counsel Assn. Wash. Bus., Olympia, 1972-73; asst. atty. gen. State of Wash., Seattle, 1973-74; v.p., gen. counsel NW Med. Rsch. Found., Seattle, 1976-86; pres. Internat. Health Found., 1986—; intern medicine U. Mich. Hosp., Ann Arbor, 1977, resident in ophthalmology, 1978-80; sr. med. staff Henry Ford Hosp., Detroit, 1981-82; dir. ophthalmology Carbondale (Ill.) Clinic, 1983-86, chmn. dept. surgery, gen. counsel, 1984-86; clin. asst. prof. ophthalmology and med. humanities So. Ill. U., Carbondale, 1983-86; clin. asst. prof. ophthalmology U. Md., Balt., 1986—92; pres., gen. counsel Internat. Inst. for Biomed. Rsch., 2002—. Med.-legal adv. com. U. Mich. Hosp. System; cons. Nat. Def. Med. Coll., China; charter coun. mem. practicing physicians adv. coun. to Sec. of U.S. Dept. Health and Human Svcs., 1992-97; lectr. in field. Assoc. editor Trauma, 1995-97, Wash. Law Rev., 1971-72; contbr. articles to profl. jours. Recipient U. Wash. Med. Thesis Award, Gold Medal Egyptian Med. Syndicate, 1986; William Wallice Wilshire Meml. scholar; Anna C. Dunlap Meml. scholar; Grad. Rsch. fellow, 1975-76; recipient Rod Rose award Soc. Rsch. Adminstrs., 1989. Fellow Am. Coll. Legal Medicine (jud. coun., model statutes com., Pres.'s award 1989), Internat. Coll. Surgeons; mem. ABA, AMA, Wash. State Bar Assn., Mich. Bar Assn., Ill. Med. Soc. (med.-legal coun.), Ill. Bar Assn., Mich. Med. Schs. Coun. Deans (med.-legal adv. com.), Mich. Ophthalmology Soc. (Rsch. award 1981), Am. Acad. Ophthalmology, D.C. Bar Assn., Phi Delta Pi, Phi Eta Sigma, Pi Sigma Epsilon. Baptist. Office: 901 N Stuart St Ste 210 Arlington VA 22203 Home: 220 108th Ave Ste 501 Treasure Island FL 33706 Personal E-mail: bioinstitute@yahoo.com. Business E-Mail: khansenmd@iibr.com.

HANSEN, KENT FORREST, nuclear engineering educator; b. Chgo., Aug. 10, 1931; s. Kay Frost and Mary (Cummins) H.; m. Katherine Elizabeth Kavanagh, June 13, 1959 (dec. Dec. 1975); children: Thomas Kay, Katherine Mary; m. Deborah Lea Hill, June 26, 1977, (div. Aug. 1991); 1 child, Gordon Benedict; m. Léonie Andrews Work, June 11, 1992. S.B., Mass. Inst. Tech., 1953, Sc.D., 1959. Sr. engr. Sylvania Electric Products, Waltham, Mass., 1957-58; asst. prof. nuclear engring. MIT, Cambridge, Mass., 1960-64, assoc. prof., 1964-68, prof., 1968—, assoc. dean engring., 1979-81, assoc. dir. energy lab., 1984-90. Bd. dirs. EG&G, Inc., Stone & Webster, Inc.; cons. to industry. Co-author: Numerical Methods of Reactor Analysis, 1964, Advances in Nuclear Science and Technology, Vol. 8, 1975. Ford postdoctoral fellow, 1960-61 Fellow Am. Nuclear Soc. (dir., Arthur Holly Compton award 1978); mem. Am. Nuclear Soc., Nat. Acad. Engring., Sigma Xi, Sigma Chi. Home: 23 Phillips Pond Rd Natick MA 01760-5643 Office: MIT Cambridge MA 02139-4325 Office Phone: 617-253-7384. Business E-Mail: kfhansen@mit.edu.

HANSEN, KRISTOPHER M., lawyer; b. 1970; BS, Fordham Univ., 1992, JD, 1995. Bar: NY 1996. Adminstrv. ptnr., fin. restructuring practice Stroock & Stroock & Lavan LLP, NYC, 1996—. Office: Stroock & Stroock & Lavan LLP 180 Maiden Ln New York NY 10038-4982 Office Phone: 212-806-6056. Office Fax: 212-806-9056. Business E-Mail: khansen@stroock.com.

HANSEN, LIBBY, broadcast executive; b. Dec. 9, 1971; m. Brett Hansen. Comml. real estate broker; with Brillstein-Grey; dir. devel. Burrow Owl Prodns. Touchstone TV; mgr. alternative series and spls. ABC, 2000—02, dir., 2002—03, exec. dir. alternative series and spls., 2003—04; head reality dept. USA Network, 2004; v.p. alternative series and spls. NBC and USA Network. Achievements include working on reality shows such as The Bachelor, The Bachelorette, Extreme Makeover, Extreme Makeover: Home Edition, Wife Swap, Nashville Star and Made in the USA. Avocation: cooking. Office: NBC 3000 W Alameda Ave Burbank CA 91523*

HANSEN, LOUISE HILL, music educator, retired application developer; b. Claudville, Va., Oct. 28, 1936; d. James Hobert Hil and Ruth Hubbard Hill; m. Gary George Hansen, Mar. 2, 1958; 1 child, Ricky Allen. AA, Sandhill CC, 1969; BA in History, West Chester State U., Pa., 1971; cert., Assumption Montessori Tchrs. Sch., 1972; student in Music, Lincoln U., 1977—95; MPA, U. Mo., 1984. Cert. tchr. 1996. Clk. The Pentagon USAF, Washington, 1955—57; tchr. Libertyville (Ill.) Montessori Sch., 1972—75; adminstrv. asst. Office Gov. Joseph Teasdale, Jefferson City, Mo., 1977—81; programmer analyst Dept. Social Svcs., Jefferson City, 1981—96; prin., owner Hansen Music Studio, Waupaca, Wis., 1997—. Organist Crystal Lake Ch., Waupaca, 2000—. Mem.: DAR, Nat. Guild Piano Tchrs., Wis. Music Tchrs. Assn., Suzuki Assn. Am. (tchr. tng. 1996, 1997, 1999—2001, 2003—04). Democrat. Avocations: exercise, travel. Home and Office: Hansen Music Studio N2237 Smith Rd Waupaca WI 54981

HANSEN, MARKA, retail executive; BA in Liberal Studies, Loyola Marymount U., LA. With Robinson's Dept. Stores, Calif.; mdse. mgr. Banana Republic women's divsn. Gap, Inc., San Francisco, 1987, v.p. men's merchandising Banana Republic, v.p. merchandising Internat. divsn., 1993—95, sr. v.p., 1995—2000, head human resources orgn., 2000—02, exec. v.p. Gap adult merchandising, 2002—03, pres. Banana Republic, 2003—07, pres. Gap brand, 2007—. Bd. mem. Gap Found. Office: Gap Inc 2 Folsom St San Francisco CA 94105 Office Phone: 650-952-4400.*

HANSEN, MATILDA, former state legislator; b. Paullina, Iowa, Sept. 4, 1929; d. Arthur J. and Sada G. (Thompson) Henderson; m. Robert B. Michener, 1950 (div. 1963); children: Eric J., Douglas E.; m. Hugh G. Hansen (dec.). BA, U. Colo., 1963; MA, U. Wyo., 1970. Tchr. history Englewood (Colo.) Sr. H.S., 1963-65; dir. Albany County Adult Learning Ctr., Laramie, Wyo., 1966-78, Laramie Plains Civic Ctr., 1979-83; treas. Wyo. Territorial Prison Corp., Laramie, 1988-93, also bd. dirs. Bd. dirs. Wyo. Territorial Pk. Author: (textbooks) To Help Adults Learn, 1975, Let's Play Together, 1978, Clear Use of Power, A Slice of Wyoming Political History, 2002. Legislator Wyo. Ho. of Reps., Cheyenne, 1975-95, minority whip, 1987-88, asst. minority leader, 1991-92, 93-94; mem. mgmt. coun. Wyo. State Legislature, Cheyenne, 1983-84; chair Com. for Dem. Legislature, Cheyenne, 1990-94, Wyo. State Dems., 1995-99; clk. Wyo. Soc. of Friends meeting, 2003-. GE fellow in econs. for high sch. tchrs., 1963; named Pub. Citizen of Yr., Wyo. Assn. Social Workers, 1980-81. Mem. LWV Wyo. (v.p. 1966-68), LWV Laramie (bd. dirs. 1966-72, Nat. Conf. State Legislators (vice chair human resources 1983, nat. exec. com.

1990-94), Laramie Area C. of C., Laramie Women's Club, Faculty Women's Club. Democrat. Avocations: gardening, mountain climbing, quilting. Home and Office: 1306 E Kearney St Laramie WY 82070-4142

HANSEN, NICK DANE, lawyer; b. Detroit, June 19, 1938; s. Nick F. and Ellen (Adelorn) H.; m. Susan Fox Cohee, Aug. 23, 1963; children: Todd Erik, Dana E. BA, Albion Coll., 1960; JD, Wayne State U., 1964; LLM, Georgetown U., 1970. Bar: Mich. 1964, Ill. 1970, Wis. 1975. Law clk. to assoc. justice Mich. Supreme Ct., Lansing, 1964-66; atty. Office of Chief Counsel IRS, Washington, 1966-70; ptnr. McDermott, Will & Emery, Chgo., 1970-74; sr. tax atty. Kimberly-Clark Corp., Neenah, Wis., 1975, tax counsel, 1975-76, staff v.p., 1976-80, v.p., tax counsel Dallas, 1980-98; cons., 1998—2001. Bd. dirs. ithought.com Mem. bd. advisor Jour. Internat. Taxation. Sec., bd. dirs. Bergstrom-Mahler Mus., Neenah, 1982-85. Mem.: ABA (chmn. com. fgn. activities tax sect. 1991—92, article editor The Tax Lawyer), Tax Execs. Inst., Wis. Bar Assn.

HANSEN, PETER REINHARD, economics professor; s. Ole Henning and Elly Hansen; m. Gridt Vig Find, Aug. 16, 2003; 1 child, Niels Vig. BS, U. Copenhagen, 1994, MS in Math. and Econ., 1995; PhD in Econ., U. Calif., La Jolla, 2000. Asst. prof. econ. Brown U., Providence, 2000—04, Stanford U., Calif., 2004—. Editor (assoc.): Jour. Applied Econometrics. Fellow Econometrics Analysis, U. Calif., 1999-2000; grantee Data Mining and Model Comparison, Danish Rsch. Agy., 2001-2002; scholar, Danish Rsch. Acad., 1997-2000; Salomon Rsch. grant, Brown U., 2001-2003, rsch. fellow, Ctr. for Rsch. in Econometric Analysis of Time Series. Mem.: Econometric Soc. Office: Stanford U 579 Serra Mall Stanford CA 94305 Office Phone: 650-725-1869.

HANSEN, RICHARD OLAF, geophysicist, educator, director; b. Ottawa, Ont., Can., Oct. 4, 1946; came to U.S., 1968; s. Hyllard Olaf and Muriel Lenora (Helson) H.; m. Kathleen Jean Thoms, June 15, 1968. BSc with honors, Carleton U., 1968; MS, U. Chgo., 1969, PhD, 1973. Rsch. assoc. U. Pitts., 1973-75; postdoctoral rsch. asst. U. Oxford, Oxford, England, 1975-76; lectr. U. Calif., Berkeley, 1976-78; staff scientist EG&G Geometrics, Sunnyvale, Calif., 1979-85; prof. Colo. Sch. of Mines, Golden, Colo., 1985-95; prin. geophysicist PRJ Inc. (formerly Pearson, de Ridder and Johnson, Inc.), Lakewood, Colo., 1995—2002, pres., 2003—06; sr. v.p. EDCON-PRJ, Inc., Lakewood, 2006—. Assoc. editor Geophysics, 1987-91, 95-99. Mem. Soc. Exploration Geophysicists (hon.), Am. Geophys. Union, Am. Phys. Soc., European Assn. Geoscientists and Engrs., Sigma Xi. Office: EDCON-PRJ Inc 171 S Van Gordon St Ste E Lakewood CO 80228 Home Phone: 303-420-3558; Office Phone: 303-987-1114, 303-980-6556. Business E-Mail: rohansen@edcon-prj.com.

HANSEN, ROBERT CLINTON, electrical engineer, consultant; b. St. Louis, 1926; married, 1952; 2 children. BS, U. Mo., 1949, DEng (hon.), 1975; MS, U. Ill., 1950, PhD, 1955. Rsch. assoc. antenna lab. U. Ill., 1950-55; sr. staff engr. microwave lab. Hughes Aircraft Co., 1955-59; sr. staff engr. telecomm. lab. Space Technol. Labs., 1959-60; dir. test mission analysis office Aerospace Corp., Calif., 1960-67; head electronics divsn. KMS Technol. Ctr., 1967-71; pres., cons. R.C. Hansen, Inc., Tarzana, Calif., 1971—. Mem. commn. B Internat. Sci. Radio Union. Editor: Microwave Scanning Antennas, 1964—65, Significant Phased Array Papers, 1973, Geometric Theory of Diffraction, 1981, Moment Methods in Antennas and Scattering, 1990; author: Phased Array Antennas, 1998, Electrically Small, Superdirective and Superconducting Antennas, 2006. Recipient Disting. Alumnus award, U. Ill. Elec. Engring. Dept., 1981, Disting. Alumnus Svc. medal, 1986. Fellow: IEEE (pres. antennas and propagation soc. 1964, 1980), Inst. Elec. Engrs. (London), Aerospace & Electronic Sys. Soc. (Barry Carlton award 1991, AP Disting. Achievement award 1994, Electromagnetics award 2002); mem.: NAE, Am. Phys. Soc. Office: RC Hansen Inc PO Box 570215 Tarzana CA 91357

HANSEN, ROBERT JOSEPH, civil engineer; b. Tacoma, May 27, 1918; s. Joseph and Olaug (Axness) H.; m. Eleanor Swaim Welch, Dec. 26, 1948; children: Eric Charles, Karen Welch. BS, U. Wash., 1940; Sc.D., MIT, 1948. Research engr. NRC, 1940-43; Princeton U., 1943-45; Arthur D. Little Co., Cambridge, Mass., 1945; NRC predoctoral fellow, 1946-47; research asso. MIT, 1947-48, mem. faculty, 1948—, prof. civil engring., 1957—, dep. dir. Project Transp., 1964-67. Ptnr. Hansen, Holley & Biggs, Inc. (cons. engrs.), Cambridge, 1955-88, prin., 1975-88; ptnr. Newmark, Hansen & Assos., Cambridge and Urbana, Ill., 1958-68; cons. biomechanics Mass. Gen. Hosp., 1956-60; mem. security resources panel Exec. Office of Pres., 1957; mem. sr. adv. panel Air Force Ballistic Div., USAF, 1958-60; mem. exec. com. Adv. Com. CD, Nat. Acad. Scis., 1959— Author: (with others) Structural Design for Dynamic Loads, 1959; also articles, chpts. in books.; editor: Seismic Design for Nuclear Power Plants, 1970. Recipient Army-Navy cert. of appreciation, 1948; Disting. Service citation Dept. Def., 1969 Fellow ASCE (Moisseiff award 1974, Raymond C. Reese research prize 1975, Innovation Civil Engring award 1989); mem. Boston Soc. Civil Engrs., Sigma Xi, Tau Beta Pi. Home: 25 Cambridge St Winchester MA 01890-3703

HANSEN, ROBYN L., lawyer; b. Terre Haute, Ind., Dec. 2, 1949; d. Robert Louis and Shirley (Nagel) Wieman; m. Gary Hansen, Aug. 21, 1971 (div. 1985); children: Nathan Ross Hansen, Brian Michael Hansen; m. John Marley Clarey, Jan. 1, 1986; 1 child, John Zender Clarey. BA, Gustavus Adolphus, 1971; JD cum laude, William Mitchell Coll. Law, 1977. Bar: Minn. 1977, U.S. Dist. Ct. Minn. 1977. Atty. Briggs and Morgan P.A., St. Paul, 1977-93, Leonard, Street and Deinard, Mpls., 1993—. Trustee Actors Theatre, St. Paul, 1980—88, Minn. Mus. Am. Art, 1994—97; active Minn. Inst. Pub. Fin., 1987—93, bd. dirs., 1993—95, pres., 1995; bd. dirs. St. Paul Downtown Coun., 1985—93, St. Paul Area Conv. and Vis. Bur., 1995—2005, chair, 1999—2001; trustee Met. State U. Found., 1993—2005, chair, 2000—02; bd. dirs. Capital City Partnership, 1997—, Pk. Sq. Theatre, 2003—, St. Paul Found., 2005—07; mem. River Ctr. Conv. and Visitors Authority, 2005—06, Minn. State Fair Found., 2005—, The Amherst H. Wilder Found., 2006—. Mem. ABA, Minn. Bar Assn., Ramsey County Bar Assn., Nat. Assn. Bond Lawyers, St. Paul Area C. of C. (bd. dirs., exec. com. 1997-99). Office: Leonard Street and Deinard 150 S Fifth St Minneapolis MN 55402 Office Phone: 612-335-1987. Business E-Mail: robyn.hansen@leonard.com.

HANSEN, SHERRI M., psychiatrist; b. Royal Oak, Wis., Mar. 7, 1965; d. Altan Hansen and Mary Katharine Bogart. BS, Mich. State U., East Lansing, 1987; MD, U. Mich., Ann Arbor, 1991. Diplomate gen. psychiatry Am. Bd. Psychiatry and Neurology, 1996. Pvt. practice psychiatrist, Capitol Assocs., LLC, Madison, Wis., 2000—. Clin. asst. prof. dept. psychiatry U. Wis. Med. Sch., Madison, 2000—. Contbr. chapters to books, articles to profl. jours. Active Wis. United for Mental Health, Madison, 2006—06. Recipient George Sternberg medal for Excellence in Preventative Medicine, U. Mich. Med. Sch., 1991, William Herdman award for Resident Tchr. of Yr., U. Mich. Med. Sch., Dept. Psychiatry, 1994, 1995, Med. Edn. Devel. and Leadership Program award, U. Wis. Med. Sch., 2000; Academic fellow, Academic Psychiatry, 1996. Mem.: State Med. Soc. Wis., Am. Psychiat. Assn. Lutheran. Avocations: Christian composer and musician, knitting, yoga. Office: Capitol Associates LLC Ste 200 440 Science Dr Madison WI 53711 Home Phone: 608-234-8570; Office Phone: 608-238-5176. Office Fax: 608-238-2727. Business E-Mail: sherrihansen@tds.net.

HANSEN, STEPHEN CHRISTIAN, banker; b. NYC, July 3, 1940; s. Norbert C. and Harriet C. H.; m. Ethel Olmsted, June 12, 1971; 1 son, Lee Christian. AB, Princeton U., 1962; LL.B., U. Va., 1966; postgrad., Brown U. Grad. Sch. Banking. Bar: N.Y. 1966. Assoc. Alexander & Green, NYC, 1966-68; mem. N.Y. State Legislature, 1968-70; spl. asst. to undersec. HUD, Washington, 1970-73; spl. asst. to chmn. FDIC, Washington, 1973-76; sr. v.p. Dollar Bank FSB, Pitts., 1976-78, pres., 1978—82, pres., CEO, 1982—2007, chmn. emeritus, 2007—. Chmn. Regional Indsl. Devel. Corp.; bd. dirs. Am. Respiratory Alliance, World Affairs Coun. Active Regional Air Svc. Partnership; trustee Carnegie Inst.; bd. dirs. Carnegie Sci. Ctr.; bd. dir. Cleve. Dist. Pitts. Fed. Res. Mem.: Regional Investors Coun., NY State Bar Assn., Allegheny Conf. on Cmty. Devel. Office: Dollar Bank PO Box 987 Pittsburgh PA 15230-0987

HANSEN, THOMAS J., engineering executive; BS in Mktg., No. Ill. U., DeKalb, 1971; MA in Bus. Adminstrn., Govs. State U., Univ. Park, Ill., 1978. Zone sales mgr. GE; various positions including regional sales mgr. and plant mgr. Singer Controls; sales and mktg. mgr. Shakeproof Indsl. Products businesses Ill. Tool Works (ITW), Glenview, 1980—83, gen. mgr. Shakeproof Indsl. Products divsn., 1983—86, v.p., gen. mgr. North Am. Indsl. Metal Fastener and Buckle divsns., 1986—90, pres. North Am. Indsl. and Automotive Fastener businesses, 1990—93, pres. Metal Fasteners and Components businesses, 1993, exec. v.p., 1998—2006, vice chmn., 2006—. Mem. adv. bd. Century Moving and Storage. Active United Way, Jr. Achievement. Mem. GM Supplier Coun., Indsl. Fastener Inst., Elgin Country Club. Office: Ill Tool Works 3600 W Lake Ave Glenview IL 60026-1215 Office Phone: 847-724-7500. Office Fax: 847-657-4572.*

HANSEN, THOMAS NANASTAD, hospital administrator, pediatrician; b. Neenah, Wis., Oct. 11, 1947; m. Cheryl Bailey, June 9, 1979; children: Elaine Christ, William Thomas. BS in Physics summa cum laude, Tex. Christian U., 1970; MD, Baylor Coll. Medicine, 1973. Diplomate Am. Bd. Pediatrics. Intern in pediatrics Baylor Coll. Medicine, Houston, 1973-74, resident in pediatrics, 1974-76, postdoctoral fellow in neonatal perinatal medicine, 1976-78; postdoctoral fellow in pediatric pulmonary disease U. Calif., San Francisco, 1978-81; asst. prof. pediatrics Baylor Coll. Medicine, 1978-84, assoc. prof. pediatrics, 1984-89; prof. pediatrics and cell biology Tex. Children's Hosp. Found., Houston, 1989-95; head sect. on neonatology Baylor Coll. of Medicine, 1987-95, vice-chmn. rsch. dept. pediatrics, 1994-95, dir. child health rsch. ctr., 1994-95, co-dir. ctr. for tng. in molecular medicine, 1994-95; chmn. pediat., CEO Children's Hosp., Columbus, Ohio, 1995—2005; pres., CEO Children's Hosp. and Regional Med. Ctr., Seattle, 2005—. Mem. exam com. Am. Bd. Pediatrics, 1982—, sub-bd. neonatal-perinatal medicine, 1992—, chmn. credentials com., 1993—, chmn.-elect sub-bd. neonaatal perinatal medicine, 1994. Contbr. numerous articles to profl. jours. Trustee Tex. Women's Hosp., 1988-91. Mem. Western Soc. for Pediatric Rsch., So. Soc. for Pediaatric Rsch., Soc. for Pediatric Rsch. (sec.-treas. 1986-91, chmn. student rsch. com. 1990—, trustee internat. chpt. 1992—), Am. Physiol. Soc., Am. Pediatric Soc., Am. Fedn. for Clin. Rsch., Am. Thoracic Soc., Am. Acad. of Pediatrics, N.Y. Acad. of Scis., Am. Soc. for Cell Biology, Assn. of Med. Sch. Pediatric Dept. Chmn., Sigma Xi. Office: Children's Hosp and Regional Med Ctr PO Box 5371 Seattle WA 98105-0371

HANSEN, VAGN KEITH, political science educator, college administrator; b. Jackson, Miss., Jan. 24, 1944; s. Vagn Aage and Elizabeth Eleanor (Keith) H.; m. Marleen Kibler Berry, June 7, 1969; 1 child, Vagn Keith II. BA cum laude, Tulane U., 1966; MA, U. Va., 1969, PhD, 1971. Asst. prof. history and polit. sci. Va. Mil. Inst., Lexington, 1971-74; with Delta State U., Cleveland, Miss., 1974-85, prof. polit. sci., 1979-85, chmn. div. social scis., 1981-85; Jefferson-Pilot prof. polit. sci. High Point U., NC, 1985—2000; provost, v.p. acad. affairs Miss. U. for Women, Columbus, 2000—03, acting pres., 2001; coord. acad. rsch. and svc. Miss. Instns. Higher Learning, Jackson, 2003—04; dean Coll. Arts and Scis. U. N. Ala., Florence, 2004—. Author: Mississippi State and Local Government, 1988; contbr. articles to profl. jours. Pres. Community Concert Assn., High Point, 1990-92; bd. dirs. Community Action Program, Cleveland, 1976-80; chair govtl. affairs com. High Point C. of C., 1998-2000; mem. Leadership Shoals, Florence, 2004-05 Mem. Phi Beta Kappa, Omicron Delta Kappa. Avocations: travel, running, music. Home: 408 7th St S Columbus MS 39701-5752 Office: UNA Box 5021 Florence AL 35632 Business E-Mail: vkhansen@una.edu.

HANSEN, W. LEE, economics professor; b. Racine, Wis., Nov. 8, 1928; s. William R. and Gertrude M. H.; m. Sally Ann Porch, Dec. 26, 1955; children— Ellen J., Martha L. BA, U. Wis., Madison, 1950, MA, 1955; PhD, Johns Hopkins U., 1958. Asst. prof. econs. UCLA, from 1958, assoc. prof., to 1965; assoc. prof. econs. U. Wis., Madison, from 1965, prof., prof. emeritus, 1996—. Sr. staff economist Pres.'s Coun. Econ. Advisers, Washington, 1964-65; trustee Nat. Coun. on Econ. Edn., N.Y.C., 1976-2000, sec., 1996-2000; mem. bd. founders NCEE, 2000—. Author: Benefits, Costs, and Finance of Public Higher Education, 1969, Education, Income, and Human Capital, 1970, The Labor Market for Scientists and Engineers, 1973, Perspectives on Economic Education, 1977, A Framework for Teaching Basic Economic Concepts, 1984, The End of Mandatory Retirement, 1989, Unemployment Insurance: The Second Half-Century, 1990, Academic Freedom on Trial: 100 Years of Sifting and Winnowing at the University of Wisconsin, 1998, Discussing Economics, 2005; contbr. articles to profl. jours. Sgt. US Army, 1951—53. Recipient Amoco Disting. Tchg. award U. Wis., 1982, Hilldale award, 1988, Disting. Svc. award Nat. Coun. on Econs. Edn., 1991, Marvin Bower award, 1994, , Henry H. Villard Rsch. award, 2000, Tchr. Acad. U. Wis., 1994, Outstanding Postsecondary Educator award nat. Fedn. Ind. Bus. Found., 1992, Leavey award for excellence in pvt. enterprise edn. Freedoms Found., 1996; Guggenheim fellow, 1969-70; Fulbright sr. scholar, Australia, 1988. Mem. AAUP (chair com. on the econ. status of the profession 1979-86, mem. nat. coun. 1980-82, retirement com. 1985-95), Am. Econ. Assn. (chmn. com. on econ. edn. 1983-88, exec. sec. commn. grad. edn. econs. 1988-91), Indsl. Rels. Rsch. Assn., Midwest Econs. Assn. (pres. 1987), Phi Beta Kappa. Unitarian Universalist. Office: U Wis Dept Econs 1180 Observatory Dr Madison WI 53706-1320 Business E-Mail: wlhansen@wisc.edu.

HANSEN, WALTER EUGENE, insurance executive; b. Woodland, Wash., May 15, 1929; s. August Hans and Esther Johanna (Johnson) H.; m. Barbara Inez Cowart, Oct. 12, 1950; m. Donna Carol Phillips, Aug. 1, 1953; children: Larry, Lindsey, Monty, Gena, Martin, Lori, Bradley, Walter Eugene Jr. Grad. high sch. Farmer, logger, 1943-51; svc. mgr. Sears Roebuck & Co., L.A. and Portland, Oreg., 1951-57; agt. various ins. cos., 1957-63; dist. mgr. Bankers Life & Casualty Co., 1960-61; state mgr. Protective Security Life Ins. Co., 1963-65; regional mgr. Amn. Pacific Life Ins. Co., 1963-72; owner Pacific N.W. Ins. Svc., Portland, 1963—, Am. Pacific Svcs., Portland, 1970—, N. Fork Motors, Woodland, Wash., 1987—. Owner Nat. Rsch. Assocs., Seattle, 1968—, N. Fork Ranch, 1962—. Mem. editl.bd. Longview Daily News, 1999-00. Past Boy Scouts Am.; chmn. Community USA Bicentennial Commn., 1976; mem. Wash. State Centennial Com., 1989; commr. Woodland Recreation Dist., 2000-2002; mem. Woodland Urban Growth Com., 1999-2002; historian City Woodland Centennial, Wash., 2006. Mem. Internat. Platform Assn., Nat. Assn. Life Underwriters, Nat. Trust Hitoric Preservation, Libr. Congress, Wa. Trust Hist. Preservation, Accident and Health Underwriters Assn., Smithsonian Assocs., Navy League of U.S, Woodland Downtown Revitalazation, Inc. (historian, v.p., dir.), Woodland Planter Days, Inc. (treas.). Home: PO Box 2000 Woodland WA 98674-1900 Office Phone: 503-236-5236. Personal E-mail: weh.1@netzero.com.

HANSEN, WAYNE W., lawyer; b. Clintonville, Wis., June 7, 1942; s. William W. and Berniece M. (Kuehn) H.; m. Carolyn M. Lemke, Dec. 21, 1969; children: Drew D., Janna J. BBA, U. Wis., 1965, JD, 1967. Bar: Wis. 1967, U.S. Dist. Ct. (we. dist.) Wis. 1971, U.S. Ct. Appeals (7th cir.) 1972, U.S. Dist. Ct. (ea. dist.) Wis. 1975, Wash. 1979, U.S. Dist. Ct. (we. dist.) Wash. 1979, U.S. Ct. Appeals (9th cir.) 1982, U.S. Dist. Ct. (ea. dist.) Wash. 1986. Atty. NLRB, Mpls., 1967-70, Schmitt Nolan Hansen & Hartley, Merrill, Wis., 1970-79; ptnr. Lane Powell Spears Lubersky, Seattle, 1979-98; mng. ptnr. Seattle office Jackson Lewis LLP, 1998—. Contbg. author: Developing Labor Law, 1971, Doing Business in Washington State*Guide for Foreign Business, 1989. Office: Jackson Lewis LLP 600 University St Ste 2900 Seattle WA 98101-4174 Office Phone: 206-626-6400. Business E-Mail: hansenw@jackson.law.com.

HANSEN, WILLIAM D., educational consultant, former federal agency administrator; b. Pocatello, Idaho; m. Kasi Hansen; 6 children. BS in Econs., George Mason U. Legis. asst. US Dept. Edn., Washington, 1981, acting asst. sec. legis. and congl. affairs, dep. asst. sec. elem. & secondary edn., acting dep. under sec. for planning, budget & evaluation, 1990—91, asst. sec. mgmt. & budget, CFO, 1991—93; dep. dir. pub. affairs US Dept. Commerce; head Office Intergovtl. and Industry Affairs US Dept. Energy; pres., CEO Edn. Fin. Coun., 1993—2001; dep. sec. US Dept. Edn., Washington, 2001—03; sr. v.p., mng. dir. Affiliated Computer Svcs. (ACS), Dallas, 2003—05; sr. mng. dir. Chartwell Education Group LLC, NYC, 2005—. Mem. nat. bds. and commns. on sch. reform; mem. Nat. Commn. on Cost of Higher Edn. Office: Chartwell Education Group LLC Empire State Bldg Ste 7506 New York NY 10118

HANSEN-DABERKOW, MICHELLE LEN, elementary school art educator; d. Gene Dale and Janet Kay Hansen; m. James Lowell Daberkow, Dec. 20, 1997; 1 child, Callum Hanz Daberkow. BA in Art Tchg., Bethany Coll., Lindsborg, Kans., 1991; MS in Art Edn., Wayne State U., Nebr., 1996. K-12 art educator Beemer Pub. Schs., Nebr., 1991—94, Stanton Cmty. Schs., Nebr., 1993—96; k-5 art specialist Lincoln Pub. Sch., Nebr., 1996—. Tchr. adult classes Norfolk (Nebr.) Arts Ctr., 1993—94; artist in residence Stone House Gallery, Fredonia, Kans., 1991. Co-leader, chair after sch. program United Luth. Ch., Lincon, 1998—2002. Recipient award, Berry Co., Lincon, 2004. Mem.: Nat. Art Edn. Assn., Nebr. Art Tchr. Assn., Guild Natural Sci. Illustrators. Republican. Lutheran. Avocations: bicycling, quilting, gardening, writing, cello. Office: Lincoln Pub Schs Kahoa Elem 7700 Leighton Ave Lincoln NE 68507

HANSEN-FLASCHEN, JOHN HYMAN, medical educator, researcher; b. Hamilton, Ohio, June 25, 1950; s. Steward Samuel and Joyce (Davies) Flaschen; m. Susan Lauretta Hansen, Aug. 22, 1951; children: Lynn, Lauren. AB, Brown U., 1972; MD, NYU, 1976. Diplomate in internal medicine, pulmonary medicine, critical care medicine Am. Bd. Internal Medicine. Resident in medicine U. Pa., Phila., 1976-79, chief resident in medicine, 1980-81, pulmonary fellow, 1979-80, 81-82, attending physician, 1982—, asst. prof. medicine, 1982-87, assoc. prof., 1988-98, prof., 1999—, dir. edn. and tng. programs in pulmonary and critical care, 1983-90, dir. pulmonary and critical care divsn., 1990-98, chief pulmonary, allergy and critical care divsn., 1998—, dir. Penn Lung Ctr., 1996—. Mem. editl. bd. Clin. Pulmonary Medicine, Respiratory Medicine, UpToDate; editor Pulmonary and Critical Care MKSAP 13, ACP; contbr. articles to profl. jours. Steering com. Nat. Emphysema Treatment Trial, 1997—2003. Recipient Spl. Investigator award Am. Heart Assn., 1982-84, Lindback Tchg. award U. Pa., 1999, others; Measey Found. fellow, 1982-83. Fellow ACP, Am. Coll. Chest Physicians, Coll. Physicians Phila.; mem. Am. Thoracic Soc. (chmn. postgrad. edn. com. 1995—, clin. problems long range planning com. 1997-99, Clinician Educator award 2004), Soc. for Critical Care Medicine, Soc. for Bioethics Consultation, Laennec Soc. Phila. (pres. 1990-91), Drinker Soc. for Critical Care in Phila. (founder, 1st pres. 1988-90), Sigma Xi, Alpha Omega Alpha. Democrat. Home: 365 Penn Rd Wynnewood PA 19096-1401 Office: Hosp U Pa 873 Mahoney Bldg 3400 Spruce St Philadelphia PA 19104-4206 Office Phone: 215-662-6003.

HANSEN-NORD, JØRGEN, Danish agency administrator; b. Oksbøl, Denmark, Jan. 1, 1954; s. Jørgen and Ingerlin Klevan Hansen-Nord; m. Ulla Kabbelgaard Mikkelsen, Apr. 6, 1985 (div. 2002); children: Christian, Louise, Maria Amalie. Grad., Danish Mil. Acad., 1978, grad. Jr. Officers Command and Staff Course, 1982, grad. Gen. Command and Staff Course, 1986, grad. Higher Command and Staff Course, 1996; student, Naval Justice Sch., Newport, RI, 1998, George C. Marshall European Ctr. Security Studies, Garmisch-Partenkirschen, Germany, 1999. Commnd. Danish Guard of Hussars, 1972; advanced through ranks to Brigadier Gen. Danish Army; comdr. Tank Battalion, 1996, Danish Battalion to SFOR, 1997; comdg. officer Danish Reaction Brigade, NATO Rapid Reaction Forces, 1997—2000; head divsn. Danish Ministry of Def., 1992—95; dep. permanent sec. state for def. Denmark; nat. armaments dir. Danish Ministry of Def., Copenhagen; chmn. Danish Maritime and Aero. Rescue Coun., 2000—04; Danish nat. liaison rep. to Supreme Allied Comdr. Transformation Norfolk, Va., 2004—07; dir. Joint Analysis and Lessons Learned Ctr., Lisbon, Portugal, 2007—. Decorated Officer 1st degree Order of Dannebroge. Avocations: golf, sports. Office: Avenida Tenente Martins Monsanto 1500 589 Lisbon Portugal Office Phone: 351217717001. Office Fax: 351217717099.

HANSHAW, JAMES BARRY, pediatrician, educator; b. Scarsdale, NY, Dec. 23, 1928; s. George Lee and Kathryn Frances (Reilly) H.; m. Marian Christine Kernan, Aug. 14, 1954; children: Thomas, Lee, Elizabeth, John, Margaret. AB, Syracuse U., NY, 1950; MD, SUNY, Syracuse, 1953, DSc (hon.), 1991. Intern Cin. Gen. Hosp., 1953-54; resident pediatrics U. Rochester Med. Center, 1956-58; Nat. Found. postdoctoral fellow virology Harvard U. Sch. Pub. Health, 1958-60; academic medicine, specializing in pediatrics Rochester, NY, 1960-75; instr. to prof. pediatrics and microbiology U. Rochester Sch. Medicine, 1960-75; prof., chmn. dept. pediatrics U. Mass., Worcester, 1975-85, interim vice chancellor, acad. dean, 1985-86; interim chancellor, 1987; provost, dean U. Mass., 1986-89, dean and provost emeritus, prof. pediatrics, 1989—, interim chmn. dept. pediatrics, 1997-98; chmn. dept. pediatrics Meml. Health Care, 1993-98. Lectr. pediatrics Harvard U. Med. Sch., 1975-2002; vis. prof. Inst. Child Health, London U. and Hosp. for Sick Children, London, 1971-72; coll. health physician WPI, 1990—. Author: (with J.A. Dudgeon) Viral Infections Fetus and Newborn, 1978, 2d edit. (with Dudgeon and W.C. Marshall), 1985. Served with USAF, 1953-56. Recipient Career Rsch. Devel. award NIH, 1962-72, Disting. Alumnus award Upstate Med. U., 2003, Career Achievement award Worcester Dist. Med. Soc., 2004, Disting. Resident Alumnus award U. Rochester Med. Ctr., 2006; Buswell fellow U. Rochester, 1960-62; NIH grantee, 1962-75. Mem. AMA, Am. Pediatric Soc., Soc. Pediatric Research, Am. Acad. Pediatrics, Infectious Diseases Soc. Am., New Eng. Pediatric Soc., Sigma Xi, Alpha Omega Alpha. Home: 18 Baypath Dr Boylston MA 01505-1427 Home Phone: 508-869-6038; Office Phone: 508-869-6038. Personal E-mail: jhans76271@aol.com.

HANSLEY, LEE, art dealer; b. Roanoke Rapids, NC, Jan. 11, 1948; s. Lonnie L. and Kathleen (Crumpler) H. Student, U. N.C., 1966-70. City editor The Daily Herald, Roanoke Rapids, 1970-73; editor The Northampton News, Jackson, NC, 1973-75, Roanoke-Chowan News-Herald, Ahoskie, NC, 1976, Halifax (N.C.) County This Week, 1976-78, The Suburbanite Newspaper, Winston-Salem, NC, 1978-80; exhbns. curator Southeastern Ctr. Contemporary Art, Winston-Salem, 1980-86; pub. rels. dir. WUNC Radio, Chapel Hill., NC, 1986-91; ind. cons. Durham (N.C.) Arts Coun., 1992; proprietor Lee Hansley Gallery, Raleigh, NC, 1993—. Cons. art exhibits Duke U. Law Sch., Durham, 1995—. Curator: Edith London: A Retrospective, 1992; editor: (exhbn. catalogs) Award in Visual Arts, 1981, 83, 84, 85, 86, Durham Art Guild 50th Anniversary Catalogue, 1998, Charlotte Robinson: A Retrospective, 2007. Mem. Raleigh Arts Commn., 1989-95, chmn., 1991-93; mem. Durham Art Guild, 1991-97; bd.

dirs. City Gallery, Raleigh, 1989-93, Theatre Devel. Bd., N.C. State U., 1986-91, 99—, N.C. State U. Gallery of Art and Design, 2003—; pub. rels. bd. Nat. Pub. Radio, Washington, 1989-91; mem. City of Raleigh Pub. Art Com., 1989-2003; founder, chmn. bd. Mus. Contemporary Art of N.C., 2003—; founding mem. Roanoke Rapids H.S. Alumni and Friends Assn., 2002. Recipient Gen. Excellence award N.C. Press Assn., Chapel Hill, 1978, Investigative Reporting award, 1978, Lee Hansley Gallery Scholarship N.C. Sch. Arts award, City of Raleigh medal of Arts, 2005; named Tar Heel of the Week, The News & Observer, Raleigh, 2007. Mem. N.C. Mus. Art., Mus. Modern Art, Smithsonian Instn., Gianini Soc. N.C. Sch. Arts, Weatherspoon Gallery, Ackland Art Mus. Democrat. Avocations: gardening, non-fiction, art collecting, music. Home: 804 N King Charles Rd Raleigh NC 27610-1628 Office: Lee Hansley Gallery 225 Glenwood Ave Raleigh NC 27603-1404 Home Phone: 919-755-0351; Office Phone: 919-828-7557. Personal E-mail: leehansley@bellsouth.net.

HANSMAN, ROBERT G., artist, educator; BFA, U. Kans., 1970. Asst. prof. Washington U., St. Louis. Instr. dept. parts and recreation Project Artspark, 1993, Arts Connection/City Faces, 1994—; instr. juvenile detention program Children's Art Cir., 1995; established Jermaine Lamond Roberts Meml. Art Studio, clinton-Peabody Pub. Housing, 1997. One-man shows include St. Louis C.C. at Forest Park, 1988, MJF Arts Studio Gallery, 1990, University City Pub. Libr., 1992, 1995, Bonsack Gallery, 1995. Mem. pub. housing revitalization focus group Darst-Webbe, 1995. Named Reader's Poll Best Local Artist, The Riverfront Times, 1995; recipient First Pl. award/Best of Show, St. Louis Artists Guild, 1988, 1992, Componere Gallery, 1990, Not Just An Art Dirs. Club, 1990, The Gallery Connection, 1991, Art St. Louis Gallery, 1991, World of Difference award City Faces, 1996, Mo. Arts award, Mo. Arts Coun., 1997, Excellence in Tchg. award, Emerson Electric, 2000, Disting. Faculty award, 2001, honoree, Colin Powell's Am. Promise, 1999, Mo. Ho. of Reps., 1997; grantee, Bi-State Arts in Transit Project, 1995, 1996, 1999. Office: Washington U Sch Arch Campus Box 1079 One Brookings Dr Saint Louis MO 63130 E-mail: hansman@architecture.wustl.edu.

HANSMANN, HENRY BAETHKE, law educator; b. Highland Park, Ill., Oct. 5, 1945; s. Elwood Hansmann and Louise Frances (Baethke) Moore; m. Marina Santilli, 1992; 1 child, Lisa Santilli. BA, Brown U., 1967; JD, Yale U., 1974, PhD, 1978. Asst. prof. law U. Pa. Law Sch., Phila., 1975-81, assoc. prof. law, econs. and pub. policy, 1981-83; prof. law Yale U., New Haven, 1983—2003, Augustus E. Lines prof. law, 2004—; George T. Lowy prof. law NYU, 2003—04. Author: The Ownership of Enterprise, 1996. John Simon Guggenheim Found. fellow, 1985-86. Mem. Am. Acad. Arts and Scis., Am. Econs. Assn., Am. Law and Econ. Assn. Office: Yale Law Sch PO Box 208215 New Haven CT 06511 Home: 1136 Fifth Ave Apt 2B New York NY 10128 Office Phone: 203-432-4966. Business E-Mail: henry.hansmann@yale.edu.

HANSMANN, RALPH EMIL, investment executive, director; b. Utica, NY, May 25, 1918; s. Emil C. and Friedericka (Fuchs) H.; m. Doris Macdonald, Oct. 16, 1943; children: Robert E., Jane C. AB, Hamilton Coll., 1940, LLD, 1992; MBA, Harvard, 1942. Investment assoc. Harold F. Linder, William T. Golden, NYC, 1945-48, 53—; staff Gen. Am. Investors Co., Inc., 1949-52. Emeritus trustee Inst. Advanced Study, Princeton, N.J.; life trustee Hamilton Coll., Clinton, N.Y., N.Y. Pub. Libr. Served as lt. USNR, 1942-45. Mem. Ridgewood (N.J.) Country Club, Harvard Club (N.Y.C.), Phi Beta Kappa. Home: 385 Manchester Rd Ridgewood NJ 07450-1212 Office: 500 Fifth Ave New York NY 10110 Office Phone: 212-391-8960. Business E-Mail: rhansmann@lingold.net.

HANSON, ARNOLD PHILIP, retired lawyer; b. Berlin, NH, July 11, 1924; s. Arnold H. and Evelyn (Renaud) H.; m. Della Ann Lavernoich, June 26, 1948; children: Arnold Philip, Caryl Hanson Brensinger, Julie E. Hanson Mook. BA, U. N.H., 1948; JD, Boston, 1951. Bar: N.H. 1951. Pvt. practice, Berlin, NH, 1951-60; ptnr. Bergeron & Hanson, Berlin, 1960-80, Bergeron & Hanson, P.A., Berlin, 1980-87, Bergeron, Hanson & Bornstein, P.A., Berlin, 1988-91; county atty. Coos County, NH, 1952-56; ret. Mem. ct. accreditation com. State of N.H., 1970-77, Regional Criminal Justice Planning Coun., 1978-88; ptnr. North Country TV Cable Co., Groveton, N.H., 1962-89; chmn. bd., chmn. exec. com. Berlin City Bank, 1975-87. Chmn. city Republican Conv., Berlin, 1952-54; bd. dirs. Rep. State Com., 1958-60; del. Rep. Nat Com., 1964; trustee A.V. Hosp., 1976-85, mem. coms., 1976-86; area chmn. fundraising campaigns including ARC, U. N.H. Centennial Fund, Crippled Children, N.H. Children's Aid Soc., Boy Scouts Am., Boston U. Law Sch. Centennial Fund, St. Paul's Sch. Advanced Studies Program, A.V. Hosp. Bldg. Fund maj. gifts program, Frank Kenison Fund Boston U. Law Sch.; mem. U. N.H. 50th Reunion Fund Raising Class of 1948, 1996-98. Served with USN, 1943-46. Recipient Silver Shingle award Boston U. Sch. Law, 1977, Alumni Meritorius award U. N.H., 1986, U. N.H. Hubbard Family award for svc. to philanthropy, 2004. Fellow Am. Bar Found.; mem. N.H. Bar Assn. (pres. 1974-75, bd. govs. 1973-76), Coos County Bar Assn. (pres. various yrs.), Tri-Legal County Svcs., N.H. Alumni Assn. (bd. dirs. 1974-77), Boston U. Alumni Assn., Am. Legion (post judge adv. 1952-64), VFW (post judge adv. 1952-93), Nashua Country Club (Nashua, N.H.), Seven Lakes Country Club (Ft. Myers, Fla.), Kiwanis (pres. 1966). Lutheran. E-mail: dahanson@aol.com.

HANSON, ARTHUR STUART, physician, consultant; b. Mpls., Mar. 10, 1937; s. Arthur Emanuel and Frances Elenor (Larson) H.; m. Gail Joan Taylor, June 16, 1963; children: Marta Eileen, Peter Arthur. BA, Dartmouth Coll., 1959; MD, U. Minn., 1963. Diplomate Am. Bd. Internal Medicine, Am. Bd. Pulmonary Disease. Intern Hennipen County Med. Ctr., 1963-64; resident in internal medicine U. Minn., 1964-65, 68-70, fellow pulmonary disease, 1970-71; cons. in pulmonary and critical care medicine Park Nicollet Clinic, Mpls., 1971—, med. dir., 1975-82, v.p. legis. and cmty. affairs, 1982-86; dir. med. edn. Park Nicollet Med. Found., Mpls., 1982-86; pres., CEO Park Nicollet Inst., Mpls., 1986—2002. Bd. dirs. Minn. Health Data Inst., 1993-03. Pres., bd. chair Minn. Smoke Free Coalition, 1985-88, 96-98, 2005-07; vice chair Minn. Partnership for Action Against Tobacco, 1998-2003; chmn. bd. Smoke Free Generation Minn., 1984-90. Recipient Cmty. Leadership award, Am. Lung Assn. Hennepin County, 1987, Harvey H. Rogers Meml. award, Minn. Pub. Health Assn., 1988, award for excellence in health promotion, Minn. Health Commr., 1989, Physician of Excellence award, Park Nicollet Health Svcs., 2000, Lynn Smith 25-Yr. award, Am. Cancer Soc., 2001, Harold S. Diehl Lifetime Achievement award, U. Minn. Med. Found., 2007. Fellow ACP, AMA (del., chmn.), Am. Coll. Chest Physicians; mem. Minn. Med. Assn. (pres. 1992-93, Stop the Violence award 1994, Disting. Svc. award 1998), Minn. Healthcare Coalition on Violence, Hennepin County Med. Soc. (pres. 1990-91, Charles Bolles Bolles-Rogers award 1998). Unitarian Universalist. Avocations: birding, gardening, physical fitness, reading, travel. Office: Park Nicollet Clinic Ste 300 6490 Excelsior Blvd Minneapolis MN 55426 Home Phone: 612-676-1591; Office Phone: 952-993-3242. Business E-Mail: hansoa@parknicollet.com.

HANSON, CAREY B., costume designer, educator; b. Plainveiw, Tex., July 23, 1970; d. Jerry Alton and Tommie L. Blackerby; m. David B. Hanson, Aug. 17, 1991; children: Tori E., Sydney Hanson Aiden Hanson. MFA, Utah Sate U., Logan, 2000. Asst. prof. costume design No. Ariz. U., Flagstaff, 2000—04, U. Miss., Oxford, 2004—. Costume designer numerous theatre prodns. including The Crucible, Our Town, A Midsummer's Night Dream, Les Liaisons Dangerouse, A Winter's Tale, The Tempest, The Mikado. Grantee Rsch. grant, U. Miss., 2007. Mem.: Inst. Theatre Tech. (sightlines editl. liaison 2006—07). Democrat-Npl. Mem. Lds Ch.

HANSON, CURTIS, film director, scriptwriter; b. Reno, Mar. 24, 1945; Dir., screenwriter (film) Sweet Kill, 1972, The Bedroom Window, 1988; dir., co-producer (film) The Little Dragons, 1977; dir. (films) The Arousers, 1970, Losin' It, 1983, Bad Influence, 1990, The Hand That Rocks the Cradle, 1992, The River Wild, 1994; dir., prodr., screenwriter (films) L.A. Confidential, 1997; dir., prodr. (film) Wonder Boys, 1999, 8 mile, 2002, In Her Shoes, 2005, Lucky You, 2007; screenwriter: The Dunwich Horror, 1970, The Silent Partner, 1978, White Dog, 1982, Never Cry Wolf, 1983; actor (TV) Hitchcock: Shadow of a Genius, 1999; (film) Adaptation, 2002. Office: United Talent Agy 9560 Wilshire Blvd Fl 5 Beverly Hills CA 90212-2400*

HANSON, DALE S., retired bank executive; b. Milw., Nov. 11, 1938; s. Yngve Holger and Evelyn (Johnson) H.; m. Joan Benton, July 15, 1961; children— Thomas S., Tim B. BA in Econs., Carlton Coll., 1960; postgrad. Exec. Program, Credit and Fin. Mgmt. Stanford U., 1966-67. Asst. cashier First Bank, St. Paul, 1964-66, asst. v.p., 1966-68, v.p., 1968-82, sr. v.p., 1982-83, exec. v.p., 1983-84, pres., 1984-88; pres., mng. ptnr. FBS Mcht. Banking Group, 1987-90; mng. ptnr. Matrix Leasing Internat., 1989-90; exec. v.p. 1st Bank System, Mpls., 1984-91; v.p., treas., chief fin. officer C.H. Robinson Co., Mpls., 1991-98, also bd. dirs.; ret., 1998. Bd. dirs. W.A. Lang Co., Edwards Mfg. Co. Mem. Corp. Health One, Inc.; bd. dirs. St. Paul Chamber Orch., Twin City Pub. TV, St. Paul Riverfront Devel. Corp., 1985-91. 1st lt. USNG, 1961-67. Mem. Robert Morris Assocs. (pres. 1982-83), Fin. Execs. Inst. (bd. dirs. Twin Cities chpt.), Somerset Golf Club, Mpls. Club, Minn. Club (St. Paul). Republican. Presbyterian. Avocations: skiing, sailing, golf, photography. Office: care C H Robinson Co 8100 Mitchell Rd Ste 200 Eden Prairie MN 55344-2178

HANSON, DAN LEWIS, music educator, composer; b. Lamesa, Tex., Mar. 28, 1953; s. Harvey James and Jerri Hanson; m. Judy Fawn Leatherwood, June 28, 2001; children: Erin Taylor, Kim Aline Zahn, Mallory Jaymes. MusB, Tex. Tech U., 1975, MusM, 1981; MusD, U. North Tex., 1987. Asst. prof. music South Plains Coll., Levelland, Okla., 1977—84; prof. music U. Sci. and Arts Okla., Chickasha, Okla., 1987—. Composer: (songs) A Triumphal Procession, (plays) The History of American Education in Song, 2002. Recipient Faculty Superior Tchg. award, U. Sci. and Arts Okla., 2005. Mem.: Okla. Music Theory Roundtable (pres. 2002—03), Okla. Music Educators Assn., Lions Club (pres. 2006—), Phi Mu Alpha Sinfonia. Democrat. Avocations: reading, travel. Home: 7 Misty Glenn Dr Chickasha OK 73018 Office: Univ of Science and Arts of Oklahoma 1727 West Alabama Chickasha OK 73018 Home Phone: 405-224-5874. Personal E-mail: dhanson3@suddenlink.net. E-mail: dhanson@usao.edu.

HANSON, DAVID ALAN, music educator; b. Bryan, Ohio, Dec. 6, 1945; s. Chester Adams and Mary Adele (Daenitz) Hanson; m. Lori Ray Stelzer, Aug. 16, 1960. MusB, Bowling Green State Univ., 1968; MusM, Univ. Mich., 1972. Cert. Permanent Tchng. Certificate Ohio. Music ed. Findlay City Sch., Findlay, Ohio, 1968—2003, Heidelberg Coll., Tiffin, Ohio, 1974—, Bluffton Coll., Bluffton, Ohio, 2000—. Prin. double Bass Lima Symphony, Lima, Ohio, 1968—74. Author: (7 music articles) Triad, (4 music articles) The Instrumentalist; composer: (compositions) 18 for brass, full orchestra, choir, guitar, double Bass- two publ. Recipient Outstanding Young Educator Award, Findlay Jaycees/ Findlay, OH, 1977, Tchr. Golden Apple Award, Findlay Rotary Club/Findlay, OH, 1996, D. Robert Baker Award, Findlay City Sch./Findlay, OH, 1999, Tchr. of Yr. award, Ohio String Tchrs. Assn., 1995. Mem.: Ohio Music Ed. Assoc. (NW Region Chair), Music Ed. Nat. Conf., Findlay Arts Coun. Avocations: lepidoptera study, reading, photography, bicycling. Home: 1709 Forest Park Findlay OH 45840 Personal E-mail: dahanso@woh.rr.com.

HANSON, DAVID JAMES, lawyer; b. Neenah, Wis., July 20, 1943; s. Vernon James and Dorothy O. Hanson; m. Diana G. Severson, Aug. 25, 1965 (div. Sept. 1982); children: Matthew Vernon, Maja Kirsten, Brian Edward; m. Linda Hughes Bochert, May 28, 1983; children: Scott Charles, Sarah Katherine. BS, U. Wis., 1965, JD, 1968. Bar: Wis. 1968, U.S. Dist. Ct. (we. dist.) Wis. 1968, U.S. Dist. Ct. (ea. dist.) Wis. 1969, U.S. Ct. Appeals (7th cir.) 1970, U.S. Supreme Ct. 1971. Asst. atty. gen. State of Wis. Dept. of Justice, Madison, 1968-71, dep. atty. gen., 1976-81; asst. chancellor, chief legal counsel U. Wis., Madison, 1971-76; ptnr. Michael, Best & Friedrich LLP, Madison, 1981—. Lectr. Law Sch., U. Wis., Madison, 1972-75; bd. dirs., chair govt. law sect. State Bar Wis., Madison, 1979-88. Contbr. articles to profl. jours. Bd. dirs. Sand County Found., Madison, 1988—, Wis. Ctr. for Academically Talented Youth, Madison, 1991-94, Access Cmty. Health Ctrs., 2004—, Wis. Law Alumni Assn., 2000—, chair 2004—, trustee Edgewood Coll., Madison, 1997—, chair 2003-05, Great Lakes Higher Edn. Corp. and affiliates, 2000—. Mem. ABA, Madison Club, Blackhawk Country Club. Democrat. Unitarian Universalist. Avocations: canoeing, skiing, golf, bicycling, hunting. Office: Michael Best & Friedrich PO Box 1806 Madison WI 53701-1806 Office Phone: 603-257-3501. E-mail: djhanson@michaelbest.com.

HANSON, DENNIS MICHAEL, retired health facility administrator; b. Cleve., Aug. 20, 1943; s. John Joseph and Victoria (Tucholski) H. BBA, Cleve. State U., 1971; MPH, U. Pitts., 1974. Asst. adminstr. Huron Rd. Hosp., Cleve., 1974—76; adminstr. asst. Mt. Sinai Med. Ctr., Cleve., 1976—80; dir. radiology U. Louisville, 1980—84, assoc. prof., 1982—86; sr. cons. Honeywell, Mpls., 1986—87; mgr. radiology U. N.C., Chapel Hill, 1987—90; mgr. diagnostic imaging Kaiser Hosp., Honolulu, 1990—97; cons. Dowdy Mgmt. and Consulting, Cocoa Beach, Fla., 1999—2000; radiol. technician Norton Healthcare, Louisville, 2000—04; ret., 2005. Councilman City of Meadowbrook Farm, Ky., 1982-86. With USAF, 1961-65. Named Ky. Colonel, 1984. Fellow Am. Coll. Healthcare Execs.; mem. Am. Hosp. Radiology Adminstrs. Home: Unit 103 3901 Yardley Ct Louisville KY 40299-7355 E-mail: dmhansonmph@aol.com.

HANSON, FLOYD BLISS, mathematician; b. Bklyn., Mar. 9, 1939; s. Charles Keld and Violet Ellen (Bliss) Hanson; m. Ethel Louisa Hutchins, July 27, 1962; 1 child, Lisa Kirsten. BS, Antioch Coll., Yellow Springs, Ohio, 1962; MS, Brown U., Providence, 1964, PhD, 1968. Space technician Convair Astronautics, San Diego, 1961; applied mathematician Arthur D. Little, Inc., Cambridge, Mass., 1961; physicist Wright-Patterson AFB, Dayton, Ohio, 1962; assoc. rsch. scientist Courant Inst., NYC, 1967-68; asst. prof. U. Ill., Chgo., 1969-75, assoc. prof., 1975-83, prof., 1983—2005, assoc. dir. Lab. for Advanced Computing, 1990—2005, assoc. dir. Lab. for Control & Info., 1993—2005, prof. emeritus, 2005—. Faculty rsch. participant Argonne Nat. Lab., Ill., 1985-87, faculty rsch. leave, 1987-88, rsch. assoc., 1988—; vis. prof. divsn. applied math. Brown U., 1994; vis. faculty Sch. Civil and Environ. Engring., Cornell U., 1995; vis. prof. stochastics Indian Inst. Sci, Bangalore, India, 2007. Assoc. editor-in-chief Applied and Computational Control Signals and Circuits, 1996-2005; contbr. articles in field to profl. jours., chpts. to books. Recipient Tchr. Recognition award, UIC CETL, 1999, Excellence in Tchg. award, Premier UIC, 2001—02; grantee, NSF, 1970—83, 1988—2006, 1973, Nat. Ctr. Supercomputer Applications, 1986—2004, Los. Alamos Nat. Lab., 1990—97, Cornell Theory Ctr., 1993—96, Pitts. Supercomputer Ctr., 1993—98, 2003—04, San Diego Supercomputer Ctr., 1998—2002. Mem. IEEE (tech. com. on control edn. appt. 200—2), Soc. Indsl. and Applied Math., Computer Soc. of IEEE, Control Sys. Soc. of IEEE, Resource Modeling Assn. Home: 5435 S East View Park Chicago IL 60615-5915 Office: U Ill Dept Math Stats and Computer Sci M/C 249 851 S Morgan St Rm 322 Chicago IL 60607-7042 Business E-Mail: hanson@uic.edu.

HANSON, GAIL G., physicist, researcher; b. Dayton, Ohio, Feb. 22, 1947; married 1968 (div. 1998); 2 children. BS in Physics, MIT, 1968, PhD in Exptl. High Energy Physics, 1973. Rsch. assoc. Stanford Linear Accelerator Ctr., 1973-76, physicist, continuing staff mem., 1976-84, physicist, permanent staff mem., 1984-89; prof. physics Ind. U., Bloomington, 1989-97, disting. prof., 1997—. Mem. subpanel High Energy Physics Adv. Panel, 1989-90; mem. physics adv. com. Univs. Rsch. Assn. Fermilab, 1990-94, mem. bd. overseers, 1991-97, dir. rev. panel, 1993-94, mem. vis. com., 1995-97; mem. com. examiners GRE Physics Test, 1992-2000; mem. collaboration exec. com. U.S. ATLAS, 1994-95. Guggenheim fellow, 1995. Fellow AAAS (mem. electorate nominating com. physics sect. 1996—), Am. Phys. Soc. (W.K.H. Panofsky prize 1996). Office: Ind U Dept Physics Bloomington IN 47405 E-mail: gail@indiana.edu.

HANSON, GARY A., lawyer, educator, academic administrator; b. Santa Fe, Sept. 30, 1954; s. Norman A. Hanson and Mary Gene (Moore) Garrison; m. Tracey J. Tannen, Mar. 11, 1982; children: Paul, Carly, Sean. BS magna cum laude, U. Utah, 1976; JD, Pepperdine U., 1980. Bar: Calif. 1980, U.S. Dist. Ct. (cen. dist.) Calif. 1980, U.S. Ct. Appeals (9th cir.) 1980. Pvt. practice, Westlake Village, Calif., 1980-82; assoc. gen. counsel Pepperdine U., Malibu, Calif., 1982-83, acting gen. counsel, 1983-84, univ. gen. counsel, 1984—2000, v.p., gen. counsel, 2000—. Adj. prof. law Pepperdine U., Malibu, 1982—, lectr. bus. law, 1986—; pro bono atty. San Fernando Valley Christian Sch., L.A., 1982-83; mem. Pro Bono Estate Adv. Svc., San Diego, 1983-86; cons. West Ednl. Pub. Co., 1988. Contbr. articles to profl. jours.; pres. Ind. Colls. and Univs. jour., 1989. Recipient Pres.'s award San Diego Christian Found., 1984. Mem. ABA, L.A. County Bar Assn., Nat. Assn. Coll. and Univ. Attys. Republican. Office: Pepperdine U 24255 Pacific Coast Hwy Malibu CA 90263-4607

HANSON, GERALD WARNER, retired county official; b. Alexandria, Minn., Dec. 25, 1938; s. Lewis Lincoln and Dorothy Hazel (Warner) H.; m. Sandra June Wheeler, July 9, 1960; 1 child, Cynthia R. AA, San Bernardino Coll., Calif., 1959; BA, Redlands U., Calif., 1979; MA, U. Redlands, 1981; EdD, Pepperdine U., 1995. Cert. advanced metrication specialist. Dep. sealer San Bernardino (Calif.) County, 1964-80, div. chief, 1980-85, dir. weights and measures, 1985-94; CATV cons. City of Redlands, 1996—2004, City of Yucaipa, 1998-99, ret., 1994. Substitute tchr. Redlands Unified Sch. Dist., 2003-04. Chmn. Redlands Rent Rev. Bd., 1985-99; bd. dirs. House Neighborly Svc., Redlands, 1972-73, Boys Club, Redlands, 1985-86; mem. Redlands Planning commn., 1990-98. With USN. Fellow U.S. Metric Assn. (treas. 1986-88, 92—); mem. NRA (life), Nat. Conf. on Weights and Measures (life, asst. treas. 1986-94), Western Weights and Measures Assn. (life, pres. 1987-88), Calif. Assn. Weights and Measures Ofcls. (life, 1st v.p. 1987), Calif. Rifle and Pistol Assn. (life), Masons, Shriners, Kiwanis (treas. Redlands club 1983-95), Over the Hill Gang (San Bernardino, newsletter editor 1998-2000). Avocations: golf, digital photography, mechanics, microcomputers. Home: 225 E Palm Ave Redlands CA 92373-6131 Personal E-mail: doctorjer@hotmail.com.

HANSON, HAROLD PALMER, physicist, editor, academic administrator, government official; b. Virginia, Minn., Dec. 27, 1921; s. Martin Bernhard and Elvida Elaine (Paulsen) H.; m. Mary Jean Stevenson, June 22, 1944; children: Steven Bernard, Barbara Jean. BS, Superior State Coll., Wis., 1942; MS, U. Wis., 1944, PhD, 1948. Mem. faculty U. Fla., 1948-54, dean grad. sch., 1969-71, v.p. acad. affairs, 1971-74, exec. v.p., 1974-78, exec. v.p. emeritus, 1990—; mem. faculty U. Tex., Austin, 1954-69, prof. physics, 1961-69, chmn. dept., 1962-69; provost Boston U., 1978-79; exec. dir. Com. on Sci. and Tech., U.S. Ho. of Reps., Washington, 1979-82, 84-90; provost Wayne State U., Detroit, 1982-84. Summer rsch. physicist Lincoln Labs., MIT, 1953, Gen. Atomic Co., San Diego, 1964; vis. lectr. U. Wis., 1957; Fulbright rsch. scholar, Norway, 1960-61. Editor DELOS, 1991—. Bd. dirs. N. Central Fla. Health Planning Coun.; steering com. Fla. Ednl. Computer Network. With USNR, 1944-46. Decorated St. Olav's medal Norway, Order of North Star 1st class Sweden; U. Fla. presdl. scholar, 1976 Fellow Am. Phys. Soc.; mem. Sigma Xi, Sigma Pi Sigma, Omicron Delta Kappa. Clubs: Town and Gown (Austin); Rotary. Business E-Mail: hanson@phys.ufl.edu.

HANSON, HEIDI ELIZABETH, lawyer; b. Portsmouth, Ohio, Nov. 13, 1954; BS, U. Ill., 1975, JD, 1978. Bar: Ill. 1978, U.S. Dist. Ct. (no. dist.) Ill., U.S. Ct. Appeals (7th cir.). Atty. water, air and land pollution divs. Ill. EPA, Springfield, Ill., 1978-85, atty. water pollution div. Maywood, Ill., 1985-86; assoc. Ross & Hardies, Chgo., 1987-89, ptnr., 1990-94; founder H.E. Hanson Law Offices, Western Springs, Ill., 1994—. Named hon. Ky. Col., 2000. Mem.: Indsl. Water, Waste and Sewer Group, Air and Waste Mgmt. Assn., Chgo. Bar Assn., Chicagoland C. of C. Avocation: gardening. Office: 4721 Franklin Ave Ste 1500 Western Springs IL 60558-1720 Personal E-mail: heh70@hotmail.com.

HANSON, JANET TIEBOUT, investment company executive; b. Sept. 6, 1952; m. Jeffrey R. Hanson; children: Meredith, Christopher. BA in Govt., Wheaton Coll., 1974; MBA in Fin. in Fin., Columbia U. Sch. Bus. Various positions including v.p. and co-mgr. of money market sales Goldman, Sachs & Co., 1977—94; v.p. mktg. Goldman Sachs Asset Mgmt., 1991; founder Milestone Capital Mgmt., 1994—. Founder 85 Broads, 1999—. Trustee Wheaton Coll., Christopher Reeve Found., Miles To Go; assoc. fellow Pierson Coll. at Yale U.; adv. bd. U. Rochester's Simon Sch. of Bus., Ctr. Exec. Women, Kellogg Sch. of Mgmt., Ctr. for Work-Life Policy's Hidden Brain Drain Task Force. Recipient Forbes Trailblazer award, 2004, Isabel Benham award, Women's Bond Club of NY, 2003, Disting. Entrepreneur award, Fin. Women's Assn., Trailblazer award, Women in Hedge Funds Network, 2003. Office: Milestone Capital Mgmt 115 E Putnam Ave Greenwich CT 06830*

HANSON, JEAN ELIZABETH, lawyer; b. Alexandria, Minn., June 28, 1949; d. Carroll Melvin and Alice Clarissa (Frykman) Hanson; children: Catherine Jean, Benjamin Colman (twins). BA, Luther Coll., 1971; JD, U. Minn., 1976. Bar: NY 1977, U.S. Dist. Ct. (so. dist.) 1977. Probation officer Hennepin County, Mpls., 1972-73; law clk. Minn. State Pub. Defender, Mpls., 1975-76; assoc. Fried, Frank, Harris, Shriver & Jacobson, NYC, 1976-83, ptnr., 1983-93, 94—. Gen. counsel U.S. Treasury, Washington, 1993—94; mem. bd. regents Luther Coll., Concordia Coll.; mem. bd. visitors Law Sch. U. Minn. Recipient Disting. Svc. award Luther Coll., 1991, Outstanding Achievement award U. Minn., 1999. Mem. ABA, N.Y. State Bar Assn., Assn. of Bar of City of N.Y. (securities regulation com. 1991-98, mem. task force women in the profession 1995-98), U. Minn. Law Alumni Assn. Democrat. Lutheran. Office: Fried Frank Harris Shriver & Jacobson One New York Plaza New York NY 10004 Home Phone: 914-793-0267; Office Phone: 212-859-8198. E-mail: jean.hanson@friedfrank.com.

HANSON, JO, artist, educator, writer; b. Carbondale, Ill. d. Thomas A. and Carrie M. H. MA in Art, San Francisco State U.; MA in Edn, U. Ill. Past instr. sculpture U. Calif., Berkeley, Calif. Coll. Arts and Crafts, Oakland. Participant art panels Women's Caucus for Art and Coll. Art Assn., 1979, 81, 89, 91, 93, 99, Exploratorium Symposium, "Rising Above Our Garbage", San Francisco, 1994; co-curator Living in Balance, San Francisco Internat. Airport and Richmond Art Ctr., 1993, 94, Dear Mother Earth, Marin County Civic Ctr., 1998; moderator Bioneers Conf. panels on art and ecology, 1999—; presenter Soc. for Ecol. Restoration, 1999; subject of "Life Messages" book by Josephine Carleton, Andreus McMeel, 2002. Author: Artists' Taxes, The Hands-on Guide, 1987; co-prodr. Women Environment Artists Directory, 1996—; contbr.: Women, Art and Technology, MIT Press, 2003; one-woman shows of sculpture and installations include, Corcoran Gallery Art, Washington, 1974, Pa. Acad. Fine Arts, Phila., 1976, Utah Mus. Fine Arts, Salt Lake City, 1977, San Francisco Mus. Modern Art, 1976, 80, Internat. Sculpture Conf., San Francisco, 1982, Internat. Conf. Healthy Cities, San Francisco, 1993, Dublin (Calif.) Civic Ctr., 1994, Fresno Art Mus., 1998; exhibited in group shows at San Francisco Mus. Modern Art, 1978, Museau de Arte Contemporanea da U. de São Paulo, Brazil, 1980, Pratt Manhattan Center, N.Y.C., 1981, Auckland City Art Gallery, N.Z., 1985, Municipal Art Soc., N.Y. 1990, John F. Kennedy U., San Francisco, 2001, Yerba Buena Ctr., San Francisco, 2002, Thoreau Ctr., 2005, Fresno Art Mus., 2006, Peninsula Mus. Art, Belmont, Calif., 2007; represented in permanent collections including Herbert F. Johnson Mus. Cornell U., Fresno (Calif.) Art Mus., Mills Coll., Oakland, Calif., Oakland Mus. of Art, San Francisco Arts Commn., San Francisco Mus. Modern Art, Knoxville Mus. Art, Tenn., Fine Arts Museums of San Francisco; numerous pvt. collections. San Francisco Arts commr., 1982-89; adv. bd. artist-in-residence Exploratorium, San Francisco, 1983-91; originator, advisor artist-in-residence program San. Fill Co., San Francisco, 1989—; advisor art and ecology Bioneers Conf., 1999-2006, EarthLight Mag., 1999—2006. Recipient citation San Francisco Bd. Suprs., 1980, San Francisco mayor, 1989, Honor award Bioneers Conf., 2000, Honor award Calif. Lawyers for the Arts, 2004; named Disting. Woman Artist of Yr., Fresno (Calif.) Art Mus., 1998, 2006; Nat. Endowment for Arts fellow, 1977, grantee, 1980. Mem. Coll. Art Assn. (co-chair panel art and ecology 1999), Women's Caucus for Art (Regional Lifetime Achievement award 1992, Nat. Lifetime Achievement award 1997), Pacific Rim Sculptors Group. Office Phone: 415-864-7139.

HANSON, JODY ELIZABETH, special education educator; b. Milw., Mar. 28, 1958; d. Alfred Herbert and Barbara Ann Bopp; m. Bryan Richard Hanson, Oct. 20, 1979; children: Keith Richard, Melissa Beth. BS in Edn., U. Wis., Whitewater, 1980, M in Spl. Edn., 1990, lic. SLD, 1994. Tchr. spl. edn. grades 9-12 Waterford Union H.S., Wis., 1989—. Chair spl. edn. dept. Waterford Union H.S., Wis., mem. staff acad. stds. com., 1998—; adviser Students Against Destructive Decisions, Waterford, 1993—. Pres., softball coach Mukwonago (Wis.) Comty. Athlete Assn., 1974—2002. Mem.: CEC, Wis. Divsn. for Learning Disabled (Tchr. of Yr. 2003), Wis. Coun. for EBD, Wis. Coun. for Exceptional Children, Coun. for Children with Behavioral Disorders. Avocations: camping, golf, reading, motorcycling. Office: Waterford Union H S 100 Field Dr Waterford WI 53185-4116 Business E-Mail: JHanson@waterforduhs.k12.wi.us.

HANSON, JOHN J., retired lawyer; b. Aurora, Nebr., Oct. 22, 1922; s. Peter E. and Hazel Marion (Lounsbury) H.; m. Elizabeth Anne Moss, July 1, 1973; children from their previous marriages— Mark, Eric, Gregory. AB, U. Denver, 1948; LL.B. cum laude, Harvard U., 1951. Bar: N.Y. bar 1952, Calif. bar 1955. Asso. firm Dewey, Ballantine, Bushby, Palmer & Wood, NYC, 1951-54; ptnr. firm Gibson, Dunn & Crutcher, LA, 1954—, mem. exec. com., 1978-87, adv. ptnr., 1991—2004, ret., 2004. Contbr. articles to profl. jours. Trustee Palos Verdes (Calif.) Sch. Dist., 1969-73. Served with U.S. Navy, 1942-45. Fellow Am. Coll. Trial Lawyers; mem. Am. Bar Assn., Los Angeles County Bar Assn. (chmn. antitrust sect. 1979-80), Bel Air Country Club. Home: 953 Linda Flora Dr Los Angeles CA 90049-1630 Office: Gibson Dunn & Crutcher 333 S Grand Ave Ste 4400 Los Angeles CA 90071-3197

HANSON, JOHN M., civil engineering and construction educator; b. Brookings, SD, Nov. 16, 1932; m. Mary Josephson, Jan. 16, 1960 (dec. 1999). BSCE, S.D. State U., 1949; MS in Structural Engring., Iowa State U., 1957; PhD in Civil Engring., Lehigh U., 1964. Profl. engr. Ill., N.C., Colo., Oreg., Mich. Structural engr. J.T. Banner & Assoc., Laramie, Wyo., 1957-58, Phillips, Carter, Osborn, Denver, 1958-60; research inst. prof. Lehigh U., Bethlehem, Pa., 1960-65; engr., asst. mgr. structural devel. Portland Cement Assn., Skokie, Ill., 1965-72; rsch. dir., v.p., pres. Wiss, Janney, Elstner Assocs., Northbrook, Ill., 1972-92; disting. prof. civil engring. and constrn. N.C. State U., Raleigh, 1993-2000, cons. engr., 2000—. Contbr. articles to profl. jours. Served to lt. USAF, 1953-55, Korea. Recipient Disting. Engr. award, S.D. State U., 1979, Profl. Achievement citation, Iowa State U., 1980, Parmer award, Structural Engring. Assn. Ill., 2005. Fellow Prestressed Concrete Inst. (bd. dirs. 1977-80, 93-95, Korn award 1978); mem. ASCE (hon., State of Art award 1974, Reese award 1976, 88, T.Y. Lin award 1979, Boase award 1995, Forensic Engring. award 1999), Am. Concrete Inst. (hon., bd. dirs. 1981-84, 88-94, v.p. 1988-89, pres. 1990, Bloem award 1976, Henry Crown award Ill. chpt. 1993), Internat. Assn. Bridge and Structural Engring. (hon., pres. 1993-97), Internat. Concrete Repair Inst. Lutheran. Office Phone: 919-637-0839. E-mail: jmhanson@nc.rr.com.

HANSON, JOHN NILS, industrial high technology manufacturing company executive; b. Berwyn, Ill., Jan. 22, 1942; s. Robert and Stephanie Ann (Kazluskas) H.; m. Stephanie Morgan, June 5, 1965; children: Laurel, Mark Nils. BS in Chem. Engring., MIT, 1964, MS in Nuclear Engring., 1965; PhD in Nuclear Sci. and Engring., Carnegie-Mellon U., 1969. Sr. scientist Bettis Atomic Power Labs., Westinghouse Electric Corp., West Mifflin, Pa., 1965-70; fellow White House, Washington, 1970-71; exec. asst. to U.S. Sec. Labor, Washington, 1971; asst. to gen. mgr. advanced test core Bettis Atomic Power Labs., Westinghouse Electric Corp., West Mifflin, Pa., 1971-73; asst. to pres. Gould Inc., Rolling Meadows, Ill., 1973-74, pres., gen. mgr. electric motor div. St. Louis, 1974-78, group v.p. elec. products Rolling Meadows, 1978-80; pres. Solar Turbines Internat., San Diego, 1980; v.p. Internat. Harvester, 1980-81, Caterpillar Tractor Co., Peoria, Ill., 1981—90; pres., COO Joy Technologies, 1990—94; pres. Joy Mining Machinery unit Harnischfeger Industries (renamed Joy Global Inc.), 1994—95; exec. v.p., COO Joy Global Inc., Milw., 1995—96, pres., COO, 1996—98, pres., CEO, 1998—2006, chmn., 2000—. Contbr. articles on indsl. tech. to profl. jours. Vice chmn. Friends of Scouting Fundraising-Boy Scouts Am., San Diego council, 1983—; mem. Judge Wallace Longrange planning com., 1983— , vice chmn. fin. adv. com., 1983—; mem. cabinet fund drive United Way, San Diego County Chpt., 1982—; mem. exec. fin. com. Pete Wilson for Senate campaign, San Diego, 1982; vice chmn. Children's Hosp. Research Ctr., 1983—; mem. vis. com. sponsored research MIT, Cambridge, 1978—; mem. Pvt. Industry Council, 1983. Mem. White House Fellows Assn., Greater San Diego C. of C. (bd. dirs.) Office: Joy Global PO Box 554 Milwaukee WI 53201*

HANSON, JON D., law educator; b. Houston, Dec. 24, 1960; BA in Economics & Pub. Policy, Rice U., 1986; JD, Yale U., 1990. Law clk. to US Dist. Judge Jose A. Cabranes; asst. prof. law Harvard Law Sch., Cambridge, Mass., 1992—97, prof., 1997—. Office: Harvard Law Sch 1563 Massachusetts Ave Cambridge MA 02138 Office Phone: 617-496-5207. Office Fax: 617-496-5156. Business E-Mail: hanson@law.harvard.edu.

HANSON, KAREN, philosopher, educator; b. Lincoln, Nebr., Apr. 11, 1947; d. Lester Eugene and Gladys (Diessner) H.; m. Dennis Michael Senchuk, Aug. 22, 1970; children: Tia Elizabeth, Chloe Miranda. BA summa cum laude, U. Minn., 1970; MA, PhD, Harvard U., 1980. Lectr. to assoc. prof. Ind. U., Bloomington, 1976-91, prof. philosophy, 1991—, Rudy prof., 2001—, adj. prof. Am. studies, gender studies and comparative lit., 1991—, chair philosophy, 1997—2002, dean E. L. Hutton Honors Coll., 2002—07, provost, exec. v.p., 2007—. Mem. governing bd. Ind. U. Inst. for Advanced Study, Bloomington, 1992-95, Ind. U. Soc. for Advanced Study, 2001-02; mem. editl. bd. Peirce Edition Project, Indpls., 1982-89, 90—. Author: The Self Imagined, 1986; co-editor: Romantic Revolutions, 1990; assoc. editor Jour. Social Philosophy, 1982-86; mem. editl. bd. Philosophy of Music Edn. Rev., 1992—, Notre Dame Philosophical Reviews, 2001-, Essays in Philosophy, 2000-, Symploke, 1998-; editl. cons. Am. Philos. Quar., 1995-99; contbr. articles to profl. books and jours. Del. Am. Coun. Learned Socs., 1993-98 (exec. com., 1994-98); officer John Dewey Found., 1989—. Recipient Disting. scholar award, Office Women's Affairs, 1995. Mem. Am. Philos. Assn. (exec. officer 1986-91, 2000-03, program com. 1984-91, nominating com. 1993-94, 95-96, chair com. priorities and problems 1998-2000, acting chair bd. officers 2004-05), Am. Soc. Aesthetics (program com. 1989-90, 98-2000, trustee 1997-2000), Soc. Women in Philosophy, Phi Beta Kappa (exec. com. Gamma Ind. chpt. 1993-97, 2002—, officer 1995-97, 2002—, pres. 1996-97, 2004-2005). Home: 3678 Sterling Ave Bloomington IN 47401-4448 Office: Ind U Bryan Hall 100 Bloomington IN 47405 also: Ind U Dept of Philosophy Sycamore 026 Bloomington IN 47405 Office Phone: 812-855-9011. Business E-Mail: provost@indiana.edu.

HANSON, KAREN NOBLE, financial holding company executive; b. Rochester, NY, June 17, 1943; d. Joseph L. and Kathryn C. Noble; children by previous marriage: Tammy C. Tobin, Scott R. Tobin, Robert L. Tobin; m. Thomas L. Hanson, May 7, 1977; step: Timothy. BA cum laude, U. Rochester, 1970, postgrad., 1972; LHD, St. Augustine's Coll., 1986; attended, Dept. Agr. Sr. Exec. Svc. Devel. Program, 1981. Tchg. fellow U. Rochester, 1971, grad. tchg. asst., 1971—72; dir. agrl. manpower Cornell U., 1972—73; exec. dir. Program Funding, Inc., Rochester, 1973—77; dir. Farmer's Home Adminstr., U.S. Dept. Agr., NY and US VI, 1977—81, spl. asst. to adminstr. Wash., 1981; v.p. Genesee Mgmt., Inc. (mgmt. holding co. for Wilmorite, Inc.), Rochester, 1981—99; canon, CFO Episcopal Diocese of Rochester, 1999—. Trustee U. Rochester; bd. mem. N.Y. Job Devel. Authority, N.Y. Ch. Ins., Mon County Cultural Ctr. Commn. Recipient Disting. Svc. award, United Way/Rochester, 1976, Special Svc. award, Nat. Assn. Farm Workers, 1982, Athena award, Rochester C of C, 1994. Democrat. Episcopalian. Office: Episcopal Diocese 935 East Ave Rochester NY 14607 Office Phone: 585-473-2977. E-mail: knhanson@aol.com.

HANSON, KENT BRYAN, lawyer; b. Litchfield, Minn., Sept. 17, 1954; s. Calvin Bryan and Muriel (Wessman) H.; m. Barbara Jane Elenbaas, Aug. 24, 1974; children: Lindsay Michal, Taylor Jordan, Chase Philip. AA with high honors, Trinity Western Coll., 1974; BA, U. B.C., Vancouver, 1976; JD magna cum laude, U. Minn., 1979. Bar: Minn. 1979, U.S. Dist. Ct. Minn. 1980, U.S. Ct. Appeals (8th cir.) 1980, U.S. Dist. Ct. (we. dist.) Wis. 1983, Wis. 1985, U.S. Ct. Appeals (9th cir.) 1989, U.S. Dist. Ct. Ariz. 1992, Ohio 1993, Calif. 1994. Assoc. Grossman, Karlins, Siegel & Brill, Mpls., 1979-81, Gray, Plant, Mooty, Mooty & Bennett, Mpls., 1981-85; ptnr. Bowman & Brooke, Mpls., 1986-95; CEO Hanson, Marek, Bolkcom & Greene, Ltd., Mpls., 1996—. Bd. dirs. Inner City Boys Club, Ctrl. Free Ch., Mpls., 1979-81; 12th ward del. Mpls. Dem. Farmer Labor Com. Conv., 1982; exec. bd. Ctrl. Free Ch., Mpls., 1986; chair exec. bd. Ctrl. Cmty. Ch., 1993-96. Mem. ABA, State Bar Assn. Wis., Minn. Def. Lawyers Assn., Minn. State Bar Assn., Hennepin County Bar Assn., Calif. State Bar Assn., State Bar of Ohio, Def. Rsch. Inst. Avocations: classical music, golf, tennis, computers, motorcycles. Office: Hanson Marek Bolkcom & Greene Ltd 2300 Rand Tower 527 Marquette Ave Minneapolis MN 55402-1302 Home Phone: 612-377-2158; Office Phone: 612-342-2880. Business E-Mail: khanson@hmbglaw.com.

HANSON, KERMIT OSMOND, business administration educator, retired dean; b. Troy Twp., Iowa, May 14, 1916; s. Gerhard Severin and Sunniva Fosmark (Borge) H.; m. Jane Elizabeth Haugen, Aug. 17, 1940; children: James Stephen, Katherine Jane, Paul Richard, Daniel Gerhard. AB cum laude, Luther Coll., Decorah, Iowa, 1938; MS, Iowa State U., 1940, PhD, 1950; D.Sc. (hon.), Luther Coll., 1981. Ops. analyst Fed. Land Bank, Omaha, 1941-43; chief statis. service sect. VA br. office, Seattle, 1946-47; mem. faculty Sch. Bus. Adminstrn., U. Wash., Seattle, 1948-81, prof. acctg., finance and statistics, 1954-81, chmn. dept. accounting, finance and statistics, 1955-60, assoc. dean, 1959-64; dean Sch. Bus. Adminstrn., U. Wash. (Grad. Sch. Bus. Adminstrn.), 1964-81, dean emeritus, 1981—; John F. Mee Disting. prof. Sch. Bus. Adminstrn. Pacific Luth. U., 1985-86. Instr., ednl. dir. Pacific Coast Banking Sch., 1948-81, bd. dirs.; exec. dir Pacific Rim Bankers Program, 1977-89, vice chmn. bd. dirs., 1979-98, chmn. emeritus, 1998—; bd. dirs. Pacific Horizon Funds, Inc., 1982-98, Wash. Fed. Savs. & Loan Assn., 1966-2004, Seafirst Retirement trust, 1993-97, Safeco Corp., 1976-81; cons. GAO, 1970-78; chmn. Wash. Gov.'s Adv. Coun. on Productivity, 1974-75; bd. adv. Naval Postgrad. Sch., Monterey, Calif., 1976-84. Author: Managerial Statistics, 1955, 2d edit. (with G. Brabb), 1961, (with M. Tomich) (monograph) Pacific Rim Bankers Program—A Brief History—The First Ten Years 1977-1986, 1987, The Pacific Coast Banking School—The First 50 Years, 1988. Mem. adv. com. Chief Seattle coun. Boy Scouts Am., 1958-2004, pres., 1967-69; bd. trustees Horizon House, 1990-96, pres., 1994-96; mem. adv. bd. U. Miami (Fla.) Sch. Bus., 1983-88, Pacific Luth. U. Sch. Bus., Tacoma, 1987-90, Seattle Pacific U. Sch. Bus., 1985-90; bd. dirs. Journey for Perspective Found., 1964-76. Lt. USNR, 1943-46. Recipient Silver Beaver award Seattle Coun. Boy Scouts Am., 1963, Disting. Svc. award U. Wash., 1981, Pioneer Meml. award Luther Coll., 1997. Mem. Am. Assn. Collegiate Schs. Bus. (pres. 1971-72), Am. Accounting Assn., Am. Finance Assn., Financial Execs. Inst., Beta Gamma Sigma, Beta Alpha Psi, Alpha Kappa Psi. Lutheran. Home: 17760 14th Ave NW Shoreline WA 98177-3207

HANSON, MARK S., bishop; b. Mpls., Dec. 2, 1946; m. Ione Agrimson; children: Aaron Hanson , Alyssa, Rachel, Ezra, Isaac, Elizabeth. Grad., Minnehaha Acad., 1964; B Sociology, Augsburg Coll., 1968; Rockefeller fellow, Union Theol. Sem., 1969, MDiv, 1972; student, Luther Sem., 1973—74; Merrill fellow, Harvard U., 1979. Ordained 1974. Pastor Prince of Glory Luth. Ch. , Mpls., 1973—79, Edina Cmty. Luth. Ch., Edina, Minn., 1979—88, U. Luth. Ch. , Hope, Mpls. , 1988—95; bishop St. Paul Area Synod Evang. Luth. Ch. Am. , 1995, presiding bishop, 2001—. Pres. Minn. Coun. Chs., 1998—2000. Author: Faithful Yet Changing: The Church in Challenging Times. Office: Evang Luth Ch Am Office of Bishop 8765 W Higgins Rd Chicago IL 60631 E-mail: bishop@elca.org.

HANSON, MARTIN PHILIP, mechanical engineer, farmer; b. Watseka, Ill., Feb. 4, 1937; s. Philip Andrew and Mary Jane (Martin) Hanson; m. Virginia Ann Garfield, Jan. 2, 1960; children: Martin Philip Jr., Adam Gunnar. BS, US Naval Acad., 1959. Registered profl. engr., Mich., Ill. Commd. ensign USN, 1959, advanced through grades to lt. comdr., 1968; reactor mech. asst. USS Enterprise (CVAN-65), Alameda, Calif., 1968-69; resigned, 1969; project engr. Consumers Power Co., Jackson, Mich., 1969-74; project engring. mgr. United Engrs. and Constructors Inc., Phila., 1974-77, Seabrook, N.H., 1977-82, Glen Rose, Tex., 1982-83, Washington, 1983-87; project control specialist Systematic Mgmt. Svcs., Argonne, Ill., 1987-92; project engr. Mac Tech. Svcs. Co., Argonne, 1992-95; sr. project mgmt. specialist Aguirre Engrs., Inc., Argonne, 1995-97; v.p. RERC Environ., Inc., Chgo., 1997-99. Sec. repository coordination group Dept. Energy, Washington, 1983—85, sec. repository change control, 1985—87. Capt. USNR, 1969—92, comdr. res. regts. USNR. Mem.: SAR, ASME (past chmn. New Eng. sect.), Organ Transplant Support (past dir.-at-large). Achievements include organizing new programs for continuous fiber ceramic composites and other technologies. Avocations: automobiles, opera, classical music. Home: 1009 Troutlilly Ln Darien IL 60561-8819 Personal E-mail: navy59@comcast.net.

HANSON, NORMA LEE, farmer; b. Brainerd, Minn., Feb. 3, 1930; d. Fred Christian Kruckow and Lena Belle Sawyer; m. Lynn Curtis Hanson; 1 child, Michael Lynn. Student, Mpls. Sch. Bus., 1949—50; grad., Northland C.C., 1972. File clk. and predetermining mortgage payments Investors Diversified Svcs., Mpls., 1949—53; social reporter Thief River Falls Times, 1954—63; office mgr. Kiewel Products Co., 1963—70; lobbyist Minn. Farmers Union, St. Paul, 1970—72, columnist, 1973—76; asst. farm mgr. Good-Vue Ayr Farms, Goodridge, 1976—. Chmn. Senate Dist. 1, Minn., 1990—, Northwest Minn. Women's Fund, 2001—. Mem.: NW Minn. Dairy Assn. (sec., treas. 2000—), Am. Dairy Assn. (pres. 1986—2001), Midwest Dairy Assn. (bd. dirs. 1995—2000, sec., treas. N.W. Minn. chpt. 2000—), Am. Agrl. Women (chmn. dairy com. 1999—), Hort. Soc. (pres. 13th dist. 2000—), Goodridge Area Hist. Soc. (pres. 1980—, founder). Democrat. Lutheran. Avocations: horticulture, horseback riding, reading, writing, snowmobiling. Home: 21625 330th Ave NE Goodridge MN 56725

HANSON, PAULA, sports association executive; BJ, U. Colo. Dir. promotions Denver Nuggets, 1974—79, v.p., asst. gen. mgr. bus. ops., 1979—85; v.p. team svcs. NBA, 1985—96, sr. v.p. team ops., 1996—99; sr. v.p., COO WNBA, NYC, 1999—2003, sr. v.p. team business devel. Denver, 2003—. Office: WNBA Olympic Tower 645 5th Ave Fl 10 New York NY 10022-5986*

HANSON, PERRY, library and information scientist; BA, Middlebury Coll., 1964; MS, Northwestern U., PhD in Geography, 1972. Dir. Office of Info. Sys. Clark U., Worcester, Mass., 1984—87; dir. Info. Sys. and Telecommunications Wellesley Coll., Mass., 1992—96; chief tech. officer Williams Coll., Williamstown, Mass., 1996—99; chief info. officer, assoc. provost academic tech. Brandeis U., Waltham, Mass., 1999—2005, v.p., vice provost Librs. and Info. Tech., 2005—. Asst. prof. geography SUNY, Buffalo, 1971—78; asst. prof., chmn. Dept. Geography Middlebury Coll., 1978—82; vis. asst. prof. to adj. assoc. prof. to adj. prof. geography Clark U., 1982—90. Mem.: EDUCAUSE Learning Tech. Leadership Inst. Avocations: bicycling, hiking. Office: Libr & Tech Svcs MS 045 Brandeis U PO Box 549110 Waltham MA 02454-9110 Office Phone: 781-736-4588. Office Fax: 781-736-4803. E-mail: phanson@brandeis.edu.*

HANSON, POLLY (PAULINE) MAE EARLY, librarian; b. Danville, Ill., Sept. 20, 1927; d. Jesse Alonzo and Mamie Viola Mapes Early; m. Carl Ludwig Hanson, June 18, 1950; children: Eric Alan, Wendy Sue Hanson Martin, Julie Marie Hanson-Geist. BA in English Lit., U. Mich., 1949; MLS, U. Wash., Seattle, 1967. Asst. children's libr. Seattle Pub. Libr., 1950—51; children's libr. King County Libr. Sys., Wash., 1967, Mercer Island Libr., Wash., 1967—71; br. mgr. Issaquah Libr., Wash., 1971—75; asst. libr. dir., pub. services Whatcom County Libr. Sys., Wash., 1975—78, libr. dir., 1978—83; founding libr. dir. NW Indian Coll., Lummi Indian Nation, Wash., 1985—95; owner-mgr. West Shore Farm Bed & Breakfast, Lummi Island, Wash., 1984—. Founder Skyway Br. Libr. King County Libr. Sys., 1951—56. Author: (newspaper column) Skyway Community Column, Renton News Record, 1951—56. Founding bd. mem. Parent Coop. Nursery Sch., Skyway, Wash., 1954—56, Lummi Island Conservancy, 1988—2002; elected cemetery bd. commr. Lummi Island Cemetery Dist., Wash., 1995—; bd. dirs. Lummi Island Cmty. Land Trust, 1998—2005; mem. Lummi Island Subarea Plan com., Whatcom County, Wash., 2000—04; Lummi Island precinct com. officer Whatcom County Democrats, 2000—04; mem. Dem. Ctrl. Com., Whatcom County, Wash., 1990—; bd. mem. Young Women's Christian Assn., Bellingham, Wash., 1980—82; founding bd. mem. Lummi Island Hist. and Preservation Soc., 1978. Recipient Photographer award, Seattle Pub. Libr., 1995, 10-yr. svc. wall plaque, NW Indian Coll., 1995. Mem.: Uppity Women's Book Club and Writing Cir. (life). D-Liberal. Unitarian Universalist. Achievements include first to develop natural childbirth breast feeding movement leading to Childbirth Education Association; member of the Mercer Island environmental committee that re-designed Highway I-90 on Mercer Island to meet community and environmental needs. Avocations: organic and native plants, birdwatching, tai chi, gardening. Home: 2781 West Shore Dr Lummi Island WA 98262-8715 Office: WestShore Farm Bed and Breakfast 2781 West Shore Dr Lummi Island WA 98262-8715 Home Phone: 360-758-2600; Office Phone: 360-758-2600. Personal E-mail: westshorefarm@msn.com.

HANSON, RANDALL A., lawyer; b. Charleston, W.Va., Dec. 18, 1960; s. William F. and Lilly Sue Hanson; m. Cynthia Brann, May 22, 1982; 1 child, Alexander Trent. AB, U. NC, 1983, JD with honors, 1985. Bar: DC 1985, NC 1993. Assoc. Winston & Strawn, Washington, 1985-88, Piper & Marbury, Washington, 1988-93, Womble Carlyle Sandridge & Rice PLLC, Winston-Salem, NC, 1993-95, mem., 2000—01, Greensboro, NC, 2001—, mng. mem. Greensboro office; assoc. gen. counsel, corp. sec., gen. counsel Mexican ops. Burlington Industries, Inc., Greensboro, NC, 1995—2000. Bd. dirs. Cmty. Theatre of Greensboro, The Nussbaum Ctr. for Entrepreneurship. Mem.: ABA (bus. law sect. com. negotiated acquisitions), Internat. Bar Assn., NC Bar Assn. (bus. law sect.). Democrat. Avocations: college basketball, tv and radio production, travel. Office: Womble Carlyle Sandridge & Rice PLLC PO Box 21104 Greensboro NC 27402-6025 Office Phone: 336-574-8070. Office Fax: 336-574-4515. Business E-Mail: rhanson@wcsr.com.

HANSON, RICHARD E., paper company executive; BS in Indsl. Mgmt., U. Oreg., 1965. With Weyerhaeuser Co., Tacoma, 1969—, v.p., western timberlands, 1996—98, sr. v.p., timberlands, 1998—2002, exec. v.p., timberlands and international, 2002—03, exec. v.p., COO, 2003—. Bd. dirs. Oreg. Forest Industries Coun., also operating com.; adv. com. Oreg. State U. Forest Rsch. Lab. Trustee Oreg. Zoo; mem. founder's cir. Stop Oreg. Litter & Vandalism. Office: Weyerhaeuser PO Box 9777 Federal Way WA 98063-9777*

HANSON, ROBERT DUANE, engineering educator; b. Albert Lea, Minn., July 27, 1935; s. James Edwin and Gertie Hanson; m. Kaye Lynn Nielsen, June 7, 1959; children: Craig Robert, Eric Neil. Student, St. Olaf Coll., Northfield, Minn., 1953-54; BSE, U. Minn., 1957, MS in Civil Engring., 1958; PhD, Calif. Inst. Tech., Pasadena, 1965. Registered profl. engr., Mich., N.D. Design engr. Pitts.-Des Moines Stel, Des Moines, 1958-59; asst. prof. U. N.D., Grand Forks, 1959-61; rsch. engr. Calif. Inst. Tech., 1965; asst. prof. U. Calif.-Davis, 1965-66; from asst. prof. to prof. civil engring. U. Mich., Ann Arbor, 1966—2001, prof. emeritus, 2001—, chmn. dept. civil engring., 1976-84; sr. earthquake engr. Fed. Emergency Mgmt. Agy., 1994-2000. Vis. prof., dir. Earthquake Engring. Rsch. Ctr., U. Calif., Berkeley, 1991; dir. BCS divsn. NSF, Washington, 1989-90; cons. NSF, 1979-88, 92-94; cons. Bechtel Corp., Ann Arbor, 1976-87, Sensei Engrs., Ann Arbor, 1977-90, Bldg. Seismic Safety Coun., 1988-94, Fed. Emergency Mgmt. Agy., 1992-94, 2000-05, applied tech. coun., 2005—. Contbr. articles to profl. jours. Recipient Reese Rsch. award ASCE, 1980; recipient Disting. Svc. award U. Mich., 1969; tchg. award Chi Epsilon, 1985, Attwood Engr. Excellence award, 1986. Fellow ASCE (life; com. chmn. 1975-94); mem. NAE, Earthquake Engring. Rsch. Inst. (hon., v.p. 1977-79, bd. dirs. 1976-79, 88-92, pres.-elect 1988, pres. 1989-91, past pres. 1991-92). Lutheran. Home: 2926 Saklan Indian Dr Walnut Creek CA 94595-3911 Home Phone: 925-946-9463. Personal E-mail: rdhanson2@aol.com.

HANSON, RONALD WILLIAM, lawyer; b. Aug. 3, 1950; s. Orlin Eugene and Irene Agnes Hanson; m. Sandra Kay Cook, Aug. 21, 1971; children: Alec Evan, Corinn Michele. BA summa cum laude, St. Olaf Coll., 1972; JD cum laude, U. Chgo., 1975. Bar: Ill. 1975, U.S. Dist. Ct. (no. dist.) Ill. 1975, U.S. Ct. Appeals (7th cir.) 1978, U.S. Ct. Appeals (10th cir.) 1989. Assoc. Sidley & Austin, Chgo., 1975-83, ptnr., 1983-88, Latham & Watkins, Chgo., 1988—, chmn. audit com., 1998—2005. Ofcl. advisor to Nat. Conf. of Commrs. on Uniform State Laws; lectr. Ill. Inst. Continuing Legal Edn., Springfield, Am. Bankruptcy Inst., Washington, Banking Law Inst., Practicing Law Inst., Am. Law Inst. Contbr. articles to profl. jours.

Mem. ABA, Ill. Bar Assn., Chgo. Bar Assn., Order of Coif, Met. Club, Phi Beta Kappa. Republican. Lutheran. Home: 664 W 58th St Hinsdale IL 60521-5104 Office: Latham & Watkins Sears Tower Ste 5800 Chicago IL 60606-6306 Office Phone: 312-876-7700. Business E-Mail: ronald.hanson@lw.com.

HANSON, SAMUEL LEE, state supreme court justice; b. Mankato, Minn., Aug. 26, 1939; s. Lester Kenneth and Margaret Dorothy (Brockmeyer) H.; m. Beret Elizabeth Brown, July 28, 1962 (div. Apr. 1976); children: Greta E., Chrystina E., Benjamin D.; m. Mirja Pirkko Karikosky, Sept. 23, 1977; children: Leif O., Luke A., Jai N. BA, St. Olaf Coll., 1961; LLB, William Mitchell Coll. Law, 1965. Bar: Minn. 1965, U.S. Dist. Ct. Minn. 1966, U.S. Ct. Appeals (8th cir.) 1966, U.S. Supreme Ct. 1971. Law clk. to hon. Douglas K. Amdahl Hennepin County Dist. Ct., Mpls., 1965; law clk. to hon. Robert J. Sheran Minn. Supreme Ct., St. Paul, 1966; assoc., shareholder Briggs and Morgan, St. Paul, Mpls., 1966—2000, pres., 1988-93; appt. Ct. of Appeals, Minn., 2000—02; justice Minn. Supreme Ct., Minn., 2002—. Mem. adv. com. Minn. Supreme Ct., St. Paul, 1984-86; adj. prof. William Mitchell Coll. Law, St. Paul, 1966-71; co-chair Minn. Legal Services State Planning Commn., 2002-; chair supreme ct. Gender Fairness Implementation Com., 2002-; liaison supreme ct. advisory com. gen. rules of practice, 2002-, supreme ct. Bd. of Legal Certification, 2002-; liaison supreme ct. adv. com. on rules of civil procedure, 2005-. Contbr. articles to profl. jours. Bd. dirs. Rural Ventures Inc., Mpls., 1981-87, Rural Tech. Partnership, St. Paul, 1987—, Global Vols., St. Paul, 1984—. Fellow Am. Coll. Trial Lawyers (chair Minn. chpt. 1991), Am. Bd. Trial Advocates, Crossroads, Inc. Avocations: rural development, organizational development. Home: 5510 Edgewater Blvd Minneapolis MN 55417-2605 Office: Minn Supreme Ct 305 Minn Jud Ctr 25 Rev Martin Luther King Jr Blvd Saint Paul MN 55155 Office Phone: 651-297-7676. Business E-Mail: sam.hanson@courts.state.mn.us.*

HANSON, STEPHEN, food service executive; Graduate, NYU Stern Sch. Bus. Mgr. Original TGIFriday's Restaurant; owner Peachtree's Nightclub, Westchester, NY; exec. Betty Hanson Designer Sportswear; owner Coconut Grill, NYC, 1987—; owner several B.R. Guest NYC restaurants including Isabella's, Atlantic Grill, Ocean Grill, Blue Water Grill, Ruby Foo's Dim Sum and Sushi Palace, Ruby Foo's Times Sq., Blue Fins, Dos Caminos, Fiamma Osteria. Mem. bd. dir. Caribou Coffee. Mem. bd. dir. Exploring Program Non-Profit. Recipient Restaurateur Yr. award, 2003. Office: BR Guest Inc 206 Spring St New York NY 10012

HANSON, THOR, retired health agency executive, retired naval officer; b. Amarillo, Tex., May 7, 1928; s. Carl Joseph Emanuel and Lillian (Nelson) H.; m. Charlotte Ann Edens, Oct. 6, 1956; children: Inge Rew, Erica Karen, Ivor Carl, Lars Jon, Ursula Edens. BS, U.S. Naval Acad., 1950; MA, Oxford U., Eng., 1954. Commd. ensign U.S. Navy, 1950, advanced through grades to vice adm., 1979, service in Korea and Vietnam, naval aide, exec. asst. to sec. Navy, 1970-72, comdg. officer Naval Sta. Pearl Harbor, 1973-74; chief U.S. Naval Mission to Brazil, 1974-76; comdr. Cruiser-Destroyer Group 8; also comdr. Attack Carrier Striking Group 2, U.S. 6th Fleet, 1976-77; mil. asst. to Sec. of Def., 1977-79; dir. joint staff Office Joint Chiefs Staff, 1979-82, ret., 1982; mil. analyst Cable News Network, 1982; pres., CEO Nat. Multiple Sclerosis Soc., 1982-92, pres. emeritus, 1992—. Chmn. Nat. Health Coun., 1991-93; hon. bd. dirs. Rsch.! Am. Bd. dirs. Empire Ranch Found., Tucson Boys Chorus; pres. Southold Citizens for Safe Roads, 1995-05. Decorated Def. D.S.M. with oak leaf cluster, Legion of Merit, Bronze Star with combat V, Meritorious Service medal, Joint Service Commendation medal; Vietnam Navy Distinguished Service medal; Brazilian Naval Order of Merit; Rhodes scholar, 1951-54 Mem. Am. Assn. Rhodes Scholars, Coun. on Fgn. Rels., U.S. Naval Inst., U.S. Naval Acad. Alumni Assn., Am. Fedn. Musicians (hon. life), Century Assn., N.Y. Yacht Club, Leander Rowing Club (England), Ends of the Earth Club, Digressionists Club. Episcopalian. Home: 3377 E Arroyo Chico Tucson AZ 85716 E-mail: vadmthor@hansonmob.net.

HANSON, TOM, state official; b. Mahnomen, Minn., Aug. 7, 1963; m. Kris Hanson; 1 child. BA in History, magna cum laude, Concordia Coll., 1985; JD, George Mason Univ., 1993. Bar: Minn. Dep. chief of staff, dir. legis., cabinet affairs Gov. Minn.; commr. fin. State of Minn., 2006—. Office: Dept Fin 400 Centennial Office Bldg 658 Cedar St Saint Paul MN 55155 Office Phone: 651-202-8000. Office Fax: 651-296-8685. Business E-Mail: tom.j.hanson@state.mn.us.*

HANSON, VICTOR HENRY, II, newspaper publisher; b. Augusta, Ga., Aug. 17, 1930; s. Clarence Bloodworth, Jr. and Elizabeth (Fletcher) H.; m. Elizabeth Stallworth, Dec. 29, 1953; children: Clarence Bloodworth III, Victor Henry III, Elizabeth Mickel, Mary Fletcher, Robert Stallworth. Grad., Choate Sch., 1949; student, U. Va., 1949-51; BA, U. Ala., 1954. With Birmingham (Ala.) News & Post Herald, 1946-54, 57—, gen. mgr., 1963-83; with advt. and prodn. dept. WAPI-TV, Birmingham, 1954-55; v.p. Birmingham News Co., 1960-79, pres., 1979-2000, pub., 1983-2000. Bd. dirs. Grace House Ministries, Art Fund, Inc.; elder Presbyn. Ch. Served to capt. USAF, 1955-57. Recipient Tree of Life award, Nat. Jewish Fund, 1991. Mem. SAR, Birmingham C. of C., Soc. of Cincinnati, N.C. Soc. of Cincinnati, Birmingham Country Club, Mountain Brook Club, The Club, Kappa Alpha. Home: 3910 Hunters Ln Birmingham AL 35243-5920 Office: 402 Office Park Dr Ste 100 Birmingham AL 35223 Office Phone: 205-879-8562. Personal E-mail: vhii@bellsouth.net.

HANSSEN, KRISTINA SCHIRM, costume designer, educator; m. Ron Charles Adams, Dec. 30, 1985. BFA, Stephens Coll., 1975; MFA, U. Mo., Kansas City, 1977. Tchr., costume designer Colo. State U., Ft. Collins, Colo., 1980—84, Sam Houston State U., Huntsville, Tex., 1985—. Costume designer Stages Repertory Theatre, Houston, 2000—. Costume designer (plays). Mem.: US Inst. Theatre Tech. (dir. at large 2006—). Office: Sam Houston State University 1740 Bobby Marks Dr Huntsville TX 77340 Office Phone: 936-294-1350. E-mail: drm_kxh@shsu.edu.

HANSSON, DAVID HEINEMEIER, application developer; b. Denmark, 1979; arrived in Chgo., 2005; B in Bus. Adminstrn. and Computer Sci., Copenhagen Bus. Sch. Freelance programmer 37Signals LLC, 2001, ptnr. Co-author: Agile Web Devel. with Rails, 2005. Named one of 50 Who Matter Now, CNNMoney.com Bus. 2.0, 2006, Top 40 Under 40, Crain's Chgo. Bus., 2006; recipient Open Source award, Best Hacker, Google and O'Reilly, 2005, Jolt award, 2006. Achievements include producing Ruby on Rails, an open-source tool that makes it easier to use the Ruby programming language. Office: 37Signals LLC 400 N May St #301 Chicago IL 60622 E-mail: david@loudthinking.com.*

HANSUK, SOHN, industrial engineer, educator; b. Seoul, Republic of Korea; s. Jik-Soo Sohn and Sang-Hee Kim; m. Jeehye Seo; 1 child, Christine Joohee Sohn. PhD, U. Iowa, Iowa City, 2004. Post-doctorate rsch. assoc. U. Iowa, Iowa City, 2004—05; asst. prof. N.Mex State U., Las Cruces, 2006—. Office: New Mexico State Univ Industrial Engring MSC 4230 Las Cruces NM 88003 Office Phone: 505-646-2957. Office Fax: 505-646-2976. Business E-Mail: hsohn@nmsu.edu.

HANTASH, BASIL M., dermatologist, educator; BS, U. Ill., Urbana-Champaign, 1992; MD with honors, PhD with honors, NJ Med. Sch., Newark, 2002. Lic. physician and surgeon Calif., 2003, Drug Enforcement Agy., 2003, diplomate Am. Bd. Dermatology, 2006. Instr. Stanford U., Calif., 2003—. Cons. ZyBas, Inc, East Palo Alto, Calif., 2002—07. Author: (poetry) Crying Inside Out, 2003 (Editor's Choice award Internat. Libr. Poetry, 2003), Merge into You, 2004 (nominee Poet of Yr. award Internat. Soc. Poets, 2004). Mem. com. task force SBIa; mem. med. adv. bd. PCRF, Kent, Ohio, 2002—07; mem. adv. coun. Greenbook Doctors. Recipient Poetry Writing award, Hollens Coll., 1989, Rsch. award, Howard Hughes Med. Inst., 1991, Hugh Grady award, NJ Med. Sch., 1998, Dean's Clin. Achievement award, 2001, Marcus T. Block MD Dermatology award, 2002; fellow, Am. Heart Assn., 1997, 1998, Stemedica Cell Techs., 2005—06; grantee, Colgate-Palmolive Rsch. Found., 1991, Stanford U., 2006—07, Minn. Jewish Found., 2006—07; scholar, NJ Med. Sch., 1996—2002, 1997—98, 2000, World Congress Dermatology, 2006; The Mary Ladanyi Hagen Meml. scholarship, NJ Med. Sch., 2001. Mem.: Soc. Investigative Dermatology, Dermatology Found., Am. Soc. Dermatologic Surgery (scholar 2005, grantee 2005), Am. Acad. Dermatology, South Bay Mobilization (founder, chmn. human rights com.), Alpha Omega Alpha, Sigma Xi Sci. Rsch. Soc. Achievements include invention of the fields of laser medicine, stem cell biology, and nanotechnology. Home: 1269 Runnymede St East Palo Alto CA 94303 Home Phone: 408-204-8946. Personal E-mail: hantasba@hotmail.com.

HANTEL, PHILIP EDWARD, lawyer; b. Los Alamos, N.Mex., Aug. 4, 1972; s. Lawrence W. and Elizabeth G. Hantel. BA in Polit. Sci., U. Wash., Seattle, 1994; JD, South Tex. Coll. Law, 1997. Bar: La. 1997, US Dist. Ct. (we., mid. and ea. dists.) La. 1997, US Ct. Appeals (5th cir.) 1997, Ariz. Bar 2006, US Ct Appeals (9th cir.) 2006, US Dist. Ct. Ariz. 2007. Staff atty. La. Indigent Defender Bd., New Orleans, 1997, juvenile atty. Harvey, La., 1998; assoc. Beevers & Beevers LLP, Gretna, La., 1998-2000; pvt. practice Phoenix, 2000—. Mem. La. Criminal Def. Lawyers Assn., La. Pub. Defenders Assn., 5th Cir. Bar Assn., Fed. Bar Assn. Home: 28939 N 111th St Scottsdale AZ 85262 Office: 710 W Roosevelt St Phoenix AZ 85007 Office Phone: 602-252-1099. Personal E-mail: philiphantel@mac.com.

HANTMAN, BARRY G., software engineer; b. Boston, May 22, 1962; s. Leonard M. and Barbara R.; m. Susan Chapman, June 2, 1985; 1 child, Noam Seth. BA, Brandeis U., 1984; postgrad., Fitchburg State Coll., 1984-86. Cons. Wicat Sys., Waltham, Mass., 1982-84; mgr. validation and BMC3I software Raytheon Co., Tewksbury, Mass., 1984—. Open Software Found. primary rep. Raytheon Co., Tewksbury, 1991-93, CAD Framework Initiative primary rep., 1993-94, program mgr. Dept. Def. Microwave/Millimeter Advanced Computational Environ. Program, 1992-97, Dept. Def. Mfg. Automation and Design Engring. Program, 1996. Lodge chief Order of Arrow, Stoneham, Mass., 1979-81; chmn. Town of Danville (N.H.) Planning Bd.; chmn. Cable TV Com., Rockingham County (N.H.) Planning Commn. Mem. IEEE Computer Soc., U.S. Holocaust Meml. Coun., African Wildlife Found., World Wildlife Fund, Wildlife Conservation Soc., Assn. Computing Machinery, Mentor Graphics User Group (pres. 1988-90, v.p. 1987-88, mem. steering com. 1985-87, 90-92). Avocations: foreign travel, video editing.

HANUS, JEROME GEORGE, archbishop; b. Brainard, N.E., May 26, 1940; Student, Conception Sem., Mo., St. Anselm U., Rome, Princeton Theol. Sem., Princeton U. Ordained priest Roman Cath. Ch., 1966. Abbot Conception Abbey, 1977—87; pres. Swiss Am. Benedictine Congregation, 1984—87; bishop Diocese of St. Cloud, Minn., 1987—94; co-adjutor archbishop Dubuque, Iowa, 1994—95; archbishop, 1995—. Office: Archdiocese of Dubuque 1229 Mt Loretta Ave Dubuque IA 52004

HANUSHEK, ERIC ALAN, economics professor; b. Lakewood, Ohio, May 22, 1943; s. Vernon F. and Ruth (Hostetler) H.; m. Nancy L. Keleher, June 11, 1965 (div.); children: Eric Alan, Megan E.; m. Margaret E. Raymond, Oct. 10, 2003. BS, U.S. Air Force Acad., 1965; PhD in Econs., MIT, 1968. Sr. staff economist Coun. Econ. Advisers, Washington, 1971-72; assoc. prof. USAF Acad., Colo., 1972-73; sr. economist Cost of Living Coun., Washington, 1973-74; assoc. prof. econs. Yale U., New Haven, 1975-78; dir. pub. policy analysis U. Rochester, N.Y., 1978-83, prof. econs. and polit. sci. NY, 1978-2000, chmn. dept. econs. NY, 1982-87, 88-90, dir. W. Allen Wallis Inst. Polit. Economy NY, 1992-99; rsch. assoc. Nat. Bur. Econ. Rsch., 1996—; Hanna sr. fellow Hoover Instn. Stanford (Calif.) U., 2000—; sr. rsch. fellow Green Ctr. U. Tex., Dallas, 2000—; sr. fellow Stanford Inst. for Econ. Policy Rsch., 2003—. Dep. dir. Congl. Budget Office, Washington, 1984-85; mem. com. nat. stats. Nat. Rsch. Coun., 1992-98, adv. coun. on Edn. Statistics, 2002; cons. World Bank 1984-95, U.S. Com. on Civil Rights, 1986-89; chair exec. bd. Tex. Schs. Project, U. Tex., Dallas, 2003—; mem nat. bd. for edn. scis. U.S. Dept. Edn., 2005—; rsch. prof. IFO Inst. Econ. Rsch., U. Munich. Author: Education and Race, 1972, (with J. Jackson) Statistical Methods for Social Scientists 1977, (with C. Citro) Improving Information for Social Policy Decisions, 1991, (with R. Harbison) Education Performance of the Poor, 1992, Making Schools Work, 1994, (with J. Banks) Modern Political Economy, 1995, (with N. Maritato) Assessing Knowledge of Retirement Behavior, 1996, (with Dale W. Jorgenson) Improving America's Schools, 1996, (with Constance F. Citro) Assessing Policies for Retirement Income, 1997, The Economics of Schooling and School Quality, 2003, Courting Failure, 2006, (with Finis Welch) Handbook of Economics of Education, 2006. Served to capt. USAF, 1965-74. Disting. vis. fellow Hoover Instn., Stanford U., 1999-2000. Fellow Internat. Acad. Edn. (bd. dirs. 2002—), Nat. Acad. Edn., Soc. Labor Econs., Assn. Pub. Policy Analysis and Mgmt. (v.p. 1986-87, pres. 1988-89), Am. Econ. Assn., Econometric Soc., Soc. Labor Economists, Am. Edn. Fin. Assn. (bd. dirs. 2006—). Office Phone: 650-736-0942. Business E-Mail: hanushek@stanford.edu.

HANVY, PHILLIP WAYNE, benefits compensation analyst; b. Columbia, Tenn., May 24, 1966; s. Bobby Gene and Rachel Hanvy. BA, Samford U., Birmingham, 1988. Disability examiner ii Disability Determinations Svcs., Nashville, 1990—96, disability counselor St. Louis, 1996—97, sr. disability adjudicator Wilmington, Del., 1997—99; disability quality reviewer office quality assurance Social Security Adminstrn., Balt., 1999—2000, Boston, 2000—03, sr. program analyst insp. gen., 2003—. Recipient Citation, Social Security Assn. Commr., 1995, Regional Commr. Citation, Social Security Regional Commr., 1999, Team award, Pres. Coun. on Integrity and Efficiency, 2004, Social Security Commr. Citation, 2007. Mem.: The Inst. Internal Auditors, Am. Guild Organists, Boston Gay Mens Chorus. Avocations: music, travel, cooking. Personal E-mail: philliphanvy@aol.com.

HANWAY, DONALD GRANT, retired agronomist, educator; b. Broadwater, Nebr., Aug. 6, 1918; s. Frank Pierce and Emma Terrissa (Twist) H.; m. Blanche Elizabeth Larson, Sept. 26, 1942 (dec. Aug. 1996); children: Donald Grant, Wayne Edward, Janice Kay; m. Susanne Ruth Pennington, Apr. 10, 1999 (dec. Sept. 2004). BS, U. Nebr., 1942, MS, 1948; PhD, Iowa State Coll., 1954. Tchr. rural schs., Morrill County, Nebr., 1936-40; mem. faculty dept. agronomy U. Nebr., Lincoln, 1947-84, chmn. faculty dept. agronomy, 1955-76, prof. emeritus, 1984—, also extension agronomist, chief of party univ. mission to Ataturk U. Erzurum, Turkey, 1965-67. Agronomic cons., Nigeria, Columbia, Morocco, Tunisia; mem. Plant Variety Protection Adv. Bd., 1987-90. Contbr. articles to profl. jours. Mem. Nebr. Commn. on Status of Women, 1986-89. With USAAF, 1942-46. Honoree Nebr. Hall of Agrl. Achievement, 1988. Fellow AAAS, Am. Soc. Agronomy, Crop Sci. Soc.; mem. Soil Sci. Soc. Am., Soil and Water Conservation Soc., Am. Inst. Biol. Scis., Phi Beta Kappa, Sigma Xi, Alpha Zeta, Gamma Sigma Delta. Episcopalian. Home: 5600 Pioneers Blvd Apt 214 Lincoln NE 68506-5175

HANWAY, H. EDWARD, insurance company executive; m. Ellen Hanway. BA, Loyola Coll., Balt., 1974; MBA, Widener U., Wilmington, Del., 1984. CPA Pa. Asst. contr. Ins. Co. N.Am., 1978; v.p. ops. CIGNA Corp., 1986-88; pres. CIGNA Internat., 1989—96, CIGNA Healthcare, Phila., 1996—99; pres., COO CIGNA Corp., Phila., 1999—2000, chmn., CEO, 2000—. Chmn. bd. dirs. MedUnite; past chmn. Coun. Affordable Quality Healthcare. Bd. trustees Healthcare Leadership Coun., Loyola Coll. Balt., Eisenhower Exch. Fellowships; bd. advisors March of Dimes Found.; bd. dirs. Phila. Orch. Mem.: Bus. Roundtable, Pa. Inst. CPA, AICPA. Office: CIGNA Corp Two Liberty Pl 1601 Chestnut St Philadelphia PA 19192-1550 Office Phone: 215-761-1000.*

HANZALEK, ASTRID TEICHER, public information officer, consultant; b. NYC, Jan. 6, 1928; d. Arthur Albin and Luise Gertrude (Funke) Teicher; m. Frederick J. Hanzalek, Nov. 11, 1955. A, Concordia Coll., 1947; BA, U. Pa., 1949. Cons., Suffield, Conn., 1960—; state rep. Conn. Gen. Assembly, Hartford, 1970-80, asst. majority leader, 1973-74, asst. minority leader, 1975-80. Corporator Conn. Childrens Med. Ctr., 1986—95; mem. Conn. Nitrogen Credit Adv. Bd., 2001—. Contbr. articles to profl. jours. Mem. Conn. State Coun. Environ. Quality, Hartford, 1980—93; chmn. Conn. State Ethics Commn., Hartford, 1985—93; commr. New Eng. Interstate Water Pollution Control Commn., 1993—; mem. Conn. Greenways Commn., 1992—; mem., chair history com. Conn. Commn. on Culture and Tourism, 2003—; trustee Priscilla Maxwell Endicott Scholarship Fund, 1972—; vice chmn. Bd. State Acad. awards, 1996—; chmn. Conn. Energy Found., Hartford, 1986—96; vice-chmn. Bradley Internat. Airport Commn., 1972—2002, Greater Hartford chpt. ARC, 1975—82; mem. Conn. Inter Agy. Libr. Planning Com., Hartford, 1975—85; bd. dirs. Riverfront Recapture, Inc., 1986—, Conn. Water Co., 1985—2006; chmn. Conn. River Watershed Coun., Greenfield, Mass., 1980—92; pres. Conn. Sr. Intern Program, Bridgeport, 1980—90; sec. Conn. Humanities Coun., Middletown, 1980—92. Named Panelist of the Yr., Auto. Consumer Action Panel, 1975—85; recipient Man of the Yr. award, Conn. Jaycees, 1972, Suffield Citizenship award, 1996. Mem.: Nat. Order Woman Legislators, Suffield Land Conservancy (bd. dirs. 1965—98, founder), Conn. Coun. Environ. Quality, Conn. Forest and Pk. Assn. (v.p., bd. dirs. 1975—), Antiquarian and Landmarks Soc. (v.p. 1974—95, pres. 1996—2002, bd. dirs., sec. 2003—). Republican. Lutheran. Avocations: musical activities, sports, culinary arts. Home: 31 Abraham Ter Suffield CT 06078-2167

HANZLIK, RAYBURN DEMARA, lawyer; b. LA, June 7, 1938; s. Rayburn Otto and Ethel Winifred (Membery) H.; m. Marilyn Burnap; children: Kristina, Rayburn N., Alexander, Geoffrey. BS, Principia Coll., 1960; MA, Woodrow Wilson Sch. Fgn. Affairs, U. Va., 1968; JD, U. Va., 1974. Bar: Va. 1975, D.C. 1977. Staff asst. to Pres. U.S., Washington, 1971-73; assoc. dir. White House Domestic Council, 1975-77; atty. Danzansky Dickey Tydings Quint & Gordon, Washington, 1977-78, Akin Gump Strauss Hauer & Feld, Washington, 1978—80, Darling, Rae & Gute, LA, 1980—81; adminstr. Econ. Regulatory Adminstrn., Dept. Energy, Washington, 1981-85; ptnr. Heidrick and Struggles, Inc., 1985-91, McKenna & Hanzlik, Irvine, Calif., 1991-92; chmn. Lanxide Sports Internat., Inc., San Diego, 1992-95, Stealth Propulsion Internat., Ltd., San Diego, Calif. and, Melbourne, Australia, 1994-97; exec. v.p. Commodore Corp., NYC and McLean, Va., 1997—99; atty. Trainum, Snowdon & Deane, Washington, 1999—; mng. dir. Washington Technology Strategies, 2002—. Contbg. author: Global Politics and Nuclear Energy, 1971, Soviet Foreign Relations and World Communism, 1965. Alt. del. Republican Nat. Conv., 1980; dir. Calif. Rep. Victory Fund, 1980; candidate U.S. Senate, 1980. Served to lt. USN, 1963-68, Vietnam. Republican. Christian Scientist. Office: Ste 350 1317 F St NW Washington DC 20004 Home Phone: 703-931-0065; Office Phone: 202-783-4350. Personal E-mail: rayburn.hanzlik@verizon.net. Business E-mail: rayburn@washstrategies.com.

HAO, CHUNHAI, pathologist, researcher; s. Chang Cheng and Song Hao; 1 child, Jason Z. MD, Jilin Med. Coll., China, 1982; MSc, Norman Bethune U. Med. Scis., Chang Chun, China, 1985; PhD, U. Sask., Can., 1991. Resident neuropathology U. We. Ontario, Canada, 1992—97; asst. prof., pathologist U. Alta. and Hosps., Edmonton, Canada, 1997—2002, assoc. prof., pathologist, 2002—04; assoc. prof., neuropathologist Emory U. and Hosp., Atlanta, 2004—. Named Disting. scholar, Ga. Cancer Coalition, 2005—. Fellow: Royal Coll. Physicians & Surgeons Can. (licentiate). Achievements include research in brain tumors. Office: Emory Univ Winship Cancer Inst 1365-C Clifton Rd NE Atlanta GA 30322 Office Phone: 404-778-4776. Office Fax: 404-778-5550. Business E-Mail: chao@emory.edu.

HAO, LAWRENCE KAHOLO, state official, clinical hypnotherapist; b. Paahau, Hawaii, Aug. 24, 1937; s. Louis Kanoa and Mona Doris (Kaholo) H.; m. Ramona Kay Newton, Apr. 15, 1960; children: Debra Lynn Kelani, Melanie Pualani, Lance Kanoa, Sean Lani Newton. BS, Ind. U., 1962, MS, 1970. Cert. internat. travel agt., pvt. pilot, scuba, charter boat capt., USCG. Recreational therapist Beatty Meml. Hosp., Westville, Ind., 1962-63; tchr. Russiaville (Ind.) Elem. Sch., 1963-65; tchr. phys. edn. Western Elem. Sch., Russiaville, 1965-67; aquatic dir. Ea. H.S., Greentown, Ind., 1967-69; grad. asst. Ind. U., Bloomington, 1969-70; asst. prof. Western Ill. U., Macomb, 1970-72, U. Hawaii, Honolulu, 1973-76; asst. coord. hwy. safety Hawaii Dept. Transp., Honolulu, 1972-76, adminstr. motor vehicle safety, 1976—. Mem., chmn. Med. Adv. Bd. Hawaii, 1972—, Hawaii Hwy. Safety Coun., 1972—, Lt. Sheriff reserve program Sheriff Dept. State of Hawaii, 1984—. With USAR, 1956-62. Mem. MADD (profl.), Am. Assn. Motor Vehicle Adminstrs. (profl., regional rep. 1978—), Nat. Hwy. Traffic Safety Adminstrn. (profl., regional rep. 1972—). Avocations: swimming, spear and sport fishing, scuba diving, ukulele. Fax: 808-832-5830.

HAOUDI, ABDELALI, science educator; b. Casablanca, Morocco, July 19, 1966; s. Hassan Haoudi and Zoubida Moumen; m. Halima Bensmail, Feb. 14, 2003; children: Elias Nabel children: William Mehdi, Kevin Hassan. PhD, Pierre and Marie Curie U., Paris, 1992—96. Vis. scientist NIH, Research Triangle Park, NC, 1997—2000; rschr., prof. Ea. Va. Med. Sch., Norfolk, 2000—. Founder, pres. Internat. Coun. Biomedicine and Biotechnology, Va., 2003—. Exec. editor Jour. Biomedicine and Biotechnology. Recipient Fogarty Internat. award, NIH, 1997—2000, Biosafety Conf. award, Ministry of Environ. and Water Resources, Sultanate of Oman, Soc. Photochemistry and Photobiology, 2005; grantee, Commonwealth Health Rsch. Bd. Va., 2001—02, Elsa U. Pardee Found., 2004—05. Mem.: AAAS, European Assn. Cancer Rsch., Am. Assn. Cancer Rsch. Office: Ea Virginia Med Sch 700 W Olney Rd Norfolk VA 23507 Home Phone: 757-332-1606; Office Phone: 757-446-5682. Personal E-mail: haoudi@i-council-biomed-biotech.org. Business E-Mail: haoudia@evms.edu.

HAPGOOD, ROBERT DERRY, language educator; b. Lompoc, Calif., Dec. 11, 1928; s. Arthur Richard and Elsie Rachel (Brown) H.; m. Marilyn Janelle Oliver, July 16, 1950; children— Miranda Kristin, Susanna Elizabeth. BA with highest honors, U. Calif., Berkeley, 1950, MA, 1951, PhD, 1955. Instr. English Ind. U., 1955-57; vis. prof. Am. lit. and civilization Dijon (France) U., 1957-58; instr. U. Calif., Berkeley, 1958-59, asst. prof. Riverside, 1959-65; mem. faculty U. N.H., Durham, 1965—, prof. English, 1969-95; prof. emeritus English, 1996—; chmn. dept. U. N.H., 1972-75, dir. London program, 1986-89; dir. U. N.H./Cambridge U. summer program, 1982-85; exchange prof. Osaka (Japan) U., 1977-79. Vis. prof. Shoin Women's U., Japan, 1992; dir. Shakespeare Workshop, Bowdoin Coll., summers 1972-75. Author: Shakespeare the Theatre-poet, 1988; editor: Hamlet - Shakespeare in Production, 1999; mem. editorial bd. Univ. Press New Eng., 1975-77. Served with AUS, 1953-55. Recipient essay prize English Inst., 1968, Lindberg award for Outstanding Scholar-Tchr., 1990; fellow Inst. Renaissance Studies, Ashland, Oreg., 1961; Mellon postdoctoral fellow, 1964-65; fellow Southeastern Inst. Medieval and Renaissance Studies, Chapel Hill, N.C., 1969; Am. Coun. Learned

Socs. fellow, 1979-80, Folger Inst. fellow, 1987, NEH summer fellow, 1994. Mem. MLA. Home: 1730 Traver Rd Ann Arbor MI 48105 Office: U NH English Dept Hamilton Smith Hall Durham NH 03824 Personal E-mail: HapgoodR@aol.com.

HAPNER, MARY LOU, securities trader, writer; b. Ft. Wayne, Ind., Nov. 9, 1937; d. Paul Kenneth Brooks and Eileen (Summers) H. BS with honors, Ariz. State U., 1966, MS, 1967. Stockbroker Young, Smith & Peacock, Phoenix, 1971-76, v.p., 1976-89, Peacock, Hislop, Staley & Given, Phoenix, 1989-90, 1st v.p., 1990—. Author: Career Courage, 1984; (poems) The Power of Forgiveness, 1995, Take Someone's Hand, 1997, Cherubs, 1997, Self Portrait, 1998, Vision, 1999, Millenium, 2000, Walk with Me, 2001, Lullabies at Night, 2004. Chmn. March of Dimes, Sun City, Ariz., 1983; trustee St. Lukes, Phoenix, 1978; mem. fin. com. YWCA, Phoenix, 1975; mem. dean's coun. of 100, Ariz. State U. Coll. Bus., 2000-03; chair budget com. Ch. of Beatitudes, Phoenix, mem. exec. coun., 1991; bd. dirs. Ariz.'s Children Found., 1998; founder Ariz. Biltmore Country Club Women's Orgn., 1976, champion 1976-83. Recipient Spirit of Philanthropy award, 1997, Impact award for Enterprising Women, 2001, Arthritis Angel award, 2002, Rookie of Yr. award Arthritis Found., 2003. Mem. Charter 100 (chair membership 1979-81, pres. 1980, pres. 1982, v.p. 1981, treas., membership chair 1995, v.p. 2003—, chair 25th Anniversary 2004). Republican. Lutheran. Avocations: golf, singing with concert choirs, poetry. Business E-Mail: mlhapner@phs&g.com.

HAPP, HARVEY HEINZ, electrical engineer, educator; b. Berlin, June 27, 1928; came to U.S., 1947, naturalized, 1953; s. Harry and Hertha (Friedmann) H.; m. Ruth Hollander, Nov. 17, 1951; children: Deborah Ann, Sandra Eva. BS in Elec. Engring, Ill. Inst. Tech., 1954; M.E.E., Rensselaer Poly. Inst., Troy, NY, 1958; D.Sc., U. Belgrade, Yugoslavia, 1962. Registered profl. engr., N.Y. With Gen. Electric Co., 1954-88, sr. application engr. Schenectady, 1968-72, mgr. analytical engring. services, 1972-77, mgr. advanced system tech., 1977-82, mgr. system analysis, 1982-87, cons., 1987-88, also mem. faculty power system engring. course; with N.Y. State Dept. Pub. Service, 1988—. Lectr. colls. Author: Diakoptics and Networks (translated into Russian and Romanian), 1971, Piecewise Methods and Applications to Power Systems (translated into Chinese), 1980; editor: Gabriel Kron and Systems Theory, 1973; mem. editorial bd. Procs. IEEE, 1979-84; contbr. numerous articles and book revs. to profl. jours., chpts. to tech. books. Fellow IEEE (life; Prize Paper award Region 5 1962, power sys. engring. com. 1977, Region 1 award 1980); mem. Tensor Soc. Gt. Britain (v.p. 1972-82), Conf. Internat. des Grands Reseaux Electrique a Haute Tension, Internat. Power Sys. Computations Conf. (co-founder 1962), Gen. Electric Co. Engrs. and Scientists Assn. (chmn. policy com. 1968-70), Ill. Inst. Tech. Alumni Assn., Sigma Xi, Tau Beta Pi, Eta Kappa Nu. Home: 2211 Webster Dr Niskayuna NY 12309-3930 Office: NY State Dept Pub Svc 3 Empire State Plz Albany NY 12223-1000 Office Phone: 518-486-2939. Business E-Mail: harvey_happ@dps.state.ny.us.

HAQUE, MALIKA HAKIM, pediatrician; b. Madras, India; arrived in US, 1967; d. Syed Abdul and Rahimunisa (Hussain) Hakim; m. C. Azeez Haque, Feb. 5, 1967; children: Kifizeba Haque Akbar, Masarath Haque Khan, Asim Zayd Haque. MBBS, Madras Med. Coll., 1967. Diplomate Am. Bd. Pediatrics. Rotating intern Miriam Hosp. Brown U., Providence, 1967-68; resident in pediatrics N.J. Coll. Medicine Childrens Hosp., 1968-70; fellow in devel. disabilities Ohio State U., 1970-71; acting chief pediat. Nisonger Ctr., 1973-74; staff pediatrician Children and Youth Project Children's Hosp., Columbus, Ohio; clin. asst. prof. pediatrics Ohio State U., 1974-80, clin. assoc. prof. pediatrics, 1981-99, clin. assoc. prof. dept. internat. health Coll. Medicine, 1993-99, clin. prof. pediatrics and internat. health Coll. Medicine, 1999—. Pediatrician Children's Hosp. Physician Health Ctrs. Children's Hosp., Columbus, 1982—; dir. Pediat. Academic Assn., 1992-2002; cons. Ctrl. Ohio Head Start Program, 1974-79; med. cons. Bur. Rehab. and Devel. Disabilities for State of Ohio, 1990—. Contbr. articles to profl. jours. and newspapers. Charter founder Ronald Reagan Rep. Ctr.; trustee Asian Am. Health Alliance Network, Columbus, 1994-01; bd. trustees Islamic Found. Ctrl. Ohio, 2006—. Recipient Physician Recognition award, AMA, 1971—86, 1988—99, 2002—05, Gold medals in surgery, radiology, pediat. and ob-gyn., Presdl. medal of Merit, Pres. Ronald Reagan, 1982, Nat. Leadership award, Nat. Rep. Congl. Com., 2001, Physician of the Yr. award, 2003, Outstanding Svc. award, CAIR Ohio, 2005, IMANA, 2005. Fellow Am. Acad. Pediatrics; mem. Islamic Med. Assn. (Outstanding Svc. and Contbn. award 2005), Am. Assn. Physicians Indian Origin, Pediat. Acad. Assn. (dir. 1992-02), Ambulatory Pediat. Assn., Ctrl. Ohio Pediatric Soc. Achievements include research on enuresis and tumors caused by human papilloma viruses. Office: 700 Childrens Dr Columbus OH 43205-2664 Home: 5095 Noor Park View Dublin OH 43016 Office Phone: 614-722-4955.

HAQUE, REZAUL, design engineer; s. Mohibbul Hoque and Hanufa Khatun; m. Shaista Kaiser; 1 child, Ridwanul. MS in Engring., U. Ill., Urbana-Champaign, 1999. Instrumentation engr. Beximco Synthetics Ltd., Dhaka, Bangladesh, 1992—94; rsch. assoc. Space Dynamics Lab., Logan, Utah, 1995—96, U. Ill., Urbana, 1997—99; design mgr. Intel Corp., Folsom, Calif., 1999—. Design flash memory circuits Intel Corp., Folsom, 1999. Contbr. articles to profl. jours. Recipient Chancellor's award, Govt. Bangladesh, 1985, DE Operational Excellence award, FPG, Intel Corp., 2003. Achievements include design of IO in first RWW flash memory; patents in field.

HARA, ERIC, chef; b. 1981; Chef Citronelle, Downey's, Santa Barbara, Calif., Restaurant Mimosa, Ritz-Carlton Laguna Niguel, Fairmont Chateau Lake Louise, Canada; exec. chef Chez Josephine; chef de cuisine David-burke & Donatella, NYC. Named one of NYC's Rising Stars, StarChefs.com, 2007. Office: Davidburke & Donatella 133 E 61st St New York NY 10021*

HARA, TADAO, educational administrator; b. Shimonoseki, Japan, Oct. 21, 1926; s. Ikuhisa and Chitose Hara; m. Suzuko Hara, May 12; children: Nobumichi, Izumi. BA, Tamagawa U., Machida, Japan, 1952; MA in Bibl. Theology, N.W. Coll., 1958; MA in Ednl. Psychology, Calif. State U., Long Beach, 1965; HHD (hon.), Newport Asi Pacific U., 2001; LittD (hon.), Northwest Coll., 1990. Ordained to ministry Assembly of God Ch. Fgn. student counselor Calif. State U., Long Beach, 1965-68; prof. edn. Tamagawa U., 1969-79, dean students, 1973-77, dir. internat. edn., 1976-79; founder, chmn. bd., pres. Internat. Bilingual Sch., Palos Verdes Estates, Calif., 1979—2000, emeritus, 2000—03, ret., 2003; dir. Mesa Verde United Meth. Ch., Japanese Lang. Fellowship, Costa Mesa, 2003—. Mem. adv. bd. Calif. State U. Long Beach Coll. Edn., 1985-88. Recipient Disting. Alumnus award Edn., Calif. State U., Long Beach, 1994. Mem. Delta Upsilon Chi. Home: 3992 Toland Cir Los Alamitos CA 90720-2261 Office: Mesa Verde UMC 1701 Baker St Costa Mesa CA 92626-3645 E-mail: haraxii@socal.rr.com.

HARACZ, STEPHEN M., lawyer; BS, MS, Fordham U., 1980; JD cum laude, NY Law Sch., 1985. Bar: NY 1986. Ptnr., co-leader Intellectual Property Client Svc. Group Bryan Cave LLP, NYC. Spkr. in field. Office: Bryan Cave LLP 1290 Ave of the Americas New York NY 10104 Office Phone: 212-541-1271, 212-904-0511. E-mail: smharacz@bryancave.com.

HARAD, GEORGE JAY, retired manufacturing executive; b. Newark, Apr. 24, 1944; m. Beverly Marcia Harad, June 12, 1966; children: Alyssa Dawn, Matthew Corde. BA, Franklin and Marshall Coll., 1965; MBA with high distinction, Harvard Bus. Sch., 1971. Staff cons. Boston Cons. Group, 1970-71; asst. to sr. v.p. housing Boise Cascade Corp., 1971, asst. to v.p. Palo Alto, Calif., 1971; fin. mgr. Boise Cascade Realty Group, Palo Alto, Calif., 1972-76; mgr. corp. devel. Boise Cascade Corp., Boise, Idaho, 1976—80, dir. retirement funds, risk mgmt., 1980—82, v.p., contr., 1982—84, sr. v.p., CFO, 1984—89, exec. v.p., CFO, 1989—90, exec. v.p. paper, 1990—91, pres., COO, 1991—94, pres., CEO, 1994—95, chmn., bd. dirs., 1995, CEO, chmn., 1995—2004; exec. chmn. OfficeMax Inc., Itasca, Ill., 2004—05, interim pres., CEO, 2005. Bd. govs. Nat. Coun. for Air and Stream Improvement Inc., 1994—2004; bd. dirs. US West, 1997—2000, Dial Corp., 2003—04, The Clorox Co., 2006—. Founder, pres. Boise Coun. for Gifted and Talented Students, 1977—79; bd. dirs. Boise Philharm. Assn., 1983—84; dir. bd. trustees Coll. Idaho, 1986—91. Recipient George F. Baker scholar, 1970—71; Grad. Prize fellow, Harvard Grad. Sch. Arts and Scis., 1965—69, Frederick Roe fellow, Harvard U. Sch. Bus., 1971. Mem.: NAM (bd. dirs), Am. Forest and Paper Assn. (bd. dirs., mem. exec. com. 1994—2004, chmn. 2004—05), Century Club (Boston), Arid Club, Crane Creek Country Club. Office: Harad Capital Mgmt 877 W Main St Ste 606 Boise ID 83702 Office Phone: 208-429-0606.

HARADA, NORIO, software engineer, researcher, educator; b. Aichi, Japan, Feb. 12, 1945; s. Iwao and Tomiko Harada; m. Reiko Harada, Oct. 31, 1971; children: Shin, Satoshi. BS, Nagoya U., Nagoya-Shi, Japan, 1967, MS, 1969; DEng, Kyoto U., Kyoto-Shi, Japan, 1979. Rschr. Nippon Electric Co. Ltd., Kawasaki-Shi, Kanagawa, Japan, 1969-82, rsch. supr., 1982-84; rsch. mgr. NEC Corp., Kawasaki-Shi, 1984-87, mgr. Minato-Ku, Tokyo, 1987-91, chief engr., 1991-96; prof. computer sci. Takushoku U., Tokyo, 1996—. Contbr. articles to profl. jours. Recipient Yonezawa Meml. Paper award, 1985. Mem. IEEE, AAAS, Assn. Computing Machinery, Math. Soc. Japan, Inst. Electronics, Info. and Comm. Engrs. Japan (Excellent Paper award 1985, 88), Info. Processing Soc. Japan, NY Acad. Scis. Buddhist. Avocations: mathematics, tennis, reading, research. Home: 18-5 Yokoyamadai 1-Chome Sagamihara-Shi Kanagawa 229-1121 Japan Office: Takushoku U 815-1 Tatemachi Hachioji-Shi Tokyo 193-0985 Japan Business E-Mail: nharada@cs.takushoku-u.ac.jp.

HARAGAN, DONALD ROBERT, academic administrator, geologist, educator; b. Houston, Apr. 15, 1936; s. Donald William and Mary (Thompson) H.; m. Willie Mae O'Berry, July 2, 1966; children— Shannon Lea, Shelley Jo. BS, U. Tex., 1959, PhD, 1969; MS, Tex. A & M U., 1960. Registered profl. engr., Tex. Research asst. Tex. A & M U., College Station, 1959-60; research scientist U. Tex., Austin, 1960-66, instr., 1966-69; asst. prof. Tex. Tech. U., Lubbock, 1969—72; assoc. prof. Tex. Tech U., 1972—78, prof. geosci., 1978—, dept. chmn., 1972—77, 1980—83, interim dean, 1985, interim v.p., 1985—86, v.p. for acad. affairs and research, 1986—88, exec. v.p., provost, 1988—; interim pres. Tex. Tech. U., 1996, pres., 1996—2000, pres. emeritus, 2000—, interim chancellor, 2006. Contbr. articles in field to profl. jours. Mem. Am. Soc. Civil Engrs., AAAS, Am. Meteorol. Soc., Am. Water Resources Assn., Tex. Acad. Sci. Home: 6914 Nashville Dr Lubbock TX 79413-6002 Office: Tex Tech U Honors Coll Lubbock TX 79409 Office Phone: 806-742-0031.

HARALICK, ROBERT MARTIN, electrical engineering educator; b. NYC, Sept. 30, 1943; s. David and Yetta (Stier) H.; m. Joy Gold, Aug. 20, 1967 (div. July 1977); 1 child, Tammy-Beth; m. Linda G. Shapiro, Feb. 12, 1978 (div. Aug. 1992); 1 child, Michael Aaron; m. Ihsin T. Phillips, Dec. 1993. BA, U. Kans., 1964, BS, 1966, MS, 1967, PhD, 1969. Asst. prof. elec. engring. U. Kans., Lawrence, 1969-71, assoc. prof., 1971-75, prof., 1975-78, Va. Poly. Inst. and State U., 1979-84; v.p. rsch. Machine Vision Internat., Ann Arbor, Mich., 1984-86; Boeing Clairmont Egtvedt prof. elec. engring., adj. prof. computer sci. U. Wash., Seattle, 1986-2000; pres. Mnemonics Inc., 1979—; disting. prof. computer sci. Grad. Ctr. CUNY, 2001—. Co-dir. NATO Advanced Study Inst. Image Processing, 1978; co-chmn. NATO Advanced Study Inst. on Image Processing, 1980, Robust Computer Vision Workshop, 1990, 92, 94; vice chmn. 5th Internat. Conf. on Pattern Recognition, Miami, 1980; dir. NATO Advanced Study Inst. on Pictorial Data Analysis, 1982; adj. prof. Ctr. Bioengring. U. Wash., Seattle, 1988—; program chmn. 10th annual ICPR Conf. on Pattern Recognition Systems and Applications, 1990; program co-chmn. Internat. Conf. on Document Analysis and Recognition, 1991, vice chmn., 1997; co-chmn. Evaluation and Validation of Computer Vision Algorithm, 1998, chmn., 2001. Author: (with T. Creese) Differential Equations for Engineers, 1977; Pictorial Data Analysis, 1983, (with L. Shapiro) Computer and Robost Vision, Vol I and II, 1992, The Inner Meaning of Hebrew Letters, 1995, (with M. Glazerson) The Torah Codes and Israel Today, 1996, (with M. Glazerson, Joel Gallis and Robert Wolf) Light Out of Darkness, 2005, (with Eliyahu Rips and Matityahu Glazerson) Torah Codes: A Glimpse of the Infinite, 2005; editor: (with J. C. Simon) Issues in Digital Image Processing, 1980, Digital Image Processing, 1981; assoc. editor Computer Vision, Graphics and Image Processing, 1975-93, Pattern Recognition, 1977-93, Communication of the ACM, Image Processing, 1982-92, Jour. of Electronic Imaging, 1994—; mem. editl. bd. Machine Vision and Applications, 1987—, Real Time Imaging, 1994—, mem. adv. bd.; mem. adv. program com. Structural & Syntactic Pattern Recognition, 1990; contbr. over 525 articles to profl. jours.; digital computer art exhbns. include William Rockhill Nelson Gallery, Kansas City, Mo., 1971, Nat. History Mus., U. Kans., 1971, Dulin Gallery Art, 1971 (2 purchase awards), Nat. Invitational Print Show, U. R.I., 1972, Fla. State U., 1972, San Diego State Coll., 1972; author more than 550 books, book chpts., others. Recipient Dow Chem. Young Outstanding Faculty award Am. Soc. Engring. Educators, 1975, Outstanding Young Elec. Engrs. Honorable Mention award Eta Kappa Nu, 1975, Best Paper award 5th Ann. Symposium on Automatic Imagery Pattern Recognition, 1975, Best Paper award Pattern Recognition Soc., 1989; NSF faculty fellow, 1977-79. Fellow IEEE (assoc. editor IEEE Transactions on Systems, Man and Cybernetics, 1979-88, IEEE Transactions on Image Processing, 1992-96, mem. editl. bd. IEEE Transactions on Pattern Analysis and Machine Intelligence, 1981-84, IEEE Expert, 1986-90), IAPR; mem. IEEE Computer Soc. (chmn. pattern analysis and machine intelligence tech. com. 1975-82, acoustics, signal and speech processing, sys., man and cybernetics, pattern recognition tech. subcom. 1975-81, data structures and pattern recognition subcom. 1975-81, biomed. pattern recognition subcom. 1975-81, internat. assn. for pattern recognition gov. bd. 1986-2000, pres. 1996-98, program com. pattern and image processing conf. 1978, 4th internat. joint conf. on pattern recognition 1978, conf. B-pattern recognition methods and sys. program com. 11th internat. conf. on pattern recognition 1992, structural and syntactic pattern recognition 1992, 2d internat. conf. on document analysis and recognition 1993, chairperson various workshops and confs., Cert. Appreciation award 1978, 84), Pattern Recognition Soc., Internat. Assn. for Pattern Recognition (pres. 1996-98), Am. Assn. Artificial Intelligence, Assn. Computing Machinery. Avocation: hammered dulcimer. Home: 1515 East 8th St Brooklyn NY 11230 Home Phone: 347-742-5871; Office Phone: 212-817-8192. Personal E-mail: haralick@netscape.net. Business E-Mail: haralick@ptah.gc.cuny.edu.

HARARI, ELI, computer company executive; BS in Physics with honors, Manchester Univ.; MA, Princeton Univ., PhD in Solid State Scis. Technical mgmt. positions Hughes Aircraft, Honeywell; co-founder, pres., CEO Wafer Scale integration; founder, pres., CEO SanDisk Corp., Sunnyvale, Calif., 1988—2006, chmn., CEO, 2006—. Patentee in field.*

HARATANI, JOAN MEI, lawyer; b. Redwood City, Calif., Aug. 2, 1957; d. Donald R. Chambers and Claire Meiko Haratani Chambers; m. Ralph Gregory Latza, Jan. 6, 2002. BA in Philosophy, St. John's Coll., 1979; JD, U. Calif.-Davis, 1984. Bar: all Calif. state cts., no. and ctrl. fed. cts. 1985. Assoc. Crosby Heafey Roach & May, Oakland, Calif., 1984—90, ptnr., 1990—2002, Shook Hardy & Bacon, San Francisco, 2002—05, Morgan, Lewis & Bockius, 2005—. Chair The Asian Pacific Fund, San Francisco, 1999—; sec. Lawyers Commn. of Civil Rights, 1999; mem. bd. Leukemia & Lymphoma Soc., 2006—; pres. Bar Assn. of San Francisco, 2004—06; past pres. Asian Am. Bar Assn. of the Greater Bay Area, 2000; mem. Claremont Resort. Named a Super Lawyer of No. Calif., San Francisco mag., 2004, 2005, 2006; named one of 500 Most Influential Asians in Am., Ave. Asia mag., 2003; recipient Top Rainmaker, Calif. Law Bus., 1996—97, 1999, Advocate of Yr. Joe Morozumi award, Asian Am. Bar Assn of No. Calif., 2001, Female Litigator on the Rise, Diversity & the Bar (publ. of Minority Corp. Counsel Assn.), 2004. Mem.: Bar Assn. San Francisoc, Nat. Asian Pacific Am. Bar Assn., Assn. Managing Counsel. Achievements include completing Ironman triathlon race, 2000. Avocations: triathlete, cooking, reading. Office Phone: 415-442-1000. Office Fax: 415-442-1001. Business E-Mail: jharatani@morganlewis.com.

HARB, MAC, Canadian senator; BSc, U. Ottawa, Ont., Can., 1979, M in Elec. Engring., 1983. Alderman City of Ottawa, 1985—88, dep. mayor, 1987—88; mem. parliament Ho. of Commons, Ottawa, 1988—2003, sec. to min. for internat. trade, 1993—95, chmn. internat. trade com., vice chair pub. account com., chair adv. group on reconstrn. Lebanon, co-chair nat. task force on infrastructure Ottawa, senator, 2003—. Mem. banking, fin., scrutiny of regulation coms. Can. Senate. Former vice-chmn. Ottawa Non-Profit Housing Corp, Ottawa Econ. Affairs Com.; bd. mgmt. Preston St. bus. improvement bd. Mem.: UNESCO Pariamentary Assn. (chair), Assn. Profl. Engrs. Ont. Avocations: cooking, gardening, travel. Office: Sen of Canada Rm 376 East Block Ottawa ON K1A OA4 Canada

HARBATER, DAVID, mathematician; b. NYC, Dec. 19, 1952; s. Maurice and Marilyn (Haber) H. AB summa cum laude, Harvard U., 1974; MS in Math., Brandeis U., 1975; PhD in Math., MIT, 1978; MA (hon.), U. Pa., 1984. Asst. prof. U. Pa., Phila., 1978-83, assoc. prof., 1983-91, prof., 1991-96, E. Otis Kendall prof. math., 1996—. Contbr. articles to profl. jours. Fellow NSF, 1975-78, 82-83, Sloan Found., 1984-87, Lindback award for disting. tchg. U. Pa., 1995. Mem. Am. Math. Soc. (postdoctoral fellow 1978-79, Frank Nelson Cole Prize in Algebra, 1995), Phi Beta Kappa, Sigma Xi. Democrat. Jewish. Home: 1711 Lombard St Philadelphia PA 19146 Office: U Pa Dept Math 209 S 33rd St Dept Math Philadelphia PA 19104-6317 E-mail: harbater@math.upenn.edu.

HARBAUGH, DANIEL PAUL, lawyer; b. Wendell, Idaho, May 18, 1948; s. Myron and Manuelita (Garcia) Harbaugh. BA, Gonzaga U., 1970, JD, 1974. Bar: Wash. 1974, U.S. Dist. Ct. (ea. dist.) Wash. 1977, U.S. Ct. Appeals (9th cir.) 1978. Asst. atty. gen. State of Wash., Spokane, 1974-77; ptnr. Richter, Wimberley & Ericson, Spokane, 1977-83, Harbaugh & Bloom, P.S., Spokane, 1983—. Bd. dirs. Spokane Legal Svcs., 1982—86; bd. govs. LAWPAC, Seattle, 1980—92. Bd. dirs. Spokane Ballet, 1983-88; chpt. dir. Les Amis du Vin, Spokane, 1985-88; mem. Spokane County Civil Svc. Commn., 1991-03, chmn., 1999-03, Gonzaga U. Pres'. Coun., 1991-00; mem. found. bd. Gonzaga Law Sch., 2007-. Mem. ATLA, Wash. State Bar Assn. (spl. dist. counsel 1982-95, mem. com. rules for profl. conduct 1989-92, mem. legis. com. 1995-96), Spokane County Bar Assn. (chair med.-legal com. 1991), Wash. State Trial Lawyers Assn. (v.p. 1988-89, co-chair worker's compensation sect. 1992, 93, spl. select. com. on workers' corp. 1990—, forum 1994-06, vice-chmn. 1994-97, mem. legis. com. 1995-98), Nat. Orgn. Social Security Claimants Reps., Internat. Wine and Food Soc. (pres. local chpt. 1989-91, cellar master 1994-96, 04-, cellar com. 2001—), Spokane Enol. Soc., Spokane Club, Spokane Country Club (adminstrv. com. 1995-98, chmn. 1997-98, trustee 1996-99, sec.-treas. 1997-98, pres. 1998-99, ex-officio 1999-00, long range planning com. 1999-01, nominating com, 2000-06), Alpha Sigma Nu, Phi Alpha Delta. Roman Catholic. Office: Harbaugh & Bloom PS PO Box 1461 Spokane WA 99210-1461 Business E-Mail: dan@hblaw2.com.

HARBAUGH, JANICE M., counselor, consultant; b. Carroll, Iowa, Aug. 17, 1949; d. Robert William and Bernice Kuehl; m. Gaylon L. Harbaugh, Feb. 10, 1973. BSc in Edn., Drake U., Des Moines, Iowa, 1971, MSc in Edn., 1973, EdS, 1979, EdD, 1984. Lic. Tchr. Iowa, 1971. Tchr. Iowa State Tng. Sch., Mitchellville, 1972—82, Colfax-Mingo Cmty. Sch., Iowa, 1982—98; with psychology dept. Woodward State Hosp. Sch., Iowa, 1982; pvt. counseling practice Newton, Iowa, 2001—. Chairperson Foster Care Rev. Bd., Des Moines, 1987—88; ct. apptd. spl. adv. 5th Jud. Dist., Iowa, 1988; cons. HomeSch. Unlimited, Newton, Iowa, 2005—. Author: (children's book) Captain Duffy and the Kid Who Threw Eggs, 1985, (play) Put On Your Brand New Bonnet, 1995; publisher: ednl. materials Down Home Press, 1985—90. Founder Weaver St. Irregulars, Colfax, 1986—98; entertaining as Tapper T. Bear, 1991—; pvt. counselor crime victims Dept. Justice, 2007—; lay eucharistic min. Iowa Women's Correctional Facility, Mitchellville, 2002—03; cons. counselor Pauls Episc. Ch., Grinnel, Iowa, 2007—; spl. edn. adv. in pvt. practice, Iowa, 1995—. Recipient Gov.'s Vol. award, Iowa, 1988. Mem.: US Chess Fedn. Episcopalian. Achievements include research in the use of bibliotherapy with female juvenile delinquents; and archiving of materials concerning James Baird Weaver. Avocations: chess, piano. Home Phone: 515-967-5091; Office Phone: 515-669-6984.

HARBAUGH, JIM (JAMES JOSEPH HARBAUGH), college football coach, retired professional football player; b. Toledo, Dec. 23, 1963; m. Miah Harbaugh (div.); children: Jay, James Jr., Grace. BA in Comm., U. Mich., 1987. Quarterback Chgo. Bears, 1987-93, Indpls. Colts, 1994-98, Balt. Ravens, 1998-99, San Diego Chargers, 1999—2000, Carolina Panthers, 2001; offensive asst. Oakland Raiders, 2002—03; head football coach U. San Diego, 2004—06, Stanford U., 2006—. Named to Am. Football Conf. Pro Bowl Team, 1995; named NFL Comeback Player of Yr., 1995 Achievements include inducted into the Indpls. Colts Ring of Honor, 2005. Office: Stanford U Athletics Stanford CA 94305*

HARBAUGH, JOHN WARVELLE, geologist, educator; b. Madison, Wis., Aug. 6, 1926; s. Marion Dwight and Marjorie (Warvelle) H.; m. Josephine Taylor, Nov. 24, 1951 (dec. Dec. 25, 1985); children: Robert, Dwight, Richard; m. Audrey Wegst, Oct. 21, 2000. BS, U. Kans., 1948, MS, 1950; PhD, U. Wis., 1955. Prodn. geologist Carter Oil Co., Tulsa, 1951-53; prof. geol. sci. Stanford U., Calif., 1955—99, prof. emeritus, 1999—. Mgr. Harbaugh Mineral Lands LLC. Author: (with G. Bonham Carter) Computer Simulation in Geology, 1970, (with D.M. Tezlaff) Simulating Clastic Sedimentation, 1989, (with P. Martinez) Simulating Nearshore Environments, 1993, (with R. Slingerland and K. Furlong) Simulating Clastic Sedimentary Basins, 1994, (with J.C. Davis and J. Wendebourg) Computing Risk for Oil Prospects: Principles and Programs, 1995, (with J. Wendebourg) Simulating Oil Entrapment in Clastic Sequences, 1997. Recipient Haworth Disting. Alumni award U. Kans., 1968, Krumbein medal Internat. Assn. Math. Geologists, 1986, U. Wis.-Madison Disting. Alumni award, 2003. Fellow Geol. Soc. Am.; mem. Am. Assn. Petroleum Geologists (Levorsen award 1970, Disting. Svc. award 1987, Disting. Edn. award Pacific sect. 1999, 2001). Independent. Home: 683 Salvatierra St Stanford CA 94305-8539 Office Phone: 650-723-3365. Business E-Mail: harbaugh@pangea.stanford.edu.

HARBECK, WILLIAM H., lawyer; b. Grand Haven, Mich., May 2, 1955; AB magna cum laude, Harvard U., 1977, JD, 1980. Bar: Wis. 1980, US Ct. Appeals (7th cir.), US Dist. Ct. (ea. & we. dist.) Wis. Ptnr. Quarles & Brady LLP, Milw. Mem. State Bar Wis., Milw. Bar Assn. (Milw. bar alternative dispute resolution sect., environ. sect.) Office: Quarles & Brady 411 E Wisconsin Ave Ste 2550 Milwaukee WI 53202-4497 Office Phone: 414-277-5853. Office Fax: 414-978-8853. E-mail: whh@quarles.com.

HARBERGER, ARNOLD CARL, economist, educator; b. Newark, July 27, 1924; s. Ferdinand C. and Martha (Bucher) H.; m. Ana Beatriz Valjalo, Mar. 15, 1958; children: Paul Vincent, Carl David. Student, Johns Hopkins U., 1941-43; MA, U. Chgo., 1947, PhD, 1950; D (hon.), U. Tucuman, 1979, Cath. U. Chile, 1988, Tech. U. Cen. Am., 1989, U. Francisco Marroquin, 2004, Instituto Tecnológicó Autonomo Mex., 2006, U. Americana, 2006. Asst. prof. polit. economy Johns Hopkins U., 1949-53; asso. prof. econs. U. Chgo., 1953-59, prof., 1959—, chmn. dept., 1964-71, 75-80, Gustavus F. and Ann M. Swift disting. svc. prof., 1977-91, prof. emeritus, 1991—, dir. Ctr. Latin Am. Econ. Studies, 1965-92. Vis. prof. MIT Ctr. Internat. Studies, New Delhi, 1961-62, Econ. Devel. Inst., IBRD, 1965, Harvard U., 1971-72, Princeton U., 1973-74, UCLA, 1983, 84, U. Paris, 1986; prof. econs. UCLA, 1984—; cons. IMF, 1950, 89, 2002-06, U.S. Pres.'s Materials Policy Commn., 1951-52, U.S. Treasury Dept., 1961-75, Com. Econ. devel., 1961-78, Planning Commn., India, 1961-62, 73, Pan Am. Union, 1962-76, Dept. State, 1962-76, USAID, 1976—, Ctrl. Bank, Chile, 1965-70, Dominican Republic, 1989, China, 1995, Ecuador, 1996, Planning Dept., Panama, 1963-77, Colombia, 1969-71, Nicaragua, 1990, Indonesia, 1997-01; cons. Ford Found., 1967-77, Planning Commn., El Salvador, 1973-75, Budget and Planning Office, Uruguay, 1974-75, Can. Dept. Regional Econ. Expansion, 1975-77, Econ. Min. Argentina, 1994-2000, Fin. Ministry, Bolivia, 1976, Mex., 1976—; cons. Can. Dept. Employment and Migration, 1980-82, Indonesian Ministry Fin., 1981-82, 86, 97-2000, Can. Dept. Fin., 1982-88, Can. Dept. Industry, Sci. and Tech., 1991-99, Chinese Ministry Fin., 1983; ministry fin., Malawi, 1988, Venezuela, 1989, Colombia, 1991, 94, 02, 06, Dominican Republic, 1996, 97, Egypt, 2002, Madagascar, 2005, Panama Canal Authority, 2005-06; mem. internat. adv. coun. Inst. Internat. Studies, Stanford U., 1991-99; v.p., chmn. adv. coun. Inst. for Policy Reform; cons. Office Econ. Adviser to the Pres. Russia, 2000-04; chief econ. advisor US Agy. Internat. Devel., 2006—. Author: Project Evaluation, 1972, Taxation and Welfare, 1974; editor: Demand for Durable Goods, 1960, The Taxation of Income from Capital, 1968, Key Problems of Economic Policy In Latin America, 1970, World Economic Growth, 1985; (with Glenn P. Jenkins) Cost-Benefit Analysis, 2002, On the Process of Growth and Economic Policy in Developing Countries, 2005; contbr. sci. papers to profl. jours. With AUS, 1943-46. Guggenheim fellow; Fulbright scholar; faculty rsch. fellow Social Sci. Rsch. Coun.; Ford Found. faculty rsch. fellow, 1968-69. Fellow Econometric Soc., Am. Acad. Arts and Scis., Am. Econ. Assn. (mem. exec. com. 1970-72, v.p. 1992, pres.-elect 1996, pres. 1997, disting. fellow 1999), Western Econ. Assn. (v.p. 1987-88, pres. 1989-90), Royal Econ. Soc., Nat. Tax Assn. (Holland medal 2001), NAS, Phi Beta Kappa. Home: 136 Buckskin Rd Bell Canyon CA 91307-1125 Office: UCLA PO Box 951477 405 Hilgard Ave Los Angeles CA 90095-1477 Office Phone: 310-825-1011. Business E-Mail: harberger@econ.ucla.edu.

HARBERS, REBECCA ANN, physical education educator; d. Robert Franklin Jr. and Roberta Elizabeth Harbers. BS, Quincy Coll., Ill., 1976; MS, We. Ill. U., Macomb, 1989. Tchr. phys. edn. Metamora Grade Sch., Ill., 1976—. Mem.: Ill. Assn. Health, Phys. Edn., Recreation and Dance (Quarter Century Club award 2001), Heart of Ill. Chorus/Sweet Adelines Internat. Office: Metamora Grade Sch 815 E Chatham Metamora IL 61548 Home: 109 Castle Ln East Peoria IL 61611 Office Phone: 309-367-2361. Office Fax: 309-367-2364.

HARBERT, TED (EDWARD W. HARBERT III), broadcast executive; b. 1955; m. Susan Harbert; children: Emily, William. Degree in Comm., Boston U., 1977. Prodr. news dept. WHDH Radio, Boston, 1976—77; feature film coord. ABC Entertainment, 1977—79, feature film and late night programming supr., 1979, asst. to v.p. of program planning and scheduling, 1979—81, dir. program planning and scheduling, 1981—83, v.p. program planning and scheduling, 1983, v.p. of motion pictures, 1986—87, v.p. of motion pictures and scheduling, 1987—88, v.p. prime time, 1988—89, exec. v.p. prime time, 1989—93, pres., 1993—96, chmn., 1996—97; prodr. DreamWorks TV, 1997—99; pres. NBC Studios, 1999—2003; prodr. 20th Century Fox TV, 2003—04; pres., CEO E!Networks, 2004—06, Comcast Entertainment Group, 2006—. Mem. dean's adv. bd. U. So. Calif. Sch. of Theater, Film and TV; mem. TV adv. coun. U. So. Calif. Sch. of Cinema-TV; exec. com. Boston U. Sch. Comm.; bd. govs. UCLA Ctr. for Comm. Policy; bd. dirs. Friends of the LA Free Clinic. Recipient Disting. Alumni Award, Boston U., 1999.*

HARBESON, JOHN WILLIS, political science professor; b. New Brunswick, NJ, Sept. 14, 1938; s. Robert Willis and Gladys (Evans) H.; m. Ann Elizabeth Warmoth, Aug. 25, 1963; children: Eric John, Kristen Lynne. BA cum laude, Swathmore Coll., Pa., 1960; MA, U. Chgo., 1962; PhD, U. Wis., 1970. From asst. prof. to prof. polit. sci. U. Wis.-Parkside, Kenosha, 1967-85; prof. polit. sci. CUNY, 1985—. Lectr. U. Nairobi, Kenya, 1966-67; vis. prof. Addis Ababa U., Ethiopia, 1973-75; prof. Land Tenure Ctr., U. Wis., Madison, 1976-85; sr. social sci. analyst Agy. Internat. Devel., 1979-82; professorial lectr. Johns Hopkins U., Washington, 1980-82; adj. prof. Columbia U., NYC, 1990-91; sr. adv. Agy. for Internat. Devel. for Democracy and Governance Issues in Ea. and So. Africa, 1993-95; Jennings Randolph sr. fellow US Inst. of Peace, 1998-99; vis. fellow Princeton U. Ctr. Internat. Studies, 2001-02; chmn. divsn. social scis., U. Wis., 1975-79, dir. internat. studies, 1977-79, 82-85; dir. internat. studies, CUNY, 85-88, chmn. dept. polit. sci., 1999-2001. Author: Nation Building in Kenya, 1973, Ethiopian Transformation, 1988; author, editor: Military in African Politics; author, co-editor: Africa in World Politics, 1991, 3d edit., 2000, Civil Society and the State in Africa, 1993, Responsible Government: The Global Challenge, 1993; contbr. over 75 articles to profl. jours. Chairperson Congl. campaigns, Racine, Wis., 1970, 72, Dem. Party, Croton-On-Hudson, N.Y., 1989-91, 2000-01; elected village trustee Croton-on-Hudson, 1991-93; pres.'s coun. U. Ill., 1992—. Recipient Meritorious Svc. award Agy. of Internat. Devel., 1980, Rsch. award J.D. and C.T. MacArthur Found., 1991; fellow Am. Coun. of Learned Socs., 1989, Rockefeller Found., 1966. Mem. ACLU (sec. Racine-Kenosha chpt. 1972-74), Am. Polit. Sci. Assn. (governing coun. 2003-2005, co-founder, chmn. comparative democratization sect. 2001-03, area studies liaison com., founder, chmn. African politics conf. group, 2001-07), African Studies Assn. (co-chmn. nat. program 2006), Nat. Urban League (bd. dirs. Racine chpt. 1971-73), Am. Polit. Sci. Assn. Episcopalian. Avocations: tennis, organ and piano playing, reading, singing. Home: 5 Valley Trl Croton On Hudson NY 10520-2213 Office: Convent and 138th Cuny New York NY 10031 Office Phone: 212-650-5246. Personal E-mail: jwharbeson@aol.com.

HARBIN, DUANE, library and information science director, theology educator; BA in Linguistics, Northwestern U., Evanston, Ill., 1977; MDiv, Yale U. Sch. Div., New Haven, Conn., 1981; MLS, So. Conn. St. U., New Haven, Conn., 1989. Libr. asst., searching dept. Northwestern U. Libr., Evanston, Ill., 1977—78; cataloging asst. Yale U. Div. Libr., New Haven, 1981—82, acquisitions supervisor, 1982—85, sys., planning mgr., 1985—90, info. svc. libr., 1990—95; assoc. libr. Birdwell Libr., Perkins Sch. Theology So. Meth U., 1995—, asst. dean instr. tech., rsch., 2001—. Mem.: Am. Theological Libr. Assn. (chmn., comm. automation and tech., steering com. 1989—93, chmn., tech. advisory comm. 1999—2001, joint ATLA/ATS comm. digital standards and projects 1999—, dir. 2004—, v.p. 2005—06, pres. 2006—). Office: Perkins Sch Theology Southern Methodist U Dallas TX 75275-0113 Office Fax: 214-768-2117.

HARBISON, ED, state legislator, broadcast journalist, motivational speaker; b. Prattville, Ala., Aug. 25, 1941; m. Cecilia Harbison; children: Edward, Ladena. Grad., Career Acad. Sch. Broadcasting, 1969, Troy State U., Ala. Broadcast journalist, pub. rels. cons., Columbus, Ga., 1994—; mem. Ga. Senate, Atlanta, 1993—, also mem. def. and vets. affairs com., mem. ethics com., mem. reapportionment com., mem. ethics and corrections coms., banking and fin. instns. com., health and human svcs. com. Second v.p. Muscogee County Sch. Bd., Columbus, 1985—; former mem. Columbus Charter Rev. Commn., Mayor's Com. for Drug-Free Columbus, Community Task Force on Gangs, Columbus Cable TV Study Commn.; grad. Leadership Columbus, 1990; bd. dirs. A.J. McClung YMCA; chmn. Ga. Legis. Black Caucus, 2003—. Sgt. USMC, 1963-67. Recipient numerous awards for profl. accomplishments and community svc., including Dr. John W. Townsend award, ann. award for best regularly scheduled TV newscast AP, PUSH Excellence award, award of support Bambino League, honored by Alpha Kappa Alpha, citation NAACP, 1989, award for outstanding contbns. to African-Ams., Columbus Times, Outstanding Man of Yr. award Men's Progressive Club, 1994; named One of 50 Most Influential African-Ams. in Columbus, Phenix City, Ft. Benning, Ga., Among 50 Most Influential African Am. in Ga., Ga. Forum Newspaper, 2004. Mem. Ga. Assn. Newscasters (former officer). Democrat. Mem. African-Methodist-Episcopal Ch. Home: PO Box 1292 Columbus GA 31902-1292 Office Phone: 404-656-0074.

HARBISON, JOHN, composer; b. Orange, NJ, Dec. 20, 1938; m. Mary Rose Harbison. BA, Harvard U., 1960; MFA, Princeton U., 1963; studied with Boris Blacher, Berlin; studied with Roger Sessions and Earl Kim Choth, Princeton U.; degree (hon.), New Eng. Conservatory, 1995. Instr. MIT, 1969-82; condr. Cantata Singers, 1969-73, 80-82, L.A. Philharm., The Boston Symphony, Speculum Musicae; creative chair St. Paul Chamber Orch., 1990—92. Composer-in-residence Pitts. Sympnony, L.A. Philharmonic, The Tanglewood, Santa Fe Chamber Festivals, Am. Acad., Rome., Aspen Music Festival, Ojai Music Festival, Calif., 1991; former music dir. Cantata Singers, Boston; instr. CalArts, Boston U.; prin. guest condr. Emmanuel Music; guest condr. Seattle Symphony, 2003. Composer: (operas) The Winter's Tale, 1974, Full Moon in March, 1977; (ballets) Ulysses' Raft, 1983, Ulysses' Bow, 1983; (symphonies/orchestral) Sinfonia, 1963, Diotima, 1976, Descant-Nocturne, 1976, Piano Concerto, 1978, Violin Concerto, 1978-80, Snow Country, 1979, Symphony No. 1, 1981, Deep Potomac Bells, 1983, Concerto for Clarinet, Oboe, and Strings, 1985, Remembering Gatsby: A Foxtrot for Orchestra, 1986, Symphony No. 2, 1987, Concerto for Double Brass Choir and Orchestra, 1988, Concerto for Viola and Orchestra, 1989, Symphony No. 3, 1990; (chamber/instrumental) Duo, 1961, Verses, 1964, Confinement, 1965, Four Preludes, 1967, Serenade, 1968, Parody-Fantasia, 1968, Piano Trio, 1969, Bermuda Triangle, 1970, Die kurze, 1970, Amazing Grace, 1972, Quintet for Woodwinds, 1979, Organum for Paul Fromm, 1981, Piano Quintet, 1981, Variations, 1982, Exequiem for Calvin Simmons, 1982, Overture: Michael Kohlhaas, 1982, String Quartet No. 1, 1985, Twlight Music, 1985, Four Songs of Solitude, 1985, Music for Eighteen Winds, 1986, Christmas Concerto, 1987, String Quartet No. 2, 1987, Piano Sonata, 1987, Magnum mysterium, 1988, Two Choral Preludes, 1988, Fantasy Duo, 1988, November 19, 1828, 1989; (vocal/choral) Autumnal, 1965, Shakespeare Series, 1965, Music, 1966, Five Songs of Experience on Poems of William Blake, 1971, Elegiac Songs, 1974, Book of Hours and Seasons, 1975, Moments of Vision, 1975, Three Harp Songs, 1975, The Flower-fed Buffaloes, 1976, Samuel Chapter, 1978, Nunc dimittis, 1980, Motetti di Montale, 1980, Mirabai Songs, 1982, The Flight into Egypt, 1986 (Pulitzer Prize for music 1988), The Natural World, 1987, The Three Wise Men, 1988, Simple Daylight, 1988, Words from Paterson, 1989; commissions include Balt. Symphony, the Juilliard String Quartet, The Met. Opera, 1999. Paine travelling fellow Harvard U., Guggenheim fellow, 1978, MacArthur fellow, 1989; recipient Kennedy Ctr. Friedheim award, 1980, Heinz award for the arts and humanities, 1998, Harvard Arts medal, 2000, Letter of Distinction, Am. Music Ctr., 2000, Disting. Composer award Am. Composer's Orch., 2002. Mem. Am. Acad. and Inst. of Arts and Letters, 1992. Office: 479 Franklin St Cambridge MA 02139-3115

HARBORDT, CHARLES MICHAEL, forest products executive; b. Houston, Apr. 8, 1942; s. Charles and Mary Lydia (Shumard) H.; m. Jackie Ward, June 23, 1960; children: Michelle, Katherine, Julie. BS, Stephen F. Austin U., Nacogdoches, Tex., 1963; MS, So. Meth. U., 1965; PhD, Tex. A&M U., 1970. Cert. environ. profl., Nat. Assn. Environ. Profls., Nat. Registry Environ. Profls. Assoc. chemist Texaco, Inc., Bellaire, Tex., 1965-67, sr. chemist, 1970-71; environ. dir. Temple Industries, Diboll, Tex., 1971-75, Temple-Eastex Inc., Diboll, 1975-80, energy, environ. and individual hygiene dir., 1980-90; v.p. Temple-Inland Forest Products Corp., Diboll, 1990—, Temple-Inland, Diboll, 1996-2000, dir. environment and sustainable forestry, 2000—. Mem. oper. com. Nat. Coun. Air and Stream Improvement, 1994-2000, 03—, chmn. chem. health effects and mgmt., 1994-97; mem. sr. adv. coun. Global Environ. Mgmt. Initiative, 1998—. Apptd. Tex. Regional Water Devel. Bd., 1998; chair forestry Chgo. Climate Exch., 2004—; mem. Pineywoods Groundwater Dist., 2004—; v.p. United Fund, Lufkin, Tex., 1976; mem. adminstrn. bd. Lufkin Meth. Ch., chmn. bd. trustees, 1989-91, trustee, 1996—; chmn. career edn. com. Lufkin H.S., 1980-86; trustee Stephen F. Austin U. Found., 1996-99—; bd. dirs. Stephen F. Austin U. Real Estate Found., 1997-99, Bus. Coun. for Sustainable Devel., Gulf of Mexico, 1993—. Robert A. Welch Found. fellow, 1963-65, Stephen F. Austin U. Disting. alumnus, 1994. Fellow Am. Inst. Chemists; mem. Am. Hardboard Assn. (chmn. environ. com. 1982-85, chmn. environ. com. 1983-85), TAPPI, Air Pollution Control Assn., Water Pollution Control Fedn., Diboll Jaycees, Angelina County (Tex.) C. of C. (bus. com. 1979, mem. edn. coun. 1984), Phi Kappa Phi, Phi Lambda Upsilon. Avocations: hunting, photography, reading, travel. Office: Temple Inland Inc PO Drawer N Diboll TX 75941

HARBOTTLE, GARMAN, chemist; b. Dayton, Ohio, Sept. 25, 1923; s. William Edwin and Susan (Garman) Harbottle; m. Naomi Perkiss, June 10, 1949; 1 child, Laura. BS, Calif. Inst. Tech., 1944; PhD, Columbia U., 1949. Chemist Brookhaven Nat. Lab., Upton, N.Y., 1949—; dir. Internat. Atomic Energy Agy., Vienna, Austria, 1965-67; rsch. collaborator Met. Museum of Art, 1990—. Adj. prof. SUNY, Stony Brook, 1985—93, Stony Brook, 1999—; guest prof. U. Sci. Tech. China, Hefei, 1997; interviewed for PBS program Nova, 2005. Assoc. editor: Archaeometry Jour., 1981—96, Jour. Radioanalytical Chemistry, 1982—2001. Trustee Vanderbilt Mus, Centerport, NY, 1979—87, Inc Village of Old Field, NY, 1980—86. Recipient George von Hevesy Medal, 1983, Glenn T Seaborg Medal, Am Nuclear Soc, 1995, Roald Fryxell medal, Soc. Am. Archaeology, 1994, Pomerance medal, Am. Inst. Archaeology, 2002; fellow Postdoctoral, Atomic Energy Comn, 1951—52, Guggenheim, 1957—58. Mem.: Soc. Archaeological Scis. (pres 1987), Metro. Mus. Art (assoc.). Office: Brookhaven Nat Lab Upton NY 11973-5000 Office Phone: 631-344-4387. Personal E-mail: garmanhb@aol.com. Business E-Mail: garman@bnl.gov.

HARBOTTLE, HEATHER C., microbiologist, researcher; PhD, La. State U., Baton Rouge, 2003. Rsch. microbiologist ctr. vet. medicine US FDA, Laurel, Md., 2004—. Recipient Best Paper award, Jour. Aquatic Animal Health, 2006. Mem.: Am. Soc. Microbiology. Office: US FDA Ctr Vet Medicine 8401 Muirkirk Rd Laurel MD 20708 Office Phone: 301-210-4246. Business E-Mail: heather.harbottle@fda.hhs.gov.

HARBOUR, PAMELA JONES, commissioner, lawyer; m. John Harbour; 3 children. BMus, Ind. U., Bloomington, 1981; JD, Ind. U., 1984. Asst. counsel NY State Dept. Trans., Albany, NY; atty. antitrust bur. NY State Atty. Gen., 1987—96, dep. atty. gen. pub. advocacy, 1997—99; ptnr. litig. dept. Kaye Scholer LLP, NY, 1999—2003; commr. FTC, Washington, 2003—. Recipient Antitrust Section Svc. award, NY State Bar Assn., 2005. Office: FTC 600 Pennsylvania Ave. NW Washington DC 20580

HARBOUR, TED IRA, lawyer, construction executive; b. 1957; BS, JD, Tex. Tech U., Lubbock. Bar: Tex. 1982. Sr. v.p. D.R. Horton, Inc., Ft. Worth, chief legal officer. Mem.: State Bar Tex. (mem. intellectual property law sect.). Office: DR Horton Inc DR Horton Tower 301 Commerce St Ste 500 Fort Worth TX 76102-4178 Office Phone: 817-856-8200. Office Fax: 817-856-8249. E-mail: tharbour@drhorton.com.*

HARBURY, PEHR A.B., biochemist, educator; BA, Harvard U., 1987, PhD, 1994. Postdoctoral fellow U. Calif., Berkeley, 1995—97; assoc. prof. Stanford U., 1997—. Contbr. articles to profl. jours. Named a MacArthur fellow, John D. and Catherine T. MacArthur Found., 2005; recipient Dir.'s Pioneer Award, NIH, 2005. Office: Stanford Univ Sch Medicine Dept Biochemistry Stanford CA 94305-5401 Office Phone: 650-725-7989. Office Fax: 650-723-6783. E-mail: harbury@cmgm.stanford.edu.

HARCLEROAD, FRED FARLEY, education administrator, consultant; b. Cheyenne, Wyo., Nov. 22, 1918; s. Fred Farley and Ina Mary (Livermore) H.; m. Moyne Payne, Dec. 20, 1942; children: Patricia Irene, Fred Douglass. AB, U. No. Colo., 1939, MA, 1942; PhD in Higher Edn., Stanford U., 1948. Tchr., coach Ault High School, Colo., 1939-42, prin. Colo., 1942-43; tchr., coach, counselor Menlo Sch. and Jr. Coll., 1943-46; asst., acting instr. Stanford U., summers 1944, 45; staff San Diego State U., 1946-52, coordinator audio-visual service, 1947-50, co-ordinator secondary edn., 1949-51, chmn. div. edn., 1951-52; dean instrn. San Jose Jr. Coll., 1952-53, San Jose State U., 1952-57, dean of coll., 1957-59; founding pres. Calif. State U., East Bay, 1959-67; prof. higher edn. U. Iowa, Iowa City, 1968-74; pres. Am. Coll. Testing Program, 1967-74; founding dir. Ctr. for Study Higher Edn., U. Ariz., Tucson, 1974-80, prof. higher edn., 1974-84; Disting. prof., cons. Pima CC, 1984—2003. Mem. Pacific Coast com. Am. Council Edn., 1955-58; pres.-elect Am. Assn. State Colls. and Univs., 1967, bd. dirs., 1965-68, chmn. com. internat. edn., 1964-80, mem. com. on purposes and policies, 1966-76; commr. Edn. Commn. of the States, 1967-68; chmn. accreditation commn. Nat. Home Study Council, 1977-85; mem. bd. Council on Postsecondary Accreditation, 1981-83; nat. adv. council on nurse tng. U.S. Dept. Health and Human Services, 1982-86; cons., Coun. Higher Edn. Accreditation, 1998-2007; cons. in field. Co-author: International Education in the Developing State Colleges and Universities, 1966, Audio-Visual Instruction: Technology, Media and Methods, 1959, rev. edits., 1964, 69, 73, 77, 83, Educational Auditing and Voluntary Institutional Accreditation, 1975, Partners for Quality, 1986; sr. author: The Developing State Colleges and Universities: Historical Background, Current Status, and Future Plans, 1969, Continuing Studies Program in the Mass. State College System, 1972, Regional State Colleges and Universities Enter the 1970's, 1973; editor: (with William Allen) Audio Visual Administration, 1951, The Education of the Audio Visual Communication Specialist, 1960, Learning Resources in Colleges and Universities, 1964, Issues of the Seventies: The Future of Higher Education, 1970, Higher Education: A Developing Field of Study, 1974, Educational Auditing and Accountability, 1976, (with others) The Regional State Colleges and Universities in the Middle Seventies, 1976, Financing Postsecondary Education in the 1980's, 1979, Voluntary Organizations in America and the Development of Educational Accreditation, 1980, Accreditation: History, Process, and Problems, 1980, The Comprehensive Public State Colleges and Universities in America, 1983, Colleges and Universities for Change, 1987; contbr. articles to mags.; contbr. chpts. to books. Named to U. No. Colo. Alumni Hall of Fame, one of Top 100 Alumni of the Century, 1890-1990. Mem. Assn. Collegiate Bus. Schs. and Programs (bd. dirs. 1990-95, cons. evaluator 1997-2000, Hall of Fame 1996), Western Coll. Assn. (bd. dirs. 1963-67), Assn. Study Higher Edn. (pres.-elect, pres., past pres. 1973-75), N.E.A. (dept. audio visual instrn. com. on profl. edn. 1951-53, mem. adv. bd. Ednl. Policies Commn. 1961-63, 65-68), Assn. Ind. Colls. and Schs. (pub. mem. accrediting commn. 1986-88, mem. rev. bd. appeals 1989-90), Am. Acad. Liberal Edn. (cons. evaluation com. 1998-01), Calif. Audio-Visual Edn. Assn. (pres. So. sect. 1950-51, sec. 1951-52), Calif. Council Tchr. Edn. (chmn. ednl. TV com. 1951-52), Phi Delta Kappa, Phi Alpha Theta, Kappa Delta Pi, Phi Kappa Phi (hon.), Phi Mu Alpha, Sinfonia, Blue Key. Clubs: Rotary, Commonwealth. studies of 16 state systems of higher education, and 12 regional and national accrediting associations. Home and Office: 5950 N Fountains Ave Apt 4101 Tucson AZ 85704-7860 Office Phone: 520-297-5521. *When we gather to settle problems in the field of education, especially at impasse, we must ask, and answer, the key question. How can we decide this issue so that the students will be better able to learn?.*

HARCROW, EDWARD EARL, lawyer; b. Carrizozo, N.Mex., Mar. 4, 1954; s. James Earl and Nettie (McInnes) H.; m. Julie A., Apr. 16, 1987; children: Ashley Nicole, James Earl. BS, Tex. Tech. U., 1976, JD, 1979. Bar: Tex. 1979, U.S. Dist. Ct. (no. dist.) Tex., U.S. Ct. Appeals (5th cir.) 1979. Asst. dist. atty. Lubbock (Tex.) Dist. Atty. Office, 1979-80, Tarrant Dist. Atty. Office, Ft. Worth, 1980-83; ptnr. Shannon, Gracey, Ratliff & Miller, Ft. Worth, 1985-99, mng. ptnr., 1995-96, ptnr. in charge of tech., 1996-99; ptnr. Haynes & Boone, Ft. Worth, 1999—; gen. counsel Dallas Ft. Worth Med. Ctr., 1990—99. Bd. dirs. Planned Parenthood North Tex., 1987-92; fellow Tex. Bar Found., 1991—. Office: Haynes and Boone LLP 201 Main St Ste 2200 Fort Worth TX 76102-3126 Office Phone: 817-346-6646. Business E-Mail: earl.harcrow@haynesboone.com.

HARDAGE, PAGE TAYLOR, elementary school educator; b. Richmond, Va., June 27, 1944; d. George Peterson and Gladys Odell (Gordon) Taylor; 1 child, Taylor Brantley. AA, Va. Intermont Coll., Bristol, 1964; BS, Richmond Profl. Inst., 1966; MPA, Va. Commonwealth U., Richmond, 1982. Cert. tchr., Va. Competent toastmaster, dir. play therapy svcs. Med. Coll. Va. Hosps., Va. Commonwealth U., Richmond, 1970-90; dir. Inst. Women's Issues, Va. Commonwealth U., U. Va., Richmond, 1986-91; adminstr. Scottish Rite Childhood Lang. Ctr. at Richmond, Inc., 1991-99. Bd. dirs. Richmond Bus. Coun. Math. and Sci. Ctr. Found., Richmond, Emergency Med. Svcs. Adv. Bd., Richmond. Treas. Richmond Black Student Found., 1989—90, Leadership Metro Richmond Alumni Assn.; group chmn. United Way Greater Richmond, 1987; bd. dirs. Maggie L. Walker Hist. Found., Richmond YWCA, 1989—91, Capital Area Health Adv. Coun.; commr. Mayors Commn. of Concerns of Women, City of Richmond. Mem.: ASPA, NAFE, Va. Assn. Fund Raising Execs., Va. Recreation and Park Soc. (bd. dirs.), Internat. Mgmt. Coun. (exec. com.), Adminstrv. Mgmt. Soc., Rotary Club of Hanover. Unitarian Universalist. Avocations: bridge, target shooting, aerobics.

HARDAWAY, ERNEST, II, oral and maxillofacial surgeon, public health service officer; BS, Howard U., 1957, DDS, 1966, cert. in oral and maxillofacial surgery, 1972; MPH, Johns Hopkins U., 1973. Intern, then chief resident oral and maxillofacial surgery Howard U. Med. Ctr., Washington, 1969-72; asst. prof., mem. attending staff Howard U. Coll. Medicine and Med. Ctr., Washington, 1974—; with Bur. Quality Assurance, HHS, Washington, 1974-77; various adminstrv. positions Bur. Med. Services and Health Services Adminstrn., USPHS, 1977-80; dep. commr., then commr. pub. health City of Washington, 1982-84; acting v.p. fin. and adminstrv. affairs Mile Sq. Health Ctr., Inc., 1984; asst. to regional health adminstr. Fed. Employee Occupl. Health Program, 1985, dir., 1986—89, Chgo. and Kansas City, 1989—90; mem. CFO coun. com. on entrepreneurial govt. Office Mgmt. and Budget, Washington, 1991—2001; chmn. com. on acad. affairs Coll. Bus. U. Ill., 2001—. Profl. staff Com. on Ways and Means, U.S. Ho. of Reps., 1972; spl. asst. to dir. Office Policy Planning and Evaluation, HEW, 1973; presenter in field. Contbr. articles to profl. jours. Mem. D.C. Emergency Med. Care Adv. Com., D.C. Long-Term Planning Group, 1983, D.C. Health Coordinating Council, D.C. Commn. on Homelessness, 1984; mem. adv. bd. Rosemont Health Ctr., 1984; sec. D.C. Commn. on Licensure to Practice Healing Art, 1983; bd. dirs. United

Black Fund, 1984, Potomac Valley Myastenia Gravis Found., 1984; mem. com. human rsch. Instnl. Rev. Bd., Chgo., 1994-2001; chmn. com. acad. affairs U. Ill., 2002. Global Community Health fellow HEW, 1971, Louise C. Ball fellow, 1969; recipient Meritorious Service award USPHS, 1982, J.B. Johnson Nursing Ctr. award, 1983, Outstanding Service placque D.C. Village Choir, 1984, Disting. Service cert. Concerned Citizens for Alcohol Abuse, 1984, Whitman-Walker award for AIDS effort, 1984, Exceptional Accomplishment award Regional Health Adminstr., 1987. Fellow Am. Assn. Oral and Maxillofacial Surgeons (ho. of dels. 1977-80), Internat. Coll. Dentistry, Royal Soc. Health, Acad. Dentistry Internat., Am. Coll. Dentistry; mem. ADA (cons. council hosp. dental care 1976-77), D.C. Soc. Oral and Maxillofacial Surgeons (sec.-treas. 1979-81), Nat. Dental Assn. (Dentist of Yr. 1983, 1st ann. Disting. Service award 1984), Omicron Kappa Upsilon, Chi Delta Mu, Sigma Pi Phi. Home: 88 W Schiller St Apt 1204 Chicago IL 60610-2037 Personal E-mail: drehardaway@aol.com.

HARDAWAY, ROBERT MORRIS, III, retired surgeon; b. Camp John Hay, The Philippines, Jan. 9, 1916; s. Robert Morris and Olive (Gray) Hardaway; m. Lee H. Harkey, June 12, 1939; children: Robert Morris IV, Elizabeth J., Thomas G. II, Christopher L. AB, U. Denver, 1936; postgrad., U. Colo. Med. Sch., 1935-37; MD, Washington U., St. Louis, 1939. Diplomate Am. Bd. Surgery. Commd. 1st lt., M.C. U.S. Army, 1939, advanced through grades to brig. gen., 1970; ward officer, surg. svc. Fitzsimons Gen. Hosp., Denver, 1940-41, resident surgery, 1949-50; ward officer, surg. svc. N. Sector Gen. Hosp., Hawaii, 1941-43; tchr. Med. Field Service Sch., Carlysle Barracks, Pa., 1943-45; surg. trainee Nichols Gen. Hosp., Louisville, 1945-46; resident surgery Madigan Gen. Hosp., Tacoma, 1946-47; chief surg. service 34th Gen. Hosp., Republic of Korea, 1947-49, Sta. Hosp., Ft. Belvoir, Va., 1950-54; chief surg. svc. 97th Gen. Hosp., Frankfurt, Germany, 1954-58, comdg. officer, 1967-70; chief surg. service Martin Army Hosp., Ft. Benning, Ga., 1958-60; dir. divsn. surgery Walter Reed Army Inst. Rsch., Washington, 1960-67; comdg. gen. William Beaumont Army Med. Ctr., El Paso, 1970-75; prof. surgery Tex. Tech U. Sch. Medicine, El Paso, 1976—2002; staff R.E. Thomason Gen. Hosp., El Paso, 1975—2002; ret., 2002. Author: Syndromes of Disseminated Intravascular Coagulation, 1966, Clinical Management of Shock, Surgical and Medical, 1968, Capillary Perfusion in Health and Disease, 1981, Shock-the Reversible Stage of Dying, 1988, Treatment of Wounded in Vietnam, 1988, Blood Problems in Critical Care, 1989; contbr. articles to profl. jours. Decorated Legion of Merit with oak leaf cluster, DSM; recipient 2d prize for exhbn., AMA, 1964, Silver award exhibit, Am. Soc. Clin. Pathologists-Coll. Am. Pathologists, 1964, cert. of Outstanding Achievement, U.S. Army Sci. Conf., 1964. Fellow: ACS, Microcirculation Assn., Am. Assn. Surgery Trauma, Am. Coll. Angiology; mem.: AMA, Assn. Mil. Surgeons U.S., Alpha Omega Alpha. Episcopalian. Achievements include research in intravascular coagulation and hemorrhagic shock. *Nothing we know, (or think we know) is the ultimate truth.*

HARDAWAY, TIMOTHY DUANE, professional basketball player; b. Chgo., Sept. 1, 1966; m. Yolanda Hardaway; 2 children. Grad., U. Tex. at El Paso, 1989. With Golden State Warriors, 1989—95, Miami Heat, 1995—2001, Dallas Mavericks, 2001, Denver Nuggets, 2001—02, Ind. Pacers, 2002—03; player/coach Am. Baseketball Assn. Fla. Pitbulls, 2005—06. Named to NBA All-Rookie team, 1990, All-Star team, 1991, 1992, 1993.*

HARDBERGER, PHILLIP DUANE, mayor, judge, lawyer, journalist; b. Morton, Tex., July 27, 1934; s. Homer Reeves and Bess (Scott) H.; m. Linda Morgan, May 1968; children: Amy, Kimberlea Moser. BA, Baylor U., 1955; MS, Columbia U., 1960; LL.B., Georgetown U., 1965. Reporter Waco (Tex.) News Tribune, 1952-54; press rep. Tex. Baptist Conv., 1958-59; assoc. editor Mil. Pub. Inst., NYC, 1961; exec. sec. Peace Corps, 1962-66; spl. asst. to dir. OEO, 1967-68; trial lawyer, 1968-94; chief justice Fourth Ct. of Appeals, State of Tex., San Antonio, 1994—2003; mayor City of San Antonio, San Antonio, 2005—. Author: Texas Courtroom Evidence, Texas Workers' Compensation Trial Manual; contbr. articles to profl. jours. Served to capt. USAF, 1955-58. Home: 319 W Hollywood Ave San Antonio TX 78212-2211 Office: City Hall Office PO Box 839966 San Antonio TX 78283-3966 Business E-Mail: mayorphilphardberger@sanantonio.gov.

HARDCASTLE, MARCIA E. (MARCIA E. TEMME), retired journalist; b. Oakland, Calif., Nov. 28, 1945; d. Charles Frederick and Lillian Callita (Johnson) Temme; children: Glenn Arthur Hardcastle, Jason Roger Hardcastle. BA, San Jose State U. Society editor Los Altos (Calif.) News, 1967-70; reporter, lifestyle editor Santa Maria (Calif.) Times, 1979-82; adminstrv. asst. sr. Diablo Canyon Nuclear Power Plant, Calif., 1983-86; lifestyle editor 5-Cities Times Press Recorder, Arroyo Grande, Calif., 1987-98; arts and entertainment features editor Pulitzer Cmty. Newspapers, 1998-2000. Chair bd. dirs. publicity Am. Heart Assn., San Luis Obispo, Calif.; freelance photographer, writer, artist. Co-author: poetry.com. Press sec. Assemblyman Eric Seastrand, Calif.; co-founder Five Cities Women's Network, 1987; mem. Girl Scouts Am. Recipient Cmty. Svc. award Santa Maria Mental Health Assn., 1980, Media award Calif. Mental Health Assn., 1980, Hon. Mention award Nat. Newspaper Assn., 1989, 2d Place award Best Lifestyle/Family Life Pages Calif. Newspaper Assn., 1991, Editor's Choice award for outstanding achievement in poetry Internat. Libr. Poetry, 2003. Mem.: Bus. and Profl. Women, Internat. Order Rainbow for Girls (worthy advisor), Theta Sigma Phi. Avocations: photography, painting, travel. E-mail: marcia_hardcastle@yahoo.com.

HARDEN, ANITA JOYCE, nurse; b. Jackson, Tenn., May 17, 1947; d. Percy Lawrence and Marjorie (Robinson) H.; 1 child, Brian Robinson Weir. BSN, Ind. U., 1968, MBA, 1989; MSN, Ind. U.-Purdue U., Indpls., 1973. Staff nurse Indpls. Hosps., 1968-71; instr. Ind. U. Sch. Nursing, 1973-75; dir. continuing care Gallahue Mental Health Ctr., Indpls., 1975-80; mgr. psychiatry Cmty. Hosp., Indpls., 1980-87, product line mgr. for psychiat. and mental health svcs., 1986—; dir. psychiat. svcs. Cmty. Hosp. North, 1987-89, v.p., 1990-94; exec. dir. mental health svcs. Cmty. Hosps. of Ind., Inc., 1989-90; exec. dir. mental health St. Vincent-Cmty. Health Network, 1994-96; exec. dir. behavioral care svcs. Cmty. Hosps. Indpls., 1996-2001, v.p. behavioral health, 2001—03; pres. Cmty. Hosp. East, 2003—. Clin. asst. prof. Ind. U., 1977-82, clin. assoc. prof., 1982—; clin. assoc., trainer Suicide Prevention Svc., Indpls., 1974-77; chmn. adv. bd. deinstitutionalization project Cen. State Hosp., Indpls., 1978-79; bd. dirs. Safe Sitter, Behavioral Sys. LLC, InteCare; adj. assoc. prof. Ind. U. Sch. Nursing, 1998—. Contbr. articles to profl. jours. Active Ind. County Cmty. Mental Health Ctr., 1979-80; bd. dirs. Marion County Mental Health Assn., Indpls. Zoo, Alternatives in Madison County, Jackson-Peoples Living Ctr.; bd. trustees Christian Theol. Sem., 2005—. Recipient Outstanding Achievement in Professions award Ctr. Leadership Devel., 1981, Clin. Excellence award Ind. U. Sch. Nursing, 1989. Mem. Ind. U. Alumni Assn., Christian Women's Fellowship, 500 Festival Assocs., Greater Indpls. Orgn. Nurse Execs. (v.p.), Coalition 100 Black Women (bd. dirs.), Neal-Marshall Aumni Club, Alpha Kappa Alpha, Sigma Theta Tau, Chi Eta Phi. Home: 7607 Newport Bay Dr Indianapolis IN 46240-3370 Office: 7150 Clearvista Dr Indianapolis IN 46256-1695 Office Phone: 317-355-5526. Business E-Mail: aharden@ecommunity.com.

HARDEN, ANNETTE C., recreation director; b. Peoria, Ill., July 17, 1976; d. D. Michael and Peggy A. Hutchison, Suzan Hutchison (Stepmother); m. Kenneth L. Harden Jr., July 27, 2002; 1 child, Kennedi C. BS in Sport Adminstrn., U. Indpls., 1998; MS in Sport Mgmt. with honors (hon.), Ind. State U., Terre Haute, 2000. Customer svc. mgr. Ind. U.-Purdue U. Indpls., 2000—02; asst. recreation dir. intramurals Butler U., Indpls., 2002—; sales assoc. Wooden Key Hallmark Gold Crown, Indpls., 1999—. Mem.: AAHPERD (Excellent Student Profl. award 1998), Nat. Intramural Recreation Sport Assn. Avocations: shopping, swimming. Office: Butler University 330 W 49th St Indianapolis IN 46208 Home Phone: 317-465-9453; Office Phone: 317-940-8514. E-mail: aharden@butler.edu.

HARDEN, JON BIXBY, publishing executive; b. Fitzgerald, Ga., Mar. 7, 1944; s. William Harmon and Mary Bixby (Brewster) H.; m. Lynne Ann Lumsden, May 3, 1986; children: Gregory Ross, Heather Lynne. AAS, Rochester Inst. Tech., 1965; BS, Univ. Rochester, 1967; MBA, U Pa., 1969. Research analyst Doubleday & Co., Inc., NYC, 1969-72, mgr. corp. research, 1972-74, pub. group mgr., 1974-77; dir. bus. devel. McGraw-Hill Book Co., NYC, 1977-80, dir. planning and devel. Internat. div., 1980-84; v.p. corp. devel. and strategic planning Simon & Schuster, Inc., NYC, 1984-85; pres. Dodd, Mead & Co., Inc., NYC, 1985-88; gen. mgr. Romaine Pierson Pubs., Inc., Port Washington, 1988-89; pres. JBH Comm., Inc., 1989—; editor, pub. The Hartford News, Conn., 1989—; pub. Greater Hartford mag., 1996—; with Gamut Pub., Hartford, Conn., 2006—. Bd. dirs. SCAN Vol. Parents Aids Assn., Inc., 1980—89, v.p., 1985—89; treas. Ancient Burying Ground Assn., 2000—02, v.p., 2002—; bd. dirs. Cmty. Ptnrs. in Action, 2000—; bd. mgrs. West Side YMCA, 1985—89, vice-chmn., 1987—89. Mem. The Hartford Club, The Hartford Golf Club. Home: 16 Oak Ridge Ln West Hartford CT 06107-3505 Office: Garmat Publishing 99 Hanmer St Ste A Hartford CT 06114-3071 Office Phone: 860-296-6128. Personal E-mail: jonh1@aol.com.

HARDEN, MARCIA GAY, actress; b. La Jolla, Calif., Aug. 14, 1959; m. Thaddaeus D. Scheel, July 9, 1996; children: Eulala Grace Scheel, Hudson Harden Scheel, Julitta Dee Harden Scheel. BA in Theatre, U. Tex., 1980; MFA, NYU. Actor: (plays) Simpatico, 1994, Angels in America: Millennium Approaches/A Gay Fantasia on National Themes, 1993 (Tony nomination); (films) The Imagemaker, 1986, Miller's Crossing, 1990, Crush, 1992, Used People, 1992, Safe Passage, 1994, The Spitfire Grill, 1996, The Daytrippers, 1996, Spy Hard, 1996, The First Wives Club, 1996, Far Harbor, 1996, Flubber, 1997, Desperate Measures, 1998, Meet Joe Black, 1998, Curtain Call, 1999, Space Cowboys, 2000, Pollock, 2000 (Acad. award for best supporting actress, N.Y. Film Critics Circle award for best supporting actress), Gaudi Afternoon, 2001, Mystic River, 2003 (Acad. Award nomination for best supporting actress, 2004), Casa de los babys, 2003, Mona Lisa Smile, 2003, Just Like Mona, 2003, Welcome to Mooseport, 2004, Bad News Bears, 2005, Am. Dreamz, 2006, The Hoax, 2006, The Dead Girl, 2006, Canvas, 2006, The Invisible, 2007; (TV films) Kojak: None So Blind, 1990, In Broad Daylight, 1991, Fever, 1991, Sinatra, 1992, Talking with, 1995, Convict Cowboy, 1995, Path to Paradise: The Untold Story of the World Trade Center Bombing, 1997, Labor of Love, 1998, Spenser: Small Vices, 1999, Thin Air, 2000, See You In My Dreams, 2000, From Where I Sit, 2000, Walking Shadow, 2001, King of Texas, 2002, She's Too Young, 2003; (TV series) The Education of Max Bickford, 2001; (TV miniseries) Guilty Hearts, 2002. Office: Creative Artists Agy 9830 Wilshire Blvd Beverly Hills CA 90212-1825*

HARDEN, MARVIN, artist, educator; b. Austin, Tex. s. Theodore R. and Ethel (Sneed) H. BA in Fine Arts, UCLA, 1959, MA in Creative Painting, 1963. Prof. art Calif. State U., Northridge, 1967-97, prof. emeritus, 1997—; Tchr. art Santa Monica City Coll., Calif., 1968; mem. art faculty UCLA Extension, 1964-68; instr. art LA Harbor Coll., Calif., 1965—68. Mem. visual arts fellowship, painting panel NEA, 1985. One-man shows include Ceeje Galleries, LA, 1964, 66, 67, LA City Coll., 1968, Occidental Coll., LA, 1969, Whitney Mus. Am. Art, NYC, 1971, Eugenia Butler Gallery, LA, 1971, Rath Mus., Geneva, Switzerland, 1971, Irving Blum Gallery, LA, 1972, LA Harbor Coll., 1972, David Stuart Galleries, LA, 1975, Coll. Creative Studies, U. Calif., Santa Barbara, 1976, James Corcoran Gallery, LA, 1978, Newport Harbor Art Mus., Survey, 1979, L.A. Mcpl. Art Gallery, Major Retrospective, 1982, Conejo Valley Art Mus., 1983, Simard Gallery, L.A., 1985, maj. retrospective at The Armory Ctr. for the Arts, Pasadena, Calif., 1994, Ventura (Calif.) Coll. Art Gallery, 1997, Louis Stern Gallery, L.A., 1998, Armory Ctr. for Arts, Pasadena, Calif., 2005; group shows include US State Dept. Touring Exhbn., USSR, 1966, Oakland (Calif.) Mus. Art, 1966, UCLA, 1966, Mpls. Inst. Art, 1968, San Francisco Mus. Art, 1969, Phila. Civic Ctr. Mus., 1969, Mus. Art, RI Sch. Design, 1969, NJ State Mus., 1969, Everson Mus. Art, Syracuse, 1969, La Jolla (Calif.) Mus., 1969, 70, High Mus. Art, Atlanta, 1969, Flint (Mich.) Inst. Arts, 1969, Ft. Worth Art Center Mus., 1969, Contemporary Arts Assn., Houston, 1970, U. N.Mex., 1974, U. So. Calif., 1975, Bklyn. Mus., 1977, L.A. County Mus. Art, 1977, 95, Newport Harbor Art Mus., 1977, Frederick S. Wight Gallery, UCLA, 1978, Cirrus Editions, Ltd., L.A., 1979, 81, 82, Franklin Furnace, NYC, 1980, Art Ctr. Coll. Design, L.A., 1981, Alternative Mus., NYC, 1981, Laguna Beach Mus. (Calif.), 1982, Cirrus, 1982, L.A. Inst. Contemporary Art, 1983, Mus. Contemporary Art, Chgo., 1983, Mint Mus., Charlotte, NC, 1983, DeCordova and Dana Mus. and Park, Lincoln, Mass., 1983, Equitable Gallery, NYC, 1984, L.A. Mcpl. Art Gallery, 1984, 1985, Cirrus, L.A., 1986, 1990, Heal the Bay, Surfboard Art Invitational, 1990, Pasadena Armory Ctr. for the Arts, 1992, Claremont Coll. West Gallery, L.A., 1992, Grolier Club, NYC, 1993, Calif. State U., San Luis Obispo, 1994, Cheney Cowles Mus., Spokane, Wash., 1995, Louis Stern Fine Art, L.A., 1995, Porter Troup Gallery, San Diego, 1995, Armory Ctr. for the Arts, Pasadena, 1996, 97, Tel Aviv Mus. Art, 1998, Gail Harvey Gallery, Santa Monica, Calif., 1998, Palos Verdes Art Ctr., 1999, L.A. City Coll., 1999, Davis and Cline Gallery, Ashland, Oreg., 2002, Hunsaker/Schlesinger Fine Art, Santa Monica, 2002, Glendale Coll. Art Gallery, 2002, Davis and Cline, Ashland, Oreg., 2003, Harriet and Charles Luckman Fine Arts Complex, L.A., 2004, Schneider Mus. Art, Ashland, Oreg., 2004, Smithsonian Inst. Archives Am. Art, others; represented in permanent collections include Whitney Mus. Am. Art, NYC, Mus. Modern Art, NYC, Smithsonian Inst. Archives of Am. Art, NY Pub. Libr. Spence Collection, Getty Ctr. for Arts and Humanities, L.A. County Mus. Art, Atlantic Richfield Co. Corp. Art Coll., Grunwald Ctr. Graphic Arts UCLA, City of L.A., Metromedia, Inc., L.A., San Diego Jewish Cmty. Ctr., Berkeley (Calif.) U. Mus., Home Savs. & Loan Assn., L.A., also pvt. collections. Bd. dir. Images & Issues, 1980-86; mem. artists adv. bd. LA Mcpl. Art Gallery Assn., 1983-86. Recipient UCLA Art Coun. award, 1963, Disting. Prof. award Calif. State U. Northridge, 1984, Exceptional Merit Svc. award Calif. State U. Northridge, 1984; Nat. Endowment Arts fellow, 1972; Awards in Visual Arts fellow, 1983; Guggenheim fellow, 1983. Mem. LA Inst. Contemporary Art (co-founder 1973). Home: Inwardness Ranch PO Box 1793 Cambria CA 93428-1793 Office Phone: 805-238-9163.

HARDEN, MARY LOUISE, human resources consultant, real estate broker, real estate appraiser; b. Natchez, Miss., Mar. 27, 1942; d. John Charles and Dorothy Louise (Reynolds) Brown; m. Billy Gene Redd, Mar. 12, 1957 (div. 1961); children: Andre Ranier, Allison Lawanda, Robin Yvette; m. Percy Lawrence Harden Jr., Aug. 31, 1968; children: Darrell Lawrence, Craig Robison. Student, Ball State U., 1975—76, Ind. U., Purdue U., 1983—88; BSBA, Ind. Wesleyan U., 1989; postgrad., U. S.C., 1990; MA, Ball State U., 1995; grad. in Diversity Leadership, Acad. Greater Indpls., 2003. Editor-in-chief U.S. Army Fin. and Acctg. Ctr., Indpls., 1974-81, pers. mgmt. specialist, 1981-87, pub. affairs officer, 1987-91; pers. mgmt. specialist Def. Fin. and Acctg. Svc., 1991-99; fed. women's program mgr. U.S. Army Fin. and Acctg. Ctr., Indpls., 1981-85; appraiser OAS Land Acquisition Group, Carmel, Ind., 1999—. Minority advisor United Way of Ctrl. Ind., Indpls., 1985—2000; active Ind. Fever Adv. Team, 2001—, Ind. Consortium to Eliminate Achievement Gaps, 2003; bd. dirs. Nat. Coalition of 100 Black Women, Indpls., 1986—, pres., 2002—03, chair nat. program com., 2004—06; bd. dirs. Urban Mission YMCA, 2002—, Madame C.J. Walker, 2001—, YMCA Greater Indpls., 2005—; exec. bd. Pres.'s Roundtable, 2004—, chair, 2006—. Named Madame C.J. Walker Outstanding Woman of Yr., Ctr. for Leadership Devel. and Indpls. C. of C., 1988, Sarah Lewis Lifetime Achievement award, United Way Ctrl. Ind., 2003. Fellow: Dept. Def. Exec. Leadership Program; mem.: AARP, Nat. Assn. Ret. Fed. Employees, Am. Soc. Mil. Comptrs., Federally Employed Women. Presbyterian. Avocations: photography, real estate, reading.

HARDEN, NEVA NINETTE, writer, consultant; d. Fred Newell and Annette Ida Stevens; children: Paul M., Janelle E., Eric N. BA, Mich. State U., 1948; MA, U. Denver, 1962. Instr. So. Colo. State Coll., Pueblo, Colo., 1964—66; assoc. prof., adv. fgn. students Adams State Coll., Alamosa, Colo., 1966—76; coord. Ctr. Handicapped San Luis Valley, 1970—71; prin., owner Horizon Comms., Albuquerque, 1982—; exec. dir. Recreation, Health and Occupl. Ctr., 1994. Writer and cons. in juvenile corrections, 2005—. Author: Survival Skills: A Job Finding Guide, 1998, rev. edit., 2006, Grantsmanship: Taming the Beast, 2001, rev. edit., 2005; editor and publisher: Blacks in the Workforce, 1987, Architecture and Children, 1991, The Era of Allan R. Phillips: A Festscrift, 1997, Ola Anfenson: Pioneer Photographer, 1997, publisher: Wildlife Rehabilitation Coloring and Activity Book, 1995. Presbyterian. Home and Office: Horizon Communications 2710 San Diego SE Albuquerque NM 87106-3027

HARDEN, OLETA ELIZABETH, literature educator, academic administrator; b. Jamestown, Ky., Nov. 22, 1935; d. Stanley Virgil and Myrtie Alice (Stearns) McWhorter; m. Dennis Clarence Harden, July 23, 1966. BA, Western Ky. U., 1956; MA in English, U. Ark., 1958, PhD, 1965. Teaching asst. U. Ark., Fayetteville, 1956-57, 58-59, 61-63; instr. S.W. Mo. State Coll., Springfield, 1957-58, Murray (Ky.) U., 1959-61; asst. prof. English Northeastern State Coll., Tahlequah, Okla., 1963-65; asst. prof. Wichita (Kans.) State U., 1965-66; asst. prof. English Wright State U., Dayton, Ohio, 1966-68, assoc. prof., 1968-72, prof., 1972-93, asst. chmn. English dept., 1967-70, asst. dean, 1971-73, assoc. dean, 1973-74, exec. dir. gen. univ. services, 1974-76, pres. of faculty, 1984-85, prof. emerita, 1993—, coord. Irish studies, 2006—07. Author: Maria Edgeworth's Art of Prose Fiction, 1971, Maria Edgeworth, 1984; editor: The Extension, 1999—. Grantee, Ford Found., 1971. Mem. MLA, AARP (impact alliance leader Ohio, 2001—), AAUP, Coll. English Assn., Women's Caucus for Modern Langs., Am. Conf. for Irish Studies (presenter 1989, 91, 94, 95), Wright State U. Retiree Assn. (pres. 1995-96), Elizabeth McWhorter Harden Forensics Alumni Assn. (founder, pres. We. Ky. U. chpt. 2004—). Office: Wright State U Dept English 7751 Colonel Glenn Hwy Dayton OH 45431-1674 Home: 2618 Big Woods Trl Dayton OH 45431-8704 Office Phone: 937-775-2777. Personal E-mail: oharden@aol.com.

HARDEN, PATRICK ALAN, journalist; b. Twickenham, Eng., Aug. 13, 1936; s. Ernest William and Annie Ceridwen (Jones) H.; m. Connie Marie Graham, Nov. 2, 1963; children: Marc Graham, Ceri Marie. Cert. in journalism, Ealing Tech. Coll., Eng., 1957. With UPI, 1960-78, regional exec. London, 1968-69, European picture mgr. London and Brussels, 1969-72, regional exec. Detroit, 1973-75; gen. mgr. UPI Can. Ltd., Montreal, 1976-78, UP Can., Toronto, 1979-82, dir., sec., 1979-82; treas. UPI Can. Ltd.; gen. mgr. Edmonton (Alta.) Sun, 1982-84, pub., 1984-92; v.p. Toronto Sun Pub. Corp., 1989-94; v.p., bur. chief Washington, 1992-94; Washington columnist Toronto Sun Pub. Corp., 1994-97; freelance writer, 1997-98; Washington bur. chief LRP Pubs., Arlington, Va., 1998—. Office Phone: 703-516-7002. E-mail: pharden@lrp.com.

HARDER, ROBERT CLARENCE, state official; b. Horton, Kans., June 4, 1929; s. Clarence L. and Olympia E. (Kubik) H.; m. Dorothy Lou Welty, July 31, 1953; children: Anne, James David. AB, Baker U., Baldwin, Kans., 1951; MTh, So. Meth. U., 1954; ThD in Social Ethics, Boston U., 1958; LHD (hon.), Baker U., 1983, Ottawa U., 1991. Ordained to ministry Meth. Ch., 1959; pastor East Topeka Meth. Ch., 1958-64; mem. Kans. Ho. of Reps., 1961-67; rsch. assoc. Menninger Found., Topeka, 1964-65; instr. Washburn U., Topeka, 1964, 68, 69; dir. Topeka Office of Econ. Opportunity, 1965-67; tech. asst. coordinator Office of Gov. of Kans., 1967-68; dir. community resources devel. League of Kans. Municipalities, 1968-69; dir. Kans. Dept. Social Welfare, Topeka, 1969-73, sec., 1973-87; projects adminstr. Topeka State Hosp., 1987-89. Adj. prof. pub. adminstrn. Kans. U., 1987-95, instr. Sch. Social Welfare, 1971-87; cons. Menninger Topeka, 1991-92; sec. Kans. Dept. Health and Environment, 1992-95. Contbr. articles to profl. jours. Recipient Disting. Svc. award East Topeka Civic Assn., 1963, Romana Hood award, 1965, Cert. of Recognition, State of Kans., 1979, 87, Spl. Commendation award Kans. Senate, 1987, Spl. Commendation, Kans. Ho. of Reps., 1987, Outstanding Alumnus award Perkins Sch. Theology, So. Meth. U., 1994, M. L. King Jr. Living the Dream Humanitarian award, 1997, Disting. Svc. award Kans. Children's Svc. League, 1998, Grant award for Exceptional Volunteerism, 1999, Advocacy award Disability Caucus, 2003, cert. appreciation Scott Sch., 2003, award of excellence Friends Edn. Award, 2004, Cmty. Leader award Topeka Pub. Schs., 2004, others; named Outstanding Pub. Ofcl. of the Yr., 1987. Mem. Am. Soc. Public Adminstrs. (Public Adminstr. of Yr. Kans. chpt. 1980), Am. Public Welfare Assn., Kans. Health Care Commn., Kans. Conf. Social Welfare (Outstanding Person of Yr. 1987). Democrat.

HARDER, ROLF PETER, graphic designer, painter; b. Hamburg, Germany, July 10, 1929; came to Can., 1955; s. Henry and Henriette (Loeffler) H.; m. Maria-Inger Rumberg, May 3, 1958; children— Christopher, Vivian Student, State Art Sch. (Acad. Fine Arts), Hamburg, 1948-52. Designer Rolf Ruehle Werbung, Hamburg, 1952-55; designer Schneider Cardon Ltd, Montreal, Que., Canada, 1955-56; art dir. George Ferguson Assocs., Montreal, 1956-57; visualizer Lintas GmbH, Hamburg, 1957-59; designer, owner Rolf Harder Design, Montreal, 1959-65; co-founder, designer Design Collaborative, Montreal, 1965-77; pres., designer Rolf Harder & Assocs., Montreal, 1977—. Mem. internat. adv. bd. Typos Mag., London, 1979—; co-organizer exhibition The Visual Image of the Munich Games, Mus. Fine Arts, Montreal, 1972 Co-publisher Pitseolak: Pictures Out of My Life, 1972, Arts of the Eskimo: Prints, 1974; Represented in permanent collections Nat. Archives of Can., Ottawa, Libr. of Congress, Washington, Musee de La Publicité, Palais du Louvre, Paris, Die Neue Sammlung, Munich, AGI Archives, Essen, Germany, Mus. Arts and Crafts, Hamburg, Germany, Mus. Modern Art, N.Y.C., San Francisco, Design Austria, Vienna, U. Reading, Eng., U. Que., Musee De Quebec, The Montreal Mus. Fine Arts, McGill U., Rare Books Dept. Coach Beaconsfield Soccer Assn., Montreal, 1966-70. Recipient design awards including World Logo Design award, Internat. Trademark Ctr., Belgium, 1998. Fellow Soc. Graphic Designers of Can.; mem. Royal Canadian Acad. Arts, Alliance Graphique Internationale (past pres. Can. group). Clubs: Clearpoint Tennis, West-Island Tennis (Montreal). Avocations: tennis, music. Home: 43 Lakeshore Rd Beaconsfield PQ Canada H9W 4H6 E-mail: rolf@rolfharder.ca.

HARDER, WENDY WETZEL, communications executive; b. Oceanside, Calif., Feb. 14, 1951; d. Burt Louis and Marjorie Jean (Evans) W.; m. Peter N. Harder, Dec. 1, 1984; 1 child, Jonathan Russell. AA, Palomar Coll., 1971; BA in Comm., U. So. Calif., 1973; MBA, Pepperdine U., 1988. Pub. rels. dir. Orange County Cmty. Devel. Coun., Santa Ana, Calif., 1975-76; assoc. prodr. Sta. KOCE-TV, Huntington Beach, Calif., 1976-77, reporter, 1977-79, anchor, assoc. prodr., 1979-82; sr. adminstr. comm. Mission Viejo (Calif.) Co., 1983-84, mgr. corp. affairs, 1984-85, dir. corp. affairs, 1985-91, v.p. corp. affairs, 1991-93, v.p. mktg. and corp. comm., 1993-97; dir. cmty. rels. Soka Univ. Am., 1998—. 1st v.p. Aliso Viejo (Calif.) Cmty. Found., 1988-93, 03-04, pres., 1993-97, Saddleback Coll. Found., Mission Viejo, 1989-94; co-chmn. The Ctr. on Tour-Schs. Com., Orange County, Calif., 1989-92; v.p. Found. for Vocat. Visions, 1996-02, pres., 2000-03; bd. dirs. Dunaj Internat. Dance Ensemble, Orange County, 1985-00; den leader Pack 709 Cub Scouts, 2001-05; mem. troop com. 1602 Boy Scouts Am., 2005—, asst. scout master, 2006-; bd. dirs. Mt. of Olives

Found., 2003-. Co-recipient Golden Mike award, Radio & TV News Assn., 1979; recipient, 1981. Mem. Pub. Rels. Soc. Am. (co-recipient Best Spl. Event award 1986), Aliso Viejo C. of C. (bd. dirs. 2002-2005), Laguna Niguel C. of C. (bd. dirs. 2006-), Anaheim/Orange County Conv. & Visitors Bur., Orange County Press Club (Best Feature Release award 1983), Phi Beta Kappa. Republican. Lutheran. Avocations: folk dancing, reading. Office: Soka Univ Am 1 University Dr Aliso Viejo CA 92656 Office Phone: 949-480-4081. Business E-Mail: wwharder@soka.edu.

HARDESTY, DAVID CARTER, JR., law educator, former academic administrator; b. Philadelphia, Miss., Sept. 20, 1945; m. Susan B. Hardesty, 1968; children: Ashley, D(avid) Carter III. AB, W.Va. U., 1967; MA, Oxford U., Eng., 1969; JD, Harvard U., 1973. Bar: W.Va. 1973. Tax commr., sec. Econ. Devel. Authority, State of W.Va., Charleston, 1977-80, chmn. Mcpl. Bond Commn., 1977-80; assoc. Bowles Rice McDavid Graff & Love, Charleston, 1973-77, ptnr., 1981-95; pres. W.Va. U., Morgantown, 1995—2007, prof. law Coll. Law, 2007—. Chmn. W.Va. Tax Study Commn., 1982-84; mem. W.Va. Asian Trade Missions, 1978-79, 95; chmn. W.Va. Roundtable, Inc., 1994-95; mem. adv. bd. Nat. Security Higher Edn., 2005—; frequent spkr. at govt., edn. and bus. group meetings. Chancellor United Meth. Ch., W.Va., 1986-95; trustee Univ. Sys., 1989-95, 1st chmn., 1989-91; trustee W.Va. Wesleyan Coll., 1986-94, Nat. 4-H Coun., 2000—, chair bd. trustees, 2004—; mem. Gov.'s Energy Task Force, 2001—; mem. W.Va. Rhodes Scholar Selection Com., 1980-2000, sec., 1991-98; bd. advisors W.Va. U., 1980-89, chmn. bd. advisors, 1987-89; bd. dirs. United Meth. Charities W.Va., 1978-94; bd. dirs. Greater Kanawha Valley Found., 1980-89, chmn., 1988-90. Rhodes scholar, 1969. Mem.: ABA, Nat. Assn. State Univs. and Land Grant Colls., Nat. Assn. Coll. and Univ. Attys., Am. Coun. on Edn., 4th Cir. Jud. Conf., W.Va. Bar Assn. Office: WVa U Coll Law PO Box 6130 Morgantown WV 26506-6130 Office Phone: 304-293-5531. E-mail: David.Hardesty@mail.wvu.edu.*

HARDESTY, JAMES, state supreme court justice; b. Reno, Nov. 28, 1948; m. Sandy Hardesty, 1971; 2 children. BS in Acctg., U. Nevada, Reno, 1970; JD, U. Pacific McGeorge Sch. of Law, 1975. Bar: Nev. 1975, U.S. Dist. Ct. Nev. 1975, U.S. Tax Ct. 1976, U.S. Ct. of Appeals, Ninth Circuit 1980. Atty. priv. practice, 1978—80; prtnr. Breen, Young, Whitehead, Belding & Hardesty, 1980—84, Anderson, Pearl, Hardesty, Lyle and Murphy, 1991—95; judge Nev. Second Jud. Dist. Ct., 1999—2001, chief judge, 2001—04; justice Nev. Supreme Ct., 2005—. Prof. Nat. Jud. Coll., 2002—; former lecturer media law U. Nev. Donald Reynolds Sch. of Journalism; co-chair Nev. Supreme Ct. Task Force to Create Bus. Ct., 2000; mem. Nev. Supreme Ct. Task Force Multi-Jurisdictional Practice of Law, 2001, Nev. Supreme Ct. Commn. on Jud. Funding, 2003—, Nev. State Bd. of Ed., 1983—84. Mem.: ABA, Am. Inns of Ct., Assn. of Trial Lawyers of Am., Nev. Dist. Judges Assn. (bd. trustees pres. 2000, bd. trustees 2000—04), Washoe County Bar Assn. Office: Nev Supreme Ct 201 S Carson St Carson City NV 89701*

HARDESTY, ROBERT LYNCH, surgeon, educator; b. New Brighton, Pa., Sept. 12, 1940; s. Robert and Cora Belva (Cable) H.; m. Catherine Ann Steward, Oct. 3, 1965; children: Lara Ann, Derek John, Kieran Steward. Student, U. Pitts., 1958-59, MD, 1966; BS, Allegheny Coll., 1962. Diplomate Am. Bd. Surgery, Am. Bd. Thoracic Surgery. Resident in surgery U. Pitts., 1966-71, resident in cardiothoracic surgery, 1971-72, asst. prof. surgery, 1974-80, assoc. prof., 1980-86, prof., 1986, prof. emeritus dept. surgery, Sch. Medicine, vice chmn. Instl. Rev. Bd., 2001, dir. Instl. Rev. Bd., 2003. Author: Extracorporeal Membrane Oxygenation (ECMO) for Neonatal Pulmonary Insufficiency, 1974, Cardiac Transplantation, 1981, Cardiac and Pulmonary Transplantation, 1982. Maj. USAF, 1972-74. Recipient Man of Yr. award Pitts. Acad. Medicine, 1986, Man of Yr. award in sci. vectors Alpha Omega Alpha, 1987. Fellow Am. Soc. for Artificial Internal Organs; mem. Am. Surg. Assn., Am. Assn. Thoracic Surgery, Soc. Univ. Surgeons, Transplantation Soc., Phi Eta Sigma. Republican. Roman Catholic. Avocation: woodworking. Office: Univ Pittsburgh Dept Surgery F1281.2 PUH 200 Lothrop St Pittsburgh PA 15261

HARDGROVE, JAMES ALAN, lawyer; b. Chgo., Feb. 20, 1945; s. Albert John and Ruth (Noonen) H.; m. Kathleen M. Peterson, June 15, 1968; children: Jennifer Anne, Amy Kristine, Michael Sheridan. BA, U. Notre Dame, 1967; cert. English law, U. Coll. Law, 1969; JD, U. Notre Dame, 1970. Bar: Ill. 1970, U.S. Ct. Appeals (7th cir.) 1970, U.S. Dist. Ct. (no. dist.) Ill. 1970, U.S. Dist. Ct. (cen. dist.) Ill. 1978, U.S. Supreme Ct. 1980. Law clk. to presiding justice U.S. Ct. Appeals (7th cir.), Chgo., 1970-71; assoc. Sidley Austin Brown & Wood LLP, Chgo., 1971-76, ptnr., 1977—. Mem. ABA, Ill. Bar Assn., Chgo. Bar Assn., Legal Club. Home: 948 Ridge Ave Evanston IL 60202-1720 Office: Sidley Austin LLP One S Dearborn St Chicago IL 60603-2000 Home Phone: 847-475-5570; Office Phone: 312-853-7464. E-mail: jhardgrove@sidley.com.

HARDIE, GEORGE GRAHAM, casino executive; b. Cleve., Aug. 19, 1933; s. William M. and Helen (Graham) H.; children: George Graham Jr., Jennifer. With sales dept. Hardie Bros., Pitts., later various mgmt. positions, operator dist. sales agys.; owner, driver, trainer, racer standardbred horses, 1963—; owner, mgr. Profile, Inc., Las Vegas, 1973—; founder, mng. ptnr. Bell Gardens Bicycle Club Casino, 1984-94; mayor City of Cathedral City, Calif., 1988-90, mayor pro tem, 1990-92; owner, mgr. Profile Comm. Inc., 1990—, Hardie's Korn Kettle Inc., 1990—, Hardie's Korn Kettle Gold, 2003; owner Las Vegas Hotel & Casino, Belize. Owner, mgr. investment and acquisitions co. Lodestar Internat. Inc. (formerly The Hardie Group), 1990—; owner Emerald Meadows Ranch, 1989—. Active cmty. and civic affairs. Recipient Congl. award, 1987; commendation L.A. County Suprs., 1987, L.A. County Office Dist. Atty., 1987; resolution Calif. Senate, 1987, cert. of recognition City of Bell Gardens, 1987; named Man of Yr. Variety Boys & Girls Club of the Desert, 1996. Mem. Calif. Harness Drivers Guild (past pres.), Western Standardbred Assn. (past bd. dirs.), Golden State Greyhound Assn. (organizer, pres. 1973), Bell Gardens C. of C. (pres. 1986). Achievements include owner of largest casino in Central America. Office: Lodestar Internat Inc 1350 E Flamingo Rd # 347 Las Vegas NV 89119 Home Phone: 702-262-6773; Office Phone: 702-891-5252. E-mail: gghardie@aol.com.

HARDIE, JAMES CARL, academic administrator, consultant; b. Pitts., June 10, 1922; s. Stanley Frank and Helen Katherine (Wassel) H.; m. Emma Kathryn Cepko, Jan. 28, 1956; children: James Matthew, Lynn Anne BA, U. Pitts., 1943, ML, 1948. Counselor U. Pitts., 1946, dir. athletic publicity, 1947—48; dir. housing, head men's dormitories Carnegie Inst. Tech., Pitts., 1946—47; dir. campaign Ketchum, Inc., Pitts., 1948—57; dir. devel., v.p. Case Inst. Tech., Cleve., 1957—67; v.p. Case We. Res. U., Cleve., 1967—69; cons. to more than 60 non-profit instns. Cleve., 1969—. Author: Fred Crawford and Fifty Golden Years of Philanthropy, 2005. Chmn. bd. Jennings Found. Yardstick Project, 1968-81; founder Corp. 1% Program for Higher Edn., 1961-69; trustee George S. Dively Found., 1985-97. Lt. U.S. Army, 1943-45 Decorated Purple Heart; recipient Disting. Svc. award Ohio Coun. Fund-Raising Execs., 1988, Citation Coun. Fin. Aid to Edn., 1979; named Outstanding Profl. Nat. Soc. Fund-Raising Profls., 1991 Mem. Union Club Cleve., Grenelefe Country Club Fla., Omicron Delta Kappa, Delta Sigma Rho Republican. Avocations: golf, reading, gardening, piano, writing. also: 1508 Ocean Dr Apt 103 Vero Beach FL 32963-5346

HARDIE, JAMES HILLER, retired lawyer; b. Pitts., Dec. 1, 1929; s. James H. and Elizabeth Gillespie (Alcorn) H.; m. Frances P. Curtis, Dec. 5, 1953; children: J. Hiller, Janet Hardie Harvey, Andrew G., Michael C., Rachel Hardie Share. AB, Princeton U., 1951; LL.B., Harvard U., 1954. Bar: Pa. 1955. Assoc. Reed Smith LLP, Pitts., 1954-62, ptnr., 1962-99, of counsel, 1999—2005, ret., 2005. Mem. ABA, Am. Law Inst., Pa. Bar Assn. E-mail: jhardie@reedsmith.com.

HARDIE, MICHAEL HOWARD, mathematician, educator; b. Marysville, Calif., Sept. 4, 1949; s. Howard Keith and Barbara Jane Hardie; m. Lynda Lee Morrison, Sept. 26, 1970 (div. Sept. 1996); children: Stephanie Rebecca, Virginia Catherine; m. Joseph Henry Edson, June 17, 2000. BS in Math., U. Santa Clara, 1971; EdM, U. Idaho, 1976, MS in Math., 1977; EdD, U. Nev., 1990. Tchr. Prairie H.S., Cottonwood, Idaho, 1972—74, Pullman (Wash.) H.S., 1976—81; prof. Western Nev. Coll., Carson City, 1981—. Recipient Horizon award, Phi Theta Kappa, 1992; Brown fellow, U. Santa Clara, 1971—72. Mem.: Nev. Math. Assn. Two-Yr. Colls. (pres. 2003—05).

HARDIMAN, JOSEPH RAYMOND, security firm executive; b. Salisbury, Md., May 27, 1937; s. Leonard Roy and Virginia Mildred (Darden) H.; m. Katherine McCampbell, Mar. 23, 1963; children: Katherine Hughes, Elizabeth Gore. BA, U. Md., Coll. Pk., 1959; LLB, U. Md., Balt., 1962. Bar: Md. 1962. Law clk. to Hon. Hall Hammond Md. Ct. of Appeals, 1962-63; assoc. Miles & Stockbridge, Balt., 1963-68; exec. v.p., sec., dir. Robert Garrett & Sons, Inc., Balt., 1968-75; gen. ptnr. Alex. Brown & Sons, 1975-87, mng. dir., COO, 1984-87; pres., CEO, dir. Nat. Assn. Securities Dealers, Inc., 1987-97, Nasdaq Stock Market, Inc., 1987-97. Bd. dirs. Franklin Resources, Inc., Brown Investment Adv. and Trust Co. Bd. dirs. Arthritis Found., Md., 1975-79, pres., 1976-78; bd. dirs. Balt. Urban Coalition, 1975-78, U. Md. Med. Sys., 1980-86, Fund for Ednl. Excellence, 1984-91, Ctr. for the Study of the Presidency, 1992-97, U. Md. Found., 1992-2000, U. Md. Balt. Found., 2000—; steering com. Baltimore County Charter Rev. Commn., 1977-78; trustee St. Paul's Sch. for Girls, 1978-86, Balt. Sch. for the Arts, 2002-06, Balt. Chesapeake Bay Outward Bound, 2005-07, Securities Industry Found. Econ. Edn., 1988-96; adv. bd. U. Calif. Securities Regulation Inst., 1988-97; bd. visitors U. Md. Sch. Law, 1990—; active Am. Bus. Conf., Con. on Competitiveness, 1994-97. Mem. Md. Club, Elkridge Club (Balt.), Gulfstream Club (Fla.), Order of Coif, Phi Delta Theta, Omicron Delta Kappa. Home: 540 Old School Rd Delray Beach FL 33483

HARDIMAN, THOMAS MICHAEL, federal judge; b. Winchester, Mass., July 8, 1965; s. Robert and Judith Hardiman; m. Lori Hardiman; 3 children. BA, U. Notre Dame, 1987; JD, Georgetown U. Law Ctr., 1990. Assoc. Skadden, Arps, Slate, Meagher & Flom LLP, Washington, 1990—92, Titus & McConomy LLP (formerly Cindrich & Titus), Pitts., 1992—96, ptnr., 1996—99, Reed Smith LLP, 1999—2003; judge US Dist. Ct. (we. dist.) Pa., Pitts., 2003—07, US Ct. Appeals (3rd cir.), Phila., 2007—. Hearing officer Disciplinary Bd., Pa. Supreme Ct., 1995—99, alt. hearing mem., 1999—2003. Dir. Big Brothers Big Sisters of Greater Pitts., Inc., 1995—, pres., 1999—2000. Recipient Nancy B. Zappala Svc. award, Big Brothers Big Sisters of Greater Pitts., Inc., 2002. Mem.: ABA (mem. Ho. Delegates 1996—98), Pa. Bar Assn. (mem. professionalism com. 1999—2003), Allegheny County Bar Assn., DC Bar Assn., Mass. Bar Assn. Office: US Ct Appeals 601 Market St Philadelphia PA 19106*

HARDIN, ADLAI STEVENSON, JR., judge; b. Norwalk, Conn., Sept. 20, 1937; s. Adlai S. and Carol H. BA, Princeton U., 1959; LLB, Columbia U., 1962. Bar: N.Y. 1963, U.S. Dist. Ct. (so. and ea. dists.) N.Y. 1965, U.S. Supreme Ct. 1967, U.S. Ct. Appeals (2d cir.) 1965, U.S. Ct. Appeals (5th cir.) 1974, U.S. Ct. Appeals (3d cir.) 1977, U.S. Ct. Appeals (9th cir.) 1982, U.S. Ct. Appeals (4th and D.C. cirs.) 1985, U.S. Ct. Appeals (7th cir.) 1988. Assoc. Milbank, Tweed, Hadley & McCloy, NYC, 1963, ptnr., 1971; judge U.S. Bankruptcy Ct., 1995—. Judge Bankruptcy Appellate Panel for 2d Circuit, 1996-2000. Trustee Spence Sch., 1981-87; former elder, trustee Madison Ave. Presbyn. Ch. With USAR, 1962-68. Mem. ABA (past chmn. N.Y. State membership com., antitrust sect., litigation sect.), Fed. Bar Coun. (trustee 1983-92, v.p. 1986-88, chmn. bd. dirs. 1990-92), Fed. Bar Found. (pres. 1992-94), N.Y. State Bar Assn. (mem. com. on profl. ethics, mem. jud. election monitoring com., mem. internat. litigation com.), Assn. of Bar of City of N.Y. (sec. 1979-82, chmn. com. on profl. and jud. ethics 1970-73, mem. spl. com. on lawyers role in securities transactions, mem. spl. com. to cooperate with ABA in revision of Canons of Ethics, mem. nominating com., mem. com. on membership, mem. com. on profl. discipline), Nat. Conf. Bankruptcy Judges, Am. Bankruptcy Inst., Westchester County Bar Assn. Office: US Bankruptcy Ct US Courthouse 300 Quarropas St White Plains NY 10601-4150

HARDIN, ANN, marriage and family therapist; b. Findlay, Ohio, Aug. 2, 1947; d. Richard Clair and Ethelyn Lois (Miller) Webber; m. John Westley Hardin, Dec. 6, 1969; children: David Jason, Christopher John. AA in Mgmt./Supervision, L.A. Met. Coll., Guam, 1981; BSW, U. Mo., 1984, MSW, 1985. Cert. clin. social worker. Bookkeeper, cashier Pub. Fin. Corp., Findlay, Ohio, 1965-66; office mgr. Grange Mut. Casualty Co., Findlay, 1967-68; exec. br. fed. govt., Washington, 1969; office mgr. Animals Hosps., Inc., Vallejo, Calif., 1970-73; dir. Option, Inc./Project Concern Internat., San Diego, 1975-78; counselor Navy Family Svc. Ctr., Guam, 1985-92; family therapist client svcs. and family counseling divsn. Superior Ct. Guam, 1992—2005. Faculty U. Guam/Sch. of S.W., 1990-91, 96-97, 98-99; mem. Gov.'s Task Force on Child Sexual Abuse, 1986-90, Gov.'s Task Force on Suicide, Guam, 1990, Gov.'s Task Force on Domestic Violence, 1993-2005; presenter confs. in field, including Joint World Congress of Internat. Fedn. Social Workers and Internat. Assn. Schs. of Social Work, 1996. Adult leader Young Christian Life, Guam, 1985-91; team presentor Cath. Engaged Encounter, Guam and Mo., 1982-92; founder Sexually Assaulted Female Enrichment Group, Multiagy. Sexual Abuse Treatment Group, Women Survivors of Ptnr. Abuse Group, Sexually Assaulted Female Edn. and Recovery Group. Named Outstanding Grad. Student, Sch. Social Work, Columbia, Mo., 1985, Woman of Yr. Bur. Women's Affairs Guam, 2002. Mem. NASW (clin. social worker, conf. presenter 2001, Lifetime Achievement award Guam chpt. 2004), Guam Assn. of Social Workers (Social Worker of Yr. 1991, v.p. 1993-94, conf. chairperson 1994, 98), Guam Assn. Marriage and Family Therapists (v.p. 1990-91), Acad. Cert. Social Workers, Mizzou Alumni Assn. Roman Catholic. Home: 1501 Vista Cir Copperas Cove TX 76522 Personal E-mail: ajhardin@hotmail.com.

HARDIN, BONIFACE, academic administrator; Student, St. Meinrad Coll., 1955, MDiv, 1959; postgrad., U. Notre Dame, 1963; LHD (hon.), Gov.'s State U. Ordained, 1959. Pres. Martin U., Indpls. Prodr., co-host (radio program) WIAN and WFYI-FM, 1971-91, (tv program) Afro-American, 1974-79; editor Afro-Am. Jour., Martin U. Mem. St. Meinrad Archabbey, 1953—; vol. fireman St. Meinrad Fire Dept., 1954-60; bd. dirs. Pres. Benjamin Harrison Home, Indpls. (Ind.) Project Against Aids for Minorities; adv. bd. mem. Indpls. (Ind.) Salvation Army; active Indpls. (Ind.) Children's Choir, Voluntary Adv. Corps, Ind. State Penal Reform Com.; bd. mem. Rsch. Role of Pub. Defender, Indpls. Bar Assn. Commn.; chmn. Nat. Sickle Cell Confidentiality Com.; co-chairperson Indpls. Black Coalition; adv. Reforms in Police Cmty. Rels. Recipient Dirs. award Ctr. for Leadership Devel., Disting. and Valuable Svc. to Humankind award Eta Chi Sorority, Scroll of Merit award Nat. Med. Assn., Appreciation cert. Mt. Pisgah Bapt. Ch. and the Brightwood Cmty., Appreciation cert. Richard Roudebush, VA Med. Ctr., The African-Am. Subcom. of the EEO Adv. Com., Appreciation cert. U.S. Dept. HUD, Ecumenical Svc. award Ind. Black Expo, Pres. Image award Urban League of Madison County, Inc., many others. Office: Martin Univ Office of the President 2171 Avondale Pl Indianapolis IN 46218-3878

HARDIN, BRIDGETTE EVERHART, educational research analyst; d. Arnold Alonzo and Twyla Gale Everhart; m. Eric Robert Hardin, Aug. 30, 1992. BA in Psychology, Met. State Coll. Denver, 1992, BA in Comm., 1992; MS in Occupl. Career Tng. Devel., Tex. A&M U., Corpus Christi, 2002. State master PRIDE train the trainer Tex. Dept. Protective and Regulatory Svcs., 1999, works welfare advisor Dept. Human Sevcs., Tex., 1996; cert. mgmt. devel. Governor's Ctr. Mgmt. Devel., Tex., 2003. Social worker Tex. Dept. Human Svcs., Corpus Christi, 1996—99; adj. psychology prof. Del Mar C.C., Corpus Christi, 1997—99; foster, adopt master pride trainer Tex. Dept. Protective and Regulatory Svcs., Corpus Christi, 1999—2002, leadership devel. coord., 2002—03; rsch. analyst, cons. Tex. A&M U., Corpus Christi, 2003—; pres. South Tex. Consortium for Instnl. Rsch., 2005—. Author: (children's story) Zachary's Special Gift; contbr. assessment guide. Named to V.P. George Bush's Honor Roll, US Dept. Edn., 1989—92; recipient Thinking Out of the Box award, Tex. Dept. Protective and Regulatory Svcs., 2000, Dean of Senate Collegiate Recognition award, State of Tex. Sen. Carlos Truan, 2002, State of Tex. Commendation award, Gov. and State of Tex. through Tex. Dept. Protective and Regulatory Svcs., 2003, Above and Beyond medallion, Tex. A&M U., Corpus Christi, 2004, Celebrating Excellence medallion, EEOC- Tex. A&M U., Corpus Christi, 2004; scholar, Coll. Edn., Tex. A&M U., Corpus Christi, 2005; Youth Leadership Devel. grantee, Ctr. for Edn. Devel. and Edn. Rsch., 2005. Mem.: Am. Soc. Tng. Devel. (assoc.), South Tex. Consortium Instl. Rsch. (assoc.), Tex. Assn. Instl. Rsch. (assoc.). Achievements include design of Texas state employee wellness program; motivation organization model for Texas state employees. Home Phone: 361-949-1910; Office Phone: 361-825-5989.

HARDIN, CHRISTOPHER DEMAREST, medical educator; b. Syracuse, NY, July 31, 1961; BS in Biology, Cornell U., 1983; MS in Physiology, U. Rochester, 1986; PhD in Physiology and Biophysics, U. Cin., 1989. Sr. fellow Dept. Radiology U. Wash., Seattle, 1989-91, rsch. asst. prof. dept. radiology, 1991—93; asst. prof. physiology U. Mo., Columbia, 1993—99, assoc. prof. physiology, 1999—. Tutor, mentor, spkr. and cons. in field. Mem. internat. adv. bd. Physiological Research, 1997-; reviewer numerous jours.; guest reviewer 29 jours. in field; contbr. articles to profl. jours.; contbr. chpts. to books. Albert J. Ryan fellow, 1986-89, Tng. Grant fellow U. Cin.,. 1985-86, Univ. Grad. fellow U. Rochester, 1983-85; recipient Jeffrey D. Doane Meml. award, 1987, Nat. Rsch. Svc. award, 1989-92, Dorsett L. Spurgeon Disting. Med. Rsch. award, 1999, other numerous awards and grants. Mem. AAAS, Internat. Soc. Heart Rsch. (N.Am. sect), Am. Physiol. Soc. (Harold Lamport award outstanding young investigator 1995), Biophysical Soc., Am. Physiological Soc. (elected fellow 2002, awards com. 2005-), Metabolomics Soc., Biophys. Soc., Am. Assn. Advancement Sci., Am. Heart Assn. (mem. sci. coun. basic sci. 1995-). Home: 4480 Roemer Rd Columbia MO 65202-7060 Office: Univ Mo Dept Physiology MA415 Med Sci Bldg Columbia MO 65212-0001 Business E-Mail: harding@missouri.edu.

HARDIN, DALE WAYNE, political science professor; b. Peoria, Ill., Sept. 9, 1922; s. James P. and Lucille Maureen (Elgin) H.; m. Sandra L. Gorzen, July 3, 1939; children: Bradley J., Stacy Alexander, Rebecca Kuplas, J. Scott Keaton. AB in Polit. Sci., George Washington U., 1949, JD, 1951. Bar: Va. 1951, D.C. 1951, U.S. Dist. D.C. 1951, U.S. Ct. Appeals (D.C. cir.) 1951. Assoc. Mills & Partridge, Washington, 1951; spl. agent FBI, Washington, 1951-54; fin. counsel ICC, Washington, 1954-55, legis. counsel, 1955-64, presdl. appointee as commr., 1967-77, vice chmn., acting chmn. agy., 1971-73, chmn. rates divsn., 1975-77; Presdl. appointee, mem. Adminstrv. Conf. U.S., 1969-72; dir. dept. transp. and comm. U.S. C. of C., Washington, 1964-66; v.p. govt. affairs Overmeyer Co., Washington, 1966-67; spl. counsel Am. Trucking Assn., Washington, 1967; assoc. prof. polit sci. S.W. Tex. State U. (now Tex. State U.), San Marcos, Tex., 1977—, assoc. prof. emeritus, 1989—2006, acting dean sch. liberal arts., 1986-87, chmn. dept. home econs., 1990-92; ret. law educator, 2000. Gen. counsel Transp. Assn. Am., Washington, 1959; exec. v.p. GC Wheaton Van Lines, Indpls., 1981-82; moderator 14th Ann. Seminar, State Bar Tex., 1982, moderator profl. devel. program gen. paralegal skills, 1988, standing com. on legal assts., 1988-00; chmn. Tex. forum IV Conf. Legal Asst. Educators, 1985, chair forum VII, 1988; presenter papers in field. Bus. sec. George Washington U. Sch. Law Rev., 1951. Bd. dirs. U. Christian Ch., 2006—. With USMC, 1942—46, PTO. Mem. Soc. Former Spl. Agents FBI. Fed. Bar Assn., Va. State Bar., D.C. Bar, Phi Delta Phi. Avocation: golf. Home: 54 Rainey St #406 Austin TX 78701-4311 E-mail: docnsand@austin.rr.com.

HARDIN, EDWARD LESTER, JR., lawyer; b. Wetumpka, Ala., Mar. 29, 1940; s. Edward Lester and Katherine (Williams) H.; m. Lila Manor, June 10, 1962; children: Leigh Hardin Hancock, Caroline Hardin Butler, Laura Elizabeth, Edward Lester III. BA, Birmingham So. Coll., 1962; JD, U. Ala., 1965. Bar: Ala. 1965, U.S. Dist. Ct. (no., mid. and so. dists.) Ala. 1965, U.S. Ct. Appeals (11th cir.), U.S. Supreme Ct. Pvt. law practice, 1965—98; exec. v.p., gen. counsel, bd. dirs. Caremark Rx, Inc., Nashville, 1998—2007. Bd. trustees Birmingham So. Coll. Mem. editl. bd. U. Ala. Law Rev., 1964-65 Trustee Birmingham So. Coll. Mem. ABA, Am. Bd. Trial Advs., Ala. Bar Assn., Ala. Trial Lawyers Assn. (exec. com., pres. 1975-76), Omicron Delta Kappa, Phi Alpha Delta. Methodist. Avocations: marlin fishing, golf. Home Phone: 615-463-3009; Office Phone: 615-743-6615. Business E-Mail: ed.hardin@caremarkrx.com.*

HARDIN, EUGENE BROOKS, JR., bank executive; b. Wilmington, NC, Oct. 18, 1930; s. Eugene Brooks Hardin and Roberta Gilmour (Sterling) Demme; m. Olivia Lynch, Aug. 16, 1958; children: John Haywood II, Olivia Cary. BS, U. N.C., 1952. With Wachovia Bank & Trust Co., Wilmington, 1956—, asst. v.p., 1957-60, v.p., 1962-68, sr. v.p., 1969-72, sr. v.p., regional exec. Raleigh, 1972-79, regional v.p., 1979-95; cashier Burlington, NC, 1961-62; ret., 1995. Bd. dirs. Wachovia Bank, Raleigh, N.C. Pres., bd. dirs. Babies Hosp., Wilmington, 1968-72; pres. United Fund, 1970; treas., trustee Episcopalian Diocese East Carolina, 1965-72; chmn. Raleigh Civic Center Authority, 1978-81; chmn. Raleigh-Durham Airport Authority, 1981-82; chmn. bd. trustees St. Mary's Coll., 1979-85; bd. dirs. Children's Home Soc. N.C. Served with USNR, 1948-49; to lst lt. USAF, 1952-56. Mem. Robert Morris Assos. Clubs: Civitan (pres. Wilmington 1971-72); Carolina Yacht (Wrightsville Beach); Carolina Country (Raleigh); Cape Fear Country (Wilmington); Land Fall (Wilmington). Home: 404 Drummond Dr Raleigh NC 27609-7006

HARDIN, HAL D., lawyer, judge, former US attorney; BA, Middle Tenn. State U.; JD, Vanderbilt U., 1968. Bar: Tenn., D.C., Tex., Ky., U.S. Ct. Claims, U.S. Tax. Ct., U.S. Ct. Mil. Appeals, U.S. Supreme Ct. Dir. St. Louis Job Corps Ctr.; vol. Peace Corps; asst. dist. atty.; pvt. practice; presiding judge Nashville Trial Cts., 1976-77; spl. judge Ct. of Appeals, 1977; U.S. atty. Middle Dist. Tenn., 1977-81; practice law Nashville, 1981—. Adj. prof. Aquinas Coll., Tenn. State U., 1975—76; faculty emeritus Nashville Sch. Law, 1993—. Bd. dirs. Nat. Assn. Former U.S. Atty., 1993—96, Leadership Nashville, 1983, Capital Case Resource Ctr., 1988—95, Leadership Alumni Assn., 1985. Master: Inns of Ct.; fellow: Tenn. Bar Found.; mem.: Washington D.C. Bar Assn., Ky. Bar Assn., Nat. Peace Corps Assn. (bd. dirs. 2001—04), Am. Bd. Trial Advs. (sec. Tenn. chpt. 1987, nat. bd. dirs. 1988—89, pres. Tenn. chpt. 1990), 6th Cir. Jud. Coun. (life), Tenn. Criminal Def. Attys. Assn., Nat. Criminal Def. Attys. Assn., Tex. Bar Assn., Tenn. Bar Assn. (gen. counsel 1982—90), Nashville Bar Assn. (bd. dirs. 1983—85, v.p. 1985, Criminal Law Excellence award 2006). Office Phone: 615-369-3377.

HARDIN, HARRY S., III, lawyer; b. New Orleans, June 7, 1945; s. Harry Simms and Evelyn Louise (Kelleher) H.; m. Ellen Lutz; children: Simms, Elizabeth, Allison. BA cum laude, Harvard U., 1967; JD, Tulane U., 1971. Bar: La. 1971, U.S. Dist. Ct. (ea., we. and mid. dists.) La. 1971, U.S. Ct. Appeals (5th cir.) 1971, U.S. Supreme Ct. 1975, U.S. Dist. Ct. (we. dist.) La. 1979, U.S. Ct. Appeals (11th cir.) 1981, U.S. Ct. Appeals (fed. cir.) 1985. Assoc. Jones, Walker, Waechter, Poitevent, Carrère & Denegre, New Orleans, 1971-76; ptnr. Jones, Walker, Waechter, Poitevent, Carrère & Denègre, New Orleans, 1976—. Mem.long range planning com. La. Supreme Ct. 1975-78, com. time standards for dist. cts., ex-officio mem. com. judicial ethics, 1993; instr. Loyola Law Sch., 1987-93; adv. com. La. Pub. Broadcasting Project Legal Ease, 1992. Co-author: Managed Care and Antitrust: The PPO Experience, 1990. Past chmn. Ptnrs. in Art, New Orleans Mus. Art; past bd. dirs. Met. Safety Coun., Garden Dist. Assn., past pres.; trustee United Way, Greater New Orleans, 1986-92, chmn. unit III, 1986, pacesetter chmn., 1987, chmn. campaigns, 1988, admissions, sr. mgrs. speakers bur., long range planning com., 1989—, cultivation group, 1990, mem. exec. campaign cabinet; bd. dirs. pro bono project, New Orleans, 1987-93; bd. dirs. Met. Area Com., 1991-92, exec. com., legis. issues com., chmn. local govt. fin. com., exec. com. MAC/MAC Found.; La. vol. lawyer for arts; chmn. stewardship St. Charles Presbyn. Ch., 1992, elder, 1993; regional co-chmn. Harvard Coll. Fund, class agent; bldg. com. Tulane Law Sch. Recipient Ten Outstanding People honor Inst. Human Understanding, 1992. Fellow La. Bar Found. (ex-officio bd. dirs. 1987-93, exec. com. interest on lawyers' trust accts. grants com. 1992-93); mem. ABA (anti-trust sect. 1974—, com. fed. procedure, healthcare com., patent and trademark sect. 1975—, litigation sect. 1978—, com. intellectural properties litigation, corp. counsel subcom., law practice mgmt. sect. 1991—, ann. meeting adv. com. 1994—, bd. govs, 2005-), Internat. Assn. Def. Counsel (com. bus. litigation 1990-93, toxic and hazardous substance litigation, 1990-93), Nat. Assn. Railroad Trial Counsel, Am. Soc. Hosp. Attys., La. State Bar Assn. (ho. dels. 1980-87, 89-91, bd. govs. 1987-89, 91-92, sec.-treas. 1987-89, editor jour. 1987-89, pres. exec. com. 1987-89, chmn. uniform admissions com. 1988-89, com. to evaluate interest on lawyers trust accts. 1988-90, implementation com. 1990-91, vice-chmn. spl. com. malpractice ins. 1988-91, chmn. com. bar governance 1989-92, liaison bd. govs. various coms. 1991-92, pres.-elect 1992-93, pres. 1993-94), La. Judicial Coll. (ex-officio bd. govs.), La. State Law Inst. (coun. 1993—), La. Soc. Hosp. Attys., La. Assn. Defense Coun., New Orleans Def. Counsel Assn., Defense Rsch. Inst., Harvard Alumni Assn. (regional bd. dirs., sec.), Harvard Club La. (pres., chmn. schs., scholarship com.). Avocations: golf, tennis, sailing, gardening, philanthropic activities. Office: Jones Walker Waechter 201 Saint Charles Ave Ste 5200 New Orleans LA 70170-5100

HARDIN, JAMES CARLISLE, III, lawyer, educator; b. Charlotte, NC, Sept. 12, 1948; s. James Carlisle Jr. and Mary Gene (Roberts) H.; m. Sally M. Drennan, June 6, 1968 (div. Dec. 1973); 1 child, Christine M.; m. Caryle Wilson (dec. June 1986); 1 child, James Carlisle IV; m. Katharine C. Harrison, May 2, 1992. AB, Wofford Coll., 1969; MA in History, U. Va., 1970, postgrad., 1970-71; JD, Duke U., 1974. Bar: S.C. 1974, U.S. Dist. Ct. S.C. 1976, N.C. 1989; U.S. Dist. Ct. (we. dist.) N.C. 1989; cert. legal specialist in estate planning and probate law, SC, NC. Ptnr. Roddey, Carpenter & White, P.A., Rock Hill, SC, 1974-86, Kennedy Covington Lobdell & Hickman, Charlotte & Rock Hill, SC, 1986—2005; atty. James C. Hardin III and Assocs., PLLC, 2005—. Chmn. specialization adv. bd. S.C. Supreme Ct., 1988-90; mem. S.C. Comm. on Continuing Lawyer Competence and Specialization, 1990-97; instr. Winthrop Univ., Rock Hill, 1979-91; mem. sect. coun. Probate Estate Planning and Trust Sect. S.C. Bar, 1997—, chmn., 1981, 91, 2003; bd. dirs. Rock Hill Econ. Devel. Corp., chmn. 1998-2000. Mem. bd. dirs. Rock Hill YMCA, 1986-89, S.C. Meth. Found., 1986—; bd. dirs. St. John's United Meth. Ch., Rock Hill, 1997—; bd. dirs. Piedmount Med. Ctr., 1994—2000, chmn., 1996. Fellow Am. Coll. Trust and Estate Coun. (state chmn. 1991-); mem. Rock Hill C. of C. (bd. dirs. 1991-95), Kiwanis (bd. dirs. Rock Hill 1978-80), Rock Hill Country Club, Phi Beta Kappa. Avocations: golf, swimming. Office: James C Hardin III & Assocs PLLC 113 E Main St Rock Hill SC 29730 Office Phone: 803-329-7601.

HARDIN, JAMES NEAL, language educator, writer; b. Nashville, Feb. 17, 1939; s. James N. and Ina M. (Anderson) H.; m. Anne Farr. AB summa cum laude, Washington and Lee U., 1960; postgrad., U. Berlin, 1960-61; PhD, U. NC, 1967. Prof. German lit. U. S.C., Columbia, 1969—98. Pres. Hardin Pub. Inc. Author: Co-founder, Camden House, imprint published by Boydell & Brewer Ltd., Johann Beer, 1983, Johann Beer Bibliographie, 1984, Christian Gryphius Bibliographie, 1985, J.C. Ettner Bibliographie, 1988; editor: Der Verliebte Oesterreicher, 1977; editor/co-editor: Dictionary of Lit. Biography, Vols. 59, 66, 69, 81, 85, 90, 94, 97, 118, 124, 129, 133, 138, 148, 194 and 168, Goethe's Wilhelm Meister's Travels, 1991; founder, co-editor: Studies in German Language, Literature and Linguistics, Works of Christian Gryphius, 2 vols., 1985; contbr. articles to profl. jours. and mags. Capt. U.S. Army, 1967-69. Decorated Army Commendation medal; recipient Alexander von Humbolt award, 1974-75, Russell award for scholarship, 1979, German-Am. Friendship award, 2004; Fulbright scholar, 1960-61 Mem. MLA, South Atlantic MLA. Home Phone: 864-235-7571; Office Phone: 864-235-7571. Personal E-mail: jamesnhardin@bellsouth.net.

HARDIN, JAMES W., botanist, educator, herbarium curator; b. Mar. 31, 1929; BS, Fla. So. Coll., 1950; MS, U. Tenn., 1951; PhD, U. Mich., 1957. Instr. U. Mich., 1956-57; from asst. prof. to prof. N.C. State U., Raleigh, 1957-68, prof., 1968-96, emeritus prof., 1996—, curator herbarium, 1957-96. Vis. prof. Mountain Lake Biological Sta. U.Va., summers 1962, 64, 83, U. Okla. Biological Sta., summers 1967, 70; mem. exec. com. Flora Southeastern U.S., 1966-97; endangered species com. N.C. Dept. Natural & Econ. Resources, 1973-74, natural areas adv. com., 1973-79; mem. plant conservation sci. com. N.C. Dept. Agriculture, 1980-97, chmn. 1987-97; mem. endangered species com. N.C. Wildlife Resources Commn., 1976-78, N.C. State Mus. Natural Hist., 1975-78; pres. Highlands Biological Station, Inc., 1963-69, trustee, 1958-69, sec., 1960-63; invited symposium speaker. Author: Human Poisoning, 1974, Textbook of Dendrology, 2001; editor ASB Bull., 1980-86; mem. editorial com. Am. Jour. Botany, 1964-66; mem. editorial bd. Brittonia, 1964-67, Brimleyana, 1975-97; reviewer jours. in field. Trustee Highlands Biol. Found., 1976—2005. Recipient Outstanding Tchr. award, NC State U., 1966—67, 1969—70. Mem. Am. Soc. Plant Taxonomists (pub. policy com. 1976-78, editorial bd. 1964-67, editor-in-chief Systematic Botany 1985-91, pres. elect 1991-92, pres. 1992-93, past pres. 1993-94, Cooley award 1958), Southern Appalachian Botanical Club (v.p. 1959-60, pres. 1964-65, Bartholomew award 1994), Botanical Soc. Am. (editorial com. 1964-66, chair southeastern sect. 1968-69), Assn. Southeastern Biologists (Meritorious Teaching award 1991, chmn. local arrangements 1966, 77, v.p. 1968-69, pres. 1979-80, editor 1980-86), Soc. Economic Botany (chmn. local arrangements 1979), Phi Kappa Phi, Sigma Xi (exec. com. N.C. chpt. 1962-63, sec. 1965-66, treas. 1966-67, v.p. 1967-68, program chmn. 1968-69, pres. 1969-70). Home: 204 Furches St Raleigh NC 27607-4056 E-mail: jwhardin@mindspring.com.

HARDIN, JANET BECKER, gifted and talented educator, music educator; b. Knoxville, Tenn., Oct. 26, 1952; d. M. Carl and Mary Evelyn (Carruth) Becker; m. Richard Vardry Hardin, Aug. 3, 1974; children: Patrick Vardry, Richard Nathaniel, Michael Joseph. MusB, Carson-Newman Coll., Jefferson City, TN, 1974; MA in Elem. Edn., Furman U., Greenville, SC, 2002. Cert. music edn. K-12 SC, elem. edn. SC, gifted edn. SC. Math asst. A.R. Lewis Elem. Sch., Pickens, SC, 1993—94; tchr. music and gifted and talented Ambler Elem. Sch., Pickens, SC, 1994—, tchr. art, 1995—98, sch. web mgr., 1998—; gifted and talented tchr. Holly Springs Elem., Pickens, SC, 1998—99; choral dir. Lakes and Mountains Sch. Arts, Pickens, SC, 2005—. Editor, author (oral history collection) Ambler Elementary School: Our Heritage, Ambler Elementary School: Our Legacy. Publicity chmn. PTO Ambler Elem. Sch., Pickens, 1991—92, pres. PTO, 1992—94; co-dir. Arts and CATS Spring Arts Festival, Pickens, 1995—; dir. children's choir Saluda Hill Bapt. Ch., Cleveland, SC, 1974—81, adult choir dir., 1974—, ch. pianist, 1974—. Named Tchr. of Yr., Ambler Elem. Sch., 2002; grantee, Humanities Coun. SC, 2004—05, SCEIA, 2006—07; Robinson grantee, Constl. Rights Found., 2003—04. Mem.: SC Music Educators Assn., Music Educators Nat. Conf., SC Consortium for Gifted Edn. Baptist. Achievements include discovery of Ambler's history. Avocations: playing dulcimer, singing. Office: Ambler Elem Sch 838 Ambler Sch Rd Pickens SC 29671 Home Phone: 864-836-8540; Office Phone: 864-898-5588. Office Fax: 864-898-5589; Home Fax: 864-836-5282. Business E-Mail: hardinjb@pickens.k12.sc.us.

HARDIN, LOWELL STEWART, retired economics professor; b. nr. Knightstown, Ind., Nov. 16, 1917; s. J. Fred and Mildred (Stewart) H.; m. Mary J. Cooley, Sept. 21, 1940; children: Thomas Stewart, Joyce Ann, Peter Lowell. BS, Purdue U., 1939, DAgr (hon.), 1990; PhD, Cornell U., 1943. Grad. asst., instr. Cornell U., 1939-43; instr., asst. and assoc. prof., prof. Purdue U., 1943-65, adj. prof. agrl. econs., 1965-66, prof., 1981-84, emeritus prof., asst. dir. internat. programs, 1984—, acting head dept. agrl. econs., 1954-57, head dept., 1957-65; also dir. Purdue Work Simplification Lab. Program adviser agr. Ford Found., 1965-66, program officer agr., 1966-81; former trustee Internat. Food Policy Rsch. Inst., Washington, Internat. Ctr. for Agrl. Rsch. in Dry Areas, Aleppo, Syria, Internat. Svc. for Nat. Agrl. Rsch., The Hague, The Netherlands, Winrock Internat. Inst. for Agrl. Devel., Little Rock, Ark. Author: (with L.M. Vaughan) Farm Work Simplification, 1949. Fellow AAAS, Am. Agrl. Econ. Assn. (pres. 1963-64); mem. Internat. Assn. Agrl. Economists, Sigma Xi, Alpha Gamma Rho, Phi Kappa Phi, Alpha Zeta, Sigma Delta Chi. Federated Church. Home: 2628 Calvin Ct W Lafayette IN 47906-1402 Office Phone: 765-494-8460.

HARDIN, MARK A., legal association administrator; b. Portland, Oreg., Sept. 13, 1945; s. Keith and Leah Hardin; 1 child, Nicole Stenson. BA in Polit. Sci., U. Calif., Berkeley, 1967; JD, U. Oreg., Eugene, 1972. Atty. Multnomah County Legal Aid Svcs., Portland, Oreg., 1974—77; rsch. assoc. in law Regional Rsch. Inst. Human Svcs., Portland State U., Oreg., 1978—80; dir. Nat. Child Welfare Ctr. on Children and Law ABA, Washington, 1980—. Spkr. on child welfare topics; tchg. asst. polit. sci. dept. UCLA, 1973—74; tchg. asst. Sch. Law, U. Oreg., 1971—72; mem. faculty Sch. Social Work, Portland State U., 1978—79; adj. prof. Sch. Social Work, Howard U., Washington, 1991—96. Author (with Ann Shalleck): Court Rules to Achieve Permanency for Foster Children: Sample Rules and Commentary, 1985; author: (with Lisa Granik, Claire Cunningham and David Colley) Ohio Child Welfare Legal Manual for Attorneys, 1990; author: Establishing a Core of Services for Families Subject to State Intervention: A Blueprint for Statutory and Regulatory Action, 1992, Judicial Implementation of Permanency Planning: One Court That Works, 1992, How to Work With Your Court: A Guide for Child Welfare Administrators, 1993; author: (with Ted Rubin and Debra Ratterman Baker) A Second Court that Works: Judicial Implementation of Permanency Planning Reforms, 1995; author: (with Robert Lancour) Early Termination of Parental Rights: Developing Appropriate Statuatory Grounds, 1996; author: (with G. Diane Dodson) On-Time Services to Preserve Families: A Guide for Child Protection Agency Administrators and Policymakers, 1997; Making Sense of the ASFA Reguations: A Roadmap for Effective Implementation, 2001; author (with Diane Boyd Rauber): How to Work With Your Court: A Guide for Child Welfare Administrators, 2005; author: (with Susan Koenig) Court Performance Measures in Child Abuse and Neglect Cases: A Technical Guide, 2006; contbr. articles to profl. jours., chpts. to books. Recipient award for outstanding nat. leadership, Nat. Foster Care Resource Ctr., Nat. Resource Ctr. Spl. Needs Adoption and Nat. Resource Ctr. Family Based Svcs., 1993, Outstanding Legal Advocacy award, Nat. Assn. Counsel for Children, 1997, Mitchell Wendell Jurist award, Assn. Adminstrs., Interstate Compect for Placement of Children, APHA, 1999, Adoption Excellence award, US Sec. Health and Human Svcs., 1999. Home: 200 N Maple Ave Apt 500 Falls Church VA 22046

HARDIN, MARTHA LOVE WOOD, civic leader; b. Muncie, Ind., Aug. 13, 1918; d. Lawrence Anselm and Bonny Blossom (Williams) Wood; m. Clifford Morris Hardin, June 28, 1939; children: Susan Hardin Wood, Clifford Wood, Cynthia Hardin Milligan, Nancy Hardin Rogers, James Alvin. Librarian U. Chgo., 1939-40. Co-author Genealogy: Ancestors of Lawrence Anselm Wood, Genealogy Ancestors of Bonny Williams Wood; contbr. articles to profl. jours. Chair Nebr. Heart Fund, 1967; vol. worker Lincoln Gen. Hosp., 1965, Clarkson Hosp., 1966; hon. chair Symphony Ball, Washington, 1970; met. bd. YWCA, Washington, 1969-71, St. Louis, 1973-95; women's com. Pres.'s Com. on Employment of Handicapped, 1970-91, bd. dirs., 1970—; co-chmn. nat. fund-raising campaign U. Nebr. Found., 1977-80. Mem. DAR, PEO, Soc. Mortar Bd., Lincoln Country Club, Wednesday Club, Phi Beta Kappa, Pi Beta Phi. Home: 6525 Lone Tree Dr Lincoln NE 68512-2405

HARDIN, MARY L., interior designer; d. William Alexander and Mary Louise (Murphy) Prosser; m. R. McCurdy, 1954 (dec.); children: Terry L. McCurdy, Lynn R. McCurdy; m. O. Hardin, 1977 (dec.). BS, Clayton Coll., 2000. Missionary oblates, Ill., 1970; mem. presdl. task force U.S. Govt, Wash., DC, 1987, 1991. Mem.: Nat. Writers Club, Sierra Club, Lourdes Prayer League, Peale Ctr. for Christian Living, World Wildlife Fund, Dinshah Health Soc., Natural Resource Def. Coun., Nat. Trust for Historic Preservation, Nat. Mus. Women in the Arts, Nat. Pks. Conservation Assn., Acad. Am. Poets, Nat. Arbor Day Found., Defenders of Wildlife, Smithsonian Instn., The Oxford Club (life). Avocations: writing, painting, poetry, antiques.

HARDIN, MELORA, actress; b. Houston, Tex., June 29, 1967; d. Jerry and Diane Hardin; m. Gildart Jackson, 1997; 1 child, Rory; 1 child, Piper. Actor: (films) Iron Eagle, 1986, Soul Man, 1986, Big Man on Campus, 1989, The Rocketeer, 1991, Chameleon, 1995, Absolute Power, 1997, Seven Girlfriends, 1999, Certain Guys, 2000, The Hot Chicks, 2002, Thank You for Smoking, 2005, The Violin, 2006, Drive-Thru, 2006; (TV series) Dirty Dancing, 1989, Cover Me: Based on the True Life of an FBI Family, 2002, Monk, 2004—05, The Office, 2005— (winner Outstanding Performance by an Ensemble in a Comedy Series, SAG awards, 2007). Office: NBC 30 Rockefeller Plz New York NY 10112*

HARDIN, PAUL, III, law educator; b. Charlotte, NC, June 11, 1931; s. Paul and Dorothy (Reel) Hardin; m. Barbara Russell, June 8, 1954; children: Paul Russell, Sandra Mikush, Dorothy Holmes. AB, Duke U., 1952, JD, 1954; LHD (hon.), Clemson U., 1970, Coker Coll., 1972; LittD (hon.), Nebr. Wesleyan U., 1978; LLD (hon.), Adrian Coll., 1987, Monmouth Coll., 1988; HHD (hon.), Wofford Coll., 1989; LLD (hon.), Rider Coll., 1990; LHD (hon.), Duke U., 1994. Bar: Ala. 1954. Practiced in, Birmingham, 1954, 1956—58; asst. prof. Duke Law Sch., 1958—61, assoc. prof., 1961—63, prof., 1963—68, univ. trustee, 1969—74, 1995—2001; pres. Wofford Coll., Spartanburg, SC, 1968—72, So. Methodist U., Dallas, 1972—74, Drew U., Madison, NJ, 1975—88; chancellor U. NC, Chapel Hill, NC, 1988—95, chancellor emeritus, prof. law, 1995—; interim pres. U. Ala., Birmingham, Ala., 1997. Vis. prof. U. Tex., 1960, U. Pa., 1962—63, U. Va., 1974; dir. Smith Barney mut. funds. Author (with Sullivan, others): The Administration of Criminal Justice, 1966; author: (with Sullivan) Evidence, Cases and Materials, 1968; contbr. articles to profl. jours., law revs. Chmn. Human Rels. Com., Durham, NC, 1961—62; pres. Nat. Assn. Schs. and Coll. of United Meth. Ch., 1984; mem. gen. conf. United Meth. Ch., 1968, 1976, 1980, 1984; chmn. Nat. Commn. on United Meth. Higher Edn., 1975—77. Served with CIC US Army, 1954—56. Mem.: Order of Coif, Carnegie Found. for Advancement Tchg. (bd. dirs. 1990—98), Phi Beta Kappa. Personal E-mail: thehardins@nc.rr.com.

HARDIN, SUSAN JEAN, social studies educator, department chairman; b. Canton, Ill., June 1, 1951; d. Eugene Max Bavery and Mary Anabel Heisler; m. Steven Leon Hardin, Oct. 5, 1973; 1 child, James Steven Eugene. BA, MacMurray Coll., Jacksonville, Ill., 1973; MS in Edn., So. Ill. U., Edwardsville, 1987. Tchr. Jacksonville Dist. 117, Ill., 1976—. Honest Abe Merit Badge counselor Boy Scouts Am., 1973—; program coord. Adolescent in West Ctrl. Ill., 1999; co-program developer Digital Jacksonville Project, 2005—. Recipient Educator of Yr. award, 1998, Bill Russell Excellence in Edn. award, Jacksonville Dist. 117, 1997, Ill. Mus. in the Classroom, Ill. State Bd. Edn., 1997, Outstanding Tchr., Nat. Soc. DAR, 1998, Nat. Tchr. of Yr., Daus. of Colonial Wars, 2004; Keizai Koha Japanese fellow, 1998, Fulbright grantee to Russia, 1996. Mem.: Nat. Coun. for the Social Studies, Ill. Coun. for the Social Studies (rep. region III), Jacksonville Edn. Assn., NEA, Am. Legion (Bishop Post #1). Republican. Roman Catholic. Avocation: historic preservation. Office: Turner Jr HS 664 S Lincoln Ave Jacksonville IL 62650 Business E-Mail: shardin@jax117.morgan.k12.il.us.

HARDIN, TERRENCE ARMSTRONG, former radio broadcasting manager; b. Cin., Sept. 10, 1961; s. Oliver Wendell and Carol Lockwood H.; m. Dayna Lynn Glasson, Oct. 8, 1994. BFA in Radio, TV Comms., So. Meth. U., 1985. Cert. radio mktg. cons. Nat. sales mgr. Sta. WBAP and Sta. KSCS-FM, Dallas, 1986-88; gen. sales mgr. Sta. WMJI-FM, Cleve., 1988-90, Stas. KCBQ-AM-FM and Sta. KIHI-FM, Denver and San Diego, 1990-92, Sta. WPNT-FM, Chgo., 1992-95; v.p., gen. mgr. Stas. KYOT-FM, KZON-FM, KOY and KISO, Phoenix, 1995-99; gen. mgr. WLIT, 1999—. Guest speaker Ariz. State U., Tempe, 1995; advisor Glaser Capital, Cin., 1990—. Mem. awards com. Medallion of Merit Scholarship Found., Ariz. State U., Tempe, 1995-96; fund raiser Children's Cancer Ctr., Phoenix, 1995-96; exec. coun. Boys and Girls Club of Met. Phoenix. Mem. Am. Diabetes Assn. Avocations: travel, golf, mountain biking. Office: Wlit Fm Radio 233 N Michigan Ave Ste 2800 Chicago IL 60601-5704

HARDIN, WILLIAM DOWNER, retired lawyer; b. Newark, Sept. 27, 1926; s. Charles R. and Emma (Downer) H.; m. Rosemarie Koellhoffer, Jan. 19, 1952 (dec. Mar. 1996); m. Ruth M. Johnson, May 29, 1999; children: William Downer, David Gerth, Peter Roe. AB, Princeton, 1948; LL.B., Columbia, 1951. Bar: N.J. 1951. Law clk. N.J. Superior Ct., 1951-52; assoc. firm Pitney, Hardin, Kipp & Szuch, Newark and Morristown, 1952—57, mem. firm, 1957—96. Mem. N.J. Bd. Bar Examiners, 1964-68, chmn., 1968; mem. local draft bd. SSS, 1953-74, chmn., 1970-74; mem. Family Svc. Bur., Newark, 1953-75, pres., 1960-66; mem. Family Svc. Morris County, 1976-85, 87-98, pres., 1979-82, 95-97, v.p., 1992-95; mem. membership com. Family Svc. Assn. Am., 1965-78, dir., 1971-79, 89-95; mem. Nat. Budget and Consultation Com., 1966-71, Coun. on Accreditation Svcs. for Families and Children, 1978-80. Trustee Newark Acad., 1952-85, pres., 1969-72, chmn., 1976-78; mem. Legal Svcs. of N.J., 1983-2002, chmn., 1990-96; mem. Legal Aid Soc. of Morris County, N.J., 1984-93, pres., 1989-90. With USNR, 1944-46. Mem. ABA, Fed. Bar Assn., N.J. Bar Assn., Essex County Bar Assn., Morris County Bar Assn., Morristown Club, Nassau Club, Coral Beach and Tennis Club, Short Hills Club, Princeton Club of N.Y., Morris County Golf Club, Rockaway River Country Club. Episcopalian. Home: 15 Gapview Rd Short Hills NJ 07078-2077 Office: 200 Campus Dr Florham Park NJ 07932-1007 Home Phone: 973-376-0300; Office Phone: 973-966-8100.

HARDING, BETH ANN, middle school educator; d. Frederick W. and Margaret A. Harding. BA in History, U. Mass., Amherst, 1988; MEd, Worcester State Coll., Mass., 1993, postgrad. Cert. tchr. history 5-9, tchr. history 9-12, tchr. mid. sch. 5-9. Tchr. Mountview Mid. Sch., Holden, Mass., 1991—94, Lexico, Burlington, Mass., 1993; tchr. history Worcester Pub. Schs., 1994—. Mem. curriculum knowing social scis. team Clark U., 1998—2000, mentor, 1999—2002, guest lectr., 1999, supr. student tchr., 2000; ednl. cons. Harding Consulting, Holden, 1999—; cyber mentor Ill. State U., 2000—; supervising practitioner Assumption Coll., 2006—; presenter in field. Contbr. articles to profl. jours. Leader, gold award advisor, asst. Girl Scouts U.S., Worcester, Plymouth, Mass., 1984—; advisor Kids' Fair Worcester Hist. Mus., 1995—2001; asst. coach Worcester Swim Club, 1991—94; mem. Small Schs. Transition Com., 2002, Sullivan's Sch. Improvement Plan Com., 2005, Forest Grove's Instrnl. Leadership Team; founder, co-leader The Girls, 2003—; del., com. mem. 1st Congl. Ch., Holden, 2000—. Mem.: NEA, ASCD, Mass. Tchrs. Assn., Edn. Assn. Worcester, Nat. Coun. History Edn., Nat. Coun. Social Studies, Ctrl. Mass. Coun. Social Studies (v.p., bd. dirs., history day judge 1998—), Coun. Social Studies, New Eng. History Tchrs. Assn., New Eng. Assn. Schs. and Colls. (mem. vis. com. commn. pub. mid. schs. 2005), Phi Alpha Theta. Avocations: travel, sailing, scrapbooks. Office: Worcester Pub Schs Irving St Worcester MA 01605 Personal E-mail: hardingb@rocketmail.com.

HARDING, FANN, retired science administrator; b. Henderson, Ky., Jan. 29, 1930; d. James Hilary and Lucy (Caldwell) H. Student, Western Coll. for Women, Oxford Ohio, 1947—48; AB in Biology, Coker Coll., Hartsville, SC, 1951; MS in Anatomy, Med. U. S.C., Charleston, 1954, PhD, 1958. Research and teaching asst. dept. anatomy Med. U. S.C., 1951-53, teaching fellow, 1953-55, research fellow, 1955-58; analyst pub. health research program, research and tng. grants br. Nat. Heart Inst., Bethesda, Md., 1958-61, scientist adminstr. research and tng. grants br., 1961-64, chmn. nat. adv. heart council statements com., 1961-64, sr. health scientist adminstr. research grants br. (sect. chief), 1964-69, sr. health scientist adminstr. thrombosis and hemorrhagic diseases br. (acting chief), extramural program, also arteriosclerosis program, 1969-72; mem. Nat. Heart Inst. (Fellowship Bd.), 1966-68; sr. health scientist adminstr. thrombosis and hemorrhagic diseases program (acting chief), div. blood diseases and resources Nat. Heart and Lung Inst. (name changed to Nat. Heart, Lung and Blood Inst. 1976), Bethesda, 1972-74; asst. to dir. div. blood diseases and resources Nat. Heart, Lung and Blood Inst., 1974—, program dir. extramural research tng. and career devel. in blood diseases and transfusion medicine, exec. sec. blood diseases and resources adv. com., 1974-95; asst. coordinator U.S.-USSR Health Exchange Program, 1974-95; ret., 1996. Women's Action Program adv. coun. HEW, 1971-72; cons. James H. Mitchell Found., Washington, 1962-67, Washington VA Hosp., 1968-70; environ. cons. Henderson (Ky.) Citizens Com., 1974-76; initiated and implemented concept of transfusion medicine, 1982—; adv. bd. Psychoceramic Found., 2001—. Editorial bd.: Lupus News, 1988—. Organizer NIH Orgn. for Women, 1970; bd. dir. Assn. Women in Sci. Edn. Found., 1973-77, Lupus Found. Am., 1985-88; bd. visitors Coker Coll., 1974-78; bd. dir., sec., treas. Nat. Children's Choir, Washington, 1981-91; bd. advisors Psychoceramic Found., 2002; mem. Woman's Nat. Dem. Club, 2004. Recipient Ruth Patrick award, 1951, NIH sustained performance award, 1973, Nat. award Fedn. Orgns. for Profl. Women, 1977, Disting. Svc. award Transfusion Medicine Acad. Award Program, Am. Assn. Blood Banks, 1990, Disting. Alumni award Coker Coll., 1992, award of Merit, NIH, 1993, Founder's award, Fedn. Orgns. for Profl. Women, 1995, Foremother award, Nat. Rsch. Ctr. Women and Children, 2005. Fellow Sigma Delta Epsilon; mem. AAAS (panel on women in sci. 1973-77), Nat. Women's Polit. Caucus (charter), Assn. Women in Sci. (founding mem. 1971, exec. bd. 1973-75), Fedn. Orgn. Profl. Women (founding pres., exec. bd. 1972—), Nat. Microcirculatory Soc. (charter), Reticuloendothelial Soc. (charter), Am. Assn. Blood Banks, Internat. Soc. Thrombosis & Haemostasis, Internat. Soc. Blood Transfusion, Internat. Soc. Lymphology, Womans Party Sewell-Belmont Ho. and Mus. (bd. dir. 1981-2005, corr. sec. 1989-91, rec. sec. 1991-96, chair audit com. 2005), Woman's Nat. Dem. Club. Avocation: sculpting. Home: 1661 Crescent Pl NW Apt 305 Washington DC 20009-4066 Home Fax: 202-265-3267. Personal E-mail: ffharding@aol.com.

HARDING, JOHN HIBBARD, retired insurance company executive; b. Plainfield, NJ, Jan. 12, 1936; s. Ernest Reginald and Emily (Hibbard) H.; m. Joan Edith Tarro, Nov. 29, 1973; children— David, Philip, Robert, Brooke, Ashley. BA, Princeton U., 1958. Asst. actuary Nat. Life Ins. Co., Montpelier, Vt., 1965-67, assoc. actuary, 1967-69, actuary R&D, 1969-72, v.p., actuary, 1972-80, sr. v.p., chief actuary, 1980-83, exec. v.p., 1983-85, vice chmn. bd., dir., 1985-87, pres., COO, 1987-96; v.p., chief actuary Blue Cross-Blue Shield of Vt., 1997-2000. Chmn., CEO Adminstrv. Svcs., Inc.; dir. Equity Svcs., Inc., Nat. Life Investment Mgmt. Co., Sentinel Advisors, Inc., 1987-96. Fellow Soc. Actuaries (bd. govs. 1993-95); mem. Am. Acad. Actuaries (bd. dirs. 1982-85, v.p. 1988-90, pres.-elect 1991-92, pres. 1992-93, immediate past pres. 1993-94). Home: 25822 N Primo Circle Rio Verde AZ 85263 Personal E-mail: hardingcalais@aol.com.

HARDING, MARIE, ecological executive, artist; b. Glen Cove, NY, Nov. 13, 1941; d. Charles Lewis and Marie (Parish) H.; m. John P. Allen, Jan. 29, 1965 (div. Oct., 1991); 1 child, Eden A. Harding. BA, Sarah Lawrence Coll., 1964; postgrad., Arts Students League, NYC, 1965. Founder Synergia Ranch Ctr. for Innovation, Retreats and Confs., Santa Fe, 1969; founding mem., actress Theater of All Possibilities, Santa Fe, 1971-86; founding mem., dir. Inst. Ecotechnics, Santa Fe, also London, 1974—; bd. dirs., founding mem. Savannah Systems Pty., Ltd., Kimberly region, Australia, 1976—, Outback Sta. Pty. Ltd., Kimberly region, Australia, 1976-94; chair, dir. EcoWorld, Inc., Santa Fe, 1982-94; dir., founding mem., CFO Space Biospheres Ventures, Biosphere 2, Ariz., 1984-94; chair, CEO Oceans Expdns., Inc., 1986-92; pres. ecol. and biosphere R&D/implementation project Global Ecotechnics Corp., Santa Fe, 1994—; pres. Decisions Team, Inc. Ecol. Project Mgmt., Ariz., 1994—, Silver Hills Ranch Homeowners Assn., 1996—2006; pres., mng. mem. Synergia Ranch, LLC, Santa Fe; mem. San Marcos Dist. Planning Co., 2004; chmn. Tropic Seas Rsch. Co., 2006—, sec., 2006—. Participant in constrn. and fin. Capt. R. Heraclitus Rsch. Vessel, Oakland, Calif., 1974; bd. dirs. Synergetic Press, London and Ariz.; chmn., sec. Tropic Seas Rsch. Co., 2006. Exhibitions include Biosphere 2, Ariz., 1979-93, Biosphere 2, October Gallery, London, 1996, 2003-04, Berlin, 2003, Peoples Bank N.Mex., 2003; project dir., artist mural project History of Jazz, Dance, Theater, Ft. Worth, 1982-83, San Marcos Studio Tours, 1999-2004; prodr., dir. (films) Bryon Gysin Loves ya, Project Charlie, The Search, Planet Earth Conf Vol. Swallows, Madras, India, 1964, Project Concern, Vietnam, Hong Kong, 1964-65; artist, founder, trustee October Gallery Trust, London, 1979; pres. Short Hills Ranch Homeowners Assn., 1996—; bd. dirs. Tropic Ventures Edn. & Rsch. Found., 2006. Mem.: Silver Hills Reach Homeowners Assn. (pres. 1996—). Avocations: painting, gardening. Home and Office: 26 Synergia Rd Santa Fe NM 87508-4438 Home Phone: 505-471-2573; Office Phone: 505-471-2573.

HARDING, RAY MURRAY, JR., retired judge; b. Logan, Utah, Nov. 23, 1953; s. Ray M. Sr. and Martha (Rasmussen) H.; m. Rebecca H.; children: Michelle, Nicole, Justin. BS, Brigham Young U., 1975; JD, J. Reuben Clark Law Sch., 1978. Bar: Utah 1978. Ptnr. Harding & Harding, American Fork and Pleasant Grove, Utah, 1978-85; owner Harding & Assoc., American Fork and Pleasant Grove, 1986-95; judge Utah County 4th Jud. Dist. Ct., Provo, 1995—2002; ret. Atty. Lindon City and Pleasant Grove City, Utah, 1983-95, Alpine City, 1985-94, American Fork, Utah, 1985-95. Bd. trustees Utah Valley State Coll., 1986-95, chmn., 1991-93. Named Businessman of Yr., Future Bus. Leaders of Am., 1983. Avocations: skiing, scuba diving, hiking, hunting, travel.

HARDING, SUSAN M., language educator; b. Norman, Okla., Aug. 29, 1952; d. Henry and Jean Munde; m. Jack Harding, 1982; children: Christopher, Jason, Jennifer. BA, U. Okla., Norman, 1977; MA, U. Am., Mexico City, 1977. Cert. NBPTS, 2003. Spanish tchr. Putnam City H.S., Oklahoma City, 1994—; adj. instr. Spanish U. Ctrl. Okla., Edmond, 1995—. Tchr. McAllen Ind. Sch. Dist., McAllen, Tex., 1977—81; Spanish and ESL tchr. John Marshall H.S., Oklahoma City, 1981—89; spanish tchr. Yukon H.S., Okla., 1989—94; ESL tchr. Am. Sch., Mexico City. Recipient Tchr. Yr., Putnam City H.S., 2000, Okla. Fgn. Lang. Tchr. Yr., Okla. Fgn. Lang. Tchrs. Assn., 2005. Office: Putnam City High Sch 5300 N W 50th Oklahoma City OK 73122 Home Phone: 405-787-5925; Office Phone: 405-789-4350. Business E-Mail: sharding@putnamcityschools.org.

HARDING, WARREN GAMALIEL, III, surgeon; b. Columbus, Ohio, Apr. 21, 1941; s. George Tryon Harding, III and Mary Virginia Harding; m. Barbara Crawford, Oct. 6, 1974; children: Warren Gamaliel Harding, IV, James Shafor, Andrew Crawford. MD, Loma Linda U., Calif., 1963—67. Lic. Am. Bd. Orthopaedic Surgery, 1974, ACS, 1978. Orthopaedic surgeon Wellington Orthopaedic & Sports Medicine, Inc., Cin., 1975—; asst. prof. orthopaedic surgery U. Cin., Cin. Editor: (book) Our Common Country. Bd. mem. Indian Hill-Madeira Joint Fire Dist., Ohio, 2002—06. Lt. comdr. USN, 1973—75, Naval Regional Medical Ctr., San Diego. Fellow: Am. Orthopaedic Assn.; mem.: Camargo Club. R-Liberal. Presbyn. Avocations: golf, history, gardening. Home: 8430 Shawnee Run Rd Cincinnati OH 45243 Office: Wellington Orthopaedic & Sports Medicine 4701 Creek Rd Cincinnati OH 45242 Home Phone: 513-561-5739. Home Fax: 513-561-5739. Personal E-mail: wharding1@cinci.rr.com.

HARDIS, STEPHEN ROGER, retired manufacturing company executive; b. NYC, July 13, 1935; s. Abraham I. and Ethel (Krinsky) H; m. Sondra Joyce Rolbin, Sept. 15, 1957; children: Julia Faye, Andrew Martin, Joanna Halley. BA with distinction, Cornell U., 1956; M.P.A. in Econs., Woodrow Wilson Sch. of Pub. and Internat. Affairs Princeton U., 1960. Asst. to controller Gen. Dynamics, 1960-61; fin. analyst Pfaudler Permutit Inc., 1961-64; staff asst. to controller, 1964; mgr. corp. long-range planning Ritter Pfaudler Corp., 1965-68, dir. corporate planning, 1968; treas. Sybron Corp., Rochester, NY, 1969—, v.p. fin., 1970-77, exec. v.p. fin. and planning, 1977-79; vice chmn., chief fin. and adminstrv. officer Eaton Corp., Cleve., 1979—, vice chmn., CEO, 1995, chmn., CEO, 1996-2000; ret., 2000; dir. Axcelis Techs., 2000—. Bd. dirs. Progressive, Nordson Corp., Lexmark Corp., Marsh & McLennan, Steeris, Am. Greetings. Past mem. Gov.'s Task Force on High Tech. Industry; past mem. bd. dirs. Rochester Area Hosp. Corp., Rochester Area Ednl. TV Sta., Genesee Hosp.; trustee Cleve. Clinic. With USNR, 1956-58. Mem. Phi Beta Kappa.

HARDISON, CYNTHIA ANN STOLTZE, retired hematologist, oncologist; d. Norris Sanborn Stoltze and Frances Willard Virtue; m. Joseph Hammond Hardison, Jr., Apr. 8, 1961; children: Joseph III, Sanborn Stoltze, Anna Katharine. BS, Stanford U., Calif.; MS, U. Minn., Mpls.; MD, Northwestern U., Evanston, Ill. Intern Evanston Hosp., Ill., 1954—55; fellow Mayo Clinic, Rochester, Minn., 1955—59, cons. in hematology, 1959—64; founder and prin. Raleigh Internal Medicine Assoc., NC, 1964—89; ret., 1989. Cons. Jour. AMA, 1964—69. Bd. dir. N.C. Symphony Found., 1983—86. Mem.: Am. Coll. Gastroenterology Auxilliary (pres. 1981), Monday Luncheon and Literacy Soc., Olla Podrida Book Club. Republican. Presbyterian. Avocations: painting, travel. Home: 1612 Oberlin Rd 7 Raleigh NC 27608

HARDISON, KADEEM, actor; b. NYC, July 24, 1965; m. Chante Moore (div.); 1 child. Actor: (TV series) ABC Afterschool Specials, 1981, The Cosby Show, 1984, Spenser: For Hire, 1987, A Different World, 1987—93 (NAACP Image award, 1991, 1992), Roc, 1992, Living Single, 1995, Touched by an Angel, 1997, Between Brothers, 1997, The Love Boat: The Next Wave, 1998, Fantasy Island, 1998, The Crow: Stairway to Heaven, 1998—99, Just Shoot Me, 2000, Static Shock, 2000—03, Livin' Large, 2002, Abby, 2003, One on One, 2005, Just for Kicks, 2006, My Name Is Earl, 2006, House, 2006, Girlfriends, 2007; (TV films) House of Dies Drear, 1984, Go Tell It on the Mountain, 1985, Dream Date, 1989, Words Up!, 1992, Fire & Ice, 2001, Red Skies, 2002, Life Is Not a Fairytale: The Fantasia Barrino Story, 2006 (NAACP Image award, 2007); (films) Rappin', 1985, Enemy Territory, 1987, School Daze, 1988, I'm Gonna Git You Sucka, 1988, Def by Temptation, 1990, White Men Can't Jump, 1992, Gunmen, 1994, Renaissance Man, 1994, Wes Craven's Vampire in Brooklyn, 1995, Panther, 1995, The Sixth Man, 1997, Drive, 1997, Blind Faith, 1998, Dancing in September, 2000, Thank Heaven, 2001, Thirty Years to Life, 2001, Instinct to Kill, 2001, Showtime, 2002, Face of Terror, 2003, Biker Boyz, 2003, Dunsmore, 2003, The Cassidy Kids, 2006, Love Hollywood Style, 2006; dir.: (TV series) A Different World, 1992—93; writer: TV series A Different World, 1992—93.*

HARDT, NANCY SISSON, pathology and laboratory medicine educator; b. Ill., May 17, 1952; married; 2 children. BA in Modern Lang. (magna cum laude), Sweet Briar Coll., Va., 1974; MD, Loyola U. Stritch Sch. Medicine, Ill., 1977. Cert. of added qualification in cytopathology Am. Bd. Pathology, 1990, diplomate Am. Bd. Pathology in Anatomic and Clin. Pathology, 1989, Am. Bd. Obstetrics/Gynecology, 1984, cert. Am. Registry of Diagnostic Med. Sonographers, 1983. Intern, obstetrics/gynecology U. Ky., Coll. Medicine, 1977—78, resident, obstetrics/gynecology, 1978—81; clin. fellow, divsn. maternal/fetal medicine, dept. obstetrics/gynecology U. Fla., Coll. Medicine, 1981—83, med. dir., reproductive ultrasound lab., dept. obstetrics/gynecology, 1983—86, asst. prof., obstetrics/gynecology, 1983—86, resident, anatomic and clin. pathology, dept. pathology, 1986—89, fellow, gynecologic pathology and cytopathology, 1989—90, asst. prof., pathology and lab. medicine, 1990—93, assoc. prof., obstetrics/gynecology, 1993—2000, assoc. prof. with tenure, pathology and lab. medicine, 1993—2000, prof., obstetrics/gynecology, 2000—02, prof. with tenure, pathology and lab. medicine, 2000—02, adj. prof., dept. obstetrics/gynecology, 2002—06, adj. prof., dept. pathology, 2002—06, clin. prof. pathology and lab. medicine, 2006—; prof., dept. obstetrics/Gynecology U. Tenn. Coll. Medicine, 2004—06, prof. with tenure, dept. preventative medicine, 2002—06; dir., Inst. for Women's Health U. Tenn. Health Sci. Ctr., 2002—05, Methodist Endowed chair for women's health, 2002—05; med. dir., physician services LabDoc, 2006—. Mem. admissions com. Loyola U., Stritch Sch. Medicine, 1975—77; mem. phase B curriculum com., dept. pathology U. Fla. Coll. Medicine, 1991—98, mem. surgical case review com., 1991—94, faculty coun. rep., 1992—94, faculty coun. v.p., 1993—94, chair faculty coun. task force on the office for faculty development, 1993, women faculty assn. pres., 1993—94, mem. search com. for chair of anatomy and cell biology, 1994—95, faculty coun. pres., 1994—95, mem. curriculum com. task force on integration reproductive services, 1994, mem. assoc. prof. promotion and tenure com., 1995—96, past pres., faculty coun., 1995—96, mem. faculty capital campaign steering com., 1995, mem. Dean's task force on early retirement, 95, mem. Dean's task force on diversity and comm., 95, mem. dept. pathology and lab. medicine, variable compensation com., 1996—2002, mem. contract adv. com., dept. pathology, managed care, 1996—2001, mem. faculty group practice bd. dirs., 1996, mem. faculty compensation mem., 1996—97, co-chair, cash collections and billing design team, adminstrv. reassignment, 1996—97, rep. to the Health Sci. Ctr. Libr. adv. bd., 1996—97, assoc. med. dir., cytopathology, dept. pathology, immunology and lab. medicine, 1997—98, mem. faculty group practice ops. com., 1997, mem. faculty group practice bd. dirs., 1998—2002, mem. exec. com., dept. pathology, 1998—2002, com. mem., chair faculty compensation, 1998—99, asst. dean, clin. affairs and managed care, 1998—99; coord. Chancellor's hours U. Tenn., 2004—05, mem. bd. dir. com. on Outreach, 2003—05; mem. student conduct standards com. U. Fla., Health Sci. Ctr., 1996—2002, co-dir., Ctr. for Rsch. on Women's Health, 1998—2002, faculty senate mem., edn. policy com., 2003—, faculty senate chair legis. resource com., 2003—04; assoc. chair for Step 3 computer-based case simulation com. Nat. Bd. Med. Examiners, 1999, mem. Step 3 com., 2001—, bd. dir., 2001—, mem. fin. com., 2001—, chair, Step 3 Test Material Develop. Com. for computer- based case stimulations, 2001—05, group leader for scripting for the step 3 computer-based case stimulation com., 2000—05; coord. Memphis City Schools Svc. Learning Project, 2002—05, Mini Med. Sch., 2003, 04, 05; mem. State Tenn. SIDS Advisory, 2004—, Governor's TennCare Advisory, 2003—04, Women's Health Adv. Com. State Commr. of Health, 2003—06; spkr. in field; invited lectr. in field. Guest editor Jour. Fla. Med. Assn.; contbr. articles to profl. jours., chapters to books. Chair, health com. New Pathways, 2004—06, bd. dir., 2003—06; co-chair, rsch. com. Cmty. Inst. for Early Childhood, 2003—04; regional health coun. mem. 0-5 Com., 2002—06; chair, Infant Mortality Prevention Com. Regional Health Coun., 2002—06, mem. exec. com., 2002—04; bd. chair Memphis Challenge, 2004—06; mem. Memphis Area Women's Coun. Bd., 2002—06, pres., 2005—06. Named one of 50 Women Who Make a Difference (Memphis), 2005; recipient Young Investigators award, Am. Acad. Pediatrics Perinatal Pediatrics Sect., 1983, Gender Equity award, Am. Med. Writers Assn., 1997, Alachua and Bradford Counties (Fla.) Women of Distinction award, 1998, Great Apple award, Memphis City Schools, 2005, Disting. Svc. award, Nat. Bd. Med. Examiners, 2006; Am. Cancer Soc. Nat. Clin. Oncology fellowship, 1989—90, Robert Wood Johnson Health Policy Fellow, IOM, 2006. Fellow: Am. Coll. Obstetrics and Gynecology, Coll. Am. Pathologists (First prize, Residents Rsch. Competition (awarded jointly with Anatomic Pathology Divsn. Am. Soc. Clin. Pahtology) 1988); mem.: Alachua County Med. Soc., Am. Inst. Ultrasound in Medicine, Am. Soc. Clin. Pathologists, US and Canadian Acad. Pathology (Residents Rsch. Competition, Stowell Orbison award 1989), Internat. Soc. Gynecological Pathologists, Am. Assn. Med. Colleges (women liason officer 1994—2001), AMA (coll. medicine delegate 1995), Exec. Leadership in Academic Medicine (adv. bd. 1997—99), Am. Coll. Physician Executives, Med. Group Mgmt. Assn., Soc. for Exec. Leadership in Academic Medicine (fellow 1995—96, pres. 1997—99, bd. dir. 1997—2001), Soc. for Women's Health Rsch. (mem. steering com., Women's Health Rsch. Coalition 1999—), Phi Beta Kappa, Alpha Sigma Nu. Achievements include co-inventing Surface Modified Silicone Drug Depot. Office: U Fla Coll Medicine Dept Pathology Immunology & Lab Medicine Rocky Point Lab Rm 1153 4800 SW 35th Dr Gainesville FL 32607 also: Dept Pathology Immunology & Lab Medicine U Fla Coll Medicine PO Box 100275 Gainesville FL 32610-0275 Office Phone: 352-265-0111 ext 7-2054. Office Fax: 352-265-9901. Business E-Mail: hardt@pathology.ufl.edu.

HARDWAY, WENDELL GARY, retired academic administrator; b. Bolair, W.Va., Mar. 5, 1927; s. Ressie Bruce and Elsie Clennen (Miller) H.; m. Hannah Lou Garrett, July 12, 1950. BS, W.Va. U., 1949, MS, 1953; PhD, Ohio State U., 1959. Tchr. Troy (W.Va.) High Sch., 1949-54; asst. prof. sci. Glenville (W.Va.) State Coll., 1954-57, assoc. prof. edn., 1959-61, prof., chmn. div. edn., dir. student teaching, 1961-66; pres. Bluefield (W.Va.) State Coll., 1966-73, Fairmont (W.Va.) State Coll., 1973-88, ret., 1988. Pres. United Way, Fairmont, 1976; mem. Glenville City Council, 1958-64; pres. W.Va. Intercollegiate Athletic Conf., 1977-78. Served with AUS, 1945-46. Named Man of Yr., Bluefield Jaycees, 1969, Disting. Pioneer, Glenville State Coll., 1985, Outstanding Alumnus, W.Va. U. Coll. Agr., 1987. Hardway Libr. at Bluefield State Coll. and Hardway Hall (adminstrn. bldg.) at Fairmont State Coll. named in his honor. Mem. Phi Delta Theta, Gamma Sigma Delta, Phi Delta Kappa, Kappa Delta Pi. Methodist. Home: 4 Bel Manor Dr Fairmont WV 26554 Personal E-mail: hlg@aol100.com.

HARDWICK, CATHERINE R., lawyer; B in Bus. Admin., Western Mich. State Univ.; JD, Ariz. State Univ. Coll. Law. Former atty. Meyer, Hendricks, Victor, Osborn and Maledon, Phoenix; law compliance dept. Viasoft, Inc., Phoenix, Avnet, Inc., Phoenix, Phelps Dodge, Phoenix, now gen. coun., corp. sec. Office: Phelps Dodge One North Central Ave Phoenix AZ 85004

HARDWICK, DAVID FRANCIS, pathologist; b. Vancouver, BC, Can., Jan. 24, 1934; s. Walter H. W. and Iris L. (Hyndman) H.; m. Margaret M. Lang, Aug. 22, 1956; children: Margaret F., Heather I., David J. MD, U. B.C., 1957, LLD (hon.), 2001. Intern Montreal (Que., Can.) Gen. Hosp., 1957-58; resident Vancouver Gen. Hosp., 1958-59, Children's Hosp., Los Angeles, 1959-62; research assoc. U. So. Calif., 1961-62; clin. instr. U. B.C., Vancouver, 1963-65, asst. prof. pathology, 1965-69, assoc. prof., 1969-74, prof., 1974—, head dept. pathology, 1976-90, assoc. dean rsch. and planning, 1990-96; dir. labs. Children's Hosp., Vancouver, 1969-92, Vancouver Gen. Hosp., 1976-90; chmn. M.A.C., Children's Hosp., 1970-87; interinstitutional planning U. B.C. Medicine, 1996-98, spl. advisor on planning, 1999—. Adj. prof. Chinese U. Hong Kong; mem. U. B.C. Senate, 1966-71. Author: Acid Base Balance and Blood Gas Studies, 1968, Intermediary Metabolism of Liver, 1971, Directing the Clinical Laboratory, 1990, Laboratory Supervision and Management, 2d edit., 2002; contbr. numerous articles to profl. publs. Bd. dirs. Children and Family Rsch. Inst., BC, 1998—, Women's Hosp. Found., 1997-2000, BC Transplant Found., 1993-2006. Recipient Queen's Centennial medal Govt. Can., 1978, U. B.C. Faculty Citation Teaching award, 1987, Wallace Wilson Leadership award, 1990, William Boyd Lectureship award Canadian Assn. Path, 1994, Sydney Israels Founders award B.C. Rsch. Inst. Children and Family, 1997, Univ. medal for Outstanding Svc., U. B.C., 1997; Sydney Farber lectr., Soc. Ped. Path., 1998, other awards. and honors Fellow Royal Coll. Physicians (Can.), Coll. Am. Pathologists; mem. Internat. Acad. Pathology (pres. 1996, v.p. N.Am. 1998—, Gold medal 2002, sec. 2006-), Can. Med. Assn., BC Assn. Lab. Medicine, BC Med. Assn., NY Acad. Sci., Soc. Pediat. Pathology, Internat. Acad. Pathology (sec. 2006-, Disting. Svc. award 1994, Gold Medal award 2004), US and Can. Acad. Pathology (Pres.'s award 2004), U BC Alumni (Lifetime Achievement award 2007), BC Transplant Found. (chmn. bd. 2000—06), Med. Student and Alumni Ctr. Soc. (chair 2001—), Alpha Omega Alpha. Home: 727 W 23rd Ave Vancouver BC Canada V5Z 2A7 Office: U BC Dept Pathology 2211 Wesbrook Mall Vancouver BC Canada V6T 1W5 Business E-Mail: david.f.hardwick@ubc.ca.

HARDWICK, ELIZABETH, writer; b. Lexington, Ky., July 27, 1916; d. Eugene Allen and Mary (Ramsey) H.; m. Robert Lowell, July 28, 1949 (div. Oct. 1972); 1 child, Harriet. AB, U. Ky., 1938, MA, 1939; postgrad., Columbia U., 1939-41. Adj. assoc. prof. Barnard Coll. Author: The Ghostly Lover, 1945, The Simple Truth, 1955, A View of My Own, 1962, Seduction and Betrayal, 1974, Sleepless Nights, 1979, Bartleby in Manhattan, 1983, Sight Readings, 1998, Herman Melville, A Life, 2000; editor: The Selected Letters of William James, 1960; adv. editor: NY Rev. Books Recipient George Jean Nathan award for dramatic criticism, 1966, Gold medal for criticism, Am. Acad. Arts and Letters, 1993; Guggenheim fellow, 1947. Mem. Am. Acad. and Inst. Arts and Letters, Acad. Arts and Scis. Home: 15 W 67th St New York NY 10023-6226

HARDWICKE, CATHERINE HELEN, film director, set designer; b. McAllen, Tex., Oct. 21, 1955; d. John Benjamin III and Jamee Alberta (Bennett) H. BArch with highest honors, U. Tex., 1979; postgrad., UCLA. Prodn. designer: (films) Tapeheads, 1988, I'm Gonna Git You Sucka, 1988, Martins Go Home, 1990, Passed Away, 1992, Posse, 1993, Freaked, 1993, Tombstone, 1993, Car 54, Where Are You, 1994, Tank Girl, 1995, 2 Days in the Valley, 1996, SubUrbia, 1996, Mad City, 1997, The Newton Boys, 1998, Three Kings, 1999, Antitrust, 2001, Vanilla Sky, 2001, Laurel Canyon, 2002, (theatre) Carnage, Methusalem, Alagazam--After the Dog Wars; dir.: (films) Thirteen, 2003 (also writer), Lords of Dogtown, 2005, The Nativity Story, 2006; art dir.: (films) Hunk, 1987, Mr. Destiny, 1990 Recipient Card Walker Animation award Disney Studios, 1984, Nissan Focus award, 1984, Joseph Jefferson award Chgo. Non-Equity Theatre, 1990, others.*

HARDWIDGE, PHILIP ROSS, microbiologist, educator; b. Kalamazoo, Mich., Feb. 26, 1976; BS in Microbiology, U. Ill., 1997; PhD, Mayo Clinic, Rochester, Minn., 2002. Postdoctoral fellow U. BC, Vancouver, Canada, 2002—05; asst. prof. microbiology SD State U., Brookings, 2005—. Avocation: acting. Office: SD State Y 1119 North Campus Drive Brookings SD 57007 Home Phone: 605-691-9137; Office Phone: 605-688-5259. Office Fax: 605-688-6003. Personal E-mail: hardwidg@gmail.com.

HARDY, ASHTON RICHARD, lawyer; b. Gulfport, Miss., Aug. 31, 1935; s. Ashton Maurice and Alice (Baumbach) H.; m. Katherine Ketelsen, Sept. 4, 1959; children: Karin H. Wood, Katherine H. Foster. BBA, Tulane U., 1958, JD, 1962. Bar: La. 1962, FCC, 1976. Ptnr. Jones, Walker, Waechter, Poitevent, Carrere & Denegre, New Orleans, 1962-74, 76-82; gen. counsel FCC, Washington, 1974-76; ptnr. Fawer, Brian, Hardy, Zatzkis, New Orleans, 1982-86, Hardy & Popham, 1986-88, Walker, Bordelon, Hamlin, Theriot & Hardy, New Orleans, 1988-92, Hardy, Carey & Chautin, New Orleans, 1992—. Gen. counsel La. Assn. Broadcasters, 1976-86, Greater New Orleans Assn. Broadcasters, 1976—, La. Assn. Advt. Agys., 1982-86; lectr. in field; advance rep. to Pres. U.S., 1971-74. Bd. dirs. New Orleans Mission, 1989—, Met. Crime Commn. New Orleans, 1993—, vice-chmn., 1997-2002, United Christian Charities, 1993-99, Prison Fellowship/La., 1976—. Lt. USN, 1958-60. Named to Hall of Fame, Greater New Orleans Broadcasters Assn., 2001. Mem. La. Bar Assn. (del. ho. of dels. 1987-92), FCC Bar Assn., Nat. Religious Broadcasters (nat. bd. dirs. 2003— bd. dirs. S.W. chpt. 1983-2003), Christian Legal Soc., Metairie Country Club (pres. 1986), Comm Club. Home: 306 Cedar Dr Metairie LA 70005-3902 Office: Hardy Carey & Chautin LLP Ste 300 110 Veterans Memorial Blvd Metairie LA 70005-4960 Office Phone: 504-830-4646. E-mail: arhardy@bellsouth.net.

HARDY, BEN(SON B.), orchid nursery executive; b. Oakland, Calif., Nov. 22, 1920; s. Lester William and Irene Isabell (Bliss) H. Student pub. schs., Oakland, Calif., Concord, Calif.; grad. photo, Intelligence Sch., Denver, 1949. Served as enlisted man U.S. Navy, 1942-48; joined USAF, 1948; advanced through grades to capt., 1957; with 67th Reconnaisance Squadron Korea, 1951-52; Hdqrs. Squadron Thule AFB, 1956; resigned, 1957; material requirements analyst-coord. Teledyne Ryan Aero. Co., San Diego, 1958-73, 83-98, ret., 1998. Dispatcher-coord. Cubic Western Data Co., San Diego, 1977-80; owner-ptnr. orchid nursery. Pres. Exotic Plant Soc., 1976-78, 81-84, San Diego Gesneriad Soc., 1978; dir. 23d Western Orchid Congress, 1979. Author: (with John Klemme) The Orchid Badge Collector's Guide, 1993, (with Duane Hall) Photographic Aerial Reconnaissance and Interpretation Korea 1950-1952, 2004. Decorated Bronze Star; recipient Letter of Commendation NASA, also others. Mem. Am. Orchid Soc. (life), N.Z. Orchid Soc., San Diego County Orchid Soc. (life, pres. 1972-73, 75-76), Hoya Soc. Internat. (pres. 1981-83, 95-2002), Orchid Digest Corp., Auckland Orchid Club, Orchid Badge Club Internat. (found. 1988, pres. 1991—), Dirs. Club, San Diego Zool. Soc., Korean War Vets. Assn. (life), VFW (life). Home: 9443 E Heaney Cir Santee CA 92071-2919 Personal E-mail: Cptdlttl@aol.com.

HARDY, CHESTER ALFRED, engineer; b. El Paso, Tex., Nov. 17, 1929; m. Evelyn Anne Moore, June 22, 1955; 1 child, Clinton Alfred (dec.). BS in Engring., U. Tex., El Paso, 1955; MS in Engring., So. Meth. U., 1959, MS in Engring. Adminstrn., 1961. Registered profl. engr., Tex. Mgr. Gen. Dynamics, Fort Worth, Tex., 1980-87; dir. Lockheed Martin, Fort Worth, 1987—2001; ret. Chmn. corp. R&M panel Gen. Dynamics, 1976; lectr. Agard Nato, Munich, London, N.Y., 1976; tchr. bus. sch. Tex. Christian U., Ft. Worth, 1968. Contbr. articles to profl. jours. With USN, 1948-52. Named to, Lockheed Martin Aero. Hall of Fame. Mem. Tex. Soc. Profl. Engrs., Moslah Shrine, Colonial Country Club, Petroleum Club, Soc. of the Cincinnati, Soc. Sons of Bench and Bar, Soc. Mayflower Desces., Jamestowne Soc., Ancient and Hon. Arty. Co. of Mass., SAR, Flagon and Trencher, Colonial Order of the Crown, Magna Charta Barons, Soc. Knights of the Garter, Soc. Descs. of Colonial Clergy, Nat. Huguenot Soc., Nat. Soc. Sons and Daus. of Pilgrims, Plantagenet Soc. Episcopalian. Avocations: tennis, skiing.

HARDY, CLARENCE EARL, JR., government, nonprofit and corporate sector executive; b. Edenton, NC, July 2, 1944; m. Mae A. Brewer; children: Clarence, Melva. BA in Polit. Sci. and Econs., N.C. Ctrl. U., 1967; MPA in Pub. Adminstrn., Syracuse U., 1969; diploma in sr. mgrs. in govt. program, Harvard U., 1990. Pers. mgmt. analyst Atomic Energy Commn., 1971-73; pers. officer, mgmt. analyst Atomic Energy Commn. Energy Rsch. and Devel. Adminstrn., 1973-75, sr. mgmt. analyst, program evaluation officer, 1975-76, chief hqrs. pers. ops. br., 1976-77; pers. officer Fed. Energy Regulatory Commn., 1978; chief pers. mgmt. svcs. Dept. Energy Hqrs., 1977-78, dep. dir. hqrs. pers. ops. divsn., 1978-79; chief pers. divsn. Nat. Bur. Standards, 1979; dir. pers. mgmt. EPA, 1979-88, dep. dir. Office of Human Resources Mgmt., 1988-97; dir. Office Cooperative Environ. Mgmt., 1997—2001; exec. dir. Combined Fed. Campaign of Nat. Capital Area, 2001—03; pres. & CEO DQC Consultants, 1994—. Prof. George Mason U., 1998—99. Recipient Disting. Fed. Career award, 2001; N.C. Ctrl U. Polit. Sci. scholar, 1966, 67, Presdl. rank award, 1998; Maxwell fellow, 1968, 69, Congl. fellow Brookings Instn., 1996. Mem. Internat. Pers. Mgmt. Assn., Internat. Platform Assn., Am. Soc. Pub. Adminstrn., Am. Mgmt. Assn., Am. Judicature Soc., Acad. Polit. and Social Sci., Am. Polit. Sci. Assn., World Future Soc., Acad. Mgmt., Nat. Assn. Environ. Profls. Office Phone: 301-869-2909. Personal E-mail: cehardy44@aol.com.

HARDY, DEBORAH LEWIS, dean, educator, dental hygienist; b. Nov. 11, 1963; Student, Christopher Newport Coll., 1982-84; BS in Dental Hygiene, Old Dominion U., 1989, cert. in gerontol. studies, 1991, MS in Dental Hygiene, 1991; postgrad., U. Tex., Dallas, 1993. Cert. ADA Joint Commn. on Nat. Dental Exam.; lic. S.E. Regional Va., Tex., Va.; cert. in cardiopulmonary resuscitation. Assoc. prof. Caruth Sch. Dental Hygiene Baylor Coll., Dallas, 1991-95; assoc. dean health occupations-dental N.E. Wis. Tech. Coll., Green Bay, 1995-97, assoc. dean health and cmty. svc., 1997—. Dental asst. Dr. William Griffin, Newport News, Va., 1989; dental asst., dental hygienist Dental Power, Inc., Newport News, 1988-90; dental hygienist Dr. John Caudill, Virginia Beach, 1990-91, Drs. Cash and Weisburg, Norfolk, Va., 1990-91; dental hygienist, educator Riverside Regional Convalescent Ctr., Newport News, 1991; part-time dental hygienist East Dallas Clinic, 1992-95, Nelson-Tebedo Dental Clinic, Dallas, 1995, Oneida (Wis.) Dental Clinic, 1997; cons., educator Skilled Nursing Facility, Collins Hosp., Baylor U. Med. Ctr., Dallas, 1992; lectr. and spkr. in field. Author: (book) Preventive Oral Health Services Provided by Nurses' Aides to Nursing Home Residents, 1991, (book chpt.) Oral Health and the Older Adult, 1995; editor: (newsletter) Oral Examiner, 1993-95; mem. editl. bd. Profl. Devel. Quar. PDQ, 1994-95; contbr. numerous articles and abstracts to profl. jours. Dental hygienist, educator Operation Smile Internat., Ghana Med. Mission, Accra, 1989; vol. Ea. Va. Med. Sch.-Ea. Shore, 1988, Girls Inc., Dallas, 1992; coord. Spirit of Christmas Program, Caruth Sch. Dental Hygiene, 1991, Sr. Student Oral Health Edn., St. Philip's Episcopal Sch. and Comty. Ctr., Dallas, 1993, Health Fair, Dallas Marriott Quorum Hotel, 1993. Recipient Acad. Dentistry for the Handicapped award, 1989, award for phenomenal achievement and leadership Women Dentists' Awards Luncheon, 1993; fellow Old Dominion U., 1990; also numerous rsch. grants in field. Mem. Am. Vocat. Assn., Nat. Dental Hygienists' Assn., Am. Dental Hygienists' Assn., Am. Assn. Dental Schs., Student Nat. Dental Assn. (faculty facilitator 1992-95), N.E. Wis. African Am. Assn. (membership chair 1997), Dallas Dental Hygienists' Soc. (Mem. of Month 1993, 95), Sigma Phi Alpha. Office: NE Wis Tech Coll PO Box 19042 2740 W Mason St Green Bay WI 54303-4966

HARDY, DORCAS RUTH, business and government relations executive; b. Newark, July 18, 1946; d. C. Colburn and Ruth (Hart) H.; m. Samuel V. Spagnolo. BA, Conn. Coll., 1964-68; MBA, Pepperdine U., 1976. cert. sr. advisor. Legis. rsch. asst. U.S. Senator Clifford P. Case, Washington, 1970; spl. asst. White House Conf. Children and Youth, Washington, 1970-71; exec. dir. Health Svcs. Industry Commn., Cost of Living Coun., Washington, 1971-73; asst. sec. Calif. Dept. Health, Sacramento, 1973-74; assoc. dir. U. So. Calif. Ctr. Health Svcs. Rsch., 1974-81; asst. sec. human devel. svcs. HHS, Washington, 1981-86; commr. Social Security Washington, 1986-89; pres. Dorcas R. Hardy & Assocs., Spotsylvania, Va., 1989—; exec. v.p. Pub. Issue Mgmt., Washington, 2001—03. Chmn. bd., CEO Work Recovery, Inc., Tucson, 1996-98; bd. dirs. First Coast Svc. Options, Inc.; chmn. Ind. Trustees Wright Investors Svc. Managed Funds; Social Security Advisory Bd.; chmn. vocat. rehab. and employment task force VA, 2003-04; chmn. policy com. 2005 White House Conf. on Aging, 2004-06. Author: Social Insecurity: The Crisis in America's Social Security System and How to Plan Now for Your Own Financial Survival, 1992. Active Girl Scouts USA, friends of Our chalet com; Va. Bd. Rehab. Svcs., 1998-2002, bd. dirs. Com. on Developing Am. Capitalism; former chmn. Pres.'s Task Force on Legal Equity for Women. Mem.: Soc. Cert. Sr. Advisors. Office: Washington Metro Office 11407 Stonewall Jackson Dr Spotsylvania VA 22553-4608

HARDY, EVA TEIG, energy executive; B in Polit. Sci., Hood Coll., Frederick, Md.; M in Govt. and Pub. Adminstrn., Am. U. Urban planner City of Portsmouth, Va.; sec. health and human resources for Gov. Gerald L. Baliles State of Va., 1986—90; with Dominion, Richmond, Va., 1990—, sr. v.p. Va. Power, 1997, sr. v.p. external affairs & corp. comm., 1999—2006, exec. v.p. external affairs & corp. comm., 2007—. Mem. State Coun. Higher Edn. Va., 2005—. Named one of Outstanding Women of Greater Richmond in Govt. and Politics, YMCA; recipient Lifetime Achievement award, Urban League of Greater Richmond, Flame Bearer of Edn. award, United Negro Coll. Fund, Wilder Sch. Pub. Svc. award, Va. Commonwealth U., 2005. Office: Dominion PO Box 26532 Richmond VA 23261-6532*

HARDY, HARVEY LOUCHARD, retired lawyer; b. Dallas, Dec. 2, 1914; s. Nat L. and Winifred F. (Fouraker) H.; m. Edna Vivian Bedell, Feb. 14, 1948; children: Victoria Elizabeth Hardy Pursch, Alice Anne Hardy Gannon. Bar: Tex. 1936, US Dist. Ct. (so. and we. dists.) Tex. 1946, US Ct. Appeals (5th cir.) 1946, US Supreme Ct. 1949. First asst. dist. atty. Bexar County, San Antonio, 1947-50, acting dist. atty., 1950-51; city atty. San Antonio, 1952—53, Castle Hills, Tex., 1967—96, Helotes, Tex., 1984-96, Fair Oaks Ranch, Tex., 1973-96; legal adviser bd. trustees Fireman and Policemen's Pension Fund of San Antonio, 1956-96; ret. Legal advisor Grey Forest Utilities, 1986-96. Author: A Lifetime at the Bar: A Lawyer's Memoir, 1999. 1st lt. inf. US Army, 1941-45. Decorated Bronze Star with cluster. Fellow Tex. Bar Found.; mem. Tex. Bar Assn., San Antonio Bar Found., Tex. Assn. City Atts., San Antonio Bar Assn. Methodist. Home: 215 Atwater Dr San Antonio TX 78213

HARDY, HUGH, architect; b. Mallorca, Spain, July 26, 1932; s. Gelston Hardy and Barbara Hardy LaVenture; m. Tiziana Spadea, Jan. 29, 1966; children: Sebastian, Penelope. B.Arch., Princeton U., 1954, M.F.A. in Architecture, 1956. Archtl. asst. to Jo Mielziner, NYC, 1958-62; founder Hugh Hardy & Assocs., NYC, 1962-67; ptnr., owner Hardy Holzman Pfeiffer Assocs., NYC and L.A., 1967—. Davenport vis. prof. archtl. design Yale U., 1976; Saarinen vis. prof. Yale U., 1987; past chmn. Design Arts Adv. Panel Nat. Endowment for the Arts; apptd. to Nat. Council on the Arts by Pres. of U.S., 1992; cons., lectr. in field. Designer: Orchestra Hall, Mpls., 1974, Cooper-Hewitt Mus., N.Y.C., 1976, St. Louis Art Mus., 1977, The Joyce Theater, N.Y.C., 1982, Rizzoli Bookstore, N.Y.C., New Victory Theater, 1995, Bryant Park Restaurant, 1995, Windows in the World, 1996, New Amsterdam Theater, 1997, U.S. Customs and Immigration Ctr. Rainbow Bridge, Niagara Falls, N.Y., 1998, Radio City Music Hall, N.Y.C., 1999, Bridgemarket, N.Y.C., 2000. Bd. dirs. Isamu Noguchi Found., Mcpl. Art Soc. N.Y., N.Y.C., 1976—, v.p., 1981—, lifetime dir., 1992—; bd. mem. N.Y.C. Hist. House Trust, 1989—. Recipient D'Amato prize Princeton U., 1954, Brunner prize in architecture Nat. Inst. Arts and Letters, 1974, Benjamin West Clinedinst medal Artists' Fellowship Inc., 1988. Fellow AIA (N.Y. chpt. medal of honor 1978, Archtl. Firm award 1981, several honor awards); mem. Archtl. League N.Y. (v.p. for architecture 1977-81, bd. dirs. 1987—), Nat. Acad. Design (assoc.), Am. Acad. Arts and Letters, Century Assn. Office: Hardy Holzman Pfeiffer Assocs 902 Broadway Fl 19 New York NY 10010-6082

HARDY, JIM, JR., food products executive; BS in Indsl. Engring., U. Fla., Gainesville. With Procter & Gamble; v.p. product supply Clorox Co., 2001—05, head global mfg.; sr. v.p. enterprise mfg. to exec. v.p. product supply ConAgra Foods, Inc., Omaha, 2005—. Nuc. reactor operator on submarines USN. Office: ConAgra Foods Inc 1 ConAgra Dr Omaha NE 68102-5001 Office Phone: 402-595-4000.*

HARDY, JOHN, artist; b. Tours, France, Mar. 23, 1923; s. Charles Crum Hardy and Jacqueline Blanche Marie Gadois; m. Elizabeth Blackman (div.); children: Jacqueline, André, Michael, Blanche; life ptnr. Joan Semmel. B in Visual Arts, Ga. State U., Atlanta, 1969. One-man shows include Brentwood Gallery, Calif., 1972, Aronson-Midtown Gallery, Atlanta, 1972, 1975, Sardoni Gallery, Wilkes Coll., Wilkes-Barre, Pa., 1978, Genesis Gallery, NYC, 1978, La. State U., Baton Rouge, 1979, Rice U., Houston, 1979, Stanley and Schenke Gallery, Atlanta, 1982, Armstrong Gallery, NYC, 1984, Lamar Dodd Art Ctr., LaGrange Coll., Ga., 1985, Macon Mus. Arts and Scis., 1986, Mus. of Western Va., Roanoke, 1987, Huntington Mus., W.Va., 1988, Cress Fine Arts Ctr., U. Tenn., Chattanooga, 1988, MacIntosh Gallery, Atlanta, 1989, Haines Lundberg Waehler Architecture Gallery, NYC, 1990, Ratner Gallery, Chgo., 1993, Bologna-Landi Gallery, East Hampton, NY, 1993, J. Gibson/Hemphill Fine Arts, Washington, 1993, Michael Walls Gallery, NYC, 1993, Hurlbutt Gallery, Greenwich, Conn., 1994, Undwercroft Gallery, St. Ann's Sch., Bklyn., 2000, DFN Gallery, NYC, 2002, 2006, Frances Aronson Fine Art, Atlanta, 2004, Elaine Baker Gallery, Boca Raton, Fla., 2004, Mason Murer Fine Arts, Atlanta, 2007, 2-person shows, Joanna Dean Gallery, NYC, 1982, Ga. Mus. Art, Athens, 1987, Brenda Taylor Gallery, NYC, 1996, exhibited in group shows at Piano Gallery, Hilton Head, SC, 1972, Aronson Midtown Gallery, Atlanta, 1972, Brentwood Gallery, Calif., 1973, Dalton Galleries/Agnes Scott Coll., Atlanta, 1973, Mus. Arts and Scis., Macon, 1974, Le Moyne Found. Gallery, Tallahassee, Fla., 1974, High Mus., Atlanta, 1974, Roko Gallery, NYC, 1975, Paul Kessler Gallery, Provincetown, Mass., 1976, Root Art Ctr., Hamilton Coll., Clinton, NY, 1977, Genesis Gallery, NYC, 1977, Nat. Collection Fine Art, Washington, 1979, Mint Mus., Charlotte, NC, 1980, Bklyn. Mus., 1980, Arts for Living Ctr., Henry St. Settlement, NYC, 1981, Arbitrage Gallery, 1983, Stephen Rosenberg Gallery, 1983, Sid Deutch Gallery, 1983, Fay Gold Gallery, Atlanta, 1984, Jerald Melberg Gallery, Charlotte, 1984, Tweed Gallery, Plainfield, NJ, 1984, Armstrong Gallery, NYC, 1984, Die Techische U., Berlin, 1984, Nexus Mattress Factory, Atlanta, 1986, Artists' Union, Kiev, Ukraine, 1988, Uddo Gallery, NYC, 1989, Brenda Taylor Gallery, 1996, Swann Coach Ho. Gallery, Atlanta, 2001, Lisan Tops Gallery, East Hampton, 2001, 2003, DFN Gallery, NYC, 2002, 2003, 2004, 2007, Hampton Rd. Gallery, Southampton, NY, 2003, NY Hist. Soc., 2004, Whitney Mus. Am. Art, NYC, 2006, ACA Gallery, 2007, Krasdale Galleries, Bronx, NY, 2007, Represented in permanent collections Bklyn. Mus., High Mus., Mint Mus., Nat. Mus. Am. Art, Mus. Western Va., US State Dept., Art in Embassies Program, Ga. Coun. Arts, Greenville County Mus., SC, Hunter Mus. Am. Art, Morris Mus., Macon Mus. Art and Scis., Guild Hall Mus., Ogden Mus., New Orleans, Rockefeller Coillection, Morris Brown Coll., Columbia U. Law Sch., La. State U., NYU, Ga. State U., Ga. Inst. Tech., La Grange Coll., Mus. Art U. Iowa, Rice U., U. Tenn., Chattanooga, U. Va. Law Sch., Southerland Asbill & Brennan Law Firm, Atlanta, Cousins Devel. Corp., Carter & Assocs. Real Estate, Kilpatrick Cody Law Firm, Kutak Rock Campbell Law Firm, King & Spalding Law Firm, The Mead Collection, Paul Weiss Rifkind Wharton & Garrison Law Firm, NYC, Reader's Digest Lila Acheson Wallace Found. Fund, Near North Agys., Chgo., NY Hist. Soc. Mus. Contemporary Art, Ga., numerous pvt. collections. Master sgt. Air Corps US Army, 1940—45, ETO. Home: 109 Spring St 2d Fl New York NY 10012

HARDY, JOHN CHRISTOPHER, physicist, researcher, educator; b. Montreal, Que., Can., July 10, 1941; s. Noel Woodburn and Ethel May (Collins) H.; m. Lynn Helen Frederick, June 3, 1964 (div.); children: Ericka, Kirsten, Bruce, Alana; m. June Dennie, July 5, 1997; stepchildren: Benjamin, Samantha. BSc, McGill U., Montreal, 1961, MSc, 1963, PhD, 1965. NRC Can. postdoctoral fellow Oxford Nuc. Physics Lab., 1965—67; Miller rsch. fellow Lawrence Radiation Lab., Berkeley, Calif., 1967—69, staff physicist, 1969—70; assoc. rsch. officer Atomic Energy Can. Ltd., Chalk River, Ont., 1970—74, sr. rsch. officer, 1975—83, head nuc. physics br., 1983—86, asst. v.p., 1986—89, dir. tandem accelerator superconducting cyclotron divsn., 1989—97; prof. physics Tex. A&M U., College Station, 1997—2006, disting. prof., 2006—. Sci. assoc. CERN, Geneva, 1976-77; program adv. coms. Oak Ridge Nat. Lab., UNISOR, 1979-85, HHIRL, 1991-92, HRIBF, 1999-2006, chmn., 2000-06; program adv. coms. Lawrence Berkeley Lab., Super HILAC, 1983-86, Cyclotron, 1994-99, chmn., 1995-99; program adv. com. Nat. Superconducting Cyclotron Lab., 1990-93; mem. adv. bd. TRIUMF, 1992-98, U. Chgo. rev. com. physics divsn. Argonne Nat. Lab., 1999, program adv. com ATLAS, 2007-; mem. sci. policy com. HRIBF, Oak Ridge Nat. Lab., 2002—. Contbr. articles to profl. jours. and books; editor North Renfrew Times, 1972-97; mem. editl. bd. Nuc. Physics News Internat., 1995-97, Phys. Rev. C. Jour., 1980-82, 95-97. Chmn. bd. dirs., co-founder Deep River Sci. Acad., 1986-97, trustee 1997—. Recipient D.W. Ambridge prize, McGill U., 1965, Disting. Achievement award for rsch., Assn. Former Students, Tex. A&M U., 2006. Fellow: Am. Phys. Soc. (DNP program com. 1999—2001, exec. com. DNP 2002—04, chair DNP publs. com. 2003—04, Tom W. Bonner prize 2006), Royal Soc. Can. (v.p. acad. III 1992—95, chmn. fundraising com. 1994—97, Rutherford medal in physics 1981); mem.: Can. Assn. Physicists (Herzberg medal 1976). Office: Tex A&M U Cyclotron Inst College Station TX 77843-3366 Office Phone: 979-845-1411. E-mail: hardy@comp.tamu.edu.

HARDY, JOHN EDWARD, language educator, writer; b. Baton Rouge, Apr. 3, 1922; s. Roger Barlow and Mary (McCoy) H.; m. Marie Elam, Dec. 30, 1942 (div.); children: Margot (Mrs. Timm Ferguson), Leonore (Mrs. David Dvorkin), Catherine, Laura, Anne, Eve; m. Willene Schaefer, June 25, 1969. BA, La. State U., 1944; MA, State U. Iowa, 1946; PhD, Johns Hopkins U., 1956. Mem. English faculties U. Detroit, 1945-46, Yale U., 1946-48, U. Okla., 1948-52, Johns Hopkins U., 1952-54; mem. faculty U. Notre Dame, 1954-66, prof. English, 1964-66, mem. acad. council, 1963-66, grad. council, 1963-66; prof. English, chmn. dept. U. South Ala., 1966-69; prof. English U. Colo., Boulder, 1969-70; prof. English, chmn. dept. U. Mo., St. Louis, 1970-72; dir. grad. studies in English U. Ill.-Chgo., 1972-75, prof. English, 1972-92; prof. emeritus, 1992—; head dept. English U. Ill.-Chgo., 1984-89, mem. grad. coll. exec. com., 1974-76, 81-82. Author: (with Cleanth Brooks) Poems of Mr. John Milton, 1951, The Curious Frame, 1962, Man in the Modern Novel, 1964, Katherine Anne Porter, 1973, Certain Poems, 1958, The Fiction of Walker Percy, 1987; Editor: The Modern Talent, 1964, (with Seymour L. Gross) Images of the Negro in American Literature, 1966. Fulbright prof. Am. lit. U. Munich, Germany, 1959-61; Ford Faculty Study fellow, 1952-53; Rockefeller fellow poetry, 1954; fellow Inst. for Humanities U. Ill. Chgo., 1989-90. Mem. MLA, Phi Beta Kappa. Home: 6033 Riverbend Lakes Dr Baton Rouge LA 70820-5050

HARDY, JOSEPH A., SR., wholesale distribution executive; b. 1923; BS in Engring., U. Pitts. Retail jeweler Hardy & Hayes Corp., Pitts., 1946—52; founder Green Hills Lumber, 1952—56; founder, chmn., CEO 84 Cash & Carry Inc. (now 84 Lumber Co.), Eighty Four, Pa., 1956—; pres. 84 Lumber Co., 1956-93. Vice chmn. Fayette County Bd. Commissioners. With U.S. Army, 1942-46. Recipient Philanthropist of the Year award, Assn. Fundraising Professionals, 2004, Golden Hammer award, Home Channel News, 2004, Fayette Chamber of Comm. Citizen Yr. award, Am. Legion Citizen Yr. award, 2004. Office: 84 Lumber Co 1019 Rt 519 Eighty Four PA 15330

HARDY, MICHELE, literature and language professor; b. La Plata, Md. MA, Johns Hopkins U., Balt., 1998. Assoc. prof. English U. Md. U. Coll., College Park, 1998—, Prince George's CC, Largo, Md., 2000—. Mem.: Coll. English Assn. (exec. bd. mem. 2004—06), NCTE.

HARDY, RALPH W. F., biochemist; b. Lindsay, Ont., Can., July 27, 1934; s. Wilbur and Elsie Hardy; m. Jacqueline M. Thayer, Dec. 26, 1954; children: Steven, Chris, Barbara, Ralph(dec.) , Jon. BSA, U. Toronto, 1956; MS, U. Wis.-Madison, 1958, PhD, 1959; DSc (hon.), U. Guelph, 1997. Asst. prof. U. Guelph, Ont., Can., 1960-63; research biochemist DuPont deNemours & Co., Wilmington, Del., 1963-67, research supr., 1967-74, assoc. dir., 1974-79, dir. life scis., 1979-84; pres. Bio Technica Internat., Inc., Cambridge, Mass., 1984-86; pres., CEO Boyce Thompson Inst., Inc., Ithaca, NY, 1986-95, pres. emeritus, 2000—; dep. chmn. Bio Technica Internat., Inc., 1986-90, cons., bd. dirs., 1990-99; pres. Nat. Agrl. Biotech. Coun., Ithaca, 1996—. Mem. exec. com. bd. agr. NRC, 1982—88, mem. commn. life scis., 1984—90, bd. biology, 1984—90, mem. com. on biotech., 1988—95, chmn. com., 1993—94, bd. sci. technol. internat. devel., 1990—93, chmn. com. on biol. control, 1992—95, chmn. com. on biol. nitrogen fixation, 1992—94, chmn. com. on natural products, 1996—97; mem. com. genetic experimentation Internat. Coun. Sci. Union, 1981—95; chmn., founder Nat. Agrl. Biotech. Coun., 1988—93; mem. sci. adv. com. U.S. Dept. Energy, 1991—95; mem. alt. agr. rsch. comml. bd. USDA, 1992—96, mem. and corp. sec. alt. agrl. rsch. comml. corp., 1996—2000; mem. Can. reallocations com. NSERC, 1997—98; mem. sci. adv. bd. Foragen, Guelph, Ont., Canada, 1999—; bd. dirs. BioCap, Canada, BioProducts, Can. Author: Nitrogen Fixation, 1975, A Treatise on Dinitrogen Fixation, 3 vols., 1977—79; contbr. articles to profl. jours. Mem. biotechnology exec. bd. Cornell U., 1986—95, mem. adv. coun. Vet. Coll., 1989—96; mem. gov. bd. Cornell Ctr. Environment, 1991—95. Recipient Gov. Gen.'s Silver medal, 1956, Sterling Henricks award, 1986; WARF fellow, 1956—58, DuPont fellow, 1958—59. Mem.: Am. Soc. Microbiology, Am. Soc. Agronomy, Am. Soc. Plant Biology (mem. exec. com., treas. 1974—77), Am. Soc. Biol. Chemists and Molecular Biologists, Am. Chem. Soc. (mem. exec. com. biol. chemisty divsn. 1978—81, Del. award 1969), Agr. Rsch. Inst. (bd. govs. 1988—91), Indsl. Biotechnology Assn. (bd. dirs. 1986—89). Episcopalian.

HARDY, RICHARD ALLEN, mechanical engineer, engineering executive; b. Cleve., Sept. 16, 1928; s. Harry and Mae Hardy; m. Lois L. Fawcett, May 16, 1953 (dec. Dec. 1990); children: Pamela, Richard, James, Thomas. BSME, Case Inst. Tech., 1952. Founder, CEO Fluid Mechanics Inc., Cleve., 1957—. Cpl. U.S. Army, 1946-48. Recipient Weatherhead 100 award Cleve., 1989. Mem. Assn. of Diesel Specialists (various coms. 1960—). Roman Catholic. Achievements include helped design and build largest dynamic fuel-injection pump test stand in Western hemisphere. Avocations: racquetball, scuba. Home: 26875 Hilliard Blvd Cleveland OH 44145-3213

HARDY, RICHARD ALLEN, JR., psychologist, educator; b. Danville, Va., Feb. 11, 1944; s. R. Allen and Jeanne Arthur Hardy; 1 child from previous marriage, Monica. BA, Fla. State U., Tallahassee, 1966; MS, Auburn U., Ala., 1968, PhD, 1971, postdoctoral student, 1979—81. Rsch. assoc. HumRRO, Columbus, Ga., 1971—73; unit psychologist Partlow State Sch. and Hosp., Tuscaloosa, Ala., 1973—79; psychologist dept. corrections Marion Correctional Inst., Ocala, Fla., 1986—94, Tomoka Correctional Inst., Daytona Beach, Fla., 1994; tchr. Duvl County Sch. Bd., Jacksonville, Fla., 1995—. Internat. sports cons.; mem. Assn. for Internat. Cultural Exch. Programs. Author: (book, tng. manual) Innovative Olympic Training, 1996. VIP 25th Olympiad, Barcelona; co-capt. Team USA World Fitness Festival, Moscow, 1991—92; capt. Team USA, 1992; amb. Mel Whitfield, Washington, 1995; goodwill amb. First African Games, Zimbabwe, 1995; capt. Team USA, 1992; mem. Team USA vs. Team USSR Adult Fitness Competition, Moscow, 1990, Team USA vs. Team Spain Family Fitness Tour, Madrid; performer World's Fair, Seville, Spain. Capt. USAR, 1967—68. Mem.: Runners For Christ, World Fitness Fedn. (founder), Sigma Xi. Republican. Avocations: running, track and field. Office Phone: 904-743-3322.

HARDY, RICHARD EARL, rehabilitation counseling educator; b. Victoria, Va., Oct. 11, 1938; s. Clifford E. and Louise (Hamilton) H.; 1 son, Jason Elliott. BS, Va. Poly. Inst. and State U., 1960, MS, 1962, EdD, 1966. Rehab. counselor State of Va., Richmond, 1961-63; rehab. advisor HHS, Washington, 1964-66; chief psychologist S.C. Dept. Rehab., Columbia, 1966-68; prof. chmn. dept. rehab. counseling Med. Coll. Va., Richmond, 1968-96, chmn., prof. emeritus, 1996—. Former bd. mem. S.C. State Bd. Psychology, former ABPP candidate examiner; internat. cons. to numerous countries including Turkey, Iraq, Peru, Uruguay, South Africa, Brazil, Thailand Author, editor: International Rehabilitation: Approaches and Programs, Hemingway: A Psychological Portrait, 1988, Gestalt Psychotherapy, 1991, Hispaniola Episode: A Mental Health Allegory, 1992, (with J.G. Cull) The Brass Chalice: Drug Prevention Stories and Information for Children and Youth, 1994, Counseling in the Rehabilitation Process, 1999, Woodpeckers Don't Get Headaches: The Psychology of Stress, Relationships, and Addiction, 2001, numerous others. Recipient Nat. award Nat. Rehab. Assn., 1976; recipient Nat. award Am. Assn. Workers for Blind, 1976, Outstanding Grad. award Med. Coll. Va./Va. Commonwealth U., Dept. Rehab. Counseling, 1997, Richard E. Hardy endowed scholarship Med. Coll. Va., 1998, Outstanding Scholar award U. Md. Sch. Edn., 2006. Fellow Am. Psychol. Soc., Assn. Allied & Preventive Psychology; mem. Am. Assn. Vol. Action Scholars, Phi Kappa Phi. Office: Va Commonwealth U 6962 Forest Hill Ave Richmond VA 23225

HARDY, SEAN, chef; Grad., Culinary Inst. Am., NYC. Exec. sous chef Four Seasons Hotel, Palm Beach, Fla.; lead chef instr. New England Culinary Inst.; exec. chef The Lodge at Koele, Lanai City, Hawaii; food and beverage mgr. Peninsula Hotel, Beverly Hills; exec. chef The Belvedere, Peninsula Hotel, Beverly Hills. Named one of LA's Rising Stars, StarChefs.com, 2006. Office: The Belvedere at The Peninsula Hotel 9882 South Santa Monica Blvd Beverly Hills CA 90212 Office Phone: 310-551-2888.*

HARDY, THOMAS CRESSON, insurance company executive; b. Hoisington, Kans., 1942; s. C.C. and Delia Hardy; children: Jay C., Glenn W. BA, U. Kans., 1963; MBA, Wharton Sch., U. Pa., 1965. CLU, CPCU, FLMI. With Exxon Corp., NYC, 1965-69; treas. Keene Corp., NYC, 1969-73; exec. v.p. fin. Fidelity Union Life Ins. Co. (co. acquired by Allianz of Am.), Dallas, 1973-79; v.p. Allianz of Am.; pres. Allianz Investment Corp., Dallas, 1979-82; pres., CEO Gt. Am. Res. Ins. Co., 1983-88; exec. v.p., COO Provident Life & Accident Ins. Co., Chattanooga, 1988-94; pres., CEO, bd. dirs. Loewen Life Ins. Group, 1997—2000, Mayflower Nat. Life Ins. Co., 1997—2000, Unity Fin. Life Ins. Co., 2001—. Chmn. bd. dirs. Security Instnl. Co., 1997-2000; pres., CEO, bd. dirs. Nat. Capitol Life, 1997-2000. Bd. dirs., pres. Chattanooga Symphony & Opera Assn., 1989-97, La. Philharm. Orch., 1999-2001; pres. Cin. Fire Mus., 2006; bd. dirs. exec. com. Chattanooga Allied Arts, 1992-97; mem. adv. bd. U. Kans. Bus. Sch., bd. dirs. 1994—; bd. visitors Berry Coll., 1992-99; trustee Huebner Found., 2005-. Mem. Fin. Execs. Inst. (chpt. pres., nat. bd. dirs.). Office: Unity Financial Life Ins Co 11311 Cornell Park Dr Ste 200 Cincinnati OH 45242 Office Phone: 513-247-0711. Business E-Mail: thardy@uflife.com.

HARDY, VICTORIA ELIZABETH, finance educator; b. Marion, NC, Feb. 26, 1947; d. Milton Victor Roth and Bertha Jean (Norris) R.; m. Michael Carrington Hardy, June 19, 1983 (div. 1993); 1 child, Christopher. BS in Edn., U. Mo., 1970; postgrad., So. Ill. U., 1974-75; postgrad. Mgmt. Devel. Program, Stanford U., 1980-81; MA in Mgmt., Aquinas Coll., 1999. Cert. facility mgr. Pub. sch. tchr. English and Theater, 1970-75; gen. mgr. Miss. River Festival, Edwardsville, Ill., 1975-77; dir. events and svcs. Stanford (Calif.) U., 1977-83; exec. dir. Meadowlands Ctr. for the Arts, Rutherford, N.J., 1983-87; pres., chief exec. officer Music Hall Ctr. for the Arts, Detroit, 1987-89; prin. AMS Planning & Rsch., Conn., 1989-94; prof. facility mgmt. Ferris State U., Big Rapids, Mich., 1994—2003; acad. dept. head Wentworth Inst. Tech., Boston, 2003—. Contbr. to various publs. Mem. USICA study team to China, 1981; bd. dirs. Internat. Facility Mgmt. Assn., 1994-97, standing coms. recognition and profl. devel.; mem. People to People facilities del. to Australia and New Zealand, 1996; bd. dirs., chair IFMA Found., 1998-2004. Named Disting. Educator of Yr., Internat. Facility Mgmt. Assn., 2001, Disting. Mem. of Yr., 2005, Educator of Yr., Boston Internat. Facility Mgmt. Assn., 2005; named to Creativity in Business Doubleday, 1986; recipient Gold medal for Cmty. Programs, Coun. for Advancement and Support of Edn., Stanford, 1985. Democrat. Avocations: skiing, gardening. Office: Acad Dept Head Design & Facilities Wentworth Inst Tech 550 Hungtington Ave Boston MA 02115 Office Phone: 617-989-4050.

HARDY, WALTER NEWBOLD, physics professor, researcher; b. Vancouver, BC, Mar. 25, 1940; s. Walter Thomas and Julia Marguerite (Mulroy) H.; m. Sheila Lorraine Hughes, July 10, 1959; children: Kevin James, Steven Wayne. BSc in Math and Physics with honors, U. B.C., 1961; PhD in Physics, Univ. B.C., 1965. Postdoctral fellow Centre d'Etudes Nucleaires de Saclay, France, 1964-66; mem. tech. staff N.Am. Rockwell, Thousand Oaks, Calif., 1966-71; assoc. prof. physics U. B.C., 1971-76, prof., 1976—. Vis. scientist Ecole Normale Superieure, Paris, 1980-81, 85, 95. Contbr. articles to sci. jours.; patentee precision microwave instrumentation. Recipient Stacie prize NRC of Can., 1978, Gold medal B.C. Sci. Coun., 1989, Killam prize Can. Coun., 1999, Fritz London Prize, 2002, Brockhouse Can. prize for interdisciplinary rsch. in sci. and engring, 2006; Rutherford Meml. scholar, 1964; Alfred P. Sloan fellow, 1972-74; Can. Coun. Rsch. fellow, 1984-86. Fellow Am. Phys. Soc.; mem. Can. Assn. Physicists (Herzberg medal 1978, gold medal for achievement in physics, 1993, Brockhouse medal 1999). Office: U BC Dept Physics Astronomy Vancouver BC Canada V6T 1Z1

HARDY, WAYNE RUSSELL, insurance and investment broker; b. Denver, Sept. 5, 1931; s. Russell Hinton and Victoria Katherine (Anderson) H.; m. Carolyn Lucille Carvell, Aug. 1, 1958 (July 1977); children: James Russell Hardy, Jann Miller Hardy. BSCE, U. Colo., 1954; MS in Fin. Svcs., Am. Coll., 1989. CLU; chartered fin. cons. Mgr. we. dist. Fenestra, Inc., San Francisco, 1956—63; ins. and investment broker John Hancock Fin. Svs., Denver, 1963—, Wayne R. Hardy Assocs., Denver, 1963—. Speaker convs. and sales seminars, 1977, 81, 84, 85, 89; v.p. CLU assn. John Hancock, 1979-80, chmn. agt.'s adv. com., 1983-84; active State of Colo. Ins. Adv. Bd., 1991-93; profl. model, actor J.F. Images Agy., Denver, 1964-89. Chmn. Colo. Coun. Camera Clubs, Denver, 1962; bd. dirs. Porter Charitable Found., Denver, 1983-85; deacon, class pres. South Broadway Christian Ch., 1961-65; mem. Denver Art Mus., Denver Botanic Gardens, Rocky Mountain Estate Planning Coun., Mensa, Alliance Francaise. Capt. U.S. Army, 1954-56, Korea, USAR, 1956-80. Named to, U. Colo. Athletic Hall of Fame, 2004. Mem. Am. Soc. CLU and ChFC (pres. Rocky Mountain chpt. 1990-91), Nat. Assn. Life Underwriters (pres. Denver chpt. 1983-84, Nat. Quality award 1968—, expert witness ins. litigation, Disting. Life Underwriters award 1970-83), Screen Actors Guild, Million Dollar Round Table (life), U. Colo. Alumni (bd. dirs. 1990-92), U. Colo. Alumni C Club (bd. dirs. 1972-74), Univ. Club, Greenwood Athletic Club, Village Tennis Club, Rocky Mountain Optimist Club (pres. 1984-85). Republican. Avocations: tennis, photography, foreign languages, art, travel. Home and Office: 6178 E Hinsdale Ct Englewood CO 80112 Office Phone: 303-292-6402.

HARDY, WILLIAM ROBINSON, lawyer; b. Cin., June 14, 1934; s. William B. and Chastine M. (Sprague) H.; children: Anita Christina, William Robinson Jr. AB magna cum laude, Princeton U., 1956; JD, Harvard U., 1963. Bar: Ohio 1963, U.S. Supreme Ct. 1975. Life underwriter New Eng. Mut. Life Ins. Co., 1956-63; assoc. Graydon, Head & Ritchey, Cin., 1963-68, ptnr., 1968-98. Mem. panel comml. and constrn. industry arbitrators Am. Arbitration Assn., 1972—, mem. panel large complex case program, 1993—, comml. arbitrator tng. faculty, 1998—; reporter joint com. for revision of rules of US Dist. Ct. for So. Dist. Ohio, 1975, 80, 83, mem., 1990—2003. Bd. dirs. Cin. Union Bethel, 1968-82, pres., 1977-82, emeritus, 1982—; bd. dirs. Ohio Valley Goodwill Industries Rehab. Ctr., Cin., 1970—, pres., 1981-92; mem. Cin. Bd. Bldg. Appeals, 1976-2001, vice chmn., 1983, chmn., 1983-2001; pres. Hamilton County (Ohio) Alcohol and Drug Addiction Svcs. Bd., 1990-92; trustee Substance Abuse Mgmt. and Devel. Inc., 1998-99. Capt. USAR, 1956-68; maj. gen. Ohio Mil. Res., comdr., 1996-2001. Recipient award of merit Ohio Legal Ctr. Inst., 1975, 76, Ohio Commendation medal, 1999. Mem. ABA, AAAS, AAJ, Ohio Bar Assn., Cin. Bar Assn., Ohio Acad. Trial Lawyers, Am. Arbitration Assn., Assn. for Conflict Resolution, 6th Cir. Jud. Conf. (life), Soc. Lees Va., Assn. Former Intelligence Officers, Diplomatic and Consular Officers Ret., Ohio Soc. Colonial Wars (gov. 1979), Princeton (NYC) Club, Bankers Club (Cin.), Phi Beta Kappa. Mem. Ch. Of Redeemer. Office: 432 Walnut St Ste 206 Cincinnati OH 45202-3909 Office Phone: 513-621-4220. Personal E-mail: wmrhardy@earthlink.net.

HARDYMON, DAVID WAYNE, lawyer; b. Columbus, Ohio, Aug. 22, 1949; s. Philip Barbour and Margaret Evelyn (Bowers) H.; m. Monica Ella Sleep, Mar. 13, 1982; children: Philip Garnet, Teresa Jeanette. BA in History, Bowling Green State U., 1971; JD, Capital U., Columbus, Ohio, 1976. Bar: Ohio 1976, U.S. Dist. Ct. (so. dist.) Ohio 1976; U.S. Supreme Ct. 1980, U.S. Ct. Appeals (6th cir.) 1982, Ky. 1999, U.S. Dist. Ct. (no. dist.) Ohio 1999, W.Va. 2000, U.S. Dist. Ct. (so. dist.) W.Va. 2000. Asst. prosecuting atty. Franklin County Prosecuter's Office, Columbus, Ohio, 1976-81; assoc. Vorys, Sater, Seymour & Pease, Columbus, 1981-86, ptnr., 1987—. Mem. Chmn's. Club Franklin Country Rep. Orgn., 1983. Fellow Columbus Bar Found.; mem. Ohio State Bar Assn., Columbus Bar Assn. Avocations: sailing, archery. Office: Vorys Sater Seymour & Pease LLP PO Box 1008 52 E Gay St Columbus OH 43215-3161 Office Phone: 614-464-5651.

HARE, DAVID, playwright; b. St. Leonards, Sussex, Eng., June 5, 1947; s. Clifford Theodore and Agnes (Gilmour) H.; m. Margaret Matheson, Aug. 1970 (div. 1980); children: Joe, Lewis, Darcy; m. Nicole Farhi, 1992. MA, Cambridge U., 1968. Founder Portable Theatre, 1968, Joint Stock Theatre Group, 1974, Greenpoint Films, 1983; assoc. dir. Royal Nat. Theatre, London, 1984-88, 89-97. Author: (plays) Slag, 1970 (Evening Standard Drama award 1970), The Great Exhibition, 1972, (with Howard Brenton) Brassneck, 1973, Knuckle, 1974 (John Llewlyn Rhys award 1975), Teeth 'n' Smiles, 1975, (with others) Deeds, 1978, Plenty, 1978 (N.Y. Drama Critics Circle Best Fgn. Play award 1983, Best Play Tony award nominee 1983), A Map of the World, 1982 (Dramalogue award), (with Brenton) Pravda, 1985 (Evening Standard Drama award 1985, Plays and Players best play award 1985, City Limits best play award 1985), The Bay at Nice, 1986, Wrecked Eggs, 1986, The Knife, 1987, The Secret Rapture, 1988 (Plays and Players Best Play award 1988, Drama mag. Best Play award 1988, Drama Desk Best Play award nominee 1990), Racing Demon, 1990, 93, 95 (Olivier Best Play award 1990, Time Out (Theatre award 1990, Plays and Players best play award 1990, London Critics Circle Best Play award 1990, Tony award nominee 1996), Murmuring Judges, 1991, 92, 93, The Absence of War, 1993, Skylight, 1995, 96, 97 (Olivier Best Play award), Amy's View, 1996, 97, 98, 99, The Judas Kiss, 1997, 98, Via Dolorosa, 98, 99, The Breath of Life, 2002, The Permanent Way, 2003, Stuff Happens, 2004; (adaptations) Fanshen (William Hinton), 1975, Rules of the Game (Luigi Pirandello), 1971, 92, The Life of Galileo (Bertolt Brecht), 1994, Mother Courage and Her Children (Brecht), 1995, Ivanov (Anton Chekhov), 1997, The Blue Room (Schnitzler), 1998, The House of Bernarda Alba (Łorca), 2005; plays performed U.S.-Broadway, Pub. Theatre, N.Y.C., Goodman Theatre, Chgo., Arena Theatre, Washington, Lincoln Ctr., and other places; (TV films) Man Above Men, 1973, Licking Hitler (Brit. Acad. Film and TV Arts Best Play award 1978), Dreams of Leaving, 1980, Saigon: Year of the Cat, 1983, Heading Home, 1990, The Absence of War, 1995; (screenplays) Plenty, 1985, Wetherby, 1985 (Golden Bear award best film Berlin Film Festival 1985), Paris By Night, 1988, Strapless, 1989, Damage, 1992, The Secret Rapture, 1993, Feasting with Panthers, 1995; (essays) Writing Lefthanded, 1991, Asking Around, 1993, The Hours, 2003; dir: (theatre) Inside Out, 1968, Christie in Love, 1969, Purity, 1969, Fruit, 1970, Blow Job, 1971, England's Ireland, 1972, Brassneck, 1973, The Pleasure Principle, 1973, The Provoked Wife, 1973, The Party, 1974, Teeth 'n' Smiles, 1975, Weapons of Happiness, 1976, Devil's Island, 1977, Plenty, 1978, Total Eclipse, 1981, A Map of the World, 1983, Pravda, 1985-86, King Lear, 1986, The Bay at Nice and Wrecked Eggs, 1986-87, The Knife, 1987, The Secret Rapture, 1989, The Designated Mourner, 1996; (films) Wetherby, 1985, Paris by Night, 1989, Strapless, 1989, (TV) Licking Hitler, 1978, Dreams of Leaving, 1980, Heading Home, 1992, The Designated Mourner, 1996, Heartbreak House. 1997; (opera libretto) The Knife, 1988; author: (books) Writing Lefthanded, 1991, Asking Around, 1993, Acting Up, 1999; plays, dir. include include Slag, Hampstead, 1970, Royal Court and N.Y. Shakespeare Festival, 1971, The Great Exhibition, Hampstead, 1972, Brassneck, Nottingham Playhouse (with Howard Brenton), Knyuckle, Comedy Theatre, 1974, Fanshen, ICA and Hampstead, 1975, Nat. Theatre, 1992, Teeth 'n' Smiles, Royal Court, 1975, Wyndhams, 1976, Plenty, 1978, 1982, 1999, A Map of the World, 1983, 85, Pravda, 1985, others; screenplays, actor, and dir. include Wetherby, 1985, Paris by Night, 1989, Strapless, 1990, Plenty, 1985, Lee Miller, 2001, Via Dolorosa, 2000, The Secret Rapture, 1993, others; films, dir. assoc. producer for TV include Licking Hitler (BBC), 1978, Dreams of Leaving (BBC), 1979, Saigon: Year of the Cat (Thames), 1983, Heading Home (BBC), 1991, The Absence of War (BBC), 1995; adaptations include The Rules of the Game-Pirandello, 1992, The Life of Galileo, 1994, Mother Courage and Her Children, 1995, Ivanov, 1997, 98, others; opera libretto, dir. include The Knife, 1988; author: Writing Lefthanded, 1991, Asking Around, 1993, Acting Up, 1999; dir. plays include Christie in Love (by Howard Brenton), 1969, Fruit (by Howard Brenton), 1970, Blowjob, 1971, England's Ireland (by seven writers, co-dir.), 1972,The Provoked Wife (by John Vanburgh), 1973, The Pleasure Principle (by Snoo Wilson), 1973, The Party (by Trevor Griffiths), 1974; dir. films, producer include The Designated Mourner (by Wallace Shawn), 1996. Fellow Royal Soc. Lit.; mem. Officiers de l″ordre des Artes et Lettres, Dramatists Club. Office: c/o Casarotto Ramsay 60 Wardour St London W1 England

HARE, HENRY PHILLIP, JR., psychiatrist; b. Paris, Tex., Apr. 4, 1925; s. Henry P. and Bertha (McIntosh) H.; children: Elizabeth Anne, John Keble. Student, Rice U., Houston, 1941-43; BA, U. Tex., Galveston, 1945, MD, 1947. Diplomate Am. Bd. Psychiatry and Neurology. Rotating intern U.S. Marine Hosp., Balt., 1947-48; fellow in psychiatry Menninger Sch., Topeka, 1951; staff to chief psychiatry USPHS Hosp., Ft. Worth, 1951-54; dir. psychotherapy Beverly Hills Clinic, Dallas, 1954-60; lectr. psychiatry Mansfield Coll., U. Oxford, Eng., 1960-61; assoc. to dir. Tulsa Psychiat. Found., 1961-63; pvt. practice Nix Med. Ctr., San Antonio, 1963—; clin. prof. psychiatry U. Tex. Health Sci. Ctr., San Antonio, 1965—; med. dir., chief profl. staff San Antonio State Hosp., 1989-93, forensic psychiatrist, 1993-97; mem. rev. bd. on manifest dangerousness TDMHMR, 1993—2003. Psychiat. examiner to Episcopal Bishop W. Tex., San Antonio, 1963—; psychiat. rep. to med. bd. Humana Met. Hosp., San Antonio, 1989-90. Contbr. articles to profl. jours. Mem. Bexar County Bd. Trustees for Mental Health and Mental Retardation, San Antonio, 1969-74; mem. distbns. com. San Antonio Area Found., 1975-78. Capt. USPHS, 1947—. Named Layman of Yr., Episcopal Diocese Dallas, 1959; named to Most Venerable Order of the Hosp. of St. John Jerusalem, 2001. Fellow Am. Psychiat. Assn. (disting. life), So. Psychiat. Assn., Royal Soc. Health; mem. Bexar County Psychiat. Soc. (pres. 1967-68), Alcuin Club. Democrat. Avocations: sailing, stamp collecting, ecclesiology and ecumenics. Home: 10314 Severn Rd San Antonio TX 78217-3945 Office: 1122 Nix Med Ctr San Antonio TX 78205 Home Phone: 210-655-6599; Office Phone: 512-222-1409. E-mail: henryhare@aol.com.

HARE, NORMA Q., retired school system administrator; b. Dadeville, Mo., July 10, 1924; d. James Norma and Mary Delia (Blakemore) Quarles; m. John Daniel Hare, June 27, 1944 (dec.); children: J. Daniel, Thomas C. BA, Calif. State U., Fresno, 1958, MA, 1963. Cert. tchr., sch. adminstr. Elem. tchr. Parlier Sch. Dist., Calif., 1956-57, Sanger Sch. Dist., Calif., 1958-66, S. San Francisco Schs., 1966-67, elem. edn. specialist, 1967, elem. sch. principal, 1967-81; ret., 1981. Dir. Title I, Spruce Sch. ESEA, El Rancho Sch. Early Childhood edn. program, sch. dist. mgmt. negotiator, S. San Francisco Schs., 1977-79. Author: Who is Root Beer, 1977, Wish Upon A Birthday, 1979, Mystery at Mousehouse, 1980, Puritans, Pioneers and Planters, 1995; co-author: The Magatagans, 1998. Mem.: DAR, AAUW, Colonial Dames XVII Century (treas. 1995—98, pres. Sierra de Santa Lucia chpt. 2003—05), Soc. Mayflower Descs. (gov. San Francisco/Peninsula colony 1983—86, govs. award 1988, 1992). Avocations: genealogy, travel. Personal E-mail: nqhare@aol.com.

HARE, PETER HEWITT, philosophy educator; b. NYC, Mar. 12, 1935; s. Michael Meredith and Jane Perry (Jopling) Hare; m. Daphne Joan Kean, May 30, 1959 (dec. Aug. 1995); children: Clare Kean, Gwendolyn Meigs; m. Susan Howe, Nov. 1, 2000. BA, Yale U., 1957; MA, Columbia U., 1962, PhD, 1965. Lectr. philosophy SUNY, Buffalo, 1962-65, from asst. prof. to prof., 1965-97, disting. svc. prof., 1997—, asst. chmn. dept., 1965-68, chmn. dept., 1971-75, 85-94, assoc. dean divsn. undergrad. edn., 1980-82, prof. emeritus, 2001—. Vis. prof. Moscow State U., 1989; bd. advisors Peirce Edition Project, INd. U./Purdue U., 1989—. Author (with others): Evil and the Concept of God, 1968, Causing, Perceiving and Believing, 1975; author: A Woman's Quest for Science, 1985; editor: Doing Philosophy Historically, 1988; editor: (with others) History, Religion and Spiritual Democracy, 1980, Naturalism and Rationality, 1986, Frontiers of Philosophy, 1986—; photo illustration Susan Howe, Kidnapped, 2002, The Midnight, 2003, mem. editl. bd. Am. Philos. Quar., 1978—87, Jour. Speculative Philosophy, 1987—, Streams of William James, 1999—2005, William James Studies, 2005—; mem. editl. bd.: Philo, 2005—. Fellow: Ctr. Inquiry; mem.: William James Soc. (v.p. 2005, pres. 2006), Josiah Royce Soc. (mem. exec. com. 2003—06), Soc. Advancement Am. Philosophy (mem. exec. com. 1977—80, pres. 1988—90, Herbert W. Schneider award 1996), N.Y. State Philos. Assn. (pres. 1975—77), Peirce Soc. (editor Transactions 1974—, pres. 1975—76), Am. Philos. Assn. (mem. nominating com. eastern divsn. 1990—92, mem. program com. 1993—95, chmn. program com. 1994—95, nat. bd. officers 1996—99, chmn. com. career opportunities 1996—99, ombudsman 1996—99, chair Romanell lectr. com. 2000—01), Elizabethan Club. Home and Office: 115 New Quarry Rd Guilford CT 06437-1621 Office Phone: 203-453-9517. Business E-Mail: phhare@buffalo.edu.

HARE, PHIL (PHILIP G. HARE), congressman; b. Galesburg, Ill., Feb. 21, 1949; m. Rebecca Hare; children: Amy, Louis. Attended, Black Hawk C.C., 1967—68. Laborer Seaford Clothing Factory, Rock Island, SC, 1969—82; staff mem. to Rep. Lane Evans US Congress, 1983—2006; mem. US Congress from 17th dist., 2007—; mem. edn. & labor com., vets affairs com., congl. progressive caucus. Former pres. UNITE HERE Local 617. Served in USAR, 1969—75. Democrat. Roman Catholic. Office: 1118 Longworth House Office Bldg Washington DC 20515 also: 1535 47th Ave #5 Moline IL 61265

HARE, ROBERT YATES, musicologist, educator; b. McGrann, Pa., June 14, 1921; s. Robert Deemar and Beulah (Yates) H.; m. Constance King Rutherford, Mar. 31, 1948; children: Stephen, Beverly, Madeleine. MusB, U. Detroit, 1948; MA, Wayne State U., 1950; PhD, U. Iowa, 1959. Instr. Marietta (Ohio) Coll., 1949-51, Del Mar Coll., Corpus Christi, Tex., 1951-55; adj. instr. U. Tex., 1953—55; prof., chmn. grad. studies San Jose (Calif.) State U., 1956-65; prof., dean Eastern Ill. U. Music, 1965-74; prof. music history and lit. Ohio State U., Columbus, 1974-86, prof. emeritus, 1986—, dir. Sch. Music, 1974-78, dir. audio-rec. engring., 1979-82, arts adminstr. rsch. and faculty devel., 1982-86. Cons., lectr. in field; mem. coun. music edn. in higher edn. Ill. Music Educators Assn., 1969-74. Condr. coll. symphony band, 1956-63, San Jose Youth Symphony, 1957-59, univ. symphony, 1968-74, Ea. Ill. U. Symphony, 1968-74; French horn recitals, Carnegie Music Hall, Pitts., 1940, 42; French hornist, Pitts. Symphony Orch., 1941-44, Buffalo Philharm., 1943-44, Cin. Summer Opera Co., 1945, Indpls. Symphony Orch., 1945-46, San Antonio Symphony Orch., 1947-49; orchestrator, San Antonio Symphony Orch., 1947-49; recs. include Pitts. Symphony Orch., Indpls. Symphony Orch. (as French hornist), San Jose State U. Symphonic Band (as condr.); contbr. articles to profl. jours. Mem. com. grad. and profl. edn. in arts and humanities Ill. Bd. Higher Edn., 1969-70; mem. performing arts commn. Ill. Sesquicentennial, 1967; mem. exec. bd. Greater Columbus Arts Coun., 1974-76, Ohio Alliance for Arts in Edn., 1974-76; trustee Columbus Symphony Orch., 1975-79. Profl. Promise scholar Carnegie-Mellon U., 1939. Mem. Music Educators Nat. Conf. (publs. planning com. 1970-76), Am. Musicol. Soc., Coll. Music Soc., Masons, Shriners, Phi Mu Alpha, Sinfonia (hon.), Pi Kappa Lambda (hon.), Delta Omicron (hon.). Office: Ohio State U Coll Arts 305 Mershon Auditorium Columbus OH 43210 E-mail: rhare4@cox.net.

HAREN, DAN (DANIEL JOHN HAREN), professional baseball player; b. Monterey Park, Calif., Sept. 17, 1980; Student, Pepperdine U., Malibu, Calif. Draft pick St. Louis Cardinals, 2001, pitcher, 2003—04, Oakland Athletics, Calif., 2004—. Named to Am. League All-Star Team, 2007. Mailing: Oakland Athletics McAfee Coliseum 7000 Coliseum Way Oakland CA 94621*

HAREN, ELIZABETH GAYE, counselor; b. Port Hueneme, Calif., Dec. 7, 1970; d. Larry Dale and Cecilia Gay Haren; m. Ted Shelton, Jan. 15, 1999. BA, Emory U., 1993; MA, East Tenn. State U., 1998. Lic. profl. counselor mental health svc. provider Tenn., 2003, nat. cert. counselor Nat. Bd. Cert. Counselors, 1999. Pub. rels. staff Preferred Internet, Blountville, Tenn., 1996—98; dir. support svcs. Tri-Cities Online, Blountville, 1997—98; mobile crisis response therapist Frontier Health, Gray, Tenn., 1998—, crisis response supr., 2001—, clin. liaison frontier mobile crisis response, 2003—06; clin. dir. Camelot Schs., 2006—. Cert. applied suicide intervention skills trainer Tenn. Suicide Prevention Network/Living Works, Nashville, 2002—; cert. question persuade refer trainer Tenn. Suicide Prevention Network, Nashville, 2004—, apptd. mem. adv. com., 2004, chair N.E. region, Johnson City, 05; critical incident stress debriefer Internat. Critical Incident Stress Found., Ellicott City, Md., 2003—; team mem. Tenn. Pub. Safety Network, Gray, 2003. Recipient NE Tenn. Suicide Prevention award, Tenn. Suicide Prevention Network, 2005, Cert. Appreciation For Support Work During Ops. Desert Shield and Dessert Storm, US Dept. Army, 1991, Heroes in the Fight award, 2006. Mem.: Am. Psychotherapy Assn., Assn. for Specialists in Group Work, Internat. Assn. Addictions and Offender Counselors, Am. Counseling Assn., Internat. Critical Incident Stress Found., Registry Interpreters for the Deaf (assoc.), Kappa Delta Pi, Phi Kappa Phi (life). Avocations: scuba diving, camping, music, art, photography. Home Phone: 423-477-6426.

HAREZI, ILONKA JO, medical technology research executive; b. Princeton, Ind., Jan. 17, 1949; d. Joseph and Helen Marie Fullop; m. John O. Schofield, Dec. 14, 1971 (div. Dec. 1982); 1 child, Franceska; m. Courtland Reeves, Nov. 26, 1986; children: Bryan, Katharine. PhD, Chgo. Sch. Design, 1969. Mktg. ptnr. Fullop and Assocs., 1983-85; founder, sec., treas. Kinetic Energy Ltd., 1985-90; freelance set designer Ilonka Creative Environments, 1974-84; founder, v.p. Harezi Internat., 1980-84; founder, sec., treas. Elf Cocoon Corp., 1984-86; founder, pres., chmn. Elf Cocoon Internat. Ltd., 1985-92; founder, pres. Elfworks, Inc., 1991-94, Elfworks, Nev., 1994-96; pres., dir. Allied Fund for Capital Appreciation, Inc., 1994—98; v.p. Phillip Stein Teslar, 2001—; pres. Nanogy, Inc., 2003—. Interviewed by radio, TV, and newspapers on design and extremely low frequency electromagnetic tech.; presenter tech. sems. on ELF, the Quantum and scalar phenomena. Author: The Resonance in Residence, (DVD) A Soul, Breathing and Steppin' into the Rain, 2007; contbr. articles to profl. jours. Bd. dirs. Inst. for Higher Human Learning Potential, Phila., 1979. Fellow N.Y. Acad. of Sci.; mem. NAFE, ACLU, AAAS, Am. Inst. Interior Designers, Women's Internat. League for Peace and Freedom, Nat. Assn. Against Health Fraud, Nat. Narcotics Officers Assns. Coalition, N.Y. Acad. Sci., UN-USA Bus. Coun., Knights of Malta (dame), Knights of Africa (dame), U.S. Acad. Polit. Sci., Am. Craft Coun. Achievements include patents pending for transdermal pump and teslar chip. Office: 169 E Flagler 17th Fl Miami FL 33101 also: 17555 Collins 2705-06 Sunny Isles Beach FL 33160 Office Phone: 618-948-2393, 305-398-7690, 305-933-6768. Personal E-mail: ilonkaharezi@aol.com.

HARFF, CHARLES HENRY, retired lawyer, manufacturing executive; b. Wesel, Germany, Sept. 27, 1929; s. Philip and Stephanie (Dreyfuss) H.; m. Marion Haines MacAfee, July 19, 1958; children— Pamela Haines, John Blair, Todd Philip BA, Colgate U., 1951; LLB, Harvard U., 1954; postgrad., U. Bonn, 1955. Bar: N.Y. 1955. Assoc. Chadbourne & Parke, NYC, 1955—64, ptnr., 1964—84; sr. v.p., gen. counsel, sec. Rockwell

Internat. Corp., Pitts., 1984—94, sr. v.p., spl. counsel, 1994—96, ret., 1996. Cons., 1996—2001; bd. dirs. Arvin Meritor, Inc., 1997—2006. Trustee Christian A. Johnson Endeavor Found., N.Y.C., 1984-2001; bd. dirs. Atlantic Legal Found., 1989-98, Fulbright Assn., 1995-2002, pres., 2001. Fulbright scholar U. Bonn, Germany, 1954-55. Mem. ABA, N.Y. State Bar Assn., The Assn. Gen. Counsel, Harvard Club of N.Y.C., Duquesne Club, Allegheny Country Club, Farm Neck Golf Club (Martha's Vineyard, Mass.)(founder, pres.).

HARFORD, JAMES, writer; b. Jersey City, Aug. 19, 1924; s. Thomas William and Jane Hume (Henderson) H.; m. Mildred Rita Waters, Apr. 19, 1952; children: Susan Gately, James Joseph, Peter Benedict (dec.), Jennifer, Christopher. BSME, Yale U., 1945. Sales engr. Worthington Corp., 1946-49; assoc. editor Modern Industry, 1950-52; free-lance writer Europe, 1952-53; exec. sec. Am. Rocket Soc., 1953-63; exec. dir. Am. Inst. Aeros. and Astronautics, 1963-88, exec. dir. emeritus, 1988—. V.p. Internat. Astronautical Fedn., 1988—90. Author: Korolev (How One Man Masterminded the Soviet Drive to Beat America to the Moon), 1997, (with others) China Space Report, 1979, Merton and Friends A Joint Biography of Thomas Merton, Robert Lax and Edward Rice, 2006. Mem. 1945W class coun. Yale U.; trustee Friends of Princeton Pub. Libr., 1996—2002. Lt. (j.g.) USNR, 1945—46. Recipient NASA Pub. Svc. award, 1985, Air Force Exceptional Svc. award, 1987, Nat. Space Club Robert Goddard Hist. Essay prize, 1995, Internat. Astron. Fedn. award, 1997; Verville fellow Nat. Air and Space Mus., 1989-92. Fellow AIAA (Disting. Svc. award 1988, Internat. Coop. Aerospace award 1995), AAAS, Brit. Interplanetary Soc., Royal Aero. Soc. (assoc.); mem. Internat. Acad. Astronautics, Cosmos Club, Nassau Club. Home and Office: 601 Lake Dr Princeton NJ 08540-5634 E-mail: j.harford@att.net.

HARFORD, JOE B., federal agency administrator; Assoc. dir. spl. projects Nat. Cancer Inst., now dir. Office Internat. Affairs. Office: Office Internat Affairs Nat Cancer Inst 6130 Executive Blvd Ste 100 Bethesda MD 20892-7301 Office Phone: 301-496-5534. E-mail: harfordj@mail.nih.gov.

HARFORD, ROBERT R., dermatologist; s. Victor and Cossil Harford; m. Ruby Harford; 1 child, Mercedes. BS, Ala. A&M U., 1980; MD, SUNY, Bklyn., 1988. Diplomate Am. Bd. Dermatology, Am. Bd. Pathology and Dermatology. Commd. officer USN, 1981—2005, advanced through grades to comdr.; head med. dept. Naval Med. Clinic, Antarctica, 1989—90; health sci. rsch. med. officer, clin. investigator Naval Med. Rsch. Inst., Bethesda, Md., 1991—93; resident in dermatology Nat. Naval Med. Ctr., Bethesda, Md., 1993—96, head dermatopathology, 2000—02; head dermatology Naval Hosp. Guam, Agana, 1996—99, dir. med. svcs., 1998—99; head dermatopathology, dir. dermatology mohs micrographic surgery lab. Naval Med. Ctr., San Diego, 2002—05. Asst. prof. dermatology Uniformed Services U. of the Health Sciences, Bethesda, 2001—; asst. clin. prof. medicine U. Calif., San Diego, 2003—. Cons. for first ann. women health fare Soroptimist Internat. Guam, Agana, 1998; med. advisor Este Magi Le Atua Care, San Jose, Calif., 2005; physician vol. Cheyenne River Reservation, Eagle Butte, SD, 1992. Decorated Meritorious Svc. medal, Navy Commendation medal (5), Achievment medal USN. Fellow: Am. Acad. Dermatology; mem.: Assn. Mil. Surgeons of the US (life). Achievements include research in relationship between changes in serum thyrotropin and lipoprotein cholesterol with prolonged antarctic residence; effects of cold weather on memory, thyroid function, and oxygen consumption. Avocation: travel. Home Phone: 310-489-1501.

HARGADON, BERNARD JOSEPH, JR., retired consumer goods company executive; b. Ardmore, Pa., Dec. 27, 1927; s. Bernard Joseph and Anna Mendenhall (Lancaster) H.; m. Jill Dinwiddie, Dec. 15, 1990; children from previous marriage: Geoffrey, Robert, Louise, Lawrence (dec.), David. BS, Drexel U., 1952, MBA, 1959; PhD (hon.), Golden Gate U., 1995. Auditor Gen. Motors Corp., 1955-57; prof. acctg. Drexel U., 1957-59; with AID, Colombia, 1960-63, McKesson, San Francisco, 1964—; pres. McKesson Internat., 1980-95, ret., 1995. Adj. prof. internat. bus. Golden Gate U. Author: in Spanish Principles of Accounting, 1964, Principles of Cost Accounting, 1971. Bd. dirs. World Affairs Coun. No. Calif., Opera Carolina, Charlotte, N.C., WDAV, Davidson, N.C.; mem. Pacific Coun. Internat. Policy. With USN, 1945-48 E-mail: bhargadon@aol.com.

HARGENS, CHARLES WILLIAM, III, electrical engineer, consultant; b. Phila., Oct. 21, 1918; s. Charles William Jr. and Marjorie (Garman) H.; m. Mary K. Johnson, June 14, 1941; children: William Garman, Mary Van Deusen, Roger Snow. SB, MIT, 1941. Registered profl. engr., Pa. Design engr. Lockheed Aircraft, Burbank, Calif., 1941-42; group engr. Gilfillan Bros., LA, 1942-43; vis. staff mem. MIT Radiation Labs., Cambridge, 1942-44; group engr. RCA, Camden, NJ, 1945-47; sr. engr., tech. dir., inst. fellow Franklin Inst. Labs., Phila., 1947-88; assoc. prof. Temple U., Phila., 1976-77, Drexel U., Phila., 1978-87; noise control cons. air mgmt. div. City of Phila., 1978—. Rsch. assoc. Wills Eye Hosp., 1970; cons., prof. acoustics; invited lectr. U. Wis., 1962, 63, 64. Co-author: Studies in Medicine, Physics and Voice, 1968, (chpts.) Bioengineering and the Skin, 1981, Handbook of Noninvasive Methods and the Skin, 1994; contbr. articles to Jour. Ophthalmic Surgery, Jour. Acoustical Soc. Am., Investigative Dermatology, Indsl. Rsch., Electronics Jour. Instrument Soc. Am., Jour. Franklin Inst., IEEE Transactions. Mem. adv. com. Spring Garden Coll., Phila., 1972-76; rsch. assoc. Bd. of City Trusts, 1970. Recipient Diploma, War Manpower Commn., 1944, Citation Mayor City of Phila., 1974. Fellow IEEE (Phila. Sect. Appreciation award 1972, Benjamin Franklin Key award 2003); mem. ASTM (Citation 1982), Franklin Inst. (com. sci. and arts 1981-99), MIT Alumni Assn. (life, Bronze Beaver award 1976), Numerical Control Soc. (founder), Sigma Xi. Episcopalian. Achievements include 12 patents for radio, electronics, computation, instrumentation optics and measurement; development of specialized instruments for dermatologists, brain tissue and other researchers. Home and Office: 718 Radcliff Ct Lansdale PA 19446-5895 Home Phone: 484-991-1105; Office Phone: 484-991-1105. *Never retire completely from your profession, unless health forces it upon you. It is foolish to give up all the experience, knowledge, and associations acquired over a productive lifetime.*

HARGESHEIMER, ELBERT, III, lawyer; b. Cleve., Jan. 4, 1944; s. Elbert and Agnes Mary (Heckman) H.; children: Heather Leigh, Elbert IV, Jon-Erik, Piper Elizabeth, Kevin R. Cross, Mark R. Dziob. AB, Cornell U., 1966; JD, SUNY, Buffalo, 1969. Bar: N.Y. 1970, U.S. Dist. Ct. (we. dist.) N.Y. 1971. Assoc. Miller, Bouvier, O'Connor & Cegielski, Buffalo, 1970-73, ptnr., 1973-74, Godinho & Hargesheimer, Hamburg, N.Y., 1974-84; pvt. practice law Hamburg, 1984—. Chief counsel Joint Legis. Commn. to Revise Bus. and Corp. Law, N.Y. State Assembly and Senate, 1974-75; prosecutor Village of Blasdell (N.Y.), 1978-80, 83-87, village atty. 1980-82; fund chmn. South Towns Hosp. Found., Inc., 1973-76, fin. chmn., bd. dirs., 1976-77, v.p., 1978-82; chmn. Hamburg Town Rep. Com., 1978-88; coord. Erie County Pretrial Svcs. Program, 1987-88; counsel Erie County Rep. Com., 1980-92; mem. Erie County Bd. Ethics, 1979-89, chmn. 1983.; charter mem., counsel S.W. Hamburg Taxpayers Assn. Named Mr. Rep., Town of Hamburg Rep. Club, 1982, Rep. of Yr., Hamburg Town Rep. Com., 1988. Mem.: Theta Chi. Methodist. Home and Office: 22 Buffalo St Hamburg NY 14075-5002 Office Phone: 716-648-4202. E-mail: ehiii44@aol.com.

HARGITAY, MARISKA MAGDOLINA, actress; b. LA, Jan. 23, 1964; d. Mickey Hargitay and Jayne Mansfield; m. Peter Hermann, Aug. 28, 2004; 1 child, August Miklos Friedrich Hermann. Student, UCLA. Actor: (films) Ghoulies, 1985, Welcome to 18, 1986, Jocks, 1987, Mr. Universe, 1988, The Perfect Weapon, 1991, Strawberry Road, 1991, Hard Time Romance, 1991, Bank Robber, 1993, Leaving Las Vegas, 1995, Lake Placid, 1999, Perfume, 2001; (TV films) Finish Line, 1989, Blind Side, 1993, Gambler V: Playing for Keeps, 1994, The Advocate's Devil, 1997, Plain Truth, 2004; (TV series) Downtown, 1986—87, Falcon Crest, 1988, Tequila and Bonetti, 1992, Can't Hurry Love, 1995—96, Prince Street, 1997, Law & Order: Special Victims Unit, 1999— (Golden Globe award for best actress TV series - drama, 2005, Emmy award for outstanding lead actress in a drama series, 2006); (TV miniseries) Night Sins, 1997, (TV appearances include) Falcon Crest, 1984, In the Heat of the Night, 1988, Freddy's Nightmares, 1988, Baywatch, 1989, Wiseguy, 1990, Thirtysomething, 1990, Booker, 1990, Gabriel's Fire, 1990, Key West, 1993, Seinfeld, 1993, Hotel Room, 1993, All-American Girl, 1995, Ellen, 1996, The Single Guy, 1996, Cracker, 1997, ER, 1997—98. Office: Law and Order SVU NBC 30 Rockefeller Plaza New York NY 10112

HARGRAVE, RUDOLPH, state supreme court justice; b. Shawnee, Okla., Feb. 15, 1925; s. John Hubert and Daisy (Holmes) H.; m. Madeline Hargrave, May 29, 1949; children: Cindy Lu, John Robert, Jana Sue. LLB, U. Okla., 1949. Bar: Okla. 1949. Pvt. practice, Wewoka, Okla., 1949—64; asst. county atty. Seminole County, 1951-55; judge Seminole County Ct., 1964-67, Seminole County Superior Ct., 1967-69; dist. judge Okla. Dist. Ct., Dist. 22, 1969—78; justice Okla. Supreme Ct., Oklahoma City, 1978—, former vice chief justice then chief justice. Former v.p. Nat. Conference of Chief Justices; mem. Okla. Jud. Conference. Mem. Seminole County Bar Assn., Okla. Bar Assn., ABA Lodges: Lions; Masons. Democrat. Methodist. Office: Okla Supreme Ct State Capitol Bldg Room 202 Oklahoma City OK 73105*

HARGRAVE, SARAH QUESENBERRY, consulting company and public relations executive; b. Mt. Airy, NC, Dec. 11, 1944; d. Teddie W. Quesenberry and Lois Knight Quesenberry Stout. Student, Radford Coll., 1963-64, Va. Poly. Inst. and State U., 1964-67. Mgmt. trainee Thalhimer Bros. Dept. Store, Richmond, Va., 1967-68; Cen. Va. fashion and publicity dir. Sears Roebuck & Co., Richmond, 1968-73, nat. decorating sch. coord. Chgo., 1973-74, nat. dir. bus. and profl. women's programs, 1974-76; v.p., treas., program dir. Sears-Roebuck Found., Chgo., 1976-87, program mgr. corp. contbns. and memberships, 1981-84, dir. corp. mktg. and pub. affairs, 1984-87; v.p. personal fin. svcs. and mktg. Northern Trust Co., Chgo., 1987-89; pres. Hargrave Consulting, 1989—. Spkr., seminar leader in field. Bd. dirs. Am. Assembly Collegiate Schs. Bus., 1979-82, mem. vis. com., 1979-82, mem. fin. and audit com., 1980-82, mem. task force on doctoral supply and demand, 1980-82; mem. Com. for Equal Opportunity for Women, 1976-81; chmn., 1978-79, 80-81; mem. bus. adv. coun. Walter E. Heller Coll. Bus. Adminstrn., Roosevelt U., 1979-89; co-dir. Ill. Internat. Women's Yr. Ctr., 1975. Named Outstanding Young Women of Yr. Ill., 1976; named Women of Achievement State Street Bus. and Profl. Woman's Club, 1978 Mem. ASTD, Profl. Women's Network, Profl. Coaches and Mentors Assn. Home and Office: 34 Fairlawn Ave Daly City CA 94015-3425 Personal E-mail: shargrave@earthlink.net.

HARGRAVES, WILLIAM FREDERICK, II, mathematics and computer science professor; b. Cin., Aug. 18, 1932; s. William Frederick and Annie Leona (Thomas) H.; m. Maurine Collins, July 5, 1957; children: William Frederick III, Jock Frederick, Charles Frederick. BS in Edn. with honors, Miami U., Oxford, Ohio, 1954, MA in Physics, 1961. Commd. 2d lt. USAF, 1954, advanced through grades to col., ret., 1982, comdr. 20th mil. airlift squadron, 1955-59, air liaison officer Wright-patterson AFB, Ohio, 1959-61; rsch. scientist USAF, Weapons Rsch. Ctr., Kirtland AFB, N.Mex., 1961—65; aircraft comdr., instr. pilot 22 mil. airlift command USAF, Tachikawa, Japan, 1965-70, air liaison officer 1st ARVAN Divsn. Vietnam, 1970-71, asst. prof. air sci., AFROTC program, Miami U. Oxford, Ohio, 1971-74, chief flight deck devel., R&D Wright Patterson AFB, 1978, dep. divsn. chief, US Pentagon Washington, 1978-82, ret., 1982; asst. prof., asst. dean arts and scis. Cen. State U., Wilberforce, Ohio, 1982—. Asst. track and field coach Cen. State U., 1993—. Founder Pilgrim Bapt. Chr. Men's Choir, Hamilton, Ohio, 1980, Grant Chapel Ave. Ch., Albuquerque, 1962; trustee Bethel AME Ch., 2002—. Decorated Dist. Flying Cross 72, Air medal, Air Force commendation medal with 2 oak leaf clusters, Vietnam Service medal with 5 bronze stars, Nat. Def. Svc. medal; named to Covington Black Hall of Fame, Ky., 1992. Mem. Am. Registry of Outstanding Profls. (life; honors), Phi Beta Kappa, Omicron Delta Kappa, Kappa Delta Pi, Pi Mu Epsilon, Sigma Pi Sigma. Methodist. Home: 123 W Walnut St Oxford OH 45056-1721 Office: Cen State U 1400 Brush Row Rd Wilberforce OH 45384 Office Phone: 937-376-6179. Business E-Mail: whargraves@centralstate.edu.

HARGREAVES, DAVID WILLIAM, retired communications company executive; b. Akron, Ohio, May 4, 1943; s. William B. and Helen Grace (Slusser) H.; m. Sandra Jean Tessier, Sept. 4, 1965; children: Kristen Elizabeth, Cinda Anne, Gregory David. BSEE, U. Maine, Orono, 1965; MBA, U. Rochester, 1967. Sales engr. Mobile Communications div. Gen. Electric, Lynchburg, Va., 1970-74, mgr. systems projects, 1974-75, mgr. systems bids/proposals, 1975-78; mgr. internat. mktg. Gen. Electric Powerline Carrier Bus., Lynchburg, 1978-80; gen. mgr. Gen. Electric Microwave Link Operation, Owensboro, Ky., 1980-84; mng. dir. Alpha Telecom div. Alpha Industries, Methuen, Mass., 1984-86; pres. Dynatech Tactical Comms. Inc. (formerly Controlonics Corp.), Nashua, N.H., 1986-97; pres., CEO DTC Comms. Inc., Nashua, 1997—2004. Condr. seminars in field. Contbr. articles to profl. jours. Chmn. bd. Gen. Electric United Way Pacesetter campaign, Lynchburg, 1978; advisor Jr. Achievement project bus., Owensboro, 1982, 83. Served to capt. U.S. Army, 1968-70, Vietnam. Decorated Bronze Star, D.S.C.; named N.H. High Tech. Coun. Entrepreneur of Yr., 2003. Mem.: Am. Mktg. Pres.'s Assn., Massibesic Yacht Club, Tau Beta Pi, Eta Kappa Nu. Republican. Avocations: sailing, skiing, amateur radio. Home: 191 Buttrick Rd Hampstead NH 03841-2183 Personal E-mail: david.hargreaves@comcast.net.

HARGREAVES, GEORGE HENRY, civil and agricultural engineer, researcher; b. Chico, Calif., Apr. 2, 1916; s. Carey and Luella May (Raymond) H.; m. Elizabeth Ann Gardner, Aug. 9, 1941 (dec. Dec. 1948); 1 child, Margaret Ann Hargreaves Stolpmann; m. Sara Etna Romero, Jan 6, 1951; children: Mark Romero, Sonia Maria Hargreaves Hart, George Leo. BS in Soils, U. Calif., Berkeley, 1939; BSCE, U. Wyo., 1943. Civil engr. U.S. Bur. Reclamation, Sacramento, 1946-48; reclamation engr. U.S. Army C.E., Greece, 1948-49; engr. AID, Greece, Peru, Haiti, Philippines, Brazil and Colombia, 1950-68; chief civil engr. engring. br. Natural Resources divsn. Inter-Am. Geodetic Survey, Ft. Clayton, 1968-70; rsch. engr. in irrigation Utah State. U., Logan, 1970-86; rsch. Internat. Irrigation Ctr., 1980-86, rsch. prof. emeritus, 1986—. Author: World Water for Agriculture, 1977; co-author: Irrigation Fundamentals, 1998, Fundamentos Del Riego, 2000; contbr. numerous articles to profl. jours. Lt. (j.g.) USNR, 1943-46, PTO. Recipient Royce J. Tipton award, 1997. Fellow: ASCE; mem.: Internat. Commn. Irrigation and Drainage (chmn. U.S. Com. on crops and water use 1992—96, drainage and flood control 1999—2003, chmn. U.S. com. on history of irrigation), Am. Soc. Agrl. Engrs. (chmn. Rocky Mountain sect. 1974). Achievements include development of methodology used by the International Water Management Institute in the IWMI World Water and Climate Atlas, providing worldwide climate data and an index of rainfall adequacy for agricultural production. Home: 1660 E 1220 N Logan UT 84341-3040 Office: Utah State U Internat Irrigation Ctr Dept Biol Irrigation Engring Logan UT 84322-4150

HARGROVE, ERWIN CHARLES, JR., political science professor; b. St. Joseph, Mo., Oct. 11, 1930; s. Erwin Charles and Gladys Lenore (France) H.; m. Lynne Douglas, Apr. 10, 1961 (div. Jan., 1991); children: John, Amy, Sarah; m. Julia Mosher, Sept. 21, 1991. BA, Yale U., 1953, PhD, 1963. From asst. prof. to prof. polit. sci. Brown U., Providence, 1960—76, prof., dept. chair polit. sci., 1971—73; sr. fellow Urban Inst., Washington, 1973—76; prof. polit. sci., dir. Inst. for Pub. Policy Studies Vanderbilt U., Nashville, 1976-85, chmn. dept. polit. sci., 1992-96, prof. polit. sci. emeritus, 2000—, lectr. dept. history, 2003—. Author: Presidential Leadership, Personality and Political Style, 1966, Professional Roles in Society and Government: The English Case, 1972, The Power of the Modern Presidency, 1974, The Missing Link: The Study of Implementation of Social Policy, 1975, Jimmy Carter as President, Leadership and the Politics of the Public Good, 1988 (Richard E. Neustadt award, 1988), Prisoners of Myth: Leadership of the Tennessee Valley Authority, 1933-1990, 1994, The President as Leader: Appealing to the Better Angels of Our Nature, 1998, The Effective Presidency: Lessens on Leadership From John F. Kennedy to George W. Bush, 2007; co-author (with Michael Nelson): Presidents, Politics and Policy, 1984; editor: The Future of the Democratic Left in Industrial Democracies, 2003; co-editor (with Paul Conkin): TVA, Fifty Years of Grass Roots Bureaucracy, 1983; co-editor: (with Samuel Morley) The President and the Council of Economic Advisers: Interviews with CEA Chairmen, 1984; co-editor: (with Jameson Doig) Leadership and Innovation: A Biographical Perspective on Entrepreneurs in Government, 1987; co-editor: (with John Glidewell) Impossible Jobs in Public Management, 1990; co-editor: (with John E. Owens) Leadership in Context, 2003, The Effective Presidency, 2007. With U.S. Army, 1954-56. Democrat. Episcopalian. Home: 662 Timber Ln Nashville TN 37215-1120 E-mail: Erwin.C.Hargrove@Vanderbilt.edu.

HARGROVE, JOHN RUSSELL, lawyer; b. Chgo., Jan. 20, 1947; s. John Francis and Dolly (Arzich) H.; m. Mary Cheryl Fuller, Feb. 12, 1972; children: John Ashby, James Fuller. BS, Butler U., 1969; JD magna cum laude, Ind. U., 1972. Bar: Ind. 1972, Fla. 1974, U.S. Tax Ct. 1975, U.S. Supreme Ct. 1976. Law clk. to Hon Roy L. Stephenson U.S. Ct. Appeals Ind., 1971-72, U.S. Ct. Appeals (8th cir.), 1972-74; mng. dir. and shareholder Heinrich, Gordon, Hargrove, Weihe & James, P.A., Ft. Lauderdale, Fla., 1985-91. Lead articles and book rev. editor Ind. Law Rev., 1971-72. Bd. visitors Ind. U. Sch. Law, 1995—; bd. dirs. EV Ready Broward, 1996-98; nat. co-chair Franciscan Games, 1996. Schofield scholar. Recipient Faculty award Ind. U. Sch. of Law, 1972. Fellow Fla. Acad. Probate and Trust Litigation; mem. ABA, Fed. Bar Assn. (Broward County Fla. chpt., exec. com. 1979-80, v.p. 1980-81, pres. 1981-82), Fla. Bar Assn., Ind. Bar Assn. (mem. bd. vis. Sch. of Law 1995—). Roman Catholic. Office: 500 E Broward Blvd Ste 1000 Fort Lauderdale FL 33394-3087 Home: 338 Royal Palm Way Boca Raton FL 33432-7944

HARGROVE, MIKE (DUDLEY MICHAEL HARGROVE), former professional baseball team manager; b. Perryton, Tex., Oct. 26, 1949; m. Sharon Rupprecht, Dec. 12, 1970; children: Kimberly Denise, Melissa Kathryn, Pamela Christine, Andrew Michael, Cynthia Michelle. BS in Phys. Edn. and Social Scis., Northwestern Okla. State U. First baseman Tex. Rangers, 1974-78, San Diego Padres, 1979, Cleve. Indians, 1979-85, coach minor league team, 1986, mgr. minor league team, 1987-89, coach, 1990-91, mgr., 1991-99; mgr., coach Balt. Orioles, 1999—2003; sr. adv., baseball ops. dept. Cleve. Indians, 2003—05; mgr. Seattle Mariners, 2005—07. Named Am. League Rookie of Yr. Baseball Writers' Assn. Am., 1974, Am. League Rookie Player of Yr. Sporting News, 1974; named to Am. League All-Star team, 1975, Am. League Mgr. of Yr. Sporting News, 1995.*

HARI, KENNETH STEPHEN, painter, sculptor, writer; b. Perth Amboy, NJ, Mar. 31, 1947; s. Stephen John and Jeannette Anna (Matuszewsky) H. Diploma, Newark Sch. Fine and Indsl. Arts, 1966; BFA, Md. Inst. Art, 1968, Yale U., 1970; postgrad., NYU, 1988. Cons. various cos. One man exhbns. include ctrl. Ala., 1996, Beijing, 1996; group exhbns. include Trave Exhibit, 2004, Beijing Mus. Fine Art, 2004, Md. State Mus., 1967, Union Coll., Schenectady, 1969, Monmouth (N.J.) Coll., 1970, Newark Mus., 1971, Trenton State Coll., 1972, one-man exhbns. include C.C. Price Gallery, N.Y.C., H.S. Graphics, Ltd., Keasbey, N.J.; represented in permanent collections of over 390 mus. throughout world, including Vatican, Lincoln Ctr. Gallery for Performing Arts, N.Y.C., Va. Poly. Inst., Blacksburg, N.J. State Mus., Trenton, Grand Ole Opry House, Nashville, Xiaoyi Liu collection, Met. Mus. Art, N.Y.C., Mus. Kenneth Hari, Beijing, China, established 1991, other pub. and pvt. collections; important works include portraits of W.H. Auden, N.Y.C., 1969, M. Moore, N.Y.C., 1969, Pablo Casals, Marlboro, Vt., 1970, Andres Segovia, N.Y.C., 1972, James Michener, Piperville, Pa., 1973, Marcel Marceau, N.Y.C., 1973, Donald Delue, N.Y.C., 1973, Dr. Allan Callow, Boston, 1973, Kurt Vonnegut, Jr., 1973, Buckminster Fuller, 1973, Lord Hailsham, London, 1978, Dr. Linus Pauling for Pauling Inst., Menlo Park, Calif., 1979, Paul Robeson for Paul Robeson Ctr., Rutgers U., Newark, 1979 (Hay award recipients.); Zhao Peng Fei, Beijing, Philip Johnson, N.Y.C., Paul Roache, Spain, Chen Chi, N.Y.C., Liu Zongyu, Beijing, Zhongguo Shengj, Living Treasure of China, 1999, Hiroko Seta, Tokyo, Japan, 1999, Rosemary Clooney, Beverly Hills, Calif., 1999, Paul Robeson exhbn. Rutgers U., 2003; exhibited at Johnson & Johnson, New Brunswick Travel Exhbn., The Angel of Revelation Mural, N.J., 1990; Original lithographs pub. Prophet, 1971, Lovers of Our Time, 1971, Vermont, 1972, Folk Singer, Marcel Marceau, 1973, Abraham, 1973, Ernest Hemingway, 1978, Homage to Virginia, 1980, Tropical Ladies, 1981, The Pearl, 1999, Lorin Pierucci Collection, 2004, Xiaoyi Liu Collection, Beijing Mus. Fine Arts, 2004, Ajeenah Collection of Paintings and Drawings, 2004, Lorin Piervcci Collection, Art Is the Soul of Man, and Without It He Is Lost. Bd. dirs. N.J. Art Festival, 1973-. Office: Eastman & John Watson Galleries c/o Dr John Eastman PO Box 243 Keasbey NJ 08832-0243 Office Phone: 732-442-8031. Personal E-mail: kennethhari@msn.com. *Art is the soul of man, and without it he is lost.*

HARI, RIITTA KYLLIKKI, neuroscientist; b. Mikkeli, Finland, Jan. 16, 1948; d. Paavo E. and Tuovi K. (Tervola) Karkiainen; m. Pertti K. J. Hari; children: Kaisa H., Tuomo T. MD, U. Helsinki, 1974; D Med. Scis., 1980, specialist in Clin. Neurophysiology, 1981; doctorate (hon.), U. Lisbon, Portugal, 2003, U. Kuopio, Finland, 2005. Prof. Acad. Finland, 1991—96, 1999—2004, Helsinki U. Tech., 1996—. Recipient award for Advancement of European Sci. Körber Found. Germany, 1987, Matti Äyräpää prize for medicine in Finland, 2001, Justine et Yves Sergent prize for cognitive sci., Can., 2002, Louis-Jeantet prize for medicine, Switzerland, 2003. Mem. Acad. Europa, Finnish Acad. Scis. and Letters, NAS (fgn. assoc.). Office: Helsinki U Tech Low Temperature Lab Brain Rsch Unit 02015 HUT Espoo Finland E-mail: hari@heuro.hut.fi.

HARIADI, JOHN WESLEY, otolaryngologist, surgeon; BS, U. Calif., LA, 1993; MD, Temple U., 1997. Lic. physician Hawaii, 1999, Ala., 2002, aviation med. examiner FAA, 2003. Transitional intern William Beaumont Army Med. Ctr. Tex. Tech U. Affiliated Hosps., El Paso, Tex., 1997—98; officer-in charge North Camp Med. Treatment Facility UN, El-Gorah, Egypt, 1998—99; resident in otolaryngology/head and neck surgery Madigan Army Med. Ctr. U. Wash. Affiliated Hospitals, Tacoma, 1999—2001; chief Dept. Aviation Medicine Aeromedical Ctr. U.S. Army, Fort Rucker, Ala., 2001—04; flight surgeon, med. officer Aviation Tng. Ctr. USCG, Mobile, Ala., 2004—05, sr. med. officer Aviation Tng. Ctr., 2005—. Instr. Def. Med. Readiness Tng. Inst., San Antonio, 1998—; space shuttle med. support officer Dept. Def. Manned Space Flight Office NASA, Patrick AFB, Fla., 2003—. Contbr. articles to profl. jours. Adv. coll. admissions Arcadia (Calif.) H.S., 1991—92; ministry asst. The Genesis Fellowship Cottage Hill Bapt. Ch., Mobile, Ala., 2004—06; co-pres. The Promise Fellowship Puyallup (Wash.) Foursquare Ch., 2000—01; pres. Coll. Fellowship Mandarin Bapt. Ch. L.A., Alhambra, Calif., 1991—92. Lt. comdr. U.S. Pub. Health Svc. US Army, 2004—06. Decorated Joint Svc.

Commendation medal U.S. Army, Army Achievement medal, Army Achievement medal with oak leaf cluster, Meritorious Svc. medal; recipient Myers Excellence award, Temple U. Sch. Medicine, 1997; scholar, 1993—95; F.Edward Hebert Health Professions scholarship, U.S. Army, 1996—97. Mem.: AMA, Assn. U.S. Mil. Surgeons, Commd. Officer Assn. U.S. Pub. Health Svc., Soc. U.S. Army Flight Surgeons (named Theodore Lyster Flight Surgeon of Yr. 2004), Am. Acad. Facial Plastics and Reconstructive Surgery, Am. Acad. Otolaryngic Allergy, Am. Acad. Otolaryngology and Head and Neck Surgery, Polo Pl. Ct. Homeowner's Assn. (pres. 2005—). Avocations: travel, water sports. Office: USCoast Guard Aviation Training Center 8501 Tanner Williams Road Mobile AL 36608 Home Phone: 251-776-6752; Office Phone: 251-441-6725. Personal E-mail: harriadi@hotmail.com. Business E-Mail: jhariadi@atc.uscg.mil.

HARICOMBE, LORRAINE, library director, dean; BA, U. of Western Cape, South Africa, MLS with honors; MLS, U. Ill., Urbana-Champaign, D in Libr. and Info. Sci. Libr. adminstr. U. and Peninsula Technikon, South Africa, No. Ill. U.; dean librs. Bowling Green U., Ohio, 2001—06, U. Kans., 2006—. Mem.: ALA, Assn. Am. Univ. Women, Libr. Adminstrn. and Mgmt. Assn., Assn. Coll. and Rsch. Librs. Office: U Kan Watson Libr Lawrence KS 66045 Office Phone: 785-864-4711. E-mail: ljharic@ku.edu.*

HARIJAN, RAM, technology transfer researcher; b. Keecheri, Kerala, India, June 3, 1938; s. Narayanan and Devaki (Amma) Nambiar; m. Lakshmi VP, Aug. 19, 1977; 1 child, Pooja Devi. BA with honors, Madras U., India; MA with award, Southampton U., Eng.; PhD, Reading U., Eng. Lectr. Kerala (India) U.; mining officer Singareni Collieries, India; sch. tchr. Barnstaple Grammar Sch., Eng.; lectr. Bosworth Coll., Eng.; tutor cons. Open U., Eng.; researcher Centre for Studies in Tech. Transfer, Eng. Involved in rsch. which influenced the computerisation policies of Indian Govt., 1982-96; vis. prof. U. Madras, 1982, Calicut U., 1985. Chmn. North Devon Dist. Labour Party, 1972-77, North Devon Assn. Racial Equality, 1978-80; vol. social worker Helping the Disabled and Disadvantaged. Avocations: bridge, chess. Home: 30 Norfolk Rd Desford Leicester LE9 9HR England Personal E-mail: drramofindia@yahoo.com.

HARING, ELLEN STONE, philosophy educator; b. LA, 1921; d. Earl E. and Eleanor (Pritchard) Stone; m. Philip S. Haring, Dec. 1942 (div. June 1951). BA, Bryn Mawr Coll., 1942; MA, Radcliffe Coll., 1943, PhD (AAUW fellow), 1959. Adminstrv. worker ARC, Boston, 1943; mem. faculty Wheaton Coll., Norton, Mass., 1944-45, Wellesley Coll., 1945-72, assoc. prof., 1958-64, prof. philosophy, 1964-72, U. Fla., Gainesville, 1972-93, prof. emerita, 1993—, chmn. dept., 1972-80. Mem.: Am. Philos. Assn., Metaphys. Soc. Am. E-mail: ellenharing@netzero.net.

HARING, EUGENE MILLER, lawyer; b. Washington, May 16, 1927; s. Horace E. and Edith (Miller) H.; m. Janet K. Marshall, Apr. 10, 1971. AB summa cum laude, Princeton U., NJ, 1949, AM, 1951; LLB, Harvard U., Cambridge, Mass., 1955. Bar: N.J. 1955, U.S. Dist. Ct. N.J. 1955, U.S. Ct. Appeals (3d cir.) 1962, U.S. Supreme Ct. 1969, N.Y. 1983, U.S. Dist. Ct. (so. and ea. dists.) N.Y. 1992. Asst. in instrn. Princeton U., 1950-52; assoc. McCarter & English, Newark, 1955-61, ptnr., 1961-97, chmn. exec. com., 1982-97, of counsel, 1997—. Cert. mediator U.S. Dist. Ct., 1994—; mediator CPR Inst. for Dispute Resolution, N.J. Panel, 1994—; mem. roster of mediators Judiciary of State of N.J; mem. civil justice reform act adv. com. U.S. Dist. Ct. N.J., 1997—2000. Contbr. articles to profl. jours. Chmn. Princeton Twp. Zoning Bd. Adjustment, 1979-80, mem. bd., 1975-79; vestryman Trinity Episc. Ch., Princeton, 1975-79, 97-2000, warden, 1980-84; mem. com. on constn. and canons Episc. Diocese of N.J., 1980-87, chancellor, 1983-94, 99—2006, hon. canon (life), 2001—; trustee Gen. Theol. Sem., N.Y., 1987-90; mem. vis. com. Rutgers U. Law Sch., 1994-2000; trustee N.J. Jersey Shore Found., 1988-92. Served with USNR, 1945-46. Woodrow Wilson fellow, Princeton U., 1949—50. Fellow Am. Bar Found. (life), Lawyers Adv. Com. (U.S. Ct. Appeals 3d cir. 1990-93, U.S. Dist. Ct. N.J. 1997—); mem. ABA, N.J. State Bar Assn. (emeritus), N.J. State Bar Found. (trustee 1986-87, v.p. 1987-88, chmn. 1988-90), Essex County Bar Assn. (Spl. Merit award 1998), Mercer County Bar Assn., Am. Law Inst. (life), Harvard Law Sch. Assn. N.J. (pres. 1971-72, nat. v.p. 1972-73), Hist. Soc. U.S. Dist. Ct. for Dist. N.J. (trustee 1987-90, 97—), Hist. Soc. 3d Cir. Ct. Appeals (bd., dirs. 1993-2000), Nassau Club, Princeton, Springdale Golf Club, Princeton, Monmouth Hunt Club, Phi Beta Kappa. Avocation: golf. Home: 75 Rosedale Ln Princeton NJ 08540-2417 Office: McCarter & English Gateway 4 100 Mulberry St Newark NJ 07102-4004 Office Phone: 973-622-4444. Business E-Mail: eharing@mccarter.com.

HARING, ROBERT WESTING, newspaper editor; b. Salem, Mo., Nov. 13, 1932; s. Arthur S. and Martha I. (Westing) H.; m. Jo M. Houser, June 1, 1957 (dec. Nov. 1991); children: Robert A., Joel B., Jon G.; m. Carolyn Scudder, May 20, 1995. AA, Kans. City CC, Mo., 1951; BJ, BA in History, U. Mo., 1954. Reporter So. Illinoisan, Carbondale, Ill., 1954-55, city editor, 1957-59; writer AP, Little Rock, 1959-61, corr. Tulsa, 1961-64, asst. bur. chief Columbus, Ohio, 1964-67, bur. chief Newark, 1967-71, exec. NYC, 1971-75; Sunday editor Tulsa World, 1975-81, exec. editor, 1981-95; ret., 1998. Chmn. Goodwill Industries, Tulsa, 1990-94; bd. dirs. River Parks Authority, Tulsa, 1985-93; pres. Tulsa Zoofriends, 1994-96; chmn. Tulsa Mentoring Coun., Tulsa Lit. Coalition, 1996-98; initiated price earnings ratio in newspaper stock tables, 1973. With U.S. Army, 1955-57. Avocations: running, walking, bicycling. Home: 1620 S Detroit Ave Tulsa OK 74120-6214 Personal E-mail: harings2@sbcglobal.net.

HARING-SMITH, TORI, academic administrator; b. Chgo., Jan. 1, 1953; d. Philip Smyth and Jacqueline (Kolle) Haring; m. Robert Henry Smith, June 1, 1974; 1 child, Whitney Patrick Haring-Smith. BA, Swarthmore Coll., 1974; MA, U. Ill., 1977, PhD, 1980. Tchg. asst. U. Ill., Urbana, 1975-80; asst. prof. Brown U., Providence, 1980-86, assoc. prof. English, 1986—96, assoc. prof. theatre, 1987—96, dir. writing fellows program, 1980—90; prof. theatre Am. U., Cairo, 1996—99, chair dept. performing and visual arts, 1996—99; exec. dir. Thomas J. Watson Found., 1999—2001; dean Coll. Liberal Arts Willamette U., 2001—02, v.p. acad. affairs, 2002—04; pres. Washington & Jefferson Coll., Pa., 2005—. Freelance edn. cons., Providence, 1981—; theatre dir., Providence, 1986—; artistic dir. Wallace Theatre, Cairo, 1996—99. Author: A.A. Milne, 1982, A Guide to Writing Programs, 1984, From Farce to Melodrama, 1985, Learning Together, 1992, Writing Together, 1993, Monologues for Women by Women, 1994, (translation) Napoli Milionaria, 1995, More Monologues for Women by Women, 1996, Scenes for Women by Women, 1998, also numerous on pedagogy, lit. and theatre, (book) New Monologues for Women by Women, 2004. Recipient sr. class citation Brown U., 1984, 85, 86; fellow Watson Found., 1974, Lilly Found., 1981, Wriston fellow Brown U., 1984. Mem.: Assn. Am. Colls. and Univs., Am. Coun. Acad. Deans., Assn. for Theatre in Higher Edn. Office: Washington & Jefferson Coll 60 S Lincoln St Washington PA 15301 Office Phone: 724-223-6000. Business E-Mail: president@washjeff.edu, tharingsmith@washjeff.edu.

HARING-SMITH, WHITNEY, political science scholar; s. Robert H. and Tori Haring-Smith. BS, MS in Polit. Sci., Yale Univ., grad. cert. in security studies, 2007; PhD student in Politics, Oxford Univ., 2007—. Dep. policy dir. DeStefano for Conn. Founder, dir. New Haven Action, 2005. Rhodes Scholar. Achievements include working with Oregon Department of Education, UN High Commissioner for Refugees, the US Department of Defense, the UN Development Program on weapons and ammunition collection in Afghanistan, and for the Mayor of New Haven.

HARINGTON, CHARLES RICHARD, vertebrate paleontologist; b. Calgary, Alta., Can., May 22, 1933; s. Charles Frederic and Florence Katherine (Shillington) H.; m. Gail Doreen Rice, Sept. 15, 1994. BA, U. Alta., 1954, BSc, 1957, PhD, 1977, DSc (hon.), 2004; MSc, McGill U., 1961. Wildlife biologist Can. Wildlife Svc., Ottawa, Ont., 1960-65; vertebrate paleontologist Can. Mus. Nature, Ottawa, 1965—98; coord. climatic change in Can. program Nat. Mus. Natural Scis., Ottawa, 1977—92; curator Quaternary zoology emeritus, rsch. assoc. Can. Mus. Nature, Ottawa, 1998—. Chmn. Can. Com. on Climatic Fluctuations and Man, Ottawa, 1985-90. Author: Quaternary Vertebrate Faunas of Canada and Alaska, 1978; editor: Climatic Change in Canada, 5 vols., 1980-85, Canada's Missing Dimension: Science and History in the Canadian Arctic Islands, 1990, The Year Without a Summer?: World Climate in 1816, 1992, Annotated Bibliography of Quaternary Vertebrates of Northern North America, 2003; contbr. articles to profl. jours., popular publs. and revs. Decorated officer Order of Can.; recipient Can. Assn. Geographers prize, 1957, Meritorious Svc. award, Yukon Govt., 1998, Lifetime Achievement Heritage award, Yukon Hist. and Mus. Assn., 2002, The Queen's Golden Jubilee medal, 2002. Fellow Royal Geog. Soc. (Eng.), Royal Can. Geog. Soc. (Massey medal 1987), Arctic Inst. N.Am., Soc. Vertebrate Paleontology (hon.). Avocations: travel, camping, reading, canoeing, bicycling. Office: Paleobiology Can Mus of Nature Ottawa ON Canada K1P 6P4 Office Phone: 613-364-4052. E-mail: dharington@mus-nature.ca.

HARIRI, ROBERT JOSEPH, neurosurgeon, research scientist; m. Maggie Meade; 3 children. Grad., Columbia Coll., Columbia U. Sch. Engring. and Applied Sciences; PhD, MD, Cornell U. Founder Anthrogenesis Corp. (acquired by Celgene Corp.), 1997—2002; surgical tng. NY Hosp.-Cornell Med. Ctr.; CEO Celgene Cellular Therapeutics Divsn., Celgene Corp., pres.; founder LifebankUSA, a Celgene Co., Cedar Knolls, NJ, 1998, chmn., chief scientific officer, pres. Bd. dir. Semorex, Inc., Vemics, Plasmasol Corp.; advisor to many pharma. and med. device enterprises. Exec. prodr. (with wife): Off the Black, 2006; guest appearance MSNBC, Connected Coast to Coast, ABC, World News Tonight. Achievements include being a recognized leader in the development of new human cellular and tissue therapeutics; development of proprietary technological solutions to enhance the processes involved in the collection, testing and storage of umbilical cord blood cells; patents pending for in all areas of cell processing and surgical devices and techniques. Avocation: avid pilot, Rocket Racing League. Office: LifebankUSA 45 Horsehill Rd Cedar Knolls NJ 07927*

HARIRI, V. M., arbitrator, mediator, educator; BS, Wayne State U.; JD, Detroit Coll. Law; LLM, London Sch. Econs. and Polit.Sci.; diploma arbitration, Reading U., Eng. Pvt. practice internat. and U.S. bus. law, Detroit. Drafting com. Republic of Kazakhstan Code on Arbitration Procedure, Free Econ. Zone Legislation, Republic of Belarus; instr. internat. comml. arbitration Chartered Inst. Arbitrators, Am. Arbitration Assn. Fellow Chartered Inst. Arbitrators (exec. com. N.Am. br., founding com. and expert advisor); mem. ABA, Internat. Bar Assn., Am. Soc. Internat. Law, Am. Arbitration Assn., London Ct. Internat. Arbitration, World Jurist Assn., Mich. Trial Lawyers Assn. Office: 143 Cady Centre Ste 352 Northville MI 48167-1244 E-mail: vhariri@msn.com.

HARISH, ZIV, allergist, immunologist; b. Jerusalem, July 2, 1954; MD, Ben-Gurion U. Med. Sch., Israel, 1983. Diplomate Am. Bd. Allergy and Immunology, Am. Bd. Pediat. Intern Morristown (N.J.) Meml. Hosp., 1985—86; resident in pediat. Albert Einstein Coll. Medicine, Bronx, NY, 1986—88, fellow, 1988—91, asst. prof., 1991—; pvt. practice Englewood, NJ. Mem. staff Englewood Hosp., 1993—, Bronx-Lebanon Hosp., 1993—; attending physician Pascack Valley Hosp., Westwood, NJ, 1996—. Named one of Top Drs. in N.Y. Metro Area, Castle Connolly, 2003, Top Drs. 2003, N.J. Monthly Mag. Mem.: Am. Acad. Asthma, Allergy and Immunology, Am. Coll. Asthma, Allergy and Immunology. Office: Englewood Hosp and Med Ctr 200 Engle St Ste 18 Englewood NJ 07631

HARITON, LORRAINE JILL, information technology executive; b. NYC, Nov. 7, 1954; d. Martin and Barbara (Jaffee) H.; m. Stephen Alan Weyl June 17, 1979; children: Eric, Laura. BS in Math Sci., Stanford U., 1976; MBA, Harvard U., 1982. Sales rep. IBM, NYC, 1977-80, regional rep. San Francisco, 1982-84, sales mgr. Oakland, Calif., 1984-86; mgr. pricing Rolm, Santa Clara, Calif., 1986-87, adminstrv. asst. to v.p. sales, 1987-88, br. mgr., 1988-90, product line mgr., 1990-92; dir. mktg. Verifone, Inc., Redwood City, Calif., 1992-93; v.p. mktg. Network Computing Devices, Mountain View, Calif., 1993—99; pres., CEO Beatnik Inc., San Mateo, Calif., 1999—2003, chmn., 2003—; pres., CEO Apptera, Inc., San Bruno, Calif., 2003—05. Business E-Mail: chariton@applera.com.

HARJO, PATTIPEG SNYDER, language educator; b. Albuquerque, May 19, 1949; d. Floyd Winfield Snyder and Margaret Florence Clark; m. Robert Rivera, Jan. 15, 1982; children: Robert Mario Rivera, Patrick Sean Rivera. BS in Anthropology, U. Tulsa, Okla., 1976, MA in Urban Studies, 1979; BA in Spanish, U. Okla., Norman, 2002. Diploma de Español como Lengua Extranjera Cervantes Inst., Spain, 2006, cert. Spanish tchr. grades K-12 Okla. Dept. Edn., 2002. Urban planner Tulsa Urban Renewal Authority, Okla., 1978—82; kindergarten tchr. Pumpkin Shell Sch., Norman, Okla., 1988—2002; spanish tchr. Norman North H.S., 2002—. Active Tulsa Indian Youth Coun., 1976—79; chair various coms. Sickle Cell Anemia Rsch. Found., Inc., Tulsa, 1978—82, Domestic Violence Intervention Svc., Tulsa, 1982—84; pres. PEO, Norman, 1991. Grantee, NEH, 2004. Mem.: SW Conf. on Lang. Tchg., Okla. Fgn. Lang. Tchrs. Assn., Am. Coun. on the Tchg. Fgn. Langs., Am. Assn. Tchrs. Spanish and Portuguese, Phi Delta Kappa Internat. Liberal. Roman Catholic. Avocations: travel, quilting, gadgets. Office: Norman North High School 1809 Stubbeman Ave Norman OK 73060 Home Phone: 405-821-4781; Office Phone: 405-366-5954. Personal E-mail: pattipeg1@yahoo.com. Business E-Mail: pharjo@norman.k12.ok.us.

HARK, WILLIAM HENRY, retired federal agency administrator, aerospace physician; b. Charleston, W.Va., Nov. 1, 1932; s. Zundel and Esther Sylvia (Henry) H.; m. Claudette Berkley Watson, Apr. 14, 1961; 1 child, William Tucker. AB, W.Va. U., 1954, BS, 1955; MD, Med. Coll. Va., 1957; MPH, Harvard U., 1963. Diplomate Am. Bd. Preventive Medicine. Intern Walter Reed Gen. Hosp., Washington, 1957-58; resident in aerospace medicine U.S. Army, 1962-65, advanced through grades to col., physician, aviation med. cons., 1957-76, ret., 1976; mgr. med. specialties divsn. FAA, Washington, 1980-92, dep. fed. air surgeon, 1992-99. Adv. group for aerospace R&D, NATO, Brussels, 1969-71; mem. joint com. on aviation pathology Dept. of Def., Washington, 1969-71. Decorated Legion of Merit, Air medal, Bronze Star, Vietnam Campaign medal U.S. Army, 1968. Fellow Am. Coll. Preventive Medicine, Aerospace Med. Assn.; mem. Assn. Mil. Surgeons U.S. Avocations: photography, computers. Home: 4317 Southwood Dr Alexandria VA 22309-2822

HARKER, BRIAN J., tobacco company executive; b. Kabwe, Zambia, Apr. 30, 1950; MBA, Cranfield U., Eng., 1981. Chartered acct., 1974. V.p. Monk-Austin Inc., sr. v.p. internat. ops., 1991-95; sr. v.p. DIMON Inc., Danville, Va., 1995-96, exec. v.p., CFO, 1996-99, pres., COO, 1999—2003, pres., CEO, 2003—05, chmn., 2003—05; chmn., CEO Alliance One Internat., Inc., Morrisville, NC, 2005—06, chmn., 2007—. Office: Allliance One Internat Inc 8001 Aerial Ctr Pwy PO Box 2009 Morrisville NC 27560-2009 Office Phone: 919-379-4300.

HARKER, PATRICK TIMOTHY, academic administrator, systems engineer, educator; b. Camden, NJ, Nov. 19, 1958; s. Orris William and Jennie S. (Gaworek) Harker; m. Emily Grace Saaty, June 13, 1981; children: Thomas Patrick, Michael Francis, Meghan Emma. BSE, MSE, U. Pa., 1981, MA in econ., 1983, PhD in civil and urban engring., 1983. Product support analyst Sun Info. Svcs. Inc., 1979; engr. Louis T. Klauder and Assocs., 1980—81; asst. prof. geography U. Calif., Santa Barbara, 1983—84; asst. prof. decision scis. Wharton Sch., U. Pa., Phila., 1984—87, assoc. prof. decision scis., 1987—91, UPS transp. prof. of pvt. sector, 1991—2000, dir. Fishman-Davidson Ctr. for Study of the Svc. Sector, 1989—94, chmn. dept. opers. and info. mgmt., 1997—99, dep. dean, 1999—2000, interim dean, 1999—2000, Reliance prof. of mgmt. and pvt. enterprise, 2000—07, dean, 2000—07; prof. sys. engring., chmn. dept. sys. engring., Sch. Engring. and Applied Sci. U. Pa., Phila., 1994—96; pres. U. Del., Newark, 2007—. Editor-in-chief Jour. Ops. Rsch., 1995—99; editl. bd. Internat. Studies in the Svc. Economy, 1990—, Computational Optimization and Applications, Jour. of Svc. Rsch.; spcl. asst. to dir. FBI, 1991—92; trustee Goldman Sachs Trust, 2000—, Goldman Sachs Variable Ins. Trust, 2000—; bd. managers Goldman Sachs Hedge Fund Partners Registered Fund LLC, 2004—; mem. adv. bd. Juniper Bank, 2000—, Mobility Technologies, 2001—; mem. diocesan fin. coun. Diocese of Camden. Author: Predicting Intercity Freight Flows, 1987, Service Quality and Productivity Challenge, 1995; co-editor: Performance of Financial Institutions, 2000; contbr. of more than 80 profl. articles. V.p. St. Peter Celestine Sch. Bd., Cherry Hill, NJ, 1993—. Named a Presdl. Young Investigator Award, NSF, 1986; recipient David W. Hauck Award for Outstanding Tchg. in the Undergraduate Divsn., 1998; fellow, White House, 1991—92. Republican. Roman Catholic. Achievements include patents in field of of railroad control systems. Avocations: bicycling, woodworking, weightlifting, sailing. Office: U Del Office of Pres Hullihen Hall Newark DE 19716 E-mail: 53775@udel.edu.*

HARKER, VICTORIA D., electric power industry executive; b. NYC, Oct. 24, 1964; d. Paul A. and Mary Ellen (Duva) Dux; m. Drew Alan Harker, June 24, 1989; children: Zachary Paul, Ethan, Benjamin. BA, U. Va., 1986; MBA, Am. U., 1990. Fin. analyst Arnold & Porter, Washington, 1986-89; from fin. mgr. to sr. mgr. bus. analysis & devel. MCI, 1990, dir. mass markets bus. analysis and planning, v.p. fin. mass markets, 1996; CFO MCI Group WorldCom Inc., 1998—2000; various mgmt. positions including acting CFO, sr. v.p. corp. fin. and treas. MCI; exec. v.p., CFO AES Corp., 2006—. Mem. Mt. Vernon Coll. Inst. on Women in Work, Washington, 1992-94; adv. Am. U. MBA Alumni Coun., Washington, 1993-94. Mem. Am. Mgmt. Assn., Women's Golf Assn., Jr. League Assn. No. Va. (chair placement com. 1991-93). Avocations: golf, reading, travel. Office: AES Corp 4300 Wilson Blvd 11th Fl Arlington VA 22203

HARKER, WILLIAM R., lawyer; Atty. Wachtell Lipton Rosen & Katz, 2000—05; v.p., chief counsel Sears Holdings Corp., Hoffman Estates, Ill., 2005—06, gen. counsel, sec., 2006—. Office: Sears Holdings Corp 3333 Beverley Rd Hoffman Estates IL 60179*

HARKEY, JOHN NORMAN, judge; b. Russellville, Ark., Feb. 25, 1933; s. Olga John and Margaret (Fleming) H.; m. Willa Moreau Charlton, May 24, 1959; children— John Adam, Sarah Leigh. AS, Marion Inst., Ala., 1952; LLB, BS, BSL, U. Ark., 1959, JD, 1969. Bar: Ark. 1959. Since practiced in, Batesville; pros. atty. 3d Jud. Dist. Ark., 1961-65; ins. commr. Ark., 1967-68; chmn. Ark. Commerce Commn., 1968-69; spl. justice Ark. Supreme Ct., 1988; judge juvenile divsn. Ark. 16th Dist., 1989-90; sr. ptnr. Harkey, Walmsley and related firms, Batesville, 1970-92; chancery and probate judge 16th Jud. Dist., Batesville, Ark., 1993-98, circuit and chancery judge, 1999-2001, circuit judge, 2001—. 1st lt. USMCR, Korea. Named Outstanding Trial Judge, Ark. Trial Lawyers Assn., 2005. Mem. Ark. Bar Assn., Am. Bar Register, U.S. Marine Corps League. Home: 490 Harkey Rd Batesville AR 72501-9294 Office: PO Box 2656 Batesville AR 72503-2656 Home Phone: 870-793-5849; Office Phone: 870-793-8890.

HARKEY, ROBERT SHELTON, retired lawyer; b. Charlotte, NC, Dec. 22, 1940; s. Charles Nathan and Josephine Lenora (McKenzie) H.; m. Barbara Carole Payne, Apr. 2, 1983; 1 child, Elizabeth McKenzie. BA, Emory U., 1963, LLB, 1965. Bar: Ga. 1964, U.S. Dist. Ct. (no. dist.) Ga. 1964, U.S. Ct. Appeals (1st, 5th, 7th, 9th and 11th cirs.) 1964-86, U.S. Supreme Ct. 1964. Assoc. Swift, Currie, McGhee & Hiers, Atlanta, 1965—68; atty. Delta Air Lines, 1968—74, gen. atty., 1974—79, asst. v.p. law, 1979—85, assoc. gen. counsel, v.p., 1985—88, gen counsel, v.p., 1988—90, gen. counsel, sr. v.p., 1990—94, gen. counsel, sr. v.p., sec., 1994—2003; ret., 2004. Coun. mem. Emory U. Law Sch., 1997—2003; bd. adv. Emory U. Med. Sch., 2004—. Unit chmn. United Way, Atlanta, 1985; trustee Woodruff Arts Ctr., 1995-2001; bd. vis. Emory U., 1999-2000; bd. dirs. Chris Kids, Inc., chmn., 2004. Lt. jg. USNR, 1968-79 Mem. ABA (com. gen. counsels), Air Transport Assn. (chmn. law coun. 1996-98), State Bar Ga. (chmn. corp. counsel sect. 1992-93), Atlanta Bar Assn., Corp. Counsel Assn. Greater Atlanta (bd. dirs. 1990), Cherokee Town and Country Club. Presbyterian. Avocations: tennis, reading. Office: Ford and Harrison 1275 Peachtree St Atlanta GA 30329 Personal E-mail: bobharkey@comcast.net.

HARKIN, THOMAS RICHARD, senator; b. Cumming, Iowa, Nov. 19, 1939; s. Patrick and Frances H.; m. Ruth Raduenz, 1968; children: Amy, Jenny. BS in Govt. and Economics, Iowa State U., 1962; JD, Cath. U. Am., 1972. Bar: Iowa 1972. Mem. staff Ho. of Reps. Select Com. U.S. Involvement in S.E. Asia, 1970; mem. 94th-98th Congresses from 5th Iowa Dist., mem. sci. and tech. com., mem. agr., nutrition and forestry coms.; US Senator from Iowa, 1985—; atty. Polk County Legal Aid Soc., 1973—74. Prin. author Americans with Disabilities Act; mem. com. agr., nutrition and forestry US Senate, com. appropriations, com. health, edn., labor and pensions, com. small bus. and entrepreneurship. Co-author: (with C.E. Thomas) Five Minutes to Midnight: Why the Nuclear Threat is Growing Faster than Ever, 1990. Dem. candidate for Presidency of U.S., 1992. Served with USN, 1962—67, served with USNR, 1968—74. Named Outstanding Young Alumnus Iowa State U. Alumni Assn., 1974; recipient Excellence in Public Svc. award Am. Acad. Pediatrics, 1991, Disting. Public Svc. award Med. Libr. Assn., 1995, William Steiger Meml. award Am. Conf. Govtl. Indsl. Hygienists, 1996, President's award Nat. Corn Grower's Assn., 2001, Richard and Barbara Hensen Leadership award and Disting. Lectureship U. Iowa Coll. Public Health, 2001, Friend of Seniors award Nat. Com. to Preserve Social Security and Medicare, 2002, Morris K. Udall award public svc. Parkinson's Action Network, 2002, Chronicles of Courage award VSA Arts, 2002, Spl. Recognition award AHA, 2003, Capitol Dome award Am. Cancer Soc., 2003, Disting. Cmty. Health Champion Nat. Assn. Cmty. Health Centers, 2005, Fred Rogers Integrity award Campaign for Commercial-Free Childhood, 2005. Mem.: Am. Legion. Democrat. Roman Catholic. Office: US Senate 731 Hart Senate Bldg Washington DC 20510-0001 also: Federal Bldg Ste 733 210 Walnut St Des Moines IA 50309-2106 Office Phone: 202-224-3254, 515-284-4574. Office Fax: 202-224-9369, 515-284-4937.*

HARKINS, JOHN GRAHAM, JR., lawyer; b. Phila., May 9, 1931; s. John Graham and Elizabeth Taylor (Bowers) H.; m. Beatrice Gibson McIlvain, June 30, 1955 (dec. Aug. 2002); children: John Graham III, Alida McIlvain (dec.). BA cum laude, U. Pa., 1953, LL.B. summa cum laude, 1958. Bar: Pa. 1959, U.S. Supreme Ct. 1971. Assoc. firm Pepper, Hamilton & Scheetz, Phila., 1958-63, partner, 1963-92, co-chmn., 1982-86, chmn., 1986-92; ptnr. Harkins Cunningham, Phila., 1992—. Instr. U. Pa., 1956-58, lectr. Law Sch., former bd. overseers-law, 1981-95; mem. adv. com. Inst. Law and Econs., 1981—, com. chmn., 1981-91. Editor-in-chief: U. Pa. Law Rev, 1957-58. Supr. Easttown Twp., Pa., 1972-77; past bd. dirs.

Chester County Hosp.; past trustee Curtis Inst. Music; trustee U. Pa., 1987-97, trustee emeritus, 1998—; trustee U. Pa. Health Sys., 1988-2001, vice chmn., 1991-2001; mem. bd. overseers U. Pa. Med. Sch., 1990-2001, chmn., 1991-2001; dir. Citizens for Pa.'s Future, 2001-. With U.S. Army, 1953-55. Fellow Salzburg Seminar in Am. Studies, 1961 Fellow Am. Coll. Trial Lawyers; mem. Am. Law Inst., Am. Bar Assn., Pa. Bar Assn., Phila. Bar Assn., Jud. Conf. U.S. Ct. of Appeals for 3d Circuit, Order of Coif, Phi Beta Kappa. Clubs: Merion Cricket, Radnor Hunt. Home: Lowbrook PO Box 813 Devon PA 19333-0813 Office: Harkins Cunningham 2800 One Commerce Sq 2005 Market St Philadelphia PA 19103-7075 Home Phone: 610-688-5453; Office Phone: 215-851-6701. Office Fax: 215-851-6710. Business E-Mail: jharkins@harkinscunningham.com.

HARKINS, PATRICK NICHOLAS, III, lawyer; b. Jackson, Miss., Apr. 27, 1941; s. Patrick Nicholas and Mary Ruth (Gammon) H.; m. Mary Elizabeth Wilson, Apr. 12, 1969; children: Elizabeth Glenn, DeMatt Henderson. BBA, U. Notre Dame, 1963; JD, U. Miss., 1965. Bar: Miss. 1965, U.S. Dist. Ct. (no. and so. dists.) Miss. 1965, U.S. Ct. Appeals (5th cir.) 1965, U.S. Supreme Ct. 1968. Legis. asst. U.S. Congressman G.V. Montgomery, 1967-68; assoc. atty. Watkins, Pyle, Ludlam, Winter & Stennis, Jackson, Miss., 1969; atty. Watkins & Eager PLLC, Jackson, 1970—, ptnr., 1973—. Served to capt. U.S. Army, 1965-67. Named to Midsouth Super Lawyers, 2006. Fellow Am. Coll. Trial Lawyers, Am. Bar Found., Miss. Bar Found. (pres. 1992-93); mem. ABA, DRI (pres.2001-2002), Miss. Bar Assn., Miss. Def. Lawyers Assn. (bd. dirs. 2003), Fedn. of Def. and Corp. Counsel, Assn. Def. Trial Attys., Internat. Assn. Def. Counsel (chair products liability 1995-97, dir. def. counsel trial acad. 1998), Hinds County Bar Assn., Jackson Country Club. Roman Catholic. Home: 2060 Sheffield Dr Jackson MS 39211-5848 Office: Watkins & Eager PLLC 400 E Capitol St Jackson MS 39201 Office Phone: 601-965-1957. Business E-Mail: nharkins@watkinseager.com.

HARKLEROAD, JO-ANN DECKER, special education educator; b. Wilkes-Barre, Pa., Oct. 22, 1936; d. Leon Joseph Sr. and Beatrice Catherine (Wright) Decker; m. A. Dwayne Harkleroad; 1 child, Leon Wade. AS, George Washington U., 1960, BS in Health, Phys. Edn. and Recreation, minor in Spl. Edn., 1968, MA in Spl. Edn. and Ednl. Diagnosis and Prescription, 1969, postgrad., 1997-99. Recipient Appreciation cert. Fairfax County (Va.) Police Dept., 1987, Meritorious Svc. medal Pres. Com. on Employment of People with Disabilities, 1988. Instr. Cath. U. Am., Washington, 1960-61; tchr. Bush Hill Day Sch., Franconia, Va., 1961-63; ednl. diagnostician Prince William County Schs., Manassas, Va., 1969-71, supr. title I, 1971-72; writer, editor Sta. WNVT-TV, Fairfax, Va., 1980-82; dir. spl. edn. Highland County Schs., Monterey, Va., 1987-90. Author: (novels) Horse Thief Trail, 1981, 3d edit., 1986, Blood Atonement, 2004, Ketch Colt, 2005, Swep Culhane, 2007; columnist op-ed page The Recorder; radio broadcaster Sta. WVMR, Frost, W.Va. Ruling elder Presbyn. Ch., McDowell, Va., Clifton, Va.; mem. divsn. Faith in Action Hunger com. Shenandoah Presbytery; dir. McDowell Presbyn. Ch. Choir; rotating dir. Highland County Cmty. Choir; past pres. Highland County Pub. Libr. Bd. Mem.: Presbyn. Women (life), Stonewall Women's Club (past pres. 1990—92). Avocations: hiking, camping, rifleshooting, reading, gardening. Home: Windy Ridge Farm 218 Davis Run Rd Mc Dowell VA 24458-9704

HARKNESS, JOHN CHEESMAN, retired architect; b. NYC, Nov. 30, 1916; s. Albert and Sara Arden (Cheesman) H.; m. Sarah Pillsbury, June 14, 1941 (separated); children: Sara Harkness Super, Joan Harkness Hantz, Nell, Timothy (dec.), Alice, Frederick, John Pillsbury. BFA cum laude, Harvard U., 1938, BArch, MArch, 1941. Registered architect Maine, Mass., R.I. Architect Saarinen and Swanson, Birmingham, Mich., Harrison, Fouilhoux and Abramovitz, N.Y.C., Skidmore, Owings and Merrill, N.Y.C., prior to 1945; prin. The Architects Collaborative, Cambridge, Mass., 1945-95, pres., 1966-67, 77-84, also bd. dirs., chmn. bd. prins., 1984-86; ret., 2003. Mem. design faculty Harvard Grad. Sch. Design, 1946-50, mem. vis. com.; mem. vis. com. R.I. Sch. Design; mem. capitol area planning bd., Minn. State; archtl. advisor Boston Redevel. Authority for Park Pla., Mass. Design Competition. Author: Encyclopedia of Architecture, 1989; prin.-in-charge projects Martin County Libr., Fla., Creative Arts Ctr., master plan, Squires addition Student Activities Ctr., Biology Bldg., all at Va. Poly. Inst. and State U., Blacksburg, Univ. Ctrs., Coll. William and Mary, Va., Sci. Bldg. Middlebury (Vt.) Coll., Hillside Office Bldg., Waltham, Mass., CBS Office Bldg., Mt. Pleasant, N.Y., master plan and 6 med. bldgs. Children's Hosp. Med. Ctr., Boston (Harleston Parker medal Boston Soc. Architects, Honor award AIA), hdqrs. CIGNA, Bloomfield, Conn. (award N.Eng. Regional Coun. AIA, award excellence Am. Inst. Steel Constrn. 1985), Hoffman Lab. Exptl. Geology (Boston Arts Festival award 1964), athletic facilities, addition Mus. Comparative Zoology, med. sch. Lab. Reprodn. and Reproductive Biology, all at Harvard U., master plan indsl. complex, Jubail, Saudi Arabia, master plan and office bldg. Summit at Westchester, Mt. Pleasant, Cen. Nat. Mus., Riyadh, Saudia Arabia, hdqrs. Shawmut Bank Boston, Amoskeag Bank, Manchester, N.H., Montego Bay (Jamaica) Hosp., Ainsworth Gymnasium Smith Coll., Northampton, Mass. (honor award N.Eng. Regional Coun. AIA), U. Tunis Libr. and Sch. Law, Econs., and Bus. Adminstrn., Tunisia, James L. Hanley Edn. Ctr., Providence (award), New Trier Twp. High Sch., Winnetka, Ill, Blue Hills Regional Vocat. Sch., Canton, Mass., Wayland (Mass.) High Sch. Ambulance driver Am. Field Svc., 1943-44. Pvt. U.S. Army, 1945, ETO, NATOUSA, bronze cross of merit with swords from Polish Rep. for action at the Battle of Casino, Italy. Recipient various competition and archtl. design awards including 6 awards Am. Assn. Sch. Adminstrs., 1960-67, William Ware award, Boston Soc. Architects honor award, 1993; named Harvard Athletic Hall of Fame, NCAA Wrestling champion, 1938, lifetime svc. to wrestling award Mass. and Nat. Wresting Hall of Fame, 1999. Fellow AIA (archtl. juror various design programs, 2d award alt. to Appleton Travelling fellowship); mem. NAD, Boston Soc. Architects (past pres., 1st prize 1940), Mass. State Assn. Architects (past pres.), Archtl. League N.Y., Harvard Grad. Sch. Design Alumni Assn. (past pres.), Harvard U. Alumni Assn. (former dir. 1988), Phi Beta Kappa. Office: Fletcher Harkness Cohen Moneyhun Inc 46 Waltham St Boston MA 02118-2436

HARKNESS, MARY LOU, librarian; b. Denby, SD, Aug. 19, 1925; d. Raleigh Everette and Mary Jane (Boyd) Barker; m. Donald R. Harkness, Sept. 2, 1967. BA, Nebr. Wesleyan U., 1947; AB Libr. Sci., U. Mich., 1948; MS, Columbia U., 1958. Jr. cataloger U. Mich. Law Library, 1948—50; asst. cataloger Calif. Poly. Coll., 1950—52; asst. cataloger, then head cataloger Ga. Inst. Tech., 1952—57; head cataloger U. South Fla., Tampa, 1958—67, dir. libraries, 1967—87, dir. emeritus, 1987—. Cons. Nat. Library Nigeria, 1962—63. Bd. dirs. Southea. Libr. Network, 1977—80. Recipient Alumni Achievement award Nebr. Wesleyan U., 1972 Mem. ALA, Fla. Library Assn., Athena Soc. Democrat. Presbyterian. Home: 12401 N 22d St Apt E-104 Tampa FL 33612-4623 E-mail: marylouh@tampabay.rr.com.

HARKNESS, NANCY P., lawyer; b. 1959; BA in Econs., Cornell U., 1980; JD, Fordham U., 1985. Bar: NY, Calif. With Internat. Broadcasting, LA; cons. Olympic Regional Devel. Authority, Lake Placid; head bus. & legal affairs dept. Motown Record Co. LP, 1995—97; named v.p. bus. & legal affairs Universal Studios Consumer Products Group, 1997; sr. v.p. bus. affairs Digital Entertainment Network Inc.; sr. counsel Akin, Gump, Strauss, Hauer & Feld, LLP; of counsel Sonnenschein Nath & Rosenthal, LA. Office: Sonnenschein Nath & Rosenthal LLP 601 S Figueroa St, Ste 1500 Los Angeles CA 90017 Office Phone: 213-892-5151. Office Fax: 213-623-9924. Business E-Mail: nharkness@sonnenschein.com.

HARKRIDER, JOHN DAVID, lawyer; b. Providence, Aug. 21, 1966; s. David Garrison Harkrider and Merilyn Grace Neher; m. Anja Kroencke; children: June E., Rose E. BA in Polit. Sci. with highest honors, U. Mich., 1988; JD cum laude, U. Calif., San Francisco, 1991. Bar: NY 1992. Assoc. Skadden, Arps, Slate, Meagher & Flom, NYC, 1991—95; ptnr. Axinn, Veltrop & Harkrider, NYC, 1997—. Co-editor: (book) Econometrics in Antitrust, 2005; dir.: (film) Mitchellville, 2005. Named one of Ten to Watch, Variety Mag., 2005. Mem.: ABA (vice chair econ. com 2004), Order of Coif. Office: Axinn Veltrop and Harkrider 1370 6th Ave 19th Fl New York NY 10019

HARKS, HELENE LOUISE, elementary school educator; b. Wisconsin Dells, Wis., Dec. 25, 1928; d. Daniel Albert and Catherine Irene Greenwood; children: Mary Pamela Bailey, Mary Ann Buckley, Christine Helene Wallace, William Robert, Jeannette Marie Grant. BS, U. of Wis., 1947—52. Calif. lifetime tchr. credential gen. elem. Tchr. Livermore (Calif.) Unified Sch. Dist., 1959—; prodr. -musical theatre Diablo Light Opera Co., Walnut Creek, Calif., 1965—. Mus. docent Blackhawk Mus., Danville, Calif. Active Blackhawk Mus. Guild, Danville, Calif.; mem., prodr. Diablo Light Opera Co., Walnut Creek, Calif. Recipient Shellie award, Diablo Light Opera Co., 2005. Home: 728 Old Creek Rd Danville CA 94526 Home Phone: 925-820-3945. Home Fax: 925-820-1378. E-mail: heleneharks@sbcglobal.net.

HARL, NEIL EUGENE, economist, educator, lawyer, writer; b. Appanoose County, Iowa, Oct. 9, 1933; s. Herbert Peter and Bertha Catherine (Bonner) H.; m. Darlene Ramona Harris, Sept. 7, 1952; children: James Brent, Rodney Scott. BS, Iowa State U., 1955, PhD, 1965; JD, U. Iowa, 1961. Bar: Iowa 1961. Field editor Wallace's Farmer, 1957-58; research assoc. U.S. Dept. Agr., Iowa City and Ames, Iowa, 1958-64; from assoc. prof. to prof. Iowa State U., Ames, 1964—2004, Charles F. Curtiss dist. prof., 1976—, prof. emeritus, 2005—, dir. Ctr. Internat. Agrl. Fin., 1990—2004. Mem. adv. group to commr. IRS, 1979-80; mem. adv. com. Heckerling Inst. on Estate Planning, Miami, Fla., 1983-96; mem. adv. com. Office Tech. Assessment, U.S. Congress, 1988-95, vice chair, 1992-93, chair, 1993-94; mem. exec. bd. U.S. West Comms., Iowa, 1989-90; mem. adv. com. on agrl. biotech. USDA, 2000-02; mem. Fed. Commn. on Payment Limitations in Agr., 2002-03; lectr. in field. Author: Farm Estate and Business Planning, 1973, 15th edit., 2001, Legal and Tax Guide for Agricultural Lenders, 1984, supplement, 1987, Agricultural Law, 15 vols., 1980—81, Agricultural Law Manual, 1985;: rev. edit., 2006, The Farm Debt Crisis of the 1980s, 1990, Arrogance and Power: The Saga of WOI-TV, 2001, Farm Income Tax Manual, 2006; co-author: Farmland, 1982, Principles of Agricultural Law, 1997, Taxation of Cooperatives, 1999, Reporting Farm Income, 2000;: rev. edit., 2006, Family Owned Business Deduction, 2001, The Law of the Land, 2002; contbr. articles to profl. jours. Trustee Iowa State U. Agrl. Found., 1969-85; bd. dirs. Henry A. Wallace Birthplace Found., 2007-. 1st lt. AUS, 1955—57. Recipient Outstanding Tchr. award Iowa State U., 1973, Disting Svc. to Agr. award Am. Soc. Farm Mgrs. and Rural Appraisers, 1977, Iowa sect. 1996, Faculty Svc. award Nat. Univ. Ext. Assn., 1980, Disting. Svc. award Am. Agrl. Editors Assn., 1984, Disting. Achievement citation Iowa State U., 1985, Disting. Svc. to State Govt. award Nat. Gov.'s Assn., 1986, Disting. Svc. award Iowa State U., 1986, Farm Leader of Yr. award Des Moines Register, 1986, Henry A. Wallace award, 1987, Superior Svc. award USDA, 1987, Disting. Svc. to Iowa Agr. award Iowa Farm Bur., 1992, Faculty Excellence award, Iowa Bd. Regents, 1993, Charles A. Black award Coun. Agrl. Sci. Tech., 1997, Excellence in Internat. Agr. award Iowa State U., 1999, Disting. Svc. to Agr. award Chgo. Farmers Club, 1999, Exceptional Svc. to Agr. award Iowa Master Farmers, Wallaces Farmer, 2000, Pres.'s award disting. svc. Iowa State U., 2002, Lifetime Achievement award Iowa Farmers Union, 2003, Svc. to Am. and World Agr., Nat. Assn. County Agrl. Agts., 2006; named Seminar Leader of Yr. Nat. Assn. Accts., 2000. Fellow: Iowa State Bar Found., ABA Rsch. Found., Am. Coll. Trusts and Estates Counsel, Am. Agrl. Econs. Assn. (exec. bd. 1979—85, pres. 1983—84, Am. Agrl. Econs. Found. pres. 1993—94, Outstanding Ext. Program award 1970, Excellence in Communicating Rsch. Results award 1975, Disting. Undergrad. Tchr. award 1976); mem.: ABA, Iowa Barn Found. (bd. dirs. 1997—2005, v.p. 1999—2001), Am. Agrl. Law Assn. (pres. 1980—81, Disting. Svc. award 1984), Iowa Bar Assn. (Pres. award 1991), Golden Key. Home: 2821 Duff Ave Ames IA 50010 Home (Winter): 78-261 Manukai St # 3001 Kailua Kona HI 96740 Office: Iowa State U Dept Econs 381 Heady Hall Ames IA 50011-1070 Office Phone: 515-294-6354. Business E-Mail: harl@iastate.edu.

HARLAN, LEONARD MORTON, merchant banker; b. Newark, June 1, 1936; s. Harold Robinson and Doris Harriet (Siegler) H.; children: Joshua, Noah. BME, Cornell U., 1959; MBA with distinction, Harvard U., 1961, DBA, 1965. Lic. real estate broker, N.Y., N.J. V.p. Donaldson, Lufkin & Jenrette, Inc., 1968-69; founder, chmn. bd. The Harlan Co., Inc., NYC, 1969-96; bd. dirs. Ryland Group, Inc., 1984—; pres. Castle Harlan, Inc., 1987—; gen. ptr. Legend Capital Group, 1987—; pres. Castle Harlan Ptnrs. II, 1992—, Castle Harlan Ptnrs. III, 1997—. Bd. dirs. Tradesco Molding, Inc., Matrix Global Investments, Inc.; guest lectr. Harvard U. and Columbia U. Grad. Schs. Bus. Adminstrn., 1968—; adj. prof. banking and real estate NYU Real Estate Inst., 1968-93, Grad. Sch. Bus. Adminstrn., 1976-80; adj. prof. bus. adminstrn. Columbia U. Grad. Sch. Bus. Adminstrn., 1980-93; trustee North Country Sch./CTT, 1989-95. Mem. editl. bd. Real Estate Rev. Jour., 1971-84; mem. bd. advisors Jour. Pvt. Equity, 1997—; contbr. articles to profl. jours. Mem. Pres.'s Com. on Indsl. Innovation, 1978; mem. Urban Devel. Action Grant Task Force, HUD, 1984; mem. nat. leadership coun. Am. Jewish Com.; 1993—, mem. exec. com. Ctrl. N.J. chpt., 1980—, treas., 1988-96, bd. govs., 1996—, nat. budget com., 1986-87; trustee N.Y.C. Citizens Budget Commn., 1988—; mem. Cranbury (N.J.) Mcpl. Planning Bd., 1987-93; mem. vis. com. Harvard Bus. Sch., 1992—. Recipient Charles B. Shatuck Meml. award Am. Inst. Real Estate Appraisers, 1967, 72; Disting. Tchr. award NYU, 1979; Ford Found. fellow, 1964-65; Zurn fellow, 1962-63. Mem. Harvard Bus. Sch. Alumni Assn. (v.p. 1991-93, bd. dirs. 1989-93), Harvard Club N.Y. (admissions com. 1973-75), Harvard Bus. Sch. Club Greater N.Y. (v.p. N.Y.C. chpt. 1977-79, bd. dirs. 1989-98), Harvard Club of Princeton, Cornell Club of Princeton. Office: Castle Harlan Inc 150 E 58th St Fl 37 New York NY 10155-3799

HARLAN, LINDA CAROL, epidemiologist; b. Glasgow, Mont., Feb. 24, 1950; d. Norman Joseph Mavencamp and Bernice Audrene Klingler; m. William Robert Harlan, Aug. 23, 1980; 1 child, Nicole Porter. BSN, Mont. State U., 1972; MPH, U. Mich., 1981, PhD, 1985. RN Calif., 1972. Project coord. U. Calif., Davis, 1973—80; sr. rsch. analyst Westat, Inc., Rockville, Md., 1981—82; rsch./tchg. asst. U. Mich., Ann Arbor, 1983—84, postdoctoral fellow, 1985—87; biostatistician, epidemiologist Henry Ford Hosp., Detroit, 1984—85; cancer epidemiologist Nat. Cancer Inst., Bethesda, Md., 1987—; mem. Am. Coll. Sugeons Commn. on Cancer, 2005. Mem. editl. bd.: Jour. Clin. Oncology, 2003—06; contbr. articles to profl. jours. Mem.: ACS (Commn. on Cancer 2005—). Office: Nat Cancer Inst Ste 4005 6130 Executive Blvd Bethesda MD 20892-7344 Business E-Mail: lh50w@nih.gov.

HARLAN, MARY ANN, lawyer; BA, Skidmore Coll.; JD, Case Western Reserve U. Ptnr. Calfee, Halter & Griswold LLP; asst. gen. counsel J.M. Smucker Co., gen. counsel, asst. sec., 2002—, v.p., gen. counsel, sec., 2005—. Office: JM Smucker Co 1 Strawberry Lane Orrville OH 44667

HARLAN, NEIL EUGENE, retired health facility administrator; b. Cherry Valley, Ark., June 2, 1921; s. William and Mary Nina (Ellis) H.; m. Martha Almlov, Sept. 27, 1952; children: Lindsey Beth, Neil Eugene, Sarah Ellis. Student, U. Edinburgh, Scotland, 1946; BS, U. Ark., 1947, LLD, 1969; MBA, Harvard U., 1950, DBA, 1956. Mem. faculty Grad. Sch. Bus. Adminstrn. Harvard U., 1951-62, asst. prof., 1954-58, assoc. prof., 1958-61, prof., 1962; asst. sec. Air Force Washington, 1962-64; exec. v.p. Anderson, Clayton & Co., 1964-67; dir. McKinsey & Co., Inc., 1967-74, McKesson Corp., San Francisco, 1974-93, chmn., CEO. Author: Management Control in Air Frame Subcontracting, 1956, Managerial Economics, 1962. Chmn. San Francisco Ballet, 1982-85; trustee exec. com. World Affairs Coun. No. Calif., 1983—; chmn., dir. Nat. Park Found., 1986-92; bd. govs. San Francisco Symphony, 1985-88; mem. Calif. Com. on Campaign Fin., Calif. Bus. Roundtable, 1984-87; pres. San Francisco Pvt. Industry Coun. Served with AUS, 1943-46. Mem. Webhannet Golf Club, Bohemian Club, Pacific Union Club. Office: McKesson Corp One Post St San Francisco CA 94104-5292 Home: 21 Admirals Way Kennebunk ME 04043

HARLAN, NORMAN RALPH, construction executive; b. Dayton, Ohio, Dec. 21, 1914; s. Joseph and Anna (Kaplan) H.; m. Thelma Katz, Sept. 4, 1955; children: Leslie, Todd. Indsl. Engring. degree, U. Cin., 1937. Chmn. Am. Constrn. Corp., Dayton, 1949, Harlan, Inc., realtors. Mem. Dayton Real Estate Bd., Ohio Real Estate Assn., Nat. Assn. Real Estate Bds., C. of C., Pi Lambda Phi. Home: 303 Glenridge Rd Kettering OH 45429-1631 Office: Am Constrn Corp 2451 S Dixie Dr Dayton OH 45409-1861

HARLAN, RAYMOND CARTER, special investigator, writer, retired communication executive, educator, and military officer; b. Shreveport, La., Nov. 13, 1943; s. Ross E. and Margaret (Burns) H.; m. Nancy K. Munson, 1966 (div. 1978); children: Kathleen Marie, Patrick Raymond; m. Sarah J. Kinzel, 1979 (div. 1982); m. Linda Frances Gerdes, Mar. 30, 1985; stepchildren: Kimberly Jo Gillis, Kellie Leigh Raffa, Ryan William Gerdes. BA Speech and Drama cum laude, Southwestern U., 1966; MA English, U. Tex., 1968; MA Speech & Theatre Arts, Bradley U., 1976. Commd. 2d lt. USAF, 1968, advanced through grades to maj., 1980, ret., 1988, missile launch officer, instr. Malmstrom AFB, Mont., 1968—72. Asst. prof. Bradley U., Peoria, Ill., 1972-76; instr., asst. prof., course dir. Air Force Acad., Colorado Springs, 1976-81; chief instrnl. sys. divsn., chief codes divsn. F.E. Warren AFB, Wyo., 1981-85; mgr. Minuteman Edn. Program, asst. prof. Air Force Inst. Tech., Dayton, 1985-88; pres. ComSkills Tng., Aurora, Colo., 1988-2000; internat. trainer Inst. for Internat. Rsch., London, 1990-92; mgr. doc and tng. AT&T Broadband, 2000-01; instr. Program Afloat Coll. Edn., 2002-03; spl. investigator U.S. Investigations Svcs., 2003—; scriptwriter Progressive Lang., Inc., 2002-05. Author: The Confident Speaker, 1993; co-author: Telemarketing That Works, 1991, Interactive Telemarketing, 1995; contbr. articles and revs. to profl. jours. Decorated Air Force Commendation medal with three oak leaf clusters, Air Force Meritorious Svc. medal with one oak leaf cluster; recipient George Washington Honor Medal Freedom Found., 1983, Leo A. Codd award Am. Def. Preparedness Assn., 1975, 1st prize Ariz. State Poetry Soc., 1979. Mem.: Soc. Children's Book Writers and Illustrators, Assn. Air Force Missileers. Lutheran. Avocations: writing, skiing, bicycling, gardening. Office Phone: 303-903-8666. E-mail: rayha2@comcast.net.

HARLAN, ROBERT DALE, library and information scientist, educator, academic administrator; b. Hastings, Nebr., Aug. 4, 1929; s. Hugh Allan and Madge Keister (Newmyer) H. BA, Hastings Coll., 1950; MA in Library Sci., U. Mich., 1956, MA, 1958, PhD, 1960. Head book order sect. Library U. Mich., Ann Arbor, 1956-58, lectr., 1960; asst. prof. Sch. Library Sci. U. So. Calif., Los Angeles, 1960-63; asst. prof. library and info. studies U. Calif., Berkeley, 1963-70, assoc. prof., 1970-76, prof., 1976-94, prof. emeritus, 1994—; assoc. dean Sch. Library and Info. Studies, 1971-74, 77-82; acting dean Sch. Library and Info. Studies U. Calif., Berkeley, 1985-86. Vis. assoc. prof. Sch. Libr. Sci. UCLA, summer 1973; cons. NEH, Washington; proprietor Park Hills Press. Author: John Henry Nash, 1970, Bibliography of the Grabhorn and Grabhorn-Hoyem Presses, 1977, George L. Harding, 1978, The Colonial Printer: Two Views, 1978, Chapter Nine, 1982, William Doxey's Publishing Venture: At the Sign of the Lark, 1983, The Two Hundredth Book, 1993; chmn. edit. bd. catalogues and bibliographies series U. Calif. Press, 1982-99; contbr. numerous articles and revs. to profl. jours. Rackham pre-doctoral fellow, U. Mich., 1958-60, summer faculty fellow U. Calif., Berkeley, 1964; grantee Assn. Coll. and Research Libraries, 1960, 63. Mem. Will Cather Pioneer Meml. Soc., Fine Press Book Assn., Book of Calif. Club (bd. dirs. 1982-88, sec. bd. 1987-88, Lewis award 2004). Office: U Calif Sch Info 102 South Hall Berkeley CA 94720-4600 Office Phone: 415-642-4375. Business E-Mail: rharlan@sims.berkely.edu.

HARLAN, ROBERT ERNEST, professional football team executive; b. Des Moines, Sept. 9, 1936; m. Madeline Harlan; children: Kevin, Bryan, Michael. BJ, Marquette U., 1958. Former gen. reporter UPI, Milw.; sports info. dir. Marquette U., Milw., 1959; dir. community rels. St. Louis Cardinals baseball team, 1966-68, dir. pub. rels., 1968-71; asst. gen. mgr. Green Bay (Wis.) Packers, 1971-75, corp. gen. mgr., 1975-81, corp. asst. to pres., 1981-88, exec. v.p. adminstrn., 1988-89, pres., chief exec. officer, 1989—. Bd. dirs. Firstar Bank, Green Bay. Mem. exec. bd. Packer 65 Roses Sports Club. Served with U.S. Army. Mem. bd. of trustees, St. Norbert Coll., Wis. Avocation: golf. Office: Green Bay Packers 1265 Lombardi Ave Green Bay WI 54304-3997 also: Green Bay Packers Lambeau Field PO Box 10628 Green Bay WI 54307-0628

HARLAN, WILLIAM ROBERT, JR., internist, educator, researcher; b. Richmond, Va., Nov. 1, 1930; s. William Robert and Helen J. (Weaver) H.; m. Linda Carol Mavencamp, Aug. 23, 1980; children: Elizabeth, William, Christopher, Nicole. BA, U. Va., 1951; MD magna cum laude, Med. Coll. Va., 1955. Diplomate Am. Bd. Internal Medicine, Am. Bd. Family Practice. Intern U. Wis., Madison, 1955-56; resident in medicine Duke U. Hosp., Durham, NC, 1958-62; dir. Clin. Rsch. Ctr., Med. Coll. Va., 1963-70; asso. dean U. Ala. Med. Sch., 1970-72; prof. medicine and community health scis. Duke U., 1972-74; prof. medicine and postgrad. medicine U. Mich., Ann Arbor, 1974-88, asst. dean Med. Sch.; dir. div. epidemology and clin. applications Nat. Heart, Lung and Blood Inst., 1988-91; assoc. dir. for disease prevention NIH, Bethesda, 1991—2002; expert NIMH, 2001—06, sr. advisor, 2001—05; cons. Nat. Libr. Medicine, 2006—. Cons. World Bank; mem. sci. adv. bd. U.S. Air Force; mem. Armed Forces Epidemiology Bd., NIH study sects. and adv. councils. Contbr. articles to med. jours. Lt. USMC, 1956—58, US Naval Sch. Aerospace Medicine. Fellow ACP, Am. Coll. Preventive Medicine, Am. Acad. Family Practice, Am. Heart Assn.; mem. N.Y. Acad. Sci., Sigma Xi, Alpha Omega Alpha (Markle Scholar in Acad. Medicine). Democrat. Episcopalian. Avocations: tennis, golf, skiing. Home: 3503 Windsor Pl Chevy Chase MD 20815-4001 also: 155 N Sea Pines Dr Hilton Head Island SC 29928-5804 Personal E-mail: wharlan@starpower.net.

HARLANDER, RONALD STANLEY, JR., pharmacist; b. Chisholm, Minn., Apr. 17, 1976; s. Ronald Stanley Harlander, Sr. and Catherine Marie Harlander; m. Kelly Sue Arms, Aug. 4, 2001; children: Katlyne Marie, Mckenzie Jo, Ronald Stanley III. AS, AA, Hibbing C.C., Minn., 1996; BA in Chemistry, St. Cloud State U., Minn., 1999, BS in Genetics, 1999, BS in Microbiology, 1999; MS in Molecular Biology, U. Wyo., Laramie, 2002; PharmD, U. Minn., Mpls., 2006. Registered pharmacist Minn., 2006, cert. medication therapy mgmt. provider Minn., 2006. Tchg. and rsch. assoc. U. Wyo., Laramie, 1999—2002, microbiology lab. instr., 2000—01; pharmacist Walgreens, Duluth, Minn., 2002—, St. Mary's Duluth Clinic, 2006—; clin. pharmacist St. Mary's Duluth Clinic Internal Medicine, Duluth, 2006—. Cons. in field. Contbr. articles to profl. jours. Scholar, St. Cloud State U., 1996; Transfer scholar, Hibbing C.C., 1994, Claude A. Mather scholar, U. Minn., 2002. Mem.: Am. Coll. Clin. Pharmacists (assoc.), Am.

Assn. Diabetes Educators (assoc.), Minn. Rural Health Assn. (assoc.), Am. Soc. Health-System Pharmacists (assoc.), Nat. Cmty. Pharmacist Assn. (assoc.), Am. Pharmacist Assn. (assoc.), Pharmacy Students for Pharm. Care (assoc.), Minn. Pharmacist Assn. (assoc.), Molecular Biology, Cell Physiology, and Microbiology Club (assoc.; sec. 1999—2002), Phi Theta Kappa, Alpha Epsilon Delta, Kappa Epsilon (assoc.; coll. bd. rep. 2002—04). Achievements include research in infectious disease. Avocations: medication therapy management, travel, swimming. Home: 4380 Grouse Ridge Dr Hermantown MN 55811 Office: 1700 Miller Trunk Hwy Duluth MN 55811 Home Phone: 218-729-9496; Office Phone: 218-727-8157.

HARLASS, FREDERICK E., obstetrician, gynecologist; b. Butte, Mont., Feb. 14, 1947; s. June Rena and Edward Gustave Harlass; m. Penny M. Wylie, Feb. 22, 1952; children: Steven Bruce, Scott Alexander, Sarah Lynn. MD, U. of Wash., 1980. Maternal-Fetal Medicine Am. Bd. of Obstetrics & Gynecology, 1996. Obstetrician, gynecologist U.S. Army, Ft. Wainwright, Alaska, 1984—86, chief, ambulatory care Ft. Lewis, Wash., 1986—87, fellow perinatal medicine, 1987—89, chief divsn. of obstetrics El Paso, 1989—91; residency dir. Tex. Tech U., El Paso, 1991—95, chmn., dept. of obstetrics & gynecology, 1995—2000, prof., 2000—. Chief dept. obstetrics, and gynecology, med. dir. for labor and delivery Del Sol Med. Ctr., El Paso, 2000—. Author numerous textbooks. Bd. mem. Lay Midwifery Commn., El Paso, 1993—97. Lt. col. U.S. Army and USN, 1966—99. Decorated 14 awards U.S. Army and USN. Fellow: FACOG (assoc.). Achievements include research in Diabetes in pregnancy. Avocations: golf, travel. Home: 5637 Buckley Dr El Paso TX 79912 Personal E-mail: frederick.harlass@ttuhsc.edu.

HARLE, THOMAS STANLEY, radiologist; b. Detroit, Aug. 17, 1932; s. Edward John and Daisy Odell (Bacon) H.; m. Barbara Janette Chrestman, Oct. 15, 1960; children: Blair Thomas, Timothy John. Student, Mich. State U., 1950-53; BS, Northwestern U., 1954; MD, Northwestern U., Chgo., 1957. Diplomate Am. Bd. Radiology (trustee 1987-99). Intern Passavant Meml. Hosp., Chgo., 1957-58; radiology resident Brooke Army Med. Ctr., San Antonio, 1958-61, asst. chief radiology, 1964-65; radiologist Ft. Detrick, Frederick, Md., 1961-62, Kelsey Seybold Clinic, Houston, 1965-66; chief of radiology Irwin Army Hosp., Ft. Riley, Kans., 1962-64; asst. prof., then assoc. prof. Baylor Coll. Medicine, Houston, 1966-69; assoc. prof. Duke U. Med. Ctr., Durham, NC, 1969-71; prof. U. Tex. Med. Sch., Houston, 1975-78, 80-82, chmn. dept. radiology, 1975-78; prof. Mich. State U., East Lansing, 1978-80, U. Tex. M.D. Anderson Cancer Ctr., Houston, 1982-1997, asst. v.p. acad. affairs, 1982-90, assoc. v.p. acad. affairs, 1990-94; prof. dept. radiology Wake Forest U., Winston Salem, NC, 1997—, Isadore Meschan disting. prof. radiology, 2001—. Contbr. articles to profl. jours., chpts. to books. Maj. U.S. Army, 1958-65. Fellow Am. Coll. Radiology; mem. Assn. Univ. Radiologists (pres. 1983-84), Radiol. Soc. N.Am. (pres. 1993), European Assn. Radiologists (hon.), Faculty of Radiologists, Royal Coll. Surgeons in Ireland (hon.), Brit. Inst. Radiology (hon.). Republican. Baptist. Avocation: architecture. Office: Wake Forest U Medical Center Blvd Winston Salem NC 27157-0001 Home Phone: 336-768-3221; Office Phone: 336-716-4316. Business E-Mail: tharle@wfuhmc.edu.

HARLEM, SUSAN LYNN, librarian; b. LA, Oct. 1, 1950; d. Frank Joseph and Esther Frances (Bomell) H.; m. Anthony Stephen Hacsi, Aug. 31, 1990. BA, UCLA, 1972, MLS, 1976. Libr. U. Md., College Park, 1976-79, U.S. Dept. Edn., Washington, 1979-82, GSA, Washington, 1982-87, NLRB, Washington, 1988—. Tutor Washington Lit. Coun., 1992—. Co-author: Washington on Foot, 1984. Office: NLRB Libr 1099 14th St NW Washington DC 20570-0001 Business E-Mail: susan.harlem@nlrb.gov.

HARLEMAN, ANN, literature educator, writer; BA in English, Douglass Coll., 1967; PhD in Linguistics, Princeton U., 1972; MFA in Creative Writing, Brown U., 1988. Asst. prof. dept. English, Rutgers U., New Brunswick, NJ, 1973-74, U. Wash., Seattle, 1974-79, assoc. prof., 1979-84; vis. assoc. prof., rsch. affiliate writing program MIT, Cambridge, 1984-86; vis. scholar program in Am. civilization Brown U., Providence, 1986—; Cole disting. prof. Wheaton (Mass.) Coll., 1992-93; prof. English, RISD, Providence, 1994—. Fulbright-Hays lectr., 1980-81. Author: Graphic Representation of Models in Linguistic Theory, 1976, (with Bruce A. Rosenberg) Ian Fleming: A Critical Biography, 1989, Happiness, 1994, Bitter Lake, 1996, Thoreau's Laundry: Stories, 2007, The Year She Disappeared, 2008; translator: Mute Phone Calls, 1992; contbr. over 50 articles to scholarly publs., transls. and revs., poems and short stories to lit. mags. Recipient Raymond Carver prize, 1986, Nelson Algren runner-up award Chgo. Tribune, 1987, 3d prize Judith Siegal Pearson award, 1988, Chris O'Malley fiction prize Madison Rev., 1990, Judith Siegal Pearson award, 1991, syndicated fiction award PEN, 1991, Iowa short fiction award, 1993, spl. mention, Pushcart prize, 1998, Zoetrope Fiction award, 2002, O'Henry prize, 2003, Goodheart prize, 2004, Rona Jaffe Writer's award, 2004; Guggenheim fellow, 1976-77, fellow Huntington Libr., 1979-80, MacDowell Colony, 1988, 99, 2004, Am. Coun. Learned Socs., 1992, Wurlitzer Found., 1992, R.I. Coun. Arts, 1989, 97, 2006, Berlin fellowship in Lit., 2000, Civitella Ranieri fellowship 2006; sr. scholar Am. Coun. Learned Socs./IREX, 1976-77; grantee NEH, 1988, Rockefeller Found., 1989, Bogliasco Found., 1998, 2004, Civitella Ranieri, 2006. Mem. PEN Am. Ctr., PEN New Eng. (exec. bd. mem.). Address: 18 Imperial Pl #5 Providence RI 02903 Office Phone: 401-272-7987. E-mail: ann_harleman@brown.edu.

HARLER, DONNA, voice educator; b. Hartford, Conn., May 22, 1944; d. Walter Joseph Dehner and Bess Laing Humphries; m. Alan Harler (div.); m. Charles Minor Smith, Feb. 29, 1992. BA, Denison U., Granville, Ohio, 1966; MusM, U. Cin., 1968. Adj. prof. Holyoke Cmty. Coll., Springfield, Mass., 1968—69; vis. instr. U. Mass., Amherst, 1970—71; owner New Record Store, Amherst, 1970—75; vis. instr. Amherst Coll., 1971—76; prof. U. Nebr., Lincoln, 1976—. Adjudicator NATS, 1978—; advisor TADA, Lincoln, 2000—. Performer: Lincoln Symphony, 2006. Lector St. Planks Episcopal Ch., Lincoln, 2004. Recipient Outstanding Tchr. award, UNL, 2002, Outstanding Tchr. Humanities award, 2002. Mem.: Phi Beta Kappa.

HARLESS, KATHERINE J., telecommunications industry executive; m. Skip Harless; children: Skip Jr., Ely, Bill. B in Acctg., U. Tex., 1972. With GTE, 1973—, regional pres. telephone ops. Tex. and Mexico, 1994-96, pres. airfone, 1996—2000; pres. info. services Verizon Communications, 2000—06; pres., CEO Idearc Inc., Dallas, 2006—. Vice chmn. Yellow Pages Assn., 2005—06, chmn., 2002, 2006—; bd. dir. Toro Co. Mem. adv. bd. McCombs Sch. Bus. Univ. Tex. Mem. Com. of 200 (tres. com. 200 found. bd.), Chgo. Network, Internat. Women's Forum, Execs. Club Chgo., Barbara Bush Found. (mem. celebration of reading com.), Leadership Am. Office: Idearc Inc 2200 W Airfield Dr Dallas TX 75261

HARLEY, HALVOR LARSON, bank executive, lawyer; b. Atlantic City, Oct. 7, 1948; s. Robison Dooling and Loyde Hazel (Gochnauer) Harley. BSc, U. SC, 1971, MA, 1973; JD, Widener U., 1981. Bar: Pa. 1982, DC 1989, US Ct. Appeals (3d cir.) 1987, US Dist. Ct. (ea. dist.) Pa. 1987, US Supreme Ct. 1988, US Ct. Appeals D.C. 1989. Staff psychologist Columbia Area Mental Health Ctr., SC, 1971—73; dir. Motivational Rsch. Cons., Columbia, 1973—79; psychologist Family Ct. Del., Wilmington, 1979; pvt. practice law Phila., 1982; v.p. investment banking Union Bank, LA, 1982—88; v.p., mgr. Tokai Bank, Newport Beach., Calif., 1988—94; first v.p., regional mgr. Mellon Pvt. Asset Mgmt., Newport Beach, 1994—97, first v.p., 1994—2004; regional sales mgr. So. Calif. Pvt. Asset Mgmt., 1994—2004; mng. dir. Deutsche Bank Pvt. Wealth Mgmt., LA, 2004—. Contbr.; author: Help for Herpes, 1982; cinematographer:. Fundraiser Orange County Performing Art Ctr., 1983—84; trustee, exec. com. Orange County Mus. Arts; vol. Hosp. Ship HOPE, Sri Lanka, 1968—69; bd. dirs., v.p. exec. com. Alzheimers Assn. Orange County; bd. dirs. Lido Sands Homeowners Assn., Newport Beach, 1984—85, So. Calif. Entrepreneurship Acad., pres./bd. dirs.; bd. dirs. United Cerebral Palsy of Orange County; chmn. Bastile Day Com.; bd. govs. Cedar-Sinai Hosp., LA. Mem.: ATLA, World Trade Ctr. Assocs. Orange County (directing com. 1983—85), Indsl. League Orange County (membership com. 1983—84), Calif. Bankers Assn., Am. Bankers Assn., Am. Judicature Soc., Orange County Performing Arts Fraternity (trustee), Calif. Club (LA), Psi Chi (chpt. pres. 1971—73). Home: 5015 Lido Sands Dr Newport Beach CA 92663-2403 Office: Deutsche Pvt Wealth Mgmt 650 Town Ctr Dr 17th Fl Costa Mesa CA 92626 Business E-Mail: Hal.Harley@DB.com.

HARLEY, ROBISON DOOLING, JR., lawyer, educator; b. Ancon, Panama, July 6, 1946; s. Robison Dooling and Loyde Hazel (Goehenauer) Harley; m. Suzanne Purviance Bendel, Aug. 9, 1975; children: Arianne Erin, Lauren Loyde. BA, Brown U., 1968; JD, Temple U., 1971; LLM, U. San Diego, 1985. Cert.: Calif. Bd. Legal Specialization (criminal law specialist since 1981), Nat. Bd. Trial Advocacy (criminal trial adv. since 1982), bar: Pa. 1971, Calif. 1976, NJ 1977, DC 1981, US Dist. Ct. (cen. and so. dists.) Calif. 1976, US Dist. Ct. NJ 1977, US Dist. Ct. (ea. dist.) Pa. 1987, US Ct. Appeals (9th cir.) 1982, US Ct. Appeals (3rd cir.) 1986, US Supreme Ct. 1980, US Ct. Mil. Appeals 1972. Asst. agy. dir. Safeco Title Ins. Co., LA, 1975—77; ptnr. Cohen, Stokke & Davis, Santa Ana, Calif., 1977—85; prin. Harley Law Offices, Santa Ana, 1985—. Adj. prof. Orange County Coll. Trial Advocacy; adj. prof. paralegal program U. Calif.; instr. trial adv. programs US Army, USN, USAF, USMC; judge pro-tem Orange County Cts. Author: Orange County Trial Lawyers Drunk Driving Syllabus; contbr. articles to profl. jours. Trial counsel, def. counsel, mil. judge, asst. staff judge adv. USMC, 1971—75, regional def. counsel Western Region, 1986—90; bd. dirs. Orange County Legal Aid Soc. Lt. col. JAGC USMCR. Decorated Nat. Def. Svc. medal, Res. medal, Navy Commendation medal; named a Super Lawyer, So. Calif., 2004, 2005, 2006, 2007. Mem.: ATLA, ABA, Orange County Criminal Lawyers Assn. (found. com.), Orange County Trial Lawyers Assn., Orange County Bar Assn. (judiciary com., criminal law sect., adminstrn. of justice com.), Assn. Specialized Criminal Def. Advs., Nat. Assn. for Criminal Def. Attys., Calif. Pub. Defenders Assn., Calif. Attys. for Criminal Justice, Calif. Trial Lawyers Assn., Marine Corps Assn., Marine Corps Res. Officers Assn., Res. Officers Assn. Republican. Avocations: sports, physical fitness, reading. Home: 31211 Paseo Miraloma San Juan Capistrano CA 92675-5505 Office: Harley Law Offices 825 N Ross St Santa Ana CA 92701-3419 Home Phone: 949-489-9666; Office Phone: 714-972-8441. Personal E-mail: robharley@earthlink.net.

HARLEY, RUTH, artist, educator; b. Phila. children: Peter W. Bressler, Victoria Angela. Student, Pa. State U., 1941; BFA, Phila. Coll. Art, 1945; postgrad., U. N.H., 1971, Hampshire Coll., 1970. Instr. Phila. Mus. Art, 1946-59; art supt. Ventnor (N.J.) City Bd. Edn., 1959-61. Art tchr. Print Club, Phila., Allens Ln. Art Ctr., Phila., Suburban Ctr. Arts, Lower Merion, Pa., Radner (Pa.) Twp. Adult Ctr., 1949—59, Atlantic City Adult Ctr., 1959—60. One-woman shows include Dubin-Lush Galleries, Phila., 1956, Contemporary Art Assn., 1957, Vernon Art Exhbns., Germantown, Pa., 1958, Detroit Inst. Arts, 1958, Phila. Mus. Art, 1957, 1959, Moore Inst., Phila., 1962—68, Greenhill Galleries, 1974, Phila. Civic Ctr., 1978, Natal Rio Grande du Norte, Brazil, 1979, Galerie Novel Esprit, Tampa, Fla., 1992—95, Mind's Eye Gallery, St. Petersburg, Fla., 1993, Ga. Tech. Art Ctr., 1998, Robert Ferst Ctr. for Arts Ga. Inst. Tech., 1998—99, exhibited in group shows at Group 55, Phila., 1955, Print Club, 1955, Nat. Tours, 1956—59, Pa. Acad. Fine Arts, 1957, Vernon Art Exhbns., 1958, Detroit Inst. Arts, 1958, Phila. Mus. Art, 1959, Moore Inst., 1962, Phila. Civic Ctr. Mus., 1975, Galerie Nouvel Esprit Assemblage Russe, 1992, Kenneth Raymond Gallery, Boca Raton, 1992—93, Mind's Eye Gallery, 1993, Polk Mus. Art, Lakeland, Fla., 1993, Don Roll Gallery, Sarasota, Fla., 1994—95, Las Vegas (Nev.) Internat. Art Expo, 1994, Heim Am. Gallery, Fisher Island, Fla., 1996, McLean Gallery, Malibu, Calif., 1997—99, Robert Ferst Ctr. for Arts Ga. Inst. Tech., 1998—99, Christina Gallery, Atlanta, 1999, Adrian Howard Gallery, St. Petersburg, 2000—02, 2004, Melrose (Fla.) Bay Art Gallery, 2001, Red River Valley Mus., Vernon, Tex., 2001, Kirkpatrick Mus., Okla., 2001, Airport, Gainesville, Fla., 2001, In Celebration of Art, 2004, Represented in permanent collections U. Villanova (Pa.) Mus., Temple U. Law Sch., Pa., Woodmere Mus., Phila.; included in Art in Am. Ann. Guide, 2000—01, 2002; commd. sculpture, Phila. Re-Devel. Authority. Contbr. art prize Ventnor N.J. Sch. Sys. Personal E-mail: harleyruth@aol.com.

HARLIN, MARILYN MILER, marine botany educator, researcher, consultant; b. Oakland, Calif., May 30, 1934; d. George T. and Gertrude (Turula) Miler; m. John E. Harlin II, Oct. 25, 1955 (dec. Feb. 1966); children: John E. III, Andrea M. Harlin Cilento. AB, Stanford U., 1955, MA, 1956; PhD, U. Wash., 1971. Instr. Am. Coll. Switzerland and Leysin, 1964-66; asst. prof. Pacific Marine Sta., Dillon Beach, Calif., 1969; asst. prof. marine biology U. R.I., Kingston, 1971-75, assoc. prof., 1975-83, prof., 1983-2000, prof. emerita, 2000—, chair botany dept., chair dept. biol. scis. Guest scientist Atlantic Regional Lab., Halifax, N.S., Can., 1973-78; hon. vis.prof. LaTrobe U., Bundoora, Victoria, Australia, 1984; resource person R.I. Coastal Resource Mgmt. Coun., 1980-2000, R.I. Dept. Environ. Mgmt., 1980; cons. Applied Sci. Assocs., Narragansett, R.I., 1988-98, Western Australia Water Authority, Perth, 1994; rsch. assoc. U. Calif., Santa Cruz, 1993. Co-editor: Marine Ecology, 1976, Freshwater and Marine Plants of Rhode Island, 1988. Bd. dirs. Westminster Unitarian Ch., East Greenwich, R.I., 1987; bd. govs. Women's Ctr., Kingston, 1989-90. Grantee NOAA, 1975-81, Dept. Environ. Mgmt./EPA, 1989-91, U.S. Fish and Wildlife, 1995. Mem. Internat. Phycological Soc., Phycological Soc. Am. (editor newsletter 1982-84, editorial bd. 1988-90), Union Concerned Scientists (nat. adv. bd. 2004—), N.E. Algal Soc. (exec. com.), Sigma Xi (pres., sec. 1979-82). Avocations: yoga, hiking, reading, writing, gardening. Personal E-mail: mharlin@macforcego.com.

HARLIN, RENNY (RENNY LAURI MAURITZ HARJOLA), film director; b. Riihimaki, Finland, Mar. 15, 1959; m. Geena Davis, Sept. 18, 1993 (div. Jun. 21, 1998); 1 child. Dir. (films) A Nightmare on Elm Street 4: The Dream Master, 1988, Deep Blue Sea, 1999, Exorcist: The Beginning, 2004, The Covenant, 2006, (TV films) T.R.A.X., 2000; dir., writer: (films) Huostaanotto, 1980, Born American, 1986, Prison 1988, Die Hard 2, 1990, The Adventures of Ford Fairlane, 1990; dir., prodr.: (films) Cliffhanger, 1993, Cutthroat Island, 1995, Long Kiss Goodnight, 1996, Deep Blue Sea, 1999, Driven, 2001; prodr.: (films) Rambling Rose, 1991, Speechless, 1994, Blast From the Past, 1999; dir., prodr., writer: (TV series) Gladiaattorit, 1993; exec. prodr.: (TV films) Mistrial, 1996; exec. prodr., dir: (TV films) Mindhunters, 2004.

HARLING, BARBARA JEAN, social worker; b. Raleigh, NC, July 21, 1939; d. Edwin Alexander and Margaret Brice Harling; 1 child, Christopher Parr Addams. BA in History, Wilson Coll., Chambersburg, Pa., 1961; MA in Am. History, Seton Hall U., South Orange, NJ, 1967; MSW, Cath. U., Washington, 1973; DSW, Cath. U., 1988. LCSW D.C., diplomate in psychotherapy Am. Assn. for Psychotherapy, 1998. Caseworker Cath. Charities, Washington, 1960—75; clin. dir. Ctr. for Mental Health Inc., Washington, 1973—2004; psychotherapist in pvt. practice Washington, 1976—; clin. dir. Anchor Mental Health, Washington, 2004, Woodley House Behavioral Healthcare Svc. Cons., mentor Clin. Social Wk. Inst., Inc., Washington, 1999—; instr. for advanced supervision course Greater Washington Soc. for Clin. Social Wk., 1989—; tchg. affiliate Va. Commonwealth U.; adj. clin. asst. prof. U. Md., Balt.; lectr., presenter in field; condr. seminars in field. Mem. Dupont Cir. Citizens Assn., Washington, 1968—86, Glover Park Citizens Assn., Washington, 1990—; mem. grandparent initiative adv. group AARP, 2003. Named Outstanding Practitioner/Supr., Chi Sigma Iota, Rho Theta chpt., 1999—2000. Mem.: NASW (diplomate in clin. social wk. 1993—), Internat.l Soc. for Psychol. Treatment of Schizophrenias and Other Psychoses, Am. Group Psychotherapy Assn., Nat. Alliance for the Mentally Ill, Am. Psychotherapy Assn., Coun. on Social Wk. Edn., Greater Washington Soc. for Clin. Social Wk. (tchr. 1980—), Nat. Network for Social Work Mgrs. Democrat. Avocations: reading, music, needlepoint. Home and Office: 2221 38th St NW Washington DC 20007 Office Phone: 202-337-9219. Business E-Mail: bharling@woodleyhouse.org.

HARLOW, FRANCIS HARVEY, physicist, anthropologist, research scientist, artist; b. Seattle, Jan. 22, 1928; m. Patricia Jean Nystuen, June 21, 1952; children: Catherine, Carol Muiznieks, Celia, Keith. BS, U. Wash., Seattle, 1949, PhD in Theoretical Physics, 1953. Staff mem. Los Alamos Nat. Lab., N.Mex., 1953—2003, guest scientist T-3, 2003—. Group leader T-3 Los Alamos Nat. Lab., Los Alamos, N.Mex., 1959—73; assoc. editor Jour. Computational Physics; sci. advisor Russian Jour. Computational Physics; adv. editor Computer Methods in Applied Mech. and Engring.; editl. adv. bd. Ann. Rev. Numerical Fluid Dynamics and Heat Transfer; vol. editor AIAA Selected Reprint Series; doctoral dissertation rsch. advisor U. N. Mex., U. Wash., Rice U., Princeton U., MIT, Monash U., U. Ill., U. Tex., Arlington, N. Mex. State U., Tex. A&M U.; Am. Indian ceramics expert and painter. Author: Historic Pueblo Indian Pottery, 1970, Modern Pueblo Pottery 1880-1960, 1977, Particle Methods in Fluid Dynamics and Plasma Physics, 1988, Two Hundred Years of Pueblo Pottery: The Gallegos Collection, 1990; co-author (with A.A. Amsden): Fluid Mechanics 2d edit., 1971; co-author: (with L. Frank) Historic Pottery of the Pueblo Indians 1600-1880, 1974; co-author: (with J. Silverman) Pueblo Indian Pottery, 2001, large folio edit., 2001; co-author: (with D. Lanmon) The pottery of Zia Pueblo, 2003, The Pottery of Cochiti and Santa Domingo Pueblos, 2004; co-author: (with D. Anderson and D. Lanmon) The Pottery of Santa Ana Pueblo, 2005; co-author: The Pottery of Zuni Pueblo, 2007; co-editor (with H.J. Shepard): Theory in Action, Highlights in the Theoretical Divsn. at Los Alamos, 1943-2003, 2003; contbr. chapters to books, scientific papers, articles to profl. jours.; exhibitions include Jamison Gallery, Santa Fe, Mendosa Gallery, Taos, N.Mex., Cliff Dwellers Gallery, Los Alamos, Represented in permanent collections Mus. N.Mex., County Los Alamos, pvt. collections. Invited lectr. seminar on Southwestern Native Am. ceramics Millicent Rogers Mus., Santa Fe, 1981. 1st lt. US Army, 1945—54. Named Rsch. Assoc., Sch. Am. Rsch., Sr. Rsch. Assoc., Mus. N. Mex.; named to Dad's Club Hall of Fame, Bremerton H.S., 1984; recipient Computational Mechanics award, Japan Soc. Mech. Engrs., 2001, R&D-100 award, 2003, LAAP Achievement award, Los Alamos Nat. Lab., 2003, Los Alamos Nat. Lab. medal, 2004, Disting. Performance award (4), Los Alamos Nat. Lab.; fellow, 1981—; scholar, NSF, 1952, Sebastian Karrar Grad. award, U. Wash., 1951. Fellow: Am. Phys. Soc.; mem.: Sigma Xi, Phi Beta Kappa. Achievements include development of FIRETEC: a Physics-Based Wildfire Model; Particle-in-Cell (PIC) analysis method for strong distortions in adjacent materials; Marker-and-Cell (MAC) method for implicit analysis of incompressible flows with free surfaces; generalized implicit (ICE) technique, which served as basis for numerous methods of analysis of fluid flow without Mach number restrictions; Particle-and-Force (PAF) method for complex fluid-flow problems; Dynamics-of-Contours (DOC) method, whose extensions form basis for much numerical analysis of vortex dynamics; Implicit-Multiphase-Flow (IMF) method for flows with material interpenetration, phase transitions, and speeds ranging from incompressible to fully relativistic; research in numerical solution of complicated material-dynamic problems involving strongly non-linear processes evolving with time in several space dimensions; basic mathematical represntations for turbulence transport theory; application of stochastic analysis techniques to investigation of biological and sociological problems; introduction of pattern-activity concept for generalized mental dynamics activity in advanced living organism; research in brachiopoda from upper Carboniferous rocks of north central N.Mex. Avocations: Pueblo Indian studies, painting. Office: Theoretical Divsn Los Alamos Nat Lab Mail Stop B216 Los Alamos NM 87545 Home: 1407 11th St Los Alamos NM 87544 Business E-Mail: fhharlow@lanl.gov.

HARLOW, RUTH, lawyer; b. 1961; AB, Stanford U., 1983; JD, Yale U., 1986. Bar: 1988. Law clk. hon. Walter K. Stapleton US Ct. of Appeals (3rd cir.), 1986—87; assoc. Vladeck, Waldman, Elias & Engelhard, NY, 1987—90; atty. ACLU, 1990—91; staff counsel dir. Am. Civil Liberties Union, 1990—93, assoc. dir., 1993—96; atty. Lambda Legal Def. and Edn. Fund, 1996—2000; deputy legal dir. Lambda Legal Defense and Fund, NY, 2000—00; legal dir. Lambda Legal Def. and Edn. Fund, 2000—03; atty. pvt. practice, 2003; counsel White & Case, 2004—06, Linklaters, NYC, 2006—. Recipient Lawyer of the Year, Nat. Law Journal, 2003. Mem.: Phi Beta Kappa. Office: Linklaters 1345 Ave of Americas New York NY 10105 Office Phone: 212-903-9210. Office Fax: 212-903-9100. Business E-Mail: ruth.harlow@linklaters.com.

HARMAN, DONNA AKERS, trade association administrator; b. Elkhart, Kans., Aug. 6, 1959; d. Donald E. and Pearl Duvall Akers; m. John R. Harman III, Aug. 20, 1988; children: Caitlin, Caroline. BA in Pub. Affairs and Econs., Anderson U., 1981; JD, Am. U., 1988. Bar: D.C. 1989. Fin. dir. La. Rep. Com., Baton Rouge, 1981-83; legis. aide to Rep. W. Henson Moore US Congress, Washington, 1983-85; mgr. govt. rels. The Dow Chem. Co., Washington, 1985-89; dir. govt. rels. Champion Internat., Washington, 1989-99, counsel govt. affairs, 1999—2001; v.p., congl. affairs Am. Forest & Paper Assn., Washington, 2001—06, sr. v.p., policy & govt. affairs, 2006—07, acting pres., 2007, pres., 2007—. Chairperson Alternative Minimum Tax Coalition, Washington, 1993—; bd. co-chair Tax Coalition, Washington, 1996. Bd. dirs. Nat. Presbyn. Ch., Washington, 1998—; leader Girls Scouts Am. Avocation: girls soccer. Office: Am Forest & Paper Assn 1111 19th St NW Ste 800 Washington DC 20036*

HARMAN, GEORGE GIBSON, physicist, consultant; b. Norfolk, Va., Dec. 7, 1924; s. George Gibson and Annie Wall (Baldwin) Harman; m. Ann Worischek, Jan. 31, 1953 (div. 1985); children: Joyce Catherine, Arthur Lawrence, Stewart Thomas; m. Donna K. Williamson, 1986. BS in Physics, Va. Poly. Inst., 1949; MS in Physics, U. Md., 1959. With Nat. Inst. Stds. and Tech. (formerly Nat. Bur. Stds.), Washington, 1950—, sr. rsch. scientist, 1976-93, fellow, 1993—2003, dean of staff, 2001—. Rsch. fellow Reading U., England, 1962—63. Author: 2 books; contbr. articles to profl. jours. With US Army, 1943—46. Recipient Silver medal, U.S. Dept. Commerce, 1973, Gold medal, 1979, Achievement award, Internat. Electronics Packaging Soc., 1988. Fellow: IEEE (chmn. fellows and awards com. 1989—, Centennial medal 1984, Outstanding Contbns. award 1992, 1993, 15-Yr. Outstanding Contbns. to ECT Conf. 1993, Harry Diamond Meml. award 1996, Third Millennium medal 2000, Outstanding Sustained Tech. Contbns. award 2001), Soc. Mfg. Engrs. (Excellence in Electronic Mfg. award 2001), Internat. Microelectronics Packaging Soc. (regional dir. 1698—1987, chpt. pres. 1980—82, chmn. nat. tech. program com. 1990—92, nat. pres. 1995, chmn. found. grants com., Tech. Achievement award 1981, Lewis F. Miller award 1984, Disting. Svc. award 1986, 1987, Daniel C. Hughes award 1989, DVS European Electronic Packaging award 1998, Lifetime Achievement award 2006); mem.: ASTM (chmn. com. 2001—), Am. Phys. Soc., Cosmos Club Washington, Sigma Pi Sigma, Sigma Xi. Achievements include patents in field. Home: 4719 Dorset Ave Bethesda MD 20815-5445 Office: Nat Inst Stds and Tech Div 812 Gaithersburg MD 20899-0001

HARMAN, GILBERT HELMS, philosophy educator; b. East Orange, NJ, May 26, 1938; s. William Henry and Marguerite Variel (Page) H.; m. Lucy Newman, Aug. 14, 1970; children: Elizabeth, Olivia. BA, Swarthmore Coll., 1960; PhD, Harvard U., 1964. With dept. philosophy Princeton (N.J.) U., 1963—, prof., 1971—, acting chair, 2001—02, chair cognitive studies program, 1992-97. Author: Thought, 1973, The Nature of Morality, 1977, Change in View, 1986, Skepticism and the Definition of Knowledge, 1990, (with Judith Jarvis Thomson) Moral Relativism and Moral Objectivity, 1996, Reasoning, Meaning, and Mind, 1999, Explaining Value and Other Essays in Moral Philosophy, 2000, (with Sanjeev Kulkarni) Reliable Reasoning, 2007; editor: On Noam Chomsky, 1974, (with Donald Davidson) Semantics of Natural Language, 1971, (with Donald Davidson) The Logic of Grammar, 1975, Conceptions of the Human Mind, 1993. Recipient Jean Nicod prize, 2005. Fellow: Cognitive Sci. Soc.; mem.: Am. Acad. Arts and Scis., Linguistic Soc. Am., Philosophy Sci. Soc., Assn. for Psychol. Sci., Am. Philos. Assn. Home: 106 Broadmead St Princeton NJ 08540-7216 Office: Princeton Univ Dept Philosophy Princeton NJ 08544-1006 Business E-Mail: harman@princeton.edu.

HARMAN, JANE, congresswoman; b. NYC, June 28, 1945; d. A. N. and Lucille (Geier) Lakes; m. Sidney Harman, Aug. 30, 1980; children: Brian Lakes, Hilary Lakes, Daniel Geier, Justine Leigh. BA, Smith Coll., 1966; JD, Harvard U., 1969. Bar: D.C. 1969, U.S. Ct. Appeals (D.C. cir.) 1972, U.S. Supreme Ct. 1975. Spl. asst. Commn. of Chs. on Internat. Affairs, Geneva, 1969-70; assoc. Surrey & Morse, Washington, 1970-72; chief legis. asst. Senator John V. Tunney, Washington, 1972-73; chief counsel, staff dir. Subcom. on Rep. Citizen Interests, Com. on Judiciary, Washington, 1973-75; adj. prof. Georgetown Law Ctr., Washington, 1974-75; chief counsel, staff dir. Subcom. on Constl. Rights, Com. on Judiciary, Washington, 1975-77; dep. sec. to cabinet The White House, Washington, 1977-78; spl. counsel Dept. Def., Washington, 1979; ptnr. Manatt, Phelps, Rothenberg & Tunney, Washington, 1979-82, Surrey & Morse, Washington, 1982-86; of counsel Jones, Day, Reavis & Pogue, Washington, 1987-92; mem. US Congress from 36th Calif. dist., 1993—99, 2001—; mem. nat. security com., intelligence com. 103rd-105th Congresses; mem. energy and commerce com., intelligence com. 107th Congress, 2001—; mem. Nat. Commn. on Terrorism, 1999—2000. Regents prof. UCLA, 1999-2000; mem. vis. coms. Harvard Law Sch., 1976-82, Kennedy Sch. Govt., 1990-96. Vice-chmn. Ctr. for Nat. Policy, Washington, 1981—90; trustee Smith Coll.; counsel Dem. Platform Com., Washington, 1984; chmn. Dem. Nat. Com. Nat. Lawyers' Coun., Washington, 1986—90; bd. dirs. Planned Parenthood, 1998—2000, Venice (Calif.) Family Clinic, 1998—2000. Mem. Phi Beta Kappa. Democrat. Office: US Ho Reps 2400 Rayburn Ho Office Bldg Washington DC 20515-0536 also: Dist Office Ste 3270 2321 Rosecrans Ave El Segundo CA 90245-4932

HARMAN, JENNIFER (JENNIFER HARMAN-TRANIELLO), professional poker player; b. Reno, Nevada, Nov. 29, 1964; m. Marco Traniello. BS in Biology, U. Nev., Reno. Profl. poker player World Series Poker Cir. Founder Creating Organ Donation Awareness. Achievements include invention of winning No Limit Deuce to Seven World Series Poker Bracelet, 2000; winning Texas Hold 'Em 5k World Series Poker Bracelet, 2002; total winnings over over 1.5 mil; generally considered to be the best female poker player in the world.*

HARMAN, MARYANN WHITTEMORE, artist, educator; b. Roanoke, Va., Sept. 13, 1935; d. John Weed and Clifford Kelly Whittemore; m. Roger Walke, Aug. 25, 1984; children: Mary Kelly, John Whittemore, Phillip Mears. BA, Mary Washington Coll., 1955; MA, Va. Poly. Inst., 1974. Faculty Va. Poly. Inst., Blacksburg, 1963—, prof. art, 1981—2001, prof. emeritus, 2001—. Guest artist Emma Lake Art Workshop, U. Sask., 1985. One-woman shows include Andre Emmerich Gallery, NYC, 1976, 78, Rubiner Gallery, Detroit, 1977-78, 80, 90, Meredith Long Gallery, NYC, 1980, Theodore Haber Gallery, NYC, 1981-82, 84-85, Osuna Gallery, Washington, 1982, 84, 87, 91, Wade Gallery, LA, 1986-87, 89, 91, Ulysses Gallery, 1990, 94, Martha Mabey Gallery, 1994, Gallery K, Washington, 1996, Armory Art Gallery VATECH, Va., 1997, 2002, Art Pannonia, Blacksburg, Va., 2003, Va. Commonwealth U. Anderson Gallery, 2004; exhibited in group shows at Va. Mus. Art, Richmond, 1973-75, 80-81, 2003, Southeastern Ctr. for Contemporary Art, Winston Salem, NC, 1963, 65, 67, 71, 76, Boston Mus. Fine Arts, 1981, 84, Roanoke (Va.) Mus., 1963-79, Butler Inst. Contemporary Art, Youngstown, Ohio, 1969, 72, Anita Shapolsky Gallery, NYC, 1988, C.S. Schulte Gallery, East Orange, NJ, 1998-07, Sandy Carson Gallery, Denver, 1995-07, Gallery One, Toronto, 1990-07, Studios in the Sq., Va., 2000-07, So. Landscape Ptnrs. Group Show, Lee Hansley Gallery, Raleigh, NC, 2006; represented in permanent collections Boston Mus., Gen. Motors, Detroit, Hunter Mus., Chattanooga, Roanoke Mus., Phillip Morris Corp., Richmond and NYC, Mfrs. Hanover Trust, NYC, Charlotte, NC, Am. Can Corp., NYC, Shawmut Bank of Boston, Mint Mus., CSX Corp., Ethyl Corp., Capital One, U. Richmond, others. Mem. Coll. Art Assn., Nat. Hon. Art and Architecture Soc., Tau Sigma Delta. Episcopalian. Personal E-mail: maryannwalke@mindspring.com.

HARMAN, REBECCA HOWARD, educator; b. Frederick, Md., Dec. 4, 1917; d. Harry Milton and Fannie Irene Howard. BA, Towson State U., Md., 1938; MEd, U. Md., 1976; D, Carroll C.C., Westminster, Md., 2000. Tchr., 1938—75. Dir. choir St. Paul's Meth. Ch., New Windsor. Mem.: VFW Ladies Aux. (legis. chair), Delta Kappa Gamma.

HARMAN, SIDNEY, audio and video company executive; b. 1918; BS, CCNY, 1939; PhD, Union Inst., 1973. Co-founder Harman-Kardon Inc. (now div. of Harman Internat. Industries), 1952; dep. sec. U.S. Dept. Commerce, 1977—80; chmn. bd., CEO Harman Internat. Industries, 1980—2000, exec. chmn., 2000—, interim CEO, 2006—07. Co-author (with Daniel Yankelovich): Starting With the People, 1988; author: Mind Your Own Business, 2003; contbr. articles to newspapers & magazines. Mem. adv. com. John F. Kennedy Sch. Govt., Harvard Univ.; chmn. prog. com. Aspen Inst.; chmn. exec. com. Pub. Agenda Found.; trustee Carter Ctr., Emory Univ.; bd. mem. Leadership Inst., Univ. So. Calif. Fellow: Am. Acad. Arts & Sciences; mem.: Council on Competitiveness, Council on Fgn. Rels., Bus. Executives for Nat. Security (chmn. exec. com.). Office: Harman International Industries Ste 1010 1101 Pennsylvania Ave NW Washington DC 20004*

HARMAN, WALLACE PATRICK, lawyer; b. El Paso, Tex., Jan. 22, 1949; s. Wallace Irvin and Dorothy Louise (Pearson) H.; m. Gina Marie Ries, Dec. 31, 1988; children: Loren Patrick, Claire Marie. BA, Stanford U., 1972; JD, U. Calif., 1977. Bar: Calif. 1977, US Ct. Appeals (9th cir.) 1977, N.Mex. 1978, US Dist. Ct. N.Mex. 1978, US Ct. Appeals (10th cir.) 1978. Zone adminstrn. mgr. Am. Motors Corp., Burlingame, Calif., 1972-74; atty., shareholder Sutin, Thayer & Browne, APC, Albuquerque, N.Mex., 1977-87, group leader comml. group, 1985-87; atty., shareholder, mng. ptnr., leader bus. group The Payne Law Firm, P.C., Albuquerque, 1987-91; atty., ptnr. Hisey & Wainwright, P.A., Albuquerque, 1991-92; atty., pres., chief exec. officer The Harman Law Firm, P.C., Littleton, CO, 1992—. Mem. N.Mex. Supreme Ct. Med.-Legal Panel, Albuquerque, 1978-80, 91—; mem. N.Mex. Supreme Ct. Lawyers Assistance Com., Albuquerque, 1991—; area rep. The Taft Sch., Watertown, Conn., 1992—; mem. mentorship program Hatings Coll. Law. Co-author: Recent Developments in Commerical Law, University of New Mexico Law Review, 1989. Bd. advisors Lovelace Med. Ctr., Albuquerque, 1980-89; mem. state bd. trustees The Nature Conservancy, N.Mex., 1984-88; adv. bd. Assistance League Albuquerque, 1982-89, Jr. League Albuquerque, 1984-87, Make-a-Wish Found. of N.Mex., Inc., 1996-97. Recipient AV Rating award Martindale-Hubbell, 1990. Mem. ABA, Albuquerque Bar Assn. Democrat. Avocations: photography, sports, computers, landscaping, writing.

HARMAN, WILLARD NELSON, malacologist, educator; b. Geneva, NY, Apr. 20, 1937; s. Samuel Willard and Mary Nelson (Covert) H.; m. Susan Beth Mead, June 12, 1968 (div. 1980); children: Rebecca Mary, Willard Wade; m. Barbara Ann Stong, June 8, 1981; children: Jessica Mary, Samuel Willard. Student, Hobart Coll., 1954—55; BS, Coll. Environ. Sci. and Forestry, SUNY, 1965; PhD, Cornell U., 1968; postgrad., Marine Biol. Lab., Woods Hole, Mass., 1968. Asst. prof. SUNY, Oneonta, 1968-69, assoc. prof., 1969-76, prof. biology, 1976—2002, chmn. dept. biology, 1981-89, dir. Biol. Field Sta., 1989—, disting. svc. prof., 2002—. Resource advisor N.Y. State Dept. Environ. Conservation, Albany, 1980—. Contbr. articles to profl. jours. Rep. Otsego County Rep. Com., N.Y., 1973-76; chmn. planning bd., Springfield, N.Y., 1984-96. Served with USN, 1956-61. Recipient Chancellor's award SUNY, 1974-75, Quality award EPA, 1989, Excellence award SUNY, 1990. Mem. Soc. Limnology and Oceanography, N.Am. Benthological Soc., Soc. for Exptl. and Descriptive Malacology, Am. Malacological Union, Otsego County Conservation Assn. (bd. dirs. 1970—, pres. 1974-78, 80-81, chmn. lake com. 1981—). Episcopalian. Avocations: sailing, fishing, scuba diving, skiing. Home: RR 2 Box 829 Cooperstown NY 13326-9327 Office: Biol Field Sta 5838 St Hwy 80 Cooperstown NY 13326-9330 Home Phone: 607-547-5262; Office Phone: 607-547-8778. Business E-Mail: harmanwn@oneonta.edu.

HARMAN, WILLIAM BOYS, JR., lawyer; b. Newport News, Va., June 5, 1930; s. William Boys and Helen (Conner) H.; children: Susan Carol, Thomas Scott, Ann Carrington. AB, Coll. William and Mary, 1951; JD, Coll. William and Mary Marshall-Wythe Sch. Law, 1956; LLM in Taxation, Georgetown U. Law Ctr., 1960. Bar: Va. 1956, D.C. 1961. Tax atty. Gen. Motors Corp., Detroit, 1956-58; atty. Office Chief Counsel, IRS, Washington, 1958-59, Office of Tax Legis. Counsel, U.S. Treasury Dept., Washington, 1959—61; atty. firm Cummings & Sellers, Washington, 1961-62; asso. gen. counsel Am. Life Conv., Washington, 1962-67, gen. counsel, 1968-72; v.p. law Am. Life Ins. Assn., 1973-75; exec. v.p., gov. rels. Am. Council Life Ins., 1976-78; partner Sutherland, Asbill & Brennan, Washington, 1978-85; partner firm Davis & Harman LLP, Washington, 1985—. Served with USCGR, 1952-54. Mem. ABA, Va. State Bar, D.C. Bar Assn., Assn. Life Ins. Counsel, Am. Law Inst., SAR, Nat. Acad. Social Insurance (bd. dir., sec.), William and Mary Law Sch. Assn., Order of Coif, Washington Golf and Country Club, Metropolitan Club, Phi Beta Kappa, Phi Alpha Delta, Sigma Alpha Epsilon. Office: Davis & Harman LLP The Willard Office Bldg Ste 1200 1455 Pennsylvania Ave NW Washington DC 20004 Office Phone: 202-347-2230. Office Fax: 202-393-3310. E-mail: wbharman@davis-harman.com.

HARMAN, YOLANDA MICHELLE, science educator; b. New Brighton, Pa., June 12, 1965; d. Peter Bernard Forno and JoAnn Virginia Speranza-Forno; m. Keith Edward Harman (div.); 1 child, Blake Edward. BS in Biology, Gannon U., 1987; student, Hood Coll., 1987, Pa. State U., 1987; M in Secondary Adminstrn. and Supervision, Frostburg U., 2005. Cert. secondary tchr. Md. Tchr., chair dept. sci. No. Garrett County H.S., Accident, Md., 1990—. Proofreader Holt Rinehart and Winston, Tex., 1999—; mentor tchr. MINT, 2002—03; biology reader Advanced Placement, Clemson, SC, 2000—, Lincoln, Nebr., 2000—; presenter in field. Instr. Nat. Youth Sci. Camp, Bayard, W.Va., 2000. Named Phi Eta Sigma Outstanding Educator, Frostburg State U., 1994, 1997, 1998, 1999, Disting. Instr., Hood Coll., 1997, Outstanding Sci. Instr., Md. Sci. Ctr., Blended Instrn., 1998, Outstanding Educator, MIT, 1999, Md. Outstanding Biology Tchr., 2000, 2001, Tchr. of Yr., Oakland Elks, 2001; recipient Justham award, ARC, 1999, Ray Kroc Tchr. Achievement award, 1999, 2000, Third Team Tchr. award, USA Today, 2001, Subaru Tchr. Recognition Hon. Mention award, 2001; grantee, Manekin, 2005; scholar, Md. Gov.'s Acad., 1998; Chesapeake Bay grantee, Potomac Watershed Study, 2000, Adminstrn. and Supervision Grad. Study scholar, Nat. Bd. Cert., 2000. Mem.: NEA, Garrett County Edn. Assn., Nat. Assn. Secondary Sch. Prins., Nat. Assn. Biology Tchrs. (Md. Biology Tchr. of Yr.), Nat. Sci. Tchrs. Assn. (judge Toshiba Exploration 2001—03, key leader county building a presence), Md. Assn. Sci. Tchrs. (mem. exec. bd.), Md. Assn. Biology Tchrs. (mem. exec. bd.), Delta Kappa Gamma (regional rep. Alpha Alpha chpt.). Home: 258 Bowser Ln Grantsville MD 21536 Office: Garrett County BOE 2d Street Oakland MD 21550

HARMATUK, FRANCES A., retired psychiatrist, anesthesiologist; d. William Harmatuk and Frances Koleczek; m. Nicholas W. DiMinno, Jan. 19, 1961 (dec.). AB magna cum laude, Syracuse U., 1937, MD cum laude, 1941. Diplomate Am. Bd. Anesthesiology, Am. Bd. Psychiatry and Neurology in Psychiatry and in Child Psychiatry. Rotating intern Meadowbrook Hosp., Hempstead, NY, 1941—42; resident in anesthesiology Bellvue Hosp., NYC, 1942—44; resident in psychiatry Bellevue Hosp., NYC, 1958—61; anesthesiologist St. Clares Hosp. and Midtown Hosp., NYC, 1944—57; child psychiatrist Lower Fifth Ave. Hosp., NYC; chief psychiatrist Cath. Charities Guidance Clinic, Bronx, NY, Holy Cross, Imperial Point Coral Ridge Hosp., Ft. Lauderdale, Fla., 1974—77; psychiatrist Henderson Clinic, Pompano Beach, Fla., 1975—76, Valley Psychiat. Hosp., Chattanooga, 1978—79; pvt. practice Virginia Beach, Va., 1979—90; ret., 1990. Clin. instr. psychiatry NY Med. Coll., 1972—74; dir. dept. anesthesiology Midtown Hosp., NYC, 1952—58. Founding mem. Wood Libr. Mus. Anesthesiology. Fellow: Am. Acad. Child Psychiatry, NY Acad. Medicine; mem.: AMA, Soc. Med. Jurisprudence, Am. Soc. Anesthesiologists, NY County Med. Soc., NY State Med. Soc., NY Soc. Clin. Psychiatry, Phi Kappa Phi, Bus. and Profl. Women's Club, Phi Beta Kappa. Avocation: organ. Personal E-mail: frha@suddenlink.net.

HARMEL, HILDA HERTA See PIERCE, HILDA

HARMEL, MEREL HILBER, anesthesiologist, educator; b. Cleve., May 19, 1917; s. Louis and Hermine (Greenbaum) H.; m. Armide Chilcoat, July 2, 1944 (dec. 1988); children: Nancy Armide, Ruth Courtney, Priscilla Gover, Mary Louise; m. Ernestine Friedl Levy, Dec. 27, 1990. BA, Johns Hopkins U., 1938, MD, 1943. Diplomate Am. Bd. Anesthesiology. Fellow in anesthesiology NRC; anesthesiologist-in-chief Albany Med. Ctr., 1948-52, Kings County Med. Ctr., Bklyn., 1952-68, pres. med. bd., 1958-62, chmn. exec. com., 1964-65; cons. L.I. Jewish, St. Albans Naval, Maimonides, St. John's Episcopal, VA hosps., N.C. Eye and Ear Hosp., Durham; assoc. prof. anesthesiology (surgery) Albany Med. Coll., 1948-52; prof., chmn. dept. anesthesiology SUNY Downstate Med. Ctr., 1952-68, Pritzker Sch. Medicine, U. Chgo., 1968-71; prof. anesthesiology Duke Med. Ctr., Durham, NC, 1971—, chmn. dept. anesthesiology ctr., 1971-83, prof. anesthesiology, 1983-87, Merel H. Harmel prof. anesthesiology, 2002, prof. emeritus, 1987—; prof. anesthesiology Duke U. Med. Ctr., Durham, 2002—. Vis. prof. dept. anesthesiology Sch. Medicine, Johns Hopkins U., 1985—. Contbr. articles to profl. jours. Named Disting. Med. Alumnae Johns Hopkins Sch. Medicine, 2003; Commonwealth fellow Oxford U., 1961-62, hon. mem. Sr. Common Rm., Pembroke Coll., 1961; named Merel Harmel vis. lectureship in his honor Duke U. Med. Ctr., 1983, Merel H. Harmel chair dept. anesthesiology in his honor, 2003. Fellow Am. Coll. Anesthesiology (bd. govs.), Royal Coll. Anaesthesia Faculty; mem. AMA, Am. Soc. Anesthesiologists (Living History Series), Assn. Univ. Anesthetists, Duke U. Med. Ctr. Founders Soc., Johns Hopkins U. Soc. Scholars, Japan Soc. Anesthesiologists (hon.), Assn. Anesthesiologists Français (hon.), Oxford Soc. Carolinas (hon. sec. 1990—, W.G. Anlyan Lifetime Achievement award 1999). Business E-Mail: harme001@mc.duke.edu.

HARMELINK, HERMAN, III, minister, writer, religious studies educator; b. Sheldon, Pa., Dec. 26, 1933; s. Herman, II and Thyrza (Eringa) Harmelink; m. Barbara Mary Conibear, Aug. 11, 1959; children: Herman IV, Alan, Lindsay Alexandra. BA cum laude, Central Coll., 1954; MA, Columbia U., 1955; postgrad., U. London, 1955; MDiv, New Brunswick Theol. Sem., 1958; World Coun. Chs. scholar, U. Heidelberg, 1959; STM magna cum laude, Union Theol. Sem., NYC, 1964, MPhil, 1978. Ordained to ministry Ref. Ch. Am., 1959. Min. Cmty. Ch., Glen Rock, NJ, 1959-64, Woodcliff Cmty. Ch., Woodcliff-on-Hudson, NJ, 1964-71, Reformed Ch., Poughkeepsie, NY, 1971—; ecumenical officer Internat. Coun. Cmty. Chs., 2000—. Adj. faculty philosophy SUNY, Marist Coll.; chaplain Holland-Am. Line; chmn. interch. rels. Ref. Ch. Am., 1964—71; pres. Synod of NJ, 1969; vice chmn. Nat. Coun. Chs., 1976—79, mem. commn. regional and local ecumenism, 1981—84, del. Gen. Assembly, 1999—, mem. faith and order commn., mem. exec. bd., 2000—; chmn. ecumenical rels. commn. Internat. Coun. Cmty. Chs., 1994—; del. 18th Plenary Consultation Cmty. Chs., St. Louis, 1999; mem. steering com. reconciliation ministries task force Chs. Uniting in Christ, 2002—; pres. Dutchess Interfaith Coun., 1977—78, devel. retirement cmty. com., 1989—, bd. dirs.; del. gen. coun. World Alliance Ref. Chs., Frankfurt, 1964, Nairobi; adv. Gen. Assembly World Coun. Chs., Uppsala, Sweden, 1968; US del. 50th Anniversary Faith and Order Commn., Lausanne, Switzerland, 1977; del. gen. assembly World coun. Chs., Porto Allegre, Brazil, 2006. Author: Ecumenism and the Reformed Church, 1968, The Reformed Church in New Jersey, 1969, Another Look at Frelinghuysen and His Awakening, 1969; contbg. author: Concord Makes Strength, 2002, Piety and Patriotism, 1976, Vision from the Hill, 1984, The Livingston Legacy, 1987. Nat. bd. dirs. Literacy Vols. Am.; participant US-South African Leader Exch. Program, 1971; bd. dirs. Dutchess County Arts Coun., 1976—80, Bardaven 1869 Opera House, 1978—79; mem. allocation and planning divsn. United Way. Dutchess County; mem. Dutchess County Execs. Com. Med. Ethics; sec. bd. dirs. Rehab. Programs, Inc., 1977—79; bd. dirs. Anderson Ednl. Found., Collingwood Repertory Theatre, 1978—80, Mid-Hudson Meml. Soc., 1981—84; pres. Poughkeepsie Generating Cmty., 1974—; bd. dirs. Literacy Vol. Dutchess County, pres., 1987—89; bd. dirs. Literacy Vols. Am., NY, chmn. pers. comm., mem. program com., pres.-elect, 1992—93, pres., 1993—96, Ranfurly Libr. Svc. NY Inc.; adv. bd. Wartburg Luth. Svcs., 1993—; chmn. Anderson Sch. Wine Showcase; pres. Town of Poughkeepsie Dem. Com., Dutchess County Dem. Com.; ecumenical adv. del. Presbyn. Ch. Gen. Assembly, Long Beach, Calif., 2000, Episc. Gen. Conv., Mpls., 2003, Columbus, 2006, United Meth. Gen. Conf., 2004; trustee Peter A. Lindsay Trust Imperial Coll. U. London; trustee St. Francis Hosp., mem. exec. com. bd.; bd. dirs. Poughkeepsie Rural Cemetery, chmn. fin. com. Lt. USNR, 1957—61. Decorated knight Order of the Temple of Jerusalem; Fulbright Travel grantee, Germany, 1958—59. Mem.: Co. of Pastors, Presbyn. Hist. Soc., Am. Soc. Ch. History, N.Am. Acad. Ecumenists, Nat. Ecumenical Officers Assn. (sec. 2007—), Dutchess County Hist. Soc. (life; bd. dirs. 1974—78), Ctr. Lifetime Study, Mil. Order Fng. Wars US (life), Fulbright Assn. (life), English Speaking Union, Dutchess Interfaith Coun., Poughkeepsie C. of C., Fjord Club, The Club, Circumnavigators Club (NYC), Poughkeepsie Social Reading Club (past pres.), Dutchess county Clergy Club, Travelers Century Club (life), Witherspoon Soc., Royal Overseas League (London), Chevalier du Tastevin (France), Lumanites (sec.-treas.), Poughkeepsie Rotary (pres. 1977—79, sec. 1979—, sec. Dist. 721 1980—81, gov. 1982—83, chmn. World Cmty. Svc., Internat. Coun. Legis. 1983, internat. pres.'s rep. to dist. confs. 1984, 1988, sect. leader internat. conv. 1990, Paul Harris fellow), Friends St. George's and Descs. Knights of Garter (life), St. George's Soc. NY (life). Office: 70 Hooker Ave Poughkeepsie NY 12601 *In the words of John Bunyan, "He who would valiant be 'gainst all disaster, let him in constancy follow the Master. There's no discouragement shall make him once relent his first avowed intent to be a pilgrim.".*

HARMON, BARBARA SAYRE, artist; b. Yerington, Nev., Aug. 8, 1927; d. Ruth (Barker) and Fred Grayson Sayre; m. Cliff Franklin Harmon, July 7, 1948; 1 child, Jonathan Henry. Student, Bisttram Sch. Fine Art, 1945—48, Black Mountain Coll., 1950; studied book binding with Johanna Jalowitz, studied etching with Lawton Parker, 1951. Sales rep. Taos Founders La Fonda Gallery, 1948—52; founder, mgr. Children's Gallery, Taos, 1963—, Children's Gallery Press, Taos, 1967—; co-dir. Torreon Gallery, Taos, 1980—. Dir. First County Wide Craft Show, Taos, 1949. Movie, played by Tony Curtis in The Great Race, 1960, exhibitions include Southwestern Galleries, 1963—, Oak Cliff Restoration Project, Dallas, 2005, Blair Galleries Ltd., Santa Fe, —, Baker Gallery, Lubbock, Tex., —, Stables Gallery, Taos, —; author, illustrator Tabbigail's Garden, 1967, Little People's Counting Book, 1968, This Little Pixie, 1969, Monday's Mouse, 1970, The Tumphee Wood Acorn Book, 1977, Thimbly Hill, 1980, cover designer, illus. N.Mex. mag. Christmas story, 1981; Represented in permanent collections Stanford U. Libr., Palo Alto, U. N.Mex. Libr., Albuquerque, Taos Pub. Libr., Taos Art Mus.; works appear in mags. and books; author (book sculpture for archival presentation): Black Mtn. Coll. Mus. and Art Ctr., 2006. Home: PO Box 202 6584 NDCBU Taos NM 87571-0202 Office Phone: 505-758-2826.

HARMON, DANIEL PATRICK, classics educator; b. Chgo., May 3, 1938; s. Bernard Leonard and Dorothy Mildred (Lesser) H. AB, Loyola U., Chgo., 1962; MA, Northwestern U., 1965, PhD, 1968; postgrad., Am. Sch. Classical Studies, Athens, Greece, 1975. Acting asst. prof. U. Wash., Seattle, 1967-68, asst. prof. classics, 1968-75, assoc. prof., 1975-76, assoc. prof. classics and comparative lit., 1976-84, prof. classics, 1984—2004, prof. emeritus, 2004—, chmn. classics, 1976-91; dir. U. Wash. Rome Ctr., 1992-2000. Contbr. articles and revs. to profl. jours. Mem. Am. Philol. Assn., Archaeol. Inst. Am., Société des Études Latines, County Louth (Ireland) Archaeol. and Hist. Soc., Classical Assn. Pacific Northwest (pres. 1974-75). Avocations: painting, photography, music. Home: 3149 NE 83rd St Seattle WA 98115-4751 Office: U Wash Dept Classics PO Box 353110 Seattle WA 98195-3110 Business E-Mail: dph@u.washington.edu.

HARMON, ETHEL JO See HARMON, JOANNA

HARMON, GAIL MCGREEVY, lawyer; b. Kansas City, Kans., Mar. 15, 1943; d. Milton and Barbara (James) McGreevy; m. John W. Harmon, June 11, 1966; children: James, Eve Bould. BA cum laude, Radcliffe Coll., 1965; JD cum laude, Columbia U., 1969. Bar: Mass. 1970, D.C. 1976, U.S. Dist. Ct. D.C. Assoc. Gaston Snow & Ely Bartlett, Boston, 1970-75, Steptoe & Johnson, Washington, 1975-76, Roisman, Kessler & Cashdan, Washington, 1976-77; ptnr. Harmon, Curran & Tousley, Washington, 1977-90, Harmon, Curran, Spielberg & Eisenberg, Washington, 1990—. Pres. Women's Legal Def. Fund, 1982-84; bd. dirs. Population Svcs. Internat., 1998—, D.C. Libr. Found. Mem. Population Svcs. Internat. (bd. dirs.) Democrat. Episcopalian. Home Phone: 202-363-3463; Office Phone: 202-328-3500. Business E-Mail: gharmon@harmoncurran.com.

HARMON, GEORGE MARION, academic administrator; b. Memphis, Aug. 12, 1934; s. George Marion and Madie P. (Foster) H.; m. Bessie W. Porter, Dec. 27, 1958; children: Nancy R., Mary K., Elizabeth T., George Marion III. BA, Rhodes Coll., 1956; MBA, Emory U., 1957; DBA, Harvard U., 1963. Market rsch. analyst Continental Oil Co., Houston, 1957; rsch. assoc. Harvard U., 1960-63; asst. prof. Coll. Bus. Adminstrn., dir. Salzberg Meml. Transp. Program Syracuse U., NY, 1963-66; sr. assoc. sys. econs. divsn. Planning Rsch. Corp., Washington, 1966-67; prof., chmn. dept econs. and bus. adminstrn., dir. continuing edn. program in econs. and bus. adminstrn. Rhodes Coll. (formerly Southwestern at Memphis), Memphis, 1967-74; prof., dean divsn. bus. and mgmt. W.Va. Coll. Grad. Studies, Charleston, 1974-75; prof., dean Sch. Bus. and Mgmt. Saginaw Valley State Coll., University Center, Mich., 1975-78; pres. Millsaps Coll.,

Jackson, Miss., 1978-2000, pres. emeritus, sr. counsel spl. projects, 2000—; mem. faculty fin. Sch. Banking of the South, La. State U., 1968-72; dir. Audio Visual Sys., Inc., Tenn., 1970-72; v.p., treas. Allen Industries, Inc., Tenn., 1970-72; co-founder, v.p. Computer Survey Sys., Inc., Tenn., 1972-73. Bd. dirs., chmn. exec. compensation com. MacCarty Farms, Inc., Magee, Miss., 1982-95; bd. dirs. Entex, Inc., Houston, 1981-99; mem. So. Regional Edn. Bd., Atlanta, 1994-98; bd. dirs. Regions Bank of Miss. Contbr. articles on bus. adminstrn. to profl. jours. Bd. dirs. Fayetteville-Manlius (N.Y.) Ctrl. Sch. Dist., 1961—63, John Houston Wear Found., Jackson, 1979—2000, Eudora Welty Found., 1999—2003, Jackson Symphony Orch. Assn., 1981—85, Miss. Opera Assn., 1981—86, Cath. Charities of Miss., 2002—, Madison County Libr. Found., 2002—04, St. Catherine's Village Retirement Ctr. Found., 2002—; trustee, chmn. pers. and labor rels. com. Saginaw Osteo. Hosp., 1977—78; chmn. So. Colls. and Univs. Union, 1983—86, Miss. Found. Ind. Colls., 1982; com. and sec. Jackson Internat. Airport Authority, 1991—97; chmn., bd. dirs. Jackson Med. Edn. Dist., 1998—2000; bd. dirs. Jackson Acad., 2005—; univ. senate United Meth. Ch., 1990—2000; bd. dirs., mem. exec. com. Cath. Found., Diocese of Miss., 2005—. Decorated knight Equestrian Order Holy Sepulchre Jerusalem. Mem. NCAA (coun. 1986-92), KC, Jackson C. of C. (bd. dirs. 1981-84), Newcomen Soc. Miss. (pres. 2001-, chmn. 2001-), Soc. Internat. Bus. Fellows, Jackson Country Club, Univ. Club, Capitol City Club, Harvard Club (NYC), Rotary, Phi Beta Kappa, Beta Gamma Sigma, Omicron Delta Kappa, Kappa Sigma (Pres.'s Commn. 2000—). Roman Catholic. Home and Office: 104 Adderbury Ct Ridgeland MS 39157-8709 Office Phone: 601-898-1800. Home Fax: 601-898-1801. Business E-Mail: harmon@millsaps.edu.

HARMON, HARRY WILLIAM, architect, former university administrator; b. San Francisco, Feb. 8, 1918; s. Harry A. and Isabel (Quagelli) A.; m. Lois Anna Holtin, July 28, 1953; children: Bruce Gregory, Mark Brian, Patricia Andree. B.Arch., U. So. Calif., 1941. Draftsman Kaufmann, Lippincott & Eggers (architects), Los Angeles, 1945-48; project architect UCLA, 1948-50, sr. architect, 1952-62; chief coll. facilities planning Calif. State Colls., Inglewood, Calif., 1962-67, asst. vice chancellor Los Angeles, 1967-69; vice chancellor phys. planning, devel. Calif. State Univs., 1969-75, exec. vice chancellor, 1975—83, exec. vice chancellor emeritus, 1983—. Spl. cons. FAO; mem. Nat. Panel Arbitrators. Chmn. bd. visitors USAF Installation Devel. for USAF Directorate of Engring. Svcs., 1989—. Lt. USNR, 1942-45; lt. comdr. 1950-51; capt. Res. ret. Fellow AIA (nat. dir. 1977-80, sec. 1981-85, Disting. Svc. award Calif. coun. 1985, Edward C. Kemper award 1986, chair nat. jud. coun. 1986-88, mem. coun. 1986-93), Assn. U. Archs.; mem. Coun. Ednl. Facility Planners Internat., Soc. Coll. and U. Planners, Am. Arbitration Assn., U. So. Calif. Alumni Assn., Blue Key, Alpha Rho Chi. Home: 1410 La Plaza Dr San Marcos CA 92078-4712 E-mail: hharmon@owl.csusm.edu.

HARMON, HORACE ELMER, JR., museum director, consultant; b. Columbia, SC, Jan. 9, 1946; s. Horace Elmer Harmon and Ruth Tabitha Wilson. AB in History, Newberry Coll., 1968; student in History, U. S.C., 1972—74. Dir. Lexington (SC) County Mus., 1974—. Field appraiser mus. assessment program Am. Assn. Mus., 1984—85; rsch. fellow dept. history U. SC, 1988—; pres. Pineview Ruritan Club, West Columbia, 1989, SC Fedn. Mus., 1990, Confedn. SC Local Hist. Socs., 2004—06. Editor: Uncle Josh, Reminiscing of Old Lexington, 1989. With USCG, 1968—72. Named Businessman of Yr., Pineview Ruritan Club, 2000; recipient Profl. Svc. award, Confedn. SC Local Hist. Socs., 2001, SC Fedn. Mus., 2005. Mem.: Lexington County Hist. Soc. (treas. 1976—), Southeastern Mus. Conf., SC Hist. Soc., South Caroliniana Soc. Independent. Lutheran. Avocations: historical research, reading, hiking, gardening, horseback riding. Home: 2700 Leaphart Rd West Columbia SC 29169 Office Phone: 803-359-8369. Business E-Mail: museum@lex-co.com.

HARMON, JANE, theater producer; With Jane Harmon Assocs., NYC. Prodr. The Last Night of Ballyhoo (by Alfred Uhry), Tony award Best Play, Driving Miss Daisy (by Alfred Uhry, Pulitzer prize), also nat. and internat. tours and Broadway, Buried Child (by Sam Shepard), A Life in the Theatre (by David Mamet), The Robber Bridegroom (by Waldman/Uhry); co-prodr. Asinamali!, Beloved Friend. Bd. dirs. Young Playwrights Inc.; mem. League of Am. Theatres and Prodrs. Inc., Off Broadway Theatre League, League of Profl. Theatre Women. Office: Jane Harmon Assocs One Lincoln Plaza Ste 280 New York NY 10023 Home Phone: 212-879-1077; Office Phone: 212-362-6836.

HARMON, JOANNA KIMBALL (ETHEL JO HARMON), retired archivist, writer; b. Mt. Ayr, Iowa, Mar. 4, 1942; d. Earnest Ira Kimball and Mary Louise Athey; m. Richard Carl Harmon (div.); 1 child, Eric John. AA, Southwestern Jr. Coll., Chula Vista, Calif., 1970; BA, N.Mex. State U., Las Cruces, 1982, MA, 1986; post. grad., Archival Inst. Cath. U. Am., Washington, 2001. Cert. pastoral lay leadership Cath. Diocese Las Cruces, 2004. Rschr. N.Mex. State U., 1986—89; vol. archives Cath. Diocese Las Cruces, 1993—97, fin. clerk, 1997—2006, archivist, 2000—06; ret., 2006. Bd. mem. Agua Viva Cath. Newspaper, Las Cruces, 2003—06, columnist, 2001—05; archivist of record Lone Mountain Archeol., Las Cruces, 2002—06. Author: Raining Sacred Rivers, 2001. Vol. archivist, N.Mex., 2006—; vol. Mariachi Conf., Las Cruces, 1997—2006, Golf Fund Raiser, Las Cruces, 1998—2005, Dem. Party, Las Cruces, 2004. With WAC US Army, 1961—63. Mem.: Assn. Cath. Diocesan Archivists, Phi Alpha Theta. Democrat. Roman Catholic. Avocations: writing, reading, needlecrafts, fabric art. Home and Office: Apt C 65 Darlene Rd SE Rio Rancho NM 87124

HARMON, LYNN ASTRID, announcer, writer; b. Wenatchee, Wash., Jan. 19, 1947; d. Maurice A and Betty Tipler Harmon; m. Bruce K Lumpkin, Feb. 17, 1973 (dec. May 1999); children: Tad W Lumpkin, Elin L Griffin. BA in radio, TV, film, U. Ky., 1969. Program coord. Internat. Telecable Productions, Balt., 1970—71; prod., show hostess WBKY-FM, Lexington, Ky., 1966—70; instr. Broadcasting Inst. of Md., 1971—88; sales promotion mgr. WBFF-TV, Balt., 1971—76; pub. rels., mktg. dir. Chattanooga Theatre Ctr., 1995—98; dir. underwriting and partnership develop. Thurston Cmty. TV, Olympia, Wash., 2002—, comty. rels. and outreach dir., 2004—. Freelance writer, 2001—; freelance broadcast talent, 1970—; performing arts reporter, critic The Sitting Duck, Olympia, 2003; bd. dirs. Capital Playhouse, Olympia, Wash., 2005—. Author: Two Rings Around the Moon, 2000, Notes on Parenting, 2001, (plays) All for One: A Forum, 2004. Publicist Concert Artists of Balt., 1990—91; pres., gen. mgr. Harmony Unlimited, 1985—86; mem. Balt. Symphony Chorus, Chattanooga Theatre Ctr. Mem.: South Sound Partners in Philanthropy. Democrat. Avocations: theater, films, skiing, music. Office: Thurston Cmty TV 440 C Yauger Way Olympia WA 98502

HARMON, MONICA RENEE, music educator; b. Greenville, Ohio, June 3, 1960; d. William Neil Harmon and Julie Ann Erk; m. Ronald Burk Lummis, Apr. 3, 1999. MusB magna cum laude, Morehead State U., 1983; BS, W.Va. State Coll., 1986; MusM, U. Miami, 1996. Profl. Tchr. Cert. Nat. Bd. for Profl. Tchg. Stds., 2002. Permanent substitute tchr. South Charleston (W.Va.) Jr. High, 1987—88; music tchr. Coconut Grove (Fla.) Elem., 1988—90; music dir. George Wash. Carver Mid. Sch., Miami, Fla., 1990—, dept. head electives, 1996—. Children's choir dir. Coral Gables (Fla.) Congl. Ch., 1991—94, Plymouth Congl. Ch., Coconut Grove, 1995—96; vocalist Coral Gables Chamber Symphony and Opera Co., 2003—, Polyphony, Renaissance Ensemble, 2004—. Choir mem. St. Thomas Episc. Parish, 2002—. Mem.: Am. Choral Dirs. Assn., Fla. Orch. Assn., Fla. Vocal Assn., Fla. Bandmasters Assn., Music Educators Nat. Conf. Home: 9720 SW 146th St Miami FL 33176 Office: George Washington Carver Middle School 4901 Lincoln Dr Miami FL 33133 Office Phone: 305-444-7388. Personal E-mail: harmonlummis@yahoo.com. E-mail: harmonm@gwcm.dadeschools.net.

HARMON, PATRICIA MARIE, retired special education educator; b. Bklyn., May 16, 1942; d. Richard Francis and Rita Ann (Baker) Sullivan; m. James Floyd Harmon Jr., June 30, 1984. BS, Molloy Coll. for Women, Rockville Centre, NY, 1972; cert. in spl. edn., SUNY, Brookville, 1978, MS, 1978. Cert. tchr., spl. edn. tchr., NY, Va.; cert. interior decorater. Tchr. Long Beach Cath. Sch., NY, 1960-65, St. Martin's Parish Sch., Amityville, NY, 1965-70, St. Ignatius Parish Sch., Hicksville, NY, 1970-75; adminstr. St. Joseph Parish, Monticello, NY, 1975-76, Holy Redeemer Parish, Freeport, NY, 1976-77; reading specialist Smithtown Reading Clinic, NY, 1977-78; tchr. spl. edn. St. Christopher's Home, Sea Cliff, NY, 1978-79, Buckingham Sch., Bayside, NY, 1979-81, Northampton Pub. Schs., Va., 1981—, Accomack County Pub. Schs., Va., 1987—2005, ret. Va., 2005—. Presenter programs Rockville Centre Diocese, NY, 1970-75, religious cons. Girl Scouts, 1974; safety patrol supr. Pungoteague Elem. Sch., 1995-05. Coun. mem. Local Adv. Com., Nassau County, NY, 1970-73; phone counselor Birthright, Levittown, NY, 1975; founder Ea. Shore Va. chpt. Big Bros./Big Sisters, Belle Haven, 1986-91; active Right to Life Accomac County, 1988; mem. Richmond Diocese Pastoral Coun., 1984-86; mem. social action com. St. Peter's Ch., 1989—, parish sacristan, 1991-01, mem. parish coun., 1992-94, retreat coord., 1999—, Bible study facilitator, 2000—, alt. presider, 2003—, coord. commn. ministers, 2001-. Grantee Va. Dept. Social Svcs., 1989, Ea. Shore Soil and Conservation, Accomac, 1990, 91, 92, Delmarva Power, 1991. Mem. NEA, Va. Edn. Assn., Coun. Excpetional Children, Va. Coun. Learning Disabilities, Women's Aglow Fellowship (corr. sec.1991, v.p. 1993, pres. 1995—). Avocations: reading, sewing, gardening, canning, doll collecting. Office: Pungoteague Elem Sch RR 1 Box 409 Melfa VA 23410-9801 Personal E-mail: pmharmon@earthlink.net.

HARMON, PATRICK, historian, retired editor, commentator; b. St. Louis, Sept. 2, 1916; s. Jack and Laura (Duchesne) H.; m. Anne M. Worland, Aug. 31, 1940; children— Michael, Timothy, Kathleen, Daniel, John, Sheila, Peggy, Brigid, Kevin, Teresa, Christopher. AB, U. Ill., Urbana, 1939. Sports editor News-Gazette, Champaign, Ill., 1942-47, Gazette, Cedar Rapids, Iowa, 1947-51, Post, Cin., 1951-85; ret., 1985; sports commentator Sta. WCPO-TV, 1953-56, Sta. WKRC, 1958, Sta. WLW-TV, 1958-68; curator, historian Coll. Football Hall of Fame, Kings Island, Ohio, 1986-95; historian Nat. Football Found., Morristown, NJ, 1994—2005; ret., 2005. Contbg. sports editor: World Book, 1959—2004. Recipient Fred Hutchinson Meml. award for community service, 1969; named Internat. Churchmen's Sports Writer of Year, 1973 Mem. Sigma Chi. Home and Office: 608 Maple Trace Cincinnati OH 45246 Home Phone: 513-782-6457.

HARMON, PHILLIP LOUIS, lawyer; b. Bourne, Mass., Sept. 8, 1954; s. Russell Sanborn and Patsy (Bilger) H.; m. Kang Sung Ae, 1997. BS in Bus. Mgmt., Cornell U., Ithaca, NY, 1976; JD, Capital Law Sch., Columbus, Ohio, 1980. Bar: OH, 1980, DC, 1981, US Dist. Ct. (so. dist.) OH, 1981, US Dist. Ct. DC, 1982, US Ct. Appeals (DC cir.), 1982, US Ct. Appeals (6th cir.), 1986, US Supreme Ct., 1993. Law clk. to presiding justice Franklin County Probate Ct., Columbus, Ohio, 1976-78; bank officer Huntington Bank, Columbus, 1978-81; mgr. internat. loan syndications Nat. Bank of Washington, 1981—82; asst. v.p., Energy Dept. Shawmut Bank, Boston, 1983—85; pvt. practice Columbus and Washington, 1985—; gen. counsel USA Rugby, 1989—98; sec. multiple entities, 1985—. Fin. advisor Elliott Richardson for US Senate, Boston, 1984; chmn., gen. counsel Progress with Economic and Environmental Responsibility, Inc., 2003-05; candidate US House of Reps. 2000, Ohio 12th Cong. Dist., 2000, Ohio City Coun., Columbus, 2005; sec. Franklin County Forum, 2006-. Mem. ABA, OH State Bar Assn., Columbus Bar Assn. Republican. Methodist. Avocations: scuba diving, swimming, reading, politics, travel. Office: 6649 N High St Ste 105 Columbus OH 43085-4004 Office Phone: 614-433-9502. Personal E-mail: philharmon@msn.com.

HARMON, RICHARD WINGATE, management consultant; b. Exeter, NH, July 16, 1958; BS in Adminstrn., U. N.H., 1981; MBA in Adminstrn., N.H. Coll., 1986. Lic. comml. pilot and flight instr. Owner, pres. Harmon-Waters, Exeter, NH, 1982—, Harmon Realty Investments, Exeter, 1985—; founder, owner Harmon Aviation, Exeter, 1988—, Exeter Storage Depot, Inc., 1989—. Venture capital cons.; constrn. mgmt. cons.; bus. turnaround cons.; bus. start-up cons. Mem.: Seaplane Pilots Assn., Exptl. Aircraft Assn., U. NH Alumni Assn., Aircraft Owners and Pilots Assn., NH Coll. Alumni Assn., Sigma Alpha Epsilon. Avocations: music, golf, skiing, travel, aviation. Office: Harmon-Waters 95 High St Exeter NH 03833-2927

HARMON, ROGER E., environmentalist; b. Henderson, Nev., May 20, 1956; s. Elwood C. and Ivy P. Harmon; m. Tammy C. Cox, May 15, 1999; children: Nichole, Tyler, Danielle. AS, Longview CC, 1976; BS, Ctrl. Mo. State U., 1979, MS, 1980. Registered Sanitarian Nat. Environ. Health Assn., 1985, Registered Environmental Health Specialist Joint Commn. for the Credentialing of Sanitarians, Kans., 1993, Certified Professional Sanitarian Mo. Bd. of Certification for Environ. Health Professionals, 1993. Consumer and compliance insp. Wyo. Dept. of Agr., Casper, 1982—84; environ. health specialist ii Casper - Natrona County Health Dept., Wyo., 1984—89; food and dairy insp. Oreg. Dept. of Agr., Tillamook, 1989—90; environ. health dir. Pacific County Health and Human Services Dept., South Bend, Wash., 1990—91; environ. compliance mgr. Johnson County Environ. Dept., Olathe, Kans., 1991—. Chmn. Joint Commn. for the Credentialing of Sanitarians, Kans., 2004—05; com. mem. Kans. Water Environ. Assn., 1993—; com. mem. solid waste adv. bd. Wash. Dept. of Environ. Quality, Wash., 1990—91. Recipient Eagle Scout, Boy Scouts of Am., 1970. Mem.: Kans. Water Environ. Assn., Water Environ. Fedn., Nat. Environ. Health Assn (licentiate). Home: 408 Sugarland Dr Pleasant Hill MO 64080-1933 Office: Johnson County Environ Dept 11811 S Sunset Dr Ste 2700 Olathe KS 66061 Office Phone: 913-715-6900. Office Fax: 913-715-6970. Business E-Mail: roger.harmon@jocogov.org.

HARMON, TERESA WILTON, lawyer; b. 1968; BS, U. Ala., 1990, MBA, 1991; JD, U. Chgo., 1994. Bar: Ill. 1994. Clk. for Hon. Phyllis Kravitch, U.S. Ct. Appeals (11th cir.), 1994; with Sidley Austin LLP, Chgo., 1995—, ptnr., 2003—. Adj. prof. U. Ill. Coll. Law. Mem.: ABA (sect. bus. law and uniform comml. code com.), Am. Law Inst., Chgo. Bar Assn. (co-chair comml. fin. and transactions com.). Office: Sidley Austin LLP Bank One Plz One S Dearborn St Chicago IL 60603

HARMON, WILLIAM E., nephrologist; b. Cleve., July 31, 1943; s. J. Leo and Frances Harmon; m. Diane J. Harmon, June 26, 1977; children: Elizabeth A., Michael D. AB, Holy Cross Coll., Worcester, Mass., 1967; MD, Case Western Res. U., Cleve., 1971; MA (hon.), Harvard U., Boston, Mass. Diplomate pediat. Am. Bd. Pediat., 1976. Dir. pediat. nephrology Children's Hosp. Boston/Harvard Med. Sch., 1987—. Editor: (medical textbook) Pediatric Nephrology Volumes 4 & 5, Pediatric Solid Organ Transplantation Volumes 1 & 2. Active United Network for Organ Sharing, Richmond, Va., 2004—07; mem. adv. com. on organ transplantation DHHS, Washington, 2000—05. Lt. comdr. USPHS, 1973—75. Recipient Henry L. Barnett award, Am. Acad. Pediat., 2007. Mem.: Am. Soc. Transplantation (pres. 2002—03, Career Clin. Sci. award 2001). Achievements include research in pediatric kidney transplantation. Office: Childrens Hospital Boston 300 Longwood Ave Boston MA 02115 Home Phone: 617-277-9084; Office Phone: 617-355-6129. Office Fax: 617-730-0657.

HARMS, DAVID B., lawyer; b. Whittier, Calif., 1954; BA, SUNY, Purchase, 1978; JD, NYU, 1984. Bar: NY 1985. Law clk. Judge Edward Weinfeld US Dist. Ct. (so. dist.) NY, 1984—85; assoc. Sullivan & Cromwell LLP, NYC, ptnr., co-mng. ptnr. gen. practice group, 2006—. Editor-in-chief: NYU Law Rev., 1983—84. Office: Sullivan & Cromwell 125 Broad St Fl 30 New York NY 10004-2489 Office Phone: 212-558-4000. Office Fax: 212-558-3588. Business E-Mail: harmsd@sullcrom.com.

HARMS, ELIZABETH LOUISE, artist; b. Milw., May 26, 1924; d. Frederick George and Veva (Sanderson) H.; m. Douglas Derwood Craft, Sept. 8, 1951. Diploma, Sch. Art Inst. Chgo., 1950, BFA, 1963, MFA, 1964. One-man shows: 55 Mercer St., N.Y.C., 1980, Fischbach Gallery, N.Y.C., 1975, Carnegie Inst. Mus. Art, 1969, Condeso/Lawler, 1982, 84, 85, 86, 90, 93, Gallery Jupiter, Little Silver, N.J., 1987, Jersey City Mus., 1988, Paul McCarron, N.Y.C., 2001, DVA, Narrowsberg, N.Y., 1996, 2002; group shows include Moravian Coll., Bethlehem, Pa., 1978, Jersey City Mus., 1980, 86, North of New Brunswick, South of N.Y., Rutgers-Newark, 1981, Coll. of New Rochelle, 1982, T. Bell Invitational, Condeso/Lawler, 1985, Montclair (N.J.) Art Mus., 1984, 86, Robeson Mus., Rutgers, Newark, 1988, Invitational Acad. & Inst. for Arts & Scis., N.Y.C., 1992, Skidmore Coll., Saratoga Springs, N.Y., 1993, So. Allegheny Mus. Art, Loretto, Pa., 1994, NAD Invitational, N.Y.C., 2004. Recipient Armstrong prize, Art Inst. Chgo., 1962; grantee, Tiffany Found., 1977. Home: PO Box 245 Jeffersonville NY 12748-0245

HARMS, JOHN KEVIN, lawyer; b. Bitburg Air Base, Germany, Oct. 19, 1960; s. William Robert and Catherine Dorothy (Heslin) H.; m. Pamela Tinkham, 1988; children: William Cameron Harms, Wade Devlin Harms. Student Wash. Seminar in Econ. Policy, Am. U., 1981; BPA magna cum laude, Loyola U., New Orleans, 1982; JD, Northwestern U., 1985; MBA, Western New Eng. Coll., 1989; postgrad., US Army Command and Gen. Staff Coll., 1997, USAF Air War Coll., 1997, US Navy Coll. Continuing Edn.; M in Strategic Studies, US Army War Coll., 2006. Bar: Ill. 1985, U.S. Army Ct. Mil. Review 1986, U.S. Ct. Mil. Appeals 1991, Mass. 1994. Commd. 2d lt. USAR, 1982, advance through grades to col., 1982—2005, comdr. 151st Legal Support Orgn. Alexandria, Va., 2005—; aide-de-camp to commdg. gen. 33d Inf. Brigade, Army Nat. Guard, Ill., 1983—85; rsch. asst. Am. Bar Found., Chgo., 1985; mem. North Western Law Review, 1985; legal assistance atty. Office Staff Judge Adv., Ft. Devens, Mass., 1986, atty.-adv., environ. law specialist, 1992—95; trial def. counsel US Army Trial Def. Svc., Ft. Devens, 1986—87, sr. def. counsel, 1987—90; mem. 1st del. of Am. criminal lawyers People to People Internat., 1987; deputy staff judge adv. Mil. Traffic Mgmt. Command Ea. Area, Bayonne, NJ, 1990—92; internat. ops. atty. Third Mil. Law Ctr., USAR, Boston, 1992—95; chief counsel Devens Res. Forces Tng. Area, Mass., 1995—96; atty., adv. govt. contracts, chief environ. law Electronic Sys. Ctr., Hanscom AFB, Mass., 1996—2003; adminstrv. and contract law atty. 94th Regional Support Command, USAR, Ft. Devens, 1996—2000, dep. staff judge adv., 2000—04; assoc. gen. counsel environment, basic realignment and closure Defense Logistics Agy., Fort Belvoir, Va., 2003—05, joint ops. law atty. Joint Reserve Forces, 2004—05, assoc. gen. counsel environment, installations and enterprise support, 2005—. Aide-de-camp to commdg. gen. 33d Inf. Brigade, Army Nat. Guard, Ill., 1983—85; rsch. asst. Am. Bar Found., Chgo., 1985; mem. North Western Law Review, 1985; legal assistance atty. Office Staff Judge Adv., Ft. Devens, Mass., 1986, atty.-adv., environ. law specialist, 1992—95; trial def. counsel US Army Trial Def. Svc., Ft. Devens, 1986—87, sr. def. counsel, 1987—90; mem. 1st del. of Am. criminal lawyers People to People Internat., 1987; deputy staff judge adv. Mil. Traffic Mgmt. Command Ea. Area, Bayonne, NJ, 1990—92; internat. ops. atty. Third Mil. Law Ctr., USAR, Boston, 1992—95; chief counsel Devens Res. Forces Tng. Area, Mass., 1995—96; atty., adv. govt. contracts, chief environ. law Electronic Sys. Ctr., Hanscom AFB, Mass., 1996—2003; adminstrv. and contract law atty. 94th Regional Support Command, USAR, Ft. Devens, 1996—2000, dep. staff judge adv., 2000—04; assoc. gen. counsel environment, basic realignment and closure and property Defense Logistics Agy., Fort Belvoir, Va., 2003—05, joint ops. law atty. Joint Reserve Forces, 2004—05, assoc. gen. counsel environment, installations and enterprise support, 2005—. Cubmaster Cub Scout Pack 50, Boy Scouts Am., 1999—2001; leader den Weblos/Boy Scouts Am., 2001—03; mem. sixth ring U.S. Olympic Com., 2003; silver level U. S. Olympic Com., 2006; trustee N. Ctrl. Charter Essential Sch., Fitchburg, Mass., 2002—04, sec., 2003—04. Named Outstanding Young Man Am., 1988. Mem. ABA, Fed. Bar Assn., Assn. U.S. Army, Navy League U.S., Boston Bar Assn. (mem. environ. law sect.), Bluekey Nat. Honor Fraternity, Alpha Sigma Nu, Delta Sigma Pi, Beta Gamma Sigma. Avocations: walking, writing, Karate. Office: Office Gen Counsel Defense Logistics Agency 8725 John J Kingman Rd Ste 1644 Fort Belvoir VA 22060 Office Phone: 703-767-6066. Business E-Mail: john.harms@us.army.mil.

HARMS, NANCY ANN, nursing educator; d. Orval M. and Ruth Marie (Nelson) H.; m. Gerhart J. Wehrbein. Diploma, Bryan Meml. Hosp., 1971; BS in Natural Sci., Nebr. Wesleyan U., 1971; BSN, U. Nebr., 1975, MSN, 1977, PhD, 1988. RN, Nebr. Staff nurse, asst. supr., ins. coord. Brewster Hosp., Holdrege, Nebr., 1971-72; instr. Immanuel Sch. Nursing, Omaha, 1972-75; coord. nursing care plan devel. Hosp. Info. Sys. U. Nebr. Med. Ctr., Omaha, 1975; asst. chair dept. Coll. St. Mary, Omaha, 1975-80; curriculum coord. Midland Luth. Coll., Fremont, Nebr., 1980-88, chair nursing divsn., 1988—. Mem. ANA (mem. Ho. of Dels.), Nebr. Nurses' Assn. (Nurse Excellence award, Excellence in Writing award jour., adv. Nebr. Student Nurses Assn., mem. various coms.), Nat. League Nursing, Sigma Theta Tau (theta omega, gamma pi chpts.).

HARMS, ROBERT THOMAS, linguist, educator; b. Peoria, Ill., Apr. 12, 1932; s. Wilbert Erwin and Mildred Matilda (Thomas) H.; m. Sirpa Helina Aaltonen, July 1, 1956; children: Kirsti Maria, Ritva Helena, Eerik Thomas, Timo Kalevi. AB, U. Chgo., 1952, A.M. in Slavic Langs, 1956, PhD in Linguistics, 1960; postgrad. (Fulbright scholar), U. Helsinki, Finland, 1954-56; U.S.-Soviet exchange, Leningrad State U., 1962-63. Instr. U. Tex., Austin, 1958-61, asst. prof. linguistics, 1961-64, asso. prof., 1965-67, prof., 1967—, prof. emeritus, 2006—, chmn. dept. linguistics, 1973-77. Vis. asst. prof. Columbia U., 1960, vis. asso. prof., 1965; vis. asso. prof. Ohio State U., 1964; U.S.-Hungary exchange prof. U. Szeged (Hungarian Acad. Scis.), Budapest, 1967-68 Author: Estonian Grammar, 1962, Finnish Structural Sketch, 1964, Introduction to Phonological Theory, 1968; Editor: (with Emmon Bach) Universals in Linguistic Theory, 1968. Fulbright research grantee Finland, 1968; Nat. Acad. Scis. exchange prof. Acad. Scis. USSR and Estonian Acad. Scis. Mem. Linguistic Soc. Am., Finno-Ugrian Soc., Phi Beta Kappa. Lutheran. Home: 2609 Deerfoot Trl Austin TX 78704-2715

HARN, AMY HELEN, music educator, director; b. Waverly, Iowa, Mar. 17, 1970; d. Connie Jo and Terry David Van Laningham; m. Timothy J. Harn, June 23, 1992; children: Amanda, Brittany, Connor. BME, Wartburg Coll., Waverly, Iowa, 1992. Choral dir. Forreston HS, Forreston, Ill., 2001—. Recipient Ill. State Sweepstakes Championship, Ill. HS Assn., 2003, 2004, 2005, 2006. Mem.: Ill. Music Educators Assn., Music Educator Nat. Conf. Office: Forreston HS 601 E Main St Forreston IL 61030 Business E-Mail: aharn@fvdistrict221.org.

HARNACK, DON STEGER, retired lawyer; b. Milw., June 19, 1928; s. Benjamin John and Katherine (Steger) H.; m. Rosemarie Ball, Oct. 17, 1959; children: Christopher Wallen, Gretchen Marie, Scott P. (dec.), Pamela Ann. BS, U. Wis., 1950; LLB, Harvard U., 1953. Bar: Wis. 1953, U.S. Dist. Ct. (ea. dist.) Wis. 1955, U.S. Tax Ct. 1957, Ill. 1959, U.S. Dist. Ct. (no. dist.) Ill. 1962, U.S. Ct. Appeals (6th and 7th cirs.) 1963, U.S. Ct.

Claims 1966, U.S. Ct. Appeals (8th cir.) 1971, U.S. Supreme Ct. 1972. Assoc. Quarles, Spence & Quarles, Milw., 1955-57; trial atty. regional counsel IRS, Chgo., 1957-61; assoc. Dixon, Todhunter, Knouf & Holmes, Chgo., 1961-65; ptnr. McDermott, Will & Emery, Chgo., 1965-96, of counsel, 1997-98; ret., 2001. Contbr. articles to profl. jours. Active Winnetka (Ill.) Zoning Bd., 1971-75; park bd. atty. Winnetka Park Dist., 1978-83; pres. N.E. Ill. coun. Boy Scouts Am., 1982-83; life trustee ULC Boys and Girls Club, Chgo., UL Civic and Arts Found.; trustee Village of Winnetka, 1984-88. Served with U.S. Army, 1953-55, USNR, 1959-69. Recipient Silver Beaver award Boy Scouts Am., 1984, named distinguished Eagle Scout, 1996. Mem. ABA, Ill. Bar Assn., Wis. Bar Assn., Union League Club (bd. dirs., officer, v.p. 1981-87, pres. 1987-88). Republican. Avocations: fishing, golf, reading. E-mail: bigcoho2@aol.com.

HARNDEN, EDWIN A., lawyer; BA, Columbia U., NYC, 1969, JD, 1972. Mng. ptnr. Barran Liebman LLP, Portland, Oreg.; pres. Oreg. State Bar, 2001—02. Past pres. Profl. Liability Fund. Fellow: Am. Coll. of Labor and Employment Lawyers, Am. Bar Found. (life). Office: ODS Tower 601 SW 2d Ave Ste 2300 Portland OR 97204-3159 Home Phone: 503-292-6490; Office Phone: 503-276-2101. Business E-Mail: eharnden@barran.com.

HARNEDY, JOAN CATHERINE HOLLAND, retired systems analyst; b. Hackensack, NJ, May 31, 1936; d. John Joseph and Marion Rita (Sexton) Holland; m. Edmund Richard Harnedy, Dec. 29, 1962; children: Richard J., Julia Ann. BS, Coll. New Rochelle, 1957. Adminstrv. asst. Ford Found. funded, Rockefeller Found. funded, 1957—59; sys. analyst IBM, White Plains, NY, 1960—65; publicity chair YWCA, White Plains, NY, 1966—69; ret., 1969. Travel cons., photographer, White Plains, 1970—92. Mem.: NAFE, Ocean Conservancy, NY Pub. Libr., United Spinal Assn., Wildlife Fedn., Defenders Wildlife, Nat. Audubon Soc., Nature Conservancy, Nat. Parks Conservancy, Children's Cancer Soc., Met. Mus. Art, Phi Chi. Avocations: writing, gardening, art history, photography, gourmet cooking.

HARNER, JAMES LOWELL, language educator; b. Washington, Ind., Mar. 24, 1946; s. Thomas Lloyd and Ruth Ellen (Clark) H.; m. Darinda Jane Wilson, Aug. 26, 1967; 1 child, Lenée Francais. BS magna cum laude, Ind. State U., 1968; MA, U. Ill., 1970, PhD, 1972. Prof. English Bowling Green (Ohio) State U., 1971-88, Tex. A&M U., College Station, 1988—. Author: Literary research Guide, 1989 (Choice Mag. Outstanding Acad. Book 1990), 4th edit., 2002, English Renaissance Prose Fiction, 1978, 3d edit., 1992, On Compiling an Annotated Bibliography, 1983-2000, Samuel Daniel and Michael Drayton, 1980, Directory of Scholarly Presses, 1991, (online database) World Shakespeare Bibliography Online, 1996—, (Besterman medal 1997, Besterman/McColvin medal, 2001, hon. mention MLA Disting. Bibliograpy prize, 2006); editor World Shakespeare Bibliography, 1988—, Essential Bibliographies Series, 1985-96; mem. editl. bd. Seventeenth-Century News, 1973-92, Lit. Rsch., 1984-99, Shakespeare Yearbook, 1992—, Shakespeare Quar., 1993—, Literature Online, 2006—. Mem. MLA, The Bibliog. Soc., Shakespeare Assn. of Am., Internat. Shakespeare Assn., Bibliog. Soc. Am. Democrat. Presbyterian. Avocations: book collecting, travel, manuscript collecting. Home: 4736 Stonebriar Cir College Station TX 77845 Office: World Shakespeare Bibliog Tex A&m U Dept English College Station TX 77843-4227 Home Phone: 979-690-9353; Office Phone: 979-845-3400. Business E-Mail: j-harner@tamu.edu.

HARNER, MICHAEL JAMES, anthropologist, educator; b. Washington, Apr. 27, 1929; s. Charles Emory and Virginia (Paxton) H.; m. June Knight (Kocher), 1951; children: Teresa J., James E.; m. Sandra Ferial (Dickey), 1966. AB, U. Calif., Berkeley, 1953, PhD, 1963; PhD (hon.), Calif. Inst. of Integral Studies, 2003. Asst. prof. Ariz. State U., 1958—61; from sr. mus. anthropologist to assoc. rsch. anthropologist and asst. dir., Hearst Mus. Anthropology U. Calif., Berkeley, 1961—66; from vis. assoc. prof. to assoc. prof. Columbia U., NYC, 1966—70; from assoc. prof. to prof. grad. faculty New Sch. U., NYC, 1970—87, chmn. dept. anthropology, 1973—77; internat. tchr. Shamanism, 1977—; founder, dir. Ctr. for Shamanic Studies, Norwalk, Conn., 1980—87; founder, pres., trustee Found. for Shamanic Studies, Mill Valley, Calif., 1985—. Field rsch. Upper Amazon Basin, 1956-57, 60-61, 64, 69, 73, Western North Am., 1948, 51-53, 59, 65, 76, 78, Lapland, 1983, 84, Can. Arctic, 1987; vis. assoc. prof. U. Calif., Berkeley, 1971, 72, vis. prof., 1975; vis. assoc. prof Yale U., 1970. Author: Population Pressure and the Social Evolution of Agriculturalists, 1970, The Jivaro: People of the Sacred Waterfalls, 1972, 2d edit., 1984, Scarcity, the the Factors of Production, and Social Evolution, 1975, The Ecological Basis for Aztec Sacrifice, 1977, The Way of the Shaman, 1980, 3d edit., 1990; co-author: Cannibal, 1979, Core Practices in the Shamanic Treatment of Illness, 1999; editor: Hallucinogens and Shamanism, 1973. Fellow Social Sci. Rsch. Coun., Doherty Found., Am. Mus. Nat. History fellow; honored as great shaman, Siberian shamans, Russia, 1999. Fellow Am. Anthrop. Assn., Royal Anthrop. Inst. G.B. and Ireland, NY Acad. Scis. (former co-chmn. anthropology sect.); mem. Am. Ethnol. Soc., Soc. Ethnohistory, Internat. Transpersonal Assn. (bd. dirs. 1982-85, 89-91), Assn. for the Anthropology of Consciousness, Internat. Soc. Shamanistic Rsch., Soc. for Anthropology of Lowland South America. Office: Found Shamanic Studies PO Box 1939 Mill Valley CA 94942-1939 Office Phone: 415-389-7222. E-mail: michaelharner@shamanism.org.

HARNESS, WILLIAM EDWARD, tenor; b. Pendleton, Oreg., Nov. 26, 1940; s. Edward Cleo and Edna Margaret (Senn) H.; m. Anna Marie Ward, Jan. 11, 1964; children: Janine Kay, Heidi Maurine, William Edward, Shaana Marie, Shane Michael. Student pub. schs., Spokane, Wash. Gen. carpenter Rainway Mfg. Co., Spokane, 1958-61; with Wash. Water Power Co., Spokane, 1961-62; tech. service rep. Nat. Cash Register Co., Seattle, 1962-73. Concert and opera tenor various opera cos. and symphonies, 1973—; profl. debut, San Francisco Opera Co., 1973, debut with NYC Opera, 1976, Met. Opera, NYC, 1977, Hamberg (West Germany) Opera, 1978, maj. symphony debuts include Vancouver (B.C., Can.), Seattle, Los Angeles Philharm., San Francisco, Minn., Milw. Symphonies, sacred concert artist, 1978—; roles include: Edmondo in Manon Lescaut, Tonio in Daughter of the Regiment, Alfredo in La Traviata, Rodolfo in La Boheme, Count Almaviva in The Barber of Seville, Tamino in The Magic Flute, Faust in Faust, Cauaradossi in Tosca, Prince Calof in Turandot, Riccardo in Un Ballo in Maschera; sacred concert and recording artist (13 sacred recordings), US and Can., South Africa, Latvia, Romania, Croatia, Latvia, India; tenor The Way Things Used to be, 2007. Recipient V.I.P. award Nat. Cash Register Co., 1970; Florence Bruce award San Francisco Opera, 1972; Enrico Caruso award, 1973; Cecilia Schultz award Seattle Opera, 1972; Distinguished Citizen award State of Wash., 1974; Nat. Opera Inst. fellow, 1973-74; Martha Baird Rockefeller grantee, 1974-76 Address: PO Box 328 Washougal WA 98671-0328 Business E-Mail: whsc@pobox.com.

HARNETT, JOSEPH DURHAM, oil industry executive; b. Paterson, NJ, Aug. 23, 1917; s. James Harold and EMily (Steele) H.; m. Wilhelmina Nordstrom, June 21, 1941 (dec. July 1958); children: Gordon D., Linda C., Ralph H., David S.; m. Nancy Beam. BS, Purdue U., 1939. With Consol. Edison Co., NYC, 1939, Worthington Pump & Machinery Corp., 1940, Standard Oil Co., Cleve., 1941-80, v.p., 1957-68, sr. v.p., 1968-70, exec. v.p., 1970-77, pres., 1977-80. Mem. Am. Petroleum Inst. (bd. dirs.), Country Club Cleve., Pepper Pike Club, Everglades Club, Lost Tree Club. Presbyterian. Home: 11090 Turtle Beach Rd # 204 North Palm Beach FL 33408-3423 Office: Moore and Ellrich 4400 P G A Blvd Ste 400 Palm Beach Gardens FL 33410-6557

HARNEY, KATHRYN ANN, opera singer; b. Lincoln, Nebr., Sept. 8, 1955; d. Herman and Sylvia (Korbel) H. Fellowship Artist, Hochschule fur Musik, Munich, 1979; Diploma in Opera, Hartt Coll. of Music, Hartford, Conn., 1975; BMus, U. Nebr., 1972, MMus, 1973. Faculty U. So. Miss., Hattiesburg, 1975-77, Shepherd Sch. of Music/Rice U., Houston, 1977; opera singer/mezzo-soprano various roles in Europe, 1977—; opera singer/debut Conn. Opera, Hartford, 1974. Opera roles include: Charlotte in Werther, Baba the Turk in Rakes Progress, La Principessa di Bouillon in Adriana Lecouvreur, Der Komponist in Ariadne Auf Naxos, Venus in Tannhausser, Dorabella in Cosi Fan Tutte. Mem. Sigma Alpha Iota. Methodist. Avocations: cooking, interior decorating. Home: PO Box 15374 Hattiesburg MS 39404-5374 Office: Artist Mgmt Owen-Evans Ltd London England

HARNOIS, VERONICA, psychologist, educator; d. John Joseph and Vera Shannon D'Urso; children: Kent, Kathleen Duquette, Sheila Foley, Carol Recor, Jeanne, John. BA, Merrimack Coll., North Andover, Mass., 1957; MEd, Am. Internat. Coll., Springfield, Mass., 1971, cert. advanced grad. studies, 1991, D of Edn., 2003. Cert. sch. psychologist Mass., lic. ednl. psychologist Mass. Substitute tchr., tchr. Springfield Pub. Schs., 1958—69; co-dir., cons., tchr. Miss Barker's Sch., 1969—75; ednl. dir., tchr. Osborn Day Sch., Agawan, 1975—83; vocat. counselor, examiner Urban League, Springfield, 1984—85; clin. specialist, sch. psychologist Kolburne Sch., New Marlborough, 1986—94; dir. sch. program Brightside, Inc., Springfield, 1994—96; cons., psychol. examiner May Inst., West Springfield, 1997—98; sch. psychologist Springfield Pub. Schs., 1998—. Instr. psychology spl. edn. Am. Internat. Coll., 1991—. Author: The Harnois Program, 1994. Mem.: Pioneer Valley Reading Coun. (bd. dirs. 1988—), Nat. Assn. Sch. Psychologists, Western Mass. Counseling Assn., Delta Kappa Gamma. Roman Catholic. Avocation: reading. Home: 38 Nassau Dr Springfield MA 01129 Office: Springfield Pub Schs 195 State St Springfield MA 01103 Personal E-mail: harnoisv@verizon.net.

HAROLD, KATHLEEN T., elementary school educator; b. Oak Park, Ill., Sept. 6, 1963; d. James Joseph Neville and Joan Esther (O'Keefe); children: Neil Austin, Leah Elizabeth. BS in Edn., Bradley U., 1985; MEd in Lang. and Lit., Nat.-Louis U., 1996. Cert. tchr., Ill. Tchr. 3d grade St. Thecla Elem., Chgo., 1985—87; tchr. 2d grade Avon Sch. Dist. # 47, Lake Villa, Ill., 1987—89; tchr. 1st grade Grayslake Sch. Dist. # 46, Ill., 1989—2002, info. specialist sch. libr., 2002—. Mem.: Ill. Sch. Libr. Media Assn. Avocations: crafts, reading, scrapbooks. Office: Avon Ctr Sch 1617 N Rte 83 Round Lake Beach IL 60073 Home: 18145 W Twin Lakes Blvd Grayslake IL 60030-2044 Office Phone: 847-223-3530. Business E-Mail: harold.kathleen@d46.org.

HAROLDS, JAY ALAN, radiologist, nuclear medicine physician; s. Louis R. and Jeanette P. Harolds; m. Melinda Elizabeth Eddins, Apr. 17, 1977; children: Jennifer Lynn, Amanda Roslyn, Laura Beth. BA in Biology, SUNY, Binghamton, 1967; MD, U. Buffalo, 1971. Diplomate Am. Bd. Med. Examiners, 1972, in diagnostic radiology Am. Bd. Radiology, 1975, with spl. competence in nuc. medicine Am. Bd. Radiology, 1979, Am. Bd. Nuc. Medicine, 1980, cert. Certification Bd. Nuc. Cardiology, 1997. Med. dir. dept. radiology Baptist Med. Ctr., 1988—95; med. dir. ultrasound tech. program U. Okla., 1989—, med. dir. nuc. medicine tech. program, 1996—, adj. assoc. prof., 2007—. Dir. radiology residency Integris Bapt. Med. Ctr., Okla. City, 1985—2002, dir. Dept. Radiology, 1988—95; asst. prof. Vanderbilt U, Nashville, 1979; examiner Am. Bd. Radiology, Tucson, 1987—2004, mem. nuc. medicine exam com.; rep. nuclear medicine exam com Am. Registry Radiological Tech., 2005—; reviewer profl. jours.; presenter in field. Contbr. over 40 articles to profl. jours. Mem. Soc. of Chiefs of Academic Radiology Depts., 1994—96; sec. Am. Registry of Radiologic Technology, 2007—, bd. mem., 2007—. Maj. US Army, 1975—77. Recipient Disting. Svc. award, Am. Bd. Radiology, 2003. Fellow: Am. Coll. Nuc. Physicians (chmn. program 2005—06, mem. bd. regents 2005—, bd. regents 2005—, sec. 2006—, sec./treas. 2006—07, treas. 2006—, Pres.'s award 2006), Am. Coll. Radiology (alt. councilor 1991—93, edn. liason officer 1992—98, councilor 1993—98, Okla. councilor 1993—98, chmn. com. edn. for commn. nuc. medicine 1999—2006, councilor 2004—, Okla. councilor 2004—07, mem. reference com., radiation oncology, med. physics, nuc. medicine 2005, mem. reference com. I 2005, rep. nuc. medicine exam com. 2005—, rep. nuc. medicine exam com., Am. Registry Radiol. Technologists 2005—, mem. academic and pvt. practice task force 2005—, coun. steering com. 2006—, oral examiner com. 2007, mem. reference com. II 2007, alt. councilor from Assn. Program Dir. Radiology); mem.: Ctrl. Okla. Nuclear Medicine Soc. (sec./treas. 1984—85, v.p. 1985—86, pres. 1986—87), Radiology Assocs. Inc., Am. Bd. Radiology Maintenance Cert. Com. (mem. maintenance of competence com. 2006—, mem. oral exam com. 2007—), Radiol. Soc. N.Am. (Okla. counselor 1998—), Assn. Program Dirs. Radiology (3rd dir. at large 1997—98, 2nd dir. at large 1998—99, 1st dir. at large 1999, sec./treas. 1999—2000, program chmn. 2000—01, pres.-elect 2000—01, pres. 2001—02, past pres., chmn. nom. com. 2002—03, chair ad hoc nuc. medicine com. 2005—), Ctrl. Okla. Radiol. Soc. (sec. and treas. 1984—85, v.p. 1985—86, pres. 1986—87, 1993), Okla. State Radiol. Soc. (mem. at large 1986—87, sec./treas. 1987—88, v.p. 1988—89, pres. 1989—90, edn. liason officer 1992—98), Soc. Nuc. Medicine (trustee, southwestern chpt. 1993—2000, program chmn., southwest chpt. 1996—97, pres.-elect, southwest chpt. 1998—99, pres., southwest chpt. 1999—2000, past pres., chmn. nom. com., southwest chpt. 2000—01, historian, southwest chpt. 2000—03, mem. edn. com. 2004—, v.p., program dir. academic coun. Soc. Nuc. Medicine 2005—06, pres. academic coun. 2006—, 2006—07, Disting. Svc. award 2006). Avocations: ballroom dancing, tennis, writing. Office: Radiology Associates 3330 NW 56 Street Oklahoma City OK 73112 Home Phone: 405-755-3288.

HARON, DAVID LAWRENCE, lawyer; b. Detroit, Sept. 24, 1944; s. Percy and Bess (Holland) H.; m. Pamela Kay Colburn, May 25, 1969; children: Eric, Andrea. BA, U. Mich., 1966, JD, 1969. Bar: Mich. 1969, U.S. Dist. Ct. (ea. dist.) Mich., 1969, U.S. Supreme Ct. 1974, U.S. Ct. of Appeals (6th cir.) 1996. Law clk. to chief judge Mich. Ct. Appeals, Detroit, 1969-70; assoc. Barris, Sott, Denn & Driker, Detroit, 1970-74; sr. ptnr. Josephson, Tennen, Haron, Weiner and Navarro, Southfield, Mich., 1974-90; prin., shareholder, sr. v.p. Frank, Haron, Weiner and Navarro, Troy, Mich., 1990—; arbitrator Mich. Prudential Securities, Inc. Expedited Arbitrations, 1994-96. Cons. Universe Computer Software, 1985; pres., bd. dirs. S&H Licensing Corp., Southfield; panelist Ct. TV Law Ctr. Bar Assn.; spkr. in field. Mem. editl. bd. Prospectus Jour. Law Reform, 1969, (newsletter) Atty.'s Mktg. Report, 1986-88; contbr. articles to profl. jours. Active Farmington Hills Planning Commn., 1996—, vice-chair, 2000-01, chair, 2001-03; vol. handicap parking enforcement officer Farmington Hills Police Dept., 1990-93; bd. dirs. Forest Elem. Sch. PTO, 1983, 87-88; v.p. North Farmington Baseball for Youth, 1984; active Sta. WTVS Auction, Detroit, 1985-88; trustee C.A.T.C.H., 1996—, Temple Israel, West Bloomfield, Mich., 1987-93, tchr. Sunday Sch., 1986-88, chmn. Ritual com., 1988-93, advisor youth group, 1987-90; chmn. Farmington Hills Com. to Increase Voter Participation, 1987-89; bd. dirs. Met. Detroit chpt. Zionist Orgn. Am., 1987-90; pres. North Farmington H.S. Parent Club, 1989-95; bd. advisors Farmington Hills Corps.-Salvation Army, 1997-00; site selection com. South Oakland County Habitat for Humanity; chair Cardozo Law Soc. of the Jewish Fedn. Met. Detroit, 1999-02; bd. dirs., treas. Mich. Psychoanalytic Found., 2003-04, pres., 2004-07. Named Mich. Super Lawyer Law & Politics, 2007; recipient Outstanding Alumnus award Mumford HS, Detroit, 1985, cert. recognition City of Farmington Hills, 1986. Fellow Roscoe Pound Found.; Mich. State Bar Found., Oakland County Bar Found. (trustee, treas. 2003-04, v.p. 2004-05, pres. 2005-06); mem. ABA (com. on comml. leasing 1987-94, real property, probate and trust law sect., bus. law sect. com. on fed. regulation of securities, subcom. on alternative dispute resolution, SEC enforcement matters), ASTM (com. on environ. assessment 1992-2006), ATLA, Nat. Arbitration Forum (arbitrator), Assn. Health Lawyers Am., Mich. Trial Lawyers Assn., Am. Soc. Writers on Legal Subjects, Internat. Assn. Jewish Lawyers and Jurists, Million Dollar Advocates Forum, State Bar Mich. (pro bono com. real property sect. 1996-98, professionalism com. 1994-2002, chmn. professionalism com. 1996-98, chmn. unauthorized practice of law com. 1990-92, unauthorized practice of law com. 1999-02, chmn. Ct. Appeals com. 1977-78, mem. rep. assembly 1999-2006), Nat. Assn. Securities Dealers (mediator), Am. Arbitration Assn. (arbitrator, mediator), Oakland County Bar Assn. (participant Mich. law-related edn. project 1988-89, real estate com. 1990—, environ. law com. 1992-95, lawyer dispute conciliator, chmn. professionalism com. 1995-97, Cir. Ct. facilitator, master Inn of Ct. 1997-2005, master emeritus, Professionalism award, 2003), U. Mich. Alumni Assn., U. Mich. Victor's Club, Franklin Hills Country Club (bd. dirs. 2004-06, treas. 2004-05, v.p. 2005-06), Zionist Orgn. (bd. dirs. Detroit 1987-90), Tau Epsilon Rho Legal Soc., Tau Delta Phi. Jewish. Home: 34685 Old Timber Rd Farmington Hills MI 48331-1436 Office: Frank Haron Weiner and Navarro 5435 Corporate Dr Ste 225 Troy MI 48098-2624 Office Phone: 248-952-0400. Office Fax: 248-952-0890. Business E-Mail: dharon@fhwnlaw.com.

HARP, JOHN ANDERSON, lawyer; b. Helena, Ark., Nov. 30, 1950; s. Bert Seth and Mary Eleanor (Jolley) H.; m. Jane Van Cleave, Apr. 26, 1980; children: Anderson, Elizabeth, William, Hamilton. BA, Am. U., Washington, 1973; JD, Mercer U., Macon, Ga., 1980. Bar: Ga., Ala. Ptnr. Harp & Callier, Columbus, Ga., 1985—. Co-author: Litigating Head Trauma Cases, 1991; bd. editors Neurolaw Letter, 1991—, Topics in Spinal Cord Injury Rehab., 1994—; issues editor Topics in Spinal Cord Injury Rehabilitation, vol. 6, no. 4, 2001; contbr. articles to profl. jours. Reservist USMCR with Office of Asst. Sec. of Def., The Pentagon, 1996-2000. Col., USMCR, 1995-2000, Marine Forces Pacific G-3, 2000-02. Mem. ABA, ATLA, Ga. Bar Assn., Ala. Bar Assn., Nat. Spinal Cord Assn. (bd. dirs. 1987-95), Acad. Rail Labor Attys. (bd. dirs. 2004), Marine Corps Res. Officers Assn. (bd. dirs. 1995-98, nat. pres. 1997-98, vice-chmn. bd. dirs. 1998-99, Non Sibi Sed Patriae award), Mercer U. Law Sch. Alumni Assn. (nat. v.p. 1997-98, nat. pres.-elect 1998-99, nat. pres. 1999—). Avocations: running, skiing. Office: Harp & Callier 233 12th St Ste 900 Columbus GA 31901-2449 Office Phone: 706-323-7711.

HARPEN, SHAWN M., lawyer; BA, U. Toledo, 1990, JD, 1998. Bar: Calif. Ptnr., bus. litigation McDermott Will & Emery, Irvine, Calif. Named a Rising Star, So. Calif. Super Lawyers, 2004—06. Mem.: ABA, Calif. Bar Assn., Fed. Bar Assn., LA County Bar Assn., Orange County Bar Assn., Order of the Coif. Office: McDermott Will & Emery Ste 500 18191 Von Karman Ave Irvine CA 92612 Office Phone: 949-757-6061. Office Fax: 949-851-9348. Business E-Mail: sharpen@mwe.com.

HARPER, A(LFRED) J(OHN), II, lawyer; b. El Paso, Tex., Aug. 11, 1942; s. Mosely Lloyd and Marion M. (McClintock) H.; m. Cynthia Newkam; children: A. John, Leslie J. BA, North Tex. State U., 1964; LLB cum laude, So. Meth. U., 1967. Bar: Tex. 1967, US Dist. Ct. (so. dist.) Tex. 1967, US Dist. Ct. (no. dist.) Tex. 1975, US Dist. Ct. (we. dist.) Tex. 1976, US Dist. Ct. (ea. dist.) Tex. 1995, US Ct. Appeals (5th cir.) 1968, US Ct. Appeals (9th cir.) 1976, US Ct. Appeals (11th cir.) 1982, US Ct. Appeals (10th cir.) 1984, US Ct. Appeals (6th cir.) 1990, US Ct. Appeals (1st cir.) 1991, US Ct. Appeals (2d cir.) 1995, US Ct. Appeals (8th cir.) 2002, US Supreme Ct. 1971. Assoc. Fulbright & Jaworski, LLP, Houston, 1967-74, ptnr., 1975—, and head, labor and employment law dept. Cert. labor and employment law specialist State Bar Tex. bd. legal specialization. Editor Jour. Air Law and Commerce, 1966-67; contbr. articles to profl. jours. With USMCR, 1960-66. Named a Tex. Super Lawyer, Tex. Monthly Mag., 2003—06; named to The Best Lawyers in Am., 2002—06, Chambers USA, 2005—06. Fellow Coll. Labor and Employment Lawyers; mem. ABA (past coun., labor and employment law sect., past mgmt. co-chmn. com. on devel. law under Nat. Labor Rels. Act, past mgmt. co-chmn. meetings and insts. com., labor law sect.), Tex. Bar Assn., Order of Coif, Houston Country Club. Republican. Methodist. Office: Fulbright & Jaworski LLP Ste 5100 1301 McKinney St Houston TX 77010-3031 Office Phone: 713-651-5151. Office Fax: 713-651-5246. Personal E-mail: ajharper@fulbright.com.

HARPER, BARBARA CLARA, educational program administrator, counselor; b. NYC, Aug. 9, 1932; d. James Gullins and Irene Christine (Robinson) H.; m. William C. Booth, Apr. 24, 1951 (div. 1958); 1 child, James Alan; m. Washington Mays, Jan. 1, 1959 (div. 1987). AA, Mattaluck Community Coll., 1978; BS, N.H. Coll., 1987, MS, 1989. Cert. profl. counselors inc. Conn. Bd., lic. profl. counselor, foster mother. Gen. office staff Avnet Electronics, Bronx, NY, 1955-59; sec., gen office staff PHA, Waterbury, Conn., 1959-64; pers. interviewer Scovill Mfg. Co., Waterbury, 1964-66; caseworker, ctr. dir. New Opportunities for Waterbury, 1966-68; coord. Waterbury Cmty. Sch., 1969-94; clinician Child Guidance Clinic Greater Waterbury, Inc., 1963—. Part-time instr. Displaced Housewives and Work Incentive Programs, 1975-80; mem. clerical staff Mattaluck C.C., Waterbury, 1974-80. Mem. Drug Free Sch., 1984; vol. leader Coop. Ext. Svc., USDA 4-H, 1984-91; com. leader Boy Scouts Am., 1974-76, Girl Scouts, 1962; sec. Northeastern Heights Coun., 1971, The Promoters Club of Wilson Sch., 1980; bd. dir. NOW Inc., 1964; vol. organist, choir dir. St. Cecilia's Ch., 1960. With USAF, 1950-52. Recipient Silver Clover award Coop. Extension Svc., U. Conn. 1989, Cert. of Appreciation award Youth Svc. Bur., Dedicated Svc. Appreciation award Boy Scouts of Am. Troop 223, 1975. Mem.: Conn. Assn. Marriage and Family Counselors (sec. 1998—99, pres. 2001—02), Nat. Polit. Congress of Black Women (sec. 1998—99, pres.-elect 1999—2001, pres. 2001—02), Long Hill Cmty. Club (sec.), Waterbury Black Dem. Club. Democrat. Home and Office: 165 Traverse St Waterbury CT 06704-3229

HARPER, BILL J., floral designer, consultant, educator; b. Freeman, Mo., Aug. 15, 1944; s. Oscar Raymond Harper and Fay Elizabeth Duncan Harper. Grad., Midway HS, Freeman, Mo., 1962. Grower Archie Greenhouse, Sedalia, Mo., 1963—67; designer, merchandiser Blantons' Flowers, Houston, 1967—70; designer, mgr. Jones/Trapp Flowers, Kansas City, Mo., 1970—74; design instr. Floral Tech. and Design, Kansas City, 1974—78; design cons. Flowerama Am., Waterloo, Iowa, 1978—79; design instr., dir. Stuppy Floral Design Sch., Kansas City, 1979—. Floral. design cons.; lectr. in field; guest design instr. Musa Sch. Floral Design, Yokohama, Japan, 1990—97; floral team coord. for rededication Statue of Liberty, 1986. Design work featured in numerous nat. and internat. publs. Recipient award of merit, Florist Transworld Delivery, 1974. Fellow: Am. Inst. Floral Designers (nat. and internat. membership chmn. 1985—89, bd. dirs. 1985—93, v.p. 1989—90, pres.-elect 1990—91, pres. 1991—92, rep. World Flower Coun. Congress 1992, 1997, Outstanding Svc. award 1996); mem.: Florist Acad. Mo. (charter), Kans. State Florist Assn. (assoc.), Ozark Florist Assn. (assoc. Outstanding Achievement award 1990), Soc. Am. Florists (assoc.), Mo. State Florist Assn. (assoc.), Am. Acad. Florists. Avocations: gardening, wildlife preservation, conservation, travel. Home and Office: 6205 E Pony Creek Rd Cleveland MO 64734 Office Phone: 816-250-2559. Personal E-mail: bill081544@aol.com.

HARPER, CHARLES MICHEL, food products executive, director; b. Lansing, Mich., Sept. 26, 1927; s. Charles Frost and Alma (Michel) Harper; m. Joan Frances Bruggema, June 24, 1950; children: Kathleen Harper Wenngatz, Carolyn, Charles Michel, Elizabeth Harper Murphy. BS in Mech. Engring, Purdue U., 1949; MBA, U. Chgo., 1950; LHD (hon.), U. Nebr., 1986; degree (hon.), Coll. St. Mary, 1986; JD (hon.), Law Coll. St. Mary, 1986; DEng (hon.), Purdue U., 1989; LHD (hon.), Kearney State U., 1990, Bellevue Coll., 1993, Creighton U., 1993. Supr. methods engring.

Oldsmobile divsn. Gen. Motors Corp., Detroit, 1950—54; indsl. engr. Pillsbury Co., Mpls., 1954—55, dir. indsl. engring., 1955—60, dir. engring., 1961—66, v.p. rsch., devel. and new products, 1965—70, group v.p.-poultry, food svc. and venture bus., 1970—74; exec. v.p., COO, dir. ConAgra Inc., Omaha, 1974—76, pres., CEO, 1976—81, chmn. bd., CEO, dir., 1981—93; chmn. bd., CEO RJR Nabisco Holdings Corp., NYC, 1993—95, chmn. bd., 1995—96, ret., 1996. Mem. exec. com. Nat. Commn. on Agrl., Trade and Export Policy, 1984—86; bd. dirs. Burlington Northern Inc., 1985—91, Norwest Bank Holding Co., 1987—97, DuPont, 1992—98, Valmont Industries, Inc., Peter Kiewit Sons, Inc., ConAgra, Inc. Pres. Mid-Am. Coun. Boy Scouts Am., 1983—84; mem. coun. Village of Excelsior, Minn., 1965—70, mayor Minn., 1974. Served US Army, 1946—48. Named Alumnus of Yr., U. Chgo. Grad. Sch. Bus., 1991. Mem.: U. Nebr. Lincoln Coll. Bus. Adminstrn. Alumni Assn. (hon. life mem.), Ak-Sar-Ben (gov.), Omaha C. of C. (chmn. 1979), U.S. C. of C. (bd. dirs., chmn. food and agrl. com.), Beta Theta Pi. Personal E-mail: olemike@west.com.

HARPER, CONRAD KENNETH, lawyer; b. Detroit, Dec. 2, 1940; s. Archibald Leonard and Georgia Florence (Hall) H.; m. Marsha Louise Wilson, July 17, 1965; children: Warren Wilson, Adam Woodburn. BA, Howard U., 1962; LLB, Harvard U., 1965; LLD (hon.), CUNY, 1990, Vt. Law Sch., 1994. Bar: NY 1966. Law clk. NAACP Legal Def. and Ednl. Fund, NYC, 1965-66, staff lawyer, 1966-70; assoc. Simpson Thacher & Bartlett, NYC, 1971-74, ptnr., 1974—93, 1996—2002, of counsel, 2003—; legal adv. US Dept. of State, Washington, 1993-96. Lectr. law Rutgers U., 1969-70; vis. lectr. law Yale U., 1977-81; cons. HEW, 1977; chmn. admissions and grievances com. U.S. Ct. Appeals, 2d cir., 1987-93; co-chmn. Lawyers' Com. for Civil Rights Under Law, 1987-89; mem. Permanent Ct. of Arbitration, The Hague, 1993-96, 1998—2004, Adminstrv. Conf. US, 1993-95, Harvard Corp., 2000-05; bd. dirs. NY Life Ins. Co., Pub. Svc. Enterprise Group. Trustee William Nelson Cromwell Found., 1990—, chmn. bd. 2005—, NY Pub. Libr., chmn. exec. com., 1990-93, vice-chmn. bd. trustees, 1991-93, Inst. Internat. Edn., 1992-93, Met. Mus. of Art, 1996—,Greenwall Found., 2006—; bd. mgrs. Lewis Walpole Libr., 1989-93; bd. visitors Fordham Law Sch., 1990-93, CUNY, 1989-93; vestryman Ch. of St. Barnabas, Irvington, NY, 1982-85; bd. dirs. Phi Beta Kappa Assocs., 1992-93; chancellor The Episc. Diocese of NY, 1987-92; bd. legal advisors Martindale-Hubbell, 1990-93. Recipient Lifetime Achievement award, Am. Lawyer mag., 2006. Fellow Am. Bar Found., NY Bar Found., Am. Coll. Trial Lawyers, Am. Acad. Arts and Scis.; mem. Am Philos. Soc. (v.p. 2005-), ABA (bd. editors jour. 1980-86), Nat. Bar Assn., NY State Bar Assn., Assn. Bar City N.Y. (chmn. exec. com. 1979-80, pres. 1990-92), Am. Law Inst. (mem. coun. 1985—, 2d v.p. 1998-2000, 1st v.p. 2000-04), Am. Assn. for Internat. Commn. Jurists (bd. dirs. 1988-93), Am. Soc. Internat. Law (mem. exec. coun. 1997-2000, exec. com. 1998-2000, counselor 2000-05), Acad. Polit. Sci. (bd. dirs. 1998—), Coun. Fgn. Rels., Grolier Club (coun. mem. 1993, 1997—2004), Century Assn., Harvard Club (mem. bd. mgrs. 1993), Phi Beta Kappa. Democrat. Episcopalian.

HARPER, DAVID TAYLOR, civilian military employee; b. LA, Feb. 3, 1959; s. Clarence Bluford Harper and Myrtle Marie Sparks, Dwain Sparks (Stepfather); m. Joyce Lee Van Leuvan, Jan. 15, 1996 (dec. Aug. 2004); m. Barbara Christine Jecz, Aug. 13, 1982 (div. Sept. 1, 1990); 1 child, Benjamin; stepchildren: Donald Drorbaugh, Deborah Drorbaugh. AAS, C.C. of the Air Force, Maxwell AFB, Ala., 1984; AA, U. Md., 1985; BS with honors, Calif. State U., Sacramento, 1988; MPA, Calif. State U., Carson, 1999. Spl. agt. Air Force Office Spl. Investigations, NYC, 1988—89, El Segundo, Calif., 1989—2005, spl. agent-in-charge Hanscom AFB, Mass., 2004—. Instr. criminal justice U. Phoenix, 2002—04. Tech., sgt. USAF, 1976—85. Mem.: ASPA, Acad. Polit. Sci., Am. Polit. Sci. Assn. (assoc.), Pi Alpha Alpha. Avocations: computers, writing, travel. Office: USAF Office Spl Investigations Detachment 102 Hanscom Afb MA 01731 Office Phone: 781-377-4607. Personal E-mail: dtharper@verizon.net.

HARPER, DONALD VICTOR, retired transportation and logistics educator, consultant; b. Chgo., Mar. 27, 1927; s. Victor Rudolph and Mildred Victoria (Safbom) H.; children: Christine Ann, Diane Elizabeth, David Victor. Student, Wright Jr. Coll., 1945, 46-47; BS in Journalism, U. Ill., Urbana, 1950, PhD in Econs., 1957. Instr. Coll. Commerce and Bus. adminstrn. U. Ill., Urbana, 1953-56; lectr. Carlson Sch. Mgmt. U. Minn., Mpls., 1956, asst. prof. Carlson Sch. Mgmt., 1956-59, assoc. prof., 1959-65, prof. transp. and logistics, 1965-97, chmn. dept. mgmt. and transp., 1967-70, dir. MBA and PhD programs, 1970-79, dir. PhD program, 1979-80, chmn. dept. mktg. and logistics mgmt., 1991-96; prof. emeritus, 1997—; cons. to bus. and govt. agys. Author: Economic Regulation of the Motor Trucking Industry by the States, 1959, Price Policy and Procedure, 1966, Transportation in America: Users, Carriers, Government, 2d edit, 1982; contbr. articles to profl. jours. Served with USN, 1945-46. Mem. Am. Econ. Assn. (Disting. Mem. award transp. and pub. utilities group 1988), Am. Mktg. Assn., Transp. Research Forum, Am. Soc. Transp. and Logistics, Transp. Club Mpls. and St. Paul, Assn. Transp. Law, Logistics and Policy. Home: 2451 Sheldon St Saint Paul MN 55113-3138 Office: U Minn Carlson Sch Mgmt 321 19th Ave S Minneapolis MN 55455-0438 Office Phone: 612-624-5833. Business E-Mail: dharper@csom.umn.edu.

HARPER, DOREEN C., nursing educator; Student, Albertus Magnus Coll., 1966-68; BSN, Cornell U., 1971; MSN, Catholic U., 1974; PhD in Human Devel., U. Md., 1980. Cert. adult nurse practitioner ANA. Home care nurse Child Devel. Ctr. R.I. Hosp., Providence, 1971; pub. health nurse Fairfax County Health Dept., Fairfax, Va., 1971-72; charge nurse adolescent mental health unit The Bancroft Inst., Falls Church, Va., 1973; college health nurse Trinity Coll., Washington, 1973-84; asst. prof. nursing dept. nursing George Mason U., Fairfax, Va., 1974-77, assoc. prof. nursing dept. nursing, 1980-82, 1987—, project dir. adult and gerontological nurse practitioner trg. grant, 1988-91, adult nurse practitioner student health svcs., 1990—, coord. nurse practitioner program Coll. Nursing and Health Scis., 1991—; adult nurse practioner Kaiser/Georgetown Cmty. Health Plan, Springfield, 1979-81; chair RN to BSN program, asst. prof.Sch. Nursing U. Md., Catonsville, 1982-86; adult nurse practitioner OB-GYN Assocs., Alexandria, Va., 1987-1990; dir. nurse practitioner program Sch. Medicine and Health Scis. George Washington U., Washington, 1994—; prof. nurse practitioner Univ. Mass. Med. Sch. Cons. in field; principal investigator Nat. Ctr. Nursing Rsch. NIH, 1989-92; presenter in field; mem. nursing task force Va. Area Health Edn. Ctrs., 1993—. Editor: Nursing Connections, 1987-89; editl. review bd. Advances in Nursing Sci., 1989-93; contbr. numerous chpts., articles to profl. jours. and books. Predoctoral rsch. fellow Nursing Rsch. Svcs. Adminstrn.U. Md., 1977-80; recipient: Nat. Inst. Mental Health traineeship award Dept. Health, Edn. and Welfare Catholic U. Am., 1972-74. Fellow Am. Acad. Nursing (nat. peer review com. 1980-88); mem. Va. Nurses Assn. (dist. VIII Outstanding Nurse of the Year award 1975, del. 1976, 81 conv., mem. joint med./nursing practice com. 1976-78, dist. 8 chmn. nominating com. 1981-82), Sigma Theta Tau (Kappa chpt. nominating com. 1978-79, Epsilon Zeta chpt. 1987—, nominating com. 1989-91). Home: 159 Robbins Rd Thompson CT 06277-2846 Office: Univ Mass Worcester 55 Lake Ave N Worcester MA 01655

HARPER, EMERY WALTER, lawyer; b. Hackensack, NJ, Feb. 25, 1936; s. Walter Van Saun and Dorothy Charlotte (Schmidt) H.; m. Judith Van Nest Hover, Sept. 9, 1961 (div. 1991); 1 child, Caroline Curry BA cum laude, Amherst Coll., 1958; LLB, Yale U., 1961. Bar: N.Y. 1962. Assoc. Lord Day & Lord, Barrett Smith, NYC, 1961-69, ptnr., 1970-93, Schnader, Harrison, Segal & Lewis, NYC, 1993-96, chmn. internat. maritime group, 1993-95; pres. Harper Cons., Inc., NYC, 1997—; of counsel Inman Deming LLP, 1998—2003, Law Offices Harry A. Inman, 2003—. Bd. dirs. The Shipping Network, Inc.; bd. dirs., founding mem. The Admiralty/Fin. Forum, Inc.; lectr. on maritime law Dalian, PRC, 1984; advisor U.S. del. to joint working group on liens and mortgages Internat. Maritime Orgn., 1st, 2d, 5th and 6th sessions UN Conf. on Trade and Devel., 1986-89; lectr. on admiralty and maritime financing; lectr. on ship fin. topics, Mex., Panama, Chile, Thailand, 1993-95; course dir. practice and techniques Financing Marine Assets and Ops., N.Y., 1995; organizer, pres. Am. Corps. in Coastwise Trade; participant U.S. Delegation to IMO/UNCTAD Joint Diplomatic Conf. on Maritime Liens and Mortgages, Geneva, 1993; cons. Inman Deming Internat., LLC, Washington, 1998—2003; del. to diplomatic conf. arrest of ships Internat. C. of C., 1999. Co-author: Essays on Maritime Liens and Mortgages and on Arrest of Ships, 1985; contbr. articles to profl. publs. Trustee The Gateway Sch., N.Y., 1975-83; deacon Brick Presbyn. Ch., 1970-76, elder, 1976-82, trustee, corp. sec., 1982-88; mem. legal adv. com. Liberian Shipowners Coun., 1988-2000; chmn. Subcom. on Liberian Maritime Law Revision, 1993-99; chmn. Marshall Islands Roundtable, 1999-2001; mem. Seatransport com. U.S. Coun. for Internat. Bus., 1987-91; dir. Cmty. Living Corp. Found., Inc., 2002—; bd. dirs. CLC Found., Inc., 2002—. With USAFR, 1961-67. Mem. ABA (chmn. admiralty and maritime law com., sect. internat. law), Assn. of Bar of City of N.Y. (mem. admiralty com. 1974-80, 90-93, 98-2000, chmn. 1977-80), Maritime Law Assn. (founding chmn. com. on Marine financing 1978—), Com. Maritime Internat. (internat. subcom. on maritime liens and mortgages), Marine Soc. City of NY, N.Y. Amherst Alumni Assn. (pres. 1975-77), Pilgrims Soc., Union Club, Down Town Club. Office: East Tower 1301 K St NW Ste 700 Washington DC 20005-3373 Home and Office: 200 E 57th St #18N New York NY 10022 Home Phone: 212-355-5114; Office Phone: 212-317-0686. Personal E-mail: eharper974@aol.com.

HARPER, GEORGE DANIEL, retired art educator; b. Glenville, W.Va., Jan. 14, 1947; s. Lewis Michael and Gladys Sadie Harper; m. Sharon Ann Harper. Cert. tchr. W.Va., 1970. Prof. emeritus Glenville State Coll., 1998—. Exhibitions include Farmyard Geometry (Named one of Top 100 Paint Am. Artist, 2006). Pub. newspaper cartoonist Glenville Dem., 1999. Scholar Tchg. Assistantship, W.Va. U., 1970—71. Mem.: W.Va. Artists & Craftsmen Guild (life), W.Va. Watercolor Soc. (life; region v trustee 1997). Democrat-Npl. Avocations: photography, political cartooning, travel. Home and Office: Harper Home Gallery 401 White Ave Harrisville WV Business E-Mail: georgeharper@zoominternet.net.

HARPER, GERARD EDWARD, lawyer; b. NYC, Feb. 2, 1953; s. Eugene Walter and Muriel (Drumgoole) H.; children: Amanda, Julia. BA, Rutgers U., 1975; JD, NYU, 1978. Bar: N.Y. 1980, U.S. Supreme Ct. 1986, D.C. 1989, U.S. Ct. Appeals (9th cir.) 1988), U.S. Ct. Appeals (2d cir.) 1991, U.S. Dist. Ct. (so. and ea. dists.) 1980, N.Y. 1985, U.S. Dist. Ct. (no. dist.) Calif., U.S. Dist. Ct. (D.C. cir.). Law clk. to hon. Judge George MacKinnon US Cir. Ct., Washington, 1978-79; assoc. Paul, Weiss, Rifkind, Wharton & Garrison, LLP, NYC, 1979-86, ptnr., 1986—. Gen. counsel, chmn. law com., mem. exec. com. NY Dem. State Com., NYC, 1987—, presl. elector, 1988; mem. rules com. Dem. Nat. Conv., 1996, 2000, 04. Editor-in-chief NYU Law Rev., 1977-78. Mem. ABA, N.Y. State Bar Assn., N.Y. County Lawyers' Assn., Assn. of Bar of City of N.Y., Order of Coif. Roman Catholic. Office: Paul Weiss Rifkind Wharton & Garrison LLP 1285 Avenue Of The Americas Fl 21 New York NY 10019-6028 Office Phone: 212-373-3000. E-mail: gharper@paulweiss.com.

HARPER, HENRY H., retired military officer; b. Ft. Benning, Ga., Aug. 24, 1934; s. H.M. and Frances Louise (Hearn) Harper; m. Helen Harpe, Apr. 2, 1960; children: Cynthia Jane, Linda Leigh BS, U. Md., 1964; MA, George Washington U., 1965; Disting. grad., Indsl. Coll. Armed Forces, 1973. Commd. officer U.S. Army, 1954, advanced through grades to maj. gen., 1980, dep. comdg. gen. Armaments Command Rock Island, Ill., 1977-79, dir. logistics U.S. European Command Stuttgart, Fed. Republic Germany, 1979-82, comdg. gen. Depot System Command Chambersburg, Pa., 1982-86, ret., 1986; corp. sr. v.p. Synovus Fin. Corp., Columbus, Ga., 1986-95; ret., 1995. Dir. Ga. State Golf Assn., 1999—. Chmn. bd. dirs. Easter Seals West Ga., Inc.; chmn., bd. dirs. Goodwill Industries, Springer Opera House; bd. dirs. Universal Bank. Mem. Assn. U.S. Army (bd. govs., dir. Chambers Fort chpt. 1982-85), Columbus C. of C. (bd. dirs.). Episcopalian. Avocations: golf, jogging. Personal E-mail: g2mmhm@knology.net.

HARPER, HILL (FRANK HARPER), actor; b. Iowa City, Iowa, May 17, 1966; BA cum laude, Brown Univ.; JD cum laude, Harvard Univ., MPA. Theater: Black Folk's Theater Co., Boston; Actor: (Films) Confessions of a Dog, 1993, Pumpkinhead II: Blood Wings, 1994, Drifting School, 1995, One Red Rose, 1995 (also writer), Get on the Bus, 1996, Hoover Park, 1997, Steel 1997, Hav Plenty, 1997, He Got Game, 1998, Park Day, 1998, The Nephew 1998, Beloved, 1998, Slaves of Hollywood, 1999, In Too Deep, 1999, Box Marley, 2000, The Skulls 2000, The Visit, 2000 (Best Actor, Method Fest, 2000), Higher Ed, 2001, Rockboy, 2002, The Badge, 2002, Love, Sex and Eating the Bones, 2003, Andre Royo's Big Scene, 2004, America Brown, 2004, My Purple Fur Coat, 2004, Constellation, 2005, Whitepaddy 2006, Max and Joshm 2006 (also writer), Premium, 2006, The Breed, 2006, 30 Days, 2006, TV movies: Zooman, 1995, Mama Flora's Family, 1998, Loving Jezebel, 1999, Lackawanna Blues, 2005; TV series: Holla, 2002, CSI: NY, 2004-; Author: Letters to a Young Brother, 2006 (NAACP Image award for best debut author, 2007). Named one of Sexiest Men Alive, People Mag., 2004; recipient W.E.B. DuBois Scholar award, 13th Annual Inner City Awards. Office: CSI: NY CBS TV City 7800 Beverly Blvd Los Angeles CA 90036*

HARPER, JAMES EDWARD, JR., academic administrator; b. Newnan, Ga., Apr. 6, 1964; s. James Edward and Lois Mae Harper; m. Jacqueline Sharon Layne, Aug. 4, 1984; children: James Edward III, Jessica Sharon. BA, Lee Coll., Cleve., Tenn., 1986; MDiv, Ch. of God Theol. Sem., Cleve., Tenn., 1990; D of Ministry, Fuller Theol. Sem., Pasadena, Calif., 2002. Ordained Minister Ch. of God, Cleve., Tenn., 1984. Min. of youth Princeton Ch. of God, NC, 1990—91, Farmington Heights Ch. of God, Wilson, NC, 1991—94, Coastal Cathedral Ch. of God, Savannah, Ga., 1994—97; sr. pastor Eastwood Ch. of God, Swainsboro, Ga., 1997—98; assoc. pastor Live Oak Ch. of God, Hinesville, Ga., 1998—2000; instr. in youth and family ministry Lee U., Cleve., Tenn., 2000—01, campus pastor and dir. of campus ministries, 2001—. Author: (text book) Launching A Forever Faith, 2004 (AIM/CTC Book of Yr., 2005). Min. Lee U., Cleve., 2000. Mem.: Nat. Youth Leaders Assn. (assoc.), Assn. Of Christians in Student Devel. (assoc.), Assn. of Youth Ministry Educators (assoc.), Alpha Gamme Chi (life). Conservative. Church Of God. Avocation: sports. Office: Lee Univ 1120 North Ocoee St Cleveland TN 37320-3450 Home Phone: 423-339-1352; Office Phone: 423-614-8420.

HARPER, JAMES WELDON, III, finance consultant; b. Frederick, Md., Mar. 3, 1937; s. James Weldon Jr. and Mildred Mary (Conaway) H. Student, Duke U. Coll. rep. Time, Inc., 1955-59; jr. exec. trainee Merrill Lynch Pierce Fenner and Smith, NYC, 1959-60; v.p. fin. planning Haight and Co., Inc., Washington, 1961-72; pres. fin. cons. Weldon Enterprises Ltd., Washington, 1973-95; founder, chmn., CEO emeritus Enviro Tek Corp. Internat., Waterford, Va., 1994—2003; founder, CEO Argicell.com, Inc., 2000—02; v.p. corp. devel. Matrix Tech., Va., 2003—. Former pres. U.S. Energy Conservation Service, Inc.; cons. Aries Corp.; nat. coord. Nat. Planned Giving Assocs., Inc., 1983-92; bd. dirs. 6 cos., 1962-91; involved with 115 corps., 98 partnerships; conservator Nat. Real Estate Trust for Health Care, Inc., 1987-92. Author 3 manuals. With U.S. Army, 1959. Methodist. Office Phone: 202-365-1515.

HARPER, JENNIFER, elementary school educator; BA, Castleton State Coll.; MA, Univ. Vt. Tchr., 1992—; state math. network leader, 1999—; tchr. Cavendish Town Elem. Sch., Proctorsville, Vt. Named Vt. Tchr. of Yr., 2006; recipient Presdl. award for Excellence in Math. and Sci. Tchg., 2003. Office: Cavendish Town Elem Sch 573 Main St PO Box 236 Proctorsville VT 05153 Business E-Mail: Jharper@fc.windsorsw.k12.vt.us.*

HARPER, JUDSON MORSE, retired university administrator, consultant, educator; b. Lincoln, Nebr., Aug. 25, 1936; s. Floyd Sprague and Eda Elizabeth (Kelley) H.; m. Patricia Ann Kennedy, June 15, 1958; children: Jayson K., Stuart H., Neal K. BS, Iowa State U., 1958, MS, 1960, PhD, 1963. Registered profl. engr., Minn. Instr. Iowa State U., Ames, 1958-63; dept. head Gen. Mills, Inc., Mpls., 1964-69, venture mgr., 1969-70; prof., dept. head agrl. and chem. engring. Colo. State U., Ft. Collins, 1970-82, v.p. rsch. and info. tech., 1982-2000, interim pres., 1989-90, spl. asst. to the pres., 2000—04. Cons. USAID, Washington, 1972-74, various comml. firms., 1975—; Lady Davis scholar Technion, Haifa, Israel, 1978-79. Author: Extrusion of Foods, 1982, Extrusion Cooking, 1989; editor newsletter Food, Pharm. & Bioengring. News, 1979-83, LEC Newsletter, 1976-89; contbr. articles to profl. publs.; patentee. Mem. sch. bd. St. Louis Park, Minn., 1968-70. Recipient Disting. Svc. award Colo. State U., 1977, Fulbright-Hayes scholar, 1978, Svc. award Centro de Investigaviones y Asistencia Technologica de Estado de Chihuahua, Chihuahua, Mex., 1980, Food Engring. award Dairy and Food Industry Supply Assn. and Am. Soc. Agrl. Engrs., 1983, Cert. of Merit, USDA Office Internat. Coop. and Devel., 1983, Cert. of Merit, Consejo Nacional de Ciencia y Technologie en Mexico, Mexico City, 1984, Profl. Achievement Citation Iowa State U., 1986, Cert. Appreciation Chinese Inst. of Food Tech., 1987, Charles Lory Pub. Svc. award, 1993, Hammer award The Nat. Performance Rev., 1994. Fellow: AAAS, Inst. Food Technologists (Internat. award 1990); mem.: Am. Soc. Engring. Edn. (com. chmn. 1976—77), Am. Chem. Soc., Am. Soc. Agrl. Engrs. (com. chmn. 1973—78, hon. engr. Rocky Mountain region), Am. Inst. Chem. Engring. (dir. 1981—84), Rotary Internat. Ind. United Meth. Ch. Home and Office: 1818 Westview Rd Fort Collins CO 80524-1891 Personal E-mail: judson.harper@colostate.edu.

HARPER, LAURA LEE, principal; b. Apr. 22, 1959; d. M. Herman and Mary Jo Walters; m. Greg Noel Harper, Dec. 25, 1959. BA, Fort Lewis Coll., Durango, Colo., 1989; MA, N. Mex. State U., Las Cruces, 1995. Tchr. Kirtland (N.Mex.) Ctrl. Sch., 1989—95; vice prin. Aztec H.S., 1995—98, prin., 1998—2004, Dolores (Colo.) Secondary Sch., 2004—. Mem. adv. bd. Sch. to Career Program, Farmington, N.Mex., 1997—2000; bd. mem. San Juan Family Preservation, 1989—2004; cons. Svc. Learning, Dolores, Colo., 2004—, Continuous Improvement, 2004—. Recipient Prin. of Yr., 2000, Quality N. Mex. Piñon recognition, Quality N. Mex. Road Runner recognition. Mem.: Kiwanis, Rotary. Office: Dolores Secondary 1301 Ctrl Ave Dolores CO 81323 Office Phone: 970-882-7289.

HARPER, LYNN D., biologist; BA, MS in Cell and Molecular Biology, U. Bridgeport. Tech. writer, asst. mgr. Bionetics Corp., Washington, 1982—83; tech. dir. space sys. divsn. Gen. Electric Mgmt. and Tech. Svcs. Co., Washington, 1983—86; program mgr. advanced missions and spl. projects space life scis. divsn. NASA, 1986—89; chief advanced life support divsn. NASA Ames Rsch. Ctr., 1990—93, acting chief advanced life support divsn., 1993—94, sr. sys. engr. space scis. divsn., 1994—96, lead, integrative studies. Office: NASA Ames Rsch Ctr MS 239-15 Bldg 244 Rm 148 Moffett Field CA 94035

HARPER, MARSHA WILSON, religious organization administrator; b. Wilmington, Del., Apr. 14, 1942; d. Woodrow and G. Lucille (Watson) Wilson; m. Conrad Kenneth Harper, July 17, 1965; children: Warren Wilson, Adam Woodburn. BA, Boston Coll., 1964; student, NYU, New Sch. Social Rsch., 1966—67. Cert.: (mediator); paralegal. Jr. caseworker Boston Redevel. Authority, 1964—65; caseworker F. Shervier Home Hosp., Riverdale, NY, 1965—68; exec. dir. Westchester Putnam chpt. ACLU, White Plains, NY, 1971—76; cons., conf. planner Westchester County Women's Ctr.-Minority Women's Conf.; devel. cons. Congregations Linked Urban Strategy Effect Renewal, Yonkers, NY, 1979—81, assoc. dir., 1981, exec. dir., 1982—87; cons., 1987—93; Diocesan deployment officer Episcopal Diocese Washington, 1993—96; faculty CREDO Inst., 1997—2007. Bd. dir. Assn. Episcopal Colls., NYC, 1988—92; interim cons. Diocese N.Y., 1991—93, transition cons., 1996—2005, former chair social concerns com.; trustee Va. Theol. Sem., 1999—2007; vestry St. Barnabas Episcopal Ch., Irvington, NY, 1986—90, Ch. Epiphany, NYC, 2006—. Mem. NAACP. Mem.: Jane Austen Soc. N.Am., Bronte Lit. Soc., Edith Wharton Lit. Soc. Democrat. Episcopalian.

HARPER, MARVIN BRUCE, pediatrics educator, hospital administrator; MD, U. Calif., San Francisco, 1986. Asst. prof. pediats. Harvard Med. Sch., Boston, 1986—; assoc. dir. clin. computing Children's Hosp. Boston, 2004—. Office: 300 Longwood Avenue Boston MA 02115 Office Phone: 617-355-6624.

HARPER, MARY SADLER, wealth advisor and relationship manager; b. Farmville, Va., June 15, 1941; d. Edward Henry and Vivien Morris (Garrett) Sadler; m. Joseph Taylor Harper, Dec. 21, 1968; children by previous marriage: James E. Hatch III, Mary Ann Hatch Czajka. Cert., Fla. Trust Sch., U. Fla., 1976. Registered securities rep., Fla., gen. securities prin., fin. and ops. prin., options prin., mcpl. securities prin., investment mgmt. advisor, wealth adv. specialist. Dep. clk. Polk County Cts., Bartow, Fla., 1964-67; rep. Allen & Co., Lakeland, Fla., 1967-71; with First Nat. Bank, Palm Beach, Fla., 1971-89, sr. v.p., 1984-86, S.E. Bank N.A., Palm Beach, 1986-89, 1st United Bank, 1997-98; pres., CEO Palm Beach Capital Svcs., Inc., 1986-88; mng. dir. Investment Svcs., Palm Beach Capital Svcs. Divsn., 1988; v.p. investments, trustee J.M. Rubin Found, Palm Beach, 1983—; v.p. sec., sr. v.p. investment divsn. Island Nat. Bank & Trust Co., 1989-97; chair, dir., pres., CEO Island Investment Svcs., Inc. (A Wachovia Co.), Palm Beach, 1989-98; also bd. dirs., mng. exec., sr. v.p. Wachovia Investments, Palm Beach, 1998-2000; sr. v.p. Wachovia Bank N.A., 1999-2000; sr. v.p., investment mgmt. advisor Wachovia Securities, Inc., 2000—05; sr. v.p. investments, wealth adv. specialist Legg Mason, Wood, Walker, Inc., 2000—05; dir. pvt. banking Credit Suisse Securities, LLC, 2005—. Adv. coun. Nuveen, 1987-99, pres.'s coun., 2001, chmn.'s coun., 2002-05; adv. bd. Kidsanctuary, Inc. Adv. panel Palm Beach County YWCA, 1985, mem. endowment com., 1990—93; mem. pres.'s club Jupiter Med. Ctr. Found., 1989—; life mem. Juno Beach Civic Assn.; profl. endowment com. Rehab. Ctr. for Children and Adults, 1998—2002; chmn. Palm Beach adv. bd. Palm Beach Nat. Bank & Trust Co., 2000—01; dir., v.p. Friends of Abused Children, 2001—03; mem. Fla. History Mus.; dir. Ctr. for Family Svcs., 2003—; bd. dirs. Biomotion Found., 2002—05, pres., 2004—05; mem. Palm Beach Hist. Soc., 2004—. Mem. Inst. CFPs (assoc.), Nat. Assn. Securities Dealers (dist. com. 1995-98), Fin. Planners Assn., Fin. Women Internat., Fla. Securities Dealers Assn., Exec. Women of Palm Beaches (fin. com. 1985-92), Internat. Soc. Palm Beach (treas., trustee 1986—), Jupiter Med. Ctr. Found. (pres.'s club 1989—), Loxahatchee Hist. Soc. (bd. dirs. 1991-93, chair devel. com. 1992-93), Sebring, Fla. Hist. Soc. (life), Jupiter/Tequesta C. of C. (assoc.), United Daus. of Confederacy, Gov.'s Club, Pub. Securities Assn. (exec. rep.), Jonathans Golf Club, Rotary (Palm Beach Found. com. 1990—, bd. dirs. 1992-94, 2001-, co-chair, 1997, chair Rotary Internat. Found., Palm Beach 1998-2006, Paul Harris fellow 1992), Lighthouse Ctr. for the Arts (life), Norton Art Mus. (patron), Palm Beach Yacht Club, Ritz Carlton Spa and Club (Jupiter), Palm Beach County Hist. Soc., Palm Beach Preservation Found. Democrat. Baptist. Avocations: reading, history. Home: 800 Ocean Dr PH

4 Juno Beach FL 33408-1730 Office: Credit Suisse 420 Royal Palm Way Ste 200 Palm Beach FL 33480 Office Phone: 561-366-2501. Home Fax: 561-626-7978. Business E-Mail: mary.harper@credit-suisse.com.

HARPER, RICHARD HENRY, film producer, director; b. San Jose, Calif., Sept. 15, 1950; s. Walter Henry and Priscilla Alden H.; m. Ann Marie Morgan, June 19, 1976; children: Christine Ann, Paul Richard, James Richard. Show designer Walt Disney Imagineering, Glendale, Calif., 1971-76; motion picture producer, dir. Harper Films, Inc., La Canada, Calif., 1976—. Producer, dir. (films) Impressions de France, Disney World, Fla., 1982, Magic Carpet Round the World, Disneyland, Tokyo, 1983, American Journeys, Disneyland, Calif., 1985, Collecting America, Nat. Gallery Art, Washington, 1988, Hillwood Mus., Washington, 1989, Journey Into the 4th Dimension for Sanrio World, Journey Into Nature for Sanrio World, Japan, 1990, Masters of Illusion, Nat. Gallery of Art, Washington, 1992. Recipient more than 150 awards world-wide for outstanding motion picture prodn. including Silver trophy Cannes Internat. Film Festival, 2 Gold awards Internat. Festival of the Ams., 1981, 82, 14 Golden Eagle C.I.N.E. awards, 1977-92, Emmy award Nat. Acad. TV Arts and Scis., 1993-. Mem. Acad. of Motion Picture Arts and Scis.

HARPER, ROBERT, actor; b. NYC, May 19, 1951; BA in English with high distinction, Rutgers U., 1974. Mem. repertory co. Arena Stage, Washington, 1974-76. Guest artist Rutgers U., New Brunswick, NJ, 1977, New Brunswick, 84. Actor: Long Wharf Theater, 1978, 1984, Theater for a New City, 1981; (Broadway plays) Once in a Lifetime, 1978, The Inspector General, 1978, The American Clock, 1980; (TV films) J. Edgar Hoover, The Wrong Man, Not Quite Human, Payoff, Running Mates, The Story of Bill W, Paper Angels, Ruby Ridge; (TV series) Newhart, Roseanne, Murphy Brown, Wiseguy, L.A. Law, NYPD Blue, Law and Order, Philly, Frank's Place, Commander-in-Chief; (films) Creepshow, 1982, Once Upon a Time in America, 1984, Amazing Grace and Chuck, 1987, Twins, 1989, Final Analysis, 1992, Deconstructing Harry, 1997, The Insider, 1999. Adviser charity events The Laugh Factory, Hollywod, 1981—. Named commencement spkr., Rutgers U., 2007; recipient Kennedy Ctr. award, Am. Coll. Theater Festival, 1974; Regents fellow, U. Calif., 1974. Mem.: SAG, ACLU (sponsor Garden Event 1994), MLA (spkr. conv. 1996), Actor's Equity Assn., Am. Soc. Aesthetics, Acad. TV Arts and Scis., Acad. Motion Picture Arts and Scis. Office: 8721 Santa Monica Blvd West Hollywood CA 90069-4507

HARPER, ROBERT AUGUSTUS, lawyer; b. Fla., Aug. 15, 1946; s. Robert Augustus Sr. and Ida Frances (Allen) H.; m. Jill Beth Levin, June 2, 1977; children: Robert Augustus III, Myriah Beth, Alexandra Rose. BA, U. Fla., 1968, JD, 1970. Bar: Fla. 1970, US Ct. Appeals (5th cir.) 1973, US Dist. Ct. (no., mid. and so. dists.) 1973, US Supreme Ct. 1976, US Dist. Ct. (so. dist.) Tex. 1977, US Ct. Appeals (2d cir.) 1978, US Ct. Appeals (3d cir.) 1980, US Ct. Appeals (11th cir.) 1981, US Dist. Ct. (so. dist.) Ala. 1983, US Dist. Ct. (ea. dist.) Mich. 1987, US Ct. Appeals (1st cir.) 1987, US Ct. Appeals (9th cir.) 1987, US Dist. Ct. (no. dist.) Ga. 1988, US Ct. Appeals (7th cir.) 1988, Ga. 1988, US Ct. Appeals (6th and 4th cirs.) 1989, US Dist. Ct. (so. dist.) Ill. 1990, US Tax Ct. 1994, US Dist. Ct. (mid. dist.) Ga. 1996. Pvt. practice, Tallahassee, Fla. Expert witness Fla. Legislature, 1996—2000; chmn. jud. nominating commn., First Dist. Ct. Appeal, Fla., 1999-2000; guest lectr. U. Fla., Fla. State U.; moot ct. judge Contbr. articles to profl. publs. Ret. capt. USAR. Named one of Florida's Legal Elite, 2005, Best Lawyers in America, Legal Elite, 2006; named to America's Top Lawyers, 2006. Mem. Fla. Bar, Am. Inns of Ct. (master lawyer), Alpha Tau Omega (pres.). Democrat. Presbyterian. Avocations: gardening, law. Office: Harper & Harper Law Firm PA 325 W Park Ave Tallahassee FL 32301-1413 Home Phone: 850-224-8600; Office Phone: 850-224-5900. Office Fax: 850-224-9800. Business E-Mail: harperlaw@harperlawfirm.com.

HARPER, ROBERT WALTER, III, museum director; b. Tallahassee, Apr. 8, 1945; s. Robert Walter Harper, Jr. and Dorothy Peters Harper; m. Alicia Anne Von Hoefling, Oct. 29, 1972; children: Robert Walter Harper, IV, Wiley Martel. BA in Art History, Fla. Atlantic U., Boca Raton, 1972. Curator Hist. St. Augustine Preservation Bd., Fla., 1973—80; exec. dir. Lightner Mus., St. Augustine, 1980—. Contbr. articles to profl. jours. Mem.: Fla. Trust Hist. Preservation (bd. mem. 1989—92), Hist. Archtl. Rev. Bd. (licentiate; chmn. 1992—98), St. Augustine Art Assn. (assoc.; bd. mem. 1979—82), Nat. Trust Hist. Preservation (assoc.), Am. Assn. Museums (assoc.). Democrat-Npl. Episc. Avocations: sailing, gardening, reading, travel, art. Home: 232 Saint George Saint Augustine FL 32084 Home Phone: 904-824-2874. Business E-Mail: lightner@aug.com.

HARPER, SANDRA STECHER, academic administrator; b. Dallas, Sept. 21, 1952; d. Lee Roy and Carmen (Crespo) Stecher; m. Dave Harper, July 6, 1974; children: Justin, Jonathan. BS in Edn., Tex. Tech. U., 1974; MS, U. N. Tex., 1979, PhD, 1985; grad. mgmt. devel. program, Harvard U., 1992. Speech/reading tchr. Nazareth H.S., Tex., 1974-75; speech/English tchr. Collinsville H.S., Tex., 1975-77, Pottsboro H.S., Tex., 1977-79; instr. comm. Austin Coll., Sherman, Tex., 1980-82; rsch. asst. U. N. Tex., Denton, 1982-84; from asst. prof. to assoc. prof. comm. McMurry Coll., Abilene, Tex., 1985-95; dean Coll. Arts and Scis. McMurry U., Abilene, 1990-95, asst. dir. NEH univ. core curriculum project; v.p. for acad. affairs Oklahoma City U., 1995-98; provost, v.p. for acad. affairs Tex. A&M U., Corpus Christi, 1998—2006, prof. comm., 1998—2006; pres. Our Lady of the Lake Coll., Baton Rouge, 2006—. Vis. instr. comm. Austin Coll., Sherman, 1985; CIES mentor for Russian adminstr. from Moscow State U., Ulyanovsk, 1995-96; mem. adv. bd. Coll. Am. Indian Devel., 1995-98; critic judge Univ. Interscholastic League, Austin, 1980-93; mem. adv. bd. Univ. Rsch. Consortium, Abilene, 1990-95; mem. formula adv. com., mem. instrn. and operation formula study com. Tex. Higher Edn. Coordinating Bd., 1999-2004, mem. adv. com. AA in Tchg., 2003-04; mem. working group Am. Assn. State Colls. and Univs. Am. Democracy Project, 2002-06; mem. student fin. assistance commn. and tuition trust authority, La., 2006—, master plan postsecondary edn. workforce devel. workgroup, 2007—. Contbr. articles to profl. jours.; author: To Serve the Present Age, 1990; co-author U.S. Dept. Edn. Title III Grant; mem. editl. bd. Soc. for the Advancement of Mgmt. Jour., 1999—. Planner TEAM Abilene, 1991; del. Tex. Commn. for Libr. and Info. Svcs., Austin, 1991; chair Abilene Children Today: Life and Cmty. Skills Task Force, 1994-95; del. Oklahoma City Ednl. TV Consortium, 1997-98; bd. dirs. South Tex. Pub. Broadcasting, 1998-2004, Leadership Corpus Christi; mem. gov.'s exec. devel. program Class XVIII, LBJ Sch. Pub. Affairs, U. Tex., Austin, 1999, S. Tex. Regional Leaders Forum, 2001-02. Media Rsch. scholar Ctr. for Population Options, 1989; recipient Corpus Christi YWCA Women in Careers Secondary Edn. award, 2000. Mem. Nat. Comm. Assn., Am. Assn. Higher Edn., Tex. Pub. Univ. Chief Acad. Officers Assn. (v.p. 2003-04, pres. 2004-05), Soc. for Advancement of Mgmt. (Mgmt. Excellence award 2005). Democrat. Roman Catholic. Office: Our Lady of Lake Coll 7434 Perkins Rd Baton Rouge LA 70808 Office Phone: 225-768-1710. Business E-Mail: sandra.harper@ololcollege.edu.

HARPER, SEAN, medical products executive; MD, U. Calif., San Francisco. Postdoctoral fellow Phillip A. Sharp Lab. MIT, 1991—96; sr. dir. clin. genomics Merck Rsch. Labs.; v.p. devel. Amgen, Inc., 2002, v.p. global regulatory affairs and safety, sr. v.p. global devel., corp. chief med. officer, 2007—. Mem. PhRMA Regulatory Affairs Coordinating Com. Office: Amgen Inc One Amgen Center Dr Thousand Oaks CA 91320-1799 Office Phone: 805-447-1000. Office Fax: 805-447-1010.*

HARPER, SHIRLEY FAY, nutritionist, educator, consultant, lecturer; b. Auburn, Ky., Apr. 23, 1943; d. Charles Henry and Annabelle (Gregory) Belcher; m. Robert Vance Harper, May 19, 1973 (dec. Mar. 2000); children: Glenda, Debra, Teresa, Suzanna, Cynthia. BS, Western Ky. U., 1966, MS, 1982. Cert. nutritionist and lic. dietitian, Ky. Dir. dietetics Logan County Hosp., Russellville, Ky., 1965-80; cons. Western State Hosp., Hopkinsville, Ky., 1983-84, instnl. dietetic adminstr., 1984-88; dietitian Rivendell Children's Psychiat. Hosp., Bowling Green, Ky., 1988-90; instr. nutrition Western Ky. U., Bowling Green, 1990-92. Cons. Auburn (Ky.) Nursing Ctr., 1976-95, Belle Meade Home, Greenville, Ky., 1980—, Brookfield Manor, Hopkinsville, 1983—, Sparks Nursing Ctr., Ctrl. City, Ky., 1983—, Muhlenberg Cmty. Hosp., Greenville, 1989-2000, Russellville Health Care Manor, 1978-83, 92-, Westlake Cumberland Hosp., Columbia, Ky., 1993-, Franklin-Simpson Meml. Hosp., Franklin, Ky., 1993-2003, Lakeview Health Care Ctr., Morgantown, Ky., 2001-03, Morgantown Care and Rehab. Ctr., 2003-, Trigg County Personal Care Home, Cadiz, 2002-, Gainsville Manor, Hopkinsville, 2002-; nutrition instr. Madisonville (Ky.) C.C., 1995-98. Mem. regional bd. dirs. ARC of Ky., Frankfort, 1990-96; vice chair ARC of Logan County, 1992-93, chmn., 1993-96, 97—; bd. dirs. Logan County ARC United Way, 1993—; co-chair adv. coun. devel. disabilities Lifeskills, 1992-93, adv. coun. Lifeskills Residential Living Group Home, 1993-2000, human rights adv. coun., 1994-2000; chair Let's Build our Future Campaign; nutrition del. Citizen Am. Program to USSR, 1990; adv. chair for vocat. edn., Russellville; mem. adv. coun. for home econs. and family living, We. Ky. U., 1990-93; bd. dirs. ARC of Logan County for United Way, 1993—; del. 24th Internat. Congress on Arts and Comm., Oxford (Eng.) U., 1997. Recipient Outstanding Svc. award Am. Dietetic Assn. Found., 1993, Outstanding Svc. award Barren River Mental Health-Mental Retardation Bd., 1987, Svc. Appreciation award Logan-Russellville Assn. for Retarded Citizens, 1987, Internat. Woman of Yr. award for contbn. to Nutrition and Humanity, Internat. Biog. Assn., 1993-94, World Lifetime Achievement award Am. Biog. Inst., 1995; inaugurated Lifetime Dep. Gov., Am. Biog. Rsch. Bd., 1995, Pres.'s award ARC of Logan County, 1996, award of excellence Oxford, Eng. Internat. Congress on Arts and Comm., Internat. Sash of Acad., Am. Biog. Inst., 1997. Mem. Am. Dietetic Assn., Nat. Nutrition Network, Ky. Dietetic Assn. (pres. Western dist. 1976-77, Outstanding Dietitian award 1984), Bowling Green-Warren County Nutrition Coun., Nat. Ctr. for Nutrition and Dietetics (charter), Ky. Nutrition Coun., Logan County Home Economist Club (sec. 1994-95, 1999-2000, v.p. 1995-96, 2000-01, pres. 1996-97, 2001—), Internat. Biog. Assn., Internat. Platform Assn., Diabetes Care and Edn., Dietitians in Nutrition Support, Cons. Dietitians in Health Care, Phi Upsilon Omicron (pres. Beta Delta alumni chpt. 1994-96, Outstanding Alumni award 1997). Avocations: music, drawing and art, poetry, reading, cake decorating. Home and Office: 443 Hopkinsville Rd Russellville KY 42276-1286

HARPER, STEVEN R., finance educator; b. Kingsville, Tex. s. Lorren Harper and Ann Wickstrom; m. Sara Greer, Aug. 0, 1991; children: Nicholas, Emily, Leslie. BS in Engring. Physics, U. Calif., Berkeley, 1981; MEE, U. Va., Charlottesville, 1988; MA in Nat. Security and Strategic Studies, Naval War Coll., Newport, RI, 1994; MBA, U. Ill., Urbana-Champaign, 2003, PhD in Sys. and Entrepreneurial Engring., 2006. Naval submarine officer USN, Washington, 1981—2001; asst. prof. mgmt. James Madsion U., Harrisonburg, Va., 2007—. Exec. officer USS Springfield, Groton, Conn., 1994—96. Comdr. USN, 1996—2001. Decorated Joint Merritorious medal Ballistic Missile Def. Orgn. Office: James Madision Univ Zane Showker Hall Harrisonburg VA 22807 Home Phone: 217-351-7606; Office Phone: 540-568-3232. Business E-Mail: harpersr@jmu.edu.

HARPER, TERRANCE G., journalism organization administrator; Exec. dir. Phi Kappa Psi Frat., 1990—99; fin. advisor UBS PaineWebber Inc., 1999—2001; dir. fundraising Kiwanis Internat. Found., Indpls., 2001—02; exec. dir. Soc. Profl. Journalists & Sigma Delta Chi Found., Indpls., 2002—. Office: Soc Profl Journalists Eugene S Pulliam Nat Journalism Ctr 3909 N Meridian St Indianapolis IN 46208 Office Phone: 317-927-8000 ext. 220. E-mail: tharper@spj.org.*

HARPER, WILLIARD FLEMMETT, language educator; b. Cleve., Aug. 1, 1924; s. Huel and Annie Mae (Benton) H. BA, Morehouse Coll., 1947; MA in Langs., Case Western Res. U., 1948; cert. d'etudes, McGill U., Montreal, Can., 1949; PhD, Sorbonne, Paris, 1954. Prof. French and Spanish Wiley Coll., Marshall, Tex., 1948-50; prof., chmn. humanities Dillard U., New Orleans, 1950-54, Albany (Ga.) State Coll., 1954-59; Smith-Mundt and Fulbright scholar U.S. Govt., 1959-65; UNESCO expert Kinshasa, Zaire, 1965-68, Institut Pedagogique, Butare, Rwanda, 1968-70; staff devel. program UN, NYC, 1970-84; cons. UN Devel. Program, NYC, 1984—; U.S. lang. escort, UN resident coord., UNDP resident rep., escort officer U.S. Dept. State, Washington, 1987—. Adj. prof. Cuyahoga Community Coll., Cleve., 1989—. Mem. adv. com. Notre Dame Coll., Cleve., 1989; apptd. humanities coun., Gov. Ohio; bd. trustees Cleve. Mus. Nat. History; bd. dirs. Am. Sickle Cell Anemia Assn.; trustee The Cleve. Mus. Natural History, bd. dirs.; coord. UN, Africa. Staff sgt. U.S. Army, 1941-43. Ford Found. fellow, 1951-52. Mem. Huachucans (treas. 1987-90). Baptist. Avocations: bridge, chess, reading, classical music. Home: 2202 Acacia Park Dr Lyndhurst OH 44124-3858

HARPHAM, VIRGINIA RUTH, violinist; b. Huntington, Ind., Dec. 10, 1917; d. Pyrl John and Nellie Grace (Whitaker) Harpham; m. Dale Lamar Harpham, Dec. 25, 1938; children: Evelyn, George. AB, Morehead State U., 1939. Violinist Nat. Symphony Orch., Washington, 1955-90, prin. of second violin sect., 1964-90; mem. Lywen String Quartet, 1960-69, Nat. Symphony String Quartet, 1973-82. Named to Hall of Fame, Morehead State U., 2003. Episcopalian. Home: 5354 43d St NW Washington DC 20015-2008 Personal E-mail: vharp.13@verizon.net.

HARR, LUCY LORAINE, public relations executive; b. Sparta, Wis., Dec. 2, 1951; d. Ernest Donald Harr and Dorothy Catherine (Heintz) Harr Vetter BS, U. Wis., Madison, 1976, MS, 1978. Lectr. U. Wis., Madison, 1977-82; from asst. editor to editor Everybody's Money Everybody's Money Credit Union Nat. Assn., Madison, 1979-84, mgr. ann. report, 1984-92, v.p. pub. rels., 1984-93, sr. v.p. credit union devel., 1993-96, sr. v.p. consumer rels. and corp. responsibility, 1996-97; owner Providing Solutions, Stoughton, Wis., 1997—; ptnr. Fourth Lake Comm., LLP. Dir. consumer appeals bd. Ford Motor Co., Milw., 1983-87. Author: Credit Union Basic Guide to Retirement Planning, 1998. Bd. dirs. Madison Area Crimestoppers, 1982-84; Midwest coord. of ofcls. USA Triathlon, 2003. Recipient Clarion award, 1982. Mem. Women in Comm. (pres. Madison profl. chpt. 1982-83, nat. v.p. programs 1986-87, vice-chair/sec. nat. interim bd. 1996-97, chair nat. bd. dirs. 1997-2001), Internat. Assn. Bus. Communicators (program chair dist. meeting 1981), Am. Soc. Assn. Execs. (Gold Circle award 1984) Avocations: bicycling, reading. E-mail: lharr@providing-solutions.com.

HARRAL, JOHN MENTEITH, lawyer; b. Ancon, Panama Canal Zone, June 25, 1948; s. Brooks Jared and Sara (Mumma) H.; m. Marjorie Van Fosson, Aug. 15, 1970; children: Alyse, Jessica. BBA, U. Miss., 1971, JD, 1974. Bar: Miss. 1974, U.S. Dist. Ct. (so. dist.) Miss. 1974, U.S. Ct. Appeals (5th cir.) 1977. Law clk. to Judge J.P. Coleman, U.S. Ct. Appeals (5th cir.), New Orleans, 1978-79; ptnr. White & Morse, Gulfport, Miss., 1979-92, Eaton & Cottrell, P.A., Gulfport, 1993-97; sole practitioner Gulfport, 1997—2002; mem. Butler, Snow, O'Mara, Stevens & Cannada, PLLC, Gulfport, 2002—. Mem. Miss. Gov.'s Jud. Nominating Com., 1990-93; instr. bus. law William Carey Coll.; mem. adv. bd. dirs. Whitney Nat. Bank. Mentor Gulfport Schs., 1991—; lay eucharistic min. St. Mark's Episcopal Ch., Gulfport, 1980, vestryman, sr. and jr. warden, Sunday sch. tchr.; chmn. Episc. Svcs. for Aging, Mississippi Gulf Coast, 1981—85, also bd. dirs.; bd. dirs. Make-A-Wish Found., Miss., Walter Anderson Mus. Art, Ptnrs. for Stennis, vice chair, 2006; founder, pres. Gulfport Excellence, 1991—; bd. dirs. Christmas in April, Harrison County, 1994—2000, pres., 1995—96; bd. dirs. Lynn Meadows Discovery Ctr., 1996—, sec., exec. com., 1997—2000; pres. Gulfport Downtown Assn., Inc., 1997—98, 2004, dir., 1998—2001; Miss. commr. Nat. Conf. Commrs. on Uniform State Laws, 2000—04; mem. exec. com. Gulf Coast Bus. Coun., 2006—; bd. dirs. Gulfport Main St., 2006—, pres. Lt. JAGC USNR, 1974—78. Named to South Miss. Leadership Hall of Fame, 2002. Fellow: Miss. Bar Found. (trustee 2002—05); mem.: ABA, Gulf Coast Law Inst. (bd. dirs. 1988—93), Harrison County Bar Assn. (pres. young lawyers sect. 1982, pres. 1987—88), Miss. Bar Assn. (bd. dirs. young lawyers divsn. 1982—84, commr. 1991—94), Miss. Coast C. of C. (bd. dirs.), Gulfport C. of C. (bd. dirs. 1995—97, pres. 1997, John Harral Spirit of Edn. award 2004), Gulfport Bus. Club (pres. 2001—02, founder), Bayou Bluff Tennis Club, Rotary (pres. 2002—03). Republican. Home: 12 Old Oak Ln Gulfport MS 39503-6210 Office Phone: 228-575-3000. E-mail: john.harral@butlersnow.com.

HARRELD, JAMES BRUCE, information technology executive; b. Gallipolis, Ohio, Dec. 12, 1950; s. James Baldwin and Ann Elizabeth (Lascu) Harreld; m. Mary E. Gillilan; children: Sara Elisabeth, Kelly Lynn, James Christopher, Matthew Parker. BS, Purdue U., 1972; MBA, Harvard U., 1975. Asst. to exec. sec. Sigma Chi, Evanston, Ill., 1972—73; asst. to pres. Epsilon Data Mgmt., Boston, 1973—74; v.p., dir. Boston Cons. Group, Boston, Munich, Chgo., 1975—82; v.p. Dart & Kraft, Northbrook, Ill., 1982—84; sr. v.p. strategy and devel. Kraft, Inc., Glenview, Ill., 1984—89, sr. v.p., chief info. officer, 1988—89, Kraft Gen. Foods, Glenview, 1989—92, sr. v.p. mktg. svcs. and info. systems, 1992—93; pres. and dir. Boston Chicken, Inc., Golden, Colo., 1993—95; sr. v.p., chief strategist IBM, Armonk, NY, 1995—2005, sr. v.p., chief mktg. officer, strategist, 2006—. Adj. prof. mgmt. Kellogg Grad. Sch. Bus. Adminstrn. Northwestern U., 1993—95. Co-author: Survival Manual, 1973. Recipient Balfour Province award, Sigma Chi, 1972, Significant Sig award, 1989, recipient Disting. Engring. Alumnus award, Purdue U., 1991. Mem.: Bachelor Gulch Club, Stanwich Club, Amelia Island Plantation Club, Amelia Island Club, Hot Springs Club, Harvard Club (Boston), Denver Country Club, Alpha Pi Mu, Tau Beta Pi. Republican. Presbyterian. Avocations: reading, golf. Office: IBM New Orchard Rd Armonk NY 10504 Home Phone: 203-972-2683; Office Phone: 914-499-5443. Business E-Mail: harreld@us.ibm.com.

HARRELL, BEVERLY ELLEN, mathematics professor; b. Stillwater, Okla., July 1, 1940; d. Floyd Henry Davis and Vera Althea Taylor; m. Gerold Lee Harrell, June 3, 1960; children: Gerold Lee Jr., Roy Henry. MEd, Ctrl. State U., Edmond, Okla., 1968. Math tchr. grades 9-12 Milfay HS, Okla., 1963—64; math tchr. grades 8-12 Jones HS, Okla., 1964—67; math tchr. grades 7-12 Luther HS, Okla., 1967—72; substitute tchr. grades 9-12 Okla. City Pub. Schs., 1974—76; math tchr. grades 7-12 Ctrl. City Bapt. Ch., Oklahoma City, 1976—78; coll. math. prof. Rose State Coll., Midwest City, Okla., 1978—. Ch. mem. Kingspark Bible Bapt. Ch., Oklahoma City, 1976—. Recipient Leadership award, Nat. Inst. Staff and Orgnl. Devel., U. Tex., 1995. Mem.: Okla. Coun. Tchrs. Maths. Democrat. Baptist. Avocations: photography, swimming. Office: Rose State College 6420 SE 15th St Midwest City OK 73110 Home Phone: 405-277-3360. Business E-Mail: bharrell@rose.edu.

HARRELL, CARL RANDALL, plastic surgeon; b. Waycross, Ga., Sept. 27, 1952; MD, Med. Coll. Ga., Augusta, 1983. Cert. Am. Bd. Plastic Surgery, 1991. Resident gen. surgery Baylor Coll. Medicine, Houston, 1983—86, fellow microsurgery, 1986—87, resident plastic surgery, 1987—89; with Mease Hosp., Fla., Helen Ellis Hosp., Fla., Clearwater Cmty. Hosp., Fla.; founder, dir. Fountain of Youth Inst. Featured Harrell's Instant Facelift: (TV series) Entertainment Tonight. Fellow: Am. Coll. Surgeons; mem.: AMA, So. Med. Assn., Am. Soc. Laser Medicine, Am. Soc. Plastic Surgeons, Am. Soc. Aesthetic Plastic Surgery. Achievements include patents for Humallagen, a dermal filler for facial wrinkles. Office: Fountain of Youth Inst 34156 US Hwy 19 N Palm Harbor FL 34684 Office Phone: 813-781-0818. Office Fax: 727-787-7512.

HARRELL, CARLTON (BENJAMIN CARLTON HARRELL), retired editor, writer; b. Mamie, NC, Oct. 1, 1929; s. Taylor Smith Jr and Nellie Augusta (Gallop) Harrell; m. Audrey Jeanine Tarkenton, Apr. 26, 1952; children: Melissa Ann, Sheila Lynn. Student, U. N.C., 1947-49. Reporter Daily Advance, Elizabeth City, N.C., 1950-52, 53-56, Goldsboro (N.C.) News-Argus, 1956-57, Durham (N.C.) Sun, 1957-64, state editor, 1964-65, asst. city editor, 1965-69, city editor, 1969-72, mng. editor, 1972-90; assoc. editor Herald-Sun, Durham, 1991-96, editor emeritus, columnist, 1996—. 2d lt US Army, 1952—53. Mem.: Hist Preservation Soc Durham, Res Officers Asn, Am Soc Newspaper Eds. Home and Office: 410 Argonne Dr Durham NC 27704-1428

HARRELL, CHARLES LYDON, JR., retired lawyer; b. Norfolk, Va., Oct. 22, 1916; s. Charles Lydon Sr. and Ethel Theresa (Toone) H.; m. Martha de Weese Guild, Feb. 5, 1943 (dec. March 1991); children: Charles Lydon III, John Morgan, Marshall Guild, deWeese Toone; m. Lynn Aikens Johnson, July 13, 1993. BA, Randolph-Macon Coll., Ashland, Va., 1938; LLB, U. Richmond, 1941. Bar: Va. 1940, US Dist. Ct. (ea. dist.) Va. 1946, US Bankruptcy Ct. (ea. and we. dist.) Va. 1946, US Ct. Appeals (4th cir.) 1947, U.S. Ct. Internat. Trade 1950, US Supreme Ct. 1952. Ptnr. Harrell & Landrum, Norfolk, 1947-76; pvt. practice Norfolk, 1987—2004; ret., 2003. Commr. in chancery Cir. Ct. Princess Anne County, 1950—76; commr. in chancery City Norfolk, 1955—76; spl. justice Princess Anne County, 1952—65. Mem. health care consumer coun. Naval Hosp., Portsmouth, 1980-90; mem. coun. of ch. Ghent United Meth. Ch., 1950-2004, tchr. Bible class, 1966—, master, mem. com. Boy Scouts of Am., Sea Scouts; mem. Coun. of Ministries, 1955-88, chmn. commn. on Christian concerns Meth. Ch., 1971-76; co-founder, chmn., pres. bd. dir. Ghent Venture, Inc.; v.p. Norfolk Seaman's Soc., 1970-, bd. dir., 1990—, v.p.; bd. dir. Handicaps Unltd. of Va., legis. chmn., legal advisor; vol. prayer counsellor Christian Broadcast Network, 1977-93; co-founder, bd. dir. Va. Assn. of Blind, 1981—; dir. Norfolk Interfaith Coalition for the Elderly, Tidewater Christian Outreach Project; pres. Mobility on Wheels, Inc., 1980-83, bd. dir., 1977—, v.p. 2000—; mem. com. therapeutic recreation of handicapped people City of Norfolk, 1991-98; co-founder, v.p., dir. New Life Devel.; pro bono counsel Tidewater Legal Aid Soc., 1941—. Comdr. USN, to 1962. Decorated 9 campaign medals, 5 combat stars; recipient Cross Mil. Svc., UDC. Mem. ABA, Norfolk-Portsmouth Bar Assn., Va. State Bar Assn. (Lawyers Helping Lawyers), Va. Bar Assn., Jud. Soc., Christian Legal Soc., Am. Legion, VFW (past comdr.), Jr. C. of C., Jesus to the World Evangelistic Assn. (co-founder, bd. dirs., v.p., chmn. bd.), Christian Legal Soc., Gideons, Masons, Shriners, Kiwanis, Ret. Officers Assn., The Fleet Res., Tin Can Sailors Assn., Mine Warfare Assn., The Caine Mutineers, McNeil Law Soc., Phi Beta Kappa, Omicron Delta Kappa (sec. Tidewater Alumni chpt.), Tau Kappa Alpha. Avocations: swimming, scuba diving, spear fishing. Home: 4464 Ocean View Ave Virginia Beach VA 23455

HARRELL, EDWARD HARDING, wine festival executive; b. Richmond, Va., Dec. 1, 1939; s. Emmett Livingston Harrell and Martha Mason (Harding) Harrell Owen; m. Diane Greer Dickerson, July 18, 1965 (dec.); children: Sara Wesley, Katherine Harding Cole. BA, U. Va., 1962. Advt. salesman Richmond Newspapers, 1963-68, asst. advt. dir., 1975-82; gen. mgr. Westover Pub., Richmond, 1968-71; mktg. dir. Media Gen. Fin., Richmond, 1971-74; asst. gen. mgr. Pitts. Press, 1982-86; pres. Harrell Assocs., 1986-89, Tribune Rev., 1989—2006, Pitts. Wine Festival, 2006—. Bd. dirs. Conv. and Vis. Bur., Pitts., 1985—87, Pitts. Dance Coun., 1985—2000; pres., bd. dirs. Sweetwater Arts Ctr., Sewickley, Pa.,

1985—94, Va. Mus. Natural Hist., 1987—94, Pitts. Downtown Partnership, 1994—2004, Pitts. Cultural Trust Bd., 1994—, Phipps Conservatory, 1997—2004, Opportunities Made Equal Bd., 1997—99, Press Club Western Pa., 1995—; pres. City Theatre, 1994—. Capt. US Army, 1962—66. Mem. Newspaper Assn. Am., Duquesne Club (Pitts.), Edgeworth Club (Sewickley). Democrat. Episcopalian. Avocations: sailing, reading. Office: 20 Stanwix St Pittsburgh PA 15222 Office Phone: 412-281-2681. Personal E-mail: eharrell@pittsburghwinefestival.com.

HARRELL, GARY PAUL, lawyer; b. Texas City, Tex., July 8, 1952; s. James Eugene Jr. and Mary Alice Harrell. BS, U. Tex., 1977, MA, 1979; cert. mgmt. healthcare facilities, UCLA, 1984; JD cum laude, Lewis & Clark Coll., Portland, Oreg., 1991. Bar: Oreg. 1991, Wash. 2006, Calif. 2006, U.S. Dist. Ct. (fed. dist.) Oreg. 1991; diplomate Am. Coll. Healthcare Execs. Staff/charge nurse Healthcare Facilties, Austin, Tex., 1972-78; gen. mgr. Nursing Support Svcs., Austin, 1978-80; dir. edn. Downey (Calif.) Cmty. Hosp., 1980-84; v.p. patient care Grande Ronde Hosp., La Grande, Oreg., 1984-88; assoc. Lane Powell Spears Lubersky, Portland, Oreg., 1990-94; ptnr. Harrell & Nester, LLP, Portland, 1994—2006; sr. counsel Cath. Healthcare West, Sacramento, 2006—. Adj. prof., asst. prof. Calif. State U., Long Beach, 1980-84; pres. Oreg. State Bd. Nursing, Portland, 1987-90. Contbr. chapters to books. With USNR, 1970-74. Recipient Am. Jurisprudence award, 1989. Fellow: Am. Coll. Health Care Adminstrs. (past pres. Oreg. chpt.), Healthcare Fin. Mgmt. Assn. (past pres. Oreg. chpt.); mem.: Wash. State Bar, Calif. State Bar, Am. Health Lawyers Assn., Oreg. Assn. Nurse Attys. (past pres.), Oreg. State Bar (chair, past chair health law section). Avocations: flying, sailing, motorcycling. Office: Cath Healthcare West Legal Dept 3400 Data Dr Rancho Cordova CA 95670 Office Phone: 916-851-2000.

HARRELL, GLENN T., JR., judge; BA, U. Md., 1967, JD, 1970. Bar: Md. 1970. Assoc. O'Malley, Miles & Harrell, 1973—76, ptnr., 1977—91; assoc. county atty. Prince George's County, 1971—73; judge at large Ct. Spl. Appeals, 1991—99; judge Md. Ct. Appeals, Prince George's County, Md., 1999—. Chair bd. dirs. Jud. Inst. Md., 2006—; chair Commn. on Jud. Disabilities, 1996-98; mem. exec. com. Md. Jud. Conf., 1997-99; adj. prof. legal writing Sch. Law U. Balt., 1997-2005; lectr. in field. Mem. Md. Bar Assn., Prince George's County Bar Assn., Md. Bar Found., J. Franklyn Bourne Bar Assn. Office: Ct Appeals PO Box 209 Upper Marlboro MD 20773-0209 Office Phone: 301-952-2716. Business E-Mail: glenn.harrell@courts.state.md.us.

HARRELL, HENRY HOWZE, tobacco company executive; b. Richmond, Va., Sept. 18, 1939; s. Theron Rice and Susan Howze (Haskell) H.; m. Jean Covington Camp, Feb. 7, 1970; children— Susan Hampton, Shelby Madison AB, Washington and Lee U. V.p. Universal Leaf Tobacco Co., Inc., Richmond, 1974-81, sr. v.p., 1981-82, exec. v.p., 1982-86, pres., 1986-88, pres., chief exec. officer, 1988-91; chmn., chief exec. officer Universal Corp. (formerly Universal Leaf Tobacco Co., Inc.), 1991—2002; chmn., dir. Universal Corp. Bd. dirs. Jefferson Bankshares Inc., Charlottesville, Va.; mem. bd. visitors James Madison U., Harrisonburg, Va. Mem. Forum Club, Commonwealth Club, Phi Beta Kappa, Omicron Delta Kappa. Clubs: Country of Va., Deep Run Hunt (bd. dirs. 1981-83), Ocean First Golf, Sunningdale Golf, Kinloch, Foundry Golf. Republican. Episcopalian. Avocations: fishing, gardening.

HARRELL, JERRY DEWITT, ophthalmologist, director; b. Port Arthur, Tex., Sept. 13, 1930; s. Jerry DeWitt and Carrie Belle (Sterrett) Harrell; m. Elizabeth Jane Cooke, Aug. 29, 1952; children: Kathleen Harrell Storm, Deborah Harrell Reining, David DeWitt. BA, Wheaton Coll., 1952; MA, U. Pa., 1957; MD, Jefferson Med. Coll., 1961; DTM & H, London Sch. Hygiene and Tropical Medicine, 1990. Diplomate Am. Bd. Ophthalmology. Fellow Mayo Clinic, Rochester, Minn., 1966—68; med. missionary Wycliffe Bible Translators, Yarinacocha, Peru, 1968—71, Bolivia, 1974—75; resident in ophthalmology Gorgas Army Hosp., Balboa, Panama, 1971—74; col., chief surgery US Army Hosps., 1975—90; med. dir. Lighthouse For Christ Eye Ctr., Mombasa, Kenya, 1990—. Contbr. articles to profl. jours. Med. officer US Army, 1961—65. Decorated Legion of Merit; recipient Hon. Pub. Svc. award, Panama Canal Co., 1985, Humanitarian award, Soc. Mil. Ophthalmologists, 1998. Fellow: ACS, Royal Soc. Tropical Medicine and Hygiene, Am. Acad. Ophthalmology. Republican. Presbyterian. Avocations: tennis, target shooting, reading. Home: 411 Whitefield Ave Saint Simons Island GA 31522 Office: Lighthouse for Christ Eye Ctr Abdel Nasser Rd Mombasa Kenya

HARRELL, JOHN MICHAEL, military officer; b. Newport News, Va., Feb. 12, 1963; s. Jack Harrell and Ellen Arnold. BA in Polit. Sci., Va. Tech, Blacksburg, 1984—86; attended, Va. Commonwealth U., Richmond, 1993. Cert. surface warfare officer USN, 1990. USN tchr. Surface Warfare Officers Sch., USS Juneau (LPD-10), San Diego, 1986—91; USN reservist, 1992—; sales assoc. Richmond, 1994—95; comml. real estate property mgr. Carey Winston Co., JBG Properties, TrizecHahn Properties, DC, 1995—2001; dep. dir., pub. safety Naval Dist. Wash., USN, DC, 2001—03; action officer J5, US European Command, USN, Stuttgart, Germany, 2003—04; facilities support specialist Comdr., Navy Installations, DC, 2004—05; adminstrv. officer Topographic Engrng. Ctr., ERDC, USACE, Alexandria, Va., 2005—; commdg. officer NR Naval Security Force, Indian Head, 2005—. Coord. combined fed. campaign USS Juneau (LPD-10), San Diego, 1989, coord. naval relief soc., 1989; coord. combined fed. campaign Topographic Engrng. Ctr., Alexandria, Va., 2005—06. Decorated Navy Achievement medal Navy Res. Ctr., Navy Commendation medal Naval Dist. Wash., Joint Svc. Achievement medal US European Command. Mem.: US Naval Inst. (corr.), Res. Officers Assn. (life), Naval Res. Assn. (life), Cadets Alumni Assn. (corr.; Va. Tech Corps.), Orders & Medals Soc. Am. (corr.), Am. Polit. Items Collectors (corr.), VFW (corr.), Am. Legion (corr.). Independent. Roman Cath. Home Phone: 703-379-4548.

HARRELL, RAY EVANS, performing company executive, conductor, educator; b. Ada, Okla., Dec. 3, 1941; s. Ray E. and Cleo Mae Harrell, William O.A. Rockko; m. Stephanie Rose Weems, June 27, 2005; 1 child, Jane Angela. BA, U. Tulsa, 1964; MM, Manhattan Sch. Music, 1973. Cert. in Rubenfeld synergy method Rubenfeld Ctr., NYC, 1979. Commd. piano tchr. Tulsa (Okla.) U., 1962—64; vocal soloist U.S. Army Field Band, Fort George G. Meade, Md., 1964—66, US Army Chorus, Washington, 1966—70; tchr. voice, performance, opera and vocal anatomy Manhattan Sch. Music, NYC, 1978—86; founder, artistic dir. Magic Cir. Opera Repertory Ensemble Inc., NYC, 1978—; master voice tchr. Magic Cir. Tng., NYC, 1978—; summer opera dir. Mannes Coll. Music, NYC, 1987—89; artistic dir., prodr. Am. Masters Arts Festival Biennial, NYC, 2003—. Lectr. on Donald Schoen Tchrs. Coll., Columbia U., NYC, 1988—89; co-leader MCORE Florentine Conf. on Arts and Econs. in Am., Washington, 2004; singer Miramax Films - Naqoyqatsi, 2001—02; rec. prodr. Magic Cir. Opera Repertory Ensemble, NYC, 1990—; dir. Magic Cir. Awards. Singer: (movie) Pocahontas, 1994 (Oscar, Grammy, Golden Globe awards, 1995); author: (libretto) A Gypsy Carmen. Lectr., panel mem. non-govtl. orgns. UN, NYC, 2000; Cherokee priest Nuyagi Keetoowah Soc., Inc., NYC, 1988—2005. Served with US Army, 1964—70. Regional Finalist, Met. Opera, 1969. Mem.: The Rec. Acad. (life mem.), Phi Mu Alpha. Liberal. Traditional Cherokee Keetoowah. Achievements include design of Magic Circle American Arts centers; Magic Circle training for chamber opera; America's first traditional Cherokee University; Cirque du Soleil approved artist listing. Office: Magic Circle Opera Repertory Ensemble 200 W 70th St Ste 6-C New York NY 10023 Home Phone: 212-724-2398; Office Phone: 212-724-2398. Personal E-mail: mcore@nyc.rr.com.

HARRELL, RICHARD GODWIN, alcohol/drug abuse services professional; s. Raliegh Clinton and Valarie Charmaine Harrell; m. Thanom Buathanong, Apr. 15, 2006. MS, Georgetown U., Washington, D.C., 1978; MA, San Jose State U., Calif., 2002. Cert. Calif. Assn. Alcohol and Drug Abuse Counselors, 2002. Addictions rsch. assoc. Stanford U., Calif., 1978—2000; adolescent program dir. Camp Recovery Ctrs., Scotts Valley, Calif., 2000—. Ednl. cons. Adolescent Placement Svcs., Los Gatos, Calif., 1998—. Author: The Adolescent Recovery Process (Therapeutic Counselor of Yr., 2004). Mem. Big Bros. Big Sisters, Los Gatos, Calif., 1992, Santa Cruz Mental Health Adv. Bd., Calif., 1996—2004; elections officer State of Calif., Los Gatos, 1998; mem. ACA, LA. Capt. US Army, 1969—73, US/Viet Nam. Achievements include research in high cortisol levels associated with teen suicide. Home Phone: 408-661-6943. Personal E-mail: rgh4u2u2@yahoo.com.

HARRELL, SAMUEL MACY, agribusiness executive; b. Indpls., Jan. 4, 1931; s. Samuel Runnels and Mary (Evans) H.; m. Sally Bowers, Sept. 2, 1958 (div.); children: Samuel D., Holly Evans, Kevin Bowers, Karen Susan, Donald Runnels, Kenneth Macy. BS in Econs., Wharton Sch., U. Pa., 1953. Pres., chmn. bd., chief exec. officer, chmn., exec. com. Early & Daniel Industries, Cin., 1971—; chmn. bd., chmn. exec. com. Early & Daniel Co., Cin., 1971—; chmn. bd., chief exec. officer, chmn. exec. com. Tidewater Grain Co., Phila., 1971—. Dir. Harriman Inst. Columbia U.; bd. dirs. Wainwright Bank & Trust Co., Wainright Abstract Co., Nat. Grain Trade Council, U.S. Feed Grains Council; mem. Chgo. bd. Trade Contbg. author: The Status of Agribusiness in Russia and the CIS. Dir. Harriman Inst., Columbia U. With AUS, 1953-55. Mem. Nat. Assn. Cert. Valuation Analysts, Inst. Bus. Appraisers, Am. Soc. Farm Mgrs. & Rural Appraisers, Am. Soc. Agrl. Cons., Internat. Bus. Brokers Assn., Young Pres.'s Orgn., U. Pa. Alumni Assn. (past pres.), Terminal Elevator Grain Mchts. Assn. (dir.), Millers Nat. Fedn. (dir.), Assn. Operative Millers, Am. Soc. Bakery Engrs., Am. Fin. Assn., Council on Fgn. Relations, Fin. Exec. Inst., N.Am. Grain Export Assn. (dir.), Mpls. Grain Exchange, St. Louis Mchts. Grain Exchange, Buffalo Corn Exchange, Delta Tau Delta (Past prs. Ind. alumni) Clubs: Columbia, Indpls. Athletic, Woodstock, Traders Point Hunt, Dramatic, Players, Lambs (Indpls.); Racquet (Phila.); University (Washington and N.Y.C.). Lodges: Masons, Rotary. Presbyterian. Office: EDI Internat Inc 3200 Teton Pines Dr Wilson WY 83014 Home: 15787 Imperial Point Ln Wellington FL 33414-7114 Office Phone: 307-734-6504. E-mail: samharrell@hotmail.com.

HARRELSON, CLYDE LEE, retired secondary school educator; b. Baton Rouge, Nov. 20, 1946; s. Hezzie Clyde and Marguerite Lucille (Tucker) Harrelson. BA, Southeastern La. U., 1968; MA, La. State U., 1974, EdS, 1980, postgrad., 1981, So. U., 1982. Cert. social studies and English tchr., prin., supr. La. Tchr. English East Baton Rouge Parish Sch. Bd., 1970—2003, McKinley Mid. Magnet Sch., Baton Rouge, 1982—2001, dean of students, 1998—2001; tchr. social studies Ctrl. HS, 2002—03; ret., 2003; tchr. practitioner advisor/mentor Teach La. Consortium/La. Resource Ctr. for Educators, 2003—. Mem. Arts Coun. Greater Baton Rouge, Found. Hist. La., La. Preservation Alliance, Nat. Trust Hist. Preservation, Colonial Williamsburg Found., NCCJ, La. Dem. Com., Nat. Dem. Com.; mem. exec. com. East Baton Rouge Parish Dems., 1981—85, 1996—2004. Mem.: Smithsonian Instn., Mus. Modern Art, Met. Mus. Art, New Orleans Mus. Art, Baton Rouge Gallery, La. Endowment for the Humanities, Old State Capitol Assocs., La. Arts and Sci. Ctr., La. State U. Mus. Art, Kiwanis, Phi Delta Kappa. Episcopalian. Home: 3101 Highland Rd 109 Baton Rouge LA 70802-7814

HARRELSON, KEN, sports broadcaster; b. Woodruff, SC, Sept. 4, 1942; married Profl. baseball player Kansas City Athletics, 1963-66, 67; profl. baseball player Washington Senators, 1966-67, Boston Red Sox, 1967-69, Cleve. Indians., 1969-71; profl. golfer, 1971; baseball broadcaster Boston Red Sox, 1975-81; exec. v.p. baseball ops. Chgo. White Sox, 1985-86; Guest reporter Sta. WMAQ-TV, Chgo., 1981-85; broadcaster N.Y. Yankees, NYC, 1987-90; baseball broadcaster Chgo. White Sox, 1981—85, 2001—. Office: care Chicago White Sox 324 W 35th St Chicago IL 60616-3622

HARRELSON, WALTER JOSEPH, minister, educator; b. Winnabow, NC, Nov. 28, 1919; s. Isham Danvis and Mabel (Rich) H.; m. Idella Aydlett, Sept. 20, 1942; children: Marianne McIver, David Aydlett, Robert Joseph. Student, Mars Hill Coll., NC, 1940-41, Litt.D. (hon.), 1977; AB, U. NC, 1947, Litt.D. (hon.), 1994; B.D., Union Theol. Sem., 1949, Th.D., 1953; postgrad., U. Basel, Switzerland, 1950-51, Harvard, 1951-53; D.D. (hon.), U. of South, 1974, Christian Theol. Sem., 1992. Instr. philosophy U. N.C., 1947; ordained to ministry Baptist Ch., 1949; tutor asst. Union Theol. Sem., 1949-50; prof. Old Testament Andover Newton Theol. Sch., 1951-55; dean, assoc. prof. Old Testament U. Chgo. Div. Sch., 1955-60; prof. Old Testament Div. Sch., Vanderbilt U., Nashville, 1960-75, chmn. grad. dept. religion, 1962-67, dean, 1967-75, Disting. prof. Hebrew Bible, 1975-90, prof. emeritus, 1990—, dir. Lilly Ministry Project, 1990-94; interim dean Disciples Div. House, 1993-94; prof. Wake Forest U., 1994-96, adj. univ. prof. Divinity Sch., 1996—. Dir. Ecumenical Inst. Advanced Theol. Studies, Jerusalem, 1977-78, 78-79; chmn. transl. com. New Rev. Standard Version of the Bible, 2000; vis. prof. Brite Div. Sch. Tex. Christian U., 1992, Boston Coll., 1991, 93; mem. ch. rels. com. U.S. Holocause Meml. Mus. Author: Jeremiah, Prophet to the Nations, 1959, Interpreting the Old Testament, 1964, From Fertility Cult to Worship, 1969, 80, The Ten Commandments and Human Rights, 1980, rev. edit., 1997, (with Rabbi R.M. Falk) Jews and Christians: A Troubled Family, 1990, (with Bruce M. Metzger and Robert C. Dentan) The Making of the New Revised Standard Version of the Bible, 1991, (with Rabbi R.M. Falk) Jews and Christians: In Pursuit of Social Justice, 1996, Festschrift, Passion, Vitality, and Foment: The Dynamics of Second Temple Judaism, 2001; co-author, editor: Teaching the Biblical Languages, 1967, New Interpreter's Study Bible, 2003; editor, contbr.: Israel's Prophetic Heritage, 1962; editl. chmn. Religious Studies Rev., 1974-80; assoc. editor Mercer Dictionary of the Bible, 1990; assoc. editor Mercer Commentary on the Bible, 1995. Dir. project to film Ethiopian Manuscripts, NEH, 1972-84; bd. dirs. Dead Sea Scrolls Found., 1991—, Planned Parenthood Assn., Nashville; active ch. rels. com. U.S. Holocaust Meml. Coun. Traveling fellow Union Theol. Sem., 1949; Am. Coun. Learned Socs. fellow, 1950-51, 70; exch. fellow U. Basel, 1950-51; fellow Inst. Internat. Edn., 1950-51; Fulbright rsch. scholar, Rome, 1962-63; Harvie Branscomb Disting. prof. Vanderbilt U., 1977-78, Alexander Heard Disting. Svc. prof., 1985-86; NEH fellow, Rome, 1983-84; recipient Thomas Jefferson prize, 1987-88, Alumni/ae award Vanderbilt U., 1989, Festschrift, Justice and the Holy, 1989, Union Theol. Sem., N.Y.C., 2003, NC award for Literature, 2004. Mem. NAS (mem. ethics com. Inst. Medicine), Soc. for Values in Higher Edn. (pres. 1972-74), Soc. Bibl. Lit. (pres. 1972), Am. Acad. Religion, Cath. Bibl. Assn., Phi Beta Kappa. Home and Office: 3605 Bechler Ln Winston Salem NC 27106 Office Phone: 336-655-2940. Personal E-mail: walterharrelson@bellsouth.net.

HARRELSON, WOODY, actor; b. Midland, Tex., July 23, 1961; s. Charles Voyde Harrelson & Diane Lou Oswald; m. Nancy Simon, June 29, 1985 (div. 1986); m. Laura Louie, Jan. 11, 1998; children: Deni Montana, Zoe Giordano, Makani Ravello. BA in Theater Arts and English, Hanover Coll., Ind. Actor (TV series) Cheers, 1985-93 (Emmy nomination 1986, 87, 89, 91, Emmy award 1988); (TV movies) Bay Coven, 1987, Killer Instinct, 1988, Mother Goose Rock 'n' Rhyme, 1990; (films) Wildcats, 1986, Eye of the Demon, 1987, Cool Blue, 1990, Doc Hollywood, 1991, Ted and Venus, 1991, L.A. Story, 1991, White Men Can't Jump, 1992, Indecent Proposal, 1993, The Cowboy Way, 1994, I'll Do Anything, 1994, Natural Born Killers, 1994, The Sunchaser, 1996, The People vs. Larry Flynt, 1996, Kingpin, 1996, Wag the Dog, 1997, The Thin Red Line, 1998, The Hi-Lo Country, 1998, Edtv, 1999, Austin Powers: The Spy Who Shagged Me, 1999, Grass (voice), 1999, Play It to the Bone, 1999, American Saint, 2000, Scorched, 2002, Anger Management, 2003, She Hate Me, 2004, After the Sunset, 2004, North Country, 2005, The Prize Winner of Defiance, Ohio, 2005, A Prarie Home Companion, 2006, (voice) Free Jimmy, 2006, A Scanner Darkly, 2006; (TV appearances) Will & Grace, 2001; (TV host) Comedy Club All-Star IV, 1990; understudy Broadway prodn. Biloxi Blues; starred in Off-Broadway prodns. The Boys Next Door, 1987, The Zoo Story; actor, playwright Two on Two, Furthest From the Sun, 1993. Avocations: sports, writing, juggling, chess, playing guitar, Elvis Presley, playing piano. Office: Creative Artists Agy 9830 Wilshire Blvd Beverly Hills CA 90212-1825

HARRIBANCE, SEAN LALSINGH, parapsychologist; b. Fyzabad, Trinidad and Tobago, Nov. 11, 1939; arrived in U.S., 1969; s. Harribance Singh and Sampatia Batchasingh; m. Christine Ann Comyn, Feb. 28, 1971; children: Linnea Christine, Sean Lalsingh Jr. Cashier Trinidad Bus Svc., San Fernando, 1959—69; part-time rschr. Parapsychology Lab., Dr. Hamlyn Dukhan, Trinidad, 1966—69; parapsychol. rsch. subject Found. for Rsch. on Nature of Man, Durham, NC, 1969—73; part-time rsch. subject Psychical Rsch. Found., Durham, NC, 1969—73, 1980; pres. Sean Harribance Inst. for Parapsychology, Inc., 1980—. Part-time parapsychology rsch. subject Laurentian U., Sudbury, Ont., Can., 1996, 97, 2000; hon. dir. Sean Harribance Inst. for Parapsychology Rsch., Inc., Tex., Sean Harribance Inst. Parapsychology Found., Trinidad; affiliated with engring. dept. Duke U., 1975. Co-author: This Man Knows You, 1976; contbr. articles to profl. jours. including Internat. Jour. Psychophysiology, Internat. Jour. Neuroscience, Perceptual and Motor Skills, Jour. Parapsychology, Jour. Am. Soc. for Psychical Rsch., Jour. Neuropsychiatry and Clin. Neuroscience, Procs. Parapsychol. Assn., Rsch. in Parapsychology. Named Hon. Citizen, recipient Key to City, City of Baton Rouge, 1975, hon. lt. col. aide-de-camp, Ala. State Militia, 1975. Home: PO Box 908 Sugar Land TX 77487-0908 Office Phone: 281-980-3860. Personal E-mail: harribance@yahoo.com.

HARRIELL, KYSHA, athletic trainer, educator; b. Washington, July 25, 1973; d. Fred and Patricia Ann Harriell. BS in Athletic Tng., U. Pitts., 1996; MS in Edn. in Sports Medicine, U. Miami, 1999, MS in Edn. in Sports Adminstrn., 2001. Cert. athletic trainer Nat. Athletic Tng. Assn. BOC, lic. Fla. Asst. athletic trainer U. Miami, Coral Gables, Fla., 1997—, adj. prof., 1999—2005. Mem. Ethnic Diversity Adv. Coun., Dallas, 1997—2004. Mem.: Amnesty Internat., Delta Sigma Theta (assoc.). Democrat. Avocations: travel, sports, reading. Home: 7355 SW 82d St # 7 Miami FL 33143 Office: U Miami 5821 San Amaro Dr Coral Gables FL 33146 Home Phone: 305-665-7584; Office Phone: 305-284-4131. Office Fax: 305-284-3008. Personal E-mail: harriell@bellsouth.net. E-mail: kharriell@miami.edu.

HARRIES, JAMES THEODORE, psychologist; b. Buffalo, June 25, 1930; s. James Theodore Harries and Lula Anna Willer-Harries; m. Karen Louise Davies, June 27, 1964 (dec. June 1997). Student, Art Inst. Buffalo, 1948-50, Albright-Knox Art Sch., 1955-58; BFA, U. Buffalo, 1958; MEd, SUNY, Buffalo, 1960, PhD, 1970. Lic. psychologist, ednl. psychology, Mass.; health svc. provider cert. Mass. Bd. Registration Psychologists. Cert. sch. psychologist Amherst (N.Y.) Sch. Sys., 1966-67; adj. prof. Canisius Coll. Grad. Sch., Buffalo, 1968-69; dir. doctoral program sch. psychology Boston U., 1969-73; dir. Mental Health Ctr. Salem (Mass.) Coll., 1973-77, coord. grad. studies in counseling, 1977; pres. Behaviorl Devel. Assocs., P.C., Brookline, Boston, 1977—. Pres. Western N.Y. Pers. and Guidance Assn., Buffalo, N.Y., 1966-68; vis. prof. U. Heidelberg, Germany, 1971; resident prof. U.S. Dept. Def., Boston U., Karlsruhe, Germany, 1971. Author: Psychological Dimensions of Prostate Cancer, 1999; editor: 38 Psychological Measures: A Reference for Counselors, 1969; editor The Counselor, 1964-65, Jour. N.Y. State Counselors Assn., 1967-68. Active Buffalo Soc. Artists, 1954-69; bd. mem. Mental Health Assn. Erie County, Buffalo, 1966; co-founder N.Y. State Sch. Counselors Assn., 1966. Recipient George E. Hutcherson Hon. award State N.Y. Counselors Assn., 1968. Mem. APA, Am. Coll. Forensic Examiners, Inc., Am. Assn. Clin. Counselors, Nat. Assn. Sch. Psychologists (nat. dir. New Eng. region 1975-77, nat. bd. mem. 1975-77), Prescribing Psychologists' Register Inc. (charter), Mass. Sch. Psychologists Assn. (pres. 1974-76, Presdl. award 1976), Phi Delta Kappa (life). Avocations: travel, architecture, painting. Home: Sea Cliff Walk Folly Point Rd Gloucester MA 01930 Office: Behavioral Devel Assocs PO Box 389 Rockport MA 01966-0489

HARRIES, KARSTEN, philosophy educator, researcher; b. Jena, Thuringia, Germany, Jan. 25, 1937; came to U.S., 1951; s. Wolfgang and Ilse (Grossmann) H.; m. Elizabeth Wanning, July 4, 1959; children: Lisa, Peter, Martin; 2d m., Elizabeth L. Langhorne, Mar. 14, 1991. BA, Yale U., 1958, PhD, 1962. Instr. Yale U., New Haven, 1961-63, asst. prof. philosophy, 1965-66, assoc. prof., 1966-70, prof., 1970—, Mellon prof., 1986-91, Brooks and Suzanne Ragen prof.; asst. prof. U. Tex., Austin, 1963-65. Lectr. U. Bonn, Fed. Republic Germany, winters 1965-66, 68-69. Author: The Meaning of Modern Art, 1967, The Bavarian Rococo Church, 1983, The Broken Frame, 1989, The Ethical Function of Architecture, 1996 (Winner of 8th Ann. AIA Internat. Architecture Book award for criticism), Infinity and Perspective, 2001; editor: (with Christoph Jamme) Martin Heidegger: Kunst, Politik, Technik, 1992, Martin Heidegger: Politics, Art, and Technology, 1994; contbr. numerous articles and revs. to profl. jours. Recipient Disting. Teaching Effectiveness award U. Tex., 1964; Morse fellow Yale U., 1965-66, Guggenheim fellow, N.Y.C., 1971-72. Mem. Soc. for Eighteenth Century Studies, Renaissance Soc. Am., Cusanus Soc. Home: 16 Morris St Hamden CT 06517-3423 Office: Yale U Dept Philosophy New Haven CT 06520 Business E-Mail: karsten.harries@yale.edu.

HARRIFF, SUZANNA ELIZABETH BAHNER, media consultant; b. Vicksburg, Miss., Dec. 30, 1953; d. David S. and F. Suzanne (McElwee) Bahner; m. James R. Harriff, Sept. 10, 1977; 1 child, Michael James. BA summa cum laude, SUNY-Fredonia, 1976; postgrad., Cornell U. Law Sch., 1981; MDiv with distinction, Colgate Rochester Div. Sch., 1995. Ordained to ministry Am. Bapt. Chs. USA, 1995. Media asst. Comstock Advt., Syracuse, NY, Buffalo, 1976-77; media buyer/planner G. Andre Delporte, Syracuse, 1979-81; media dir. Roberts Advt., Syracuse, 1982; dir. media svcs. Signet Advt., Syracuse, 1982-84; owner, pres. MediaMarCon, Syracuse, 1984—. Interim dir. mktg. and comm. Onondaga CC, 1998—99; adj. prof. Newhouse Sch. Syracuse U., 2001—02; pub. rels. cons. Syracuse Symphony Orch., 2000—01, 2005. Singer: Aspen Dreams, 1996—2005. Vol. pub. TV auction drive, chair media divsn. Sta. WCNY-TV, 1986—97, 2004, gen chair, 1994, chair media divsn., 1986—97, 2004—06; Pheresis donor ARC, 1987—2005; accompanist musicals and chorus Manlius-Pebble Hill Sch., 1991—96; resource devel. chair Winterfest, Syracuse, 1992; cmty. liason Cmty. United Way, 2000—01; media panelist Hugh O'Brien Youth Leadership Conf., 2003, 2004; bd. dirs. Westminster Manor, 2004—; music dir., pianist Manlius (N.Y.) United Meth. Ch., 1983—92, youth dir., 1983—85; co-chair St. Nicholas Ecumenical Festival, 1992—98, Am. Bapt. Ch. Nat. Biennial Conf., 1995; dir. music First Bapt. Ch., Manlius, 1993—96; assoc. pastor Andrews Meml. United Meth. Ch., 1996—99; workshop leader United Meth. Ch., 1997—; interim pastor Oswego First United Meth. Ch., 2000; pastor Apulia and Onativia United Meth. Chs., 2000—02; interim pastor Hannibal (N.Y.) Cmty. Ch., 2003—04; tchr. Am. Bapt. Chs., Syracuse; tchr. NY state lay studies program Bethel Bible Inst., Syracuse; music min. Northminster Presbyn. Ch., 2006—. Recipient 500 Hour Svc. pin, WCNY, 1996, Gold Medallion of Excellence, Upstate N.Y. Dist., 1999, Bronze and Silver Paragon awards, Nat. Coun. Mktg. and Pub. Rels., 2000, Women in Bus. award, 2001. Mem.: NAFE, Irish-Am. Cultural Inst. Syracuse, Syracuse Advt. Club (bd. dirs. 1985—88, program chair 1986—88, pres. 1988—89), Phi Beta Kappa. Democrat. Avocations: music, theater. Home: 8180 Bluffview Dr Manlius NY 13104-9740 Home Phone: 315-682-9492; Office Phone: 315-423-0226. Business E-Mail: sharriff@mediamarcon.com.

HARRIGAN, ANTHONY HART, author; b. NYC, Oct. 27, 1925; s. Anthony Hart and Elizabeth Elliott (Hutson) H.; m. Elizabeth McP. Ravenel, Aug. 16, 1950; children: Anthony Hart, Elizabeth Chardon, Elliott McP., Mary Ravenel. Student, Bard Coll., Kenyon Coll., Gambier, Ohio, U. Va. Reporter Virginian-Pilot, Norfolk, 1953-55, Charleston (S.C.) News & Courier, assoc. editor, 1957-70; exec. v.p. U.S. Indsl. Coun., Nashville, 1970-78, pres., 1978-90. Pres. U.S. Bus. and Indsl. Coun. Ednl. Found., 1978-90; trustee, rsch. fellow Nat. Humanities Inst.; lectr. Harvard U., Nat. War Coll., Vanderbilt U., U. Colo.; past mem. rsch. com. S.C. Commn. Higher Edn. Author: Ten Poets Anthology, 1947, The Editor and the Republic, 1952, Red Star Over Africa, 1964, The New Republic, 1965, Defense Against Total Attack, 1966, A Guide to the War in Vietnam, 1965, American Perspectives, 1974, American Perspectives II, 1977; co-author: The Indian Ocean and the Threat to the West, 1976, The Southern Oceans and the Security of the Free World, 1978, Putting America First, 1987, American Economic Pre-eminence, 1989; co-author or editor other works, 1978; editl. adv. bd. Modern Age, 1955—; author newspaper column, 1970-90, also numerous articles in nat. jours. Trustee Nat. Humanities Inst. Served with USMCR, World War II. Recipient Mil. Rev. award U.S. Army Command and Gen. Staff Coll., 1965; grantee Relm Found., 1966, Wilbur Found., 1992, 95, Earhart Found., 1993. Mem. Soc. Colonial Wars in S.C., Carolina Yacht Club. Anglican.

HARRIGAN, JOHN THOMAS, JR., physician, obstetrician, gynecologist; b. Perth Amboy, NJ, Apr. 20, 1929; s. John T. and Mary E. (Czapp) H.; m. Marlene Lulka, Apr. 14, 1961 (div.); children: John, Alisa, Edmund; m. Karen Tiejen, Aug. 23, 1992. Student, U. Va., 1946-49; MD, George Washington U., 1953. Diplomate Am. Bd. Ob-Gyn. Intern Doctors Hosp., Washington, 1953-54; resident in ob-gyn Luth. Hosp., Balt., 1954-55, Providence Hosp., Washington, 1957-58, Free Hosp. for Women, Boston, 1958-59; practice medicine specializing in ob-gyn, sub specialist in maternal-fetal medicine Jersey City, 1960-65, Colonia, NJ, 1962-70, Madison Twp., NJ, 1965-70; asst. attending in ob-gyn Margaret Hague Hosp., Jersey City, 1960-65; attending physician in ob-gyn Rahway Hosp., N.J., 1962-70, South Amboy Hosp., N.J., 1965-73, sec. to med. staff, 1970; attending in ob-gyn Martland Hosp. Unit, Newark, 1970-74; dir. dept. ob-gyn Monmouth Med. Ctr., Long Branch, NJ, 1974-76, dir. regional perinatal edn. program, 1975-78; dir. Monmouth Perinatal Ctr., Long Branch, 1975-78; sr. attending in ob-gyn St. Peter's Med. Ctr., 1978—; assoc. prof. ob-gyn Hahnemann Med. Coll., Phila., 1975-78; prof. dir. div. maternal-fetal medicine Rutgers Med. Sch., Piscataway, NJ, 1978—, prof. ob-gyn., dir. div. maternal-fetal medicine, 1978-86, U. Medicine and Dentistry N.J., Robert Wood Med. Sch., 1986—. Cons. in maternal-fetal medicine to physicians, Eastern N.J.; mem. maternal and infant care services com. N.J. Dept. Health, 1975—; dir. statewide premature delivery prevention project; med.-legal expert cons.; tech. adv. panel Healthstart program, N.J. Health Dept. Contbr. articles to med. jours.; reviewer med. jours. Mem. task force on biomed. causes and pub. rels. Gov.'s Coun. on Prevention Mental Retardation, N.J., task force on genetics and fetal defects, 1984—; mem. pub. affairs com. MOD Birth Defects Found.; pres. Perinatal Assn. N.J., 1991-93; mem. N.J. Commn. of Health and Parental and Child Health adv. Com., 1993—, vice chair, 1995—. Capt. M.C. U.S. Army, 1955-57. Fellow ACOG (vice chmn. N.J. sect. 1979-82, chmn. N.J. sect. 1982—, nat. adv. coun. 1982—, legis. rep., treas. dist. III 1986); mem. AMA, Med. Soc. N.J. (maternal infant care com. 1988—), Am. Inst. Ultrasound in Medicine (legis. com. 1994), Am. Fertility Soc., N.J. Perinatal Assn. (v.p. 1980-90, pres. 1990), N.J. Perinatal Tech. adv. Com. Baker channing Soc., N.J. Ob-gyn. Soc. (coun.), N.J. Maternal Fetal Medicine Soc. (pres. 1994-95). Democrat. Roman Catholic. Home: 301 Sussex Ave Spring Lake NJ 07762-1231 Office: Jersey Shore Med Ctr Perinatal Inst 301 Sussex Ave Spring Lake NJ 07762-1231 Personal E-mail: j.harrigan@verizon.net.

HARRIGAN, ROSANNE CAROL, medical educator; b. Miami, Fla., Feb. 24, 1945; d. John H. and Rose (Hnatow) Harrigan; children: Dennis, Michael, John. BS, St. Xavier Coll., 1965; MSN, Ind. Univ., 1974, EdD in Nursing and Edn., 1979. Staff nurse, recovery rm. Mercy Hosp., Chgo., 1965, evening charge nurse, 1965—66; head nurse Chgo. State Hosp., 1966—67; nurse practitioner Health and Hosp. Corp. Marion County, Indpls., 1975—80; assoc. prof. Ind. U. Sch. Nursing, Indpls., 1978—82; nurse practitioner devel. follow up program Riley Hosp. for Children, Indpls., 1980—85; prof. Ind. U. Sch. Nursing, Indpls., 1982—85; chief nursing sect. Riley Hosp. Child Devel. Ctr., Indpls., 1982—85; chmn., prof. maternal child health Loyola U., Niehoff Sch. Nursing, Chgo., 1985—92; dean sch. nursing U. Hawaii, Honolulu, 1992—2002; nurse practitioner Waimanalo Health Ctr., Hawaii, 1998—2002; Frances A. Matsuda chair women's health John A. Burns Sch. Medicine U. Hawaii Manoa, Honolulu, 2000—, chair faculty devel., 2002—, chair dept. Complementary and Alternative Medicine, 2002—, prof. pediat., 2003—. Lectr. Ind. U. Sch. Nursing, 1974-75, chmn. dept. pediat., family and women's health, 1980-85; adj. prof. of pediat. Ind. U. Sch. Med., 1982-85; editl. bd. Jour. Maternal Child Health Nursing, 1984-86, Jour. Perinatal Neo-natal, 1985—, Jour. Perinatology, 1989—, Loyola U. Press, 1988-92; adv. bd. Symposia Medicus, 1982-84, Proctor and Gamble Rsch. Adv. Com. Blue Ribbon Panel; sci. rev. panel NIH, 1985; mem. NIH nat. adv. coun. nursing rsch., 2000-; cons. in field. Contbr. articles to profl. journals. Bd. dir. March of Dimes Ctrl. Ind. Chpt., 1974-76, med. adv., 1979-85; med. and rsch. adv. March of Dimes Nat. Found., 1985—, chmn. Task Force on Rsch. Named Nat. Nurse of Yr. March of Dimes, 1983; faculty rsch. grantee Ind. U., 1978, Pediatric Pulmonary Nursing Tng. grant Am. Lung Assn., 1982-85, Attitudes, Interests, and Competence of Ob-Gyn. Nurses Rsch. grant Nurses Assn. Am. Coll. Ob-Gyn., 1986, Attitudes, Interests, and Priorities of Neo-natal Nurses Rsch. grant Nat. Assn. Neonatal Nurses, 1987, Biomedical Rsch. Support grant, 1988; Doctoral fellow Am. Lung Assn. Ind. Tng. Program, 1981-86. Mem. AAAS, ANA (Maternal Child Nurse of Yr. 1983), Assn. Women's Health, Obstetrical and Neonatal Nursing (chmn. com. on rsch. 1983-86), Am. Nurses Found., Nat. Assn. Neo-natal Nurses, Nat. Perinatal Assn. (bd. dir. 1978-85, rsch. com. 1986), Midwest Nursing Rsch. Soc. (theory devel. sect.), Ill. Nurses Assn. (commn. rsch. chmn. 1990-91), Ind. Nurses Assn., Hawaii Nurses Assn., Ind. Perinatal Assn. (pres. 1981-83), N.Y. Acad. Sci., Ind U. Alumni Assn. (Disting. Alumni 1985), Sigma Xi, Pi Lambda Theta, Sigma Theta Tau (chpt. pres. 1988-90). Home Phone: 808-728-2904. Business E-Mail: harrigan@hawaii.edu.

HARRIMAN, GERALD EUGENE, retired business administrator, economics professor; b. Dell Rapids, SD, May 30, 1924; s. Roy L. and Margaret (Schrantz) H.; m. Eileen Bernadine Bensman, June 10, 1950; children— G. Peter, Mary K., Margaret C., Elizabeth A. BS, U. Notre Dame, 1947; A.M., U. S.D., 1949; PhD, U. Cin., 1957. Expediter Minn. Mining & Mfg. Co., 1947-48; from instr. to asst. dean, chmn. dept. bus. adminstrn. and finance Xavier U., 1949-66; prof. bus. adminstrn., chmn. div. bus. and econs. Ind. U., South Bend, 1966-75, prof. bus. adminstrn. and econs., 1975-89, prof. emeritus, 1989—, dean faculties, 1975-87, acting chancellor, 1979, vice chancellor acad. affairs, 1987-89; ret., 1989. Vis. prof. fin. U. S.D., 1962; chmn. acad. deans Ind. Conf. Higher Edn., 1981-82; cons. in field. Mem. citizens adv. coun. long range fin. planning Coun. of City of Cin., 1963; mem. Community Edn. Roundtable, 1984—; mem. Scholarship Found. of St. Joseph County, Inc., 1992. Served with USNR, 1942-45. Mem.: Am. Econs. Assn., Am. Fin. Assn., Beta Gamma Sigma. Home: 16600 Gerald St Granger IN 46530-9579 Office: 1700 Mishawaka Ave South Bend IN 46615-1408

HARRIMAN, JOHN HOWLAND, retired lawyer; b. Buffalo, Apr. 14, 1920; s. Lewis Gildersleeve and Grace (Bastine) H.; m. Barbara Ann Brunmark, June 12, 1943; children— Walter Brunmark, Constance Bastine, John Howland. AB summa cum laude, Dartmouth, 1942; JD, Stanford U., 1949. Bar: Calif. 1949. Assoc. firm Lawler, Felix & Hall, LA, 1949-55; asst. v.p., then v.p. Security Pacific Nat. Bank, LA, 1955-72, sr. v.p., 1972-85; ret., 1985. Sec. Security Pacific Corp., 1971-85; dir. Master Metal Works; mem. nat. adv. coun. The Pub. Svc., 1992-93. Mem. L.A. adv. coun. Episcopal Ch. Found., 1977-79; mem. Republican Assocs., 1951-72 , trustee, 1962-72; mem. Calif. Rep. Central Com., 1956-69, 81— , exec. com., 1960-62, 81-84; mem. L.A. County Rep. Central Com., 1958-70, exec. com., 1960-62, vice chmn., 1962; chmn. Calif. 15th Congl. Dist. Rep. Central Com., 1960-62, Calif. 30th Congl. Dist. Rep. Central Com., 1962; treas. United Rep. Fin. Com. L.A. County, 1969-70; chmn. L.A. County Reagan-Bush campaign, 1980, co-chmn., 1984; exec. dir. Calif. Rep. Party, 1985-86. With USAAF, 1943-46. Mem. Am. Bar Assn., State Bar Calif., Phi Beta Kappa, Theta Delta Chi, Phi Alpha Delta. Clubs: California (Los Angeles); Lincoln, Breakfast Panel (pres. 1970-71).

HARRIMAN, RICHARD LEE, performing arts association administrator, educator; b. Independence, Mo., Sept. 10, 1932; s. Walter S. and M. Eloise (Faulkner) Harriman. AB, William Jewell Coll., 1953, LittD (hon.), 1983; MA, Stanford U., 1959. Instr., asst. prof. English U. Dubuque, Iowa, 1960—62; asst. prof. English William Jewell Coll., Liberty, Mo., 1962, acting head English dept., 1965—69, dir. fine arts program, 1965—2003, assoc. prof., 1966—. Artistic dir. Harriman-Jewel Series, Liberty, 2003—. Treas. Kansas City Arts Coun., 1980, sec, 1981, Kansas City Am. Arts Festival, 1988—89. With AUS, 1953—55. Woodrow Wilson fellow, 1957. Mem.: AAUP, MLA, Assn. Performing Arts Presenters (nat. exec. bd. 1975—78), Shakespeare Assn. Am., Internat. Soc. Performing Arts, Alpha Psi Omega, Sigma Tau Delta, Lambda Chi Alpha. Methodist. Home: 1043 E Hwy H Liberty MO 64068-4303

HARRINGTON, ANTHONY ROSS, radio announcer, educator; b. Sanford, NC, Feb. 18, 1958; s. Refus Roy and Pauline (Kelly) H. Diploma, Cen. Carolina Tech. Coll., 1977; AGE, Cen. Carolina C.C., 1983; BS summa cum laude, Campbell U., 1985, MEd, 1988, EdS, 1993; EdD, N.C. State U., 1995-2000. Cert. tchr., N.C.; lic. FCC radiotelephone operator. News announcer Sandhills Community Broadcasters, Southern Pines, N.C., 1977-78; announcer, engr. Harnett Broadcast, Inc., Lillington, N.C., 1978-88; bus driver Harnett County Schs., Lillington, 1974-76, instr. social studies, 1985—; mgr. radio sta., instr. radio-TV, mem. transfer adv. bd. Ctrl. Carolina C.C., 1988-99, lead history instr., 1999—, chmn. dept. pub. svcs., 2000, instrnl. coord., 2004—06. Campus rep. Ctrl. Carolina C.C. Found., 2002-2003; mem. Ctrl. Carolina C.C. Tri-County English Alliance, 1989—; support N.C. Dems., Raleigh, 1986—; pres. Campbell U. Friends of Libr., 2003-04. Pres.'s scholar Campbell U., 1983-85, Coates-Rodgers History scholar Campbell U., 1983-85. Mem. ASCD, NEA, Nat. Assn. Secondary Sch. Prins., Orgn. Am. Historians, N.C. Assn. Educators, N.C. C.C. Faculty Assn., N.C. Assn. Historians, N.C. Distance Learning Assn., N.C. Assn. Broadcasters, Nat. Coun. Social Studies, Century Club (N.C.), Campbell U. Century Club, Masons (chaplain 1983, jr. steward 1984, sr. steward 1990, sec. 1991-97), Ctrl. Carolina C.C. Century Club, Profl. Educators of N.C., Masons (32 degree), Shriners. Presbyterian. Avocations: photography, singing popular and religious music. Home: 4224 Mount Pisgah Church Rd Broadway NC 27505-8506 Office: Ctrl Carolina CC 1105 Kelly Dr Sanford NC 27330-9059 Office Phone: 919-718-7322.

HARRINGTON, ANTHONY STEPHEN, lawyer, diplomat, business executive; b. Taylorsville, NC, Mar. 9, 1941; s. Atwell Lee and Louise (Chapman) H.; m. Hope Reynolds, Sept. 25, 1971; children: Adam Reynolds, Michael Addison. AB, U. N.C., 1963; LLB, Duke U., 1966. Asst. dean Duke Law Sch., Durham, NC, 1966-68; assoc. Hogan & Hartson, Washington, 1968-73, ptnr., 1974-99; U.S. amb. to Brazil, 2000-01; pres. Stonebridge Internat. LCC, 2001—; chmn. Civitas Group LLC, 2005—. Bd. dirs. Ovation, Inc., Ctr. for Democracy, SouthernNet Inc., Southeastern Metal Products, Rosemount Ctr., PRE Holdings Inc., Kenan Inst. Pvt. Enterprise; co-chair Nat. Alliance to End Homelessness; vice-chmn. Pres. Fgn. Intelligence Adv. Bd., 1993-99; mem. Commn. on Roles and Capabilities of Intelligence Cmty., 1995; chmn. Pres. Intelligence Oversight Bd., 1994-99. Gen. Counsel Dem. Nat. Com., Washington, 1981-85. Episcopal. Club: Met. Avocations: politics, reading, gardening, tennis. Home: Ratcliffe Manor 7768 Ratcliffe Manor Ln Easton MD 21601-7432 also: 701 Pennsylvania Ave NW Washington DC 20004-2608 Office: Stonebridge Internat 555 13th St NW Washington DC 20004-1109

HARRINGTON, BRUCE MICHAEL, lawyer, investor; b. Houston, Mar. 12, 1933; s. George Haymond Harrington and Doris (Gladden) Maginnis; m. Anne Griffith Lawhon, Feb. 15, 1958; children: Julia Griffith, Martha Gladden, Susan McIver BA, U. Tex., 1960, JD with honors, 1961. Bar: Tex. 1961, U.S. Dist. Ct. (so. dist.) Tex. 1962, U.S. Ct. Appeals (5th cir.) 1962, U.S. Supreme Ct. 1973. Assoc. Andrews & Kurth and predecessor firm, Houston, 1961-73, ptnr., 1973-84. Dir. Offenhauser Co., Houston, Allied Metals, Inc., Houston Trustee St. John's Sch., Houston, 1981-92, chmn. bd., CEO, 1986-92; chmn. bd. Covenant House, Tex., 1991-95; trustee St. Luke's Episcopal Hosp., Tex. Med. Ctr., Houston, 1983-86; bd. dirs. YMCA Bd. Mgmt., Am. Cancer Soc., 1992-94, Ctr. for Hearing and Speech, 1993, chmn. bd., 1995-98; vice chmn. Gateway Found., 1993-95; mem. adv. com. Assn. Governing Bds. of Colls. and Univs. Mem. ABA, Nat. Assn. Ind. Schs. (chmn. trustee com.), Ind. Schs. Assn. S.W. (chmn. trustee com., bd. exec. com.), Tex. Bar Assn., Houston Bar Assn., The Mil. and Hosp. Order of St. Lazarus (grand prior), The Venerable Order of St. John (U.K.), Houston Country Club, Petroleum Club, Houston Club, Phi Delta Phi, Order of Coif. Republican. Episcopalian. Home: 3608 Overbrook Ln Houston TX 77027-4128

HARRINGTON, CAROL A., lawyer; b. Geneva, Ill., Feb. 13, 1953; d. Eugene P. and M. Ruth (Bowersox) Kloubec; m. Warren J. Harrington, Aug. 19, 1972; children: Jennifer Ruth, Carrie Anne. BS summa cum laude, U. Ill., 1974, JD magna cum laude, 1977. Bar: Ill. 1977, U.S. Dist. Ct. (no. dist.) Ill. 1977, U.S. Tax Ct. 1979. Assoc. Winston & Strawn, Chgo., 1977—84, ptnr., 1984—88, McDermott, Will & Emery, Chgo., 1988—, pvt. client dept. chair, 2006—. Adv. com. Heckerling Inst. Estate Planning; speaker in field. Co-author: Generation-Skipping Tax, 1996, Generation-Skipping Transfer Tax, Warren, Gorham & Lamont, 2000. Fellow Am. Coll. Trusts and Estate Coun. (bd. regents 1999-2005); mem. ABA (chmn. B-1 generation skipping transfer com. 1987-92, coun. real property, probate and trust law sect. 1992-98), Ill. State Bar Assn., Chgo. Bar Assn., Chgo. Estate Planning Coun. Office: McDermott Will & Emery 227 W Monroe St Ste 3100 Chicago IL 60606-5096 Office Phone: 312-984-7794.

HARRINGTON, CLIFFORD M., lawyer; b. Lafayette, La., Nov. 20, 1947; BA with distinction, Univ. Southwest La., 1969; JD, Univ. Colo., 1972. Bar: Colo. 1972, DC 1975, US Ct. Appeals (DC cir.), US Supreme Ct. Atty., Office of Opinions & Review FCC, 1972—74; ptnr., chmn. Comm. group Pillsbury Winthrop Shaw Pittman, Washington. Mem.: ABA, Fed. Comm. Bar Assn., DC Bar Assn. Office: Pillsbury Winthrop Shaw Pittman 2300 N St NW Washington DC 20037-1128 Office Phone: 202-663-8525. Office Fax: 202-663-8007. Business E-Mail: clifford.harrington@pillsburylaw.com.

HARRINGTON, DAN WILLIAM, state senator; b. Butte, Mont., Feb. 12, 1938; m. Pat Harrington; children: Kathleen, Dan, Kevin. BS, Western Mont. Coll., 1960. Cert. tchr., Mont. Tchr. Sch. Dist. No. 1, Butte, 1961-97; Dem. rep. dist. 38 Mont. Ho. of Reps., 1976-2000; Dem. senator dist. 38 Mont. State Senate, 2000—. Majority whip Mont. Ho. of Reps., 1983, minority whip, 1995-99; pres. pro-tem. Mont. Senate, 2005-. Pres. Silver Bow Young Dems., 1960-62; del. Mont. Constl. Conv., 1971-72; chair Silver Bow County Dem. Com., 1970-90; pres. Silver Bow Dem. Burrows Club, 1997-01. Mem. Butte Tchrs. Union. Roman Catholic. Office: 1201 N Excelsior Ave Butte MT 59701-8505 also: Mont State Senate Capitol Station Helena MT 59620 Business E-Mail: dznwharrington@in-tch.com.

HARRINGTON, DIANE, librarian, writer; d. G. Robert and Jane Coupe Harrington; m. Bradley Kent Purvis, Mar. 21, 1981; 1 child, Megan Susan Purvis. BA in English, Wellesley Coll., 1968; MA in English, Columbia U., 1971. Cert. adminstr. Fordham U., 1981, lib. media specialist Palmer Sch. Info. Sci., 1999. Sr. fellow, instr. Columbia U., NYC, 1971—73; media specialist, lead tchr. New Rochelle Sch. Dist., NY, 1973—75; instr. CUNY, 1975—77, adj. instr., 1977—79; spl. specialist Office of Chancellor NYC Pub. Schs., 1984; ednl. writer United Fed. Tchrs., 1986—91; adj. instr. Westchester CC, NY, 1993—95; English tchr. Nyack HS, 1995—96; lib., media specialist White Plains HS, NY, 1996—2005; libr. media specialist Rye HS, NY, 2005—. Edl. cons., 1980—96; freelance writer, editor, 1980—. Co-author (with Laurette Young): School Savvy, 1993, lib. website; developer HS rsch. handbook; contbr. articles to. profl. jours. Unitarian Universalist. Avocations: singing, reading. Office: Rye HS Parsons St Rye NY 10580 Office Phone: 914-967-6100 1960. Business E-Mail: harringd@ryeschools.lhric.org.

HARRINGTON, DONALD JAMES, university president; b. Bklyn., Oct. 2, 1945; s. John Joseph and Ruth Mary (Cummings) H. BA, Mary Immaculate Sem., Northampton, Pa., 1969, MDiv, 1972, ThM, 1973; LLD (hon.), St. John's U., 1985; postgrad., U. Toronto, 1980—82; PhD (hon.), Fu Jen U., Taipei, Taiwan, 1994; HHD (hon.), Am. U. Rome, 1994, Dowling Coll., 1996; D of Pedagogy (hon.), St. Thomas Aquinas Coll., Sparkhill, NY; STD (hon.), Niagara U., 2000; STD, Kokushikan U., 2002. Ordained priest Roman Catholic Ch., 1973. Instr. Niagara U., NY, 1973-80, dir. student activities NY, 1974-77, dean student activities NY, 1977-80, exec. v.p. NY, 1981-84, pres. NY, 1984-89, St. John's U., Jamaica, NY, 1989—. Bd. dirs. The Bear Stearns Cos., Inc., 1993—, Commn. Ind. Colls. and Univs., Albany, N.Y., 1987-89, 91-94, 2003-; mem. bd. Cath. edn. Diocese of Buffalo, 1987-89. Trustee Niagara U., 1984-89, emeritus bd. mem., 2002-, St. John's U., 1986—, DePaul U., 1988-91, Sem. Immaculate Conception, 1990-97, Res. Group, 1988—, Sisters Hosp., Buffalo, 1988-89; chair adv. com. Love Canal Land Use, 1988-89; chair Big East Athletic Conf., 1994-97; mem. sanctity of life com. Diocese of Bklyn., 1990-96; chair Western N.Y. Consortium for Higher Edn., 1988-89, mem. exec. com., 1985-89; mem. adv. bd. New Yorkers Caring for N.Y.-N.Y. Med. Coll., 1998-. Recipient Pro Ecclesia et Pontifice, Pope John Paul II, 1989. Mem. Assn. Cath. Colls. and Univs. (bd. dirs. 1997-2003). Office: St John's U Office of Pres 8000 Utopia Pkway, Newman Hall Rm 318 Jamaica NY 11439-0001

HARRINGTON, GARY BURNES, retired controller; b. Parkville, Mo., Nov. 8, 1934; s. George Burnes and Ethel May (Burge) H.; m. Doris Ann Scott, Oct. 28, 1953; children: Gary Burnes Jr., Sherri Ann, Michael Scott, John Patrick, Heather May. Student, Oklahoma City U., 1962-67. Acctg. supr. CIT Fin. Svcs., Oklahoma City, 1952-76; sr. auditor CIT Fin. Corp., NYC, 1976-83, sr. supervising auditor Livingston, NJ, 1983-86; audit officer Mfrs. Hanover Corp., NYC and Atlanta, 1986-88, The CIT Group/Sales Fin., Livingston and Oklahoma City, 1988-89; asst. contr. The CIT Group/Sales Financing, Livingston and Oklahoma City, 1989-95, ret., 1995. Various positions from Webelo leader to dist. commr. Boy Scouts Am., Oklahoma City and Norman, Okla., 1967—. Staff sgt. USAF, 1947-48, USAFR. Mem. Inst. Internal Auditors (1st v.p. 1979-80, pres. 1980-81, bd. chmn. 1981-82, Dist. Svc. award 1982), Am. Legion. Republican. Baptist. Avocations: woodworking, fishing, camping, hunting. Home: 13609 Calistoga Dr Oklahoma City OK 73170-5111

HARRINGTON, GEORGE FRED, retired air transportation executive; b. Killingly, Conn., July 29, 1923; s. George Whitman and Beatrice Evelyn (Sheldon) H.; m. Ruth Lydia Saarinen, June 7, 1947; children: Joanne Ruth, George Lauri, Julie Ann. BS, U.S. Mil. Acad., 1947; MBA, Harvard U., 1957; grad., Armed Forces Staff Coll., 1961, Indsl. Coll. of Armed Forces, 1967. Commd. 2d lt. USAF, 1947, advanced through grades to col., 1968, ret., 1977; mgr. market devel. Beech Aircraft, Washington, 1978-81, gen. mgr. internat. div. Wichita, 1981-82, v.p., 1982-85; cons. Gen. Aviation, Arlington, Va., 1986—. Cons. in field. Past pres. Collingwood Libr. and Mus. on Americanism, Alexandria, Va.; overseer Plimoth (Mass.) Plantation; trustee US Mil. Acad. Assn. Grads Decorated D.S.M., Legion of Merit with oak leaf cluster. Mem. Air Force Assn., Ret. Officers Assn., Harvard Bus. Sch. Club of Washington (pres. 1988-89), Masons, Shriners, Nat. Sojourners (past nat. pres.). Republican. Methodist. Avocations: gardening, music. Home and Office: 1300 Crystal Dr # 304 Arlington VA 22202-3234

HARRINGTON, JAMES TIMOTHY, lawyer; b. Chgo., Sept. 4, 1942; s. John Paul and Margaret Rita (Cunneen) H.; m. Roseanne Strupeck, Sept. 4, 1965; children: James Timothy, Roseanne, Maris Zajdela. BA, U. Notre Dame, 1964, JD, 1967. Bar: Ill. 1967, Ind. 1968, U.S. Dist. Ct. (no. dist.) Ill. 1967, U.S. Dist. Ct. (no. and so. dists.) Ind. 1968, U.S. Ct. Appeals (7th cir.) 1969, U.S. Ct. Appeals (4th cir.) 1977, U.S. Ct. Appeals (8th cir.) 1979, U.S. Ct. Appeals (3d cir.) 1981, U.S. Supreme Ct. 1979, U.S. Ct. Appeals (D.C. cir.) 1993. Law clk. U.S. Dist. Ct. (no. dist.) Ind., 1967—69; assoc. Rooks, Pitts & Poust, Chgo., 1969—75, ptnr., 1976—87, Ross & Hardies, Chgo., 1987—2003, McGuireWoods, LLP, 2003—. Adj. prof. environ. mgmt. Ill. Inst. Tech., 2004—, Stuart Grad. Sch. Bus.; lectr. environ. law and mgmt., fed. procedures, adminstrv. law, 1960—. Vice chmn. Mid Am. Legal Found., 1998—; past chmn., bd. dirs. Ill. Safety Coun., 2002-05; chmn., bd. adv. masters in environ. mgmt. program Ill. Inst. Tech. Sch. Bus. Fellow Am. Bar Found.; mem. Ill. Bar Assn., Ind. Bar Assn., Chgo. Bar Assn. (environ. law com.), Indsl. Water Waste and Sewer Group (past chmn.), Air and Waste Mgmt. Assn. (sec. Lake Mich. sect.), Assn. Environ. Law Inst., Lawyers Club Chgo., Union League Club Chgo. Roman Catholic. Home: 746 Foxdale Ave Winnetka IL 60093-1908 Office: McGuireWoods LLP 77 W Wacker Dr Ste 4400 Chicago IL 60601 Office Phone: 312-849-8252. Business E-Mail: jharrington@mcguirewoods.com.

HARRINGTON, JEAN PATRICE, academic administrator; b. Denver; d. James Michael and Katherine Ann (Holl) H. BA, Coll. Mt. St. Joseph, 1953; MA, Creighton U., 1958; PhD, U. Colo., 1967; LHD (hon.), Xavier U., 1983, Ohio Dominican Coll., 1988; LLD (hon.), St. Thomas Inst., Cin., 1985, Coll. Mt. St. Joseph, 1988, Hebrew Union Coll., 1990; D. Tech. Studies (hon.), Cin. Tech., 1988; LLD (hon.), No. Ky. U., 1996, U. Dayton, 1999. Joined Sisters of Charity of Cin., 1940; prin. St. Rose of Lima, Denver, 1953-56; tchr. Cathedral H.S., Denver, 1956-58, prin., 1958-68; dir. instl. rsch. Coll. Mt. St. Joseph, Cin., 1968-69, pres., 1977-87; exec. dir. Cin. Youth Collaborative, 1988-90; interim pres. Cin. State Coll., 1997. Bd. dirs. Penrose Hosp., Colorado Springs, 1976-86, St. Mary Corwin Hosp., Pueblo, Colo., 1972-80, Cin. Bicentennial Commn., 1982-89, Samaritan Health Resources, Inc., 1983-96, St. Rita Sch. for Deaf, 1983-86, United Appeal Cabinet, 1983, Cin. Cmty. Chest, 1988-95, Dan Beard coun. Boy Scouts Am., 1988-91; trustee Good Samaritan Hosp. and Health Ctr., Dayton, Ohio, 1978-80, 89-97, bd. dirs., 1989-96; trustee Miami U., 1989-97, chmn. 1994-97; bd. dirs. Coll. of Mt. St. Joseph, 1995-2002; trustee U. Dayton, 1999-2002. Recipient Disting. Svc. citation NCCJ, 1987, Women Helping Women award Soroptimist Internat., 1990, Statesman award Cin. Assn. Execs., 1988, St. Francis award Friars Club, 1994, Daniel Ransahoff Initiative award, 1994, Lincoln award No. Ky. U., 1994, Gt. Living Cincinnatian award C. of C., 1996, Svc. to Edn. award Ohiana Libr. Assn., 1998, Children's Advocate award Beech Acres; named Career Woman of Achievement YWCA, 1981, Disting. Bus. and Profl. Woman of Yr., 1982; inductee Hall of Excellence of Ohio Fedn. of Ind. Colls., 1990, Ohio Women's Hall of Fame, 2000, Pres.' award Children's Def. Fund, 2003. Mem. Nat. Assn. Ind. Colls. and Univs., Assn. Cath. Colls. and Univs. (bd. dirs.), Ohio Found. Ind. Colls., Greater Cin. Consortium Colls. and Univs. (vice chmn. 1980-82), Coun. Ind. Colls. (bd. dirs. 1981-85), Cin. C. of C. (bd. dirs. 1978-84, trustee 1981-85, sec. 1979-85, named Great Living Cincinnatian 1996). Roman Catholic. Personal E-mail: jphsc@juno.com.

HARRINGTON, JEREMY THOMAS, priest, publishing executive; b. Lafayette, Ind., Oct. 7, 1932; s. William and Ellen (Cain) H. BA, Duns Scotus Coll., 1955; postgrad., U. Detroit, 1955, Marquette U., 1961; MA, Xavier U., Cin., 1965; MS in Journalism, Northwestern U., 1967; LHD (hon.), St. Bonaventure U., 1999. Ordained priest Roman Cath. Ch., 1959. Joined Order Friars Minor, 1950; tchr. Roger Bacon High Sch., Cin., 1960-64; assoc. editor St. Anthony Messenger, Cin., 1964-66, editor, 1966-81, pub., 1975-81, pub., CEO, 1991—2007; mem. bd. Franciscan Province Cin., 1969-72, 75-81, chief exec. bd., 1981-90; ret., 2007. Author: Your Wedding: Planning Your Own Ceremony, 1974; editor: Conscience in Today's World, 1970, Jesus: Superstar or Savior?, 1972. Mem. Catholic Press Assn. (pres. 1975-77, dir.), Kappa Tau Alpha. Home: 1615 Vine St Cincinnati OH 45202 Office: St Anthony Messenger 28 W Liberty St Cincinnati OH 45202 Business E-Mail: jeremyh@franciscan.org. *My success has been made by others. As a priest, as well as an editor and publisher, my challenge is to discover, recognize, encourage and make available to others the talents of authors and artists. To me, that's a parable of life. The more we can discover, appreciate and foster the good qualities and strengths of others, the more "successful" we are. Success in life is realizing how many gifts are made available to us by God and our fellow human beings.*

HARRINGTON, JOEY (JOHN JOSEPH HARRINGTON), professional football player; b. Portland, Oreg., Oct. 21, 1978; s. John and Valerie Harrington; m. Emily Hatten, Mar. 10, 2007. BS in Bus. Admin., U. Oreg., 2002. Quarterback Detroit Lions, 2002—06, Miami Dolphins, 2006—07, Atlanta Falcons, 2007—. Founder Joey Harrington Challenge for Kids, 2004; vol. Feed The Children. Named to All-American Team, USA Today, 2002. Office: Atlanta Falcons 4400 Falcon Parkway Flowery Branch GA 30542*

HARRINGTON, JOHN MICHAEL, JR., lawyer; b. Boston, July 5, 1921; s. John Michael and Marie Bernadine (Ratchford) H.; m. Ellen Patricia White, May 12, 1951; children— John Michael III, Marc W., Francis X. B., Ellen M., Matthew J., Patrick W. AB, Harvard U., 1943, LL.B., 1949. Bar: Mass. 1949, U.S. Dist. Ct. (Mass.) 1950, U.S. Ct. Appeals (1st cir.) 1956, U.S. Supreme Ct. 1968. Law clk. Supreme Jud. Ct. Mass., Boston, 1949-50; assoc. Ropes & Gray LLP, Boston, 1950-55, 57-61, ptnr., 1961-93, counsel, 1994—; asst. U.S. atty. Dist. of Mass., Boston, 1955-57. Trustee Winchester Sav. Bank, Mass., 1966-91; mem. Mass. Jud. Conduct Commn., Boston, 1978-81. Trustee Roxbury Latin Sch., Boston, 1962-67, St. Sebastian's County Day Sch., Needham, Mass., 1973-86; mem. fin. com. Town of Winchester, 1959-62. Served to capt. field arty. U.S. Army, 1943-46, ETO. Fellow Am. Coll. Trial Lawyers, Am. Bar Found.; mem. ABA (standing com. on fed. judiciary 1st cir. 1978-84), Boston Bar Assn. Clubs: Union (v.p. 1982-86, pres. 1986-88), Curtis, Harvard (Boston). Democrat. Roman Catholic. Home: 19 Cabot St Winchester MA 01890-3501 Office: Ropes & Gray LLP One International Pl Boston MA 02110-2624 Office Phone: 617-951-7000.

HARRINGTON, JOHN TIMOTHY, retired lawyer; b. Madison, Wis., May 26, 1921; s. Cornelius Louis and Emily (Chisholm) H.; m. Deborah Reynolds, May 23, 1948; children— Elizabeth Chisholm, Samuel Parker, Hannah Quincy, Jane McRae BS, Harvard U., 1942, LL.B., 1948. Bar: Wis. 1949. Assoc. Quarles & Brady and predecessor firms, Milw., 1948-58, ptnr., 1958-91; ret., 1991—. Served to lt. comdr. USNR, 1942-46, PTO Home: 924 E Juneau Ave Milwaukee WI 53202-2748 Office: Quarles & Brady 411 E Wisconsin Ave Ste 2550 Milwaukee WI 53202-4497 Home Phone: 414-291-8885. Personal E-mail: jtharrington_4@sbcglobal.net.

HARRINGTON, JOHN TOLAN, medical educator, internist, nephrologist, retired dean; b. Fall River, Mass., Dec. 30, 1936; s. John J. and Elizabeth C. (Tolan) Harrington; m. Gertrude Rose Hargraves, Aug. 27, 1960; children: Gertrude, Kathleen, Daniel, Ann, John, Mark, Timothy. BA magna cum laude, Coll. of the Holy Cross, 1958; MD cum laude, Yale U., 1962. Diplomate Am. Bd. Internal Medicine. Intern, resident in internal medicine N.C. Meml. Hosp., Chapel Hill, 1962-65; clin. and rsch. fellow in nephrology New Eng. Med. Ctr., Boston, 1965-68, nephrologist, dir. hemodialysis unit, 1971-81, chief gen. medicine divsn., 1981-86, sr. nephrologist, 2003—; chmn. dept. medicine Newton (Mass.)-Wellesley Hosp., 1986-94; dean academic affairs Tufts U. Sch. Medicine, Boston, 1994-95, asst. prof. medicine, 1971-75, assoc. prof. medicine, 1975-79, prof. medicine, 1979—, dean ad interim, 1995-96, dean, 1996—2002, dean emeritus, 2003—. Author: Acid-Base, 1982; editor: Nephrology Forum Kidney Internat., 1979—2005; contbr. articles to profl. jours. Pres. Hummocks Cmty. Orgn., Portsmouth, RI, 1978—80, Nat. Kidney Found., Mass., 1988. Master: ACP (gov. Mass. chpt. 1989—93); fellow: Royal Irish Coll. Physicians (hon.); mem.: Am. Soc. Nephrology, Internat. Soc. Nephrology, Holy Name Soc. Democrat. Roman Catholic. Avocations: sailing, swimming, Irish poetry and drama, baseball. Office Phone: 617-636-9439. Personal E-mail: gertrudeharrington123@comcast.net. Business E-Mail: jharrington@tufts-nemc.org.

HARRINGTON, JOHN VINCENT, retired communications executive, engineer, educator; b. NYC, May 9, 1919; s. John Joseph and Dorothy (Neisel) H.; m. Frances Cullinane, Jan. 23, 1943; children: John F., Nancy Harrington Higgins, Jeffrey, Richard, Brian. B.E.E., Cooper Union, 1940; M.E.E., Poly. Inst. Bklyn., 1948; Sc.D., Mass. Inst. Tech., 1957. Research engr. U.S. Air Force Cambridge Research Lab., Mass., 1946-51; leader data transmission group Lincoln Lab., M.I.T., Cambridge, 1951-56, asso. div. head aircraft control and warning, 1956-58, head radio physics div., 1958-63; prof. aeros., astronautics and elec. engring., 1st dir. Center Space Research, M.I.T., 1963-73; v.p. research and engring. Communications Satellite Corp., Washington, 1973-79; sr. v.p. research and devel., dir. COMSAT Labs., Clarksburg, Md., 1979-84. Dir. Epsco, Inc., 1964-72, Shawmut County Bank, Cambridge, 1964-73, COMSAT Gen. Telesystems, Inc., Washington, 1973-81, Environ. Research and Tech., Inc., Concord, Mass., 1981-82; mem. Space Applications Bd., NRC, 1975-81 Contbr. articles to profl. jours. Lt. USNR, 1942-46. Recipient Exceptional Civilian Service medal U.S. Air Force, 1952, Exceptional Profl. Achievement citation Cooper Union, 1965, Gano Dunn award Cooper Union, 1983. Fellow IEEE, AAAS, AIAA. Home: 11657 Asbury Cir Solomons MD 20688

HARRINGTON, JOSEPH FRANCIS, educational company executive, history educator; b. Boston, Oct. 24, 1938; s. Joseph Francis and Mary Virginia (Lynch) H.; m. Brenda Marie Crowley, Sept. 3, 1966; children: Megan Marie, Christopher Joseph John. BS, Boston Coll., 1960; MA, Georgetown U., 1963, PhD, 1971. Instr. Framingham State Coll., Mass., 1966-68, asst. prof., 1968-70, assoc. prof., 1970-72, prof., 1972—2003, chmn. dept. history, 1972—82, prof. emeritus, 2004—; pres. Learning, Inc., Stoughton, 1979—2003, bd. dirs.; pres. J.C. Enrichment. Program, 2003—. Treas. East European Rsch. Ctr., 1990-2007. Author: Masters of War, Makers of Peace, 1985, Powers, Pawns and Parleys, 1978, Tweaking the Nose of the Russians: American-Romanian Relations, 1940-90; American-Romanian Relations: From Pariah to Partner, 1989-2004; editl. bd. dirs. New England Jour. of History, 1991—2004, editor, 1995-2004; editor: The Creative Child and Adult Quar., 1991-94; contbr. articles to profl. jours. Mem. Stoughton, Mass. Sch. Com., 1971-77, 82-87, 91-94. With U.S. Army, 1962-65. Tchg. fellow Georgetown U., Washington, 1960-62, 65-66, hon. fellow Kennedy Presdl. Libr., 1986-93. Mem. Mass. Assn. for Advancement of Individual Potential (bd. dirs., pres. 1987-89, 90-92, v.p. for R&D 1989), Nat. Assn. Creative Children and Adults (bd. dirs. 1985-92, editor The Creative Child and Adult Quar. 1991-93), New Eng. Slavic Assn. (v.p. 1990-91, treas. 1991-98), Soc. for Romanian Studies (pres. 1994-97, bd. dirs. 1997-2000), Kennedy Libr. Acad. Adv. Coun. Roman Catholic. Avocation: reading. Home: 119 Holmes Ave Stoughton MA 02072-1926 Office: Framingham State Coll State St Framingham MA 01701 Office Phone: 781-344-7174. Personal E-mail: cacg1@aol.com.

HARRINGTON, KATHLEEN M., public relations company executive, former federal agency administrator; BA, Colgate U., 1972; MA in Psychology, The Cath. U. Am., 1977. Adminstrv. asst. to Rep. Jim Dunn US Ho. Reps., Washington, 1981—83, 1983—87; asst. adminstr. pub. affairs FAA, Washington; asst. sec. congrl. and intergovtl. affairs US Dept. Labor, Washington, 1989—93; v.p. govt. rels. Aetna, Inc.; dir. Office of Elizabeth Dole Dole-Kemp Campaign, 1996; sr. v.p. pub. affairs and advocacy Health Ins. Assn. Am.; asst. sec. pub. affairs US Dept. Labor, Washington, 2002—03; sr. v.p. pub. affairs, dir. policy outreach Porter Novelli, Washington, 2003—. Office: Porter Novelli 1909 K St NW Washington DC 20006

HARRINGTON, KEVIN PAUL, lawyer; b. Paterson, NJ, Jan. 1, 1951; s. James John and Theresa Elizabeth (Giblin) H. BA, Niagara U., 1973; JD, N. E. Sch. Law, Boston, 1978. Bar: NJ 1978, US Dist. Ct. NJ 1978, US Supreme Ct. 1983. Judicial clerkship to hon. Thomas R. Rumana, Paterson, NJ, 1978-79; asst. prosecutor Passaic County Prosecutor's Office, Paterson, 1979-80; assoc. DeYoe & Guiney, Paterson, 1980-87; ptnr. Catania & Harrington, N. Haledon, NJ, 1987-99, Harrington and Lombardi, LLP, Wayne, 2000—. Recipient Civil Trial Atty. cert., Supreme Ct. NJ, 1986—; named NJ Super Lawyer NJ Monthly Mag., 2005, 06, 07. Master Am. Inns of Ct.; mem. NJ Def. Assn., NJ Bar Assn., Passaic County Bar Assn. (pres.), Def. Rsch. Inst. Avocations: sports, golf, scuba diving. Office: 508 Hamburg Tpke #207 Wayne NJ 07470-8482 Office Phone: 973-790-8900.

HARRINGTON, MARY EVELINA PAULSON (POLLY), writer, educator; b. Chgo. d. Henry Thomas and Evelina (Belden) Paulson; m. Gordon Keith Harrington, Sept. 7, 1957; children: Jonathan Henry, Charles Scranton. BA, Oberlin Coll., 1946; postgrad., Northwestern U., Evanston, Ill., Chgo., 1946-49, Weber State U., Ogden, Utah, 1970s, 80s; MA, U. Chgo.-Chgo. Theol. Sem., 1956. Publicist Nat. Coun. Chs., NYC, 1950-51; mem. press staff 2d assembly World Coun. Chs., Evanston, Chgo., 1954; mgr. Midwest Office Communication, United Ch. of Christ, Chgo., 1955-59; staff writer United Ch. Herald, NYC, St. Louis, 1959-61; affiliate missionary to Asia, United Ch. Bd. for World Ministries, NYC, 1978-79; freelance writer and lectr., 1961—; corr. Religious News Svc., 1962—. Prin. lectr. Women & Family Life in Asia series to numerous librs., Utah, 1981, 1981—82; pub. rels. coord. Utah Energy Conservation/Energy Mgmt. Program, 1984—85; tchr. writing Ogden Cmty. Schs., 1985—89; adj. instr. writing for publs. Weber State U., 1986—; instr. Acad. Lifelong Learning, Ogden, 1992—95, Eccles Cmty. Art Ctr., Ogden, 1993—94; dir. comm. Shared Ministry, Salt Lake City, 1983—97; chmn. comm. Intermountain Conf., Rocky Mountain Conf. Utah Assn. United Ch. of Christ, 1970—78, 1982—, Ind. Coun. Chs., 1960—63, United Ch. of Christ, Ogden, 1971—; dir. comm. United Chs., 1971—78, Christ Congl., Ogden, , 1980—; chmn. comm. Ch. Women United Utah, 1974—78, Ogden rep., 1980—, hostess Northern Utah, 1998. Editor: Sunshine and Moonscapes: An Anthology of Essays, Poems, Short Stories, 1994; (booklet) Family Counseling Service: Thirty Years of Service to Northern Utah, 1996; contbr. articles to profl. jours. Pres. T.O. Smith Sch. PTA, 1976-78, Ogden City Coun. PTA, 1983-85; assoc. dir. Region II, Utah PTA, Salt Lake City, 1981-83, mem. State Edn. Commn., 1982-87; chmn. state internat. hospitality and aid Utah Fedn. Women's Clubs, 1982-86; v.p. Ogden dist., 1990-92, pres. Ogden dist., 1992-96, state resolutions com., 1996—; trustee Family Counseling Svc. No. Utah, Ogden, 1983-95, emeritus trustee, 1995—; Utah rep. to nat. bd. Challenger Films, Inc., 1986—; state pres. Rocky Mountain Conf. Women in Mission, United Ch. of Christ, 1974-77, sec., 1981-84, vice moderator Utah Assn., 1992-94; chair pastor-parish rels. com. United Ch. of Christ Congl., Ogden, 1999-03, chair search com., 1995-96, mission com., 2002—, chmn. mission com., 2006—; Interfaith Works!, rep. Interfaith Cmty., North Utah. Recipient Ecumenical Svc. citation Ind. Coun. Chs., 1962, Outstanding Local Pres. award Utah PTA, 1978, Outstanding Latchkey Child Project award, 1985, Cmty. Svc. award City of Ogden, 1980-82, Celebration of Gifts of Lay Woman Nat. award United Ch. of Christ, 1987, Excellence in the Arts in Art Edn. award Ogden City Arts Commn., 1993, Spirit of Am. Woman in Arts and Humanities award Your Cmty. Connection, Ogden, 1994, Heart and Hand award United Ch. of Christ, Ogden, 2001; Utah Endowment for Humanities grantee, 1981-82. Mem. Nat. League Am. Penwomen (chmn. Utah conv. 1973, 11 awards for articles and essays 1987-95, 1st pl. news award 1992, 1st pl. short stories 1997, 3d pl. articles 1997), AAUW (state edn. rep. 1982-86, parliamentarian Ogden br. 1997—, membership v.p. Ogden br. 2003—, Disting. Woman award 2006), League of Utah Writers (Publ. Quill award 1998). Democrat. Home and Office: 722 Boughton St Ogden UT 84403-1152 E-mail: gkharrington1@comcast.net.

HARRINGTON, PATTI, school system administrator; BA, MEd, Brigham Young U.; PhD in Edml. Adminstrn., U. Utah. Prin. Provo HS, Utah; asst. supt. Provo; supt., 2001; assoc. supt. State of Utah, 2002—04, supt. of pub. instrn., 2004—. Recipient Secondary Sch. Prin. of Yr., 1997. Office: Utah Office of Edn 250 E 500 S PO Box 144200 Salt Lake City UT 84114-4200 Office Phone: 802-538-7500. Office Fax: 801-538-7768.*

HARRINGTON, PAUL, apparel executive; BA, Clark Univ.; MBA, Babson Grad. Sch. Bus. Mgr. prod. planning & fin. Ford Motor Co.; dir. footwear forecasting & inventory Reebok Internat., Canton, Mass., 1995—98, v.p. worldwide footwear & apparel ops., 1998—2000, sr. v.p. supply chain, 2000—03; sr. v.p. worldwide supply chain Levi Strauss & Co., San Francisco, 2003—04; sr. v.p. global ops. & chief supply chain officer Reebok Internat., Canton, Mass., 2004—06, pres. Reebok brand, 2006—. Office: Reebok Internat 1895 JW Foster Blvd Canton MA 02021

HARRINGTON, RICK, psychology professor; s. Keith S. and Grace L. Harrington; m. Cynthia A. Thompson, June 17, 1985. BA, U. Tex., Austin, 1975; PhD, U. Tex., Arlington, 1981. Lic. psychologist Tex. State Bd. Examiners Psychologists, 2007. Pvt. practice, Houston, 1984—87; prof. psychology U. Houston, Victoria, 1987—. Contbr. articles to profl. jours. Recipient Tchg. Excellence award, U. Houston, Victoria, 1990—91; fellow, U. Houston, 1981—84. Mem.: APA, Victoria Area Psychol. Assn. (pres. 1990—91), Psi Chi, Phi Beta Kappa. Avocation: running. Office: U Houston 3007 N Ben Wilson Victoria TX 77901-5731 Office Phone: 361-570-4205. Business E-Mail: harringtonr@uhv.edu.

HARRINGTON, ROBERT DUDLEY, JR., retired printing company executive; b. Worcester, Mass., Dec. 19, 1932; s. Robert Dudley and Anne Victoria Harrington; m. Melissa Banks Hubner, Mar. 25, 1978 (div.). AB, Brown U., 1955; MBA, Columbia U., 1957. With Morgan Guaranty Trust Co., NYC, 1957-59; v.p. Faulkner, Dawkins & Sullivan, NYC, 1959-69; ret., 1999. Hon. trustee, hon. mem. Woods Hole Oceanographic Instn. Corp. Mem.: Edgartown Reading Rm., Sail Newport, Round Hill Club, Edgartown Yacht Club, NY Yacht Club, Guiding Lights Lodge, Pilgrims, Holland Lodge. Personal E-mail: rdhmagic@aol.com.

HARRINGTON, ROGER FULLER, electrical engineering educator, consultant; b. Buffalo, Dec. 24, 1925; s. Henry Bassett and Emilie (Fuller) H.; m. Juanita L. Crawford, Aug. 7, 1954; m. Sandra, Judith, Alan, Laura. BS, Syracuse U., 1948, MS, 1950; PhD, Ohio State U., 1952. Instr. Syracuse U., NY, 1948-50, asst. prof. NY, 1952-56, assoc. prof. NY, 1956-60, prof. NY, 1960-94, dir. Electromagnetics Ctr. NY, 1982-94. Vis. prof. U. Ill., Urbana, 1959-60, U. Calif., Berkeley, 1964, E. China Normal U., 1983, Ecole Poly. Fédéral de Lausanne, Switzerland, 1991; guest prof. Tech. U. Denmark, Lyngby, 1969; cons. in field. Author: Introduction to EM Engineering, 1956, Time-Harmonic EM Fields, 1961, Field Computation by Moment Methods, 1968. Served with USN, 1944-46. Rsch. fellow Ohio State U., Columbus, 1950-52; Fulbright lectr., Denmark, eng., 1969; named Disting. Alumni Ohio State U., 1970; recipient Chancellor's Citation Syracuse U., 1984, URSI van der Pol Gold medal, 1996, jubilee medal Nicola Tesla Found., 1998. Mem. IEEE (Centennial medal 1984, Disting. Achievement award 1989, Electromagnetics award 2000, Third Millennium medal 2000), AAUP, Sigma Xi, Sigma Nu. Home: 5424 N Strada De Rubino Tucson AZ 85750-6061 Office: U Ariz Dept Elec Computer Engring Tucson AZ 85721-0001

HARRIS, A. BROOKS, physicist, researcher; b. Boston, Mar. 25, 1935; s. Frank Ephraim and Wilhelmina (Sellers) Harris; m. Margaret Marie Rees, Aug. 23, 1958; children: Katherine Margaret Harris Gray, William Brooks, Thomas Andrew. AB, Harvard U., 1956, MA, 1959, PhD, 1962. Mem. faculty to prof. physics emeritus U. Pa., Phila., 1965—; Alfred P. Sloan postdoctoral fellow, 1967—69. Prog. co-chmn. Magnetism and Magnetic Materials Conf., 1969; vis. scientist UK Atomic Energy Authority, 1965, Brookhaven Nat. Lab., 1972, Sandia Labs., 1974, Oxford U., Eng., 1986, Tel Aviv U., 1987; Schlumburger-Doll rschr., 1983 Contbr. articles to sci. jours.; co-editor: Magnetic Material Digest, 1968. John Simon Guggenheim fellow, 1972-73; recipient Lars Onsager prize, Am. Phys. Soc., 2007. Mem.: Internat. Lawn Tennis. Home: 117 Bair Rd Berwyn PA 19312-1403 Office: Dept Physics U Pa Philadelphia PA 19104 E-mail: harris@dept.physics.upenn.edu.*

HARRIS, AARON, management consultant; b. Birmingham, Ala., Oct. 27, 1930; s. Moses and Fannie (Williams) H.; m. Edna Mabel Turner, May 13, 1954; children: Kevin Brian, Edwin Maurice. BA, Talladega Coll., 1952; MS, Columbia U., 1959; postgrad., Princeton U., 1961. Trainee Bklyn. Pub. Library, 1956-59; asst. librarian Burroughs Wellcome Co., Tuckahoe, NY, 1959-64; assoc. librarian IBM Corp., East Fishkill, NY, 1964-66; library mgr. IBM Research Lab., San Jose, Calif., 1966-73; personnel exec. IBM Corp., San Jose, 1973-77; v.p. Discovery Sys., Inc., 1974—; data processing mgr. IBM, 1977-80, mgr. tng. and devel., 1980-84, mgr. human resources info. systems, 1985-88; program mgr. mgmt. devel. Rolm Systems, Santa Clara, Calif., 1988-91. Adv. instr. IBM Mgmt. Inst., 1992; cons.; pres. Amistad Assocs. Gen. chmn. Citizens Com. on Schs., San Jose, 1969-71; mem. San Jose CSC, 1974-78; foreman pro tem Santa Clara County Grand Jury, 1979-80; candidate San Jose Sch. Bd., 1969, 73; past bd. dirs. Santa Clara chpt. ARC, Mus. Art, San Jose; bd. dirs. Opera San Jose, 1986-92, Santa Clara County Urban League, 1984-87; San Jose Planning Commr., 1989-92; bd. dirs. Am. Civil Liberties Union Ala., 1996-99; conf. pres. laymen's coun. AME Zion Ch., trustee. With AUS, 1952-55. Recipient Citizen of Year award Omega Psi Phi, 1970, Outstanding Contbn. award Omega Psi Phi, 1991. Mem. Talladega Coll. Alumni Assn. (pres. Birmingham chpt. 1995-2000, Outstanding Contbn. award 2000, Outstanding Alumnus award Talladege Coll. 2005). Mem. AME Zion Ch. Home and Office: 341 Turnberry Rd Birmingham AL 35244-3291 E-mail: AaronAt75@yahoo.com. *Those who have presented obstacles for failure have been overwhelmed by my confidence. Those who longed for my success have been supportive with encouragement and opportunity. The principles embodied in the golden rule are my constant aim.*

HARRIS, ADAM C., lawyer; b. East Orange, NJ, 1960; BA, Emory U., 1982; JD magna cum laude, Georgetown U., 1986. Bar: NY 1987, US Dist. Ct. (So. and Ea. Districts of NY) 1987, US Ct. Appeals (2nd Cir.). Ptnr. Schulte Roth & Zabel LLP, NYC. Mem.: Assn. Bar City of NY. Office: Schulte Roth & Zabel LLP 919 Third Ave New York NY 10022 Office Phone: 212-756-2253.

HARRIS, ALICE, linguist, educator; b. Columbus, Ga., Nov. 23, 1947; d. Joseph Clarence and Georgia (Walker) H.; m. James Vaughan Staros, Aug. 7, 1976; children: Joseph Vaughan, Alice Carmichael. BA, Randolph-Macon Woman's Coll., 1969; MA, U. Essex, Eng., 1972; PhD, Harvard U., 1976. Tchg. fellow linguistics Harvard U., Cambridge, Mass., 1972-74, 75-76, lectr. linguistics, 1976-77, rsch. fellow linguistics, 1977-79; rsch. asst. prof. linguistics Vanderbilt U., Nashville, 1979-84, assoc. prof. linguistics, 1985-91, assoc. prof. anthropology, 1986-92, prof. linguistics, 1991—2002, prof. anthropology, 1992—2002, chair dept. Germanic, Slavic langs., 1993—2002; prof. linguistics SUNY, Stony Brook, 2002—, dir. grad. program, 2005—. Chair faculty coun. Coll. Arts and Scis., 1995-96; vice chair grad. faculty coun., 1993-94, sec. faculty senate, 1993-94; assoc. rsch. U. Tbilisi, USSR, 1974-75; tutor linguistics Dunster House, Harvard U., Cambridge, 1975-77; cons. to Simon and Schuster; Erskine vis. prof. U. of Canterbury, Christchurch, New Zealand, 1999; adv. bd. Pubs. MLA, 1995-98. Author: (book) Georgian Syntax, 1981, Diachronic Syntax, 1985, The Indigenous Languages of the Caucasus, 1991, Endoclitics and the Origins of Udi Morphosyntax, 2002; co-author: Historical Syntax in Cross-Linguistic Perspective, 1995 (Leonard Bloomfield book award, 1998); assoc. editor (jour.) Language, 1988—89, mem. editl. bd. Diachronica, 1994—2002, Natural Language and Linguistic Theory, 1987—90, Linguistic Typology, 2003—; contbr. articles to profl. jours. Sinclair Kennedy fellow Harvard U., 1974-75, NSF Nat. Needs Postdoctoral fellow, 1978-79; grantee Internat. Rsch. and Exch. Bd., 1973, 74-75, 77, 81, 89, 92, Linguistic Soc. Am., 1981, NSF 1980-83, 81-83, 83-85, 85-89, 97-99, 2001-03, 02-05, 02-07, NEH, 1990-91, Deutscher Adademischer Austausch Dienst, 1994; scholar Harvard U. 1972-73, Georgetown U., 1973; recipient Mellon Found. Regional Faculty Devel. award 1981, ACLS travel award, 1988, venture fund Vanderbilt U., 1987, 92, 94, Earl Sutherland prize for rsch. Vanderbilt U., 1998. Mem. Internat. Soc. Hist. Linguistics (mem. exec. com. 1995-01), Linguistic Soc. Am. (cons., com. status women in linguistics, nominating com., com. endangered langs. and preservation), Southeastern Conf. Linguistics, Soc. for Study of Caucasia (exec. coun. 1990-98), Societas Caucasologica Europaea (v.p. 1990-92, exec. com. 1992-94, 1994-2000), Phi Beta Kappa. Office: SUNY Dept Linguistics Stony Brook NY 11794-4376 Office Phone: 631-632-7758. Business E-Mail: alice.harris@stonybrook.edu.

HARRIS, ANDREW BENNETT, artist, writer, producer; b. Geneva, NY, Sept. 4, 1944; s. Earle Harold and Muriel (Lipsett) H.; m. Ronnie Sue Shenkman, Dec. 29, 1968 (div. May 1979); m. Ann Marcia Silverglit, May 17, 1985. AB, U. Chgo., 1967; MPhil, Columbia U., 1976, PhD, 1981; CIB, NYU, 1985. Jr. exec. Greystone Press, NYC, 1971-73; tchg. asst. theatre divsn. Columbia U., NYC, 1974-75, rsch. assoc., 1975-76, asst. prof., 1977-84, chmn., 1981-83; exec. dir. Riverside Shakespeare Co., NYC, 1984; chmn. theatre dept. So. Meth. U., Dallas, 1985-88, Tex. Christian U., Ft. Worth, 1989-93; pres. ABH Prodns., Inc., McKinney, Tex., 1993—. Bd. advisors Broadway Theatre Inst., N.Y.C., 1989—; bd. dirs. Jubilee Theatre, Ft. Worth, New Dramatists, N.Y.C. Author: Broadway Theatre, 1993 (Excellence Edn. award 1994), (play) Erasmus, 1967;

compiler: (play) Albee's Women, 1993; producer (play) Better Half Dead, 1995, Chgo., 1996, Idol Hill, 1994. Active Trinity Art Guild, 1998—. Recipient Founders award, 1st pl. Collin County Art Show, 2001, 1st pl. Mid-Cities Fine Arts, Hurst, Tex., 1998; Creative Work grantee Goldring Found. Tex. Christian U., 1991, 90, 89, NationsBank grantee, 1990, travel grantee, IREX, 1981, 83, 84, 86. Mem. Players Club, Art Club of McKinney (pres. 2002). Home and Office: ABH Prodns 514 W Hunt St Mc Kinney TX 75069-3837

HARRIS, ANN BIRGITTA SUTHERLAND, art historian; b. Cambridge, Eng., Nov. 4, 1937; came to U.S., 1965, naturalized, 1996; d. Gordon B.B.M. and Gunborg Elizabeth (Wahlström) Sutherland; m. William Vernon Harris, July 13, 1965 (div. Oct. 1999); 1 son, Neil William Orlando Sutherland. BA with 1st class honours, Courtauld Inst., U. London, 1961, PhD, 1965. Asst. lectr. U. Leeds (Eng.), 1964-65; asst. prof. art history Columbia U., NYC, 1965-71, Hunter Coll., NYC, 1971-73; assoc. prof. SUNY, Albany, 1973-77; chmn. for acad. affairs Met. Mus. Art, NYC, 1977-80; part-time faculty Juilliard Sch., NYC, 1978-84; prof. U. Pitts., 1984—. Founder, 1st pres. Women's Caucus for Art, 1973-76; disting. vis. prof. U. Tex.-Arlington, fall 1982; Mellon prof. history of art U. Pitts., spring 1984; vis. prof. history of art So. Meth. U., Dallas, fall 1993. Author: Andrea Sacchi, 1977, Selected Drawings of Gian Lorenzo Bernini, 1977, Seventeenth Century Art and Architecture, 2004; co-author: Die Zeichnungen von Andrea Sacchi und Carlo Maratta, 1967, Women Artists: 1550-1950, exhbn. catalogue, 1977, Landscape Painting in Rome, 1575-1675, exhbn. catalogue, 1985, Italian, French, English and Spanish Drawings and Watercolors in the Detroit Institute of Arts, 1992. Fellow Guggenheim Found., 1971, Ford Found., 1975-76, NEH, 1981-82, rsch. fellow Getty Mus. Art, 1988. Mem. Coll. Art Assn., Women's Caucus for Art. Office: U Pittsburgh Dept History of Art Pittsburgh PA 15260 Office Phone: 412-648-2408. Business E-Mail: ash@pitt.edu.

HARRIS, ARLENE, lawyer; b. Buffalo, Dec. 29, 1944; d. Yetta (Kerner) Cramer; m. Ira S. Harris, Dec. 25, 1971; children: Elliot, David, Sara. BA cum laude, Bklyn. Coll., 1965; JD, NYU, 1968. Bar: NY 1969, US Tax Ct. 1971. Assoc. trusts and estates dept. Paul, Weiss, Rifkind, Wharton & Garrison, 1968-75; asst. atty. gen. NY State Dept. Law, 1975-76; law asst.-referee NY County Surrogate's Ct., 1976-78, chief law asst., 1978-90; ptnr. trusts and estates dept. Shea & Gould, NYC, 1990-93; spl. counsel, chair Wills & Estates Dept. Kaye Scholer, LLP, NYC, 1993—. Mem. Internat. Acad. Estate and Trust Law, Estate's Discussion Grps.; bd. dirs. Estate Planning Coun.; adj. prof. law St. John's U. Sch. Law, 1984-92; instr. NYU Sch. Continuing Edn., 1991—; lectr. estate planning, trusts and estates ABA Nat. Inst., World Trade Inst., NY County Lawyer's Assn., Acad. Trial Lawyers, United Jewish Appeal Am. Estates Conf., Practising Law Inst. Contbr. chpt. to book, articles to legal publs. and procs. Bd. dirs. East Bay Civic Assn., Inc., 1974-87. Named one of Top 100 Attys., Worth mag., 2006; John Norton Pomeroy scholar, NYU, 1968. Fellow Am. Coll. Trusts and Estate Counsel; mem. NY State Bar Assn. (chmn. legislation com., former mem.-at-large trusts and estates sect., lectr. trusts and estates law sect., chmn. trusts and estates law sect.), Assn. of Bar of City of NY (mem. trusts, estates and surrogate's cts. com. 1979-81, 2005—), Order of Coif. Avocations: gardening, reading, boating. Office: Kaye Scholer LLP 425 Park Ave New York NY 10022-3598 Office Phone: 212-836-8816. E-mail: aharris@kayescholer.com.*

HARRIS, BARBARA CLEMENTINE, bishop; b. Phila., 1930; Grad., Charles Morris Price Sch. Advt. and Journalism, Phila.; student, Villanova U., Urban Theology Unit, Sheffield, Eng.; D in Sacred Theology (hon.), Hobart and William Smith Colls., 1981; DD (hon.), Gen. Theol. Sem., 1989, Episc. Div. Sch., 1989, Amherst Coll., 1989. Ordained to ministry Episcopal Ch. as deacon, 1979, as priest, 1980. Pres. Joseph V. Baker Assocs., Phila., 1958-68; sr. staff cons., mem. community rels. dept. Sun Oil Co.; priest-in-charge St. Augustine of Hippo, Norristown, Pa.; interim rector Ch. of the Advocate, Phila.; exec. dir. Episc. Ch. Pub. Co., 1984-88; suffragan bishop Episcopal Diocese of Mass., Boston, 1989—. Trustee Episc. Div. Sch. Address: Episc Diocese of Mass 138 Tremont St Boston MA 02111-1318

HARRIS, BARBARA S., publishing executive, editor-in-chief; BS in Phys. Edn., Fla. State U., 1978; Masters, N.E. Mo. State U. Editor-in-chief Weider Publ., Woodland Hill, Calif., 1987—2003; exec. v.p. Am. Media, Woodlands Hills, 2003—. Current advisor Calif. Gov.'s Coun. on Phys. Fitness and Sports; past chmn. bd. dirs. Am. Coun. on Exercise; mem. adv. bd. Fitness Cert. program U. Calif., LA; nat. women's wellness expert and presenter. Appearances on Oprah, Today Show, CNN, MSNBC, Access Hollywood, Entertainment Tonight. Achievements include climbing 20,000 foot mountain in the Bolivian Andes, Mt. Rainier and Mt Kilimanjaro. Avocations: running, weight training, kayaking, photography, rock climbing. Office: Am Media 21100 Erwin St Woodland Hills CA 91367-3712 Business E-Mail: bharris@weiderpub.com.

HARRIS, BEN M., education educator; b. Chgo., Feb. 8, 1923; s. Eva Mae (Barber) Sands; m. Mary Lee Christian, Sept. 28, 1948; children: Kim Christian, Tamara Lee. AA, Glendale Coll., 1943; BA, UCLA, 1948, MEd, 1951; EdD, U. Calif., Berkeley, 1958. Cert. elem. tchr., secondary tchr., prin., sch. adminstr., Calif. Chemist Desert Chem. Co., Twenty Nine Palms, Calif., 1943-44; tchr. Burbank Jr. HS, Calif., 1948-51; curriculum coordinator Inyo County Schs., Independence, Calif., 1951-54; tchr. Lafayette Elem. Sch., Calif., 1954-55; dir. curriculum Lafayette Sch. Dist., 1955-56, dir. pers., 1956-57; acad. asst. dept. edn. U. Calif., Berkeley, 1957-58; asst., then assoc. prof. U. Tex., Austin, 1958-68, prof. edn. adminstrn., 1968-87, M.K. Hage Centennial prof. edn., 1987, prof. emeritus, 1988—. Cons. Ministry Edn., Venezuela, 1973, Bahrain, 1985, Effective Border Schs. R&D Initiative, 1995-96, U. Sch. Collaborative project, Austin Pub. Schs., 1995-97; vis. prof. U. Wash., Seattle, 1976, U. Tex., San Antonio, 1989, U. Tex. Pan Am., Edinburg, 1992, 1997-2002; planning cons. Ministry of Edn., Egypt, 1987, Venezuela, 1973, 75, Malaysia, 1989, 91; UNESCO advisor U. Cordoba, Spain, 1971, U. Petroleum and Minerals, Dharan, 1979; advisor Lagoven, S.A. Venezuela Petroleum, 1991-92, Am. 2000 New Generation Schs. Project, Austin, 1991-92; vis. lectr. Taiwan Tchrs. Coll., Taichung/Kaochsfungand, 1994; dir. evaluation effective schs. border project, Edinburgh, 1995-97; co-dir. Visioning the Future Project Austin (Tex.) Ind. Sch. Dist., 2004. Author: Supervisory Behavior in Education, 1963, 3d edit., 1985, Developmental Teacher Evaluation, 1986, Inservice Education for Staff Development, 1980, 2d edit., 1989; (with others) Inservice Education: A Guide to Better Practice, 1969, Personnel Administration in Education, 1980, 3d edit., 1992, Invention*Developmental Teacher Evaluation Kit; co-developer Diagnostic Executive Competency Assessment System, 1988, Performance Criteria for School Executives, 1991, Summary Report on Formative Evaluation of Partner School Progress, 1997; mem. editl. bd. Handbook of Rsch. on School Supervision, 1998; co-author: Visioning the Future for Austin Senior High Schools, 2004, Cooperative Superintendency Project, 2004; contbr. chpts. to books and articles to profl. jours. Served with USNR, 1944-46. Fulbright scholar U. Teheran, Iran, 1962-63, Bahrain, 1985. Mem. ASCD (nat. bd. dirs. 1973-75, 80-82), Am. Edn. Rsch. Assn., Coun. Profs. of Instrnl. Supervision (pres. 1976-77), Sam Bass Theatre Assn., Trad. Jazz Club, Fulbright Alumni Assn., Phi Delta Kappa. Avocations: country and western dancing, singing, gardening. Office: U Tex Austin Dept Ednl Adminstrn D5400 George Sanchez Bldg 310 Austin TX 78712 Home Phone: 512-248-9284. Office Fax: 512-471-5975.

HARRIS, BENJAMIN HARTE, JR., lawyer; b. Sept. 12, 1937; s. Ben H. and Mary Cade (Aldridge) H.; m. Martha Elliott Lambeth, Aug. 26, 1961; children: Benjamin Harte, Wayt. AB, Davidson Coll., NC, 1959; JD, U. Ala., 1962. Bar: Ala. 1964, US Dist. Ct. (so. dist.) Ala. 1965, US Ct. Appeals (5th cir.) 1981, US Supreme Ct. 1971, US Ct. Appeals (11th cir.) 1981, US Tax Ct. 2000. Assoc. Johnstone, Adams, Bailey, Gordon & Harris (formerly Johnstone, Adams, May, Howard & Hill, LLC), Mobile, Ala., 1964-70; mem. Johnstone, Adams, Bailey, Gordon & Harris, Mobile, 1971. Chmn. Atty's Ins. Mut. Ala., bd. dirs. Past bd. dirs., past pres. Boys' Club, 1989-95; past chmn., past trustee UMS Prep Sch.; past v.p., bd. dirs. Gordon Smith Ctr.; past mem. stds. com. United Way; past sr. warden, All Saints Episc., mem. vestry, 2005—, treas., 2007—. Fellow: Ala. Bar Found. (past. pres., past trustee, past pres.), Am. Bar Found. (life); mem.: Nat. Conf. Bar Pres. (past exec. coun.), 11th Cir. Ct. Appeals Hist. Soc. (trustee, v.p.), Ala. Jud. Commn., Am. Arbitration Assn., Am. Judicature Soc., Ala. Def. Lawyers Assn., Ala. Law Sch. Found. (past pres., trustee, Pipes Disting. Alumnus award 2003), Ala. Law Inst., Ala. State Bar (bd. commrs. 1978—87, mem. exec. com., trustee bar found., past chmn. disciplinary commn., past pres.), Mobile County Bar Assn. (exec. com. 1980—87), ABA (past ho. of dels., past bd. govs.), Athelstan Club, Murray House (pres. 2003—04, past dir. 2006—), Mobile Rotary Club (Paul Harris fellow), Brook Inn of Ct. (pres. 1996—98). Episcopalian. Office: PO Box 1988 Mobile AL 36633-1988 Office Phone: 251-441-9205. Business E-Mail: bhh@johnstoneadams.com.

HARRIS, BEVERLY HOWARD, retired mathematics professor, genealogist; b. Lee's Summit, Mo., Aug. 22, 1927; s. Howard Kennedy Harris and Mattie Orman Beggs; m. Zorene Pruitt, May 21, 1950; children: Susan Annette Spurgeon, Steven Howard, Joy Aileen Crow. AA, SW Bapt. U., 1947; BS in Edn., Mo. State U., 1949; MA, U. Mo., 1953, EdD, 1963. Math. and sci. tchr. Humansville (Mo.) H.S., 1949—51; asst. instr. math. U. Mo., Columbia, 1951—52, instr. math., 1962—63, SW Bapt. U., Bolivar, 1952—64, prof. math., 1965—89, chmn. math. dept., 1965—89. Ofcl. basketball scorekeeper SW Bapt. U., Bolivar, 1954—89, chmn. scholarship com., 1975—84; supr. math. instrs. freshman math. U. Mo., Columba, 1962—63. Co-organizer State Tng. Ctr. for Handicapped, Bolivar, 1963—64; sec. bd. Bolivar Sheltered Workshop, 1978—93; organizer tennis tournaments Bolivar Tennis Assn., 1980—94; treas. bd. Polk County Christian Social Ministries, Bolivar, 1985—2006, organizer Share Your Christmas, 1989—2005. Sgt. US Army, 1946—47. Named Disting. Prof. Math., SW Bapt. U., 1980; named to Hall of Fame, Bolivar H.S., 2000; recipient Adults Sportsmanship award, Mo. Valley Tennis Assn., 1994, Disting. Alumni award, SW Bapt U., 1997; Full Curators scholar for grad. study, U. Mo., Columbia, 1962—63. Mem.: Math. Assn. Am. (life), Kappa Mu Epsilon (hon.). Republican. Baptist. Achievements include solved advanced mathematics problem Convergence of an Infinite Series. Avocations: genealogy, writing religious devotionals. Home: 910 E Division PO Box 66 Bolivar MO 65613-0066 Home Phone: 417-326-5338. Personal E-mail: bharris2x@alltel.net.

HARRIS, BRECK ANTHONY, business educator, writer, researcher; b. Denver, Aug. 2, 1953; s. Bobby Elywn Harris and Patricia Rosebrook (Stepmother), Joyce Schroeder; m. Dora Argyropoulos, Sept. 15, 1984; children: Jason John, Nikolas Bobby. AA, Coll. Alameda, Calif., 1978; BS, San Francisco State U., 1980, MBA, 1982; cert., Boeke Kenshu Ctr., Inst. Internat. Studies and Tng., Fujinomiya Shi, Japan, 1981; Ed. D., U. La Verne, Calif., 2000. Elec. engring. sales rep. Sq. D. Corp., Pleasanton, Calif., 1988—92. Cons. Internat. Exch. Corp., Oakland, Calif., 1982; spkr., presenter in field. Contbr.: coll. textbook Great Ideas for Teaching Marketing, 2002; musician (percussionist): (CD) Let Your Spirit Fall, 2003, Pistevo, 2007. Amb. Chamber of Commerce, Fresno, Calif.; bd. of trustees mem. Fresno Pacific U., 2003—04. With USN, 1972—76. Recipient Bus. award, Bank of Am., 1978, Alameda First Nat. Bank, 1978, Internat. Studies Grad. Fellowship award, San Francisco State U., 1981, Sigma Phi Award for Scholastic Achievement award in field of fgn. trade, San Francisco Propeller Club. Mem.: Nat. Soc. Exptl. Edn., Coun. Adult and Exptl. Learning, Adult Higher Edn. Alliance, Christian Adult Higher Edn. Assn., Beta Gamma Sigma. Avocations: travel, backpacking, running, music. Office: Fresno Pacific U 1717 S Chestnut Ave Fresno CA 93702 Office Phone: 559-453-2288. E-mail: baharris@fresno.edu.

HARRIS, CARL G., music educator; b. Fayette, Mo., Jan. 14, 1935; s. Carl G. Harris Sr. and Frances M. (Harris) Harris. BA, Philander Smith Coll., 1956; MA, U. Mo., 1964; Mus D, U. Mo., Conservatory of Music, 1972. Dir. of choirs Philander Smith Coll., Little Rock, 1959—69; prof., chair, dir. of choirs Va. State U., Petersburg, Va., 1971—84, Norfolk State U., Norfolk, Va., 1984—97; prof. of music, organist Hampton U., Hampton, Va., 1997—. Min. of music Bank St. Meml. Bapt. Ch., Norfolk, 1984—2004; min. of music emeritus bank St. Meml. Bapt. Ch., Norfolk, 2005—; organist Gillfield Bapt. Ch., Petersburg, Va., 1971—84, Centennial United Meth. Ch., Kans. City, Mo., 1968—71. Contbr. articles various profl. jours. Recipient Disting. Alumnus award, U. Mo., 1980, Alumnus award, Philander Smith Coll., 1975. Mem.: Lions, Kappa Delta Pi in Edn., Alpha Kappa Mu Nat., Tau Beta Sigma Hon. Band Soc., Phi Delta Kappa Edn., Kappa Kappa Psi Hon. Band, Phi Mu Alpha Sinfonia Music, Omega Psi Phi Fraternity, Inc. Democrat. Episcopalian. Home: 171 Atlantic Ave A Hampton VA 23664 Office: Hampton U Dept of Music Hampton VA 23668 Office Phone: 757-727-5702. Personal E-mail: charris54@cox.net.

HARRIS, CARLA ANN, investment company executive; m. Victor Adrian Franklin, Aug. 11, 2001. BA in economics, Harvard U., 1984, MBA, 1987. Joined Morgan Stanley, NYC, 1987, mergers, acquisitions, and restructuring dept., 1987—91, joined equity capital markets dept., 1991, mng. dir. global capital markets, head equity pvt. placements and retail capital markets. Singer: (albums) Carla's First Christmas, 2000, Joy is Waiting, 2005. Funded Carla Harris Scholarship at Harvard U. and Bishop Kenny H.S., Jacksonville, Fla.; exec. bd. Food for Survival, NYC Food Bank, St. Charles Borromeo Cath. Sch., Sponsors for Ednl. Opportunities, A Better Chance Inc.; bd. dirs. Boy Scouts Am., Manhattan; bd. mem. Apollo theater. Named Most Powerful African Am., Fortune Mag.; recipient Bethune Award, Nat. Coun. Negro Women, Ron Brown Trailblazer Award, St. John's U. Sch. Law, Women of Distinction Award, Girl Scouts of Greater Essex and Hudson Counties, Frederick Douglass Award, NY Urban League, 2003.

HARRIS, CHARLES EDISON, banker, lawyer; b. Ft. Lauderdale, Fla., Sept. 16, 1946; s. Thomas Edison and Margaret (Bailey) H.; m. Jeanne Dammas, June 17, 1969; children: David Edison, Ginger Suzanne, Brian Charles. BA, U. Fla., 1969; JD, Harvard U., 1972. Bar: Fla. 1972, D.C., 1987, U.S. Dist. Ct. (mid. dist.) Fla. 1978, U.S. Supreme Ct. 1978. Assoc. Maguire, Voorhis & Wells PA, Orlando, Fla., 1972-73; gen. counsel, sec. Sun Banks, Inc., Orlando, 1973-75, sr. v.p. adminstrn., sr. v.p. legal affairs and sec., 1976-81; asst. prof. law U. Fla., Gainesville, 1975-76; pvt. practice Orlando, 1981-84; ptnr. Arky, Freed, Stearns, Watson, Greer, Weaver & Harris, P.A., Orlando, 1984-85, Smith, Mackinnon, Mathews, Harris & Christiansen, P.A., Orlando, 1985-89; chmn. bd. Mid-State Fed. Savs. Bank, Ocala, Fla., 1987—; vice chmn., cfo Starwood Vacation Ownership Inc.; chief exec. officer Mid-State Fed. Savs. Bank, Ocala, 1988—, acting pres., 1988-89; ceo Allen C. Ewing & Co; chmn., pres. Synagen Capital Ptnrs., Inc., Orlando, 1989—; investor & dir. Intellon, Ocala, Fla., 1994, chmn. & pres., 2001, ceo, 2002—. Author: Business Negotiating Power: Optimizing Your Side of the Deal, 1983; co-author: Computer Contract Negotiations, 1981, Major Equipment Procurement, 1983. Served to capt. U.S. Army Res., 1969-77. Mem. ABA, Fla. Bar Assn., D.C. Bar Assn. also: Synagen Capital Ptnrs Inc PO Box 568589 Orlando FL 32856-8589 Office: Intellon 5100 W Silver Springs Blvd Ocala FL 34482 Office Phone: 352-237-7416. Office Fax: 352-237-7616.

HARRIS, CHARLES ELMER, retired lawyer; b. Williamsburg, Iowa, Nov. 26, 1922; s. Charles Elmer and Loretto (Judge) H.; m. Marjorie Clark, Jul. 9, 1949 (div. June. 1969); m. Linda Rae Slaymaker, Nov. 25, 1992; children: Martha Ann, Julie Ann, Charles Elmer III. Student, St. Ambrose Coll., 1940-42; BSc, U. Iowa, 1946, JD, 1949. Bar: Iowa 1949. Mem. firm Brody, Parker, Roberts, Thoma & Harris, Des Moines, 1949-66, Herrick, Langdon, Belin Harris, Langdon & Helmick, Des Moines, 1966-78, Belin Harris Helmick, P.C., Des Moines, 1978-91, Belin, Harris, Lamson, McCormick, P.C., Des Moines, 1991-96; pvt. practice, Des Moines, 1997-99; ret., 1999. Lectr. tax schs., meetings, 1951, 55, 67, 69, 77-84, 90, 91. Comments editor: Iowa Law Rev., 1948-49. Bd. dirs. NCCJ, 1964-67, Iowa Bar Found., 1977-92, Iowa Law Sch. Found., 1977-90, United Way Found., 1981-89. Lt. (j.g.) USNR, 1943-46. Fellow Am. Coll. Trust and Estate Counsel; mem. ABA, Iowa Bar Assn. (bd. govs. 1973-80, Merit award 1980), Polk County Bar Assn. (pres. 1972-73), Polk County Jr. Bar Assn. (pres. 1952-53), Order of Coif, Sigma Chi, Delta Theta Phi. Roman Catholic. Home: 5141 Robertson Dr Des Moines IA 50312-2170 Personal E-mail: harris5141@aol.com.

HARRIS, CHARLIE J., JR., lawyer; b. Fayetteville, NC, July 25, 1956; BA, Tarkio Coll., 1978; JD, U. Mo., Kans. City, 1995. Bar: Mo. 1995, Kans. 1996, US Dist. Ct. (We. Dist. Mo.) 1995, US Dist. Ct. (Ea. Dist. Mo.), US Dist. Ct. (Dist. Kans.), US Dist. Ct. (No. Dist. Ill.), US Ct. Appeals (8th Cir.). Law clk. to Hon. Fernando J. Gaitan Jr. US Dist. Ct. (We. Dist. Mo.), 1995—97; atty. Shook, Hardy & Bacon LLP, Kans. City, Mo.; ptnr. Berkowitz Oliver Williams Shaw & Eisenbrandt LLP, Kans. City, Mo., 1999—. Recipient Pat Kelly Disting. Alumni award, U. Mo. at Kans. City Law Sch., 2005. Mem.: Mo. State Bar (pres.-elect 2006—07), Jackson County Bar, ABA. Office: Berkowitz Oliver Williams Shaw & Eisenbrandt LLP Ste 1200 2600 Grand Blvd Kansas City MO 64108 Office Phone: 816-627-0223. Office Fax: 816-561-1888. E-mail: charris@bowse-law.com.

HARRIS, CHRISTOPHER, editor, writer, illustrator, graphics designer; b. Plainfield, NJ, June 7, 1933; s. Maynard Lawrence and Edith Johnson (Bushnell) H.; m. Linda Martin Robinson, Oct. 8, 1955 (dec. 1967); children— Katherine Hamilton, Stephen Christopher, Andrea Lawrence; m. Sarah Pickett Hargrove Sullivan, Aug. 18, 1977. BA, Yale U., 1955. Book mfg. coordinator Rand McNally & Co., Hammond, Ind., and NYC, 1955-60; mng. editor Studio Books div. Viking Press, NYC, 1960-70; editor, pres. Chatham Press, Riverside and Old Greenwich, Conn., 1970-76; dir. design and prodn. Yale U. Press, New Haven, 1977-88; dir. Summer Hill Books, 1978—; editor Proctor Libr. Newsletter, Weathersfield, Vt., 1996—; auditor Town of Weathersfield, 1996-97. Chmn., Weathersfield Dem. Town Com., 2000-03; trustee Proctor Libr., 2003—; mem. Weathersfield Conservation Commn. Democrat. Home and Office: 304 Beaver Pond Rd Perkinsville VT 05151-9558

HARRIS, CHRISTY FRANKLIN, lawyer; b. Greensboro, NC, Dec. 8, 1945; s. Luther Franklin and Rebecca Ann (Bluster) H.; children: Stacey Lynn, Aubrey Leigh. AA, Oxford Coll., Emory U.; BA, U. Fla., Gainesville, 1967; JD with honors, U. Fla., 1970. Bar: Fla. 1970, U.S. Dist. Ct. (mid. dist.) Fla. 1970, U.S. Ct. Mil. Appeals 1971, U.S. Ct. Appeals (11th cir.) 1984. Assoc. Holland & Knight, Lakeland, Fla., 1970, 1973—74; pres. Canan & Harris P.A., Lakeland, 1974—76; pres., sr. atty. Harris, Midyette & Clements P.A., Lakeland, 1976—89, Harris & Midyette, P.A., Lakeland, 1989—91, Harris, Midyette, Geary, Darby & Morrell, P.A., Lakeland, 1991—98, Harris, Midyette & Darby, P.A., Lakeland, 1998—2000; shareholder Peterson & Myers, P.A., Lakeland, 2000—03; of counsel Kinsey, Vincent, Pyle, L.C., Daytona Beach, Fla., 2003—. Mem. 10th cir. Grievance Com., Lakeland, 1976—79, Lakeland, 1983—86, vice chmn., 1979, chmn., 86; mem. Unauthorized Practice of Law Com., 1983—86; bd. dirs. Internat. Speedway Corp., 1984—. Bd. dirs. Program to Aid Drug Abusers, Lakeland, 1975-76, Campfire, 1979-85. Served to capt. USMCR, 1968-73, mil. judge, 1972-73 Named to Hon. Order of Ky. Cols., 1974 Mem. Volusia County Bar Assn., Attys. Title Ins. Fund, Grand Am. Rd. Racing Assn., LLC (founding mem.), Order of Coif, Art League Daytona Beach, Phi Beta Kappa, Phi Kappa Phi. Republican. Avocations: motor sports, art collecting. Home: 6022 S Williamson Blvd Port Orange FL 32128 Office: Kinsey Vincent Pyle LC 150 S Palmetto Ave Box A Daytona Beach FL 32114 Business E-Mail: cfh@kvplaw.com.

HARRIS, CIARA PRINCESS See CIARA

HARRIS, CLIFFORD JOSEPH, JR., (T.I., TIP HARRIS), rap artist; b. Atlanta, Sept. 25, 1980; children: Messiah, Damani Uriah, Deyjah, King. Launched film prodn. co. Grand Hustle Films, 2005—; founder & co-CEO Grand Hustle Records, 2005—. Singer: (albums) I'm Serious, 2001, Trap Muzik, 2003, Urban Legend, 2004, King, 2006 (Billboard Music award for Best Album of Yr., 2006, BET Hip Hop CD of Yr., 2006), In Da Streets, 2007, T.I. vs T.I.P., 2007, (songs) What You Know, 2006 (BET Hip Hop Video of Yr., 2006, Grammy award for Best Rap Solo Performance, 2007), (with Justin Timberlake) My Love, 2006 (Grammy award for Best Rap/Sung Collaboration, 2007); co-exec. prodr. (film soundtracks) Hustle & Flow, 2005; actor: (films) ATL, 2006 (BET award for Best Hip Hop Movie, 2006). Recipient Lisa Lopez award for Comty. Svc., 2005, Most Stylish Male award, Black Entertainment TV (BET) Awards, 2005, Best Male Hip Hop Artist award, 2006—07, Hip Hop MVP of Yr., BET Hip Hop Awards, 2006, Rap Artist of Yr., Rap Album Artist of Yr., Rap Songs Artist of Yr., & Videoclips Artist of Yr., Billboard Music Awards, 2006. Office: Grand Hustle PMB 161 541 10th St Atlanta GA 30318 E-mail: info@grandhustle.com.*

HARRIS, CONNIE, gifted and talented educator; d. Thomas Lloyd and Mary Margaret Coker; m. Barry Eugene Harris, May 15, 1983; children: Brian Limbaugh, Lara Landry, Melissa, Todd, Brittany. BS, U. Ala., Birmingham, 2000. Cert. edn. Fla., 2001. Gifted edn. tchr. Three Oaks Mid. Sch., Fort Myers, Fla., 2000—. Renaissance sponsor Three Oaks Mid. Sch., Fort Myers, 2000—06, Odyssey of the Mind sponsor, 2006—; county spelling bee coord. Lee County Schs., Fort Myers, 2006—. Smarter with Smart Tech. grantee, Found. for Lee County Sch. Dist. Mem.: Phi Theta Kappa. Home: 17509 Phlox Dr Fort Myers FL 33967 Office: Three Oaks Middle School 18500 Three Oaks Pkwy Fort Myers FL 33967 Home Phone: 239-482-7457; Office Phone: 239-267-5757.

HARRIS, CURTIS CRAIG, medical researcher; BA in Zoology, U. Kans., 1965, MD, 1969. Intern Dept. Medicine UCLA Hosp., 1969—70; resident and trainee in clin. oncology VA Hosp., Washington, 1973—76; rsch. assoc. Lung Cancer Inst. Divsn. Cancer Cause and Prevention, Nat. Cancer Inst., NIH, Bethesda, Md., 1970—72, head Ultrastructure Unit, Pathogenesis Sect., Lung Cancer Br., 1972—75, head Human Tissue Studies Sect., Lab. Exptl. Pathology, 1975—81, assoc. chief Lab. Exptl. Pathology, 1979—81; chief Lab. Human Carcinogenesis Ctr. Cancer Rsch., Nat. Cancer Inst., NIH, Bethesda, Md., 1981—, head Molecular Genetics and Carcinogenesis Sect., 1981—. Clin. prof. medicine and oncology Georgetown U. Sch. Medicine. Recipient Alton Ochsner Award Relating Smoking and Health, Alton Ochsner Med. Found. and Am. Coll. Chest Physicians, 1993, Walter Hubert Award and Lectr., Brit. Assn. Cancer Rsch., 1995, DSM, USPHS, 1999. Fellow: AAAS; mem.: Internat. Assn. for Study of Lung Cancer, Am. Soc. Differentiation, Am. Assn. Cancer Rsch., Am. Soc. Clin. Investigation, Internat. Soc. Gastroent. Carcinogenesis (Charles Heidelberger Award 1999). Office: NIH Nat Cancer Inst Lab Human Carcinogenesis Bldg 37 Rm3068A 37 Convent Dr Bethesda MD 20892 Office Phone: 301-496-2048. Office Fax: 301-496-0497. E-mail: curtis_harris@nih.gov.

HARRIS, CURTIS DEAN, financial consultant; s. Dean and Marilyn Harris; m. Rebecca Harris, Aug. 12, 2006. BBA in Fin., Tex. A&M U., College Station, 1994. Wealth mgr. HFG Advisors, LLC, Dallas, 1995—2006. Office: HFG Advisors LLC 12750 Merit Dr Suite 900 Dallas TX 75251 Home Phone: 214-353-9999; Office Phone: 972-386-5050.

HARRIS, CYNTHIA VIOLA, principal; b. San Francisco, Aug. 18, 1948; d. Gilbert and Mary Lee (barnes) H. BA in Speech, San Francisco State U., 1970, MA in Counseling, 1975; EdD, Nova U., 1987. Cert. tchr., adminstr., Calif. Tchr. Martin L. King Elem. Sch., Oakland, Calif., 1971-74; tchg. v.p. Peratta Yr. Round Sch., Oakland, 1974-80, prin., 1980-86, coord. staff devel., 1986-90, dir. staff devel., 1990-91, coord. recruitment, 1991—, asst. coord. to supt. cmty., parents, bus. ptnrships, 1992—; prin. Nystrom Magnet Sch., 2003—06; regional supt. Portland Pub. Sch., Oreg., 2006—. Mgmt. cons. year-round educ., leadership; guest lectr. Mills Coll., LaVerne U; coord. Community, Parents and Bus. Partnership; coord. coaches West Contra Costa Unified Sch. Dist., 2002-03; devel. dir. Help Other People Evolve; mem. Head Start commn. panel City of Oakland. Author: (tchg. manual) All About Us, 1980. Bd. dirs. Wiley Manuel Law Found., Charles Harrison Mason Scholarships; chiar minority caucus New Oakland Com. Nominated Outstanding Woman of Am., Alpha Kappa Alpha, 1981; recipient Capwell's Networker award, 1985; named Outstanding Youth Leader, Nat. Bus. and Profl. Bd., 1981; named to Alameda Edn. Hall of Fame, 2001. Mem. Nat. Assn. Female Execs., Nat. Assn. Prins., Nat. Ch. of God in Christ Bus. and Profl. Women, United Adminstrs. Oakland, Alliance Black Educators, Black Summit (internat. enrollment mgr.), Glamor Working Women's Panel, Coalition of 100 Black Women, Phi Delta Kappa. Democrat. Mem. Pentacostal Ch. Home: The Merrick 1231 NE Martin Luther King Blvd #509 Portland OR 97232 Office Phone: 503-916-5415. Personal E-mail: harriscynthia@hotmail.com. Business E-Mail: charris@pps.k12.or.us.

HARRIS, CYRIL MANTON, physicist, acoustical engineer, engineering and architecture educator; b. Detroit; s. Bernard O. and Ida (Moss) H.; m. Ann Schakne; children: Nicholas Bennett, Katherine Anne. BA, UCLA, 1938, MA, 1940; PhD, MIT, 1945; Sc.D. (hon.), N.J. Inst. Tech., 1981, Northwestern U., 1989. Rsch. asst. Carnegie Instn. Washington, 1941; mem. staff Bell Telephone Labs., 1945-51; cons. Office Naval Research, London, Eng., 1951; Fulbright lectr. Tech. U., Delft, Holland, 1951-52; Charles Batchelor prof. elec. engring., prof. architecture and past chmn. div. archtl. tech. Columbia U.; now prof. emeritus. Vis. Fulbright prof. U. Tokyo, 1960; acoustical cons. Met. Opera House, N.Y.C., John F. Kennedy Ctr. Performing Arts, Washington, Krannert Ctr. Performing Arts, U. Ill., Powell Symphony Hall, St. Louis, Nat. Acad. Scis. Auditorium, Washington, Minn. Orch. Hall, Mpls., Nat. Ctr. Performing Arts, Bombay, Symphony Hall, Salt Lake City, Benaroya Hall, Seattle; past dir. Inst. Theatre Tech.; mem. noise control group, mem. com. on undersea warfare NRC, 1955-57, mem. bldg. adv. bd., 1977-79; mem. coun. hearing and bio-acoustics Armed Forces-NRC, 1953-55; mem. adv. panel 213 to Nat. Bur. Standards, 1966-69, chmn., 1969-71. Author: (with V.O. Knudsen) Acoustical Designing in Architecture, 1950, rev., 1980, Handbook of Noise Control, 1957, 2d edit., 1979, 3d edit retitled Handbook of Acoustical Measurements and Noise Control, 1991, Dictionary of Architecture and Construction, 3d edit., 2000; Historic Architecture Sourcebook, 1977, Illustrated Dictionary of Historic Architecture, 1983; Handbook of Utilities and Services for Buildings, 1990, Noise Control in Buildings, 1993, American Architecture: An Illustrated Encyclopedia, 1998, Shock and Vibration Handbook 5th edit., 2002; mem. editl. adv. bd.: Physics Today, 1955-66; contbr. articles to profl. jours. Hon. trustee St. Louis Symphony Soc., 1977—; mem. nat. adv. bd. Utah Symphony Orch., 1976-85. Recipient Franklin medal, 1977; Emile Berliner award, 1977; Hon. award U.S. ITT, 1977; Wallace Clement Sabine medal, 1979; AIA medal, 1980; Gold Medal Audio Engring. Soc., 1984; award of honor for sci. and tech. City of N.Y., 1985; Alumni award UCLA, 1989, Pupin medal Columbia U., 1998. Fellow IEEE, Acoustical Soc. Am. (pres. 1964-65, assoc. editor jour. 1959-70, Gold medal), Audio Engring. Soc. (hon.); mem. NAS, NAE, Am. Inst. Physics (governing bd. 1965-66), N.Y. Acad. Scis. (pres. 1991-93, chmn. bd. 1992-94), Am. Philos. Soc., Century Assn., Sigma Xi, Tau Beta Pi.

HARRIS, DALE HUTTER, retired judge; b. Lynchburg, Va., July 10, 1932; d. Quintus and Agnes (Adams) Hutter; m. Edward Richmond Harris Jr., July 24, 1954; children: Mary Fontaine, Frances Harris Russell, Jennifer Harris Haynie, Timothy Edward. BA, Sweet Briar Coll., 1953; MEd in Counseling and Guidance, Lynchburg Coll., 1970; JD, U. Va., 1978; LLD (hon.), Wilson Coll., 1988; LHD (hon.), Lynchburg Coll., 2002. Bar: Va. 1978, U.S. Dist. Ct. (we. dist.) Va. 1978, U.S. Ct. Appeals (4th cir.) 1978. Admissions asst. Sweet Briar Coll. (Va.), 1953-54; caseworker Winchester/Frederick Dept. Welfare, Va., 1954-55; vis. lectr. Lynchburg Coll., Va., 1971; assoc. Davies & Peters, Lynchburg, 1978-82; substitute judge 24th Dist. Gen. Dist., Juvenile and Domestic Rels. Dist. Ct., Va., 1980-82; judge Juvenile and Domestic Rels. Dist. Ct., Lynchburg, 1982—2003; ret., 2003. Judge Family Ct. Pilot Project, Va., 1990—91; lectr. law U. Va. Law Sch., 1986—98; pres. Va. Coun. Juvenile and Family Ct. Judges, 1994—96; mem. panel of experts and adv. com. Child Protection and Custody Resource Ctr., 1994—2001; mem. Commn. on Future of Va.'s Jud. Sys., 1987—89; mem. adv. bd. Hilton Project on Model State Laws about Family Violence. Vice chmn. bd. dirs. Sweet Briar Coll., 1976-86; vol. coord. vols. in probation with Juvenile and Domestic Ct., 1971-73; chmn. steering com. for establishment Youth Svc. Bur., Lynchburg, 1972-73; chmn. bd. dirs. Lynchburg Youth Svcs., 1973-75; mem. adv. bd. Juvenile Ct., 1957-60, 62-68, sec., 1966-68; bd. dirs. Family Svc. Lynchburg, 1967-69; Lynchburg Fine Arts Ctr., 1965-67, Seven Hills Sch., 1966-73, Greater Lynchburg United Fund, 1963-65, Lynchburg Assn. Mental Health, 1960-61, Miller Home, 1980-82, Lynchburg Gen.-Marshall Lodge Hosps., Inc., 1980-82; v.p. Lynchburg Mental Health Study Commn., 1966; bd. dirs. Lynchburg Sheltered Workshop for Mentally Retarded Young Adults, 1965-69; bd. dirs. Lynchburg Guidance Ctr., 1959-61, v.p., 1970, pres., 1961; bd. dirs. Hist. Rev. Bd. Lynchburg, 1978-82; adv. bd. study of effectiveness of civil protection orders Nat. Ctr. State Cts., 1994-97; chair Va. State Bar Access to Legal Svcs. com., 2006-. Mem.: ABA, Am. Prosecutors Rsch. Inst., Nat. Coun. Juvenile and Family Ct. Judges (mem. child custody edn. com. 1993—98, chair family violence commn. 1998—2000, trustee 1998—2001, chair custody com. 1999—2001), Lynchburg Bar Assn., Va. State Bar (bd. govs. criminal law sect. 1988—90, bd. govs. family law sect. 1989—91, chair access to legal svcs. spl. com. 2006—07), Va. State Bar Assn., Phi Beta Kappa.

HARRIS, DALE RAY, lawyer, arbitrator, mediator; b. Crab Orchard, Ill., May 11, 1937; s. Ray B. and Aurelia M. (Davis) H.; m. Toni K. Shapkoff, June 26, 1960; children: Kristen Dee, Julie Diane. BA in Math., U. Colo., 1959; LLB, Harvard U., 1962. Bar: Colo. 1962, U.S. Dist. Ct. Colo. 1962, U.S. Ct. Appeals (10th cir.) 1962, U.S. Supreme Ct. 1981. Assoc. Davis, Graham & Stubbs, Denver, 1962-67, ptnr., 1967—, chmn. mgmt. com., 1982-85. Spkr. instr. in field; civil litigation editl. adv. bd. Bradford Pub. Co., 2005—. Mem. campaign cabinet Mile High United Way, 1986—87, chmn., atty. adv. com., 1988, sec., legal counsel, trustee, 1989—94, 1996—2001, mem. exec. com., 1989—2001, chmn. bd. trustees, 1996, 1997; trustee The Spaceship Earth Fund, 1986—89, Legal Aid Found. Colo., 1989—95, 2000—01; mem. devel. coun. U. Colo. Arts and Scis. dept., 1985—93; area chmn. law sch. fund Harvard U., 1978—81; bd. dirs. Colo. Jud. Inst., 1994—2003, vice chair, 1998; bd. dir. Colo. Lawyers Trust Account Found., 1996—2001; steering com. Youth-At-Work, 1994; School-To-Work, 1995; mem. jud. adv. coun. Colo. Supreme Ct., 2001—; bd. dirs. Rocky Mountain Arthritis Found., 2002—, Qualife Wellness Cmty., 2002—; mem. cmty. leadership bd. Mile High Montessori Early Learning Ctr., 2006—. With reserves USAR, 1962—68. Recipient Williams award Rocky Mountain Arthritis Found., 1999. Fellow: Am. Coll. Trial Lawyers, Am. Bar Found. (Colo. state chmn. 1998—2005); mem.: ABA (antitrust and litigation sects.), Colo. Assn. Corp. Counsel (pres. 1973—74), Denver Bar Assn. (chmn. centennial com. 1990—91, bd. trustees 1992—95, pres. 1993—94, Merit award 1997), Colo. Bar Assn. (coun. corp. banking and bus. law sect. 1978—83, chmn. antitrust com. 1980—84, bd. govs. 1991—95, chmn. family violence task force 1996—2000, pres.-elect, co-chair multi-disciplinary practice task force 1999—2000, bd. govs. 1999—2002, pres. 2000—01, chmn. transitions com. 2001—03, chmn. profl. reform initiative task force 2001—, chmn. transitions com. 2006—), Colo. Bar Found. (award of merit 2002), Rotary (Denver), Denver Law Club (pres. 1976—77, Lifetime Achievement award 1997), Univ. Club, Colo. Forum, The Two Percent Club (exec. com. 1994—), Citizens Against Amendment 12 Com. (exec. com. 1994), Phi Beta Kappa. Home: 2032 Bellaire St Denver CO 80207-3722 Office: Davis Graham & Stubbs 1550 17th St Ste 500 Denver CO 80202-1202 Home Phone: 303-377-8926; Office Phone: 303-892-9400. Business E-Mail: dale.harris@dgslaw.com.

HARRIS, DALE WILLIAM, systems engineer; b. Bethesda, Nov. 15, 1958; s. Dale Spear Harris and Gloria Ruth Karle; m. Zelia Goncalves Martins, May 5, 2006; m. Dionisia Ana Claudia Ghislieri (dec.). BA in Econs. and Math., U. Va., Charlottesville, 1981, M of Sys. Engring., 1982. Software developer ENSCO, Inc., Springfield, Va., 1982—90, Digital Sys. Resources, Fairfax, Va., 1990—96, TRW, Fairfax, 1996—98, mgr. software evaluation team, 1998, developer fingerprint software, 1998—2001; test and evaluation analyst, leader Northrop Grumman, Alexandria, Va., 2001—05, mgr. support to Army evaluation, 2005—. Del. Rep. Party Va., 1978—88; bd. dirs. Oakwood Condominium, Burke, Va., 1990—94. Mem.: IEEE, Internat. Test and Evaluation Assn., Am. Numismatic Assn. Republican. Methodist. Avocations: coin collecting/numismatics, architecture. Office: Northrop Grumman Mission Systems 4501 Ford Ave Ste 401 Alexandria VA 22302 Home: 1462 Cedar Ave Mc Lean VA 22101 Office Phone: 703-575-0771. Business E-Mail: dale.harris@ngc.com.

HARRIS, DANIEL MARK, lawyer; b. Chgo., May 23, 1951; s. Irving David and Tobie Gertrude (Zion) H.; m. Faith Bressler, Sept. 2, 1978; children: David, Rachel, Joseph, Talia, Tobie. BA, Johns Hopkins U., 1972; JD magna cum laude, Harvard U., 1977. Bar: Ill. 1978, DC 1980, Calif. 1980, US Dist. Ct. (no. dist.) Ill. 1981, US Ct. Appeals (7th cir.) 1982, US Supreme Ct. Law clk. to presiding justice U.S. Ct. Appeals (9th cir.), 1977-78; law clk. to assoc. justice Brennan U.S. Supreme Ct., Washington, 1978-79; assoc. O'Melveney & Myers, 1979-80; asst. atty. gen. State of Ill., 1980-82; from assoc. to ptnr. Mayer, Brown & Platt, Chgo., 1982; mem. Law Offices of Daniel Harris. Mem. nat. legal affairs com. Anti Defamation League. Recipient Sears Prize. Mem. ABA, Ill. Bar Assn. Lodges: B'nai B'rith (anti defamation league), Phi Beta Kappa. Republican. Jewish. Office: Law Offices of Daniel Harris 150 N Wacker Dr Ste 3000 Chicago IL 60606 Office Phone: 312-960-1803. Office Fax: 312-960-1936. Business E-Mail: lawofficedh@yahoo.com.

HARRIS, DARRYL WAYNE, publishing executive; b. Emmett, Idaho, July 29, 1941; s. Reed Ingval and Evelyn Faye (Wengreen) H.; m. Christine Sorenson, Sept. 10, 1965; children: Charles Reed, Michael Wayne, Jason Darryl, Stephanie, Ryan Joseph. BA, Brigham Young U., 1966. Staff writer Deseret News, Salt Lake City, 1965, Post-Register, Idaho Falls, 1966-67; tech. editor Idaho Nuc. Corp., Idaho Falls, 1967-68; account exec. David W. Evans & Assocs. Advt., Salt Lake City, 1968-71; pres. Harris Pub., Inc., Idaho Falls, 1971—; pub. Potato Grower of Idaho mag., 1972—, SnoWest Mag., 1974—, Sugar Prodr. mag., 1974—, Blue Ribbon mag., 1987-90, Modstock mag., 1992—, SnowAction mag., 1987—2000, Western Guide to Snowmobiling, 1988—, Houseboat Mag., 1990—, Pontoon and Deck Boat Mag., 1995—, Mountain Turf mag., 2001—, Idaho Falls mag., 2001—, SnoWest Canada mag., 2001—, Today's Playground mag., 2001—, SkatePark Mag., 2001—, Sledheads Mag., 2001—, River Jet Mag., 2004—. Campaign mgr. George Hansen for Congress Com., 1974, 76; campaign chmn. Mel Richardson for Congress Com., 1986; 1st counselor to pres. Korean Mission, Ch. Jesus Christ of Latter-day Saints, Seoul, Korea, 1963, area pub. comm. dir., Ea. Idaho, 1976-86; pres. Korea Seoul Mission, 1997-2000; High Priest, LDS Ch., 1987-2002, Bishop BYU, Idaho 27th Ward, 2003—, high coun. Idaho Falls Ammon Stake, 1987-91, Ammon 8th Ward Bishopric, 1991-96; founder Blue Ribbon Coalition, 1987; v.p. Teton Peaks coun. Boy Scouts Am., 1987-92; publicity chmn. Upper Snake River Scout Encampment, 1988; founder, pres. Our Land Soc., 1989-92. Mem. Agr. Editors Assn., Internat. Snowmobile Industry Assn. (Best Overall Reporting journalism award 1979, 80), Western Publs. Assn., World Champion Cutter and Chariot Racing Assn. (historian 1966-80), Nat. Snowmobile Found. (founder 1988), Kappa Tau Alpha, Pres. Club (award 1978), Idaho Falls Kiwanis (Disting., pres. 1978). Office: Harris Pub Inc 360 B St Idaho Falls ID 83402

HARRIS, DAVID ALAN, not-for-profit organization executive; b. Santa Monica, Calif., Sept. 23, 1949; s. Eric Albert and Nelly (Chender) H.; m. Giulia Boukhobza, Jan. 14, 1979; children: Daniel, Michael, Joshua. BA, U. Pa., 1971; MS, London Sch. Econs., 1972, postgrad., 1975—77, Oxford U., Eng., 1977—78; PhD (hon.), Hebrew Union Coll., 2003. Dir. govt. and internat. affairs Am. Jewish Com., NYC, 1987-90, exec. dir., 1990—. Nat. coord. Freedom Sunday for Soviet Jewry rally, Washington, 1987; pub. mem. U.S. Del. to Conf. on Security and Coop. in Europe; vis. scholar Johns Hopkins U., 2000-02. Author: The Jokes of Oppression, 1988, Entering a New Culture, 5th edit., 1989, The Jewish World, 1989, In The Trenches, Vol. 1, 1999, Vol. 4, 2006; contbr. over 100 articles to mags. and newspapers. Trustee Conn. Coll., 1999-2002. Cited by Lifestyles mag., Avenue mag., and Jewish monthly as Jewish leader; honored by govts. of Bulgaria, France, Germany and Poland. Mem.: Coun. Fgn. Rels. Office: Am Jewish Com 165 E 56th St New York NY 10022-2709 E-mail: harrisd@ajc.org.

HARRIS, DAVID FORD, management consultant, retired federal official; b. Hillsboro, Mo., Feb. 14, 1931; s. Walter Dunklin and Nelle (Landrigan) H.; m. Erna Beckmann, Mar. 5, 1964; children: Christopher Beckmann, Stefanie Ford. BS, U.S. Mil. Acad., West Point, 1954; MBA, Stanford U., 1961. Budget officer Post Office Dept., Washington, 1964-68, spl. asst. postmaster gen., 1968-70; chief adminstrv. officer, sec. Postal Rate Commn., Washington, 1970-83; sec. to bd. govs. U.S. Postal Svc., Washington, 1983-95; ret., 1995; mgmt. cons. representing N.Am. for CB Group, Santiago, Chile, 1996—. Capt. U.S. Army, 1954-64. Mem. West Point Alumni Assn., Stanford Alumni Assn., Alexandria Sportsman's Club. Roman Catholic. Home and Office: 3643 Trinity Dr Alexandria VA 22304-1840 Office Phone: 703-751-6945.

HARRIS, DAVID HENRY, retired life insurance company executive; b. NYC, May 7, 1924; s. Julian A. and May L. (Wilenski) H.; 1 child, Jean Harris Haig; m. Cassandra Sturman, Feb. 20, 1987. Student, Sherborne Sch., Eng., 1937-40. With Prudential Ins. Co. Am., 1940-43, Equitable Life Assurance Soc. U.S., NYC, 1946-86, exec. v.p., 1973-77, exec. v.p., chief adminstrv. officer, 1977-80, exec. v.p., chief staff, 1981-86, bd. dirs., 1977-86; pres. Equitable Found., 1986-88. Chmn. bd. Equimatics, Inc., 1971-73, Informatics, Inc., 1974-75; vice chmn. Equitable Variable Life Ins. Co., 1975-76, chmn., 1976-77. Bd. dirs. Can. Life of Am. Series Fund, 1989-2000; trustee Chappaqua Libr., 1991-94. With AUS, 1943-46. Fellow Soc. Actuaries. Home: 130 E 67th St New York NY 10065

HARRIS, DAVID M., information technology executive; Grad. in Chem. Engring., Howard U., Washington; MS in Real Estate Devel. and Investment, NYU. Various mgmt. positions Pepsi-Cola, Ameritech; sr. dir. workplace resources advanced planning group Sun Microsystems, Inc., Santa Clara, Calif., 2000, sr. v.p. workplace resources, sr. v.p. global bus. svcs. Office: Sun Microsystems Inc 4150 Network Cir Santa Clara CA 95054 Office Phone: 650-960-1300.*

HARRIS, DAVID THOMAS, immunology educator; b. Jonesboro, Ark, May 9, 1956; s. Marm Melton and Lucille Luretha (Buck) Harris; m. Francoise Jacqueline Besencon, June 24, 1989; children: Alexandre M., Stefanie L., Leticia M. BS in Biology, Math. and Psychology, Wake Forest U., 1978, MS, 1980, PhD in Microbiology and Immunology, 1982. Fellow Ludwig Inst. Cancer Rsch., Lausanne, Switzerland, 1982-85; rsch. asst. prof. U. NC, Chapel Hill, 1985-89; assoc. prof. U. Ariz., Tucson, 1989—2004, prof., 1996—. Cons. Teltech, Inc. Mpls., 1990—, Advanced Biosci. Resources, 1994-95; bd. sci. advisors Cryo-Cell Internat., 1992-95; bd. dir. Ageria, Inc., Tuscon; dir. Cord Blood Stem Cell Bank, 1992—; mem. Ariz. Cancer Ctr., Steele Meml. Children's Rsch. Ctr., Ariz. Arthritis Ctr. Program, sci. adv. bd. Cord Blood Registry, Inc., chief sci. div. Cord Blood Registry, Inc.; founder ImmuneRegen BioScis., Inc., 2002, Advanced Genetic Tools (Quregen, Inc.), 2004. Co-author chpts. to sci. books, articles to profls. jour.; reviewer sci. jour.; co-holder 9 scientific patents. Grantee numerous grants, 1988—. Mem. AAAS, Am. Assn. Immunologists, Reticuloendothelial Soc., Internat. Soc. Hematotherapy and Graft Engring., Internat. Soc. Devel. and Comparative Immunology, Scandanavian Soc. Immunology, Sigma Xi, Democrat. Church Of Christ. Avocations: tennis, hiking, jogging, skiing, travel. Office: U Ariz Dept Immunology Life Sci North 1501 N Campbell Ave Tucson AZ 85724 Office Phone: 520-626-5127. Business E-Mail: davidh@U.Arizona.edu.

HARRIS, DAVID W., academic administrator; m. Linda Harris; two children. Grad., Ea. N.Mex. U., 1971. Trainee analyst Legis. Fin. Com., 1972; asst. fin. dir. State Hwy. Dept.; dir. property control divsn. Dept. Fin. and Adminstrn., sec. natural resources dept.; sec. fin. and adminstrn. N.Mex. Dept. Fin. and Adminstrn., 1995—2000; dep. chief of staff N.Mex State Govt., 2001—03; exec. dir. N.Mex Fin. Authority, 2003—04; exec. v.p. adminstrn. U. N.Mex., Albuquerque, 2004—, acting pres., 2006—07. Exec. officer State Bd. Fin.; mem. State Investment Coun., Pub. Sch. Capital Outlay Coun., N.Mex. Fin. Authority, N.Mex. Cmty. Assistance Coun. With USAF, Korea. Recipient N.Mex. Disting. Pub. Svc. award, 1997. Office: U New Mexico MSC05 3350 1 Univ of New Mexico Albuquerque NM 87131*

HARRIS, DIANA KOFFMAN, sociologist, educator; b. Memphis, Aug. 11, 1929; d. David Nathan and Helen Ethel (Rotter) Koffman; m. Lawrence A. Harris, June 24, 1951; children: Marla, Jennifer. Student, U. Miami, 1947-48; BS, U. Wis., 1951; postgrad., U. Oxford, Eng., 1968-69. Advt. and sales promotion mgr. Wallace Johnston Distbg. Co., Memphis, 1952-54; welfare worker Tenn. Dept. Pub. Welfare, Knoxville, Tenn., 1954-56; instr. sociology Maryville (Tenn.) Coll., 1972-75, Fort Sanders Sch. Nursing, Knoxville, 1971-78, U. Tenn., Knoxville, 1967—; series editor Garland Pub., Inc., 1989—. Author: Readings in Social Gerontology, 1975; author: (with Cole) The Elderly in America, 1977; author: The Sociology of Aging, 1980, 3d edit., 2007; co-author: Sociology, 1984, Annotated Bibliography and Sourcebook: Sociology of Aging, 1985, Dictionary of Gerontology, 1988, Teaching Sociology of Aging, 1991, 5th edit., 2000, Maltreatment of Patients in Nursing Homes: There Is No Safe Place, 2006; co-editor: Encyclopedia of Ageism, 2005; aging series editor Garland Pub., Inc., 1989—; contbr. articles to profl. jours. Chmn. U. Tenn. Coun. on Aging, 1979—; organizer Knoxville chpt. Gray Panthers, 1978; mem. Govnr.'s Task Force on Preretirement Programs for State Employers, 1973, White Ho. Conf. on Aging, 1981; bd. mem. Knoxville-Knox County Coun. on Aging, 1976, Sr. Citizens Info. and Referral, 1979, Sr. Citizens Home-Aide Svc., 1977; del. E. Tenn. Coun. on Aging, 1977. Recipient Meritorious award Nat. U. Continuing Edn. Assn., 1982, Pub. Svc. award Nat. Alumni Assn., 1992, Appreciation award Assn. Gerontology in Higher Edn., 1994, Appreciation award for excellent scholarly contbn. to ednl. gerontology lit. Ednl. Gerontology jour., 1996; grantee Retirement Rsch. Found., 1997—. Mem. Am. Sociol. Assn., AAAS, Gerontol. Soc. Am., Popular Culture Assn., So. Sociol. Soc., So. Gerontol. Soc. (pres.'s award 1984), N. Central Sociol. Assn., London Competitor's Club, Nat. Contest Assn., Knoxville Kontestars. Home and Office: U Tenn Dept Sociology PO Box 50546 Knoxville TN 37950-0546 Business E-Mail: dharris@utk.edu.

HARRIS, DIANE CAROL, merger and acquisition consulting firm executive; b. Rockville Centre, NY, Dec. 25, 1942; d. Daniel Christopher and Laura Louise (Schmitt) Quigley; m. Wayne Manley Harris, Sept. 30, 1978. BA, Cath. U. Am., 1964; MS, Rensselaer Poly. Inst., 1967. With Bausch & Lomb, Rochester, NY, 1967-96, dir. applications lab., 1972-74, dir. tech. mktg. analytical systems divsn., 1974-76, bus. line mgr., 1976-77, v.p. planning and bus. programs, 1977-78, v.p. planning and bus. devel. Soflens divsn., 1978-80, corp. dir. planning, 1980-81, v.p. corp. devel., 1981-96; v.p. RID-N.Y. State, 1980-83; pres. Hypotenuse Enterprises, Inc., 1994—. Mem. adv. bd. Merger Mgmt. Report, 1986—92; internat. bd. dirs. Assn. Corp. Growth, v.p. corp. mem. affairs, 1993—94, v.p. internat. expansion, 1994—95, pres.-elect, 1996—97, pres., 1997—98, immediate past pres., 1998—99; bd. dirs. Flowserve Corp., chmn. audit com., 2001—04, mem. fin. com., 2005—; bd. dirs. Monroe Fund, Venture Capital Group. Contbr. articles to profl jours. Pres Rochester Against Intoxicated Driving, 1979—83, chmn polit action comt, 1983, 1986; bd dirs, chmn long range planning comt Rochester area Nat Coun Alcoholism, 1980—84; mem Stop DWI Adv Panel to Monroe County Legis, 1982—87, NY State Coalition for Safety Belt Use, 1984—85; mem. key exec. group Rensselaer Poly. Inst., 1993—96; mem. Com. 200, 1993—2002; mem ACG Speakers Bur, 1993—; mem adv comt Catalyst, 1995; bd dirs Rochester Rehab Ctr, 1982—84, Friends of Bristol Valley Playhouse Found, 1983—87. Named one of 50 Women to Watch in Corp Am, Bus Week Mag, 1987, 1992, 100 Women to Watch, Duns Bus Rev, 1988; recipient Distinguished Citizen's Award, Monroe County, 1979, Tribute to Women in Indust and Serv Award, YWCA, 1983, Pres's 21st Century Leadership Award, Women's Hall of Fame, 1995; grantee NSF, 1963. Mem.: Assn. Corp. Growth (Meritorious Svc. award 1995), Internat. Alliance Com. and Rochester Women's Network (com. of 200 1993—2002), Nat. Assn. Women Bus. Owners, Fin. Execs. Inst., Am. Mgmt. Assn., C. of C. (pub safety com. Rochester area chpt, task force on hwy. safety 1981—86, High Tech. Rochester adv. panel 1989—91, 1999—2000), Phi Beta Kappa, Delta Epsilon Sigma, Sigma Xi. Home: 60 Mendon Center Rd Honeoye Falls NY 14472-9363 Office: Hypotenuse Enterprises Inc 1545 East Ave Rochester NY 14610-1614 Office Phone: 585-473-7799. E-mail: harris@hypot.com.

HARRIS, DOLORES M., retired academic administrator, adult education educator; b. Camden, NJ, Aug. 5, 1930; d. Roland Henry, Sr. and Frances Anna (Gatewood) Ellis; m. Morris E. Harris, Sr., 1948 (div. 1987); children: Morris E. Jr., Sheila Davis, Gregory M. Sr. BS, Glassboro Coll., NJ, 1959, MA, 1966; EdD, Rutgers U., 1983. Tchr., reading specialist Glassboro Bd. Edn., 1958-68, dir. aux. svcs., 1968-70; supr. adult edn. Camden Welfare Bd., summer 1968; Head Start dir. Glassboro SCOPE, summer 1969-70; assoc. dir. Jersey City State Coll., summer 1971; dir. adult edn. Glassboro State Coll., 1970-74, dir. continuing edn. dept., 1989-90, acting assoc. v.p. acad. affairs, 1989-91; ret., 1991. Cons. Mich. State Dept. Edn., Lansing, 1973; examiner N.Y. State Civil Svc. Commn., 1976—; chmn. adv. bd. Women's Ednl. Equity Comm. Network Project, San Francisco, 1977—78; cons. crossroads project Temple U., Phila., 1977; bd. dirs. Glassboro State Coll. Mgmt. Inst.; cons. corrections project Va. Commonwealth U., Richmond; vice-chmn. comm. Accrediting Coun. Continuing Edn. and Tng., Richmond, 1985—89, chmn., 1989—. Author: (book) How to Establish ABE Programs, 1972; author: (with others) Black

Studies for ABE and GED Programs in Correction, 1975; founding editor: newsletter For Adults Only, 1970; contbr. articles to profl. jours. Founder, trustee, chair bd. trustees Glassboro Child Devel. Ctr., 1974—87; bd. dirs. Gloucester County United Way, NJ, 1977—, sec. bd. dirs. NJ, 1980, pres. bd. dirs. NJ, 1983—85; charter mem., bd. dirs. Glassboro Glass Mus., 1979—87; vice chair, chair, mem. Gloucester County Commn. Women, NJ, 1983—87; trustee Frederick Douglas Meml. and Hist. Assn., 2000—. Named Woman of the Yr., Gloucester County Bus. and Profl. Women's Club, 1985, Woman of Achievement, Gloucester County Commn. Women, 1987, Counselor of Yr., Svc. Corps Ret. Execs., 2003; named one of Outstanding Citizens, Holly Shores Girl Scouts U.S., 1987, 100 Most Influential Black Ams., Ebony Mag., 1989—92; named to Legion of Honor, Chapel of Four Chaplains, 1983; recipient Disting. Alumnae award, Glassboro State Coll., 1971, Disting. Svc. award, Camden County, 1974, Holly Shores Girl Scouts U.S., 1979, N.J. Woman of Achievement award, 1991. Mem.: AAUW (v.p. membership com. Gloucester County chpt. 1986—87), NEA, Ea. Montgomery County Svc. Corps Ret. Execs. (chair seminars, workshop programs 2001—, Counselor of Yr. 2003), NJ Edn. Assn., Women Greater Phila. (bd. dirs.), Soc. Docta (bd. dirs. 1987—), N.J. Adult Edn. Assn. (life; pres. 1973—74), South Jersey Links Club (v.p. 1982—84, pres. 1984—86), Links Club, Nat. Assn. Colored Women's Clubs, Inc. (pres. 1988—92), Northeastern Fedn. Women's Clubs (v.p.-at-large 1983—85, parliamentarian 1985—), NJ State Fedn. Colored Women's Clubs (pres. 1976—80). Presbyterian. Avocations: reading, fitness exercises.

HARRIS, DON VICTOR, JR., lawyer; b. Nottingham Twp., Ind., Jan. 16, 1921; s. Don Victor and Nellie Florence (Dukes) H.; m. Joan Elliott Haffler, Aug. 15, 1959; children: Leigh Elliott Hay, Meghan St. Clair Zeisser. AB, DePauw U., 1943; JD, Harvard U., 1945. Bar: DC 1947. Law clk. to judge U.S. Ct. Appeals 2d Cir., 1945-46; assoc. firm Covington & Burling, Washington, 1946-57, ptnr., 1957—. Lectr. in law George Washington U., 1963-64; lectr. tax insts.; mem. IRS Commr.'s Adv. Group, 1976. Contbr. articles to law jours.; case editor: Harvard Law Rev. Fellow Am. Coll. Tax Counsel, Am. Bar Found. (life); mem. Am. Law Inst. (life), ABA (chmn. sect. taxation 1976-77), DC Bar Assn., Fed. Bar Assn., Am. Camellia Soc. (judge), Met. Club, Chevy Chase Club, Phi Beta Kappa, Beta Theta Pi. Episcopalian. Home: 2803 P St NW Washington DC 20007-3067 Office: Covington & Burling 1043-C 1201 Pennsylvania Ave NW Washington DC 20004-2401 Home Phone: 202-338-7284; Office Phone: 202-662-5330. Personal E-mail: ursa1921@aol.com. Business E-Mail: dharris@cov.com.

HARRIS, DONALD, composer; b. St. Paul, Apr. 7, 1931; s. Barney William and Hattie (Paper) H.; m. Marilyn Hackett, 1983; children: Daniel, Jeremy. Mus.B., U. Mich., 1952, Mus.M., 1954. Music cons. Am. Cultural Center, USIS, Paris, 1965-67; asst. to pres. for acad. affairs New Eng. Conservatory Music, Boston, 1967-71, v.p., 1971-74, exec. v.p., 1974-77, mem. teaching faculty depts. composition and music lit., 1967-77; composer-in-residence, prof. music, chmn. composition and theory Hartt School of Music, U. Hartford, Conn., 1977-80, dean, 1981-88; dean Coll. of the Arts The Ohio State U., 1988-97, prof. composition, 1997—. Vis. prof. music George Washington U., 1998; pres. Internat. Coun. Fine Arts Deans, 1994-96. Composer: Piano Sonata, 1956, Fantasy for Violin and Piano, 1957, Symphony in Two Movements, 1961, String Quartet, 1965, Ludus for 10 Instruments, 1966, Ludus II for 5 Instruments, 1973, Charmes for Voice and Orchestra, 1977, On Variations, 1976, For the Night to Wear (Hortense Flexner), mezzo-soprano and 7 instruments, 1978, Balladen for solo piano, 1979, Of Hartford in a Purple Light (Wallace Stevens) for soprano and piano, 1979, Prelude to a Concert in Connecticut, 1981, Les Mains (Marguerite Yourcenar) for mezzo-soprano and piano, 1983, Meditations for Solo Organ, 1984, Three Fanfares for Four Horns, 1984, Canzona & Carol for Double Brass Quintet and Timpani, 1986, Pierrot Lieder (soprano & 5 instruments), 1988, Mermaid Variations (chamber orch.), 1993, Second String Quartet, 2002, Lyric Fanfare (orch.), 2003, Five Tempi, 2004; recs., CRI, Delos, Golden Crest Records; co-editor: The Correspondence Between Arnold Schoenberg and Alban Berg, 1986. Recipient commns. from Serge Koussevitzky Music Found., 1977, Elizabeth Sprague Coolidge Found., 1977, Goethe Inst., 1978, Conn. Commn. Arts, 1979, French Nat. Radio, 1972, Festival Contemporary Am. Music at Tanglewood, 1965, Boston Musica Viva, 1973, Cleve. Orch., 1975, Arnold Schoenberg Inst., 1988, Cleve. Chamber Orchestra, 1991, Jefferson Acad., 2001; recipient Louisville Orch. award, 1954, Prince Rainier of Monaco Composition prize, 1960, award Am. Acad. and Inst. Arts and Letters, 1991; grantee-in-aid Rockefeller Found., 1969; grantee-in-aid Chapelbrook Found., 1970; fellowship grantee Nat. Endowment for Arts, 1974; Fulbright scholar, 1956; Guggenheim fellow, 1965. Mem. ASCAP (Deems Taylor award 1989, others 1973—). Address: 5257 Courtney Pl Columbus OH 43235-3474 E-mail: harris.27@osu.edu.

HARRIS, DOUGLAS CLAY, retired newspaper executive; b. Owensboro, Ky., Oct. 9, 1939; s. Marvin Dudley and Elizabeth (Adelman) H. BS, Murray State U., 1961; MS, Ind. U., 1964, EdD, 1968; grad. advanced mgmt. program, Harvard U., 1987. Counselor, asst. to dean of students Ind. U., Bloomington, 1965-68; mgmt. appraisal specialist United Air Lines, Elk Grove Village, Ill., 1968-69; dir. manpower div. Computer Age Industries, Washington, 1969; area personnel dir. Peat Marwick Mitchell & Co., NYC, 1969-72; v.p. personnel Knight-Ridder, Inc., Miami, Fla., 1972-85, v.p., sec., 1986-98. Served to capt. U.S. Army, 1961-62. Republican. Home and Office: 218 Fairchild Dr Highlands Ranch CO 80126-4751 E-mail: drdoug.harris@comcast.net.

HARRIS, ED (EDWARD ALLEN HARRIS), actor; b. Englewood, NJ, Nov. 28, 1950; s. Bob L. and Margaret Harris; m. Amy Madigan, 1983; 1 child, Lilly. Student, Columbia U., 1969-71, U. Okla., Norman, 1972-73; BFA, Calif. Inst. of Arts, Valencia, 1975. Appeared in plays A Streetcar Named Desire, Sweet Bird of Youth, Julius Caesar, Hamlet, Camelot, Are You Lookin?, Time of Your Life, Learned Ladies, Kingdom of Earth, Grapes of Wrath, Present Laughter, Balaam, Killers' Head, Fool for Love (Obie award 1983), Prairie Avenue (L.A. Drama Critics Circle award 1981), Scar, 1985 (San Francisco Critics award), Precious Sons, 1986 (Theater World award), Simpatico, 1994, 95, Taking Sides, 1996, Wrecks, 2006; (repertory plays) Servant of Two Masters, Ohio, Claptrap, Cambridge, Mass., 1985, Pirates of Penzance at N.Y. Shakespeare Festival, Glass Menagerie, Long Wharf, New Haven, 1986, Bobby Gould in Hell, 1989; appeared in films including Coma, 1978, Borderline, 1978, Knightriders, 1980, Dream On, 1980, Creepshow, 1981, The Right Stuff, 1982, Swing Shift, 1982, Under Fire, 1982, Places in the Heart, 1983, A Flash of Green, 1984, Alamo Bay, 1984, Sweet Dreams, 1985, Code Name: Emerald, 1985, Walker, 1987, To Kill a Priest, 1988, Jacknife, 1989, The Abyss, 1989, State of Grace, 1990, Glengarry Glen Ross, 1992, Needful Things, 1993, The Firm, 1993, China Moon, 1994, Milk Money, 1994, Apollo 13, 1995 (Acad. award nominee for best supporting actor 1996, SAG award 1996), Just Cause, 1995, Eye for an Eye, 1995, Nixon, 1995, The Rock, 1996, Absolute Power, 1997, Stepmom, 1998, The Truman Show, 1998 (Golden Globe award, 1999), The Third Miracle, 1999, Waking the Dead, 2000, The Prime Gig, 2000, Enemy at the Gates, 2001, Buffalo Soldiers, 2001, A Beautiful Mind, 2001, Just a Dream, 2002, The Hours, 2002, Masked and Anonymous, 2003, The Human Stain, 2003, Radio, 2003, A History of Violence, 2005 (Best Supporting Actor, Nat. Soc. Film Critics award, 2006), Winter Passing, 2005; acted, dir., prodr., Pollock, 2000; TV movies include The Amazing Howard Hughes, 1977, The Seekers, 1979, The Aliens Are Coming, 1980, The Last Innocent Man, 1987, Paris Trout, 1991, Running Mates, 1992, The Stand, 1994 (unbilled cameo), Riders of the Purple Sage (also exec. prodr), 1997; TV miniseries Empire Falls, 2005; TV appearances The Rockford Files, 1978, Lou Grant, 1979, 80, 81, Barnaby Jones, 1979, CHiPs, 1981, Hart to Hart, 1981, Cassie and Co., 1982, Frasier, 1995. Trustee Calif. Inst. of Arts, Valencia, 1985—. Mem. Screen Actors Guild, Equity. Address: 22031 Carbon Mesa Rd Malibu CA 90265-5008*

HARRIS, EDWARD DAY, JR., physician; b. Phila., July 7, 1937; children: Ned, Tom, Chandler. AB, Dartmouth Coll., 1958, grad. with honors, 1960; MD cum laude, Harvard U., 1962. Diplomate Am. Bd. Internal Medicine and Rheumatology (chmn. subsplty. bd. in rheumatology 1986-88). Intern Mass. Gen. Hosp., Boston, 1962-63, asst. resident, 1963-64, sr. resident, 1966-67, clin. research fellow arthritis unit, 1967-69; asst. prof. Harvard Med. Sch., Boston, 1970; from asst. prof. to prof. Dartmouth Med. Sch., Hanover, NH, 1970-83, Eugene W. Leonard prof., 1979-83, chief connective tissue disease sect., 1970-83; mem. staff Mary Hitchcock Meml. Hosp., 1970-83; chief med. service Middlesex Gen. U. Hosp., New Brunswick, NJ, 1983—; asst. prof. Harvard U. Med. Sch., Boston, 1970; prof., chmn. medicine U. Medicine and Dentistry N.J.-Rutgers U. Med. Sch., New Brunswick, 1983-88; Arthur L. Bloomfield prof. medicine Stanford U. Sch. Medicine, 1988-95, chmn. dept. medicine, 1988-95, George DeForest Barnett prof. medicine, 1988—2003, George DeForest Barnett prof. medicine emeritus, 2003—; acad. sec. to Stanford U., 2002—07. Chief med. svc. Stanford U. Hosp., 1988-95; dir. Ctr. for Musculoskeletal Diseases, Stanford, 1996-99, emeritus, 2003—; pres. med. staff, Stanford U. Hosp., 1997-99; med. dir. Internat. Med. Svc., 1997—2002. Master: ACP (gov. No. Calif. chpt. 2000—), Am. Coll. Rheumatism (numerous coms. 1967—, pres. 1985—86, Dist. Rheumatism award 2004); fellow: Royal Soc. Medicine; mem.: Alpha Omega Alpha (exec. sec. 1997—, editor The Pharos 1997—). Office: Alpha Omega Alpha 525 Middlefield Rd Ste 130 Menlo Park CA 94025 Office Phone: 650-320-9875. Business E-Mail: madera@stanford.edu.

HARRIS, ELAINE K., medical consultant; b. NYC, Mar. 17, 1924; d. Julius and Bertha (Wecker) Kirschbaum; m. Herbert Harris, Aug. 1, 1948; children: Gail, Linda, Geoffrey. AB Bus. Economics cum laude, Hunter Coll.; AM Bus. Edn., Columbia U. Lic. tchr. bus. NY. Founder, pres. Sjogren's Syndrome Found., 1983-91, exec. dir., 1991-94. Cons. in field; v.p. exec. bd. Nat. Alliance for Oral Health; developer Sjogren's Syndrome Ednl. Symposia for lay and profls., nat. and internat. support group network. Editor: Moisture Seekers Newsletter, 1984-94, Sjogren's Syndrome Handbook: An Authoritative Guide for Patients, 1989; editor: The New Sjogren's Syndrome Handbook, 1998; contbg. author: Sjogren's Syndrome: Clinical and Immunologic Aspects, 1987, Self-Help, Concepts and Applications, 1992; contbr. articles to profl. jours. Founded Nassau-Suffolk Chpt. Hunter Coll. Alumni Assn., 1949; past treas. Youth Employment Svc., Great Neck (N.Y.) Pub. Schs., former chair Broader Horizons Com., PTA, Great Neck Pub. Sch., others; active Jewish communal field. Recipient Women's Living Legacy, Women's Internat. Ctr., 1994, Third Internat. Conf. on Sjogren's Syndrome, Greece, 1991; elected to Hunter Coll. Hall of Fame, 1989. Avocations: gardening, baking, photography, duplicate bridge. Personal E-mail: elaine.hh@verizon.net.

HARRIS, ELEANOR LYNNE K., theology studies educator; b. Villa Park, Ill., July 07; d. Robert Carl and Karin Elizabeth (Peterson) Karlström. BA, MA, U. Chgo.; MDiv, No. Bapt. Theol. Sem., 1975; D of Ministry, Chgo. Theol. Sem., 1980; PhD, NYU, 1980. Ordained min. United Ch. of Christ, 1987. From instr. to prof. U. Ill., Chgo., 1970—2006, prof. emerita, 2006—. Interim min. Union Congl. Ch., Moline, Ill., 1997; min. Glen Ellyn (Ill.) Congl. Ch., 1987-89; night ministry, Chgo., 1999, 2000, 01; adj. faculty religious studies Loyola U., Chgo., U. St. Francis; adj. faculty English Ind. U. Northwest, DePaul U., Ill. Benedictine U.; sec. Bd. Christian Witness in Soc., 1984-88; mem. seminaries com. Chgo. Met. Assn., United Ch. Christ, 2000-03; active Night Ministry, Chgo., summers 1999-2001; presenter, cons. adult edn. St. Pauls Ch., 2002; instr. creative writing Covenant, Plantation, Fla., 2007—; preaching and pastoral counseling, 2007—; contbr. poetry to Kavya Bharati; presenter in field; preacher SE conf. United Ch. Christ. Author: The Mystic Spirituality of A.W. Tozer, A Twentieth Century American Protestant, 1992; contbr. poems and articles to profl. jours. Recipient Lucia Queen of Light award City of Chgo., 1970. Mem. MLA, Am. Acad. Religion, Soc. Sci. Study Religion, Am.-Scandinavian Found., Chgo. Metro. Assn. (seminaries com.), Mensa. Avocations: art, music, travel, folk dancing, camping. Home: PO Box 16154 Plantation FL 33318-6154

HARRIS, EMILY LOUISE, special education educator; b. New London, Conn., Nov. 16, 1932; d. Frank Sr. and Tanzatter (McCleese) Brown; m. John Everett Harris Sr., Sept. 10, 1955; children: John Everett Jr., Jocelyn E. (dec.). BS, U. Conn., 1955; MEd, Northeastern U., 1969. Cert. tchr. elem. spl. subject sci., Mass., spl. subject reading, secondary prin., elem. prin. Tchr. New Haven Sch. Dept., 1957-59, Boston Sch. Dept., 1966-68, Natick (Mass.) Sch. Dept., 1969-72; cert. nurse's asst. The Hebrew Rehab. Ctr., Roslindale, Mass., 1973-75; spl. edn. educator Boston Sch. Dept., 1975-76, 78—, support tchr., 1976-78. Site coord. Tchr. Corps., 1977-81; leader, co-leader Harvard U. Student Tchrs. at Dorchester H.S. Sem., 1995—; tchr. adviser Future Educators Am. Dorchester H.S. Editor, compiler: Cooking With the Stars, 1989. Mem.-del. Mass. Fedn. Tchrs., Boston, 1993-96; elected rep. AFL-CIO (Boston Tchrs. Union), 1986-96; registrar of voters Dorchester (Mass.) H.S., 1986—; adv. bd. New England Assn. Schs. and Colls., 1980-93; 1st v.p., bd. dirs. League of Women for Comty. Svcs., Boston, 1976-80, Cynthia Sickle-Cell Anemia Fund, Boston, 1976-80. Recipient Tchg. award Urban League Guild Mass., 1993. Mem. AAUW, Zeta Phi Beta (Zeta of Yr. 1994), Alpha Delta Kappa, Kappa Delta Pi, Order Ea. Star (past worthy matron Prince Hall chpt. 1983-84), Delta Omicron Zeta, Phi Delta Kappa. Baptist. Avocations: reading, sewing. Home: 36 Dietz Rd Hyde Park MA 02136-1134

HARRIS, EMMYLOU, singer; b. Birmingham, Ala., Apr. 2, 1947; d. Walter and Eugenia; children: Hallie, Meghann. Student, U.N.C.-Greensboro. Singer, 1967; assisted Gram Parsons on album GP, Grievous Angel, 1973; toured with Fallen Angels Band, performed across Europe and U.S.; recording artist on albums for Reprise Records, Warner Bros. Records, Electra/Asylum Records; appeared in rock documentary The Last Waltz, 1978; albums include The Gliding Bird, 1969, Pieces of the Sky, 1975, Elite Hotel, 1976 (Grammy award), Luxury Liner, 1977, Quarter Moon In A Ten Cent Town, 1978, Profile: Best of Emmylou Harris, 1978, Blue Kentucky Girl, 1979, Light of the Stable, 1979, Evangeline, 1981, Last Date, 1982, White Shoes, 1983, Profile II: Best of Emmylou Harris, 1984, The Ballad of Sally Rose, 1985, Thirteen, 1986, Trio (with Dolly Parton, Linda Ronstadt), 1987 (Grammy award), Angel Band, 1987, Bluebird, 1988, Duets, 1990, Cowgirl's Prayer, 1993, Songs Of The West, 1994, Wrecking Ball, 1995 (Grammy award 1996), Spyboy, 1998, The Horse Whisperer, 1998, Singin' with Emmy Lou Harris, Vol. 1, 2000, Vol. 2, 2003, Red Dirt Girl, 2000, Anthology: The Warner-Reprise Years, 2001, Nobody's Darling But Mine, 2002, Stumble Into Grace, 2003, The Very Best of Emmylou Harris: Heartaches & Highways, 2005 (Grammy award 2006 for The Connection); co-writer, co-prodr.: (with Paul Kennerley) The Ballad of Sally Rose, 185. Pres. Country Music Found., 1983. Recipient of 12 Grammy awards, 1979, 80, 81, 84, 87, 92, 96, 98, 99, 2000, 2001, 2006, Orville H. Gibson Lifetime Achievement award, 1996, Patrick J. Leahy Humanitarian award-Americana Music awards Lifetime Achievement Performer, 2002; named Female Vocalist of Yr., Country Music Assn., 1980, Golden Plate award, Acad. Achievement, 2004; co-recipient (with Dolly Parton and Linda Ronstadt) Album of Yr. award Acad. Country Music, 1987; named to Ala. Music Hall of Fame, 2003. Office: Vector Management 1607 17th Ave S Nashville TN 37212-2875*

HARRIS, EON NIGEL, dean, rheumatologist, internist; b. Georgetown, Guyana, S.Am. came to U.S., 1987; s. T. Wilson and Cicely H.; m. Yvette Williams, 1981; children: Zaman Rashid, Tamia Alisha, Sandhya Caroline. BS, Howard U., 1968; MPhil, Yale U., 1970; MD, U. Pa., 1976; PhD in Medicine, U. West Indies, Kingston, Jamaica, 1982. Diplomate Am. Bd. Internal Medicine, Am. Bd. Rheumatology. Intern U. of the West Indies, Kingston, Jamaica, 1977, resident, 1978-81; lectr. U. West Indies, Kingston, 1981-83; rheumatology fellow Hammersmith Hosp., London, 1983-85; dir. Lupus rsch. lab. St. Thomas Hosp., London, 1985-87; asst. prof. U. Louisville, Ky., 1987-91, assoc. prof., 1991—93, prof., 1993—96; dean, sr. v.p. acad. affairs Morehouse Sch. of Medicine, Atlanta, prof. dept. medicine, 1996—2004; vice chancellor U. West Indies, Mona, Jamaica, 2004—. Chief div. rheumatology U. Louisville; med. adv. bd. Lupus Found. Am.; sci. adv. bd. Alliance for Lupus Rsch. Editor: Phospholipid Binding Antibodies, 1991; contbr. articles to profl. jours. Recipient Internat. League Against Rheumatism prize Ciba-Geigy, 1993. Fellow Am. Coll. Rheumatology (chmn. antiphospholipid study group 1993—); mem. Phi Beta Kappa, Alpha Omega Alpha. Office: Univ West Indies Kingston 7 Mona Jamaica Office Phone: 876-927-2406.

HARRIS, ERIC, accountant, auditor; Acct., auditor Office Depot, Delray Beach, Fla., 1996—. Mem.: Nat. Notary Assn. (assoc.). Home: 1081 SW Alcantarra Blvd Port Saint Lucie FL 34953 Home Phone: 561-889-1141. Personal E-mail: eric_harris@bellsouth.net.

HARRIS, ERICA RENEE, researcher; d. Lewis Kirk and Linda Harlow Harris. BA, U. Va., Charlottesville, 2001; MPH, Boston U., 2005. Cert. notary pub. NC, 2002. Rsch. asst. med. ctr. dept. neurology U. Va., Charlottesville, 2000—01; data technician med. ctr. dept. psychiatry Duke U., Durham, NC, 2001—03; rsch. asst, health educator ctr. infectious diseases Boston Med. Ctr., 2004; tchg. asst. Boston U., 2004—06; lab supr. Boston U. Sch. Medicine, 2005—. Contbr. articles to profl. jours. Advisor Peer Advisor Program, Boston, 2004—05; mem. very important person crew Fenway Cmty. Health, Boston, 2004; mentor Haven Ho. 'YES' Program, Raleigh, NC, 2002—03; crisis counselor Interact Battered Women's Shelter, Raleigh, 2002—03; vol. Boston Cares, 2007—. Mem.: Am. Acad. Neurology. Office Phone: 857-364-5007. Business E-Mail: erh8x@bu.edu.

HARRIS, ETHAN S., diversified financial services company executive; married; 2 children. BA, Clark U.; PhD in Econs., Columbia U. Internat. polit. economist JP Morgan; sr. economist, mgr. domestic rsch. div. Fed. Res. Bank N.Y., 1990—96; mng. dir, deputy chief economist Lehman Bros., Inc., NYC, 1996, chief U.S. economist, 2003—. Avocations: history, Boston Red Sox. Office: Lehman Brothers Inc 745 Seventh Ave New York NY 10019

HARRIS, FRED R., political scientist, educator, retired senator; b. Walters, Okla., Nov. 13, 1930; s. Fred Byron and Alene (Person) Harris; m. LaDonna Crawford, Apr. 8, 1949 (div. 1981); children: Kathryn, Byron, Laura; m. Margaret S. Elliston, Sept. 5, 1982. BA, U. Okla., 1952, JD, 1954. Bar: Okla. 1954. Founder, sr. partner firm Harris, Newcombe, Redman & Doolin, Lawton, Okla., 1954-64; mem. Okla Senate, 1956-64, U.S. Senate from Okla., Washington, 1964-73; prof. polit. sci. U. N.Mex., Albuquerque, 1976—. Author: (book) Alarms and Hopes, 1969, Now is the Time, 1971, The State of the Cities: Report of the Commission on Cities in the 70's, 1972, Social Science and National Policy, The New Populism, 1973, Potomac Fever, 1977, America's Democracy, 1980, America's Democracy, 3d edit., 1985, Readings on the Body Politic, 1987, Deadlock or Decision, 1993, In Defense of Congress, 1994, Coyote Revenge, 1999, Easy Pickin's, 2001, Following the Harvest, 2004, The Baby Bust, 2006; co-author: America's Legislative Processes, 1983, Understanding American Government, 1988, Quiet Riots, 1988, America's Government, 1990, Locked in the Poor House, 1998. Mem. Nat. Adv. Commn. Civil Disorders, 1967—68; chmn. Dem. Nat. Com., 1969—70. Mem.: Order of Coif, Phi Beta Kappa. Office: U New Mexico Dept Polit Sci Albuquerque NM 87131-0001 Business E-Mail: fharris@unm.edu.

HARRIS, FREDERICK JOHN, foreign language and literature educator; b. NYC, July 29, 1943; s. Frederick and Anna (Guttmann) H. BA, Fordham U., 1965; MA, Columbia U., 1966, PhD, 1969. Asst. prof. Fordham U., NYC, 1970—79, assoc. prof., 1979—84, prof. French and comparative lit., 1984—, chmn. divsn. humanities, 1979—85, chmn. dept. modern langs. and lits. (bi-campus), 1995—99. Bd. dirs. Fordham U. Press, NYC; mem. adv. com. Krieg und Literatur/War and Literature. Author: André Gide-Romain Rolland: Two Men Divided, 1973, Encounters with Darkness: French and German Writers on World War II, 1983, Friend and Foe: Marcel Proust and André Gide, 2002; contbr. articles to profl. jours. Mem. MLA, PEN Am. Ctr. (translation com. 1999-2004), Am. Assn. Tchrs. French, Internat. Comparative Lit. Assn., Am. Comparative Lit. Assn., Coll. English Assn., Assn. des Amis d'André Gide, Société des Professeurs Français et Francophones d'Amérique (bd. dirs. 1995-98), Stewart Hall (v.p. 1989-90, bd. dirs.). Roman Catholic. Office: Rose Hill Campus Lincoln Center Campus Fordham U New York NY 10023 Office Phone: 212-636-6790. E-mail: fharris@fordham.edu.

HARRIS, GAYLE ELIZABETH, bishop; b. Cleve., Feb. 12, 1951; m. Peter W. Peters; 3 children. BA in history, Lewis and Clark Coll., Portland, 1978; MDiv, Ch. Div. Sch. of the Pacific, Berkeley, Calif., 1981. Ordained deacon, 1981, priest, 1982; priest-in-charge Holy Communion Ch., Washington, 1984—92; rector St. Luke and Simon Cyrene, Rochester, NY, 1992—2002; consecrated bishop, 2003; bishop suffragen Episcopal Diocese of Mass., Boston, 2003—. Episcopalian. Office: Episcopal Diocese of Mass 138 Tremont St Boston MA 02111

HARRIS, GERALD DAVID, surgeon; b. Olney, Ill., July 3, 1947; s. Gerald Craver and Juanita Harris; m. Mary Josephine Burke, Sept. 6, 1970. MD, U. Ill., Chgo., 1973; MBA, Northwestern U., Evanston, Ill., 1995. Resident Northwestern U., Chgo., 1973—79; asst. Northwestern Meml. Hosp., Chgo., 1978—79; asst. clin. prof. Northwestern U., Chgo., 1980—98, assoc. clin. prof., 1999—. Asst. clin. prof. dept. surgery Northwestern U., Chgo., 1980—98, assoc. clin. prof. dept. surgery, 1998—. Contbr. chpts. to books and articles to profl. jours. Fellowship, U. Calif., San Francisco, 1979. Mem.: Soc. for Reconstructive Microsurgery, Am. Soc. for Surgery of the Hand. Avocations: weightlifting, aerobics, team sports. Home: 800 N Michigan Apt 3801 Chicago IL 60611 Office: Drs Bell Stomberg Harris Nagle et al 737 N Michigan Chicago IL 60611 Office Phone: 312-337-6960. Office Fax: 312-337-3961. Business E-Mail: gharris@chicagohandsurgery.com.

HARRIS, GODFREY, public policy consultant; b. London, June 11, 1937; came to U.S., 1939, naturalized, 1945; s. Alfred and Victoria H.; m. Barbara DeKovner-Mayer, Nov. 5, 1984; children: Gregrey, Kennith, Mark. BA with gt. distinction, Stanford U., 1958; MA (disting. mil. grad.), UCLA, 1960. Fgn. svc. officer U.S. State Dept., Germany, 1962—65; mgmt. analyst Office mgmt. and Budget, Washington, 1965-67; spl. asst. to pres. IOS Devel. Co., Geneva, 1967-68; pres. Harris/Ragan Mgmt. Group, LA, 1968—. Lectr. Rutgers U., 1960-61. Author: History of Sandy Hook, N.J, 1961, (with F. Fielder) The Quest for Foreign Affairs Officers, 1966, Panama's Position, 1973, (with C. Sonabend) Commercial Translations, 1985, (with B. DeKovner-Mayer) From Trash to Treasure, 1985, (with K. Katz) Promoting International Tourism, 1986, 2d edit., 1996, The Panamanian Perspective, 1987, The Ultimate Black Book, 1988, (with Kenneth Harris), 2d edit., 1996, Concentration, 1997, Don't Take Our Word for It!, 1998, (with D. Behar) Ivasion, 1990, The Fascination of Ivory, 1991, (with

Gregrey Harris) Talk is Cheap, 1991, How to Generate Word of Mouth Advertising, 1995, (with Guillermo de St. Malo Arias) The Panamanian Problem, 1993, (with Adelheid Hasenknopf and Hans Jorgen Groll) European Union Almanac, 1995, 96, Grandparenting, 2002, Corruption, 2003, Civility, 2003, The Hottest Ideas in Word of Mouth Advertising, 2004, (with Jeffrey I. Barke) The Definitive Southern California Diet, 2004, What A Great Idea!, 2005, Leonardo's Quotebook, 2006, The Legacy of Leonardo daVinci, 2007, The Essential Event Planning Kit, 2007; founder, editor Almanac of World Leaders, 1957-62, Consultants Directory, 1975-76; curator The DaVinci Experience Exhibit. Mem. adv. com. on gifted Santa Monica Unified Sch. Dist. (chmn. 1978-79); bd. dir. Beverly Hills (Calif.) Internat. Music Festival; former exec. dir. Internat. Pubs. Alliance, Friends Assisting Friends. 1st lt. U.S. Army, 1958-60 Decorated Commendation medal. Fellow Am. Acad. Cons.'s; mem. Assn. Mgmt. Cons.'s, Stanford U. Alumni Assn Democrat. Jewish. Office: Harris Ragan Mgmt Group Ste 404 9200 W Sunset Blvd Los Angeles CA 90069-3506 also: Harris Ragan Mgmt Group 654 N Sepulveda Blvd Ste 1 Los Angeles CA 90049-2070 Home Phone: 818-784-7366; Office Phone: 310-278-8037. Personal E-mail: hrmg@mac.com.

HARRIS, GREGORY SCOTT, state representative; b. Denver, June 5, 1955; s. Herbert E. and Marna Jean (Raabe) H. BS in Journalism with honors, U. Colo., 1977. Dir. public relations IMPACT Internat., Inc., Chgo., 1977-78; dir. edn. Nat. Home Furnishings Assn. (NHFA), Chgo., 1978-79, v.p. industry affairs, 1981-87, exec. v.p., chief operating officer, 1987-88; exec. dir. Interior Design Soc., Chgo., 1979-82; sec. NHFA Service Corp., 1986-87, v.p., 1986-87, pres., 1987-91, also bd. dirs.; pres. Open Hand: Chgo. Found., 1988-91; chief of staff Chgo. City Coun., 1992—2006; mem. Ill. Gen. Assembly, 2006—. Mem. Devel. Adv. Coun. City of Chgo., 1990-92; bd. dirs. Nonprofit Fin. Ctr.; mem. advocacy and pub. policy com. AFC, Ctr. Halsted Fin. com., 2003—. Trustee Design Found., Chgo., 1980-88; chmn. bd. dirs. AIDS Walk Found., 1990-91; bd. dirs. AIDS Legal Coun., 1992-94, Heartland Alliance for Human Needs and Human Rights; fin. dir. Simpson for Congress Com., 1991-92; mem. adv. bd. The Neofuturists, 2000. Recipient Leadership in Mktg. award Newspaper Pubs. Assn., 1983, Outstanding Young Chicagoan award Chgo. Jaycees, 1992, Outstanding Svc. to Immigrant and Refugee Cmty. award, 1996, Uptown C. of C. Ann. award, 1996, Voice of People Cmty. award, 1994, Equality award Human Rights Campaign, 1997, W. Clement Stone award, 1998, Biggest Heart award Hearts Found., 1999, Food For Life award, Florence Bezazian Citizenship award, 1999, Greater Chgo. Com. Humanitarian Efforts award, 2000, Inst. Cultural Affairs USA cert. of appreciation, 2000, Svc. award Cambodian Buddhist Assn., 2002, Chgo. House Pub. Svc. award, 2002, Hopeful Spirit award Names Project, 2005; named to City of Chgo. Hall of Fame, 1996. Office: 1967 W Montrose Chicago IL 60613 Office Phone: 773-348-3434. Business E-Mail: greg@gregharris.org.

HARRIS, HAROLD STEPHEN, JR., lawyer; b. Nashville, June 9, 1955; s. Harold Stephen Sr. and Aline (Broadway) H.; m. Shigeko Ikeda, May 20, 1989; 1 child, Lee Ikeda. AB, Cornell U., 1977; JD with honors, Columbia U., 1982, cert. with honors. Bar: Ga. 1982, U.S. Dist. Ct. (no., so. and mid. dists.) Ga. 1982, U.S. Ct. Appeals (11th, 4th, 5th cirs.) 1982. Ptnr. Alston & Bird LLP, Atlanta, 1982—, chmn., antitrust group and global svcs. task force. Mem. ABA (antitrust law sect., internat. law sect.), Japan-Am. Soc. Ga., Internat. Bar Assn. (competition and trade com.). Office: Alston & Bird LLP 1 Atlantic Ctr 1201 W Peachtree St NW Ste 4200 Atlanta GA 30309-3449 Office Phone: 404-881-7197. Office Fax: 404-881-7777. Business E-Mail: sharris@alston.com.

HARRIS, HARRIET, actress; b. Ft. Worth, Jan. 8, 1955; Grad., Juilliard. Actor: (TV series) The Five Mrs. Buchanans, 1994, Union Square, 1997—98, Stark Raving Mad, 1999, The Beast, 2001, It's All Relative, 2003, Desperate Housewives, 2005; (plays) Hamlet, 1986—, Four Baboons Adoring the Sun, 1992, Jeffrey, 1993—, The Man Who Came to Dinner, 2000, The Dining Room, 2005, On the Town, 2006 (LA Ovation award featured actress in a musical, 2006), (Broadway musical) Thoroughly Modern Millie, 2002— (Tony award, 2002), Old Acquaintance, 2007; (films) Memento, 2000, Nurse Betty, 2000.

HARRIS, HARVEY ALAN, lawyer; b. St. Louis, Nov. 5, 1936; s. Irvin S. and Sylvia Zelda (Goodman) H.; m. Gloria Goldman, Aug. 14, 1960; children: Stephen J., David A., Linda A.; m. Linda Ruth Everett, Mar. 17, 1977; m. Judith A. Stackhouse, Dec. 19, 1992. AB magna cum laude, Harvard U., 1958, JD, 1961. Bar: Mo. 1961, U.S. Dist. Ct. (ea. dist.) Mo. 1963, U.S. Ct. Appeals (8th cir.) 1979, U.S. Supreme Ct. 1979. Ptnr. and chmn. The Stolar Partnership and predecessors, St. Louis, 1961—. Cons. Office Policy Devel. and Rsch., HUD; owner, ptnr. Fox Assocs., LLC, Metrotix, Fox Theatricals, LLC. Author: Schumpeter's Theory of Innovation, 1958. Commr., treas., trustee St. Louis Sci. Ctr.; former chmn. St. Louis bi-state chpt. ARC; chmn. emeritus Sta. KETC-TV, St. Louis; commr., former chmn. Bi-State Transit Authority Met. St. Louis; former pres. St. Louis Jewish Fedn.; pres. Grand Ctr. Assn. Off the Cuff; chair Barnes-Jewish Coll. Nursing; bd. dirs. Jewish Fedn. St. Louis, Barnes Jewish Hosp., St. Louis, St. Louis Symphony. Mem.: ABA, St. Louis Bar Assn., Mo. Bar Assn., Harvard of St. Louis (v.p. 1983), Noonday, Westwood (pres.), St. Louis Racquet, Phi Beta Kappa. Democrat. Home: 31 Westmoreland Pl Saint Louis MO 63108-1227 Office: 911 Washington Ave 7th Floor Saint Louis MO 63101 Office Phone: 314-231-2800. Personal E-mail: harveystl@aol.com. Business E-Mail: hah@stolarlaw.com.

HARRIS, HAZEL LYNN, medical/surgical nurse; b. Taylor, Tex., Apr. 29, 1953; d. L.B. Clark, Doris Evelyn Clark; m. James Paul Harris; 1 child, Jonathan. BSN, Tex. Woman's U., 1974. RN Tex., cert. orthopedic nurse. Student nurse Parkland Health & Hosp. Sys., Dallas, 1973—74, staff nurse, 1974—80, unit mgr., 1982—. Clin. instr. Am. Tng. Ctr., Dallas, 1988—90; mem. nursing peer rev. Parkland Health & Hosp. Sys., Dallas, 1999—99. Contbr. Book Decision Making in Medical / Surgical Nursing, 1990. Polit. action com. Am. Heart Assn., Dallas, 2000—03. Finalist Tex. Nurses Excellence award Cmty. Svc., Nurseweek, 2000; named one of Great 100 Nurses, Dallas/Ft. Worth Hosp. Coun. and Dists. Three and Four of Tex. Nurses Assn., 1998. Mem.: ANA, Tex. Nurses Assn., Nat. Assn. Orthopedic Nurses (treas. Dallas chpt. 1982—90), Nat. Coun. Negro Women (life; rec. sec. Greater Trinity sect. 1999—2003), Chi Eta Phi Sorority- Xi Phi Chapter (Tamiochus 2001—03, Basileus 2003). Methodist. Avocations: shopping, travel, walking. Home: 5606 Shady Crest Trail Dallas TX 75241-1803 Office: Parkland Health & Hosp Sys 5201 Harry Hines Blvd Dallas TX 75235 Home Phone: 214-374-8755. Home Fax: 214-374-0823. Personal E-mail: hazelharrisrn@aol.com. Business E-Mail: hlharr@parknet.pmh.org.

HARRIS, HENRY WILLIAM, physician; b. Catawba, NC, Jan. 6, 1919; s. Henry William and Katie (Coulter) H.; m. Margaret Ann Roberts, Nov. 29, 1950; children: Henry William, John R., James P. BA, U.N.C., 1940; MD cum laude, Harvard U., 1943. Diplomate: in pulmonary disease Am. Bd. Internal Medicine. Intern Harvard Med. Service, Boston City Hosp., 1944-45, asst. resident medicine, 1945-46; resident fellow Thorndike Meml. Lab., 1944, 46; resident chest service Bellevue Hosp., NYC, 1947; staff physician Gundersen Clinic, LaCrosse, Wis., 1948-53; asst. prof. medicine U. Utah Coll. Medicine, 1955-59, asso. prof., 1959-60; chief pulmonary disease service VA Hosp., Salt Lake City, 1955-60; prof. chmn. dept. medicine Woman's Med. Coll. of Pa., 1960-67; chmn. dept. medicine Catholic Med. Center Bklyn. and Queens, 1967-70; asso. prof. clin. medicine N.Y.U. Sch. Medicine, 1969-70, prof., 1970—. Adj. staff chest svc. Bellevue Hosp., N.Y.C.; hon. staff Tisch Hosp., N.Y.C.; sr. coms. Bur. Tb, Dept. of Health, N.Y.C., 1989-2005. Mem. editorial bd.: Annals of Internal Medicine, 1976-80; Contbr. articles to profl. publs. Bd. dirs. Am. Lung Assn., 1961-79, v.p., 1972-73; bd. dirs. N.Y. Lung Assn., 1974-95, v.p., 1983—, pres. 1987-90; bd. dirs. Am. Bur. Med. Advancement in China, 1978-2005, v.p., 1983-87, pres. 1987-92, chmn. H. Wm. Harris vis. prof. com., 1986-96. Served to capt., M.C. AUS, 1953-55. Fellow ACP; mem. Am. Thoracic Soc. (pres. 1962-63). Home: 4 Birchwood Ct Apt 3L Mineola NY 11501-4513 Office: Chest Service Bellevue Hosp 1st Ave New York NY 10016

HARRIS, HOLTON EDWIN, plastics machinery manufacturing executive; b. NYC, Aug. 24, 1923; s. David William and Mildred (Stoutenborough) H.; m. Jeanne Deming, Feb. 22, 1963; children: Walter Deming, Dorothy Stoutenborough. BSEE, MIT, 1947, MSEE, 1948. Engr. GE, Syracuse, NY, 1948-49, sect. sales mgr. Schenectady, NY, 1949-52; asst. to pres. R.W. Cramer Co., Centerbrook, Conn., 1952-53; sales mgr. Ea. Air Devices, Dover, NH, 1953-54; mgr. comml. products Reeves Instrument Corp., Carle Place, NY, 1954-58; pres. Harrel, Inc., Norwalk, Conn., 1958—. Lectr. in field. Author: Extrusion Control; contbg. author: Modern Plastics Ency., 1990, Blow Molding Handbook, 1989; patentee in field; contbr. numerous articles to profl. jours. Mem. Representative Town Meeting, Westport, Conn., 1965-75, 93-97, 99-2001, dep. moderator, 1973-75, chmn. fin. com.; chmn. Rep. Town. Com., Westport; mem. Charter Revision Com., Westport. 1st lt. U.S. Army Signal Corp., 1943-46, South Pacific. Recipient award in recognition of meritorious svc., Town of Westport, Conn. Mem. IEEE (life), Soc. Plastics Engrs. (sr.), Instrument Soc. Am. (sr.). Avocation: amateur radio. Home: 5 Newtown Tpke Westport CT 06880-1802 Office: Harrel Inc 16 Fitch St Norwalk CT 06855-1392 E-mail: info@harrel.com, harrish@harrel.com.

HARRIS, IRVING, lawyer; b. Cin., May 23, 1927; s. Albert and Sadye H.; m. Selma Schottenstein, June 18, 1950; children: Jeffrey Philip, Jonathan Lindley (dec.), Lisa Ann Hollister. Undergrad. degree, U. Cin., 1948, LLB, 1951. Bar: Ohio 1951, US Dist. Ct. Ohio 1952, US Ct. Appeals (6th cir.) 1952, US Supreme Ct. 1960. Ptnr. Cors, Hair & Hartsock, 1954-81, Hartsock, Harris & Schneider, Cin., 1981-82, Porter, Wright, Morris & Arthur, Cin., 1982-89; ptnr. firm Harris, Harris, Field Schacter & Bardach Ltd., Cin., 1989-2000. Mem. Ohio Trade Mission to Orient, 1973, to Eng. and Germany, 1974; spl. counsel to Atty. Gen. Ohio, 1963-71; life mem. 6th Cir. Jud. Conf.; lectr. Advising, Oper. and Rebuilding the Financially Distressed Co., 1991; sponsor Disting. Visitor Series of Lectures, U. Cin. Coll. Law; bd. dirs. HRC Ltd. Partnership Hyatt Regency Cin. Mem. Ohio Devel. Financing Comm., 1974—84, vice-chmn., 1978—79; spl. counsel Ohio Atty. Gen.'s Office for the Police and Firemen's Disability and Pension Fund, 1994—97; trustee Skidmore Coll., 1976—90, trustee emeritus, 1991—, Big Bros.; trustee Cin. Symphony Orch., 1989—96; bd. overseers U. Cin. Law Sch., 1998—; arbitrator Ct. of Common Pleas of Hamilton County, 2001—; mediator US Dist. Ct. (so. dist.) Ohio Western divsn., 1999—2000. Mem. ABA (Sherman act com., sect. on antitrust and bus. law 1969-2000, subcoms. on derivative actions, bankruptcy, litigation of bus. and corp. litigation 1992-2000), Ohio Bar Assn., Cin. Bar Assn., Am. Judicature Soc., Potter Stewart Inn of Ct. (master of the bench), Queen City Club, Univ. Club, Cin. Tennis Club, Roaring Fork Country Club, Ocean Reef Club. Home: 18 Grandin Ln Cincinnati OH 45208-3365 Office: 3801 Carew Tower 441 Vine St Cincinnati OH 45202-2806

HARRIS, J. GEORGE (JACOB GEORGE HARRIS), health products executive; b. Kings Mountain, NC, Sept. 5, 1938; s. James A. and Carolyn (Hord) H.; m. Sondra Gilbert, Mar. 29, 1959; children: Cynthia, Susan, David. BA in Math., Duke U., 1960. With Am. Hosp. Supply Corp., 1960-84, region mgr. South San Francisco, 1964-67, pres. Port Credit, Ont., Canada, 1967-70, v.p. ops. Evanston, Ill., 1970-71, pres. dietary products div. McGaw Park, Ill., 1971-74, corp. v.p. Evanston, 1974-78, exec. v.p., 1978-84; chmn., chief exec. officer Health Group Inc., Nashville, 1984-85; founder, pres., CEO Pinnacle Care Corp. (merged Mariner Health Group), 1985-94; pres., COO Mariner Health Group, 1994; ret., 1994; formerly bd. dirs. Mariner Health Group. Bd. dirs. Union Spl. Corp., Chgo., Monoclonal Antibodies, Inc., Mountain View, Calif., Electro Neucleonics Inc., Health Group, Electro-Biology Inc., Dialogic Comm. Corp. Bd. dirs. Highland Park (Ill.) Hosp., 1981-84; trustee McCormick Sem., Chgo. Mem. Scientific Apparatus Mfrs. Assn. (bd. dirs.), Richland Country Club. Home: 1204 Beddington Park Nashville TN 37215-5810 Office Phone: 615-370-9191. Personal E-mail: bocaj1938@aol.com.

HARRIS, JACK F., police chief; b. 1950; m. Connie Harris. BA in Polit. Sci., Ariz. State U., 1977, grad. cert. pub. mgr. program; M in human resources, Ottawa U., 2000; grad., FBI Nat. Acad. Patrol officer Phoenix Police Dept., 1972, spl. investigations, undercover, vice and narcotics, 1981—84, sgt. patrol divsn., 1984—88, sgt. tng. acad. and street crimes, 1985—88, lt. patrol and motorcycle divsn., 1988—89, unit comdr. spl. assignments unit (SWAT team), 1989—95, city mgr. liaison, 1996—97, comdr. Desert Horizon Police Precinct, 1997—99, comdr. profl. standards divsn. (internal affairs), 1999—2000, asst. police chief North Divsn., 2000—04, interim police chief, 2004, chief of police, 2004—. Achievements include development of the first community policing station in the Palomino area of northeast Phoenix. Office: 620 W Washington St Phoenix AZ 85003 Office Phone: 602-262-7626. Business E-Mail: jack.harris@phoenix.gov.

HARRIS, JACQUELINE MYERS, speech/language pathology services professional; b. Phila., Oct. 22, 1949; d. Murray Irving Myers and Gladys Markovitch; m. Joseph Steven Harris, Dec. 31, 1994. BA, L.I. U., 1971; postgrad., U. South Fla., 1973—75, Nova U., 1980—81. Cert. speech/lang. therapy Fla., hearing correction Fla. Sec. Sch. Adv. Bd., Hollywood, Fla., 1995—97; lead speech pathologist Hollywood Hills Speech Zone, 2002—06; peer rev. mem. So. Assn. Colls. and Schs., Fla., 2003—05; founder Children Helping Children food drive Broward City Schs., 1993—94, founder Student Ct. for Elem. Schs., 1997—98, founder Hard Bound Book Program for Speech/Lang. Students, 2001—04. Co-author: Manual for Conflict Mediation in the Elementary Schools, 1992—93, The Slide Therapy Technique for Fluency, 2005; author: If I Could Change the World, 1998, I'll Love You Forever Today, 2005. Founding mem. bd. dirs. Maestro Broward Philharmonic, Ft. Lauderdale, Fla., 1992—93; com. mem. Winterfest, Ft. Lauderdale, 1993—95; active Haddasah, West Palm Beach, Fla., 1994—; vol. Boca Raton (Fla.) Mus. Art, 2003—. Mem.: Broward Tchrs. Union, Am. Found. Suicide Prvention (bd. mem. 2001—). Avocations: dance, art, music, charitable projects. Office: Stoneman Douglas HS 5901 Pine Island Rd Parkland FL 33076 Office Phone: 754-322-2150 ext. 3095. Business E-Mail: jacqueline.harris@browardschools.com.

HARRIS, JAMES BRAXTON, retired humanities educator, freelance/self-employed writer; b. Reidsville, NC, Apr. 30, 1929; s. Whitelaw Reid and Willie Zoie (Kelly) Harris; m. Gertrude Lawrence, Dec. 24, 1950; children: Lorraine, Helen, Joseph, Kelene, Lawrence. BA, Lenoir-Rhyne Coll., 1949; MA, Appalachian State U., 1956; EdD, Ind. U., 1960. Tchr. English and history Pub. Schs., Hildebran, Francisco and Hickory, NC, 1949—50, 1953—57; prof., vice chancellor Appalachian State U., Boone, NC, 1958—64, 1970—90, prof. emeritus, 1991—; dean Brevard (NC) Coll., 1964—68; dir. pre-svc. tchr. edn. NC Dept. Pub. Instrn., Raleigh, 1968—70; freelance writer Hendersonville, NC, 1991—. Tech. tng. cons. Naval Sea Sys. Command USN, Washington, 1985—89; cons. to colls., univs. and profl. orgns. Author: Lyrics for Three Julies: Song Lyrics for Three Musical Plays, 1992, Lyrics for Three Lovers: Song Lyrics for Three Musical Plays, 1993, Bittersweet Lyrics: Song Lyrics for Three Musical Plays, 1994, The Bolejack Chronicle, 2000, The Stokesburg Trilogy, 2000, The Dorian Chronicle, 2000, The Boldorian Chronicle, 2000, The Trinity Trilogy, 2000, The Chronicle of Scale, 2000, The Technics Trilogy, 2000, The C (sic) cycle: Precis and Personae, 2000, Dalton's Folly, 2003, Bay's Book: Being Benign Bagatelles Befitting Beneficent Bards, 2003, Lyrical Eyes: Song Lyrics for Three Musical Plays, 2004, Brooke Lyrics: Song Lyrics For Three Musical Plays, 2004, Ray's Way, 2004, Romance Gone Blue: Song Lyrics for Three Musical Plays, 2006; contbr. articles to profl. jours. Bd. dirs. Western Carolina Cmty. Action, Hendersonville and Brevard, 1966—68. 1st lt. USAF, 1950—53, Capt. USAFR, 1953—61. Grantee, Appalachian State U., 1972—73. Avocations: designing houses and small buildings, beekeeping. Home: 37 Jeter Mountain Rd Hendersonville NC 28739

HARRIS, JAMES CAROL OVERTON, JR., psychiatrist, pediatrician; b. Birmingham, Ala., Nov. 6, 1940; s. James Carol and Mary Virginia (Respess) H. BS, Univ. Md., 1962; MD, George Washington U., 1966. Cert. Am. Bd. Pediat., Am. Bd. Psychiatry, Am. Bd. Child Psychiatry. With Peace Corps, Thailand, 1967-70; dir. devel. neuropsychiatry Johns Hopkins U., Balt., 1976—; pres. med. staff Kennedy Krieger Inst., Johns Hopkins U., Balt., 1986-88; asst. prof. Johns Hopkins U., Balt., 1976-82, interim dir. divsn. of child and adolescence psychiatry, 1978-82, dir. consultation/liason svc., 1978-82, dir. edn. divsn. of child and adolescence psychiatry, 1982-89, assoc. prof. psychiatry, mental hygiene, pediat., 1982—97, prof., 1997—, co-dir. autism clinic, 1983—, co-dir. sleep disorder clinic, 1983—, joint appointment dept. of mental hygiene, 1985—. Adj. scientist Ctr. for Brain Evolution and Behavior, Poolesville, Md., 1978—84, Lab. Comparative Ethology, 1984—93; mem. White House conf. on Mental Health, 1999; cons. Joseph P. Kennedy Jr. Found., 2000—; mem. Pres.'s Com. on Mental Retardation, 2001—02; vis. scholar dept. psychiatry U. Chgo., 2001—02, vis. rsch. scientist Inst. for Mind and Biology, 2001—02; cons. U of Ill, Brain and Body Inst., 2003—. Author: Developmental Neuropsychiatry Fundamentals, 1995, Developmental Neuropsychiatry: Assessment, Diagnosis and Treatment, 1995 (Med. Book of Yr. award 1995), Intellectual Disability, 2006; mem. editl. bd. Jour. Child Neurology, 2001—; art and cover editor Archives of Gen. Psychiatry, 2002—; contbr. articles to profl. jours. Recipient NIMH Trainee award, 1964—65, Pollen award, 1965—66, R-01 Rsch. award, Nat. Inst. Child Health and Human Devel.; Fgn. fellow, Assn. Am. Med. Colls.-Smith Kline & French, 1965. Fellow: Am. Acad. Child and Adolescent Psychiatry, Am. Psychiat. Assn. (Disting., Agnes Purcell McGawn award 2007); mem.: Am. Coll. Psychiatry, Soc. Profs. Child and Adolescent Psychiatry (pres. 1998—2000), Soc. Study Behavioral Phenotypes, Am. Assn. Psychiatry and the Law, Soc. Neurosci., Am. Assn. Dirs. Psychiat. Residency Tng., Md. Psychiat. Soc., Am. Coll. Neuropsychopharmacology. Avocation: foreign travel. Home: 3704 N Charles St Apt 105 Baltimore MD 21218 Office: Johns Hopkins U Sch Medicine CMSC 343 600 N Wolfe St Baltimore MD 21287-0005 Address: 505 N Lakeshore Dr Ste 416 Chicago IL 60611 Office Phone: 410-955-6181. Personal E-mail: jamesharris@erols.com. Business E-Mail: jharrisd@jhmi.edu.

HARRIS, JAMES DEAN, computer scientist, educator; s. James Clifford and Edith Dean Harris; m. Strelsa Jean Bonham; children: James Randolph, Jason Bonham, Joseph Douglas. BA, Kans. U., Lawrence, Kans., 1964; MA, Coll. William and Mary, Williamsburg, Va., 1967; PhD, U. Va., Charlottesville, 1970. MCSE 2000, cert. network+ Computer Industry Assn., 2000, info. sys. security profl. 2003, info. security assessment methodology 2004. Data sys. analyst NASA, Hampton, Va., 1964—71; assoc. prof. Tenn. Technol. U., Cookeville, Tenn., 1971—79; u. prof. Pitts. State U., 1979—. Contbr. articles to profl. jours. Bd. moderator First Christian Ch., Pitts., 2004. Mem.: IEEE Computer Soc., ACM, Info. Sys. Audit and Control Assn., Computer Security Inst., Kiwanis. Office: Pittsburg State Univ 1701 S Broadway Pittsburg KS 66762 Home Phone: 620-231-5196; Office Phone: 620-235-4541. Business E-Mail: jdharris@pittstate.edu.

HARRIS, JAMES MICHAEL, sales executive; b. San Francisco, Mar. 24, 1947; s. Alfred James and Pearl Olga (Slavich) H.; m. Vivian Toni Ferrara, Mar. 20, 1987 (div. Mar. 1992); 1 child, Michael James. BA, San Diego State U., 1971. Rsch. assoc. San Diego State U., 1971-73; assoc. dir. San Diego Taxpayers Assn., 1973-75, exec. dir., 1976-79; govt. rels. dir. Rohr Industries, San Diego, 1975-76; chief of staff City of San Diego, 1979-83; CEO Harris & Lee, San Diego, 1983-90; exec. dir. San Diego Auto Mus., 1990-96; dir. corp. sales Rely, Inc., San Diego, 1996—99; mng. dir. WFW Capital Engine LLC, Escondido, Calif., 1999—; v.p. sales Capital Engine Group, La Jolla, Calif., 2000—. Cons. Souplantation Restaurants, San Diego, 1977-83, Fuego Zero, San Diego, 1989-90, Couveé Comm., San Diego, 1989-90, Deanna Kay Products, Carlsbad, Calif., 1989-90, SJ Lynde LLC, Escondido, 2001--, Chemtroxx Rsch. Group Corp., San Diego, 2002--, Phoenix Displays, L.A., 2003--; bd. dirs. Ctrl. Balboa Park Assn., Inter-Mus. Promotional Coun. Rschr. (book) Public Finance in the San Diego S.M.S.A., 1972, Shifting Public Functions and the Distribution of Tax Burden by Economic Class, 1972. Bd. dirs. Alumni Assn. San Diego State U., 1977-79; San Diego county coord. Yes on Lottery Campaign, Woodward/McDowell, San Diego, 1984; expert witness San Diego County Grand Jury, 1977, 78; charter rev. com. mem. San Diego County, 1984. Recipient 20 Outstanding Young Citizens of San Diego award San Diego Jr. C. of C., 1977, Man of Distinction award San Diegans Inc., 1979. Avocation: old cars. Office: 1610 Windsor St San Diego CA 92103

HARRIS, JAMES ROBERT, structural engineer; Founder, pres. J.R. Harris & Co., Denver. Investigator Structural Engring. Inst. Contbr. articles to profl. jours. Mem.: NAE, ASCE, Bldg. Seismic Safety Coun., Am. Inst. Steel Construction, Am. Concrete Inst. Office: JR Harris & Co Ste 1100 1776 Lincoln St Denver CO 80203

HARRIS, JAMES THOMAS, III, college administrator, educator; b. Findlay, Ohio, July 31, 1958; s. James Thomas II and Carolyn Sue (Cairns) H.; m. Mary Catherine Kurdila, June 27, 1981; children: Zachary James, Braden Gerald. BE in Secondary Edn., U. Toledo, 1980; MEd in Ednl. Adminstrn., Edinboro U., 1983; D in Edn., Pa. State U., 1988; postgrad. Inst. Ednl. Mgmt., Harvard U., 1993. Pres. Defiance (Ohio) Coll., 1994—2002; pres., prof. Widener U., Chester, Pa., 2002—. Chmn. bd. dirs. Pa. Campus Compact, 2004—06, Mid. Atlantic Conf., 2004—; adv. bd. higher edn. Pa. Dept. Edn., 2004—06; faculty adv. presdl. svc. corps. Widener U., 2003—, faculty adv. cir. leadership and excellence, 2003-04, faculty adv. Omicron Delta Kappa, 2004—; bd. dirs. U. Tech. Pk. Contbr. articles to profl. jours. Chair, founder Vol. Connection of Defiance County, 1995-2002; vol. Leadership Defiance, Defiance, Ohio, chair, 1992-94; bd. dirs. Defiance County United Way, 1998-2001; vol. ARC, Cin., 1988-91; trustee Ohio Found. Ind. Colls., 1994-2002; mem. exec. com. Ohio Campus Compact, 1998-2002; bd. dirs. Chester Arts and Cultural Ctr., 2003—; sec. bd. dirs. Nat. Assn. Ind. Colls. and Univs., 2006. Recipient Excellence in Edn. award Pa. State U., 2000, Alumni Leadershiip and Svc. award Pa. State U., 1996, Disting. Alumni award U. Toledo, 1999, Cmty. Leadership award NAACP N.W. Ohio Chpt., 1999, Bud Williams Humanitarian award NAACP N.W. Ohio Chpt., 2003, CASE Stueben Apple award, 2004, Excellence in Edn. award Boy Scouts Am., 2005, Excellence in Edn. award March of Dimes, 2005; named to Top 50 Coll. and Univ. Presidents Templeton Found, 1999; Alumni Fellow, Pa. State U., 2003. Mem. NAACP, Nat. Assn. Ind. Colls. and Univs. (sec., bd. dirs. Pa. chpt. 2006—), Assn. Ind. Colls. and Univs. Pa. (bd. dirs.), Am. Assn. Higher Edn., Nat. Collegiate Athletic Assn. (pres. coun. 2006), Coalition Urban and Met. Univs. (mem. exec. com. 2006), Am. Coun. on Edn. (com. on advancement of racial and ethnic equity 2006), Delaware County C. of C. (bd. dirs.

2003—06), Pa. State U. Alumni Assn., Rotary, Young President's Orgn., Alpha Kappa Delta, Pi Lambda Theta. Roman Catholic. Avocations: reading, blues music, walking, travel, boating. Office: Widener Univ 1 University Pl Chester PA 19013 Home Phone: 610-565-5125; Office Phone: 610-499-4100.

HARRIS, JAY TERRENCE, communications educator; b. Washington, Dec. 3, 1948; s. Richard James and Margaret Estelle (Burr) H.; m. Eliza Melinda Dowell, June 14, 1969 (div.); 1 child, Taifa Akida; m. Anna Christine Harris, Oct. 25, 1980; children: Jamarah Kai, Shala Marie. BA, Lincoln U., 1970, LHD (hon.), 1988. Reporter Wilmington (Del.) News-Jour., 1970-73, spl. project editor, 1974-75; instr. journalism and urban affairs Medill Sch. Journalism, Northwestern U., Evanston, Ill., 1973-75, asst. prof., 1975-82, asst. dean, 1977-82; nat. corr. Gannett News Service, Washington, 1982-84, columnist Gannet newspapers and USA Today, 1984-85; exec. editor Phila. Daily News, 1985—88; v.p. Phila. Newspapers, Inc., 1987—94; chmn., pub. San Jose Mercury News, 1995—2001; Annenberg prof. journalism & comm. Annenberg Sch. for Comm., USC, 2001—. Asst. dir. Frank E. Gannett Urban Journalism Ctr., Northwestern U., 1977-82; founder, exec. dir. Consortium for Advancement of Minorities in Journalism Edn., Evanston, 1978-81; dir. Dow Jones Newspaper Fund, Princeton, N.J., 1980—; bd. visitors John S. Knight Profl. Journalism Fellowships, Palo Alto, Calif., 1982—; head Minorities and Communication Div. Assn. for Edn. in Journalism, 1982-83; journalist in residence Notre Dame, 2002-03; bd. mem. Deep River Assocs., 2002—. Author: (annual census) Minority Employment in Daily Newspapers, 1978-82; co-author series articles on drug trafficking in Wilmington, 1972 (Pub. Service awards AP Mng. Editors Assn. 1972, Greater Phila. chpt. Sigma Delta Chi 1973) Past mem. bd. advisors Sch. Journalism U. Mo. Frank E. Gannett Urban Journalism fellow, 1973-74; recipient Pub. Service award Greater Phila. chpt. Sigma Delta Chi, 1973; Pub. Service award AP Mng. Editors Assn., 1972; Spl. Citation Nat. Urban Coalition, 1979; Par Excellence Disting. Service in Journalism award Operation PUSH, 1984; Drum Maj. for Justice award Southern Christian Leadership Conf., 1985; Robert C. Maynard Fellow, 2001—. Mem. Am. Soc. Newspaper Editors (chmn. readership and rsch. com.), Women in Communication, Nat. Assn. Black Journalists, Omega Psi Phi Office: San Jose Mercury News 750 Ridder Park Dr San Jose CA 95190-0001

HARRIS, JEFF M., waste management executive; BS in Natural Resources, Ohio State U., Columbus. With Ohio EPA, Browning Ferris Industries, Inc., Waste Mgmt., Inc., 1999—, pres. Can. Waste Svcs. Inc., area v.p. Mich., SW Ont. and Greater Toronto Market areas, sr. v.p. Midwest Group, 2006—. Office: Waste Mgmt Inc 720 E Butterfield Rd Lombard IL 60148*

HARRIS, JEFFREY, lawyer; b. Bklyn., Mar. 20, 1944; s. Herman and Pearl (Herman) H.; m. Joyce Rosa Meckler, June 22, 1975; 1 child, Daniela Rose. BS, NYU, 1965; JD, Syracuse U., 1968. Bar: N.Y. 1969, U.S. Supreme Ct. 1976, D.C. 1977, Va., 1990. Asst. U.S. atty. So. Dist. N.Y., U.S. Dept. Justice, NYC, 1972-76; chief investigation rev. unit. U.S. Dept. Justice, Washington, 1976-77; dep. chief counsel U.S. Ho. of Reps., Korean Investigation, Washington, 1977-79; asst. dir. FTC, Washington, 1979-81; exec. dir. Atty. Gen.'s Task Force on Violent Crime, U.S. Dept. Justice, Washington, 1981; dep. assoc. atty. gen. U.S., Washington, 1981-83; sr. v.p. Capital Bank N.A., Washington, 1983-85; sr. v.p., counsel Capital Bancorp, Miami, Fla., 1983-85; ptnr. Sachs, Greenebaum & Tayler, Washington, 1985-90, Rubin, Winston, Diercks, Harris & Cooke, LLP, Washington, 1990—. Instr. Advocacy Inst., U. Calif. Hastings Coll. Law, San Francisco, 1979-83; adj. asst. prof. George Washington U., Washington, 1980 Lt. (j.g.) USN, 1968—71. Named Meritorious Exec. Pres. of U.S.; recipient Spl. Commendation, Att. Gen. of U.S.; decorated Navy Commendation medal, Vietnam Cross of Gallantry. Mem. ABA Office: Rubin Winston Diercks Harris & Cooke LLP 6th Fl 1155 Connecticut Ave NW Washington DC 20036-4306 Home Phone: 301-465-0527; Office Phone: 202-861-0870. E-mail: jharris@rwdhc.com.

HARRIS, JEFFREY SAUL, physician, consultant, health facility administrator; b. Pitts., Mar. 13, 1949; s. Aaron Wexler and Janet Mary (Wexler) Harris; m. Mary V. Anderson, Jan. 2, 1981; children: Sarah Ariel, Noah Aaron, Susannah Leia. BS in Molecular Biophysics/Biochemistry, Yale U., New Haven, Conn., 1971; MD, U. N.Mex., Albuquerque, 1975; MPH, U. Mich., Ann Arbor, 1982; MBA, Vanderbilt U., Nashville, 1988. Diplomate Am. Bd. Preventive Medicine in Occupl. Medicine and Gen. Preventive Medicine, Am. Bd. Emergency Medicine, Am. Bd. Medicine Quality, Am. Bd. Ind. Med. Exam. Gen. med. officer USPHS, Juneau, Alaska, 1976-78; clin. dir. S.E. Alaska Native Health Corp, Juneau, 1978-79; asst. to commr. Tenn. Dept. Health and Environ., Nashville, 1980—83; dir. health care mgmt. Northern Telecom Inc., Nashville, 1983—88; pres. HDM, Inc., Nashville, 1988—90; med. dir. Aetna Health Plans of Tenn., Nashville, 1990-91; nat. practice leader, health strategy Alexander & Alexander Cons. Group, San Francisco, 1991-94; chief prevention, health and disability officer Indsl. Indemnity, San Francisco, 1994-97; pres. J. Harris Assocs., Inc., Mill Valley, Calif., 1979—; CEO Med-Fx, LLC, 1999—2004; sr. physician Permanente Med. Group, San Rafael, Calif., 2000—. Pres., chmn. Collaborative for Excellence in Occupl. Medicine, Mill Valley, Calif., 2005—. Author: Strategic Health Management, 1994, Evidence-Based Occupational Medicine, 2007; author, editor: Managed Care in Occupational Medicine, 1998, Quick Reference to Practice Guidelines in Occupational Medicine, 1999, author, co-editor: Occupational Medicine Practice Guidelines: Evaluation and Management of Common Health Problems and Functional Recovery in Workers, 1997, 2004, 2007, Integrated Health Management, 1998, Managing Employee Health Care Costs, 1992, Manual of Occupational Health and Safety, 1992, 1996, 2004—, Health Promotion in the Work Place, 1994, 2001, 2003, mem. editl. bd.: Am. Jour. Health Promotion, 1985—, Occupl. Environ. Med. Report, 1988—2005, editl. reviewer: JAMA, BMJ, Am. Jour. Pub. Health, Internat. Jour. Occupl. Environ. Health, Occupl. Medicine, Arch. Internat. Med., JOEM, Cochrane Collaborative, ACP, Am. Pain Soc.; contbr. articles to profl. jours., chapters to books. Fellow Am. Coll. Occupl. Environ. Medicine (dir. 1982-, chmn. practice guidelines com. 1992-98, Presdl. award 1996, Felton Authorship award 1998, Achievement award, 2004), Western Occpl. Environ. Med. Assn. (Authorship award 1997, Rutherford B. Johnstone award 2006), Am. Coll. Preventive Medicine, Am. Coll. Med. Quality, Am. Bd. Ind. Med. Examiners. Avocations: skiing, running, music, painting, writing. Home: 386 Richardson Way Mill Valley CA 94941-4053 Personal E-mail: jharrismvl@aol.com.

HARRIS, JEREMY, former mayor; b. Wilmington, Del., Dec. 7, 1950; s. Ann Harris; m. Ramona Sachiko Akui. BA, BS in Biology, U. Hawaii, 1972; MS in Population and Environ. Biology, U. Calif., Irvine, 1973. Lectr. oceanography, biology Kauai C.C.; marine advisor Sea Grant Program, U. Hawaii; del. Hawaii Constl. Conv., 1978; chmn. Kauai County Council, 1979—81; exec. asst. to mayor City and County of Honolulu, 1984—86, dep. mng. dir. of Honolulu, 1986-94, mng. dir., 1986—94, acting mayor, 1994, mayor, 1994—2004. Founder, chair Mayors' Asia-Pacific Environ. Summit, 1999; established Pacific Islands Environmental Symposium, China-US Conf. of Mayors and Bus. Leaders, Asia-Pacific Urban Tech. Inst. Am.-Nat. chair Japan-Am. Conf. of Mayors and C. of C. Presidents, 1996—. Mem.: Am. Planning Assn. (Disting. Leadership award 2002), Internat. Downtown Assn. (Merit award), Am. Soc. Pub. Adminstrn. (Pub. Adminstr. of Yr. 1993, 1994), Am. Inst. Archs. (hon.).

HARRIS, JOE FRANK, former governor; b. Cartersville, Ga., Feb. 16, 1936; s. Grover Franklin and Frances (Morrow) H.; m. Elizabeth Carlock Harris, June 25, 1961; 1 son. Joe Frank, Jr. BBA, U. Ga., 1958; LLD (hon.), Woodrow Wilson Coll. Law, 1981, Asbury Coll., 1983, Morris Brown Coll., 1983, LaGrange Coll., 1987, Mercer U., 1987. Sec.-treas. Harris Cement Products, Inc., Cartersville, 1958-79; pres. Harris Georgia Corp., Cartersville, 1979-83; mem. Ga. Gen. Assembly, 1965-83; gov. State of Ga., 1983-91; prof., Disting. Exec. fellow Ga. State U., Atlanta, 1993—. Bd. regents Univ. Sys. Ga., 1999—2006. With US Army, 1958. Democrat. Methodist.

HARRIS, JOEL B. (JOEL BRUCE HARRIS), lawyer; b. NYC, Oct. 15, 1941; s. Raymond S. and Laura (Greene) H.; m. Barbara J. Rous, June 13, 1965 (div.); 1 child, Clifford S.; m. Deborah Sherman, Apr. 1, 1986 (div.); children: Sydney Anne, Cassidy Raye; m. Marcia E. Haddad, Aug. 18, 1999. AB, Columbia U., 1963; LLB, Harvard U., 1966; LLM, U. London, 1967. Bar: N.Y. 1968, U.S. Dist. Ct. (so. dist.) N.Y. 1970, U.S. Ct. Appeals (2d cir.) 1970, U.S. Dist. Ct. (ea. dist.) N.Y. 1975, U.S. Supreme Ct. 1976, U.S. Ct. Appeals (3d cir.) 1980, U.S. Dist. Ct. (we. dist.) N.Y. 1981. Assoc. Simpson, Thacher & Bartlett, NYC, 1967-70; asst. U.S. atty. So. Dist. N.Y., 1970-74, chief civil rights unit, 1973-74; assoc. Weil, Gotshal & Manges, NYC, 1974-76, ptnr., 1976-86, Thacher, Proffitt & Wood, NYC, 1986—; chmn. litigation dept., Latin Am. practice group. Speaker, panelist, moderator confs. Contbr. articles to profl. jours. Knox Meml. fellow, 1966-67. Fellow Am. Bar Found.; mem. ABA (chmn. com. internat. litigation 1981-84, chmn. com. personal rights litigation 1984-87), N.Y. State Bar Assn. (mem. internat. law and practice sect., sect. chair 1997-98, mem. exec. com. 1990—, chmn. internat. dispute resolution com. 1990-93, chmn. seasonal meeting 1993, 2001), Assn. Bar City N.Y., Inter-Am. Bar Assn., N.Y. County Lawyers Assn. (bd. dirs. 2004—, treas. 2005—, mem. exec. com. 2005—), Fed. Bar Coun., Am. Soc. Internat. Law, Internat. Law Assn., Am. Judicature Soc. Home: 40 Prince St New York NY 10012-3426 Office: Thacher Proffitt & Wood Two World Fin Ctr New York NY 10281 Home Phone: 212-941-0272; Office Phone: 212-912-7785. Business E-Mail: jharris@tpw.com.

HARRIS, JOHN BORGESON, plastic surgeon; b. Lincoln, Ill., Sept. 10, 1956; B, Vanderbilt U., Nashville, 1978; MD, So. Ill. U., 1981. Cert. Am. Bd. Plastic Surgery, 1991, Am. Bd. Surgery. Intern Mayo Clinic Grad. Sch. Medicine, Rochester, Minn., 1981—85, resident, 1985—88, head plastic surgery, asst. prof. plastic and reconstructive surgery Jacksonville, Fla., 1988—2001; fellow cosmetic surgery Mt. Sinai Hosp., Miami, Fla.; fellow microsurgery Royal Melbourne Hosp., Australia; with St. Luke's Hosp., Jacksonville, Baptist Beaches Hosp., Ponte Vedra Medspa Plastic Surgery & Laser Ctr., Fla. Contbr. articles to med. jours. Fellow: Am. Coll. Surgeons; mem.: Am. Soc. Plastic Surgeons. Office: Ponte Vedra Medspa Plastic Surgery & Laser Ctr 50 A1A North Ste 103 Ponte Vedra Beach FL 32082 Office Phone: 904-285-7202. Office Fax: 904-285-3931.

HARRIS, JOHN F., editor-in-chief; m. Ann O'Hanlon; children: Liza, Griffin, Nikki. Grad. with degree in Am. History, Carleton Coll., Northfield, Minn., 1985. Intern The Washington Post, 1985, reporter, Va. and Washington region stories, 1985—90, reporter, Va. state govt. and politics Richmond, 1990—94, reporter, Washington and nat. staff Washington, 1994—95, reporter, Clinton White House, 1995—2001, polit. editor, nat. polit. editor, 2005—06; co-founder, editor-in-chief The Politico, Arlington, Va., 2006—; editor-in-chief Politico.com, Arlington, Va., 2007—. Author: The Survivor: Bill Clinton in the White House, 2005; co-author (with Mark Halperin): The Way to Win: Clinton, Bush, Rove and How to Take the White House in 2008, 2006; guest panelist Washington Week and other radio shows, guest appearances Face the Nation. Recipient Aldo Beckman award, White House Corr. Assn., 1999, prize for Disting. Reporting on the Presidency, Gerald R. Ford Libr., 2001; Guest Scholar, Brookings Institution, 2003. Office: The Politico 1000 Wilson Blvd Ste 601 Arlington VA 22209 Office Phone: 703-647-7998.*

HARRIS, JOHN T., IV, religious organization administrator; b. Green Bay, Wis., Oct. 18, 1974; s. John T. Harris III and Carol A. Harris; m. Lori L. Foerster, Aug. 19, 2006. DD (hon.), Progressive Universal Life Ch., Sacramento, Calif., 2006; PhD in Theological Studies (hon.), Rose Ministries, Las Vegas, Nev., 2006. Pres. Divine Inspiration, LLC, De Pere, Wis., 2003—06; pres., CEO Heavenscent Therapeutic Oils, LLC, De Pere, Wis., 2005—06, St. John's Whole Life Inst., Inc., Green Bay, 2006—, St. John's Ch. of Light, Green Bay, 2006—. Fellow: Am. Assn. Integrative Medicine. Achievements include first to new system of integrative medicine called Celestial Healing Therapy. Office: St John's Whole Life Inst Inc 518 Greene Ave Green Bay WI 54301 Home Phone: 920-403-7808; Office Phone: 920-445-0404. Business E-Mail: dr.john@stjohnswholelife.org.

HARRIS, JOHN WILLIAM, historian, educator; b. Jacksonville, Fla., Oct. 18, 1946; s. Jack W. and Louise Pollard Harris; m. Terry Kay Rockefeller; children: Logan, Kathryn Cox, Hannah. BS, MIT, 1968; PhD, Johns Hopkins U., 1982. Prof. Dept. History U. N.H., Durham, NH, 1985—. Author: Deep Souths: Delta, Piedmont, and Sea Island Society in the Age of Segregation, 2001 (Pulitzer Prize for History finalist, 2002). Co-recipient Rawley prize, Orgn. Am. Historians, 2002; recipient Theodore Saloutos prize, Agrl. History Soc., 2002. Office: Department of History Univ of New Hamp Durham NH 03824

HARRIS, JOSEPH MCALLISTER, retired chemist; b. Pontiac, Ill., July 27, 1929; s. Fred Gilbert and Catherine Marguerite (McAllister) H.; m. Margot Jeanette L'Hommedieu, Feb. 17, 1952; children: Timothy, Kaye, Paula, Bruce, Anne, Martha, Rebecca. BA, Blackburn Coll., Carlinville, Ill., 1952; postgrad., So. Ill. U., 1953-54, U. Ill., 1956-61. Technician Olin Ind., Inc., Energy, Ill., 1953-54; quality control staff Union Starch and Refining Co., Granite City, Ill., 1954; rsch. asst. Ill. State Geol. Survey, Urbana, 1954-61; chemist II Water Pollution Control Bd., Annapolis, Md., 1961-63; phys. chemist Ball Bros. Rsch., Inc., Muncie, Ind., 1963-66; engr. Radio Corp. Am., Marion, Ind., 1966-70; chemist OA Labs., Inc., Indpls., 1973-86, OA Labs. & Rsch., Inc., Indpls., 1986-93, cons., 1993—. Bd. dirs. Tri-County Hearing Assn. for Children, Muncie, 1967-70. Mem. Am. Chem. Soc., AAAS, Soc. Applied Spectroscopy. Republican. Presbyterian. Avocations: gardening, camping. Home: 800 E Washington St Muncie IN 47305-2533 Personal E-mail: berrijoe@aol.com.

HARRIS, JUDITH ANN WHITE, occupational health nurse, educator; b. Springfield, Ohio, Mar. 6, 1939; d. Willis and Tennessee Belle (Poole) Martin; m. Allen G. Harris, Mar. 21, 1986; 1 child by previous marriage, Denise Marian Womble. Student, U. South Fla., 1978-85, BS/MS in Psychology, 2000. RN, Fla.; cert. tchr., Fla. Nurse Dr. Robert Tapogna, Springfield, Ohio, 1960-62, Springfield City Hosp., 1962-65, Dr. Robert Beam, Springfield, 1965-75; edn. coord., instr. med. assisting Sarasota Vocat. Ctr., Fla., 1977-82, instr. med. assisting program, chmn. dept., 1982-84, 89-91, instr. health svc. occupations, placement coord. health occu, 1985-88; dept. chmn. Allied Health, 1989-95. Bd. dirs. Fla. Bd. Inc.; pres. J.W. Harris Pub. Co.; cruise ship lectr. for Princess, Royal Caribbean and Celebrity Cruise Lines; v.p., sec. Al Harris Pest Control, Inc. 1996-; dir. adv. & mktg., 2000-. Author: J.W. Harris Medical Assisting Review Manual, 1995, Templin, 2002; contbr. articles to profl. jours. Vol. Children's Breath Clinic, Sarasota, 1977-79, Kidney Found., Sarasota, 1982, ARC, Sarasota, 1976-88; dir. Spl. Care Unit, 1984-88; v.p. Sons of Norway, 1993-95; choir soloist Beneva Christian Ch., 1989—, deaconess, 1993-96, elder 1997—; chmn. Health Care Svcs. Dept., 1996—, vice chmn. bd. dirs., 2001-02, chmn. bd., 2002—; asst. state dir. Fla. Good Sons, 1993-94; bd. dirs. Fla. Bd. Camping Assn., Inc., sec., 1999-, newsletter editor, 1996—; chmn. FVA Leadership Forum, 1992—; parish nurse and chmn. health svcs. dept. Beneva Christian Ch., 1995—; pres. FVA Post Pres.'s Club, 1999—; 1st v.p. Sarasota Bay Republican Women's Club Federated, 1998-2001; mem. Sarasota Tiger Bay Club, 1999—, Sarasota Homebuilders Assn., 1999—; sec. Acorn Glass Bowling League, 2000—. Named Outstanding Vocat. Tchr. Sarasota County Sch. Bd., 1985, Woman of Impact for Edn., Sarasota County Commn. on the Status of Women, 1995. Mem. Am. Vocat. Assn. (Outstanding Vocat. Tchr. region II 1985, Vocat. Tchr. Yr. 1987), Health Occupations Educators (vice chmn. policy com. 1985-86), Nat. Assn. Health Occupations Tchrs. (v.p. region II 1984-86, pres. elect 1988, pres. 1989-91), Fla. Vocat. Assn. (bd. dirs. 1983-85, pres. 1987-88, Pres. award 1984, Outstanding Vocat. Educator region 23 award 1982, Sarasota Mayors award 1984, Gov.'s Proclamation for Outstanding Tchg. 1987, chmn. leadership forum 1993—), Health Occupations Educators Assn. Fla. (pres. 1983-84, chmn. legis. com. 1985-93, Outstanding Tchr. 1983), Sarasota County Vocat. and Adult Edn. Assn. (pres. 1978-80, editor newsletter 1978-83), Am. Assn. Med. Assts., Good Sams Inc. Fla. (asst. state dir. dist. 12 1993-95), Fraternal Order of Eagles Aux. (dist. 3 auditor 1995-96, eagle nurse 1995-97, chair health care dept. 1995—, condr. 1996—), Sarasota Bay Republican Women's Club (life; v.p. 1998—), Women's Coun. Realtors (ways and means chair 2002-, corr. sec. 2003, rec. sec. 2004), Sarasota Assn. Realtors, Sunrise Rotary Club (Paul Harris fellow, 2002-, Rotary Internat. Sustaining Mem. 2002-), Tiger Bay Club, Delta Kappa Gamma, Phi Kappa Phi. Avocations: swimming, camping, knitting, sewing, biking. Home: PO Box 7278 Sarasota FL 34278 Office: 6100 Palmer Blvd Sarasota FL 34232 E-mail: alharrispestcontrol@netzero.net.

HARRIS, JUDITH E., lawyer; b. Apr. 28, 1945; AB, Mount Holyoke Coll., 1967; JD, Howard U., 1970. Bar: Pa. 1971. City solicitor City of Phila., 1992-93; ptnr. Morgan, Lewis & Bockius LLP, Phila. Office: Morgan Lewis & Bockius LLP 1701 Market St Philadelphia PA 19103-2903 Office Phone: 215-963-5028. Business E-Mail: jeharris@morganlewis.com.

HARRIS, JULIE (ANN), actress; b. Grosse Pointe Park, Mich., Dec. 2, 1925; d. William Pickett and Elsie (Smith) Harris; m. Jay I. Julien, Aug. 12, 1946 (div. 1954); m. Manning Gurian, Oct. 21, 1954 (div. 1967); 1 child, Peter; m. Erwin Carroll, Apr. 26, 1977 (div. 1982). Student, Perry Mansfield Theatre Work Shop, 1941-43, Yale Drama Sch., 1944-45. Theater debut in It's a Gift, N.Y.C., 1945; appeared in plays Playboy of the Western World, 1946, Oedipus, 1946, Henry IV-Part II, 1946, Alice in Wonderland, 1947, We Love A Lassie, 1947, Macbeth, 1948, Sundown Beach, 1948 (Theatre World award 1949), The Young and Fair, 1948-49, Magnolia Alley, 1949, Montserrat, 1949, The Member of the Wedding, 1950-51 (Donaldson award 1950), I Am a Camera, 1951-52 (Tony award 1952, Donaldson award 1952, Variety-N.Y. Drama Critics Poll 1952), Mademoiselle Colombe, 1954, The Lark, 1955 (Tony award 1956), The Country Wife, 1957, The Warm Peninsula, 1959, Little Moon of Alban, 1960, Romeo and Juliet, 1960, King John, 1960, A Shot in the Dark, 1961, Marathon 33, 1964 (Tony nomination 1964), Hamlet, 1964, Ready When You Are, C.B, 1964, The Hostage, 1965, Skyscraper, 1965 (Tony nomination 1969), A Streetcar Named Desire, 1967, Forty Carats, 1968 (Tony award 1969, Antoinette Perry award for best actress), The Women, 1970, And Miss Reardon Drinks A Little, 1971-72, Voices, 1972, The Last of Mrs. Lincoln, 1972 (Tony award 1973, Antoinette Perry award for best actress), The Au Pair Man, 1973 (Tony nomination 1974), In Praise of Love, 1974, Break a Leg, 1979, On Golden Pond, 1980, Mixed Couples, 1980, Under the Ilex, 1983, Tusitala, 1988, (nat. co.) Driving Miss Daisy, Love Letters, 1989, The Belle of Amherst, 1977 (Grammy award 1977, Tony award 1977), Currier Bell, Glass Menagerie, 1994, Ellen Foster, 1997, Love is Strange, 1999, Fossils, 2001; one-woman theater presentations include Lucifer's Child, 1991; film debut in The Member of the Wedding, 1952 (Acad. award nomination); other films include The East of Eden, 1955, I Am A Camera, 1955, The Truth About Women, 1958, Poacher's Daughter, 1960, Requiem for a Heavyweight, 1962, The Haunting, 1963, The Moving Target, 1966, You're a Big Boy Now, 1966, Harper, 1966, Reflections in a Golden Eye, 1967, Tarzan and the Perils of Charity Jones, 1967, Tarzan and the Four O'Clock Army, 1968, The Split, 1968, Journey into Midnight, 1968, The People Next Door, 1970, The Hiding Place, 1975, Voyage of the Damned, 1976, The Bell Jar, 1979, The Prostitute, 1980, The Nutcraker: The Motion Picture, 1986, Gorillas in the Mist, 1988, Housesitter, 1992, The Dark Half, 1993, Little Surprises, 1995, Carried Away, 1996, Bad Manners, 1997, Gentle into the Night, 1998, The Way Back Home, 2005; TV series include Thicker Than Water, 1973, The Family Holvak, 1975, Knots Landing, 1979-87; TV movies include Wind From the South, 1955, The Good Fairy, 1956, The Lark, 1957, Johnny Belinda, 1968, Little Moon of Alban, 1958 (Emmy award 1959), A Doll's House, 1959, Victoria Regina, 1961 (Emmy award 1962), The Power and the Glory, 1961, The Heiress, 1961, Pygmalian, 1964, Hamlet, 1964, The Holy Terror, 1965, Anastasia, 1967, The House on Green Apple Road, 1970, How Awful About Alan, 1970, Home for the Holidays, 1972, The Greatest Gift, 1974, The Belle of Amherst, 1976, The Last of Mrs. Lincoln, 1976, Stubby Pringle's Christmas, 1978, Backstairs at the White House, 1979, The Gift, 1979, The Christmas Wife, 1979, The Annihilator, 1986, The Woman He Loved, 1988, Too Good To Be True, 1988, Single Women, Married Men, 1989, They've Taken Our Children: The Chowchilla Kidnapping Story, 1993, When Love Kills: The Seduction of John Nearn, 1993, One Christmas, 1994, Scarlett, 1994, Little Surprises, 1995, Secrets, 1995, The Christmas Tree, 1996, James Dean: A Portrait, 1996, Carried Away, 1996, Bad Manners, 1997, Ellen Foster, 1997, The First of May, 1998, Love is Strange, 1999, (voice) Frank Lloyd Wright, 1998; author: (with Barry Tarshis) Julie Harris Talks to Young Actors, 1971. Recipient Nat. Medal of the Arts, 1994, Tony award for lifetime achievement in theatre, 2002, Drama Desk Career Achievement award for commitment to excellence in theatre, 2005, Kennedy Ctr. Honor, John F. Kennedy Ctr. for Performing Arts, 2005. Office: William Morris Agy c/o Samuel Liff 1325 Avenue of the Americas New York NY 10019

HARRIS, JUNE LEATRICE, education coordinator, administrator; b. South Mills, NC; d. Charlie Cyphus and Emma Jane (Griffin) H. BS, N.C. Ctrl. U.; MA, Atlanta U.; PhD, U. Md. Profl. staff Com. Edn. and Labor Rep. William L. Clay, Washington, 1983-94; tchr. Balt. Pub. Schs., Mo. Coll., St. Louis, Mo., U. D.C., Washington, Elizabeth City (N.C.) State U.; edn. policy coord. Com. on Edn. and the Workforce, 1994—. Author: Excellence in Education. Recipient Recognition award State Occupl. Info. Coordinating, Salt Lake City, 1990. Mem. Mich. Edn. Assn., D.C. Vocat. Edn., Phi Delta Kappa, Delta Sigma Theta. African Methodist Episcopal Zion Church. Avocations: basketball, golf, reading. Office: US Ho Reps 1107 Longworth Bldg Washington DC 20515-0004

HARRIS, K. DAVID, senior state supreme court justice; b. Jefferson, Iowa, July 29, 1927; s. Orville William and Jessie Heloise (Smart) H.; m. Madonna Theresa Coyne, Sept. 4, 1948; children: Jane, Julia, Frederick. BA, U. Iowa, 1949, JD, 1951. Bar: Iowa 1951, U.S. Dist. Ct (so. dist.) Iowa, 1958. Sole practice Harris & Harris, Jefferson, 1951-62; dist. judge 16th Judicial Dist., Iowa, 1962-72; justice Iowa Supreme Ct., Des Moines, 1972-99, sr. justice, 1999—; ret., 2005. Served with U.S. Army, 1944-46, PTO. Mem. VFW, Am. Legion, Rotary. Roman Catholic. Avocation: poetry. Office: Iowa Supreme Ct State Capitol Bldg Des Moines IA 50319-0001 Office Phone: 515-386-4321.

HARRIS, KAMALA D., prosecutor; b. Oakland, Calif., 1964; BA, Howard U.; JD, U. Calif. Bar: 1990. Dep. dist. atty. Office Dist. Atty., Alameda County, Calif., 1990—98, mng. atty. career criminal unit San Francisco, 1998—2000, head city atty.'s divsn. on families and children, 2000—04, dist. atty., 2004—. Co-chair Lawyers' Com. Civil Rights; pres. bd. dirs. Partners Ending Domestic Abuse; founder mentoring program San Francisco Mus. Modern Art; founder Coalition to End Exploitation of Kids. Named Child Advocate of Yr., San Francisco Child Abuse Prevention

Coun., 2004; named one of Top 20 Young Lawyers Calif., Daily Journal, 1998; recipient award, Crime Victims United, County Counsel Assn. Calif., Thurgood Marshall award, Nat. Black Prosecutors Assn., 2005. Office: San Francisco Dist Attys Office 850 Bryant St Rm 322 San Francisco CA 94103

HARRIS, KATHERINE H., former congresswoman, former state official; b. Key West, Fla., Apr. 5, 1957; m. Anders Ebbeson; 1 child Student, U. Madrid, 1978; BA in History, Agnes Scott Coll., 1979; MPA in Internat. Trade, Harvard U., 1996. Mem. Fla. State Senate from 24th dist., 1994—98; sec. state State of Fla., Tallahassee, 1999—2002; mem. US Congress from 13th Fla. dist., 2003—07. Vice chmn. banking and ins. com. Fla. State Senate, vice chmn. govtl. reform and oversight com., chmn. commerce and econ. opportunities com. Congl. intern U.S. Senate and U.S. Ho. of Reps., 1978; vice chmn. Sarasota County Legis. Del.; mem. Supreme Ct. Gender Bias Commn.; vice chmn. Fla. Am. Legis. Exch. Coun.; mem. arts and tourism com. Nat. Conf. State Legislators; former mem. adv. coun. Mote Marine Lab., Women's Resource Ctr., Sarasota County Arts Coun.; mem. Leadership Sarasota, Leadership Tampa; former vice chmn. bd. trustees Ringling Mus.; mem. nominating com. Pub. Svc. Commn.; active Habitat for Humanity, New Coll., Fla. Rep. Exec. Com. Recipient Disting. Leadership Alumni award, Leadership Sarasota, 1994, Arts Advocacy award, Sarasota County Arts Coun., 1995, Best Govt. Ofcl. award, Sarasota Mag., 1995—2002, Legislator of Yr. award, Sarasota Opera, 1996, Ind. Funeral Dirs. of Fla., 1996, Fla. Optometric Assn., 1996, Legis. Appreciation award, Dept. Labor and Employment Security, 1996. Mem. Sarasota C. of C. (Disting. Leadership Alumni award 1994), Englewood C. of C., Charlotte C. of C., Venice C. of C., Jaycees. Republican. Presbyterian. Avocations: reading, sailing, painting, skiing, skeet shooting.*

HARRIS, KATHERINE SAFFORD, speech and hearing educator; b. Lowell, Mass., Sept. 3, 1925; d. Truman Henry and Katherine (Wardwell) Safford; m. George Harris, Oct. 2, 1952; children: Maud White, Louise. BA, Radcliffe Coll., 1947; PhD, Harvard U., Cambridge, Mass., 1954. Rsch. assoc. Haskins Labs., New Haven, 1952-85, v.p., 1985—; prof. CUNY, NYC, 1970—, disting. prof., 1982—. Active U.S./Israeli Speech Program Littauer Found., N.Y.C., 1986. Author: (with Borden and Raphael) Speech Science Primer, 1970, 5th edit., 2006, (with Baer and Sasaki) Phonatory Control, 1986. Active U.S./Israeli Speech Program Littauer Found., NYC, 1986. Nat. Inst. Deafness and Other Comm. Disorders grantee. Fellow AAAS, Acoustical Soc. Am. (pres. 2000-01, Silver medal in speech commn. 2006, Rossing prize in acoustics edn. 2006, Gold medal in acoustics, 2007), Am. Speech Hearing Assn., N.Y. Acad. Scis. Office: CUNY Grad Sch 415 5th Ave New York NY 10016 Personal E-mail: loumau2003@yahoo.com.

HARRIS, LARRY, professional sports team executive; s. Del Harris; children: Zachary, Janaya. Grad. in Math., Eastern N.Mex. U. Actuary Wyatt Corp., Dallas; scout/video coord. Milw. Bucks, 1988—96, dir. scouting, 1996—98, dir. player pers., 1998—2001, asst. gen. mgr., 2001—03, gen. mgr., 2003—. Office: Milw Bucks 1001 N Fourth St Milwaukee WI 53203*

HARRIS, MARGARET T., school system administrator; b. Boston, Feb. 22, 1944; d. Michael Cotter and Margaret Murnane; m. James M. Harris Jr., May 28, 1966; children: Troy, Jason, Damien, Gillian. BSEd, U. Mass., Boston, 1966; MLS, Boston U., 1973; MSc, Syracuse U., 1989; EdD, U. Mass., Amherst, 2003. Cert. tchr. Nat. Bd. Edn., 2003. Tchr. Boston Schs., 1966—67; tchr. history and social studies Martha's Vineyard Schs., Oak Bluffs, Mass., 1976—2003, dir. curriculum and instrn. Tisbury, Mass., 2003—04, head history dept., 1980—2003, asst. supt. curriculum, 2004—. Contbr. articles to profl. publs. Mem. Martha's Vinehard Libr. Commn., Oak Bluffs, 1977—80, Martha's Vineyard Conservation Commn., Oak Bluffs, 1978—82. Fulbright fellow, Brazil, 1993, Japan, 1997, South Africa, 2001. Mem.: AAUW, Orgn. Am. History (mem. various coms.), Phi Beta Kappa. Democrat. Avocations: dogs, music, dance, reading, knitting, walking. Business E-Mail: margaret_harris@fc.mv.k12.ma.us.

HARRIS, MARK R., film producer; Prodr.: (TV films) Dog's Best Friend, 1997, The Twilight of the Golds, 1997, Doomsday Rock, 1997, Sweet Deception, 1998, Crash and Byrnes, 1999, Sanctimony, 2000, Britannic, 2000, A Woman's a Helluva Thing, 2001; (films) Error in Judgment, 1998, Gods and Monsters, 1998, Red Team, 1999, Kiss of a Stranger, 1999, I'll Remember April, 1999, Big Monster on Campus, 2000, Nostradamus, 2000, Maze, 2000, Crash, 2004 (Spirit award best first feature, 2006); exec. prodr.: (TV series) EZ Streets, 1996, Family Law, 1999; (TV films) Panic in the Skies!, 1996, EZ Streets, 1996, When Time Expires, 1997—, Ghost of a Chance, 1998—, Storm Chasers: Revenge of the Twister, 1998; (films) Loyal Opposition, 1998, Tejing xinrenlei 2, 2000, I Saw Mommy Kissing Santa Claus, 2002, A Good Night to Die, 2003, Conversations with Other Women, 2005.

HARRIS, MARK W., mayor, lawyer; b. Evanston, Wyo., May 17, 1957; m. Diane Harris; children: Bryan, Cameron. BS, U. Wyo., 1979, JD, 1982. Bar: Wyo. 1982. Atty. Harris Law Firm PC, Evanston, Wyo.; city atty. Evanston, Wyo., 1983—87; spl. asst. atty. gen. Wyo.; ct. commr. and magistrate Uinta County Circuit Ct., Wyo., Third Jud. Dist. Ct., Wyo.; mayor City of Evanston, 2003—07. Adj. instr. We. Wyo. CC, Evanston. Past chmn. Evanston Urban Renewal Agency; past pres. Uinta Med. Found. Bd. Mem.: Wyo. State Bar (commr. 1994—97, sec., treas. 1997—2002, pres. 2004). Office: Harris Law Firm 927 Main St Evanston WY 82930-3440 Office Phone: 307-789-3210. Office Fax: 307-789-0410. E-mail: mayor@allwest.net.*

HARRIS, MARY LYNN, science educator, consultant; b. Kalamazoo, Mich., July 20, 1949; d. Robert Eugene and Margaret Marie Coe; m. William Arthur Harris, June 19, 1971; children: Jennifer Lynn, Jonathan William. BA in Biology and Chemistry, No. Mich. U., Marquette, 1971. Student tchr. No. Mich. U., Marquette, 1967—71; substitute tchr. Escanaba (Mich.) Area Pub. Schs., 1971—73, 1978—84, Gladstone (Mich.) Area Pub. Schs., 1971—73, 1978—84, Bark River (Mich.)-Harris Pub. Sch., 1971—73, 1978—84, Holy Name Cath. Sch., Escanaba, 1973—84; adult edn. tchr. North Cen. Area Schs., Powers, 1988—92; sci. tchr. grades 8-12 Nah-Tah-Wahsh Pub. Sch. Acad., Wilson, Mich., 1984—86, 1988—. Mem. environ. protection com. Hannahville Indian Comty., Wilson, 1988—92; sci. edn. adviser Delta-Schoolcraft Ind. Sch. Dist., Escanaba, 1988—2006; sci. coord. K-12 Nah Tah Wahsh PSA, Wilson, 1990—2001; coord., coach Native Am. Sci. Bowl Team, 1999—2004; grantwriter in field. Named Sci. Tchr. of Yr., No. Mich. Univ. chpt. Sigma Xi, 1998, Outstanding Conservation Tchr., Menominee Conservation Soc., 1998; recipient Native Am. Cultural award, Hannahville Indian Sch., 1998, Beyond the Books Outstanding Educator award, 1990—91, 1997—98. Mem.: VFW, Native Am. Sci. and Engring. Soc., Mich. Sci. Tchrs. Assn. (presenter conf. 1999—2000), Nat. Wildlife Fedn. Avocations: gardening, travel, crocheting, birdwatching. Home: 1005 Lake Shore Dr Escanaba MI 49829 Office: Nah-Tah-Wahsh Pub Sch Acad N 14911 Hannahville B-1 Rd Wilson MI 49896

HARRIS, MEL (MARY ELLEN HARRIS), actress; b. Bethlehem, Pa., July 12; m. David Hume Kennerly (div. 1988); 1 child, Byron; m. Cotter Smith, Oct., 1988; 1 child; m. Mike Toomey, 2001. Student, Columbia U.; studies with Lee Strasberg, Betty Cashman, Milton Katselas. Appeared in films Wanted: Dead or Alive, 1987, Cameron's Closet, 1989, K-9, 1989, Raising Cain, 1992, Suture, 1993, Desperate Motive, 1993, The Pagemaster, 1994, The Secretary, 1995, What Kind of Mother Are You?, 1996, Sonic Impact, 1999, Firetrap, 2001, Dynamite, 2002, Hangman's Curse, 2003, Purple Heart, 2005, Arc, 2005;(TV films) Harry's Hong Kong, 1987, Cross of Fire, 1989, My Brother's Wife, 1989, The Burden of Proof, 1992, Grass Roots, 1992, Child of Rage, 1992, With Hostile Intent, 1993, Desperate Journey: The Allison Wilcox Story, 1993, Ultimate Betrayal, 1994, The Spider and The Fly, 1994, The Women of Spring Break, 1995, Sharon's Secret, 1995, The Secretary, 1995, A Case for Life, 1996, Out of Time, 2000, The Retrievers, 2001, Another Pretty Face, 2002, Out of the Woods, 2005;(TV series) thirtysomething, 1987-91; guest appearances The Wizard, 1986, Rags to Riches, 1987, Something So Right, 1996, Dawson's Creek, 1999, Touched By an Angel, 2001, Strong Medicine, 2002, The West Wing, 2005, Stargate-SG-1, 2005, Jake In Progress, 2005, JAG, 2005, Cold Case, 2006, House M.D., 2006. Office: care UTA 9560 Wilshire Blvd Fl 5 Beverly Hills CA 90212-2401

HARRIS, MERLE WIENER, college administrator, educator; b. Hartford, Conn., July 25, 1942; d. Irving and Leah (Glasser) Wiener; m. David R. Harris, June 23, 1963; children: Jonathan, Rebecca. BS, Ctrl. Conn. State U., 1964, MS, 1973; EdD, U. Mass., 1988. Clk., edn. com. Conn. Gen. Assembly, Hartford, 1971-72; career edn. coordinator Bloomfield (Conn.) Pub. Schs., 1973-78; asst. to commr. Dept. of Higher Edn., Hartford, Conn., 1978-82, asst. commr., 1982-88, deputy commr., 1988-89; pres. Charter Oak State Coll., New Britain, Conn., 1989—; exec. dir. Bd. for State Acad. Awards, New Britain, Conn., 1989—; interim pres. Cen. Conn. State U., 1995-96. Cons.on career edn. U.S. Dept. Edn., Washington, 1974; fellow Inst. for Ednl. Leadership, 1980; bd. dirs. Old State House, 1996—2003, Conn. Hist. Soc., 2003—07, Conn. Literacy Vols., 1991—98, Conn. Humanities Coun., 1991—97, Conn. Acad. for Edn. in Math., Sci. and Tech., 2000—, vice chmn., 2002—05, chmn., 2005, Joint Com. Ednl. Tech., 1991—98; mem. Conn. Commn. Ednl. Tech., 2000—. Mem. New Eng. Assn. Schs. and Colls. (bd. dirs. 1997-2003), Am. Coun. on Edn. (commr. on ednl. credit and credentials 1995-98). Democrat. Jewish. Avocations: gardening, cooking. Home Phone: 860-521-0557; Office Phone: 860-832-3875. Business E-Mail: mharris@charteroak.edu.

HARRIS, MICALYN SHAFER, lawyer, arbitrator, mediator, educator, consultant; b. Chgo., Oct. 31, 1941; d. Erwin and Dorothy Shafer. AB, Wellesley Coll., 1963; JD, U. Chgo., 1966. Bar: Ill. 1966, Mo. 1967, US Dist. Ct. (ea. dist.) Mo. 1967, US Supreme Ct. 1972, US Ct. Appeals (8th cir.) 1974, NY 1981, NJ 1988, US Dist. Ct. NJ, US Ct. Appeals (3d cir.) 1993. Law clk. US Dist. Ct., Mo., 1967-68; atty. May Dept. Stores, St. Louis, 1968-70, Ralston-Purina Co., St. Louis, 1970-72; atty., asst. sec. Chromalloy Am. Corp., St. Louis, 1972-76; pvt. practice St. Louis, 1976-78; atty. CPC Internat., Inc., 1978-80; divsn. counsel CPC N.Am., 1980-84, asst. sec., 1981-88; gen. counsel S.B. Thomas, Inc., 1983-87; corp. counsel CPC Internat., Englewood Cliffs, NJ, 1984-88; assoc. counsel Weil, Gotshal & Manges, NYC, 1988-90; pvt. practice, 1991; v.p., sec., gen. counsel Winpro, Inc., 1991—. Arbitrator Am. Arbitration Assn., NYSE, NASD; adj. prof. Lubin Sch. Bus. Pace U.; expert cons., mediator. Mem. editl. bd.: Wall St. Lawyer. Mem. Met. Mus. of Art, Mus. Modern Art, Lincoln Ctr. Theater, Philharmonic-Symphony NY. Mem.: ABA (Ctr. Profl. Responsibility, bus. law sect., past chair corp. counsel com., past chair subcom. counseling mktg. function, mem. securities law com., tender offers proxy statements subcom., chair task force e-mail privacy, task force electronic contracting, task force conflicts interest, ad hoc com. tech., profl. responsibility com., profl. conduct com. task force on revised code of jud. conduct), Am. Law Inst. (mem. consultative groups restatement of agy. 3d intellectual property, prins. governing jurisdiction & judgements, internat. enforcement of judgements), NYC Bar Assn. (mediation coach), NJ Bar Assn. (computer law com.), NY State Bar Assn. (securities regulation com. and legis. com., past chair internet tech. law com., past chair subcom. on licensing, task force shrink-wrap licensing, electronic comm. task force), Asia Soc., Lotos Club. Avocations: ballroom dancing, piano, reading, theater, travel. Mailing: 625 N Monroe St Ridgewood NJ 07450-1206

HARRIS, MICHAEL GENE, optometrist, lawyer, educator; b. San Francisco, Sept. 20, 1942; s. Morry and Gertrude Alice (Epstein) H.; m. Dawn Block; children: Matthew Benjamin, Daniel Evan, Ashley Beth, Lindsay Meredith. BS, U. Calif., 1964, M in Optometry, 1965, D in Optometry, 1966, MS, 1968; JD, John F. Kennedy U., 1985. Bar: Calif., U.S. Dist. Ct. (no. dist.) Calif. Assoc. practice optometry, Oakland, Calif., 1965-66, San Francisco, 1966-68; instr., coord. contact lens clinic Ohio State U., 1968-69; asst. clin. prof. optometry U. Calif., Berkeley, 1969-73, dir. contact lens extended care clinic, 1969-83, chief contact lens clinic, 1983—, assoc. clin. prof., 1973-76, from asst. chief to assoc. chief contact lens svc., 1970—, from lectr. to sr. lectr., 1978—, vice chmn. faculty Sch. Optometry, 1983-85, 95—, prof. clin. optometry, 1984-86, clin. prof., 1986—, dir. residency program, 1993-95, asst. dean, 1994-95, assoc. dean, 1995—, acting dean, 2000, dir. policy and planning, 2003—. Peter's Meml. lectr. U. Calif. Sch. Optometry, 2000; vis. prof. City U., London, 1984; vis. rsch. fellow U. NSW, Sydney, 1989; sr. vis. rsch. scholar U. Melbourne, Victoria, Australia, 1989, Victoria, 92; mem. ophthalmic devices panel med. device adv. com. FDA, 1990—, interim chmn., 1994; lectr., cons. in field; mem. regulation rev. com. Calif. Bd. Optometry; cons. hypnosis Calif. Optometric Assn., Am. Optometric Assn.; cons. Nat. Bd. Examiners in Optometry, Soflens divsn. Bausch & Lomb, 1973—, Barnes-Hind Hydrocurve Soft Lenses, Inc., 1974—87, Pilkinton-Barnes Hind, 1987—94, Contact Lens Co., 1977—2001, Palo Alto, Va., 1980, Primarius Corp., Cooper Vision Optics, 1979—, Alcon, 1980—, CIBA, 1976—, Vistakon, 1980—2000; co-founder Morton D. Sarver Rsch. Lab., 1986. Editor current comments sect. Am. Jour. Optometry, 1974-77; editor Eye Contact, 1984-86; assoc. editor The Video Jour. Clin. Optometry, 1988-92; cons. editor Contact Lens Spectrum, 1988—; author: Contact Lenses: Treatment Options for Ocular Disease, Contact Lenses for Pre & Post-Surgery; editor: Problems in Optometry, Special Contact Lens Procedures; Contact Lenses in Ocular Disease, 1990; mem. editl. bd. Contact Lens and Anterior Eye Jour.; contbr. chpts. to books, articles to profl. jours. Planning commnr. Town of Moraga, Calif., 1986, vice-chmn. Calif., 1987—88, chmn., 1988—90; mem. Town Coun., Moraga, 1992—96; mem. adv. planning commn. Medi-Cal., 1993—95, chmn., 1994—96, with managed care commn., 1995—, chmn. managed care commn., 1996—98; life mem. Bay Area Coun. for Rescue & Recovery, 1976—; grantor Michael G. Harris Family Endowment Fund U. Calif., Dr. Michael G. Harris Tchg. award U. Calif.; commr. Sunday Football League Contra Costa County, 1974—78; planner, fin. advisor College Pk. HS Track Project; mem. Pleasant Hill C. of C., Friends of Rodgers Ranch, Friends of Libr.; mem. adv. bd. Mt. Diablo Regional YMCA, 2003—; vice-mayor Town Coun., Moraga, 1994—95; city county rels. com. Contra Costa County, Calif.; planning commr. City of Pleasant Hill, Calif., 1999—2002, coun. mem. Calif., 2002—; vice chair Redevel. Agy., Pleasant Hill, 2002—, vice mayor, 2003—, mayor, 2004—05; founding mem. Young Adults divsn. Jewish Welfare Fedn., 1965—69, chmn., 1967—68; charter mem. Jewish Cmty. Ctr. Contra Costa County; founding mem. Jewish Cmty. Mus. San Francisco, 1984; para-rabinnic Temple Isaiah, Lafayette, Calif., 1987; bd. dirs., 1990, Jewish Cmty. Rels. Coun. Greater East Bay, 1979—83, Campolindo Homeowners Assn., 1981—85, League of Calif. Cities East Bay Divsn., 2002—; bd. dirs. East Bay divsn. League of Calif. Cities. Named Alumnus of Yr., U. Calif. Sch. Optometry, 1999, John F. Kenndey Univ. Sch. of Law, 2005; recipient Eminent Svc. award, Am. Acad. Opometry, 2003; U. Calif. fellow, 1971, Calif. Optometric Assn. scholar, 1965, George Schneider meml. scholar, 1964, Disting. scholar, Nat. Acad. Practice in Optometry, 2004. Fellow: Prentice Soc. (pres.-elect 1994—96, pres. 1996—98), Assn. Schs. and Colls. Optometry (coun. on acad. affairs), British Contact Lens Assn., Am. Acad. Optometry (diplomate cornea and contact lens sect., chmn. contact lens papers, mem. contact lens com. 1974—, vice-chmn. contact lens sect. 1980—82, chmn. sect. 1982—84, immediate past chmn. 1984—86, chmn.jud. com. 1989—2001, chmn. bylaws com. 1989—, ethics taskforce 1999—, Eminent Svc. award 2003); mem.: ABA, Nat. Acads. of Practice (Distin. Scholar 2004—), Contra Costa Bar Assn., Calif. Acad. Sci., Calif. State Bd. Optometry (regulation rev. com.), Internat. Soc. Contact Lens Rsch., Mex. Soc. Contactology (hon.), Nat. Coun. on Contact Lens Compliance, Am. Optometric Found., Internat. Assn. Contact Lens Educators, Assn. Optometric Contact Lens Educators, Calif. Optometric Assn., Am. Optometric Assn. (proctor 1969—79, cons. on hypnosis, mem. contact lens sect., position papers com., mem. com. on opthalmic stds., subcom. on testing and certification, cons. editor Jour.), Internat. Assn. Contact Lens Educators, Robert Gordon Sproul Assn. U. Calif., Benjamin Ide Wheeler Soc. U. Calif., JFK U. Sch. Law Alumni Assn., U. Calif. Optometry Alumni Assn. (life), Pleasant Hill C. of C. Democrat. Office: U Calif Sch Optometry Berkeley CA 94720-2020 Business E-Mail: mharris@berkeley.edu.

HARRIS, MITCHEL BRION, orthopedist, surgeon; b. Chgo., Dec. 19, 1958; MD, U. Ill., 1984. Cert. Orthop. Surgery, 1992. Intern surgery U. Ill. Hosps., Chgo., 1984—85; resident orthop. surgery Dartmouth Hitchcock Med. Ctr., Hanover, NH, 1989, Sunnybrook & Womens Coll. Health Scis. Ctr., 1990; attending U. Hosp., La. State U., New Orleans, 1990, Charity Hosp., New Orleans, 1990; chief orthop. trauma Brigham and Women's Hosp., Boston. Asst. prof. La. State U., 1990—95, assoc. prof., 1995; spkr. in field. Contbr. articles to med. jours. Named a Top Doctor, Boston mag., 2006. Office: Brigham and Women's Hosp Dept Orthopedic Surgery 75 Francis St Boston MA 02115 Office Phone: 617-732-5322. Office Fax: 617-732-6937.*

HARRIS, NANCY LEE, special education educator, behavior analyst; b. West Point, NY, Dec. 25, 1955; d. Richard Lee and Joan Patricia (Corbett) Sandison; 1 child. Student, Lesley Coll., 1975—78; AA, Cape Cod Cmty. Coll., Barnstable, Mass., 1976; BS, U. Mass., Boston, 1987; postgrad., Salem State, 1992. Cert. elem. edn. and learning disabilities and emotionally disturbed Fla., N.C., elem. disabilities and learning and mentally and physically challenged Pa., nat. bd. cert. assoc. behavior analyst, cert. elem. edn. and learning disabilities Mass. Spl. edn. tchr. St. Anne's Home, Methuen, Mass., 1987, Mass. Cerebral Palsy, Methuen, 1988, IFFL, Danvers, Mass., 1989—91; LD tchr. Janus Sch., Lancaster, Pa., 1991—93; ED/LD tchr. PS Jones Mid. Sch., Washington, NC, 1993—97, Devereux Viera, Fla., 1998—2001, Milestones Charter Sch., Palm Bay, Fla., 2002—; with Indian River County Schs., Fla., 2002—. Home Phone: 772-562-5950; Office Phone: 772-913-0604. Personal E-mail: nancileeh@yahoo.com.

HARRIS, NEIL, historian, educator; b. Bklyn., 1938; s. Harold and Irene Harris. AB, Columbia U., NYC, 1958; BA, Cambridge U., Eng., 1960; PhD, Harvard U., 1965. From instr. to asst. prof. history Harvard U., Cambridge, Mass., 1965-69; assoc. prof. U. Chgo., 1969-72, prof., 1972-90, Preston and Sterling Morton prof. of history, 1990—, dir. Nat. Humanities Inst., 1975-77, chmn. dept. history, 1985-88. Mem. adv. bd. Temple Hoyne Buell Ctr., Columbia, 1984-89; mem. adv. com. dept. architecture Art Inst. Chgo., 1982—; mem. Smithsonian Council, 1978-84, chmn. 1984-92; visiting prof. Yale U., 1974; dir. d'etudes Ecole des Hautes Etudes en Sci. Sociales, Paris, 1985. Author: Artist in American Society, 1966, Humbug: The Art of P.T. Barnum, 1970, Cultural Excursions, 1990, Building Lives, 1999, Chicago Apartments, 2004; editor: Land of Contrasts, 1970, the WPA Guide to Illinois, 1983; bd. editors New Eng. Quar., 1982—, Winterthur Portfolio, 1978-80, 85-88. Frederick Law Olmsted Papers, 1973, Am. Scholar, 1994-2000; mem. editorial adv. bd. History Today, 1978-86. Trustee H.F. DuPont Winterthur (Del.) Mus., 1978-87, Newberry Libr.; mem. Nat. Mus. Svcs. Bd., Washington, 1977-84; vis. com. J. Paul Getty Mus., 1995—; bd. dirs. Nat. Mus. Am. History, 1997-2000, Terra Found. for Arts, 2002—. Am. Coun. Learned Socs. fellow, 1972-73, NEH fellow, 1980-81, Guggenheim fellow, 1999-2000; Getty scholar, 1991, Nat. Mus. Am. Art scholar, 1995-96; Boucher lectr. Johns Hopkins U., 1971, Cardozo lectr. Yale U., 1974, Tandy lectr. Whitney Mus. Am. Art, 1982, Kemper lectr. Pitzer Coll., 1980, Buell lectr. Columbia U., 1993; recipient Joseph Henry medal Smithsonian Instn., 1991. Fellow Am. Acad. Arts and Scis.; mem. Am. Antiquarian Soc., Am. Coun. Learned Socs. (vice chmn. N.Y. 1978-89, chmn. 1989-93), Phi Beta Kappa (senator united chpts. 1985-97, vis. lectr. 1985-86). Home: 4950 S Chicago Beach Dr Chicago IL 60615-3207 Office: U Chgo Dept History 1126 E 59th St Chicago IL 60637-1580 Office Phone: 773-702-8380. Business E-Mail: nh16@uchicago.edu.

HARRIS, NEIL PATRICK, actor; b. Albuquerque, June 15, 1973; s. Ron and Sheila H. Harris. Actor: (TV series) Doogie Howser, 1989—92 (People's Choice award, 1989, Young Artists award best young actor in series, 1989, 1990, 1991, 1992, Golden Globe nominee best actor, 1992), (voice only) Captain Planet and the Planeteers, 1990, Spider-Man, 2003, How I Met Your Mother, 2005—; (TV films) Too Good to be True, 1988, Home Fires Burning, 1989, Cold Sassy Tree, 1989, A Stranger in the Family, 1991, Sudden Fury: A Family Torn Apart, 1993, Snowbound: The Jim and Jennifer Stolpa Story, 1994, The Man in the Attic, 1994, Not Our Son, 1995, Legacy of Sin: The William Coit Story, 1995, My Antonia, 1995, The Christmas Wish, 1998, Joan of Arc, 1999, The Wedding Dress, 2001, Sweeney Todd: The Demon Barber of Fleet Street in Concert, 2001, The Christmas Blessing, 2005; (films) Clara's Heart, 1988 (Golden Globe nominee), The Purple People Eater, 1988, Animal Room, 1995, Starship Troopers, 1997, The Proposition, 1998, The Next Best Thing, 2000, The Mesmerist, 2001, Undercover Brother, 2002, Mesmirist, 2002, Harold and Kumar Go to White Castle, 2004, (voice only) The Golden Blaze, 2005,; (TV appearances) B.L. Stryker, 1989, Blossom, 1991, Roseanne, 1992, (voice only) Capitol Critters, 1992, Quantum Leap, 1993, Murder, She Wrote, 1993, The Outer Limits, 1996, Homicide: Life on the Streets, 1997, Will & Grace, 2000, Stark Raving Mad, 1999, (voice only) Static Shock, 2001, Son of the Beach, 2001, Ed, 2001, (voice only) Spider-Man: The Animated Series, 2002, Justice League, 2002, Touched By An Angel, 2002, (TV appearance) Boomtown, 2003, (TV appearances) Law & Order: Criminal Intent, 2004, Numb3rs, 2005, Jack & Bobby, 2005; (plays) Luck, Pluck & Virtue, (musicals) Fiddler on the Roof, 1991, Rent, 1997—98, Sweeney Todd; (plays) Romeo and Juliet, The End of the Day, A Fair Country. Office: William Morris Agy Inc 151 El Camino Dr Beverly Hills CA 90212

HARRIS, NICHOLAS GEORGE, publisher; b. Salisbury, Eng., Sept. 8, 1939; s. George Ivan and Phyllis Dorothy (Porter) H.; m. Margaret Jane Darling, Feb. 3, 1968; children: Nicola, Gregory. Sales rep. Collins Pubs., London, 1963-67, Montreal, 1967-72, sales dir. Toronto, 1972, exec. v.p., 1973; pres. William Collins Sons & Co., Can. Ltd., 1974-87; chmn., pres. Collins Pubs. N.Am., 1986-87; mng. dir. McClelland & Stewart, 1988-89; pres. Wright Harris, Inc., 1990; v.p., gen. mgr. Grolier, Ltd., 1990-92; pres. Nick Harris Assocs., 1993—, Harris Sorensen Internat. Inc., 2003—. Trustee Markham Pub. Lib., 1994-2000. Served to 1st lt. Brit. Army, 1958-63. Mem.: Donalda Club (Toronto). Anglican. E-mail: nickharris@sympatico.ca.

HARRIS, NORMAN EDWIN, food scientist, consultant; b. Riverside, NJ, Oct. 20, 1929; s. George Martin and Hilda Edith Harris; m. Patricia Ann Stiles, Sept. 15, 1956; children: Steven, Christopher, Juli, Jeffrey. BS, Mich. State U., East Lansing, 1957, MS, 1960. Food technologist Lever Bros. Rsch. & Devel., Edgewater, NJ, 1960—62; rsch. asst. Union Carbide Devel. Co., Tarrytown, NY, 1962—64; food technologist Corn Products, Waltham, Mass., 1964—68, U.S. Army Rsch. & Devel. Ctr., Natick, Mass., 1968—93. Bd. dirs. Piscataquis Golf Course, Guilford, Mass., 2000—, pesticide mgr., 2000—. Co-author: Formulary of Candy Products, 1991,

1998; contbr. over 30 sci. jour. food articles to profl. jours., chapters to books. Mem. Hist. Soc., Riverton, NJ, 2000. Airman 1st class USAF, 1950—54. Mem.: Svc. Corps. of Retired Execs. (chair 2000—02), Sigma Xi. Achievements include patents in field; fortified Tang with calcium used in NASA moon landing, July 1969; discovery in sensory taste tests that sucrose was sweeter than fructose in many food applications, contradicting establised literature values. Avocations: walking, reading, gardening, golf. Home: 83 Douty Hill Rd Sangerville ME 04479-3103 Office: Harris Consulting 83 Douty Hill Rd Sangerville ME 04479-3103 Office Phone: 207-876-4166.

HARRIS, PAUL, sculptor; b. Orlando, Fla., Nov. 5, 1925; Student, U. N.Mex., New Sch. Social Research, Hans Hofmann Sch. Fine Arts. Fulbright prof. sculpture Universidad Catolica de Chile, 1961-62; later faculty San Francisco Art Inst., Calif. Coll. Arts and Crafts, Oakland; artist-in-residence Rinehart Sch. Sculpture, Md. Inst. Art, 1981, U. Ariz., Tucson, 1986. Vis. critic, lectr. U.S.F.S. Ctrs., Valparaiso and Concepcion, Chile, 1962, Rinehart Sch. Sculpture, spring 1981, Md. Inst. Art, (9 times) 1963-86, U. Oreg., Eugene, 1968, Newark (N.J.) State U., 1970, Mont. State U., Bozeman, 1970, 74, State U. N.Mex., Las Cruces, 1971, Montclair (N.J.) State U., 1973, Commonwealth U. Va., 1975, 76, 95, Clemson U., 1975, Haverford Coll., 1977, Phila. Coll. Art, 1977, R.I. Sch. Design, 1977, U. Ariz., Tucson, 1986. One-man shows include Poindexter Gallery, N.Y.C., 1957, 1960, 1963, 1967, 1970, Lanyon Gallery, 1965, Berkeley Gallery, 1965, William Sawyer Gallery, San Francisco, 1969, 1971, 1986, 1987, Galerie Thelen, Essen, 1970, San Francisco Mus. Art, 1972, U. Calif., Santa Barbara, 1972, U. N.Mex., 1973, Ark. Arts Ctr., 1973, Loch Haven Art Ctr., Orlando, 1981, Stanford U. Art Mus., Calif., 1982, Greenville County Mus. Art, S.C., 1982, Iannetti-Lanzone Gallery, San Francisco, 1989, Fuller Goldeen Gallery, 1983, C. Grimaldis Gallery, Balt., 1989, Galerie Redmann, Berlin, 1990, 1995, Michael Himowitz Gallery, Sacramento, 1993, Bolinas (Calif.) Mus., 1999, Fresno (Calif.) Art Mus., 1999, 2003, The Coll. of Marin Gallery, Kentfield, Calif., 2000, Yellowstone Art Mus., Billings, Mont., 2001, Holter Mus. Art, Helena, Mont, 2003, Wiegand Gallery, Notre Dame de Namur U., Belmont, Calif., 2004, exhibited in group shows at Mus. Modern Art, N.Y.C., 1958, 1963, N.Y. World's Fair, 1965, Art Inst. Chgo., 1965, Md. Inst. Art, 1966, Mus. Contemporary Crafts, 1966, 1973, São Paulo Bienal, 1967, Crocker Art Gallery Assn., Sacramento, 1968, Smithsonian Instn. Traveling Exhibn., 1969, Phila. Inst. Art., San Francisco Mus. Art, N.J. State Mus., L.A. County Mus., 1973, Brandeis U., A.C.A. Gallery, 1972, Contemporary Art Ctr. Cin., 1973, Coll. Marin Galleries, 1974, JPL Gallery, London, 1975, Yellowstone Art Ctr., Billings, Mont., 1976, Renwick Gallery, Nat. Coll. Fine Arts, Washington, 1976—77, Falkirk Ctr., San Rafael, Calif., 1980, Transam. Bldg. Gallery, San Francisco, 1982, San Francisco Mus. Modern Art, 1983, Otis Art Inst. Parsons Sch. Design, 1984, Fendrick Gallery, 1984, William Sawyer Gallery, San Francisco, 1985, 1993, Iannetti Lanzone Gallery, 1987, Meml. Union Art Gallery, U. Calif., Davis, 1988, Civic Arts Gallery, Walnut Creek, Calif., 1988, Constantine Grimaldis Gallery, Balt., 1988, Gallery, San Francisco, 1989, Cologne (Germany) Art Fair, 1989, 1992, 1995, 1997, Galerie Redmann, Berlin, 1990, 1993, 1994, Bolinas Mus., Calif., 1990, Wolk Gallery, St. Helena, Calif., 1993, 1994, Oliver Art Ctr., Calif. Coll. Arts and Crafts, Oakland, Calif., 1993, Orlando (Fla.) History Mus., 1994, Sheldon Meml. Art Gallery, U. Nebr., 1996, Western Book Exhibit, San Francisco, 1996, The Woodson Art Mus., Wausaw, Wis., 1997—98, 871 Fine Arts Gallery, San Francisco, 2005, Wregard Gallery, Notre Dame U., Namur U., Belmont, Calif., 2007, Oakland Mus. Art, 2007, Coll. Marin Gallery, 2007, others, Wrongtree Press, 1973, on aspects of ballet A False Alarm on the Nightbell Once Answered-It Cannot Be Made Good, Not Ever, Art in Am. Illus. Torso (Dorothy Schmidt), 1974, Paul Harris (Dennis Leon, Harry Abrams), 1975, drawings, for Pas d'Une, 1979; writer, artist (drawings) Phases of the Moon, 1995, designer (book) Motives and Cues by Marguerite Harris, 1993; lithographs, Paradise: Variations, 1996, Paul Harris, drawings, 1998, sculpture, 1999. Recipient Longview Found. grant, 1960, Neallie Sullivan award, 1967; Tamarind fellow, 1969-70; named Miembro Academico de la Facultad de Bellas Artes Universidad Catolica de Chile, 1962; resident Macdowell Colony, 1977; grantee Lebovitz Fund, 1978; Guggenheim fellow 1979. Address: PO Box 930 Bolinas CA 94924-0930

HARRIS, PAUL LYNWOOD, retired aerospace transportation executive; b. Richmond, Va., May 30, 1945; s. Paul Lynwood Sr. and Marjorie (Southward) H.; m. Susan Lee, Sept. 20, 1969; children: Meredith Lynn, Joanna Lee. AA, Ferrum Coll., 1965; BS, U. Richmond, 1967. CPA, Va. Staff acct. Price Waterhouse & Co., Washington, 1967-71, sr. acct., 1971-73; v.p. fin. Universal Restoration Inc., Washington, 1973-76; treas. Hawker Siddely Aviation Inc., Washington, 1976-78, Brit. Aerospace Inc., Herndon, Va., 1978-81, v.p. fin., 1981-86, sr. v.p. fin., 1986-88; fin. dir. Brit. Aerospace Comml. Aircraft, Hatfield, Eng., 1988-92; sr. v.p. adminstrn. Brit. Aerospace, Inc., Herndon, Va., 1992-93; sr. v.p., gen. mgr. Brit. Aerospace N.Am., Inc., Herndon, Va., 1993-99; ret., 2000; chmn. Ferrum Coll., 2002—. Bd. trustees Ferrum Coll., 1999-2000. Bd. dirs. Reflectone, Inc., Cheshire Homes No. Va., Arlington, 1986, Washington Dulles Task Force, 1993-2001, Dulles Area Transport Assn., 1993-95; chmn. fin. com. United Christian Parish, Reston, Va., 1979. Mem. AICPA, Nat. Aviation Club (pres. 1995-96), Fin. Execs. Inst. Methodist. Home: PO Box 636 2006 Pumpkin Hill Rd Burgess VA 22432 E-mail: paulsusan2000@yahoo.com.

HARRIS, PAUL N., lawyer; BA, U. Chgo., 1980; JD, Stanford Law Sch., 1983. Assoc. to ptnr.-in-charge Thompson Hine, LLP, Cleve., 1983—88, with, 1997—2003; sr. counsel Revco DS Inc. (now CVS), 1988—97; exec. v.p., sec., gen. counsel, mem. mgmt. com., mem. exec. coun. Keycorp, Cleve., 2003—. Trustee, past pres. bd. trustees Friends of Cleve. Sch. of the Arts; trustee Hawken Sch., Cuyahoga Cmty. Coll. Found., Children's Mus. Cleve., City Club Cleve.; mem. vis. com. Cleve.-Marshall Coll. Law. Mem.: Cleve. Bar Assn., Soc. Corp. Secs. and Governance Profls. Office: Keycorp 127 Public Sq Cleveland OH 44114-1306 Office Fax: 216-689-0840.

HARRIS, PAUL SMITH, human resources professional; b. Santa Monica, Calif., Nov. 29, 1935; s. Wallace Albert and Henrietta (Smith) H.; m. Jill B. Hall, Sept. 15, 1956 (div. June 1974); children: Gregory A., Geoffrey A.; m. Nancy Lynn Cherry, Sept. 9, 1975; 1 child, Doug B. BA in Psychology, U. Utah, 1958; postgrad., UCLA, 1961-63. Mgr. employment Western Airlines Inc., LA, 1956-64; mgr. selection Am. Airlines Inc., NYC, 1964-66; mgr. adminstrn. IBM, Princeton, N.J., 1966-72; dir. orgn. planning and devel. CNA Fin. Corp., Chgo., 1972-76; v.p. human rsch. developer W.E. Walker Stores Inc., Jackson, Miss., 1976-80; pres. Harris Cons., Inc., Salt Lake City, 1980-83; dir. pers. Americas divsn. Intercontinental Hotels, Washington, 1983-88; v.p. human rsch. devel. Showboat Casino and Hotel, Atlantic City, 1988-93; exec. v.p. Showboat Devel. Co., Atlantic City, 1993-98; ret., 1998. Bd. dirs. C. of C., Middlesex County, N.J., 1970-71, Chgo. Alliance of Businessman, 1974-75. Mem. Masons (master mason Mt. Moriah # 2 Utah, 32 degree). Republican. Christian Scientist. Avocations: tennis, skiing, flying. Business E-Mail: paulsharris@cox.net.

HARRIS, PENNY SMITH, fundraising consultant; b. Old Town, Maine, Apr. 6, 1941; d. Owen Halbert and Louise Marion (Whitten) Smith; m. Parker Fred Harris, June 22, 1963 (div. 1992); children: Susan Leslie, Nancy Lynne. BS in Sociology, U. Maine, 1963; MS in Bus. Mgmt., Husson Coll., Bangor, Maine, 1984. Cert. fund raising exec. Social worker Elizabeth Lund Home, Burlington, Vt., 1964—65; pub. sch. tchr. Essex Junction, Vt.; asst. dir. devel., corp. support mgr. Maine Pub. Broadcasting Network, Bangor, 1985—89; dir. devel. Ea. Maine Healthcare, Bangor, 1989—94; dir. healthcare campaign N.E. Health, Rockland, Maine, 1994—97; sr. assoc. Copley Davenport Co., Inc., Wenham, Mass., 1997—98, M. Davenport Assocs., 1998—; pres. PS Harris Assocs., Portland, Maine, 2001—. Trustee Maine Pub. Broadcasting Corp., 1991—95, Ctr. for Maine Contemporary Art, 1993—, U. Maine Sys., 1991—2001; mem. task force on campaign fin. Senator George Mitchell, Augusta, Maine, 1983; mem. All Am. City selection award jury, Nat. Civil League, NYC, 1987; chmn. bd. dirs. Ctr. for Maine Contemporary Art, 2003—; bd. dirs. Greater Bangor United Way, 1990—93. Mem. LWV (pres. Bangor-Brewer chpt. 1979-81, state pres. 1982-85, nat. bd. dirs. 1986-88, sec. nat. bd. dirs. 1988-90, project dir. TV polit. debates Bangor 1982, project dir. Nat. Security and You Conf., Portland, Maine 1983), U. Maine Alumni Assn. (v.p. bd. dirs. 1991-93), Greater Portland C. of C. Democrat. Methodist. Avocations: skiing, travel, hiking, bicycling. Home and Office: PO Box 2862 South Portland ME 04116 Personal E-mail: penny.harris2@verizon.net. Business E-Mail: penny@harrisfundraising.com.

HARRIS, PHILIP JOHN, retired engineering educator; b. Montreal, Que., Can., Mar. 22, 1926; s. Thomas Percival and Gladys Marion (Gillett) H.; m. Norma Joyce Maynard, May 23, 1953; children: Elizabeth Joyce Harris Richardson, Janet Constance. B.Sc., U. Man., 1948; M.Eng., McGill U., 1949, PhD, 1964. Structural designer Dominion Bridge Co. Ltd., Lachine, Que., 1949-51; chief civil engr. C.D. Howe Co., Ltd., Montreal, 1951-58; asst. prof. dept. civil engring. McGill U., Montreal, 1958-59, assoc. prof., 1959-73, prof. dept. civil engring., 1973-91, chmn. dept., 1977-84, bd. govs., 1975-82, prof. emeritus, 1993—; prof. dept. civil engring. McMaster U., Hamilton, Ont., 1991-95. Cons. structural and found. engring., 1958-91; cons. engr., 1991-99. Contbr. articles to profl. jours. NRC Can. grantee, 1965-79; Natural Scis. and Engring. Research Council grantee, 1979-87. Fellow Can. Soc. Civil Engring., Engring. Inst. Can.; mem. ASCE (life). Anglican. Home: 408 Swanson Ct Burlington ON Canada L7R 4G6 E-mail: pjharris@idirect.com.

HARRIS, PHILIP ROBERT, management and space psychologist; b. Bklyn., Jan. 22, 1926; s. Gordon Roger and Esther Elizabeth (Delahanty) H.; m. Dorothy Lipp, July 3, 1965 (dec. 1997); m. Janet Belport, Feb. 14, 2001. BBA, St. John's U., 1949; MS in Psychology, Fordham U., 1952, PhD, 1956; spl. student, NYU, 1948-49, Syracuse U., 1961. Lic. psychologist U. of State of N.Y., 1959, N.Y. Dir. guidance St. Francis Prep. Sch., NYC, 1952-56; dir. student personnel, v.p. St. Francis Coll., NYC, 1956-63; exec. dir. Assn. Human Emergency-Thomas Murray Tng. Program, 1964-66; vis. prof. Pa. State U., 1965-66; vis. prof., cons. Temple U.; sr. assoc. Leadership Resources Inc., 1966-69; v.p. Copley Internat. Corp., La Jolla, Calif., 1970-71; pres. Mgmt. and Orgn. Devel. Inc. (now Harris Internat. Ltd.), La Jolla, 1971—; edn. dir. Air/Space Am., 1988; sr. scientist Netrologic, Inc., La Jolla, Calif., 1990-93; prof. Calif. Sch. Internat. Mgmt., 2005—. Rsch. assoc. Calif. Space Inst., U. Calif., San Diego, 1984-90; adj. prof. Pepperdine U., U. No. Colo., Calif. Sch. Internat. Mgmt., 2005-07; acad. adv. Command Coll., Commn. on Peace Officers Stds. and Tng. State of Calif., Dept. Justice, 1986-94; past cons. Westinghouse, N.V. Philips, I.B.M., Computer Sci. Corp. Control Data, govt. agys.; chmn. bd. dirs. United Socs. in Space, Inc., 1993-97 Author, vols. including: Effective Management of Change, 1976, Improving Management Communication Skills, 1978, Managing Cultural Differences, 1979, 7th edit., 2007, New Worlds, New Ways, New Management, 1983, Managing Cultural Synergy, 1982, Management in Transition, 1985, Living and Working in Space, 1992, 2d edit., 1996, High Performance Leadership, 2d edit., 1994, New Work Culture, 1998, Launch Out, 2003, Managing the Knowlege Culture, 2005; co-author: Transcultural Leadership, 1993, Developing Global Organizations, 1993, 2d edit., 2001, Multicultural Management 2000, 1998, Multicultural Law Enforcement, 1995, 4th edit., 2007, Managing the Knowledge Culture, 2005; editor: Innovations in Global Consultation, 1980, Global Strategies in Human Resource Development, 1983; author (series) New Work Culture, 3 vols., 1994-98; co-editor Manging Cultural Differences Series Butterworth-Heinemann/Elsevier Sci., 1979-2007; mem. editl. bd. European Bus. Rev., 1996-2006; founding editor emeritus Space Governance Jour., 1993-98; contbr. 235 articles to profl. jours. V.p. Bklyn. Downtown Renewal Effort, 1957-59. Recipient Literati Club award for excellence, 2005; named to Gulf Pub. Author Hall of Fame, 1999; Fulbright prof. to India U.S. State Dept., 1962; NASA faculty fellow, 1984. Fellow AIAA (assoc.); mem. ASTD (Torch award 1975), Aviation Space Writers Assn. (journalism awards 1986, 88, 89, 93), World Bar Assn. (Space Humanitarian award1992), Nat. Space Soc., United Socs. in Space (dir. emeritus), Soc. for Human Performance in Extreme Environments, La Jolla Beach and Tennis Club, Literati Club Independent. Home and Office: 2702 Costebelle Dr La Jolla CA 92037-3524 Office Phone: 858-453-2271. E-mail: philharris@aol.com.

HARRIS, PHILLIP H., lawyer; BS, Ind. U.; JD, Georgetown U. Solicitor US Catholic Conf.; assoc. counsel Evangelical Lutheran Church Am., Chgo., 1995—96, gen. counsel, 1996—, chmn. elections com. Mem.: Md. Bar Assn., DC Bar Assn. Office: Evangelical Lutheran Church 8765 W Higgins Rd Chicago IL 60631 E-mail: phil.harris@elca.org.

HARRIS, QUEEN WIGGS, mathematician, educator; b. Goldsboro, NC, Feb. 18, 1948; d. Frederick Calvin and Josephine James Wiggs; m. Clayton Harris Jr., June 25, 2005; 1 child, Kenneth S. Tollett Jr. BS, Bennett Coll., 1970; MS, Howard U., 1972; postgrad., Md. U., 1972—75, Am. U., 1984—85. Asst. prof. U. DC, Washington, 1973—97; adj. prof. NC Wesleyan Coll., Rocky Mount, NC, 1995—97, Ga. Perimeter Coll., Dunwoody, 2005—, Oglethorpe U., Atlanta, 2006; asst. prof. Shaw U., Raleigh, NC, 1999—2003; tchr. NC Sch. Sci. and Math., Durham, 2003—05. Proposal reviewer NSF, 1990—92; AP calculus cons. Coll. Bd., 2002—; table leader AP calculus AP Readings, 2007—. Contbg. author: Precalculus/Calculus Short Course, 1997. Bd. dirs. Project R.E.S.C.U.E., Wilson, NC, 1999; mem. Wilson Med. Ctr. Aux., 1999—2001. Mem.: AAUW (treas. Wilson chpt. 1997), Delta Sigma Theta. Home: 2019 Emerald Dr Jonesboro GA 30236 Personal E-mail: qewiggs@msn.com. Business E-Mail: qharris@gpc.edu.

HARRIS, RAYMOND CLEMENT, nephrologist, educator; b. Nashville, Tenn., Mar. 26, 1952; s. Raymond Clement and Elizabeth Lay Harris; m. Paula Jean Messenheimer, Sept. 26, 1982; children: Matthew Clement, William Alexander. BS, Yale U., 1974; MD, Emory U., 1978. Intern U. Calif., San Francisco, 1978—79, med. resident, 1979—81; renal fellow Brigham & Women's Hosp., Boston, 1982—86; asst. prof. Vanderbilt U. Hosp., Nashville, 1986—91, assoc. prof., 1991—98, prof., 1998—, dir. divsn. nephrology & hyptertension; dir. Vanderbilt O'Brien Ctr. for Study of Kidney Disease, Nashville. Office: Vanderbilt U Med Ctr Medicine Dept D-3100 Med Ctr N Nashville TN 37232-0001 Home Phone: 615-385-4575; Office Phone: 615-322-2150.

HARRIS, RAYMOND JESSE, retired federal official; b. Van Buren, NY, Dec. 28, 1916; s. Francis Elbert and Anna Marie (Selinsky) H.; m. Rosalba Emilia Prestianni, Jan. 7, 1950 (dec. 1989). AB, Harvard U., 1940, postgrad., 1940-42, U. Pa., 1952-54, 59-60. Corr. drafter U.S. State Dept., Washington, 1947; vice consul Am. consulate palermo, Italy, 1947-50, Munich, Germany, 1950-51; personnel technician, information officer City of Phila., 1952-59, administrv. asst. to water commr., 1959-79; ret., 1979; Republican committeeman 59th ward City of Phila., 1986-98. Served with USAAF, 1942-45; ETO. Named Water Dept. Supr. of Year, 1971, 72, 73, 76; recipient Ted Moses award Pa. Water Pollution Control Assn., 1978. Mem. Am. Water Works Assn., Archeol. Inst. Am., Amnesty Internat. USA, Nat. Trust Historic Preservation, Pa. Hist. Soc., Acad. Polit. Sci., Am. Anti-Vivisection Soc., Planetary Soc., Harvard of Phila. Club, Preservation Alliance Greater Phila. Home: 275 W Tulpehocken St Philadelphia PA 19144-3209

HARRIS, REGINALD MERVYN, JR., librarian, writer; b. Annapolis, Md., June 25, 1960; s. Reginald Mervyn and Ellen Felicia (Powell) H. BA, Randolph-Macon Coll., 1982. Mgmt. trainee Tandy Corp./Radio Shack, Balt., 1987-89, mgr., 1989; credit liaison Balt. Mag., 1989; part-time libr. circulation asst. Soper Libr., Morgan U., Balt., 1992-93; libr. assoc. Enoch Pratt Free Libr., Balt., 1990-97, info. tech. support specialist, 1997-99, info. tech. tng. mgr., 1999—2001, mem. program planning guideline com. PC supportingsubcom., 1993, head info. tech. support dept., 2001—; rep. to Balt. mayor's web page subcom., 1996; interim dir. comm. Enoch Pratt Free Libr., Balt., 2006—07. Program planning guildeline com., PC support and tng. subcom., 1993. Author: Ten Tongues: Poems, 2002; bd. dirs.: Jour. of Arts, exec. bd. mem.: Link: A Jour. of Arts, 2003—, bd. pres.:, 2005—. Mem. cmty. adv. bd. Study to Help the AIDS Rsch. Effort, Johns Hopkins Hosp., Balt., 1989-92; adv. coun. Learning Bank of Coil, Inc., 2004—; judge Publishing Triangle Poetry awards, 2004, judge spriritualty category, Lambda Lit. Awards, 2004, Gay Men's Fiction Category, 2005, erotica category, 2006, anthology category, 2007; pres. bd. dirs. Link: A Jour. of the Arts, 2005—. With US Coast Guard, 1983—87. Recipient Individual Artist award in fiction Md. State Arts Coun., 2000, Individual Artist award in poetry, 2001 Mem. Pratt Staff Assn. (bd. govs. 1991-93); bd. dirs., Fire & Ink., Inc. Office: Enoch Pratt Free Libr Info Tech Support Dept 400 Cathedral St Baltimore MD 21201 Office Phone: 410-545-6341. Office Fax: 410-396-3722. Personal E-mail: rmharris2001@hotmail.com.

HARRIS, REUBEN, wholesale distribution executive; BS in Mech. Engring., Antioch Coll., 1969; MBA, U. Rochester, 1972; PhD, Stanford U., 1972. V.p. R&D Tom Peters Group, 1985—91; cons. C&S, 1988—2001; vice chmn. C&S Wholesale, Brattleboro, Vt., 2001—; dir. C&S Holdings, 1992—. Bd. dirs. Bulab Holdings, Inc., 1997—; mem. mgmt. faculty Naval Postgrad. Sch., Monterey, Calif., 1978—2001, dean Grad. Sch. Bus. and Pub. Policy, 1995—2001; faculty mem. Coll. Bus. Adminstrn. U. Calif., Berkeley; faculty mem. Alfred P. Sloan Sch. Mgmt., MIT, Irish Mgmt. Inst., Dublin. Author 2 books; contbr. articles to profl. jours. Trustee Antioch U. Office: C&S Wholesale 7 Corporate Dr Keene NH 03431

HARRIS, RICHARD EUGENE VASSAU, lawyer; b. Detroit, Mar. 16, 1945; s. Joseph and Helen Harris; m. Milagros A. Brito; children: Catherine, Byron. AB, Albion Coll., 1967; JD, Harvard U., 1970; postdoctoral, Inst. Advanced Legal Studies, London, 1970-71. Bar: Calif. 1972. Assoc. Orrick, Herrington, Rowley & Sutcliffe, San Francisco, 1972-77; ptnr. Orrick, Herrington & Sutcliffe, San Francisco, 1978-98; pvt. practice Richard E. V. Harris Law Office, Oakland, Calif., 1998—. Faculty Calif. Tax Policy Conf., 1987, 95; spkr. univ., govtl. and profl. groups. Knox fellow, Harvard U., 1970—71. Mem.: ABA (litig. sect. corp. counsel com., subcom. chmn. 1980—82, antitrust law sect. state action com. 1981—, vice chmn. 1982—83, vice chmn. govt. liability com. 1982—84, co-chmn. Nat. Insts. Antitrust Liability 1983, Boulder task force 1983—84, coun. urban state and local govt. sect. 1983—88, litig. sect. corp. counsel com., subcom. chmn. 1983—, co-chmn. Nat. Insts. Antitrust Liability 1985, bus. law sect., SEC investigation atty.-client privilege waiver task f 1988, profl. conduct com., tax sect., state and local taxes com. 1989—, tax litig. com. 1992—, conflicts of interest task force 1993—96, internat. com. 1994—, corp. counsel com. 1995—, conflicts of interest com. 1996—2000, ad hoc com. on ethics 2000, com. profl. conduct 2001—, Ctr. Profl. Responsibility, ABA Ethics 2000 adv. group), Bar Assn. San Francisco (ethics com. 1980—, state bar conf. del. 2003), Am. Law Inst. (cons. restatements of law unfair competition 1991—94, governing lawyers com. 1991—2000, torts com. 1993—, agy. com. 1996—2006, trusts com. 1996—). E-mail: richardevh@aol.com.

HARRIS, RICHARD LEE, engineering executive, retired military officer; b. Bellevue, Pa., Dec. 26, 1928; s. Everett Lee and Marjorie Anna (Messer) H.; m. Patricia Ann Walton, Dec. 12, 1953; children: Sandra Jo, Carole Jill, William Walton, Robert Lee. BS, U.S. Mil. Acad., West Point, NY, 1951; student, Army Engr. Sch., 1951-59; MS, MIT, 1956; grad., Oak Ridge Sch. Reactor Tech., 1957, Command and Gen. Staff Coll., 1963, Nat. War Coll., 1967. Designated sr. parachutist, nuclear reactor comdr. registered profl. engr., Pa., Tex. Commd. 2d lt. U.S. Army, 1951, advanced through grades to maj. gen., 1973; with (32d Engrs. Combat Bn.), 1951; co-comdr. (13th Engrs. Combat Bn., 7th Inf. Divsn.), Korea, 1952-53; res. engr. (Phila. Engrs. Dist.), 1953-54; engrs. supply officer Columbus Depot, 1954-55; tech. ops. officer AEC, NYC, 1957-59; officer in charge (SM-1A Nuclear Power Plant), Alaska, 1960-62; with (U.S. STRIKE Command), 1963-65; bn. comdr. (20th Engrs. Combat Bn.), Vietnam, 1965-66; with Office Chief of Staff, U.S. Army, 1967-68, Hdqrs. U.S. Army Pacific, 1968-70; comdr. divsn. support command (1st Cav. Divsn.), Vietnam, 1970-71; asst. comdt. Army Engrs. Sch., 1971-73; dir. mgmt. info. sys. Office Chief Staff Army, Hdqrs. Dept. Army, 1973-76; comdr. U.S. Army Tng. Ctr.-Engr. and Ft. Leonard Wood, Mo., 1976-78; divsn. engr. North Ctrl. Engr. Divsn., 1978-80; ret., 1980; v.p. Radian Corp., Austin, 1980-93; ret., 1993. Decorated D.S.M., Legion of Merit with 4 oak leaf clusters, Bronze Star with 2 oak leaf clusters, Air medal with 4 numerals, Joint Services Commendation medal, Purple Heart. Fellow: Soc. Am. Mil. Engrs.; mem.: Mil. Officers Assn., Assn. U. S. Army, Phi Kappa Phi. Home: 8817 Balcones Club Dr Austin TX 78750-3042

HARRIS, RICHARD W., lawyer, educator, accountant; b. Arlington, Va., Aug. 4, 1952; s. Glendal W. and Jean K. Harris; m. Deborah Lynn Weber, Nov. 22, 1987; children: Lindsey, Taylor, Cameron. BS in acctg., U. Md., Coll. Pk., 1974, MBA, 1976; JD with honors, U. Md., Balt., 1981; LLM tax, Georgetown Law Ctr., Washington, 1989. CPA Md., 1975; bar: Md. 1982, U.S. Supreme Ct. 1984. Assoc. Levitan, Ezrin, West & Kerxton, Bethesda, Md., 1981—84; pvt. practice Lanham, Md., 1984—89; asst. prof. taxation Am. U., Washington, 1989—95; prof. taxation Grand Valley State U., Grand Rapids, Mich., 1995—. Dir. grad. tax program Grand Valley State U., 1995—2002, L. William Seidman chair of acctg. and taxation, 1995—, chair MST adv. bd., 1995—2002; chair West Mich. Tax Symposium, Grand Rapids, Mich., 1995—; adj. instr. Mich. State U., Lansing, 2004—. Contbr. articles to profl. jours. Co-founder and dir. Grand Rapids Vol. Income Tax Assistance Program, 1997—. Mem.: ABA, Mich. Assn. of CPA's, Md. State Bar Assn. Avocations: pvt. pilot, basketball coach, motorhome travel. Home: 3751 Oak Creek Ct Grand Rapids MI 49546 Office: Grand Valley State Univ 401 W Fulton Grand Rapids MI 49504 Office Phone: 616-331-7399. Business E-Mail: harrisr@gvsu.edu.

HARRIS, ROBERT A., retired music educator; b. Rich Hill, Mo., May 8, 1928; s. Archie L. and Edith Jeannette (Bailey) H. AA in Music, Joplin Jr. Coll., 1948; MusB, Kans. State Tchrs. Coll., 1950, MS in Edn., 1953; student, Rosina Lhevinne. Pianist, organist 1st United Meth. Ch., Carthage, 1946—; pvt. tchr. piano Carthage, Mo., 1947—; tchr. music, choir dir. Coll. Our Lady of the Ozarks, Carthage, 1949-53, 55-57; prof. music Mo. So. State U., Joplin, 1971-95, ret. Piano adjudicator; presenter piano and organ recitals. Cpl., chaplain's asst. US Army, 1953-55. Mem. Nat. Guild Piano Tchrs., Nat. Fedn. Music Clubs (local v.p.), Fellowship of United Meths. in Music and Worship Arts, Music Tchrs. Nat. Assn. (permanent profl. piano cert.), Am. Coll. Musicians, Mo. State Tchrs. Assn., Mo. Federated Music Club (ch. musician yr. 1993). Avocation: collectibles. Personal E-mail: raharris9@yahoo.com.

HARRIS, ROBERT DALTON, retired history professor, researcher, writer; b. Jamieson, Oreg., Dec. 24, 1921; s. Charles Sinclair and Dorothy (Cleveland) H.; m. Ethel Imus, June 26, 1971. BA, Whitman Coll., Walla Walla, Wash., 1951; MA, U. Calif., Berkeley, 1953, PhD, 1959. Tchg. asst. U. Calif., Berkeley, 1956-59; instr. history U. Idaho, Moscow, 1959-61, asst. prof., 1961-68, assoc. prof., 1968-74, prof. history, 1974-86, prof. emeritus, 1986—. Author: Necker, Reform Statesman of Ancient Regime, 1979, Necker & Revolution of 1789, 1986 1st lt., U.S. Army, 1942-46; Ballet Folk of Moscow, Idaho, (bd. dirs., 1971-73), Historian, First United Methodist Church, Moscow, Idaho, 1989—. Mem.: AAUP, Am. Hist. Assn. Democrat. Methodist. Avocations: social dancing, violinist. Home: Apt 318 640 N Eisenhower St Moscow ID 83843-9588

HARRIS, ROBERT LAIRD, minister, theology educator emeritus; b. Brownsburg, Pa., Mar. 10, 1911; s. Walter William and Ella Pearl (Graves) H.; m. Elizabeth Krugar Nelson, Sept. 11, 1937 (dec. 1980); children: Grace Sears, Allegra Smick, Robert Laird; m. Anne Paxson Krauss, Aug. 1, 1981. BSChemE, U. Del., Newark, 1931; postgrad, Washington U., 1931-32; ThB, Westminster Theol. Sem., 1935, ThM, 1937; MA in Oriental Studies, U. Pa., 1941; PhD, Dropsie Coll., 1947. Ordained to ministry Presbyn. Ch. Am., 1936; instr. Faith Theol. Sem., Phila., 1937-43, asst. prof. Bibl. Exegesis, 1943-47, prof. Bibl. Exegesis, 1947-56; prof. Covenant Theol. Sem., St. Louis, 1956-81, dean, 1964-71, prof. emeritus, 1981—; prof. Winona Lake Summer Sch. of Theology, 1964, 66-67, Near East Sch. Archaeology and Bible, Jerusalem, 1962; vis. prof. China Grad. Sch. Theology, Hong Kong, 1981, Freie Theologische Akademie, Giessen, Fed. Republic Germany, 1982-85, Tyndale Theol. Sem., Amsterdam, The Netherlands, 1986-2000, Bibl. Theol. Sem., Hatfield, Pa., 1992, J. Manoel Conceicao Presbyn. Sem., Sao Paulo, Brazil, 1995. Vis. lectr. Wheaton Coll., Ill., 1957-61; lectr. Japan, Korea, 1965, India, 1981, Australia, 1989; moderator Presbyn. Ch. in Am., 1982. Author: Introductory Hebrew Grammar, 1950, Inspiration and Canonicity of the Bible, 1957, 2d edit., 1995, Man-God's Eternal Creation, 1971, You and Your Bible, 1990; editor: Theological Wordbook of the Old Testament, 2 vols., 1981, Leviticus in Expositor's Bible Commentary, Vol. 2, 1990; mem. editorial bd. New Internat. Version of Bible, 1965-2000, chmn., 1970-74; contbg. author various books. Trustee Bibl. Theol. Sem., Hatfield, Pa., 1985-2000. DuPont fellow U. Del., 1930-31; recipient first prize Zondervan Textbook Contest, 1955; Foxwell Lecture lectureship Tokyo Christian Theol. Sem., 1981. Mem. Evang. Theol. Soc. (pres. 1961), Tau Beta Pi, Phi Kappa Phi Republican. Home and Office: 625 Robert Fulton Hwy Quarryville PA 17566 Personal E-mail: laird_harris@paonline.com. *In my ministry of over 60 years I have seen a distressing erosion of national morals and decency. But there has also been a counter-resurgence of evangelical faith. As part of this movement, I am gratified to have had a part in producing the New International Version of the Bible.*

HARRIS, ROBERT L(EE), judge; b. Spokane, Wash., Oct. 3, 1934; s. Roy L Harris, Celia A Reed; m. Mary Jo Bourke; children: Joanna, Marie, Robert. BA, Wash. State U., 1955; JD, U. Wash., 1958. Bar: Wash. 1958. Judge Superior Ct. of Wash., Vancouver, 1979—. Presiding judge Supreme Ct. Com. Capitol Def. Qualifications, 1997—; mem. project 2001 bd. jur. adminstrn. Task Force, 1999—2001; justice in jeopardy Bd. Judicial Adminstrn. Task Force, 2001—. Pres. St. Joseph Cmty. Hosp., Vancouver, 1967—74. Mem.: Wash. Judges' Found. (pres. 2003—), Superior Ct. Judges Assn. (chair criminal law com. 1996—97, trustee 1998—2000, pres. 2000—01). Achievements include first to use therapists to debrief jurors following their trial to help provide psychological assistance in gruesome trials. Avocation: youth sports. Office: Superior Court PO Box 5000 Vancouver WA 98666 Office Phone: 360-397-2017. Business E-Mail: robert.harris@clark.wa.gov.

HARRIS, ROBERT LEE, JR., history professor; b. Chgo., Apr. 23, 1943; s. Robert L. Sr. and Ruby L. (Watkins) H.; m. Anita B. Campbell, Nov. 14, 1964; children: Lisa M., Leslie S., Lauren Y. BA, Roosevelt U., 1966, MA, 1968; PhD, Northwestern U., 1974. Tchr. 6th grade St. Rita Elem. Sch., Chgo., 1965-68; instr. Miles Coll., Birmingham, Ala., 1968-69; asst. prof. U. Ill., Urbana, 1972-75, Cornell U., Ithaca, NY, 1975-82, assoc. prof. history, 1982—2004, dir. Africana studies, 1986-91, vice provost, 2000—, prof., 2004—. Mem. tech. adv. com. Grad. Record Exam., Princeton, N.J., 1988-94; cons. Cicada Films, N.Y.C., 1988-89, Cin. Pub. Sch. System, 1990-91; chair adv. com. for U.S. history Coun. for Internat. Exch. of Scholars, Washington, 1992-94; mem. N.Y. State adv. com. U.S. Commn. on Civil Rights, 1999-2002. Author: Black Studies in the United States, 1990, Teaching African-American History, 1992, Columbia Guide to African-American History Since 1939, 2006; also articles. Bd. dirs. NY Coun. Humanities, NYC, 1983-87; trustee DeWitt Hist. Soc., Ithaca, 1994-99; bd. trustees Nat. Hist. Ctr., 2006—. NEH fellow, 1974-75, Ford Found. fellow, 1983-84; W.E.B. DuBois Inst. fellow Harvard U., 1983-84; Rockefeller Humanities fellow SUNY, Buffalo, 1991-92. Mem. Am. Hist. Assn. (life, chmn. program com. 1995), Assn. Study Afro-Am. Life and History (life, pres. 1991-92), Nat. History Ctr. (bd. trustees 2007-), Orgn. Am. Historians (life, chair com. on minority history and historians 1999)), Soc. History of Edn. (bd. dirs. 1996—), Alpha Phi Alpha (nat. historian 1999—). Avocations: music, gardening, jogging, basketball. Office: Cornell U Africana Studies Rsch Ctr Ithaca NY 14850 Office Phone: 607-255-5358.

HARRIS, ROBERT NORMAN, advertising executive, educator; b. St. Paul, Feb. 11, 1920; s. Nathan and Esther (Roberts) H.; m. Paula Nidorf, May 2, 1992; children: Claudia, Robert Norman, Randolph B. BA, U. Minn., 1940. A founder Toni Co., div. Gillette Co., 1940-55; exec. v.p. Lee King & Ptnrs., Chgo., 1955-60, Allen B. Wrisley Co., Chgo., 1960-62, North Advt., Chgo., 1962-72; pres. Robert Piguet, Ltd., Chgo., 1972-73, Westbrook/Harris, Inc., Chgo., 1973-77; exec. v.p., gen. mgr. Creamer Inc., Chgo., 1977-81; pres. The Harris Creative Group, Inc., 1981—; prof. advt. and mass communications San Jose State U. (Calif.), 1983-92. Bd. dirs. KTEH Pub. Broadcasting Sys. Found., San Jose, 1987-99, CHM Villages Golf and Country Club CATV Sys., 1995-99. Mem. NATAS, Am. Mktg. Assn., Am. Advt. Fedn., Am. Assn. Advt. Agys., Sons in Retirement (bd. dirs. 1986-90). Office Phone: 310-474-0302. Personal E-mail: zugmir11@aol.com.

HARRIS, ROBERT SHIELDS, finance educator; b. Eden, NC, Nov. 6, 1949; married; 2 children. BA in economics summa cum laude, Davidson Coll., 1971; PhD in economics, Princeton U., 1977. Faculty Wharton Sch. Bus., U. Pa., 1975-78, Kenan-Flagler Bus. Sch., U. NC, Chapel Hill, 1978—88, U. Va. Darden Sch. Bus., Charlottesville, 1988—, assoc. dean faculty, 1990—93, Charles C. Abbott prof. bus. adminstrn., dean, 2001—05, C. Stewart Sheppard prof. bus. adminstrn., 2005—; v.p., chief learning officer United Tech. Corp., 1998—2001. Vis. prof. London Grad. Sch. Bus.; vis. scholar Oxford U.; cons. and expert witness in field. Assoc. editor: Fin. Mgmt., Jour. Fin. Rsch., Fin. Review, Jour. Applied Fin., author: books, articles, cases and tutorials. Mem.: Fin. Mgmt. Assn. (v.p. fin. edn.). Office: U Va Darden Sch Bus PO Box 6550 Charlottesville VA 22906-6550 Office Phone: 434-924-4823. Business E-Mail: HarrisR@darden.virginia.edu.

HARRIS, ROGER CLARK, psychiatrist, consultant; b. Washington, Aug. 27, 1938; s. Lester Wilbur and Margaret Elizabeth (Gilligan) H.; m. Ann Marie Dorman, Sept. 22, 1962; children: Laura Colleen, Gregory Scott Henry. BS, U. Md., 1961, postgrad., 1961—62, MD, 1968. Diplomate Am. Bd. Med. Examiners, Am. Bd. Psychiatry and Neurology. Intern Washington Hosp. Ctr., 1968—69; resident in psychiatry U. Md. Med. Sch., 1969—72; staff psychiatrist Portsmouth Psychiat. Ctr., Va., 1972—73, Larry H. Dizmang and Assoc., Annapolis, Md., 1973—74; pvt. practice Annapolis, 1974—75; prin. Roger C. Harris Group Practice of Psychiatry and Assocs., Annapolis, 1975—; pres. Chesapeake Comprehensive Counseling Ctrs., Inc., Washington and Balt., 1988—96. Co-founder Psychiatry Consultation Svc. of Baltimore City Police Dept., 1970-72; chief psychiatry svc. Anne Arundel Gen. Hosp., Annapolis, 1978-81; asst. clin. prof. psychiatry U. Md. Sch. Medicine, 1973—; acting dir. of outpatient clinic U. Md. Emergency Psychiat. Svcs., 1971-72, chief resident, 1971-72; primary founder psychiatry dept. Anne Arundel Gen. Hosp. Mem. Disability Rev. Bd. for Anne Arundel County, 1985-87, Orgn. of Physicians for Social Responsiblity, 1985—. Recipient Cert. Appreciation Arundel Lodge, Inc., Annapolis, 1988, Mitchell Scholarship, Alpha Tau Omega Social Fraternity, College Park, Md., 1960. Mem. Chesapeake Bay Psychiat. Soc., Am. Psychiat. Assn., Md. Psychiat. Soc., Anne Arundel County Med. Soc., Am. Group Psychotherapy Assn., Orthopsychiat. Assn., Epping Forest Boat Club, Young Foresters Orgn., Alpha Tau Omega (sec. 1958-60). Democrat. Presbyterian. Avocations: boating, swimming, body surfing, bodyboard surfing, classical music. Home: 212 Eareckson Ln Stevensville MD 21666-3040 Office: 1511 Ritchie Hwy Ste 201 Arnold MD 21012-2410 Home Phone: 410-643-1262; Office Phone: 410-757-1511.

HARRIS, ROGERS SANDERS, bishop; b. Anderson, SC, Feb. 22, 1930; s. Wilmot Louis and Sarah Elizabeth (Sanders) H.; m. Anne Marshall Stewart, Mar. 28, 1953; children: Katherine Anne, Frances Elizabeth, Rebecca Susan. BA, U. of South, 1952, MDiv, 1957, DD (hon.), 1986; D Ministry, Va. Theol. Sem., 1977, DD (hon.), 1986. Ordained deacon Episcopal Ch., 1957, priest, 1958, bishop, 1985. Vicar Grace Episcopal Ch., Ridge Spring, SC, 1957-59, St. Paul's Episcopal Ch., Batesburg, SC, 1957-59; rector Ch. of Good Shepherd, Greer, SC, 1959-69, St. Christopher's Ch., Spartanburg, SC, 1969-85; suffragan bishop Diocese of Upper S.C., Columbia, SC, 1985-89; bishop Diocese of S.W. Fla., St. Petersburg, 1989-97. V.p. Province IV of Episcopal Ch., 1991-94, pres., 1994-97; mem. Presiding Bishop's Coun. of Advice, N.Y.C., 1994-97. Trustee U. of South, Sewanee, Tenn., 1985—; trustee, v.p. Bishop Gray Inn, Davenport, Fla., 1989-97. 1st lt. USMC, 1952-54, Korea. Mem. Order of Holy Cross (assoc.). Episcopalian.

HARRIS, RONALD DAVID, chemical engineer; b. Norman, Okla., Apr. 9, 1938; s. Loyd Ervin and Maurine Cora (Dill) H.; m. Judith Anne Wright, July 28, 1962 (div.); children: Todd David (dec.), Scott Howard, Susanna Katherine. B.Chem. Engring., Ohio State U., 1961, M.Sc., 1961; MBA, U. Cin., 1970; student, Chase Law Sch., Cin., 1970-71. Chem. engr. Procter & Gamble Co., Cin., 1961-62, process devel. group leader, 1964-71; mgr. food product devel. Clorox Co., Oakland, Calif., 1971-73, dir. R & D Pleasanton, Calif., 1973-77; v.p. R & D Anderson Clayton Foods, Dallas, 1977-87; v.p. tech. Kraft Inc., Glenview, Ill., 1987-90; v.p. Kraft U.S.A. Tech., 1990-94; v.p. sci. rels. Kraft Foods, Inc., 1994-96; exec. v.p. R & D, Nabisco, Inc., Hanover, NJ, 1999-2001; mng. gen. ptnr. Harris Mgmt. LLC, 1998—. Instr. Keller Grad. Sch. Mgmt., 1995—; assoc. dir. exec. edn., sr. lectr. Ohio State U., 1996-99, 2001—; adj. prof. food sci., lectr. mgmtm. sci. Ohio State U., 1996—. Patentee process for adsorbent bleaching oils, dry prepared fluffy frosting mixes. Trustee San Ramon Valley Unified Sch. Dist., 1977; mem. Richardson City Planning Commn., 1980-83, Richardson City Coun., 1983-87, Lake Forest Bldg. Rev. Bd., 1993-99; bd. dirs. Richardson Symphony Orch., 1982-85, Heard Natural Sci. Mus., 1985-87, Richardson br. YMCA, 1984-87, 1st United Meth. Ch., Richardson, 1986-87, Chilled Foods Assn., 1988-94, 1st Presbyn. Ch., Lake Forest, 1988—; bd. dirs. Hull House Assn., 1988-96, vice chmn., 1993-96; mem. citizens adv. com. North Tex. Mcpl. Water Dist., 1980; mem. adv. com. doctorate in chemistry program U. Tex., Dallas, 1983-89; mem. adv. bd. dept. food sci. U. Minn., 1984-96; mem. adv. bd. dept. chem. engring. Ohio State U., 1991—, pres. Chem. Engring. Alumni Soc., 1998-99, alumni assn. adv. coun. Ohio State U., 2000—, mem. Pres.' Club; mem. adv. bd. Masters in Ops. and Tech. Ill. Inst. Tech., 1995-99; mem. Leadership Richardson, 1984-87; life mem. Julian C. Hyer Youth Camp; mem. Littlefield Soc., U. Tex., Austin, 1991—. Officer U.S. Army, 1962-64. Named Disting. Alumnus, Ohio State U., 1992, Meritorious Svc. award, 2000. Fellow Inst. Food Technologists, Am. Chem. Soc.; mem. Am. Oil Chemists Soc., Richardson C. of C. (1st v.p., dir., pres. 1982), Richardson Hist. Soc., Tex. Mcpl. League, Columbus Athletic Club, Lake Forest Club, Lions (bd. dirs., pres. 1982-83), Columbus Rotary, Symposiarchs, Tau Beta Pi, Phi Eta Sigma (past chpt. pres.), Phi Lambda Upsilon, Delta Mu Delta, Kappa Sigma (past chpt. pres., alumnus advisor 1996-99, house corp. 2001—). Home: 1051 Urlin Ave Columbus OH 43212 E-mail: hiyoron@aol.com.

HARRIS, ROSE M., academic administrator; b. Shreveport, La., Oct. 26, 1967; d. Artis T. Harris, Sr. and Lessie B. Hardman Harris. BA in Polit. Sci., So. U., Baton Rouge, La., 1989; MA in Polit. Sci., Howard U., Washington, 1991; PhD, Rutgers U., New Brunswick, NJ, 1999. Part-time lectr. Rutgers U., New Brunswick, NJ, 1993—95; coord. of planning and devel. So. U., Shreveport, La., 1996; vis. scholar U. of Houston, 2000—01; chancellor's post-doctoral fellow and adj. asst. prof. of polit. sci. U. of Ill. at Champaign-Urbana, Champaign, Ill., 2001—02; asst. prof. Ohio State U., Columbus, 1997—2002; dir. The La. Ctr. for Women and Govt. at Nicholls State U., Thibodaux, La., 2002—. Assoc. program dir. (head staff, staff mem. and counselor) La. Girls State, Baton Rouge, 1984—98. Editor: (book) Women in Louisiana Politics: Essays on Race, Gender and Politcs in the Bayou State, Louisiana's Political Women, 1930-2006, The African American Political Woman: A Reader. Apptd. by the gov. as a commn. mem. (former vice-chair of the commn.) La. Women's Policy & Rsch. Commn., Baton Rouge, 2003, 2004; co-founder The Assn. for the Study of Black Women in Politics, Thibodaux, La. Named a 2005 Pacesetter as a Proven Woman Leader, Stennis Ctr. Pub. Svc.; recipient Houston's Prominent Woman Table Talk, U. of Houston, Women's Studies, 2001; fellow NSF Minority Grad. fellow, The NSF, 1990—91, 1992—94, Excellence fellow, Rutgers U., 1994—96. Mem.: Nat. Conf. of Black Polit. Scientists (Sammy D. Young Award 1989), Women's Caucus for Polit. Sci., So. Polit. Sci. Assn., Am. Polit. Sci. Assn. Non-Denominational Christian. Avocations: bible study and bible teaching, reading, running. Office: The Louisiana Center for Women & Govt PO Box 2062 Nicholls State University Thibodaux LA 70310 Office Phone: 985-448-4770. Office Fax: 985-448-4771. E-mail: lcwg-info@nicholls.edu.

HARRIS, ROY JAY, JR., editor, business journalist; b. St. Louis, Oct. 2, 1946; s. Roy Jay and Ruth Dorothy (Schofer) H.; m. Andrea McKenna (dec.); children: David McKenna Harris, Roy Jay Harris III; m. Eileen Carol McIntyre. BS in Journalism, Northwestern U., 1968, MS in Journalism, 1971. Staff reporter The Wall Street Jour., Pitts., 1971-74, LA, 1974-88, dep. bur. chief, 1988—94; sr. editor CFO Mag., Boston, 1996—. James C. Millstone Meml. lectr. Emerson Coll., St. Louis U., 2002, adj. prof., 04. Contbg. author: Best Practices of the Business Press, 2004; author: Pulitzer's Gold, 2007. Bd. dirs. Atlantic Symphony Orch., 2006-. With U.S. Army, 1969-70. Mem. Am. Soc. Bus. Publ. Editors (nat. v.p. 2003-04, nat. pres. 2005-07), Soc. Am. Bus. Editors and Writers, Soc. Profl. Journalists. Office: CFO Mag 253 Summer St Fl 3 Boston MA 02210-1118 E-mail: royharris@cfo.com.

HARRIS, S. BUDDY, architect, interior designer; b. NYC, Jan. 4, 1927; s. Edward and Lola Taylor; m. Phyllis Frank, July 8, 1951; children: Robert I., Richard Craig. BBA, CCNY, 1948. Exec. dir. Redevel. Agy., Woodbridge, NJ, 1960—64; dir. dept. planning and devel. City of Woodbridge, 1964—67; v.p. and mng. dir. Gruen Assocs., Washington, 1966-84, ptnr., 1984—88, pres., 1986-88, ret., 1988. Guest lectr. Sch. Arch., Va. Poly. Inst., 1978, Sch. Arch., Cath. U., 1979; founder Inst. Econ. and Environ. Balance, 1976-84; dir. Greater Washington Bd. Trade, 1980-86, vice chmn. Cmty. Devel. Bur., 1979-84. Editor, pub.: USAF Aux. Fla. Facts Mag., 1995—2004, mem. editl. adv. bd., tech. dir.: USAF Aux. CAP Vol. Nat. Mag., 2005—07, pub.: USAF Aux. Vol. Mag., 2006—. V.p. Washington Bldg. Congress, 1978; house com., chmn. design com. Jewish Ctr. Marco Island, 1989; active Collier County Beach Renourishment Adv. Com., 1990; chief of staff Marco Island CAP Squadron, 1990, Fla. wing staff officer, 1997—2005, nat. hdqs. staff officer, 2005—06; chmn. blue ribbon task force, faculty SE Region USAF Aux. Staff Coll., 2003—06; spl. advisor to Maj. Gen. Pineda, Nat. Comdr. USAF Aux., 2006; participant AARP study NIH, 2006—; participant Parkinson's Disease study Nat. Inst. Environ. Health Scis., 2006—; mem. ACTS Pres.'s Coalition, 2007—, ACTS SE Region Pres.'s Coalition; chmn. DC Met. Planning Com., 1975—79, DC Water Resources Com., 1977—84; vice chmn. We The People, Inc.; chmn. Blue Ribbon tech. com. Hurricane Evacuation Plan for Barrier Free Islands, 1993—94. Lt. col. USAF Aux., 1990—2007, col. USAF Aux., 2007—, nat. staff advisor USAF Aux., 2005—. Mem.: EPE Residents Assn. (pres., bd. dirs.), Resident's Assn. (bd. dirs. 2002—06, treas. 2002—06, pres. bd. dirs. 2007—), Edgewater Point Estates Computer Club (chmn. 2002—,). Home: Apt B509 23343 Blue Water Cir Boca Raton FL 33433-7025 E-mail: sbharris@cap.gov.

HARRIS, SCOTT BLAKE, lawyer; b. NYC, June 18, 1951; s. Stanley Robert and Adele Jean (Ganger) Harris; m. Barbara Straughn, Aug. 5, 1978. AB magna cum laude, Brown U., 1973; JD magna cum laude, Harvard U., 1976. Bar: DC 1977, U.S. Ct. Appeals (DC cir.) 1978, U.S. Supreme Ct. 1983. Law clk. to presiding justice U.S. Dist. Ct., Washington, 1976-77; assoc. Williams & Connolly, Washington, 1977-84, ptnr., 1984-93; chief counsel Bur. Export Adminstrn., U.S. Dept. Commerce, Washington, 1993-94; chief internat. bur. FCC, 1994-96; ptnr. Gibson, Dunn & Crutcher, Washington, 1996-98; mng. ptnr. Harris, Wiltshire & Grannis LLP, Washington, 1998—. Mem. adv. bd. Ctr. Wireless Tech., Va. Tech. U., 1996—2004, Satellite Comm. Mag., 1996—2000, Critical Infrastructure Fund, LLP, 1999—2000, Telecom. Reports Internat., 2000—02, Morphics Tech., Inc., 2000—02; adj. prof. Georgetown U. Law Ctr., 1996, 2001—02. Columnist: Aviation Week, 2000—01, Space News, 2001—05. Trustee Fed. Comm. Bar Assn. Found., 1997—2000. Recipient Marconi-Bell award, Nat. Assn. Radio and TV Engrs., 2004. Mem.: ABA (co-chair telecom. com., sect. internat. law 1999—2002), US ITU Assn. (bd. dirs. 1999—2003), Fed. Comm. Bar Assn. (co-chair online comm. com. 2000—02, co-chair legislation com. 2004—05), Phi Beta Kappa. Home: 3409 Fulton St NW Washington DC 20007-1436 Office: Harris Wiltshire & Grannis LLP 1200 18th St NW Washington DC 20036-2506 Office Phone: 202-730-1330. Business E-Mail: sharris@harriswiltshire.com.

HARRIS, SHIRLEY, elementary and secondary and adult education school educator; b. Chgo., Aug. 14, 1945; BA in Behavioral Sci., Nat. Louis U., 1985; MS in Edn., Chgo. State U., 1993. Cert. in curriculum and instr. Legal sec. Friedman/Rochester, Chgo. and Portland, Oreg., 1974; supr., clerical positions Model Cities, Chgo. and Portland, Oreg., 1973-75; bd. sec. Portland Comm., 1976-78; tchr., clerical positions Portland O.I.C., 1975-76; tchr., juvenile/youth counselor Yaun Youth Ctr., Portland, 1978-80; pres. Flexible Temps, Chgo., 1980—. Part-time prof. Wright Jr. Coll., 1999, Northeastern Ill. U., 1999—, Robert Morris Coll., 2000, DeVry Inst. Tech., 2000; adj. prof. U. St. Francis, Chgo., 2005; cons. in field, Chgo., 1983; typing tchr., Chgo., 1983; pers. recruiter, Chgo., 1974-75. Author: (poetry and lyrics) True Covenant Not Mine; contbr. poetry to anthologies. Bd. dirs. Operation Probe, Chgo., 1990-93. Mem. NAFE, ASCD, Internat. Platform Assn. Baptist. Avocations: movies, reading, writing, poetry. Home: 28 E Jackson Blvd Ste S805 Chicago IL 60604 Office Phone: 312-714-7896. Office Fax: 312-922-6964. Personal E-mail: educator8503@yahoo.com.

HARRIS, STANLEY S., retired judge, arbitrator, mediator; b. Washington, Oct. 19, 1927; s. Stanley Raymond and Elizabeth (Sutherland) H.; m. Rebecca Ashley, Aug. 1, 1964; children: Scott Sutherland, Todd Ashley, Mark Ashley. BS, U. Va., 1951, JD, 1953. Bar: D.C. 1953, U.S. Supreme Ct. 1964. Assoc., then ptnr. Hogan & Hartson, Washington, 1953-70; judge Superior Ct. D.C., 1971-72, D.C. Ct. Appeals, 1972-82; U.S. atty. for D.C. Dept. Justice, 1982-83; judge U.S. Dist. Ct. D.C., 1983—, sr. judge, 1996—2001; ret., 2001; arbitrator, mediator. Mem. com. on criminal law Jud. Conf. U.S., 1988-94, chmn. com. intercircuit assignments, 1994-2000. Served with U.S. Army, 1945-47. Recipient Judiciary award Assn. Fed. Investigators, 1982. Mem. Bar Assn. D.C. (bd. dirs. 1970-72, Lawyer of Yr. award 1982, Disting. Career award 1996), Lawyers' Club of Washington (pres. 1998-99). Republican. Home: 4982 Sentinel Dr Apt 406 Bethesda MD 20816-3579 Personal E-mail: stanley.s.harris@verizon.net.

HARRIS, STEVEN M., urologist; b. Port Chester, NY, Aug. 19, 1952; s. Jules Franklin and Belle Diane Harris; m. Chantal Harris, Aug. 26, 2001; children: Hillel, Adena, Rafi, Rebecca. BA in Physics, SUNY, Buffalo, 1973; MD, Albert Einstein Coll. Medicine, Bronx, 1976. Resident urology Mt. Sinai Sch. Medicine, NYC, 1981; chief urology Long Beach Med. Ctr., NY, 1996—. Pres. med. staff LBMC, NY, 2005—06, pres. med. bd., 2007—. Physician liaison Future Physician Club, Long Beach HS, 1984—. Mem.: Profl. Tennis Registry (instr. 1996—2006). Avocations: tennis, golf. Office: 309 W Park Ave Long Beach NY 11561 Office Phone: 516-431-9800.

HARRIS, T. GEORGE, editor; b. Hillsdale, Ky., Oct. 4, 1924; s. Garland and Luna (Byrum) Harris; m. Sheila Hawkins, Oct. 31, 1952 (dec. Jan. 1977); children: Amos, Anne, Crane, Gardiner; m. Ann Rockefeller Roberts, Mar. 3, 1979 (div. Apr. 1993); children: Clare, Joseph, Mary Louise, Rachel Pierson; m. Jeannie Pinkerton, Sept. 12, 1998; 1 child, Arthur Joseph Clancy. Student, U. Ky., 1946; BA, Yale U., 1949. Reporter Clarksville (Tenn.) Leaf-Chronicle, 1942; corr. Time, Dallas, Atlanta and Washington, 1949—55; Chgo. bur. chief Time-Life-Fortune, 1955-58, San Francisco bur. chief, 1960-62; sr. editor Look mag., 1962-68; editor in chief Psychology Today mag., 1969-76, 88-90, US, 1977; founding editor Am. Health mag., Behavior Today, AH Fitness Bull., Spirituality & Health, 1980-90; exec. editor Harvard Bus. Rev., Boston, 1992-93; cons. Beliefnet.com, 1993—, Procter & Gamble Creative Svcs. Group, 1993—; editor UCSD-Connect Hi-tech. Weekly Online, 2000—03. Sci. adv. ABC's 20/20 Program, Inst. Advancement of Health. Editor: WGBH Bodywatch on PBS; cons. editor Sci. & Spirit, Next, Runner, Somatics, Aware, Indistry Week, Psychologia Contemporanea, Man the Mystery, Japan, Modern Maturity, Psychologie Heute mags., Addison-Wesley Pub. Co., Abby Press of Benedictine Order, Age Wave, editor-in-residence U. Calif., San Diego, columnist, cons. Beliefnet.com. Bd. dirs. Am. Health Found., Ch. Soc. for Coll. Work, Nat. Vol. Ctrs., Rockefeller Bros. Fund, Go Code Corp.; med. adv. com. Nat. YMCA; regent Cathedral of St. John the Divine, NYC. Staff sgt. US Army, WWII. Decorated Commissioned for leadership under fire Battlefield at Bostogne. Mem.: Time-Life Alumni, Century Assn., Yale Club N.Y.C., UCSD Faculty Club, La Jolla Beach and Tennis Club, Phi Beta Kappa. Episcopalian. Home and Office: 8115 Paseo Del Ocaso La Jolla CA 92037-3140 Office Phone: 858-459-5694. Personal E-mail: tgeorgeh@aol.com.

HARRIS, TERRELL LEE (TERRY HARRIS), delivery services company executive, former prosecutor; b. 1961; BA, Rhodes Coll.; JD, U. Miss. Assoc. Kirkpatrick, Kirkpatrick and Efird, Memphis, 1986—87; asst. dist. atty. gen. Shelby County Dist. Atty.'s Office, 1987—2001; US atty. (we. dist.) Tenn., US Dept. Justice, Memphis, 2001—05; v.p. customer security services FedEx Express Corp., Memphis, 2005—. Office: FedEx Express Corp 3610 Hacks Cross Rd Memphis TN 38125

HARRIS, THERESA, lawyer; b. Bronx, NY, July 25, 1957; BSN, Coll. Mt. St. Vincent, Riverdale, NY, 1979; JD, Pace U., 1995. Bar: NY 1995, NJ 1995, US Dist. Ct. Ea. Dist. NY, US Dist. Ct. So. Dist. NY. Ptnr. Wilson, Elser, Moskowitz, Edelman & Dicker LLP, NYC. Mem.: ABA, NY State Bar Assn. Office: Wilson Elser Moskowitz Edelman & Dicker LLP 23rd Fl 150 E 42nd St New York NY 10017-5639 Office Phone: 212-490-3000 ext. 2776. Office Fax: 212-490-3038. Business E-Mail: harrist@wemed.com.

HARRIS, THOMAS, writer; b. Jackson, Tenn., 1940; s. William Thomas and Polly Harris; BA in English, Baylor U., 1964. News reporter, editor AP, NYC, 1968—74. Author: Black Sunday, 1975, Red Dragon, 1981, The Silence of the Lambs, 1988 (Bram Stoker award for Best Novel, 1988), Hannibal, 1999, Hannibal Rising, 2006 Office: c/o Random House 20 Vauxhall Rd London SW1V 2SA England

HARRIS, THOMAS L., public relations executive; b. Dayton, Ohio, Apr. 18, 1931; s. James and Leona (Blum) H.; m. JoAnn K. Karch, Apr. 14, 1957; children: James Harris, Theodore Harris. BA, U. Mich., 1953; MA, U. Chgo., 1956. Exec. v.p. Daniel J. Edelman Inc., Chgo., 1957-67; v.p. pub. rels. Neddham Harper & Steers, Chgo., 1967-72; pres. Foote Cone & Belding Pub. Rels., Chgo., 1973-78, Golin-Harris Communications Inc., Chgo., 1978-89, also vice chmn.; adj. prof. Medill Sch. Journalism, Northwestern U., Evanston, Ill., 1987—2002; mng. ptnr. Thomas L. Harris & Co., Highland Pk., Ill., 1992—. Served with U.S. Army, 1953-55. Mem. Public Relations Soc. Am. (Gold Anvil award 2000). Office: Thomas L Harris & Co 600 Central Ave Highland Park IL 60035-3211 Office Phone: 847-266-1020. E-mail: ttlhco@aol.com.

HARRIS, VENITA VAN CASPEL, retired financial planner; b. Sweetwater, Okla. d. Leonard Rankin and Ella Belle (Jarnagin) Walker; m. Lyttleton T. Harris IV, Dec. 26, 1987. Student, Duke, 1944-46; BA, U. Colo., 1948, postgrad., 1949-51, N.Y. Inst. Fin., 1962. CFP. Stockbroker Rauscher Pierce & Co., Houston, 1962-65, A.G. Edwards & Sons, Houston, 1965-68; founder, pres., owner Van Caspel & Co., Inc., Houston, 1968—87, Van Caspel Wealth Mgmt.; owner, mgr. Van Caspel Planning Svc., Van Caspel Advt. Agy.; sr. v.p. investments Raymond James and Assocs., 1987-95; ret., 1995. Moderator PBS TV show The Money Makers and Profiles of Success, 1980; 1st women mem. Pacific Stock Exchange. Author: Money Dynamics, 1978, Money Dynamics of the 1980's, 1980, The Power of Money Dynamics, Money Dynamics for the 1990's, 1988; editor: Money Dynamics Letter. Bd. dirs. Horatio Alger Assn.; trustee Northwood U.; founding mem. Com. of 200. Recipient Matrix award Theta Sigma Phi, 1969, Horatio Alger award for Disting. Americans, 1982, Disting. Woman's medal, Northwood Univ., 1988, George Norlin award U. Colo. Alumni Assn., 1987. Mem. Internat. Assn. Fin. Planners, Inst. Cert. Fin. Planners, Phi Gamma Mu, Phi Beta Kappa. Presbyterian. Home: 4 Saddlewood Estates Dr Houston TX 77024-6841

HARRIS, WALTER EDGAR, chemistry professor; b. Wetaskiwin, Alta., Can., June 9, 1915; s. William Ernest and Emma Louise (Humbke) H.; m. Phyllis Pangburn, June 14, 1942; children: Margaret Anne, William Edgar. BS, U. Alta., 1938, MS, 1939; PhD, U. Minn., 1944; DSc (hon.), U. Waterloo, 1987, U. Alta., 1991. Research fellow U. Minn., 1943-46; prof. analytical chemistry U. Alta., Edmonton, 1946-80, chmn. dept. chemistry, 1974-79, chmn. Pres.'s Adv. Com. on Campus Revs., 1980-90. Author: (with H.W. Habgood) Programmed Temperature Gas Chromatography, 1965, (with B. Kratchovil) Chemical Separations and Measurements, 1974, Teaching Introductory Analytical Chemistry, 1974, An Introduction to Chemical Analysis, 1981, Risk Assessment, 1997, (with H.A. Laitinen) Chemical Analysis, 1975; contbr. numerous articles to profl. jours. Decorated Order of Can.; recipient Outstanding Achievement award U. Minn., 1973; Govt. Alta. Achievement award, 1974, Associated Honor award U. Alta. Alumni, 2003. Fellow AAAS, Royal Soc. Can., Chem. Inst. Can. (hon., Fisher Sci. Lecture award 1969, Chem. Edn. award 1975, hon. fellow, 2001); mem. Am. Chem. Soc., Sigma Xi. Home: Ste 515 11148-84 Ave Edmonton AB Canada T6G 0V8 Office: U Alta Dept Chem Edmonton AB Canada T6G 2G2 Home Phone: 780-433-8220; Office Phone: 780-492-3252. Business E-Mail: Walter.Harris@ualberta.ca.

HARRIS, WARREN LYNN, computer engineer; b. Albuquerque, May 8, 1966; s. Jerry Dale and Viola Guadalupe (Gutierrez) H., m. Clarissa Cosgrove, Apr. 1, 1998, 1 child: Tiffany Bellan. BS, Ariz. State U., 1988. Programming mgr. I.P.C. Computer Svcs., Inc., Tempe, Ariz., 1985-89; software sys. engr. Intel Corp., Chandler, Ariz., 1990; dir. software R & D Pics, Inc., Tempe, 1990-91; dir. software R & D parics divsn. Ansoft Corp., Tempe, 1991-94, devel. engr. Phoenix, 1994—2002; software engr. Neolinear, Inc., Tempe, 2002—04; mem. cons. staff Cadence Design Systems, Tempe, 2004—. Contbr. articles to profl. jours. Mem. IEEE, Assn. for Computing Machinery, Mortar Bd., Golden Key, Upsilon Pi Epsilon. Avocations: racquetball, model building, chess, pool, star trek collecting. Office: Cadence Design Sys Inc 1620 W Fountainhead Pkwy Ste 219 Tempe AZ 85282

HARRIS, WARREN WAYNE, lawyer; b. Houston, Nov. 5, 1962; BBA, U. Houston, 1985, JD, 1988. Bar: Tex. 1988, U.S. Ct. Appeals (5th cir.) 1989, U.S. Ct. Appeals (fed. cir.) 1995, U.S. Ct. Appeals (8th, 10th and 11th cirs.) 1996, U.S. Ct. Appeals (9th cir.) 2004, U.S. Ct. Appeals (2d and 9th cirs.) 2005, U.S. Dist. Ct. (so., no., ea. and we. dists.) Tex. 1990, U.S. Supreme Ct. 1991; bd. cert. civil appellate law Tex. Bd. Legal Specialization. Briefing atty. Tex. Supreme Ct., Austin, 1988-89; ptnr. Bracewell & Giuliani LLP, Houston, 1996—. Adj. prof. U. Houston Law Ctr., 2001—05, U. Tex. Sch. Law, 2006—07. Editor-in-chief: Houston Lawyer mag., 1991-92; assoc. editor: The Appellate Advocate, 1992-97; editor: The Appellate Lawyer, 1994-96; chair editl. bd. Tex. Bar Jour., 2002—06. Fellow: Houston Bar Found., Tex. Bar Found. (chair dist. 4 nominating com. 2006—); mem.: ABA (chair tort and ins. practice sect. appellate advocacy com. 1990—), Houston Lawyer Referral Svc. (trustee 1994—95), Houston Young Lawyers Assn. (pres. 1999—2000), Houston Bar Assn. (coun. appellate practice sect. 1993—, chair appellate practice sect. 1998—99, Pres.'s award 1993—94), Tex. Young Lawyers Assn. (bd. dirs. 1994—98, outstanding dir. 1995—96, Pres.'s award 1996—97), State Bar Pro Bono Coll., State Bar Coll. (bd. dirs. 1994—95), State Bar Tex. (appellate sect. 1988—, coun. 1997—, chmn. 2005—06), Houston Livestock Show and Rodeo (steer auction com. 2001—05, capt. 2003—05), Stages Repertory Theatre (pres., chmn. 1994—95, bd. dirs., WineFest com. chair 1994—96), Order of Barons, Order of Barristers, Phi Delta Phi. Republican. Office: Bracewell & Giuliani LLP 711 Louisiana St Ste 2300 Houston TX 77002-2770 Office Phone: 713-221-1490. Business E-Mail: warren.harris@bgllp.com.

HARRIS, WESLEY L., aeronautical engineer, educator; b. Richmond, Va., Oct. 29, 1941; s. William M. and Rosa P. (Minor) Harris; m. Myrtle Ann Satterwhite, June 14, 1960 (div. Mar. 1985); children: Wesley Jr., Zelda, Marcus, Kamau, Kalomo, Eletha; m. Sandra Maria Butler, Sept. 21, 1985; 1 child, Tosha. B in Aero. Engring. with honors, U. Va., 1964; MA in Aero. Scis., Princeton U., 1966, PhD in Aero. Scis., 1968; PhD (hon.), U. Pretoria, 2006; LHD (hon.), Lane Coll., 1994; DEng (hon.), Milw. Sch. Engring., 1994; DSc (hon.), Old Dominion U., 1995. Asst. prof. aerospace engring. U. Va., 1968-70, assoc. prof., 1971-72; assoc. prof. physics Southern U., 1970-71; dir. office min. edn., 1975—78; assoc. prof. aeronautics & astronautics/ocean engring. MIT, Cambridge, 1973-79, assoc. prof. aeronautics and astronautics, 1980-81, prof., 1981-85, 1996—2001, Charles Stark Draper prof. of aeronautics and astronautics, 2001—, head dept. aeronautics and astronautics, 2003—; mgr. computational methods Office Aeronautics & Space Tech. NASA Hdqs., Washington, 1979-80, assoc. administr. Office of Aeronautics, 1993-96; dean sch. engring. U. Conn., Storrs, 1985-90; v.p. U. Tenn. Space Inst., Tullahoma, 1990-93. Mem. adv. groups Nat. Rsch. Coun. Commn. Engring. and Tech. Sys., Bd. Engring. Edn., Bd. Army Sci. and Tech., Air Force Studies Bd., Com. Aero. Techs.; mem. adv. com. NSF, U.S. Army Sci. Bd.; advisor univs.; nat. adv. com. dept. engring. Hampton U., 1989—96. Contbr. scientific papers to profl. jours. Trustee Sci. Mus. Conn., 1985—90, Princeton (N.J.) U., 2001—05; adv. bd. dirs. Am. City Bank, Tullahoma, 1990—93; bd. vis. sch. engring. Duke U., 1991—99; vis. com. dept. aeronautics and astronautics MIT, 1988—95. Named Milton Pikarsky Meml. lectr., CCNY Sch. Engring., 1990, Barry Goldwater chair, Am. Instns. Ariz. State U., 2000—01; recipient Herbert S. and Jane Gregory Disting. Lectr. award, Coll. Engring. U. Fla., 1992, Dr. Martin Luther King Leadership award, MIT, 2001. Fellow: AIAA, Am. Helicopter Soc.; mem.: NAE, AAAS, Nat. Tech. Assn., Math. Assn. Am., Am. Phys. Soc. Democrat. Avocation: squash. Office: MIT Dept Aeronautics 33-207 77 Mass Ave Cambridge MA 02139-4307 Office Phone: 617-253-0911. Business E-Mail: weslhar@mit.edu.

HARRIS, WHITNEY ROBSON, lawyer, educator, military officer, volunteer; b. Seattle, Aug. 12, 1912; s. Olin Whitney and Lily Harris; m. Jane Freund Foster, Feb. 14, 1964 (dec.); 1 child, Eugene Whitney; m. Anna Galakatos, Jan. 8, 2000. AB magna cum laude, U. Wash., 1933; JD, U. Calif., 1936; LHD (hon.), McKendree Coll., 1999; LHD (hon.), U. Mo., 2001. Bar: Calif. 1936, U.S. Supreme Ct. 1945, Tex. 1953, U.S. Ct. Mil. Appeals 1955, Mo. 1964. Pvt. practice, LA, 1936-42; trial counsel at trial of maj. German war criminals, Nuremberg, Germany, 1945-46; chief legal advice br. U.S. Mil. Govt. for Germany, 1946-48; prof. law So. Meth. U., 1948-54; staff dir. legal service and proc. Com. Orgn. Exec. Br. Govt., 1954; exec. dir. ABA, 1954-55; solicitor for Tex. Southwestern Bell Telephone Co., Dallas, 1955-63, gen. solicitor St. Louis, 1963-65; pvt. practice St. Louis, 1965-89; arbitration judge, 1993—. Sr. counselor Mo. Bar Assn., 1987—; lectr. UCLA, Stanford U., Washington U., Wellesley Coll., U. Denver, Reed Coll., U. Wash., Claremont Coll., Boston Coll., Williams Coll., So. Meth. U., U. Mo., McKendree Coll., Ga. State Coll., Slippery Rock U., others; trustee McKendree Coll. Author: Family Law, 1953, Tyranny On Trial, 1954, 3rd. edit., 1999, Legal Services and Procedure, 1955, The Tragedy of War, 2004, Murder by the Millions, 2005; author: (with others) Law, Culture and Values, 1989; contbr. articles to profl. jours., Ency. Brit., 1954, Whitney Robson Harris collection on Third Reich Washington U., 1980. Capt. USN, 1942—46, WWII. Decorated Legion of Merit, Order of Merit Officer's Class (Germany), Medal of the War Crimes Commn. (Poland); named nat. outstanding fund raising vol. Nat. Soc. Fund Raising Execs., 1985, Disting. Lawyer St. Louis Bar Assn., 2005. Mem. ABA (chmn. internat. law sect. 1953-54, chmn. adminstrv. law sect. 1960-61), Naval War Coll. Found. (grad. level), Order of Coif, Phi Beta Kappa, Phi Kappa Psi, Delta Theta Phi. Achievements include establishment of Whitney Robson Harris Collection on Third Reich of Germany, Washington U., 1980; Whitney R. Harris Inst. Global Legal Studies, Washington U., 2002; Whitney and Anna Harris Conservation Forum at the University of Missouri, St. Louis, 2004; Whitney R. Harris World Ecology Center at University of Missouri, St. Louis, 2006. Home: 2818 Stonington Pl Saint Louis MO 63131-3417 E-mail: whitneyharris@msn.com. *Tyranny leads to inhumanity, and inhumanity to death. Let us resolve that tyranny shall not extend its sway, nor war become its game— placing our faith in the cause of justice, in the freedom of man, and in the mercy of God.*

HARRIS, WILLIAM JAMES, JR., retired science administrator; b. South Bend, Ind., June 17, 1918; s. William James and Elizabeth M. (Scott) H.; m. Ruth Laubinger, Aug. 26, 1944 (dec. 1977); children: June Elizabeth Sherren, William James III, Debbie Shafer Hayden, Britta Shafer Kreuger, Barkley Shafer.; m. Elizabeth Dotten Shafer, June 24, 1978. BS in Chem. Engring; MS in Engring, Purdue U., 1940, D.Engring. (hon.), 1978; Sc.D., M.I.T., 1948. Head ferrous alloys br. metallurgy div. Naval Research Lab., 1947-51; exec. sec. materials adv. bd. Nat. Acad. Sci.-NRC, 1951-54, exec. dir., 1957-60, asst. sec., planning div. engring., 1960-62; asst. to dir. Battelle Meml. Inst., 1954-57, asst. to v.p., 1962-67; asst. dir. tech. Columbus Labs., 1967-69; v.p. research and test dept. Assn. Am. Railroads, 1970-85; E.B. Snead and Disting. prof. transp. engring. Tex. A&M U., 1985-95; assoc. dir. Tex. Transp. Inst., 1987-95, sr. rsch. engr., 1995—97; disting. prof. emeritus/Snead prof. emeritus Tex. A&M U., 1995—97; commr. Pres.'s Commn. on Critical Infrastructure Protection, 1997-98, sr. exec., 1998-99; cons. CIAO, 1999—2002. Hon. prof. China Acad. Ry. Scis., 1987; pres. W. J. Harris, Inc., 1985-98; pres., chmn. bd. Piscataway Co., Accokeek, Md., 1958-63; mem. Nat. Exec. Res. Dept. Transp., 1983—; sr. tech. advisor UN Devel. Orgn., 1987-91. Editor: (with others) Perspectives in Materials Research, 1963; co-author: Guildelines for Best Heavy Haul Practices, 2002; contbr. (with others) articles to tech. publs. Mem. nat. materials adv. bd. Nat. Acad. Sci., 1967— , chmn., 1969-70; sec. Pres.'s Com. on Hwy. Safety, 1969; mem. high speed ground transp. adv. com. U.S. Dept. Transp., 1972-74, Md. Gov.'s Sci. Adv. Com., 1972-76, Md. Gov.'s Energy Council, 1974-76; pres. Moyoane Assn., 1951-53, 58; pres., chmn. bd. Alice Ferguson Found., 1966-68; chmn. exec. com., disting. profs. Tex. A&M U. Served to lt. comdr. USNR, 1941-45. Decorated Naval letter of commendation; recipient Disting. Svc. award (Carey award) Transp. Rsch. Bd., NRC, 1977, Roy Crum award for disting. rsch., 1989; Disting. Rsch. award Transp. Rsch. Forum, 1986; named R.R. Man of Yr., 1976; inducted into Cooperstown Conf. R.R. Hall of Fame, 1993, Batteile Meml. Inst. Transp. Hall of Fame, 1994, Internat. Heavy Haul of Fame, 1999. Fellow Am. Soc. Metals, ASME, Metall. Soc. (pres. 1970), Nat. Acad. Engring., elected 1977, (chair program com. 1995-98, chmn. audit com. 1982, fin. com. 1995-98); mem. Intelligent Transp. Soc. Am. (hon. mem., coord. coun. 1990-97, bd. dirs. 1997—, chmn. N.Am. steering com. 1993-95, chmn. clearinghouse and publ. speech com., world congress bd. dirs., Spl. award for Internat. Congress Leadership 1995), Am. Inst. Mining, Metall., and Petroleum Engrs. (dir. 1964-69, v.p. 1964-67, chmn. inst. metals divsn. 1960, Mathewson medal 1950), Engrs. Joint Coun. (bd. dirs. 1965-70, pres. 1968-70), Engring. Found. (chmn. rsch. conf. com. 1964-67, bd. dirs. 1968-70), Am. Ordnance Assn. (chmn. materials divsn. 1966-68), Nat. Security Indsl. Assn. (chmn. exec. planning com. 1965-67, chmn. rsch. and devel. adv. com. 1967-69), Transp. Rsch. Bd. (exec. com. 1977-85, 87-90, chmn. coun. 1989-95, emeritus internat. transp. sys. com. of transp. rsch. bd. com.), Nat. Def. Transp. Assn. (life, chmn. com. on engring. tech.), Found. on Engring. Techs. (chmn. 1990-97), Internat. Heavy Haul Assn. (chmn. 1982-89), Alice Ferguson Found. (hon. life mem.), Sigma Xi, Alpha Sigma Mu, Tau Beta Pi, Phi Lambda Upsilon, Sigma Delta Chi. Home: 1200 N Nash St Apt 1140 Arlington VA 22209-3682

HARRIS, WILLIAM NORMAN, music educator; b. Washington, Sept. 8, 1952; s. Clarence Norman and Helen Lucy (Holsey) H. BMEd, Millikin U., Decatur, Ill., 1974; postgrad., various univs. Elem. gen. music tchr. Montgomery County Pub. Schs., Rockville, Md., 1974—. Prodr., dir. spring musical theatre, Poolesville Jr./Sr. H.S., Md.1986-91, Way Off Broadway Dinner Theatre, Frederick, Md., 2005-06; leader, tenor/baritone soloist St. John's Episc. Ch., Bethesda, Md., 1995, U. Md. Chorus; baritone soloist Montgomery Coll. Chorus, 1995. Former mem. Montgomery County Masterworks Chorus, U. Md. Chorus; actor, singer Montgomery Coll., Summer Dinner Theatre, Rockville, 1988, 89, 90; artistic dir., choral master Damascus (Md.) Theatre Co.; singer U.S. Postal Svc. (Black History Month's Observances) Hdqrs., Washington, 1986-88; dir. children's chorus for PYE Panda Earth Day Expo '90. Fellow NEA, Music Educators Nat. Conf.; mem. Md. Music Educators Assn. (pres. south ctrl. region), Phi Mu Alpha Sinfonia, Beta Theta chpt. (treas. 1972-74). Democrat. Methodist. Avocations: interior decorating, white-water rafting. Home: 19256 Misty Meadow Ter Germantown MD 20874-5367 Office Phone: 301-972-7960. E-mail: billharristenor@aol.com, Bill_N_Harris@mcpsmd.org.

HARRIS, WILLIAM VERNON, history professor; b. Nottingham, Eng., Sept. 13, 1938; naturalized; 1982; s. K. W. F. and Elizabeth H.; m. Silvana Patriarca; 1 child, Neil BA, Oxford U., 1961, MA, 1964, D.Phil., 1968. Instr. history Columbia U., NYC, 1965-68, asst. prof., 1968-71, assoc. prof., 1971-76, prof., 1976—, William R. Shepherd prof. history, 1995—, chmn. history dept., 1988-94, acting chair, 2005. Mem. adv. council Am. acad. in Rome, 1976— , resident, 1978, 82; dir. NEH summer seminars, 1979, 81; mem. Inst. Advanced Study, Princeton, N.J., 1970-71, 78; Gray lectr. Cambridge U., 1998. Author: Rome in Etruria and Umbria, 1971, War and Imperialism in Republican Rome, 1979, Ancient Literacy, 1989, Restraining Rage: The Ideology of Anger-Control in Classic Antiquity, 2002 (James Henry Breasted prize Am. Hist. Assn.); editor: (series) Columbia Studies in the Classical Tradition, 1976—, The Imperialism of Mid-Republican Rome, 1984, The Inscribed Economy, 1993, The Transformations of Urbs Roma in Late Antiquity, 1999, Rethinking the Mediterranean, 2005; co-editor (with G. Ruffini): Ancient Alexandria between Egypt and Greece, 2004. Fellow, NEH, 1978, Guggenheim Found., 1982—83, Nat. Humanities Ctr., 1998, vis. fellow, All Souls Coll., Oxford U., Eng., 1983, St. John's Coll., Oxford U., 2002; fellow, Am. Coun. of Learned Soc., 1970—71, 2005—. Fellow AAAS, Soc. Antiquaries (London), Finnish Soc. Scis.; mem. Academia Europaea (fgn.), Archaeol. Inst. Am., Am. Philol. Assn., Am. Hist. Assn., Assn. Ancient Historians, Century Assn. Office: Columbia U 624 Fayerweather Hall New York NY 10027 E-mail: wvh1@columbia.edu.

HARRIS-BARBER, DAISY, elementary school educator; d. Mable Harris and Edward Harris, Sr.; m. Craig Barber; children: Brandi J. Barber children: Cory Cormier. BA, So. U., Baton Rouge, La., 1977; postgrad., McNeese U., Lake Charles, La., 1983. Tchr. 1st grade tchr., Lake Charles, La., 1977—2002, 7th grade tchr., 2002—. Home Phone: 337-474-1052. E-mail: d82455@cox-internet.com.

HARRIS-OFFUTT, ROSALYN MARIE, counselor, consultant, mental health nurse, writer; b. Memphis; d. Roscoe Henry and Irene Elnora (Blake) Harris; 1 child, Christopher Joseph. RN, St. Joseph Cath. Sch. Nursing, Flint, Mich., 1965; student, Hurley Med. Ctr. Sch. of Anesthesia, 1970; BS in Wholistic Health Scis., Columbia-Pacific U., 1984, postgrad., 1985—. RN; cert. registered nurse in anesthesia; nat. bd. cert. addiction counselor; cert. psychiat. nursing Kalamazoo State Hosp.; lic. profl. counselor, N.C.; cert. detoxification acupuncturist; bd. cert. med.-legal nurse cons. Staff nurse anesthetist, clin. instr. Cleve. Clinic Found., 1981-82; pvt. practice psychiat. nursing and counseling; assoc. counselor human svcs. Shaker Heights, Ohio, 1982-84; ind. contractor anesthesia Paul Scott & Assocs., Cleve., 1984, Via Triad Anesthesia Assocs., Thomasville, NC, 1984-85; sec. Cons. Psychology Counseling, P.A., 1984-86; pvt. practice psychiat. nursing and counseling Greensboro, NC, 1984-86; pvt. practice psychiat. nursing, counseling, psychotherapy UNA Psychol. Assocs., 1986—; staff cons. Charter Hills Psychiat. Hosp. in Addictive Disease, 1991—98. Nat. resource cons. Am. Assn. Nurse Anesthetists on Addictive Disease; cons. Ctr. for Substance Abuse Prevention, also advisor to assoc. and clin. med. dir. Ctr. Substance Abuse Prevention. Contbr. chpt. to book, also articles and columns in health field. Co-sponsor adolescent group Jack and Jills of Am., Inc., Bloomfield Hills, Mich., 1975; co-sponsor Youth of Unity Ctr., Cleveland Heights, Ohio, 1981-84; vol. chmn. hospitality Old Greensboro Preservation Soc., 1985; bd. dirs. Urban League, Pontiac, Mich., 1972; apptd. mem. gov's. coun. on alcohol and other drug abuse State of N.C., 1989—, gov's. coun. women's issues of addiction, 1991—; apptd. advisor to assoc. clin., med. dir. Ctr. for Substance Abuse Prevention, Dept. Health and Human Svcs. U.S., 1991—, nat. spkrs. bur., 1991—, cons.; apptd. legis. com., mental health study commn. on child and adolescent substance abuse State of N.C., 1992—; lay speaking min. United Meth. Ch.; mem. Triad United Meth. Native Am. Ch. Mission. Columbia-Pacific U. scholar, 1983. Fellow Soc. Prevention Nutritionists; mem. Am. Assn. Profl. Hypnotherapists (registered profl. hypnotherapists, adv. bd.), Am. Assn. Nurse Anesthetists (cert.), Nat. Alaska Native Am. Indian Nurses Assn., Assn. Med. Educators and Rsch. in Substance Abuse, Nat. Acupuncture Detoxification Assn., Am. Assn. Counseling and Devel., Assn. for Med. Edn. and Rsch. in Substance Abuse, Am. Assn. Clin. Hypnotists, Am. Assn. Wholistic Practitioners, Am. Acad. Experts Traumatic Stress, Am. Nurse Hypnotheray Assn. (state pres. 1992-93), Am. Nurse Assn., Am. Holistic Nurses Assn. (charter mem.), Guilford Native Am. Assn., Negro Bus. and Profl. Women Inc. (v.p., parliamentarian 1961-83, 2001-03), Oakland County Coun. Black Nurses (v.p. 1970-74), Assn. Med. Educators (rschr. substance abuse, ad hoc com. mem. cultural diversity 1994—), Zeta Phi Beta (Nu Xi Zeta chpt. 2d anti-basilevs 1992-93, Beta Nu Zeta chpt. Greensboro). Republican. Avocations: music, nature, reading, egyptian history, metaphysics. Office: UNA Psychol Assocs and Prima Med-Legal Nurse Cons 620 S Elm St Ste 371 Greensboro NC 27406-1398 Home Phone: 336-698-9191; Office Phone: 336-370-0655. E-mail: rharrisoffutt@cs.com.

HARRISON, ANDRE L., education educator, director; b. Montgomery, Nov. 1, 1970; s. Willie James and Inez McCall Harrison; m. Monica Harrison, June 3, 1995; 1 child, Aundrea LaMonica. B in Lang. Arts and English Edn., Ala. State U., Montgomery, 1993, M in English Edn., 1995; EdS, Auburn U., Ala., 2005, D in Ednl. Adminstrn., AA in Ednl. Adminstrn., Auburn U., Ala., 2005. Class A cert. libr. media tech. Ala. State U., 1999, Class A cert. ednl. adminstrn. Ala. State U., 2000. Instr., supr. Ctr. Ala. Skills Ctr., Montgomery, 1993—99; lang. arts tchr., dept. chmn., tech. coord. Wetumpka Jr. HS, Ala., 1993—98, interim prin., 2003; English tchr. Elmore County Bd. Edn., Wetumpka, Ala., 1993—, libr. media specialist, 1998—2000, dir. instr., 2000—; adj. instr. English Ala. State U., 1995—2003, adj. instr. libr. media tech., 1999—2003, adj. instr. curriculum and instr., 2006—; prin. Wetumpka Intermediate Sch., 2003—04; adj. instr. ednl. leadership Auburn U., 2005. Coord. curriculum and instrn. Elmore County Bd. Edn., Ala.; ednl. cons. Ctrl. Ala. Regional In-Svc. Ctr., Montgomery, East Ala. Regional In-Svc. Ctr., Auburn U., Ala. State Dept. Edn., Classroom Improvement Sect.; lectr., guest spkr. grad. level curriculum courses. Mem. Profl. Devel. Adv. Com. and Subcom., Tech. Com., Title III Com., Lang. Arts Curriculum Com., Lang. Arts Textbook Com., Title IV Adv. Com., Sect. 504 Screening Com.; chairperson Student Handbook Com. Mem.: NEA, Ala. Coun. Tchrs. English, Ala. Edn. Assn., Phi Delta Kappa Internat., Sigma Tau Delta Internat.

HARRISON, BETTY CAROLYN COOK, retired education educator, administrator; b. Cale, Ark., Jan. 11, 1939; d. Denver G. and Minnie (Haddox) Cook; m. David B. Harrison, Dec. 31, 1956; children: Jerry David, Phyllis Lynley. BSE, Henderson State Tchrs. Coll., Arkadelphia, Ark., 1961; MS, U. Ark., 1971; PhD, Tex. A&M U., 1975. Tchr. secondary schs., McCrory, Ark., 1962-64, Taylor, Ark., 1964—69, Shongaloo, La., 1969-73, Minden, La., 1974-76, 77-80; adminstrv. intern La. Dept. Edn., 1974; cooperating tchr., supr. student tchrs. Grambling State U., La., 1974-76, La. Tech. U., Ruston, 1974-76, 78-80; asst. prof. vocat. edn. Va. Poly. Inst. and State U., Blacksburg, 1976-77; asst. prof. vocat. edn. Coll. Agr., La. State U., Baton Rouge, 1980-85, assoc. prof. Sch. Vocat. Edn., 1985-90, prof. vocat. edn., 1990—2001, prof. emeritus, 2001. Prof. career devel. specializing in instrnl. methodologies and brain-based learning, edn. and tng., edn. educator, sect. leader home econs. edn. La. State U., 1982-85, head dept. home econs. edn. and bus. edn., 1985-87, dir. La. Job Link Ctr., 1988-91, mem. univ. grad. coun., 1990-96, dir. Sch. Vocat. Edn., 1993-94, courses and curriculum sch. and coll., 1989-92. Contbr. articles to profl.

jours. HEW fellow, 1973; grantee Future Homemakers Am., 1956, Coll. Acads., 1956, Ark. Edn. Assn., 1966-69, Internat. Paper Co., 1966-68, La. Dept. Edn., 1972, others. Mem. NEA (nat. assembly del.), ASTD (v.p. comm. 1991-92, sec. 1993-94), Am Vocat. Edn. Assn., Nat. Assn. Vocat. Spl. Needs Pers., Am. Vocat. Edn. Rsch. Assn., Am. Home Econs. Assn., La Home Econs. Assn. (bd. dirs., pres.-elect), La. Vocat. Assn. (bd. dirs.), La. Assn. Vocat. Home Econs. Tchrs. (pres.), Nat. Assn. Vocat. Home Econs. Tchrs., Nat. Assn. Vocat. Home Econs. Tchr. Educators, (newsletter editor), Home Econs. Edn. Assn. (regional dir., nat. v.p., editor and chair publs. 1987-93), Family Rels. Coun. La. (edn. chmn. officer) Phi Delta Kappa, Delta Kappa Gamma (chpt. v.p., rsch. chair 1978-86), Gamma Sigma Delta (historian, sec., treas. 1984-93). Democrat. Baptist. Home: 37 Broadmoor Dr Magnolia AR 71753-4381

HARRISON, CECIL W., JR., lawyer; b. New Bern, NC, July 29, 1947; BA, Univ. NC, 1969, JD, 1973. Bar: NC 1973, US Supreme Ct. 1979. Mng. ptnr., comml. & appellate litigation, employment law, mem. mgmt. com. Poyner & Spruill LLP, Raleigh, NC. Mem.: ABA, NC Bar Assn., Wake County Bar Assn. Office: Poyner & Spruill LLP 3600 Glenwood Ave Raleigh NC 27612 Office Phone: 919-783-2814. Office Fax: 919-783-1075. Business E-Mail: cwharrison@poynerspruill.com.

HARRISON, CHARLES MAURICE, retired lawyer, communications executive; b. Anderson, SC, Aug. 30, 1927; s. Emmitte Smallwood and Jessie Maysel (Hawkins) H.; m. Lorna Jean Tomalty, June 27, 1970; children: Suzanne Elizabeth, Linda Jean. AB, Marshall U., 1949; JD, W.Va. U., 1952. Bar: W.Va. 1952, D.C. 1958, N.Y. 1965, N.J. 1972. Legal asst. W.Va. Dept. Ins., Charleston, 1952-54; hearing examiner Pub. Svc. Commn., Charleston, 1954-57; atty. Chesapeake and Potomac Tel. Co., Washington and Charleston, 1957-64, Western Electric Co., NYC, 1964-69; gen. atty., sec., treas. Bellcomm, Inc., Washington, 1969-71; asst. gen. counsel, asst. sec. Bell Tel. Labs., Murray Hill, N.J., 1971-75, gen. atty., sec., 1975-76, sec., gen. counsel corp. matters, 1976-84; asst. sec., asst. gen. counsel AT&T Bell Labs, 1985-87; gen. atty. AT&T, Berkeley Heights, N.J., 1987-89; of counsel Ventantonio & Wildenhain, Warren, NJ, ret., 2004. Bd. dirs. Somerset County C. of C. (chmn. 1990-92). Trustee Family Counseling Svcs. Somerset County, N.J., 1976-94, pres., 1978-81; chmn. R&D Coun. N.J., 1985-87, Bridgewater (N.J.) Commn. Substance Abuse, 1986-89, Bridgewater Mcpl. Facilities Commn., 1988-89, Bridgewater Twp. Alliance Com. on Alcoholism, 1989-99; bd. dirs. Martin Luther King Youth Ctr., 1984-90, Somerset Alliance for Future, 1992, N.J. affiliate Am. Heart Assn., 1991-94, Somerset County Coalition on Affordable Housing, 1995—; bd. dirs., pres. Somerset Treatment Svcs., 1992-99, bd. dirs., 2002—; mem. Bridgewater-Raritan Youth Svcs. Commn., chmn., 1989-90; mem. Bridgewater Planning Bd., 1989-94, chmn., 1992-94; mgmt. com. Ridewise Traffic Mgmt. Assn., 1992-96; mem. Somerset County Local Adv. Com. on Alcohol and Drug Abuse, 1992-99, Bridgewater Twp. Operation (police-pub.) Cooperation, 1992—, 200 Club of Somerset County, 1990—; trustee Henderson Meml. Scholarship Fund, 1993-99; mem. Twp. Coun., 1994-2001, coun. pres., 1996, 2000; mem. Bridgewater Zoning Bd. of Adjustment, 2002-, Bridgewater Econ. Devel. Adv. Com., 2005-. With AC, U.S. Army, 1945-46, W.Va. Air N.G., 1955-57, UsAFR, 1955-62. Named Somerset County Citizen of Yr., 1996. Mem. Rotary (pres. Somerville and Bridgewater, 2000-01, treas. 2005-06), Somerville Elks, Am. Legion. Republican. *Regardless of profession, career, occupation, or trade, success in life can only be achieved if a significant part of one's effort includes the gift of one's personal talent, energy, and time to his or her community. In this part of one's life, financial reward, public recognition, or even results, do not count as much as dedication and sincerity, but the opportunities for creativity and personal satisfaction are enormous.*

HARRISON, CHRISTOPHER EUGENE, graphics designer, artist, consultant; b. Springfield, Ohio, Aug. 27, 1965; s. Eugene and Marylene Anne Harrison; m. Camiile Margurite Boone, Apr. 28, 1995. BFA, Columbus Coll. Art and Design, 1987. Graphic designer Mpls. Spokesman-Recorder, 2004—; graphic artist/illustrator Harrison Art Properties, Robbinsdale, Minn., 2005—06. Bd. dirs. Northside Arts Collective, Mpls. Cultural Cmty. Partnership grantee, Minn. State Arts Bd., 2005. Mem.: TAWU Artist Group (assoc.), Visual Artist Focus Group (assoc.). Achievements include design of Bridge of Dreams public art project. Home: 3855 York Ave North Robbinsdale MN 55422 Office: Harrison Art Properties 3855 York Ave North Robbinsdale MN 55422 Home Phone: 763-522-6837; Office Phone: 763-522-6837. Personal E-mail: charrchr@yahoo.com.

HARRISON, CLIFFORD JOY, JR., banker; b. Nashville, Feb. 21, 1925; s. Clifford Joy and Rosa Lee (Bennett) H.; m. Saralu Fondren, May 3, 1957; children: Julia Lee, Clifford Joy III, John Fondren. BA, Vanderbilt U., 1949; postgrad., Law Sch., 1949-50, Nashville Sch. Law, 1950-53; LLB, Rutgers U., 1963; student, Advanced Mgmt. Program, Harvard U., 1975. With 3d Nat. Bank, Nashville, 1950-88, ret. vice chmn. in charge trust divsn., retail divsn. and pvt. banking, 1988. Past pres. Estate Planning Coun.; past pres. trust divns. Tenn. Bankers Assn. Past pres. YMCA Found. Bd.; past chmn. bd. trustees Tenn. Nature Conservancy. 1st lt. USAAF, 1943-46. Decorated Air medal with oak leaf cluster. Mem. Exch. Club, City Club (past pres.), Belle Meade Country Club, Beta Theta Pi, Phi Alpha Delta. Episcopalian. Home: 102 Abbottsford Nashville TN 37215-2437 E-mail: cliffharrison@comcast.net.

HARRISON, CRAIG DONALD, water rights broker, real estate and land use planner; b. Balt., May 9, 1956; s. Charles R. and Iris (Gable) H.; m. Carol Ann Hharrison, June 24, 2005; children: Craig Russell, Charles Marshall. Grad. high sch., Balt. Lic. real estate broker, Colo. V.p. Russell William Ltd., Balt., 1974-80; sole proprietor Harrison Land Co., Ft. Collins, Colo., 1980-82; pres. Harrison Resource Corp., Ft. Collins, 1982—, Terra Resource Corp., Fort Collins, 1991—; gen. ptnr. Gateway Farms, 1990—, Highland Farms, 1990—96; pres. Harrison Data Sets, Inc., 1995—; sole proprietor Harrison Land & Cattle Co., Ft. Collins, 1995—; mng. dir. Connor Creek Ranch LLC, 1997—; pres. Landnet Corp., 1998—; mng. dir. Tinnatti Lands LLC, 2005—, Suerpior Lands LLC, 2005—. Mem. Colo. Water Congress. Republican. Methodist. Avocations: ranching, mountain sports, music, art. Home: 5329 S County Road 3F Fort Collins CO 80528-9577 Office: Harrison Resource Corp 2725 Rocky Mtn Ave Ste 400 Loveland CO 80538

HARRISON, CYNTHIA L., librarian; m. David Harrison; 2 children. With Kitsap Regional Libr., Wash., 1990—, br. mgr. Bainbridge Island, Wash., 1991—. Recipient NY Times Libr. award, 2006. Office: Bainbridge Island Libr 1270 Madison Ave N Bainbridge Island WA 98110-2721 Office Phone: 206-842-4162. Office Fax: 206-780-5310. E-mail: cindyh@krl.org.

HARRISON, DONALD CAREY, academic administrator, cardiologist, educator; b. Blount County, Ala., Feb. 24, 1934; s. Walter Carey and Sovola (Thompson) H.; m. Laura Jane McAnnally, July 24, 1955; children: Douglas, Elizabeth, Donna Marie. BS in Chemistry, Birmingham So. Coll., 1954; MD, U. Ala., 1958. Diplomate Am. Bd. Internal Medicine (cardiovascular disease). Intern, asst. resident Peter Bent Brigham Hosp., 1958-60; fellow in cardiology Harvard U., 1961, NIH, 1961-63; mem. faculty Stanford U. Med. Sch., 1963-86, chief div. cardiology, 1967-86, prof. medicine, 1971-86; chief cardiology Stanford U. Hosp., 1967-86, William G. Irwin prof. cardiology, 1972-86; sr. v.p., provost for health affairs U Cin. Med. Ctr., 1986—2003; sr. v.p., provost for health affairs, emeritus U. Cin. Med. Ctr.; prof. medicine, cardiology U. Cin. Coll. Medicine; CEO U. Cin. Med. Ctr., 1987—2003. Cons. to local hosps., industry and govt.; mng. dir. Charter Life Sci. Venture Fund; bd. dir. Med. Edn. and Consultation, AtriCure Med., Uterine Muscle Dysfunction, Inc., Kendle Industries, Entero Medics, Inc., Am. Heart Assn., U. Cin. Physicians. Mem. editorial bd. Brit. Jour. Clin. Practice, 1993—; mem. editorial bd. Drugs, 1980—, Am. Jour. Cardiology, 1984—; contbr. articles to med. jours., chpts. to books. Served with USPHS, 1961-63. Fellow Interam. Soc. Cardiology (v.p. 1980-86), Am. Coll. Cardiology (mem. chmn., v.p. 1972-73, sec. 1969-70, trustee 1972-78), Am. Heart Assn. (fellow coun. circulation, clin. cardiology and basic sci., chmn. program com. 1972-76, nat. chmn. publs. com. 1976-81, pres.-elect 1980-81, pres. 1982-83); mem. ACP, Am. Soc. Clin. Investigation, Am. Fedn. Clin. Rsch., Am. Assn. Physicians, Assn. U. Cardiologists, Am. Clin. and Climatol Assn., Brit. Cardiac Soc., Acad. Medicine Cin., Assn. Acad. Health Ctrs. (past chmn.). Home: 9250 Old Indian Hill Rd Cincinnati OH 45243-3438 Office: U Cin Med Ctr ML 0669 3130 Highland Ave Cincinnati OH 45267-0669 Office Phone: 513-558-6397. Business E-Mail: don.harrison@uc.edu.

HARRISON, EARL DAVID, lawyer, real estate company officer; b. Bryn Mawr, Pa., Aug. 25, 1932; 1 child. BA, Harvard U., 1954; JD, U. Pa., 1960. Bar: DC 1960. Pvt. practice, Washington; exec. v.p. Washington Real Estate Corp., Washington, 1986-94; pres. EDH Assocs., Inc., 1994—. Capt. US Army, 1954—57. Decorated Order of Rio Branco Brazil, Order of Merit Italy. Mem.: ABA, Met. Washington Restaurant Assn., Nat. Restaurant Assn., Nat. Assn. Realtors, Greater Washington Comml. Assn. Realtors, Washington Assn. Realtors, DC Bar Assn., U. Pa. Club, Nat. Press Club, Harvard Club. Office: 1077 30th St NW Ste 706 Washington DC 20007-3834 Office Phone: 202-333-6776. Business E-Mail: david@edhlaw.com, david@edhassoc.com.

HARRISON, EMMETT BRUCE, JR., public relations counselor; b. Lanett, Ala., Apr. 3, 1932; s. Emmett Bruce and JeNelle (Williams) H.; m. Patricia DeStacy, Aug. 26, 1973; children by previous marriage: Susan, Emmett, Joe. AB, U. Ala., 1954; postgrad., Cath. U. Am., 1966-67. Mng. editor Talladega (Ala.) News, 1955; polit. reporter Columbus (Ga.) Ledger, 1956; adminstrv. asst. to U.S. Rep. K.A. Roberts Washington, 1957-61; pub. rels. dir. Mfg. Chemists' Assn., Washington, 1961-69; v.p. Freeport Minerals Co., NYC, 1969-73; pres. Harrison Assocs., Washington, 1973-77; pres., chmn. E. Bruce Harrison Co., Inc., Washington, 1978—97; chmn., CEO EnviroComm Internat., 1992—. Instr. bus. studies George Washington U.; bd. dirs. PR News. Author: Going Green: How to Communicate Your Company's Environmental Commitment, 1993; prodr. plays at Dramarena, N.Y.C., and Washington Theatre Club, Arena Stage, 1966-69. Asst. press mgr. J.F. Kennedy campaign Ala., 1960; mem. U.S. Coun. Internat. Bus.; del. UN Conf. on Environ., Rio de Janiero, 1992, People to People Amb. to China, 2005. Named Outstanding Journalism Grad., U. Ala., 1954; recipient AP Radio award, 1956, Nat. Endowment of Arts Play award, 1969. Fellow Pub. Rels. Soc. Am. (named Top 100 People 20th Century award 2000, Washington PR Hall Fame 2000), Counselors Acad. (chair 1990—), Arthur W. Page Soc. (bd. 1989-96, sec. 1994-96, exec. dir. 1997-98), Nat. Press Club, Senate Press Secs. Club, Chemists Club N.Y., Soc. Profl. Journalists (bd. 2003-06), Guest Svcs. Inc. (bd. 1998-2001), Washington Golf and Country Club, Sigma Delta Chi (bd. com. 1991-93), Omicron Delta Kappa, Pi Kappa Phi. Methodist. Home: 3201 N Vermont St Arlington VA 22207-4480 Office Phone: 202-789-2424. Business E-Mail: bruceharrison@envirocomm.com.

HARRISON, FAYE VENETIA, anthropologist, educator, writer; b. Norfolk, Va., Nov. 25, 1951; d. James and Odella Blount (Harper) Harrison; m. William Louis Odelia Conwill, May 17, 1980; children: Giles Harrison-Conwill, L. Mondlane Harrison-Conwill, Justin Harrison-Conwill. AB, Brown U., 1974; MA, Stanford U., 1977, PhD, 1982. Asst. prof. anthropology U. Louisville, 1983-89; assoc. prof. U. Tenn., Knoxville, 1989-97, prof., 1999—2004; prof., grad. dir. women's studies U. S.C., Columbia, 1997-99; prof. anthropology and African Am. studies U. Fla., Gainesville, 2004—, dir. African-Am. studies, 2007—. Author: Outsider Within: Reworking Anthropology in the Global Age, 2007; editor, contbg. author: Black Folks in Cities Here and There, 1988, Decolonizing Anthropology, 1991, 2d edit., 1997, W.E.B. DuBois and Anthropology, 1992, American Anthropologist Contemporary Forum: Race and Racism, 1998, African-American Pioneers in Anthropology, 1999, Resisting Racism and Xenophobia, 2005, assoc. editor: Urban Anthropology, 1992—99, cons. editor: Women and Aging, 1990—96, Identities: Global Studies of Culture and Power, 1992—99; mem. editl. com. Critique of Anthropology, 1995—99, Annual Rev. Anthropology, 1995—2000, Am. Anthropologist, 2000—05, mem. editl. bd. U. Tenn. Press, 1996—97, mem. adv. com. Womanist Theory and Research, Transforming Anthropology, 1990—2004; author, performer: (one woman show) The Other Side of Paradise; Three Women; One Struggle; contbr. articles to profl. jours. Mem. Nat. Alliance Against Racist and Polit. Repression, 1970—, Black Women Organized for Power, Louisville, 1984—86, Alliance Against Women's Oppression, Lousiville, 1988—89, E. Tenn. Coalition Against State Killing, 1995—97, 1999—2004, So. Human Rights Organizers Network, 2000—; organizer Ky. Rainbow Coalition, Lousiville, 1987—89; mem. Sister Song Reproductive Health & Rights Collective, 2002—, Sister Love Women of Color Coalition for Reproductive Rights, 2003—; mem. adv. bd. Knoxville Roman Cath. Diocese's Justice, Peace, Integrity of Creation, 1996—97. Recipient cert. of Merit, U. Louisville Pres. Office, 1989, Phi Beta Kappa U. Tenn. chpt., 1993, Hardy Liston, Jr. Symbol of Hope award for Promotion Cultural Diversity, U. Tenn. Commn. Blacks, 2003, award for Disting. Contbn. to Study of N.Am., Soc. Anthropology N.Am., 2004, Zora Nealethurston award for mentoring, svc. and scholarship, So. Anthrop. Soc., 2007; Ford Found. fellow, 1987—88. Mem.: Internat. Union Anthrop. and Ethnol. Scis. (co-chair commn. anthropology women 1993—98, chair commn. anthropology women 1998—), Assn. Black Anthropologists (pres. 1989—91), Am. Anthrop. Assn. (exec. bd. dirs. 1990—91, 1999—2001, ann. meeting exec. program chair 2007). Office: Univ Fla Turlington Hall Gainesville FL 32611 Personal E-mail: fevenetia@yahoo.com.

HARRISON, FRANK, former university president; b. Dallas, Nov. 21, 1913; s. Frank and Ruby (Davison) H.; m. Elsie Claire Redfearn, June 26, 1946; children— Frank, Susan Claire, James Redfearn. BS, So. Methodist U., 1935; MS, Northwestern U., 1936, PhD, 1938; MD, U. Tex. Southwestern Med. Sch., 1956. Mem. faculty U. Tenn. med. units, Memphis, 1938-51, prof., 1946-51, chief divsn. anatomy, 1946-51; prof. anatomy U. Tex. Southwestern Med. Sch., Dallas, 1952-68, assoc. dean, 1956-68; assoc. dean grad. studies U. Tex. at Arlington, 1965-68, acting pres., 1968-69, pres., 1969-72, Health Sci. Ctr., San Antonio, 1972-85, dir. Inst. Biotech., 1985, pres. emeritus. Named Distinguished Alumnus So. Meth. U., 1971 Mem. Am. Assn. Anatomists, Am. Physiol. Soc., Tex. Philos. Soc., Biophys. Soc., IEEE, Soc. Exptl. Biology and Medicine, Phi Beta Kappa, Alpha Omega Alpha, Kappa Sigma, Alpha Kappa Kappa. Home: 4168 Valley Ridge Rd Dallas TX 75220-1924 Personal E-mail: lsfh@msn.com.

HARRISON, FRANK W., JR., geologist; b. Bastrop, La. BS in Petroleum Geology, La. State U. Draftsman, geol. scout, geologist Union Producing Co.; geologist Seaboard Oil Co., New Orleans; dist. geologist Transtex Drilling Co., Lafayette, La., 1956—57; head geologist Am. Natural Gas Prodn. Co., Lafayette, 1957—59; ind. geologist Lafayette, 1959—; pres., owner Optimistic Oil Co., Lafayette. Mem. adv. bd. dirs. Entergy La.; dir. La. State U. Found., Am. Geol. Inst. Found.; bd. dirs. La. Oil and Gas Assn. Contbr. articles to sci. jours. Served in US Army. Recipient Ben H. Parker award Am. Inst. Profl. Geologists, 1994, Col. Edwin L. Drake Legendary Oilman award Drake Found. Mem.: Am. Geol. Inst. (past pres.), Am. Assn. Petroleum Geologists (past pres.), Soc. Ind. Profl. Earth Scientists, Ind. Petroleum Assn. Am., Geol. Soc. Am., Lafayette Geol. Soc. (hon.; past pres.). Office: Optimistic Oil Co 200 Audubon Blvd PO Box 51943 Lafayette LA 70503-2609 Office Phone: 337-232-4031. Office Fax: 337-235-5333. E-mail: f.harrison.jr@worldnet.att.net, FrankH@OptimisticOil.com.*

HARRISON, GAIL G., public health educator; M in Nutritional Scis., Cornell U.; PhD in Biol. Anthropology, U. Ariz. Mem. faculty Coll. Medicine, founding dir. program in internat. health, prof. family and cmty. medicine U. Ariz., 1976—92; chair, prof. dept. cmty. health scis. UCLA Sch. Pub. Health, 1992—; asst. program dir. program for health and at-risk populations UCLA/Jonsson Comprehensive Cancer Ctr. Mem. Food and Nutrition Bd., Nat. Acad. Scis./Inst. Medicine; cons. WHO, UNICEF. Mem.: Inst. Medicine. Office: UCLA Ctr for Health Policy Rsch Ste 1550 10960 Wilshire Blvd Los Angeles CA 90024 Business E-Mail: gailh@ucla.edu.

HARRISON, GEORGE BROOKS, engineer, researcher, retired military officer; b. Greenville, SC, July 30, 1940; s. William Henry and Mary Carter (Ogburn) Harrison; m. Pennie Maria Jenkins, Nov. 29, 1963; children: Taylor Leigh, Todd Henry, Tracy Elizabeth. BS in Pub. Policy, USAF Acad., 1962; MBA, U. Pa., 1970. Cert. flight instr. single and multi-engine instrument glider, lic. airline transport pilot. Commd. 2d lt. USAF, 1962, advanced through grades to maj. gen., 1989; fighter pilot, forward air contr. and instr. 557th and 436th Tactical Fighter Squadron, Fla., Vietnam, 1963—69; joint exercise planner U.S. Readiness Command, MacDill AFB, Fla., 1971-74; grad. Armed Forces Staff Coll., Norfolk, Va., 1974; ops. officer 13th and 25th Tactical Fighter Squadron, Udorn, Thailand, 1974-75; comdr. 4485th Test Squadron, Eglin AFB, Fla., 1975-78; grad. Air War Coll., Montgomery, Ala., 1979; wing comdr. 479th Tactical Tng. Wing, Holloman AFB, N.Mex., 1982-86; chief joint ops. divsn. Orgn. of Joint Chiefs of Staff, Washington, 1984-86; dept. chief staff plans USAF Europe, Ramstein AFB, Germany, 1986-89, dep. chief staff ops., 1991-92; asst. chief staff studies and analyses Hdqrs. USAF, Washington, 1989-91; comdr. Air Warfare Ctr., Eglin AFB, Fla., 1992-93; comdr. combined/joint task force USAF, S.W. Asia, 1993; comdr. Air Force Operational Test and Evaluation Ctr., Kirtland AFB, N.Mex., 1994-97; prin. rsch. engr., dir. rsch. ops. Ga. Tech Rsch. Inst., 1997—; mil. affairs cons. CNN, 1997—. Mem. sci. adv. bd. USAF, Washington, 1998—; sponsor Mil. Ops. Rsch. Soc., 1989—91; U.S. del. NATO Adv. Group Aerospace R & D, Paris, 1989—91; lectr. to mil., tech. and civic groups, 1982—. Contbr. articles to mil. jours. Mem., lt. col. CAP, SC, N.Mex., Ga., 1978—; dist. commr. Boy Scouts Am., Germany, 1986—89, coun. commr., 1991—92, exec. coun. N.Mex., 1995—97; exec. v.p., bd. dirs. Air Warrior Courage Found., 1998—; bd. dirs. Nat. Mus. Aviation, 1998—, Ga. Aviation Hall of Fame, 2005. Decorated DSM with oak leaf cluster, DFC, Air medal with eleven oak leaf clusters, Legion of Merit with one oak leaf cluster, Def. Superior Svc. medal; recipient Lt. Gen. Glen Kent Leadership award, USAF, 2005. Fellow: Beta Gamma Sigma; mem.: Air Force Assn., Quiet Birdmen, Order of Daedalians (flight capt. 1987—89, 2003—05). Baptist. Avocation: aviation. Office: Ga Tech Rsch Inst 400 10th St CRB 225 Atlanta GA 30318-5712 Home: 104 Middleton Dr Peachtree City GA 30269 Home Phone: 770-487-7742; Office Phone: 404-407-7136. Business E-Mail: george.harrison@gtri.gatech.edu.

HARRISON, GEORGE HARRY, III, (HANK HARRISON), publishing executive, author; b. Monterey, Calif., June 17, 1940; s. Edith Cooke; 1 child, Courtney Love. BA in Psychology, San Francisco State Univ., Calif., 1965; postgrad., U. London, 1978-81. Mgr. Grateful Dead (formerly Warlocks), Palo Alto, Calif., 1965-66, 70-73; founder, counselor LSD rescue founder Inst. Contemporory Studies, San Francisco, 1967; pvt. practice counselor San Francisco, 1967-78; pub., founder Arkives Press, San Francisco, 1979—. Writer-in-residence Montalvo Ctr. Arts, Saratoga, Calif., 1974; founder Media Assocs., Los Altos, Calif., 1991—; presenter, expert witness, lectr. in field; co-owner Epona Equestrian Ctr., Wilton, Calif, 1995; story cons., contbg. editor NBC prodn. The Search for the Unicorn Killer, 1999; co-developer Adobe Acrobat, Irish Govt.; cons. in field; lectr. in field. Author: The Dead Trilogy, 1972-97, Quest for Flight, 1975, 2nd edit., 1995, The Cauldron and the Grail, 1992, The Stones of Ancient Ireland, 2007, Ace of Cups: The Grail in Tarot, 1998, Hamburger Zen, 2001, The Grail in the Troubadour World, 2006, Love Kills: The Assassination of Kurt Cobain, 2007; contbr. VSD (Paris), San Francisco Oracle, The Berkeley Barb, The Ga. Straight and L.A. Free Press, Dragon's Quest, E Channel, Court TV, True Hollywood Story: Courtney Love, 2003; editor emeritus Doctor Dobb's Jour.; tech., staff writer Info World Apple Plus Mag., radio, TV guest including Geraldo, Am. Jour., Inside Edition, Hard Copy, Maury Povitch Show, America's Most Wanted, Fox News Contribution, 1998; editor: Vancouver Mag., 1974-75, Las Vegas Sun, 1976-77, Jour. Psychedelic Drugs, 1967; contbg. editor High Times, 1996-97; prodr. (CD) Garcia: The Lost Concert, 1999; commentator Mystery of the Holy Grail Sacred Mysteries (The Learning Channel), Crown of Stars: The Grail in the Troubadour World, 2004; editor, pub.: (book and CD) A Guide to Fractional and Civil War Currency, 2003; editor, co-author Kravitz Guide to Fractional Currency, 2003; contbr. Dateline Feature: Was Kurt Coban Murdered?, 2004. Served USN, 1958-61. Rocky Mountain Writers Conf. scholar, 1968, Frances Yates scholar Warburg Inst. U. London, 1978-80; Francis Gates fellow, Warburg Inst., London, 1980. Mem. Press Club, Ind. Pub. Assn., San Francisco Press Club, Las Vegas Press Club, Sacramento Press Club, Masons. Democrat. Avocations: horse breeding, dog breeding. Home and Office: PO Box 46 Wilton CA 95693-0046 Home Phone: 800-373-1897. Office Fax: 800-373-1897. Personal E-mail: zendogg@gmail.com, hankharrison916@hotmail.com, hank@hankharrison.com.

HARRISON, GORDON RAY, engineering executive, consultant, research scientist; b. Wister, Okla., Dec. 14, 1931; s. Trannie Gordon and Isah Lee (Ray) H.; m. Barbara Ann Herndon, June 22, 1957; children: William Andrew, Melissa Leigh, Lori Jeanne, Amanda Ray. BS in Physics, U. Central Ark., 1952; MS, Vanderbilt U., 1954, PhD, 1958. Sr. staff engr. and engrng. mgr. Sperry Microwave, Clearwater, Fla., 1957-71; prin. research scientist to lab. dir. Engrng. Expt. Sta., Ga. Inst. Tech., Atlanta, 1971-83; v.p. Electromagnetic Scis., Inc., Atlanta, 1983-91; ind. cons. tech., bus., 1991—. Contbr. chpt. to book, numerous articles to profl. jours.; patentee microwave ferrimagnetic garnets. Fellow IEEE; mem. Soc. Microwave Theory and Techniques, Magnetics Soc., Mustang Club Am., Sigma Xi. Democrat. Methodist. Personal E-mail: bahgrh@bellsouth.net.

HARRISON, GUY NEWELL, lawyer; b. Longview, Tex., Dec. 14, 1946; s. Guy Franklin and Margaret Louise (Newell) H.; m. Lucinda Dodson, July 5, 1969; children: Parker Trigg Harrison, Worth McKinley Harrison. BBA, So. Meth. U., 1968, JD, 1974. Bar: Tex., U.S. Dist. Ct. Tex., U.S. Supreme Ct. Ptnr. Green & Harrison, Longview, Tex., 1974—. Pres. Longview YMCA, 1976-78; bd. dirs. YMCA of the USA, 1990-91, Good Shepherd Hosp. Found., Longview, 1989-91. Sgt. U.S. Army, 1968-70, Vietnam. Recipient Lowell Linnes award YMCA of the Midwest, 1979; named Atty. of Yr. Longview Legal Secs. Mem. Gregg Bar Assn., Tex. Trial Lawyers Assn., Tex. State Bar Assn. (bd. dirs. 1995-, chmn. 1997-98, pres.-elect 2001-02, pres. 2002-03); fellow (life) Tex. Bar Found. (trustee 1998-). Office: 100 W Methvin Longview TX 75601

HARRISON, HENRY STARIN, real estate appraiser, educator, entrepreneur; b. New Haven, June 19, 1930; s. Julius and Helen (Starin) H.; m. Minna Snyder, Apr. 16, 1960 (div. 1970); children: Julie, Eve; m. Ruth Lambert, May 30, 1976; children: Kate, H. Alex. BS in Econs., U. Pa., 1952; MA, Goddard Coll., 1974. Asst. to pres. Charlton Press, Derby, Conn., 1954-56; assoc. Harris Weissbuck Co., New Haven, 1956-57; pres. Harrison Appraisal Co., New Haven, 1958-90, H & R Ins. Agy., 1975-88,

Health Care Mgmt. Co., 1964-86, The H2 Co., New Haven, 1986-95, H Squared Co., 1995—, A&A World Travel, New Haven, 1989-94; treas., v.p. Forms & Worms, Inc., 1989-97; pub. NAFFA, Inc., New Haven, 1985—. Appraisal cons. Nat. Assn. Environ. Risk Auditors, Bloomington, Ind., 1989-94. Author: Houses, Houses, Houses, 1974, URAR-Illustrated Guide, 1975, Appraising Single Family Residences, 1978, Home Buying-The Complete Illustrated Guide, 1980, Small Income Property-Illustrated Guide, 1980, Dictionary of Real Estate Appraisal, 1982, Condominium-Illustrated Guide, 1984, Review Appraisers Handbook, 1987, Appraising Residences and Income Properties, 1989, ARIP Student Workbook, 1989, NAERA Environmental Manual, 1989, Environmental Risk Screening, 1990, 1001 Q & A Appraisal Exam Preparation, 1990, Standards of Professional Appraisal Practice and Ethics, 1991, ARIP General Property Supplement, Real Estate 2055 Evaluation Illustrated Guide, 2005, Real Estate Principles and Practices Plus, 1994, Russian Appraisal Textbook, 1994, Advanced Appraisal Methods, 1994, Guide to New Haven, Connecticut, 1995, How To Make an FHA Single Family Appraisal, 1999, How To Pass the HUD/FHA Appraisal Qualification Examination, 1999, Spanish and English Dictionary of Real Estate and Appraisal, 2000, Hopkins History and Chronicles (1660-2000), 2004, Small Residential Income Property Appraisal Report-Mini Guide, 2005, Uniform Residential URAR Appraisal Report-Mini Guide, 2005, Exterior Inspection Only Appraisal Report, 2005, Basic Appraisal Principles, 2006, Basic Appraisal Procedures, 2006; pub.: Real Estate Valuation Mag., 1985—; contbr. articles, chapters to books, audio-visual materials; patentee: Perpetual Birthday and Anniversary Reminder Calendar, —. Alderman City of New Haven, 1961-63; pres. Young GOP, New Haven, 1960, Real Estate Edn. Found., 1980—, Greater New Haven Arts Coun., 1989-91; trustee Goddard Coll., 1976-78. 1st lt. USAF, 1952-54. Recipient Real Estate Educators Assn. award, 1995. Fellow Am. Coll. Health Care Adminstrs. (award 1984); mem. Am. Inst. Real Estate Appraisers (pres. Conn. chpt. 1975-76, Profl. recognition award 1976, 78, MAI award 1980), Am. Soc. Appraisers (award 1987), Soc. Real Estate Appraisers (nat. vice gov. 1980), Columbia Soc. Appraisers (award 1959), Greater New Haven Real Estate Bd. (Realtor of Yr. award 1976, Educator of Yr. 1992), Lawn Club. Jewish. Avocations: water sports, travel. Home: Carriage House 315 Whitney Ave New Haven CT 06511-3715 Office: Harrison Cos Carriage House 315 Whitney Ave New Haven CT 06511-3772 Office Phone: 203-562-3159. Personal E-mail: henryhsq@aol.com.

HARRISON, HOLLY A., lawyer; b. 1958; BA, U. Denver, 1981; JD, Boston U., 1984. Bar: Mass. 1984, Ill. 1985. Law clk. to Hon. Raymond J. Pettine, U.S. Dist. Judge Dist. R.I., 1984—85; with Sidley Austin Brown & Wood, Chgo., 1985—, ptnr., 1992—. Office: Sidley Austin Brown & Wood Ste 900 1 S Dearborn St Chicago IL 60603-2310

HARRISON, JAMES FRANCIS, chemistry professor, researcher; b. Phila., Jan. 19, 1940; s. Albert and Ann Jane Harrison; m. Jane I. Moore, Dec. 2, 1995; m. Jane Ann Kuczynski, Oct. 9, 1965 (div. Jan. 1, 1985); children: Christopher James, Kenneth Andrew. BS, Drexel Inst. Tech., Phila., 1962; AM, Princeton U., NJ, 1964, PhD, 1966. Rsch. asst. USDA, Wyndmore, Pa., 1958—62; lab. instr. Drexel Inst. Tech., Phila., 1962; postdoctoral fellow Ind. U., Bloomington, 1966—68; asst. prof. chemistry Mich. State U., East Lansing, 1968—73, assoc. prof. chemistry, 1973—81, prof. chemistry, 1981—. Scientist in residence Argonne Nat. Lab., Ill., 1980—81; cons. AMOCO Corp., Napervile, Ill., 1987—95; assoc. chmn. undergraduate studies Mich. State U., East Lansing, 1987—93. Contbr. articles to profl. jours. Recipient Disting. Faculty award, Coll. Natural Sci., Mich. State U., 1995; Food Fair scholar, Drexel Inst. Tech., 1957—62, Am. Machine and Foundry fellow, Princeton U., 1963—64, NASA fellow, 1964—66, NSF fellow, Ind. U., 1966—68, Camille and Henry Drefus Tchr. scholar, Camille and Henry Drefus Found., 1972—77. Mem.: Am. Phys. Soc., Am. Chem. Soc. (chair Mich. State U. sect. 1972—76, Scholastic Achievement award Phila. sect. 1962), Phi Kappa Phi, Sigma Xi (pres. Mich. State U. sect. 2004—05). Home: 6054 Skyline Dr East Lansing MI 48823 Office: Chemistry Dept Michigan State University East Lansing MI 48824 Office Phone: 517-355-9715 295. Office Fax: 517-353-1793; Home Fax: 517-353-1793. Business E-Mail: harrison@chemistry.msu.edu.

HARRISON, JEREMY THOMAS, dean, law educator; b. San Francisco, Dec. 23, 1935; s. James Gregory and Agnes Johanna (Patrick) H.; m. Roseanne E. Thomas, Dec. 29, 1962 (dec. Oct. 1983); children: James, Amelia, Roseanne, Jeremy, Alexandra, Nadya, Rachel; m. Laura Ellen Marrack, Apr. 28, 1990; children: Robert, Peter, Paul, Philip, John. BS, U. San Francisco, 1957, JD, 1960; LLM, Harvard U., 1962. Bar: Calif. 1961, Hawaii 1987. Assoc. Brobeck, Phleger & Harrison, San Francisco, 1960-61; law clk. to assoc. justice U.S. Ct. Claims, Washington, 1962-63; lectr. law U. Ghana, Accra, 1963-64, U. Ife, Ibadan, Nigeria, 1964-66; prof. law U. San. Francisco, 1966-85; dean Sch. Law U. Hawaii, Honolulu, 1985-94; dean Mich. State U. Coll. Law, East Lansing, 1996-98, prof. law, 1998—. Vis. prof. law Haile Sellassie I U., Addis Ababa, Ethiopia, 1971-74, U. Hawaii, 1977-79; Elips Disting. prof. law Gadjah Mada U., Yogyakarta, Indonesia, 1995-96. Author: Cases and Materials on Evidence, Africa, 1967, Cases and Materials on Ethiopian Civil Procedure, 1974. Counsel citizen's panel Hawaii's Jud. Adminstrn., Honolulu, 1985-86; bd. dirs. Straub Found., Honolulu; pres. Pacific Health Rsch. Inst., Honolulu, 1993-95. Mem. ABA, Am. Bar Found., Calif Bar Assn., Hawaii Bar Assn. Office: Mich State U Coll Law 465 Law College Bldg East Lansing MI 48824-1300 Business E-Mail: jharriso@law.msu.edu.

HARRISON, JOHN COLLIER, law educator; b. Columbus, Ohio, July 9, 1956; s. James Collier and Margaret Eva (Bradenburgh) H. BA, U. Va., 1977; JD, Yale U., 1980. Bar: DC 1980. Assoc. Patton, Boggs & Blow, Washington, 1980-82; law clk. to Hon. Robert H. Bork US Ct. Appeals DC Cir., Washington, 1982-83; with US Dept. Justice, Washington, 1983—93, dep. asst. atty. gen. Office Legal Counsel, 1990—93; assoc. prof. U. Va. Sch. Law, 1993—98, prof., 1998—, now David Lurton Massee, Jr. prof. law, Horace W. Goldsmith rsch. prof. Mem. Soc. for Am. Baseball Research. Office: U Va Sch Law 580 Massie Rd Charlottesville VA 22903-1789 Office Phone: 434-924-3093. E-mail: jh8m@virginia.edu.

HARRISON, JOHN CONWAY, retired state supreme court justice; b. Grand Rapids, Minn., Apr. 28, 1913; s. Francis Randall and Ethlyn (Conway) H.; m. Ethel M. Strict; children: Nina Lyn, Robert Charles, Molly M., Frank R., Virginia Lee. LLD, George Washington U., 1940. Bar: Mont. 1947, U.S. Dist. Ct. 1947. County atty. Lewis and Clark County, Helena, Mont., 1934-60; justice Mont. Supreme Ct., Helena, 1961-98, ret., 1998. Pres. Mont. TB Assn., Helena, 1951-54, Am. Lung Assn., N.Y.C., 1972-73, Mont. coun. Boy Scouts Am., Great Falls, Mont., 1976-78. Col. U.S. Army Mem. ABA, Mont. Bar Assn., Kiwanis (pres. 1953), Sigma Chi. Home: 215 S Cooke St Helena MT 59601-5143 Office Phone: 404-442-5833.

HARRISON, JOHN D., state agency administrator; m. Barbara Harrison; 5 children. B in Bus. Adminstrn. and Mktg., Troy U., 1967; grad., La. State U. Grad. Sch. Banking, 1988. Ptnr., v.p. C&H Trucking Co., Inc., 1976—97; owner, pres. Crenshaw Land and Timber Co., 1981—; CEO First Citizens Bank of Luverne, 1983—2003; mayor Luverne, Ala., 1988—2003; dir. Ala. Dept. Cmty. and Econ. Affairs, 2003—05; supt. Ala. State Banking Dept., 2005—. Bd. trustees Ala. Forestry Assn. Forest Fund. Bd. trustees Troy U. Named Alumnus of Yr., Troy U., 1992. Office: Ala State Banking Dept PO Box 4600 Montgomery AL 36103-4600 Office Phone: 334-242-3585. Office Fax: 334-242-3500. E-mail: john.harrison@banking.alabama.gov.

HARRISON, JOHN RAYMOND, foundation administrator, retired publishing executive; b. Des Moines, June 8, 1933; s. Raymond Harrison and Dorothy (Stout) Harrison Cohen; m. Lois Cowles, June 24, 1955 (div. Apr. 1981); children: Gardner Mark, Kent Alfred (dec.), John Patrick, Lois Eleanor; m. Mary Gee MacQueen, Sept. 5, 1981 (div. 2000); m. Bonnie Lynne Anderson, Aug. 26, 2000; stepchildren: Jennifer Alicia Anderson, Michael Christopher Anderson. Grad., Phillips Exeter Acad., 1951; AB, Harvard U., 1955, postgrad. Sch. Bus., 1955-56; DHL (hon.), Fla. So. Coll. With various papers throughout the U.S.; vice pres. N.Y. Times Co., ret.; chmn. Harrison Charitable Found., Sarasota, Fla. Dir. Internat. Herald-Tribune, Paris, 1974-91. Bd. dirs. Ft. Pierce (Fla.)-St. Lucie County Indsl. Devel. Coun., 1959-62, Ft. Pierce Meml. Hosp., 1959-62, Lincoln Pk. Child Care Ctr., Ft. Pierce, 1959-62, Gainesville United Fund, 1965, Boys Club Gainesville, 1965, U. Fla. Found., 1967, YMCA Greater Lakeland, 1967-69, Human Rels. Coun. Lakeland, 1967-69, Boys Club Lakeland, ARC, 1967-69; trustee Robert H. Anderson Found., Ridge Sch., Bartow, Fla., High Mus., 1988-94; mem. Pres.'s Resources Coun. Wellesly (Mass.) Coll.; mem. bd. counsellors Fla. So. Coll., 1974; mem. bd. visitors Emory U., 1984, pres., 1986; trustee Westminster Schs., 1989-92, Kennesaw State Coll. Found.; mem. bd. councillors Carter Presdl. Ctr.; mem. bd. overseers Harvard U., 1995-2001; bd. trustees Ringing Sch. Art and Design, 2003. Recipient Pulitzer Prize for editl. writing, 1965, Nat Headliners award for pub. svc. editl. writing, Nat. Headliners Club, 1972, Walker Stone award for editl. writing Scripps-Howard Found., 1974, 76, Silver Gavel award for pub. svc. editls. ABA, 1977, Sigma Delta Chi Bronze medal, 1970, 73. Mem. Greater Lakeland C. of C. (dir. 1966-67), Associated Harvard Alumni (dir. 1979-82), Spee Club, Hasty Pudding Inst. 1770 (grad. dir.), Harvard Club (N.Y.C., Boston, Ga. bd. dirs.), Oaks Club-Sarasota, Fla.

HARRISON, JOHNNIE SHEPPARD, religious organization administrator; b. Jacksonville, Fla., Oct. 16, 1947; d. John and Sarah Sheppard; m. Augustine Richard Harrison, Sr., Aug. 11, 1969; children: Rezella Delourse, Augustine Richard Harrison, Jr.; children: Kyle Harold Taylor, Deltris Quinn Sheppard. AA, Brevard C.C., Melbourne/Cocoa, Fla., 1983; AS, BA, Living Word Bible Coll. & Sem., Maryland Heights, MO, 1986; BS, Orlando Coll., 1996; MBA, Nova Southeastern U., 1999; postgrad. Nova Southeastern U., 2003—. Title clk. Dept. of Interior, Big Cypress, Naples, Fla., 1977—78; resources control clk. NASA, Kennedy Space Ctr., Fla., 1978—85; postal worker USPS, Melbourne, Fla., 1985—90; dir. Kids at Risk Programs and Svcs. ministry Outreach, Melbourne, Fla., 2002—; pres., CEO Outreach Mission Internat., Melbourne. Author: (book) Strategies for Constructive Leadership (Cert. of Achievement, 2001). Supr. of women Ch. of God in Christ, Inc., Memphis, 1998. Mem.: So. Brevard Ministerial Alliance, Inc. (assoc.; parliamentarian 2002—03). Home: 626 Reddick St Melbourne FL 32901-7112 Office: Ch of God In Christ Inc PO Box SS 6281 Np Nassau The Bahamas Home: PO Box 2487 Melbourne FL 32902-2487 Office Fax: 484-231-3400. Personal E-mail: johnnie_harrison714@hotmail.com.

HARRISON, JOSEPH HEAVRIN, lawyer; b. Evansville, Ind., July 23, 1929; s. Homer William and Lillie Isabelle (Heavrin) H.; m. Sharon Jeanene Miller, June 30, 1957 (div. 1976); children: Joseph Heavrin, Jr., Sara Ann; m. Julie Anne Gerard, Dec. 10, 1976; 1 child, Meghann. BA in Econs., U. Notre Dame, Ind., 1952; JD cum laude, U. Notre Dame, 1953. Bar: Ind. 1953, U.S. Dist. Ct. D.C. 1953, U.S. Dist. Ct. (so. dist.) Ind. 1953, U.S. Ct. Appeals (7th cir.) 1968, U.S. Tax Ct. 1984. Mng. ptnr., chmn. Bowers Harrison and predecessors, Evansville, Ind., 1955. Pres. Sandy's Assocs., Inc. (14 Hardee's franchised restaurants). Dir. Vanderburgh County Legal Aid Soc., Evansville, 1958—68, pres., 1964—65; Ind. counsel Bush Presdl. campaign, 1988; co-chair Ind. Lawyers for G.W. Bush, 2000—; chmn. Vanderburgh County Election Bd., 1979—90, Vanderburgh Rep. Fin. Com., 1982—89; mem. Evansville Econ. Devel. Commn., 1991—2002, pres., 1995—2001; Ind. commr. Ohio River Valley Water Sanitation Commn., 1982—, chmn., 1987; commr. Vanderburgh County Conv. & Vis. Bur., 1997—2001; bd. dirs. Arbor Hosp., 1991—94. With US Army, 1953—55. Fellow Ind. Bar Found.; mem. ABA, Evansville Bar Assn., Ind. Bar Assn., Am. Judicature Soc., Evansville Country Club (pres. 1976), Oak Meadow Country Club. Republican. Roman Catholic. Avocations: golf, flying. Office: Bowers Harrison LLP PO Box 1287 25 NW Riverside Dr Evansville IN 47708-1255 Office Phone: 812-426-1231. Business E-mail: jhh@bowersharrison.com.

HARRISON, LOIS SMITH, hospital executive, educator; b. Frederick, Md., May 13, 1924; d. Richard Paul and Henrietta Foust (Menges) Smith; m. Richard Lee Harrison, June 23, 1951; children: Elizabeth Lee Boyce, Margaret Louise Wade, Richard Paul. BA, Hood Coll., 1945, MA, 1993, Columbia U.; LHD (hon.), Hood Coll., 1993. Counselor CCNY, 1945-46; founding adminstr., counselor, instr. psychology and sociology Hagerstown (Md.) Jr. Coll., 1946-51, registrar, 1946-51, 53-54, instr. psychology and orienta, 1954-56; registrar, instr. psychology Balt. Jr. Coll., 1951-54; bus. mgr., acct. for pvt. med. practice Hagerstown, 1953-2000; trustee Washington County Hosp., Hagerstown, 1975-97, chmn. bd., 1986-88, 95—; mem. bd. Washington County Health Sys. Inc., 1997—. Chmn. Home Fed. Savs. Bank, Hagerstown, 1997-99; chmn. acute care Health Sys. Bd., 1997—; chmn. bd. dirs. Home Fed. Savs. Bank, 1998-2000, emeritus, 2001—; spkr. ednl. panels, convs. hosp. panels and seminars Author: The Church Woman, 1960-65, With Courage and Vision: Christ's Reformed Church Celebrate 150 Years, 2004. Trustee Hood Coll., Frederick, 1972—, chmn. bd., 1979-95; mem. Md. Gov.'s Commn. to Study Structure and Ednl. Devel. Commn., 1971-75; pres. Washington County Coun. Ch. Women, 1970-72; appointee Econ. Devel. Commn., County Impact Study Commn. Bd.; bd. dirs. Md. Hosp. Assn., 1988-98, Md. Chs. United, 1975—; chmn. bd. dirs. Md. Hosp. Edn. Inst., 1978-98; mem. Christ's Reformed Ch., 1935—; pres. Ch. Consistory; chmn. Chesapeake Healthcare Forum, 1995-97; chmn. Centennial Celebration, Washington County Hosp. Bd. Recipient Alumnae Achievement award Hood Coll., 1975, Washington County Woman of Yr. award, AAUW, 1984, Md. Woman of Yr. award, 1984, Md. Woman of Yr. award Francis Scott Key Commn. for Md.'s 350th Anniversary, 1984; named one of top 10 women Tri-State area, Herald-Mail Tri-State newspaper, 1990, Zonta Internat. Woman of Yr., 1994, Outstanding Woman of the Yr., Woman At the Table award, 2002, Citizen of Yr. award Herald-Mail, 2006. Mem. Hagerstown C. of C. Republican. Home: 12835 Fountain Head Rd Hagerstown MD 21742-2748 Office: Washington Cty Hosp Off Chmn Bd Hagerstown MD 21740 Office Phone: 301-790-8107. Personal E-mail: lorichco@aol.com.

HARRISON, LOUIS S., lawyer; b. Evanston, Ill., 1959; BA magna cum laude in Math., Colgate U., 1981; MBA with honors in Fin., U. Chgo., 2002; JD with high honors, Duke U., 1984. Bar: Ill. 1984. Ptnr.-in-charge Lord, Bissell & Brook Wealth Preservation Grp.; ptnr. Harrison & Held, LLP, Chgo. Adj. prof. law DePaul U. Law Sch., Ill. Kent Sch. Law, Northwestern U. Contbr. articles to profl. publs.; sr. editor: Duke-Alaska Law Rev., 1983—84; co-author: Sorting Out Life's Complexities: What You Really Need to Know about Taxes, Wills, Trusts, Powers of Attys. and Health Care Decisions, 1992, Ill. Estate Planning Forms and Commentary. Named one of Top 100 Attys., Worth mag., 2005. Fellow: Am. Coll. Trust and Estate Counsel; mem.: Chgo. Estate Planning Coun., ABA, Ill. State Bar Assn., Chgo. Bar Assn. (mem. fed. taxation com., past chair estate and gift tax divsn., mem. trust law com.). Office: Harrison & Held LLP 333 W Wacker Dr Chicago IL 60606-1218 Office Phone: 312-332-5440. Office Fax: 866-456-8494. E-mail: lharrison@harrisonheld.com.*

HARRISON, LUVADA A., voice educator, singer; d. Theodore R. and Monterey R Harrison. MusM, Binghamton U., Binghamton, New York, 1991; MusD, Fla. State U., 2007. Singer: (Operas) Le Nozze di Figaro, Suor Angelica, Doktor Faustus, Aida, The Consul, Albert Herring, Scourge of the Hyacinths, Il Trovatore, Messiah, Beethoven's Ninth Symphony, Rossini-Petit Misse Solenelle, Beethoven Missa Solemnis, Verdi Requiem, Elijah, Rossini - Stabat Mater. Recipient Friedrich award, Binghamton U., 1991; fellow, Fla. State U., 2004—05; scholar, Fla. State U., Barga Inst., Italy, G, Binghamton U., 1989—91, Fla. State U., 2003—04; Verdian Concoursa Study grant, Bel Canto Soc. Chgo., 1988. Mem.: Coll. Music Soc., Nat. Assn.Tchrs. of Singing, Pi Kappa Lambda. Office: Dept Music Florida A&M Univ Tallahassee FL 32307 Home Phone: 850-942-2035; Office Phone: 850-561-2317. E-mail: luvada.harrison@famu.edu.

HARRISON, MARION EDWYN, lawyer; b. Phila., Sept. 17, 1931; s. Marion Edwyn and Jessye Beatrice (Cilles) H.; m. Carmelita Ruth Deimel, Sept. 6, 1952; children: Angelique Marie (Mrs. Kevin B. Bounds), Marion Edwyn III, Henry Deimel. BA, U. Va., 1951; LLB, George Washington U., 1954, LLM, 1959. Bar: Va. 1954, DC 1958, US Supreme Ct. 1958. Spl. asst. to gen. counsel PO Dept., 1958-60, mem. bd. contract appeals, 1958-61, assoc. gen. counsel, 1960-61; ptnr. firm Harrison, Lucey & Sagle (and predecessors), Washington, 1961-78, Barnett & Alagia, 1978-84; ptnr. Scott, Harrison & McLeod, 1984-86, Law Offices Marion Edwyn Harrison, Washington, 1986—; pres. Free Congress Rsch. and Edn. Found., Inc., 2002—. Mem. coun. Adminstrv. Conf. US, 1971—78, sr. conf. fellow, 1984—88; mem. DC Law Revision Commn., 1975—92; adv. dir. Nations-Bank, N.A., 1987—93; lectr. Nat. Jud. Coll., Reno, 1979, La. State U. Law Sch., Aix-en-Provence, 1987, Aix-en-Provence, 89, Tulane U. Law Sch., Crete, 1997, Thessaloniki, 2001, Rhodes, 04, Hofstra U. Law Sch., Nice, France, 1999, Nice, 2003, Sorrento, 06, Pa. State U. Dickinson Law Sch., Vienna, 2000, St. Mary's U. Law Sch., Innsbruck, Austria, 2002, Innsbruck, 07, U. Kans. Law Sch., Istanbul, 2005. Contbr. articles to profl. publs.; editor-in-chief Fed. Bar News, 1960-63; mem. editl. bd. Adminstrv. Law Rev., 1976-89. Trustee AEFC Pension Fund, Chgo., 1986-92; pres. Young Rep. Fedn. Va., 1954-55; mem. Va. Rep. Ctrl. Com., 1954-55; bd. visitors Judge Adv. Gen. Sch., Charlottesville, Va., 1976-78; chmn. Wolf Trap Assn., 1984-87; bd. dirs. Wolf Trap Found., 1984-88; pub. mem. USIA Mission, Argentina, 1971; mem. bd. visitors JAG's Sch., 1974-76. Officer AUS, 1955-58. Decorated Commendation medal. Fellow: Am. Bar Found. (life); mem.: ABA (chmn. sect. adminstrv. and reg. law 1974—75, ho. of dels. 1978—88, chmn. lawyers in govt. com. 1980—82, bd. govs. 1982—86, chmn. com. on fgn. and internat. orgns. 1986—87), Bar Assn. DC (chmn. adminstrv. law sect. 1970—71, bd. dirs. 1971—72), Inter-Am. Bar Assn., Fed. Bar Assn. (nat. coun. 1966—82), Coun. for Nat. Policy, Supreme Ct. Hist. Soc., Federalist Soc., George Washington U. Law Assn. (pres. 1974—77), Smithsonian Instn. (nat. bd. dirs. 1991—97), Soc. Mayflower Desc., Farmington Country Club (Charlottesville, Va.), Gainey Ranch Golf Club (Scottsdale, Ariz.), Met. Club, Washington Golf and Country Club, Knight of Malta. Republican. Roman Catholic. Home: 4111 N Ridgeview Rd Arlington VA 22207-4617 Address: 7222 E Gainey Ranch Rd Scottsdale AZ 85258-1529 Office: 717 Second St NE Washington DC 20002

HARRISON, MARJORIE FREEMAN, secondary education educator, librarian; b. Yonkers, NY, Dec. 26, 1952; d. Burton Morton and Sandra (Firestone) Freeman; m. Fred Harrison, Mar. 31, 1974; 1 child, Alexander. Student, U. Rochester, 1970—72; BA cum laude, Columbia U., 1974; MLS, L.I. U., Greenvale, NY, 1975; PhD, Columbia U., 2005. Cert. tchr. secondary social studies, libr. media specialist, N.Y. Tchr., libr. Portledge Sch., Locust Valley, NY, 1975-77; tchr. history various LI HS, 1977-82; tchr., libr. rsch. tchr. Lawrence HS, Cedarhurst, NY, 1982—. Contbr. chpts. in books and articles to mags. and newspapers. Vice chair N.Y. Dem. Com., N.Y.C. and Albany, 1982-94; mem. del. selection com. N.Y. State Dem. Com., N.Y.C., 1987, 91; bd. dirs. Citizen Action in N.Y., 1990—94; mem. Gov. Cuomo's Fact-Finding Panel on the Shoreham Nuclear Power Plant, 1983-84; chair L.I. Citizens in Action, 1978—; convenor L.I. Pub. Power Project, chair, 1980-88; mem. L.I. Studies Coun.; bd. dirs. L.I. Progressive Coalition, 1979-88. Named Citizen Activist of Month, Ralph Nader's Pub. Citizen, 1984; recipient Leadership award L.I. Progressive Coalition, 1987, others. Mem. N.Y. Hist. Soc., Lawrence Tchrs. Assn. (v.p., press officer, local polit. action dir., v.p.), N.Y. State United Tchrs./Am. Fedn. Tchrs. (union del. 1988—92, mem. com., chmn. adv. coun. Nassau sch. libr. sys., 1997-2000). Avocations: walking, travel, reading, writing, politics. Home: 62 Elinore Ave Merrick NY 11566-4214 Personal E-mail: marjhar@optonline.net.

HARRISON, MARK B., lawyer; b. Bronx, NY, Feb. 20, 1953; BA, SUNY, 1973; JD, Rutgers U., 1977. Bar: Pa. 1977, US Ct. of Customs and Patent Appeals 1977, DC 1982, US Dist. Ct., DC, US Patent and Trademark Office. Former examining atty. US Patent and Trademark Office, 1977—81; ptnr., chair trademark group Venable LLP, Washington, 1982—. Mem.: ABA, Pa. Bar Assn., DC Bar Assn. Office: Venable LLP 575 7th St NW Washington DC 20004 Office Phone: 202-344-4019. Office Fax: 202-344-8300. Business E-Mail: mbharrison@venable.com.

HARRISON, MARK ISAAC, lawyer; b. Pitts., Oct. 17, 1934; s. Coleman and Myrtle (Seidenman) H.; m. Ellen R. Gier, June 15, 1958; children: Lisa, Jill. AB, Antioch Coll., Yellow Springs, Ohio, 1957; LLB, Harvard U., Cambridge, Mass., 1960. Bar: Ariz. 1961, Colo. 1991. Law clk. to justices Ariz. Supreme Ct., 1960-61; ptnr. Harrison, Harper, Christian & Dichter, Phoenix, 1966-93, Bryan Cave, LLP, Phoenix, 1993—2003, Osborn Maledon, P.A., Phoenix, 2004—. Adj. prof. U. Ariz. Coll. Law, 1995-97, Ariz. State Coll. Law, 2001—; nat. bd. visitors, 1996—; judge pro tem Ariz. Ct. Appeals, Maricopa County Superior Ct. Co-author: Arizona Appellate Practice, 1966; editl. bd. ABA/BNA Lawyers Manual on Profl. Conduct, 1983-86; contbr. articles to profl. jours. Chmn. Phoenix City bond Adv. Commn., 1976—79; pres. Valley Commerce Assn., 1978, Ariz. Friends of Talking Books, Inc., 2000—01; vice chmn. Maricopa County Dem. Cen. Com., 1967—68, Ariz. Dem. Com, 1969—70, legal counsel, 1970—72; del. Dem. Nat. Conv., 1968; bd. dir. Careers for Youth, 1963—67, pres., 1966—67; bd. dir. Planned Parenthood of Cen. and No. Ariz., 1992—98, pres., 1995; bd. dir. Ariz. Policy Forum, 2000—03. Recipient Peggy Goldwater award, Planned Parenthood, 2003, Planned Parenthood of Ctrl. and No. Ariz., 2003, Good Guys award, Ariz. Women's Polit. Caucus, 2004, Learned Hand Cmty. Svc. award, Am. Jewish Com., 2005, Disting. Hon. Alumni award, U. Ariz. Fellow: Am. Acad. Appellate Lawyers (pres. 1993—94), Am. Bar Found.; mem.: ABA (standing com. profl. discipline 1976—84, chmn. 1982—84, chmn. com. pub. understanding law 1984—87, chmn. coord. com. on professionalism 1987—89, com. on women in the profession, 1996-98, ethics com. 1999—2002, commn. Brown v. Bd. of Edn. 2003—04, chmn. joint com. Code of Judicial Conduct 2003—07, Michael Franck Profl. Responsibility award 1996), Justice for All (founding mem. 2005, pres. 2005—), Lawyers Com. for Civil Rights Under Law (bd. dirs.), Law Coll. Assn. U. Ariz. (bd. dir. 1999—2004, pres. 2002—03), Am. Law Inst. (lawyers com. for human rights nat. coun. 1995—), Harvard Law Sch. Assn. (nat. exec. coun. 1980—84), Ariz. Civil Liberties Union, Am. Judicature Soc. (exec. com. 1983—86, bd. dir. 1983—87), Western States Bar Conf. (pres. 1978—79), Nat. Conf. Bar Pres. (pres. 1976—77), Am. Inns of Ct. (master, pres. Sandra Day O'Connor chpt. 1993—94), Ariz. Bar Found. (pres. 1991, Walter E. Craig Disting. Svc. award 2002), State Bar Ariz. (bd. govs. 1971—77, pres. 1975—76), Am. Bd. Trial Advocates, Maricopa County Bar Assn. (pres. 1970), Assn. Profl. Responsibility Lawyers (pres. 1992—93). Office: Osborn Maledon PA 2929 N Central Ave Ste 2100 Phoenix AZ 85012 Office Phone: 602-640-9324. Personal E-mail: ellenmark1@cox.net. Business E-Mail: mharrison@omlaw.com.

HARRISON, MARVIN, professional football player; b. Phila., Aug. 25, 1972; s. Linda Harrison; 1 child, Marvin Jr. BS in Retailing, Syracuse U., NY, 1995. Wide receiver Indpls. Colts, 1996—. Named to Am. Football

Conf. Pro Bowl Team, 1999—2006, NFL All-Pro Team, 1999—2007. Achievements include holding NFL record for most receptions in one season (143), 2002; leading NFL in receptions, 2000, 2002, recieving yards, 1999, 2002; being the only player in NFL history to have four consecutive 100 or more reception seasons. Office: Indpls Colts 7001 W 56th St Indianapolis IN 46254*

HARRISON, MICHAEL, opera company director; b. Augusta, Ga., June 22, 1940; s. Oscar T. and Helen (Harrison) Smith. BA, Vanderbilt U., 1962; postgrad., Yale U., 1962-64. Actor, singer Broadway, Regional Opera and Theatres, 1964-80; gen. dir. Providence Opera Theatre, 1979-81, Opera/Columbus, Columbus, Ohio, 1983-89, Balt. Opera Co., 1989—. Pres. Harrison/Connor Consultants, L.A., 1981—83. Mem.: Md. Club., Rotary, Ctr. Club. Episcopalian. Office: Baltimore Opera Co Inc 110 W Mount Royal Ave Ste 306 Baltimore MD 21201-5732*

HARRISON, MICHAEL GREGORY, judge; b. Lansing, Mich., Aug. 4, 1941; s. Gus and Jean D. (Fuller) H.; m. Deborah L. Dunn, June 17, 1972; children: Abigail Ann, Adam Christopher, Andrew Stephen. AB, Albion Coll., Mich., 1963; JD, U. Mich., 1966; postgrad., Hague Acad. of Internat. Law, George Washington U. Bar: Mich. 1966, U.S. Dist. Ct. (ea. and we. dists.) Mich. 1967, U.S. Ct. Appeals (6th cir.). Asst. pros. atty. County of Ingham, Lansing, 1968-70, corp. counsel, 1970-76; judge 30th Jud. Cir. State of Mich., Lansing, 1976-2000; chief judge 30th Jud. Cir. State of Mich., Lansing, 1980-91; judge Ct. of Claims, 1979-2000; of counsel Foster, Swift, Collins and Smith, Lansing, 2000—. Counsel Capital Region Airport Authority, Lansing, 1970-76, Ingham Med. Ctr., Lansing, 1970-76; chmn. Ingham County Bldg. Authority, Mason, Mich., 1971-76; adj. prof. Thomas M. Cooley Law Sch., Lansing, 1976—. Editor Litigation Control, 1996; contbr. chpt. to Michigan Municipal Law, Actions of Governing Bodies, 1980; contbr. articles to profl. jours. Mem. shared vision steering com. United Way-C. of C.; mem. adv. bd. Hospice of Lansing; pres. Greater Lansing Urban League, 1974-76, Lansing Symphony Assn., 1974-76; chmn. Mid. Mich. chpt. ARC, Lansing, 1984-86; bd. dirs., sec. St. Lawrence Hosp., Lansing, 1980-88; bd. dirs. ARC Gt. Lakes Regional Blood Svcs., 1991-95, Lansing 2000, 1987-2000, Greater Lansing Symphony, 2002-, Mich. Supreme Ct. Hist. Soc.; mem. exec. bd. Chief Okemos coun. Boy Scouts Am., pres., 2003-05; mem. criminal justice adv. com. Olivet Coll.; hon. bd. dirs. Lansing Area Safety Coun.; mem. State Bar Bd. Commrs., 1993-96; chair State Bar Rep. Assembly; mem. felony sentencing guidelines steering com., chmn. caseflow mgmt. coordinating com., mem. juror use and mgmt. task force Mich. Supreme Ct.; mem. Mich. Supreme Ct. Hist. Soc.; mem. Mayor's Lansing Metro Regional Initiative. Recipient Disting. Citizens award Boy Scouts Am., Disting. Vol. award Ingham County Bar Assn., award of judicial excellence ABA, Disting. Alumni award Albion Coll., Mich. Super Lawters; named to Best Lawyers in Am. Fellow: Mich. Bar Found., Am. Bar Found.; mem.: ABA (Fund for Justice and Edn. coun. 2003—06, coun. mem. judicial divsn., coun. mem. tort and ins. practice sect., award of jud. excellence), Mich. State Bar Found. (pres. 1991—2000), Nat. Conf. State Trial Judges (exec. com. 1991—94, vice chmn. 1995—96, chmn. 1997—98), Mich. Judges Assn. (treas. 1991, sec. 1992, 2d v.p. 1993, 1st v.p. 1994, pres. 1995), Mich. State U. Am. Inn of Ct. (pres. 2001—03, master), Am. Judicature Soc. (bd. dirs. 1996—2002), Rotary Club, Lansing (pres. 2001—02), Country Club, Lansing. Avocations: skiing, golf, tennis, travel, photography. Office: 313 S Washington Sq Lansing MI 48933-2193 Office Phone: 517-371-8162. Business E-Mail: mharrison@fosterswift.com.

HARRISON, MICHAEL JAY, physicist, researcher; b. Chgo., Aug. 20, 1932; s. Nathan J. and Mae (Nathan) H.; m. Ann Tukey, Sept. 1, 1970. AB, Harvard, 1954; MS, U. Chgo., 1956, PhD, 1960. Fulbright fellow and H. Van Loon fellow in theoretical physics U. Leiden, Netherlands, 1954-55; NSF fellow U. Chgo., 1957-59; research fellow math. physics U. Birmingham, Eng., 1959-61; asst. prof. Mich. State U., East Lansing, 1961-63, assoc. prof., 1963-68, prof., 1968—, faculty grievance officer, 1972-73, dean Lyman Briggs Coll., 1973-81, adj. prof. epidemiology, 1993—, adj. prof. pediatrics and human devel., 2004—. Vis. research physicist Inst. Theoretical Physics, U. Calif., Santa Barbara, 1980-81; with Air Force Cambridge Research Center, summer 1953, M.I.T. Lincoln Lab., summer 1954, RCA Sarnoff Lab., summers 1961-63; physicist Westinghouse Labs., summer 1956; cons. RCA Lab., 1961-64, United Aircraft Co., 1964-66, U.K. Atomic Energy Authority, Harwell Lab., summer 1960, Thailand project in Bangkok, Mich. State U.-AID, summer 1968; vis. research affiliate theoretical biology and biophysics, Los Alamos Nat. Lab., 1987-88. Contbr. articles to U.S., fgn. profl. jours. Am. Council on Edn. fellow U. Calif., Los Angeles, 1970-71. Fellow Am. Phys. Soc.; mem. AAUP (chpt. treas. 1966-67), N.Y. Acad. Scis., Harvard Club of Ctrl. Mich. (pres. 1988-93), Rotary, B'nai B'rith, Phi Beta Kappa, Sigma Xi. Jewish. Avocations: hiking, travel, photography. Home: 277 Maplewood Dr East Lansing MI 48823-4746 Office: Mich State U Physics Dept East Lansing MI 48824 Home Phone: 517-337-7007; Office Phone: 517-355-9200 2205. E-mail: harrison@pa.msu.edu.

HARRISON, NEDRA JOYCE, surgeon; b. Buffalo, Apr. 16, 1951; d. Herman Lloyde and Gertrude (Newsom) H. BS, Rosary Hill Coll., 1973; MD, SUNY, Buffalo, 1977. Diplomate Am. Bd. Surgery. Resident in surgery Millard Fillmore Hosps., Buffalo, 1977-82, mem. active attending staff in gen. surgery, 1983—2000; practice medicine specializing in gen. surgery Buffalo, 1982—2000; courtesy staff Scottsdale (Ariz.) Healthcare, 2000—. Cons. staff Bry-Lyn Hosp., 1986-89; provisional staff in gen. surgery St. Joseph Intercommunity Hosp., 1986-87, active staff, 1995-2000; courtesy staff Scottsdale (Ariz.) Healthcare, Shea, Ariz., 2001—, Osborn, Ariz., 2001— Chmn. United Thank Offering, Episcopal Ch., Buffalo, 1982; bd. dirs. Niagara Luth. Home, 1987-2000; mem. alumni bd. dirs. SUNY at Buffalo Sch. Medicine, 1986-92. Recipient Best Rsch. Paper in Gen. Surgery award Millard Fillmore Hosps., 1978, 81. Fellow ACS; mem. AMA, Am. Med. Women's Assn., Maricopa County Med. Soc., Christian Med. Soc., Delta Epsilon Sigma. Episcopalian. Office: 10210 N 92nd St Scottsdale AZ 85258 Office Phone: 480-551-2528.

HARRISON, PATRICIA DE STACY, broadcast executive, former federal agency administrator; b. NYC; m. Emmett Bruce Harrison; 3 children. BA, Am. U., 1968; MA, George Mason U.; PhD (hon.), Am. U., 2002. V.p. Holly Realty Co., Arlington, Va., 1965-69; co-founder, ptnr. E. Bruce Harrison Co., Washington, 1973—96; former pres. AEF/Harrison Internat., Washington; asst. sec. edn. & cultural affairs U.S. Dept. State, Washington, 2001—05, acting sec. pub. diplomacy & pub. affairs, 2004; pres., CEO Corp. for Pub. Broadcasting, Washington, 2005—. Keynote spkr. U.S. Dept. Labor del. to Israel and Greece, Indsl. Devel. Authority of Ireland Conf./Women Execs. in Mgmt., U.S. Info. Agy./WorldNET program for entrepreneurs via satellite to 7 countries, Export Expo '90, Seattle, Nat. Govs. Conf., U.S. SBA Fin. Mgmt. Conf. in 9 states, mgmt. and tng. program for women entrepreneurs Budapest, Hungary (Alliance Decade for Democracy series); guest lect. Thomas Colloquium on Free Enterprise, 1989; trustee Guest Svcs., Inc.; mem. adv. coun. Avon Products, Inc. Author: Inside and Out: The Story of a Hostage, 1981, (with Margaret Mason, editor) The Washington Post Pocket Style Plus, 1983-84, America's New Women Entrepreneurs, 1986. Bd. dirs. Med. Coll. Pa. Recipient Librs.' and Tchrs.' award for play produced at Kennedy Ctr., 1980, Del. award Insieme per La Pace, Rome, 1988, Disting. Woman award Northwood Inst., 1991; named Washington Woman of Yr., Washington Women Mag., 1985, Entrepreneur of Yr., Washington, Arthur Young Co. and Venture mag., 1988, Women of Enterprise award. Mem. Nat. Women's Econ. Alliance Found., Pres.'s Export Coun., SBA Nat. Adv. Coun. (co-chmn., exec. com.), SBA Women's Network for Entrepreneurial Tng. (adv. coun.), Nat. Coal Coun. (exec. com.), Women in Internat. Trade, Nat. Fedn. Press Women (ex-officio, communication award 1979, bus. communicator of yr. 1988), Capital Press Women (ex-officio, named bus communicator of yr. 1988, journalist award for non-fiction 1988), Pub. Rels. Soc. Am. (counsellors acad.), Internat. Pub. Rels. Assn. Office: Corporation Public Broadcasting 401 Ninth St NW Washington DC 20004-2129 Office Phone: 202-879-9600.

HARRISON, PATRICK WOODS, lawyer; b. St. Louis, July 14, 1946; s. Charles William and Carolyn (Woods) Harrison; m. Rebecca Tout, Dec. 23, 1967; children: Heather Ann, Heath Aaron. BS, Ind. U., 1968, JD, 1972. Bar: Ind. 1973, U.S. Dist. Ct. (so. dist.) Ind. 1973, U.S. Supreme Ct. 1977, U.S. Dist. Ct. Nebr. 1982. Assoc. Goltra, Cline, King & Beck, Columbus, Ind., 1972-73; ptnr. Goltra & Harrison, Columbus, 1973-78; pvt. practice Columbus, 1979-80; ptnr. Cline, King, Beck and Harrison, Columbus, 1980-85, Beck Harrison (formerly Beck, Harrison & Dalmbert), Columbus, 1985—. Ind. Nominating Commn. nominee Ind. Supreme Ct., 1984. With US Army, 1968—70. Fellow: Ind. Trial Lawyers Assn. (bd. dirs. 1984, emertitus dir. 1999, Co-Trial Lawyer of the Yr. 1999); mem.: Am. Trial Lawyers Assn. Republican. Baptist. Avocation: golf. Home: 14250 W Mount Healthy Rd Columbus IN 47201-9309 Office: Beck Harrison 320 Franklin St Columbus IN 47201-6732 Office Phone: 812-372-8858. Personal E-mail: pharrison@hughes.net. Business E-Mail: woodyh@beckharrison.com.

HARRISON, PAULA JEAN, church musician; b. Kansas City, Mo., May 9, 1949; d. Lester Irving and Isabelle Marie (Entsminger) Mast; m. Gerald Wayne Waltz, Aug. 23, 1970 (div. Nov. 1992); children: Matthew Amos Waltz, Amy Elizabeth Waltz; m. Paul Douglas Harrison, Dec. 20, 1997. Student, Ind. U., 1970, Perkins Sch. Theology, 2004—, Our Lady of Lake U., 2005—. Ordained minister United Meth. Ch., 2005. Tchr. piano, flute Paula Waltz Music Studio, Houston, 1982—92; tchr. music The Kinkaid Sch., Houston, 1983—89; accompanist Houston Bapt. U., 1989—90; dir. music Richmond Plaza Bapt. Ch., Bellaire, Tex., 1990—92; accompanist Tex. Music Educators Assn. Dist. IX Honor Choir, 1994—97; choir accompanist Conroe H.S., Tex., 1992—98; tchr. piano Paula Harrison's Music Studio, Conroe, 1992—2004; organist, chirldrens choir dir. First United Meth. Ch., Conroe, 1996—2004; rehearsal pianist Montgomery County Choir Soc., Conroe, 1996—2004; dir. music and fine arts Cedar Bayou United Meth. Ch., Baytown, Tex., 2004—. Flutist Webster Groves Symphony Orch., 1966—67, performer, flutist St. Louis All-County Double Woodwind Quintet, 1966—67, performer, accompanist Annie - Class Act Productions, 1998, performer, flutist Gypsy - Crighton Theater, 1996, Nunsense - Crighton Theater, 1995. Fl. gov. Ind. U. Wilkie Dorm, 1968—69, female v.p., 1969—70; mem. childrens and dirs. workshop planning com. An August Adventure; active Baytown Area Missionary Alliance; chaplain Sigma Alpha Iota, Ind. U., 1968—69; organist Grace Luth. Ch., Conroe, Tex., 1992—95; bd. dirs. Tex. Conf. Choir Clinic, Baytown Interfaith Hospitality Network. Recipient Am. Band Master's award, Phi Beta Mu-Lambda Chpt., 1966. Mem.: Tex. Conf. Choir (bd. dirs.), Tex. Music Educators Assn., Jr. Music Club, Tex. Fedn. of Music Clubs, Houston Chorister Guild (pres. 2004—), Huntsville Music Tchrs Assn. (pres. 2001—04), Am. Assn. of English Handball Ringers, Sigma Alpha Iota, Ind. U. (pres. 1969—70). Republican. Methodist. Avocations: reading, needlecrafts, walking, swimming. Home: 2205 French Pl Baytown TX 77520

HARRISON, PETE (ROBERT E. HARRISON), tobacco company executive; b. 1954; BA, High Point, 1976; MBA, Wake Forest, 1978. With R.J. Reynolds Tobacco Internat., 1978—95; sr. v.p., CFO Standard Comml. Corp., 1995—98, pres., CEO, 1996—2005, chmn., 2003—05; pres. Alliance One Internat., Inc., Morrisville, NC, 2005—, COO, 2005—06, CEO, 2007—. Bd. dirs. Alliance One Internat., Inc., 2005—. Office: Alliance One International Inc 8001 Aerial Ctr Pkwy PO Box 2009 Morrisville NC 27560-2009 Office Phone: 919-379-4300. Office Fax: 919-379-4346.*

HARRISON, PRESTON ERSHEL, JR., neurologist; b. Houston, Aug. 6, 1944; s. Preston Ershel Harrison Sr. and Melba Kathyrin Tipton; m. Marsha Sue Yarberry, June 21, 1971; children: Kristofer Lee, Robert Randle. BA, Tex. Tech U., Lubbock, 1966; MD, Baylor U., Houston, 1970. Diplomate Am. Bd. Psychiatry and Neurology, Am. Bd. Electrodiagnostic Medicine. Clin. prof. neurology Southwestern Med. Sch., Dallas, 1973—78; clin. practice neurology East Tex. Neurology, Tyler, 1978—. Named Tex. Super Dr., Tex. Monthly, 2005, 2006. Mem.: Tex. Neurol. Soc. (pres.), Tex. Med. Assn. Methodist. Avocations: amateur radio, mathematics, electronics. Home: 2104 Parkway Pl Tyler TX 75701 Office: East Tex Neurology 1301 Doctors Dr Tyler TX 75701

HARRISON, RACHEL, artist; b. NYC, 1966; One-woman shows include Posh Floored as Ali G Tackles Beck, Galerie Arndt & Ptnr., 2004, Brides & Bases, Oakville Galleries, Can., 2002, Look of Dress-Separates, Greene Naftali Gallery, NYC, 1997, Should Home Windows, Arena Gallery, Bklyn., 1996, exhibited in group shows at Dreams & Conflicts: Dictatorship of Viewer, La Biennale di Venezia, Venice, 2003, Experimenters, Lombard-Freid Fine Arts, NYC, 1997, Rachel Harrison & Michael Lazarus, Feature, NYC, 1996, Space, Mind, Place, Andrea Rosen Gallery, NY, 1996, Summer Exhbn., Greene Naftali Gallery, NY, 1996, Sex, Drugs & Explosives, New London Art Forms, London, 1996, Sculpture Incorporating Photog., Feature Gallery, NY, 1996, Post Hoc, Stark Gallery, NY, 1996, Facing the Millennium: The Song Remains the Same, Arlington Mus., Tex., 1996, Oy, 121 Greene St., NY, 1995, High Anxiety, 66 Crosby, NY, 1995, Looky Loo, Sculpture Ctr., NY, 1995, Dark Room, Stark Gallery, NY, 1995, Unsuccess, 479 Broome St., NY, 1994, Tight, Tannery Gallery, London, 1994, Dirty, John Good Gallery, NY, 1994, I Could Do That, 109 Spring St., NY, 1994, Poverty Pop: Aesthetics of Necessity, Exit Art, NY, 1993, Resurrections, William Benton Mus. Art, U. Conn., 1993, Benefits for Four Walls Gallery, David Zwirner Gallery, NY, 1993, Shooting Blanks, 81 Greene St., NY, 1993, 1920: Subtlety of Subversion, Continuity of Intervention, Exit Art, NY, 1993, Simply Made in Am., Aldrich Mus. Contemporary Art, 1993, I Was Born Like This, Mulberry St. Gallery, NY, 1993, Morality Cafe, Postmasters Gallery, NY, 1993, Unlearning, 142 Greene St., NY, 1991, Open Bar, Flamingo East, NY, 1991. Mailing: c/o Greene Naftali Gallery 526 West 26th St New York NY 10001

HARRISON, RICHARD WAYNE, lawyer; b. Marfa, Tex., June 23, 1944; AA, Schreiner U., 1964; BBA, U. Tex., Austin, 1966; JD, U. Tex. Sch. Law, 1968. Ptnr. Florence & Harrison, Hughes Springs, Tex., 1968-69; pvt. practice Hughes Springs, Tex., 1969-73; asst. atty. gen. Atty. Gen.'s Office of Tex., Austin, 1973-74, chief tax divsn., 1974-76, spl. asst. atty. gen., 1976-78; ptnr. McGinnis, Lochridge & Kilgore, Austin, 1978-87, Jones, Day, Reavis & Pogue, Austin, 1987-94; mng. ptnr. Harrison & Rial LLP, Austin, 1994—2000; owner Rick Harrison & Assocs., Austin, 2000—02; ptnr. Fritz, Byrne, Head & Harrison LLP, Austin, 2002—. Pres. Hughes Springs Indsl. Found., 1970; Cass County chmn. Salvation Army, 1970—72; chmn. Hughes Springs United Fund Drive, 1972; mem. Austin Convocation Cursillo Steering Com., 1983—86, chmn., 1985—86; precinct chmn. Cass County Dem. Com., 1969—73; area coord. Lloyd Bentsen for Senate Com., 1970; trustee, treas. St. Andrew's Episcopal Sch., Austin; sr. warden St. Luke's-on-the-Lake Episcopal Ch., 1984. Named a Tex. Super Lawyer Comml. Litig., 2007; named one of 500 Leading Plaintiffs Lawyers in Am., 2007; named to Best Lawyers in Am., 2007. Fellow: Tex. Bar Found. (life); mem.: Schreiner Coll. Former Student Assn. (bd. dirs. 1984—88), Cass County Bar Assn. (past pres.), Travis County Bar Assn., State Bar of Tex. (fed. jud. com. 1980—83, bar jour. com. 1980—83), Barton Creek Country Club, Masons. Democrat. Home: 1730 Camp Craft Rd Austin TX 78746-7317 Office: Fritz Byrne Head & Harrison LLP 98 San Jacinto Blvd Ste 2000 Austin TX 78701 Office Phone: 512-476-2020.

HARRISON, ROBERT ALLEN, retired operations research analyst; m. Joyce Eleanor Amirikian, Sept. 9, 1961; children: Lynda Joy, Robert Amirikian. AB, Harvard U., 1951; MS, George Washington U., Washington, 1982. Ops. rsch. analyst, editor, writer, 1956—90; pres. Harrison and Co., Fairfax, Va., 1990—97, Harrison Aerospace Corp., Fairfax, 1997—2001; ret., 2001. Dir. Am.-Russian Tech. Exch. Ctr., Washington, 1991—93; investor, 2001—. Author: Analysis of Future Naval Weapons Systems, 1969, Aircraft Production and Development Schedules, 1982, Prediction and Prevention of Failures of Avionics and Sensors, 1990; editor: Handbook of Reliability Engineering, 1994. Fellowship, U. Rochester, 1970—71. Mem.: Inst. Ops. Rsch. and Mgmt. Sci., Cavalier Golf and Yacht Club, Harvard Club of Washington (v.p. 1994—95). Home: 8909 Glenbrook Rd Fairfax VA 22031 Home (Summer): 303 Atlantic Ave Virginia Beach VA 23451 Office Phone: 703-280-2202. Personal E-mail: raha888@cox.net.

HARRISON, ROBERT POGUE, literature educator; b. Izmir, Turkey; BA in Humanities, Univ. Santa Clara, 1976; PhD in Romance Studies, Cornell Univ., 1984. Vis. asst. prof., dept. French, Italian Stanford Univ., 1985—86, asst. prof., 1986—92, prof., 1995—97, Rosina Pierotti Chair, 1997—, and chmn., dept. French, Italian, 2002—. Fellow: Am. Acad. Arts & Scis. Office: 121 Pigott Hall Stanford Univ 515 Gerona Rd Stanford CA 94305 Office Phone: 650-723-4204. Business E-Mail: harrison@stanford.edu.*

HARRISON, ROBERT WARD, retired surgeon; b. Toledo, July 18, 1927; s. Robert William and Margaret Ward Harrison; m. Lynette Gene Baumann, Aug. 1, 1949; children: Robert Wayne(dec.) , Renee Lynn Ryan, Lisa Gene Shvart, Randal Ward. BA in Zoology, State U. Iowa, Iowa City, 1949, MS in Physiology, 1953, MD, 1953. Intern U. Chgo. Clinics, 1953—54, resident gen. surgery, 1954—58, resident thoracic surgery, 1958—60, asst. prof. surgery, 1960—62; pvt. practice thoracic and cardiovasc. surgery Grand Rapids, Mich., 1962—96; ret., 1996. Med. dir. Hospice Western Mich., Grand Rapids, 1990—96. With USN, 1945—47. Recipient Frederick Christopher award, Chgo. Surg. Soc., 1960. Fellow: ACS (Rsch. scholar 1960); mem.: Soc. Thoracic Surgeons (sr.), Am. Assn. Thoracic Surgeons (sr.). Home: 2044 Lake Pointe Dr SE East Grand Rapids MI 49506 Office: Western Mich Cardio-Thoracic Surgeons 1900 Wealthy St SE Grand Rapids MI 49506

HARRISON, S. DAVID, lawyer; b. NYC, Jan. 29, 1930; s. Louis and Molly (Ginsburg) Harrison; m. Joan S. Horowitz, Mar. 23, 1958 (dec. May 1993); children: Andrew L., Rachel E.; m. Roberta S. Karmel, Oct. 29, 1995. AB, Harvard U., 1951, LLB, 1954; LLM, NYU, 1959. Bar: NJ 1955, NY 1968. Law sec. to Hon. William J. Brennan, Jr. N.J. Supreme Ct., 1954-55; from assoc. to ptnr. Platoff, Platoff & Heftler, Union City, NJ, 1955-65; corp. counsel Beaunit Corp., NYC, 1965-71, corp. sec., 1966-71; asst. sec. Tyrex, Inc., 1969-71; dir. Man-Made Fibers Prodrs. Assn., 1970-71; pvt. practice law NYC, 1971—; of counsel Rosen & Livingston. Bd. dirs. various corps.; mem. panel arbitrators N.Y. Stock Exch. Chmn. zoning bd. Village Hastings-on-Hudson, 1988—98; bd. dirs. Am. Friends Sarah Herzog Hosp. Jerusalem, 1992—; trustee Gallery at Hastings, NY, 1993—97. Mem.: ABA, Am. Arbitrators Assn., Nat. Panel Arbitrators, N.Y. State Bar Assn., Harvard Club Westchester, Harvard Club N.Y., Masons. Home: 66 Summit Dr Hastings On Hudson NY 10706-1215 Office: 275 Madison Ave New York NY 10016

HARRISON, STANLEY L., editor, educator, writer; s. Frank Imwold Harrison and Thelma Emma Baer; m. Frances June Keane, Nov. 22, 1956. BA, U. Md., College Park, 1955, MA, 1962; PhD, Am. U., DC, 1967. Sr. leader Inst. Def. Analyses, Washington, 1960—63; sr. analyst Rsch. Analysis Corp., Chevy Chase, Md., 1963—70; legis. asst. Ho. of Reps., Washington, 1971—73; assoc. editor Nat. Jour., Washington, 1973—76; dir., corp. comm. Corp. for Pub. Broadcasting, Washington, 1976—85; prof. comms. U. Miami, Coral Gables, Fla., 1986—; editor Enoch Pratt Free Libr., Balt., 1999—. Author: (book) Cavalcade of Journalists 1900-2000, Mencken Revisited: Author, Editor & Newspaperman, Editorial Art of Edmund Duffy, Florida's Editorial Cartoonists; editor: a.k.a. H.L. Mencken: Selected Pseudonymous Writings, Menckeniana, 2002, Robert Benchley's The Wayward Press, 2007. Chmn. Dem. State Ctrl. Com., Howard County, 1960—63. Airman 1st class USAF, 1950—53. Decorated Silver Medal award US Naval Inst.; recipient Writer of Merit, Mil. Rev., 1965, Gov.'s Citizenship award, Gov. of Md., 1974; Wilton Pk. Fellow, Fgn. Office, 1969, Pub. Affairs Fellowship, Stanford U., 1970-72. Mem.: Internat. Inst. for Strategic Studies, Nat. Press Club, Mencken Soc., Pi Sigma Alpha, Pi Delta Epsilon, Pi Alpha Theta, Omicron Delta Kappa, Sigma Delta Chi. Protestant. Avocation: reading. Home: 5783 SW 40th St 221 Miami FL 33155 Office Phone: 305-284-2265. Personal E-mail: menckeniana@earthlink.net.

HARRISON, STEPHEN COPLAN, biochemist, educator; b. New Haven, June 4, 1943; s. Harold E. and Helen Miriam (Coplan) H. AB in Chemistry and Physics, Harvard Coll., 1963; PhD in Biophysics, Harvard U., 1968. Helen Hay Whitney postdoctoral rsch. fellow Children's Cancer Rsch. Found., Boston, 1967—68, rsch. assoc. pathology, 1969—71; rsch. fellow biophysics Harvard U., 1967—68, jr. fellow Soc. Fellows, 1968—71, asst. prof. biochemistry, 1971—75, assoc. prof., 1975—77, prof. biochemistry and molecular biology, 1977—98, prof. biol. chemistry and molecular pharmacology, 1996—, Higgins prof. biochemistry, 1998—2002; investigator Howard Hughes Med. Inst., 1987—; dir. Ctr. Structural Biology Harvard Med. Sch., 1996—2002, prof. pediat., 1996—; head Lab. Molecular Medicine Children's Hosp., Boston, 1996—, dir. Ctr. Molecular and Cellular Dynamics, 2002—. Vis. rsch. assoc. biophysics Max-Planck Inst., 1971—72; vis. prof. biology U. Heidelberg, 1971—72; non-resident tutor Lowell House Harvard U., 1971—, chmn. bd. tutors biochemical scis., 1971—96, chmn. dept. biochemistry and molecular biology, 1988—92; vis. fellow commoner Trinity Coll., Cambridge, England, 1977; vis. scientist MRC Lab. Molecular Biology, Cambridge, England, 1977; acting head tutor biochemical scis., 2000—01. Contbr. articles to sci. jours.; mem. editl. bd.: Structure, 1993—, Cell, 2001—. Recipient Wallace P. Rowe award, Nat. Inst. Allergy and Infectious Diseases, 1988, Louisa Gross Horwitz prize, Columbia U., 1990, ICN Internat. Prize in Virology, 1998, Paul Ehrlich and Ludwig Darmstaedter prize, 2001, U. Calif. San Diego/Merck Life Scis. Achievement award, 2007. Fellow Am. Acad. Arts & Scis.; mem. AAAS, NAS, Am. Philos. Soc., Am. Soc. Microbiol., Am. Soc. Virology, Am. Crystallographic Assn., European Molecular Biology Orgn. (assoc.). Office: BCMP Harvard Med Sch Seeley G Mudd 130 250 Longwood Ave Boston MA 02115 Fax: 617-432-5600. E-mail: schadmin@crystal.harvard.edu.*

HARRISON, THOMAS FLATLEY, lawyer, environmental consultant; b. NYC, Jan. 11, 1942; s. John P. and Mary F. (Flatley) H.; m. Lorraine Brereton, Aug. 16, 1969; children: John J., Jane C., Ann B., Peter T. AB, Holy Cross Coll., 1963; JD, Fordham U., 1966. Bar: N.Y. 1967, Ill. 1979, Ohio 1981, D.C. 1988, Conn. 1989. Asst. counsel NYC Dept. Rent and Housing, 1966-69; asst. atty. gen. NY State Dept. Law, 1969-74; chief enforcement N.Y. region US EPA, 1974-76, regional counsel Chgo., 1976-80; sr. corp. counsel B.F. Goodrich Co., Akron, Ohio, 1980-87; ptnr. Manatt, Phelps, Rothenberg & Evans, Washington, 1987-88; ptnr., co-chmn. environ. and land use dept. Day, Berry & Howard LLP, Hartford, Conn., 1988—2006; environ. cons. The Hartford Ins. Group, 2007—.

Faculty Practising Law Inst. Contbr. articles to profl. jours. Mem. 49th Assembly Dist. Rep. Orgn., N.Y.C., 1963-73, bd. govs., 1969-73; active Silver Lake, Ohio, Rep. Orgn., 1981-87; mem. Rep. Town Com., Avon, Conn., 1991—, Inland Wetlands Commn., Avon, 1992-95; mem. Bd. Fin. 1995—, chmn., 2002—; mem. Conn. Coun. on Environ. Quality, 1997—, chmn., 2004—; mem. Conn. Small Bus. Compliance Adv. Panel, 1996—; bd. dirs. Conn. League of Conservation Voters, 2000—, Nat. Audubon Conn. 2001-07. Recipient Outstanding Performance award EPA, 1976. Mem. Conn. Bar Assn. (exec. com. environ. law sect. 1989—, sect. chair 1998-99, Clyde Fisher award 2006). Republican. Roman Catholic. Home: 51 Briar Hill Rd Avon CT 06001-4007 Office Phone: 860-547-4864. Personal E-mail: tfh101@sbcglobal.net.

HARRISON, TODD A., lawyer; b. Duarte, Calif., Apr. 16, 1962; BS magna cum laude, U. Houston, Clear Lake, 1989; JD with honors, U. Tulsa Coll., 1993. Bar: Tex. 1993, Md. 1994, DC 1999. Ptnr. Buchanan Ingersoll PC, Washington; ptnr., food and drug group Venable LLP, Washington, 2004—. Author: (articles) Introducing New Dietary Ingredients, 2002, The Cholestin Case: The Ongoing Saga, 2002, FDA's Proposed Rule for Dietary Supplement cGMPs, 2003. Recipient Am. Jurisprudence award. Office: Venable LLP 575 7th St NW Washington DC 20004 Office Phone: 202-344-4724. Office Fax: 202-344-8300. Business E-Mail: taharrison@venable.com.

HARRISON, WALTER ASHLEY, physicist, researcher; b. Flushing, NY, Apr. 26, 1930; s. Charles Allison and Gertrude (Ashley) H.; m. Lucille Prince Carley, July 17, 1954; children: Richard Knight, John Carley, William Ashley, Robert Walter. B. Engring. Physics, Cornell U., 1953; MS, U. Ill., 1954, PhD, 1956. Physicist Gen. Elec. Research Labs., Schenectady, 1956-65; prof. applied physics Stanford (Calif.) U., 1965-2001, prof. emeritus, 2001—, chmn. applied physics dept., 1989-93, prof. emeritus, 2001—. Scientific adv. bd. Max Planck Inst., Stuttgart, Germany, 1989-92. Author: Pseudopotentials in the Theory of Metals, 1966, Russian transl., 1968, Solid State Theory, 1970, Chinese transl., Polish transl., 1976, Electronic Structure and the Properties of Solids, 1980, Russian transl., 1983, Japanese transl., 1986, Elementary Electronic Structure, 1999, revised edit., 2004, Applied Quantum Mechanics, 2000; editor: the Fermi Surface, 1960, Proceedings of the International Conference on the Physics of Semiconductors, 1985, Proceedings of the International Conference on Materials and Mechanisms of High-Temperature Superconductivity, 1989. Guggenheim fellow, 1970-71; recipient von Humboldt sr. U.S. scientist award, 1981, 89, 94; vis. fellow Clare Hall, Cambridge U., 1970-71. Fellow Am. Phys. Soc.; mem. European Phys. Soc. Home: 817 San Francisco Ct Stanford CA 94305-1021 Office: Stanford U Dept Applied Physics Stanford CA 94305-4045 Home Phone: 650-857-0807; Office Phone: 650-723-4224. E-mail: walt@stanford.edu.

HARRISON, WALTER LEE, university president; b. Pitts., May 15, 1946; s. Lester Maurice and Alice Hagedorn (Cohen) H.; m. Dianne Ellen Mintz, June 22, 1970. BA, Trinity Coll., 1968; MA, U. Mich., 1969; PhD, U. Calif., Davis, 1980. Lectr. Johannes Gutenberg U., Mainz, Germany, 1976-77; instr. Iowa State U., Ames, 1978-80, Colo. Coll., Colorado Springs, 1980-82, dir. coll. rels., 1982-85; pres. Gehrung Assocs., Keene, NH, 1985-89; exec. dir., v.p. univ. rels. U. Mich., Ann Arbor, 1989-98; pres. U. Hartford, West Hartford, 1998—. Vis. prof. Colo. Coll., 1988-91; adj. prof. U. Mich., 1991-98. Contbr. articles to profl. jours. Trustee Fountain Valley Sch., 1990-99; bd. dirs. Univ. Musical Soc., 1990-98, Mich. Journalism Fellow Program, 1991-98; dir. St. Francis Hosp. and Med. Ctr., 1998—, Hartford Stage Co., 2000-07, Hartford Symphony Orch. 1998-; trustee Suffield Acad., 2002-; bd. dirs. divsn. I, NCAA, 2002-07, chair com. on acad. performance, 2004-, chair exec. com., 2005-07. Mem. Phi Kappa Phi. Avocations: baseball, recreational sports. Office: Univ of Hartford 200 Bloomfield Ave West Hartford CT 06117-1599 Office Phone: 860-768-4417. Business E-Mail: horky@hartford.edu.

HARRISON, WILLIAM BURWELL, JR., retired diversified financial services company executive; b. Rocky Mount, NC, Aug. 12, 1943; s. William Burwell and Katherine (Spruill) Harrison; m. Anne MacDonald Stephens, Dec. 7, 1985; children: Katherine Adams, Anne Stephens. AB in Econs., U. N.C., Chapel Hill, 1966, spl. student in bus. adminstrn., 1966-67; Sr. Mgmt. Program, Harvard Bus. Sch., Vevey, Switzerland, 1979. Trainee Chem. Bank, NYC, 1967-69, Mid-South corp. and corr. banking group, 1969-74, West Coast corp. and corr. banking group, 1974-76, dist. head, Western regional coord. San Francisco, 1976-78, regional coord., sr. v.p. London, 1978-82, sr. v.p., divsn. head Europe, 1982-83, exec. v.p. U.S. corp. divsn. NYC, 1983-87, group exec. banking and corp. fin. group, 1987-90, vice chmn. instl. banking, 1990—94; vice chmn. Global Bank, NYC, 1992—99, Chase Manhattan Corp., NYC, 1995—99, pres., CEO, 1999, chmn., CEO, 2000; pres., CEO J.P. Morgan Chase & Co., NYC, 2000—01, CEO, 2001—05, chmn., 2001—06. Bd. dirs. Merck & Co., Inc., Whitehouse Station, NJ, Cousins Properties, Inc., Atlanta; mem. bd. advisors N.C. Outward Bound Sch., Asheville. Bd. overseers Sloan-Kettering Cancer Ctr., 1999—; bd. visitors Kenan Flagler Bus. Sch. Mem.: Bus. Coun., Fin. Svcs. Roundtable, Augusta Nat. Golf Club, Nat. Golf Links Am., Golf Club Purchase, Field Club Greenwich, Links Club, Racquet Club, Blind Brook Club, Round Hill Club. Episcopalian. Avocations: athletics, travel.*

HARRISON, WILLIAM HENRY, retired medical educator; b. Aberdeen, SD, Feb. 24, 1924; s. William Henry Sr. and Catherine Marie (McMasters) Harrison; m. Mary Anne Peavy (div.); children: Karen, William, Thomas, Kenneth. Student, Washington U., St. Louis, 1943—44, Harvard U., 1944—45; BA in Chemistry, U. Minn., 1948, MS in Biochemistry, 1952, PhD in Biochemistry, 1954; postgrad., Columbia U., 1958—62. Sr. biochemist Eli Lilly Rsch. Lab., Indpls., 1954—58; neurochemistry rschr. NIH, Bethesda, Md., 1963—64; asst. prof. Chgo. Med. Sch., 1963—64, U. Ill., Chgo., 1964—68; assoc. prof. Rush Med. Ctr., Chgo., 1968—71, Rush. Med. Coll., Chgo., 1971—73, prof., 1973—98, prof. emeritus, 1998—. Asst. dir. minority med. edn. programs Chgo.-Rush-Robert Wood Johnson Ill. Inst. Tech., 1987—96. Contbr. chapters to books, articles to profl. jours. With USAAF, 1943—46. Recipient Mark Lepper MD Soc. Tchrs. award, Rush Med. Coll., 1986, James Campbell MD Disting. Svc. Alumni award, 1997; Rsch. grantee, NIH, 1963—88, Chgo. Heart Assn., 1963—69. Avocations: camping, fishing, dance, reading, writing. Home: 11715 Olde English Dr Apt A Reston VA 20190 Personal E-mail: wharr0224@yahoo.com.

(PICKETT) HARRISON FLINT, NANCY ELIZABETH, retired medical administrator; b. Worcester, Mass., Feb. 24, 1941; d. Thornton Webster and Dorothy Stearns (Gallagher) Pickett; m. Albert Gordon Flint, June 20, 1992; m. George Couper Harrison, Dec. 23, 1961; children: David George Harrison, Susan Elizabeth Fothergill Harrison, Paul Richard Harrison. Degree, Lasell Coll., Newton, Mass., 1961. Cert. tchr. med. assisting and med. office mgmt. The Bryman Sch., Brookline, Mass. Adminstr. continuing med. edn. courses Harvard Med. Sch. tchg. hosps. Mass. Gen. Hosp., Boston, 1980—96; ret., 1996. Notary pub. Notary Law Inst., Mass., Fla.; secret security clearance The Mitre Corp., Bedford, Mass.; chpt. pres. Profl. Sec. Internat., Boston; tchr. med. terminology divsn. continuing edn. Marian Ct. Jr. Coll., Swampscott, Mass.; ret.; state regent Fla. State Soc., Daughters Am. Colonists; past regent DAR, Colonial Dames XVII Century. Mem. Air Response Team SW Fla, Cape Coral; vol. officer Cape Coral Police Dept.; dir. Woodcrest Comm. Corp., Chelmsford, Mass.; with grand chpt. Mass. Order Ea. Star Mass., Newton; elected dir. Charitable Found. Inc., Newton; elected dir. edni. found. Order Ea. Star Mass., past matron Puritan Ch. Lowell, past matron Laurel Hill Ch. Newburyport. Mem.: Bus. and Profl. Women's Assn., DAR, Colonial Dames of the XVII Century, Daughters of Am. Colonists. R-Conservative. Protestant Congregational. Home: 3827 S E 2nd Pl Cape Coral FL 33904-4816 Home Phone: 239-549-0995. Personal E-mail: nanphf@aol.com.

HARRISON-JERVAY, EVELYN YVONNE, publishing executive; b. Macon, NC, Mar. 7, 1945; d. John Andrew and Sallie Elizabeth (Somerville) Harrison; m. Paul Reginald Jervay, July 24, 1989; children: Nikki, Shenay, Adria, Kelvin; m. Roy Dunston, Jan. 28, 1961 (div. Apr. 1980); children: Sylvia, Sharon, Kerry, Sonja. AA, Am. Coll., 1972, AA survey of adv. sales, 1974, AA bus. taxation, 1976; div. requirement, Shaw Div. Sch., 1985. Supr. First Nat. City Bank, NY, 1963—72; ins. agt. Mut. of NY, 1972—76; self employed Evelyn's, Raleigh, NC, 1977—80; founder Nay-Kel Edn. Ctr., Raleigh, NC, 1980—, Nay-Kel Ministries, Warrenton, NC, 2001—; co-pub. Carolinian Newspaper, Raleigh, 1997—; pub. The Carolina Call, Raleigh, NC, 1994—. Recipient Trailblazer in Media award, 2d Dist. Ch., Va., 2003, Outstanding Media award, Am. Minority Media, 1998. Avocations: reading, tennis, art, thrift shopping. Office Phone: 919-834-5558. Office Fax: 919-832-3243. Personal E-mail: carolinian@mindspring.com.

HARRISS, CYNTHIA THERESE (CYNTHIA THERESE CLARKE), retail executive; b. Huntington, W. Va., June 12, 1952; d. Forbes Richard and Arlene (Will) Clarke. Buyer Scripps McCartney, Canton, Ill., 1972—73; store mgr. Paul Harris Stores, Cin., 1973—75, dist. mgr. St. Louis, 1975—77, regional mgr. Chgo., 1977—82, v.p. stores operation Indpls., 1982—85, v.p. div. mdse. mgr., 1985—89; sr. v.p. sales, Walt Disney Stores The Walt Disney Co., Glendale, Calif., 1992—97; sr. v.p. park ops. Disneyland Resort, The Walt Disney Co., Glendale, Calif., 1997—99, exec. v.p., 1999, pres., 1999—2003; pres., Gap Outlet stores The Gap Inc., San Francisco, 2004—05, pres., Gap Brand, 2005—. Bd. trustees Laguna Beach Playhouse. Recipient Internat. Disting. Leadership award, Jewish Nat. Fund, Tree of Life award, 2000. Mem.: Women's Leadership Bd., Harvard U., JFK Sch. Govt. Roman Catholic. Office: Gap Inc Two Folsom St San Francisco CA 94105

HARRIS-STOKES, JOYCE A., secondary school educator; b. Detroit, Dec. 22, 1954; d. Willie L. Sr. and Mary L. (Hightower) H.; m. Daniel T. Taylor, July 17, 1980 (div.); m. Vernon L. Stokes, July 11, 2002. BS in Math., Columbus State U., Ga., 1977, BS in Edn. and Math., 1979, MPA, 2007. Cert. math. tchr., Ga. Pvt. practice math. tutor, Columbus, Ga., 1974-78; news and sports editor The Saber, Columbus, 1975-77; math. tchr. Russell County Bd. Edn., Phenix City, Ala., 1979—, math. chairperson, 1981—. Adv. Jr. Honor Soc., 1980—84; dist. dir. SECME, 2000—; advisor Mu Alpha Theta, 2006—. Storyteller:; author: Zap Pow Pop-An Interdisciplinary Unit on Energy, 1992, Talents in Russell County; co-author: Tales and Poems from Grandma Tempie, 2003; co-author: (with Mary L. Hightower-Harris) Tales and Poems from Grandma Tempie-Angels, 2004, Tales and Poems from Grandma Tempie-Talents, 2006. Mem. Juvenile Justice Com., Russell County Com. for Change; vol. United Hospice, Ronald McDonald House. Mem.: ASCD, NEA (del. 2007), Russell County Edn. Assn. (pres.), Ga. Edn. Environ. Coun., Environ. Edn. Assn. Ala., Ala. Edn. Assn. (del. 2004—), Am. Math. Soc., Math. Assn. Am., Chattahoochee Coun. Tchrs. of Math., Ala. Coun. Tchrs. of Math. (adv. coun.), Nat. Fedn. State Poetry Socs. (legis. contact team), Ga. Poetry Soc. Baptist. Avocations: designing, photography, basketball, sewing, writing. Office: Russell County HS 4699 Old Seale Hwy Seale AL 36875-4006

HARROLD, BERNARD, lawyer; b. Wells County, Ind., Feb. 5, 1925; s. James Delmer and Marie (Mounsey) H.; m. Kathleen Walker, Nov. 26, 1952; children— Bernard James, Camilla Ruth, Renata Jane. Student, Biarritz Am. U., 1945; AB, Ind. U., 1949, LLB, 1951. Bar: Ill. 1951. Since practiced in, Chgo.; assoc., then mem. firm Kirkland, Ellis, Hodson, Chaffetz & Masters, 1951-67; sr. ptnr. Wildman, Harrold, Allen & Dixon, 1967—. Note editor: Ind. Law Jour, 1950-51; contbr. articles to profl. jours. Served with AUS, 1944-46, ETO. Fellow Am. Coll. Trial Lawyers, Acad. Law Alumni Fellows Ind. U. Sch. Law; mem. ABA, Ill. Bar Assn. (chmn. evidence program 1970), Chgo. Bar Assn, Lawyers Club, Univ. Club, Order of Coif, Phi Beta Kappa, Phi Eta Sigma. Home: 809 Locust St Winnetka IL 60093-1821 Office: Wildman Harrold Allen & Dixon 225 W Wacker Dr Fl 30 Chicago IL 60606-1229 *I try to see people and events for what they really are, apply my talents, work hard, and pay good attention to fairness.*

HARROLD, JOHN ANDREW, education educator, consultant; b. Ft. Wayne, Ind., July 11, 1937; s. Virgil Odell and Naomi Roth Harrold; m. Anna Margaret Kaserman; children: John Andrew Jr., Rebekah Ann Overbey. BS in Edn., Ind. U., 1961, MA in Geography & Sociology, 1967, MA in Polit. Sci., 1971; diploma in Civil Affairs, Civil Affairs Sch., US Army, 1966. Instr. and evaluation officer U. S. Army Q.m. Sch., Petersburg, Va., 1962—63; social studies tchr. Martinsville (Ind.) H.S., 1964—67; tchr. and dept. chair MSD of Lawrence Twp., Indpls., 1967—72; state social studies cons. Ind. Dept. Edn., Indpls., 1972—76, dir. of curriculum, 1976—85, spl. asst. for long-range planning, 1985—91, performance-based edn. cons., 1991—98; pres. 21st Century Learning Cmtys., Indpls., 1998—. Fellow social studies field agt. tng. program Ind. U., Bloomington, 1970—72; instr. Ind. U., Purdue U., Indpls., 1973—74; co-dir. Egypt studies program Ind. Consortium for Internat. Programs, Terre Haute, 1973—75; chairperson textbook adoptions Ind. State Bd. Edn., Indpls., 1984—90, exec. dir. 21st century schooling, 1984—91; prin. Gary (Ind.) Consulting Group, 1994—98; mgr. fwy. sch. program Ind. Dept. Edn., Indpls., 1996—98; edn. chairperson Indpls. Regional Transp. Coun., 1998—; dir. learning systems and techs. Keyway Assocs., Inc., Indpls., 1999—; bd. mem. East Ctrl. Ind. Chambers Partnership, Greenfield, 2000—; dir., cmtys. and new econs. Am.'s Nat. Rd. Corridors of Learning, Indpls., 2003—. Councilman, coun. pres., utilities bd. chair Cumberland (Ind.) Town Coun., 1995—2002; bd. mem. Hancock Econ. Devel. Coun., Greenfield, 1999—; redevel. task force Hancock Econ. Coun., 2006—; bd. dirs Soc. Advanced Study, Indian U., 2006—; candidate state supt. pub. instrn. Rep. Party, Ind., 1991—92. Maj. USAR, 1962—81. Named to Sagamore of the Wabash, Gov. State of Ind., 1998; recipient Exceptional Svc. award, Ind. Coun. Social Studies, 1977, Outstanding Leadership award, Gov. State of Ind., 1987, Outstanding Svc. award, Ind. State Bd. Edn., 1990, Outstanding Contbns. award, Ind. Coun. Econ. Edn., 1998. Home: 12256 Dunbar Cir S Indianapolis IN 46229-3262 Office: 21st Century Learning Cmtys LLC 10535 E Washington St Ste 177 Indianapolis IN 46229-2609 Office Phone: 317-894-3595. Office Fax: 317-894-7743. Personal E-mail: learning21stclc@aol.com.

HARROLD, RONALD THOMAS, research scientist; b. Fulham, London, Eng., Apr. 4, 1933; arrived in U.S., 1963; s. John and Cicely Helen (Eddenden) H.; m. Ann Marie Whitley, Dec. 3, 1955; children: Lesley Ann, Linda Jane. BS, Chelmsford Coll. Tech., Eng., 1962, Twickenham Coll. Tech., 1955. Student apprentice Brit. Thomson-Houston Co., Willesden, London, England, 1950-55; lectr. radar tech. Army Sch. Electronics, Arborfield, Berkshire, England, 1955-57; devel. engr. English Electric Valve Co., Chelmsford, Essex, England, 1957-61; rsch. engr. Sylvania-Thorn Color TV Labs., Enfield, Middlesex, England, 1961-63; adv. rsch. scientist Westinghouse Sci. and Tech. Ctr., Pitts., 1963-96, cons., 1996—. Contbr. articles to profl. jours. Fellow: IEEE (life); mem.: Instn. Engring. and Tech., Club 4 Life. Republican. Episcopalian. Achievements include 30 U.S. patents in field of vapour mist dielectrics, acoustic waveguide monitoring. Home: 4052 Benden Cir Murrysville PA 15668-1336 Office: George Westinghouse Rsch and Tech Park 1310 Beulah Rd Pittsburgh PA 15235-5098 Personal E-mail: rharrold_777@comcast.net.

HARROLD, THOMAS J., JR., lawyer; b. Athens, Ga., July 22, 1944; s. Thomas J. and Virginia Harris Harrold; m. Constance P. Harrold, May 1, 1971; 1 child, Elizabeth Virginia. BA in History, Columbia U., 1966; JD, U. Ga., 1969. Bar: Ga. 1969, U.S. Dist. Ct. (no. dist.) Ga. 1969. From assoc. to ptnr. Fortson, Bentley, Griffin, Athens, Ga., 1969—76; dep. commr. Ga. Dept. Revenue, Atlanta, 1976—78; ptnr. Cofer, Beauchamp, Hanes & Harris, Atlanta, 1978—85, Glass, McCullough, Sherrill & Harrold, Atlanta, 1985—97, Miller & Martin, LLP, Atlanta, 1997—. Author: Starting and Operating a Business in Georgia, 1986. Pres. World Law Group, 1995—97; bd. trustees Ga. Econ. Devel. Found., Atlanta, 1988—; bd. dirs. German Am. C. of C., Atlanta, 1995—, Japan Am. Soc., Atlanta, 1992—. Capt. Ga. Air NG, 1969—75. Democrat. Methodist. Avocations: reading, jogging, travel. E-mail: tharrold@millermartin.com.

HARROP, DANIEL SMITH, III, psychiatrist; b. Warwick, RI, June 15, 1954; s. Daniel Smith and Dorothy Jane (Hickey) H. BA, Brown U., 1976, MD, 1979; MBA, Edinburgh Bus. Sch., Scotland, 1997. Diplomate Am. Bd. Med. Examiners, Am. Bd. Psychiatry and Neurology, Am. Bd. Geriatrics, Am. Bd. Forensic Examiners, Nat. Registry Cert. Group Psychotherapists. Resident in psychiatry Brown U., Providence, 1983; med. dir. East Bay Cmty. Mental Health Ctr., Barrington, R.I., 1983-87; asst. unit chief Butler Hosp., Providence, 1988-89, chief gen. treatment unit, 1989-93; clin. asst. prof. psychiatry Brown U., Providence, 1985—; physician advisor Magellan Behavioral Health, Balt., 1991-2000, 2003—; collaborator lab. for clin. and exptl. psychopathology Harvard Med. Sch., Fall River, Mass., 2000—02. Med. dir. Corrigan Ctr., Fall River, Mass., 1996-2002; cons. Harvard Pilgrim Healthcare, 2004—, Pacificare Behavioral Health, 2005—, Focus Behavioral Health, 2006—; chmn. utilization rev. Butler Hosp., Providence, 1985-93; instr. dept. psychiatry Harvard U., 1997-2003; physician advisor Value Options, Reston, Va., 2003—, Am. PsychSystems, Bethesda, Md., 1997—; bd. dirs. Operation Happy Birthday, 2006—. Pres. parish coun. St. Joseph's Ch., Providence, 1987-91, trustee, 1991—; bd. gov.'s Associated Alumni Brown U., Providence, 1988-92; pres. Assn. Class Officers Brown U., Providence, 1988-92; chair Libertarian Party of RI, 2000—05; bd. dirs. Hendicken H.S., Warwick, RI, 2004—, pres. alumni assn., 2004-06; bd. dirs. Found. for Intellectual Diversity Brown U., 2006—. Fellow: Am. Assn. Integrative Medicine; mem.: SAR, KC (grand knight 1998, 2002, faithful navigator 2004), AMA (life), Cath. Med. Assn. (pres. RI guild 2007—), Mass. Med. Soc. (med. edn. com. 1999—), Am. Group Psychotherapy (Assembly 1989—97), RI Group Psychotherapy Soc. (pres. 1989—91), RI Psychiat. Soc. (pres. 1989—90), RI Med. Soc. (med. edn. com. 1989—), Am. Psychiat. Assn. (com. on quality care 2003—), Mil. Order Fgn. Wars U.S., Roman Cath. Alumni Assn. Brown U. (pres. 1982—83, 1993—97), R.I. Hist. Soc. (life), Soc. Sons & Daus. The Pilgrims (R.I. br. gov. 2006—), Ancient Order of Hibernians (divsn. pres. 2003—), Sons of Union Vets. of Civil War, Brown Club of RI (pres. 2007—), Serra Internat., Sierra Club, Providence Art Club, Faculty Club of Brown U. (pres. 1994—95), Galilee Beach Club (Narragansett, R.I.) (pres. 1995—98), Internat. Order of Odd Fellows, Masons (worshipful master 2001—03), Sigma Chi (grand coun. 1981—), Sigma Xi. Roman Catholic. Office Phone: 401-331-7778. Personal E-mail: danharrop@hotmail.com.

HARROP, THOMAS, publishing company executive; b. Salt Lake City, Apr. 30, 1954; s. Raymond William and Fern Pearse (Wheelwright) H.; m. Diane Louise Hokans, July 15, 1995; children: Anne Rochelle, Catherine Lindsay, Kyle. BA, Brooks Inst., 1983, MS, 1994. Mng. editor Petersenis Photographic, LA, 1983-84; photographer NASA, Edwards AFB, Calif., 1987-88; editl. dir. Cameras & Darkroom, LA, 1988-92; mng. editor Outdoor Photograph, LA, 1992-93; pub., editor PhotoWork, Whitefish, Mont., 1996—. Author: (book) Getting Info Print, 1996 Mem. Am. MENSA Soc. Avocations: photography, web design, book publishing.

HARROP, WILLIAM CALDWELL, retired ambassador; b. Balt., Feb. 19, 1929; s. George A. and Esther (Caldwell) H.; m. Ann G. Delavan, Aug. 22, 1953; children— Mark D., Caldwell, Scott N., George H. AB, Harvard U., 1950; postgrad., Grad. Sch. Journalism U. Mo., 1953-54; fellow, Woodrow Wilson Sch., Princeton U., 1968-69. Fgn. Service officer, 1954-93; vice consul Palermo, 1954-55; 2d sec. Rome, 1955-58; internat. relations officer Dept. State, 1958-63; 1st sec. Brussels, 1963-66; consul Lubumbashi, Congo, 1966-68; dir. Office Research for Africa, Dept. State, Washington, 1969; dep. chief mission Am. embassy, Canberra, Australia, 1973-75; U.S. ambassador to Guinea, 1975-77; dep. asst. sec. of state for Africa, 1977-80; ambassador to Kenya and Seychelles, 1980-83; insp. gen. Dept. State and Fgn. Service, 1983-86; ambassador to Zaire, 1987-91; ambassador to Israel, 1992-93; ret., 1994. Bd. dirs. Am. Fgn. Svc. Assn., 1970-73, Assn. for Diplomatic Studies and Tng. Bd. dirs. Population Svcs. Internat. Humane Soc. Washington D.C., Henry L. Stimson Ctr. Served with USMCR, 1951-52. Recipient Dept. State Merit Service award, 1968, Presdl. Disting. Service award, 1985, State Dept. Disting. Service award, 1987. Mem.: Chevy Chase (Md.) Club, Met. Club (Washington), Fly Club (Cambridge, Mass.). Address: 3615 49th St NW Washington DC 20016-3214 E-mail: HarropBill@mac.com.

HARROUN, DOROTHY SUMNER, artist; b. El Paso, Tex., Nov. 29, 1935; d. Daniel Stuart and Eleanor (Flowers) H. BFA, U. N.Mex., 1957; postgrad., U. Paris Sorbonne, 1957—58; MFA, U. Colo., 1960. Art dir. Wood-Reich Advt. Agy., Boulder, 1960—61; lectr. U. Colo., Boulder, 1961—62, San Francisco State Coll., 1964—65; art tchr. Langley-Porter Neuropsychiat. Inst. U. Calif., 1963; tchr. Art Ctr. Sch., Albuquerque, 1975—79; tchr. watercolor, drawing U. N.Mex., 1980—81; invited participant THROUGH HER EYES, 2006. One-woman shows include The Gondolier Gallery, Boulder, Colo., 1961—62, Sta. KAFE-FM Gallery, San Francisco, 1963—64, Lovelace-Bataan Hosp., Albuquerque, 1976, 1979, Ea. N.Mex. U., 1981, Rathaus, Kelkheim, Germany, N.Mex. State U., United World Coll., Montezuma, N.Mex., 2002, Back St. Bistro, Santa Fe, 2006, exhibited in group shows at Whitte Mus., San Antonio, 1960, Hyannis, Mass., Waterbury, Conn., Newport, R.I., 1964—65, Mus. N.Mex., Santa Fe, 1966, Ogunguit Art Ctr., Maine, 1977, Am. Watercolor Soc., NYC, 1979, Coos Art Mus., Coos Bay, Oreg., 1980, We. Slope Show, Montrose, Colo., 1981—82, Ga. Watercolor Soc. Open, 1983, We. Fedn. Watercolor Socs., Albuquerque, 1984—88, Sun Carnival Art Show, El Paso, Tex., 1984, 12th Ann. Interna.t Biog. Ctr. Internat. Arts. Congress, Budapest, Hungary, 1985, UN World Conf. on Women Art, Nairobi, Kenya, 1985, El Paso Mus. Art, 1987, Gov.'s Gallery, N.Mex., 1988, State Fair Fine Arts Gallery, Albuquerque, 1988, Ch. Farm House Mus., London, 1988—89, St. John's Coll., Santa Fe, 1991, Gallery of the Rep., 1993, On Water, 1994, Fuller Lodges, Los Alamo, N. Mex., 2003, Carlsbad Mus. Fine Arts, N.Mex., 2004 (award), Represented in permanent collections Nat. Mus. Women in the Arts, Washington, U. N.Mex., U. Colo., Fine Arts Mus., Carlsbad, N.Mex., N.Mex. State Capitol, Santa Fe, also pvt. collections, exhibitions include El Paso Mus. Art, 1987, juried shows, Tucson Mus. Art, 1988, Boston, 1993, Painted Violin Gala and Auction, Santa Fe Symphony, 2006; author, illustrator Take Time to Play and Listen, 1963, Phun-y Physics, 1975, illustrator Mini Walks on the Mesa, 1989. Pres. fine arts alumni bd. U. N.Mex., 1989—90; bd. dirs. Santa Fe Desert Chorale, 1986—92. Recipient Lobo award, U. N. Mex., 2000; Fulbright scholar. Mem.: AAUW (state cultural dir.), Santa Fe Concert Assn. (bd. dirs. 1996—2007), N.Mex. Watercolor Soc. (v.p. 1984, pres. 1985), Nat. League Am. Pen Women (pres. Albuquerque br. 1982—83), Artist Equity Assn. (pres. Albuquerque chpt. 1977—79). Home: 1365 Thunder Rdg Santa Fe NM 87501-8875

HARROW, JEFFREY JOHN, spinal cord injury physician; s. Lee and Phyllis Harrow; m. Anita Kolek; 1 child, Jason. BS, Calif. Inst. Tech., Pasadena, 1974; MEE, Rice U., Houston, 1976; MD, Baylor U., Houston,

1979; PhD, U. Utah, Salt Lake City, 1985; M Strategic Studies, Army War Coll., Carlisle, Pa., 2006. Diplomate in spinal cord injury medicine Am. Bd. Phys. Medicine and Rehab., 1999, Am. Bd. Internal Medicine, 1990. Transitional intern LDS Hosp., Salt Lake City, 1985—86; resident in anesthesiology Mass. Gen. Hosp., Boston, 1986—87; resident in internal medicine U. Utah Med. Ctr., Salt Lake City, 1988—90; commd. US Army, 1989, advanced through grades to col., served Operations Enduring Freedom, Iraqi Freedom, Desert Shield and Storm; staff physician Vets. Hosp., Palo Alto, Calif., 1991—94; career devel. physician VA Rehab. R & D, Tampa, Fla., 2003—; staff physician, spinal cord injury svc. James A. Haley Veterans Hosp., Tampa, 1999—2006. Cons. BD Drake Willock, Salt Lake City, 1983—85, Organon Technika, Salt Lake City, 1983—85. Contbr. articles to profl. jours. Decorated Meritorious Svc. medal; recipient Coll. of Engring. Patent award, U Utah, 1984, Med. Records Charting award, LDS Hosp., Salt Lake City, 1986, Career Devel. award, VA Rehab. R & D, 2003—06; fellow, Hertz Found., 1974—76; Nat. Merit scholarship, 1970—74, clin. fellow end stage renal disease, Divsn. Artificial Organs, U. Utah, 1981—83, rsch. fellow bioengring., 1981—83, Prin. Investigator grantee, VA Rehab. R & D, 2003—05, co-investigator grantee, VA Health Svcs. R & D, 2004—. Fellow: ACP; mem.: Am. Paraplegia Soc., Assn. Mil. Surgeons US, Assn. US Army Flight Surgeons (life). Achievements include patents for subcutaneous catheter for peritoneal insulin administration. Avocation: scuba diving. Home Phone: 813-632-2710; Office Phone: 813-558-3938.

HARROW, MARTIN, psychologist, educator; b. NYC, Aug. 22, 1933; s. Morris Harrow and Thelma Black; m. Helen M. Kramer, Aug. 19, 1956; children: Jean Libera, Wendy Donovan, Barbara Perez, Ellen. BA, CUNY, 1955; PhD, Ind. U., 1960. Lic. psychologist Ill., diplomate in clin. psychology. Asst. prof. Yale U., New Haven, 1964—69, assoc. prof., 1969—73; chief psychologist Yale-New Haven Hosp., 1968—73; prof. U. Chgo., 1973—89; chief psychologist Michael Reese Med. Ctr., Chgo., 1973—95; prof. U. Ill., Chgo., 1989—, dir. psychology, dept. psychiatry, 1989—. Mem. sci. adv. bd. Schizophrenia Bull., 1995—2004. Author (with J.F. Goldberg): Bipolar Disorders: Clinical Course and Outcome, 1999; mem. editl. bd.: Jour. Abnormal Psychology, 1979—89, Clin. Psychology Rev., 1985—; contbr. more than 240 sci. articles to profl. jours. Recipient Outstanding Contbn. to Psychology award, Ill. Psychol. Assn., 1990, Gralnick award, Am. Assn. Suicidology, 1998, Merit award, NIMH, 1997, Zubin award for Lifetime Contbns. to Understanding of Psychopathology, Soc. for Rsch. Psychopathology, 2005; grantee, NIMH, 1975—2002, 2004—. Fellow: APA; mem.: Soc. for Rsch. in Psychopathology, Midwestern Psychol. Assn. Achievements include former U.S. chess master, placed in top 7 in U.S. Open Chess Championship three times; Conn. Chess Champion, 1965, New England Chess Champion, 1967, Ill. Chess Champion, 1974; two draws in tournament chess games against Bobby Fischer. Office: U Ill Coll Medicine Dept Psychiatry 1601 W Taylor St MC 912 Chicago IL 60612 Office Phone: 312-996-3585. Business E-Mail: mharrow@psych.uic.edu.

HARROW, NANCY (MRS. JAN KRUKOWSKI), editor, composer, singer; b. NYC, Oct. 03; d. Benjamin and Frances (Kirschenbaum) H.; m. Jan Krukowski; children: Damon, Anton. BA, Bennington Coll. From copy editor to editor William Morrow & Co., NYC; editor Am. Jour., NYC, 1972-73, editor-at-large, 1974—. Vocalist Tommy Dorsey Orch., 1958; singer Jazz Gallery, Café Au Gogo, Mars Club, N.Y.C. and Paris, 1961-64, Cookery, Plaza Hotel, Upstairs at Cecil's, NYC, 1975-76, Rachel's, Lush Life, Freddy's, Blues Alley, NYC and Washington, 1984-85; singer WDR Big Band, Cologne, Brussels, Holland, NYU Highlights in Jazz, Mazur Theatre, 1986; singer Jan Wallman's NYC, 1987, 89, Stockholm Jazz Festival, 1988, Michael's Pub, 1990, Judy's Supper Club, The Salon, NYC, 1995-96; The Marble Faun, 1999, The Salon, NYC, 2006, Music Roots 77, Tokyo; Maya the Bee Puppet Show, 2000-06, 45 Bleecker Theater, NYC, 2007, 55 Mercer Theater, 2007; The Cat Who Went to Heaven Puppet Show 55 Mercer Theater, NYC. Recording artist (albums) Wild Women Don't Have the Blues, 1961, You Never Know, 1963, Anything Goes, 1979, The John Lewis Album for Nancy Harrow, 1981, Two's Company: Nancy Harrow with Jack Wilkins, 1984, You're Nearer, 1986, Street of Dreams, 1990, The Beatles and Other Standards, 1990, Two's Company: Nancy Harrow with Jack Wilkins, 1991, Secrets, 1992, Lost Lady, 1994, You're Nearer, 1998, The Marble Faun, 1999, Maya the Bee, 2000, Winter Dreams, 2003, The Cat Who Went to Heaven, 2005; recording artist: albums An Intimate Evening with Nancy Harrow, 2007, songwriter: (John Lewis music) As Long As It's About Love, Distant Lover, 1981; composer: (Nancy Harrow music and lyrics) 5 songs for Secrets album, 1992, 12 songs for the Lost Lady album, 1994, (Raymond Patterson lyrics) A Little Blue, 1990, (Nancy Harrow music and lyrics) 21 songs for Maya the Bee, 2000, 13 songs for The Marble Faun, 1999, 11 songs for Winter Dreams, 2003, 16 songs for The Cat Who Went to Heaven, 2005. Mem.: Century Assn. Address: 130 E End Ave New York NY 10028-7553 Office Phone: 212-249-4376. E-mail: nancyjazz@mac.com.

HARRY, DEBORAH ANN, singer; b. Miami, Fla., July 11, 1945; d. Richard Smith and Catherine (Peters) H. AA, Centenary Coll., 1965. Singer, songwriter rock group Blondie, 1975-83. Albums include Blondie, 1976, Plastic Letters, 1977, Parallel Lines, 1978, Eat to the Beat, 1979, Autoamerican, 1979, The Best of Blondie, 1981, The Hunter, 1982; (solo) Koo Koo, 1981, Rockbird, 1981, Def, Dumb & Blond, 1989, Debravation, 1993, Blonde and Beyond, 1993, Jazz Passengers - In Love, 1994, Rapture, 1994, The Platinum Collection, 1994, Virtuosity, 1995, Los Fabulosos Caillacs-Rey Azucar, 1995, Blodie-Atomic, 1995, Rockbird, 1996, Der Einziger Weg, 1999; songs include Heart of Glass, 1978 (ASCAP award), Call Me, Tide is High, Rapture, 1980; film appearances include Union City Blues, 1980, Videodrome, Roadie, 1980, Hairspray, 1988, Tales From the Darkside: The Movie, 1990, Joe's Day, 1999, Zoo, 1999, Six Ways to Sunday, 1999, Ghost Light, 2000, Dueces Wild, 2000, Red Lipstick, 2000; TV appearances include Saturday Night Live, The Muppet Show, Tales from the Darkside, Wiseguy; appeared on Broadway Teaneck Tanzi, The Venus Flytrap, 1983; (movie) Satisfaction, New York Stories, 1989, Wigstock: The Movie, 1995, Heavy, 1995, Copland, 1997. Recipient Gold, Silver and Platinum records; named to Rock and Roll Hall of Fame, 2006. Mem. ASCAP, AFTRA, Screen Actors Guild, Equity. Office: c/o 10th St Entertainment Ste G410 700 San Vicente Blvd West Hollywood CA 90069

HARRY, VICKIE DIANE, education educator; b. Oil City, Pa., Jan. 18, 1951; d. John Phillip and Myrtle Mildred (Rex) Smith; m. Richard Keith Harry, Sept. 3, 1983; children: Brian M. Fry, Thomas C. Fry, Richard J., Lance C., Amanda E. Corrigan. BS in Elem. Edn., Clarion U., Pa., 1981, MEd in Sci. Edn., 1986; PhD in Sci. Edn., Pa. State U., University Park, 1996. Cert. tchr. Pa. Tchr. Oil City Area Schs., 1977—93; tchr. asst. Pa. State U., 1993—94; prof. Clarion U., 1994—. Cons. in field. Contbr. articles, revs. to profl. publs. Dir. children's program Good Shepherd United Meth. Ch., Leeper, Pa., 1993—2000; mem. choir, tchr. 1st United Meth. Ch., Clarion, 2000—05, chmn. mission com. Franklin, Pa., Sunday sch. tchr., 2005—. Finalist Pa. Tchr. of Yr., Pa. Dept. Edn., 1993; named Disting. Alumni award, Clarion U., 1996. Mem.: Assn. Math. Tchrs. NW Pa. (program chmn. 1998—2001), Pa. Sci. Tchrs. Assn. (regional rep. 2000—04), Phi Delta Kappa (pres. 1999—2002). Office: Clarion U 112 Stevens Hall Clarion PA 16214 Office Phone: 814-393-1868.

HARRYMAN, RHONDA L., special education educator; b. Perry, Okla., Apr. 1, 1954; d. Otis Issac Jr. and Jeanette Roberta (Creacy) Shelley; m. Gilbert Wayne Harryman, Mar. 19, 1978. BS in Edn. cum laude, U. Ctrl. Okla., 1975, M in Spl. Edn., 1979; postgrad., Okla. State U., 1992—. Cert. learning disabilities, mentally handicapped, physically handicapped, emotional disturbance, elem. sch. adminstrs., Okla. Asst. workshop coord. for trainable mentally handicapped, physically handicapped Edmond (Okla.) ARC, 1974-76; instr. educable mentally handicapped, physically handicapped, emotionally disabled Edmond Pub. Schs., 1976-77, instr. spl. edn., emotionally disabled, educable mentally handicapped, physically handicapped, visually and hearing impaired, 1977-91; univ. coord., supr. practicums, instr. spl. edn. U. Ctrl. Okla., Edmond, 1992—. Edn. advisor tchrs. undrepresented populations in Shawnee, Okla. Three Feathers Assn., Norman, Okla. 1983; pvt. teaching, parent counseling learning disabilities, 1982-87; instr. spl. edn. Okla. Christian U., 1992—, mem. tchr. edn. adv. coun.; co-moderator New Eng. Joint Conf. Specific Learning Disabilities, Boston, 1991; edn. rep. Okla. Joint Conf. Juvenile Justice; edn. del. Okla. Japan-Am. Grassroots Coun., Tokyo, 1991; conducted workshops, presented insvcs., speaker in field. Editorial rev. bd. Teaching Resources, Dayton, Ohio. Counselor Edmond Youth Advocacy Bd.; mem. Gov.'s Round Table on Edn. and Bus., Edmond Juvenile Crime Commn.; sponsor Ala-Teen, Boys Ranch Town. Named Okla. Tchr. of Yr. by Okla. State Dept. Edn., 1992. Mem. Orton Dyslexia Soc., Coun. Exceptional Child, Kappa Delta Pi. Home: 3816 Deason Dr Edmond OK 73013-7742 Office: U Ctrl Okla Dept Spl Svcs 100 N University Dr Edmond OK 73034-5207

HARSANYI, JANICE, retired soprano, educator; b. Arlington, Mass., July 15, 1929; d. Edward and Thelma (Jacobs) Morris; m. Nicholas Harsanyi, Apr. 19, 1952; 1 son, Peter Michael. BMus, Westminster Choir Coll., 1951; postgrad., Phila. Acad. Vocal Arts, 1952-54. Voice tchr. Westminster Choir Coll., Princeton, NJ, 1951-63, chmn. voice dept., 1963-65; lectr. music Princeton Theol. Sem., 1956-63; voice tchr. summer sessions U. Mich., 1965-70; artist-in-residence Interlochen Arts Acad., 1967-70; voice tchr. N.C. Sch. Arts, Winston-Salem, 1971-78; music faculty Salem Coll., 1973-76; condr. voice master classes, choral clinics various colls., 1954—; prof. voice Fla. State U., Tallahassee, 1978—, chmn. dept., 1979-83; ret., 2005. Concert singer, 1954— , debut, Phila. Orch., 1958; appearances with, Am., Detroit, Houston, Minn., Nat., Symphony of Air orchs., Bach Aria Group, 1967-68, maj. music festivals, U.S., 1960—; toured with, Piedmont Chamber Orch., 1971-78, concerts and recitals, in major U.S. cities, also in Belgium, Eng., Ger., Italy, Switzerland and Sweden; rec. artist, Columbia, Decca, CRI records. Mem. Nat. Assn. Tchrs. Singing, Music Tchrs. Nat. Assn., Coll. Music Soc., Riemenschneider Bach Inst., Sigma Alpha Iota, Pi Kappa Lambda. Home: 2116 Trescott Dr Tallahassee FL 32308-0732

HARSH, ANTOINETTE MOLLETT, investor; b. Glendale, Calif., Nov. 21, 1946; d. Byron Hendrix Mollett and Margaret Louise Hunter; children: Casey, Brent, Troy, Danielle. Student, Cambridge U., 1967; BS cum laude in History, U. So. Calif., 1968, MS in Edn., 1969. Edn. asst. L.A. County Mus. Natural History, 1968—70; tchr. Washoe County Sch. Dist., Reno, 1970—72; ptnr. Valley Bldg. Co., Glendale, Calif., 1975—, bd. dir., 1st v.p., 2002—. Owner Profl. Filing Svcs., Reno, 1989—2000; sr. v.p. Kirby-Smith and Assocs., Quarreyville, Pa., 1998—2001. Mem. Human Resources Consortium, Reno, 2002—04; Fin. Adv. Bd. Reno, 1998—2000; bd. dirs. Reno Regional Govt., 2002—04; liason Arts and Culture Commn., Reno, 2000—04, Hist. Resources Commn., Reno, 2000—04, Parks & Rec. Commn., Reno, 2000—04; liaison Urban Forestry Commn., Reno, 2002—04, Citizens Traffic Adv. Com., Reno, 2002—04; pres. Voices Truckee Meadows, PAC, 2004—07; coun. mem. Reno City Coun., 2000—04; pres. Truckee Meadows Heritage Trust, Reno, 1999; mem. Reno Sr. Aux. Vol. Effort, 2004—05, bd. dirs. Ret. and Sr. Vol. Program, 2005—; vice-chmn. Salvation Army, Reno, 2005—; bd. dirs. Scenic Nev., 2005—, Reno Tahoe Winter Games Com., 2005—07. Recipient Hero award, Scenic Nev., 2003. Mem.: U. So. Calif. Alumni, Delta Delta Delta (pres. Reno chpt. 1996—98). Republican. Avocations: history, rafting. Address: PO Box 2327 Reno NV 89505 Office Phone: 775-846-1910. Personal E-mail: toniharsh@charter.net.

HARSHA, PHILIP THOMAS, retired aerospace engineer; b. NYC, Feb. 22, 1942; s. Palmer and Catherine (Redinger) H.; m. Jean Ann Quinn, Oct. 23, 1965; children: Peter Charles, Evan Michael. BS in Engring. Sci., SUNY, Stony Brook, 1962, MS in Engring. Sci., 1964; PhD in Aerospace Engring., U. Tenn., 1970. Combustion rsch. engr. GE, Cin., 1964—67; lead rsch. engr. Aro, Inc., Arnold Engring. Devel. Ctr., Tenn., 1969—74; rsch. specialist R & D Assoc., Marina Del Rey, Calif., 1974—76; divsn. mgr. Sci. Applications Internat. Corp., Chatsworth, Calif., 1976—85; chief aero. scientist Lockheed Aero. Sys. Group, Burbank, Calif., 1985—88; chief project engr. Rocketdyne divsn. Rockwell Internat., Canoga Park, Calif., 1988—90; dep. program dir. Nat. Aero-Space Plane Program, 1990—95; program mgr. The Boeing Co., Huntington Beach, Calif., 1994—2004, Boeing Tech. fellow, 2002—. Contbr. articles to profl. jours. Recipient Disting. Alumnus award U. Tenn. Space Inst., 1984. Mem. AIAA, ASME, N.Y. Acad. Sci., Sigma Xi. Republican. Methodist. Home: 677 Oak Glade Dr Fallbrook CA 92028-3693 Home Phone: 760-728-7863. E-mail: harsha322@adelphia.net.

HARSHBARGER, RICHARD B., retired economics professor; b. Lafayette, Ind., May 6, 1934; s. Albert E. and Olive M. (Shambaugh) M.; m. Jane L. Newcomer, Aug. 24, 1958; children: Lisa, Jon. BS, Manchester Coll., 1956; MA, Ind. U., 1958, PhD, 1964. Fuels economist Tenn. Valley Authority, Chattanooga, 1958; econ. prof. Manchester Coll., North Manchester, Ind., 1960-99, ret., 1999. Vis. prof. Pasadena (Calif.) Coll., 1968-69, Eastern Nazarene Coll., Quincy, Mass, 1977-78. Active Manchester (Ind.) Park Bd., 1972—76, Manchester Sch. Bd., 1972—76, Town Forum, 1986—2004, Indsl. Policy Com., North Manchester, 1990—; pres. Shepherd Ctr., 2002—04; fin. com. Cmty. Svcs. North Manchester, 2005—; active Meals on Wheels, North Manchester, 2002; bd. dirs. Bethany Theol. Sem., Oak Brook, Ill., 1987—92, Camp Mack, Milford, Inc., 1986—92, 2001—07, One World Shop, 2007—; fin. com. Wabash County Found., 1997—. Fellow NSF, 1958-59, grad: fellow Ind. U., 1956-58. Mem. Am. Econ. Assn., Midwest Econ. Assn., Ind. Acad. Social Sci. (dir. 1965-66), Ind. Econ. Forum (pres. 1973-74), Rotary (pres. 1979-80). Democrat. Mem. Ch. of Brethren.

HARSTAD, CAROLYN AUDREY, writer, educator, photographer; b. Albert Lea, Minn., Oct. 25, 1936; d. Walter H. and Emma Frankson Schneider; m. Peter T. Harstad, Aug. 10, 1957; children: Linda C. Becker, Karen D. Scislow, Mark P., Kristen E. Vehling, David G. AB, Bethany Luth. Coll., 1956; BS, U. Minn., 1957. Author: Go Native! Gardening With Native Plants and Wildflowers, 1999, Got Shade? A Take It Easy Approach For Today's Gardener, 2003. Office Phone: 952-435-6988. Personal E-mail: carolynharstad@yahoo.com.

HART, ANGELA, insurance company executive; BBA in Acctg., Columbus State U., Ga. Comptr. so. divsn. Aflac Broadcast Group AFLAC Inc., Columbus, Ga., 1980, second v.p. risk mgmt., 1991, v.p. corp. svcs., v.p., asst. dir. human resources, 1996—97, v.p., dir. human resources, 1997—98, sr. v.p., 1998—2001, sr. v.p. cmty. rels., 2001—. Chairwoman bd. trustees Muscogee County Libr. Found.; Aflac rep. bd. dirs. Cmty. Found. Chattahoochee Valley, Inc., United Way Chattahoochee Valley. Office: AFLAC Inc 1932 Wynnton Rd Columbus GA 31999 Office Phone: 706-323-3431.*

HART, ANN WEAVER, academic administrator; b. Salt Lake City, Nov. 6, 1948; d. Ted Lionel and Sylvia (Moray) Weaver; m. Randy Bret Hart, Sept. 12, 1968; children: Kimberly, Liza, Emily, Allyson. BS in History, U. Utah, 1970, MA in History, 1981, PhD in Ednl. Adminstrn., 1983. Tchr. pub. schs., Salt Lake City, 1970-73, 80-81; jr. high sch. prin. Provo Pub. Schs., Utah, 1983-84; prof. ednl. adminstrn. U. Utah, Salt Lake City, 1984—98, assoc. dean Grad. Sch. Edn., 1991-93, dean Grad. Sch., 1993—98; provost, v.p. acad. affairs Claremont Grad. U., Calif., 1998—2002; pres. U. NH, Durham, 2002—06, Temple U., Phila., 2006—. Bd. dirs. Citizens Bank N.H. Author: Principal Succession: Establishing Leadership in Schools, 1993, The Principalship, 1996, Designing and Conducting Research, 1996; editor: Ednl. Adminstrn. Quar., 1990-92; contbr. articles to profl. jours. Grantee U. Utah, State of Utah, U.S. Dept. Edn. Mem. Am. Ednl. Rsch. Assn., Am. Coun. on Edn., Phi Beta Kappa, Phi Kappa Phi. Avocations: skiing, backpacking, hiking, kayaking, bicycling. Office: Temple Univ Office of Pres 200 Sullivan Hall 1330 W Berks St Philadelphia PA 19122 Office Phone: 215-204-4405. Business E-Mail: president@temple.edu.

HART, ANTONIO MAURICE, musician, educator; b. Balt., Sept. 30, 1968; s. Berthenia and Floyd Davis (Stepfather). BA in Music Edn., Berklee Coll. Music, Boston, 1991; MFA, CUNY, Flushing, NY, 1993. Saxophonist Roy Hargrove Quintet, NY, 1990—93; leader Antonio Hart Quintet, NY, 1993—; lead saxophonist Dizzy Gillespie Alumni Big Band, NY, 1994—; saxophonist Nat Adderley Quintet, NY, 1994—98; lead saxophonist Dave Holland Big Band, NY, 2002—. Asst. prof. jazz saxophone Queens coll. CUNY, Flushing, 2000—; pvt. tchr. New Sch., NY, 2005—; sub. tchr. jazz for teens NJ PAC, Newark, 2006—. Musician: (albums) Dear Ella, 1997 (Grammy award, 1997); composer Hear I Stand, 1998 (Best Jazz Solo Composition nomination Grammys, 1998); musician What Goes Around, 2002 (Best Large Ensemble Album award Grammys, 2002), Overtime, 2005 (Best Large Ensemble Album award Grammys, 2005), over 80 recordings. Bd. dirs. Harmony Program, NY, 2006—07. Mem.: Alpha Phi Alpha (life). Democrat. Avocations: martial arts, reading, travel. Office: Queens Coll CUNY 65-30 Kissena Blvd Flushing NY 11367-1597 Office Phone: 718-997-3809. Office Fax: 718-997-3849. Personal E-mail: hart20@aol.com.

HART, ARTHUR ALVIN, historian, author; b. Tacoma, Feb. 13, 1921; s. Albert Arthur and Erma Lola (Maltby) H.; m. Novella D. Cochran, Feb. 26, 1944; children: Susanna, Robin, Catherine, Allison. BA, MFA, U. Wash., Seattle, 1948; postgrad., Biarritz Am. U., Hans Hofmann Sch. Fine Arts, U. Calif., Berkeley; HHD (hon.), Coll. Idaho, 1985. Head art dept., chmn. divsn. fine arts Albertson Coll. (formerly Coll. of Idaho), Caldwell, 1948—53; instr. art Colby Jr. Coll. Women, New London, NH, 1953-54; head art dept., dir. adult edn. Bay Path Jr. Coll., Longmeadow, Mass., 1955-69; dir. Idaho Hist. Mus., Boise, 1969-75, Idaho Hist. Soc., 1975-86. Lectr. Am. architecture Boise State U., 1970—86; mem. Boise Allied Arts Coun., 1970—78, Idaho Historic Preservation Coun., 1971—87, Boise Bicentennial Commn., 1975—76, Idaho Centennial Commn., 1985—90, Idaho Humanities Coun., 1985—86, Idaho Abraham Lincoln Bicentennial Commn., 2006—; mem. adv. bd. Snake River Regional Studies Ctr., 1969—, Boise Redevel. Agy., 1986—87, Basque Mus. and Cultural Ctr., 1985—, Idaho Aviation Hall of Fame, 1990—. Author: Steam Trains in Idaho, 1971, Space, Style and Structure: Building in Northwest America, 1974, Fighting Fire on the Frontier, 1976, Historic Boise, 1979, The Boiseans: At Home, 1984, Idaho, Gem of the Mountains, 1985, Basin of Gold, 1986, Life in Old Boise, 1989, Camera Eye on Idaho: Pioneer Photography 1863-1913, 1990, Wings Over Idaho: An Aviation History, 1991, Boise Baseball: The First 125 Years, 1994, The Boise Children's Home, 1996, Barns of the West: A Vanishing Legacy, 1996, The Arid Club, Its Life and Times, 1997, Centennial History of the Western Idaho Fair, 1897-1997, 1997, To Protect and To Serve: Law Enforcement in Boise, Idaho, 1863-2000, 2000, Boise: An Illustrated History, 2000, Chinatown: Boise, Idaho, 1870-1970, 2002, Echoes from the Ada County Courthouse, 1938-2001, 2005 (Preservation Idaho Orchid award, 2006, AASLH Merit award, 2006), Life in Eagle: A History, 2007; contbg. author: Encyclopedia of American Forest and Conservation History, 1983, Dictionary of American Medical Biography, 1984; weekly columnist (newspaper) Idaho Statesman, 1970—95, Boise Weekly, 1995—97, Idaho Mag., 2002—07. Mem. Mayor's Boise 2000 Com. Recipient Idaho Statesman Disting. Citizen award, 1973, Allied Arts Coun. award for hist. writing, 1972, Phoenix award for leadership in conservation, Am. Travel Writers, 1982, Idaho Bar Assn. award, 1985, James C. Howland Urban Enrichment award, 1990, Disting. Preservationist award, Idaho Hist. Preservation Coun., 1999, Disting. Achievement in the Humanities award, Idaho Humanities Coun., 2000, Esto Perpetua award, Idaho State Hist. Soc., 2003. Mem. AIA (hon.), AAUP, Coll. Art Assn., Soc. Archtl. Historians (pres. No. Pacific Coast chpt. 1974-76), Am. Assn. Museums (mem. council 1980-82, pres. Western regional conf. 1979-81), Am. Assn. for State and Local History.

HART, BROOK, lawyer; b. NYC, Aug. 24, 1941; s. Walter and Julie H.; divorced; children: Morgan M., Leilani L., Ashley I., Ariel I. BA, Johns Hopkins U., 1963; LLB, Columbia U., 1966. Bar: N.Y. 1966, U.S. Ct. Appeals (9th cir.) 1967, Hawaii 1968, U.S. Supreme Ct. 1972, Calif. 1973. Law clk. to chief judge U.S. Dist. Ct. Hawaii, 1966-67; chief pub. defender Legal Aid Soc. Hawaii, 1970—72; assoc. Greenstein and Cowan, Honolulu, 1968-70; co-founder, ptnr. Hart, Leavitt, Hall and Hunt, Honolulu, 1972-80, Hart and Wolff, Honolulu, 1980-96; sr. ptnr. Law Offices of Brook Hart; pvt. practice. Instr. course U. Hawaii, 1972-73, lectr. Sch. Law, 1974—; apptd. Nat. Commn. to Study Def. Svcs., 1974, Planning Group for U.S. Dist. Ct. Hawaii, 1975; spl. counsel City Coun. of City and County of Honolulu, 1976-77, spl. investigative counsel to trustee in bankruptcy THC Fin. Corp., 1977; mem. Jud. Coun. State of Hawaii com. on revision state penal codes, 1984—; lectr. schs., profl., civic groups; mem. com. to select Fed. Pub. Defender Dist. Hawaii, 1981, 95; guest commentator Court TV, 1995, 99, 2002, 03, 04; with faculty Hawaii Inst. Continuing Legal Edn., 1988, Hawaii Pub. Defender Advocacy Inst., 1993-. Contbr. chpts. to books, articles to profl. publs. Named Bencher, Am. Inn of Ct., Hawaii, 1982—. Fellow Am. Bd. Criminal Lawyers; mem. ABA, Hawaii Bar Assn., State Bar Calif., Am. Judicature Soc., Nat. Legal Aid and Defender Assn. (Reginald Herber Smith award Outstanding Pub. Defender in Nation, 1971), Nat. Assn. Criminal Def. Lawyers, Calif. Attys. for Criminal Justice. Office: Ste 610 Melim Bldg 333 Queen St Honolulu HI 96813-4726 Office Phone: 808-526-0811. Office Fax: 808-531-2677. E-mail: hartlaw@hawaii.rr.com.*

HART, BUSTER CLARENCE, lawyer; b. Promise City, Iowa, Mar. 19, 1923; s. Harry H. and Alfreda (DeBolt) H.; m. Jean E. Hart, July 7, 1933; children: Nannette, Kyle, Charles, Charlotte. AB, U. Iowa, 1947; JD, Harvard U., 1950. Bar: Minn. 1951, U.S. Ct. Mil. Appeals 1956, U.S. Supreme Ct. 1956. Ptnr. Briggs and Morgan, P.C., St. Paul, 1951-76, pres., 1976-83, Hart, Bruner, O'Brien & Thornton and predecessors, Mpls., 1983—; ptnr. Fabyanske, Westre & Hart, 1983—. V.p. Downtown St. Paul, 1956—59; bd. dirs. Lakewood Coll. Found., 1974—76; mem. Minn. Citizens Com. for Voyageurs Nat. Park, 1975—; co. chmn. United Fund, bd. dirs., 1958—61, 1981—; mem. midwest regional adv. com. Nat. Park Svc. Lt. col. USAR. Fellow: Am. Bar Found.; mem.: ABA (chmn. tort and ins. practice sect. 1980—81, Martin J. Andrew Lifetime Achievement award, Tips Andrew Hecker Lifetime Achievement award), ATLA, Forum on the Constrn. Industry (Cornerstone award), Harvard Law Sch. Assn. (state pres. Minn., nat. v.p.), Am. Coll. Constrn. Lawyers (past pres.), Am. Bd. Trial Advocates (state pres. 1973), Am. Coll. Trial Lawyers, Internat. Assn. Ins. Counsel, Ramsey County Bar Assn., Fed. Bar Assn., Minn. Bar Assn. (chmn. ct. rules com. 1973—77), Minn. Club (bd. dirs. 1980—86), St. Paul Athletic Club, Phi Beta Kappa. Office: Fabyanske Westra Hart & Thomson Ste 1900 800 LaSalle Ave Minneapolis MN 55402 E-mail: bchart@minnlaw.com.

HART, CECIL WILLIAM JOSEPH, otolaryngologist, surgeon; b. Bath, Somerset, Eng., May 27, 1931; came to U.S., 1957. s. William Theodore Hart and Paulina Olive (Adams) Gilmer; m. Brigid Frances Molloy, June 15, 1957 (dec. Nov. 1984); children: Geoffrey Arthur, Paula Mary, John Adams; m. Doris Crystel Katharina Alm, Mar. 14, 1987; children:

Kristen-Linnea Alm, Erik Alm, Britt-Marie Alm. BA, Trinity Coll., Dublin, Ireland, 1952, MB, BCH, BAO, 1955, MA, 1958. Diplomate Am. Bd. Otolaryngology. Intern Dr. Steevens Hosp., Dublin, Ireland, 1956, Little Co. Mary Hosp., Evergreen Park, Ill., 1957, mem. staff, 1958-59; resident in otolaryngology U. Chgo. Hosp. and clinic, 1959-62; instr. U. Chgo. Med. Sch., 1962-64, asst. prof., 1964-65; practice medicine specializing in otolaryngology Chgo., 1958—; mem. staff Northwestern Meml. Hosp., 1972-97, Rehab. Inst. Chgo., 1965-97, Children's Meml. Hosp., 1972-97, Little Co. of Mary Hosp., 1977-94, LaGrange (Ill.) Comty. Meml. Hosp., 1977-94, Loyola U. Med. Ctr., 1997—. Tchg. assoc. Cleft Palate Inst., 1968, dir. otolaryngology, 1969-92; asst. prof. dept. otolaryngology-head and neck surgery Northwestern U. Med. Sch., 1965-75, assoc. prof., 1975-92, prof., 1992-97, prof. emeritus, 1997—; lectr. dept. otorhinolaryngology Loyola U., 1972, prof. otolaryngology, head and neck surgery, 1997-2001; med. adv. bd. So. Hearing and Speech Found., Nat. Inst. of Deafness and Other Communicative Disorders, 1989-95. Producer videos, movie; contbr. numerous articles to profl. jours. and mags.; also guest appearances various radio and TV talk shows. NIH fellow U. Chgo., 1962-63; NIH grantee, 1985-88. Fellow Am. Neurotology Soc. (pres. 1974-75, chmn. editorial review & publ. com. 1978-79, constn. and bylaws com. 1979-97), Am. Acad. Otolaryngology-Head and Neck Surgery (chmn. subcom. on Equilibrium 1980-86, computer com. 1987-90), ACS, Inst. Medicine Chgo., Soc. for Ear, Nose and Throat Advances in Children; mem. AMA, Brit. Med. Assn., Ill. State Med. Soc., Chgo. Med. Soc., Am. Cleft Palate Assn., Am. Council Otolaryngology, Am. Otological Soc., Chgo. Laryngological and Otological Soc. (v.p. 1975-76), Northwestern Clin. Faculty Med. Assn. (vice chmn. 1976-78, pres. 1979-81), Barany Soc., Royal Soc. Medicine, Irish Otolaryngological Soc., So. Hearing and Speech Found (med. adv. bd.), Chgo. Hearing and Balance Assn. (pres.), Sigma Xi. Roman Catholic. Avocations: travel, baroque music, symphony, opera, tennis. E-mail: cwjhart@aol.com.

HART, C(HARLES) W(ILLARD), JR., zoologist, curator; b. Farmville, Va., Jan. 30, 1928; s. Charles Willard and Etta Catharine (Sawyer) H.; m. Margaret Waddell Gordon, Sept. 17, 1957 (div. Jan. 1958); m. Nancy Dabney Gardner, June 9, 1962. BA, Hampden-Sydney Coll., Va., 1949, BS, 1950; postgrad., Fla. State U., 1950-52, 53-54; MA, U. Va., 1951. Instr. biology Washington Coll., Chestertown, Md., 1954-55, Randolph Macon Woman's Coll., Lynchburg, Va., 1955-56; med. editor Smith, Kline & French Labs., Phila., 1956-58; editor sci. publs. Acad. Natural Scis., Phila., 1958-70, dir. water pollution studies, 1968-74; asst. to dir. Natural History Mus., Smithsonian Instn., Washington, 1974-79, curator dept. invertebrate zoology, 1979-92, chmn. dept., 1988-91, rsch. scientist, curator, 1992-96, rsch. scientist emeritus, 1996—. Author: A Dictionary of the Non-Scientific Names of Freshwater Crayfishes, 1994; (with Janice Clark) An Interdisciplinary Bibliography of Freshwater Crayfishes from Aristotle Through 1987, 1989; editor: (with P. Holt and R. Hoffmann) The Distributional History of the Biota of the Southern Appalachians, Part I: Invertebrates, 1969, (with S.L.H. Fuller) Pollution Ecology of Freshwater Invertebrates, 1974, Pollution Ecology of Estuarine Invertebrates, 1979, (with Dabney G. Hart) The Ostracod Family Entocytheridae, 1974; contbr. numerous articles to profl. jours. Mem. Phila. Rep. City Com., 1966-68; bd. dirs. Archbold Ctr. for Tropical Rsch., Dominica, 1987-96. Fellow AAAS; mem. Am. Soc. Zoologists (com. on rsch. in systematic biology 1974-78), Crustacean Soc. (treas. 1981-85), Biol. Soc. Washington (editor Procs. Biol. Soc. Washington 1978-80, sec. 1986-88), Assn. Southeastern Biologists (editor ASB Bull. 1961-72, pres. 1970-71), Coun. Biology Editors (treas. 1968-71), Explorers Club, Cosmos Club Washington (mem., chair, program com. 1996-98), Cosmos Club Found. (trustee 1998-2005, advisor 2005-), Phi Beta Kappa, Sigma Xi. Episcopalian. Avocations: web page design and maintenance, flying, sailing, jewelry design and fabrication, cartography of Bermuda. Home: 6449 Walters Woods Dr Falls Church VA 22044-1424 E-mail: winston@patriot.net.

HART, CHRISTOPHER ALVIN, lawyer; b. Denver, June 18, 1947; s. Judson Duncan and M. Murlee (Shaw) H.; children: Adam Christopher, Brooke Corinne; m. Leeann Moore, 2002; B.S. in Aerospace Engring., Princeton U., 1969, M.S. in Aerospace Engring., 1971; J.D., Harvard U., 1973. Bar: D.C. 1973, U.S. Dist. Ct. D.C. 1973, U.S. Ct. Appeals (D.C. cir.) 1973, U.S. Ct. Appeals (8th cir.) 1981, U.S. Supreme Ct. 1985. Assoc. Peabody, Rivlin & Lambert, Washington, 1973-76, Dickstein, Shapiro & Marin, Washington, 1979-81; gen. atty. Air Transport Assn., Washington, 1976-77; dep. asst. gen. counsel U.S. Dept. Transp., Washington, 1977-79; charter, prin. firm Hart & Chavers, Washington, 1981-90; mem. Nat. Transp. Safety Bd., 1990-93; dep. adminstr. Nat. Highway Traffic Safety Adminstrn., 1993-94; assoc. adminstr. for system safety Fed. Aviation Adminstrn., 1994—. Bd. dirs. Howard U. Hosp. Cancer Ctr., Washington, 1983-88, WPFW (Pacific Found.)-FM, 1984-90, Nat. Sleep Found., 1997—. Recipient Superior Performance award U.S. Dept. Transp., 1979. Mem. D.C. Bar (com. ethics 1983-89, mem. bd. profl. responsibility 1989-94), Washington Bar Assn., Fed. Bar Assn., Fed. Communications Bar Assn., Lawyer-Pilots Bar Assn., Black Princeton Alumni (dir. N.Y.C. 1981-87). Democrat. Episcopalian. Home: 1612 Crittenden St NW Washington DC 20011-4218 Office: Fed Aviation Adminstrn 800 Independence Ave SW Washington DC 20591-0001 Home Phone: 202-882-5393; Office Phone: 202-267-5205. Business E-Mail: chris.hart@faa.gov.

HART, CLARE, information company executive; b. Morristown, NJ, Sept. 22, 1960; m. Greg Baer. BS in Finance and Computer Systems Mgmt., Drexel U., 1983; MBA, Rider U., 1986. Programmer, analyst applications dept. Dow Jones & Co., 1983—90, sr. programming analyst to program mgr. advanced systems group; joined Desktop Data (renamed NewsEdge in 1998), Mich., 1991—92; regional sales dir. US Central region and Canada Dow Jones & Co., Mich., 1992, dir. corp. news products Dow Jones Interactive NYC, 1995, dir. enterprise mktg., 1996, exec. dir. enterprise products, 1999; v.p., dir. Global Sales Dow Jones Reuters Business Interactive LLC (now Factiva), 1999; pres., CEO Factiva, 2000—06, chmn. bd., 2006—; exec. v.p. Dow Jones & Co., 2006—; pres. Dow Jones Enterprise Media Group, 2006—. Recipient NY Ten Awards, Exec. Coun., 2005. Mem.: Special Libraries Assn., Soc. Competitive Intelligence Professionals (bd. dirs. 1999—2000), Software and Info. Industry Assn. (bd. dirs.). Avocations: horseback riding, theater. Office: Dow Jones & Co 1 World Financial Ctr 200 Liberty St New York NY 10281*

HART, CLIFFORD HARVEY, lawyer; b. Flint, Mich., Nov. 12, 1935; s. Max S. and Dorothy H. (Fineberg) H.; m. Alice Rosenberg, June 17, 1962; children: Michael F., David E., Steven A. AB, U. Mich., 1957, JD, 1960. Bar: Mich. 1960, U.S. Dist. Ct. (ea. and we. dists.) Mich. 1962; cert. civil trial advocate. Assoc. Stevens & Nelson, Flint, 1960-62; ptnr. White, Newblatt, Nelson & Hart, Flint, 1962-64, Dean, Dean, Segar & Hart, P.C. and predecessor firms, Flint, 1965-97; pvt. practice Law Offices Clifford H. Hart, 1997—. Adj. assoc. prof. Flint Sch. Mgmt., U. Mich., 1972—; lectr. Inst. Continuing Legal Edn., Mich.; lectr. Mich. Jud. Inst. Pres. Vis. Nurse Assn., Flint, 1967; pres. Temple Beth El, 1973-75; trustee United Way Genesee County, 1981—, chmn. bd., 1990-91, sec., 1988-89, chmn. bd. dirs. Genesee County and Lapeer County, 1990-91; chair corp. adv. bd. U. Mich., Flint, 1988-93; mem. faculty Inst. Continuing Legal Edn., Ann Arbor, Mich., 1984—. Fellow: Roscoe Pound Found., Mich. Bar Found., Mich. Bar Found. (life); mem.: ATLA (bd. govs. 1979—, exec. com. 1984—85, chmn. elections com. 1984—87, lectr., budget com. 1987—2004, chair 1989—91, nat. parliamentarian 1990—91, exec. com. 1990—93, chair 1990—93, nat. treas. 1991—92, exec. com. 1998—2004, chair 1998—2004), ABA, Nat. Bd. Trial Advocacy (cert.), Am. Judicature Soc., Genesee County Bar Assn. (pres. 1975—76), Mich. Trial Lawyers Assn. (pres. 1977—78, lectr.), Mich. State Bar Assn. (rep. assembly 1975—81, chmn. negligence law sect. 1981—82, Mich. Super Lawyer 2006—07), B'nai B'rith (past pres.). Democrat. Office: 1410 Mott Found Bldg 503 S Saginaw St Flint MI 48502-1807 Office Phone: 810-235-5631. Business E-Mail: clhart@umich.edu.

HART, DANIEL ANTHONY, bishop; b. Lawrence, Mass., Aug. 24, 1927; s. John J. and Susan M. (Tierney) H. BSBA, Boston Coll., 1956; MEd, Boston State Coll., 1972; MDiv, St. John's Sem., Brighton, Mass., 1974. Priest Roman Cath. Ch., 1953. Asst. pastor, Lynnfield, Mass., 1953—54, Wellesley, Mass., 1954—56, Malden, Mass., 1956—64; vice-chancellor Archdiocese of Boston, 1964—70; asst. pastor Peabody, Mass., 1970—76; titular bishop of Tepelta, aux. bishop of Boston, 1976—95; regional bishop S. region, 1976—95; archdiocesan vicar for pastoral devel., 1976—85; bishop of Norwich Conn., 1995—2003; bishop emeritus of Norwich, 2003—. Pres. Boston Senate of Priests, 1972—74; mem. exec. bd. Nat. Fedn. Priests' Couns., 1973—75. Roman Catholic. Address: 213 Broadway Norwich CT 06360-4307 E-mail: dahart@sbcglobal.net.

HART, DON LEE, academic administrator, writer; b. Vinita, Okla., Mar. 11, 1953; s. Roy Junior and Iona Mae Hart; m. Lisa Anne Hilburn, Apr. 21, 1961; children: Nicholle Michelle, Matthew Sterling, Katharine Elizabeth. BA, U. N.Mex, 1979, MA, 1984. Cert. distance learning adminstr. Teletraining Inst./Stillwater, Okla., 2000. Libr. U. N.Mex, Albuquerque, 1983—85; dir. Woolworth Pub. Libr., Jal, 1985—86; libr. Nickerson H.S., Nickerson, Kans., 1986—93; tchr. Reno County Edn. Coop, Hutchinson, 1993—94; reporter Sterling Bull., 1994—94, Hutchinson News, 1994—97; dir. learning resources Pratt C.C., 1997—. Presenter League Innovation C.C., Orlando, 2000—00, Mpls., 2001—01. Author: Year of the Rat, (short stories) Smith Magazine; contbr. articles in Vietnam magazine. With USN, 1971—73. Mem.: U.S. Distance Learning Assn., Phi Alpha Theta. Avocations: creative writing, photography, fishing. Office: Pratt Community College 348 Northeast State Road 61 Pratt KS 67124 E-mail: donh@prattcc.edu.

HART, EDWARD LEROY, poet, educator; b. Bloomington, Idaho, Dec. 28, 1916; s. Alfred Augustus and Sarah Cecilia (Patterson) H.; m. Eleanor May Coleman, Dec. 15, 1944 (dec. Dec. 1990); children: Edward Richard, Paul LeRoy, Barbara, Patricia; m. Leah Yates Bryson, Apr. 30, 1993 (dec. Aug. 2001); m. Frances Cannon Lee, June 7, 2002. BS, U. Utah, 1939; MA, U. Mich., 1941; DPhil (Rhodes scholar), Oxford U., Eng., 1950. Instr. U. Utah, Salt Lake City, 1946; asst. prof. U. Wash., Seattle, 1949-52, Brigham Young U., Provo, Utah, 1952-55, assoc. prof., 1955-59, prof., 1959-82, prof. emeritus, 1982—. Vis. prof. U. Calif., Berkeley, 1959-60, Ariz. State U., summer 1968. Author: Minor Lives, 1971, Instruction and Delight, 1976, Mormon in Motion, 1978; (poems) To Utah, 1979, Poems of Praise, 1980; More Than Nature Needs, 1982, God's Spies, 1983; contbr. articles to profl. jours. Lt. USNR, 1942—46. Am. Philos. Soc. grantee, 1964; First prize in poetry and biography Utah State Arts Coun., 1973, 75; Fulbright-Hays sr. lectr. Pakistan, 1973-74; recipient Charles Redd award Utah Acad., 1976, Coll. Humanities Disting. Faculty award Brigham Young U., 1977, presdl. citation Brigham Young U. Commencement, 1998. Fellow Am. Coun. Learned Socs., Found. Econ. Edn.; mem. Phi Beta Kappa, Phi Kappa Phi. Democrat. Mem. Lds Ch. Home: 1401 Cherry Ln Provo UT 84604-2848 Office: Brigham Young U Dept English Provo UT 84602 *As a young writer in graduate school, I made the shocking discovery one day that I had written some things I did not really believe. I wanted to be a writer, but I made a vow in my journal that I would not do so at the expense of my integrity: that I would never write anything again that I did not believe and accept with all my being. I have kept that promise, and at the same time have tried to be creative and resourceful. I do not believe that my writing has suffered from the attempt to be honest, but if it has, that is a small price to pay for self-respect.*

HART, ERIC MULLINS, consumer products company executive; b. Clanton, Ala., May 6, 1925; s. Eric and Myrtle (Mullins) H.; m. Joy Porter, May 16, 1953; children: Anne Porter, Eric Mullins. BS, U. Ala., 1946; grad., Harvard Advanced Mgmt. Program, 1970. With Internat. Paper Co., 1946-69, asst. to v.p.-treas., 1962-64, comptroller, 1964-69; treas. Red River Paper Mill, Inc., 1964-69; fin. v.p. Lever Bros. Co., 1969-83, dir., 1969-83, Unilever U.S. Inc., 1981-83, Macmillan, Inc., 1975-88; exec. in residence Columbia U. Bus. Sch., 1983-88. Trustee King Sch., Stamford, Conn., 1970-76. Mem. Union League Club (N.Y.C.), Lakewood Golf Club, Fairhope Yacht Club, Sigma Alpha Epsilon. Home: 2267 Pesnell Ct B Mobile AL 36695-3710

HART, FREDERICK MICHAEL, law educator; b. Flushing, NY, Dec. 5, 1929; s. Frederick Joseph and Doris (Laurian) H.; m. Joan Marie Monaghan, Feb. 13, 1956; children: Joan Marie, Ellen, Christiane, F. Michael, Margaret, Andrew, Brigid, Patrick. BS, Georgetown U., 1951, JD, 1955; LL.M., N.Y. U., 1956; postgrad., U. Frankfurt, Germany, 1956-57. Lectr., dir. food law program N.Y. U., NYC, 1957-58, asst. prof., 1958-59; prof. law Albany Law Sch., Union U., 1959-61, Boston Coll., 1961-66, Law Sch., U. N.Mex., Albuquerque, 1966—, dean, 1971-79, acting dean, 1985-86; dir. Law Sch., U. N.Mex. (Indian Law Center), 1967-69; vis. prof. U. Calif., Davis, spring 1981. Pres., chmn. bd. trustees Law Sch. Admission Test Council, 1974-76 Author: Forms and Procedures Under the Uniform Commercial Code, 1963, Uniform Commercial Code Reporter-Digest, 1965, Handbook on Truth in Lending, 1969, Commercial Paper Under the U.C.C, 1972, Student Guide to Secured Transactions, 1985, Student Guide to Sales, 1987, (with Nathaliie Martial) Emanual Guide to Secured Transaction, 2006; editor: Am. Indian Law Newsletter, 1968-70. Served to lt. USAF, 1951-53. Mem. ABA (law sch. accreditation com. 1986-93, skills tng. com. 1995-98, nominating com. 1987), Order of Coif, Phi Delta Phi. Roman Catholic. Home: 1505 Cornell Dr NE Albuquerque NM 87106-3703 Office: U NMex Sch Law 1117 Stanford Dr NE Albuquerque NM 87131-1431 Office Phone: 505-277-4737. Business E-Mail: hart@law.unm.edu.

HART, GARY W., retired senator, lawyer; b. Ottawa, Kans., Nov. 28, 1936; m. Lee Ludwig, 1958; children: Andrea, John. BA, Bethany Nazarene Coll., Okla., 1958; BD, Yale Div. Sch., 1961; JD, Yale U., 1964; D.Phil. in Politics, Oxford U., 2001. Bar: Colo. 1964. Began career as atty. U.S. Dept. Justice, Washington; then spl. asst. to sec. U.S. Dept. Interior; practiced in Denver, 1967-70, 72-74; nat. campaign dir. Senator George McGovern Democratic Presdl. Campaign, 1970-72; U.S. senator from Colo., 1976-84; of counsel Davis, Graham & Stubbs, Denver, 1985; of counsel, strategic and legal advisor, internat. law Coudert Brothers, San Francisco, 1988—; co-chmn. US Commn. Nat. Security/21st Century Dept. of Def., 1998—2001. Founder, 1st chmn. Environ. Study Conf., 1975; congl. adviser Salt II Talks, 1977; adviser UN Spl. Session on Disarmament, 1978; chmn. Nat. Commn. on Air Quality, 1978-81; founder Congl. Mil. Reform Caucus, 1981 Author: Right From the Start, 1973, A New Democracy, 1983, America Can Win, 1986, The Strategies of Zeus, 1987, Russia Shakes the World, 1991, The Good Fight: The Education of an American Reformer, 1993, The Patriot, 1996, The Minuteman, 1998, Restoration of the Republic, 2002, The Shield & The Cloak, 2006; co-author: The Double Man, 1985. Student vol. John F. Kennedy Presdl. Campaign, 1960; vol. organizer Robert F. Kennedy Presdl. Campaign, 1968; bd. visitors U.S. Air Force Acad., 1975—, chmn., 1978-80; nat. co-chmn. Share Our Strength, 1985; candidate for Democratic presdl. nomination, 1983-84, 87-88.*

HART, GURNEE FELLOWS, investment counselor; b. Chgo., Apr. 26, 1929; s. Percival Gray and Marguerite May (Fellows) H.; m. Marjorie Walker Leigh, Apr. 23, 1966 BA cum laude, Pomona Coll., 1951; MBA, Stanford U., 1955; vis. scholar, Jesus Coll., Cambridge, Eng., 1994-95. With Willis & Christy, LA, 1955-65; investment counsel Scudder, Stevens & Clark, Inc., LA, 1965-67; with Scudder, Stevens & Clark, NYC, 1967—, ptnr., 1972-85, mng. dir., 1985-94, adv. mng. dir., 1994—2002. Bd. dirs. Lincoln Ctr. for the Performing Arts, Inc., 1981-86, 2004—, NY Philharmonic, 1974—, vice-chmn., exec. com., 1976-96, trustee, 1988-2005; chmn. Friends of NY Philharm., 1975-82; bd. dirs., v.p. Berkshire Farm Ctr. and Svcs. for Youth, 1972-83; trustee Pomona Coll., 1982-2000, trustee emeritus, 2000—; bd. dirs., treas. Am. Friends of Cambridge U., 1997-2000; bd. dirs. Cambridge U. Devel. Office in U.S., Inc., 1998-2000; chmn. Cambridge in Am., 2000-2004; trustee The Cambridge Found., U.K., 2001-04; adv. bd. Yale Ctr. Parliamentary Hist., 2003- 1st lt. inf. USAR, 1951—53, Korea. Decorated Bronze Star. Mem. St. Andrew's Soc. State of N.Y., Soc. Mayflower Desc., Century Assn., Univ. Club, Knickerbocker Club, Indian Harbor Yacht Club (Greenwich, Conn.), Phi Beta Kappa Republican. Episcopalian. Home: 133 E 64th St New York NY 10075-7045

HART, HERBERT MICHAEL, military officer; b. St. Louis, Oct. 19, 1928; s. Herbert Malcom and Helen Genevieve (Quigley) Hart; m. Teresa Keating, Oct. 13, 1958 (dec. Sept. 11, 2002); children: Bridget, Erin, Bret, Tracy, Megan, Michael, Patrick. BS in Journalism, Northwestern U., Evanston, Ill., 1951. Commd. 2d lt. USMC, 1951, advanced through grades to col., 1972, infantry platoon, co. and bn. comdg. officer Republic of Korea, 1952—53, 1957—60, Vietnam, 1969-70; Arab, Israeli, Persian plans officer US Strike Command, Mid. East and Tampa, Fla., 1967-69; head profl. edn. Dept. Navy, Washington, 1977-78; head hist. br. Marine Corps. Hqrs., Washington, 1973-77, dep. dir. pub. affairs, 1978-80, dir. pub. affairs, 1980-81, ret., 1981—99; dir. pub. affairs Res. Officers Assn. of US, Washington, 1982-94. Cons. office of History US Army Corps Engrs., 1981-94; mem. adv. bd. ad hoc com. Nat. Park Svc., 1985-94; mem. com. on Cemeteries and Memls. VA, 1987-92; mem. coun. advisors Nat. Park Conservation Assn., 1992-99. Author 9 mil. history books; editor ROA Nat. Security Report, 1983-94; mem. editl. bd. Mil. History mag., 1983-95; asst. editor Leatherneck Mag., Washington, 1946-47; editor-in-chief Daily Northwestern, Evanston, Ill., 1949-51. Decorated 2 Purple Heart medals, 2 Legion of Merit medals; recipient Award of Merit Am. Assn. State and Local History, 1976, Cultural Achievement award Sec. of Interior, 1979, Conservation Svc. award Sec. Interior, 1986, named Hon. Ky. Col. by Gov. of Ky. Fellow Co. Mil. Historians; mem. Potomac Westeners (pres. 1974-75, 84-85), Res. Officers Assn. U.S. (life), Marine Corps Res. Assn. (life), Marine Corps Combat Corres. Assn. (life), Marine Corps Hist. Found. (charter, bd. dirs. 1983-87), Assn. US Army, Army. Hist. Found. (charter), Nat. Pk. Svc. Employee and Alumni Assn. (life), VFW (life), Am. Legion (life), Mil. Order Purple Heart (life), Civil War Preservation Trust (charter mem.), Mil. Officers Assn. (life), 1st Marine Divsn. Assn. (life), 3rd Marine Divsn. Assn. (life), Coun. Am. Mil. Past (co-founder 1966, exec. dir. 1971-2007, exec. dir. for life emeritus 2007-), Western History Assn. (charter), Nat. Assn. Uniformed Svcs. (life), Coast Def. Study Group, Naval and Maritime Corrs. Circle, State Hist. Soc. SD (life), Ft. Adams, R. Trust (charter), Ft. Douglas, Utah, Mus. Assn. (life), Civil War Fortifications Study Group (charter), Friends of Ft. Davis, Tex. (life), Battlefield Preservation Coalition (dir. 1991-2003), Friends of Ft. Ward, Va. (charter), Friends of Manassas Battlefield, Va. (charter), Nat. Trust Hist. Preservation, Theodore Roosevelt Assn., Va. Hist. Soc., Order of Indian Wars (companion), Apollo Soc. (bd. dirs. 1983-87), Am. Civil Def. Assn. (bd. advisors 1991-2000), Soc. Mil. History (trustee 1978-83), Ft. Phil Kearny/Bozeman Trl. Assn. (life), Ft. DeRussy La. Friends, Ft. Point and Presidio Assn. (life), Mil. Order of Carabao, US Cavalry Assn. (life), K.C., Soc. Profl. Journalists, Theta Xi (life). Republican. Roman Catholic. Avocation: photography. Home: 7510 Gambrill Rd Springfield VA 22153-1809 Office Phone: 703-912-6124.

HART, JAMES WARREN, retired athletic administrator, professional football player; b. Evanston, Ill., Apr. 29, 1944; s. George Ezrie and Marjorie Helen (Karsten) H.; m. Mary Elizabeth Mueller, June 17, 1967; children: Bradley James and Suzanne Elizabeth (twins), Kathryn Anne BS, So. Ill. U., 1967. Quarterback St. Louis Cardinals Profl. Football Team, 1966—83, Washington Redskins Profl. Football Team, 1984; radio sports personality Sta. KMOX, 1975—84, Sta. KXOK, 1985—86; sports analyst Sta. WGN Radio, Chgo., 1985—89; athletics dir. So. Ill. U., Carbondale, 1988—99, assoc. chancellor for external affairs, 1999—2000; head coach So. Ill. Spl. Olympics, 1973—90, Mo. Spl. Olympics, 1976—78; co-owner Dierdorf & Hart's Steak House (2 locations), St. Louis; spl. asst. to vice chancellor for instnl. devel. So. Ill. U., 1999—2002. Co-author: The Jim Hart Story, 1977. Gen. campaign chmn. St. Louis Heart Assn., 1974-88; hon. chmn. St. Louis Sr. Olympics, 1986-88 Named Most Valuable Player in Nat. Football Conf., 1974, Most Valuable Player with St. Louis Cardinals, 1973, 1975, 1978, Man of Yr., St. Louis Dodge Dealers, 1975—76, Miller High Life, 1980; named to So. Ill. U. Sports Hall of Fame, 1978, Mo. Sports Hall of Fame, 1998, Mo. Valley Conf. Hall of Fame, 2001, Chicagoland Sports Hall of Fame, 2003; recipient Brian Piccolo Nat. YMCA award for most civic minded profl. athlete, 1980. Mem.: AFTRA, NFL Players Assn. (Byron Whizzer White award 1976), Fellowship Christian Athletes. Republican.

HART, JAMES WHITFIELD, JR., retired public relations executive, lawyer; b. Greenwood, Fla., Dec. 20, 1935; s. James Whitfield Sr. and Lela (Cox) H.; m. Patricia Ann Landrum, Mar. 11, 1961; children: William Gordon, Melanie Ann. AA, Chipola Coll., 1956; JD, U. Ala., 1973; MBA, MIT, 1982. Bar: Ala. 1974, Colo. 1976; cert. flight instr. News dir., anchorman Sta. WTVY-TV, Dothan, Ala., 1958-60, Sta. WSFA-TV, Montgomery, Ala., 1960-62; exec. dir. Am. Petroleum Inst., Montgomery, 1962-75; mgr. pub. affairs Gulf Oil Corp., Atlanta, 1975-76, dir. pub. affairs Denver, 1976-81, sr. dir. pub. affairs Pitts., 1981-85; sr. v.p. Blue Cross/Blue Shield, Jacksonville, Fla., 1985-86; sr. v.p., gen. mgr. Hill & Knowlton, Denver, 1986-88; v.p. pub. affairs PanEnergy Corp., Houston, 1988-97; v.p. Duke Energy Corp., 1997-99; ret. Res. dir. pub. affairs Office Sec. Air Force, 1988-95; bd. dirs. Vita-Living, Inc.; chmn. interstate natural gas Am. Pub. Affairs Com., 1994. Adv. bd. City of Sugar Land Airport; former pres. Ala. N.G. Assn.; bd. dirs. Opportunity Fla., Boy Scouts Am.; pres. Chipola Jr. Coll. Found. Brig. gen. USAFR, 1990-95. Decorated Disting. Svc. medal, Legion of Merit, Meritorious Svc. medal, Air Force Commendation medal; recipient Meritorious Svc. award and Disting. Svc. award State of Ala., Outstanding Young Man of Am. award U.S. Jaycees, 1965, Outstanding Pub. Rels. Practitioner award, 1991, Pub. Rels. Practitioner of Yr., 1996; named Alumnus of Yr., Chipola Coll., 2007. Mem. ABA, Pub. Rels. Soc. Am., Tex. Pub. Rels. Assn. (bd. dirs., chmn. pub. affairs coun. 1996, pres. 1996, Gold Spur award 1999), Coun. Assn. Execs. (former pres.), Am. Petroleum Inst., Am. Gas Assn., Pub. Affairs Coun. (past chmn.), Res. Officers Assn. (life), Air Force Assn. (life), Tex. Coun. Econ. Edn. (bd. dirs.), Tex. Rsch. League (bd. dirs.), Forum Club Houston, Houston Club, Univ. Club Houston, Rotary, Sigma Delta Kappa (former chancellor). Baptist. Home: 7371 Cox Rd Bascom FL 32423-9411 E-mail: jimwhart@digitalexp.com.

HART, JOHN CLIFTON, lawyer; b. Chgo., Apr. 29, 1945; s. Clifton Edwin and Eleanor (Zielinski) H.; m. Dianne Lynn Wenzel, Jan. 18, 1969; children: David Clifton, Steven Philip, Kristin Dianne. BS, Loyola U., Chgo., 1967; postgrad., Northwestern U. Sch. Law, Evanston, Ill., 1967—69; JD, U. ND, Grand Forks, 1972. Bar: Minn. 1973, US Dist. Ct. Minn. 1973, Tex. 1979, US Dist. Ct. (no. dist.) Tex. 1979, US Dist. Ct. (we dist.) Tex. 1981, US Dist. Ct. (ea. dist.) Okla. 1981, US Dist. Ct. (ea. dist.) Tex. 1984, US Dist. Ct. (no. dist.) Okla. 1999, US Ct. Appeals (5th and 8th cirs.) 1980, US Supreme Ct., 1997. Ptnr. Robins, Zelle, Larson & Kaplan, Mpls., 1973-81; v.p. Gollaher & Hart, Dallas, 1981-84; pres. Hart & Engen, Dallas, 1984-87, Hart & Assocs., Dallas, 1987-88; mng. ptnr. SW regional office Robins, Kaplan, Miller & Ciresi, 1988-93; ptnr. Cantey & Hanger LLP, 1993-98, Brown, Dean, Wiseman, Proctor, Hart & Howell LLP, Fort Worth, 1998—. Contbr. articles to profl. jours. Maj. USAF, 1969-73. Mem.: ABA, Loss Exec. Assn., Fedn. Def. and Corp. Counsel, Tarrant County Bar Assn., State Bar Tex. Republican. Lutheran. Office: Brown Dean Wiseman Proctor Hart & Howell LLP Ste 200 306 W 7th St Fort Worth TX 76102-4905 Office Phone: 817-820-1112. Business E-Mail: jhart@browndean.com.

HART, JOHN EDWARD, lawyer; b. Portland, Oreg., Nov. 21, 1946; s. Wilbur Elmore and Daisy Elizabeth (Bowen) H.; m. Bianca Mannheimer, Mar. 29, 1968 (div. 1985); children: Ashley Rebecca, Rachel Bianca, Eli Jacob; m. Serena Callahan, Nov. 9, 1991; 1 child, Katelyn Elizabeth. Student, Oreg. State U., 1965-66; BS, Portland State U., 1971; JD, Lewis and Clark Coll., 1974. Bar: Oreg. 1974, U.S. Dist. Ct. Oreg. 1974, U.S. Ct. Appeals (9th cir.) 1975. Ptnr. Schwabe, Williamson and Wyatt, Portland, 1973-92, Hoffman, Hart & Wagner, Portland, 1992—. Adj. faculty U. Oreg. Dental Sch., 1987—; legal cons. Oreg. Chpt. Obstetricians, Gynecologists, Portland, 1985—, Am. Cancer Soc. Mammography Project, 1987—. Contbr. articles to profl. jours. Co-chmn. Alameda Sch. Fair, Portland, 1983. With U.S. Army, 1967-68. Mem. ABA, Am. Coll. Trial Lawyers, Am. Bd. Trial Advocates (pres. 1995) Am., Inns of Ct., Oreg. State Bar Assn., Oreg. Assn. Def. Counsel (pres. 1989), Multnomah Athletic Club. Democrat. Presbyterian. Avocations: jogging, weightlifting, outdoor activities. Office: Hoffman Hart & Wagner 1000 SW Broadway Ste 2000 Portland OR 97205-3072

HART, JOHN WILLIAM, theology and ecology educator; b. NYC, Oct. 5, 1943; s. Thomas Esmond and Veronica Frances (Merz) H.; m. Jane Helen Morell, Aug. 16, 1975; children: Shanti, Daniel. BA, Marist Coll., 1966; STM, Union Theol. Sem., 1972, MPhil, 1976, PhD, 1978. Dir. Heartland Project, Midwestern Cath. Bishops, 1979-81; prof. religion various acad. instit. in NY, Conn., Tex. and S.D., 1975—83; assoc. prof. religious studies Coll. of Gt. Falls, Mont., 1983-85; prof. theology Carroll Coll., Helena, Mont., 1985—2004; prof. Christian ethics Boston U. Sch. Theology., 2004—. Vis. asst. prof. religion Howard U., Washington, 1978-79; project writer Columbia River Pastoral Letter, 1998-2001; dir., founder environtl. studies program Carroll Coll., 1997—2004; lectr. in field in 28 states in US, Brazil, Can., Italy, Switzerland, Eng., Nepal, 1980—; dir., founder ecol. ethics doctoral program Boston U., 2005-. Author: The Spirit of the Earth: A Theology of the Land, 1984, Ethics and Tech.: Innovation and Transformation in Cmty. Contexts, 1997, What Are They Saying About.Environmental Theology?, 2004; ghost author: various ch. documents on theology and ecology; contbr. articles to profl. publ., periodicals, and encys., chpt. t. Del. Internat. Indian Treaty Coun., Geneva, 1987, 90, UN Internat. Human Rights Commn., Templeton Oxford Sems. in Sci. and Christianity, 1999-2001, Earth Charter, Italy, 2002, Amsterdam, 2005; assoc. Ctr. for Maximum Potential Bldg. Sys., Austin, Tex., 2002-. Recipient Templeton Sci.-Religion award, 1995; Danforth Found. fellow, 1973-74; NEH grantee, 1985, 86, 2003; AAR/Lilly Tchg. Scholar in Religion, 1997-98. Mem. Soc. Christian Ethics, Am. Acad. Religion, Mont. Wilderness Assn., Mont. Environ. Info. Ctr. (pres., bd. dirs.), Alternative Energy Resources Orgn., Sierra Club. Democrat. Office: Boston U Sch of Theology Boston MA 02215 Office Phone: 617-353-3032. Business E-Mail: drjhart@bu.edu. *Humanity has been entrusted with a sacred intergenerational responsibility: to care for creation and the common good and to conserve the common ground of the biotic community in its Earth home.*

HART, KAREN ANN, advertising executive; b. Olean, NY, July 11, 1943; d. John Eugene and Lillian Lila (Gardner) H. BSN, D'Youville Coll., Buffalo, 1965. RN, Ohio, N.Y., Calif. Staff nurse, head nurse, supr. Montefiore Med. Ctr., Bronx, N.Y., 1965-77; nurse recruiter L.A. New Hosp., 1978-79, Midway Hosp., LA, 1979-80; dir. nurse recruitment Akron (Ohio) City Hosp., 1980-87; exec. dir. Nat. Assn. Health Care Recruitment, Akron, 1987-96; sr. v.p. health care divsn. Bernard Hodes Group, NYC, 1996—. Contbr. articles to profl. jours. Recipient Women in Comm. award Women Aware Program, 1986. Mem. Nat. Assn. Health Care Recruitment (past officer, Disting. Mem. award 1986, 87), Northeastern Ohio Assn. Health Care Recruitment (past officer), Sigma Theta Tau. Democrat. Roman Catholic. Avocations: travel, writing, reading, swimming. Home: 201 N Hawkins Ave Akron OH 44313-6425 Office: 220 E 42nd St New York NY 10017 E-mail: khart@ny.hodes.com.

HART, KAREN E., psychologist, consultant; b. Nassau, Bahamas; d. Neville E. and Henrietta Hart. AA, Coll. Bahamas, Nassau, 1989—91; BA magna cum laude, Spelman Coll., Atlanta, 1991—93; MEd, Ga. State U., Atlanta, 1995—96, EdS, 1996—97; PhD student, Prairie View A&M U., Tex., 2004—. Cert. gen. mgr. Inst. Cert. Profl. Mgrs., 2003. Tchr. Ministry Edn., Nassau, Bahamas, 1993—95; guidance counselor Hawksbill Sr. Secondary Sch., Freeport, Grand Bahama Island, 1993—95; psychology internship Atlanta Pub. Schs., 1995, DeKalb County Schs., Ga., 1996—97; coord. counseling svcs., lectr. Coll. Bahamas, Freeport, 1997—2003; psychologist trainee Inst. Rehab. & Rsch., Houston, 2005—06; psychology intern Houston Ind. Sch., 2007—. Bahamas regional ednl. advisor Edn. USA, 2001—03; grad. tchg., rsch. asst. Prairie View A&M U., 2004—07. Contbr. articles to profl. jours. Mental health worker for hurricane survivors Disaster Recovery Ctr., Houston, 2005; lead pronouncer Dist. Scripps Howard Spelling Bee, Freeport, Bahamas, 1998—2002; sch. liaison Sch. Welfare Com., Freeport, 1993—95. Recipient Mortar Bd. award, Sr. Honor Soc., 1993. Mem.: NASP, APA, Nat. Orgn. Victims Assistance, Union Tertiary Educators Bahamas (trustee 1998—2003), Assn. Black Psychologists, Internat. Neuropsychological Soc., Ga. Assn. Sch. Psychologists, Nat. Scholars Honor Soc., Psi Chi, Golden Key, Kappi Delta Pi. Personal E-mail: edspecialist@hotmail.com.

HART, KAREN JEAN, special education educator; b. Elizabeth, NJ, July 6, 1952; d. Santo Joseph and Florence (Machrone) Materia; m. Thomas Raymond Hart, June 28, 1975; children: Brian, Kimberly. BA, Kean Coll. of N.J., 1974, MA, 1981. Cert. elem. tchr. of reading, reading specialist, tchr. of handicapped and learning disabilities, supr. Elem. tchr. Harding Sch., Kenilworth, N.J., 1970-74; adj. faculty Kean Coll., Union, N.J., 1981-87; supplemental instr. Bridgewater (N.J.) -Raritan, 1987-91; tchr. of the handicapped Somerset County Vo-Tech, Bridgewater, 1991—2005; learning disabilities tchr. cons. Somerset County Vocat. Tech., NJ, 2005—. Yearbook fin. advisor Sch. Yearbook, 1993-95; advisor, state officer team mgr. NJ SkillsUSA, 2000—. Den leader Boy Scouts Am., Bridgewater, 1989-91, cubmaster, 1991-92, advancement chair, Martinsville, 1993-97; sec., cultural arts chair PTO, Bridgewater, 1991—. Recipient Citation State Legis., State of N.J., 1992. Mem. Coun. of Exceptional Children, Assn. Learning Cons., Kappa Delta Pi, Phi Delta Kappa, Epsilon Pi Tau Home: 282 Carber St Bound Brook NJ 08805-1529 Office: Somerset County VoTech HS North Bridge and Vogt Bridgewater NJ 08807 Office Phone: 908-526-8900. Business E-Mail: khart@scettc.org.

HART, LEROY BANKS, systems administrator, director; b. July 12, 1954; s. Bill and Helen (Lauver) Hart; m. Virginia Sattazahn, June 26, 1976; children: Peter, Timothy, Michael, Evan. BS, Kutztown State U., 1976; postgrad., Pa. State U., 1978—79, St. Joseph's Coll., 1979—81. Acct. Security of Am. Life., Reading, Pa., 1976—78, EDP coord., 1978—80, asst. v.p., contr., 1981—82; exec. v.p. Eastern Software Corp., 1984—88; pres. Hart Fin. Svcs., 1982—84, 1988—, ERA Ulrich Realty Co., 1990—97, Hart Software, Inc., 1990—99; staff info. sys. Lancaster Bible Coll., 1999—2004, dir. info. sys., 2004—05; COO, Hart Software, Inc., 2005—. Trustee Zion Evang. Congl. Ch., 1978—84, Lakeside Evang. Congl. Ch., 1987—88, Evang. Sch. Theology, 1991—2001, Twin Pines Camp Conf. and Retreat Ctr., 1990—, Mohn's Hill Meml. Evang. Congl. Ch., 1994—. Fellow: Life Office Mgmt. Assn. Home: 5 Buck Run Mohnton PA 19540-1220 Office: 708 Centre Ave Reading PA 19601 Home Phone: 610-777-3174.

HART, LORING EDWARD, academic administrator; b. Bath, Maine, Sept. 22, 1924; s. Joseph Edward and Elizabeth (Hayes) H.; m. Marilyn Louise Cummings, Jan. 7, 1950; children: Ellen Louise, Matthew Cummings. BA, Bowdoin Coll., Brunswick, Maine, 1948; MA, U. Miami, Coral Gables, Fla., 1951; PhD, Harvard U., Cambridge, Mass., 1961; degree (hon.), Norwich U., Northfield, Vt., 1982, Bowdoin Coll., 1982, St. Joseph's Coll., Maine, 2004. Teaching fellow Harvard U., 1954-56; instr. English U. Ky., 1956-57; from asst. prof. to prof. Norwich U., Northfield, Vt., 1957-83, head dept. English, 1961-68, dean of faculty, 1968-69, v.p., dean, 1969-72, pres., 1972-82; assoc. dir. devel. campaign Bowdoin Coll., Brunswick, Maine, 1983-86; pres. St. Joseph's Coll., Standish, Maine, 1987-95. With armored inf. AUS, World War II, ETO. Decorated Bronze Star, Combat Inf. badge; recipient Outstanding Civilian Svc. award Air Force, Army. Mem. SAR, Sons of Colonial Wars, 4th Armored Divsn. Assn., Phi Beta Kappa, Sigma Nu. Address: PO Box 13 Yarmouth ME 04096-0013 E-mail: bas745@gwl.net.

HART, MARNIE R., art educator; b. Monterey, Calif., Feb. 7, 1971; d. Larry Kim Hart and Sylvia George. BA in Fine Art, Salisbury State U., Md., 1992; cert. in K-12 art edn., Towson State U., Md., 1995; MPS in Humanistic and Multicultural Edn., SUNY, New Paltz, 2001. HS art tchr. Rondout Valley Ctrl. Sch. Dist., Accord, NY, 1996—2006; art tchr. Hays Cen. Ind. Sch. Dist., 2006—. Art club advisor Rondout Valley Ctrl. Sch. Dist., 2000—, art dept. liaison, 2002—04. Organizer art dept. donation Heiffer Internat. and Rochester Food Pantry, 2002, 2004—05. Nominee NY State Tchr. of Yr., 2001. Avocations: clay, sculpting, painting. E-mail: marnie01@austin.rr.com.

HART, MARY, television talk show host; b. Sioux Falls, SD, Nov. 8, 1951; m. Burt Sugarman, Apr. 8, 1989; 1 child. BA, Augustana College, 1972. Co-host, prodr. Danny's Day, Oklahoma City, Iowa; co-host PM Mag., LA, 1978, The Regis Philbin Show, NYC, 1981-92, Entertainment Tonight, Hollywood, 1982—; co-owner Customer's Last Stand. Host: Tournament of Roses Parade, Macy's Thankgiving Day Parade; other TV appearences include (miniseries) Hollywood Wives, 1985, Circus of the Stars, Good Morning America, Blossom, Coach; exec. prodr., host Mary Hart Presents: Love in the Public Eye, 1990, Mary Hart Presents: Power in the Public Eye, 1990; musical debut Dolly, ABC-TV; headliner, dancer, singer, Las Vegas debut Golden Nugget, 1988, Resorts Internat., Atlantic City; videos include: Shape Up with Mary Hart, 1989, Mary Hart: Fit and Firm, 1990. Office: Paramount TV 5555 Melrose Ave Los Angeles CA 90038-3112

HART, MARY T., lawyer; BA, Georgetown U., 1991; JD, Fordham U., 1995. Bar: NY, US Dist. Ct. So. Dist. NY, US Dist. Ct. Ea. Dist. NY. Ptnr. Wilson, Elser, Moskowitz, Edelman & Dicker LLP, NYC. Mem.: Assn. of the Bar of the City of NY. Office: Wilson Elser Moskowitz Edelman & Dicker LLP 23rd Fl 150 E 42nd St New York NY 10017-5639 Office Phone: 212-490-3000 ext. 2113. Office Fax: 212-490-3038. Business E-Mail: hartm@wemed.com.

HART, MATTHEW J., hotel and recreation executive; married; 3 children. BA cum laude, Vanderbilt U., 1974; MBA, Columbia U., 1976. Mktg. rsch. assoc. Merrill Lynch; lending officer Bankers Trust Co., NYC; from mgr. project fin. to exec. v.p., CFO Marriott Corp., 1981—92; exec. v.p., CFO Host Marriot Corp., 1992—95; sr. v.p., treas. Walt Disney Co., 1995—96; CFO, exec. v.p. Hilton Hotels Corp., Beverly Hills, Calif., 1996—2004, pres., COO, 2004—. Bd. dir. Hilton Hotels Corp., 2007—, Kilroy Realty Corp., Am. West Airlines. Bd. dirs. Heal the Bay, Westside Breakers. Office: Hilton Hotels Corp PO Box 5567 9336 Civic Center Dr Beverly Hills CA 90210-3604*

HART, MELISSA ANNE, former congresswoman; b. Pitts., Apr. 4, 1962; d. Donald P. and Albina Simone Hart. BA, Washington & Jefferson Coll., 1984; JD, U. Pitts., 1987. Mem. Pa. State Senate, 1991—2000, US Congress from 4th Pa. dist., 2001—07, mem. ways and means com., standards ofcl. conduct com., 2005—07. Bd. trustees Washington & Jefferson Coll., U. Pitts, CC Allegheny County, Vietnam Vets. Leadership Prog., Pitts. Film Office, Pitts. Ballet Theatre. Named Guardian of Small Bus., Nat. Fedn. Ind. Bus.; recipient Hero of the Taxpayer award, Ams. for Tax Reform, Legislator of Yr. award, Am. Legis. Exch. Coun., Eagle award, Associated Builders and Contractors, Pres.'s medal, Chatham Coll., Thomas Jefferson award, Food Distbrs. Internat., Advocacy award, Nat. Epilepsy Assn., Spirit of Enterprise award, US C. of C., People Leading Change award, Pa. Leadership Coun., Status of Women award, Zonta Internat., Women of Spirit award, Carlow Coll. Mem.: North Suburban Builders Assn., Allegheny County Bar Assn., Pa. Bar Assn. Republican.*

HART, MELISSA JOAN CATHERINE, actress; b. Smithtown, NY, Apr. 18, 1976; m. Mark Wilkerson, July 19, 2003; 1 child, Mason Walter. Appeared in TV series, including Clarissa Explains It All, Sabrina The Teenage Witch; appeared in TV movies, including Kane and Able, Christmas Show, The Tale of the Frozen Ghost, Family Reunion, Twisted Desire, Sabrina The Teenage Witch, Two Came Back, Sabrina Goes to Rome, Silencing Mary; appeared in feature film Can't Hardly Wait, Drive Me Crazy, 1999, Recess: School's Out (voice), 2001, Hold On, 2002, Rent Control, 2002, Jesus, Mary and Joey, 2003; appeared in plays, including Besides Herself, Imagining Brad, The Crucible; actress (TV movie) The Voyage to Atlantis: The Lost Empire, 2001; actress, prodr. (TV movie) Sabrina, Down Under, 1999. Office: Creative Artists Agy 9830 Wilshire Blvd Beverly Hills CA 90212

HART, OLIVER D'ARCY, economics professor; b. London, Oct. 9, 1948; came to U.S., 1984; s. Philip D'Arcy and Ruth D'Arcy (Meyer) H.; m. Rita B. Goldberg, June 9, 1974; children: Daniel S., Benjamin P. BA, Cambridge U., 1969; MA, Warwick U., Eng., 1972; PhD, Princeton U., 1974; PhD (hon.), Free U. Brussels, 1992, U. Basel, Switzerland, 1994. Lectr. econs. U. Essex (Eng.), 1974-75, Cambridge (Eng.) U., 1975-81; prof. econs. London Sch. Econs., 1981-85, MIT, Cambridge, 1984-93, Harvard U., Cambridge, 1993—, Andrew E. Furer prof. econs., 1997—. Marvin Bower fellow Harvard U. Bus. Sch., Boston, 1988-89; Centennial vis. prof. London Sch. Econ., 1997—. Author: Firms, Contracts, and Financial Structure, 1995; editor Rev. Econ. Studies, 1979-83; contbr. articles to profl. jours. Guggenheim fellow, 1987-88. Fellow Econometric Soc. (coun. 1983—, Fisher-Schultze lectr 1988), Am. Acad. Arts. and Scis., Brit. Acad. (corr.); mem. Am. Law and Econ. Assn. (pres. 2006-07), Am. Econ. Assn. (v.p. 2006). Avocation: listening to music. Office: Harvard U Dept Econs Cambridge MA 02138 Home Phone: 781-862-2258; Office Phone: 617-496-3461. Business E-Mail: ohart@harvard.edu.

HART, PAUL VINCENT, JR., emergency and acute care physician, inventor; b. Estherville, Iowa, Sept. 28, 1950; s. Paul Vincent and Florence Mary (Gehringer) H. BS, Iowa State U., 1972; MD, Creighton U., 1976. Diplomate Am. Bd. Emergency Medicine. Resident in gen. surgery U. Minn., Mpls., 1976-77; emergency physician Wheeling (W.Va.) Med. Ctr., 1977-79; pvt. practice Kansas City, Kans., 1979-84, Westwood, Kans., 1985—. V.p. Organ Design & Mfg., Westwood, 1989—; cons. Hepatocyte Transformation Lab. Hannover (Germany) U. Med. Sch., 2000—. Mem. Am. Acad. Family Physicians. Republican. Roman Catholic. Achievements include patent for transformed kidney cells for renal assist device; patent pending for bioartifical kidney; co-patentee for liver assist devices.

HART, RICHARD BANNER, lawyer; b. Winston-Salem, NC, Apr. 9, 1932; s. Samuel Bruce and Cordia M. (Lamb) H.; m. Jean Elizabeth Shinn, Apr. 28, 1956; 1 dau., Fabra. AB in Polit. Sci, U. NC, 1957, JD, 1959. Bar: N.C. 1959, Tenn. 1970, U.S. Supreme Ct. 1991; CLU. Assoc. counsel Jefferson Standard Life Ins. Co., Greensboro, NC, 1959-70; with NLT Corp. and Nat. Life and Accident Ins. Co., Nashville, 1970-73, asst. v.p., counsel, 1973-75, sec., counsel, 1975-84; v.p., sec., assoc. gen. counsel Am. Gen. Ins. Cos., Nashville, 1982-88; v.p., sec., gen. counsel Intereal Co., 1984-85; spl. counsel Bowne of Nashville, Inc., 1988-94; pvt. practice, 1988—; judge City of Belle Meade, Nashville, 2003—06. Lectr. in field; adv. com. U.S. Dist. Ct. (mid. dist.) Tenn. Civil Justice Reform Act 1990. Bd. editors U. N.C. Law Rev., 1958-59. Budget com. Guilford County United Fund, N.C., 1968-69; bd. dirs. Guilford County Mental Health Assn., 1968-69; nat. bd. dirs. Joint Action in Cmty. Svc., Washington, 2005-06; treas. Nashville Exch. Club Charities, 1987-88; chmn. adminstrv. bd. West End United Meth. Ch., 2007; vol. The Talking Libr.; bd. govs. Shakespeare on the Cumberland, 2004-06. With U.S. Army, 1953-55. Mem. Assn. Life Ins. Counsel, Am. Corp. Counsel Assn. (pres., chmn. bd. dirs. Tenn. chpt. 1990-92), Am. Soc. Corp. Secs. (exec. com., pres. S.E. region 1979-81), Tenn. Mcpl. Judges Assn., Nashville Com. Fgn. Rels., English Speaking Union U.S. (bd. dirs. 1998-2007, pres. Nashville br. 1999-2001) , Phi Delta Phi, Phi Kappa Sigma (nat. officer, exec. bd. 1971-77), Phi Kappa Sigma Ednl. Fund, Inc. (trustee 1997-2000), Exch. Club (Nashville) (bd. dirs. 1984-85), Univ. Club Nashville (bd. dirs. 2003-06), Belle Meade Country Club. Home: 2815 Kenway Rd Nashville TN 37215-1903

HART, ROBERT M., lawyer; b. NYC, Nov. 7, 1944; s. Charles John and Helen Ann (Hammond) H.; m. Dale Elizabeth McConaughy, Nov. 21, 1970; children: Michael, Jonathan, Bryan. BA, Marist Coll., 1966; JD, Duke U., 1969. Bar: N.Y. 1969, U.S. Ct. Appeals (2d cir.) 1970, U.S. Dist. Ct. (so. dist.) N.Y. 1979. Assoc. Donovan Leisure Newton & Irvine, NYC, 1969-71, 74-77, London, 1972-73, ptnr. NYC, 1977-84, 88-94, Dorsey & Whitney, NYC, 1984-88; sr. v.p., gen. counsel, sec. Alleghany Corp., NYC, 1994—; dir., chmn. comp.com. Chgo. Title Corp., 1998-2000. Sr. lectr. law Duke U., Durham, NC, 1986—. Contbr. articles to profl. jours. Sr. fellow, Duke U., 1983—. Mem. ABA (securities regulation com. 1981—), N.Y. State Bar Assn., Assn. Bar City N.Y. (securities regulation com. 1979-82), Am. Law Inst. Office: 7 Times Sq Tower 17th Flr New York NY 10036-1356 Office Phone: 212-752-1356. Personal E-mail: rhart@alleghany.com.

HART, RONALD WILSON, radiobiologist, educator, toxicologist, business adviser; b. Syracuse, NY, Mar. 23, 1942; s. Wilson and Annabell Hart. BS, Syracuse U., 1967; MS, U. Ill., 1970, PhD, 1971; postgrad. (Nat. Cancer Inst. trainee), Oak Ridge Nat. Lab., 1973. USPHS trainee, 1970-71; asst. prof. dept. radiology Ohio State U., Columbus, 1971-75, dir. radiation biology rsch. divsn., 1971-82, assoc. prof. depts. biology, biophysics, preventive medicine, 1976-78, assoc. prof. pharmacology, medicinal chemistry dept. preventive medicine, 1977-78, dir. chem., biomed. environ. rsch. group dept. preventive medicine, 1977-82, prof. depts. radiology, preventive medicine, pharmacology, medicinal chemistry, vet. pathobiology, 1978-82; dir. Nat. Ctr. for Toxicological Rsch., Jefferson, Ark., 1980-92, Disting. scientist in residence, 1992-2000; rsch. prof. Strang Cancer Prevention Rsch. Ctr. Rockefeller U., 2000—04. Disting. prof. U. Poona, India, 1978—2004, Cairo U., 1989—; disting. prof. carcinogenesis Guang Zhou Med. Coll., China, 1988—; adj. prof. U. Ark. Med. Sci., 1980—, U. Tenn. Health Scis., 1983—; adj. prof. pharmacology Coll. Pharmacy U. Ark., 1997—; cons. Oak Ridge Nat. Lab., 1971—75, Brookhaven Nat. Lab., 1975—78, Argonne Nat. Lab., 1975—78, EPA, 1976, 78, Am. Indsl. Health Coun., 1978, PPG Industries, 1978, Informatics, 1978—80, FDA, 1980; mem. NAS/NRC Bd. Toxicology and Environ. Health Hazards, 1976—82; mem. insteragy. staff group Office Sci. and Tech. Policy Exec. Office of Pres., 1982—85, chmn., 1983—85; chmn. bd. dirs. Ark. Sci. and Tech. Authority, 1983—84, mem., 1985—88; bd. dirs. Miltos Pharms., Water Chef, Inc., SpectRX Immunovative, Inc.; adv. bd. Miss. State U., 1987—96, Petrotech, 1991—92, 2006—, VoiceNet, 1998—99, Waterchef, Inc., 2001—03, Micromed Labs., 2002—06, Biomed, 2002—. Applied DNA Sci., Inc., 2003—05, Fla. A&M U. Rsch. Ctr., 1985—2004, Omega Foods, 2004—05, Met. Area Networks, 2004, Ship OK, LLC, 2004—, Biophora, Inc., 2005, Neogenix Ind., 2006—; bd. visitors Memphis State U., 1984—90; chair task force risk assessment/risk mgmt. HHS, 1985, chmn. com. coordinate environ., health and related programs, 1985—88; chmn. sci. panel Agt. Orange working group, 1986—88; mem. USAF toxicology rev. panel, 1987; chmn. intergovtl. Task Force Tech. Transer, 1987—88, DHHS Task Force Tech. Transfer, 1987—88; mem. Inter Govt. Commn. Competitiveness, 1987—94; apptd. del. US-USSR Emerging Leaders Summit; chmn. Sci. and Tech. Commn., 1988; disting. adj. prof. Moscow State U., 1989—, Guanzou Med. U., China, 1988—, U. Udina, Italy, 1999—2002; chmn. Ark. Sch. Math. and Sci. Found., 1997—2003. Editor-in-chief: Toxicology Indsl. Health, 2000—; contbr. chapters to books, articles to profl. jours. Named Outstanding Alumnus, Syracuse U., 1976; recipient Hopkins award for grad. rsch., 1971, Japanese Med. Assn. award, 1978, Karl-August-Forester award, West Germany, 1980, award of merit, FDA, 1982, 1985, 1986, Sr. Exec. Svc. award, 1982, 1984, 1985, Commr.'s Spl. citation, 1987, Superior Svc. award, USPHS, 1983, Gov.'s award Outstanding Svc., State of Ark., 1985, Letter of Commendation, Pres. of US, 1985, Pres. Rank award Outstanding Accomplishment, Guangzhou Med. Coll., 1988, Bose medal, Bose Inst., 1994, Ednl. medal, U. Ark., 2005. Fellow: AAAS, Am. Assn. Clin. Chemistry, Risk Analysis Soc., Gerontol. Soc., Am. Coll. Toxicology (past pres.); mem.: Sr. Execs. Assn., Photochem. and Photobiol. Soc., Biophys. Soc., Radiation Rsch. Soc., Sigma Xi. Office: 4821 Crestwood Little Rock AR 72207 Personal E-mail: rhart99@comcast.net.

HART, RUSSELL HOLIDAY, retired lawyer; b. Chgo., May 1, 1928; s. Russell Holiday and Allegra (Prince) H.; m. Mary Gehres, June 16, 1951; children: Holiday Hart McKiernan, Robert Russell, Andrew Richard. AB, DePauw U., 1950; JD, Ind. U., 1956. Bar: Ind. 1956, U.S. Dist. Ct. (no. and so. dists.) Ind. 1956, U.S. Ct. Appeals (7th cir.) 1965, U.S. Supreme Ct. 1973. Assoc. Stuart & Branigin, Lafayette, Ind., 1956-61, ptnr., 1961-99; ret., 1999. Lectr. Ind. Continuing Legal Edn. Forum; tchr. trial lawyers Nat. Inst. for Trial Advocacy. Served with U.S. Army, 1951-53. Fellow: Acad. Law Alumni Ind. U. Sch. Law;, Ind. Bar Found. (sec., v.p. 1985), Internat. Acad. Trial Lawyers, Am. Coll. Trial Lawyers, Am. Bar Found., Internat. Soc. Barristers; mem.: ABA (del.), Nat. Assn. Railroad Trial Counsel (past pres.), Def. Trial Counsel of Ind. (past pres.), Ind. Def. Trial Counsel (diplomate), Tippecanoe County Bar Assn. (past pres.), Ind. Bar Assn. (pres.-elect 1986—87, pres. 1987—88, bd. mgrs., former treas., chmn. trial lawyers sect.). Office: Stuart & Branigin PO Box 1010 Lafayette IN 47902-1010 Home Phone: 765-463-1238; Office Phone: 765-423-1561.

HART, STANLEY ROBERT, geochemist, educator; b. Swampscott, Mass., June 20, 1935; s. Robert Winfield and Ruth Mildred (Standley) H.; m. Joanna Smith, Sept. 1, 1956 (div. Dec. 1978); 1 dau., Jolene Kaweah; m. Pamela Coulouras Shepherd, Nov. 4, 1980; children: Elizabeth Ann, Nathaniel Charles. BS, MIT, 1956, PhD, 1960; MS, Calif. Inst. Tech., 1957; Dr. honoris causa, U. Paris, 2005. Staff mem. Carnegie Instn., Washington, 1960-75; prof. dept. earth and planetary sci. Mass. Inst. Tech., Cambridge, 1975-89; sr. scientist Woods Hole (Mass.) Oceanographic Instn., 1989—2007, C.O. Iselin chair, emeritus, 2007—; mem. U.S. Nat. Com. for Geochemistry, 1973-76, chmn., 1975; mem. ocean crust panel

Internat. Phase of Ocean Drilling, 1974-76; mem. U.S. nat. com. Internat. Geol. Correlations Program, 1974-76; ocean studies bd. Nat. Rsch. Coun., 2003—05. Assoc. editor: Jour. Geophys. Rsch., 1966-68, Revs. of Geophysics, 1970-72, Geochimica et Cosmochimica Acta, 1970-76; editorial bd.: Physics of the Earth and Planetary Interiors, 1977-92, Earth and Planetary Sci. Letters, 1977-87, Chem. Geology, 1985—; contbr. articles in field to profl. jours. Fellow Am. Acad. Arts and Scis., Geol. Soc. Am., Am. Geophys. Union (Harry H. Hess medal 1997), Geochem. Soc. (councillor 1981-83, v.p. 1983-85, pres. 1985-87, V.M. Goldschmidt award 1992), European Assn. Geochemistry; mem. NAS. Office: Woods Hole Oceanographic Inst Dept Geology & Geophysics Woods Hole MA 02543 *I view science, the search for truth and understanding, as an infinitely long road; getting to the end is not as important as how we get there.*

HART, TERRY JONATHAN, communications executive; b. Pitts., Oct. 27, 1946; s. Jonathan Smith Hart and Lillian Dorothy (Zugates) Hart Pierson; m. Mary Jane McKeever, Aug. 13, 1999; children: Amy, Lori. B of Mech. Engring., Lehigh U., 1968, DEng (hon.), 1988; MS, MIT, 1969; MEE, Rutgers U., 1978. Mem. tech. staff AT&T Bell Labs., Whippany, N.J., 1968-69, 73-78, supr., 1984—, head cellular systems strategic planning, 1989—; astronaut NASA Johnson Space Ctr., Houston, 1978-84, captured solar maximum satellite, 1984, div. mgr. Telstar 4 Satellite Program; pres. Loral Skynet, Bedminster, N.J., 1997—. Patentee in field. Served to lt. col. USAF Air N.G., 1969-90. Recipient N.J. Disting. Service medal, NASA Space Flight medal, Pride of Pa. medal; named N.J. Aviation Hall Fame. Mem. IEEE, Sigma Xi, Tau Beta Pi. Avocations: skiing, golf. Office: Loral Skynet 500 Hills Dr 3rd Fl Bedminster NJ 07921-1538

HART, WILLIAM C., underwriter, educator, writer; b. Orange, NJ, Jan. 6, 1947; s. William Gerard and Etchen (Alsberg) Hart; m. Wendy Clarkson, Oct. 14, 1978 (div.); m. Charlotte R. Wagner, Oct. 7, 1989. AB, Fla. So. Coll., 1969; MBA, Ashbourne U., 1973; diploma in real estate fin., NYU, 1975; profl. garden tng. program, Longwood Garden, Kennett Sq., Pa., 1976; postgrad., Dale Carnegie Inst., 1994. Cert. land title profl. Land Title Inst. Va. Regional underwriter Chgo. Title Ins. Co., Dallas, 1980—83; sr. adv. title officer Lawyers Title Ins. Corp., New Brunswick, NJ, 1983—85; chief title officer Am. Title Ins. Co., Miami, Fla., 1985—92; chief title underwriter emeritus T. A. Title Ins. Co., Media, Pa., 1993—; prin. Title Law Assocs., Phila., 1999—; editor in chief Title Mgmt. Today, 2003—. Lectr. NJ Land Title Sch., Upsala Coll., East Orange, NJ, 1972, Land Title Sch., Austin, 1982, NJ Lawyers Title Inst., Summit, 1984—85, Land Title Inst. Va., 1990, 91; instr. Neumann Coll. CLE Cert., 1995—97, NBI, Inc., 2003—. Author: (book) Standard Title Underwriting Practices, 1991, Creditors Rights and Title Insurance, Questionable Title, Remedies & Extra-Hazardous Risks, 1991, Title Insurance Underwriting Principles and Exception Language, 1992, Instructions as the Use of Title Insurance Endorsements, 1992, Title Insurance Underwriting Process, 1994, The Law of Titles in Florida, 1996, The Law of Titles in New York, 1996, The Law Titles in Pennsylvania, 1998; editor: New Jersey Titles Annotated, 1986, Alta Title Counsel, 1989—, Title Law Annotated, 2000—, The Law of Titles, 2002, Title Management Today, 2003—; contbg. editor: book Patton & Palomar on Land Titles, 2003, contbg. author: Thompson/Westgroup. Mem.: USGA (assoc.), Internat. Platform Assn., Internat. Platform Assn., Pa. Land Title Assn. (mem. forms com. 1989—92, 1994), NJ Land Title Assn. (chmn. title officers com. 1987—88), Pa. Sheriffs Assn., Fraternal Order Police (assoc.), Standard and Poor's Vista Rsch. Soc. Industry Leaders, World Affairs Coun. Phila., Golden Horshoe Golf & Country Club, Ashbourne Country Club, Sigma Phi Epsilon. Republican. Avocations: martial arts (black belt), golf, stamp collecting/philately, gardening. Home: 612 Boyer Rd Cheltenham PA 19012-1610 Office: Tttle Law Assocs PO Box 7137 Elkins Park PA 19027-0137 Personal E-mail: TitleLaw@comcast.net.

HART, WILLIAM THOMAS, federal judge; b. Joliet, Ill., Feb. 4, 1929; s. William Michael and Geraldine (Archambeault) H.; m. Catherine Motta, Nov. 27, 1954; children: Catherine Hart Maher, Susan Hart DaMario, Julie Hart Boesen, Sally Hart Collins, Nancy Hart McLaughlin. JD, Loyola U., Chgo., 1951. Bar: Ill. 1951, U.S. Dist. Ct. 1951, U.S. Ct. Appeals (7th cir.) 1954, U.S. Ct. Appeals (D.C. cir.) 1977. Asst. U.S. atty. U.S. Dist. Ct. (no. dist.) Ill., Chgo., 1954-56; assoc. Defrees & Fiske, 1956-59; spl. asst. atty. gen. State of Ill., 1957-58; assoc. then ptnr. Schiff, Hardin & Waite, 1959-82; spl. asst. state's atty. Cook County, Ill., 1960; judge U.S. Dist. Ct. Ill., 1982—; now sr. judge. Mem. exec. com. U.S. Dist. Ct. (no. dist.) Ill., 1988-92; mem. com. on adminstrn. fed. magistrates sys., Jud. Conf. U.S., 1987-92, 7th cir. Jud. Coun., 1990-92; mem. edn. com. Fed. Jud. Ctr., 1994-99; chair No. Dist. Ill. Ct. Hist. Assoc., 1998—. Pres. adv. bd. Mercy Med. Ctr., Aurora, Ill., 1980-81; v.p. Aurora Blood Bank, 1972-77; trustee Rosary H.S., 1981-82, 93-98; bd. dirs. Chgo. Legal Asst. Found., 1974-76. Served with U.S. Army, 1951-53. Decorated Bronze Star; named to Joliet/Will County Hall of Pride, 1992; recipient Disting. Jurist award Loyola U., Chgo., 2005. Mem. 7th Cir. Bar Assn., Law Club, Legal Club, Soc. Trial Lawyers, Union League Club of Aurora, Ill. (hon.), Inn of Ct., Serra Club of Aurora (v.p. 2000). Office: US Dist Ct No Dist Ill US Courthouse Rm 2246 219 S Dearborn St Chicago IL 60604-1702

HARTE, ANDREW DENNIS, transportation company executive, travel agent; b. Bronx, NY, Jan. 23, 1946; s. Bernard and Gertrude (Romm) H. BA, CUNY-Hunter Coll., 1968; MS in Spanish, SUNY, New Paltz, 1975, MS in English, 1979; MA in French, NYU, 1975; MS in Reading, L.I. U., 1979. Cert. tchr., 48 states. Tchr. Hendrick Hudson Sch., Montrose, N.Y., 1968-69, Mahopac Schs., N.Y., 1969-70, Croton-Harmon Schs., N.Y., 1970-83; pres., owner Dominion Limousine Corp., Peekskill, N.Y., 1989—. Mem. local com. N.E. Conf. on Tchg. Fgn. Langs., N.Y.C., 1979-83. Mem. Am. Assn. Tchrs. French (life), Am. Assn. Tchrs. Spanish and Portuguese (life), N.Y. State Assn. Fgn. Lang. Tchrs. (life, bd. dirs. 1983-86), Mensa (life), The Intertel Soc., Phi Delta Kappa (life, editor, historian). Avocations: foreign and domestic travel, language study, stamp collecting/philately, reading, current events. Office: Dominion Limousine Corp PO Box 328 Peekskill NY 10566-0328 Business E-Mail: aharte@dominionlimo.com.

HARTE, JOHN HERMAN, artist; b. Omaha, June 11, 1927; s. William Drexel Harte and Arlina Carncross; m. Dorothy Beatty Harte, June 29, 1957. BA in Comml. Art, U. Wyo., Laramie, 1955. Comml. artist Continental Can Co., Chgo., 1949—53, NYC, 1953—56; clk. US State Dept., Washington, 1956—57; sec. to pres., office mgr. Chevron, San Francisco, 1957—78; ret., 1978. Artist mem. Art League Fla. State U., Tallahassee, 1999—2001. Represented in permanent collections County Civic Ctr., San Rafael, Calif., exhibitions include Lucien Labaudt Gallery, San Francisco, 1964, U. Calif. Morgan Hall, Berkeley, 1965, Frank Lloyd-Wright Marin County Civic Ctr., San Rafael, Calif., 1977, Grand Canyon Nat. Pk., Ariz., 1984, Death Valley Nat. Pk., Calif., 1985, Chapin Mesa Mus. Auditorium, Mesa Verde Nat. Pk., 1986, Channel Islands Nat. Pk., Calif., 1987, Chevron Corp., San Francisco and Concord, Calif., 1988, Govs. Gallery State Capitol, Tallhassee, 1999, Tallahassee Natural History Mus., 2000, LeMoyne Art Found. Hoover Gallery, Tallahassee, 2001, Pfizer, Inc., NYC, 2003, Interior Motives, St. Petersburg, Fla., Red Cloud Art Gallery, St. Petersburg, 2007, Soho Myriad Gallery, Atlanta, 2007, Tree Studio Arts and Antiques, Chgo., Represented in permanent collections Palm Springs Desert Mus., Riverside Mus., Oakland Mus. Bd. dirs. Downtown Neighborhood Assn., St. Petersburg, 2006, Marin Soc. Artists, Ross, Calif. With USN, 1945—46. Mem.: Salvadore Dali Mus. St. Petersburg, Mus. Fine Arts St. Petersburg, Art Ctr. St. Petersburg. Democrat. Avocations: travel, hiking, swimming, reading.

HARTELIUS, CHANNING JULIUS, lawyer; b. Gt. Falls, Mont., Oct. 2, 1946; s. Chester Werner and Hildegarde Margaret (Kehm) Hartelius; children: Rhonda, Kerry, Chanin, Courtney. BA with honors, U. Mont., 1968; JD with honors, George Washington U., 1971. Bar: Va. 1971, Mont. 1971. Asst. atty. gen., Mont., 1971; ptnr. Wuerthner & Hartelius, Gt. Falls, 1972—73, Hartelius & Lewin, Gt. Falls, 1973—78, Hartelius & Assocs., P.C., Gt. Falls, 1978—87, Hartelius, Ferguson, Baker and Kazda, P.C., 1987—. Asst. city atty., Gt. Falls, 1972—76; instr. Coll. Gt. Falls, 1980. Author: Understanding Bankruptcy, A Guide, 1981, Montana Handbook on Contract for Deeds, 1982; co-author: Law and the Municipal Ecology, 1971; contbr. articles to legal jours. Participant Leadership Gt. Falls, 1983; bd. dirs. Selective Svc., 1995—. Served to capt. USAR, 1971—82. Recipient Presdl. award of excellence, U.S. Jaycees, 1976. Mem.: ATLA, ABA, Cascade County Bar Assn. (pres. 1997), Mont. Bar Assn., Mont. Hist. Soc. Lutheran (pres. Ch. 1996, 1997), Gt. Falls Jaycees (pres. 1976), Meadow Lark Country Club, Toastmasters (pres. 1975, 1997). Home: 825 4th Ave N Great Falls MT 59401-1511 Office: PO Box 1629 Great Falls MT 59403-1629

HARTELL, HOLLY, school librarian; b. Spartanburg, SC; BA, Converse Coll., Spartanburg, SC, 1997; MLIS, U. SC, 1999. Cert. Nat. Bd. Profl. Teaching Standards, 2003. Media specialist Parcolet (SC) Elementary Sch., 1999—; assessor & media specialist Nat. Board Profl. Teaching Standards. Named Pacolet Elementary Teacher of Yr.; recipient Ann T. White award, Spartanburg County, 2004, Info. Tech. Pathfinder award, Am. Assn. Sch. Librarians, 2007; grantee EIA Unit Grant, SC Dept. Edn. Office: Parcolet Elementary Sch 150 McDowell St Pacolet SC 29372 Office Phone: 864-474-4060. Office Fax: 864-474-4065. E-mail: hharte@spa3.k12.sc.us.

HARTER, DONALD HARRY, neurologist, medical educator; b. Breslau, Germany, May 16, 1933; came to U.S., 1940; naturalized, 1945; s. Harry Morton and Leonor Evelyne (Goldmann) H.; m. Lee Grossman, Dec. 18, 1960 (div. 1976); children: Kathryne, Jennifer, Amy, David; m. Rikki Horne, May 18, 1985 (div. 1986); m. Marjorie Brandt Dahlin, Oct. 12, 1990. AB, U. Pa., 1953; MD, Columbia U., 1957. Diplomate Am. Bd. Psychiatry and Neurology. Intern in medicine Yale-New Haven Med. Center, 1957-58; asst. resident, then resident neurology N.Y. Neurol. Inst., 1958-61; guest investigator Rockefeller U., 1963-66; mem. faculty Columbia Coll. Physicians and Surgeons, 1960-75, prof. neurology and microbiology, 1973-75; vis. fellow Clare Hall, Cambridge, England, 1973-74; attending neurologist N.Y. Neurol. Inst., Presbyn. Hosp., 1973-75; Charles L. Mix prof. Northwestern U., 1975-85, Benjamin and Virginia T. Boshes prof. neurology, 1985-87, chmn. dept. neurology, 1975-87, Northwestern Meml. Hosp., Chgo., 1975-87; dir. rsch. scholars program Howard Hughes Med. Inst./NIH, Bethesda, 1989-2000; with dept. neurology George Washington U. Med. Ctr., Washington, 1987—. Vis. sci. officer Howard Hughes Med. Inst., 1986—87, sr. sci. officer, 1987—2000; clin. prof. neurology George Washington U. Sch. Medicine and Health Scis., 1987—2001, prof. emeritus clin. neurology, 2001—03; prof. emeritus neurology in residence George Washington U., 2004—; vis. rsch. fellow Dept. Pathology U. Cambridge, England, 1973—74, 2000—01; vis. life mem. Clare Hall, 2000—01; mem. adv. com. on fellowships Nat. Multiple Sclerosis Soc., 1976—79, chmn., 1977—79, rsch. programs adv. com., 1989—94; mem. Nat. Commn. on Venereal Disease, HEW, 1970—72; mem. med. adv. bd. Am. Parkinson Disease Assn., 1976—90, Myasthenia Gravis Found., 1980—87; mem. sci. adv. coun. Nat. Amyotrophic Lateral Sclerosis Found., 1978—85; mem. bd. sci. counselors Nat. Inst. Dental Rsch. NIH, 1990—95; sr. sci. advisor Amyotrophic Lateral Sclerosis Assn., 1992—2000. Mem. editorial bd. Neurology, 1976-82, Anns. of Neurology, 1983-89; mem. adv. bd. Archives of Virology, 1975-81. Recipient Joseph Mather Smith prize Columbia U., 1970, Lucy G. Moses award, 1970, 72, Donald W. Mulder award The ALS Assn., 1998; Am. Cancer Soc. scholar, 1973-74; USPHS spl. fellow, 1963-66, Guggenheim fellow, 1973. Fellow: AAAS, Am. Acad. Neurology, Infectious Diseases Soc. Am.; mem.: Am. Soc. Virology, Am. Soc. Microbiology, Deutsche Gesellschaft fur Neurologie (corr.), Am. Neurol. Assn., Am. Soc. Clin. Investigation, Univ. Club Washington, Yale Club N.Y.C., Cosmos Club, Phi Beta Kappa, Sigma Xi. Office: George Washington U Med Ctr Ste 7-404 2150 Pennsylvania Ave NW Washington DC 20037-3201 Business E-Mail: dharter@mfa.gwu.edu.

HARTER, HUGH ANTHONY, foreign language educator; b. Columbus, Ohio, Dec. 13, 1922; s. Anthony Hugh and Georgiana (Hayes) H.; m. Driscilla Escher, Aug. 31, 1959 (div. 1961); m. Frances D. Reichman, Oct. 7, 1970 (dec. Feb. 16, 2006). Student, Ohio Wesleyan U., 1940-41, Hamilton Coll., 1943, Ecole du Syndicat de la Haute Couture, Paris, 1947, NYU, 1975, New Sch. Social Research, 1975; BA cum laude, Ohio State U., 1947, PhD, 1959; MA cum laude, Mexico City Coll., U. Ams., 1951. Student teaching asst. Ohio State U., 1946-47, grad. teaching asst., 1951-53; asst. to prof. French Mexico City Coll., U. Ams., 1951; instr., asst. prof. Romance langs. Wesleyan U., Middletown, Conn., 1953-59; assoc. prof. Elmira Coll., 1959-60; Andrew Mellon postdoctoral fellow U. Pitts., 1960-61, spl. lectr., 1963-64, NDEA Insts. fellow, 1962, 63; assoc. prof. Chatham Coll., 1961-64, Loyola U., Chgo., 1964-66; prof. Ohio Westeyan U., Delaware, 1966-84; chmn. dept. Romance langs. Ohio Wesleyan U., Delaware, 1966-80, Robert Hayward prof. modern fgn. langs. Delaware, 1976-84, dir. Internat. Inst. of Spain, 1984-87, prof. emeritus. Pres. Vitalicio, Fundacion Juan Ruiz, Segovia, Spain, 1971-86, Horizons for Learning, Delaware, Ohio, 1974—, Cursos Americanos e Internacionales, Segovia, 1986-1998; acct. Columbus Coated Fabrics Corp., Columbus, 1941-42; auditor European Post Exchange System, Bad Nauheim, Germany, 1948; co-owner John Anthony Studios, Columbus, 1954-64; v.p., dir. Von Mock Assocs., N.Y.C., 1969-70; spl. lectr. U. Catolica de Santa Maria, Arequipa, Peru, 1969; dir. Acad. Program in Segovia, 1969-1998. Author: Gertrudis Gomez de Avellaneda, 1981, Tangier and All That, 1993, reissue, 1997, D'Utah Beach aux Ardennes: Itiéraires 1944-1994, 1996, Return to Patton's France 1944's Odyssey Retraced, 1999, The Countess, 2004, Juan Ramon Jiminez's Diary of a Newlywed Past, 2004; co-author (with J. D. Mitchell): Staging a Spanish Classic: El hospital de los locos, 1990; translator, author The Scavenger, 1962, Femmes/Hommes, 1977, The Butts (Driss Chraïbi), 1983, Mother Comes of Age (Driss Chraïbi), 1983, Mother Spring (Driss Chraïbi), 1989, Past Tense (Driss Chraïbi), 1990, The Distant Friend (Claude Roy), 1990, Shadow of Paradise: Vicente Aleixandre, 1987, Remembrance of a Time Just Past, 1993, Shattered Vision (Rabah Belamri), 1994, translator, editor A History of Spanish Literature, 1971; co-editor (with Willis Barnstone): Riconenete y Cortadillo, 1960; co-editor: (with R.C. Allen, Jr.) A First Spanish Handbook for Teachers in Elementary Schools, 1961; co-editor: A Second Spanish Handbook for Teachers in Elementary Schools, 1963; lyricist More About the Pear Tree, The Death of the Soldier Guard, 1976; translator: Diary of a Newlywed Poet, 2004, Rochambeau and America's Independence, 2005. Bd. dirs. Centro Segovia, 1971-80; v.p. Delaware (Ohio) Heritage Inc., 1973-75, bd. dirs., 1975-78, pres., 1978-80; pres. Delaware Shakespeare Soc., 1980-81. Served with M.I. 3d Army, Normandy, No. France, then Air Transport Command, U.S. Army, ETO. Recipient medals of St. Calais, Vendome, Blois, Dombasle, Utah Beach, Avranches, Blois, St. Calais, Ouzouer, 1994, medaille d'Honneur of Confedn. Europeene des Anciens Combattants, 1992, 93; named Hon. Citizen City of Segovia, 1976; summer rsch. grantee Andrew Mellon Found., Morocco, 1973; spl. grantee Govt. of Morocco, 1975; spl. langs. grantee Mellon Mediterranean Studies, Algeria and Tunisia, 1977. Mem.: AAUP, MLA, ASCAP, Am. Assn. Tchrs. Spanish and Portuguese, Authors' Guild, Coll. Lang. Assn., La Academia de San Quirce (Segovia corr.). Home: 135 Bow St #8 Portsmouth NH 03801 Office Phone: 603-373-8000. Personal E-mail: hharter@comcast.net.

HARTER, JAMES LESTER, academic administrator, consultant; b. Lima, Ohio, Feb. 2, 1959; s. Lester Rudolph and Patricia Lou (Pryer) Harter; m. Cynthia Ann Whitaker, Dec. 18, 1981; children: Joshua James, Jennifer Leigh, Jonah Reed. BS in Edn., Bowling Green State U., Ohio, 1981, MA in Coll. Student Pers., 1982. Head resident Bluffton (Ohio) Coll., 1981—82; hall dir., complex coord. Bowling Green (Ohio) State U., 1982—84; dir. student life SUNY, Purchase, NY, 1984—85; dir. residence life Franklin (Ind.) Coll., 1985—89; v.p. student affairs, dean students Defiance (Ohio) Coll., 1989—94; tchr. Paulding (Ohio) H.S., 1994—95; dean student affairs Mercy Coll. N.W. Ohio, Toledo, 1995—2004, v.p. adminstrv. svcs., 2004—. Cons. Partners in Planning, Grand Rapids, Ohio, 1996—2002. Mem. adv. com. Toledo (Ohio) Housing Ct., 2004—05; pres. bd. edn. Otsego Local Schs., Tontogany, Ohio, 1999—2006; bd. dirs. Nieghborhoods in Partnership, Toledo, 2004—06, UpTown Assn., Toledo, 2002—06; chmn. devel. com. Habitat for Humanity Wood County, Bowling Green, 2006. Mem.: Am. Coll. Pers. Assn. (assoc.), Mercy Children's Hosp. Kiwanis (assoc.; pres. 2003—06). Republican. Avocations: travel, walking, reading. Home: 17090 Wapakoneta Road Grand Rapids OH 43522 Office: Mercy College of Northwest Ohio 2221 Madison Avenue Toledo OH 43624-1132 Home Phone: 419-832-0918; Office Phone: 419-251-1786. Office Fax: 419-251-1570. E-mail: james.harter@mercycollege.edu.

HARTER, JOHN J., economic analyst; b. Canyon, Tex., Jan. 31, 1926; s. Ralph E. and Grace S. Harter; m. Irene T. Harter, May 25, 1957 (dec. Feb. 2002); children: Tian, Tonia, Lal; m. Evelyn Bland Harter, Sept. 19, 2004. BA, U. So. Calif., LA, 1948, MA, 1953; M of Econs., Harvard U., Cambridge, Mass., 1963. Lectr. in history U. So. Calif., LA, 1948-53; fgn. svc. officer, various fgn. assignments Geneva, South Africa, Chile, Thailand, Dept. of State, Washington, 1954-83; oral historian Washington, 1983—2007; conf. affairs officer Am. Fgn. Svc. Assn., Washington, 1989-96; freelance writer, cons. Washington, 1983—; declassifier Agy. for Internat. Devel., Washington, 1998—. Author: The Language of Trade, 1984. Sec., mem. vestry Am. Ch., Geneva, 1969-70. Mem. Diplomatic and Consular Officers Ret., Am. Fgn. Svc. Assn. Democrat. Episcopalian. Home: 12109 Kershaw Pl Glen Allen VA 23059-6978 Office Phone: 301-837-0764. Personal E-mail: jjitharter@aol.com.

HARTER, LAFAYETTE GEORGE, JR., retired economics professor; b. Des Moines, May 28, 1918; s. Lafayette George and Helen Elizabeth (Ives) H.; m. Charlotte Mary Toshach, Aug. 23, 1950; children— Lafayette George III, James Toshach, Charlotte Helen. BA in Bus. Adminstrn, Antioch Coll., 1941; MA in Econs, Stanford, 1948, PhD, 1960. Instr. Menlo Coll., Menlo Park, Calif., 1948-50; instr. Coll. of Marin, Kentfield, Calif., 1950-60; prof. econs. dept. Oreg. State U., 1960-85, prof. emeritus, 1985—, chmn. dept., 1967-71. Mem. panel arbitrators Fed. Mediation and Conciliation Svc., 1965-84, Oreg. Conciliation Svc., 1967-84; mem. Univ. Ctrs. for Rational Alternatives. Author: John R. Commons: His Assault on Laissez-faire, 1962, Labor in America, 1957, Economic Responses to a Changing World, 1972; editorial bd. Jour. Econ. Issues, 1981-84. Assoc. campaign chmn. Benton United Good Neighbor Fund, 1970-72, campaign chmn., v.p., 1972-73, pres., 1973-74, vice chmn.; pub. mem. Adv. Commn. on Unemployment Compensation, 1972, 73, chmn., 1974-78; Bd. dirs. Oreg. Coun. Econ. Edn., 1971-89; pub. mem. local profl. responsibilities Oreg. State Bar Assn., 1980-83; pub. mem. Oreg. Coun. on Ct. Procedures, 1985-93, bd. mem. Community Econs. of Corp., Community Econ. Stabilization Corp. Lt. comdr. USNR, 1941-46. Mem. AAUP, Am. Arbitration Assn. (pub. employment disputes panel 1970-92), Am. Western Econ. Assns., Indsl. Rels. Rsch. Assn., Am. Assn. for Evolutionary Econs., Oreg. State Employees Assn. (v.p. faculty chpt. 1972, pres. 1973), Am. Assn. Ret. Persons (pres. local chpt. 1992-93), Corvallis Retirement Village (fin. com., bd. dirs.). Democrat. Mem. United Ch. of Christ (moderator 1972, 73; mem. fin. com. Oreg. conf. 1974-82, dir. 1978-81, mem. personnel com. 1983-85). Home: 4123 SW Comus St Portland OR 97219

HARTER, PHILIP J., lawyer, educator; b. Columbus, Ohio, Apr. 14, 1942; s. Joseph M and Edith R. Harter; m. Nancy B. Gammel, Aug. 22, 1964; 1 child, Alexa. AB, Kenyon Coll., 1960—64; MA in Math., U. Mich., Ann Arbor, 1965—66, JD, 1966—69. Bar: D.C. 1971, Supreme Ct. U.S. 1979. Vis. prof. of law Vt. Law Sch., South Royalton, Vt., 1999—2003; dir. program on democracy and governance; mediator The Mediation Inst., Washington, 1998—2003; Earl F. Nelson prof. law U. Mo., Columbia, 2003—. Author: Negotiating Regulations: A Cure for Malaise, 1981. Recipient Gellhorn award, Federal Bar Assn., 1998, award for Outstanding Contribution to the Pub. Policy of fostering the use of ADR, Soc. of Profls. in Dispute Resolution, 1992, award for Outstanding Achievement for Excellence and Innovation in Alternative Dispute Resolution, Ctr. for Pub. Resources, 1992. Mem.: ABA (chmn. sect. adminstrv. law and regulatory practice 1995—96, chmn. working group on regulatory reform 1995—98, chmn. environ. com., sect. dispute resolution 2004—). Avocation: bicycling. Address: 201 S Glenwood Ave Columbia MO 65211 Office: U Missouri Hulston Hall Columbia MO 65211 Office Phone: 573-884-3614. Business E-Mail: harterpj@missouri.edu.

HARTER, RALPH MILLARD PETER, lawyer, minister, educator; b. Auburn, NY, Mar. 15, 1946; s. Donald Robert and Ruth (Ashdown) H.; m. Robin Ann Bampton, June 29, 1968 (div. Oct. 1994); m. Leslie J. Teague, Sept. 13, 1997; children: Robin Brooke, Donald Bampton. BA, Hobart Coll., 1968; JD, Cornell U., 1972; MDiv, Colgate Rochester Div. Sch., 2007; postgrad., Bexley Hall Episcopal Sem., 2007—. Bar: Pa. 1972, U.S. Dist. Ct. (ea. dist.) Pa. 1972, N.Y. 1981, U.S. Dist. Ct. (we. dist.) N.Y. 1981; ordained deacon Episcopal Ch., 2007. Assoc. Duane, Morris & Heckscher, Phila., 1972-81, Harter, Secrest & Emery, Rochester, N.Y., 1981-83; ptnr. Goldstein, Goldman, Kessler & Underberg, Rochester, 1983-91, Sutton, DeLeeuw, Clark & Darcy, Rochester, 1991-94; mng. ptnr. Burke, Albright, Harter & Reddy, LLP, Rochester, 1994—2003; of counsel Burker, Albright, Harter & Reddy LLP, Rochester, 2003—. Educator elder law issues, right to die, ethics, trusts and estates issues; transitional deacon Episcopal Diocese of Rochester, 2007. V.p., gen. counsel, bd. dirs. Otetiana council Inc., Boy Scouts Am., Rochester, 1982-2000; mem. various coms. Episcopal Diocese and Ch., Phila. and Rochester, 1972—; chair bd. dirs. Episcopal Sr. Life Cmtys., 1997-99, bd. dirs., 1995—; trustee Colls. of Seneca (Hobart & William Smith Colls.), 1987-96; bd. dirs. Allendale Columbia Sch., 1991-96; trustee Sigma Phi Ednl. Found., N.Y.C., 1990—; pres., gen. coun., bd. dirs. Rochester chpt. Alzheimer's Assn., 1981-2003. Served with USAR, 1969-75. Mem. ABA, N.Y. State Bar Assn. (various sects., lectr.), Pa. Bar Assn., Phila. Bar Assn., Monroe County Bar Assn., Nat. Acad. Elder Law Attys., Rochester Area C. of C. (United Way coms. 1984-96), Alzheimer's Disease and Related Disorders Assn. Inc. (pres., gen. counsel, bd. dirs. 1981—), Assn. of Adirondack Scout Camps (bd. dirs. 1986-93), Cornell U. Law Sch. Assn., Hobart Coll. Alumni Assn. and Alumni Council (pres. 1984-86), Hobart Coll. Statesmen Athletic Assn. (gen. counsel, bd. dirs. 1983-2003), Hobart Coll. Club of Rochester (pres. 1984-86), The Genesee Valley Club (Rochester), Webhannet Golf Club (Kennebunkport, Maine), Delta chpt. Sigma Phi. Republican. Avocations: fly fishing, duck decoy carving, white-water rafting, canoeing, golf. Home: Tuckaway Farm 98 Canfield Rd Pittsford NY 14534-9709 Office: 1800 Hudson Ave Rochester NY 14617-5128 E-mail: peteharter@rochester.rr.com.

HARTER, THEO C., music educator, composer; d. Edward Hegeler and Dorothy Blouke Carus; m. Robert Handley Hold, Oct. 31, 1960 (div.); m. Robert Lyle Harter, Jan. 1, 1949 (div.); children: George Carus, Edward Bixby, Katherine Hegeler. Studied, U. Wash., 1941—43, Goodman Theatre, 1943—44, New Sch., 1945—46; studied composition, Meyer Kupferman, NYC, 1951—52; studied piano and composition, Macio Williams, NYC, 1958—60; studied composition, Hall Overton Studio, 1969, Art Murphy Studio, 1969. Dance accompanist Martha Graham Sch. Dance, NYC, 1946—47, New Dance Group, NYC, 1947—48; pianist, singer various night clubs, NY and NJ, 1957—60; coord., editor music program Open Ct. Pub. Co., LaSalle, Ill., 1970—74, dir., editor music program, 1974—86; founder, dir. TurnAbout Songs-Children's Music Workshop, NYC, 1986—. Actor, tchr. Summer Stock, West Newbury, Mass., 1947; owner, performer duo-piano Nirvana Coffee Ho., NYC, 1961—63; vol. tchr. composition Bronx Cmty. Ctr., NYC, 1968—69; vol. music composition Peekskill Cmty. Ctr., Peekskill, 1970; music literacy tchr. St. John, the Bapt. Elem. Sch., Yonkers, NY, 1972—73; tchr. music literacy Pub. Sch. 91, Bklyn., 1972—74; music literacy tchr. Pub. Sch. 153, NYC, 1981—82; inter-age music tchr. youth program Bank St. Sch., NYC, 1992; tchr. inter-age music literacy Duke Ellington, NYC, 1994—95; dir., tchr. West End Collegiate Ch. Summer Arts Project, NYC, 1995—96; dir. Ctrl. Presbyn. Summer Project for Arts, NYC, 1997—99; supr. PowellFest TurnAbouts Program, Peru, Ill., 2001—04; supr. Summer Project Arts West Pk. Presbyn. Ch., NYC, 2001—02, 2001—04; pianist, singer solo and duo Night Clubs, NY, NJ, 1957—60, 2004. Composer: The Marriage Broker of Nirvana, 1961, The Legend of Sleepy Hollow, 1963, I, Robot, 1965, The Terribly Tonic Tiger, 1972, The Thirsty Crow, 1972, Circus Rhapsody, 1974, Windy City Suite, 1976; editor (prodr.): (songbook) Let's Sing This-a-Way, 1971—72, Field Guide, Reader, Writer: Levels D, E; prodr.: (tchrs. guide and cassettes) Open Court Music Program. Levels 1, 2, 3, 1971—72; dir.: Children's Music Workshop, Level A-Singing Program, 1988, Children's Music Workshop, Level C Beginning Music Literacy, 1995, Children's Music Workshop, Level B, Music Literacy Readiness, 1991. Mem.: Dramatists Guild (assoc.), Am. Guild of Authors and Composers (assoc.). Avocations: mathematics, bicycling, philosophy, reading. Home: 315 Riverside Dr #7C New York NY 10025 Office: TurnAbout Songs Inc 315 Riverside Dr #7C New York NY 10025 Office Phone: 212-932-8621. Personal E-mail: turnaboutsongs@verizon.net.

HARTFORD, MAUREEN A., academic administrator; m. Jay Hartford. BA in French and History, U. N.C., Chapel Hill, MA in coll. tchg.; EdD in higher edn. adminstrn., U. Ark. Dean of student affairs Case Western Res. U., Cleve., 1982—86; vice provost student affairs Wash. State U., 1986—92; v.p. student affairs U. Mich., Ann Arbor, 1992—99; pres. Meredith Coll., Raleigh, NC, 1999—. Faculty Ctr. Study of Higher and Post-Secondary Edn., Ann Arbor, Mich., 1992—99. Mem. governing bd. LeaderShape; bd. trustees Wake Edn. Partnership; bd. dir. Greater Raleigh C. of C., N.C. Triangle United Way; bd. of governors Capital City Club. Recipient Women in Bus., Bus. Jour., 2002, Dist. Scholar award, N.C. Coll. Pers. Assn., 2002. Office: Meredith Coll Adminstrn Bldg 3800 Hillsborough St Raleigh NC 27607 Office Phone: 919-760-8511. E-mail: hartfordm@meredith.edu.*

HARTGER, BARBARA J., marketing professional; b. Grand Rapids, Mich., June 14, 1950; d. Harold Vos Hartger and Marjorie Hartger Bjork. AA, Pine Manor Jr. Coll., 1970; BFA, Sch. of Art Inst. Chgo., 1974; MBA, Baylor U., 2006. Animator, audio-visual dir., tech. dir., multimedia producer Wernecke Studios, Greyhound Exposition Svcs., Chgo., 1974—79; comm. specialist Spl. Events IBM, 1979—83, staff comm. specialist Exec. Briefing Ctr. Dallas, 1983—89, sr. comm. specialist Office Systems Mktg. Southlake, 1989—95, sr. mktg. specialist Worldwide Channel Mktg. Dallas, 1995—97, sr. mktg. support rep. Branding and Naming, Software Group, 1997—2003. Pres. Country Villas Homeowners Assn., Carrollton, Tex., 2002—; pub. info. chmn. United Way of Olmsted County, 1982—83. Recipient Gold award, United Way Am., 1980, Vol. Recognition award, State of Minn., 1983, cert. of appreciation, Dallas County Juvenile Dept., 1988, Appreciation award, Rochester Area C. of C., 1979. Mem.: Apple Corps, SMAA Oratorio Choir, Leadership Tex., Frank Reaugh Art Club. Episcopalian. Avocations: theater, travel, symphony, choral music, skiing.

HARTH, MARSHALL STEPHEN, psychology professor, psychotherapist; b. NYC, Aug. 19, 1943; s. Martin and Rochelle Harth; m. Diane Harth, Mar. 20, 2000; children: Cara Elizabeth, David Gregory, Bernadette Josephine Williams, Jarret Jon Schumacher. PhD, Rutgers U., Newark, 1970. Lic. psychologist NY, 1976; NJ, 2006. Prof. Ramapo Coll. NJ, Mahwah, 1972—. Mem. bd. edn. Chester Union Free Sch. Dist., NY, 1974—76; cmty. adv. bd. mem. Ednl. Opportunity Fund Adv. Bd. Ramapo Coll., Mahwah, NJ, 1997—2004; bd. dirs. Ctr. for Holocaust and Genocide Studies Ramapo Coll., Mahwah, 1987—99, Hurley Camp Fund, NYC, 1992. Fellow, NIMH, 1964—69, Nat. Inst. Child Health and Human Devel., 1970—72; grantee, NSF, 1973. Mem.: APA, Am. Assn. Sex Educators, Counselors and Therapists (cert. 1979), NY Acad. Sci., Animal Behavior Soc., Rockland County Psychol. Assn. (v.p. 1988—96), NY State Psychol. Assn., Sigma Xi, Psi Chi (pres. 1963—64). Office: Ramapo Coll NJ 505 Ramapo Valley Rd Mahwah NJ 07430 Home Phone: 201-684-0942; Office Phone: 201-684-7757. Office Fax: 201-684-0941. Business E-Mail: mharth@ramapo.edu.

HARTH, SIDNEY, musician, educator; b. Cleve., Oct. 5, 1929; s. Leonard and Anne (Dunnire) H.; m. Teresa Testa, July 7, 1949; children: Laura, Robert. Mus.B., Cleve. Inst. Music, 1947; studied with, Joseph Knitzer, Mishel Piastro, Georges Enesco. Assoc. prof. U. Louisville, 1953-58; faculty DePaul U., 1959-62; chmn. dept. music, A.W. Mellon disting. prof. Carnegie-Mellon U., Pitts., 1963-73; mem. faculty Aspen (Colo.) Music Festival, 1963-74; exchange artist Les Jeunesses Musicales de France, 1952; with Mrs. Harth nat. tour, 1952; concertmaster Louisville Orch., 1953-58, Chgo. Symphony, 1959-62; condr. Evanston (Ill.) Orch., 1960-62; assoc. condr., concertmaster Los Angeles Philharm., 1973-79; chief guest condr. Jerusalem Symphony, 1975-77; music dir. Puerto Rican Symphony, 1977-79; condr. Can. Nat. Chamber Orch., 1979, 80; concertmaster N.Y. Philharm., 1980-81; orch. dir. Mannes Coll. of Music, 1981-84; prof. SUNY, Stony Brook, 1981-82, Yale U., 1982-99; prin. condr. Natal Symphony Orch., Durban, South Africa, 1994-99. Dir. orchestral activities Hartt Sch. Music, U. Hartford, 1991-93; violin Wieniawski competition laureate, Poland, 1957; orch. dir., vis. prof. U. Houston, 1985; dir. orchestral studies Carnegie-Mellon U., Pitts., 1989-90; faculty, Carnegie-Mellon U., 2000—, dir. Orchestral Sch. Music and condr. orch., Duquesne U., Pitts., 2001—. Ann. internat. tours including Yugoslavia, Poland, Belgium, Austria, Eng., USSR, Poland, Czechoslovakia, Romania, Switzerland, Holland., Vanguard, Iramac, Concert Hall Soc., Stradivari Records; contbr. articles to nat. mags. Recipient Ysaye medal; Wieniawski medal. Home: 135 Westland Dr Pittsburgh PA 15217-2538 Office Phone: 412-396-6079.

HARTH-BEDOYA, MIGUEL, conductor; b. Lima, Peru, 1968; Degree, Curtis Inst. Music, Juilliard Sch. Music dir. Eugene (Oreg.) Symphony Orch.; now music dir. Ft. Worth Symphony Orch.; assoc. dir. L.A. Philharmonic Orch. Music dir., condr. N.Y. Youth Symphony Carnegie Hall; guest condr. N.Y. Philharm., L.A. Philharm., Fla. Orch., Seattle Symphony, Colo. Symphony, Que. Symphony, Auckland Philharm., New Zealand, Puerto Rico Symphony, Buenos Aires Philharmonia, Evansville Philharm. Orch., Ind.; condr. Juilliard Orch. tour, France, 1993, Japan, 95, St. Luke's Orch., 1995; founder, artistic dir. New Opera Co. Peru, Orquestra Filarmonica de Lima; mem. conducting faculty Juilliard Sch. Condr. opera Il Tutore Burlato, Italy, 1994, rec. artist, 1995, musical dir. (plays) Show Boat, 2007. Office: Fort Worth Symphony Orch 330 E 4th St Ste 200 Fort Worth TX 76102-4019*

HARTIGAN, CAROL, orthopedist; b. 1958; MD, U. Va. Sch. of Medicine, 1987. Cert. Fellow Am. Bd. Physical Med & Rehabilitation. Intern Framingham Union Hospital, 1988; resident Tufts U. Sch. of Medicine in Physical Medicine & Rehabilitation, 1991; with New England Baptist Hospital, 1993—, med. dir., Physical Medicine and Rehabilitation, spine physician; staff mem. Beth Israel Deaconess Med. Ctr.; asst. clinical prof. of Physical Medicine and Rehabilitation Harvard Med. Sch. Mem. Pub. Edn. Com., Surgical Care Com., Scientific Program Com., Multidisciplinary Patient Care Com. Fellow: North Am. Spine Soc. Office: Spine Center New England Baptist Hospital 125 Parker Hill Avenue Boston MA 02120 Office Phone: 617-754-5246. Home Fax: 617-754-6332. E-mail: chartiga@caregroup.harvard.edu.*

HARTIGAN, KARELISA VOELKER, classics educator; b. Stillwater, Okla., Mar. 5, 1943; d. Charles Henry and Elsie Florence Voelker; m. Barry Hartigan, Apr. 21, 1966 (div. Feb. 1978); 1 child, Timothy Lawrence; m. Kevin Michael McCarthy, Dec. 22, 1992. BA in Classics, Coll. of Wooster, 1965; AM in Classics, U. Chgo., 1966, PhD in Classics, 1970. Asst. prof. St. Olaf Coll., Northfield, Minn., 1969-73; asst. prof., assoc. prof. Greek studies U. Fla., Gainesville, from 1973, prof., 1991—, co-dir. Ctr. for Greek Studies, 1980—, assoc. dir. honors program, 1989-95. Author: The Poets and the Cities, 1979, Ambiguity and Self-Deception, 1991, Greek Tragedy on the American Stage, 1995, Myths Behind Our Words, 1998, Muse on Madison Avenue, 2001; editor Text and Presentation jour., 1983-94; editor spl. issues Classical and Modern Lit.; Classical Reflections, 1980. Recipient Excellence in Tchg. award Am. Philol. Assn., 1985; Disting. Alumni Prof. award U. Fla., 1987-89, Univ.-Wide Tchg. award, 1990, Tchg. award, 1994, Disting. Prof. award, 2001. Mem. Modern Greek Studies Assn. (sec. 1983-1986), Classical Assn. Mid. West and South (pres. so. sect. 1986-88, nat. pres. 1992-93). Avocations: bicycling, swimming, travel, cooking, dogs. Office: University of Florida Ctr Greek Studies PO Box 117435 Gainesville FL 32611-7435 Home Phone: 352-377-2178. E-mail: kvhrtgn@classics.ufl.edu.

HARTIL, KIRSTEN, research scientist; b. Irvine, Scotland, Dec. 8, 1974; d. John Davidson and Jean Adams Hartil. BSc, Aberdeen U., Scotland, 1996; PhD, Cambridge U., Eng., 2000. Rsch. assoc. Albert Einstein Coll. Medicine, Yeshiva U., Bronx, NY, 2001—. Mem.: Am. Diabetes Assn. (Menor Based fellow), NY Acad. Sci. (assoc.), Am. Heart Assn. (assoc.). Office: Albert Einstein Coll Medicine 1300 Morris Park Ave Bronx NY NY104 Home Phone: 917-679-4701; Office Phone: 718-430-2853. Office Fax: 718-430-8676. E-mail: khartil@aecom.yu.edu.

HARTING, HARRY LLOYD, JR., government agency administrator, retired military officer; b. Clark AFB, Phillipines, Aug. 31, 1953; s. Harry Lloyd and Virginia Maude (Lipps) Harting. BS in Fgn. Svc., Georgetown U., 1976; MBA, Western New Eng. Coll., 1981; BS in Mgmt., Park Coll., 1988; MPA, Northeastern U., 1990. Commn. 2d lt. USAF, 1976, promoted through ranks to lt. col., 1997; ret. USAFR, 2006; civil servant USCG and IRS, 1989—92, U.S. Customs Svc., U.S. Immigration Svc., 1992—99; contract specialist U.S. Army Garrison, Ft. Myer, Va., 1999—2000, Hdqs. Def. Logistics Agy., Ft. Belvoir, Va., 2000—01, U.S. Army Space and Missile Def. Command, Ft. Dietrich, Md., 2001—03; ops. support staff officer Hdqs. U.S. European Command, Stuttgart, Germany, 2003—04; contract mgr. U.S. Army Ctr. Mil. History, Ft. McNair, 2004—06. Lt. col. CAP, USAF Aux.; vol. firefighter, EMT Ashburn Vol. Fire and Res. Dept. Mem.: Nat. Contract Mgmt. Assn. (cert. profl. contracts mgr.), Masons. Republican. Avocations: private pilot, historical reenactments. Home: 20400 Elm Grove Terr Ashburn VA 20147 Office: US Army Surface Devel and Hdqs Distbn Command 200 Stovall St Alexandria VA 22332 Office Phone: 703-428-2084. Personal E-mail: hlharting@comcast.net.

HARTL, ROGER, physician, researcher; b. Wunsiedel, Germany, June 2, 1965; came to U.S., 1993; s. Ulf Härtl and Graziella Lazzarin. MD, Ludwig-Maximilians U., Munich, 1993. Rsch. fellow Brain Trauma Found., NYC, 1993-95; fellow neurosurgery dept. Charité Hosp., Berlin, 1996; resident in neurosurgery Allegheny Gen. Hosp., Pitts., 1997-99, Cornell U., NYC, 1999; fellow complex spine surgery Barrow's Neurological Inst., Phoenix; attending surgeon Dept. Neurosurgery Weill Coll., Cornell U. Contbr. articles to profl. jours. Named one of Medical Marvels, New York Mag., 2006. Mem. Internat. Neurotrauma Soc. (charter mem.), Internat. Soc. Cerebral Blood Flow and Metabolism, Am. Assn. Neurol. Surgeons, Congress Neurol. Surgeons. Avocations: climbing, skiing, running. Office: Divsn Neurosurgery Weill Med College Cornell Univ 525 E 68th St New York NY 10021-4870 Office Phone: 212-746-2152. Office Fax: 212-746-7732. E-mail: roh9005@med.cornell.edu.

HARTLAND, JAMES ROBERT, retired minister; b. Johnstown, Pa., June 21, 1920; s. Walter Daniel Hartland and Alice Maude Wilson; m. Helen Jane Croft, Sept. 7, 1947 (dec. 1997). AB, Mt. Union Coll., 1947; MST, Boston U. Sch. Theology, 1950; MEd, U. Pitts., 1958. Ordained to ministry Meth. Ch., 1950. Student pastor Meth. Ch., Winona, Ohio, 1945—47, Aqawam, Mass., 1947—50; pastor Irwin, Pa., 1950—52, Concord Ch., Beaver Falls, Pa., 1952—54, Whitaker Cmty. Ch., Pa., 1954—57, 1st Meth. Ch., Rochester, Pa., 1957—58; min. of edn. Lakewood Meth. Ch., Ohio, 1958—61; pastor 1st Sylvania Meth. Ch., Ohio, 1961—66, 1st Sidney Meth. Ch., Ohio, 1966—70, Christ Columbus Ch., Ohio, 1970—75, United Meth. Ch., Tipp City, Ohio, 1975—82, First Urbana United Meth. Ch., Ohio, 1982—86; ret., 1986. Contbr. articles to profl. jours. Aux. Sch. Bd., Sidney, Ohio; chair bd. edn. West Ohio Conf., 1970—80; chaplain Civil Air Patrol, 1972—; active Libr. Bd., Sylvania, Ohio. Mem.: Ret. Pastors West Ohio Conf., Psi Kappa Omega, Pi Gamma Nu. Avocations: travel, workshop leader. Home: 61 Brookhill Woods Ln Tipp City OH 45371

HARTLE, ROBERT WYMAN, retired literature and language professor; b. Kongmoon, China, Sept. 1, 1921; s. Jacob Everett and Margaret (Wyman) H.; m. Ann Dorothy Mordhorst, Jan. 5, 1980; 1 son, Robert Wyman, Jr.; children by previous marriage: Shirley Ann (Mrs. Jan McDaniel), John Wyman. BA, MA, U. Tex., 1947; AM, Princeton U., 1949, PhD, 1951. Instr. French Princeton U., 1950-53, asst. prof., 1953-60; assoc. prof. modern langs. U. Oreg., 1961-63; asst. prof. Romance langs. Queens Coll. (now CUNY-Queens Coll.), NYC, 1960-61, prof., chmn. dept. Romance and Slavic langs., 1963-65, assoc. dean faculty, 1964-65, dean faculty, 1965-70, prof., 1972-87, prof. emeritus, 1987—, chmn. ad hoc legal affairs com., mem. univ. acad. senate, 1979-81, dir. PhD program in France, 1970-72, mem. senate. Founder, dir. programs of study abroad, 1963-70; vis. prof. Inst. Liberal Arts, Emory U., 1985-93. Author: Index du vocabulaire du théâtre classique: Racine, 8 vols, 1956-64; transl. Tartuffe (Molière), 1963; contbr. articles on the iconography of Alexander the Great, 17th century French art and architecture, Hellenistic Art, 1955—; French translator Papers of Robert Morris, 1973-84; French cons. Papers of Thomas Jefferson, Princeton U. Press, 1986—. Bd. dirs. Am. Ctr. for Students and Artists, Paris, 1970-78; eucharistic minister Atlanta VA Med. Ctr., 2007-. Decorated officer Ordre des Palmes Académiques (France), knight Order of Merit (Italy), officer's cross Order of Merit (Germany). Mem. MLA, AAUP (pres. chpt. 1975-80) Home: 1803 Westminster Way NE Atlanta GA 30307-1134 E-mail: rwhartle@comcast.net.

HARTLEY, BOB, professional hockey coach; b. Hawkesbury, Ont., Can., Sept. 7, 1960; m. Micheline; children: Kristine, Steve. Coach Hawkesbury Hawks, 1987-91; head coach Laval Titans, 1991-93, Cornwall Aces, 1993-94, 1994-95, Colo. Avalanche, 1998—2002; coach Hershey Bears, 1996-98; head coach Atlanta Thrashers, 2003—. Office: c/o Atlanta Thrashers Centennial Tower, Ste 1900 101 Marietta Street NW Atlanta GA 30303

HARTLEY, CELIA LOVE, retired nursing educator, administrator, consultant, writer; b. Colfax, Wash., Oct. 25, 1935; d. Thomas Warren and Ella Marie (Kerkman) Love; m. Lawrence Dosser (div.); children: Laurie Denise Draper, Byron Garth Dosser; m. Gordon E. Hartley, Dec. 17, 1972. Diploma, Deaconess Hosp. Sch. Nursing, Spokane, Wash., 1956; BSN, U. Wash., Seattle, 1965, MSN, 1968. RN, Wash., Calif. Staff nurse Deaconess Hosp., Spokane, 1956-62; charge nurse Northgate Gen. Hosp., Seattle, 1963-65; hosp. supr. Stevens Meml. Hosp., Edmonds, Wash., 1965-66; prof. nursing Shoreline C.C., Seattle, 1967-73, dir. nursing edn., asst. div. chmn. health occupations, 1973-92; chair health sci. divsn. Coll. of the Desert, Palm Desert, Calif., 1992-99, prof. emerita, 1999—; nursing curriculum cons. Pres. Coun. on Nursing Edn. in Wash. State, 1992; adv. com. Antioch West and Seattle U., 1979-81, Nursing Edn. Com. Higher Edn. Coordinating Bd., 1990, Western Wash. U. Nursing, 1984, Seattle Pacific U. Nursing, 1992; other coms. various orgns., 1979—; presenter in field. Author: (with Janice Ellis) Nursing in Today's World; Challenges, Issues, and Trends, 1980, 9th rev. edit., 2007, Managing and Coordinating Patient Care, 1991, 4th edit., 2005; mem. editl. bd. Assoc. Degree Nurse, 1987-91, Jour. Nursing Edn., 1991—; contbr. articles to profl. jours.; chpts. to books. Mem. Nat. League of Nursing (bd. dirs. 1981-84, appeal panel Coun. AD Programs 1988-91, 95-98, chmn.-vice chmn. various coms.), Wash. Constituent League (v.p. 1986-87, chmn. nominating com. 1984-85, chmn. membership com. 1985-86), Sigma Theta Tau. Methodist. Home: 3234 Mabana Rd Camano Island WA 98282 Office Phone: 360-387-0822. Personal E-mail: cegohart@wavecable.com.

HARTLEY, JAMES EDWARD, lawyer; b. Orange, NJ, Nov. 4, 1949; s. George and Carolyn (Stewart) H.; m. Judy Franklin, Mar. 1, 1986; 1 child, Jonathan. BA, U. Calif., Berkeley, 1971, JD, 1974. Bar: Colo. 1974, U.S. Dist. Ct. Colo. 1974, U.S. Ct. Appeals (10th cir.) 1975, U.S. Supreme Ct. 1981, U.S. Ct. Appeals (Fed. cir.) 1993. Assoc. Holland & Hart, Denver, 1974-80, ptnr., 1980—. Adj. prof. Denver U. Law Sch., 1985-86. Co-author: Private Litigation Under Section 7 of the Clayton Act: Law and Policy, 1989, Antitrust Pitfalls in Outpatient Services, 1992, Rule of Reason Monograph, 1999, State Antitrust Practice and Procedure, 1999; asst. editor: ABA Antitrust Law Jour., 1994-98. Mem. ABA (coun. antitrust law sect. 2003—06), Colo. Bar Assn., Denver Bar Assn., Order of Coif, Phi Beta Kappa (named one of Best Lawyers in Am. 2004-). Home: 2540 Briarwood Dr Boulder CO 80305-6804 Office: Holland & Hart LLP 555 17th St Ste 3200 Denver CO 80202-3950

HARTLEY, JAMES R., musician, writer; b. Washington, Dec. 23, 1948; s. James Aaron Hartley and Ruth Virginia Pope; m. Lisa Graffen, Dec. 28, 2005. AA TV, Radio, Montgomery Coll., Rockville, Md., 1981. Tech. asst. Montgomery County Pub. Schs., Rockville, Md., 1968—84; musician self-employed, Md., 1980—, Va., 1980—. Newsletter editor / pub. Wash. Baseball Hist. Soc., Silver Spring, Md., 2001—. Author: Washington's Expansion Senators (1961-1971), 1998, Baseball Is Back: The Washington Nationals 2005 Inaugural Season. Recipient award, Phi Theta Kappa, 1981. Mem.: Soc. Am. Baseball Rsch., Washington Baseball Hist. Soc. (newsletter editor, pub. 2001—). Democrat. Avocations: baseball history, golf. E-mail: natnative7@aol.com.

HARTLEY, MICHAEL J., travel company executive; CEO Cheap Tickets, Inc., Honolulu, 1986—. Recipient Hawaii Ernst & Young Entrepreneur of Yr. award, 2000. Office: Cheap Tickets Inc Po Box 291987 Nashville TN 37229-1987

HARTLEY, PAUL E., insurance company executive; Grad., U. Sheffield & Hallam, Eng. Cert. FCA Inst. Chartered Accts. England and Wales. Fin. contr. Caribbean region CIGNA Internat., 1985, country head Hong Kong Life ops., COO Life, Property & Casualty businesses Asia Pacific, 1996, CEO Asia Pacific Ops., pres., 2005—. Mem.: Brit. Inst. Mgmt. Office: CIGNA Internat Two Liberty Pl 1601 Chestnut St Philadelphia PA 19192-1550 Office Phone: 215-761-1000. E-mail: paul.hartley@CIGNA.com.*

HARTLEY, THOMAS Y., gas industry executive; Grad. in Bus., Ohio U., Athens, 1955. CPA. Various positions up to mng. ptnr. Las Vegas, Reno, Phoenix and Tucson offices Deloitte Haskins and Sells (now Deloitte & Touche), 1959—88; bd. dirs. SW Gas Corp., 1991—, chmn., 1997—. Bd. dirs. Rio Hotel and Casino, Inc., 1990—98, Sierra Health Svcs., Inc., 1992—, Ameritrade Holdings Corp., 1996—2002. Office: Southwest Gas 5241 Spring Mt Rd Las Vegas NV 89193*

HARTLYN, JONATHAN, political scientist, educator; BA magna cum laude, Clark U., 1974; MPhil, Yale U., 1976, PhD, 1981. Asst. prof. Vanderbilt U., Nashville, 1981-87, assoc. prof., 1987-88, U. NC, Chapel Hill, 1988-97, prof., 1997—, chair dept. polit. sci., 2000—05, dir. Inst. Latin Am. Studies, 1997—2000. Author: The Politics of Coalition Rule in Colombia, 1988, The Struggle for Democratic Politics in the Dominican Republic, 1998; co-author: Latin America in the Twenty-First Century,2003; co-editor: Latin American Political Economy, 1986, The United States and Latin America in the 1990s, 1992, Democracy in Developing Countries: Latin America, 2d edit., 1999; contbr. articles to profl. jours. Tinker Found. fellow, 1985-86. Mem. Am. Polit. Sci. Assn. (chair comparative democratization sect. 2005-07), Latin Am. Studies Assn., Phi Beta Kappa. Office: U NC Dept Polit Sci Cb 3265 Hamilton Hl Chapel Hill NC 27599-3265 Office Phone: 919-962-3041. E-mail: hartlyn@unc.edu.

HARTMAN, ALAN, investment banker; b. 1965; married. Joined Merrill Lynch & Co. Inc., NYC, 1993—, head healthcare practice, also head US mergers and acquisitions practice, 2006—. Named a Top Dealmaker in healthcare, Dealmaker mag., 2006. Office: Merrill Lynch & Co Inc 4 World Fin Ctr 250 Vesey St New York NY 10080 Office Phone: 212-449-8585.*

HARTMAN, ALAN ROY, surgeon, educator; b. NYC, Feb. 9, 1955; s. Jerome and Lillian Hartman; m. Britt Rolfsson, Sept. 23, 1986; 1 child, Justin Eric. BA summa cum laude, U. Rochester, NY, 1976; MD, Mt. Sinai Sch. Medicine, 1979. Cert. Am. Bd. Surgery, Am. Bd. Thoracic Surgery. Intern surgery Bellevue Hosp. Ctr., NYU, NYC, 1979—80, resident cardiothoracic surgery, 1980—84, fellow cardiothoracic vascular surgery, 1984—86; asst. prof. surgery Stony Brook U., NY, 1986-90, clin. assoc. prof., 1990—96; chief cardiovasc. surgery divsn. Univ. Hosp. Stony Brook; ptnr. Cardiothoracic Surg. Group Winthrop Univ. Hosp., 1996—2002; chmn. dept. cardiovasc. and thoracic surgery North Shore Univ. Hosp., Manhasset, NY, 2002—. Contbr. articles to profl. jours. Mem. NY State Cardiac Adv. Com. Fellow: ACS, Am. Coll. Chest Physicians, Soc. Critical Care Medicine, Soc. Thoracic Surgery, Am. Coll. Cardiology. Office: North Shore Univ Hosp 300 Community Dr Manhasset NY 11030 Office Phone: 516-562-4970. Office Fax: 516-562-3786.*

HARTMAN, CHARLES HENRY, transportation and not-for-profit executive, educator; b. Red Lion, Pa., Feb. 1, 1933; s. Earl Eugene and Jeannette (Kline) Hartman; m. Patricia A. Cooper, Aug. 3, 1956 (div. May 1974); children: Elizabeth Jean, Amy Joan; m. Catherine M. Wheeler, June 7, 1975 (div. Apr. 1994); children: Eric Michael, Jennifer Leigh, David Wheeler, Scott Andrew; m. Andrea S. Anderson, July 8, 2000. BS, Millersville U., 1954; MA, Mich. State U., 1958, EdD, 1962. Cert. assn. exec. Tchr. Hollidaysburg Pub. Schs., Pa., 1956—57; assoc. prof. Ill. State U., Normal, 1959—62; vis. lectr. edn. U. Wis., Madison, 1962—63, Milw., 1963—64; dir. edn. Automotive Safety Found./Hwy. Users Fedn., Washington, 1964—70; dep. adminstr. Nat. Hwy. Traffic Safety Adminstrn., U.S. Dept. Transp., Washington, 1970—73; pres. Motorcycle Safety Found., Irvine, Calif., 1973—84; also pres. Touchstone Mgmt. Svcs., Delta, Pa.,

1984—88; exec. v.p. AAHPERD, Reston, Va., 1988—90; exec. dir. Am. Coll. Health Assn., Balt., 1990—98; pres. Nonprofit Orgn. Mgmt. and Consultation, 1998—2002; dir. transp. and support svcs. Red Lion Area Sch Dist., Pa., 2003—04; office mgr. Andrea S. Anderson Law Offices, 2004—. Cons. Nat. Assn. Women Hwy. Safety Leaders, Md. State Dept. Edn., 1969—70; dir. Nat. Safety Coun., Chgo., 1976—79; vice chmn. traffic conf., 1976—78; presdl. appointee Nat. Hwy. Safety Adv. Commn., Washington, 1977—80; gov.'s appointee Pa. Task Force Alcohol and Hwy. Safety, 1981—82; vice chmn. Alliance Traffic Safety, 1981—83, chmn., 1983—85; mem. policy com. Hwy. Users Fedn.; lectr. bus. adminstrn. Capitol Campus Pa. State U., Middletown, 1987—88; bd. dirs. Lincoln Intermediate Unit # 12, 1987—89, 1991—93; sr. cons. York Nonprofit Mgmt. Devel. Ctr., 1998—2000; spkr. in field. Sch. dir. Red Lion (Pa.) Area Schs., 1986—2003, pres. sch. bd., 1988, 1996—2003, v.p., 1989—95; mem. York 2000 Commn.; trustee Nat. Motorcycle Fund; pres. Howard County C. of C., Columbia, Md., 1985—87. With US Army, 1954—56. Named to Hall of Fame, Red Lion Area Sch. Dist., 1993; recipient Traffic Safety Educator of the Yr. award, Wis. Traffic Edn. Assn., 1972, Sec.'s award, U.S. Dept. Transp., 1973. Fellow: Am. Acad. Safety Edn.; mem.: NEA, Pa. Sch. Bds. Assn., Assn. Advancement Automotive Medicine, Am. Driver and Traffic Safety Edn. Assn., Pres. Assn./Am. Mgmt. Assn., Soc. Automotive Engrs., Am. Soc. Assn. Execs. (vice-chmn. evaluation com. 1984—85, chmn. 1985—86), Phi Delta Kappa. Republican. Home: 122 E McKinley Rd Delta PA 17314 Office: 901 Delta Rd Red Lion PA 17356-9179 Business E-Mail: charley@asa-law.com.

HARTMAN, DAVID G., actuary; b. Evanston, Ill., July 10, 1942; s. Fred E. and Martha Hartman; m. Katherine A. Holmes; children: Timothy, Andrew. Student, Ripon Coll., 1960-62; BBA, U. Mich., 1964, M in Actuarial Sci., 1965. With Kemper Ins. Co., Chgo., 1966—71; mng. dir., sr. v.p., chief actuary Chubb & Son, Warren, NJ, 1971—2005. Trustee Overlook Hosp., Summit, NJ, 1993—2002, Overlook Hosp. Found., Summit, 1999—; elder New Providence Presbyn. Ch., NJ, 1973—75, 1986—88. Fellow: Casualty Actuarial Soc. (v.p. 1985—86, pres. 1987—88, cert.), Can. Inst. Actuaries; mem.: Actuarial Studies in Non-Life (chair 2003—07), Actuarial Stds. Bd. (bd. dirs. 1996—2001, chmn. 1998—99), Internat. Actuarial Assn. (coun. 1996—, pres.-elect 2007), Am. Acad. Actuaries (v.p. 1983—85, pres.-elect 1992—93, pres. 1993—94, cert.).

HARTMAN, DEANNA MEARS, retired family counselor, addiction counselor; b. Norfolk, Va., Aug. 11, 1937; d. James Gordon Jr. and Sarah Talmadge (Johnson) Mears; m. David Luther Brinkley Jr. (div.); children: Kim Brinkley Hebebrand, David III, Jeffrey Lawrence Brinkley; m. Shirish Ramachandra Pandya, June 7, 1978 (dec.). AA, U. Akron, 1980; BA, Va. Wesleyan, 1983; MA, Antioch U., 1994. Cert. cognitive behavioral therapist; nat. cert. counselor. Dir. edn. svcs. Va. Coun. on Alcoholism, Drugs, Norfolk, 1985-87, exec. dir., 1990-93; outpatient program specialist Maryview Psychiat. Hosp., Portsmouth, Va., 1988-89; clin. therapist City of Portsmouth, 1988-89; educator, therapist City of Va. Beach, 1984-86, 93-95; mental health counselor Glasgow High Wellness Ctr., Newark, Del., 1995; family counselor, addiction specialist Williamsburg Pl., Farley Ctr., Williamsburg, Va., 1997—. Founder Survivors of Suicide, Virginia Beach, 1982-86, vol. educator AARP Bear, Del., 1995. Contbr. articles to profl. jours., various presentations. Bd. dirs. Hospice of Virginia Beach, 1983-85, Safe Place, 1988-90, Civitan Internat., 1990-92, comty. adv. coun. for curriculum Coll. of Edn., Old Dominion U., Norfolk, 1991-92. Named Rookie of Yr., Civitan Internat., 1991; recipient Disting. Svc. award Va. Alcohol and Drug Abuse Counselors, 1992. Avocations: reading, writing, walking, birdwatching. Home: 932 Anna St Norfolk VA 23502-3314 Personal E-mail: dhartman@cavtel.net.

HARTMAN, EARL KENNETH, writer; b. Chgo., Jan. 31, 1943; s. Ferdinand Frederick and Betty Marie (Sjerslee) H.; m. Linda Lee Griffin, July 10, 1981 (div. June 1988); m. Beatrice Gail Adams, Mar. 11, 1989. BA, Fla. Atlantic U., 1980, B of Edn., 1981. Promotion mgr., spl. issues editor Asheville Citizen-Times, NC, 1966—67; reporter Shelby Daily Star, NC, 1967; copy editor Palm Beach Post-Times, West Palm Beach, Fla., 1968—69; dist. exec. Boy Scouts Am., West Palm Beach, 1973—76, Albany, Ga., 1983—84; tchr., asst. dir. Unity Sch., Delray Beach, Fla., 1981—83; tchr. Tift County Bd. Edn., Ga., 1984—85; sr. reporter Island Reporter, Sanibel Island, Fla., 1985—87; free-lance writer Fort Myers, Fla., 1987—2005; creator, devel. Family Choice, Etowah, NC, 2000—05, prin., owner, 2005—. Mem. Nat. Eagle Scout Assn. E-mail: nightjack6-choice@yahoo.com.

HARTMAN, FREDERICK COOPER, retired biochemist; b. Memphis, Aug. 17, 1939; s. Fred Francis and Raymie Constance (Cooper) H.; m. Patricia Jean Ballard, Sept. 7, 1961; children: Patricia Suzanne, Sheila Katherine. BS in Chemistry, Memphis State U., 1960; MS in Biochemistry, U. Tenn., 1962, PhD in Biochemistry, 1964; postgrad., U. Ill., 1964-66. Sr. rsch. biochemist Oak Ridge (Tenn.) Nat. Lab., 1966—99; group leader protein chemistry Oak Ridge Nat. Lab., 1972-99, sect. head molecular and cellular scis., 1975-88, dir. biology divsn., 1988-97; prof. dept. biochemistry U. Tenn., Knoxville, 1999—2004; ret., 2004. Mem. editl. bd. Jour. Biol. Chemistry, BioSci., Jour. Protein Chemistry; contbr. numerous articles to profl. jours. Grantee Dept. Agr., 1978—, NSF, 1980-87; fellow USPHS, 1962-64, NIH, 1963, 65. Fellow AAAS; mem. Am. Chem. Soc. (Pfizer award 1979, nominating com. 1982), Am. Soc. Biol. Chemists (nominating com. 1979, 81), Am. Soc. Plant Physiologists, Protein Soc., Sigma Xi. Home: 9172 Sugarland Dr Jacksonville FL 32256 Personal E-mail: fredchartman@aol.com.

HARTMAN, GEORGE EITEL, architect; b. Ft. Hancock, NJ, May 7, 1936; s. George Eitel and Evelyn (Ritchie) H.; m. Ann Burdick, May 22, 1965 (div. Oct. 2000); children— Sarah, Joshua; m. Jan Cigliano, Jan. 21, 2001. BA, Princeton, 1957, M.F.A., 1960. Registered arch., Md., Washington, Va. Pvt. practice architecture, 1964-65; ptnr. Hartman-Cox Architects, Washington, 1965—; Design critic Cath. U. Am., 1964-69, U. Md.; Kea Disting. prof. architecture N.C. State U., 1973-74, prof. architecture, 1977. Chmn. adv. coun. Princeton U. Sch. Architecture, 1985-87; mem. architecture rev. panel Fgn. Bldg. Office, Dept. State, 1991—, mem. architecture adv. bd. Works include EURAM office bldg, Washington, Waterfront Center, Washington; Brewer residence, Chevy Chase, Md., Conant residence, Potomac, Md., Nat. Humanities Center, Raleigh, N.C., Nat. Permanent Bldg., Washington, 1001 Pennsylvania Ave, Washington; Folger Shakespeare Library, Washington, Immanuel Presbyn. Ch., McLean, Va., Sumner Sch., Washington, H.E.B. hdqrs., San Antonio, Market Square, Washington, Franklin Sq., Washington, Pa. Plaza, Washington, U.S. Embassy, Kuala Lumpur, Malaysia, Chrysler Mus., Norfolk, Va., 555 11th St., Washington. Served to 2d lt. F.A., AUS, 1957. Recipient Louis Sullivan award arch., 1972, 100 Nat., State and Local Design awards, 1967—; fellow Am. Acad. Rome, 1977-78. Fellow AIA (pres. Washington chpt. 1975, chmn. nat. capitol com. 1976, chmn. nat. com. on design 1977, AIA Nat. Honor award 1970, 71, 81, 83, 89, 94, AIA Firm award 1988, fellow 1975); mem. U.S. Commn. Fine Arts, Cosmos Club (pres. 1985, Washington Chpt. Centennial award 2005). Office: Hartman Cox Architects 1074 Thomas Jefferson St NW Washington DC 20007-3832

HARTMAN, GEORGE M., retired engineering contracts manager; b. May 26, 1926; BME, City Coll. NY, 1950; MBA, Baruch Sch. Bus., 1961. Lic. profl. engr., SUNY, 1960. Design engr. Island Equipment Corp., Long Island City, NY, 1950—54; sr. engr. Arma Corp., Garden City, NY, 1954—59, Unisys Corp. (formerly Sperry Corp.), Great Neck, NY, 1959—80, engr. contracts mgr., 1980—89; pres. Contract Advisor Corp., Plainview, NY, 1989—91. Author: How to Negotiate a Bigger Raise, 1991, Making the Deal, Quick Tips for Successful Negotiating, 1992, How to Negotiate a Raise Without Losing Your Job, 1997. With USN, 1944—46, USS Mo. Recipient Alumni Svc. award, CCNY, 2006. Fellow: Nat. Contract Mgmt. Assn.; mem.: Palm Beach County Alumni Assn. (pres. 1999—).

HARTMAN, JAMES AUSTIN, retired geologist; b. Lanark, Ill., Jan. 29, 1928; s. Llewelyn John and Gladys Mae (Doyle) Hartman; m. Zoe Marie Wiley (dec. Dec. 1996); children: Victoria Lynn, Lester James; m. Merilyn J. Gerlich, Dec. 30, 2005. BS, Beloit Coll., Wis., 1951; MS, U. Wis., 1955, PhD, 1957. Geologist Reynolds Jamaica (W.I.) Mines, Jamaica, W.I., 1951-53, Union Carbide Ore Co., Parimaribo, Surinam, 1956-57; various positions Shell Oil Co., New Orleans, 1957-86; cons. New Orleans, 1986-94; ret., 1994. Bd. mgmt. YMCA, Metairie, 1972-74; pres. Jefferson Com. for Better Schs., Metairie, 1961-63, pres. Westgate PTA, Kenner, La., 1964-65. With U.S. Army, 1946-47. Union Carbide Rsch. fellowship U. Wis., 1954-56. Mem. Am. Assn. Petroleum Geologists (hon., sec. 1981-83, Disting. Svc. award 1985), New Orleans Geol. Soc. (hon., 2d v.p. 1975-76, pres.-elect 1984-85, pres. 1985-86, Outstanding Mem. 1977), Gulf Coast Assn. Geol. Socs. (hon., v.p. 1987, pres. 1988), Sigma Xi. Republican. Methodist. Achievements include research in heavy minerals in Jamaican Bauxite, titanium mineralogy of Bauxites, petroleum geology. Home: 4916 Jule Dr Panora IA 50216-8620

HARTMAN, JOAN EDNA, retired literature educator, dean, provost; b. Bklyn., Oct. 5, 1930; d. H. Graham and Edna (Kuebler) H. BA, Mt. Holyoke Coll., 1951; MA, Duke U., 1952; postgrad., Oxford U., 1958-59; PhD, Radcliffe Coll., 1960. Instr. Washington Coll., Chestertown, Md., 1952-54, Wellesley Coll., 1959-62, asst. prof., 1962-63, Conn. Coll., New London, 1963-66, CUNY-Queens Coll., Flushing, 1967-70, CUNY-S.I. C.C., 1970-72, assoc. prof., 1972-76; prof. CUNY-Coll. S.I., 1976-98, acting dean humanities and social scis., 1995-98; ret., 1998. Vis. prof. Am. U. of Rome, 1991, 99, 2001, 03, acting provost, 2005—06. Editor: Women in Print I, II, 1982, (En)Gendering Knowledge, 1991, The Norton Reader, 2000, Structures and Subjectivities, 2006; contbr. articles to profl. jours. Fellow, AAUW, NEH, Mellon Found., Folger Shakespeare Libr. Mem.: MLA, Renaissance Soc. Am., Women's Caucus for the Modern Langs., Soc. Study of Early Modern Women, Nat. Arts Club. Home: 201 E 21st St Apt 17C New York NY 10010-6423 Personal E-mail: hartman@mail.csi.cuny.edu.

HARTMAN, JOAN EVANS, educational consultant; b. Gibson, Tenn., Sept. 30, 1935; d. William Slaton and Helen (Mann) Evans; children: John Scott, Edwin Evans, Mary Lane Hartman McKinney. BA, Lambuth U., Jackson, Tenn., 1957; MA, Peabody C. Vanderbilt U., 1958; EdD, Memphis State U., 1991. Tchr. Davidson County Schs., Nashville, 1958-60, pvt. kindergartens, Memphis and Ripley, Tenn., 1971-74, Lauderdale County Schs., Ripley, 1982-90, supr. fed. projects, 1990—2006. Mem. evaluation teams So. Assn. Coll. and Schs., Memphis, 1985-88. Author: Sam's Special Cookie, 2006. Recipient Grad. Rsch. Symposium award Memphis State U., 1989, Career Ladder III Tenn. State Dept. Edn., Nashville, 1988-2006. Mem. Western Tenn. Edn. Assn. (v.p. 1985-88), Tenn. Edn. Assn., NEA, ASCD, Tenn. Assn. for Supervision and Curriculum Devel., Kappa Delta Pi. Methodist. Avocations: reading, needlepoint, travel. Address: 111 Lankford Dr Ripley TN 38063 Home Phone: 731-635-9470; Office Phone: 731-635-9470. Personal E-mail: hartbeat@bellsouth.net.

HARTMAN, MARY SUSAN, historian, educator; b. Mpls., June 25, 1941; married. BA, Swarthmore Coll., 1963; MA, Columbia U., 1964, PhD, 1970. From instr. to asst. prof. Rutgers U., 1968-75; from assoc. prof. to prof. history Douglass Coll., Rutgers U., 1975—; dean Douglass Coll. Rutgers U., 1982-94; dir. Inst. for Women's Leadership Douglass Coll., 1994—; prof. Rutgers U., 1994—. Author: Clio's Consciousness Raised, 1974, Victorian Murderesses, 1978; editor: Talking Leadership: Conversations with Powerful Women, 1999, The Household and the Making of History: A Subversive View of the Western Past, 2004. Office: 162 Ryders Ln New Brunswick NJ 08901-8555 Office Phone: 732-932-1463 ext. 648. Business E-Mail: msh@rci.rutgers.edu.

HARTMAN, ROBERT LEROY, artist, educator; b. Sharon, Pa., Dec. 17, 1926; s. George Otto and Grace Arvada (Radabaugh) H.; m. Charlotte Ann Johnson, Dec. 30, 1951; children: Mark Allen, James Robert. BFA, U. Ariz., 1951, MA, 1952; postgrad., Colorado Springs Fine Arts Ctr., 1947, postgrad., 1951, Bklyn. Mus. Art Sch., 1953—54. Instr. architecture, allied arts Tex. Tech. Coll., 1955-58; asst. prof. art U. Nev., Reno, 1958-61; mem. faculty dept. art U. Calif., Berkeley, 1961—, prof., 1972-91, prof. emeritus, 1991—, chmn. dept., 1974-76. Mem. Inst. for Creative Arts, U. Calif., 1967-68. One-man shows include Bertha Schafer Gallery, N.Y.C., 1966, 69, 74, Santa Barbara Mus. Art, 1973, Cin. Art Acad., 1975, Hank Baum Gallery, San Francisco, 1973, 75, 78, San Jose Mus. Art, 1983, Bluxome Gallery, San Francisco, 1984, 86, U. Art Mus., Berkeley, 1986, Instituto D'Arte Dosso Dossi, Ferrara, Italy, 1989, Victor Fischer Galleries, San Francisco, 1991, Triangle Gallery, San Francisco, 1992, 93, 95, 97, 99-2002, 04, 06, Augusta State U., 1998, Mary Pauline Gallery, Augusta, Ga., 2001, Oakland Mus., 2002, Viewpoint Photographic Art Ctr., Sacramento, CAlif., 2006; group exhbns. include Richmond Mus., 1966, Whitney Mus. Biennial, 1973, Oakland Mus., 1976, San Francisco Arts Commn. Gallery, 1985 (award), Earthscape Expo '90 Photo Mus., Osaka, Japan, 1990, In Close Quarters, American Landscape Photography Since 1968, Princeton Art Mus., 1993, Facing Eden: 100 Years of Landscape Art in The Bay Area, de Young Mus., San Francisco, 1995, Colorado Springs Fine Arts Ctr., 1998; represented in permanent collections, Nat. Collections Fine Arts, Colorado Springs Fine Arts Ctr., Corcoran Gallery, Roswell Mus., Princeton Art Mus. U. Calif. humanities rsch. fellow, 1980. Office: U Calif Dept Art Berkeley CA 94720-0001

HARTMAN, ROME, television producer; b. West Palm Beach, Fla. married; 2 children. Grad., Duke U., 1977. Desk asst., reporter, cameraman, film editor, prodr. WPEC-TV, West Palm Beach, Fla., 1977—80; prodr. WJLA-TV, Washington, 1980—83; with CBS News, 1983—2007; White Ho. prodr. CBS Evening News, Washington, 1986—89, sr. prodr., 1989—91; prodr. 60 Minutes, 1991—2007; sr. prodr. 60 Minutes II, 2005; exec. prodr. CBS Evening News, 2005—07; prodr. BBC Am./BBC World, 2007—. Recipient 2 Emmy awards, Robert F. Kennedy Journalism award, Gerald Loeb award for Bus. Journalism, UCLA Anderson Sch. Mgmt., 2005, David Kaplan award, Overseas Press Club Am., 2007. Office: BBC Worldwide Americas PO Box 6266 Florence KY 41022-6266*

HARTMAN, RONALD G., lawyer; b. Harrisburg, Pa., Aug. 13, 1950; s. Manny and Helene L.; m. Leslie Ann Golomb, May 31, 1980; children: Molly, Samuel. BA, U. Pitts., 1972, JD, 1975. Bar: Pa. 1975, U.S. Dist. Ct. (we. dist.) Pa. 1975. Assoc. and ptnr. Baskin & Sears, Pitts., 1975-84; ptnr. Reed Smith LLP, Pitts., 1985—. Bd. dirs. Citizens League Southwestern Pa., Pitts., 1988; bd. dirs. Am. Cancer Soc.-Greater Pitts. Unit, exec. com., 1990—, chair, 2003—05; bd. dirs. Jewish Family and Children's Svc. of Pitts., pres. 1995-97; bd. dirs. United Jewish Fedn. Greater Pitts., 1995-97, 98-2000, co-chmn. bus. and profl. divsn., 1989-91, mem. steering com. atty. divsn., 1992—; chair Cardoza Soc., 1999-2001; bd. dirs. Jewish Chronicle, 1997-2000. Mem.: ABA, Pa. Bar Assn., Allegheny County Bar Assn. Jewish. Avocations: jogging, reading. Home: 500 Glen Arden Dr Pittsburgh PA 15208-2809 Office: Reed Smith LLP 435 6th Ave Pittsburgh PA 15219-1886 Office Phone: 412-288-3092. Business E-Mail: rhartman@reedsmith.com.

HARTMAN, ROSEMARY JANE, retired special education educator; b. Gainesville, Fla., Aug. 24, 1944; d. John Leslie and Irene (Bowen) Goddard; m. Alan Lynn Gerber, Feb. 1, 1964 (div. 1982); children: Sean Alan, Dawn Julianne Silva, Lance Goddard; m. Perry Hartman, June 27, 1992. BA, Immaculate Heart Coll., 1967; MA, Loyola U., 1974. Cert. resource specialist. Tchr. L.A. Unified Schs., 1968-78; resource specialist Desert Sands Unified Sch. Dist., Palm Desert, 1978-83, Palm Springs Unified Schs., 1983-99, ret., 1999. Facilitator Phobics Anonymous World Svc. Ctr. Author: Jesus, My Higher Power, 2005; co-author: The Twelve Steps of Phobics Anonymous, 1989, One Day At A Time in Phobics Victorious, 1992, The Twelve Steps of Phobics Victorious, 1993; founder Phobics Victorious, 1992. Mem. Anxiety Disorders Assn. Am. Business E-Mail: rosemaryjane@dc.rr.com.

HARTMAN, THOMAS BENNETT, mechanical engineer; b. Rochester, NY, Oct. 25, 1942; m. Angela Cebula, Aug. 22, 1999; children: Katherine Joy, Thomas Bennett. BS in Mech. Engring., Mich. State U., E. Lansing, 1964. Cert. profl. engr., State Bd. Registration, Wash., 1979, Oreg. State Bd. Engring. Examiners, 1979, Bd. Registration Profl. Engrs., Calif., 1981, Assn. Profl. Engrs. and Geoscientists-BC, 1993, Bd. Engrs. & Architects, Nebr., 2000, Tex. Bd. Profl. Engring., 2003, Bd. Profl. Engrs. & Land Surveyors, NJ, 2003, State Bd. Profl. Engrs. & Land Surveyors, Nev., 2004, State Bd. Archtl. & Engring. Examiners, Tenn., 2006. Prin. engr. Hartman Co., Georgetown, Tex., 1970—. Sci. coll. advisor Edmonds Cmty. Coll., Edmonds, Wash., 1980—84. Author: (book) Direct Digital Control for HVAC Systems, 1993. Recipient Efficient Bldg. award, Energy User News, 1994. Mem.: Am. Soc. Heating, Refrigerating and Air-conditioning Engrs. (corr.; publs. com. 1988—2007, Jour. Paper award 2002, Tech. award 2003). Achievements include research in the principles of physics; patents in field. Office: Hartman Co 755 County Rd 247 Georgetown TX 78633 Office Phone: 254-793-0120. Office Fax: 254-793-0121. Business E-Mail: thc@hartmanco.com.

HARTMANIS, JURIS, computer scientist, educator; b. Riga, Latvia, July 5, 1928; arrived in US, 1950, naturalized, 1956; s. Martins and Irma (Liepins) Hartmanis; m. Ellymaria Rehwald, May 16, 1959; children: Reneta, Martin, Audrey. Student, U. Marburg, 1947-49; MA, U. Kansas City, 1951; PhD, Calif. Inst. Tech., Pasadena, 1955; LHD (hon.), U. Dortmund, Germany, 1995; D, DHL, U. Mo., 1999. Instr. Cornell U., Ithaca, NY, 1955-57, prof., 1965—, Walter R. Read prof. engring., 1980—, chmn. dept. computer sci., 1965-71, 77-82, 92-94. Asst. prof. Ohio State U., 1957—58; rsch. mathematician GE R&D Ctr., Schenectady, 1957—65; asst. dir. NSF Computer and Info. Sci. & Engring., Arlington, Va., 1996—99. Author (with R. E. Stearns): (book) Algebraic Structure Theory for Sequential Machines, 1966; author: Feasible computations and Provable Complexity Properties, 1978; editor: SIAM Jour. Computing; assoc. editor: Jour. Computer and Sys. Scis., 1966—, Jour. Math. Sys. Theory, 1966—89; co-editor: Springer-Verlag Lecture Notes in Computer Sci., 1973—2004. Recipient Turing award, 1992, B. Bolzano Gold medal, Acad. Scis. Czech Republic, 1995, Grand medal, Latvian Acad. of Sci., 2001. Fellow: AAAS, Computing Machinery, Am. Acad. Arts and Scis.; mem.: NAE, Latvian Acad. Sci. (fgn., Grand medal 2001), Assn. N.Y. Acad. Scis., Am. Math. Soc., Sigma Xi. Home: 324 Brookfield Rd Ithaca NY 14850-2008 Office: Cornell Univ Upson Hall Ithaca NY 14853 Office Phone: 607-255-9208. Business E-Mail: jh@cs.cornell.edu, jh111@cornell.edu.

HARTMANN, ANN WILSON, financial planner; b. Detroit, Mar. 5, 1941; d. Robert Allan and Eunice Elizabeth (Seitz) Wilson; m. James Cline Hartmann, July 18, 1970 (dec.); m. Richard W. Brockmeyer, Oct. 1, 1994 (div. 1999); m. Frank Snug, Sept. 11, 2004. BA, Montclair State Coll., 1962; MBA in Fin., Rutgers U., 1975. CLU, ChFC. Tchr. Bloomfield Bd. Edn., NJ, 1962-63; administr. Girl Scouts USA, Pa., 1963-72, Mich., 1963—72, YWCA of Am., NJ, 1972-77, Ohio, 1972—77; dir. fin. and field personnel Sycor, Inc., Ann Arbor, Mich., 1977-79; sr. cons. Health Systems Group, Ann Arbor, 1979-80; fin. planner Hartmann & Assocs., Toledo, 1980—. Adj. faculty U. Toledo, 1983-87, Lourdes Coll., Sylvania, Ohio, 1987-98; faculty Cigna/Lincoln Nat. Edn. Events, 1984—; speaker in field. Editor: (newletter) Money Talks, 1982—. 1st v.p. Girls Clubs Am., NYC, 1985—87; pres. Maumee Valley coun. Girl Scouts U.S.A., Toledo, 1990—97; trustee Spiritual Counselling and Edn. Ctr., 2002—05, pres., 2004—05; trustee Friendly Ctr., 2005—, Zonta Club Toldeo I Found. Bd., 2003—; treas. Z Found., 2004—; trustee Friendly Ctr. Found., 2005—, treas., 2005—; nat. aquatic sch. staff instr., trainer ARC, Mich., 1974—80, Pa., 1974—80. Named Hines award Honoree Nat. Bd. Child Welfare, 1986; recipient Disting. Accredited Estate Planner, Nat. Assn. Estate Planners and Couns., 2006, Disting. Cmty. Woman of the Yr. Girl Scouts Maumee Valley Coun., 2007. Mem.: NASD (arbitrator), Soc. Fin. Svcs. Profls. Found. (pres. 2001—03), Toledo Estate Planning Coun. (bd. dirs. 1992—98), Toledo Assn. Life Underwriters (v.p. 1991—94, pres. elect 1994, pres. 1995), Soc. Fin. Svc. Profls. (pres. Toledo chpt. 1988—90, nat. bd. dirs. 1993—96, nat. nominating com. 1996—97, sec. 1998—99, treas. 1999—2000, pres.-elect 2000—01, pres. 2001—02, immediate past pres. 2002—03, pres. Toledo chpt. 2005—06), Am. Arbitration Assn. (comml. panel, arbitrator), Zonta Club Toledo (bd. dirs. 1987—88). Republican. Methodist. Avocations: sailing, bridge, needlecrafts. Office: Hartmann & Assocs 6635 W Central Ave Toledo OH 43617-1029 Office Phone: 419-841-5331. Business E-Mail: ann.hartmann@lfg.com.

HARTMANN, CARL JOSEPH, lawyer, consultant; b. Rochester, NY, Apr. 21, 1954; s. Carl Joseph and Mary (Ercel) H.; m. Kimberly Lynn Japinga, Feb. 15, 1998. JD, Antioch Coll., 1979. Bar: N.Mex. 1980, US Dist. Ct. N.Mex. 1981, US Ct. Appeals (10th cir.) 1982, US Supreme Ct. 1985, US Ct. Appeals (3d cir.) 1988, US Ct. Appeals (fed. cir.) 1993, VI 1993. Jud. intern U.S. Supreme Ct., Washington, 1979; jud. clk. N.Mex. Ct. Appeals, Santa Fe, 1980-81; asst. prof. law Antioch Coll. Sch. Law, Washington, 1982-85; ptnr. Law Offices of Carl Hartmann, Albuquerque, 1985-87; assoc. Campbell, Arellano & Rich, St. Thomas, V.I., 1988-89; special counsel Merrill Lynch Pvt. Capital, NYC, 1989-91; ptnr. Law Offices of Carl Hartmann, NYC, 1991—; of counsel Law Offices of Lawrence H. Schoenbach, NYC, 1991—. Gen. counsel Emerging Comms., Inc., St. Croix, V.I., 1997-98, Innovative Comms., Corp., St. Croix, 1998-2003; spl. counsel U.S. Park Svc., Santa Fe, 1987. Author: Legal Analysis for Clinical Students, 1981; co-author: Private Law: An Introduction to Torts, 1980, Clinical Perspectives on Fair Employment, 1979; co-editor-in-chief Antioch Sch. Law--Law Rev., 1979. Adv. bd. Our Lady of Czestochowa Sch., Paulus Hook, N.J., 1998-2001. Mem. Assn. of the Bar of the City of N.Y., V.I. Bar Assn., Virgin Islands Bar Assn., State Bar of New Mex. Roman Catholic. Avocations: fencing, flying, scuba, skiing, golf. Home: 126 Sussex St Jersey City NJ 07302-6405 Office: Trinity Bldg 111 Broadway 13th Fl New York NY 10006 Home Phone: 201-434-1738; Office Phone: 212-595-0959. E-mail: carl@carlhartmann.com.

HARTMANN, FREDERICK HOWARD, retired political science professor; b. NYC, July 6, 1922; s. Frederick Herman and Grace (McNamara) H.; m. Regina Lou Kiracofe, Dec. 26, 1943; children: Lynne Merry, Vicky Carol, Peter Howard. AB, U. Calif., Berkeley, 1943; MA, Princeton, 1948, PhD, 1949; student, Grad. Inst. Internat. Studies, U. Geneva, Switzerland, 1947. Instr. politics Princeton, 1947; from asst. prof. to prof. polit. sci. U. Fla., 1948-66; dir. Inst. Internat. Relations, 1963-66; Alfred Thayer Mahan prof. maritime strategy U.S. Naval War Coll., 1966-88, prof. emeritus, 1988—, spl. acad. advisor, 1966-86. Vis. prof. Wheaton (Mass.) Coll., part-time, 1966-69, Brown U., part-time, 1968-69, U. R.I., part-time, 1970-71, Tex. Tech U., 1974-75; vis. prof. polit. sci. U. Calif., Berkeley, 1979-80, Middle East Tech. U., Ankara, Turkey, 1988. Author: The Relations of Nations, 4th edit., 1973, 5th edit., 1978, 6th edit., 1983,

Spanish edit., 1986, The Swiss Press and Swiss Foreign Affairs, 1960, Germany Between East and West, 1965, The New Age of American Foreign Policy, 1970, Naval Renaissance: The U.S. Navy in the 1980s, 1990, (Chinese transl. 1994), America Under Threat, 2002; (with Robert L. Wendzel) To Preserve the Republic, 1985, Defending America's Security, 1988, America's Foreign Policy in a Changing World, 1994; editor: Basic Documents of International Relations, 1951, Readings in International Relations, 1952, World in Crisis, 4th edit., 1973; contbr. to: System for Educating Military Officers in the U.S., 1976, The Conservation of Enemies, 1981. U. Fla. rep. Fla. Bd. Control Com. Acad. Freedom, 1961-62; mem. Fulbright Nat. Selection Com., 1954-56; U.S. del. 4th Conf. Naval War Colls. Am., 1966, 6th Conf., 1970, 10th Conf., 1980, 12th Conf., 1985. Served to lt. (j.g.) USNR, 1943-46; capt. Res. Recipient Meritorious Civilian Service medal Dept. Navy, 1985; Fulbright research prof. U. Bonn, Germany, 1953-54; Rockefeller grantee, 1959; Exxon Corp. grantee, 1973 Mem. AAUP (pres. U. Fla. chpt. 1959-60, mem. nat. council 1963-66), Am. Polit. Sci. Assn., Internat. Studies Assn. (pres. New Eng. div. 1971-72), New Eng. Polit. Sci. Assn. (exec. com. 1982-84), Fla. Blue Key, Pi Sigma Alpha, Delta Phi Epsilon. Home: 8457 Twin Rocks Rd Granite Bay CA 95746-8123

HARTMANN, FREDERICK WILLIAM, newspaper editor; b. Wilmington, Del., Feb. 3, 1928; s. William and Louise (Askani) H.; m. Mary Lucille Nelson, Oct. 16, 1954; children: Michele Mary, Randi Lucille, Frederick Andrew, Eric William, Adam Nelson BA, U. Del., 1951; postgrad., Am. U., 1952; MS, Columbia U. Grad. Sch. Journalism, 1953. Reporter AP, NYC, 1954; dir. news and sports WDEL Radio, Wilmington, 1954-56; reporter Morning News, News-Jour. Co., Wilmington, 1956-60, asst. city editor, 1961-62, city editor, 1962-64, Morning and Evening Jour., 1964-67, met. editor, 1967-72, asst. to pres., 1972-74, dir. corp. mktg., 1974-75, exec. editor, 1975-80, v.p., 1977-80; mng. editor Fla. Times-Union, Jacksonville, 1980-83; exec. editor Times-Union/Jacksonville Jour., Jacksonville, 1983-88, Times-Union, Jacksonville, 1988-98, ret., 1998. Lectr. U. Del., 1971, 72; Pulitzer prize juror, 1981, 82 Mem. budget com. United Way of Del., 1973, 74; v.p. Brandywine Little League, 1973; bd. dirs. United Cerebral Palsy Assn. of Del., 1970-72. Served with AUS, 1946-48 Mem.: Theta Chi. Home: 3852 Mcgirts Blvd Jacksonville FL 32210-4337 Personal E-mail: freditor39@bellsouth.net.

HARTMANN, GEORGE HERMAN, retired manufacturing executive; b. NYC, Nov. 6, 1927; s. Herman George Dietrich and Margaret Bertha (Winkler) Hartmann; m. Anne Katharine Hartmann, July 9, 1960; children: Michael George, Steven Herman, Katharine Margaret, Elizabeth Anne. AB cum laude, Dartmouth Coll., 1949, MS in Mech. Engring, 1950. With Gen. Electric Co., 1950-70; v.p. mfg. Gen. Signal Corp., 1970-71; exec. v.p., then pres. GE Espanola, 1971-74; pres. Davol Co. (subs. Internat. Paper Co.), 1975-78, corp. v.p. human resources, then v.p. materials, 1979-80; pvt. investor, 1980-81; group v.p. Textron Inc., Providence, 1981-92; ret., 1992. Trustee RI Coun. Econ. Edn., 1977, vice chmn. 1983-92; trustee Am. Sch., Bilbao, Spain, 1972-74, chmn., 1973-74; trustee Joint Coun. Econ. Edn., 1986-91, Nat. Security Indsl. Assn., 1988-92, Calvin K. Kazanjian Econs. Found., Inc., 1996-; zoning bd. mem. Lyme, NH, 2002- , chmn. 2004-2006; U.S. del. NATO Indsl. Adv. Group, 1989-92; mem. adv. com. Lebanon (NH) Airport, 2000-07, vice chmn., 2005-06. Served to lt. USNR, 1955-60. Mem. NAM (dir. 1977-80), NH/Vt. Vis. Nurse/Hospice Assn. (trustee 2007—), RI C. of C. (dir. 1977-78), Greater Providence C. of C. (dir. 1976-78), NY Yacht Club, Cruising Club Am. (Parkinson Meml. Trophy for Transoceanic Passage 1993, 97). Independent.

HARTMANN, ROBERT ELLIOTT, retired manufacturing executive; b. Bklyn., Apr. 10, 1926; s. James and Edna Mae (Schroeder) H.; m. Anne Marie Mongiello, Feb. 15, 1948; children: Barbara Hartmann Kaszor, Donna Hartmann Dow. BS, Miami U., Oxford, Ohio, 1946. CPA, N.Y. Acct. Price, Waterhouse & Co., NYC, 1948-57; mgr. fin. acctg. Air Products & Chems., Allentown, Pa., 1957-58; v.p. Alpha Portland Cement Co. divsn. Alpha Portland Industries, Inc., Easton, Pa., 1958-82. Sec. Slattery Group, Inc. (formely Alpha Portland Industries, Inc.), Easton, 1962-89; sec., treas. Energy and Resource Recovery Corp., until 1982; sec., treas., dir. H.O.H. Corp., until 1982; past pres. Moravian Book Shop, Inc. Bd. dirs. Bethlehem Area Moravians. Served to lt. Supply Corps USNR, World War II. Mem. Inst. Mgmt. Accts. (pres. Lehigh Valley chpt. 1973-74), Financial Execs. Inst. (treas. N.E. Pa. chpt. 1972-74), Am. Inst. C.P.A.s. Mem. Moravian Ch. Home: 285 Bridle Path Rd Bethlehem PA 18017-3867

HARTMANN, ROBERT SANKEY, health facility administrator, not-for-profit fundraiser; b. June 9, 1948; s. Robert Trowbridge and Roberta (Sankey) H.; m. Ruth Eva Satterthwaite, Dec. 2, 1978; children: Daniel Satterthwaite, David Trowbridge. BA in Speech/Drama cum laude, Occidental Coll., 1969, MA in Speech/Drama, 1971; student, Guildhall Sch. Music & Drama, 1970; mgmt. devel. course, Harvard Bus. Sch., 1974. Spl. asst. to chmn. Nat. Endowment for Arts, Washington, 1973—78; lobbyist for Daniel J. Edelman Washington, 1978; creative dir., lobbyist Hill and Knowlton, Washington, 1978—81; sr. v.p. Ruder Finn & Rotman, Washington, 1981—84; dir. pub. rels. World Wildlife Fund, Washington, 1984—86; sr. v.p. and dir. pub. rels. Abramson Assocs., Inc., 1986—90; v.p. pub. affairs, mktg. and devel. Nat. Rehab. Hosp., Washington, 1990—. Chmn. bd. dirs. Met. Meth. Nursery Sch., 1989—94. Named Outstanding Young Man Am., 1983. Mem. Pub. Rels. Soc. Am. (Thoth award 1984), Internat. Assn. Bus. Communicators (Gold Quill award 1984), Westmoreland Citizens Assn. (pres. 1992-93), Nat. Press Club, Capitol Hill Club. Home: 5023 Worthington Dr Bethesda MD 20816-2748 Office: Nat Rehab Hosp 102 Irving St NW Washington DC 20010-2949 Office Phone: 202-877-1776. Business E-Mail: robert.s.hartmann@medstar.net.

HARTNETT, JAMES PATRICK, engineering educator; b. Lynn, Mass., Mar. 19, 1924; s. James Patrick and Anna Elizabeth (Ryan) H.; m. Shirley Germaine Carlson, July 14, 1945 (div. 1969); children: James, David, Paul, Carla, Dennis; m. Edith Zubrin, Sept. 10, 1971. BS in Mech. Engring, Ill. Inst. Tech., 1947; MS, MIT, 1948; PhD, U. Calif., Berkeley, 1954. Engr. gas turbine div. Gen. Electric Co., 1948-49; rsch. engr. U. Calif., Berkeley, 1949-54; asst. prof. to prof. mech. engring. U. Minn., 1954-61; Guggenheim fellow, vis. prof. U. Tokyo, Japan, 1960; cons. ICA, Seoul, Korea, 1960; Fulbright lectr., cons. mech. engring. U. Alexandria, Egypt, 1961; H. Fletcher Brown prof. mech. engring., chmn. dept. U. Del., 1961-65; engring. cons., 1954-74; prof., head dept. energy engring. U. Ill., Chgo., 1965-74; dir. Energy Resources Ctr., 1974-98. Sci. exch. visitor, Romania, 1969; vis. prof. Israel Inst. Tech., 1971; cons. Asian Inst. Tech., Bangkok 1977; 1st Dr. Arcot Ramachandran prof. heat transfer Indian Inst. Tech., Madras, 1995-96. Editor: Recent Advances in Heat and Mass Transfer, 1961; co-editor: Internat. Jour. Heat and Mass Transfer, 1960—, (with T.F. Irvine, Jr.) Advances in Heat Transfer, 1963—, Heat Transfer-Japanese Research, Soviet Research, 1971, Fluid Mechanics-Soviet Research, 1971; contbr. articles on heat transfer, fluid mechanics, energy to tech. jours. Mem. organizing com. and sci. coun. Internat. Centre Heat and Mass Transfer, Ankara, Turkey, 1969—; mem., sec. Ill. Energy Resources Commn., 1974-85; mem. sci. coun. Regional Center for Energy, Heat and Mass Transfer for Asia and Pacific, 1976—; sec. Midwest Univs. Energy Consortium, 1980—. Recipient Profl. Achievement award Ill. Inst. Tech. Alumni Assn., 1977; recipient Luikov medal Internat. Ctr. Heat and Mass Transfer, 1981; Japan Soc. for Promotion of Sci. fellow, 1987. Fellow ASME (Meml. award heat transfer divsn. 1969, 40th Anniversary award 1989, AIChE-ASME Max Jakob Meml. award 1989), Indian Nat. Acad. Engring., Japanese Soc. Mech. Engrs. (hon.); mem. Internat. Higher Edn. Acad. of Scis./Moscow (Disting. prof. 1997), Sigma Xi, Tau Beta Pi, Pi Tau Sigma. Address: Univ of Ill 1919 W Taylor St Chicago IL 60612-7246

HARTNETT, JOSH, actor; b. San Francisco, July 21, 1978; s. Daniel and Molly Hartnett (Stepmother). Student, SUNY, Purchase. Actor: (films) Halloween: H2O, 1998, The Faculty, 1998, The Virgin Suicides, 1999, Here on Earth, 2000, Blow Dry, 2001, Member, 2001, Town & Country, 2001, Pearl Harbor, 2001, O, 2001, Black Hawk Down, 2001, The Same, 2001, 40 Days and 40 Nights, 2002, Hollywood Homicide, 2003, Wicker Park, 2004, Sin City, 2005, Mozart and the Whale, 2005, Lucky Number Slevin, 2006, The Black Dahlia, 2006, Resurrecting the Champ, 2007; (TV films) Debutante, 1998; (TV series) Cracker, 1997—98. Named ShoWest Male Star of Tomorrow, 2002. Office: Patricola Lust Pub Relations Inc 8383 Wilshire Blvd Ste 530 Beverly Hills CA 90211-2404*

HARTNETT, WILL FORD, lawyer; b. Austin, Tex., June 3, 1956; s. James Joseph and Emily (High) Hartnett; m. Tammy Lynn Cotton, Dec. 7, 1996; children: Will, Winston, Warner. BA, Harvard U., 1978; JD, U. Tex., 1981. Bar: Tex. 1981, U.S. Ct. Appeals (5th cir.) 1985, U.S. Supreme Ct. 1985; cert. in Estate Planning and Probate Law Tex. Bd. Legal Specialization. Assoc. Turner & Hitchins, Dallas, 1981-82; ptnr. The Hartnett Law Firm, Dallas, 1982—. Bd. dirs. Tex. Guaranteed Student Loan Corp., Austin, 1987-90. Co-author: Annual Survey of Wills and Trusts, 1986. Mem. Tex. Ho. of Reps., 1991—, Tex. Jud. Coun.; vice chmn. Ho. Judiciary Com., 1995-02, chmn., 2003-. Fellow: Tex. Bar Found., Am. Coll. Trust and Estate Coun.; mem.: SAR, Tex. Jud. Coun., Dallas Bar Assn., Order of Malta, Mensa, St. Nicholas Soc., Harvard Club Dallas (bd. dirs., treas. 1983—95, 2006—). Republican. Roman Catholic. Home: 4722 Walnut Hill Ln Dallas TX 75229-6354 Office: 2920 N Pearl St Dallas TX 75201 Office Phone: 214-742-4655. Business E-Mail: will@hartnettlawfirm.com.

HARTNETT, WILLIAM M., lawyer; b. NYC, Feb. 23, 1954; BA cum laude, Rider U., 1976; JD cum laude, Fordham U., 1979. Bar: NY 1980. Ptnr., Corp. Fin and Mergers & Acquisitions Practice Areas Cahill Gordon & Reindel LLP, NYC, mem. exec. com. Mem. Fordham Law Rev., 1978—79. Office: Cahill Gordon & Reindel LLP 80 Pine St New York NY 10005-1702 Office Phone: 212-701-3847. Office Fax: 212-378-2198. Business E-Mail: whartnett@cahill.com.

HARTOG, JOHN A., lawyer; b. Scarsdale, NY, Jan. 27, 1952; BA cum laude, Pomona Coll., 1974; JD, U. Calif. Hastings Coll. Law, 1979; LLM in Taxation, Golden Gate U., 1984. Bar: Calif. 1979, US Tax Ct. 1984, US Ct. Appeals DC 1997, NY 2002, US Ct. Appeals (3rd cir.), Adj. prof. Golden Gate U. Sch. Tax. Contbr. articles to profl. publs.; co-author: California Trust Practice, 1996. Named one of Top 100 Attys., Worth mag., 2005—06. Fellow: Am. Coll. Trusts and Estates Counsel; mem.: Calif. Trust and Estate Counselors, State Bar Calif. (mem. trusts and estates law and taxation sects.), ABA (mem. taxation, real property, probate and trust law sects.), Alameda County Bar Assn. (chair estate planning com. of probate sect.). Office: John A Hertog Inc Bldg B Ste 250-B 4 Orinda Way Orinda CA 94563 Office Phone: 925-253-1717. Office Fax: 925-253-0334. E-mail: jahartog@calteclaw.com.*

HARTRICK, JANICE KAY, lawyer; b. Baytown, Tex., Oct. 15, 1952; BA, Rice U., 1974; JD, U. Houston, 1976. Bar: Tex. 1977, La. 1980. With contracts sect. Texaco Corp., Houston, 1977-78; asst. gen. counsel Cities Exploration Co., Watson Oil Corp., Houston, 1978-79; sr. atty. Coastal Corp., Houston, 1979-87; chief counsel, v.p. Seagull Energy Corp., Houston, 1987-97; gen. counsel, sr. v.p. EEX Corp., Houston, 1997-2000; v.p., assoc. counsel Apache Corp., 2000—. Coun. Thompson and Knight, LLP, Houston. Contbg. editor Regulation of the Natural Gas Industry, 1980-84. Vice chair adv. bd. Internat. Oil and Gas Ednl. Ctr., Southwestern Legal Found.; trustee Rocky Mountain Mineral Law Found. Mem. ABA (chair oil and gas exploration and prodn. 2000-2002), Tex. Bar Assn., State Bar of Tex. (oil, gas and mineral law sect. chair 1999), La. Bar Assn. Avocation: track. Office: Apache Corp 2000 Post Oak Blvd Ste 100 Houston TX 77056-4400

HARTSFIELD, JAMES KENNEDY, JR., orthodontist, geneticist; b. Decatur, Ala., Feb. 12, 1955; s. James Kennedy and Shirley Joann (Bridwell) H.; m. Karen Lee Whitaker, May 8, 1977; 1 child, Kennedy Whitaker. BS, U. SC, 1977; DMD, Med. U. SC, 1981; MS, Ind. U., 1983; M in Med. Sci., Harvard U., 1987; PhD, U. South Fla., 1993. Diplomate Am. Bd. Med. Genetics., Am. Bd. Orthodontics. Intern Hillsborough Dental Rsch. Clinic, Tampa, Fla., 1981-82; clin. fellow Ind. U., Indpls., 1982-83; rsch. fellow Harvard U., Boston, 1983-86, Mass. Gen. Hosp., Boston, 1984-86; clin. fellow U. South Fla., Tampa, 1986-87, asst. prof., 1987-93; assoc. prof. Sch. Dentistry and Sch. Medicine, Ind. U., Indpls., 1993—99, prof. Sch. Dentistry and Sch. Medicine, 1999—. Dir. Teratogen Info. Svc., U. South Fla., 1987-93; dir. oral facial genetics divsn. Sch. Dentistry Ind. U., 1993-, acting chmn. oral facial devel., 1998-99, chmn., 1999-2002, interim chmn. orthodontics and oral facial genetics, 2007—; pres. Meridian Orthodontics, PC, 2003-. Mem. editl. bd. Jour. Dental Rsch., 2007-; contbr. articles to profl. jours. Med. adv. coun. Osteogenesis Imperfecta Found., 2007—. Recipient Physician-Scientist award NIH, 1989, 1st Ind. Rsch. Support and Transition award, 1996, B.F. Dewell Meml. Biomed. Rsch. award Am. Assn. Orthodontists Found., 2001, Disting. Faculty award Ind. U. Sch. Dentistry Alumni Assn., 2003; named Outstanding Faculty of Yr., Ind. Dental Assn., 2004 Fellow Am. Coll. Med. Genetics (founding), Am. Coll. Dentists, Coll. of Diplomates of Am. Bd. Orthodontics; mem. ADA, Am. Soc. Human Genetics, Am. Assn. for Dental Rsch., Internat. Assn. Dental Rsch. (v.p. craniofacial biology group 2003-04, pres. 2005-06), Internat. Coll. Dentists, Soc. Craniofacial Genetics (pres. 1989-90), Am. Dental Edn. Assn., Am. Cleft Palate Assn., Am. Assn. Orthodontists, Harvard Soc. for Advancement of Orthodontics (v.p. 2006-, mem. bd. dirs. for Confs. on Orthodontic Advances in Sci. and Tech. 2006-). Presbyterian. Avocations: music, boating. Home: 8095 Sunfish Ct Indianapolis IN 46236-8887 Office: Ind U Schs Dentistry and Medicine 1121 W Michigan St Indianapolis IN 46202-5186: 13590 B North Meridian Ste 205 Carmel IN 46032 Home Phone: 317-823-9254; Office Phone: 317-278-1148.

HARTSOCK, LANGDON ALL, medical educator, department chairman, physician; b. Charlotte, June 1, 1961; s. Theodore Glenn and Sarah Mills Hartsock; married. MD, Duke U., Durham, 1987. Cert. Orthopaedic Surgery Am. Bd. Orthop. Surgery, 1996. Assoc. prof., chmn. Med. U. SC, Charleston, 2000—. Lt. comdr. USMC, 1989—97. Office: Med U SC 96 Jonathan Lucas St Charleston SC 29425 Office Phone: 843-792-3934. Office Fax: 843-792-3674.

HARTSOCK, LINDA SUE, retired management consultant; b. St. Joseph, Mo., Feb. 20, 1940; d. Waldo Emerson and Martha (Skelkop) H. BS, Ctrl. Meth. Coll., Fayette, Mo., 1962; MEd, Pa. State U., 1965, D in Edn., 1971. Cert. assn. exec. Am. Soc. Assn. Execs. Tchr. Jr. High Sch. (North Kansas City (Mo.) Pub. Sch. Sys.), 1962; sr. resident Pa. State U., 1963—64, asst. coord. residence halls, 1964—65, residence hall coord., 1965—66, asst. dean women, 1966—68, asst. dean students, 1968—71; rschr. Ctr. for Study Higher Edn., 1971, dir. new student programs, 1971—72; nat. dir. program AAUW, 1972—76; exec. dir. Adult Edn. Assn., 1976—80; CEO Integrated Options, Inc., Assn., Edn. and Mgmt. Svcs., Alexandria, Va., 1980—2000, ret., 2000. CEO Hartburn Prodns. LLC; v.p. fin. Com. for Full Finding Edn., 1979; first adv. panel convened future directions of learning soc. project Coll. Entrance Exam. Bd., 1978, planning group for Course-By-Newspaper exam. project, 1979; mem. White House Conf. on Aging Com., 1979; nat. adv. bd. Nat. Ctr. Higher Edn. Mgmt. Sys. Project to Develop a Taxonomy for the Field of Adult Edn., 1978; nat. adv. coun. on adult edn. Futures and Amendments Project, 1977; adv. Collection of Census Data, Nat. Ctr. Ednl. Stats., 1977; pub. policy com., program com. chmn. Adv. Coun. Nat. Orgns. to Corp. for Pub. Broadcasting, 1976; adv. devel. New Mediated Programs, Office Instructional Resources, Miami Dade C.C., 1976; innovative awards com. Nat. Univ. Ext. Assn., 1977; field reader U.S. Dept. Edn. Title III Grants, 1981-83 Mem. editl. bd. Off to Coll. mag, 1972-74; co-author: Voices of the Chincoteague-Memories of Greenbackville and Franklin City, 2007; contbr. articles to profl. jours. Womans aux. Greenbackville Va. Fire Dept., 2000—02; instr. water exercise Lower Shore YMCA, Pocomoke City, Md., 2002—; tour guide Chincoteague Nat. Wildlife Refuge, 2002—06; chair family and friends forum Hartley Hall Nursing Home; bd. mgrs. Lower Shore YMCA, 2004—07, chair fin. devel. com., 2005—06; chair media rels. Greenbackville Old Tyme Days. Recipient Disting. Alumni award Ctrl. Meth. Coll., 1978. Mem. Am. Soc. Assn. Execs. (individual membership coun. 1979-81, edn. com. 1985-88, 92-94, univ. affairs commn. 1989-92, awards com. 1991), Washington Women's Forum (budget, program and exec. coms. 1978-82), Alumni Soc. Coll. Edn. Pa. State U. (bd. dirs., chairperson strategic planning com. 1986, Outstanding Alumni award). E-mail: ioinc@verizon.net.

HARTSOUGH, GAYLA ANNE KRAETSCH, management consultant; b. Lakewood, Ohio, Sept. 16, 1949; d. Vernon W. and Mildred E. (Austin) Kraetsch; m. James N. Heller, Aug. 20, 1972 (div. 1977); m. Jeffrey W. Hartsough, Mar. 12, 1983; 1 child, Jeffrey Hunter Kraetsch. BS, Northwestern U., Evanston, Ill., 1971; EdM, Tufts U., Medford, Mass., 1973; MEd, U. Va., Charlottesville, 1978; PhD, U. Va., 1978. Vol. VISTA, Tenn., 1970-71; asst. tchr. Perkins Sch. for the Blind, Watertown, Mass., 1971-72; resource tchr. Fairfax (Va.) County Pub. Schs., 1972-76; asst. dir. ctr. U. Va., Charlottesville, 1976-78; sr. program officer Acad. Edn. Devel., Washington, 1978-80; mng. cons. Cresap/Towers Perrin, Washington, LA, 1980-86; pres. KH Consulting Group, LA, 1986—. Mem. nat. adv. coun. Sch. Comm. Northwestern U., Evanston, Ill., 1992—2005. Contbr. articles to profl. jours. Co-founder LA Higher Edn. Roundtable, 1987—94; mem. nat. adv. coun. Northwestern U., 1992—2005, mem. coun. of 100, 1999—. Recipient Outstanding Women of Achievement award, Century City C. of C., 1991. Mem.: Orgn. Women Execs. Home: 15624 Royal Ridge Rd Sherman Oaks CA 91403-4207 Office: KH Consulting Group 1901 Ave Of Stars Ste 1900 Los Angeles CA 90067-6020 Office Phone: 310-203-5417. Office Fax: 310-203-5419. Personal E-mail: khcggak@aol.com.

HARTSTEIN, HAROLD HERMAN, psychology educator, consultant; b. NYC, Jan. 9, 1921; s. Samuel and Margaret Amanda (Wussow) H.; m. Marion Elizabeth Shea, Apr. 11, 1953; children: Marion Farnham Korzec, Margaret Ann. BGS, U. Nebr.-Omaha, 1971; MA, U. South Fla., 1972; EdD, Nova U., 1978. Enlisted U.S. Army, 1942, commd. 2d lt., 1948, advanced through grades to lt. col., 1967, served in ETO, 1944-45, Japan, 1949-50, Republic of Korea, 1950-51, Germany, 1955-57, Vietnam, 1960-61, Taiwan, 1963—65; with 3d Inf. Honor Guard, Washington, 1951-54; comdg. officer Signal Battalion, Korat, Thailand, 1967-68; gen. staff officer Hdqrs., U.S. Army Strategic Comm. Commd., Ft. Huachua, Ariz., 1968-70; ret., 1970; prof. psychology Hillsborough CC, Tampa, Fla., 1973-91; ret., 1991. Cons. textbook pubs. Decorated Legion of Merit, Bronze Star medal, Army Commendation medal. Mem. NEA, VFW, Ret. Officers Assn., Am. Assn. Ret. Persons, Am. Legion, Common Cause, U. Nebr. at Omaha Alumni Assn., U. South Fla. Alumni Assn., Nova U. Alumni Assn., Friends of Tampa Mus. Art. Democrat. Mem. United Ch. of Christ. Personal E-mail: harion@prodigy.net.

HARTT, GROVER, III, lawyer; b. Dallas, Apr. 12, 1948; s. Grover Jr. and Dorothy June (Wilkins) H. BA with high honors, So. Meth. U., 1970, LLM in Tax, 1986; JD with high honors, Tex. Tech U., 1973. Bar: Tex. 1973, U.S. Dist. Ct. (no. dist.) Tex. 1974, U.S. Dist. Ct. (we. dist.) Tex. 1975, U.S. Ct. Appeals (5th cir.) 1975, U.S. Dist. Ct. (ea. dist.) Tex. 1999, U.S. Dist. Ct. (so. dist.) Tex. 2005, U.S. Ct. Fed. Claims, 2005, U.S. Supreme Ct. 1976. Law clk. to presiding justice Ct. Criminal Appeals Tex., Austin, 1973-75; atty. Hartt and Hartt, Dallas, 1975-79; atty., advisor Office Spl. Counsel U.S. Dept. Energy, Dallas, 1979-80, dep. chief counsel, 1981-83; trial atty. tax divsn. U.S. Dept. Justice, Dallas, 1983-86, dep. atty.-in-charge tax divsn., 1986-95, asst. chief southwestern region civil trial sect. tax divsn., 1995—2006, sr. litigation counsel, 2006—. Nat. spkr. on taxation, bankruptcy and litig. Contbg. author: Collier on Bankruptcy; contbr. articles to profl. jours. Recipient Atty. Gen's award for disting. svc., 1996; named a Super Lawyer, Tex. Monthly Mag., 2006. Fellow Am. Coll. Bankruptcy; mem. ABA (mem. ct. procedure com. tax sect., chmn. bankruptcy litig. subcom. 1995-2003, Dept. of Justice liaison 2003—, mem. bus. bankruptcy com. bus. law sect., vice chmn. tax and fed. claims subcom. 1996-2000, chmn. 2000-06), Tex. Bar Assn., Dallas Bar Assn. (tax sect. sec.-treas. 2007), Am. Bankruptcy Inst., Coll. of State Bar of Tex., John C. Ford Am. Inn of Ct. (master of bench 2000-06). Office: US Dept Justice Tax Divsn 717 N Harwood St Ste 400 Dallas TX 75201-6506 Home Phone: 214-522-3653; Office Phone: 214-880-9733. Business E-Mail: grover.hartt@usdoj.gov.

HARTWELL, ALFRED STEDMAN (ASH HARTWELL), international relations educator, consultant; b. Boston, Nov. 1, 1940; s. Alfred Stedman and Nancy Herrick Hartwell; m. Patricia Martin-Jenkins, Jan. 28, 1967; children: Meredith, Elina, Ruhiyyih. BA, Dartmouth Coll., 1963; EdD, U. Mass., 1972. Vol. Peace Corps, Ethiopia, 1963—65; sr. lectr. Makerere U., Uganda, 1972—75; project dir. edn. planning UN-UNESCO, Uganda, 1975—79, Lesotho, 1979—85; project dir. secondary edn. project Fla. State U., USAID, Botswana, 1985—89; tng. advisor planning project Acad. Edn. Devel., Egypt, 1989—92; sr. edn. advisor Am. Inst. Rsch., USAID Africa, 1992—99, Edn. Devel. Ctr. Africa, 1999—2004; prof. Ctr. Internat. Edn., U. Mass., Amherst, 2004—. Edn. policy advisor Edn. Devel. Ctr., USAID, 2004—. Author: Basic Education in Africa, 1995, USAID's Strategic Framework for Basic Education in Africa, 1998; editor: Outgrow War, 2002. Mem.: Coop. Internat. Edn. Assn., Am. Edn. Rsch. Assn., Profl. Ski Instrs. Assn. Home: 130 Red Gate Ln Amherst MA 01002 Office: Ctr Internat Edn Hills House S Amherst MA 01003

HARTWELL, LELAND HARRISON (LEE HARTWELL), geneticist, educator; b. LA, Oct. 30, 1939; s. Majorie (Taylor) H.; m. Theresa Naujack. BS, Calif. Inst. Tech., 1961; PhD, MIT, 1964. Postdoctoral fellow Salk Inst., 1964-65; asst. prof. U. Calif., Irvine, 1965-67, assoc. prof., 1967-68, U. Washington, Seattle, 1968-73, prof. genome sciences, 1973—, adj. prof. of medicine, 2003; pres., dir. Fred Hutchison Cancer Rsch. Ctr., Seattle, 1997. Named rsch. prof. of genetics Am. Cancer Soc., 1990; chmn. sci. adv. bd., Canary Fund. Recipient Eli Lilly award, 1973, NIH Merit award, 1990, GM Sloan award, 1991, Hoffman LaRoche Mattia award, 1991, Gairdner Found. Internat. award, 1992, Simon Shubitz award U. Chgo., 1992, Brandeis U. Rosenstiel award, 1993, Sloan Kettering Cancer Ctr. Katherine Berkan Judd award, 1994, Genetics Soc. of Am. medal, 1994, MGH Warren Triennial prize, 1995, Keith Porter award Am. Soc. Cell Biology, 1995, Carnegie Mellon Dickson award, 1996, Louisa Gross Horwitz prize Columbia U., 1995, Albert Lasker Basic Med. Rsch. award Albert and Mary Lasker Found., 1998, Brinker Internat. award for basic sci. Susan G. Komen Breast Cancer Found., 1998, Disting. Alumni award Calif. Inst. Tech., 1999, City of Medicine award, 1999, medal of honor Am. Cancer Soc., 1999, Léopold Giffuel prize Assn. pour la Recherche sur le Cancer, France, 2000, The Massry prize The Meira and Shaul G. Massry Found., Nobel prize in Physiology or Medicine, 2001, Wash. Medal of Merit, 2003; Guggenheim fellow, 1983-84; Am. Bus. Cancer Rsch. grantee, 1983—; Am. Cancer Soc. scholar; laureate Passano Found., 1996. Mem. NAS, AAAS, Am. Soc. Microbiology, Am. Soc. Cell Biology, Genetics Soc. Am. (pres. 1990). Office: Hutchinson Cancer Rsch Ctr D1-060 1100 Fairview Ave N PO Box 19024 Seattle WA 98109-1024

HARTWELL, STEPHEN, investment company executive; b. Phila., Apr. 10, 1915; s. Stephen Warren and Elizabeth (Thompson) Hartwell; m. Elizabeth van Laer Speer, Feb. 21, 1946 (div. Jan. 1973); children: Stephen Warren II, Robert van Laer; m. Norma Bostick, Dec. 9, 1978. BS in Adminstrv. Engring., Lafayette Coll., 1936. Investment analyst Pa. Co. Banking & Trusts, 1936-41; procurement officer electronic equipment CAA, 1947-48; indsl. specialist AEC, 1948-49, chief progress and stats. sect., prodn. div., 1949-51, chief constr. engring. reports br., 1951-54; exec. v.p. Atomic Devel. Securities Co. (and successor cos.), 1954-68; v.p. Washington Mut. Investors Fund, Inc., 1968-81, pres., 1981-85, chmn., 1985—2001, chmn. emeritus, 2001—. Pres. Washington Investment Advisers Inc., 1992—2002; chmn. Tax Exempt Bond Fund Md., Tax Exempt Bond Fund Va., 1986—97, chmn. emeritus, 1997—; pres. Colchester Corp., Woodbridge, Va., 1971—, bd. dirs.; chmn. WMIF Mgmt. Corp., Washington, 1986—, Hartick LLC, 1997—; bd. dirs. Wentz Corp., Wilmington, Del., Johnston Lemon Group Inc.; trustee Ameribanc Investors Group, 1985—95. Mem. Fairfax County Planning Commn., 1961—67, chmn., 1964—66; mem. No. Va. Regional Planning and Econ. Devel. Commn., 1963—64; bd. govs. Gunston Hall Sch.; active Mt. Vernon Life Guards, 1992—, chmn., 1998—2005; trustee Am. U., 1983—88, trustee emeritus, 1988—; trustee Woodlawn Found., 1983—89; trustee, treas. Found. for Mid. East Peace, 1993—, Fairfax Hosp. Assn., 1986—93, Inova Health Sys., 1987—96, chmn. investment and pension com., 1997—; chmn. Jefferson Hosp., Alexandria, Va., 1986—92, Va. Coll. Bldg. Authority, Richmond, 1994—2001; mem. Commonwealth Coun., Richmond, 1998—, Fairfax County Rep. Com., 1955—61, 1966—70, 1979—81. Maj. US Army, 1941—45. Mem.: NASD (Dist. 10 com. 1968—71), SAR, Nat. Economists Club, Washington Soc. Investment Analysts, Met. Club, Mt. Vernon Country Club, Phi Alpha (pres.), Zeta Psi (trustee Ednl. Found. 1997—2005, pres. 1999—2000). Home: Riversedge PO Box 33 Mount Vernon VA 22121-0033 Office: AMA Bldg 1101 Vermont Ave NW Fl 6 Washington DC 20005-3583 Office Phone: 202-842-5670. Personal E-mail: stephcom@msn.com.

HARTWELL, WILLIAM GERSHAM, III, retired music educator; s. William Gersham Hartwell Jr. and Barbara Lillian Parker Hartwell; m. Janis Louese Quier, Jan. 15, 1982; children: Ted, Susanne, John Harrison, Brian Harrison, Mark Harrison. BA in Music, Whitman Coll., 1961; MMus in Voice and Pedagogy, Ind. U., 1964. Instr. music Ea. Wash. State, Cheney, 1963—66; asst. prof. music Whitworth Coll., Spokane, 1967—68; assoc. instr. music Ind. U., Bloomington, 1969—71; asst. prof. music Alma (Mich.) Coll., 1971—72; assoc. prof. music Tex. Tech U., Lubbock, 1973—2004, adj. prof., 2004—, prof. emeritus, 2005—. Dirigent Spokane German Chorale, 1964—69; dir. music Millwood Presbyn. Ch., Spokane, 1964—68, Ch. of the Cross, Bloomington, 1970—71, St. John's United Meth. Ch., Lubbock, 1974—82, Asbury Meth. Ch., Lubbock, 1996—; dir. Sweet Adelines Chorus, Spokane, 1968—69, Lubbock, Tex., 1974—75. Contbr. (CD-ROM) Liberty, Equality, Fraternity, 2001; numerous vocal performances in recitals, musicals, operas. Mem.: Nat. Assn. Tchrs. of Singing, Beta Theta Pi, Phi Mu Alpha, Phi Delta Kappa, Pi Kappa Lambda. Republican. Avocations: fishing, hunting, golf, bowling, reading. Home: 3204 68th St Lubbock TX 79413 Office: Tex Tech Sch Music PO Box 42033 Lubbock TX 79409 Office Phone: 806-799-2034. E-mail: wghartwell@sbcglobal.net.

HARTWIG, ROBERT PAUL, insurance institute executive, economist; b. Providence, Mar. 26, 1964; s. Robert Joseph and Rachel Aileen (Morin) H.; m. Laura Michelle Warner, May 19, 1990; 1 child, Jordan Alexander. BA in Econs. cum laude, U. Mass., 1986; MS in Econs., U. Ill., 1988, PhD in Econs., 1993. Instr. econs. U. Ill., Urbana-Champaign, 1986-89, rsch. asst. Bur. Econ. and Bus. Rsch., 1988-91, project coord. Bur. Econ. and Bus. Rsch., 1989-91; statistician Directorate for Epidemiology U.S. Consumer Product Safety Commn., Washington, 1991-93; sr. economist, instr. Nat. Coun. on Compensation Ins., Boca Raton, Fla., 1993-97; sr. economist Swiss Reinsurance Group, NYC, 1997; dir. econ. rsch. Nat. Coun. Compensation Ins., Hoboken, NJ, 1998; v.p., economist Ins. Info. Inst., NYC, 1998—99, v.p., chief economist, 1999—2002, sr. v.p., chief economist, 2002—06, pres., 2007—. Adj. prof. econs. Fla. Atlantic U., 1996-97; econ. cons. Office of Pres., U. Ill., Urbana, 1990-91, Aerosol Industry Devel. Assn., Niles, Ill., 1990-91, Office of Atty. Gen., State of Ill., Springfield, summer 1989. Contbr. articles to profl. jours. Mem. Am. Econ. Assn., Am. Risk and Ins. Assn. E-mail: info@iii.org.*

HARTY, JAMES D., former manufacturing company executive; b. Bridgeport, Conn., Oct. 5, 1929; s. John S. and Catherine (Lee) H.; m. Margaret O'Connor, June 4, 1955; children: Shaun, Kevin, Maura, Megan. Grad., U.S. Army Officer Candidate Sch., Ft. Bliss, Tex., 1952; degree in indsl. engring, U. Bridgeport, 1962. Analyst E.I. DuPont, 1947-51; prodn. control mgr. Sikorsky Aircraft, 1954-62; plant mgr. Stanley Works, 1962-68; corp. mgr. prodn. and inventory control ITT, 1968-70; corp. dir. mfg. projects Singer Co., NYC, 1970-74; pres., chief operating officer Raymond Corp., Greene, NY, 1974-84, also dir., now ret.; owner, cons. J.D. Harty Assocs., Hilton Head Island, SC, 1984-94. Mem. engring. tech. adv. com. and M.B.A. adv. bd. SUNY-Binghamton, mem. found.; mem. Sch. Bd. Found., Hilton Head Island, S.C. 1st lt. U.S. Army, 1951-53, Korea. Recipient Corp. Leadership award MIT, 1987. Mem. Am. Mgmt. Assn. (Internat. Svc. award), Am. Prodn. and Inventory Control Soc. (past internat. v.p. edn. and rsch., Disting. Svc. award), Hilton Head Island Computer Club, Country Club of Hilton Head. Home: 4 Herring Gull Ln Hilton Head Island SC 29926-2655 Personal E-mail: jdharty@gmail.com.

HARTY, JAMES QUINN, lawyer; b. Phila., Dec. 10, 1925; s. William Lawrence and Marie Sarita (Quinn) H.; m. Ann Elizabeth McGeeney, July 23, 1955; children: Michael, Martha Harty Scheines, Christopher, Patrick, Mark, Paul. AB, LaSalle Coll., 1949; MBA, U. Pa., Phila., 1952, LLB, 1959. Bar: Pa. 1961. Personnel mgr. Corning (N.Y.) Glass Works, 1952-56; lectr. Wharton Sch. U. Pa., Phila., 1956-59; assoc. Reed, Smith, Shaw & McClay, Pitts., 1961-70, ptnr., 1971-95, Plummer DeWalt & Linn, Pitts., 1995—. Author: Table Talk, Trying Times; rsch. editor: Office Management Handbook, 1958. Mem. Thornburg Zoning Rev. Bd., Thornburg Borough Coun., Pitts., 1968-76. With USN, 1943-46, PTO, CBI. Fulbright lectr. U. Kanazawa, Japan, 1959-60. Mem. Pa. Bar Assn. (chmn. labor sect. 1982), Allegheny Bar Assn., Pitts. Athletic Assn. Clubs: Pitts. (gov. 1986-87), Chartiers Country (Pitts.). Roman Catholic. Avocation: golf. Home: Keevican Weiss et al Federated Industries Tower 11th Fl 1001 Liberty Ave Pittsburgh PA 15222 Home Phone: 412-687-1835; Office Phone: 412-355-8152. Business E-Mail: jharty@kwbhlaw.com.

HARTY, THOMAS H., publishing executive; Advt. dir. Reader's Digest; assoc. pub. TV Guide, NYC, 1998—99, v.p., publisher, 1999—2001; sr. v.p., gen. mgr. Golf Digest Cos., Trumbull, Conn., 2002—04; joined Meredith Pub. Group, NYC, 2004, exec. v.p., 2006—. Office: Meredith Pubublishing Group 125 Park Ave New York NY 10017 Office Fax: 212-557-6600.

HARTZ, HARRIS L, judge; b. Balt., Jan. 20, 1947; s. Alvin Sidney and Muriel (Abrams) H.; children: Jacob Cameron, Andrew Samuel. A.B. summa cum laude, Harvard U., 1967, J.D. magna cum laude, 1972. Bar: N. Mex. 1972, US Dist. Ct. N.Mex. 1972, US Ct. Appeals (10th cir.) 1973. Asst. US atty. Dept. Justice, Albuquerque, 1972-75; asst. prof. Coll. Law, U. Ill., Champaign, 1976; atty., exec. dir. Gov.'s Organized Crime Prevention Commn., Albuquerque, 1976-79; assoc. Poole, Tinnin & Martin, P.A., Albuquerque, 1979-82; assoc. Miller, Stratvert, Torgerson & Brandt, Albuquerque, 1982-83, ptnr., dir., 1983-88; judge N. Mex. Ct. Appeals, 1988-99; judge U.S. Court Appeals (10th cir.) Albuquerque, 2001-. Case and devels. editor Harvard Law Rev., 1971-72, editor 1970-71; bd. editors Litigation Mag., 1983-86. Mem. exec. com. Bernalillo County Republican Party, Albuquerque, 1982-83; Rep. nominee for N.Mex. Supreme Ct. elections, 1986, 92, 96; chmn. N.Mex. Racing Commn., 1987-88; bd. dirs. Appellate Judges Edn. Inst., 2003-; mem. com. on rules of practice and procedure U.S. Jud. Conf., 2003-. Recipient Founders' award Nat. Kidney Found., N.Mex., 1997; nominee Joan Pew award Nat. Assn. State Racing Commrs., 1988. Mem. ABA (mem. adv. com. standing com. law and nat. security 1995-97, chmn. appellate judges conf. 2004-05), Am. Law Inst. (advisor restatement law agy. 1996-05), Albuquerque Com. on Fgn. Rels. (chmn. 1981-82), Am. Judicature Soc., Rotary Club of Albuquerque (pres. 1996-97), Phi Beta Kappa. Office: 201 3d St NW # 1870 Albuquerque NM 87102-4391 Office Phone: 505-843-6196. Business E-Mail: judge_harris_hartz@ca10.uscourts.gov.*

HARTZ, MICHAEL O., lawyer; b. Flint, Mich., July 24, 1953; BA, Kalamazoo Coll, 1975; JD, U. Detroit, 1978; LLM in Taxation, U. Fla., 1979. Bar: Mich. 1978, Fla. 1979, Ill. 1980. Ptnr. estate planning Katten Muchin Rosenman LLP, Chgo. Fellow: Am. Coll. of Trusts and Estates Counsel. Office: Katten Muchin Rosenman LLP 525 W Monroe St Ste 1900 Chicago IL 60661 Office Phone: 312-902-5279. Office Fax: 312-577-8789. E-mail: michael.hartz@katenlaw.com.

HARTZ, RICHARD ALLEN, research scientist; s. Jacob Allen and Fannie Mae Hartz. BS in Chemistry, Ea. Mennonite U., Harrisonburg, Va., 1988; PhD in Organic Chemistry, U. Pa., Phila., 1996. Postdoctoral fellow Ind. U., Bloomington, Ind., 1996—97, U. Mich., Ann Arbor, Mich., 1997—98; sr. rsch. scientist DuPont Pharm. Co., Wilmington, Del., 1998—2001; sr. rsch. investigator Bristol-Myers Squibb Co., Wallingford, Conn., 2001—. Contbr. articles various profl. jours. Mem.: NY Acad. Sci, Am. Chem. Soc. Avocations: bicycling, skiing. Office: Bristol-Myers Squibb Co 5 Rsch Pkwy Wallingford CT 06492

HARTZ, STEVEN EDWARD MARSHALL, lawyer, educator; b. Cambridge, Mass., July 11, 1948; s. Louis and Stella (Feinberg) H.; m. Janice Lindsay, June 12, 1976. AB magna cum laude, Harvard Coll., 1970; JD, U. Chgo., 1974. Bar: N.Y. 1975, U.S. Dist. Ct. (so. and ea. dists.) N.Y. 1975, U.S. Ct. Appeals (2d cir.) 1975, Fla. 1979, U.S. Dist. Ct. (so. dist.) Fla. 1979, U.S. Tax Ct. 1979, U.S. Ct. Appeals (5th cir.) 1979, U.S. Supreme Ct. 1979, U.S. Ct. Appeals (11th cir.) 1981, U.S. Dist. Ct. (mid. dist.) Fla. 1984. Assoc. Cleary, Gottlieb, Steen & Hamilton, NYC, 1974-79; asst. U.S. atty. U.S. Dept. Justice, Miami, Fla., 1979-82, dep. chief criminal divsn., chief fraud and pub. corruption sect., 1981-82; sole practice Miami, Fla., 1982-90; of counsel Akerman, Senterfitt & Eidson, P.A., Miami, 1980, ptnr., shareholder, 1991—. Lectr. dept. English, U. English, U. Miami, 1984, adj. assoc. prof., 1985-86. Co-author: Housing, A Community Handbook, 1973. Vol. atty. Mobilization for Youth Legal Svcs., N.Y.C., 1978. Recipient Dirs.' award U.S. Dept. Justice, 1981; Fulbright Hays scholar, 1970. Mem. ABA, FBA, Fla. Bar Assn., N.Y. State Bar Assn., N.Y.C. Bar Assn., Dade County Bar Assn., Phi Beta Kappa. Office: One Southeast 3rd Ave 28th Fl Miami FL 33131-4943 Business E-Mail: steven.hartz@akerman.com.

HARTZELL, ANDREW CORNELIUS, JR., retired lawyer; b. Balt., Nov. 5, 1927; s. Andrew Cornelius and Mary Frances (Milholland) H.; m. Mary Leontine McPhillips, July 31, 1954; children: Andrew Cornelius III, Stephen Carroll, Mary Leontine, James Francis, John Michael, Peter Milholland. BA, Yale U., 1950, LLB, 1953. Bar: NY 1953, Ohio 1955, US Supreme Ct. Law clk. Fed. Judge Irving R. Kaufman, NYC, 1953—54; assoc. Thompson, Hine & Flory, Cleve., 1954—63, Debevoise, Plimpton, Lyons & Gates, NYC, 1963—65; ptnr. Debevoise & Plimpton and predecessor firms, 1966—96, chmn. litig. dept., 1989—92, of counsel, 1996—98. Author: The Treacherous Snows, 1993; contbr. articles to legal jours. and to Antitrust Advisor, McGraw-Hill Pub. Co., 1971, 78; Note and Comment editor Yale Law Jour, 1952-53. Mem. bd. archtl. rev. Village of Scarsdale, NY, 1965-67; mem. Adv. Coun. on Environ. Conservation, 1986-90, chmn., 1987-89; mem. Sch. Facilities Adv. Com., 1988-90; bd. dirs. Friends of Scarsdale Parks, 1991-2000; mem. Scarsdale Bowl com., 2001-02; Bd. Assessment Review, 1998-2003; Rep. candidate for Congress 18th dist. NY, 1994. With US Army, 1946-48. Fellow Am. Coll. Trial Lawyers; mem. ABA, Union Internat. des Avocats, Scarsdale Golf Club, Yale Club NY, Town and Village Club (Scarsdale), Am. Alpine Club. Roman Catholic. Home: 7 Eastwoods Ln Scarsdale NY 10583-6401 Office: Debevoise & Plimpton LLP 919 Third Ave New York NY 10022-3904 Office Phone: 212-909-6397. Business E-Mail: achartzell@debevoise.com.

HARTZELL, CHARLES R., science foundation director, cell biologist, biochemist; b. Butler, Pa., Aug. 12, 1941; s. Charles R. and Ada Grace (Giles) H.; m. Marguerite K. Getty; children: Scott David, Amy Lynette. BS, Geneva Coll., 1963; PhD, Indiana U., 1967; MDiv, Union Theol. Sem., 2002. Post-doctoral fellow Ind. U., Bloomington, 1967; rsch. fellow Commonwealth Sci. and Industry Rsch. Orgn., Melbourne, Australia, 1967-68; rsch. fellow, asst. rsch. prof. U. Wis., Madison, 1968-71; asst. prof. Pa. State U., University Park, 1971-75, assoc. prof., 1975-78; sr. rsch. scientist Alfred I. DuPont Inst., Wilmington, Del., 1978-80, dir. rsch., 1981-97, Nemours Children's Clinics, Fla., 1987—2001; rsch. mgr. The Nemours Found., Jacksonville, 1987—2001; prof. pediat. Jefferson Med. Coll., Phila., 1989—; dir. Cross Heart Ministries, Inc., Wilmington, 2002—. Contbr. articles to profl. jours. NIH fellow, 1968-70; established investigator Am. Heart Assn., 1970-75. Presbyterian. Avocations: ballroom dancing, music, exercise, cabinet making. Office: Cross-Heart Ministries Inc 34 Colefax Ct Wilmington DE 19804-2950 Office Phone: 302-636-0190. Personal E-mail: chartzell1@verizon.net. Business E-Mail: chartzell@juno.com.

HARTZELL, IRENE JANOFSKY, retired psychologist; d. Leonard S. and Annelies Janofsky. BA, U. Calif., Berkeley, 1963, MA, 1965; PhD, U. Oreg., 1970. Psychologist Lake Washington Sch. Dist., Kirkland, Wash., 1971-72; staff psychologist VA Med. Ctr., Seattle, 1970-71, Long Beach, Calif., 1973-74; dir. parent edn. Children's Hosp., Orange, Calif., 1975—78; clin. psychologist Kaiser Permanent, Woodland Hills, Calif., 1979—94; clin. instr. pediats. Coll. Medicine U. Calif., Irvine, 1975—78; ret., 1994. Author: The Study Skills Advantage; contbr. articles to profl. jours. Intern Oreg. Legis., 1974—75. U.S. Vocat. Rehab. Adminstrn. fellow, U. Oreg., 1966—67, 1969. Personal E-mail: drijh@earthlink.net.

HARTZELL, KARL DREW, retired dean, historian; b. Chgo., Jan. 17, 1906; s. Morton C. and Bertha V. (Drew) Hartzell; m. Anne Lomas, Sept. 7, 1935; children: Karl Drew, Richard Lomas, Julian Crane; m. Elizabeth Farnum Guibord, Oct. 2, 1993. PhB cum laude, Wesleyan U., 1927; AM, Harvard U., 1928, PhD, 1934. Mem. faculty European history and Western civilization Carleton Coll., 1930-31; mem. faculty European history and western civilization dept. Ga. Sch. Tech., 1935-40; with SUNY, Geneseo, 1940-47, exec dean SUNY Ctrl. Adminstrn., acting chief adminstrv. officer Stony Brook, 1962-65, adminstrv. officer, 1965-71; archivist, historian N.Y. State War Coun., 1945-46; adminstrv. officer Brookhaven Nat. lab., 1947-52; dean Cornell Coll., Iowa, 1952-56, Bucknell U., 1956-62; libr. Inst. Advanced Studies World Religions, cons.; ret., 1972. Author: The Empire State at War: World War II, 1949, Opportunities in Atomic Energy, 1950, A Philosophy for Science Teaching, 1957, The Laws of the Living: American Values in Action, 2005; editor: The Upperclass Student and His Curriculum, 1955; co-editor: The Study of Religion on the Campus of Today, 1967. Wilbur Fisk scholar, Wesleyan U. Fellow: Soc. Values Higher Edn. (sr.); mem.: Soc. Christian Ethics, Phi Beta Kappa. Republican. Personal E-mail: kdh27@comcast.net.

HARTZLER, GEOFFREY OLIVER, retired cardiologist; b. Goshen, Ind., Nov. 6, 1946; s. Robert Willis and Emma Irene (Blosser) H.; m. Lois Anne Kauffman, June 1967 (div. May 1983); children: Abigail, Christine, Amanda; m. Dorothy Eloise Arnn, July 1985. BA, Goshen Coll., 1968; MD with honors, Ind. U., 1972. Diplomate Am. Bd. Internal Medicine, Bd. in Cardiovascular Disease. Intern Mayo Grad. Sch. Medicine, Rochester, Minn., 1972—73, fellow in medicine, 1973—74, fellow in cardiology, 1974—76; assoc. cons. internal medicine and cardiovascular disease Mayo Clinic, Rochester, 1976—77; instr. medicine Mayo Med. Sch. and Grad. Sch. Medicine, Rochester, 1976—79; cons. cardiovasc. disease and internal medicine Mayo Clinic and Mayo Found., Rochester, 1977—80; dir. invasive diagnostic electrophysiology Mayo Clinic, Rochester, 1979—80; cardiologist Cardiovasc. Cons., Inc., Kansas City, Mo., 1980—93; clin. prof. medicine U. Mo., Kansas City, 1985—95. Cons. cardiologist Mid-Am. Heart Inst., Kansas City, 1980-95; dir. advanced angioplasty fellowship program St. Luke's Hosp., Kansas City, 1985-92, med. dir. cardiovasc. clin. rsch. ctr. Mid-Am. Heart Inst., 1993-95; cons. Advanced Cardiovasc. Sys., Inc., Santa Clara, Calif., 1983-95; past mem. editl. or rev. bd. Am. Jour. Cardiology, Jour. Am. Coll. Cardiology, Cath. and CV Diagnosis, others; co-founder Ventritex, Inc., Sunnyvale, Calif., 1985-88, Triax Internat., Inc., Lenexa, Kans., 1989-96; prin., bd. dirs. Kustom Signals, Inc., Lenexa, 1990-96, LMP Steel & Wire Co., Maryville, Mo., Hartz Properties, Inc., Prairie Village, Kans., Lett Electronics, Inc., Topeka, 1995-98, Intraluminal Therapeutics, Inc., Carlsbad, Calif., 1997-2006, Cardiovasc. Sys., Mpls., 2002—. Contbr. articles to profl. jours., chpts. to books; made TV presentations to lay people on aspects of cardiology. Recipient K.K. Chen award, 1970, E.V. Allen scholarship, 1971, Osler award U. Miami, 1986, 1st Ann. Career Achievement award Cardiol. Rsch. Found., 1994. Fellow Am. Coll. Cardiology, Coun. on Clin. Cardiology of Am. Heart Assn., Soc. for Cardiac Angiography; mem. AMA, Mo. State Med. Assn., Jackson County Med. Assn., Am. Heart Assn., Alpha Omega Alpha. Avocations: music, motorcycling, reading, travel. Office: 2118 W 116th St Leawood KS 66211 Home: 2118 W 116th St Leawood KS 66211

HARUTUNIAN, ALBERT T(HEODORE), III, judge; b. San Diego, May 15, 1955; s. Albert Theodore Jr. and Elsie Ruth H.; m. Rebecca Blair, 1999. BA, Claremont McKenna Coll., 1977; JD, U. Calif., Berkeley, 1980. Bar: Calif. 1980, U.S. Dist. Ct. (so. dist.) Calif. 1980, U.S. Ct. Apppeals (9th cir.) 1982, U.S. Supreme Ct. 1984. Law clk. to Hon. Howard B. Turrentine U.S. Dist. Ct., San Diego, 1980-81; assoc. Luce, Forward, Hamilton & Scripps, San Diego, 1982-87, ptnr., 1988-95; judge San Diego Mcpl. Ct., 1995-98, San Diego Superior Ct., 1998—. Spl. counsel standing com. on discipline U.S. Dist. Ct. Calif., San Diego, 1983-85; chmn. San Diego Bar Labor and Employment Sect., 1988-89; chmn. fed. cts. com. Calif. State Bar, 1989-90. Bd. dirs. ARC San Diego chpt., 1992-2002, Crime Victims Fund, 1995-97; bd. govs. Muscular Dystrophy Assn., San Diego, 1985; grad. LEAD Inc., San Diego, 1986; planning com. San Diego United Way, 1986-92. Named one of Outstanding Young Men of Am., 1983; recipient Outstanding Service award 9th Cir. Jud. Conf., 1986. Mem. ABA, Calif. State Bar Ct. (referee 1985-88), Am. Arbitration Assn. (arbitrator 1986-95), Calif. Judges Assn. (mem. criminal law and procedure com. 1997-2000), Boalt Hall Alumni Assn. (bd. dirs. 1994-97), Claremont McKenna Coll. Alumni Assn. (founding dir. San Diego chpt. 1984-2000), Rotary (bd. dirs. San Diego club 1995—). Republican. Avocations: music, golf. Office: San Diego Superior Ct PO Box 122724 San Diego CA 92112-2724

HARUTYUNYAN, ARMINE, billing company executive; b. Yerevan, Armenia, July 24, 1979; arrived in US, 1998; d. Hrachy Shakhnazaryan and Neli Khachikoghlyan; m. Harutyun Harutyunyan, Oct. 3, 1998; 1 child, Eric. Assoc. in Liberal Arts, LA Valley Coll., Van Nuys, Calif., 2004; B Psychology, Calif. State U., Northridge, 2006. Med. labs. supr. Health Line Clin. Labs., Burbank, Calif., 2002—05; mng. Phoenix Med. Billing, LA, 2004—; mgr. Sirin Billing, Van Nuys, 2006—. Mem.: APA, Multicultural Psychol. Assn., Internat. Neuropsychol. Assn. Home: 6223 Mary Ellen Ave Van Nuys CA 91401

HARVEY, ADIA M., sociology professor; d. William B. and Brenda N. Harvey. BA in English, Spelman Coll., Atlanta, 1998; MA in Sociology, Johns Hopkins U., Balt., 2000, PhD in Sociology, 2004. Asst. prof. Hollins U., Roanoke, Va., 2004—06, Ga. State U., Atlanta, 2006—. Contbr. articles to profl. jours. Vol. D.C. Rape Crisis Ctr., Washington, 2002—04, Big Bros. Big Sisters, Roanoke, Va., 2005—06; bd. mem. Planned Parenthood Blue Ridge, Roanoke, 2004—06. Mem.: Soc. Study Social Problems, Am. Sociological Assn., Sociologists for Women in Soc. Avocations: tap and Latin dance, reading, running. Office: Ga State Univ Dept Sociology PO Box 5020 Atlanta GA 30302-5020 Office Phone: 404-463-9664. Office Fax: 404-651-1712. Business E-Mail: aharvey@gsu.edu.

HARVEY, ALBERT C., lawyer; b. Knoxville, Tenn., June 30, 1939; m. Nancy Rutherford; children: Anne, Elizabeth. BS, U. Tenn., 1961, JD, 1967. Law clk. Tenn. Supreme Ct.; asst. to pub. defender Shelby County, 1969-71; ptnr. Thomason, Hendrix, Harvey, Johnson & Mitchell, Memphis. Instr. med. and dental jurisprudence U. Tenn., Memphis. Bd. editors Tenn. Law Rev. Pres. Goodwill Boys Club, 1983-85; active YMCA, Arthritis Found., Citizens Assn. Memphis and Shelby County, Shelby County War Memls.; sr. warden of vestry Calvary Episcopal Ch. Maj. gen. USMCR, comdg. gen. 4th Marine divsn. Recipient Sam A. Myar, Jr. award Tenn. Bd. Law Examiners, 1978. Fellow: Am. Coll. Trial Lawyers, Tenn. Bar Found. (pres. 1993—94), Am. Bar Found. (life); mem.: Memphis Area C. of C. (pres. mil. affairs coun.), Am. Inns. of Ct., Memphis Bar Assn. (v.p. 1989, pres. elect 1990, pres. 1991, pres. young lawyers divsn.), Tenn. Bar Assn. (pres. 2002—03), Am. Bd. Trial Advocates (adv.), Am. Judicature Soc. (nat. bd. dirs.), ABA (bd. govs., ho. dels. charter mem. and coun. sect. litigation, young lawyers sect., fellow young lawyers divsn., com. on ethics and profl. responsibility, chair standing com. on law and nat. security, ethics 2000 spl. com.), Navy League, U. Tenn. Nat. Alumni Assn. (pres. Memphis chpt., nat. bd. govs.), Ctrl. Garden Area Assn. (pres.), Memphis Rotary Club (officer, bd. dirs.), Univ. Club Memphis (pres.), Kiwanis, Phoenix Club (1st v.p.). Office: Thomason Hendrix Harvey Johnson & Mitchell 29th Fl 1 Commerce Sq Memphis TN 38103 Home Phone: 901-529-4339; Office Phone: 901-525-8721. Business E-Mail: Harveya@ThomasonLaw.com.

HARVEY, ALEXANDER, II, retired federal judge; b. Balt., May 3, 1923; s. Fred B. and Rose (Hopkins) H.; m. Mary E. Williams, Feb. 24, 1951; children: Elizabeth H., Alexander IV. BA, Yale U., 1947; LLB, Columbia U., 1950. Bar: Md. 1950. Assoc. Ober, William, Grimes & Stinson, Balt., 1950-66, ptnr., 1953-66; asst. atty. gen. Md., 1957-58; judge U.S. Dist. Ct. Md., 1966-86, chief judge, 1986-91, sr. judge Balt., 1991—2004. Mem. Gov.'s Com. To Study Blue Sky Law of Md., 1961; mem. character com. Ct. Appeals Md. for 8th Jud. Cir. Bd. dirs. Balt. Symphony Assn., 1966-68; pres., dir. Balt. Opera Guild, 1960; bd. dirs. Balt. Coun. Social Agys., 1957-63; trustee Ch. Home and Hosp., Balt., 1952-71. 1st lt. AUS, World War II, ETO. Mem. Am., Md., Balt. bar assns., Phi Beta Kappa. Episcopalian (vestry 1967-70). Home: 7300 Brightside Rd Baltimore MD 21212-1011 Office: US Dist Ct 101 W Lombard St Ste 404 Baltimore MD 21201-2605

HARVEY, ALLISON CHARMAINE, chemist; b. Port-of-Spain, Trinidad and Tobago, Oct. 11, 1961; d. Clyde Francis and Frances Hosanna Harvey. BA, U. Ill., Champaign-Urbana, 1984. Cert. hazardous waste site worker EPA. Biologist/organic data reviewer Lockheed-Martin, Contractor to USEPA, Chgo., 1990—2001; assoc. chemist Alion Sci. and Tech., Contractor to USEPA, Chgo., 2001—06; sr. organic data reviewer Techlaw, Contractor to USEPA, Chgo., 2006—. Office: Techlaw Environ Consultants 536 S Clark St Chicago IL 60605 Home Phone: 773-723-1994; Office Phone: 312-353-2960. Office Fax: 312-353-8307. Personal E-mail: trinicharm@earthlink.net, trinicharm@earthlink.com. E-mail: aharvey@techlawinc.com.

HARVEY, AUBREY EATON, III, industrial engineer; b. Charlottesville, Va., Oct. 20, 1944; s. Aubrey Eaton Jr. and Jaquelin Ambler (Nicholas) H.; m. Elizabeth Dillard Pettit, June 6, 1964; children: Eleanor Taylor, Philip Ambler. BS, U. Ark., 1966; MA, U. Va., 1970; PhD, U. Ark., 1974. Asst. prof. indsl. engring. dept. Tex. A&M U., College Station, 1973-74; asst. prof. dept. systems analysis Miami U., Oxford, Ohio, 1974-78; analyst computer svc. Norfolk and Western Railway, Roanoke, Va., 1978-80, systems analyst computer svc., 1980-83; ops. rsch. analyst Norfolk (Va.) Southern Corp., 1983-90, sr. ops. rsch. analyst, 1991; rsch. assoc. Va. Polytech Inst. and State U., Blacksburg, 1991-93, rsch. scientist, 1993-94; sr. ops. rsch. analyst Rsch. Mgmt. Cons., Inc., McLean, Va., 1994-95; adv. knowledge engr. Elec. Data Systems Corp., Herndon, Va., 1995-99, sr. sys. analyst, 1999—2002, sr. sys. engr., 2002—04, Optimal Solution and Techs., Inc., Washington, 2005—. Cons. Ark. Dept. Labor, Little Rock, 1971-72, Ark. Health Systems Found., Little Rock, 1972-73; adj. faculty Va. Polytech Inst. and State U., 1980-85. Contbr. articles to profl. jours. Pres. U. Va. Law and Grad. Young Reps., Charlottesville, 1969; treas. Va. Young Reps., Richmond, 1970, 71. Recipient Hammer award HUD/REAC SASS System. Mem. Inst. Ops. Rsch. and Mgmt. Scis., Inst. Indsl. Engrs. (divsn. dir. 1983-84), Disting. Svc. award 1985), Sigma Xi, Alpha Pi Mu, Omega Rho. Episcopalian. Achievements include development of track quality index, consensus measure; immigration and naturalization service compensation expert system and attorney scheduling system; design of patent application immaging system; numerous systems for the FAA and other government agencies. Home: 11019 Saffold Way Reston VA 20190-3804 Business E-Mail: aubrey.ctr.harvey@faa.gov.

HARVEY, BIRT, retired pediatrician, educator; b. Teheran, Iran, Nov. 24, 1928; five children. BA, Johns Hopkins U., 1948; MD, N.Y.U., 1952. Pvt. practice, 1958-88; prof. pediat. emeritus Stanford U., Palo Alto, Calif., 1995—. Past sr. fellow Inst. Health, Policy Studies, U. Calif., San Francisco. Mem. Inst. Med. Nat. Acad. Scis. (emeritus), Am. Acad. Pediatrics (past pres.), Am. Pediat. Soc. (emeritus).

HARVEY, CHRISTINE LYNN, publishing executive; b. Bklyn., Dec. 7, 1962; AS in Liberal Arts, Nassau C.C., 1982; BA in Comm. Arts, Adelphi U., 1985. Cert. EMT, 1983-86. Franchise mgr. N.Y. Daily News, Mineola, 1981-84; copywriter, vido prodr., 1984-85; pub. rels. assoc. King Features Syndicate, NYC, 1986; account exec. Promotional Broadcasting Svc., Babylon, NY, 1986-87; sr. account mgr. L.I. Bus. News, Ronkonkoma, NY, 1987-91; sr. ptnr. Karen Saeger Assocs., Stony Brook, NY, 1990—; editor The Steuben News, Ridgewood, NY, 1992—; founder, pub., editor-in-chief New Living, Stony Brook, 1991—; pub. rels. cons. Am. Health Found., Valhalla, NY, 1994—96; radio prodr./dir./host New Living Prodns., Stony Brook, 1997—98. Clin. hypnotherapist, Reiki master, 1999; TV prodr. Outlook Mag., 1985; TV news reporter, field prodr. LI News Tonite, 1984. Avocations: running, swimming, bicycling, hiking, golf. Office: New Living 1212 Route 25A Ste 1B Stony Brook NY 11790-1919

HARVEY, CHRISTOPHER P., lawyer; b. 1961; BA summa cum laude, Boston Coll., 1983, JD magna cum laude, 1986. Bar: Mass. 1986. Ptnr., co-chmn. investment mgmt. group Wilmer Cutler Pickering Hale and Dorr LLP, Boston. Editor: Boston Coll. Law Rev. Mem.: Mass. Bar Assn., Boston Bar Assn., Phi Beta Kappa. Office: Wilmer Cutler Pickering Hale and Dorr LLP 60 State St Boston MA 02109 Office Phone: 617-526-6532. Office Fax: 617-526-5000. Business E-Mail: christopher.harvey@wilmerhale.com.

HARVEY, D. PETER, lawyer, educator; b. Charlotte, NC, June 22, 1947; s. Irvine Dillard and Virginia McCartney Harvey; m. Susan Mack Harvey, June 5, 1971; children: Thomas Andrews, Peter McCartney, Douglas Reed. AB, Cornell U., Ithaca, NY, 1969; JD, Yale U., New Haven, Conn., 1972. Bar: Calif. 1973. Assoc. Pillsbury, Madison & Sutro, San Francisco, 1972—80; ptnr. Ream, Train, Horning, Maxwell, Ellison & Roskoph, San Francisco, 1980—83, Horning, Janin & Harvey, San Francisco, 1983—95, Carr, Mussman & Harvey LLP, San Francisco, 1996—99, Harvey Siskind LLP, San Francisco, 2000—. Adj. prof. Sch. Law U. San Francisco, 2000—. Bd. dirs. Episcopal Ch. Diocese of Calif., San Francisco, 2001—06, Episcopal Charities, San Francisco. Avocations: squash, golf. Office: Harvey Siskind LLP 4 Embarcadero Center Suite 3950 San Francisco CA 94111-4106 Home Phone: 510-652-5242; Office Phone: 415-354-0100. Office Fax: 415-391-7124.

HARVEY, DAVID R., chemical company executive; With Sigma-Aldrich Corp., St. Louis, 1981—; v.p. Europe Aldrich Chem. Co.; COO Sigma Aldrich Corp., S. Louis, Mo., 1986—99; pres., CEO Sigma-Aldrich Corp., St. Louis, 2000—05, chmn., 1999—. Bd. dir. CF Industries. Trustee St. Louis Sci. Ctr. Office: Sigma-Aldrich Corp 3050 Spruce St Saint Louis MO 63103*

HARVEY, DAVID W., humanities educator; b. Gillingham, Kent, Eng., Oct. 31, 1935; s. Frederick Hercules and Doris Maud Harvey; m. Haydee Salmun, Dec. 23, 1998; 1 child, Delfina Eva. BA, St. Johns Coll., Cambridge, England, 1957, MA, PhD, St. Johns Coll., Cambridge, England, 1962; PhD (hon.), Buenos Aires U., Argentina, 1997, Roskilde U., Denmark, 1992, Uppsala U., Sweden, 2000, Ohio State U., 2004. Lectr. U. Bristol, England, 1961—69; from assoc. prof. to prof. Johns Hopkins U., Balt., 1969—90; prof. Oxford U., England, 1987—93; prof. geography Johns Hopkins U., Balt., 1993—2001; prof. anthropology CUNY, 2001—. Author: (book) Explanation in Geography, Social Justice & the City, The Limits to Capital, The Urbanisation of Capital, Consciousness and the Urban Experience, The Condition of Postmodernity, The Urban Experience, Justice, Nature, and the Geography of Difference, Spaces of Hope, Spaces of Capital, The New Imperialism, 2003; book, Paris, Capital Modernity, 2003, A Brief History of Neoliberalism, 2005. Recipient Patron's medal, Royal Geog. Soc., 1995, Anders Retzius Gold medal, Sweden, 1989; Guggenheim fellow, 1987. Fellow: Am. Acad. Arts & Scis. Home: 30 East End Avenue Apt 5A New York NY 10028-7053 Office: CUNY Graduate Center 365 Fifth Avenue New York NY 10016 E-mail: dharvey@gc.cuny.edu.*

HARVEY, DONALD, artist, educator; b. Walthamston, Eng., June 14, 1930; s. Henry and Annie Dorothy (Sawell) H.; m. Elizabeth Clark, Aug. 9, 1952; children— Shan Mary, David Jonathan. Art tchrs. diploma, Brighton Coll. Art, 1951. Art master Ardwyn Grammar Sch., Wales, 1952-56; mem. faculty dept. art U. Victoria, B.C., Canada, 1961-95, now prof. emeritus painting. One man exhbns. include, Albert White Gallery, Toronto, 1968, retrospective, Art Gallery of Victoria, 1968; represented in permanent collections, Nat. Gallery Can., Montreal Mus. Contemporary Art, Albright-Knox Mus., Seattle Art Mus. Mem. accessions com. Art Gallery of Victoria, 1969-72. Can. Council fellow, 1966 Mem. Royal Can. Acad. of Arts (full academician), Can. Group Painters, Can. Painters and Etchers. Home: 1025 Joan Crescent Victoria BC Canada V8S 3L3 E-mail: doharvey@telus.net.

HARVEY, DOUGLASS COATE, retired photographic company executive; b. Batavia, NY, Aug. 28, 1917; s. Homer A. and Della S. Harvey; m. Elizabeth Kellas, June 27, 1942; children: Robert, Anne, Katharine (dec.), Douglass Coate Jr. BSME with highest distinction, Purdue U., 1939, DEng (hon.), 1982. With Eastman Kodak Co., Rochester, NY, 1939-82, dir. corp. product devel., 1970-73, v.p., gen. mgr. apparatus divsn., 1973-77; exec. v.p., gen. mgr. Eastman Kodak Co. (mgr. U.S. and Canadian photog. divns.), 1977-82; ret., 1982. Commr. Monroe Co. Case Commn. Former trustee Alfred (N.Y.) U.; former exec. bd. Otetiana (N.Y.) coun. Boy Scouts Am.; former chmn. bd. dirs. Rochester and Monroe County YMCA, nat. bd. dirs., 1979-81; ret. chmn. engring. adv. coun. Clarkson U., Potsdam, N.Y.; former bd. mgrs. Meml. Art Gallery; Adirondack Pk. Inst., Inc. Named Outstanding Mech. Engr., Purdue U., 1991. Mem. Nat. Acad. Engring., Optical Soc. Am., Photog. Soc. Am., Soc. Photog. Scientists and Engrs., Rochester Engring. Soc., Nat. Security Indsl. Assn. (ret., trustee 1973-78), Rochester Country Club (former mem. bd. stewards), Genesee Valley Club, Lake George Club (Diamond Point, N.Y.), Rotary, Tau Beta Pi, Pi Tau Sigma. Republican. Personal E-mail: dch25@juno.com.

HARVEY, ELEANOR JONES, museum curator; b. Washington, Sept. 20, 1960; d. Charles Roy Jr. and Margaret McChesney (Jeffries) Jones; m. Stephen Jay Harvey, Oct. 10, 1992. BA with distinction summa cum laude, U. Va., 1983; MA, Yale U., 1985, MPhil, 1987, PhD, 1998. Asst. curator Am. paintings Mus. Fine Arts, Boston, 1989-91; assoc. curator Am. art Dallas Mus. Art, 1992-98, cons. curator Am. art, 1996—99, curator Am. art, 1999—2002; cons. curator Nat. Mus. Wildlife Art, 1996—99; curator Luce Foundation Center for American Art, Washington, 2003; chief curator Smithsonian American Art Museum, Washington, 2003—. Lectr. in field. Author: The Painted Sketch: American Impressions from Nature, 1830-1880, 1998, In Context: Painting in Dallas 1889-1945, 1999, Thomas Moran and the Spirit of Place, 2001, The Voyage of the Icebergs: Frederic Church's Arctic Masterpiece, 2002, An Impressionist Sensibility: The Halff Collection, 2006; co-author: Albert Pinkham Ryder, 1990, The Lure of Italy, 1992, Dallas Museum of Art: A Guide to the Collection, 1996, Cosmos: From Romanticism to the Avant Garde 1801-2001, 1999, Hudson River School Visions Landscapes of Sanford R. Gifford, 2003; contbr. articles to profl. jours. Bd. dirs. Wood Turning Ctr., Phila., 1998—; mem. ann. giving adv. coun. U. Va.; mem. U. Va. Assocs. of Libr., 1998—. Henry S. McNeill fellow in Am. decorative arts Yale U., 1985-87, Smithsonian predoctoral fellow Nat. Mus. Am. Art, 1988-89; Henry Luce Found. grantee, 1987-88. Mem. Am. Assn. Mus., Am. Craft Guild, Coll. Art Assn. Office: Smithsonian American Art Museum MRC 970 PO Box 37012 Washington DC 20013-7012 Home Phone: 703-528-4026; Office Phone: 202-633-8377. Business E-Mail: harveye@si.edu.

HARVEY, FRANCIS J., former civilian military employee; b. Latrobe, Pa., July 8, 1943; m. Mary Harvey; 2 children. BS in Metallurgical Engring. & Material Sci., U. Notre Dame, 1965; PhD in Metallurgy & Material Sci., U. Pa., 1969. Spl. asst. to sec. US Dept. Def., Washington, 1978; with Westinghouse Electric Corp., 1969—99, engring. mgr. Marine Div., gen. mgr. Electrical Sys. Div., gen. mgr. Marine Div., v.p. Sci. & Tech., 1993—94, pres. Govt. & Environ. Svcs. Co., 1994—95, pres. Electronics Sys. Group, 1995—96, chmn., CEO Industry & Tech. Group, 1996—99; dir., vice chmn. Duratek Inc., 1999—2004; sec. Dept. of Army US Dept. Def., Washington, 2004—07. Dir. IT Group, Inc., Gardner Technologies, Inc., Bridge Bank, Kulman Electric Corp.; mem. Army Sci. Bd., 1999—2001. Mem. bd. regents Santa Clara U.; co-chair Campaign for Santa Clara. Named White House Fellow, 1978—79.

HARVEY, GLENN FRANCIS, management consultant; b. Tarentum, Pa., May 10, 1940; s. Howard F. and Evelyn H.; m. Linda M. Herr, Mar. 19, 1960; children: Jeffrey Howard, Lisa Anne. BSEd., Slippery Rock State Coll., 1961; M.Ed., Duquesne U., 1964; MBA, U. Pitts., 1975. Tchr. Fox Chapel Area Schs., Pitts., 1961-67; exec. dir. Instrument Soc. Am., Research Triangle Park, NC, 1967-99; cons., 1999—2003; exec. dir. Am. Ceramic Soc., Westerville, Ohio, 2003—06; cons., 2006—. Mem. Am. Soc. of Assn. Execs., Coun. Engring. and Sci. Soc. Execs. Republican. Personal E-mail: glennharvey@charter.net.

HARVEY, GREGORY MERRILL, lawyer; b. Morris Twp., NJ, Jan. 6, 1937; s. Merrill Piercy and Dorothy Ceola (Gregory) H.; m. Emily Mitchell Wallace, June 14, 1969. AB, Harvard U., 1959; JD, Harvard Law Sch., 1962. Bar: Pa. 1963. Assoc. Morgan, Lewis & Bockius, Phila., 1962-69, ptnr., 1969-99, Montgomery, McCracken, Walker & Rhoads, Phila., 1999—2007, sr. counsel, 2007—. Chmn. City of Phila. Bd. Ethics, 1984-91; trustee Fairmount Park Art Assn., Phila., 1981—, The Phila. Award, 2007-; co-chmn. 8th Ward Dem. Exec. Com., Phila., 1984—; bd. dirs. Ams. for Dem. Action Southeastern Pa. chpt., 1966—, bd. dirs. Conservation Ctr. Art and Historic Artifacts, Phila., 1995—. Recipient James Madison award Soc. Profl. Journalists, 1986, Judge Learned Hand Human Rels. award Am. Jewish Com., 1991. Fellow Am. Coll. Trial Lawyers; mem. ABA, Pa. Bar Assn., Phila. Bar Assn., Phila. Club, Franklin Inn (Phila.), Merion Cricket Club (Haverford, Pa.), Racquet Club (Phila.), Phi Beta Kappa. Home: 1939 Panama St Philadelphia PA 19103-6609 Office: Montgomery McCracken et al 123 S Broad St Philadelphia PA 19109-1099 Office Phone: 215-772-7684. Business E-Mail: gharvey@mmwr.com.

HARVEY, J. BRETT, energy executive; B mining engring., Univ. Utah. With Kaiser Steel Corp.; pres., CEO Interwest Mining Co., 1993—98; v.p. PacifiCorp Fuels, 1993—98; pres., CEO PacifiCorp Energy Inc., 1995—98; pres., CEO, dir. CONSOL Energy Corp., 1998—. Bd. dir. Barrick Gold Corp., CNX Gas Corp.; chmn. Nat. Mining Assn.; vice-chmn. World Coal Inst.; mem. IEA Coal Industry Adv. Bd.; bd. dir. Bituminous Coal Operators Assn.; mem. bd., exec. com. Ctr. for Energy & Econ. Develop.; mem. exec. adv. bd. Va. Coalfield Develop. Authority; mem. Nat. Coal Council; mem. CEO group Coal-Based Generation Stakeholders. Mem.: Assn. Devel. Inland Nav. in America's Ohio Valley (chmn.). Office: CONSOL Energy 1800 Washington Rd Pittsburgh PA 15241-1421*

HARVEY, JAMES A., lawyer; b. Heidelburg, Germany, Sept. 18, 1961; BA in Econ., Univ. Ark., 1983; JD with honors, Univ. NC, 1988. Bar: Ga. 1988. Ptnr., tech. group Alston & Bird LLP, Atlanta. Editl. bd. Internet & Computer Lawyer, GigaLaw.com; contbr. articles to profl. jours. Mem.: Computer Law Assn., Phi Beta Kappa. Office: Alston & Bird LLP One Atlantic Ctr 1201 W Peachtree St NW Atlanta GA 30309-3424 Office Phone: 404-881-7328. Office Fax: 404-881-7777. Business E-Mail: jharvey@alston.com.

HARVEY, JAMES MATHEWS, JR., public relations administrator; b. Detroit, Dec. 5, 1964; s. James M. and Leotha (Frazier) Harvey; m. Leesa Ann Hatch, June 10, 2000; 1 child, James (Trey) III. BS, Troy State U., 1987. Media assoc. Ctr. for Environ. Rsch., Troy, Ala., 1987-88; prodr., dir. Coop. Ext. Svc. (became Coop. Ext. Sys. 1995), Auburn, Ala., 1988—99; media coord. Ala. Indsl. Devel. Tng., Montgomery, 1999—2001; pub. comm. specialist Shelby County Ala. Govt., Columbiana, 2001—03; comm. dir. Chatham County Pub. Schs., Savannah, Ga., 2003—05; media ctr. dir. Sch. Vet. Med. Tuskegee U., Ala., 2006—07; pub. rels. dir. Ctrl. Ga. Tech. Coll., Macon, 2007—. Dir. videos including: Nature's Way, 1988, Red Drum: A Struggle for Survival, 1989, Pond Management, 1991; slide series including: Nature's Way, 1988, Beach Mice and Their Habitat, 1989; dir., editor Safety in the Logging Woods series, 1989-95, Forestry in Alabama, 1993, Small Business Resources Series, 1995, Adult Education Principles for Loggers, 1996, Multiple Use Management, 1996; assoc. producer, dir. Extension Today, 1990; assoc. producer satellite programs Principles of Parenting and State of Our Environment, 1991, White-Tailed Deer Management, 1991-92, Residential Landscaping, 1992, Small Business Resources, 1994, Wildlife Damage Management, 1995, Alabama Forest Resources Today, 1996; creator, prodr. Ala. 4-H Congress Video, 1990-99, 4-H Performing Arts Video, 1993-99; prodr., dir. Street Trees and Sewing Update for Entrepreneurs, 1994, Tax Fraud Prevention, 1995, AU Presents, 1998; guest columnist The Messenger, 1993-94. Mem. agrl. adv. com. Pike County H.S., Brundidge, Ala., 1983-95, pres. 1995-2000; bd. dirs. Pike County Agrl. Complex Bd., 1996. Mem. Nat. Assn. County Info. Officers, Troy State U. Journalism Alumni Assn, Nat. Sch. Pub. Rels. Assn. Baptist. Avocations: music, movies, tennis, model trains. Home: 1332 Waxwing Trl Alabaster AL 35007-9027

HARVEY, JANE HULL, church administrator; BA with high honors, Scarritt Coll., Nashville, 1958; MA in Spl. Edn. with highest honors, Columbia U., 1972; grad., Tokyo Sch. Japanese Lang., 1966; Tchg. Cert., Sogetsu Japanese Ikebana Inst., Tokyo, 1969. Tchr. remedial English lang. arts Englewood (N.J.) Pub. Schs.; tchr. Head Start learning disabled children Ctrl. Harlem, NYC; person in mission United Meth. Ch., Korea, Japan, Okinawa, 1958-60, 64-69, 1975-80; office mgr. ednl. TV office Pub. Broadcasting Svc., Washington, 1980-81; program coord., asst. dir. dept. social/econ. justice Gen. Bd. Ch. and Soc. of United Meth. Ch., 1981-86, program coord. Justice for women project, 1986-88, dir. dept. human welfare, 1988-92, asst. gen. sec., 1992—. Lectr. in field. Contbr. articles to profl. jours.; asst. to editor Japan Christian Activity News, Tokyo, 1975-79; editl. asst. AMPO Mag., Tokyo, 1975-79. Chair bd. dirs. Interfaith IMPACT for Justice and Peace, 1995—; chair Washington Interreligious Staff Cmty., 1983-85, 89-91; co-chair Interreligious Coalition on Smoking or Health, 1992—; founding mem. World Alliance for Breast-feeding Action, Internat. Conf., Penang, Malaysia, 1990—; liaison to Gen. Commn. on Status and Role of Women, 1988—; chief staff Infant Formula Task Force, 1988-94; advisor Korean Legal Aid Ctr. for Family Rels., 1980-87; co-chair religion and race com. Dumbarton United Meth. Ch., Washington, 1986-88; founding mem., advisor Co-Madres, 1982; bd. dirs. Ptnrs. for Global Justice, 1982-87, Ctr. for Reproductive and Sexual Health, N.Y.C., 1973-75; co-founder Judson Health Project for Working Women, N.Y.C., 1973-75; adult counselor Youth March Against Hunger, Englewood, 1972-74; vol. adminstrv. asst. Greater Englewood Housing Authority, 1972-74; co-coord. United Farm Workers Boycott, Englewood, 1972-74; campaign coord., speech writer Dem. Mayoral Campaign, Englewood, 1972; co-dir. McGovern for Pres. campaign, Englewood, 1972. Office: United Meth Ch Gen Bd Ch Soc 100 Maryland Ave NE Washington DC 20002-5625

HARVEY, JOHN ADRIANCE, psychologist, educator, pharmacologist, researcher; b. NYC, Oct. 14, 1930; s. John Adriance Harvey and Paula Ann (Truhar) Oestreich; m. Rhoda S. Sadigur, Dec. 20, 1958; children: David Alexander, Andrew Martin, Michael Allen. AB, U. Chgo., 1955, PhD, 1959. Research assoc. U. Chgo., 1959-61, asst. prof., 1961-67, assoc. prof., 1967-68; prof. psychology and pharmacology U. Iowa, Iowa City, 1968-88; prof. pharmacology and physiology, chief div. behavioral neurobiology Drexel U. Coll. Medicine, Phila., 1988—, chair dept. pharmacology and physiology, 2006—. Guest worker Maudsley Hosp., London, 1966-67; chmn. biopsychology rsch. rev. com. NIH, 1983-85; chmn. behavioral neurobiology rsch. rev. com. NIMH, 1986-90, mem. adv. panel; mem. extramural sci. adv. bd. Nat. Inst. on Drug Abuse, 1990—. Author: Behavioral Analysis of Drug Action, 1971, (with Barry Kosofsky) Cocaine: Effects on the Developing Brain; editor Jour. Pharmacology and Exptl. Therapeutics, 1990-98; contbr. numerous articles to profl. jours. Recipient Rsch. Devel. award, NIMH, 1963—68, Rsch. Scientist award, 1969—74. Fellow APA (pres. divsn. 28 1984-85), Am. Coll. Neuropsychopharmacology; mem. Am. Soc. for Pharmacology and Exptl. Therapeutics (editl. adv. bd.), Soc. for Neurosci. (fin. com.), Soc. for Neurochemistry, European Soc. for Neurochemistry, Pavlovian Soc., Soc. for Biol. Psychiatry, Behavioral Pharmacol. Soc. (pres. 1996-98). Office: Drexel U Coll Medicine Dept Pharmacology/Physiol 245 N 15th St Mail Stop 488 Philadelphia PA 19102 Home: 2401 Pennsylvania Ave 11B24 Philadelphia PA 19130 Office Phone: 215-762-2369. Business E-Mail: john.harvey@drexel.edu.

HARVEY, JOHN ARTHUR, nuclear physicist; b. Saskatoon, Sask., Can., Dec. 14, 1921; naturalized U.S. citizen; married; 2 children. BSc, Queen's U., Ont., Can., 1945; PhD in Physics, MIT, 1950. Physicist Atomic Energy Can., Ltd., 1945-46; rsch. asst. MIT, 1946-50; assoc. physicist Brookhaven Nat. Lab., 1951-55; physicist Oak Ridge Nat. Lab., 1955-93, dir. linear accelerator, 1965-93, retired, 1993, cons., 1993—. Rsch. prof. U. Tenn., 1995—. Fellow Am. Phys. Soc. (sec.-treas. divsn. nuc. physics 1966-86). Home: 108 Ogontz Ln Oak Ridge TN 37830-3905 Office: Oak Ridge Nat Lab PO Box 2008 Oak Ridge TN 37831-6354 E-mail: harveyjm@icx.net.

HARVEY, JOHN COLLINS, internist, educator; b. Youngstown, Ohio, Sept. 11, 1923; s. J. Paul and Mary J. (Collins) H.; m. Adele Dillon, Nov. 26, 1949; children: Elizabeth V.R. (Mrs. Charles Yon), John Collins Jr., William Charles II, Amy L.R. (Mrs. L. F. Reese), Margaret J.B. (Mrs. Gregory Granitto). Grad., Phillips Exeter Acad., 1941; BS, Yale U., 1944; MD, Johns Hopkins U., 1947; DSc (hon.), Barry U., 1952; MLA, Johns Hopkins U., 1968; MAS, Johns Hopkins, 1974; MA, St. Mary's U., 1975, PhD in Theology, 1988. Diplomate Am. Bd. Internal Medicine, 1992. Successively house officer, asst. resident, resident Osler Med. Service, Johns Hopkins Hosp., 1947-53, physician, 1953-73; successively instr., asst. prof., asso. prof., prof. medicine Johns Hopkins, 1953-73; prof. medicine Georgetown U., Washington, 1973-89, prof. medicine emeritus, 1989—; sr. rsch. scholar Kennedy Inst. of Ethics, Georgetown U., Washington, 1989—, Ctr. for Clin. Bioethics, Georgetown Med. Ctr., 1993—. Vis. prof. medicine U. Ibadan, Nigeria, 1964; hon. assoc. prof. medicine Guy's Hosp., London, 1973 Co-editor: Catholic Perspectives on Medical Morals, Catholic Studies in Bioethics; Contbr. articles to profl. publs. Mem. various local, state and nat. govt. med. adv. coms.; trustee emeritus Washington Home for Incurables; mem. emeritus med. adv. com. Sacred Congregation for Causes of Saints, Holy See, Vatican City. Col. (ret.) M.C., USAR. A. Blaine Brower Traveling fellow ACP to Guy's Hosp. London, 1956; sr. scholar Kennedy Inst. Ethics, Georgetown U., 1973-89. Fellow ACP (master); mem. AAAS, AMA, Am. Clin. and Climatol. Assn., Biophys. Soc., Johns Hopkins Soc. Scholars, Tudor and Stuart Club (Balt.), Cosmos Club, Knights of St. Gregory, Knights of Malta, Phi Beta Kappa, Sigma Xi, Alpha Omega Alpha. Republican. Roman Catholic. Home: 12610 Three Sisters Rd Potomac MD 20854-6359 Office Phone: 202-687-1160. Office Fax: 202-687-8955. Personal E-mail: jcviola@aol.com. Business E-mail: harveyjc@georgetown.edu.

HARVEY, JOHN COLLINS, JR., military officer; b. Balt., Nov. 17, 1951; s. John Collins and Adele Dillon Harvey; m. Mary Ellen Swift, Dec. 27, 1980; children: Sarah Swift, David Dillon. BS in Polit. Sci., US Naval Acad., 1973; MPA, Harvard U., 1988. Vice adm. USN, Washington, 2000—. Decorated Def. DSM Sec. Of Def. Mem.: US Naval Inst. Roman Catholic. Avocations: reading, travel. Office: Dep for Warfare Integration (N7F) 2000 Navy Pentagon Rm 5C469 Washington DC 20350-2000 Home Phone: 202-678-2757; Office Phone: 703-614-1101. E-mail: john.c.harvey1@navy.mil.

HARVEY, JONATHAN MATTHEW, lawyer; b. Worcester, Mass., July 6, 1955; s. Irwin and Hannah H.; m. Lyssa Lynn Kligman, Dec. 17, 1977; children: Laurel Eden, Jordane Mills, Kyle Michael. BA cum laude, U. Ga., 1977; JD, U. S.C., 1981. Bar: SC 1981, US Dist. Ct. SC 1982, US Ct. Appeals (4th cir.) 1992. Asst. solicitor Fifth Judicial Circuit Solicitor's Office, Columbia, SC, 1982-83; asst. atty. gen. Office of the Atty. Gen., Columbia, SC, 1983-86; lawyer pvt. practice, Columbia, 1986—. Vice chair Richland Sch. Dist. Ednl. Found., 2001—02; fin. dir. Richland County Dems., Columbia, SC, 1987—88, mem. exec. com., 1987—90, 1998—2000; commr. East Richland County Pub. Svc. Dist., 1990—99, chmn., 1999—2000. Mem.: ATLA, S.C. Trial Lawyers Assn., S.C. Assn. Criminal Def. Lawyers (bd. dirs. 5th jud. cir. 1998—2001, treas. 2002—),

S.C. Bar Assn., Richland County Bar Assn. Democrat. Avocations: tennis, outdoor activities. Office: 1804 Bull St Columbia SC 29201-2506 Home Phone: 803-787-7331; Office Phone: 803-779-3363.

HARVEY, JOSEPH PAUL, JR., orthopedist, educator; b. Youngstown, Ohio, Feb. 28, 1922; s. Joseph Paul and Mary Justinian (Collins) H.; m. Martha Elizabeth Toole, Apr. 12, 1958; children: Maryalice, Martha Jane, Frances Susan, Helen Lucy, Laura Andre. Student, Dartmouth Coll., 1939—42; MD, Harvard U., 1945. Diplomate Nat. Bd. Med. Examiners. Intern Peter Bent Brigham Hosp., Boston, 1945-46; resident Univ. Hosp., Cleve., 1951-53, Hosp. Spl. Surgery, NYC, 1953-54; instr. orthopedics Cornell Med. Coll., NYC, 1954-62; mem. faculty Sch. Medicine, U. So. Calif., Los Angeles, 1962-92; prof. orthopedic surgery U. So. Calif., 1966-92, prof. emeritus, 1992—; chmn. sect. orthopedics Keck Sch. Medicine, U. So. Calif., 1964-78. Dir. dept. orthopedics U. So. Calif.-LA County Med. Ctr., 1964-79, staff, 1979— Editor-in-chief: Contemporary Orthopedics, 1978-96. Served to capt. AUS, 1946-48. Exchange orthopedic fellow Royal Acad. Hosp., Upsala, Sweden, 1957 Fellow Western Orthop. Assn., Am. Acad. Orthop. Surgery, A.C.S., Am. Soc. Testing Materials; mem. AMA, Calif. Med. Assn., Los Angeles County Med. Assn., Am. Rheumatism Assn., Am. Orthop. Assn., Internat. Soc. Orthopedics and Traumatology. Clubs: Boston Harvard. Home: 432 Arlington Dr Pasadena CA 91105-2850 Address: The Athenaeum 551 South Hill Ave Pasadena CA 91106 Business E-Mail: harvey@usc.edu.

HARVEY, KENNETH L., lawyer; b. Mesa, Ariz., Oct. 29, 1961; BS, So. Utah State Coll., 1986; JD, Columbia U., 1990. Bar: Mass. 1990. Ptnr. Holland & Knight, LLP, Boston. Named one of Top 100 Attys., Worth mag., 2006. Mem.: ABA (real property, probate and trust law sects.), Mass. Bar Assn. (probate and taxation sect.), Boston Bar Assn. Office: Holland & Knight LLP 10 St James Ave 11th Fl Boston MA 02116 Office Phone: 617-573-5814. E-mail: ken.harvey@hklaw.com.*

HARVEY, KENT M., utilities executive; B in Econs., Stanford U., Calif., M in Engring. - Econ. Systems. Engr. PG&E Corp., San Francisco, 1982, various positions including corp. sec., dir. fin. analysis, dir. investor rels., v.p., and treas., sr. v.p., CFO, treas. Pacific Gas and Electric Co., sr. v.p., chief risk and audit officer, 2005—. Treas., trustee Am. Conservatory Theater; dir. North Bay Coun. Office: PG&E Corp One Market Spear Tower Ste 2400 San Francisco CA 94105-1126 Office Phone: 415-267-7070. Office Fax: 415-267-7268.*

HARVEY, LYNNE COOPER, broadcast executive, civic worker; b. near St. Louis; d. William A. and Mattie (Kehr) Cooper; m. Paul Harvey, June 4, 1940; 1 child, Paul Harvey Aurandt. DHL (hon.), Rosary Coll., 1996; D (hon.), Washington U., 1988. Broadcaster ednl. program KXOX, St. Louis, 1940; broadcaster-writer women's news WAC Variety Show, Ft. Custer, Mich., 1941-43; gen. mgr. Paul Harvey News ABC, 1944—. Pres. Paulynne Prodn., Ltd., Chgo., 1968—, exec. prodr. Paul Harvey Comments, 1968—; pres. Trots Corp., 1989—; editor, compiler The Rest of the Story. Pres. women's bd. Mental Health Assn. Greater Chgo., 1967-71, v.p. bd. dirs., 1966—; pres. woman's aux. Infant Welfare Soc. Chgo., 1969-71, bd. dirs., 1969—, benefits hon. chmn., 1994, 96; mem. Salvation Army Woman's Adv. Bd., 1967; reception chmn. Cmty. Lectures; women's com. Chgo. Symphony, 1972—; pres. Mothers Coun., River Forest, 1961-62; charter bd. mem. Gottlieb Meml. Hosp., Melrose Park, Ill.; mem. adv. bd. Nat. Christian Heritage Found., 1964—; mem. USO woman's bd., 1983, woman's bd. Ravinia Festival, 1972—; trustee John Brown U., 1980—; bd. dirs. Mus. Broadcast Comms., 1987—; adv. coun. Charitable Trusts, 1989—; mem. Joffrey Ballet Com.; chmn. Brookfield Zoo Whirl, 2000. Named to, Mus. Broadcast Comm.-Radio Hall of Fame; recipient Heritage of Am. award, 1974, Little City Spirit of Love award, 1987, Salvation Army Others award, 1989, disting. friend award, NCPCA, disting. alumni award, Washington U., Friske Meml. award, USO, 2000, Lynne Harvey scholarship named in her honor, Musicians Club of Women.

HARVEY, MARC S(AN), lawyer, historian, educator; b. NYC, May 4, 1960; s. M. Eugene and Coleen (Jones) H. BA with highest honors, So. Ill. U., 1980; Pre-Law, Wash. U., 1980; JD, Southwestern U., 1983; MBA, Loyola Marymount U., LA, 1984-86; postgrad., Oxford U., Christ Ch. Coll., 1994—97. Bar: Calif., U.S. Supreme Ct. Counsel U.S. SBA, LA, 1982-83; counsel enforcement div. U.S. SEC, LA, 1983-84; counsel State Farm Ins. Co., LA, 1984-85, 20th Century Ins. Co., Woodland Hills, Calif., 1985-86; pvt. practice Encino, Calif., 1986—. Lectr. in field. Contbr. articles to profl. jours. Judge pro tem Culver Mcpl. Ct.; charter mem., trustee Rep. Presdl. Task Force, Washington, 1981—; mem. Nat. Rep. Senatorial Com., Washington, 1983—, Rep. Congl. Leadership Coun., Washington, 1987—, Rep. Senatorial Inner Cir., Washington, 1988—. Named Vol. of Yr., L.A. County, 1992; recipient 1st pl. essay award, VFW, 1976, Judge Pro Tem of Yr. award, Culver Mcpl. Ct., 1991. Mem.: SAG, AFTRA, ATLA, ABA, L.A. Trial Lawyers Assn., Calif. Trial Lawyers Assn., Nat. Thespian Soc., Themis Soc., U.S. Supreme Ct. Hist. Soc.

HARVEY, MARK SUMNER, composer, educator, retired minister, musician; b. Binghamton, NY, July 4, 1946; s. Robert Mark and Marjorie Grace (Tolley) H.; m. Kate Matson, Aug. 14, 1983. AB, Syracuse U., 1968; ThM, Boston U., 1971, PhD, 1983. Ordained to ministry United Meth. Ch. as deacon, 1970, as elder, 1975. Intern min. Old West United Meth. Ch., Boston, 1969-71, staff mem., assoc. min., 1971-73; min. with jazz and arts cmty. Emmanuel Ch., Boston, 1974—93, 2003—05, Harvard-Epworth United Meth. Ch., 1993—2003; ret., 2005. Mem. music faculty MIT, Cambridge, Mass., 1981—; founder, music dir. Aardvark Jazz Orch., 1973—, New Am. Music Ensemble, 1969— Composer chamber, choral, jazz orch. pieces; 9 CD recs. of original compositions and arrangements; contbr. articles to profl. jours. Pres., founder The Jazz Coalition, inc., Boston, 1971-83; trustee Mass. Cultural Alliance, Boston, 1971-73, 81-87; mem. music adv. panel Mass. Coun. on the Arts and Humanities, Boston, 1971-75, 79-82, Meet the Composer/Reader's Digest Commissioning Program, 1989; mem. arts adv. com. Harvard U. Ctr. for Study of World Religions, 1994-97. Fellow NEH, 1987, The Whiting Found., 1986; recipient Contbn. to Cultural Activity award Mass. Cultural Alliance, 1987, City of Boston, 1980. Fellow Soc. for the Arts, Religion, and Contemporary Culture (chmn. 1991-95, bd. dirs. 1986—); mem. ASCAP, Am. Acad. Religion, Soc. for Am. Music, Duke Ellington Soc., Am. Studies Assn., Boston Athenaeum, Theta Chi Beta. Office: PO Box 8721 JFK Sta Boston MA 02114 Office Phone: 617-452-3205. Business E-Mail: mharvey@mit.edu.

HARVEY, MORRIS LANE, lawyer; b. Madisonville, Ky., Apr. 22, 1950; s. Morris Lee and Margie Lou (Wallace) H.; m. Mary Topel Harvey; children: Morris Lane Jr., John French, Laura Kathleen, Adam, Kim. BS, Murray State U., 1972; JD, U. Ky., 1974. Bar: Ill. 1975, US Dist. Ct. (so. dist.) 1979, US Ct. Appeals (7th cir.). Assoc. Hanagan & Dousman, Mt. Vernon, Ill., 1975-77; ptnr. Feiger, Quindry, Molt & Harvey and successor firms, Fairfield, Ill., 1977-85; sole practice Fairfield, 1986-97, Mt. Vernon, 1997—2003; ptnr. Harvey and Bradley, Mount Vernon, 2004—07; proprietor Morris Lane Harvey Law Offices, Mount Vernon, 2007—. Instr. Frontier C.C., Fairfield, 1977-79; spl. asst. atty. gen. State of Ill., Fairfield, 1977-82; alternate delegate, Republican Nat. Convention, 1988, 2004. Contbr. articles to profl. jours. Pres. Mt. Vernon Rotary Club, 2006—07; bd. mem. United Way of Southern Ctrl. Ill., 2002—. Recipient Outstanding Young Man Am. U.S. Jaycees, 1978, 81, 89. Mem. ABA, Ill. Bar Assn., Assn. Trial Lawyers Am., Ill. Trial Lawyers Assn., Woodmen of World Life Ins. Soc. (pres. Ill. chpt. 1985-87, nat. fraternal com., 1987-89, 2000-02, nat. legis. com., 1989-93, nat. jud. com., 1993-97, nat. dir. 2005—) Republican. Home: 5 Webster Hill Est Mount Vernon IL 62864-2346 Office: 2029 Broadway St Mount Vernon IL 62864-2910 Office Phone: 618-244-9544.

HARVEY, NORMAN RONALD, retired finance company executive; b. Rahway, NJ, Aug. 17, 1933; s. George Henry and Jennie Louise (Proudfoot) H.; m. Gail Molitor, May 26, 1962 (dec.); 1 dau., Anne. BA in Econs., Cornell U., 1955; MBA in Investments, NYU, 1962. Security analyst Bankers Trust Co., NYC, 1958-61, Anchor Corp., Elizabeth, NJ, 1961-64; dir. research Auerbach, Pollak & Richardson, NYC, 1964-75; chief investment officer E.W. Axe & Co., Inc., Tarrytown, NY, 1975-82; sr. v.p., equity funds investment officer Merrill Lynch Asset Mgmt., Princeton, NJ, 1982-99; ret. Served to 1st lt. USAR, 1957-58. Corson Meml. scholar, 1951 Mem. NY Soc. Security Analysts, The Union League NY, Edgcomb Tennis Club,Eagle Rock Yacht Club. Republican. Home: 39 Florence Ln Princeton NJ 08540-2631

HARVEY, PAUL, commentator, writer, columnist; b. Tulsa, Sept. 4, 1918; s. Harry Harrison and Anna Dagmar (Christensen) Aurandt; m. Lynne Cooper, June 4, 1940; 1 child, Paul Harvey. LittD (hon.), Culver-Stockton Coll., 1952, St. Bonaventure U., 1953; LLD, John Brown U., Ark., 1959, Mont. Sch. Mines, 1961, Trinity Coll. Fla., 1963, Parsons Coll., 1968; HHD, Wayland Bapt. Coll., 1960, Union Coll., 1962, Samford U., 1970, Howard Payne U., Tex., 1978, Sterling Coll., 1982; Degree (hon.), Rosary Coll., 1996; LHD (hon.), Hillsdale Coll., Mich., 2000. Announcer radio sta. KVOO, Tulsa; sta. mgr. Salina, Kans.; spl. events dir. radio sta. KXOK, St. Louis; program dir. radio sta. WKZO, Kalamazoo, 1941-43; dir. news and information OWI, Mich., Ind., 1941-43; news commentator, analyst ABC, 1944—; syndicated columnist Los Angeles Times Syndicate (formerly Gen. Features Corp.), 1954—; TV commentator, 1968. Author: Remember These Things, 1952, Autumn of Liberty, 1954, The Rest of the Story, 1956, You Said It, Paul Harvey, 1969, Our Lives, Our Fortunes, Our Sacred Honor; Album rec. Yesterday's Voices, 1959, Testing Time, 1960, Uncommon Man, 1962. Bd. dirs. John D. and Catherine T. MacArthur Found.; mem. bd. govs. Orchestral Assn. Chgo. Symphony Orch. Recipient citation DAV, 1949, 11 Freedoms Found. awards, 1952-76, radio award Am. Legion, 1952, citation of merit, 1955, 57, Cert. of merit VFW, 1953, Bronze Christopher's award, 1953, award of honor Sumter Guards, 1955, nat. pub. welfare services trophy Colo. Am. Legion, 1957,Great Am. KSEL award, 1962, Spl. ABC award, 1973, Ill. Broadcaster award, 1974, John Peter Zenger Freedom award Eagles, 1975, Am. of Year award Lions Internat., 1975, Outstanding Broadcast Journalism award, 1980, Gen. Omar N. Bradley Spirit of Independence trophy, 1980, Man of Yr. award Chgo. Broadcast Advt. Club, 1981, Golden Radio award Nat. Radio Broadcasters Assn., 1982, Best Speaking Voice award Am. Speech, Lang. and Hearing Assn., 1982, Horatio Alger award, 1983, Outstanding Broadcast Personality award Advt. Club Balt., 1984, Meritorius Svc. award Am. Acad. Family Physicians, 1984, Cert. of Appreciation Humane Soc. of U.S., 1985, Genesis award The Fund for Animals, 1986, Okla. Assn. Broadcasters award, 1987, Henry G. Bennett Disting. Svc. award Okla. State U., 1987, James Herriot award Humane Soc. U.S., 1987, Lowell Thomas award, 1989, Gold medal Internat. Radio & TV Soc., 1989, Others award Salvation Army, 1989, Journalism award Internat. Radio Festival, 1989, 5 Marconi awards Network Personality of Yr., 1989, 91, 96, 98, 2002, Dante award, 1990, William Booth award Salvation Army, 1990, Journalism award Chgo. Hall of Fame, 1990, Bd. of Dirs. award Nat. Religious Broadcasters, 1991, Great Am. Race Legend's award Interstate, 1991, Good Guy award Am. Legion, 1992, Outstanding Pub. Spkr. award Toastmasters Internat., 1992, Paul White award Radio T.V. News Dirs., 1992, Peabody award 1993, 94, Spirit of Broadcasting award NAB, 1994, Silver award Am. Advertising Fedn., 1994, Hall of Fame award Broadcasting & Cable Mag., 1995, Am. Spirit award USAF, 1996, Lifetime Achievement award Radio Mercury, 1997, Lifetime Achievement award Gold Angel, 1998, Lifetime Achievement award Radio Mercury, 1997, Tex McCrary award Journalism from Congl. Medal Honor Soc., 2000, Lifetime Achievement A.I.R. award Radio Broadcasters Chgo., 2001, R&R News/Talk Radio Lifetime Achievement award, 2003, NY Festivals World Gold Medal award best personality network/syndicated, 2004; Presdl. Medal of Freedom, The White House, 2005; elected to Okla. Hall of Fame, 1955, Nat. Assn. Broadcasters Hall of Fame, 1979; named Top Commentator of Yr. Radio-TV Daily, 1962, Father of Yr. Father's Day Coun., 1980, Laureate Lincoln Acad. of Ill., 1987 (Ill. highest honor); to Emerson Radio Hall of Fame, 1990; one of The Men of the Century Broadcast and Cable Mag., 1999; among 20th Century's Most Significant Americans George Mag., 1998. Mem. Washington Radio and Television Corrs. Assn., Aircraft Owners and Pilots Assn. Clubs: Chicago Press. Achievements include having broadcasts and columns reprinted in Congressional Record 102 times. Office: 333 N Michigan Ave Ste 1600 Chicago IL 60601-4005 Office Phone: 312-899-4085.

HARVEY, PAUL H., evolutionary biologist, researcher; b. Worcestershire, Eng., Jan. 19, 1947; s. Edward Walter and Eileen Joan (Pagett) H.; children: Joseph Edward, Benjamin Mark. BA, U. York, 1968, DPhil, 1971; MA, Oxford U., Eng., 1985, DSc, 1989. Lectr. U. Wales, Swansea, 1971-73, U. Sussex, Brighton, 1973-84, reader, 1984-85; lectr., then prof. Harvard U., Boston, 1978-80; prof. Princeton (N.J.) U., 1984-85; lectr., reader, then prof. Oxford (Eng.) U., 1985-98; head zoology dept. Oxford (England) U., 1998—. Rsch. fellow Wellcome Trust, Oxford, 1993—96. Author: The Comparative Method in Evolutionary Biology, 1991. Recipient Sci. medal Zool. Soc., 1986, Visitors medal U. Helsinki, 1994, NAS award for Scientific Reviewing, 1997. Fellow Royal Soc. London (mem. coun. 2000-02); mem. Zool. Soc. London (sec. 1999—). Avocations: walking, gardening. Office: Oxford U Dept Zoology South Parks Rd Oxford OX1 3PS England Office Phone: 44(0)01865271259. Business E-Mail: paul.harvey@zoo.ox.ac.uk.

HARVEY, PETER C., lawyer, former state attorney general; b. NYC, Feb. 2, 1958; married; 3 children. BA in Polit. Sci., Morgan State U., 1979; JD, Columbia U., 1982. Bar: N.Y. 1984, D.C. 1985, N.J. 1989. Law clk. to Hon. Dickinson R. Debevoise US Dist. Ct. NJ, 1982—83; assoc. Kaye Scholer, Fierman, Hays & Handler, 1983—86; asst. U.S. atty. Dist. NJ US Dept. Justice, 1986—89; spl. asst. to atty. gen. State of NJ, 1989—90; assoc. Riker, Danzig, Scherer, Hyland and Perretti LLP, Morristown, NJ, 1990—93, ptnr., 1993—2002; 1st asst. atty. gen., dir. divsn. criminal justice State of N.J., Trenton, 2002—03, acting atty. gen., 2003, atty. gen., 2003—06; ptnr. Patterson, Belknap Webb & Tyler LLP, NYC, 2006—. Mediator U.S. Dist. Ct., NJ, N.J. Supreme Ct.; mem. lawyers' adv. com. U.S. Dist. Ct. for the Dist. N.J., U.S. Ct. of Appeals (3d cir.). Named Lawyer of the Year, NJ State Law Jour., 2003. Office: Patterson Belknap Webb & Tyler LLP 1133 Ave Americas New York NY 10036

HARVEY, RICHARD DUDLEY, marketing consultant; b. Atlanta, Sept. 24, 1923; s. Robert Emmett and June (Dudley) H.; m. Donna Helen Smith, Oct. 12, 1944 (dec. Mar. 1990); 1 child, Louise Dudley; m. Catherine M. McFarland, Nov. 13, 1993. BA, U. Denver, 1947; postgrad., Harvard U., Stanford U. Various positions in sales, sales promotion & mktg. The Coca-Cola Co., St. Louis, Denver, Atla., 1948-60, v.p., brand mgr., mktg. mgr., mktg. dir. Atlanta, 1965-70, v.p. orgn. & mktg. devel., 1970-75; sr. v.p. mktg. Olympia Brewing Co., Seattle, 1975—78; pres. Sound Mktg. Svcs., Inc., 1978—93, Harvey Mktg. Corp., Mountain Lakes, NJ, 1994—. Vice chmn. bd. Roman Meal Co., Tacoma, Washington, 1990—; dir. Lone Star Brewing Co., San Antonio, 1976-78. Trustee Episcopal Radio-TV Found., Atlanta, 1961-88, vice chmn., 1975-84, emeritus trustee, 1988—; bd. dir. Oreg. Shakespearean Festival Assn., 1982-86; vol. Nat. Exec. Svc. Corps., N.J., N.Y.C., 1997—; chmn. mktg. com., trustee Seattle Symphony, 1983-88; mem. gov.'s adv. com. bus. devel. and job retention, State of Wash., 1988-92; mem. Montclair Hist. Preservation Commn., 1998-2000; mem. cmty. adv. bd. Montclair State U., 2002—03. Served with USAAF, 1942-45. Fellow Inst. Mgmt. Cons. (pres. N.J. chpt 1995-96); mem. Am. Mktg. Assn. (pres. Seattle chpt. 1983-84), Arc of N.J. (bd. dir. 1997-98, exec. com. 1998-99), Mktg. Comm. Execs. Internat. (pres. Seattle chpt. 1984-85), Mountain Lakes Club, Seattle Tennis Club, Phi Beta Kappa, Omicron Delta Kappa. Personal E-mail: dickharvey10@optonline.net.

HARVEY, RONALD GILBERT, research chemist; b. Ottawa, Ont., Can., Sept. 9, 1927; arrived in U.S., 1948; s. Gilbert and Adeline (LeClair) H.; m. Helene H. Szpara, May 18, 1952; 1 child, Ronald Edward. BS in Biology, UCLA, 1952; MS in Chemistry, U. Chgo., 1956, PhD in Chemistry, 1960. Project leader Sinclair Rsch. Labs., Harvey, Ill., 1956-58; instr. U. Chgo., 1960-63, asst.prof., 1964-68, assoc. prof., 1968-75, prof., 1975-97, prof. emeritus, 1997—; postdoctoral fellow Imperial Coll., London, Eng., 1963-64. Cons. Nat. Cancer Inst., Washington, Farmacon Corp., Oakbrook, Ill., CIDAC, Palo Alto, Calif., 1978-80; OMNI Research Mayaguex, P.R., 1973-74, Nat. Inst. Environ. Health Sci., Washington, Am. Cancer Soc., Atlanta, U.S.-Israel Binational Sci. Found. Author: Polycyclic Aromatic Hydrocarbons Chemistry and Carcinogenesis, 1991, Polycyclic Aromatic Hydrocarbons, 1997; editor: Polycyclic Hydrocarbons and Carcinogenesis; mem. editl. bd. Polycyclic Aromatic Compounds (1990-), Mini Reviews in Organic Chemistry (2003-); contbr. more than 450 articles to profl. jours. Recipient ISPAC award for rsch. in polycyclic hydrocarbon chemistry, 1995, Ochsber award Am. Coll. Chest Physicians, 2006. Fellow Royal Chem. Soc., Am. Inst. Chemists; mem. AAAS, Am. Chem. Soc., Am. Assn. Cancer Rsch., Sigma Xi. Achievements include patents for synthesis of alpha-olefins, anti-androgen compounds. Home: 10550 Golf Rd Orland Park IL 60462-7420 Office: U Chgo Ben May Inst for Cancer Rsch 929 E 57th St Chicago IL 60637 Business E-Mail: rharvey@huggins.bsd.uchicago.edu.

HARVEY, SCOTT DOUGLAS, chemist, researcher; b. Denver, Aug. 22, 1955; s. Wells Fox Harvey, Jr. and Isabelle Simpson Harvey; m. Colleen Sue Stoker, July 6, 1985. BA with honors, U. Colo., Boulder, 1977, MS, 1981; PhD, Ind. U., Bloomington, 1988. Toxicologist on call Swedish Hosp., Englewood, Colo., 1978; tchg. asst. U. Colo., Boulder, 1978—81; assoc. instr. Ind. U., Bloomington, 1981—86, instr., 1987; rsch. scientist Pacific N.W. Nat. Lab., Richland, Wash., 1988—90, sr. rsch. scientist, 1990—2005, staff scientist, 2006—. Contbr. over 40 articles to profl. jours., over 35 scientific reports. Nominee Esther L. Kinsley Dissertation award, Ind. U., 1989; recipient Outstanding Performance award, Pacific N.W. Nat. Lab., 1991, 1994, 1998, 2004, Significant Publications award, 2003, 2007. Mem.: AAAS, Am. Orchid Soc., Soc. Molecular Imprinting, Am. Chem. Soc. (mem. labguide adv. bd. jour. Analytic Chemistry 1995—2002), Phi Beta Kappa. Achievements include over 23 scientific invention disclosures; patents in field. Avocations: orchid culture, parrot training and breeding, photography, gardening. Office: Pacific NW Nat Lab PO Box 999 Richland WA 99352 Home Phone: 509-735-9810; Office Phone: 509-372-1144. Office Fax: 509-376-5433. Business E-Mail: scott.harvey@pnl.gov.

HARVEY, SHEILA MCCAFFERTY, lawyer; b. Ridgewood, NJ, June 28, 1954; AB summa cum laude, Bryn Mawr Coll., 1976; JD, Univ. Mich., 1979. Bar: DC 1979. Ptnr., co-chmn. Environ. Land Use & Natural Resources practice Pillsbury Winthrop Shaw Pittman, Washington. Mem.: ABA, Environ. Law Inst. Office: Pillsbury Winthrop Shaw Pittman 2300 N St NW Washington DC 20037-1128 Office Phone: 202-663-8224. Office Fax: 202-663-8007. Business E-Mail: sheila.harvey@pillsburylaw.com.

HARVEY, STEVEN JOHN, not-for-profit developer; b. Buffalo, Feb. 22, 1971; s. Donald Marley and Patricia Harvey; m. Kathleen Sarah Ertel, May 31, 1997; children: Grace Elizabeth, Noah David. BS, U. Buffalo, 1993, MEd, 1995, PhD, 1997. Prin., owner The Ctr. Ednl. and Career Advancement, Inc., Buffalo, 1992—; sr. career devel. assoc. U. Buffalo, 1993—2001; dir. rsch. and nat. programs Every Person Influences Children, Buffalo, 2001—. Adj. faculty Buffalo (N.Y.) State Coll., 2004—; adj. faculty mem. U. Buffalo, 1997—2001. Author: College to Career: How 4 Years of College Determines 40 Years of Career, 1999, Beating the Odds: How the Select Few Earn a College Degree, 1997, A Qualitative Research Manual for Doctorate Students, 1999, The Quality Job Search Made Quick and Easy; contbr. articles to profl. jours. Chmn. mkt. and devel. com. Nativity of Mary Sch., Williamsville, NY, 2005—06; steering com. mem. Buffalo (N.Y.) Reads Literacy Coalition, 2004—06; mem. best practices com. Care Mgmt. Coalition, Buffalo, 2004—06; adv. com. Early Childhood Edn. and Econ. Devel. Initiative, Buffalo, 2005—06. Grantee, U.S. Dept. Health and Human Svcs., 2005—, The Margaret Wendt Found., 2006, The John R. Oishei Found., 2006. Achievements include research in Presented research on vocational theory, educational theory, male athletes, and masculinity development at several national venues (Orlando, Philadelphia, Cleveland, Houston, and Buffalo). Avocation: writing. Home: 4350 Arondale Road Williamsville NY 14221 Office: EPIC Every Person Influences Children 1000 Main Street Buffalo NY 14202 Home Phone: 716-633-9194; Office Phone: 716-332-4100. Personal E-mail: harvey1510@msn.com. Business E-Mail: harveysj@epicforchildren.org.

HARVEY, THOMAS EDWARD, federal agency administrator; b. Evanston, Ill., Nov. 9, 1941; s. John Thomas and Margaret (Carey) H.; m. Cathleen Black, May 20, 1982; children: Duffy, Alison BA, U. Notre Dame, 1963, JD, 1966; LLM, NYU, 1980. Bar: Ill., Ind., N.Y., D.C. Atty. Milbank, Tweed, Hadley, & McCloy, NYC, 1972-77; White House fellow CIA, Washington, 1977-78; dep. asst. sec., Dept. of Army US Dept. Def., Washington, 1978-79, dep. asst. sec. Dept. of Navy, 1979-81; staff Veterans Affairs Com. US Senate, Washington, 1981-83; gen. counsel US Info. Agy., Washington, 1983-86; dep. adminstr. Veterans Adminstrn. US Dept. Veterans Affairs, Washington, 1986—89; sr. counsel govtl. affairs Inst. Internat. Edn. (IIE), NYC; sr. adv. to sec. US Dept. Veterans Affairs, Washington, 2005—07, acting asst. sec. pub. & intergovernmental affairs, 2005, acting asst. sec. congl. & legis. affairs, 2005—07, asst. sec. congl. affairs, 2007—. Served with U.S. Army, 1966-71, Vietnam. Decorated Silver Star, Purple Heart, others. Mem. White House Fellows Found. Clubs: Capitol Hill, St. Alban's Tennis. Republican. Roman Catholic. Office: US Dept Veterans Affairs 810 Vermont Ave NW Rm 500 Washington DC 20420-0001 E-mail: thomas.harvey@va.gov.*

HARVEY, WILLIAM BRANTLEY, JR., lawyer, retired lieutenant governor; b. Walterboro, SC, Aug. 14, 1930; s. William Brantley and Thelma (Lightsey) H.; m. Helen Coggeshall, Dec. 30, 1952; children: Eileen L., William Brantley, III, Helen C., Margaret D., Warren C. AB in Polit. Sci., The Citadel, Charleston, SC, 1951, LLD (hon.), 1978; JD magna cum laude, U. S.C., Columbia, 1955. Bar: SC 1955. Since practiced in, Beaufort, SC; sr. ptnr. Harvey & Battey; mem. S.C. Ho. of Reps. from Beaufort County, 1958-74, chmn. rules com., mem. constl. revision com.; lt. gov. State of S.C., 1974-78. Bd. dirs., past chmn. Carolina Motor Club (AAA); mem. exec. com. Assoc. Marine Inst., past chmn.; bd. dirs., sec. Beaufort Marine Inst.; past chmn. Beaufort County Transp. Com.; pres. SC Bar, 1986—87; mem., vice chmn. SC State Bd. Tech. and Comprehensive Edn.; mem. AMI Found. Former commr. S.C. Dept. Hwys. and Pub. transp.; former commr., vice chmn. S.C. Parks, Recreation and Tourism Commn.; mem. Coastal Caroline coun. Boy Scouts Am.; mem. adv. bd. The Salvation Army Beaufort Unit; pres. Beaufort Indsl. Park, Beaufort County Devel. Corp.; bd. dirs. The Citadel Found.; Lowcountry Habitat for Humanity, Mustard Seed Found. Lt. artillery US Army, 1952—54. Decorated Order of Palmetto Gov. James B. Edwards, SC. Mem. ABA, S.C. Bar Assn., Beaufort County Bar Assn., Rotary, Phi Beta Kappa, Kappa Alpha, Phi Delta Phi, Omicron Delta Kappa. Presbyterian (elder). Avocations:

sailing, hunting, fishing, reading. Home: 501 Pinckney St Beaufort SC 29902-4739 Office: Harvey & Battey Attys PO Box 1107 1001 Craven St Beaufort SC 29902-5577 Office Phone: 843-524-3109. Office Fax: 843-524-6973. Business E-Mail: wbharvey@islc.net, wbharvey@harveyandbattey.com.

HARVEY, WILLIAM D., utilities executive, lawyer; BA in Econs., U. Wis., Madison, 1971, JD, 1974. Solo practice, 1974—76; prin. Wheeler, Van Sickle, Anderson, Norman & Harvey, S.C., 1976—86; v.p. and assoc. gen. counsel Wis. Power & Light (now Alliant Energy Corp.), 1986—89, v.p. and gen. counsel, 1989—92, v.p. natural gas and gen. counsel, 1992—93, sr. v.p., 1993—98; exec. v.p. generation Alliant Energy-Wis. Power & Light Co. (now Alliant Energy Corp.), 1998—2004; pres. and COO Alliant Energy Corp., Madison, Wis., 2004—05, pres., CEO, 2005—06, chmn., pres., CEO, 2006—. Bd. dir. Am. Transmission Co.; chair bd. dir. Wis. Utilities Assn. Bd. dir. United Way of Dane County, 1993—2001, campaign chair, 2001, mem. cmty. bldg. com., 1996—2000; bd. dir. Greater Madison C. of C., 1993—, Madison Symphony Orch., 1998—2001; exec. com. Dane County Econ. Summit Coun.; bd. dir. Wis. Botechnology Assn., 1998—2001, Riverlands Conservancy, Inc. Office: Alliant Energy Corp 4902 N Biltmore Ln Madison WI 53718*

HARVEY, WILLIAM ROBERT, university president; b. Brewton, Ala., Jan. 29, 1941; s. Willie D. C. and Mamie Claudis (Parker) H.; m. Norma Baker, Aug. 13, 1966; children: Kelly Renee, William Christopher, Leslie Denise. BA, Talladega Coll., 1961; EdD, Harvard U., 1972. Asst. govt. affairs to dean Harvard U. Grad. Sch. Edn., 1969-70; adminstrv. asst. to pres. Fisk U., Nashville, 1970-72; v.p. student affairs/dir. planning Tuskegee (Ala.) Inst., 1972-76, v.p. adminstrv. services, 1976-78; pres. Hampton (Va.) U., 1978—; owner Pepsi-Cola Bottling Co., Houghton, Mich., 1986—. Chmn., bd. dirs. Fund for the Improvement of Post Secondary Edn.; mem. Coun. Presidents, Assn. Gov. Bds. of Univs. and Colleges; bd. dirs. Nat. Assn. for Equal Opportunity in Higher Edn., Newport News Savs. Bank; former bd. mem. Trigon Blue Cross Blue Shield Va., Newport News Shipbuilding, Fannie Mae. Contbr. articles to profl. jours. Bd. dirs. United Way, Peninsula Econ. Devel. Council; vice-chmn. President's nat. adv. council ESEA; mem. Harvard U. Alumni Council; mem. nat. adv. com. Woodrow Wilson Nat. Fellowship Found. Served with U.S. Army, 1962-65. Woodrow Wilson Martin Luther King fellow, 1968-70; Woodrow Wilson Found. intern fellow, 1970-72; Harvard U. Higher Edn. Adminstrv. fellow, 1968-70 Mem. Am. Coun. Edn., Am. Assn. Higher Edn., Nat. Assn. Equal Opportunity in Higher Edn. (chmn., bd. dirs.), Va. Assn. Higher Edn., 100 Black Men (charter mem. Newport News chpt.), Nat. Guardsmen (Norfolk chpt.), Peninsula C. of C. (dir.), Coun. Ind. Colls. in Va., Omega Psi Phi, Phi Delta Kappa, Sigma Pi Phi. Baptist. Office: Hampton U Office of Pres Hampton VA 23668 E-mail: presidentsoffice@hamptonu.edu. *It is very important today for people to have the opportunity to do some thinking about ethics and morals. It is my firm belief that decency is as important as degrees and this means not only being good doctors, lawyers, professors, engineers and nurses, but good moral leaders who have a sense of community and service as well.*

HARVEY, WILLIAM TARVER, biomedical engineer, chronic disease physician; b. Liberty, Miss., Aug. 9, 1937; s. Thomas Elijah Harvey and Cordelia Williams; m. Pat Harvey, June 6, 1962. BS in Engring. Scis. with honors, USAF Acad., 1962; MS in Elec. Engring., USAF, Dayton, Ohio, 1965; MD, Case We. Res. U., Cleve., 1974; MPH, U. Tex., Houston, 1977. Cert. in aerospace medicine Am. Bd. Preventive Medicine, 1978. Biomed. engr. USAF Manned Orbital Lab., Space Command Headquarters, Calif., 1965—70; med. internship Wilford Hall USAF Hosp., San Antonio, 1974—75; flight surgeon Randolph AFB, Tex., 1975—76; resident aerospace medicine USAF Sch. Aerospace Medicine, San Antonio, 1977—78; chief aerospace medicine Osan Air Base, Republic of Korea, 1978—79; clinician Flight Medicine Evaluation Function, USAF Sch. Aerospace Medicine, Tex., 1979—82; dir. space medicine rsch. USAF Sch. Aerospace Medicine, Brooks AFB, Tex., 1982—85; med. dir. Lockheed Space Sta. Program, Sunnyvale, Calif., 1985—89; writing sabbatical Santa Fe, 1989—90; med. dir. Pantex Nuc. Facility, Amarillo, Tex., 1990—93; locum tenens N.Mex. Health Resources, 1993—95; dir. occupl. medicine Huguley Med. Ctr., Ft. Worth, 1995—96; med. dir. Wyle Life Scis., NASA Joshson Space Ctr., Tex., 1997—2000; chronic disease physician Diversified Med. Practices, Houston, 2000—04; gen. medicine staff Family Medicine Clinic, Del Rio, Tex., 2004—06; chronic disease physician Rocky Mt. Chronic Disease Specialists, Colo. Springs, 2006—. Contbr. scientific papers in field. Chmn. Morgellons Found., Timonium, Md., 2006—07. Officer USAF, 1962—85. Recipient Writing Achievement award, USAF, 1962. Mem.: Space Found. Achievements include development of an advanced high-altitude pressure suit; a space flight medical monitoring system; a high-g centrifuge training program. Avocation: flying. Office: Rocky Mtn Chronic Disease Specialists 3010 N Circle Dr Ste 120 Colorado Springs CO 80909 Office Fax: 719-234-0024.

HARVICK, KEVIN, race car driver; b. Bakersfield, Calif., Dec. 8, 1975; m. DeLana Linville, Feb. 28, 2001. Student, Bakersfield Jr. Coll., 1997. Racecar driver Richard Childress Racing, Welcome, NC, 2000—. Named Rookie of the Yr., Busch Series, 2000, Winston Cup Raybestos, 2001, champion, NASCAR Winston West, 1998, Busch Series, 2001, 2006, Brickyard 400, 2003, Daytona 500, 2007. Achievements include becoming the first driver in NASCAR history to run full-time on both the Busch and Winston Cup series, a total of 70 races, in one season (2001); first to be named Winston Cup rookie of the year the same season that he earned the Busch Series Championship (2001). Avocations: riding ATV's and go karts, video games, remote control cars, skeet shooting. Office: c/o Richard Childress Racing PO Box 1189 Welcome NC 27374-1189*

HARVIE, CRAWFORD THOMAS, lawyer; b. NYC, Mar. 28, 1943; s. William Mead and Barbara Adele (Johnson) H.; m. Iris Ruth Alofsin, June 10, 1972; children: Katherine, Edward. AB, Stanford U., 1965; LLB, Yale U., 1968; cert. advanced mgmt. prog., Harvard U., 1992. Bar: NY 1969. Assoc. Debevoise & Plimpton, NYC, 1971-75; counsel TRW, Inc., Cleve., 1976-77, sr. counsel, 1978-79, asst. gen. counsel, v.p., 1980-83; v.p. law TRW Automotive, Cleve., 1983-90; v.p., assoc. gen. counsel TRW, Inc., 1990-95; sr. v.p., gen. counsel, sec. Goodyear Tire and Rubber Co., Akron, Ohio, 1995—. Trustee Cleve. Inst. of Music, 1989—; bd. overseers Blossom Music Ctr. Mem. Am. Corp. Counsel Assn., Assn. Gen. Counsel, Chief Legal Officer Roundtable-US. Home: 6537 Thornbrook Cir Hudson OH 44236-3552 Office: Goodyear Tire and Rubber Co 1144 E Market St Akron OH 44316-0001

HARVIN, DAVID TARLETON, lawyer; b. Houston, Feb. 15, 1945; s. William Charles and Ruth Helen (Beck) H.; m. Sarah Ann Hartman, Apr. 21, 1973; children: Kimberly Kate, William Hartman, John Andrew. BA magna cum laude, Yale U., 1967; JD with high honors, U. Tex., 1970. Bar: Tex. 1970, US Dist. Ct. (so. dist.) Tex. 1972, US Dist. Ct. (ea. dist.) Tex. 1977, US Dist. Ct. (no. dist.) Tex. 1979, US Dist. Ct. (we. dist.) Tex. 1988, US Ct. Appeals (5th cir.) 1971, US Supreme Ct. 1977. Law clk. U.S. Ct. Appeals (5th cir.), 1970-71; assoc. Vinson & Elkins L.L.P, Houston, 1971-77, ptnr., 1977—, mgmt. com., 2000—05. Trustee Episcopal Theol. Sem. of S.W., 1995-2002, Stehlin Found. for Cancer Rsch., 1986-96, Kinkaid Sch., 1997-2003; vice-chancellor Episcopal Diocese of Tex. Fellow Am. Coll. Trial Lawyers, Tex. Bar Found., Houston Bar Found.; mem. ABA, Houston Country Club, The Downtown Club, Old Baldy Club, Phi Beta Kappa. Home: 111 Maple Valley Rd Houston TX 77056-1007 Office: Vinson & Elkins LLP 1001 Fannin St Ste 2500 Houston TX 77002-6706 Office Phone: 713-758-2368. Business E-Mail: dharvin@velaw.com.

HARWARD, DONALD WEST, retired academic administrator; m. Ann Harward; 2 children. B, Maryville Coll.; M, Am. U.; PhD, U. Md. Prof. U. Del., 1968—82; v.p. acad. affairs Coll. Wooster, Ohio, until 1989; pres. Bates Coll., Lewiston, Maine, 1989—2002, pres. emeritus, 2002—. Chmn. and co- founder LA Excels. Fellow: Assn. of Am. Colleges and Universities (sr.). Office: PO Box 152 Corea ME 04624-0152

HARWELL, DAVID WALKER, retired judge; b. Florence, SC, Jan. 8, 1932; s. Baxter Hicks and Lacy (Rankin) H.; married; children: Robert Bryan, William Baxter. LL.B., JD, U. S.C., 1958; HHD (hon.), Frances Marion U., 1987; D in Pub. Svc. (hon.), Coastal Carolina U., 2006. Bar: S.C. 1958, U.S. Dist. Ct. S.C. 1958, U.S. Ct. Appeals 1964, U.S. Supreme Ct. 1961. Circuit judge 12th Jud. Ct. S.C., 1973-80; justice S.C. Supreme Ct., 1980-91, chief justice, 1991-94; ret., 1994; spl. counsel Nelson, Mullins, Riley and Scarborough. Mem. S.C. Ho. of Reps., 1962-73. Served with USNR, 1952-54. Mem. Am. Bar Assn., Am. Trial Lawyers Assn., S.C. Bar Assn., S.C. Trial Lawyers Assn. (Portrait and Scholarship award 1986). Presbyterian. Office: PO Box 2459 Myrtle Beach SC 29578-2459 Office Phone: 843-448-3500. Business E-Mail: david.harwell@nelsonmullins.com.

HARWELL, DENISE, researcher; BA in Psychology, U. Ala., Huntsville, 1992, MA in Psychology, 1996. Rsch. asst. U. Ala., 1992, 1993; psychiatric tech. Crestwood Hosp., Huntsville, 1995—97, Huntsville Hosp., 2004—07; resident asst. Morningside of Madison, 2001—04; care mgr. Harbor Chase of Huntsville, 2006. Rsch. asst. U. Ala., Huntsville, 1993. Named Assoc. of the Quarter, Morningside, 2003; recipient Angel on Earth award, 2003. Mem.: Nat. Inst. Mental Health, Alzheimer's Assn., Ala. Psychological Assn. (assoc.), Am. Psychological Assn. (assoc.). Personal E-mail: 102740.1756@compuserve.com.

HARWELL, KENNETH E., chemist, researcher, consultant; b. Bell Springs, Tex., Sept. 11, 1921; s. Samuel Franklin and Hettie Mae (King) H.; m. Joye Murphy, Dec. 19, 1961. BS in Chemistry, Baylor U., 1945; MA in Organic Chemistry, U. Tex., 1947, PhD in Organic Chemistry, 1952. Spl. problems chemist Union Carbide Chems. Co., Texas City, Tex., 1947-48; rsch. scientist Cotton Rsch. Com. of Tex., Austin, 1948-50; rsch. chemist Celanese Corp. of Am., Clarkwood, Tex., 1951; project supr., rsch. chemist, electronics engr. Tex. A&M Rsch. Found., College Station, 1952-54; asst. prof., assoc. mem. grad. faculty Tex. A&M Coll., College Station, 1952-54; sr. rsch. chemist Jefferson Chem. Co., Austin, 1954-58; owner, mgr. Tex. Fine Chems. Co., Austin, 1958-59; dir., mgr., treas. Quality Chems. Corp., Austin, 1960; rsch. chemist, exploratory rsch. sect. petrochems. divsn. Continental Oil Co., Ponca City, Okla., 1961-65; sr. rsch. chemist plastics divsn. Gulf R & D Corp., Merriam, Kans., 1965-72; rsch. chemist R&D dept. Cook Paint and Varnish Co., Kansas City, Mo., 1972-79; owner, mgr. Merriam Chem. Devel. Co., Edwardsville, Kans., 1979-89; cons. Skiatook, Okla., 1989—. R & D cons. Nalle Plastics, Inc., Austin, 1958-59. Author 1 book; contbr. articles to profl. jours.; patentee in field. Mem. AAAS, AIChE, NRA, Am. Chem. Soc., Sigma Xi, Phi Lambda Upsilon. Avocations: photography, writing, travel. Home: PO Box 158 Skiatook OK 74070-0158

HARWELL, WILLIAM EARNEST (ERNIE HARWELL), retired commentator; b. Washington, Ga., Jan. 25, 1918; s. Davis Gray Harwell; m. Lula Tankersley, Aug. 30, 1941; children: William Earnest, Jr., Gray Neville, Julie, Carolyn. AB, Emory U., 1940; LittD (hon.), Adrian Coll., 1985; LHD (hon.), No. Mich. Coll., 1990. Sports dir. Sta. WSB, Atlanta, 1940-43; announcer Atlanta Crackers, 1946-48, Bklyn. Dodgers, 1948-49, N.Y. Giants, 1950-53, Balt. Orioles, 1954-59, Detroit Tigers, 1960—91, 1993—2002; ret., 2002. Announcer All-Star games, World Series, NBC, CBS Radio, pro football Balt. Colts, N.Y. Giants; broadcaster Master's golf tournament, NBC, 1942, 46. Author: Tuned to Baseball, 1985, Diamond Gems, 1991, The Babe Signed My Shoe, 1994, Stories From My Life in Baseball, 2001, Life After Baseball, 2004, Ernie Harwell's Audio Scrapbook, 2006; composer songs including I Don't Know Any Better, Move over Babe, Only a Fool, One-Room World, One Dream, Sing Every Song. With USMC, 1942—46. Recipient Lowell Thomas Broadcast award, 1985, Alvin Foon award Mich. Jewish Sports Hall of Fame, 1988, 90, Big Mac award Detroit News, 1989, Golden Compass award Campfire Inc., 1989, Life Directions Enrichment award, 1989, Nat. Lifetime Nat. Achievement award March of Dimes, 1991, Joe Louis award, 1991, Ken Hubbs Meml. award, 1991, Stanley Kresge award, 1994, U. Detroit Jesuit Magis award, 1995; named Most Durable Baseball Announcer, Guinness Book Records, 2003-07; named to Baseball Hall of Fame, Cooperstown, 1981, Mich. Sports Hall of Fame, Emory U. Hall of Fame, Nat. Sportscasters and Sportswriters Hall of Fame, Am. Sportscasters Hall of Fame, Catch Hall of Fame, Ga. Broadcasters Hall of Fame, Nat. Radio Hall of Fame, 1998, SAE Leadership Hall of Fame, 2001. Mem.: ASCAP, Sigma Alpha Epsilon.

HARWICK, WAYNE THOMAS, economist; b. Oakland, Calif., Feb. 29, 1948; s. Burton Thomas and Betty Corinne (Burns) H. BA in Econs., Calif. State Univ., Northridge, 1970, MA in Econs., 1975; BA in Math., Calif. State Univ., LA, 1983. Cert. tchr. in econ. 1975. Planner Ventura (Calif.) County Schs., 1975-76; labor market economist Calif. Employment Data Rsch., LA, 1976-83; cost analyst TRW, Redondo Beach, Calif., 1983-88; cost engr., bus. economist Northrop-Grumman, El Segundo, Calif., 1988-92, 96—; cost economist Aerojet, Azusa, Calif., 1992-94; sr. assoc. Mgmt. Consulting Rsch., Thousand Oaks, Calif., 1994-95, JAG Oceaneering, 2007—. Instr. Oxnard (Calif.) Coll., 1995-98; owner Industry Metrics, Torrance, Calif., 1995-99; rep. Space Systems Cost Analysis Group for Northrop Grumman Corp.; co-owner dot com bus., 2004; spkr. in field. Bd. dirs. Homeowners Assn., Torrance, 1993-95, 97-99; mem. Crystal Cathedral Choir, 2005—. Mem. Soc. Cost Estimating Analysis (cert. cost analyst), Internat. Soc. Parametric Analysts (So. Calif. bd. dirs. 1997). Lutheran. Achievements include patents pending. Avocations: weightlifting, swimming, applied mathematics, astronomy, economic history. Office: Northrop Grumman Corp 1 Hornet Way El Segundo CA 90245-2804 Home: 536 Via Almar Palos Verdes Estates CA 90274-1230 Office Phone: 310-332-0262. Personal E-mail: wtharwick@earthlink.net.

HARWIN, S. MARTIN, pediatrician; b. Paterson, NJ; s. Nathan Harwin; children: Jonathan Eric, Wendy Lynn Harwin Bates. MD, NYC, NYC, 1961. Sr. pediatrician Grove Hill Med. Ctr., New Britain, Conn., 1966—2004; pediatrician New Britain Gen. Hosp., New Britain, Conn., 2006—. V.p. Mooreland Hill Sch., Kensington, Conn., 1990—2007. Lt. cmdr. USPHS, 1953—55. Named a Top Doc in Conn., Conn. Mag. Home: 89 Edgewood Rd Kensington CT 06037 Home Phone: 860-828-5371. Personal E-mail: mharwin@comcast.net.

HARWIT, MARTIN OTTO, astrophysicist, writer, educator, museum director; b. Prague, Czechoslovakia, Mar. 9, 1931; came to US, 1946, naturalized, 1953. s. Felix Michael and Regina Hedwig (Perutz) Haurowitz; m. Marianne Mark, Feb. 1, 1957; children: Alex, Eric, Emily. BA in Physics, Oberlin Coll., 1951; MA in Physics, U. Mich., Ann Arbor, 1953; PhD in Physics, MIT, 1960. NATO postdoctoral fellow U. Cambridge, England, 1960-61; NSF fellow Cornell U., Ithaca, NY, 1961-62, asst. prof. astronomy, 1962-64, assoc. prof., 1964-68, prof., 1968-87, prof. emeritus, 1988—, chmn. dept. astronomy, 1971-76, co-dir. prog. for hist. and philosophy of sci. and tech., 1985-87; dir. Nat. Air and Space Mus. Smithsonian Instn., Washington, 1987-95. E.O. Hulburt fellow Naval Rsch. Lab., Washington, 1963-64; NAS exch. visitor Czechoslovak Acad. Sci., Prague, 1969-70; v.p., dir. Spectral Imaging Inc., Concord, Mass., 1971-77; external mem. Max Planck Soc., Inst. Radioastronomy, Bonn., Germany, 1979—; cons. NASA.; chair for space hist. Nat. Air and Space Mus., Smithsonian Instn., 1983; chmn. astrophysics mgmt. ops. working group, NASA, 1985-87; Adriaan Blaauw prof. U. Groningen, The Netherlands, 2002; cons. James Clerk Maxwell Telescope Bd., 2005. Author: Astrophysical Concepts, 1973, 4th ed., 2006 (transl. into Chinese 1981), (with N.J.A. Sloan) Hadamard Transform Optics, 1979, Cosmic Discovery-The Search, Scope and Heritage of Astronomy, 1981 (transl. into German and French 1982), (with the mus. staff) Treasures of the National Air and Space Museum, 1995, An Exhibit Denied: Lobbying the History of Enola Gay, 1996 (transl. into Japanese 1997): editor: (with M. G. Hauser) The Extragalactic Infrared Background and its Cosmological Implications, International Astronomical Union Symposium 204, 2001. With US Army, 1955-57. Recipient Alexander von Humboldt Found. sr. US scientist award Max Planck Inst. Radioastronomy, 1976-77, Catherine Wolfe Bruce Gold medal Astron. Soc. of the Pacific, 2007; NSF grantee, 1963-68; Rsch. Corp. grantee, 1970-75; NASA grantee, 1965—; Air Force Cambridge Rsch. Labs. grantee, Mass., 1969-74. Fellow AAAS (chmn. sect. on astronomy, 2001-02, coun. mem. 2002-03), Am. Phys. Soc. (chmn. divsn. hist. of physics 1986-87, chmn. astrophysics divsn. 1988-89), Royal Astron. Soc.; mem. Soc. for Hist. of Tech., Am. Astron. Soc.

HARWOOD, HAROLD JAMES, JR., biochemist; b. New Haven, July 27, 1954; s. Harold James and Gloria Maxine (Rogers) H.; m. Janice Kay Gill, Mar. 19, 1977; children: Katryn Renee, William Bradley. BS in Chemistry, U. Akron, 1976, BS in Biology, 1977; PhD in Biochemistry, Purdue U., 1982. Lab. asst. Inst. Polymer Sci., Akron (Ohio) U., 1971-72, rsch. assoc. applied rsch. divsn., 1976-77; demonstration rm. technician Monsanto Chem. Co., 1973-76; grad. rsch. assoc. dept. biochemistry Purdue U., West Lafayette, Ind., 1977-82; postdoctoral fellow in medicine U. Fla., Gainesville, 1982-84, rsch. asst. prof. dept. medicine and pharmacology, 1984-86; from rsch. scientist dept. metabolic diseases to prin. rsch. investigator Pfizer Cen. Rsch., Groton, Conn., 1986—2007; chief cons. Delphi Biomed. Cons., 2007—. Music programmer Conn. Coll. Broadcasting Assn., 1997—. Musician: Pfizer Chamber Orch., 1999—. Coach Ledyard (Conn.) Soccer Club, 1990-97, Gainesville Youth Soccer Orgn., 1984-86; USSF Referee, 1996-, referee assignor, 1996-2004; mem. coun. on basic scis. Am. Heart Assn.; projectionist Akron Inst. Civic Edn., 1974-77; guitarist Prophet's Town Band, Battleground, Ind., 1981-82; referee USSF, 1996—. Recipient New Investigator Rsch. award, Nat. Cancer Inst., 1985—88; David Ross fellow, Purdue U., 1979—81. Mem. Am. Chem. Soc., Am. Fedn. Clin. Rsch., Am. Soc. Biochemistry, Assn. Molecular Biology, Am. Diabetes Assn., Am. Heart Assn. (peer rev. com. 1989-2002, rsch. com. 2002—), Purdue Alumni Assn., Alpha Chi Sigma. Avocations: music, soccer, camping, hiking, gardening. Home and Office: 10 Eska Dr Ledyard CT 06339-1344 Home Phone: 860-464-9653; Office Phone: 860-271-9001. Business E-Mail: h.james.harwood@gmail.com.

HARWOOD, JERRY, market research executive; b. Jersey City, June 19, 1926; s. Louis and Dorothy (Cohen) Horowitz; m. Ruthella Zimmerman, June 25, 1950; children: Robin Jill, Dean Brook. BA cum laude, L.I. U., 1949; MA, NYU, 1953. Tech. instr. U.S. Bur. Census, 1950-51; v.p., assoc. research dir. Kenyon & Eckhardt Advt., NYC, 1962-66; sr. v.p., dir. research Needham, Harper & Steers Advt., NYC, 1966-73; sr. v.p., group research dir. Benton & Bowles Advt., NYC, 1975-88; mktg. cons. Short Hills, NJ, 1988—; mem. Census Adv. Com., 1976-83. Adj. assoc. prof. NYU Grad. Sch. Bus., 1984-85 Pres. Temple B'nai Jeshurun, 1980-82, Jewish Family Svc. of MetroWest, 1984-87, N.J. Jewish News, 1992-95; v.p. Mental Health Assn. Essex County, 1992-99; mem. Essex County Child Placement Rev. Bd., 1988—; bd. dirs. Am. Jewish Com., 1996—, v.p., 2005; trustee Hebrew Immigrant Aid Soc., 1997-98. Mem. Am. Mktg. Assn. (pres. N.Y.C. chpt. 1970-71, nat. v.p. pub. policy and issues 1973, nat. v.p. mktg. rsch. 1981-82, mem. editl. bd. 1992-98, chmn. Marketing Hall of Fame 1995-98), Nat. Assn. Jewish Family and Children Agys. (pres. 1997-99). Home and Office: 22 Athens Rd Short Hills NJ 07078-1312 Personal E-mail: jandrharwood@comcast.net. *The individual who respects the rights, opinions and needs of others is the individual who manages his own life most productively and successfully.*

HARWOOD, JOHN H., II, lawyer; b. Sept. 20, 1945; BA, Harvard Univ., 1967; JD, Columbia Univ., 1973; LLM, Georgetown Univ., 1974. Bar: DC 1973. Ptnr., chmn. Comm. & E-Commerce dept. Wilmer Cutler Pickering Hale & Dorr, Washington. Adj. prof. Georgetown Univ. Law Ctr., 1978; past fellow & acting dep. dir. Inst. for Pub. Interest Representation. Contbr. articles to profl. jours. Served USMC, 1967—70. Mem.: ABA, Fed. Comm. Bar Assn., DC Bar. Office: Wilmer Cutler Pickering Hale & Dorr 1801 Pennsylvania Ave NW Washington DC 20006 Mailing: Wilmer Cutler Pickering Hale & Dorr 2445 M St NW Washington DC 20037 Office Phone: 202-663-6333. Office Fax: 202-663-6363. Business E-Mail: john.harwood@wilmerhale.com.

HARWOOD, JULIUS J., metallurgist, educator; b. NYC, Dec. 3, 1918; m. Naomi Beitner, 1983; children: Dane L., Gail A., Caren L., Rochelle. BS, CCNY, 1939; MS, U. Md., 1953; D of Engring. (hon.), Mich. Tech. U., 1986. Materials engr. U.S. Naval Gun Factory, 1940-46; metall. Off Naval Rsch., 1946-60; mgr. metall. sci. lab. Ford Motor Co., Dearborn, Mich., 1960-69, mgr. rsch. planning engring. and rsch. staff, 1969—71, dir. Material Sci. Lab, engring. and rsch. staff, 1971—83; prof. engring. Wayne State U., Detroit, 1984; pres. Ovonic Synthetic Material Co., Troy, 1984—87, Harwood Cons., West Bloomfield, 1987—. Adj. prof. Wayne State U., Detroit, 1975. Editor 5 books on materials; contbr. articles to profl. jours. Fellow AAAS, TMS, Metall. Soc. (pres. 1973), Am. Soc. Metals (John H. Shoemaker award 1977, Disctinction award), Engring. Soc. of Detroit (Gold Medal award 1983); mem. Am. Inst. Mining, Metall. and Petroleum Engrs. (hon., pres. 1976), Am. Ceramic Soc. (Orton lectr. 1978), Nat. Acad. Engrs. (life). Office: 5023 Pheasant Cv West Bloomfield MI 48323-2093 Office Phone: 248-681-6747.

HARWOOD, ROBERT BERNARD, JR., former state supreme court justice; b. Oct. 17, 1939; Student, U. of the South, 1958—59; BS in Commerce and Bus. Adminstrn., U. Ala., 1962, JD, 1963. Spl. asst. atty. gen. State of Ala., 1969—75; dep. city judge City of Tuscaloosa, Ala., 1975—80; cir. judge Tuscaloosa County, 1991—2001; assoc. justice Ala. Supreme Ct., 2001—06. Lectr. law and trial advocacy U. Ala., 1979—83, 1989—99. Mem. exec. bd. Black Warrior coun. Boy Scouts Am., 1976—, pres., 1993; mem. leadership assn. United Way Tuscaloosa County; mem. Carroll Creek Vol. Fire Dept.; bd. dirs. FOCUS on Sr. Citizens of Tuscaloosa County. Recipient Silver Beaver award, Black Warrior Coun. Boy Scouts Am., 1994. Mem.: ABA, Am. Coll. Trial Lawyers, Am. Bd. Trial Advocates, Am. Bar Found., Am. Judges Assn., Tuscaloosa County Bar Assn. (pres. 1978—79), Tuscaloosa Inn of Ct. (pres. 1991—92), Ala. Bar Assn., Tuscaloosa County Cattlemen's Assn., Ala. Cattlemen's Assn., Order of the Coif. Republican. Episcopalian. Home Phone: 205-345-7953. E-mail: bernarwood@comcast.net.

HARWOOD, STANLEY, retired judge, lawyer, arbitrator, mediator; b. NYC, June 23, 1926; s. Benjamin and Hannah (Schwartz) H.; m. Deborah Weinerman, June 18, 1950 (dec. 1995); children: Richard, Ellen Harwood Jacobs, Michael, Jonathan; m. Cathleen Hamilton, May 25, 1997. AB, Columbia U., 1949, LLB, 1952. Bar: N.Y. 1954, U.S. Dist. Ct. (ea. and so. dists.) N.Y. 1956, U.S. Supreme Ct. 1960. Atty. Dept. of Navy, Washington, 1952—53; assoc. Benjamin Harwood, Bklyn., 1953—56; pvt. practice Levittown, NY, 1956—61; law clk. to justice N.Y. Supreme Ct., Mineola, 1961—65, justice, 1982—92, judge appellate divsn., 1987—92; ptnr. Mishkin, Miner, Harwood & Semel, Mineola, 1965—69, Shayne, Dachs, Stanisci & Harwood, Mineola, 1969—81, Bower & Gardner, NYC, 1992—94; counsel Jaspan, Schlesinger & Hoffman, 1994—. Mem. N.Y. State Assembly, 1966-72; chmn. Nassau County Dem. Com., 1973-81; commr. elections Nassau County Bd. Elections, 1976-81; bd. dirs. Nat.

Conf. Christians and Jews, 1993-98. With USNR, 1944-46, U.S. Merchant Marines. Mem. N.Y. State Bar Assn., Nassau County Bar Assn. (chmn. cts. com. 1971-73, chmn. pro bono com. 1988-90, bd. dirs. 1997-2000, Nassau-Suffolk Law Svs. Committment to Justice medal 2002), Mill River Club. Jewish. Home: 2 Bull Calf Ln Centerport NY 11721-1669 Office: Jaspan Schlesinger & Hoffman 300 Garden City Plz Garden City NY 11530-3324 Office Phone: 516-746-8000. Office Fax: 516-393-8282. Business E-Mail: sharwood@jshllp.com.

HARYONO, IGNATIUS WIBISONO, writer; s. Henricus Harjono Martodirjo and Anastasia Kusmaria Soemodirjo; m. Wijakti Karlina Harlim, Dec. 24, 1943. PhD, Rosevelt U., Brussels, 1980; DD, Rosevelt U. Belgium, Brussels, 1981. Philosophy docent Pajajaran State U., Bandung, W. Java, Indonesia, 1968—73; u. prof. Parahyangan Cath. U., Bandung, 1972—79; prof. State and Cath. U., Bandung, 1972—78; asst. to provincial Order of the Holy Cross, Bandung, 1975—79; asst. to bishop Diocese of Bandung, 1978—80; asst. to chaplain Cath. Ch., LA, 1990—. Dir. USA Today, Glendale, 1985—90; postal worker Burbank Post Office, Calif., 1989—90; religious cons. (prvt.), 2000—. Author: (book) Was Mary Also Redeemed, 1989, poems in Nat. Libr. of Poetry; contbr. articles to religious publs. Dir. religious edn. Indonesian Cath. Cmty. of Archdiocese, LA, Calif., 1994—2000; dir., leader Bible Readers Club, 1995; mem. Lumen Christi Indonesian Cath. Bible Study. Lt. col. titular chaplaincy Indonesian Army, 1972—79. Recipient Presdl. award, W. Java Cath. Youth Orgn., 1973, 1979, Moderator award, Cathedral Youth Orgn., 1978, 1979, Indonesian Cath. Cmty. award, 2001, award, KKIA Inc., 2001. Master: Iggy LLC (immigrants helper 2000—01, pres., owner). Populist. Roman Catholic. Avocation: travel. Office Phone: 818-737-0013. E-mail: iharyono@aol.com, yhwhigna@yahoo.com.

HASALONE, ANNETTE LEONA, radio personality, research and development company executive; d. Glenn Allen Greene and Betty Leona Palmer; m. Mark Joseph Eve, Sept. 24, 2002; m. Cipriano Ramirez, May 24, 1977 (div. Sept. 0, 1985); children: Elizabeth Leona Ramirez, Dominic Earl Ramirez, Jerrod Emmett Ramirez. D in Naturopathy, Trinity Coll. Natural Healing, Warsaw, Ind.ana, 2003. Pres. Elemental Rsch., LLC, Post Falls, Idaho, 1999—; R&D cons. Eniva Corp., Blaine, Minn., 1999—2003. Case mgr. Homeless Mental Health Program, Oroville, Calif., 1984—86; account clk. I GAIN, Woodland, Calif., 1986—88; drug and alcohol specialist Health and Human Svcs., Woodland, 1988—89; DUI edn. counselor AK Bean Found., Fairfield, Calif., 1988—89; mgr./cons. WaterOz, Grangeville, Idaho, 1997—99; radio talk show host WGTG, Ga., 1998—2000, WHJM, Knoxville, Tenn., 1998—2000; product knowlege liaison Shagoi/Lanea Rx Larrea Corp., 2005; radio talk show host KLAV, 2006—, KTAC, Wash., 2006—, KTRW, Wash., 2007, Idaho, 07. Author: (educational book) Mono-Atomic Minerals Information and Reference Guide, 1999, Off Balance, 2003, (educational booklet) Essential Information Booklet, (audio tape) Naturally Healthy With Mono-Atomic Minerals, (protocols for natural healing) Protocols Booklet. Campaign mgr. Ted Gunderson for Pres., Las Vegas, Nev., 1996—96. Recipient Outstanding Achievement in Poetry award, Internat. Libr. Poetry and Poetry.com, 2001, Outstanding Contbn. award, Enira Corp., 2001. Mem.: NAFE (assoc.), Internat. Ozone Soc. (assoc.). Republican. Achievements include invention of proprietary process for cell ready, ionic, liquid, water-soluble mineral supplements. Avocations: skiing, art, research and development, guitar, poetry. Office: Elemental Research LLC 4353 E Poleline Ave Post Falls ID 83854 Office Phone: 800-314-2884. Business E-Mail: annette@elementalresearchllc.com. E-mail: ahasalone@gmail.com.

HASANYAN, DAVRESH, research scientist, educator; b. Kurdish, Armenia, Apr. 18, 1959; s. Javo and Gulizar Hasanyan; m. Jalil Armanj. PhD, Yerevan State U., Armenia, 1985. Sr. rsch. scientist Inst. Mechancis, Yerevan, Armenia, 1985—; rsch. prof. Va. Tech., Blacksburg, Va., 2001—.

HASDAY, ROBERT JOEL, lawyer; b. NYC, Apr. 30, 1949; s. Isaac and Dora (Ariewitz) Hasday; m. Carol Minette Rosenfelt, June 18, 1970; children: Jill Elaine, Michael Jonathan, Lisa Robin. BA magna cum laude, Brandeis U., 1970; MBA, U. Chgo., 1972; JD, Yale U., 1975. Bar: NY 1976. Assoc. Shea & Gould, NYC, 1975-83, ptnr., 1984-94, Duane Morris LLP, NYC, 1994—, mng. ptnr. NY office, 1994—, mem. partners bd., 1998—. Bd. dirs. Apple Bank for Savings, NYC, 1991—. Mem. Assn. Bar City of NY (com. securities regulation 1987-90), Phi Beta Kappa, Beta Gamma Sigma. Office: Duane Morris LLP 1540 Broadway New York NY 10036-4086 Office Phone: 212-692-1010. Office Fax: 212-692-1020. Business E-Mail: rjhasday@duanemorris.com.

HASE, DAVID JOHN, lawyer; b. Milw., Feb. 27, 1940; s. John Henry and Catherine Charlotte (Leekley) H.; m. Penelope Sue Pritchard, Sept. 2, 1964; children: Jeffrey David, Jennifer Anne, John Paul. AB, Dartmouth Coll., 1962; LLB, U. Wis., 1965. Bar: Wis. 1965, U.S. Dist. Ct. (ea. dist.) Wis. 1965, U.S. Ct. Appeals (7th cir.) 1971, U.S. Ct. Appeals (D.C. cir.) 1975, U.S. Ct. Appeals (9th cir.) 1989, U.S. Supreme Ct. 1975. Assoc. Grootemaat, Cook & Franke, Milw., 1965-67, ptnr., shareholder, 1968-70; shareholder Cook & Franke S.C., Milw., 1970-73; legal counsel to gov. Wis., Madison, 1973-74; dep. atty. gen. State of Wis., Madison, 1974-76; assoc. Foley & Lardner, Milw., 1976-77, ptnr., 1977-94; shareholder Cook & Franke S.C., Milw., 1994—. Mem. Sch. Bd., Mequon, Wis., 1971-94, treas., 1973-75, pres., 1975-94' trustee Frank L. Weyenberg Libr., 2004—. Mem. ABA. Democrat. Home: 2108 W Raleigh Ct Mequon WI 53092-5416 Office: Cook & Franke SC 660 E Mason St Ste 401 Milwaukee WI 53202-3877 Office Phone: 414-227-1281. E-mail: hase@cf-law.com.

HASEK, DOMINIK, professional hockey player; b. Pardubice, Czech Republic, Jan. 29, 1965; m. Alena Hasek; children: Michael, Dominika. Goaltender Chgo. Blackhawks, 1990—92, Buffalo Sabres, 1992—2001, Detroit Red Wings, 2001—02, 2003—04, 2006—, Ottawa Senators, 2004—06. Goaltender Czech Republic, Nagano Olympics, 1998, Czech Republic, Salt Lake City Olympics, 2002. Named Best Goaltender, Nagano Olympic Games, 1998; named to NHL All-Star Game, 1996—99, 2001—02, NHL First All-Star Team, 1994, 1995, 1997—99, 2001; recipient Vezina Trophy, 1994, 1995, 1996, 1997, 1998, 2001, Hart Trophy, 1997, 1998, Lester B. Pearson, 1997, 1998, William M. Jennings Trophy, 2001. Achievements include being a member of gold medal Czech Republic hockey team, Nagano Olympics, 1998, and bronze medal team, Torino Olympics, Italy, 2006; being a member of Stanley Cup Championship team, Detroit Red Wings, 2002. Office: Detroit Red Wings Joe Louis Arena 600 Civic Center Dr Detroit MI 48226

HASELMANN, JOHN PHILIP, management consultant; b. Summit, NJ, Feb. 25, 1940; s. John and Elizabeth Haselmann; divorced; children— Terri Lee, Karen Lynn, Guy Philip BSEE, N.J. Inst. Tech., 1961; MBA in Indsl. Mgmt., Ops. Research and Mgmt. Sci., U. Pa., 1963. Asst. dir. Behavior Systems, Phila., 1961-63; prof. econs. Union Coll., 1964-66; mgr. mgmt. sci. div. Western Electric Co., Princeton, NJ, 1970-73; mgr. mktg. sci. div. AT&T Long Lines, Bedminster, NJ, 1974-78; pres., founder, chmn. of bd. Info. Mgmt. Group, Morristown, NJ, 1978-83; pres. Trinet Inc., Morristown, NJ, 1984-85; pres., founder, chmn. of bd. Entity Advt. and Graphics, Inc., Florham Park, NJ, 1986-88, Integrated Mktg. Svcs., Inc., Parsippany, NJ, 1989—; founder, mng. ptnr. COB and Intergrated Mgmt. Svcs. Inc., Morristown, NJ, 1989—; founder and exec. dir. Am. Employers Assn., Washington, 1989—95; co-founder, vice chmn., exec. v.p., bd. dirs. TCI Comm. Mgmt. Corp., Parsippany, NJ, 1991-95; pres., founder, chmn. bd. Computer Tech. Integration, 1995—; founder, exec. dir. Assn. for the Adv. Knowledge-Mgmt., Morristown, NJ, 2001—. Guest lectr. on application of sci. to problems in mtkg. Columbia Grad. Sch. Bus., Sloan Sch. MIT, Wharton Grad. Sch. U. Pa. Author: Computers and Data Processing Applied to a Personnel Processing System as a Management Tool, 1963, How to Improve the Effectiveness of Your Advertising/Marketing/Sales Investment, 1987, How to Lower the Cost of Getting an Order and Increase Revenues through Improved Market Analysis and Sales Management, 1990. Mem. Am. Mgmt. Assn., Am. Soc. Assn. Execs., Am. Soc. Profl. Cons. Republican. Lutheran. Avocations: golf, sailing. Office: PO Box 339 Morristown NJ 07963-0339 Office Phone: 973-715-7771. Personal E-mail: jhaselmann@rcn.com. E-mail: jhaselmann@integratedmgt.com.

HASELTINE, FLORENCE PAT, obstetrician, gynecologist, medical association administrator; b. Phila., Aug. 17, 1942; d. William R. and Jean Adele Haseltine; m. Frederick Cahn, Mar. 12, 1964 (div. 1969); m. Alan Chodos, Apr. 18, 1970; children: Anna, Elizabeth. BA in Biophysics, U. Calif., Berkeley, 1964; PhD in Biophysics, MIT, 1969; MD, Albert Einstein Coll. of Medicine, 1972. Diplomate Am. Bd. Ob-Gyn., Am. Bd. Reproductive Endocrinology. Intern U. Pa.; resident Brigham and Women's Hosp., Boston; asst. prof. dept. ob-gyn. and pediatrics Yale U., New Haven, 1976—82, assoc. prof. dept. ob-gyn. and pediatrics, 1982—85; dir. Ctr. for Population Research, Nat. Inst. Child Health and Human Devel. NIH, Bethesda, Md., 1985—; founder Haseltine System, Inc., Products for the Disabled, 1995—. Founding sr. editor Jour. Women's Health. Co-author: Woman Doctor, 1976, Magnetic Resonance of the Reproductive System, 1987; co-editor: 25 books on reproductive scis. Bd. dirs. Older Women's League, 1998—, Am. Women in Sci., 1998—. Fellow: AAAS; mem.: Soc. Cell Biology, Soc. for Women's Health Rsch. (founder 1990, bd. dirs.), Soc. Gynecol. Investigation, Inst. of Medicine. Office: NIH/NICHD Ctr Population Rsch Executive Bldg Rm 8B07 6100 Executive Blvd Bethesda MD 20892-7510 Office Phone: 301-496-1101. E-mail: haseltif@mail.nih.gov.

HASELTINE, JAMES LEWIS, artist, consultant; b. Portland, Oreg., Nov. 7, 1924; s. William Ambrose and Clara Thusnelda (Scharpf) H.; m. Jane Winsberg, Nov. 14, 1948 (div. 1953); m. Margaret Ann Wilson, Aug. 15, 1955; children: Thomas, Jean, Kay, Suzanne, Angela. Student, Ark. State Coll., 1943—44, Reed Coll., 1946—47, Mus. Art Sch., 1947, student, 1949, Art Inst. Chgo., 1947—48, Bklyn. Mus. Sch., 1950—51. Dir. Salt Lake Art Ctr., Salt Lake City, 1961—67; exec. dir. Wash. State Arts Commn., Olympia, 1967—80, prof. art, 1950—. Vis. lectr. art history U. Utah, Salt Lake City, 1964-65; panel mem. Nat. Endowment for Arts, Washington, 1969-80; cons. in field. Author: 100 Years of Utah Painting, 1965 (Mormon History Assn. award 1965); paintings and prints represented in permanent collections Portland Art Mus., Oakland Art Mus., Mus. Art U. Oreg., Mus. Fine Arts U. Utah, Tacoma Art Mus., Willamette U., Salem, Oreg Mem. search com. for pres. Evergreen State Coll., Olympia, 1984; trustee Portland Art Mus., 1953-55. With U.S. Army, 1942-46, ETO. Mem. We. Assn. Art Mus. (pres. 1964-66), Artists Equity Assn. (nat. dir. 1955-58, chmn. Oreg. chpt. 1953-55), We. States Arts Found. (bd. dirs. 1975-77), Brit.-Am. Art Assn. (trustee 1980-84) Home and Office: 3820 Sunset Beach Dr NW Olympia WA 98502-3542

HASELTINE, WILLIAM ALAN, virology educator, former biopharmaceutical company executive; b. St. Louis, Oct. 17, 1944; s. William R. and Jean (Ellsberg) H.; m. Patricia Gercik; children: Mara, Alexander; m. Gale Hayman, Feb. 16, 1991. BA, U. Calif., Berkeley, 1966; PhD, Harvard U., 1973. Fellow MIT, Cambridge, 1973-74; asst. prof. Harvard Med. Sch., Dana Farber Cancer Inst., Cambridge, 1975-78, assoc. prof., 1979-88, prof. Boston, 1988-95; assoc. prof. Harvard Sch. Pub. Health, Boston, 1979-88, chief, prof. divsn. human retrovirology, 1988, prof., 1988; founder, former chmn. bd., CEO Human Genome Scis., Inc., Rockville, Md., 1992—2004. AIDS exec. com. NIH, 1986. Assoc. editor Cancer Rsch., 1985-93, Leukemia Rsch., 1986; editor in chief Jour. AIDS, 1987—; contbg. author: The Microverse: The Genetic Code, 1989; contbr. articles to Sci. Am., Jour. AIDS. Trustee Leukemia Soc. Am. (Disting. svc. award 1987). Recipient Faculty Rsch. award Am. Cancer Soc., 1978-82, AIDS Recognition award Goiv. of Mass., 1986; grantee Bristol-Myers Squibb Co., 1991. Mem. Am. Fedn. AIDS Rsch., Coun. Nat. Inst. Allergy and Infectious Diseases. Office: Harvard Med Sch Dana Farber Cancer Inst 44 Binney St Boston MA 02115-6013

HASELTON, RICK THOMAS, lawyer; b. Albany, Oreg., Nov. 5, 1953; s. Shirley (Schantz) H. AB, Stanford U., 1976; JD, Yale U., 1979. Chair Oreg. State Bd. Bar Examiners, 1988-89, bd. dirs., 1986-88; mem. adv. com. on rules of practice 9th Cir. Ct., 1991-93. Law clk. U.S. Ct. Appeals (9th cir.) Oreg., Portland, 1979-80; from assoc. to ptnr. Lindsay, Hart, Neil & Weigler, Portland, 1979-93; sole practice Portland, 1993-94; assoc. judge Oreg. Ct. Appeals, Salem, 1994—. Chair Multnomah County Legal Aid, Portland, 1985-86, bd. dirs., 1982-87. Mem. ABA, Oreg. Bar Assn., ACLU (cooperating atty. 1982-94), Phi Beta Kappa. Jewish. Office: 300 Justice Blvd Salem OR 97310-0001

HASEN, BURTON STANLEY, painter; b. NYC, Dec. 19, 1921; s. Herman Harold and Mina (Leibowitz) H. Student, Art Students League, 1940-42, 46, H. Hoffmann Sch. Fine Arts, 1947-48, Acad. dela Grande-Chaumiere, Paris, 1948-50, Acad. delle Belle-Arti, Rome, 1959-60. Tchr. Sch. Visual Arts, NYC, 1953-2000, Mpls. Sch. Art and Design, 1966 One-man shows include Galerie 8, Paris, 1950, Grand Ctrl. Moderns, NYC, 1958-61, DArcy Gallery, NYC, 1964, Landmark Gallery, NYC, 1976, T'Pandje Gallerie, Belgium, 1981, Anita Shapolsky Gallery, 1987, 1992, 94, Gallery 1100-Niagara, Buffalo, 1993, Staller Ctr. for Arts, SUNY, Stony Brook, 1995, Hamilton Coll., Clinton, NY, 1996, Hugode Pagano gallery, NYC, 1997, Nat. Jewish Mus., Washington, 1997, Islip Art Mus., NY, 2003, Retrospective Southeast Mo. State Regional Mus., Cape Girardeau, 2005; group shows include Mus. Modern Art, Paris, 1951, Whitney Mus. Am. Art, NYC, 1964, Corcoran Gallery Art, Washington, 1959, Kresge Art Center, U. So. Ill., 1961, Krannert Art Mus.-U. Ill., Urbana, Am. Acad. Arts and Letters, NYC, 1965, Berlin Acad. Arts, 1956, W.G. Picker Gallery, 1969, Colgate U., Hamilton, NY, 1969, Mus. Modern Art, NYC, 1966, Met. Mus. Art, N.Y.C., 1952, Worcester (Mass.) Art Mus., 1968, Walker Art Center, Mpls., 1966, Bklyn. Mus., 1954, Artist Choice Mus., NYC, NAD, NYC, 1985, Anita Shapolsky Gallery, 1989, 90, 92, 2000, Neo Persona Gallery, 1989, 90, Rider Coll., 1992, Albright-Knox Mus., 1992, Islip Art Mus., 1992, Cleve. Inst. Art, 1993, Swiss Cultural Inst., 1993, David Anderson Gallery, Buffalo, 1993, Henry St. Settlement, NYC, 1993, Sordoni Art Gallery, Wilkes-Barre, Pa., 1994, Nat. Acad., 1995, 96, 97, 99, 00, 01, 03, 05, Alysia Duckler Gallery, Portland, 1996, Pagano Gallery, NYC, 1997, 98, Studio 18 Gallery NYC, 2002, 04, Studio 18 Gallery Graphics Show, Sheldon Meml. Art Gallery, U. Nebr., Lincoln, 2003, Brooms Street Gallery, NYC, Denise Bibro Gallery, NY, Lohin Geduld Gallery, NY, 2005, NY Soc. Etchers, Studio 12N, NYC, NAD, NYC, Terrain Gallery, NYC, Artist's Equity Gallery, NYC, Hunterdon Art Ctr., Clinton, NJ, 2007; represented in permanent collections Walker Art Center, Worcester Art Mus., Hampton Inst., CIBA-GEIGY Co., Bibliotheque Nationale, Paris, NY Pub. Library, Princeton U., Columbia U., Mus. Fine Art, Portland, Maine, NY Crestview Coll., Muhlenberg, Fine Prints Dept., SUNY, Buffalo, 1989, CCNY, Rider U., Lawrenceville, NJ, 1993, Islip Mus., East Islip, NY, Hamilton Coll., Clinton, NY, Nat. Jewish Mus., Washington, Southeast Mo. State U., Cape Giradeau, Mo., Birmingham So. Coll., Ala., Hudgens Ctr. Arts, Duluth, Ga., High Mus., Miami, Fla., Newberger Mus. Art, Purchase, NY, Libr. Congress, Fine Print Collection, Smithsonian, Washington, Jules Sherman Collection, NY, Robert Blackburn Collection, Elizabeth Found., NY, The Lowe Art Mus., U. Miami, U. Chgo.; illustrator books, 1959-89, Beyond the Furies, 1985, Franklin Mint, Phila., 1991, The Flame Charts, 2002; archives include Smithsonian Mus. Am. Art, Centre Georges Pompidou, Musée d'Art Moderne, Paris. With AUS, 1942—46. Recipient Emily Lowe Found. Purchase prize, 1955; grantee Fulbright Found., 1959-60, NY Found. Arts, 1990, Richard Florsheim Art Fund , 1993, 96, 97, Nat. Acad. Design, 2001; Pollack Krasner fellow 1995-96, 1999-2000, 2003, 04, Am. Acad. Arts & Letters, 2000, 01, 02, 03. Mem.: NY Artists Equity (hon. pres. 2005), Nat. Acad. Design, Fulbright Alumni Assn. *The motivating force of my life has been the desire to paint meaningful paintings that express my innermost feelings. Art for me is the exhilarating experience of discovering new worlds. Each work is a projection of myself into the cosmic universe. This compulsion to paint my fantasy has never faltered or been self-deceptive.*

HASEN, MICHAEL, engineering company executive, civil engineer; s. Hans Helmut and June Katherine Hasen; m. Sandra Susan Scurlock, May 23, 1991; 1 child, Alexander Hans. BS in Civil Engring., U. Ill., Urbana-Champaign, Ill., 1980; MS in Civil Engring., U. Calif., Berkeley, Calif., 1981; MBA, U. Houston, Tex., 1992. Registered profl. engr., Calif., 1984, Tex., 1985, La., 2005. Project engr. McClelland-Suhami, Ltd., Dammam, Saudi Arabia, 1982—85, Converse Consultants, Pasadena, Calif., 1986—87; project mgr. Fugro-McClelland Marine Geosciences, Inc., Houston, 1987—92; ops. mgr. HVJ Assocs., Inc., Houston, 1992—2000, v.p. corp. devel., 2000—02, exec. v.p., 2002—. Chmn. sections and branches coun. Geo-Inst., Washington, 2004—06. Editor: Expansive Clay Soils and Vegetative Influence on Shallow Founds., 2001. Asst. scoutmaster Troop 441, Sugar Land, Tex., 2004—06; bd. mem. Assocs. First Colony, Sugar Land, 2004—06. Mem.: Houston Consulting Engineers Coun. (chmn. geotechnical com. 1999—2000), Ft. Bend C. of C. (bd. dirs. 2000—03, vice chmn. infrastructure planning divsn. 1998—99), Tau Beta Pi. Methodist. Achievements include design of freeway reconstruction; ship channel widening and deepening; cruise terminal; port; outfall and inter-island tunnel. Office: HVJ Associates Inc 6120 S Dairy Ashford Road Houston TX 77072 Office Phone: 281-933-7388.

HASENFUS, HAROLD JOSEPH, retired mechanical engineer, naval technical director; b. NYC, Apr. 9, 1921; s. Joseph Vincent and Ethel Elizabeth (Galvan) Hasenfus; m. Mary Margaret Boone, Nov. 7, 1945; children: James Joseph, Stephen Francis, Jean Marie, Edward Harold. BSME, CCNY, 1943; MSEE, Va. Tech., 1981, MS in physics, 1986. Cert. Vatican's Cert. of Recognition St. Joan of Arc's Roman Cath. /MD, 1959. Rsch. asst.-Manhattan Project U of Chgo., Chgo., 1944; project engr., Manhattan Project Fercleve Corp., Oak Ridge, Tenn., 1945; ordnance engr. Ballistic Rsch. Lab., Aberdeen Proving Ground, Md., 1946—52; chief Ballistic Rsch. Lab., rocket br., Aberdeen Proving Ground, Md., 1952—60; head,satellite applications div. Naval Weapons Lab., Dahlgren, Va., 1960—61; tech. dir. Naval Space Surveillance Sys., Dahlgren, Va., 1961—86, tech. dir. emeritus, 1986—. Cons. Nat. Def. Indsl. Assoc., 1955—60; cons., satellite detection Naval Space Surveillance Sys., Dahlgren, Va., 1986—88; del., Tripartite Conf. on armaments U.S. Army, Quebec, Canada, 1959; del., Tripartite Conf. on artificial Earth satellites U.S. Navy, 1971. Author: (poem) John Adams' Reward, 2002. Chmn., Cub Scout Com. Boy Scouts of Am., Dahlgren, Va., 1971—86. Decorated Group Achievement Dept. of the Navy; recipient Tech. Dir. emeritus, Naval Space Surveillance Sys. Mem.: ASME (life), AIAA (sr.), Am Inst. for Aeronautics and Astron. (Dir. 1960—62), Am. Rocket Soc., MD Sect. (Pres. 1959), Com. on Guidance for MD, Am. Math. Soc. (hon.), Res. Officers Assoc. (life), Nat. Def. Indus. Assoc. (life), Am. Assoc. for the Advancement of Sci. (life). Democrat. Roman Catholic. Achievements include development of rocket weapons; oversaw advances in the understanding of rockets as artillery weapons. Avocations: singing, languages, acting, poetry, pen and ink drawing. Home: 311 Ingleside Drive, Fredericksburg VA 22405-2344

HASHIMOTO, KEN, dermatologist, educator; b. Niigata City, Japan, June 19, 1931; came to U.S., 1956; m. Noriko Sakai, Oct. 3, 1961; children: Naomi, Martha, Eugene, Amy. MD, Niigata U., 1955. Cert. Am. Bd. Dermatology, 1968, Dermatopathology, 1972. Asst. prof. dermatology Tufts U. Sch. Medicine, Boston, 1965-68; assoc. prof. medicine, anatomy U. Tenn., Memphis, 1968-70, prof. medicine, assoc. prof. anatomy, 1970-77, dir., dermatopathology, prof., 1975-77; prof., dir. dermatology, prof. anatomy Wright State U., Dayton, Ohio, 1977-80; chief, dermatology sect., dir. elec. microscopy lab. VA Med. Ctr., Dayton, 1977-80; dermatologist in chief Detroit Med. Ctr., 1987—; prof., chmn. dermatology Wayne State U., Detroit, 1980-99, prof. emeritus, 1999—. Mem. dermatol. drugs adv. com. FDA. Fulbright scholar, 1956-59; participant med. investigatorship career devel. program VA, 1969-77. Mem. Am. Soc. Dermatopathology (pres. 1986-87), Nat. Bd. Med. Examiners, Japanese Soc. Investigative Dermatology (hon.), Memphis Dermatological Soc. (pres. 1973-74), Soc. Investigative Dermatology (v.p. 1980-81, chmn. program com. 1985-86), Soc. Francaise de Dermatologie et de Syphilographie (corr. 1989), Japanese Assn. Dermatology (hon.). Office: Wayne State U Sch Medicine Dept Dermatology 540 E Canfield St Detroit MI 48201-1928

HASHIMOTO, TADAO, engineering company executive; b. Toyonaka, Osaka, Japan, Nov. 7, 1968; B Engring. in Elec. Engring., Kyoto U., Japan, 1991, M Engring. in Elec. Engring., 1993; PhD in Materials, U. Calif., Santa Barbara, 2005. Engr. Matsushita Electronic Corp., Takatsuki, Osaka, Japan, 1993—99; rschr. U. Calif., Santa Barbara, 2001—; pres. SixPoint Materials, Inc., 2006—. Contbr. articles to profl. jours. Achievements include 15 patents in compound semiconductor research; research and development of the ammonothermal growth of gallium nitride. Office: SixPoint Materials Inc 37 Industrial Way Unit 106 Buellton CA 93427 Office Phone: 805-686-3900. Business E-Mail: tadao@azurescript.com.

HASHMI, SAJJAD AHMAD, finance educator, dean; b. India, Dec. 20, 1933; m. Monica Ruggiero; children: Serena, Jason, Shawn, Michelle. BA, U. Karachi, 1953, MA, 1956; PhD in Ins., U. Pa., 1962. Lectr. Ohio State U., Columbus, 1962-64; asst. prof. Roosevelt U., Chgo., 1964-66; prof. Ball State U., Muncie, Ind., 1966-83, chmn. dept. fin., 1973-83; Jones disting. prof., dean emeritus Sch. Bus. Emporia (Kans.) State U., 1983—. Tech. advisor Ind. Arts Commn.; vice chmn. bd. trustees Kans. Ins. Edn. Found.; appeared on TV and radio programs, testified before NY, Kans. and Ind. legis. coms.; cons., spkr. in field. Author: Insurance is a Funny Business, 1972, Automobile Insurance, 1973, Contemporary Personal Finance, 1985, Make Every Second Count, 1989, Strategies for The Future, 1990; contbr. articles to profl. jours. Named Prof. of Yr., Ball State U. Students, 1971, Outstanding Tchr. of Yr., Ball State U., 1970. Mem. Am. Risk and Ins. Assn., Midwest Fin. Assn., Fin. Mgmt. Assn., Emporia C. of C., Emporia Country Club, Rotary, Beta Gamma Sigma, Sigma Iota Epsilon, Alpha Kappa Psi, Gamma Iota Epsilon, Phi Kappa Phi. Home: 7187 Boca Grove Pl # 204 Bradenton FL 34202 Personal E-mail: shashmi1@tampabay.rr.com.

HASIJA, SAMEER, finance educator, consultant; B in Tech., Indian Inst. Tech., Madras, India, 2002; MS, U. Rochester, NY, 2007, student, 2002—. Engring. intern Cochin Shipyard Ltd. India, 1998; mgmt. intern We. India Shipyard, Vasco, India, 2001; instr. MBA lab. U. Rochester, 2004—, course instr., 2007—; mgmt. intern Sutherland Global Svcs., Rochester, 2005. Vis. rsch. specialist Tuck sch. bus. Dartmouth Coll., Hanover, NH, 2006; cons. in field. Contbr. articles to profl. jours. Fellow, U. Rochester, 2002—06. Mem.: Informs. Achievements include design of high speed motor launch. Office Phone: 585-273-4827.

HASKAYNE, RICHARD FRANCIS, retired petroleum company executive; b. Calgary, Alta., Can., Dec. 18, 1934; s. Robert Stanley and Bertha (Hesketh) H.; m. Lee Mary Murray, 1958 (dec. 1993); m. Lois P. Heard, 1995. B Comm., U. Alta., 1956; postgrad., U. We. Ont., 1968, LLD, U. Calgary, U. Alta. Chartered acct., Alta. With Riddell, Stead & Co., chartered accts., Calgary, 1956—60; corp. acctg. supr. to v.p. fin. Hudson's

Bay Oil & Gas Co., Ltd., Calgary, 1960—73; comptr. Can. Arctic Gas Study Ltd., 1973—75; sr. v.p. to pres. Hudson's Bay Oil & Gas Co. Ltd., Calgary, 1975—81; pres., CEO Home Oil Co., Ltd., Calgary, 1981—91; chmn. bd. NOVA Corp., Calgary, 1992—98; ret., 1998. Pres., CEO Interprovencial Pipe Line Co., 1987—91, Interhome Energy, 1989—91; bd. dirs. Fording Inc., chmn. bd., 2001—03; past chmn. bd. dirs. TransCanada Corp., 1998—2005; chmn. bd. TransAlta Corp., 1998—2005, TransCan Corp., 1998—2005, MacMillan Bloedel Ltd., 1996—99; dir. emeritus CIBC. Chmn. emeritus bd. govs. U. Calgary. Recipient award Officer Order of Can., 1997, Woodrow Wilson Corp. Citizenship award; named to Can. Bus. Hall of Fame, Calgary Bus. Hall of Fame, Petroleum Hall of Fame Fellow Fin. Execs. Inst., Inst. Corp. Dirs.; mem. Calgary Petroleum Club (past pres.), Calgary Golf and Country Club, Earl Grey Golf Club, Ranchmen's Club, U. Calgary Chancellor's Club, The York Club, Libr. Club, Commerce Club, Alta Inst. Chartered Accts., Kappa Sigma Office: 3845 Bankers Hall 855 2d St SW Calgary AB Canada T2P 4J8 Office Phone: 403-265-5931.

HASKELL, ANNE, secondary school educator; b. Emporia, Kans., Sept. 24, 1949; d. Mary Haskell-Hansen and Bill Hansen (Stepfather); m. Fred Brockman, June 28, 1997; children: Jamál Currie, Táhirih Currie. BS, U. Wis., Menomonie, 1976, MS, 1977. Tchr. Sch. Dist. Palm Beach County, West Palm Beach, Fla., 1981—. Home visitor Cmtys. in Schs. Palm Beach County, Fla., 1987—2001. Coach state champion black history brain bowl team Glades Ctrl. Cmty. HS, Belle Glade, Fla. Named Tchr. of Yr., Cmtys. in Schs. Fla., 1998, Vol. of Yr., Children's Home Soc. Palm Beach County, 1998, Tchr. of Yr. Fla. Region, Juvenile Justice Edn. Inst., 2005; recipient Spl. Recognition award, Urban League Palm Beach County, 1998, I Make A Difference award, The Palm Beach Post, 2000, Spl. Recognition award, Belle Glade, Fla. C. of C., 2004. Mem.: NAACP (life; mem. exec. com. 2000—07, Diversity award Glades Area br. 2003, Humanitarian award 2004), Fla. Coun. Social Studies (named Palm Beach County Social Studies Tchr. of Yr. 1992, 2005), Nat. Coun. Social Studies. Bahá'I.

HASKELL, ARTHUR JACOB, retired water transportation executive; b. Newark, Apr. 16, 1926; s. Isidore David and Elena (Greenbaum) H.; m. Amparo Serrano, Dec. 31, 1958 (div.); children: Amparo Rocio, Vincent Isidore, Joaquin Arthur; m. Marge Gibson, June 8, 1986. BS, U.S. Naval Acad., 1947; profl. naval engr., MIT, 1953. Sr. procurement engr. Nat. Bulk Carriers, NYC, 1956-62; asst. plant mgr. Western Gear Corp., Belmont, Calif., 1962-64; project engr. Matson Nav. Co., San Francisco., 1964-70, v.p., 1970-73, sr. v.p., 1973-91, ret., 1991. Mem. marine bd. NRC, 1981-85; bd. mgrs. Am. Bur. Shipping, 1988-92; bd. dirs., budget officer Nat. Liberty Ship Meml. Bd. dirs. San Francisco Marine Exchange, 1975-78, v.p., 1976-77, pres., 1977-78. Served to comd. USN, 1947-56. Mem. Soc. Naval Architects and Marine Engrs. (chmn. No. Calif. sect. 1971-72, v.p. 1973-83, exec. com. 1977-80, 83-96, hon. v.p. for life 1983—, pres. 1989-91), Assn. for Preservation of Presdl. Yacht Potomac (bd. govs. 1984—, co-pres. 1993-99). Home: 287 Sheridan Rd Oakland CA 94618-2717 Personal E-mail: arthur.haskell@alum.mit.edu.

HASKELL, BARBARA, curator; b. San Diego, Nov. 13, 1946; d. John N. and Barbara (Freeman) H.; m. Leon Botstein; children: Clara Haskell Botstein, Maxim Haskell Botstein. BA, UCLA, 1969. Asst. registrar Pasadena (Calif.) Art Mus., 1969, curatorial asst., 1970, asst. curator, 1970, assoc. curator, 1970-72, curator painting and sculpture, 1972-74, Whitney Mus. Am. Art, NYC, 1975—. Author: Arthur Dove, 1974, Marsden Hartley, 1980, Milton Avery, 1982, Blam! The Explosion of Pop, Minimalism and Performance 1958-64, 1984, Georgia O'Keefe: Works on Paper, 1985, Ralston Crawford, 1985, Charles Demuth, 1987, Red Grooms, 1987, Donald Judd, 1988, Burgoyne Diller, 1990, Agnes Martin, 1992, Joseph Stella, 1994, The Am. Century: Art and Culture 1900-1950, 1999, Edward Steichen, 2000, Elie Nadelman, 2002, Oscar Bluemner, A Passion for Color, 2005. Recipient award for scholarly excellence in field of Am. art history Archives of Am. Art, 2003; named Woman of Yr., Mademoiselle mag., 1973. Office: Whitney Mus Am Art 945 Madison Ave New York NY 10021-2701 Home Phone: 212-925-2454; Office Phone: 212-570-3606. Business E-Mail: barbara_haskell@whitney.org.

HASKELL, BARRY GEOFFRY, computer engineer, researcher; b. Lewiston, Maine, 1941; s. George Raymond and Dorothy H.; m. Ann Kantrow, Sept. 13, 1964; children: Paul Eric, Andrew. AA, Pasadena City Coll., 1962; BSEE, U. Calif., Berkeley, 1964, MSEE, 1965, PhD, 1968. Electronics engr. Lawrence Livermore Lab., Calif., 1965; rsch. asst. Electronics Rsch. Lab. U. Calif., Berkeley, 1965-68; mem. tech. staff AT&T Bell Labs., Holmdel, NJ, 1968-76, head radio comm. rsch. dept., 1976-83, visual comm. cons., 1984-86, head visual comm. rsch. dept., 1987-95; head image processing rsch. dept. AT&T Labs., Middletown, NJ, 1996-99; sr. scientist Apple Computer, Inc., Cupertino, Calif., 2002—. Adj. prof. Rutgers U., New Brunswick, NJ, 1976-79, CCNY, 1983-84, Columbia U., NYC, 1987, 93; negotiator Internat. Stds. Orgn., Am. Nat. Stds. Inst., Internat. Telecom. Union - Telecom Sector. Co-author: Image Transmission Tech., 1979, Digital Pictures, 1988, 2d edit., 1995, Digital Video—An Introduction to MPEG-2, 1996; contbr. articles to profl. jours.; patentee in field. Recipient Elec. Engring. Dept. Outstanding Alumnus award U. Calif., Berkeley, 1998; co-recipient Japan's Computer and Comm. prize, 1997, NJ Inventor Hall of Fame Inventor of Yr., 2000; AT&T fellow, 1998; picture coding symposium award for leadership, pioneering rsch., 2006. Fellow: IEEE (life), Phi Beta Kappa. Avocations: sailing, skiing, guitar playing. Office: Apple Computer 302-3KS 2 Infinite Loop Cupertino CA 95014

HASKELL, DONALD MCMILLAN, lawyer; b. Toledo, July 2, 1932; s. Irwin Wales and Grace (Lee) H.; m. Carol Jean Ross, June 19, 1954; children: Deborah Lee, Catherine Jean, David Ross. BA, Coll. of Wooster, 1954; JD, U. Mich., 1957. Bar: Ill. 1957, U.S. Dist. Ct. (no. dist.) Ill. 1958, U.S. Ct. Appeals (7th cir.) 1960, U.S. Supreme Ct. 1963, U.S. Ct. Appeals (10th cir.) 1974, Oreg. 1990. Ptnr. McKenna, Storer, Rowe, White & Haskell and predecessors, Chgo., 1957-75; sr. ptnr. Haskell & Perrin, Chgo., 1975-89, of counsel, 1989-2000. Commr. Clatsop County, Oreg., 1991-94; bd. dirs. N.W. Oreg. Econ. Alliance, 1993-98; bd. dirs. Oreg. Bd. Bar Examiners, 1991-94, chmn. 1993-94. Trustee Columbia River Maritime Mus., 1991—; chmn. Clatsop County Rep. Com., 1994-95; mem. Astoria Planning Commn., 1999-2002, chmn., 2001-02. Fellow Am. Bar Found., Ill. Bar Found.; mem. ABA (ho. of dels. 1982-92, bd. govs. 1987-90), Lawyers Club Chgo., Astoria Country Club. Lutheran. Home: 600 W Lexington Ave Astoria OR 97103-5726

HASKELL, JOHN HENRY FARRELL, JR., investment company executive; b. NYC, Jan. 24, 1932; s. John Henry Farrell and Paulette (Heger) H.; m. Francine G. Le Roux, June 30, 1955; children: Michael J., Christopher E., Diana F. T. BS, U.S. Mil. Acad., 1953; MBA with distinction, Harvard U., 1958. Assoc. Dillon, Read & Co., NYC, 1958-61, mgr. European office Paris, 1961-66; v.p Dillon, Read & Co. (now UBS Securities, LLC), NYC, 1964-75, mng. dir., 1975-99, sr. advisor, 2000—04. Pres., CEO The France Fund, Inc., 1986—89; bd. dirs. Pall Corp.; mem. adv. coun. Overseas Pvt. Investment Corp., 1972—75. Bd. dirs. Belgian-Am. Ednl. Found.; co-chmn. bd. trustees French Inst./Alliance Francaise; mem. adv. coun. Lycee Francais de N.Y.; bd. trustees St. Paul's Sch., Concord, N.H. Decorated Legion of Honor, Ordre National du Merite France; recipient Presdl. Recognition award For Cmty. Svc., 1986. Mem. Coun. Fgn. Rels., Assn. Grads. of U.S. Mil. Acad. (trustee 1984-87), Am. Soc. French Legion of Honor (bd. dirs., v.p.), Links Club, Univ. Club, Meadow Brook Club (Jericho, N.Y.), Bohemian Club (San Francisco), Eagle Springs Golf Club (Wolcott, Colo.). Home: 120 East End Ave New York NY 10028-7552 Office: 535 Madison Ave 4th Fl New York NY 10022 Office Phone: 212-906-7810. Business E-Mail: jhaskell05@yahoo.com.

HASKELL, PETER ABRAHAM, actor, director; b. Boston, Oct. 15, 1934; s. Norman Abraham and Rose Veronica (Golden) H.; m. Ann Compton, Feb. 27, 1960 (div. 1974); m. Dianne Tolmich, Oct. 26, 1974; children: Audra Rosemary, Jason Abraham. BA, Harvard U., 1962; student, N.Y. Law Sch., 1982-83. Actor (plays) The Love Nest, 1963, The Seagull, 1979, A Rich Full Life, 1985, Jenny, 2002, One Step Over, 2006, A Couple of Horses Asses, 2006, Leash on Life, 2006, (films) Finnegans Wake, 1965, Legend of Earl Durand, 1972, Christina, 1974, Forty Days of Musa Dagh, 1982, Riding the Edge, 1987, Child's Play II, 1990, Child's Play III, 1991, Robot Wars, 1993; (TV series) Bracken's World, NBC, 1969-71, Rich Man Poor Man, Book II, ABC, 1976-77, Ryan's Hope, ABC, 1982-83, Search for Tomorrow, NBC, 1983-85, Rituals, Metromedia, 1985, The Law and Harry McGraw, CBS, 1987-88; (TV films) Love, Hate, Love, 1970, The Eyes of Charles Sand, 1972, Mandrake, 1977, The Cracker Factory, 1979, Christine Cromwell, 1990, Columbo, 1991, Maid for Each Other, 1992, Faces of Deception, 1993, Never Talk to Strangers, 1997; dir. (plays) Nightgames, 2000, Mrs. Warren's Profession, 2004, What are Friends For, 2006, The Wedding Night, 2006, Mark on Society, 2007. Active duty 11th and 101st Airborne Divsn. US Army, 1954—56, with USAR, 1956—62. Mem. SAG, AFTRA, Actors Equity. Democrat. Avocations: photography, skiing. Office: Upward Mobility 19924 Acre St Northridge CA 91324-3201 Home Phone: 818-998-7493; Office Phone: 818-772-1137. Personal E-mail: peterahaskell@sbcglobal.net.

HASKELL, WYATT RUSHTON, lawyer; b. Birmingham, Ala., May 15, 1940; s. Preston Hampton and Mary Wyatt (Rushton) H.; m. Susan Porter Nabers, June 1, 1968; children: John Howze, Henry Devereux, Samuel Drayton. AB, Amherst Coll., 1961; LLB, Yale U., 1965. Bar: Ala. 1965. Assoc. Bradley, Arant, Rose & White, Birmingham, 1966-71; staff atty. So. Natural Gas Co., Birmingham, 1971-73; ptnr. Haskell, Slaughter, Young & Rediker, LLC, Birmingham, 1973—. Vis. rsch. asst. U. Muenster, Germany, 1965—66; vis. prof. U. Ala. Law Sch., 1970—73. Contbr. articles to profl. jours. Bd. dirs. Ala. Shakespeare Fest, Montgomery, Folger Shakespeare Libr., Washington, Birmingham Mus. Art, Ala. Symphony Assn., Alys Stephens Ctr.; chmn. State of Ala. Ballet, 1992—2000. Thomas Pope fellow Trinity Coll., Oxford; named to Assn. Fundraising Profls., Birmingham, 2005, Outstanding Philanthropist, Birmingham, 2005. Mem. ABA, Ala. Bar Assn., Birmingham Bar Assn., Mountain Brook Club. Presbyterian. Home: 2964 Cherokee Rd Birmingham AL 35223-2609 Office: Haskell Slaughter et al 1400 Park Place Tower 2001 Park Place North Birmingham AL 35203 Office Phone: 205-254-1415. Business E-Mail: wrh@hsy.com.

HASKETT, DIANNE LOUISE, retired mayor, lawyer, consultant; b. London, Ont., Can., Mar. 4, 1955; d. Allan Douglas and Frances Shirley (Crone) Haskett; m. Jack Kotowicz; 1 child, Annie Kotowicz. BA, U. Waterloo, Ont., 1974; LLB, U. Western Ont., 1977; LLM, London Sch. Econs., 1979, George Washington U., 2005. Bar: DC 2005. Lawyer Law Soc. Upper Can., Ont., 1980—; founding ptnr. Haskett, Menear Assoc., Law Firm, 1980—94; speechwriter, internat. cons., and pub. rels. advisor Washington Contact, 2001—; estate and bus. coord. Living Trust Atty. Ltd., Fairfax, Va.; Senate and Congl. campaign advisor. V.p. London Urban Alliance Race Rels.; pres., editor-in-chief Believe Books, Washington. Contbr. articles to profl. jours. Founder Open Homes Can., London, 1992; founding mem. London Citizens Com., 1980—84; v.p. Ark Aid St. Mission Inc., London, 1986—88; city councillor London City Coun., 1991—94; mayor City of London, 1994—2000. Recipient Pericles award, Am. Hellenic Ednl. Prog. Assn., 1999; Grad. scholar, Rotary Internat., 1978—79, Paul Harris fellow, Rotary Club London, 1998. Mem.: Law Soc. Upper Can. Avocations: journalism, speech making. Home: 2970 Kildare Ln Fairfax VA 22031

HASKIN, J. MICHAEL, lawyer; b. Kansas City, Mo., Sept. 25, 1949; s. Harley V. and Geraldine E. (Porterfield) H.; m. Pamela J. Lutz, May 22, 1999. BA, Baker U., 1971; JD, U. Mo., 1976. Bar: Kans. 1976, Mo. 1987, U.S. Fed. Tax Ct., U.S. Supreme Ct. Ptnr., atty. Haskin, Hinkle, Slater & Snowbarger, Olathe, Kans., 1976-83, Dietrich, Davis, Dicus, Rowlands, Schmitt & Gorman, Kansas City, Mo., 1984-88; pres., atty. J. Michael Haskin, PA, Olathe, 1989—. Bd. dirs., exec. com., The Assn. K-10 Corridor Devel., Inc., Lawrence, 1993-95. City councilman-at-large City of Olathe, 1989-93, mayor, 1993-95; mem., vice chmn., chmn. Stormwater Mgmt. Adv. Coun., Johnson County, Kans., 1989-95, Olthe Sesquicentennial Com., 2005-; bd. dirs. Olathe Pub. Libr., 1989-90, 93-95; bd. dirs. Hidden Glen Arts Festival, vice chmn., chmn., 1990—); mem. Mid-Am. Regional Coun. Perimeter Transp. Com., 1995—. Recipient Boss of Yr. award Johnson County Legal Secs. Assn., 1991-92, Cmty. Leadership award Olathe Area C. of C., 1992. Mem. Kans. Bar Assn., Mo. Bar Assn., Olathe Rotary Club (bd. dirs., pres. 1981—, Paul Harris award 1992, Olathe Rotarian of Yr. 1995), Olathe Arts Alliance (pres. 1988), Kaw Valley Philological Soc. Republican. Methodist. Avocations: golf, sailing. Office: PO Box 413 100 E Park St Ste 203 Olathe KS 66061-3463 Office Phone: 913-782-0706. E-mail: haskinlawoffice@aol.com.

HASKINS, DEBRA MAY, academic administrator, educator; d. John Albert and Norma W. Haskins; m. Lee Mead; children: Julia, Kerry, Donna, Gavin, Jacqueline. BA, SUC Cortland, NY, 1975; MA, SUNY, Stony Brook, 1991; student, Coll. New Rochelle, NY, 1992—94, St. John's U., Jamaica, NY, 1995—2005. Cert. social studies educator, grades 7-12, sch. dist. adminstr. Pub. rels. position Taylor Wine Co., Hammondsport, NY, 1973—75; realtor Carriage Home Realty, Smithtown, NY, 1979—81; social studies tchr. Baldwinsville Acad., NY, 1975—79, Sachem Schs., Holbrook, NY, 1983—84, Huntington Unified Sch. Dist., NY, 1981—83, 1984—98, chairperson social studies, 1998—. Exec. bd. tchr. ctr. Huntington Tchr. Ctr., 1999—; exec. bd. mem. Long Island Coun. Social Studies, NY, 2001—03. Women's advocate Chosin Few, LI, 1996—2003. Mentoring Grant for Tchrs., Huntington, NY, 1999—2002, Art and Architecture grant, NEA, 2002—04, Taft scholar, Freedoms Found. Mem.: ASCD, Nat. Coun. Social Studies. Independent. Avocations: painting, writing, reading, travel, dream interpretation. Home: 96 Summit Dr Smithtown NY 11787 Personal E-mail: debhaskins@aol.com.

HASKINS, JAMES P., finance educator, consultant; b. Estevan, Saskatchewan, Canada, Apr. 6, 1951; arrived in U.S., 1952; s. Kenneth R. and O. Dee (Christopherson) Haskins; m. Nancy A. Walker, July 13, 1974; 1 child, Jason P. BS in Agrl. Econs., ND State U., Fargo, 1974, MS in Agrl. Econs., 1978; PhD in Econs., Colo. State U., Ft. Collins, 1991. Cert. in risk mgmt. 2006. Asst. prof. fin. U. No. Colo., Greeley, 1987—93; asst. prof. Colo. State U., Ft. Collins, 1993—95; pres. and prin. investigator Haskins Enterprises, Ft. Collins, 1993—95; controller, property mgr. Albrecht Cos. Inc., Ft. Collins, 1995—98; adj. prof. bus. Embry-Riddle Aeronautical U., various locations, 1998—2004; asst. prof. fin. Minot State U., ND, 1998—99, U. N.D., Grand Forks, 1999—. Trustee, officer, acctg. and bus. advisor, bus. practices coord. B.P.O.E. #804 and Colo. and Nat. Lodges B.P.O.E., Ft. Collins, 1994—99. Author: (articles) Jour. Applied Bus. and Econs, Jour. Fin. Svc. Profls. Chmn. bds., leadership positions many not-for-profit orgns., Colo., ND, 1968—; academic advisor Mortor Bd., Inc. (Nat. Sr. Honor Soc.), Grand Forks, 2002—06; coun. advisor Order of DeMolay, Ft. Collins, Colo., 1994—96; trustee, officer, acctg. & bus. advisor BPOE, Ft. Collins, 1994—99; bd. dirs. No. Tier Fed. Credit Union, Minot, 1999—2000. Recipient Meml. Union award for Outstanding Student Orgn. Advisor, U. N.D., 2003, Excellence in Advisory award, Mortar Bd., Inc., 2004, numerous awards and grants, various orgns. and locations, 1973—. Mem.: Am. Acctg. Assn., Ops. Mgmt. and Entrepreneurship Assn., N.Am. Acctg. Soc., Acad. Fin. Svcs., Assn. Fin. Profls., Fin. Mgmt. Assn., Nat. Bus. and Econs. Soc., Acad. Fin. (sec., program chair 2004—), Knights Templar of York Rite, Scottish Rite of Freemasonry, El Jebel Shriners, numerous collegiate nat. hon. socs. in agr., econs., bus., mgmt. and acctg. Avocations: golf, research. Home: 1410 S 40th St Grand Forks ND 58201 Office: Univ ND Dept Finance Gamble Hall Rm 310F 293 Centennial Dr Stop 7096 Grand Forks ND 58202 Business E-Mail: jim.haskins@mail.business.und.edu.

HASKO, JUDITH ANN, lawyer; b. Waterbury, Conn., Feb. 11, 1964; BA, Vassar Coll., 1986; MPhil, U. Sussex, Brighton, Eng., 1988; JD, U. Wis., 1994. Bar: Wis. 1995, Calif. 1995, US Patent and Trademark Office 1998. Rsch. assoc. Genentech Inc., South San Francisco, Calif., 1988-92; ptnr. Cooley Godward, Palo Alto, Calif., 1994—2006, Latham & Watkins, Menlo Park, Calif., 2006—. Articles editor Wis. Law Rev., 1993-94. Mem.: ABA. Office Phone: 650-463-3065. Business E-Mail: judith.hasko@lw.com.

HASKVITZ, ALAN PAUL, elementary school educator, consultant; b. Mpls., Sept. 7, 1942; s. Harry and Rose (Portugal) H.; married, Apr. 1, 1970; children: Anna, Maxwell Harry. AA, Chaffey Coll., 1963; MS, Calif. State U., LA, 1965, MA, 1970; BE, Meml. U., St. John's, Newfoundland, 1972. Cert. secondary tchr., adminstr., Calif.; cert. tchr., Ont., Newfoundland, N.Y.; cert. cmty. coll. instr., Calif.; cert. audio-visual. Tchr. Cornwall Sch. Bd., Ont., Canada, 1970-78, Corono Sch. Sys., Calif., 1980-81, Walnut Sch. Dist., 1987—; vice prin. Quest School for the Gifted, Oshawa, Ont., 1978-80; cons. Edn. Strategies, Alta Loma, Calif., 1981—. Pres.-elect Nat. Coun. for the Social Scis.; mem. Nat. Critical Thinking Com., Coun. of Chief State Sch. Officers, Nat. Assessment of Ednl. Progress, Nat. Responder Com. on Tchrs. and Schs., Constl. Rights Found., Western States Accreditation Commn., Cal Poly Master Tchr. Com. on Student Tng. Programs; evaluator imagination in edn. Nat. Coun. for Accreditation of Tchr. Edn.; spkr. in field; lectr. in field; US rep Internation Jr. Global Tech. Competition, Rome, 2007. Author: Motorvation: Math for the Difficult to Motivate, 2007, Resources for Social Studies Educators; syndicated automobile journalist: The Car Family, features in: Futures videos, Project citizen video, Time, Newsweek, CNN, ABC, CBS, NBC, NPR, numerous textbooks; contbr. columns to websites, numerous articles to profl. jours. Commr. City of Rancho Cucamonga, 1986—; pres. United Counties Sports, Cornwall, 1980-84; bd. advisors Americans All. Named USA Today All Am. Educator, 2000; named one of 100 Most Influential Educators in Am.; named to Nat. Tchrs. Hall of Fame, 1997; recipient Golden Bell award, Calif. Sch. Bd. Assn., 1987, 1997, 2007, Presdl. award for environ. edn., 1988, Calif. Dept. Water Agencies, Cmty. award, Walnut Valley Water Dist., 1989, Am.'s Profl. Best Tchr. award, Learning mag., 1989, Nat. Coun. for Social Studies, 1992, George Washington medal, Freedom Found., 1992, Nat. Bicentennial Tchg. award, Bicentennial Com., 1993, Outstanding Citizen award, LA County Supr., 1994, Nation's Best Program, 1994, Calif. Agr. in Classroom award, 1995, Agr. Tchr. of Yr., Nat. Coun. for Social Studies, 1995, Calif. Water Environ. Edn. award, Calif., 1995, Christa McAuliffe award, 1996, Busch Environ. award, 1996, Nation's Outstanding Mid. Sch. Tchr., 1996, Spirit of Edn. award, NBC, 1997, Crystal Apple award, 1998, Robert Cherry Internat. Tchr. of Yr., 1997, Leavey award for pvt. enterprise edn., 1998, Daus. of Am. Colonies, 1999, Heroes in Edn. award, Reader's Digest, Outstanding Tchr. award, Baylor U., Top Ten Tchrs. in Am. award, Campbell's, Disney Regional Winner, Nat. Garden award, George Washington award, Freedom Found., Agy. for Water Edn., Calif. History Tchrs. of Yr., numerous awards for sch. programs. Achievements include development of Reach Every Child. Home: 9655 Carrari Ct Alta Loma CA 91737-1653 E-mail: freealan@yahoo.com.

HASL, RUDOLPH CARL, dean, law educator; b. Aug. 30, 1942; BA, Xavier U., 1964; JD, St. Louis U., 1967; LLM, NYU, 1973. Bar: Ill. 1967. Law clk. 5th Dist. Appellate Ct., Ill., 1966—67, Ill., 1971; teaching fellow NYU, 1967—68; asst. prof. St. Louis U., 1971—73, assoc. prof., 1973—77, asst. dean Sch. Law, 1973—76, acting dean, 1976, prof., 1977—91, assoc. dean, 1976—78, dean, 1979—91; prof. St. John's U. Sch. Law, 1991—2000, dean, 1991—98, Seattle U. Sch. Law, 2000—05. Co-author: Missouri Law of Evidence, 1984; author: The Internationalization of Law Practice: Issues of Access and Education, 1994. Capt. US Army, 1968—71. Mem.: ABA, Alpha Sigma Nu. Home: 100 Harbor Dr # 5 San Diego CA 92101-6844 E-mail: hasl@seattleu.edu.

HASLAG, KAREN CHRISTINE, art educator, musician; b. Jefferson City, Mo., Aug. 27, 1948; d. Leonard Frank and Alice Christine Kliethermes Haslag; m. Roger William Hurlbert, Nov. 6, 1982. BA, Benedictine Coll., 1970; MA, San Francisco State U., 1981. Cert. music edn. tchr. Lincoln U., 1972, edn. tchr San Francisco State U., 1985. Tchr. St. Stanislaus Sch., Wardsville, Mo., 1970—72, St. Charles, San Francisco, 1973—78, Our Lady of Mercy Sch., Daly City, Calif., 1978—86, 1989—96, St. James Sch., San Francisco, 1987—89; music dir., organist Trinity Episcopal Ch., Sonoma, Calif., 1998—99, Our Lady of Mercy Ch., Daly City, Calif., 1994—97, St. Elizabeth Roman Cath. Ch., San Francisco, 1999—2004; music tchr., band dir. Sonoma Charter Sch., 2004—05, Kenwood Elem. Sch., 2006—. Treas. Friends of Calligraphy, San Francisco, 1984—86, vol. coord., 1986—87. Grantee, Nat. Endowment for Humanities, 1986—87, Nat. Cath. Educators Assn., 1992. Mem.: Nat. Pastoral Musicians, Choristers Guild, Am. Guild Organists (bd. dirs. 1999—2002, hospitality chair 2000—03, Dean's award 2003). Office: 190 Bonnie Way Glen Ellen CA 95442

HASLAM, DENNIS V., professional sports team executive, lawyer; b. Salt Lake City, Sept. 19, 1948; m. Deborah Haslam; children: Peter, Carter, Madeleine. BA magna cum laude in Hist., U. Utah, 1973, JD, 1976. Bar: Utah 1976, US Ct. Appeals (10th cir.) 1984, US Supreme Ct. 1985. Co-founder Winder & Haslam, 1983—97, of counsel Salt Lake City; pres., COO sports and entertainment divsn. Larry Miller Group, 1997—; pres. Utah Jazz, Salt Lake City, 2000—. Adj. prof. U. Utah Coll. Law, 1994—96; chair Access to Justice Found. Active Utah Jud. Coun., Utah Sports Authority, 2002 Winter Olympics venues. Mem. Utah State Bar (chmn. character and fitness com. 1981-90, mem. ethics and discipline screening panel 1987-90, mem. admission rules com. 1989, bd. commrs. 1990-95, pres. 1995-96), Utah Bar Found. Office: Utah Jazz 301 W South Temple Salt Lake City UT 84101-1216*

HASLAM, GERALD WILLIAM, writer, educator; b. Bakersfield, Calif., Mar. 18, 1937; s. Fredrick Martin and Lorraine Hope (Johnson) H.; m. Janice Eileen Pettichord, July 1, 1961; children: Frederick W., Alexandra R., Garth C., Simone B., Carlos V. BA, San Francisco State U., 1963, MA, 1965; PhD, Union Grad. Sch., 1980. Instr. English San Francisco State U., San Francisco, 1966-67; asst. prof. English Sonoma State U., Rohnert Park, Calif., 1967-70, assoc. prof. English, 1970-74, prof. English, 1971-97, emeritus prof. English, 1997—; prof. Fromm Inst./U. San Francisco, 2001—. Adj. prof. Union Grad. Sch., Cin., 1984—, The Nat. Faculty, Atlanta, 1984—; prof. Oscher Lifelong Learning Inst., Sonoma State U., 2003—. Editor various anthologies; author various booklets, monographs, film scripts, (fiction) Okies: Selected Stories, 1973, Masks: A Novel, 1976, The Wages of Sin: Collected Stories, 1980, Hawk Flights: Visions of the West, 1983, Snapshots: Glimpses of the Other California, 1985, The Man Who Cultivated Fire and Other Stories, 1987, That Constant Coyote: California Stories, 1990, Condor Dreams and Other Fictions, 1994, The Great Tejon Club Jubilee, 1996, Manuel and the Madman, 1999, Straight White Male, 2000, Haslam's Valley, 2005, (fiction/non-fiction) Voices of a

Place, 1987, Coming of Age in California, 1990, The Other California, 1990, The Great Central Valley: California's Heartland, 1993, Workin' Man Blues: Country Music in California, 1999, Coming of Age in California, 2d enlarged edit., 2000, Grace Period, 2006; contbg. writer West (LA Times' mag.). With U.S. Army, 1958-60. Creative Writing fellow Calif. Arts Coun., 1989; recipient Benjamin Franklin award, 1993, Bay Area Book Reviewers' Non-fiction award, 1994, Commonwealth Club medal for Calif., 1994, Merit award Assn. State & Local History, 1994, Commendation citation, 2001; Fulbright sr. lectr., 1986-87, Josephine Miles award, 1990, Ralph J. Gleason award, 2000, Carey McWilliams award, 2001, Western States Book Fiction award, 2001, Sequoia - Giant of the Valley award, 2003, Cert. of Commendation, Calif. Arts Coun., 2004, Delbert and Edith Wyler award, 2005, Josephine Miles award, 2006. Mem. Great Valley Ctr. (adv. bd.), Western Lit. Assn. (bd. dirs., past pres., Disting. Achievment award 1999, Delbert and Edith Wylder award 2005), Calif. Studies Assn. (steering com., founding mem.), Calif. Hist. Assn., Calif. Tchrs. Assn., San Francisco State U. Alumni Assn. (life), Union Inst. Alumni Assn., Multi-Ethnic Lit. of U.S. (founding mem.), Robinson Jeffers Assn. (founding mem.), Sierra Club, The Nature Conservancy, Calif. Trout (founding mem.), Tulare Basin Archeology Group, Defenders of Wildlife, Common Cause, Soc. of the Third Infantry Divsn., Yosemite Assn. (bd. dirs.). Roman Catholic. Avocations: bicycling, hiking, fishing. Office: PO Box 969 Penngrove CA 94951-0969 Office Phone: 707-792-2944. Personal E-mail: ghaslam@sonic.net.

HASLAM, ROBERT THOMAS, III, lawyer; b. Taunton, Mass., May 4, 1946; s. Robert Thomas and Marcella Neale (Compton) H.; children: Laurel Ashley, Julia Compton; m. Molly Haslam. BS Aeronautics and Astronautics, MIT, 1968; JD, Hastings Coll., 1976. Bar: Calif., 1976. Atty., ptnr. Heller, Ehrman, Menlo Park, Calif., 1976—. Capt. USAF 1969-73. Mem. ABA (co-chair litigation, intellectual property sect. 1993—). Avocations: tennis, soccer. Office: Heller Ehrman 275 Middlefield Rd Menlo Park CA 94025-3506 Home: 1410 Enchanted W San Mateo CA 94402 Office Phone: 650-324-7073.

HASLANGER, PHILIP CHARLES, journalist; b. Menominee, Mich., May 11, 1949; s. Harry LeRoy and Agnes Gertrude (Seidl) H.; m. Rosemary Ann Raasch Carta, May 27, 1972 (div.); children: Brian David, Sarah Marie; m. Ellen Jean Reuter, Apr. 9, 1983; children: Michael Kenneth, Julia Jane. BA in Sociology, U. Wis., 1971, MA in Journalism, 1973. With The Capital Times, Madison, Wis., 1973—, mng. editor, 1998—2006, contbg. editor, 2006—. Author: Stories of Call, 1998. Authorized lay pastor United Ch. of Christ, 2004—. Mem. Nat. Conf. Editl. Writers (bd. dirs. 1993, 94, 97, 2003, officer 1999-2002), New Media Fedn. Avocations: reading, music, hiking, theology. Home: 5409 Vicar Ln Madison WI 53714-3443 Office: The Capital Times 1901 Fish Hatchery Rd Madison WI 53713-1248 E-mail: phaslanger@madison.com.

HASLER, WILLIAM ALBERT, electronics executive; b. Los Angeles, Nov. 22, 1941; s. Albert Ernst and LaDella (Stewart) H.; m. Janet Louise Kindstrom, June 10, 1963; children— Claire, Laura, James BA, Pomona Coll., 1963; MBA, Harvard U., 1967. C.P.A., Calif. Ptnr. Peat, Marwick, Mitchell & Co., Los Angeles, 1972-76, ptnr.-in-charge, 1976-81, NYC, 1981-84; vice chmn., dir., mem. operating com. Peat, Marwick, Main & Co., San Francisco and NYC, 1984-91; dean Haas Sch. Bus., U. Calif., Berkeley, 1991-98; co-CEO Aphton Corp., Miami, 1998—2003, vice chmn., 2003; chmn. Solectron, 2003—. Mem. council KPMG Internat., 1985— Mem. editorial adv. bd. Jour. Accountancy Fellow Huntington Library, San Marino, Calif.; treas. Harvard U. Bus. Sch. Alumni Bd.; trustee Pomona Coll.; bd. dirs. Nat. Ctr. Fin. Services; mem. Pacific Basin Econ. Council Mem. Am. Inst. C.P.A.s, Calif. Soc. C.P.A.s, Calif. C. of C. Clubs: Calif. (Los Angeles); Union League (N.Y.C.); University (bd. dirs.); St. Francis Yacht. Avocations: sailing, skiing, diving. Office: Solectron 847 Gibraltar Dr Milpitas CA 95035 also: Aphton Corp 444 Brickell Ave Ste 51-507 Miami FL 33131-2403*

HASLER-REID, LINDA, elementary school educator; b. St. Louis; m. Michael Reid; 4 children. BA in English Edn., summa cum laude, Northeastern State Univ. Cert. in World Lang. Nat. Bd. Tchg. Standards. Tchr. Muskogee (Okla.) Pub. Schs., 1995—, Muskogee 7th & 8th Grade Ctr. Named Okla. Tchr. of Yr., 2007; grantee Fund for Teachers fellow, Forester Inst., San Jose, Costa Rica. Mem.: Okla. Fgn. Lang. Tchr. Assn. (v.p.). Office: Muskogee 7th & 8th Grade Ctr 402 North S St Muskogee OK 74403 E-mail: michael_linda@cox.net.*

HASLETT, JARED WOODDELL, physicist, educator; b. Akron, Ohio, Oct. 11, 1930; s. George William and Mildred W. H.; m. Winona Rose Goss, 1954 (div.); children: Jonathan, Joel, Jeanne; m. Diane Margaret Crowley, Sept. 4, 1965; children: Ethan, Benjamin. MS, Ill. Inst. of Tech., 1955. Physicist U. Chgo., 1956-57; educator U. Ill., Chgo., 1959-94. Dir. undergrad. studies dept. physics U. Ill., Chgo.; resident rsch. assoc. Argonne (Ill.) Nat. Labs., 1959—65; rsch. physicist Chgo. Wesley Meml. Hosp., 1966; cons. physicist Michael Reese Hosp., Chgo., 1966—67; cons. on Rudolf Steiner's works to various libraries, 1998—. Author: Works of Rudolf Steiner in English Translation, 1998. Treas. Waldorf Sch. of Chgo., 1975-77; libr. Rudolf Steiner Group Anthroposophical Soc. in Am., 1971-75. Faculty fellowship NSF, 1988, 89. Mem. AAAS (life), Anthroposophical Soc., Bioelectromagnetics Soc., Am. Mensa Ltd.(life), Am. Radio Relay League, Agni Yoga Soc., Moose (life), Sigma Pi Sigma, Sigma Xi (life). Espicopalian. Avocations: chess, amateur radio. E-mail: JHaslett@uic.edu.

HASLETT, JIM, professional football coach; b. Pittsburgh, Pa., Dec. 9, 1955; BA in Elem. Edn., Ind. U. of Pa., 1978. Profl. football player Buffalo Bills and NY Nets, 1979-87; asst. football coach U. Buffalo, 1988-89; asst. coach Los Angeles Raiders, 1993-94, Pittsburgh Steelers, 1996-99; head coach New Orleans Saints, 2000—05; defensive coord. St. Louis Rams, 2006—. Named NFL Coach of the Yr., 2000; named to Coll. Football Hall of Fame, 2001. Office: c/o St Louis Rams 1 Rams Way Saint Louis MO 63045

HASS, LAWRENCE JOEL, lawyer; b. NYC, Dec. 1, 1946; s. Nathan Harold and Helen Bernice (Goldin) H.; children: Joanna Sheri, David Brian, Lindsay Jill. BA, U. Pa., 1967; JD, Bklyn. Law Sch., 1971. Bar: NY 1972, DC 1977. Atty. SEC, Washington, 1971-75, U.S. Dept. Labor, Washington, 1975-76; spl. asst. to adminstr. Pension & Welfare Benefit Program, Washington, 1976-77; prin. Groom & Norberg, Chartered, Washington, 1977—87; ptnr. Akin, Gump, Strauss, Hauer & Feld, Washington, 1987—92, Paul Hastings Janofsky & Walker, NYC, 1992—, mem. policy com. Bd. dirs., gen. counsel Pension Real Estate Assn., Hartford, 1985—; chmn. Broadcast Capital Fund, Washington, 1995-2002. Author: The Annotated Fiduciary, 1981. Mem. ABA, DC Bar Assn. Avocations: tennis, jogging. Office: Paul Hastings Janofsky & Walker LLP 75 E 55th St First Floor New York NY 10022 Office Phone: 212-318-6401. Business E-Mail: larryhass@paulhastings.com.

HASS, ROBERT L., writer, literature educator; b. San Francisco, 1941; Prof. Dept. English U. Calif., Berkeley. Author: (books of poetry) Sun Under Wood: New Poems, 1996, Human Wishes, 1989, Praise, 1979, Field Guide, 1973; co-translator vols. of poetry with Czeslaw Milosz including: Facing the river, 1995; author/editor essays and translation including: The Essential Haiku: Versions of Basho, Buson, and Issa, 1994, Twentieth Century Pleasures: Prose on Poetry, 1984 (Nat. Book Critics Circle award); editor: Best American Poetry, 2001. Bd. dirs. Internat. Rivers Network. Apptd. Poet Laureate of U.S., 1995-97; MacArthur "Genius" fellow; named Educator of the Yr., N.Am. Assn. on Environ. Edn., 1997, chancellor Acad. Am. Poets, 2000. Office: Steven Barclay Agy 321 Pleasant St Petaluma CA 94952-2648 E-mail: bobhass@uclink4.berkeley.edu.

HASSAN, AFTAB SYED, education specialist, writer, editor; b. Lahore, Punjab, Pakistan, Apr. 20, 1952; came to U.S., 1976; s. Maqsud Syed and Saliha Akhtar Hassan. BSCE with distinction, U. Engring. and Tech., Lahore, 1973; postgrad. in aerodyns., Colo. State U., 1976; MS, George Washington U., 1977; PhD, Columbia Pacific U., 1985. Scientist in ocean, coastal and environ. engring. George Washington U., 1977-84, grad. tchg. asst. Washington, 1979-84, asst. prof., 1980-85; chmn. math. and sci. Emerson Prep. Inst., Washington, 1979-89; acad. coord. Ctr. for Minority Student Affairs Georgetown U. Med. Sch., Washington, 1983-87; v.p. Met. Acctg. Assocs., Washington, 1987-88; acctg. mgr. Washington Info. Group, 1988-91; owner Met. Acctg. and Rsch., Washington, 1988-91; sr. tech. editor and author Betz Pub. Co., Rockville, Md., 1991-94, designer new products, dir. sci. rsch., 1991-94, v.p. acad. devel. Williams and Wilkins Ednl. Svcs. div., 1994-96, v.p. acad. devel. Betz Sci. Rsch. div., 1994-96; v.p. acad. devel., strategic planning Metro Acad. Rsch., Washington, 1996—. Adj. prof., clin. coord. Harlem Hosp. Ctr. Physicians Asst. program, The Sophie Dairs Sch. Biomed. Edn., 1998—. Author, dir. sci. rsch.: A Complete Preparation for the MCAT, 7th edit., 1996, Preparing for the D.A.T., 1992, Dental Admission Test--The Betz Guide, 1993, Optometry Admission Test--The Betz Guide, 1993, Problem Solving Software for the MCAT-Biological Sciences and Physical Sciences, 1994, Pharmacy College Admission Test--The Betz Guide, 1994, Allied Health Professions Admission Test--The Betz Guide, 1994, Veterinary Entrance Tests--The Betz Guide, 1995. Bd. dirs. Ctr. for Edn. Achievement, Charles R. Drew U. Medicine and Sci., Ebon Internat. Acad., Forsythe, Ga.; ednl. specialist Am. Physician Asst. Programs; curriculum advisor statewide programs for minority health professions State of Pa.; curriculum and ednl. specialist for ACCESS, statewide program at Priarie View (Tex.) A&M U. Recipient Merit award Nat. Assn. Chiefs of Police, Leaders in Cmty. Svc. award Am. Biog. Inst. 1990, Bell award Nat. Assn. Black Sch. Educators Found. Mem. ASCE, NSPE, Am. Soc. Engring. Edn., Am. Inst. Profl. Bookkeepers, Soc. Am. Mil. Engrs., Nat. Soc. Tax Profls., Nat. Coun. for Testing and Measurement, Nat. Law Enforcement Acad. (hon.), Nat. Assn. Advisors for Health Professions, Nat. Assn. Fgn. Student Advisors, Nat. Sci. Tchrs. Assn., Nat. Assn. Profl. Educators, Nat. Assn. Minority Med. Educators, Am. Ednl. Rsch. Assn., Soc. Tchrs. Family Medicine, N.Y. Acad. Scis., Soc. Competitive Intelligence Profls., Assn. Am. Med. Colls. (assoc.), Acad. Physician Assts. (assoc.). Avocations: exotic cooking, swimming, collecting currency. Address: Americian Soc Landscape Asso 636 I St NW Washington DC 20001-3736

HASSAN, FRED, pharmaceutical executive; b. Pakistan, Nov. 12, 1945; arrived in US, 1970; s. Syed Fida and Zeenat (Hussain) Hassan; m. Noreen Shah, Mar. 15, 1969. BS in Chem. Engring. with honors, Imperial Coll. of Sci. and Tech., 1967; MBA, Harvard U., 1972. Chem. engr., sales mgr. Dawood Corp., Lahore, Pakistan, 1967-70; sales rep. Richardson-Vicks, NYC, 1970; project mgr., corp. planning Sandoz Pharms. Corp., East Hanover, NJ, 1972-74; mgr. planning Dorsey Labs. div. Sandoz Pharms. Corp., Lincoln, Nebr., 1974-76, dir. mktg., 1975-80; CEO Sandoz Pakistan, Karachi, Pakistan, 1980-83; gen. mgr. Sandoz Pharms. Corp., East Hanover, NJ, 1984—86, COO, 1986—87, CEO, 1987-89; pres. Wyeth Ayerst Labs., St. David's, Pa., 1989-93; sr. v.p. global pharm. Am. Home Products, Madison, NJ, 1993—95, exec. v.p., 1995-97; CEO Pharmacia Corp., Peapack, NJ, 1997—2003, chmn., 2001—03; chmn., CEO Schering-Plough Corp., Kenilworth, NJ, 2003—. Bd. dirs. Avon Products, Inc., 1999—, Schering-Plough Corp., 2003—; chmn. Health Care Inst. of NJ. Named CEO of Yr. in global pharmaceutical industry, Financial Times, 1999. Mem.: Pharm. Rsch. & Mfrs. Am. (former chmn.), Alliance for Aging Rsch. (former bd. dir.). Office: Schering-Plough Corp 2000 Galloping Hill Rd Kenilworth NJ 07033*

HASSAN, IBNE, lawyer, diplomat, political philosopher, international strategist; b. Najibabad, India, Jan. 2, 1938; s. Alhaj M. Abdul Aziz and Hasrat Jehan Begum. BA in Pub. Law and Govt., Purdue U., 1963; MA in Internat. Rels., Fordham U., 1964; PhD in Polit. Econ., Columbia U., 1966; PhD in Pub. Adminstrn., NYU, 1968; PhD in Internat. Rels., Oxford U., Eng., 1972; LLB, LLM, PhD in Internat. and Comparative Law, Cambridge U., Eng., 1977. CEO Fgn. Devel. Corp., NYC, London, Geneva, 1965-81; dir. gen. Kalos World Order Found., NYC, 1971-81; prin. assessor Found. New World Edn., Geneva, 1972-77; sr. assoc. Fletcher Sch. Law and Diplomacy, Tufts U., Medford, 1978-79; permanent rep. to UN Ctr. Devel. Policy, Washington, 1981-85; spl. rep. Inst. Internat. Security Studies, Washington, 1981-85; chief commr. Commn. Mid. Ea. Affairs, Washington, 1981-85; disting. prof. Sch. Advanced Internat. Studies, Johns Hopkins U., Washington, 1981-83; regional pres. Internat. Law Chambers, Washington, Hague, Islamabad, 1986—. Sr. fellow UN, NYC, 1970-71, spl. advisor, 1983-85, mission assessor, 1994-96, spl. rep., 1998—; dir. Oxford Conf. Internat. Affairs, 1970, Philip Jessup Moot Internat. Law, Cambridge, Eng., 1975; faculty bd. law, Cambridge U., Eng., 1974-77; vis. assoc. Grad. Inst. Higher Internat. Studies, Geneva U., 1971-72; adv. bd. World Peace News, NYC, 1977-81; sr. fellow, vis. scholar Harvard U., Cambridge, Mass., 1977-78, 86-87; vis. scholar Yale U., New Haven, 1978-79, Columbia U., NYC, 1996-98; vis. fellow Princeton U., 1979-80; regional rep. World Fedn. UN Assns., 1970-71, Internat. Students Movement for the UN, 1970-71; legal assoc. Internat. Law Commn., 1971-72; jud. asst. Internat. Ct. Justice, 1973-74; chief commr., ambassador extraordinary and plenipotentiary Cisri-Isp Permanent Observer Mission to UN, NYC, 2005—; chmn. Commn. on Conflict Prevention, Peacebuilding and Sustainable Devel., NYC, 2005—; pres. Overworld Mercantile Corp. Contbr. numerous treatises and articles to pol., legal, econ. and adminstrv. pubs. Chmn. Culture of Peace Commn., NYC, 2005—; coord. Millennium Devel. Goals, NYC, 2005—; spl. advisor, goodwill amb. Spirulina Conv., Rome, 2005—. Recipient Hyder Meml. award of merit, Aligarh U., 1951, Lit. award of merit, Majlis-i-Ilmistan, 1958, Internat. award of merit, Purdue U., 1962, Purdue Calumet award, 1962, Goldrush Medallion award, 1963, Acad. Excellence award, Purdue Hassars, 1963, Student of Yr. award, Internat. Reporter, 1962, Quaid-i-Azam award of merit, Oxford U. Pakistan Soc., 1968, Meritorious Achievement award, New World Edn. Found., 1972, World Peace award, World Peace News, 1977, World Order award, Kalos World Order Found., 1978, Disting. Achievement award, WAFUNIF, 2001, Wall of Tolerance award, Campaign for Tolerance, 2004; fellow, UN, 1968, 1970, Hague Acad. Internat. Law, 1972, 1974—75, 1994, Internat. Inst. Human Rights, 1975—76, Inst. Internat. Law & Rels., 1976—77, 1979, 1981, 1986, 1994, 1996; Disting. scholar, Inst. World Affairs, 1964—65, Litigious fellow, European Ct. Human Rights, 1972—73. Fellow World Lit. Acad., Acad. of Polit. Sci.; mem. Am. Soc. Internat. Law, Global Policy Forum, Internat. Polit. Sci. Assn., Internat. Bar Assn., Internat. Peace Bur., Punjab Bar Coun., Internat. Soc. for Mil. Law, UN Assn. (UK, USA, Pakistan), Internat. Law Assn., Internat. Econ. Soc., Internat. Devel. Coun., Soc. for Internat. Devel., Royal Commonwealth Soc., Royal Inst. Internat. Affairs, Pakistan Inst. Internat. Affairs, Internat. Inst. Strategic Studies, Fedn. Internat. des Avocats, Carnegie Coun., Am. Polit. Sci. Assn., World Jurist Coun., Rhodes Scholars Assn., Oxford Soc., Oxford Union Soc., Cambridge Soc., Cambridge Union Soc., Harvard Alumni Assn., Harvard Coun. Internat. Rels., Harvard Grad. Soc., Harvard Law Soc., World Inst. Achievements, Oxford Mgmt. Soc., Pi Sigma Alpha. Avocations: gardening, painting, photography, music, riding. Office Phone: 212-963-3110. Personal E-mail: ibnehassan_un@yahoo.com. Business E-Mail: wafunif@wafunif.org.

HASSAN, SAYED MOHAMMED, chemist; b. Cairo, Oct. 18, 1944; came to US, 1988; s. Mohammed Hassan Ali; m. Souad Ali Shaaban, July 12, 1973; children: Wael, Ghada, Hany. B in Pharmacy and Pharm. Chemistry, U. Cairo, 1966, M in Pharm. Sci., 1973, PhD in Pharm. Sci., 1975. Drug control analyst Nile Co. for Pharms., Cairo, 1966-67, Drug Control and Rsch. Ctr., Cairo, 1967-74; asst. lectr. to prof. and head dept. analytical chemistry Faculty of Pharmacy, Al-Mansoura, Egypt, 1974-88; prin. rsch. chemist DynCorp/U.S. EPA, Athens, Ga., 1988-95; mgr. chem. instrumentation dept. crop and soil scis. Coll. Agrl. and Environ. Scis., U. Ga., Athens, 1996-99; assoc. rsch. scientist, dir. lab. for environ. analysis Dept. Crop & Soil Scis., U. Ga., Athens, 2000—. Cons. Nat. Orgn. Drug Control and Rsch., Cairo, 1976-88, Kahira Co. for Chem. and Pharm. Industries, Cairo, 1987-88. Contbr. articles, revs. to profl. jours. Recipient Abdul Hameed Shoman award Shoman Found., Jordon, 1984. Mem. AAAS, Am. Chem. Soc., NY Acad. Scis., Assn. Ofcl. Analytical Chemists, Egyptian Biochem. Soc., Chem. Soc. Egypt, Pharm. Soc. Egypt, Sigma Xi. Avocations: stamp collecting/philately, fishing, walking, chess, computer programming. Office Phone: 706-227-7993. Business E-Mail: shassan@uga.edu.

HASSE, JOHN EDWARD, music curator; b. Aberdeen, SD, Nov. 20, 1948; s. Merten Milton Hasse and Gladys Irene Elizabeth Johnson; 1 child, Leanne Alexandra. BA cum laude with distinction, Carleton Coll., 1971; MA, Ind. U., 1975, PhD, 1981; LHD (hon.), Walsh U., 2001. Cert. in Bus. Adminstrn. U. Pa., 1981. Founder, campaign mgr. Minnesotans for McGovern, Mpls., 1971—72; rsch. asst. Ind. U., Bloomington, 1973—74, assoc. instr., 1974—75, project coord., 1979—81; brand asst. Procter & Gamble, Cin., 1982—83; dir. Sounds of Ind. Project, Cin., 1983—84; curator Am. music Nat. Mus. Am. History, Smithsonian Instn., Washington, 1984—. Chief advisor legends of Am. music stamp series US Postal Svc., 1989—99; founder Smithsonian Jazz Masterworks Orch., 1991, exec. dir., 1991—99; co-dir. Am.'s Jazz Heritage, 1992—96; pub. spkr. in field, 1993—; mem. New Orleans Jazz Commn., 1996—; founder Jazz Appreciation Month; interviewee in field. Co-prodr., co-annotator: Indiana Ragtime: A Documentary Album, 1981 (ASCAP Deems Taylor award, 1982); editor: Ragtime: Its History, Composers, and Music, 1985 (ASCAP Deems Taylor award, 1986), Jazz: The First Century, 2000; author, prodr.: book, compact disc set The Classic Hoagy Carmichael, 1988 (Grammy Award nominations for Best Hist. Album, Best Album Notes, 1989, Best Hist. Popular Album award by Music Retailers' Assn., 1989), curator: traveling exhbn. Beyond Category: The Musical Genius of Duke Ellington, 1993—2000; author: Beyond Category: The Life and Genius of Duke Ellington, 1993, (book) I Love You When, 2000; author, assoc. prodr.: booklet, compact disc set Beyond Category, 1995; co-curator Ella Fitzgerald: First Lady of Song, 1997—. Del. Dem. Nat. Conv., Miami Beach, 1972. Recipient Disting. Alumni Achievement award, Carleton Coll., 1996;, Danforth Found. fellow, 1975—78. Mem.: Soc. Am. Music (mem. bd. trustees 1991—93), Nat. Acad. Recording Arts and Scis. (mem. hall of fame elections com. 1990—96), Internat. Assn. Jazz Edn. (sec. 2002—04), Am. Musicological Soc. (cultural diversity com. 1995—97), Soc. Ethnomusicology (life; editl. bd. mem. 1974—78). Business E-Mail: hasse@si.edu, john@johnedwardhasse.com.

HASSE, WILMA HAHN, retired English professor; b. West Haven, Conn., July 21, 1926; d. William Russell and Ruth Haines Hahn; m. Raymond William Hasse, June 17, 1950; children: Lizbeth Lynn, Michael Raymond, Andrew Raymond. BA, U. Conn., Storrs, 1947; M of Art of Tchg., Conn. Coll., New London, 1975. Cert. secondary edn. tchr. Conn., 1950. Tchr. English and social studies Old Saybrook H.S., Conn., 1947—52; substitute tchr. Ledyard HS, Waterford, Cohanzie Elem. Sch., Waterford, 1952—76; assoc. prof. English Mitchell Coll., New London, 1976—2003; ret., 2003. Fgn. student advisor and asst. advisor Mitchell Coll., New London, 1976—89. Editor: The Short Prose Reader, 1991, The Enjoyment of Literature, 1993, Bedford Introduction to Drama, 1996. Deacon Second Congl. Ch., New London, 1956—2006, choir mem., 1956—2006, com. mem., 1956—2006. Recipient Monte Cristo award, Playwrights Theater and Monte Cristo Cottage, Pres.'s award, Mitchell Coll.; Yale-Mellon vis. faculty fellow, 1984—85. Mem.: Nat. Coun. Tchrs. English (assoc.; presenter, chair, recorder), Alumni Club Conn. Coll., Phi Beta Phi. Congregationalist. Avocations: travel, swimming, singing, reading, cooking. Home: 145 Old Colchester Rd Box 313 Quaker Hill CT 06375 Personal E-mail: wilma@hasse.com.

HASSELBACH, KARLHEINZ, retired literature educator; b. Giessen, Germany; arrived in US, 1965; s. Adolf and Elisabeth Hasselbach; m. Ingrid Tiesler, June 10, 1972. PhD, Philipps U., Marburg, Germany, 1971. Asst. prof. Fla. State U., Tallahassee, 1965—72; assoc. prof. Tulane U., New Orleans, 1974—86, prof., 1986—2005, chmn. dept. Germanic and Slavic languages, 1978—82, dept. chair Germanic and Slavic languages, 1989—95, emeritus, 2005. Author: The Dialects of the Region of the Central Vogelsberg in Germany (vol. 76 of Deutsche Dialekt- Geographie), 1971, Thomas Mann: Doktor Faustus, 1978, 1986, Thomas Mann: Doktor Faustus, vol. 24 of Oldenbourg-Interpretationen, 1988, 1996, Georg Büchner: Lenz, 1986, Georg Büchner: Lenz, vol. 5 of Oldenbourg-Interpretationen, 1988, Bertolt Brecht: Kalendergeschichten, vol. 32 of Odlenbourg-Interpretationen, 1990, 1997, Georg Büchner, Reclam, 1997, 2d rev. edit., 1999; contbr. articles to profl. jours. on Thomas Mann, Ernst Jünger, romanticism, and socio-linguistics. Home: 7325 Maple St New Orleans LA 70118 Personal E-mail: hasselk@tulane.edu.

HASSELBECK, MATT, professional football player; b. Westwood, Mass., Sept. 25, 1975; m. Sarah Hasselbeck, 2000; 2 children. Grad., Boston Coll. Player Green Bay Packers, 1999—2001; quarterback Seattle Seahawks, 2001—. Named to Pro Bowl, 2003. Named to NFC Pro Bowl Team, 2005. Achievements include became the Seahawks all-time, highest-rated passer (83.9) in 2003. Has 1,282 career attemps and 769 completions for 9,084 yards, 50 touchdowns, and 33 interceptions. Office: Seattle Seahawks Qwest Field 800 Occidental Ave S Seattle WA 98134

HASSELHOFF, DAVID, actor; b. Balt., July 17, 1952; m. Catherine Hickland Mar. 24, 1984 (div. Mar. 1, 1989); m. Pamela Bach, Dec. 8, 1989 (div. May 4, 2006); children: Taylor-Ann, Hayley Amber. Actor: (TV series) The Young and the Restless, 1975-82, Semi-Tough, 1980, Knight Rider, 1982-86; actor, exec. prodr. (TV series) Baywatch, 1989-2000, Baywatch Nights, 1995-97; actor: (TV films) Griffin and Phoenix: A Love Story, 1976, Pleasure Cove, 1979, The Cartier Affair, 1984, Bridge Across Time, 1985, Perry Mason: The Case of the Lady in the Lake, 1988, Knight Rider the Movie, 1988, Panic at Malibu Pier, 1989, Knight Rider 2000, 1990, Ring of the Muskateers, 1992, Avalanche, 1994, Gridlock, 1996, NightMan, 1997, Nick Fury: Agent of Shield, 1998, Shaka Zulu: The Citadel, 2001, Baywatch: Hawaiian Wedding, 2003; (films) Starcrash, 1979, Starke Zeiten, 1988, W.B. Blue and the Bean, 1989, The Final Alliance, 1989, Legacy, 1998, The Big Tease, 1999, The Target Shoots First, 2000, Layover, 2001, The Spongebob Squarepants Movie, 2004, Dodgeball: A True Underdog Story, 2004, Click, 2006, Kickin It Old Skool, 2007; judge (TV series) America's Got Talent, 2006-; singer (albums) Looking for Freedom, 1989 (Platinum), Crazy for You, 1991 (Gold), David, 1991 (Gold), Everybody's Sunshine, 1992 (Gold), You Are Everything, 1993 (Gold), Du, 1994, Best of David Hasselhoff, 1995, David Hasselhoff, 1995, Hooked on a Feeling, 1997, Magic Collection, 2000; (video) Baywatch: Forbidden Paradise, 1995; Broadway plays Jekyll and Hyde, 1998; regional theatre The Producers, 2007; author: Making Waves: The Autobiography, 2006, Don't Hassel the Hoff: The Autobiography, 2007 Recipient Star, Hollywood Walk of Fame, 1996.*

HASSELL, GERALD L., bank executive; b. Coral Gables, Fla., Oct. 7, 1951; s. Spencer R. and Geraldine A. (Denault) H.; m. Anita-Agnes Ortiz Luis, May 25, 1985; children: Alyssa O., Jarred S. BA in Econs., Duke U., 1973; MBA in Fin., NYU, 1979. Mgmt. positions with Bank of NY, NYC, 1973—90, exec. v.p., 1990—94, sr. exec. v.p., chief comml. banking officer, 1994—98, pres., 1998—2007, Bank of NY Co., Inc., NYC, 1998—2007, Bank of NY Mellon Corp., 2007—. Vice chmn. Big Bros. of N.Y.C.; active Jr. Achievement, N.Y.C.; mem. bd. visitors Fuqua Sch. Bus., Duke U., 1999-, chmn., 2005-; bd. dirs. Pvt. Export Funding Corp. Presbyterian. Avocations: squash, tennis, scuba diving, biking. Office: The Bank of NY Mellon Corp One Wall St New York NY 10286*

HASSELL, LEROY ROUNTREE, SR., state supreme court chief justice; b. Norfolk, Va., Aug. 17, 1955; BA in Govt. and Fgn. Affairs, U. Va., 1977; JD, Harvard U., 1980. Bar: Va. Former ptnr. McGuire, Woods, Battle and Boothe; assoc. justice Va. Supreme Ct., Richmond, 1989—2003, chief justice, 2003—. Former mem. Va. gen. assembly task force to study violence on sch. property. Former mem. adv. bd. Massey Cancer Ctr.; mem. policy com., former chmn. Richmond Sch. Bd.,; former bd. dirs. Richmond Renaissance, Inc., Richmond chpt. ARC, Garfield childs Fund, Carpenter Ctr. for Performing Arts, St. John's Hosp., Legal Aid Ctrl. Va.; vol. Richmond Pub. Schs., Hospice vol.; elected sch. bd. chmn. 4 terms. Recipient Liberty Bell award 1985, 86, Black Achievers award, 1985-86, Outstanding Young Citizen award Richmond Jaycees, 1987, Outstanding Young Virginian award Va. Jaycees, 1987; one of youngest persons to both serve on the Richmond Sch. Bd. and to serve as bd. chmn. Mem. Va. Trial Lawyers Assn., Assn. Trial Lawyers Am., Va. Assn. Def. Attys., Old Dominion Bar Assn., Va. Bar Assn. Office: Supreme Ct of Virginia PO Box 1315 Richmond VA 23218-1315*

HASSELL, STEPHEN C., information technology executive; BS, US Naval Acad., Annapolis, 1988; MBA, Kellogg Sch., Northwestern, Chgo., 1995. Mgr. Newport News Shipbuilding, 1995—98, dir., process innovation, CIO, 1998, v.p., 2000; pres. & CEO Naptheon Inc. (subs. Newport News); chief info. officer Invensys; v.p. & chief info. officer Emerson Elec. Co., St. Louis, 2004—. Decorated Navy Commendation medal; recipient CIO 100 award, CIO Mag. Office: Emerson Elec Co 8000 W Florissant Ave PO Box 4100 Saint Louis MO 63136–850

HASSELMAN, RICHARD B., retired rail transportation executive; b. Jersey City, Nov. 28, 1926; s. Benjamin R. and Clara A. (Borchert) H.; m. Mildred E. Schaber, May 29, 1954; children: Richard Dwight, James Christopher. BME, Yale U., 1947; MBA, NYU, 1949. Student engr. N.Y. Ctrl. R.R., 1947-49, trainee, 1949—52, brakeman, 1952-53, signalman, freight agt., 1953; transp. insp. Ea. region Syracuse, NY, 1953-55; trainmaster Mohawk divsn. Albany, NY, 1955-57; divsn. trainmaster Syracuse divsn., 1957; divsn. supt. Boston & Albany divsn. Springfield, Mass., 1957-59; dist. transp. supt. Western region Cleve., 1959-60; gen. supt. yards and terminals N.Y. Ctrl. Sys., NYC, 1960-63; gen. mgr. Ind. Harbor Belt and Chicago River & Ind. R.R., Hammond, Ind., 1963; gen. mgr. No. Region N.Y. Ctrl. R.R., Detroit, 1964, gen. mgr. So. Region Indpls., 1964-66, gen. mgr. Western Region Cleve., 1967; asst. v.p. transp. N.Y. Ctrl. Sys., NYC, 1967-68; v.p. transp. Penn. Ctrl., Phila., 1968-76; pres. Ind. Harbor Belt R.R., 1968-87; sr. v.p. ops. Consol. Rail Corp., Phila., 1976-89; transp. cons., 1989—. Home: 5289 Ladyfinger Lake Rd Sanibel FL 33957-2436

HASSELMEYER, EILEEN GRACE, medical researcher; b. Bklyn., May 23, 1924; d. Edwin Allen and Margaret Grace (Cody) H. RN, Bellevue Sch. Nursing, 1946; BS, NYU, 1954, MA, 1956, PhD, 1963. Mem. staff Pediatric Metabolic and Nutritional Rsch. Svc., NYU Children's Med. Svc., Bellevue Hosp., NYC, 1946-56, study coord., 1951-56; rsch. nursing supr. Met. Hosp., NYC, 1951; lectr. pediatric nutrition rsch. U. Tex. Sch. Nursing, 1952-53; nursing dir. nutritional rsch. studies Children's Hosp. of John Seely Hosp. (U. Tex. Med. Br.), Galveston, 1952-53; lectr. and nursing rsch. assoc. nutritional svc. pediat. dept. Hosp. Infantile, Mexico City, 1953; nursing dir. rsch. unit Willowbrook State Sch., SI, 1953-54; commd. USPHS, 1956, advanced through grades to asst. surgeon gen.-rear adm., 1981; ret. 1989; nurse cons. Divsn. Nursing Resources, Bur. Med. Svcs., USPHS, Washington, 1956-59; prin. investigator Handling and Premature Infant Behavior project, NYU, NYC, 1961-63; sr. nurse cons. Div. Nursing, Bur. State Svcs., USPHS, Washington, 1963; spl. asst. for prematurity Office of Dir., Nat. Inst. Child Health and Human Devel., Bethesda, Md., 1963-66, acting dir. perinatal biology and infant mortality program, extramural programs, 1967-68, dir., 1969-74, asst. to dir. for perinatology, 1974-80; chief pregnancy and infancy br. Ctr. for Rsch. for Mothers and Children, 1974-79, acting chief clin. nutrition and early devel. br., 1979-80; assoc. dir. for sci. rev. Office of Dir., 1979-89; spl. asst. to dir. N.C. for Nursing Rsch., 1986-89; exec. dir. Uniform Svcs. U. Health Sci., Fed. Coll. Nursing Feasability Study Task Force, 1989-92. Annie W. Goodrich vis. prof. Yale U. Sch. Nursing, New Haven, 1968-69; asst. surgeon gen. USPHS, Dept. Health and Human Svcs., 1981-89, chmn. interagy. panel on sudden infant death syndrome, 1974-82, others. Contbr. articles to profl. jours. Recipient NICHD Recognition of Outstanding Performance, 1973, plaque for 25 yrs. dedicated svc., 1987, Chief Nurse Officer's medal USPHS, 1989; USUHS Commendable Svc. medal, 1990; USPHS Surgeon Gen.'s Cert. of Appreciation, 1990; HEW-USPHS Commendation medal, 1975; recipient Perinatal Research Soc. award, 1979; NYU Sch. Edn., Health, Nursing and Arts Professions Creative Leadership award, 1980; Achievement award Nat. Sudden Infant Death Syndrome Found., 1987, Eileen G. Hasselmeyer Disting. Sci. Achievement award Sudden Infant Death Syndrome Alliance, 1990; Outstanding Performance award NCNR, 1987, Meritorious Svc. medal HHS-USPHS, 1989; cert. appreciation NIH-NCNR, 1989; Nat. League for Nursing Commonwealth fellow, 1959-62; NIH fellow, 1962-63; Am. Nurses Found. grantee, 1962-63; State of Conn. Maternal and Infant Program grantee, 1969; Sigma Theta Tau research grantee, 1969-71; Yale U. Sch. Nursing developmental grantee, 1969; disting. alumnae award Bellevue Alumnae Assn., 1997. Mem. Pub. Health Svc. Commd. Officers Assn., Bellevue Alumnae Assn.

HASSELMO, ANN HAYES DIE, executive recruiter, consultant, psychologist, educator, retired academic administrator; b. Baytown, Tex., Aug. 15, 1944; d. Robert L. and Dorothy Ann (Cooke) Hayes; 1 child, Meredith Anne. BS with highest honors, Lamar U., 1966; MEd, U. Houston, 1969; PhD, Tex. A&M U., 1977. Lic. psychologist. Asst. prof. dept. psychology Lamar U., Beaumont, Tex., 1977—82, assoc. prof., dir. Psychol. Clinic, 1982—86, prof., dir. Psychol. Clinic, 1986—88, Regents prof. psychology, 1986, dir. grad. programs in psychology, 1981—86, pres. faculty senate, 1985—86; pvt. practice clin. psychology Beaumont, 1979—87; prof. Tulane U., New Orleans, 1988—92, dean Newcomb Coll., 1988—92, assoc. provost, 1991—92; pres., prof. psychology Hendrix Coll., Conway, Ark., 1992—2001, pres. emerita, 2001—; v.p., ptnr. higher edn. practice A.T. Kearney, Inc., Alexandra, Va., 2001—02; mng. dir. Acad. Search Consultation Svc., Washington, 2002—06; pres. Am. Acad. Leadership Inst., 2006—. Adminstr. adolescent residential unit Mental Health/Mental Retardation S.E. Tex., 1979-80, mem. cmty. adv. com., 1981-87; cons. in field; coordinating bd. Tex. Coll. and Univ. Sys. Internship, 1986, chair, bd. dirs. Ednl. and Instl. Ins. Adminstrs., 2000-02; bd. dirs. Nat. Merit Scholarship Corp., Acxiom Corp., Found. for Ind. Higher Edn., Air U., USAF. Contbr. articles to profl. jours. Mem. cmty. adv. com. Beaumont State Ctr. Human Devel., 1981-88; chair So. Collegiate Athletic Conf., 1996-97; participant Nat. Identification Program for Women, Am. Coun. on Edn., 1985, mem. govt. rels. commn., 1993-96, chmn., 1994-96, chmn. coun. of fellows, 1995-96, bd. dirs., 1997-2000; bd. dirs. Beaumont Civic Opera, Lamar U. Wesley Found., Tulane U. Wesley Found.; bd. govs. Isidore Newman Sch., 1991-92; trustee Robert Morris Coll., 1990-98, chmn. edn. com., 1990-94, chmn. pers. com., 1994-98, mem. exec. com., 1990-98; mem. univ. senate United Meth. Ch., 1993-01, chair commn. on instnl. rev., 1997-01; 1st v.p. Nat. Assn. Schs. & Colls. United Meth. Ch., 1996, pres. 1997-98; bd. dirs. Ouachita coun. Girl Scouts U.S., 1996-2000; mem. bd. visitors Air U., USAF, 1999—; mem. Internat. Women's Forum, 1995—, Ark. Women's Leadership Forum, 1999-02, pres. 2000-01; mem. Ark. Commn. to Streamline State Govt., 1996-98; mem. pres. commn. NCAA, 1997-01, chmn. div. III, 1999-2001, mem. exec. com. 1999-2001; chair Assoc. Coll. of the South, 1997-99; bd. dirs. Ark. Repertory Theatre, 2000-01, United Way of Faulkner County, 2000-01. Am. Coun. Edn. fellow Coll. William and Mary, 1986-87; recipient Regents Merit award, 1979, Coll. Health and Behavioral Sci. Merit award, 1982, Lamar U.; named one of Top 100 Women in Ark., Ark. Bus., 1995-99. Mem. APA, Southwestern Psychol. Assn., Family Svcs. Assn. (bd. dirs. 1988-89), Tex. Psychol. Assn. (dir. divsn. acad. psychologists 1986), S.E. Tex. Psychol. Assn. (treas. 1978-80, pres. 1983), Mental Health Assn. Jefferson County, Nat. Register Health Svc. Providers in Psychology, Nat. Assn. Ind. Colls. and Univs. (bd. dirs., vice chmn. 1995, chair 1996). Address: 1825 K St NW Ste 705 Washington DC 20006

HASSELMO, NILS, retired academic administrator, linguist; b. Kola, Sweden, July 2, 1931; arrived in U.S., 1956; s. A. Wilner and Anna Helena (Backlund) Hasselmo; m. Patricia June Tillberg, Oct. 25, 1958 (dec. Dec. 30, 2000); children: Nils Peter, Michael Erik, Anna Patricia; m. Ann Hayes, Nov. 8, 2003. Fil. mag., Uppsala U., 1956; BA, Augustana Coll., Ill., 1957; PhD, Harvard U., 1961; Fil. lic., Uppsala U., 1962, PhD (hon.), 1979; LHD (hon.), North Park Coll. Theol. Sem., 1992; DHL (hon.), Augustana Coll., Ill., 1995. Asst. prof. Swedish Augustana Coll., Rock Island, Ill., 1958—59, 1961—63; assoc. prof. to prof. Scandinavian langs. and lit. U. Minn., Mpls., 1965—83, 1988—97, chmn. Scandinavian langs. and lit., 1970—73; dir. U. Minn. Ctr. for N.W. European Langs. and Area Studies, Mpls., 1970—73; assoc. dean U. Minn. Coll. Liberal Arts, Mpls., 1973—78; v.p. for adminstrn. and planning U. Minn., Mpls., 1980—83, pres., 1988—97; sr. v.p. acad. affairs, provost U. Ariz., Tucson, 1983—88, prof. English and linguistics, 1983—88; pres. Assn. Am. Univs., Washington, 1998—2006. Vis. com. dept. Germanic langs. and lit. Harvard U., Cambridge, Mass., 1981—86; trustee Nat. Merit Scholarship Corp., 1992—97. Author: Amerikasvenska, 1974, Swedish America: An Introduction, 1976; editor: Perspectives on Swedish Immigration, 1978. Active Gov.'s Task Force on Tech. and Improvement of Employment, Minn., 1982—83; trustee Am. Scandinavian Found., 1992—; bd. dirs. Swedish Coun. Am., 1978—2004, chmn. bd., 1999—2001; bd. dirs. Walker Art Ctr., 1989—95; bd. overseers Mpls. Coll. Art and Design, 1982—83; bd. dirs. Carnegie Found. for Advancement of Tchg., 2002—05, Coun. Libr. and Info. Resources, 1999—2006. Sgt. Royal Signal Corps Swedish Army, 1951—54. Decorated Royal Order of North Star Sweden; named Swedish-Am. of Yr., Swedish Govt. and Vasa Order Am., 1991; recipient King Carl XVI Gustaf's Bicentennial medal in Gold, Sweden, 1976, Ellis Island medal of honor, 1993, Great Swedish Heritage award, Swedish Coun. Am., 2007; Fulbright-Hays fellow, 1968—69. Mem.: MLA, Nat. Acad. Forum Info. Tech. and Rsch. U., Univ. Rsch. Assn. (trustee 1993—97), Nat. Assn. State Univs. and Land Grant Colls. (exec. com. acad. affairs coun. 1986—88, chmn. coun. pres. and chancellors 1992—93, chair bd. 1994—95), Swedish-Am. Hist. Soc. (chmn. bd. 1984—86), Royal Gustavus Adolphus Acad., Vetenskaps-Soc., Linguistic Soc. Am., Soc. for Advancement Scandinavian Study (pres. 1971—73).

HASSENFELD, ALAN GEOFFREY, consumer products company executive; b. Providence, Nov. 16, 1948; s. Merrill Lloyd and Sylvia (Kay) H.; married. BA, U. Pa., 1970. Asst. to pres. Hasbro, Inc., Pawtucket, RI, 1970—72, v.p. internat. ops., 1972-78, v.p. mktg. and sales, 1978-80, exec. v.p., 1980-84, pres., 1984-89, chmn., CEO, 1989—2003, chmn., 2003—. Dir. Hasbro, Inc., 1978; dir. exec. com. Internat. Tennis Hall Fame, 1998; dir. Salesforce.com, 2004. Dir. Hasbro Children's Found., Shoah Found., Milken Family Found., Jewish Fedn. RI, 1989, Refugees Internat., 1992; bd. gov. Miriam Hosp., 1984, Operation Smile, 2002; bd. overseers (dean's coun.) Sch. Arts and Sci., U. Pa., 1986, Kennedy Sch. Govt., Harvard, 1995, mem. exec. com., 2003; bd. overseers (dean's coun.) Harvard Sch. Pub. Health, 1997, Rosenberg Inst. Brandeis, 2002; trustee Deerfield Acad., 1996, U. Pa., 1999, US Coun. Internat. Bus., 2002, Save the Bay, 2003, Bryant Coll., 2004; trustee emeritus Brown U.; mem. adv. com. Big Brothers RI, Internat. Inst. RI; mem. exec. com. Brown U. Civic Leadership Coun., Commodores RI; chmn. Right Now! Coalition, 1991, World Scholar Athlete Games, 1996, RISOP, 2002, Jerusalem Found., 2004. Office: Hasbro Inc 1027 Newport Ave Pawtucket RI 02862 Office Phone: 401-727-5103.

HASSENGER, JAMES MICHAEL, writer, retired small business owner; b. Sioux City, Iowa, Dec. 9, 1926; s. Ralph Joseph and Eva Sylvia Hassenger; m. Joann C. Bendixen, Nov. 14, 1951 (div. Oct. 14, 1983); children: Susan, Michael, Timothy, Juliana, Elizabeth, James, Daniel. BS, Creighton U., 1948; MA, U. S.D., 1993. Sales exec. Hassenger Bros. Ins., Sioux City, 1948—50; owner Quality Beverage, Sioux City, 1950—52, Hassenger Import Motors, Sioux City, 1952—63, Citizens Loan and Thrift, Sioux City, 1963—80, KBCM FM radio sta., Sioux City, 1973—83; author, pub. Marriage Enhancement Ctr., Sioux City, 1988—. Pres. Iowa Consumer Loan Assn., 1981—83. Author: (book) Marriage Enhancement Guide, 2001, Marriage #101, 2004. Divsn. mgr. Sioux City C of C., 1979; pres. Mariners Swim Club, Sioux City, 1980; active Jr. Chamber of Sioux City C. of C. Midshipman USN, 1944—46. Mem.: ACA. Avocations: flying, golf. Home and Office: Marriage Enhancement Ctr 520 Buckwalter Dr Sioux City IA 51104 Office Phone: 712-239-2347.

HASSERT, DERRICK LAWRENCE, psychology professor; s. Earl Edward Hassert and Diane June Bahor; m. Sara Marie Christen-Hassert, June 3, 2000. BA, So. Ill. U., Carbondale, 1994, MA, 1998, PhD, 2000. Postdoctoral rschr. U. Va., Charlottesville, Va., 2001—03; assoc. prof. psychology Trinity Christian Coll., Palos Heights, Ill., 2003—. Mem.: Internat. Neuropsychological Soc., Assn. Psychol. Sci. Anglican. Office: Trinity Christian Coll 6601 West Coll Dr Palos Heights IL 60463 Office Phone: 708-239-4862. Business E-Mail: derrick.hassert@trnty.edu.

HASSETT, JOSEPH MARK, lawyer; b. Buffalo, May 1, 1943; m. Carol A. Melton, June 23, 1984; children: Matthew, Meredith. BA summa cum laude, Canisius Coll., 1964; LL.B. cum laude, Harvard U., 1967; MA with 1st class honors, Univ. Coll. Dublin, 1981, PhD, 1985. Bar: N.Y. 1967, D.C. 1970, U.S. Supreme Ct. 1976. Assoc. Hogan & Hartson, Washington, 1970-74, ptnr., 1974—. Bd. trustees Canisius Coll. Author: Yeats and the Poetics of Hate, 1986; contbr. articles to profl. publs. Mem.: ABA, D.C. Bar Assn. Office: 555 13th St NW Washington DC 20004-1109 Home: 1230 27th St NW Washington DC 20007 Office Phone: 202-637-5600. Business E-Mail: jmhassett@hhlaw.com.

HASSETT, VALERIE JANE, interior designer, architect, educator; b. San Diego, Dec. 22, 1962; d. Roger John and Cecelia Virginia (Cibarich) H. Student, U. Tenn., Knoxville, 1982—86; BFA in Interior Design, Va. Commonwealth U., Richmond, 1988; MArch, Va. Poly. U., Alexandria, 1993. Registered profl. interior designer, Va., cert. constrn. documents technologist, registered profl. architect, Va., cert. Nat. Coun. Archtl. Registration Bds., LEED accredited, Nat. Coun. Interior Design Qualification, cert. U.S. Green Bldg. Coun. Interior arch. Washington Area Transit Authority, 1988-90, 91-92, Prince William County Va. Govt., 1993-96, RTKL, Balt., 1996-97; instr. Mt. Vernon Coll. at George Washington U., Washington, 1997-99; project arch., head interior design dept. Sharadan, Behm, Eustice and Assocs. Ltd., Arlington, Va., 1997—; assoc. prof. No. Va. C.C., 2000—. Mem. professions fellowship rev. panel AAUW, 2003—. Exhibitions include Nat. Bldg. Mus., 1995, 1996. Chmn. women in architecture film festival Nat. Mus. Women in the Arts, 1998, 2000; Va. State Govt. & Industry Affairs Commn., 2003—06. Mem. AIA (bd. dirs., 1998-, v.p. 2003, chair women in architecture com. No. Va. chpt. 1993—2005, pres.-elect, 2007-), Internat. Interior Design Assn. (past pres. Mid-Atlantic chpt., Herb Ginsburg Leadership award 2005), Neighborhood Design Ctr. Balt. Avocation: paper making. Office: Sheridan Behm Eustice Assoc 3508 Lee Hwy Arlington VA 22207-3717 Business E-Mail: studio@valeriehassett.com.

HASSEY, L. PATRICK, metal products executive; married; 6 children. Degree, Calif. State U., Long Beach, Calif. From mgr. sales and mktg. to exec. v.p Alcoa Inc., 1990—2000, exec. v.p., 2000—03, group pres. Alcoa Indsl. Components, 2000—03; cons. Allegheny Technologies Inc., Pitts., 2003, pres., CEO, 2003—, chmn., 2004—. Bd. dir. Ryder System. Office: Allegheny Technologies Inc 1000 Six PPG Pl Pittsburgh PA 15222*

HASSIBI, ARJANG, engineering educator, director; b. Kitchener, Can., Nov. 5, 1975; arrived in US, 1999; s. Jamshid Hassibi and Farzaneh Naraghipour. BS, U. Tehran, 1997; MS, Stanford U., Calif., 2001, PhD, 2005; postdoctoral diploma, Calif. Inst. Tech., Pasedena, 2006. Lab. supr. Iranian Army Rsch. Ctr., Tehran, 1997—99; dir. engring. Xagros Geromics, Inc., Mountain View, Calif., 2002—04. Rsch. cons. Panorama Rsch. Inst., Mountain View, 2004—05. 2d lt. US Army, 1997—99. Home: 4700 W Guadalupe St #A403 Austin TX 78751 Office: U Tex 1 University Station C8800 Austin TX 78712

HASSID, SAMI, architect, educator; b. Cairo, Apr. 19, 1912; came to U.S., 1957, naturalized, 1962; s. Joseph S. and Isabelle (Israel) H.; m. Juliette Mizrahi, June 29, 1941; children: Fred, Muriel. Diploma in Architecture with distinction, Sch. Engring., Giza, Egypt, 1932; BA in Architecture with honors, U. London, Eng., 1935; M.Arch., U. Cairo, 1943; PhD in Architecture, Harvard U., 1956. Tchr. Alexandria (Egypt) Tech. Sch., 1932-34; successively tchr., lectr., asst. prof. U. Cairo, 1934-56; prof. architectural theory and design U. Ein-Shams, Cairo, 1957; mem. faculty U. Calif., Berkeley, 1957—, prof. architecture, 1964-79, prof. emeritus, 1979—; also assoc. dean U. Calif. (Coll. Environ. Design), 1977-83, faculty asst. to vice-chancellor for campus planning, 1980-85, dir. campus planning office, 1983-84; archtl. practice Cairo, 1932-57, Berkeley, 1957-85; from draftsman to sr. designer office Ali Labib Gabr (architect), Cairo, 1935-47; ptnr. Sami Hassid and Youssef Shafik, Cairo, 1947-57, Hassid and Kelemen, Berkeley, 1963-65. Author: The Sultan's Turrets, 1939, Architectural Construction Details, 1954, Development and Application of a System for Recording Critical Evaluations of Architectural Works, 1964, Architectural Education U.S.A, 1967, (with others) Innovations in Housing Design and Construction Techniques as Applied to Low-Cost Housing, 1969, Surface Materials in Architecture, 1970, Doctoral Studies in Architecture, 1971, Methods for the Development of Shipboard Habitability Design Criteria, 1974, Fire Safety in Buildings, A Course Offering Package, 1976, (with others) The Berkeley Campus Space Plan, 21 publs., 1981-83; Proc. Workshop on Seismic Upgrading of Existing Bldgs., NSF, 1982; prin. works include Hill House; student hostel, Am. U. Cairo, 1952. Commr. Calif. Bd. Archtl. Examiners, 1961-71. Fulbright grantee, 1954-56; recipient First prize Al-Chams Competition, Cairo, 1947, First prize San Francisco AIA Hdqrs. Competition, 1963 Fellow AIA; mem. Bldg. Research Inst., Assn. Collegiate Schs. Architecture. Democrat. Jewish (trustee temple; v.p. East Bay synagogue council 1970-71). Home: 1866 San Miguel Dr # 221 Walnut Creek CA 94596

HASSLER, DONALD MACKEY, II, English language educator, writer; b. Akron, Ohio, Jan. 3, 1937; s. Donald Mackey and Frances Elizabeth (Parsons) H.; m. Diana Cain, Oct. 8, 1960 (dec. Sept. 1976); children: Donald, David; m. Sue Smith, Sept. 13, 1977; children: Shelly, Heather. BA (Sloan fellow), Williams Coll., 1959; MA (Woodrow Wilson fellow), Columbia U., 1960, PhD, 1967. Instr. U. Montreal, 1961-65; instr. English Kent State U., Ohio, 1965-67, asst. prof., 1967-71, assoc. prof., 1971-76, prof., 1977—, acting dean honors and exptl. coll., 1979-81, dir., 1973-83, chmn. undergrad. studies, 1987-91, chair NEOMFA hiring com., 2007—. Coord. writing cert. program Kent State U., Ohio, 1986—91, dir. Wick poetry competition, 1987—91, coord. maj. program, 1991—94, sec. faculty senate, 1996—, mem. selection com. NE Ohio MFA faculty, 2005—, chair, chair review com., 2007—. Author: Erasmus Darwin, 1974, The Comedian as the Letter D: Erasmus Darwin's Comic Materialism, 1973, Asimov's Golden Age: The Ordering of an Art, 1977, Hal Clement, 1982, Comic Tones in Science Fiction, 1982, Patterns of the Fantastic, 1983, Patterns of the Fantastic II, 1984, Death and the Serpent, 1985, Isaac Asimov, 1991; mng. editor Jour. Extrapolation, 1986-87, co-editor, 1987-89, editor, 1990-2001, exec. editor, 2002—; co-editor (with Sue Hassler) Letters of Arthur Machen and Montgomery Evans, 1923-1947, 1993, (with Clyde Wilcox) Political Science Fiction, 1997, (with Clyde Wilcox) New Boundaries Political Science Fiction, 2007; adv. editl. bd. Hellas, 1988—; editl. bd. Paradoxa, 1994—. Co-chmn. Kent Am. Revolution Bicentennial Commn., 1974-77; deacon Presbyn. Ch., 1971-74, elder, 1974-77; sec. Kent State Faculty Senate, 1996—, chancellor's faculty adv. com., 1996—, univ. priorities and budget adv. coun., 1998—; spkr. Smithsonian Yesterday's Tomorrow's exhibit, 2003; mem. Kent State U. Press Bd., 2004—; trustee Covington Hist. Soc., 2005—. Recipient J. Lloyd Eaton award, Eaton Libr. Collection U. Calif., Riverside, 1993. Mem. Sci. Fiction Rsch. Assn. (treas. 1983-84, 2005—, pres. 1985-86, Thomas D. Clareson award 2001), Kiwanis (bd. dirs. 1974-76), Phi Beta Kappa (pres. 1983-84). Home: 1226 Woodhill Dr Kent OH 44240-2832 Office Phone: 330-672-1778. Business E-Mail: extrap@kent.edu.

HASSON, ADAM ISAAC, lawyer; b. NYC, Aug. 15, 1974; BA, Binghamton U., 1996; MS, Hofstra U., 1999; JD, Boston Coll. Law Sch., 2002. Assoc. Kronish Lieb Weiner & Hellman LLP, NYC, 2002—05; legal counsel Sidney Frank Importing Co., New Rochelle, NY, 2006—. Author: Domestic Implementation of International Obligations: The Quest for World Patent Law Harmonization; editor-in-chief Boston Coll. Internat. & Comparative Law Review, 2001—02. 1st lt. USMC, 1994—98. Office: Sidney Frank Importing Co Inc 20 Cedar St New Rochelle NY 10801

HASSON, JAMES KEITH, JR., lawyer, educator; b. Knoxville, Tenn., Mar. 3, 1946; s. James Keith and Elaine (Biggers) Hasson; m. Jayne Young, July 27, 1968; 1 child, Keith Samuel. BA, Duke U., 1967; JD, 1970. Bar: Ga. 1971, DC 1971. Assoc. Sutherland, Asbill & Brennan, Atlanta, 1970—76; ptnr., 1976; prof. law Emory U., Atlanta, 1976—94; chmn. bd. dir. House-Hasson Hardware Co., Knoxville, 2000—. Editor: Jour. Taxation; contbr. articles profl. jour. Mem. Atlanta Civilian Rev. Bd.; trustee Met. Atlanta Crime Commn., chmn., 1986—87; trustee Foxfire Fund, 1988—2001, chmn. bd. dirs.; chmn. bd. trustees Reinhardt Coll., 2001—06. Recipient Pres. Disting. Svc. award, 1980. Mem.: ABA (com. chmn. 1983—85), Atlanta Bar Assn. (counsel 1977—80), Leadership Atlanta, Lawyers Club. Presbyterian. Home: 3185 Chatham Rd NW Atlanta GA 30305-1101 Office: Sutherland Asbill & Brennan 999 Peachtree St NE Ste 2300 Atlanta GA 30309-3996 Office Phone: 404-853-8083. Business E-Mail: jim.hasson@sablaw.com.

HASSON, KIRKE MICHAEL, lawyer; b. East St. Louis, Ill., Oct. 25, 1949; s. David S. and Audrey (Leber) Hasson. BA magna cum laude, Yale U., 1971; JD cum laude, Harvard U., 1974. Bar: Calif. 1974, U.S. Dist. Ct. (all dist. Calif.), US Ct. Appeals (2d, 5th, 9th cir.). Assoc. Pillsbury Winthrop Shaw Pittman LLP (formerly Pillsbury Winthrop LLP), San Francisco, 1974—81, ptnr., 1982—2007, ptnr., chmn. life sci. and tech.

group, 2007—. Office: Pillsbury Winthrop Shaw Pittman LLP 50 Fremont St San Francisco CA 94105 Office Phone: 415-983-1077. Office Fax: 415-983-1200. E-mail: kirke.hasson@pillsburylaw.com.

HAST, ADELE, historian, editor, writer; b. NYC, Dec. 6, 1931; d. Louis and Kate (Miller) Krongelb; m. Malcolm Howard Hast, Feb. 1, 1953; children: David Jay, Howard Arthur. BA magna cum laude, Bklyn. Coll., 1953; MA, U. Iowa, 1969, PhD, 1979. Rsch. assoc. Atlas Early Am. History Project, Newberry Library, Chgo., 1971-75; assoc. dir. Atlas Great Lakes Indian History Project, 1976-79, Hist. Boundary Data File Project, 1979-81; editor in chief Marquis Who's Who, Inc., Chgo., 1981—86; survey dir. Nat. Opinion Rsch. Ctr., U. Chgo., 1986-89; rsch. fellow Newberry Libr., Chgo., 1989-95, scholar in residence, 1995—; exec. editor St. James Press, Chgo., 1990-92; mng. editor Hist. Ency. of Chgo. Women U. Ill., Chgo., 1991-93, dir., editor Hist. Ency. of Chgo. Women project, 1993-2001, sr. rsch. assoc. Ctr. for Rsch. on Women and Gender, 1999—2002. Mem. faculty Newberry Libr. Summer Inst. Cartography, 1980; cons. NEH planning grant Addams' Hull-House Mus., 2006. Author: Loyalism in Revolutionary Virginia, 1982, American Leaders Past and Present: The View from Who's Who in America, 1985, Hyman Libbie Henrietta (1988-1969) in Jewish Women in America: An Historical Encyclopedia, 1998; compiler: Iowa, Missouri, vol. 4 of Historical Atlas and Chronology of County Boundaries, 1788-1980, 1984; editor: International Directory of Company Histories, vols. 3-5, 1991-92, Women Building Chicago 1790-1990: A Biographical Dictionary, 2001, Libbie Hyman in Jewish Women: A Comprehensive Historical Encyclopedia, 2006; assoc. editor: Atlas of Great Lakes Indian History, 1987; curator exhibit on Chgo. history Spertus Inst. of Jewish Studies, 2002-03; contbr. articles to profl. jours. Mem. profl. adv. grad. program pub. history Loyola U., 1986—; treas., bd. dirs. Chgo. Map Soc., 1980-81, 93-95; mem. New Trier Twp. H.S. Bd. Caucus, 1972-74; mem. acad. coun. Am. Jewish Hist. Soc., 1985—; pres. Chgo. Jewish Hist. Soc., 1980-81, bd. dirs., 1977—. Recipient Alumna of Yr. award Bklyn. Coll., 1984, Colonial Williamsburg Found. grantee-in-aid, 1975, Brit. Acad. rsch. fellow, 1979; Am. Coun. Learned Socs. grantee-in-aid, 1980; NEH rsch. grantee, 1985, 87, 93-95, 97-98, fellow Jewish Women's Archive, 2003-04. Fellow Royal Hist. Soc., Phi Beta Kappa, Kappa Delta Pi; mem. Am. Hist. Assn., Orgn. Am. Historians, Chgo. Area Women's History Coun. (sec., treas. 1994-2004, bd. dirs. 1990—), Caxton Club (coun. 1990-93, 2003—, v.p. 2005—). Office: Newberry Library 60 W Walton St Chicago IL 60610-3380

HAST, MALCOLM HOWARD, biomedical scientist, educator; b. NYC, May 28, 1931; s. Irving William and Rose Lillian (Berlin) H.; m. Adele Krongelb, Feb. 1, 1953; children: David Jay, Howard Arthur. BA, Bklyn. Coll., 1953; postgrad., U. So. Calif., LA, 1955—57; MA, Ohio State U., Columbus, 1958; PhD (NIH fellow), Ohio State U., 1961; CBiol, FIBiol, Gt. Britain, 1991. Instr. U. Iowa, 1961-63; NIH spl. fellow U. Iowa Coll. Medicine, 1963-65, asst. prof., 1965-69; assoc. prof. otolaryngology-head and neck surgery Northwestern U. Feinberg Sch. Medicine, Chgo., 1969—74, prof., 1974—; dir. research otolaryngology Northwestern U. Med. Sch., Chgo., 1969-93, prof. cell and molecular biology (anatomy), 1977—2001; prof. basic and behavioral scis. Northwestern U. Dental Sch., 1989-2001; assoc. med. staff Northwestern Meml. Hosp., 1969-90, health profl., 1990-93; rsch. assoc. zoology Field Mus. Natural History, 1995—; assoc. editor Clinical Anatomy, 1995—. Mem. faculty appeals panel Northwesten U., 1974-83, chmn., 1999-2001, med. sch. appt. promotion and tenure com., 1986-91, gen. faculty benefits com., 2004—; mem. exec. com. of med. admissions com. Feinberg Sch. Medicine, 1991-, chmn., 1998-2003; mem. task force on new materials Am. Bd. Otolaryngology, 1969-72; dir. Ill. Soc. Med. Rsch., 1973-77; guest scientist Max Planck Inst. für Psychiatrie, 1976, Zoologisches Forchungsinstitut und Mus. A. Koenig, 1988; mem. Internat. Anat. Nomenclature Com., 1983-91; mem. exec. admissions com. MSTP, 2002-; Brodel meml. lectr. Assn. Med. Illustrators, 1995; mem. Chgo. Clin. Ethics Programs; vis. prof. Royal Coll. Surgeons Eng., 1980-86, U. Edinburgh, 1987. Editor Annotated Translation of Vesalius' Fabrica, 1995-, elec. edit., 2003; contbr. articles to profl. jours., chpts. to books. Mem. adv. bd. Ctr. Deafness, 1977-80; bd. dirs. Cliff Dwellers Arts Found., 1979-82; trustee Wilmette Libr. Bd., 1982-83, Wilmette Bd. Health, 1999-2007. Served with US Army, 1953-55. NATO sr. fellow in sci. Oxford U., Eng., 1978; NIH rsch. grantee, 1964-84, 95—2004, NSF rsch. grantee, 1975-77, NEH grantee, 1995-2002; recipient Gould Internat. award, 1971, Disting. Alumnus award of Honor, Bklyn. Coll., 1977, Alumnus of Yr. award, 1984; Arnott demonstrator Royal Coll. Surgeons Eng., 1985. Fellow AAAS, Linnean Soc. London, Inst. Biology, Am. Speech-Hearing Assn., Royal Soc. Medicine; mem. AMA, AAUP (chpt. pres. 1977-82), Am. Physiol. Soc. (animal care and experimentation com. 1976-82), Am. Assn. Clin. Anatomists, Chgo. Laryngol. and Otol. Soc. (coun. 1988-89), Am. Soc. Mammalogists, Anat. Soc. Gt. Britain and Ireland, Am. Assn. History Medicine, Soc. Med. History Chgo., Amnesty Internat. (coord. Chgo. Health profls. group 1986-87), Am. Assn. Anatomists, Nat. Eagle Scout Assn., Sigma Xi (chpt. pres. 1971-72), Sigma Alpha Eta. Achievements include research on neuromuscular physiology, embryology and comparative anatomy of the larynx, history of medicine. Office: 303 E Chicago Ave Chicago IL 60611-3008

HASTAD, DOUGLAS NOEL, academic administrator, physical education educator; b. Fargo, ND, Dec. 18, 1949; s. Harold Noel and Olive Adelaide (Nugent) H.; m. Nancy Jo Seljevold, June 11, 1972; children: Jacob Noel, Rebekah Josie. BA, Concordia Coll., 1971; MS, Wash. State U., 1972; EdD, Ariz. State U., 1980; postgrad., Harvard U., 1992. Elem. phys. edn. specialist Moorhead Pub. Schs., Minn., 1972-76; instr. Concordia Coll., Moorhead, 1976-78; grad. assoc. Ariz. State U., Tempe, 1976-79; asst. prof. No. Ill. U., DeKalb, 1979-84; dept. chmn., assoc. prof. Tex. Christian U., Ft. Worth, 1984-89, interim dean, 1987-89; prof., dean dept. health, phys. edn. and recreation U. Wis., La Crosse, 1989—98, dean, human devel. programs, coll. health, phys. edn. and recreation, 1997—98, interim provost, vice chancellor academic affairs, 1998—99, provost, vice chancellor academic affairs, 1999—2000, interim chancellor, 2000—01, chancellor, 2001—06; acting pres. Carroll Coll., Waukesha, Wis., 2006—07, pres., 2007—. Coordinator statewide fitness evaluation project for youth, DeKalb, 1980-84; cons. U. Tex. Med. Br., Galveston, 1985-86. Author: Fitness in the Elementary School, 1986, 2d edit., 1989, Measurement and Evaluation in Physical Education and Exercise Science, 1989, 2d edit., 1994; editl. bd.: The Physical Educator, 1984—; contbr. articles to profl. jours. Vol. Spl. Olympics/Sr. Olympics, DeKalb, 1982-84; vice chmn. program com. Am. Heart Assn. Tex. br., Ft. Worth, 1985-86; dir. conf. on future directions for fitness Tarrant County Med. Soc., Ft. Worth, 1985, pub. sch. adv. bd., 1984-86; bd. dirs. Rotary Internat. Fellow Bush Foundation (hon.); mem. Am. Alliance for Health, Phys. Edn., Recreation and Dance, Golden Key Honor Soc. Home: N2166 Valley Rd La Crosse WI 54601-7118 Office: Carroll Coll Office of Pres 100 N East Ave Waukesha WI 53186*

HASTEN, JOSEPH ERWIN, bank executive; b. Feb. 25, 1952; m. Jane Hasten, 1977; 3 children. B, Fairfield U., 1974; MBA, Northwestern U., 1978. Head, Midwest ops. Std. Chartered Bank, 1984—91; CEO Std. Chartered's South Korean and Indonesian Bus., 1991—95; pres., St. Louis bank Mercantile Bancorp, 1995—99; vice chmn. Firstar, now U.S. Bancorp, 1995—2001; vice chmn., corp. banking US Bancorp, St. Louis, 2001—05; pres., CEO ShoreBank Corp., Chgo., 2007—. Office: ShoreBank Corp 7054 S Jeffery Blvd Chicago IL 60649*

HASTERT, DENNIS (JOHN DENNIS HASTERT), congressman; b. Aurora, Ill., Jan. 2, 1942; m. Thelma Jean Kahl, 1973; children: Joshua John, Ethan Allen. BA in Econ., Wheaton Coll., 1964; MS in Philosophy of Edn., No. Ill. U., 1967. Tchr., coach Yorkville (Ill.) High Sch., 1964—80; mem. Ill. House Reps., Springfield, 1980-86, US Congress from 14th Ill. dist., 1987—, chief dep. majority whip, 1994-99, spkr. of the House, 1999—2007, mem. commerce com., govt. reform and oversight com. Permanent chair Rep. Nat. Conv., 2000; mem. bd. dirs. Aurora Family Support Ctr. Author: Speaker: Lessons from Forty Years of Coaching and Politics, 2004. Named Ill. Coach of the Year, 1976, Guardian of the Seniors Rights, 60 Plus Assn., 1999; named an Outstanding Am., Nat. Wrestling Hall of Fame, 2000; named one of The 20 Top Legislators, Chgo. Sun Times, 1985; recipient Build Life award, Nat. Coalition for Athletic Equity, 1999, Taxpayer Hero award, Americans for Tax Reform, 1999, Disting. Citizen award, Three Fires Coun. (St. Charles, Ill.) Boy Scouts of Am., 2000, Alumnus of the Year award for Disting. Svc. to Society, Wheaton Coll., 2002, Golden Plate award, Acad. Achievement, 2004. Mem.: US Wrestling Assn., IL Wrestling Coaches Assn. (pres. 1977—78), US Olympic Com., US Olympic Movement, Farm Bureau, Lions (Yorkville). Republican. Protestant. Office: US Ho of Reps 235 Cannon House Office Bldg Washington DC 20515-1314*

HASTIE, JOHN DOUGLAS, lawyer; b. Guthrie, Okla., Dec. 9, 1939; BA, U. Okla., 1961, LLB, 1964. Bar: Okla. 1964. Atty. Hastie and Kirschner, Oklahoma City, 1974-96, Andrews Davis Legg Bixler Milsten and Price, Oklahoma City, 1996-2001, Phillips McFall McCaffrey McVay & Murrah, P.C., Oklahoma City, 2001—. Adj. prof. U. Okla. Coll. Law, 1982—90, 2000—02; cons., lectr. in field. Mem. editl. bd.: The Practical Real Estate Lawyer; contbr. articles to profl. jours. Capt. US Army, 1964—66. Mem. ABA, Okla. Bar Assn., Cleve. County Bar Assn., Assn. Bar City NY, Am. Coll. Real Estate Lawyers (gov. 1990-2000, exec. com. 1992-2000, pres. 1999, Frederick S. Lane award 2002), Anglo-Am. Real Property Inst., Am. Law Inst., Am. Coll. Mortgage Attys. Home: 914 Living Springs Trail Goldsby OK 73093 Office: Phillips McFall McCaffrey McVay & Murrah 401 W Main St Ste 444 Norman OK 73069-1319 Office Phone: 405-292-4445. Business E-Mail: jdhastie@hastielaw.com.

HASTIE, REID, psychology professor; BS, Stanford U., Calif., 1968; MA, U. Calif., San Diego, 1970; PhD in Pysch., Yale U., 1973. Asst. prof. to assoc. prof. dept. psych. Harvard U., 1973—80; prof. dept. psych. Northwestern U., 1980—88, U. Colo., 1988—2002; Robert S. Hamada prof. behavioral sci. grad. sch. bus. U. Chgo., 2001—. Fellow Ctr. Advanced Study in Behavioral Scis. Stanford U., 1986—87; dir. Ctr. Rsch. on Judgment and Policy U. Colo., adj. prof. Contbr. articles to profl. jours., chapters to books; consulting editor: Jour. Exptl. Social Psych., 1976—83, 1989—94, Social Cognition, 1981—83, Law and Soc. Rev., 1983—85, Jour. Exptl. Psych.: Learning, Memory, and Cognition, 1984—86, 1999—, Jour. Exptl. Psych.: Gen., 1985—86, 1988—92, 1995—, Psychol. Rev., 1988—94, Orgnl. Behavior and Human Decision Processes, 1988—92, 2001—, Memory, 1991—95, Jour. Consumer Psych., 1996—2002, Jour. Psych. and Fin. Markets, 2000—, Law, Probability, and Risk, 2000—, assoc. editor: Jour. Personality and Social Psych., 1977—79, consulting editor:, 1979—83, assoc. editor: Psychonomic Bull. & Rev., 1993—97, Psychol. Sci., 2004—; co-author: Social Psych. in Court, 1978, Rational Choice in an Uncertain World, 2001; author: Person Memory: The Cognitive Basis of Social Perception, 1980; editor: Inside the Juror: The Psych. of Juror Decision Making, 1993; co-editor: Decision Making from a Cognitive Perspective, 1995. Fellow: Am. Acad. Arts & Scis., Am. Psychol. Soc.; mem.: Soc. Exptl. Psychologists, Soc. Exptl. Social Psych., Psychonomic Soc., Judgement and Decision Making Soc., Cognitive Sci. Soc., APA. Office: Grad Sch Bus U Chgo 5807 S Woodlawn Ave Chicago IL 60637 E-mail: reid.hastie@gsb.uchicago.edu.

HASTINGS, ALCEE LAMAR, congressman, retired judge; b. Altomonte Springs, Fla., Sept. 5, 1936; s. Julius C. and Mildred L. H.; 3 children BA, Fisk U., 1958; postgrad., Howard U. Sch. Law, 1958-60; JD, Fla. A&M U., 1963. Bar: Fla. 1963. Mem. firm Allen and Hastings, Ft. Lauderdale, 1963-66; pvt. practice law Ft. Lauderdale, 1966-77; judge Cir. Ct. Broward County, Fla., 1977-79, U.S. Dist. Ct. (so. dist.) Fla., 1979-89; mem. U.S. Congress from 23d Fla dist., 1993—; mem. rules com., intelligence com. Adj. prof. criminal justice dept. Nova U.; lectr. So. Regional Council on Black Am. Affairs; lectr., cons. Internat. Juvenile Officers Assn., Peace Corps Vols. in Avon Park, Fla., 1966; legal counsel Community Action Migrant Program, Broward County Classroom Tchrs.; mem. Gov.'s Conf. on Criminal Justice, State of Fla.; lectr., cons. to elem. and secondary public and pvt. schs., chs., synagogues, social orgns., civic orgns., colls. and univs. in U.S.; co-propr. Tri-City News Host TV program: Pride, Sta. WPLG; columnist: West Side Gazette. Atty. various civic assns., Broward County and State of Fla.; mem. Bi-Racial Adv. Commn., Broward County Personnel Adv. Commn.; sec. Fla. Council on Aging; chmn. Broward Youth Services Task Force; mem. State of Fla. Edn. Commn., Task Force on Crime, Democratic Exec. Com; candidate for Fla. Ho. of Reps., Fla. Senate, U.S. Senate, Fla. Public Service Commn.; bd. dirs. Urban League of Broward County, Child Advocacy, Inc., The Starting Place, Broward County Sickle Cell Anemia Found., Fla. Voters League, Broward County Council on Human Relations; trustee Mt. Hermon A.M.E. Ch., Ft. Lauderdale, Broward Community Coll., Bethune Cookman Coll. Recipient numerous awards and honors including; Humanitarian award Broward County Young Democrats, 1978; Citizen of Year award Zeta Phi Beta, 1978; Sam Delevoe Human Rights award Community Relations Bd. of Broward County, 1978; Glades Festival of Afro Arts award Zeta Phi Beta, 1981; named Man of Year, Com. Italian Am. Affairs, 1979-80; Judge Alcee Hastings Day proclaimed for City of Daytona Beach in his honor on Dec. 14, 1980; named one of 100 Most Influential Black Americans, Ebony mag., 2006. Mem. ABA (standing com. profl. discipline), Nat. Bar Assn. (Chmn.'s award 1981), Am. Trial Lawyers Assn., Fla. Bar Assn., U.S. Dist. Judges Council., A.M.E. Ch. Clubs: Elks, KP. Democrat. Office: US Ho of Reps 2353 Rayburn Ho Office Bldg Washington DC 20515-0923 Office Phone: 202-225-1313. E-mail: alcee.pubhastings@mail.house.gov.*

HASTINGS, DANIEL, aeronautical engineer, educator; b. Chardstock, Devon, Eng. BA in Math., Oxford U., 1967; SM in Aeronautics and Astronautics, MIT, 1978, PhD in Plasma Physics, 1980. Rsch. scientist Physical Sciences Inc., Andover, Mass., 1980—81, Oak Ridge Nat. Lab., Tenn., 1981—85; asst. prof. aeronautics and astronautics MIT, 1985—88, assoc. prof. aeronautics and astronautics, 1988—93, prof. aeronautics and astronautics, 1993—, dir. Space Grant Prog., 1990—93, assoc. dept. head of rsch., dept. aeronautics and astronautics, 1993—96, dir., Space Engring. Rsch. Ctr., 1996—97, prof. engring. systems, 2000—, dir. technol. and policy prog., 2000—03, assoc. dir. engring. sys. divsn., 2001—03, co-dir. engineering systems div., assoc. dean engring. systems, 2003—04, dir. engineering systems div., 2004—. Vis. scientist Phillips Lab., 1993—94; chief scientist US Air Force, Washington, 1997—99; mem. Applied Physics Lab Sci. and Technol. Advisory Bd.; mem. bd. dir. Nat. Sci. Bd., 2002—; chair Air Force Scientific Advisory Bd.; mem. MIT Lincoln Lab. Advisory Com.; bd. trustees Aerospace Corp. Contbr. articles to profl. jours. Recipient Martin Marietta Superior Publ. award, 1988, Air Force Disting. Civilian award, 1997, 1999, Bur. Eagle award, Nat. Guard, 1999. Fellow: AIAA; mem.: Internat. Acad. Astronautics. Achievements include research in tethers, plasma conductors, and high voltage arching on solar arrays; research in new design paradigms for space systems, collaborating distributed satellite systems, changing the nature of the space economy and strategic space policy. Avocations: reading, walking. Office: MIT Engring Systems Divsn 77 Massachusetts Ave Bldg E40-251 Cambridge MA 02139-4307

HASTINGS, DEBORAH, bass guitarist; b. Evansville, Ind., May 11, 1959; d. Mortimer Winthrop Hastings and Margaret Hooper (Smith) Zimmerman. Student music, U. Wis. Bass guitarist, NYC and Madison, Wis., 1975—; freelance photographer Madison, 1976-81; band leader Bo Diddley, 1992—; founder A/Prompt Computer Telepromting Svcs., Inc., 1994—. Featured bassist with Duck Dunn for Bush inauguration, performing with Billy Preston, Dr. John, Koko Taylor, Willie Dixon, Carla Thomas, Eddie Floyd, Ron Wood, Steve Cropper, Bo Diddley, Jerry Lee Lewis, Chuck Berry, Joe Louis Walker; has also performed with Ben E. King, Little Anthony, Sam Moore, John Lee Hooker, Mick Fleetwood, Al Kooper, James Cotton; TV shows include Legends of Rock and Roll Live from Rome; appeared on David Letterman Show, 2003; subject of PBS Spl., 2003. Bass player TV shows Joan Rivers, 1987, Classics of Rock and Roll, 1988, Gunslingers tour Live from the Ritz with Ron Wood & Bo Diddley, 1988, Live from the Ritz, 1989, Legends of Rock and Roll (live from Australia), Legends of Guitar from Seville, Spain, 1991, Showtime at the Apollo, 1992, N.Y. at Night, 1992; performed Into The Night, 1991 (TV show) Nashville Now, 1991, American Musicshop, 1991, Johnny Carson Show, 1990, Pat Sajak Show, 1990, Carla Thomas, 1991, Arts & Entertainment Revue, 1990, (Madison Sq. Garden) Tribute to John Lee Hooker, 1990, Richard Nader's 25th Anniversary Show, 1994, Conan O'Brien Show, 1996; recordings include Bo Diddley's Grammy Nominated Album "A Man Amongst Men", 1996; performer in concert video "A Man Amongst Men", 1996; tours in Europe, Australia and Japan; performed at inaugurations of Pres. George Bush, 1989, Pres. Bill Clinton, 1997; performed with Bo Diddley opening of Seattle Music Experience Mus., 2000, Edgar Winter, 2003, Buffy Saint-Marie, 2003, Rock n'Roll Hall of Fame, 2005, with Eric Clapton, Robbie Robertson, Bo Diddley. Fundraiser, bassist polit. campaigns, Madison. Recipient numerous awards for pottery, award Arts Coun., Madison, Arts Coun., Ann Arbor, Mich.; played at Rock and Roll Hall of Fame Mus. Johnnie Johnson in Buenos Aires, Argentina, 2003. Mem. Musicians Union (local 802). Democrat. Avocations: computers, photography, graphics design, video. Office: Talent Cons Internat 1560 Broadway Ste 1308 New York NY 10036-1518 Office Phone: 212-730-2701.

HASTINGS, DOC (RICHARD NORMAN HASTINGS), congressman; b. Spokane, Wash., Feb. 7, 1941; m. Claire Hastings; 3 children. Student, Columbia Basin Coll., 1958—61, Ctrl. Wash. U., 1964. Mem. Wash. State Ho. Reps., 1979-87, asst. majority leader; pres. Columbia Basin Paper & Supply, 1983-94; mem. US Congress from 4th Wash. dist., 1995—, mem. rules com., chmn. rules and orgn. of the house, chmn. stds. ofcl. conduct com., 2005—, chair Congl. Nuc. Cleanup Caucus, asst. majority whip. Bd. dirs. Yakima Fed. Savings & Loan; chmn. Franklin County Rep. Com., 1974-78 Del. Rep. Nat. Conv., 1976—84. Served in USAR, 1963—69. Republican. Office: US Ho Reps 1323 Longworth Ho Office Bldg Washington DC 20515-0001 Office Phone: 202-225-5816.*

HASTINGS, DONALD FRANCIS, actor, writer; b. Bklyn., Apr. 1, 1934; s. Charles Benedict and Hazel May (Kirk) H.; m. Noretta Kennedy, Dec. 29, 1956 (div. Feb. 1980); children: Jennifer, Julie Ann, Matthew; m. Leslie Denniston, June 7, 1980; 1 dau., Katharine Scott. Student pvt., pub. schs., NY. Appeared on network radio shows, 1940-53, including Cavalcade of Am; appeared in plays including Life With Father, 1941-43, I Remember Mama, 1944-45, On Whitman Avenue, 1946, Young Man's Fancy, 1947, Summer and Smoke, 1948; various TV shows, from 1947, including Captain Video, 1949-55, Studio One, 1955, Big Story, 1959, Chevrolet on Broadway, 1948, Edge of Night, 1956-60, As The World Turns, 1960—; author: scripts of As The World Turns, 1972-73, Guiding Light, 1974, 77, (films) Prisoner at Gilbert House, 1976, Decoys, 2003, Engaged to Kill, 2005. Recipient Lifetime Achievement award, Nat. TV Acad., 2004. Mem. AFTRA (AMEE award 2005, Ken Harvey award 2006), SAG, Actors Equity. Roman Catholic. Office: 549 Tripp Rd Millerton NY 12546-4751

HASTINGS, DOUGLAS ALFRED, lawyer; b. Oak Park, Ill., July 28, 1949; s. Douglas A. and Elaine M. (Schramm) H.; m. Virginia Joslin, May 28, 1982; children: Corey, Douglas. BA, Duke U., 1971; JD, U. Va., 1981. Bar: D.C. 1981. Assoc. dir. Inst. for Govt. Studies, Memphis State U., 1976-77; adminstrv. intern Fed. Exec. Inst., Charlottesville, Va., 1977-78; project coord. Assn. Acad. Health Ctrs., Charlottesville, 1978-80; cons. Shenandoah PSRO, Charlottesville, 1980-81; ptnr. Epstein Becker & Green, Washington, 1981—. Vis. lectr. dept. health adminstrn. Duke U., Durham, N.C., 1985-90. Contbr. articles to profl. jours. Mem. ABA, Washington Coun. Lawyers, Am. Health Lawyers Assn. (bd. dirs. 1991—, pres. 2001-02), Inst. of Med. (bd. health svs. 2001—), Order of Coif, Phi Beta Kappa. Democrat. Unitarian Universalist. Avocations: baseball, tennis, basketball. Home: 5301 Burke Dr Alexandria VA 22309-3310 Office: Epstein Becker & Green 1227 25th St NW Fl 7 Washington DC 20037-1156 Home Phone: 703-619-6372; Office Phone: 202-861-1807. E-mail: dhastings@ebglaw.com.

HASTINGS, EDWARD WALTON, theater director; b. New Haven, Apr. 14, 1931; s. Edward Walton and Madeline (Cassidy) H. BA, Yale, 1952; postgrad., Royal Acad. Dramatic Art, London, 1953, Columbia U., 1955-56. Bd. dirs. Eugene O'Neill Found., 1993; guest instr. Shanghai Drama Inst., 1984. Dir. Australian premiere Hot L Baltimore, 1975, Shakespeare's People nat. tour, 1983, Nothing Sacred, Hong Kong, 1992, Come Back Little Sheba, Gogol Theater, Moscow, 1995, Dial M for Murder nat. tour, 1995, Beggars Opera, Santa Fe Opera, 2000, H.M.S. Pinafore, Santa Fe Opera, 2001, Italian Girl, 2005, Oliver!, St. Louis Mcpl. Opera, 2005, others; exec. dir. Am. Conservatory Theatre, San Francisco, 1965-80, artistic dir., 1986-92; freelance dir., 1980-86. Mem. Santa Fe Arts Commn. Served with U.S. Army, 1953-55. Recipient Tao House award, Eugene O'Neill Found. Mem. Coll. of Fellows of the Am. Theatre. Clubs: Elizabethan (New Haven). Office: Am Conservatory Theatre 30 Grant Ave San Francisco CA 94108-5800 Home: 945 Acequia Madre Santa Fe NM 87505

HASTINGS, GEORGE L., federal official; b. Detroit, July 24, 1953; BA magna cum laude, U. Mich., 1974; JD cum laude, U. Mich. Law Sch., 1977. News editor Good Morning Mich., 1975; atty. tax divsn., appellate sect. US Dept. Justice, 1978—85, asst. chief claims ct. sec. tax divsn., 1985—89; spl. master US Ct. Fed. Claims, 1989—. Recipient Tax Divsn. Outstanding Atty. award, 1981, 1984, Atty. Gen. Spl. Commendation, 1983. Mem.: US Supreme Ct. Bar, Mich. State Bar. Office: US Ct Fed Claims Office Spl Masters 717 Madison Pl NW Washington DC 20005 Office Phone: 202-357-6400.

HASTINGS, HILL, surgeon; m. Bettie Hastings; children: Peiper, Laurel. BA, Williams Coll., Williamstown, Mass., 1970; PhD in Medicine, U. So. Calif., LA, 1974. Diplomate Am. Bd. Orthop. Surgery. Pvt. practice, Vail, Colo., 1977; ptnr. Ind. Hand Ctr., Indpls., 1981—. Clin. prof. orthop. surgery Ind. U. Med. Ctr., Indpls., 2003—. Contbr. articles to profl. jours. Named Disting. Physician, St. Vincent Hosp., Indpls., 2001; named one of Top Drs. in Indpls., Indpls. Monthly, 1995—; grantee, Found. for Hand Rsch. and Edn., Indpls., 2000. Mem.: Am. Shoulder & Elbow Surgery, Am. Soc. for Surgery of the Hand, Am. Acad. Orthop. Surgeons. Achievements include discovery of elbow bionet. Avocations: horseback riding, skiing, travel, photography, kayaking. Office: Ind Hand Ctr 8601 Harcourt Rd Indianapolis IN 46260 Office Phone: 317-870-5125.

HASTINGS, JOHN JACOB, writer, lyricist, consultant, activist; b. Walla Walla, Wash., Oct. 7, 1953; s. Frederic William and Margaret Mary (McElliggot) Hastings. AA, Walla Walla C.C., 1976; BFA, Ea. Wash. U., 1979. Mgr. Monroe Cigar Co., Chgo., 1980-83; prof. Harry Truman C.C., Chgo., 1981; farmer Touchet, Wash., 1986-99. Author: Four Score Seven, 1995; (poetry) Playing Possum, 1995, Back on the Stack, 1998, Linda's Lullaby in Heaven, 1998, Penultimate Glory, 1998, Excellent annus, 1998, Eiriecalm, 2000, Moods, Anew, 2001; lyricist: Hilltop Records, Hollywood, Calif., 1997-98. Moderate Nat. Orgn. Dems., 1975-2005; precinct com. mem. Walla Walla (Wash.) County Dem. Ctrl. Com., 1992-99, mem. Dem. Nat. Com., 1998, 2005, Dem. Senatorial Campaign, 1998, 2000, 01, 02, 05, Westchester County Dem. Party, 2000-2005; activist Peace Movement, Walla Walla and Bellingham, Wash., 1977-86; mem. MADD, ACLU. Recipient Man of the Yr., Am. Biog. Inst., 2006. Mem. Nat. Geographic Soc., Nat. Trust for Hist. Preservation, Walla Walla Pioneers Hist. Soc. (faculty mem.), Nat. Assn. Women in Arts (assoc.), Smithsonian Instn., Libr. Congress (assoc.), Ea. Wash. U. Alumni, Nat. Parks and Conservation Assn. Wilson Ctr., Handyman's Club Am., Nature Conservancy, Hastings Art Entertainment Ltd. (pres, C.L.O.), N.Y. Acad. Polit. Sci., N.Y. Acad. Sci., Metro. Registry, Manhattan Club. Roman Catholic. Avocations: conservationist, tree planter, advocate, writing.

HASTINGS, JOHN WOODLAND, biologist, educator; b. Salisbury, Md., Mar. 24, 1927; s. Vaughan Archelaus and Kathrine (Stevens) H.; m. Hanna Machlup, June 6, 1953; children: Jennifer, David, Laura, Karen. BA, Swarthmore Coll., 1947; MA, Princeton U., 1950, PhD, 1951; MA, Harvard U., 1966. AEC postdoctoral fellow Johns Hopkins, 1951-53; instr. to asst. prof. biol. scis. Northwestern U., 1953-57; from asst. prof. to prof. biochemistry U. Ill. at Urbana, 1957-66; prof. biology Harvard, 1966-87, Paul C. Mangelsdorf prof. natural scis., 1987—; master Pforzheimer House, 1976-96. Summer rsch. participant Oak Ridge Nat. Lab., 1958; vis. lectr. biochemistry Sheffield (Eng.) U., 1961-62; instr. physiology Marine Biol. Lab., Woods Hole, Mass., 1961-66, dir., 1962-66, dir. marine ecology, 1989-91, mem. corp., 1961, trustee, 1966-74, exec. com., 1968-74; guest prof. Rockefeller U., 1965-66, Inst. Biol. Phys. Chemistry Paris, 1972-73, U. Konstanz, Ger., 1979-80, Nat. Biology Inst., Okazaki, Japan, 1986, U. Munich, 1993; Disting. vis. scientist Calif. Inst. Tech., 2000, Jet Propulsion Lab., 2000--; mem. panel molecular biology NSF, 1963-66, mem. adv. com. biology and medicine, 1968-71; com. postdoctoral fellowships chemistry Nat. Acad. Scis., 1965-67, com. photobiology, 1965-71, com. on phototherapy, 1971-73, com. on low frequency radiation, 1975-77; mem. Commn. Undergrad. Edn. in Biol. Scis., 1965-66; space biology com. NASA, 1966-71; biochemistry tng. com. Nat. Inst. Gen. Med. Scis., 1968-72; mem. internat. adv. bd. Marine Biol. Lab., Eilat, Israel, 1968—; faculty assoc. Calif. Inst. Tech., 2000. Contbr. profl. jours. With USN, 1944—45. Guggenheim fellow, 1965-66, NIH fellow, 1972-73, Yamada Found. fellow, Osaka, Japan, 1986, Humboldt fellow, 1993, recipient Alexander von Humboldt prize, 1979, Lifetime Achievement award, Am. Soc. Photobiology, 2003, Peter C. Farrell Sleep Medicine prize, Harvard Med. Sch., 2006. Fellow AAAS, Am. Soc. Biol. Chemists, Biophys. Soc., Soc. Am. Microbiologists, Am. Soc. Photobiology (pres. 1999-2001), Soc. Gen. Physiology (pres. 1963-65), Soc. Chemi- and Bio-luminescence (founding pres. 1994-98), Pierian Found. (pres. 1999—2001), Johns Hopkins Soc. Scholars, mem. Nat. Acad. Scis., Am. Acad. Arts and Scis. Home: 14 Concord Ave Cambridge MA 02138-2356 Office: 16 Divinity Ave Cambridge MA 02138-2020 Home Phone: 617-492-8374; Office Phone: 617-495-3714. Business E-Mail: hastings@fas.harvard.edu.

HASTINGS, KERRY P., lawyer; b. Cin., Oct. 27, 1971; BA, U. Mich., 1993; JD, Harvard U., 1996. Bar: Ohio 1996. Ptnr. Taft, Stettinius & Hollister LLP, Cin. Named one of Ohio's Rising Stars, Super Lawyers, 2005, 2006. Mem.: Cin. Acad. Leadership for Lawyers (class of 2006), Harvard Law Sch. Assn., ABA (mem., Labor and Employment Law Sect.), Cin. Bar Assn. (mem., Unauthorized Practice of Law Com.), Harvard Club Cin. Office: Taft Stettinius & Hollister LLP 425 Walnut St Ste 1800 Cincinnati OH 45202-3957 Office Phone: 513-381-2838. Office Fax: 513-381-0205.

HASTINGS, LINDSAY MARIE, industrial engineer; b. Glenshaw, Pa., Feb. 25, 1982; d. Albert and Linda Hastings. BS in Indsl. Engring., Pa. State U., State College, 2005, M in Indsl. Engring. and Ops. Rsch., 2007. Labor maintenance analyst Wald Disney World, Lake Buena Vista, Fla., 2004—06; indsl. engr. Fed Ex Ground, Pitts., 2007—. Mem.: Inst. Ops. Rsch. and Mgmt. Sci., Inst. Indsl. Engrs.

HASTINGS, L(OIS) JANE, architect, educator; b. Seattle, Mar. 3, 1928; d. Harry and Camille (Pugh) H.; m. Norman John Johnston, Nov. 22, 1969. B.Arch., U. Wash., Seattle, 1952, postgrad. in Urban Planning, 1958. Architect Boeing Airplane Co., Seattle, 1951-54; recreational dir. Germany, 1954-56; architect (various firms), Seattle, 1956-59, pvt. practice architecture, 1959-74; instr. archtl. drafting Seattle Community Coll., part-time 1969-80; owner/founder The Hastings Group Architects, Seattle, 1974—; lectr. design Coll. Architecture, U. Wash., 1975; incorporating mem. Architecta (P.S.), Seattle, 1980, pres., from 1980. Mem. adv. bd. U. Wash. YWCA, 1967—69; mem. Mayor's Com. on Archtl. Barriers for Handicapped, 1974—75; chmn. regional public adv. panel on archtl. and engring. services GSA, 1976; mem. citizens adv. com. Seattle Land Use Adminstrn. Task Force, 1979—; AWIU guest of Soviet Women's Con., 1983; spkr. Pacific Rim Forum, Hong Kong, 1987; guest China Internat. Conf. Ctr. for Sci. and Tech. of the China Assn. for Sci. and Tech., 1989; mem. adv. com. Coll. architecture and urban planning U. Wash., 1993; mem. accreditation team U. Oreg. Coll. Architecture, 1991, N.J. Inst. Tech. Sch. Architecture, 1992; juror Home of the Yr. ann. award AIA/Seattle Times, 1996; mem. architect selection com. Wash. State capital carillon project, Pratt Art Ctr. new bldg., 2001. Design juror for nat. and local competitions, including Red Cedar Shingle/AIA awards, 1977, Current Use Honor awards, AIA, 1980, Exhibit of Sch. Architecture award, 1981; Contbr. to: also spl. features newspapers, articles in profl. jours. Sunset mag. Mem. bd. Am. Women for Internat. Understanding, del. to, Egypt, Israel, USSR, 1971, Japan and Korea, 1979, USSR, 1983; mem. Landmarks Preservation Bd. City of Seattle, 1981-83; mem. Design Constrn. Rev. Bd. Seattle Sch. Dist., 1985-87; mem. mus. con. Mus. History and Industry, 1987—; leader People to People del. women architects to China, 1990. Recipient AIA/The Seattle Times Home of Month Ann. award, 1968; Exhbn. award Seattle chpt. AIA, 1970; Environ. award Seattle-King County Bd. Realtors, 1970, 77,; AIA/House and Home/The American Home Merit award, 1971, Sp. Honor award Wash. Aggregates and Concrete Assn., 1993, Prize bridge Am. Inst. Steel Contrn., 1993; Honor award Seattle chpt. AIA, 1977, 83; Women Achievement award Past Pres. Assembly, 1983, Washington Women and Trading Cards, 1983; Nat. Endowment for Arts grantee, 1977; others; named to West Seattle High Sch. Hall of Fame, 1989, Woman of Achievement Matrix Table, 1994; named Woman of Distinction, Columbia River Girl Scout Coun., 1994. Fellow AIA (pres. Seattle chpt. 1975, pres. sr. coun. 1980, state exec. bd. 1975, N.W. regional dir. 1982-87, Seattle chpt. found. bd. 1985-87, Bursar Coll. Fellows 1989-90, Coll. of Fellows historian 1994—, internat. rels. com. 1988-92, vice chancellor 1991, chancellor 1992, Seattle chpt. medal 1995, Northwest & Pacific region Medal of Honor 2002, Leslie N. Boney Spirit of Fellowship award 2003, Richard Upjohn Fellows medal), Internat. Union Women Architects (v.p. 1969-79, sec. gen. 1985-89, del. UIA Congress, Montreal 1990), Am. Arbitration Assn. (arbitrator 1981—), Coun. of Design Professions, Assn. Women Contrs., Suppliers and Design Cons., Allied Arts Seattle, Fashion Group, Tau Sigma Delta, Alpha Rho Chi (medal). *It is not the quantity but the quality of space that is important.*

HASTINGS, MARY JANE, minister; b. NYC, July 23, 1949; d. Lucy Lake and Charles Thomas Hastings. BS in Bus. Adminstrn., Caldwell Coll., 1998; MDiv, Luth. Theol. Sem., Phila., 2002. Sec. TV Bur. Advt., NYC, 1968—72; exec. asst. to pres. TeleRep, Inc., 1972—80; v.p. ops. TV Program Enterprises divsn. TeleRep, Inc., 1980—93; exec. v.p. and ptnr. Al Masini Productions, 1993—94; dir. sales and mktg. The Mediacenter, 1994—96; pastor St. Mark Luth. Ch., Morristown, 2002—. Co-pres. Morris Area Clergy Coun., Morristown, 2006—. Writer (short drama) The Trial of Judas, The Sacrificing Samaritan, Second Chance, The Wives of the Disciples, Mary Magdalene - A Personal Reflection. Recipient Tracy L. Maul award, Luth. Theol. Sem., Phila., 1999. Mem.: Delta Epsilon Sigma, Kappa Gamma Pi, Alpha Chi. Lutheran. Avocations: travel, walking, old movies, exercise, reading. Home: 100 James St Morristown NJ 07960 Office: St Mark LuthCh 100 Harter Rd Morristown NJ 07960 Home Phone: 973-889-0682; Office Phone: 973-538-3939. Office Fax: 976-538-6223. Personal E-mail: pastormj@optonline.net.

HASTINGS, REED, film rental company executive, former education association administrator; b. 1960; BA, Bowdoin Coll., 1983; MS in Computer Sci., Stanford U., 1988. High sch. math tchr. US Peace Corps, Swaziland, 1983—86; founder, CEO Pure Atria Software, 1991—97; CEO Tech. Network, 1998—99; co-founder, chmn., CEO Netflix, Inc., Los Gatos, Calif., 1998—, pres., 1998—. Bd. dirs. Microsoft Corp., 2007—. Pres. Calif. State Bd. Edn., 2000—04; founding mem. NewSchools.org, Aspire Pub. Schs., Pacific Collegiate Sch., EdVoice.net. Named one of World's 100 Most Influential People, Time Mag., 2005. Office: NetFlix com Inc 970 University Ave Los Gatos CA 95032*

HASTINGS, SAMANTHA KELLY, library and information science professor, director; BA, U. Ariz.; MLS, U. South Fla.; PhD in Libr. and Info. Sci., Fla. State. U., 1994. Asst. med. libr. Tucson Med. Ctr. Libr., 1970—77; tchr. English and math. Flowing Wells HS, 1977—80; ind. cons. Bradenton, Fla., 1982—86, Tallahassee, 1989—92; reference, circulation and evening supr. Manatee CC Libr., Bradenton, 1986—87; tech. svcs. libr. Jane Bancroft Cook Libr. U. South Fla./New College, Sarasota, 1987—89; libr. Fla. Dept. of Natural Resources Marine Fisheries Commn., Tallahassee, 1990—92; adj. instr. Sch. Libr. and Info. Studies Fla. State U., Tallahassee, 1991—94; libr. program specialist Fla. Dept. State, Div. Libr. and Info. Svcs., Bur. Libr. Devel., Tallahassee, 1992—95; assoc. prof. Sch. Libr. and Info. Scis., U. North Tex., Denton, 2000—06, interim dean, 2004—05; dir., prof. Sch. Libr. and Info. Sci., U. SC, Columbia, 2006—. Cons. Bur. Libr. Devel., State of Fla. Fellow Tex. Ctr. for Digital Knowledge. Mem.: Am. Soc. of Info. Sci. and Tech. (pres. 2004). Office: Sch Libr and Info Sci Coll Mass Comm and Info Studies U SC Columbia SC 29208 Office Phone: 803-777-3858. E-mail: hastings@sc.edu.*

HASTINGS, SUSAN C., lawyer; b. Mpls., 1959; BA, U. Iowa, 1980, JD with distinction, 1985. Bar: Ohio 1985, registered: US Dist. Ct. (No. Dist.) Ohio, US Ct. Appeals (6th cir.). Ptnr. Squire, Sanders & Dempsey LLP, Cleve., chmn., Labor & Employment Practice Group. Mem.: ABA (Labor & Employment Law Sect.), Ohio State Bar Assn. (Labor & Employment Law Sect.), Nat. Sch. Bd. Assn., Ohio Coun. of Sch. Bd. Attys. Office: Squire Sanders & Dempsey LLP 4900 Key Tower 127 Public Sq Cleveland OH 44114-1304 Office Phone: 216-479-8723. Office Fax: 216-479-8780. Business E-Mail: shastings@ssd.com.

HASTINGS, VIVIEN N., lawyer; b. Havana, Cuba, Dec. 22, 1951; BA, U. Conn., 1973; JD, Wash. U., 1977. Bar: Ill. 1977, Fla. 1990. Assoc. Winston & Strawn, 1977—82; v.p., co-gen. counsel Merrill Lynch Hubbard, Inc., 1982—89; various positions WCI Communities Ltd. Partnership; sr. v.p., gen. counsel WCI Communities Ltd. Partnership (now WCI Communities, Inc.), Bonita Springs, Fla. Office: WCI Communities Inc 24301 Walden Ctr Dr Bonita Springs FL 34134 Office Phone: 239-947-2600. Office Fax: 239-498-8277.*

HASTINGS, WILLIAM CHARLES, retired state supreme court chief justice; b. Newman Grove, Nebr., Jan. 31, 1921; s. William C. and Margaret (Hansen) H.; m. Julie Ann Simonson, Dec. 29, 1946; children—Pamela, Charles, Steven. B.Sc., U. Nebr., 1942, JD, 1948; LHD (hon.), Hastings Coll., 1991. Bar: Nebr. 1948. With FBI, 1942-43; mem. firm Chambers, Holland, Dudgeon & Hastings, Lincoln, 1948-65; judge 3d jud. dist. Nebr., Lincoln, 1965-79, Supreme Ct. Nebr., Lincoln, 1979-88, chief justice, 1988-95; ret., 1995. Bd. dir. Nat. Conf. Chief Justices, 1989-91. Pres. Child Guidance Ctr., Lincoln, 1962, 63; v.p. Lincoln Community Coun., 1968, 69; vice chmn. Antelope Valley coun. Boy Scouts Am., 1968, 69; pres. 1st Presbyn. Ch. Found., 1968—; mem. Lincoln Parks and Recreation Adv. Bd., Govs. task force correctional dept. medical svcs., 2000; mem. Nebr. Pub. Employees Retirement Bd. With US Army, 1943—46. Named to Nebr. Jaycee Hall of Fame, 1998, U. Nebr. Lincoln-Greek Hall of Fame, 2005; recipient Merit award, Acacia Nat. Frat., 2004. Mem. ABA, Nebr. Bar Assn. (George H. Turner award 1991, Pioneer award 1992), Am. Jud. Soc., Lincoln Bar Assn., Nebr. Dist. Judges Assn. (past pres.), Nat. Conf. Chief Justices (past bd. dirs.), Am. Judicature Soc. (Herbert Harley award 1997), Phi Delta Phi. Republican. Presbyterian (deacon, elder, trustee). Club: East Hills Country (pres. 1959-60). Home: 1544 S 58th St Lincoln NE 68506-1407 Personal E-mail: hwchastings@aol.com.

HASTINGS, WILMOT REED, lawyer, writer; b. Salem, Mass., May 29, 1935; s. Abner Horace and Florence (Hylan) H.; m. Joan Amory Loomis, Aug. 30, 1958; children: W. Reed, Jr., Melissa H., Claire A. AB magna cum laude, Harvard U., 1957, LL.B. magna cum laude, 1961; postgrad., U. Paris, 1957-58. Bar: Mass. 1961. Law clk. Chief Justice Raymond S. Wilkins, Boston, 1961-62; assoc. firm Bingham, Dana & Gould, Boston, 1962-68; 1st asst. and dep. atty. gen. Mass., 1968-69; spl. asst. and exec. asst. to undersec. state, 1969-70; gen. counsel HEW, 1970-73; ptnr. Bingham, Dana & Gould (now Bingham McCutchen), Boston and London, 1973-90; writer, 1990—. Home and Office: 45 Ward Ave Northampton MA 01060 Personal E-mail: hastings@crocker.com.

HASTRITER, MICHAEL WAYNE, medical entomologist; b. Nampa, Idaho, 1945; m. Pauline Lorraine Butler, Mar. 16, 1968; children: Michael Larkin, Eric Vance, Natasha Marne, Anya Rene, Kimberly Jewel, Celestia Marcine. BS in Zoology, Brigham Young U., 1971, MS in Entomology, 1973; grad., US Army Commd. and Gen. Staff Coll., 1985. Entomologist US Army Med. Lab., St. Louis, 1973—75, US Army Environ. Hygiene Agy., Aurora, Colo., 1975—79, chief entomology divsn., dir. radiation entomologic scis. Aberdeen Proving Ground, Md., 1990—92; entomologist US Army Med. Dept. Activity, Ft. Leonardwood, Mo., 1984—90; chief entomology sect. Walter Reed Army Inst. Rsch., Silver Spring, Md., 1979—82; adjutant, rsch. entomologist US Army Med. Rsch. Unit, Kuala Lumpur, Malaysia, 1982—84; med. entomologist Mo. Dept. Health, Jefferson City, 1994—95; entomologist Monte L. Bean Life Sci. Mus. Brigham Young U., Provo, Utah, 1995—. Rsch. assoc. Nat. Mus. Nat. History, Smithsonian Instn., Washington, 2000—, Carnegie Mus. Nat. History, Pitts., 2000—. Contbr. articles to profl. jours., chapters to books. Lt. col. US Army, 1973—92. Decorated Bronze Star with v device USN, Meritorious Svc. medals (4) US Army, Army Commendation medal. Mem.: Entomol. Soc. Washington. Mem. Lds Ch. Achievements include assembly and compilation of disease vector ecology profiles for Colombia, Ecuador, Peru and Bolivia. Avocations: bow hunting, fishing, woodworking, genealogy. Home: 1955 E Oregon Ave Provo UT 84606 Office: Monte L Bean Life Sci Mus Brigham Young U PO Box 20200 Provo UT 84602 Office Phone: 801-422-3193. Personal E-mail: michaelhastriter@comcast.net.

HASWELL, CARLETON RADLEY, banker; b. Milw., May 18, 1939; s. Clayton Lyman and Jane (Radley) H.; m. Almut Haberkamp, Dec. 10, 1966; children— Angela, Robin. BS, Northwestern U., 1961; MBA, NYU, 1967. Chief internat. credit officer Chem. Bank, NYC, 1963-87; dir. Chem. Internat. Inc., NYC, 1981-86, Chem. Internat. Fin., NYC, 1981-84; pres. Carleton Haswell Assocs., 1987—. Treas. P.G. Islanders; counselor S.C.O.R.E. With US Army, 1961—63. Republican. Home and Office: Villa 514 2645 W Marion Ave Punta Gorda FL 33950-5979

HATADA, KAZUYUKI, mathematician, educator; b. Maebashi, Gunma, Japan, Dec. 23, 1951; s. Kiyoshi and Tokiko Hatada; m. Kumiko Yoshikawa, Dec. 15, 1985; 1 child, Hidehiko. BS, U. Tokyo, 1974, MS, 1976; DSc, U. Tokyo, 1979. Rsch. fellow faculty sci. U. Tokyo, 1979-80; assoc. prof. dept. math. faculty edn. Gifu U., Gifu City, Japan, 1981-99, prof., 1999—. Vis. prof. U. Paris XI, 1993, Nagoya U., 2001-03. Contbr. articles to profl. math. jours. Recipient Insignia of Dedications, Cambridge, 1988, Internat. Cultural Diploma of Honor, 1988, Silver medal, 1989, Gold medal for 1st 500, 1990, Internat. Order of Merit, 1990, Internat. Man of Yr. award, 1991-92, 95-96, 20th Century award for Achievement, 1993, Global Distinction award, 1994-95, Golden Scroll of Excellence, 1997, Am. Medal of Honor, 2002, Lifetime Achievement award for contbns. to Generalized Ramanujan Conjecture, 2005, Archimedes award, 2006; named Man. of Yr., 2000, Internat. Personality of Yr., 2001, Internat. Scientist of Yr. award, 2002; named one of Top 100 Scientists, 2005; named to Dir. Gen.'s Roll of Honor, 2007; Albert Einstein Internat. Acad. Found. honoree, 1998. Mem. World Inst. Achievement (life), Math. Soc. Japan (councilor 2001, rep. 2002), Am. Math. Soc. (reviewer), Math. Assn. Am. Achievements include proofs of the 10 new congruences enjoyed by all the eigenvalues of Hecke operators on SL(2,Z); discovery that the Hecke rings as representations act naturally on the integral homology groups and l-adic cohomology groups of suitable smooth projective toroidal compactifications of the higher dimensional modular varieties through correspondences and the investigation of properties on this; gave new sharp estimates of all the eigenvalues of Hecke operators on Siegel cusp forms; expressed any modular form of nebentypus of level Np**m as a p-adic modular form of level N; obtained the new expressions of the local zeta functions of the compactified Hilbert modular schemes in terms of the action of the Hecke rings; study of l-adic modular forms and mod l Galois representations; study of the parabolic cohomology; characterized Siegel cusp forms as holomorphic differential forms on certain compact varieties, others. Home: 6-2 Chiyoda 2 chome Maebashi Gunma 371-0022 Japan Office: Gifu U Dept Math Fac Edn 1-1 Yanagido Gifu 501-1193 Japan Office Phone: 058-293-2235.

HATAMIYA, LON SHOSO, consultant, former state official; m. Nancy Hatamiya; 2 children. BS in Economics, Harvard U.; MBA in Internat. Bus. & Entrepreneurial Studies, UCLA; JD, UCLA Sch. of Law. Former atty. Procter & Gamble Co., Cincinnati, Ohio, Sony Corp., Tokyo; administrator Agricultural Mktg. Svc., USDA, 1993—97, Foreign Agricultural Svc., USDA, 1997—99; secy. Calif. Techn., Trade and Commerce Agy., 1999—2003; dir. LECG, 2004—. Mem. Calif. Rural Economic Develop. Infrastructure Panel; exec.-in-residence U. Calif. Grad. Sch. of Bus., Davis, 2004. Office: LECG 333 S Grand Ave Ste 3750 Los Angeles CA 90071

HATCH, DENNY (ALDEN DENISON), publishing executive, writer; b. NYC, Aug. 15, 1935; s. Alden R. Hatch and Ruth Brown Hatch Elwell; m. Margaret Cook, July 12, 1970. AB in English, Columbia U., 1958. Sales mgr. Franklin Watts, Inc., Pubs., NYC, 1961—64; mem. staff advt. sales Libr. Jour. Mag., NYC, 1965—66; copywriter, dir. new products Grolier Enterprises, NYC, 1966—68; dir. book club Macmillan, NYC, 1968—69; dir. book clubs Meredith Corp., Manhasset, NY, 1970—71; v.p., account exec. Walter Weintz & Co., Stamford, Conn., 1972—75; pres. Denison Hatch Assocs., Inc., 1976—. Editor, pub. Who's Mailing What! newsletter, 1984—95; editor Target Mktg. mag., 1992—97; contbg. editor Tarket Mktg., Catalog Success, Fundraising Success mags., 1997—. Author: Million Dollar Mailings, 1992, Method Marketing, 1999, Priceline.com: A Layman's Guide to Manipulating the Media, 2004, Cedarhurst Valley, 2005; co-author (with Don Jackson): 2,239 Tested Secrets for Direct Marketing Success, 1998; editor: www.businesscommonsense.com. With AUS, 1958—60. Mem.: Union League Club Phila., Delta Kappa Epsilon. Home and Office: 310 Gaskill St Philadelphia PA 19147-1503 Home Phone: 215-627-9103; Office Phone: 215-627-9103. Personal E-mail: dennyhatch@yahoo.com.

HATCH, FREDERICK TASKER, research scientist; b. Boston, Aug. 27, 1924; s. Frederick Southard and Beatrice (Tasker) H.; m. Virginia Weeks, Mar. 3, 1946; children: Daniel F., Daphne A., Deborah J., Douglas E. BA, Dartmouth Coll., 1944; MD, Harvard U., 1948; PhD, MIT, 1960. Diplomate Nat. Bd. Med. Examiners. Intern Roosevelt Hosp., NYC, 1948-49; rsch. fellow Columbia U., NYC, 1949-52; established investigator Am. Heart Assn./Mass. Gen. Hosp., Boston, 1960-65; sr. scientist, sect. leader Lawrence Livermore Nat. Lab., Calif., 1965-80, asst. assoc. dir. Calif., 1980-87, cons. Calif., 1987—2006. Mem. lipid metabolism adv. com. Nat. Heart, Lung and Blood Inst., Bethesda, Md., 1968-73. Assoc. editor Lipids Jour., 1964-73; author chpts. in books; contbr. numerous articles to profl. jours. Sec. Land Conservation Task Force, Meredith, N.H., 1989-90, chmn. Transp. Adv. Com., 1994—. Capt., Army Nutrition Lab., Denver, USAR, 1952-55. Fellow Am. Inst. Chemists; mem. Am. Chem. Soc., Am. Soc. Biochemistry and Molecular Biology, Environ. Mutagen Soc., Arteriosclerosis, Thrombosis and Vascular Biology, Coun. of Am. Heart Assn. (exec. com. 1971-73). Lipid and lipoprotein metabolism; coronary heart disease risk factors; satellite DNA structure; mutagens and carcinogens in cooked foods; genetic toxicology of heterocyclic and aromatic amines. Home and Office: 27 Pease Rd Meredith NH 03253-5506 Office Phone: 603-279-5142. Personal E-mail: fhatch@emailmv.com.

HATCH, GEORGE CLINTON, television executive; b. Erie, Pa., Dec. 16, 1919; s. Charles Milton and Blanche (Beecher) Hatch; m. Wilda Gene Glasmann, Dec. 24, 1940; children: Michell Arnow, Diane Glasmann Orr, Jeffrey Beecher, Randall Clinton, Deepika Hatch Avanti. AB, Occidental Coll., 1940; MA in Econs., Claremont Coll., 1941; HHD (hon.), So. Utah U., 1988. Pres. Comms. Investment Corp., Salt Lake City, 1945-95; chmn. Double G Comm. Corp., Salt Lake City, 1956—; dir. Republic Pictures Corp., Los Angeles, 1971-94; pres. Sta. KVEL, Inc., 1978-94. Pres. Standard Corp., Ogden, 1993-98, Hatch Family LLC, 1998—; past mem. Salt Lake adv. bd. First Security Bank Utah; past chmn. Rocky Mountain Pub. Broadcasting Corp.; past chmn. bd. govs. Am. Info. Radio Network; past bd. govs. NBC-TV Affiliates. Past pres. Salt Lake Com. on Fgn. Relations; past mem. Utah Symphony Bd., Salt Lake City; past chmn. and mem. Utah State Bd. Regents, 1964-85. Recipient Svc. to Journalism award U. Utah, 1966, silver medal Salt Lake Advt. Club, 1969, Disting. Svc. award Utah Tech. U., 1984, Disting. Utahan Centennial Yr. award Margaret Thatcher U.K., Utah Festival, 1996. Mem. Nat. Assn. Broadcasters (past pres., radio bd. dirs., ambassador to Inter-Am. mtgs. in Latin Am. 1962), Utah Broadcasters Assn. (past pres., Mgmt. award 1964, Hall of Fame award 1981), Salt Lake City Advt. Club (silver medal 1969), Phi Beta Kappa, Phi Rho Pi (life). Democrat. Avocations: hiking, rock art. Office: Hatch Family LLC 1537 Chandler Dr Salt Lake City UT 84103-4220

HATCH, HELEN DAVIS, architect; BA, Agnes Scott Coll., Decatur, Ga.; MArch, Harvard Grad. Sch. Design. Arch. Thompson, Ventulett, Stainback & Assocs., Atlanta, 1973, positions up to mem. prins. adv. group, v.p. client rels., 1994—; prin., dir. hospitality design Cooper Carry, Atlanta, 1985—94. Adj. faculty mem. U. Hawaii Sch. Architecture, Manoa. Past chair Atlanta Dist. Coun. Urban Land Inst., trustee, dist. coun. counselor, mem. policy and practice com.; chair Mayor's Walkable Atlanta Task Force; bd. mem. Beltline Partnership; mem. alumni coun. Harvard Grad. Sch. Design; mem. adv. coun. Savannah Coll. Art and Design; mem. steering com. Metro Atlanta C. of C., mem. environ. com. Named Outstanding Alumnus, Agnes Scott Coll. Fellow: AIA. Office: TVS Internat 2700 Promenade Two 1230 Peachtree St NE Atlanta GA 30309-3591 Office Phone: 404-888-6600. Office Fax: 404-888-6700. E-mail: hhatch@tvsa.com.

HATCH, LORI S., physical education educator; b. Maquoketa, Iowa, Apr. 29, 1960; d. Don M. and Rochelle A. Busch; m. Jay P. Busch, June 24, 1966; children: Emily Jordan, Erin Riley. Degree in Phys. Edn. (hon.), William Penn Coll., Oskaloosa, Iowa, 1982; MA in Athletic Adminstrn., U. Iowa, Iowa City, 1989. Cert. tchr. Iowa, 1982. Tchr. Bettendorf Cmty. Sch. Dist., Bettendorf, Iowa, 1982—. Personal com. mem. St. Paul Luth. Ch., Davenport, Iowa, 2005—07. Mem.: Nat. Coun. for Social Studies (assoc.). Home: 5205 Amesbury Dr Davenport IA 52807 Office: Bettendorf Mid Sch 2030 Middle Rd Bettendorf IA 52722 Home Phone: 563-355-0001; Office Phone: 563-359-3686. Personal E-mail: hatch2103@aol.com.

HATCH, MICHAEL WARD, lawyer; b. Pittsfield, Mass., Nov. 19, 1949; s. Ward Sterling and Elizabeth (Hubbard) H.; m. Lisa Schilling, June 8, 1974; children: Stuart, Andrew, Gillian. AB in Econs., St. Lawrence U., 1971; JD, Yale U., 1974. Bar: Wis. 1974, N.Y. 1980. Ptnr. Foley & Lardner LLP, Milw., 1974—, chmn. real estate practice group. Mem. ABA, N.Y. State Bar Assn., Wis. Bar Assn., Milw. Bar Assn., Am. Coll. Real Estate Lawyers, Urban Land Inst., Nat. Multi Housing Coun., Mortgage Bankers Assn. Wis., Bldg. Owners and Mgrs. Assn., Local Initiatives Support Corp., Milw. Athletic Club, Town Club. Avocations: architecture, historic preservation. Office: Foley & Lardner LLP 777 E Wisconsin Ave Ste 3800 Milwaukee WI 53202-5367 Office Phone: 414-297-5706. Office Fax: 414-297-4900. Business E-Mail: mhatch@foley.com.

HATCH, MIKE, former state attorney general; m. Patti Hatch; 3 children. BS in Polit. Sci. with honors, U. Minn., Duluth, 1970; JD, U. Minn., 1973. Commr. of commerce State of. Minn., 1983—89; pvt. practice law; atty. gen. State of Minn., 1999—2007. Democrat. Mailing: 320 E 135th St Burnsville MN 55337*

HATCH, NATHAN ORR, academic administrator; b. May 17, 1946; m. Julia Gregg; 3 children. AB summa cum laude, Wheaton Coll., 1968; AM, Washington U., 1972, PhD, 1974. Postdoctoral fellow Johns Hopkins U., 1974-75; from asst. prof. to prof. history U. Notre Dame, South Bend, Ind., 1975-88, dir. grad. studies dept. history, 1980-83, assoc. dean Coll. Arts and Letters, dir. Inst. for Scholarship in the Liberal Arts, 1983-89, acting dean Coll. Arts and Letters, 1988-89, v.p. for grad. studies and rsch., 1989-96, prof., 1989, provost, 1996—2005, Andrew V. Tackes prof. history, 1999—2005; pres. Wake Forest U., Winston-Salem, NC, 2005—. Author: The Sacred Cause of Liberty: Republican Thought and the Millennium in Revolutionary New England, 1977, The Democratization of American Christianity, 1989 (Albert C. Outler prize Am. Soc. Ch. History 1989, 1989 Book prize Soc. for Historians of Early Am. Republic, co-winner John Hope Franklin Publ. prize Yale U. Press 1990); also articles; editor: The Professions in American History, 1988; co-editor: The Bible in America: Essays in Cultural History, 1982, Jonathan Edwards and the American Experience, 1988. Bd. dirs. United Way St. Joseph County, Ind., 1987-92; trustee St. Joseph's Med. Ctr., 1994, chair bd. trustees, 1997-99; mem. nat. adv. bd. Salvation Army, 1997-99; trustee Fuller Theol. Sem., 1998—; mem. Nat. Coun. Humanities, 2000—. Recipient Paul Fenlon Teaching award U. Notre Dame, 1981; Am. Coun. Learned Socs. fellow, 1976, Fred Harris Daniels fellow Am. Antiquarian Soc., 1977, Charles Warren fellow Harvard U., 1977-78; grantee Lilly Endowment, 1979, Ind. Com. for the Humanities, 1981-82, NEH, 1981-85. Mem. Johns Hopkins Soc. Scholars, Am. Soc. Ch. Hist. (pres. 1993), Phi Beta Kappa. Office: Wake Forest U 211 Reynolds Hall Box 7226 1834 Wake Forest Rd Winston Salem NC 27109 Office Phone: 336-758-5112. E-mail: hatch@wfu.edu.*

HATCH, ORRIN GRANT, senator; b. Homestead Park, Pa., Mar. 22, 1934; s. Jesse and Helen (Kamm) H.; m. Elaine Hansen, Aug. 28, 1957; children: Brent, Marcia, Scott, Kimberly, Alysa, Jess. BS in History, Brigham Young U., 1959; JD, U. Pitts., 1962; LLD (hon.), U. Md., 1981; MS (hon.), Def. Intelligence Coll., 1982; LLD (hon.), Pepperdine U., 1990, So. Utah State U., 1990. Bar: Pa. 1962, Utah 1962. Ptnr. firm Thomson, Rhodes & Grigsby, Pitts., 1962-69, Hatch & Plumb, Salt Lake City, 1976; US Senator from Utah, 1977—. Mem. com. fin. US Senate, com. health, edn., labor, and pensions, com. judiciary, joint com. tax, select com. intelligence. Author: The Equal Rights Amendmen: Myths and Realities, 1983, Understanding the Doctrines of Christ, 1995, Square Peg: Confessions of a Citizen Senator, 2003; contbr. articles to newspapers and profl. jours. Recipient Excellence in Public Svc. award Am. Acad. Pediatrics, 1988, Senator of Yr. award Nat. Multipule Sclerosis Soc., 1996, Lifetime Achievement award Asian Assn. Utah, 1998, Small Investor Empowerment award Nat. Assn. Real Estate Investment Trusts, 2001, Campbell award, Am. Soc. Law Enforcement Tng., 2002, Elmer P. Martin Public Svc. award Great Blacks in Wax Mus., 2003, Legis. of Yr. award biotechnology Industry Orgn., 2003, Nat. Leadership award, Coalition for Juvenile Justice, 2004. Mem. ABA., Nat. Bar Assn., Utah Bar Assn., Pa. Bar Assn., Am. Judicature Soc. Republican. Mem. Lds Ch. Avocations: golf, poetry, piano playing, composer lyrics. Office: US Senate 104 Hart Senate Office Bldg Washington DC 20510-0001 also: Federal Bldg Rm 8402 125 S State St Salt Lake City UT 84138-1191 Office Phone: 202-224-5251, 801-524-4380. Office Fax: 202-224-6331, 801-524-4379.*

HATCH, RICHARD, actor; b. Santa Monica, Calif., May 21, 1945; 1 child, Paul Michael. Student, Harbor Coll. Actor: (plays) Love Me, Love My Children, P.S., Your Cat is Dead, (TV series) The Streets of San Francisco, 1976-77, Forever Fernwood, 1977-78, Mary Hartman, Mary Hartman, 1977-78, Battlestar Galactica, 1978-79, Santa Barbara, 1990, Battlestar Galactica, 2004-06; (TV films) The Last of the Belles, 1974, The Hatfields and The McCoys, 1975, Deadman's Curve, 1978, The Hustler of Muscle Beach, 1980, (films) Charlie Chan and the Curse of the Dragon, 1981, Prisoners of the Lost Universe, 1983, Heated Vengeance, 1985, Leathernecks, 1988, Dark Bar, 1988, Party Line, 1988, The Hitch-Hikers, 1989, Ghetto Blaster, 1989, Mal d'Africa, 1990, Delta Force Commando II: Priority Red One, 1990, Renaissance, 1994, Iron Thunder, 1998, Unseen Evil, 1999, Big Shots, 2001, The Ghost, 2001, The Great War of Magellan, 2005, The Rain Makers, 2005; host: (radio show) Love on the Edge.*

HATCHELL, SYLVIA R., women's college basketball coach; b. Gastonia, NC, Feb. 28, 1952; m. Sammy Hatchell; 1 child, Van. BS cum laude in Phys. Edn. and Health, Carson-Newman Coll., 1974; MS, U. Tenn., 1975. Coach jr. varsity women's team U. Tenn.; head coach Francis Marion Coll., 1976, U. NC, Chapel Hill, 1986—. Asst. coach US World U. Games team, 1983, 85, coach, 1995; ct. coach US Olympic basketball try-outs, 1984, 92; basketball event staff Olympic Games, LA, 1984; asst. coach US team 1988 Olympic Games, Goodwill Games and World Championships. Named Nat. Coach of Yr., USA Today, 1994, Coll. Sports Mag., 1994, Converse Nat. Assn. Intercollegiate Athletics Regional Coach of Yr., 1986, AMFVoit Championship Coach, 1986, Coll. Basketball Coach of Yr., Athletes Internat. Ministries, 1995, Carson-Newman Disting. Alumnus of the Yr., 1994; named to Francis Marion U. Athletic Hall of Fame, 1993, Women's Basketball Hall of Fame, 2004; recipient Naismith award, 2006. Mem. Women's Basketball Coaches Assn. (pres. 1996-97, past bd. dirs.), Amateur Basketball Assn. US (women's games com.). Office: U NC Dept Athletics PO Box 2126 Chapel Hill NC 27514-2126 Office Phone: 919-962-5187. E-mail: shatchel@email.unc.edu.*

HATCHER, BARBARA A., lawyer; BA, U. NH, 1977; JD, Wake Forest U., 1980. Atty. Squire, Sanders & Dempsey, Washington; asst. gen. counsel Burlington Industries; v.p., gen. counsel GNB Technologies Inc.; group counsel transp. bus. group Exide Technologies, Alpharetta, Ga., 2000—04, dep. gen. counsel, asst. sec., 2004—06, exec. v.p., gen. counsel, 2006—. Office: Exide Technologies Bldg 200 13000 Alpharetta Pkwy Alpharetta GA 30004*

HATCHER, CHARLES ROSS, JR., surgeon, health facility administrator; b. Bainbridge, Ga., June 28, 1930; s. Charles Ross and Vivian Elizabeth (Miller) Hatcher; m. Phyllis Gregory Slappey, July 9, 1988; children from previous marriage: Marian Barnett Thorpe, Charles Hatcher III. BS magna cum laude, U. Ga., 1950; MD cum laude, Med. Coll. Ga., 1954. Intern Johns Hopkins Hosp., Balt., 1954-55; resident surgery Peter Bent Brigham Hosp., Boston, 1955-56, Johns Hopkins Hosp., 1958-62; prof. surgery, chief cardiothoracic surgery Emory U. Sch. Medicine, Atlanta, 1971-90; dir., CEO Emory Clinic, Atlanta, 1976-84; v.p. health affairs, dir. Woodruff Health Scis. Ctr., Emory U., 1984-96, dir. emeritus; chmn., CEO Emory HealthCare, 1995-96. Bd. dirs. Life of the South Corp., Japan Am. Soc. Contbr. Capt. US Army, 1956—58. Mem.: ACS, So. Thoracic Surg. Assn. (pres. 1984), So. Surg. Assn., Am. Cancer Soc., Soc. Thoracic Surgeons (pres. 1986—87), Am. Assn. Thoracic Surgery, Am. Surg. Assn., Am. Coll. Chest Physicians (bd. regents 1977—81, bd. govs. 1974—77), Am. Coll. Cardiology (bd. govs. 1976—80), Johns Hopkins Soc. Scholars, Gov.'s Club Tallahassee, Fla., Bainbridge Country Club, Piedmont Driving Club, Rotary Club (bd. dirs. Atlanta chpt. 1976—80), Capital City Club, Alpha Omega Alpha, Sigma Xi, Phi Beta Kappa. Methodist. Home: 1105 Lullwater Rd NE Atlanta GA 30307-1245 Office: Emory U Woodruff Health Scis Ctr 1365 A Clifton Rd NE Ste 5036 Atlanta GA 30322-1013 Office Phone: 404-778-5860. Business E-Mail: charles.hatcher@emoryhealthcare.org.

HATCHER, JAMES A., lawyer; b. Macon, Ga., Feb. 20, 1952; BA, Furman U., 1974; JD, U. SC Sch. Law, 1977. Assoc. Sell & Melton, Macon, Ga., 1977—79; corp. legal counsel, sec. Cox Comm. Inc., Atlanta, 1979—92, v.p., gen. counsel, 1992, v.p. legal & regulatory affairs, 1995—99, sr. v.p. legal & regulatory affairs, 1999—; sec., gen. counsel Cox Enterprise (parent co. of Cox Communications), 1987—93. Recipient Diversity Champion award, Walter Kaitz Found., 2005. Mem.: Ga. Bar Assn., SC Bar Assn., Bd. Dir. Diversity Com. State Bar Assn. Ga. Office: Cox Comm Inc 1400 Lake Hearn Dr Atlanta GA 30319 Office Phone: 404-843-5000. E-mail: jim.hatcher@cox.com.*

HATCHER, JOE BRANCH, management consultant; b. Ft. Worth, July 28, 1936; s. W. Joe and Jessie Mae Hatcher; m. Irma Gail Collins, Apr. 18, 1957; children: Gregory Layne, Geoffrey Alan, Gailyn. BA, U. Wichita, 1960; MA, U. Kans., 1967, PhD, 1968. Mem. English lit. faculty Baker U., Baldwin City, Kans., 1966-74; asst. to pres. Park Coll., Kansas City, Mo., 1974-75; v.p. Albion (Mich.) Coll., 1976-81; pres. Hendrix Coll., Conway, Ark., 1981-91; vice chmn. 1st Comml. Bank, Little Rock, 1992-95, also bd. dirs., 1992-95; cons. Hatcher & Assocs., Conway, 1995—. Mem.: Conway C. of C. Methodist. Avocation: tennis. Office: 916 Heather Cir Conway AR 72034-9395 Office Phone: 501-269-3185. Personal E-mail: jhatcher@cyberback.com.

HATCHER, KENDRA, advertising executive; b. 1972; V.p. brand planner Westwayne, Inc., Atlanta; planning dir. Global Hue; sr. v.p., dir. of consumer context planning Mediavest USA, 2003—. Named Who's Who Among Black America; named one of 40 Under 40, Advt. Age, 2007. Office: MediaVest Worldwide 757 Third Ave New York NY 10018 Office Phone: 212-868-0920.*

HATCHER, ROBERT DEAN, JR., geologist, educator; b. Madison, Tenn., Oct. 22, 1940; married; 2 children. BA in Geology and Chemistry, Vanderbilt U., 1961, MS in Geology, 1962; PhD in Structural Geology, U. Tenn., Knoxville, 1965. Registered profl. geologist Ga., Tenn., SC; registered engrng. geologist SC. Tchg. asst. Vanderbilt U., Nashville, 1960-62, U. Tenn., Knoxville, 1962-65; mem. staff Humble Oil and Refining Co., New Orleans, 1965—66; asst. prof. geology Clemson U., SC, 1966-70, assoc. prof. geology, 1970-76, prof. geology, 1976-78, Fla. State U., Tallahassee, 1978-80, U. SC, Columbia, 1980-86; staff mem. Oak Ridge Nat. Lab., Tenn., 1986—2000; mem. faculty, disting. scientist, prof. tectonics and structural geology U. Tenn., Knoxville, 1986—. Part-time geologic mapping Tenn. Divsn. Geology, 1961-64, SC Divsn. Geology, 1966-82, Ga. Geol. Survey, summer, 1970, NC Divsn. Mineral Resources, 1974-80; mem. rev. panel NSF, 1982, 85, 95, Ednl. Geologic Mapping Prog., 1995; mem. NAS Bd. Radioactive Waste Mgmt., 1990-96; mem. nuc. reactor safety com. NRC, 1993-95; mem. Nat. Coop. Geologic Mapping Prog. Adv. Com., 1996-. Contbr. articles to profl. jours.; co-author: Phys. Geology: Principles, Processes and Problems, 1976, Lab. Manual for Structural Geology, 1990, US Appalachian and Quachita Orogens, 1990; co-editor: Geol. Soc. Am. Bull., 1981—88, Contbns. to the Tectonics and Geophysics of Mountain Chains, 1983, Variscan-Appalachian Dynamics: The Building of the Late Paleozoic Basement, 2002, Four-D Framework of Continental Crust, 2007; author: Structural Geology: Principles, Concepts and Problems, 1990. Grantee NSF, 1968-70, 70-72, 76-78, 78-79, 79-87, 89-92, Duke Power Co., 1974-75, Westinghouse Elec. Corpn., 1974-75, Nuc. Regulatory Commn., 1978-79, Dept. Energy, 1993-2005, US Geol. Survey, 1997-2007; named hon. citizen of W.Va., 1998. Fellow: Geol. Assn. Can., Geol. Soc. Am. (chmn. exec. com. 1991—92, pres. 1992—93, found. bd. trustees, exec. com. 1999—2007, bd. chair 2005—07, Disting. Svc. award 1988, Penrose medal 2006), AAAS; mem.: Ga. Geol. Soc., East. Tenn. Geol. Soc., Carolina Geol. Soc., Am. Geophys. Union, Am. Assn. Petroleum Geologists (I.C. White Meml. award (eastern sect.) 1997, John T. Galey award from Eastern Sect. 2001), Am. Geol. Inst. (pres. 1995—96, Ian Campbell medal 2006), Sigma Xi. Office: U Tenn Dept Earth and Planetary Scis 1412 Circle Dr 306 Earth and Planetary Scis Bldg Knoxville TN 37996-1410 E-mail: bobmap@utk.edu.

HATCHER, TERI, actress; b. Sunnyvale, Calif., Dec. 8, 1964; d. Owen and Esther Hatcher; m. Marcus Leithold, June 4, 1988 (div. 1989); m. Jon Tenney, May 27, 1994 (div. Mar. 2003); 1 child, Emerson Rose. Student, Deanza Jr. Coll., Am. Conservatory Theater. Spokeswoman Clairol Nice 'n Easy hair color. Actor: (films) Tango and Cash, 1989, The Big Picture, 1989, Soapdish, 1991, Straight Talk, 1992, Heaven's Prisoners, 1996, Two Days in the Valley, 1996, Dead Girl, 1996, Tomorrow Never Dies, 1997, Since You've Been Gone, 1998, Fever, 1999, Spy Kids, 2001, The Chester Story, 2003; (TV films) Dead in the Winter, 1991, The Brotherhood, 1991, Running Mates, 2000, Jane Doe, 2001, Say Uncle, 2001, Momentum, 2003; (TV series) The Love Boat, 1985-86, Capitol, 1986-87, Karen's Song, 1987, Lois and Clark: The New Adventures of Superman, 1993-97, Desperate Housewives (Golden Globe Award for best actress in a TV series - musical or comedy, 2005, Screen Actors Guild Award for outstanding performance by a female actor in a comedy series, 2005, Screen Actors Guild Award for outstanding performance by an ensemble in a comedy series, 2005, 2006), 2004-; Author: Burnt Toast: And Other Philosophies of Life, 2006 Named one of The Most 10 Fascinating People of 2005, Barbara Walters Special. Address: Desperate Housewives Touchtone Television 100 Universal City Plaza Bldg 2128 Ste G Universal City CA 91608

HATCHETT, EDWARD BRYAN, JR., lawyer; b. Glasgow, Ky., Aug. 8, 1951; s. Edward Bryan and Leona Katherine (Azbill) Hatchett; m. Judie Etta James, Aug. 3, 1973; children: Catherine Wade, Elizabeth Black, James Edward Bryan. BA, Centre Coll., Danville, Ky., 1973; JD, U. Louisville, 1976; diploma Nat. Grad. Trust Sch., Northwestern U., 1980; diploma Stonier Grad. Sch. Banking, U. Del., 1986; diploma Ky. Mgmt. Inst., Western Ky. U., 1988. Bar: Ky. 1976. Editorial asst. Dept. Agr., Washington, 1971; edn. rsch. asst. Ky. Legis. Rsch. Commn., Frankfort, 1972; law clk. Dept. Law, City of Louisville, 1973-76; pvt. practice Glasgow, 1978-88; v.p., trust officer New Farmers Nat. Bank, Glasgow, 1980-88, sec., 1986-88; asst. gen. counsel Ky. Dept. Fin. Instns., Frankfort, 1977, commr., 1988-94, dir. securities divsn., 1992-94; auditor pub. accts. Commonwealth of Ky., 1996—2004; counsel Blue Spring Creek, LLC, 2001—, mng. ptnr., 2006—. Chmn. Ky. Fin. Instns. Bd., Frankfort, 1988—94; bd. dirs. Commonweath Preservation Advs., Inc., Frankfort. Pres. Mammoth Cave Area 4-H Found., Glasgow, 1981; gov.'s appointee Ky. Heritage Coun., Frankfort, 1985—88; pres. Estate Planning Coun. So. Ky., Bowling Green, Ky., 1988; elected Ky. Auditor Pub. Accts., 1995, 1999; lay reader Ch. Ascension, Ky., 1988—, treas., 2006—. Named Nat. Pub. Speaking Champion, Future Farmers Am., 1970. Mem.: Nat. Assn. State Auditors, Contrs. and Treas. (mem. bond com. 1997—2004), N.Am. Securities Adminstrs. Assn., Rotary. Democrat. Episcopalian. Avocations: historical research, golf. Home: 454 Chinook Trail Frankfort KY 40601-1602 Personal E-mail: ebhatchett@aol.com.

HATCHETT, JOSEPH WOODROW, lawyer, former federal judge; b. Clearwater, Fla., Sept. 17, 1932; s. John Arthur and Lula Gertrude (Thomas) H.; children: Cheryl Nadine, Brenda Audrey. AB, Fla. A. and M. U., 1954; JD, Howard U., 1959; JD certificate mil. judge course, U.S. Naval Justice Sch., Newport, RI, 1973; LLD, Fla. A&M U., 1996; LLD (hon.), Howard U., 1998. Bar: Fla. 1959, U.S. Ct. Appeals (5th and 11th cirs.). Pvt. practice, Daytona Beach, 1959-66; asst. US atty. (mid. dist.) Fla. US Dept. Justice, Jacksonville, Fla., 1966-70; magistrate (mid. dist.) Fla. US Dist. Ct., Jacksonville, Fla., 1971-75; justice Fla. Supreme Ct., Tallahassee, 1975-79; judge US Ct. Appeals (5th Cir.), Tallahassee, 1979-81, US Ct. Appeals (11th Cir.), Tallahassee, 1981-99, chief judge, 1996—99; shareholder Akerman Senterfitt, Tallahassee, 1999—. Cooperating atty. N.A.A.C.P. Legal Def. Fund, 1960-66; gen. counsel Masons of Fla., 1963-66; cons., mem. staff dept. urban renewal, Daytona Beach, 1963-66, spl. asst. to city atty., 1964; Mem. com. selection for Jacksonville Naval Res. Officer Tng. Corps, 1971. Contbr. articles to profl. jours. Mem. John T. Stocking Meml. Trust, med. sch. scholarships, 1961-66; Co-chmn. United Negro Coll. Fund of Volusia County, Fla., 1962; bd. dirs. Jacksonville Opportunities Industrialization Center, 1972-75. Served to 1st lt. AUS, 1954-56, Germany. Recipient Mary McCloud Bethune medallion for community service Bethune-Cookman Coll., 1965, medallion for human relations, 1975, Tampa Urban League Accolade, 1975, Postgraduate Achievement award Howard U., 1977, Medal of Honor, Fla. Bar Assn., 2000, Leroy Collins Lifetime Achievemet award, Leadership Fla., 2001, Anti-Defamation League Jurisprudence award, 2003, Spirit of Excellence award, ABA Commn. on Racial & Ethnic Diversityin the Professoion, 2007. Mem. Am., Nat., Fla., Jacksonville, D. W. Perkins, Fed. bar assns., Am. Judicature Soc., Nat. Council Fed. Magistrates, V.F.W., Omega Psi Phi. Baptist (trustee). Club: Fla-Jax (Jacksonville) (Man of Year 1974). Office: Akerman Senterfitt Highpoint Ctr 12th Fl 106 E Coll Ave Tallahassee FL 32301

HATELEY, J. MICHAEL, human resources executive; BA in Psychology, U. Calif. Mgr. human resources Monogram Industries, ITT; v.p. pres. human resources Mil. Aircraft, Elec., Aircraft Northrop Grumman, Inc., LA, 1976-99, corp. v.p. personnel, 1999; corp. v.p., chief human resourve Northrop Grumman Corp., LA, 2000—. Mem. human resources adv. coun. conf. bd. USC Marshall Sch. Bus., mem. corp. adv. bd. Bd. dirs. Ind. Colls. So. Calif. Office: Northrop Grumman Corp 1840 Century Park E Los Angeles CA 90067-2101 Office Phone: 310-553-6262.

HATFIELD, BARBARA SCOTT, academic administrator; d. Jim Seth and Marie Miller Scott; m. Steven Hunter Hatfield, Dec. 28, 1985. BS, Miss. State U., 1971; MEd, U. So. Miss., 1976; EdS, Miss. State U., 1980; PhD, U. Ky., 1991. Tchr. math. grades 7, 9, 11, and 12 Meridian Pub. Sch., Miss., 1971—83; mem. adj. faculty Meridian C.C., 1981—82; Va Felder vis. instr. U. So. Miss., Hattiesburg, 1982—83; tchg. asst., fellow U. Ky., Lexington, 1983—90; rsch. assoc. U. Utah, Salt Lake City, 1989; asst. prof. U. Rio Grande, Ohio, 1990—94, assoc. prof., 1994—98, prof. math., 1998—, chair, Sch. Scis., 1997—99, coord. semester conversion, 1999—2002, interim dean, Coll. Liberal Arts and Scis., 2002—04, dean, Coll. Liberal Arts and Scis., 2004—05, interim provost, v.p. acad. affairs, 2005—. Co-coord. title III grantee Rio Grande CC, 2003—06; leadership team SE Ohio Ctr. Excellence in Math. and Sci., Athens, 2004—06; module devel. Ohio Math. Acad. Program Math Sci. Learning Network, Columbus, 2004—06. Named Tchr. of the Week, U. So. Miss. Student Newspaper, 1982; recipient Donna Chen Women's Equity award, Ohio U., 2000. Mem.: Am. Conf. Acad. Deans, Assn. Am. Colls. and Univs., Nat. Coun. Tchrs. English, Math. Assn. Am., Delta Kappa Gamma (pres. 1997—2002, Beta Alpha chpt., internat. scholar 1985), Phi Alpha Theta, Delta Gamma (treas. 1968—70). Achievements include founding co-director of Girls Emerging in Math and Science program. Office: U Rio Grande Office Academic Affairs 218 N Coll Ave PO Box 500 Rio Grande OH 45674 Home Phone: 740-441-1024; Office Phone: 740-245-7215. Business E-Mail: hatfield@rio.edu.

HATFIELD, BENNETT K., mining executive; BS in Mining Engrng., Va. Polytechnic Inst. and Univ. Exec. v.p. El Paso Energy Coastal Coal Co., 2001—03; exec. v.p., COO Massey Energy Co., 1998—2001; pres., eastern ops. Arch Coal, inc., 2003—05; pres., CEO Internat. Coal Group, Inc., Ashland, Ky., 2005—, also bd. dir. Office: Internat Coal Group Inc 2000 Ashland Dr Ashland KY 41101

HATFIELD, DONALD GENE, retired art educator; b. Detroit, May 23, 1932; s. Floyd Myrl Hatfield and Helen Regina Nehmer; m. Marilyn Ann Grindstuen, Sept. 10, 1960 (dec.); children: Suzanne Valadon, John Thomas(dec.) , Kathleen Marie. AA, Northwestern Mich. Coll., 1958; BA, Mich. State U., 1960, MA, 1961; MFA, U. Wis., 1962. Elem. art supr., art tchr. Auburndale Elem., Jr. and Sr. HS, Wis., 1962—64; asst. prof. art Auburn U., Ala., 1964—71, assoc. prof., 1971—81, prof., 1981—94, prof. emeritus art, 1994. Instr. history architecture and art Tuskegee Inst., Ala., 1968—69; art accreditation team mem. So. Assn. Colls. and Schs., 1973—81; dep. art accreditation team mem. Nat. Assn. Schs. Art & Design, Arlington, Va., 1975, mem. comm., 76; spkr. in field. One-man shows include Home Savings & Loan, Madison, Wis., 1962, Parker Co., Madison, 1962, La Cross State Coll., Wis., 1963, Unitarian House, Auburn, Ala., 1966, Auburn U., Bradley Lounge, 1967, Columbus Mus. Arts and Crafts, Ga., 1968, Birmingham Mus. Art, 1968, Savannah Arts Assn. Gallery, 1969, Birmingham So. Coll., 1970, Montgomery Mus. Art., 1972, LaGrange Coll., Ga., 1972, Eufaula Bank and Trust Co., Mezzanine Gallery, 1972, Telfair Peet Theater, Auburn U., 1976, 1980, Chattahoochee Valley State Coll., Phenix City, Ala., 1983, others, exhibited in group shows at Greater River Fall Art Assn., Fall River, Mass., 1964—65, Birmingham Mus. Art, 1965—66, 1968—72, Callaway Gardens, Pine Mountain, Ga., 1968, Montgomery Mus. Art, 1969, 1973, 1979—81, Columbus Mus. Art, 1969, Greater Birmingham Arts Alliance Gallery, 1976—77, 1980, Auburn U., 1983, Marble Gallery, Charleston, SC, 1983, Del Mar Coll., Corpus Christi, Tex., 1983, Columbia Coll., Mo., 1983, numerous others, marble sculpture, Gov.'s Mansion, Montgomery, Ala., 1973. Art awards judge Chattanoochee Valley Fair, Columbus, Ga., 1966—90; v.p. Ala. Art League, Montgomery, 1969—70, pres., 1970—72; bd. trustees Opelika Arts Assn., Inc., Ala., 1971—73. Served with USN, 1952—56. Recipient Merit award and Kelly Fitzpatrick award, Centennial Painting Exhbn., Montgomery, 1972, Purchase award, Opelika Arts Festival, 1972, 5th Ann. Miniworks, Jackson State U., 1983, numerous other purchase and exhbn. awards; grantee, Auburn U., 1985, 1986; Faculty Improvement grantee, 1990—91. Mem.: Nat. Soc. Sons of Am. Revolution, Mil. Order of Cootie (life; Ala. grand comdr. 1994—95, 2005—07, vet. affairs vol svc rep. to Tuskegee Vets Hosp. 1988—2007), Elks (vet. affairs vol. svc. rep. to Tuskegee Vets. Hosp. 1989—95), VFW (life; quartermaster post 5404 all state team 1991—92, 1996—97). Avocations: genealogy, artifacts, gardening, reading. Home: 550 Forest Pk Cir Auburn AL 36830 Personal E-mail: dghatprof@charter.net.

HATFIELD, FRED (FREDERICK WILLIAM HATTFIELD), former commissioner; b. Calif. BA in History summa cum laude, Calif. State Univ., Fresno, 1977. Chief of staff to Rep. Tony Coelho US Congress, 1980—89; dep. commr. gen. US Pavilion Worlds Fair, Lisbon, Portugal, 1998; chief of staff to Senator John Breaux US Senate, Washington; commr. Commodity Futures Trading Commn., Washington, 2004—06; ptnr. Patton Boggs LLP, Washington, 2007—. Recipient Outstanding Alumni award, Fresno U., 2006. Office: Patton Boggs LLP 2550 M St NW Washington DC 20037

HATFIELD, JACK KENTON, lawyer, accountant; b. Medford, Okla., Jan. 26, 1922; s. Loate L. and Cora (Walsh) H.; m. D. Ann Keltner, Dec. 5, 1943 (dec. Sept. 1988); children: Susan Kathryn Hatfield Bechtold, Sally Ann Hatfield Clark; m. K. Dean Walker, Aug. 7, 1997; m. Dores Hamaker, Aug. 9, 2000. BS in Bus. Adminstrn., Phillips U., Enid, Okla., 1947, BA, 1953; LLB, JD, Oklahoma City U., 1954. Bar: US Dist. Ct. (we. dist.) Okla. 1954, US Supreme Ct. 1961, US Dist. Ct. (no. dist.) Okla. 1967, US Ct. Appeals (10th cir.) 1968; CPA 1954. Pvt. practice, Enid, Okla., 1954-58; with Dept. Interior, Tulsa, 1958-77; pvt. practice, Tulsa, 1977—. Mem.: AICPAs, ABA, Okla. Bar Assn., Tulsa Bar Assn., Okla. Soc. CPAs, Petroleum Club. Avocations: photography, tennis. Home: 4013 E 86th St Tulsa OK 74137-2609

HATFIELD, JERRY LEE, plant physiologist, agricultural meteorologist; b. Wamego, Kans., May 1, 1949; s. Virgil H. and Elsie L. (Fischer) H.; m. Patricia JoAnne Reigle, Sept. 1, 1968; children: Mark E., Andrew J. BS, Kans. State U., 1971; MS, U. Ky., 1972; PhD, Iowa State U., 1975. Biometeorologist U. Calif., Davis, 1975-83; plant physiologist USDA-Agrl. Rsch. Svc., Lubbock, Tex., 1983-89; lab. dir. Nat. Soil Tilth Lab., USDA-Agr. Rsch. Svc., Ames, Iowa, 1989—. Scientific quality review officer Agrl. Rsch. Svc., 2005—06. Editor: Biometerology and Integrated Pest Management, 1982, Limitations to Plant Root Growth, vol. 19, Advances in Soil Science, 1992, Soil Biology: Impacts on Soil Quality, Advances in Soil Science, 1993, Crops Residue Management, Advances in Soil Science, 1994, Utilization of Manure as a Soil Resource, Advances in Soil Science, 1998, Innovative Weed and Soil Management, Advances in Soil Science, Nitrogen in the Environment, 2001, Micrometeorogy in Agricultural Systems, 2005, The Farmers Decision: Balancing Economic Successful Agriculture Production with Environmental Quality, 2005, The Farmer's Decision, 2005; contbr. over 340 articles to profl. jours. Recipient Arthur S. Flemming award for outstanding svc. to fed. govt., 1997, Disting. Svc. award in agr., Kans. State U., 2002. Fellow Soil Sci. Soc. Am., Am. Soc. Agronomy (editor jour. 1989-95, editor-in-chief 1996-2002, pres.-elect 2006, pres. 2006-07, Agronomic Svc. award 1999), Crop Sci. Soc. Am.; mem. Am. Geophys. Union, Am. Meteorol. Soc. (chair agrl./forest com. 1980-81, agrl. and forest meteorology com. 1999-2002), Indian Agrometeorol. Soc. (hon.), Soil and Water Conservation Soc. (program chair 1997-98, bd. dirs. 2005—, Pres. Leadership award 1998, 2005, Presdl. Rank award 2005), Phi Kappa Phi, Gamma Sigma Delta (Outstanding Alumni award 2005). Republican. Avocations: golf, reading, photography, landscaping. Office: USDA Agrl Rsch Svc Nat Soil Tilth Lab 2150 Pammel Dr Ames IA 50011-0001 Home Phone: 515-232-1963; Office Phone: 515-294-5723. Business E-Mail: jerry.hatfield@ars.usda.gov.

HATFIELD, JULIE STOCKWELL, journalist; b. Detroit, Mar. 22, 1940; d. William Hume and Ruth Reed (Palmer) Stockwell; m. Philip Mitchell Hatfield, Aug. 1, 1964 (div. 1979); children— Christian Andrew, Juliana, Jason David; m. Timothy Leland, Nov. 23, 1984; stepchildren— Christian Bourso, London Chamberlain BA, U. Mich, 1962. Staff reporter Women's Wear Daily, NYC, 1962-64; freelance feature writer Bath-Brunswick Times, Wis. State Jour., 1964-68, Quincy Patriot Ledger, Mass., 1968-77; freelance music critic, fashion editor Boston Herald, 1977-79; fashion editor Boston Globe, 1979-95, living/arts writer, 1995-96, soc. columnist, 1996-2001, travel writer, 2001, bus. columnist, 2005—; freelance travel writer, 2001—. Author: (with others) Guide to the Thrift Shops of New England, 1982, Felix, 2004; contbg. editor The Boston (Mass.) Courant, The Lawrence Eagle - Tribune, AAA Horizons mag.; contbr. columns to newspapers. Recipient Lulu award, Men's Fashion Assn., 1985, Atrium award for Outstanding Writing on Fashion, U. Ga., 1987, 1992; Nat. Endowment Arts grantee, 1973. Mem.: Soc. of Am. travel writers. Episcopalian. Avocation: piano. Office Phone: 781-934-2624.

HATFIELD, MARK ODOM, former senator; b. Dallas, Oreg., July 12, 1922; s. Charles Dolen and Dovie (Odom) H.; m. Antoinette Kuzmanich, July 8, 1958; children: Mark, Elizabeth, Theresa, Charles. AB, Willamette U., 1943; AM, Stanford U., 1948. Instr. Willamette U., 1949, dean students, assoc. prof. polit. sci., 1950-56; mem. Oreg. Ho. of Reps., 1951-55, Oreg. Senate, 1955-57; sec. State of Oreg., 1957-59, gov., 1959-67; U.S. senator from Oreg., 1967-97. Chmn. appropriations com., energy and natural resources com., rules and adminstrn. com., joint printing com., joint libr. com., select com. Indian Affairs, Republican Policy Com.; chmn. Appropriations subcom. on transp. & related agencies. Author: Not Quite So Simple, 1967, Conflict and Conscience, 1971, Between A Rock and A Hard Place, 1976; co-author: Amnesty: The Unsettled Question of Vietnam, 1976, Freeze! How You Can Help Prevent Nuclear War, 1982, The Causes of World Hunger, 1982; co-author: What About the Russians, 1984, Vice Presidents of the United States 1789-1993, 1997. Lt. (j.g.) USN, 1943-45, PTO. Recipient over 100 hon. degrees Republican. Baptist. Office: PO Box 2 Marylhurst OR 97036 E-mail: bjhart52@aol.com.

HATFIELD, RENEE S.J., music educator; b. Worcester, Mass., July 15, 1962; d. Raymond S.Y. and Ramona Mok Chin; m. Jeffery Allen Hatfield, Oct. 5, 1986; children: Aria Jenee, Tyler Allen. B in Music Edn., Campbellsville Coll., Ky., 1985; M of Creative Arts in Learning, Lesley U., 2006. Lic. tchr. pre K-12 Mass. Gen. music tchr. Jacob Hiatt Magnet Sch. Blue Ribbon, Worcester, 1985—. Chair Campbellville Coll. Handbook, 1984—86; sec. student found. Campbellsville Coll., 1983—84. Singer: Campbellsville Coll., 1982—83. Mem. Campbellsville Handbell Choir, 1980—85, Campbellsville Coll. Singer, 1982; ch. pianist, worship leader, diversity leader First Bapt. Ch., Shrewsbury, Mass., 1970—; ch. pianist, worship leader Faith Bapt. Ch., Auburn, Mass., 2003—. Mem.: Boston Am. Kodaly Educators, Music Educators Nat. Conf. Home: 33 Neptune Rd Worcester MA 01605 Office: Jacob Hiatt Magnet Sch Worcester Pub Sch Systems 772 Main St Worcester MA 01610 Office Phone: 508-799-3601 ext 3002. Personal E-mail: hatfieldrenee@hotmail.com, hatfieldrenee33@verizon.net.

HATFIELD, STACEY, elementary school educator; d. Curt and Susan Franz; m. Jason Hatfield, June 19, 1999; 1 child, Jaron. BS in Multidisciplinary Studies, Tex. Tech U., Lubbock, 1996. Provisional tchg. cert. Tex., 1996. 5th grade math., sci. and social students tchr. Lamesa Elem. Sch., Tex., 1997—98; 6th grade math. Blalack Mid. Sch., Carrollton, Tex., 1998—2000; 6th grade gifted and talented and 7th grade pre advanced placement math. Ruth Dowell Mid. Sch., McKinney, Tex., 2000—. Mem.: Assn. Tex. Profl. Educators. Home Phone: 214-505-2640.

HATFIELD, TINKER L., architect, apparel designer, product designer; b. Hillsboro, Oreg., Apr. 30, 1952; married; 3 children. BArch, U. Oreg., 1976. Independent architect, Eugene, Oreg.; architect Balzhiser Group; with Nike, Inc., Beaverton, Oreg., 1981—, corporate architect, 1981—85, designer, product design, 1985—90, creative dir., product design, 1990, v.p., innovation design & spl. projects. Spkr. in field. Contbr. articles to Harvard Bus. Review. Vol. coach for track team. Named one of 100 Most Influential People in the sports bus., Sportstyle Mag., 1993, 1996, 100 Most Influential Designers of the Century, Fortune Mag., 1998, 25 Masters of Innovation, BusinessWeek; recipient Internat. Design award for Air Huarache, 1993, Leo Harris award, Dept. Intercollegiate Athletics, U. Oreg., 1996, Portland Alumni Spotlight award, U. Oreg. Alumni Assn., 1997. Achievements include design of new Air Jordon shoe each year, since number III to XV; brought about the idea of Brand Jordon as a separate brand & division within Nike with the involvement of Michael Jordan; some design work for Air Jordon line is included in the Smithsonian Museum for Design; design of designs shoes for Kobe Bryant, Lance Armstrong, Gabrielle Reece, and Picabo Street; designed the first pole vault shoe for former world record holder Stacy Dragila; designed the original Air Pack Series (including the first Visi-Air shoe, the Air Max), Pete Sampras tennis shoes, Andre Agassi footwear and apparel and the original Air Huarache; creates environmentally preferred shoes and track & field spikes; designed for Air Mowabb and Michael Johnson's gold track shoes; created the first LeBron James shoe; served as creative director for all LeBron James projects; invention of the first cross-trainer, the Air Trainer; mentors young Nike designers. Avocations: water-skiing, bicycling, cross country skiing, downhill sking. Office: Nike Inc One Bowerman Dr Beaverton OR 97005-6453 Office Phone: 503-671-6453. Office Fax: 503-671-6300. Business E-Mail: tinker.hatfield@nike.com.

HATFULL, GRAHAM F., microbiologist, educator; BSc in biological sci., Westfield Coll., Univ. London; PhD in molecular biology, Edinburgh Univ., Scotland, 1981; postdoctoral studies, Yale Univ., Cambridge Univ., UK. Prof. to Eberly Family Prof. U. Pitts., 1988—, chmn. Dept. Biological Sci. Mem. editl. bd. Jour. of Bacteriology, jour. Molecular Microbiology, jour. Molecular Microbiology & Biotechnology. Grantee professorship, Howard Hughes Med. Inst., 2002—. Office: 376 Crawford Hall U Pitts 4249 5th Ave Pittsburgh PA 15260 Office Phone: 412-624-6975, 412-624-6976. Office Fax: 412-624-4870. E-mail: gfh+@pitt.edu.

HATGIL, PAUL PETER, artist, sculptor, educator; b. Manchester, NH, Feb. 18, 1921; s. Peter and Katina (Karkadou) H.; m. Katherine Haritos. BS, Mass. Coll. of Art, 1950; MFA, Columbia U., 1951. Instr. art U. Tex., Austin, 1951-54, asst. prof., 1954-56, assoc. prof., 1956-67, prof., 1967-85, prof. emeritus, 1985—, design curator Archer M. Huntington Gallery Mus., 1965-68. Vis. instr. Columbia U. (summer) 1958; designed and installed Tex. Pavilion Exhbn., N.Y. World's Fair; coord. for Gov. John Connolly's Exhbn. of Art and Conf. on the Arts; aux. edn. officer Dist. 8 U.S. Coast Guard, 1965-74; bd. dirs. AHEPA Nat. Ednl. Found., 2003—. Author: Establishing Residency in Greece. 1988, (autobiography) Apostolos, The Immigrant's Son, 1990; (book) Contemporary Encaustic Painting, 1994; contbr. numerous articles and papers to profl. jours. One man shows include Baylor U. Gallery, Bass Concert Hall, U. Tex.; exhbns. include: 42 annual faculty exhbns. U. Tex., Austin, 2d, 3d, 4th Internat. Invitational Exhbn. of Ceramic Art Smithsonian Mus., Washington, 2d, 3d and 7th Nat. Decorative Arts Exhbns., Wichita, Kans., Internat. Invitational Exhbn. of Ceramic Art Iowa State U., Ceder Rapids, Flatbed Print Gallery, 1985-2003, St. Stephen's Emeriti Exhbn., Tex., Austin (Tex.) Mus. Fine Arts; pvt. collections including St. Paul's Luth. Ch., U. Tex. Bus. Adminstrn. Bldg., Huston Tillotson Coll., Seguin Luth. Coll., U. Tex. Faculty Club, U. Tex. Coll. Fine Arts, Woodlands Corp., Houston, Zapata Corp., Houston, Warren Cravens Corp., Houston, U.S. Mil. Ins. Corp., Harry Litwin Industries, Wichita, Kans., Coopers & Lybrand Corp., Houston, Cesar Design Inc., Cleve., Abilne (Tex.) 1st Nat. Bank, Tchr. Retirement Sys., Austin, FAA, Panama C.Z., Austin (Tex.) Mus. Art, Fox Collection, Austin, Tex., Voutsinas Collection, Elgin, Tex., Iatrou Collection, Austin, Tex.; videos collections include Ceramic History 1951-1976, Baylor U. Archives, Art in Texas - 1951-2000, Baylor U.; work featured in Encaustic Painting, 2000. With USAAF, 1943-45, PTO. Recipient Estelle Grey Meml. prize in art, Margaret Flowers prize in art, White Mus., San Antonio, Wolff and Marx prize in art, Dallas Mus. of Fine Arts; purchase prizes Dallas Mus. of Art, Laguan Gloria Mus. Austin; grantee U. Tex. Mem. Am. Hellenic Ednl. and Progressive Assn. (pres. Stephen F. Austin chpt. 312, dist. gov., 1999-2002, mem. nat. ednl. found. bd.). Home: 2203 Onion Creek Pky Unit 7 Austin TX 78747-1648 Business E-Mail: propph@mail.utexas.edu.

HATHAWAY, ANNE, actress; b. Bklyn., Nov. 12, 1982; d. Gerard Hathaway and Kate McCauley. Actor: (TV series) Get Real, 1999—2000; (films) The Princess Diaries, 2001, The Other Side of Heaven, 2001, (voice) The Cat Returns, 2002, Nicholas Nickleby, 2002, Ella Enchanted, 2004, The Princess Diaries 2: Royal Engagement, 2004, (voice) Hoodwinked, 2005, Havoc, 2005, Brokeback Mountain, 2005, The Devil Wears Prada, 2006, Becoming Jane, 2007.*

HATHAWAY, CARL EMIL, investment company executive; b. Boston, Aug. 12, 1933; s. Carl Barbour and Tekla (Neumaier) H.; m. Gail Humphries Oglee, Dec. 6, 1958 (div. Oct. 23, 1996); children: Brian Kent, Carl Nichols, Andrew Oglee; m. Martha Livingston, Jan. 1, 1999. BA, Harvard U., 1955; MBA, Cornell U., 1959. With Morgan Guaranty Trust Co. N.Y., 1959-81, sr. v.p. pension investments, vice chmn. trust and investments dept., 1969-81; pres. Hathaway & Assocs. Ltd. (instl. investment mgmt.), Rowayton, Conn., 1981—, Hathaway Ptnrs., Inc., Rowayton, Conn., 1994—. Served to lt. (j.g.) USNR, 1955-57. Mem.: Shorehaven Golf Club, Eastward Ho Country Club, Harvard Club, Blind Brook Club. Home: 526 Flax Hill Rd Norwalk CT 06854-2317 Office: Hathaway & Assocs Ltd Rowayton Ave Norwalk CT 06853

HATHAWAY, DEREK C., mining products executive; Founder, chmn. Dartmouth Investments (aquired by Harsco 1979), divsn. pres., 1979-84; group v.p. ops. Harsco Corp., Camp Hill, Pa., 1984-86, sr. v.p. ops. for engineered products group, 1986-91, pres., COO, 1991-94, chmn., pres., CEO, 1994—2006, chmn., CEO, 2006—. Office: Harsco Corp PO Box 8888 350 Poplar Church Rd Camp Hill PA 17011*

HATHAWAY, GERALD THOMAS, lawyer; b. Frankfurt, Federal Republic of Germany, Aug. 5, 1954; came to U.S., 1955; s. Robert Ernest Hathaway and Jacqueline Anne (Hughes) Gouin; m. Kathleen Ann McCauley, Dec. 27, 1980; children: Michael, Anne, Thomas. BA, LaSalle U., 1976; JD, U. Pitts., 1979. Bar: Pa. 1979, NJ 1980, NY 1983, US Dist. Ct. (ea. dist.) Pa. 1980, US Dist. Ct. NJ 1980, US Ct. Appeals (3d cir) 1980, US Dist. Ct. (ctrl. dist.) Ill. 1981, US Dist. Ct. (so. and ea. dists.) NY 1984, US Supreme Ct., 1988, US Ct. Appeals (2d cir.) 1988. Assoc. Cunniff, Bray & McAleese, Phila., 1979-82, Holtzmann, Wise & Shepard, NYC, 1982-86, ptnr., 1987-91, Marks & Murase, L.L.P., NYC, 1991-97, Bingham McCutchen LLP, NYC, 1997—2003; shareholder Littler Mendelson PC, NYC, 2003—. Author: (musical play) Ire, 1984; contbg. editor: The Developing Labor Law, 1987, 4th edit., 2005; contbr. articles to profl. jours. Vol. dir. NYU Grad. Sch. Bus., 1983-87; asst. sec. Riverside Opera Ensemble, NYC, 1984-91; pres. Barrow Group, NYC, 2000—. Mem. ABA, N.Y. State Bar Assn., Assn. Bar of City of N.Y. Episcopalian. Avocations: writing, theater, photography. Office: Littler Mendelson PC 885 Third Ave New York NY 10022-4614 Office Phone: 212-583-9600. Business E-Mail: ghathaway@littler.com.

HATHAWAY, JAMES C., law educator; JSD, LLM, Columbia U.; LLB with honors, York U. James E. and Sarah A. Degan Prof. Law U. Mich. Law Sch., Ann Arbor, dir. Refugee and Asylum Law Prog. Sr. vis. rsch. assoc. Refugee Studies Prog., Oxford U.; vis. prof. U. Tokyo, U. Calif., U. Cairo, U. Melbourne, U. Macerata. Author: The Law of Refugee Status, 1991, Reconceiving International Refugee Law, 1997, The Rights of Refugees Under International Law, 2005; editor: Jour. Refugee Studies, Immigration and Nationality Law Reports. Office: U Mich Law Sch 970A Legal Research 625 S State St Ann Arbor MI 48109 Office Phone: 734-764-2359. Office Fax: 734-764-8309. E-mail: jch@umich.edu.

HATHAWAY, PETER S., corporate financial executive; Auditor Arthur Anderson, LLP, 1979—91; contr. and fin. dir. BFI, 1991—95; chief acctg. officer Allied Waste Industries, Phoenix, 1995—2001, treas., 1996—97, v.p., 1996—2000, sr. v.p., fin., 2000—03, exec. v.p., CFO, 2003—. Office: Allied Waste Industries Inc 18500 N Allied Way Phoenix AZ 85054*

HATHAWAY, RICHARD DEAN, retired language educator; b. Chillicothe, Ohio, Aug. 8, 1927; s. Dale and Edith (Hart) H.; m. Viola Hale, Apr. 16, 1978; children by previous marriage: Linda Hathaway Ellis, Bruce. AB summa cum laude, Oberlin Coll., 1949; AM, Harvard U., 1952; PhD, Western Res. U., 1964. Instr. English Oberlin Jr. H.S., 1949-50; chief interviewer U.S. Bur. of Census, Boston, 1952-53; exec. sec. New Eng. Fellowship of Reconciliation, Boston, 1953-55; instr. in English, Rensselaer Poly. Inst., Troy, NY, 1957-62; from asst. prof. to assoc. prof. SUNY, New Paltz, 1962-69, prof., 1970—2001; ret., 2001. Assoc. prof. Millsaps Coll., Jackson, Miss., 1965-66. Author: Sylvester Judd's New England, 1981, The Henry James Scholar's Guide to Web Sites, 1997; (computer software) Text: A Program About Literature, 1990; contbr. articles to profl. jours. Chair legis. com. SCLC Poor People's Campaign, 1968. Served with USNR, 1945-46. Mem. MLA. Mem. Religious Soc. of Friends. Home: Apt 112 141 Fulton Ave Poughkeepsie NY 12603

HATHAWAY, ROBIN, writer; married; 2 children. BA in English, Smith Coll. Owner Barnhouse Press. Author: (novels) (Dr. Fenimore series) The Doctor Digs a Grave, 1998 (Malice Domestic Agatha award for best first novel, 1998), The Doctor Makes a Dollhouse Call, 2000, The Doctor and the Dead Man's Chest, 2001, The Doctor Dines in Prague, 2003, The Doctor Rocks the Boat, 2006, (Jo Banks series) Scarecrow, 2003, Satan's Pony, 2004. Mailing: Author Mail St Martin's Minotaur 175 Fifth Ave New York NY 10010 Office Phone: 212-725-1319. Personal E-mail: robdoneit@aol.com.

HATHCOCK, BONITA CATHERINE (BONNIE HATHCOCK), managed health care company executive; b. Chambersburg, Pa., Oct. 30, 1948; d. John McGillis Gentry and Lola Vaneda (Showaker) Wood; m. Lindsay Levoy Hathcock, Apr. 14, 1984. BS in Bus., Shippensburg State U., 1971; MBA, Nova Southwestern U., 1989; grad. Exec. Human Resource Program, Stanford U. Instr. bus. Cen. Pa. Bus. Sch., Summerdale, 1972-75; with Xerox Corp., various locations, 1975-84, product planning mgr. Dallas, 1982-84; dir. mktg. edn. Datapoint Corp., San Antonio, 1984-85, sr. dir. corp. edn., 1985, sr. dir. worldwide edn., 1985-87; various positions including dir. corp. tng. and v.p. human resources Siemens-Rolm, Boca Raton, Fla.; v.p. human resources U.S. Airways; joined Humana Inc., Louisville, 1999, now sr. v.p., chief human resources officer. Prin. bcG Enterprises (profl. awareness tng. co.) Dallas, 1982-84. Avocations: cooking, swimming, reading, walking, writing. Office: Humana Inc The Humana Bldg 500 W Main St Louisville KY 40202

HATHCOCK, JOHN EDWARD, vocalist; b. Memphis, Sept. 6, 1955; BA in Psychology, Memphis State U., (now U. Memphis), 1986; studied with Dr. David Williams, U. Memphis, 1992-97; studied with Ethel Maxwell, 1982-98; AAS in Graphic Art Tech. summa cum laude, S.W. Tenn. C.C., 2001; MA in Music summa cum laude, Am. World U., Iowa City, Iowa, 2001; PhD in music, Canbourne U., 2004; student, Am. U., 2004—. Cert. Internet Webmaster 2003. Singer, performer, composer opera and sacred classical music; vocal coach, 1999—. Pres. Positron Prodns., 1988-90; pres., founder Soaring Spirit Music, 1996—. Author: Seasons of Wonder, 1995; author poems; patentee in field; exec. prodr., vocal performer Grace: The Eternal Song. Mem. Bellevue Choir, 1991-92, Memphis Vocal Arts Ensemble, 1993, The Heritage Found. Recipient Mr. Wheelchair Am. award, 1990, Man of Yr. award, Happi Internat. Talent, 1990, Trailblazer award, City of Memphis, 1990. Mem.: Internat. Soc. Poets, Beethoven Club (dir. pub. rels. 1993), Phi Theta Kappa (Nat. Dean's List 1999—2000, 2000—01). Baptist.

HATHEWAY, JOHN HARRIS, advertising agency executive; b. Waterbury, Conn., Aug. 9, 1926; s. Fred Whipple and Louise (Wood) H.; m. Patricia Mary Flaherty, Sept. 24, 1955; children: John Harris, Geoffrey Mills, Sara Wood. AB, Dartmouth Coll., 1948; MBA, Amos Tuck, 1950. With Young and Rubicam Inc., NYC, 1950-89, sr. v.p., mgmt. supr., 1968-74, sr. v.p., group dir., 1974-83, exec. v.p., group dir., 1983-87, exec. v.p., western regional dir., 1987-89, also dir. Bd. overseers Hanover Inn, N.H., 1968-78, 94—. Mem. editl. bd. Dartmouth Life, 1991—. Mem. Coun. of Alumni Dartmouth, 1968—90, mem. alumni awards com., 1982—86, chmn., 1986—90, chmn. pub. affairs adv. com., 1990—; pres. Dartmouth Class 1948, 1994—98; assembly overseers Dartmouth-Hitchcock Med. Ctr., 1996—; mem. Dean's Coun., Dartmouth Med. Sch., 2001—; mem. com. Parents' Fund, U. Vt., 1981—86; overseer Hanover Inn, 1998—; mem. Diocesan Mission Com.; bd. dirs. Chappaqua Summer Sch. Program, Horace Greeley Ednl. Fund, 1978—85, Upper Valley Hostel, 1999—2005, Friends of Hopkins and Hood, 1990—. Served with AUS, 1945—46. Recipient Alumni award Dartmouth Coll., 1980 Mem.: Dartmouth Coll. NY Alumni Assn. (pres. 1965—66, bd. dirs. 1958—64, 1967—70, 1972—87), Dartmouth Club Upper Valley (dir. 1994—2001), Hanover Country Club, Manchester (Vt.) Country Club, Waccabuc Country Club, Phi Beta Kappa. Episcopalian (vestryman, warden). Home: 10 Buell St Hanover NH 03755-2416 Office: Young and Rubicam Inc 285 Madison Ave New York NY 10017-6486

HATHORNE, GAYLE GENE, musician, family historian; b. Concordia, Kans., Sept. 3, 1953; d. Richard and R. Virginia (Huscher) Hathorne; 1 child, Amanda Kimberly. BMusic, Manhattan Sch. Music, NYC, 1976; Artist's Diploma, Karajan Akademie, Berlin Philharm. Orch., 1980. Backstage hornplayer Bayreuth Festival, 1977; 3d/1st solo hornist Stadt. Orch., Solingen, Germany, 1980-88; genealogy instr. Blue Ridge C.C., 1999—2002; dir. membership, office mgr. N.Y. Geneal. and Biog. Soc., 2002—05; adminstrv. asst. Legal Lang. Svs., Leawood, Kans., 2006—. Substitute tchr. music and German, Henderson County Pub. Schs., 1988-98; pvt. horn tchr., Hendersonville, 1989—; mem. Schola Cantorum, Kansas City, Kans., 2006—, Summer Singers of Kansas City, 2007. Sr. editor Tarheel Tattler, 1994-96, River Ramblings, 1994-96; editor Kuykendall Gazette, 1996-97; performer on CDs/cassettes; extra in film 28 Days, 1999, The Departed, 2006. Mem. William Baker Summer Singers, Kansas City, 2007—. Nat. Fedn. Music Clubs nat. scholar, 1971. Mem. DAR (state pub. rels. N.C. Soc. 1997-99, organizing regent Abraham Kuykendall chpt. 1996), Children of Am. Revolution (organizing sr. pres. French Broad River Soc. 1992, state libr. 1996-98), Schola Cantorum. Democrat. Avocations: genealogy, photography, travel, writing, listening to opera. Personal E-mail: gaylegenehath@yahoo.com.

HATKOFF, CRAIG MITCHELL, real estate executive, educator; b. Albany, NY, Mar. 19, 1954; s. Leon and Doris (Wildove) H. BA magna cum laude, Colgate U., 1976; MBA, Columbia U., 1978. Mng. dir. Chem. Bank, NYC, 1978-89; mng. ptnr. Victor Capital Group, NYC, 1989—; co-founder Tribeca Film Festival, 2002—. Adj. prof. bus. Columbia U., N.Y.C., 1990—. Author: (children's book) Owen and Mzee, 2006. Mem. Albany Academy (nat. adv. bd.), Columbia Bus. Sch. Alumni Assn. (bd. dirs.), Phi Beta Kappa. Avocations: collecting guitars, tennis, waterskiing.

HATLER, PATRICIA RUTH, lawyer; b. Las Vegas, Nev., Aug. 4, 1954; d. Houston Eugene and Laurie (Danforth) Hatler; m. Howard A. Coffin II; children: Sloan H. D. Coffin, Laurie H. M. Coffin. BS magna cum laude in Cognitive Psych., Duke U., 1976; JD, U. Va., 1980. Bar: Pa. 1980, Ohio 2002. Assoc. Dechert, Price & Rhoads, Phila., 1980-83; assoc. counsel Independence Blue Cross, Phila., 1983-86, sr. v.p., gen. counsel, corp. sec.,

1987-99; exec. v.p., chief legal, governance officer Nationwide, Columbus, Ohio, 1999—. Office: Nationwide One Nationwide Plz Columbus OH 43215-2220 Office Phone: 614-677-8754. E-mail: hatlerp@nationwide.com.*

HATT, CLIFFORD VAN, school system administrator, psychologist; b. Buffalo, Feb. 17, 1949; s. Clifford Milton and Mary Eileen Hatt; m. Cynthia Kay Ellis, July 21, 1979; children: Gregory Gerard Clifford, Catherine Marie. BA, Canisius Coll., Buffalo, 1969—71; MEd, Fla. Atlantic U., Boca Raton, 1973—75; EdD, U. No. Colo., Greeley, 1977—81. Diplomate in School Psychology Am. Bd. Profl. Psychology, 2004, Am. Bd. Med. Psychotherapists, 1998, cert. sch. psychologist Nat. Assn. Sch. Psychologists, 1989, lic. clin. psychologist Va. Bd. Psychology, 1987. Tchr. Cardinal Newman H.S., West Palm Beach, Fla., 1972—76; adj. assoc. prof., psychology Coll. William and Mary, Williamsburg, Va., 1988—; sch. psychologist Va. Beach City Pub. Schs., 1979—89, coord., psychol. svcs., 1989—, dir, doctoral psychology internship tng., 1997—; adj. prof., psychology Norfolk State U., Va., 1995—. Contbr. articles to profl. jours., chapters to books. Fellow: Am. Acad. Sch. Psychology; mem.: NASP, APA, Va. Acad. Clin. Psychologists, Va. Acad. Sch. Psychologists (pres. 1990—91), Va. Psychol. Assn. (pres. 1992—93). Roman Catholic. Avocations: music, travel, racquetball. Home: 1310 Plantation Lakes Cir Chesapeake VA 23320-8110 Office: Va Beach City Pub Schs 1413 Laskin Rd Virginia Beach VA 23451 Home Phone: 757-479-1113; Office Phone: 757-437-7589. Office Fax: 757-437-7596. Personal E-mail: chatt@vbschools.com.

HATT, DAVID, application developer, composer; b. Douglas, Ariz., July 10, 1954; s. Frank Hatt; m. Carol Teal Johnson, Nov. 8, 2003. MusB, Calif. State U., San Bernardino, 1975; MA in Music, U. Calif., Riverside, 1978. Organ builder Raymond Garner and Co., Crestline, Calif., 1976—82; software adaptation specialist FAA, Fremont, Calif., 1982—. Organist, choirmaster First Presbyn. Ch., San Fernando, Calif., 1980—82, Trinity Episc. Ch., Hayward, Calif., 1986—96; radio host KKUP-FM, Santa Clara, Calif., 1993—97; concert organist, 1995—; asst. organist St. Mary's Cathedral, San Francisco, 1998—. Musician: College Music Society National Conference, San Francisco Lyric Chorus, San Francisco Symphony, 2006, (albums) New Lights on Old Channels, 1977, As It Was, Song, 1978, Marty Walker, Clarinets, 1984, Ashen Light, 1986, Baroque Sampler, 1988, The Coefficient of Restitution, 1989, Desert Dreams, 1990, (CD) St. Mary's Catherdral Organ Recitals, 1994, Yearbook, Vol. 1, 1995, Streets and Sounds of San Francisco Bay Area, 2006. Vol. Pets Are Wonderful Support (PAWS), San Francisco, Calif. Mem.: Coll. Music Soc., Am. Guild Organists (dean San Jose chpt. 1997—99), Soc. Composers, Inc. Home: 44 Macondray Ln 1W San Francisco CA 94133 Office: St Marys Cathedral 1111 Gough St San Francisco CA 94115 Office Phone: 415-756-2020. Personal E-mail: dave_hatt@juno.com.

HATTAR, JACQUELINE, lawyer; b. Yonkers, NY, Sept. 24, 1967. BA cum laude, Fordham U., Bronx, NY, 1988; JD, Pace U., White Plains, NY, 1991. Bar: NY 1992, US Dist. Ct. (ea. and so. dists.), NY 1993, US Ct. Appeals (2d cir.) 1993. Asst. dist. atty. Bronx (N.Y.) County Dist. Atty.'s Office, 1991—97; sr. trial atty. Goodman & Jacobs, NYC, 1997—2001; in-house counsel Frontier Ins. Co., Rock Hill, NY, 2001; atty. Wilson, Elser, Moskowitz, Edelman, Dicker, LLP, White Plains, NY, 2001—. Mem. CPLR com. NY Bar Assn., 2002—. Mem.: ABA, NY State Trial Lawyers, Westchester County Bar Assn., Westchester County Women's Bar Assn., NY County Lawyers Assn., NY State Bar Assn. (civil practice law and rules com., stds. atty. conduct com., tort, ins. & compensation law sect.). Cath. Avocations: reading, art, theater, sailing. Office: Wilson Elser Moskowitz Edelman & Dicker LLP 3 Gannett Dr White Plains NY 10604-3407 Office Phone: 914-323-7000. Office Fax: 914-323-7001. Business E-Mail: jacqueline.hattar@wilsonelser.com.

HATTAWAY, KAREN ANN, literature and language professor; d. William N. and Hildur A. Kennett; m. David R. Hattaway, Jan. 20, 1968; children: Elizabeth Ann, William David. BA, U. Mo., Columbia, 1966; MA, U. Okla., Norman, 1967; PhD, Rice U., Houston, 1981. Cert. online instr. Virtual Coll. of Tex., 2004. Prof. of English San Jacinto Coll. N., Houston, 1968—. Grant dir. Eisenhower grant: count on reading, Houston; gearup grant profl. devel. coord. and tchr. trainer San Jacinto Coll. N., Houston; reaffirmation self-study chair San Jacinto Coll. Dist., 1987—89, interim planning dir., 1989—95, chair, core-curriculum rev., 2002—04; divsn. chair, lang. arts San Jcinto Coll. N., 1987—98. Musician handbell choir dir. Coun. on ministries, mem. bd. of edn. Houston East Dist. of the Tex. Conf. of the United Meth. Ch. Named Outstanding Tchr., Nat. Inst. for Orgn. and Staff Devel., 2000, 2006, Nat. Inst. for Staff and Orgnl. Devel., 2000—06, 2006; fellow summer tchr. inst. at UC Santa Cruz: Dickens the Crisis Years, NEh, 2004; grantee Co-Dir. Reacher Quality: Mid. Sch. Math, Tex. Higher Edn. Coordinating Bd., 2004—05, Dir. Tchr. Quality: Inquiry Learning Beats the Word Problem Blues, 2003—04, Eisenhower grantee, 2000—03. Mem.: Phi Beta Kappa, Delta Kappa Gamma (chpt. pres. 1980—82, chpt. achievement award 1985). Democrat-Npl. Methodist. Achievements include first to Learning community instruction pairing developmental reading and developmental mathematics. Avocations: quilting, gardening, piano. Office: San Jacinto College North 5800 Uvalde Road Houston TX 77049 Home Phone: 713-453-3747; Office Phone: 281-458-4050 7212. Office Fax: 281-459-7602. E-mail: karen.hattaway@sjcd.edu.

HATTEBERG, LARRY MERLE, photojournalist; b. Winfield, Kans., June 30, 1944; s. Merle Lawrence and Mary Dorothy (Early) H.; m. Judy Beth Keller, June 6, 1965; children: Sherry Renee, Susan Michelle. Student, Kans. State Tchrs. Coll., 1962-63, Emporia-Wichita State U., 1963-66. Photographer Sta. KAKE-TV, Wichita, Kans., 1963, photojournalist, 1966-67, chief photographer, 1967-81, assoc. news dir., 1981-87, exec. news dir., 1987-88, co-anchor 5 p.m. newscast, 1988-92; co-anchor Evening News broadcasts KAKE-TV, Wichita, Kans., 1992—. Co-chmn. faculty Nat. Press Photographers TV Workshop, U. Okla., 1975—. Author: Larry Hatteberg's Kansas People,1991; developed Hatteberg's People series for TV, 1974. Served with USAR, 1966-72. Regional semi-finalist NASA Journalist-in-Spece Program; recipient Brotherhood award Kans. region NCCJ, 1995, regional lifetime Emmy award TV segment Hatteberg's People, Regional Emmy, 2000, 04. Life mem. Nat. Press Photographers Assn. (Nat. TV News Photographer of Yr. award 1975, 77, Joseph Sprague award 1983, Joseph Costa award 1991). Office: 1500 N West St Wichita KS 67203-1323

HATTEN, WILLIAM SEWARD, manufacturing executive, consultant; b. Chgo., Apr. 7, 1917; s. William Seward and Margaret (Ahearn) H.; m. Marjorie Popp, Dec. 29, 1939; 1 dau., Patricia Marie (Mrs. Dudley D. Pendleton III) BA, Lawrence Coll., 1939; MBA, Northwestern U., 1944; PhD, Kennedy-Western U., 2000. Indsl. engr. Sears, Roebuck & Co., 1940-43; mgr. control div. Chgo. Ordnance Dist., 1943-45; owner Eskimo Ice Cream Co., Tucson, 1945-50; gen. mgr. Utica Knitting Co., NY, 1950-54; cons. Worden & Risberg, Phila., 1954-64; pres., chief exec. officer, dir. Clayton Mark & Co., Evanston, Ill., 1964-67; chmn. bd. Ken-Ray Brass Products, Inc., Vermont, Ill., 1964-67; pres., chief exec. officer, dir. Harper-Wyman Co., Hinsdale, Ill., 1967-69; exec. v.p. Warner Electric Brake & Clutch Co., Beloit, Wis., 1969-72; group v.p. engines and generators Kohler Co., Wis., 1973—80; pres. Hatten & Assocs., Lakeland, Fla., 1980—. Mem. Am. Ordance Assn., Northwestern U. Grad. Bus. Alumni Assn., Lone Palm Golf Club (Lakeland, Fla.), Lakeland Yacht and Country Club (Lakeland, Fla.), Union League (Chgo.), Phi Delta Theta. Episcopalian. Office: Hatten & Assocs 4010 Cheverly Dr E Lakeland FL 33813-1207 Office Phone: 863-680-4117. Business E-Mail: whatten@flsouthern.edu.

HATTER, RICHARD WAYNE, foundation administrator, artist; b. Mangum, Okla., June 30, 1953; s. Travis Wayne and Catherine Elzora (Rozell) H. BS, Okla. State U., 1975; MPA, U. Colo., Colorado Springs, 1980. Mgr. lab. svcs. El Paso County Health Dept., 1975—80; adminstrv. mgr. civil rights divsn. State of Colo., 1980—81; schistosomiasis rschr. Acad. Natural Scis., Phila., 1982—84; grants mgr. dept. radiation therapy and nuclear medicine Thomas Jefferson U., Phila., 1984-86; dir. sponsored projects-rsch. Office for Instl. Advancement, Phila. Coll. Pharmacy and Sci., 1986-88; dir. devel. Courant Inst. Math. Scis., Office Univ. Devel., NYU, NYC, 1988-90, dir. corp. and found. rels., 1988-90, dir. devel. faculty arts and sci., 1990—93, sr. dir., asst. dean for devel., faculty arts and scis., 1993—96; v.p. for devel. Am. Acad. in Rome, 1996-97; dir. devel. and pub. rels. John Simon Guggenheim Meml. Found., NYC, 1997—. One-man shows include Phila. Art Alliance, 1988; exhibited in group shows at Williamsburg Art and Hist. Ctr., Bklyn., 2003-05. Mem. Planned Giving Group of Greater N.Y. Recipient cert. of recognition Sigma Xi, 1988. Mem.: Assn. Fund Raising Profls. Home: 310 E 23d St Apt 9G New York NY 10010-4706 Office: John Simon Guggenheim Meml Found 90 Park Ave New York NY 10016-1301 Office Phone: 212-687-4470. E-mail: rh@gf.org.

HATTERSLEY-SMITH, GEOFFREY FRANCIS, retired government research scientist; b. London, Apr. 22, 1923; s. Wilfred Percy Ashby and Ethel Mary (Willcocks) H.-S.; m. Maria Kefallinou, May 12, 1955; children: Kara Mary, Fiona Anastasia Student, Winchester Coll., Eng., 1937-41; BA, Oxford U., Eng., 1948, MA, 1951, DPhil, 1956. Base leader Falkland Islands Dependencies Survey, 1948-50; def. sci. staff officer Def. Rsch. Bd., Ottawa, Ont., Canada, 1951-73; prin. sci. officer Brit. Antarctic Survey, Cambridge, England, 1973-91. Sec. Antarctic place-names com. Fgn. and Commonwealth Office, London, 1975-91. Author: North of Latitude Eighty, 1974, Present Arctic Ice Cover, 1974, The History of Place Names in the Falkland Islands Dependencies, 1980, The History of Place Names in the British Antarctic Territory, 1991, Geographical Names in the Ellesmere Island National Park Reserve, 1998; editor: Proceedings of International Symposium on Glacier Mapping, 1967, The Norwegian with Scott, 1984. Sub-lt. Royal Navy, 1942-46. Fellow Royal Soc. Can. (Acad. Scis.), Royal Geog. Soc. (Founder's Gold medal 1966), Arctic Inst. N. Am. (gov. 1963-66), Arctic Circle Club (pres. 1967-69), Arctic Club (pres. 1976), Antarctic Club (London) (com. mem. 1983-85, Polar medal, 2006). Avocations: history, gardening. Home: The Crossways Kent Cranbrook TN17 2AG England

HATTERY, ROBERT RALPH, radiologist, educator; b. Phoenix, Dec. 15, 1939; s. Robert Ralph and Goldie M. H.; m. D. Diane Sittler, June 18, 1961; children: Angela, Michael. BA, Ind. U., 1961, MD, 1964; cert. in diagnostic radiology, Mayo Grad. Sch. Medicine, 1971. Diplomate Am. Bd. Radiology. Intern Parkland Meml. Hosp.-Southwestern Med. Sch., Dallas, 1964-65; fellow Mayo Clinic, Rochester, Minn., 1967-70, cons., 1970-81, chmn. dept. diagnostic radiology, 1981-86; instr. radiology Mayo Med. Sch., 1973-75, asst. prof. radiology, 1975-78, assoc. prof. radiology, 1978-82, prof. radiology, 1982—. Chair Mayo Group Practice Bd., 1991-93; chmn. bd. govs Mayo Clinic, Rochester, 1994-98; trustee Mayo Found., 1992-2002; trustee Am. Bd. Radiology. Author numerous jour. articles and abstracts, book chpts. Capt. USAF, 1965-67, Willford Hall Hosp., San Antonio. Fellow Am. Coll. Radiology; mem. Radiol. Soc. N.Am. (bd. dirs. 1999—), Am. Roentgen Ray Soc., Soc. Computed Body Tomography (pres. 1982-83), Soc. Genitourinary Radiography (pres. 1986-88), Am. Bd. Radiology (exec. dir.). Office: American Bd Radiology 5441 E Williams Blvd Tucson AZ 85711 Home Phone: 520-219-8599. Business E-Mail: rhattery@theabr.org.

HATTERY, ROBERT WILBER, political science educator; b. Chgo., Jan. 5, 1925; s. Wilber and Ruth (Adolphus) H.; m. Carolyn Potschke, Feb. 2, 1957 (dec. Feb. 1979); children: David Wilber, Lor Ruth, John Furer; m. Eleanor Lorraine Evans, Dec. 28, 1984. PhB, U. Chgo., 1948, MA, 1954, PhD, 1961. From lectr. to asst. prof. U. Wis., Madison, 1955-62; from asst. to assoc. prof. Ind. U., Bloomington, 1962-87; founding mem., acting dir. Ind. U., West European Studies, 1969—71; assoc. prof. emeritus polit. sci. and continuing edn. Ind. U., Bloomington, 1987—. Asst. dir. Salzburg Sem., Austria, 1960-61; mem. adv. bd. Emeritus Coll., Coll. St. Scholastica, Duluth, Minn., 1994-2002; founder and acad. chmn. North Shore Pub. Discussion Opportunities, Grand Marais, Minn., 1992—, emeritus, 2006; mem. planning com. Upper Deck Forum, Grand Marais, 1989—; mem. adv. bd. Cook County, Minn. Cmty. Edn., 2000-07, U. Minn. Ext. Svc., Cook County, 2001-04. Reviewer books; contbr. articles to profl. jours. Bd. dirs. UN Assn., Duluth, 1991-94. Pvt. inf. AUS, 1943-45. Decorated Purple Heart, 2 Bronze Battle Stars. Mem. AAAS, Am. Polit. Sci. Assn., Nat. U. Continuing Edn. Assn. bd. dirs. 1986-87), Ind. Acad. Social Scis. (life, sr. dir. studies 1980's), Univ. Continuing Edn. Assn. (bd. dirs. 1986-87, emeritus key holder 1987—). Avocation: canoeing. Home: 144 Devil Track Rd Grand Marais MN 55604-2273 Personal E-mail: bhatt@boreal.org. Business E-Mail: rhattery@indiana.edu.

HATTIN, DONALD EDWARD, geologist, educator; b. Cohasset, Mass., Nov. 16, 1928; s. Edward Arthur and Una Vestella (Whipple) H.; m. Marjorie Elizabeth Macy, July 15, 1950; children: Sandra Jane, Ronald Scott, Donna Jean. BS, U. Mass., 1950; MS, U. Kans., 1952, PhD (Shell fellow), 1954. Asst. instr. geology U. Kans., 1950-52, instr., 1953-54; asst. prof. geology Ind. U., Bloomington, 1954-60, assoc. prof., 1960-67, prof., 1967-95, prof. emeritus, 1995—; asst. geologist Kans. Geol. Survey, 1952, research assoc., 1959-68, 70-74, 77-82, 86-87. Vis. prof. Ernst-Moritz-Arndt U., Greifswald, German Dem. Republic, 1985; geologist Ind. Geol. Survey, 1957-58; cons. in field; mem. N.Am. Commn. on Stratigraphic Nomenclature, 1987-94; vis. disting. prof. U. Kans., 1991. Author: Stratigraphy of the Wreford Limestone, 1957, Stratigraphy of the Carlile Shale, 1962, Stratigraphy of the Graneros Shale in Central Kansas, 1965, Stratigraphy and Depositional Environment of Greenhorn Limestone of Kansas, 1975, Upper Cretaceous Stratigraphy and Depositional Environments of Western Kansas, 1978, Stratigraphy and Depositional Environment of Smoky Hill Chalk, Niobrara Chalk, Western Kansas, 1982, W. Ferdinand Macy, 1852-1901: Painter of New England Landscapes, 2004, Tales of a New England Boyhood: Scituate, Massachusetts, 1931-1946, 2006 Trainman, steam locomotive restoration specialist Ind. Railway Mus., French Lick. Capt. reserves USAF, 1950—59, lt. USAF, 1955—57. Recipient Erasmus Haworth Disting. Alumni honors in geology U. Kans., 1976, Alumni Disting. Tchg. award Coll. Arts and Scis. Ind. U., 1988, Disting. Tchg. and Mentoring award Grad. Sch. Ind. U., 1995; NSF grantee, 1975-77, 88-90, Am. Chem. Soc. grantee, 1978-80, 84-86; NSF fellow, 1969. Fellow: Geol. Soc. Am. (grantee 1975); mem.: Paleontol. Soc., Soc. Econ. Paleontologists Mineralogists, Am. Assn. Petroleum Geologists (Outstanding Educator award Ea. sect. 1993), Ind. Soc. Mayflower Descendants (chmn. scholarship com.). Office: Ind U Dept Geol Scis Bloomington IN 47405 Personal E-mail: hattin@indiana.edu.

HATTON, BARBARA R., academic administrator; b. La Grange, Ga., June 4, 1941; d. William H. and Katye (Tucker) H.; 1 child, Kera M. Washington. BS, Howard U., 1962; MA, The Atlanta U., 1966; MEA, Stanford U., 1971, PhD, 1976. Assoc. dir. Stanford (Calif.) U., 1970-72, asst. prof. edn. adminstrn. and policy studies, 1976-79; chair Dept. Adminstrn. & Supervision, acting assoc. dean The Atlanta U., 1979-80; dean, prof. Tuskegee U., Ala., 1984-88; dep. dir. The Ford Found., NYC, 1988; scholar-in-residence So. Edn. Found., Atlanta, 1992—; pres. S.C. State U., Orangeburg, 1993—, Knoxville Coll., 1997—. Mem. adv. com. Tchr. Edn. Project Assn. Am. Colls.; mem. review panel Fifth Yr. Non-Trad. Edn. Programs Ala. Dept. Edn.; mem. futures task force Am. Assn. Colls. for Tchr. Edn.; noms. com. New Deans Orientation Com. Trainer New Dean's Inst. Am. Assn. of Colls. of Tchr. Edn.; commn. on ednl. quality So. Regional Edn. Bd.; mem. Math. Standardization Com. Atlanta Pub. Schs.; reader Jour. Ga. Ednl. Rsch. Assn.; chmn. subcommittee on provisional certification and reciprocity, exec. com. Bd. Regents and State Bd. of Edn., State of Ga. Mem. S.C. Humanities Coun., Orangeburg C. of C.; bd. dirs. Assn. Presbyn. Colls. and Univs., Tenn. Rsch. Valley, Knoxville Symphony; active Met. Drug Com., Coll. Bds. Equity 2000 Project. Fellow NDEA, EPDA; recipient The Rose award U. S.C., 1993, Drum Major for Justice awards, 1993. Mem. Am. Ednl. Rsch. Assn., Am. Assn. Sch. Adminstrs., Exec. Women's Assn., Rotary Knoxville, Alpha Kappa Alpha Sorority Inc., Phi Chi Hon. Soc., Phi Delta Kappa Hon. Soc.

HATTON, VINCENT PAUL, lawyer; b. Hartford, Conn., June 2, 1950; s. Leo William and Rose J. (Delaura) H.; m. Anne Louise Sweet, Aug. 22, 1972; children: Sarah Anne, Matthew Thomas, Daniel Leo, Michael Robert. BA cum laude, U. Pa., 1972, JD cum laude, 1975. Bar: Pa. 1975, N.Y. 1982. Assoc. Ballard, Spahr, Andrews and Ingersoll, Phila., 1975-81; asst. corp. counsel, divsn. counsel, asst. gen. counsel Corning (N.Y.) Inc., 1981-95, asst. gen. counsel, dir. legal dept., 1995-97, v.p., 1998—2003, sr. v.p., 2003—07, sr. v.p., gen. counsel, 2006. Mem. ABA (bus. law sect.), Am. Corp. Counsel Assn., Nature Conservancy, Atlantic Salmon Fedn., Trout Unltd., Rockwell Mus., Corning Glass Mus., Am. Chestnut Found. Republican. Roman Catholic. Avocation: fly fishing. Office: Corning Inc One Riverfront Plz Corning NY 14831 Office Phone: 607-974-8382. Business E-Mail: hattonvp@corning.com.

HATTORI, NAOZO, science educator; b. Ashikaga, Tochigi, Japan, Apr. 13, 1938; s. Eigorou and Kou Hattori; m. Takako Mitsutomi, Nov. 1, 1967; children: Miki Ooya, Nobuko Tanaka. B of Physics, U. Tokyo, 1963, M of Physics, 1965, DEng, 1980. Rschr. Inst. Space and Aero. Sci., U. Tokyo, 1965—76; sr. staff engr. Power Reactor and Nuc. Fuel Devel. Corp., Tokyo, 1976—88; prof. Sci. U. Tokyo, Noda/Chiba, 1988—2004. Chmn. dirs. Soc. Housing Devel., Tokorozawa, Japan, 1988. Mem.: Heat Transfer Soc. Japan, Atomic Energy Soc. Japan, Japan Soc. Mech. Engrs. Avocations: oil painting, classical music, golf. Office: Sci Univ Tokyo 2641 Yamazaki Noda Chiba 278-8510 Japan Home: 104-1-301 2-1 Kotesashiminami 6-choume Tokorozawa 359-1146 Japan Office Phone: 04 7124 1501. Business E-Mail: n-hatto@qf7.so-net.ne.jp.

HATZIAVRAMIDIS, KATIE, lawyer; d. Dimitri Hatziavramidis and Susan Osuch. BA, Kans. State U., Manhattan, 2001; jd, U. Tex., Austin, 2005. Bar: Ill. 2006. Vol. atty. Chgo. Vol. Legal Svcs., Chicago, Ill., 2006—. Legal and bus. cons., English instr. Englishworks, Inc., Plano, Tex., 2005—; law clk. litig. divsn. EEOC, Houston, 2004; law clk., hotline vol. Jane's Due Process, Austin, 2003—04. Article and notes editor: Texas Internat. Law Jour.; author: (poetry) How to Survive the Loss of a Loved One: A Primer in 12 Easy Steps (Editor's Choice award Outstanding Achievement in Poetry, Internat. Libr. of Poetry, 2005). Presdl. scholar, Kans. State U., 1999—2000, Endowed Presdl. scholar, U. Tex. Sch. Law, 2002—03. Mem.: ABA (mem. labor and employment law sect. 2003—07), Ill. State Bar Assn., Am. Mensa, Ltd., Golden Key Internat. Honor Soc. (life). Avocations: charitable work, writing, reading, travel, creative arts. Office: Chgo Vol Legal Svcs 100 N LaSalle Ste 900 Chicago IL 60602 also: Englishworks Inc 8401 Custer Rd Ste 126 Plano TX 75023 also: EEOC Mickey Leland Fed Bldg 1919 SMith St 6th Fl Houston TX 77002 Personal E-mail: kshlaw@gmail.com.

HAUBIEL, CHARLES W., II, lawyer; b. July 1965; m. Michele R. Haubiel. B, Purdue U.; JD, Ohio State U. Bar: 1992. Atty. Vorys, Sater, Seymour & Pease; sr. staff counsel Big Lots Inc. (previously Consolidated Stores Corp.), Columbus, Ohio, 1997—99, dir., corp. counsel, asst sec., 1999—2000, v.p., gen. counsel, corp. sec., 2000—04, sr. v.p., gen. counsel, corp. sec., 2004—. Office: Big Lots Inc 300 Phillipi Rd Columbus OH 43228*

HAUCK, FREDERICK HAMILTON, retired military officer, retired astronaut, aerospace executive; b. Long Beach, Calif., Apr. 11, 1941; s. Philip and Virginia (Hustvedt) H.; m. Dolly Bowman, Aug. 27, 1962 (div.); children: Whitney Irene, Stephen Christopher; m. Susan Cameron Bruce, June 27, 1993. BS in Physics, Tufts U., 1962; MS in Nuclear Engring., MIT, 1966; D of Pub. Svc. (hon.), Tufts U., 2007. Commd. ensign USN, 1962, advanced through grades to capt., 1983; pilot Attack Squadron 35, USS Coral Sea, 1968-70; instr. pilot Attack Squadron 42, Oceana, Va., 1970-71; test pilot Naval Air Test Ctr., Patuxent River, Md., 1971-74; ops. officer Carrier Air Wing 14, Miramar, Calif., USS Enterprise, 1974-76; exec. officer Attack Squadron 145, Wash., 1976-78; astronaut NASA, Houston, 1978-89; space shuttle pilot shuttle transp. system mission 7, 1983; space shuttle comdr. STS-51A, 1984; assoc. adminstr. for external rels. NASA, 1986; space shuttle comdr. STS-26, 1988; dir. Navy Space Systems (OP-943), Washington, 1989-90, ret., 1990; pres., CEO AXA Space (formerly Internat. Tech. Underwriters), Bethesda, Md., 1990—2005. Comml. space transp. adv. com. Dept. Transp., 1990-98, chmn. COMSTAC task group on Soviet entry into world space markets; mem. comml. programs adv. com. NASA, 1991-92, mission rev. group on spacecraft salvage and repair, 1992; mem. panel on space launch industry U.S. Congress Office Tech. Assessment, 1994-95; chmn. NASA External Ind. Readiness rev. group for Second Hubble space Telescope Servicing Mission, 1995-97; mem. aeronautics and space engring. bd., Nat. Rsch. Coun., 1996-2002, internat. space sta. meteoroid/debris risk mgmt. com., 1995-97, chair space shuttle meteoroid/debris risk mgmt. com., 1996-97; chair bd. overseers Schs. Arts and Scis., Tufts U.; mem. adv. coun. Inst. Nuc. Power Ops., 2005-; mem. NASA Adv. Coun., 2005—; space commentator and analyst NBC News, 2005-06. Trustee Tufts U., 1987-2002, emeritus, 2003—; bd. govs. St. Albans Sch., 1989-95; bd. dirs. U.S. Space Foun., 2006—, Astronaut Scholarship Foun., 2005—. Decorated Def. D.S.M. (2), Def. Superior Svc. medal, Legion of Merit, DFC, Air medal (9), Navy Commendation Medal with Gold Star and Combat V, NASA D.S.M, NASA medal for Outstanding Leadership, NASA Space Flight medal (3), Presdl. Cost Saving Commendation; named to U.S. Astronaut Hall of Fame, 2001; recipient AIAA Haley Space Flight award, Disting. Svc. award, Tufts U. Alumni Assn., 2000. Fellow: AIAA, Am. Astron. Soc. (bd. govs. 1997—2000), Soc. Exptl. Test Pilots; mem.: Astronaut Scholarship Found. (bd. govs.), Nat. Assoc. Nat. Academies, Early and Pioneer Naval Aviators Assn., Assn. Space Explorers (v.p. 1991—93, bd. govs. 2000), Winter Harbor Yacht Club (Maine).

HAUCK, LINDSAY BETH, elementary school educator; b. Pitts., Oct. 8, 1982; d. Paul Tracey Lucas and Nancy Elizabeth Lukacs; m. Bill Joseph Hauck, June 18, 2005. BS in Elem. Edn., Pa. State U., University Park, 2000—03. Elem. edn. tchr. Shenango Area Sch. Dist., New Castle, Pa., 2003—. Mem.: Pa. State Edn. Assn. Home: 532 Sarah Dr Cranberry Township PA 16066 Home Phone: 724-772-4541. Business E-Mail: l_hauck@shenango.k12.pa.us.

HAUCK, WILLIAM EDWARD, retired education educator; b. Pa., July 5, 1932; s. Lewis William and Margaret Alice (Freas) H. BS in Math. and Physics, U. Pitts., 1954, MEd in Edn. Psychology, 1962; PhD in Counseling & Edn. Psychology, U. Wis., Madison, 1969. Cert. tchr. in English, math., phys. scis., social studies; cert. sch. psychology, counseling, Pa.; lic. psychologist, Pa. Dir., overseas adult edn. Armed Svcs., Kassel, Fed. Republic Germany, 1954-57; tchr., math. and English Churchill Area Schs., Pitts., 1957-61; rsch. assoc. Bucknell U., Lewisburg, Pa., 1961-63; rsch. assoc., teaching asst. U. Wis., Madison, 1963-67; assoc. coord., Project SESAME-Title III Bucknell U., Lewisburg, Pa., 1967-69, from prof. edn. to prof. emeritus, 1969—95, prof. emeritus, 1995, chair dept. edn., 1989—95; psychologist Five-County Psychol. Svcs., Lewisburg, Pa.,

1985—. Author: Fractions, 1966, Decimals and Percents, 1966, Review of Trigonometry, 1968; co-author: (manual) Brief Algebra Review Manual, 1967, Algebra Review Manual, 1967; reviewer Harper Collins Publishers, 1990—; contbr. numerous rsch. articles to refereed jours. With U.S. Army, 1954-56. Recipient Lindback award, Bucknell U. Mem. Am. Ednl. Rsch. Assn. (div. rsch. and instrn., div. counseling), APA (div. sch. psychology, div. counseling), Nat. Assn. Sch. Psychologists. Avocations: travel, skiing, reading. Home: 117 Oakwood Dr Winfield PA 17889 Office: 115 Farley Cir Ste 304 Lewisburg PA 17837 Office Phone: 570-523-6224. Personal E-mail: wehauck@dejazzd.com.

HAUENSTEIN, GLEN W., air transportation executive; BBA in Fin., Stetson U., DeLand, Fla., 1982. Internat. contr. Continental Airlines, 1987, v.p. scheduling, 1998—2001, sr. v.p. scheduling, 2001—03, sr. v.p. network, 2003; vice gen. dir., chief comml. officer, COO Alitalia, 2003—05; exec. v.p., chief network and revenue mgmt. Delta Air Lines, Inc., Atlanta, 2005—06, exec. v.p. network planning and revenue mgmt., 2006—. Office: Delta Air Lines Inc PO Box 20706 Atlanta GA 30320-6001 Office Phone: 404-715-2600.*

HAUER, ERWIN FRANZ, sculptor, educator; b. Vienna, Austria, Jan. 18, 1926; s. Johann and Margarete (Maehner) H.; m. Helen Takacs, Feb. 28, 1961; children— Nicholas James, Laura Leslie. M.F.A., Acad. Applied Arts, Vienna, 1954; M.F.A. (hon.), Yale U., 1983. Mem. faculty Yale U., New Haven, 1956-60, 63-90, prof. art, 1983-90, ret., 1990; artist in residence Dartmouth Coll., Hanover, N.H., 1976; vis. critic R.I. Sch. Design, 1963-64, U. Pa., 1979; vis. artist U. Mich., 1982, U. Maine, Orono, 1983; originator, sculpture Project Calif. Condor traveling exhbn. 1978-83. Author: Erwin Hauer Continua, 2004; one-man shows Old Dominion Coll., Norfolk, Va., 1964, Am. Mexican Inst. Cultural Relations, Mexico City, 1963, Yale U., 1964, 65, Dartmouth Coll., Hanover, N.H., 1976, Sindin Galleries, N.Y.C., 1977, Mid Hudson Arts and Sci. Ctr., Poughkeepsie, N.Y., 1981, Smithsonian Instn., 1981, U. Conn., Storrs, 1981, Hartford Childrens Mus., 1982, 1708 E Main St., Richmond, Va., 1983, Nat. Soaring Mus., Elmira, N.Y., 1984, Creative Arts Workshop, New Haven, 1998; exhibited in group shows Vienna, Rome, Italy, Boston, Cleve., Ann Arbor, Hartford, Manchester, N.H., Yale U., Galerie Chalette, N.Y.C., 1961, 68, Sculptors Guild, N.Y.C., 1983, 84, Silvermine Collection, Westport, Conn., 1984, Arrowwood, Purchase, N.Y., Smithsonian Mus., 1984, Bklyn. Mus., 2001, Frist Ctr., Nashville, Tenn., 2002, San Diego Mus. Art, 2002, De Cordova Mus., Lincoln, Mass., Nat. Acad. Design, NYC, 2005, Walker Art Ctr., Mpls., 2007; sculpture commns. and indsl. designs in Austria, Can., Italy, Mexico, Netherlands-Antilles, US, Venezuela; represented in permanent collections Bklyn. Mus. Art, Yale U. Art Gallery, Josef Albers Found., Am. Mexican Cultural Inst., Mexico City, Chase Manhattan Bank, N.Y.C., 1st Nat. Bank Chgo., Mus. Art, Basel, Switzerland, Wadsworth Atheneum, Hartford, Conn., Art Inst. Chgo., Nat. Soaring Mus.; prin. works include sculpture Conn. Superior Ct., New London, Köln, Taschen Verlag, 2006; author: Erwin Hauer Continua, 2004; contbr. to numerous printed works and publs. Recipient Design award Indsl. Designers Inst. Chgo., 1959, Editor's prize Internat. Contemporary Furniture Fair, NYC, 2006; Fulbright grantee, 1955; Morse fellow, 1968. Mem. AAUP, Nat. Acad. Design, Sculptors Guild, Soaring Soc. Am. Avocations: soaring. Office Phone: 203-393-3076. Business E-Mail: erwin.hauer@yale.edu.

HAUER, JAMES ALBERT, lawyer; b. Fond du Lac, Wis., Apr. 3, 1924; s. Albert A. and Hazel M. (Corcoran) H.; children: Stephen, John, Paul, Christopher, Patrick. BCE, Marquette U., 1948, LLB, 1949; bank mgmt. cert., Columbia U., 1957, U. Wis., 1959. Bar: Wis., U.S. Dist. Ct. (ea. dist.), U.S. Ct. Appeals (9th cir.), U.S. Dist. Ct. (fed. dist.) 1958. Patent counsel Ira Milton Jones, Milw., 1949; chief counsel Wauwatosa Realty, Milw., 1950-57; v.p. Wauwatosa (Wis.) State Bank, 1957-67; pres. Milw. We. Bank, 1967-69, Prem Constrn. Co., Milw., 1969-73; pvt. practice Elm Grove, Wis., 1973-86, Sun City, Ariz., 1986—. Pres., bd. dirs. Sunshine Svc., Sun City, Meals on Wheels, Sun City. With USMCR, 1942-45. Mem. Wis. Bar Assn., Ariz. Patent Law Assn. (charter). Home and Office: 9915 W Royal Oak Rd Apt 1098 Sun City AZ 85351-3161 Personal E-mail: jimhauerscaz@juno.com.

HAUFLER, CHRISTOPHER HARDIN, botany educator; b. Niskayuna, NY, Apr. 20, 1950; s. J. Hervie and Patricia (DeLearie) Haufler. BA, Hiram Coll., 1972; MA, Ind. U., 1974, PhD, 1977. Assoc. instr. Ind. U., 1972—76, asst. prof, 1977; postdoctoral fellow Gray Herbarium, Harvard U., 1977-78; NEA postdoctoral fellow Mo. Bot. Garden, St. Louis, 1978-79; asst. prof. U. Kans., Lawrence, 1979-84, assoc. prof., 1984-90, chmn. dept. botany, 1985, prof., 1990—. Faculty sponsor undergraduate biology club, 1980—, search com., 1980—, field facilities com., 1980-92, curriculum com., 1980—, greenhouse com., 1980—, chair, 1984-88, honors and awards com., 1980-87, space com., 1980-86, chair departmental admissions and awards com., 1981-84, biology core rev. com., 1983-85, biol. scis. resource ctr., 1984-87, biol. scis. exec. com., 1985—, stewart Evolutionists, 1985, sec., 1986; mem. panel systematic biology NSF, 1987-93. Reviewer Index to Plant Chromosome Numbers, 1979-89; presenter papers in field. William R. Ogg Departmental fellow, 1976-77; Rsch. fellow Gray Herbarium, 1977-78. Mem. Bot. Soc. Am. (mem. nominating com. for officers pteridological sect. 1981, 82, sec.-treas. 1983-89, prog. organizer 1985, 87, 89, chair 1991-93, symposium organizer 1984, 85, 87, editor Ann. Bibliography Am. Pteridology 1978-82, assoc. editor Am. Jour. Botany 1994—, sec. 1991—, pres. 2006-, Best Paper award 1979, 80, 82, 83, 84, 92, 93), Am. Fern Soc. (mem. nominating com. for officers 1980, 83, assoc. editor Am. Fern Jour. 1986—), Am. Inst. Biol. Scis., Am. Soc. Plant Taxonomists (rsch. awards com. 1989-91, prog. dir. 1990-93, editl. bd. Systematic Botany 1985-87, assoc. editor 1994—), Nat. Geog. Soc., Soc. Systematic Biologists (editl. bd. 1992—), Internat. Assn. Pteridologists (sec. 1987—, compiler Internat. Report Pteridological Rsch. 1984-88), Brit. Pteridological Soc., Soc. for Study Evolution, Sigma Xi. Office: U Kans Dept Ecology and Evolutionary Biology 2041 Haworth Hall 1200 Sunnyside Ave Lawrence KS 66045 Office Phone: 785-864-3255. Office Fax: 785-864-5294. E-mail: vulgare@ku.edu.*

HAUG, WARREN R., research and development consultant; b. Milw., May 26, 1938; s. Ernst Friedrich and Emily Leone Haug; m. Karen Ann Nichols, July 20, 1968; children: Erin, Michael, Kevin. BS in Chem. Engring., U. Wis., 1961; MS in Chem. Engring., Northwestern U., 1963, PhD in Chem. Engring., 1965. With Procter & Gamble, Cin., 1965—96, dir. R & D, 1981—87, v.p. R & D, 1987—96; cons. Global Innovation, 1996—. Adj. prof. Northwestern U., Evanston, Ill., 1996—; sr. fellow Wharton Sch., U. Pa., Phila., 1996—. Recipient Disting. Svc. citation, U. Wis., 1992, Alumni Merit award, Northwestern U., 1995, Alumni Svc. award, 2006, Faculty of the Yr. award for master of product development program, 2005. Home and Office: 11281 Longwater Chase Ct Fort Myers FL 33908

HAUGEN, CHRISTINE, plastic surgeon; b. Newport Beach, Calif., Aug. 20, 1968; d. Bjorn Hugo and Margit Haugen; m. Frederick Martin Haddad, Sept. 20, 2003; 1 child, Hunter Haugen Haddad. Student, U. So. Calif., 1986—87; AB in English Lit. cum laude, Bryn Mawr Coll., 1990; MD Med. Coll. Pa., 1994. Diplomate Am. Bd. Plastic Surgery. Resident in gen. surgery Brown U., Providence, 1994—97; resident in plastic surgery U. Miami, Fla., 1998—2000; plastic surgeon Advanced Cosmetic Laser Ctr., Ft. Lauderdale, Fla., 2000—01; pvt. practice Ft. Lauderdale, 2001—03; med. dir. Med. Spa Ft. Lauderdale, 2003—04, Radiance Med. Spa, Palm Beach Gardens, Fla., 2006—. Contbr. articles to profl. jours. Active Hospice Hundred, Ft. Lauderdale, 2002—, Goodwill Amb., Ft. Lauderdale, 2004—. Hannah E. Longshore Meml. scholar, Bryn Mawr Coll., 1990. Mem.: Am. Soc. Plastic Surgeons. Avocations: skiing, surfing, travel. Office: 4800 N Federal Hwy Ste C-101 Boca Raton FL 33431

HAUGEN, JANE S., elementary school educator; b. Dubuque, Iowa, Feb. 18, 1950; d. Wilfrid L. and Frances E. Welter; m. Daryl A. Haugen, Aug. 9, 1974; 1 child, Alex M. BS, U. Wis., Platteville, 1972; MA, Clarke Coll., 1975. Cert. tchr. Iowa. Tchr. elem. sch. We. Dubuque (Iowa) Schs., Epworth, 1972—73, Dubuque (Iowa) Cmty. Schs., 1973—. Cons. Kendall Hunt co., Dubuque, Iowa, 2005. Recipient Tchg. award, Izaak Walton League, 1996, Excellence in Math. Sci. Tchg. award, Pres. U.S., 2000; fellow, FINE Found., 2004—05. Mem.: NEA, Internat. Reading Assn., Nat. Sci. Tchrs. Assn., Iowa Acad. Sci. (facilitator projects 1999—, Excellence in Elem. Sci. Tchg. award 1999), Soc. Elem. Presdl. Awardees, Nat. Coun. Tchrs. Math., Iowa Coun. Tchrs. Math., Iowa State Edn. Assn., Dubuque Edn. Assn., Phi Delta Kappa (v.p. membership 2000—01, pres. 2001—02, treas. 2002—03). Democrat. Roman Catholic. Avocations: reading, gardening. Home: 2989 Olde Country Ln Dubuque IA 52001 Office: Kennedy Elem 2135 Woodland Dr Dubuque IA 52002 Business E-Mail: jhaugen@dubuque.k12.ia.us.

HAUGEN, JANET B., corporate financial executive; B in Econ. magna cum laude, Rutgers U. Ptnr. Ernst & Young LLP; corp. v.p., contr. Unisys Corp., Blue Bell, Pa., 1996—2000, sr. v.p., CFO, 2000—. Mem.: Conf. Bd. Coun. of CFOs, Fin. Exec. Inst., Forum Exec. Women. Office: Unisys Corp Unisys Way Blue Bell PA 19424*

HAUGEN, MARY MARGARET, state legislator; b. Camano Island, Wash., Jan. 14, 1941; d. Melvin Harry and Alma Cora (Huntington) Olsen; m. Basil Badley; children: Mary Beth Fisher, Katherine Heitt, Richard, James. Mem. Wash. Ho. Reps., Olympia, 1982-1992, past mem. natural resources com., transp. com., mem. joint legis. com. on criminal justice system; mem. Wash. Senate, Dist. 10, Olympia, 1993—, chair transp. com., mem. rules com. Mem. LWV, Stanwood Camano Soroptomists. Lodges: Order Ea. Star. Democrat. Methodist. Avocations: fishing, reading, collecting antique clothing. Office: Wash Senate Legis Bldg PO Box 40482 Olympia WA 98504-0482 E-mail: haugen_ma@leg.wa.gov.

HAUGHEY, JAMES MCCREA, lawyer, artist; b. Courtland, Kans., July 8, 1914; s. Leo Eugene and Elizabeth (Stephens) H.; m. Katherine Hurd, Sept. 8, 1938; children: Katherine (Mrs. Lester B. Loo), Bruce Stephens, John Caldwell. Student, Deep Springs Coll., Dyer, Calif., 1930-31; LLB, U. Kans., Lawrence, 1939. Bar: Kans. 1939, Mont. 1943. Landman Carter Oil Co., 1939-43; practice in Billings, Mont., 1943-98; ptnr. Crowley, Haughey, Hanson, Toole & Dietrich, 1950-86, counsel, 1986-98; ret. dir. Mont.-Dakota Resources Group Inc., 1998. One-man shows include, U. Kans., U. Mont., Mont. State U., Concordia Coll., Nebr., C.M. Russell Mus., Great Falls, Mont., Boise Mus. Art, Mont. State Mus., Helena, Sandzen Gallery, Bethany Coll., Lindsborg, Kans., Yellowstone Art Mus., Billings, Mont., also numerous group shows. Pres. Rocky Mountain Mineral Law Found., 1957-58, trustee, 1955—; pres. Mont. Inst. Arts Found., 1965-67; pres. Yellowstone Art Center Found., 1969-71, trustee, 1964-81; mem. Mont. Ho. of Reps., 1960-64, Mont. Senate, 1966-70, senate minority leader, 1969-70. Recipient Gov.'s award Arts, 1981 Fellow Mont. Inst. Arts (Permanent Collection award 1960), Am. Artists Profl. League; mem. ABA, Am. Coll. Real Estate Lawyers, Yellowstone County Bar Assn. (pres. 1960-61), U. Kans. Law Soc. (bd. govs. 1989-92), Am. Watercolor Soc. (Midwest v.p. 1978-82), N.W. Watercolor Soc. (life), Midwest Watercolor Soc., Kans. Watercolor Soc. (hon.), Mont. Watercolor Soc. (hon.), Yellowstone Art Mus. (Pres.'s award svc. to Arts, 2005, Philanthropist of Yr.), Phi Delta Theta, Phi Delta Phi. Republican. Episcopalian. Office: Crowley Haughey Hanson Toole & Dietrich TranswWestern Pla II 490 N 31st St Ste 500 Billings MT 59101-1256 Personal E-mail: jimhoy@bresnan.net. Business E-Mail: jhaughey@crowleylaw.com.

HAUGHT, JAMES ALBERT, JR., journalist, editor; b. Reader, W.Va., Feb. 20, 1932; s. James Albert and Beulah (Fish) H.; m. Nancy Carolyn Brady, Apr. 22, 1958; children: Joel, Jacob, Jeb, Cassie Student, Morris Harvey Coll., 1950—52; part-time, W.Va. State Coll., 1960—63. Apprentice printer Charleston Daily Mail, 1951—53; reporter Charleston Gazette, 1953—, varied positions as night and weekend city editor, music and film critic, govt., schs., suburban, religion and investigative reporter, 1970—82, assoc. editor, 1983—92, editor, 1992—. Author: Holy Horrors, 1990, Science in a Nanosecond, 1990, The Art of Lovemaking, 1992, Holy Hatred, 1994, 2000 Years of Disbelief, 1996, Honest Doubt, 2007, Amazon Moon, 2007; sr. editor: Free Inquiry mag., 1996— Recipient award Headliners Club, 1971, 1st Ann. Consumer Writing prize Nat. Press Club, 1973, Nat. Hwy. Safety Writing award Uniroyal Tire Co., 1975, First Amendment award Sigma Delta Chi, 1977, People for Am. Way, 1986, Merit award ABA, 1977, Consumer Writing prize Nat. Press Club, 1979, 83, Spl. award Religion Newswriters Assn., 1980, Health Journalism award Am. Chiropractic Assn., 1981, 83, Nat. award for edn. reporting Edn. Writers Assn., 1989, Hugh M. Hefner First Amendment award Playboy Found., 1989, Benjamin Fine award for edn. reporting Nat. Assn. Secondary Sch. Prins., 1990, Clarion award Women in Comm., 2000, 02-03, Nat. Headliners award, 2001, Green Eyeshade award, 2003 Democrat. Unitarian Universalist. Home: 15 Killen Hollow Dr Cross Lanes WV 25313-3516 Office: Charleston Gazette 1001 Virginia St E Charleston WV 25301-2895 Office Phone: 304-348-5199. Personal E-mail: haught@wvinter.net. Business E-Mail: haught@wvgazette.com.

HAUGHT, WILLIAM DIXON, lawyer, writer; b. Kansas City, Kans., June 12, 1939; s. Walter Dixon and Florence Louise (Rhoads) H.; m. Julia Jane Headstream, July 22, 1967; 1 dau., Stephanie Jane. BS, U. Kans., 1961; LL.B., U Kans., 1964; LL.M., Georgetown U., 1968. Bar: Kans. 1964, Ark. 1971. Assoc. Stanley, Schroeder, Weeks, Thomas & Lysaught, Kansas City, Kans., 1968-70; ptnr. Wright, Lindsey & Jennings, Little Rock, 1970-91; pvt. practice Little Rock, 1991-95; ptnr. Haught & Wade, 1996—. Author: Arkansas Probate System, 1977, 7th ed. 2005, (with others) Probate and Estate Administration: The Law in Arkansas, 1983. Served to capt. USAR, 1964-68, Korea, Washington. Mem. ABA (coun. chmn. coms.), Am. Coll. Trust and Estate Counsel (regent, editor studies program, chmn. editl. bd., state chair), Internat. Acad. Estate and Trust Law, Am. Law Inst., Am. Counsel Assn., Ark. Bar Assn. (chmn. probate law sect., chmn. econs. of law practice com., chmn. agrl. law com., chmn. juris law reform com.), Ctrl. Ark. Estate Coun., Pulaski County Bar Assn., Ark. Bar Found., Country Club of Little Rock. Presbyterian. Office: Haught & Wade 111 Center St Ste 1320 Little Rock AR 72201-4405 Office Phone: 501-375-5257. Business E-Mail: wdh@haughtwade.com.

HAUGLAND, SUSAN WARRELL, education educator, consultant; b. Portland, Oreg., Aug. 29, 1950; d. George William and Commery Wallace (Coleman) Warrell; children from previous marriage: Charles, Michael. BS in Child Devel., Oreg. State U., Corvallis, 1972; PhD in Psychology, Saybrook Inst., 1976. Cert. family and consumer scis. Dir., head tchr. Lafayette Co-op Nursery Sch., Detroit, 1973-75; handicapped svcs. coord. OutWayne County Head Start, Wayne, Mich., 1975-76; asst. prof. child devel. Va. Poly. Inst. and State U., Blacksburg, 1976-79; prof. emeritus child devel. S.E. Mo. State U., Cape Girardeau, 1979-99, prof. emeritus, 1999—; pres. K.I.D.S. & Computers, Inc., Cape Girardeau, 1999—; prof. early childhood edn. The Met. State Coll. of Denver, 2000—. Dir. Ctr. for Child Studies, Cape Girardeau, 1979-99, Kids Interacting with Devel. Software, Cape Girardeau, 1985—; chair Human-Environ. Studies, Cape Girardeau, 1990-93; judge Developmental Software Awards, 1991—, Child Mag. Awards, 1992-99. Author: Helping Young Children Grow, 1980, Developmental Evaluations of Software for Young Children, 1990, Young Children and Technology: A World of Discovery, 1997, Haugland Developmental Software Scale, 1997, Haugland/Gertzog Developmental Scale for Web Sites, 1998; dept. editor Early Childhood Education Jour., 1992—; contbr. numerous articles to profl. jours. Chair Clayton Found. Partnership; exec. bd. Tech. and Young Children Interest Forum. Grantee numerous orgns.; recipient Gov.'s award for Teaching Excellence, 1996. Mem. Assn. for Childhood Edn. Internat., Nat. Assn. for Edn. Young Children, Nat. Assn. for Early Childhood Tchr. Educators, Tech. and Young Children Caucus, Omicron Nu. Democrat. Methodist. Avocations: reading, travel, cooking, bicycling. E-mail: susanhaugland@hotmail.com.

HAUGNER, CAROLYN M., elementary school educator; b. Appleton, Wis., Aug. 16, 1948; d. Joseph A. and Rosemary A. (Probst) Suess; m. John C. Haugner Jr., June 22, 1974; children: Krista Haugner Sieg, John C. III. BA in Elem. Edn., St. Norbert Coll., West De Pere, Wis., 1970; MS in Edn., U. Wis., Oskkosh, 1976. Tchr. grades 3-4 Hilbert Pub. Schs., Wis., 1970—71; tchr. grades 4-6 Hortonville Pub. Schs., 1971—74; tchr. grade 1 Kettle Moraine Schs., Delafield, 1974—86, reading specialist, 1986—. Bd. mem. St. Bruno Sch. Com., Dousman, Wis., 1992—96, 2002—06; vol. St. Bruno Parish, 1974—. Recipient Leadership award, Kettle Moraine Sch. Dist., Wales, Wis., 1990; fellow, Herb Kohl Ednl. Found., Wis., 2005. Mem.: NEA, Internat. Reading Assn. (Celebrate Literacy award 2006), Wis. State Reading Assn., Wis. Edn. Assn., Waukesha County Reading Coun. (pres. 1998—99, 2001—02, sec. 2004—07). Roman Catholic. Avocations: travel, reading. Home: S15 W37060 Willow Springs Dr Dousman WI 53118 Office: Cushing Sch 227 Genesee St Delafield WI 53018

HAUK, BETH MACKENZIE, elementary school educator, writer; b. Beaver Falls, Pa., Dec. 5, 1952; d. James W. and Laura A. MacKenzie; m. Timothy G. Hauk; children: Kelly, Eric. BA with honors, U. Redlands, Calif., 1974; postgrad., Calif. State U., San Bernardino, 2003. Cert. lang. devel. specialist Calif., 1994, administrv. Calif., 2000, primary reading Calif., 2002. 4th and 5th grade tchr. Corona-Norco Unified Sch. Dist., Calif., 1974—79; home-hosp. tchr. Brea-Olinda Unified Sch. Dist, 1979—87, Yucaipo-Calimesa Joint Unified, 1988—89; substitute tchr. Ctrl. Sch. Dist., Rancho Cucamonga, 1989—90; kindergarten and 1st grade tchr. Apple Valley Unified Sch. Dist., 1990—94, 1998—2007, lang. devel. specialist, 1994—98. Commr. Calif. Commn. Tchr. Credentialing, Sacramento, 2001—04; master tchr. Cal State U., various locations, Calif., 1977—2001, Chapman U., 1977—2001. Author: Heartless, 2006; contbr. articles to mags. Planning commr. City of Hesperia, Calif., 1997—98; candidate mgr. for Timothy G. Hauk Calif. State Assembly, 1994; canditate Hesperia City Coun., 1996. Mem.: Calif. Tchrs. Assn. (site rep. 2001—06). Avocations: travel, genealogy, gardening, walking, art. Home: 15473 Cardiff Ln Victorville CA 92394

HAUN, JOHN DANIEL, petroleum geologist, educator; b. Old Hickory, Tenn., Mar. 7, 1921; s. Charles C. and Lydia (Rhodes) H.; m. Lois Culbertson, June 30, 1942. AB, Berea Coll., 1948; MA, U. Wyo., 1949, PhD, 1953. Registered profl. engr., Colo. Geologist Stanolind, Amoco, Vernal, Utah, 1951-52; v.p. Petroleum Research Corp., Denver, 1952-57; mem. faculty dept. geology Colo. Sch. Mines, Golden, 1955-80, prof., 1963-80, part time, 1980-85, emeritus prof., 1983—; cons. Barlow & Haun, Inc., Evergreen, Colo., 1957-90. Cons. Potential Gas Agy., 1966-78, mem. com., 1978—; mem. adv. com. Colo. Water Pollution Control Commn., 1969-70; mem. adv. council Kans. Geol. Survey, 1971-76; del. Internat. Geol. Congress, Sydney, Australia, 1976; U.S. rep. Internat. Com. on Petroleum Res. Classification UN, N.Y.C., 1976-77; mem. oil shale adv. com. Office of Tech. Assessment, Washington, 1976-79, mem. U.S. natural gas availability adv. panel, 1983; mem. Colo. Oil and Gas Conservation Commn., 1977-87, vice-chmn., 1983-85, chmn. 1985-87; mem. energy resources com. Interstate Oil and Gas Compact Commn., 1978—; mem. exec. adv. com. Nat. Petroleum Coun., 1968-70, 79-89, mem. com. on unconventional gas sources, 1978-80; com. on Arctic oil and gas resources, 1980-81; mem. U.S. Nat. Com. on Geology Dept. Interior and NAS, 1982-89, chmn., 1985-87; mem. com undiscovered oil and gas resources, 19881-91, com. status and rsch. objectives in solid-earth scis.: critical assessment, 1988-92, Nat. Rsch. Coun.; del. Internat. Geol. Congress, Paris, 1980, Moscow, 1984; mem. Colo. Oil and Gas legis. com., 1993-94. Editor: The Mountain Geologist, 1963-65, Future Energy Outlook, 1969, Methods of Estimating the Volume of Undiscovered Oil and Gas Resources, 1975; asst. editor: Geologic Atlas of the Rocky Mountain Region, 1972; co-editor: Subsurface Geology in Petroleum Exploration, 1958, Symposium on Cretaceous Rocks of Colorado and Adjacent Areas, 1959, Guide to the Geology of Colorado, 1960; contbr. articles to profl. jours. Served with USCG, 1942-46. Recipient Disting. Svc. award Am. Assn. Petroleum Geologists, 1973, Mines medal Colo. Sch. Mines, 1995. Fellow Geol. Soc. Am., AAAS; mem. Am. Assn. Petroleum Geologists (editor 1967-71, pres. 1979-80, hon. mem. 1984, Sidney Powers Meml. award 1995, Disting. Educator award 2000), Am. Inst. Profl. Geologists (hon. mem., v.p. 1974, pres. 1976, exec. com. 1981-82, Ben H. Parker Meml. award 1983), Am. Geol. Inst. (governing bd. 1976, 79-82, sec.-treas. 1977-78, v.p. 1980-81, pres. 1981-82, Ian Campbell medal 1988, William B. Heroy Jr. award 1996), Rocky Mountain Assn. Geologists (sec. 1961, 1st v.p. 1964, pres. 1968, hon. mem. 1974), Soc. Econ. Paleontologists and Mineralogists, Am. Petroleum Inst. (com. exploration 1971-73, 78-88), Nat. Assn. Geology Tchrs., Wyo. Geol. Assn. (hon. life), Colo. Sci. Soc. (hon. life), Sigma Xi, Sigma Gamma Epsilon, Phi Kappa Phi. Home: 1238 Kerr Gulch Rd Evergreen CO 80439-6397

HAUNER, DAVID, economist; b. Vienna, Aug. 25, 1976; arrived in U.S., 2003; MA in Internat. Policy Studies, Stanford U., Calif., 2001; PhD in Econ., U. Vienna, 2002. Economist Munich Reinsurance Co., 2002—03, Internat. Monetary Fund, Washington, 2003—. Contbr. articles to profl. jours. Recipient Fulbright scholarship, 2000—01. Mem.: Austrian Econ. Assn., Rotaract Internat. (Vienna) (treas. 1998—2000). E-mail: hauner@stanfordalumni.org.

HAUPT, ROBERT J., hotel and real estate developer; b. St. Louis, July 1, 1957; s. Robert Gene and Shelby Joan (Huffman) H.; m. Robin Lynn Bowling, Sept. 22, 1986; children: Lauren Elisabeth, Nicholas Elliott. BA in Psychology, Okla. Bapt. U., 1977; BA in Japanese Studies, Seinan Gakuin U., Fukuoka, Japan, 1979; MA in Social Sic., U. Chgo., 1981. Cert. hotel adminstr. Corp. contr. Ing and Ing, Inc., Oklahoma City, 1983-85; v.p., gen. mgr. SunBay Mgmt. Co., Inc., Hot Springs, Ark., 1985-88; pres. Ctr. Properties, Inc., Hot Springs, 1988—. Chmn. Hot Springs Advt. and Promotion Commn., 1988—. Named Restauranteur of Yr., Ark. Times, Little Rock, 1991. Mem. Ark. Hospitality Assn. (officer, Golden Key award 1989), Diamond Lakes Travel Assn. (officer 1986—), Hot Springs C. of C. (bd. dirs. 1986—), Rotary. Avocations: tennis, golf, swimming. Office: Ctr Properties Inc 1801 Central Ave Hot Springs National Park AR 71901-6848

HAUPT, ROGER A., advertising executive; Joined Leo Burnett (became Leo Group), Chgo., 1984—2000; exec. v.p. Leo Group, 1989—97, 1999—2000, pres., CEO, 2000, COO, 1999; CAO Leo Group (became BCom3), 1997—99; chmn., CEO BCom3 (became Publicis Groupe SA), 2000—02; pres., COO Publicis Groupe SA, Chgo, 2002—04; chmn. Publicis Groupe Media.

HAUPTMAN, GREGORY B., lawyer; b. Washington, Apr. 5, 1951; AB, Washington U., 1973; JD with honors, George Washington U., 1976. Bar: Md. 1976, DC 1977. Ptnr., real estate group Venable LLP, Washington.

Mem.: ABA (mem. real property section), Md. Bar Assn., DC Bar Assn. Office: Venable LLP 575 7th St NW Washington DC 20004 Office Phone: 202-344-8528. Office Fax: 202-344-8300. Business E-Mail: gbhauptman@venable.com.

HAUPTMAN, HERBERT AARON, mathematician, educator, researcher; b. NYC, Feb. 14, 1917; s. Israel and Leah (Rosenfeld) Hauptman; m. Edith Citrynell, Nov. 10, 1940; children: Barbara, Carol Hauptman Fullerton. BS in Math., CCNY, 1937; MA, Columbia U., 1939; PhD, U. Md., 1955, PhD (hon.), 1985, CCNY, 1986, U. Parma, Italy, 1989, D'Youville Coll., 1989, Bar-Ilan U., Israel, 1990, Columbia U., 1990, Tech. U., Lodz, Poland, 1992, Queen's U., Kingston, Ont., Can., 1994, Niagara U., 1996, U. Toledo, 1999, Medaille Coll., 2002. Statistician U.S. Census Bur., Washington, 1940—42; civilian instr. electronics and radar U.S. Army Air Force, Boca Raton, Fla., 1942—43; physicist, mathematician Naval Rsch. Lab., Washington, 1947—70; mathematician Hauptman-Woodward Med. Rsch. Inst., 1970—72, exec. v.p., rsch. dir., 1972—85, pres., rsch. dir., 1985—87, pres., 1988—, also bd. dirs.; prof. biophys. scis. SUNY, Buffalo, 1970—, prof. computer scis., 1992—, disting. prof. structural biology, 2001—. Chmn. N.Y. State Inst. on Superconductivity, 1988—98; mem. sci. adv. bd. Biocryst, 1989—; math. instr. U. Md., 1958—70; chmn. Intercongress Symposium Direct Methods in Crystallography, Buffalo, 1976; pres. Assn. Ind. Rsch. Insts., 1979—80; mem. U.S. Nat. Com. for Crystallography, 1979—81, 1982—85, 1988—89; mem. sci. adv. bd. Biophan, 2001—04. Author (with J. Karle): Solution of the Phase Problem, 1953; author: Crystal Structure Determination: The Role of the Cosine Seminvariants, 1972; editor: Direct Methods in Crystallography, Proceedings of the 1976 Intercongress Symposium, 1978; contbr. chapters to books, articles to profl. jours. Trustee Buffalo Gen. Hosp., 1990—96; chmn. comm. com. Philos. Soc. Washington, 1966—67, corr. sec., 1967—69. Lt. (j.g.) USNR, 1943—46. Named Western N.Y. Man of Yr., Buffalo C. of C., 1986, YMCA Dinner, 1986, 90th Nobel Ann. Dinner, 1991; named to Nobel Hall Mus. Sci. and Industry, 1986, Townsend Harris Hall of Fame, 1989, U. Md. Alumni Hall of Fame, guest of honor Roswell Park Meml. Inst., 1985, YMCA Luncheon, others, invited guest Am. Nobel Convocation, 1987, 1988, Weizmann Nat. Dinner, 1998, others; recipient Belden prize (Gold medal) in Math., 1935, RESA award in Pure Scis., 1959, Citizen of Yr. award, Buffalo Evenings News, 1986, Schoelkopf award, Am. Chem. Soc., 1986, Gold Plate award, Am. Acad. Achievement, 1986, Nat. Libr. Medicine medal, 1987, Law Sch. award, Maimonides Chabad House, 1986, others, (with J. Karle) Patterson award, 1984, Nobel Prize in Chemistry, 1985; grantee, NSF, 1972—92, NIH, 1992—2006, Human Frontier Sci. Program Orgn., 2006—; Sr. fellow, NATO, 1973. Fellow: Jewish Acad. Arts and Scis. (medal 1986), Washington Acad. Scis.; mem.: NAS, AAAS, Math. Assn. Am., Am. Crystallographic Assn. (mem. Fankuchen award com. 1988), Am. Phys. Soc., Am. Math. Soc., Saturn Club (guest of honor 1985), Cosmos Club, Sigma Xi (sec. Buffalo chpt. 1971—72), Phi Beta Kappa. Avocation: stained glass art, swimming, hiking. Office: Hauptman Woodward Med Rsch Inst 700 Ellicott St Buffalo NY 14203 Business E-Mail: hauptman@hwi.buffalo.edu.

HAUPTMANN, RANDAL MARK, biotechnologist; b. Hot Springs, SD, July 6, 1956; s. Ivan Joy and Phyllis Maxine (Pierce) H.; m. Beverly Kay Suko, May 22, 1975; 1 child, Erich William. BS, S.D. State U., 1979; MS, U. Ill., 1982, PhD, 1984. Postdoctoral rschr. Monsanto Corp. Rsch., St. Louis, 1984-86; vis. rsch. scientist U. Fla., Gainesville, 1986-88; asst. prof. No. Ill. U., DeKalb, 1988-90, dir. plant molecular biology ctr., 1989-90; sr. rsch. scientist Amoco Life Sci. Techs., Naperville, Ill., 1990-94; dir. advanced tech. Seminis Vegetable Seeds, Woodland, Calif., 1994-98; gen. mgr. Ball Helix, West Chicago, Ill., 1998—2003; pres. Varro Inc., Chgo.; head raw product rsch. Fresh Express, Salinas, Calif. Author: (with others) Methods in Molecular Biology, 1990; contbr. articles to profl. jours. Mem. Internat. Assn. Plant Tissue Culture, Internat. Soc. Plant Molecular Biology, Am. Soc. Plant Physiologists, Tissue Culture Assn. (Virginia Evans award 1982), Sigma Xi, Gamma Sigma Delta. Democrat. Office Phone: 831-772-6054. Business E-Mail: randalhauptmann@varroinc.com.

HAURI, PETER J., psychology professor, researcher; b. Sirnach, Switzerland, June 25, 1933; arrived in US, 1960, naturalized, 1969; s. Rudolf and Verena Hauri; m. Cynthia A. Cleveland, Sept. 25, 1992; 1 child, Matthew R.; m. Debbie Jo Rea-Hauri (div. 1989); children: Heidi J., David J., Katrin J. Sekundar lehr patent, SLS St. Gallen, Switzerland, 1958; PhD, U. Chgo., 1966. Bd. cert. sleep disorders medicine; lic. psychologist Minn. Bd. Profl. Psychology. Tchg. prin. Pestalozzi Children's Village, Trogen, Switzerland, 1956—59; asst. prof. psychology Sacramento State Coll., 1966—68; assoc. prof. psychology U. Va., Charlottesville, 1968—71; prof. psychology Dartmouth Coll., Hanover, NH, 1971—88, Mayo Med. Sch., Rochester, Minn., 1988—2000, prof. emeritus, 2000—. Adminstrv. dir. Mayo Sleep Disorders Ctr., Rochester, Minn., 1988—2000, chair com. revise internat. classification sleep disorders, Chgo., 2002—05; chair divsn. behavioral medicine Mayo Clinic, 1993—2000. Author: No More Sleepless Nights, 1990, The Sleep Disorders (and revisions), 1977—98; contbr. articles to profl. jours. Scoutmaster Boy Scouts Am., Hanover, NH, 1980—88; vol. Habitat Humanity, Rochester, Minn., 2001—03; soccer coach Rochester Youth Hockey, 2002—03; bd. mem. The Sleep Found., Chgo., 1992—96. Lt. Swiss Army, 1952—59. Recipient Kleitman Disting. Svc. award, Am. Sleep Disorders Assn., 1989. Mem.: APA, Am. Acad. Sleep Medicine (bd. mem. 1988—92), Sleep Rsch. Soc. (pres. and exec. sec. 1974—75). Democrat. Achievements include research in insomnia; first to descibe psychophysiological insomnia, the most common type of insomnia. Avocations: skiing, history, outdoor sports, gardening. Home: 422 Seventh Ave SW Rochester MN 55902 Office Phone: 507-266-7603. Personal E-mail: cphauri@charter.net. Business E-Mail: hauri.peter@mayo.edu.

HAUSCHILD, DOUGLAS CAREY, optometrist; b. Manchester, Conn., Oct. 3, 1955; s. Vernon Francis and Barbara Gwendolyn (Rose) H.; 1 child, Chelsea Anna. BA in Biology magna cum laude, Wesleyan U., 1977; OD, New Eng. Coll. Optometry, 1981. Clinician Boston Eye Clinic, 1978-81; assoc. Drs. Todd, Todd & Hauschild, Hendersonville, NC, 1981-84; owner, optometrist Weaverville (N.C.) Eye Assocs., 1984—, Asheville (N.C.) Eye Care Assocs., 1985—2005. Clinician Walter Reed Army Med. Ctr., 1980, West Roxbury VA Med. Ctr., 1981, NEWENCO Pediatric/Geriatric Sply. Clinic, 1981; nominee Buncombe County Bd. of Health. Contbr. health articles to newsletters; singer New Day Singers, 2000-02. Mem. Henderson County Bd. Health, 1983—85; instr. phys. edn. Evangel. Chapel Christian Acad., Asheville, 1985—86; v.p. Asheville Choral Soc., 2007—; mem., soloist Bent Creek Bapt. Ch. Choir; leader Bent Creek Bapt. Ch. Care Group, 1987—91; choir mem., soloist, cantor St. Eugene's Roman Cath. Ch., 1992—; mem. St. Eugene's Pastoral Coun., 1995—98, chair, 1997—98; bd. dirs. Asheville Choral Soc., 2002—07; actor Asheville Cmty. Theatre, 1988—; mem., soloist Asheville Choral Soc. and New Day Singers, 2000—; soloist Midday Musicals, 2002—05. Mem. Am. Optometric Assn., So. Coun. Optometrists, N.C. State Optometric Soc., Mtn. Dist. Optometric Soc., Am. Pub. Health Assn., Lions (past pres.), KC (grand knight 2000-02), Elks, Beta Sigma Kappa, Delta Tau Delta. Republican. Avocations: photography, gardening, theater, coin collecting/numismatics. Office: Weaverville Eye Assocs PO Box 1620 Weaverville NC 28787-1620 E-mail: eyecheckup@aol.com.

HAUSDORFER, GARY LEE, management consultant; b. Indpls., Mar. 26, 1946; s. Walter Edward and Virginia Lee (Bender) Hausdorfer; children: Lisa Ann Turner, Janet Lee Fortner. AA, Glendale Coll., 1966; BS, Calif. State U.-L.A., 1968. Rsch. officer Security Pacific Bank, LA, 1968-73; v.p., mgr. W. Ross Campbell Co., Irvine, Calif., 1973-81; sr. v.p. Weyerhaeuser Mortgage Co., Irvine, 1982-87; exec. v.p., ptnr. L.J. Melody & Co. of Calif., 1987-89; pres. Hausdorfer Co., 1989—, The Diamond Group, 1994—; chmn., CEO Cofiroute USA, 2003—. Councilman, City of San Juan Capistrano, 1978-94, mayor, 1980-81, 84-85, 88-90; chmn. Capistrano Valley Water Dist., 1980-81, San Juan Capistrano Redevel. Agy., 1983-84, 85-86, South Orange County Leadership Conf.; bd. dirs. Orange County Trans. Corridor Agy., Orange County Transit Dist.; chmn. Orange County Transp. Authority. Recipient cert. of commendation Orange County Bd. Suprs., 1981, congl. commendation, 1985, Theodore Roosevelt Conservation award Pres. Bush, 1990. Republican. Personal E-mail: ghausdorfer@cofiroutusa.com.

HAUSELT, DENISE ANN, lawyer; BS, Cornell U., 1979, JD, 1983. Bar: N.Y. 1984, Ill. 1984, U.S. Dist. Ct. (we. dist.) N.Y. 1984, U.S. Bankruptcy Ct. 1984. Summer assoc. Wildman, Harrold, Allen & Dixon, Chgo., 1982; assoc. Nixon Peabody LLP, Rochester, N.Y., 1983-86; asst. counsel Corning (N.Y.) Inc., 1986-93, divsn. counsel, 1993-99, asst. gen. counsel, 1999-2000, asst. gen. counsel, asst. sec., 2000—01, corp. sec., 2001—. Adv. coun. Cornell Law Sch.; sec. Corning Inc. Found., Corning Mus. of Glass. Recipient Am. Jurisprudence Constl. Law prize, Cornell U., 1981. Mem.: ABA, Soc. Corp. Secs. and Governance Profls., Cornell Law Assn., Assn. Corp. Counsel. Republican. Avocations: sailing, skiing. Office: Corning Inc Riverfront Plz Mp Hq E2 Corning NY 14831-0001

HAUSER, BERNICE WORMAN, director; m. A. Daniel Hauser; children: Mitchell Alan, Lisa Ann. BA cum laude, Hunter Coll., 1953, MS, 1956; MS in Adminstrn. and Supervision, CUNY, 1978. Tchr. Yonkers Pub. Schs., NYC, 1953-54, N.Y. Pub. Schs., NYC, 1954-60; primary sci. tchr., cons. Pub./Parochial/Ind. Schs., NYC, 1960-72; tchr., primary sci. chair Walden Sch., NYC, 1972-80, coord. student tchrs., 1980-88, curriculum cons., prin. sci. chair, 1988-91; asst. to headministress Horace Mann Sch., NYC, 1991-93, dir. inter-campus acitivities, 1993—. Cons. Scholastic Publs., N.Y.C., 1980—; bd. dirs. CUNY Pub.-Pvt. Schs. Partnership Coun. Author: How to Help Your Child at Home with Science, 1991, The Cat in the Hat Comes Back, 1997, You're the Apple of My Eye, 1998, (adoption issues) Am. Baby, 1984; primary corres. articles Tchr. Clearinghouse for Sci., 1987—; editor: Horace Mann Bull., 1993—; contbr. articles to Ind. Sch., Bull. of Sci. Tech & Soc., Parents League Bull., others. Mem. parks coun. Ctrl. Park Conservancy, 1970—; mem. Citizens Com. For Better N.Y., N.Y.C., 1980—; cons., spkr. and writer Adoptive Parents Com., N.Y.C., 1975—; trustee, v.p., nominating chair Louis Wise Svcs. for Children, N.Y.C., 1976—. Recipient Impact II award Exxon, 1987, Jeremy Rifkin award NASTS, 1991; honoree United Jewish Appeal for Disting. Vol. Svc. to Louise Wise Svcs., 1998; named to Hunter Coll. Hall Fame, 2003. Fellow Phi Delta Kappa; mem. AAUW, ASCD, NSTA (presenter 1985—), Nat. Assn. Ind. Schs., Nat. Assn. Sci. Tech. and Soc., Assn. Tchr. Ind. Schs. (program chairperson), N.Y. Assn. Ind. Schs. (liaison), Hunter Coll.H.S. Alumni Assn. (past pres. 1982-1988), Phi Beta Kappa, Epsilon Pi Tau, Cum Laude Soc. Avocations: gardening, theater, opera, reading, writing. Office: Horace Mann Sch 231 W 246th St Bronx NY 10471-3430 Office Phone: 718-432-3831. Business E-Mail: Bernice_Hauser@horacemann.org.

HAUSER, CHRISTOPHER GEORGE, lawyer; b. Syracuse, NY, May 15, 1954; s. W. Dieter and Nancy (Keating) H. BA, Washington & Jefferson Coll., 1976; JD, Dickinson Sch. Law, 1979. Bar: Pa. 1979, U.S. Dist. Ct. (we. dist.) Pa. 1981, N.Y. 1987, U.S. Supreme Ct. 1992. Legal asst. Pa. Dept. of Justice, Harrisburg, 1978-79; assoc. McDowell, McDowell, Wick & Daly, Bradford, 1979-83; ptnr. McDowell, Wick, Daly, Gallup, & Hauser, and predecessor firm McDowell, McDowell, Wick & Daly, Bradford, 1983—; broker, owner Re/Max Alpine Sales, Ellicottville, N.Y., 1991-93. Pres./owner Alpine Sales and Rental Mgmt., Inc., Ellicottville, N.Y., 1987-94. Chmn. campaign Bradford Area United Way, 1984, v.p., 1987—89, pres., 1990—92; chmn. Downtown Bradford Revitalization Corp., 1986—, Bradford Parking Authority, 1986—94, 1999—; pres. Allegheny Highlands coun. Boy Scouts Am., Falconer, NY, 1986—88; dir. Bradford Econ. Devel. Corp., 1987—, Exch. Club, 1989—91; sec., treas. Bradford Redevel. Authority, 1992—96, chmn., 1992—96, 1996—; active Bradford Area Citizens Adv. Com., 1992; dir. N.W. divsn. Pa. Economy League, 1997—2002; dir., sec. Bradford Area Alliance, 1997—98, solicitor, 1998—; bd. dirs. Rt. 219 Assn., 1996—98; v.p. Continental One, 1998—, pres., 2000—; magistrate dist. judge McKean County, Pa., 2000—06; dir. Bradford Regional Med. Ctr., 2000—. Recipient Outstanding Svc. award Bradford Area United Way, 1985, Silver Beaver award Alleghany Highlands coun. Boy Scouts Am., 1990, Founder's award Order Arrow Boy Scouts Am., 1991, Cmty. Svc. award City of Bradford Office Econ. and Cmty. Devel., 1995; named Bus. Person of Yr. Bradford C. of C., 1986, One of Outstanding Young Men Am. U.S. Jaycees, 1983. Mem. N.Y. Bar Assn., Pa. Bar Assn., McKean County Bar Assn. (v.p. 1992-93, pres. 1994-96), Bradford Area Jaycees (pres. 1983-85), Pennhills Club (sec. 1985-90, 99-2000, pres. 1990-92, 2000—02, chmn. exec. com. 2002—), Bradford Club. Republican. Episcopalian. Home: 110 Congress St Bradford PA 16701-2228 Office Phone: 814-362-5519. E-mail: cghauser@atlanticbb.net, mwdlaw@atlanticbb.net.

HAUSER, DAVID L., energy executive; b. 1951; m. Nancy Hauser; 3 children. BA in Bus. Adminstrn., Furman U., SC; MBA, U. NC, Charlotte; grad. in Exec. Prog. of Profl. Mgmt. Edn., U. NC, Chapel Hill. CPA; cert. purchasing mgr. With Duke Energy, 1973—, various acctg. positions including contr., v.p. procurement svcs. and materials, sr. v.p. global asset devel., 1997—98, sr. v.p., treas., 1998—2003, acting CFO, 2003—04, group v.p., 2004—06, CFO, 2004—, group exec., 2006—. Bd. dirs. Fairpoint Comm., Enpro Industries. Trustee NC Blumenthal Performing Arts Ctr.; mem. bus. adv. coun. U. NC, Charlotte. Mem.: AICPA, NC Assn. CPA. Office: Duke Energy 526 S Church St Charlotte NC 28202-1904 Office Phone: 704-594-6200.*

HAUSER, GEORGE, biochemist, educator; b. Vienna, Dec. 13, 1922; came to U.S., 1939. s. Hans Joseph and Juliane Therese (Gleissner) H.; m. Louise Jean Russo, July 2, 1955. BS, Ohio State U., 1949; PhD, Harvard U., 1955. Mem. faculty Harvard Med. Sch., Boston, 1952-55, from rsch. assoc. to prof., 1955-93, prof emeritus, 1993—; from asst. biochemist to biochemist McLean Hosp., Belmont, Mass., 1957-93, sr. biochemist, 1993—; rsch. affiliate Mass. Inst. Tech., 2000—. Mem. editl. bd. Neurochem. Rsch; adv. and editl. bd. Jour. Neurochemistry, 1977-86, dep. chief editor, 1986-92; interim dir. Ralph Lowell Labs., McLean Hosp., Belmont, 1983-93; reviewer many sci. jours.; cons. NIH, NSF, MIT. Co-editor: Inositol & Phosphoinositides: metabolism & metabolic regulation. Mem., treas. Dem. Ward Com., Newton, Mass., 1976—. With U.S. Army, 1943-48. Recipient Austrian Cross Honor Sci. and Art, 2000; grantee Nat. Insts. Health, 1965-92, Nat. Sci. Found., 1980-82; fellow Japan Soc. for the Promotion of Sci., 1988. Mem. Biochem. Soc., Am. Soc. Biochemistry and Molecular Biology, Internat. Soc. Neurochemistry, Am. Soc. Neurochemistry (coun. 1983-87), Soc. Neurosci. Democrat. Jewish. Home: 47 Windermere Rd Auburndale MA 02466-2521 Office: McLean Hosp 115 Mill St Belmont MA 02478-1048 Office Phone: 617-855-2408. Business E-Mail: george_hauser@hms.harvard.edu.

HAUSER, GUSTAVE M., media specialist; b. Cleve., Sept. 3, 1929; s. Abraham and Stella H.; m. Rita Abrams, June 10, 1956; children: Glenvil A., Patricia A. AB, Western Res. U., Cleve., 1950; JD, Harvard U., Cambridge, Mass., 1953; LLM, NYU, 1957; diploma in law, U. Paris, 1958. Bar: Ohio 1953, N.Y. 1957. Instr. Harvard U. Law Sch., Cambridge, Mass., 1955-56; counsel internat. affairs Office Sec. Def., Washington, 1958-60; v.p. Gen. Telephone & Electronics Internat., NYC, 1960-71; exec. v.p. Western Union Internat., NYC, 1971-73; pres., CEO Warner Cable Corp., NYC, 1973-75, chmn., chief exec. officer, 1975-79, Warner Amex Cable Communications, Inc., NYC, 1979-83; chmn., CEO Hauser Comm., Inc., NYC, 1983—. Chmn, bd. dirs. Orion Network Sys., Inc., Washington, 1996-98. Author: A Guide to Doing Business in the European Common Market, 1960. Chmn., bd. dirs. Hauser Found., Inc., 1989—; trustee Steep Rock Land Trust, 1992—; trustee, vice-chmn. The Mus. TV and Radio, 1992—; exec. com. Harvard U., com. on univ. resources, 1997—; bd. dirs. The Cable Ctr., 1997—. Served with AUS, 1953-55. Named to, Cable Hall of Fame, 2003. Mem. Nat. Cable TV Assn. (dir. 1976-84, exec. com. 1978-84, vice chmn. 1983-84). Office: Hauser Comm 712 5th Ave New York NY 10019-4108

HAUSER, JOHN REID, electrical engineering educator; b. Advance, NC, Sept. 19, 1938; s. Reid R. and Lillian (Sheek) H.; m. Ann Covington, June 15, 1962; children: John R. Jr., James W., Daniel R. BS, N.C. State U., 1960; MS, Duke U., 1962, PhD, 1964. Mem. tech. staff Bell Telephone Labs., Winston-Salem, NC, 1960-62; rsch. engr. Rsch. Triangle Inst., Rsch. Triangle Pk., NC, 1963-66; asst. prof. N.C. State U., Raleigh, 1966-68, assoc. prof., 1968-73, Disting. prof., 1983—, prof., 1973—. Dir. Solid State Electronics Lab., N.C. State U., 1984—. Author: Fundamentals of Silicon Internal Devel. Tech., vol. II, 1968; contbr. over 150 articles to profl. jours. Recipient R.J. Reynolds Indsl. award for excellence N.C. State U., 1982, Univ. Rsch. award, Semiconductor Ind. Assn., 2002. Fellow IEEE (Outstanding Engr. in N.C. award, 1978); mem. Am. Phys. Soc., Am. Soc. for Engring. Edn. Home: 233 Baines Ct Cary NC 27511

HAUSER, JOHN RICHARD, marketing and management science educator; b. Scranton, Pa., Apr. 19, 1949; s. Jesse Ransberry and Muriel Florence (Myers) H.; m. Marija Danüte Eiva Hauser, June 9, 1979; children: Marius John, Aleksas Jonas, Rolandas Aras. SB in Elec. Engring., MIT, 1973, SM in Elec. Engring. and Civil Engring., 1973, ScD in Ops. Rsch., 1975. Asst. prof. mktg. and transp. Northwestern U., Evanston, Ill., 1975-80; assoc. prof. mgmt. sci. MIT, Cambridge, Mass., 1980-84, prof. mgmt. sci., 1984-89, Kirin prof. mktg., 1989—, head mgmt. sci., 1988—2003, co-dir. Internat. Ctr. Rsch. on Mgmt. of Tech., 1993-2000, rsch. dir. Ctr. for Innovation in Product Devel., 1997-2000; Marvin Bower fellow Harvard U., Cambridge, Mass., 1987-88; prin. Applied Mktg. Sci., Waltham, Mass., 1989—. Vis. lectr. European Inst. Bus. Adminstrn., Fontainbleau, France, 1985; trustee Mktg. Sci. Inst., Cambridge, Mass., 2003—; spkr., lectr. in field; expert witness in field; cons. in field. Author: Applying Marketing Management: Four Simulations, 1986, (with others) Essentials of New Product Management, 1986, Design and Marketing of New Products, 2nd edit., 1993, Enterprise: An Integrating Management Exercise, 1989; editor-in-chief Mktg. Sci., 1989-94; contbr. articles to profl. jours. NSF fellow, 1971-74; grantee in field; recipient Parlin award, 2001. Fellow Inst. Ops. Rsch. and Mgmt. Sci.; mem. Am. Mktg. Assn. (1st Pl. Thesis Supervision award 1981, Paul D. Converse award 1996, MSI award 1996, Parlin award 2001), European Mktg. Acad., Inst. Mgmt. Sci. (1st Pl. Best Paper award 1982, 83, 93, 2003), Product Devel. and Mgmt. Assn., Tau Beta Pi, Eta Kappa Nu, Sigma Xi. Episcopalian. Avocations: sailing, skiing, basketball. Office: MIT E56-314 38 Memorial Dr Cambridge MA 02142-1347 Business E-Mail: jhauser@mit.edu.

HAUSER, JOYCE ROBERTA, marketing professional; b. NYC; d. Abraham and Helen (Lesser) Frankel; divorced; children: Mitchell, Mark, Ellen BA, SUNY, 1976; PhD, Union Inst. and U., 1987. Editor Art in Flowers, 1956-58; pres. Joyce Advt., 1958-65; ptnr. Hauser & Assocs., Pub. Rels., 1966-75; dir. broadcasting Bildersee Pub. Rels., 1973-75; pres. Hauser & Assocs., Inc., Pub. Rels., 1975-78; COO, pres. Hauser-Roberts, Inc., Pub. Rels./Mktg., NYC, 1978—85; pres. Mktg. Concepts & Communications Inc., NYC, 1985-92; moderator show Perceptions Sta. WEVD, 1975-77, Speaking of Health Sta. WNBC, 1977-89, 97 Health Line, Sta. WYNY, 1980-83, Conversations with Joyce Hauser, Sta. WNBC, 1975-86, What's on Your Mind, Sta. WYNY, 1983-84, Talk-Net, 1983-90; entertainment critic Sta. NBC, 1986-92. Instr. Baruch Coll., CCNY, 1980—85; assoc. prof. NYU, 1987—, prof. edn., 1992—. Sr. editor Art & Leisure News Svc., 1988—; editor-in-chief N.Y. State Comms. Annual, 1999—; contbg. editor Alive, 1976-77; author: Good Divorces, Bad Divorces: A Case for Divorce Mediation, 1995; contbr. 70 articles to profl. jours., chpts. to books. Mem. Citywide Health Adv. Coun. on Sch. Health, 1970-88, treas., 1980-92; mem. adv. bd. degree programs NYU Sch. Continuing Edn.; mediator/arbitrator Victim Svcs. Agy., 1986-87, Inst. Mediation and Conflict Resolution, 1985-86. Named one of 10 Top Successful Women, Cancer Soc., 1976, Tchr. of Yr., Zeta Beta Tau, 1989-90, one of 20 Top Women in Pub. Rels., 1981, Prof. of Yr. Sch. of Edn., 1999, Prof. of Yr., NYU Sch. Edn., 1999-2000; recipient Professionalism award Sta. WNBC, 1980; John E. Wilson fellow, 1996-97. Mem. AFTRA, Pub. Rels. Soc. Am., Nat. Assn. Communicators, Nat. Assn. Scholars, NY State Communicators (treas., v.p. 1996, pres. 1997), NY State Comms. Assn. (editor annual 1998), Acad. Family Mediators, Soc. Am. Travel Writers, Soc. Profl. Dispute Resolutions, Drama Desk (bd. dirs. 2004), Outer Critics Cir., NY Press Club. Office Phone: 212-772-1625.

HAUSER, MARC D., psychology professor, educator; b. Boston, Oct. 25, 1959; m. Lilan Basse; children: Alexandra, Sofia. BS, Bucknell Univ., Lewisburg, Pa., 1981; PhD, Univ. Calif., LA, 1987. Hon. lectr., dept. zoology Makerere Univ., Kampala, Uganda, 1987—89; postdoctoral fellow, evolution and human behavior prog. Univ. Mich., 1987—88; postdoctoral fellow Rockefeller Univ Field Rsch. Ctr., 1988—89; postdoctoral fellow, dept. zoology Univ. Calif., Davis, 1989—92, lectr., rsch. assoc., dept. psychology & zoology, 1991—92; asst. prof., dept. anthropology, psychology & prog. in neuroscience Harvard Univ., 1992—94, assoc. prof., dept. anthropology, psychology and prog. in neuroscience, 1995—98, mem. interdisciplinary faculty, Mind, Brain & Behavior prog., 1996—, prof., dept. psychology & prog. in neuroscience, 1998—, adj. prof., grad. sch. edn., 2001—, co-dir., Mind, Brain & Behavior prog., 2003—, faculty assoc., prog. for evolutionary dynamics, 2003—, faculty mem., dept. organismic and evolutionary biology, 2005—, faculty mem., dept. biol. anthropology, 2005—; mem. interdisciplinary faculty for the Speech & Hearing Sciences prog. Mass. Gen. Hosp.-Harvard-MIT, 1995—. Fellow Ctr. for Ethics; dir. Cognitive Evolution Lab.; mem. scientific bd. Fyssen Found., Paris, 1998—2003. Cons. editor American Journal of Primatology, 1989—2000, cons. Bradford Books/MIT Press, 1995—2001, series editor Aldine deGruyter Press, Evolutionary Foundations of Human Behavior, 1996—2003, mem. editl. bd. Animal Cognition, 1997—, Cognition, 1997—2001, Trends in Cognitive Science, 1998—, Evolutionary Psychology, 2001—, Review of General Psychology, 2002—, Language Learning & Development, 2003—, Social Neuroscience, 2005, reviewer for several peer-reviewed jours.; author: The Evolution of Communication, 1996, Wild Minds: What Animals Really Think, 2000, Moral Minds: How Nature Designed our Universal Sense of Right and Wrong, 2006; co-author: The Design of Animal Communication, 1999, From Monkey Brain to Human Brain, 2005, People, Property & Pets, 2005; contbr. over 200 articles to profl. jours. Recipient Tchg. Innovation award, Harvard U., 1992, 1997, Professorship Chair for Distinction in Tchg. and Rsch., Harvard Coll., 2002, Young Investigator award, NSF, 1993, Sci. medal, Coll. France, Paris, 2006; Guggenheim fellowship, 2005. Mem.: Animal Behavior Soc., Acoustical Soc. Am. (mem. animal bioacoustics technical com. 1991—), Internat. Behavioral Ecology Soc., Am. Primatological Soc., Internat. Soc. for Infant Studies, Cognitive Neuroscience Soc., Neuroethology Soc. Avocations: running, skiing, snowboarding, squash, gourmet cooking. Office: Harvard Univ Dept Psychology 33 Kirkland St Cambridge MA 02138 Office Phone: 617-496-7077. Business E-Mail: mdh@wjh.harvard.edu.*

HAUSER, MICHAEL GEORGE, astrophysicist; b. Chgo., Dec. 3, 1939; s. Julius and Sylvia Ann (Gross) Hauser; m. Miriam Freedman, Sept. 11, 1960 (div. May 1977); children: Karen Celia(dec.) , Gerald Paul; m. Deanna Grove, May 8, 1981; stepchildren: Lisa Dawn Greening, Amy Lynne Canby, Elizabeth Ann Grove. B.Engring. Physics with distinction, Cornell U., 1962; PhD in Physics (NSF fellow), Calif. Inst. Tech., 1967. Instr. Princeton U., 1967-70, asst. prof. physics, 1970-72; sr. rsch. fellow in physics Calif. Inst. Tech., 1972-74; head infrared astronomy group lab. for high energy astrophysics Goddard Space Flight Center, Greenbelt, Md., 1974-77, head sect. infrared astrophysics Lab. for Extraterrestrial Physics, 1977-85, head infrared astrophysics br. Lab. Extraterrestrial Physics, 1985-87, head infrared astrophysics br. Lab. Astronomy and Solar Physics, 1987, chief Lab. Astronomy and Solar Physics, 1988-95; dep. dir. Space Telescope Sci. Inst., Balt., 1995—. Mem. joint sci. working group Infrared Astron. Satellite, 1977-84; prin. investigator Diffuse Infrared Background Experiment, Cosmic Background Explorer, 1977-97; mem. NASA Space Sci. Adv. Com., 1994-97; adj. prof. dept. physics and astronomy Johns Hopkins U., 1997—. Vice pres. PTA, Kensington (Md.) Jr. High, 1977-78, mem. exec. bd., 1978-79. Recipient Exceptional Sci. Achievement medal, NASA, 1984, 1991, John C. Lindsay award, Goddard Space Flight Ctr., 1986, Award of Merit, 1995, Meritorious Exec. award, Exec. Svc., 1994, AURA Sci. award, Assn. Univs. for Rsch. in Astronomy, 1998, Cosmology prize, Gruber Found., 2006; Hon. Woodrow Wilson fellow, 1962. Fellow Am. Phys. Soc., AAAS; mem. Am. Astron. Soc., Internat. Astron. Union (v.p. commn. 21, 1991-94), Sigma Xi Achievements include rsch. in elem. particle physics, astronomy, and cosmology. Office: Space Telescope Sci Inst 3700 San Martin Dr Baltimore MD 21218-2464 Office Phone: 410-338-4730. E-mail: hauser@stsci.edu.

HAUSER, RAY LOUIS, engineer, researcher, entrepreneur; b. Litchfield, Ill., Apr. 16, 1927; s. A. Vernon and Grace (Gregg) H.; m. Consuelo Wright Minnich, Sept. 2, 1951; children: Beth, Cynthia, Dewi, Chris. BS, U. Ill., 1950; M in Engring., Yale U., 1952; PhD, U. Colo., 1957. Registered profl. engr., Colo., safety engr., Calif. Sr. project engr. Conn. Hard Rubber Co., New Haven, 1950-52; rsch. staff U. Colo., Boulder, 1954-57; material tech. staff Martin Co., Denver, 1957-61; owner, mgr. Hauser Labs., Boulder, 1961-89; materials/process cons., expert witness Ray Hauser Expertise, Boulder, 2000—. Bd. dirs. Surface Solutions Inc.; vis. lectr. U. Colo., Boulder, 1957-63. Pres. Boulder Civic Opera, 1971-72. Sgt. U.S. Army, 1952-54. Recipient U. Colo. medal, 1995, Gold medal Colo. Engring. Coun., 1999. Fellow AAAS, Soc. Plastics Engrs. (bd. dirs. 1959-62, 2004—); mem. AIChE, Assn. Cons. Chemists and Chem. Engrs. (bd. dirs. 1986), Am. Assn. Lab. Accreditation (bd. dirs. 1986-91), Rotary (bd. dirs. 1975-77). Home and Office: 5758 Rustic Knolls Dr Boulder CO 80301-3029 Business E-Mail: ray@rayhauser.com.

HAUSER, RICHARD ALAN, lawyer, foundation administrator; b. Litchfield, Ill., Feb. 26, 1943; s. Melvin Henry and Helen Maxine (Roberts) H.; m. Carol E. Clampett, Jan. 2, 1965 (div. 1974); children: Jennifer Macey, Sarah Hampton; m. Karen Rolow Allen, July 26, 1977; children: Kristin Anne, Erica Christine, Alissa Marie. BS, U. Pa., 1965; JD cum laude, U. Miami, 1968. Bar: Fla. 1968, D.C. 1972, Va. 1978. Law clk. U.S. Dist. Ct. (so. dist.) Fla., Miami, 1968-70; asst. U.S. atty. U.S. Dept. Justice, Miami, 1970-71, atty. adviser Dept. Atty. Gen.'s Office Washington, 1971-73, asst. dir. Office of Policy Planning, 1974-75; assoc. counsel The White House, Washington, 1973-74, dep. counsel to pres., 1981-86; pvt. practice Washington, 1975-81; ptnr. Baker & Hostetler, Washington, 1986—2001; gen. counsel US Dept. HUD, Washington, 2001—04; pres. Nat. Legal Ctr. for Pub. Interest, Washington, 2004—. Chmn. Pennsylvania Ave. Devel. Corp., 1988-96; mem. Internat. Ctr. Settlement of Investment Disputes, 1986-94; chmn. bd. dirs. The Luther Inst., Washington; bd. dirs. Thrivent Fin. Luths.; v.p., asst. gen. counsel Washington and internat. ops. Boeing Co. Bd. dirs. Washington Hosp. Ctr., 2000—. Recipient Spl. Asst. U.S. Atty. award for Superior Performance, Dept. Justice Mem. Fla. Bar Assn., D.C. Bar Assn., Va. Bar Assn., Chevy Chase Club, Met. Club (bd. govs.). Office: Nat Legal Ctr Pub Interest Ste 800 1776 K St NW Washington DC 20006 also: Boeing Co 1200 Wilson Blvd MC RS 00 Arlington VA 22209

HAUSER, RITA ELEANORE ABRAMS, lawyer; b. NYC, July 12, 1934; d. Nathan and Frieda (Litt) Abrams; m. Gustave M. Hauser, June 10, 1956; children: Glenvil Aubrey, Ana Patricia. AB magna cum laude, CUNY Hunter Coll., 1954; D in Polit. Economy with highest honors, U. Strasbourg, France, 1955; Licence en Droit, U. Paris, 1958; student, Harvard U., 1955-56; LLB with honors, NYU, 1959; LLD (hon.), Seton Hall U., 1969, Finch Coll., 1969, U. Miami, Fla., 1971, Colgate U., 1995. Bar: D.C. 1959, N.Y. 1961, U.S. Supreme Ct. 1967. Atty. U.S. Dept. Justice, 1959-61; pvt. practice NYC, 1961-67; ptnr. Moldover, Hauser, Strauss & Volin, 1968-72; sr. ptnr. Stroock & Stroock & Lavan, NYC, 1972-92, of counsel, 1992—; pres. The Hauser Found., NYC, 1990—; apptd. mem. fgn. intelligence bd. Pres., 2001—04. Handmaker lectr., Louis Brandeis Lecture Series, U. Ky. Law Sch.; lectr. internat. law Naval War Coll. and Army War Coll.; lectr. St. Anthony's Coll., Oxford (England) U., 2002; Mitchell lectr. in law SUNY, Buffalo; USIA lectr. constl. law Egypt, India, Australia, New Zealand; U.S. chmn. Internat. Ctr. for Peace in Middle East, 1984-92; bd. dirs. Internat. Peace Acad., chair 1993—; U.S. pub. del. to Vienna follow-up meeting of Conf. on Security and Cooperation in Europe, 1986-88; mem. adv. panel in internat. law U.S. Dept. State, 1986-92, Am. Soc. Internat. Law Award to honor Women in Internat. Law; mem. Pacific Coun. on Internat. Policy, 1998-00; bd. dirs. The Rand Corp., Internat. Inst. Strategic Studies, London, The Lowy Inst. Internat. Policy, Sydney, The Ctr. Internat. Governance Innovation, Can.; chair internat. adv. bd. The Internat. Crisis Group, 2004; chair Am. Ditchley Found., 2006-. Contbr. articles to profl. jours. U.S. rep. to UN commn. on Human Rights, 1969-72; mem. U.S. del. to Gen. Assembly UN, 1969; vice chmn. U.S. Adv. Com. on Internat. and Cultural Affairs, 1973-77; mem. N.Y.C. Bd. Higher Edn., 1974-76, Stanton Panel on internat. info., edn., cultural rels. to reorganize USIA and Voice of Am., 1974-75, Mid. East Study Group Brookings Inst., 1975, 87-88, U.S. del. World Conf. Internat. Women's Yr., Mexico City, 1975; co-chair Com. for Re-election Pres., 1972, Presdl. Debates project LVW, 1976, Coalition for Regan/Bush; adv. bd. Nat. News Coun., 1977-79; bd. dirs. Bd for Internat. Broadcasting, 1977-80, Internat. Peace Acad., The Aspen Inst., The RAND Corp.; chair internat. adv. bd. Internat. Crisis Group, 2005; trustee Lincoln Ctr. Performing Arts; adv. bd. Ctr. For Law and Nat. Security, U. Va. Law Sch., 1978-84; vis. com. Ctr. Internat. Affairs Harvard U., 1975-81, John F. Kennedy Sch. Govt., Harvard U., 1992—, chair adv. bd. Hauser Ctr. for Non-Profit Orgns. at Harvard U.; co-chair dean's bd. advisors Harvard Law Sch., 1996—, vice-chair, nat. co-chair univ. fund-raising campaign, 1997-2000, vice chmn. com. on univ. resources, 2002-; bd. advisors Mid. East Inst., Harvard U.; bd. trustees NYU Law Sch.; bd. visitors Georgetown Sch. Fgn. Svc., 1989-94; chmn. adv. panel Internat. Parlimentatry Group for Human Rights in Soviet Union, 1984-86; mem. Lawyers Com. for Human Rights, 1995—; mem. spl. refugee adv. panel Dept. State, 1981; bd. fellows Claremont U. Ctr. and Grad. Sch., 1990-94; former trustee Internat. Legal Ctr., Legal Aid Soc. N.Y., Freedom House; mem. Lawyers Comm. Human Rights, 1996—. Fulbright grant U. Strasbourg, 1955; Intellectual Exch. fellow Japan Soc.; recipient Jane Addams Internat. Women's Leadership award, 1996, Women in Internat. Law award Am. Soc. Internat. Law, 1995, Fulbright award for Fulbright Alumni, 1997, Servant of Justice award, Legal Aid Soc. N.Y., 2000, Vanderbilt medal NYU Law Sch., 2004, Albert Gallatin medal, NYU, 2006. Fellow ABA (life, mem. standing coms. on law and nat. security 1979-85, standing com. on world order under law 1969-78, standing com. on jud. selection, tenure, compensation 1977-79, coun. sect. on ind. rights and responsibilities 1970-73, advisor bd. jour. 1973-78); mem. Am. Soc. Internat. Law (v.p. 1988—, mem. exec. com. 1971-76), Am. Fgn. Law Assn. (bd. dirs.), Am. Arbitration Assn. (past bd. dirs.), Ams. Soc. (bd. dirs. 1988—), Coun. Fgn. Rels. (bd. dirs.), Internat. Inst. for Strategic Studies (London, bd. dirs. 1994—), Internat. Adv. Bd., Jaffee Ctr. for Strategic Studies, Tel Aviv Univ. (1999—), Am. Coun. on Germany, The Atlantic Coun. U.S., Friends of the Hauge Acad. Internat. Law (bd. dirs.), Assn. of Bar of City of N.Y., Catalyst (bd. dirs. 1989-96). Republican. Office: Stroock & Stroock & Lavan 180 Maiden Ln Fl 17 New York NY 10038-4937 also: The Hauser Found Office of Pres 712 5th Ave New York NY 10019-4108

HAUSER, WILLIAM BARRY, historian, educator; b. Washington, May 2, 1939; s. Philip Morris and Zelda Barnett (Abrams) H.; children: Benjamin Lester, Aaron Davidson, Zachary Barnett. SB in Math., U. Chgo., 1960; MA in East Asian Studies, Yale U., 1962, PhD in History, 1969. Lectr., asst. prof. U. Mich., Ann Arbor, 1967-69, 70-74; asst. prof. history U. Rochester, NY, 1974-77, assoc. prof. history NY, 1977-83, prof. history NY, 1983—, chmn. dept. history NY, 1979-85. Author: Economic Institutional Change in Tokugawa Japan, 1974, (with Jeffrey P. Mass) The Bakufu in Japanese History, 1985; contbr. articles and revs. to profl. publs. Fellow Fulbright-Hays fellow, U.S. Dept. State, Osaka, Japan, 1964—66, NEH fellow, 1972—73, 1982—83, Mellen Faculty fellow, U. Rochester, 1977, Japan Found. fellow, 1976, 1982. Mem. Assn. for Asian Studies (chmn. adv. com. Bibliography of Asian Studies 1984-96). Avocations: cooking, gardening. Home: 425 Westminster Rd Rochester NY 14607-3231 Office: U Rochester Dept History Rochester NY 14627-0070 Home Phone: 585-442-0952; Office Phone: 585-275-9359. Business E-Mail: wbha@mail.rochester.edu.

HAUSERMAN, JACQUITA KNIGHT, management consultant; b. Donalsonville, Ga., Apr. 23, 1942; d. Lendon Bernard and Ressie Mae (Robinson) Knight; m. Mark Kenny Hauserman, July 8, 1978 (div. Mar. 1998). BS in Math., U. Montevallo, Ala., 1964; MA in Tchg. Math., Emory U., 1973; MBA in Fin., Ga. State U., 1978. Fin. analyst Cleve. Electric Illuminating Co., 1982-83, gen. supr. employment svc., 1983-85, sr. corp. planning advisor, 1985-86, dir. customer svc., 1986-88, v.p. adminstrn., 1988-90; v.p. customer svc. & cmty. affairs Centerior Energy Corp., Independence, Ohio, 1990-93, v.p. customer support, 1993-95, v.p. bus. svcs., 1995-97; v.p., chief devel. officer Summa Health Sys., Akron, Ohio, 1999-2000; prin. Arcadia Consulting, Pepper Pike, Ohio, 2000—. Home and Office: 2901 Greenflower Ct Bonita Springs FL 34134-4387 E-mail: jhauserman@johnrwood.com.

HAUSFELD, MICHAEL D., lawyer; b. Bklyn., 1946; AB cum laude, Bklyn. Coll., 1966; JD with honors, George Washington U., 1969. Bar: Washington, DC 1969. Sr. ptnr. Cohen, Milstein, Hausfeld & Toll, P.L.L.C., Washington. Mem., bd. editors George Washington Law Rev., 1969—69; adj. prof. Georgetown U. Law Ctr., 1980—87, mem. adv. bd., Inst. Law and Econs., 1980—; adj. prof. George Washington U. Law Sch., 1996—98, bd. dirs., 1998—. Named one of 75 Best Lawyers in Washington, Washingtonian survey mag., Top 100 Influential Lawyers in Am., Nat. Law Jour., 2000, 2006; recipient Humanitarian of Yr. award, B'Nai Brith, 2002, Simon Wiesenthal Ctr. award for Disting. Svc., Human Spirit award, U.S. Dept. Energy. Mem.: Order of the Coif. Office: Cohen Milstein Hausfeld & Toll PLLC Ste 500 W 1100 New York Ave NW Washington DC 20005-3964*

HAUSLER, RUDOLF HEINRICH, research chemist; b. Zurich, Switzerland, Apr. 9, 1934; came to U.S., 1963; s. Robert Ruppert and Elsa (Figi) H.; m. Joyce Ann Partridge, Sept. 19, 1998; 1 child, Natasha Louise. diploma chem. engring., Swiss Fed. Inst. Tech., Zurich, 1958, D.Tech.Scis., 1961. Research chemist, project leader Battelle Meml. Inst., Geneva, 1961-63; research chemist, research assoc. Universal Oil Products Co., Des Plaines, Ill., 1963-76; tech. dir. Gordon Lab., Inc., Great Bend, Kans., 1976-79; sr. research chemist corp. research and devel. Petolite Corp., St. Louis, 1979-81, prin. investigator, 1981-86, research fellow, 1986-91; sr. engring. advisor Mobil R&D Corp., Dallas, 1991-96; co-owner, v.p. tech. BJB Co., Post, Tex., 1996—; pres. Corro-Consulta; cons. in field of corrosion in nuc. energy generation, in oil and gas prodn.; investor in oil and gas prodn.; horse farmer, 2001; lectr. in field. Registered profl. engr., Calif. Author, co-author 3 books. Mem. Electrochem. Soc. (chmn. Chgo. sect. 1967-68, councilor 1972—), Nat. Assn. Corrosion Engrs. (chmn. Chgo. sect. 1974-75, Outstanding Achievement award 1990, fellow 2003), Chgo. Tech. Socs. Council (chmn. 1974-75), Am. Chem. Soc., Am. Soc. Metals. Unitarian-Universalist. Author, patentee in field. Office: 8081 Diane Dr Kaufman TX 75142-4607 Office Phone: 972-962-8287.

HAUSLER, WILLIAM JOHN, JR., microbiologist, educator, public health service officer; b. Kansas City, Kans., Aug. 31, 1926; s. William John and Clifton (McCambridge) H.; m. Mary Lois Rice, Apr. 19, 1949 (dec. 1999); children: Cheryl Kaye Johnson, Kenneth Randall, Eric Rice, Mark Clifton. AB in Microbiology, U. Kans., 1951, MA in Microbiology, 1953, PhD in Microbiology and Math., 1958. Diplomate Am. Bd. Med. Microbiology (chmn. 1979-82, Profl. Recognition award 1995). Asst. instr. U. Kans., Lawrence, 1951-56, rsch. asst., 1956-58; assoc. bacteriologist Iowa State Hygienic Lab., Iowa City, 1958-59, asst. dir., prin. bacteriologist, 1959-65, dir., 1965-95; dir. emeritus, 1995—; asst. prof. U. Iowa Coll. Medicine, Iowa City, 1959-66, assoc. prof., 1966-90, prof., 1990—95, emeritus prof., 1995—; assoc. prof. U. Iowa Coll. Dentistry, 1966-90, prof., 1990—95, emeritus prof., 1995—. Cons. to Iran WHO, 1969, U.S. EPA, 1970-72, CDC, 1965—, People's Republic China WHO, 1990, WHO Western Pacific Region, 1991, UNDP India, 1992; cons. to industry; mem. mil. infectious diseases rsch. program Am. Inst. Biol. Scis., 2002. Editor: Standard Methods for the Examination of Dairy Products, 1972, Manual Clinical Microbiology, 3d edit., 1980, 5th edit., 1991, Compendium of Methods for the Microbiological Examination of Foods, 1980, 2d edit., 1984, Diagnostic Procedures for Bacterial Mycotic and Parasitic Infections, 1981, Laboratory Diagnosis of Infections Diseases: Principles and Practice, 1988; co-editor: Topley & Wilson's Microbiology and Microbial Infections, 9th edit., 1997; mem. editl. bd. various profl. jours.; contbr. articles to profl. jours. Councilman City Govt., University Heights, Iowa, 1966-69; commr. Iowa Air Pollution Control Commn., 1967-74; mem. exec. com. Iowa Dept. Environ. Quality, 1974-80, Nat. Com. for Clin. Lab. Standards, bd. dirs., 1987-93. Lt. comdr. USNR, 1944-67. Recipient Henry Albert Meml. award Iowa Pub. Health Assn., 1974. Fellow APHA, Am. Acad. Microbiology (chmn. 1983-89, Profl. Recognition award 1995); mem. Am. Soc. Microbiology, Assn. State and Territorial Pub. Health Lab. Dirs. (pres. 1984-85, Lifetime Achievement award 1998), Sigma Phi Epsilon, Rotary (Paul Harris fellow). Avocations: photography, woodworking, wilderness backpacking. Home: 11 The Woods NE Iowa City IA 52240-7986 Office: U Iowa Hygienic Lab Oakdale Hall Iowa City IA 52242 Office Phone: 319-335-4500. Personal E-mail: iahausler@yahoo.com.

HAUSMAN, ARTHUR HERBERT, electronics company executive; b. Chgo., Nov. 24, 1923; s. Samuel Louis and Sarah (Elin) H.; m. Helen Mandelowitz, May 19, 1946; children: Susan Lois, Kenneth Louis, Catherine Ellen. BSEE, U. Tex., 1944; MS, Harvard U., 1948. Electronics engr. Engring. Rsch. Assocs., St. Paul, 1946-47; supervisory electronics scientist U.S. Dept. Def., Washington, 1948-60; now advisor, v.p., dir. rsch. Ampex Corp., Redwood City, Calif., 1960-63, v.p. ops., 1963-65, group v.p., 1965-67, exec. v.p., 1967-71, exec. v.p., pres., CEO, 1971-83, chmn. bd., 1981-87, chmn. bd. emeritus, 1987—. Chmn. tech. adv. com. computer peripherals Dept. Commerce, 1973-75; mem. Pres.'s Export Coun.; chmn. Subcom. on Export Adminstrn., 1984-88; bd. dirs. Lasercard Inc., Vista Advanced Tech. Group Inc., Calamp, Inc. Trustee United Bay Area Crusade.; mem. vis. com. dept. math. MIT; bd. dirs. Bay Area Coun. Served with USNR, 1944-54. Recipient Meritorious Civilian Svc. award Dept. Def. Mem. IEEE, Army Ordnance Assn. (dir. chpt. 1969-71), Am. Electronics Assn. (dir.), Cosmos Club.

HAUSMAN, C. MICHAEL, lawyer; b. Chgo., Oct. 4, 1940; s. Charles Martin and Evelyn (Partridge) H.; children: Laura, Sarah, Craig, Karen, Richard, Ronald, Charles, Ashley, Courtney Megan. BS, Marquette U., 1962, JD, 1967. Bar: Wis. 1967, U.S. Dist. Ct. (ea. dist.) Wis. 1967, U.S. Supreme Ct. 1972. Ptnr. Frisch, Dudek & Slattery, Ltd., Milw., 1967-88; mcpl. judge City of Delafield, Wis., 1983—; ptnr. Slattery & Hausman, Ltd., Waukesha, Wis., 1988—2001, C. Michael Hausman and Assocs. Ltd., Delafield, Wis., 2001—. Lectr. State Bar of Wis. Family Law Seminars, Am. Acad. Matrimonial Lawyers; bd. dirs. Collaborative Family Law Coun. Wis., Inc., 2001—. Named Outstanding Young Man Brookfield (Wis.) Jaycees, 1975. Fellow: Am. Acad. Matrimonial Lawyers (pres. Wis. chpt. 1988—89), Internat. Acad. Matrimonial Lawyers; mem.: ATLA, Brookfield C.of C. (pres. 1977—78), Milw. Jr. Bar Assn. (bd. dirs. 1969—71), State Bar Wis., Wis. Acad. Trial Lawyers, Am. Arbitration Assn., Brookfield Rotary (pres. 1980—81). Avocations: fishing, hiking, stamp and coin collecting. Home and Office: 329 GeneseeSt Delafield WI 53018

HAUSMAN, HARRIET SECELEY, administrator; b. Chgo., Apr. 8, 1924; d. Samuel and Lena Rubin; m. Martin C. Hausman, June 30, 1946 (dec. Apr. 1988); children: Daniel, Barbara. Student, U. Ill., 1941—42, Northwestern U., 1943—45; BS, Rosary Coll., 1972. Asst. tchr. Winfield (Ill.) Sch., 1945; psych testing Hines Vet. Hosp., Maywood, Ill., 1972-74; social worker Cook County Hosp., Chgo., 1973; pres. Power Parts Co., Chgo., 1947-87, CEO, 1987-92. Author: Reflections, A History of River Forest, 1975. Trustee River Forest (Ill.) Twp., 1978-90; bd. dirs. ACLU, 1988—, v.p.; bd. dirs. Jewish Childrens Bur., pres. 1970-92, v.p., 1992—; v.p., bd. dirs. Bldg. Better Futures (BBF), 1992-96, v.p. BBF Scholarship Bd., 1997-; vice chmn. scholarship com., 1998-; adv. bd. Bus. and Profl. People for Pub. Interest, 1999—; plannig commn. Oak Pk. Temple, 2001—. Named Woman Entrepreneur of Yr., 1992, U.S. Transp. Cmty. Svc. award Oak Park and River Forest, 1980, 96, 90, 92, 96, 99, Carl Winter Svc. award, 1972, Lifetime Achievement award, 2005. Democrat. Jewish. Achievements include one of 4 who est. River Forest Cmty. Ctr. Avocations: symphony, opera, drama, gardening, travel.

HAUSMAN, HOWARD, electronics executive; b. NYC, July 4, 1945; s. Edward A. and Bella H.; children: Lawrence Stuart, Bradley Russel. BSEE, Poly. Inst. N.Y., 1967, MSEE, 1971. Computer programmer Harry Kahn Assocs., Great Neck, N.Y., 1965-67; engr. Airborne Instruments Lab., Deer Park, N.Y., 1967-72; dept. head Miteq Inc., Hauppauge, N.Y., 1972-81; pres. Syncom Industries Inc., Bohemia, N.Y., 1981—; chief scientist Microphase Systems Inc., Hauppauge, N.Y., 1992—; v.p. engring. Miteq Inc., Hauppage, 1996—; pres. Syncom Industries, Bohemia, 1999—. Mem. tech. cons. com., v.p. local adv. counsel 1st supervisory dist. Bd. Coop. Ednl. Services, Suffolk County, N.Y., 1986—; cons. Arista Devices, Inc., Ronkonkoma, N.Y., 1974-81; prof. Hofstra U., Hempstead, N.Y., 1996; adj. prof. Polytech. U., Farmingdale, N.Y., 1978—. Contbr. articles to profl. jours. Mem. IEEE (sr.), AIAA (sr.), AAAS, Nat. Contracts Mgmt. Assn., N.Y. Acad. Scis., Am. Inst. Aeronautics and Astronautics (sr.). Office: MITEQ Inc 100 Davids Dr Hauppauge NY 11788-4 Home: 25 Maple Run Dr Jericho NY 11753-2828 Business E-Mail: hhausman@miteq.com. E-mail: h.hausman@ieee.org. *As we acquire more knowledge we realize how little we know. It is a very humbling experience that tends to limit our creativity. It is important that we realize the subliminal negative feedback effects inherent in our learning experience and consciously focus our energies on piercing the envelope of the psychologically comfortable known universe.*

HAUSMAN, KEITH LYNN, health facility administrator, physical therapist; b. Cleve., Nov. 20, 1949; s. Harold Herbert and Betty (Reed) H.; 1 child, Sierra Dawn. BS, Loma Linda U., 1972, MA in Pub. Health, 1975. Lic. real estate broker; cert. instrument multiengine flight instr., air transport pilot. Acting adminstr. Thomas Rehab. Hosp., Asheville, NC, 1976-77; pres. Marion County Hosp., Jefferson, Tex., 1977-81, Jellico (Tenn.) Cmty. Hosp., 1981-91; health care cons., 1991—; pres. Premier Rehab., Inc., 1994—, Premier Vending, Inc., 2000—, Premier Vending Wholesale, Inc., 2002—, Med. Sales & Supplies of Tenn., Inc., 2006—. Bd. dirs. Pvt. Indsl. Coun. SDA4, Tenn., 1989-2000, Ardmore Adventist Hosp., 1977-81, Meml. Hosp., Manchester, Ky., 1981-91, Takoma Adventist Hosp., Greenville, Tenn., 1981-91. Fellow Am. Coll. Health Care Execs.; mem. Tenn. Hosp. Assn. (bd. dirs. 1991, pres. Mid-East dist. 1991), Campbell County C. of C. (bd. dirs. 1989-92). Republican. Seventh-Day Adventist. Home: PO Box 541 Jellico TN 37762-0541 Office Phone: 423-784-4704. E-mail: flyboy@2geton.net.

HAUSMAN, STEVEN JACK, health science association administrator; b. Phila., May 20, 1945; s. Leo and Bella Hausman. BA, U. Pa., 1967, MS, 1968, PhD, 1972. Postdoctoral fellow Inst. for Cancer Rsch., Phila., 1972-75; staff fellow Nat. Inst. on Aging, Balt., 1975-77; spl. asst. to assoc. dir. Nat. Inst. Arthritis, Metabolism and Digestive Diseases, Bethesda, Md., 1977-78, dir. ctrs. program, 1978-86; dep. dir. extramural program Nat. Inst. Arthritis and Musculoskeletal and Skin Diseases, Bethesda, 1986-90, dep. dir., 1990—2007, dir. extramural program, 1997—2002; pres. HausmanTech Consulting, 2007—. Mem. AAAS, Am. Assn. Immunologists, Soc. In Vitro Biology, Am. Chem. Soc., Am. Soc. for Cell Biology. Office: NIAMS-NIH 31 Center Dr Msc2350 Bldg 31 Bethesda MD 20892-0001 Office Phone: 301-402-1691.

HAUSMAN, WILLIAM RAY, fund raising and management consultant; b. Bradford, Pa., Apr. 22, 1941; s. Raymond Harvey and Eleanor Janet (Freeman) H.; m. Rosalyn Schmidt, Aug. 16, 1963; children: Valerie Noelle, Stephanie Carol. AB, Wheaton Coll., 1963; MA, Trinity Evang. Div. Sch., 1966, DD (hon.), 1981; postgrad., North Park Theol. Sem., 1968—69; EdM, Harvard U., 1977. Ordained to ministry Evang. Covenant Ch., 1971. Min. Christian edn. Glen Ellyn (Ill.) Covenant Ch., 1966-69; from registrar, dir. admissions to assoc. dean Trinity Evang. Div. Sch., Deerfield, Ill., 1969-80; pres. North Park Coll. and Theol. Sem., Chgo., 1980-86; from cons. to group mgr. Donald A. Campbell & Co., Inc., Chgo., 1986-94, v.p. ea. regional mgr., 1994—, sr. v.p., 1995—. Dir. Rockport Chamber Music Festival. Mem. Assn. Fundraising Profls., Lehigh County Hist. Soc., Coun. Advancement and Support Edn., New Eng. Hist. Geneal. Soc. Office: Campbell & Co Ea Regional Office 85 Eastern Ave Ste G104 Gloucester MA 01930-1869 Home Phone: 978-546-0135; Office Phone: 978-281-1235. E-mail: wrh@campbellcompany.com.

HAUSMANN, CHARLES STEWART, retired funeral director; b. Orange, NJ, Oct. 18, 1922; s. Charles Franklin Hausmann and Christina Becker; m. Lillian Helen D'Addario, Aug. 6, 1944; children: Charles S., Steven C., Christine Redy. AB with highest honors, Upsala Coll., East Orange, NJ, 1945, BS in Edn., 1946; MA in Sch. Adminstrn., Montclair State U., NJ, 1952; grad., NY Coll. Mortuary Sci.; LHD, Cin. Coll. Mortuary Sci., 1985; postgrad., Rutgers U. Cert. funeral svc. practioner, lic. comml. pilot. Tchr. Irvington Pub. Schs., NJ; funeral dir. Charles Hausmann and Son, Irvington, 1954—72; exec. dir. NJ. State Funeral Dirs. Assn., Manasquan, NJ, 1975—85; ret. Dir., v.p. Supreme Savings and Loan Assn., Irvington, 1969—77; founding dir. Investor Savings Bank, Millburn, NJ, 1977—85. Editor: (monthly mag.) The Forum. Pres. Irvington Bd. Edn., 1958—65; mem. bd. estimate Essex County Coll., Newark, 1969—70, Essex County Vocational Schs., NJ, 1969—71; mem. Brielle Environ. Commn., 1980—81; chmn. Brielle Planning Bd., NJ, 1981—90; adv. bd. mem. Mercer County Coll., 1985—2000; freeholder Essex County

NJ, Newark, 1966—72, freeholder, dir., 1968—69; del. Rep. Nat. Convention, 1968, 1972; councilman Borough Brielle, 1995—98; pres. Borough Brielle Coun., 1998; chmn. Essex County Hosp. Ctr., Cedar Grove, NJ, 1969—71, Essex County Geriatrics Ctr., Belleville, NJ, 1969—71. With USAF, 1942—45. Decorated Air Force Wings medal USAF; recipient Christian Churchman of Yr., Coun. Chs., 1961, Citizen Yr., Irvington Jewish War Vets., 1964, Disting. Layman award, Essex County Edn. Assn., 1964, Citizen citation, Irvington B'nai B'rith, 1965, Svc. Youth award, Newark, 1968, Alumnus of Yr. award, Irvington H.S., 1970. Mem.: Irvington C. of C. (former dir.), Vail Dean Sch. (former trustee), Irvington Hist. Soc., Irvington Cmty. Welfare Coun., United Fund (past cmty. chmn.), Am. Legion (past comdr.), Lions Club (past pres.).

HAUSMANN, RICARDO, economics professor, director; BSc, Cornell U., MA, 1980, PhD in Econs., 1981. Prof. econs. Instituto de Estudios Superiores de Administracion, Caracas, 1985—91, founder Ctr. for Pub. Policy; min. of planning Govt. of Venezuela, 1992—93; chief economist Inter-Am. Devel. Bank, 1994—2000, founder Rsch. Dept.; prof. practice of econ. develop John F. Kennedy Sch. Govt., Harvard U., Cambridge, Mass., 2000—, dir. Ctr. for Internat. Devel., 2005—. Mem. Bd. of Ctrl. Bank of Venezuela, 1992—93; chair IMF-World Bank Devel. Com., 1993. Co-author: Government Spending and Income Distribution in Latin America, 1993, Volatile Capital Flows: Consequences for Latin American Economic Reform, 1996, Banking Crises in Latin America, 1997, Wanted: World Financial Stability, 2000; editor: Democracy, Decentralisation and Deficits in Latin America, 1998, Other People's Money: Debt Denomination and Financial Instability in Emerging Market Economies, 2005; contbr. articles to profl. jours. Fellow Oxford U., 1988—91. Office: John F Kennedy Sch Govt Rubenstein-414 79 John F Kennedy St Cambridge MA 02138 Office Phone: 617-496-3740. Office Fax: 617-496-8753. E-mail: ricardo_hausmann@harvard.edu.

HAUSNER, JOHN HERMAN, retired judge; b. Detroit, Oct. 31, 1932; s. John E. and Anna (Mudrak) Hausner; m. Alice R. Kieltyka, Aug. 22, 1959. PhB cum laude, U. Detroit, 1954, MA, 1957, JD summa cum laude, 1966. Bar: Mich. 1967, US Ct. Appeals (6th cir.) 1968, US Supreme Ct. 1971, US Tax Ct. 1976, US Ct. Claims 1976, US Ct. Mil. Appeals 1976. Tchr. Detroit Pub. Schs., 1954, 56-59; tchg. fellow U. Cin., 1959-61; instr. U. Detroit, 1961-74; pvt. practice Detroit, 1967-69; asst. US atty., 1969-73; chief asst. US atty. Ea. Dist. Mich., 1973-76; judge 3rd Jud. Cir. Mich., Wayne County, 1976-94; ret., 1994. Lectr. law sch.; faculty adviser Nat. Jud. Coll., 1978—79. Author: Sebastian, The Essence of My Soul, 1982, 2007; contbr. articles to profl. jours. With US Army, 1954—56. Mem.: State Bar Mich., Fed. Bar Assn. (mem. exec. bd. Detroit chpt. 1976—82), Mich. Ret. Judges Assn., Blue Key, Alpha Sigma Mu. Republican. Home: 22433 Louise St Saint Clair Shores MI 48081-2034 also: 8420 E Desert Palm Tucson AZ 85730-4723

HAUSRATH, DAVID L., lawyer; m. Debra Hausrath; 3 children. BSEE, Va. Tech., 1974; JD, U. Richmond, 1979. Law clk. Va. Supreme Ct.; project engr. DuPont, 1974—76; from lawyer to sr. v.p. Ashland, Inc., Covington, Ky., 1980—2004, gen. counsel, 1999—2004, sec., 2004—06, sr. v.p., gen. counsel, 2004—. Bd. adv. Salmon P. Chase Coll. Law, No. Ky. U.; mem. coun. chief legal officers The Conf. Bd. Mem.: ABA, Va. Bar Assn., Ky. Bar Assn., Am. Soc. Corp. Secs., Am. Corp. Counsel Assn. Office: Ashland Inc 50 E RiverCenter Blvd Covington KY 41012-0391 Home Phone: 859-441-9711. Business E-Mail: dlhausrath@ashland.com.

HAUSSLER, DAVID H., molecular biologist, educator; BA in Math., Conn. Coll., New London, 1975; MS in Applied Math., Calif. Poly. State U., San Luis Obispo, 1979; PhD in Computer Sci., U. Colo., Boulder, 1982. Asst. prof. math. computer sci. U. Denver, 1982—86; asst. prof. computer sci. U. Calif., Santa Cruz, 1986—89, assoc. prof., 1989—93, prof., 1993—2004, prof. biomolecular engring., 2004—. Investigator Howard Hughes Med. Inst., 2000—; presdl. chair computer sci. U. Calif., 2000—03; dir. Ctr. Biomolecular Sci. and Engring. Contbr. articles to sci. jours.; internat. lectr.; assoc. editor: Machine Learning, 1988—97, Jour. Computational Biology, 1996—, Pub. Libr. Sci. Computational Genomics, 2005—, mem. editl. bd.: Jour. Artificial Intelligence Rsch., 1993—95, Jour. Neurocomputing, 1995—2002, Neural Computing Surveys, 1996—2002, Drug Discovey Today, 2001—. Recipient Disting. Scientist of Yr. award, Boston Biomedical/Clinical Ligand Assay Soc., 2003, Tech. award, San Jose Tech. Mus. Innovation, 2003, Dickson prize, Carnegie Mellon U., 2006. Fellow: World Tech. Network (World Tech. Network award (IT Software) 2005), Am. Acad. Arts and Scis., AAAS, Am. Assn. Artificial Intelligence (Allen Newell award (also from Assn. Computing Machinery) 2004, Classic Paper award 2005), Calif. Acad. Scis.; mem.: NAS. Achievements include selection as Scientist of Yr., Rsch. and Devel. Mag., 2001; selection as Featured Scientist, Incyte Genomics, 2001. Office: 501A Engring 2 Bldg U Calif 1156 High St MS: CBSE/ITI Santa Cruz CA 95064

HAUTMAN, PETE (PETER MURRAY), writer; b. Berkeley, Calif., 1952; V.p. mktg. Crowd Caps Inc., Minneapolis, 1981—88; owner Hautman Mktg. Svcs., 1988—91; writer, 1991—. Author: Drawing Dead, 1993 (selected NY Times Book Review Notable Books), Short Money, 1995, Mortal Nuts, 1996 (selected NY Times Book Review Notable Books), Mr. Was, 1996 (nominated Edgar Allan Poe Award, 1997), Ring Game, 1997, Stone Cold, 1998, Mrs. Million, 1999, Rag Man, 2001, Hole in the Sky, 2001 (Wis. Libr. Assn. Award, 2002), Doohickey, 2002, Sweetblood, 2003 (Best Young Adult Book of Yr., Mich. Libr. Assn., 2004), Godless, 2004 (Nat. Book Award for Young People's Lit., 2004). E-mail: pete@petehautman.com.

HAUVER, CONSTANCE LONGSHORE, lawyer; b. Abington, Pa., Oct. 9, 1938; d. Malcolm Rettew and Margaret Evans (Lyon) L.; m. Arthur R. Hauver, 1962 (div. Mar. 1979); 1 child, Sian; m. Giles Toll, 1990. BA with high honors, Swarthmore Coll., 1960; MA, UCLA, 1962; JD magna cum laude, U. Denver, 1967. Bar: Colo. 1968, U.S. Dist. Ct. Colo. 1968, U.S. Tax Ct. 1970. Libr. Friends Com. on Nat. Legis., Washington, 1960-61; lectr. U. Hawaii, Honolulu, 1963-64; assoc. Sherman & Howard, Denver, 1968-73, ptnr., 1973-91; vol. naturalist Lookout Mountain Nature Ctr., 1998—. Mem. grievance com. Colo. Supreme Ct., 1981—86. Co-contbr. legal articles. Trustee Rocky Mountain Women's Inst., Denver, 1987-90, Swedish Med. Ctr. Found., Denver, 1978-85; bd. dirs. Women's Forum Colo. Inc., Denver, 1988-89, Girls Count, Denver, 1995-2000, pres., 1996-97. Named New Vol. Naturalist of Yr., Lookout Mountain Nature Ctr., 1998, Vol. Naturalist of Yr., 2001; recipient Athena award, Alliance Profl. Women, 1987. Fellow Am. Coll. Probate Counsel; mem. Colo. Bar Assn. (chair probate and trust law sect. 1982-83), Denver Bar Assn. (del. to ABA Ho. of Dels. 1986-88), Rocky Mountain Estate Planning Coun. (pres. 1980-81). Democrat. Mem. Soc. Of Friends. Avocations: mountain climbing, kayaking, skiing, reading, learning Spanish.

HAVEL, RICHARD JOSEPH, physician, educator; b. Seattle, Feb. 20, 1925; s. Joseph and Anna (Fritz) Havel; m. Virginia Johnson, June 25, 1947; children: Christopher, Timothy, Peter, Julianne. BA, Reed Coll., 1946; MS, MD, U. Oreg., 1949. Intern Cornell U. Med. Coll., NYC, 1949—50, resident in medicine, 1950—53; clin. assoc. Nat. Heart Inst., NIH, 1953—54, rsch. assoc., 1954—56; faculty Sch. Medicine, U. Calif., San Francisco, 1956—, prof. medicine, 1964—; assoc. dir. Cardiovasc. Rsch. Inst., 1961—73, dir., 1973—92. Chief metabolism sect., dept. medicine Sch. Medicine, U. Calif., San Francisco, 1967—97; dir. Arteriosclerosis Specialized Ctr. Rsch., 1971—96; mem. bd. sci. counselors Nat. Heart, Lung and Blood Inst., 1976—80; chmn. food and nutrition bd. NRC, 1987—90; pres. Lipid Rsch., Inc., 1999—. Editor: Jour. Lipid Rsch., 1972—75; assoc. editor: Am. Jour. Clin. Nutrition, 1997—2007, mem. editl. bd.: Jour. Biol. Chemistry, 1981—85, Jour. Arteriosclerosis, 1980—; contbr. chapters to books, articles to profl. jours. Established investigator Am. Heart Assn., 1956—61, chmn. coun. on arteriosclerosis, 1977—79. With USPHS, 1951—53. Recipient Disting. Achievement award, Am. Heart Assn., 1993, Bristol-Myers award for nutrition rsch., 1989, Gold medal, Charles U., Prague, Czech Republic, 1996. Fellow: AAAS (Theobald Smith award 1960), Am. Inst. Nutrition; mem.: NAS, Western Soc. Clin. Investigation (Mayo Soley award 1997), Am. Soc. for Clin. Investigation, Assn. Am. Physicians, Am. Soc. Clin. Nutrition (McCollum award 1993), Am. Acad. Arts and Scis., Inst. Medicine of NAS, Alpha Omega Alpha, Phi Beta Kappa. Office: U Calif San Francisco Cardiovascular Rsch In San Francisco CA 94143-0130 Home Phone: 415-461-8583. Business E-Mail: richard.havel@ucsf.edu.

HAVEL, RICHARD W., lawyer; b. Fairmont, Minn., Sept. 20, 1946; s. Thomas Earl and Elizabeth (Shiltz) H.; m. Arlene Havel, July 6, 1968; children: Stephanie, Derek. BA, Notre Dame U., 1968; JD, UCLA, 1971. Bar: Calif., U.S. Dist. Ct. (no., ea., cen. and so. dists.) Calif., U.S. Ct. Appeals (9th cir.). Atty. Shutan & Trost, LA, 1971—80, Sidley Austin LLP, LA, 1980—. Adj. prof. law Loyola Law Sch., 1975-80; bd. govs. Fin. Lawyers Conf., 1991-94, 95-98, officer, 1998-01; spkr., panelist Bankruptcy Litigation Inst., 1989-95, ALI-ABA, 1989, 90, 91; chmn. L.A. City Indsl. Devel. Authority, 1993-98, bd. dirs., 1998-00. Contbr. articles to profl. jours. Trustee Jonsson/UCLA Cancer Ctr., 1998—; bd. dirs. Dollars for Scholars, So. Calif. region, 1999-05. Fellow Am. Coll. Bankruptcy, 1997; mem. ABA, Calif. Bar Assn., L.A. County Bar Assn. (comml. law and bankruptcy sect. bankruptcy subcom. 1986-89, exec. com. 1987-90, lawyer assistance com. 1985-90), UCLA Law Alumni Assn. (trustee 1996—2001). Office: Sidley Austin LLP 555 W 5th St 40th Fl Los Angeles CA 90013-1010 Office Phone: 213-896-6017. Business E-Mail: RHavel@Sidley.com.

HAVEMANN, JOEL, editor; b. NYC, 1943; BA in Math., Harvard U., 1965. Gen. assignment reporter Portland Oregonian, 1965-67; edn. reporter Chicago Sun-Times, 1967-73; budget reporter National Journal, 1973-78, dep. ed., 1978-83; econ. reporter L.A. Times, 1983-84, projects editor, 1984-90, Brussels bur. chief, 1990-93, DC projects editor, news editor, 1993—. Author: (book) Congress and the Budget, 1978.

HAVENS, ARNOLD I., lawyer; b. 1947; m. Debra Hardy; 3 children. BA in History, U. Ill., 1969, JD, 1973. Assoc. counsel, Office Legis. Affairs. US Ho. Reps., 1973—79, assoc. minority counsel subcommittee on Commerce, Transp. & Tourism, 1981—83, assoc. minority counsel & staff dir., Energy & Commerce Com., 1983—86; asst. to chmn. Railroad Retirement Bd., Chgo., 1979—81; spl. asst. for legis. affairs The White House, Washington, 1991—93; sr. v.p. Pagonis and Donnelly Group, Washington, 1993—94; pres. Havens Group, Inc., 1994—95; v.p., Washington counsel CSX Corp., Washington, 1995—97, v.p. fed. affairs, 1997—2001, sr. v.p. govt. affairs, 2001—03; gen. counsel US Dept. Treasury, Washington, 2003—06, acting dep. sec., 2005. Pres. Bus.-Govt. Rels. Coun.; bd. dirs. Bryce Harlow Found.

HAVENS, CHARLES WILLIAM, III, retired lawyer; b. Balt., Mar. 22, 1936; m. Lucille Bowman; children— Charles W. IV, Jessica Madaline AB, Franklin and Marshall Coll., Lancaster, Pa., 1958; LL.B., U. Va., Charlottesville, 1961. Bar: DC 1961, Va. 1961, US Supreme Ct. Assoc. Covington & Burling, Washington, 1961-66; spl. asst. to gen. counsel Dept. Def., Washington, 1966-67, spl. asst. to asst. sec. def., 1967-70; gen. counsel then pres. Reins. Assn. Am., Washington, 1970-81; ptnr. LeBoeuf, Lamb, Leiby & MacRae, Washington, 1981—2000; ret., 2000. Contbr. articles to profl. jours. Mem. AIDA Reins. and Ins. Arbitration Soc. (founding, bd. dirs.), St. John's Island Club, Metropolitan Club (Washington). Avocation: golf. Home: # 396 1000 Beach Rd Vero Beach FL 32963 Home (Summer): 4045 Mansion Dr NW Washington DC 20007 Personal E-mail: cwhavensIII@aol.com.

HAVENS, HARRY STEWART, retired federal official, management consultant; b. Little Rock, Dec. 18, 1935; s. Ralph Murray and Catherine Clara (Clark) H.; m. Frances Jones, June 12, 1960. BA in Econs. magna cum laude, Duke U., 1957; BA in Philosophy, Politics, Econs., Oxford U., England, 1959, MA, 1963. Economist U.S. Budget Bur., Washington, 1964-66, budget examiner, 1966-70, chief housing br., 1970-72; chief income maintenance br. U.S. Office Mgmt. and Budget, Washington, 1972-74, dep. dir. human resources divsn., 1972—74; dir. program analysis divsn. U.S. GAO, Washington, 1974-80, asst. comptroller gen., 1980-93; pvt. practice cons. Washington, 1993—. Cons. Orgn. Econ. Coop. & Devel., Paris, 1993—, U.S. GAO, 1993-96, Supreme Soviet of Russian Fedn., 1992-93, State Duma of Russian Fedn., 1994. Contbr. articles to profl. jours.; contbr. book chpts. Rhodes scholar, 1957. Home and Office: 4515 Neptune Dr Alexandria VA 22309-3129 Personal E-mail: havensh@aol.com.

HAVENS, JASON EDWARD, lawyer; s. Edward A. and Mary Jane Havens; m. Daphne K. McDermit, June 1, 1996. BA magna cum laude, Lipscomb U., 1996; JD, U. Tenn., 1999; LLM in Estate Planning, U. Miami, 2000; LLM in Internat. Taxation, Regent U., 2003. Bar: Fla. 2000, Tenn. 2006. Summer assoc. Henderson, Franklin, Ft. Myers, Fla., 1998—99, assoc. atty., 2000—01; shareholder atty. Hall & Runnels, P.A., Destin, Fla., 2002—03; pvt. practice Havens & Miller, PLLC, Destin, 2003—, Niceville, Fla., 2004—. Legal adv. bd. Capital Trust Co., Wilmington, Del., 2004—06; bd. dirs. Estate Plan Coun. Emerald Coast, Destin, pres., 2004—06; spkr., presenter in field. Contbr. articles to profl. jours. Chmn. Planned Giving com. Sacred Heart Hosp. Found., Destin, 2003—05; bd. dirs. The Able Trust, 2004—, Boys and Girls Club, Ft. Walton Beach, Fla., 2002—04. Fellow: ABA (editor Probate & Property mag., Best Article award 2004); mem.: Tenn. Bar Assn., Fla. Bar Assn., Christian Legal Soc. (v.p. gift, estate and trust sect. 2004—). Republican. Presbyterian. Office: Havens & Miller PLLC 4400 East Hwy 20 Ste 211 Niceville FL 32578 also: Ste 101 1223 Airport Rd Destin FL 32541 Office Phone: 850-897-6733. Business E-Mail: jasonhavens@abanet.org.

HAVENS, LESTON LAYCOCK, psychiatrist, educator; b. Bklyn., July 31, 1924; s. Valentine Britton and Nellie Falk (Laycock) H.; m. Susan Elizabeth Miller, May 19, 1973; 1 child, Emily E.; children by previous marriage: Christopher W., Jeffry B. (dec.), Jennifer F., Sarah B. BA, Williams Coll., 1947; MD, Cornell U., 1952; MA (hon.), Harvard U., 1987; LHD, Mass. Sch. Profl. Psychology, 1993. Intern N.Y. Hosp., 1952-53, asst. resident internal medicine, 1953-54; resident, chief of svc. Mass. Mental Health Ctr., Boston Psychopathic Hosp., 1954-58, staff visit and asst. clin. dir., 1958-62, prin. investigator studies in visual word perception, 1960-66, program dir. psychiat. rehab. internship program, 1962-68, program dir. med. student teaching, 1964-81; asst. prof. psychiatry Harvard Med. Sch., Boston, 1963-64, assoc. clin. prof. psychiatry, 1965-71, psychoanalyst, 1967—, prof. psychiatry, 1971—. Cargnegie vis. prof. humanities MIT, 1968; H. B. Williams traveling prof. Australian and New Zealand Coll. of Psychiatrists, 1975; chief psychiat. cons. Mass. Rehab. Commn., 1959-65; mental health adminstr. Region VI, Mass. Dept. Mental Health, 1968-69; dir. residency tng. Cambridge Hosp., 1987-96, co-dir. edn., 1996—. Author: Approaches to the Mind, 1973, Participant Observation, 1977, Making Contact, 1986, A Safe Place: Laying the Groundwork of Psychotherapy, 1989, Coming to Life, 1993, Learning To Be Human, 1994, The Real Life Guide to Psychotherapy Practice, 2000; contbr. articles to profl. jours. Served to 2d lt. AUS, 1944-46. Recipient H.C. Solomon award, 1977, Benjamin Rush award, APA, 1995; Leston Havens award for excellence in tchg., Cambridge Hosp., 2003. Mem. Am. Psychiat. Assn., Soc. Biol. Psychiatry (A.E. Bennett award 1958), Mass. Soc. for Rsch. in Psychiatry (McCurdy prize 1962), Mass. Psychiat. Soc. (Lifetime Achievement award 2004), Phi Beta Kappa, Alpha Omega Alpha. Home: 151 Brattle St Cambridge MA 02138-2243 Office: Cambridge Hosp 1493 Cambridge St Cambridge MA 02139-1099

HAVENS, MURRAY CLARK, political scientist, educator; b. Council Grove, Kans., Aug. 21, 1932; s. Ralph Murray and Catherine Clara (Clark) H.; m. Agnes Marie Scharpf, July 5, 1958 (dec. 1969); children: Colin Scott, Theresa Agnes; m. Carolyn Trost, May 5, 1997. BA, U. Ala., 1953; MA, Johns Hopkins U., 1954, PhD, 1958. Postdoctoral fellow Brookings Instn., Washington, 1958-59; asst. prof. polit. sci. Duke U., 1959-61; from asst. prof. to prof. U. Tex., Austin, 1961-73; vis. lectr. U. Sydney (Australia), 1966; prof. polit. sci. Tex. Tech U., Lubbock, 1973-98, chmn. dept., 1975-83, prof. emeritus, 1999—. Author: City Versus Farm?, 1957, The Challenges to Democracy, 1965, The Politics of Assassination, 1970, Assassination and Terrorism, 1975, Texas Politics Today, 1995; book rev. editor Jour. Politics, 1971-83; contbr. numerous articles to profl. jours. With AUS, 1954—56. Mem.: AAUP, Am. Polit. Sci. Assn., So. Polit. Sci. Assn., Southwestern Polit. Sci. Assn. (pres. 1983—84), Phi Beta Kappa. Home: 804 Deer Foot Ct Nashville TN 37221

HAVENS, TIMOTHY JOHN, physicist; b. Bismark, ND, Feb. 1, 1956; s. Harold Lloyd and Luanne Virginia (Cowan) H.; m. Janine Louise Ley, June 19, 1981; children: Garrett Wade, Stanley McKay, Luke Timothy. BS, Eckerd Coll., 1980; PhD, Coll. of William and Mary, 1985. Asst. prof. physics Francis Marion U., Florence, SC, 1985-90; summer rsch. fellow Med. U. S.C., Charleston, 1986; functional sys. mgr. GE Med. Systems, Florence, SC, 1990—. Contbr. articles to Phys. Rev. Letters, IEEE Trans. on Mag., Jour. of Applied Sci.; patentee in field. Grantee NSF, 1990, Fed. Edn. for Scon. Security Act. Mem.: SC Acad. Sci., Am. Phys. Soc. Home: 1208 Madison Ave Florence SC 29501-4254 Office: GE Med Systems PO Box 100539 Florence SC 29501-0539 Office Phone: 843-664-1616. Personal E-mail: sc_havens@yahoo.com. Business E-Mail: timothy.havens@med.ge.com.

HAVER, JURGEN F., marketing consultant; b. Joliet, Ill., July 16, 1932; s. Elmer William and Hermina (Peters) H.; m. Judith Costello, May 19, 2001; children: Jason, Kyra, Peter, Brigit. BA, Wartburg Coll., 1956. Feature writer Daily Peoples Press, Owatonna, Minn., 1959-60; editor Lyon County Independent, Marshall, Minn., 1960-62; asst. advt. dir. Burpee Seed Co., Phila., 1962-66; advt. mgr. for Organic Gardening, Theater Crafts and Quinto Rodale Press, Emmaus, Pa., 1966-67; promotion of electronics mag. staff Kiver Pubs., Chgo., 1968-69; advt. dir. Henry Regnery Co., Chgo., 1969-70; pub. rels. dir. Hess's Dept. Stores, Allentown, Pa., 1970-76; cons. Haver Mktg., Moriarty, N.Mex., 1976—; spl. cons. Gov. N.Mex., 1995—2003; v.p. thedailychristian.com. Co-founder U. N.Mex. Inst. for Entrepreneurial Success; faculty mktg. Moravian Coll., U. Pa. Sch. Dentistry, Pa. State U. Author: Personalized Guide to Marketing Strategy, 1982, Zen Parenting, 2004; contbr. articles to profl. jours. Mem. Internat. Bus. Writers (past pres.), Am. Mktg. Assn. (past pres.). Address: PO Box 70 Moriarty NM 87035- Home Phone: 505-832-9158. E-mail: jurgenh@nmia.com.

HAVER-ALLEN, ANN, communications director; d. Vivian Faye Haver; m. William Allen, June 21, 1986; children: Jason Allen, Summer Allen. BA in Journalism, Thomas Edison State Coll., Trenton, NJ. Reporter Angleton Times, Tex., 1985—86; mng. editor Princeton Packet Group, NJ, 1986—90, Engel Pub. Ptnrs., West Trenton, NJ, 1990—92; dir. engring. comm. Princeton U., NJ, 1992—2004; dir. pub. rels. and mktg. Prescott Coll., Ariz., 2004—05; founder aha Creative Ink, 2005—; mng. editor The Rim Country Gazette, 2006—. Editor: EQuad News at Princeton U., Transitions at Prescott Coll. Commr. Red Heart Coastal Mvskoke Clan, Robertsdale, Ala., 2001—; bd. dirs. Cmtys. for Compassion and Justice, Prescott. Recipient APEX award for publ. excellence, 2002—04, Communicator award, 2002, Communicator award design/logo, 2004, Award of Merit, Internat. Assn. Bus. Communicators, 2002, 2004, Silver Quill award, Assn. Bus. Communicators, 2003, Crystal Award of Excellence, 2003, Clarion award, Assn. Women Comm., 2003—04, Magnum Opus Gold award in Best Rewrite category, Mo. Sch. Journalism and industry comm. profls., 2004, Merit award, Dalton Pen Comms., 2004. Mem.: NAFE, N.J. Press Assn. (hon. mention), Nat. Newspaper Assn. (Blue Ribbon Excellence 1988), Internat. Assn. Bus. Communicators (IRIS Award of Excellence 2002, IRIS award 2004), Women in Comm., Ednl. Press Assn. Am., Coun. for Advancement and Support of Edn. Office Phone: 928-717-2412. Personal E-mail: editoraha@yahoo.com.

HAVERTY, MICHAEL R., rail transportation executive; Pres, COO Atchison, Topeka and Santa Fe Railway Co., 1989—91; ind. exec. transp. advisor, 1991—93; chmn., CEO Haverty Corp., 1993—95; exec. v.p. Kans. City So., 1995—2000, bd. dirs., 1995—, pres., CEO Kans. City So. Railway Co. subs., 1995, bd. dirs. Kans. City So. Railway Co. subs., 1995—, chmn. bd. Kans. City So. Railway Co. subs., 1999—, pres., CEO, 2000, chmn., CEO, 2001—, chmn. bd., CEO Kans. City So. de Mex., chmn., dir. Tex.-Mex. Railway, 2005—. Dir., chmn. exec. com. Grupo Transportacion Ferroviaria Mexicana, S.A. de C.V., TFM, S.A. de C.V.; dir. Mexrail, Inc., 1995—, Panama Canal Railway Co., 1996—, co-chmn., 1999—, Panarail Tourism Co., 2000—; dir., chmn. nominating com., mem. audit rev. and human resources coms. MGP Ingredients Inc., Atchison, Kans., 1999—2004. Office: Kans City Southern PO Box 219335 Kansas City MO 64121-9335 Office Phone: 816-983-1303. Office Fax: 816-556-0297.*

HAVIGHURST, CLARK CANFIELD, law educator; b. Evanston, Ill., May 25, 1933; s. Harold Canfield and Marion Clay (Perryman) H.; m. Karen Waldron, Aug. 28, 1965; children: Craig Perryman, Marjorie Clark. BA, Princeton U., 1955; JD, Northwestern U., 1958. Bar: Ill. 1958, N.Y. 1961. Assoc. Debevoise Plimpton Lyons & Gates, NYC, 1958, 61-64; assoc. prof. law Duke U., Durham, NC, 1964-68, prof., 1968-86, William Neal Reynolds prof., 1986—2002, emeritus, 2005—; interim dean Duke U. Sch. Law, 1999. Dir. Program on Legal Issues in Health Care Duke U., 1969-88; adj. scholar Am Enterprise Inst. Pub. Policy Rsch., 1976-2005; resident cons. FTC, Washington, 1978, Epstein, Becker & Green, Washington, 1989-90; scholar in residence Inst. Medicine of NAS, Washington, 1972-73, RAND Corp., Santa Monica, 1999. Author: Deferred Compensation for Key Employees, 1964, Regulating Health Facilities Construction, 1974, Deregulating the Health Care Industry, 1982, Health Care Law and Policy, 1988, 2d edit., 1998, Health Care Choices: Private Contracts as Instruments of Health Reform, 1995; editor Law and Contemporary Problems jour., 1965-70. With U.S. Army, 1958-60. Mem. Inst. Medicine of Nat. Acad. Sci., Order of Coif Home: 1109 Fearrington Post Pittsboro NC 27312 Office: Duke U Sch Law PO Box 90360 Durham NC 27708-0360 Office Phone: 919-613-7061. Business E-Mail: hav@law.duke.edu.

HAVILAND, DAVID SANDS, retired architectural educator, researcher, administrator; b. Rome, NY, Apr. 26, 1942; s. William Erwin and Barbara Hannon (Huguenin) H.; m. Kathleen Anne Kelly, July 8, 1973; children: Kelly Sands, Wallace Sands. BS, Rensselaer Poly. Inst., 1964, BArch, 1965, MArch, 1967. Rsch. asst., instr. Rensselaer Poly. Inst., Troy, NY, 1965-67, asst. prof. architecture, 1967-70, assoc. prof., 1970-79, prof., 1979—2006, dean Sch. of Architecture, 1980-90, v.p., student life, 1994-2000, v.p. Inst. Advancement, 2000—06; ret. Vis. prof. constrn. mgmt. and engring. U. Reading, Eng., 1990-96. Editor: The Architect's Handbook fo Profl. Practice, 12th edit., 1994; contbr. articles to profl. jours. V.p. Arts Ctr. Capital Region; pres. Howard and Bush Found. Recipient James L. Haecker award for disting. rsch. leadership, 1996, medal R.P.I Trustees,

2005, Disting. Svc. award R.A.A., 2007; numerous rsch. grants. Mem. AIA (Inst. award 1989), N.Y. State Assn. Architects. Home: 63 Pinewoods Ave Troy NY 12180-4701

HAVLICEK, FRANKLIN J., communications executive; b. NYC, July 18, 1947; s. Raymond Joseph and Rosalia Maria (Zona) H.; m. Louise Sferrazza, Dec. 21, 1980. BA, Columbia U., 1968, JD, 1973, MA, 1977, MPhil, 1980; cert., Internat. Inst. Human Rights, Strasbourg, France, 1972. Bar: N.Y. 1974, U.S. Dist. Ct. (so. and ea. dists.) N.Y. 1974, U.S. Ct. Appeals (2d cir.) 1975, U.S. Supreme Ct. 1979, D.C. 1990. Atty. Battle & Fowler, NYC, 1973-78; spl. advisor to Mayor of N.Y.C., 1978-82; ptnr. Seham, Klein, Zelman, NYC, 1982-84; dir. labor rels. NBC, NYC, 1984-88; v.p. personnel, indsl. rels. and environ. svcs. Washington Post, 1988-97; pres. stratagem adv. svcs. Washington, 1997-98; with Internat. Monetary Fund, Washington, 1998—. Adj. prof. internat. & pub. affairs Columbia U., N.Y.C., 1978-88, Sch. Pub. Affairs & Sch. Internat. Svc., Am. U., Washington, 1999—. Editor: Collective Bargaining, 1979, Presidential Selection, 1982, Election Communications, 1984; contbr. numerous articles on law, govt., communications to mags., newspapers. Exec. com. N.Y. Gov.'s Task Force in Schs. and Bus., 1986-88; counsel Vietnam Vets. Meml. Commn., 1982-85, State Commn. on Dioxin, 1983-85; candidate for U.S. Senate in N.Y., 1986; mem. U.S. U.S.S.R. Emerging Leaders Summit, 1988, 90; bd. dirs. World Affairs Coun., 1991-97, Washington Performing Arts Soc., 1995-97, Internat. Peace Acad., 1989-90, World Media Colloquium UNESCO, 1989; U.S. Tech. expert ILO, 1990; cons. to UN High Commr. for Human Rights in Bosnia, 1992; study grant on media and communications European Cmty., 1994; cons. Cath. Relief Svcs., Kosovo, 1999. With U.S. Army, 1968-70. Ford Found. fellow, 1977; study grantee on media and comms. European Cmty., 1994. Mem. ABA, Assn. of Bar of City of N.Y., Am. Polit. Sci. Assn., Am. Acad. Polit. Sci., N.Y. Acad. Scis. Clubs: City N.Y. (trustee 1985-87). Roman Catholic. Avocations: tennis, running, climbing, films, architecture. Home: 6024 Western Ave Chevy Chase MD 20815-3344 Office: Internat Monetary Fund 700 19th St NW Washington DC 20431 Office Phone: 202-623-7732. Personal E-mail: fhavlicek@aol.com. Business E-Mail: fhavlicek@imf.org.

HAVLIN, JOHN LEROY, soil scientist, educator; b. Chgo., May 8, 1950; 1 child, Jonathon Cary. MS, Colo. State U., 1980, PhD, 1983. Asst. prof. U. Nebr., Scottbluff, 1983-85, Kans. State U., Manhattan, 1985-90, prof. dept. agronomy, 1990-96; prof. N.C. State U., Raleigh, 1996—. Author: Soil Fertility and Fertilizers; contbr. articles articles to profl. pubs., chapters to books. Named Rschr. of Yr., Nat. Fertilizer Solutions Assn., 1989; recipient Werner L. Nelson Rsch. award, 1991, R.E. Wagner award, 2003, Honors award, USDA, 2004; fellow Tchr. fellow, Nat. Assn. Coll. Tchrs. of Agr., 1994. Fellow: Soil Sci. Soc. Am. (pres. 2005, Edn. award 2002), Am. Soc. Agronomy; mem.: Soil and Water Conservation Soc., Phi Kappa Phi, Sigma Xi, Gamma Sigma Delta (Outstanding Tchr. award 1992). Republican. Presbyterian. Achievements include research in advancement of dryland soil and crop managment technologies to improve productivity and profitability; crop rotation and tillage effects on soil organic matter and productivity; dryland fertilizer managment and precision farming. Office: NC State U Dept Soil Sci Raleigh NC 27695-0001 Home: 2512 Wheeler Bluff Dr Raleigh NC 27606-8955 Home Phone: 919-859-6502; Office Phone: 919-513-4411. Business E-Mail: havlin@ncsu.edu.

HAWASS, ZAHI, archaeologist, educator, writer; b. Damietta, Egypt, May 28, 1947; BA in Greek and Roman Archaeology, Cairo U., 1967, diploma in Egyptology, 1979; MA in Egyptology and Syro-Palestinian Archaeology, U. Pa., Phila., 1983, PhD in Egyptology, 1987; PhD (hon.), Am. U., Cairo, 2005. Insp. antiquities Italian Expedition, Sikh Abada, Minia, 1969, Pa. Yale Expedition, Abydos, 1969, We. Delta, Alexandria, 1970, Embaba, Giza, Cairo, 1972—74, Abu Simbel, 1973—74, Pa. Expedition, Malkata, Luxor, 1974, Boston Mus. Fine Arts, Giza Pyramids, 1974—75; first insp. antiquities Giza Pyramids, Embaba, Bahria Oasis, 1974—79; chief insp. Giza Pyramids, Cairo, 1980; gen. dir. Giza Pyramids, Saqqara, Bahria Oasis, 1987—97; undersec. of State Giza Monuments, 1998—2002. Adj. prof. UCLA, 2000—. Author: Pyramids of Ancient Egypt, 1990, Secrets of the Sphinx, 1998, Valley of the Golden Mummies, 2000, Silent Images, 2000, Hidden Treasures of the Egyptian Museum, 2003, Hidden Treasures of Ancient Egypt, 2004, The Golden Age of Tutankhamun, 2004, Curse of the Pharoahs, 2004 (Blue Ribbon Nonfiction Book award), Mountains of the Pharoahs, 2006, (children's books) Tutankhamun, 2005. Named Disting. Scholar of Yr., Assn. Egyptian-Am. Scholars, 2000; named an Explorer-in-Residence, Nat. Georgraphic, 2001; named one of Five Pioneers of Egypt, Egyptological Soc. of Spain, 2002, 100 Most Influential People, Time Mag., 2006; recipient Golden Plate award, Am. Acad. Achievement, 2000, Silver Medal and membership, Rusian Acad. Natural Sci., 2001, award for contributions to Egyptian soc. and the archaelogical cmty. worldwide, Mansoura Univ., 2001; grantee Mellon Fellowship, Univ. Pa., 2000. Office: 3 El Adel Abu Bakr St Zamalek Cairo Egypt also: Supreme Coun Antiquities 42 Aden St Mohandiseen Cairo Egypt Office Phone: 7365645, 6859253. Office Fax: 6831117. E-mail: lyramiza2004@yahoo.com.

HAWAUX, ANDRÉ J., food products executive; B in Acctg., Pace U., NY; MBA, So. NH U., Manchester. CPA. V.p. fin. China bus. unit Pepsi-Cola Internat., 1995—2005; v.p. fin., CFO Pepsi-Cola N.Am., 2000—05; sr. v.p. worldwide strategy and corp. devel. PepsiAmericas, 2005—06; exec. v.p., CFO ConAgra Foods, Inc., Omaha, 2006—. Office: ConAgra Foods Inc 1 ConAgra Dr Omaha NE 68102-5001 Office Phone: 402-595-4000.*

HAWE, DAVID LEE, manufacturing consultant, venture capitalist; b. Columbus, Ohio, Feb. 19, 1938; s. William Doyle and Carolyn Mary (Hassig) H.; m. Margret J. Hoover, Apr. 15, 1962; children: Darrin Lee, Kelly Lynn. Lic. real estate broker, Calif. Project mgr. ground antenna systems W.D.L. Labs., Philco Corp., 1960-65; credit mgr. for Western U.S. Am. Hosp. Supply Corp., Burbank, Calif., 1965-74; owner, mgr. Hoover Profl. Equipment Co., Contract Health Equipment Co., Guasti, Calif., 1974-75; pres. Baslor Care Svcs.; owner convalescent homes Santa Ana, Calif., 1975-80; pres. Application Assocs., 1980-2000; CEO Xiron Inc., 1985—2004; owner Tripro Assocs.; chmn. bd. C-Squared Inc., Anaheim, Calif., 2002—. Bd. dirs., chmn. bd. dirs. Xiron, Inc.; bd. dir. Medisco Co., Casa Pacifica, Broadway Assocs., C-Squard Inc., Xiron Corp., C and C Group, Application Assocs. Inc. Bd. dirs. Santa Ana Cmty. Convalescent Hosp., 1974-79, pres. 1975-79. With USN, 1954-56. Mem. Am. Vacuum Soc. Republican. Roman Catholic. Home: 18082 Hallsworth Cir Villa Park CA 92861-4503 Office Phone: 714-999-2791. Personal E-mail: triproassoc@att.net.

HAWES, BESS LOMAX, retired folklorist; m. Baldwin Hawes; children: Corey, Naomi, Nicholas. BA, Bryn Mawr U., 1941; MA, U. Calif., 1970; PhD (hon.), Kenyon Coll., 1994, U. N.C., 1995. With music divsn. N.Y. Pub. Libr.; prof. anthropology Calif. State U., Northridge, 1963—74, Smithsonian Instn., 1974—76; dir. Folk Arts Program Nat. Endowment for Arts, 1977—92; ret., 1992. Recipient Nat. Medal of Arts, Pres. Clinton, 1993.

HAWES, CLAY ERIK, lawyer; b. Murfreesboro, Tenn., Dec. 10, 1969; s. Clayton E. Hawes and Kathleen Joan Nelson; m. Melissa Kaye Giles, May 18, 2004; 1 child, Hayden Carter. BS in Econs., U. Minn., 1992, JD, 1995. Bar: Minn. 1995, Nev. 2001, Tex. 2003. Assoc. Larkin, Hoffman, Daly & Lindgren, Mpls., 1995—2000, Morris, Pickering & Sanner, Las Vegas, 2001; sr. assoc. Fulbright & Jaworski, LLP, Mpls., 2002, Houston, 2003—05, ptnr., 2006—. Mem.: ABA, Am. Intellectual Property Law Assn., Fed. Cir. Bar Assn. Avocations: running, travel, scuba diving, skiing, Tae Kwon Do. Office: Fulbright & Jaworski LLP Ste 5100 1301 McKinney Houston TX 77010 Office Phone: 713-651-5151.

HAWES, SUE, lawyer; b. Washington, Mar. 30, 1937; d. Alexander Boyd and Elizabeth (Armstrong) H.; m. James E. Brodhead, June 21, 1963; children: William James Pusey Brodhead, Daniel Alexander Hawes Brodhead. BA, Sarah Lawrence Coll., 1959, MA, 1963; JD, Whittier Sch. Law, Calif., 1983. Bar: Calif. 1988, U.S. Dist. Ct. (ctrl. dist.) Calif. 1990. Dancer and choreographer, NYC, Washington, Latin Am., Europe, 1959-62; instr., dir. dance program dept. theatre and phys. edn. Smith Coll., Northampton, Mass., 1963-65; instr. dept. dance UCLA, 1973-75; freelance script supr. LA, 1976-80; prin. Law Office of Sue Hawes, LA, 1988-96. Articles editor Whittier Law Rev., 1982-83. Active Santa Barbara Symphony League; mem. Santa Barbara Women's Polit. Com.; Bd. dirs. Nuc. Age Peace Found., 2003—. Mem. State Bar Calif., Actors' Equity Assn. Democrat. Avocations: music, gardening, politics.

HAWES, WILLIAM KENNETH, communication educator, author; b. Grand Rapids, Mich., Mar. 6, 1931; s. William Kenneth and Cora Elizabeth (Tibble) H.; m. Ella Margaret Plant, Aug. 13, 1961 (dec. 1998); children: William III, Robert Ernest. AB, Eastern Mich. U., 1955; AM, U. Mich., 1956, PhD, 1960. Tchg. asst. U. Mich., Ann Arbor, 1956-57; instr. English and speech Eastern Mich. U., Ypsilanti, 1956-60; asst. prof., mgr. KTCU Tex. Christian U., Ft. Worth, 1960-64; vis. assoc. prof., mgr. WUNC U. N.C., Chapel Hill, 1964-65; assoc. prof., mgr. KUHF U. Houston, 1965-76, prof., 1976—. Admissions bd. Biomed. Program, Sch. Allied Health Scis., U. Tex. Health Sci. Ctr., Houston, 1974-95; prof. U. Houston program, London, 1984, 94; J. William Fulbright lectr. Nat. Chenghi U., Taipei, Taiwan, 2001; resident Rockefeller Found., Bellagio, Italy, 2003. Author: The Performer in Mass Media, 1978, American Television Drama, 1986, Television Performing, 1991, 2007, Ante La Cámara, 1993, Chinese edit., 1999, Public Television: America's First Station, 1996, 2007, Live Television Drama, 1946-1951, 2001, Filmed Television Drama, 1952-1958, 2002; contbg. author: Understanding Radio, 1967, 85, La Radio: Une Carrière, 1970, Understanding Television, 1978, Television Station Management and Operations, 1989; editor: Pornography Cinema Community Standards, 1975, 4th edit., 2006; prodr., creator TV series including Video Workshop, 1967—2006; film guest Fed. Republic of Germany, 1981. Active Houston Pub. TV, Fulbright Found.; established William Hawes Family scholarship U. Mich., 2006, U. Houston, 2007. Recipient Avery Hopwood award U. Mich., 1957, Rockwell award, 1996, Gulf Coast Film and Video award, 2004; grantee U. Houston and/or NEH, 1981, 83, 86-87, 91, 2003; Jack LeRoy Bush Meml. scholar U. Mich., 2007. Mem.: ACLU, Acad. TV Arts and Scis., Mus. of Fine Arts Houston, Am. Film Inst., Smithsonian Instn., Nat. Trust Historic Preservation. Home: Parc V-902 3600 Montrose Blvd Houston TX 77006-4658 Office: U Houston Sch of Comm Houston TX 77204-4072 Office Phone: 713-743-2863. Office Fax: 713-743-2604. Business E-Mail: whawes@uh.edu.

HAWK, A.J., professional football player; b. Centerville, Ohio, Jan. 6, 1984; s. Keith and Judy. Graduated, Ohio St. Univ., 2006. Linebacker Ohio State Univ., 2002—06, Green Bay Packers (NFL), 2006—. Recipient Defensive MVP, Tostitos Fiesta Bowl, 2003, Lombardi award, 2005. Achievements include 5th overall selection in NFL Draft by Green Bay Packers, 2006. Office: Green Bay Packers 1265 Lombardi Ave Green Bay WI 54304

HAWK, ERNEST T., federal agency administrator; BS, MD, Wayne State U., Detroit; MPH, Johns Hopkins U., 1994. From intern to resident to sr. accoc. medicine Emory U. Sch. Medicine, Atlanta, 1985—91; fellow in med. oncology U. Calif., San Francisco, 1991—93; cancer prevention fellow Nat. Cancer Inst., NIH, 1993, various positions in Chemoprevention Br., chief Gastrointestinal and Other Cancers Rsch. Group, Divsn. Cancer Prevention, 1999—2004, dir. Office of Centers, Training and Resources, 2004—. Office: Nat Cancer Inst Office Centers Training and Resources 6116 Exec Blvd Rm 7001 Rockville MD 20852 Office Phone: 301-594-2664. Office Fax: 301-435-6344. E-mail: eh51p@nih.gov.

HAWK, GEORGE WAYNE, retired electronics company executive; b. Warren, Ohio, Feb. 21, 1928; s. Oscar Wilmer and Morda Irene (Klingensmith) H.; m. Charline Hines Bond, Feb. 12, 1955; children: George Wayne, David James, John Robert. BS in Aero. Engring, Purdue U., 1951; MSME, U. So. Calif., 1955; postgrad., U. Tenn. Registered profl. engr., Ind. Asst. R & D officer gas dynamics facility Arnold Engring. Devel. Ctr., Tullahoma, Tenn., 1951-53; project engr. Hughes R & D Lab., Culver City, Calif., 1953-56; sr. rsch. engr. Goodyear Aircraft Corp., Akron, Ohio, 1956-57; with Moog Inc., East Aurora, N.Y., 1957-81, v.p. aerospace divsn., 1968-69, exec. v.p., dir., gen. mgr. controls divsn., 1969-76, exec. v.p., dir. pres. controls group, 1976-81; pres. G.W. Hawk Inc., 1981-86; pres., CEO Acme Electric Corp., 1986-91, chmn. bd. dirs., CEO, 1992-94; chmn. bd. dirs. Comptek Rsch. Inc., 1983-87, M.H.P. Machines, Inc., Buffalo, 1983-92. Chmn. bd. dirs. B.I.S. Ptnrs.; bd. dirs. Comptek Rsch., Inc., Western N.Y. Tech. Devel. Corp., past chmn. Contbr. articles profl. jours.; patentee in field. Past chair and vice chair bd. dirs. Buffalo Philharm. Orch., lifetime dir.; past pres. Greater Niagara Frontier coun. Boy Scouts Am.; past chmn. bd., pres. Greater Buffalo Devel. Found.; past trustee, treas. Buffalo Gen. Hosp. Found.; pres. Niagara Aerospace Mus.; bd. dirs. Niagara Luth. Home Found.; past bd. dirs. Fluid Power Ednl. Found.; past bd. regents emeritus Canisius Coll. With US Army, 1946—48, 1st lt. USAF, 1951—53. Inducted into Niagara Frontier Aviation Hall of Fame. Fellow AIAA (assoc.); mem. Air Force Assn. (pres. Larry D. Bell chpt. 1978), Navy League, Am. Def. Preparedness Assn., Nat. Fluid Power Assn. (past chmn. bd.), Nat. Conf. on Fluid Power (past conf. dir.) Buffalo C. of C. (past vice chmn.). Avocations: private pilot (twin engine-instrument), skiing, golf, fishing. Home: 380 Schultz Rd Elma NY 14059-9257 E-mail: hawkwabunk@msn.com.

HAWK, PHILLIP MICHAEL, service corporation executive; b. Oklahoma City, June 14, 1939; s H. M. and Rosetta (Cross) H.; m. Nancy Batton, Aug. 13, 1966; children— Tabatha Lynn, Phillip Michael BBA, U. Okla., 1961. Pub. rels. exec. Coca Cola Co., Dallas, 1961-63; salesman svc. Reynolds Metals Co., Dallas, 1963-65; corp. dir. mktg. Cole Pubs. Co., Dallas, 1965-71; sr. v.p. Club Corp. of Am., Dallas, 1972-90; pres. Interclub Corp., Blackwell, Tex., 1990-93, CEO club acquisiton and devel., 1993—2006; CEO Clubnet, Kingwood, Tex., 1996—2001. Bd. dirs. Club Corp. Mex. Exec. v.p. United Golf Group, N.Y.C., 1998-2000; v.p. Acquisitions Renaissance Golf Group, LLC, 2001-. Republican. Avocation: golf. Office: 5362 Keswick Dr Frisco TX 75034 Office Phone: 281-853-7167. E-mail: phawk281@aol.com.

HAWK, TONY, professional skateboarder; b. San Diego, May 12, 1968; s. Frank and Nancy Hawk; m. Cindy Dunbar, 1990; 1 child, Riley; m. Erin Lee, Sept. 28, 1996; children: Spencer, Keegan; m. Lhotse Merriam, Jan. 12, 2006. Profl. skateboarder, 1983—; founder Tony Hawk Found., Vista, Calif., 2002. Founder Tony Hawk's Demolition Radio, Sirus Satellite Radio. Actor: (films) Thrashin', 1986, Police Academy 4: Citizens on Patrol, 1987, Gleaming the Cube, 1989, xXx, 2002, Haggard: The Movie, 2003; (TV films) The Contest, 1989, Reunion X, 2004, (video) Destroying America, 2001, CKY 3, 2001, Dogwoton and Z-Boys, 2002, Lords of Dogtown, 2005, (guest appearances): (TV series) Arli$$, 1999; (TV series, voice) The Simpsons, 2003; (TV series) CSI: Miami, 2005; prodr.: (soundtrack for Tony Hawk's Underground) T.H.U.G. (MTV Music award, 2004); actor(guest appearances): (TV series) Extreme Home Makeover, 2005. Recipient 6 gold medals for skateboarding, ESPN X Games, 16 medals, No. 1 Vertical Skateboarder in the World, 1984—96, 4 time Favourite Male Athlete, Nickelodeon Kids Choice Awards, 3 time Male Athlete, Fox Teen Choice, Lifetime Achievement award, ESPN ESPY. Achievements include first skateboarder in history to do "The 900" skateboarding trick; Video Game Series is the top selling sports video game franchise in history. Office: Tony Hawk Found 1611-A Melrose Dr 360 Vista CA 92081 Office Phone: 760-477-2479.

HAWKE, BERNARD RAY, planetary scientist, researcher; b. Louisville, Oct. 22, 1946; s. Arvil Abner and Elizabeth Ellen (Brown) H. BS in Geology, U. Ky., 1970, MS, 1974, Brown U., 1977, PhD in Planetary Geology, 1978. Geologist U.S. Geol. Survey, 1967-68; researcher U. Ky., 1972-74, Brown U., 1974-78; planetary scientist Hawaii Inst. Geophysics, U. Hawaii, Honolulu, 1978—; dir. NASA Pacific Regional Planetary Data Ctr., 1981—; prin. investigator NASA grants. Assoc. dir. Hawaii Space Grant Coll. Author papers in field. Served with USAR, 1970-72. Decorated Bronze Star Mem. Geochem. Soc., Meteoritical Soc., Am. Geophys. Union, Am. Chem. Soc., Geol. Soc. Am., Sigma Xi, Sigma Gamma Epsilon, Alpha Tau Omega. Republican. Office: U Hawaii SOEST Hawaiian Inst Geophysics Honolulu HI 96822

HAWKE, ETHAN GREEN, actor; b. Austin, Tex., Nov. 6, 1970; m. Uma Thurman, May 1, 1998 (div.); children: Maya Ray Thurman-Hawke, Roan. Co-founder & artistic dir. Malaparte Theatre Co., NYC, 1992—. Actor: (plays) Casanova, 1991, A Joke, The Seagull, 1992, Sophistry, Henry IV, 2003—04, Hurlyburly, 2005, The Coast of Utopia, 2006; (TV series) Alias, 2003; (films) Explorers, 1985, Lion's Den, 1988, Dead Poet's Soc., 1989, Dad, 1989, White Fang, 1991, Mystery Date, 1991, A Midnight Clear, 1992, Waterland, 1992, Alive, 1993, Rich in Love, 1993, Floundering, 1994, Reality Bites, 1994, White Fang II, 1994, Quiz Show, 1994, Before Sunrise, 1995, Search & Destroy, 1995, Gattaca, 1997, Great Expectations, 1998, The Newton Boys, 1998, The Velocity of Gary, 1998, Joe the King, 1999, Snow Falling on Cedars, 1999, Tell Me, 2000, Hamlet, 2000, (voice) Waking Life, 2001, Tape, 2001, Training Day, 2001, The Jimmy Show, 2001, (dir., voice) Chelsea Walls, 2001, (& author) Before Sunset, 2004, Taking Lives, 2004, Assault on Precinct 13, 2005; dir.: Straight to One, 1994; dir., writer, actor (films) The Hottest State, 2007; author: (novels) The Hottest State, 1996, Ash Wednesday, 2002. Mailing: c/o Creative Arts Agency 9830 Wilshire Blvd Beverly Hills CA 90212*

HAWKE, JOHN DANIEL, JR., former federal official; b. NYC, June 26, 1933; s. John Daniel and Olga (Buchbinder) H.; m. Marie Reddan, June 15, 1962 (dec. Mar. 1991); children: Daniel, Caitlin, Anne, Patrick BA, Yale U., 1954; LL.B., Columbia U., 1960. Bar: D.C. 1961, U.S. Supreme Ct. 1968. Law clk. to judge U.S. Ct. Appeals (D.C. cir.), Washington, 1960-61; counsel Select Subcom. on Edn., U.S. Ho. of Reps., Washington, 1961-62; assoc. Arnold & Porter, Washington, 1962-66, ptnr., 1967—75, 1978—95, 2004—; gen. counsel bd. govs. Fed. Res. System, Washington, 1975-78; under sec. for domestic fin. US Dept. Treasury, Washington, 1995-98, comptroller of the currency, 1998—2004; dir. Fed. Deposit Ins. Corp., Washington, 1998—2004. Adj. prof. law Georgetown U., Washington, 1971-87; lectr. law Columbia U., N.Y.C., 1979; bd. advisers Morin Ctr. for Banking Law Studies, Boston U. Sch. Law, 1982—, lectr., 1984-88; mem. Shadow Fin. Regulatory Com., 1986-95, 2004—; lectr. in field. Author: Commentaries on Banking Regulation, 1985; chmn. editorial adv. bd. Banking Policy Report, 1982-95; contbr. numerous articles to profl. jours., chpt. to book. Mem. Fed. City Coun., 1990-95; trustee Found. for Nat. Capital Region, 1992-98; trustee Washington Opera, 1992-96; mem. Pres.'s Com. on the Arts and Humanities, 1996-2001. 2d lt. USAF, 1955-57. Mem. Fed. Bar Assn. (banking law com., chmn. 1976-78), Cosmos Club, Exchequer Club, Econ. Club, Yale Club, Vineyard Haven Yacht Club.

HAWKE, ROBERT FRANCIS, dentist; b. Pasadena, Calif., Oct. 26, 1946; s. George Herbert and Mildred Estelle (Wood) H.; m. Emily Sue Wilkins, Aug. 17, 1973; 1 child, Kristen. BA, U. Ariz., 1969; DDS, Baylor U., Dallas, 1973. Assoc. B.J. Barber, Tucson, 1976-78; ptnr. Barber-Hawke, P.C., Tucson, 1978-87; pvt. practice Tucson, 1987—. Bd. dirs., pres. Delta Dental Ariz., Phoenix, 1985-91. Mem. Tucson Bus. Alliance, 1981—, pres., 1983, 94, Comty. Auto Immune Deficiency Syndrome Adv. Coun., Tucson, 1987-90, Auto Immune Deficiency Syndrome Edn. Project, Tucson, 1988-90. Maj. U.S. Army. Fellow Am. Coll. Dentists, Internat. Coll. Dentists; mem. ADA (alt. del. 1988-92, del. 1994-2000, 14th dist. chmn. polit. action com. 1995-98), Ariz. State Dental Assn. (trustee 1988, v.p. 1991, pres.-elect 1992-93, pres. 1993-94, past pres. 1994-95, mem. legal liaison com. 1993-94, chmn. coun. on constitution and bylaws 1996-97, chmn. coun. on budget planning 1992-93, chmn. coun. on ins. 1998-2003, Svc. award 2002), So. Ariz. Dental Soc. (bd. dirs. 1983-89, pres. 1987-88), Pierre Fauchard Acad., Acad. Laser Dentistry, Acad. Gen. Dentistry, Tucson Advanced Cosmetic & Restorative Study Club, World Clin. Laser Inst., Give Kids a Smile Day (So. Ariz. chmn. 2003-04), Rotary (Paul Harris fellow), Beta Beta Beta. Republican. Evangelical. Avocations: golf, jogging, tennis, racquetball, reading. Home: 6745 E Tivani Dr Tucson AZ 85715-3348 Office: 1575 N Swan Rd Ste 200 Tucson AZ 85712-4068 Office Phone: 520-323-3842. Personal E-mail: robertfhawke@comcast.net. Business E-Mail: hawkerobertf@qwest.net.

HAWKE, ROGER JEWETT, lawyer; b. NYC, July 2, 1935; s. John Daniel and Olga (Buchbinder) H.; m. Rose Marie Ferri, Aug. 15, 1964; children— Christopher, Allison, John. BA cum laude, Amherst Coll., 1956; LL.B., Columbia U., 1959. Bar: NY 1960, U.S. Supreme Ct. 1976. Assoc. Donovan, Leisure, Newton & Irvine, NYC, 1960, 62-65; asst. U.S. atty. U.S. Atty.'s Office, So. Dist. N.Y., NYC, 1965-69; assoc. Brown, Wood, Ivey, Mitchell & Petty LLP, NYC, 1969-71, ptnr., 1971—2001, Sidley Austin Brown & Wood LLP, NYC, 2001—05, Sidley Austin LLP, NYC, 2006—. Arbitrator Nat. Assn. Securities Dealers. Acting village justice Village of Lloyd Harbor, NY,1977-83, trustee, 1983-00; police commr., 1983-99, dep. mayor, 1983-99. With U.S. Army, 1961-62. Fellow: Am. Coll. Trial Lawyers; mem.: ABA, Am. Law Inst., NY Law Inst. (treas. 1989—2005, exec. com.), Assn. of Bar of City of NY, Lloyd Neck Bath (pres. 1981). Office: Sidley Austin LLP 787 Seventh Ave New York NY 10019

HAWKER, KENO, mayor, trucking company executive; BA, Wis. State U.; MBA, U. Wis. Owner & pres. Hawker Trucks & Materials, Inc.; mem. coun. City of Mesa, Ariz., 1986—94, 1998—2000, vice mayor, 1990—92, mayor, 2000—. Mem. U.S. Conf. Mayors, Ariz. League of Cities and Towns Bd., Williams Gateway Authority, Regional Public Transportation Authority, Regional Aviation System Policy Com., Ariz. Mcpl. Water Users Assn., Nat. League of Cities Transp. TEA 21 Reauthorization Task Force, Nat. League of Cities Transp. Infrastructure and Svcs. Steering Com., Nat. League of Cities, Maricopa Assn. Govt.'s, Mesa Chamber of Commerce, Valley Metro Rail Bd.; chair Maricopa Assn. Govt.'s Regional Coun., Regional Coun. Transp. Subcom.; pres. Ariz. Mcpl. Water Users Assn.; ex-officio mem. adv. bd. City of Mesa Econ. Develop. Mem.: Maricopa Assn. Govts. (treas.), Mesa HoHoKams, Mesa Baseline Rotary. Avocations: biking, hiking, climbing, rappelling, travel, rollerblading, owns his own palne and is a lic. pilot, dirt bike racing, river rafting, motorcycle riding. Office: Mesa City Plaza 20 E Main St Mesa AZ 85201 Address: Hawker Trucks and Materials Inc 315 S Morris Mesa AZ 85210 Office: Office of Mayor PO Box 1466 Mesa AZ 85211-1466 E-mail: mayor_hawker@ci.mesa.az.us.*

HAWKES, CAROL ANN, academic administrator; b. NYC; d. Howard N. and Lavinia M. (Lally) H. BA, Barnard Coll., 1943; MA, Columbia U., 1944, PhD, 1949. Dir. acad. English liberal arts div. Katharine Gibbs Sch., NYC, 1950-57; prof. English, chmn. dept. English and comparative lit. Finch Coll., NYC, 1957-75; v.p. for ednl. affairs, dean of coll. Hartwick

Coll., Oneonta, NY, 1975-80; pres. Endicott Coll., Beverly, Mass., 1980-87; assoc. v.p. for acad. affairs, founding dean Sch. Visual and Performing Arts Western Conn. State U., Danbury, 1987—. Trustee Norwich U., Hartwick Coll. Author: Master's Degree Programs and the Liberal Arts College, 1968. Harvard Sch. Dental Medicine fellow. Mem. MLA, LWV, Modern Humanities Rsch. Assn., Princeton Club (N.Y.C.), Columbia U. Club New Eng., Phi Beta Kappa. Office: Western Conn State U Academic Affairs Danbury CT 06810 Home Phone: 203-744-7236; Office Phone: 203-837-8851. Business E-Mail: hawkesc@wcsu.edu.

HAWKES, MARY NEWGEON, retired minister, educator; b. Thessaloniki, Greece, June 27, 1934; arrived in U.S., 1937; d. William Emory and Jessie Newgeon Hawkes. AB in Music, Doane Coll., 1956; MA in Religious Edn., Hartford Sem., 1958; EdD in Religious Edn., Columbia U. Tchrs. Coll./Union Theol. Sem., 1983. Ordained to ministry United Ch. of Christ, 1980. Dir. Christian edn. United Chs. of Christ, Middletown and Hartford, Conn., 1958—67; ecumenical ch. worker German Protestant Ch., Hamburg/Berlin, 1967—69; dir. Christian edn. United Chs. of Christ, Conn., NY, and Mich., 1969—76, interim min. Conn., NY, Vt., 1986—88, 1994—98, pastor North Bennington, Vt., 1988—94; sec. edn. programs United Ch. Bd., Homeland Min., NYC, 1981—85; pastor 1st Congl. Ch., Deer River United Cmty. Ch., Carthage, NY, 1998—2002. V.p., pres. Village Ecumenical Min, Carthage, NY, 1999—2002; resource person United Ch. of Christ N.Y. Women, 1999—2002. Mem. editl. bd.: hymnal Sing of Life and Faith, 1963—67, content editor: religious songbook Sing to God, 1981—84, co-author, editor: Festivals of Christmas, 1981—83. Mem. family life com. Bennington (Vt.) Pub. Schs.; bd. dirs. Adult Day Care Program, Bennington, 1990—93; editor newsletter, v.p. Adam Hawkes Family Assn., Saugus, Mass., 2002—; v.p. Greater Hartford Coun. Chs., 1963—66; mem., chair Task Force on the Homeless, Bennington, 1989—94; annuitant visitor UCC Pension Bds. for So. Vt., 2004—. Recipient Doane Builder award, Doane Coll., 1981. Mem.: AAUW (scholarship com. 2004, sec. 2006—), Alban Inst., Ptnrs. in Edn. United Ch. of Christ, Children's Def. Fund, Habitat for Humanity, Common Cause, So. Poverty Law Ctr., Amnesty Internat., N.H. Peace Found., Kappa Delta Pi. Democrat. United Ch. Of Christ. Avocations: music, travel. E-mail: mellyhaw@sover.net.

HAWKEY, G. MICHAEL, lawyer, real estate developer; b. Apr. 17, 1941; m. Frances Tripp, Feb. 27, 1971; children: Samuel, Eliza, MacKenzie. AB, Princeton U., 1963; postgrad., Columbia Bus. Sch., 1964; LLB, Cornell U., 1967. Bar: Mass. 1967. Atty. Sullivan & Worcester LLP, Boston. Founder Sun Valley Properties, Ketchum, Idaho, Mettowee Valley Properties, Pawlet, Vt.; lectr. Mass. Restaurant Assn. Bd. dirs. Pacific. Internat. Inst., Lewiston, Idaho, 1992—97, St. Lukes Cancer Rsch. Found., Cork, Ireland, 1994—97; N.Am. bd. Michael Smurfit Grad. Sch. Bus., Univ. Coll., Dublin, 1994—98; trustee Maruzen Hawthorne Coll., Antrim, NH, 1991—92; bd. govs. Wianno Club, Osteville, Mass., 1982—98; bd. dirs. Greyhawk Village Assn., Ketchum, 2001—. Mem. Internat. Coun. Shopping Ctrs., Mass. Real Estate Fin. Assn. (bd. dirs. 1989-92), Sr. Execs. Club of Mass. Real Estate Fin. Assn., The Country Club (Brookline, Mass.), Wianno Club (Osterville, Mass.). Home: 26 Arlington Rd Wellesley MA 02481-6129 Office: Sullivan & Worcester LLP 1 Post Office Sq Ste 2300 Boston MA 02109-2129 Personal E-mail: mhawkey@sandw.com.

HAWKING, STEPHEN WILLIAM, astrophysicist, mathematician, educator; b. Oxford, England, Jan. 8, 1942; s. Frank and Isobel Hawking; m. Jane Wilde, 1965 (div. 1991); 3 children; m. Elaine Mason, 1995 (div. 2007). BA, Oxford U., DSc (hon.), 1978; PhD, Cambridge U.; DSc (hon.), U. Chgo., 1981, Notre Dame U., 1982, NYU, 1982, Leicester U., 1982. Research asst. Inst. Astronomy, Cambridge, Eng., 1972-73, research asst. dept. applied maths. and theoretical physics, 1973-75, reader in gravitational physics, 1975-77, prof., 1977-79, Lucasian prof. math., 1979—. Author: The Large Scale Structure of Space-Time, 1973 (with G.F.R. Ellis), 300 Years of Gravity, 1987 (with W. Israel), A Brief History of Time: From the Big Bang to Black Holes, 1988, Black Holes and Baby Universes, 1993, Hawking on the Big Bang and Black Holes, 1993; The Universe in a Nutshell, 2001, The Theory of Everything: The Origin and Fate of the Universe, 2002; also author numerous jour. articles. Decorated comdr. Brit. Empire, 1981; recipient Eddington medal Royal Acad. Sci., 1975, Pius XI Gold medal Pontifical Acad. Sci., 1975, Danne Heinemann prize for math. and physics Am. Phys. Soc.-Am. Inst. Physics, 1976, William Hopkins prize Cambridge Philos. Soc., 1976, Maxwell medal Inst. Physics, 1976, Einstein award Strauss Found., 1978, Albert Einstein medal Albert Einstein Soc. of Berne, 1979, Wolf Prize in physics, 1988, Britannica award, 1989, Julius Edgar Lilienfield prize, Am. Physical Soc., 1999, Michelson Morley award, Case Western U., 2003, Copley medal of the Royal Soc., 2006 Fgn. mem. Am. Philos. Soc., AAAS; fellow Royal Soc. (Hughes medal 1976, Copley medal, 2006). In April 2007, partook in a zero-gravity flight by Zero Gravity Corporation. Plans to go into space in 2009 on Virgin Galactic SpaceShipTwo. Address: Dept Applied Math and Theoretical Physics Ctr Math Sci Wilberforce Rd Cambridge CB3 0WA England

HAWKINS, BARBARA REED, mental health nurse; b. Burghettstown, Pa., July 20, 1945; d. John Francis Reed and Iona Eleanor Spring; m. Hal Kenneth Hawkins, Sept. 6, 1969; children: David, Heidi, Brian, Russell. BS in Nursing, Duke U., 1968; MSN, U. N.C., 1973; postgrad., Houston Montessori Ctr., 1992—95. RN N.C., 1968. Staff nurse pediatrics Duke U. Med. Ctr., 1968—69; psychiatric nurse, group co-therapist Durham County Mental Health Ctr., 1971—72; counselor Durham Crisis and Suicide Ctr., 1972—73; lectr. psychiat. nursing U. N.C., Sch. Nursing, Chapel Hill, 1972; lectr. U. N.C., 1972—73, instr., 1973—77; therapist Psychiat. Assocs. Chapel Hill, 1975—79; head nurse, nursing supr., acting unit dir. Ga. Mental Health Inst., 1979—80; coord. career devel. Emory U. Hosp., 1980—81; tchr. Sugar Creek Children's Montessori Sch., Sugarland, Tex., 1992—95. Cons. in field. Contbg. author Patterson Family Favorites, 1998. Vol. Tex. Wildlife and Rehab. Ctr., 1983—2004; vol. cons. in counseling crisis intervention, 2000—. Avocations: shell collecting, gourmet cooking, gardening, interior decorating, crafts. Home: 5500 N Braeswood Blvd Apt 198 Houston TX 77096

HAWKINS, BRANDON JAMES, podiatrist, surgeon; b. Murray, Utah, July 13, 1972; s. Lorin Robert and Evelyn Schoenfeld Hawkins; m. Jessica Ann Barron, Mar. 18, 1995; children: Nicholle, Emma, Micah. BS in BioChemistry, U. Utah, 1997; BS in Biol. Scis., Scholl Coll. Podiatric Medicine, 1998; D Podiatric Medicine, Finch U., 2001. Diplomate Am. Bd. Podiatric Medicine. Intern Lebanon DVAMC/Pa. State U., Lebanon, 2001—02; resident Hu Hu Kam Meml. Hosp., Sacaton, Ariz., 2002—03; chief resident South Western Podiatry Program, San Juan Capistrano, Calif., 2004—. Team surgeon Bakersfield Condors Hockey Team, 2005—06; podiatrist Calif. Foot Drs. Pride Podiatry, 2005—; team surgeon Bakersfield Blitz Arena Football, 2005—, Bakersfield Jam Football Team, 2006—, Bakersfield Coll., 2006—, Taft Coll., Calif., 2006—, Coll. Sequoias, Visalia, Calif., 2006—, Fresno Pacific U., Calif., 2006—. Contbr. articles to profl. publs. Regional dir., scoutmaster Boy Scouts Am., Salt Lake City and Chgo., 1995—2001. Scholar, Scholl Coll. Podiat. Medicine, 1999. Mem.: Am. Podiatric Med. Assn., Am. Profl. Wound Care Assn. Home: 9809 Treetop Ave Bakersfield CA 93312-2348 Office: Calif Foot Drs Pride Podiatry 4000 Stockdate Hwy Ste C Bakersfield CA 93309

HAWKINS, BRETT WILLIAM, retired political science professor; b. Buffalo, Sept. 15, 1937; s. Ralph C. and Irma A. (Rowley) H.; m. Linda L. Knuth, Oct. 31, 1974; 1 child, Brett William. AB, U. Rochester, 1959; MA, Vanderbilt U., 1962, PhD, 1964. Instr. polit. sci. Vanderbilt U., 1963; instr. in polit. sci. Washington and Lee U., 1963-64, asst. prof., 1964-65, U. Ga., Athens, 1965-68, assoc. prof., 1968-70, U. Wis., Milw., 1970-71, prof., 1971-99, ret, 2000. Author: Nashville Metro, 1964, The Ethnic Factor in American Politics, 1970, Politics in the Metropolis, 2d edit, 1971, Politics and Urban Policies, 1971, The Politics of Raising State and Local Revenue, 1978, Professional Associations and Municipal Innovation, 1981; contbr. articles to profl. jours., chpts. in edited vols. Mem. Phi Beta Kappa, Iota of N.Y. Home: 5318 N Kent Ave Whitefish Bay WI 53217-5109 Personal E-mail: bretthwk@yahoo.com.

HAWKINS, BRIAN LEE, educational association administrator; b. Lafayette, Ind., Aug. 5, 1948; s. Robert H. and Marjorie Joan (Bradley) H.; m. Lisa Ellen Herrick, Dec. 30, 1970; children: Timothy, Steven. BA, Mich. State U., 1970, MA, 1972; PhD, Purdue U., 1975. Asst. prof. U. Tex., San Antonio, 1975—76, asst. dean bus., 1976—81; assoc. v.p. academic affairs Drexel U., Phila., 1981—86, assoc. v.p. computing and telecom., 1984—86; v.p. Brown U., Providence, 1986, spl. asst. to pres., assoc. provost academic planning, 1990—92, v.p. academic planning and adminstrn., 1992—96, sr. v.p. academic planning and adminstrv. affairs, 1997—98; pres., CEO EDUCAUSE, 1998—. Trustee EDUCOM, Washington, 1986-90, chmn. bd., 1989-90; trustee U. Richmond, 1999-2003; dir. Forum for Future of Higher Ed., 1999-, Am. Coun. Edn., 2005-. Author: Managerial Communications, 1981; editor: Managing & Organizing Information Resources on Campus, 1990, The Mirage of Continuity: Reconfiguring Academic Information Resources in the 21st Century, 1998; Tech. Everywhere, 2002. Bd. dirs. CAUSE, 1992-96. Office: EDUCAUSE Ste 206 4772 Walnut St Boulder CO 80301-2538 Office Phone: 303-939-0335. E-mail: hawkins@educause.edu.*

HAWKINS, DAVID G., lawyer; b. Hartford, Conn., 1945; married. BA English, Yale U., New Haven, Conn., 1965; JD magna cum laude, Columbia U. Law Sch., NY, NY, 1970. Staff atty. Stern Comm. Law Firm, Washington, 1970—71, Natural Resources Defense Coun. (NRDC), Washington, 1971—77; asst. adminstr. Air, Noise, and Radiation at EPA, Washington, 1977—81; co-dir. Clean Air Program NRDC, Washington, 1981—90, dir. Air and Energy Program, 1990—2001, dir. Climate Ctr., 2001—. Named one of 100 Most Influential Lawyers, Nat. Law Jour., 2006. Office: Natural Resources Defense Council 1200 New York Ave NW Washington DC 20005

HAWKINS, DAVID RAMON, psychiatrist, writer, researcher, spiritual teacher; b. Milw., June 3, 1927; s. Ramon Nelson and Alice-Mary (McCutcheon) H.; m. Susan Humphrey; children: Sarah Humphrey. BS, Marquette U., 1950; MD, Med. Coll. Wis., Milw., 1953; PhD, Columbia Pacific U., 1995. Med. dir. North Nassau Mental Health Ctr., Manhasset, NY, 1956-80; dir. rsch. Brunswick Hosp., LI, NY, 1968-79; pres. Acad. Orthomolecular Psychiatry, NYC, 1970-80; dir. Inst. Spiritual Rsch., Sedona, Ariz., 1979-88, The Rsch. Inst., Sedona, 1988—. Chmn. Inst. Advanced Theoretical Rsch., 1993—; guest on TV shows including McNeal-Lehrer, Barbara Walters, Today; chief of staff Mingus Mountain RTC, 1995; lectr. in field; cons. in field. Author (with Linus Pauling): Orthomolecular Psychiatry, 1973; author: Power vs. Force, 1995, The Eye of the I, 2001, I, 2002, Truth vs. Falsehood, 2005, Transcending the Levels of Consciusness, 2006, Devotional Non-Duality, 2006. With USN, 1945—46. Nominee Templeton prize, 2006; named knight, Sovereign Order St. John of Jerusalem, Tae Ryoung Sun Kak Tosun, Mount Bo Jing and Radasanti Meditation Ctr., 2006; recipient Mosby Book award, 1953. Mem. AMA, APA, Ariz. Med. Soc., Ariz. Psychiat. Soc., Alpha Omega Alpha. Avocations: inventing, designing, architecture. Office: Rsch Inst PO Box 3516 W Sedona Ave Sedona AZ 86340 Business E-Mail: info@veritospub.com. *Our lives are created more by our vision of the future then they are by the details of our past.*

HAWKINS, DAVID ROLLO, SR., psychiatrist, educator; b. Springfield, Mass., Sept. 22, 1923; s. James Alexander and Janet (Rollo) H.; m. Elizabeth G. Wilson, June 8, 1946; children: David Rollo Jr., Robert Wilson, John Bruce, William Alexander. BA, Amherst Coll., 1945; MD, U. Rochester, NYC, 1946. Intern Strong Meml. Hosp., Rochester, 1946-48; Commonwealth Fund fellow in psychiatry and medicine U. Rochester, 1950-52; instr. psychiatry U. N.C. Sch. Medicine, 1952-53, asst. prof., 1953-57, asso. prof. psychiatry, 1957-62, prof., 1962-67; prof., chmn. dept. psychiatry U. Va. Sch. Medicine, 1967-77, Alumni prof. psychiatry, 1967-79, asso. dean, 1969-70; psychiatrist-in-chief U. Va. Hosp., 1967-77; prof. psychiatry Pritzker Sch. Medicine, U. Chgo., 1979-90, U. Ill., 1990—; clin. prof. psychiatry U. N.C., Chapel Hill, 1992—. Dir. liaison and consultation svcs. dept. psychiatry Michael Reese Hosp., Chgo., 1979-87, chmn., 1987-92; assoc. attending physician N.C. Meml. Hosp., Chapel Hill, 1952-62, attending physician, 1962-67; cons. Watts Hosp., Durham, 1952-67, VA Hosp., Fayetteville, N.C., 1956-67, Eastern State Hosp., Williamsburg, Va., 1971—, VA Hosp., Salem. Va., 1969-79, mem. deans com., 1971-77; spl. rsch. fellow Inst. Psychiatry, U. London, 1963-64, Fogarty internat. rsch. fellow, 1976-77, U.S.-USSR and Romania health exch. fellow, 1978. Rev. editor Psychosomatic Medicine, 1958-70; assoc. editor Psychiatry, 1970-92. Mem. small grants com. NIMH, 1958-62; mem. nursing rsch. study sect. NIH, 1965-67; mem. Gov.'s Commn. Mental, Indigent and Geriatric Patients, 1968-72; mem. rsch. evaluation com. Va. Dept. Mental Hygiene and Hosps., 1970-73; mem. behavioral sci. test com. Nat. Bd. Med. Examiners, 1970-73. Served as capt. M.C., AUS, 1948-50. Fellow Am. Coll. Psychoanalysts (charter bd. regents 1979-81, treas. 1989-91, pres.-elect 1992, pres. 1994), Am. Psychiat. Assn.; mem. AAUP, Am. Psychosomatic Soc. (mem. coun. 1959), AMA, Group for Advancement Psychiatry (bd. dirs. 1987-89), Assn. Am. Med. Colls. (coun. acad. socs. 1973-78), Am. Psychoanalytic Assn., Am. Coll. Psychiatrists, AAAS, Va. Psychoanalytic Soc., Washington Psychoanalytic Soc., Chgo. Psychoanalytic Soc., N.C. Psychoanalytic Soc., Ill. Psychiat. Soc. (coun. 1981-82, pres.-elect 1987, pres. 1988-90), Soc. Neurosci., Am. Assn. Chmn. Depts. Psychiatry (sec.-treas. 1971-73, pres. 1974-75), Sleep Rsch. Soc., Nat. Bd. Med. Examiners (exam. com. 1983-87), Phi Beta Kappa, Sigma Xi, Alpha Omega Alpha. Home: 235 Cedar Club Cir Chapel Hill NC 27517

HAWKINS, EDWARD J., retired lawyer; b. Fall River, Mass., June 24, 1927; s. Edward Jackson and Harriet (Sherman) H.; m. Janet Schwerdt; children: Daniel, George, Robert, Harriet. Grad., Phillips Acad., Andover, Mass., 1945; AB summa cum laude, Princeton U., 1950; LLB magna cum laude, Harvard U., 1953. Bar: Ohio 1954, D.C. 1990. Assoc., ptnr. Squire, Sanders & Dempsey, Cleve., 1953-78, ptnr. Cleve. and Washington, 1982-96, counsel, 1997-99; ret., 2000. Chief tax counsel U.S. Senate Fin. Com., Washington, 1979-80, minority tax counsel, 1981; gen. chmn. Cleve. Tax Inst., 1969. Contbr. articles to profl. jours. With U.S. Army, 1945-46. Mem. ABA (vice chmn. govt. rels. tax sect. 1987-89), D.C. Bar Assn., Phillips Acad. Alumni Assn. (alumni coun. 1967-70), Quadrangle Club. Democrat. Home: 1843 Westerham St Keswick VA 22947 E-mail: ejhawkins2@earthlink.net.

HAWKINS, ELEANOR CARROLL, veterinary educator; b. Balt., Apr. 18, 1957; d. Elbert Stewart and Elizabeth Eleanor (Howard) H. BS, U. Md., 1978; DVM, Ohio State U., 1982. Diplomate Am. Coll. Vet. Internal Medicine. Intern small animal medicine and surgery Animal Med. Ctr., NYC, 1982-83; resident small animal medicine U. Calif., Davis, 1983-85; asst. prof. internal medicine Purdue U., West Lafayette, Ind., 1985-91, assoc. prof. internal medicine, 1991; asst. prof. small animal medicine N.C. State U., Raleigh, 1991-93, assoc. prof. small animal medicine, 1993—2000, prof. small animal medicine, 2000—. Author: (with others) Textbook of Veterinary Internal Medicine, 1989, 3d edit., 1995, Current Veterinary Therapy X, 1989, Small Animal Internal Medicine, 1992, 3d edit., 2003, Current Veterinary Therapy XI, 1992, Current Veterinary Therapy XII, 1995, Current Veterinary Therapy XIII, 2000, others; sect. editor The 5 Minute Veterinary Consult, 2d edit., 1998; contbr. articles to profl. jours. Mem. AVMA, Am. Coll. Vet. Internal Medicine (cert. exam. com. 1994-98, chair 1998, pres. splty. of internal medicine 2003-2006), Comparative Respiratory Soc. (bd. dirs. 1991-94), Phi Beta Kappa, Phi Zeta. Achievements include research in techniques to perform bronchoalveolar lavage in cats and dogs with minimal equipment needs; characterization of BAL cytology in cats and dogs in health and disease; educational video of abnormal breathing patterns in dogs; characterization of chronic bronchitis in dogs. Office: NC State U Coll Vet Medicine 4700 Hillsborough St Raleigh NC 27606-1428

HAWKINS, ELINOR DIXON (MRS. CARROLL WOODARD HAWKINS), retired librarian; b. Masontown, W.Va., Sept. 25, 1927; d. Thomas Fitchie and Susan (Reed) Dixon; m. Carroll Woodard Hawkins, June 24, 1951; 1 child, John Carroll. AB, Fairmont State Coll., 1949; BS in Libr. Sci., U. N.C., 1950. Children's libr. Enoch Pratt Free Libr., Balt., 1950-51; head circulation dept. Greensboro (N.C.) Pub. Libr., 1951-56; libr. Craven-Pamlico Libr. Svc., New Bern, N.C., 1958-62; dir. Craven-Pamlico-Carteret Regional Libr., New Bern, N.C., 1962-92. Storyteller children's TV program Tele-Story Time, 1952-58, 63—; bd. dirs. Triangle Bank of New Bern. Mem. New Bern Hist. Soc., 1973—, Tryon Palace Commn., 1974—; mem. adv. bd. Salvation Army. Mem. N.C. Assn. Retarded Children, Pilot Club (pres. 1957-58, v.p. 1962-63). Baptist. Home: PO Box 57 Cove City NC 28523-0057

HAWKINS, ELLIS DELANO, manufacturing, insurance company, gaming executive; b. Princeton, Ark., Feb. 13, 1941; s. Eddie and Anne Beadie (Smith) H.; m. Vera Mae Smith, Aug. 19, 1969 (div. Sept. 1979); children: Angela, Stacey, Rhonald. AA, Shorter Jr. Coll., 1958; BBA, Calif. Coast U., 1981, MBA, 1983. Cert. in statis. process control; lic. ins. agt., Ill. Operator drill press Choctaw Inc., Poyen, Ark., 1962-65; supr. Chrysler Corp., Detroit, 1965-76, Alcan Aluminum, Terre Haute, Ind., 1976-86; Borg-Warner, Chgo., 1986-91, ins. exec., 1991—; pres., chief exec. officer Jes-El-Ed Inc., Chgo., 1980—, also bd. dirs. Bd. dirs., sec. Idlewild Civic Investment, Inc.; prodn. mgr., photographer St. James Trumpet, 1989; mem. bd. rsch. advisors ABS Inc., 1993; spkr. in field. Scoutmaster Boy Scouts Am. Troop 53, Malvern, Ark., 1962; solicitor United Found., Detroit, 1971; life mem. NAACP. With USN, 1958-62. Recipient Commendation Letter Tribune Star, 1986, Appreciation Letter, M.L. King Convocation Com., 1986. Mem. Am. Legion (chmn. Spl. Olympics 1982-89, Plaque 1985, Cert. of Appreciation 1989), Idlefellows Social Club. Democrat. Avocations: golf, bowling, writing, photography. *Personal philosophy: To care and be concerned for others. Be willing to help someone by sharing yourself including information and or assistance. You have to believe and give thanks.*

HAWKINS, GREGORY J., consumer products company executive; BSBA, Oreg. State U. With J.C. Penney, GTE, Mitel Corp.; v.p. sales Ingram Micro., Inc., v.p. major accounts div. consumer markets, sr. v.p. global sales; CEO, chmn. Buy.com, 1999—2000; CEO BMS, Inc., 2001—04, bd. dirs., 2004—. Office: BMS Reimbursement Mgmt 2058 Mills Ave PMB 201 Claremont CA 91711

HAWKINS, H. RALPH, architectural firm executive; BArch, U. Tex., Arlington; MPH, U. Tex. Health Scis. Ctr.; MArch, Rice U. Registered Ala., Ariz., Calif., D.C., Fla., Ga., La., Mich., Miss., Nev., N.J., N.C., Ohio, Pa., Tex., Utah, Va. Pres., CEO HKS, Inc., Dallas. Adj. prof. U. Tex., Arlington, Tex. Recipient Best Exec.-Bus. Svcs., Am. Bus. Awards, 2007. Fellow: AIA (pres. Acad. Arch. for Health 2003), Forum for Health Planning, Am. Coll. Healthcare Archs. Office: HKS Inc 1919 McKinney Ave Dallas TX 75201 Home Phone: 972-791-1207; Office Phone: 214-969-5599. E-mail: rhawkins@hksinc.com.*

HAWKINS, HAL K(ENNETH), pathologist; b. Bartlesville, Okla., Aug. 11, 1945; s. Guy Rodgers and Sarabeth (Barbour) H.; m. Barbara Patterson Reed, Sept. 6, 1969 (div. Apr. 1992); children: David, Heidi, Brian, Russell. PhD, Duke U., 1971, MD, 1972. Asst. prof. Duke U. Med. Sch., Durham, N.C., 1973-79, Emory U. Sch. Medicine, Atlanta, 1979-83, Baylor Coll. Medicine, Houston, 1983-93; assoc. prof. U. Tex. Med. Br., Galveston, 1993—2002, prof., 2002—. Pathologist Shriners Burns Hosp., Galveston, 1996—. Mem. U.S. Canadian Acad. of Pathology. Avocation: sailing. Office: Shriners Burns Hosp/Path 815 Market St Galveston TX 77550-2725 Office Phone: 409-770-6635. Business E-Mail: hhawkins@utmb.edu.

HAWKINS, HAROLD STANLEY, pastor, school director, police chaplain; b. Santa Ana, Calif., Oct. 16, 1927; s. Henry Jesse and Susan Brown (Young) H.; m. Paula Juanita Paeschke, Feb. 19, 1949 (dec. June 1999), m. JoAnn Faron, Feb. 12, 2005; children: Bert Stanley, Harold Paul, Kathleen Faith Meulstee. Grad., L.I.F.E. Bible Coll., 1950; cert., So. Bay Regional Police Acad., 1978; DD, Hawthorne Christian Sch./Coll., 1978. Pastor Internat. Ch. of the Foursquare Gospel, Redondo Beach, Calif., 1949-58, 69-97, Reseda, Calif., 1958-66; staff mem. Oral Roberts U., Tulsa, 1966-67; pastor Internat. Ch. of the Foursquare Gospel, Bell, Calif., 1967-69; chaplain Redondo Beach Police, 1978-98, res. police officer, 1978-88; master police chaplain L.A. Police Dept. Acad., 1988-92. Dir. Camp Cedar Crest, Running Springs, Calif., 1961-81, Wings of Mercy, Santa Ana, 1966-70, Hawthorne (Calif.) Christian Schs., 1973-96. Mem. Redondo Beach Round Table, 1974-2000, pres. 1991-92; commr. Harbor Commn., Redondo Beach, 1982-92, planning commn., 1996-2000. With USN, 1944-46, World War II. Mem.: Rotary (pres. 1982—83). Republican. Home Phone: 951-924-7200; Office Phone: 951-924-1073. E-mail: revhal@allvantage.com. *We live in exciting days! America needs a great revival to start the new millennium!.*

HAWKINS, JAMESETTA See JAMES, ETTA

HAWKINS, JASPER STILLWELL, JR., architect; b. Orange, NJ, Nov. 10, 1932; s. Jasper Stillwell and Bernice (Ake) H.; m. Patricia A. Mordigan, Mar. 22, 1980; children: William Raymond, John Stillwell, Karen Ann, Jasper Stillwell III. B.Arch., U. So. Calif., 1955. Registered architect, Calif., Ariz., N.Mex. Founder, prin. Hawkins & Lindsey & Assocs., LA, 1958-90, Hawkins Lindsey Wilson Assocs., L.A. and Phoenix, 1978-85; pres. Fletcher-Thompson Assocs., 1981-84; prin. Jasper Stillwell Hawkins, F.A.I.A., architect, Phoenix, 1990—. Bd. visitors Nat. Fire Acad., 1978-80; bd. dirs. Nat. Inst. Bldg. Scis., 1976-85, chmn. bd. dirs., 1981-83, consultative council, 1978—; mem. com. protection of archives and records centers GSA, 1975-77; mem. archtl. adv. panel Calif. State Bldg. Standards Commn., 1964-70; mem. U.S. del. to UN Econ. Commn. for Europe Working Party on Bldg., 1978-84; mem. U.S. presdl. del. to Honduran Presdl. Elections, 1985; mem. com. standards and evaluation Nat. Conf. States on Bldg. Codes and Standards, 1971-74; mem. Am. Arbitration Assn., 1992-2002; trustee Underwriter's Labs., 1984-2002, mem. nat. coun. Archtl. Registration Bds., 1971—; participant and speaker numerous confs. Contbr. articles to profl. jours.; maj. works include Valley Music Theatre, L.A., Houston Music Theatre, Sundome Theatre and R.H. Johnson Ctr., Sun City West, Ariz., Bell Recreation Ctr., Sun City, U. Calif. at Irvine Student Housing, Oxnard (Calif.) Fin. Ctr., condominium devels., Lakes Club, Sun City. Mem. Nev. Gov.'s Commn. Fire Safety Codes, 1980-81, Pres. Reagan's Commn. on Housing, 1981-82, City of Phoenix ACDC Task Force, 1985-86, ACDC Aesthetics Commn., 1986-89, City of Phoenix Camelback East Village Planning Com., 1983-89; mem. fire rsch. panel Nat. Bur. Stds., 1978-81; chmn. NAS fire assessment rev. com., 1987-88, com. on analytical methods for designing bldgs. for fire safety, 1977-78; chmn. bldg. seismic safety coun. ind. rev. panel San Francisco War Meml. Opera House, 1995; bd. dirs. Jazz in Ariz.,

2004—. Recipient design awards from Ariz. Rock Products Assn., Theater Assn. Am., Nat. Food Facilities, House and Home Mag., Practical Builders Mag., Am. Builders Mag., Nat. Inst. of Bldg. Sci. Inst. award, 1995, others. Mem. AIA (mem. codes and stds. com. 1970—, chmn. 1970-73, nat. liaison commn. with Assoc. Gen. Contractors 1969-70, chmn. nat. fire safety task force 1972-74, chmn. Calif. coun. AIA state code com. 1964-68, chmn. nat. conf. industrialized constrn. 1969-70, nat. com. bldg. industry coordination 1969-70, nat. rep. to Internat. Conf. Bldg. Ofcls. 1969, state Calif. AIA codes com. 1960-70, chmn. 1965-70, nat. AIA codes and stds. com. 1970-80, chmn. 1970-74, nat. crisis adv. com. 1988-89, coll. of fellows 1976—), ASCE (task force bldg. codes 1971-74), ASTM, Nat. Fire Protection Assn. (com. bldg. heights and areas 1965-72, chmn. 1968-72, fire prevention code com. 1974-76, bd. dirs. 1985-93, chmn. nat. model codes coordinating com. 1983-86, stds. coun. 1996—, bldg. code task force 2000—), Nat. Fire Acad. (bd. regents 1980-83), Nat. Bur. Stds. Fire (rsch. adv. com. 1979-82), Nat. Acad. Forensic Engrs., Ariz. C. of C. (policy com. 1983-84), Ariz. Biltmore Village Estates Homeowners Assn. (pres. 1981-83), Phoenix C. of C. (chmn. Water task force 1982-83), So. Calif. Phoenix Alumni Club (chmn. scholar com. 1997—). Office: 5332 N 24th Pl 220 Phoenix AZ 85016

HAWKINS, JEFF, information technology company executive; b. LI, NY, June 1, 1957; BSEE, Cornell U., 1979; student, U. Calif., 1986—88. Key tech. positions Intel Corp., 1982; with GRiD Sys. Corp., 1982—92, v.p. rsch.; co-founder Palm Computing (sold to US Robotics in 1995, in 1997 sold to 3Com Corp., now palmOne Inc.), 1992, with, 1992—98; co-founder Handspring, Inc. (merged with Palm Hardware Group to create new co. palmOne, Inc., 2003, now called Palm. Inc., 2005), 1998, chief product officer, bd. mem., 1998—2003; CTO palmOne, Inc. (now called Palm, Inc.), Milpitas, Calif., 2003—; founder Redwood Neuroscience Inst., Menlo Park, Calif., 2002, exec dir, chmn.; co-founder Numenta, Inc., Menlo Park, Calif., 2005—. Mem. sci. bd. dirs. Cold Spring Harbor Labs; mem. adv. bd. Redwood Ctr. for Theoretical Neuroscience, U. Calif. Berkeley. Co-author (with Sandra Blakeslee): (non-fiction) On Intelligence, 2004 (Wired Mag RAVE award, 2005). Named one of Digital 50 with Donna Dubinsky, Time Mag., 1999; named to Innovators Hall of Fame with Donna Dubinsky. Mem.: NAE. Achievements include invention of architect for the original PalmPilot, 1994 and Treo smart phone, 2001; patents for nine various handheld devices and features; prin. architect and designer for GRiDPad (1989) and GRiD Convertible; Numenta Inc. is creating a new pattern recognition software called Hierarchical Temporal Memory modeled on the human brain's neocortex. Avocations: sailing, playing musical instruments. Office: Palm Inc 950 W Maude Ave Sunnyvale CA 94085 also: Numenta Inc 1010 El Camino Real Ste 380 Menlo Park CA 94025 Office Phone: 408-503-7000, 650-321-8282. Fax: 408-503-2750; Office Fax: 650-321-8585.

HAWKINS, JOHN DONALD, JR., lawyer; b. Bronxville, NY, Dec. 30, 1956; s. John Donald and Lucille Phyllis (Sassano) H.; m. Alice Sherron Harward, May 17, 1980; children: Alison Lyn, Megan Leigh. BA cum laude in Govt. and Econ., Lehigh U., 1977; JD with honors, U. N.C., 1980. Bar: N.Y. 1981, U.S. Dist. Ct. (so. dist.) N.Y. 1983, U.S. Ct. Appeals (2d cir.) 1983, Conn. 1998. Ptnr. Mudge Rose Guthrie Alexander & Ferdon, NYC, 1980—, Paul, Hastings, Janofsky & Walker LLP, chmn. global project practice. Mem. N.Y. State Bar Assn., Assn. of Bar of City of N.Y., Phi Beta Kappa. Roman Catholic. Office: Paul Hastings Janofsky & Walker LLP 1055 Washington Blvd Stamford CT 06901 Office Phone: 203-961-7486. Office Fax: 203-674-7686. Business E-Mail: johnhawkins@paulhastings.com.

HAWKINS, JOHN N., education educator, writer; b. Sterling, Ill., May 18, 1944; m. Judith Ayami Takata, Aug. 12, 1967; children: Marisa Harumi, Larina Yasuko. BA with honors, U. Hawaii, 1967; MA, U. BC, Vancouver, Can., 1969; PhD, Vanderbilt U., 1973. Dean internat. studies and overseas programs UCLA, chair dept. edn., dir. curriculum inquiry ctr., prof. comparative and internat. edn., dir. ctr. internat. devel. and edn., 2006—. Author (with T. LaBelle): Education and Intergroup Relations: An International Perspective, 1988; author: Education and Social Change in the People's Republic of China, 1983; author: (with B. Koppel) The Future Work in Rural Asia, 1993; author: Changing Education, 2007; co-editor: Transnational Competence: Rethinking the US-Japan Educational Relationship, Values Education for Dynamic Societies. Mem. internat. adv. com. Exxon Edn. Found.; bd. dirs., found. bd. UCLA, East West Ctr. Named Chevalier dans l'Ordre Palmes Academiques, French Govt., 1997; recipient numerous grants; fellow, NDEA, Internat. Studies Ministry of Edn., Japan; U. BC, Mombusho Fgn. scholar. Mem. AERA, Comparative and Internat. Edn. Soc. (bd. dirs., pres.), Am. Ednl. Studies Assn., Omicron Delta Kappa., Phi Delta Kappa. Home: 3847 Daguerre Ave Calabasas CA 91302-5816

HAWKINS, JOSEPH ELMER, JR., physiologist, educator; b. Waco, Tex., Mar. 4, 1914; s. Joseph Elmer and Maude Burke (Schlenker) H.; m. Jane Elizabeth Daddow, Aug. 24, 1939 (dec. Sept. 2002); children: Richard Spencer Daddow, Peter Douglas Huntington, James Marion Davis, William Alexander Parmley, Priscilla Ann (Mrs. Philip A. Leach). Student, Altes Realgymnasium, Munich, 1929-30; AB, Baylor U., 1933; postgrad., Brown U., 1933-34; BA in Physiology, U. Oxford, 1937, MA, 1966, DSc in Clin. Medicine, 1979; PhD in Med. Sci., Harvard U., 1941. Tchg. fellow in physiology Harvard Med. Sch., 1937-41, instr., 1941-45; asst. investigator Nat. Def. Rsch. Com.-Office Sci. Rsch. & Devel., Harvard U., 1941-43; spl. rsch. assoc. Harvard Psycho-Acoustic Lab., Cambridge, Mass., 1943-45; asst. prof. physiology Bowman Gray Sch. Medicine, Wake Forest Coll., Winston-Salem, NC, 1945-46; rsch. assoc. neurophysiology Merck Inst. for Therapeutic Rsch., Rahway, NJ, 1946-56; assoc. prof. otolaryngology NYU Sch. Medicine, 1956-63; prof. physiol. acoustics U. Mich., Ann Arbor, 1963-84, prof. otolaryngology emeritus, 1984—, chmn. grad. program in physiol. acoustics, 1969-81. Disting. vis. prof. biology Baylor U., Waco, Tex., 1985-93; mem. NIH sensory diseases study sect., 1958-61, communicative disorders rsch. tng. com., 1965-69, communicative scis. study sect., 1975-79; mem. Nat. Libr. Medicine Communicative Disorders Task Force, 1977-79; lectr. Armed Forces Inst. Pathology, 1969-74; cons. various pharm. cos. Contbr. to: Ency. Brit., 1974, 86, 99, Ency. Neuroscience, 1987, 99, 2003; editor: (with M. Lawrence and W.P. Work) Otophysiology, 1973, (with S.A. Lerner and G.T. Matz) Aminoglycoside Ototoxicity, 1981; contbr. sci. articles to profl. jours. Mem. Bd. Edn., Cranford, NJ, 1958—61. Rhodes scholar Tex. and Worcester Coll., U. Oxford, 1934-37; USPHS spl. fellow Öronkliniken, Sahlgrenska Sjukhuset U. Göteborg, Sweden, 1961-63; NAS exch. lectr. to Yugoslavia and Bulgaria, 1977; Chercheur étranger de l'INSERM, Lab. d'Audiologie Expérimentale, U. Bordeaux II, 1978; recipient Disting. Achievement award Baylor U., 1982, City of Pleven, Bulgaria medal, 1982, U. Bordeaux medal, 1983, Humboldt Rsch. award for sr. U.S. scientists U. Würzburg, 1991, Hon. Citizen award, Bordeaux, 1991, Disting. Alumnus award Baylor U., 1996. Fellow AAAS, Acoustical Soc. Am.; mem. Am. Physiol. Soc., Assn. for Rsch. in Otolaryngology (award of merit 1985, Presdl. citation 2004), Collegium Oto-rhino-laryngologicum Amicitiae Sacrum, Bárány Soc., European Workshop for Inner Ear Biology, Am. Assn. for History of Medicine, Am. Otol. Soc. (assoc.), Prosper Menière Soc. (hon., Gold medal for basic sci. 1998), Pacific Coast Oto-ophthalmol. Soc. (hon.), Connétablie de Guyenne (Bordeaux, assoc.), Phi Beta Kappa, Sigma Xi. Anglican. Democrat. Achievements include research in ototoxic, noise-induced, and presbyacusic hearing loss; history of otolaryngology; masking of speech by noise. Avocations: Germanic and Romance languages and literature, gardening. Home: Glacier Hills Apt 258 1200 Earhart Rd Ann Arbor MI 48105 Office: U Mich Med Sch Kresge Hearing Rsch Inst Ann Arbor MI 48109-0506 Office Phone: 734-764-0215. Business E-Mail: josehawk@umich.edu.

HAWKINS, KATHERINE ANN, hematologist, educator, lawyer; b. Teaneck, NJ, Oct. 25, 1947; d. Howard Robert and Helen Ann (Foley) Hawkins; m. Paul Jonathan Chrzanowski, June 29, 1974; children: Eric, Brian. AB, Manhattanville Coll., Purchase, NY, 1969; MD, Columbia U., 1973; JD, Fordham U., Sch. of Law, 2002. Intern Presbyn. Hosp., NYC, 1973, Roosevelt Hosp., NYC, 1974-75, resident, 1975-77; fellow NYU, 1977-79; attending hematologist Sickle Cell Ctr. St. Luke's Hosp., NYC, 1985-87; assoc. attending physician St. Luke's - Roosevelt Hosp. Ctr., NYC, 1989—; asst. clin. prof. medicine Columbia U., NYC, 1987-94, assoc. clin. prof., 1994—96; assoc. dir. dept. medicine, dir. med. edn. St. Luke's Hosp., NYC, 1991-96; assoc. residency program dir. Beth Israel Med. Ctr., NYC, 1996—; assoc. prof. clin. medicine Albert Einstein Coll. Medicine Yeshiva U., NYC, 1996—. Mem. attending staff Beth Israel Hosp., N.Y.C., St. Luke's-Roosevelt Hosp. Ctr., N.Y.C. Contbr. articles to profl. jours. Fellow ACP, Am. Coll. Legal Medicine; mem. ABA, Am. Soc. Hematology, Am. Soc. Clin. Oncology Roman Catholic. Office: Gair Gair Conason Steigman and Mackauf 80 Pine St New York NY 10005 Office Phone: 212-943-1090.

HAWKINS, LAWRENCE CHARLES, management consultant, educator; b. Greenville County, SC, Mar. 20, 1919; s. Wayman and Etta (Brockman) H.; m. Earline Thompson, Apr. 29, 1943; children: Lawrence Charles Jr., Wendell Earl. BA, U. Cin., 1941, BEd, 1942, MEd, 1951, EdD, 1970; AA (hon.), Wilmington Coll., 1979; LittD (hon.), Cin. Tech. and CC; LHD (hon.), Mt. St. Joseph Coll. Cert. sch. supt. Ohio. Elem./secondary tchr. Cin. Pub. Schs., 1945-52, sch. prin./dir., 1952-67, asst. supt., 1967-69; dean U. Cin., 1969-75, v.p., 1975-77, sr. v.p., 1977-83; vis. asst. prof. Eastern Mich. U., Ypsilanti, summers 1955-60; mem. Cincinnatus Assn., 1971-87. Vice chair Student Loan Funding Corp., 1982-98; mem. cmty. rels. panel Cin. Mayors, 1979—, others; cons. US Dept. Justice, Dept. Edn.; bd. dirs. We. and So. Fin. Group. Bd. dirs. exec. com. Ohio Citizens Coun. Health and Welfare, 1966-73; vice chair Ohio Valley Regional Med. Program, 1972-77, bd. trustees Cmty. Chest and Coun. Cin. Area Inc., 1970-72; bd. dirs. Wilmington Coll., Ohio, 1980-90, Bethesda Hosp., Cin., 1980-90; trustee Children's Home of Cin., 1978-90, Coll. Mt. St. Joseph, 1989-93; pres., CEO Omni-Man, Inc., 1981-96; bd. dirs. emeritus Nat. Underground R.R. Freedom Ctr., 1994-98; owner The L.C.H. Resource; vice chmn. Greater Cin. TV Ednl. Found., WCET-TV, 1983; co-chmn. Cin. area NCCJ 1980-87; nat. bd. dirs. Inroads, 1982-87; bd. trustees Knowledge Works Found., 1999-2002. Served to lt. USAAF, 1943-45 (an original Tuskegee Airman). Recipient award of Merit, Cin. Area United Appeal, 1955, 73, cert. Pres.'s Coun. on Youth Opportunity, 1968, City Cin., 1968, Disting. Svc. citation Greater Cin. NCCJ, 1988; named Great Living Cincinnatian, Greater Cin. C. of C., 1989. Mem. NEA (life), ASCD, Am. Assn. Sch. Adminstrs. (conv., Golden Eagles Lifetime Achievement award 1998), Nat. Congress Parents and Tchrs. (hon. life; chmn. com.), Phi Delta Kappa, Kappa Delta Pi, Kappa Alpha Psi, Sigma Pi Phi. Home: 3544 Sherbrooke Dr Cincinnati OH 45241-3831 Home Phone: 513-563-8387; Office Phone: 513-563-8387.

HAWKINS, LORETTA ANN, retired secondary school educator, playwright; b. Winston-Salem, NC, Jan. 1, 1942; d. John Henry and Laurine (Hines) Sanders; m. Joseph Hawkins, Dec. 10, 1962; children: Robin, Dionne, Sherri. BS in Edn., Chgo. State U., 1965; MA in Lit., Governor's State U., 1977, MA in African Cultures, 1978; MLA in Humanities, U. Chgo., 1998. Cert. tchr., Ill. Tchr. Chgo. Bd. Edn., 1968—2002; lectr. Chgo. City Colls., 1987-89; tchr. English, Gage Park H.S., Chgo., 1988—2002; ret., 2002. Mem. steering com. Mellon Seminar U. Chgo., 1990; tchr. adv. com. Goodman Theatre, Chgo., 1992, mem. cmty. adv. coun., 1996—; spkr. in field; creator 5-4-3-2-1- Essay Writing Method, 1997. Author: (reading workbook) Contemporary Black Heroes, 1992, (plays) Of Quiet Birds, 1993 (James H. Wilson award 1993), Above the Line, 1994, Good Morning, Miss Alex, (work books) 5-4-3-2-1 ESSAY!: A Holistic Writing Program Book 1 & 2; contbr. poetry, articles to profl. publs.; featured WYCC-TV-Educate, 1996. Mem. Chgo. Tchg. Connections Network, DePaul U. Ctr. Urban Edn., 2001; mem. Chgo. Pub. Schs. Mentoring and Induction of New Tchrs. Program. Fellow Santa Fe Pacific Found., 1988, Lloyd Fry Found. 1989, Andrew W. Mellon Found., 1991, Ill. Arts Coun., 1993; grantee Cmty. Arts Assistance Program Award, Chgo. Dept. Cultural Affairs; recipient Feminist Writers 3d pl. award NOW, 1993, Zora Neale Hurston-Bessie Head Fiction award Black Writer's Conf., 1993, Suave Tchr. Plus award, 2002; numerous others. Mem. AAUW, Nat. Coun. Tchrs. English (spkr. conv.), Am. Fedn. Tchrs., Women's Theatre Alliance, Dramatists Guild of Am., Internat. Women's Writing Guild. Avocations: films, coins, reading, walking. Home: 8928 S Oglesby Ave Chicago IL 60617-3047

HAWKINS, MARY ELLEN HIGGINS, retired state legislator, public relations executive; m. James H. Hawkins, Feb. 13, 1960 (div. 1971); children: Andrew Higgins, Elizabeth, Peter Hixon. Student, U. Ala., Tuscaloosa, 1945-47. Congl. aide to several mems. U.S. Ho. Reps., 1950-60; instr. art Sumter County Schs., Americus, Ga., 1971-72; staff writer Naples (Fla.) Daily News, 1972-74; prin. Daniels-Hawkins, Naples, 1982-84; mem. Fla. Ho. Reps., Tallahassee, 1974-94; vice chmn. Banc-Florida Fin. Corp., Naples, 1979-91, pres., CEO, 1991-92, chmn., 1991-93, also. bd. dirs. Columnist, contbr. articles to local newspapers. V.p. Naples Philharm., 1984-91; life mem., vice chair Big Cypress Basin bd. South Fla. Water Mgmt. Dist., 1999-05; mem. adv. com. Lower Gulf Coast Water Supply Plan, 1999; trustee CREW Land and Water Trust, 2002-, treas., 2004-; vice chair Fla. Children's Campaign, 1997—; various offices Rep. Party Ga., Americus, 1965-71; literacy vol., 2005—. Mem. Zonta Internat. Avocation: painting. Office Phone: 239-262-4932. Personal E-mail: mhawk26249@aol.com.

HAWKINS, MICHAEL DALY, federal judge; b. Winslow, Ariz., Feb. 12, 1945; s. William Bert and Patricia Agnes (Daly) H.; m. Phyllis A. Lewis, June 4, 1966; children: Aaron, Adam. BA, Ariz. State U., 1967, JD cum laude, 1970; LLM, U. Va., 1998. Bar: Ariz. 1970, US Ct. Mil. Appeals 1971, US Supreme Ct. 1974. Pvt. practice law, 1973—77; US atty. Dept. Justice, Phoenix, 1977—80; pvt. practice law, 1980—94; judge US Ct. Appeals (9th cir.), Phoenix, 1994—. Mem. Appellate Cts. Jud. Nominating Commn., 1985—89. Staff editor: Ariz. State U. Law Jour., 1968—70. Mem. Ariz. Lottery Commn., 1980—83, Commn. on Uniform State Laws, 1988—93. Capt. USMC, 1970—73. Recipient Alumni Achievement award, Ariz. State U., 1995. Mem.: ABA, Nat. Assn. Former U.S. Attys. (pres. 1989—90), Adminstrv. Conf. U.S. (pub. mem. 1985—94), Phoenix Trial Lawyers Assn., Ariz. Trial Lawyers Assn. (bd. dirs. 1976—77, state sec. 1976—77), State Bar of Ariz. (James Walsh Outstanding Jurist Award 2003), Maricopa County Bar Assn. (bd. dirs. 1975—77, 1981—89, pres. 1987—88). Office: US Ct Appeals 9th Cir Sandra Day O'Connor Cthse 401 W Washington St Ste 510 Phoenix AZ 85003-2151 Office Phone: 602-322-7310.*

HAWKINS, PAMELA LEIGH HUFFMAN, biochemist; b. Washington, Oct. 7, 1950; d. Lauria Carl and Maryalice (Flinner) Huffman; m. James Lee Hawkins, Mar. 7, 1981 (div. Aug. 1993). BS in Biochemistry, Va. Polytech. Inst. & State U., Va., 1972; MS in Biochemistry, Pa. State U., Pa., 1975. Sci. info. specialist Inform., Inc., Rockville, Md., 1972; asst. rsch. scientist Union Carbide Corp., Tarrytown, NY, 1975; assoc. rsch. scientist Am. Hosp. Supply Corp., Gibbstown, NJ, 1976-78, rsch. scientist Miami, Fla., 1978-85; R & D scientist Baxter Healthcare Corp., Miami, Fla., 1985-95, sr. rsch. scientist, 1993-95; prin. scientist Sigma Diagnostics, St. Louis, 1995—2002; sr. scientist Biotech. Rsch. and Devel., Sigma-Aldrich, 2002—04; prin. scientist Instrumentation Lab., Orangeburg, NY, 2004—. Contbr. articles to profl. jours. Recipient Baxter Diagnostics Tech. award for Thromboplastin-IS, 1990, Baxter Internat. Tech. award, 1991. Mem. Mortar Bd., Phi Sigma, Gamma Sigma Delta, Phi Lambda Upsilon. Lutheran. Achievements include US and one European patent for fresh blood (unfixed) hematology control, 3 US and 1 European patents for improved extraction methods for preparing thromboplastin reagents, patent for thromboplastins for recombinent tissue factor, US patent for thromboplastin reagents based on recombinent technology, production of thromboplastin IS, Innovin, Two US patents-US Pat. No. 6,528,273, 2003, Methods for Quality Control of Prothiombin Thromboplastin Time (PT) and Activated Partial Thromboplastin Time (APTT) Assays using coagulation controls for coagulation controls for prothrombin time and activated partial thromboplastin time, others. Office: Instrumentation Lab 526 Route 303 Orangeburg NY 10962

HAWKINS, PHILIP LINTON, real estate executive; b. Phila., Dec. 27, 1955; s. Robert Bruce and Nancy (Perry) H.; m. Elizabeth Porter, June 28, 1980; children: Robert Bruce II, Jennifer Louise. BA, Hamilton Coll., 1978; MBA, U. Chgo., 1980. New products mgr. Avery Internat., Cleve., 1980-82; v.p., gen. mgr. LaSalle Ptnrs., Cin., 1982-85, v.p., regional mgr. Dallas, 1985—; pres., COO CarrAmerica Realty, Wash., DC; die. SBA Comm. Avocations: golf, sailing, skiing. Home: 7713 Crossover Dr Mc Lean VA 22102-2507 Office: CarrAmerica Realty 1850 K St NW Ste 500 Washington DC 20006

HAWKINS, RICHARD ALBERT, medical educator, administrator; b. Greenwich, Conn., Mar. 27, 1940; s. Albert Rice and Florence Marie Elizabeth (Hansen) H.; m. Enriqueta Elias, May 9, 1964; children: Richard Alfred, Paul Andrés. BSc magna cum laude, San Diego State U., 1963; PhD, Harvard U., 1969; LHD (hon.), U. Phoenix, 1994. Rsch. fellow Metabolic Rsch. Lab. Radcliffe Infirmary, Oxford (Eng.) U., 1969-71; staff fellow in neurochemistry St. Elizabeth Hosp., Washington, 1971-72, NIMH/NIAAA sr. staff fellow in neurochemistry, 1972-74; chief phys. sci. br. FDA, Rockville, Md., 1974-76; assoc. prof. neurosurgery and physiology NYU Med. Ctr., NYC, 1976-77; prof. anesthesia and physiology Pa. State U., Hershey (Pa.) Med. Ctr., 1977-88; prof., chmn. physiology and biophysics The Rosalind Franklin U. Medicine and Sci., North Chicago, Ill., 1988-93, prof., 1988—; exec. v.p. acad. affairs, chief academic officer Herman M. Finch U. Health Scis./Chgo. Med. Sch., North Chicago, Ill., 1993-98, provost, 1998, pres., CEO, 1999—2003. Hon. prof. U. Valencia, Spain, 1989—. Contbr. numerous articles to profl. jours. Recipient Meritorious Rsch. award Morris Parker Found., 1992. Fellow Am. Heart Assn.; mem. Am. Physiol. Soc., Am. Soc. Neurochemistry, Biochem. Soc., Soc. for Neurosci., Alpha Omega Alpha. Home: 950 N Michigan Ave Chicago IL 60611 Office: Rosalind Franklin U Med and Sci 3333 Green Bay Rd North Chicago IL 60064-3037 Home Phone: 847-615-1826; Office Phone: 847-578-3218. Business E-Mail: rah@post.harvard.edu.

HAWKINS, RICHARD MICHAEL, lawyer; b. Nevada City, Calif., July 23, 1949; s. Robert Augustus and Virginia June (Hawke) H.; m. Linda Lee Chapman, Sept. 27, 1975; child, Alexandra Michelle. BS in Math., U. Calif., Davis, 1971; JD, U. Calif., San Francisco, 1974; LLM in Taxation, U. Pacific, 1983. Bar: Calif. 1974, U.S. Dist. Ct. (ea. dist.) Calif. 1974, U.S. Dist. Ct. (no. dist.) Calif. 1982, U.S. Ct. Claims 1982, U.S. Tax Ct. 1982, U.S. Ct. Appeals (9th cir.) 1982, U.S. Supreme Ct. 1982. From assoc. to ptnr. Larue & Francis, Nevada City, 1974-76; ptnr. Larue, Roach & Hawkins, Nevada City, 1977-78; of counsel Berliner & Ellers, Nevada City; ptnr. Berliner, Spiller & Hawkins, Nevada City, 1981; sole practice Grass Valley, Calif., 1981—. Bd. dirs. 49er Fire Dist., Nevada City, 1977-81, 89-98, asst. fire chief, 1981-83, fire chief, 1983-89. Mem. ABA, Calif. State Bar (cert. specialist in estate planning, trust and probate law 1990), Nevada County Bar Assn. (v.p. 1976), Order of Coif, Phi Kappa Phi, Am. Morgan Horse Inst. (bd. trustees 1997-; treas. 2004-06, pres. 2006-). Republican. Roman Catholic. Avocations: running, showing Morgan horses. Home: 14762 Banner Quaker Hill Rd Nevada City CA 95959-8813 Office: 563 Brunswick Rd Ste 2 Grass Valley CA 95945-7801 Office Phone: 530-272-6733. Fax: (530) 272-7861. E-mail: rhawk53@aol.com.

HAWKINS, ROBERT B., think-tank executive; PhD, U Wash. Chmn. Adv. Commn. on Intergovt. Rels., Washington, 1982-93; dir. Am. pub. policy program Woodrow Wilson Internat. Ctr. for Scholars, Washington; pres., CEO Inst. for Contemporary Studies, Oakland, Calif. Tv co-host, That's Politics, 1987-91; radio California Political Review; Books American Federalism: A New Partnership for the Republic, Self-government by District: Myth and Reality. Office: Institute For Contemporary Studies 3100 Harrison St Oakland CA 94611-5526

HAWKINS, TRIP, electronics executive; Chmn. bd. dirs., CEO 3DO, Redwood City, Calif. Office: The 3do Company 345 California St Ste 1150 San Francisco CA 94104-2664

HAWKINS, VIVIAN AGATHA, mental health nurse, educator; b. NYC, Dec. 18, 1917; d. Joseph Emanuel Williams and Naomi Adorcus Wallace; m. William Hawkins, Dec. 13, 1949 (dec.). BSN, M Sociology, M Cmty. Health, L.I. U.; cert. in group therapy, Washington Sq. Inst. Psychotherapy, 1982. Lectr., clin. instr. fundamental nursing NY Tech. Coll., Bklyn., 1972—77; clin. instr. psychol./med. surg. nursing Kings County Sch. Nursing, Bklyn., 1972—77; supr. psychiatry partial hospitalization and cmty. outreach Met. Hosp. Ctr., NYC, 1977—79; psychiat. nurse clinician Kings County Hosp. Ctr., Bklyn., 1979—82; clin. group psychiatrist Washington Sq. Inst. Psychotherapy and Mental Health, 1982—86; adj. prof. Manhattan C.C., NYC, 1985—86; clin. nurse instr. Clara Barton H.S., Bklyn., 1988—91; supr. Sheepshead Nursing Home, Bklyn., 1992—94; PMR surveyor First Mental Health Inc., Nashville, 1994—95; adj. prof. clin. psychiatry Borough of Manhattan C.C., 1995. Author, actor: (video) Remotivation Technique, 1984. Grief counselor Project Liberty. Mem.: Am. Group Psychotherapy Assn. (cert.). Avocations: travel, reading, cooking, sports, knitting. Home: 801 E 52d St Brooklyn NY 11203-5913 E-mail: vivaga@aol.com.

HAWKINS, WILLIAM A., III, medical products executive; b. 1954; BS, Duke U., 1976; MBA, U. Va., 1982. Corp. v.p., pres. Sherwood Davis & Geck div. Am. Home Products Corp., 1997—98; pres., CEO Novoste Corp., 1998—2002; sr. v.p., pres. vascular Medtronic Inc., Mpls., 2002—04, pres., COO, 2004—07, pres., CEO, 2007—. Bd. dir. DeLuxe Corp. Mem. bd. vis. Enging. Sch., Duke Univ.; trustee Darden Sch. Found., Univ. Va.; bd. mem. Guthrie Theatre. Office: Medtronic Inc 710 Medtronic Pkwy Minneapolis MN 55432-5604*

HAWKINS, WILLIAM DAVID, marketing executive; b. Ft. Worth, May 7, 1960; s. William Edward and Woola Dean Hawkins; m. Ursula Rae Crutsinger, June 30, 1984; 1 child, William Barrett. BA in Theology, Abilene Christian U., Tex., 1982, MA in Theology, 1986; MBA in Mktg., Dallas Bapt. U., 1997; postgrad., North Ctrl. U., Prescott, Ariz. Mngr. inventory control M&D Distr., Dallas, 1987—93; owner Whistle Stop Day Care and Pvt. Sch., Dallas, 1993—2000; pres., CEO Bottom Line Mktg., Irving, Tex., 2000—. Adj. instr. U. Phoenix, Dallas, 2001—. Bd. dirs. Las Colinas Symphony Orch., 2001—, pres. bd., 2001—. Mem.: Mensa, Alpha Mu Alpha. Office: Bottom Line Mktg PO Box 1075 Irving TX 75017

HAWKINS, WILLIAM E. N., newspaper editor; b. NYC, Dec. 4, 1943; s. Frank Nelson and Lottie (Norton) H.; m. Diane Taylor, Apr. 1, 1967; children: William E.N. Jr., Geoffrey W.T. BA, Cornell U., 1966. Reporter Patriot-News, Harrisburg, Pa., 1968-73, Balt. Evening Sun, 1973-78, city editor, 1978-83, asst. mng. editor, 1983-88; exec. editor The Herald-Sun, Durham, N.C., 1988—; v.p. The Durham Herald Co., 1994—. Vis. media fellow Duke U., 2002. Mem. bicentennial adv. com. U. N.C., 1992-93. 1st lt. U.S. Army, 1966-68, Vietnam. Decorated Bronze Star. Mem. Am. Soc. Newspaper Editors, AP Mng. Editors, N.C. Press Assn. (pres. 2001-2002, bd. dirs. 1992-96), N.C. Press Found., Soc. Profl. Journalists, Americal Divsn. Vets. Assn. Presbyterian. Avocation: skiing. Home: 7 Hartley Pl Durham NC 27707-2437 Office Phone: 919-419-6678.

HAWKINS, WILLIAM H., II, lawyer; b. Cin., July 18, 1948; BS, U. Cin., 1970, MEd, 1974; JD, No. Ky. U., 1978. Bar: Ohio 1978, Ky. 1979. Atty. then ptnr. Frost & Jacobs (now Frost Brown Todd); assoc. gen. counsel, sec. Convergys Corp., Cincinnati, Ohio, 1999—2001, gen. counsel, sec., 2001—03, sr. v.p., gen. counsel, corp. sec., 2003—. Office: Convergys Corp PO Box 1638 Cincinnati OH 45201*

HAWKINS DE GOLIER, DANIELLE, political activist; b. Valhalla, NY, Dec. 6, 1947; d. Daniel Livingston and Lucy Ann (Collesano) Wilson; m. David Frederick DeGolier, Apr. 8, 1967 (div. 1984); children: Jeffrey David De Golier, Amyjo Meloon; m. Charles Edward LaGreca, Feb. 14, 1986 (div. May 1993); m. Steven Tracey Moore, July 7, 1996 (div. 1998); m. Robert Michael Hawkins, Oct. 16, 2004. AA in Liberal Arts Human and Social Scis., Niagara County C.C., 1991. Founder, pres. Citizens Against Pollution Niagara County, 1980—82; founder, facilitator Love Addicts Anonymous Niagara Falls, 1982—88; prof. dancer, 1998—2003. Author: (children's book) A Lap for Leonard, 1977; columnist The Niagara Gazette, 1975-76, Nat. Women's Polit. Caucus, 1978, Just Ask Danni, The Niagara Falls Reporter, 2000-2002. Lobbyist state/fed. upgrade adoption laws granting adopted adults access to med. info. via anonymous computer network, 1975; founder, pub. rels. dir. Peoples Animal Lovers Soc., 1975-76; pres. Niagara Area chpt., pub. rels. dir. Animal Birth Control Soc. Western N.Y., 1976; founder, pres. Citizens Against Pollution, Niagara County, 1980-82, Love Addicts Anonymous, Niagara Falls, 1982-89; lobbyist state/fed. stalkers act., Niagara Falls, 1991-93, fed. sponsorship to upgrade domestic violence laws, 1990-94. Statue erected in honor of her Citizens Against Pollution work, Lewiston, N.Y., 1982. Mem. NOW (pres. Niagara County chpt. 1993-94); People Animal Lovers Soc. (founder, pub. rels. dir. 1975-76), Animal Birth Control Soc. Western N.Y. (pres. Niagra County chpt., pub. rels. dir. 1975-77. Avocation: writing. Home: 550 Main St #2 Niagara Falls NY 14301

HAWKINSON, LORRAINE A., librarian; b. Stoughton, Wis., Oct. 2, 1922; d. Parker Lynn and Myrtle A. Lee; m. Carroll Stanley Hawkinson, July 20, 1941; children: Dennis, Donna Hawkinson Ross. Student, U. Wis., Whitewater, 1958—59, U. Wis., Madison. Writer on staff Stoughton Courier-Hub, 1954—59; asst. libr. Stoughton H.S. Libr., 1959—61; libr. technician U. Wis. Meml. Libr., Madison, 1961—88; libr., rschr. Vesterheim Geneal. Ctr. and Naeseth Libr., Madison, 1991—. Questionnaire editor U.S. Census, Madison, 1990; freelance writer, photographer, 1955—. Columnist: Stoughton Courier-Hub, 1955—60. Mem. Town of Dunn Planning Commn., Dane County, Wis., Sr. Ctr. Commn. on Aging, Stoughton, 1995—. Recipient Gov.'s Spl. award for 27 yrs. svc. to state of Wis., Notable Norwegian award, Norwegian Am. Fest, 1998, Local History award of merit, Wis. State Hist. Soc., 1997, Winning Entry award, Wis. Sesquicentennial Com., 1998, Com. Appreciation award, Stoughton City, 1996, Stewardship award, Town of Dunn. Mem.: Norwegian-Am. Hist. Assn., Wis Regional Writers Assn. (historian 1980—, Svc. award 1993). Democrat. Lutheran. Office: Vesterheim Geneal Ctr and Naeseth Libr 415 W Main St Madison WI 53703

HAWKINSON, TIM, sculptor; b. San Francisco, 1960; married. Grad., San Jose State U.; MFA, UCLA, 1989. Prin. works include Egg, 1997, Bird, 1997, Shatter, 1998, Aerial Mobile, 1998, Pentecost, 1999, Bear, U. Calif. San Diego Stuart Collection, 2005, Uberorgan, Mass. Mus. Contemporary Art, exhibitions include Venice Biennale, 1999, Mass. Mus. Contemporary Art, 2000, Power Plant, Toronto, Can., 2000, Whitney Biennial, 2002, Corcoran Biennial, Washington, 2003, Akira Ikeda Gallery, Japan, Serpentine Gallery, London, Cartier Found., Paris, Whitney Mus. Am. Art, 2005, LA County Mus. Art, 2005. Mailing: c/o Stuart Collection 0010 U Calif San Diego 9500 Gilman Dr La Jolla CA 92093-0010

HAWKS, BARRETT KINGSBURY, lawyer; b. Barnesville, Ga., July 13, 1938; s. Paul K. and Nettie Glenn (Barrett) H.; m. S. Kathleen Pafford, Apr. 3, 1965 BBA, Emory U., 1960, LL.B., 1963; LL.M., Harvard U., 1964. Bar: Ga. Clk. Supreme Ct. Ga., 1963; Assoc. Gambrell, Russell, Moye & Richardson (now Smith, Gambrell & Russell), Atlanta, 1961-65; assoc. Sutherland, Asbill & Brennan, Atlanta, 1965-70, ptnr., 1970-82, 93—, Paul, Hastings, Janofsky & Walker, 1982-93. Served to lt. comdr. USNR. Mem. ABA (mem. coun. group pub. utility, transp. and comms. law sect.), State Bar Ga. (bd. govs. 1981-88), Atlanta Bar Assn., D.C. Bar Assn., Emory Law Sch. Alumni Assn. (pres. 1996-97), Emory Law Sch. Coun. (chmn., 1997-98), Capital City Club, Highlands Country Club. Presbyterian. Office: Sutherland Asbill & Brennan 999 Peachtree St NE Ste 2300 Atlanta GA 30309-3996 Office Phone: 404-853-8164. Business E-Mail: barrett.hawks@sablaw.com.

HAWKS, HOWARD L., energy executive; b. Bruning, Nebraska, June 2, 1935; m. Myrna Kleen, Sept. 3, 1955 (dec. Jan. 24, 2001); children: Troy, Neal, Tim; m. Rhonda Hawks, Nov. 30, 2002; 2 stepchildren. B in Acctg. and Bus. Adminstrn., U. Nebr., Lincoln, 1957; MBA, U. Nebr., Omaha, 1971. With GM, 1957—66; joined InterNorth, 1966, v.p. adminstrn., 1977, pres., No. Plains Natural Gas, 1980, pres., No. Liquid Fuels Co., 1982, pres., No. Natural Resources Co., 1985; pres., Enron Resources Enron Corp. (formerly InterNorth), pres., Enron Devel., 1986; co-founder, CEO, chmn. Tenaska, Inc., Omaha, 1987—. Bd. dirs. McCarthy Co. Founder, chmn. Hawks Family Found.; bd. trustees Omaha Zool.; adv. bd. Assistance League of Omaha; bd. dirs. Mid Am. Coun. Boy Scouts of Am., Joslyn Mus., Omaha Henry Doorly Zoo, Knights of Ak-Sar-Ben, Creighton U., Nebr., 2003—; bd. regents U. Nebr., 2002—, vice chmn. bd. regents, 2004, chmn., 2005. Named to Omaha Bus. Hall of Fame, 2002; recipient Disting. Alumnus award, U. Nebr. at Omaha Coll. Bus., 1999. Mem.: N. Am. Electric Reliability Coun. (past vice chair Stakeholder Com.). Mailing: Tenaska Energy Inc 1044 North 115th St Ste 400 Omaha NE 68154-4446 Office Phone: 402-938-1604. E-mail: hhawks@nebraska.edu.*

HAWLEY, ANNE, museum director; b. Iowa City, Nov. 3, 1943; d. Marshall Newton and Leone Ardith (Wilson) Hawley; m. Bruce Ivor McPherson, Sept. 4, 1977; 1 child, Katherine Black. BA, U. Iowa, 1966; MA, George Washington U., 1969; LHD (hon.), Lesley Coll, 1987; LHD (hon.), Williams Coll., 1989, Babson Coll., 1990, sr. exec. prog., Kennedy Sch. Govt, Harvard Univ., Intern in edn., Washington, 1967-69; research assoc. Nat. Urban League, Washington, 1969-71, Ford Found. Study Leadership in Pub. Edn., Washington, 1971-73; exec. dir. Cultural Edn. Collaborative, Boston, 1974-77, Mass. Council Arts/Humanities, Boston, 1977-89; mus. dir. Isabella Stewart Gardner Mus., Boston, 1989—; resident Nat. Hist. Soc. 1993—; adv. com. Nat. Trust of Historic Preservation, 1993—; vis. com. Fitchburg Art Mus., 1992-94. Bd. dirs. New Eng. Found. for Arts, 1978-89, Nat. Assembly/State Arts Agencies, Washington, 1981-83, Greater Boston Arts Fund, 1984-89, Boston Archtl. Found., 1986-89, Nat. Art Stabilization Fund, 1990-95, Boston Fenway Program, 1990-93. Trustee Inst. Contemporary Art, Boston, 1990—, Old Sturbridge Village, 1991-94; vis. comm. Sch. Mus. Fine Arts, Boston, 1989—, adv. bd. Mass. Coll. Art, 1979-81. Fulbright scholar, 1986; recipient Design Travel Grant, Women's Travel Club, Boston, Mass., 1982, Polaroid travel grant, 1987, Fund for Mutual Understanding travel grant to USSR, 1988, Art award Mass. Coll. Art, 1987, Lyman Ziegler award Commonwealth of Mass., 1988. Mem. Nat. Endowment for Arts (mus. panel 1978-81, task force on trng. and devel. of artists and art edu., 1978, dance panel 1982-84, design panel 1978-81, 88—, Pres. Clinton's transition team for arts and humanities, 1992-93), Boston Soc. Architecture (hon. mem. 1989); Radcliffe Alumnae Career Svcs. (adv. comm. 1974). Office: Isabella Stewart Gardner Mus 280 The Fenway Boston MA 02115-5807

HAWLEY, EDMUND S. (KIP), federal agency administrator; s. Edmund Blair and Greta (Crocker) H.; m. Janet Isak. AB, Brown U.; JD, U. Va., 1980; postgrad., Harvard U. Legis. asst. to Senator John Chafee U.S. Senate, Washington, 1977-78; assoc. Gaston, Snow and Ely Bartlett, Boston, 1980-81; dep. asst. sec. for govt. affairs US Dept. Transp., Washington, 1981-83; dep. asst. to the Pres. for intergovernmental affairs The White House, Washington; v.p. Union Pacific R.R.; asst. sec., Transp. Security Adminstrn. US Dept. Homeland Security, Washington, 2005—. Republican. Congregationalist. Office: US Dept Homeland Security E Bldg 601 S 12th St Arlington VA 22202

HAWLEY, ELLIS WAYNE, historian, educator; b. Cambridge, Kans., June 2, 1929; s. Pearl Washington and Gladys Laura (Logsdon) H.; m. Sofia Koltun, Sept. 2, 1953; children— Arnold Jay, Agnes Fay. BA, U. Wichita, 1950; MA, U. Kans., 1951; PhD (research fellow), U. Wis., 1959. Instr. to prof. history North Tex. State U., 1957-68; prof. history Ohio State U., 1968-69, U. Iowa, 1969-94, prof. emeritus, 1994—, chmn. dept. history, 1986-89. Hist. cons. Pub. Papers of the Presidents: Hoover, 1974-78. Author: The New Deal and the Problem of Monopoly, 1966, The Great War and the Search for a Modern Order, 1979, (with others) Herbert Hoover and the Crisis of American Capitalism, 1973, Herbert Hoover as Secretary of Commerce, 1981, Federal Social Policy, 1988, Herbert Hoover and the Historians, 1989; contbr. articles to profl. jours., essays to books Investigator Project to Study Hist. in Iowa Pub. Schs., Iowa City, 1978-79; cons. Quad Cities hist. project Putnam Mus., Davenport, 1978-79. Served to 1st lt. inf. AUS, 1951-53 North Tex. State U. Faculty Devel. grantee, 1967-68, U. Iowa, 1975-76. Mem. Am. Hist. Assn., Orgn. Am. Historians, So. Hist. Assn., AAUP (mem. exec. coun. Iowa chapt. 1982-84), Iowa Hist. Soc. Democrat. Home: 2524 E Washington St Iowa City IA 52245-3724 Personal E-mail: ellis.hawley@mchsi.com.

HAWLEY, FRANK JORDAN, JR., venture capital executive; b. Roanoke Rapids, NC, Oct. 3, 1927; s. Frank Jordan and Mary (Miller) H.; m. Alethea Wood, Sept. 12, 1959; children: Frank J. III, Mark R., Andrew D., Stuart W., Alethea S. BS in Physics, U. N.C., 1949; MBA, Harvard U., 1955. Rsch. analyst Eaton & Howard, Inc., Boston, 1955-59; banking assoc. Lazard Freres, NYC, 1959-64; portfolio mgr. Stein, Roe & Farnham, NYC, 1964-69; exec. v.p. Laidlaw Coggeshall, Inc., NYC, 1969-74; gen. ptnr. Foster Mgmt. Co., NYC, 1974-82; mng. ptnr. Saugatuck Capital Co., Stamford, Conn., 1982—. Chmn. bd. Floor & Decor. Inc., Atlanta; bd. dirs. Tharpe Corp., Statesville, NC. Chmn. bd. Waterloo Rest. Ventures, Inc., Vancouver, Oreg.; vice pres., treas. New Canaan (Conn.) YMCA, 1981-85; trustee Chocorua Chapel Assn., Squam Lake, N.H.; bd. visitors U. N.C., Chapel Hill, 1990-94; trustee Kenan Inst. Pvt. Enterprise of U. N.C. Lt. (j.g.) USN, 1950-53, Korea. Mem. Links Club, Harvard Club (N.Y.C.), New Canaan Country Club, Mill Reef Club (Antigua), Bald Peak Club (N.H.), Phi Beta Kappa. Republican. Episcopalian. Avocations: tennis, fly fishing, hunting. Office: Saugatuck Capital Co 1 Canterbury Grn Stamford CT 06901-2032 Office Phone: 203-348-6669.

HAWLEY, HAROLD PATRICK, educational consultant; b. Paducah, Ky., Jan. 8, 1945; s. Mathew Mark and Mae (Herndon) H.; m. Ann Dunbar, 1971 (dec. 1998); m. Lucrecia Thomas, Aug. 27, 1983; children: Cherise, Charlotte. AA, Paducah Jr. Coll., 1965; BA, U. Ky., 1968; MS, Ind. U., New Albany, 1974; EdD, Ind. U., Bloomington, 1977; postgrad., Mary Baldwin Coll., 1988, Ala. A&M U., 1996. Liaison to adjutant gen. 5th army U.S. Army, Ft. Carson, 1970, Bien Hoa, Vietnam, 1969-70; diversity rschr. (with Christine Bennett) Indpls. Pub. Sch., 1977; English tchr. Southwestern Consol. Schs., Hanover, Ind., 1971-73; asst. prin. Whitewater Consol. Sch., Lyons, Ind., 1978-80; assoc. prof., dir. secondary edn. Birmingham (Ala.)-So. Coll., 1980-86, chmn. freshman seminar, 1984-86; 1988-95 Ga. Dept. Edn., Atlanta, 1988-95; evaluator So. Assn. Schs. and Colls., 1988—; ednl. cons. Ga. Dept. Edn., Atlanta, 1988-95; chmn. Effective Sch. Rsch. Program, 1991; asst. prof. elem. edn. program Ala. A&M U., 2000—01, asst. prof. secondary edn. and multicultural edn., 2001—, advisor svc. frat., 2003; dir. Harlem Renaissance Project, Lee H.S., 2003. Adj. prof. Ind. U., Bloomington, 1975-80, Samford U., 1980-84, Auburn U., 1987, U. Ala., Gadsen, 1984-85, Brenau U., Gainesville, Ga., 1988-96, Reinhardt Coll./Brenau Coll. Collaboration, 1995—; adj. prof. Ala. A&M U., 1999, univ. supr., 1996—; cons. Intervarsity Beach Project, 1982—, Ford Ednl. Found., Parker H.S., Birmingham, Ala., 1981-85, Christian Acad., Cornerstone, Baton Rouge, 1983-84, FCA, 1983, Happy Valley Elem., Fairview Elem. Schoolwide Project, 1995, Walker County Curriculum Specialist, 1995-96, Nicholas Soc., 1997—; tech. advisor Polk County Schoolwide Projects, 1995, Floyd County Schoolwide Project, 1995—, Dade County Schoolwide Project, 1996; ednl. cons. Ga. Dept. Edn., Atlanta, 1988-95, Attention Deficit Disorder/HD, 1995—, Effective Schs. Rsch./Authentic Ins.; coord. 9th Dist. Schs. of Excellence, Ga., 1988-92; team leader sch. improvement teams Ga. Dept. Edn., Calhoun, 1995; dir. 1st State Remedial Edn. Conf., Lafayette, Ga., 1994, 1st statewide instrnl. conf. ESEA, 1995-96, Title I Northwest Ga. Instrnl. Conf., 1996, Lone Oak Edn. Svcs. 1999—, Regional Writers Conf., 2007; student tchr. supr. Covenant Coll., Chattanooga, 1996—; rsch. asst. North Ala. Tchr. Exch., Normal, 2000—; dir. Impact Ministries, Hist. Black Colls. and Univs., 2004—, Stone Mid. Sch. Project, Impact Ministries, 2007; featured presenter Midwouth Rsch. Assn., Gatlinburg, 2005, Regional Writers Conf., 2006; presenter in field. Author: (with Don Manlove) Classroom Climate Teacher-Student Relations, Expectancy Effects, 1976; rsch. asst. (with Floyd Coppedge) Binford Middle School Project, Bloomington, Ind., 1976, Individual Instrn. Project, 1975, Lebanon High Sch. Project, 1975-76, Katherine Hamilton Rsch. Project, New Albany, Ind., 1974 (with Carol Lewis). Bd. dirs. Boys Club Am., Paducah, 1963-65; tech. adv. Polk County Consol. Schs., 1995-96, Dade County Consol. Schs., 1995. Named among top 5 profs. Ala. A&M U., 2005, 06; Basketball scholar, 1965, attention deficit rsch. scholar univ. supr., Ala. A&M U., 1997—; nominee Oxford U. Roundtable, 2006; Spenser grantee, 1981, Mellon grantee, 1985; grad fellow Okla. State Sch. Supt., 1975-77, Nat. Study Sch. Evaluation fellow Ind. U., 1977. Mem. ASCD (Egypt Symposium nominee, 2007), Ga. Com. Leaders Assn., Internat. Platform Assn., Phi Delta Kappa. Achievements include music and brain research. Avocations: jogging, basketball, camping. Home: 117 Darlington Rd NE Huntsville AL 35801-1513 Office Phone: 256-372-4589. Business E-Mail: phawley@aamu.edu. E-mail: loneoakknight@gmail.com.

HAWLEY, JANA MARIE, educator, department head; b. Beloit, Kans., Oct. 1, 1955; d. Dale Dewey and Nadine Marlene Adams; m. Neil Kent Hawley, Aug. 2, 1975 (div. 1988); children: Adam Charles, Grant Cameron. BS, Ft. Hays State U., Hays, Kans., 1975; MS, Okla. State U., Stillwater, 1989; PhD, U. Mo., Columbia, 1993. Asst. prof. Ind. U., Bloomington, 1992—97; resident asst. San Antonio, 1997—98; asst. prof. U. North Tex., Denton, 1998—2000; assoc. prof. U. Mo., Columbia, 2001—07; prof., dept. head apparel, textile and interior design Kans. State U., Manhattan, 2007—. Recipient Kemper award for Excellence in Tchg., U. Mo., 2005; grantee, Fulbright-Hays to India, 2007. Mem.: Internat. Textile and Apparel Assn. (assoc.; v.p. ops. 2003—). Achievements include research in textile recycling and sustainability. Office: 224 Justin Hall Manhattan KS 66506 Business E-Mail: hawleyj@ksu.edu.

HAWLEY, JEFFREY LANCE, investments executive, accountant; b. Shreveport, La., Aug. 28, 1948; s. Eugene E. Jr. and Opal Marie (Hitchcock) H.; m. Pam Haley, Mar. 7, 1970; children: Suzanne, Allison. BS in Acctg., La. Tech. U., 1970; MBA, N.E. La. U., 1978. CPA, La.; registered securities rep.; cert. personal fin. specialist. Sr. acct. Peat, Marwick, Mitchell and Co., Houston, 1970-74; budget dir. Olinkraft, Inc., West Monroe, La., 1974-77; v.p., treas., CFO Palomar Fin., San Diego and Monroe, La., 1977—83; v.p., investment broker Legg Mason Wood Walker, Inc., Monroe, 1983—99; br. mgr. Morgan Stanley Dean Witter, Monroe, 1999—2001; v.p. A.G. Edwards & Sons, 2002—. Bd. trustees Our House. Mem. Am. Inst. CPA's, Soc. La. CPA's (com. chmn. 1986—, past pres. local chpt. 1981-84), Monroe Athletic Club, Rotary (bd. dirs.), English Speaking Union (past pres.). La. Tech. Alumni Assn. (bd. dirs.). Republican. Baptist. Avocation: tennis. Office: 2407 Broadmoor Blvd Monroe LA 71201 Office Phone: 318-387-6575. Personal E-mail: jhawleycpa@aol.com.

HAWLEY, JOSEPH. B., property management executive, educator; b. Red Bank, NJ, May 1, 1963; s. Bart J. and Genevieve M. Hawley. BA, Kean Coll. N.J., 1986; MA, Rutgers U., 1989, PhD, 1998. V.p. Bay Haven Property Mgmt., Atlantic Highlands, NJ, 1985—. Founding mem. Kean U. Peace Edn. Resource Ctr., trustee, 1986—90; pres. Genevieve M. Hawley Meml. Found., 2002—; chmn. Atlantic Highlands Dem. Exec. Com., 1990—92, 1996—; mem. Atlantic Highlands Planning Bd., N.J. Dem. State Com., Trenton, 1994—. Henry Hudson Regional Bd. Edn., Highlands, NJ, 1986, Atlantic Highlands Bd. Edn.; pres. Kean U. Class of 1986, 1985—86, Kean U. Student Orgn., Inc., 1984—85. Mem. Kiwanis (pres. Phila. chpt. 1989-90), Phi Alpha Theta. Roman Catholic. Avocations: long distance running, weightlifting. Home: 25 Ocean Blvd Atlantic Highlands NJ 07716 Office: Bay Haven Property Mgmt 25 Ocean Blvd Atlantic Highlands NJ 07716 Office Phone: 732-291-2962.

HAWLEY, KIMRA, computer company executive; BS in Psychology, Pitts. State U. Founding prin. MarketBound, Inc., Silicon Valley, Calif.; various mktg. mgmt. positions Amdahl Corp.; imaging mktg. dir. Action Point Software (formerly Cornerstone Imaging), 1992-96, gen. mgr. software divsn., pres., CEO, chmn. bd., 2001—04; interim CEO, pres. iUniverse, Inc., 2004, bd. dirs., 2005—. Office: iUniverse Inc 2021 Pine Lake Rd Ste 100 Lincoln NE 68512 Office Phone: 402-323-7800. Office Fax: 402-323-7824.

HAWLEY, NANCI ELIZABETH, professional society administrator; b. Detroit, Mar. 18, 1942; d. Arthur Theodore and Elizabeth Agnes (Fylling) Smisek; m. Joseph Michael Hawley, Aug. 28, 1958; children: Michael, Ronald, Patrick (dec.), Julie Anne. Pres. Tempo 21 Nursing Svcs., Inc., Covina, Calif., 1973-75; v.p. Profl. Nurses Bur., Inc., LA, 1975-83; owner, CEO Hawley & Assocs., Covina, 1983-87; exec. v.p. Glendora C. of C., Calif., 1984-85; dir. membership West Covina C. of C., Calif., 1985-87; exec. dir. San Dimas C. of C., Calif., 1987-88; mgr. pub. rels. Soc. for Advancement of Material and Process Engrs., Covina, 1988-92; small bus. rep. South Coast Air Quality Mgmt. Dist., 1992-94; bus. counselor Commerce and Trade Agy., Small Bus. Devel. Ctr., 1994; exec. v.p. Ontario C. of C., Calif., 1994-97; CEO, RMH Elec. Contractors, Colorado Springs, Colo., 1997-98; exec. v.p. Teen Resources, Inc., Colorado Springs, 1998; meetings mgr., registrar Am. Birding Assn., Colorado Springs, 1999—2006; co-owner, pres. 719 Day Spa and Salon, Colorado Springs, 2006—. V.p. Sangabriel valley chpt. Women in Mgmt. Recipient Youth Motivation award Foothill Edn. Com., Glendora, 1987. Mem. NAFE, Colo. Assn. Nonprofit Orgns., Pub. Rels. Soc. Am., Soc. Nat. Assn. Publs., Am. Soc. Assn. Execs., Nat. Assn. Membership Dirs., Profl. Communicators Assn. So. Calif., Profl. Conf. Mgrs. Assn., West End Bus. Assn. (pres. 1997-99), Western Assn. Chamber Execs. (Spl. merit award for mag. pub. 1995), Profl. Conv. Mgrs. Assn., Bus. Network Internat., eWomen Network, Kiwanis (sec. 1989-90, pres. West Covina 1990-91, Kiwanian of Yr. 1989), Rotary. Avocations: reading, walking, painting, gardening, birdwatching. Office: 719 Day Spa and Salon # 205 5969 N Academy Blvd Colorado Springs CO 80918 Office Phone: 719-535-9300. Business E-Mail: nhawley@719dayspa.com.

HAWLEY, PHILIP METSCHAN, retired retail executive, management consultant; b. Portland, Oreg., July 29, 1925; s. Willard P. and Dorothy (Metschan) H.; m. Mary Catherine Follen, May 31, 1947; children: Diane (Mrs. Robert Bruce Johnson), Willard, Philip Metschan Jr., John, Victor, Edward, Erin (Mrs. Kevin Przybocki), George. BS, U. Calif., Berkeley, 1946; grad. advanced mgmt. program, Harvard U., 1967. With Carter Hawley Hale Stores, Inc., LA, 1958-93, pres., 1972-83, chief exec. officer, 1977-93, chmn., 1983-93. Bd. dirs. Weyerhaeuser Co. Trustee Calif. Inst. Tech., U. Notre Dame; chmn. L.A. Energy Conservation Com., 1973-74. Decorated hon. comdr. Order Brit. Empire, knight comdr. Star Solidarity Republic Italy; recipient Award of Merit L.A. Jr. C. of C., 1974, Coro Pub. Affairs award, 1978, Medallion award Coll. William and Mary, 1983, Award of Excellence Sch. Bus. Adminstrn. U. So. Calif., 1987, Bus. Statesman of Yr. award Harvard Bus. Sch., 1989, 15th ann. Whitney M. Young Jr. award L.S. Urban League, 1988; named Calif. Industrialist of Yr. Calif. Mus. Sci. and Industry, 1975. Mem. Calif. Retailers Assn. (chmn. 1993-95, dir.), Beach Club, Calif. Club, L.A. Country Club, Bohemian Club, Pacific-Union Club, Newport Harbor Yacht Club, Multnomah Club, Links Club, Phi Beta Kappa, Beta Alpha Psi, Beta Gamma Sigma. Office: 800 W 6th St Ste 920 Los Angeles CA 90017

HAWLEY, PHILLIP EUGENE, investment banker; b. Tecumseh, Mich., Dec. 9, 1940; s. Paul P. and Vadah Arlene (Lawhead) H.; m. Linda Darlene Miller, Feb. 14, 1957; children: Pierre Lee, Paul Marvin, Danny Parke, David Eugene, Martin Edward. Student mgmt., Yale U., New Haven, Conn., 1959—63; BSBA, Northwestern Coll., Tulsa, 1980. With Credit Bur. Ft. Myers Inc., Fla., 1956—; chmn. bd. dirs., regional mgr. Credit Bur. Internat. Corp., Ft. Myers, 1993—; pvt. investigator Transworld Investigators, Inc., 1964, now v.p.; mgr., founder real estate co. Gold Coast Devel. Corp., 1965, pres., Phillip Hawley Investment Banking Co. Bd. dirs. Caribbean Industries Internat. Corp., Future Investment Corp. Author: Law and It's Alternative to Chaos, 1958, The Happiest Man in the World, 1970, The Best Buys in Fort Myers, 1982. Mem. Praise Tabernacle Cmty. Ch. Named Outstanding Individual, Fla. Fedn. Young Reps., 1971; recipient Presdl. Sports award, 1979. Mem. Am. Collectors Assn. (scholar degree Collection Bus. Acad. 1994, fellow degree 1996), Fla. Collectors Assn. (Outstanding Spkr. 1967), Assn. Credit Burs. Am., Med.-Dental Hosp. Burs. Am., Fla. Assn. Mortgage Brokers, Fla. Assn. Pvt. Investigators, Am. Numismatic Assn., Gideons Internat., Collier-Lee Wrestling Assn. (cofounder, bd. dirs. 1974—). Office: Internat Collection Svc Inc 255 Tamiami Trl S Nokomis FL 34275-3136 Home: 13391 Shire Ln Fort Myers FL 33912-0375 Personal E-mail: philhawley@earthlink.net.

HAWLEY, RAYMOND GLEN, pathologist; b. Cambridge, Kans., Jan. 13, 1939; s. Pearl Washington and Gladys Laura (Logsdon) H.; m. Phyllis Ann Williams, Aug. 25, 1963; children: Bradford, Anthony, Douglas. BS, Kans. State U., 1961; MD, U. Kans., 1965. Intern Wesley Med. Ctr., Wichita, 1965-66; pathology resident Riverside Meth. Hosp., Columbus, Ohio, 1966-70; pathologist St. Joseph Hosp., Concordia, Kans., 1973-75, St. Joseph Med. Ctr., Wichita, 1975—82, Via Christi Regional Med. Ctr., Wichita, 1983—2000; with Coffeyville (Kans.) Regional Med. Ctr., 2000—, chief of staff, 2004, 2005. Maj. U.S. Army, 1970-73. Fellow Am. Coll. Pathologists; mem. AMA, Am. Soc. Clin. Pathologists, Kans. Soc.

Pathology (sec.-treas. 1989-99, pres. 2004—06). Home: 512 Spruce St Coffeyville KS 67337-4834 E-mail: rhawley@cox.net.

HAWLEY, ROBERT C., JR., pathologist; b. Denver, Mar. 3, 1947; s. Robert C. Hawley, Sr. and Mary E. Hawley; m. Cathy I. Cogan, July 15, 1989. MD, Loma Linda U., Calif., 1977. Diplomate Am. Bd. Pathology. Hematopathologist Henry Ford Hosp., Detroit, 1983—. Assoc. dir. labs. Henry Ford Health Sys., 1983—; cons. in field. Fellow, Am. Cancer Soc., 1979—80. Fellow: Coll. Am. Pathologists; mem.: Alpha Omega Alpha. Office: Henry Ford Hosp 2799 West Grand Blvd Detroit MI 48202 Office Phone: 313-916-1577. Business E-Mail: rhawley1@hfhs.org.

HAWLEY, ROLLIN JAMES, neurologist; s. Rollin James Hawley and Janice Sedgwick Hawley-Kopf; m. Mary Frances Daly, Sept. 17, 1966; children: Rollin James, Mark Sedgwick, Brien Joseph. AB in Biology, Fordham Coll., 1963; MD, Drexel U. Sch. Medicine, 1967. Lic. MD D.C., Ohio, Md., Va., N.C., 1968, diplomate geriatrics Am. Bd. of Internal Medicine, 1976, Am. Bd. of Neurology and Psychiatry, 2002, Am. Acad. of Sleep Medicine, 2002. Intern and resident Georgetown U. Hosp., Washington, 1967—69; neurology resident, neuropathology fellow Cleve. Met. Gen. Hosp., 1971—74; neurology and neurophysiology registrar Inst. Neurol. Scis., Glasgow, Scotland, 1974; chief, neuromuscular sect. DC Veterans Adminstrn. Med. Ctr., Washington, 1974—92; physician muscular dystrophy assn. clinic Georgetown U., Washington, 1974—92; neurology cons. Carilion New River Valley Med. Ctr., Christiansburg, Va., 1992—. Med. dir. Mobile Med. Care (for the indigent), Rockville, Md., 1986—92. Pres. med. ctr. Assembly of Physicians and Dentists, Washington, 1985—92; tchr. Sunday sch. Holy Redeemer and St. Jude's Parishes, Christiansburg, 1976—2006. Capt. US Army Preventive Medicine Corps, 1969—71. Decorated Commendation Medal U.S. Army; recipient award, Okinawa Pub. Health Assn., 1971, awards, Muscular Dystrophy Assn. Am., 1977, award, 1992, 1993, Montgomery County Govt., 1988, 1993; fellow neurology, Nat. Inst. Health, 1971—74. Mem.: Am. Acad. Electrodiagnostic and Neuromuscular Medicine (licentiate), Am. Acad. Neurology (licentiate), AMA (life), Assn. Mil. Surgeons U.S. (life), Kennedy Inst. Ethics (life). Roman Catholic. Avocations: reading, writing, walking, swimming, travel. Office: Neurology Consultant 2900 Lamb Circle Ste 350 Christiansburg VA 24073 Office Phone: 540-731-1677. Office Fax: 540-731-0387.

HAWN, GOLDIE, actress; b. Washington, Nov. 21, 1945; d. Edward Rutledge and Laura (Steinhoff) H.; m. Gus Trinkonis, May 16, 1969 (div. 1976); m. Bill Hudson, July, 1976 (div. 1979); children: Oliver, Kate; 1 child (with Kurt Russell), Wyatt Russell. Student, Am. U.; Ph.D (hon.), Loyola Marymount U., 2004. Co-head (with Kurt Russell, Kate Hudson, Oliver Hudson) Cosmic Entertainment, 2003—. Profl. dancer, 1965; profl. acting debut in Good Morning, World, 1967-68; mem. company TV series Laugh-In, 1968-70; film appearances include: The One and Only Genuine Original Family Band, 1968, Cactus Flower, 1969 (Acad. award best sup. actress, 1969, Golden Globe best sup. actress, 1969), There's A Girl In My Soup, 1970, $ (Dollars), 1971, Butterflies Are Free, 1971, The Sugarland Express, 1974, The Girl from Petrovka, 1974, Shampoo, 1975, The Duchess and the Dirtwater Fox, 1976, Travels with Anita, 1978, Foul Play, 1978, Seems Like Old Times, 1980, Lovers and Liars, 1981, Best Friends, 1982, Swingshift, 1984, Overboard, 1987, Bird on a Wire, 1989, Deceived, 1991, Housesitter, 1992, Death Becomes Her, 1992, Crisscross, 1992, The First Wives Club, 1996, Everyone Says I Love You, 1996, The Out of Towners, 1999, Town and Country, 1999, The Banger Sisters, 2002; actor, exec. prodr. (films) Private Benjamin, 1980, Protocol, 1984, Wildcats, 1986; exec. prodr.(films) My Blue Heaven, 1990, Something to Talk About, 1995; exec. prodr. (TV films) When Billie Beat Bobby, 1991, The Matthew Shepard Story, 2002; exec. prodr., dir. (TV films) Hope, 1997; host TV spl. Pure Goldie, 1970, Goldie Hawn Special, 1978, Goldie and Liza Together, 1980, Goldie and Kids: Listen to Us!, 1982; Author: (memoir) Goldie: A Lotus Grows in the Mud, 2005 (NY Times Bestseller list, 2005). Named Woman of the Year, Hasty Pudding Theatricals, 1999; recipient Women in Film Crystal award, 1997. Office: 9465 Wilshire 6th fl Beverly Hills CA 90212

HAWORTH, DANIEL THOMAS, chemistry professor; b. Fond du Lac, Wis., June 27, 1928; s. Arthur Valentine and Mary Lena (Wattawa) H.; m. Mary Hormuth, Dec. 27, 1952; children: Daniel G., M. Judith, Steven T. BS, U. Wis., Oshkosh, 1950; MS, Marquette U., 1952; student, Oak Ridge Sch. Reactor Tech., 1952; PhD, St. Louis U., 1959. Nuclear chemist Bur. of Ships, Washington, 1952-53; rsch. chemist All-Chalmer Mfg. Co., Milw., 1958-60; instr. chemistry Marquette U., Milw., 1955, from asst. prof. to assoc. prof., 1960-68, prof., 1968—. Vis. prof. chemistry U. Wis.-Milw., 2001—02. Contbr. numerous articles to profl. jours.; patentee in field. Served as cpl. U.S. Army, 1953-55. Recipient Pere Marquette award for tchg. excellence Marquette U., 1971, Nicolos Salgo Outstanding Tchr. award, 1971. Mem. Am. Chem. Soc. (emeritus), N.Y. Acad. Scis., Wis. Acad. Arts/Scis./Letters, Sigma Xi (emeritus). Roman Catholic. Avocation: stamp collecting/philately. Home: 3483 N Frederick Ave Milwaukee WI 53211-2902 Office: Marquette Univ Dept Chemistry PO Box 1881 Milwaukee WI 53201-1881 Home Phone: 414-332-3048; Office Phone: 414-288-3534. Business E-Mail: daniel.haworth@marquette.edu.

HAWORTH, JAMES CHILTON, pediatrics educator; b. Gosforth, Eng., May 29, 1923; emigrated to Can., 1957, naturalized, 1972; s. Walter Norman and Violet Chilton (Dobbile) H.; m. Eleanor Marian Bowser, Oct. 18, 1951; children— Elizabeth Marian, Peter Norman James, Margaret Jean, Anne Ruth. M.B., Ch.B, U. Birmingham, Eng., 1945, MD, 1960. House physician Birmingham Gen. and Children's Hosps., 1946-47; fellow Cin. Children's Hosp., 1949-50; house physician Hosp. for Sick Children, London, 1951; pediatric registrar Alder Hey Children's Hosp., Liverpool, Eng., 1951-52; sr. registrar Sheffield Children's Hosp., 1953-57; pediatrician Winnipeg (Man., Can.) Clinic, 1957-65; asst. prof. dept. pediat. U. Man., Winnipeg, 1965-67, assoc. prof., 1967-70, prof., 1970-94, head dept. pediat., 1979-85, senate mem., 1985-90, prof. human genetics, 1987-94, prof. emeritus, 1994—, sr. scholar dept. biochemistry and med. genetics, 1999—2005. Mem. active staff Health Scis. Centre-Children's, 1957-93; cons. staff St. Boniface Hosp., 1974-93; hon. staff Health Sci. Ctr., 1993—. Contbr. articles to profl. jours. Bd. dirs. Man. Med. Svc. found., 1988—, exec. dir., 1995-2004. Served with Royal Naval Vol. Res., 1947-49. Fellow Royal Coll. Physicians (Can., London), Can. Coll. Med. Geneticists (hon.); mem. Can. Soc. Clin. Investigation, Am. Pediatric Soc., Soc. Pediatric Rsch., Can. Pediatric Soc. Home: 301 Victoria Crescent Winnipeg MB Canada R2M 1X8 Office: Childrens Hosp Dept Pediatrics 678 William Ave Winnipeg MB Canada R3E 0W1

HAWORTH, LAWRENCE LINDLEY, philosophy educator; b. Chgo., Dec. 14, 1926; s. Lawrence Lindley and Ruth Ethyl (Johnson) H.; children: Lawrence Lindley III, Ruth Ellis. BA with highest distinction, Rollins Coll., 1949; MA, U. Ill., 1950, PhD (Univ. fellow), 1952. Asst. prof. U. Ala., 1952-54, asst. dean, 1953-54; asst. prof. Purdue U., 1954-59, assoc. prof., 1959-65; prof. philosophy U. Waterloo, Ont., Can., 1965-96, disting. prof. emeritus Ont., 1996—, dir. Ctr. for Soc., Tech. and Values, 1984-86, chmn. dept. philosophy, asso. dean grad. studies, assoc. dean computing and rsch., 1967-70, 88-89. Author: The Good City, 1963, Decadence and Objectivity, 1977, Autonomy, 1986, Value Assumptions in Risk Assessment, 1991, A Textured Life: Empowerment and Adults with Developmental Disabilities, 1999; contbr. articles to profl. jours. Served with AUS, 1945-46. Purdue U. rsch. fellow, 1956, 59, 64; U. Waterloo rsch. fellow, 1967, 68, 69, 70; Can. Coun. leave fellow, 1971-72; Can. Coun. rsch. grantee, 1973-75, 81-83, 85-87, Social Sci. and Humanities Rsch. Coun. leave fellow, 1985-86, rsch. grantee 1981-84, 85-87, 91—. Fellow Royal Soc. Can.; mem. Canadian Philos. Assn., Phi Beta Kappa. Office: U Waterloo Dept Philosophy Waterloo ON Canada N2L 3G1 Office Phone: 519-888-1211. Personal E-mail: lhaworth@uwaterloo.ca.

HAWORTH, MICHAEL ELLIOTT, JR., aerospace company executive; b. Pitts., Dec. 18, 1928; s. Michael E. and Margarett (Thomas) Haworth; m. Elizabeth Jean Evans, Dec. 20, 1949; children: Michael Elliott III, Jean Evans. Student, U. Ala., 1946-50; BS, Samford U., 1958. Gen. mgr. Haworth Engring. & Mfg. Co., Birmingham, Ala., 1954-56; chief contract negotiator U.S. Army Ordnance, Birmingham, 1956-61; dir. procurement Kennedy Space Center NASA, 1961-67; v.p., sec. Hayes Internat. Corp., Birmingham, 1967-86, pres., chief exec. officer, 1986-88, also bd. dirs.; pvt. investor, 1989-99. Life mem. Bapt. Med. Ctr.-Montclair Aux. With Q.M. Corps, U.S. Army, 1952-54. Mem. Am. Def. Indsl. Assn. (life, chpt. pres. 1969-71, 82-85), Nat. Aerospace Svcs. Assn. (dir. 1971-74, chmn. 1972-73), Coun. Def. and Space Industry Assns. (vice chmn. 1973-74, chmn. 1974-75), Nat. Contract Mgmt. Assn. (bd. dirs. Birmingham area chpt. 1976-78, lifetime cert. profl. contracts mgr.), Birmingham Urban League (dir. 1971-75), Phi Gamma Delta, Country Club of Birmingham. Home: 4805 Mill Springs Cir Birmingham AL 35223-1682

HAWORTH, RANDAL DIGBY, plastic surgeon; b. LA, Sept. 19, 1961; s. William and Annalise Haworth. BA in Biology, U. Calif., Santa Cruz, 1982, BA in Chemistry, 1982; MD, U. So. Calif., LA, 1988. Diplomate bd. cert. Am. Bd. Plastic Surgeons. Resident gen. surgery Cornell N.Y. Hosp., 1988—93; fellow plastic surgery UCLA Med. Ctr., 1993—95; pvt. practice Beverly Hills, Calif., 1995—. Contbr. articles to profl. jours.; contbg. editor: Fitness Mag., Swan Mag.; exhibitions include 2 shows in L.A., 2006. Bd. dirs. Sheba Med. Ctr.; Mem. Pres.'s Cir. The Thalians, Cedars Sinai Med. Ctr., 1999—; Mem. L.A. Mus. Art, Mus. Contempory Art, LA. Named one of Best Surgeons in Am., Rsch. Coun. Am. Mem.: Am. Soc. Plastic Surgeons, Alpha Omega Alpha. Avocations: art, music, skiing. Office: Ste 105 436 N Bedford Dr Beverly Hills CA 90210 Office Phone: 310-273-3000. Personal E-mail: rdhaworth@sbcglobal.net.

HAWORTH, RICHARD G. (DICK HAWORTH), office furniture manufacturer; b. 1942; With Haworth, Inc., Holland, Mich., chm. bd., 1975—. Office: Haworth Inc 1 Haworth Ctr Holland MI 49423-8820

HAWRYLYCZ, MICHAEL, information scientist; PhD in Applied Math. in Combinations, MIT, 1981. Post-doctoral researcher in computer rsch. and applications group Los Alamos Nat. Lab.; dir., informatics, Allen Brain Atlas project Allen Inst. for Brain Sci. Spkr. in field. Co-recipient Rave award-Science, WIRED Mag., 2007. Office: Allen Inst Brain Sci 551 N 34th St Seattle WA 98103

HAWS, ELIZABETH ANNE, psychologist, director; b. Willingboro, NJ, Mar. 30, 1970; d. William Joseph and Mary Ruth (Datko) Haws. BA in Edn. of the Handicapped, Kean U., 1992; MA in Sch. Psychology, Rowan U., 1998, supr. curriculum and instrn., 2000, EdS, 2001, EdD, 2007. Spl. edn. tchr. Willingboro Bd. Edn., 1992—98, peer mediation supr., 1994—95, peer mediation coord., 1996—98, sch. psychologist, 1998—2000, Mt. Laurel (NJ) Bd. Edn., 2005—; supr. Union County ESC, Westfield, NJ, 2000—03; dir. spl. svcs. Eastampton Bd. Edn., NJ, 2003—05; cons. sch. psychologist, 2005—. Mem. crisis response team Burlington County Sch.; mem. Burlington County Red Cross Disaster Relief Team. Mem.: NASP, N.J. Prin. and Supr. Assn., N.J. Assn. Sch. Psychologists, Coun. Exceptional Children (chpt. 461 programming com. 1988—89, pres. 1989—91, treas. 1991—92), Profl. Assn. Dive Instructors, Cara Irish Soc., Alpha Epsilon Lambda, Sigma Beta Chi. Republican. Roman Catholic. Avocations: writing, bicycling, walking, travel, golf, scuba diving. Home: 202 E Union St Burlington NJ 08016-1717 Personal E-mail: lizhaws@aol.com. Business E-Mail: ehaws@mountlaurel.k12.nj.us.

HAWS, ROBERT JOHN, lawyer; b. Highland Park, Ill., Aug. 1, 1947; s. Robert Willim and Ardyth E. (Meintzer) Haws; children: Benjamin Robert, Theodore Matthew. BA, Rutgers U., 1969; JD, Seton Hall U., 1976. Bar: N.J. 1976, U.S. Ct. N.J. 1976, U.S. Supreme Ct. 1986, cert.: (civil trial atty.). Dep. atty. Dep. Atty. Gen. State of N.J., Trenton, 1977—83; pvt. practice Milltown, NJ. Mem.: ATLA, ABA, Middlesex County Bar Assn., N.J. State Bar Assn., N.J. Trial Lawyers Assn. Democrat. Roman Catholic. Avocations: skiing, travel, mountain biking. Office: 86 Washington Ave Milltown NJ 08850 Home: 40 Washington Ave Unit 21 Milltown NJ 08850 Office Phone: 732-246-7000. Business E-Mail: rjhaws@rjhaws.com.

HAWTHORNE, BARBARA L., anthropologist, educator; b. Denver, Colo., Mar. 13, 1949; d. Virgil James Moore and Doris Ann Matteson-Moore; m. H. Douglas Hawthorne, Mar. 9, 1990. MA in Anthropology, Colo. State U., 1995, cert. with hons. in Women's Studies, 2005, PhD with hons. in Edn. and Anthropology, 2005. Prin., owner Moss Bay Design, Inc., Kirkland, Wash., 1985—95; tchr. Lake Wash. Vocat. Sch., Kirkland, 1990—95; prof. U. No. Colo., Greeley, Colo., 2003—. Dir. Kaplan-Hoover Archaeology Preserve, Windsor, Colo., 2003—; prof. Front Range C.C., Ft. Collins, Colo., 2005—06, Aims C.C., Greeley, Colo., 1998—; instr. Lake Wash. VoTech, Kirkland, Wash., 1990—95. Contbr. articles to profl. jours. Named Most Influential Tchr., U. No. Colo., 2006; recipient Disting. Tchg. award, Aims C.C., 2004, 2005, 2006, Excellence in Tchg. award, 2006; Patsy Boyd scholarship, Women's Studies Colo. State U., 2004. Mem.: AAUW (assoc.), Windsor-Severance Hist. Soc. (pres.), High Plains Applied Anthropology Assn., Archaeology Conservancy (assoc.), Colo. Hist. Soc. (assoc.), Visual Anthropology Assn. (assoc.), Am. Anthropology Assn. (assoc.). Avocations: drawing, photography, swimming, nature, bicycling. Home: 401 Locust Street Windsor CO 80550 Office: University of Northern Colorado Greeley CO Home Phone: 970-686-6423. Business E-Mail: barbara.hawthorne@unco.edu.

HAWTHORNE, BRUCE N., lawyer, former telecommunications industry executive; b. Dearborn, Mich., Sept. 21, 1949; BBA with distinction, U. Mich., 1971; MBA, U. Detroit, 1972; JD, Vanderbilt U., 1975. Bar: Ga. 1975. Atty., ptnr. King & Spalding LLP, Atlanta; lead outside counsel Sprint Corp., Overland, Kans., exec. v.p., chief staff officer, 2003—04; exec. v.p., gen. counsel, sec. Electronic Data Systems Corp., Plano, Tex., 2004—05. Mng. editor Vanderbilt Law Rev., 1974-75. Mem. ABA (fed. regulation of securities com., corp., banking and bus. law sect. 1983—), State Bar Ga., Atlanta Bar Assn., Order of the Coif, Beta Gamma Sigma.

HAWTHORNE, MARION FREDERICK, chemistry professor; b. Ft. Scott, Kans., Aug. 24, 1928; s. Fred Elmer and Colleen (Webb) Hawthorne; m. Beverly Dawn Rempe, Oct. 30, 1951 (div. 1976); m. Diana Baker Razzala, Aug. 14, 1977. BA, Pomona Coll., Claremont, Calif., 1949, DSc (hon.), 1974; PhD (AEC fellow), UCLA, 1953; PhD (hon.), Uppsala U., Sweden, 1992. Rsch. assoc. Iowa State Coll., 1953-54; rsch. chemist Rohm & Haas Co., Huntsville, Ala., 1954-56, group leader, 1956-60, lab. head Phila., 1961; prof. chemistry U. Calif., Riverside, 1962-68, UCLA, 1968—98, univ. prof. chemistry, 1998—2006; univ. prof. chemistry emeritus U. Mo., Columbia, 2006—, dir. Internat. Inst. Nano and Molecular Medicine, 2006—. Vis. lectr. Harvard U., 1960, vis. prof., 68; vis. lectr. Queen Mary Coll., U. London, 1963; vis. prof. U. Tex., Austin, 1974; mem. sci. adv. bd. USAF, 1980—86, NRC Bd. Army Sci. and Tech., 1986—90; disting. vis. prof. Ohio State U., 1990; 1st Anton Burg lectr. U. So. Calif., 2004; mem. dir.'s external adv. bd. divsn. M Los Alamos Nat. Lab., N.Mex., 1991—94; lectr. in field. Editor-in-chief: Inorganic Chemistry, 1969—2000, assoc. editor:, 1966—69. Decorated Meritorious Civilian Svc. medal USAF; named Sr. Scientist Alexander von Humboldt Found., Inst. Inorganic Chemistry U. Munich, 1990—96, Centenary lectr., Royal Soc. Chemistry, London, 1998, Lloyd B. Thomas lectr., U. Mo., Columbia, 2007; recipient Chancellors Rsch. award, 1968, Herbert Newby McCoy award, 1972, Am. Chem. Soc. award Inorganic Chemistry, 1973, Glenn T. Seaborg medal, 1997, Tolman Medal award, 1986, Nebr. sect. Am. Chem. Soc. award, 1979, Disting. Svc. Advancement of Inorganic Chemistry award, Am. Chem. Soc., 1988, Disting. Achievements in Boron Sci. award, 1988, Bailar medal, 1991, Polyhedron medal and prize, 1993, Chem. Pioneer award, Am. Inst. Chemists, 1994, Willard Gibbs medal, Am. Chem. Soc., 1994, Internat. award in Polyhedral Borane Chemistry, Internat. Com. on Boron Chemistry, 1996, Basolo medal, Am. Chem. Soc., 2001, King Faisal Internat. Sci. prize, 2003; fellow Sloan Found., 1963—65, Japan Soc. Promotion Sci., 1986, Disting. Vis. scholar, Chinese U. Hong Kong, 2001. Fellow: AAAS; mem.: Nat. Acad. Sci. Bd. Army Sci. and Tech., Internat. Soc. Neutron Capture Therapy for Cancer (mem. exec. com. 1992—2000, pres. 1996—98), Am. Acad. Arts and Scis., US Nat. Acad. Scis. (award in chem. scis. 1997), Göttingen Acad. Scis. (corr.), Aircraft Owners and Pilots Assn. (named Col. Confederate Air Force 1984), Cosmos Club, Sigma Nu, Alpha Chi Sigma, Sigma Xi (Monie A. Ferst award 2003). Home: 1616 Glenbrook Ct Columbia MO 65203-5203 Business E-Mail: hawthornem@health.missouri.edu.

HAWTHORNE, ROY JOHN, retired music educator; b. Cleve., Sept. 26, 1944; s. Clyde Schaefer and Helen Jean Hawthorne; m. Frances Carol Foote, Mar. 6, 1965; children: David Scot, Carol Jean. BS in Edn., Ohio State U., 1966; MA, Case Western Res. U., 1970. Permanent cert. Ohio Dept. of Edn. Music specialist South Euclid-Lyndhurst City Schs., Lyndhurst, Ohio, 1966—95. Choir dir. So. Euclid Hillcrest United Meth. Ch., 1968—86. Arranger (band) Four Scottish Songs, Happy Bros. (Vesili Bratri), Rapid Transit Rag, A Burns Medley; composer: (band compositions) Red Shirt waltz, Prelude, Waltz And Rondo, Karlin polka, Polka Sine Nomine, Bo and John polka, Brittany's Waltz, Ernie's Polka, DTJ polka, Freedom and Justice march, Ohio 200 march, When I Survey the Wondrous Cross, Here Comes the Band. Mem.: NEA (life), Ohio Edn. Association (life; ret. mem.), Phi Mu Alpha Sinfonia (life), Kappa Kappa Psi (life). Avocation: music performance. Home Phone: 440-461-4507.

HAWTHORNE, SARAH BECK, reading educator; b. Macon, Ga. d. James Edward Beck, Sr. and Margaret (Wall) Beck; m. W. Fleming Hawthorne, Jr.; 1 child, Jennifer Smith. BA, Mercer U., 1964; MEd, U. Ga., 1972, EdD, 1985. Tchr. Houston County Schs., Warner Robins, Ga., 1964—66; tchr./ reading specialist Gainesville City Schs., 1970—75; reading specialist Bibb County Schs., Macon, 1975—79, dir. regional assessment ctr., 1980—91; curriculum dir. Wilkinson County Schs., Irwinton, Ga., 1993—96; pres. AlphaSkills, Inc., Jeffersonville, Ga., 1997—. Adj. prof. Mercer U., 1980—89. Author: (tchr. tng. materials) Read with Sarah, Modeled Comprehension Strategies, I Tri Tutoring, Language, Listening and Literacy Learning: Birth to Five. Chairperson downtown devel. authority City of Jeffersonville, 2004—05; mem. Macon Jr. Womans Club; counselor Stake Relief Soc.; primary pres. LDS Ch., Macon; mem. Macon Arts Alliance. Named an Outstanding Young Women of Am., 1978; recipient Tchr. of the Yr., Runner Up, Ga. Dept. of Edn., 1975, Reading Tchr. of Yr., Ga. Coun. of Internat. Reading Assn., 1978, Annette P. Hopson Svc. award, 1983. Mem.: Internat. Reading Assn. (com. mem.), Delta Kappa Gamma (v.p.), Phi Delta Kappa (v.p.), Ga. Reading Assn. (pres. 1982—83), Chi Omega. Achievements include development of guided reading program for kindergarten through ninth grade; one-to-one tutoring program for kindgarten through fifth grade; literacy program for children from birth to five years old; Alpha Skills Family Literacy Program. Office: AlphaSkills Inc PO Box 188 Jeffersonville GA 31044 Office Phone: 478-945-3915.

HAWTHORNE, SIR WILLIAM REDE, aerospace and mechanical engineer, educator; b. May 22, 1913; s. William and Elizabeth H.; m. Barbara Runkle, 1939; 1 son, 2 daus. Student, Trinity Coll., Cambridge, MIT. Devel. engr. Babcock & Wilcox Ltd., 1937-39; sci. officer Royal Aircraft Establishment, 1940-44; seconded to Power Jets, 1940-41; with Brit. Air Commn., Washington, 1944; dep. dir. engine rsch. Ministry of Supply, 1945; assoc. prof. mech. engring. MIT, 1946, George Westinghouse prof. mech. engring., 1948-51, Jerome C. Hunsaker prof. aero. engring., 1955-56; master Churchill Coll., Cambridge, 1968-83, now fellow; Hopkinson and ICI prof. applied thermodynamics U. Cambridge, 1951-80, head dept. engring., 1968-73. Chmn. Home Office Sci. Adv. Council, 1967-76, Adv. Council Energy Conservation, 1974-79; dir. Cummins Engine Co., Inc., 1974-86, dir. Dracone Devels. Ltd. Bd. govs. Westminster Sch., 1956-76. Recipient Royal medal Royal Society, 1982, R. Tom Sawyer award ASME, 1992. Fellow AIAA (hon.), ASME (hon.), Royal Soc., Royal Acad. Engring.; mem. NAE (fgn. assoc.), NAS (fgn. assoc.). Office: Churchill Coll Cambridge CB3 0DS England also: 19 Chauncy St Cambridge MA 02138-2549

HAWVER, DENNIS A., psychologist, consultant; s. Carl F. and Frances J. H.; m. Anne M. Augustyn, 1961 (div. Oct. 1974); children: Timothy, Laura, Derek; m. Judith M. Anderson, Jan. 28, 1977. BA, U. Akron, 1964, MA, 1965; PhD, Temple U., Phila., 1964-70. Dir. rsch. Temple U., Phila., 1964-70, instr. Grad. Sch., 1968-70, internal cons., 1964-70; mng. ptnr. Cardall Assocs., Princeton, N.J., 1970-72; nat. program dir. The RHR Inst., NYC, 1972-80; pres. The Hawver Group, NYC and Princeton, 1980—. Pres. The Hawver Group, N.Y.C. and Princeton, 1980-; pres. Princeton chpt. Inst. Mgmt. Cons. Author: How to Improve Your Negotiating Skills, 1983; contbr. to bus. and profl. jours.; developer rsch. and tng. programs; internat. cons. in exec. identification and devel. and bus. negotiations. Chmn. Leadership Devel. Com. of Princeton C. of C. Mem. APA, Soc. Indsl. and Organizational Psychology, Internat. Assn. Applied Psychology, Inst. Mgmt. Cons. (CMC), Soc. Assessment Sys. Practitioners, Internat. Pers. Mgmt. Assn. Assessment Coun. Office: The Hawver Group 21 Park Place W Cranbury NJ 08512-3224 E-mail: hawvergrp@aol.com.

HAXO, FRANCIS THEODORE, marine biologist; b. Grand Forks, ND, Mar. 9, 1921; s. Henry Emile and Florence (Shull) H.; m. Judith Morgan McLaughlin, Apr. 15, 1961; children: John Frederick, Barbara, Philip, Francis Theodore, Aileen. BA, U. N.D., 1941; PhD, Stanford U., 1947. Teaching, research asst. Stanford U., 1941-44, acting instr., 1943; research asst. Calif. Inst. Tech., 1946; research asso. Hopkins Marine Sta., Pacific Grove, Calif., 1946-47; from instr. to asst. prof. plant physiology Johns Hopkins U., 1947-52; mem. faculty U. Calif. Scripps Inst. Oceanography, La Jolla, 1952-88, prof. biology, 1963-88; prof. emeritus, 1988—; chmn. marine biology dept. U. Calif. Scripps Inst. Oceanography, 1960-65, chmn. marine biology research div., 1960-77; instr. marine botany Marine Biol. Lab., Woods Hole, Mass., 1949-52, 70. Vis. faculty botany U. Calif. at Berkeley, 1957, U. Wash. Marine Lab., Friday Harbor, 1963 Abraham Rosenberg fellow Stanford U., 1945. Fellow AAAS, San Diego Zool. Soc.; mem. Am. Soc. Photobiology, Phycological Soc. Am., Western Soc. Naturalists, Internat. Phycological Soc., Phi Beta Kappa, Sigma Xi. Achievements include spl. rsch. photosynthesis, plant pigments, physiology of algae. Home: 6381 Castejon Dr La Jolla CA 92037-6933 Business E-Mail: fhaxo@ucsd.edu.

HAY, AUSTIN (GEORGE A. HAY), actor, artist, musician, writer; b. Johnstown, Pa., Dec. 25, 1915; s. George and Mary Louise (Austin) H. BS, U. Pitts., 1938; postgrad., U. Rochester, 1939; MLitt, U. Pitts., 1948; MA, Columbia U., 1948. Dir. Jr. League hosp. shows, NYC, 1948-53. *As a legacy from his physician and surgeon father, Austin Hay has enjoyed a regimen of lifelong healthfulness. In his youth, he became inspired by two young local figures: an obscure endlessly exuberant, surprisingly skilled, astonishingly agile, indefatigable teacher in his hometown--namely Gene*

Kelly; and a lanky assistant to a prestidigitator in a neighboring town--unknown Princeton student, James Stewart. To a youngster, this exemplified magical adventureland. From such extraordinary influences, a career in theater and movies followed. Through ensuing times, friendships continued with notables in the field, among them, "the most trusted man in America," Walter Cronkite. In a lively saga of effort to broaden horizons and enhance the quality of life, he performs in a variety of disciplines, is productive in different fields of creative endeavor. Being born on Christmas day, he helps nurture in a joyous way a continuing ethic of integrity, and healthful living. Producer, dir. off-Broadway prodns., 1953-55; motion picture casting dir. for Dept. Def. films, Astoria Studios, NY, 1955-70, motion picture producer-dir., US Dept. Transp., Washington, 1973—, Office Presdl. Personnel, The White House, 1993—; group exhbns. of paintings and sculpture include, Lincoln Ctr., NYC, 1965, Parrish Art Mus., Southampton, NY, 1969, Carnegie Inst., 1972, Duncan Galleries, NYC, 1973, Bicentennial Exhbn. Am. Painters, Paris, 1976, Chevy Chase Gallery, 1979, Watergate Gallery, 1981, Le Salon des Nations a Paris, 1983; rep. permanent collections, Met. Mus. Art, NYC, Library Congress, also, pvt. collections; bibliog. reference to works pub. in History of Internat. Art, 1982; author, illustrator: Seven Hops to Australia, 1945, The Moving Image, A Career in Pictures, 1990; Dir.: Bicentennial documentary Highways of History, 1976; dir.: film World Painting in Museum of Modern Art, 1972; Composer: Rhapsody in E Flat for piano and strings, 1950; writer: TV program Nat. Council Chs., 1965; Broadway appearances include: What Every Woman Knows, 1954; original Broadway run of Inherit the Wind, 1955-57; created role of Prof. Fiveash in premiere of The Acrobats, White Barn Theater, Westport, Conn., 1961; feature films include: North by Northwest, 1959, Murder, Inc., 1960, Pretty Boy Floyd, 1960, The Landlord, 1970, Child's Play, 1971, Chekhov's The Bet, 1978, Being There, 1980, No Way Out, 1986, Her Alibi, 1988, Air Force One, 1997, Guarding Tess, 1994, Contact, 1997 The Contender, 2000, Head of State, 2003; TV appearances include Am. Heritage, 1961, Americans-A Portrait in Verses, 1962, Naked City, 1962, US Steel Hour, 1963, Another World, 1965, Edge of Night, 1968, As the World Turns, 1969, Love Is a Many-Splendored Thing, 1972, The Adams Chronicles, 1976, A Woman Named Jackie, 1991; piano soloist in concerts and recitals, 1937; performer Cruise Ship, Europe, 1938; author, illustrator: The Arts Scene; contbr. articles to periodicals. App. time adv. panel, pres.'s coun. Col. William and Mary; mem. World Affairs Coun., Am. Archit. Found.; bd. govs. Home of Pres. James Monroe; trustee Home of Pres. James Monroe; mus. donor turn-of-century doctor's office from estate of surgeon father; With AUS, 1942—46; PTO; bd. dirs. Washington Film Coun. Recipient Loyal Svc. award Jr. League, 1953, St. Bartholomew's Silver Leadership award, 1966, Gold medal Accademia Italia, 1980, Smithsonian Instn. Pictorial award, 1982; Fed. Govt. Honor award in recognition 50 yrs. dedicated svc., 2005, with presdl. commendation; subject of biog. work: Austin Hay, Adventures of a Christmas Child, 1970. Mem. NATAS, AFTRA, SAG, Am. Artists Profl. League, Allied Artists Am., Internat. Bach Soc., Rachmaninoff Soc., Beethoven Soc. (bd. dirs.), Nat. Soc. Arts and Letters (bd. dirs.), Music Libr. Assn., Nat. Symphony Orch. Assn., Actors Equity Assn., Nat. Trust Hist. Preservation, SAR, Nat. Parks and Conservation Assn., Shakespeare Oxford Soc., St. Andrew's Soc., Victorian Soc. (bd. dirs.), Cambria County Hist. Soc., Am. Philatelic Soc., Am. Mus. Moving Image, Jimmy Stewart Mus. (Indiana, Pa.), English Speaking Union (bd. dirs.), Nat. Arts Club (NYC), Players Club (NYC), Nat. Travel Club, Columbia U. Club, Nat. Press Club, Arts Club of Washington, Cosmos Club, Classic Car Club Am., Nat. Naval Med. Command, Sigma Chi, Phi Mu Alpha Office Phone: 202-366-9127.

HAY, DENNIS LEE, lawyer; b. LA, Feb. 18, 1958; s. Frank Henry, Jr. and Kyoko (Sukuya) H.; m. Kerry Lynne Hatfield, Aug. 11, 1984; children: Michelle, Jason, Katheryne. BS in Fin., San Jose State U., 1984; JD, U. Honolulu, 1988. Bar: Calif. 1989. Law clk. Legal Aid Soc. of Alameda Co., Hayward, Calif., 1985-87, Cohn, Becker & Jacquint, Hayward, Calif., 1987, Souza, Coats, McInnis, Mehlhaff & Hay, Tracy, Calif., 1987-89, assoc. counsel atty., 1989-92; ptnr. Mehlhaff & Hay, Tracy, Calif., 1992—2006; judge pro tem San Joaquin Superior Cts.; hearing officer City of Stockton, 2006—; ptnr. Willbankes, Hay & Wood, 2006—. Prof. law U. Honolulu Law Sch., Modesto, Calif.; hearing officer City of Stockton, 2006-. Mem. Calif. Bar Assn., San Joaquin County Bar Assn. (chairperson bus. litig. sect. com. 1997-98, judicial liaison com. 2002-2003, chmn. judicial liaison com. 2004-05, mem. bd. gov. 2007-). Republican. Presbyterian. Avocations: dog racing, horse back riding, raquetball. Office: 1047 S Tracy Blvd Tracy CA 95376 Office Phone: 209-830-9191. Business E-Mail: dhay@whw-law.com.

HAY, ELIZABETH DEXTER, embryologist, educator; b. St. Augustine, Fla., Apr. 2, 1927; d. Isaac Morris and Lucille Elizabeth (Lynn) H. AB, Smith Coll., 1948; MA (hon.), Harvard U., 1964; ScD (hon.), Smith Coll., 1973, Trinity Coll., 1989; MD, Johns Hopkins U., 1952, LHD (hon.), 1990. Intern in internal medicine Johns Hopkins Hosp., Balt., 1952-53; instr. anatomy Johns Hopkins U. Med. Sch., Balt., 1953-56, asst. prof., 1956-57, Cornell U. Med. Sch., NYC, 1957-60, Harvard Med. Sch., Boston, 1960-64, Louise Foote Pfeiffer assoc. prof., 1964-69, Louise Foote Pfeiffer prof. embryology, 1969—, chmn. dept. anatomy and cellular biology, 1975-93; prof. dept. cell biology, 1993—. Cons. cell biology sect. NIH, 1965-69; mem. adv. coun. Nat. Inst. Gen. Med. Sci., NIH, 1978-81; mem. sci. adv. bd. Whitney Marine Lab., U. Fla., 1982-86; mem. adv. coun. Johns Hopkins Sch. Medicine, 1982-96; chairperson bd. sci. counselors Nat. Inst. Dental Rsch., NIH, 1984-86; mem. bd. sci. counselors Nat. Inst. Environ. Health Sci., NIH, 1990-93. Author: Regeneration, 1966; (with J.P. Revel) Fine Structure of the Developing Avian Cornea, 1969; editor: Cell Biology of Extracellular Matrix, 1981, 2d edit., 1991; editor-in-chief Developmental Biology Jour., 1971-75; contbr. articles to profl. jours. Mem. Scientists Task Force of Congressman Barney Frank, Massach, 1982-92. Recipient Disting. Achievement award N.Y. Hosp.-Cornell Med. Ctrl. Alumni Coun., 1985, award for vision rsch. Alcon, 1988, Excellence in Sci. award Fedn. Am. Socs. Exptl. Biology. Mem. Soc. Devel. Biology (pres. 1973-74, E.G. Conklin award 1997), Am. Soc. Cell Biology (pres. 1976-77, legis. alert com. 1982—, E.B. Wilson award 1989, chair 40th anniversary 2000), Am. Assn. Anatomists (pres. 1981-82, legis. alert com. 1982—, Centennial award 1987, Henry Gray award 1992), Am. Acad. Arts and Scis., Johns Hopkins Soc. Scholars, Nat. Acad. Sci., Inst. Medicine, Internat. Soc. Devel. Biologists (exec. bd. 1977, keynote spkr. 1st Australian EMT conf. 2003), Boston Mycol. Club. Home: 14 Aberdeen Rd Weston MA 02493-1733 Office: Harvard Med Sch Dept Cell Biology 220 Longwood Ave Boston MA 02115-5701 Home Phone: 781-899-8668; Office Phone: 617-432-1651. Business E-Mail: ehay@hms.harvard.edu.

HAY, GEORGE ALAN, law and economics educator; b. NYC, Feb. 4, 1942; s. George N. and Marjorie H. (Prote) H. BS, Le Moyne Coll., 1963; MA, Northwestern U., 1967, PhD, 1969. From asst. to assoc. prof. econs. Yale U., New Haven, 1967-74; dir. econs. antitrust div. U.S. Dept. Justice, Washington, 1973-79; prof. law and econs. Cornell U., Ithaca, N.Y., 1979-92, Edward Cornell prof. law, prof. econs., 1992—. Vis. prof. law U. Sydney, 1992, vis. fellow Balliol Coll., Oxford, 2001. Contbr. articles on antitrust to profl. jours. Fulbright scholar Oxford U., 1984-85. Mem. ABA, Am. Econ. Assn., Assn. Am. Law Schs. (chmn. antitrust sect. 1985-87). Office: Cornell Law Sch 214 Myron Taylor Hall Ithaca NY 14853-4901

HAY, HOWARD CLINTON, lawyer; b. Portland, Maine, Apr. 16, 1944; s. Willis and Ruth (Clark) H.; m. Carol Anne Newsome, Dec. 21, 1968; children: Mark, David, Scott. AB (with distinction), Duke U., 1966; JD magna cum laude, U. Mich., 1969. Bar: U.S. Supreme Ct. 1977, Calif. 1970. Law clerk U.S. Ct. Appeals, Boston, 1970; atty. NLRB; ptnr. Paul, Hastings, Janofsky & Walker, Costa Mesa, Calif., 1971—. Program chmn. Certificate in Employee Rels. Law; instr. U. S.C. Grad. Sch. Bus. Editor Mich. Law Review; contbr. articles to profl. jours. Mem. State Bar Calif. (exec. com. labor and employment sect.), Calif. Bar Assn. Office: Paul Hastings Janofsky & Walker 695 Town Center Dr Fl 17 Costa Mesa CA 92626-1924 Office Phone: 714-668-6266. E-mail: howardhay@paulhastings.com.

HAY, JESS THOMAS, retired finance company executive; b. Forney, Tex., Jan. 22, 1931; s. George and Myrtle Hay; m. Betty Jo Peacock, 1951; children: Deborah Hay Spradley, Patricia Hay. BBA, So. Meth. U., 1953, JD magna cum laude, 1955. Bar: Tex. Assoc. Locke, Purnell, Boren, Laney & Neely, 1955-61, partner, 1961-65; pres., chief exec. officer Lomas Fin. Corp., Dallas, 1965-69, chmn. bd., chief exec. officer, 1969-94; chmn. bd., chief exec. officer, trustee Lomas & Nettleton Mortgage Investors, 1969-92; chmn., CEO Capstead Mortgage Corp. (formerly Lomas Mortgage Corp.), 1985-91. Chmn. HCB Enterprises Inc, 1996-2007; bd. dirs. Trinity Industries, Inc., Viad Corp., Money Gram Internat.; former bd. dirs. Exxon Corp., SBC Comm., M Corp., Republic Fin. Svcs., Allied Fin. Co. Former mem. Dem. Nat. Com., also former nat. fin. chmn.; former chmn. bd. regents U. Tex. Sys.; former mem. Dallas Citizens Coun., Dallas Assembly; mem. Greater Dallas Planning Coun.; mem. WWII Meml. Adv. Bd.; bd. dirs. Tex. Rsch. League, North Tex. Food Bank, Child Care Partnership Dallas, Dallas County Hist. Found.; chmn. bd. Tex. Found. for Higher Edn.; trustee Southwestern Med. Found. Recipient Disting. Service award Assn. Governing Bds. of Univs. and Colls., 1987, Disting. Alumnus award So. Meth. U., Santa Rosa award, U. Tex. Austin, 1991. Mem. ABA, Dallas Bar Assn., Tex. Bar Assn., Am. Judicature Soc., Newcomen Soc. N.Am., U.S. C. of C. Methodist. Home: 7236 Lupton Cir Dallas TX 75225-1737 Office: 7236 Lupton Cir Dallas TX 75225-1737 Home Phone: 214-368-4059.

HAY, JOHN LEONARD, lawyer; b. Lawrence, Mass., Oct. 6, 1940; s. Charles Cable and Henrietta Dudley (Wise) H.; m. Ruth Murphy, Mar. 16, 1997; 1 child, Ian. AB with distinction, Stanford U., Calif., 1961; JD, U. Colo., 1964. Bar: Colo. 1964, Ariz. 1965, DC 1971. Assoc. Lewis and Roca, Phoenix, 1964-69, ptnr., 1969-82, Fannin, Terry & Hay, Phoenix, 1982-87, Allen, Kimerer & LaVelle, Phoenix, 1987-94, Gust Rosenfeld, Phoenix, 1994—; judge pro tem Ariz. Ct. Appeals, Phoenix, 1999—2000. Bd. dirs. Ariz. Life and Disability Ins. Guaranty Fund, 1984-95, chmn., 1993-95. Co-author: Arizona Corporate Practice, 1996, Representing Franchisees, 1996. Mem. Dem. Precinct Com., 1966-78, Ariz. State Dem. Com., 1968-78; chmn. Dem. Legis. Dist., 1971-74; mem. Maricopa County Dem. Cen. Com., 1971-74; bd. dirs. ACLU, 1973-78; bd. dirs. Community Legal Svcs., 1983-89, pres., 1987-88; bd. dirs. Ariz. Club, 1994-96; mem. Ariz. Town Hall, 2006-; mem. law alumni bd. U. Colo., 2007-. Mem. ABA, Ariz. Bar Assn., Maricopa County Bar Assn. (bd. dirs. 1972-85), Assn. Life Ins. Counsel, Ariz. Licensors and Franchisors Assn. (bd. dirs. 1985—, pres. 1988-89), Ariz. Civil Liberties Union (bd. dirs. 1967-84, 95-2002, pres. 1973-77, 97-2000, Disting. Citizen award 1979), Phoenix C. of C. (chmn. arts and culture task force 1997-99). Home: 201 E Hayward Ave Phoenix AZ 85020-4037 Office: Gust Rosenfeld 201 E Washington St Ste 800 Phoenix AZ 85004- Office Phone: 602-257-7468. Personal E-mail: johnlhay@cox.net. Business E-Mail: jhay@gustlaw.com.

HAY, LEROY E., school system administrator; BA in Secondary English Edn., SUNY, Cortland, 1966; MA in Theatre, U. Conn., 1971, 6th-yr. cert. in adminstrn., 1977, PhD in Secondary Edn., 1978. Tchr. English, Marcellus (N.Y.) High Sch., 1966-68, Manchester (Conn.) High Sch., 1968-89, chmn. dept., 1983-89, interim. vice prin., 1988-89; asst. supt. schs. East Lyme (Conn.) Pub. Schs., 1989-92, acting supt., 1990; supt. schs. Windsor Locks (Conn.) Pub. Schs., 1992-93; asst. supt. schs. Wallingford (Conn.) Pub. Schs., 1993—2003; founding faculty mem. MS program in edn. innovation and tech. Walden U., 1994—; pres. ASCD, Alexandria, Va., 2000—01; dir. Conn. alt. rte. to cert. program Dept. Higher Edn., Hartford, Conn., 2003—. Adj. instr. Boston Coll., 1987—, U. Conn., Sacred Heart U., Bridgeport, Conn., Manchester C.C. cons. on English teaching Granby (Conn.) Pub. Schs., 1988; mem. English adv. bd. Conn. Dept. Edn., 1987-90; mem. adv. bd. Conn. Inst. for Tchr. Evaluation, 1987-89; mem. Presdl. Scholars Commn., 1983-84; grant reviewer U.S. Dept. Edn.; mem. nat. adv. bd. Project 6 Found., Nat. Ctr. for Innovative Ednl. Media., 1987-93. Author: (with Richard Zboray) Complete Communication Skills, 1992; contbg. author: The Shape of Things to Come: Employment and Higher Education to the Year 2000, 1988; editor: (with Arthur Roberts) Curriculum For the New Millennium, 1988, 2d edit., 1994; mem. editorial adv. bd. Edn. Digest, 1984-86; contbr. articles to profl. publs. Mem. Conn. Gov.'s Commn. on Equity and Excellence in Edn., 1984-85, Congl. Task Force on Merit Pay, 1984; judge Birmingham Internat. Ednl. Film Festival, 1984. Named Nat. Tchr. of Yr., 1983, Disting. alumnus SUNY at Cortland and U. Conn. Mem. ASCD (bd. dirs. 1990—, exec. coun. 1996-99, pres.-elect 1999—), nat. conv. adv. com. 1990-92), Conn. ASCD (bd. dirs. 1988-90, v.p. 1990-92, pres. 1992-94), World Future Soc., U. Conn. Alumni Assn., Phi Delta Kappa. Home: 33 Risley Rd Vernon Rockville CT 06066-5924 Office: Dept Higher Education 61 Woodland St Hartford CT 06105-2326*

HAY, LEWIS, III, utilities executive; b. 1955; BSEE, Lehigh U., Bethlehem, Pa., 1977; M in Indsl. Adminstrn., Carnegie-Mellon U., Pitts., 1982. Gen. foreman US Steel Corp., Pitts., 1977-80; v.p., mng. ptnr. strategy practice Strategic Planning Assocs., Washington, 1982-91; exec. v.p., CFO US Foodservice Inc., Columbia, Md., 1991-99; pres. FPL Energy, 2000—01; CFO FPL Group Inc., Juno Beach, Fla., 1999—2000, pres., 2001—06, CEO, dir., 2001—, chmn., 2002—; chmn., CEO Fla. Power & Light Co., 2002—. Bd. dirs. Capital One Fin. Corp., Harris Corp.; mem. exec. com. Nuc. Energy Inst. Office: FPL Group Inc 700 Universe Blvd Juno Beach FL 33408-0420*

HAY, PETER HEINRICH, law educator; b. Berlin, Sept. 17, 1935; s. Edward and Margot (Tull) H.; 1 child, Cedric. BA, JD, U. Mich., 1958. Prof. law U. Ill., Champaign, 1963-91, dean Coll. Law, 1979—89; L.Q.C. Lamar prof. law Emory U., Atlanta, 1991—, interim dean, chief exec. and acad. officer, 2001—02. Hon. prof. U. Freiburg, Germany, 1976—; prof. U. Dresden, Germany, 1994-2000. Author: Law of the United States, 2002, 2d edit., 2005, Internationales Privatrecht, 3d edit., 2007; co-author: Conflict of Laws, 4th edit., 2004; contbr. over 70 articles to profl. jours. Recipient Rsch. prize von Humboldt Found., Germany, 1990; Fulbright rsch. prof., 1992; Jean-Monnet prof., Bonn, Germany, 1994. Mem. Am. Law Inst., Am. Acad. Fgn. Law, Internat. Acad. Comparative Law. Office: Emory U Sch Law G523 Gambrell Hall 1301 Clifton Rd Atlanta GA 30322-2770 Office Phone: 404-727-6896. Business E-Mail: phay@law.emory.edu.

HAYAKAWA, KAN-ICHI, retired food scientist; b. Shibukawa, Gumma, Japan, Aug. 12, 1931; arrived in U.S., 1961, naturalized, 1974; s. Chyogoro and Kin (Hayakawa) H.; m. Setsuko Maekawa, Feb. 18, 1967. BS, Tokyo U. Fisheries, 1955; PhD, Rutgers U., 1964. Rsch. fellow Canners' Assn. Japan, 1955—60; asst. prof. food sci. Rutgers U., New Brunswick, NJ, 1964—70, assoc. prof. food sci., 1970—77, prof. food engring., 1977—82, Disting. prof. food engring., 1982—99, prof. emeritus, 1999—. Cons. to food processing cos.; organizer, chmn., participant NSF sponsored U.S.-Japan Coop. Conf., Tokyo, 1979; lectr. Industry R&D Inst. and Nat. Taiwan U., 1982, Wuxi Inst. Light Industry, China, 1986, Tokyo U. Fisheries, 1992. Co-editor: Heat Sterilization of Food, 1983; contbr. articles to books, profl. jours. and encys.; developer new math methods for predicting safety of food processes; found theoretical and exptl. theorems on heat and mass transfer in biol. material with or without strain--stress formation. Rsch. grantee USPHS, 1966-73, Nabisco Found., 1975-76, NSF, 1981-82, travel grantee NSF, 1972, Rutgers Rsch. Found., 1977, rsch. grantee Advanced Food Tech. Ctr., 1985-89, John von Neumann Nat. Supercomputer Ctr., 1989-90, Pitts. Nat. Supercomputer Ctrs., NSF, 1990-97, Cray Rsch. Inc., 1993-95, U.S. Army Natick R & D Ctr., 1992-95, USDA, 1994-98. Fellow Inst. Food Technologists; mem. ASHRAE (life, chmn. tech. com. on thermophys. property values of food 1981-85, mem. com. 1981-96).

HAYASHI, TETSUMARO, retired literature educator, writer, editor; b. Sakaide City, Japan, Mar. 22, 1929; arrived in U.S., 1954, naturalized, 1969; s. Tetsuro and Shieko (Honjyo) Hayashi; m. Akiko Sakuratani, Apr. 14, 1960; 1 child, Richard Hideki. BA, Okayama U., Japan, 1952; MA, U. Fla., 1957; MALS, Kent State U., 1959, PhD, 1968; LHD (hon.), Wilmington Coll., Ohio, 2005. Instr., asst. prof. English and libr. sci. Culver-Stockton Coll. Libr., Canton, Mo., 1959-63; instr. English Kent State U., Ohio, 1965-68; from asst. prof. to assoc. prof. Ball State U., Muncie, Ind., 1968—77, prof., 1977-93; dir. Steinbeck Rsch. Inst., 1981-93; vis. grad. prof. Kwassui Women's Coll., Japan, 1993-96; v.p., grad. prof. English Yasuda Women's U., Hiroshima, Japan, 1996-2001, dir. grad. studies in English, 1997-99; ret., 2001. Sr. editl. cons. Steinbeck Yearbook, 2001—03; sr. cons. Steinbeck Soc. Japan, 1976—, The New Steinbeck Soc. of Am., 2003—, Steinbeck Rev., 2004—; cons. in field; ret. Author: (book) Sketches of American Culture, 1960, John Steinbeck: A Concise Bibliography, 1967, Arthur Miller Criticism, 1969, Robert Greene Criticism, 1971, Shakespeare's Sonnets: A Record of 20th Century Criticism, 1972, Index to Arthur Miller: Criticism, 1976; editor: A Looking Glass for London and England (Thomas Lodge, Robert Greene), An Elizabethan Text, 1970, Steinbeck's Literary Dimension, 1973, Steinbeck's Literary Dimension, Series II, 1991, A Study Guide to Steinbeck: A Handbook of His Major Works, 1974, 1979, 1993, 24 others; editor: (with Richard Astro) Steinbeck: The Man and His Work, 1971, John Steinbeck: A Dictionary of His Fictional Characters, 1976; founder, editor-in-chief: Steinbeck Quar., 1968—93, Steinbeck Monograph Series, 1971—91; contbr. articles to profl. jours. Executor Pruis Award Fund and Burkhardt Award Fund, Ball State U. Found., Muncie, 1978—. Named Disting. English Alumnus, Kent State U., 2002; grantee, Am. Philos. Soc., 1975, 1981, Am. Coun. Learned Socs., 1976, Bernard Boyd Meml. Found., 1986, Lyndon B. Johnson Found., 1987, others; Rotary Internat. Jr. fellow, U. Fla., 1957, Folger Sr. fellow, 1972. Mem.: MLA, Steinbeck Soc. Japan, New Steinbeck Soc. Am., Shakespeare Assn. Am., Am. Lit. Assn. Home: 636 Nurttal St Westfield IN 46074

HAYCOCK, CHRISTINE ELIZABETH, retired medical educator; b. Mt. Vernon, NY, Jan. 7, 1924; d. John B. and Madeline (Sears) H.; m. Sam Moskowitz, July 6, 1958 (dec. Apr. 1997). SB, U. Chgo., 1948; MD, SUNY, Bklyn., 1952; MA in Polit. Sci., Rutgers U., 1981. RN, N.J.; diplomate Am. Bd. Surgery. Intern Walter Reed Army Med. Ctr., Washington, 1952-53; resident in surgery St. Barnabas Med. Ctr., Newark, 1954-58, St. John's Episcopal Hosp., Bklyn., 1958-59; pvt. practice Newark, 1959-68; asst. prof. surgery, N.J. Med. Sch. U. Med. and Dentistry N.J.-N.J. Med. Sch., Newark, 1968-75; assoc. prof. surgery, N.J. Med. Sch. UMDNJ, Newark, 1975-89, prof. clin. surgery, 1989-92; prof. emeritus, 1992—. Chief GYN Svc., VA Hosp., East Orange, NJ Trauma Soc.; pres. Med. Amature Radio Coun., 1981, bd. dirs. (Coun. award 1978); adv. com. NJ Phys. Conditioning of the Police Tng. Commn., 1984-96. Editor: Trauma and Pregnancy, 1985, Sports Medicine for the Athletic Female, 1980; mem. editl. bd. Jour. NJ Med. Soc., 1979-95, The Physician and Sports Medicine, 1975-98, The Main Event, 1987; contbr. articles to profl. jours. Chmn. bd. Essex County chpt. Am. Cancer Soc., West Orange, N.J., 1978-79, bd. mgrs., Livingston, N.J., 1962—, hon. life mem., 1992. With U.S. Army, 1947-86, col. Res. ret. Recipient Outstanding Alumnae award Bloomfield Coll., 1971, Res. Forces Achievement award, 1974, Distinguished Lecturer award Downstate Med. Ctr., 1976, Dr. Frank L. Babbott Meml. award SUNY Alumni Assn., 1982, Pres. Honor citation, N.J. Assn. Phys. Edn. and Health Tchrs., 1982, Commendation medal, 1982, Meritorious Svc. medal, 1986, Presdl. Citation, N.J. Assn. for Health, Phys. Edn. and Recreation, 1984, Med. Bd. Svc. award Newark City Hosp., 1986, Bertha Van Hoosen award Am. Med. Women's Assn., 1997, Alma Dea Morani MD Renaissance Women of Yr. award Found. for History of Women in Medicine, 2004; named to Nutley Hall of Fame, 2005; grantee Abbott Labs, 1981-82. Fellow ACS (hon., life, N.J. com. on trauma 1970-91), Am. Coll. Sports Medicine (trustee 1978-80), Photog. Soc. Am. (chmn. video/motion picture divsn. 1993-95; Silver medal jour. award 2000, 02); mem. AMA, Am. Med. Women's Assn. (bd. dirs. 1976-86, pres. 1980, hosp. assn. com. 1985—, Silver Medallion award 1980), Zonta Internat., Assn. Women Surgeons (treas. 1989-91, chair found. com. 1991-95, sec. 1995-99, Disting. Surgeon award 1990), N.J. Women's Assn. (pres. 1976, treas. 1989-92, Woman of Yr. 1987), Amateur Radio Relay League. Avocations: photography, dog training and showing, sports, collecting elephants, amateur radio. Home: 361 Roseville Ave Newark NJ 07107-1721 Personal E-mail: chrish2@juno.com.

HAYCOCK, KENNETH ROY, academic administrator, educator, consultant; b. Hamilton, Ont., Can., Feb. 15, 1948; s. Bruce Frederick T. and Doris Marion P. (Downham) H.; m. Sheila Tripp, Jan. 28, 1990. BA, U. Western Ont., 1968, diploma in edn., 1969; specialist cert., U. Toronto, Can., 1971; MEd, U. Ottawa, Can., 1973; AMLS, U. Mich., 1974; EdD, Brigham Young U., 1991; MBA, Royal Roads, 2004. Tchr., dept. head Glebe Collegiate Inst., Ottawa, 1969-70, Col. By Secondary Sch., Ottawa, 1970-72; cons. Wellington County Bd. Edn., Guelph, Ont., 1972-76; coord. libr. svcs., supr. instrn. Vancouver (B.C.) Sch. Bd., Canada, 1976-84, acting mgr., elem./secondary edn. Canada, 1984-85, dir. instrn., head program svcs., 1985-89, 91-92; prin. Waverley Elem. Sch., 1989-91; prof. Sch. Libr., Archival and Info. Studies U. B.C., Vancouver, 1992—2005, dir., 1992—2002; prof. Sch. Libr. and Info. Sci., dir. San Jose State U., 2005—. Instr. univs. and colls.; pres. Ken Haycock and Assocs., Inc. Editor Tchr. Libr., 1978-2004; contbr. articles to profl. jours. Trustee Guelph Pub. Libr., 1975-76; trustee West Vancouver Sch. Bd., 1993-99, chair, 1994-97, councilor Dist. of West Vancouver, 1999-2002; trustee West Vancouver Pub. Libr., 1999-2000. Recipient award Beta Phi Mu, 1976, Queen Elizabeth Silver Jubilee medal, 1977. Fellow: Can. Coll. Tchrs.; mem.: ASCD (urban curriculum leaders 1985—92, internat. panel 1990—94), ALA (life; coun. 1995—2003, exec. bd. 1999—2003, coun. 2004—07, Herbert and Virginia White Advocacy award 2001), Coun. for Can. Learning Resources (pres. 1995—98), Internat. Assn. Sch. Librarianship (dir. N.Am. 1993—95, exec. dir. 1995—2000, Ken Haycock Leadership Devel. award named in his honor 2001), B.C. Libr. Assn. (Ken Haycock Student Conf. award named in his honor 1999, Helen Gordon Stewart Outstanding Contbns. award 2005), Assn. for Libr. and Info. Sci. Edn. (sec. coun. dean and dirs. 1993—96, pres. 2005—06), Can. Libr. Assn. (life; pres. 1977—78, Outstanding Svc. award 1991, Ken Haycock award for promoting librarianship named in his honor 2005), Ont. Libr. Assn. (life), B.C. Tchr. Libr. Assn. (Ken Haycock Profl. Devel. award named in his honor 1984, Disting. Svc. award 1989), Can. Sch. Libr. Assn. (pres. 1974—75, Margaret B. Scott award of merit 1979, rsch. award 1984, Disting. Sch. Adminstr. award 1989, rsch. award 1995), Am. Assn. Sch. Librs. (pres. 1997—98, Baker and Taylor Disting. Svc. award 1996), Internat. Fedn. Libr. Assns. and Instns. (sect. on Edn. and Tng. 1997—2005, chair 1999—2001), Phi Delta Kappa (Young Leader in Edn. award). Office: San Jose State U One Washington Sq San Jose CA 95192-0029 Home and Office: 46 W Julian St Ste 229 San Jose CA 95110 Home Phone: 408-293-9791; Office Phone: 408-924-2491. Business E-Mail: khaycock@slis.sjsu.edu.

HAYDEN, CARLA DIANE, library director, educator; d. Bruce Kenard and Colleen (Dowling) Hayden. BA, Roosevelt U., 1973; MA in Libr. and Info. Sci., U. Chgo., 1977, PhD, 1987; LHD (hon.), U. Balt., 2000, Morgan State U., 2001. Children's and young adult libr. Chgo. Pub. Libr., 1973-81;

asst. prof. Sch. Libr. and Info. Sci. U. Pitts.; libr. svcs. coord. Mus. Sci. and Industry, Chgo., 1982-87; mem. faculty Sch. Libr. and Info. Sci., Pitts., 1987-91; 1st dep. commr., chief libr. Chgo. Pub. Libr., 1991-93; exec. dir. Enoch Pratt Free Libr., Balt., 1993—. Adj. prof. U. Md., College Park, 1995—; faculty mem. LI U., NY, 1994, Columbia U., NYC, 1990, 91. Contbr. numerous articles to profl. jours. Bd. dirs. Md. African Am. Mus. Corp., Balt. City Hist. Soc., Balt. Reads, Goucher Coll., Md., Greater Balt. Cultural Alliance, Franklin and Eleanor Roosevelt Inst. and Libr., NYC, Balt., Mercy Hosp. , mem. adv. bd. Women's Ctr., Nat. Aquarium, mem. nat. adv. bd., Balt., PALINET, Sinai Hosp., U. Pitts. Sch. Info. Scis. Named Libr. of Yr. Libr. Jour., 1995, One of Md.'s Top 100 Women Warfield Bus. Record 1996, Daily Record, 2003, Woman of Yr. Ms. mag., 2003; recipient Legacy of Literacy award DuBois Cir., 1996, Torch Bearer award Coalition of 100 Black Women, 1996, Andrew White medal Loyola Coll., 1997, Pres.'s medal Johns Hopkins U., 1998, Pro Urbe award Coll. Notre Dame Md., 2004, Whitney M. Young Jr. award Greater Balt. Urban League, 2004, Leader award YWCA, Balt, 2004, Medal of Distinction Barnard Coll., 2005. Mem.: Md. Libr. Assn., Pub. Libr. Assn., ALA (pres.-elect 2002—03, pres. 2003—04, immediate past pres. 2004—05, chmn. com. on accreditation and spectrum initiative). Office: Enoch Pratt Free Libr 400 Cathedral St Baltimore MD 21201-4401 E-mail: chayden@prattlibrary.org.*

HAYDEN, DOLORES, author, architecture educator; b. NYC, Mar. 15, 1945; d. J. Francis and Katharine (McCabe) H.; m. Peter Horsey Marris, May 18, 1975; 1 child, Laura Hayden Marris. BA, Mt. Holyoke Coll., 1966; diploma in English studies, Cambridge U., Eng., 1967; LHD (hon.), Mt. Holyoke Coll., 1987; MArch, Harvard U., 1972; MA (hon.), Yale U., 1991. Registered architect. Lectr. U. Calif., Berkeley, 1973; assoc. prof. MIT, Cambridge, 1973-79; prof. UCLA, 1979-91, Yale U., New Haven, 1991—. Author: Seven American Utopias, 1976, The Grand Domestic Revolution, 1981, Redesigning the American Dream, 1984 (notable book award ALA, 1984, award for outstanding publ. in urban planning Assn. Collegiate Schs. of Planning 1986), rev. edit., 2002, The Power of Place: Urban Landscapes as Public History, 1995 (Assn. Am. Pubs. award), Playing House, 1998, Line Dance, 2001, Building Suburbia, 2003, A Field Guide to Sprawl, 2004, American Yard, 2004; also articles (Best Feature Article award Jour. Am. Planning Assn. 1994). Fellow Guggenheim Found., 1981, Rockefeller Found., 1980, ACLS/Ford Found., 1989, NEH, Ctr. Advanced Study Behavioral Scis., Stanford, Calif., 2006-07ow; recipient Radcliffe Grad. Soc. medal, 1991, Preservation award L.A. Conservancy, 1986, Vesta award Woman's Bldg., L.A., 1985, Design Rsch. award NEA, The Writer/Emily Dickinson award Poetry Soc. Am., 2001, Boyle Farber award New Eng. Poetry Club, 2004; Feminist Arts scholarship. Mem. Am. Studies Assn., Orgn. Am. Historians, Am. Planning Assn. (Diana Donald award 1987, various awards L.A. and Calif. chpts.), Urban History Assn. (dir. 1991-93), Soc. Am. City and Regional Planning History. Avocations: travel, poetry. Office: Yale Univ Sch Architecture PO Box 208242 180 York St New Haven CT 06520-8242 Office Phone: 203-432-4782. E-mail: dolores.hayden@yale.edu.

HAYDEN, HARROLD HARRISON, communications executive; b. Cin., Jan. 16, 1942; s. Harold Richard and Blanche Marie (Sargent) H. BA, Millikin U., Decatur, Ill., 1964; MA, DePaul U., Chgo., 1970. Dir. mktg. tng. Automatic Electric, Northlake, Ill., 1968-70; dir. Universal Tng. Co., Wilmette, Ill., 1970-80; pres. Performance Achievement Group, Chgo., 1980-85; v.p. Lead Mgmt. Service, Chgo., 1985-90, Qualified Lead Systems, Chicago Heights, Ill., 1990—; pres. Intramark, Chicago Heights, Ill., 1992-94, chmn., 1995-97, 2000—; pres. Pace Airline Svcs. USA, Chgo., 1994—97, 2000—01, v.p. Synergistic Networks, 2001—. Exec dir. Internat. Meetings Inst., 1997-2000. Author: (multimedia package) Successful Telephone Selling, 1979, Santa Fe Railroad Data, 1975, Best Ill. award, 1975; editor Secrets of Successful Telemarketing, 1985. Mem. Ohlmstead Hist. Soc., Riverside, Ill., 1985; bd. dirs. 44th Ward Bus. Com., Chgo,. 1985-86; exec. mgr. British Consortium, 1989-91; bd. dirs. North Park Village, 1993-96; bd. dirs. Ill. Acad. Criminology, 1996-2000, pres., 2002-2003; vols. v.p. Am. Police Ctr. and Mus., 1996—; bd. mem. House Crosses, Inc., 2006—. Recipient award Best Condo Bldg., Northside Real Estate Bd., Chgo., 1985, Book of Honor award World Trade Ctr. Assn., 2001. Mem. Am. Mgmt. Assn. (spkr. 1979-85), Pine Point Ski Club, Simply Singles (CEO). Avocations: sailing, skiing. Office: Intramark 200 E Randolph 22d Fl Chicago IL 60601-6433 Office Phone: 630-993-0460 ext. 3904. Personal E-mail: hhh55@aol.com.

HAYDEN, I. JILL, secondary school educator; d. Vernon Thomas and Vonna May Anderson; m. Phillip G. Hayden, Aug. 8, 1980. BA in Secondary Edn. Math., N.W. Nazarene Coll., 1973. Cert. tchr. Oreg. Tchr. Mountain Home (Idaho) AFB Jr. High, Idaho, 1973—83, Crook County Middle Sch., Prineville, Oreg., 1983—98, The Dalles (Oreg.) Middle Sch., 1998—, math. dept. head, mem. various coms., 1998—; bookkeeper, corp. sec. Juniper Heating, Inc., The Dalles, 2003—. Mem. State Math Content and Assessment Panel, Oreg., 2003—. Coord. PJ's Childrens Ministries, The Dalles, 1984—. Finalist Presdl. Math. and Sci. Tchg. Excellence award, Abimai Sci. Found., 1998; named Tchr. of Yr., Mountain Home Sch. Dist., 1979. Mem.: NEA, Dalles Edn. Assn. (bldg. rep. 1998—2003), Oreg. Coun. Tchrs. Math., Oreg. Math. Tchrs., Nat. Coun. Tchrs. Math., Oreg. Edn. Assn., Fellowship Christian Magicians. Republican. Avocations: balloon creations, walking, camping. Office: The Dalles Middle Sch 1100 E 12th St The Dalles OR 97058 Office Phone: 541-296-4616. Business E-Mail: haydenj@nwasco.k12.or.us.

HAYDEN, JEREMY A., lawyer; b. Henderson, Ky., Apr. 17, 1974; BA, Western Ky. U., 1996; MSBA in Taxation, U. Cin., 2002; JD, U. Ky., 2000. Bar: Ky. 2000, Ohio 2002. Sr. assoc. Frost Brown Todd LLC, Cin. Mem., Planning Com. Southwestern Ohio Tax Inst.; founding bd. mem., gen. counsel Cin. Real Estate Club; co-chair Roebbing Murals Merchandising project, Legacy Grp. Mentor Williams Coll. Bus., Xavier U.; bd. mem., gen. counsel Southbank Fund, 2004—06; co-chair Opening Doors Event, 2005; mem., Fin. Com. Diocesan Children's Home; mem. Northern Ky. Chamber Exec. Roundtable; mem., Adv. Bd. NKU Family Bus. Ctr. Named one of Ohio's Rising Stars, Super Lawyers, 2005, 2006, 40 Under 40, Cin. Bus. Ctr., 2006. Mem.: ABA (Sect. on Taxation), Northern Ky. Bar Assn. (Bus. and Tax Sect.), Ky. Bar Assn., Ohio State Bar Assn., Cin. Bar Assn. (Sect. on Taxation), Phi Delta Phi. Office: Frost Brown Todd LLC 2200 PNC Ctr 201 E Fifth St Cincinnati OH 45202-4182 Office Phone: 513-651-6800. Office Fax: 513-651-6981.

HAYDEN, JOHN OLIN, English literature educator, writer; b. LA, Dec. 18, 1932; s. John Ellsworth and Norah Elizabeth (Bussens) H.; m. Mary Kathleen Garland, Dec. 18, 1965; children— Michael, John, Mark, Ann BA, U. Calif.-Santa Barbara, 1958; MA, Columbia U., 1959, PhD, 1965. Asst. prof. U. Colo., Boulder, 1964-66; assoc. prof. English lit. U. Calif.-Davis, 1966-75, prof. English lit., 1975-94, prof. emeritus, 1994—. Author: Romantic Reviewers, 1969, Polestar of the Ancients, 1979, William Wordsworth and the Mind of Man, 1993, Why the Great Books are Great, 1998; editor: Sir Walter Scott, 1970, Wordsworth: The Poems, 1977, Wordsworth: The Prose, 1988, Wordsworth: Selected Poetry, 1994. Served with USAF, 1951-55 E. J. Noble Found. fellow Columbia U., N.Y.C., 1959-61; fellow NEH, 1971, Am. Council Learned Socs., 1984 Republican. Roman Catholic. Avocation: coin collecting/numismatics. Home: 25199 Carlsbad Ave Davis CA 95616-9434 Office: U Calif English Dept Davis CA 95616 E-mail: johayden@ucdavis.edu.

HAYDEN, JOSEPH A., JR., lawyer; b. Newark, Apr. 2, 1944; s. Joseph A. and Mary (Giblin) H.; m. Donna Heinrich, Aug. 26, 1967; children: Kathryn Elizabeth, Patrick Joseph; m. Katharine Jackson Sweeney, July 19, 1987. BA, Boston Coll., 1966; JD magna cum laude, Rutgers U., 1969. Bar: N.J. 1969, U.S. Dist. Ct. N.J. 1969, U.S. Ct. Appeals 3rd cir. 1975, N.Y. 1981. Law sec. to chief justice N.J. Supreme Ct., Trenton, 1969-70; dep. atty. gen. organized crime and spl. prosecution sect. Div. Criminal Justice, Atty. Gen.'s Office, Trenton, 1970-73; mem. Walder Hayden & Brogan, Roseland N.J. Notes & Comments ed. Rutgers Law Rev. 1968-69; mem. editl. bd. N.J. Law Jour., 1998—. Counsel to Essex County Dems., 1976-80; mem. lawyers adv. comm. U.S. Dist. Ct. N.J.; mem. lawyers adv. comm. U.S. Ct. Appeals 3rd cir. Named to Top 10 of Super Lawyers, 2005, 2007; recipient outstanding contbn. to trial work award, NJ Criminal Def. Attys., 2000, Trial Bar award, Trial Attys. of N.J., 2001, Whipple award for Excellence in Criminal Law, N.J. State Bar, 2004, Prof. Lawyer of the Yr., Criminal Law, N.J. Commn. Professionalism in Law, 2004. Fellow: Am. Bar Found., Am. Coll. Trial Lawyers; mem.: Essex County Bar Assn., Hudson County Bar Assn., Internat. Acad. Trial Attys., Assn. Criminal Def. Lawyers N.J. (trustee 1985—, founder, 1st pres.), N.J. State Bar Assn. (prosecutorial and jud. appointment com. 1992—97, trustee 1998—99), Assn. of Fed. Bar (trustee 1996—99, pres. 2005). Democrat. Avocations: exercise, theater, movies. Office: Walder Hayden & Brogan PA 5 Becker Farm Rd Roseland NJ 07068

HAYDEN, JOSEPH PAGE, JR., finance company executive; b. Cin., Oct. 8, 1929; s. Joseph Page and Amy Dorothy (Weber) H.; m. Lois Taylor, Dec. 29, 1951; children: Joseph Page III, William Taylor, John Weber, Thomas Richard. BS in Bus, Miami U., Oxford, Ohio, 1951; student, U. Cin. Law Sch., 1952; DL (hon.), Miami U., 1986. With mobile home div. Midland-Guardian Co., Cin., 1952-61, v.p., 1954-60; pres., chief exec. officer, dir. Midland Co., Cin., 1961-80, chmn. bd., CEO, dir., 1980-98, chmn. exec. com., bd. dirs., 1998—. Former bd. mem. Firstar Corp. (now U.S. Bank); former Cin. mem. bus. adv. com. Miami U., Oxford, Ohio; former mem. pres.'s council Xavier U., Cin.; former trustee Miami U. Found. Mem. Met. Club (Cin., Ohio), Comml. Club (Ohio), Boca Bay Pass Club (Fla.), Lemon Bay Golf (Fla.), Useppa Island Club (Fla.), Sigma Chi. Clubs: Queen City, Hyde Park Golf and Country, Cincinnati, Ohio. Office: 7000 Midland Blvd Amelia OH 45102-2608

HAYDEN, (JOHN) MICHAEL, state official, former governor; b. Colby, Kans., Mar. 16, 1944; s. Irven Wesley and Ruth (Kelley) H.; m. Patti Ann Rooney, Aug. 26, 1968; children: Chelsi, Anne. BS, Kans. State U., 1966; MS, Ft. Hays State U., 1974. Exec. mgr. Rawlins County Promotional Council, Atwood, Kans., 1973-77; agt. E.C. Mellick Agy., Atwood, 1977—; mem. Kans. Ho. of Reps., 1973—87, spkr., 1983—87; gov. State of Kans., Topeka, 1987—91; sec. Kans. Dept. Wildlife & Parks, Topeka, 2002—; asst. sec. fish, wildlife & parks US Dept. Interior, Washington, 1991—93. Acting chmn. Migratory Bird Commn., 1991—93; mem. N. Am. Wetlands Conservation Coun., 1993—96; pres. Am. Sportfishing Assn. Former pres. U.S. Hwy. 36 Assn. Served to 1st lt. AUS, 1967-70, Vietnam. Recipient Chevron-Times Mirror Conservation award, 1995, Hunting Heritage award, Nat. Wild Turkey Fedn., 1996, 2004. Mem. Am. Legion, VFW, Ducks Unltd., Rotary. Republican. Methodist. Office: Kans Dept Wildlife & Parks 512 SE 25th Ave Pratt KS 67124

HAYDEN, MICHAEL VINCENT, CIA Director, career military officer; b. Pitts., Mar. 17, 1945; s. Harry V. Hayden Jr.; m. Jeanine Carrier; children: Margaret, Michael, Liam. BA in History, Duquesne U., 1967, grad. Res. Officer Tng. Corps, 1967, MA in Am. History, 1969; postgrad., Acad. Instr. Sch., Maxwell AFB, Ala., 1975, Squadron Officer Sch., 1976, Air Command and Staff Coll., 1978, Def. Intelligence Agy., Bolling AFB, DC, 1980, Armed Forces Coll., Norfolk, Va., 1983, Air War Coll., Maxwell AFB, Ala., 1983. Commd. 2d lt. USAF, 1967, advanced through grades to gen., 2005, analyst, briefer Hdqrs. Strategic Air Command Offutt AFB, Nebr., 1970-72, chief intelligence divsn. Hdqrs. 8th Air Force Andersen AFB, Guam, 1972-75; acad. instr., cadet comdt. Res. Officer Tng. Corps St. Michael's Coll., Winooski, Vt., 1975-79; chief intelligence 51st Tactical Fighter Wing USAF, Osan Air Base, South Korea, 1980-82; air attache U.S. Embassy, Sofia, Bulgaria, 1984-86; politico-mil. affairs officer Strategy Divsn. USAF, Washington, 1986-89; dir. for def. policy and arms control NSC, Washington, 1989-91; chief Sec.'s Staff Group Office Sec. Air Force USAF, Washington, 1991-93, dir. intelligence directorate Hdqrs. U.S. European Command Stuttgart, Germany, 1993-95, spl. asst. to comdr. Hdqrs. Air Intelligence Agy. Kelly AFB, Tex., 1995, comdr. Air Intelligence Agy., dir. Joint Command Control, 1996-97; dep. chief of staff UN Command, U.S. Forces Korea, 1997—99; dir. Nat. Security Agy./Ctrl Security Svc., Ft. Meade, Md., 1999—2005; prin. dep. dir. Office Nat. Intelligence, Washington, 2005—06; dir. CIA, 2006—. Decorated Air Force Achievement medal, Def. Disting. Svc. medal, Def. Superior Svc. medal with oak leaf cluster, Legion of Merit, Bronze Star, Meritorious Svc. medal with two oak leaf clusters, Air Force Commendation medal. Office: CIA Office of Dir Washington DC 20505*

HAYDEN, PAUL ALLAN, speech pathology educator, consultant, researcher; b. Williston, ND, Jan. 29, 1949; s. George L. Hayden and Ortense M. Bernier; m. Elaine Margret Stauder, Aug. 19, 1975; children: Dan, Jessica. BA in Speech Pathology summa cum laude, Moorhead State U., Minn., 1971, MS in Speech Pathology, 1972; PhD in Speech Pathology, Purdue U., 1975. Cert. speech pathologist; other mediation St. Olaf Coll., Minn., 2004, family law mediation, 2005, domestic issues, 2005, arbitration, 2005. Prof. communicative disorders dept. U. Wis., River Falls, 1975—. Dept. chmn., 1988-2003; cons. area hosps., Wis., 1980—. Mem. Am. Speech Lang. and Hearing Assn. (presenter confs.), Wis. Speech Lang. and Hearing Assn., Phi Eta Sigma, Phi Kappa Phi. Home Phone: 715-792-5156. Fax: 715-425-3800. Personal E-mail: phayden@redwing.net. E-mail: paul.a.hayden@uwrf.edu.

HAYDEN, TIM, marketing executive; BA in polit. sci., S.W. Tex. U., 1995. Co-founder & pres. GamePlan Mktg. & Events, LLC, Austin, Tex., 2003—. Mem. communication coun. Greater Austin C. of C., 2000—, chair media relations task force, 2004—06, vice-chair comm., 2006—; amb. Capital City African-Am. C. of C., 2003—05; bd. dirs. & exec. com. Meals on Wheels & More, 2003—; chair Ballet Austin Mktg. Coun., 2006—. Recipient Communication Vol. of Yr. award, Greater Austin C. of C., 2005, Austin Under 40 award for Bus./Entrepreneurship, 2006. Mem.: Sigma Phi Epsilon. Office: GamePlan Mktg & Events LLC Ste 207 200 E 6th St Austin TX 78701 Office Phone: 512-275-1336. Office Fax: 512-275-1339. E-mail: info@gpexperience.com.

HAYDEN, WILLIAM ROBERT, lawyer; b. Chgo., May 22, 1947; s. Robert George and Dorothy (Honan) H.; m. Carol Ann Brock, Aug. 12, 1978; 1 child, Nathaniel. BA, Kans. State U., 1969; JD with honors, George Washington U., 1972. Bar: D.C. 73, U.S. Dist. Ct. D.C. 75, U.S. Ct. Appeals (D.C. cir.) 75, Ariz. 78, U.S. Dist. Ct. Ariz. 78, U.S. Ct. Appeals (9th cir.) 79, U.S. Ct. Appeals (10th cir.) 97, U.S. Ct. Appeals (11th cir.) 01, Colo. (U.S. Dist. Ct.) 2002. Mem. gen. counsel's staff NLRB, Washington, 1973-75; assoc. O'Donoghue and O'Donoghue, Washington, 1975-78, Snell and Wilmer, Phoenix, 1978-82, ptnr., 1982—. Contbg. editor: Developing Labor Law, 1974, Employment Discrimination Law, 1989. Mem. ABA (labor and employment law sect.), Nat. Panel, Am. Arbitration Assn. (employment dispute resolution), Ariz. Bar Assn. (exec. com., past chmn. labor and employment law sect. 1984-89, employment civil jury instructions com.), Maricopa County Bar Assn., D.C. Bar Assn., Ariz. C. of C. (employee rels. subcom.). Avocations: tennis, softball, skiing. Office: Snell & Wilmer 1 Arizona Ctr Phoenix AZ 85004 Office Phone: 602-382-6000. Business E-Mail: bhayden@swlaw.com.

HAYDON, MICHAEL, obstetrician, gynecologist; b. Bellflower, Calif. m. Vena Haydon. MD, U. Calif., Irvine, 2000, postgrad., 2004—07. Clin. instr. U. Calif. Irvine Med. Ctr., Orange, 2004—. Mem.: ACOG (jr. fellow chmn. 2006—07). Office: Univ Calif Irvine Med Ctr 101 The City Dr Orange CA 92868 Home Phone: 714-488-6690; Office Phone: 714-456-5967. Personal E-mail: haydon.michael@gmail.com.

HAYEK, CAROLYN JEAN, financial consultant, retired judge; b. Portland, Oreg., Aug. 17, 1948; d. Robert A. and Marion L. (DeKoning) H.; m. Steven M. Rosen, July 21, 1974; children: Jonathan David, Laura Elizabeth. BA in Psychology, Carleton Coll., 1970; JD, U. Chgo., 1973. Bar: Wash. 1973; cert. webmaster Lake Washington Tech. Coll., 2000. Assoc. Jones, Grey & Bayley, Seattle, 1973-77; pvt. practice Federal Way, Wash., 1977-82; judge Federal Way Dist. Ct., 1982-95; ret., 1995. Task force Alternatives for Wash., 1973-75; mem. Wash. State Ecol. Commn., 1975-77; columnist Tacoma News Tribune Hometown Sect., 1995-96; bus. law instr. Lake Washington Tech. Coll., 2000-01; exec. dir. People's Meml. Assn., Seattle, 2002-03; owner Hayek Svcs., 2003-. Bd. dirs. 1st Unitarian Ch., Seattle, 1986-89, vice-chair 1987-88, pres. 1988-89; ch. adminstr. Northlake Unitarian Universalist Ch.; treas. Eastshore Unitarian Universalist Ch. Women's Perspective, 2001-02; den leader Mt. Rainier coun. Boy Scouts Am., 1987-88, scouting coord., 1988-89; bd. dirs. Twin Lakes Elem. Sch. PTA; v.p. Friends of the Libr. Kirkland, 2000-05; mem. City of Kirkland Planning Commn., 2002—, chair, 2005—06; regional liaison Nat. Girls Collaboration Project, 2007—. Recipient Women Helping Women award Fed. Way Soroptimist, 1991, Martin Luther King Day Humanitarian award King County, 1993, Recognition cert. City of Fed. Way Diversity Commn., 1995. Mem.: ABA, AAUW (pres. Federal Way br. 1978—80, chair state level conf. com. 1986—87, pres. Federal Way br. 1990—92, diversity com. 1991—98, state bd. 1995—97, co-pres. Kirkland-Redmond br. 1999—2000, co-v.p. Lake Washington br. 2001—03, Wash. State pres. 2004—06, dir. ESL project), Nat. Assn. Women Judges (dist. bd. dir. 1984—86, chmn. rules com. 1988—89, chmn. bylaws com. 1990—91, nat. bd. dir.), Elected Wash. Women (dir. 1983—87), King County Dist. Ct. Judges Assn. (treas. exec. com. 1990—93, chair and rules com. 1990—94), Wash. State Bar Assn., Wash. Women Lawyers, Plz. on State Owners Assn. (pres. 1997—99, bd. dir. 1997—2000, sec. 1999—2000, webmaster 2000—), Eliot Inst. (bd. dir. 1996—2000, vice chair 1998—99, bd. chair 1999—2000, webmaster 1999—2002), Unitarian Universalist Women's Fedn. (chair bylaws com. 1996), Greater Federal Way C. of C. (dir. 1978—82, sec. 1980—81, v.p. 1981—82), Fed. Way Women's Network (bd. dir. 1984—91, pres. 1985, program co-chair 1989—91, bd. dir. 1995—97, co-editor newsletter), Wash. Women United (bd. dir. 1995—97), Rotary (Sunrise Fed. Way chpt.) (membership com. 1991—96, youth exch. officer 1994—95, comty. svc. chair, bd. dir.). Office Phone: 425-822-2794. Personal E-mail: hayekservices@aol.com.

HAYEK, SALMA, actress; b. Coatzacoalcos, Veracruz, Mexico, Sept. 2, 1968; d. Sami Hayek Domingues and Diana H. CEO Ventanazul, 2007—. Actress: (films) Mi Vida Loca, 1993, Four Rooms, 1995, Desperado, 1995, Fair Game, 1995, From Dusk Til Dawn, 1996, Fled, 1996, Fools Rush In, 1997, Follow Me Home, 1997, Breaking Up, 1997, Sister Diastole, 1997, The Velocity of Gary, 1998, The Faculty, 1998, 54, 1998, Dogma, 1999, Wild Wild West, 1999, No One Writes to the Colonel, 1999, Shiny New Enemies, 2000, Timecode, 2000, Chain of Fools, 2000, Living It Up, 2000, Traffic, 2000, Hotel, 2001, Frida (also prod.), 2002, Spy Kids 3-D: Game Over, 2003, Once Upon a Time in Mexico, 2003, After the Sunset, 2004, Sian Ka'an, 2005, Bandidas, 2006, Ask the Dust, 2006, Lonely Hearts, 2006; actress, prodr. (films) Frida, 2002; actress (TV films) Roadracers, 1994, The Hunchback, 1997, In the Time of the Butterflies, 2001 (also exec. prodr.); dir, sr. exec. prod.: The Maldonado Miracle, 2003; (TV appearances) Un Nuevo amanecer, 1988, Teresa, 1989, Dream On, 1992, Street Justice, 1992, Nurses, 1992, The Sinbad Show, 1993, Roadracers, 1994, El Vuelo del aguila, 1996, The Hunchback, 1997, Action, 1999, Ugly Betty, 2006-07 (also exec. prodr.) Named one of 25 Most Influential Hispanics, Time Mag., 2005. Office: Creative Artists Agy 9830 Wilshire Blvd Beverly Hills CA 90212

HAYES, ALICE BOURKE, academic administrator, biologist, researcher; b. Chgo., Dec. 31, 1937; d. William Joseph and Mary Alice (Cawley) Bourke; m. John J. Hayes, Sept. 2, 1961 (dec. July 1981). BS, Mundelein Coll., Chgo., 1959; MS, U. Ill., 1960; PhD, Northwestern U., Evanston, Ill., 1972; DSc (hon.), Loyola U., Chgo., 1994; HHD (hon.), Fontbonne Coll., St. Louis, 1994; LHD (hon.), Mount St. Mary Coll., 1998; DSc (hon.), St. Louis U., 2002; EdD (hon.), Providence Coll., 2004; DLH (hon.), U. San Francisco, 2006. Rschr. Mcpl. Tb San., Chgo., 1960-62; faculty Loyola U., Chgo., 1962-87, chmn. dept., 1968-77, dean natural scis. divsn., 1977-80, assoc. acad. v.p., 1980-87, v.p. acad. affairs, 1987-89; provost, exec. v.p. St. Louis U., 1989-95; pres. U. San Diego, 1995—2003, pres. emerita, 2003—. Mem. space biology program NASA, 1980—86; mem. adv. panel NSF, 1977—81, Parmly Hearing Inst., 1986—89; del. Bot. Del. to South Africa, 1984, to People's Republic of China, 1988, to USSR, 1990; reviewer Coll. Bd. and Mellon Found. Nat. Hispanic Scholar Awards, 1985—86; bd. dirs. Jack-in-the-Box, ConAgra; mem. Ill. Bd. Higher Edn., 2004. Co-author books; contbr. articles to profl. publs. Campaign mem. Mental Health Assn. Ill., Chgo., 1973-89; trustee Chgo.-No. Ill. divsn. Nat. Multiple Sclerosis Soc., 1981-89, bd. dirs., 1980-88, com. chmn., sec. to bd. dirs., vice chmn. bd. dirs.; trustee Regina Dominican Acad., 1984-89, Civitas Dei Found., 1987-92, Rockhurst Coll., Loyola U., Chgo., San Diego Found.; trustee St. Ignatius Coll. Prep. Sch., bd. dirs., 1984-89, sec., vice chmn.; bd. dirs. Urban League Met. St. Louis, St. Louis Sci. Ctr., 1991-95, Cath. Charities St. Louis, 1992-95, St. Louis County Hist. Soc., 1992-95, Cath. Charities San Diego, 1996—2003, San Diego Hist. Soc., 1996—2003; bd. dirs., trustee Old Globe Theater, 1996—2003. Named to Tchrs.' Hall of Fame Blue Key Soc.; fellow in botany U. Ill., 1959-60; fellow in botany NSF, 1969-71; grantee Am. Orchid Soc., 1967; grantee HEW, 1969, 76; grantee NSF, 1975; grantee NASA, 1980-85. Mem. AAAS, AAUP (corp. rep. 1980-85), Am. Assn. for Higher Edn., Am. Assn. Univ. Adminstrs. (mem. program com. nat. meeting 1988), Am. Soc. Gravitational and Space Biology, Assn. Midwest Coll. Biology Tchrs., Am. Soc. Plant Physiology, Bot. Soc. Am., Am. Inst. Biol. Scis. Acad., Chgo. Network, Soc. Ill. Microbiologists (edn. com. 1969-70, Pasteur award com. 1975, pub. rels. com. 1974, chair speakers' bur. 1974-79), Chgo. Assn. Tech. Socs. (acad. liaison 1982-85, awards com. 1984-89), Am. Coun. on Edn. (corp. rep. higher edn. panel), Ctr. Rsch. Librs. (nominating com. 1986), N.C. Assn. Colls. and Schs. (cons., evaluator Commn. on Higher Edn. 1984-95, commr.-at-large 1988-94), Mo. Women's Forum Club, North Ctrl. Assn. Schs. and Colls., Western Assn. Schs. and Colls., N.W. Assn. Schs. and Colls., Sigma Xi, Delta Sigma Rho, Sigma Delta Epsilon, Phi Beta Kappa, Alpha Sigma Nu. Roman Catholic. Home: 6801 N Loron Chicago IL 60646

HAYES, ANDREW WALLACE, II, consumer products company executive; b. Corning, Ark., Aug. 21, 1939; s. Andrew Wallace and Helen (Latimer) H.; m. Sandra Smith, Dec. 28, 1963; children: Andrew Wallace III, Helen Cathleen, Benjamin Bailey. AB, Emory U., 1961; MS, Auburn U., 1964, PhD, 1967. Diplomate Am. Bd. Toxicology, Am. Bd. Forensic Medicine, Am. Bd. Forensic Examiners; cert. nutrition specialist; Eurotox registered toxicologist. NIH postdoctoral fellow, rsch. assoc. div. toxicology Vanderbilt U. Sch. Med., Nashville, 1966-68; asst. prof. dept. microbiology U. Ala., Tuscaloosa, 1968-71, assoc. prof. dept. microbiology, 1971-75, prof. depts. microbiology and biochemistry, 1975; assoc. prof. dept. pharmacology and toxicology U. Miss. Med. Ctr., Jackson, 1975-76, prof. dept. pharmacology and toxicology, 1976-80, program dir. NIEHS tng. program in environ. toxicology, 1977-80; dir. toxicology rsch. Rohm and Haas Co., Spring House, Pa., 1980-84, dir. regulatory affairs, agrl. chems. (worldwide) Phila., 1984; corp. toxicologist RJR Nabisco Inc., Winston-Salem, NC, 1984; corp. toxicologist, dir. biochem. and biobehavioral rsch., Bowman Gray Tech. Ctr. R.J. Reynolds Tobacco Co., Winston-

Salem, NC, 1984-86, corp. toxicologist, group dir. biochem. and biobehavioral rsch., 1986-87, corp. toxicologist, v.p. biochem. and biobehavioral rsch., 1987-92; prof. Bowman Gray Sch. Medicine Wake Forest U., Winston-Salem, 1992; v.p. corp. product integrity The Gillette Co., Boston, 1993—2002; prin. Gradient Corp., Cambridge, Mass., 2002—03. Vis. sr. scientist biochemistry dept. Cen. Vet. Lab., New Haw, Weybridge, Surrey; Eng., 1977; disting. lectr. U. Calif., 1979; vis. prof. dept. vet. pub. health Tex. A&M U., 1979-91; rsch. prof. dept. physiology and biophysics Sch. Dentistry, Temple U., 1981-84, Phila. Coll. Pharmacy and Sci., 1982-84, dept. medicine and toxicology program Duke U., 1986-2001, dept. pharmacology and toxicology Med. Coll. Va., 1987—, Sch. Vet. Med., Va. Poly. Inst., 1988—, Sch. Pub. Health U. Mass, Armherst, 1994—, dept. pharmacology and toxicology Sch. Medicine, U. Louisville, 1997—; mem. faculty Wayne State U., 1987; vis. scientist Harvard U. Sch. Pub. Health, Boston, 2003—; collaborator Interlab. Collaborative Study for Aflatoxin B1, FDA, 1977, Aflatoxin Check Sample Survey, Internat. Agy. Rsch. on Cancer, 1978; mem. Target Organ Toxicity Conf. Steering Com., 1978-88, Panel on Equivalent Safety Concept of Maritime Hazardous Materials, Nat. Materials Adv. Bd., NAS, 1979-82, Safe Drinking Water Com., Bd. Toxicology and Environ. Health Hazards, NAS, 1979-81, Environ. Health Scis. Rev. Com. NIEHS, 1981-85, sci. program com. Internat. Congress Toxicology, 1982-83, Testing Task Group, CMA, 1981-84, Chem. Systems Lab. Toxin Def. Group Rev. Panel, U.S. Army, 1982, TDB/CIS User Assessment Panel Life Scis. Rsch. Office, FASEB, Bethesda, Md., 1982; alt. del. Internat. Union Toxicology, 1982-83; advisor U.S. Army Med. Command, 1982-84; del. Internat. Union Toxicology, 1984-86; cons. Walter Reed Army Inst. Rsch., 1984-86; mem. selection com. Immunotoxicology Found., 1986, Commn. on Comm., Internat. Union Toxicology, 1986-89, program com. Toxicology Forum, 1986-87, toxicology adv. bd. Raven Press, N.Y.C., 1982-96; mem. external adv. bd. La. Inst. Toxicology, 1996—; bd. dirs. Toxicology Edn. Found., 1997-2001, 2005—, pres., 1998-2000; mem. sci. adv. bd. Inst. In Vitro Scis., 1997-2002; commn. strategic devel. IUTOX, 1997, sec.-gen., 2004—; bd. dirs. Ctrs. for Alternatives to Animal Testing; sci. adv. com. on alternative toxicol. methods NIEHS, 2002-05; mem. sci. expert panel for environ. water monitors U.S. Army, 2004—; sci. adv. panel EPA FIFRA, 2004, 05; trustee Scientists Ctr. for Animal Welfare, 2004—. Author: Mycotoxin Teratogenicity, 1981; editor: Toxicology of the Eye, Ear and Other Special Senses, 1985, Extrapolation of Dosimetric Relationships for Inhaled Particles and Gases, 1989, Prinicples and Methods of Toxicology, 5th edit., 2007, Human and Experimental Toxicology, 1993—, Jour. Toxicology, Cutaneous and Ocular Toxicology, 2001—; co-author: Loomis's Essentials of Toxicology, 4th edit., 1996; co-editor: Target Organ Toxicity Series, 1989—; founding editor Comments of Toxicology, 1986—2003; assoc. editor Regulatory Toxicology and Pharmacology, 1986—, Toxicology and Applied Pharmacology, 1980, editor, 1981-86, mem. editl. bd., 1978-80; mem. editl. bd. Archives Environ. Contamination and Toxicology, 1987-2000, Environ. Toxin Series, 1987-95, Toxicology, 1978-83, Jour. Toxicology and Environ. Health, 1979—, Food and Chem. Toxicology, 1987—; mem. editl. coun. Toxicon, 1980-90; contbr. articles to profl. jours., chpts. to books. Mem. adv. coun. Auburn U., 1987—97; mem. dept. environ. health Harvard Sch. Pub. Health, 1997—; mem. nat. coun. Fla. Coll., 1980—97, bd. dirs., 1998—; trustee Scientists Ctr. for Animal Welfare, 2004—; bd. dirs. Join Hands--The Health and Safety Alliance, 1995—2001; trustee Am. Assn. for Accreditation of Lab. Animal Care, Chgo., 1984—89. Named Exec. of Yr., Winston-Salem chpt. Profl. Secs. Internat., 1989-90; recipient cert. of merit, EPA, 1981, Rsch. Career Devel. award NIH, 1973-78. Fellow Acad. Toxicological Scis. (bd. dirs. 1993-2001), Inst. Biology, Am. Coll. Forensic Examiners; mem. Inst. Toxicology (external adv. bd. 1996—), Soc. Toxicology (co-chmn. tech. com. 1978, chmn. 1978-79, pres. Mid-Atlantic chpt. 1983-84, v.p. mech. sect., 1981-82, 82-83, chmn. animals in rsch. com. 1999-99, bd. dirs. toxicology edn. found. 1996-07, pres. 1998-2000, Merit award 2006), Am. Coll. Toxicology (edn. com. 1996-99, coun. 2003-05, v.p. 2006, pres.-elect 2007), Cosmetic, Toiletry, and Fragrance Assn. (sci. adv. exec. com. 1999-2002), Am. Soc. Pharmacology and Exptl. Therapeutics (chmn. com. on environ. pharmacology 1981-82, coun. sect. toxicology), Internat. Union Toxicology (sec. gen. 2004—), Am. Chem. Soc. (com. on chemistry and pub. affairs task force on TSCA Interagy. Testing Com.'s Preliminary List of Chem. Substances, 1977-80), Am. Soc. for Nutritional Scis., Am. Soc. for Microbiology (environ. microbiology com. 1975-76), Internat. Union Pharmacology (sect. on toxicology), Internat. Soc. Regulatory Toxicology and Pharmacology, Interant. Itamesis Soc. (chair exec. com. 2005—), Sigma Xi. Mem. Ch. of Christ. Avocation: fishing. Office: Harvard Sch Public Health Harvard Univ Boston MA 02142 Office Phone: 978-409-1153. Personal E-mail: awallacehayes@comcast.net.

HAYES, ANGELA MARIW, psychologist; b. Jan. 11, 1979; M, Calif. U. Pa., 2004. Sch. psychologist Morgantown County Bd. Edn., W.Va. Mem.: W.Va. Assn. Sch. Psychologists, Nat. Assn. Sch. Psychologists. Office: Morgantown County Schs 13 S High Morgantown WV 26501

HAYES, ANN CARSON, computer company executive; b. Hamlin, Tex., Apr. 25, 1941; d. Fred Elbert and Nona Faye (Riddle) Carson; m. James Russell Brown, May 7, 1959 (div. July 1973); children: James Allen Brown, Daniel Russell Brown, Robert Anthony Brown, Debra Faye Brown; m. Robert Lee Hayes, Nov. 15, 1975. AAS, Howard Coll., Tex., 1972; student, Regents Coll., NYC, 1986. Lic. ins. agt. Nat. Assn. Self-Employed. Freelance artist, Big Spring, Tex., 1956-76; real estate agt. Century 21, Littleton, Colo., 1976-78, Huntsville, Ala., 1978-79; art dir. Hayes and Co., Splendora, Tex., 1979—; CEO Hayes Enterprises, New Caney, Tex., 2000—. Executor Hayes Tax Svc., New Caney, 1992. Mem.: NAFE. Democrat. Episcopalian. Avocations: sculpting, glass etching. Home and Office: 20152 Split Oak Dr New Caney TX 77357-3565 Personal E-mail: achayes1@yahoo.com.

HAYES, BYRON JACKSON, JR., retired lawyer; b. LA, July 9, 1934; s. Byron Jackson and Caroline Violet (Scott) H.; m. DeAnne Saliba, June 30, 1962; children: Kenneth Byron, Patricia DeAnne. Student, Pomona Coll., 1952-56; BA magna cum laude, Harvard U., LLB cum laude, 1959. Bar: Calif. 1960, U.S. Supreme Ct. 1963. Assoc. McCutchen, Black, Verleger & Shea, LA, 1960-68, ptnr., 1968-89, Baker & Hostetler, 1990-97; ret., 1998. Gov. bd. Fashion Inst. Design & Mdse., 2003—. Trustee LA Urban Found., 1996—, CFO, 1998-00, v.p., CFO, 2000—; trustee LA Ch. Ext. Soc. United Meth. Ch., 1967-77, pres., 1974-77, chancellor ann. conf. Pacific and S.W., 1979-86, dir. 1010 devel. corp., 1993—, v.p., 1995-05, chmn. bd., 2005-06; dir., pres. Pacific and S.W. United Meth. Found., 1978-84; dir., v.p. Padua Hills, Inc., 1999—; dir. South Park Neighborhood Ctr., 2005-06, CEO, 2005-06. Named Layperson of Yr. Pacific and S.W. Ann. Conf., United Meth. Ch., 1981; recipient Bishop's award, 1992, 2000, Disting. Alumni Svc. award Pomona Coll., 2006, Hutchinson Green award 2007. Mem. Am. Coll. Mortgage Attys. (regent 1984-93, pres. 1993-94), Calif. Bar Assn., Los Angeles County Bar Assn. (chmn. real property sect. 1982-83, Outstanding Real Estate Lawyer award 2007), Toluca Lake Property Owners Assn. (sec. 1990-94), Toluca Lake C. of C. (dir. 2001—), Pomona Coll. Alumni Assn. (pres. 1984-85), Pomona Coll. Torchbearers (pres. 2001-2003), Lakeside Golf Club. Office Phone: 818-752-4653. Personal E-mail: bhayes@earthlink.net.

HAYES, CAROL SUE, elementary school educator; b. Martinsburg, W.Va., Oct. 16, 1949; d. John S. and Harriet C. Beard; children: Kevin, Brian, Christopher. BASE, Shepherd U., Shepherdstown, W.Va., 1975; MA, W.Va. U., Morgantown, 1978; ESL, Marshall U., Huntington, W.Va., 2005. Tchr. Berkeley County Bd. Edn., Martinsburg, 1975—. County mem. Staff Devel. Coun., Martinsburg, 1980—. Mem.: BCEA (rep.), NEA. Republican. Roman Catholic. Avocations: photography, reading, dance. Home: 915 S Raleigh St Martinsburg WV 25401 Office: Berkeley County South Middle Sch Bulldog Blvd Martinsburg WV 25401

HAYES, CATHERINE DAVIS, elementary school educator; Grad., RI Sch. Design; M in Tchg., Tufts Univ. Cert. Nat. Bd. Tchg. Standards. Former comml. artist; visual arts tchr. Oakland Beach Elem. Sch., Warwick, RI, 1995—. Vol. RI Sch. for Deaf. Named RI Tchr. of Yr., 2007; recipient Humanitarian award, RI Bus. Volunteers for Arts for work at Hasbro Children's Hosp. Office: Oakland Beach Elem Sch 383 Oakland Beach Ave Warwick RI 02889 E-mail: cdh1@mac.com.*

HAYES, CHARLES FRANKLIN, III, retired museum director; b. Boston, Mar. 6, 1932; m. Nannette J. Rhodes; children: Marna Brewster Dove, Tavia Frances. AB in Anthropology, Archaeology, and Ethnography, Harvard U., 1954; MA in Anthropology, U. Colo., 1958. Rsch. asst. Glen Canyon Archeol. Survey U. Utah., 1957; rsch. asst. Shoshone Indian Land Claims U. Colo., 1957; jr. anthropologist Rochester (N.Y.) Mus. and Sci. Ctr., 1959-61, assoc. curator anthropology, 1961-66, curator anthropology, 1966-79, coord. curator, mus. dir., 1970-79, dir. rsch., 1979-97, also instr. Sch. Sci. and Man; ret., 1997. Asst. lectr. U. Rochester, 1961-69, assoc. lectr., 1970-73; lectr. anthropology St. John Fisher Coll., 1986, 89, rsch. cons. 1997—; cons. Rochester Hist. Soc., 2003 Contbr. 70 publs. on museology and archeology. Trustee Seneca Iroquois Nat. Mus., Salamanca, N.Y., 1977-2002; mem. restoration com. New City Hall, Rochester, 1977. 2nd lt. USAF, 1954-56, USAFR, 1956-67. Fellow N.Y. State Archeol. Assn. (sec. 2 yrs., v.p. 2 yrs., pres. 1967-69, chair publs. 1965-67, editor rschs. and transactions 1966-67, co-editor 1976-77, editor The Bull. 1983—, chmn. awards and fellowships com. 1975-77, sec. Lewis H. Morgan chpt. 2 yrs., pres. 4 yrs., exec. com. 20 yrs.).

HAYES, CLAUDE QUINTEN CHRISTOPHER, research scientist, inventor; b. NYC, Nov. 15, 1945; s. Claude and Celestine (Stanley) H.; m. Solvi Wold, 2002. BA in Chemistry and Geol. Sci., Columbia U., NYC, 1971, postgrad., 1972-73, N.Y. Law Sch., 1973-75; JD, Thomas Jefferson Law Sch., 1978. Cert. community coll. tchr. earth scis., phys. sci., law, Calif. Tech. writer Burroughs Corp., San Diego, 1978-79; instr. phys. scis. Nat. U., San Diego, 1980-81; instr. bus. law, earth scis. Miramar Coll., 1978-82; sr. systems analyst Gen. Dynamics Convair, 1979-80, advanced mfg. technologist, sr. engr., 1980-81; pvt. practice sci. and tech. cons. Calif., 1979—; instr. phys. sci., phys. geography, bus. law San Diego Community Coll. Dist., 1976-82, 85-90; U.S. Dept. Def. contractor Def. Nuclear Agy., Strategic Def. Initiative Agy., USAF, Def. Advance Rsch. Projects Agy., 1986—, U.S. Army, 1991—, USN, 1995-2000. Adj. prof. phys. chemistry San Diego State U., 1986-87; bus. and computer sci. def. rsch. contractor to Maxwell Labs., Honeywell Inc., Naval Ocean Sys. Ctr.; tech. cons. Pizza Hut, Inc., Carts of Colo., Smiths Industries; guest lectr. in endothermics applied to protective devices and clothing; lectr. in field of invention and patent commercial litigation Contbr. articles to profl. jours.; patentee in field. Mem. Am. Chem. Soc., N.Y. Acad. Sci., Am. Inst. Aero. and Astronautics, Princeton Columbia Barnard Club. Avocations: travel, technical, ancient history, art, people. Home and Office: 3737 3rd Ave Apt 308 San Diego CA 92103-4133

HAYES, COLLEEN BALLARD, journalist, photographer, writer; b. Kansas City, Mo. d. Charles Richard and Mary Frances (Ballard) Hayes. BA in English, U. Kans., 1972. Assoc. editor, reporter Johnson County (Kans.) Sun newspapers, 1967—68; editor, writer press releases and pub. rels. Met. Plan Agy., 1968-70; writer speeches, Freedom of Info. and other letters for Pres. U.S., U.S. Senators, U.S. Reps., midwest govs., EPA, 1972—82. Contbr. articles (with photography) Elle Mag., Travel-Holiday, Country Inns Mag., Archtl. Digest publs., Confederate Veteran Mag., The Boston Globe, The Phila. Inquirer, Chgo. Tribune, LA Times, The Balt. Sun, Odyssey, San Francisco Examiner, The Denver Post, Christian Science Monitor, The Detroit News, The Orlando Sentinel, St. Petersburg Times, St. Louis Post Dispatch, The Kansas City Star, San Jose Mercury News, NY Daily News, The Plain Dealer, Chicago Sun-Times, Des Moines Register, Richmond (Va.) Times-Dispatch, Women's Sports and Fitness, The Calgary Herald, others; co-author: Anthology Am. Holidays; author numerous poems; contbr. Nat. Scholastic Mag. (recipient writing award), Mo. Hist. Rev., others; lead in drama prodns. at regional theaters and Topeka Civic Theater; commentator WIBW-TV, performed role of Medea on KTWU Pub. TV, guest interview KCUR-FM, others. Named to, Honorable Order Ky. Cols.; recipient 1st Prize Bethany Coll. Creative Writing award, Key to City of St. Joseph, Mo., City and Regional Tennis awards, numerous awards. Mem. Jackson County Hist. Soc., Quantrill Hist. Soc., Pony Express Hist. Soc., St. Andrew Scottish Soc., Woodside Racquet Club. Avocations: history, international and adventure travel, lap swimming, tennis, golf. Personal E-mail: bcolin77@hotmail.com.

HAYES, CYNTHIA ANN (C.A. HAYES), writer; b. LA, Sept. 11, 1954; d. Lafayette and Verna (O'Gee) H.; 1 child, LaLaunie Charisse. Student, U. Calif., LA, 1972-75. Author: The My Family Collection, 1985, That Lovely Piece of Art, 1997, The Death of Lillie Maroe, 1998, The Night Aunt Ives Went to Sleep, 1999. Donor The Brotherhood Crusade, The Donor's Welfare Plan. Mem. U. Calif. L.A., The Duvall Found. Democrat. Baptist. Avocations: sewing, creating graphic designs, sailing, bicycling, attending concerts and theater.

HAYES, DAUN L., music educator; b. San Diego, Apr. 28, 1964; d. Kenneth Ludwick and Eleanor M. Hyatt; m. Kevin C. Hayes. BS in Music Edn., Western Bapt. Coll., Salem, Oreg., 1993; MusM in Vocal Performance, U. Oreg., Eugene, 1998. Instr. singing Western Bapt. Coll., Salem, Oreg., 1997—99, U. Oreg., Eugene, 1999, Simpson U., Redding, Calif., 2000—, Calif. State U., Chico, 2000—. Singer (soloist): Chico Bach Festival, Carmina Burana, Beethoven Choral Symphony, Mozart Requiem, Poulenc Gloria. Recipient Outstanding Grad. Music Performer award, U. Oreg., 1999, Outstanding Grad. Performance in Voice, 1999; Grad. Tchg. fellow, 1996—98. Mem.: Nat. Assn. Tchrs. of Singing (pres. Sierra North chpt. 2004—). Home Phone: 530-893-0138; Office Phone: 530-898-6127.

HAYES, DAVID JOHN, lawyer; b. Rochester, NY, Oct. 7, 1953; s. John E. and Helen E. (Hendrick) H.; m. Elizabeth Haile, Oct. 2, 1982; children: Katherine, Stephen, Molly. AB summa cum laude, U. Notre Dame, 1975; JD, Stanford U., 1978. Bar: D.C. 1978. Law clk. to hon. William Jones U.S. Dist. Ct. D.C., Washington, 1978-79; assoc. Hogan & Hartson, Washington, 1979-86, ptnr., 1986-90, Latham & Watkins, Washington, 1990—97, ptnr., global chair, environmental land and resources dept., 2001—; dep. sec. US Dept. of Interior, Washington, 1997—2001. Past chmn. bd. dirs. Environ. Law Inst., bd. dir. RESOLVE, Am. Rivers, Natural Heritage Inst., chair; bd. visitors Stanford Law Sch. Contbr. articles to profl. jours. Mem. ABA, Phi Beta Kappa. Office: Latham & Watkins Ste 1000 555 11th St NW Washington DC 20004-1304 Home Phone: 703-528-4119; Office Phone: 202-637-2204. Business E-Mail: david.hayes@lw.com.

HAYES, DAVID JOHN ARTHUR, JR., legal association executive; b. Chgo., July 30, 1929; s. David J.A. and Lucille (Johnson) H.; m. Anne Huston, Feb. 20, 1963; children— David J.A. III, Cary AB, Harvard U., 1952, JD, 1961. Bar: Ill. Trust officer, asst. sec. First Nat. Bank of Evanston, Ill., 1961-63; gen. counsel Ill. State Bar Assn., Chgo., 1963-66; asst. dir. ABA, Chgo., 1966-68, div. dir., 1968-69, asst. exec. dir., 1969-87, v.p., 1987-88, assoc. exec. v.p., 1989-90, sr. assoc. exec. v.p., 1990, exec. dir., 1990-94, exec. dir. emeritus, 1994—; exec. dir. Naval Res. Lawyers Assn., 1971-75; asst. sec. gen. Internat. Bar Assn., 1978-80, 90—, Inter-ABA, 1984—. Contbr. articles to profl. jours. Capt. JAGC, USNR Fellow Am. Bar Found. (life); mem. Ill. State Bar Assn. (ho. of dels. 1972-76), Nat. Orgn. Bar Counsel (pres. 1967), Chgo. Bar Assn., Michigan Shores Club. Home: 908 Pontiac Rd Wilmette IL 60091-1349 Office: ABA 750 N Lake Shore Dr Chicago IL 60611-4403 E-mail: djahayes@aol.com.

HAYES, DAVID MICHAEL, lawyer; b. Syracuse, NY, Dec. 2, 1943; s. James P. and Lillie Anna (Wood) H.; m. Elizabeth S. Tracy, Aug. 26, 1972; children: Timothy T., AnnElizabeth S. AB, Syracuse U., 1965; LLB, U. Va., 1968. Bar: Va. 1968, N.Y. 1969. Assoc. Hiscock & Barclay, Syracuse, 1968-72; asst. gen. counsel Agway Inc., Syracuse, 1972-81, gen. counsel, sec., 1981-87, v.p., gen. counsel, sec., 1987-92, sr. v.p., gen. counsel, sec., 1992-2001; of counsel Bond, Schoeneck & King, Syracuse, 2001—. Adj. prof. law Syracuse U. Coll. Law, 1995—; former chmn. Nat. Coun. of Farmer Coops. Legal Tax and Acctg. Com. Bd. dirs., former pres. Boys and Girls Club of Syracuse; pres. Legal Aid Soc. Mid-NY, Inc., Legal Svcs. of City of NY, Inc. With Army N.G., 1968-74. Mem.: ABA, Va. State Bar, N.Y. State Bar Assn. (ho. dels. 1995—99, exec. com. of antitrust sect. 2001—, ho. dels. 2002—, v.p. 5th dist. 2006—), Onondaga County Bar Assn. (pres. 1998), N.Y. Bar Found., Skaneateles Country Club, Century Club. Democrat. Office: BS&K One Lincoln Ctr Syracuse NY 13202-1355 Office Phone: 315-218-8188. E-mail: dhayes@bsk.com.

HAYES, DAVID RYAN, mathematics professor; b. Raleigh, NC, July 14, 1937; s. Woodrow Rufus and Eleanor Ruth (Crocker) H.; m. Carla Ann Bradshaw, Sept. 2, 1961 (div. 1980); children: Robert, Christopher, Jonathan; m. Irene P. Brown, Nov. 6, 2004. AB, Duke U., 1959, PhD, 1963. Asst. prof. U. Tenn., Knoxville, 1963-65, assoc. prof., 1965-67, U. Mass., Amherst, 1967-72, prof., 1972—2002, Emeritus prof., 2002—. Visiting prof. Oxford (Eng.) U., 1974-75, Harvard U., Cambridge, Mass., 1981, U. Calif., San Diego, 1983, Imperial Coll. of Sci. and Tech., London, 1989. Contbr. numerous articles to profl. jours. NSF postdoctoral fellow Harvard U., 1966-67. Mem. Am. Math. Soc., Math. Assn. Am. Democrat. Personal E-mail: cftheorie@aol.com.

HAYES, DAVID VINCENT, sculptor; b. Hartford, Conn., Mar. 15, 1931; s. David Vincent and Adelaide (Brown) H.; m. Julia Moriarty, June 22, 1957; children: David Matthew, Brian James, Mary Judith, John Mark. AB, U. Notre Dame, 1953; MFA, Ind. U., 1955. Vis. lectr. visual and environ. studies Harvard U., 1972-73; regent U. Hartford, 1992-94. One man shows include Ind. U., 1955, Wesleyan U., Middletown, Conn., 1958, Mus. Modern Art, 1959, Willard Gallery, N.Y.C., 1961-64, 66, 69, 71, U. Notre Dame-Ind. U., 1963, Root Art Center, Clinton, N.Y., 1963, Galerie David Anderson, Paris, France, 1966, Columbus (Ohio) Mus., 1974, Martha Jackson Gallery, N.Y.C., 1974, Everson Mus., Syracuse, N.Y., 1975, DeCordova Mus., Lincoln, Mass., 1977, Springfield (Mass.) Mus., 1978, SUNY, Albany, 1978, Dartmouth Coll., 1979, Amherst Coll., 1979, Nassau County (N.Y.) Mus., 1979, Saratoga Performing Arts Center, Sarasota Springs, N.Y., 1980, Old State House, Hartford, 1981, Shippee Gallery, N.Y.C., 1984, 86, Elaine Benson Gallery, Bridgehampton, N.Y., 1993, Anderson Gallery, Buffalo, 1994, Prudential Ctr., Boston, 1996, U. New Haven, 1997, Orlando City Hall, Boca Raton Mus., 1998, Colgate U., Hamilton, N.Y., 1999, Sasaki Assocs., Watertown, Mass., 2000, Fordham U., New York, 2000, Denise Bibro Gallery, New York, 2000, Sculpture 2000, New London, Conn., Lyric Theatre, Stuart, Fla., 2001, U. Ctrl. Fla., Orlando, 2004, Fla. Internat. U., Miami, 2004, Michner Mus., Doylestown, Pa., 2004, City of Fort Pierce, Fla., 2004, Krasle Art Ctr., St. Joseph, Mich., 2005, City of Erie, Pa., 2005, La. State U. Mus., Baton Rouge, 2006, Longview Mus. Fine Arts, Tex., 2006, Hartwick Coll., Oneonta, NY, Mobile Mus. Art, others; numerous group shows, 1959—; represented in permanent collections Albertus Magnus Coll., New Haven Ct., 2007, City of Syracuse, NY, Everson Mus., Syracuse, 2007, Vero Beach Mus., Fla., 2007, Mus. Modern Art, Guggenheim Mus., Carnegie Inst., Hirshhorn Mus., Washington, U. Notre Dame, Mus. Fine Arts, Houston, Wadsworth Atheneum, Hartford, Addison Gallery Am. Art, Andover, Mass., Currier Gallery Art, Manchester, N.H., Williams Coll., Dartmouth Coll., Harvard U., Colgate U., Hartwood Acres, Pitts., Hartford Pub. Library, Snite Mus., Notre Dame, Ind., Western Mich. U., Kalamazoo, U. Hartford, Hamilton Coll., Clinton, N.Y., Krasle Art Ct., St. Joseph, Mich., Erie Art Mus., others. Regent, U. Hartford, Conn., 1992-96. Recipient Logan medal Art Inst. Chgo., 1960; Fulbright research grantee, 1961; Guggenheim fellow, 1961; grantee Nat. Inst. Arts and Letters, 1965. Mem. Sculptors Guild N.Y. (bd. dirs. 1994-2000). Office Phone: 806-742-9687. E-mail: dvhayes@snet.net.

HAYES, DENNIS COURTLAND, civil rights association executive, lawyer; b. Jan. 29, 1951; BS in Am. History, Ind. U., Indpls., 1973; JD with high honors, Ind. U., 1977. Bar: Ind. 1977, U.S. Dist. Ct. (so. dist.) Ind. 1977. With Law Offices of Brooks and Schwartz, 1976-77; pvt. practice law Indpls., 1977—85; asst. gen. counsel NAACP, Balt., 1985—89, gen. counsel, 1989—, interim pres., CEO, 2005. Bd. dirs. Ind. Black Expo, Community Svcs. Addiction Agy.; asst. dir. Nat. Rsch. Inst., Washington; dir. Guide Right Program; trustee First Bapt. Ch., Indpls., mem. Mass Choir, Male Chorus. Mem. Marion County Bar Assn. (pres. 1980-81), Black Am. Law Student Assn. (pres.), Kappa Alpha Psi. Avocations: swimming, reading, guitar, backgammon. Office: NAACP 4805 Mount Hope Dr Baltimore MD 21215-3297

HAYES, DEWEY, lawyer; b. Ga., July 27, 1923; s. J.C. and Mary (Walsh) H.; m. Margaret Haley, June 16, 1951; children: Dewey Jr., Franklin, Candy. AB, Mercer U., JD, 1949. Bar: Ga. 1949, U.S. Supreme Ct. 1966. Mem. Ga. Ho. of Reps., 1953-56; dist. atty. Waycross Jud. Cir., Ga., 1957-80; sole practice Douglas, Ga., 1980—. Instr. law South Ga. Coll., 1973. Author: You and the Law, 1970, Georgia Warrants, 1972; Miranda, 1973; Search and Seizure, 1973. Mem. Ga. State Crime Commn., 1973-74. Served with U.S. Army, 1942-46, ETO, PTO. Mem. Nat. Dist. Atty.'s Assn., Dist. Attys. Assn. Ga. (pres. 1972), Am. Legion, V.F.W., Douglas Bar Assn. (pres. 1962—), Delta Theta Phi (pres. 1949), Kappa Sigma. Lodges: Elk, Lion, Woodman of World. Methodist. Office: 107 Madison Ave S Douglas GA 31533-5321

HAYES, EDDIE (EDWARD W. HAYES), lawyer; b. 1947; married; 2 children. BA, U. Va.; JD, Columbia Law Sch. Bar: 1973. Asst. dist. atty. homicide bureau Bronx Dist. Atty. Office; ptnr. Sullivan & Cromwell LLP; pvt. practice; co-anchor Both Sides, Court TV, 2000—. Co-author (with Susan Lehman): Mouthpiece: A Life in--and Sometimes Just Outside--the Law, 2006. Office: Court TV 600 Third Ave 3rd Fl New York NY 10016

HAYES, ELVIN ERNEST, retired basketball player; b. Rayville, La., Nov. 17, 1945; Grad., U. Houston, 1968. Basketball player San Diego Rockets, 1968-71, Houston Rockets, 1971-72, 81-83, Balt. Bullets, 1972-74, Capital Bullets, 1973-74, Washington Bullets, 1974-75. Named to Basketball Hall of Fame, 1989, All-NBA 1st Team, 1975, 77, 79, All-NBA 2d Team, 1973, 74, 76, NBA All-Defensive 2d Team, 1974, 75, NBA All-Rookie Team, 1969; record-holder single season most minutes played by rookie, 1969, NBa Finals single-game record most offensive rebounds, 1979; recipient Coll. Player of Yr. sporting News, 1968, All-Am. 1st Team, 1967, 68, All-Am. 2d Team, 1966. Home: 252 Piney Point Rd Houston TX 77024-7325

HAYES, ERNEST M., podiatrist; b. New Orleans, Jan. 21, 1946; s. Ernest M. and Emma Hayes; m. Bonnie Ruth Beigle, Oct. 16, 1970. BA, Calif. State U., Sacramento, 1969; BS, Calif. Coll. Podiat. Medicine, San Francisco, 1971, DPM, 1973. Diplomate Am. Coun. Cert. Podiatric Physicians and Surgeons. Resident in surg. podiatry Beach Cmty. Hosp., Buena Pk., Calif., 1973-74, dir. residency program, 1974-75; pvt. practice

Anaheim, Calif., 1974-80, Yreka, Calif., 1980-95, Machias, Lubec and Calais, Maine, 1995—. Courtesy staff Down East Cmty. Hosp., 1997—2004; sr. clin. instr. So. Calif. Podiatric Med. Ctr., LA, 1975—78; vice chmn. podiatry dept. Good Samaritan Hosp., Anaheim, Calif., 1978—79; mem. med. staff Mercey Med. Ctr., Mt. Shasta, Calif.; CEO, Siskiyou Foot Group, Yreka, 1980—95, Nature's Pace, 1995, Underground Food and Seed, LLC, 1995; pres. Down East Podiatry, Machias, Maine, 1995—. Registrar POSM Horse Registry, 2000; bd. dir. Little Bogus Ranches Home Owners Assn., 1981—83, pres., 1983—84. Fellow: Nat. Coll. Foot Surgeons; mem.: Am. POSM Horse Assn. (trustee 1995), Am. Assn. Podiatric Physicians and Surgeons, 1989. Baptist. Home: PO Box 538 Lubec ME 04652-0538

HAYES, GERALD JOSEPH, lawyer; b. Bronx, NY, July 24, 1950; s. James Joseph and Gladys (Guest) H.; m. Diane Elizabeth Willoughby, July 21, 1984; children: Erin Jane, Thomas Joseph, Cara Elizabeth. BA, U. Mass., 1972; JD, U. Miami, 1978. Bar: NY 1979, U.S. Dist. Ct. (so. dist.) NY 1979. Assoc. Baker & McKenzie, NYC, 1978-85, ptnr., 1985—, mng. ptnr., 1995, 1997, 1999—2006, mem. policy com., 1997—2006, nominating com., 2002—06. Mem. Bus. Coun. for UN, 1990-95. Nat. alumni adv. bd. U. Miami Sch. Law, 1992-1994. Mem. ABA (atomic energy com. pub. utility law sect. 1983, vice chair internat. tort and ins. law com., tort and ins. practice sect. 1997-2006), Assn. Bar City of NY (com. on nuc. tech. and law 1979-82, 85-88, com. on ins. law 1983-84), Nat. Assn. Ins. Commrs. (adv. com. on internat. law 1989-90), Nat. Risk Retention Assn. Office: Baker & McKenzie 1114 Avenue of the Americas New York NY 10036 Office Phone: 212-626-4100. Business E-Mail: gerald.j.hayes@bakernet.com.

HAYES, GREGORY J., corporate financial executive; B econ., Purdue Univ. CPA. Acct. Arthur Andersen; fin. mgmt. positions through v.p. fin. & info. sys. aerospace Sundstrand Corp., 1989—99; v.p., controller United Technologies Corp., Hartford, Conn., 1999—2004, v.p. acctg. & control, 2004—. Office: United Technologies United Technologies Bldg Hartford CT 06101*

HAYES, ISAAC, rhythm and blues singer, composer; b. Covington, Tenn., Aug. 20, 1942; s. Isaac Hayes Sr. and Eula Hayes; m. Mignon Harley (div.); m. Adjowa Hayes, 2005; 1 child, Nana Kwadjo. Formerly singer rhythm and blues recs., Stax Records; albums recorded included Hot Buttered Soul, 1969, Isaac Hayes Movement, 1970, Enterprise, 1970, Black Moses, 1971, Hotbed, 1978, Don't Let Go, 1979, U-Turn, 1986, Love Attack, 1988, Greatest Hit Singles, (with Dionne Warwick) A Man and A Woman, And Once Again, 1980, Lifetime Thing, 1981, Back to Back (with Barry White), Branded, 1995, Raw and Refined; (with Donald Dunn and Al Jackson Jr.), 1995); composer: musical score film Shaft (Grammy and Oscar awards); actor: voice of Jerome 'Chef' McElroy on TV series South Park, 1997-2006, (TV films) Betrayed by Innocence, 1986, Hammer, Slammer, & Slade, 1990, Acting On Impulse, 1993, Hallelujah, 1993, Soul Survivors, 1995, Book of Days, 2003, Anonymous Rex, 2004, (films) Truck Turner, 1974, Tough Guys, 1974, It Seemed Like a Good Idea at the Time, 1975, Escape from New York, 1981, Counterforce, 1987, Dead Aim, 1987, I'm Gonna Git You Sucka, 1988, Guilty as Charged, 1991, Prime Target, 1991, Final Judgement, 1992, Deadly Exposure, 1993, CB4, 1993, Posse, 1993, Robin Hood: Men in Tights, 1993, Oblivion, 1994, It Could Happen to You, 1994, Once Upon a Time.When We Were Colored, 1995, Oblivion 2: Backlash, 1996, Flipper, 1996, Illtown, 1996, Uncle Sam, 1997, Six Ways to Sunday, 1997, Blues Brothers 2000, 1998, Ninth Street, 1999, (voice) South Park: Bigger, Longer & Uncut, 1999, Reindeer Games, 2000, (voice) Dr. Dolittle 2, 2001, Dodge City: A Spaghetto Western, 2004, Dream Warrior, 2004, Return to Sleepaway Camp, 2005, Hustle & Flow, 2005. Named to Rock and Roll Hall of Fame, 2002, Songwriters Hall of Fame, 2005. Office: ILH Entertainment Inc 113 Pavonia Ave # 376 Jersey City NJ 07310

HAYES, JACK IRBY, historian, educator; b. Danville, Va., Aug. 13, 1944; s. Jack Irby and Minnie Lee (Conner) H.; m. Bernadine Joy Arnn, June 5, 1966; children: Emily Wilson, Julia Arnn. BA in History, Hampden-Sydney Coll., 1966; MA in History, Va. Poly. Inst. and State U., 1968; PhD in History, U. S.C., 1972; BS in Bus., Averett Coll., 1987. Dir. continuing edn. U. S.C., Columbia, 1972-74; asst. prof. history Averett Coll., Danville, 1974-77, assoc. prof., 1977-82, prof., 1982-90, W.C. Daniel prof. history and polit. sci., 1990—, chmn. dept. history, 1976—. Adj. prof. grad. sch. Va. Poly. Inst. and State U., Blacksburg, 1977-79; archival cons. Dibrell Bros., Inc., Danville, 1990-91. Author:Dan Daniel and the Persistence of Conservatism in Virginia, 1997, South Carolina and the New Deal, 2001, The Lamp and The Cross: A History of Averett College, 1859-2001, 2004, Jud. ethics adv. com. Commonwealth Va., 1999-2007; bd. dirs. Womack Found., 1982-90, Danville Mus. Fine Arts and History, 1992-98, 2004-06; pres. Hughes Meml. Home, 1999-2006; mem. Danville Dem. Com., 1977-90; elder, trustee First Presbyn. Ch., Danville; past pres. Citizens Bd., Danville Corps., Salvation Army. Grantee Va. Found. for Humanities and Pub. Policy, Charlottesville, 1976-87, Commn. on Bicentennial of U.S. Constn., Washington, 1989, 90; Westmoreland Davis Meml. Found. fellow, 1967-68, Seminar for Hist. Adminstrs. fellow, Colonial Williamsburg, Va., 1967, Louis P. Jones fellow, U. S.C., 1998; named one of Outstanding Young Men of Am., 1977. Mem. So. Hist. Assn., Assn. for Preservation of Va. Antiquities (life), Kiwanis (lt. gov. div. 2 capital dist. 1991-92, pres. Danville club 1989, sec.,1998—), So. Assn. Colls. and Schs. (mem. re-accreditation com. 1986-99), German Club Danville, Danville Golf Club. Avocations: tennis, golf. Home: 245 Linden Dr Danville VA 24541-3523 Office: Averett Coll 420 W Main St Danville VA 24541-3612

HAYES, JANET GRAY, retired management consultant, mayor; b. Rushville, Ind., July 12, 1926; d. John Paul and Lucile (Gray) Frazee; m. Kenneth Hayes, Mar. 20, 1950; children: Lindy, John, Katherine, Megan. AB, Ind. U., 1948; MA magna cum laude, U. Chgo., 1950. Psychiat. caseworker Jewish Family Svc. Agy., Chgo., 1950-52; vol. Denver Crippled Children's Service, 1954-55, Adult and Child Guidance Clinic, San Jose, Calif., 1958-59; mem. San Jose City Coun., 1971-75, vice mayor, 1973-75; mayor San Jose, 1975—82; co-chmn. com. urban econs. U.S. Conf. Mayors, 1976-78, co-chmn. task force on aging, mem. sci. and teck task force, 1976-80, bd. trustees, 1977-82; bd. dirs. League Calif. Cities, 1976-82, mem. property tax reform task force, 1976-82; chmn. State of Calif. Urban Devel. Adv. Com., 1976-77; mem. Calif. Commn. Fair Jud. Practices, 1976-82; client-community relations dir. Q. Tech., Santa Clara, Calif., 1983-85; bus. mgr. Kenneth Hayes MD, Inc., 1985-88; CEO Hayes House, Book Distbr., 1998—. Mem. Dem. Nat. Campaign Com., 1976; mem. Calif. Dem. Commn. Nat. Platform and Policy, 1976; del. Dem. Nat. Conv., 1980; bd. dirs. South San Francisco Bay Dischargers Authority; chmn. Santa Clara County Sanitation Dist.; mem. San Jose/Santa Clara Treatment Plant Adv. Bd.; chmn. Santa Clara Valley Employment and Tng. Bd. (CETA), League to Save Lake Tahoe adv. bd., 2000—; past mem. EPA Aircraft/Airport Noise Task Group; bd. dirs. Calif. Center Rsch. and Edn. in Govt, Alexian Bros. Hosp., 1983-92; bd. dirs., chmn. adv. council Public Tech. Inc.; mem. bd. League to Save Lake Tahoe, 1984-2000; pres. bd. trustees San Jose Mus. Art, 1987-89; founder, adv. bd. Calif. Bus. Bank, 1982-85; polit. advisor Citizens Against Airport Pollution, 2003—. AAUW Edn. Found. grantee. Mem. Assn. Bay Area Govts. (exec. com. 1971-74, regional housing subcom. 1973-74), LWC (pres. San Francisco Bay Area chpt. 1968-70, pres. local chpt. 1966-67), Mortar Bd., Phi Beta Kappa, Kappa Alpha Theta.

HAYES, JIMMY W., media company executive; BA in Acctg., M in Acctg., U. Ga. Audit mgr. Price Waterhouse & Co., Atlanta; acctg. mgr. Cox Enterprises Inc., Atlanta, 1980, asst. contr., 1981, corp. officer, 1982-89; v.p. fin. Cox Cable, Atlanta, 1989-92, sr. v.p. fin., 1992-95; sr. v.p. fin., CFO Cox Comm. Inc., Atlanta, 1995-99, exec. v.p. fin. adminstrn., CFO, 1999—2005; pres., COO Cox Enterprises Inc., Atlanta, 2005—. Trustee Mighty Eighth Air Force Mus., Savannah, Ga. Mailing: Cox Enterprises PO Box 105357 Atlanta GA 30348 Office: Cox Enterprises 6205 Peachtree Dunwoody Rd Atlanta GA 30328

HAYES, JOANNA, Olympic track and field athlete; b. Williamsport, PA, Dec. 23, 1976; Grad., UCLA, 1999. Mem. U.S Olympic Track Team, Athens, 2004. SMART Moves Coord. Jackie Joyner-Kersee Youth Center, East St. Louis, Ill., 2001—02. Achievements include being NCAA Champion, 400m hurdles, 1999; winning gold medal, 400m hurdles, Pan American games, 2003; winning gold medal, 100m hurdles, Athens Olympic games, 2004. Office: c/o USOC 1 Olympic Plaza Colorado Springs CO 80909

HAYES, JOHN C., JR., lawyer; b. Utica, NY, 1947; BA, Williams Coll., 1969; JD with honors, George Washington U., 1973. Bar: DC 1973, Md. 1982, US Supreme Ct., US Ct. Appeals (DC, Fed., Fourth, Tenth and Eleventh Cirs.), US Dist. Ct. DC, US Dist. Ct., Dist. Md., US Ct. Fed. Claims, US Tax Ct. Ptnr. Nixon Peabody LLP, Washington, DC. Mem.: ABA, Defense Rsch. Inst., Internat. Assn. Defense Counsel, The Barristers, Md. Bar Assn., DC Bar Assn. Office: Nixon Peabody LLP Ste 900 401 Ninth St NW Washington DC 20004-2128 Office Phone: 202-585-8345. Office Fax: 202-585-8080. E-mail: jhayes@nixonpeabody.com.

HAYES, JOHN D., diversified financial services company executive; Grad. in Mktg. and Comm., Seton Hall U. Pres. Lowe & Ptnrs./SMS; various positions Geer DuBois, Saatchi & Saatchi Compton; exec. vp. global advt. and brand mgmt. Am. Express, NYC, 1995—, chief mktg. officer, 2004—. Mem. planning and policy com. Am. Express; mem. Tiger Wood Found. Mem.: Assn. Nat. Advertisers (chmn. 2000—01, vice chmn. 2002—). Office: Am Express World Fin Ctr 200 Vesey St New York NY 10285*

HAYES, JOHN FRANCIS, lawyer; b. Salina, Kans., Dec. 11, 1919; s. John Francis and Helen (Dye) H.; m. Elizabeth Ann Ireton, Aug. 10, 1950; children: Carl Ireton, Ann Chandler. AB, Washburn Coll., 1941, LLB, 1946. Bar: Kans. 1946, Mo. 1987. Pvt. practice, Hutchinson, Kans., 1946—; dir. Gilliland & Hayes, P.A. (and predecessors), 1946—. Mem. Commn. Uniform State Laws, 1975—; bd. dirs. Cen. Bank and Trust Co., Hutchinson, Cen. Fin. Corp., Waddell & Reed Funds. Mem. Kans. Ho. of Reps., 1953-55, 67-79, majority leader, 1975-77. Served as capt. AUS, 1942-46. Fellow Am. Bar Found., Am. Coll. Trial Lawyers; mem. Hutchinson C. of C. (pres. 1961), Kans. Assn. Def. Counsel (pres. 1972-73), Internat. Assn. Def. Counsel. Republican. Office: 20 W 2nd Ave Fl 2 Hutchinson KS 67501 also: 1211 Penntower Bldg 3100 Broadway St Kansas City MO 64111-2406 also: Epic Ctr 301 N Main Ste 1300 Wichita KS 67202 also: 900 Massachusetts Ste 400 Lawrence KS 66044-2868 Home Phone: 620-662-7359; Office Phone: 620-662-0537. E-mail: johnh@gh-hutch.com.

HAYES, JOHN FREEMAN, architect; b. Media, Pa., June 16, 1926; s. James Alfred and Katharine Stoddard (Williams) H.; m. Anne Gitt Fox, Apr. 5, 1952; children: John Fox, Thomas Freeman, Anne Clarke. Grad., Haverford Sch., 1944; BArch, U. Pa., 1950. With various cos., 1954-60; ptnr. Hayes & Hough Archs., Phila., 1960-95; sr. cons. Blackney Hayes Archs., Phila., 1995—. Pres. The Carpenters Co. of the City and County of Phila., 1993. Served with USNR, 1944-46; served with USAF, 1951-53. Fellow AIA (John Harbeson Svc. award 1995); mem. Martins Dam Club, Phila. Curling Club. Episcopalian. Office: Blackney Hayes Architects 105 S 12th St Philadelphia PA 19107-4809

HAYES, JOHN PATRICK, electrical engineering and computer science educator, consultant; b. Newbridge, Ireland, Mar. 3, 1944; s. Patrick Joseph and Christine (Duggan) H.; m. Joan Benson, June 7, 1969; children: Thomas, Michael. BE in Elec. Engring., Nat. U. Ireland, Dublin, 1965; MS in Elec. Engring., U. Ill., 1967, PhD in Elec. Engring., 1970. Systems engr. Royal Dutch Shell Co., The Hague, The Netherlands, 1970-72; asst. prof. elec. engring. and computer sci. U. So. Calif., LA, 1972-77, assoc. prof., 1977-82; prof. U. Mich., Ann Arbor, 1982—2002, Shannon prof. engring. sci., 2002—. Cons. in field. Author: Computer Architecture and Organization, 1978, 3d edit., 1998, Digital System Design and Microprocessors, 1984, Hierarchical Modeling for VLSI Circuit Testing, 1990, Layout Minimization for CMOS Cells, 1992, Introduction to Digital Logic Design, 1993; contbr. articles to profl. jours. Fellow: IEEE (assoc. editor jour. 1989—94), Assn. Computing Machinery (assoc. editor jour. 1978—81); mem.: Sigma Xi. Office: U Mich Dept Elec Engring & Computer Sci Ann Arbor MI 48109 Office Phone: 734-763-0386. Business E-Mail: jhayes@eecs.umich.edu.

HAYES, JOHN PATRICK, retired manufacturing company executive; b. Manistee, Mich., May 9, 1921; s. John David and Daisy (Davis) H.; m. Margaret Barbara Butler, Apr. 12, 1947; children: John Patrick, Timothy Michael. BS, U. Detroit, 1947. With Nat. Gypsum Co., 1947-90, group v.p., 1970-75, pres., 1975-90, chmn. bd., chief exec. officer, 1983-90, also bd. dirs. Served to 1st lt. AUS, 1942-45.

HAYES, KEVIN J., literature educator; b. Toledo, Ohio, Nov. 14, 1959; s. Richard Allen and Carole Joan Hayes; m. Myung Sook Park, May 8, 2000. BA, U. Toledo, Ohio, 1981, MEd, 1983; MA, U. Del., Newark, 1989, PhD, 1991. Prof. U. Ctrl. Okla., Edmond, 1991—. Author: (book) The Cambridge Introduction to Herman Melville, 1991, Melville's Folk Roots, 1994, A Colonial Woman's Bookshelf, 1996, Folklore and Book Culture, 1997, The Library of William Byrd of Westover, 1997 (History award Va. Libr., 1999), Poe and the Printed Word, 2000, The Library of John Montgomerie, Colonial Governor of New York and New Jersey, 2000, An American Cycling Odyssey, 1887, 2002, Stephen Crane, 2004, Captain John Smith: A Reference Guide, 2007, A Peep into Korea, 2007; co-author: Checklist of Melville Reviews, 2000, The Library of Benjamin Franklin, 2006; editor: The Critical Response to Herman Melville's Moby-Dick, 1994, Henry James: The Contemporary Reviews., 1996, Itinerant Observations in America, 1998, Maggie: A Girl of the Streets (A Story of New York), 1999, The Cambridge Companion to Edgar Allan Poe, 2002, Conversations with Jack Kerouac, 2005, Martin Scorsese's Raging Bull, 2005, Charlie Chaplin: Interviews, 2005. Recipient Disting. Svc. award, Assn. Documentary Editing, 1998; Mellon fellowship, Va. Hist. Soc., 1991, William Reese Co. fellowship, Libr. Co. Phila., 2004—05. Mem.: Cosmos Club. Avocation: bicycling. Office: Univ Ctrl Okla 100 N Univ Dr Edmond OK 73034 Home Phone: 405-525-3663; Office Phone: 405-974-2000. Personal E-mail: kjhayes59@hotmail.com. Business E-Mail: khayes@ucok.edu.

HAYES, LARRY B., retired lawyer; b. Atlanta, Oct. 4, 1939; s. Luther F. and Ruby (Thomas) H.; m. Rebecca Thomason, Feb. 7, 1959; children: Laura Alison, Lawrence Bruce. BS in Pharmacy, U. Fla., 1962; JD, St. Mary's U., 1977. Bar: Tex. 1978, U.S. Dist. Ct. (we. dist.) Tex. 1979, U.S. Ct. Appeals (5th cir.) 1979; cert. personal injury trial law, Tex. Trial counsel Windle Turley PC, Dallas, 1978-82; ptnr. Ware & Hayes, Dallas, 1982-83; sr. trial atty. Green, Hayes & Ryan, Dallas, 1983-86; ptnr. Cantey & Hanger, Ft. Worth, 1986—2006; ret., 2006. Mem. Tex. Bar Assn., Tex. Assn. Def. Counsel, Def. Rsch. Inst., Tarrant County Bar Assn., Tarrant County Civil Trial Lawyers Assn., Phi Delta Phi. Home: 1155 Oceanshore Blvd Unit 305 Ormond Beach FL 32176 Office Phone: 817-929-4625.

HAYES, LINDA MARIE, middle school educator; b. Honolulu, Mar. 9, 1957; d. Jerome Donald and Rose Marie (Davalos) H. Student, Southwest Tex. State U., 1975-80; BS in Edn., George Mason U., Fairfax, Va., 1990, EdM, 1997. Swim coach Prince William Swim Club, Dale City, Va., 1986—2000; tchr. Parkside Mid. Sch., Manassas, Va., 1990—. Instr. ARC, Fla., Tex., Va., 1982—. With USN, 1980-86, mem. Res. Mem. Internat. Reading Assn., Va. Edn. Assn., Kappa Delta Pi, Delta Psi Kappa. Baptist. Avocations: rugby, fencing, music, poetry, reading. Office: Parkside Mid Sch 8602 Mathis Ave Manassas VA Office Phone: 703-361-3106. Business E-Mail: hayeslm@pwcs.edu.

HAYES, MARY DIANNE WIXTED, lawyer; b. Danbury, Conn., Jan. 4, 1942; d. Francis Joseph and Mary (Zwyner) Wixted; m. Paul P. Hayes, Jr., June 18, 1966. BA in Economics, Regis Coll., Weston, MA, 1961—64; JD, Suffolk U. Law Sch., Boston, 1968, LLM, 1968—70; MEd in Religious Edn., Boston Coll., Chestnut Hill, MA, 1989, MA in Theology, 1990—97; STL, Weston SJ Sch. of Theology, Cambridge, MA, 1997—2002. Bar: Mass. 1970, U.S. Dist. Ct. (Mass.) 1971, U. S. Supreme Ct. 1973, U.S. Ct. Appeals (1st cir.) 1979. Ptnr. Hayes and Hayes, Quincy, Mass., 1970—; vol. atty. Irish Pastoral Centre, 1998—, mem. adv. bd., 2004—. Town meeting mem. Town of Milton, Milton, Mass., 1977—93; mem. Secular Franciscan Order, Boston, 1985—. Mem.: Am. Immigration Lawyers Assn., Mass. Real Estate Bar Assn., Mass. Assn. Women Lawyers (pres. 1993—94), Mass. Bar Assn. (chair probate law sect. coun. 1995—97), S. Shore Regis Club, Weston, Mass. (pres. 1973—75). Roman Catholic. Office: Hayes and Hayes 31 Newcomb Street Quincy MA 02169-4507 Office Phone: 617-773-2800. Personal E-mail: Wixtedhaye@aol.com.

HAYES, MARY ESHBAUGH, editor, writer; b. Rochester, NY, Sept. 27, 1928; d. William Paul and Eleanor Maude (Sievert) Eshbaugh; m. James Leon Hayes, Apr. 18, 1953; children: Pauli, Eli, Lauri Le June, Clayton, Merri Jess Bates. BA in English and Journalism, Syracuse U., NYC, 1950. With Livingston County Republican, Geneseo, NY, summers, 1947-50, mng. editor, 1949-50; reporter Aurora Advocate, Colo., 1950—52; reporter-photographer Aspen Times, Colo., 1952-53, columnist, 1956—, reporter, 1972-77, assoc. editor, 1977-89, editor-in-chief, 1989-92, contbg. editor, 1992—. Instr. Colo. Mountain Coll., 1979; Aspen corr. Reuters, 1997—. Author, editor: The Story of Aspen, 1996 (1st prize, 1996); contbg. editor: Destinations Mag., 1994—97, Aspen Mag., 1996—, Aspen Sojourner Mag., 2005—; editor: Aspen Pot Pourri, 1968 (1st prize, 1990), rev. edit., 2002 (1st prize, 2002). Recipient Living Landmark award, Aspen Hist. Soc., 2002. Mem.: Colo. Press Women's Assn. (writing award 1974—75, 1978—85, sweepstakes award for writing 1977—78, 1984—85, 1991—2003, 2d pl. award 1976, 1979, 1982—83, 1994—95, Woman of Achievement 1986), Nat. Fedn. Press Women (1st prize in writing and editing 1976—80, 1st prize in adv. photography 1998). Home: PO Box 497 Aspen CO 81612-0497 Office: Box E Aspen CO 81612 Personal E-mail: meh@sopris.net.

HAYES, MICHAEL J., retail executive; Mgmt. positions through mng. dir., exec. v.p. corp. fin. & financial svcs. Oppenheimer & Co. Inc., 1976—85; bd. dir. Fred's Inc., Memphis, 1987—, mng. dir., CEO, 1989—2002, chmn., CEO, 2002—. Office: Fred's Inc 4300 New Getwell Rd Memphis TN 38118*

HAYES, PATRICIA ANN, health facility administrator; b. Binghamton, NY, Jan. 14, 1944; d. Robert L. and Gertrude (Congdon) H. BA in English, Coll. of St. Rose, 1968; PhD in Philosophy, Georgetown U., 1974. Tchr. Cardinal McCloskey H.S., Albany, NY, 1966-68; tchg. asst. Georgetown U., Washington, 1968-71; instr. philosophy Coll. of St. Rose, Albany, 1973-75, instr. bus., 1981, adminstrv. intern to acad. v.p., 1973-74, dir. admissions, 1974-78, dir. adminstrn. and planning, 1978-81, v.p. adminstrn. and fin., treas., 1981-84; pres. St. Edward's U., Austin, Tex., 1984-98; exec. v.p., COO Seton Healthcare Network, Austin, 1998—2001, 2003—, interim pres., CEO, 2001—02. Bd. dirs. Tex. Assn. Pub. and Nonprofit Hosps., Topfer Family Found. Roman Catholic. Office: Seton Med Ctr 1201 W 38th St Austin TX 78705-1006 Office Phone: 512-324-1102. Business E-Mail: phayes@seton.org.

HAYES, PATRICIA THORNTON, music educator, retired director; m. Raymond S. Hayes, Jr., Nov. 28, 1959; children: Rhett S., Amber. BA, W.Va. U. Inst. Tech., 1956; MS in Edn., Old Dominion U., 1970. Dir. music Clendenin HS Kanawha County Schs., Charleston, W.Va., 1956—57; dir. music Shelton Pk. Elem. Sch., Va. Beach, Va., 1957—58, Suburban Pk. Elem. Sch., Norfolk, Va., 1958—60, Bayview Elem. Sch., Norfolk, 1958—60; tchr. music and spl. edn. Mt. Zion Elem. Sch., Suffolk, Va., 1970—71; dir. choral and orch. Portsmouth City Schs., Va., 1973—96; specialist music Portsmouth Diagnostic Ctr., 1993—2005; ret., 2005. Dir. music programs, festivals, theater prodns. various schs., Va.; judge Doris Sahr Meml. Piano Competition, Chesapeake, Va. Composer: (songs) We're Supporting You All The Way Student - Farrah Fales, 1991; dir.: (chorus) Mayor's Breakfast, Seawall Festival, Manor HS Award Banquet, NAVSEA and CG. Recipient Proclamation award, Fine Arts Commn., Chesapeake, Va., 1981—89, Oustanding Music Works awards, Portsmouth City Sch. Bd., 1992.

HAYES, PAUL ROBERT, retired field and clinical experiences coordinator; b. Shelby County, Ind., Apr. 30, 1939; s. J. Robert and Evelyn Hayes; m. Rhoda Stuenkel, 1979; children: Robert, Susan, Adam. AB, Franklin Coll., 1964; MS, Ind. U., 1967, EdS, 1973. Tchr. Southwestern Sch. Dist., Shelbyville, Ind., 1964-67; prin. Noble Twp. Sch., St. Paul, Ind., 1967-72, Woodstock Cmty. Sch. Dist., Ill., 1972-80; supt. Sandoval Sch. Dist., Ill., 1980-83; prin. Macomb Sch. Dist., Ill., 1983-93; instr., grad. field experience supr. Western Ill. U., Macomb, 1994—2005, coord. field and clin. experiences, 2001—05. Student tchg. oversight com. State Bd. of Edn., 1989-93, 94, evaluator of new pub. schs. Editor: Allying the Arts in Education, 1987. Founding bd. mem. Habitat for Humanity, Macomb, 1995-2001; chairperson, mem. Wesley Day Care Ctr., Macomb, 1993—2001; mem., com. chair Lions Club, Macomb, 1990—. Recipient Assoc. award Ill. State Bd. of Edn., 1992, Mem. award, 1994. Mem. Nat. Assn. Elem. Prins. (fellowship 1984, 85, 87), Coun. for Exceptional Children, Ill. Assn. Sch. Adminstrs., Internat. Reading Assn. Avocations: travel, gardening, bear hunting, archaeology. Office: Western Ill Univ Ednl and Interdisciplinary Studies Dept Macomb IL 61455 Business E-Mail: pr-hayes@wiu.edu.

HAYES, PAULA FREDA, federal agency administrator; b. Apr. 5, 1950; d. Ario Louis and Elena Marguerite (Gentile) Freda; m. Robert J. Hayes, Sept. 6, 1975; children: Brendan Michael, Lauren Ann. BA magna cum laude, R.I. Coll., 1972; MPA, Syracuse U., 1973. Criminal justice planner City of Syracuse, NY, 1973—75, asst. coord. crime control, 1975—77; specialist supervisory grants Nat. Endowment Arts, Washington, 1977—78; analyst criminal justice program Dept. Justice, Washington, 1978—79, mgr. arson discretionary grant program, 1979—80, sr. analyst mgmt., 1980—81; dir. legis. and analysis divsn. Office of Insp. Gen., Dept. Agr., Washington, 1981—89, asst. insp. gen. for policy devel. and resources mgmt., 1989—2003, asst. insp. gen. for planning and spl. projects, 2003—04, asst. insp. gen. for mgmt. USAID, 2004—05, acting dep. insp. for gen. USAID, 2005—06, asst. insp. mgmt., 2006; asst. dean, dep. dir. IG Inst. George Mason U., Fairfax, Va., 2006; asst. insp. mgmt. US AID, Washington, 2006—07, insp. gen. mgmt., 2007—. Roman Catholic. Office Phone: 202-712-0010. Business E-Mail: phayes@usaid.gov.

HAYES, PHILIP HAROLD, lawyer; b. Battle Creek, Mich., Sept. 1, 1940; s. Robert Harold and Maurine (Page) H.; m. Robin Hayes, May 20, 1995; 1 child, Rian; children from previous marriage: Elizabeth, Courtney. AB, Ind. U., 1963, JD, 1967. Bar: Ind. 1967, U.S. Dist. Ct. (so. dist.) Ind. 1967, D.C. 1977, U.S. Ct. Appeals (7th cir.) 1992. Dep. prosecutor Vanderburgh County, Evansville, Ind., 1967-68; ptnr. Cox & Hayes, Evansville, 1969-72; senator State of Ind., Evansville, 1971-74; pvt. practice Evansville, 1973-74, 77-79, 1980—; mem. U.S. Ho. of Reps., Washington, 1975-77; ptnr. Hayes & Young, Evansville, 1980-90, Hayes & Tornatta, Evansville, 1990-92. Legal counsel Airport Authority Dist., Evansville, 1980-84, Redevel. Commn., Evansville, 1984-88, Health and Hosp. Corp., Evansville, 1984-88, Vanderburgh County Atty., 2001-02. Mem. Evansville Bar Assn., D.C. Bar Assn., Seventh Cir. Bar Assn. Home: 218 Glenview Dr Evansville IN 47710-3737 Office: 555 Sycamore St Evansville IN 47708 Office Phone: 812-425-1000. Business E-Mail: hayes@philiphayeslaw.com. E-mail: hayeslegal@sbcglobal.net.

HAYES, RANDY ALAN, family therapist, process improvement specialist; b. Johnston City, Ill., Jan. 12, 1950; s. Clarence Lee Jr. and Mable Marie (McClain) H.; m. Donna Faye Carriker, Oct. 9, 1971; 1 child, Colin. BA, So. Ill. U., 1972; postgrad., U. Dubuque Theol. Sem., 1973-74; MS, No. Ill. U., 1975; post grad., Columbia Pacific U., 1996. Cert. rational emotive therapy, family life educator; cert. substance abuse counselor; ordained as deacon United Meth. Ch., 1973; lic. local pastor United Meth. Ch.; lic. clin. profl. counselor; nat. cert. counselor; clin. cert. mental health counselor. Day sch. dir. Village of Progress, Oregon, Ill., 1974-76; team coord. Children's Devel. Ctr., Rockford, Ill., 1976-78; career counselor Highland C.C. CETA, Freeport, Ill., 1978-79; family therapist, clin. dir. Stephenson County Assn. for Prevention of Child Abuse, Freeport, 1979-92; dir. quality assurance Sinnissippi Ctrs., Inc., 1992—2006; pastor Zion United Meth. Ch., Mendota, Ill., 1996-98, Brookville-Elkhorn United Meth. Chs., Polo, Ill., 1996-98, 2004—06; leader Weith Watchers, 2005; sr. v.p. Timberline Knolls, LLC, Lemont, Ill., 2006—. Pre-marriage cons. Rochelle (Ill.) United Meth. Ch., 1985—91; mem. adminstrv. bd. Polo United Meth. Ch., 1975—90; cons. quality assurance, 1998; guest faculty mem. Family Info. Svcs., 2001—; lectr. Joint Commn. Resources, 2000—. Pub.: Handbook of Quality Training and Implementation, 2001, Behavior Health Mgmt., 2000—, The Evidence Based Practice, 2004; contbr. JCAHO Advisor. Vol. Ogle County Hospice Assn., Oregon, 1990; campaign coord. Am. Cancer Assn., Polo, 1987-93; bd. dirs. Ogle County Mental Health Assn., Oregon, 1974-76; den leader Polo Cub Scouts, 1988-91; violinist Sauk Valley Coll. String Orch., 1992-96. Mem.: Ill. Counselors Assn., Ill. Coun. Family Rels. (bd. dirs. 1990—2000, pres. 1993, immediate past pres. 1994), Nat. Coun. Family Rels. Avocations: collecting asian art, crafting fiber and textile art, poetry. Home: 401 N Congress Ave Polo IL 61064-1306 Office: 40 Timber Line Dr Lemont IL 60439 Home Phone: 815-622-5118; Office Phone: 630-343-2407. Business E-Mail: rhayes@timberlineknolls.com.

HAYES, REGGIE, actor; b. Chgo., July 15, 1969; BA in Theatre, Ill. State Univ. Actor: (films) A Family Thing, 1996, Chicago Cab, 1998, Being John Malkovich, 1999, Charlie's Angels, 2000; (TV series) Space: Above and Beyond, 1996, Nick Freno: Licensed Teacher, 1996, Something So Right, 1997, The Pretender, 1997, Getting Personal, 1998, Party of Five, 1999, Roswell, 1999, Girlfriends, 2000— (Best Supporting Actor in a Comedy Series, NAACP Image awards, 2006, Supporting Actor in a Comedy Series, NAACP Image Awards, 2007), Kimpossible, 2003—.*

HAYES, RICHARD J., JR., engineering company executive; b. Evanston, Ill., Jan. 8, 1964; s. Richard J and Mary L Hayes; m. Danette G Kauffman, Aug. 25, 1990; children: David A Cansler, Makayla M Cansler, Kelly Ms. BA, U. Kans., 1982—86; grad. CGSOC, US Army Command and Gen. Staff Coll., 1998—2002; MBA in Mil. Mgmt., Touro U. Internat., 2005; postgrad., U.S. Army War Coll., 2005—. Cert. hazardous materials manager, Inst. of Hazardous Materials Mgmt., 2000. Constrn. mgr. Hall Kimbrell, Lawrence, Kans., 1987—89; officer, US Army 1-127 FA Kans. Army N.G., Ottawa, Kans., 1987—89; project mgr. Fluor Daniel, Chgo., 1989—93; officer, US Army 2-122 FA Ill. Army N.G., Chgo., 1989—2002; v.p. RMS Inc., Mnpls., 1993—97, Profl. Svc. Industries, Inc., Hillside, Ill., 1997—2004; lt. col. -comdr. 2-122 F.A. Ill. Army N.G., Chgo., 2002—05; lt. col., asst. chief staff US Army 35th Inf. Divsn., Leavenworth, Kans., 2005—. Bd. mem. Ill. Assn. of Environ. Professionals, Chgo., 2002—. Co-author: Asbestos Control and Replacement Guidelines for the Electric Industry. Com. mem. Ill. Legislature Joint Task Force on mold in indoor environments. Home: 1140 Gail Dr Buffalo Grove IL 60089 Office: Patrick Engring Inc 4970 Varsity Dr Lisle IL 60532 Personal E-mail: rihayes@yahoo.com.

HAYES, RICHARD JOHNSON, association executive, retired lawyer; b. Chgo., May 25, 1933; s. David John Arthur and Lucille Margaret (Johnson) H.; m. Mary R. Lynch, Dec. 2, 1961; children: Susan, Richard, Jr., John, Edward. BA, Colo. Coll., 1955; JD, Georgetown U., 1961. Bar: Ill. 1961. Assoc. firm Barnabas F. Sears, Chgo., 1961-63, Peterson, Lowry, Rall, Barber and Ross, Chgo., 1963-65; staff dir. Am. Bar Assn., Chgo., 1965-70; exec. dir. Internat. Assn. Def. Counsel, Chgo., 1970—99; instr. various legal programs, 1966—98; pres. Aegis Group Chgo., 1997—2002, Heritage Resource Mgmt. Group, 1997—99, Tri Star Corp., 1997—; dir. nat. jury innovations program Internat. Assn. Def. Counsel, Chgo., 1998-99, ret., 1999. Dir. Def. Counsel Trial Acad., 1973-99; exec. dir. Nat. Pre-Suit Mediation, 1991-2000, pres. Hamilton Enterprizes, 2003-. Editor: Antitrust Law Jour., 1969-71. 1st lt. USAR, 1955-57. Mem. ABA (chmn. various coms. 1977-2003), Ill. Bar Assn., Chgo. Bar Assn., Jr. Bar (chmn. 1965), Am. Multicastles (chmn. 2001-04), Am. Soc. Assn. Execs., Nat. Conf. Lawyers and Ins. Cos. (bd. dirs. 1983-1995), Rotary/One, Monroe Club, Met. Club, Mich. Shores Club, Boulder Country Club. Home: 7173 Old Post Rd Boulder CO 80301 Office Phone: 303-516-9198. Personal E-mail: richardhys@yahoo.com.

HAYES, ROBERT BRUCE, former college president, educator; b. Clarksburg, W.Va., Nov. 15, 1925; s. Bruce and Ruby (Hitt) H.; m. Ruth Harrison, July 19, 1947 (dec.); children: Steven, Ruthann, Mark; m. Kathleen Peters. Student, Fairmont State Coll., W.Va.; BA, Asbury Coll., Wilmore, Ky., 1950; MEd, U. Kans., 1956, EdD, 1960. Tchr., prin. elem. and secondary schs., Kans., 1951-57; chmn. dept. edn. and psychology Asbury Coll., Wilmore, Ky., 1957-59; dir. tchr. edn. Taylor U., Upland, Ind., 1959-65; dean Coll. Edn. Marshall U., Huntington, W.Va., 1965-74, pres., 1974-83; prof. ednl. adminstrn. Coll. Edn., Marshall U., 1983-90; exec. v.p. Warner So. Coll., Lake Wales, Fla., 1991-92; interim dean coll. bus. Marshall U., Huntington, W.Va., 1992-93, coord. accreditation, 1993-95, pres. emeritus, 1992-95, provost, 1996-97, 99; interim v.p. Cmty. & Tech. Coll., 1995-97; interim pres. Marshall Cmty. and Tech. Coll., 2006—07. Mem. W.Va. Adv. Com. Tchr. Edn., 1965-74; dir. Twentieth St. Bank Editor, contbr.: 1966 Yearbook of Assn. Student Teaching. Bd. dirs. Cabell-Wayne United Way, 1981; chmn. bd. Green Acres, 1983; commr. Cabell County (W.Va.), 1983-88. Served with USMCR, 1944-46. Recipient Green Acres award for contbn. to mentally retarded, 1972, Golden Knight award Nat. Mgmt. Assn., 1981 Mem. Huntington Area C. of C. (dir. 1974-83), Phi Delta Kappa, Kiwanis. Methodist. Home: 347 Bradley Foster Dr Huntington WV 25701-9451 Office: Marshall Cmty and Tech Coll Huntington WV 25755-0001 Office Phone: 304-696-3064.

HAYES, ROBERT FRANCIS, lawyer; b. Boston, Jan. 1, 1941; s. Robert Francis and Miriam Frances (Comfrey) H.; m. Nancy Hite Roach, Apr. 26, 1969; children: Robert Francis III, Katherine M., Rebecca C. AB, Harvard U., 1962, JD, 1965. Bar: Mass. 1965. With Ropes & Gray, Boston, 1966—2006, of counsel, 2006—. Trustee Thayer Acad., Braintree, Mass., 1985-96, Duxbury, Mass. Beach Reservation, Inc, 1986-; trustee, dir. Jordan Hosp., Inc., Plymouth, Mass., 1984-2004, Duxbury, Mass. Beach Reservation, Inc., 1986—2006. Office: Ropes & Gray One International Pl Boston MA 02110 Office Phone: 617-951-7381. Business E-Mail: RHayes@Ropesgray.com.

HAYES, ROBERT HERRICK, technology management educator; b. Wakeeney, Kans., July 17, 1936; s. Daniel Frank and Ruth Dee (Herrick) H.; m. Priscilla Jane Alden, Aug. 25, 1963; children: Melissa, Jonathan, Michelle. BA, Wesleyan U., 1958; MS, Stanford U., 1962, PhD, 1966; AM (hon.), Harvard U., 1973. Prof. Harvard U., Boston, 1966-91, Caldwell prof. bus. adminstrn., 1991-2000, sr. assoc. dean, 1992-98, emeritus, 2000—. Bd. dirs. Applera Corp., Norwalk, Conn. Co-author: Restoring our Competitive Edge, 1984 (Assn. Am. Pubs. award 1984), Dynamic Manufacturing, 1988, Manufacturing Renaissance, 1995, Strategic Operations, 1996, Operations, Strategy, and Technology: Pursuing the Competitive Edge, 2004. Trustee Wesleyan U., Middletown, Conn., 1985-88. Recipient McKinsey award 1980, 81, 82, Outstanding Alumnus award Wesleyan U., 1983. Fellow: Prodn. and Ops. Mgmt. Soc. (life). Avocations: sailing, reading, travel. Office: Harvard Bus Sch Soldiers Fld Boston MA 02163-1317 Office Phone: 617-495-6330. Business E-Mail: rhayes@hbs.edu.

HAYES, ROBIN (ROBERT CANNON HAYES), congressman; b. Concord, NC, Aug. 14, 1945; m. Barbara; children: Winslow, Bob. BA in Hist., Duke U., 1967. With Lease A Plane, 1972, Ctrl. Motor Lines, 1973—74, Palmer Mountain Farms, 1974—83, Coleville Environ. Svcs., 1983—90, Mack Sales Birmingham, 1984—88, Arctic So. Turbines, 1986—92; owner-operator Mt. Pleasant Hosiery Mills, 1989—; mem. NC State Ho. Reps., 1992—96, US Congress from 8th NC dist., 1999—, mem. transp. and infrastructure com., mem. agr. com., ranking mem. livestock, dairy and poultry subcommittee, mem. armed svcs. com., chmn. spl. ops. forces caucus, asst. whip. Mem. Concord Bd. Aldermen, 1978-81; Wildlife Resources Commn., Coun. on Drug Abuse, Prison Fellowship in NC, 1994-; chmn. Cabarrus County Drug Task Force, 1998-; Nominated 1996 as Rep. candidate for gov. of NC; Mem. 1st Presbyn. Ch. Concord. Recipient Charles Dick Medal of Merit, Nat. Guard Assn. US, 2000, Guardian of Small Bus., Nat. Fedn. Ind. Bus., 2002, Legis. Achievement award, Seniors Coalition, 2002, Spirit of Enterprise award, US C. of C., 2002; named Legislator of Yr. by Nat. Rep. Legislator's Assn., 1996. Republican. Presbyterian. Office: US House Reps 130 Cannon House Office Bldg Washington DC 20515-0001 Office Phone: 202-225-3715. Office Fax: 202-225-4036.*

HAYES, SAMUEL LINTON, III, business educator; b. Phila., Feb. 23, 1935; s. Samuel L. and Ann Walsh (Barclay) H.; m. Barbara Frances Lloyd, Dec. 21, 1963; children: Elizabeth Ann, Susan Lloyd, Judith Linton. AB, Swarthmore Coll., 1957; MBA with distinction, Harvard U., 1961, DBA, 1966. Asst. prof. bus. adminstrn. Columbia U., NYC, 1965-68, assoc. prof., 1968-70; vis. assoc. prof. Harvard U., Cambridge, Mass., 1970-72, prof., 1972-75, Jacob Schiff prof. investment banking, 1975—98, Jacob Schiff prof. emeritus, 1999—, chmn. faculty Research and Mgmt. Ctr. Vevey, Switzerland, 1979-81. Bd. dirs. Tiffany & Co., 1984—2007, Eaton Vance Mut. Funds, 1984—2007, Telect, Inc., Yakima, Inc., 2000—; adv. dir. Am. U. Beirut Sch. Bus., 2002—; cons. in field. Mem. editorial bd. Harvard Bus. Rev., 1976-84, Harvard Bus. Sch. Press, 1986-89; contbr. articles to profl. jours. Mem. Mass. Fin. Adv. Bd., 1976-87, chmn., 1978-87; trustee Swarthmore Coll., 1983-94, 96—, New Eng. Conservatory, 1989—; hon. dir. Nat. Scoliosis Found. With USN, 1957-59. Mem.: Am. Guild Organists, Fin. Mgmt. Assn., Dedham Country and Polo Club, Harvard Club (N.Y.C.). Office: Harvard U Sch Bus Cumnock Hall 300 Soldiers Field Rd Boston MA 02163 Office Phone: 617-495-6240. Business E-Mail: shayes@hbs.edu.

HAYES, SEAN (SEAN PATRICK HAYES), actor, comedian; b. Chgo., Ill., June 26, 1970; s. Ron and Mary Hayes. Attended, Ill. State Univ. Music dir. Pheasant Run Theatre, Chgo., comedian Second City Improvisational Comedy Group, stand-up comedian in clubs in LA and Chgo.; actor: (TV films) A & P, 1996; (films) Billy's Hollywood Kiss, 1998, Sin City Spectacular (Episode: Penn & Teller's Sin City Spectacular), 1999, Martin and Lewis, 2002, Pieces of April, 2003, Win a Date with Tad Hamilton!, 2004; (TV series) Silk Stalkings (Episode: Services Rendered), 1996, Will & Grace, 1998—2006 (Emmy award for Outstanding Supporting Actor in a Comedy, 2000, Outstanding Performance by an Ensemble in a Comedy Series, Screen Actors Guild award, 2001, Outstanding Performance by a Male Actor in a Comedy Series, Screen Actors Guild award, 2002, 2003, 2006), Scrubs (Episode: My Super Ego), 2001; voice Buzz Lightyear of Star Command: The Adventure Begins, 2000, Cats & Dogs, 2001, The Cat in the Hat, 2003, host (TV series) Saturday Night Live, 2001; exec. prodr.: (TV series) Situation: Comedy, 2005.

HAYES, STEPHEN KURTZ, writer; b. Wilmington, Del., Sept. 9, 1949; s. Ira Maurice and Carolyn (Kurtz) H.; m. Rumiko Urata, Apr. 14, 1980; children: Reina Emily, Marissa Christine. BA, Miami U., Oxford, Ohio, 1971. Ordained Tendai sect Japanese Esoteric Buddhist priest, 1991. Adj. prof. master bus. mgmt. program McGregor Sch., Antioch U. Author: The Ninja and Their Secret Fighting Art, 1981, Ninjutsu: Art of the Invisible Warrior, 1984, The Mystic Arts of the Ninja, 1985, Ninja: Spirit of the Shadow Warrior, Vol. I, 1980, Warrior Ways of Enlightenment, Vol. II, 1981, Warrior Path of Togakure, Vol. III, 1983, Legacy of the Night Warrior, Vol. IV, 1984, Wisdom from the Ninja Village of the Cold Moon, 1984, Ninja Realms of Power, 1986, Tulku, 1985, Ancient Art of Ninja Warfare, 1988, Lore of the Shinobi Warrior, Ninja Vol. V, 1989, Action Meditation, 1992, Enlightened Self-Protection, 1992, How to Own the World, 2000, Secret Scrolls of the Warrior Sage, Ninja Vol. VI, 2007. Bd. mem. Tibetan Cultural Ctr.; founder Stephen K. Hayes' Quest Ctr. for Martial Arts Tng., 1996. Named to Black Belt Hall of Fame, Black Belt. mag., 1985. Mem. Tibetan Med. Inst. (life), Togakure Ryu Ninjutsu (10th degree black belt), To-Shin Do (founder 1997). Home: PO Box 326 Bellbrook OH 45305-0326 Office: PO Box 291947 Dayton OH 45429-0947 E-mail: daytonquest@skhquest.com.

HAYES, STEPHEN MATTHEW, librarian; b. Detroit, Sept. 30, 1950; s. Matthew Cleary and Evelyn Mary (Warren) H. BS in Psychology, Mich. State U., 1972; MLS, Western Mich. U., 1974; MS in Adminstrn., U. Notre Dame, 1979. Cons. Western Mich. U., Kalamazoo, 1974; libr. U. Notre Dame, Ind., 1974-76, ref. and pub. documents libr. Ind., 1976-94; libr. Bus. Svcs. Libr., 1994—. Adv. bd. Ebsco's Bus. Sch., 2003—. Author/contbr.: What is Written Remains: Historical Essays on the Libraries of Notre Dame, 1994; editor: Environmental Concerns, 1975; contbr.: Depository Library Use of Technology: A Practitioner's Perspective, 1993. Apptd. mem. Depository Libr. Coun. to Pub. Printer, 1994—97; citizen appointee, com. on info. and tech. South Bend City Coun., 2006. Recipient Rev. Paul J. Foik award, 1998. Mem. AAUP, ALA (govt. documents roundtable 1978—, chair 1987-88, chair pubs. com. 1989-91, coord. com. on access to info. 1989-90, 93-95, exec. bd. dirs. 1988-91, awards com. 1991-93, chair Godort orgn. com. 1991-93, Godort legis. com., 1999-2002, bus. ref. and svc. sect. 1994—, bus. & adult ref. roundtable 1995—, edn. com. 1996-98, resolution com. 1997-99, task force or restrictions on access to govt. info. 2002-03), Assn. Pub. Data Users (census com., steering com. 1987-96), Indigo (fed. rec. commn. chair 1992-93, provosts task force libr. 2004-2005). Roman Catholic. Avocations: horseback riding, quilting, gardening. Home: PO Box 6032 South Bend IN 46660-6032 Office: U Notre Dame L012 Mendoza Coll Of Business Notre Dame IN 46556-5646 Office Phone: 574-631-5268. Business E-Mail: shayes1@nd.edu.

HAYES, STEVEN CHARLES, psychologist, educator; b. Aug. 12, 1948; s. Charles Aloysius and Ruth Esther (Dryer) Hayes; m. Angela Fe Butcher (div.); 1 child, Camille; m. Linda Jean Parrott (div.); children: Charles Frederick, Esther Marlena; m. Jacqueline Pistorello; 1 child, Steven Joseph. BA cum laude in Psychology, Loyola U., 1970; postgrad., Calif. State U., San Diego, 1971-72; MA in Clin. Psychology, W.Va. U., 1974, PhD, 1977. Lic. psychologist, N.C., Nev. Intern psychology Brown U. Sch. Medicine, Providence, 1975-76; asst. prof. U. N.C., Greensboro, 1976-82, assoc. prof., 1982-86; prof. U. Nev., Reno, 1986—, dir. clin. tng., 1994—. Found. prof. W.Va. U. Author: The Effects of Monthly Feedback, Rebate Billing and Consumer Directed Feedback on the Residential Consumption of Electricity, 1977; Abnormal Psychology, 1979; (with J.D. Cone) Environmental Problems/Behavioral Solutions, 1980; (with D.H. Barlow and R.O. Nelson) The Scientist Practitioner: Research and Accountability in Clinical and Educational Settings, 1984, (with R.O. Nelson) Conceptual Foundations of Behavioral Assessment, 1986, Rule-Governed Behavior, 1989, (with L.J. Hayes) Understanding Verbal Relations, 1992, (with others) Varieties of Scientific Contextualism, 1993, Behavior Analysis of Language and Cognition, 1994, Acceptance and Change, 1994, Scientific Standards of Psychological Practice, 1995, (with K. Strosahl and K.G. Wilson) Acceptance and Commitment Therapy, 1999, (with E. Heiby) Prescription Privileges for Psychologists, 1998, (with D.H. Barlow & R.O. Nelson-Gray) The Scientist-Practitioner: Research & Accountability in the Age of Managed Care, 1999, 2d edit., (with D. Barnes-Holmes and B. Roche) Relational Frame Theory, 2001, (with W. O'Donohue, D. Henderson, J. Fisher and L. Hayes) A History of the Behavior Therapies, 2001, (with N. Cummings, W. I'Donohue and V. Follette) Intergrated Behavioral Healthcare, (with E.T. O'Donohue and J.E. Fisher) Cognitive Behavior Therapy, 2003, (with V.M. Follette & M.M. Linehan) Mindfulness and Acceptance: Expanding the Cognitive Behavioral Tradition, 2004, (with R. Lappalainen, T. Lehtonen, S. Batten, E. Gifford, K. Wilson, N. Afari, and S.M. McCurry) Applying Acceptance and Commitment Therapy, 2004, (with K. Strosahl) A Practical Guide to Acceptance and Commitment Therapy, 2005, (with J. Dahl, K. Wilson, and C. Luciano) Acceptance and Commitment Therapy for Chronic Pain, 2005, (with S. Smith) Get Out of Your Mind and Into Your Life, 2005, (with D. Barnes-Holmes, F. Bond, and J. Austin) Acceptance and mindfulness at work: Acceptance and Commitment Therapy, Relational Frame Theory, and organizational behavior management, 2006, (with J. Luoma and R. Walser) Learning ACT, 2007; contbr. chpts. to books, articles to profl. jours.; editor APS Observer, 1988-89, The Scientist Practitioner, 1990-92; assoc. editor Jour. Applied Behavior Analysis, 1982-85; editl. bd. Behavioral Assessment, Behavior Modification, Jour. Cons. and Clin. Psychology, The Behavior Analyst, Behaviorism, Jour. Experimental Analysis of Behavior, The Psychological Record. Found. Inc. grantee, 1975; NIMH grantee, 1976-77; U. NC grantee, 1976-77, 77-78, 81-82, 82-83, NSF 1992, NIDA, 1994-2003, 2005—, NCI, 2000-02, Nat. Adv. Coun. on Drug Abuse, NIH, 2000-04, Clin. Trials Network Adv. Coun., NIDA, 2000-02, U. Nev. Found. grantee, 1992-94, 97—; named 30th highest impact psychologist in world Inst. Sci. Info, 1986-90; recipient Don F. Hake award APA, 2000, Rschr. of Yr. award U. and Cmty. Coll. Sys. of Nev. Regents, 2000, Disting. Alumni award W.Va. U., 2000, Rschr. of Yr. award U. Nev. Reno, 1997, Psychologist of Yr., Nev. Psychol. Assn., 2006, Impact of Sci. on App. award, Soc. for Advancement of Behavior Analysis, 2007. Fellow Assn. Psychol.Sci. (sec.-treas. 1988-89), Assn. Applied and Preventive Psychology (exec. com., mem.-at-large, bd. dirs., 1992-96, v.p. 1993, pres. 1994-96), Western Psychol. Assn.; mem. AAAS, Am. Psychol. Assn. (divsn. 25 student affairs coord., 1977, 78, continuing edn. chmn., 1980-82, program co-chmn., 1980-82, chmn. long-term planning com. 1982, mem.-at-large 1982-85, pres. 1987, council of reps., 1988-89, fellow divsn. 12, 24, and 25), Assn. Behavior Analysis, Assembly of Sci. and Applied Psychology (sec.-treas. 1987-88), Assn. Behavioral and Cognitive Therapy (student affairs coord. 1978, assoc. program chmn. 1979, program chmn. 1980, chmn. task force student involvement 1980-81, pres.-elect, 1996-97, pres. 1997-98, Lifetime Achievement award 2007), Assn. for Contextual Behavioral Sci. (pres.-elect 2007); Soc. Exptl. Analysis Behavior (sec. 1985, pres.-elect, 1996—, co-chmn. practice guidelines coalition 1997—, co-chair practice guidelines coalition 1996-2001), Southeastern Assn. for Behavior Analysis (sec. 1985-86), Sigma Xi. Democrat. Avocations: guitar, boating. Home: 933 Gear St Reno NV 89503-2729 Business E-Mail: hayes@unr.edu.

HAYES, SYLVIA RICHMOND, music educator; b. Lawrenceburg, Tenn.; d. Edward David and Blanche Audrey (Sells) Richmond; m. Gene Edwin Hayes; B.S., George Peabody Coll. Tchrs., M.Mus. Edn., 1968; postgrad. Tenn. State U.; postgrad. in data processing Columbia State Community Coll. Band dir., tchr. English, high sch., Loretto, Tenn.; dir. band, tchr. music Coffman Sch., Lawrenceburg, 1972—89, Leoma (Tenn.) Sch., 1989-94; tech. coord. Lawrence County Sch. Sys., 1994—. Choir and music dir., sec. Immanuel Baptist Ch. Mem. Bus. and Profl. Women's Club (Career Woman of Yr. 1972), Lawrence County Edn. Assn. (treas. bd. dirs., sec. 1988-98, pres. 1998-99), Midele Edn. Assn. (Tenn.), Tenn. Edn. Assn., NEA, Middle Band and Orch. Assn., Music Educators Nat. Conf. Democrat. Club: Lioness (pres. 1977-78). Office: Lawrence County Bd Edn 700 Mahr Ave Lawrenceburg TN 38464

HAYES, TIMOTHY GEORGE, lawyer, consultant; b. New London, Conn., June 27, 1954; s. George Melen and Lauretta C. (Bresnahan) Hayes; m. Barbara Joan White, Jan. 27, 1983; children: Laura Katherine, Kevin Michael. BS, Fla. State U., 1976, MS, 1977; JD, Stetson Coll. Law, 1982. Bar: Fla. 1982, U.S. Dist. Ct. (mid. dist.) Fla. 1983. Legis. aide Fla. State Rep. George H. Sheldon, Tallahassee, 1978-79; assoc. Alice K. Nelson, P.A., Tampa, Fla., 1982-83; ptnr. Cotterill, Gonzalez & Hayes, Lutz, Fla., 1983-84, Cotterill, Gonzalez, Hayes & Grantham, Lutz, 1984-88; sr. ptnr. Hayes & McClelland, Lutz, 1988-90, Hayes, Winick & Albrechta, Lutz, 1990-91, Hayes & Albrechta, P.A., Lutz, 1991-93, Hayes & Assocs., Lutz, 1993—. Task force Tampa-Orlando High-Speed Transp. Study, 1992—94; adv. bd. Pasco-Hernando C.C., 1994—95; citizens adv. com. Pasco County Parks and Recreation, 1999—2002, Pasco County Natural Gas Pipeline, 2000; pres. United Soccer Assn., 2000—02; adv. bd. Gulf and Lake Acad., 2002—; co-chmn. Penny for Pasco Sales Tax Referendum, 2003—04; v.p. Hillsborough County Young Dems., Tampa, 1978, pres., 1979; bd. dir. Tampa Bay Commuter Rail Authority, Tampa, 1990—97, Pasco County Econ. Devel. Coun., Land O'Lakes, Fla., 1990—92, 2004—, Heritage Park Found., 1998—, Pasco Edn. Found., Inc., 2004—, Ctrl. Pasco Chamber of Commerce, 2001—; bd. dir., chmn. bd. Suncoast Harvest Food Bank, 2003—06; bd. dir., coach Ctrl. Pasco United Soccer Assn., 1995—2003, pres., 1996—98; chmn. Govt. Affairs Com., 2003—. Named Outstanding Young Man in Am., Jaycees, 1980, Citizen of Yr., Ctrl. Pasco C. of C., 2002; recipient Sam Walton Bus. Leader award, 1998. Mem.: ABA (real property, probate and trust law sect.), Fla. Bar Assn. (environ. and land use law sect., real property, probate and trust law sect.), Ctrl. Pasco C. of C. (chmn. 2003—05), Land O' Lakes C. of C. (v.p. 1988—89, pres. 1991—92, chmn. bd. 1992—93, bd. dirs.). Roman Catholic. Avocations: soccer, bicycling, camping, gardening. Office: Hayes & Assocs 21859 State Road 54 Ste 200 Lutz FL 33549-6986 Home Phone: 813-849-7057; Office Phone: 813-949-6525. E-mail: tghayes@mindspring.com.

HAYES, WILBUR FRANK, retired biology professor; b. Rhinelander, Wis., Nov. 10, 1936; s. Wilbur Mead and Evelyn (Stritesky) H.; m. Dawn Olivia Waldorf, July 21, 1979 (div. Feb. 1991); stepchildren: Lynn, Robert, Dana, Richard, Gary, Kevin. BA, Colby Coll., Waterville, Maine, 1959;

MS, Lehigh U., Bethlehem, Pa., 1961, PhD, 1965. Postdoctoral fellow Yale U., New Haven, 1965-67; asst. prof. biology Wilkes Coll., Wilkes-Barre, Pa., 1967-71, assoc. prof., 1971-99, assoc. prof. emeritus, 2000—. Vis. prof. Northeastern U., Boston, 1987-88. Contbr. articles to profl. jours. Chmn. bd. dirs. N.E. Pa. chpt. Am. Heart Assn., Wilkes-Barre, 1986-87. Mem. Soc. for Integrative and Comparative Biology, Pa. Acad. Sci., Microscopy Soc. Am., Sigma Xi (pres. Wilkes Coll. chpt. 1976-77, sec.-treas. 1984-87, 88-91). Republican. Congregationalist. Avocations: downhill skiing, photography, travel, colonial american history. Home: 47 Stanley St Wilkes Barre PA 18702-2308 Office: Wilkes U Dept Biology Wilkes Barre PA 18766

HAYES, WILLIAM MEREDITH, pilot, retired military officer; b. San Antonio, Mar. 28, 1947; s. Oscar Junior and Mary Kathryn (Leuthart) Hayes; m. Beverly Jeanne Lowe, May 20, 1972; children: Loren Elaine, Colin Meredith. BA, Western Ky. U., 1971. Cert. naval aviator, airline transport pilot FAA. Commd. ensign USCG, 1973, advanced through grades to capt., 1994; asst. ops. officer USCG Base, Honolulu, 1973-74; pub. affairs officer USCG Air Sta., Mobile, Ala., 1975-78; tng. officer USCG Group/Air Sta., Corpus Christi, Tex., 1978-81; head Falcon jet tng. USCG Aviation Tng. Ctr., Mobile, 1981-87; air ops. officer USCG Air Sta., Miami, Fla., 1987-92, exec. officer Elizabeth City, NC, 1992-94; commdg. officer USCG Activities, San Diego, 1994-97; chief office of ops. 8th C.G. Dist., New Orleans, 1997; pilot Humana, Inc., Louisville, 1997—. Bd. dir. USO, San Diego, Armed Svcs. YMCA, San Diego; mem. mil. adv. coun. C. of C., San Diego, 1994—. Contbr. articles to profl. jours. Recipient Humanitarian Svc. medal USCG, Corpus Christi, 1978, Commendation medal USCG, Miami, 1992, Achievement medal USCG, Elizabeth City, 1994, Meritorious Svc. medal, 1997. Mem. SCV, Amateur Radio Relay League, Sons of the Am. Revolution, Delta Tau Delta (life, chpt. v.p. 1969-70). Avocations: fishing, amateur radio, golf. Home: 2420 Napoleon Blvd Louisville KY 40205-2011 Office: Humana 1180 Standiford Ct Louisville KY 40213-2019 Office Phone: 502-580-0452. Personal E-mail: wmhayes@bellsouth.net. Business E-Mail: wmhayes@humana.com.

HAYFLICK, LEONARD, cell biologist, biogerontologist, microbiologist, educator, writer; b. Phila., May 20, 1928; s. Nathan Albert and Edna H.; m. Ruth Louise Heckler, Oct. 3, 1954; children: Joel, Deborah, Susan, Rachel, Anne. BA in Microbiology and Chemistry, U. Pa., 1951, MS in Med. Microbiology, 1953, PhD in Med. Microbiology and Chemistry, 1956. McLaughlin rsch. fellow in infection and immunity, dept. microbiology U. Tex. Med. Br., Galveston, Tex., 1956-58; assoc. mem. Wistar Inst. Anatomy and Biology, Phila., 1958-68; asst. prof. rsch. medicine U. Pa., Phila., 1966-68; prof. med. microbiology Stanford U. Sch. Medicine, Calif., 1968-76, senator-at-large, Basic Med. Scis., 1970-73, chmn. gen. rsch. support grant com., 1972-74; sr. rsch. cell biologist Children's Hosp., Oakland, Calif., 1976-81; prof. zoology, prof. microbiology and immunology U. Fla., Gainesville, 1981-87, dir. Ctr. for Gerontol. Studies, Coll. Liberal Arts and Scis., 1981-87; prof. anatomy U. Calif. Sch. Medicine, San Francisco, 1988—. Mem. subcom. on mycoplasmataceae Internat. Com. Bacteriol. Nomenclature, 1965-78; mem. steering com. cell and devel. biology film program MIT, 1970-73; chmn. Calif. State Com. Health White Ho. Conf. Aging, 1971-72, Calif. state rep., 1972; Nat. Cancer Planning Com. Nat. Cancer Inst., NIH, 1972; chmn., adult devel. and aging rsch. and tng. com. Nat. Inst. Child Health and Human Devel., NIH, 1972-73; non-resident fellow Inst. Higher Studies, Santa Barbara, Calif., 1973—; mem. Argonne Nat. Lab. rev. com. biol. and med. rsch. div. Argonne Nat. Lab., 1973-76; mem. rsch. adv. com. Tchrs. Ins. and Annuity Assn. Am.-Coll. Retirement Equities Funds, NYC, 1974-80; founding mem. Nat. Adv. Coun. on Aging, Nat. Inst. on Aging, NIH, Bethesda, Md., 1975; cons. Office of Dir. Nat. Cancer Inst., Bethesda, 1963-74; vis. scientist Ctr. for Aging Weizmann Inst. Sci., Rehovoth, Israel, 1980, 86; mem. adv. bd. Internat. Exchange Ctr. Gerontology, Fla. Univ. System, Tampa, 1982-86; mem. jury for Sandoz prize in gerontology and geriatrics, 1985-89; bd. dirs. Ctr. for Climacteric Studies, Inc., Gainesville, 1985-88; expert cons. various coms. US Congress, vis. prof. Oita Med. U., Japan, 1991-95, U. Parma, Italy, 1991, Kurume U. Med. Sch., Japan; lectr. in field. Author: How and Why We Age, 1996; editor: Biology of the Mycoplasmas, 1969, Handbook of the Biology of Aging, 1977; sr. editor Biol. Scis. Microfiche Collection Info. on Gerontology and Geriatric Medicine Univ. Microfilms Internat., Ann Arbor, Mich., 1984-98; editor-in-chief Exptl. Gerontology, 1984-98; asst. editor In Vitro jour. Tissue Culture Assn., 1969-75; editor biol. scis. sect. Jour. Gerontology, 1975-80; assoc. editor Cancer Rsch., 1972-80; mem. editorial bd. Jour. Bacteriology, 1964-72, Jour. Virology, 1967-70, Infection and Immunity jour., 1968-78, Exec. Health Report, 1970—, Mechanisms of Aging and Devel., 1972—, Gerontology and Geriatrics Edn., 1980—, A Revista Portuguesa de Medicina Geriatrica, 1987—; mem. adv. com. Bergey's Manual of Determinative Bacteriology, 1965-78; bd. dirs., mem. editorial bd. Bollettino Dell Instituto Sieroterapico Milanese, Archivo de Microbiologia ed Immunologia, Milan, Italy, 1968—; contbr. numerous articles in field to profl. jours. Staff sgt. US Army, 1946-48. Recipient Samuel Roberts Noble Found. Rsch. Recognition award, 1984; co-recipient Sandoz prize Internat. Assn. Gerontology, 1991, Biomed. Scis. & Aging award U. So. Calif., 1974, Rsch. Recognition award Samuel Roberts Noble Found., 1984; Karl-Forster lectr. Acad. Sci. and Lit., Mainz, Germany, 1983, Hoffman-LaRoche lectr. Waksman Inst. Microbiology Rutgers U., 1984, Wadworth Meml. Fund lectr. Rush-Presbyn.-St. Luke's Med. Ctr., Chgo., 1984, hon. lectr. Rosenfield Program Pub. Affairs Grinnell Coll., 1989, invited speaker Sandoz lectrs. in Gerontology, Basle, Switzerland, 1986, 92, numerous other lectureships U.S.A., Can. and Europe, 1970—, Career Devel. award Nat. Cancer Inst., NIH, 1962-70, Lifetime Achievement award Soc. In Vitro Biology, 1996, Van Wezel prize Euro. Soc. Animal Cell Technology, 1999, Lord Cohen of Birkinhead medal Brit. Soc. Rsch. on Aging, 1999, Life Extension prize, Regenerative Medicine Secretariat, 2001. Fellow AAAS, Gerontol Soc. Am. (program and awards com. 1972-77, chmn., exec. com. biol. scis. sect. 1972-74, com. on internat. rels. 1980-82, pub. policy com. 1980-82, pres. 1982-83, ann. Robert W. Kleemeier award 1972, Brookdale award 1980); mem. Am. Soc. for Microbiology, Tissue Culture Assn. (hon., trustee 1966-68, program com. 1970, mem. coun. 1972-74, v.p. 1974-76, pres. Calif. chpt. 1971-73), Soc. for Exptl. Biology and Medicine (councillor 1984-88), Assn. for Advancement of Aging Rsch. (adv. coun. 1970-71), Am. Aging Assn., Am. Cancer Soc. (virology and cell biology study sect. 1974-76), Internat. Assn. Microbiol. Standardization (sec. cell culture com. 1963-73, chmn. 1985—, mem. coun. 1987-89), Internat. Orgn. for Mycoplasmology (Presdl. award 1984), Am. Gerontol. Soc. (v.p., coun. 1972-74, 81-83, program com. 1977-79, bdu. dirs. 1981-83), Am. Fedn. Aging Rsch. (bd. dirs., exec. com., rsch. adv. com. 1981—, chmn. study sect. 1987—, v.p. 1988—, Leadership award 1983), Fedn. Am. Socs. for Exptl. Biology, Aging Prevention Rsch. Found. (sci. adv. bd. dirs.), Am. Assn. for Cancer Rsch., Am. Soc. Pathologists, Calif. Found. for Biomed. Rsch., Am. Longevity Assn. (sci. adv. bd. dirs. 1981—), Western Gerontology Assn. (coun. 1972-74, bd. dirs. 81-83), Internat. Assn. Gerontology (mem. Am. exec. com. 1972-75, treas., exec. com. 1985-89, co-recipient Sandoz award gerontology 1991), Found. on Gerontology (sci. adv. bd. 1985—), Soc. Medicine and Natural Sci., Ukrainian Acad. Med. Scis. (fgn., Academician 1991, 2005), French Biol. Soc. (fgn.), Euro. Soc. Animal Cell Tech. (Van Wezel prize), Brit. Soc. Rsch. on Aging (Lord Cohen of Burkinhead medal), France Soc. Biology. Achievements include prototype of inverted microscope acquisitioned by Smithsonian Natural Museum of American History in 2006. Office: U Calif 36991 Greencroft Close PO Box 89 The Sea Ranch CA 95497-0089 Business E-Mail: lenh38@aim.com.

HAYGOOD, ALMA JEAN, elementary school educator; d. John Thomas and Alma Perry Haygood. BS, Ala. A&M U., 1978; MA, George Mason U., 2001. Kindergarten tchr. Talladega (Ala.) County Pub. Schs., 1978—80; adult edn. tchr. Ft. Carson (Colo.) Mil. Base, 1980—82; day care ctr. tchr. KinderCare Learning Ctrs., Colorado Springs, Colo., 1982—84; child care ctr. dir. Open Hands Preschool, Colorado Springs, Colo., 1984—85; preschool tchr. Gum Springs Child Devel. Ctr., Alexandria, Va., 1985—87; tchr. Fairfax County Pub. Schs., Springfield, Va., 1987—. Cons., tutoring-mentoring program Lomax Ch., Arlington, Va., 1989—95. Sch. union rep. Fairfax Edn. Assn., Fairfax, Va., 2001—. Tchr. tng. grantee, Fairfax Edn. Assn., 2003. Mem.: Kappa Delta Pi (assoc.; mem. 2002—). Democrat. Baptist. Avocations: piano, singing, exercise. Home: 5318 Harbor Court Dr Alexandria VA 22315-3934 Office: Mount Vernon Woods Elem Sch 4015 Fielding St Alexandria VA 22309 Personal E-mail: hhaggard86@aol.com. E-mail: Alma.Haygood@fcps.edu.

HAYGOOD, EITHEL MARINELLA, artist, educator; b. Ohio County, Ky., Nov. 18, 1926; d. Lloyd Urbin and Alma Alice (Simpson) Miller; m. James Richard Haygood, June 12, 1955; children: James Steven, Russell Alan, Marcus Llyod, Susan Marinella. BA, Ark. State Coll., 1952. Art and speech tchr. Bell City (Mo.) Consol., 1952—54; art and English tchr. Lamar Consol. Ind. Sch. Dist., Rosenberg, Tex., 1954—55, 1964—88. Founding mem. Visual Arts Com. Scholar, Ark. State Coll., 1949. Mem.: Tex. Ret. Tchrs. Assn., Tex. State Tchrs. Assn., Nat. Mus. Women in Arts, Ret. Tchrs. Assn., S.W. Artisans Soc. (founding mem.), Art Exchg. Baptist. Avocations: singing, gardening, photography, birdwatching, reading. Home: 1423 Gardenia Cir Rosenberg TX 77471

HAYHURST, JAMES FREDERICK PALMER, career and business consultant, inspirational speaker, writer; b. Toronto, Can., May 24, 1941; s. W. Palmer and Jean E. (Hunnisett) H.; children: Cindy, Jim, Barbara. H.BA, U. Western Ont., 1963. Brand man Procter & Gamble, Toronto, 1963-66, exec. v.p., 1975-82; pres. Hedwyn Communications Inc., Toronto, 1983-86; chmn. Saatchi & Saatchi Compton Hayhurst, Toronto, 1983-86; owner Wyldwyn Holdings Ltd., Toronto, 1986—; pres. The Hayhurst Career Ctr., Toronto, 1988—, The Right Mountain Crew, 1994—. Author: The Right Mountain, 1996, Where Have I Gone Right?, 2004. Chmn. Outward Bound Can., 1985-87; founding co-chmn. Trails Youth Initiatives. Mem. Toronto Golf Club, Olde Fla. Golf Club (Naples), Osler Brook Golf Club. Office: The Right Mountain Inc 1788 Avenue Rd Ste E F Toronto ON M5M 321 Canada Business E-Mail: jim@therightmountain.com. *True success is the attainment of purpose without compromising your core values.*

HAYLEY, KATHRYN, consulting company executive; BS applied computer sci., Ill. State U., 1979; MBA Fin. in Mgmt., Northwestern U. Kellogg Sch. of Mgmt., 1984. Joined Deloitte Consulting LLP, 1984; mng. dir. Midwest regional, Deloitte Consulting LLP; CEO Aon Corp., US, 2006—. Mem. bd. dirs. Gateway Found., The Chgo. Shakespeare Theater, The Civic Cons. Alliance, Deloitte & Touche U.S. Named one of 25 Women to Watch, Crain's Chgo. Bus., 2007. Office: Aon Corp 200 E Randolph St Chicago IL 60601 Office Phone: 312-381-1000.

HAYMAN, HARRY, professional society administrator, electrical engineer; b. Lewistown, Pa., Mar. 20, 1917; s. Sidney and Nettie (Hirsch) H.; m. Edith Harriet Levitz, Mar. 18, 1946; children: Gail A., Beth (Mrs. Stanley Truman), Sidney F., Stuart A. BS, NYU, 1938; postgrad., George Washington U., 1947—50. Engr. FCC, Washington, 1940-54; pres., gen. mgr. radio sta. WPGC, Morningside, Md., 1954-55; project mgr. U.S. Navy and FAA, Washington, 1956-60; program mgr. NASA project Apollo, Washington, 1960-71; chmn. IEEE Computer Soc., Washington, 1965, exec. sec. NYC, 1971-82, dir. confs. and tutorials Silver Spring, Md., 1982-89, coord. robotics and automation divsn., 1988—. Vice pres. Nat. Childrens Ctr., 1960; pres. Henryton State Hosp. Assn., 1970, 74; Bd. dirs. D.C. Assn. Retarded Children, 1956-70, pres. Washington chpt., 1953-55; pres. Gt. Oaks Aux., 1975-78. Served with USNR, 1944-46. Recipient Apollo Achievement award 1969. Mem. IEEE (treas. Computer Soc. Internat. Conf. 1970, treas. Internat. Conf. on Computer Comm. 1972, spl. asst. to chmn. Conf. on Computer Comm. 1974, coord., treas. Internat. Conf. on Robotics and Automation 1980-96). Home: 3037C Exeter Dr Boca Raton FL 33434

HAYMAN, MARTIN ARTHUR, psychiatrist, educator; b. NYC, Dec. 5, 1929; s. Louis and Cecelia (Klatzkin) H.; m. Traude E. Sighartner, June 9, 1957; children: Douglas, Kenneth. BA cum laude, NYU, 1951, MD, 1955. Diplomate Am. Bd. Psychiatry and Neurology, Nat. Bd. Med. Examiners. Intern Meadowbrook Hosp., East Meadow, NY, 1955-56; pvt. practice Nassau County, 1959-73; sr. physician VA Med. Ctr., Northport, 1973; resident in psychiatry SUNY Med. Ctr., Stony Brook, 1974-77, asst. prof. clin. psychiatry, 1977—. Dir. psychiatry South Brookhaven Health Ctr., Patchogue, NY, 1977—91; attending physician Brookhaven Meml. Hosp. Med. Ctr., 1977—91. Reviewer jour.; contbr. articles to profl. jours. Mem. ad hoc com. Helping Older People Emotionally, Suffolk County, 1981-82. Capt. M.C., USAF, 1956-58. Fellow Acad. Psychosomatic Medicine; mem. AMA (Physician's Recognition awards 1970—), Am. Psychiat. Assn., Med. Soc. N.Y., Suffolk County Med. Soc., Phi Beta Kappa, Beta Lambda Sigma (vice chancellor 1951). Home and Office: 20 Redwood Dr PO Box 626 Great River NY 11739-0626 Personal E-mail: mhayman@pol.net, mthayman@optonline.net.

HAYMAN, RANDY E., lawyer; b. St. Louis, Sept. 24, 1963; s. Robert B.E. and Roen Hayman. BA, U. Mich., 1985; JD, Georgetown U., 1989. Bar: Mo. 1995, Pa. 1990, D.C. 1990, U.S. Dist. Ct. (ea. dist. Mo.) 1999, U.S. Dist. Ct. (we. dist. Mo.) 1995, U.S. Supreme Ct. 1997. Intern ABC News, 1984; reporter KMOX Radio News CBS, St. Louis, 1985—86; law clk. Nat. Pub. Radio, Washington, 1987; assoc. Wilkes, Artis, Hedrick & Lane, Washington, 1989—92; counsel NAACP Legal Def. Fund, Inc., Washington, 1992—93; asst. atty. gen. Mo. Atty. Gen.'s Office, Jefferson City, Mo., 1994—96; assoc. Stinson, Mag & Fizzell PC, Kansas City, St. Louis, 1996—2000; gen. counsel Met. St. Louis Sewer Dist., 2000—. Mem. Leadership St. Louis, 2002; bd. dirs. Crime Solvers, Washington, 1991—94, pres., 1993—94; bd. dirs. Build a Future Found., 1989—97, Trailnet, 2005—, Herbert Hoover Boys and Girls Club, 2006—, Assn. Corp. Coun. St. Louis chpt., 2006—, Crime Stoppers, 2006—. Named to, Herbert Hoover Boys and Girl's Club Hall of Honor, 2006; recipient Yes I Can Achievement award, Met. Sentinel Jour. Newspaper, 2006. Mem.: ABA, Mo. Bar Young Lawyers' Coun. (bd. dirs. young lawyer's coun. 1998), Lawyers' Assn. Kansas City (bd. dirs. Young Lawyers divsn. 1997—98), Am. Met. Sewer Assn., Water Environment Fedn., Am. Corp. Counsel Assn., Bar Assn. Met. St. Louis (bd. dirs. Young Lawyers divsn. 1998—2001). Avocations: guitar, radio talk show host, public speaking. Office: Met St Louis Sewer Dist 2350 Market St Saint Louis MO 63103

HAYMAN, RICHARD WARREN JOSEPH, conductor; b. Cambridge, Mass., Mar. 27, 1920; s. Fred Albert and Gladys Marie (Learned) Hayman; m. Maryellen Daly, June 25, 1960; children: Suzanne Marie, Olivia Kathryn. D Hum. (hon.), Detroit Coll. Bus., 1980. Freelance composer, arranger 20th Century Fox, Warner Bros., MGM, Universal Film Studios; music arranger, dir. Vaughn Monroe Orch. records and TV show, NYC, 1945-50; chief arranger Arthur Fiedler and Boston Pops Orchestra, 1950-95; mus. dir. Mercury Record Corp., NYC, 1950-65, Time-Mainstream Records, NYC, 1960-70; prin. pops condr. Detroit Symphony Orchs.; prin. pops condr., McDonnell Douglas chair St. Louis, 1976—; prin. pops condr. Birmingham (Ala.), Hartford (Conn.), Calgary (Can.), Grand Rapids (Mich.) Symphony Orch., London (Ont., Can.) Orch. Composer: No Strings Attached, Dansero, Skipping Along, Carriage Trade, Serenade to a Lost Love, Olivia, Suzanne, Freddie the Football; rec. artist Naxos Internat. Records, 1991—. Recipient Best Instrumental Record award, Sta. WERE, Cleve., 1963, McDonnell Douglas award, 2000, Star dedicated, Hollywood Blvd. Walk of Fame. Mem.: ASCAP, NARAS (Best TV Comml. Jingle award 1960), Am. Fed. Musicians. Roman Catholic. Office: Richard Hayman Prodns 784 US Highway 1 Ste 22B North Palm Beach FL 33408-4411*

HAYMET, ANTHONY DOUGLAS-JOHN, research scientist, chemistry educator; b. Sydney, Feb. 5, 1956; came to US, 1978; s. William Brian and Coral Elizabeth (Snaden) H.; m. Nan Christine Jackson, Nov. 21, 1984. BSc with honors, U. Sydney, 1977; PhD in Chemistry, U. Chgo., 1981; DSc, U. Sydney, 1997. Postdoctoral rsch. fellow Harvard U., Cambridge, Mass., 1981-83; asst. prof. chemistry U. Calif., Berkeley, 1983-88; assoc. prof. chemistry U. Utah, Salt Lake City, 1988-91, adj. prof. chemistry, 1991—95; prof. chemistry U. Sydney, Australia, 1991—98, vis. prof., 1998—99; dep. dir. physical sciences CAUT Ctr. Ednl. Software in Sci., Sydney, 1994—97; chmn. physical chemistry divsn. U. Houston, 1998—2001, founder Environ. Modeling Inst., 2000—02, disting. U. prof. chem., 1998—2002; hon. rsch. prof. chemistry U. Tasmania, 2002—06; dir. sci. & policy Australian Commonwealth Sci. & Indsl. Rsch. Orgn. (CSIRO), 2005—06, chief marine & atmospheric rsch., 2006; vice chancellor marine sciences U. Calif. San Diego, 2006—, dean Grad. Sch. Marine Sciences & dir. Scripps Instn. Oceanography, 2006—. Affiliate staff scientist Pacific N.W. Nat. Lab., 1996—2002; mem. faculty W.M. Keck Ctr. Computational Biology, Washington, 1998—2002; adv. bd. Environ. Inst. Houston, 2001—02; bd. dirs. Coop. Rsch. Ctr. Antarctic Climate & Ecosystems, Tasmania, 2003—06; mem. founding group Western Australia Marine Sci. Instn., 2005—06. Recipient Student Disting. Svc. award, U. Utah, 1990, Antarctic Svc. medal, US Dept. Navy & Nat. Sci. Found., 1994, Disting. Young Chemist award, Fedn. Asian Chem. Socs., 1997. Mem. Am. Chem. Soc., Am. Phys. Soc., AAAS, Royal Australia Chem. Inst. (Masson medal, 1977, Rennie medal, 1988). Avocations: running, cross country skiing, hiking. Office: U Calif San Diego #0210 9500 Gilman Dr La Jolla CA 92093-0210 Office Phone: 858-534-2827. Office Fax: 858-453-0167. E-mail: thaymet@ucsd.edu.

HAYMON, CHADRON ZONELLE, music educator, minister; b. Denver, June 28, 1974; s. Ronald Zonelle and Sheila Jo Haymon; m. Andrea Michelle Bunch, May 23, 1998; 1 child, Joya Isabelle. BA in Music Edn., Metro State Coll., Denver, 1997. Cert. music edn. K-12 vocal and instrumental Va. Bd. Edn., 2002. Music pastor Capital Cmty. Ch., Ashburn, Va., 1997—; orch. dir. Marsteller Mid. Sch., Bristow, Va., 1998—2005. Min. of music Capital Cmty. Ch., Ashburn, Va., 1997—. Mem. steering com. Heart of Worship Ministries, Stockton, Calif., 2003—. Mem.: Music Educators Nat. Conf. (licentiate). Republican. Pentecostal. Avocations: music, skiing. Home: 608 Nathan Pl Leesburg VA 20176 Office: Capital Comty Ch 20430 Ashburn Village Blvd Ashburn VA 20147 Home Phone: 571-258-1288; Office Phone: 703-393-7608. E-mail: haymoncz@pwcs.edu.

HAYNER, HERMAN HENRY, lawyer; b. Fairfield, Wash., Sept. 25, 1916; s. Charles H. and Lillie (Reifenberger) H.; m. Jeannette Hafner, Oct. 24, 1942; children: Stephen, James K., Judith A. BA, Wash. State U., Pullman, 1938; JD with honors, U. Oreg., Eugene, 1946. Bar: Wash. 1946, Oreg. 1946, US Dist. Ct. Wash. 1947, US Ct. Appeals (9th cir.) 1947. Asst. US atty. US Dept. Justice, Portland, Oreg., 1946-47; atty. City of Walla Walla, Wash., 1949-53; ptnr. Minnick-Hayner, Walla Walla, 1949—. Mem. Wash. State exec. bd. U.S. West, Seattle, 1988-95. Regent Wash. State U., Pullman, 1965-78; dir. YMCA, Walla Walla, 1956-67. Lt. col. Infantry, 1942-46. Decorated Bronze Star medal and four Battle Stars; recipient Disting. Svc. award Jr. C. of C., 1951, Wash. State U. Alumni award, 1988. Fellow ABA, Am. Coll. Trust & Estate Counsel; mem. Wash. State Bar Assn., Walla Walla County Bar Assn. (pres. 1954-55), Walla Walla C. of C. (merit award 1977, dir. 1973-88), Rotary (pres. 1956-57), Walla Walla Country Club (pres. 1956-57). Republican. Presbyterian. Avocation: golf. Home: PO Box 454 Walla Walla WA 99362 Office: Minnick-Hayner PO Box 1757 Walla Walla WA 99362 Personal E-mail: hhhayner2@aol.com.

HAYNES, BARTON FORD, medical educator; b. Memphis, Tenn., July 13, 1947; BS, U. Tenn., 1969; MD, Baylot Coll. Medicine, 1973. Cert. Internal Medicine, Allergy & Immunology, Pediatric Infectious Diseases, Clin. & Lab. Immunology. Intern, medicine Duke U. Sch. Medicine, Durham, NC, 1973—74, resident, 1975, dir., Human Vaccine Inst., 2002—; resident Nat. Inst. Allergy and Infectious Diseases, Bethesda, Md., 1975—78, dir., Ctr. for HIV-AIDS Vaccine Immunology; fellow HIH/Nat. Inst. Allergy and Infectious Diseases, Bethesda, Md., 1975—78; prof. medicine, chief divsn. rheumatology, allergy and clin. immunology Duke U. Med. Ctr., Durham, NC, 1987—95, chmn., dept. medicine, 1995—2002, Frederic M. Hanes Prof. Medicine and Immunology. Chmn. Nat. Inst. Allergy and Infectious Diseases AIDS Vaccine Research Working Group; served on Nat. Inst. Allergy and Infectious Diseases Blue Ribbon Committees on Bioterrorism and Emerging Infections, 2002. Contbr. articles to profl. jours. Fellow: Infectious Disease Soc. Am., Am. Acad. Arts & Scis.; mem.: Assn. Am. Physicians, NAS Inst. Medicine (chmn. Roundtable for Develop. for Drugs and Vaccines Against AIDS). Office: Duke U Med Ctr DUMC Box 3258 Durham NC 27710 Office Phone: 919-684-5384. Business E-Mail: hayne002@mc.duke.edu.*

HAYNES, CALEB VANCE, JR., geology and archaeology educator; b. Spokane, Wash., Feb. 29, 1928; m. Elizabeth Hamilton, Jan. 11, 1954 (dec. 2004); 1 child, Elizabeth Anne. Student, Johns Hopkins U., 1947-49; degree in geol. engring., Colo. Sch. Mines, 1956; PhD, U. Ariz., 1965. Mining geology cons., 1958-60; sr. project engr. Am. Inst. Research, Golden, Colo., 1956-60; sr. engr. Martin Co., Denver, 1960-62; geologist Nev. State Mus. Tule Springs Expedition, 1962-63; research asst. U. Ariz., Tucson, 1963-64, asst. prof. geology, 1965-68, prof. geoscis., anthropology, 1974-99, Regents prof., 1991-99, Regents prof. emeritus, 1999; assoc. prof. So. Meth. U., Dallas, 1968-73, prof., 1973-74. With USAF, 1951—54. Guggenheim fellow 1980-81, Smithsonian sr. post doctoral fellow, 1987; grantee NSF, Nat. Geographic Soc., others. Fellow: AAAS, Geol. Soc. Am. (Archaeol. Geology award 1984, Kirk Bryan award 2003); mem.: Soc. Am. Archaeology (Fryxell award 1978), Am. Quaternary Assn. (pres. 1976—78, Disting. Career award 2002), Nat. Acad. Sci., Sigma Xi. Office: U Ariz Dept Anthropology Tucson AZ 85721-0001 Office Phone: 520-621-6307.

HAYNES, CORNELL **See NELLY**

HAYNES, GARY ALLEN, photojournalist, editor; b. Beloit, Kans., Jan. 25, 1936; s. Blair W. and Evelyn H. (Allen) F.; children by previous marriage: Stephanie L., Philip A., Emily L.; m. Audrey M. (Edwards); stepchildren: Jane Kelly, Katie Kelly. BS in journalism, Kans. State U., 1957. Staff photographer Salina (Kans.) Jour., Salina, Kans., 1957; photographer UPI, Detroit, 1958, mgr. picture bur. Phila., 1959-62, Atlanta, 1962-63, spl. projects photographer NYC, 1964, mgr. picture bur. LA, 1964-68; photographer Internat. Olympic Photo Pool, Tokyo, 1964; mgr. divsn. news pictures UPI, Chgo., 1968-70, asst. to mng. editor newspictures NYC, 1970-71; nat. picture editor N.Y. Times, NYC, 1971-74; photo editor San Francisco Examiner, San Francisco, 1974; dir. graphic arts Phila. Inquirer, Phila., 1974-95, asst. mng. editor; with Photography weekly column, syndicated by Knight Newspapers (later Knight Ridder), 1976-87; cons. N.Y. Times, NYC, 1996—. Photographer NASA Photo Pool, 1962-63; spkr., del., USA,USSR Photo Summit, Moscow, 1990, Washington, 1991. Contbg. photographer: (book) Four Days-The Historical Record of Death of President Kennedy, 1963, A Week at Kansas State, 1988; author:

Picture This! The Inside Story and Classic Photos of UPI Newspictures, 2006; picture editor: Assignment Am.-N.Y. Times, 1972, A Day In the Life of Calif., 1989; contbr. articles to profl. jours.; judge, W.R. Hearst photojournalism competition, San Francisco, 1986-88; lectr., photography and photo editing, Am. Press Inst., Reston, Va., 1987-96, The New Sch., 1991, Internat. Ctr. Photography, NY., 1990, U. Arts, Phila., 1989-91, Kans. State U., Manhattan, 1989-99, 2000, 04, Kans. State U., photo workshop, Salina, 2002, 04, Temple U., Phila., 1992. Capt., Adj. Gen. Corps, U.S. Army, 1957-58. Recipient 1st and 3d pl. pictures of yr. gen. news, News Pictures of Yr. 18th ann. competition, 1961, 1st pl. award, Look mag., Sports Photo Contest, 1962, 1st and Best of Show awards, The White Ho. News Photographers Assn., 1962, Photo awards, World Press Photo, 1964, Sweepstakes award, Atlanta Press Assn., 1964, Sweepstakes 1st and 3d pl. awards, Gen. News, 1964, Best Use of Pictures in a Newspaper award, Nat. Press Photog. Assn., 1978, Judges Spl. award for newspaper picture editing, 1979, Berman award for advances in photojournalism, Nat. Press Photog. Assn., 1979, Best Use of Photos in a Newspaper Zoned Edit, Nat. Press Photog. Assn./Pictures of Yr. Competition, Silver medal mag. photo editing, Soc. Newspaper Design, 1988. Mem., Nat. Press Photographer's Assn., Sigma Delta Chi. Home: 1473 N Ill Rte 2 Oregon IL 61061 Home Phone: 815-732-9119. Personal E-mail: garyhaynes1@verizon.net.

HAYNES, JOHN MABIN, retired utilities executive; b. Albany, NY, Apr. 22, 1928; s. John Mabin and Gladys Elizabeth (Phillips) H.; m. Marion Enola Hamilton, Apr. 7, 1956; children: John David, Douglas Hamilton, Robert Paul. BS, Utica Coll., Syracuse U., 1952. Accountant Price Waterhouse & Co., NYC, Syracuse, NY, 1953-61; successively auditor, adminstrv. asst., asst. treas., treas., treas. and v.p., sr. v.p. Niagara Mohawk Power Corp., Syracuse, 1961-88; past pres., chmn., dir. N.Y. Bus. Devel. Corp., Albany. Past dir., pres. N M Uranium, Inc.; past dir., treas. Canadian Niagara Power Co. Ltd.; past treas. Moreau Mfg. Co., St. Lawrence Power Co.; past treas. Empire State Power Resources, Inc.; past dir. and treas. Beebee Island Corp.; past bd. dirs. treas. Opinac Investments Ltd., Opinac Energy Ltd., Opinac Holdings Ltd.; past mng. dir. Niagara Mohawk Fin. N.V. Mem. Westhill Cen. Sch. Bd. Edn., 1968-73, pres., 1969-71; treas. Henderson County Humane Soc., 1989-90. With AUS, 1945-47. Mem. Nat. Assn. Accountants (past dir.), Am. Gas Assn. (fin. com.), Fin. Execs. Inst. Clubs: Bond of Syracuse (past dir.), Masons. Home: Apt 352 400 Wesley Dr Asheville NC 28803 Personal E-mail: jack_hay352@msn.com.

HAYNES, LEONARD L., III, director; b. Boston, Jan. 26, 1947; s. Leonard L. Haynes Jr. and Leila Louise (Davenport) H.; m. Mary Jane Sensley, Aug. 10, 1968; children: Leonard IV, Eboni Michelle, Jabari Kenyatta, Bakari Ali. BA, So. U., Baton Rouge, 1968; MA, Carnegie-Mellon U., 1969; PhD, Ohio State U., 1975, LLD (hon.), 1990, Ala. A&M U., 1990; DHL (hon.), Wiley Coll., 1990; LLD (hon.), Richard Stockton U., NJ, 1991. Instr. history So. U., 1969-70, exec. v.p., 1982-85, prof., 1985-88; edn. policy fellow Dept. Edn. State of Ill., Springfield, 1972-73; staff asst. to pres. Ohio State U., Columbus, 1974-75, asst. to provost, 1975-76; dir. desegregation policy Inst. Svcs. Edn., Washington, 1976-79; dir. Office Advancement Pub. Black Colls., Washington, 1979-82; asst. supt. acad program Dept Edn. State of La., Baton Rouge, 1988-89; asst. sec. U.S. Dept. Edn., Washington, 1989-91; pres. Haynes the Third and Assocs., Silver Spring, Md., 1993-94; sr. asst. to pres. The Am. V., 1994-95; spl. asst. to pres. Fine Host Corp., 1995—. Cons., HHS, Washington, 1991—; cons., dir. acad. programs USIA, Washington, 1991-93; vis. scholar edn. policy U. Md., 1994; sr. asst. to pres. Am. U., 1994—; dir. Fund for Improvement of Postsecondary Edn. US Dept. Edn., 2001—; acting pres. Grambling State U., 1997-1998; sr. adv. to supr. DC Pub. Schs., 1999-2001. Author: A Critical Examination-Adams Case, 1978; editor: An Analysis-Arkansas and Georgia Desegregation Plans, 1979; editorial bd. Jour. Negro Edn. Mem. fam. com. United Way, Baton Rouge, 1985-88; bd. dirs. NCCJ, Baton Rouge, 1988. Recipient Meritorious citation Pres.'s Bd. Advisors Black Colls., 1991, Nat. Svc. award S.C. State Coll., 1991, Disting. Alumni award So. U., 1991. Mem. Jack and Jill Inc., So. U. Nat. Lettermen's Club (pres. 1987-88), Ohio State U. Alumni Assn., So. U. Alumni Assn., Washington Cosmos Club, Washington Rotary Inernat, Hist. Makers, Inc., Omega Psi Phi, Phi Delta Kappa. Methodist. Avocation: competitive sports. Home: 1346 Atwood Rd Silver Spring MD 20906-2087

HAYNES, PETER LANCASTER, utilities executive; b. Ellsworth, Maine, July 8, 1939; s. Charles A. and Hazel G. (Giles) H.; m. Judith A. Bates, Aug. 26, 1961; children: Jeffrey, Timothy, Christopher. BS, U. Maine, 1961; MBA, Cornell U., 1963. Registered profl. engr., Vt. V.p. switched svcs. New Eng. Telephone, Boston, 1978-83, v.p. mktg., 1983-85; pres., CEO Nynex Enterprises, NYC, 1985-90, Quality Logistics Mgmt., Inc., Bedford, NY, 1991-92, Consumers Water Co., Portland, Maine, 1992-99. Bd. visitors U. Maine, 2007—. Chmn. Boys and Girls Club Am., 1999—2001, bd. govs.; pres. Portland Symphony, 2002—04; chmn. Maine Med. Ctr., 2002—05, MaineHealth, 2005—. Mem.: Cornell Club N.Y. Home: 98 Starboard Reach Yarmouth ME 04096-6158 Home Phone: 207-846-7807; Office Phone: 207-846-4561. Personal E-mail: plhaynes@aol.com.

HAYNES, R. MICHAEL, lawyer; b. Safford, Ariz., Oct. 3, 1940; s. Rodman and Angeline (Fragale) H.; m. Anne Marie de Almeida, Aug. 15, 1972; 1 child, Michelle Chloe. BA, Rutgers U., 1963, JD with honors, 1968. Bar: N.Y. 1969, N.J. 1977, D.C. 1992, U.S. Dist. Ct. (so. and ea. dists.) N.Y. 1973, U.S. Ct. Appeals (2d cir.) 1973, U.S. Supreme Ct. 1973, U.S. Dist. Ct. N.J. 1977, U.S. Dist. Ct. D.C. 1992. Assoc. Cooper, Ostrin, DeVargo & Ackerman, NYC, 1968-69; asst. dist. atty., dep. chief rackets bur. N.Y. County Dist. Atty.'s Office, NYC, 1969-74; exec. asst. dist. atty. spl. narcotics Prosecutor's Office, NYC, 1974-76; asst. U.S. atty. Dist. N.J., Newark, 1976-79; minority counsel Com. on Small Bus., U.S. Senate, Washington, 1979-81, chief counsel, 1981-86; gen. counsel Nat. Assn. Small Bus. Investment Cos., Washington, 1986-90; founding ptnr. Law Offices R. Michael Haynes, Washington, 1990—2000; prin. Semmes, Bowen & Semmes, P.C., Washington, 2000—. Adj. prof. L.I. U., 1975-76; instr. N.Y. State Commn. Investigation, 1974-75, Atty. Gen.'s Adv. Inst., Dept. Justice, 1978-79; counsel White House Conf. on Small Bus., 1980 Advisor Washington Internat. Sch. Mock Trial Team, 1991-95. Recipient Atty. Gen.'s Spl. Achievement award, 1977 Mem. ABA (chmn. SBIC subcom. small bus. com. 1986-89), Fed. Bar Assn. (chmn. small bus. com. fin. insts. and economy sect. 1988-89), U.S. C. of C. (small bus. coun. 1987-89), SEC Govt. Bus. Forum on Capital Formation (exec. com. 1988-89). Republican. Office: 3509 Idaho Ave NW Washington DC 20016-3151 Office Phone: 202-966-5102. E-mail: mhaynes@semmes.com. *The law holds everyone equally accountable, but requires of a lawyer a higher duty to honor the principles that the law prescribes while at the same time serving the people whom it governs. To that end, a lawyer must insure that the law itself remains just and fair and that those who make and enforce the law do so with integrity.*

HAYNES, RICHARD (RACEHORSE HAYNES), lawyer; b. Houston, Apr. 3, 1927; BBA, U. Houston, 1951, JD, 1956. Bar: Tex. 1956. Pvt. practice, 1956—. Adj. prof. law U. Houston, 1972—73; mem. permanent tchg. faculty Nat. Coll. for Criminal Def. Charter mem. Coll. Edn., Challenge Club, U. Houston; chmn. bd. regents Nat. Coll. for Criminal Def., 1980—81; mem. Nat. Neurofibromatosis Found.-Tex. Chpt.; bd. mem. Coll. Edn. Found. Bd., U. Houston. Paratrooper officer. Named one of Top Criminal Def. Lawyers, The Best Lawyers in Am., 5th edit. (book), 10 Best Trial Lawyers, The Trial Lawyers (book); recipient Tex. Lifetime Achievement award, Mexican Am. Bar Assn., 2004, Outstanding Alumni award, U. Houston, Law Alumni award, Golden Plate award, Am. Acad. Achievement. Fellow: Internat. Acad. Trial Lawyers, Tex. Bar Found.; mem.: ABA, Houston Law Found. (bd. dirs.), Houston Bar Assn. (bd. dirs.), Harris County Criminal Lawyers Assn. (bd. dirs., named Lawyer of Yr. 1999), Tex. Trial Lawyers Assn., Tex. Criminal Def. Lawyers Assn. (bd. dirs.), Tex. Bar Assn. (bd. dirs.), Nat. Assn. Criminal Def. Lawyers, Am. Judicature Soc., Am. Bd. Trial Advs., Internat. Soc. Barristers, Phi Alpha Delta (alumni advisor 1979—80). Office: Richard Haynes & Assocs PC 4300 Scotland Houston TX 77007-7394 Office Phone: 713-868-1111.*

HAYNES, ROBERT VAUGHN, retired academic administrator, historian; b. Nashville, Nov. 28, 1929; m. Martha Farr, Dec. 25, 1952; children: Catherine Anne, Carolyn Alice, Charles Allen. BA, Millsaps Coll., 1952; MA, Peabody Coll., 1953; PhD, Rice U., 1959. Mem. faculty U. Houston, 1956-84, prof. history, 1967-84, acting dir. Afro-Am. studies, 1969-71, interim dir. libraries, 1976-78; dir. libraries U. Houston central campus, 1978-80, assoc. provost, 1980-81, dep. provost, 1981-84; v.p. acad. affairs Western Ky. U., Bowling Green, 1984-96; ret., 1996. Vis. prof., Black studies cons. U. Ala., 1970; dir. Inst. Cultural Understanding, 1971; mem. adv. planning com. Tex. Conf. on Library and Info. Services, 1978-79 Author: A Night of Violence: The Houston Riot of 1917, 1976, The Natchez District and the American Revolution, 1976; editor: The Houston Rev., 1981-84; Contbr. articles to profl. jours. Mem. Houston United Campus Christian Life com., 1973-81; chmn. ch. and soc. com. Synod of Tex., Presbyn. Ch. U.S.A., 1970-73; treas. Houston Com. on the Humanities, 1978-79. Served with USAF, 1950-51. Danforth assoc., 1969, Carnegie fellow, 1952—53, Nat. Endowment Humanities fellow, 1973. Mem. Am. Hist. Assn., Orgn. Am. Historians, So. Hist. Assn., Miss. Hist. Soc., Inst. Early Am. History and Culture, Tex. Assn. Coll. Tchrs. (past chpt. pres.), Phi Kappa Phi (past pres.). Democrat. Office: Dept History Western Ky U Bowling Green KY 42101 Office Phone: 270-745-4090. Business E-Mail: robert.haynes@wku.edu.

HAYNES, RUTH ELAINE, accountant; b. Cranesville, Pa., Sept. 21, 1943; d. Jack and Viola Emma (Drury) Gelvin; m. Jim D. Haynes, Aug. 26, 1962 (div. July 1974); children: Christine Haynes-Rollins, Jim Michael. AA summa cum laude, Del Mar Coll., 1973; BBA summa cum laude (Warren Found. scholar), Tex. A&I U. Corpus Christi, 1976; MBA summa cum laude, Corpus Christi State U., 1977; PhD in Fed. Taxation, U. Tex., Arlington, 1995. CPA Tex. Tax acct. Tex. Comptroller Public Accounts Dept., Ft. Worth, 1976—83; supr. Chgo. , Ill. State Tex. Audit Office, 1983—84, Ft. Worth Audit Office, 1984—86; pvt. practice acctg. Richland Hills, Tex., 1986—. Grad. assoc. U. Tex., Arlington, 1988—93; adj. instr. Tarrant County Jr. Coll., 1980—83, 1985—88, Dallas Bapt. U., 1993—95; spkr. ind. bus. seminars. Mem. Am. Inst. CPAs, Mid Cities Assn. CPAs, Am. Soc. Women in Acctg. (legis. chair Tarrant County br.), Altrusa (corresponding sec. Arlington chpt.), Network Exec. Women, Phi Theta Kappa, Ft. Worth Girls Club (bd. dirs.). Democrat. Lutheran. Avocations: reading, swimming, camping, travel, art. Office: 7232 Glenview Dr Richland Hills TX 76180-8612 Office Phone: 817-590-0300. Personal E-mail: rhaynes262@aol.com.

HAYNES, ULRIC ST. CLAIR, JR., retired dean; b. Bklyn., June 8, 1931; s. Ulric St. Clair and Ellaline (Gay) H.; m. Yolande Toussaint, Sept. 20, 1969; children: Alexandra, Gregory. BA, Amherst Coll., 1952; JD, Yale U., 1956; LLB (hon.), Ind. U., 1981, John Jay Coll., 1981, Fisk U., 1982, Ala. State Coll., 1982; JD, Butler U., 1988; LLB (hon.), Mercy Coll., 1994. Exec. asst. N.Y. State Dept. Commerce, Albany, 1956-57; adminstrv. officer UN European Office, Geneva, 1959-60; asst. to rep. Ford Found., Lagos, Nigeria, Tunis, Tunisia, 1960-63; asst. officer in charge Moroccan affairs Dept. State, Washington, 1963, officer in charge Southwest Africa and High Commn. Ters. Affairs, 1963-64; mem. NSC staff White House, 1965-66; pres. Mgmt. Formation Inc., NYC, 1966-70; sr. v.p., ptnr. Spencer Stuart and Assocs. Mgmt. Consultants, NYC, 1970-72; v.p. for mgmt. devel. Cummins Engine Co., Columbus, Ind., 1972-74, v.p. for Mid-East and Africa, 1974-77, v.p. internat. bus. planning, 1981-83; ambassador to Algeria Am. Embassy, Algiers, Algeria, 1977-81; acting pres. SUNY/Coll. at Old Westbury, 1985-86; pres. AFS Intercultural Programs, NYC, 1986-88; cons. NYC, 1989-91; exec. dean Hofstra U. Sch. Bus., Hempstead, NY, 1991-96; exec. dean internat. rels. Hofstra U., Hempstead, NY, 1996—2003; adj. prof. internat. rels Rollins Coll. and U. Ctrl. Fla., 2004—05. Bd. dirs. Pall Corp. Contbr. articles to profl. publs. Selection com. Henry Luce Found. Asian Scholars Program; internat. adv. bd. KidsRights, 2005—; trustee Deep Springs Coll., 1999-04. Root-Tilden scholar; John Hay Whitney scholar; Leopold Schepp Found. scholar. Mem. Coun. Fgn. Rels., Yale Club of N.Y.C., Am. Acad. Diplomacy, Atlantic Coun. US. Democrat. Episcopalian. Home: 2403 Timothy Ln Kissimmee FL 34743 Personal E-mail: uhaynesjr@yahoo.com.

HAYNES, VICTORIA F., science administrator; Chief tech. officer, v.p. Advanced Tech. Group, BFGoodrich Co., 1992—99; pres., CEO Rsch. Triangle Inst., Research Triangle Park, NC, 1999—. Bd. dir. Ziptronix Bd., Lubrizol Corp., Nucor Corp., MCNC, N.C. Biotech. Ctr., N.C. Bd. Sci. and Tech., PPG Ind.; appt. to Kans. Bioscience Authority, 2004—. Office: c/o Rebecca Switzer Rsch Triangle Inst Internat PO Box 12194 Research Triangle Park NC 27709-2194

HAYNES, WILLIAM JAMES, II, lawyer; b. Waco, Tex., Mar. 30, 1958; s. William James and Caroline H.; m. Margaret Frances Campbell, 1982; 3 children. BA, Davidson Coll., 1980; JD, Harvard U., 1983; LLD (hon.), Stetson U., 1999. Bar: NC 1983, Ga. 1989, DC 1990. Law clk. to Hon. James B. McMillan US Dist. Ct. NC, Charlotte, 1983-84; assoc. Sutherland, Asbill & Brennan, Washington, 1989; spl. asst. to gen. counsel US Dept. Def., Washington, 1989-90, gen. counsel Dept. Army, 1990-93; ptnr. Jenner & Block LLP, Washington, 1993-96; v.p., assoc. gen. counsel Gen. Dynamics Corp., Falls Church, Va., 1996-98; gen. counsel Gen. Dynamics Marine Grp., 1997-98; ptnr. Jenner & Block, Washington, 1999—2001; gen. counsel, dir. def. legal services agy. US Dept. Def., Washington, 2001—. Capt. US Army, 1984-88. Mem. ABA, NC Bar Assn., DC Bar Assn., Ga. Bar Assn. Presbyterian. Avocation: tennis. Office: Gen Counsel US Dept Def 1600 Defense Pentagon Washington DC 20301 Office Phone: 703-695-3341. Office Fax: 202-693-7278.*

HAYNIE, THOMAS POWELL, III, physician; b. Hearne, Tex., Aug. 9, 1932; s. Thomas Powell Jr and Sue Cummings Haynie; m. Bette Flossel, Mar. 10, 1956 (dec. Apr. 2002); children: David Powell, Amy Cummings, Sue Cummings, Garner Powell; m. Charlotte Peters, Dec. 18, 2004. Student, U. South, Sewanee, Tenn., 1949-51, U. Tex., Austin, 1951-52; MD, Baylor U., 1956. Diplomate Am Bd Internal Med, Am Bd Med Oncology, Am Bd Nuclear Med. Intern, then resident in internal medicine U. Mich. Med. Center, Ann Arbor, 1956-60, instr., 1960-62; asst. prof. medicine, dir. nuclear med. service U. Tex. Med. Br., Galveston, 1962-65; assoc. prof. medicine U. Tex.-M.D. Anderson Cancer Ctr., Houston, 1965-75; prof. U. Tex.-M.D. Anderson Hosp. and Tumor Inst., Houston, 1975-95, James E. Anderson prof. nuclear medicine, 1988-95, prof. emeritus of nuclear medicine, 1995—, chief sect. nuclear medicine, 1967-84, chmn. dept. nuclear medicine, 1984-93, head dept. internal medicine, 1977-84. Adj prof radiology Baylor Col Med, Houston, 1996—; pres Am Col Nuclear Med, 1993—94; consult in field. Contbr. articles in field, chapters to books; editor: Jour Nuclear Med, 1985—89. Mem.: AMA, ACP, AAAS, Am. Coll. Radiology, Tex. Assn. Physicians Nuclear Medicine, Tex. Med. Assn., Soc. Nuclear Medicine, Assn. Univ. Radiologists, Am. Thyroid Assn., Radiol. Soc. N.Am., Am. Coll. Nuclear Medicine, Am. Coll. Nuclear Physicians, Order St. Lazarus of Jerusalem, Sigma Xi, Phi Gamma Delta. Episcopalian. Home: 1222 Ripple Creek Dr Houston TX 77057 Office: U Tex-MD Anderson Cancer Ctr 1515 Holcombe Blvd Houston TX 77030-4009 Personal E-mail: thaynie@swbell.net. Business E-Mail: thaynie@mdanderson.org.

HAYNIE, TONY WAYNE, lawyer; b. Houston, Sept. 26, 1955; BA, U. Okla., 1978; postgrad., Boston U., Heidelberg Br., Fed. Republic Germany, 1980-81; JD, U. Tulsa, 1984; MBA, Okla. State U., 1993. Bar: Okla. 1985, US Dist. Okla. 1985, US Ct. Appeals (10th cir.) 1987, US Ct. Appeals (5th cir.) 1992, US Ct. Appeals (7th and DC cirs.) 1998, US Supreme Ct. 1990. Assoc. Conner & Winters, Tulsa, 1984-90, ptnr., 1991—; pres., CEO The Colonneh Co., Tulsa, 1991—. Arbitrator NY Stock Exch., 1991—93; trustee Transvoc, Inc., 1995—2000, pres. bd. trustees, 1998—99; adj. prof. Coll. Law U. Tulsa, 2002—. Mem. adv. bd. Tulsa Area United Way, 1998-99; bd. dirs. Big Bros. and Big Sisters of Green Country, 2004—, chmn. elect, 2007. 1st lt. US Army, 1978—82. Mem. ABA (sect. bus. law and litig., chair subcom. on expert witness on trial evidence com. of litig. sect. 1991-94), Am. Inns of Ct. (master Hudson-Hall-Wheaton chpt.), Okla. Bar Assn., Okla. Bar Found., Tulsa County Bar Assn. (chmn. fee arbitration com. 2006—, bd. dirs. 2006—), Tulsa County Bar Found., Phi Delta Phi. Democrat. Methodist. Office: Conner & Winters 4000 One Williams Ctr Tulsa OK 74172 Office Phone: 918-586-8954. Business E-Mail: thaynie@cwlaw.com.

HAYNOR, PATRICIA MANZI, nursing educator, consultant; children: Kelly Christine, Craig; m. Donald C. Maaswinkel. Diploma in nursing, Grasslands Hosp., Valhalla, NY; BSN, Fairleigh Dickinsn U., 1967; MSN in Nursing Adminstrn., U. Pa., 1969; D Nursing Sci., Widener U., 1989. RN, Pa., N.J., N.Y., Del. Asst. dir. surg. nursing Thomas Jefferson U. Hosp., Phila., 1972-74; asst. dir. nursing care depts. Our Lady of Lourdes Hosp., Camden, NJ, 1974-76; assoc. dir. nursing West Jersey Hosp., Camden, 1976-79; dir. nursing West Jersey Health System, Camden, 1979-81, corp. dir. nursing, 1981-82; v.p. nursing Crozer-Chester (Pa.) Med. Ctr., 1982-85; coord. nursing adminstrn. program, asst. prof. Widener U., Chester, 1985-87; v.p. for nursing St. Francis Med. Ctr., Trenton, NJ, 1987-90; asst. prof. U. Del. Coll. Nursing, 1990-92; assoc. prof. Villanova (Pa.) U. Coll. Nursing, Phila., 1992—. Cons. Nurse Assocs., West Deptford, N.J., 1985—; spkr. in field. Contbr. articles to profl. publs. Mem. Am. Orgn. Nurse Execs., Am. Coll. Healthcare Execs., S.E. Pa. Orgn. Nurse Leaders. Office: Villanova U Coll Nursing Villanova PA 19085 Home: 301 Lentz Rd Thorofare NJ 08086 Office Phone: 610-519-7751. E-mail: patriciahaynor@villanova.edu.

HAYNSWORTH, HARRY JAY, IV, law educator; b. Greensboro, NC, Apr. 9, 1938; s. Harry J. Jr. and Ruth (Eberhardt) H. AB, Duke U., 1961, JD, 1964; postgrad., U. Denver Law Center, 1972; MAR, Luth. Theol. So. Sem., 1989; LLD (hon.), William Mitchell Coll. Law, 2004. Bar: SC 1965, Minn. 2005, U.S. Supreme Ct. 2005. Assoc. Haynsworth, Perry, Bryant, Marion & Johnstone, Greenville, SC, 1964-69, ptnr., 69-71; assoc. prof. law U. SC, 1971-74, prof., 1974-90, assoc. dean, 1975-76, 85-86, acting dean, 1976-77; of counsel Nexson, Pruet, Jacobs & Pollard, Columbia, SC, 1986-90, Briggs & Morgan, Mpls., 2005—; dean, prof. law So. Ill. U., Carbondale, 1990-95; dean, pres. William Mitchell Coll. Law, St. Paul, 1995—2004; dean emeritus William Mitchell Coll. Law, 2004—. Vis. prof. U. Leeds, Eng., 1978-79; commr. Nat. Conf. Commrs. on Uniform State Laws, 1992—; mem. S.C. Legis. Consumer Law Com., 1975-80. Author: Comments, S.C. Consumer Protection Code, 1983, 2d edit. 1990, Organizing a Small Business Entity, 1986, Marketing and Legal Ethics: The Rules and Risks, 1990, others; contbr. articles to profl. jours.; mem. editorial bd.: Am. Bar Assn. Jour, 1977-83, chmn. editorial bd., 1982-83. Chmn. bd. S.C. Commn. for Blind, 1973-75; bd. dirs. Greenville County Housing Commn., S.C., 1970-71; v.p., dir. United Speech and Hearing Ctr., Greenville, 1970-71; trustee Heathwood Hall, 1976-86, Randolph-Macon Women's Coll., Lynchburg, Va., 1970-75, Minn. Zoo, 1999—, chair, 2006—; trustee Episc. Diocese Minn., 2006—. Mem. ABA (small bus. com., spl. cons. corp. laws com. 1978-82, coun. sect. bus. law 1988-92), S.C. Bar Assn. (vice chmn. consumer and comml. law com. 1975-78, sec., exec. com. 1972-75, exec. dir. 1971-72), Minn. State Bar Assn., Am. Law Inst., 4th Cir. Jud. Conf., S.C. Bar Assn. Office: Briggs and Morgan 2200 IDS Ctr Minneapolis MN 55402 Home Phone: 651-433-3312; Office Phone: 612-977-8298. Business E-Mail: hhaynsworth@briggs.com.

HAYO, GEORGE EDWARD, management consultant; b. LA, Nov. 2, 1934; s. George Edward Hayo Sr. and Esther Marie (Goodman) Arthur; m. Nixie Joanne Hunt, Aug. 4, 1956; children: Michael Edward, Kenneth Marvin, Michelle Virginia. BS in Applied Math., Calif. State U., 1960; MBA in Mgmt., U. Denver, 1968. Cert. mgmt. cons. Mathematician U.S. Naval Civil Engring. Lab., Port Hueneme, Calif., 1961-63; corp. systems planner No. Natural Gas Co., Omaha, 1963-66; asst. to pres. C.A. Norgren Co., Littleton, Colo., 1966-68; sr. staff cons. Emerson Electric, St. Louis, 1968-71; dir. adminstrn. Fisher Radio, NYC, 1971-72; v.p., dir. The Emerson Cons., NYC, 1973-87; pres. The Hayo Cons., Albuquerque, 1988—. Arbitrator Am. Arbitration Assn., N.Y., 1985—. Contbr. articles to profl. jours. Mem. Inst. Mgmt. Cons., Am. Inst. Plant Engrs., Am. Prodn. and Inventory Control Soc. Avocations: running, sailing, golf. Home and Office: The Hayo Cons 335 Pinon Creek Tr SE Albuquerque NM 87123-4123 Office Phone: 505-237-0313. Personal E-mail: hayocon@aol.com.

HAYON, ELIE M., chemist, educator; b. Cairo, May 15, 1932; came to U.S., 1965; s. Mayer E. and Regina (Cohen); m. Nina Mokady, 1982; 1 child, Rona B.Sc., U. Strathclyde, Glasgow, Scotland, 1954; PhD, Durham U., Newcastle-upon Tyne, Eng., 1957. Brit. Empire Cancer Research fellow Kings Coll., Newcastle-upon Tyne, 1957-58, Brookhaven Nat. Lab., Upton, NY, 1958-60, Cambridge (Eng.) U., 1960-62, Centre Nucleare Studies, Saclay, France, 1963-65; head phys. chemistry Natick (Mass.) Labs., 1966-75, Gen. Foods Corp., Tarrytown, NY, 1976-78; dean grad. studies and research, prof. chemistry Queens Coll., City U.N.Y., 1978—. Contbr. articles to profl. jours. Mem. numerous profl. assns. in U.S. and U.K. Home: 240 E 82nd St New York NY 10028-2703 Office: 6 Einstein St Ra'anana Israel

HAYS, DENNIS K., former ambassador; b. Calif., June 1, 1953; married; 4 children. B.Am. studies, U. Fla.; MPA, Harvard U.; grad., Nat. War Coll., 1993. Staff mem. Congressman Charles E. Bennett, Fla.; with U.S. Fgn. Svc., 1976—, dep. chief of mission Bujumbura, Burundi, 1985-88, dep. chief of mission, then charge d'affaires Georgetown, Guyana, 1988-93; coord. Cuban Affairs US Dept. State, 1993-95, dir. Office for Mex. Affairs, 1995-96, US amb. to Suriname Paramaribo, 1997—2000; pres. Fgn. svc. Assn., 1982-85; exec. v.p. Cuban Am. Nat. Found., 2000—. Advance man for presdl. and vice-presdl. visits overseas. Recipient Superior Honor award Dept. of State, 1981, 87, 91, 95, Meritorious Honor award, 1979.

HAYS, HOWARD H. (TIM HAYS), editor, publisher; b. Chgo., June 2, 1917; s. Howard H. and Margaret (Mauger) H.; m. Helen Cunningham, May 27, 1947 (div. Dec. 1988); children: William, Thomas; m. Susie Gudermuth, Sept. 1992. BA, Stanford U., 1939; LLB, Harvard U., 1942. Bar: Calif. 1946. Spl. agt. FBI, 1942-45; reporter San Bernardino Sun, Calif., 1945-46; asst. editor Riverside Daily Press, Calif., 1946-49, editor, 1949-65, editor, co-pub., 1965-83, editor, pub., chief exec. officer, 1983-88, editor, chmn., chief exec. officer, 1989-92, chmn. bd., 1992-97, chmn. emeritus, 1997—. Mem. Pulitzer Prize Bd., 1976-86; mem. AP Bd., 1980-89, vice chmn. 1988-89. Mem. nat. com. Wash. U. Sch. of Art, 1992—2003; bd. visitors John S. Knight Fellowships for Profl. Journalists, Stanford U., 1983—98. Recipient Dist. award Calif. Jr. C. of C., 1951, William J. Brennan Def. of Freedom award, 2003; named Pub. of Year Calif. Press Assn., 1968 Mem.: New Directions for News (bd. dirs. 1982—86), Am. Press Inst. (bd. dirs. 1973—, chmn. 1978—83), Internat. Press. Inst. (chmn. Am. Com. 1971—72, mem. exec. bd. 1977—83), Am.

Soc. Newspaper Editors (dir. 1969—76, pres. 1974—75), Calif. Bar Assn., Tower Grove Pk. (bd. dirs. 1999—, vice chmn. 2000—), Stanford Alumni Assn. (dir. 1970—74). Home: 3724 Utah Pl Saint Louis MO 63116-4831 Office Phone: 314-773-8082.

HAYS, JAMES FRED, geologist, educator; b. Little Rock, July 10, 1933; s. Orren Lee and Virginia (Russell) H.; m. Diane Lee Huntoon, Dec. 22, 1956; 1 dau., Lee Anne. AB, Columbia U., 1954; MS (NSF fellow), Calif. Inst. Tech., 1961; PhD, Harvard U., 1966. Geologist U.S. Geol. Survey, 1961; guest investigator Geophys. Lab., Carnegie Instn. of Washington, 1965; Soc. Fellows jr. fellow Harvard U., 1963-66, asst. prof. geology, 1966-69, assoc. prof., 1969-72, prof., 1972-84, chmn. dept. geol. scis., 1981-82; dir. div. earth scis. NSF, 1982-87, sr. sci. advisor, 1987-91, dir. earth scis. div., 1991-95. Cons. NASA Astronaut Tng. Program, 1969-73; mem. NASA Lunar Sample Analysis Planning Team, 1973-76, chmn. Lunar and Planetary Rev. Panel, 1978-81; prin. investigator Apollo Lunar Sample Program; vis. prof. chemistry and geology Ariz. State U., 1978-79; adminstrs. bd. Harvard and Radcliffe Colls., 1976-78; mem. Harvard Ctr. for Earth and Planetary Physics, 1970-84, sci. adv. bd. Mt. St. Helens Nat. Volcanic Monument, 1983-87, adv. com. on mining and minerals rsch. Dept. Interior, 1983-85, Working Group for U.S.-Peoples' Republic of China Agreement for Cooperation in Earth Scis., 1982-87, Space Grant Rev. Panel NASA, 1992-95; NRC com. on Rsch. Opportunities and Priorities for EPA, 1995-97; exec. sec. Pres.'s Com. on Nat. Medal Sci., 1987-91; vis. scholar U. Ariz., 1997—. Assoc. editor: Nature of the Solid Earth, 1970, Jour. Geophys. Research, 1978-80, 83-85. Served to capt. USNR, 1954-59. Recipient Presdl. Rank award U.S. Govt., 1994; NSF grantee, 1974-82, NASA grantee, 1971-82. Fellow AAAS (councilor 1989-92), Geol. Soc. Am. (councilor 1988-91), Mineral. Soc. Am.; mem. Am. Geophys. Union, Geol. Soc. Ariz. (councilor 2004—), Am. Ornithologists Union, Naval Res. Assn., Harvard Club, Cosmos Club, Phi Beta Kappa, Sigma Xi. Rsch. and publs. on exptl. petrology and geochemistry. Home: 3381 W Foxes Den Dr Tucson AZ 85745-5107 Personal E-mail: jhays@post.harvard.edu.

HAYS, MARGUERITE THOMPSON, nuclear medicine physician, educator; b. Bloomington, Ind., Apr. 15, 1930; d. Stith and Louise (Faust) Thompson; m. David G. Hays, Feb. 4, 1950 (div. 1975); children: Dorothy Adele, Warren Stith Thompson, Thomas Glenn. AB cum laude, Radcliffe Coll., 1951; postgrad., Harvard U. Med. Sch., 1954; MD, UCLA, 1957; ScD (hon.), Ind. U., 1979. Diplomate Am. Bd. Internal Medicine, Am. Bd. Nuc. Medicine. Intern UCLA Sch. Medicine, 1957-58, resident, 1958-59, 61-62, USPHS postdoctoral trainee, 1959-61, USPHS postdoctoral fellow, 1963-64, asst. prof. medicine, 1964-68, SUNY-Buffalo, 1968-70, asst. prof. biophys. sci., 1968-74, assoc. prof. medicine, 1970-76, clin. assoc. prof. nuc. medicine, 1973-77; asst. chief nuc. medicine VA Med. Ctr., Wadsworth, Calif., 1967-68; chief nuc. medicine Buffalo VA Med. Ctr., 1968-74, assoc. chief of staff for rsch., 1971-74; dir. med. rsch. svc. VA Ctrl. Office, Washington, 1974-79, asst. chief med. dir. for R & D, 1979-81; chief of staff Martinez VA Med. Ctr., Calif., 1981-83; prof. radiology Sch. Medicine U. Calif., Davis, 1981-93, prof. medicine and surgery, 1983-91, assoc. dean, 1981; clin. prof. radiology Stanford U. Sch. Medicine, 1990—; assoc. chief of staff for rsch. Palo Alto (Calif.) VA Med. Ctr., 1983-97, staff physician, 1997-99, cons., 1999—2001. Vis. rsch. scientist Euratom, Italy, 1962-63; chmn. radiopharm. adv. com. FDA, 1974-77; co-chmn. biomedicine com. Pres.'s Fed. Coun. on Sci., Engring. and Tech., 1979-81; mem. rsch. restructuring adv. com. Va. R & D Office, 1995-96, chair task group to restructure R & D Career Devel. Program, 1996-97; chmn. coop. studies evaluation com., Med. Rsch. Svc., VA, 1990-93; mem. sci. rev. and evaluation bd. Health Svcs. Rsch. and Devel. Svc., VA, 1988-91, chmn. career devel. com., 1991-99, chmn. career devel. com. Rehab. Rsch. and Devel. Svc., 1997-2003. Rsch. grantee VA, 1968-2003. NIH grantee, 1964-71; recipient Exceptional Svc. award Sec. Vets. Affairs, 2000. Fellow ACP; mem. Soc. Nuc. Medicine (chmn. publs. com., trustee, v.p. 1983-84), Am. Thyroid Assn. (bd. dirs. 1993-96), Endocrine Soc., Western Assn. Physicians. Home: 270 Campesino Ave Palo Alto CA 94306-2912 Office: 3801 Miranda Ave Palo Alto CA 94304-1207 E-mail: ritahays19@yahoo.com.

HAYS, PATRICK GREGORY, healthcare executive; b. Kansas City, Kans., Sept. 9, 1942; s. Vance Samuel and Mary Ellen (Crabbe) H.; m. Penelope Ann Hall, July 3, 1976; children: Julia L., Jennifer M., Emily J., Drew D. BS in Bus. Adminstrn, U. Tulsa, 1964; M.H.A., U. Minn., 1971; postgrad., U. Mich. Grad. Sch. Bus. Adminstrn., 1977. Mfg. analyst N.Am. Rockwell Corp., Tulsa, 1964-66; asst. adminstr., adminstr. for ops. Henry Ford Hosp., Detroit, 1971-75; exec. v.p. Meth. Med. Ctr. of Ill., Peoria, 1975-77; adminstr. Kaiser Found. Hosp., Los Angeles, 1977-80; pres. Sutter Community Hosps. and Sutter Health, Sacramento, 1980-95; pres., CEO Blue Cross Blue Shield Assn., Chgo., 1995—2000; faculty, School of Policy, Planning and Devel. U. So. Calif., Los Angeles. Trustee Cen. Area Teaching Hosps., Inc., L.A., 1977-79; mem. exec. com. St. Jude Children's Rsch. Hosp. Midwest Affiliate, Peoria, 1975-77; past chmn. adv. bd. grad. program in health svcs. adminstrn. U. So. Calif., Sacramento; regent Am. Coll. Healthcare Execs., 1989-95, 90-96, founding pres. Sacramento Regional Purchasing Coun., bd. govs., 1998-02; mem. adv. bd. the Governance Inst.; mem. civil justice reform act com., U.S. Dist. Ct., Ea. Calif.; adj. faculty Ariz. State U.; bd. dirs. Trinity Health, Novi, Mich., chmn. HR and compensation com.; vice chmn. bd. dirs. Trinity Health, Novi, Mich., commr. accrediting commn. edn. in health adminstrn., adv. to mgmt. Contbr. articles on health services to publs. Mem. Pvt. Industry Coun., Sacramento Employment and Tng. Agy., 1984-85; bd. dirs. Consumer Credit Counselors Sacramento, 1984-87, Sacramento Area United Way, campaign chair, 1992-93; bd. dirs. Comstock Club, 1986-89; pres. Sacramento Camellia Festival Assn., 1987-88; chmn. Whitney M. Young Jr. Award, 1987; pres. Sacramento Regional Purchasing Coun., 1989-90. With U.S. Army, 1966-69. Decorated Army Commendation medal, cert. of appreciation Dept. Army; recipient Commendation resolution Calif. Senate, 1979, Whitney M. Young award Sacramento Urban League, 1983; named Chief Exec. Officer of Yr., Soc. for Healthcare Planning and Mktg. of Am. Hosp. Assn., 1991; USPHS fellow, 1969-71, Calif. Assn. Hosps. and Health Systems Walker fellow, 1989. Fellow Am. Coll. Healthcare Execs. (Calif. regent, Gold medal for career excellence 2003); mem. Calif. Assn. Hosps. and Health Systems (chmn. bd. dirs. 1991), Sacramento-Sierra Hosp. Assn. (exec. com., bd. dirs., pres. 1984), Royal Soc. Health (U.K.), Am. Mgmt. Assn. (Pres. Club), Hollywood C. of C. (revitalization com. 1979), Sacramento C. of C. (bd. dirs. 1982-85, 87-88), Vol. Hosps. Pacific (bd. dirs.), Rotary (bd. dirs. Sacramento 1987-89), Rotary Club (Las Vegas), Kappa Sigma (treas.). Presbyterian. *Personal philosophy: Most people want to excel at what they do. Management's job, at its essence, is to remove the barriers to their success.*

HAYS, RICHARD R., lawyer; b. Tulsa, Okla., Mar. 25, 1960; AB, Harvard Univ., 1982; MSc., Univ. Edinburgh, Scotland, 1984; JD, Vanderbilt Univ., 1986. Bar: Ga. 1986. Co-chair, litig., trial practice group Alston & Bird LLP, mngmt. com., 2005, deputy mng. ptnr., mng. ptnr. elect, 2006. Editor: Vanderbilt Law Rev.; co-author: Georgia Appellate Practice Handbook; contributing author Litigation Year 2000 Cases, 1999. Bd. mem. Ga. Shakespeare, Harvard of Ga., Vanderbilt Law Sch., United Way, Alexis de Tocqueville Soc. Rotary scholar. Office: Alston & Bird LLP One Atlantic Ctr 1201 W Peachtree St NW Atlanta GA 30309-3424 Office Phone: 404-881-7360. Office Fax: 404-881-7777. Business E-Mail: richard.hays@alston.com.

HAYS, ROBERT WILLIAM, communications educator, consultant, writer; b. Atlanta, Oct. 17, 1925; s. Calvin Samuel and Elizabeth (Green) H.; m. Rebecca Copeland, June 15, 1950; children: Michael, David, William. Student, Duke U., Durham, NC, 1943-44; AB summa cum laude, Presbyn. Coll., SC, 1947; MEd, Emory U., Atlanta, 1957. Comml. mgr. Sta. WSFT-AM, Thomaston, Ga., 1947-48, Sta. WLBG, Clinton, SC, 1948; co-owner Clinton Plastic Co., 1948-49; instr. English So. Tech. Inst. (now So. Polytechnic State U.), Chamblee, Ga., 1950-51; supr. of tng. course devel. Lockheed Aircraft Corp., Marietta, Ga., 1951-52; asst. prof. So. Tech. Inst. (now So. Polytechnic State U.), Chamblee, Ga., 1952-57, head English dept. Marietta, 1953-73, assoc. prof., 1958-60, prof., 1960-85, prof. emeritus, 1985; ret. Comm. cons., Marietta, 1965—, Mid. East, 1968—70; trainer Coll. Officer Tng. Salvation Army, 1991; cons. Atlanta Exec. Svc. Corps, 1991—92; part time cons., lectr. Ga. Sch. Profl. Psychology, 1997—98. Author: Pacific Parodies, 1947, Principles of Technical Writing, 1965, Practically Speaking in Business, Industry and Government, 1969, Guide to Technical Writing, 1970, (with others) Getting Your Message Across, 1981; author poetry; contbr. numerous articles to profl. jours. Program dir. Marietta History Mus./Kiwanis Culture Capsule, 1999; mem. Cobb Arts Commn., 1988—90; mem. adv. bd. Salvation Army, Marietta, 1996—. Served to lt. (j.g.) USNR, 1943—46. Hixson fellow Kiwanis, 1996; recipient Arthur Williston award, 1967, Internat. Tech. Communications Conf. Honor, 1980, 83, Cmty. Svc. award King Ctr., 1994, 95. Fellow: Soc. for Tech. Comm. (life Disting. award 1993, Author one of 13 most significant articles 1954-2004); mem.: Mensa, VFW, Ga. Poetry Soc., Kiwanis (program dir. 1991—2006). Home: 3360 Trickum Rd Marietta GA 30066-4683 Office Phone: 678-445-7649. Personal E-mail: haysr@aol.com.

HAYS, RONALD JACKSON, career officer; b. Urania, La., Aug. 19, 1928; s. George Henry and Fannie Elizabeth (McCartney) H.; m. Jane M. Hughes, Jan. 29, 1951; children: Dennis, Michael, Jacquelyn. Student, Northwestern U., 1945-46; BS, U.S. Naval Acad., 1950; HHD (hon.), Northwestern State U. Commd. ensign U.S. Navy, 1950, advanced through grades to adm., 1983; destroyer officer Atlantic Fleet, 1950-51; attack pilot Pacific Fleet, 1953-56; exptl. test pilot Patuxent River, Md., 1956-59; exec. officer Attack Squadron 106, 1961-63; tng. officer Carrier Air Wing 4, 1963-65; comdr. All Weather Attack Squadron, Atlantic Fleet, 1965-67; air warfare officer 7th Fleet Staff, 1967-68; tactical aircraft plans officer Office Chief Naval Ops., 1969-71; comdg. officer Naval Sta., Roosevelt Roads, P.R., 1971-72; dir. Navy Planning and Programming, 1973-74; comdr. Carrier Group 4, Norfolk, Va., 1974-75; dir. Office of Program Appraisal, Sec. of Navy, Washington, 1975-78; dep. and chief staff, comdr. in chief U.S. Atlantic Fleet, Norfolk, Va., 1978-80; comdr. in chief U.S. Naval Force Europe, London, 1980-83; vice chief naval ops. Dept. Navy, Washington, 1983-85; comdr. in chief U.S. Pacific Command, Camp H.M. Smith, Hawaii, 1985-88; pres., chief exec. officer Pacific Internat. Ctr. for High Tech. Rsch., Honolulu, Hawaii, 1988-92; tech. cons., 1992—. Chmn. Pacific Aviation Mus Pearl Harbor Bd. Decorated D.S.M. with 3 gold stars, Silver Star with 2 gold stars, D.F.C. with silver star and gold star, Legion of Merit, Bronze Star with combat V, Air Medal with numeral 14 and gold numeral 3, Navy Commendation medal with gold star and combat V; recipient Disting. Eagle Scout award, 1987. Republican. Baptist. Home and Office: 869 Kamoi Pl Honolulu HI 96825-1318 Home Phone: 808-739-7770. Personal E-mail: rjhayshawaii@msn.com.

HAYS, SHARON LYNN, federal official; married. BA in Molecular Biology, U. Calif., Berkeley; PhD in Biochemistry, Stanford U., Calif., 1997. AAAS Congl. Sci. fellow Office of Rep. Vernon Ehlers, 1997—99; staff mem. basic rsch. subcommittee to staff mem. space and aeronautics subcommittee US Ho. Reps. Com. on Sci., Washington, 1999—2001, staff dir. rsch. subcommittee, 2001—02; mem. staff tech. divsn. to chief of staff Office Sci. & Tech. Policy, Exec. Office of the Pres., Washington, 2002—06, assoc. dir., 2006—. Bd. dirs. Women in Aerospace, 2003. Office: Office Sci & Tech Policy Exec Office of the Pres 725 17th St Rm 5228 Washington DC 20502 Office Phone: 202-456-6130. E-mail: shays@ostp.eop.gov.*

HAYS, STEPHEN ROBERT, pediatrician; b. Syracuse, NY, Dec. 17, 1964; MS, Yale U., 1987; MD, John Hopkins U., 1991. Cert. Pediatrics, Pediatric Critical Care Medicine. Intern. pediatrics John Hopkins U., Balt., 1991—92, resident, pediatrics, 1992—94, resident, anesthesia, 1994—97, fellow, pediatric anesthesia, 1996—99, fellow, pediatric critical care medicine, 1996—99; dir., pediatric pain services Vanderbilt Children's Hosp., 2003—; asst. prof. anesthesia and pediatrics Vanderbilt U. Med. Ctr., Nashville, 1999—. Office: Vanderbilt Children Hosp 2200 Children's Way RM 3115 Nashville TN 37232 also: Vanderbilt U Rm 3115 VCH 2201 West End Ave Nashville TN 37235 Office Phone: 615-936-0023. Office Fax: 615-936-4294. Business E-Mail: stephen.hays@vanderbilt.edu.

HAYS, THOMAS S., medical educator, researcher; b. Winter Haven, Fla., Dec. 20, 1954; married. BS in Zoology, U. N.C., 1976, PhD in Cell Biology, 1985. Rsch. asst. dept. zoology U. N.C., Chapel Hill, 1975—76; rsch. asst. dept. biol. scis. Duke U., Durham, NC, 1976—79; asst. instr. quantitative and analytical microscopy Marine Biol. Lab., Woods Hole, Mass., 1981—83; asst. instr. optical microscopy U. Calif., Santa Cruz, 1982; postdoctoral fellow dept. molecular, cellular and devel. biology U. Colo., Boulder, 1985—89; asst. prof. dept. genetics and cell biology U. Minn., St. Paul, 1989—95, assoc. prof. dept. genetics and cell biology, 1995—. External reviewer NSF, 1989—. Reviewer: Jour. Cell Biology, Jour. Biol. Chemistry, Molecular Biology of the Cell, Molecular Cell Biology, Proceedings Nat. Acad. Sci. USA, Cell Motility and the Cytoskeleton, Jour. Cell Sci., Genetics; contbr. articles to profl. jours. Recipient Basil O'Connor Scholar award, March of Dimes, 1993, Establishe Investigator award, Am. Heart Found., 1996; fellow H.V. Wilson, U. N.C., 1983, R.J. Reynolds, 1983, Postdoctoral, NIH, 1985—88; grantee Tng., 1991—95, 1995—, Rsch. Tng., NSF, 1991—95, March of Dimes, 1995—; scholar Founders, Marine Biol. Lab., 1980. Mem.: Genetics Soc. Am., Am. Soc. Cell Biology. Office: U Minn Dept Genetics Cell Biology & Devel 6-160 Jackson Hall 321 Church St SE Minneapolis MN 55455

HAYS, WILLIAM GRADY, JR., corporate financial and banking consultant; b. Covington, Ga., July 9, 1927; s. William Grady and Ella Maude (Wofford) H.; m. Emily Ann Holcombe, Aug. 1, 1954; children: Woodfrin Grady, Steven Gregory, William Danfield. BS, U. Ga., 1949; M.Litt., U. Pitts., 1950. Pres. First So. Corp., Atlanta, 1955-57; v.p. Comml. Trust Co., 1957-59; pres., CEO Comml. Acceptance Corp., 1959-74; fin. cons. William G. Hays & Assocs., Inc., 1974—; cons., CEO N.Am. Acceptance Corp., 1974—; cons. Kaleidoscope, Inc., 1979—, Speir Ins. Agy., Inc., 1982—; CEO United Am. Fin. Corp., Knoxville, Tenn., 1983—. Cons. Banque Nationale De Paris, Nat. Westminister Bank, PLC, United Bank of Kuwait, PLC, Security Pacific Nat. Bank, First Nat. Bank of Boston; trustee Beacon Fin. Group, Inc., 1986; cons. Micro Mart, Inc., 1987; examiner World Bazaar Franchise Corp., 1992; spl. master Hannover Corp. Am., 1991; spl. agt. Diversified Growth Corp., 1989; trustee Internat. Trading Inc., 1993, Aledo Fin. Svcs., Inc., 1985, Flexel, Inc., RDM Sports Inc. Contbr. articles to profl. jours. Mem. Kappa Delta Pi. Clubs: Cherokee Town and Country, Univ. Yacht. Republican. Presbyterian. Home: 2755 Normandy Dr NW Atlanta GA 30305-2822 Office: 1100 Spring St NW Ste 450 Atlanta GA 30309-2847

HAYSBERT, DENNIS, actor; b. San Mateo, Calif., June 2, 1954; s. Charles and Gladys Haysbert; m. Lynn Griffith, 1989 (div. 2001); children: Charles, Katherine. Grad., Am. Acad. Dramatic Arts, Coll. San Mateo. Spokesperson Allstate Ins. Actor: (TV series, guest appearances) The White Shadow, 1979, Laverne & Shirley, 1979, The Incredible Hulk, 1980, Galactica 1980, 1980, Quincy, 1980, 1981, Buck Rogers in the 25th Century, 1980, 1981, The A-Team, 1983, Dallas, 1984, Riptide, 1984, Magnum P.I., 1985, Growing Pains, 1985, 1987, 1988, What's Happening Now!, 1986, Fall Guy, 1986, 227, 1986, Scarecrow and Mrs. King, 1986, Knots Landing, 1987, Valerie, 1987, Our House, 1987, The Facts of Life, 1987, Crime Story, 1988, Night Court, 1989, Soul Food, 2001, The Outer Limits, 2001; (TV series) Off the Rack, 1984, Just the Ten of Us, 1988—89, Now and Again, 1999 (Saturn Award for TV Supporting Actor, 2000), 24, 2001—06, The Unit, 2006—, (voice) Duckman: Private Dick/Family Man, 1996, Batman: Gotham Knights, 1998, The New Batman Superman Adventures, 1998, Static Shock, 2001, 2002, 2003, Justice League, 2001, 2003,: (TV films) Code Red, 1981; (TV miniseries) Queen, 1993, Return to Lonesome Dove, 1993; (TV films) Grambling's White Tiger, 1981, The Return of Marcus Welby, M.D., 1984, A Summer to Remember, 1985, K-9000, 1991, Hallelujah, 1993, Widow's Kiss, 1996, The Writing on the Wall, 1996; (films) Major League, 1989, Navy Seals, 1990, Mr. Baseball, 1992, Love Field, 1992, Major League II, 1994, Waiting to Exhale, 1995, Heat, 1995, Insomnia, 1996, Amanda, 1996, Absolute Power, 1997, Standoff, 1998, How to Make the Cruelest Month, 1998, Major League: Back to the Minors, 1998, The Minus Man, 1999, The Thirteenth Floor, 1999, Random Hearts, 1999, What's Cooking, 2000, Love & Basketball, 2000, Far from Heaven, 2002 (Washington Film Critics Award for Best Supporting Actor, 2002, Black Reel Theatrical Award for Best Supporting Actor, 2003, Golden Satellite Award for Best Performance by an Actor in a Supporting Role, 2003), Ticker, 2002, (voice) Sinbad: Legend of the Seven Seas, 2003, Jarhead, 2005, Goodbye Bafana, 2007, Breach, 2007; host/narrator (documentaries) Secrets of Pearl Harbor, 2004. Office: The Gersh Agency 232 N Canon Dr Ste 201 Beverly Hills CA 90210*

HAYSBERT, JOANN WRIGHT, academic administrator; b. Kingstree, SC; d. Norwood and Lillie Mae (Scott) Wright; m. Barral Stanley Hershel Haysbert; children: Andre, Nineveh, Nazareth, Jordan, Samaria. BA, Johnson C. Smith U., Charlotte, NC, 1969; MEd, Auburn U., 1974, EdD, 1978. Coordinator rsch. and program planning Macon County Pub. Sch. System, Tuskegee, Ala., 1971-76; title IX coordinator Auburn (Ala.) U., 1976-78; instr. psychology Alexander City (Va.) State Jr. Coll., 1977-78; asst. prof. edn. Va. State U., Petersburg, 1978-80, prin. lab. sch., 1979-80; dir. women and minorities program Hampton (Va.) U., 1981-82, asst. v.p. acad. affairs, dir. summer session, various positions including asst. provost, provost, prof. and dean, acting pres., 2003—04; pres. Langston U., Langston, Okla., 2005—. Cons. in field. Author ednl. materials. Mem. Va. Nat. Identification Program for Advancement of Women in Higher Edn. Adminstrn. Ford Found. fellow, 1973. Mem. Nat. Assn. Women Deans, Adminstrs. and Counselors, Nat. Assn. Summer Sessions (chmn. com. 1986-88), Assn. Univ. Summer Sessions, AAUW, Phi Delta Kappa. Avocations: reading, music. Office: Langston Univ PO Box 907 Langston OK 73050 Office Phone: 405-466-3201. Office Fax: 405-466-3461. Business E-Mail: jwhaysbert@lunet.edu.

HAYSE, RICHARD FRANKLIN, lawyer; b. Kansas City, Mo., Sept. 6, 1943; s. Lewie Frank and Elizabeth Bronson (Humfreville) H.; m. Linda Rae Fairchild, Aug. 8, 1964; children: Adrienne Jennifer, Thomas Bronson. BA in Speech, Kansas State U., 1964; JD, Washburn Law Sch., 1969. Bar: Kans. 1969, U.S. Dist. Ct. Kans. 1969, U.S. Ct. Appeals (10th cir.) 1969, U.S. Supreme Ct. 1990. Broadcast journalist WIBW-TV-AM-FM, Topeka, 1964-68; asst. atty. gen. State of Kansas, Topeka, 1969-70; fgn. svc. info. officer U.S. Info. Agy., Washington, 1971-75; lawyer Eidson, Lewis, Porter & Haynes, Topeka, Kans., 1975-89, Hayse Law Offices, Topeka, 1989-90; ptnr. Morris, Laing, Evans, Brock & Kennedy, Chartered, Topeka, 1991—. Editor in chief Washburn Law Jour., author, 1969, co-author, 1970; contbr. chpts. to books. Pres. Topeka Lions Club, 1983-84, Topeka Youth Project, 1990-91, Topeka Symphony Soc., 1993-94, Cornerstone of Topeka, Inc., 1998-99. Mem. ABA, Kans. Bar Assn. (pres. 2005-06), Topeka Bar Assn. (dir. 1986-91). Avocations: gardening, sailing. Home: 1724 SW Collins Ave Topeka KS 66604-3219 Office: Morris Laing Evans Brock & Kennedy Chartered 800 SW Jackson St Ste 1310 Topeka KS 66612-1216 Office Phone: 785-232-2662.

HAYTER, ANTHONY, finance educator, department chairman; b. Eng. MA, Cambridge U., 1982; PhD, Cornell U., 1985. Prof., dept. chair U. Denver, 2006—. Author: (textbook) Probability and Statistics for Engineers and Scientists. Office: Univ Denver 2101 S University Blvd Denver CO 80208 Business E-Mail: anthony.hayter@du.edu.

HAYTHE, WINSTON MCDONALD, lawyer, real estate investor, educator; b. Reidsville, NC, Oct. 10, 1940; s. McDonald Swann and Henrietta Elizabeth (East) H.; m. Glenann Leigh Rogers, Aug. 17, 1963 (div. 1977); children: Sheila Elaine, Kevin McDonald, Rhonda Leigh. BS, Mo. State U., 1963; JD, Coll. William and Mary, 1967; postgrad., U. Va., 1968—69; grad., Command and Gen. Staff Sch., Ft. Leavenworth, Kans., 1982, U.S. Def. U., 1984; LLM, U.S. Army JAG Sch., 1976. Bar: Va. 1967, D.C. 1969. Assoc. Rhyne & Rhyne, Washington, 1969-72; sr. trial atty. AEC, Washington, 1972-73; asst. gen counsel, sr. atty. Consumer Produce Safety Commn., Washington, 1973-82; staff dir. legal office EPA, Washington, 1982-83, sr. atty. for enforcement policy, 1985-91, sr. atty. Nat. Enforcement Tng. Inst., 1991-94, asst. dir., 1994-96, sr. legal counsel, 1996-2001; sr. counsel Office of Criminal Enforcement, Forensics and Tng., 2001—05; chief counsel Nat. Enforcement Tng. Inst., 2005—. Legis. fellow US Senate, Washington, 1983-85; adv. coun. paralegal studies U. Md., 1980-95, chmn., 1992-95, adj. prof. law, 1978-94; law faculty US Army Judge Adv. Gen.'s Sch., Charlottesville, Va., 1969-94, Nat. Advocacy Ctr. US Dept. Justice, Columbia, SC, 1999—; cons. Barrister Ent., Washington, 1978—; elected mem. undergrad. programs adv. coun. U. Md., 1993-95; guest lectr. George Washington U. Sch. Law, 1999-2002, adj. prof. law, 2002—; mem. Strayer U. Bus. Admin. Program Adv. Coun., 2003—, Fed. Dispute Resolution Conf. Adv. Bd., 2004—. Trustee Georgetown Presbyn. Ch., 1995-98, v.p. trustees, 1996, pres. trustees, 1997-98, elder, mem. session, 2000-03, clk. of session, 2003-07. Col. JAGC, USAR, 1967-94, ret. Fellow: Found. Fed. Bar Assn. (life); mem.: St. Andrews Soc. Washington, Fed. Bar Assn. (fed. career svcs. divsn. 1974—90, nat. coun. 1998—, coun. mem. found. 2003—), DC Bar Assn., Va. State Bar Assn., Coll. William and Mary Law Sch. Assn. (bd. dirs. 1988—95), Social List Washington, English Speaking Union, Cosmos Club, Knights Templar, Kappa Mu Epsilon. Presbyterian. Avocations: playing organ, piano, theater, concerts, reading. Home: 2141 P St NW Apt 402 Washington DC 20037-1031 Office: EPA (MC-2235A) 1200 Pennsylvania Ave NW Washington DC 20460-0001 Office Phone: 202-564-6057. Business E-Mail: haythe.winston@epa.gov.

HAYUTIN, DAVID LIONEL, lawyer; b. Phoenix, Apr. 19, 1930; s. Henry and Eva (Gaines) H.; m. Lee June Rodgers, June 15, 1951. AB, U. So. Calif., 1952, JD, 1958. Bar: Calif. 1958. Assoc. Pillsbury Winthrop Shaw Pittman LLP and predecessor firms, LA, 1958-67, ptnr., 1967—. Author: Distributing Foreign Products in the United States, 1988, revised edit., 2000; assoc. editor So. Calif. Law Rev.; contbr. legal articles to profl. jours. Served to lt. (j.g.) USN, 1952-55. Mem. ABA, Internat. Bar Assn., Calif. Bar Assn., Maritime Law Assn. Republican. Avocations: opera, golf. Office: Pillsbury Winthrop Shaw Pittman LLP 725 S Figueroa St Los Angeles CA 90017-5524 Office Phone: 213-488-7351. Business E-Mail: dhayutin@pillsburylaw.com.

HAYWARD, EDWARD JOSEPH, lawyer; b. Springfield, Mo., Dec. 4, 1943; s. Joseph Hunter and Rosemary Hayward; m. Ellinor Duffey, Aug. 30, 1968; children: Jeffrey, Stephen, Susan. Student, U. d'Aix Marseille, Aix-en-Provence, France, 1963-64; AB, Stanford U., 1965; JD magna cum laude, Harvard U., 1971. Bar: N.Y. 1972, Minn. 1980. Assoc. Cleary, Gottlieb, Steen & Hamilton, NYC and Brussels, 1971-74, Oppenheimer Wolff & Donnelly, LLP, Brussels, 1975-79, ptnr. Mpls., 1978—. Pres. pres.

Twin Cities Fgn. Trade Zone Inc., Mpls., 1983—84. Chmn. legis. com. Minn. World Trade Assn., Mpls., 1984—87. Served to capt. US Army, 1965—68. Mem.: ABA, Minn. Bar Assn. (councillor internat. law sect. 1983—, sec. 1986—88, vice chmn. 1988—89, chmn. 1989—90), Dist. Export Coun. (chmn. 1996—), German-Am. C. of C. (bd. dirs. 1994—99, 2000—), French-Am. C. of C. (bd. dirs. 1983—, pres. 1985—87, 1996—2001, nat. sec. 1988—). Republican. Presbyterian. Avocations: languages, sports. Home: 6625 W Shore Dr Minneapolis MN 55435-1528 Office: Oppenheimer Wolff & Donnelly LLP 45 S 7th St Ste 3300 Minneapolis MN 55402-1609 Office Phone: 612-607-7280. Business E-Mail: ehayward@oppenheimer.com.

HAYWARD, FREDRIC MARK, social reformer; b. NYC, July 10, 1946; s. Irving Michael and Mildred (Feingold) Hayward; m. Ingeborg Beck, Aug. 18, 1971 (div. 1974); 1 child, Jack. BA, Brandeis U., Waltham, Mass., 1967; MA, Fletcher Sch. Law & Diplomacy, Medford, Mass., 1968, MALD, 1969. Exec. dir. Men's Rights, Inc., Boston, 1977—. Vis. lectr. Tufts U., Medford, Mass., 1979; conductor workshops in field; mem. adv. bd. Ctr. for Men's Studies, 1988-93; host, prodr. The SacraMENshow; founder Nat. Coalition Just Draft; co-founder Free Men Boston; co-founder, v.p. Children's Rights Coun. Sacramento, Stop Abuse for Everyone; co-founder, treas. Fathers' Symposium, 1996—; lectr. in field Contbg. editor: The Liberator, Forest Lake, Minn., 1988-89; contbr. Spectator, Berkeley, Calif., 1988-2001; contbr. articles to profl. jours. Farrell Fellowship on Men, 1989, Fletcher Sch. Law and Diplomacy fellow, 1967-69; recipient award of Excellence Nat. Coalition of Free Men, 1993, award Western Access Video Excellence, 1995. Mem. JBANTA (vice chmn. bd. dirs. 2003-04, Fatherhood Pioneer award 2005), Nat. Congress for Men (bd. dirs. 1981-90), Am. Fedn. TV and Radio Artists, Men. Internat. (bd. dirs. 1982-86). Office: Mr Inc PO Box 163180 Sacramento CA 95816-9180 Office Phone: 916-484-7333.

HAYWARD, JEAN, artist, musician, interior designer; b. LA, Apr. 4, 1917; d. Herbert Hastings Eastwood and Irma Isabel Arundell; m. William Hayward (dec.); m. George R. Collins (dec. Sept. 26, 1939); children: Julia Ann, Stephen, George, Mark. BA, U.C.L.A., LA, 1938. Mime story telling with orchestras, all around the world; designer clothing line of denim for Bullock's Willshire; architecture and design houses, Santa Barbara. Contbr. articles to profl. jour.; performer symphony soloist. Vol. Jr. League, Santa Barbara, Calif., 1946—70. Mem.: Birnam Wood Golf Club. Republican. Episcopalian. Avocation: horseback riding. Home: 300 Hot Springs Rd Santa Barbara CA 93108

HAYWARD, LANI, bank executive; 2 children. Grad., Univ. Ariz. Mgmt. positions through sr. v.p. mktg. Umpqua Bank, Portland, Oreg., 1998—2005, exec. v.p. creative strategy group, 2005—. Named a Rising Star, Fin. Mktg. Mag., 2001; named Advt. Profl. of the Yr., Portland Advt. Fedn., 2006; named one of 25 Most Powerful Women in Banking, US Banker mag., 2006. Office: Umpqua Holdings Corp Ste 1200 Umpqua Plz 1 SW Columbia Portland OR 97258*

HAYWARD, ROBERT M., lawyer; s. Thomas Z. and Sally M. Hayward; m. Elizabeth R. Richards, June 15, 1971; children: Trevor R., Charlie N. BS, Northwestern U., 1994, JD, 1997. Bar: Ariz. 1997, U.S. Dist. Ct. Ariz. 1997, Ill. 1998, U.S. Dist. Ct. (no. dist.) Ill. 1998. Assoc. Snell & Wilmer LLP, Phoenix, 1997—2000, Kirkland & Ellis LLP, Chgo., 2000—03, ptnr., 2003—. Dir. Northwestern Gridiron Network, Evanston, Ill., 2003—; trustee Music Inst. Chgo., Winnetka, Ill., 2003—; mem. adv. bd. TheCorporateCounsel.net, Washington, 2003—; co-chair class gift Northwestern U. Alumni Assn., Evanston, 2003—. Contbr. articles to profl. jours. Mem. Northwestern U. Leadership Cir. Named one of Best Lawyers in Am., Securities, 2005. Mem.: ABA, Chgo. Bar Found. (dir. young profls. bd. 2004—), Ariz. Bar Assn., Chgo. Bar Assn., Econ. Club Chgo., Lawyers Club Chgo. Office: Kirkland & Ellis LLP 200 East Randolph Dr Chicago IL 60601 Office Phone: 312-861-2000. Office Fax: 312-861-2200.

HAYWARD, RONALD HAMILTON, surgeon; b. Wellington, N.Z., Nov. 7, 1927; s. Frederick Howard and Emma Mathilde (Hannibal) H.; m. Elizabeth Ruth Wells, Sept. 16, 1961; children— Maureen, John, Gregory, Jennifer. Student, Wellington Coll., 1941-45; M.B., Ch.B., U. Otago, 1951; PhD in Surgery, U. Minn., 1961. Resident Mayo Clinic, Rochester, Minn., 1956-62; practice medicine specializing in thoracic and cardiovascular surgery Ft. Worth, 1962-65, Scott & White Clinic, Temple, Tex., 1965-93; prof., chmn. dept. surgery Tex. A&M Med. Sch., 1979-89. Recipient Alumni award Mayo Clinic, 1959 Mem. AMA, Tex. Med. Assn., Tex. Surg. Soc., So. Thoracic Surg. Assn., Soc. Thoracic Surgeons, Sigma Xi. Republican. Episcopalian. Patentee in field. Office: Scott & White Clinic Temple TX 76508-0001

HAYWARD, SAM, chef; b. Ohio, 1950; Kitchen mgr. oceanog. lab. Appledore Island, Maine, 1974; owner, exec. chef 22 Lincoln, Brunswick, Maine, 1981—91, Fore Street Grill, Portland, Maine, 1996—. Featured in Atlantic Monthly, Saveur, Food Arts, Wine Spectator, NY Times, Gourmet Mag. Named Best Chef in Northeast, James Beard Found., 2004, Best Chef, Casco Bay Weekly. Mem.: Maine Organic Farmers and Gardeners Assn. Avocations: gardening, writing, backpacking, canoeing. Office: Fore Street Grill 288 Fore St Portland ME 04101-4109*

HAYWARD, THOMAS ZANDER, JR., lawyer; b. Oct. 21, 1940; s. Thomas Z. and Wilhelmina (White) H.; m. Sally Madden, June 20, 1964; children: Thomas Z., Wallace M., Robert M. BA, Northwestern U., 1962, JD, 1965; MBA, U. Chgo., 1970. Bar: Ill. 1966, Ohio 1966, U.S. Dist. Ct. (no. dist.) Ill. 1966, U.S. Supreme Ct. 1970. Assoc. Defrees & Fiske, Chgo., 1965-69, ptnr., 1969-81, Boodell, Sears, Giambalvo & Crowley, Chgo., 1981-87, Bell, Boyd, Lloyd, Chgo., 1987—. Mem. mgmt. and exec. coms. Bell, Boyd, Lloyd. Trustee Northwestern U., 1980-84, 97—, vice-chmn., 2000—; bd. dirs. Ill. Continuing Legal Edn., 1987-92, Chgo. Area Found. for Legal Svcs., 1983—; bd. dirs. Nat. Cowboy and Western Heritage Mus., 2004—; pres. Sigma Alpha Epsilon Found., 2005—. Recipient Northwestern U. Alumni Svc. award, 1973. Mem. ABA (ho. of dels. 1984—, fed. jud. com. 1993-97, bd. govs., exec. com. 1998-2001, chmn. fin. com. 2000-01), ABA/Am. Law Inst. (pres. continuing profl. edn. 2005—), Fed. Judiciary Com. (chmn. 2003-05), Ill. State Bar Assn., Chgo. Bar Assn. (pres. 1983-84), Chgo. Bar Found. (bd. dirs., pres. 2003—), Chgo. Club, Casino Club, Barrington Hills Country Club (pres. 1985-87). Republican. Presbyterian. Home: 8 W County Line Rd Barrington IL 60010-2613 Office: Bell Boyd & Lloyd 3 1st Nat Plz 70 W Madison St Ste 3100 Chicago IL 60602-4284 Office Phone: 312-807-4340. Business E-Mail: thayward@bellboyd.com.

HAYWOOD, BRUCE, retired academic administrator; b. York, Eng., Sept. 30, 1925; came to U.S., 1951, naturalized, 1957; s. Joseph Edgar and Eva (Street) H.; m. Isona Gretchen Shelley, June 21, 1947; children—Anne Margaret, Elizabeth Shelley. Student, U. Leeds, Eng., 1947-48; BA, McGill U., 1950, MA, 1951; PhD, Harvard, 1956. Mem. faculty Kenyon Coll., 1954, prof. German lit., 1960-63, dean coll., 1963-67, provost, 1967-80; pres. Monmouth (Ill.) Coll., 1980-94; ret., 1994. Author: The Veil of Imagery, 1959, The Essential College, 2006, Allerton Bywater, 2007. Served with Brit. Army, 1943-47. Mem. Am. Assn. Tchrs. of German. Home: 311 E Simmons St Apt 706 Galesburg IL 61401

HAYWOOD, H(ERBERT) CARL(TON), psychologist, educator; b. Taylor County, Ga., July 2, 1931; s. Howard Chapman and Rosebud (Smith) H.; m. Nancy Patricia Roberts, Oct. 5, 1951 (div. Mar. 1971); children: Carlton, Terence, Elizabeth, Kristin; m. Dona June Wooldridge Tapp, Sept. 6, 1993 (div. Mar. 2000). AB, San Diego State Coll., 1956, MA, 1957; PhD, U. Ill., 1961. Lic. clin. psychologist Tenn. Mem. faculty George Peabody Coll. (merged with Vanderbilt U. 1979), Nashville, 1962—94, Alexander Heard disting. svc. prof., 1993-94, prof. psychology, 1969-93, prof. spl. edn., 1975-79, prof. emeritus, 1994—, dir. mental retardation rsch. tng. program, 1968-70; dir. Inst. Mental Retardation and Intellectual Devel., 1970-73, Office Rsch. Adminstrn., 1974-76, John F. Kennedy Ctr. Rsch. Edn. and Human Devel., 1971-83; prof. neurology Vanderbilt U. Sch. Medicine, 1971-93; prof. psychology and edn., dean grad. sch. edn. & psychology Touro Coll., NYC, 1993-2000. Vis. prof. U. Toronto, 1965-66; sr. fellow Vanderbilt Inst. Pub. Policy Studies, 1983-88; chmn. Nat Mental Retardation Research Center Dirs., 1979-82; adv. bd. Ill. Inst. Developmental Disabilities, Chgo., 1970-78, Eunice Kennedy Shriver Center Mental Retardation, Waltham, Mass., 1973-80, Tenn. Dept. Mental Health, 1964-92; mem. nat. child health and human devel. council NIH, 1983-88; cons. President's Com. on Mental Retardation, 1968-73; mem. sci. rev. com., health research facilities br., div. edn. and research facilities NIH, 1967-71 Author (with Brooks and Burns): Bright Start: Cognitive Curriculum for Young Children, 1992; editor: Brain Damage in School Age Children, 1968; author (with Lidz): Dynamic Assessment in Practice, 2007; editor: Social Cultural Aspects of Mental Retardation, 1970; editor: (with Begab and Garber) Prevention of Retarded Development in Psychosocially Disadvantaged Children; editor: (with J.R. Newbrough) Living Environments for Developmentally Retarded Persons, 1981; editor: (with D. Tzuriel) Interactive Assessment, 1992; editor: (with S. Friedman) Developmental Follow-Up: Domains, Concepts, and Methods, 1994; editor: Am. Jour. Mental Deficiency, 1969—79, Jour. Cognitive Edn. and Psychology, 1999—2006; mem. editl. bd.: Jour. Abnormal Child Psychology, 1973—89, Contemporary Psychology, 1982—85, Acta Paedologica, 1983—87, Jour. Mental Deficiency Rsch., 1984—2001, Internat. Rev. Rsch. in Mental Retardation, 1982—97; contbr. articles on child devel., motivation, cognitive edn., psycho assessment and mental retardation to profl. jours. Trustee Am. U. Rome, 2000—04. With USN, 1950-54. Recipient Myrtle Wreath Citation of Honor, So. Region Hadassah, 1979. Fellow Am. Assn. Mental Retardation (v.p. psychology 1975-77, 1st v.p. 1978-79, pres. 1980-81, Leadership award, 1985, Rsch. award, 1989), APA (pres. Div. 33 1978-79, mem. Coun. of Reps. 1980-82, Edgar A. Doll award, 1988), Assn. for Psychol. Sci.; mem. Internat. Assn. Cognitive Edn. (pres. 1988-92, Disting. Svc. award, 1995), Soc. Rsch. in Child Devel., Inst. Medicine. Democrat. Episcopalian. Avocations: piano, organist, choral conductor. Business E-Mail: carl.haywood@vanderbilt.edu. *Dominant values include enthusiasm for scholarship, equal parts of dedication to science for its own sake and concern for social progress, and the conviction that self-concern and self-seeking constitute the most dangerous threat to the collective goals of humanity. The future lies in education designed to stretch minds and develop processes of critical thought rather than to impart job-oriented skills.*

HAYWOOD, J. WILLIAM, oil industry executive; B, Miami U., Ohio; B in Civil Engring., Ohio State U.; MBA, Pepperdine U., Malibu, Calif. Gen. mgr. Wilmington refinery Ultramar Diamond Shamrock Corp., Calif., 1997—2000, regional v.p., 2000—02; sr. v.p. Tesoro Corp., San Antonio, 2002, pres. Calif. region Tesoro Refining and Mktg. Co., 2002, sr. v.p. refining. Office: Tesoro Corp 300 Concord Plz San Antonio TX 78216-6999 Office Phone: 210-283-2000.

HAYWOOD, L. JULIAN, cardiologist, educator; b. Reidsville, NC, Apr. 13, 1927; s. Thomas Woodly and Louise Viola (Hayley) H.; m. Virginia Elizabeth Paige, Dec. 3, 1953; 1 child, Julian Anthony. BS, Hampton Inst., 1948; MD, Howard U., DC, 1952. Intern St. Mary's Hosp., Rochester, NY, 1952-53; resident L.A. County Hosp., 1956-58; fellow cardiology White Meml. Hosp., 1959-61; traveling fellow U. Oxford, England, 1963; instr. medicine Loma Linda (Calif.) U., 1960-61, asst. prof., 1961-73, assoc. clin. prof., 1973-82, clin. prof., 1982—; asst. prof. medicine U. So. Calif., 1963-67, assoc. prof., 1967-76, prof., 1976—; dir. EKG dept. L.A. County/U. So. Calif. Med. Ctr. Past dir. coronary care unit, physicians tng. program Regional Med. Programs L.A. County/U. So. Calif. Med. Ctr, 1970-75; cons. Los Angeles County Coroner, Indsl. Accident Bd. Calif., Health Care Tech. Divsn., USPHS, Nat. Heart and Lung Inst.; past mem. cardiology adv. com. divsn. heart and vascular diseases; bd. dirs., pres. Sickle Cell Diseases Found.; mem. Armed Forces Epidemiol. Bd., 1996-2006; active U. So. Calif. Salerni Collegium, 1997-98; bd. dirs. Charles Drew U. Medicine and Scis., 1999—. Contbr. articles profl. jours.; Mem. editorial bds.: Jour. Nat. Med. Assn. Past pres., hon. mem., bd. dirs. Am. Heart Assn. Greater L.A., 1989—. With M.C. USNR, 1954-56. Recipient award of merit L.A. County Heart Assn., 1968, 69, 73, 75, 78, 79, 95, Disting. Alumnus award Howard U. Sch. Medicine, 1982, Disting. Svc. award, 1996, Disting. Health Educator award, 2003, Louis B. Russel award Am. Heart Assn., 1988, Merit award, 1991, Heart of Gold award Am. Heart Assn./Greater L.A. Affiliate, 1989, Dedicated Svc. award, 1991, 93, Award of Achievement in Rsch., 1994, 20th Anniversary Founder's award Assn. Black Cardiologists, 1994, Cert. of Appreciation, Armed Forces Epidemiology Bd., 2001, Eagle Cert. of Excellence award Nat. Med. Fellowships, N.Y.C., 2004, Cert. of Appreciation, Office of Def., 2006, Disting. Svc. award Black History Month, LA County/U. So. Calif. Med. Ctr., 2007; J.B. Johnson Meml. lectr., 1975, 88; honoree Internal Medicine sect. Nat. Med. Assn., 1988; named Alumnus of Yr.-at-Large, Hampton U., 1993; nat. med. fellow Gala West 2004, 2004. Fellow ACP, AAAS (Disting. Svc. award 2007), L.A. Acad. Medicine, Am. Coll. Cardiology (Disting. Svc. award 2001, Cert. of Merit 2003, Cert. of Appreciation 2003), Am. Heart Assn. (coun. on clin. cardiology, coun. on atherosclerosis, exec. com. coun. on epidemiology, long range planning com., dir., past sec., v.p. Greater L.A. affiliate, pres.); mem. AMA, AAUP, Am. Fedn. Clin. Rsch., Western Soc. Clin. Investigation, Assn. Advancement Med. Instrumentation, Nat. Med. Assn. (Charles Drew Med. Soc.), N.Y. Acad. Scis., Hampton Inst. Alumni Assn. (past pres. L.A. chpt.), Med. Faculty Assn. U. So. Calif. Sch. Medicine (past pres.), Assn. Physicians L.A. County Hosp. (pres. 1991-2006), Western Assn. Physicians, Fedn. Am. Scientists, Assn. Black Cardiologists (Walter Booker Innovation award 1990), Assn. Acad. Minority Physicians (councilor, pres.-elect 1992-93, pres. 1993-94), Alpha Omega Alpha, Am. Coll. Physicians (Laureate award So. Calif. Region I 1997). Office: LACt USC Med Ctr 1200 N State St Rm 8305 Los Angeles CA 90033-1029 Office Phone: 323-226-7116. Business E-Mail: jhaywood@hsc.usc.edu.

HAYWOOD, MARY GWENDOLYN, music educator; b. Eufaula, Ala., Feb. 15, 1962; d. Wayne Clevester and Sara Dean Cosson. MusB in Edn., Samford U., 1985; MusM in Ch. Music, Southwestern Bapt. Theol. Sem., 1988. Min. music Omega (Ga.) Bapt. Ch., 1989; tchr. music Omega (Ga.) Elem., 1990—92, Tifthea Acad., Tifton, Ga., 1990—95, Turner County Schs., Ashburn, Ga., 1995—96, Berrien County Schs., Nashville, Ga., 1996—. Min. music Unity Bapt. Ch., Sylvester, Ga., 1994—99; dir. music Alapaha (Ga.) Cmty. choir, 2000—; dir. children's choir First Bapt. Ch., Tifton, Ga., 1990—, adult ensemble, 1990—. Singer: Samford U. Acapella Choir, 1982—83, Acapella Alumni Choir, 1996, 1998. Orch. flutist First Bapt. Ch., Tifton, Ga., 1998. Scholar Camerata T.D. scholar, Camerata Chorus, 1980. Mem.: NEA, Ga. Music Educators, Ga. Assn. Educators, Nat. Fedn. Music Clubs, Tifton Choral Soc., Tifton Music Club (pres. 1994). Republican. Baptist. Avocations: piano, flute, violin, reading, exercise. Home: 104 Maple St PO Box 742 Omega GA 31775 Office: Berrien Elementary 305 N Anne st Nashville GA 31639

HAYWOOD, THEODORE JOSEPH, physician, educator; b. Monroe, NC, Feb. 13, 1929; s. Jesse Beman and Mary (McDonald) H.; m. Nancy Hume Ferguson, Dec. 21, 1959; children: Elizabeth Linscott, Keene McDonald, Mark Shepard. BS, The Citadel, 1948; MD, Vanderbilt U., 1952. Diplomate: Am. Bd. Pediatrics, Am. Bd. Allergy and Immunology. Pvt. practice allergy, Houston, 1958—; mem. staff Tex. Children's Hosp., 1958—, mem. active staff Pediatrics, 1963—; mem. faculty Baylor U. Coll. Medicine, 1958—, clin. assoc. prof. pediatrics and allergy, 1977—. Assoc. mem. U. Tex. McDonald Obs., 2000—, bd. visitors dept. astronomy, 2007—. Served with M.C. AUS, 1955-57. Fellow Am. Coll. Allergists, Am. Acad. Allergy and Immunology, Am. Acad. Pediatrics; mem. Sigma Xi. Clubs: River Oaks Country (Houston). Republican. Episcopalian. Home: 2923 Ferndale Pl Houston TX 77098-1117 Office: McGovern Allergy & Asthma Clinic 4710 Bellaire Blvd Ste 200 Bellaire TX 77401-4505 Home Phone: 713-522-5600; Office Phone: 713-661-1444. Business E-Mail: mac@mcgovernallergy.com.

HAYWORTH, J.D. (JOHN DAVID JR.), former congressman; b. High Point, NC, July 12, 1958; s. John David and Gladys Ethel (Hall) H.; m. Mary Denise Yancey, Feb. 25, 1989; children: Nicole Irene, Hannah Lynne, John Micah. BA in Speech and Polit. Sci., N.C. State U., 1980. Sports anchor, reporter Sta. WPTF-TV, Raleigh, N.C., 1980-81, Sta. WLWT-TV, Cin., 1986-87; sports anchor Sta. WYFF-TV (formerly Sta. WFBC-TV), Greenville, S.C., 1981-86, Sta. KTSP-TV, Phoenix, 1987-94; mem. US Congress from 5th Ariz. dist., Washington, 1995—2007, mem. ways and means com., mem. resources com., asst. whip. Co-author: (With Joseph J. Eule) Whatever It Takes: Illegal Immigration, Border Security, and the War on Terror, 2006 Dist. committeeman Ariz. Rep. Com., Scottsdale, 1988-89; bd. dirs. Am. Humanics Found., Ariz. State U., Tempe, 1991-92; chmn. Scout-A-Rama, Theodore Roosevelt coun. Boy Scouts Am., 1991-92. Recipient honor roll award Atlantic Coast Conf., 1977, Young Am. award Unharrie coun. Boy Scouts Am., 1979, Friend of Edn. award Sch. Dist. Greenville County, 1985, Sch. Bell/Friend of Edn. award S.C. Dept. Edn., 1985. Mem. Rotary (bd. dirs. Phoenix 1989-90). Republican. Baptist. Avocations: reading, running, bible study, public speaking, television trivia.

HAYWORTH, SCOTT DAVID, physician; b. NYC, Apr. 4, 1956; s. Henry Charles and Anne (Sinnreich) H.; m. Nan Alison Sutter, June 21, 1981; children: William, John. AB, Princeton U., 1978; MD, Cornell U., 1984. Diplomate Am. Bd. Ob/Gyn., Nat. Bd. Med. Examiners. Intern Mt. Sinai Hosp., NYC, 1984-85, resident physician, 1985-87, chief resident, 1987-88; physician Mt. Kisco (N.Y.) Med. Group, 1988—, v.p., 1995-96, pres., 1996—, acting med. dir., 1996-98, CEO, 1998—. Co-chmn. laser com. No. Westchester Hosp., 1991-95, mem. pharmacy and therapeutics com., 1990-04, mem. med. cabinet, 2002-04; found. bd., 2005-; mem. nat. physician adv. bd. Aetna, 2004-; clin. asst. prof. Mt. Sinai Sch. Medicine, NYC, 2005—. Consulting editor Contemporary Ob-Gyn., 2006—; contbr. chpt. to book and articles to profl. jours. Bd. dirs. No. Westchester Hosp. Found., 2005—. Recipient award of merit Vis. Nurse Assn. Hudson Valley, 2005; NIH fellow, 1981, David Bar fellow, 1981. Fellow Am. Coll. Ob-Gyn. (chmn. Hudson Valley sect. 2000-01, sec. Dist. II-NY 2002, treas. Dist. II-NY 2002-04, vice chair Dist. II-NY 2004—, Dist. Svc. award 2002); mem. Westchester Obstet. and Gynecol. Soc. (sec.-treas. 1995-96, co-pres. 1996-97, pres. 1997-99), Internat. Soc. Gynecol. Endoscopy, Gynecol. Laser Soc., Am. Med. Group Assn. (bd. dir. 2005—, chmn. membership com. 2005—, found. bd. dirs. 2006-). Office: Mt Kisco Med Group 90 S Bedford Rd Mount Kisco NY 10549-3412 Office Phone: 914-241-1050.

HAZAN, MARCELLA MADDALENA, writer, educator, consultant; b. Cesenatico, Italy, Apr. 15, 1924; d. Giuseppe and Maria (Leonelli) Polini; m. Victor Hazan, Feb. 24, 1955; 1 child, Giuliano. Dr. in Natural Scis., U. Ferrara, 1952, Dr. in Biology, 1954. Rschr. Guggenheim Inst., 1955-58; prof. math. and biology Italian State schs., 1963-66; founder Sch. of Italian Cooking, NYC, 1969-94, Marcella Hazan Sch. of Classic Italian Cooking, Bologna, Italy, 1976-94, Master Classes in Classic Italian Cooking, Venice, Italy, 1986-98. Pres. Hazan Classic Enterprises, Inc., 1978-99. Author: The Classic Italian Cookbook, 1973, More Classic Italian Cooking, 1978, Marcella's Italian Kitchen, 1986, Essentials of Classic Italian Cooking, 1992, Marcella Cucina, 1997, Marcella Says, 2004. Decorated knight Presdl. Order Star of Italian Solidarity. Roman Catholic. Address: 1211 Gulf Of Mexico Dr # 109 Longboat Key FL 34228 Fax: (941) 387-0183.

HAZAN, SCOTT L., lawyer; b. NYC, Sept. 13, 1948; s. Jacob and Mildred Hazan; m. Lorraine Hazan, June 25, 1972; children: Jeremy, Alissa. BA, Queens Coll., 1970; JD cum laude, Bklyn. Law Sch., 1973. Assoc., ptnr. Otterbourg, Steindler, Houston & Rosen, P.C., NYC, 1973—. Mem. adv. bd. LLM program St. John's U. Law Sch. With USAR, 1969—75. Mem.: ABA (bus. bankruptcy com., chpt. 11 subcom., claims trade subcom., task force on profl. compensation subcom.), Comml. Law League of Am., Turnaround Mgmt. Assn., Am. Bankruptcy Inst. (exec. com. for NYC Day), Bankruptcy Bar Assn. City of NY, NY State Bar Assn. (subcom. on bankruptcy, former chmn. subcom. on revisions to the Debtor and Creditor Law State), Bklyn. Law Sch. Alumni Assn. (officer and dir.). Office: Otterbourg Steindler Houston & Rosen PC 230 Park Ave New York NY 10169 Office Phone: 212-905-3625.

HAZARD, CHRISTOPHER WEDVIK, international business executive; b. NYC, Aug. 9, 1943; s. Herbert Ray and Ellen Clausine (Wedvik) H.; m. Sally Grace Woodruff, Sept. 1, 1966; children: Mark Alexander, Julie Lynne. BA, Ohio State U., 1965; MPA, U. Colo., 1973; postgrad., U. Pa., The Wharton Sch. Lt. col. USAF, 1965-86; near east region dir. ops. Def. Security Assistance Agy., Washington, 1982-86; v.p. Bofors, Inc., 1986—; exec dir. internat. mktg. BAE Sys., Land and Armaments, Arlington, Va., 1986—. Active Neighborhood Friends of Mt. Vernon Recipient Def. Superior Svc. award, Sec. of Def., 1986, Joint Svc. Achievement award, Dept. of Def., 1984; decorated Air Force Meritorious Svc. medal. Mem.: Mt. Vernon Citizens Assn. (pres. 1984—85), Soc. Am. Period Furniture Makers. Avocations: international affairs, historic preservation, gardening, woodworking. Office Phone: 703-312-6119. Business E-Mail: chris.hazard@baesystems.com.

HAZARD, GEOFFREY CORNELL, JR., law educator; b. Cleve., Sept. 18, 1929; s. Geoffrey Cornell and Virginia (Perry) H.; m. Elizabeth O'Hara; children: James G., Katherine W., Robin P., Geoffrey Cornell III. BA, Swarthmore Coll., 1953, LLD (hon.), 1988; LLB, Columbia U., 1954; LLD (hon.), Gonzaga U., 1985, U. San Diego, 1985, Ill. Inst. Tech., 1990, Republica Italiana, 1998. Bar: Oreg. 1954, Calif. 1960, Conn. 1982, Pa. 1994. Assoc. Hart, Spencer, McCulloch, Rockwood & Davies, Portland, Oreg., 1954-57; exec. sec. Oreg. Legis. Interim Com. Jud. Adminstrn., 1957-58; assoc. prof. law, then prof. U. Calif., Berkeley, 1958-64; prof. law U. Chgo., 1964-71, Yale U., 1971-94, prof. mgmt., 1979-83, acting dean Sch. Orgn. and Mgmt., 1980-81, Sterling prof. law, 1986-94; trustee prof. U. Pa., Phila., 1994—; disting. prof. U. Calif. Law, Hastings, 2005—. Mem. Adminstrv. Conf. U.S., 1971-78; cons. jud. conf. U.S. com. on rules practice and procedure, 2004. Author: (Law text) Research in Civil Procedure, 1963, Ethics in the Practice of Law, 1978; author: (with D.W. Louisell, C. Tait, W. Fletcher) Pleading and Procedure, 1972; author: 9th rev. edit., 2005; author: (with M. Taruffo) (Law text) American Civil Procedure, 1994; author: (with S. Koniak, R. Cramton and G. Cohen) Law and Ethics of Lawyering, 4th edit., 2004; author: (with W.W. Hodes) Law of Lawyering 3d edit., 2000; author: (with F. James and J. Leubsdorf) Civil Procedure 5th rev.edit., 2001; author: (with A. Dondi) Legal Ethics: A Comparative Study, 2004; editor: (Law text) Law in a Changing America, 1968; editor: (with D. Rhode) Legal Profession: Responsibility and Regulation, 2006; contbr. articles to profl. jours. Served with USAF, 1948-49. Fellow Am. Bar Found. (exec. dir. 1964-70, rsch. award 1986); mem. ABA (cons. code jud. conduct 1970-72, reporter stds. jud. adminstrn. 1971-77, reporter model rules of profl. conduct 1978-83), Am. Law Inst.

(reporter restatement of judgments 1973-81, dir. 1984-99, dir. emeritus, 1999-), Am. Acad. Arts and Scis., Am. Philos. Soc., Nat. Legal Aid and Defender Assn., Am. Judicature Soc., Selden Soc., Calif. State Bar, Phi Beta Kappa. Episcopalian. Avocations: tennis, history, golf.

HAZARD, ROBERT CULVER, JR., hotel executive; b. Balt., Oct. 23, 1934; s. Robert Culver and Catherine B. H.; m. Mary Victoria Cranor, Jan. 2, 1981; children by previous marriage: Alicia W., Letitia A., Robert Culver, III, Thomas E.J., Anne. BA cum laude, Woodrow Wilson Sch., Princeton U., 1956; postgrad., Johns Hopkins U., U. Denver. Mktg. rep. IBM Corp., Denver, 1959-68; with Am. Express Co., 1968-74, v.p. exec. accounts, 1973-74; CEO Best Western Internat., 1974-80; CEO, retired chmn. Choice Hotels Internat., Silver Spring, Md., 1980-96; chmn. Creative Hotel Assocs., Rockville, Md., 1996—. Capt. USAF, 1956-59. Recipient Man of Yr. award Motel Brokers Assn. Am., 1976, Silver Plate award Hospitality mag., 1979, Albert E. Koehl award HSMA, 1992, Cecil B. Day Hospitality award AAHOA, 1993, Silver Plate award Lodging Hospitality Mag., 1995. Mem.: Am. Hotel and Lodging Assn. E-mail: roberthazard@msn.com.

HAZBOUN, VIVECA, psychiatrist; b. Ramallah, Jordan, Nov. 2, 1949; arrived in U.S., 1966; d. Albert Anthony and Helen Hazboun. BS in Chemistry, Immaculate Heart Coll., LA, 1970; MD, U. So. Calif., 1976. Diplomate in adult psychiatry Am. Bd. Psychiatry and Neurology, 1980, in child psychiatry Am. Bd. Psychiatry and Neurology, 82. Tchg. asst. Grad. Sch. U. So. Calif., LA, 1970—72; intern in internal medicine Huntington Meml. Hosp., Pasadena, Calif., 1976—77; resident in adult psychiatry Los Angeles County-U. So. Calif. Med. Ctr., 1977—79, fellow in child and adolescent psychiatry, 1979—81, chief child resident, 1980—81, asst. prof. clin. psychiatry, 1981—85, clin. instr., 1980—81; practice adult, child and adolescent psychiatry LA, 1980—; supr. mental health UN Relief and Work Agy., 1990—95; dir. adult and child psychiatry and neurology Guidance and Tng. Ctr., 1994—. Ward chief children's inpatient Los Angeles County-U. So. Calif. Med. Ctr. Psychiat. Hosp., 1981—85; cons. staff Edgemont Psychiat. Hosp., LA, 1982—85; cons. Medecins sans Frontieres, Jerusalem, Medecins du Monde, Jerusalem; project dir. World Vision; founder Guidance and Tng. Ctr. for the Child and Family, 1994—, dir., 1994—. Contbr. articles to med. jours. Recipient Papal award, Rome, 1968, recognition awards Child Guidance Clinic, 1980, Women in Data Processing, 1983; fellow Child Guidance Clinic, 1980. Mem. WHO (steering com., thematic group, 2003—), Am. Acad. Child Psychiatry, So. Calif. Psychiat. Soc., So. Calif. Soc. Child Psychiatry, Internat. Assn. Child and Adult Psychiatry (sci. com.), Ea. Mediterranean Child and Adult Psychiatry Assn. (ethics com.), Am. Arab Univ. Grads. Office: PO Box 51399 Jerusalem Israel Business E-Mail: gtc@p_ol.com.

HAZEKAMP, PHYLLIS WANDA ALBERTS, retired library director; b. Chgo. d. John Edward and Mary Ann (Demski) Wojciechowski. BA, De Paul U., 1947; MSLS, La. State U., 1959; postgrad., Santa Clara U., U. Chgo. Cert. tchr., Calif., Ariz. Libr. Agrl. Experiment Sta., U. Calif., Riverside, 1959-61; tech. libr. Lockheed Tech. Libr., Palo Alto, Calif., 1962-63; asst. law libr. Santa Clara (Calif.) U. Law Sch., 1963-72; libr. dir. Carmelite Seminary, San Jose, Calif., 1973-78; reference libr. San Jose State U., 1978-79; libr. dir. SAI Engrs., Santa Clara, 1980-81, Palmer Coll. Chiropractic, San Jose, 1981-90, Camp Verde (Ariz.) Cmty. Libr., 1990-98; ret., 1998. Mem. Cultural Commn., Santa Clara, 1968-72; pres. Santa Clara Art Assn., 1973-74; cons., lectr. in field. Co-editor: Beaver Creek Adult Ctr. Newsletter, 2007—. Bd. dirs. Camp Verde Art Commn., 1994—; spkr. Ho. of Ruth, 2000—02; chmn. Montezuma Chapel Ladies Guild, 2003—04; bd. dirs. Beaver Creek Adult Ctr., 2000—02; vol. various orgns.; pres. Book Rev. Club, 2003—; vol. Camp Verde Christian Sch. Avocations: writing articles, painting, teaching, giving talks to groups.

HAZEL, MARY BELLE, university administrator; b. Orange, NJ, May 30, 1932; d. Morris M. Sr. and Robena (Brinkley) Thomas; m. James H. Hazel, Sept. 28, 1958 (div. Sept. 1976); children: Sharon Marie Hazel-Griggs, James Thomas. BSBA, Seton Hall U., South Orange, NJ, 1992, MA in Edn. cum laude, 1998. Publs. asst. advt. and pub. rels. dept. Foster Wheeler Corp., NYC, 1969-87; ind. contractor, 1987-92; adminstrv. coord. dean's office Univ. Medicine and Dentistry NJ Sch. Health Related Professions, Newark, 1992—. Elder Elmwood United Presbyn. Ch. Mem. AAUW, NAFE, Smithsonian Nat. Assn., Soc. Allied Health Professions NJ, YWCA, NJ Performing Arts Ctr., Jersey Ednl. Opportunity Fund Profl. Assn., Newark Mus. Assn., YWCA of Essex and West Hudson (NJ).

HAZELIP, LINDA ANN, musician, small business owner, executive assistant; b. El Campo, Tex., Oct. 20, 1952; d. Al Gareth and Annabelle (Black) Braswell; m. Richard Chris Hazelip, July 28, 1972 (div. Aug. 30, 1984). *It is only by God's grace I live a normal life, developing and using the talents given me. Born with a dislocated hip, I was chosen by a team of doctors from around the world to try to help. I learned to walk three times before age five. At age three, Jesus told me three times in a dream that I could walk. With childlike faith, I did walk while continuing my rehabilitation; a miracle in medical history. My continual prayer is for my life to be a living testimony of what is possible with God if we only believe.* Diploma in computer programming and data processing, Massey Bus. Coll., 1972. Cert. tchr. progressive series intermediate level piano St. Louis Conservatory Music, 1971. Tchr. basic music and piano, 1971—79; bookkeeper Millar Instruments, Houston, 1973—74; sec. St. Andrew's United Meth. Ch., Houston, 1975—79; various positions as exec. asst., mgmt. asst., exec. sec., adminstr. , and other adminstrv. positions Houston, 1979—; bus. owner, organist/choirmaster, pianist, vocalist sacred occasions, select secular spl. occasions Met. Area, Houston, S.E. Tex., 1986—; dir., exec. sec. Exponet Trading Co., Houston, 1983—86; exec. sec. InterFirst Bank Post Oak, Houston, 1986; sec., adminstr., mgmt. asst. Halliburton Energy Svcs., Houston, 1991—96; tchr. voice, organ, piano, 2000—. Organist, vocalist, pianist, children's music dir. Faith United Methodist Ch., South Houston, 1972—77; organist, vocalist, children's music dir. Old River Ter. United Methodist Ch., Channelview, Tex., 1978—80; organist, vocalist, music dir. St. John's United Methodist Ch., Baytown, Tex., 1980—84; organist, vocalist St. Stephens United Methodist Ch., Houston, 1983—85; organist, choir dir., vocalist Parker Meml. United Methodist Ch., Houston, 1984—85; choir dir., vocalist Reid Meml. United Methodist Ch., Houston, 1985, Covenant United Methodist Ch., Houston, 1985—86. Vocalist, pianist Open Door Mission, Houston, 1997—; mem. First United Meth. Ch., Houston, 1986—. Mem.: NAFE, Chorister's Guild, Houston Area League PC Users, Am. Bus. Women's Assn. (Skyscraper chpt., Woman of Yr. 1993—94), Am. Guild Organists, Nat. Honor Soc., Nat. Math. Honor Soc. Republican. Methodist. Avocation: holy land study tours. Office: 2501 Westridge 241 Houston TX 77054-1519 Office Phone: 713-668-2248. Business E-Mail: lhazelip@hal-pc.org.

HAZELRIGG, GEORGE ARTHUR, JR., systems engineer, educator; b. Summit, NJ, Oct. 28, 1939; s. George Arthur Hazelrigg and Dorothy Hetty (Howell) Orr; m. Lauretta Blanche Powell, Aug. 31, 1968; children: George A. III, Geoffrey A. BS, N.J. Inst. Tech., 1961, MS, 1963; MA, Princeton U., 1966, MSE, 1968, PhD, 1969. Cert. glider flight instr. Engr. Curtiss-Wright, Wood Ridge, NJ, 1961-63, Jet Propulsion Lab, Pasadena, Calif., 1966-67; staff sci. Gen. Dynamics, San Diego, 1968-71; rsch. staff Princeton U., 1971-75; dir., systems engr. Econ, Inc., Princeton, 1976-82; dep. dir. divsn. NSF, Arlington, Va., 1982—; prof. of systems engring. (sabbatical) Inst. for Advanced Engring., Seoul, 1993. Dir. ECON, Inc., Princeton, 1974-84; cons. Princeton Synergetics, Inc., 1986-2000. Author: Systems Engineering: An Approach to Information-Based Design, 1996; editor: Opportunities for Academic Research in a Low Gravity Environment, 1986; assoc. editor Jour. Spacecraft and Rockets, 1977-82. Named Disting. Alumnus, N.J. Inst. Tech., Newark, 1989. Fellow ASME; mem. AIAA, Am. Soc. for Engring. Edn., Tau Beta Pi. Avocation: commercial pilot. Home: 8427 Idylwood Rd Vienna VA 22182-5309 Office: NSF 4201 Wilson Blvd Arlington VA 22230-0001 E-mail: ghazelri@nsf.gov.

HAZELTINE, BARRETT, electrical engineer, educator; b. Paris, Nov. 7, 1931; came to U.S., 1932; s. L. Alan and Elizabeth (Barrett) H.; m. Mary Frances Fenn, Aug. 25, 1956; children: Michael B., Alice W., Patricia F. BSE, Princeton U., 1953, MSE, 1956; PhD, U. Mich., 1962; ScD (hon.), SUNY, Stony Brook, 1988. Registered profl. engr., R.I. Asst. prof. engring. Brown U., 1959—66, assoc. prof., 1966—72, prof., 1972—; asst. to dean Brown U. (The Coll.), 1962—63, asst. dean, 1968—74, assoc. dean, 1974—93; Robert Foster Cherry chair for disting. tchg. Baylor U., 1991—92; prof. U. Botswana, 1993. Lectr., vis. prof. U. Zambia, Lusaka, 1970-71, 76-77; vis. prof. U. Malawi-Poly., Blantyre, 1980-81, 83-84, 88-89, Africa U. Mutare, Zimbabwe, 1996-97, 2000; asst. to mgr. rsch. labs., space and info. sys. divsn. Raytheon Co., 1964-65, cons., 1965-67; cons. R.I. Utilities Commn., 1977-80, others. Author: Introduction to Electronic Circuits and Applications, 1980, Appropriate Technology: Tools, Choice and Implications, 1998, Field Guide to Appropriate Technology, 2003; editor: The Weaver, 1982—90. Trustee Stevens Inst. Tech. Recipient award for excellence in instrn. Western Electric, 1968; grantee NSF, Dept. Edn.; grantee Met. Life Ins. Ednl. Found.; Fulbright fellow 1988-89, 93. Mem. IEEE (sr., chmn. Providence sect. 1971-72), Providence Engring. Soc. (pres. 1977-78), Am. Soc. Engring. Edn., Sigma Xi, Tau Beta Pi. Congregationalist (deacon). Clubs: Providence Art, Providence Review. Achievements include patents for color recognition system. Home: 60 Barnes St Providence RI 02906-1502 Office: Brown U Divsn Engring Providence RI 02912-0001 Office Phone: 401-863-2673. Business E-Mail: Barrett_Hazeltine@brown.edu.

HAZELTINE, JOYCE, former state official; b. Pierre, SD; m. Dave Hazeltine; children: Derek, Tara, Kirk (dec.). Student, Huron Coll., SD, No. State Coll., Aberdeen, SD, Black Hills State Coll., Spearfish, SD. Former asst. chief clk. SD Ho. of Reps.; former sec. SD State Senate; sec. of state State of SD, Pierre, 1987—2003. Bd. dirs. S.D. Bankers Found.; chair SD Bankers Found., 2004—; bd. dirs. Chiesman Ctr. Democracy, Black Hills Playhouse. Adminstrv. asst. Pres. Ford Campaign, SD; Rep. county chmn. Hughes County SD; state co-chair Phil Gramm for Pres., 1996; mem. Custer Co. Rep. Women; chair bd. dirs. Black Hills Playhouse. Mem. Nat. Assn. Secs. of State (exec. bd., pres.), Women Execs. in State Govts. (bd. dirs.). Republican.

HAZELTON, PENNY ANN, law librarian, educator; b. Yakima, Wash., Sept. 24, 1947; d. Fred Robert and Margaret (McLeod) Pease; m. Norris J. Hazelton, Sept. 12, 1971; 1 child, Victoria MacLeod. BA cum laude, Linfield Coll., 1969; JD, Lewis and Clark Law Sch., 1975; M in Law Librarianship, U. Wash., 1976. Bar: Wash. 1976, U.S. Supreme Ct. 1982. Assoc. law libr., assoc. prof. U. Maine, 1976-78, law libr., assoc. prof., 1978-81; asst. libr. for rsch. svcs. U.S. Supreme Ct., Washington, 1981-85, law libr., 1985, U. Wash., Seattle, 1985—, prof. law, assoc. dean libr. and computing svcs., 1985—. Tchr. legal rsch., law librarianship, Indian law; cons. Maine Adv. Com. on County Law Librs., Lawyers Coop. Pub., 1993-94, Marquette U. Sch. Law, 2002, Georgetown U. Law Ctr., 2004. Author: Computer Assisted Legal Research: The Basics, 1993; author: (with others) Washington Legal Researcher's Deskbook, 3d edit., 2002; contbr. articles to legal jours.; gen. editor Specialized Legal Rsch. (Aspen). Recipient Disting. Alumni award U. Wash., 1992. Mem. ABA (sect. legal edn. and admissions to bar, chair com. on librs. 1993-94, vice chair 1992-93, 94-95, com. on law sch. facilities 1998—), Am. Assn. Law Schs. (com. law librs. 1991-94), Law Librs. New Eng. (sec. 1977-79, pres. 1979-81), Am. Assn. Law Librs. (program chmn. ann. meeting 1984, exec. bd. 1984-87, v.p. 1989-90, pres. 1990-91, program co-chair Insts. 1983, 95), Law Librs. Soc. Washington (exec. bd. 1983-84, v.p., pres. elect 1984-85), Law Librs. Puget Sound, Wash. State Bar Assn. (chair editl. adv. bd.), Wash. Adv. Coun. on Librs., Westpac. Office: U Wash Marian Gould Gallagher Law Libr William H Gates Hall Box 353025 Seattle WA 98195 Home Phone: 206-363-1174; Office Phone: 206-543-4089. Business E-Mail: pennyh@u.washington.edu.

HAZEN, PAUL MANDEVILLE, banker; b. Lansing, Mich., 1941; married. BA, U. Ariz., 1963; MBA, U. Calif., Berkeley, 1964. Asst. mgr Security Pacific Bank, 1964-66; v.p. Union Bank, 1966-70; chmn. Wells Fargo Realty Advisors, 1970-76, with San Francisco, 1979—2001, exec. v.p., mgr. Real Estate Industries Group, 1979-80, mem. exec. office Real Estate Industry Group, 1980, vice-chmn. Real Estate Industries Group, 1980-84, pres., chief oper. officer Real Estate Industries Group, 1984—, also dir. Real Estate Industries Group, 1984—; pres., treas. Wells Fargo Mortgage & Equity Trust, San Francisco, 1977-84; with Wells Fargo & Co., San Francisco, 1978—2001, from exec. v.p. to vice-chmn., pres., chief operating officer, 1981—95, chmn, CEO, 1995-2001, chmn. bd. dirs., Accel-Kohlbert, Kravis, Roberts and Co., Menlo Park, Calif., 2001—. Trustee Wells Fargo Mortgage & Equity Trust; bd. dirs. Pacific Telesis Group, Safeway Inc., Phelps Dodge Corp., Xstrata AG, E.piphany; dep. chmn. Vodafone. Office: Accel Kohlberg Kravis Roberts and Co 2500 Sand Hill Rd Ste 100 Menlo Park CA 94205

HAZEN, ROBERT MILLER, research scientist, writer; b. Rockville Centre, NY, Nov. 1, 1948; s. Dan Francis and Dorothy Ellen (Chapin) Hazen; m. Margaret Hindle, Aug. 9, 1969; children: Benjamin Hindle, Elizabeth Brooke. BS, SM, MIT, 1971; PhD, Harvard U., 1975. NATO fellow U. Cambridge, England, 1975—76; rsch. sci. Geophys. Lab., Carnegie Instn., Washington, 1976—; Robinson prof. earth sci. George Mason U., Washington, 1990—. Author: Comparative Crystal Chemistry, 1982, Music Men, 1987, The Breakthrough, 1988, Keepers of the Flame, 1991, Why Aren't Black Holes Black?, 1997, The Diamond Makers, 1999, The Sciences, 2000, Physics Matters, 2003, Genesis: The Scientific Quest for Life's Origins, 2005; co-author: Science Matters, 1990; contbr. articles to profl. jours.; musician (trumpeter): Nat. Gallery Orch., Nat. Philham., also recs. Recipient Deems Tayor award, ASCAP, 1989, Wood Sci. Writing prize, 1998. Fellow: AAAS, Mineral Soc. Am. (editor, coun. pres., Mineral Soc. Am. award 1982, Disting. Lectr.); mem.: Internat. Guild Trumpeters, History of Sci. Soc., Am. Chem. Soc. (Ipatief prize 1985), Am. Geophys. Union, Phi Lambda Upsilon, Sigma Xi. Avocations: volleyball, ballroom dancing, string quartets. Office: Geophys Lab 5251 Broad Branch Rd NW Washington DC 20015-1305 Office Phone: 202-478-8962. Business E-Mail: rhazen@gl.ciw.edu.

HAZLEHURST, ROBERT PURVIANCE, JR., lawyer; b. Spartanburg, SC, Jan. 7, 1919; s. Robert Purviance and Lottie Lee (Nicholls) H.; m. Mary Kierulff, Feb. 20, 1947 (dec. July 1971); children: Ellen Hazlehurst Courtney, Charlotte Hazlehurst Leonesio, Anne Hazlehurst Goldberg; m. Dorothy Wilson Deemer, Jan. 7, 1972. AB, Princeton U., 1940; LL.B., Yale U., 1947. Bar: N.J. 1947. Since practiced in Newark and Morristown; ptnr. Pitney, Hardin, Kipp & Szuch, 1952-89. Bd. dirs. Princeton Fund, 1966-71, chmn. ann. giving campaign, 1967-68 Sec., trustee Greater Newark Hosp. Devel. Fund; trustee Kent Pl. Sch., Summit, N.J., 1960-70; trustee, v.p. Silver Hill Found., New Canaan, Conn., 1973-85; trustee United Hosps. Newark, 1958-73, pres., 1970-73. Served to capt. USAAF, 1942-45. Mem.: Short Hills (N.J.), Nassau (N.J.). Home and Office: 38 Sinclair Ter Short Hills NJ 07078-1714

HAZLETT, DAVID LAWRENCE, social studies educator; b. Rock Island, Ill., Nov. 20, 1956; s. Albert Dale and Orpha Ellen Hazlett; m. Theresa Ann Wright, June 21, 1997; children: Dahlton, Jennifer. BSc with distinction, U. So. Colo., Pueblo, 1978, BA with spl. distinction, 1980; MA, U. Colo., Colo. Springs, 1984. Cert. Colo. Profl. Tchrs. Lic. Social studies tchr. El Paso County Sch. Dist. 8, Fountain, Colo., 1980—. Mentor tchr. El Paso County Sch. Dist. 8, Fountain, Colo., 1997—; adj. lectr. US history, history of S.W., Colo. State U., Pueblo, 2000—; in-svc. workshop presenter Fountain-Ft. Carson HS, Fountain, Colo., 2004. Vol. coach Colo. Springs Sch. Dist. 11, 1992—96, El Paso County Sch. Dist. 8, Fountain, Colo., 2002—. Named Disting. Tchr., El Paso County Sch. Dist. #8, 2005; named one of Am.'s Outstanding Tchrs., Nat. Honor Roll, 2006; recipient Tchr. Yr., Wal-Mart, 2002. Mem.: Orgn. History Tchrs., Am. Hist. Assn., Colo. HS Coaches Assn. (Svc. award 2000, 2004). Non-Denom. Christian. Avocations: travel, reading. Home: 11115 Peaceful Valley Rd Colorado Springs CO 80925 Office: Fountain Ft Carson HS 900 Jimmy Camp Rd Fountain CO 80817 Business E-Mail: dhazlett@ffc8.org.

HAZLETT, MARK A., lawyer; b. NYC, Aug. 18, 1948; BA, Stanford U., 1970, JD, 1973. Bar: Hawaii 1973. Ptnr. Cades Schutte LLP, Honolulu. Adv. com. to Commr. of Fin. Insts., 1984-86; adj. prof. law U. Hawaii Law Sch., 19952—2001. Co-editor: Hawaii Commercial Real Estate Manual, 1988; co-editor, co-author: Hawaii Real Estate Financing Manual, 1990, Hawaii Real Estate Law Manual, 1997. Mem. ABA, Hawaii State Bar Assn. (dir. fin. svcs. divsn. 1982-83, chmn. real property and fin. svcs. sect. 1984, bd. dirs. 1982-98), Waikiki Yacht Club (commodore 2007). Office: Cades Schutte LLP PO Box 939 1000 Bishop St Honolulu HI 96808 Office Phone: 808-521-9224.

HAZZARD, SHIRLEY, author; b. Sydney, Jan. 30, 1931; d. Reginald and Catherine (Stein) Hazzard.; m. Francis Steegmuller, Dec. 22, 1963 (dec. Oct. 1994). Student, Queenwood Sch., Sydney, 1946. With Spl. Ops. Intelligence, Hong Kong, 1947—48, U.K. High Commr. Office, Wellington, New Zealand, 1949—50, UN (gen. svc. category), NYC, 1952—61. Boyer lectr., Australia, 1984, 88. Author: Cliffs of Fall and other stories, 1963; (novels) The Evening of the Holiday, 1966, People in Glass Houses, 1967, The Bay of Noon, 1970, The Transit of Venus, 1980, History Defeat of an Ideal: A Study of the Self Destruction of the UN, 1973, History Countenance of Truth, 1990; (novel) The Great Fire, 2003 (Nat. Book award, 2003); (memoir) Greene on Capri, 2000. Trustee N.Y. Soc. Libr. Named Hon. Citizen Capri, 2000, Libr. Lion, N.Y. Pub. Libr., 2006; recipient Lit. Award, Nat. Inst. Arts and Letters, 1966, First prize, O. Henry Short Story Awards, 1976, Cir. Award for Fiction, Nat. Book Critics, 1981, Clifton Fadiman Medal for Lit., 2001, Nat. Book Award for Fiction, 2003, Medal of Honor, Nat. Arts Club Lit., 2004, Mary McCarthy award, Bard Coll., 2004, Miles Franklin award, Australia, 2004; Guggenheim Fellow, 1974. Fellow Royal Soc. Lit.; mem. AAAL (William Dean Howells medal 2005), Nat. Arts and Sci., Century Club N.Y.C. Address: 200 E 66th St Apt C1705 New York NY 10021-9187

HAZZARD, WILLIAM RUSSELL, geriatrician, educator; b. Ann Arbor, Mich., Sept. 5, 1936; s. Albert Sidney and Florence Bernice (Woolsey) Hazzard; m. Ellen Bennett Friedman, June 10, 1961; children: Susan Lovejoy Roque, Russell Holden, Rebecca Cornell Oliver, Daniel Bennett. AB, Cornell U., 1958, MD, 1962. Diplomate Am. Bd. Internal Medicine, Am. Bd. Geriatrics. Resident in internal medicine U. Wash. Sch. Med. and Affiliated Hosps., Seattle, 1966—67, fellow in endocrinology and metabolism, 1965—66, 1967—69; from instr. to prof. medicine U. Wash., Seattle, 1969—82, dir. Northwest Lipid Rsch. Clinic, 1972—78; investigator Howard Hughes Med. Inst., U. Wash., Seattle, 1972—80; chief divsn. gerontology and geriatric medicine, 1978—82; prof. medicine, assoc. dir. dept. medicine Johns Hopkins Med. Instns., Balt., 1982—86, dir. ctr. on aging, 1983—86; prof., chmn. dept. internal med. Bowman Gray Sch. Medicine of Wake Forest U., Winston-Salem, NC, 1986—98; dir. J. Paul Sticht Ctr. on Aging of Wake Forest U., Winston-Salem, NC, 1987—97; sr. adv. J. Paul Ctr. On Aging of Wake Forest U., 1998—; prof. medicine U. Wash., Seattle, 1999—; dir. geriatrics and extended care VA Puget Sound Health Care Sys., 1999—. Vis. lectr., hon. sr. registrar Oxford (Eng.) U., 1977—78, St. Thomas Sch. Medicine, London, 1977—78; dir. sect. gerontology and geriatric medicine VA Puget Sound Health Care Sys., Seattle, Tacoma, Wash., 1999—. Editor: Principles of Geriatric Medicine and Gerontology, 1984, 1989, 1993, 1999, 2003; contbr. over 200 articles to jours. in field. Lt. USNR, 1963—65. Fellow: ACP; mem.: Nat. Inst. on Aging (mem. nat. adv. coun. 1995—99, aging rev. com. 1990—94, Geriatric Medicine Acad. award 1980), Am. Clin. and Climatol. Assn., Assn. Am. Physicians, Am. Soc. Clin. Investigation (mem. emeritus), Am. Fedn. Biomed. Rsch. (mem. emeritus), Am. Heart Assn. (coun.on arterosclerosis), Gerontol. Soc. Am. (chmn. clin. med. sect. 1984), Am. Geriatrics Soc. (bd. dirs. 1988—94, pres. 1993), Inst. Medicine of NAS. Avocations: gardening, conservation and nature study, music, athletics. Home: 3515 E Conover Ct Seattle WA 98122-6426 Office: VA Puget Sound Health Care Sys Geriatric Extended Care 1660 S Columbian Way Seattle WA 98108-1532 E-mail: william.hazzard@med.va.gov.

H'DOUBLER, FRANCIS TODD, JR., surgeon; b. Springfield, Mo., June 18, 1925; s. Francis Todd and Alice Louise (Bemis) H'D; m. Joan Louise Huber, Dec. 20, 1951 (dec. Dec. 1983); children: Julie H'Doubler Thomas and Sarah H'Doubler Muegge (twins), Kurt, Scott; m. Marie Ruth Duckworth, Jan. 18, 1986 Student, Washington U., St. Louis, 1943, Miami U., Oxford, Ohio, 1943-44; BS, U. Wis., 1946, MD, 1948. Intern Milw. Hosp., 1948-49; resident in surgery U.S. Naval Hosp., Oakland, Calif., 1950-51; practice medicine specializing in alternative medicine Springfield, Mo., 1952—; mem. courtesy staff St. John's Hosp., Springfield, L.E. Cox Hosp., Springfield. Bd. dirs. Union Planters Bank. Active Singing Doctors; chmn. fundraising drive YMCA, 1960-61, Sch. Bond and Tax Levy Com., 1958, Greene County Rep. Com., 1974-75; past bd. trustees Shriners Hosps., past chmn. spinal cord injury com., past chmn. rsch. com., past chmn. long range planning com., emeritus mem. rsch. com.; mem. Commn. to Reapportion Mo. Senate, 1971, Rep. State Fin. Com., 1972-75, steering com. Wilson's Creekl Battlefield Nat. Park, 1951-61, pres.'s adv. coun. Sch. Ozarks, Point Lookout, Mo., 1975-89; trustee Cottey Coll., Nevada, Mo., past bd. chmn.; bd. trustees Forest Inst. With USNR, 1943-46, 49-51. Decorated Bronze Star with V, Purple Heart with oak leaf cluster; recipient Disting. Service award Mo. Jaycees, 1959; Humanitarian award S.W. Mo. Drug Travelers Assn., 1971; named Young Man of Yr., City of Springfield, 1959 Fellow Am. Coll. Nuclear Medicine (founder's group); mem. AMA, Greene County Med. Assn., Mo. Med. Soc., Southwestern Surg. Congress, Mo. Surg. Assn., Soc. Nuclear Medicine, Am. Thyroid Assn., Springfield Jr. C. of C. (past pres.), Springfield C. of C., DAV, VFW, SAR, Am. Legion, Green Gang (co-founder), Sigma Nu (Outstanding Alumnus nat. award 1980), Nu Sigma Nu. Clubs: Hickory Hills Country. Lodges: Mason (33 deg.), Shriners (imperial potentate 1980-81), Red Cross of Constantine, Order DeMolay Legion Honor (hon.), Royal Order Scotland. Presbyterian.

HE, JUNKUN, research scientist; married, Aug. 18, 1998; children: Linda, Huang. PhD, Chinese Acad. Sci., Shanghai, 1981; postgrad., Duke U., Durhm, NC, 1986, U. Md., College Park, 1991. Rsch. asst. prof. Uniform Svc. U. Health Sci., Bethesda, Md., 1992—96; sr. scientist Naval Med. Ctr./Naval Med. Rsch. Inst., Bethesda, 1992—96, Walter Reed Army Inst. Rsch., Washington, 1997—2004; sr. rsch. scientist Armed Forces Inst. Pathology, Washington, 2004—. Contbr. articles to profl. jours. Office: Armed Forces Inst Pathology 1413 Research Blvd Rockville MD 20850

HE, LIUSHENG, biomedical researcher; s. He and Liu; m. Xiaoli Wu, Nov. 10, 1992; 1 child, Caroline. MD, Anhui Med. U., China, 1986; PhD, Colo. State U., 1996. Flow Cytometry FACS DiVa BD Bioscience, 2000. Staff scientist, dir. flow cytometry core facility Niams, Nih, Bethesda, Md., 2000—. Recipient NIH Merit award, NIH, 2004, Intramural Tng. Rsch. award; fellow, Nat. Cancer Inst., 1997—2000. Achievements include invention of flow cytometric assay to monitor three protein-protein interaction and caspase activity in living cells; development of novel FRET technologies for monitoring biological processes in living cells. Office: Niams Nih 9000 Rockville Pike Bethesda MD 20850 Business E-Mail: liusheng.he@stjude.org.

HE, MIN, mathematics professor; d. Baiwen He and Xueying Wu; m. Yidong Chen; 1 child, Kristy Xing Chen. BS (hon.), Northease Normal U., 1982, MS (hon.), 1984; PhD (hon.), So. Ill. U., 1994. Instr. Ne Normal U., Changchun, Jilin, China, 1984—88; lectr. So. Ill. U., Carbondale, 1994—95; asst. prof. Kent State U. Trumbull, Warren, Ohio, 1995—2000, assoc. prof., 2001—. Author: Stability Theory In Ordinary Differential Equations; contbr. articles to profl. jours. Pres. Chinese Assn. Greater Youngstown Area, Ohio, 2001—03. Fellow, So. Ill. U., 1991—92; grantee, Assn. Women Math., 1997. Mem.: Assn. for Women Math., Math. Assn. Am., Am. Math. Soc. Avocations: reading, music, travel, cooking, gardening. Office: Kent State University Trumbull 4314 Mahoning Avenue Nw Warren OH 44483 Business E-Mail: mhe@kent.edu.

HE, PINGAN, systems engineer; b. 1975; BS, Zhengzhou U., China, 1997; MS, U. Mo., Rolla, 2004. Rsch. asst. U. Mo., Rolla, 2002—04; powertrain controls engr. MotoTron Corp, Oshkosh, Wis., 2005—06, IAV, Inc., Ann Arbor, 2006—. Contbr. articles over ten jours. and conf. papers in field, scientific papers. Finalist Best Student Paper award, Artificial Neural Networks in Engring., 2004; recipient Automaica and IEEE Transactions on Sys., Man and Cybernatics, 2005. Mem.: Soc. Automotive engring. Office Phone: 734-971-1070. Business E-Mail: pingan.he@iav-usa.com.

HE, SHOULING, engineering educator; b. Beijing, May 29, 1959; d. Shizhen He and Jingping Yang; m. Hua Wang, Oct. 21, 1956; 1 child, Zexi Wang. PhD, U. Nuermberg, Erlangen, Germany, 2001. Asst. prof. Pa. State U., Behrend Coll., Erie, 2001—. Contbr. articles to profl. jours. Grantee, Rsch. Incentive Grant Program for Early Career Faculty, 2003. Mem.: IEEE. Achievements include research in multi-layer neural networks for solving a class of partial differential equations; Pseudospectral technique for continuation methods with application to nonlinear control problems. Home Phone: 18148248203; Office Phone: 18148986390.

HE, XIAODONG, application developer; b. Shandong, China, Oct. 1973; arrived in US, 1999, arrived in US, 1999; s. Limin He and Rusong Qin; m. Chuanhong Ma, 1999. B, Tsinghua U., Beijing, 1996; M, Chinese Acad. Scis., Beijing, 1999; PhD, U. Mo., Columbia, 2003. Mem. tech. staff Microsoft Rsch., Redmond, Wash., 2003—. Contbr. articles to profl. jours. Recipient Outstanding Academic Achievement award, U. Mo., 2001, Gold Star award, Microsoft, 2005. Mem.: IEEE, Intenrat. Assn. Sci. and Tech. for Devel. (program com. mem. 2005—), Sigma Xi. Achievements include research in computer science, machine learning, speech and natural language processing; contributed to various Microsoft speech recognition and machine translation products; patents pending in field. Office: Microsoft Research 1 Microsoft Way Redmond WA 98052 Office Phone: 425-706-4939. Office Fax: 425-936-7329. Business E-Mail: xiaohe@microsoft.com.

HE, XIAOHONG, finance educator; b. Beijing, May 15, 1953; arrived in U.S., 1984; d. DongChang He and Zhuobao Li; m. Ping Su, June 29, 1949; 1 child, Xiaowei Su. MA in Internat. Bus., U. Tex., Dallas, 1986, MS in Fin., 1989, PhD in Internat. Mgmt., 1991. Engr., rschr. China's Nat. Acad. Agr. Mechanization Scis., Beijing, 1977-84; rsch. assoc. Hass Bus. Sch. U. Calif., Berkeley, 1984-85; mgmt. cons. Greyhound Lines & China Auto Import Co., Dallas, 1985-89; v.p. China Auto Import Co., Dallas, 1989-91; dir. Far East Econ. Devel. Greyhound Lines, Dallas, 1989-91; dir. Internat. Bus. ExchangeProg. Quinnipiac U., Hamden, Conn., 1991-93, prof., chair internat. bus. and mktg. dept., 1997—2000, dir. Internat. Bus. Rsch., 1993-94, chair internat. bus., 2001—. Author: Globalization and International Business: Living Ever Closer Together, 2006; contbr. articles to profl. jours., chapters to books. Recipient Outstanding R&D award China's Machine Bldg. Min., 2d Prize, 1983, 3rd Prize 1979-81, Citation of Excellence award ANBAR Electronic Intelligence, U.K., 1998, Literati Club award for excellence, MCB Univ. Press, U.K., 1999, Excellence in Tchg. award Quinnipiac U., 2003; Mellon Vis. Faculty Fellowship Yale U., 2000-01. Fellow Soc. Global Bus. Edn.; mem. Internat. Mgmt. Devel. Assn., Assn. Global Bus., Acad. Mgmt., Assn. Internat. Trade and Fin., Acad. Internat. Bus. (Best Paper award N.E. chpt. 1992). Office: Quinnipiac U Sch Bus 275 Mount Carmel Ave Hamden CT 06518-1961

HE, ZHONGQI, chemist, researcher; b. Sichuan, China, Apr. 27, 1958; BS, Chongqing U., China, 1982; MS, South China U. Sci. & Tech., Guanzhou, 1985, U. Ga., Athens, 1992, PhD, 1996. Assoc. US Air Force Rsch. Lab, Tyndall Air Force Base, Fla.; rsch. scientist USDA-Agrl. Rsch. Svc., Orono, Maine, 2000—. Contbr. articles to profl. jours. Fellow, NRC, 1996—99, Oak Ridge Inst. Sci. and Edn., 1999—2000; scholar, NSF, 1995—96. Mem.: Internat. Humic Substance Soc., Am. Soc. Agronomy, Soil Sci. Soc. Am. Achievements include patents for Biological process for the production of ortho-aminophenols from nitroaromatic compounds using mutase. U S Patent No. 6, 797, 497; Preparation of 2-aminomuconate from 2-aminophenol by coupled enzymatic dioxygenation and dehydrogenation reactions. U S Patent No. 6, 432, 683; discovery of A Novel Ortho-Aminophenol Extradiol-Like Ring Cleavage Pathway Involved In Biodegradation Of Nitroaromatic Compounds; A novel 2-aminomuconate deaminase. Office: USDA-Agr Rsch Svc New Eng Plant Soil and Water Lab Orono ME 04469 Office Phone: 207-581-3373. Office Fax: 207-866-0464. E-mail: zhongqi.he@ars.usda.gov.

HEACOCK, DAVID, electronics executive; BS in Interdisciplinary Engring. and Mgmt., Clarkson U., Potsdam, NY, 1983; MBA, U. North Tex., Denton, 1988. With Benchmarq Microelectronics, 1990—98, Unitrode Corp., 1998, dir. portable power products; with Tex. Instruments Inc., Dallas, 1999—, mgr. battery mgmt. product line, v.p. portable power mgmt. bus. unit, 2003, sr. v.p., mgr. high-volume analog and logic, 2007—. Achievements include patents in field. Office: Tex Instruments Inc PO Box 660199 Dallas TX 75266-0199 Office Phone: 972-995-2011. Office Fax: 972-995-4360.*

HEACOCK, DONALD DEE, social worker; b. Anthony, Kans., Feb. 21, 1934; s. C.W. and Thelma Olive (Hilton) H.; m. Margaret Newberry, Sept. 4, 1953; children: Teresa Ellen, Mark Dee. AB, Washburn U., 1956; BD cum laude, United Sem., 1959; MSW, Barry Coll., 1971; ThD, Slidell Bapt. Sem., 1999. Ordained priest Episcopal Ch., 1965; diplomate in clin. social work. Parish minister St. John's Ch., Clinton, Mich., 1961-66; chaplain Margarita, Canal Zone, 1966-69; tchr. Christ Ch. Acad. Secondary Sch., Colon, Panama, 1966-69; counselor South Fla. Neighborhood Youth Corp., Miami, 1969-70; chief social svc., instr. pediat. comprehensive health care U. Miami, 1971-72; asst. dir. Alpha House, Dade County, Fla., 1972-73; field supr. Barry Coll., 1972-73; marriage and family therapist Psychiat. Assocs., Shreveport, La., 1973-75; pvt. practice social work Shreveport, 1975—. Dir. Holy Cross Child Placement Agy., Inc., 1984; lectr. sociology Centenary Coll., 1981-88. With USAF, 1959-61. Mem. NASW (Lifetime Achievement award 2007), Acad. Cert. Social Work, Masons, Phi Kappa Mu, Phi Gamma Mu. Home: 3820 Fairfield Ave # 113 Shreveport LA 71104 Office: Ste 357 910 Pierremont Rd Shreveport LA 71106-2063 Home Phone: 318-219-9188; Office Phone: 318-865-3199. Personal E-mail: domahea@aol.com.

HEAD, HAYDEN WILSON, JR., federal judge; Student, Washington and Lee U., 1962-64; BA, U. Tex., 1967, LLB, 1968. Bar: Tex. Assoc. Head & Kendrick, Corpus Christi, Tex., 1968-69, 1972-76, ptnr., 1976-81; judge US Dist. Ct. (So. Dist.) Tex., Corpus Christi, 1981—, chief judge, 0003—. Chmn. 5th Cir. Com. on Criminal Pattern Jury Instr., 1986—; mem. jud. conf. U.S. Com. on Security and Facilities, 2002—06; mem. U.S. Jud. Conf., 1998—2006. Fellow: Tex. Bar Found.; mem.: State Bar Tex. Office: US Dist Ct 1133 N Shoreline Blvd Corpus Christi TX 78401 Office Phone: 361-888-3148.

HEAD, JAMES WILLIAM, III, geological sciences educator; b. Richmond, Va., Aug. 4, 1941; BS, Washington and Lee U., 1964; PhD, Brown U., 1969; DSc (hon.), Washington and Lee U., 1995. Employee NASA/Bellcomm, Inc., Washington, 1968—72; interim dir. Lunar Sci. Inst., Houston, 1973—74; asst. prof. Brown U., Providence, 1973—74, assoc. prof., 1974—80, prof. geol. scis., 1980—95, Louis and Elizabeth Scherck disting. prof., 1995—. Vis. assoc. Calif. Inst. Tech., Pasadena, 1990-91; prof. Universidad Complutense, Madrid, 1997. Contbr. chpts. to books, more than 300 articles to profl. jours. Recipient medal for exceptional sci. achievement NASA, pub. svc. medal; award Alpha Circle of Omicron Delta Kappa, 1990. Fellow AAAS, Am. Acad. Arts & Scis., Am. Geophys. Union, Geol. Soc. Am. (G.K. Gilbert award 2002), Meteoritical Soc.; mem. Am. Astron. Soc., European Geophys. Union. Office: Dept Geol Scis Brown U Box 1846 Providence RI 02912 Business E-Mail: james_head@brown.edu.

HEAD, JONATHAN FREDERICK, cell biologist; b. Syracuse, NY, Nov. 23, 1949; s. Arthur Everard and Lillian Myrtle (Hendra) H.; m. Priscilla Catherine Tambone, July 28, 1984; 1 child, Catherine Elizabeth. BS in Zoology, Syracuse U., 1971; MA in Biology, Bklyn. Coll., 1977; PhD in Biology, Fordham U., 1985. Rsch. asst. Naylor Dana Inst. Disease Prevention/Am. Health Found., Valhalla, NY, 1974-78, Cornell U. Med. Coll., NYC, 1978, Mt. Sinai Sch. Medicine, NYC, 1978-84, rsch. assoc., 1984-86, rsch. asst. prof., 1986-87; dir. tumor cell biology Ctr. Clin. Scis./Internat. Clin. Labs., Nashville, 1986-89; pres. Mastology Rsch. Inst., Baton Rouge, 1989—, Oncbiomune, LLC, Baton Rouge, 2005—. High Complexity Clin. Lab. dir. Am. Bd. Bioanalysis, 1988—; med. lab. dir. Clin. Chemistry, State of Tenn., 1988—; clin. lab. scientist/specialist, State of La., 1995—; adj. assoc. prof. Tulane U. Sch. Medicine, New Orleans, 1989—, La. State U. Vet. Sch., Baton Rouge, 2005-; adj. prof. Delta State U., Cleve., Miss., 1992—; dir. R&D Med. Thermal Diagnostics, Baton Rouge, 1995-2001, Innovative Dug Techs., Edmond, Okla., 1999-2005; rschr. and lectr. in field of cancer. Contbr. articles, abstracts and chpts. to sci. publs. Mem. State of La. Adoption Cmty. Adv. Bd., 1992-95. Mem. AAAS, Am. Assn. Cancer Rsch., Am. Soc. Clin. Oncology, Am. Acad. Thermology, Internat. Soc. Biol. Therapy Cancer, Am. Soc. Breast Disease, European Soc. Med. Oncology, NY Acad. Scis. Methodist. Home: 6144 Hagerstown Dr Baton Rouge LA 70817-3917 Office: Mastology Rsch Inst 17050 Med Ctr Dr 4th Fl Baton Rouge LA 70816 Home Phone: 225-753-4939; Office Phone: 225-755-3070. Business E-Mail: jhead@eehbreastca.com.

HEAD, WILLIAM IVERSON, SR., retired chemical company executive; b. Tallapposa, Ga., Apr. 4, 1925; s. Iverson and Ruth Britain (Hubbard) H.; m. Mary Helen Ware, June 12, 1947; children: William Iverson, Connie Suzanne Head Toohey, Alan David. BS, Ga. Inst. Tech., 1949; D in Textile Engring. (hon.), World U., 1983; PhD in Indsl. Mgmt., Columbia Pacific U., 1988. Textile engr. Tenn. Eastman Co., Kingsport, 1949-56, quality control-mfg. sr. textile engr., 1957-67, dept. supt., 1968-74; supt. acetate yarn dept., bus. team, chem. divsn. Eastman Kodak Co., Kingsport, 1975-85; ret., 1985. Info. officer U.S. Naval Acad., 1983-97; adv. bd., rsch. assoc. Point One Adv. Group, Inc., 1988-2005. Capt. USNR, 1943-83. Mem.: VFW, Mil. Order of Stars and Bars, Internat. Soc. Philos. Enquiry (pers. cons. 1978—79, v.p. 1979—80, sr. rsch. fellow and internat. pres. 1980—85, diplomate, trustee 1986—, chmn. bd. trustees 1987—2002, Whiting Meml. award 1993), Wisdom Soc. (Award of Honor 2000), Mil. Officers Assn. Am., SCV, Res. Officers Assn. (pres. Tenn. dept. 1981—82, nat. councilman 1991—98, nat. coun. steering com. 1993—97), Assn. Naval Aviation, Prometheus Soc., Naval Res. Assn., Mil. Order World Wars, Sons of Revolution, Mensa (pres. Upper East Tenn. 1976—79). Achievements include patents for textured yarn technology in U.S., Great Britain, Federal Republic of Germany, Japan and France. Home: 4035 Lakewood Dr Kingsport TN 37663-3374

HEADDEN, SUSAN M., editor; Formerly reporter Indpls. Star, Indpls.; sr. editor to asst. mng. editor, spl. projects U.S. News & World Report, Washington, mng. editor, spl. projects, 2004—. Recipient Pulitzer prize for investigative reporting, 1991. Office: US News and World Report 1050 Thomas Jefferson St NW Washington DC 20007 Office Phone: 202-298-0485.

HEADLAM, BRUCE, editor; With NY Times, 1998—, Monday bus. tech. & media sect. editor, mktg. & media editor for bus. sect., 2007—. Office: New York Times 229 W 43d St New York NY 10036 Office Phone: 212-556-1474. Office Fax: 212-556-1448. Business E-Mail: headlam@nytimes.com.*

HEADLEY, MARK J., lawyer; s. Richard and Carol H. BA in Philosophy magna cum laude, Yale U., 1981; JD, Columbia U., 1986. Bar: N.Y. 1987, U.S. Dist. Ct. (so. and ea. dists.) N.Y., U.S. Ct. Appeals (2d and DC cirs.), U.S. Supreme Ct. Law clk. to Hon. Pierre N. Leval, NYC, 1986-87; assoc. Kramer, Levin, Naftalis & Frankel, NYC, 1987-95; ptnr. Kramer Levin Naftalis & Frankel LLP, NYC, 1996—. Editor-in-chief Columbia Law Rev., 1985-86; contbr. articles to profl. jours. James Kent scholar Columbia U. Mem. ABA, N.Y. State Bar Assn., Assn. of Bar of City of N.Y. Office: Kramer Levin Naftalis & Frankel LLP 1177 Ave of Americas New York NY 10036 Home Phone: 212-362-7440; Office Phone: 212-715-9119. Business E-Mail: mheadley@kramerlevin.com.

HEADRICK, THOMAS EDWARD, lawyer, educator; b. East Orange, NJ, June 28, 1933; s. Lewis Barnard and Marian Elizabeth Headrick; m. Mary Margaret Shontz, June 27, 1957; children— Trevor, Todd. BA, Franklin and Marshall Coll., 1955; LittB, Oxford U., Eng., 1958; LLB, Yale U., 1960; PhD, Stanford U., 1975. Bar: Conn. 1960, Calif. 1962. Asst. dir. Ansonia (Conn.) Redevel. Agy., 1959-60; law clk. to justice Wash. State Supreme Ct., Olympia, 1960-61; assoc. firm Pillsbury, Madison & Sutro, San Francisco, 1961-64; mgmt. cons. Emerson Cons., London, 1964-66, Baxter, McDonald & Co., Berkeley, Calif., 1966-67; asst. dean Stanford U. Law Sch., 1967-70; v.p. acad. affairs Lawrence U., 1970-76; dean law sch. U. at Buffalo, 1976-85, prof. law, 1976—, interim dean arts and letters faculty, 1990, disting. svc. prof., 1993—, provost, 1995-99, sr. counselor to pres., 1999, interim dean architecture and planning, 1999. Cons. NEH, NSF; legal commentator Sta. WKBW-TV, 1978-80. Author: The Town Clerk in English Local Government, 1962; co-editor Law and Policy, 1988-92. Named to, Franklin and Marshall Sports Hall of Fame, 2002. Mem. Phi Beta Kappa. Office: University at Buffalo 411 O'Brian Hall Buffalo NY 14260-1100 Business E-Mail: headrick@buffalo.edu.

HEADRICK, TODD CHRISTOPHER, mathematical statistician, educator; s. Robert Frank Headrick and Sally Marie Proctor. BS, Ea. Mich. U., 1984, MA, 1986; PhD, Wayne State U., 1997. Assoc. prof. So. Ill. U., Carbondale, Ill., 1999—. Co-dir. Midwest Applied Cognition and Stats. Lab, Carbondale, 2002—. Contbr. articles to profl. jour. Mem.: APA, Am. Edn. Rsch. Assn., SIG/Ednl. Statisticians, Psychometric Soc., Math. Assn. of Am., Am. Statis. Assn., Internat. Assn. for Statis. Computing, Inst. of Math. Stats. Conservative. Roman Cath. Avocations: travel, outdoor activities. Office: So Ill Univ 223 Wham Bldg Mail Code 4618 Carbondale IL 62901-4618 Office Phone: 618-453-1818. Business E-Mail: headrick@siu.edu.

HEADY, EUGENE JOSEPH, lawyer; b. Poughkeepsie, NY, Jan. 25, 1958; s. William and Margaret Patricia Heady; m. Lisa Dupre, Dec. 31, 2004; children: Anthony Ray, Emily Rene, Katie Shanell, Megan Whyte, Joseph Whyte, Jacob Whyte. BS in Engring., U. Hartford, 1981; JD cum laude, Tex. Tech. U., 1996. Bar: Tex. 1996, Ga. 1997, Colo. 1997, Fla. 1998, Supreme Ct. Ga. 1997, U.S. Dist. t. (no. dist.) Ga. 1997, U.S. Ct. Appeals Ga. 1997, U.S. Dist. Ct. (no. dist.) Tex. 2001, U.S. Dist. Ct. (so. dist.) Tex. 2006. V.p. Heady Electric Co., Inc., Poughkeepsie, NY, 1980—83; project mgr. ANECO, Inc., West Palm Beach, Fla., 1987—93; assoc. Smith, Currie & Hancock LLP, Atlanta, 1996—2002, ptnr., 2003—. Editor-in-chief: Tex. Tech Law Rev. vol. 27, 1995-96; student editor: Tex. County Ct. Bench Manual, 1996, Bench Book for the Tex. Jud., 1996; editor: Tex. Tech Legal Rsch. Bd., 1995-96; co-author: Ga. Suppl. to Fifty State Construction Lien and Bond Law, 1996, 97, 98, 01, 02, 03, Ga. chpt. Fifty State Construction Lien and Bond Law, 2000; author: chpts. in Alternative Clauses to Standard Construction Contracts, 1998, 99, 00, 01, 02, 03, 04, 05, 06; contbr. numerous articles to profl. jours. Fellow Am. Bar Found.; mem. ABA (forum on the constrn. industry, vice-chmn. region IV sect. of pub. contract law), Scribes-The Am. Soc. Writers on Legal Subjects. Avocations: writing, reading. Home: 362 Grassmeade Way Snellville GA 30078 Office: Smith Currie & Hancock LLP 2700 Marquis One Tower 245 Peachtree Center Ave NE Atlanta GA 30303-1227 Office Phone: 404-521-3800. Office Fax: 404-688-0671. Business E-Mail: gjheady@smithcurrie.com.

HEAGARTY, MARGARET CAROLINE, retired pediatrician; b. Charleston, W.Va., Sept. 8, 1934; d. John Patrick and Margaret Caroline (Walsh) H. BA, Seton Hill Coll., 1957; BS, W.Va. Sch. Medicine, 1959; MD, U. Pa., 1961; DSc honoris causa, Iona Coll., 1989. Diplomate: Am. Bd. Pediatrics. Intern Phila. Gen. Hosp., 1961—62; resident in pediatrics St. Christopher's Hosp. for Children, Phila., 1962—64; dir. pediatric ambulatory care services N.Y. Hosp.-Cornell Med. Ctr., NYC, 1969—78; dir. pediatrics Harlem Hosp. Ctr. Columbia U., NYC, 1978—2000, prof. pediatrics coll. physicians & surgeons, 1987—2000, prof. emerita coll. physicians and surgeons, 2000—. Cons. Dept. HEW Promotion of Child Health, Washington; mem. Com. Community Oriented Primary Care Inst. Medicine, Washington; mem. Robert Wood Johnson Found. Program for Prepaid Managed Health Care, 1984; mem. governing council Inst. Medicine, Nat. Acad. Scis., 1986 Author: Changing the Medical Car System-Report of an Experiment, 1974, Medical Sociology: A Systems Approach, 1975, Child Health: Basics for Primary Care, 1980. Grantee Commonwealth Found., 1981, Robert Wood Johnson Found., 1983, Ctr. for Disease Control, 1985, Health Rsch. and Svc. Adminstrn., 1988, Nat. Inst. Allergy/Infectious Disease, 1988. Fellow Inst. Medicine (steering group for nat. forum on future of children and their families 1987—); mem. Ambulatory Pediatric Assn. (pres. 1976-77), Soc. Pediatric Research, Am. Pediatric Soc., Am. Acad. Pediatrics (com. on hosp. care 1988—), Assn. Pediatric Program Dirs., Nat. Bd. Med. Examiners. Home: 2520 Kingsland Ave Bronx NY 10469-6108 E-mail: mheagarty@aol.com.

HEALD, BRUCE DAY, English and music educator, historian; b. Boston, June 5, 1935; s. Henry M. and Muriel D. (Day) H. m. Helen Peaslee, May 21, 1960; children: William Forristall III, Craig, Eric Bentley, Allyson Kaye. AA, Boston U., 1956; BS in Music Edn., Lowell State U., Mass., 1959; MA, Columbia Pacific U., Calif., 1984, PhD, 1985. Supr. music Ashland-Meredith Union 2, Meredith, N.H., 1959-64; dir. music, lectr. fine arts Belknap Coll., Center Harbor, N.H., 1963-65; dir. bands Plattsburgh (N.Y.) City Schs., 1969-70; supr. music Inter-Lakes Sch. Dist., Meredith, 1965-69, dir. music edn., 1970-77; dir. instrumental music Kennebunk (Maine) High Sch., 1977-79; prodn. mgr. Annalee Mobilitee Dolls, Meredith, 1979-81; lectr. English and journalism Moultonborough Acad., 1981-86; dir. music Congl. Ch., Laconia, N.H., 1985-86; chair English dept. Holy Trinity Sch., Laconia, 1987—2000; mentor Columbia Pacific U., 1986—; instr. music N.H. Coll., Manchester, 1988—95; historian Weirstimes Pub. Co., 1992—2001. Lectr. English lit. Plymouth State Coll., 1995-97, lectr. U.S. history Plymouth State U., 1998—. Author: Follow the Mount, 1968, 70, 93, 97, 2000, Postmaster of the Lake, 1971, Mail Service on the Lake, 1980, 2000, Steamboats in Motion, 1984, New Hampshire Learnin' Days, 1987, Boats 'n Ports I and II, 1989, Landmarks and Legacy, 1990, The Boston See Party, 1991, Reminisce the Valley, 1992, Shadows in the Window, 1995, Images of America: Meredith, 1996, Images of America: The Lakes Region of New Hampshire, 1996, vol. I and II, 1998, Images of America: The Upper Merrimack to Winnipesaukee by Rail, 1997, Images of America: Boats and Ports in Lake Winnipesaukee, vol. I and II, 1998, Images of America: The White Mountains Region by Rail, 1999, Image of America: Plymouth State College, 1999, Images of America: Stereoptic Memories of the White Mountains, 2000, Images of America: Lakes and Ponds of the Granite State, 2000, Images of Rail: The Boston and Maine in the 19th Century, 2001, Images of Rail: The Boston and Maine in the 20th Century, 2001, Images of the Civil War: N.H. in the Civil War, 2001, Images of America: Around Squam Lake, 2002, History & Guide: The Franconia Gateway, 2002, Images of Rail: Boston and Maine Locomotives, 2002, The Adventures to the Great American Railroads, 2003, Images of America: Main Streets in New Hampshire, 2003, Images of America: Meredith Then and Now, 2005, Images of Rail: Boston and Maine Trains and Services, Fence Building and Apple Cider: Memories from New Hampshire's Lakes and Mountains, 2007, A New Hampshire Dynasty: B&M Railroad, 2007; composer: Kennebunk Concert March, The Hills of Old N.H., Moultonboro Concert March, Cascades, Trilogy. Commr. Parks and Playgrounds, Meredith, 1966-69; selectman Town of Meredith, 1971-76; mem. N.H. State Legislature, 2004—. Served with USMC, 1954-62. Mem. Masons. Republican. Home: PO Box 1052 Meredith NH 03253-1052 Office Phone: 603-279-8026. Personal E-mail: bheald@metrocast.net.

HEALD, MORRELL, humanities educator; b. Oak Park, Ill., July 16, 1922; s. Howard Leslie and Helen (Morrell) H.; m. Barbara Legg, June 25, 1949; children: David M., Seth G., Sarah H. AB, Yale U., 1946, A.M., 1947, PhD, 1951. Instr. history Yale, 1950-53; mem. faculty Case Inst. Tech., 1953-68, assoc. prof. history, 1958-68, chmn. dept. humanities and social studies, 1959-62; prof. Am. studies Case Western Res. U., 1968-82, Samuel B. and Virginia C. Knight prof. humanities, 1982-88, prof. emeritus, 1988—, chmn. div. spl. interdisciplinary studies, 1971-78, 79-82. Vis. prof. Am. history Indian Inst. Tech., Kanpur, 1966-67; dir. Armington Research Program on Values in Children, 1978-80, chmn. adv. com., 1978-82 Author: The Social Responsibilities of Business: Company and Community, 1900-1960, 1970, Japanese edit., 1974, 2d edit., 1988, paperback edit., 2005, Transatlantic Vistas: American Journalists in Europe, 1900-1940, 1987; (with Lawrence S. Kaplan) Culture and Diplomacy: The American Experience, 1977; editor: Journalist at the Brink, Loris P. Lochnaf in Berlin, 1922-1942, 2007; co-editor: The Aims and Organization of Liberal Studies, 1966. V.p. Cleveland Heights Your Schools Com., 1962, pres., 1965; Pres. of the First Ward Democratic Club, Cleveland Heights, 1962; active Cleve. Heights Landmarks Commn., 1987-01; publs. com. Western Res. Hist. Soc., 1981-89. With AUS, 1943-45, ETO Mem. Soc. for History Am. Fgn. Rels., Phi Beta Kappa. Episcopalian. Home: 10450 Lottsford Rd #4215 Mitchellville MD 20721

HEALEY, FRANK HENRY, retired chemicals executive; b. Worcester, Mass., Oct. 5, 1924; s. Frank H. and Elizabeth (MacGillivray) H.; m. Loretta Marguerite Finnigan, June 5, 1948; children: Steven Allan, Elaine

Elizabeth, Frank Henry. AB, Clark U., 1947, PhD, 1949. Asst. prof. chemistry Lehigh U., Bethlehem, Pa., 1949-56; with Lever Bros. Co., Edgewater, N.J., 1956-88, v.p. research and devel., 1964-73, research v.p., 1973-78, v.p. research and engring., 1978-80, research v.p., dir., 1968-88; pres. Lever Research Inc., Edgewater, 1982-88. Served to lt. (j.g.) USN, 1943-46. Mem. Indsl. Rsch. Inst. (pres. 1977-78, bd. dirs. 1972-79), Assn. Rsch. Dirs., Am. Chem. Soc., Dirs. Indsl. Rsch., Am. Oil Chemists Soc., Soap and Detergent Assn. (steering com. tech. and materials divsn.), Ridgewood Country Club (sec. 1981-82, bd. dirs. 1990-94), Hobbyists Unlimited (v.p. 1994-95, pres. 1996). Home: 255 W Ridgewood Ave Ridgewood NJ 07450-3629

HEALEY, KERRY MURPHY, former lieutenant governor; b. Omaha, Apr. 30, 1960; d. Edward Morris and Shirley (Cumming) M.; m. Sean Michael Healey, Dec. 28, 1985; children: Alexander Edward, Averill Adair. AB in Govt., Harvard Coll., 1982; PhD in Law and Polit. Sci., Trinity Coll., Dublin, Ireland, 1991. Proctor freshman dean's office, vis. reseacher Law Sch. Harvard U., Cambridge, Mass., 1985—86; legal policy analyst ABT Assocs., Inc., Cambridge, 1986—87; pub. policy cons. Bklyn. and Boston, 1990—99; mem. Mass. Rep. State Com., 1999; chmn. Mass. Republican Party, 2001—02; lt. gov. State of Mass., 2003—07. Del. UN Non-Govtl. Orgn. Assembly, 1994—95; fellow Inst. Politics Harvard Kennedy Sch. Govt., Cambridge, Mass., 2007. Author: State and Local Experience with Drug Paraphernalia Laws, 1987, Victim and Witness Intimidation: New Developments and Emerging Responses, 1995; co-author: Compendium of Federal Justice Statistics, 1989, Handbook of Drug Control in the United States, 1990, Prosecutorial Response to Heavy Drug Case Loads, 1993. Bd. dirs., Mass. Women's Polit. Caucus, 1999-2001; bd. dirs., North Shore C.C. Found., Danvers, Mass., 1999-2002, Friends of Beverly (Mass.) Hosp., 1999-2001; co-chair North Shore United Way Campaign, Beverly, 2001, bd. dirs. YWCA, N.Y.C., 1992-95, mem. YWCA World Svc. Coun., 1992—. Grad. fellow Rotary Internat., 1983-84; rsch. grantee Mark DeWolfe Howe Fund of Harvard Law Sch., 1986. Mem. Coun. on Fgn. Rels., Harvard Club N.Y.C. (mem. schs. com. 1987-95), N.Y. Jr. League (rep. N.Y.C. ednl. priorities panel 1992-95), Cosmopolitan Club (N.Y.C.), Union Club (Boston). Republican.

HEALEY, THOMAS J., former government official, brokerage house executive; b. Balt., Sept. 14, 1942; m. Margaret Sachs Healey; children—Megan, Jeremiah AB, Georgetown U., 1964; MBA, Harvard U., 1966. CFA. Mgr. project fin. group Dean Witter, 1975-82; mng. dir., mgr. corp. fin. Dean Witter Reynolds Capital Markets, 1982-83; asst. sec. domestic fin. Dept. of Treasury, Washington, 1983-85; v.p. real estate Goldman Sachs & Co, NYC, 1985-88, mng. dir. pension svcs. group, 1988-99, mng. dir. instl. sales and mktg., 1999-2000, adv. dir., 2001—; prin. Healey Devel. LLC, Morristown, NJ. Fellow, adj. lectr. John F. Kennedy Sch. Govt. Harvard U., 2001—. Trustee Rockefeller Found. Office: Healy Devel LLC 310 South St Morristown NJ 07960 Business E-Mail: tom.healey@healeydev.com.

HEALY, BERNADINE P., physician, educator, former federal official; b. NYC, Aug. 2, 1944; d. Michael J. and Violet (McGrath) Healy; m. Floyd Loop, Aug. 17, 1985; children: Bartlett Anne Bulkley, Marie McGrath Loop. AB summa cum laude, Vassar Coll., 1965; MD cum laude, Harvard Med. Sch., 1970. Diplomate Am. Bd. Med. Examiners, Am. Bd. Cardiology, Am. Bd. Internal Medicine, lic. physician Md., Ohio. Intern in medicine Johns Hopkins Hosp., Balt., 1970—71, asst. resident, 1971—72; staff fellow sect. pathology Nat. Heart, Blood & Lung Inst., NIH, Bethesda, Md., 1972—74; fellow cardiovascular div. dept. medicine Johns Hopkins U. Sch. Medicine, Balt., 1974—76, fellow dept. pathology, 1975—76, asst. prof. medicine and pathology, 1976—81, assoc. prof. medicine, 1977—82, asst. dean postdoctoral programs and faculty devel., 1979—84, assoc. prof. pathology, 1981—84, prof. medicine, 1982—84, dean Coll. Med. and Pub. Health, 1995—99, prof. internal medicine, physiology, 1995—99; active staff medicine and pathology Johns Hopkins Hosp., 1976—, dir. CCU, 1976—84; pres. ARC, 1999—2001; advisor on weapons of mass destruction & bioterrorism White House, Washington, 2001—; med. & healthcare columnist, sr. writer U.S. News & World Report, 2002—. Dep. dir. Office Sci. and Tech. Policy Exec. Office of Pres., White House, Washington, 1984—85; chmn. Rsch. Inst. The Cleve. Clinic Found., 1985—91, sr. health and sci. policy advisor, 1994—95; dean Med. Sch. Ohio State U., 1995—97; dir. NIH, Bethesda, Md., 1991—93; vice-chmn. Pres.' Coun. Advisers on Sci. and Tech., 1990—91; mem. Spl. Med. Adv. Group, Dept. Vet.'s Affairs, 1990—91, chmn. adv. panel for Basic Rsch. for 1990s, Office Tech. Assessment, 1990—91, mem. NHLBI Task Force on Atherosclerosis, 1990; mem. Vis. Com. Bd. Overseers Harvard Med. Sch. and Sch. of Dental Medicine, Boston, 1986—91; councillor Harvard Med. Alumni Assn., 1987—90; mem. Nat. Adv. Bd. Johns Hopkins Ctr. for Hosp. Fin. and Mgmt., 1987—91, Bd. Overseers Harvard Coll., 1989—; chmn. Office of Tech. Assessment Panel New Devels. in Biotech., U.S. Congress, 1986—87; mem. U.S.-Brazil Panel on Sci. and Tech., 1987, White House Sci. Coun., 1988—89; cons. Nat. Heart, Lung and Blood Inst., NIH, 1976—91; mem. adv. com. to dir. NIH, 1986—91; chmn. steering com. Post-CABG Clin. Triai, 1987—91; bd. dirs. Medtronic, Inc., Mpls., Nat. City Corp., Cleve., Nova Pharms., Balt.; mem. adv. bd. Bayer Fund for Cardiovasc. Rsch., NYC, 1987—89; trustee Edison BioTech. Ctr., Cleve., 1990—; chmn. Ohio Coun. on Rsch. and Econ. Devel., 1989—91; bd. dirs. Nat. City Corp., 1989—90, 1995—2001, 2003—. Editl. cons. numerous jours.; abstract reviewer:, editl. bd.: Jour. Cardiovasc. Medicine, 1980—91, Am. Jour. Cardiology, 1981—82, Circulation, 1981—, Jour. Am. Coll. Cardiology, 1982—84, Am. Jour. Medicine, 1986—91; contbr. articles to profl. jours. Recipient Nat. Bd. Ann. award for Medicine, Med. Coll. Pa., 1983; fellow Eloise Ellery fellow, 1965—66, Stetler Rsch. fellow, 1976—77; scholar Matthew Vassar scholar, 1962—65, Harvard Nat. scholar, 1965—70. Mem.: ACP, Inst. Medicine NAS, Am. Bd. Internatl Medicine (bd. dirs. 1983—87, bd. govs. 1986—), Am. Soc. Clin. Investigation, Assn. for Women in Sci., Am. Med. Women's Assn., Internat. Acad. Pathology, Assn. Am. Med. Colls., Am. Coll. Cardiology (bd. govs. 1979—82), Am. Heart Assn. (fellow coun. on clin. cardiology, coun. on circulation, dir. 1983—84, pres. 1988—89, award 1983—84, 1990), Am. Fedn. Clin. Rsch. (pres. 1983—84), Johns Hopkins U. Soc. Scholars, Alpha Omega Alpha, Phi Beta Kappa.

HEALY, BRIDGET M., lawyer; b. Clinton, Iowa, Feb. 14, 1955; AB with honors, Brown U., 1976; JD magna cum laude, Georgetown U. Law Ctr., 1982. Assoc. Davis, Polk & Wardwell; ptnr. Stroock & Stroock & Lavan; atty. Becton, Dickinson & Co., Franklin Lakes, NJ, 1995—97, v.p., sec., 1997, gen. counsel, 2000—05; sr. v.p., group gen. counsel The Travelers Companies, 2005—07; exec. v.p., chief legal officer ING Americas, NYC, 2007—. Mem.: Am. Soc. Corp. Sec. Inc., Am. Corp. Counsel Assn., ABA. Office: ING Americas 5780 Powers Ferry Rd Atlanta GA 30327*

HEALY, GEORGE WILLIAM, III, lawyer, mediator; b. New Orleans, Mar. 8, 1930; s. George William and Margaret Alford H.; m. Sharon Saunders, Oct. 26, 1974; children: George W. IV, John Carmichael, Floyd Alford, Hyde Dunbar, Mary Margaret. BA, Tulane U., 1950, JD, 1955. Bar: La. 1955, U.S. Supreme Ct. 1969. Assoc. Phelps, Dunbar, Marks, Claverie & Sims, New Orleans, 1955-58; ptnr. Phelps Dunbar LLP, 1958-95; of counsel Phelps Dunbar, 1996—. Mem. U.S. del. Comité Maritime Internat., Tokyo, 1969, Lisbon, 1985, Paris, 1990, Sydney, 1994, titulary mem. Mem. planning com. Tulane U. Admiralty Law Inst., dir. World Trade Ctr., 1993-2001; dir. New Orleans Pro Bono Project, 1995-97, La. Orgn. for Jud. Excellence, 1997—. Fellow Am. Bar Found., Am. Coll. Trial Lawyers, Maritime Law Assn. U.S. (mem. exec. com. 1984-87, 2d v.p. 1988-90, 1st v.p. 1990-92, pres. 1992-94), La. Bar Found.; mem. ABA (ho. dels. 1993-95, 97-2000), New Orleans Bar Assn. (pres. 1992), Def. Rsch. Inst., La. Assn. Def. Counsel, Com. Maritime Internat. Am. Found. (dir. 1990—), New Orleans Bar Assn. Inn of Ct. (master), Boston Club., La. Club, Stratford Club, Plimsoll Club, Recess Club (pres. 1978), Pinfeathers Hunting Club, New Orleans Lawn Tennis Club Republican. Episcopalian. Home: 6020 Camp St New Orleans LA 70118-5902 Office: Canal Place 365 Canal St Ste 2000 New Orleans LA 70130-6534 Office Phone: 504-581-9238. Office Fax: 504-568-9130. Business E-Mail: healyg@phelps.com.

HEALY, GERALD BURKE, otolaryngologist; b. Boston, Mar. 31, 1942; s. Gerald E. and Margaret C. (Burke) H.; m. Anne Herron, June 3, 1991; children: Elisabeth, Laurie. AB cum laude, Boston Coll., 1963; MD, Boston U., 1967; MBA (hon.), Harvard U., 1990. Diplomate Am. Bd. Otolaryngology, Am. Bd. Laser Surgery, Nat. Bd. Med. Examiners; lic. physician, Mass., Pa. Surg. intern Univ. Hosp., Boston, 1967-68, resident in surgery, 1968-69, resident in otolaryngology, 1969-72; instr. otolaryngology Boston U. Sch. Medicine, 1974-75, asst. prof., 1975-77, assoc. prof., 1977-83, prof., 1983—; assoc. dir. otolaryngology Boston VA Hosp., 1975-76; assoc. otolaryngologist-in-chief The Children's Hosp., Boston, 1976-79, otolaryngologist-in-chief, 1979—. Instr. otolaryngology Tufts U. Sch. Medicine, 1975-88; assoc. prof. otolaryngology Harvard Med. Sch., 1979-88, prof. otology and laryngology, 1988—; chief otolaryngology Valley Forge Army Med. Ctr., Phoenixville, Pa., 1972-73, William Beaumont Army Med. Ctr., El Paso, 1973-74; assoc. dir. otolaryngology Boston City Hosp., 1975-76; bd. dirs. Am. Bd. Otolaryngology, 1986, exec. v.p., 1998; mem. com. on certification Am. Bd. Med. Specialists, 1988—. Reviewer Jour. Pediatrics, 1976—, Pediatrics, 1977—, New Eng. Jour. Medicine, 1979—, Annals of Otology, Rhinology and Laryngology, 1982-88, The Laryngoscope, 1986-88; mem. editorial bd. Internat. Jour. Pediatric Otolaryngology, 1979—, The Laryngoscope, 1988—, Annals of Otology, Rhinology and Laryngology, 1988—. Maj. U.S. Army, 1972-74. Fellow ACS, Am. Coll. Chest Physicians, Am. Acad. Pediatrics; mem. Am. Bd. Emergency Medicine (bd. dirs. 1988—), Am. Soc. Pediatric Otolaryn. (pres. 1987), Am. Laryngol. Assn. (exec. coun. 1985—), Am. Broncho-Esophagological Assn. (exec. coun. 1983—, pres. 1990-91), Am. Acad. Otolaryngology-Head and Neck Surgery (chmn. outcomes com. 1991), Am. Acad. Facial Plastic and Reconstructive Surgery, Soc. Univ. Otolaryngologists, Mass. Med. Soc., New Eng. Otolaryn. Soc., Pediatric Otolaryn. Study Group, bd. regents, Am. Coll. Surgeons, 1997- (chmn., 2005-). Office: Childrens Hosp 300 Longwood Ave Boston MA 02115-5737

HEALY, J. KEVIN, lawyer; b. Bklyn., Feb. 1, 1949; s. Joseph John and Isabel Mark (O'Brien) H.; m. Carey Weiss; children: Christopher Robert, William Daniel. BS, St. Joseph Coll., Phila., 1970; JD, Forham U., NYC, 1973. Bar: N.Y., U.S. Dist. Ct. (no., ea. and so. dists.) N.Y. Atty. enforcement div. EPA, NYC, 1973-78; gen. counsel Dept. Environ. Protection City of NY, 1978-82, NY Conv. Ctr. Devel. Corp., NYC, 1982-84; assoc. Stadtmauer, Bailkin, NYC, 1984-87, Teitelbaum, Hiller, NYC, 1987; ptnr., mem. exec. com. Bryan Cave LLP, NYC. Spl. master U.S. Dist. Ct. (so. dist.) N.Y. 1990. Vice chair citizens' adv. com. Delaware River Basin Commn. Capt. USAFR. Mem. N.Y. State Bar Assn. (co-chair global warming com.,air quality com.), N.Y.C. Bar Assn. (environ. law com.). Home: 235 Corlies Ave Pelham NY 10803-1903 Office: Bryan Cave LLP 1290 Ave of the Americas New York NY 10104 Office Phone: 212-541-1078. Business E-Mail: jkhealy@bryancave.com.

HEALY, JAMES CASEY, lawyer; b. Washington, Feb. 19, 1956; s. Joseph Francis Jr. and Patricia Ann (Casey) H.; m. Kelly Anne Quinn, Nov. 4, 1995; 1 child, Caitlin Quinn. BS, Spring Hill Coll., 1978; JD, Emory U., 1982. Bar: Ga. 1983, Conn. 1983, U.S. Dist. Ct. Conn. 1984, U.S. Tax Ct. 1984, U.S. Supreme Ct. 1987. Assoc. Gregory and Adams PC, Wilton, Conn., 1982-87, ptnr., 1988-89, mng. ptnr., 1990-94, v.p., 1995—. Spl. counsel Wilton Police Commn., 1986-98; mem. Wilton Parks and Recreation Commn., 1991-2002, sec., 1991-93, chmn., 1997-2002; corporator Ridgefield Bank, 1997—; mem. Wilton Fire Commn., 2002—, sec., 2002—. Bd. dirs. Mark Lavin Meml. Offshore Med. and Safety Found., Empire, Mich., 1987—97, Village Market, Inc., 1988—90, Wilton Teen Ctr., 2001—05, Friends of Ambler Farm, Inc., 2005—; chmn. leadership giving program United Way, 1991; bd. mgrs. Wilton Children's Ctr., 1996—98; athletic fields subcom.of building com. Wilton H.S., 1998—99; steering com. Wilton Family Recreation and Activity Ctr., 2000; trustee Wilton Hist. Soc., 2001—05. Mem. Internat. Mcpl. Lawyers Assn., State Bar Ga., State Bar Conn. (exec. com., planning and zoning sect. 1992-94), Am. Planning Assn., Fairfield County Bar Assn. (law office mgmt. com. 1994-96, co-chmn. land use com. 1996—2005, real estate brokers contract com. 1997-98), Real Estate Fin. Assn., Wilton C. of C. (bd. dirs. 1994-96). Republican. Roman Catholic. Office: Gregory and Adams 190 Old Ridgefield Rd Wilton CT 06897-4023 Office Phone: 203-762-9000. E-mail: jhealy@gregoryandadams.com.

HEALY, JERRAMIAH, mayor; b. Dec. 1950; m. Maureen Healy; children: Jeremiah, Susanne, Catherine, Patrick. BA, Villanova U., 1972; JD, Seton Hall U. Atty., 1977—; asst. prosecutor Hudson County Prosecutor's Office, Jersey City, 1977—81; chief judge Jersey City Mcpl. Ct., 1991—2001; councilman City Coun., Jersey City, 2001—04; mayor Jersey City, 2004—. Office: City Hall 280 Grove St Jersey City NJ 07302 Fax: 201-547-4288. E-mail: MayorHealy@jcnj.org.*

HEALY, JODI, library services manager; With Google, 2003—, mgr. Libr. Partnership Team, ptnr. mgr. Book Search Team, 2005—. Author: Google Librarian Newsletter, 2005—. Office: Google Book Search Team 1600 Amphitheatre Pky Mountain View CA 94043 Office Phone: 650-253-5343. Office Fax: 650-253-0001. E-mail: jhealy@google.com.

HEALY, JOSEPH FRANCIS, JR., lawyer, retired air transportation executive; b. NYC, Aug. 11, 1930; s. Joseph Francis and Agnes (Kett) H.; m. Patricia A. Casey, Apr. 23, 1955; children: James C., Timothy, Kevin, Cathleen M., Mary, Terence. BS, Fordham U., 1952; JD, Georgetown U., 1959. Bar: D.C. 1959. With gen. traffic dept. Eastman-Kodak Co., Rochester, NY, 1954-55; air transp. examiner CAB, Washington, 1955-59; practiced in Washington, 1959-70, 80-81; asst. gen. counsel Air Transport Assn. Am., 1966-70; v.p. legal Eastern Air Lines, Inc., NYC and Miami, Fla., 1970-80; ptnr. Ford, Farquhar, Kornblut & O'Neill, Washington, 1980-81; v.p. legal affairs Piedmont Aviation, Inc., Winston Salem, NC, 1981-84, sr. v.p., gen counsel, 1984-89, ret., 1989; sr. v.p., gen. counsel Trans World Airlines Inc., Mt. Kisco, NY, 1993-94. Mem. bd. visitors Sch. Law Wake Forest U., 1988-96. 1st lt. USAF, 1952-54. Mem.: Nat. Aero. Assn., Phi Delta Phi, Beta Gamma Sigma. Home: 104 Overlink Ct Lynchburg VA 24503-3200

HEALY, JULIA SCHMITT, artist, educator; b. Elmhurst, Ill., Mar. 28, 1947; d. Albert Leo and Louise Anne (Tilly) Schmitt; m. Richard Healy, Apr. 6, 1973 (div. Aug. 1990); children: Patrick, Katharine; m. Pierre Tonachel, Oct. 10, 2004. BFA, Sch. of the Art Inst. Chgo., 1970, MFA, 1972; student, U. Chgo., Yale U., Dalhousie U., NYU; Sch. Dist. Adminstrn., SUNY, Stony Brook, 2003. Dir. Eye Level Gallery, Halifax, N.C., 1974-76; artist, tchr. Studio in a Sch., NYC, 1989-94; tchr. Valley Stream Sch. Dist. 13, 1994—2005; dir. related arts West Hempstead Schools, 2005—. Adj. prof. Sch. of the Art Inst. Chgo., 1970-72, Ocean County Coll., Toms River, N.J., 1979-81, Pratt Inst., Bklyn., 1991-93, CUNY/CSI, 1995-2005, CUNY/QCC, 2005-; art adv. bd. Chancellor's Bd., N.Y.C. Pub. Schs.; edn. com. Snug Harbor Cultural Ctr., Staten Island, N.Y., 1991—98; dir. Art Lab, Staten Island, 1990-93, Alice Austen House, Staten Island, 1990-99. Columnist: (syndicated) Artmakers, 1990-98; exhbns. include Staten Island Mus., 1989, Newhouse Ctr. for Contemporary Art, 1987, Soho 20, Sch. Art Inst. Chgo.; over 50 group exhbns., three maj. pub. commns.; pub. art installation Von Briesen Park, NYC, Faber Park. Mem. Community Bd. Waterfront Com., Staten Island, 1989-92; vol. Project Hospitality, Staten Island, 1989-2000. Recipient artist's grant Staten Island Coun. on the Arts, 1987, 91, Can. Coun., Ottawa, 1976-78, fellowship Yale Summer Sch. of Music and Art, 1969, Weissglass award Staten Island Mus. Mem. Artists Space, New Mus., Tibetan Mus., Mudlane Soc., Soc. for Art Religion and Contemporary Culture (bd. dirs. 2003). Home: 63 E 9th St 14R New York NY 10003 Personal E-mail: juliahealy@aol.com.

HEALY, MARK, editor-in-chief; b. 1968; married; 2 children. BA in Eng., U. Vt., Burlington. Assoc. editor Rolling Stone; sr. editor Details, GQ, articles editor, 2003—06; editor-in-chief Penthouse, 2006—. Office: Penthouse Media Group 11th Fl 2 Penn Plz New York NY 10121*

HEALY, MARTIN RUSSELL, lawyer; b. Yonkers, NY, Apr. 22, 1950; s. Thomas Joseph and Faith (DeBaun) H.; m. Joanne Ferrera, Aug. 5, 1972; children: Adam, Alexander, Craig, David. BA, Boston Coll., 1972, JD, 1975. Bar: Mass., U.S. Dist. Ct. Mass., U.S. Ct. Appeals (1st cir.). Law clk. Mass. Trial Ct., Boston, 1975-76; with Rackemann, Sawyer & Brewster, Boston, 1976—95; ptnr. Goodwin Procter LLP, Boston, 1995—. Editor, contbg. author: Massachusetts Zoning Manual, 1989. Mem. Needham (Mass.) Conservation Commn., 1983-86; trustee Capt. Robert Bennet Forbes House Charitable Trust, Milton, Mass., 1986-87. Fellow Mass. Bar Found.; mem. Mass. Bar Assn. (chmn. property law coun. 1986-88), Nat. Assn. Indsl. and Office Parks (chmn. pub. affairs com. Mass. chpt. 1990-91). Roman Catholic. Office: Goodwin Procter LLP Exchange Pl 53 State St Boston MA 02109 Office Phone: 617-570-1371. Office Fax: 617-523-1231. Business E-Mail: mhealy@goodwinprocter.com.

HEALY, NICHOLAS JOSEPH, retired lawyer; b. NYC, Jan. 4, 1910; s. Nicholas Joseph and Frances Cecilia (McCarthy) H.; m. Margaret Marie Ferry, Mar. 29, 1937; children: Nicholas, Margaret Healy Parker, Rosemary Healy Bell, Mary Louise Healy White, Donall, Kathleen Healy Hamon. AB, Holy Cross Coll., 1931; JD, Harvard U., 1934. Bar: N.Y. 1935, U.S. Supreme Ct. 1949. Pvt. practice, NYC, 1935—42; mem. Healy & Baillie (and predecessor firms), 1948—. Spl. asst. to atty. gen. U.S., 1945-48; tchr. admiralty law NYU Sch. Law, 1947-86, adj. prof., 1960-86; Niels F. Johnsen vis. prof. maritime law Tulane Maritime Law Ctr., 1986; vis. prof. maritime law Shanghai Maritime Inst. (now Shanghai Maritime U.), 1981, 86, 88. Contbr. chpts. to Ann. Survey Am. Law, 1948-87; author: (with Sprague) Cases on Admiralty, 1950; (with Currie) Cases and Materials on Admiralty, 1965; (with Sharpe) Cases and Materials on Admiralty, 1974, 3rd edit., 1998; (with Sweeney) The Law of Marine Collision, 1998; editor: Jour. Maritime Law and Commerce, 1980-90, mem. editl. bd., 1969-79, 91—; assoc. editor: American Maritime Cases; mem. scientific bd. Il Dirittimo Marittimo; contbr. to Ency. Brit. Chmn. USCG Adv. Panel on Rules of the Road, 1966-72; mem. permanent adv. bd. Tulane Admiralty Law Inst. Lt. (s.g.) USNR, 1942-45. Fellow Am. Coll. Trial Lawyers; mem. ABA (ho. of dels. 1964-66), N.Y. State Bar Assn., Assn. of Bar of City of N.Y., N.Y. County Lawyers Assn., Maritime Law Assn. U.S. (pres. 1964-66), Assn. Average Adjusters U.S. (chmn. 1959-60), Com. Maritime Internat. (exec. coun. 1972-79, v.p. 1985-91, hon. v.p. 1991—), Ibero-Am. Inst. Maritime Law (hon.). Office: Healy & Baillie LLP 61 Broadway New York NY 10006-3201 Home: 35A Jane St New York NY 10014-5129 Business E-Mail: nhealy@healy.com.

HEALY, PATRICIA COLLEEN, social worker; b. Denver, Aug. 24, 1935; d. Cecil John and Gracia Maude (Walker) Schulte; m. John Patrick Healy III, Aug. 3, 1957 (div. Jan. 1972); 1 child, Sean Patrick. BA, Sacred Heart Coll., Wichita, 1957; MSW, U. Kans., 1983; postgrad., Wichita State U., 1974, 75, 89, Emporia U., Kans., 1990, U. Kans., 1998. Lic. specialist clin. social worker, Kans.; cert. in spinal cord injury medicine. Proofreader Wichita Pub. Co., 1953; clk. typist Nat. Sales, Inc., Wichita, 1954-58, Dept. of Army, Ft. Leavenworth, Kans., 1958-60, Air Force, McConnell AFB, Kans., 1962-63; clk., typist VA Regional Office, Wichita, 1963-66; self-employed typist Wichita, 1966-70; ward clk., typist VA Regional Office and VA Med. Ctr., Wichita, 1970-73; vets. benefits counselor VARO, Wichita, 1973-83; social worker VA Med. Ctr., Wichita, 1983-2000; ret.; pvt. practice Wichita, 2000—. Author filmstrip, columns, book revs., feature stories and poetry. Former mem. Ctrl. Plains AAA Coun. on Aging; mem. Clin. Social Work Assoc., 2003—; vol. Sr. Svcs.; bd. dirs. Ind. Living Ctr. South Ctrl. Kans., 1990—96, Sedgwick County Dept. Aging Cmty. Svc. Adv. Bd. Mem.: Kans. Authors Club. Roman Catholic. Avocations: writing, reading, photography, music, knitting and sewing.

HEALY, SONDRA ANITA, consumer products company executive; b. 1939; married; 3 children. BFA, Goodman Sch. Drama, 1963; MA, Nat. Coll., 1964. Owner, chair Turtle Wax, Chgo., 1973—. Office: Turtle Wax 5655 S 73rd Ave Chicago IL 60638

HEALY, STEPHANIE LEMME, hospital organization administrator; b. 1972; Pres. Hosp. Coun. Southern Ariz. Mem. Southern Ariz. AIDS Found.; hostess Silver and Turquoise Ball; bd. mem. Juvenile Diabetes Rsch. Found.; bd. dir. Pledge-A-Job. Named one of 40 Under 40, Tucson Bus. Edge, 2006. Mem.: Pima Assn. (Governments Population Planning Com.), Ariz. Assn. for Econ. Devel., Armory Park Neighborhood Assn. Office: Southern Arizona Leadership Council 4400 E Broadway Ste 307 Tucson AZ 85711

HEALY, STEVEN MICHAEL, accountant, city official; b. Chgo., July 20, 1949; s. Daniel Francis and Angelina (Massino) H. BA, U. Ill., Chgo., 1971; MBA, Dominican U., 1984. Br. mgr. Assocs. Capital Co., Chgo., 1971-74; credit analyst Motorola, Inc., Schaumburg, Ill., 1974-76; office mgr. Triple "S" Steel Corp., Franklin Park, Ill., 1976-79; accounts payable supr. Zenith Electronics, Chgo., 1979-84; supr. acctg. Village of Oak Park, Ill., 1984-86; bus. analyst Cablevision of Chgo., Oak Park, 1986-87; dir. fin. Village of Maywood, Ill., 1988-91; dir. fin., treas. City of DeKalb, Ill., 1991-93; dir. fin. Village of Cahokia, Ill., 1993—2003; acct. III City of Ocala, Fla., 2003—. Active Friends of Oak Park Libr., Friends of the Conservatory, Oak Park Village Players Group, Cahokia Econ. Devel. Commn., Cmty. Emergency Response Team, Ocala; bd. dirs. Oak Park Employees Credit Union, Cahokia C. of C., 2000—; treas. Cahokia Assn. for the Tricentennial; pres. sch. bd. Cahokia Unit Sch. Dist. 187. Mem.: Ill. Govt. Fin. Officers Assn., Nat. Govt. Fin. Officers Assn., Dominican U. MBA Alumni Assn. (soc. com. 1984—, founder), U. Ill. Alumni Assn., Kiwanis, Village Oak Park Chess Club, Cath. Alumni Club, Rotary (sec. St. Clair Valley chpt.), Jaycees. Avocations: sports, reading, travel, writing, chess. Personal E-mail: shealy@ocalafl.org.

HEALY, THERESA ANN, retired ambassador; b. Bklyn., July 14, 1932; d. Anthony and Mary Catherine (Kennedy) H. BA, St. John's U., 1954, LLD (hon.), 1985. Tchr. elem. and secondary schs., NYC, 1951-55; with U.S. Fgn. Svc., 1955-94, amb. to Sierra Leone, 1980-83; with Ctr. for Internat. Affairs, U. South Fla., Tampa, 1983-84; faculty Nat. Def. U., Washington, 1984-86; with pers. and mgmt. policy bur. U.S. Dept. State, 1986-92; with Office of Freedom of Info., 1992-94; ret., 1994. Cons. Dept. State, 1996—, Office of Freedom Info., 1997—2005; arbitrator dispute resolution Nat. Assn. Security Dealers, 1999—. Mem. Am. Fgn. Svc. Assn., Diplomatic and Consular Officers Ret. Roman Catholic. Home: 6800 Fleetwood Rd Apt 1002 Mc Lean VA 22101-3610

HEANEY, GERALD WILLIAM, retired federal judge; b. Goodhue, Minn., Jan. 29, 1918; s. William J. and Johanna (Ryan) H.; m. Eleanor R. Schmitt, Dec. 1, 1945; children: William M., Carol J. Student, St. Thomas

Coll., 1935—37; BSL, U. Minn., 1939, LLB, 1941, LLD for Pub. Svc., 2001. Bar: Minn. 1941. Lawyer securities div. Dept. of Commerce Minn., 1941—42; mem. firm Lewis. Hammer, Heaney, Weyl & Halverson, Duluth, 1946—66; judge U.S. Ct. Appeals (8th cir.), 1966—88, sr. judge, 1988—2006. Bd. regents U. Minn., 1964—65; Mem. Dem. Nat. Com. from Minn., 1955. Capt. AUS, 1942—46. Mem.: ABA, Am. Judicature Soc., Minn. Bar Assn. Roman Catholic.

HEANUE, ANNE ALLEN, retired librarian; b. Ft. Oglethorpe, Ga., Feb. 7, 1940; d. James Edward and Mary (Dennean) Allen; m. Kevin E. Heanue, July 20, 1963; children: Mary, Brian, Patricia. BA cum laude, Dunbarton Coll., 1962; MA, Georgetown U., 1966; MS in Libr. Sci., Cath. U. Am., 1976. Libr. Deloitte Haskins and Sells, Washington, 1977—79; asst. to dir. ALA, Washington, 1979—81, asst. dir., 1981—84, assoc. dir., 1984—98; ret., 1998. Bd. dirs. Alexandria (Va.) LWV, 1967-78; chmn. Alexandria Spl. Edn. adv. com., 1978-79; mem. Alexandria Gypsy Moth Control Commn., 1991-96; vol. White House, 1999—; trustee Freedom to Read Found., 2003—; mem. cancer care com. Inova Alexandria Hosp. Found., 2003—. Recipient Fed. Librs. Round Table Achievement award, 1988. Mem. ALA, Hist. Soc. Washington, D.C., Va. Hist. Soc., Rappahannock Hist. Soc., D.C. Libr. Assn. (bd. dirs. 1994-97), Beta Phi Mu, Pi Gamma Mu. Roman Catholic. Avocations: reading, travel, theater.

HEAP, JOAN S., elementary school educator; b. Ogden, Utah, July 13, 1944; d. Ralph William Spackman and Reita Anone Ward; m. Brent Aaron Heap, Sept. 3, 1965; children: Amie Nicole, Aaron Robert, Ethan Trevor, Tucker Justin, Tyler Brent, Morgan Katie Zavala, Kellie Joan. BS, Weber State U., Ogden, Utah, 1965. Lang. arts tchr. Walhquist Jr. High, Harrisville, Utah, 1965—66, Rocky Mountain Jr. High, West Haven, 1994—99; lang. arts tchr., dept. chair N. Ogden Jr. High, Ogden, 1999—. Adv. Nat. Jr. Honor Soc., Ogden, 1999—; team mem. Utah Behavior Intervention, Salt Lake City, 2003—, Student at Risk Intervention, Ogden, 2003—. Active Cmty. Coun., 1994—. Named Utah Tchr. of Yr., 2006; recipient Tchr. of Yr., Weber Sch. Dist., Ogden, 2005. Mem.: NEA, UCTE, WEA, Utah Edn. Assn. Republican. Mem. Lds Ch. Avocations: hiking, skiing, mountain biking, marathoner. Office: North Ogden Jr High 575 E 2900 N North Ogden UT 84414*

HEAPHY, JANIS BESLER, newspaper executive; b. Kalamazoo, Oct. 10, 1951; d. Elvin Julius and Margaret Louise (Throndike) Olson; m. Douglas R. Dern, Aug. 15, 1980 (div. Nov. 1985); m. Robert Thomas Heaphy, Feb. 11, 1989; 1 child, Tanner. BS, Miami U., 1973, MEd, 1976. Tchr. Edgewood Jr. HS, Seven Mile, Ohio, 1973—75; acct. exec. LA Times, 1976—79, sr. acct. exec., 1986—87, ea. mag. mgr., 1987—89, nat. advt. mgr., 1989—92, retail advt. mgr. then sr. v.p. advt./mktg., 1992—97; acct. exec. LA Mag., 1979—82; mgr. LA Omni Mag., 1982—86; pres. & pub. Sacramento Bee, 1998—. Co-editor: Secrets of the Master Sellers, 1987. Bd. dirs. Sacramento Region Cmty. Found., Valley Vision, Sacramento; mem. Sacramento Host Com., Pride Industries Bd., Sacramento, Mountain Valley ch., Am. Leadership Forum Bd.; hon. chmn. Children's Receiving Home, Sacramento. Named one of Women Who Mean Business, Sacramento Bus. Jour.; recipient Ruth Standish Baldwin award, Sacramento Urban League. Mem.: Calif. Newspaper Publishers Assn., Advt. Club LA. Avocations: home decorating, reading, swimming, music. Office: Sacramento Bee 2100 Q St Sacramento CA 95816 Mailing: Sacramento Bee PO Box 15779 Sacramento CA 95826 Office Phone: 916-321-1885. Office Fax: 916-321-1109. E-mail: jheaphy@sacbee.com.*

HEAPHY, JOHN MERRILL, lawyer; b. Escanaba, Mich., Apr. 27, 1927; s. John Merrill and Catherine R. (Feeney) H.; m. Martha Jean Knowles, Nov. 16, 1951; children— John Merrill III, Catherine Jean Heaphy DeThorne, Barbara H. Murphy. BA, U. Mich., 1950; JD, Wayne State U., 1953. Bar: Mich. 1954. Atty. office of gen. counsel HEW, Washington, 1954-57; ptnr. Vandeveer & Garzia, P.C. and predecessor firms, Detroit, 1958-86, pres. firm, 1986-92; ret. Served with USNR, 1945-46. Fellow Am. Coll. Trial Lawyers; mem. ABA, Internat. Assn. Def. Counsel, Mich. Bar Assn., Delta Theta Phi, Alpha Sigma Phi. Republican. Home: 312 Honors Dr Shorewood IL 60404 Personal E-mail: jomhe27@sbcglobal.net.

HEAPS, MARVIN DALE, retired food services company executive; b. Boone, Iowa, June 26, 1932; s. Donald and Mary Isabel (Robson) H.; m. Martha Coleman Davis, July 4, 1957; children— Mitchell, Matthew, Martha. BA in Econs, Whitworth Coll., 1953; postgrad., George Washington U., 1957; MBA (Achievement scholar), U. Pa., 1959. Asso. McKinsey & Co. (mgmt. cons.), Washington, Geneva and NYC, 1960-66; dir. service systems engrng. Automatic Retailers of Am., Phila., 1967, v.p., 1968; sr. v.p. ARA Svcs., Inc., Phila., 1969-71; pres. ARA Food Svcs. Co., 1971-75; exec. v.p. ops. ARA Svcs., Inc., 1975-77, pres., chief operational officer, 1977-81; pres./chief exec. officer Marvin D. Heaps Assos., Inc., 1981—. Cons. to Office Edn., HEW; mem. food svc. industry adv. com. Exec. Office Pres., 1969—; chmn. bd. ACTS Retirement Life Communities, 1997-. Active Whitworth Coll.; chmn. Salvation Army. Lt. USN, 1955-59. Mem. Conf. Bd., Am. Mgmt. Assn., Assn. Internat. Devel., Nat. Automatic Mdse. Assn. (dir.), Wharton MBA Alumni Club. Republican. Presbyterian (elder). Home and Office: 1079 Kennett Way West Chester PA 19380

HEARD, CHARLES WOLFE, lawyer, consultant; b. Pitts., Nov. 15, 1931; s. Charles Clarke and Margaret Wolfe Heard; m. Corina Shattuck Higginson; children: Sarah, Drayton. BA, Yale U., New Haven, Conn., 1953; LLB, U. Mich., Ann Arbor, 1959. Bar: Mass. 1959, NH 1974. Lawyer Stackpole Stetson & Bradlee, Boston, 1959—66, Powers, Hall, Montgomery & Weston, Boston, 1966—67, Manchester, NH, 1974—81, Heard Hunter Cohen and Porch, Wolfeboro, NH, 1981—85, Cleveland Waters and Bass, P.A., Concord, NH, 1985—; trust officer South Shore Nat. Bank, Wellesley, Mass., 1974—81. Cons. Northwestern Mut. Life Ins. Co., Manchester, NH, 2001—04, Mass. Mut. Life Ins. Co., Nashua, NH, 1994—2004. Bd. dirs. Boston Estate Planning Coun., 1959—2006; pres.bd. dirs. NH Estate Planning Coun., Manchester, NH, 1975—2003. Pvt. inf. US Army, 1954—56. Fellow: Am. Coll. Trust and Estate Counsel; mem.: Harvard Club Boston, Union Club Boston. Republican. Episcopalian. Avocations: violin, viola, chamber music. Office: Cleveland Waters and Bass PA 2 Capital Plaza Concord NH 03301 Home Phone: 603-569-9510; Office Phone: 603-224-7761. Office Fax: 603-224-6457. Business E-Mail: heardc@cwbpa.com.

HEARD, EDWIN ANTHONY, banker; b. NYC, Oct. 31, 1926; s. Edwin Anthony and Frances Weaver (Taylor) H.; m. Phyllis Marie Gregory, Dec. 18, 1948; children: Elizabeth Gregory, Edwin Anthony III. AB, Princeton U., 1948; grad., Advanced Mgmt. Program, Harvard U., 1966. V.p. Irving Trust Co., NYC, 1960-71; treas. U.S. Trust Co., NYC, 1971-73, exec. v.p., 1973-76, vice chmn., 1976-89; pres. Excelsior Income Shares, Inc., 1989-92, also bd. dirs., emeritus. Trustee Trinity Episcopal Sch. Corp.; trustee emeritus Collegiate Sch., NYC. With USNR, 1944-46. Mem. Belle Meade Country Club (Nashville), Bond Club (N.Y.C.). Home: 3901 West End Ave Nashville TN 37205-1837

HEARD, JAMES HENRY, lawyer, educator, historian; b. Woburn, Mass., Sept. 28, 1940; s. James Henry Heard and Thelma Mae Bailey; m. Deloris Heard, Sept. 2, 1978; children: Patrick, Malcolm, Anthony. BS, Boston State Coll., 1963; MAT, U. Chgo., 1968; JD, DePaul U., 1974. Bar: Ill. 1975, U.S. Dist. Ct. (no. dist.) Ill. 1975, U.S. Supreme Ct. 1975. Chmn. social sci. Bloom Twp. H.S., Chgo. Heights, Ill., 1965-70; prof. of history Prarie State Coll., Chgo. Heights, 1970-71, Harold Washington Coll., Chgo., 1971—, chmn. social scis. dept., 1980-85, 90—, chmn. faculty coun., 1993—; dean applied scis. Kennedy-King Coll., Chgo., 1985-90; arbitrator Cook County Cir. Cts., Chgo., 1975—. Coord. common ground projects Harold Washington Coll., Chgo., 1995—. Contbr. to book and profl. jours.; chorister Kennedy King Coll. Cmty. Chorus, 1985—. Cantor St. Thomas the Apostle Ch., Chgo., 1985—; chmn. of adv. bd. Ill. Infant Mortality Project, 1980-85; chmn. bd. dirs. New City Health Ctr., Chgo., 1980-90. Named Educator of Yr., Comty. Coll. Assn. of Ill. and U. Mich. Consortium, 1995, Disting. Prof. Harold Washington Coll., 1995, Most Disting. Advisor, Phi Theta Kappa Internat. Honor Soc., Jackson Miss. chpt., 1995; recipient award Chgo. Urban League, 1985, Osterman Outstanding Svc. award City of Chgo., 1996. Mem. Comty. Colls. Humanities Assn. Avocations: music appreciation, running, reading.

HEARD, LARRY, real estate company executive; b. Houston; BBA in Fin., Baylor U. With devel. and leasing divsn. Joe A. McDermott, Inc., Houston, 1981—84; joined Transwestern Comml. Svcs., Inc., Houston, 1984, pres. S.W. region, 1996—2002, exec. v.p. Houston divsn., pres., CEO, 2002—, also bd. dirs. Bd. dirs. SEARCH. Adv. bd. Hankamer Sch. Bus. Baylor U.; bd. dirs. SEARCH. Mem.: Urban Land Inst. (mem. exec. com. Houston), Baylor Bear Found. (past pres. Houston chpt.), Young Pres. Orgn. (exec. com. Houston chpt.). Office: Transwestern Comml Svcs Ste 1300 1900 W Loop South Houston TX 77027*

HEARD, RONALD ROY, motion picture producer, lawyer; b. Denver, Oct. 3, 1947; s. John Arthur and Louise Marie (Smith) H.; m. Kim Widing Aug. 12, 1967 (div. 1969). BS, Colo. State U., 1969; postgrad., U. Colo., 1969-72, U. Paris/Sorbonne, 1964-65; JD, Abraham Lincoln U., 2005. Prodn. design/stage mgr. The Rolling Stones, London, 1969-99; property/set dresser Universal Studios, Universal City, Calif., 1978-79, Warner Bros. Studios, Burbank, Calif., 1979-80; producer stage plays Hollywood, 1980-85; music video cons. LA, 1984—; corres. CBS Network News, Chgo., 1971-72; writer/photographer UPI/Nat. Geographic/Denver Post, 1969-73; ptnr. Silver Screen Ptnrs. II and III, LA, 1986—; CEO, pres. Radio Safari, 1991—; pres. Brightstar Entertainment dba Liberty Tree Studios, 1994—. Owner Yankee Pride Ent., North Hollywood, Calif., 1986—, LAPD Police Cmty. rep. 1995-95, LAPD Citizen Tagger Task Force, 1995. Exec. com. Dem. Party, Larimer County, Colo., 1972-79; Dem. candidate for Ho. of Rep., 1972, 76. Named honorary citizen of S.D. by Gov. Richard Kneip, 1972. Mem. Am. Film Inst., Smithsonian Instn., Statue of Liberty/Ellis Island Cen. Commn., Rock and Roll Hall of Fame (founding mem.), Knights Templar (knight 2005). Democrat.

HEARL, PETER R., food service executive; b. Sydney; m. Helen Hearl; 3 children. BCom, Univ. New South Wales, Australia, 1973. Mgmt. positions Exxon, 1973—91; dir KFC ops. PepsiCo, Sydney, 1991—93, KFC mgmt. positions London, 1993—96; regional v.p. KFC & Pizza Hut, Sydney, 1996—97, Yum! Restaurants Internat., Hong Kong, 1997—98, exec. v.p. Dallas, 1998—2002; exec. v.p., chief people officer Yum! Brands Inc., Louisville, 2002; pres., chief concept officer Pizza Hut, Dallas, 2002—06; COO, chief develop. officer Yum! Brands Inc., Louisville, 2006—. Office: Yum! Brands 1441 Gardiner Ln Louisville KY 40213-1914*

HEARLE, DOUGLAS GEOFFREY, public relations consultant; b. NYC, Apr. 7, 1933; s. Douglas G. and Regina Irene (Booth) H.; m. Mary Elizabeth Hogan, July 13, 1957; children: Douglas, Christopher, Matthew. BA, Iona Coll., 1954, MBA, 1970. Reporter-editor N.Y. Jour.-Am., NYC, 1954-63; pub. relations mgr. Borden Inc., NYC, 1963-66; account exec. Hill & Knowlton, NYC, 1966-70, v.p., 1970-73, sr. v.p., 1973-80, exec. v.p., 1980-86, vice chmn., 1989-90, also bd. dirs.; founder, pres. Douglas G. Hearle & Co., NYC, 1993—. Pres. John W. Hill Found., N.Y.C., 1980-86; founder, pres. Douglas G. Hearle & Assoc., Inc., N.Y.C., 1986-89; pres., CEO Carl Byoir & Assocs., N.Y.C., 1990-92; adj. prof. Iona Coll., 1982-84, Coll. New Rochelle, 1996—, Fordham U., 1998-99; disting. lectr. Ball State U., 1981, U. Tex., 1984. V.p. Bd. Edn., Pelham, N.Y., 1972-78; v.p. N.Y. Newspaper Reporters Assn., 1961-63; mem. exec. coun. Boy Scouts Am., 1967-69; vice chmn. bd. trustees Coll. New Rochelle, 1989-95; bd. dirs. The Roper Ctr., U. Conn., 1990—2003; pres. Danny Fund, Pelham, N.Y., 2003-2005. Recipient Disting. Service award Asean P.R. Congress, Jakarta, Indonesia, 1981; recipient Citizen of Yr. award Pelham Men's Club, 1978, Five Most Respected award by PR Week, 1988, All Star award Inside PR Mag., 1992. Mem. Silurians, N.Y. Newspaper Reporters Assn., Asia Soc., Grenock C. of C. Lee, Mass., Sky Club of N.Y. Republican. Roman Catholic. Home: 20 Maple Ave Pelham NY 10803-2220 E-mail: santa4343@aol.com.

HEARN, BILLY RAY, recording industry executive; b. 1929; Tchr. choir, music, Tex. and Ga., 1950-68; dir. Myrth Records (a divsn. Word Inc.), Waco, Tex., 1968-75; chmn. Sparrow Corp., Brentwood, Tenn., 1975-92; CEO & co-chmn. EMI Christian Music Group, 1993-95, chmn., 1996—. Chmn. Sparrow Found. Recipient Lifetime Achievement award, Gospel Music Assn. Mem.: Gospel Music Hall of Fame. Office: EMI Christian Music Group 101 Winners Cir Brentwood TN 37027-5017 also: EMI Christian Music Group PO Box 5084 Brentwood TN 37024-5084*

HEARN, GEORGE, actor; b. St. Louis, June 18, 1934; m. Mary Harrell (div.), 1 child, David; m. Susan Babel (div.); m. Dixie Carter, 1978 (div.); m. Leslie Simons, 1985. BS Philosophy, Southwestern U. Numerous stage appearances, including: The Changing Room, 1973, An Almost Perfect Person, 1977, Sweeny Todd, 1979 (Broadway), 1980 (tour of U.S. cities, Emmy award - PBS broadcast), I Remember Mama, 1979, Watch on the Rhine, 1980, A Doll's Life, 1982, La Cage aux Folles, 1983 (Broadway, Tony award, 1984), 1986 (London, Olivier award), Sunset Boulevard, 1993-95 (Broadway, Tony award, 1995), The Diary of Ann Frank, 1997, Putting It Together, 1999, Sweeney Todd, 2000, Wicked, 2004-05, Children and Art, 2005; TV appearances include: The Silence, 1975, The Adams Chronicles, 1976, Sanctuary of Fear, 1979, A Piano for Mrs. Cimino, 1982, False Arrest, 1991, Fire in the Dark, 1991, Johnny's Golden Quest, 1993 (voice only), Deadly Secret: The Robert Bierer Story, 1993, Daisy-Head Mayzie, 1994 (voice only), Murder She Wrote, Annie: A Royal Adventure, 1995, Sarah, Plain and Tall: Winter's End, 1999; films include: See You in the Morning, 1989, Sneakers, 1992, The Vanishing, 1993, The Pagemaster, 1994 (voice only), (voice) All Dogs Go to Heaven 2, 1996, The Devil's Own, 1997, Barney's Great Adventure, 1998, Flags of Our Fathers, 2006. Named to Theatre Hall of Fame, 2007. Office: Paradigm Talent Agency 500 5th Ave Fl 37 New York NY 10110-3799*

HEARN, GEORGE HENRY, lawyer, water transportation executive; b. Bklyn., July 4, 1927; s. Henry G. and Grace A. (Flaherty) H.; m. Cecelia Anne Philbin, June 28, 1952; children: Annemarie Jude, Margaret Mary, George Henry. BA, St. Francis Coll., Bklyn., 1950; student, Fordham U., Bronx, NY, 1948; JD, St. John's U., Bklyn., 1954. Bar: N.Y. 1955, U.S. Supreme Ct. 1960, D.C. 1965. Jr. ptnr. Haight, Gardner, Poor and Havens, NYC, 1954—61; mem. CAB, 1961-64; commr. Fed. Maritime Commn., 1964-75; maritime adminstr. Govt. Sultanate of Oman, 1975-80; counsel to firm Hill, Rivkins, Carey, Loesberg & O'Brien (specializing in maritime and transp. law), NYC, 1977-82; exec. v.p. Waterman Steamship Corp., NYC, 1982—97. Lectr. transp. Georgetown U., Am. U., Tulane U., St. Francis Coll. Contbr. articles to profl. jours. Pres. Fleet Week Found., 1990—; dist. commr. Boy Scouts Am., 1958—, mem. N.Y.C. coun., 1958—61; chmn. Kings County spkrs. com. 1960 presdl. election of John F. Kennedy; vice-chmn. com. nationalists and intergroup rels. N.Y. State Dem. Com., 1960—. Served USNR, WWII, PTO. Recipient Disting. Svc. award U.S. Jr. C. of C., 1958; named Man of Yr., N.Y. Freight Forwarders and Brokers Assn., 1968, Cathedral Club of Bklyn., 1974. Mem. D.C. Bar Assn., Fed. Bar Assn., Maritime Adminstrv. Bar Assn., Maritime Law Assn., Soc. Maritime Arbitrators, U.S. Maritime Assn. Port of N.Y. and N.J. (pres., Man of Yr. 2000), India House (bd. govs.), Adminstrv. Conv. U.S., St. Patrick's Soc. Bklyn. (past pres.), Am. Com. Italian Migration (rec. sec. Bklyn. divsn.), KC. Home: 250 Lido Blvd PO Box 143 Point Lookout NY 11569 Office: 1 Whitehall St New York NY 10004-2109 Office Phone: 212-747-8550. Business E-Mail: moranjc@intship.com.

HEARN, JACKSON, church musician, educator; b. Tiptonville, Tenn., Feb. 26, 1958; s. James Alfred and Mary Maude Algee Hearn; m. Margaret Luanne Gowan, May 16, 1981 (div. Nov. 1, 1995); children: Margaret Hearn Jambard, Paul Jackson. BMus, Lambuth Coll., Jackson, Tenn., 1980; M of Sacred Music, So. Meth. U., Dallas, 1982. Dir. music, organist First Presbyn. Ch., Jackson, Tenn., 1982—86, Good Shepherd Episcopal Ch., Kingwood, Tex., 1997—; dir. music Christ United Meth. Ch., Memphis, 1986—95, Holy Apostles Episcopal Ch., Memphis, 1995—97. Adj. faculty Kingwood Coll., 2005—; musical editor The After Party mag. Musical director: Deep In The Heart. Mem.: Am. Guild Organists (dean Memphis chpt. 1993—94, sub dean Houston chpt. 2006), Chorister's Guild (pres. Houston chpt. 2003—05). Avocations: cooking, bicycling, weightlifting. Home: 1738 Redwing Ridge Dr Houston TX 77009 Office: Good Shepherd Episcopal Ch 2929 Woodland Hills Dr Kingwood TX 77339 Home Phone: 713-869-3192; Office Phone: 281-358-3154. Office Fax: 281-358-3155. Personal E-mail: pauljacksonhearn@aol.com. Business E-Mail: jacksonhearn@goodshepherdkingwood.org.

HEARN, JOYCE CAMP, retired state legislator, educator, consultant; b. Cedartown, Ga. d. J.C. and Carolyn (Carter) Camp; m. Thomas Harry Hearn (dec.); children: Theresa Hearn Potts Bailey, Kimberly Ann Johnson, Carolyn Lee Becker. Student, U. Ga.; BA, Ohio State U., 1957; postgrad., U. S.C. Former h.s. tchr.; dist. mgr. U.S. Census, 2d Congl. Dist., 1970; mem. S.C. Ho. of Reps., 1975-89. Asst. minority leader, 1976-78, 86-89; chmn., commn. alcohol beverage control, ABC, 1989-91; pres., cons. Hearn & Assocs., Columbia, S.C., 1995—. Mem. Richland County Planning Comm., 1974-76; bd. dirs. Meml. Youth Ctr. and Stage South; chmn. Sexual Assault Awareness; vice chmn. Dist. Rep. Com., 1968; Rep. chmn. 2d Congl. Dist., 1969; Rep. chmn. Richland County, 1972; del., platform com. Rep. Nat. Conv., 1980, 84; moderator Kathwood Bapt. Ch., 1979-80, former asst. Sunday Sch. tchr.; bd. dirs. Small Bus. Devel. Ctr., S.C., Columbia Coll. Bd. Vis., Columbia Urban League, Fedn. of Blind; trustee Columbia Mus. Art; apptd. to Alcohol Beverage Control Bd., 1989, apptd. chmn. commn., adminstr., judge, 1990-92, commr., 1991-94; bd. dirs. Lupus Found., 1990-94; chair nat. adv. com. Occupl. Safety and Health, Washington, DC, 1980-88. Recipient Outstanding Citizen award Columbia Rape Coalition, 1977, Disting. Svc. award Claims Mgmt. Assn., S.C., 1977, Nat. Fedn. Blind S.C., 1978, Columbia Urban League, 1983, MADD, 1985, Outstanding Legislator of Yr. award Alcohol and Drug Abuse Assn., 1980, Retarded Citizens Assn., 1982, S.C. Rehab. Assn., 1984, S.C. Assn. of Deaf, 1987, Legislator of Yr., Fedn. of Blind, 1988, Disting. Legislator, DAV, 1989; honoree Easter Seals, 1989; numerous other awards. Mem. Nat. Order of Women Legislators (v.p., pres.), Order of the Palmetto, S.C. Women's Club, Columbia Women's Club (bd. dirs.), Larkspur Garden Club, Spring Valley Country Club Golf Assn. (pres. 1973, 97), Spring Valley Country Club. Office Phone: 803-256-7255. Personal E-mail: joyce-hearn@sc.rr.com.

HEARN, THOMAS K., JR., academic administrator; b. Opp, Ala., July 5, 1937; s. Thomas H. Hearn; m. Laura Walter; children: Thomas K., William Neely, Lindsay. BA summa cum laude, Birmingham-So. Coll., 1959; BD, Baptist Theol. Sem., 1963; PhD (NDEA fellow), Vanderbilt U., 1965. Instr. Birmingham-So. Coll., 1964—65; asst. prof. Coll. William and Mary, 1965—68, assoc. prof., 1968—74; prof. philosophy U. Ala., Birmingham, 1974—83, chmn. dept. philosophy, 1974—76; dean U. Ala. Sch. Humanities, Birmingham, 1976—78; v.p. U. Ala. Univ. Coll., Birmingham, 1978—83; pres. Wake Forest U., Winston-Salem, NC, 1983—2005, pres. emeritus, 2005—. Contbr. articles to profl. jours. Chmn. bd. govs. Ctr. for Creative Leadership; chair Knight Commn. on Intercoll. Athletics, 2005—. Recipient Thomas Jefferson Teaching award, 1970; fellow, Council Philos. Studies, 1968, Coop. Program in Humanities, 1969—70; grantee, Nat. Found. Humanities, 1967, Faculty Summer grant, Coll. William and Mary, 1970, 1972—73. Mem.: AAUP, Newcomen Soc. N.Am., David Hume Soc., Am. Philos. Assn., Soc. Philosophy Religion (pres. 1974—75), So. Soc. Philosophy, Psychology (exec. council 1974—77, Jr. award), Phi Kappa Phi, Omicron Delta Kappa, Phi Beta Kappa. Home: 2730 Chatham Farm Rd Winston Salem NC 27106-5824 Office: Wake Forest U Office of Pres Emeritus PO Box 7626 Winston Salem NC 27109 E-mail: tkh@wfu.edu.

HEARON, SHELBY, writer, educator; b. Marion, Ky., Mar. 18, 1931; d. Charles Boogher and Evelyn Shelby (Roberts) Reed; m. William Halpern, Aug. 19, 1995; children from previous marriage: Anne Rambo, Reed. BA, U. Tex., 1953. Disting. vis. prof. U. Ill., Chgo., 1993, Colgate U., 1993, U. Miami, Fla., 1994, U. Mass., Amherst, 1994-96, Middlebury Coll., 1996-98. Author: Armadillo in the Grass, 1968, The Second Dune, 1973, Hannah's House, 1975, Now and Another Time, 1976, A Prince of a Fellow, 1978, Painted Dresses, 1981, Afternoon of a Faun, 1983, Group Therapy, 1984, A Small Town, 1985, Five Hundred Scorpions, 1987, Owing Jolene, 1989, Hug Dancing, 1991, Life Estates, 1994, Footprints, 1996, Ella in Bloom, 2001, Year of the Dog, 2007; mem. editl. bd. The Writer Mag.; contbr. articles, short fiction and book revs. to various publs. Pres. Tex. Inst. Letters, 1980; chair lit. panel Tex. Commn. on Arts, 1980; mem. lit. panel N.Y. Coun. on Arts, 1985. Named to, Tex. Lit. Hall of Fame, 2004; recipient Syndication prize, NEA/PEN, 1984—85, 1985, 1987, 1988, Lit. award, Am. Acad. Arts and Letters, 1990, Lifetime Achievement award, Tex. Book Festival, 2003; fellow, Guggenheim, 1982, Nat. Endowment Arts, 1983; grantee, Ingram Merrill, 1987. Mem.: PEN, Associated Writing Programs, Tex. Inst. Letters (Fiction award 1973, 1978), Poets and Writers Inc., Authors Guild. Democrat. Presbyterian. Home: 246 S Union St Burlington VT 05401-4514

HEARST, GEORGE RANDOLPH, JR., publishing executive, real estate company executive; b. San Francisco, July 13, 1927; s. George and Blanche (Wilbur) Hearst; m. Mary Thompson, Apr. 23, 1951 (dec. Dec. 1969); children: Mary, George Randolph III, Stephen T., Erin; m. Patricia Ann Bell, Nov. 30, 1969 (div. Nov. 1985) Pvt. bus., 1946-48; staff LA Examiner, 1948-50, San Francisco Examiner, 1954-56; with LA Evening Herald-Express, from 1956, bus. mgr., 1957, pub., from 1960, LA Herald-Examiner, from 1962; grp. head Hearst Real Estate; v.p. Hearst Corp., 1977—, chmn., 1996—. Pres. Hearst Found.; dir. Randolph William Hearst Found. Served with USNR, 1945-46; with AUS, 1950-54. Named one of 400 Richest Ams., Forbes mag., 2006. Mem. VFW Clubs: Burlingame Country, Jonathan, Calif., Riviera. Office: Hearst Corp 1345 Sixth Ave New York NY 10105

HEARST, JOHN EUGENE, retired chemistry professor, consultant, researcher; b. Vienna, July 2, 1935; came to U.S., 1938; s. Alphonse Bernard and Lily (Roger) Hirsch; m. Jean Carolyn Bankson, Aug. 30, 1958; children: David Paul, Leslie Jean. BE, Yale U., New Haven, Conn., 1957; PhD, Calif. Inst. Tech., Pasadena, 1961; DSc (hon.), Lehigh U., Bethlehem, Pa., 1992. Postdoctoral rschr. Dartmouth Coll., Hanover, NH, 1961-62; prof. chemistry U. Calif., Berkeley, 1962-95, prof. emeritus, 1996—, Miller rsch. prof., 1970-71; founder, dir. HRI Rsch. Inc., 1978—; sr. rsch. scientist Lawrence Berkeley Lab., 1980-99, faculty chemist, 2000—, dir. divsn. chem. biodynamics, 1986-89; founder, sr. cons. Advanced Genetics Rsch., Inc., Oakland, Calif., 1981-84; founder, dir. Steritech Inc., Concord, Calif., 1992-96; founder, dir., v.p. new sci. opportunities Cerus Corp., Concord, 1992—2004, cons., 2005—06; sci. adv. bd. Oncologics, Inc., 2007—. Disting. lectr. Purdue U., 1986; Merck

Centennial lectr. Lehigh U., 1992, Robert A. Welch Found. lectr., 1992-93; adv. bd. Pharm. and Chem. Scis. Graduate Program Univ. of the Pacific, 2000—; cons. Codon, Inc., 1993-97; scientific adv. bd. Thomas McNerney & Ptnrs., 2003—; mem. governing bd. dirs. Leonardo Internat. Soc. Arts, Sci. and Tech., 2007-. Author: Contemporary Chemistry, 1976. editor: General Chemistry, 1974; exec. editor Nucleic Acids Rsch., 1990-93; inventor, patentee in field. Bd. dirs. U. No. Calif., 1993-95, dir. Disability Policy and Planning Inst., Berkeley, 2000-2002. Recipient Sci. Profl. Devel. award NSF, 1977-78, The Berkeley citation, 1999, Mortimer Bortin award for outstanding rsch. in bone marrow transplant, 2000, Tech Mus. Discover award, San Jose, 2001; John Simon Guggenheim fellow, 1968-69, European Molecular Orgn. sr. fellow, 1973-74. Fellow AAAS; mem. Am. Chem. Soc., Biophys. Soc., Am. Soc. Biol. Chemists, Am. Soc. for Photobiology (coun., pres. elect 1990-91, pres. 1991-92, Rsch. award 1994), Am. Phys. Soc. Home: 101 Southampton Ave Berkeley CA 94707-2036 Office: U Calif Dept Chemistry Berkeley CA 94720-1460 Office Phone: 510-407-4555. Business E-Mail: jehearst@berkeley.edu.

HEARST, WILLIAM RANDOLPH, III, lawyer, former newspaper publisher; b. Washington, June 18, 1949; s. William Randolph and Austine (McDonnell) Hearst; m. Margaret Kerr Crawford, Sept. 23, 1990; children: William, Adelaide, Caroline. AB, Harvard U., 1972. Reporter, asst. city editor San Francisco Examiner, 1972-76, publisher, 1984-96; editor Outside Mag., 1976-78; asst. mng. editor LA Herald Examiner, 1978-80; mgr. devel. Hearst Corp., 1980-82, dir., 1992—; v.p. Hearst Cable Comm. Divsn., 1982-84; dir. Hearst-Argyle TV; affiliated ptnr. Kleiner, Perkins, Caufield & Byers, Menlo Park, Calif., 1995—. Pres. William Randolph Hearst Found., 2003—; bd. dirs. Akimbo, Applied Minds, Juniper Networks, Oblix, OnFiber, RGB Networks. Bd. trustees Grace Cathedral, San Francisco, Carnegie Inst. Washington, Math. Scis. Rsch. Inst. Named one of 400 Richest Ams., Forbes mag., 2006. Fellow: AAAS; mem.: Calif. Acad. Scis. (bd. trustees). Office: Kleiner Perkins Caufield & Byers 2750 Sand Hill Rd Menlo Park CA 94025 Office Phone: 650-233-2750. Office Fax: 650-233-0300.

HEASLEY, THOMAS ALLEN, composer, musician; b. Columbus, Ohio, July 26, 1956; s. Allen Sutcliffe and Bette Lorraine Heasley; m. Martina Gail Brown, Jan. 7, 2001; 1 stepchild, Erik Robert Klinger. Student, Dana Sch. Music, Youngstown State U., 1974—78. Tchr. Calif. State Summer Sch. Arts, 2006—. Guest lectr. Mills Coll., Oakland, Calif., 1997, Calif. Inst. Arts, Valencia, 2000, Timara/Oberlin Conservatory, 2001, CalArts, 2005. Freelance tubist, Youngstown, Ohio, 1974—79, L.A., 1981—84, NYC, 1985—86, San Francisco Bay, 1988—2002, tubist Charlie Haden's Liberation Orch., LA, 1983—85, Cabrillo Music Festival, Santa Cruz, Calif., 2000, composer, performer, San Francisco, 1999—2003, LA, 2003—, Meet the Composer Concerts, San Francisco, NYC, 2003, composer, performer, prodr. (CD) Where the Earth Meets the Sky, 2001; prodr.: (CD) On the Sensations Tone, 2002, Desert Triptych, 2005; featured (interview) BBC Radio 3, London, 2004; composer: (BBC TV documentary) Tough Kids, Tough Love, 2005, Stock Exchange, 2006, Tuba Mirrors, Musical Painting; performer, composer, clinician: Internat. Tuba Euphonium Conf., 2006. Grantee Am. Composers Forum, San Francisco, 2003, LA, 2005; Artists fellow musical composition, Arts Coun. Silicon Valley, San Jose, 2002. Mem.: ASCAP (writer, pub. 2001—, award 2002—07), Am. Soc. Music Arrangers and Composers, Assn. Ind. Music Publishers, Nat. Assn. Rec. Arts and Scis., Musician's Union, Soc. Composers and Lyricists, Am. Composers Forum (Subito grant chpt. San Francisco Bay area 2003, Subito grant chpt.LA area 2005), Internat. Tuba Euphonium Assn. Democrat. Avocations: travel, tennis, golf. Office: Tom Heasley Full Bleed Music 9663 Santa Monica Blvd Ste 125 Beverly Hills CA 90210 Business E-Mail: tom@tomheasley.com.

HEATH, BERTHANN JONES, educational association administrator; b. Dallas, May 4, 1938; d. James Lafayette and Allie Mae (Hudson) Jones; m. John Willie Heath, Jr., July 14, 1963 (div. 1975); 1 child, John William, III. BS cum laude, Pepperdine U., 1959; MS, UCLA, 1960. Nat. cert. family and consumer scientist. Tchr., dept. chair L.A. Unified Sch. Dist., 1960—69, tchr. dist. resource, 1972—75; counselor L.A. H.S., 1968—72; regional supr., home econ. edn. Calif. State Dept. Edn., 1975—85; program mgr., sch.-to-career transition San Diego City Sch., 1985—2000; CEO Berthann's Enterprises, 2000—, cons. Trustee Consumer Credit Counselors of San Diego and Imperial Counties, Calif., 1986-2000; mem. adv. com. Calif. State Dept. Edn. Home Econs., Sacramento, 1985-98; mem. articulation team SDUSD and San Diego C.C.s, 1987-2000. Author, contbr. to curriculum guides, pamphlets and leaflets. V.p. San Diego chpt. The Links, Inc., 1995-97, corr. sec. Inglewood Pacific chpt., 2007—; presenter TV-8 Looks at Learning and Inside San Diego, 1985-95. Recipient Appreciation/Commendation award Calif. Dept. Edn., 1987, Nat. Gourmet Cook award Nat. Assembly, Links, Inc., 1996, Fin. Literacy Program Svc. award Consumer Credit Counselors of San Diego and Imperial Counties, 1996, Am. Assn. Family and Consumer Scis. Nat. Leader of Yr. award, 1998; named Woman of Distinction, Women, Inc., 1999. Mem. Am. Vocat. Assn. (bylaws chair family and consumer scis. edn. divsn. 1993-97), Nat. Assn. Local Suprs. of Family and Consumer Scis. (pres. 1992-93), Am. Vocat. Assn. (policy and planning com. 1991-97), Calif. Assn. Family and Consumer Scis. (San Diego chpt., chair secondary edn. 1985-95, state chair edn. com. 1989-90, ex-officio mem. articulation com. 1989-96), So. Calif. Biotech. Consortium (charter 1994-96), Links, Inc., Alpha Rho Tau, Delta Sigma Theta, Kappa Omicron Nu, Phi Delta Kappa. Avocations: food design and recipe experimentation, writing, elder care research and material development. Office: Berthann's Enterprises PO Box 10823 Marina Del Rey CA 90295

HEATH, CHARLES DICKINSON, lawyer, telecommunications industry executive; b. Waterloo, Iowa, June 28, 1941; s. George Clinton and Dorothy (Dickinson) Heath; m. Carilyn Frances Cain, June 3, 1972. BBA, U. Iowa, 1962, JD, 1966; MBA, U. Ariz., 1963. Bar: Iowa 1966, Pa. 1969, Ind. 1970, U.S. Supreme Ct. 1971, Wis. 1973, Ariz. 1975, Mich. 1979, Fla. 1979, Calif. 1989. Asst. gen. counsel Kohler Co., Wis., 1973-79; securities and tax counsel Kellogg Co., Battle Creek, Mich., 1979-81; assoc. gen. counsel Universal Telephone Inc., Milw., 1981-89, also corp. sec., 1987-89; atty. CenturyTel, Inc., LaCrosse, Wis., 1989—. E-mail: charlesheath@centurytel.com.

HEATH, DWIGHT BRALEY, anthropologist, educator; b. Hartford, Conn., Nov. 19, 1930; s. Percy Leonard and Luise (Hosp) H.; 1 child, David Braley (dec.). AB in Social Rels., Harvard U., 1952; PhD in Anthropology, Yale U., 1959. Mem. faculty Brown U., 1959—, prof. anthropology, 1970—. Dir. Ctr. for Latin Am. Studies, 1984-87, 88-89; vis. prof., U.S. and abroad, cons. in field. Author: A Journal of the Pilgrims at Plymouth, 1963, 86, Land Reform and Social Revolution in Bolivia, 1969, Historical Dictionary of Bolivia, 1972, Contemporary Cultures and Societies of Latin America, 1965, 74, 3d edit., 2002, Cross-Cultural Approaches to the Study of Alcohol, 1976, Alcohol Use and World Cultures, 1980, Cultural Factors in Alcohol Research and Treatment of Drinking Problems, 1981, International Handbook on Alcohol and Cultures, 1995, Drinking Occasions, 2000; contbr. articles to profl. jours. With AUS, 1952—54. Grantee Nat. Acad. Scis., 1974, Am. Philos. Soc., 1972, Social Sci. Research Council, 1958, Doherty Found., 1956-57, Nat. Inst. Alcohol Abuse and Alcoholism, 1976-81. Mem. AAAS, Am. Anthrop. Assn., Am. Ethnol. Soc., Am. Soc. Ethnohistory, Royal Anthrop. Inst., L.Am. Studies Assn. Office: Brown U Dept Anthropology PO Box 1921 Providence RI 02912-1921 Business E-Mail: Dwight_Heath@brown.edu.

HEATH, FRED MILTON, library director, educator; b. Dothan, Ala., Aug. 26, 1944; s. Fred Milton and Mary Glenn Marsh Heath; m. Carol Jean Benton, Aug. 6, 1966; children: Laura Elizabeth Heath Case, Joseph Benton. BA in History, Tulane U., 1966; MA in History, U. Va., 1968; MLS, Fla. State U., 1973; EdD in Edn. Adminstrn., Va. Tech., 1980. Commd. 2d lt. USAF, 1968, rose through ranks to capt., 1972; reference libr. U. Richmond, Va., 1973—74; pub. svcs. libr. Radford U., 1974—80; libr. dir. U. North Ala., Florence, 1980—87, Tex. Christian U., Ft. Worth, 1987—93; dean of librs. Tex. A&M U., College Station, 1993—2003; vice provost librs. U. Tex., Austin, 2003—. Interim dir. Network Ala. Acad. Librs., Montgomery, 1984—85; chair coun. libr. dirs. Assn. Higher Edn. North Tex., 1990—93; pres. Va. Libr. Assn., 1978—79; editor Libr. Adminstrn. and Mgmt. Assn. Jour. ALA, 1992—93; founding adv. bd. SPARC, 1999—2001. Co-editor: Libraries Act on Their Libqual and Findings, 2004; mem. editl. bd. Tex. A&M U. Press., 1993—2003, mem. editl. adv. bd. Libr. Quar., 2003—. Grantee Fund for Improvement of Postsecondary Edn., 2000, NSF, 2001, Telecomm. and Informatics Task Force, Tex., 2002. Mem.: Tex. Coun. State Univ. Librs. (pres. 1998—2000), Greater Midwest Libr. Consortium (pres. 1998—99), Assn. Rsch. Librs. (pres. 2002—03). Avocations: golf, kayaking, running, photography. Home: 5909 Tom Wooten Dr Austin TX 78731 Office: U Tex at Austin Mail Stop 5400 Austin TX 78713 Office Phone: 512-495-4350. E-mail: fheath@austin.utexas.edu.*

HEATH, GARY BRIAN, manufacturing executive, engineer; b. Pueblo, Colo., Nov. 5, 1954; s. William Sidney Heath and Eleanor Aileen (Mortimer) Svedman, Donald Svedman (Stepfather); m. Denise Heath. BSME, U. So. Colo., 1979; MBA, U. Phoenix, 1984. Engr. ADR Ultrasound Corp., Tempe, Ariz., 1979-81; sr. engr. Technicare Ultrasound, Englewood, Colo., 1981-83; engring. mgr. COBE Labs., Inc., Lakewood, Colo., 1983-89; dir. mfg. Gambro BCT, Inc., Lakewood, 1989-96, v.p. mfg., 1996-2000, chief operating officer, 2000—. Mem.: Soc Plastic Engrs, Soc Mfg Engrs. Achievements include patents for fluid flow transfer device, pressure diaphragm for fluid flow device. Avocations: skiing, fishing, reading, weightlifting. Office: Gambro BCT Inc 10811 W Collins Ave Lakewood CO 80215-4409 Home: 18 Prairie Clover Littleton CO 80127-2231 Office Phone: 303-231-4337. Business E-Mail: gary.heath@gambrobct.com.

HEATH, GEORGE ROSS, oceanographer; b. Adelaide, Australia, Mar. 10, 1939; s. Frederick John and Eleanora (Blackmore) H.; m. Lorna Margaret Sommerville, Oct. 5, 1972; children: Amanda Jo, Alisa Jeanne. BSc, Adelaide U., 1960, BSc with honors, 1961; PhD, U. Calif., 1968. Geologist S. Australian Geol. Survey, Adelaide, 1961-63; asst. prof. oceanography Oreg. State U., Corvallis, 1969-72, assoc. prof., 1972-75, prof., dean, 1978-84; assoc. prof. oceanography U. R.I., Narragansett, 1974-77, prof., 1977-78; dean U. Wash., Seattle, 1984-96, prof., 1984—2006, prof. emeritus, 2006—, dean emeritus, 1996—, chair, faculty senate, 2004—05; pres., exec. dir. Monterey Bay Aquarium Rsch. Inst., Moss Landing, Calif., 1996-97. Co-chmn. exec. com. oceans and atmosphere Nat. Assn. State Univs. and Land Grant Colls., 1992-93; chmn. legis. com. Commn. on Food, Environment and Renewable Resources, 1994-96; chmn. bd. ocean sci. and policy NRC, 1984-85; bd. govs. Joint Oceanographic Instns., Inc., 1978-96, chmn., 1982-84; v.p. sci. com. on oceanic rsch. of Internat. Coun. of Sci. Unions, 1984-90; chmn. performance assessment peer rev. panel Waste Isolation Pilot Plant, 1987-98; bd. dirs. Monterey Bay Aquarium Rsch. Inst.1987-; found. com. Coll. Marine Sci. and Fisheries, Sultan Qaboos U., Muscat, Sultanate of Oman, 1994—; adv. panel Odyssey, 1990-2001, bd. govs., 1999-2000; environ. analyst Sta. KIRO-TV, Seattle, 1993; bd. govs. Consortium for Oceanographic Rsch. & Edn., 1994-98, chmn., 1996-98; bd. govs. Seattle Aquarium Soc., 1998—; mem. Nat. Sea Grant rev. panel, 2001—, vice chmn., 2006—. Contbr. articles to profl. jours. Recipient Fulbright award, 1963, medal Seattle Aquarium Soc., 2006. Fellow AAAS, Geol. Soc. Am., Am. Geophys. Union; mem. Oceanography Soc. Home: 12513 237th Way NE Redmond WA 98053 Office: U Wash Sch Oceanography PO Box 357940 Seattle WA 98195-7940 Home Phone: 425-898-7388; Office Phone: 206-543-3153. Business E-Mail: rheath@u.washington.edu.

HEATH, JAMES R., chemistry educator; BSc, Baylor U., 1984; PhD in Chemistry, Rice U., 1988. Mem. technical staff IBM Watson Labs, Yorktown Heights, NY, 1991—94; with UCLA, 1994—, asst. prof. dept. chemistry, 1994—96, tenure prof., 1996, prof. molecular & med. pharmacology, 1997—; Elizabeth W. Gilloon prof. chemistry Calif. Inst. Tech., 2004—; dir. Nat. Ctr. Inst. NSB Cancer Ctr. Founder Calif. Nanosystems Inst., 2000, dir., 2000—03; co-dir., bd. dir. Crump Inst. for Molecular Imaging, 2003—. Contbr. articles to profl. jours. Miller Fellow, Univ. Calif. Berkeley, 1988-91, Packard fellow David and Lucile Packard Found., 1994-99, Alfred P. Sloan Fellow, 1997. Achievements include being the principal student involved in the Nobel Prize winning discovery of C60 and the fullerenes; being the co-creator of world's densest memory circuit in 2007. Office: Nanosystem Biology Cancer Ctr Caltech Chemistry 127-72 1200 E California Blvd Pasadena CA 91125 Office Phone: 310-825-2836. Office Fax: 626-395-2355. Business E-Mail: heath@caltech.edu.*

HEATH, JAYNE MARIE, music educator; b. Denver, Feb. 23, 1955; d. Harold Edward and Alice Clara Walker; m. William B. Heath, Aug. 28, 1976; children: James, Jared, Jessica. B.Mus.Edn., U. No. Colo., 1976, MA, 1980. Lic. tchr. Colo. Music tchr. Cherry Creek Sch. Dist., Centennial, Colo., 1976—; mus. dir. Stage Eleven, Centennial, 1984—96, Young Actors Theatre, Centennial, 1996—. Mem.: Music Educators Nat. Conf. Avocations: softball, reading, gardening, scrapbooks. Office: Walnut Hills Elementary Sch 8195 E Costilla Blvd Centennial CO 80112

HEATH, JOHN ROBERT, music educator; b. Aurora, Ill., Dec. 16, 1951; s. John Martin and Patricia Colleen Heath. B in Mus. Edn., U. Ill., 1975, M in Mus. Edn., 1977, B in Tuba Performance, 1986. Dir. of bands Highland H.S., Ill., 1977—89, Batavia H.S., Ill., 1990—. Condr. Blue Lake Fine Arts Camp, Twin Lake, Mich., 1995—2005; music adv. bd. U. Ill., Urbana-Champaign, 2003—. Condr. Highland Mcpl. Band, Ill., 1982—89, Aurora Summer Concert Band, Ill., 1992—2005. Recipient Chicagoland Outstanding Music Educator award, Quinlan and Fabish Music Co., 1998, Those Who Excel Tchg. award, Ill. State Bd. Edn., 1984, Supt.'s award for tchg. excellence, Kane County Regional Supt. of Edn., 2004. Mem.: Ill. Music Educators Assn. (v.p. band divsn. 1999—2005), Music Educators Nat. Conf., Am. Sch. Band Dirs. Assn., Nat. Band Assn. (Citation of Excellence 1999, 2000). Achievements include guest condr. for band festivals and honor bands throughout the state of Ill; mem. St. Louis Philharmonic Orch., 1981-89. Avocations: collecting books, artwork, Boston terrier. Office Phone: 630-879-4600.

HEATH, JOSEPH NOUNNAN, retired literature and language educator, writer; b. San Francisco, May 23, 1926; s. Alfred Joseph Heath and Charlotte Amelia Hendriksen; m. Virginia Marie Grampp, Dec. 16, 1961. BA, San Francisco State Coll., 1950; MS, Old Dominion U., 1976; EdS, Nova U., 1979. Elem. tchr. San Francisco Unified Sch. Dist, 1951—54, San Rafael Sch. Dist., 1954—58; adminstr. 3R Schs., San Rafael, Calif., 1958—73, Santa Rosa, Calif., 1968—73, San Leandro, Calif., 1968—73, Delta 3R, Santa Rosa, 1979—82, Hayward Christian, 1982—83, Highland Christian, San Bruno, Calif., 1983—85; lang. arts tchr. Virginia Beach Sch. Dist., Va., 1974—76; English and journalism tchr. Glendale Ariz. Sch. Dist., 1976—79; ret., 1985. Author: 5 Self-Instructional books in Elem. Lang. Arts and Sci., 3R Approach to Phonetics, 1962, Phonetic Lessons, 1978, The How & Why of Phonetics, 1995, Sanctuary From Greed, 2001; pub.: Agape Love Messenger, 1985—2001. Seaman 1st class USNR, 1944—46. Republican.

HEATH, JOSEPHINE WARD, foundation administrator; b. San Jose, Calif., Sept. 5, 1937; d. James Hugh and Adella Ward; m. Stratton Rollins Heath Jr.; children: Stratton, Kristin Heath-Colon, Joel. BS, Ea. Oreg. State U., 1959; MS, U. Wis., 1960. Commr. Boulder County, Colo., 1982-90; tchg. fellow John F. Kennedy Sch. of Govt., Harvard U., Cambridge, Mass., 1991; spl. asst. to the dir. White Ho. Office of Nat. Svc., Washington, 1993; pres. Jurismonitor, Boulder, 1993-95; tchr., project liberty John F. Kennedy Sch. Govt., Harvard U., Cambridge, 1994-98; pres. The Cmty. Found., Boulder, 1995—. Tchr. Bad Kreuznach, Germany, 1966-67, El Paso, Tex., 1963-64, Appleton, Wis., 1961-62; regional dir. ACTION, Denver, 1977-79. Editor: Alternative Work Patterns, 1977. Candidate US Senate, Colo., 1992, 1990; commr. Met. Baseball Stadium Dist., Maj. League Colo. Rockies, 1991—; county commr. Boulder County, 1982-90; co-founder Women's Found. of Colo., 1987; trainer for elected offcls. in Ctrl. Europe, 1994-98; mem. internat. com. Coun. on Founds. Named to Colo. Women's Hall of Fame, 2000; recipient William Funk award for Statewide Cmty. Leadership, Colo. Assn. Non Profits, 2004. Mem. Internat. Women's Forum (bd. dirs. 1986-89), Women's Forum of Colo. (pres. 1991), Internat. Com. Coun. on Founds. Democrat. Avocations: skiing, hiking, sports. Home: 2455 Vassar Dr Boulder CO 80305-5728 Office: The Cmty Found 1123 Spruce St Boulder CO 80302-4001 Office Phone: 303-442-0436. Personal E-mail: JosieHeath@aol.com.

HEATH, KAREN, secondary school educator; b. Buffalo, June 18, 1961; d. Richard Eddy and Beth Montgomery Heath; m. Christopher Almy Howe; children: Ian, Sarah, Lucas. BA, Middlebury Coll., 1983; MEd, U. Vt., 1993. Cert. elem. edn. tchr., secondary edn. tchr. Tutor Ind. Learning Sch., Berkeley, Calif., 1983—84, tchr. City Roots Alternative H.S., South Boston, Mass., 1984—85, adminstrv. tchr., 1985—86; counselor, head sch. devel. Maplehill Sch., Plainfield, Vt., 1986—88, edn. dir., 1989—90, 1992—93, English tchr., 1993—99; lang. arts tchr. Barret (Vt.) City Sch., 1999—. Cons. Vt. Dept. Edn., Montpelier, 1991—92; bd. dirs. Vt. Children's Forum, Montpelier, 1990—92. Alumni interviewer Middlebury Coll., 1992—; booster pres. North Stars Gymnastics, Berien, Vt., 2003—. Named Tchr. of Yr., Vt. Dept. Edn., 2005. Mem.: Vt. NEA. Avocation: outdoor activities. Home: 280 Cutler Corner Rd Barre VT 05641 Office: Barre City Sch 50 Parkside Terr Barre VT 05641 E-mail: heathnhovue@aol.com.*

HEATH, MARIWYN DWYER, writer, legislative staff member; b. Chgo., May 1, 1935; d. Thomas Leo and Winifred (Brennan) Dwyer; m. Eugene R. Heath, Sept. 3, 1956; chilren: Philip Clayton, Jeffrey Thomas. BJ, U. Mo., 1956. Mng. editor Chemung Valley Reporter, Horseheads, N.Y., 1956-57; freelance writer, platform spkr., editor Tech. Transls., Dayton, Ohio, 1966—. Cons. Internat. Women's Commn., 1975-76; ERA coord. Nat. Fedn. Bus. and Profl. Women's Clubs, 1974-82, 92—; polit. and mgmt. coms. ERAmerica, 1976-82, exec. dir., 1982-88; pres. Miami Valley Regional Transit Authority, 1986-88; chair Regional Transit Coalition, 1991-94. Author: 75 Years and Beyond-BPW/USA, 1994. Active Gov. Ohio Task Force Credit for Women, 1973, Ohio Womens Commn., 1990-98, vice-chair, 1993-96, chair, 1996-98; midwest regional adv. com. SBA, 1976-82; task force Women Ohio Bicentennial Commn., 1999—; pres. Dayton Pres. Club, 1973-74; chmn. Ohio Coalition ERA Implementation, 1974-75; appt. joint civilian orientation conf. U.S. Dept. Def., 1988. Recipient Legion of Honor award Dayton Pres. Club, 1987, Keeper of Flame award Ohio Sec. of State, 1990; named one of 10 Outstanding Women of World Soroptimist Internat., 1982; named to Ohio Womens Hall of Fame. Mem. AAUW (dir. Dayton 1965-72, Woman of Yr. award Dayton 1974), Nat. Fedn. Bus. and Profl. Womens Clubs (pres. Dayton 1967-69, Ohio 1976-77, nat. polit. action com. 1985-98, chmn. 1988-98), Miami Valley Mil. Affairs Assn. (bd. dirs.), Ohio Women (v.p. 1983-86, bd. dirs. 1977-89), Assn. Women Execs., Women in Comm. Republican. Roman Catholic. Home: 145 Huffman Ave Dayton OH 45403-1915

HEATH, MATTHEW W., engineer; b. Rockland, Maine, May 22, 1972; s. Reginald F. and Constance L. Heath; m. Dena S. Sage, Apr. 22, 2006. BS, Worcester Poly. Inst., Mass., 1994; MS, Carnegie Mellon U., Pitts., 1996; PhD, U. Mass., Amherst, 2004. Sr. design engr. Intel Corp., Hillsboro, Oreg., 1997—. Mem.: IEEE (assoc.). Achievements include research in deterministic design of globally asynchronous locally synchronous systems. Avocations: hiking, travel. Office: Intel Corp 2111 NE 25th Ave Hillsboro OR 97124 Home Phone: 503-681-7681; Office Phone: 503-712-2977. Personal E-mail: matthew.heath@ieee.org.

HEATH, PATTI, art educator, musician; b. Syracuse, NY, Nov. 10, 1956; d. Maryann Clark; m. Steven Heath; 1 child, Sarah. MusB cum laude, Hartt Sch., Hartford, Conn., 1974—78; MusM, Manhattan Sch. Music, NYC, 1978—79. Prin. clarinet Festival of the Americas, San Jose, Costa Rica, 1984, Palm Beach Opera, West Palm Beach, 1984—93, Palm Beach Symphony, West Palm Beach, 1984—93; techg. artist Young Audiences of South Fla., West Palm Beach, 1990—93; tchg. artist Syracuse Inst. Aesthetic Edn., 1995—; artist in residence Blodgett Sch., Syracuse, 2002—05; instrumental music/visual arts tchr. St. James Sch., Syracuse, NY, 2004—, dir. after sch. programs, 2005—. Recipient Applied Music award for Outstanding Musical Achievement, Hartt Sch., 1978. Mem.: Americans for the Arts. Avocations: travel, building traditional folk instruments. Home Phone: 315-488-4953.

HEATH, RALPH D., aerospace transportation executive; BSEE, Univ. Tenn., Knoxville; MBA, Univ. tenn., Knoxville. Engring. & mgmt. positions Lockheed Martin Corp., Bethesda, Md., 1975—, v.p. bus. develop. tactical aircraft sys., 1996—99, COO aeronautics, 1999—2002, exec. v.p. & gen. mgr. F/A-22 Raptor prog, 2002—04, exec. v.p. aeronautics, 2005—. Mem. adv. council Univ. Tenn. Coll. Bus. Adminstrn.; mem. internat. bd. vis. Tex. Christian Univ. Neeley Sch. Bus. Combat engring. officer, Airborne Ranger US Army, 1971—75. Office: Lockheed Martin Corp 6801 Rockledge Dr Bethesda MD 20817*

HEATH, RICHARD EDDY, lawyer; b. NJ, Nov. 15, 1930; s. W. Eddy and Dorothy (Brown) H.; m. Beth M., June 17, 1955; children: Ellen Louise, David Montgomery, Karen Elizabeth, Deborah Anne. BA cum laude, Swarthmore Coll., Pa., 1952; LLB cum laude, Harvard U., Cambridge, Mass., 1955. Bar: NY, Fla. Tchg. fellow Harvard Law Sch., Cambridge, Mass., 1955—56; assoc. Hodgson and Russ, Buffalo, 1956—61, ptnr., 1961—. Trustee Children's Hosp., Buffalo, 1975-98; trustee U. at Buffalo Found., 1966-89, sec., 1976—. Recipient Walter P. Cooke award U. Buffalo, 1978. Office Phone: 716-856-4000.

HEATH, RICHARD RAYMOND, retired investment company executive; b. La Junta, Colo., June 22, 1929; s. Perry Stanford and Genevieve Anabelle (Whitney) H.; m. Arlene Newbrow, Nov. 3, 1961. BA in Econs., U. Colo., 1951, LLB, 1954. Bar: Colo. 1954, Calif. 1957, Ark. 1973. Mem. firm Neyhart & Grodin, San Francisco, 1957-66; dep. Peace Corps dir. Ivory Coast, 1966-68; dir., 1968-69; Peace Corps dir. Mali, 1969-72; dir. Ark. Dept. Fin. and Adminstrn.; also chief fiscal officer, commr. revenues State of Ark., mem. gov.'s cabinet, 1972-77; dir. San Francisco Internat. Airport, 1977-81; v.p., dir. mktg. AIS, Inc., 1981-84; exec. v.p., CFO United Bank, San Francisco, 1984-85; chmn., CEO Nat. Bus. Resources Inc., 1985-87; ptnr. Hakman & Co., Investment Bankers, 1987-2000; chmn., CEO Podarok Internat., Inc., 1993-96; chmn., pres. Heath Mgmt. Svcs., 1994-2000; chmn. Laser Design Internat., LLC, 1996—. Chmn., CEO 1st Calif. Bus. and Indsl. Devel. Corp., United Bus. Ventures; bd. dirs. V-Ray Imaging, Inc.; vice chmn. Multi-State Tax Commn., 1973-74, chmn., 1976-77, mem. exec. com., 1974-77; del. Conf. State Bar Dels. Bd. dirs., treas. San Francisco Midsummer Mozart Festival, 1986-92, chmn., 1999-2000; mem. nat. bd. dirs. Coalition for a Dem. Majority, 1973-76;

chmn. bd. dirs. FORUM; mem. conservative caucus nat. Tax Limitation Com., 1980—; mem. rep. presdl. task force Rep. nat. Com., 1980-91. Mem. State Bar Calif., San Francisco Bar Assn. (past chmn. indsl. accident com.), San Francisco Lawyers Club, Am., Calif. trial lawyers assns., San Francisco Planning and Urban Renewal Assn., Nat. Parks Assn., Calif. Applicants Attys. Assn. (v.p.) Clubs: Little Rock Racquet, Little Rock Athletic, San Francisco Tennis (gov.), Rotary Internat., World Trade. Home: 1904 21st Ave E Seattle WA 98112-2906 Personal E-mail: dickheath@aol.com.

HEATH, ROBERT F., lawyer; BA, Harvard U., 1969; JD, Georgetown U., 1975, MBA, 1982. Atty. Davison & Easton, Stowe, Vt.; various sr. legal positions U.S. Dept. Transp.; sr. counsel RCA Comm., 1981—84, GE Am. Com., 1984—88; assoc. gen. counsel GE Medical Systems, Milw., 1988—97; sr. v.p., gen. counsel Omnicare, 1997; gen. counsel Briggs & Stratton Corp., Milw., 1997—, asst. sec., v.p., 2001—, sec., 2002—. Office: Briggs & Stratton Corp 12301 W Wirth St PO Box 702 Wauwatosa WI 53222 Office Phone: 414-259-5333. Office Fax: 414-259-5773.*

HEATH, ROSS BRADLEY, consulting company executive; b. Geneva, Ill., June 26, 1959; s. Donald Jeremiah Heath and Louise Zalithea H. BA in English, Augustana Coll., 1982; MS in Tech. Mgmt., U. Md., 1996. Program mgr. performance engring. Getronics (formerly J.G. Van Dyke & Assocs.), Alexandria, Va., 1992-2000; cons. network architect EDS, Washington, 2001—04; network engr. Northrop Grumman, Washington, 2004—. Mem. City of Alexandria Commn. on Aging, 1989-92; master of ceremonies Annual Lighting of Nat. Christmas Tree, Ellipse, Washington, 1999. Grantee Andrew Mellon Found., 1979; recipient award of Merit City of Alexandria Commn. on Aging, 1993, Cert. of Recognition City of Alexandria, 1993, U.S. Dept. State, 2003, 2005. Mem. Toastmasters (pres. 1998-99, Schweitzer award 1998, Toastmaster of Yr. 1998-99). Avocation: composing music.

HEATHCOCK, CLAYTON HOWELL, chemistry educator, researcher; b. San Antonio, July 21, 1936; s. Clayton H. and Frances E. (Lay) H.; m. Mabel Ruth Sims, Sept. 6, 1957 (div. 1972); children: Cheryl Lynn, Barbara Sue, Steven Wayne, Rebecca Ann; m. Cheri R. Hadley, Nov. 28, 1980. BSc, Abilene Christian Coll., Tex., 1958; PhD, U. Colo., 1963. Supr. chem. analysis group Champion Paper and Fiber Co., Pasadena, Tex., 1958-60; asst. prof. chemistry U. Calif.-Berkeley, 1964-70, assoc. prof., 1970-75, prof., 1975—, Gilbert Newton Lewis prof., 2003—05, chmn., 1986-89, dean Coll. of Chemistry, 1999—2005; chief scientist Berkeley QB3 Calif. Inst. Quantitative Biosciences, 2005—. Chmn. Medicinal Chemistry Study Sect., NIH, Washington, 1981-83; mem. sci. adv. coun. Abbott Labs., 1986-97. Author: Introduction to Organic Chemistry, 1976; editor-in chief Organic Syntheses, 1985-86, Jour. Organic Chemistry, 1989-99; contbr. numerous articles to profl. jours. Recipient Alexander von Humboldt U.S. Scientist, 1978, Allan R. Day award, 1989, Prelog medal, 1991, Centenary medal Royal Soc. Chemistry, 1995. Mem. AAAS, Am. Acad. Arts and Scis., Am. Chem. Soc. (chmn. divsn. organic chemistry 1985, Ernest Guenther award 1986, award for creative work in synthetic organic chemistry 1990, A.C. Cope scholar 1990, H.C. Brown medal 2002, Paul Gassman award 2004), Nat. Acad. Scis., Royal Soc. Chemistry (Centenary medal 1995), Am. Soc. Pharmacology. Home: 5235 Alhambra Valley Rd Martinez CA 94553-9765 Office: U Calif GB3 Institute 3320 Berkeley CA 94720 Office Phone: 510-666-3316. Business E-Mail: heathcock@berkeley.edu.

HEATHERLEY, JAMES LAWRENCE, psychotherapist, educator; b. Ft. Worth, Nov. 21, 1946; s. Gordon Inez and Katherine Elizabeth (Eddins) H.; m. Elinor Parent, June 1968 (div. July 1974); 1 child, Charlotte Kelly; m. Melody Ann Jones, July 21, 1982. AAS, Tarrant County Jr. Coll., Ft. Worth, 1972; student, North Lake C.C., Irving, Tex., 1988, U. Tex., Arlington, 1972-89, Parker Coll. Chiropractic, Dallas, 1989; BA, Amber U., Garland, Tex., 1997, MA, 1999; PhD, Honolulu U., 1999. Registered radiol. technologist. Paramedic Ray Crowder, Ft. Worth and Detroit, 1968-76; instr., tutor radiation physics and tech. Parker Coll. Chiropractic and Southwestern Med. Sch., Dallas, 1989; merchandiser Walt Disney World, Buena Vista, Fla., 1990; real estate broker Ft. Worth and Orlando, Fla., 1986-93; spl. tutor St. John's Sch., Ennis, Tex., 1998; tchr. Mesquite (Tex.) Ind. Sch. Dist., 1998—, Ferris (Tex.) Ind. Sch. Dist., 1998—; fed. mediator All About Taxes, Ferris, 1993—. Radiol. technologist multiple hosps., clinics, physician's offices, Arlington, Tex., Bryan, Tex., Dallas, Ft. Worth, Kissimmee, Fla., Orlando, St. Cloud, Fla., 1972-92; adj. prof. psychology Richland Coll., Dallas, 1999—, counseling intern, 1999—. Contbr. poetry to profl. jours. Pres. Rolling Meadows Cmty. Civic Action League, Arlington, 1969-74. With USN, 1968. Recipient Am. Poet's award, 1998. Mem. ACA, Tarrant County Soc. Radiol. Technologists (sec. pro-tem 1974), Nat. Assn. Student Nurses, Tex. Assn. Student Nurses, Am. Chiropractic Assn., Mason, Scottish Rite (med. officer 1987—, Golden Trowel award 1989), York Rite (knighthood 1987—), DeMolays, Order Eastern Star. Avocations: art, music, research, outdoors, history.

HEATLEY, DANY, professional hockey player; b. Freibourg, Germany, Jan. 21, 1981; Right wing Atlanta Thrashers, 2001—05, Ottawa Senators, 2005—. Mem. Team Canada, World Cup of Hockey, 2004, Team Can., Olympic Games, Torino, Italy, 2006; player NHL YoungStars Game, 2002, NHL All-Star Game, 2003. Named to All-Rookie Team, NHL, 2002, Second All-Star Team, 2006, First All-Star Team, 2007; recipient Calder Meml. Trophy, 2002, MVP, NHL All-Star game, 2003. Achievements include being a member of World Cup Champion Team Canada, 2004. Office: Ottawa Senators Scotiabank Place 1000 Palladium Dr Kanata ON K2V 1A5 Canada*

HEATLEY, GREGG ALAN, ophthalmologist; s. Truman Beier and Elaine Moderow Heatley. BS, U. Wis., Madison, 1982, MD, 1987. Diplomate Am. Bd. Ophthalmology, 1992. Assoc. prof., vice chair, dept. ophthalmology U. Wis., Madison, 1997—. Office: Univ Wis 2870 University Ave Ste 206 Madison WI 53705 Office Phone: 608-263-1481.

HEATON, CHARLES LLOYD, dermatologist, educator; b. Bryan, Tex., May 8, 1935; BS, Tex. A&M U., 1957; MD, Baylor U., 1961; MA (hon.), U. Pa., 1973. Diplomate Am. Bd. Dermatology. Intern Jefferson Davis Hosp., Houston, 1961-62; resident Baylor U., 1962-65; sr. attending physician Phila. Gen. Hosp., 1965-69, chief of svc., 1970-77; mem. dept. dermatology U. Pa. Sch. Medicine, 1966-78; assoc. prof. dermatology U. Pa., 1973-78, U. Cin., 1978-85, prof., 1985—, interim dir. dept. dermatology, 1998. Author: Audiovisual Course in Venereal Disease, 1972, (with D.M. Pillsbury) Manual of Dermatology, 1980; contbr. 35 articles to profl. jours., 12 chpts. to books. Served to lt. comdr. USPHS, 1965-67. Named Ohio Dermatologist of Yr., 2000. Fellow ACP, AAD, Coll. Physicians of Phila.; mem. AMA, Soc. Investigative Dermatology, Am. Venereal Disease Assn., Am. Dermatol. Assn., Cin. Dermatol. Soc., Alpha Omega Alpha Home: 5534 E Galbraith Rd Apt 25 Cincinnati OH 45236-2840 Office: U Cin Coll Coll Medicine Dept Dermatology 231 Albert Sabin Way Cincinnati OH 45229-2827 Office Phone: 513-584-6060. Business E-Mail: charles.heaton@uc.edu.

HEATON, ERIC, investment banker; b. Cortland Manor, NY, 1968; 1 child. Grad., Dartmouth Coll., 1989. With Merrill Lynch & Co., NYC, 1989—, sr. v.p., mng. dir. Americas Fin. Institutions group. Named one of 40 Under 40, Investment Dealers' Digest, 2006, Crain's NY Bus., 2007. Office: Merrill Lynch & Co Inc 4 World Fin Ctr 250 Vesey St New York NY 10080 Office Phone: 212-449-1000.

HEATON, HAROLD IRVING, JR., research scientist, consultant; b. Fitchburg, Mass., July 18, 1946; s. Harold Irving and Olive Eldora Heaton; m. Rebecca Ann Cummings, Aug. 8, 1976; children: Jennifer Renee Palazzo, Megan Emily Shapero, Laura Kathleen. BA, U. Mass., Amherst, 1968, MS, 1970, PhD, 1974. Sr. scientist EG&G, Inc., Los Alamos, N.Mex., 1975—77; prin. staff scientist Johns Hopkins U. APL, Laurel, Md., 1977—, program area mgr., 1983—88, mgr. departmental programs, 1989—94, dir. environ. scis. internal R&D program, 1994—97, program mgr., 2000—03, sys. and tech. evaluator, 2004—; Merle A. Tuve fellow Space Telescope Sci. Inst., Balt., 1998—99. Author: A Montage of Ancient Histories (hon. mention Judy A. Seydoux award, 1973); contbr. articles to profl. jours; mem. editl. bd. APL Tech. Digest, 1994—98, guest editor, 1993. Decorated Coin of Excellence Asst. Sec. of the Army; grantee, FAA, 2000—01; Stuart A. Janney fellow, Johns Hopkins U. APL, 2005. Mem.: IEEE Lasers and Electrooptics Soc. (chpt. chmn. and vice-chmn. Washington/No. Va. chpt. 1993—97, Chpt. Leadership award 1998), Am. Astron. Soc., Optical Soc. Am. Avocations: travel, gardening, coin collecting/numismatics, sports. Home: 28437 Honeysuckle Dr Damascus MD 20872 Office: Johns Hopkins U APL 11100 Johns Hopkins Rd Laurel MD 20723 Home Phone: 301-253-5246; Office Phone: 240-228-5025. Office Fax: 240-228-1868. Business E-Mail: harold.heaton@jhuapl.edu.

HEATON, PATRICIA, actress; b. Bay Village, Ohio, Mar. 4, 1958; d. Chuck and Pat Heaton; m. David Hunt Oct. 10, 1990; children: Sam, John Basil, Joseph Charles, Daniel Patrick. BA in Theater, Ohio State U., 1980. Spokesperson Albertsons, Inc. supermarkets. Actor (stage) The Johnstown Vindicator, 1987, Don't Get God Started, 1987-88, Miracle in the Woods, 1997, The Scene, 2006; (TV series) Room for Two, 1992-93, Someone Like Me, 1994, Women of the House, 1995, Everybody Loves Raymond, 1996—2005 (Best Actress in Quality Comedy Viewers for Quality TV award 1998, Outstanding Lead Actress in Comedy Series Emmy award, 2000 and 2001); (TV films) Shattered Dreams: The Charlotte Fedders Story, 1990, Miracle in the Woods, 1997, A Town Without Christmas, 2001, The Goodbye Girl, 2004, The Engagement Ring, 2005 (also exec. prodr.), Untitled Patricia Heaton Project, 2006 (also exec. prodr.), The Path to 9/11, 2006, (films) Beethoven, 1992, Memoirs of an Invisible Man, 1992, The New Age, 1994, Space Jam, 1996; TV appearances include Alien Nation, 1989, Thirtysomething, 1989-91, Matlock, 1990, DEA, 1991, Party of Five, 1996, The King of Queens, 1999, (voice) Danny Phantom, 2004; prodr. (films) The Bituminous Coal Queens of Pennsylvania, 2005, Amazing Grace, 2006; author (book): Motherhood and Hollywood, 2003. Hon. chairperson Feminists for Life. Mem.: Delta Gamma. Office: United Talent Agency 9560 Wilshire Blvd Ste 500 Beverly Hills CA 90212*

HEATON, RODGER A., prosecutor; b. July 20, 1959; Attended, U. Ill.; JD, Ind. U., 1985. Prosecutor US Atty.'s Office, Springfield, Ill., 1990—2000, chief, civil divsn., 2003—05; litig. ptnr. Kirkland & Ellis LLP, Chgo., 2001—03; US atty. (ctrl. dist.) Ill. US Dept. Justice, Springfield, Ill., 2006—. Former adj. prof. U. Ill. Coll. Law. Recipient Dir.'s award, Exec. Office of US Atty., 1998. Office: US Attys Office 318 S 6th St Springfield IL 62701*

HEATON, ROGER LAURENCE, lawyer; b. Rockville Centre, NY, Sept. 18, 1949; s. Gordon W. and Anne (Davis) H.; m. Susan J. W. Heaton, May 20, 1983; children: W. Bradford, Randall A. Student, Wesleyan U., 1967-68; BS, Denison U., 1971; JD, U. San Diego, 1981. Bar: Calif. 1982, U.S. Dist. Ct. N.D. 1982, U.S. Dist. Ct. (no. dist.) Tex. 1982, U.S. Dist. Ct. S.D. 1983, U.S. Dist. Ct. (so. dist.) Calif. 1983, U.S. Dist. Ct. Hawaii 1983. Assoc. Ungerman, Hill et al, Dallas, 1982-83, Shigemura and Ching, Honolulu, 1983, McInnis, Fitzgerald et al, San Diego, 1983-87; ptnr. Gilson and Heaton, San Diego, 1987—. Instr. in legal research and writing U. San Diego , 1981-82. Mem. ABA, Calif. Bar Assn., So. Calif. Def. Counsel Assn., San Diego Bar Assn., San Diego Def. Counsel Assn. Avocations: athletics, family activities. Office: Gilson and Heaton 401 West A St Suite 1300 San Diego CA 92131*

HEATON, STUART ALAN, lawyer; b. Orange, Calif., Mar. 28, 1956; m. Carolyn T. Heaton. BA, Calif. State U., Fullerton, 1979; JD, UCLA, 1982; MBA, Vanderbilt U., 1991. Bar: Fla. 1982, Tenn. 1989. Atty. Preddy, Kutner, Rubinoff, Brown & Thompson, Dixon, Dixon, Hurst & Nicklaus, Miami; v.p., gen. counsel Thomas Nelson Inc., 1989—96; asst. gen. counsel Lockheed Martin Corp., 1997—2002; v.p., gen. counsel, corp. sec. CarMax Inc., Glen Allen, Va., 2002—. Mem.: Assn. of Corp. Counsel, Richmond Bar Assn., Va. Bar Assn., Tenn. Bar Assn., Fla. Bar Assn., ABA. Office: Carmax 12800 Tuckahoe Creek Pkwy Richmond VA 23238-1115*

HEATWOLE, MARK M., lawyer, director; b. Pitts., Jan. 28, 1948; s. Marion Grove and Phyllis Adelle (Leiter) H.; m. Sarah Ann Collier, Dec. 30, 1970; children: Mary Phyllis, Elizabeth Collier, Anna Bell. BA, Washington and Lee U., 1969, JD, 1972. Bar: Ill. 1972, U.S. Dist. Ct. (no. dist.) Ill. 1972, U.S. Ct. Appeals (7th cir.) 1977, U.S. Supreme Ct. 1980, U.S. Tax Ct. 1987. Assoc. Chadwell & Kayser, Ltd., Chgo., 1972-79, ptnr., v.p., 1979-89; ptnr. Winston & Strawn LLP, Chgo., 1990—2006; exec. v.p., gen. counsel Priva Techs., Inc., Chgo., 2006—. Treas. Lyric Opera Chgo. Guild, 1980—81, v.p., 1980—81, chmn. fundraising, 1986; vice-chmn. Gorton Cmty. Ctr., 1986; chmn. bd. Gorton Cmty. Ctr. Found., 1986—89; trustee Barat Coll., 1982—85, The Admiral, Chgo., 1988—2001, Allendale Assn., 1991—2000; mem. Art Inst. of Chgo. Old Masters Soc., 1999—; Mem. 1st ward Rep. com. on candidates Lake Forest (Ill.) Caucus, 1985—88, chmn. 1st ward, 1987—88, vice-chmn., 1989—90, chmn., 1990—91; mem. session Lake Forest Presbyn. Ch., 1978—84, chmn. ch. and society com., 1980; bd. dirs. Lyric Opera Chgo. Guild, 1976—2005, Lake Forest Symphony, 1987—91, Rehab. Inst. Chgo. Enterprises, 1991—2001, Gorton Community Ctr., 1982—88. Mem.: ABA (continuing legal edn. com. 1978—79, mem. antitrust com. young lawyers sect. 1978—81, com. on civil practice and procedure antitrust sect. 1980, bus. law sect. 1986—, patent trademark and copyright sect. 1990—), Chgo. Bar Assn. (chmn. profl. responsibility com. young lawyers sect. 1977—78, mem. exec. com. 1978—79, bd. dirs.), Valley Club Montecito, Lawyers Club, Econ. Club Chgo., Shoreacres Club (bd. govs. 1996—2004, pres. 2002—04). Republican. Office: Priva Techs Inc 875 N Michigan Ave Ste 1404 Chicago IL 60611 Home Phone: 312-643-2184; Office Phone: 312-759-3535. Business E-Mail: mark.heatwole@privatech.com.

HEAVICAN, MICHAEL G., state supreme court justice; b. 1947; BA, JD, U. Nebr. From dep. county atty. yo chief dep. county atty. Lancaster County, Nebr., 1975—81, county atty. Nebr., 1981—91; chief of criminal div. US Atty.'s Office Nebr. US Dept. Justice, Nebr., 1991—2001, US atty. Nebr., 2001—06; chief justice Nebr. Supreme Ct., 2006—. Office: State Capitol Rm 2214 Lincoln NE 68509 Office Phone: 402-471-3738. Office Fax: 402-471-2197.*

HEBARD, BARBARA ADAMS, conservator; b. Fort Dodge, Iowa, July 26, 1951; d. George D. and Bonnie J. Adams; m. Christopher G. Hebard, Jan. 10, 1981. B, U. Mass., 1975. Handbinder cert. North Bennet St. Sch., Mass., 1990. Book conservator Boston Athenaeum, 1990—. Chair alumni steering com. North Bennet St. Sch., Boston, 1998—2002, mem. corp., 2002—04, overseer, 2004—. Author: (catalogues) Boston Athenaeum Conservation Dept. Finishing Tools, King's Chapel Library, 2006; exhibitions include Roundup: Rocky Mountain chpt. Guild of Book Workers, 9th Wexford Artist Books Exhbn., Book Explorations, Arts Iowa City: Multiple Talents, Heaven on Earth: Lone Star Chapter of the Guild of Book Workers, Essence: The Art of Simplicity, Society of Arts and Crafts: Centennial Edn., Planet Dada Show, The Nurtured Spirit: Rocky Mountain Chapter of the Guild of Book Workers Exhibit, NE School of Art and Design exhibit, Bound Together: Ten Years of Bookbinding at N. Bennet St. Sch., Boston Athenaeum Mems., New England Vignettes: NE Chapter of Guild of Book Workers, Leap of Faith, 2004, 2005, 1st Internat. Collage, 2d Internat. Collage, N. Bennet St. Sch. Juried Show of Grad. Work, 2000—, San Diego Book Artists Nat. Juried Exhibit, 2006, Chgo. Pub. Libr., 2006, Biennale Mondiale de la Reliure d'Art, 2007, Cuesta Coll., 2007; contbr. articles to profl. jours., chapters to books. Mem. parish coun. St. Paul Ch., Cambridge, Mass., 2003—06. Andrew Oliver Wellspring fellow. Fellow: Internat. Inst. Conservation Hist. and Artistic Works; mem.: New Eng. Conservation Assn. (bd. mem.), Assn. Coll. and Rsch. Librs., Am. Inst. Conservation Hist. and Artistic Works (assoc.), Guild Book Workers (coord. NE chpt. exhbn.), Cultural Emergency Mgmt. Team, Ticknor Soc. Achievements include design of design binding, Grace Raymond Hebard scrapbook purchased by the Marriott Rare Book Library at the University of Utah. Office: Boston Athenaeum 10 1/2 Beacon St Boston MA 02108 Home Phone: 781-662-0675; Office Phone: 617-720-7632. Business E-Mail: hebard@bostonathenaeum.org.

HEBELER, HENRY KOESTER, retired electronics executive, aerospace engineer; b. St. Louis, Aug. 12, 1933; s. Henry and Viola O. (Koester) H.; m. Mirriam Robb, Aug. 12, 1978; children by previous marriage: Linda Ruth, Laura Ann. BS in Aero. Engring., MIT, 1956, MS, 1956, MBA, 1970. Gen. mgr. rsch./engring. Boeing Aerospace Co., Seattle, 1970-72, pres., 1980-85; v.p. bus. devel. The Boeing Co., Seattle, 1973-74, exec. coun. and corp. v.p. planning, 1988-89; pres. Boeing Engring. & Constrn. Co., Seattle, 1975-79, Boeing Electronics Co., Seattle, 1985-87. Bd. dirs. Microelectronics and Computer Tech. Corp.; mem. fusion panel Ho. of Reps., 1979-81, energy rsch. adv. bd. Dept. Energy, 1980-81, task force on internat. industry Def. Sci. Bd., 1982-84, adv. com. nat. strategic materials and minerals program U.S. Dept. Interior, 1986—. Author: Your Winning Retirement Plan, 2001, Getting Started in a Financially Secure Retirement, 2007. Bd. govs. Sloan Sch., MIT, 1980-84; bd. visitors Def. Systems Mgmt. Coll., Ft. Belvoir, Va. Recipient Mead prize for aero. engrs., 1956; Kuljian humanities award, 1954; Sperry Gyroscope fellow, 1956; Sloan fellow M.I.T., 1970 Mem. AIAA, Nat. Aeros. Assn., Assn. of U.S. Army, Armed Forces Comm. and Electronics Assn. (bd. dirs.), Aviation Hall of Fame, Ala. Space and Rocket Ctr. (sci. and adv. com. 1980-85), Nat. Space (bd. govs. 1980-85), Meridian Valley Country Club. Achievements include patents in field. Home and Office: 24600 140th Ave SE Kent WA 98042-5160

HEBENSTREIT, JAMES BRYANT, agricultural products executive, venture capitalist; b. Long Beach, Calif., Mar. 8, 1946; s. William Joseph and Jean (Stark) H.; m. Marilyn Bartlett, Aug. 23, 1986. AB, Harvard U., 1968, MBA, 1973. Pres. Terra-Light div. Butler Mfg. Co., Boston, 1980-82, Capital for Bus., Inc. (SB/C, venture capital affiliate Commerce Bancshares), St. Louis and Kansas City, Mo., 1982-87; sr. v.p. fin., CFO Commerce Bancshares, Inc., Kansas City, 1985-87, bd. dirs., 1987—; pres. Bartlett and Co., Kansas City, 1992—. Lt. USNR, 1968-71. Office: Bartlett & Co 4800 Main St Kansas City MO 64112-2510 Home: 5828 Pembroke Ct Mission Hills KS 66208-1148

HEBER-KATZ, ELLEN, research scientist, educator; BA in Med. Microbiology, U. Wis., Madison, 1969, MS in Immunology, 1972; PhD in Immunology, U. Pa., 1976. Staff fellow, Lab. Immunology Nat. Inst. Allergy and Infectious Diseases, NIH, 1977—79, 1979—82; prof., Molecular and Cellular Oncogenesis Wistar Inst., Phila. Scientific advisory bd. Ind. Univ. Ctr. for Regenerative Biology and Medicine; spkr. in field. Contbr. articles to profl. jours. Achievements include pioneering the first potent vaccine capable of stimulating T cell-mediated protection in the absence of antibodies; discovering the extraordinary ability of the MRL mouse to regenerate multiple organ systems, including cardiac muscle, cartilage and skin. Office: Wistar Inst 3601 Spruce St Philadelphia PA 19104 Office Phone: 215-898-3710. Business E-Mail: herberkatz@wistar.org.*

HEBERT, ADELAIDE, dermatologist, pediatrician; MD, Tulane U., New Orleans, 1980. Prof. dematology and pediat. U. Tex. Med. Sch., Houston, 1986—. Mem.: Am. Acad. Dermatology, Soc. Pediat. Dermatology (pres. 2006—07). Office: U Tex Med Sch Houston 6655 Travis 980 Houston TX 77030

HEBERT, BLISS EDMUND, opera director; b. Faust, NY, Nov. 30, 1930; s. Wilfrid Joseph and Merle Addasah (Bliss) H. BA, Syracuse U., 1951, M.Mus., 1952; piano pupil of, Robert Goldsand, Simone Barrere, Lelia Gousseau. Gen. mgr. Washington Opera Soc., 1960-63; guest dir. Juilliard Sch., 1975-76; mem. faculty Boston U., 1952-53, U. Wash., 1969. Stage dir., Met. Opera, N.Y.C., 1973-75, N.Y. City Opera, 1963-75, Santa Fe Opera, 1957—; dir. opera companies of, San Francisco, 1963, Houston, 1964, Seattle Opera, 1967, Toronto, 1972, San Diego, 1970, Vancouver, B.C., 1969, Ft. Worth, 1966, Washington, 1959, Cin., 1968, Portland, Oreg., 1969, Caramoor Festival, Katonah, N.Y., 1966, La Gune Festival, 1968— , New Orleans, 1970, Balt., 1972, Tulsa, 1975, Miami, Fla., 1975, Charlotte, N.C., 1975, Dallas, 1977, Shreveport, La., 1977, Chgo., 1983, Montreal, 1984, Boston, 1984, Cleve., 1988, Opera Northern Ireland, 1988, Virginia Opera, 1991, Opera Mexico City, 1993, Austin Opera, 1993, Florentine Opera, Milw., 1994, Atlanta Opera, 2005, Mich. Opera Theater, 2006; rec. artist, Columbia records; as stage dir. for Igor Stravinsky's major operas under his conducting. Served AUS, 1954-56. Mem. Lambda Chi Alpha, Phi Mu Alpha. Office: care John S Miller 2nd Fl 889 Ninth Ave New York NY 10019

HEBERT, JAY HOWELL, lawyer; b. Lake Charles, La., Jan. 31, 1961; s. John Roland and Cynthia Hope (Johnson) H.; m. Camille Renee Comeau, June 8, 1986; 1 child, Isabel Suzanne. BA summa cum laude, Rice U., 1983; JD magna cum laude, Harvard U., 1986. Bar: Tex. 1986, U.S. C. Appeals (5th cir.) 1987, U.S. Supreme Ct. 1990, D.C. 2001. Law clk. to presiding judge U.S. Ct. Appeals (5th cir.), Dallas, 1986-87; with Hughes & Luce LLP, Dallas, 1987—96, Vinson & Elkins LLP, Dallas, 1996—, ptnr. Bus. and Internat. Group Washington, DC, 1996—, chair Comm. Practice Group. Mem. Tex. Bar Assn., DC Bar Assn. Office: Vinson & Elkins LLP Ste 600 1455 Pennsylvania Ave NW Washington DC 20004 Office Phone: 202-639-6521. E-mail: jhebert@velaw.com.

HEBERT, STEVEN C., medical educator; MD, U. Fla.; MA (hon.), Harvard. C.N.H. Long prof. molecular and cellular physiology Yale U., prof. medicine, chmn. cellular and molecular physiology. Recipient Homer W. Smith award, Am. Soc. Nephrology, A.N. Richards award, Internat. Soc. Nephrology. Mem.: NAS. Office: Yale Univ FMP 107 330 Cedar St New Haven CT 06510 Mailing: Dept Internal Medicine Yale Sch Medicine PO Box 208029 New Haven CT 06510-8029 Office Phone: 203-785-4186. Office Fax: 203-785-4904. E-mail: steven.hebert@yale.edu.

HEBERT, WILLIAM N., lawyer; b. Iowa City, Iowa, Oct. 19, 1960; AB with distinction, Stanford Univ., 1983; JD, Boalt Law Sch., Univ. Calif., Berkeley, 1988. Bar: Calif. 1988, US Dist. Ct. (no., ctrl. & ea. Calif., Colo.), US Ct. Appeals, 9th cir. Ptnr., Global Litigation practice Coudert Bros. LLP, San Francisco. Mediator US Dist. Ct., no. Calif. dist. Contbr. articles to profl. jours. Mem.: Fed. Bar Assn. (mem. steering com., no. dist. Calif.). Office Phone: 415-267-6200. Office Fax: 415-977-6110. Business E-Mail: whebert@coudert.com.

HEBERTON, GEORGE H., lawyer; b. Phila., 1957; BA cum laude, Vanderbilt U., 1978; JD, U. Ga., 1981. Bar: Ga. 1981. Ptnr. Roberts, Isaf & Summers (acquired by McGuireWoods in 1999), McGuireWoods LLP, Atlanta, 1999—, mng. ptnr. Atlanta office, 2000—03, chair firm real estate

& environ. dept. Office: McGuireWoods LLP Ste 2100 1170 Peachtree St NE Atlanta GA 30309-7649 Office Phone: 404-443-5710. Office Fax: 404-443-5767. Business E-Mail: gheberton@mcguirewoods.com.

HEBRINK, BOB, publishing executive; BA, Metro State Univ. Sales & sys. engr. Data Gen. Corp.; client svc. mgr. Oracle Corp.; v.p. bus. develop. York & Associates; dir. client services Nistevo Corp.; dir. bus. develop. Midwave Corp.; sr. v.p. Sagebrush Corp.; CEO Sagebrush Books (now Tandem Library Group), Mpls., 2006—. Office: Tandem Library Group Ste 600 7900 Xerxes Ave S Minneapolis MN 55431

HECHE, ANNE (ANNE CELESTE HECHE), actress; b. Aurora, Ohio, May 25, 1969; d. Donald Heche; m. Coley Laffoon, Sept. 1, 2001 (separated, 2007); 1 child, Homer Heche Laffoon. Actress (films) An Ambush of Ghosts, 1993, The Adventures of Huck Finn, 1993, A Simple Twist of Fate, 1994, Milk Money, 1994, I'll Do Anything, 1994, The Wild Side, 1995, Pie in the Sky, 1995, Walking and Talking, 1996, The Juror, 1996, Volcano, 1997, Donnie Brasco, 1997, Wag the Dog, 1997, I Know What You Did Last Summer, 1997, Return to Paradise, 1998, Six Days Seven Nights, 1998, Psycho, 1998, The Third Miracle, 1999, Auggue Rose, 2000, Prozac Nation, 2001, John Q., 2002, Timepiece, 2003, Birth, 2004; (TV movies) O Pioneers!, 1992, Against the Wall, 1994, Girls in Prison, 1994, The Investigator, 1994, Kingfish: A Story of Huey P. Long, 1995, If These Walls Could Talk, 1996, Wild Side, 1996, SUBWAYStories: Tales from the Underground, 1997, One Kill, 2000, Gracie's Choice, 2004, The Dead Will Tell, 2004, Sexual Life, 2005, Silver Bells, 2005, Fatal Desire, 2006; (TV series) Another World, 1987-91, Murphy Brown, 1991-92, Ally McBeal, 2001, Ellen, 1998, Everwood, 2004-05, Men in Trees, 2006-; (stage) Getting Away with Murder, 1991-92; (Broadyway plays) Proof, 2002-03, Twentieth Century, 2004- (Tony nom. best actress in a play, 2004); actor, prodr. (TV movies) The Dead Will Tell, 2004; dir. (films) Reaching Normal, 2001; dir., writer (TV films) On the Edge; dir.(TV movies) If These Walls Could Talk 2, 2000; writer (short film) Stripping for Jesus, 1998; author: (autobiography) Call Me Crazy: A Memoir, 2001. Recipient Emmy award Another World; named one of the 50 Most Beautiful People in the World, People, 1998.

HECHLER, KEN, retired state official, retired congressman, writer, political science professor; b. Roslyn, NY, Sept. 20, 1914; s. Charles Henry and Catherine Elizabeth (Hauhart) H. *Grandfather George Hechler emigrated from Germany in 1854, enlisted with Union infantry at Parkersburg, West Virginia, wounded at Antietam and discharged at Wheeling, West Virginia. Great Uncle John Hechler captured at Chickamauga, died in Andersonville Prison. Father University of Missouri graduate, managed Clarence H. Mackay's 600 acre farm estate on Long Island, elected to numerous Republican county offices and President of Board of Education, secretary-treasurer of New York Guernsey Breeders' Association, bank president. Mother was a school teacher in St. Louis County, elected to numerous Republican county offices on Long Island, noted raiser and exhibitor of Chrysanthemums.* AB, Swarthmore Coll., 1935, LLD (hon.), 2001; AM, Columbia U., 1936, PhD, 1940; HHD (hon.), W. Va. Inst. Tech., 1988; LittD (hon.), U. Charleston, 1988; LHD (hon.), Marshall U., 2007. Lectr. govt. Barnard Coll., Columbia Coll., NYC, 1937-41; rsch. asst., Judge Samuel I. Rosenman, 1939-50; rsch. asst. Pres. Roosevelt's pub. papers, 1939-50; sect. chief Bur. Census, 1940; pers. technician Office Emergency Mgmt., 1941; adminstrv. analyst Bur. of Budget, 1941—42, 1946—47; spl. asst., Pres. Harry S. Truman, 1949-53; rsch. dir. Stevenson-Kefauver campaign, 1956; adminstrv. aide Senator Carroll of Colo., 1957; mem. 86th-94th Congresses from 4th W.Va. dist., 1959-77; sec. state State of W.Va., 1985-2001. Sci. and tech. com. 86th to 94th Congresses from 4th W.Va. Dist., chmn. Energy (Fossil Fuels) Subcom.; mem. Joint Com. on Orgn. of Congress, 1965-66, NASA Oversight Subcom. (US Congress); asst. prof. politics Princeton U., 1947-49; prof. polit. sci. Marshall U., Huntington, W.Va., 1957, 82-84, 2001-2003; sci. cons. US House Com. on Sci. and Tech., 1978-80; radio, TV commentator Sta. WHTN, Huntington, 1957-58, Sta. WWHY, 1978; adj. prof. polit. sci. U. Charleston, W.Va., 1981; keynote spkr. Harry Truman lecture ser. USAF Acad., 1995; disting. vis. scholar W.Va. State Coll., Institute, 2001, Bowling Green State U., 2003, Fla. Atlantic U., 2004-2005, Va. Military Inst., 2004, High Point U., NC, 2005, Truman Symposium, Key West, Fla., 2004-07, Am. History Forum, Sarasota, Fla., 2006-07, U. Western Ky., 2006, U. Fla., Gainesville, 2007, L.I. U., 2007, U. Kans., 2007; lectr. in field. *Only Congressman to march with Martin Luther King in Selma, Alabama. First Congressman sponsoring legislation to limit coal dust and provide strict safety standards in Federal Coal Mine Health and Safety Act of 1969. Fought against corruption in coal union, risked life to campaign for Jock Yablonski, insurgent candidate later murdered. Crusaded against strip mining and mountain top removal of coal. Helped mobilize secretaries of state and attorneys general in 33 states to limit campaign spending. Led campaign to more fairly appraise and tax West Virginia natural resources owned by out-of-state corporations. Cracked down on West Virginia political corruption.* Author: Insurgency: Personalities and Politics of the Taft Era, 1940, The Bridge at Remagen, 1957, rev. edit., tech. advisor of motion picture based on book, 1969, 1998, 2005, West Virginia Memories of President Kennedy, 1965, Toward the Endless Frontier, 1980, The Endless Space Frontier, 1982, Working with Truman, 1982, 3d edit., 2001, Hero of the Rhine, 2004, Supermarine, 2007; weekly columnist Cabell Record, Hampshire Rev., Elk River and Little Kananha News, W.Va. Hillbilly, 1990—2000; author (Dr. Charles Moffat): biography of Ken Hechler, 1987. Bd. dirs. W.Va. Humanities Coun., 1982-84; del. Dem. Nat. Conv., 1964, 68, 72, 80, 84; mem. W.Va. State Dem. Exec. Com., 1998-99. Served to maj. AUS, 1942—46, served to col. Res., 1947—74. Decorated Bronze Star; named W.Va. Son of Yr., W.Va. State Soc. of D.C., 1969, W.Va. Spkr. of Yr., W.Va. U., 1970, Smithsonian Instn. lectr. on 50th Anniversary of Pres. Truman, 1985, Prof. of Yr., Marshall U. student senate, 2002, Grand Marshal, Ann. Martin Luther King Parade, Huntington, 2003, 2006, 2007, Mountaineer of Yr., Graffiti Mag., 2003; recipient Conservation award, Nat. Audubon Soc., 1973, Mother Jones award, W.Va. Environ. Coun., 1995, Civil and Human Rights award, Martin Luther King Commn. W.Va., 2001, Harry S. Truman award for pub. svc., Independence, Mo., 2002, Good Samaritan award, Pinch, W.Va. Reunion Com., Ann. award, W.Va. Humanities Coun., 2005, Civil Rights award, Gov. W.Va., 2006. Mem. VFW, DAV, Am. Polit. Sci. Assn. (assoc. dir. 1953-56), Civitan, Am. Legion, Judson Welliver Soc. of Presdl. Speech-Writers, W.Va. Labor History Assn. (namedto Labor Hall Honor 2006), Elks, Golden Key Internat. Hon. Soc. (hon.). Democrat. Episcopalian. Walked 530 miles with Granny D on behalf of campaign reform, 2000. Home and Office: 101B Greenbrier St Charleston WV 25311-2130 E-mail: fesenms@wvlc.lib.wv.us.

HECHT, ALAN DANNENBERG, insurance executive; b. Balt., Aug. 31, 1918; s. Lee I. and Miriam (Dannenberg) H.; m. Margaret R. Moses, June 27, 1943 (dec. Nov. 1, 1984); children: Stephen Lee, Nancy H., Elizabeth Ann; m. Marcia Levin Oberfeld, Dec. 8, 1985. BS, Johns Hopkins U., 1940, M Liberal Arts, 1976. CLU, 1951. Solicitor Travelers Ins. Co., 1945-60; partner Hecht-Schoenfeld Ins. Agy., 1960-62; merged and formed Wolman-Hecht-Schoenfeld, Inc., 1962, v.p., 1962-64, Wolman-Hecht, Inc., 1964-91, pres., 1971-92, chmn., 1992; v.p. Tongne Brooks & Co., Inc. (merged with Wolman-Hecht, Inc.), 1992-95; founder, pres. Alan D. Hecht & Co., Inc., 1966—; gen. agt. Sunamerica Life Ins. Co. Am. and other cos., Balt., 1960—; pres. Ins., Inc., Balt., 1995—. Pres. Balt. Estate Planning Coun., 1978-79; tchr. CLU econs. and fin. Johns Hopkins U., 1954-81; mem. faculty dept. econs. Mount St. Mary's Coll., Emmitsburg, Md., 1981-84; past bd. graders Am. Coll. Life Underwriters. Pres. Balt. Jewish Council, 1971-73; life and qualifying mem. Million Dollar Round Table, 1985, mem. resolutions com., 1976; bd. dirs. Balt. chpt. Am. Jewish Com., pres., 1958-60, former mem. nat. exec. com.; trustee Sinai Hosp. of Balt., 1959-68. Served to 1st lt. AUS, 1941-45. Recipient Nat. Quality award Nat. Assn. Life Underwriters; Nat. Sales Achievement award; Szold award Temple Oheb Shalom Brotherhood, 1980; George S. Robertson award Balt. Life Underwriters Assn., 1981 Mem. Soc. Fin. Svc. Profls. (CLU, dir. 1957—, nat. sec. 1962-63, pres. 1964-65, Helen Hottenbacher award Balt. chpt. 1991), Omicron Delta Kappa, Pi Delta Epsilon. Jewish (pres. congregation 1968-70, past dir.). Home and Office: 111 Hamlet Hill Rd Apt 312 Baltimore MD 21210-1521 Office Phone: 410-753-1857. E-mail: heclev@aol.com. *With some background in economics, I believe that we can improve our life and environment only by greater productivity. Each person should accept responsibility for finishing assigned tasks at every level, no matter how menial or unimportant that task may seem. I would add that courtesy and respect for others should be a top priority for the successful growth and future of our great country.*

HECHT, DARYL L., state supreme court justice; b. Sac City, Iowa, June 25, 1952; s. Eldon E. and Darlene E. (Rubendall) H.; m. Sandra Ellen Bubke, June 16, 1973; children: Erica M., Lindsay M. BA, Morningside Coll., 1974; JD magna cum laude, U. S.D., 1977; MA in Law, U. Va. Sch. of Law, 2004. Bar: U.S, Dist. Ct. Iowa 1977, U.S. Dist. Ct. S.D. 1977. Atty. Crary, Huff, Inkster, Hecht & Sheehan, Sioux City, Iowa, 1977—99; judge Iowa Ct. of Appeals, 1999—2006; justice Iowa Supreme Ct., 2006—. Bd. dirs. Boys & Girls Home and Family Svcs., Sioux City, 1982-89. Mem. Assn. Trial Lawyers Am., Iowa Trial Lawyers Assn. (pres. 1994-95). Avocations: reading, politics. Office: Iowa Supreme Ct 1111 E Ct Ave Des Moines IA 50319 Office Phone: 515-281-5174.

HECHT, DONALD D., lawyer; b. Newark, Sept. 30, 1957; BA in Polit. Sci., Johns Hopkins U., Balt., 1979; MBA, JD, U. Md., 1984. Bar: Md. 1985, US Dist. Ct. (dist. Md.) 1986, US Ct. Appeals (4th cir.) 1988. Contract/panel atty. Pub. Defenders Office for Balt. City, 1984—92; ptnr. Leslie L. Gladstone, P.A., Balt., 1987—. Mem.: ABA, Md. Trial Lawyers Assn., Assn. Trial Lawyers of Am., Md. Bar Assn., Bar Assn. Balt. City. Office: Leslie L Gladstone PA 1040 N Calvert St Baltimore MD 21202-3856 Office Phone: 410-727-2322. Office Fax: 410-385-0311. E-mail: ddhecht@earthlink.net.*

HECHT, JENNIFER MICHAEL, poet, historian; b. Glenn Cove, NY, Nov. 23, 1965; d. Eugene and Carolyn Hecht; m. John Mitchell Chaneski, May 27, 2001; children: Jessie Leo Hecht-Chaneski children: Maxwell Joseph Hecht-Chaneski. Student, U. Caen and U. d'Angers, France, 1984—85; BA, Adelphi U., 1987; PhD, Columbia U., 1995. History instr. Mannes Coll. Music, The New Sch., NYC, 1993—94; assoc. prof. history Nassau C.C., Garden City, NY, 1994—. Author: (book) Doubt: A History, 2003, The End of the Soul: Scientific Modernity, Atheism, and Anthropology, in France, 2003 (Ralph Waldo Emerson award Phi Beta Kappa Soc., 2004), (poetry collection) The Next Ancient World, 2001 (Tupelo Press Judge's prize, 2000, Norma Farber First Book award Poetry Soc. Am., 2002, Poetry Book of Yr., ForeWord Mag., 2002), Funny, 2005 (Felix Pollak prize U. Wis. Press, 2005). Fellow: NY Inst. for the Humanities. Office: Nassau Community College 1 Education Dr Garden City NY 11530-6719 Home Phone: 718-852-0076; Office Phone: 516-572-7313. Personal E-mail: hechtjm@aol.com.

HECHT, JOEL RANDOLPH, oncologist; b. Norfolk, Va., July 23, 1960; BA, U. Va., Charlottesville, 1981; MD, Eastern Va. Med. Sch., Norfolk, 1984; studied Internal Medicine, Northwestern U. Med. Sch., Chgo., Ill., 1987; studied Gastrointestinal Rsch., U. Chgo., Ill., 1988; studied Gasteroenterology, UCLA, 1991. Lic. Calif., diplomate Nat. Bd. Med. Examiners, Am. Bd. Internal Medicine, Am. Bd. Internal Medicine (Gastroenterology), Am. Bd. Internal Medicine (Med. Oncology). Resident, internal medicine Northwestern U., Chgo., 1984—87; gastroenterology rsch. fellow U. Chgo., Ill., 1987—88; gastroenterology fellow David Geffen Sch. Medicine, UCLA, 1988—89, asst. prof. medicine in residence, divsn. digestive diseases, 1991—95, asst. clin. prof. medicine, divsn. digestive diseases, 1995—97, med. oncology fellowship, 1997, assoc. clin. prof. medicine, divsn. hematology-oncology, 1997—, dir., GI oncology program, divsn. hematology-oncology, 2003—. Mem., Jonsson Comprehensive Cancer Ctr. Signal Transduction and Therapeutics Program area David Geffen Sch. Medicine, UCLA. Contbr. articles to profl. jours. Office: UCLA Jonsson Comprehensive Cancer Ctr 8-684 Factor Bldg Box 951781 Los Angeles CA 90095-1781 Office Phone: 310-206-4303.*

HECHT, LAURENCE M., editor, political organization worker; b. Great Neck, NY, Oct. 18, 1945; s. Morton, Jr. and Marie B. Hecht; m. Marjorie Mazel, July 2, 1972. BS, Columbia U., NYC, 1972; diploma (hon.), Universal Ecol. Acad., Moscow, 1995. Polit. organizer Nat. Caucus Labor Coms., NYC, 1973—79; mng. editor New Solidarity, NYC, 1980—84; fundraiser La Rouche campaign, Lessburg, Va., 1984—90; assoc. editor 21st Century Sci. & Tech., Washington, 1991—99, editor-in-chief, 1999—. Assoc. La Rouche Polit. Action Com., Leesburg, 2004—.

HECHT, LOUIS ALAN, lawyer; b. Chgo., July 20, 1944; s. Bernard T. and Dorthe E. (Callen) H.; m. Joanne Lebow, Aug. 16, 1967; children—Jonathan D., Peter A. BS, U. Ill., JD, 1969. Bar: Ill. bar 1969. Mem. Hofgren, Wegner, Allen, Stellman & McCord, Chgo., 1969-71, Coffee & Sweeney, Chgo., 1971-74; patent counsel Molex, Inc., Lisle, Ill., 1974—77, gen. counsel, sec., 1978—. Mem. Am. Bar Assn., Ill. State Bar Assn., Chgo. Bar Assn., Am. Patent Lawyers Assn., Patent Lawyers Assn. Chgo. Office: Molex Inc 2222 Wellington Ave Lisle IL 60532-3820

HECHT, MARION B., counselor; b. Bklyn., Nov. 21, 1966; d. Herman and Selma Sonnenblick; m. Ronald J. Hecht; children: Henry, Rachel. MA, Goddard Coll., Plainfield, Vt., 1991; postgrad., Goddard Coll., 1998, Hofstra U., U. Minn., U. Iowa, Montclair State U. Lic. profl. counselor NJ, DC, mental health counselor NY, registered and bd. cert. art therapist Am. Art Therapy Assn., cert. guidance counselor, handicapped tchr. NJ Dept. Edn., cognitive behavioral therapist Nat. Assn. Cognitive Behavioral Therapists, diplomate AM. Psychotherapy Assn. Mental health specialist, gerontologist Bay Ridge Ctr. for Older Adults, Bklyn., 1989-90; art therapist Rockaway Mental Health Svcs., Far Rockaway, NY, 1990-91, Coney Island Hosp., 1991—93; pvt. practice No. NJ Counseling Svcs., 1996—; tchr. home instrn., spl. edn. Montclair & South Orange Pub. Schs., NJ, 1997-2000. Mem.: Am. Coll. Counselors. Avocations: sports, reading, computer, drawing. Office: 15 Village Plaza South Orange NJ 07079 Office Phone: 973-762-1224. Office Fax: 973-597-1357. Personal E-mail: mbshinc@comcast.net.

HECHT, MARJORIE MAZEL, editor; b. Cambridge, Mass., Dec. 21, 1942; d. Mark and Theresa (Shuman) Mazel; m. Laurence Michael Hecht, July 2, 1972 BA cum laude, Smith Coll., 1964; postgrad., London Sch. Econs., 1964-65; MSW, Columbia U., 1967. Dir. Forest Neighborhood Service Ctr., NYC, 1967-70, Wiltwyck Sch. for Boys, Bronx Center, NY, 1970-73; mng. editor Fusion Mag., Washington, 1977-87, 21st Century Sci. & Technol. Mag., Washington, 1987—; sci. editor Exec. Intelligence Rev., Washington, 1997—. Co-author: Beam Defense: An Alternative to Nuclear Destruction, 1983 (Aviation and Space Writers award 1983); editor: Colonize Space! Open the Age of Reason, 1985, The Holes in the Ozone Scare: The Scientific Evidence That the Sky Isn't Falling, 1992. Press rep. LaRouche Campaign, NYC, 1984, LaRouche PAC. Democrat. Jewish. Office: 21st Century Sci & Technol Mag PO Box 16285 Washington DC 20041-6285 Home Phone: 703-777-7893; Office Phone: 703-777-6943.

HECHT, NATHAN LINCOLN, state supreme court justice; b. Clovis, N.Mex., Aug. 15, 1949; s. Harold Lee and Mary Loretta (Byerly) H. BA, Yale U., 1971; JD cum laude, So. Meth. U., 1974. Bar: Tex. 1974, D.C. 1975, U.S. Dist. Ct. D.C. 1975, U.S. Dist. Ct. (no. and we. dists.) Tex. 1976, U.S. Ct. Appeals (D.C. cir.) 1975, U.S. Ct. Appeals (5th cir.) 1976, U.S. Supreme Ct. 1979. Law clk. to judge U.S. Ct. Appeals (D.C. cir.), 1974-75; assoc. Locke, Purnell, Boren, Laney & Neely, Dallas, 1976-80, ptnr., 1981; dist. judge 95th Dist. Ct., Dallas, 1981-86; judge Tex. Ct. Appeals (5th Dist.), 1986-89; justice Tex. Supreme Ct., Austin, 1989—. Contbr. articles to profl. jours. Bd. visitors So. Meth. U., Dallas, 1984-87; trustee Children's Med. Found., Dallas, 1983-89; bd. dirs. Children's Med. Ctr. North, Dallas, 1985-89; elder Valley View Christian Ch., Dallas, 1981—. Lt. USNR, 1971—79. Named Outstanding Young Lawyer of Dallas, Dallas Assn. of Young Lawyers, 1984. Fellow Tex. Bar Found., Am. Bar Found.; mem. ABA, Dallas Bar Assn., D.C. Bar Assn., Am. Law Inst. Republican. Avocations: piano, organ, jogging, bicycling. Office: Tex Supreme Ct PO Box 12248 201 West 14th Room 104 Austin TX 78711*

HECHT, SIDNEY MICHAEL, chemistry professor; b. NYC, July 27, 1944; AB, U. Rochester, 1966; PhD, U. Ill., 1970. USPHS fellow U. Wis., 1970-71; from asst. prof. to assoc. prof. MIT, Cambridge, 1971-79; John W. Mallet prof. chemistry U. Va., Charlottesville, 1978—; v.p. preclin. research and devel. Smith Kline & French Labs., 1981-83, v.p. chem. research and devel., 1983-86. Mem. editl. adv. bd. Anti-Cancer Drug Design, 1986—,2002 Jour. Molecular Recognition, 1991-98, Bioconjugate Chemistry, 1992—, Molecules Online, 1997—99, Current Medicinal Chemistry, 2000—, Molecular Cancer Therapeutics, 2001—, Oncology Rsch./Anticancer Drug Design, 2002—; assoc. editor Medicinal Chemistry Rsch., 1990-91; assoc. editor Jour. Am. Chem. Soc., 1992—. Alfred P. Sloan research fellow, 1975-79, John Simon Guggenheim fellow, 1977-78, AAAS, 2004; NIH research career devel. grantee, 1975-80; recipient Arthur C. Cope Scholar award Am. Chem. Soc., 1996; recipient Rsch. Achievement award Am. Soc. of Pharmacognory, 1998; named Va.'s Outstanding Scientist, 1996. Mem. AAAS, Am. Chem. Soc., Royal Soc. Chemistry, Am. Soc. Biol. Chemists, Sigma Xi Office: U Va Dept Chemistry Charlottesville VA 22901

HECHT, WILLIAM DAVID, accountant; b. NYC, Nov. 7, 1941; s. Adolph J. and Lillian (Shore) H.; m. Francine Rosen, Aug. 22, 1964; children: Peter, Dana, Allison. BS in Acctg., Queens Coll., 1962; JD, Bklyn. Law Sch., 1971; LLM in Taxation, NYU, 1974. Bar: N.Y. 1972. Ptnr., mem. mgmt. com. Weiser LLP, NYC, 1964—. Mem. faculty Found. Acctg. Edn., N.Y.C.; lectr. in field. Contbr. articles to CPA Jour. Mem. ABA, AICPA, N.Y. State Soc. CPAs, N.J. State Soc. CPAs, N.Y. State Bar Assn. Republican. Jewish. Avocations: skiing, basketball. Home: 10233 Spyglass Way Boca Raton FL 33498 Office: 135 W 50th St New York NY 10020 Home Phone: 732-254-7486; Office Phone: 732-205-2001, 212-375-6584. Business E-Mail: whecht@mrweiser.com.

HECHTER, MICHAEL NORMAN, sociologist; b. LA, Nov. 15, 1943; s. Oscar Milton and Gertrude (Horowitz) H.; children: Joshua, Eliana. AB, Columbia U., 1966, PhD, 1972. From asst. prof. to prof. U. Wash., Seattle, 1970-84; prof. sociology, dir. research group for instnl. analysis U. Ariz., Tucson, 1984—99; prof. sociology U. Wash., Seattle, 1999—2005; found. prof. global studies Ariz. State U., 2005—, interim dir. sch. global studies, 2007—. Univ. lectr., fellow New Coll., Oxford (Eng.) U., 1994-96; vis. prof. U. Bergen, Norway, 1984. Author: Internal Colonialism, 1975, Principles of Group Solidarity, 1987, Containing Nationalism, 2000; editor: The Microfoundations of Macrosociology, 1983, Social Institutions, 1989, The Origin of Values, 1993, Social Norms, 2001, Theories of Social Order, 2003. Fellow Russell Sage Found., 1988-89, Ctr. Advanced Study Behavioral Scis., 1990-91, Udall Ctr. for Studies in Pub. Policy. Fellow: Am. Acad. of Arts and Sci.; mem.: Am. Polit. Sci. Assn., Soc. for Comparative Rsch., Internat. Sociol. Assn., Sociol. Rsch. Assn., Am. Sociol. Assn. Office: School Global Studies Ariz State Univ Tempe AZ 85287 Home Phone: 206-217-0207; Office Phone: 480-727-0735. Business E-Mail: michael.hechter@asu.edu.

HECHTMAN, HOWARD, financial analyst; b. NYC, Sept. 1947; s. Charles and Pauline (Barmatz) Hechtman; m. Marsha Louise Garwin, Dec. 19, 1976 (div. 1984). BS, Bklyn. Poly. U., 1968; MS in Physics, Adelphi U., 1970, MBA in Mgmt. with distinction, 1972; cert. in labor rels., Cornell U., 1999, advanced cert. in labor rels., 2000. Grad. teaching asst. physics Computer Ctr. Adelphi U., Garden City, NY, 1970-72; from asst. to assoc. analyst N.Y.C. Transit Authority, 1973—. Capt. NY State Guard. Named Patron of Arts Soc. Theater Arts Resources, 1989—90; recipient cert. of Merit, Rep. Nat. Com., 1990. Mem.: Civil Svc. Tech. Guild (del. 1994—2007), Soc. Am. Mil. Engrs., Poly. U. Alumni Assn. (alumni bd. dirs. 1978—, life dir. 1996—). Office: NYC Transit Authority MOW Finance 7th Fl 130 Livingston St Brooklyn NY 11201-3817 Office Phone: 718-694-3039. Personal E-mail: howardusaten@yahoo.com.

HECK, ALBERT FRANK, retired neurologist; b. Balt., Oct. 9, 1932; s. Albert Franklin and Dorothy Mary Heck; divorced; children: Albert William, Karl Andrew, Robert Conrad, Paul Christopher. AB, Johns Hopkins U., 1954; MD, U. Md., 1958. Diplomate: Am. Bd. Psychiatry and Neurology. Intern Mercy Hosp., 1958-59; NIH fellow in neurology U. Md., Balt., 1959-62, faculty, instr. to prof., 1964-77; prof., chmn. dept. neurology U. Tenn. Center for Health Scis., Memphis, 1977-82, dir. neurosci. program, 1978-82; prof. neurology W. Va. U., 1982-2000, ret., 2000—. Vis. prof. Medezinische Hochschule Hannover, W. Ger., 1973-74 Contbr. writings to profl. publs. Served with M.C. U.S. Army, 1962-64. Recipient jr. investigator award NIH, 1965, U.S. sr. scientist award, 1973; Humboldt Found. prize Fed. Republic Germany, 1973-74 Fellow Am. Acad. Neurology, ACP, Stroke Council Am. Heart Assn.; mem. Am. Neurol. Assn., Alpha Omega Alpha. Achievements include research in field. Home: 10906 Baronet Rd Owings Mills MD 21117

HECK, DEBRA UPCHURCH, information technology, procurement professional; b. Valparaiso, Fla., Nov. 4, 1956; d. Robert P. and Sallaine S. (Sledge) Upchurch; m. Robert J. Heck, May 31, 1980; children: Andrew W., Jennifer A. BS in Math., Purdue U., 1978, MS in Mgmt., 1980. Analyst mgmt. sci. Monsanto Corp. Mgmt. Sci., St. Louis, 1980-81; sys. analyst Monsanto Agr. Group, St. Louis, 1981-82, sr. sys. analyst, 1982-84; sr. analyst mgmt. sci. Monsanto Polymer Products Group, St. Louis, 1984-86; total quality fundamentals instr. Monsanto Co., St. Louis, 1985-86; project mgr. Monsanto Chem. Co., St. Louis, 1986-88; group leader Monsanto Corp. MIS, St. Louis, 1988-92, sr. group leader, 1992-95; info. tech. dir. Monsanto Bus. Svcs. Fin. & Procurement, St. Louis, 1995—97, dir. strategic sourcing procurement strategic initiatives, 1997—2000; exec. dir. global procurement Pharmacia, St. Louis, 2000—03; exec. dir. global sourcing Pfizer, 2003—04; v.p. corp. procurement Express Scripts, St. Louis, 2005—. Trustee, chair fall gathering, doubles, social com. Ethical Soc., St. Louis, 1982—; mem. sci. adv. com., PTO bd. Parkway Sch. Dist., St. Louis, 1992—; vol. St. Louis Assn. for Retarded Citizens, 1978-85. Recipient Leader award, YWCA Monsanto Corp., 1999. Mem. Nat. Assn. Purchasing Mgmt., Human Resource Sys. Profls., Leadership Am. Alumni (award 1994), Winning Women. Avocations: travel, sports. Personal E-mail: debrauheck@aol.com.

HECK, HENRY D'ARCY, retired toxicologist, consultant; b. Bryn Mawr, Pa., Apr. 18, 1939; s. Harold Joseph and Lydia Suzanne (Holt) H.; m. Mercedes Casanova, Dec. 21, 1984; children: Katherine (Mrs. Daniel Troy), Julia, John Schmitz, Lara (Mrs. Daniel King). AB, Princeton U., 1962; PhD, Northwestern U., 1966. Asst. prof. chemistry U. Calif., Berkeley, 1968-72; chemist Stanford Rsch. Inst., Menlo Park, Calif.,

1972-77; scientist Chem. Ind. Inst. Toxicology, Research Triangle Park, NC, 1977-85, sr. scientist, 1985-99; ret., 1999; prin. Casaheck Cons., 2004—. Adj. assoc. prof. U. NC, Chapel Hill, 1983-99, Duke U., Durham, NC, 1987-99 Assoc. editor: Fundamental and Applied Toxicology, 1986-1991, editor-in-chief, 1991-97. Fellow NSF, NIH, EMBO, 1963-68; mem. AAAS, Am. Chem. Soc., NC Soc. Toxicology (pres. 1995-96), Soc. Toxicology (Frank Blood award 1983, Inhalation Toxicol. Paper of Yr. award 1987, 93). Home: 9536 25th Bay St Norfolk VA 23518 E-mail: casaheck@cox.net.

HECK, JAMES BAKER, retired education educator; b. Columbus, Ohio, Aug. 26, 1930; s. Arch O. and Frances (Agnew) H.; m. Jo Ann Gatton, Nov. 18, 1950; children: Janice M., Judith L., J. Jeffrey. BS in Edn., Ohio State U., 1953, MA, 1961, PhD, 1967. Comml. sales engr. Ohio Bell Tel. Co., Dayton, 1955-57; tchr. Ohio Pub. Schs., Dayton, 1957-59, sch. counselor, 1959-60; from instr. to assoc. dean Ohio State U., 1960—67, assoc. dean faculties Office Acad. Affairs, 1967-68, asst. prof. edn., 1967—68, prof., dean, dir. Mansfield campus, 1971-78; prof., dean Coll. Edn. U. Del., Newark, 1968-71; dean regional campus affairs U. South Fla., 1978-81, assoc. v.p. acad. affairs, 1981-84, prof., assoc. v.p. acad. affairs, dir. office of tech., 1984-86, prof., dean Sch. Extended Studies & Learning Techs., gen. mgr. pub. broadcasting Sta. WUSF-TV/FM, WSFP-TV/FM, spl. asst. to provost, dir. office tech., 1986-90; prof., gen. mgr. Sta. WSFP-TV/FM, 1990-96, Sta. WUSF-TV/FM, 1990—2002; exec. dir. WUSF advancement Sta. WUSF TV/FM, 2002—03; ret., 2003. Mem. bd. adminstrv. reps. U. South Fla. Pub. Broadcasting, 1999-2002; asst. state supr. for guidance svc. Ohio Dept. Edn., 1962-63; Am. Coun. on Edn. fellow in acad. adminstrn. U. Ill., 1965-66; evaluator Nat. Coun. for Accreditation Tchr. Edn., 1972-78; mem. planning com. Nat. Conf. Br. and Regional Campus Adminstrs., 1973-82, chmn., 1972, 80; chmn. planning com. Am. Coun. Edn. Acad. Fellows Working Reunion, 1972, 79, 85; vice chmn. Am. Coun. Edn. Coun. Fellows, 1980-81, chmn., 1981-82, exec. com., 1980-83, chmn. S.E. Region Conf., 1988, mem. alumni rels. com.; mem. U. South Fla. Interdisciplinary Ctr. on Digital and Computational Video, 1999-2002; co-chair Internat. Workshop on Digital and Computational Video, 1999, 2000; cons., lectr. in field. Co-author: Counseling; Selected Readings, 1962, Educational Administration: Selected Readings, 1965, 2d edit., 1971, Analysis of Educational Change in Ohio Public Schools, 1968; contbr. articles to profl. jours.; singer: Palma Ceia United Meth. Ch. Choir, 1979-. Gen. chmn. Mansfield Area United Way campaign, 1975, bd. dir., 1976-78, v.p., 1977, 78; bd. dir. Mansfield Symphony Orch., 1972-78, pres., 1978; bd. dir. Rsch. for Better Schs., Inc., 1968-71, pres., 1970-71; mem. Kiwanis Club Mansfield, 1971-78, bd. dir., 1974-78; mem. citizens adv. com. Richland County Regional Planning Commn., 1973-74, bd. dir., 1975-78, v.p.; mem. Manpower Adv. Coun. Richland and Morrow Counties, 1977-78; trustee Hillsbrough County Hosp. Authority, Tampa, Fla., 1980-84, Tampa Heart Ctr., 1982-84; sec.-treas., 1983-84; mem. Leadership Tampa, 1982-83, Leadership Tampa Alumni, 1983-2003, 2006—, Leadership Tampa Bay, 1992—2003; mem. Tampa-Hillsborough Cable adv. com., 1984-92, vice chmn., 1987-88, chmn., 1988-92; instl. rep. PBS and Nat. Pub. Radio, Am. Pub. TV Stas. 1986-2001, Legis. adv., APTS, 1995-2001; market fund adv. com. CPB, 1996; steering com. Higher Edn. Telecomm. Consortium, 1995-2001; steering com., pub. broadcasting joint licensee Consortium, 1996-2001; bd. dir. Fla. Pub. Broadcasting Svc. Inc., 1986-2001, chair Long Range Planning Com., 1988-93, treas., 1991-93, vice chair, 1993-95, chair, 1995-97, chair programs and ops. com., 1993-95, exec. com. 1991-99; bd. dir. Program Resources Group, 1993-2001, exec. com., 1995-2001, vice-chair, sec., 1995-2001; mem. Palma Ceia United Meth. Ch., 1980—, chair coun. on ministries, 1985-86, chair pipe organ com., 1985-91, chair adminstrv. bd., coun., 1987-89, 93-98; mem. pastor parish com., 1990-92, 96-98, chair, 1992; mem. Master Chorale of Tampa Bay, 1983—, mem. bd. trustees, vol. devel. officer; bd. dir. Chorale Masterworks Festival, Inc., 1987—, v.p., 1991-93, chair and pres., 1993-95, 97-99, 2000-01, exec. com., 2002—, sr. advisor, 2004-, co-chair longrange planning com., 2005-06, chair Devel. Com., 2006-; bd. dir. So. Ednl. Comms. Assn., 1986-97, mem. budget and fin. com., 1989-91. bd. dir. Nat. Edn. Telecom. Assn., 1997-2002, long range planning coun. 1997-98; mem. Tampa Bay Area Com. Fgn. Rels., 2002—. With USAF, 1953-55; USAFR, ret. 1973. Recipient Best Comprehensive Grassroots Program award, Am. Pub. TV Stas., 1999; Nat. Def. Edn. Act fellow, Ohio State U., 1961. Mem. Assn. Higher Edn. (life), Ohio State U. Assn. (life), Nat. Univ. Continuing Edn. Assn. (instnl. rep., bd. dirs. region III, honors and awards com. 1986-90), Greater Tampa C. of C. (chmn. emergency preparedness task force 1991-94), Civitan (club founding pres. 1980-82), Rotary (Downtown Tampa, chair music com. 2003-04, 06-07), Columbus North H.S. ALumni Club (life), Phi Delta Kappa (life), Kappa Delta Pi, Phi Kappa Phi. Democrat. Methodist. Personal E-mail: jim@jbheck.com.

HECK, JENNIFER LEIGH, neonatal clinical nurse specialist, educator; b. Tulsa, Okla., May 17, 1977; d. Alfred Lee and Carol Ann Tibbs; m. Allan Shane Heck, Dec. 31, 2004. BSN, U. Okla., 1999, MSN, 2004. RN Okla. Bd. of Nursing, cert. level III NICU, Nat. Certification Corp. Student nurse technician VA Med. Ctr., Oklahoma City, 1998—99; nurse Hillcrest Med. Ctr., Tulsa, 1999—, mem. unit coun. com., 2002—04, primary dayshift preceptor, 2003—04, mem. pain adv. com., 2004; nurse NormanRegional Hosp., Okla., 2005; asst. prof. nursing Bacone Coll., Muskogee, Okla., 2006—. Recipient Advanced Edn. Nurse Traineeship grant, U. Okla. Coll. of Nursing, 2000—03. Mem.: AACN, Acad. Neonatal Nursing, Assn. Women's Health, Obs. and Neonatal Nurses (scholarship Okla. sect. 2003), U. Okla Alumni Club, Sigma Theta Tau. Democrat. Baptist. Avocations: reading, travel, cooking. Office: Bacone Coll Dept Nursing 2299 Old Bacone Rd Muskogee OK 74403

HECK, ROBERTA M., poet, writer; b. Durham, NC, Oct. 13, 1954; d. Otis Walter Mc Culler and Dora Betty Ann (Tillman) McCuller; m. Roderick Orlando Heck, Sept. 23, 1957; 1 child, Ronald Ray. Sr. v.p. RnRh Pub., Jackson, NJ, 2000—; mng. ptnr. RnRh Pub. with Robert Heck Ministries, LLC, Roberta Heck Collection LLC. Author: After the Storm is Over, 2002, The Dawn of A New Day, 2003, One With God, 2005 (Poet of the Yr., 2005), Changes of the Mind: Thoughts With Sober Conclusions, 2007. Recipient Editor's Choice award, Internat. Soc. Poets, 2000, Poetic Excellence award, Poetry of Today, 2002, Shakespear Trophy of Excellence, Poet Soc., 2002. Mem.: NJ Poet Soc., Inc., Delaware Valley Poets. Avocations: fishing, boating, swimming. Home and Office: Roberta Heck Ministries RNRH Pub PO Box 57 Jackson NJ 08527 Office Phone: 732-928-1486. Business E-Mail: heckro@verizon.net, roberta@robertaheckministries.org.

HECK, TODD WILLIAM, lawyer; b. Bristol, Pa., June 9, 1955; m. Maureen Nancy McCauley. BS in Mgmt., Lehigh U., Bethlehem, Pa., 1976; JD, Villanova U. Sch. Law, 1979; LLM in Taxation, NYU, 1983. Bar: Pa. 1979, NJ 1980, NY 1990. Assoc. Basile & Testa P.A., Vineland, NJ, 1990—96, ptnr., 1996—. Counsel Citizens United to Protect the Maurice River and It's Tributaries, Inc., Millville, NJ, 1986—; instr., bus. law Cumberland County Coll., Vineland, NJ, 1992—93; solicitor Maurice River Twp. Zoning Bd., Leesburg, NJ, 1993—97, Cumberland County Improvement Auth., Millville, 2005—. Treas. Peterson Christy Smith Campaign, Vineland, NJ, 2005—06. Recipient Disting. Svc. award, Cumberland County Bd. Chosen Freeholders, 1987. Mem.: NJ. State Bar Assn., Cumberland County Bar Assn. Avocations: skiing, travel. Office: Basile & Testa PA 424 Landis Ave Vineland NJ 08360 Office Phone: 856-691-2300. Office Fax: 856-691-5655. Business E-Mail: thecknj@comcast.net.

HECKADON, ROBERT GORDON, plastic surgeon; b. Brantford, Ont., Can., Jan. 30, 1933; s. Frederick Gordon and Laura (Penrose) H.; BA, U. Western Ont., 1954, MD, 1960; postgrad. U. Toronto, 1960-66, U. Vienna, 1966; m. Camilla Joyce Russell, July 11, 1959; children: David, Louise, Peter, William, Barbara. Intern, Toronto Gen. Hosp., 1960-61; asst. resident Toronto Western Hosp., 1961, Toronto Wellesley Hosp., 1962, Toronto Gen. Hosp., 1962-63; resident in plastic surgery St. Michael's Hosp., Toronto, 1963, Toronto Western Hosp., 1964, Toronto Gen. Hosp., 1964, Toronto Hosp. for Sick Children, 1965; asst. resident orthopedics Toronto East Gen. Hosp., 1965-66; practice medicine specializing in plastic surgery, Windsor, Ont., Can., 1966-96; mem. surg. staff Hotel Dieu Grace, Windsor, Windsor Regional Hosp.; med. dir. Workplace Safety and Ins., Windsor. Served with RCAF, 1951-56. Fellow ACS; mem. Canadian Med. Assn., Ont. Med. Assn., Essex County Med. Assn., Windsor Acad. Surgery, Royal Coll. Physicians and Surgeons, Can. Soc. Plastic Surgeons.

HECKEL, JOHN LOUIS (JACK HECKEL), aerospace management executive; b. Columbus, Ohio, July 12, 1931; s. Russel Criblez and Ruth Selma (Heid) H.; m. Jacqueline Ann Alexander, Nov. 21, 1959 (div. 1993); children: Heidi, Holly, John; m. Linda Holleran, Aug. 1, 1994. BS, U. Ill., 1954; PhD with honors, Nat. U. San Diego, 1984. Divsn. mgr. Aerojet Divsn., Azusa, Calif., 1956-70, Seattle and Washington, 1956-70; pres. Aerojet-Space Gen. Co., El Monte, Calif., 1970-72, Aerojet Liquid Rocket Co., Sacramento, 1972-77; group v.p. Aerojet Sacramento Cos., 1977-81; pres. Aerojet Gen., La Jolla, Calif., 1981-85, chmn., CEO, 1985-87; pres., COO GenCorp., Akron, 1987-94, also bd. dirs. Bd. dirs. WD-40 Corp., Petritech, Corp. Bd. dirs. San Diego Econ. Devel. Corp., 1983-86, Akron Regional Devel. Bd., Akron Gen. Hosp., Summit County United Way; pres. Summit Edn. Partnership Found., Akron. Recipient Disting. Alumni award U. Ill. Ann. Alumni Conv., 1979 Fellow AIAA (assoc.); mem. Aerospace Industries Assn. Am. (gov. 1981), Navy League U.S., Am. Def. Preparedness Assn., San Diego C. of C. (bd. dirs.)

HECKEL, RICHARD WAYNE, metallurgical engineering educator; b. Pitts., Jan. 25, 1934; s. Ralph Clyde and Esther Vera (Zoerb) H.; m. Peggy Ann Simmons, Jan. 3, 1959 (dec. Apr. 1998); children: Scott Alan, Laura Ann Rowe. BS in Metall. Engring., Carnegie Mellon, 1955, MS, 1958, PhD, 1959. Sr. rsch. metallurgist E.I. duPont de Nemours & Co., Wilmington, Del., 1959—63; prof. metall. engring. Drexel U., Phila., 1963—71; head dept. materials sci. and engring. Carnegie Mellon, Pitts., 1971—76; prof. materials sci. and engring. Mich. Tech. U., Houghton, 1976—96, prof. emeritus, 1996—; tech. dir., owner Engring. Trends, Houghton, 2000—. Commr. at large Engring. Workforce Commn., 1997—, founder, tech. dir. Engring. Trends (e-commerce). Contbr. articles to profl. jours. Served as 1st lt. Ordnance Corps, U.S. Army, 1959-60. Recipient Lindback Teaching award Drexel U., 1968; Research award Mich. Tech. U., 1985 Fellow ASM Internat. (life; Bradley Stoughton Young Tchr. of Metallurgy award 1969, Phila. Ednl. Achievement award 1967); mem. The Metals, Minerals and Materials Soc., Am. Welding Soc. (Adams Meml. mem. 1966), Am. Soc. Engring. Edn., Sigma Xi, Omicron Delta Kappa, Tau Beta Pi, Phi Kappa Phi, Alpha Sigma Mu. Address: Engring Trends 1281 Hickory Ln Houghton MI 49931-1609 Home Phone: 906-482-2208; Office Phone: 906-482-1523. Personal E-mail: rheckel@chartermi.net, engtrend@up.net.

HECKELMAN, JAC C., economics professor; b. Somerset, NJ, Aug. 22, 1967; s. Sol and Sandra Heckelman. BA, U. Tex., Austin, 1989; PhD, U.Md., Coll. Pk., 1994. Vis. asst. prof. Wake Forest U., Winston-Salem, NC, 1994—95; ops. rsch. analyst Joint Warfare Analysis Ctr., Dahlgren, Va., 1995—96; asst. prof. of econ. Wake Forest U., 1996—2001, assoc. prof. of econ., 2001—, mcculloch family fellow, 2002—06. Law and Social Sciences grant, NSF, 2004—05, R. J. Reynolds Co. Rsch. Leave scholar, Wake Forest U., 2005—06. Mem.: Am. Econ. Assn., Pub. Choice Soc., So. Econ. Assn. (life). Office: Wake Forest U 110 Carswell Hall Winston Salem NC 27109 Office Phone: 336-758-5923.

HECKER, DAVID, lawyer; b. 1947; JD, Cornell Univ. Sr. v.p., gen. counsel SC Johnson & Son Inc., Racine, Wis., 2005—. Office: SC Johnson & Son 1525 Howe St Racine WI 53403 Office Phone: 262-260-2000. Office Fax: 202-260-4253.

HECKER, MICHAEL HANNS LOUIS, retired electrical engineer, speech scientist; b. Hamburg, Germany, Mar. 30, 1936; came to U.S., 1948; s. Hanns Ewald Hecker and Wilhelmine (Corinth) H. Klopfer; m. Elizabeth Ann Bowen, Sept. 3, 1960 (div.); 1 child, Serena Suzanne; m. Dorothy Louise Dunlap, Mar. 12, 1971. BSEE with honors, Northeastern U., 1959; MSEE, MIT, 1961; PhD in Speech & Hearing Scis., Stanford U., 1974. Sr. rsch. engr. Bolt Beranek and Newman Inc., Cambridge, Mass., 1964-67, SRI Internat., Menlo Park, Calif., 1967-95. Cons. forensic acoustics, Los Altos, Calif., 1967-98; retained by White House during Watergate investigation to examine presdl. tapes; sci. cons. Nat. Commn. Rev. Fed. & State Laws Relating to Wiretapping & Electronic Surveillance, 1974-76. Author: Speaker Recognition, 1971; co-editor: Speech Evaluation in Psychiatry/Medicine, 1981; contbr. articles to profl. jours., chpts. to med. books. 1st lt. U.S. Army, 1962-64. Grantee, NIH, 1982—88. Mem. Eta Kappa Nu, Tau Beta Pi, Sigma Xi. Achievements include rsch. in speech changes related to emotional states, psychological stress, and neurological disorders; developed methods of speech analysis to assess behavioral risk for coronary heart disease. E-mail: midohecker@earthlink.net.

HECKER, PETER S., lawyer; b. NYC, Sept. 4, 1949; BA, Carleton Coll., 1970; JD, U. Calif., Berkeley, 1973. Bar: N.Y. 1974, Calif. 1975, Am. Bar. Assoc. Atty. Heller, Ehrman, White & McAuliffe, San Francisco, 1975—. Mem. ABA, Order of Coif, Phi Beta Kappa. Office: Heller Ehrman White & McAuliffe 333 Bush St San Francisco CA 94104-2806 Office Phone: 415-772-6080. E-mail: phecker@hewm.com.

HECKERT, PAUL CHARLES, sociologist, educator; b. May 30, 1929; s. Paul Kester and Clara Belle (Plessinger) H.; m. Sara Mae (Raezer), Sept. 6, 1952; children: Paul Andrew, Druann Maria, Daniel Alex, Nathanael Alan, Diane Manette. BA, Catawba Coll., 1951; BD, Lancaster Theol. Sem., 1954; MS, Cornell, 1959, PhD, 1964. Ordained min. United Ch. of Christ, 1954. Missionary United Ch. of Christ, Honduras, 1954—60; clergyman of various Meth. ch. NY, 1960—64; assoc. prof. sociology, also chmn. dept. Catawaba Coll., NC, 1964—68; prof. Catawba Coll., NC, 1968—72; chmn. joint dept. sociology Livingstone Coll, Salisbury, NC; chmn. dept. sociology Frostburg State U., Md., 1972—87, prof. Md., 1987—94. Support visitor, Prison, 1995—; del. Rowan Coop. Christian ministry, 1968-72; Spanish and sociology vol. tchr. fed. prison; mem. leadership devel. com. Pa. West Conf., United Ch. of Christ, 1973-78. Bd. dir. Salisbury Rowan Cmty. Svc. Coun., 1971-72. Served with AUS, 1948-50. Ford fellow, summer 1968, NASA, ASEE summer faculty fellow, 1969, 77, AEC summer faculty fellow, 1973. Contbg. book reviews. to profl. journals. Recipient Vol. of Yr. Award, Fed. Correctional Instn., 2001; grantee, NEH, 1975, 1979, 1983, 1986. Mem. AAAS, Am. Sociol. Assn., Rural Sociol. Soc., Allegany County Ret. Tchr. Assn. (mem. chmn. 1997, pres. elect 1998, 2003, pres. 1999, 2004), Phi Kappa Phi, Alpha Kappa Delta, Sigma Delta Pi, Delta Tau Kappa. Home: 13 N Woodlawn Ave Cumberland MD 21502-7254

HECKLER, FREDERICK ROGER, plastic surgeon; b. NYC, Mar. 7, 1942; s. Frances George; children: Jeremy, Michael, Adrienne, Lauren. Student, Tufts U., 1959-62, MD, 1966. Diplomate Nat. Bd. Med. Examiners, Am. Bd. Surgery, Am. Bd. Plastic Surgery with qualification in surgery of the hand. Intern in surgery U. Chgo. Med. Ctr., 1966-67; resident in gen. surgery Tufts New Eng. Med. Ctr., Boston, 1967-69; fellow in surgery Malmo (Sweden) Gen. Hosp., 1969-70; resident in plastic surgery Wilford Hall USAF Med. Ctr., San Antonio, 1973-75; fellow in hand surgery Denver Gen. Hosp., 1976-77; chief surgery USAF Hosp., Taiwan, 1976-77; asst. prof. surgery U. Miss. Med. Ctr., Jackson, 1977-79, chief divsn. plastic surgery, 1979-82; dir. divsn. plastic surgery Allegheny Gen. Hosp., Pitts., 1982—; clin. assoc. prof. plastic surgery U. Pitts. Sch. Medicine, 1982—. Active med. staff Miss. Cripple Children's Treatment and Tng. Ctr., Miss., 1981-82; dir. cleft palate clinic Allegheny Gen. Hosp., Pitts., 1982-88; attending physician St. Margaret Meml. Hosp., Pitts., 1984-89, Montefiore Hosp., Pitts., 1986-89, Divine Providence Hosp., Pitts., 1991—, North Hills Passavant Hosp., Pitts., 1993; cons. med. staff Harmarville Rehab. Ctr., Inc., Pitts., 1985; cons. in plastic surgery VA Hosp., Pitts., 1993—, Miss. Meth. Rehab. Ctr., Jackson, 1977-82, VA Hosp., Jackson, 1977-82; dir. burn unit U. Miss. Med. Ctr., Jackson, 1979-82, co-dir. hand surgery svc., 1979-82; mem. med. staff Miss. Crippled Children's Treatment and Tng. Ctr., Jackson, 1981-82; presenter in field. Contbr. numerous articles to profl. publs., chpts. to books; assoc. editor Jour. Plastic and Reconstructive Surgery. Lt. col. USAF, 1972-76. Mem. AMA, ACS, Am. Soc. Plastic and Reconstructive Surgeons, Am. Assn. Plastic Surgeons, Assn. Mil. Plastic Surgeons, Soc. Air Force Clin. Surgeons, Am. Burn Assn., Internat. Soc. for Burn Injuries, Am. Cleft Palate Assn., Plastic Surgery Rsch. Coun., Am. Soc. for Surgery of Hand, Am. Assn. Hand Surgery, Royal Soc. Medicine, Assn. Acad. Chmn. of Plastic Surgery, Lipolysis Soc. N.Am., Allegheny County Med. Soc., Pa. Med. Soc., Ohio Valley Plastic Surg. Soc., Pitts. Surg. Soc. Office: Allegheny Gen Hosp 320 E North Ave Pittsburgh PA 15212-4756 Office Phone: 412-359-4352.

HECKLER, GERARD VINCENT, lawyer; b. Utica, NY, Feb. 18, 1941; s. Gerard Vincent and Mary Jane (Finocan) H. BA, Union Coll., 1962; JD, Syracuse U., 1970; MA in Clin. Psychology, Antioch U., 1994; postgrad., The Fielding Inst., 1995. Bar: Ill. 1971, Calif. 1980, Mass. 1986, N.Y. 1986, U.S. Supreme Ct. 1985. Assoc. Martin, Craig, Chester & Sonnenschein, Chgo., 1970—73, Goldstein, Goldberg & Fishman, Chgo., 1973—76; ptnr. Heckler & Enstrom, Chgo., 1976—80; pvt. practice law L.A., Irvine, 1980—85; sr. trial atty. Law Office of Harden Bennion, LA, 1985—87, Rafferty & Polich, Cambridge, Mass., 1987—88; trial atty. Acret, Gropman & Turner, LA, 1989—92; of counsel Lanak & Hanna PC, Santa Ana, Calif., 1992—. Instr. trial skills and evidence Calif. State Bar, 1987—; judge pro tem L.A. Mcpl. Ct., 1991—. Lt. USCG, 1964-67, Vietnam. Mem. Calif. State Bar (Bd. Govs. commendation 1986), L.A. County Bar Assn., Acad. Family Mediators, Ill. Bar Assn., Mass. Bar Assn., N.Y. Bar Assn. Avocations: sports, theater, public speaking. Office Phone: 714-550-0418. E-mail: guheckler@lanak-hanna.com.

HECKMAN, GARY WALTER, military career officer; b. Des Moines; m. Sally Mitchell; children: Wendy, Ryan, Benjamin. BA in Edn., U. No. Iowa, 1972; MPA, Troy State U., 1981; grad., Air Command and Staff Coll., 1981, Armed Forces Staff Coll., 1984, Air War Coll., 1989; M in Nat. Security and Strategic Studies, Naval War Coll., 1992. Commd. 2d lt. USAF, 1973, advanced through grades to brig. gen., 1997, C130 transport and AC-130 gunship aircrew and staff, 1974-79, with hdqs., 1979-80, 92-94, plans officer 1st spl. ops. wing, 1980-83, with hdqs. European Commandhdqrs., 1984-87, with hdqs. Air Force spl. ops., 1987-89, dep. dir. programming and policy Mil. Airlift Command Scott AFB, Ill., 1989-91, commdr. 16th Spl. Ops. Group Hurlburt Field, 1994-96; dir. resources (J8), chief of staff J7/J8 US Spec Ops Cmd., 1996—; co-dir. Air Force's base-closing analysis team, 2004—. Decorated Legion of Merit with one oak leaf cluster, Def. Meritorious Svc. medal, Meritorious Svc. medal with three oak leaf clusters, Air medal, Joint Svc. Commendation medal, Air Force Commendation medal, Air Force Achievement medal.

HECKMAN, GREGORY A., food products executive; B in Agrl. Econs., U. Ill. With ConAgra Foods, Inc., Omaha, 1984—, pres., COO Trade Group, 1998—2001, pres., COO Agrl. Products Co., 2002—03, pres., COO Ingredients Group, 2003—06, pres., COO Comml. Products, 2006—. Office: ConAgra Foods Inc 1 ConAgra Dr Omaha NE 68102-5001 Office Phone: 402-595-4000.*

HECKMAN, HENRY TREVENNEN SHICK, retired steel executive; b. Mar. 27, 1918; s. H. Raymond and Charlotte E. (Shick) Heckman; m. Helen Clausen Wright, Nov. 28, 1946 (dec. Mar. 29, 2007); children: Sharon Anita(dec.) , Charlotte Marie. AB, Lehigh U., Bethlehem, Pa., 1939. Advt. prodn. mgr. Republic Steel Corp., Cleve., 1940—42; editor Enduro Era, 1946—51, account exec., 1953—54, asst. dir. advt., 1957—65, dir. advt., 1965—82; ptnr. Applegate & Heckman, Washington, 1955—56; advt. mgr. Harris Corp., 1956—57; ret., 1982. Permanent chmn. Joint Com. Audit Comparability, 1968—93; chmn. Media Comparability Coun., 1969—83; chmn. indsl. advertisers com. Greater Cleve. Growth Assn., 1973—76; chmn. pubs. com. Lehigh U., 1971—76; pres.'s adv. coun. Ashland Coll., 1966—76; advt. adv. coun. Kent State U., 1976—81; exec. com. Cleve. chpt. ARC, 1968—74; mem. Rep. Fin. Exec. Com., 1966—87; coord. adv. coun. pub. svcs. campaign Employer Support Guard and Res., 1973—83, 1990—2003. Lt. USNR, 1942—46, comdr. USNR, 1951—53, Korea. Named Advt. Man of Yr., 1969; named to Advt. Effectiveness Hall of Fame, 1967, Cleve. Graphic Arts Coun. Hall of Distinction, 1981; recipient G.D. Crain, Jr. award, 1973, Disting. Alumnus award, Lehigh U., 1979. Mem.: SAR (pres. Western Res. Soc. 1979, Archibald Willard award 1996), New Eng. Soc. (trustee 2007), Steel Svc. Ctr. Inst. (advt. adv. com. 1965—77), Am. Iron and Steel Inst. (com. chmn. 1961—69), Assn. Nat. Advertisers (chmn. shows and exhibits com. 1966—74, dir. 1969—72), Bus. Mktg. Assn. (pres. 1968—69, Best Seller award 1966, Hall of Fame 1973), Indsl. Marketers Cleve. (past pres., Golden Mousetrap award 1968), Ctr. Mktg. Comm. (chmn. bd. 1965), Ohio Soc. SAR (Hub Scott award 1995), Mil. Order World Wars (comdr. 1980), Cleve. Grays (trustee 1980—82), Cheshire Cheese (pres. 1982), Cleve. Advt. Club (pres. 1961—62, Hall of Fame 1980), Early Settlers, Pi Delta Epsilon. Home: 6000 Nob Hill Dr Apt 401 Chagrin Falls OH 44022-3358

HECKMAN, JAMES JOSEPH, economist, educator; b. Chgo., Apr. 19, 1944; s. John Jacob and Bernice Irene (Medley) H.; m. Lynne Pettler, 1979; children: Jonathan Jacob, Alma Rachel. AB in Math. summa cum laude (Woodrow Wilson fellow), Colo. Coll., 1965, D (hon.), 2001; MA in Econ., Princeton U., 1968, PhD in Econ. (Harold Willis Dodds fellow), 1971; MA (hon.), Yale U., 1989; D (hon.), U. Chile, 2002, Universidad Autonoma del Estados de Mex., Toluca, 2003, U. Montreal, 2004; DHL (hon.), Bard Coll., 2004. From lectr. to assoc. prof. Columbia U., 1970-74; assoc. prof. econs. U. Chgo., 1973-76, prof., 1976—, Henry Schultz prof. of econ., 1985-95, prof. econs. Harris Sch. Pub. Policy, 1990—, dir. Ctr. for Program Evaluation Harris Sch. Pub. Policy, 1991—, Henry Schultz Disting. Svc. prof., 1995—, dir. Econs. Rsch. Ctr. dept. econs., 1997—, Changjiang River Scholar prof., 2004—; A. Whitney Griswold prof. econs. Yale U., New Haven, 1988-90, Sterling prof., 1990, prof. dept. stats., 1990, dir. dept. econs. Econs. Rsch. Ctr., 1997—; disting. prof. microeconometrics Univ. Coll., London, 2004—, disting. chair microeconomics, 2004—, prof. sci. and society Dublin, 2005. Rsch. assoc. Nat. Bur. Econs. Rsch., 1970-77, sr. rsch. assoc., 1977-85, 87—; Irving Fisher prof. econs. Yale U., 1984; treas. Chgo. Econ. Rsch. Assocs.; rsch. assoc. Econs. Rsch. Ctr.-NORC, 1985—; cons. in field; cons. Chgo. Urban League, 1978-86; mem. status Black Ams. com. NRC; lectr. in field.; hon. prof. U. Tucuman, Argentina, 1998, Hangzhou U. Sci. and Tech., Wuhan, China, 2001, Wuhan U., 2003. Co-author: (with Alan Krueger) Income Inequality in America: What Role for Human Capital Policy, 2004; editor Jour. Polit. Economy, 1981-87; assoc. editor Jour. Econometrics, 1977-83, Jour. Labor Econs., 1983—, Econs. Revs., 1987—, Rev. of Econs. and Statistics, 1994-2002, Jour. Econ. Perspectives, 1989-96, Labor Econs., 1992—; editor: (with B. Singer), Longitudinal Analysis of Labor Market Data, 1985; (with E. Leamer) Handbook of Econometrics, Vol. 5, 2001, vol. 6, 2005, (with

Carmen Pages) Law and Employment Lessons from the Latin America and The Caribbean, 2004; Am. editor Rev. Econ. Studies, 1982-85; contbr. articles to profl. jours. Founding faculty and curriculum com. U. Chgo. Harris Sch. Pub. Policy. Recipient John Bates Clark prize, 1983, Louis Benezet Alumni prize Colo. Coll., 1985, Nobel Prize in Econs., 2000, Paul Harris award Internat. Rotary Assn., 2002, Jacob Mincer award, 2005, Ulysses medal U. Coll. Dublin, Aigner award, 2005; J.S. Guggenheim Found. fellow, 1978-79, Social Sci. Rsch. Coun. fellow, 1977-78, Ctr. for Advanced Study in Behavioral Scis. fellow, 1978-79; NDEA fellow; NIH fellow. Fellow Am. Bar Found. (sr. rsch. affiliate 1989-91, sr. rsch. fellow 1991-), Econometric Soc. (mem. coun. 2001—), Am. Acad. Arts and Scis., Am. Statis. Assn., Soc. Labor Econs.; mem. NAS, Am. Econ. Assn. (exec. com. 2000-03), Midwest Econs. Assn. (pres.-elect 1996-97, pres. 1997-98), Western Econ. Assn. (pres.-elect 2005-), Indsl. Rels. Rsch. Assn., Econ. Sci. Assn. (founder), Econometric Soc. (coun. 2000-06), Phi Beta Kappa. Office: U Chgo Dept Econs 1126 E 59th St Chicago IL 60637-1580 Home Phone: 773-268-4547; Office Phone: 773-702-0634. Business E-Mail: jjh@uchicago.edu.

HECKMAN, JEROME HAROLD, lawyer; b. Washington, June 7, 1927; s. Morris and Pauline (German) H.; m. Margot Resh, June 16, 1948 (div. Oct. 1977); children: Eric Stephen, Carey Eugene; m. Ilona Ely Grenadier, Jan. 2, 1986. BSS, Georgetown U., 1948, LLB, 1953, JD, 1967. Bar: D.C. 1953, U.S. Supreme Ct. 1965. Assoc. Dow, Lohnes & Albertson, Washington, 1954-59, ptnr., 1959-62; sr. ptnr. Keller and Heckman, Washington, 1962—. Gen. counsel Soc. of Plastics Industry Inc., N.Y.C., Washington, 1954—2006, Broadcasting Publs. Inc. Mag., Washington (co. sold to L.A. Times), 1968-87, Disposables Assn. Inc. (now named Internat. Nonwovens and Disposables Assn.), 1958-67. Contbr. articles to profl. jours. Chmn. regional Rep. com., Md., 1966-72; pres. Plastics Acad., 1995-97. Named to Hall of Fame of Plastics Industry, 1987; recipient Spes Hominum award, Nat. Sanitation Found., 1987, William Bradbury award, Soc. Plastics, 2000, Paul R. Dean Disting. Alumni award, Georgetown U. Law Ctr., 2001, Internat. Achievement award, Internat. Soc. Regulatory Toxicologists and Pharmacologists, 2005; Dirs. citation, Ctr. Food Safety and Applied Nutrition, FDA, 2000. Mem. ABA, Bar Assn. D.C., George Town Club, Woodmont Country Club, Phi Delta Phi. Avocations: golf, tennis. Office: Keller & Heckman 1001 G St NW Ste 500 Washington DC 20001-4545 Office Phone: 202-434-4110. Business E-Mail: heckman@khlaw.com.

HECKMANN, RICHARD J., sporting goods company executive; m. Mary Heckmann; 6 children. Attended, Univ. Hawaii, Small Co. Mgmt. Prog., Harvard Bus. Sch. Founder & chmn. Tower Scientific Corp., 1971—77; assoc. adminstr. SBA, Washington, 1978—79; founding shareholder Callaway Golf Inc.; owner & dir. Smith Goggles, Sun Valley, Idaho; founder & chmn. USFilter Inc., 1990—99; chmn. Vivendi Water, 1999—2001; dir. K2 Inc., Carlsbad, Calif., 1997—, chmn., 2000—, CEO, 2002—. Trustee Eisenhower Med. Ctr., Univ. Calif., Riverside; mem. Bus. Council Univ. Notre Dame Bus. Sch.

HECKT, MELVIN DEAN, lawyer; b. Dysart, Iowa, Apr. 21, 1924; s. Wesley T. and Ada Merle(Lawyer) H.; m. Dorothy M. Simons, Sept. 4, 1948; children— Janice, Paul, Mary, Barbara, William, Thomas. B.A. in Econs., State U. Iowa, 1948, J.D., 1950. Bar: Minn., 1950, Iowa 1950, U.S. Dist. Ct. (Minn.), U.S. Supreme Ct. Assoc. Snyder, Gale, Hoke, Richards, Janes (name changed to Bassford, Heckt, Lockhart & Mullin), Mpls., 1950-55, ptnr., 1955—94, prtnr. Luther, Heckt & Cameron, 1994-. Served with USMC, 1943-45. Decorated Bronze Star. Mem. Iowa Bar Assn., Minn. Bar Assn., Am. Legion, VFW, past dir. Marine Corps Heritage Found., U.S. Marine Raider Assn. (past pres.). Republican. Lutheran. Contbr. articles to profl. jours. Address: 1905 E Wayzata Blvd Ste 115 Wayzata MN 55391-2070 Office Phone: 952-449-4145. Office Fax: 952-449-4149.

HECOX, MORRIS B., academic administrator; Grad., Colo. Coll., U. Colo. Law Sch. Lawyer, mining and natural resources law, Denver, NYC; pres., founder Cook Street Sch. of Fine Cooking, Denver, 1999—. Served in US Army. Office: Cook Street School of Fine Cooking 1937 Market St Denver CO 80202 Office Phone: 303-308-9300. Office Fax: 303-308-9400.*

HEDAHL, GORDEN ORLIN, theater educator, dean; b. Minot, ND, Jan. 2, 1946; s. Chester Owen and Delores May (Johnson) H.; m. Kathleen Josephine Sawin, Sept. 2, 1967 (div.); children: Marc Oscar, Melissa Ann; m. Jean Louise Loudon, Dec. 31, 1983. BS, U. N.D., 1968, MA, 1972; PhD, U. Minn., 1980. Postdoctoral fellow Purdue U., West Lafayette, Ind., 1981-82; prof. theater U. Wis., Whitewater, 1970-92, chair dept. theatre and dance, 1986-89, assoc. dean Coll. Arts, 1989-90, acting assoc. vice chancellor, 1991-92, dean Coll. Arts. and Scis. River Falls, 1998—; dean Coll. Liberal Arts U. Alaska, Fairbanks, 1993-98; acad. planner U. Wis. System, 1990-91. Author: (plays) Tall Tales and True, 1976, The Brothers Grimm, 1977, Land of the Rising Sun, 1979, Trolls and Other Fjord Folk, 1983, Andersen's Storybook, 1986, The Magic of Oz, 1987, African Folk Tales, 1989, Tell Me a Story, 1992; assoc. editor: Guide to Curriculum Planning in Classroom Drama and Theatre, 1989. Recipient Roseman Excellence in Teaching award U. Wis., Whitewater, U. Wis. Mem. Am. Coun. of Colls. of Arts and Scis., Am. Alliance for Theatre and Edn., Internat. Coun. of Fine Arts Deans, Theatre in Higher Edn., Rotary. Lutheran. Office: U Wis Coll Arts and Scis 410 S 3d St River Falls WI 54022-5001 Office Phone: 715-425-4896. E-mail: gorden.o.hedahl@uwrf.edu.

HEDBERG, PAUL CLIFFORD, broadcast executive; b. Cokato, Minn., May 28, 1939; s. Clifford L. and Florence (Erenberg) Hedberg; m. Juliet Ann Schubert, Dec. 30, 1962; children: Mark, Ann. Student, Hamline U., 1959-60, U. Minn., 1960-62. Program dir. Sta. KRIB, Mason City, Iowa, 1957-58, Sta. WMIN, Mpls., 1959; staff announcer Time-Life broadcast Sta. WTCN-AM-TV, Mpls., 1959-61, Crowell Collier Sta. KDWB, St. Paul, 1961-62; founder, pres. Sta. KBEW, Minn., 1963-81; founder, owner Sta. KQAD and KLQL-FM, Luverne, Minn., 1971-88; co-founder Sta. KMRS-AM, KKOK-FM, Morris, Minn., 1956-94, pres., 1974-94; founder, pres. Courtney Clifford Inc., Mpls., 1977-79; founder, owner Market Quoters Inc., Blue Earth, Iowa, 1974-96; pres. Complete Commodity Options Inc., Blue Earth, 1977-91; pres., owner Sta. KEEZ-FM, Mankato, Minn., 1977-92; founder, pres. Sta. KUOO-FM, Spirit Lake, Iowa, 1984-99; owner Sta. KRIB and KLSS-FM, Mason City, 1984-97; owner, pres. Sta. KAYL-AM-FM, Storm Lake, Iowa, 1990-99; pres. KLGA AM-FM, Algona, Iowa, 1993-99; CEO Hedberg Broadcasting Group, Blue Earth, 1976-99; pres. KSOU AM-FM, Sioux Center, Iowa, 1996-99. Pres. Blue Earth Indsl. Svcs. Corp., 1970—76, bd. dirs., Minn. Good Rds., v.p., 1976—79, pres., 1979—81; bd. dirs. Spirit Lake Industries; mem. affiliates bd. NBC Radio Network, 1990—95, chmn., 1991—95; pres., CEO Arnolds Park (Iowa) Amusement Pk., 1990—95; founder Sta. KUQQ-FM, Spirit Lake-Milford, 1996—99, Sta. KIHK-FM, Rock Valley, Iowa, 1997—99. Mem. Iowa Gt. Lakes Airport Commn., 1986—92; bd. dirs. Pavek Mus. Wonderful Wireless, St. Louis Park, Minn., 1987—. Named to, Mus. Broadcasting Hall of Fame, 2002; recipient Disting. Svc. award, Blue Earth Jaycees, 1971. Mem.: Iowa Broadcasters Assn. (Broadcaster of the Yr. 1998), Minn. AP Broadcasters (pres. 1966, bd. dirs. 1976—78), Minn. Assn. Broadcasters (radio bd. dirs. 1975—86, v.p. 1980—81, pres. 1983—84), Nat. Assn. Broadcasters (bd. dirs. 1985—89, 1993—95), Antique and Classic Boating Soc. (bd. dirs. 2003—), Iowa Lakes C. of C. (bd. dirs. 1985—86), Blue Earth C. of C. (pres. 1967, Leadership Recognition award 1967), Shriners, Masons, Grebdeh L. C. (founder 1995—). Lutheran. Home Phone: 239-434-8261. E-mail: Grebdeh@aol.com.

HEDDELL, GORDON S., federal agency administrator; b. St. Louis, Aug. 13, 1943; BA in Polit. Sci., U. Mo., 1971; MA, U. Ill. (formerly Sangamon State U.), 1975. Asst. spl. agt. in charge U.S. Secret Svc., Phila., deputy asst. dir. office tng., spl. agt. in charge v.p. protective divsn., 1995—98, asst. dir. office inspection, 1998—2000; inspector gen. U.S. Dept. Labor, Washington, 2000—. Aviator, chief warrant officer US Army, 1966—69. Former Woodrow Wilson Pub. Svc. fellow. Office: US Dept Labor S 5502 200 Constitution Ave NW Washington DC 20210 Office Phone: 202-693-5100. Business E-Mail: gheddell@oig.dol.gov.

HEDDEN, ANDREW S., lawyer; b. Hempstead, NY, June 3, 1941; BA, Hamilton Coll., 1963; LLB, Duke Univ., 1966. Bar: NJ 1966, NY 1970. Atty. Coudert Bros. LLP, NYC, 1968—, ptnr., Global Securities, Mergers & Acquisitions practices, former mem. exec. bd. Mem.: ABA, NY State Bar Assn. Office: Coudert Bros LLP 1114 Ave of the Americas New York NY 10036 Office Phone: 212-626-4422. Office Fax: 212-626-4120. Business E-Mail: heddena@coudert.com.

HEDDEN, WILLIAM JAMES, plastic surgeon; b. Mar. 10, 1963; AA with honors, Broward Cmty. Coll., Ft. Lauderdale, Fla., 1984; BS with honors in Sculpting and Anatomy, U. Fla., Gainesville, 1987; MD, U. South Fla., Tampa, 1993. Cert. Am. Bd. Plastic Surgery, 2002. Resident surgery La. State U. Med. Ctr., Shreveport, 1994—99, chief resident, 1998—99; resident plastic surgery U. Ala., Birmingham, 1999—2001; prin. Hedden Plastic Surgery, Birmingham. Diplomate Am. Bd. Surgery. Featured: magazines Birmingham Mag., 2004, 2005, 2006. Mem.: AMA, Ala. Med. Assn., So. Med. Assn., Jefferson Med. Assn., Am. Soc. Aesthetic Plastic Surgery, Am. Soc. Plastic Surgeons. Office: Hedden Plastic Surgery 111 Village St Ste 202 Birmingham AL 35242 Office Phone: 205-980-1744. Office Fax: 205-980-1334. E-mail: bill@heddenmd.com.

HEDDINGS, RAYMOND EUGENE, military officer; b. Hampton, Va., July 14, 1954; s. Raymond Andrew Jr. and Barbara Ann (Smith) H.; m. Faith Dawn Lea, Dec. 19, 1976; children: Joshua Ray, Elayne Lea. BA, U. So. Miss., 1976; MEd, No. Mont. Coll., 1984; JD, Creighton U., 1993. Commd. 2d lt. USAF, 1977, advanced through grades to lt. col., 1993, chief customer assistance sect. 2851 Air Base Group San Antonio, 1977-78, chief personnel utilization sect. 7275 Air Base Group San Vito, Italy, 1978-81, flight comdr. alternate wing command post 490 strategic Great Falls, Mont., 1981-83, missile combat crew comdr. instr. 341 strategic missile wing, 1983-84, chief ICBM ops. plans br. 321 strategic missile wing Grand Forks, N.D., 1984-88, chief ICBM timing sect. joint strategic target planning Omaha, 1988-92; nuclear survivability and security program mgr. Def. Nuclear Agy., Alexandria, Va., 1992—. Sunday sch. tchr. Chandler Acres Bapt. Ch., Omaha, 1988-90, New Life Bapt. Ch., Bellevue, Nebr., 19990-92, Lake Ridge Bapt. Ch.; mem. stewardship com. Calvary Bapt. Ch., Grand Forks, 1986-88, usher, lay reader, 1984-88. Named one of Outstanding Young Men Am., 1990. Mem. Student Bar Assn., Omicron Delta Kappa, Pi Gamma Mu, Alpha Phi Omega. Republican. Avocations: racquetball, golf, travel.

HEDER, JON, actor; b. Fort Collins, Co., Oct. 26, 1977; m. Kirsten Bales, Nov. 23, 2002; 1 child, Evan Jane. Student, BYU. Actor: (films) The Wrong Brother, 2000, Funky Town, 2000, Peluca, 2003, Napoleon Dynamite, 2004, Just Like Heaven, 2005, The Benchwarmers, 2006, School for Scoundrels, 2006, (voice) Monster House, 2006, Blades of Glory, 2007; host: (TV series) Saturday Night Live, 2005. Office: c/o Creative Artists Agy 9830 Wilshire Blvd Beverly Hills CA 90212*

HEDGE, ARTHUR JOSEPH, JR., manufacturing executive; b. Hudson County, NJ, Sept. 19, 1936; s. Arthur Joseph and Mary Cecelia (Kieran) H.; m. Julie Norton Dahm, Apr. 15, 1961; children: Arthur Joseph III, Peter Michael, Gregory Carlton. BS, St. Peter's Coll., Jersey City, 1960; MS, MIT, 1973. Several mktg. postions Data Processing divsn. IBM, NYC, 1960-68, sr. mktg. mgr. Data Processing divsn. Chgo., 1968-70, br. mgr. Data Processing divsn. NYC, 1970-73, dir. mktg. practices Data Processing divsn. White Plains, NY, 1973-74, regional mgr. Data Processing divsn. Chgo., 1974-77, v.p. mgmt. svcs. Data Processing divsn. White Plains, 1977-80, v.p. Real Estate and Constrn. divsn., 1980-85, pres. Real Estate and Constrn. divsn., 1985-87, IBM v.p. and pres. Real Estate and Constrn. divsn., 1987-88, IBM v.p. Corp. Real Estate and Constrn. divsn. Stamford, Conn., 1988-90, v.p. environ. affairs, 1990-93; pres., CEO, bd. dirs. Kroll Environ. Enterprises Inc. subs. Kroll Assocs., Stamford, 1993-97; chmn. Jannon Holdings, LLC, Stamford, 1997-2001, ABR Group, LLC, Westport, Conn., 2003—. Mem. adv. bd. Wharton Real Estate Ctr., Phila., 1988-94. Mem. vis. com. Harvard U. Grad. Sch. Design, Cambridge, 1985-91, Chgo. Crime Commn., 1974-77, Urban Gateways Exec. Com., Chgo., 1974-77, Conn. Bus. and Industry Assn. Exec. Com., Hartford, 1989-92, trustee, 1988-92; chmn. Bd. Regents Fairfield (Conn.) Coll. Prep. Sch., 1978-84; chmn. bd. dirs. White Plains Hosp. Ctr., 1985-92, trustee, bd. dirs., 1978—; chmn. bd. trustees Am. Festival Theatre, Stratford, Conn., 1988-93; trustee Coun. for Arts, White Plains, 1982-89, The Presbyn. Hosp. N.Y.C., 1993—; bd. dirs. N.Y. and Presbyn. Hosps., Inc., 1996—; vice chmn. HealthStar Network, 1996-97, 99, chmn., 1998. Alfred P.Sloan fellow MIT, 1972-73. Mem. Westchester County Assn. (vice-chmn. 1989-92, trustee bd. dirs. 1986-96), Southwestern Area Commerce and Industry Assn. of Conn. (bd. dirs. 1992-2001), Conn. Golf Club (bd. dirs. 1980-85). Roman Catholic. Avocations: golf, reading, the arts. Office: ABR Group LLC 320 Post Rd West Westport CT 06880 Office Phone: 203-221-3117.

HEDGEBETH, REGINALD D., lawyer, retail executive; BS, Pa. State U.; JD, Harvard U., 1996. Bar: Ga. 1996. Fin. analyst GE Capital Corp., Atlanta; assoc. King & Spalding LLP; v.p. legal Home Depot Inc., Atlanta; sr. v.p., gen. counsel, sec. Circuit City Stores Inc., Richmond, Va., 2005—. Mem.: State Bar Ga. Office: Circuit City Stores Inc 9950 Mayland Dr Richmond VA 23233-1464*

HEDGES, GEORGE REYNOLDS, lawyer, archaeologist; b. Phila., Feb. 26, 1952; s. Thomas Reed and Ann Hedges; m. Christy Susan Shonnard; children: George Shonnard, Duncan Fox. BA, U. Pa., Phila., MA, 1975; JD, U. So. Calif., LA, 1978. Bar: Calif. 1979. Letterhead ptnr. Quinn Emanuel Urquhart Oliver & Hedges, LA, 1998—. Pres. The Archaeology Fund, LA, 1995—. Trustee Claremont Grad. U., Calif., 2006. Recipient Commendation award, LA County Bd. Suprs., 1992. Mem.: Penn Club NY, Athenaeum, Calif. Inst. Tech. (assoc.). Achievements include discovery of ancient incense roads in Southern Arabia. Office: Quinn Emanuel Urquhart Oliver & Hedges 865 S Figueroa St Tenth Fl Los Angeles CA 90017 Office Phone: 213-443-3000. Business E-Mail: georgehedges@quinnemanuel.com.

HEDGES, HARRY GEORGE, retired computer scientist; b. Lansing, Mich., Oct. 7, 1923; s. Charles William and Elsie (Frost) H.; m. Mary J. Corbishley, June 14, 1944 (dec.); children: Susan, Martha; m. Kamla J. King, July 24, 1988. BS, Mich. State U., 1949, PhD, 1960; MS, U. Mich., 1954. Electronics engr. USAF Wright Air Devel. Center, Dayton, Ohio, 1949-51; research asso. U. Mich., 1951-54; instr. Mich. State U., East Lansing, 1954-60, asst. prof., 1960-63, asso. prof., 1963-69, prof., chmn. dept. computer sci., 1969-84, prof. emeritus, 1988—; sr. staff assoc. NSF, 1984-88, head Office Cross-Disciplinary Activities, 1988-92, program dir. undergrad. edn., 1992, program dir. exptl. and integrative activities, 1993—2003. Dir. Nat. Electronics Conf., Inc., 1968-75 Tech. editor: Analysis of Discrete Physical Systems, 1967; mem. Computer Sci. Bd, 1973-84; chmn., 1974-75. Chmn. Selective Service Bd. 264, Lansing, 1970-76. Served with AUS, 1943-46, PTO. NSF sci. faculty fellow, 1960 Mem. Am. Soc. Engring. Edn. (chmn. N.Central sect. 1968-69), IEEE (dir. 1967-69, treas. 1969, vice chmn. 1973, chmn. 1974, Southeastern Mich. sect.). Home: 4331 Embassy Park Dr NW Washington DC 20016-3607

HEDGES, JERRIS, medical educator, health services researcher; MS, MD. Chmn. dept. emergency medicine Oreg. Health & Scis. U., 1997—2005, vice-dean Sch. Medicine, 2005—. Editor: (med. jour.) Acad. Emergency Medicine, 1993—97; co-editor: (med. text) Clinical Procedures in Emergency Medicine, 4th edit. Mem.: Nat. Acad. Scis. Inst. of Medicine, Soc for Acad. Emergency Medicine. Achievements include research in the evaluation of Trauma System impact and effectiveness. Office: Oreg Health Scis U 3181 SW Sam Jackson Pk Rd Portland OR 97201-3098 Office Phone: 503-494-8220. Business E-Mail: hedgesj@ohsu.edu.

HEDGES, KAMLA KING, library director; b. Covington, Va. d. John Wilton and Rhoda Alice (Loughrie) K.; m. Harry George Hedges, July 24, 1988. AB, Coll. of William and Mary, 1968; MLS, Vanderbilt U., 1969. Law and legis. reference libr. Conn. State Libr., Hartford, 1969-74; dep. law libr. Steptoe and Johnson, Washington, 1974-78; law libr. Wilkinson, Cragun and Barker, Washington, 1978-83; corp. libr. The Bur. of Nat. Affairs, Inc., Washington, 1983-94, dir. libr. rels., 1995—. Compiler: (directories) BNA's Directory of State and Federal Courts, Judges, Clerks, 1995, BNA's State Administrative Codes and Registers, 1995; contbr. chpt. to law manual. Bd. dirs. Friends of the Law Libr. of Congress, 2000—05. Mem. Am. Assn. Law Librs. (exec. bd. dirs. 1984-87), Spl. Libr. Assn. Episcopalian. Office: Bur Nat Affairs Inc 1231 25th St NW Washington DC 20037-1197

HEDGES, MARK STEPHEN, clinical psychologist; b. Chgo., Feb. 15, 1950; s. Norman T. and Doris Mae (Walters) H.; m. Janice Finnie, Aug. 16, 1975; children: Anna, Miriam. BS, Purdue U., 1972; MA, U. S.D., 1974, PhD, 1977. Psychology intern Western Mo. Mental Health Ctr., Kansas City, 1975-76; psychologist, dir. psychol. svcs. Northeastern Mental Health Ctr., Aberdeen, SD, 1977—2003; psychologist Luth. Social Svcs., Aberdeen, SD, 2003—; sch. psychologist Aberdeen Pub. Schs., 2003—. Mem. citizens rev. panel/children's justice task force S.D. Dept. Social Svcs. Mem. APA, S.D. Assn. Sch. Psychologists, Phi Beta Kappa, Psi Chi, Phi Kappa Phi. Methodist. Office: Aberdeen Pub Sch 314 S Main St Aberdeen SD 57401 Office Phone: 605-725-7148. Business E-Mail: mark.hedges@aberdeen.k12.sd.us.

HEDGES, PATRICK ARMAND, security firm executive; b. Ft. Bragg, NC, June 2, 1948; adopted s. Harold and Marcelle Marie Julienne (Zeyen) H.; m. Penelope Ann Huff, Aug. 20, 1968 (div. Feb. 1981); children: Johnn Patrick, Sean Armand, Cristina Marie. AA, St. Leo Coll., Ft. Monroe, Va., 1985, Air Command and Staff Coll., Langley AFB, Va., 1990, Air War Coll., Kelly AFB, Tex., 1993. Computer programmer Applied Tech. Lab., Ft. Eustis, Va., 1978-81, computer sys. analyst, 1983—84; dep. dir. intelligence support Hdqrs. Tactical Air Command, Langley AFB, 1984—85, tech. advisor intelligence support, 1985—86; chief sys. application, computer sys. analyst 1912 Computer Sys. Group, Langley AFB, 1986—91; chief air force computer security Air Force Info. Warfare Ctr., San Antonio, 1991-94; chief info. protection tech. support Air Force Comm. Agy., Scott AFB, Ill., 1994—2001, chief comm. Air Force security program, 2001—. Contbr. articles to profl. jours. With U.S. Army, 1968-77, Vietnam. Decorated Bronze Star, Vietnam Cross of Gallantry Unit, Meritorious Svc. medal, Army Commendation medal with oak leaf, Vietnam Svc. medal with three campaign stars. Mem.: Vet. Foreign Wars. Avocations: collecting books, coins and stamps, woodworking. Home: 2412 Antiquity Ln Belleville IL 62221 Personal E-mail: hdgesarm1@aol.com.

HEDGES, RICHARD HOUSTON, lawyer, epidemiologist; b. Louisville, July 16, 1952; s. Houston and Frances Ruth (Zemo) H.; m. Mary Kathryn Werry. BA, U. Ky., 1974; MA, Ea. Ky. U., 1975, MPA, 1983; PhD, U. Ky., 1986; JD, Capital U. Law, 1994. Bar: Ohio 1995. Rehab. specialist Commonwealth Ky., Somerset, 1976-81, chief health planner Frankfort, 1981-82; asst. prof. U. Ky., Lexington, 1985-87; rsch. assoc. dept. med. behavioral sci. U. Ky. Coll. Medicine, Lexington, 1982-85; program adminstr. Rollman Psychiat. Inst., Cin., 1987-88; asst. prof. Ohio U., 1988-92, assoc. prof., 1992—2005; assoc. Garry Hunter, LPA, Athens, Ohio, 1997-98; ptnr. Thomas & Hedges LLC, 1998-99; pvt. practice Athens, 1999—. Asst. city atty. City Nelsonville, Ohio, 1997—2001, city pros., 1997—2001, 2004—, coord., long term care adminstrn., 2003—05; dir. divsn. aging Ohio U. Health Promotion and Rsch., 1990—92, MHA grad. program coord., 1995—96; bd. dirs. Washington County Mental Health and Addiction Recovery Svcs., 1998—99; exec. dir. pro tem Health Recovery Svcs., 1998; solicitor Village Chauncey, 2000; magistrate Village Coolville, Ohio, 2001—03, Ohio, 2004—; pros. Meigs County Asst. Pros., 2004—05. Author: Bioethics, Healthcare and the Law, 1999; contbr. articles to profl. jours. Mem. Athens County Domestic Violence Task Force, Athens County Victim's Assistance Adv. Fellow NIMH, 1984-86. Mem.: ATLA, ABA, Athens County Bar Assn., Washington County Bar Assn. (trustee at large 2000—02), Ohio Bar Assn., Am. Health Lawyers Assn., Healthcare Fin. Mgmt. Assn., Soc. Ohio Healthcare Attys., Ohio Acad. Trial Lawyers, Phi Delta Phi, Pi Sigma Alpha. Episcopalian. Avocations: backpacking, volleyball, bicycling, sailing. Home: 275 Mooreland Rd Belpre OH 45714-9702 Office: 8 N Court St Ste 507 Athens OH 45701-2450 also: Ohio U Sch Health Sci E346 Grover Ctr Athens OH 45701

HEDGES, STEPHEN BLAIR, biology professor, researcher; BSc in Biology, George Mason U., Fairfax, Va., 1981; MSc in Zoology, U. Md., 1984, PhD in Zoology, 1988. Post-doctoral rsch. dept. biology Pa. State U., 1988—92, asst. prof. dept. biology, 1992—97, assoc. prof. dept. biology, 1997—2002, prof. dept. biology, 2002—. Mem. NASA Astrobiology Inst., 1998—; rsch. assoc. Nat. Mus. Natural History, Washington, 1998—; coord. for Caribbean Global Amphibian Assessment, 2001—. Named Best News and Views, Nature, 2003; recipient Hot Paper, Inst. for Scientific Info., Darwin Lecture, Natural History Mus., London, 2001, Karling Lecture, Mycological Soc. Am., 2001, Philips Disting. Lecture, Haverford Coll., 2003. Achievements include author of 190 research articles, discoverer and co-discoverer of 65 species of amphibians and reptiles, including the smallest tetrapod and smallest amniote vertebrate; discovery of five species of butterflies; invention of a method (print clock) for dating early books and prints. Office: Pa State Univ Dept Biology 208 Mueller Lab University Park PA 16802-5301 Business E-Mail: sbh1@psu.edu.

HEDICAN, BRET, professional hockey player; b. St. Paul, Minn., Aug. 10, 1970; m. Kristi Yamaguchi; children: Keara Kiyomi, Emma Yoshiko. Defenseman St. Louis Blues, 1991—94, Vancouver Canucks, 1994—99, Florida Panthers, 1999—2002, Carolina Hurricanes, 2002—. Achievements include being a member of Stanley Cup Champion Carolina Hurricanes, 2006. Office: Carolina Hurricanes RBC Ctr 1400 Edwards Mill Rd Raleigh NC 27607

HEDIEN, COLETTE JOHNSTON, lawyer; b. Chgo., 1939; d. George A. and Catherine (Bugan) Johnston; m. Wayne E. Hedien; 3 children. BS with honors, U. Wis., 1960; JD, DePaul U., 1981. Bar: Ill. 1981. Tchr. Sch. Dist. 39, Wilmette, Ill., 1960-63, Tustin (Calif.) Pub. Schs., 1964-66; extern law clk. to judge Chgo., 1980, U.S. Atty.'s Office, Chgo., 1980; pvt. practice Northbrook, Ill., 1981—. Mem. Chgo. Appellate Law Com., 1982—83, chmn., 1987—88. Atty. Chgo. Vol. Legal Svcs.; founding dir. U. Irvine Friends of Libr., 1965—66; guidance vol. Glenbrook HS, 1984—89;

trustee Village of Northbrook, 1989—97; mem. Women's Bd. Field Mus.; bd. dirs. Ill. Project for Spl. Needs Children, 1998—; founder Am. Women of Surrey, England, 1975—77. NSF scholar, 1962. Mem. ABA (com. on real property), Ill. Bar Assn., Chgo. Bar Assn., North Shore Panhellenic Assn. (rep. 1982—), Phi Kappa Phi, Kappa Alpha Theta (bd. dirs.).

HEDLEY-WHYTE, ELIZABETH TESSA, neuropathologist; b. London, Jan. 17, 1937; came to U.S., 1960; d. George Stanley and Elizabeth Margery Waller; m. John Hedley-Whyte, Sept. 19, 1959. MB, BS, Durham U., Eng., 1960; MD, Newcastle U., Eng., 1976; AM (hon.), Harvard U., Cambridge, Mass., 1992. Diplomate Am. Bd. Pathology; cert. examiner neuropathology. Resident in pathology Children's, New Eng. Deaconess and Peter Bent Brigham Hosps., Boston, 1960-65; fellow Cerebral Palsy Found., 1965-66; asst. neuropathologist Children's Hosp., Boston, 1966-68, neuropathologist, 1968-77, cons. neuropathologist, 1977—2000; pathologist New Eng. Deaconess Hosp., 1977-81; asst. prof., assoc. prof., prof. pathology Harvard Med. Sch., Boston, 1968—; assoc. neuropathologist Mass. Gen. Hosp., Boston, 1981-83, neuropathologist, 1983—, dir. neuropathology tng., 1983—2007, dir. pathology residency tng., 1985-96; cons. neuropathologist Beth Israel Deaconess Hosp., Boston, 1977—. Cons. NIH, 1976-81; mem. residency rev. com. for pathology Accreditation Coun. on Grad. Med. Edn., 1996-2001. Mem. editl. bd. Jour. Neuropathology and Exptl. Neurology, 2000-2004, Human Pathology, 2000—; N.Am. editor Neurobiology and Applied Neurobiology, 1991-99; contbr. articles to profl. jours. Wellcome Trust fellow, 1984-85; recipient Meritorious award for contbns. to neuropathology Am. Assn. Neuropathologists, 2005. Mem. Nat. Insts. Nervous and Communicative Disorders and Stroke (chair program project com. 1979-81), Am. Assn. Neuropathologists (pres. elect 1994-95, pres. 1995-96, v.p., chair coms. 1976-90), Diagnostic Slide Session (moderator 1995-07), New Eng. Soc. Pathologists (sec., treas., pres. 1980-86), Boston Soc. Neurology and Psychiatry (pres. 1994-95). Avocations: gardening, skiing, needlecrafts.

HEDLEY-WHYTE, JOHN, anesthesiologist, educator; b. Newcastle-upon-Tyne, Eng., Nov. 25, 1933; arrived in U.S., 1960, naturalized, 1965; s. Angus and Nancy (Nettleton) H.-W.; m. Elizabeth Tessa Waller, Sept. 19, 1959. Student, Harrow Sch., 1947-52; BA (Rothschild scholar Clare Coll.), Cambridge U., 1955, MB, 1958, MA, 1959, MD, 1972; AM (hon.), Harvard U., 1967. House surgeon St. Bartholomew's Hosp., London, 1958-59; resident in anesthesia Mass. Gen. Hosp., 1960-62, hon. anesthetist, 1977—; clin. asst. anesthesia Harvard U., 1961-63, instr., 1963-65, clin. assoc., 1965-67, assoc. prof., 1967-69, prof., 1969-76, 1st David S. Sheridan prof. anaesthesia and respiratory therapy, 1976—; prof. dept. health policy and mgmt. Harvard U. Sch. Pub. Health, 1988-2000, mem. leadership coun., 2003—06; chmn. faculty seminar in health and medicine Harvard U., 1975—76, 2003—; anesthetist-in-chief Beth Israel Hosp., Boston, 1967-88, chmn. com. on rsch., 1976-82. Cons. in field; mem. tech. adv. bd. on med. devices tech. Am. Nat. Stds. Inst., 1973-83; U.S. del. Internat. Electrotech. Commn., 1989-91, 92—; leader U.S. del. Internat. Orgn. Standardization, Geneva, 1973-89, chmn. com. TC 121, SC 3 on anaesthetic and respiratory equipment, 1978—. Author: Respiratory Care, 1965, Applied Physiology of Respiratory Care, 1976, Continuous Anesthesia Vapor Monitoring, 1990, Operating room and Intensive Care Alarms and Information Transfer, 1992; contbr. articles to profl. jours. Recipient Hichens prize St. Bartholomew's Hosp., London, 1957, Cert. Appreciation, Surgeon Gen., 2007. Fellow ACP (life), German Soc. Anaesthesia and Intensive Care Medicine (hon., life), ASTM (hon., chmn. com. F29 1983-89, Merit award 1994, user vice chmn. 2000-05, membership sec. 2006—), Royal Coll. Anaesthetists (hon., life); mem. Am. Physiol. Soc., Abernethian Soc. (past pres.), Am. Soc. Anesthesiologists (chmn. com. mech. equipment 1977-82, chmn. com. on equipment and standards 1982-84), Mass. Soc. Anesthesiologists (pres. 1973-74), Am. Soc. Pharmacology and Exptl. Therapeutics, Roxbury Soc. Med. Improvement (libr. 1970-88, sec.-treas. 1988—), Mass. Med. Soc. (coun. 1975-78), Fairhaven Preservation Assn. (pres. 1990—), Boodle's Club, Carlton Club (hon., life), The Country Club, Somerset Club, Harvard Club of Boston, Harvard Travellers' Club, Vicarage Club. Democrat. Episcopalian. Achievements include discovery that human blood has a constant relative solubility for oxygen. Office: VA Med Ctr 1400 VFW Pkwy Boston MA 02132-4927

HEDLUND, ELLEN LOUISE, state agency administrator, educator; b. Omaha, Feb. 17, 1943; d. Edwin Hugo and Olga Josephine Parrish; m. Ronald David Hedlund, Aug. 22, 1964; children: Karen Marie, David Peter. BA, Augustana Coll., 1965; MA, U. Iowa, 1966; PhD, U. Wis. Milw., 1989. Cert. life cert. in guidance and counseling Wis. Dept. Pub. Instr., 1977. Counselor Clear Creek Cmty. Schs., Oxford, Iowa, 1966—67; counselor, tchr. Nicolet H.S., Glendale, Wis., 1967—72, 1979; tchr. asst., project mgr. U. Wis., Milw., 1982—89, proposal writer, 1989; cons. R.I. Coll., Providence, 1990; adj. prof. U. R.I., Kingston, 1991; assessment coord. R.I. Dept. Edn., Providence, 1991—. Ptnr., cons. Wis. Pub. Opinion Mktg. Rsch., Milw., 1976—89. Adv. bd. U. Wis., Milw. Coll. for Kids, 1980—89; Sunday sch. supr. Bay Shore Luth., Whitefish Bay, Wis., 1987—89; congl. pres. Luth. Ch. of the Good Shepherd, Kingston, RI, 1996. Named Viking of Distinction, North HS, Omaha, Nebr., 2003. Mem.: Am. Edn. Rsch. Assoc., Assoc. for Supervision and Curriculum Devel., R.I. Assoc. Supervision and Curriculum Devel. Lutheran. Avocations: reading, gardening, home decor, stained glass. Office: RI Dept Elem Secondary Edn 255 Westminster St Providence RI 02903

HEDLUND, PAUL JAMES, lawyer; b. Abington, Pa., June 26, 1946; s. Frank Xavier and Eva Ruth (Hoffman) H.; m. Marta Louise Brewer, Dec. 7, 1985; children: Annemarie Kirsten, Brooke Ashley, Tess Kara. BSME, U. Mich., 1968; JD, UCLA, 1973. Bar: Calif. 1973, D.C. 1994, U.S. Dist. Ct. (ctrl. dist.) Calif. 1977, U.S. Dist. Ct. (ea. dist.) Calif. 1991, U.S. Dist. Ct. (no. dist.) N.Y. 1994, U.S. Patent and Trademark Office 1978, U.S. Ct. Appeals (9th cir.) 1994, U.S. Supreme Ct. 1997. Staff engr. So. Calif. Edison, LA, 1968-70; ptnr. Hedlund & Samuels, LA, 1974-88, Kananack, Murgatroyd Baum & Hedlund (and predecessor firms), LA, 1988-92; shareholder Baum, Hedlund, Aristei, Goldman & Menzies, P.C., LA, 1993—. Mem. discovery and trial teams MDL 817 aircrash at Sioux City Iowa United Airlines, Chgo., 1989; mem. plaintiffs' steering com. Alaska Airlines crash off Pt. Mugu, Calif., 2000; mem. plaintiffs' exec. com. Sept. 11, 2001 Tort Litigation; lectr. in field. Named one of So. Calif. Super Lawyers, LA Mag., 2005; recipient Safety award, Nat. Air Disaster Found., 2002. Mem.: ABA (forum on air and space law com., litig. sect., tort trial and ins. practice sect.), Am. Assn. for Justice (aviation law sect.), LA County Bar Assn., Consumer Attys. LA, DC Bar Assn., State Bar Calif. Office: Baum Hedlund Aristei Goldman & Menzies PC 12100 Wilshire Blvd Ste 950 Los Angeles CA 90025-7107 Home Phone: 818-225-8744; Office Phone: 310-207-3233. Business E-Mail: phedlund@baumhedlundlaw.com.

HEDLUND, RONALD, baritone; b. Mpls., May 12, 1934; s. Cyril and Mildred H.; m. Barbara Smith, Nov. 12, 1974; children: Eric, Alexander. BA, Hamline U.; MusM, Ind. U., Juilliard Sch. Mem. faculty dept. music U. Ill., 1970—74, 1983—2006; bass soloist, instr. classical music seminar Eisenstadt and Vienna, Austria; ret., 2006. Singing voice cons. Carle Clinic Speech Ctr., Urbana, 1994—. Appeared throughout U.S. including opera cos. of San Francisco, Chgo., Houston, Miami, Seattle, Dallas, Ft. Worth, Phila., Washington, Omaha, Santa Fe, Lake George, Boston, N.Y.C. Opera, Met. Opera Nat. Co., New Orleans, Spoleto Festival, Edinburgh Festival, Vancouver Opera, Conn. Opera, Aspen Festival, R.I. Opera, Chgo. Opera Theater, Opera Theatre St. Louis, Utah Opera, Opera Ill., Ill. Opera Theatre; soloist with numerous orchs., recitals throughout U.S. Served with USNR, 1958-63. Office: 1st Choice Music Svcs 505 Eliot Dr Urbana IL 61801-6727 Office Phone: 217-244-3339. Business E-Mail: rhedlund@uiuc.edu.

HEDLUND, RONALD DAVID, academic administrator, researcher, educator; b. Joliet, Ill., June 16, 1941; s. Henry Gustav and Betty Marie (Nelson) H.; m. Ellen Louise Parrish, Aug. 22, 1964; children: Karen Marie, David Peter. BA, Augustana Coll., 1963; MA, U. Iowa, 1964, PhD, 1967. Asst. prof. U. Wis., Milw., 1967-73, assoc. prof., 1973-77, dir. social sci. rsch. facility, 1978-80, prof., 1977-89, assoc. dean of rsch. Grad. Sch., 1980-89; vice provost of rsch., prof. U. R.I., Kingston, 1989-96, acting dean grad. sch., 1995-96; prof. Northeastern U., Boston, 1996—, vice provost, 1996—2004. Co-chair rsch. network R.I. Partnership Sci. & Tech., Providence, 1990-93; bd. dirs. Econ. Innovation Ctr., Newport, R.I.; mem. R.I. legis. commn. on creating high-tech jobs and Univ. Contbr. articles to profl. jours. Mem. Kingston Fire Dist. Study Com., 1990. NSF grantee, 1967, 77, 84, 95, Ford Found. grantee, 1985. Mem. Am. Polit. Sci. Assn., Internat. Polit. Sci. Assn., Midwest Polit. Sci. Assn. (exec. coun. 1987-90), Southern Polit. Sci. Assn., Western Polit. Sci. Assn. Lutheran. Avocation: gardening. Office: Northeastern U 313 Meserve Hall Huntington Ave Boston MA 02115 Business E-Mail: r.hedlund@neu.edu.

HEDMAN, ZOE ANN, retired literature and language educator, artist; b. Seattle, Oct. 18, 1946; d. Carl John and Ethel Emma (Murden) Hedman. BA in Edn., We. Wash. U., 1968, postgrad., 1964—68, U. Wash., Antioch U., Portland State U. Lic. life tchr. State of Wash. Eng. tchr. Snohomish Sch. Dist. #201, Wash., 1968—99; ret., 1999. Legacy leader Heritage Found., Washington. Named to, We, the People Wall of Nat. Constn. Ctr., Phila., Wall of Tolerance, Montomery, Ala., Roll of Honor, Nat. D-Day Mus., New Orleans; recipient Svc. to Cmty award, Wash. Edn. Assn., 1999. Mem.: NAACP, AAUW, Wash. State Ret. Tchrs. Assn., Nat. Cathedral Assn., Amnesty Internat., Civil War Preservation Trust, World Wildlife Fund, So. Poverty Law Ctr., Nat. Trust for Historic Preservation, Georgia O'Keefe Mus., Archeol. Conservancy, U.S. Holocaust Meml. Mus., Mus. Spanish Colonial Art, 1785 Soc., Nat. Women's History Mus., Colonial Williamsburg Founder, Smithsonian Nat. Mus. Am. Indian, Nature Conservancy, Circle of Life, Nat. Pk. Trust, Humane Soc. (mem. ptnr.'s circle), Young Am. Found. (Reagan ranch mem.), Ducks Unltd., Audabon Soc. Avocations: reading, hiking, music. Home: 11311 N Cedarvale Loop Rd Arlington WA 98223-8668

HEDREEN, RICHARD C, real estate developer; Degree in Civil Engring., U. Wash., 1957. Founder, CEO, pres. R.C. Hedreen Co., 1965—. Former bd. dirs. Terabeam Corp. Bd. dirs. Benaroya Music Ctr. Hall. Named to Top 200 Collectors, ARTnews Mag., 2006.

HEDREN, PAUL LESLIE, parks director, historian; b. New Ulm, Minn., Nov. 12, 1949; s. Thomas Harry and Muriel Mary (Kunz) H.; m. Janeen Margaret Wolcott, June 19, 1974 (div. 1997); children: Ethne Olivia, Whitney Elizabeth; m. Connie Joyce Burns, Sept. 10, 2005. BA, St. Cloud State Coll., 1972. Park ranger, historian Ft. Laramie (Wyo.) Nat. Hist. Site, 1971-76; historian Big Hole Nat. Battlefield, Wisdom, Mont., 1976-78; chief ranger, historian Golden Spike Nat. Hist. Site, Brigham City, Utah, 1978-84; supt. Fort Union Trading Post Nat. Hist. Site, Williston, ND, 1984-97, Niobrara Nat. Scenic River/Mo. Nat. Recreational River, O'Neill, Nebr., 1997—. Author: First Scalp for Custer, 1980, With Crook in the Black Hills, 1985, Fort Laramie in 1876, 1988 (Best Book of 1988 Wyo. State Hist. Soc.), Campaigning with King, 1991 (Merit award State Hist. Soc. Wis. 1991), The Great Sioux War 1876-77, 1991, Traveler's Guide to the Great Sioux War, 1996, We Trailed the Sioux, 2003; contbr. articles to profl. jours. Bd. dirs. Conv. and Vis. Bur., Williston, 1984-96, pres., 1994-96. Named Supt. of Yr. for Nat. Resources Mgmt., NPS, 2004; recipient Vivian Paladin award, Mont. Hist. Soc., 2005. Mem. Western Writers Assn. (Spur award 2005), Western History Assn. (mem. coun. 1990-93). Avocations: writing, lecturing. Office: Nat Park Svc PO Box 591 Oneill NE 68763-0591 Home Phone: 402-336-2073; Office Phone: 402-336-3970. Business E-Mail: paul_hedren@nps.gov.

HEDRICH, CLEDA POLLARD, real estate broker, writer; b. Richmond, Va., July 3, 1940; d. Herschel Newton and Frances Morton Pollard; m. Norman Hedrich, Mar. 27, 1967; children: Norman Lee, Bradley Charles. BA, U. of N.C., 1960—62. Real Estate Broker State of Fla., 1974. Exec. asst. to the pres. London & Cheshire Ins. Co., London, 1962—63; exec. asst. Eurofinance, Paris, 1963—64; psychiat. asst. Emory U. (Grady Hosp.), Atlanta, Ga., 1965—66; elem. tchr. City of Chgo. Sch. Sys., Chgo., 1967—67; book editor MacMillan Pub. Co., NYC, 1967—69; editor Internat. Jour. of Psychiatry, Internat. Jour. of Child Psychotherapy, Internat. Jour. of Psychoanalytical Psychotherapy, NYC, 1970—72; real estate broker/owner Pollard & Hedrich Realty Inc., Bonita Springs, Fla., 1976—; vice pres./owner Hickory Homes, Inc., Bonita Springs, 1976—. Author: (novels) A Pl. to Go Someday, (mystery novel) Threat of a Stranger, (screenplays). Personal E-mail: cleda@hedrichgroup.com.

HEDRICK, CHAD, Olympic athlete; b. Houston, Tex., Apr. 17, 1977; Recipient Oscar Mathisen Speed Skater Yr. award, 2004, Gold Medal, 5000 m Speed Skating, Winter Olympics, 2006, Silver Medal, 10,000 meter Speed Skating, 2006. Achievements include First place, World All Roun Speed Skating Championship, 2004; World 5000 m Speed Skating Championship, 2004; Silver Medalist, World All Round Championship, 2005; 5000 m Outdoor World Record Holder, 2005. Office: c/o Ty Kilinc Ste 280 1420 W Mockingbird Ln Dallas TX 75247

HEDRICK, LOIS JEAN, investment company executive, state official; b. Topeka, Kans., Jan. 25, 1927; d. Arthur Lenard and Nellie Cecelia (Johnson) Lungstrum; m. Clayton Newton Hedrick, Apr. 26, 1949; 1 dau., Carol Beth. Student, Washburn U., Topeka, 1980-83. Cert. Strickler's Bus. Coll., Topeka, 1947. Staff sec. Kans. State Senate, Topeka, 1946-65; com. sec. Kans. House Rep.; co-owner Hedrick's Market, Topeka, 1953-67; exec. sec. to sr. legal counsel Security Benefit Life Ins. Co., Topeka, 1963-71; asst. corp. sec. Security Mgmt. Co., Topeka, 1971-92, Security Distbrs. Inc., SBL Planning Inc., SBL Fund, Security Action Fund, Security Equity Fund, Security Investment Fund, Security Ultra Fund, Security Bond Fund, Security Cash Fund, Security OmniFund, Security Tax-Exempt Fund, Security Benefit Group Ins., Security Mgmt. Co.; govs. constituents rep. State of Kans., 1987—91; mem. Kans. Adv. Coun. on Aging, 1990-93; mgmt. cons. United Way of Greater Topeka, 1981-89, pub. rels. staff, 1982—. Rep. precinct woman, organizer, chmn. Topeka and Shawnee County Crime Blockers, 1976—; vol. fundraiser Am. Heart Assn., Stormont-Vail Hosp. Expansion, 1976-77; chmn. Plant a Tree for Century III, 1976; chmn. Greater Topeka Edn. Com., 1981—; organizing staff sec., fundraiser Christian Rural Overseas Program, 1951, staff sec. USAF Supply Depot, 1951-53; vol. community and various hosps.; dir. Topeka Women's Bowling Assn., 2000—. Named Woman of Yr. Am. Bus. Women's Assn., 1970, Sec. of Yr. Profl. Secs., Internat., 1975. Mem. Greater Topeka C. of C. (chmn. edn. com. 1981—, ambassador chmn. hs honors banquet 1982—), Adminstrv. Mgmt. Soc. (dir., pres. 1976—), Zonta Inernat., Beta Sigma Phi. Republican. Home: 1556 SW 24th St Topeka KS 66611-1329

HEDRICK, WYATT SMITH, pharmacist; b. Roswell, N.Mex., Sept. 28, 1951; s. Wyatt Smith and Roberta Walker (Stuart) H. BS in Pharmacy, U. N.Mex., 1974; MS in Hosp. Pharmacy, U. Houston, 1978. Registered pharmacist, N.Mex., Tex. Pharmacy intern St. Mary's Hosp., Roswell, N.Mex., 1973, Ea. N.Mex. Med. Ctr., 1973-74, U-SAVE Drug, 1974-75; pharmacy resident U. Tex. Med. Br. Hosps., Galveston, 1977-78; staff pharmacist Meml. Gen. Hosp., Las Cruces, N.Mex., 1978, Las Palmas Med Ctr., El Paso, Tex., 1978—. Mem. Am. Soc. Health-Sys. Pharmacists, Tex. Soc. Health-Sys. Pharmacists, El Paso Area Soc. Health-Sys. Pharmacists. Avocations: reading, travel, physical fitness. Home: 1028 Quinault Dr El Paso TX 79912-1223 Personal E-mail: whedr34182@aol.com.

HEEB, MARY JO, biochemist, researcher; b. Louisville, Sept. 20, 1942; d. John J. and Mary R. (Bohn) Holzknecht; m. Michael A. Heeb, Nov. 10, 1962 (div. Sept. 1987); children: Angela L., Randall V., Derek M., Cynthia A.; m. James M. Thomas, July 2005. BS in Chemistry, U. Fla., 1966, MS in Microbiology, 1968; PhD in Biochemistry, Georgetown U., 1983. Technician U. Fla., Gainesville, 1963-65; rsch. asst. U. Miami (Fla.), 1969-71; algebra tchr. Hoggard High Sch., Wilmington, N.C., 1971-72; instr. chemistry U. N.C., Wilmington, 1973-75; rsch. group leader Hazelton Labs., Vienna, Va., 1975-78, 81-82; postdoctoral fellow Scripps Rsch. Inst., La Jolla, Calif., 1983-88, sci. assoc., 1988-92, asst. mem., 1993—99, assoc. prof., 1999—. Cons. Office of Saline Water, Dept. of the Interior, Wrightsville Beach, NC, 1972-73. Contbr. articles to profl. jours. Fellow Am. Heart Assn., 1986; recipient Wilhelm Turk prize Austrian Soc. for Hematology and Oncology, 1986. Mem. Internat. Soc. Thrombosis and Hemostasis, Am. Soc. Hematology, Am. Soc. Biochemistry and Molecular Biology, Scripps Soc. Fellows (officer 1986). Democrat. Roman Catholic. Achievements include discovery of several Plasma Protease Inhibitors of Protein C., that Protein C Inhibitor is identical to Plasminogen Activator Inhibitor-3; demonstration that Protein C is activated during Intravascular Coagulation; that protein S inhibits factors Xa and Va; that factor IXa is regulated by protein Z-dependent protease inhibitor that low protein Z levels are associated with risk of stroke. Office: Scripps Rsch Inst MEM150 10550 N Torrey Pines Rd La Jolla CA 92037-1000 Business E-Mail: heeb@scripps.edu.

HEEBNER, ALBERT GILBERT, retired economist, educator, bank executive; b. Phila., Mar. 7, 1927; s. Albert and Julia (Zwada) Heebner; m. Dorothy Mae Kiler, Aug. 16, 1952. AB, U. Denver, 1948; AM, U. Pa., 1950, PhD, 1967. Instr. econs. Coll. Wooster, Ohio, 1950-52; with Phila. Nat. Bank subs. CoreStates Fin. Corp, 1952-87, economist, 1960-87, asst. v.p., 1961-64, v.p., 1964-70, sr. v.p., 1970-73, exec. v.p., 1973-83; exec. v.p., chief economist CoreStates Fin. Corp., Phila., 1983-87; Disting. prof. econs. Eastern Coll., St. Davids, Pa., 1987-97, disting. prof. econs. emeritus, 2000—. Lectr. fin. Wharton Sch., U. Pa., 1968—69; spl. asst. to chmn. Coun. Econ. Advisers, Washington, 1971—72; vis. prof. econs. Swarthmore (Pa.) Coll., 1976; chmn. Econ. Adv. Com., Am. Bankers Assn., 1978—80; adj. prof. Ea. Coll., St. Davids, 1982; mem. Inflation Policy Task Force adv. com. to Pres.-elect Reagan, 1980; mem. investment adv. bd. to City of Phila. Bd. Pensions, 1980—85; bd. dirs. Nat. Bur. Econ. Rsch., 1983—85, Market St. Fund, 1989—2003; bd. dirs., vice-chmn. Global Interdependence Ctr., 1992—2005, dir. emeritus, 2005—. Author: (book) Negotiable Certificates of Deposit: The Development of a Money Market Instrument, 1969; contbr. articles to profl. jours. Mem. Internat. Visitors Coun. Phila.; trustee Eastern U., 2001—06, trustee emeritus, 2006—. With USNR, 1945—46. Named to Wall of Fame, N.E. HS, Phila., 1996; recipient Alumni Cmty. Svc. award, 1995. Fellow: Nat. Assn. Bus. Econs. (contbr. Econ. Policy Survey, pres. 1975—76); mem.: Phila. Coun. Bus. Economists, Fgn. Policy Rsch. Inst., World Affairs Coun. Phila., Union League Phila., Conf. Bus. Econs. (chmn. 1987—88), Am. Econ. Assn., Sunday Breakfast Club. Baptist. Home: 1515 The Fairway 471 Rydal PA 19046-1491 Personal E-mail: agheebner@aol.com. *I have always striven for excellence in everything that I undertake-reaching for the highest standards of which I am capable, not just meeting requirements. While I like to think that I have earned my way, I am deeply indebted to key people who encouraged me, mentored me, and steered me to opportunities. Thus, I do not see my career as a solo venture.*

HEED, PETER W., former state attorney general; b. West Chester, Pa., Apr. 2, 1950; s. Walter R. and Elizabeth Allen Heed; m. Patricia Longo, Oct. 3, 1983; children: Travis, Ethan. BA, Dartmouth Coll., 1972; JD, Cornell U., 1975. Bar: N.H. 1975, U.S. Dist. Ct. N.H. 1975, U.S. Ct. Appeals (1st cir.) 1976. Asst. atty. gen. State of NH, Concord, 1975-80; assoc. Cristiano and Krumphold, Keene, NH, 1980-82; sr. ptnr. Green, McMahon & Heed, Keene, NH, 1982—2001; county atty. Cheshire County, NH, 2001—03; atty. gen. State of NH, 2003—04. Instr., paralegal studies, Keene State Coll., 1980-84; bd. govs. N.H. Health & Welfare Coun., Keene, 1985-90. Co-author: Canoe Racing: The Competitor's Guide, 1992; dir./prodr. (video) The General Clinton Regatta, 1989. Moderator, Town of Westmoreland, N.H., 1998—; mem. zoning bd. adjustment, Town of Roxbury, N.H., 1989-90; bd. govs., v.p. Norris Cotton Cancer Ctr., Dartmouth-Hitchand Hosp., Lebanon, N.H., 1993—; mem. U.S. Marathon Canoe and Kayak Team, 1982-83. Mem. ATLA (sustaining mem. 1987-2000), N.H. Trial Lawyers Assn. (bd. dirs. 1987-93). Republican. Avocations: canoe and kayak racing (7 times National Marathon and Downriver Canoe Champion, World Masters Marathon Canoe Champion, Nike World Masters Games, 1998), nordic ski racing, marathon running, history.

HEEG, PEGGY A., lawyer, former gas industry executive; b. Louisville, June 25, 1959; BA with honors, U. Louisville, 1983, JD, 1986. Bar: Ky. 1986, DC 1987, Tex. 1987. Various Tenneco Energy, El Paso Corp., Houston, 1996—97, v.p., assoc. gen. counsel regulated pipelines, 1997—2001, sr. v.p., dep. gen. counsel, 2001, exec. v.p., gen. counsel, 2002—04; ptnr. Fulbright & Jaworski L.L.P., 2004—. Legal advisor to commr. Charles Stalon Fed. Energy Regulatory Commn., 1988; bd. dirs. El Paso Tenn. Pipeline Co. Mem.: ABA, Interstate Natural Gas Assn. Am., DC Bar, State Bar Tex., Ky. Bar Assn., Energy Bar Assn. Office: Fulbright & Jaworksi LLP 1301 McKinney Ste 5100 Houston TX 77010-3095 Office Phone: 713-651-5151.

HEEGER, ALAN JAY, physicist, educator; b. Sioux City, Iowa, Jan. 22, 1936; s. Peter J. and Alice (Minkin) Heeger; m. Ruthann Chudacoff, Aug. 11, 1957; children: Peter S., David J. BA with high distinction, U. Nebr., 1957; PhD in Physics, U. Calif., Berkeley, 1961; degree (hon.), U. Mons, Belgium, 1993; DTech (hon.), Linköping U., Sweden, 1996; PhD (hon.), Abo Akademie, Turku, Finland, 1998; DHL (hon.), U. Mass., 1999; DSc (hon.), U. Nebr., 1999, So. China U. Tech., Japan Adv. Inst. Sci. & Tech., Bar Ilan U., Israel, Trinity Coll., Dublin, 2005, U. Alicante, Spain, 2006. Asst. prof. U. Pa., Phila., 1962—64, assoc. prof., 1964—66, prof. physics, 1966—82, U. Calif., Santa Barbara, 1982—, dir. inst. for Polymers and Organic Solids, 1983—2000; pres. UNIAX Corp., Santa Barbara, 1990—94, chief tech. officer, 1999—2002; chmn. CBritu, Inc., 2005—; dir. Heeger Ctr. Advanced Materials Gwangju Inst. Sci. and Technology, 2005; co-founder and chief scientist Konarka Tecnologies, Inc., Lowell, Mass., 2004—; founder, vice-chmn. CytomX, Inc., 2006. Dir. Lab. Rsch. on Structure of Matter U. Pa., 1974—81; acting vice provost for rsch. U. Pa., 1981—82; Morris Loeb lectr. Harvard U., 1973. Editor-in-chief Synthetic Metals jour., 1983—2000, contbr. sci. articles to profl. jours. Recipient John Scott medal, City of Phila., 1989, Oliver P. Buckley prize, 1983, Balzan prize, Balzan Found., Italy and Switzerland, 1995, Pres. medal, U. Pa., 2000, Nobel prize in Chemistry, 2000, Italgas prize, Eni, Inc., Italy, 2007; fellow, Alfred P. Sloan, Guggenheim; grantee, Govt. Fellow: Am. Physics Soc. (Buckley prize for solid state physics 1983); mem.: NAE, NAS, Korean Acad. Scis. (fgn.). Achievements include patents in field. Avocation: skiing. Office: U Calif Dept Physics Santa Barbara CA 93106 Business E-Mail: ajhe@physics.ucsb.edu.

HEEGER, DAVID J., psychology professor; b. Berkeley, Calif., Oct. 3, 1961; s. Alan J. and Ruth (Chadacoff) H.; m. Anne Gelman, Oct. 21, 1990; 2 children. BA in Math., U. Pa., 1983, MSE in Computer Sci., 1985, PhD in Computer Sci., 1987. Postdoctoral fellow MIT Media Lab, 1987—99; rsch. scientist NASA Ames Rsch. Ctr., 1990—91; asst. prof. Stanford U., 1991—98, assoc. prof., 1998—2002; prof. psychology and neural sci. NYU, 2002—. Contbr. articles to profl. jours.; patentee in field. Rsch. fellow U. Pa., Phila., 1983-87, Vis. fellow SRI Internat., Menlo Park, Calif., 1984-85, Fairchild Found. Postdoctoral fellow, 1987, Alfred P. Sloan Rsch. Found. fellow, 1994-95; NIH Rsch. grantee, 1993; recipient David Marr prize Internat. Conf. Computer Vision, London, 1987, Troland Rsch. award in Psychology, NAS, 2002 Office: Dept Psychology and Ctr for Neural Sci NYU 6 Washington Pl New York NY 10003 Office Phone: 212-998-7868. Office Fax: 212-995-4349. Business E-Mail: david@cns.nyu.edu.

HEEKIN, JIM (JAMES ROBSON HEEKIN III), advertising executive; b. Cin., Aug. 12, 1949; s. James Robson and Jane (Jessup) H.; children: Katie, James. BA, Williams Coll., 1971; cert., N. Adams State Tchrs. Coll., 1974. V.p. account supr. J. Walter Thompson, NYC, 1975-78, exec. v.p., gen. mgr., 1986; sr. product mgr. Gen. Foods, White Plains, NY, 1978-80; exec. v.p., mgmt. dir. Bozelle Jacobs Kenton-Echardt, NYC, Detroit, 1980-85; pres. McCann-Erickson North Am., 1994-97; regional dir. for Europe McCann-Erickson, 1997—2000; chmn., CEO McCann-Erickson WorldGroup, 2000—03; pres., COO Euro RSCG Worldwide, NYC, 2003—04, chmn., CEO, 2004—05, Grey Worldwide, NYC, 2005—, Grey Global Group, NYC, 2007—. Office: Grey Worldwide NY 777 Third Ave New York NY 10017*

HEEKIN-CANEDY, SCOTT H., publishing executive; m. Anne Heekin-Canedy; 1 child, Siobhan. BA in Polit. Sci., Williams Coll., 1974; LLD, Northeastern U., 1979; MBA in Mktg. and Fin., Columbia U., 1985. Positions with Dow Jones, Doubleday; circulation acctg. mgr., fin. planning mgr. LA Times, 1989—92; circulation market planning analyst NY Times, NYC, 1987—89, circulation systems support mgr., 1989, asst. mgr. fin. planning dept., 1992—93; project mgr. to project dir. strategic planning NY Times, NYC, 1993—94; group dir. strategic planning NY Times, NYC, 1994—97, v.p. strategic planning, 1994—97, sr. v.p. circulation, 1999—2004; pres. NY Times Media Group, 2004—, gen. mgr., 2004—. Office: NY Times 229 W 43rd St New York NY 10036*

HEEL, JOE, information technology executive; b. Germany; PhD in Computer Sci., MIT, Cambridge. Ptnr. High Tech Practice McKinsey and Co., head Miami office and pvt. equity practice; sr. exec. StorageTek; with Sun Microsystems, Inc., Santa Clara, Calif., 2005—, sr. v.p. global storage practice. Contbr. articles to profl. jours. Avocations: hiking, boating, bicycling, skiing. Office: Sun Microsystems Inc 4150 Network Cir Santa Clara CA 95054 Office Phone: 650-960-1300.*

HEELAN, PATRICK AIDAN, philosophy educator; b. Dublin, Mar. 17, 1926; s. Matthew Henry and Pauline (Beirens) H. Student, Belvedere Coll., 1938-42; BA, Univ. Coll., Dublin, 1947, MA, 1948; PhD, St. Louis U., 1952; STL, Jesuit Theol. Faculty, Dublin, 1959; student, Princeton U., 1960-62; PhD, U. Louvain, 1964. Ordained priest Soc. Jesus, Roman Catholic Ch., 1958; lectr. math. physics Univ. Coll., Dublin, 1964-65; research asso. Dublin Inst. Advanced Studies, 1952-54, 64-65; asst. prof. philosophy Fordham U., 1965-67, asso. prof., 1967-70; prof. philosophy, chmn. dept. SUNY at Stony Brook, 1970-74, acting v.p. liberal studies, 1975-77, v.p. liberal studies, 1977-79, prof. philosophy, 1979-92, dean humanities and fine arts, 1990-92; exec. v.p. Georgetown U., Washington, 1992-95, William Gaston prof. philosophy, 1995—; external appraiser philosophy and arts and scis. programs U. Western Ont., Lowell U., John Carroll U., San Diego State U. Acad. adv. coun. Inst. for Advanced Cath. Studies. Author: Quantum Mechanics and Objectivity, 1965, Space-Perception and Philosophy of Science, 1983; festschrift: Hermeneutic Philosophy of Science, Van Gogh's Eyes and God: Essays in Honor of Patrick A Heelan, S.J., 2002. Fulbright fellow, 1960-62; NSF sr. fellow, 1983 Mem. AAAS, Am. Cath. Philos. Assn. (coun. 1973-75), Ctr. for Integrative Edn. (coun. 1972-74), Am. Philos. Assn. (program com. Ea. sect. 1975, nominating com. 1988), Philosophy Sci. Assn., Brit. Soc. Philosophy Sci., Soc. Phenomenology and Existential Philosophy, N.Y. Acad. Scis., Internat. Orgn. for Hermeneutics and Sci., Phi Beta Kappa, Sigma Xi. Address: 3612 O St NW Washington DC 20007-2615 Office: Georgetown Univ Philosophy Dept 234 New N Washington DC 20057-0001 Office Phone: 202-687-5222. Business E-Mail: heelanp@georgetown.edu.

HEENAN, MICHAEL TERENCE, lawyer; b. Pitts., Jan. 28, 1942; s. Paul Joseph and Helen (Chemas) Heenan; m. Maryte Victoria Narkevicius, Feb. 12, 1970 (dec. Dec. 1999); children: Garrett, Leslie, Suzanne; m. Patricia Gaw Canestra, Aug. 5, 2005. BS, Mount St. Mary's Coll., Emmitsburg, Md., 1964; JD, U. Pitts., 1967. Bar: Pa. 1967, D.C. 1972, U.S. Supreme Ct. 1974, U.S. Ct. Appeals (D.C. cir.), U.S. Ct. Appeals for Armed Forces 1974, U.S. Ct. Fed. Claims 1975, U.S. Customs Ct. 1975, U.S. Ct. Appeals (3d cir.) 1979, U.S. Ct. Appeals (Fed. cir.) 1982, U.S. Ct. Appeals (4th cir.) 1987. Atty. advisor Bd. Vets. Appeals, Washington, 1971—73; trial atty., divsn. mine safety and health Office of Solicitor, Dept. of the Interior, 1973—74; assoc. Webster, Kilcullen & Chamberlain, 1974—75; ptnr. Kilcullen, Smith & Heenan, 1975—80, Heenan, Althen & Roles, Washington, 1980—2003; shareholder Ogletree Deakins, 2003—. Instr., internat. law U.S. Navy Reserve Officers Sch., 1971—72; adj. instr. New Century Coll., 2004—, prof.; adj. instr. George Mason U. Author: Understanding MSHA, 1981, Enforcement, Administrative and Judicial Review, Coal Law and Regulation, 1983, Inspections and Investigations, Workplace Safety and Health, 1995, Employer Liability Related to Workplace Safety and Health Obligations at Cement Operations, 1996, Safety and Health at Mines: A Manual for Operators and Contractors, 1999, Federal Regulation of Mine Safety and Health, Mine Health and Safety Management, 2001, MSHA - The Mine Operator and the Law, 2003; co-author (with Ronald E. Meisburg): Federal Regulation of Mine Safety and Health, Administration, Practice and Procedure, 1986; co-author: (with C. Gregory Ruffennach) National Institute of Occupational Safety and Health: Limits of Authority in Rulemaking Under the Federal Mine Safety and Health Act of 1977, 1992; co-author: (with Lynn M. Rausch) Vicarious Liability for Contract Mine Operations: Expanding Liability for Mineral Owners and Lessees, 1994; co-author: (with William K. Doran) Employee Protections, 1995; legal editor Pit & Quarry, 1996—; with Margaret S. Lopez: Self Audits, Occupational Safety and Health Handbook, 2001. Trustee Energy & Mineral Law Found., 1996—. Lt. USN, 1968—71. Mem.: ABA (mem., labor and employment sect.), D.C. Bar Assn., Pa. Bar Assn., Nat. Stone and Gravel Assn. (coun. of counsel). Office: Ogletree Deakins Nash Smoak & Stewart PC 2400 N St NW 5th Fl Washington DC 20037 Office Phone: 202-887-0855. Business E-Mail: michael.heenan@odnss.com.

HEER, NICHOLAS LAWSON, language educator; b. Chapel Hill, NC, Feb. 8, 1928; s. Clarence and Jean Douglas (MacAlpine) H. BA, Yale U., New Haven, Conn., 1949; PhD, Princeton U., NJ, 1955. Transl. analyst Arabian Am. Oil Co., Saudi Arabia, 1955-57; asst. prof. Stanford U., Calif., 1959-62; vis. lectr. Yale U., New Haven, 1962-63; asst. prof. Harvard U., Cambridge, Mass., 1963-65; assoc. prof. U. Wash., Seattle, 1965-76, prof. Near Eastern langs. and civilization, 1976-90, prof. emeritus, 1990—; chmn. dept. Near Eastern langs. and civilization U. Wash, 1982-87. Middle East curator Hoover Instn., Stanford, Calif., 1958-62 Editor: Tirmidhi: Bayan al-Farq, 1958, Jami: Al-Durrah al-Fakhirah, 1981, Islamic Law and Jurisprudence: Studies in Honor of Farhat J. Ziadeh, 1990; translator: Jami: The Precious Pearl, 1979, (with Kenneth Honerkamp) Three Early Sufi Texts, 2003. Mem. Am. Oriental Soc., Middle East Studies Assn., Am. Assn. Tchrs. of Arabic (treas. 1964-76, pres. 1981, dir. 1982-84) Home: 1821 10th Ave E Seattle WA 98102-4214 Office: U Wash Dept Near Ea Langs & Civ PO Box 353120 Seattle WA 98195-3120 Personal E-mail: heer@eskimo.com. Business E-Mail: heer@u.washington.edu.

HEERE, KAREN R., astrophysicist; b. Teaneck, NJ, Apr. 9, 1944; d. Peter N. and Alice E. (Hall) H. BA summa cum laude, U. Pa., 1965; MA, U. Calif., Berkeley, 1968; PhD, U. Calif., Santa Cruz, 1976. Rsch. assoc. NRC NASA Ames Rsch. Ctr., Moffett Field, Calif., 1977—79; rsch. astronomer NASA Ames Rsch. Ctr., U. Calif., Santa Cruz, 1979—86, sr. analyst, 2004—; assoc. prof. San Francisco State U., 1986-87; scientist Sci. Applications Internat. Corp., Los Altos, Calif., 1974-76, 87-93; rsch. specialist Sterling Software, Redwood City, Calif., 1993-98; sr. scientist Raytheon, Moffett Field, 1998—2003, mgr. space and earth sci., 2001—03. Vis. scientist TATA Inst. for Fundamental Rsch., Bombay, 1984. Contbr. articles to profl. jours. Mem.: Am. Astron. Soc. Avocations: hiking, travel. Home: PO Box 2427 El Granada CA 94018-2427 Office Phone: 650-604-6524.

HEERENS, ROBERT EDWARD, physician; b. Evanston, Ill., July 2, 1915; s. Joseph and Karen (Larsen) H.; m. Martha Virginia Lysne, Aug. 21, 1943; children: Kisti Lyn, Martha Jill, Nancy Ann, Robin Jan, Sara Bryce. AB, Kalamazoo Coll., 1938; postgrad., U. Ala. Med. Sch., 1939-41; MD, Northwestern U., 1944. Diplomate Am. Bd. Family Practice. Intern U.S. Naval Hosp., Great Lakes, Ill., 1943-44, resident, 1946-47; gen. practice medicine Rockford, Ill., 1947—; pres. med. staff Swedish-Am. Hosp.; mem. staffs St. Anthony, Rockford hosps.; clin. assoc. prof. family medicine Rockford Sch. Medicine, also dir. ind. studies, mem. exec. com.; mem. admissions com. U. Ill. Coll. Medicine, 1970—, promotions com., 1973-75, mem. Senate Med. Ctr., 1975-77, also mem. acad. council, mem. adv. com. on family practice. Bd. dirs. Rockford Community Chest, 1954-60, Vis. Nurse Assn.; pres. Winnebago Tb Assn., 1960-61, Winnebago County Bd. Health, 1961-69; mem. Rockford Community Devel. Com.; mem. Community Action Com., 1969-71; pres. Northwestern Area Agy. on Aging, 1991-93. Served with M.C., USN, 1942-47. Recipient Disting. Svc. award Pub. Health Winnebago County Health Dept., 1997, Unique Achievement award Gov. of Ill., 1992, Betty Henry award for Cmty. Svc., 2000; Sr. of Yr. award Lifescape Cmty. Svcs., 2000, Super Sr. of Yr., 2006; Svc. Above Self award Rotary, Rockford, 2007. Mem. AMA, Am. Acad. Family Physicians (Ill. del. to congress of dels. 1959-71, mem. pub. relations com. 1967-74, chmn. pub. relations com. 1971-74, bd. dirs. 1970-73, exec. com. 1972-73, v.p. 1974), Ill. Acad. Gen. Practice (pres. 1958), Ill. Acad. Family Physicians (Pres.'s award 2000), Ill. Med. Soc. (chmn. pub. relations com. 1961-62, Pub. Svc. award 1994), Winnebago County Med. Soc. (v.p. 1965, pres. 1966), Rockford C. of C. (pres. 1962, chmn. edn. com.), Phi Beta Phi Home: 5664 Spring Brook Rd Rockford IL 61114-5553

HEESCHEN, DAVID SUTPHIN, astronomer, educator; b. Davenport, Iowa, Mar. 12, 1926; s. Richard George and Emily (Sutphin) H.; m. Eloise St. Clair, June 11, 1950; children: Lisa Clair, David William, Richard Mark. BS, U. Ill., 1949, MS, 1951; PhD, Harvard U., 1954; ScD (hon.), W.Va. Inst. Tech., 1974, New Mex. Inst. Tech., 1989. Instr. Wesleyan U., Middletown, Conn., 1954-55; lectr., rsch. assoc. Harvard U., 1955-56; scientist Nat. Radio Astronomy Obs., 1956-77, sr. scientist, 1977-92; emeritus, 1992—; dir. Nat. Radio Astronomy Obs., 1962-78; rsch. prof. astronomy U. Va., 1980-92. Cons. NASA, 1960-61, 68-72, Univs. Space Rsch. Assn., 1996-99, Nat. Radio Astronomy Obs., 1997-99; Karl Jansky lectr., 1993. Contbr. sci. jours. Bd. dirs. Fla. Keys Land and Sea Trust, 2000—, treas., 2006-07, vice chmn., 2007-. With Army Air Corp., 1944—45. G.R. Agassiz fellow Harvard Obs., 1953-54; Recipient Disting. Public Svc. award NSF, 1980, Alexander von Humboldt Sr. Scientist award 1985 Fellow AAAS; mem. NAS, Am. Acad. Arts and Sci., Am. Philos. Soc., Am. Astron. Soc. (v.p. 1969-71, pres. 1980-82), Internat. Astron. Union (v.p. 1976-82), Internat Sci. Radio Union. Personal E-mail: dheeschen@earthlink.net.

HEETER, JAMES A., lawyer; b. Monett, Mo., Oct. 28, 1948; AB with honors, U. Mo., Columbia, 1970; JD cum laude, Harvard U., 1973. Bar: Mo. 1973. Mem. Stinson, Mag & Fizzell PC, Kansas City, Mo., 1973—95; ptnr. Sonnenschein Nath & Rosenthal LLP, Kansas City, Mo., 1995—, mng. ptnr. Kansas City office, 2001—, mem. exec. com. Mem. City Coun., Kansas City, Mo., 1983—87. Mem. Civic Coun. of Greater Kansas City. Mem. ABA, Mo. Bar, Kansas City Met. Bar Assn. Office: Sonnenschein Nath & Rosenthal LLP Ste 1100 4520 Main St Kansas City MO 64111 Office Phone: 816-460-2452. Office Fax: 816-531-7545. Business E-Mail: jheeter@sonnenschein.com.

HEFEMAN, MARK, real estate broker; b. Durango, Colo., Apr. 1, 1960; s. W. C. and W. J. Hafeman. BA in Psychology and History, Georgetown U., Washington, 1982; JD, Loyola Law Sch., LA, 1984; MA in Adminstrn., Calif. State U., LA, 1989. Real estate broker W. Mark Hafeman Realty, Glendale, Calif., 1985—. Oil painging, Pasadena Find Arts, 2005. Pres. Capri Ct. II Orgns., Playa Vista, Calif., 2005—; founder CAAMP LA Mentor Project, LA, 2000—; benefactor City Beautification, Glendale, 2003. Recipient Travel award, Freedman Found., 2006. Mem.: Phi Delata Kapa. Personal E-mail: marcwaveman@earthlink.net.

HEFFELFINGER, THOMAS BACKER, lawyer, former prosecutor; b. Mpls., Feb. 13, 1948; BA in History, Stanford U., 1970; JD, U. Minn., 1975. Bar: Minn. 1976, US Dist. Ct. Minn. 1977, US Ct. Appeals (8th cir.) 1983, US Dist. Ct. (ea. dist.) Wis., 1999, Forest County Potawatomi Community Tribal Ct., 1999, US Supreme Ct., 2000, US Ct. Fed. Claims, 2000. Law clk. Office of the Hennepin County Atty., 1974-76, asst. atty. juvenile divsn., 1976, asst. atty. criminal divsn. trial sect., 1977-82, asst. atty. major offender unit, 1978-81, supr. burglary unit, 1981-82; asst. US atty. criminal divsn. US Dept. Justice, Minn., 1982-88, atty. white collar crime sect., 1982-85, supr. narcotics and firemans sect., 1985-86, US atty. Dist. Minn., 1991-93, 2001—06; ptnr. Opperman Heins & Paquin, 1988-91, Bowman & Brooke, 1993—2000, Best & Flanagan LLP, Mpls., 2000—01, 2006—. Contbr. articles to profl. jours. Candidate Hennepin County Atty., 1986; bd. dirs. Mpls. Chpt. ARC, 1987-2001, chair, 1998-; mem. Hennepin County Task Force on Youth and Drugs, 1987-88, Minn. Ho. of Reps. Rep. Caucus Drug Task Force, 1989-90, Minn. Commn. on Violent Crime, 1991; chmn. Minn. Commn. on Jud. Selection, 1990-91; mem. Flying Cloud Airport Adv. Commn., 1996-, chair, 1998-; bd. mem., Minn. Campaign Fin. & Pub. Disclosure Bd., 1998-2000; lectr. in field. Mem. ABA, Fed. Bar Assn., Minn. Bar Assn., Hennepin County Bar Assn., Minn. Am. Indian Bar Assn., Ethics Officer Assn., 1994-2001, Nat. Assn. Criminal Def. Lawyers, 1997-2001, Nat. Assn. Former US Attys., 1993-2001, 2006- Office: Best & Flanagan LLP 225 S Sixth St Ste 4000 Minneapolis MN 55402 E-mail: heffelfinger@bestlaw.com.

HEFFERAN, COLIEN JOAN, economist; b. Mpls., May 13, 1949; d. Bernard and Rosemary Arnsdorf; m. Hollis Spurgeon Summers, Oct. 14, 1987; 1 child, Margaret Vimont Summers. BS, U. Ariz., 1971; MS, U. Ill., 1974, PhD, 1976. Asst. prof. Pa. State U., University Park, 1975-79; econ., rsch. leader Agrl. Rsch. Svc., USDA, Hyattsville, Md., 1979-88; adminstr. Coop. State Rsch., Edn. and Ext. Svc., 1988—. Adj. prof. U. Md., University Park, 1982-88; chmn. Ctr. for Family, Washington, 1985-87; vis. fellow Australian Nat. U., Canberra, NSW, 1989-91. Mem. editl. bd. Jours.-Family Econ. Issues, 1987—. Recipient Outstanding Citizen award U. Ariz., 1985, Outstanding Alumni award U. Ill., 1986, Presdl. Rank award as Disting. Fed. Exec., 2000. Mem. Am. Econ. Assn., Am. Coun. on Consumer Interests. Democrat. Roman Catholic. Home Phone: 703-533-2843; Office Phone: 202-720-4423. Business E-Mail: chefferan@csrees.usda.gov.

HEFFERNAN, DEBRA JANE, administrator; b. Milw., Nov. 30, 1953; d. Joseph Jacob and Marjorie Christine (Stadler) Anheier; m. John William Heffernan, Oct. 19, 1974; 1 child, Justin Bryant. BS, U. Wis., Milw., 1979; MEd, U. Ill., Chgo., 1984; adminstrv. cert., Govs. State U., 1989; postgrad., Chgo. State U., 1990—; EdS, No. Ill. U., 2005. Cert. adminstr. Tchr. Guardian Angel Day Treatment Program, Joliet, Ill., 1981-86, Joliet Twp. Adult Edn. Program, 1982-84; instr. DeVry Inst. of Tech., Lombard, Ill., 1989; bldg. prin. Ann Rutledge Therapeutic Sch. Lincoln Way Area Spl. Edn. Coop., Frankfort, Ill., 1986—2000; spl. svcs. dir. Lincoln-Way HS, 2000—06; prin Martin P. MacKay Edn. Ctr., New Lenox, Ill., 2006—. Mem., sec., bd. dirs. Head Start, Joliet, 1985-89; adv. bd. Groundwork, Joliet, 1990—. Mem. Coun. for Exceptional Children, Ill. Coun. of Adminstrs. of Spl. Edn., Delta Kappa Gamma Soc. Internat. (v.p., 1998-2000, pres., 2002-04, 2006-). Avocations: arts and crafts, music, reading. Office: Martin P Mackay Edn Ctr 516 S Cedar New Lenox IL 60451 Home Phone: 815-254-3215; Office Phone: 815-463-8068.

HEFFERNAN, JAMES ANTHONY WALSH, language and literature educator; b. Boston, Apr. 22, 1939; s. Roy Joseph and Kathleen (Walsh) H.; m. Nancy Coffey, June 27, 1964; children: Virginia, Andrew. AB cum laude, Georgetown U., 1960; PhD, Princeton U., 1964. Instr. English U. Va., 1963-65; asst. prof. English Dartmouth Coll., Hanover, NH, 1965-70, assoc. prof., 1970-76, prof., 1976—2004, chmn. dept. English, 1978-81, Frederick Sessions Beebe prof. in art of writing, 1997—2004, prof. emeritus, 2004—. Cons. Mt. Holyoke, 1986, PMLA, 1986-87, Johns Hopkins U., 1987, NYU, 1987, 89, U. Press New Eng., 1987, U. Press Chgo., 1988, NEH, 1988, 90, Rutgers U., 1988, U. Md., 1988, Vanderbilt U., 1989, Barnard Coll., 1992; dir. summer seminar English romantic lit. and visual arts NEH/Dartmouth Coll., Hanover, 1987, 89; spkr. various seminars; lectr. in field Author: Wordsworth's Theory of Poetry: The Transforming Imagination, 1969, The Re-Creation of Landscape: A Study of Wordsworth, Coleridge, Constable and Turner, 1985, Museum of Words: The Poetics of Ekphrasis from Homer to Ashbery, 1993, reissued, 2004, Cultivating Picturacy Visual Art and Verbal Interventions, 2006; co-author: Writing: A College Handbook, 5th edit., 2000, Writing: A Concise College Handbook, 1st edit., 1996; editor: Space, Time, Image, Sign: Essays on Literature and the Visual Arts, 1987, Representing the French Revolution: Literature, Historiography and Art, 1992; contbr. articles to profl. jours Trustee Vermont Acad., 1992-01. Woodrow Wilson fellow, 1960-61, Franklin Murphy, Jr. fellow, 1961-62, R.K. Root fellow, 1962-63, Dartmouth Coll., 1968-69, NEH fellow, 1991; grantee Dartmouth Coll., 1971, 74, 87, NEH, 1984, 87, 89. Mem. MLA (evaluator essays, presenter, del. various convs.), Assn. Literary Scholars and Critics (coun. 1996-99). E-mail: jamesheff@dartmouth.edu.

HEFFERNAN, JAMES VINCENT, lawyer; b. Washington, Oct. 6, 1926; s. Vincent Jerome and Hazel Belle (Wiltfong) Heffernan; m. Virginia May Adams, June 26, 1954; children: David V., Douglas J., Alan P., Margaret L., Thomas A. AB, Cornell U., 1949, JD with distinction, 1952. Bar: DC 1953, Md. 1959, US Ct. Claims 1955, US Tax Ct. 1953, US Supreme Ct. 1958. Assoc. Sutherland, Asbill & Brennan, Washington, 1952-59, ptnr., 1959—. Adj. prof. Georgetown U., Washington, 1978—79. Contbr. articles to profl. jours. With USN, 1945—46. Mem.: ABA, Bar Assn. DC, Fed. Bar Assn., Kenwood Golf and Country Club, Met. Club (Washington), KC, Order Coif, Phi Alpha Delta. Democrat. Roman Catholic. Home: 5216 Falmouth Rd Bethesda MD 20816-2913 Office: Sutherland Asbill & Brennan LLP 1275 Pennsylvania Ave NW Washington DC 20004-2415 Personal E-mail: jvh3@cornell.edu. Business E-Mail: james.heffernan@sablaw.com.

HEFFERNAN, PETER JOHN, state official; b. Hartford, Conn., Feb. 19, 1945; s. Kenneth F. and Vivian (Lacourse) H. m. Rosemary Margaret Eagan, May 29, 1971; children: Peter John, Matthew Paul. BA, Providence Coll., 1967; MBA, George Washington U., 1971. Adminstrv. resident Waltham (Mass.) Hosp., 1970-71, asst. dir., 1971-74, v.p. adminstrn. and gen. svcs., 1974-78, exec. v.p., 1978-86; pres., chief exec. officer Cardinal Cushing Gen. Hosp., Brockton, Mass., 1986-87; regional v.p. Weatherby Health Care, Norwell, Mass., 1987-90; regional adminstr. health svcs. divsn. Mass. Dept. Correction, Jamaica Plain, 1990—2003, dep. dir., 2004—; sr. surveyor Nat. Commn. on Correctional Health Care, 1999—. Co-preceptor health care adminstrn. George Washington U., 1977; mem. faculty evening div. Stonehill Coll., 1990—. Mem. instructional conf. coun. New Eng. Hosp. Assembly Inc., 1976; bd. dirs. Waltham Boys Club, 1977, Hosp. Svcs. of New Eng., 1980-83. USPHS trainee, 1967-70. Fellow Am. Coll. Hosp. Adminstrs.; mem. Health Care Mgmt. Assn. Mass., ACHE Regents Adv. Council, 1994—, Lions. Roman Catholic. Office: Dept of Correction PO Box 426 Bridgewater MA 02324-0426 Home: 58 Benjamins Gate Plymouth MA 02360-8254

HEFFERNAN, THOMAS CARROLL, English literature and American studies educator; b. Hyannis, Mass., Aug. 19, 1939; arrived in Japan, 1984; s. Thomas (Hugh) Carroll and Mary Elizabeth (Sullivan) H.; m. Nancy Elizabeth Iler, 1972 (div. 1977). BA in English, Boston Coll., 1961; MA in English Lit., Victoria U. Manchester, Eng., 1963; PhD in English Lit., Sophia U., 1990. Asst. lectr. English U. Manchester, Eng., 1964-65, U. Bristol, Eng., 1965-66; instr. English U. Hartford, West Hartford, Conn., 1967-70, N.C. State U., Raleigh, 1971-73; poet in the schs. N.C. Dept. Pub. Instrn. and Arts Coun., Raleigh, 1973-77; lectr. English and humanities Program for Afloat Coll. Edn., USN, Norfolk (Va.) & San Diego, Calif., 1982-84; lectr. in English, history and philosophy U. Md., Asian Divsn., Tokyo, 1984-92; vis. prof. English U. Kagoshima, Japan, 1992-94; prof. English and Am. studies Kagoshima Prefectural Coll., Japan, 1994—2005; vis. prof. English and creative writing St. Andrews Presbyn. Coll., 2005—. Editor, pub., dir. Yorick Books, Boston and Hartford, 1967-71; dir., poetry instr. Martha's Vineyard Writers Workshop, Vineyard Haven, Mass., 1973-77; vis. artist in poetry N.C. Arts Coun., N.C. Dept. C.Cs., Raleigh, 1977-81; vis. artist in poetry S.C. Arts Commn., Columbia, 1981-82; editor, pub. Plover/Chidori, Okinawa, Japan, 1987-92; lectr. in field. Author: The Liam Poems, 1981 (Roanoke-Chowan 1982), Art and Emblem: Early 17th Century English Poetry of Devotion, 1991, Gathering In Ireland, 1996, Christmas Gifts in South Japan, 2002, White Edge, Curing Wave, 2003; editor (Celtic issue) Internat. Poetry Rev., 1979, CAIRN: The St. Andrews Rev., 2005—; contbr. chpts. to books and articles to profl. jours. Recipient Mainichi Internat. Haiku award in English, Mainichi Daily News, Japan, 1985, 87-93, 97, 2d pl. in English, 1999-2000, 06, Portfolio Poetry award Poetry Ctr.-Guilford Coll., Greensboro, N.C., 1983, Mainichi Culture Seminar Haiku award Mainichi Daily News/Japan Air Lines, Tokyo, 1986, Internat. Haiku award Itoen Co., Tokyo, 1990, 1995, Kusamakura Internat. Haiku Grand prize, 2006. Mem. Renaissance Inst. (Tokyo), Internat. Ezra Pound Conf., Japan Assn. Lang. Tchrs. (local chpt. v.p. 1992-94), Haiku Soc. Am., NC Haiku Soc. Avocations: singing, walking, travel. Office Phone: 910-277-5268. E-mail: thomasheffernan@yahoo.com, hefferntc@sapc.edu.

HEFFERNAN, VIRGINIA, television critic; b. Hanover, NH, Aug. 8, 1969; PhD in English lit., Harvard Coll. Fact checker New Yorker; editor Talk Magazine, NYC, 1998—2000, Slate, 2001; sr. editor Harper's, 2002; tv critic Slate, 2003, NY Times, 2003—. Contbr. VH1, MTV, Salon, New Yorker, NY Times, 1997—; author: (Documentary) Matthew's Murder, 1998; co-author: The Underminer, 2005. Named a Rising Star, Folio, 2002;

named one of Ten young editors to watch, Columbia Journalism Rev., 2002. Office: NY Times 229 W 43rd St New York NY 10036 Office Phone: 212-556-7341. Office Fax: 212-556-1516.

HEFFERON, THOMAS MICHAEL, lawyer; b. Mt. Vernon, NY, Sept. 20, 1960; s. George Joseph and Julia Theresa Hefferon; m. Elizabeth Ann Rosnagle, May 27, 1990; children: David, Margaret, Robert. BA, Trinity Coll., 1982; JD, U. Chgo., 1986. Bar: Mass. 1986, US Dist. Ct. Mass., US Dist. Ct.Md., US Dist. Ct. (ea. dist.) Va., US Dist. Ct.(no. dist.) Mich., US Dist. Ct. (we. dist.) Mich., US Dist. Ct.(no. dist.) Ill., US Ct. Appeals (1st, 2d, 3d, 4th, 5th, 6th, 9th, 11th dists.), US Supreme Ct., 1998, DC, 1999, Va. 2001. Asst. prof. Boston Coll. Law Sch., Newton, Mass., 1989-90; assoc. Goodwin, Procter & Hoar, Boston, 1986-89, 90-95; ptnr., co-chair, litig. dept. Goodwin Procter LLP (formerly Goodwin, Procter & Hoar), Washington, 1995—; chair, consumer fin. svcs. litig. practice group Goodwin Procter LLP, Washington. Mem. ABA, Boston Bar Assn., Order of Coif. Office: Goodwin Procter LLP 901 New York Ave NW Washington DC 20001 Office Phone: 202-346-4029. Office Fax: 202-346-4444. Business E-Mail: thefferon@goodwinprocter.com.

HEFFNER, DANIEL JASON, film producer; b. NYC, Mar. 30, 1956; s. Richard Douglas and Elaine Peggy (Segal) H.; m. Beth Klein, May 26, 1991; children: Jeremy Aaron, Zachary David. BS in Comm., Ithaca Coll., 1978. Prodn. exec. Columbia Pictures, LA, 1982-85; prodn. exec., prodr. Walt Disney Pictures, LA, 1985-88; v.p. prodn. Buena Vista Pictures Distbn. divsn. Walt Disney Co., LA, 1988-91; prodr. Serendipity Prodns., Inc., 1991—. Asst. dir. (film) The Big Chill, 1982; co-prodr. (film) Cocktail, 1988; exec. prodr. (film) The Good Mother, 1988; co-exec. prodr. (film) Holy Matrimony, 1993; asst. dir., 2d unit dir. (film) The Seventh Veil, 1999; line prodr., 1st asst. dir. (films) Highway 395, 1999, Sheer Bliss, 2000, Flying Virus, 2001; co-prodr. (films) George of the Jungle 2, 2002, Saw, 2003 Checking Out, 2004, Saw II, 2005; prodr. (film) Anonymous Rex, 2004; exec. prodr. Saw III, 2006. Mem.: Prodrs. Guild Am., Dirs. Guild Am. Democrat. Jewish. Home: 4119 Woodman Ave Sherman Oaks CA 91423-4331 Office Phone: 818-789-3035. Fax: 818-789-0213. E-mail: danheffner@earthlink.net.

HEFFNER, RICHARD DOUGLAS, historian, educator, communications consultant, television producer; b. NYC, Aug. 5, 1925; s. Albert Simon and Cely (Bender) H.; m. Anne de la Vergne, Dec. 14, 1946; m. Elaine Segal, July 30, 1950; children: Daniel Jason, Charles Andrew. AB, Columbia U., 1946, MA (Mitchell fellow), 1947. Tchg. asst. history U. Calif., Berkeley, 1947-48; instr. Am. history Rutgers U., 1948-50, univ. prof. comm., pub. policy, 1964—; lectr. history Columbia, 1950-52; prof. history Sarah Lawrence Coll., 1952-53; dir. pub. affairs WNBC-TV, NYC, 1955-57; dir. programs Met. Ednl. TV Assn., NYC, 1957-59; editl.l cons. CBS, Inc.; mem. editl. bd., dir. spl. projects CBS-TV Network, 1959-61; v.p., gen. mgr. ednl. TV Channel 13 WNET, NYC, 1961-63; pres. Richard Heffner Assocs., Inc., NYC, 1964—. Mem. program adv. bd. Teleprompter Corp.; dir. commn. campaign costs 20th Century Fund, 1968-69; dir. study TV's environ. messages Ford Found., 1970-72; chmn. bd. classification rating adminstrn. Motion Picture Assn. Am., 1974-94. Producer-moderator The Open Mind, NBC-TV, 1956—59, Channel 13, NYC, 1973—, moderator-host National Educational TV series People and Politics, 1964, exec. editor-host WPIX-TV From the Editor's Desk, 1981—86; author: A Documentary History of the United States, 1952, 7th 50th Anniversary edition, 2002, Conversations with Elie Wiesel, 2001, As They Saw It, A Conversational History of Modern America, 2003; editor: Alexis de Tocqueville's Democracy in America, 1956. Mem. exec. com., vice chmn. bd. NYC Police Found.; chmn. judiciary com. cameras cts. NY State, 1987-89. Sr. fellow Freedom Forum Media Studies Ctr., NYC, 1994-95. Mem. AAAS, Acad. Motion Picture Arts Scis., Am. Hist. Assn., Nat. Assn. Ednl. Broadcasters, Phi Beta Kappa. Clubs: Century. Home: 90 Riverside Dr New York NY 10024-5306 Office: 320 Park Ave New York NY 10022-6815 Office Phone: 212-224-1368. Personal E-mail: richarddheffner@aol.com, openmindtv@aol.com.

HEFFRON, HOWARD A., lawyer; s. Jack and Sophie (Malkin) H.; m. Stella Meller, July 4, 1946; children: James, Robert, Nancy. AB, Columbia U., 1948; LL.B., Harvard U., 1951. Bar: N.Y. State 1953, D.C. 1953. Practiced in, NYC and Washington, 1953-58, 61-66, 69-77, 79—; asst. U.S. atty. So. Dist. N.Y., 1953-57; 1st asst. tax div. and asst. dep. atty. gen. Dept. Justice, Washington, 1958-61; chief counsel Fed. Hwy. Adminstrn., Dept. Transp., Washington, 1967-69; apptd. by Pres. and confirmed by Senate as dir. Office Rail Pub. Counsel, Washington, 1977-79; prof. law U. Wash., Seattle, 1965-67. Cons. Pres.'s Commn. on Law Enforcement and Adminstrn. of Justice, Washington, 1965-66, Nat. Commn. on Product Safety, Washington, 1969-70 Author: Federal Consumer Safety Legislation, 1970. With U.S. Army, 1946-47.

HEFFRON, MICHAEL EDWARD, software engineer, computer scientist; b. Battle Creek, Mich., Dec. 18, 1949; s. Michael Richard and Maxine Beverly (Piper) Heffron; m. Judith M. Dole, June 22, 2002; children from previous marriage: Karen, Jennifer. BS in Computer Sci., Ariz. State U., 1986; MS in Computer Sci., Colo. Tech. U., 1998, D in Computer Sci., 2001. Engring. asst. Motorola, Inc., Scottsdale, Ariz., 1977-81; calibration lab. supr. ADR Ultrasound, Tempe, Ariz., 1982-83; engring. aide Motorola, Inc., Scottsdale, 1983-86; v.p. CyberSoft, Inc., Tempe, Ariz., 1986-90; engr. Injection Rsch. Specialists, Inc., Colorado Springs, Colo., 1990-91; software devel. mgr. Injection Rsch. Specialists Co. div. Pacer Industries, Colorado Springs, 1991-92; sr. systems engr. Computer Data Systems Inc., Rockville, Md., 1992-93; software engr. Coergon, Inc., Boulder, Colo., 1993-95, Loral Comm. Systems (purchased by Lockheed Martin 1996), Colorado Springs, Colo., 1995-96, Lockheed Martin, Colorado Springs, 1996-97; sr. software engr. L-3 Comms. Corp. (formerly Lockheed Martin Wideband Sys.), Colo. Springs, 1997-99, prin. software engr., 1999—2005, staff software engr., 2005—07; software engr. Harris Corp., Colo. Springs, 2007—. Patentee in field. Served with USAF, 1970-77. Mem. IEEE, Assn. Computing Machinery. Office: Harris Corp Tech Svcs 8955 Drennan Rd Colorado Springs CO 80925

HEFFRON, WARREN A., physician, educator; b. St. Louis, Nov. 7, 1936; s. Willard Page H. and Alma Alberta Revington; m. Rosalee Bowdish, June 10, 1961; children: Kimberly, Wanda, Kara, Arthur. AB, U. Mo., 1958, MD, 1962. Diplomate Am. Bd. Family Practice (pres. 1998—). Rotating intern U. Calif., Orange, 1962-63; physician Hosp. Castaner (P.R.), 1966-68; resident internal medicine U. N. Mex., Albuquerque, 1968-71, asst. prof., chief divsn., 1971-76; assoc. prof., asst. chair Family Cmty. and Emergency Medicine, Albuquerque, 1976-82; prof., chmn. Family Committee and Emergency Medicine, Albuquerque, 1982-93; chief med. staff U. N. Mex. Hosp., Albuquerque, 1993—. Bd. dirs. Am. Acad. Family Physicians, Am. Bd. Family Practice; dir. family Med. Residency Program, Albuquerque, 1971-82; vis. prof., cons. Dept. Cmty. Health, Punjab, India, Christian Med. Coll., Punjab U., Ludihiana; prof. Dept. Family and Cmty. Medicine, Albuquerque, 1993—; various internat. vis. professorships; internat. cons. family medicine residences in missionary settings. Contbr. numerous articles to profl. jours. Mem. free clinic Albuquerque Rescue Mission. Lt. comdr. USPHS, 1964-66. Named N. Mex. Family Physician of the Yr. 1990; recipient Recognition award Am. Med. Assn. Physicians, 1971, 74, 77, 80, 83, 86, 89, 92, 95, 98. Mem. N. Mex. Am. Acad. Family Physicians (pres. 1985, N. Mex. Family Dr. of Yr. award, chpt. svc. award 1988), Am. Bd. Family Practice (pres. 1998-99), N. Mex. Med. Soc. (pres. 1996-97, Robbins award Cmty. Svc. 1981), Soc. Tchrs. of Family Medicine (bd. dirs., treas. 1997, Smilkstein award 1998), Christian Med. and Dental Assn. (bd. dirs. 1998-06, pres. 2003-05, residency rev. com. for family practice 1999-05, Educator of Yr. award 2007), World Orgn. Family Drs. (pres. Ams. 2000-07). Methodist. Home: 2406 Ada Pl NE Albuquerque NM 87106-2550 Business E-Mail: wheffron@salud.unm.edu.

HEFLEY, JOEL MAURICE, former congressman; s. J. Maurice and Etta A. (Anderson) H.; m. Lynn Christian, Aug. 25, 1961; children: Jana, Lori, Juli. BA, Okla. Baptist U., 1957; MS, Okla. State U., 1962. Exec. dir. Community Planning and Research, Colorado Springs, Colo., 1966-86; mem. Colo. State Ho. of Reps., 1977-78, Colo. State Senate, 1979-86, US Congress from 5th Colo. dist., 1987—2007; mem. armed svcs. com.; mem. natural resources com.; mem. small bus.-SBA com.; mem. nat. security com.; chmn. stds. ofcl. conduct com., 2001—05. Mem.: Rotary, Colorado Springs Country. Republican. Presbyterian.

HEFLIN, MARTIN GANIER, diplomat, political scientist; b. Oklahoma City, July 5, 1932; s. Martin Henry and Eugenia Marie (Gabel) H.; m. Sydney Daffin Lewis, Nov. 24, 1954; children— Martin Hays, Stephanie Anne Heflin Pace BA, U. Okla., 1954, MA, 1957; postgrad., U. Redlands, 1955, U. Tex., 1958-59. Vice consul U.S. Consulate, Ponta Delgada, Portugal, 1960-62, U.S. Consulate Gen., São Paulo, Brazil, 1962-64; 2d sec. U.S. Embassy, Tokyo, Japan, 1964-68; prin. officer U.S. Consulate, Sapporo, Japan, 1968-71; fgn. affairs officer U.S. Dept State, Washington, 1971-74; consul, econ. and commerce U.S. Consulate Gen., São Paulo, 1974-76; dir. U.S. Trade Ctr. U.S. Dept. Commerce, São Paulo, 1976-78; counselor econ. and comml. affairs U.S. Embassy, New Delhi, India, 1979-83; minister-counselor, sr. Fgn. Service; prin. officer U.S. Consultate Gen., Monterrey, Mexico, 1983-87; sr. fellow Ctr. for Study of Fgn. Affairs, Fgn. Service Inst., Dept. State, 1987-89; mng. dir. The Naiad Corp., 1990—. Served to 1st lt. USAF, 1954-56. Mem. Am. Fgn. Service Assn., Am. Legion, Phi Delta Theta Roman Catholic. Avocations: golf, photography. Home: 4411 NW 12th Pl Gainesville FL 32605-5500 Personal E-mail: nikkihef@cox.net.

HEFLIN, TOM PAT, artist; s. Edward James and Mary Modell Heflin; children: Rebecca Mary, Mark Patrick, Elizabeth Eve, Eron Irish, Sarah Lynn, Sienna Blue, Kane Tom. Student, U. La., Monroe, 1955—56, Art Inst. Chgo., 1956—57. Art instr. Rock Valley Coll., Rockford, Ill., 1969—71. Author (artist): (paintings and writings) Roots And Wings 36 Year Retrospective; book, paintings and writings, Quite Places, video, The Art Of Tom Heflin, 37 year retrospective exhibition, Tranquil Heart. Artist Statue Of Liberty Restoration Project, NYC, 1976. Recipient Top Award For Painting, Nat. Soc. Of Painters In Casien And Acrylic, 1976. Fellow: Rockford Art Mus. (assoc.); mem.: Oil Painters Of Am. (assoc.). X. Avocations: fishing, birding, guitar, nature science, photography. Home: 1162 South Weldon Rd Rockford IL 61102 Office: Heflin Gallery 1162 South Weldon Rd Rockford IL 61102 Office Phone: 815-962-1835. E-mail: heflingallery@insightbb.com.

HEFLING, DEBRA L., financial representative; b. Albuquerque, Jan. 31, 1976; d. Walter W. and Nancy C. Simpson; m. Brian L. Hefling, June 22, 2002; 1 child, Scott Ian Anderson. Student in bus. fin., Am. InterContinental U., 2005—07. Payment plan specialist State Farm Ins., Dallas, 1999—2004; sport sound technician Daktronics, Brookings, SD, 2004—06; fin. rep. GE Money, Rapid City, SD, 2007—. Mem.: Gen. Fedn. Women's Clubs. Home: 709 E Anamosa Apt 312 Rapid City SD 57701 Home Phone: 605-695-9034. Personal E-mail: dhefling@rushmore.com.

HEFNER, CHRISTIE ANN, publishing executive; b. Chgo., Nov. 8, 1952; d. Hugh Marston and Mildred Marie (Williams) H. BA in English and Am. Lit., summa cum laude, Brandeis U., 1974. Freelance journalist, Boston, 1974-75; spl. asst. to chmn. Playboy Enterprises, Inc., Chgo., 1975-78, v.p., 1978-82, bd. dirs., 1979—, pres., 1982-88, COO, 1984-88, chmn., CEO, 1988—. Bd. dirs. Playboy Found., Mag. Pubs. Assn. Bd. dirs. Creative Coalition, Rush Med. Ctr., Canyon Ranch, Bus. Com. for the Arts. Named Advocate of Yr., AIDS Legal Coun., 1998, Friend for Life, Howard Brown Med. Ctr., 1998; named one of 100 Most Powerful Women in World, Forbes mag., 2005—06; named to Today's Chgo. (Ill.) Woman Hall Fame, 2002; recipient Agness Underwood award, LA chpt. Women in Comm., 1984, Founders award, Midwest Women's Ctr., 1986, Human Rights award, Am. Jewish Com., 1986, Harry Kalven Freedom of Expression award, ACLU, Ill., 1987, Spirit of Life award, City of Hope, 1988, Eleanor Roosevelt award, Internat. Platform Assn., 1990, Will Rogers Meml. award, Beverly Hills C. of C. and Civic Assn., 1993, Humanitarian award, Rainbow/PUSH Coalition, 1998, Corp. Leadership award, AIDS Pastoral Care Network, 1998, Exec. Leadership award, Nat. Soc. Fundraising Execs., 1998, Champion of Freedom award, ADL, 2000, Spirit of Hope award, John Wayne Cancer Ctr., 2001, Bettie B. Port Humanitarian award, Mt. Sinai, 2001, Christopher Reeve 1st Amendment award, Creative Coalition, 2001, Bette B. Port Humanitarian award, Sianai Health Sys., 2001, Vanguard award, Nat. Cable & Telecommunications Assn., 2002, Philanthropic Innovator Luminary award, Com. of 200, 2002, Family Bus. Coun. Leadership award, U. Ill., Chgo., 2003, Friends of Cmty. award, Diversity Healthcare, Inc., 2005, Lifetime Achievement award, 25-Yr. Club, 2005. Mem. Nat. Cable and Telecomm. Assn. (Vanguard award 2002, Interlochen's Path of Inspiration award 2003), Mus. of TV and Radio Media Ctr., Brandeis Nat. Women's Com. (life), Com. of 200, World Pres. Orgn., Chgo. Network, Sierra Club, Emilys List, Phi Beta Kappa. Democrat. Office: Playboy Enterprises Inc 680 N Lake Shore Dr Chicago IL 60611-4455

HEFNER, HUGH MARSTON, editor-in-chief; b. Chgo., Apr. 9, 1926; s. Glenn L. and Grace (Swanson) H.; m. Mildred M. Williams, June 25, 1949 (div.); children: Christie A., David P.; m. Kimberley Conrad, July 1, 1989 (div.); children: Marston G., Cooper B. BS, U. Ill., 1949. Subscription promotion writer Esquire mag., 1951; promotion mgr. Pubs. Devel. Corp., 1952; circulation mgr. Children's Activities mag., 1953; chmn. bd. HMH Pub. Co. Inc. (now Playboy Enterprises, Inc.), 1953-88; editor-in-chief Playboy mag., 1953—; pres. Playboy Clubs Internat., Inc., 1959-86; editor, pub. VIP mag., 1963-75, Oui mag., 1972-81. Film appearances include History of the World, Part I, 1981, The Comeback Trail, 1982, Beverly Hills Cop II, 1987; TV series) The Girls Next Door, 2005-. Served with AUS, 1944-46. Recipient 1st Amendment Freedom award B'nai B'rith Anti-Defamation League, L.A., 1980, Internat. Pub. award Internat. Press Directory in London, 1997; named Man of Yr. Mag. Industry Newsletter, 1967; named to Pub. Hall of Fame, 1989; honored with Hugh M. Hefner chair in study of Am. film U. So. Calif. Sch. Cinema/TV, 1996, Henry Johnson Fisher award, 2002. Mem.: N.Y. Friars Club (hon.). Office: Playboy Enterprises Inc 2706 Media Ctr Dr Los Angeles CA 90065-1733

HEFNER, LINDA P., retail executive; BS, U. North Tex., MS in Accounting; MBA, Harvard U. Mgmt. cons. Ernst & Young; with Sara Lee Corp., 1989—2004, CEO L'eggs and Hanes hosiery, CEO Underwear, Socks and L.Am. Group; exec. v.p. global strategy & bus. devel. Kraft Foods Inc., 2004—06; exec. v.p., gen. mgr. home divsn. Wal-Mart Stores, Inc., Bentonville, Ark., 2007—. Bd. dirs. Danaher Corp., 2005—06. Office: Wal-Mart Stores Inc 702 Southwest 8th St Bentonville AR 72716

HEFNER, WILLIAM JOHNSON, JR., (W. JOHN HEFNER JR.), oil and gas industry executive; b. Oklahoma City, July 29, 1952; s. William Johnson and Eloise (Wallace) H.; m. Deborah Seyan Raulston, Nov. 23, 1979; children: Margaret Leigh, Virginia Lynn. BA in Journalism, U. Okla., 1980; MBA, Oklahoma City U., 1983. Reporter city desk The Daily Oklahoman, Oklahoma City, 1978-79; field landman Gerald D. Whitfield, Oklahoma City, 1980, W.W. Blair, Oklahoma City, 1980-81; field landman, in-house landman T.S. Dudley Land Co., Oklahoma City, 1981-82; landman, part owner Arbuckle Enterprises, Inc., Oklahoma City, 1984-88; mng. ptnr. Hefner Co., Oklahoma City, 1986-93, Hefner Prodn. Co., Oklahoma City, 1986-93; leasing agt. First Resource Realty, Inc., Oklahoma City, 1987; leasing agt., property mgr. Alquest Property Corp., Oklahoma City, 1987-88; pres. Hefner Corp., Oklahoma City, 1988-93, Hefner Co., Inc., Oklahoma City, 1994—. Pres. Midtown Redevel. Corp., 2000—02; mem. steering com. Deaconess Found., 2005; mem. leadership cir. com. Casady Sch., 1994—99, co-chair leadership cir., 1994, 2001—02, mem. com. Leadership Cir., 1999; active Leadership Oklahoma City Class XI, 1993, Downtown Now, 1989—2000, Oklahoma City Art Mus., 1985—, U. Okla. Found., Norman, 1990—, YMCA, 1988—94, Com. of 100, 1993—99, bd. dirs., 1996—97; bd. visitors U. Okla. Coll. Fine Arts, 2004—, U. Okla. Pres. Assocs., 2004—; vestry mem. St. Paul's Cathedral, 1990—92, mem. Usher's Guild, 1988—97, 1999—2003; mem. St. Francis of Assisi trust bd., 2006, mem. courier, 2006, chmn. sprinkler com., 2006—07; bd. dirs. Hist. Preservation, Inc., 1983—2006, pres., 2000—03, mem. trees, pks. and beautification com., 1983—85, 1988—89, 1995, chmn. trees, pks. and beautification com., 1986, mem. projects com., 1986, 1989, 1991, 1994—99, chmn., 2002, mem. enforcement com., 1984—85, 1988, mem. long-range planning com., 1988—89, 2004, mem. oil and gas com., 1988—89, 2004, mem. fin. and budget com., 1989, 1st v.p., 1988, 2d v.p., 1989, mem. assoc. bd., 1992, chmn. pub. rels. com., 1992, mem. real estate com., 1998—99, 2005, dir. emeritus, 2006—; bd. dirs. Uptown 23 Devel. Assn., 2001—02; assoc. bd. dirs. Okla. Med. Rsch. Found., 1988—92, mem. fin. and investment com., 1991, exec. com., 1991—2001, bd. dirs., 1992—2001, Lyric Theatre, 1990—92, adv. bd. dirs., 1992—95; bd. dirs. Deaconess Hosp., 1991—2005, mem. exec. com., 1993—95, 2d v.p., 1994—95; bd. dirs. Deaconess Health Care Corp., 1994—2003, Butterfield Meml. Found., 2005—06, Children's Med. Rsch., 1992—94, Okla. Heritage Assn., 1994—99, St. Anthony Hosp. Found., 2004—, Okla. Blood Inst., 2004—, mem. audit and corp. governance com., 2005—, mem. exec. com., 2005—, chmn. search com., 2006, mem. bd. dirs. holding co., 2005, chmn. bldg. sub-com., 2007—; reporter, editor The Heritage Hills Herald, 1987—89, vice-chmn., 1993—97; participant Heritage Hills Housetour, 1982, 1987, 1993, 2005. Mem. Ind. Petroleum Assn. Am., Okla. Ind. Petroleum Assn., Chafing Dish Soc., Okla. Hist. Soc., Oklahoma City/County Hist. Soc. (life), Beacon Club, Oklahoma City Golf and Country Club, Magna Charta Barons, Lotus Club. Republican. Roman Catholic. Avocation: historical preservation. Office: Hefner Co Inc PO Box 2177 Oklahoma City OK 73101-2177

HEFTER, LAURENCE ROY, lawyer; b. NYC, Oct. 13, 1935; s. Charles S. and Rose (Postal) H.; m. Jacqulyn Maureen Miller, June 13, 1957; children: Jeffrey Scott, Sue-Anne. B.M.E., Rensselaer Poly. Inst., 1957, MS in Mech. Engring., 1960; JD with honors, George Washington U., 1964. Bar: Va. 1964, N.Y. 1967, D.C. 1973. Instr. Rensselaer Poly. Inst., Troy, NY, 1957-59; patent engr. Gen. Electric Co., Washington, 1959-63; sr. patent atty. Atlantic Research Corp., Alexandria, Va., 1963-66; mem. firm Ryder, McAulay & Hefter, NYC, 1970-73, Finnegan, Henderson, Farabow, Garrett & Dunner, LLP, Washington, 1973—. Professorial lectr. trademark law George Washington U., 1981-90; mem. adv. com. U.S. Patent and Trademark Office, 1988-92, Trademark Rev. Commn., 1986-89. Bd. govs. Brand Names Ednl. Found., 2001-05. Named one of best lawyers in intellectual property law, Best Lawyers in Am., 2005—07. Mem. ABA (chmn. patent office affairs com. patent, trademark and copyright sect. 1976-80, unfair competition com. 1980-81, governing com. franchise forum 1994-97), N.Y. State Bar Assn., D.C. Bar Assn., Va. Bar Assn. (dir. patent, trademark and copyright sect. 1976-78), Internat. Bar Assn. (chmn. trademark com. 1986-90), Am. Patent Law Assn. (chmn. trademark com. 1979-81, dir. 1981-84), U.S. Trademark Assn. (dir. 1982-84), Order of Coif, Alpha Epsilon Pi. Office: Finnegan Henderson Farabow Garrett & Dunner LLP 901 New York Ave NW Washington DC 20001-4413 Office Phone: 202-408-4053. Office Fax: 202-408-4400. Business E-Mail: larry.hefter@finnegan.com.

HEFTER, LEE, chef; Chef China Moon Cafe, San Francisco; sous chef Spago, Hollywood, Calif., exec. chef Beverly Hills, Calif.; chef Granita, LA; mng. ptnr., corp. chef Wolfgang Puck Fine Dining Grp., Wolfgang Puck Catering and Events. Nominee Rising Star, James Beard Found., 1997, Best Calif. Chef, 2003; named one of Best Young Chefs in Am., Restaurants & Instn., 1997; recipient Best New Chef, Food & Wine Mag., 1998, American Express Best Chef: California award, James Beard Found., 2005. Office: Spago 176 N Canon Dr Beverly Hills CA 90210 Office Phone: 310-385-0880.

HEFTER, MICHAEL C, lawyer; b. Bklyn., Apr. 22, 1966; BA, U. of Mich., 1988; JD, Emory U. School of Law, 1991. Bar: New York 1992, U.S. District Ct., Am. Bar Assoc. Ptnr. Dewey Ballantine LLP. Named one of Top 40 Lawyers Under 40, The National Law Journal, 2002. Mem.: U. of Mich., Dept. of Organizational Studies (Mem., Faculty Advisory Comm. 2002—), Volunteer Lawyers for the Arts (Bd. Dir. 2002—). Office: Dewey Ballantine LLP 1301 Avenue of the Americas New York NY 10019

HEFTLER, THOMAS E., lawyer; b. Jersey City, 1943; AB, Princeton U., 1965; JD cum laude, NYU, 1968. Bar: NY 1968. Mng. ptnr. Stroock & Stroock & Lavan LLP, NYC, 1996—, mem. operating exec. com. Office: Stroock & Stroock & Lavan LLP 180 Maiden Ln New York NY 10038-4925 Office Phone: 212-806-6052. Office Fax: 212-806-6006. Business E-Mail: theftler@stroock.com.

HEGAMIN-YOUNGER, CECILIA, statistician, consultant, educator; b. Calif., Apr. 1, 1967; BA in Psychology, U. Calif., San Diego, 1988; MPH in Biostatistics, U. NC, Chapel Hill, 1991; PhD, U. Iowa, Iowa City, 1995. Rsch. dir. Harcourt Assessment Inc., San Antonio, 2005—06; assoc. prof. Touro U. Internat., Cypress, Calif., 2006—. Statis. cons. Info. Decision Analysis, St. Louis, 2000—06. Active Planned Parenthood, St. Louis, 2002—07. Home Phone: 314-584-2166. Office Fax: 314-584-2166; Home Fax: 314-584-2166. Personal E-mail: chyounger@sportspi.com. Business E-Mail: info@sportspi.com.

HEGAR, REBECCA L., social worker, educator, consultant; b. San Antonio, Nov. 2, 1950; d. Joseph A. and Lucille Hegar; 1 child, Anna Natasha. BA, U. Tex., Austin, 1972, MS in Social Work, 1975; PhD, Tulane U., New Orleans, 1986. LCSW Tex. Asst. prof. So. U., New Orleans, 1984—87; assoc. prof., assoc. dean U. Md., Balt., 1987—97; prof. U. Tex., Arlington, 1997—. Author: When Parents Kidnap, 1993; editor: Kinship Foster Care: Practice, Policy & Research, 1999; assoc. editor: Brit. Jour. Social Work, 2005—. Trainer of vols. Cir. T coun. Girl Scouts USA, Ft. Worth, 2003—; mem. Families Way Impact Coun. United Way of Tarrant County, Ft. Worth, 2004—; bd. dirs. Associated Cath. Charities, Ft. Worth, 1999—2005. Lutheran. Home Phone: 817-472-7246; Office Phone: 817-272-5357. Business E-Mail: rhegar@uta.edu.

HEGARTY, GEORGE JOHN, university president, literature and language professor; b. Cape May, NJ, July 20, 1948; s. John Joseph and Gloria Anna (Bonelli) H.; m. Joy Elizabeth Schiller, June 9, 1979. Student, U. Fribourg, Switzerland, 1968-69; BA in English, LaSalle U., Phila., 1970; Cert., Coll. de la Pocatiere, Que., Can., 1970; postgrad., U. Dakar, Senegal, 1970, Case Western Res. U., 1973-74, U. N.H., 1976; MA in English, Drake U., 1977; cert., U. Iowa, 1977; DA, Drake U., 1978; Cert., UCLA, 1979, U. Pa., 1981. Tchr. English, Peace Corps vol. College d'Enseignment General de Sedhiou, Senegal, 1970-71; tchr. English Belmore Boys' and Westfields High Schs., Sydney, Australia, 1972-73; teaching fellow in English Drake U., Des Moines, 1974-76; mem. faculty English Des Moines Area CC, 1976-80; assoc. prof. Am. lit. U. Yaounde, Cameroon, 1980-83;

prof. Am. lit. and civilization Nat. U. Cote D'Ivoire, Abidjan, 1986-88; dir. ctr. for internat. programs and svcs. Drake U., Des Moines, 1983-91; prof. grad. program intercultural mgmt. Sch. for Internat. Tng., The Experiment in Internat. Living, Brattleboro, Vt., 1991-93; pres., prof. English, Teikyo Westmar U., Le Mars, Iowa, 1994-95; program dir. Am. degree program Taylor's Coll., Malaysia, 1996-97; provost, prof. English Teikyo Loretto Heights U., Denver, 1992-94, v.p. academic affairs, prof. English, 1997—2001, pres., prof. English, 2005—; rector Webster U., Thailand, 2002—03; prof. Am. lit. & civilization U. Antananarivo, Madagascar, 2003—05; pres. Okinaga Found., 2006—. Acad. specialist USIA, 1983-84; workshop organizer/speaker Am. Field Svcs., 1986; cons. Coun. Internat. Ednl. Exch., 1986; evaluator Assn. des Univ. Partiellment Entierément de Langue Francais, 1987, Iowa Humanities Bd., 1990-91, USAID's Ctr. for Univ. Coop. and Devel., 1991; Fulbright lectr., rschr. Am. Lit U., 2003-05; study leader Am. Mus. Natural History Expeditions, 2007—; cons. in field. Book reviewer African Book Pub. Record, Oxford, Eng., 1981-1996, African Studies Rev., 1990-1993; host, creator TV show Global Perspectives, 1989-91; exhibitor of African art, 1989—; contbr. articles to profl. jours. Commr. Des Moines Sister City Commn., 1984-87, 91; bd. dirs. Iowa Sister State Com., 1988-91; pres. Chautauqua Park Nat. Hist. Dist. Neighborhood Assn., 1991; bd. dirs. Melton Found., 1994-95. Drake U. fellow, 1971-72, 74-76; Nat. Endowment for Humanities grantee, 1981; Fulbright grantee, USIA, 1980-83, 86-88; Dept. of State grantee, 2003-05. Mem.: NAFSA: Assn. Internat. Educators (sectional chmn. region VI 1986—87, Vt. rep. 1992). Avocations: collecting tribal art, travel, swimming, writing. Office: Teikyo Loretto Heights U 3001 S Federal Blvd Denver CO 80236 Personal E-mail: georgehegarty@aol.com. Business E-Mail: ghegarty@tlhu.edu.

HEGARTY, JOHN F., JR., advertising executive; PhD (hon.), Buckinghamshire Chilterns Univ. Coll. Jr. art dir. Benton and Bowles, London, 1965; with John Collings & Ptnrs.; joined Cramer Saatchi, 1967; founding shareholder Saatchi & Saatchi, 1970, dep. creative dir., 1971—73; co-founder, creative dir. TBWA, London, 1973; co-founder Bartle Bogle Hegarty, 1982, chmn., worldwide creative dir. Chair NY Art Dirs. Advt. Show, 1999. Named to Creative Hall of Fame, One's Club, 2005; recipient Pres. Award, D&AD, Life Time Achievement Award, Internat. Clio Awards, 2005. Office: Bartle Bogle Hegarty 7 W 22Nd St New York NY 10010 Office Phone: 212-812-6600. Office Fax: 212-242-4110.*

HEGARTY, JOSEPH LEE, neurotologist; b. Media, Pa., Dec. 7, 1965; m. Allison Adams, July 13, 1988. MD, Jefferson Medial Coll., Phila., 1992. Diplomate Am. Bd. Otolaryngology, 1993. CEO Colo. Springs Ear Assocs., Colorado Springs, Colo., 0202—. Office: Colorado Springs Ear Assocs 1625 Medical Center Point Ste 180 Colorado Springs CO 80907 Home Phone: 719-579-5559; Office Phone: 719-667-1327.

HEGARTY, MARY FRANCES, lawyer; b. Chgo., Dec. 19, 1950; d. James E. and Frances M. (King) H. BA, DePaul U., 1972, JD, 1975. Bar: Ill. 1975, U.S. Dist. Ct. (no. dist.) Ill. 1976, U.S. Supreme Ct. 1980. Ptnr. Lannon & Hegarty, Park Ridge, Ill., 1975-80; pvt. practice Park Ridge, 1980—. Dir. Legal Assistance Found. Chgo., 1983—. Mem. revenue study com. Chgo. City Coun. Fin. Com., 1983; mem. Sole Source Rev. Panel, City of Chgo., 1984; pres. Hist. Pullman Found., Inc., 1984-85; apptd. Park Ridge Zoning Bd., 1993-94. Mem. Ill. State Bar Assn. (real estate coun. 1980-84), Chgo. Bar Assn., Women's Bar Assn. Ill. (pres. 1983-84), N.W.Suburban Bar Assn., Women's Bar Found. (v.p. 2003), Park Ridge Women Entrepreneurs, Chgo. Athletic Assn. (pres. 1992-93), Park Ridge C. of C. (pres. 2002-). Democrat. Roman Catholic. Office: 301 W Touhy Ave Park Ridge IL 60068-4204 Personal E-mail: mfhegarty@sbcglobal.net.

HEGARTY, THOMAS JOSEPH, retired history professor; b. Boston, Dec. 6, 1935; s. Thomas John and Abigail Barbara (Dunlap) H.; m. Louisa Ivanova, May, 1959; children: Alton Dunlap, Allison McAndrew. AB, Harvard U., 1957, AM, 1958, PhD, 1965; cert., Inst. Ednl. Mgmt. Harvard U., 1973. Asst. prof. history and history of ideas Brandeis U., Waltham, Mass., 1962-67; assoc. prof. history, chmn. Soviet and East European studies program Boston U., 1967-71; assoc. prof. history, dean grad. studies Boston State Coll., 1971-78; prof. history, v.p. provost SUNY-Potsdam, 1978-82; v.p. acad. affairs Butler U., Indpls., 1982-88, prof. history, 1982-89; sr. cons. Am. Assn. State Colls. and Univs., 1988-89; provost, prof. history U. Tampa, Fla., 1989—2007; prof. emeritus history, 2007—. Assoc. Russian Research Ctr., Harvard U., 1968—72; summer 2000 fellow U.S. Holocaust Meml. Mus., 2000. Mem. Tampa Bay Coun. on Fgn. Rels., 1989—; bd. dirs. Internat. Ctr., Indpls., 1983-85, Park-Tudor Sch., 1983-88; mem. 1000 Friends of Fla., 1990—. Fellow, Ford Found., 1957—61, Holocaust Ednl. Found., 1999, Inst. for Study of Conflict, Ideology and Policy U. Boston. Mem. Indpls. Coun. World Affairs (bd. dirs. 1988), Indpls. Com. on Fgn. Rels., Am. Assn. State Colls. and Univs., Resource Ctr. for Planned Change, Greater Tampa C. of C., Greater Tampa World Affairs Coun. (pres. 1992—), Japan-Am. Soc. Cen. Fla. Inc. (bd. dirs. 1990, chair edn. coun. 1993), Greater Tampa Internat. Trade Coun., Rotary, Harvard Club of West Cen. Fla., Lit. Club of Indpls., Tampa Club (mem. com. 1990—), Fla. Humanities Coun. (bd. dirs. 1986—), Phi Beta Kappa (Alpha of Harvard U. 1956), Phi Kappa Phi, Phi Alpha Theta. Office: U Tampa Box Q Tampa FL 33606-1490 Home Phone: 813-264-5091; Office Phone: 813-253-3333. Business E-Mail: thegarty@ut.edu.

HEGEDUS, L. LOUIS, chemical engineer, consultant, retired research and development company executive; arrived in U.S., 1968; s. Lajos and Anna Hegedus; m. Eva Judith Brem, Mar. 28, 1968; children: Caroline Nora, Monica Michelle. MSChemE, Tech. U., Budapest, 1964, D honoris causa, 1991; PhD, U. Calif., Berkeley, 1972. Rsch. engr. Rsch. Inst. Organic Chem. Industry, Budapest, 1964-65; group leader Daimler-Benz AG, Manheim, Germany, 1965-68; supr. catalysis rsch. Gen. Motors Rsch. Labs., Warren, Mich., 1972-80; dir. inorganic rsch. W.R. Grace Co., Columbia, Md., 1980-84, v.p. rsch. dept., 1984-94, v.p. corp. tech. divsn., 1994-96; v.p. R&D Arkema Inc., King of Prussia, Pa., 1996—2001, sr. v.p. R&D, 2001—06; cons., 2006—. Allan P. Colburn lectr. U. Del., 1976; Union Carbide lectr. SUNY, Buffalo, 1983; B.F. Dodge lectr. Yale U., 1988; J.A. Gerster lectr. U. Del., 1988, Regents lectr. UCLA, 1991, Mason lectr. Stanford U., 1991, disting. faculty lectr. U. Tex., Austin, 1992, Ashton Cary lectr. Ga. Inst. Tech., 1993, Hugh Hulburt Meml. lectr. Northwestern U., 1993, Warren K. Lewis lectr. MIT, 1994; Disting. Landegger lectr. Sch. of Fgn. Svc. Georgetown U., 1995; R.L. Pigford Meml. lectr. U. Del., 1998; mem. adv. bd. chem. thermal bioengring. divsn. NSF, 1985; mem. adv. bd. dept. chem. engring. Princeton U., 1980-92, U. Calif., Berkeley, 1988-95, U. Wis., Madison, 1987-95, Lawrence Berkeley Lab. Ctr. for Advanced Materials Surface Sci. Program, 1989-93; mem. governing bd. Coun. Chem. Rsch., 1987-90, 92-95, chmn., 1993-94; mem. bd. on chem. sci. and tech., NRC, 1991-95, chmn. com. critical techs., 1992; mem. Commn. on Phys. Scis., Math. and Applications, 1995-98; catalysis and reaction engring. award lectr. AIChE, L.A., 2000. Author: Catalyst Poisoning, 1984; editor 3 books on catalysis; mem. editl. bd. Inds. and Engring. Chem. Rsch., 1992-95, Hungarian Jour. Chemistry, 1992—, Catalysis Letters, 1993-2002, Topics in Catalysis, 1994—; contbr. articles to profl. jours. Fellow AIChE (editl. bd. jour. 1978-83, 85-88, trustee AIChE Found. 2007—, R.H. Wilhelm award 1988, Profl. Progress award 1980, Chem. Engr. of Yr. award Detroit 1978, Catalysis and Reaction Engring. Divsn. award 2000, Mgmt. Divsn. award 2006); mem. NAE (chmn. chem. engring. sect. 2000), Am. Chem. Soc. (Chemtech Leo Friend award 1981, editl. bd. Indsl. and Engring. Chemistry Rsch., 1992-95, adv. bd. Chem. and Engring. News 2004—), Md. Acad. Scis. (sci. coun. 1987-91), Hungarian Nat. Acad. Engring. (hon.). Avocation: flying. Home and Office: 1104 Beech Rd Bryn Mawr PA 19010 Personal E-mail: HegedusLL@aol.com.

HEGEL, CAROLYN MARIE, farm owner and organization executive; b. Lagro, Ind., Apr. 19, 1940; d. Ralph H. and Mary Lucile (Rudig) Lynn; m. Tom Lee Hegel, June 3, 1962. Student pub. schs., Columbia City, Ind. Bookkeeper Huntington County Farm Bur. Co-op, Inc., Ind., 1959-67, office mgr. Ind., 1967-70; twp. woman leader Wabash County (Ind.) Farm Bur., Inc., 1970-73, county woman leader, 1973-76; dist. woman leader Ind. Farm Bur., Inc., Indpls., 1976-80, 2d v.p., bd. dirs., 1980—2006, chmn. women's com., 1980—2006, exec. com., 1988—2006; agr. program coord. Ivytech State Coll., 2007—. Farmer Andrews, Ind., 1962—; dir. Farm Bur. Ins. Co., Indpls., 1980—2006, exec. com., 1988—2006, audit com., 2000—06, chmn. audit com., 2003—06; bd. dirs., spkr. in field, bd. mem. Country Way Ins., 2002—06. Women in the Field columnist Hoosier Farmer mag., 1980—2006. Mem. rural task force Gt. Lakes States Econ. Devel. Commn., 1987—88; mem. Ind. Farm Bur. Svc. Co., 1980—; active Leadership Am. Program, 1988; Sunday sch. tchr., bd. dirs. children's activities Bethel United Meth. Ch., 1965—; pres. Bethel United Meth. Women, Lagro, 1975—81; bd. dirs. Ind. Farm Bur. Found., Indpls., 1980—, Ind. Inst. Agr., Food and Nutrition, Indpls., 1982—, Ind. 4-H Found., Lafayette, 1983—86; mem. Ind. Rural Health Adv. Coun., 1993—96, Hoosier Homestead Award Cert. Com., Indpls., 1980—; organizer farm divsn. Wabash County Am. Cancer Soc. Fund Dr., 1974; bd. dirs. N.E. Ind. Kidney Found., 1984—, Nat. Kidney Found. of Ind., 1985—89. Named Big Sister of Yr., Wabash County, Ind., 2003; named one of Outstanding Farm Woman of Yr., Country Woman Mag., 1987; recipient State 4-H Home Econs. award, Ind. 4-H, 1960. Mem.: Am. Farm Bur. Fedn. (midwest rep. to women's com. 1986—93), Producers Mktg. Assn. (bd. dirs. 1980—94), Ind. Agrl. Mktg. Assn. (bd. dirs. 1980—94), Women in Comm., Inc. Republican. Home: 3330 N 650 E Andrews IN 46702-9616 Office: Ind Farm Bur Inc PO Box 1290 225 S East St Indianapolis IN 46202-4058 E-mail: chegel@omnicityusa.com.

HEGENDERFER, JONITA SUSAN, public relations executive; b. Chgo., Mar. 18, 1944; d. Clifford Lincoln and Cornelia Anna (Larson) Hazzard; m. Gary William Hegenderfer, Mar. 12, 1971 (dec. 1978). BA, Purdue U., 1965; postgrad., Calif. State U., Long Beach, 1966-67, Northwestern U., 1969-70. Tchr. English, Long Beach (Calif.) Schs., 1965-68; editl. asst. Playboy Mag., Chgo., 1968-70; comms. specialist AMA, Chgo., 1970-72; v.p. Home Data, Hinsdale, Ill., 1972-75; mktg. mgr. Olympic Savs. & Loan, Berwyn, Ill., 1975-79; sr. v.p. Golin/Harris Comms., Chgo., 1979-89; pres. JSH & A, Chgo., 1989—. Bd. dirs. Chgo. Internat. Film Festival, 1989, 90, 2005, 06. Author: Slim Guide to Spas, 1984, (video) PR Guide for Chicago LSCs, 1991; editor: Financial Information National Directory, 1972; contbr. articles to profl. jours. Co-chmn. pub. rels. com. Am. Cancer Soc., Chgo., 1984; mem. com. March of Dimes, Chgo., 1986; mem. pub. rels. com. Girl Scouts Chgo., 1989-90, bd. dirs., 1994-95; bd. dirs. Greater DuPage Women's Bus. Coun., 1992-93, Girl Scouts U.S. DuPage County, 1994—; vol. ctr. adv. com. United Way, Chgo., 1990-93; mem. cmty. svc. com. Publicity Club Chgo., 1990—. Recipient 5 Golden Trumpet awards Publicity Club Chgo., 1983, 96, 94, Silver Trumpet awards, 1984, 86, 88, Spectra awards Internat. Assn. Bus. Communicators, 1984, 85, 87, Gold Quill aard, 1985, Bronze Anvil award Pub. Rels. Soc. Am., 1985, award Nat. Creativity in Pub. Rels. award, 1995; named Influential Woman in Bus., 1998. Mem. Am. Mktg. Assn., Publicity Club Chgo., Pub. Rels. Soc. Am., Chgo. Women in Pub., Nat. Assn. Women Bus. Owners, DuPage Area Assn. Bus. Tech. (bd. dirs. 1997), Coun. on Fgn. Rels., Met. Women's Forum, Cinema Chgo. (bd. dirs. 1988-89, 2005-). Avocations: travel, photography. Office: JSH & A Ltd 2 Transam Plaza Dr Ste 450 Oakbrook Terrace IL 60181-4290 Home Phone: 630-852-3600; Office Phone: 630-932-4242. Business E-Mail: jonni@jsha.com.

HEGER, HERBERT KRUEGER, education educator; b. Cin., June 15, 1937; s. J. Herbert and Leona (Krueger) H.; m. Thyra Cleek. AS, Ohio Mechanics Inst., 1956; BS, Miami U., 1962, MEd, 1965; PhD, Ohio State U., 1969. Tchr. Marshall Jr. High Sch., Pomona, Calif., 1962—63; tchr. math. Mt. Healthy High Sch., Ohio, 1963—66; grad. asst., grad. assoc. Miami U.-Ohio State U., 1966—69; asst. prof. U. Ky., 1969—75; assoc. dir. Louisville Urban Edn. Ctr., 1971—75; vis. prof. Sch. Profl. Studies, Pepperdine U., 1975—78; dir. student teaching U. Tex., San Antonio, 1975—77, coord. curriculum and instrn., 1977—78; assoc. prof. edn. Whitworth Coll., Spokane, Wash., 1978—82, chmn. dept., 1978—79, dean Grad. Sch., 1979—82; prof. edn. U. Tex., El Paso, 1982—99, prof. emeritus, 1999—. Cons. in field Contbr. articles to profl. jours. Mem. Am. Ednl. Rsch. Assn., Nat. Soc. Study Edn., Phi Delta Kappa. Republican. Mem. Church Of Christ. Home: 2495 Tiffany Dr Las Cruces NM 88011-2008

HEGGEN, ARTHUR WILLIAM, insurance company executive; b. Eureka, Calif., Aug. 9, 1945; s. Arlo Murray and Edna Marie (Nelson) H.; m. Betty Louise Roddy, Nov. 21, 1970; children: Cherilyn, Christopher. BS in Indsl. Adminstrn., Acctg., Iowa State U., 1967. CPA, Iowa, Fla.; CPCU, FLMI, AIAF. Audit staff mgr. Ernst & Whinney, Des Moines, 1971-84; sr. v.p., treas. Am. Bankers Ins. Group, Inc., Miami, Fla., 1984-96; exec. v.p. Am. Bankers Ins. Co., Miami, 1996-99, Assurant Solutions (formerly Assurant Group), Miami, 1999—. Bd. dirs. YMCA of Greater Miami; pres. Iowa Ptnrs. of the Yucatan, Des Moines, 1984; pres., treas. Des Moines Hearing Speech Ctr., 1976-82. Capt. USMC, 1967-70, Vietnam. Fellow Life Mgmt. Inst.; mem. AICPA, Soc. CPCU, Fla. Inst. CPAs, Ins. Acct. & Sys. Assn. Office: Assurant Solutions 11222 Quail Roost Dr Miami FL 33157-6543 also: Assurant Solutions 260 Interstate North Cir NW Atlanta GA 30339-2210 Office Phone: 305-253-2244, 305-252-6916.

HEGI, FREDERICK B., JR., wholesale distribution executive; b. 1943; Grad., So. Meth. U., 1966; MBA, Harvard U., 1968; PhD, U. Tex., 1970. With First Chgo. Co., 1970-73; v.p. Cooper Industries, Dallas, 1973-82; pres. Valley View Capital, Dallas, 1982-87; founding ptnr. to prin. Wingate Ptnrs., Dallas, 1987—; chmn., pres., CEO Kevco Inc., 1999—2002; dir. United Stationers Inc., 1995—, chmn., interim pres. & CEO, 1996—97, chmn., 1997—. Bd. dir. Lone Star Tech Inc., Drew Industries Inc., Tex. Capital Bancshares Inc. Office: Wingate Partners 750 N Siant Paul St Ste 1200 Dallas TX 75201 also: United Stationers Inc 2200 E Golf Rd Des Plaines IL 60016*

HEGLEH, JOSEPH A., ophthalmologist; Student, U. South Fla., 2001. Diplomate Am. Bd. Ophthalmology. Cornea and refractive surgery fellow U. South Fla., Tampa, 2001; med. dir. Fla. Eye and Laser Inst., Pt. Charlotte, 2003—. Recipient LFO award, Am. Acad. Ophthalmology. Fellow: AMA (Achievement award), ACS. Office: Fla Eye and Laser Inst 3195 Tamiami Trail Port Charlotte FL 33952

HEGSTROM, WILLIAM JEAN, retired mathematics professor; b. Macomb, Ill., Oct. 21, 1923; s. Carl William and Thelma (Canavit) Hegstrom; m. Grace Ann Paladino, May 3, 1944 (dec. Nov. 29, 2005); children: Elizabeth Louise, William Jean II, Jean Kilbourne. Studied, Western Ill. U., 1941—42; BSc, Rutgers U., 1949, EdM, 1952; postgrad., U. Fla., 1961; MA in Tchg., Purdue U., 1964; postgrad., Fla. Atlantic U., 1965—68; EdD, U. Miami, 1971. Tchr. S. Plainfield Jr. H.S., NJ, 1949—52, Bernardsville H.S., NJ, 1952—54, Oak St. Sch., Bernardsville, NJ, 1954—55, Summit H.S., NJ, 1955—58, Delray Beach Jr. H.S., Fla., 1958—65; chmn., math. dept. John I. Leonard H.S., Lake Worth, Fla., 1965—68; dir. Palm Beach County Rsch. Project, 1966—68; adj. prof. Fla. Atlantic U., 1965—69, assoc. prof., 1969—70; counselor coord. John Leonard Adult Ctr., Lake Worth, Fla., 1965—68; supr. rsch. and evaluation Palm Beach County Sch. Bd., West Palm Beach, Fla., 1970—74; adj. prof. Palm Beach Jr. Coll., 1981—88, Palm Beach Atlantic Coll., 1984—86, asst. prof., 1986—87; cons. math. prof. Palm Beach County Sch. Bd., 1985—87; ret., 1987. Contbr. articles to profl. jours. With USAAF, 1942—46. Mem.: NEA, Am. Assn. Individual Investors. Home: 225 NE 22nd St Delray Beach FL 33444-4221

HEHIR, J. BRYAN, priest, educator, social services administrator; BA, MA, St. John's Sem., Boston; ThD in Applied Theology, Harvard Div. Sch. Ordained priest Archdiocese of Boston, 1966; served St. Elizabeth of Hungary Parish, Acton, Mass.; pastor St. Paul Parish, Cambridge, Mass.; positions with US Cath. Conf. Bishops, Washington, 1973—92, sec. dept. social devel. & world peace, dir. office internat. affairs, counselor social policy; mem. faculty Georgetown U., 1984—92; Joseph P. Kennedy Prof. Christian Ethics Kennedy Ctr. Ethics; rsch. prof. ethics & internat. politics Sch. Fgn. Svc.; mem. faculty Harvard Div. Sch., 1992—2001, chair exec. com., 1998—2001; counselor Cath. Relief Services, 1996—2001; pres. & CEO Cath. Charities USA, 2001—03; Parker Gilbert Montgomery Prof. of the Practice of Religion and Pub. Life Hauser Ctr. Nonprofit Organizations, John F. Kennedy Sch. Govt., Harvard U., 2004—; sec. social services Archdiocese of Boston, 2004—; pres. Cath. Charities Archdiocese of Boston, 2004—. Bd. dirs. Ind. Sector. Recipient 2004 Vision Award, Cath. Charities USA; MacArthur Fellow, 1984. Mem.: Arms Control Assn. (bd. dirs.), Coun. Fgn. Rels., Am. Philos. Soc., Am. Acad. Arts & Sciences. Roman Catholic. Office: Archdiocese of Boston 49 Franklin St Boston MA 02110-1304 Office Phone: 617-451-7955. Office Fax: 617-451-0337.

HEIBERG, ROBERT ALAN, lawyer; b. St. Cloud, Minn., June 29, 1943; s. Rasmus Adolph and Irene (Shaffer) H.; m. Sharon Ann Olson, Aug. 2, 1969; children— Eric Robert, Mark Alan, Maren Ann BA summa cum laude, U. Minn., 1965, JD summa cum laude, 1968. Bar: Minn. 1968. Law clk. to assoc. justice Minn. Supreme Ct., 1968-69; assoc. Dorsey & Whitney, Mpls., 1969-73, ptnr., 1974—2003, of counsel, 2004—; instr. Law Sch., U. Minn., 1968-72, instr. legal assts. program, 1972-77. Articles editor Minn. Law Rev., 1967-68 Mem. adv. com. U. Minn. Legal Assts. Program, 1977-84, bd. visitors Law Sch., 1991-96. Mem. ABA (sect. real property, probate and trust law), Minn. Bar Assn. (chmn. com. on legal assts. 1979), Hennepin County Bar Assn., Am. Rose Soc. (accredited judge 1996), Order of Coif, Phi Beta Kappa Republican. Lutheran. Home: 4510 Wooddale Ave Minneapolis MN 55424-1137 Office: Dorsey & Whitney 50 S 6th St Ste 1500 Minneapolis MN 55402-1498 Home Phone: 952-926-4762; Office Phone: 612-340-2751. Business E-Mail: heiberg.robert@dorsey.com.

HEICHEL, GARY HAROLD, agronomist, educator; b. Park Falls, Wis., Nov. 9, 1940; s. Harold H. and Bernice I. (Comp) Heichel; m. Iris Fehl Martin, Apr. 24, 1988. BS, Iowa State U., 1962; MS, Cornell U., 1964, PhD, 1968; D in Natural Scis. (hon.), Swiss Fed. Inst. Tech., Zurich, 1998. Asst. plant physiologist Conn. Agrl. Expt. Stats., New Haven, 1968-73, assoc. plant physiologist, 1973-76, plant physiologist, 1976, USDA Agrl. Rsch. Svc., St. Paul, 1976-90, acting rsch. leader, 1988-90; head agronomy dept. U. Ill., Urbana, 1990-95, interim head plant pathology dept., 1994-95, head crop scis. dept., 1995—2004, prof. emeritus, 2004—. Adj. prof. agronomy U. Minn., 1976—90; program mgr. USDA Competitive Rsch. Grants Office, 1981; bd. dirs. Coun. Agrl. Sci. and Tech., 2005—; pres. Whiting's Neck Farm Estates, Inc., 2005—. Contbr. chapters to books, articles to profl. jours. Pres., mem. adminstrv. bd. Cheshire (Conn.) United Meth. Ch., 1973—76, v.p. Cheshire Land Trust, 1975—76. Named Civil Servant of the Yr., Twin Cities Fed. Exec. Bd., St. Paul, 1984; Paul Harris fellow, Rotary Internat., 2002. Fellow: AAAS (chair sect. 0 1997—98); mem.: Coun. Agrl. Sci. & Tech., Am. Soc. Plant Physiologists (trustee 1988—90), Am. Soc. Agronomy (pres. North Ctrl. sect. 1991—93, pres. 1997—98, Svc. award 2001), Crop Sci. Soc. Am. (pres. 1991—92, Monsanto Crop Sci. Disting. Career award 2006), Urbana Rotary (bd. dirs. 1997—99). Avocations: classical music, reading, hiking, gardening. Office: U Ill Dept Crop Scis 1102 S Goodwin Ave AW-101 Urbana IL 61801-4730 Business E-Mail: gheichel@uiuc.edu.

HEICK, LEON JOSEPH, data processing executive; b. New England, ND, May 14, 1944; s. Joseph Philiph and Frances (Bosepflug) H.; m. Alicia Marie Finneman, July 13, 1968; children: Brent, Royce, Travis. BS in Bus. Adminstrn., U. Mary, Bismarck, ND, 1991, BS in Acctg., 1998. Computer operator North Ctrl. Data Corp., Mandan, ND, 1968-69, computer programmer, 1970-71, programming mgr., 1972-78, sys. mgr., 1979-83, asst. gen. mgr., 1984—, mgr. multi million dollar offshore software devel. projects, 1991—. Dir. Project Back Home Coop, Mandan, 1994—, Rural Electric and Telephone Credit Union, Bismarck, N.D., 1993—. Singer No. Lights Barbershop Chorus, Bismarck, 1991-93; active ch. choir. With U.S. Army, 1965-67, Vietnam. Mem. Am. Legion, KC, Elks, Amvets. Avocations: singing, guitar playing, golf, hunting, fishing. Office: North Ctrl Data Corp PO Box 728 Mandan ND 58554-0728

HEIDE, JOHN WESLEY, engineering executive; b. Chgo., Sept. 14, 1946; s. Frederick Bernard Heiner-Heide and Eleanor Francis (Tuttle) Heide; m. Patricia Ann Lynn, Aug. 5, 1967 (div. Jan. 1973); m. Carol G. Gutierrez, Sept. 27, 1999; children: John Wesley, Joseph Edward, Adela B., Monica, Nicholas B., Johanna M. AA, Phoenix Jr. Coll., 1972; BS, Ariz. State U., 1975. Quality assurance engr. Tex. Instruments, Dallas, 1969-70, ITT Courier, Tempe, Ariz., 1975-79; sr. project engr. GTE Comms., El Paso, 1979-83, Telxon Corp., Houston, 1983-87; engring. mgr. United Techs., Niles, Mich., 1987-91, Automotive Industries, Midland, Tex., 1991-94; divsn. quality assurance mgr. Pec Golden Triangle Plastics, El Paso, 1994-95; indsl. engring. mgr. Elcom, Inc., El Paso, 1995-97; quality assurance mgr. United for Excellence Inc., El Paso, 1997-99; TQM mgr. Dayco Inc., El Paso, 1999—. Instr. engring. Houston C.C., 1984—85; instr. plastic technology El Paso Cmty. Coll., 2003—04; superior woodwork auditor, 2004—07. Author: Reflections, 1990, Scan-It, 1991, A Step Beyond the Fog, 1992, How Cheap Is Cheap, 1993, None but the Brave Walk Alone, 1994, Beyond the Scope, 2001, Tootsie Roll Man, 2002, Saga, 2003, Behind the Scene: U.S. Economics, 2004; contbr. articles to mags. Candidate for mayor, El Paso, 1980, 82, 84; candidate for State Rep., Berrien Springs, Mich., 1990; pres. Toys for Tots, USMC, Mich., 1990. With USMC, 1965-69, Vietnam. Mem. NSPE, Soc. Plastics Engrs. (pres.), Inst. Indsl. Engring. (v.p. 1982-83), Soc. Mfg. Engrs. (v.p.), Am. Soc. Quality Control (v.p.). Republican. Lutheran. Avocations: travel, genealogy, stamp collecting/philately, coin collecting/numismatics, art. Home: 9920 Minuteman El Paso TX 79924-1647

HEIDEL, THERESA ELIZABETH, artist, educator; b. Teaneck, NJ, Aug. 16, 1950; d. Louis Edward Troise and Lorene Elizabeth Rising; m. Robert Werner Heidel, May 2, 1975. BA, St. Peter's Coll., Jersey City, 1972. Graphic artist Prentice Hall Pub. Co., Englewood Cliffs, NJ, 1973—78; art dir. Stoeger Pub. Co., South Hackensack, NJ, 1978—79; freelance artist, 1980—; artist-in-residence Cunard's Queen Mary 2 Voyage to Norway, 2007. Instr. watercolors Ridgewood Art Inst., NJ, 1995—98. Children's books, Happy Hollow Stories, Books I, II and III, 1986—87, watercolors, reproduced in To the Shore Once More, vols. I and II, 1999—2001, painting for cover of ad book, Monmouth County Cancer Soc., Rumson, NJ, 1995, series of commemorative paintings, Casino Complex, Convention Hall, Mayfair Theatre, 2004, exhibited in group shows at NJ Watercolor Soc., Lincroft, NJ, 2005, collections, Jack Till, Blue Chip Ranch, New Mex., Lawrence Waterhouse, TD Waterhouse Brokerage, NYC. Named one of 20 Emerging Watercolorists Across Nation, Watercolor Mag., 2006; recipient Mary La Greca award, Hudson Valley Art Assn., Hastings-on-Hudson, NY, 2004, award, Catharine Lorillard Wolfe Club, 2005. Roman Catholic. Avocations: piano, travel, hiking. Home and Studio: 333 Main St Ridgefield Park NJ 07660

HEIDELBERG, PAUL, writer; b. Austin, Tex., Dec. 23, 1948; s. James Martin and Alice Huebinger Heidelberg. BFA, San Francisco Art Inst., 1975. Author: (novels) Oceans Apart, 1988, Cook's Return, 1991, (literary publ.) Paris, Prague and Salzburg: A Remembrance, 1999, Chasing Freedom, 2005, poems; contbr. to jours. and mags. With USAF, 1966—70. Mem.: J.F. Kennedy Libr., Hemingway Collection, Poetry Soc. Am. Avocations: hiking, bicycling. Office: c/o Jeanette Heidelberg 245 Seford Dr San Antonio TX 78209 Home: 1956 Sattler Rd New Braunfels TX 78132-2166 E-mail: info@paulheidelberg.com.

HEIDEMAN, RICHARD D., lawyer; b. Detroit, Apr. 4, 1947; s. Theodore Samuel and Marion (Yura) H.; m. Phyllis Greenberg, June 23, 1968; children: Stefanie Jo, Elana Yael, Ariana Michal. BA, U. Mich., 1969; student, Am. U./Hebrew U., Jerusalem, 1970-72; JD, George Washington U., 1972; grad., Nat. Coll. of Criminal Def. Lawyers and Pub. Defenders, 1974. Bar: Md. 1972, Ky. 1972, U.S. Dist. Ct. (we. dist.) Ky. 1972, U.S. Ct. Appeals (6th cir.) 1974, Wyo. 1979, Ind. 1979, U.S. Dist. Ct. Wyo. 1981, U.S. Dist. Ct. (ea. dist.) Ky. 1982, U.S. Dist. Ct. (so. dist.) Ind. 1982, U.S. Ct. Mil. Appeals 1982, U.S. Supreme Ct. 1983, U.S. Ct. Appeals (D.C. cir.) 1984, U.S. Dist. Ct. Md. 1989, U.S. Dist. Ct. D.C. 1989, U.S. Ct. Internat. Trade 1990, U.S. Ct. Claims 1992, U.S. Ct. Appeals (4th cir.) 1993. Sr. counsel Heideman Nudelman & Kalik, PC, Washington, 1973—. Markham's negligence counsel, 1989; vice-chmn. legislative com. Nat. Assn. Criminal Def. Lawyers. Internat. pres. B'nai B'rith Youth Orgn., 1964-65; past chmn. bd. dirs. Am. Indoor Soccer Assn.; past mayor Spring Valley, Ky.; past gen. co-chmn. State of Israel Bonds, Louisville; past mem. Ky. Crime Commn. Juvenile Delinquency Task Force; Non-Govtl. Orgn. del. U.S. Conf. on Women, Nairobi, Kenya, 1985; del.-prime minister Israel Solidarity Conf., 1989; past bd. dirs. Health Care for Am., Inc., No. Va. Family Svcs., Inc; delegate, NGO, UN World Conf. Against Racism, Durban, S.Africa, 2001. Recipient Label A. Katz Young Leadership award, 1983, Heritage award State of Israel Bonds, 1988, Sam Beber Distinq. Alumnus award, 2001, Joseph Papp Racial Harmony award, 2005; designated People to Watch, Louisville Mag., 1986. Mem. ABA, D.C. Bar Assn. (mem. criminal law steering com.), 1997-2000, Ind. Bar Assn., Ky. Bar Assn., Md. Bar Assn., Wyo. Bar Assn. (past v.p. Teton county chpt.), Am. Trial Lawyers Assn., Am. Inst. of Parliamentarians, Main St. Assn. (past v.p.), U. Mich. Club (past pres.), Nat. Coll. of Criminal Def. Lawyers (past resident faculty), Am. Soc. of Criminology (past chmn. criminal def. com.), B'nai Brith Internat. (pres. 1998-2002, hon. pres. 2002-), Anti-Defamation League, (exec. com. 1998-2002), internat. chmn. Ctr. for Pub. Policy, 1996-98, del. 50th World Jewish Congress 1986, Iternat. Family award, 1981, Internat. Assn. Jewish Lawyers and Jurists (past bd. dirs.), Am.-Israel C. of C. Inc. (past pres.). Home: 7229 Armat Dr Bethesda MD 20817-2107 Office: Heiedeman Nudelman & Kalik PC 1146 19th St NW 5th Fl Washington DC 20036-2907 also: B'nai B'rith Perlman Intl 2020 K St NW #7700 Washington DC 20006-1806 Office Phone: 202-463-1818. Office Fax: 202-463-2999. Business E-Mail: rdheideman@hnklaw.com.

HEIDEMANN, LYLE G., retail executive; B, No. Ill. U., 1967. Asst. mgr. Sears Roebuck and Co., 1967—71, mdse. mgr., 1971—74, staff asst., 1974—76, mdse. mgr. III, 1976—79, gen. mdse. mgr. II, 1979—80, gen. mdse. mgr. IV, 1980—83, ter. gen. mdse. mgr., 1983—85; nat. mgr. mdse. sys., 1985—89; spl. assignment logistics mgmt. Sears Roebuck and Co., 1989—90, nat. logistics mgr., 1990—91, nat. mdse. mgr., 1991—92, divsn. v.p., gen. mgr. lawn and sporting goods, 1992—96, v.p., gen. mgr. home appliances, 1996—97, v.p. appliances and electronics, 1997—98, sr. v.p., appliances and electronics, 1998—99, exec. v.p., gen. mgr. hardlines, 1999—2003, exec. v.p., gen. mgr. home and off-mall stores, 2003; pres., CEO True Value Co., Chgo., 2005—. Office: True Value Co 8600 W Bryn Mawr AVe Chicago IL 60631

HEIDEMARK, GEORGE JOHN, elementary school educator; b. Neptune, NJ, Oct. 28, 1960; s. George James and Marion Heidemark; m. Susan Small, Oct. 6, 1996. BA in Hist., Glassboro State U., NJ, 1988; MA in Hist., Temple U., Phila., 2000. Tchr. Williamstown Mid. Sch., NJ, 1990—. Named Tchr. of Yr., 2000. Mem.: Nat. Coun. History Edn., Nat. Coun. Social Studies, Civil War Preservation Trust. Cath. Avocations: reading, travel. Home: 2001 Beacon Hill Dr Sicklerville NJ 08081 Office: Williamstown Mid Sch 561 Clayton Ave Williamstown NJ 08094

HEIDEN, CARA, mortgage company executive; Joined Norwest Bank Iowa, 1981, CFO, 1988—92, Norwest Mortgage, 1992—94, head, servicing and post closing, 1994—97, head, mktg. and retail direct client services, 1997—98, head, nat. consumer lending, 1998—2004; pres. nat. consumer & instl. lending Wells Fargo Home Mortgage (division of Wells Fargo Bank, N.A.), Des Moines, 2004—. Pres. Norwest Housing Found., 1996—99. Named an 25 Most Powerful Women in Banking, US Banker mag., 2006; named one of 25 Women to Watch, 2005. Office: Wells Fargo Home Mortgage 405 SW 5th St Des Moines IA 50309*

HEIDEN, CHARLES KENNETH, metal products executive, consultant, retired military officer; b. Detroit, July 7, 1925; s. Carl William and Elsie Mae (Langley) H.; m. Nancy Earle Gray, June 7, 1949; 1 son, Charles Gray. BS, U.S. Mil. Acad., 1949; MS in Mech. Engring, U. Mich., 1957; grad. mgmt. execs. program, U. Pitts., 1971. Registered profl. engr., Ky. Enlisted U.S. Army, 1943, commd. 2d lt., 1949, advanced through grades to maj. gen., 1977; services in Panama, France, Korea and Vietnam; dep. dir. ops. Nat. Mil. Command Center, Joint Chiefs of Staff, 1973-74; dir. enlisted personnel U.S. Mil. Personnel Center, Washington, 1974-76; comdr. U.S. Army Mil. Personnel Center, 1977-80; comdg. gen. U.S. Army Tng. Ctr., Ft. Dix, N.J., 1980-81; pres., dir. Montel Metals Inc., 1981-83, Cedar Lake Lodge Inc., La Grange, Ky., 1982—98, chmn. bd. dirs., 1986—98, dir. emeritus, 1998—; cons. Computer Simulation, 1987-98. Bd. dirs. Park Glen Heights Assn., Annandale, Va., 1974-76; bd. dirs. Seven Counties Svcs., 2000-07, treas., 2004-05; pres. Our Saviour Luth. Ch., Arlington, Va., 1974-76; mem. code enforcement bd. City Jeffersontown, Ky., 1998-2000. Decorated D.S.M., D.F.C., Legion of Merit with 3 oak leaf clusters, Air medal with 10 oak leaf clusters, Joint Services Commendation medal, Army Commendation medal with 2 oak leaf clusters, Meritorious Service medal with oak leaf cluster; Cross of Gallantry with silver star Vietnam; recipient Pace award Office Sec. Army, 1963. Mem. Armed Forçes Relief and Benefit Assn. (dir. 1977-81), West Point Alumni Assn., Forest Garden Assn. (chmn. and pres. 2001—04), Am. Legion, U.S. Army War Coll. Alumni Assn. Home: 10500 Forest Garden Ln Louisville KY 40223-6166 Personal E-mail: heidenck@bellsouth.net.

HEIDER, ANNE HARRINGTON, music educator; BA, Wellesley Coll., 1963; MA, NYU, 1965; DMA, Stanford U., 1981. Dir. choral ensembles Roosevelt U., Chgo., 1988; assoc. prof. Roosevelt U. Coll. Performing Arts, Chgo.; founding singer, co-dir. His Majestie's Clerkes (name changed to Bella Voce), Chgo., 1983—89, artistic dir., 1989—. Bd. dirs. Chorus Am. Recipient Tempo All-Prof. Team, Humanities award, 1993. Office: Bella Voce Ste 301 839 N Hermitage Ave Chicago IL 60622 also: Roosevelt U Coll Performing Arts 430 S Michigan Ave Chicago IL 60605 Office Phone: 312-479-1096. E-mail: email@bellavoce.org, aheider@roosevelt.edu.

HEIDER, JON VINTON, retired lawyer; b. Moline, Ill., Mar. 1, 1934; s. Raymond and Doris (Hinch) H.; m. Barbara L. Bond, Dec. 27, 1960 (div.); children: Loren P., John C., Lindsay L.; m. Mary R. Murray, Jan. 27, 1984. AB, U. Wis., 1956; JD, Harvard U., 1961; grad., Advanced Mgmt. Program, 1974; LHD (hon.), U. Akron, 2005. Bar: Pa. 1962, U.S. Dist. Ct. (ea. dist.) Pa. 1962, U.S. Ct. Appeals (3d cir.) 1962, U.S. Supreme Ct. 1991. Assoc. Morgan Lewis & Bockius, Phila., 1961-66; counsel Catalytic, Inc., Phila., 1966-68, Houdry Process & Chem. Co., Phila., 1968-70; counsel chems. group Air Products & Chems., Inc., Valley Forge, Pa., 1970-75, asst. gen. counsel, 1975-76, assoc. gen. counsel, 1976-78, gen. counsel Allentown, Pa., 1978-80; v.p. corp. affairs, sr. adminstrv. officer-Europe, Air Products Europe, Inc., London, 1980-83; v.p. corp. devel. Air Products & Chems., Inc., 1983-84; v.p., gen. counsel BF Goodrich Co., Akron, Ohio, 1984-88, sr. v.p., gen. counsel, 1988-94, exec. v.p., gen. counsel, 1994-98; ret., 1998. Trustee U. Akron, 2001-04; distbn. com. Charles E. and Mabel M. Ritchie Meml. Found.; bd. overseers Blossom Music Ctr. Lt. USNR, 1956-58. Mem. Portage Country Club, Rolling Rock Club, Key Biscayne Yacht Club. E-mail: JHeider-Fl@msn.com.

HEIDLAGE, PATSY JO, physical education educator; b. Chickasha, Okla., Oct. 21, 1937; d. Harry James and Esther Victoria Gibson; m. Robert Frederick Heidlage Sr., Aug. 9, 1959; children: Robert Frederick Heidlage Jr., Vickie Ann Heidlage-Williams, Charles James. BS, Okla. Coll. for Women, Chickasha, 1955; MEd, Northeastern State U., Tahlequah, Okla., 1991. Cert. tchr. phys. edn., sci., counseling Okla., 1959. Phys. edn. tchr. Claremore H.S., Okla., 1973—75; tennis instr. and coach Rogers State U., Claremore, 1975—77; phys. edn. tchr. Westside Elem. Sch., Claremore, 1977—. Cmty. tennis camp dir. Claremore Parks Dept., 1968—; elem. counselor Westside Sch., Claremore, 2004—; bd. dirs. Title 1 Com. / Westside Elem., Claremore, 2005—; bd. mem. and sec. Claremore Pk. Bd., 1975—81. Jump rope for heart coord. Am. Heart Assn., Claremore, 1985—2006; choir mem. Claremore Cmty. Chorus, 1995—2006; sec. Rogers County Bd. Adjustment, Claremore, 1975—80; bd. dirs. U. Sci. and Arts, 1966—, Claremore United Way, 1997—. Recipient Claremore Pub. Schs. Tchr. of the Yr., Claremore Classroom Tchrs. Assn., 1987. Mem.: AAHPERD, Okla. Tennis Coaches Assn. (pres., dir. 1998—2003, Tennis Coach of the Yr. 1998), Delta Kappa Gamma (sec. 1995—97, Scholarships 1989, 1990 and 1991), Okla. Edn. Assn., Okla. Assn. Health Phys. Edn. and Recreation, NEA. D-Conservative. Catholic. Avocations: tennis, restoration, gardening. Home: P O Box 781 Claremore OK 74018 Office: Westside Elementary School 2600 Holly Rd Claremore OK 74017 Home Phone: 918-341-4651; Office Phone: 918-341-3511. Office Fax: 918-343-6338; Home Fax: 918-343-6338. Personal E-mail: pheidlage@claremore.k12.ok.us.

HEIDRICH, ROBERT WESLEY, lawyer; b. Chgo., Aug. 1, 1927; children: John G., Robert G., Kimberly L Student, U. Wis., 1944-45, 47-48; JD, DePaul U., 1951. Bar: Calif. 1974. Atty. Brunswick Corp., Chgo., 1953-60, 65-69; v.p. Brunswick AG (Switzerland), 1960-61; dir. Brunswick Internat. Fin. AG (Switzerland), 1962-65; sec., corp. counsel Nat. Can Corp., Chgo., 1969-73; v.p., sec., gen. counsel, dir. Rohr Industries, Inc., Chula Vista, Calif., 1973-79; corp. v.p., gen. counsel Holiday Inn Hotels, Memphis, 1979-85; counsel Kaiser Steel Corp., LaVerne, Calif., 1985-87, San Diego Real Estate Devel., 1987—. Bd. dir., Am. Internat. Sch. Zurich, 1964-65. Served with U.S. Army, 1945-47 Mem. Frederick Law Olmstead Soc. (founding pres. 1967-69). Home: 5157 Long Branch Ave Apt 4 San Diego CA 92107-2032 Office: San Diego Devel PO Box 70075 San Diego CA 92167 Personal E-mail: derobdude@cox.com.

HEIDT, JEFFREY L., lawyer; b. 1945; AB in Philosophy with high honors, Brown U., 1967; JD, Harvard U., 1970. Bar: Mass. 1970. Mem. Choate, Hall & Stewart, Boston; ptnr. Ropes & Gray LLP, Boston. Author Contbd. Articles to profl. journals. Frequent lectr. at (HFMA, MCLE, hospital assn, health ins., medical soc. & bar assn sponsored events), Co-chair of Integrated Delivery Sys. Com. Mass. Chpt. HFMA, Mem. AHA Medicare Adv. Com. With Signal Corps USAR, 1970—72. Recipient William G. Folmer Merit (Outstanding Svc. Chapter Activities of HFMA), 1986, The Best Lawyers in Am., Reeves Silver Merit Award (Outstanding Svc. HealthCare Fin. Mgmt. Assn), 2000, Am. Leading Lawyers, Chambers USA, 2004—06. Mem.: Mass. Bar Assn., Boston Bar Assn., Am. Health Lawyers Assn., ABA. Office: Ropes & Gray LLP 1 International Place Boston MA 02110 Office Phone: 617-951-7000, 617-951-7390. Office Fax: 617-951-7050, 617-235-7403. Business E-Mail: jeffrey.heidt@ropesgray.com.

HEIDT-DUNWELL, DEBRA SUE, vocational school educator; b. Liberty, NY, Oct. 28, 1952; d. Charles William and Lillian Lorraine (Ball) H. AA, Sullivan County Community Coll., Lock Sheldrake, NY, 1972; BS, SUNY, Oneonta, 1974, MS in Edn., 1979. Cert. permanent math. tchr., provisional elem. tchr., N.Y. High sch. tchr. math. Downsville (N.Y.) Cen. Sch., 1980-83, Oneonta Cen. Sch., 1984-85; tutor Sullivan County Community Coll., 1985; cons. tchr. related skills for vocat. programs Sullivan County Career and Tech. Edn. Ctr., Liberty, 1985—, fin. aid adminstr. LPN program, 1995—. Conf. presenter in field; rschr. Hudson Valley Faculty Portfolio Assessment. Contbr. poetry to various publs. Recipient Golden Poet award World of Poetry Press, 1986-91. Mem. ASCD, AAUW, AMTNYS, AMS, SSMA, Sullivan Reading Coun., Nat. Coun. Tchrs. Math., Am. Career and Tech. Educators, Nat. Coun. Tchrs. English, Internat. Reading Assn., Am. Poetry Assn. (Poet of Merit award 1989), Kappa Delta Pi., Delta Kappa Gamma (Tau chpt). Home Phone: 845-482-3237; Office Phone: 845-295-4136. E-mail: rdunwell@hvc.rr.com.

HEIFERMAN, SCOTT, Internet company executive; b. Homewood, Ill., 1972; Grad., U. Iowa. Interactive mktg. frontiersman Sony Corp., 1994; founder i-traffic; co-founder Fotolog, 2002; co-founder & CEO Meetup, 2002—. Named Innovator of Yr., MIT Tech. Rev., 2004; named one of 40 Under 40, Crain's NY Bus., 2007. Office: Meetup Inc 10th Fl 632 Broadway New York NY 10012*

HEIGHT, DOROTHY I., former foundation administrator; b. Richmond, Va., Mar. 24, 1912; d. James Edward and Fannie (Burroughs) Height. BA, MA, NYU. Mem. nat. staff YWCA of the U.S.A., 33 yrs.; caseworker NYC Welfare Dept., 1934; dir. Ctr. Racial Justice YWCA, 1946; nat. pres. Nat. Coun. Negro Women Inc., 1957—97, pres. emeritus, 1998—. With Dept. Def. Adv. Com. Women, 1952—55; mem. N.Y. State Social Welfare Bd., 1958—68; bd. govs. ARC, 1964—70; pres.'s com. Employment Handicapped; mem. ad hoc com. Pub. Welfare Dept. Health Edn. and Welfare; dir. Ctr. Racial Justice YMCA. Pres. Nat. Coun. Negro Women, 1957—; hon. mem. nat. bd. dirs. YWCA of the U.S.A. Recipient Disting. Svc. award, Nat. Conf. Social Welafre, 1971, William L. Dawson award, 1974, Citizens Medal award, 1989, Camille Cosby World Children award, 1990, Amb. award, YWCA of the USA, 1993, Presdl. Freedom medal, 1994, Congl. Gold Medal, 2004, 100 Most Influential Black Americans, Ebony mag., 2006. Office: Pres Emerita Nat Coun Negro Women 633 Pennsylvania Ave NW Washington DC 20004

HEIGL, KATHERINE MARIE, actress; b. Washington, DC, Nov. 24, 1978; d. Paul and Nancy Heigl. Actor: (films) That Night, 1992, King of the Hill, 1993, My Father the Hero, 1994, Under Seige 2: Dark Territory, 1995, Wish Upon a Star, 1996, Prince Valiant, 1997, Stand-ins, 1997, Bug Buster, 1998, Bride of Chucky, 1998, The Tempest, 1998, 100 Girls, 2000, Valentine, 2001, Descendant, 2003, Zyzzyx Rd., 2005, Side Effects, 2005, The Ringer, 2005, Caffeine, 2006, Knocked Up, 2007; (TV series) Roswell, 1999—2002, Grey's Anatomy, 2005— (SAG award for Outstanding Performance by an Ensemble in a Drama Series, 2007), (guest appearance) The Twilight Zone, 2002,: (TV films) Vegas Dick, 2003, Love Comes Softly, 2003, Evil Never Dies, 2003, Critical Assembly, 2003, Wuthering Heights, 2003, Love's Enduring Promise, 2004, Romy and Michele: In the Beginning, 2005. Office: c/o Grey's Anatomy Los Feliz Tower, 4th Fl 4151 Prospect Ave Los Angeles CA 90027 also: c/o Paradigm 360 N Crescent Dr, N Bldg Beverly Hills CA 90210*

HEIKEN, JAY PAUL, physician; b. NYC, Aug. 31, 1952; s. Martin and Sylvia (Fisher) H.; m. Barbara Ellen Rayburn, Dec. 11, 1976 (div. 1982); m. Francine J. Rosen, Apr. 29, 1990 (div. 2007); 1 child, Lauren M. BA, Williams Coll., 1974; MD, Columbia U., 1978. Intern Emory U. Hosp., Atlanta, 1978-79; resident in radiology Columbia-Presbyn. Med. Ctr., NYC, 1979-82; fellow abdominal radiology Mallinckrodt Inst. Radiology, St. Louis, 1982-83; asst. prof. Washington U. Sch. Medicine, St. Louis, 1983-87, assoc. prof., 1988-93, prof., 1993—. Dir. abdominal imaging Mallinckrodt Inst. Radiology, St. Louis; mem. Washington U. Cancer Ctr. Author, editor: Manual of Clinical Magnetic Resonance Imaging, 1986, 2d edit., 1991; editor: Computed Body Tomography with MRI Correlation, 1998, 4th edit., 2006; contbr. articles to profl. jours. Mem. AMA, Radiol. Soc. N.Am., Am. Roentgen Ray Soc., Am. Coll. Radiology, Greater St. Louis Soc. Radiologists, Soc. Computed Body Tomography and Magnetic Resonance (pres. 2003-04), Internat. Soc. Magnetic Resonance in Medicine, Soc. Gastrointestinal Radiologists (bd. dirs.), Assn. Univ. Radiologists, Internat. Cancer Imaging Soc.(pres.-elect, trustee) Avocations: skiing, tennis, softball, wine tasting. Home: 157 Gay Ave Saint Louis MO 63105-3665 Office: Mallinckrodt Inst 510 S Kingshighway Blvd Saint Louis MO 63110-1076 Office Phone: 314-362-1053. Business E-Mail: heikenj@wustl.edu.

HEIL, MICHAEL LLOYD, military officer, academic administrator; BS in Engring. Scis., USAF Acad., Colo., 1975; MS in Flight Structures, Columbia U., 1976; PhD in Solid Mechanics, Air Force Inst. Tech., 1986; MS in Nat. Resource Strategy, Indsl. Coll. of Armed Forces, 1994. Registered profl. engr., Colo. Commd. 2d lt. USAF, 1975, advanced through grades to col., 1995, structural engr. F-15 Sys. Program Office Wright-Patterson AFB, 1976—79, asst. prof., exec. officer dept. engring. mechanics, 1979—83, chief C-17 Structures Divsn., C-17 Sys. Program Office Wright-Patterson AFB, Ohio, 1986—88, mgr. Advanced Cruise Missile Sys. Program Office, 1988—89, dep. dir. Astronautical Scis. Divsn., Astronautics Lab. Edwards AFB, Calif., 1989—90, dep. dir. Propulsion Directorate, Phillips Lab., 1990—93, asst. dir. countermeasures Ballistic Missile Def. Orgn., The Pentagon Washington, 1994—95, comdr. Air Force Phillips Lab. Kirtland AFB, N.Mex., 1995—97, insp. gen. HQ material comd. Wright-Patterson AFB, 1997—98, comdr. Arnold Engring. Devel. Ctr. Arnold AFB, Tenn., 1998—2001, comdt. Inst. Tech. Wright-Patterson AFB, 2001—03, dir. propulsion directorate Rsch. Lab., 2003—05, dir. Ctr. Space Studies Inst. Tech., 2005—07; pres. and CEO Ohio Aerospace Inst., 2007—. Decorated Legion of Merit with two oak leaf clusters, Air Force Commendation medal. Home: 115 Walden Ridge Dr Hinckley OH 44233 Office: Ohio Aerospace Inst 22800 Cedar Pt Rd Brookpark OH 44142 Home Phone: 330-278-2408; Office Phone: 440-962-3001. Personal E-mail: mlheil@aol.com.

HEIL, PAUL SAMUEL, radio producer; b. Reading, Pa., June 8, 1947; s. David Paul and Virginia May (Gaul) H.; m. Shelia Kay Troyer, Dec. 19, 1982; children: Jason David, Andrew Troy. BA in English, Elizabethtown Coll., 1969; LHD (hon.), Emmanuel Bapt. U., 2006. News dir. Sta. WGAL Radio, Lancaster, Pa., 1969—77; news anchor Sta. WSBA Radio, York, Pa., 1977; news dir. Sta. WGAL-TV, Lancaster, 1977—79; owner, exec. prodr. The Gospel Greats, Lancaster, 1979—; owner Springside Mktg., Lancaster, 1986—. Prodr., host weekly 2 hour nationally syndicated Gospel Greats program, 1980—. Monthly columnist Christian Music News, 1986-87, Singing News Mag., 1987-94. Recipient Fan award Singing News, 1986-05, Marvin Norcross award, 1991; named Favorite Gospel Disk Jockey So. Gospel Music News, 1984, People's Choice Favorite Disk Jockey Gospel Music News, 1985, 86, 87; inducted into Pa. So. Gospel Music Hall of Fame, 2003. Mem. So. Gospel Music Guild (founder 1986, pres. 1990-99), Gospel Music Assn. (v.p. 1991-92), So. Gospel Music Assn. (adv. bd. 1995—, Silver Mike award 1983-84). Republican. Mennonite. Office: Heil Enterprises 921 Nissley Rd Lancaster PA 17601-1456 Home Phone: 717-299-5113; Office Phone: 717-898-9100. E-mail: paul@heilenterprises.com.

HEILBORN, GEORGE HEINZ, investor; b. Cologne, Germany, Feb. 27, 1935; arrived in U.S., 1941; s. Walter and Christine (Spiegel) H.; m. Phyllis Dorothy Ehrhardt, Sept. 30, 1972; children: Stephanie, Allison. BA, Northwestern U., 1956; AM, Harvard U., 1958. With Thompson Ramo Wooldridge Products Co., El Segundo, Calif., 1958—60; project mgr. Electronics divsn. Gen. Mills, Mpls., 1960—61; project mgr. Philco Corp., Willow Grove, Pa., 1961—63; pres., chmn. Info. Processing Sys., Inc., Hackensack, NJ, 1963—92; pres. G.H. Heilborn & Co., Inc., 1992—. Bd. vis. Coll. Arts and Scis., Northwestern U., 1992—, alumni regent, 1997—; grad. sch. alumni coun. Harvard U., 1993—, chmn., 1996-98; trustee Family Counseling Svc., Ridgewood, N.J., 1992-95; fin. and investment com. Children's Aid and Family Counseling, N.J., 1996—. Mem. Computer Dealers and Lessors Assn. (founding mem., pres. 1980-82, chmn. 1982-84), Equipment Leasing Assn. Am., US-USSR Trade and Econ. Coun., N.Y. Acad. Scis., Harvard Club N.Y. Home: 385 Knollwood Rd Ridgewood NJ 07450-4814 Office: G H Heilborn & Co Inc One University Plz Hackensack NJ 07601

HEILBRON, DAVID MICHAEL, lawyer, arbitrator, mediator; b. San Francisco, Nov. 25, 1936; s. Louis H. and Delphine A. (Rosenblatt) H.; m. Nancy Ann Olsen, June 21, 1960; children: Lauren Ada, Sarah Ann, Ellen Selma. BS summa cum laude, U. Calif., Berkeley, 1958; AB first class, Oxford U., Eng., 1960; LL.B. magna cum laude, Harvard U., Cambridge, Mass., 1962. Bar: Calif. 1962, U.S. Dist. Ct. (no. dist.) Calif. 1963, U.S Ct. Appeals (9th cir.) 1963, U.S. Ct. Appeals (D.C. cir.) 1972, U.S. Ct. Appeals (8th cir.), 1985, U.S. Ct. Appeals (1st cir.) 1987, U.S. Ct. Appeals (10th cir.) 1988, U.S. Ct. Appeals (7th cir.) 1988, U.S. Ct. appeals (11th cir.) 1988, U.S. Dist. Ct. Nev. 1982, U.S. Dist. Ct. (cen. dist.) Calif. 1983, U.S. Supreme Ct. 1988, U.S. Ct. Appeals (3rd cir.) 1992, (6th cir.), 1995, U.S. Ct. Appeals (2d cir.) 1998, U.S. Ct. Appeals (5th cir.) 1998. Assoc. McCutchen, Doyle, Brown & Enersen, San Francisco, 1962-69, ptnr., 1969—, mng. ptnr., 1985-88. Vis. lectr. appellate advocacy U. Calif., Berkeley, 1981-82, 82-83. Bd. trustees Golden Gate U., 1993-97, vice chair, 1995-97; bd. dirs. San Francisco Jewish Cmty. Ctr., 1974—, Legal Aid Soc., 1974-78, Legal Assistance to Elderly, San Francisco, 1980, San Francisco Renaissance, 1982—; pres. San Francisco Sr. Ctr., 1972-75; co-chmn. San Francisco Lawyers' Com. for Urban Affairs, 1976. Rhodes scholar. Fellow Am. Bar Found.; mem. ABA, Am. Coll. Trial Lawyers, Am. Arbitration Assn. (bd. dirs. 1986-98, 2002--, adv. coun. No. Calif. chpt. 1982—, chmn. 1987, jud. coun. 1986-88, exec. bd. 1994-98, instr. and panelist arbitrator tng. programs), Am. Acad. Appellate Lawyers, State Bar Calif. (chmn. com. cts. 1982-83. bd. govs. 1983-85, mem. commn. on discovery 1984-86, pres. 1985-86), Calif. Acad. Appellate Lawyers, Coll. Comml. Arbitrators, Bar Assn. San Francisco (chmn. conf. dels. 1975-76, pres. 1980). Clubs: Calif. Tennis. Democrat. Office: Bingham McCutchen LLP 3 Embarcadero Ctr San Francisco CA 94111-4003 Office Phone: 415-393-2177. Business E-Mail: david.heilbron@bingham.com.

HEILBRUN, JAMES, economist, educator; b. NYC, Dec. 13, 1924; s. Maurice L. and Hortense (Unger) H.; m. Carolyn Gold, Feb. 20, 1945 (dec. Oct. 2003); children: Emily, Margaret, Robert. BS, Harvard Coll., 1945; MA, Harvard U., 1947; PhD, Columbia U., 1964. Asst. economist Prentice Hall Inc., NYC, 1947-50; econ. analyst Chase Manhattan Bank, NYC, 1951-55; instr. Columbia U., NYC, 1961-65, asst. prof. econs., 1965-70; assoc prof. econs. Fordham U., Bronx, 1970-74, prof., 1974-97, prof. emeritus, 1997—. Research dir. Harlem Devel. Project, Columbia U., 1967-68 Author: Real Estate Taxes and Urban Housing, 1966, Urban Economics and Public Policy, 1973, 3d edit., 1987, (with Charles M. Gray) Economics of Art and Culture, 1993, 2d edit., 2001. Served with USN,

1944-46. Fellow Com. on Urban Econs., 1960-61; fellow Ford Found., 1969-70; UCLA resident scholar, 1978. Mem. Am. Econ. Assn. Home: 151 Central Park W New York NY 10023-1514 E-mail: jheilbrun@wordnet.att.net.

HEILICSER, BERNARD JAY, emergency physician; b. Bklyn., Jan. 19, 1947; s. Murray and Esther (Dubrow) H.; m. Marcia Cherry, June 2, 1976; children: Micah, Seth, Jacob. BA, SUNY, Binghamton, 1968; MS, Hahnemann Med. Coll., Phila., 1971; DO, Coll. Osteo. Medicine/Surgery, Des Moines, 1976. Diplomate Am. Bd. Emergency Medicine. Instr. anatomy and physiology U. Pa. and Hahnemann Med. Coll., Phila., 1971-73; staff physician Va. Inst. Tech., Blacksburg, 1977-78; asst. prof. emergency medicine Chgo. Coll. Osteo. Medicine, 1979; emergency physician St. Margaret Hosp., Hammond, Ind., 1979-83, Michael Reese Med. Ctr., Chgo., 1989-91, Ingalls Hosp., Harvey, Ill., 1983—; project med. dir. South Cook County Emergency Med. Svc., Harvey, 1984—. Faculty Chgo. Osteo. Med. Ctr., 1987-99; faculty trauma nurse specialist St. James Hosp., Chicago Heights, Ill., 1980—; preceptor nurse practitioners Purdue U., Hammond, 1981-90; fellow MacLean Ctr. Clin. Med. Ethics, U. Chgo., 1993-94; chmn. ethics com., hosp. med. ethicist Ingalls Hosp., Harvey, Ill., 1994—; cons. Nat. Bd. Osteo. Med. Examiners, Harvey, 1994-95, ethics com. Am. Coll. Osteo. Emergency Physicians, 1997—; chmn. disaster com. Ill. Region 7 Emergency Med. Svcs./Trauma, 1997—; chair Ill. Region VII EMS Adv. Coun., 2001-04; adj. faculty Coll. Health Professions, Govs. State U., 1999—; lt. comdr., exec. coun. Ill. Med. Emergency Response Team, 1999—; med. advisor Combined Agy. Response Team, 1999—. Vol. fireman Flossmoor (Ill.) Fire Dept., 1985—, Matteson (Ill.) Fire Dept., 1980-90; lead physician, mgr. med. team Ill. Task Force One Urban Search and Rescue, 2004—. Fellow Am. Coll. Emergency Physicians, Am. Coll. Osteo. Emergency Physicians; mem. Am. Osteo. Assn., Nat. Assn. Emergency Med. Svcs. Physicians, Nat. Assn. Emergency Med. Technicians, Sigma Sigma Phi. Jewish. Avocations: running, basketball. Office: Ingalls Hosp One Ingalls Dr Harvey IL 60426 Office Phone: 708-915-6900. E-mail: bernardh47@yahoo.com.

HEILIGENSTEIN, CHRISTIAN ENRIC, lawyer; b. St. Louis, Dec. 7, 1929; s. Christian A. and Louisa M. (Dixon) H.; children: Christie; m. Liselotte Warbanoff, Feb. 6, 1981. BS in Law, U.Ill., 1953, JD, 1955. Bar: Ill. 1956, U.S. Dist. Ct. (so. dist.) Ill. 1956, U.S. Ct. Appeals (7th cir.) 1956, U.S. Dist. Ct. (cen. dist.) Ill. 1960, U.S. Supreme Ct. 1978. Assoc. Listeman & Bandy, East St. Louis, Ill., 1955-61; sole practice Belleville, Ill., 1962-84; ptnr., pres. Heiligenstein & Badgley, Belleville, 1984-98; pres. C.E. Heiligenstein, P.C., Belleville, 1998—. Bd. dirs. Union Planters Corp., Union Planters Bank NA, 1998-2000, audit com. 1999-2000, Magna Bank and Magna Group, Inc., 1984-98; chair audit com. Magna Group, Inc., 1994-98. Bd. visitors U. Ill. Coll. of Law, 2000. Recipient Alumni of Month award U. Ill. Law Sch., 1982; C.E. Heiligenstein Chair in Law named in his honor U. Ill., 1999. Mem. Ill. State Bar Assn., Internat. Acad. Trial Lawyers (bd. dirs. 1991-97), St. Clair County Bar Assn., St. Louis Bar Assn., Inner Circle Advs., Am. Bd. Trial Advs. (nat. bd. dirs. 1992, pres. St. Louis, So. Ill. region 1993), Am. Acad. Profl. Liabilities Attys. (Nat. bd. dirs., 1990-99), ATLA (bd. govs. 1985-87), Ill. Trial Lawyers Assn. (bd. mgrs. 1975-88, pres. 1989), Beach Club (bd. dirs. 1996, v.p. 1998, pres. 2005—), Old Guard Soc. of Palm Beach (bd. dirs. 2005). Democrat. Office Phone: 561-848-4019. Personal E-mail: l.warbanoj@aol.com.

HEILIGER, ROBERT LEE, minister; b. Milw., Nov. 14, 1948; s. Robert Bailie Heiliger and Elayne Violet Beiliger; m. Holly Lynn Baker, Nov. 1, 1986; children: Robert, Elizabeth, Evangeline, Christopher, Thomas, Tiffany, Brandy. BA, Concordia Sr. Coll., Ft. Wayne, Ind., 1970; MDiv, Concordia Seminary, St. Louis, 1974; M of Sacred Thology and Pastoral Counseling, Christ Seminary, St. Louis, 1976; D of Ministry and Pastoral Counseling, Andover Newton Theol. Sch., Newton Center, Mass., 1981. Lic. prof. clin. counselor Ohio; counselor, social worker, marriage and family therapist Ohio Therapy Bd. Vicar St. Paul Luth. Ch., Cin., 1972—73; assoc. dir. children's svcs. Luth. Svc. Assn. New England, Framingham, Mass., 1975—85; assoc. pastor Trinity Luth. Ch., Sprinfield, Ohio, 1982—84; mental health educator, therapist Mental Health Svcs. East, Cin., 1985—87; pastor St. Matthew Luth. Ch., Darrtown, Ohio, 1991—; pastoral counselor Profl. Pastoral Counseling Inst., Cin., 1985—. Cons. Mental Health Svcs. East, Cin., 1987—89; cons., advisor Ohio Govs. Refugee Adv. Coun., Columbus, Ohio, 1986—87; cons. Khmer Cultural Inst., Amherst, Mass., 1982—82; mem. Ohio Luth. Campus Ministry Adv. Bd., Columbus, 1983—84. Recipient Acad. Excellence award, 2003. Fellow: Am. Assn. Pastoral Counselors. Independent. Lutheran. Avocations: genealogy, history, classical music. Office: Profl Pastoral Counseling Inst 8035 Hasbrook Rd Ste 300 Cincinnati OH 45236

HEILMAN, JOHN EDWARD, engineering consultant; b. Chgo., Mar. 20, 1936; s. Frederick John and Kathryn Grace (Schnider) H.; m. Virginia Lois Anderson, Jan. 28, 1956; children: Wayne John, Warren Wesley. BS in Food Engring., Ill. Inst. Tech., 1961. Engr. grocery products divsn. Armour & Co., Chgo., 1959-61, lab. technician, 1958, foreman, 1958-59; process engr. Ctrl. Soya Co., Inc., Ft. Wayne, Ind., 1962-65, supt. Chgo., 1965-68; sr. process engr. Continental Grain Co., Chgo., 1968-75, dir. engring. process divsn. NYC, 1975-77, asst. v.p. process divsn., 1977-79, v.p. world oilseeds group, 1979-91; prin. Heilman Consulting Group, 1991—. Mem. Nat. Fire Protection Assn. (sectional com. solvent extraction, sectional com. agrl. dusts), Am. Oil Chemists Soc. (pres. 1998-99, Baldwin award 2007). Republican. Methodist. Home and Office: 6135 Moorfield Ave Colorado Springs CO 80919-4802 Personal E-mail: jeheilman@comcast.net.

HEILMAN, MARLIN STEPHEN, medical products executive; b. Tarentum, Pa., Dec. 25, 1933; s. Glenn Harold and Hilda Barnes; m. Drusilla Carswell, Aug. 18, 1956; children: Philip, Glenda, Carl Barnes, Stephen James, Karen. BA, U. Pa., 1955, MD, 1959. Pvt. practice, Pitts., 1963—65; cons. Westinghouse R & D, Pitts., 1965—67; pres. Medrad, Inc., Pitts., 1968—80, Intec Systems, Inc., Pitts., 1980—84; chmn., CEO Medrad/Intec, Inc., Pitts., 1984—86; chmn. bd. dirs., CEO Vascor, Inc., Pitts., 1986—, Lifecor, Inc., Pitts., 1986—. Founder Medrad, Intec, Medrad/Intec, Vascor & Lifecor; chmn. Alle-Kiski Med. Ctr. Contbr. articles to profl. jours. Capt. USAF, 1961—63. Named Entrepreneur of Yr., Arthur Young/Venture Mag., 1987; named to Nat. Inventors Hall of Fame, 2002; recipient Michel Mirowski Excellence in Cardiology award, 1992. Office: Vascor Inc 566 Alpha Dr Pittsburgh PA 15238-2912

HEILMAN, PAMELA DAVIS, lawyer; b. Buffalo, July 2, 1948; d. George Henry and Natalie (Maier) Davis; m. Robert D. Heilman, June 27, 1970. AB, Vassar Coll., 1970; JD, SUNY, Buffalo, 1975. Bar: N.Y. 1976, Fla. 1980. Assoc. Hodgson, Russ, Andrews, Woods & Goodyear, Buffalo, 1975-84, ptnr., 1984—. Bd. dirs. United Way Buffalo, 1985-97, vice chmn., 1989-92, chair, 1993-97, gen. campaign chair, 1992; bd. dirs. D'Youville Coll., Buffalo, 2001—, WNY Internat. Trade Coun., Inc., Buffalo, 2001—, Fin. Instns., Inc., Warsaw, 2002—; dean's adv. coun., SUNY at BUffalo Sch. Law, 2004-. Named to Western NY Women's Hall of Fame, 2005; recipient One Person award, United Way, 1997, Cmty. Champion award, Nat. Multiple Sclerosis Soc., 1998, Canadian Ambassador's award, 1999, Athena award, Buffalo Niagara Partnership, 2004. Mem. ABA, N.Y. State Bar Assn. (vice chmn., exec. com., sect. on internat. law and practice 1988-90), Fla. Bar Assn., Erie County Bar Assn. Office: Hodgson Russ Andrews Woods & Goodyear LLP One M&T Plz Buffalo NY 14211-1638 E-mail: pheilman@hodgsonruss.com.

HEILMANN, CHRISTIAN FLEMMING, manufacturing executive; b. Apr. 26, 1936; s. Poul Bent and Hedvig Buchwald (Moller) Heilmann; m. Marilyn Mildred Harter, July 9, 1959 (div. 1973); children: Christian Philip, Nicholas John, Claire Marie; m. Judith Lucy Tucker, Sept. 15, 1973; children: Per Flemming, Niels Henrik. MA, Cambridge U., Eng., 1957. Mng. dir., CEO Metal Box South Africa Ltd., Johannesburg, 1970-77; trustee Nat. Devel. and Mgmt. Found., South Africa, 1970-75; v.p. Continental Can Co., Stamford, Conn., 1977-78; pres. Continental Group Europe, Brussels, 1978-80, Continental Diversified Industries, Stamford, Conn., 1980-81; exec. v.p., chief administrative officer Continental Group, Inc., Stamford, Conn., 1982-84; dir., pres, CEO Am. Can Canada, Inc. (name changed to Onex Packaging Inc. 1986), Rexdale, Ont., 1984-89; N.Y. rep. Danes Worldwide, 1996; chmn., CEO Brockway Standard, Inc., Atlanta, 1989-94; dir., bd. dirs. Whitlock Packaging Co., Okla., 1998—2004. Mem. adv. coun. U. Toronto Bus. Sch., 1985—92; bd. dirs. Porter Chadburn, Inc., Porter Chadburn PLC, O'Shaughnessy Funds, Inc. U.S. rep. Nat. Olympic Com. Denmark, 1994—96; attache Paralympic Games Danish Sports Orgn. for Disabled, Atlanta, 1996; trustee Am. Scandinavian Found., 1998—, Paul Smith's Coll., St. Regis, NY, 1999—2005; mem. coun. Cornell U., 1996—2000, 2002—06; bd. dirs. Cambridge in Am., 1996—2002, Jacob Riis Settlement House, NYC, 1996—, chmn. bd. dirs., 2006; elected Wilkins fellow Downing Coll., Cambridge U., 2000. Decorated knight Order of Dannebrog (Denmark); recipient Ellis Island medal of honor, 2002. Mem.: Danish Am. C. of C. (dir. 1995—2001), Danish-Am. Soc. (bd. dirs. 1990—2003, pres. 1996—2001). Office Phone: 203-831-0367. E-mail: cfheilmann@aol.com.

HEILMEIER, GEORGE HARRY, electrical engineer, researcher; b. Phila., May 22, 1936; s. George C. and Anna I. (Heineman) Heilmeier; m. Janet Faunce, June 24, 1961; 1 child, Elizabeth. BEE, U. Pa., 1958; MS in Engring., Princeton U., 1960, MA, 1961, PhD in Solid-State Electronics, 1962; DEngring (hon.), Stevens Inst. Tech., 1995, Technion, Israel Inst. Tech., 1997. With RCA Labs., Princeton, NJ, 1958—66, dir. solid state device rsch., 1966—69, dir. device concepts, 1969—70; White House fellow, spl. asst. to sec. def. Washington, 1970—71; asst. dir. def. rsch. and engring. Office Sec. Def., 1971—74; dir. Def. Advanced Projects Agy., 1974—77; v.p. corp. rsch., devel., engring. and strategic planning Tex. Instruments Inc., 1977—83, sr. v.p., chief tech. officer, 1983—91; pres., CEO Bell Comm. Rsch., Inc., Livingston, NJ, 1991—96, chmn., CEO, 1996—97; chmn. emeritus Telecordia Techs., Inc. (formerly Bell Comm. Rsch., Inc.), 1997—. Vis. com. MIT, 1988—; leadership coun. Princeton U. Sch. Engring. and Applied Sci.; bd. overseers. Sch. Engring. and Applied Sci. of U. Pa., 1989—; adv. group on electron devices Office Undersec. of Def., 1979—91; bd. dirs. TRW, Compaq Computer Corp., Automatic Data Processing, INET Technologies, Inc., Teletech Holdings; mem. Pres.'s Com. on Nat. Medal of Sci., 1992—94, U.S. Adv.Coun. on Nat. Info. Infrastructure, 1994—; def. sci. bd. Pres.'s Nat. Security Telecom. Adv. Com., 1991—97; adv. bd. Alamos Nat. Security, 1988—91; sci. adv. bd. Nat. Security Agy., 1992—; chmn. adv. bd. GM Sci. and Tech. Bd. trustees Fidelity Funds, 1996—. Named Tech. Leader of Yr., Industry Week, 1994; named to Consumer Elec. Hall of Fame, 2006; recipient IR-100 New Product award, Indsl. Rsch. Assn., 1968—69, Disting. Civilian Svc. award, U.S. Sec. Def., 1975, 1977, Arthur Fleming award, U.S. Jaycees, 1974, Nat. medal Sci., 1991, Japan Commn. and Computing Prize, 1992, Indsl. Rsch. Inst. medal, 1993, John Fritz award, Am. Assn. Engring. Soc., 1999, Kyoto prize (Advanced Technology award), Inamori Found., 2005, Edwin Land medal, Optical Soc. Am., 2006. Fellow: IEEE (David Sarnoff award 1976, Outstanding Achievement award Dallas chpt. 1984, Philips award 1985, Founder's award 1986, Japan Computers and Comm. prize 1990, Pres. Nat. Medal of Sci. 1991, IEEE Medal of Honor 1997); mem.: NAE (Founders award 1992), Am. Acad. Arts and Scis. (John Scott award 1996), Princeton U. Grad. Alumni Assn., U. Pa. Alumni Assn., Eta Kappa Nu (Outstanding Young Engr. in U.S. 1969, Vladimir Karapetoff Eminent Mem. award 1993), Tau Beta Pi, Sigma Xi. Conservative. Methodist. Achievements include discovery of new electro-optic effects in liquid crystals leading to the development of the first liquid crystal displays for watches, calculators, and instrumentation; patents in field. Avocations: reading, sports. Personal E-mail: gheilmeier@aol.com.

HEIM, LORI JOAN, physician; b. Livermore, Calif., June 28, 1955; d. Fred Nelson and Ruth Marie Stahl; m. James Joseph Heim, Dec. 21, 1979. MD, Uniformed Svc. U. of the Health Sciences, Bethesda, Md., 1986. Diplomate Am. Bd. of Family Medicine, 2003. Commd. capt. U.S. Air Force, 1982; chief med. staff and staff physician 7241 Air Base Wing, Izmir, Turkey, 1989—90; family medicine residency staff 89 Med. Group, Andrews AFB, Md., 1990—96; asst. prof. Uniformed Services U. Health Scis., Bethesda, Md., 1996—99; family medicine residency dir. Eglin AFB Family Medicine Dept., Fla., 1999—2001; chief med. staff 96th Med. Group, Eglin AFB, 2001—02; squadron comdr., physician 43 Med. Group, Pope AFB, NC, 2002—04; dep. comdr. and chief med. staff 62d Med. Group, McChord AFB, Wash., 2004—. Contbr. chapters to books. Bd., vp, pres. elect, pres. Uniformed Services Acad. of Family Physicians, 1993—99. Decorated Def. Meritorious Svc. medal USAF, Air Force Meritorious medal. Fellow: Am. Acad. of Family Physicians (bd. dirs. 2005—). Office: 293 Olmstead Blvd Pinehurst NC 28374 Home Phone: 253-582-6800; Office Phone: 970-255-0033.

HEIMAN, MARVIN STEWART, finance company executive; b. Chgo., Sept. 16, 1945; s. Samuel J. and Mildred (Miller) H.; m. Adrienne Joy Nathan, Aug. 7, 1966; children: Scott, Michelle, Adam. Student, Roosevelt U., 1963-67. Pres. Curtom Record Co., Chgo., 1969-80, Gold Coast Entertainment, Chgo., 1980-82; ptnr. Profl. Real Estate Securities Co., Lincolnwood, Ill., 1982-86; pres., chmn. bd. Sussex Fin. Group, Inc., Deerfield, Ill., 1986—; ptnr. Spago Restaurant, Chgo., 1997—, 1997—2003. Bd. dirs. Skokie Bank, Drovers Bank, Chgo., Met. Health Care; ptnr. Cole Taylor Banks, Chgo., 1984—, bank examining com., 1986—, ptnr. Chgo. White Sox Am. League Baseball Club, 1981—, Gore/Bronson Bancorp, 1988-2005, Sun Life of Can., 1993. Mem. Rep. Nat. Com., 1980—, Simon Wiesenthal Ctr., 1988. Recipient Men of Achievement award Cambridge, Eng., Nat. Quality award Nat. Assn. Life Underwriters, 1992. Mem. Internat. Assn. Fin. Planners, Chgo. Assn. Life Underwriters, Real Estate Securities Syndication Assn. Am., Nat. Assn. Securities Dealers (registered rep.), Am. Jewish Com. (Humanitarian award 1978), Internat. Platform Assn., Million Dollar Round Table, Pres.'s Club (Am. funds com. 1992). Avocations: baseball, tennis, music. Office: Sussex Fin Group Inc 155 Pfingsten Rd Ste 370 Deerfield IL 60015

HEIMANN, JOHN GAINES, investment banker; b. NYC, Apr. 1, 1929; s. Sidney M. and Dorothy V.B. (Gainesburg) H.; m. Margaret E. Fechheimer, Dec. 2, 1956 (div.); children: Joshua Gaines, Eliza Faith; m. Maria Cristina Anzola, Oct. 17, 1989. BA in Econs., Syracuse U., NY, 1950; LLD (hon.), St. Michael's Coll., 1979. V.p. Smith, Barney & Co., NYC, 1955-66; sr. v.p., dir. E.M. Warburg, Pincus & Co., Inc., NYC, 1967-75; N.Y. State supt. banks, 1975-76; N.Y. State commr. housing and community renewal, 1976-77; compt. of the currency Washington, 1977-81; co-chmn. exec. com. Warburg, Paribas, Becker, NYC, 1981-82; dep. chmn. A.G. Becker Paribas Inc., Paribas Internat., 1982-84; vice chmn. Merrill Lynch Capital Markets, NYC, 1984-91; chmn. Europe/Middle East Merrill Lynch, London, 1988-90; chmn. global fin. instns. group office of chmn. Merrill Lynch & Co. Inc., NYC, 1991-99; chmn. Fin. Stability Inst. of the Bank for Internat. Settlements, NYC, 1999-2001; sr. advisor Fin. Stability Inst. Bank for Internat. Settlements, 2001—; sr. advisor Merrill Lynch & Co., Inc., 2001—03. Chmn. Merrill Lynch Internat. Bank; chmn. Fin. Svcs. Coun.; mem. exec. com. Inst. Internat. Fin.; chmn. Fed. Fin. Instns. Exam. Coun., 1979-81, Comml. Reinvestment Task Force, 1978-81, 20th Century Task Force on Internat. Debt Crisis; lectr. Harvard U., Yale U., Columbia U., U. Calif., NYU; chmn. Brit.-N.Am. com.; trustee Nat. Policy Assn.; vice chmn., chmn. securities subcom. Am. Banking and Securities Assn. of London; chmn. NY State Supt.'s Adv. Com. on Transnat. Banking Instns., 1981; co-chmn. Derivatives Policy Group; mem. Fed. Res. Bank of NY's Internat. Capital Markets Adv. Com.; mem. adv. com. on fin. svcs. Dept. US Treasury; mem. governing coun. Ctr. for Study of Fin. Instns.; trustee French-Am. Found.; bd. dirs. NewSmith Hedge Fund LP, Interaudi Bank, Assured Guaranty ltd., NewSmith UK Hedge Fund Ltd., URBAN Assembly. Bd. dirs., mem. Group of Thirty, Am. Ditchley Found., Inst. Internat. Fin., Chatham Ho. Found.; trustee Hampshire Coll.; mem. strategic com. France Tresor; mem. Citizens Com. for NY C.; mem. adv. coun. Ctr. Econ. Policy Rsch.; mem. Coun. Fgn. Rels.; bd. dirs. Urban Assembly. Named Housing Man of Yr. Nat. Housing Conf., 1976; recipient Bank Adminstrn. Key for Disting. Svc., 1980, Alexander Hamilton award Treasury Dept., 1981, Brotherhood award NCCJ, 1986, Pacesetter award Nat. Assn. Bank Women, Inc., 1986. Mem. Nat. Policy Assn. (vice chmn.), Fgn. Rels. Coun. Democrat. Office: Warburg Pincus 466 Lexington Ave Fl 11 New York NY 10017 Home Phone: 212-288-1384; Office Phone: 212-878-6118. E-mail: heimannjo@aol.com.

HEIMANN, M.L. (DICK HEIMANN), auto dealership executive; BS in Biology and Langs., U. Colo. Dist. mgr. Chrysler Corp., 1967—70; pres., COO Lithia Motors Inc., Medford, Oreg. Mem.: Medford New Car Dealers Assn., Jeep Dealer Coun., Oregon Auto Dealers Assn. Office: Lithia Motors Inc 360 E Jackson St Medford OR 97501

HEIMBERG, MURRAY, pharmacologist, biochemist, physician; b. Bklyn., Jan. 5, 1925; s. Gustav and Fannie (Geller) H.; children by previous marriage: Richard G., Steven A.; m. Anna Frances Langlois Knox, July 12, 1964; stepchildren: Larry M. Knox, David S. Knox. BS, Cornell U., Ithaca, NY, 1948, MNS, 1949; PhD in Biochemistry (NIH fellow), Duke, 1952; MD, Vanderbilt U., 1959. NIH Postdoctoral fellow in biochemistry Med. Sch. Washington U., St. Louis, 1952-54; research asso. physiology Med. Sch. Vanderbilt U., 1954-59, asst. prof. to prof. pharmacology, and asst. prof. medicine, 1959-74; prof., chmn. dept. pharmacology, prof. medicine U. Mo., 1974-81; prof. and chmn. dept. pharmacology, prof. medicine, endocrinology and metabolism U. Tenn., Health Sci. Ctr., Memphis, 1981-96; Van Vleet prof. pharmacology U. Tenn., Memphis, 1986-96, Disting. prof. pharmacology and medicine, 1996-99, disting. prof. pharmacology and medicine emeritus, 2000—. Cons. NSF, NIH; cons., established investigator Am. Heart Assn.; attending physician U. Tenn. Hosps. and Memphis VA Hosp.; dir. lipid metabolism clinic U. Tenn. Med. Group. Contbr. articles to profl. jours. Served with inf., AUS, 1943-45, ETO. Decorated Purple Heart, Bronze Star; recipient Lederle Med. Faculty award; research grantee. Fellow AAAS, Am. Coll. Clin. Pharmacology, Am. Heart Assn.; mem. Am. Soc. Biol. Chemistry and Molecular Biology, Am. Soc. Pharmacology and Exptl. Therapeutics, Endocrine Soc., Am. Diabetes Assn., So. Soc. Clin. Investigation. Home: 105 Devon Way Memphis TN 38111-7711 Office Phone: 901-448-4748. Personal E-mail: mheimberg1@comcast.net. Business E-Mail: mheimberg@utmem.edu.

HEIMBINDER, ISAAC, lawyer; b. Bklyn., May 15, 1943; s. David and Evelyn (Brown) H.; m. Sheila Marie Mooney, Aug. 3, 1970; children: Susan, Daniel, Erin, Michael. BS in Bus., Am. U., 1965; JD, NYU, 1968. Atty. Debevoise and Plimpton, NYC, 1969-72; corp. counsel U.S. Home Corp., Clearwater, Fla., 1973-77, v.p. legal affairs Houston, 1977-79, CFO, 1979-86, pres. COO, 1986-95, co-CEO, pres. COO, 1995-99; chmn., CEO HomeWrite Inc., Houston, 2000—01; vice chmn., pres., COO Kimball Hill Homes, 2001—06; chmn. Buildtopia, 2007—. Named one of 100 Most Influential People in Homebuilding Industry in 20th Century, Builder Mag., 1999; recipient Homebuilder of Yr. award Profl. Builder, 1994 Mem. N.Y. Bar Assn., Fla. Bar Assn., Tex. Bar Assn., Nat. Assn. Home Builders (mem. high prodn. home builders coun.), Order of Coif, Omicron Delta Kappa. Home Phone: 713-871-8555. Personal E-mail: heimbinder@aol.com.

HEIMBOLD, CHARLES ANDREAS, JR., former ambassador; b. Newark, May 27, 1933; s. Charles Andreas and Mary Joseph (Corrigan) Heimbold; m. Monka Astrid Barkvall, Sept. 22, 1962; children: Joanna, Eric, Leif, Peter. BA cum Laude, Villanova U., 1954; LLB cum laude, U. Pa., 1960; LLM, NYU, 1966; postgrad., Hague Acad. Internat. Law, 1959. Bar: N.Y. 1962. Assoc. Milbank, Tweed, Hadley & Mc Cloy, 1960-63; staff atty. Bristol-Myers Squibb Co., NYC, 1963-70, dir. corp. devel., 1970-73, v.p. planning and devel., 1981-84, sr. planning and devel., 1981-84, pres., health care group, 1984-88, pres., health care group and sr. v.p. planning and devel., 1988-89, dir., 1989, exec. v.p., 1989-92, pres., 1992-94, pres., CEO, 1994-95, chmn., CEO, 1995-2001, chmn. emeritus, 2001—; U.S. amb. to Sweden US Dept. State, Stockholm, 2001—04. Trustee U. Pa., mem. bd. overseers Law Sch. With USN, 1954—57. Mem.: Assn. Bar City of N.Y., Causeway Club, Riverside Yacht Club.

HEIMBOLD, MARGARET BYRNE, publisher, poet, consultant, realtor; came to U.S., 1966, naturalized, 1973; d. John Christopher and Anne (Troy) Byrne; m. Arthur Heimbold, Feb. 26, 1984; children: Eric Thomas Gordon, Victoria Byrne Heimbold BA, Queens Coll.; MA, Georgetown U., 2003; cert., Dale Carnegie, 1977, Psychol. Corp. Am., 1981, Wharton Sch., 1983, Stanford U., 1989. Mgr. group advt. N.Y. Times, NYC, 1978—85; pub. Am. Film, Washington, 1985—86; v.p., pub. Nat. Trust for Hist. Preservation, Washington, 1986—90; pres. Summerville Press, Inc., Washington, 1990—; realtor Long and Foster, Washington, 2005—. Pub. Metro Golf, 1992—; advisor Mag. Pubs.; mentor Women's Ctr. Va.; judge various publ. competitions. Trustee Nat. Mus. Women in Arts, Choral Arts Soc. Washington, Kidsave Internat., Irish Peace Inst. Office Phone: 202-944-8400, 202-812-2750. Business E-Mail: margaret.heimbold@longandfoster.com. E-mail: summervillemedia@erols.com.

HEIMBUCH, BABETTE E., bank executive; b. 1948; BS in Math. summa cum laude, U. Calif., Santa Barbara, 1972. Sr. v.p., CFO FirstFed. Bank Calif., Santa Monica, 1982—85, exec. v.p., CFO, 1985—87, dir., 1986—, FirstFed. Fin. Corp., 1987—; sr. exec. v.p., CFO FirstFed. Fin. Corp. & FirstFed Bank Calif, 1987—88, pres., COO, 1989—97, CEO, 1997—, chmn., 2002—. Bd. dirs. Water Pik Technologies Inc., 2002—, Scape Industries. Chair bd. advisors Santa Monica-UCLA Med. Ctr.; fin. oversight com. Santa Monica/Malibu Unified Sch. Dist. Named one of 25 Women to Watch, US Banker Mag., 2003. Office: First Fed Bank Calif 401 Wilshire Blvd Santa Monica CA 90401-1416*

HEIMES, CHARMAINE MARIE, elementary school educator, poet, writer; b. Detroit, June 28, 1960; d. Charles M. and Mary Patricia (Allen) H. BA, Olivet Coll., Mich., 1982. Cert. tchr. Tex., nat. cert. abstinence educator, cert. USA track & field ofcl. 2005. Substitute tchr. Charlotte (Mich.) Pub. Schs., 1982-84; coach jr. varsity volleyball Charlotte High Sch., 1983-84, coach jr. varsity softball, 1984; tcrh. phys. edn., coach Cigarroa Mid. Sch., Laredo, Tex., 1984—, head phys. edn. dept., 1988—. Asst. field hockey coach Olivet (Mich.) Coll., 1982-83; abstinenece master tchr. 1999-; Tex. Bess mentor, 2004-; Quest mentor Tex. A&M Internat. U., 2000-. Nominee Golden Apple, Cigarroa Mid. Sch., 2007; recipient Tamiu Dean's Extra Miler award, 2007. Avocations: coin collecting/numismatics, plates, poetry, writing, Elvis memorabilia. Office: Cigarroa Mid Sch 2600 Palo Blanco St Laredo TX 78046-8232 Office Phone: 956-795-3706. Personal E-mail: laredomac@hotmail.com.

HEIMLICH, HENRY J., physician, surgeon, educator; b. Wilmington, Del., Feb. 3, 1920; s. Philip and Mary (Epstein) Heimlich; m. Jane Murray, June 3, 1951; children: Philip, Janet, Elisabeth. BA, Cornell U., 1941, MD, 1943; DSc (hon.), Wilmington Coll., 1981, Adelphi U., 1982, Rider Coll., 1983, Alfred U., 1993. Diplomate Am. Bd. Surgery, Am. Bd. Thoracic

Surgery. Intern Boston City Hosp., 1944; resident VA Hosp., Bronx, 1946—47, Mt. Sinai Hosp., NYC, 1947—48, Bellevue Hosp., NYC, 1948—49, Triboro Hosp., Jamaica, NY, 1949—50; attending surgeon divsn. surgery Montefiore Hosp., NYC, 1950—69; dir. surgery Jewish Hosp., Cin., 1969—77; prof. advanced clin. scis. Xavier U., Cin., 1977—89; assoc. clin. prof. surgery U. Cin. Coll. Medicine, 1969—78. Pres. Heimlich Inst.; mem. Pres.'s Commn. on Heart Disease, Cancer and Stroke, 1965; pres. Nat. Cancer Found., 1963—68, bd. dirs., 1960—70; founder Heimlich Inst. Found. Author: Postoperative Care in Thoracic Surgery, 1962; author: (with M.O. Cantor, C.H. Lupton) Surgery of the Stomach, Duodenum and Diaphragm, Questions and Answers, 1965; contbr. chapters to books, articles to profl. jours.; prodr.(film): Esophageal Replacement with a Reversed Gastric Tube (Medaglione Di Bronzo Minerva, 1961), Reversed Gastric Tube Esophagoplasty Using Stapling Technique, How to Save a Choking Victim: The Heimlich Maneuver, 1976, 1982, How to Save a Drowning Victim: The Heimlich Maneuver, 1981, Stress Relief: The Heimlich Method, 1983, (video): Dr. Heimlich's Home First Aid Video, 1989 (Vira award, 1989); editl. bd. films Reporte's Medicos, 1962. Cmty. Devel. Found., 1967—70; Save the Chidlren FEdn., 1967—68; United Cancer Coun., 1967—70. Served to lt. (s.g.) USNR, 1944—46. Recipient Lasker award for Pub. Svc., Lasker Found., 1984, China-Burma-India Vets. Assn. Americanism award, 1988, 1st Heimlich Humanitarian award, Spirit of Am. Festival, 1994, Heimlich Inst. established in perpetuity by Deaconess Assns., Inc. Fellow: ACS (chpt. pres. 1964), Am. Coll. Gastroenterology, Am. Coll. Chest Physicians; mem.: AMA (cons. to jour.), Ctrl. Surg. Assn., Collegium INternat. Chirurgiae Digestive, Pan Am. Med. Assn., Am. Gastroent. Assn., Soc. Surgery Alimentary Tract, N.Y. Soc. Thoracic Surgery, Cin. Soc. Thoracic Surgery, Soc. Thoracic Surgeons (founding mem.). Achievements include development of Heimlich Operation (reversed gastric tube esophagoplasty) for replacement of esophagus; invention of Heimlich chest drain valve, Heimlich Micro-Trach (HMT) for COPD, emphysema and cystic fibrosis; development of Heimlich Maneuver to save lives of victims of food choking and drowning and prevents and overcomes asthma attacks (listed in Random House, Oxford Am. and Webster dictionaries); Computers for Peace, a program to maintain peace throughout world and A Caring World. Office: Heimlich Inst Found Inc 311 Straight St Cincinnati OH 45219 Personal E-mail: hjheimlich@fuse.net. *I have never been satisfied with existing methods and seek to simplify and improve them. After devising an operation for replacement of the esophagus, I became aware that with one such discovery I could help more people in a few weeks than in my entire lifetime as a surgeon in the operating room. The Heimlich Maneuver, which saves thousands of choking and drowning victims as well as asthmatics annually, confirmed this realization. My ultimate goal is to avoid needless death and promote well-being for the largest number of people by establishing a philosophy that will eliminate war and promote a caring world. Seeking to find a cure for cancer, AIDS, and Lyme disease through immunotherapy.*

HEIN, JAY F., federal official; b. 1965; BA, Eureka Coll.; M in Polit. Studies, U. Ill. Springfield. With Dept. Pub. Aid, Ill., Office Sec. of State, Ill. State Libr.; dir. field office Hudson Inst., Madison, Wis., exec. dir. civil soc. programs; v.p., CEO Found. Am. Renewal; founding pres. Sagamore Inst. Policy Rsch.; dep. asst. to Pres., dir. The White House Office Faith-Based and Cmty. Initiatives, 2006—. Co-author, editor: book The New Wisconsin Idea: Replacing Entitlement Welfare with Personal Empowerment, The Welfare of Britain. Office: White House Office Faith Based and Cmty Initiatives The White House Washington DC 20502 E-mail: jay@sipr.org.

HEIN, KAREN KRAMER, pediatrician, epidemiologist; b. NYC, Feb. 2, 1944; d. Irving W. and Ruth (Eisenberg) Kramer: m. Ralph Dell, Aug. 28, 1983; children: Ethan, Molly. BA, U. Wis., 1966; B of Med. Sci., Dartmouth Med. Sch., 1968; MD, Columbia U., 1970. Intern Bronx Mcpl. Hosp., Bronx Mcpl. Hosp. Ctr., 1970, resident, 1971-73; dir. adolescent AIDS program Montefiore Med. Ctr., NYC, 1987-94; prof. pediat. Albert Einstein Coll. Medicine, NYC, 1991—, prof. epidemiology and social medicine, 1993—, clin. prof. pediat., epidemiology and population health, 1995—; exec. officer Inst. Medicine NRC, Washington, 1995—98; pres. William T. Grant Found., NYC, 1998—2003. Cons. NYC Dept. Health, 1980-85, NYC Bd. Edn., 1987-93; bd. dirs. Dartmouth Med. Sch., Hanover, NH, Consumers Union, 1998-, Childfund Internat., 2005-, Internat. Rescue Com., 2005-, Nat. Bd. Med. Examiners, 2002—. Author: AIDS: Trading Fears for Facts Consumer Reports Books, 1989. Named Outstanding Physician, Dept. Health and Human Svcs., 1989, Adminstrs. Citation award, 1993. Fellow Am. Bd. Pediat.; mem. Am. Pediatric Soc., Soc. for Pediatric Rsch., Am. Acad. Pediat., Soc. for Adolescent Medicine (pres. 1992-93). Address: Box 607 Jacksonville VT 05342

HEIN, TODD JONATHAN, accountant; b. Encino, Calif., May 11, 1960; s. Walter Adolph Jr. and Valerie Wynann (Phipps) H.; 1 child, MacKenzie James. BA in Econs., UCLA, 1982; cert. in fin. planning, U. So. Calif., 1987; MS in Taxation, Golden Gate U., 2001. CPA Calif., CFP; CLU 1983. Acct. analyst Exec. Life Ins. Co., LA, 1983; acct. Satriano & Young, LA, 1983—85; personal acct. Barron Hilton; pres. Hilton Hotels Corp., Beverly Hills, Calif., 1985-86; acct. Gursey, Schneider & Co., LA, 1987-88; agent Nat. Life of Vt., LA, 1988-89; spl. agt. Northwestern Mut. Life, Woodland Hills, Calif., 1989-96; sr. acct. Gursey, Schneider & Co., LLP, LA, 1996-98; sr. staff accountant Engel, Kalvin, McMillan & Kipper, LLP, LA, 1998-99; tax mgr. Sher, Sherr, Gelb & Co., Sherman Oaks, Calif., 1999—2004, Grobstein, Horwath & Co., LLP, Sherman Oaks, 2004—. Mem. AICPA, Calif. Soc. CPAs, Inst. Cert. Fin. Planners, So. Calif. Mountaineering Assn., Sierra Club. Avocations: reading, astronomy, travel, triathlons, mountaineering. Office: Grobstein Horwath & Co LLP 15233 Ventura Blvd 9th Fl Sherman Oaks CA 91403-2201

HEINDEL, NED DUANE, chemistry professor; b. Red Lion, Pa., Sept. 4, 1937; s. Penrose Horace and Dorothy May (Strayer) H.; m. Linda Clarella Heefner, Aug. 26, 1959. BS, Lebanon Valley Coll., Annville, Pa., 1959; D.Sc. (hon.), Lebanon Valley Coll., 1985; MS, U. Del., 1961, PhD, 1963; postdoctoral studies, Princeton U., 1964; DSc (hon.), Albright Coll., 1993. Instr. chemistry U. Del., 1962-63; asst. prof. chemistry Ohio U., Ironton, 1964-65, Marshall U., Huntington, W.Va., 1964-66; asst. prof. to assoc. prof. chemistry Lehigh U., Bethlehem, Pa., 1966-73, H.S. Bunn prof., 1973—, dir. Ctr. Health Scis., 1980-88; prof. nuclear medicine Hahnemann Med. U., Phila., 1971—. Cons. Pa. State Police Crime Lab., Bethlehem, 1975-88; cons. safety program J.T. Baker Chem. Co., Phillipsburg, N.J., 1978-83; regional lectr. Mid. Atlantic region Sigma Xi. Author: Iron, Armor and Adolescents, 1982; editor: Chemistry of Radiopharmaceuticals, 1978; contbr. numerous articles to profl. jours. Trustee Keystone Jr. Coll., LaPlume, Pa., 1975-90, Ctr. for History of Chemistry, Phila., 1982—, Nat. Found. for History of Chemistry, Phila., 1988—. Recipient Alumni Assn. award Lebanon Valley Coll., 1971; fellow NSF, 1963-64; recipient numerous rsch. grants. Mem. Am. Chem. Soc. (councilor, bd. dirs., pres. 1994, Harry and Carol Mosher award 1995), Royal Soc., Soc. Nuclear Medicine, Am. Assn. Pharm. Scientists, Sigma Xi. Republican. Methodist. Home: 200 Hexenkopf Rd Easton PA 18042-9570 Office: Dept Chem Lehigh U Bethlehem PA 18015 Business E-Mail: ndh0@lehigh.edu.

HEINDL, CLIFFORD JOSEPH, physicist, researcher; b. Chgo., Feb. 4, 1926; s. Anton Thomas and Louise (Fiala) H. BS, Northwestern U., 1947, MS, 1948; AM, Columbia U., 1950, PhD, 1959. Sr. physicist Bendix Aviation Corp., Detroit, 1953-54; student rschr. Oak Ridge Nat. Lab., 1954-55; asst. sect. chief Babcock & Wilcox Co., Lynchburg, Va., 1956-58; rsch. group supr. Jet Propulsion Lab., Pasadena, Calif., 1959-65, mgr. rsch. and space sci., 1965—2005. Served with AUS, 1944-46. Mem. AIAA, Am. Nuclear Soc., Health Physics Soc., Planetary Soc., Am. Phys. Soc. Home: 179 Mockingbird Ln South Pasadena CA 91030-2047 Office: 4800 Oak Grove Dr Pasadena CA 91109-8001

HEINDL, PHARES MATTHEWS, lawyer; b. Meridian, Miss., Dec. 14, 1949; s. Paul A. and Leila (Matthews) H.; m. Linda Ann Williamson, Sept. 21, 1985; children: Lori Elizabeth, Jesse Phares, Jared Matthews. BSChemE, Miss. State U., 1972; JD, U. Fla., Gainesville, 1981. Bar: Fla. 1981, Calif. 1982, US Dist. Ct. (cen. dist.) Calif. 1983, US Dist. Ct. (mid. dist.) Fla. 1983; cert. civil trial lawyer Fla. Bar. Assoc. Lafollette, Johnson et al, LA, 1982-83, Sam E. Murrell & Sons, Orlando, Fla., 1983-84; pvt. practice Orlando, Fla., 1984-93, Altamonte Springs, Fla., 1993—. Program com. Volie Williams Jr. Inns of Ct., 2003. Precinct coord. Freedom Coun., Orlando, 1986; pres. Friends of the Wekiva River, 1999—2001. Mem. Fla. Bar Assn., Calif. Bar Assn., Seminole County Bar Assn. (pres. civil trial sect. 1998), ATLA, Christian Legal Soc. (past pres. Ctrl. Fla.), Fla. Acad. Trial Lawyers, Workers Compensation Rules Com. Republican. Avocation: kayak racing. Home: 2415 River Tree Cir Sanford FL 32771-8334 Office: The Welaka Bldg 114 W First St Ste 242 Sanford FL 32771 Office Phone: 407-936-2175. Business E-Mail: phares@heindllaw.com.

HEINEKEN, FREDERICK GEORGE, biochemical engineer; b. Chgo., Oct. 22, 1939; s. Frederick W.G. Heineken and Marie Helene Faber Heineken; divorced; 1 child, Christopher P. BS, Northwestern U., 1962; PhD, U. Minn., 1966. Sr. biochem. engr. Monsanto, St. Louis, 1966-71; postdoctoral fellow U. Colo., Denver, 1972-74, rsch. assoc., instr., 1974-76; sr. project engr. Cobe Labs., Lakewood, Colo., 1977-79, dept. head, 1979-81, therapy scientist, 1981-84; cons. Heineken & Assocs., Potomac, Md., 1985—; program dir. NSF, Washington, 1985—. Trustee 1st Universalist Ch., Denver, 1980-83, vice-moderator, 1984. Recipient Young Investigator award, NIH, 1974. Mem. AIChE, AAAS, Am. Chem. Soc. (councilor 1990—), Assn. for Advancement of Med. Instrumentation, Am. Soc. for Artificial Organs, St. Louis Ski Club (pres. 1971). Home: 7908 Turncrest Dr Potomac MD 20854-2772 Office: NSF Engring 4201 Wilson Blvd Arlington VA 22230-0001 Office Phone: 703-292-7944. Business E-Mail: fheineke@nsf.gov.

HEINEMAN, ANDREW DAVID, retired lawyer; b. NYC, Nov. 5, 1928; s. Bernard and Lucy (Morgenthau) H. BA, Williams Coll., 1950; LLB, Yale U., 1953. Bar: N.Y. 1953. Assoc. Proskauer Rose Goetz & Mendelsohn, NYC, 1953—63; ptnr. Proskauer Rose LLP, NYC, 1963—2002; ret., 2002. Pres., chmn. bd. dirs. Ernest and Mary Hayward Weir Found., N.Y.C., 1969-87, trustee Mt. Sinai Hosp. Med. Sch. and Med. Ctr., 1976—, Williams Coll., 1980-95, Abelard Found., 1976-96; Asphalt Green, 1992-96; bd. dirs. Jewish Home and Hosp. for Aged, 1967—, vice chmn. bd. dirs., 1992, chmn. bd. dirs. 1993-97; exec. asst. Citizens for Kennedy and Johnson, N.Y.C., 1960; mem. N.Y. Gov.'s Commn. on Minorities in Med. Schs., 1982; co-chmn. Mt. Sinai adv. com. the Ctr. Multicultural and Cmty. Affairs. Mem. Yale Law Sch. Assn. N.Y. (pres. 1970-73), Yale Law Sch. Alumni Assn. (v.p. 1973-76, exec. com.), Audubon Soc., North Country Bird Club, Linnaean Soc. (life), Fedn. N.Y. State Bird Clubs, Brit. Naval Photog. Club.

HEINEMAN, BEN WALTER, corporation executive; b. Wausau, Wis., Feb. 10, 1914; s. Walter Ben and Elsie Brunswick (Deutsch) H.; m. Natalie Goldstein, Apr. 17, 1935; children: Martha Heineman Pieper, Ben Walter. Student, U. Mich., 1930-33; LLB, Northwestern U., 1936; LLD (hon.), Lawrence Coll., 1959; LL.D. (hon.), Lake Forest Coll., 1966, Northwestern U., 1967; LHD, DePaul U., 1986. Bar: Ill. 1936. Pvt. practice law and govt. svc., Chgo., Washington, Algiers, 1936-56; chmn. bd. dirs. Four Wheel Drive Auto Co., 1954-57; chmn. C. & N.W. Ry. Co., 1956-72; founder, former chmn., CEO Northwest Industries, Inc., 1968-85. Dir., chmn. exec. com., bd. dirs. 1st Nat. Bank, Chgo.; chmn. orgn. com. First Chgo. Corp., 1965-86; Chmn. White House Conf. to Fulfill These Rights, 1966, Pres.'s Task Force on Govt. Orgn., 1966-67, Pres.'s Commn. Income Maintenance Programs, 1967-69 Life trustee U. Chgo.; chmn. Ill. Bd. Higher Edn., 1962-69; trustee, mem. investment com. Savs. and Profit Sharing Fund Sears Roebuck Employees, 1966-71; trustee, mem. exec. com., chmn. audit com. Rockefeller Found., 1972-78; life dir. Lyric Opera, Chgo.; life trustee Orchestral Assn.; sustaining fellow Art Inst. Chgo., 20th century acquisition com.; dir. emeritus The Corning (N.Y.) Glass Mus. Recipient Carol Fox award, Lyric Opera, Chgo., 2006. Fellow ABA, AAAS, Am. Bar Found. (life); mem. Am. Law Inst. (life), Ill. Bar Assn., Chgo. Bar Assn., Ephraim Club (Wis.), Yacht Club, Mid-Am. Club, Chgo. Club, Wayfarers Club, Std. Club (life), Quadrangle Club, Comml. Club (life), Carlton Club, Order of Coif, Phi Delta Phi (hon.). Office: 180 E Pearson St Apt 4304 Chicago IL 60611-2171 E-mail: BWH4304@hmansr.net.

HEINEMAN, BENJAMIN WALTER, JR., lawyer; b. Chgo., Jan. 25, 1944; s. Benjamin Walter and Natalie (Goldstein) H.; m. Jeanne Cristine Russell, June 7, 1975; children: Zachary R., Matthew R. BA magna cum laude, Harvard U., 1965; B.Letters, Balliol Coll., Oxford U., Eng., 1967; JD, Yale U. Law Sch., 1971. Bar: D.C. 1973, U.S. Supreme Ct. 1973. Reporter Chgo. Sun Times, 1968; law clk. to Assoc. Justice Potter Stewart U.S. Supreme Ct., 1971-72; staff atty. Center for Law and Social Policy, 1973-75; with Williams Connolly and Califano, Washington, 1975-76; exec. asst. to sec. US Dept. Health, Edn. & Welfare, Washington, 1977-78, asst. sec. for planning & evaluation, 1978-79; partner Califano, Ross & Heineman, Washington, 1979-82; mng. ptnr. Sidley & Austin, Washington, 1982-87; sr. v.p., gen. counsel, sec. Gen. Electric Co., Fairfield, Conn., 1987—2004, sr. v.p., law & pub. affairs, 2004—05; sr. fellow, Belfer Ctr. for Sci. and Internat. Affairs Harvard U., Kennedy Sch. Govt., Cambridge, Mass.; disting. sr. fellow Harvard Law Sch. Program on Legal Profession; sr. counsel WilmerHale (Wilmer, Cutler & Pickering and Hale and Dorr LLP merge to become WilmerHale in 2004), NY. Bd. dir. Transparency Internat.-USA. Author: The Politics of the Powerless: A Study of the Campaign Against Racial Discrimination, 1972, Memorandum for the President: A Strategic Approach to Domestic Affairs in the 1980's, 1981; editor-in-chief: Yale Law Jour., 1970-71. Mem. bd. managers and overseers Meml. Sloan Kettering Cancer Ctr.; trustee Nat. Constitutional Ctr.; trustee, sr. advisor Ctr. for Strategic and Informational Studies, Washington. Rhodes scholar, 1965-67; recipient Excellence in Corp. Practice award, Am. Corp. Counsel Assn., 2002, Exemplar award, Nat. Legal Aid and Defenders Assn., 2004, Welfare Law Ctr. Econ. Justice award, 2005, Lifetime Achievement award, Am. Law mag., 2005; named one of 100 Most Influential Lawyers in America, The Nat. Law Jour., 2006. Mem. Phi Beta Kappa, Am. Law Inst., Coun. Fgn. Relations; fellow Am. Acad. Arts & Sciences Address: Belfer Ctr for Sci and Internat Affairs John F Kennedy Sch Govt 79 JFK St Littauer 362 Cambridge MA 02138 Office Fax: 617-495-8163. Business E-Mail: ben_heineman@harvard.edu.

HEINEMAN, DAVID EUGENE, governor; b. Falls City, Nebr., May 12, 1948; s. Jean Trevers and Irene Larkin H.; m. Sally Ganem, 1977; 1 child, Sam. BS, U.S. Mil. Acad., 1970. Sales rep. Procter & Gamble, 1976-77; campaign mgr. Hal Daub for Congress, 1977-78; dep. dir. Policy Rsch. Office, Nebr., 1979; dir. Nebr. State Rep. Exec. Com., 1979-81; chief of staff to Congressman Hal Daub, 1983-88; office mgr. for Congressman Doug Bereuter, 1990-94; city councilman City of Fremont, Nebr., 1990-94; state treas. State of Nebr., 1994—2000, lt. gov., 2001—05, gov., 2005—. Served in US Army, 1970—75. Decorated Army Commendation medal; recipient Outstanding Rep. Vol. award Douglas County Rep. Party, 1976, Outstanding Young Am. award Jaycees, 1980. Mem. Nat. Assn. State Treas. (pres. 1999-2000), Nat. Electronic Commerce Coordinating Coun. (exec. com. 1998-2000). Republican. Office: Office of Governor PO Box 94848 Lincoln NE 68509 Office Phone: 402-471-2244. Office Fax: 402-471-6031. E-mail: dave.heineman@email.state.ne.us.*

HEINEMAN, NATALIE (MRS. BEN W. HEINEMAN), civic worker; Formerly med. social worker, Chgo.; bd. dirs. Child Welfare League Am., 1960-86, pres., 1971-74, now hon. life mem.; chmn. citizens com. Ill. Adoption Svc., 1959-71; bd. dirs. Chgo. Child Care Soc., 1959-97, pres., 1967-71, now hon. life mem.; mem. citizens' com. Juvenile Ct. of Cook County, 1984-95. Bd. dirs. Children and Family Justice Ctr., Northwestern U. Sch. Law, 1991-96; mem. women's bd. Field Mus. Natural History, U. Chgo., Northwestern U.; vis. com. U. Chgo. Sch. Social Svc., 1956-91. Bd. dirs. United Way Met. Chgo., 1975-86, United Way Am., 1974-80, Erikson Inst. for Advanced Study Child Devel., 1966-88. Address: 180 E Pearson St Chicago IL 60611-2143 Personal E-mail: bwh4304@hmansr.net.

HEINEMANN, ALLEN W., rehabilitation psychologist; PhD, U. Kans., Lawrence, 1977—82. Lic. clin. psychologist Ill., 1984. Prof. Feinberg Sch. Medicine, Northwestern U., Chgo., 1985—; dir. ctr. rehab. outcomes rsch. Rehab. Inst. Chgo., 1988—. Pres. Am. Congress Rehab. Medicine, Indpls., 2004—06. Recipient Essie Morgan Excellence award, Am. Assn. Spinal Cord Injury Psychologists & Social Workers, 2003. Fellow: Am. Congress Rehab. Medicine (Disting. Mem. award 2006); mem.: APA (pres. rehab. psychology divsn. 2004—05, Harold Yuker award for rsch. excellence 2004, Roger Barker Disting. Career award 2000). Office: Rehab Inst Chgo 345 E Superior St Chicago IL 60611

HEINEMANN, LARRY C., writer; b. Chgo., Jan. 18, 1944; s. John Hubert and Dorothy Heinemann; m. Edith Jane, Apr. 27, 1968; children: Sarah Catherine, Preston John. BA, Columbia Coll., 1971; AA, Kendall Coll., 1966. Tchr. Columbia Coll., Chgo., 1971—86; writer-in-residence U. Mass., Boston, 1991—2002, DePaul U., Chgo., 2000—02. Writer-in-residence Northwestern U., Evanston, Ill., spring 1996, U. So. Calif., L.A., fall 1996. Author: Close Quarters, 1977, Paco's Story, 1986 (Nat. Book award, 1987), Cooler by the Lake, 1992, Black Virgin Mountain: A Return to Vietnam, 2005; contbr. articles to numerous mags. Bd. dirs. City Chgo. Adv. Com. Vets. Affairs, 1988-90, Nat. Vets. Legal Svcs. Project, 1990, My Lai Peace Park Project, Madison, Wis., 1995—. Sgt. U.S. Army, 1966-68, Vietnam. Recipient Nat. Book award Nat. Book Found., 1987, Carl Sandburg award Chgo. Pub. Libr. Assn., 1987, Fiction award Soc. Midland Authors, 1987; fellow NEA, 1982, 86, Guggenheim, N.Y.C., 1988-89, Steinberg/Pen U. Pa., 1989; Regent's scholar U. Calif., Davis, spring 1995. Buddhist. Office: c/o Doubleday Random House 1745 Broadway New York NY 10019 Office Phone:.

HEINEMANN, PETER, artist, educator; b. Denver, Apr. 22, 1931; s. Arthur Mason Heinemann and Stella Irene Diana (Peckham) Cohen; m. Gisella Gross (div. Aug. 1970); children: Mark Elliot, Johanna Ellen; m. Marie Savettieier. Student, Black Mt. Coll., 1948-49. Tchr. Sch. Visual Arts, NYC, 1960—. One-person shows at Roko Gallery, 1954, 56, 59, Hacker Gallery, 1963, Gallery 120, 1983, Gallery Schlesinger, 1985, 87, 89, 92, Gallery Pehlesineer, 1994, 96, 97, 99, 2001, 03, 05; group exhbns. at Ctr. Figurative Painting, 55 Mercer St. Gallery, NY Studio Sch. Gallery, 1984, Prince St. Gallery, 1986, Lake Placid Ctr. for Arts, 1986, Visual Arts Mus. Recipient Creative Artists Program grant, 1972, 74, 77, NEA grantee, 1983, N.Y. Found. for Arts grantee, 1986; recipient Nat. Inst. Arts and Letters Childhassam Purchase award, 1972. Office: Sch Visual Arts 209 E 23rd St New York NY 10010-3994

HEINEN, JAMES ALBIN, electrical engineering educator; b. Milw., June 23, 1943; s. Albin Jacob and Viola (DeBuhr) H. BEE, Marquette U., 1964, MS, 1967, PhD, 1969. Registered profl. engr., Wis. Data analyst Med. Sch. Marquette U., Milw., 1963, teaching asst. elec. engring. dept., 1964-65, 65-66, research asst., 1966, NASA trainee, 1966-69, asst. prof., 1969—71, research assoc. Provost's Office, 1970, asst. prof. and grad. adminstr., 1971-73, assoc. prof., chmn. elec. engring. dept., 1973-76, assoc. prof., 1976-80, prof. elec. engring. and computer sci., 1980-87, prof., dir. grad. studies elec. and computer engring., 1987-95, prof. elec. and computer engring., 1995—99, rsch. prof., 1999—2000, prof. emeritus, 2000—, dir. signal processing rsch. ctr., 1990-99, co-dir. ctr. intelligent syss., controls, and signal processing, 1999—2001. Cons. in field. Contbr. numerous articles and revs. on elec. engring. and computer sci. to profl. jours. Recipient Outstanding Engring. Tchr. award Marquette U., 1979, Teaching Excellence award Marquette U., 1985. Mem. IEEE (various coms., tech. reviewer Trans. Automatic Control 1969—, Trans. Circuits and Systems Soc. 1980—, Signal Processing Soc. 1980—, sr. mem., Meml. award Milw. sect. 1981, assoc. editor Trans. Circuits and Systems 1983-85, assoc. editor Trans. Indsl. Electronics 1996-2000), Am. Soc. Engring. Edn., Sigma Xi, Tau Beta Pi, Eta Kappa Nu (Most Outstanding Elec. Engring. Tchr. in U.S. award 1974), Pi Mu Epsilon, Alpha Sigma Nu. Home: 8200 W Menomonee River Pky Wauwatosa WI 53213-2537 Office: Marquette U Haggerty Hall Rm 211 PO Box 1881 Milwaukee WI 53201-1881 Home Phone: 414-476-6367; Office Phone: 414-288-3500. Business E-Mail: james.heinen@marquette.edu.

HEINEN, JOHN TIMOTHY, environmental engineer; b. Oshkosh, Wis., Sept. 30, 1966; adopted s. Larry John and Marie Jane Heinen, s. John Paul Fink and Judith Loretta Bloedow; m. Leslie Dawn Gahagan (div. Jan. 2, 1997); children: Timothy J., Zoë N. BS in Indsl. Tech. summa cum laude, U. Wis., Platteville, 1989. Cert. hazardous waste mgmt. Lion Tech., Inc. R & D engr. Intermet Foundries, Inc., Lynchburg, Va., 1990—93; indsl. engr. Richland Ctr. Foundry Co., Richland Center, Wis., 1993—95, indsl. systems engr., 1995—2000, environ. dir., 2000—03, environ. health and safety dir., 2003—. Chmn. Richland County Local Emergency Planning Com., Richland Center, 1999—. Contbr. articles to profl. jours.; moderator for: Dennis Kucinichm, www.kucinich.us. Mem.: AAAS, Ocean Arks, Internat., Am. Foundry Soc. (sec. 1996—99, environ. com.), Gt. Lakes Pollution Prevention Roundtable, Fedn. of Environ. Techs. (cert.), Am. Chem. Soc., Nature Conservancy, Smithsonian Instn., Nat. Geog. Soc., Am. Black Holocaust Mus., Sierra Club, Epsilon Pi Tau, Phi Kappa Phi. Avocation: studies in: cosmology, philosophy, cultural anthropology, complex systems, natural & artificial intelligence and ecology. Home: 215 South Park St Richland Center WI 53581 Office: Richland Ctr Foundry Co 1000 Foundry Dr Richland Center WI 53581 Office Phone: 608-647-1420. Personal E-mail: atla201@yahoo.com. Business E-Mail: jheinen@rcfoundry.com.

HEINEY, JOHN WEITZEL, former utilities executive; b. Lancaster, Pa., Nov. 9, 1913; s. George and Gertrude G. (Weitzel) H.; m. Betty M. Horn, Apr. 12, 1941. BS in Bus. Adminstrn, Lehigh U., 1935. With various subsidiaries Am. Water Works Co., 1935-41, 46-60; pres., chief exec. officer, dir. Indiana Gas Co., Inc., Indpls., 1960-73, chmn. bd., chief exec. officer, 1973-78, chmn. bd., 1978-84; pres., dir. Ohio River Pipe Line Corp., 1964-73, chmn. bd., 1973-78; pres., chmn. Gen. Assurance Services, Ltd., 1975-84. Bd. dirs. United Fund Greater Indpls., 1960-77; bd. dirs. Community Hosp. Indpls., 1968-73, 75-81, chmn., 1972-73; bd. dirs., chmn. Community Hosps. Found., 1983-89. Served to lt. col., inf. AUS, 1941-46. Decorated Bronze Star medal; named Sagamore of Wabash, Gov. of Ind., 1997. Mem. Am. Gas Assn. (past chmn. spl. com. on consumer affairs, 1st vice chmn. 1968, chmn. 1969, dir. Disting. Svcs. award com. 1975), Ind. Gas Assn. (past pres. and dir.), Inst. Gas Tech. (trustee 1965, chmn. bd. trustees 1968), Internat. Gas Union (mem. council and bur. 1973-75), Ind. C. of C. (dir. 1973-80), Newcomen Soc. N.Am., Beta Theta Pi, Am. Legion. Clubs: Meridian Hills Country.

HEINICKE, RALPH MARTIN, science administrator, consultant; b. Hickory, NC, Sept. 3, 1914; s. Martin John and Lydia Sophia (Kurth) H.; m. Sarah Anne Hall, July 31, 1944; 1 child, Mark. BS, Cornell U., 1936; PhD, U. Minn., St. Paul, 1950. Agr. chemist Shell Oil Co., NYC, 1939-43; tech. advisor Jintan-Dolph, Osaka, Japan, 1962-86; assoc. faculty U. Hawaii, Honolulu, 1950-86; chemist Pineapple Rsch. Inst., Honolulu, 1950-55; dir. rsch. Dole Co., Honolulu, 1955-72; v.p. Biol. Control Systems, Honolulu, 1981-86; pres. Biotech. Resources Inc., Clarksville, Ind., 1990-94; cons. Morinda, Inc., 1996. Cons. various drug cos., 1972—; cons. on the xeronine-sys. Inventor, patentee on xeronine; inventor, patentee on nerve toxin insecticide, proxeronine, proxerinonase. Master sgt. U.S. Army, 1942-45, CBI. Democrat. Avocations: music, writing, philosophy. Office Phone: 502-896-1693. Personal E-mail: rheinicke@bellsouth.net.

HEINKE, REX S., lawyer; b. Ill., 1950; s. William and Versa Heinke; m. Margaret Nagle, 1978; children: William, Meghan. BA, U. Witwatersrand, Johannesburg, Republic of South Africa, 1971; JD, U. Columbia, 1975. Bar: Calif. 1975. Ptnr. Gibson, Dunn & Crutcher, LA, 1983-99, Greines, Martin, Stein & Richland, 1999—2001, Akin, Gump, Strauss, Hauer & Feld, 2001—. Office: 2029 Century Park E Ste 2400 Los Angeles CA 90067 Office Phone: 310-229-1000. Business E-Mail: rheinke@akingump.com.

HEINLE, BEVERLY DIANE, publishing executive; d. Charles William Hoffman and Beryl Dorothy Hoffman-Ferree; m. Charles A.S. Heinle, Dec. 25, 1973; children: Elisabeth Beryl, Katherine Margaretta. MA, W.Va. U., Morgantown, W. Va., 1966. Editl. sec. Ginn & Co., Boston, 1966—66; asst. to editor-in-chief Blaisdell Pub., Waltham, Mass., 1967—67; dir. distbn. Ctr. for Curriculum Devel. in Audio-Visual Lang. Tchg., Phila., 1967—72; editor-in-chief/dir. of advt. and promotion F.W. Faxon Co., Dedham, Mass., 1973—82; pres. H & H Advt., Concord, Mass., 1983—91; editor-in-chief Pimsleur Internat., Concord, Mass., 1992—97; exec. editor Pimsleur Lang. Programs/Simon & Schuster Audio, Concord, Mass., 1997—. Editor (foreign-lang. courses) 35 different Lang.:, author created model for future Pimsleur programs. Avocations: ice skating, classical music, science fiction, yoga. Home: 29 Lexington Rd Concord MA 01742 Office: Pimsleur Lang Programs 30 Monument Sq Concord MA 01742 Home Phone: 978-369-4858; Office Phone: 978-369-7525 202. Business E-Mail: beverly.heinle@simonandschuster.com.

HEINLE, RICHARD ALAN, lawyer; b. New Kensington, Pa., May 13, 1959; s. Robert Alan and Barbara Jane (Klimeck) H.; m. Sharon Eileen Farrell, Oct. 20, 1990; children: Kelly, Kyra, Casey. AB with highest honors, U. Chgo., 1981; JD cum laude, Georgetown U., 1984. Bar: Ill. 1984, Fla. 1994. Assoc. Arnstein & Lehr, Chgo., 1984-89, Foley & Lardner, Chgo., 1989-93, ptnr. Orlando, Fla., 1994—2003, Pohl & Short, P.A., Winter Park, Fla., 2003—. Counsel BBB Ctrl. Fla., Orlando, 1996-03. Bd. dirs. Better Bus. Bur. Ctrl. Fla., 2003—. Mem.: Fla. C. of C. (bd. dirs. 1999—2000), Mfrs. Assn. Ctrl. Fla. (bd. dirs. 1995—2005), Phi Beta Kappa. Roman Catholic. Avocations: golf, running. Home: 8100 Vineland Oaks Blvd Orlando FL 32835-8215 Office: Pohl & Short PA 280 W Canton Ste 410 Winter Park FL 32789 Home Phone: 407-293-1189. Business E-Mail: rheinle@alumni.uchicago.edu.

HEINLEN, DANIEL LEE, alumni organization administrator, consultant; b. Columbus, Ohio, Nov. 16, 1937; s. Calvin Xenophon and Charlotte Elizabeth (Lanman) H.; m. Roberta Bishop, Mar. 20, 1966 (div. 1975); m. Gelene Vogel Kozlowski, June 17, 1978; children: Stephanie Heinlen, Kate Kozlowski Isler, Amy Heinlen. BS in Social Work, Ohio State U., 1960. Youth program dir., ext. dir. YMCA, Pitts., 1960-65; field dir. Alumni Assn., Ohio State U., Columbus, 1965-67, assoc. dir., 1967-73, dir. alumni affairs, 1973-92; pres., CEO Ohio State U. Alumni Assn., Inc., 1992—2003, pres., CEO emeritus, 2004—; sec. Alumni Assn. Bd., 1973—2003; pub. mag. Alumni Assn., Ohio State U., 1973—2003; sr. consulting v.p. Grenzebach Glier and Assoc., Inc., Chgo., 2004—07; pres. DLH. LLC, Lewis Center, Ohio, 2004—. Ex-officio trustee Ohio State U. Found.; presdl. search com. Ohio State U., 1990, 97, 2002; trustee Coun. for Advancement and Support of Higher Edn., Washington, 1986-88, 90-94, chmn., 1992-93; chmn. 75th anniversary Colloquium, Columbus, 1988, chmn. ann. assembly alumni track, 1988, chmn. ann. assembly, 1990; chmn. Mgmt. Inst. for Alumni Assn. Execs., Chgo., 1996, pres., 1994-96, bd. dirs., 1988-96; founding bd. Coun. Alumni Assn. Execs. 1989-96, pres. 1992-93; chmn. Univ. ProNet, Inc., Palo Alto, Calif., 1996-99, chmn. alumni dirs. Big Ten, 1973, 84, 93; mem. Ohio State U. Pres.'s Coun., 1991-98; bd. dirs. River Road Hotel Corp.; founding chmn. Self-Governing Alumni Forum, 2000-2003; chmn. task force on alumni advocacy Inter Univ. Coun., 2002. Author chpts. in books. Mem. exec. com. N.W. Ordinance U.S. Constn. Bicentennial Commn., Ohio, 1986-88; bd. dirs. Non-profit Mailers Fedn., Wash., 1985-88; mem. OSU Com. on Student Fin. Aids, Columbus, 1973-99, exec. com. Acad. Disting. Tchg., 1995-2003, Newcomen Soc. N.Am., 1975-90, 93-2003. Med. specialist USAR, 1962—67, hon. discharge USAR, 1967. Recipient Ohio State U. Coll. of Social Work Disting. Svc. award, 1996, Disting. Svc. award CASE Dist. 5, 2003, Everett Reese medal Svc. in Philanthropy Ohio State U., 2003, Frank Ashmore award CASE Internat., 2004, Ohio State U. Disting. Svc. award, 2005; named Hon. Trustee Easter Seal Rehab. Ctr. of Ctrl. Ohio, Columbus, 1988-92; D.L. Heinlen award for univ. advocacy named in his honor Ohio Sate U. Alumni Assn., Inc., 1995. Mem. Rotary (bd. dirs. Columbus Club 1986, v.p. 1987-89, pres. 1989-90), U. Club (bd. dirs., 2nd v.p. 1985-88, 94-95, 1st v.p. 1996), Faculty Club (mem. bd. control 1978-80, pres.-elect 1999, pres. 2000-01), Kit Kat (exec. com. 1999-2002, sec. 2001-07), Golden Key Nat. Honor Soc. (hon.), Sphinx Coun. (convener, 1983-2003, hon. chair Sr. Hon. Centennial Celebration). Avocations: tennis, sporting clays, horseback riding. Home and Office: 2981 E Powell Rd Lewis Center OH 43035-9517 Business E-Mail: heinlen.4@osu.edu.

HEINRICH, BERND, biologist, educator; b. Bad Polzin, Poland, Apr. 19, 1940; came to US, 1950, naturalized, 1951; s. Gerd Hermann and Hildegard Maria (Bury) H. BA in Zoology, U. Maine, 1964, MS in Zoology, 1966; PhD in Zoology, UCLA, 1970; PhD (hon.), U. Maine, 1999, Unity Coll., Maine, 1986, PhD (hon.), 2000; MA in Philosophy and Human Ecology, Coll. Atlantic, 2006. Teaching and research asst. UCLA, 1966-70; asst. prof. entomology U. Calif., Berkeley, 1971-75, assoc. prof., 1975-78, prof., 1978-80; prof. biology U. Vt., Burlington, 1981—2003, prof. emeritus, 2004—. Author: Bumblebee Economics, 1979, Insect Thermoregulation, 1981, In a Patch of Firewood, 1984, One Man's Owl, 1987, Ravens in Winter, 1989, The Hot-Blooded Insects, 1993, A Year in the Maine Woods, 1994, The Thermal Warriors, 1996, The Trees in My Forest, 1998, Mind of the Raven, 1999, Racing the Antelope, 2001, Why We Run, 2001, The Winter World, 2003, The Geese of a Beaver Bog, 2003, The Snoring Bird, 2007; co-author: Biology, 1979; contbr. numerous articles to sci. jours. Recipient Burroughs, Winship and Rutstrums Author's awards, 1984, 95; Guggenheim fellow, 1976-77, von Humboldt fellow, 1988-89. Mem. Am. Ornithological Union, NAS, Sigma Xi; Fellow Am. Acad. Arts & Sciences. Office: U Vermont Dept Biology Marsh Life Science Bui Burlington VT 05405-0001

HEINRICH, DANIEL J., chemicals executive; b. Gridley, Calif. BBA, U. Calif., Berkeley, Calif.; MBA, Saint Mary's Coll. CPA. With Ford Fin. Svcs. Group; acct. Ernst and Young; sr. v.p., treas. Transamerica Fin. Corp., San Francisco; controller The Clorox Co., Oakland, Calif., 2001—03, CFO, 2003—. Office: Clorox Co 1221 Broadway Oakland CA 94612-1888

HEINRICH, RANDALL WAYNE, lawyer; b. Houston, Nov. 29, 1958; s. Albert Joseph Sr. and Beverly June Earles; m. Linda Carol Cheek, June 6, 1993; children: Angela Leigh, Conrad Randall. BA, Baylor U., 1980, postgrad., 1981, Rice U., 1981-82; JD, U. Tex., 1985. Bar: Tex. 1985. Assoc. Baker & Botts, Houston, 1985-87, Chamberlain, Hrdlicka, White, Williams & Martin, Houston, 1987-91, Norton & Blair, Houston, 1991-92; mem. Gillis Paris & Heinrich, Houston, 1992—; mng. dir. Baytree Investors, Houston, 1993-97. Mem. dirs.' circle Houston Grand Opera, 1991, The Arts Symposium, 1991, Center Stage, Alley Theater, Houston, 1992-93, Houston Entrepreneurs' Forum, 1990-91; bd. dirs. The Cadre, 1991-92; pres. Exchange Club of Bayou City, 1992-93. Mem. ABA (YLD securities law com. 1993-95, vice chmn. 1994-95), NASD Pool Securities Arbitrators, Am. Arbitration Assn. (mem. nat. panel neutrals), Houston Bar Assn., Forum Club Houston, Phi Delta Theta. Baptist. Home: 4318 Saint Michaels Ct Sugar Land TX 77479-2986 Office: Gillis Paris & Heinrich 8 Greenway Plz Ste 818 Houston TX 77046 Office Phone: 713-951-9100. E-mail: heinrich@pdq.net.

HEINRICHS, APRIL, soccer coach; b. Charlottesville, Va., Feb. 27, 1964; BA in Radio, TV and Motion Pictures, U. N.C., 1986. Lic. U.S. Soccer Federation "A" coaching license. Player U.S. Nat. Team, 1986—91; profl. soccer player Prato, Italy, 1987—92; head coach Princeton U., 1990, U. Md., 1991—95, U. Va., 1996—99; full time asst. U.S. Women's Nat. Team, 1995—97; mem. coaching staff 1995 Women's World Cup, 1995, 1996 Olympic Women's Soccer Team, 1996; head coach U.S. U-16 Nat. Team, 1997—2000; head coach, tech. dir. U.S. Women's Nat. Team, 2000—. Mem. NCAA Championship Team, 1983, 84, 86. Recipient U.S. Soccer Female Athlete of Yr. award, 1986, 89; voted female player of the 1980s Soccer America Magazine; first female inducted into Nat. Soccer Hall of Fame, 1998; named First Team All-American U. N.C. (3 times); inaugural recipient NSCAA Women's Com. award of Excellence, 2000. Achievements include coached U.S. Women's Soccer Team to Silver Medal, Sydney Olympic Games, 2000. Office: US Soccer House 1801-1811 S Prairie Ave Chicago IL 60616

HEINSOHN KROPP, HOLLY LYNN, educational consultant, history professor, researcher; b. Corpus Christi, Tex., Dec. 27, 1966; d. Earl Lowell Heinsohn and Betty Jean Winkenwerder Heinsohn; m. Richard Karl Kropp, Jan. 22, 1994; 1 child, Braden Walter Heinsohn Kropp. BA in Humanities, U. Houston, Victoria, Tex., 1992, MA in Interdisciplinary Studies, 2003. Educator cert. Tex., 1992. Ednl. cons. Nat. Evaluation Sys., Inc., Austin, Tex., 2002—; history instr. Victoria Coll., 2004—. Contbr. articles to profl. jours. Tchr. Luth. Ch., Shiner, Tex., 2007. Grantee, Honeywell Corp., 1992. Mem.: Tex. State Geneal. Soc., Lavaca County Hist. Commn. (assoc.), Tex. State Hist. Assn. (assoc.), Tex. Coun. Social Studies (assoc.), Tex. Assn. Gifted and Talented (assoc.), German-Texan Heritage Soc. (assoc.), Gamma Beta Phi (life). Personal E-mail: hheinsohn@yahoo.com.

HEINTZ, CAROLINEA CABANISS, retired home economist, educator; b. Roanoke, Va., Jan. 19, 1920; d. Luther Bertie and Emblyn Bird (Jennings) Cabaniss; m. Howard Elmer Smith, Dec. 19, 1942 (div. Aug. 1975); children: Emblyn Davis, Cynthia Shannon, Cheryl Peterson, Melyssa Sexton; m. Raymond Walter Heintz, May 21, 1977; 1 stepchild, James. BS in Home Econ. Edn., U. Ala., Tuscaloosa, 1941; vocat. home econ. degree, Montevallo Coll., Ala., 1941. Cert. vocat. home econs. tchr. Swimming instr. Camp Mudjekeewis, Centerlovel, Maine, summer 1940; home econs. tchr. Roanoke Pub. Schs., 1941-43; dietitian U. Va., Charlottesville, 1943; nutrition edn. specialist Liberty Health Ctr. Svcs., Liberty Center, Ohio, 1974-80; home economist Dayton Hudson Dept. Store, Toledo, 1980-84; splty. food instr., continuing edn. U. Toledo, 1984-85. Pres., mem. Greater Toledo Nutrition Coun., 1966-98; pres. Sunset House Aux., 1999-2001, bd. dirs., 2001—. Co-editor ch. cookbook Loaves and Fishes and Other Dishes, 2000. Spkr. United Way, Toledo, 1965-90; founder, pres. Mobile Meals Toledo, Inc., 1968-71, mem. adv. bd., 1988-2007, bd. dirs., 2005, chmn. pub. rels., 1997-99, nominating com., 2000-04, mem. long-range planning com., 2005-07, Spirit of Mobile Meals award, 1998; affiliate mem. Arts Commn., Toledo, 1976-77; chmn. Saphire Ball, Toledo Symphony Orch., Toledo Opera, 1978; adminstrv. coord. Feed Your Neighbor program Met. Chs. United, Toledo, 1979-86; deacon Collingwood Presbyn. Ch., 1969-71, elder, 1972-74, 77-79, 97-99, 2001-05, trustee, 1984-86, elder, clk. of session, 1991-94, stewardship chmn., 1996-97, del. to Maumee Valley Presbytery, 1991-99; mem. steering com. Interfaith Hospitality Network, 1992-94, bd. dirs., 1993-94; alt. del. Gen. Assembly Presbyn. Ch. U.S.A., 1993, del.-commr., 1994. Recipient Woman of Toledo award St. Vincent Hosp. and Med. Ctr. Guild, 1967, 80, Outstanding Community Svc. award United Way, 1987, Henry Morse vol. award, Greater Toledo award United Way, 1998, runner-up Nat. Vol. of the Year award Project Meal Found., Reynolds Metal Co., 1998. Mem. AAUW (bd. dirs. 1974-76, 94-96, 97-98, chmn. mem. gourmet group 1966-99, 2001, 03, edn. found. chmn. 1994-96, book sale chmn. 1998, chmn. nominating com. 2005-06), Ohio Med. Aux. (1st v.p. 1973-74), Aux. Acad. Medicine (pres. 1967-68, chmn. edn. gourmet group 1966-99, 2001-03, Health Care award 1974), Indian Trails Garden Club (pres. 1997-98), Sigma Kappa (various alumni offices). Republican. Avocations: volunteering, gourmet cooking, travel, bridge. Home: # 108 4030 Indian Rd Toledo OH 43606-2225

HEINTZ, FLORENT M., art appraiser; ThM, Harvard Univ., 1993, PhD in Classical Archaeology, 1999. Keeper of coins Harvard Univ. Art Mus.; curatorial asst. Worcester Art Mus, Mass.; antiquities specialist to asst. v.p. Sotheby's, NYC, 2001—. Author: Agnostic Magic in the Late Antique Circus, 1999. Named a Dumbarton Oaks Jr. Fellow, Harvard Univ., 1998—99. Office: Sotheby's NY 1334 York Ave New York NY 10021 Home Phone: 212-492-4277; Office Phone: 212-606-7266. Office Fax: 212-894-1371. Business E-Mail: florent.heintz@sothebys.com.

HEINTZ, JOHN EDWARD, lawyer; b. Bronxville, NY, Dec. 12, 1948; s. Howard Theodore and Ruth Janet (Brodhead) Heintz; m. Lynn Ann Ohman, June 21, 1980; children: Eric John, Jennifer Ann. BA, Cornell U., 1970; MPA, Princeton U., 1974; JD, NYU, 1977. Assoc. Covington & Burling, Washington, 1977-86; shareholder Popham, Haik, Schnobrich & Kaufman, Ltd., Washington, 1986-91; ptnr. Howrey, Simon, Arnold & White, LLP, Washington, 1991-2000, Gilbert Heintz & Randolph LLP, Washington, 2000—07, Kelley, Drye & Warren, LLP, Washington, 2007—. Contbr. articles to profl. jours. Democrat. Avocations: sailing, swimming. Office: Kelley Drye & Warren LLP 3050 K St NW Ste 400 Washington DC 20007-5108

HEINY, JAMES RAY, lawyer; b. Albert Lea, Minn., Oct. 7, 1928; s. Albin James and Lola Marguerite (Keig) H.; m. Wava Jeanine Isaacson, Sept. 2, 1951 (dec. 1980); children: Jon Carl, Jane Ellen Heiny Smith, Ann Elizabeth Heiny Hohenshell, Thomas James; m. Norma Lou West, July 24, 1982. BA, Grinnell Coll., 1950; JD, U. Iowa, 1953. Bar: Iowa 1953. Assoc. Westfall, Laird & Burington, Mason City, Iowa, 1955—58; ptnr. Heiny, McManigal, Duffy, Stambaugh & Anderson, Mason City, 1958—. Pres. Luth. Social Svcs. Iowa FODN, 1987—2001; bd. dirs. YMCA, Mason City, 1972—75; pres. Good Shepherd Geriatric Ctr., Inc., Mason City, 1960—72. With US Army, 1953—55. Mem. ABA, Iowa State Bar Assn. (bd. govs. 1986-91), Cerro Gordo County Bar Assn. (pres. 1976). Republican. Avocations: amateur radio, bird watching, sports. Home: 2040 Hunters Ridge Dr Mason City IA 50401-7500 Office: Heiny McManigal et al 11 Fourth ST NE Mason City IA 50401 Office Phone: 641-423-5154. Business E-Mail: jheiny@heinymcmanigal.com.

HEINZ, JEREMY DAVID, military officer; b. Knoxville, Tenn., Sept. 19, 1979; s. Jeff Scott Heinz and Judy Diane Yarbrough; m. Kelly Ann Heinz, May 12, 2006. Cert. CPR, self-aid buddy care instructor 72nd Med. Group, Tinker AFB, Okla., 2004. Enlisted USAF, 2002, advanced through ranks to staff sgt.; radar maintainence craftsman 34th Combat Comm. Sqaudron, Tinker AFB, Okla., 2001—. Vol. Oklahoma City Animal Shelter, 2006—07. Named Airman of Quarter, Tinker AFB, 2006; recipient Freedom Citation award, 2006. Mem.: Air Force Sgts. Assn. (assoc.). Republican. Office: 34th Combat Comms Squadron 4437 S Air Depot Blvd Tinker AFB OK 73145 Home Phone: 405-326-7230; Office Phone: 405-734-3634.

HEINZ, JOHN PETER, lawyer, educator; b. Carlinville, Ill., Aug. 6, 1936; s. William Henry and Margaret Louise (Denby) H.; m. Anne Murray, Jan. 14, 1967; children: Katherine Reynolds, Peter Lindley Murray. AB, Washington U., St. Louis, 1958; LLB, Yale U., 1962. Bar: D.C. 1962, Ill. 1966, U.S. Supreme Ct. 1967. Teaching asst. polit. sci. Washington U., St. Louis, 1958-59, instr., 1960; asst. prof. Northwestern U. Sch. Law, Chgo., 1965-68, assoc. prof., 1968-71, prof., 1971-88, Owen L. Coon prof., 1988—, dir. program law and social scis., 1968-70, dir. rsch., 1973-74, prof. sociology, 1987—. Affiliated scholar Am. Bar Found., Chgo., 1974—, vis. scholar, 1975-76, exec. dir., 1982-86, disting. research fellow, 1987—. Author: (with A. Gordon) Public Access to Information, 1979, (with E. Laumann) Chicago Lawyers, 1982, rev. edit., 1994, (with E. Laumann, R. Nelson, R. Salisbury) The Hollow Core, 1993, (with R. Nelson, R. Sandefur and E. Laumann) Urban Lawyers, 2005; contbr. articles to profl. jours. Served to capt. USAF, 1962-65 Grantee NIMH, 1970-72, NSF, 1970, 78-81, 84-86, 94-97, CNA Found., 1972, Am. Bar Found., 1974—, Russell Sage Found., 1978-80. Fellow: Am. Bar Found.; mem.: ABA, Chgo. Coun. Lawyers, Law and Soc. Assn. (Harry Kalven prize for disting. rsch. 1987). Home: 525 Judson Ave Evanston IL 60202-3083 Office: Northwestern U Sch Law 357 E Chicago Ave Chicago IL 60611-3059 Office Phone: 312-503-8473. Business E-Mail: j-heinz@law.northwestern.edu.

HEINZ, WILLIAM DENBY, lawyer; b. Carlinville, Ill., Nov. 26, 1947; s. William Henry and Margaret (Denby) H.; children: Kimberly, Rebecca, Elizabeth; m. Catherine Lamb Heinz. BS, Millikin U., 1969; JD, U. Ill., 1973. Bar: Ill. 1973, U.S. Dist. Ct. (no. dist.) Ill. 1974, U.S. Ct. Appeals (3d cir.) 1982, U.S. Ct. Appeals (5th cir.) 1973, U.S. Ct. Appeals (7th cir.) 1976, U.S. Supreme Ct. 1979. Law clk. to judge U.S. Ct. Appeals (5th cir.), Tuscaloosa, Ala., 1973-74; assoc. Jenner & Block, Chgo., 1974-80, ptnr., 1980—; mem. faculty NITA, 1981—. Adj. prof. Northwestern U. Sch. Law, 1995—; mem. bd. dir. The North Am. Co. for Life and Health Ins., 2002—; bd. visitors U. Ill. Coll. Law, 1990-93, pres.'s coun. U. Ill.; bd. dirs., chair Legal Aid Bur., Chgo.; bd. dirs. exec. com. Met. Family Svcs. Chgo; mem. bd. dirs. Ptnrs Fin. Holdings, Inc., 2003—. Recipient Disting. Grad. award U. Ill. Coll. Law, 1995. Fellow Am. Coll. Trial Lawyers; mem. ABA, Ill. Bar Assn. (civil practice and procedure sect. coun., com. on liaison with Ill. ARDC, task force on multi-disciplinary practice), Chgo. Bar Assn. (jud. evaluation com. 1990-93), ARDC Ill. Profl. Responsibility Inst., Cribbett Soc., U. Ill. Coll. Law, Legal Club (bd. dirs. 1998-2000), Westmoreland Country Club. Home: 437 Sheridan Rd Kenilworth IL 60043-1220 Office: Jenner & Block 1 E Ibm Plz Fl 46 Chicago IL 60611-3586 Office Phone: 312-923-2763. E-mail: wheinz@jenner.com.

HEINZE, MARK WILLIAM, elementary school educator; s. Raymon Heinze and Lela Rossini; m. Carrie Heinze, June 28, 1986; children: Greg, Kristin. BA, U. Calif., Santa Barbara, 1982; MA, U. Hawaii, Honolulu, 1984. Tchr. San Diego City Schs. Broadcaster acad. league instructional television San Diego County Office Edn., 2002—. Mem. So. Poverty Ctr., 2001—, PTA, 1990—. Home Phone: 619-218-5065.

HEINZELMAN, KRIS F., lawyer; b. Monroe, Wis., Jan. 9, 1951; AB, Brown U., 1973, MA magna cum laude, 1973; JD, Yale U., 1976. Bar: N.Y. 1977. Assoc. Cravath, Swain & Moore, NYC, 1976—83, ptnr., corp. dept, 1983—. Named one of 12 Dealmakers of the Yr., The Am. Lawyer, 2004. Mem.: ABA, Am. Coll. Investment Counsel, Assn. of the Bar of the City of N.Y., N.Y. State Bar Assn. Office: Cravath Swain & Moore Worldwide Plz 825 8th Ave Fl 38 New York NY 10019-7475 also: 1 Chase Manhattan Plz New York NY 10005-1401 Office Phone: 212-474-1336. Office Fax: 212-474-3700. Business E-Mail: kheinzelman@cravath.com.

HEINZEN, BERNARD GEORGE, lawyer; b. Hendricks, Minn., Sept. 18, 1930; s. Bernard Martin and Thelma Harrington (Bowers) H.; m. Maryann Mullen, Aug. 25, 1978; children from previous marraige: John Masters, Robert Kenneth (dec.), James Warren, William Martin. BA, Carleton Coll., 1953; LLB, NYU, 1956. Bar: Minn. 1956, U.S. Supreme Ct. 1969, Pa. 1978. Atty., legal adviser U.S. Dept. State, Washington, 1956-58; assoc. Dorsey & Whitney, Mpls., 1960-65, ptnr., 1966-76; spl. asst. atty. gen. State of Minn., St. Paul, 1967-70; gen. counsel Consol. Rail Corp., Phila., 1976-77; counsel Harvey, Pennington, Herting & Renneisen, Ltd., Phila., 1977-83; pres. Bernard G. Heinzen, Ltd., Phila., 1978—2004; ptnr. Stassen, Kostos & Mason, Phila., 1983-85; pres., bd. dirs. Rittenhouse Town Watch, Inc., Phila., 1993—; gen. counsel Logan Capital Mgmt., Inc., Ardmore, 1995—. Dir. Chamber Orch. of Phila., 1995—; adviser U.S. del. to Geneva Conf. on Law of Sea, 1958. Contbr. Stanford Law Rev., 1959; assoc. editor NYU Law Rev., 1955-56. Mem. Citizens Com. on Pub. Edn., Mpls., 1964-76; exec. com. state cen. com. Minn. Rep. Party, 1967-71; vestryman The Ch. of the Holy Trinity, Phila., 1998-2006. 1st lt. U.S. Army, 1957-60. Mem. ABA, Phila. Bar Assn., Minn. Bar Assn. (chmn. com. on ins. 1970-73), Am. Judicature Soc. (life), Racquet Club Phila., Merion Cricket Club (Haverford, Pa.), Union League Phila., Phi Beta Kappa. Republican. Episcopalian. Home: 1901 Walnut St Philadelphia PA 19103-4640 Office: 6 Coulter Ave Suburban Sw Ardmore PA 19003-2308 Home Phone: 215-567-4780.

HEINZERLING, LARRY EDWARD, communications executive; b. Elyria, Ohio, Aug. 28, 1945; s. Lynn Louis and Agnes Corinne (Dengate) H.; m. Sharyn Lee Jorgensen, Jan. 11, 1969 (div. 1985); children: Jesse, Kristen, Benjamin; m. Sieglinde Wolf, Aug. 1, 1985 (dec. Mar. 1998); stepchildren: Andreas Klohnen, Eva Klohnen; m. Ann Kathleen Cooper, May 12, 2001; 1 stepchild: Tom Keller. BA in Polit. Sci., Journalism, Ohio Wesleyan U., 1967; MA in Internat. Journalism, Ohio State U., 1969. Reporter AP, Columbus, Ohio, 1969-71, corr. Lagos, Nigeria, 1971-74, bur. chief Johannesburg, South Africa, 1974-78, mng. dir. Frankfurt, Germany, 1978-83, dir. world services NYC, 1983-87; dep. dir. AP World Svc., NYC, 1987-2000, also spl. asst. to AP pres., dep. internat. editor, 2000—. News coverage includes: coverage West Africa including Sahel drought, 1971-74, coverage Soweto riots, Mozambique independence, Angola, Rhodesia (now Zimbabwe); co-editor: Fundamental Analysis Worldwide: Investing and Managing Money in International Capital Markets, 1996; contbg. author: Breaking News: How the Associated Press Has Covered War, Peace and Everything Else, 2007. Trustee Ohio Wesleyan U., 1993-96, Bancroft, Inc., 1993-97, Bancroft Schs. and Cmtys., 1997-2002. Recipient Headliners award Headliners Club, Atlantic City, 1977, AP reportorial Performance award Mng. Editors, N.Y.C., 1977; nominated for Pulitzer Prize, 1976. Mem. Phi Delta Theta. Roman Catholic. Avocations: foreign affairs, history, philosophy, science. Office: AP 450 West 33rd ST New York NY 10001 Home Phone: 212-316-1801. Business E-Mail: lheinzerling@ap.org.

HEINZ KERRY, TERESA (MARIA TERESA THIERSTEIN SIMOES-FERREIRA), foundation administrator; b. Mozambique, Oct. 5, 1938; d. Jose Simoes Ferreira and Irene Thierstein; m. John Heinz, Feb. 5, 1966 (dec. Apr. 4, 1991); children: John, Andre, Christopher; m. John Kerry, May 26, 1995; stepchildren: Alex, Vanessa. BA in Romance Langs., Lit., U. Witwatersrand, Johannesburg, South Africa, 1960; grad., U. Geneva, 1963; PhD (hon.), Beloit Coll., Wis., Bank ST. Coll. Edn., NYC, Drexel U., Pa., Med. Coll. Pa. Cons. UN Trusteeship, NYC; chmn. Heinz Family Found., Pitts., Howard Heinz Endowment; trustee Vira I. Heinz

Endowment; founder Women's Inst. for Secure retirement, 1996—. Endowed creation of professorship environ. mgmt. Harvard Bus. Sch., chair environ. policy John F. Kennedy Sch. Govt.; vice chair Environ. Def.; past mem. external adv. bd. Inst. Biospheric Studies, Yale U.; mem. adv. bd. Earth Comm. Office; founder Second Nature; co-founder, bd. dirs. Alliance to End Childhood Lead Poisoning; bd. dirs. Carnegie Corp., Family Comm.; trustee Brookings Inst.; former bd. dirs., trustee Phillips Exeter Acad., St. Paul's Sch., Georgetown U.; co-founder Nat. Coun. Families TV; featured speaker Dem. Nat. Convention, Boston, 2004. Co-author (with John Kerry): This Moment on Earth: Today's New Environmentalists and Their Vision for the Future, 2007. Founding mem., co-chair Congl. Wives Soviet Jewry; trustee governing bd. Yale Art Gallery; mem. trustees coun. Nat. Gallery Art; bd. dirs. Carnegie Inst., Pitts. Women's Leadership award, Save the Children Found., 2003, World Ecology award, Internat. Ctr. for Tropical Ecology, U. Mo., 2003, Albert Schweitzer Gold medal for Humanitarianism, John Hopkins U., 2003. Fellow: Am. Acad. Arts and Sciences. Avocation: art collecting. Office: The Heinz Family Office 1101 Pennsylvania Ave NW Ste 350 Washington DC 20004-2532*

HEIPLE, JAMES DEE, state supreme court justice; b. Peoria, Ill., Sept. 13, 1933; s. Rae Crane and Harriet (Birkett) H.; B.S., Bradley U., 1955; J.D., U. Louisville, 1957; Certificate in Internat. Law, City of London Coll., 1967; grad. Nat. Jud. Coll., 1971; LLM U. Va., 1988; m. Virginia Kerswill, July 28, 1956 (dec. Apr. 16, 1995); children: Jeremy Hans, Jonathan James, Rachel Duffield. Bar: Ill. 1957, Ky. 1958, U.S. Supreme Ct. 1962; partner Heiple and Heiple, Pekin, Ill., 1957-70; circuit judge Ill., 10th Circuit 1970-80; justice Ill. Appellate Ct., 1980-90; justice Ill. Supreme Ct., 1990—, ret., 2000. V.p., dir. Washington State Bank (Ill.), 1959-66; dir. Gridley State Bank (Ill.), 1958-59; village atty., Tremont, Ill., 1961-66, Mackinaw, Ill., 1961-66; asst. pub. defender Tazewell County, 1967-70., jud. clerk Ill. Appellate Ct., 1968-70. Chmn. Tazewell County Heart Fund, 1960. Pub. Adminstr. Tazewell County, Ill., 1959-61; sec. Tazewell County Republican Central Com. 1966-70; mem. Pekin Sch. Bd., 1970; mem. Ill. Supreme Ct. Com. on Profl. Responsibility, 1978-86. Recipient certificate Freedoms Found., 1975, George Washington honor medal, 1976, Bradley Centurion award Bradley U., 1995; named Disting. Alumnus, U. Louisville, 1992. Fellow ABA (life), Ill. Bar Found. (life), Ky. Bar Found. (life); mem. Ky., Ill. (chmn. legal edn. com. 1972-74, chmn. jud. sect. 1976-77, chmn. Bench and Bar Council 1984-85), Tazewell County Bar Assn. (pres. 1967-68), Ill. Judges Assn. (pres. 1978-79), Ky., Ill., Pa. hist. socs., S.A.R., War of 1812, Sons of Union Vets., Delta Theta Phi, Sigma Nu, Pi Kappa Delta. Methodist. Clubs: Filson; Union League (Chgo.), Country (Peoria). Lodge: Masons (33 degree). Office: PO Box 10495 Peoria IL 61612-0495 Office Phone: 309-682-7242. Business E-Mail: jamesdheiple@insightbb.com.

HEIRMAN, DONALD NESTOR, training engineering company executive, consultant, educator, director, research scientist; b. Mishawaka, Ind., Aug. 16, 1940; s. Chester J. and Agnes M. Heirman; m. Lois M. Heirman. BSEE, Purdue U., West Lafayette, Ind., 1962, MSEE, 1963. Mem. tech. staff, then disting. mem. tech. staff AT&T Bell Labs., Holmdel, NJ, 1963—83; mem. tech. staff Am. Bell, Holmdel, 1983—84; supr. AT&T Info. Sys., Holmdel, 1984—88; mgr. global product compliance lab. AT&T Bell Labs., Holmdel, 1989—96, Lucent Technologies Inc., 1996—97; adj. prof., sr. rsch. scientist, assoc. dir. wireless EMC Ctr. Study Wireless EMC, U. Okla., 1997—. US tech. expert subcoms. (SC) A and I, Internat. Spl. Com. on Radio Interference, 1986—; course dir. Ctr. for Profl. Advancment, East Brunswick, NJ, 1988-2003; cons. in field, 1998—; sec. SC A, CISPR, 1998-2000, chair, 2000--; chmn. SC A, WG1, 1998-2002; pres. Nat. Coop. for Lab. Accreditation, 1999-2001; com. mem. US Nat. Com. IEC Tech Mgmt., 2000-, IEC Adv. Com. on EMC, 2001-; chmn. Am. Nat. Stds. Inst. Accredited Stds. Com. C63, 2006-, vice chair, 2002-05, chair SC I, 1986-2005. Contbr. articles to profl. jours. Cmdr. USNR, 1963—85, ret.. Named Disting. Mem. Tech. Staff, AT&T Bell Labs., 1982. Fellow IEEE (stds. bd. 1990-2003, vice chmn. 1998-99, chmn. 2000-01, bd. govs. 2001—, pres.-elect standards assn. 2004, pres. 2005-06, bd. dirs. 2005-06, mem. exec. com. 2005-06, Centennial medal 1984, Disting. Svc. award 1993, Charles Proteus Steinmetz award 1996-97, Millennium medal 2000); mem. IEEE Electromagnetic Compatibility Soc. (bd. 1981-93, 97-99, 2002—, pres. 1980-81, chmn. stds. com. 1982-2000, v.p. for stds. 1997—, Laurence G. Cumming award 1986, Stoddart award 1995), Am. Nat. Stds. Inst (Finegan medal 2003)

HEISE, JOHN IRVIN, JR., lawyer; b. Balt., Dec. 13, 1924; s. John Irvin and Ruby Belle (Carpenter) H.; m. Jacqueline Mosey Morley, Sept. 3, 1949; children: John Irvin III, Liane Des Roches, Jeff Howard, Suzanne Wolfrom. AB, U. Md., 1947; JD, U. Va., 1950. Bar: Md. 1950, D.C. 1953, U.S. Supreme Ct. 1962. Trial atty. civil divsn. Dept. Justice, Washington, 1950-52; assoc. Shea Greenman Gardner & McConnaughey, Washington, 1952-57; ptnr. Heise Jorgensen & Stefanelli, P.A., Silver Spring, Md., Gaithersburg, Md., 1957, 1968—. Committeeman, merit badge counselor, dist. chmn. sustaining mem. dr. Boy Scouts Am.; chmn. Md. Ednl. Found., Inc., 1972-92. Maj. USAF, 1942-45. Recipient Gottwals award U. Md., 1978. Mem. ABA, Fed. Bar Assn., Md. Bar Assn., D.C. Bar Assn., Montgomery County Bar Assn., Md. Alumni Assn. (pres. 1966-67), Terrapin (pres. 1961-62), Omicron Delta Kappa, Phi Kappa Phi. Republican. Episcopalian. Office Phone: 301-258-0400. E-mail: heisejacks@aol.com.

HEISENBOTTLE, RICHARD JOHN, architect; b. Rahway, NJ, Aug. 23, 1950; s. John Joseph and Marie Ann (Marchitto) H.; m. Donna Blaszak, May 5, 1979. BS, NY Inst. Tech., 1974; BArch, U. Miami, Fla., 1984. Designer S.B. Jacobs & Assocs. Archs., NYC, 1972-76; project arch. Smith Korach Partnership, Miami, Fla., 1977-79; v.p. Spillis Candela & Ptnrs., Coral Gables, Fla., 1979-87; pres., owner RJ Heisenbottle Archs., Miami, 1987—. Bd. dirs. Franklin Aviation, Miami. Prin. works include Colony Theatre, Miami Beach (AIA Fla. Honor Award of Excellence, 2007). Named Designer of Yr., QR Pub., 1990. Mem. AIA, Greater Miami C. of C., Baton Rouge Jaycees (bd. dirs. 1976), Nat. Trust for Historic Preservation. Clubs: Architecture (Miami). Democrat. Roman Catholic. Avocation: sailing. Office: RJ Heisenbottle Archs 340 Minorca Ave Coral Gables FL 33134 Office Phone: 305-446-7799. Office Fax: 305-446-9275. E-mail: rheisenbottle@rjha.net.*

HEISER, ARNOLD MELVIN, astronomer; b. Bklyn., Feb. 9, 1933; s. Hyman Samuel and Sadie (Kretchmer) H.; m. Vivian Carol Jacobs, June 6, 1964; children: Naomi Elizabeth, David Alan. AB, Ind. U., 1954, MA, 1956; PhD, U. Chgo., 1961. Rsch. asst. Ind. U., 1954-56; rsch. fellow U. Chgo., 1956-61; asst. prof. physics and astronomy Vanderbilt U., Nashville, 1961-66, assoc. prof., 1966-99, prof. emeritus, 1999—. Dir. A.J. Dyer Obs., 1972-86; H. Shapley vis. prof. Am. Astron. Soc., 1969—. Subscriptions editor Comms. of the Internat. Amateur-Profl. Photoelectric Photometry, 1993-99; contbr. articles to profl. jours. Mem. Am. Astron. Soc., Internat. Astron. Union, Tenn. Acad. Sci., Sigma Xi. Home: 6132 Gardendale Dr Nashville TN 37215-5602 Office: Vanderbilt Univ Dyer Observatory 1000 Oman Dr Brentwood TN 37027-4143 Office Phone: 615-373-4897. E-mail: a.heiser@vanderbilt.edu.

HEISER, JAMES S., manufacturing executive; b. 1956; BA in Econs., U. Va.; JD, Stanford U. Gen. counsel, v.p. Ducommun Inc., Carson, Calif., 1985—. Office: Ducommun Inc 23301 Wilmington Ave Carson CA 90745 Office Phone: 310-513-7280. E-mail: jheiser@ducommun.com.

HEISER, ROLLAND VALENTINE, former army officer, foundation administrator; b. Columbus, Ohio, Apr. 25, 1925; s. Rudolph and Helen Cecile H.; m. Gwenne Kathleen Duquemin, Feb. 26, 1949; children: Helen Heiser Sanford, Charlene Heiser Wolff. BS, U.S. Mil. Acad., 1947; MS in Internat. Affairs, George Washington U., 1965. Commd. 2nd lt. U.S. Army, 1947; advanced through grades to lt. gen., 1976; army planner Washington, 1973-74; comdr. 1st Armored divsn. Germany, 1974-75; chief of staff U.S. Army, Europe, 1975-76, U.S. European Command, 1976—78; ret., 1978; pres. New Coll. Found., Sarasota, Fla., 1979—2003. Trustee New Coll. Fla., New Coll. Found. Decorated D.S.M. with oak leaf cluster, Def. Superior Svc. medal, Legion of Merit (3), Bronze Star, others. Mem.: Mil. Officers Assn., Ret. Officers Sarasota (past pres., dir.), Masons. Republican. Episcopalian. Home: 4104 Las Palmas Way Sarasota FL 34238-4532 Personal E-mail: rvh2@comcast.net.

HEISLER, ELWOOD DOUGLAS, hotel executive; b. Wilmington, Del., June 29, 1935; s. Elwood Dean and Laura Matilda (Hutchison) H. BA, Mich. State U., 1957; postgrad., Johns Hopkins U., 1979—. Asst. mgr. Kents Restaurants, Atlantic City, 1957; innkeeper Treadway Inns Corp., NY and Mass., 1960—68, Holiday Inns, Inc., Lansing and Troy, Mich., 1969—77; gen. mgr. Quality Inns, Inc., Towson, Md., 1977—89, Quality Suites Hotel, Mt. Laurel, NJ, 1989—94, Accor Hotels, Windsor Locks, Conn., 1994—98, Best Western Inn on River, Niagara Falls, NY, 1999, Milner Hotel, Boston, 1999—2001, Wellesley Travel Inn, 2001—02, Wellesley Inn On-the-Square, 2002—. Author manual for resort ops., 1965, The Rising Sun of the Japanese Hotel Industry, 1980. Sec. Md. adv. coun. Future Bus. Leaders Am.; bd. dirs. Gunpowder Youth Camps, Inc.; mem. Balt. Coun. on Fgn. Affairs; v.p. Ea. Shore Soc. Balt. 1st lt. U.S. Army, 1957-59; assoc. mem. First Congl. Ch., Nantucket, Mass.; mem. Trinity Ch. in the City of Boston. Named Top Ten Innkeeper, Holiday Inns Internat., 1975, Md. Bus. Person of Yr., Future Bus. Leaders Am., 1981, Bus. Person of Yr. nat. chpt. 1981; recipient award of merit Baltimore County C. of C., 1982, Outstanding Svc. award Md. Future Bus. Leaders Am., 1984, Balt. Mayor's citation, 1984; Paul Harris fellow Rotary Found., 1983. Mem. Am. Hotel and Motel Assn., Mass. Lodging Assn., Hotel Sales Mgmt. Assn., Baltimore County C. of C. (v.p.), St. George Soc. N.Y., Advt. Club. Balt. (bd. govs., sec.), SAR, Soc. Sons of St. George Phila., German Soc. Md., German Soc. Pa., Amicale Soc. Francaise Balt., Welsh Soc. Phila., St. David's Soc. N.Y., St. Andrew's Soc. Conn., St. Davids Soc. Conn., Mass. Lodging Assn., German Soc. N.Y.C., Rittenhouse Family Assn., Supreme Ct. Hist. Soc., Hist. Soc. Del., Md. Hist. Soc., Nantucket Hist. Assn., Nantucket C. of C. (pres.), Trot, Mich. C. of C. (v.p.), Burlington County Hist. Soc., Md. Ret. Officers Assn., Rotary Club of Towson Md. (sec., pres.), Balt. Yacht Club, Lideerkranz Club, Williams Club (N.Y.C.), Theta Chi (pres. chpt., alumni corp. pres.). Republican. Home and Office: PO Box 812662 Wellesley MA 02482-0023 Office Phone: 781-237-0604. Personal E-mail: edouglasheisler@yahoo.com.

HEISLER, QUENTIN GEORGE, JR., lawyer; b. Jefferson City, Mo., 1943; m. Susan D.; children: Sarah, Thomas, Margaret. AB magna cum laude, Harvard U., 1965, JD, 1968. Bar: Ill. 1968, U.S. Dist. Ct. (no. dist.) Ill. 1969, Fla. 1977. Assoc. McDermott, Will & Emery, Chgo., 1968-69, 70-75, ptnr., 1975—, chmn. firm pvt. client dept., 1998—2006, ptnr. in charge, 2006—. Co-author: Working With Family Businesses, 1995; gen. editor: Trust Administration in Illinois, 1979. Chmn. Winnetka Caucus, Ill., 1983; mem. Winnetka Bd. Edn., 1985-89; trustee Shedd Aquarium, 2002—, mem. exec. com., 2004—, chmn. planned giving com., 2006—; chmn. gift planning adv. com. Art Inst. Chgo., 2005—, Hadley Sch. for the Blind, 1998-2002; bd govs. Winnetka Cmty. House, 1998-99; mem. planned giving com. Ravinia Festival, 2006—. Fellow Am. Coll. Trust and Estates Counsel; mem. Chgo. Coun. Estate Planning, Chgo. Bar Assocs., Univ. Club (Chgo.), Harvard Club (bd. dirs. Chgo. chpt. 1984-95, pres. bd. 1989-91), Skokie Country Club (Glencoe, Ill.), Racquet Club (Chgo.), Sanctuary Country Club (Sanibel, Fla.). Office: McDermott Will & Emery LLP 227 W Monroe St Ste 4700 Chicago IL 60606-5096 Home Phone: 312-335-8294; Office Phone: 312-984-7606. Business E-Mail: qheisler@mwe.com.

HEISLER, STANLEY DEAN, lawyer; b. The Dalles, Oreg., Jan. 11, 1946; s. Donald Eugene and Roberta (Van Valkenburgh) Heisler. BA, Willamette U., 1968, JD, 1972. Bar: Oreg. 1972, U.S. Ct. Claims 1972, U.S. Tax Ct. 1972, U.S. Ct. Appeals (9th cir.) 1972, D.C. 1973, U.S. Ct. Appeals (fed. cir.) 1973, U.S. Ct. Mil. Appeals 1973, N.Y. 1985, U.S. Supreme Ct. 1985. Assoc. Heisler & Van Valkenburgh, The Dalles, 1973-74; ptnr. Heisler, Van Valkenburgh & Coats, The Dalles, 1975-81, Heisler & Heisler, The Dalles, 1982-84, Cohen & Shalleck, NYC, 1985-88, Phillips, Nizer, Benjamin, Krim & Ballon, NYC, 1988-91, Squadron, Ellenoff, Plesent, Sheinfeld & Sorkin, NYC, 1991-94; mng. ptnr. Shays & Kemper, LLP, NYC, 1994-98, Shays, Rothman, & Heisler, LLP, NYC, 1999-2000, Shays, Heisler & Rosenthal, LLP, NYC, 2000-01; pvt. practice Stanley D. Heisler, PC, NYC, 2001—. Speechwriter Sec. of State Tom McCall, Salem, 1965, Gov. Tom McCall, Salem, 1966—68; speechwriter, legis. asst. U.S. Senator Bob Packwood, Washington, 1969—73; vice chmn. Pres.'s Air Quality Adv. Bd., Washington, 1973—76. Named Knight of the Order of Ss. Maurice and Lazarus, His Royal Highness Victor Emanuel The Prince of Naples and Duke of Savoy; named to Most Venerable Order of the Hosp. of St. John of Jerusalem, Her Majesty Queen Elizabeth II. Mem.: SAR, ABA, Assn. of Bar City of NY, NY State Bar Assn., Holland Soc. NY, St. Nicholas Soc. City NY, The Pilgrims of the U.S., St. Andrews Soc. of State of N.Y., Soc. Colonial Wars (mem. coun. N.Y. State chpt. 2003—), Soc. Mayflower Descs. (bd. dirs. N.Y. chpt. 2001—, capt. N.Y. chpt. 2005—), Soc. Descs. Washington's Army at Valley Forge, Soc. Promotion of Hellenic Studies, Edmund Rice (1638) Assn., New Eng. Soc. City of NY, St. George's Soc. NY, Colonial Soc. Pa., Union League Club City NY, Yale Club NYC, Nassau Club, Univ. Club (N.Y.C. and Portland, Oreg.), Arlington Club. Republican. Episcopalian. Home: 400 E 77th St Apt 8J New York NY 10021-2342 Office: 330 Madison Ave 9th Fl New York NY 10017 E-mail: s.heisler@worldnet.att.net.

HEISLER, TODD, photojournalist; b. Chgo. BA, Ill. State U., 1994. Photographer cmty. newspapers, Chgo., 1994—2001; staff photographer Rocky Mountain News, Denver, 2001—. Co-recipient Pulitzer Prize for breaking news photography, 2003; recipient Pulitzer Prize for feature photography, 2006. Office: Rocky Mountain News 100 Gene Amole Way Denver CO 80204 Office Phone: 303-892-2430, 303-892-5382. Office Fax: 303-892-5015. E-mail: heislert@rockymountainnews.com.

HEISLEY, MICHAEL E., SR., manufacturing executive, professional sports team owner; b. Washington; m. Agnes Heisley; 5 children. BA, Georgetown U., 1960. With Robertson-Ceco Corp., Toms Foods, Inc., WorldPort Comm. Inc., Pettibone Corp.; chmn., CEO Heico Cos. LLC, St. Charles, Ill., 1979—; owner Memphis Grizzlies (formerly Vancouver Grizzlies), 2000—. Chmn. Davis Wire Corp., Toms Foods, Inc. Mem. St. Patrick's Cath. Ch. Named one of 400 Richest Ams., Forbes mag., 2006. Mem. Turnaround Mgmt. Assn., Union League Club, Chgo. Club. Office: Heico Cos LLC 70 W Madison St Ste 5600 Chicago IL 60602*

HEISS, DAVID JAMES, editor; b. Siagon, Vietnam, Oct. 1972; BA in English, U. Redlands, 1995. Writer Redlands (Calif) Daily Facts, 1999—. Contbg. author: Coming of Dawn, 1993. Instr., coach volleyball Redlands YMCA, 1998—. Mem. Redlands Hort. and Improvement Soc. (newsletter editor 2000—), Town and Gown, Sigma Kappa Alpha (alumni assn. officer 2001-04), Internat. Knights of Round Table. Office: Redlands Daily Facts 700 Brookside Redlands CA 92373 Office Phone: 909-793-3221. Business E-Mail: dheiss@redlandsdailyfacts.com.

HEISS, HARRY GLEN, archivist; b. Fort Smith, Ark., Jan. 3, 1953; s. Fred William and Mary Kathryn (Hall) H. BA, U. Ark., 1975, MA, 1984; archives cert., Western Wash. U., 1979. Archives intern Oreg. State Archives, Salem, 1979; asst. archivist Smithsonian Instn. Archives, Washington, 1980-85; archivist Nat. Air and Space Mus., Washington, 1985-87, Jefferson Nat. Expansion Meml., Nat. Pk. Svc., St. Louis, 1988-91, Libr. Congress, Washington, 1991-2000, Shenandoah Nat. Park, Nat. Pk. Svc., Luray, Va., 2000—02, Bur. Pub. Debt, U.S. Dept. Treasury, Washington, 2002—. Democrat. Avocations: bicycle touring, camping. Home: 23333 Mountain Valley Rd Millboro VA 24460 Office: Bur Pub Deby US Treasury 799 9th St NW Washington DC 20239 Home Phone: 540-322-1778. Business E-Mail: Harry.Heiss@bpd.treas.gov.

HEISS, RICHARD WALTER, retired bank executive, consultant, lawyer; b. Monroe, Mich., July 8, 1930; s. Walter and Lillian (Harpst) H.; m. Nancy J. Blum, June 21, 1952; children: Kurt Frederick, Karl Richard. BA, Mich. State U., 1952; LLB, Detroit Coll., 1963, LLD (hon.), 1982; LLM, Wayne State U., 1969; cert., Stanford U. Exec. Program, 1979. Bar: Mich. 1963, U.S. Dist. Ct. (federal dist.) Mich. 1963. Asst. trust officer Mfrs. Nat. Bank of Detroit, 1960-62, trust officer, 1962-66; v.p., trust officer Mfrs. Nat. Bank Detroit, 1966-68, v.p., sr. trust officer, 1968-75, 1st v.p., sr. trust officer, 1975-77, sr. v.p., 1977-89, exec. v.p., 1989-92; vice chair Detroit Coll. Law Found., 1995—2000, chair, 2001—. Pres., CEO, Mfrs. Nat. Trust Co. Fla., 1984-88, chmn. bd., 1988-92; lectr. Inst. Continuing Legal Edn., Procknow Grad. Sch. Banking, U. Wis., Southwestern Grad. Sch. Bank, Am. Bankers Assn., Banking Sch. South; chmn. mem. exec. com. Trust Mgmt. Seminar, 1980; expert witness fiduciary law, 1993-2003. Mem. Legal-Fin. Network, Cmty. Found. S.E. Mich.; bd. dirs. Hist. Trinity, Inc., 1992—; trustee Mich. State U. Coll. Law, 1972—, pres., 1983-94; pres. Mich. State U. Bus. Sch. Alumni Bd., 1983; mem. allocation and evaluation com. United Way S.E. Mich., 1989-92. 1st lt. AUS, 1952-57. Fellow State Bar Mich. Found.; emeritus mem. Mich. Bar Assn., Am. Bankers Assn. (pres. 1981, exec. com. trust divsn., pvt. banking com. 1984-89, investment adv. com. 1984-89), Mich. Bankers Assn. (chmn. trust divsn. exec. com. 1975), Detroit Golf Club (bd. dirs., pres. 1983), Mich. Srs. Golf Assn. (bd. govs. 1994-), Club at Seabrook Island (golf and green com.), Delta Chi, Sigma Nu Phi. Republican. Lutheran. Home (Summer): 30684 Sudbury Ct Farmington Hills MI 48331-1368 Office Phone: 843-768-3678.

HEISTAD, DONALD DEAN, cardiologist; b. Chgo., Apr. 2, 1940; m. Sandra J.; children: Wendy, Dean. BS, U. Ill., 1959; MD, U. Chgo., 1963. Asst. prof. medicine U. Iowa Coll. Medicine, Iowa City, 1970-73, assoc. prof. medicine, 1973-76, prof. medicine, 1976—, prof. pharmacology, 1987—, prof. cardiology, dir. cardiovascular divsn., 1995—2003, Zahn prof. cardiology, 1999—. Bd. dirs. Iowa Ctr. on Aging. Editor: Cerebral Blood Flow: Effects of Nerves, 1982; assoc. editor: Hypertension, 1989-93, Circulation Rsch., 1980-85, consulting editor; editor-in-chief: Arteriosclerosis, Thrombosis, and Vascular Biology, 1999—; contbr. more than 400 papers to profl. jours. and chpts to books. Pres. U. Iowa Faculty Senate, Iowa City, 1980-81; vice-chair coun. on circulation Am. Heart Assn., 1994-96, chair, 1996-98. Capt. U.S. Army, 1967-70. Recipient Irving S. Wright award Stroke Coun., 1976, Harry Goldblatt award Coun. for High Blood Pressure Rsch., 1980, Merit award, 1987, Disting. Lecture award Coun. on Thrombosis, George E. Brown Meml. Lectr., Am. Heart Assn., 1999, Rsch. Achievement award, 2001; Disting. Alumni award U. Chgo., 1991, Novartis award Coun. High Blood Pressure Rsch., 1997; Landis award, Microcirculation Soc., 2001. Fellow Coun. for High Blood Pressure Rsch., Am. Soc. for Clin. Investigation, Assn. Am. Physicians, Assn. Univ. Cardiologists (sec.-treas. 1998-2001, pres. 2002-03), Am. Physiol. Soc. (chair cardiovascular sect. 1995-96, Wiggers award 1999); mem. Internat. Soc. and Fedn. Cardiologists. Democrat. Office: U Iowa Coll Medicine Dept Medicine Iowa City IA 52242 E-mail: donald-heistad@uiowa.edu.

HEIT, MARNY, lawyer; b. Miami, Fla., Nov. 22, 1976; BA, Syracuse Univ., 1998; JD, Emory Univ. Sch. Law, 2001. Bar: State of Ga. 2001. Atty., divsn. traffic and DUI Chestney-Hawkins Attys., 2001—, now ptnr. Spkr. in field. Recipient Best Speaker award, Irving R. Kaufman National Securities Moot Court Competition, 2000. Mem.: Ga. Assn. Women Lawyers, Ga. Assn. Criminal Defense Lawyers, Bar Ga. Ct. Appeals. Office: Chestney-Hawkins 448 East Paces Ferry Road Atlanta GA 30305

HEITER, MATTHEW STEPHEN, lawyer; b. Ft. Campbell, Ky., Oct. 1, 1960; m. Judy Anthony, Dec. 10, 1958; children: Emma Celeste, Charles Anthony. BA, U. of Miss., Oxford, 1982; JD, Vanderbilt U., Nashville, 1985. Bar: Tenn. 1985. Exec. v.p., gen. counsel IPIX Corp., Reston, Va., 1999—2002; chair securities practice group Baker, Donelson, Bearman, Caldwell & Berkowitz, Memphis, 2002—. Contbr. chapters to books. Named one of Top 40 Under 40, Memphis Bus. Jour., 1999; named to Best Lawyers in Am., Woodward/White, Inc., 2005, 2006. Mem.: ABA, Memphis Bar Assn., Tenn. Bar Assn. Home: 1376 Carr Ave Memphis TN 38104 Office: Baker Donelson Bearman Caldwell & Ber 165 Madison Ave Memphis TN 38103 Office Phone: 901-577-8117. Business E-Mail: mheiter@bakerdonelson.com.

HEITING, JAMES OTTO, lawyer; b. Chgo., Apr. 21, 1949; m. Cindy Heiting; 3 children. BS, Riverside Univ., 1971; JD, Western State Univ., 1975. Bar: Calif. 1976, U.S. Supreme Court and U.S. District Ct. 1977, Central Dist. of Calif., U.S. Dist. Ct., So. Dist. of Calif. 1982. Founder, partner Heiting & Irwin, 1976—. Mem. bd. dirs The Other Bar, 1998—2003, pres., chmn., 1991—93. Mem.: Calif. State Bar Assn. (v.p., treas. 2004—05, pres. 2005—06), Am. Soc. Law and Medicine, Am. Bar Assoc. Office: Heiting & Irwin 5885 Brocton Avenue Riverside CA 92506

HEITLER, GEORGE, lawyer; b. NYC, Sept. 3, 1915; s. John J. and Celia (Zeichner) H.; m. Florence A. Posner, Apr. 21, 1940; children: James B., Richard S. BS, Columbia U., 1936, JD, 1938. Bar: NY 1938, Ill. 1962. Asso. firm Cutler, Wilson & McMahon, NYC, 1938-40; spl. asst. to David L. Podell; counsel to Hays, Podell & Schulman, NYC, 1940; asso. atty. firm Coughlan & Russell; also mng. agt. and asst. sec. Central Manhattan Properties, Inc., NYC, 1940-43; chief clk., legal adviser rents and claims bd. 4th Service Command, U.S. Army, 1943-45; engaged as bus. exec., also house counsel various comml. orgns., 1946-57; asst. sec., staff counsel Blue Cross Assn., NYC, 1957-60, corporate sec., staff counsel, 1960-61; v.p., sec. Chgo., 1961-71; sr. v.p., corporate sec., gen. counsel, 1971-81; sr. v.p., legal counsel Nat. Blue Shield Assn., 1978-81; counsel to Kaye, Scholer, Fierman, Hays & Handler, NYC, 1981-85. Spl. adviser Dept. Labor, also speaker and panelist. Author articles. Mem. Am., Chgo. bar assns., Assn. Bar City N.Y. Home: 700 John Ringling Blvd Apt 1408 Sarasota FL 34236-1555 Personal E-mail: fgheitfl@comcast.net.

HEITMANN, GEORGE JOSEPH, business educator, consultant; b. NYC, Nov. 27, 1933; s. Frederick Charles and Henrietta (Boesl) H.; m. Marian Kingsley, Sept. 3, 1960; children: James, Noel, Peter. AB, Syracuse U., 1956; MA, Princeton U., 1960, PhD, 1963. Prof. mgmt. sci. Pa. State U., University Park, 1958—94, chmn. dept., 1978—87, dir. internat. programs Coll. Bus. Adminstrn., 1989—94, prof. emeritus, 1994—; prof. econs. Muhlenberg Coll., Allentown, Pa., 1994—, chmn. dept. acctg., bus. and econs., 1994—2003, dean internat. programs, 1994—2004. Econ. advisor Ministry of Planning and Devel., Govt. of Libya, Tripoli, 1964-66; cons. energy policy staff Exec. Office of Pres., Washington, 1968-70; vis. prof. Universität zu Köln, Cologne, Fed. Republic of Germany, 1974; vis. prof. Ruhr Universität, Bochum, Fed. Republic of Germany, 1970, 74, 77, W.Va. U., Morgantown, 1975, Shanghai Inst. Mech. Engring., Peoples Republic of China, 1985, U. Maastricht, 2002; cons. Helsinki Inst. Bus. Econs., Finland, 1980; Pa. State U. resident advisor U. West Indies, Kingston, Jamaica, 1987-89. Contbr. articles to profl. jours. Served as 1st lt. U.S. Army, 1957. Mem. Am. Econ. Assn., Decision Scis. Inst., Phi Beta

Kappa. Home: 930 S 24th St Allentown PA 18103-3706 Office: Muhlenberg Coll Ettinger Bldg Allentown PA 18104-5586 Home Phone: 610-776-1997; Office Phone: 484-664-3283. E-mail: heitmann@muhlenberg.edu.

HEITNER, KENNETH HOWARD, lawyer; b. Jersey City, Apr. 1, 1948; s. Charles Fred and Molly (Vogelman) H.; m. Anne Barbara Siegel, June 14, 1970; children: Douglas, Andrew, Elizabeth. BA, Rutgers U., 1969; JD, NYU, 1973, LLM in Taxation, 1977. Bar: NY 1974, US Dist. Ct. (So. and Ea. dists.) NY 1975, US Tax Ct. 1976. Assoc. Weil, Gotshal & Manges, NYC, 1973-81, ptnr., co-head tax dept., 1981—. Gen. counsel, mem. bd. trustee Central Park Conservancy. Author: (articles) Tax Lawyer and Jour. of Partnership Taxation. With US Army, 1969-75. Mem. ABA tax sect., NY State Bar Assn., (exec. com. and former chmn. of committees on bankruptcy , corps., practices and procedure and net oper. losses, reorgns.) tax sect., Assn. Bar City NY, Fairview Country Club (Greenwich, Conn., bd. govs. 1983-90), Tax Club (past pres.), Phi Beta Kappa. Office: Weil Gotshal & Manges LLP 767 5th Ave Fl Concl New York NY 10153-0119 Home Phone: 212-289-3048; Office Phone: 212-310-8288. Office Fax: 212-310-8007. Business E-Mail: kenneth.heitner@weil.com.

HEITSCH, LEONA MASON, artist, writer; b. Pontiac, Mich., Jan. 6, 1931; d. Russell Leonard and Margaret M. (Arnold) Mason; m. Charles Weyand Heitsch, July 5, 1952; children: Russell, Carrie, Grace, Charles, Irene. BA in chemistry, U. Mich., 1952. Ednl. asst. Spl. Sch. Dist., St. Louis County, Mo., 1969-81. Commentator Sta. KUMR, Rolla, Mo., 1996—. Author: (pvt. printing) Echoes of the Ridge, 1985, Get Him to St. Louis, 1983; contbg. author: (poem anthology) Seasons of the Ozarks, 1998, Missourians Write About Reading, 2002, Apples, Apples Everywhere; contbr. poetry, articles to various publs. Sec., activist Mo. Assn. Children with Learning Disabilities, St. Louis, 1973-75; fundraising, writing Friends of Foster-Dolbeer Farm, Walled Lake, Mich., 1996—; contbg. poet Wis. Breastfeeding Coalition, Lac du Flambeau, 1996—; activist Poets Against the War, 2003. Recipient honorable mention Mo. Writers Week award for poetry, 1992, 94, grand prize Artists Embassy Internat., San Francisco, 1997, Editors Challenge award Internat. Soc. Authors and Artists, Abilene, Tex., 1997, included in Memories and Memoirs, Anthology of Mo. authors, 2000; featured in Grandmother Earth IX, 2003, Grist, Mo. State Poetry Soc., 2003. Mem. St. Louis Poetry Soc., Rolla Area Writers Guild. Home and Office: Ridge Orchards 13321 Hwy N Bourbon MO 65441-9305 E-mail: clheitsc@fidnet.com.

HEITZ, KENNETH R., lawyer; b. Santa Maria, Calif., June 25, 1947; BA cum laude, UCLA, 1969; JD cum laude, Harvard U., 1972. Bar: Calif. 1972, US Dist. Ct. (so. & no. dists) Calif., US Ct. of Appeals (9th cir.), US Supreme Ct. Mem. Irell & Manella, LA; co-mng. ptnr. Irell & Manella LLP, 1997—2003, ptnr. Dep. gen. counsel Webster Commn. 1992, lead counsel Terex Audit Com., adv. (bd. dir.) SEC, FTC, IRS, FDIC, FSLIC, FHLBB, OTS , US Atty., bd. NYSE corp.& chaired compensation com., lead counsel with several major pub. co. Recipient Southern Calif 's.Super Lawyers, LA Mag., 2006, Best Lawyers in Am., 2007—08. Mem. ABA (corp., banking and bus. law sects.), State Bar Calif., Phi Beta Kappa. Office: Irell & Manella LLP 1800 Ave of Stars Ste 900 Los Angeles CA 90067-4276 Office Phone: 310-203-7980. Office Fax: 310-203-7199. Business E-Mail: kheitz@irell.com.

HEITZENRATER, JAMES F, hospital administrator; BA, Marshall U., W. Va.; MA in healthcare adminstrn., Ctrl. Mich. U. Past CEO Marcum & Wallace Meml. Hosp., Irvine, Ky.; now CEO, pres. Methodist Sugar Land Hosp. Mem. Program Planning Com. DePelchin Children's Ctr.; bd. mem. Fort Bend Econ. Devel. Coun., Fort Bend C. of C. Mem.: Am. Coll. Healthcare Exec. (diplomat). Office: Methodist Sugar Land Hosp 16655 SW Fwy Sugar Land TX 77479

HEITZMANN, RAY, education educator, athletic coach; b. Hoboken, NJ, Feb. 12, 1948; s. William Henry and Mary B. (Tolland) H.; m. Kathleen Heitzmann (div.); children: Richard, Mary. BS, Villanova U.; MAT, U. Chgo.; PhD, U. Del.; postgrad., Northeastern Calif. State U., San Jose. Cert. tchr., N.Y., Ill. Pvt. practice cons. various pub. and pvt. schs. and bus.; prof. Villanova (Pa.) U. Dir. grad. tchr. edn., dir. Writing for Pub. workshops Villanova U.; basketball, baseball, men and women's football coach, NJ, Ill., Pa., NY. Author: 50 Political Cartoons for Teaching U.S. History, 1975, American Jewish Political Behavior: History and Analysis, 1975, The Newspaper in the Classroom, 1979, 84, Educational Games and Simulations, 1987, Opportunities in Marine Sci. and Maritime Careers, 1988, 4th edit., 2006, Opportunities in Sports and Athletics, 1992, Opportunities in Sports Medicine, 1993, Careers for Sports Nuts and Other Athletic Types, 1997, 3d edit., 2004, Super Study Skills for Success, 1997, 2d edit., 1998, Opportunities in Sports and Fitness Careers, 2003, Opportunities in Marine Science and Maritime Careers, 2006; contbr. articles to profl. jours. Recipient Outstanding Alumnus award, Sch. Edn., U. Del., 1986, plaque, Weehawken (N.J.) Bd. Edn. Mem.: Pa. Coun. for Social Studies, N.J. Marine Educators, Nat. Social Sci. Assn. (Recognition award 2004), Nat. Marine Educators Assn., Nat. Maritime Hist. Soc., Nat. Coun. for History Edn., Mid. States Coun. for the Social Studies (Outstanding Rsch. award 1989, Carman award 2000), Nat. Coun. Social Studies (Outstanding Svc. award 1980), U.S. Naval Inst., Nat. Assn. Basketball Coaches, Phi Delta Kappa. Office: Villanova U Dept Edn Human Svcs Villanova PA 19085 Office Phone: 610-519-4618. Business E-Mail: ray.heitzmann@villanova.edu.

HEIVILIN, DONNA MAE, retired government executive; b. Clear Lake, Iowa, May 12, 1937; d. Nels Oliver Ouverson and Nellie Bernice (Humphrey) Ouverson-Loats; m. Thomas Stuart Heivilin, Dec. 26, 1961 (div. Dec. 1971); children: Vincent Stuart, James Edward. Student, Iowa State U., 1956-57; BA, U. Minn., 1959; MPA, George Washington U., 1974, DPA, 1988. Assoc. dir. Navy issues, nat. security and internat. affairs U.S. Gen. Acctg. Office, Washington, 1985-88, dir. logistics issues, nat. security and internat. affairs, 1988-93, dir. def. mgmt., NASA issues, 1993-95, vice chair job process reengring. team, 1995-96, dir. planning & reporting, nat. security & internat. affairs, 1996-99, dir. quality and risk mgmt., 1999-2000, dir. applied rsch. and methods, 2000—04; ret., 2004. Pres. Nat. Coun. Assn.'s Policy Scis., Washington, 1980-83. Profiler editor Pub. Budget and Fin. Jour, 1985-98. Vol. Fin. Svcs. Vol. Corps, 2006. Mem. Exec. Women in Govt. (pres. 1996-97), Am. Assn. Budget and Programming Analysts (bd. dirs. 1980-83, 98-99), Coun. Logistics Mgrs., Soc. Logistics Engrs., World Future Soc. US Nat. Capitol (region chpt., bd. dirs. 2006-), Profl. Futurists Assn., Nat. Capitol Region Futurists (bd. dirs. 2006-), The Internat. Alliance for Women (bd. dirs. 1997-2006, treas. 1998, 1st v.p. 1999, pres. 2000-01, amb. at large 2004-05), Capitol Sisters (bd. dirs. 2007-), Phi Kappa Phi. Avocations: recreational walking, plays, shakespeare, country music. Home: 5330 36th St N Arlington VA 22207-1816 Office Phone: 703-532-0610. Personal E-mail: donna.heivilin@verizon.net.

HEIZER, EDGAR FRANCIS, JR., venture capitalist; b. Detroit, Sept. 23, 1929; s. Edgar Francis and Grace Adelia (Smith) H.; m. Molly Bradley Hunt, June 17, 1952; children: Linda Heizer Seaman, Molly Hunt, Edgar Francis III. BS, Northwestern U., 1951; JD, Yale U., 1954. Bar: Ill. 1954; CPA, Ill. Mem. audit and tax staff Arthur Andersen & Co., Chgo., 1954-56; fin. analyst Kidder, Peabody & Co., Chgo., 1956-58; mgmt. cons. Booz, Allen & Hamilton, Chgo., 1958-62; asst. treas., mgr. venture capital divsn. Allstate Ins. Co., Northbrook, Ill., 1962-69; chmn., founder, CEO Heizer Corp., a venture capital & bus. devel. co., Chgo., 1969-85; venture capitalist Tucker's Town, Bermuda, 1985—; dir. Chesapeake Energy Corp., Material Sciences Corp., Elk Grove, Ill. Bd. dirs. Needham & Co., N.Y., Material Sci. Corp., Elk Grove Village, Ill., Manus Health Systems Inc., Lake Forest, Ill., Chesapeake Energy Corp., Oklahoma City, Okla.; mem. adv. bd. Kellogg Sch. Mgmt., Northwestern U.; chmn. Heizer Ctr. for Entrepreneurship at Kellogg Sch. Mgmt. Chmn. task force on capital formation for White House Conf. on Small Bus., 1978-80. Mem. Nat. Venture Capital Assn. (founder, 1st pres., chmn.), Nat. Assn. Small Bus. Investment Cos., Delta Upsilon (chmn. bd. dirs. 1985-88, chmn. ednl. found. 1990-98). Clubs: Chgo. Curling, Shoreacres, Econ. of Chgo., Coral Beach and Tennis, Mid-Ocean; Riddells Bay Golf (Bermuda). Republican. Presbyterian. Home: 28 S Shore Rd Tuckers Town HS 02 Bermuda also: 261 Bluffs Edge Dr Lake Forest IL 60045-3301

HEJDUK, MILAN, professional hockey player; b. Usti-nad Labem, Czech Republic, Feb. 14, 1976; m. Zlatuse Hejduk; children: Marek, David. Right wing Colo. Avalanche, 1998—. Mem. Czech Nat. Hockey Team, Olympic Games, Nagano, Japan, 1998, Salt Lake City, 2002, Torino, Italy, 06, Czech Nat. Hockey Team, World Cup of Hockey, 2004; player NHL All-Star Game, 2000, 01. Co-recipient Bud Light Plus/Minus Award, NHL, 2003; named to All-Rookie Team, 1999, Second All-Star Team, 2003; recipient Maurice Richard Trophy, 2003. Achievements include being a member of gold medal winning Czech Republic Hockey Team, Nagano Olympics, 1998, bronze medal team, Torino Olympics, Italy, 2006. Office: Colo Avalanche Pepsi Ctr 1000 Chopper Cir Denver CO 80204*

HEJTMANEK, DANTON CHARLES, lawyer; b. Topeka, July 22, 1951; s. Robert Keith and Bernice Louise (Krause) H.; m. Julie Hejtmanek; 1 child, Brian J. BBA in Acctg., Washburn U., 1973, JD, 1975. Bar: Kans. 1976, U.S. Dist. Ct. Kans. 1976, U.S. Tax Ct. 1976. Ptnr. Schroer, Rice, Bryan & Lykins, P.A., Topeka, 1975-86, Bryan, Lykins, Hejtmanek & Fincher P.A., Topeka, 1986—. Mem. ABA (rep. young lawyers Kans. and Nebr.), ATLA, Kans. Bar Assn. (pres. young lawyers 1985), Kans. Trial Lawyers Assn., Sertoma (pres. 1983, internat. pres. 1998-99). Republican. Presbyterian. Avocations: skiing, travel. Home: 2800 SW Burlingame Rd Topeka KS 66611-1316 Office: Bryan Lykins Hejtmanek & Fincher PA 222 SW 7th St Topeka KS 66603-3734 Home Phone: 785-357-4126; Office Phone: 785-235-5678. Business E-Mail: danhejtmanek@ksjustice.com.

HEKTNER, JOEL MARTIN, psychology professor; b. Breckenridge, Minn., Apr. 26, 1968; s. Vernon E. and Leona B. Hektner; m. Kristin M. Kessler, Aug. 28, 1993; children: Owen M., Ben J. BA, Princeton U., NJ, 1990; PhD, U. Chgo., 1996. Rsch. assoc. U. Minn., Mpls., 1997—2000; assoc. prof. ND State U., Fargo, 2000—. Author: (book) Experience Sampling Method: Measuring the Quality of Everyday Life, 2007. Mem. Kiwanis, Fargo, 2002—; coun. com. chair Boy Scouts Am., Fargo, 2002—. Recipient US Presdl. Scholar award, US Dept. Edn., Presdl. Scholars Commn., 1986. Mem.: Soc. Prevention Rsch., Soc. Rsch. in Child Devel. Lutheran. Office: ND State U 283 EML Hall Fargo ND 58105 Business E-Mail: joel.hektner@ndsu.edu.

HEL, ZDENEK, immunologist, educator; b. Policka, Czech Republic, July 5, 1967; PhD, McGill U., Montreal, Can., 1997. Asst. prof. U. Ala., Birmingham, 2003—. Mem.: Internat. AIDS Soc. Achievements include research in HIV and cancer vaccine development.

HELANDER, ROBERT CHARLES, lawyer, arbitrator; b. Chgo., Oct. 30, 1932; s. William Eugene and Grace Pauline H.; m. Betty Jane Vinson, Apr. 8, 1961; children: Diana Chaffin, Alexander Christian, Nicholas Charles. BA, Amherst Coll., 1953; JD, Harvard U., 1956, PMD, 1971. Bar: D.C. 1956, Ill. 1956, N.Y. 1979, U.S. Supreme Ct. 1960. Practice law, Chgo., 1956-62; Amherst fellow in Mid. East, 1960-61; mem. firm Helander, Farmanfarmaian & Ghany, Tehran, Iran, 1962-65; assoc. gen. counsel Internat. Basic Economy Corp., Lima, Peru, 1965-68, v.p., 1968-71, v.p. devel. and adminstrn., gen. counsel NYC, 1971-73; group v.p. and pres. Internat. Basic Economy Corp. Housing Internat., NYC, 1973-76; ptnr. firm Jones, Day, Reavis & Pogue (Surrey & Morse), NYC, 1976-93; ptnr. Kaye, Scholer LLP, NYC, 1993—2001; mng. ptnr. InterConsult., LLP, 2002—. Panelist Am. Arbitration Assn., 1986—, Internat. Ctr. for Settlement of Investment Disputes of World Bank, 2005—. Pres. Accion Internat., 1978-88; chmn. Pan Am. Soc., 1979-88, Am. Fund for Ind. Univs., 1987—, Fund for Multinat. Mgmt. Edn., 1981-91; bd. dirs. Internat. Law Inst., 1975, Ams. Soc., 1982—, Univ. Andes Found., 1983—, Overlook Hosp. Found., 2006—, Near East Found., 1977—, Bolivarian Soc., 1980—, IESA Found., 1991—, chmn. Internat. Coun. Escuela Superior Adminstrn. de Negocios, 1999—; dir. The Americas Endowment (Orgn. Am. States), 2003-; mem. bd. disting. advisors Am. Coms. on Fgn. Rels., 2006-. Named Comendador, Orden del Sol (Peru). Fellow Am. Bar Found. (life); mem. ABA (chmn. inter-Am. law com. sect. internat. law and practice 1978-83, editor-in-chief Inter-Am. Legal Materials 1983-91, del. to Inter-Am. Bar Assn.), Assn. Bar City N.Y. (inter-Am. affairs com.), Inter-Am. Bar Assn., Am. Fgn. Law Assn. (pres. 2001-04), Coun. Fgn. Rels., Carnegie Coun., Century Assn. Republican. Episcopalian. Home: 3 Mountainview Dr Mountainside NJ 07092-2510 Office: InterConsult LLP PO Box 1337 Mountainside NJ 07092 Office Phone: 917-345-8250. Business E-Mail: rch@interconsultllp.com.

HELD, HUYLER CLARK, lawyer; b. NYC, Apr. 13, 1925; s. John Seys Huyler Held and Winabeth (Clark) Woodworth. AB, Princeton U., 1948; LLB, Columbia U., 1951. Bar: N.Y. 1952, U.S. Supreme Ct. 1961. Assoc. Spence, Hotchkiss, Parker & Duryee, NYC, 1951-55, Willkie, Farr, Gallagher, Walton & Fitzgibbon, NYC, 1956-57; ptnr. Satterlee, Browne, Cherbonnier & Dickerson, NYC, 1957-62, Turk, Marsh, Kelly & Hoare, NYC, 1962-94, Bryan Cave, 1995-98, McLaughlin & Stern, 1998—. Trustee Peggy N. and Roger G. Gerry Charitable Trust, Annette Kade Charitable Trust, NY State Archives Partnership Trust, Rhodebeck Charitable Trust, NYC; trustee, treas. John Merck Fund, NYC; bd. dirs. Preservation League NY State, Albany, Friends of Upper Eastside Historic Dist., Two East 62nd St Found.; trustee, past pres. Soc. Preservation LI Antiquities, Setauket; bd. dirs. past pres. Fountain House, Inc.; bd. dirs. Nature Conservancy, NY State Bd., Albany; bd. dirs., sec., treas. Eppley Found. Rsch., Inc., NYC; bd. dirs. Cathedral St. John Divine. Ensign USNR, 1943-46. Mem. ABA, NY State Bar Assn., Assn. Bar City NY, NY County Lawyers Assn., Anglers Club NY, Ausable Club, Century Assn., Church Club NY, Cold Spring Harbor Beach Club, Pilgrims, Down Town Assn., Knickerbocker Club (bd. govs.), Nassau Club (Princeton, NJ), Univ. Club, Yeamans Hall Club (Charleston, SC), Piping Rock Club. Office: 260 Madison Ave New York NY 10016-2401 Office Phone: 212-448-6243. Business E-Mail: hheld@mclaughlinstern.com.

HELD, JOE ROGER, retired veterinarian; b. LA, June 23, 1931; s. Edward Samuel and Carmen Antoinette (Planas) H.; m. Carolyn Ann Friderich, May 26, 1956; children: Lisa Held Doseff, Robert Joseph Held, Leslie Held Barnett, Teresa Held Johnson. AA, Pasadena City Coll., 1950; BS, U. Calif., Davis, 1953, DVM, 1955; MPH, Tulane U., 1959. Lic. veterinarian, Calif. Pvt. practice, Pasadena, Calif., 1957-58; various positions USPHS, 1959-72; dir. div. rsch. svcs. NIH, Bethesda, Md., 1972-84; asst. surgeon gen. USPHS, Bethesda, 1975-84; dir. Pan Am. Zoonoses Ctr., Buenos Aires, 1984-87; coord. vet. pub. health Pan Am./WHO, Washington, 1987-89; v.p. primate ops. Charles River Labs., Arlington, Va., 1989-91, dir. Washington office, 1991; dir. Lab. Animal Health Svcs. of Microbiol. Assocs., Rockville, Md., 1992-96, ret., 1996. Cons., Arlington, 1991—; chmn. AID Rinderpest Biosafety Commn., Washington, 1991; mem. USDA, APHIS panel on sci. and tech., Washington, 1987-91; mem. Pew Health Profl. Com. adv. panel on vet. medicine, Durham, N.C., 1991. Contbr. over 70 publs. to scientific jours. Rear adm. USPHS, 1955-84. Recipient Outstanding Svc. medal Uniformed Svcs., Univ. Health Sci., Bethesda, 1985. Mem. AAAS, Am. Vet. Med. Assn. (alt. del. 1981-84, Charles River prize 1984, XII Internat. Vet. Congress prize 1989), Am. Vet. Epidemiology Soc. (pres. 1990-93, K.F. Meyer award 1982), Assn. Mil. Surgeons of U.S. (chmn. vet. med. sect. 1977, McCallam award 1990), Am. Assn. for Lab. Animal Sci., Am. Assn. for World Health, NIH Alumni Assn. (pres. 1991-93), Am. Coll. Lab. Animal Medicine (hon.). Home: 1300 Crystal Dr Apt 505 Arlington VA 22202-3234 Personal E-mail: joeheld@verizon.net.

HELD, WAYNE EDWARD, retired military officer; b. Plymouth, Mass., Dec. 26, 1950; s. Arthur Lee Held and Ruth May Reamy. Assoc. Sci., Hudson Valley CC, Troy, NY, 1994. With USN, 1972—94; adminstr. DOE Windsor Field Office, Conn., 1982—86; adminstrv. supr. Fighter Squadron 32 Naval Air Sta., Oceana, Va., 1986—89; adminstrv. officer Naval Res. Officer Tng. Corps Rensselaer Poly. Inst., Troy, 1990—94; computer testing clk. Compaq Computer, Contoocook, NH, 1994—2000. Democrat. Congragational. Avocations: camping, ATV riding, canoeing, cross country skiing. Home: 49 Red Fox Crossing Hillsboro NH 03244 Office: McLane Food Distribution 932 Maple St Contoocook NH 03229 Home Phone: 603-464-5976; Office Phone: 603-746-8000. Personal E-mail: wheld@conknet.com.

HELDER, JAN PLEASANT, JR., lawyer; b. Marysville, Calif., Jan. 18, 1963; s. Jan Pleasant Sr. and Roleane Phylis (Harrison) H.; m. Barbara Irene Loring, July 14, 1990; children: Russell Wright, Zachary Allen, David Grant. BA in Econs., Calif. State U., Sacramento, 1986; JD, Georgetown U., 1989. Bar: Mo. 1989, U.S. Dist. Ct. (we. dist.) Mo. 1989, Kans. 1990, U.S. Dist. Ct. Kans. 1990, U.S. Ct. Appeals (10th cir.) 1994, U.S. Tax Ct. 1994. Exec. asst. to pres. Sacramento Trade Exch., 1983-84; legis. asst. Calif. Postsecondary Edn. Commn., Sacramento, 1985-86; assoc. Spencer, Fane, Britt & Browne, Kansas City, Mo., 1989-94, Sonnenschein Nath & Rosenthal, Kansas City, Mo., 1994-96, ptnr., 1996-2000, Stueve Helder Siegel LLP, 2001—04; mng. ptnr. Helder Law Firm, 2004—. Judge pro tem City of Prairie Village (Kans.) Mcpl. Ct.; bd. dirs. Edn., Inc., bd. sec., 1994-95; bd. dirs. Young Audiences, vice pres., 1997-98, vice chmn., 1999-2001, sec., 2001-02. Bd. editor Bus. Torts Reporter, 1996—. Chair Calif. State Student Assn., Sacramento and Long Beach, 1984-85; mem. Leadership Mo., Jefferson City, 1992; mem. Centurions Leadership Program, 1993-95, mem. steering com., 1994-95; bd. dirs. Ivanhoe Neighborhood Coun., 2003—. Pursuit of Worthwhile Endeavors scholar Calif. State U., Sacramento, 1982. Mem. ABA (vice-chair bus. torts subcom., bus. and corp. litigation com., bus. sect. 1993-95, task force on Litigation Reform, chair bus. torts subcom. 1995—, co-chair, Task Force on Year 2000 Legislation, 1999—), co-chair, Task Force on Litigation Reform and Rule Revision, 1999—, ATLA, Nat. Inst. Trial Advocacy (western regional 1993), Am. Law Inst., 2003—, Kans. Assn. Trial Lawyers, Mo. Bar Assn., Kans. Bar Assn., Kansas City Met. Bar Assn., Johnson County Bar Assn., Greater Kansas City C. of C. (chair subcom. on labor and jud. 1990-91, fed. affairs com. 1989—), Ross T. Roberts Inn Ct. (barrister 1991-92), Am. Law Inst. Republican. Presbyterian. Avocations: jazz and classical and choral music, golf, tennis, running, politics. Home: 2216 W 63rd St Shawnee Mission KS 66208-1903 Office Phone: 816-561-5000. Business E-Mail: jan@helderlaw.com.

HELDMAN, ALAN WOHL, JR., medical educator; b. Birmingham, Ala., Oct. 28, 1962; s. Alan Wohl and Ann Bowles (Huntington) H.; m. Allison Anne Rosenberg, Dec. 29, 1991. AB in History of Sci. cum laude, Harvard Coll., 1984; MD, U. Ala., 1988. Diplomate Am. Bd. Internal Medicine, Nat. Bd. Med. Examiners. Intern and resident in Osler Med. Svc. Johns Hopkins Hosp., Balt., 1988-91; fellow in cardiology Johns Hopkins U. Sch. Medicine, Balt., 1991-95; asst. prof. medicine Johns Hopkins U., Balt., 1995—. Sci. and biotech. cons.; presenter papers Am. Gastroenterology Assn., Chgo., 1986, San Francisco, 1987, Cleve. Clinic, 1993, Am. Heart Assn., Atlanta, 1993. Contbg. author: (chpts. in books) Complications in Head and Neck Surgery, 1993, Anticoagulation, Hemostasis & Blood Preservation in Cardiovascular Surgery, 1993, Cell Behavior: Adhesion and Motility, 1993, The Cytoskeleton and Cell Function, 1993; contbr. articles to profl. jours. including Circulation Research. Interviewer Harvard Coll. Schs. Com., Balt., 1992—; vol. AmeriCares Med. Relief Airlift, Baku, Azerbaijan, 1993. Rsch. fellow Am. Heart Assn. Mem. ACP, Alpha Omega Alpha. Avocation: music. Office: Johns Hopkins U Cardiology Carnegie 565 600 N Wolfe St Baltimore MD 21287-0005 Home: 1001 Aliceanna St Apt 411 Baltimore MD 21202-4393

HELDMAN, JAMES GARDNER, lawyer; b. Cin., Mar. 7, 1949; s. James Norvin and Jane Marie (Gardner) H.; m. Wendy Maureen Saunders, Sept. 3, 1978; children: Dustin A., Courtney B. AB cum laude, Harvard U., 1971; JD with honors, George Washington U., 1974. Bar: D.C. 1975, U.S. Dist. Ct. (D.C. dist.) 1975, U.S. Ct. Appeals (D.C. cir.) 1975, U.S. Supreme Ct. 1980, Ohio 1981. Assoc. Perazich & Kolker, Washington, 1974-79, Wyman, Bautzer, Kuchel & Silbert, Washington, 1979-81, Strauss & Troy, Cin., 1981-83, ptnr., 1984—. Mem. ABA, Ohio State Bar Assn., Cin. Bar Assn. Avocations: tennis, platform tennis, biking. Office: Strauss & Troy The Fed Res Bldg 150 E Fourth St Cincinnati OH 45202-4018 Home Phone: 513-531-7221; Office Phone: 513-621-2120. Business E-Mail: jgheldman@strausstroy.com.

HELDMAN, PAUL W., lawyer, food service executive; BS, Boston U., 1973; JD, U. Cin., 1977. Bar: Ohio 1977. Assoc. Beckman, Lavercombe & Well, 1977-82; atty. The Kroger Co., Cin., 1982-86; sr. atty. Kroger Co., Cin., 1986-87, sr. counsel, 1987-89, gen. counsel, 1989-92, v.p., sec., gen. counsel, 1992-97, sr. v.p., sec., gen. counsel, 1997—2006, exec. v.p., sec., gen. counsel, 2006—. Office: The Kroger Co 1014 Vine St Ste 1000 Cincinnati OH 45202-1100*

HELENIAK, DAVID WILLIAM, diversified financial services company executive, lawyer; b. St. Paul, June 27, 1945; s. George L. and Elizabeth (Child) H.; m. Kathryn Moore, Jan. 14, 1967; children: Claire Elizabeth Moore, Charlotte Margaret Moore. AB, U. Mich., 1967; MSc in Econ., London Sch. of Econ., 1969; JD, Columbia U., 1974. Bar: NY 1975. Exec. asst. to dep. sec. US Dept. Treasury, Washington, 1977-78, asst. gen. counsel, domestic fin., 1978-79; head Shearman & Sterling LLP, Hong Kong, 1981—84, from co-head to head mergers & acquisitions group NYC, 1987—95, ptnr. mergers & acquisitions, 1995—2005, from assoc. to sr. ptnr., 1974—2001, sr. ptnr., 2001—05; vice chmn. Morgan Stanley, 2005—. Instr. in econs. U. Wis., Eau Claire, 1969-71; dir. NYC Partnership, 2001-, NYC Ballet, 2001-, NYC Investment Fund, 2007-; mem. Coun. Fgn. Rels. Contbr. articles to profl. publs. Pres. The MacDowell Colony Inc., Peterborough, NH 1987-93, also bd. dirs.; bd. visitors Columbia U. Law Sch.; chmn. London Sch. Econs. Centennial Fund.; co-chmn. Coun. for US and Italy. Mem. ABA, Bar Assn. City NY (mem. com. on securities regulation, com. to enhance diversity in the profession), Lawrence Beach Club, Century Assn. Office: Morgan Stanley 1585 Broadway New York NY 10036

HELENTJARIS, DIANE, physician; BS, MD, Mich. State U. Dir. Loudoun County Dept. Health, 1993—2000; interim dir. Lord Fairfax Health Dist., 1999—2000, dir., 2000—. Grad. Leadership Loudoun, 1995. Mem.: Am. Med. Women's Assn. (pres. 2004—05). Avocation: photography. Office: Lord Fairfax Health Dist 107 N Kent St Ste 201 Winchester VA 22601 Home Phone: 703-771-6359; Office Phone: 540-722-3480. Office Fax: 540-722-3479. Business E-Mail: diane.helentjaris@vdh.virginia.gov.

HELFAND, ARTHUR ERWIN, podiatrist; b. Phila., Jan. 12, 1935; s. Nathan H. and Esther Helfand; m. Myra Werner, May 23, 1976; children: Jennifer Bess, Lewis Aaron. MD, Temple U., 1957. Diplomate AM. Bd. Podiatric Pub. Health, Am. Bd. Podiatrics and Primary Podiatric Medicine (bd. dirs. 1992-95). Pvt. practice, Phila., 1957—2002; active staff James C. Giuffre Med. Ctr., Phila., 1958-89, coord. dept. podiatry, 1959-68, co-chief, 1968-78, chief, 1978-89, dir. podiatric edn., 1968-89; dir. clin. rsch. Pa. Coll. Podiatric Medicine, Phila., 1963-64, prof. podiatry, coord. clinics, 1964-70, prof. podiatry, chmn. dept. community health and aging, 1970—2002, prof. podiatric medicine, podiatric orthopedics, 1998—2002; prof. Sch. Podiatric Medicine Temple U., Phila., 1998—2002, prof. emeritus, 2002—. Mem. staff Thomas Jefferson U. Hosp., Phila., 1973—2002, hon. staff, Temple U. and Temple U. Children's Hosp., 2002—; cons. podiatry dept. surgery Phila. VA Hosp., 1973—82; adj. prof. depts. orthopedic surgery and medicine Jefferson Med. Coll., Phila., 1976—2002, adj. prof. orthopedic surgery, podiatry, vis. assoc. prof. cmty. health and preventive medicine, 1977—79; adj. prof. medicine Temple U., 2003—; cons. staff Willis Eye Hosp., 1980—2002; affiliate staff Joslin Ctr. Diabetes, Boston, 1993—96, Joslin Ctr. Diabetes at Wills and Jefferson, 1993—96; hon. staff Temple U. Hosp.; cons. staff Temple U. Children's Hosp.; cons. Dept. Vets. Affairs, Podiatric Svc., Washington; cons. in field. Mem. editl. bd. Rehab. Today, 1990—93; contbr. chapters to books, articles to profl. jours.; editor: 8 textbooks. Bd. dirs. Pa. Diabetes Acad., 1988—2002, treas., 1991—93, 1995—97, chmn., 1993—95; bd. dirs. Phila. Corp. Aging, 2005—. Recipient Lifetime Achievement award, Podiatry Mgmt., 1991. Fellow: ACP, Royal Soc. Health, Am. Pub. Health Assn. (emeritus, mem. task force aging), Pa. Pub. Health Assn., Am. Geriatrics Soc. (emeritus); mem.: AMA, Am. Assn. Colls. Podiatric Medicine, Internat. Acad. Preventive Medicine, Gerontol. Soc., Delware Valley Geriatrics Soc. (bd. dirs. 1989—2004, pres. 1999—2000), Am. Assn. Hosp. Podiatrists, Am. Soc. Podiatric Dermatology, Phila. County Podiatry Soc., Pa. Podiatry Assn., Am. Podiat. Med. Assn. (pres. 1982—83), Am. Soc. Podiatric Medicine (pres. 1994—95), Am. Coll. Foot Orthopedists, Temple U. Alumni Assn. Personal E-mail: aehelfand@aol.com. Business E-Mail: arthur.helfand@temple.edu.

HELFAND, EUGENE, chemist; b. Bklyn., Jan. 8, 1934; s. Saul and Helen Helfand; m. Sondra Ruth Yoskowitz, Nov. 17, 1957; children: Robin Hope, Dawn Alisa, Russ Daniel. BS summa cum laude, Poly. Inst. Bklyn., 1955; MS, Yale U., 1957, PhD, 1958. Mem. tech. staff AT&T Bell Labs., Murray Hill, NJ, 1958-60, supr. chem. computations group, 1960-83, disting. mem. tech. staff, 1983-96; cons. Lucent Techs., Bell Labs., Murray Hill, 1996-98. Adj. prof. Yeshiva U., N.Y.C., 1960-62, Poly. Inst. Bklyn., 1963-64; mem. panel on polymer sci. and engring. NRC, 1979-81. Contbr. articles to profl. jours. Guggenheim Meml. Found. fellow Stanford U., 1969-70. Fellow Am. Phys. Soc. (chmn. divsn. high polymer physics 1987-88, prize 1989); mem. Am. Chem. Soc., Soc. of Rheology, Soc. Info. Display, Sigma Xi, Phi Lambda Upsilon. Achievements include research in theory of polymers, colloids and liquid crystal displays. Office: Lucent Techs Bell Labs PO Box 636 New Providence NJ 07974-0636

HELFAND, LEONARD T., lawyer; b. Bklyn., Mar. 3, 1943; s. Harry and Sara (Radun) H.; (div. 1985); m. Julie Pestella Jan. 1, 1987; children: Melissa Ann Helfand-Pestella, Noah Joseph Helfand-Pestella, Sara May Helfand-Pestella. BA in Econs., Hobart Coll., Geneva, NY, 1964; JD, U. Miami, Coral Gables, Fla., 1966. Bar: Fla. 1967, U.S. Supreme Ct. 1972. Spl. asst. atty. gen. State of Fla., Miami, 1966, sr. atty. dept. health and rehab. services, 1977—. Sr. atty. Legal Services Greater Miami, Inc., 1967-77; legal advisor Fla. St. Council Senior Citizens, Miami, 1968-88; bd. dirs. Robert Sharp Towers Elderly Housing. Contbg. author: Mediation and Arbitration Practice. Council mem, vice-mayor City of North Miami Beach, 1973-77; mem. Dade County Dem. Exec. Com., 1975-79, 90—; asst. gen. counsel Dade County Dem. Party, 1991-92. Served to capt. USAR, 1966-72. Recipient Humanitarian award Latin Affairs Commn., 1975, City of Hope Million Dollar Club award, 1977; named One of 100 Outstanding Legal Services Lawyers in Country U.S. Office Econ. Opporutnity, 1969; recipient Special Recognition award Cedars Found., 1991. Mem. Dade County Bar Assn. (chmn. juvenile law 1983-84, vice chmn. mediation com. 1989—, Disting. Svc. award 1990, 91, 92), Fla. Bar Assn. (grievance com. 1979-81), ACLU (vice chair legal panel Ft. Lauderdale chpt. 1984-85), Sierra, B'nai Brith. Avocations: travel, canoeing, public speaking. Office: Fla Agy for Health Care Adm 401 NW 2nd Ave Ste N526 Miami FL 33128-1762

HELFAND, MARCY CAREN, lawyer; b. Chgo., Sept. 2, 1954; d. Irwin and Pauline H.; children: Eric and Alexis Weisbrod. BS with high hons., So. Meth. U., 1976, JD cum laude, 1979. Bar: Tex. 1979, U.S. Dist. Ct. (no. dist.) Tex.; cert. comml. real estate law, Tex. Bd. of Legal Specialization. Assoc. Freytag, Marshall, et al, Dallas, 1979-83, Jones, Day, Reavis & Pogue, Dallas, 1983-84; Of Counsel Morgan & Weisbrod, Dallas, 1984-94; pvt. practice Dallas, 1994—. Precinct chair Dallas Dem. Orgn., 1979—. Mem. ABA (chair remedies, miscellaneous clauses real property, probate and trust section 1993-95, chair lit. com. 2001-2003), Dallas Assn. Young Lawyers (chair continuing legal edn. com. 1983), Dallas Bar Assn., Coll. State Bar of Tex., Order of Coif. Home: 7191 Kendallwood Dr Dallas TX 75240-5510 Office: 5429 LBJ Freeway Ste 430 Dallas TX 75240 E-mail: marcy@helfandpc.com.

HELFAND, STEPHEN L., biomedical researcher, educator; b. Bklyn., Apr. 24, 1953; BSc, Stanford U., 1975; MD, Albert Einstein Coll. Medicine, Bronx, NY, 1979. Diplomate Am. Bd. Psychiatry and Neurology, 1986. Med. intern, dept. internal medicine Montefiore Hosp., Bronx, NY, 1979—80; clin. resident, neurology Mass. Gen. Hosp., Boston, 1980—83; clin. fellow, neurology Harvard Med. Sch., Boston, 1980—83; postdoctoral fellow, dept. biol. sciences Stanford U., Calif., 1983—84, postdoctoral fellow, dept. biochemistry Calif., 1984—85; assoc. rsch. scientist, dept. biology Yale U., New Haven, 1985—90; asst. prof., dept. biostructure and function, sch. dental medicine U. Conn. Health Ctr., 1990—, mem., oral biology grad. faculty, 1991—, mem., develop. biology grad. faculty, 1991—, mem., neuroscience grad. faculty, 1991—, mem. core faculty of U. Conn. Ctr. on Aging, 1993—, dir., genetics and develop. biology grad. program, 1995—2005, assoc. prof. with tenure, dept. biostructure and function, Sch. Dental Medicine, 1997—, acting head, dept. biostructure and function, 1998—; assoc. prof. with tenure U. Conn. Health Ctr., Dept. Genetics and Develop. Biol., Sch. Medicine, 1999—2003, prof. with tenure, 2003—05, clin. prof., 2005—; prof. with tenure, Dept. Molecular Biology, Cell Biology and Biochemistry, Divsn. Biology and Medicine Brown U., 2005—. Vis. scholar, neuroimmunology Queens U., Canada, 1981; vis. prof., dept. biology Univ. Coll. London, 2000; invited spkr. in field. Contbr. articles to profl. jours., chapters to books; mem. editl. bd. Ageing Cell, Faculty of 1000, contbg. editor Science of Aging Knowledge Environment, reviewer of several peer-reviewed jours. Recipient NIH Physician Scientist award, 1984—89, NSF award, 1992—95, Am. Fedn. of Aging Rsch. award, 1992, Sandoz award for Gerontolgical Rsch., 1993, Nathan W. and Margaret T. Shock Aging Found. award, 1995, Donaghue Found. Investigator Program for Health-Related Rsch. award, 2000—01, Ellison Med. Found. Sr. Investigator award in Aging, 2001—05, MERIT award, Nat. Inst. on Aging, 2004; NSF Undergraduate Fellowship, 1975, NIH Postdoctoral Fellowship, 1983—84, Ellison Med. Found. Sr. Scholar. Mem.: Soc. Develop. Biology, AAAS, NY Acad. Sciences, Mass. Med. Soc., Am. Acad. Neurology, Gerontology Soc. Am., Genetics Soc. Am. Achievements include patents in field. Office: Brown Med Sch Box G-A2 Providence RI 02912*

HELFER, MICHAEL STEVENS, lawyer, insurance company executive; b. NYC, Aug. 2, 1945; s. Robert Stevens and Teresa (Kahan) H.; m. Ricki Tigert Helfer; children: Lisa, David, Matthew. BA summa cum laude, Claremont Men's Coll., 1967; JD magna cum laude, Harvard U., 1970. Bar: DC 1971, NY 2004. Law clk. to chief judge US Ct. Appeals DC, 1970-71; asst. counsel subcom. on constl. amendments Senate Judiciary Com., 1971-73; assoc. Wilmer, Cutler & Pickering, Washington, 1973-78, ptnr., 1978-2000, mgmt. com., 1990-98, chmn., 1995-98; exec. v.p. for corp. strategy Nationwide Ins./Fin. Svcs., Columbus, Ohio, 2000—03; pres. Nationwide Strategic Investments, 2002—03; gen. counsel, corp. sec. Citigroup Inc., NYC, 2003—. Bd. dirs. Lawyers for Children Am., 1997, Lincoln Ctr. Theater, 2005—, Legal Aid Soc. NY, 2005—, mem. adv. bd. Mem. Am. Law Inst. Democrat. Home Phone: 212-573-0073; Office Phone: 212-559-5152.

HELFER, RICKI TIGERT, banking consultant; b. NC, Feb. 4, 1945; m. Michael S. Helfer; 1 child, Matthew. BA with honors, Vanderbilt U.; MA, U. N.C.; JD with honors, U. Chgo. Law. clk. to hon. John Minor Wisdom U.S. Ct. Appeals; counsel to Jud. Com. U.S. Senate, Washington, 1978-79; assoc., ptnr. Leva, Hawes, Symington, Martin and Oppenheimer, 1979-83; sr. counsel internat. fin. Treasury Dept., Washington; chief internat. lawyer Fed. Reserve Bd., 1985-92; ptnr. Gibson, Dunn & Crutcher, Washington, 1992-94; chmn. FDIC, Washington, 1994-97; nonresident sr. fellow The Brookings Inst., Washington, 1998-99; prof. law, dir. fin. instns. program Washington Coll. Law, Am. U., Washington, 2000—; cons. Am. Cmty. Bankers, Washington, 2000—. Bd. govs., chmn. audit com. Phila. Stock Exch., 1997-99; cons. internat. banking and fin. regulation. Bd. dirs. Girl Scouts U.S., 1995-99, Life Pt. Hosps., Inc., 1999—; mem. vis. com. U. Chgo. Law Sch., 1989-92, 94-97. Mem. ABA (former chair internat. banking and fin. com.), Am. Law Inst., Coun. Fgn. Rels., Washington Fgn. Law Soc. (past pres.), Basle Com. Banking Supervision.

HELFERT, ERICH ANTON, management consultant, writer, educator; b. Aussig/Elbe, Sudetenland, May 29, 1931; came to U.S., 1950; s. Julius and Anna Maria (Wilde) H.; m. Anne Langley, Jan. 1, 1983; children: Claire L., Amanda L. BS, U. Nev., 1954; MBA with distinction, Harvard U., 1956, DBA, 1958. Newspaper reporter, corr., Neuburg, Germany, 1948—52; rsch. asst. Harvard U., 1956-57; asst. prof. bus. policy San Francisco State U., 1958-59; asst. prof. fin. and control Grad. Sch. Bus. Adminstrn. Harvard U., 1959-65; internal cons., then asst. to pres., dir. corp. planning Crown Zellerbach Corp., San Francisco, 1965-78, asst. to chmn., dir. corp. planning, 1978-82, v.p. corp. planning, 1982-85; mgmt. cons. San Francisco, 1985—. Co-founding dir., chmn. Modernsoft, Inc.; mem. Dean's adv. coun. San Francisco State Bus. Sch., sch. fin. Golden Gate U.; bd. dirs., past chmn. and pres. Harvard U. Bus. Sch. No. Calif.; trustee Saybrook Inst. Author: Techniques of Financial Analysis, 1963, 11th edit., 2003, Valuation, 1966, Valley of the Shadow, 1997, (with others) Case Book on Finance, 1963, Controllership, 1965; contbr. articles to profl. jours. Exch. student fellow U.S. Inst. Internat. Edn., 1950, Ford Found. doctoral fellow, 1956. Mem. Assn. Corp. Growth (past pres., bd. dirs. San Francisco chpt.), Inst. Mgmt. Cons., Commonwealth Club, Forensic Expert Witness Assn., Phi Kappa Phi. Roman Catholic. Home: 111 St Matthews Ave No 307 San Mateo CA 94401-4519 Office Phone: 650-377-0540. E-mail: heleassoc@rcn.com.

HELFFERICH, MERRITT RANDOLPH, industry and education consultant; b. Hartford, Conn., Aug. 10, 1935; s. Reginald Humphrey and Virginia (Merritt) H.; m. Carla Anne Ostergren, July 11, 1959 (div. 1978); children: Deirdre Alida, Tryntje Bronwyn; m. April Evalyn Crosby, Aug. 24, 1985. BA in Am. lit., U. Alaska, Fairbanks, 1966; MPA in Sci. Policy, John. F. Kennedy Sch. Govt., Harvard U., Cambridge, Mass., 1990. Surveyor Golden Valley Electric Assn., Fairbanks, Alaska, 1965-66; engring. technician Geophys. Inst., U. Alaska, Fairbanks, 1966-69, field technician, rocket flight meteorologist Poker Flat Rsch. Range, 1969-76, head tech. svcs., 1976-83, asst. dir., 1986-88, assoc. dir., 1988-93; ice technician Humble Oil Co./U. Alaska, S.S. Manhattan, Northwest Passage Voyage, 1969; assoc. v.p. human resource devel. U. Alaska, Fairbanks, 1983, asst. to chancellor, 1983-86, dir. Internat. Arctic Rsch. Ctr. project, 1994-95; exec. v.p. U. Alaska Tech. Devel. Corp., Fairbanks, 1994-97; sr. cons. Innovation Consulting, Inc., 1997—, sec., treas., 1998—; distance edn. instr. Ilisagvik Coll., 2002—03, bd. mem., 1998—2005, pres., 2002—05, coord., 2006—, Consortium for Alaska Native Higher Edn. Inc. Adj. faculty Tanana Valley CC, 1972-82; legis. liaison U. Alaska, Fairbanks, 1983-86; adv. bd. NSF Polar Ice Coring Office, Fairbanks, 1989-94; bd. dirs. Internat. Small Satellite Orgn., Washington, No. Alaska Environ. Ctr., 1994-95; project mentor NSF grant Ilisagvik Coll., 1998-2000, NSF Tribal Coll. and Univs. Program Grants, Ilisagvik Coll., 2001-06; exec. bd. World Indigenous Nations Higher Edn. Consortium; cons. in field. Mem. editl. bd. U. Alaska Press, Fairbanks, 1986-94, external program evaluator, 2006—. Bd. mem., Enepu't Children's Ctr., 1970-76, Alaska Ski Corporation, 1971-74, , Fireweed Press, 1983-84, Dance Omnium, Inc., 1984-86, Women in Crisis-Counseling and Assistance, Inc., 1986-88; bd. mem., pres., Greater Fairbanks Teachers Credit Union, Inc., 1970-76; bd. mem., treas., Greater Fairbanks Family Headstart Assn., Inc., 1976-78; board mem, Fairbanks Symphony Assn., Inc., 1979-86; commr. Alaska Women's Commn., Juneau, 1988-89; proposal evaluator, Innovations in State and Local Govt., Harvard U., 1990.; mem., co-chair Main St. Fairbanks, 1990-94; mem. Fairbanks Native Cultural Ctr. Com., 1991-93; co-chair steering com., Mainstreet Fairbanks, Inc., 1992-93; commissioner, State of Alaska Subsistance Commission Board of Fish and Game, 1990-01; chair Fairbanks North Star Borough Riverfront Commn., 1992-95, 99-06, mem., 1995-06,; bd. dirs. Snedden Parks Found., 1993-2003; bd. dir., Alaska High-Tech Bus. Coun., 1995-99, Festival Fairbanks, Inc., 1996—, bd. dirs. Interior Alaska Land Trust, 1995—, Alaska Boreal Forest Coun., 2003-06, Northern Alaska Environ. Ctr., 1994-95, 97-96; mem. exec. com. World Indigenous Nations Higher Edn. Consortium, 2002—. Recipient Antarctic Svc. medal NSF, 1971, Nick Begich Scholarship Fund award, 1989, Alumni Achievement award U. Alaska Alumni Assn., 1993; Helfferich Glacier named in his honor US Bd. Geographic Names, 1971; named to Webster Groves Mo. HS Wall of Fame, 2006. Fellow Explorers Club (sec. Alaska Yukon chpt. 1999—, chair 1995-98); mem. ACLU, Soc. Rsch. Adminstrs. Internat. (travel award 2007), Rotary Club of Fairbanks, N. Alaska Environ. Ctr., Alaska Bird Observatory, Am. Sailing Assn., Big Brothers Big Sisters, Upper Gila Watershed Assn. Democrat. Avocations: collecting antiquarian arctic books, sailing, hiking, bicycling. Office: Innovation Cons Inc PO Box 80769 Fairbanks AK 99708-0769 Home Phone: 907-479-2846; Office Phone: 907-479-2846. Business E-Mail: innovate@mosquitonet.com.

HELFGOTT, ROY B., economist, educator; b. Bklyn., Oct. 27, 1925; s. Moses N. and Dorothy A. (Levine) H.; m. Gloria Wolff, July 4, 1948 (dec. June 23, 2007); 1 son, Daniel Andrew. BS in Social Sci, City Coll., NYC, 1948; MA, Columbia U., 1949; PhD, New Sch., 1957. Rsch. dir. N.Y. coat bd. Internat. Ladies Garment Workers Union, NYC, 1949—57; indsl. rels. analyst Wage Stblzn. Bd., NYC, 1952; economist N.Y. Met. Regional Study, 1957—58; asst. prof. econs. Pa. State U., University Park, 1958—60; rsch. dir. Indsl. Rels. Counselors, NYC, 1960-66, 67-68; adj. assoc. prof. Baruch Coll., 1961—68; indsl. devel. officer UN, NYC, 1966—67; head UN mission, Lower Mekong Basin, 1967; disting. prof. econs. N.J. Inst. Tech., Newark, 1968—93, disting. prof. econs. emeritus, 1993—. Cons. Orgn. Resources Counselors, Inc., N.Y.C., 1968-2005; pres. Indsl. Rels. Counselors, Inc., N.Y.C., 1996-2005. Author: Computerized Manufacturing and Human Resources, 1988, Labor Economics, 1974, 2d edit., 1980; co-author: Industrial Planning, 1969, Management, Automation and People, 1964, Made in New York, 1959; co-editor: Industrial Relations to Human Resources and Beyond, 2003; editor IR Concepts, 1993-2005. Served with AUS, 1944-46, ETO. Decorated Bronze Star with oak leaf cluster, Combat Inf. badge; fellow Inter-Univ. Inst. Social Gerontology, Berkeley, Calif., 1959; sr. Fulbright rsch. scholar U.K., 1955-56. Mem. Am. Econ. Assn., Indsl. Rels. Rsch. Assn., Met. Econ. Assn. (pres. 1978-79), Phi Beta Kappa.

HELFGOTT, SAMSON, lawyer; b. NYC, May 10, 1939; s. Benjamin Wolf and Hannah (Stern) H.; m. Joyce Ann Miller, Feb. 21, 1965; children: Yaffa, Eliezer, Batsheva, David. BEE cum laude, CCNY, 1961; MEE, NYU, 1963; JD cum laude, Fordham U., 1972; MHL, Yeshiva U., 1962, DHL, 1974. Bar: NY 1973, US Patent Office 1973, US Supreme Ct. 1978. Patent agt. Eugene S. Lovette, NYC, 1961-65, Leonard H. King, NYC, 1965-67; patent engr. IBM Corp., Rockville, Md., 1967-69; patent atty. Western Electric Co., NYC, 1971-74; patent counsel Gen. Electric Co., NYC, 1969-71, 1974-86; ptnr. Helfgott & Karas, P.C., 1986, Katten Muchin Zavis Rosenman. Editor: Foreign Patent Litigation 1983; contbr. articles to profl. jours. Patentee in communications sys. V.p. Jewish Cmty. Coun., West Lawrence, NY, 1980-84, Congregation Kneseth Israel, West Lawrence, 1982-83. Mem. ABA, Am. Patent Law Assn. (chmn. fgn. patent com., Japanese sub-com., harmonization com.), NY Patent Law Soc. (bd. dirs., chmn. fgn. com.), Internat. Patent Club (bd. dirs.), Eta Kappa Nu. Jewish. Home: 611 Caffrey Ave Far Rockaway NY 11691-5322 Office Phone: 212-940-8683. Office Fax: 212-940-8987. E-mail: samson.helfgott@kmzr.com.

HELFRICH, CORNELIUS DAVID, lawyer; b. 1939; m. Carol Helfrich. BS, Univ. Pa.; LLB, Univ. Md.; LLM, George Washington Univ. Nat. Law Ctr. Solo law practice. Recipient Pro Bono award for outstanding svc., Md. Volunteer Lawyers Svc., 1989, David Hjortsberg award. Mem.: ABA, Harford County Bar Found. (bd. dir.), Harford County Bar Assn. (pres.), Md. State Bar Assn. (pres.-elect 2003, pres. 2004, sec., bd. gov.), Md. Bar Found. (life), Am. Bar Found. (life). Office: 31 E Lee St Bel Air MD 21014 E-mail: beachrd@aol.com.

HELFRICK, ALBERT DARLINGTON, electronics engineering educator, consultant, department chairman; b. Camden, NJ, June 10, 1945; s. Eugene G. and Irma (Darlington) H.; m. Toni Venezia, May 6, 1989; children: A. Karl, Rachel. BS, Upsala Coll., East Orange, NJ, 1969; MS, N.J. Inst. Tech., 1973; PhD, Clayton U., Mo., 1988. Registered profl. engr., N.J. Sr. rsch. engr. Singer-Kearfott Div., Little Falls, NJ, 1969-72; sr. engr. Kay Elemetrics, Pine Brook, NJ, 1972-77; sr. project engr. Cessna Aircraft, Boonton, NJ, 1977-84; prin. engr. RFL Industries, Boonton, 1984-89; cons. engr. Boonton, 1989-92; prof. electronics engring. Embry-Riddle Aero. U., Daytona Beach, 1992—2003, chair engring. sci. dept., 2003—05, chair elec. and sys. dept. and mech., civil and engring. sci. dept., 2005—. Mem. com. Radio Tech. Commn. for Aeros., Washington, 1980-85, 93—; mem. adj. faculty Upsala Coll., 1972-73, Kean Coll., NJ, 1979-81, Fairleigh Dickinson U., 1986-87; instr. aerospace U. Kans., 2006-. Author: Practical Repair and Maintenance of Communications Equipment, 1983, Modern Aviation Electronics, 1984, 2d edit., 1994, Electronic Instrumentation and Measurement Techniques, 1985, Modern Electronic Instrumentation and Measurement Techniques, 1990, Electrical Spectrum and Network Analyzers, 1991, Practical Aircraft Electronic Systems, 1994, Avionics Test Equipment Handbook, 1997, Principles of Avionics, 1999, 01, 04, 07, Electronics in the Evolution of Flight, 2004; assoc. editor Jour. Aerospace Computing, Info. and Communication; tech. editor IEEE Transactions on Aerospace and Electronic Systems; also contbr. 60 articles. Bd. dirs. Aircraft Electronics Assn. Edn. Found. Sgt. U.S. Army, 1969-71, Vietnam. Recipient award RF Design mag., 1988, Excellence in Rsch. award Embry-Riddle U., 2001, Outstanding Faculty award 2006. Fellow AIAA (assoc.), Radio Club Am. (bd. dirs. 1989-90, 92-94, sec. 1990-91); mem. IEEE (sr., chmn. Daytona Beach sect., editor IEEE Transactions and Aerospace Electronics Sys., named Outstanding Faculty Educator, Fla. Coun. 2006). Achievements include patents in magnetic recording tape erasure, a method of frequency synthesis, antenna coupling device, method of coupling GPS to VHF navigation equipment. Home: 2925 Betty Dr Deland FL 32720-1945 Office: Embry-Riddle Aero U 600 S Clyde Morris Blvd Daytona Beach FL 32114-3900

HELGASON, SIGURDUR, mathematician, educator; b. Akureyri, Iceland, Sept. 30, 1927; arrived in US, 1952; s. Helgi and Kara (Briem) Skulason; m. Artie Gianopulos, June 9, 1957; children: Thor Helgi, Anna Loa. Student, U. Iceland, 1946, D (hon.), 1986; MS, U. Copenhagen, 1952, D (hon.), 1988; PhD, Princeton U., 1954; D (hon.), Uppsala U., 1996. C.L.E. Moore instr. MIT, Cambridge, 1954-56, asst. prof. math., 1960-61, assoc. prof. math., 1961-65, prof. math., 1965—; lectr. Princeton (N.J.) U., 1956-57; Louis Block asst. prof. math. U. Chgo., 1957-59; asst. prof. Columbia U., 1959-60. Vis. mem. Inst. Advanced Study, Princeton, 1964-66, 74-75, 83-84, 98, Mittag-Leffler Inst., 1970-71, 95. Author: Differential Geometry and Symmetric Spaces, 1962, Differential Geometry, Lie Groups and Symmetric Spaces, 1978, Groups and Geometric Analysis, 1984, Geometric Analysis on Symmetric Spaces, 1994, Radon Transform, 1999; editor Progress in Math., 1980-86, Perspectives in Math. Academic Press, Cambridge, 1985—; contbr. articles to profl. jours. Decorated Major Knight's Cross of Icelandic Falcon; recipient Jessen diploma, Danish Math. Soc., 1982, Gold medal, U. Copenhagen, 1951; Guggenheim fellow, 1964—65. Mem. Am. Acad. Arts and Scis., Royal Danish Acad. Scis. and Letters, Icelandic Acad. Scis., Am. Math. Soc. (Steele prize 1988). Avocations: music, photography. Office: MIT 77 Massachusetts Ave Dept Math Cambridge MA 02139-4307 Business E-Mail: helgason@mit.edu.

HELGENBERGER, MARG, actress; b. Fremont, Nebr., Nov. 16, 1958; m. Alan Roseberg Sept. 9, 1989; 1 child, Hugh. BS, Northwestern U., 1982. Appeared in TV series Ryan's Hope, 1984-86, The Shell Game, 1987, China Beach, 1988-91 (Emmy award; named Primetime Programming Individual Outstanding Supporting Actress in Drama Series, 1990, 91), CSI:Crime Scene Investigation, 2000-; co-host of New Year's Rockin' Eve, 1988, Home, 1989, (TV movies) Blind Vengence, 1990, Death Dreams, 1991, In Sickness and In Health, 1992, Through the Eyes of a Killer, 1992, When Love Kills: The Seduction of John Hearn, 1993, Stephen King's The Tommyknockers, 1993, Where Are My Children?, 1994, Lie Down with Lions, 1994, Partners, 1994, Perfect Murder, Perfect Town: Jon Benet and the City of Boulder, 2000; appeared in films Always, 1989, After Midnight, 1989, Crooked Hearts, 1991, Desperate Motive, 1993, The Cowboy Way, 1994, Bad Boys, 1995, Species, 1995, Erin Brockovich, 2000, In Good Company, 2004; TV appearances include Spenser: For Hire, 1986, Matlock, 1987, Thirtysomething, 1987, Tales from the Crypt, 1991, The Larry Sanders Show, 1995, ER, 1996, Frasier, 2000, (voice) King of the Hill, 2004.

HELGERSON, JOHN LEONARD, federal agency administrator; b. Madison, SD, Feb. 8, 1944; B, St. Olaf Coll., 1966; M, Duke U., 1968, PhD, 1970. With CIA, 1971—, deputy dir. intelligence, 1989—93, chmn. nat. intelligence coun. Washington, 2001—02; dep. dir. Nat. Imaging and Mapping Agy., 2000—01; inspector gen. CIA, 2002—. Office: CIA Office of Inspector General Washington DC 20505

HELGERSON, RICHARD, English literature educator; b. Pasadena, Calif., Aug. 22, 1940; s. Donald Theodore and Viola Dolores (Huss) H.; m. Marie-Christine David, June 8, 1967; 1 child, Jessica. BA, U. Calif., Riverside, 1963; MA, Johns Hopkins U., 1964, PhD, 1970. Prof. English Coll. Notre-Dame d'Afrique, Atakpamé, Togo, 1964-66; asst. prof. English U. Calif., Santa Barbara, 1970-76, assoc. prof., 1976-82, chair dept. English, 1989-93, prof. English, 1982—. Vis. prof. Calif. Inst. Tech., Pasadena, 1987-88; chair Huntington (Calif.) Libr. Rsch. Rev., 1986-87; faculty rsch. lectr. U. Calif., Santa Barbara, 1998. Author: The Elizabethan Prodigals, 1976, Self-Crowned Laureates, 1983, Forms of Nationhood, 1992 (James Russell Lowell prize MLA, Brit. Coun. prize in humanities), Adulterous Alliances, 2000, Joachim du Bellay, 2006, Sonnet from Carthage, 2007; contbr. articles to profl. jours. Fellow Woodrow Wilson Found., 1963-64, NEH, 1979-80, Huntington Libr., 1984-85, Guggenheim

Found., 1985-86, Folger-NEH, 1993-94, NEH, 1998-99, U. Calif. Pres.'s fellow, 1998-99, Borchard Found. fellow, 2003, Lifetime Achievement award, Internat. Spenser Soc., 2005. Mem. MLA (exec. com. English renaissance div. 1988-92), N.Am. Conf. on Brit. Studies, Renaissance Soc. Am., Spenser Soc. Am. (pres. 1988), Shakespeare Assn. Am., Western Humanities Conf. (exec. com. 1988-91). Democrat. Home: 334 E Arrellaga St Santa Barbara CA 93101-1106 Office: U Calif Dept English Santa Barbara CA 93106

HELGESON, JOHN PAUL, plant pathology and botany educator; b. Barberton, Ohio, July 25, 1935; s. Earl Adrian and Marguerite (Dutcher) H.; m. Sarah Frances Slater, June 10, 1957; children: Daniel, Susan, James. AB, Oberlin Coll., 1957; PhD, U. Wis., 1964. NSF postdoctoral fellow dept. chemistry U. Ill., Urbana, 1964-66; from asst. to prof. botany and plant pathology U. Wis., Madison, 1996—2002, prof. emeritus, 2003—. Plant physiologist USDA Argl. Rsch. Svc. plant disease resistance unit, Madison, 1966-90, rsch. leader, 1990-2003; program dir. USDA, Washington, 1982-83; vis. scientist Lab. of Cell Biology, Versailles, France, 1985-86. Lt. USAF, 1957-60. Mem. Am. Phytopathol. Soc., Am. Soc. Plant Physiologists. Achievements include development of tissue culture procedures for studying interactions of plants and fungi, of somatic hybridizations to obtain new disease resistances in plants, isolation of a gene for potato late blight resistance. Business E-Mail: jphelges@wisc.edu.

HELINSKI, DONALD RAYMOND, biologist, educator; b. Balt., July 7, 1933; s. George L. and Marie M. (Naparstek) H.; m. Patricia G. Doherty, Mar. 4, 1962; children: Matthew T., Maureen G. BS, U. Md., 1954; PhD in Biochemistry, Western Res. U., 1960; postdoctoral fellow, Stanford U., 1960-62. Asst. prof. Princeton (N.J.) U., 1962-65; mem. faculty U. Calif., San Diego, 1965—, prof. biology, 1970—, chmn. dept., 1979-81, dir. Ctr. for Molecular Genetics, 1984-95, assoc. dean Natural Scis., 1994-97, prof. emeritus, 2006—. Mem. com. guidelines for recombinant DNA research NIH, 1975-78 Author papers in field. Mem. Am. Soc. Biol. Chemists, Am. Soc. Microbiology, AAAS, Am. Acad. of Arts and Scis., Am. Acad. Microbiology, Nat. Acad. Scis., European Molecular Biology Orgn. (assoc.). Office: Bonner Hall 9500 Gilman Dr La Jolla CA 92093-0322

HELLAND, GEORGE ARCHIBALD, JR., manufacturing executive, federal official; b. San Antonio, Nov. 28, 1937; s. George Archibald and Ruth (Gorman) H.; m. Josephine Howell, June 9, 1962 (div. 1989); children: Jane Elizabeth, Thomas Gorman; m. Antonia Scott Day, Nov. 24, 1990. BS in Mech. Engring., U. Tex., 1959; MBA with distinction, Harvard U., 1961. Registered profl. engr., Tex. With Cameron Iron Works, Inc., Houston, 1961-77, asst. sales mgr., 1963, dist. sales mgr., 1964, dist. sales mgr., U.K., Africa, 1965, product mgr., 1966, plant mgr., Leeds, Eng., 1967, mgr. oil tool products, 1968, v.p., 1969-75, exec. v.p., 1975-77; with Weatherford Internat., Inc., Houston 1977-79, v.p., 1977, pres., CEO, dir., 1978-79; pres. McEvoy Oilfield Equipment Co. (name changed to Sii McEvoy div. Smith Internat., Inc. 1980), Houston, 1979-85; pres., bd. dirs. McCall Industries, Inc., Houston, 1986-87; gen. mgmt. cons., 1987-90; dep. asst. sec. of energy for export assistance U.S. Dept. Energy, Washington, 1990-93; v.p. Dreser Industries, Inc., Houston, 1993-97. Sr. assoc. Cambridge Energy Rsch. Assocs., 1997—; pres. Lockwood Corp., Gering, Nebr., 1986—91; chmn. bd. dirs. SIE Internat., Inc., Ft. Worth, 1986—87, Gas Turbine Efficiency Holdings Corp., 2002—04; prin. Innova Ptnrs., 1988—90; bd. dirs. NSGroup, Newport, Ky., 2000—06, Hunting PLC, London, Skip's Clothing, Ephrato, Pa., 2006—07; chmn. bd. dirs. Tokheim Corp., Ft. Wayne, Ind., 2001—03. Bd. dirs. Jr. Achievement Worldwide, Houston; trustee S.W. Rsch. Inst., Eurasia Found., Washington; mem. exec. com. Jr. Achievement of S.E. Tex.; mem. engring. adv. coun. U. Tex. Recipient Five Outstanding Young Texans award Tex. Jr. C. of C., 1972; named Outstanding Young Houstonian Houston Jr. C. of C., 1972; Disting. Grad. Sch. Engring. U. Tex., 1977. Mem. ASME, Am. Inst. Mining, Metall. and Petroleum Engrs., Am. Petroleum Inst. (bd. dirs.), Inst. Gas Engrs. (U.K.), Tex. Soc. Profl. Engrs., Am. Wellhead Equipment Assn. (pres. 1967), Petroleum Equipment Suppliers Assn. (pres. 1976-77), Houston C. of C., Tau Beta Pi, Phi Eta Sigma, Pi Tau Sigma, Sigma Nu, Friars Soc. Presbyterian. Home and Office: 3635 Overbrook Ln Houston TX 77027-4127 Office Phone: 713-961-4475. Personal E-mail: ghelland@worldnet.att.net.

HELLEBOID, OLIVIER, information technology executive; Degree in Engring., Ecole Nationale Superieure des Telecom. de Paris; MS, MIT. Participant in design and launch of data network for indsl. automation Telemecanique Electrique, Valbonne, France; with Hewlett-Packard, 1982—2002, mktg. mgmt. positions, gen. mgr. comml. svc. bus., v.p., gen. mgr. HP OpenView Software Bus. Unit; CEO, pres. Rainfinity; exec. v.p. corp. devel. BEA Systems, Inc., San Jose, Calif., 2002—. Office: BEA Systems Inc 2315 N First St San Jose CA 95131

HELLEINER, GERALD KARL, economics professor; b. St. Pölten, Austria, Oct. 9, 1936; s. Karl Ferdinand and Grethe (Deutsch) H.; m. Georgia Stirrett, Aug. 16, 1958; children— Jane Leslie, Eric Noel, Peter David. BA, U. Toronto, 1958; PhD, Yale U., 1962; LLD (hon.), Dalhousie U., 1988; DLitt (hon.), U. W.I., 1997; LLD (hon.), U. Guelph, 2005. Asst. prof. Yale U., 1961—65; assoc., then prof. U. Toronto, 1965—98, prof. emeritus, disting. rsch. fellow Munk Ctr. Internat. Studies, 1998—. Dir. Econ. Rsch. Bur., Dar es Salaam, Tanzania, 1966-68; vis. fellow Inst. Devel. Studies, Sussex, 1971-72, 75, Queen Elizabeth House, Oxford, 1979. Dir. Econ. Rsch. Bur., Dar es Salaam, Tanzania, 1966-68; vis. fellow Inst. Devel. Studies, Sussex, 1971-72, 75, Queen Elizabeth House, Oxford, 1979. Rsch. coord. Group of 24, 1990-98; bd. dirs., chmn. bd. trustees Internat. Food Policy Rsch. Inst., 1988-94; bd. dirs. North-South Inst., 1976-92, chmn., 1990-92; bd. dirs. Internat. Devel. Rsch. Ctr., 1985-91, Econ. and Social Rsch. Found., 1995-2000, African Capacity Bldg. Found., 1997-2003; chmn. Internat. Lawyers and Economists Against Poverty, 2003—, chmn. emeritus Guggenheim fellow, 1971-72 Fellow Royal Soc. Can.; mem. Can. Econs. Assn., Can. Assn. Study Internat. Devel., Am. Econs. Assn., Can. African Studies Assn., Order of Can. (officer). Office: 150 Saint George St Toronto ON Canada M5S 3G7 E-mail: ghellein@sympatico.ca.

HELLENBRAND, SAMUEL HENRY, lawyer; b. NYC, Nov. 11, 1916; s. Louis H. and Fannie (Cohen) H.; children: Kathy Noreen, Linda Caryn. LL.B., Bklyn. Law Sch. St. Lawrence U., 1941, LL.M., 1942. Bar: NY 1942. With NY Ctrl. R.R., NY, 1942-68, atty., asst. to gen. atty., tax atty. NY, 1947-52, gen. tax atty. NY, 1952-56, dir. taxes fin. dept. NY, 1956-63, v.p. planning and devel. NY, 1963-64, v.p. real estate NY, 1964-68; v.p. indsl. devel. and real estate Penn Ctrl. Co., 1968-70, v.p. real estate and taxes, 1970-71; pres. Pa. Co., Pa., 1970-71; v.p. exec. asst. to pres., dir. real estate affairs ITT, 1971-81; chmn. fin. com., vice-chmn. AMTRAK, 1982-90. Mem.: ABA. Home: 177 E 75th St New York NY 10021-3231

HELLENGA, ROBERT RINER, language educator, writer; b. Milw., Aug. 5, 1941; s. Theodore Edward Hellenga and Marjorie Johnson; m. Virginia K. Hellenga, Aug. 31, 1963; children: Rachel, Heather, Caitrine. BA, U. Mich., 1963; PhD, Princeton U., 1968. Tchr. English Knox Coll., Galesburg, Ill., 1968—. Co-dir. Seminar in Humanities Newberry Libr., Chgo., 1973—74; dir. Florence programs Associated Colls. of Midwest, Florence, Italy, 1982—83. Author: The Sixteen Pleasures, 1994 (Soc. of Midland Authors, 1994), The Fall for Sparrow, 1998, Blues Lessons, 2001, Philosophy Made Simple, 2006, The Italian Lover, 2007. Recipient Award, Ill. Arts Coun., 1981—2001; fellow, NEA, 1981—82. Avocations: blues guitar, Italian cooking. Office: Knox Coll Classics Dept 2 E South St Galesburg IL 61401-4999

HELLER, ADAM, chemist, researcher; b. Cluj, Romania, June 25, 1933; came to U.S., 1962; s. Ephraim and Blanche (Nissel) H.; m. Ilana Grossbard, July 26, 1956; children: Ephraim, Jonathan. MSc, Hebrew U., 1957, PhD, 1961; D honoris causa, Upsalla U., Sweden, 1991. Postdoctoral rsch. assoc. U. Calif., Berkeley, 1962-63; mem. tech. staff Bell Labs., Murray Hill, NJ, 1963-64, 75-77, GTE Labs., Bayside, NY, 1964-70, mgr. exploratory rsch. Waltham, Mass., 1970-75; head electronic materials rsch. dept. AT&T Bell Labs., Murray Hill, 1977-88; prof. chem. engring. U. Tex., Austin, 1988—. Co-founder, chief sci. advisor TheraSense Inc., 1996—2003; guest prof. Coll. de France, 1982-, The Berkeley Lectures (Chem. Engring.) 1991. Editor: Semiconductor Liquid Junction Solar Cells, 1977, Inorganic Resists, 1982; contbr. articles to profl. jours.; patentee in field. Recipient Chemistry of Materials award, ACS, 1994, Faraday medal Royal Chem. Soc., London, 1996, Spiers medal, 2000, Charles N. Reilley award, Electroanalytical Soc., 2004, Fresenius Gold medal, Soc. German Chemists, 2005, Chem. Engring. Practice award, Am. Inst. Chem. Engrs., 2005. Fellow AAS (elected), Electrochem. Soc. (elected); mem. US Nat. Acad. Engring. (elected). Jewish. Achievements include co-inventor of first substantiantially painless blood glucose monitoring system for diabetes management; subcutaneously implanted continuous glucose sensors for diabetes management; invention of lithium batteries, liquid lasers, electrochemical solar cells, photocatalytically self-cleaning windows and coatings. Business E-Mail: heller@che.utexas.edu.

HELLER, ARTHUR, advertising executive; b. Bklyn., Mar. 14, 1930; s. Max and Tecla (Jacobs) H.; m. Phyllis Olarsch, Dec. 25, 1954; children: Todd, Tracy. BA, Bklyn. Coll., 1951, MA, 1952. Speech and speech correction tchr. N.Y.C. Bd. Edn., 1951—52; v.p., assoc. media dir., media analysis and planning Benton & Bowles, Inc., 1955-66; with Ted Bates & Co., NYC, 1966—, v.p., media dir., 1966-69, v.p., assoc. dir. media-program dept., 1969-71, sr. v.p., 1971—, also account dir., 1974-78; sr. v.p., dir. media-programming-mktg. services Griffin Bacal Inc., NYC, 1978-82, exec. v.p., 1982-97, also bd. dirs.; pres. Heller Mktg. & Comms. Former dir. media programming worldwide, former gen. mgr. Griffin Bacal Can. Served with AUS, 1952-54. Mem. Actors Equity Assn.

HELLER, DAN L., lawyer; b. Spartanburg, SC, July 31, 1953; BA magna cum laude in English Lit., Yale U., 1975; JD cum laude, Harvard U., 1980. Bar: Ga. 1980. Atty. King and Spalding, Atlanta, 1980, ptnr., 1987—. Reporter: various newspapers. Mem. ABA, State Bar Ga., Atlanta Bar Assn., Phi Beta Kappa. Office: King & Spalding 1180 Peachtree St NE Atlanta GA 30309 Office Phone: 404-572-4919. Office Fax: 404-572-5100. Business E-Mail: dheller@kslaw.com.

HELLER, DEAN, congressman, former state official; b. Castro Valley, Calif., May 10, 1960; m. Lynne Brombach, children: Hilary, Harrison, Andrew, Emmy. BS with honors, U. S. Calif., 1985. Stockbroker, broker, trader Pacific Stock Exch.; chief dep., Office of State Treas. State of Nev.; mem. Nev. State Assembly, 1990—94; sec. state State of Nev., Carson City, 1995—2006; mem. US Congress from 2nd Nev. dist., 2007—, mem. edn. & labor com., nat. resources com., small bus. com. Bd. dirs. Western Nev. Cmty. Coll. Found. Mem.; We. Nev. C C. Found., Boys & Girls Club We. Nev., N.Am. Securities Adminstrs. Assn. Republican. Mem. Lds Ch. Achievements include being the first secretary of state in the nation to demand a voter-verifiable paper audit trail printer on touchscreen voting machines. Avocation: stockcar racing. Office: 405 Idaho St Ste 214 Elko NV 89801 also: 1023 Longworth House Office Bldg Washington DC 20515*

HELLER, ERIC JOHNSON, physicist, educator, digital abstract artist; b. Washington, Jan. 10, 1946; PhD, Harvard U., 1973. Camile and Henry Dreyfus tchr.-scholar, 1977—82; Alexander von Humboldt Sr. Fellow, 1985; prof. physics Harvard U., Cambridge, Mass. Digital abstract artist. Author of 130 sci. papers. John Simon Guggenheim Fellowship, 1992. Fellow: Am. Physical Soc., AAAS, Am. Acad. of Arts and Scis.; mem.: NAS, Am. Chem. Soc. (Award in Theoretical Chemistry 2005). Research involves theoretical investigation of wave behavior, chaos and quantum mechanics, and collision theory. Office: Harvard U Jefferson 352 17 Oxford St Cambridge MA 02138 Office Phone: 617-496-7537. Business E-Mail: heller@physics.harvard.edu.

HELLER, ESTHER A., writer, educator; b. Malden, Mass., Nov. 14, 1947; d. Eugene Gregory and Goldie (Stern) Heller; m. Nicholas A. Corsano, Sept. 4, 1971. BA with honors, Brandeis U., 1969; MS, Stanford U., 1971; postgrad., U. Calif., Davis, 1979. Cert. diversity trainer Equity Inst., 1995. Engr. DCA Reliability, Sunnyvale, Calif.; firmware engr. ISS/Sperry-Univac, Cupertino, Calif., 1979-81; hardware engr. Hewlett-Packard, Cupertino, 1981-86, software engr., 1986-95; ind. cons., trainer and diversity coach self employed, Menlo Park, Calif., 1995—. Author diversity columns, 1996—; staff writer Voices of New Bridges-Connections in Judaism, 1999-2003. Bd. dirs. San Francisco Bay coun. Girl Scouts U.S.A., 1988—95, troop leader, 1972—2003; trainer San Francisco Bay coun. Girls Scouts U.S.A., 1982—, subchair capital campaign, 1997—98; founding mem. Silicon Valley Partnership, 1999, co-chair, 2001—02, 2005—06; mem.-at-large Jewish Cmty. Rels. Coun., San Francisco area, 2000—; bd. dirs. Keddem Congregation, 2002—, 1st v.p., 2006—. Recipient Thanks badge San Francisco Bay coun. Girl Scouts USA, 1991, Maude Whalen award, 2003, Thanks badge II, 2007, Ora award Nat. Jewish Girl Scout Com., 1997. Fellow: Soc. Women Engrs. (chair Santa Clara Valley sect. diversity com. 1996—2006, mem. nat. multicultural com. 2000—, chair nat. Girl Scout com. 2000—, leadership coach 2003—, Disting. Svc. award 2007); mem.: Nat. Assn. Parliamentarians, Nat. Field Archery Assn. (cert. basic archery instr. 2004), King's Mountain Archery Club (staff instr. 2004—). Jewish. Avocations: needlecrafts, orienteering, photography, archery. Office: Ind Cons and Trainer 665 Gilbert Ave Menlo Park CA 94025-2731 E-mail: esther@galarc.com.

HELLER, FRANCIS HOWARD, retired law and political science educator; b. Vienna, Aug. 24, 1917; came to U.S., 1938, naturalized, 1943; s. Charles A. and Lily (Grunwald) H.; m. Donna Munn, Sept. 3, 1949 (dec. Dec. 1990); 1 child, Denis Wayne. Student in Law, U. Vienna, 1935—37; JD, MA, U. Va., 1941, PhD, 1948; DHL (hon.), Benedictine Coll., 1988. Asst. prof. govt. Coll. William and Mary, 1947; asst. prof. polit. sci. U. Kans., Lawrence, 1948-51, assoc. prof., 1951-56, prof., 1956-72, Roy A. Roberts prof. law and polit. sci., 1972-88, prof. emeritus Lawrence, 1988—, assoc. dean Coll. Liberal Arts and Scis., 1957-66, assoc. dean of faculties, 1966-67, dean, 1967-70, vice chancellor for acad. affairs, 1970-72, acting provost, 1967—68, 1969—70. Vis. prof. Inst. Advanced Studies, Vienna, 1965, U. Vienna Law Sch., 1985, 97, Trinity U., Tex., 1992. Author: Introduction to American Constitutional Law, 1952, The Presidency: A Modern Perspective, 1960, The Korean War: A 25-Year Perspective, 1977, The Truman White House, 1980, Economics and the Truman Administration, 1982, USA: Verfassung und Politik, 1987, NATO: The Founding of the Alliance and the Integration of Europe, 1992, The Kansas State Constitution: A Reference Guide, 1992, The United States and the Integration of Europe, 1996. Mem. Kans. Commn. on Constl. Revision, 1957-61, Lawrence City Planning Commn., 1957-63, ednl. adv. commn. U.S. Army Command and Gen. Staff Coll., 1969-72; bd. dirs. Harry S. Truman Libr. Inst., 1958-96, v.p., 1962-96; bd. dirs. Benedictine Coll., 1971-79; mem. nat. adv. coun. Ctr. for Study of Presidency, 1991-97. Pvt. to 1st lt. arty. AUS, 1942-47, capt. 1951-52, maj. USAR, ret. Decorated Silver Star, Bronze Star with cluster; recipient Career Teaching award Chancellor's Club, 1986, Silver Angel award Kans. Cath. Conf., 1987, Disting. Svc. citation U. Kans., 1998; Austrian Cross of Honor for Sci. and Art 1st class, 2004. Mem. Am. Polit. Sci. Assn. (exec. council 1958-60), Order of Coif, Phi Beta Kappa, Pi Sigma Alpha (mem. nat. council 1958-60) Home: 1510 St Andrews Dr Lawrence KS 66047-1634

HELLER, FREDERICK, retired mining executive;; 3 children. BA, Harvard U., 1954. With Hanna Mining Co., Cleve., 1957-87, v.p. sales, 1973-76, sr. v.p. sales and transp. Cleve., 1976-81, sr. v.p. mktg., 1981-84; sr. v.p. sales and mktg. M.A. Hanna Co., Cleve., 1984-87; dir. exec. com. Tucson Bot. Gardens, 2002—04. Trustee, exec. com. Cleve. Inst. Art, 1977-82; trustee, fin. com. McGregor Home, 1978-86. 1st lt. U.S. Army, 1954-56. Mem.: Gallery Golf Club. Home: 4825 N Camino Sumo Tucson AZ 85718-7403

HELLER, JACK ISAAC, lawyer; b. Passaic, NJ, July 12, 1932; m. Naomi Heller AB, U. Chgo., 1952; LLB, Columbia U., 1958. Teaching fellow, research asst. Internat. Program in Taxation Harvard Law Sch., 1958-61; sr. tax advisor Latin Am. Bur., US AID, 1962-65; with Office Gen. Counsel, AID, 1965-66; legal adviser AID, Brazil, 1966-67, asst. dir., 1967-68; dir. Office of Devel. Programs, Latin Am. Bur., AID, 1969-72; atty., mgr. spl. projects Office Gen. Counsel, Gen. Electric Co., 1972-74; pvt. practice Washington, 1974—; ptnr. Heller & Rosenblatt, Washington, 1991—. Co-dir. spl. programs in Latin Am. U. Ill. Coll. Law, 1975—80, co-dir. spl. programs in China, 1982—86; bd. mem. Pan Am. Devel. Found., 1986—98, pres., 1998—2000; co-founder Ukraine-US Bus. Coun., 1996, gen. counsel, 1996—; co-founder Fund for Democracy and Devel., 1993, sr. v.p., 1993—2004. Co-author: Tax Incentives for Industry in Less Developed Countries, 1963. Served with AUS, 1953-55. Avocation: photography. Home: 3431 Porter St NW Washington DC 20016-3125 Office: Heller & Rosenblatt 1101 15th St NW Washington DC 20005-5002 Office Phone: 202-466-4700. Personal E-mail: hellerji@erols.com.

HELLER, JAMES STEPHEN, law librarian, educator; b. Detroit, Apr. 11, 1950; s. Benjamin Heller and Vera Frances (Broder) Schumer; m. Janet Louise Crowther, Oct. 27, 1985; children: Benjamin William, Seth Joseph. BA, U. Mich., 1971; JD cum laude, U. San Diego, 1976; MLS, U. Calif., Berkeley, 1977. Bar: Calif. 1976, D.C. 1978. Assoc. law librarian Nat. Law Ctr., George Washington U., Washington, 1977-80; dir. Civil Library, U.S. Dept. Justice, Washington, 1980-83; dir., asso. prof. law Coll. Law Library, U. Idaho, Moscow, 1983-88; dir. Law Libr., prof. law Marshall-Wythe Sch. Law, Coll. of William and Mary, Williamsburg, Va., 1988—. Co-author: Copyright Handbook, 1984; contbr. articles to legal jours. Mem. Am. Assn. Law Librs. (chmn. copywrite com. 1982-83, 93-94, chmn. awards com. 1991-92, chair edn. com. 1994-95), Northwest Consortium Law Librs. (chmn. 1987-88), Va. Assn. Law Librs. (pres. 1994-95), Southeastern Assn. Law Librs., ACLU (v.p. Moscow-Latah com. 1987-88). Jewish. Office: William & Mary Sch Law PO Box 8795 Williamsburg VA 23187-8795 Office Phone: 804-221-3252. E-mail: heller@wm.edu.*

HELLER, JEFFREY M., data processing executive; m. Carol; children: Scott, Debbie. BBA, U. Tex. Joined engring. devel. program Electronic Data Systems Corp., 1968, systems engr. Camp Hill, Pa., 1969, mem. medicare ctrl. support group Dallas, 1969—70, participant NY Stock Exch. study, 1970, various mgmt. positions, 1970-72, mgr. regional data ctr. Dallas, 1972-73, regional mgr. health care bus. Ea. US, 1973-74, corp. v.p., 1974-79, head tech. services group, 1979-87, sr. v.p., 1987-96, pres., COO, 1996—2000, vice chmn., 1996—2002, also bd. dirs., pres., COO, 2003—06, vice-chmn., 2006—. Bd. dirs. Mutual of Omaha, Trammell Crow Co., Temple-Inland. Bd. dirs. Dallas Symphony Assn., Cotton Bowl Athletic Assn.; mem. Longhorn Found., U. Tex. Chancellor's Coun., U. Tex. McCombs Sch. Bus. Adv. Coun., U. Tex. Devel. Bd., U. Tex. Men's Athletic Coun.; trustee Southwestern Med. Found. Served to capt. USMC, 1960—66. Office: Electronic Data Systems Corp 5400 Legacy Dr Plano TX 75024 Office Phone: 972-604-6000.*

HELLER, JOHN RODERICK, III, lawyer, corporate financial executive; b. Harrisburg, Pa., Aug. 14, 1937; s. John Roderick and Susie May (Ayres) H.; children: Elizabeth, Carolynn, John. AB summa cum laude, Princeton U., 1959; AM in History, Harvard U., 1960, JD magna cum laude, 1963. Bar: D.C. 1964. Assoc. Wilmer, Cutler & Pickering, Washington, 1963-65, 68-71, ptnr., 1971-82, of counsel, 1982-85; spl. asst. to dir. for India, AID, New Delhi, 1966-67, regional legal adviser for Pakistan, 1967-68; pres. Bristol Compressors, Inc., Va., 1982-85; pres., dir. NHP, Inc., 1985-97, also bd. dirs.; chmn. Carnton Capital Assocs., Washington, 1997—. Bd. dirs. First Potomac Realty Trust, The Phillips Collection; former chmn. Civil War Trust, WETA, Nat. Capital Revitalization Corp.; prof. law George Washington U., 1976—81. Author: The Confederacy Is On Her Way Up the Spout: Letters to South Carolina 1861-64, 1992, An Upcountry Chronicle, 1998. Recipient Meritorious Honor award U.S. Dept. State, 1967. Mem. ABA, Soc. of Cincinnati, Cosmos Club, Met. Club (Washington). Presbyterian. Office: Carnton Capital Assocs 2540 Massachusetts Ave #304 Washington DC 20008

HELLER, JULES, artist, educator, writer; b. NYC, Nov. 16, 1919; s. Jacob Kenneth and Goldie (Lassar) H.; m. Gloria Spiegel, June 11, 1947; children: Nancy Gale, Jill Kay. AB, Ariz. State Coll., 1939; AM, Columbia U., 1940; PhD, U. So. Calif., 1948; DLitt, York U., 1985. Spl. art instr. 8th St. Sch., Tempe, Ariz., 1938-39; dir. art and music Union Neighborhood House, Auburn, NY, 1940-41; prof. fine arts, head dept. U. So. Calif., 1946-61; vis. asso. prof. fine arts Pa. State U., summers 1955, 57; dir. Pa. State U. (Sch. Arts), 1961-63; founding dean Pa. State U. (Coll. Arts and Architecture), 1963-68; founding dean Faculty Fine Arts York U., Toronto, 1968-73; prof. fine arts Faculty of Fine Arts, York U., 1973-76; dean Coll. Fine Arts, Ariz. State U., Tempe, 1976-85, prof. art, 1985-90; prof. emeritus, dean emeritus, 1990—. Vis. prof. Silpakorn U., Bangkok, Thailand, 1974, Coll. Fine Arts, Colombo, Sri Lanka, 1974, U. Nat. Tucumán, Argentina, 1990, U. Nat. Cuyo, Mendoza, Argentina, 1990; lectr., art juror; Cons. Open Studio, 1975-76; vis. com. on fine arts Fisk U., Nashville, 1974; co-curator Leopoldo Méndez exhbn. Ariz. State U., Tempe, 1999 One man shows include Gallery Pascal, Toronto, U. Alaska, Fairbanks, Alaskaland Bear Gallery, Visual Arts Ctr., Anchorage, Ariz. State U., Tempe, Lisa Sette Gallery, 1990, Centro Cultural de Tucumán, San Miguel de Tucumán, 1990; retrospective exhbn. Ariz. State U., Tempe, 1999, Town Hall, Paradise Valley, Ariz., 1999-00, Cattle Track Arts Compound, Scottsdale, Ariz., 2006; exhibited in group shows at Canadian Printmaker's Showcase, Pollack Gallery, Toronto, Mazelow Gallery, Toronto, Santa Monica Art Gallery, L.A. County Mus., Phila. Print Club, Seattle Art Mus., Landau Gallery, Kennedy & Co. Gallery, Bklyn. Mus., Cin. Art Mus., Dallas Mus. Fine Arts, Butler Art Inst., Oakland Art Mus., Pa. Acad. Fine Arts, Santa Barbara Mus. Art, San Diego Gallery Fine Arts, Martha Jackson Gallery, NYC, Yuma Fine Arts Assn., Ariz., Toronto Dominion Centre, Amerika Haus, Hannover, Fed. Rep. Germany, U. Md., Smith-Andersen Galleries, Palo Alto, Calif., Grunewald Ctr. Graphic Arts, L.A., Steel Pavilion, Phoenix, 2003, U. So. Fla., Tampa, Sheldon Meml. Gallery, Lincoln, Nebr., Santa Cruz (Calif.) Mus., Drake U., Iowa, Bradley U., Ill., Del Bello Gallery, Toronto, Honolulu Acad. Fine Arts, New Orleans Mus. Art, Robert Roman Gallery, Scottsdale, Ariz., 2004, Ariz. State U, 2005, Seattle Print Art, Jules Heller and Friends Cattle Track Arts Compound, Seattle, 2006; represented in permanent collections, Nat. Mus. Am. Art Smithsonian Instn., Washington, Long Beach Mus. Art, Library of Congress, York U., Allan R. Hite Inst. of U. Louisville, Ariz. State U., Tamarind Inst., U. N.Mex., Zimmerli Mus. Rutgers U., NJ, Can. Council Visual Arts Bank, also pvt. collections; author: Problems in Art Judgment, 1946, Printmaking Today, 1958, revised, 1972, Papermaking, 1978, 79; co-editor: North American Women Artists of the Twentieth Century, 1995, Codex Méndez, 1999; contbg. artist: Prints by California Artists, 1954, Estampas de la Revolución Mexicana, 1948; illustrator: Canciónes de

Mexico, 1948; author numerous articles. Adv. bd. Continental affairs com. Americas Soc., 1983-86. With USAAF, 1941-45. Can. Coun. grantee; Landsdowne scholar U. Victoria; Fulbright scholar, Argentina, 1990. Mem. Coll. Art Assn. (Disting. Teaching of Art award 1995), Authors Guild, Internat. Assn. Hand Papermakers (steering com. 1986—), Nat. Found. Advancement in the Arts (visual arts panelist 1986-90, panel chmn. 1989, 90), Internat. Assn. Paper Historians, Internat. Coun. Fine Arts Deans (pres. 1968-69), So. Graphics Coun. (printmaker emeritus award 1999). Business E-Mail: jules.heller@asu.edu.

HELLER, MARK A., lawyer; b. 1947; BA with honors, Univ. Wis., Madison, 1970, JD, 1973. Bar: Wis. 1973, DC 1981. Sr. trial atty. FTC, Washington, 1973—81; assoc. chief counsel, enforcement FDA, Washington, 1981—84, assoc. chief counsel, med. devices, 1984—91; ptnr., chmn. FDA dept. Wilmer Cutler Pickering Hale & Dorr, Washington, 1997—. Author: Guide to Medical Device Regulation; contbr. chapters to books, articles to profl. jours. Named a Top Lawyer in Washington, Washingtonian mag., 2004. Office: Wilmer Cutler Pickering Hale & Dorr 1899 Pennsylvania Ave NW Washington DC 20006 Mailing: Wilmer Cutler Pickering Hale & Dorr Willard Office Bldg 1455 Pennsylvania Ave NW Washington DC 20004 Office Phone: 202-663-6005. Office Fax: 202-663-6363. Business E-Mail: mark.heller@wilmerhale.com.

HELLER, MARY BERNITA, psychotherapist; b. Roland, Iowa, Feb. 11, 1934; d. Casper and Blanche (Hanson) Stenberg; m. John R. Heller, June 7, 1958; children: Kristen, Jonathan, Kathryn. BA, St. Olaf Coll., 1956; MSW, Fordham U., 1970. Lic. Social Worker NY, Bd. Cert. Diplomate in Social Work. Psychiat. social worker Beloit Children's Home, Ames, Iowa, 1957—58; caseworker Luth. Cmty. Svcs., NYC, 1958—59, Soc. Seamen's Children, SI, NY, 1971—75; psychiatric social worker S.I. Mental Health, 1971—75; psychotherapist Mid-Hudson Cons. Ctr., Wappinger Falls, NY, 1976—84; pvt. practice Poughkeepsie, NY, 1977—; psychotherapist Windsor Counseling Group, New Windsor, NY, 1989—2003. Supr. Luth. Cmty. Svcs., NYC, 1987-96. Bd. dirs. Children's Home of Poughkeepsie, 1983-88; resident, bd. dirs. Seafarers and Internat. House, N.Y.C., 1990-96, v.p., 2002-2005, pres., 2005—; mem. candidacy com. Met. N.Y. Synod, N.Y.C., 1986-94, v.p., 1992-2002; mem. coun. Hudson Valley Philharm., Poughkeepsie, 1983-88; mem. Mission Devel. Bd., Metro NY Squad, 2004-. Fellow Am. Orthopsychiat. Assn.; mem. NASW, Acad. Cert. Social Workers. Democrat. Lutheran. Avocations: alpine skiing, plants. Home: 24 Thornwood Dr Poughkeepsie NY 12603-4633 Office: 55 Wilbur Blvd Poughkeepsie NY 12603-3424 Home Phone: 845-473-5451; Office Phone: 845-452-3714. Personal E-mail: maryheller211@hotmail.com.

HELLER, PAUL MICHAEL, film company executive, producer; b. NYC, Sept. 25, 1927; s. Alex Gordon and Anna (Rappaport) H.; children: Michael Peter, Charles Paul. Student, Drexel Inst. Tech., 1944-45; BA, Hunter Coll., 1950. Freelance scenic designer, NYC, 1952-61; film producer, 1961—; instr. NYU, NYC, 1964-66; prodn. exec. Warner Bros., 1970-71; pres. Paul Heller Prodns. Inc., Beverly Hills, Calif., 1973—. Producer over 30 films including David and Lisa, 1962, Enter the Dragon, 1973, First Monday in October, 1981, Withnail and I, 1987, My Left Foot, 1989, The Lunatic, 1990, The Annihilation of Fish, 1999; mus. multi-media prodr. The Skirball Cultural Center Museum, 1997, The Hong Kong Museum of History, 2000. Founding mem. Com. 100, Am. Film Inst. Served with U.S. Army. Recipient spl. award Nat. Assn. Mental Health. Mem. Dirs. Guild Am., Screen Actors Guild, Actors Equity Assn., Acad. Motion Picture Arts and Scis., Brit. Acad. Film and TV Arts (bd. dirs.), Hearst Castle Preservation San Simeon (bd. dirs.), Lotos Club (N.Y.C.). Home and Office: 1666 N Beverly Dr Beverly Hills CA 90210-2316 E-mail: pheller@earthlink.net.

HELLER, PHILIP, lawyer; b. NYC, Aug. 12, 1952; s. Irving and Dolores (Soloff) Heller; married; children: Howard Philip, John Philip, Madison Irene Sarah. Attended, Harvard Coll.; BA summa cum laude, Boston U., 1976, JD, 1979. Bar: Mass. 1979, NY 1980, Calif. 1984, US Dist. Ct. Mass., US Dist. Ct. (ea. and so. dists.) NY, US Dist. Ct. (all dists.) Calif., US Ct. Appeals (1st, 2d and 9th cirs.) 1980, US Supreme Ct. 1983. Law clk. to Judge Cooper US Dist. Ct. NY, NYC, 1979; ptnr. Fagelbaum & Heller LLP, LA. Mem.: ABA (litigation sect), LA County Bar Assn., Calif. Bar Assn. Office: 2049 Century Park E Ste 4250 Los Angeles CA 90067-3168 Home Phone: 310-203-0677; Office Phone: 310-286-7666. Office Fax: 310-286-7086. Business E-Mail: ph@philipheller.com.

HELLER, ROBERT, financial executive, economist; b. Cologne, Germany, Jan. 8, 1940; m. Emily Mitchell, Dec. 5, 1970; children: Kimberly, Christopher. MA in Econs., U. Minn., 1962; PhD, U. Calif., Berkeley, 1965. Instr. U. Calif., Berkeley, 1965; assoc. prof. econs. UCLA, 1965-71; prof. U. Hawaii, Honolulu, 1971-74; chief fin. studies divsn. Internat. Monetary Fund, Washington, 1974-78; sr. v.p., dir. internat. econ. rsch. Bank of Am., San Francisco, 1978-86; mem., bd. govs. Fed. Res. System, Washington, 1986-89; exec. v.p. VISA Internat., San Francisco, 1989-91; pres., CEO VISA, U.S.A., San Francisco, 1991-93; exec. v.p. Fair, Isaac and Co., San Rafael, Calif., 1994-2001; chmn. Govs. Group, 2001—. Bd. dirs. Fair, Isaac and Co., Plus Sys. Inc., Interlink, Mcht. Bank Svcs. Corp., Bay Area Coun., San Francisco, Sonic Automotive, Bank of Marin, San Rafael, Calif., 2006—; bd. dirs., mem. adv. bd. BMW of N.Am., Inc.; vice-chmn. Fed. Fin. Instns. Exam. Coun., 1988-89; mem. Nat. Adv. Coun. Internat. Monetary and Fin. Policies, 1987-89, U.S. Coun. Internat. Bus., N.Y.C., 1979—; trustee World Affairs Coun., 1990-96; mem. adv. bd. Nat. Ctr. Fin. Svcs., U. Calif., Berkeley, 1984-90, Ctr. Fin. Sys. Rsch., Ariz. State U., Tempe, 1989, Inst. Internat. Edn., San Francisco, 1989; mem. Bay Area Internat. Forum, 1989, Bay Area Coun., 1992; dir. Am. Inst. Contemporary German Studies, Johns Hopkins U., Washington, 1989; dir. Wharton Fin. Instns. Ctr., U. Pa., 1989—2004. Author: International Trade, 1968, rev. edit. 1973, International Monetary Economics, 1974, The Economic System, 1972, Japanese Investment in the U.S., 1974; mem. editorial bd. Jour. Money, Credit and Banking, 1975-83, Internat. Trade Jour., 1985-88. Bd. dirs. Marin Gen. Hosp., 2001— Mem. Bankers Club of San Francisco, Royal Econ. Soc., Am. Econ. Assn., Western Econo. Assn. (exec. bd. 1977-81), San Francisco Yacht Club, Tiburon Peninsula Club. Avocations: sailing, skiing.

HELLER, ROBERT MARTIN, lawyer; b. NYC, Feb. 12, 1942; s. Philip B. and Mildred S. (Friedman) H.; m. Amy Wexler, July 11, 1965; children: David B., Pamela L. BA, Columbia U., 1963, LLB, 1966. Bar: N.Y. 1967, D.C. 1992, U.S. Dist. Ct. (so. and ea. dists.) N.Y. 1970, U.S. Ct. Appeals (2d cir.) 1967, U.S. Supreme Ct. 1976. Law clk. to judge U.S. Ct. Appeals (2d cir.), NYC, 1966-67; atty. adviser to commr. FTC, Washington, 1967-69; asst. to mayor for housing, city planning, transp. and model cities, sec. to cabinet City of N.Y., 1971-73; ptnr. Kramer Levin Naftalis & Frankel LLP, NYC, 1974—, mng. ptnr., 1991-94. Adj. prof. architecture Columbia U., 1975—77; bd. visitors Columbia Law Sch., 1992—2000. Chair Union for Reform Judaism, 2003—; bd. govs. Hebrew Union Coll./Jewish Inst. Religion, 1996—; pres. bd. dirs. 1056 Fifth Ave. Corp., 1994-96; trustee Rabbi Marc H. Tanenbaum Found. James Kent scholar; Harlan Fiske Stone scholar. Mem. ABA, N.Y. State Bar Assn., Assn. of Bar of City of N.Y. (com. on antitrust and trade regulation 1996-99), Phi Beta Kappa. Avocations: aerobic walking, photography. Home: 1056 5th Ave New York NY 10028-0112 Office: Kramer Levin Naftalis & Frankel LLP 1177 Ave of the Americas New York NY 10036 Office Phone: 212-715-9100.

HELLER, RONALD IAN, lawyer; b. Cleve., Sept. 4, 1956; s. Grant L. and Audrey P. (Lecht) Heller; m. Shirley Ann Stringer, Mar. 23, 1986 (dec. 2001); 1 child, David Grant. AB with high honors, U. Mich., 1976, MBA, 1979, JD, 1980. Bar: Hawaii 1980, U.S. Ct. Claims 1982, U.S. Tax Ct. 1981, U.S. Ct. Appeals (9th cir.) 1981, U.S. Supreme Ct. 1992; Trust Ter. Pacific Islands 1982, Rep. Marshall Islands 1982; CPA, Hawaii. Assoc. Hoddick, Reinwald, O'Connor & Marrack, Honolulu, 1980-84; ptnr. Reinwald, O'Connor & Marrack, Honolulu, 1984-87; stockholder Torkildson, Katz, Fonseca, Moore & Hetherington, Honolulu, 1988—2007; stockholder, bd. dirs. Torkildson, Katz, Moore & Hetherington, Honolulu, 2007—. Adj. prof. U. Hawaii Sch. Law, 1981; arbitrator ct.-annexed arbitration program First Cir. Ct., State of Hawaii; author, instr. Hawaii Taxes. Bd. dirs. Hawaii Women Lawyers Found., Honolulu, 1984-86, Hawaii Performing Arts Co., Honolulu, 1984-93; panel of arbitrators Am. Arbitration Assn., 1987-99; actor, stage mgr. Honolulu Cmty. Theatre, 1983-87, Hawaii Performing Arts Co., Honolulu, 1982-87; mem. Tax Rev. Commn., State of Hawaii, 2005. Named Hawaii Outstanding Small Bus. Vol., NFIB, 1998, Small Bus. Champion for State of Hawaii and S.W. U.S., 2004. Fellow Am. Coll. Tax Counsel; mem. AICPA (coun. 1994-96, 2002-04), ABA, Hawaii State Bar Assn. (chair tax sect. 1997-98, chair state and local tax com. 1994-95), Hawaii Soc. CPAs (chmn. tax com. 1985-86, legis. com. 1987-88, bd. dirs. 1988-2003, pres. 1994-95), Hawaii Women Lawyers. Office: Torkildson Katz Moore & Hetherington 700 Bishop St Ste 1500 Honolulu HI 96813-4187 Office Phone: 808-523-6000. E-mail: rheller@torkildson.com.

HELLERER, MARK R., lawyer; b. 1949; BA, Fordham Univ., 1971; JD, Univ. Buffalo, 1976. Bar: NY 1977, US Dist. Ct. (ea., so., we. dist. NY), US Ct. Appeals (2d cir.) DC. Law clk. Judge John T. Curtin, US Dist. Ct., We. Dist. NY, 1976—78; asst. U.S. atty. So. Dist. NY, U.S. Dept. Justice, NYC, 1983—89, chief Major Crimes unit, 1989—92; ptnr., co-chmn. Corp. Investigations & White Collar Def. practice, head NY Litigation practice Pillsbury Winthrop Shaw Pittman, NYC. Chmn. NYC Water Bd., 1995—2004. Recipient Dir. award, US Dept. Justice, 1988, John Marshall award, 1990. Mem.: ABA, Assn. Bar City of NY, Fed. Bar Coun., NY Coun. Criminal Def. Lawyers. Office: Pillsbury Winthrop Shaw Pittman 1540 Broadway New York NY 10036 Office Phone: 212-858-1787. Office Fax: 212-858-1500. Business E-Mail: mark.hellerer@pillsburylaw.com.

HELLERSTEIN, DAVID JOEL, psychiatrist, researcher, writer; b. Cleve., Dec. 30, 1953; s. Herman Kopel and Mary Leah (Feil) H.; m. Lisa Perry, Oct. 16, 1983; children: Sarah Nicole, Benjamin, Jason Samuel. AB, Harvard U., Cambridge, Mass., 1976; MD, Stanford U., Calif., 1980. Intern, then resident psychiatry NY Hosp. Cornell Med. Ctr., 1980-84; fellow pub. psychiatry Columbia Presbyn. Med. Ctr.-N.Y. State Psychiat. Inst., NYC, 1984-85; attending psychiatrist Beth Israel Med. Ctr., NYC, 1985-2000; instr. psychiatry Mt. Sinai Med. Ctr., NYC, 1985-88, asst. prof. psychiatry, 1988-93; physician in charge psychiat. outpatient svcs. Beth Israel Med. Ctr., NYC, 1989-96, chief outpatient psychiatry divsn., 1996-2000; asst. prof. psychiatry Albert Einstein Coll. Medicine, NYC, 1993-96, dir. mood disorders rsch. unit, 1994-2000, assoc. prof. psychiatry, 1996-2000; assoc. prof. clin. psychiatry Columbia U. Coll. Physicians and Surgeons, NYC, 2000—. Clin. dir. NY State Psychiatric Inst., 2000—05; dir. mood disorders rsch. unit St. Luke's Roosevelt Hosp. Ctr., 2001—; med. dir. clin. trials program Columbia Psychiatry, 2005—, dir. med. comm., 2007—. Author: (novels) Loving Touches, 1987, Stone Babies, 2000, (essay collection) Battles of Life and Death, 1986, (non-fiction) A Family of Doctors, 1994; contbr. articles to profl. jours.; contbg. editor N.Am. Rev., 1981—, Sci. Digest, 1986-87, 7 Days mag., 1988-90, M.D. Mag., 1990-95. MacDowell Colony fellow, 1984, 86, 88. Fellow APA (disting.); mem. PEN, Am. Psychiat. Assn. (editor NY County Dist. newsletter, 1989-2001; chmn. publs. com. N.Y. County chpt. 1989-2001, pres.-elect 1997-98, pres. 1998-99), Author's Guild. Democrat. Jewish. E-mail: djh102@columbia.edu.

HELLERSTEIN, LEWIS JAN, hematologist, oncologist, consultant; b. Denver, Sept. 27, 1938; s. Louis A. and Lenoara Brilliant Hellerstein; m. Peggy Henry Hellerstein, Feb. 4, 1962; children: Raymond Trent, Julia K. Connel, Kimberly Helen Segelke, Jason Lee. Student, Ohio State U., 1956—57; BA, U. Colo., 1960, MD, 1964. Diplomate Am. Bd. Internal Medicine, 1972, Am. Bd. Hematology, 1972. Extern Gen. Rose Meml. Hosp., Denver, 1962—64; intern DC Gen. Hosp. George Washington U., 1964—65, from jr. asst. resident to asst. resident in medicine, instr. phys. diagnosis, 1965—66, fellow in medicine, 1966; fellow in hematology and oncology Beth Israel Hosp., Boston, 1968—69; fellow in coagulation Beth Israel Hosp., Children's Med. Ctr., Boston, 1969—70, sr. fellow in coagulation, instr., 1970—71; assoc. in medicine Harvard Med. Sch., Boston, 1969—70, instr., 1970—71, Albany Med. Coll., NY, 1969—70; clin. instr. Baylor Coll. Medicine, Houston, 1971—80; clin. asst. prof. U. Tex. Med. Sch., Houston, 1974—76, clin. assoc. prof., 1976—. Contbr. articles to profl. jours. Med. officer USAF, 1966—68. Achievements include research in LDH isoenzyme fractionation in clinical medicine; use of Kr 95 in diagnosis of right to left shunts and pulmonary function; effects of hormones in tissue culture of cancerous and non-cancerous origin; guanethidine in spasticity; patents for intracorporal vacular prosthetic blood irradiator. Office: 11506 Habersham Ln Houston TX 77024-6518

HELLERSTEIN, WALTER, lawyer; b. NYC, June 21, 1946; s. Jerome Robert and Pauline Alice H.; m. Nina Laurie Salant, Aug. 31, 1970; children: Michael, Margaret. AB, Harvard U., 1967; JD, U. Chgo., 1970. Bar: D.C. 1970, Ill. 1976, N.Y. 1989. Law clk. U.S. Ct. Appeals (2d cir.), NYC, 1967-71; atty. Air Force Gen. Counsel's Office, Washington, 1971-73; assoc. Covington & Burling, Washington, 1973-75; asst. prof. law U. Chgo., 1976—78; assoc. prof. law U. Ga., Athens, 1978-84, prof. law, 1984-98, Francis Shackelford prof. taxation, 1999—; of counsel Morrison & Foerster, NYC, 1986-96; ptnr. Sutherland, Asbill & Brennan, Atlanta, 1996-98, of counsel Washington, 2004—, KPMG, 1999—2004. Cons. Orgn. Econ. Coop. and Devel., 1999—, UN, 2000—; trustee Am. Tax Policy Inst., 2006—. Co-author: State and Local Taxation of Natural Resources, 1986, State Taxation, vols. 1 & 2, 3d edit., 1998, Electronic Commerce and Multijurisdictional Taxation, 2001, Streamlined Sales and Use Tax, 2007 edit., State and Local Taxation, 8th edit., 2005; mem. editl. bd. Nat. Tax Jour., 1983-2004, Multistate Tax Analyst, 1986—; chmn. editl. adv. bd. State Tax Notes, 1991—, Jour. Taxation, 1993—; contbr. articles to profl. jours. Recipient Multistate Tax Commn. 25th Ann. award for outstanding contbn. 1992. Fellow Am. Coll. Tax Counsel; mem. ABA, Nat. Tax Assn. (dir. 1981-83), Ill. State Bar Assn., D.C. Bar Assn., N.Y. State Bar Assn., Am. Law Inst., Order of Coif, Phi Beta Kappa. Home: 239 Westview Dr Athens GA 30606-4731 Office: U Ga Law Sch Athens GA 30602-6012 Home Phone: 706-353-0865; Office Phone: 706-542-5175. Business E-Mail: wallyh@uga.edu.

HELLIE, RICHARD, historian, educator; b. Waterloo, Iowa, May 8, 1937; s. Ole Ingemann and Mary Elizabeth (Larsen) H.; children: Benjamin, Michael; m. Shujie Yu, Feb. 26, 1998. BA, U. Chgo., 1958, MA, 1960, PhD, 1965; postgrad., Ind. U., Bloomington, 1963, U. Moscow, 1963—64. Vis. asst. prof. Rutgers U., 1965—66; asst. prof. Russian history U. Chgo., 1966—71, assoc. prof., 1971—80, prof., 1980—2001, Thomas E. Donnelley prof., 2001—. Presenter in field; chmn. Coll. Russian Civilization course U. Chgo., 1967—, chmn. undergrad. studies in Russian Civilization, 1970—, chmn. Ea. European NDEA Title VI Area Com., 1974—78, coord. Coll. History, 1971—73, mem. Coun. U. Senate, 1976—79, mem. coll. com. academic standing, 1984—87, co-coord. Moscow exchange program, 1990—96, co-coord. Russian and Soviet studies workshop, sole coord. Russian and Soviet studies workshop, 1993—94, dir. Nat. Resource Ctr. Slavic, East European/Russian and Eurasian studies, 1997—2004, mem. faculty oversight com. on computing, 1999—2002, dir. Ctr. for East European, Russian and Eurasian studies, 1997—2004. Author: Muscovite Society, 1967, 1970, Enserfment and Military Change in Muscovy, 1971 (Am. Hist. Assn. Adams prize 1972), Slavery in Russia 1450-1725, 1982 (Laing prize U. Chgo. Press 1985, Russian translation with new post-Soviet foreword Kholopstvo v Rossii, 1450-1725, 1998), 1982, The Russian Law Code (Ulozhenie) of 1649, 1988, The Economy and Material Culture of Russia 1600-1725, 1999; editor: The Plow, the Hammer and the Knout: An Economic History of Eighteenth Century Russia, 1985, Ivan the Terrible: A Quarcentenary Celebration of His Death, 1987, The Frontier in Russian History, 1995, The Economy and Material Culture of Russia, 1999, The Soviet Global Impact 1945-1991, 2002; editor quar. jour. Russian History, 1988; translation editor: Kholopstvo v Rossii 1450-1725, 1998; contbr. numerous articles to profl. jours, presenter in field. Fgn. area tng. fellow Ford Found., 1962-65, Inter-Univ. Com. on Travel Grants award, 1963-64, Quantrell grant for Improvement of Tchg., 1969, Social Sci. Divsional Rsch. grants U. Chgo., 1970-88, 1991-94, 1996-97, 1998-99, Guggenheim fellow, 1973-74, fellow NEH, 1978-79; grantee NEH, 1982-83, summer, 1988, NSF, 1988-90, Bradley Found., 1988-91. Mem. PEN, Nat. Hist. Soc. (founding mem., bd. govs.), Am. Soc. Legal History (program com. ann. meetings 1976), Am. Assn. Advancement Slavic Studies (editl. bd. Slavic Rev. 1979-81), Econ. History Assn., Assn. Comparative Econ. Studies, Nat. Assn. Scholars, Jean Bodin Soc. Comparative Instl. History, Chgo. Consortium Slavic and East European Studies (pres. 1990-92), Nat. Hist. Soc. (founder, bd. govs. 1999-2002), Chgo. Com. Chgo. Coun. on Fgn. Rels. Office: U Chgo Dept History 1126 E 59th St Box 78 Chicago IL 60637-1580 Home: 5811 S Dorchester Ave Apt 2G Chicago IL 60637-1775 Office Phone: 773-702-8377. Business E-Mail: hell@midway.uchicago.edu.

HELLIWELL, THOMAS MCCAFFREE, physicist, researcher; b. Mpls., June 8, 1936; s. George Plummer and Eleanor (McCaffree) H.; m. Bernadette Egan Busenberg, Aug. 9, 1997. BA, Pomona Coll., 1958; PhD, Calif. Inst. Tech., 1963. Asst. prof. physics Harvey Mudd Coll., Claremont, Calif., 1962-67, assoc. prof., 1967-73, prof., 1973—2005, prof. emeritus, 2005—, chmn. dept. physics, 1981-89, chair of faculty, 1990-93, Burton Bettingen prof. physics, 1990—2004, interim dean of faculty, 2004—05. Author: Introduction to Special Relativity, 1966; author papers in field of cosmology, gen. relativity and quantum theory. Sci. faculty fellow NSF, 1968. Mem.: AAAS, Am. Phys. Soc., Am. Assn. Physics Tchrs. Avocations: music, hiking. Office: Harvey Mudd Coll Dept Physics 301 Platt Blvd Claremont CA 91711-5901

HELLKAMP, ANNE SIDLO, statistician, researcher; b. Framingham, Mass., Aug. 23, 1961; d. Clarence and Elmore Sidlo; m. Mark Hellkamp; children: Alex, Jack. MS in Zoology, NC State U., Raleigh, 1990, M in Stats., 1991. Assessment coord. Environ. Monitoring and Assessment Program, Raleigh, 1991—95; sr. statistician Duke Clin. Rsch. Inst., Durham, NC, 1995—. Contbr. articles to profl. jours. Mem.: Mu Sigma Rho, Phi Kappa Phi. Office: Duke Clin Rsch Inst PO Box 17969 Durham NC 27715 Office Phone: 425-939-0710. E-mail: anne.hellkamp@duke.edu.

HELLMAN, ARTHUR DAVID, law educator, consultant; b. NYC, Dec. 9, 1942; s. Charles and Florence (Cohen) Hellman. BA magna cum laude, Harvard U., 1963; JD, Yale U., 1966. Bar: Minn. 1967, U.S. Ct. Appeals (3d cir.) 1976, U.S. Ct. Appeals (9th cir.) 1979, U.S. Supreme Ct. 1980, Pa., 1985. Law clk. to assoc. justice Minn. Supreme Ct., 1966—67; asst. prof. William Mitchell Coll. Law, St. Paul, 1967—70, U. Conn. Sch. Law, West Hartford, 1970—72; vis. asst. prof. U. Ill. Coll. Law, Champaign, 1972—73; dep. exec. dir. Commn. on Revision Fed. Ct. Appellate Sys., Washington, 1973—75; assoc. prof. U. Pitts. Sch. Law, 1975—80, prof., 1980—, Sally Ann Semenko endowed chair, 2005—. Supervising staff atty. U.S. Ct. Appeals 9th cir., San Francisco, 1977-79, evaluation com., 1999-2001; vis. assoc. prof. U. Pa. Sch. Law, Phila., 1979; faculty Practicing Law Inst. Program on Fed. Appellate Practice, N.Y.C., 1984, Fed. Jud. Ctr. Nat. Workshop for Judges of U.S. Cts. of Appeals, 1993; planner Nat. Conf. Empirical Rsch. in Judicial Adminstrn., Tempe, Ariz., 1988; gen. editor U.S. Ct. Appeals 9th Cir. Project Improvements in Judicial Adminstrn., 1987-91; prin. investigator intercir. conflicts study Fed. Jud. Ctr., 1990; lectr., cons. and expert witness in field. Author: Laws Against Marijuana-The Price We Pay, 1975, Restructuring Justice-The Innovations of the Ninth Circuit and the Future of the Federal Courts, 1990, (with Russell Weaver) The First Amendment: Cases, Materials and Problems, 2002, The Federal Judiciary: Is There a Ned for Judges?, 2003, Ninth Circuit Court of Appeals Judgeship and Reorganization Act of 2004, 2004, (with Lauren K. Robel) Federal Courts: Cases and Materials on Judicial Federalism and the Lawyering Process, 2005, Holmes Group, The Federal Circuit, and the State of Patent Appeals, 2005; editor: Major Cases in First Amendment Law: Freedom of Speech, the Press, and Assembly, 1984; bus. editor: Yale U. Law Jour. Mem. liaison task panel on psychoactive drug use/misuse Pres.'s Commn. on Mental Health, 1977-78; conferee Pound Conf., 1976, The Future and the Courts Conf., 1990; conferee Nat. Conf. on State-Fed. Jud. Relationships, 1992; adv. bd. Western Legal History, 2001—. Recipient Chancellor's Disting. Rsch. award, U. Pitts., 2002; U. Pitts. Sch. Law disting. faculty scholar, 2001—. Fellow Am. Bar Found.; mem. ABA (subcom. on stds. of com. appellate staff attys., jud. adminstrn. divsn., future of cts. com. 1992—, conferee Nat. Conf. on State-Fed. Jud. Rels. 1992, conferee summit on civil justice improvements 1990), Pa. Bar Assn. (discovery rules com. 1995—), Am. Law Inst., Supreme Ct. Hist. Soc., Am. Judicature Soc. (drafting com. project on jud. election campaigns, bd. dirs. 1985-89, justice reform com. 1992-95, chair civil justice reform subcom. 1993-95, chair civil justice reform com. 1995-97, invited witness, hearings of the Subcommittee on Cts., the Internet and Intellectual Property of the US House Judiciary Com. on: Final Report of the Commn. on Structural Alternatives for Fed. Cts. Appeals, 1999, Fed. Jud. Discipline, 2001, unpublished jud. opinions, 2002). Office: Univ Pitts Law Sch 3900 Forbes Ave Pittsburgh PA 15260 Office Phone: 412-648-1340. E-mail: hellman@law.pitt.edu.

HELLMAN, F(REDERICK) WARREN, investor; b. NYC, July 25, 1934; s. Marco F. and Ruth (Koshl) H.; m. Patricia Christina Sander, Oct. 5, 1955; children: Frances, Patricia, Marco Warren, Judith. BA, U. Calif., Berkeley, 1955; MBA, Harvard U., 1959. With Lehman Bros., NYC, 1959-84, ptnr., 1963-84; exec. mng. dir. Lehman Bros., Inc., NYC, 1970-73, pres., 1973-75; ptnr. Hellman Ferri Investment Assocs., 1981-89, Matrix Ptnrs., 1981—; chmn. Hellman & Friedman LLC, San Francisco. Bd. dirs. DN & E Walter, Levi Strauss & Co., Offit Hall Capital Mgmt., LLC, Sugar Bowl Corp.; hon. trustee emeritus The Brookings Inst. Former chmn. The San Francisco Found., trustee; trustee emeritus The Brookings Instn.; co-chair Calif. Commn. for Jobs and Econ. Growth; mem. Governor's Coun. Econ. Advisors, Com. on JOBS; mem. adv. bd. Walter A. Haas Sch. Bus., UC Berkeley; chmn. Voice of Dance; bd. dirs. Bay Area Coun., San Francisco C. of C. Named to Am. Acad. Arts and Scis., 2005. Mem. Am. Acad. Arts and Scis., Bond Club, Century Country Club, Pacific Union Club. Office: Hellman & Friedman LLC 1 Maritime Plz Fl 12 San Francisco CA 94111-3404

HELLMAN, GEOFFREY P., philosopher, educator; AB, Harvard U.; PhD, Harvard Univ. Prof., chair, dept. philosophy Univ. Minn. Contbr. articles to profl. jours.; author: Mathematics without Numbers: Towards a Modal-Structural Interpretation, 1989; co-editor (with Richard Healey): Quantum Measurement: Beyond Paradox, Minnesota Studies in Philosophy of Science, 1998. Fellow: Am. Acad. Arts & Scis. Office: Dept Philosopy 845 Heller Univ Minn 271 19th Ave S Minneapolis MN 55455-0310 Office Phone: 612-625-8201. Business E-Mail: hellm001@umn.edu.

HELLMAN, RICHARD, endocrinologist; b. NYC, Jan. 19, 1943; s. Gabriel Michael and Rose Hellman; m. Julie Lynn Hellman, Aug. 17, 1997; children: Leslie Gayle. BA in Math., NYU, 1962; MD, Chgo. Med. Sch., 1966. Diplomate Am. Bd. Internal Medicine, Am. Bd. Endocrinology and Metabolism, Nat. Bd. Med. Examiners. Intern in straight medicine U. Kans., Kansas City, 1966-67, resident in internal medicine, 1967-68, 71-72, fellow in endocrinology and metabolism, 1972-73; asst. prof. medicine U. Mo., Kansas City Sch. Medicine, 1973-75, assoc. prof. medicine, 1975-81, clin. assoc. prof. medicine, 1981-95, clin. prof. medicine, 1998—; pvt. practice physician North Kansas City, Mo., 1981—. Chmn. adv. bd. Mo. Diabetes Control program CDC, ATlanta, 1981-86; med. dir. Midwest Diabetes Care Ctr., Kansas City, 1981-86, Diabetes Treatment Ctr., Trinity Luth. Hosp., Kansas City, Mo., 1986-94; med. dir., founder, Heart of Am. Diabetes Rsch. Found., North Kansas City, 1991—; mem. Physicians Consortium for Performance Improvement, 2000—, co-chmn. work group depression, 2001—, work group implementation, 2002—, mem. exec. com., 2005—; cons. in field. Contbr. articles to profl. jours. Active Mo. Inst. Quality Health Care Mo. Patient Care Rev. Found., 1999—; mem. cmty. adv. com. Health Care Found., Greater Kans. City, 2005-; mem. Mayor's Health Commn., Kansas City, Mo., 2001—, mem. minority health com., 2001—, mem. improvement com., 2001—; chair patient safety com. Health Commn., 2005—; mem. tech. adv. panels, Nat. Quality Forum, 2005-. Mem. AMA (accreditation program 1998-99, work group, cons. on applications of med. informatics and performance measures 2001, mem. exec. com. physicians consortium, co-chair implementation com.), Am. Assn. Clin. Endocrinologists (bd. dir. 1999—, chair continuing med. edn, 2000-01, chair legis. and regulatory com. 2001-03, strategic planning com. 2000-01, sec. 2003-04, chmn. task force on patient safety 2003—, treas. 2004-05, bd. liaison legis. and regulatory com. 2001-04, Kansas City, chair patient and safety com. 2005—, v.p. 2005-06, pres.-elect 2006-07, pres. 2007-), Am. Coll. Endocrinology (bd. dir. 2001-02, task force on cert. 2002-03, sec.-treas. 2004-05), Met. Med. Soc. Greater Kansas City (sec. 1999, bd. dir. 1999-2000, pres. 2000-01, Meritorious Svc. award 2002), Physicians Coalition (exec. com.), Nat. Diabetes Alliance (tech. expert panel), Alpha Omega Alpha. Office: 2790 Clay Edwards Dr Ste 1250 North Kansas City MO 64116 Office Phone: 816-421-3700. Office Fax: 816-421-1654.

HELLMAN, SAMUEL, radiologist, educator; b. NYC, July 23, 1934; s. Henry Sidney and Anna (Egar) Hellman; m. Marcia Sherman, June 30, 1957; children: Jeffrey, Richard, Deborah Susan. BS magna cum laude, Allegheny Coll., 1955, DSc (hon.), 1984; MD cum laude, SUNY, Syracuse, 1959, DSc (hon.), 1993; MS (hon.), Harvard U., 1968. Med. intern Beth Israel Hosp., Boston, 1959—60; asst. resident radiology Yale Sch. Medicine and Grace-New Haven Hosp., 1960—62, postdoctoral fellow radiotherapy and cancer research, 1962—64; postdoctoral fellow Inst. Cancer Research and Royal Marsden Hosp., London, 1965—66; asst. prof. radiology Yale Sch. Medicine, 1966—68; assoc. prof. radiology Harvard Med. Sch., 1968—70; dir. Joint Center for Radiation Therapy, 1968—83, assoc. prof., chmn. dept. radiation therapy, 1971, prof., chmn. dept., 1971—83, also Alvan T. and Viola D. Fuller-Am. Cancer Soc. prof.; physician-in-chief Meml. Sloan Kettering Cancer Ctr., 1983—88, Benno Schmidt chair in clin. oncology, 1983—88; dean div. biol. sci. and Pritzker Sch. Medicine, v.p. for Med. Ctr. U. Chgo., 1988—93, Pritzker prof., 1988—93, Pritzker disting. svc. prof., 1993—2006, Pritzker disting. svc. prof. emeritus, 2006—. Chmn. bd. sci. counselors divsn. cancer treatment Nat. Cancer Inst., 1980—84; bd. govs. Argonne Nat. Lab., 1990—93; trustee Brookings Inst., 1992—; bd. dirs. Varian Med. Systems Inc., Insightec; mem. sci. adv. bd. Ludwig Inst. for Cancer Rsch. Contbr. numerous articles to med. jours. Trustee Allegheny Coll., 1979—98, chmn. bd. trustees, 1987—93. Recipient Rosenthal award for cancer rsch., 1980, medal, City of Paris, 1986, award for Outstanding Contbns. to Cancer Care, Assn. Cmty. Cancer Ctrs., 1993. Fellow: AAAS; mem.: N.Y. Acad. Scis., Soc. Chmn. Acad. Radiology Depts., Inst. Medicine NAS, Assn. Am. Physicians, Am. Cancer Soc., Am. Soc. Hematology, Am. Assn. Cancer Rsch., Am. Soc. Clin. Oncology (pres. 1986, David A. Karnovsky lectr. 1994), Assn. Univ. Radiologists, Am. Coll. Radiology (gold medal 2003), Am. Soc. Therapeutic Radiologists (pres. 1983, Gold medal 1991), Am. Radium Soc., Alpha Omega Alpha, Sigma Xi, Phi Beta Kappa. Home: 1122 N Dearborn St Apt 25H Chicago IL 60610 Office: U Chgo Divsn Biol Scis 5841 S Maryland Ave Chicago IL 60637-1463 Office Phone: 773-702-4346. Business E-Mail: s-hellman@uchicago.edu.

HELLMANN, DAVID BRUCE, medical educator; b. Louisville, Mar. 2, 1951; BA magna cum laude, Yale U., 1973; MD, Johns Hopkins U., 1977. Diplomate Am. Bd. Internal Medicine, Am. Bd. Rheumatology, lic. physician Md. Intern, resident Johns Hopkins Hosp., Balt., 1977-80; fellow in rheumatology/clin. immunology U. Calif., San Francisco, 1980-82, asst. clin. prof. medicine, 1982—86; chief Moffitt Arthritis Clinics, 1984—86; acting chief divsn. rheumatology/clin. immunology U. Calif., 1985—86; dep. dir. dept. medicine Johns Hopkins U., Balt., 1986-94, exec. vice chmn. dept. medicine, 1995—2000, med. dir. Faculty Practice Ctr., 1991—93, dir. Osler Med. Housestaff Tng. Program, 1992—2000, Mary Betty Stevens prof. medicine, 1996—2006, Aliki Perrot prof. medicine, 2006—; chmn. dept. medicine Johns Hopkins Bayview Med. Ctr., 2000—, vice dean, 2005—. Assoc. physician-in-chief Johns Hopkins Hosp., Balt., 1986—94, acting physician-in-chief, 1994—95, acting dir. dept. medicine, 1994—95; lectr. in field. Assoc. editor Medicine, 1993—; co-author: Rheumatology Committee, MKSAP II, 1995—; reviewer Jour. Rheumatology, Arthritis and Rheumatism, Western Jour. Medicine, Medicine, Jour. Clin. Investigation, Jour. of AMA; contbr. articles to profl. jours. Chmn. profl. edn. com. Md. chpt. Arthritis Found., 1991, 92, 93, 94. Recipient Kaiser Award for excellence in teaching U. Calif.-San Francisco, 1986, Cert. of Distinction in Teaching, 2d Yr. Med. Sch. Class, 1986, Profl. Edn. award Md. chpt. Arthritis Found., 1991, Disting. Svc. award for profl. edn., 1993, Faculty Teaching award Osler Med. Housestaff, 1992, Johns Hopkins Minority Faculty Assn. award, 1993; Henry Strong Denison scholar, 1975. Master ACP (gov. 1998-2002), Am. Coll. Rheumatology; mem. Am. Bd. Internal Medicine (dir. 2000—), Assn. Program Dirs. Internal Medicine, Internat. Network for Study of the Systemic Vasculitides, Alpha Omega Alpha. Office: Johns Hopkins Bayview Med Ctr A-I-W 4940 Eastern Ave Baltimore MD 21224

HELLMERS, NORMAN DONALD, retired historic site director; b. New Orleans, Feb. 3, 1944; s. Leonard H. and Meta J.C. (Wegener) H.; m. Patricia I. O'Brien, May 29, 1966; children: Jennifer I., Jeffrey N. BA, Concordia U., River Forest, Ill., 1966; postgrad., U. Iowa, 1966-67, La. State U., 1968. Writer, photographer Nebr. Game and Pks. Commn., Lincoln, 1969-71; ranger nat. pks. various locations, 1972-73; dist. naturalist Shenandoah Nat. Pk., Luray, Va., 1973-76; chief interpretation Grand Portage (Minn.) Nat. Monument, 1976-81; supt. Lincoln Boyhood Nat. Meml., Lincoln City, Ind., 1981-90, Lincoln Home Nat. Hist. Site, Springfield, Ill., 1990—2003; ret., 2003. Lutheran. Avocations: photography, genealogy.

HELLMUTH, GEORGE WILLIAM, architect; b. Detroit, Nov. 21, 1942; s. George Francis and Mildred Lee (Henning) H.; m. Camille Byrns Carmody, Feb. 20, 1965 (div. 2003); children: George, Holly, Julie, Emily. BA in Architecture, Yale U., 1964; MBA, Eastern N.Mex. U., 1969; BArch, CCNY, 1979. Sr. prin. Hellmuth, Obata & Kassabaum, Washington, 1971—2006, cons., 2007—. Capt. USAF, 1965—69. Mem.: AIA, Elizabethan Club. Roman Catholic. Home: 2721 N Ohio St Arlington VA 22207 E-mail: george.hellmuth@msn.com.

HELLMUTH, PHIL (PHILLIP J. HELLMUTH JR.), professional poker player; b. Madison, Wis., July 16, 1964; s. Phillip J. Hellmuth; m. Kathy Hellmuth; children: Phillip III, Nicholas. Grad., U. Wis. Author: Play Poker Like the Pros, Bad Beats and Lucky Draws, 2004, Texas-Hold'em, 2005. Named Best All-Around Tournament Poker Player in World, 1996; named one of The Poker Power 20, Bluff Mag., 2005. Achievements include winning 11 World Series of Poker events, including becoming the youngest player to win the Main Event, 1989; winner, The World's Biggest Seven-Card Stud Tournament, Austria; winner, Late Night Poker, UK; winner, Golden Nugget's National Heads-Up Poker Tournament, 2005. Mailing: c/o Brian Balsbaugh Poker Royalty LLC 8367 W Flamingo Rd Ste 102 Las Vegas NV 89147*

HELLMUTH, STEPHEN M., sports association executive; m. Theresa Hellmuth; children: Alexandra, Nick. B in Art Hist., Princeton U., NJ, 1975. Prodn. mgr. sports divsn. NBC, NYC, 1979—87; gen. mgr. Potomac TV Comm., Washington; v.p. ops. NBA Entertainment, sr. v.p. ops. and tech. Secaucus, NJ, 2000—; sr. v.p., gen. mgr. Maj. League Baseball Prodns. Achievements include producing the Emmy-nominated telecast openings for the 1986 World Series and coordinating the production of Olympic profiles for the 1980 Moscow games. Office: NBA Entertainment 450 Harmon Meadow Blvd Secaucus NJ 07094*

HELLMUTH, THEODORE HENNING, lawyer; b. Detroit, Mar. 28, 1949; s. George F. and Mildred Hellmuth; m. Laurie Hellmuth, May 29, 1970; children: Elizabeth Ann, Theodore Henning, Sara Marie. BA, U. Pa., 1970; JD cum laude, U. Mo.-Columbia, 1974. Bar: Mo. 1974, U.S. Dist. Ct. (ea. dist.) Mo. 1974, U.S. Ct. Appeals (8th cir.) 1978. Assoc., then ptnr. Armstrong Teasdale LLP, St. Louis, 1974—2002. Author: Missouri Real Estate, 1985, 2d edit., 1998, Lease Audits: The Essential Guide, 1994; editor Distressed Real Estate Law Alert, 1987-88, Litigated Commercial Real Estate Document Reports, 1987-95. Mem.: ABA, Am. Coll. Real Estate Lawyers, Order of Coif. Office: Armstrong Teasdale LLP 1 Metropolitan Sq Ste 2600 Saint Louis MO 63102-2740 E-mail: thellmuth@armstrongteasdale.com.

HELLMUTH, WILLIAM FREDERICK, economics professor; b. Washington, Jan. 8, 1920; s. William Frederick and Sybel (Grant) H.; m. Jean A. Dieffenbach, Feb. 14, 1943; children: James (dec.), Suzanne, William L., Peter G. BA, Yale U., New Haven, Conn., 1940, PhD, 1948. Instr. econs. Yale U., 1945-48; mem. faculty Oberlin Coll., 1948-68, prof. econs., 1958-68; dean Oberlin Coll. (Coll. Arts and Scis.), 1960-67; staff economist Fed. Res. Bank, 1954—56; dep. asst. sec. treasury for tax policy, 1968-69; v.p. arts, prof. econs. McMaster U., Hamilton, Ont., Can., 1969-73, also bd. govs., 1969-73; prof. econs. Va. Commonwealth U., 1973-87, chmn. dept. econs., 1973-82; emeritus prof., 1987—. Economist Fed. Res. Bd., 1954-56; prof. U. Wis., 1959, Univ. Coll., Dar es Salaam, Tanzania, 1965, 66 Mem. Nat. Com. Taxation with Representation; mem. Oberlin City Coun., 1957-63, 67-68; pres. 1st Unitarian Ch., Richmond, 1976-78; mem. welfare adv. bd. City of Richmond, 1976-83; staff dir. Capital City Govt. Commn., 1980-81; treas. adv. bd. Richmond Cmty. H.S., 1986-92; bd. dirs. Common Cause Va., 1988-96, Shepherd's Ctr. of Richmond, 1985-91, 94-96, Va. Interfaith Ctr. for Pub. Policy, 1987-96; mem. Va. State Dem. Com., 1994-96; fin. comm., Eskaton, 2001-05. Maj. US Army, WWII. Decorated Air medal, Bronze Star. Mem. SAR, Nat. Tax Assn., Beta Gamma Sigma, Phi Beta Kappa. Democrat. Home: 3939 Walnut Ave # 187 Carmichael CA 95608-7309 Personal E-mail: bjhcool@sbcglobal.net.

HELLON, MICHAEL THOMAS, tax specialist, political organization worker; b. Camden, NJ, June 24, 1942; s. James Bernard and Dena Louise (Blackburn) H.; m. (div.); 2 children. BS, Ariz. State U., 1972. Ins. investigator Equifax, Phoenix, 1968-69; exec. v.p. Phoenix Met. C. of C., 1969-76; exec. Londen Ins. Group, 1976-78; pres. Hellon and Assocs., Inc., 1978—. Small claims hearing officer Pima County Justice Ct., 1990—; mem. Pima County Bd. Adjustments, 1993-00, Pima County Merit Commn., 2000—, Ariz. Jud. Performance Rev. Commn., 2004-; nat. def. exec. res. U.S. Dept. of Commerce, 1986-97; bd. dirs. Equity Benefit Life Ins. Co., Modern Income Life Ins. Co. of Mo., First Equity Security Life Ins. Co., Tucson Classics; mem. commn. jud. performance rev., Ariz., 2004—. Mem. Ariz. Occupl. Safety and Health Adv. Coun., 1972-76, mem. Speaker's Select Com. Auto Emissions, 1976; Phoenix Urban League, 1972-73, Area Manpower Planning coun., 1971-72, Phoenix Civic Plaza Dedication Com., 1972, Phoenix Air Quality Maintenance Taks Force, 1976; pres. Vis. Nurse Svc., 1978-79; Rep. precinct capt., 1973—; state campaign dir. Arizonans for Reagan Com., 1980; alt. del. Rep. Nat. Conv., 1980, 84, 88; mem. staff Reagan-Bush Nat. Conv., 1984; campaign mgr. for various candidates, 1972-82; mem. exec. com. Ariz. Rep. Party, 1989-90, chmn., 1997-99; mem. Rep. Nat. Com., 1992-04, mem. exec. com., 1997-04; bd. dirs. ATMA Tng. Found., 1981-84. Served with USAF, 1964-68. Decorated Bronze Star medal, Purple Heart; Recipient George Washington Honor medal Freedom's Found., 1964; commendation Fed. Bar Assn., 1973. Mem. U.S. C. of C. (pub. affairs com. western divsn. 1974-76), Inst. of Property Taxation, Internat. Assn. Assessing Officers, U.S. Dept. Commerce Exec. Res., Ariz. C. of C. Mgrs. Assn. (bd. m em. 1974-76), Tucson C. of C., Trunk 'N Tusk Club, Catalina Soccer Club (bd. dirs. 1984-88). Home: 1261 W Hopbush Way Tucson AZ 85704-2647

HELLRUNG, STEPHEN ANDREW, lawyer; b. St. Louis, July 7, 1947; s. J. W. and Alice T. Hellrung; m. Margaret M. Frailey; children: Margaret, Carolyn, Joseph, Leigh. AB, U. Notre Dame, 1969, JD, 1972. Bar: Mo. 1972, U.S. Dist. Ct. (ea. dist.) Mo. 1972, Ill. 1978, N.Y. 1983, Minn. 1998, N.C. 2000. Assoc. Rassieur, Long, Yawitz & Schneider, 1972—78; asst. gen. counsel A.E. Staley, Decatur, Ill., 1978—82; sr. v.p., sec., gen. counsel Bausch & Lomb, Inc., Rochester, NY, 1983—97; sr. v.p., gen. counsel, sec. Pillsbury Co., Mpls., 1997—98, Lowe's Cos., Inc., 1999—2003, Graphic Packaging Corp., Marietta, Ga., 2003—. Mem.: Am. Corp. Counsel Assn., Mo. Bar Assn., NC State Bar Assn., Ill. State Bar Assn., NY State Bar Assn., Minn. State Bar Assn. Office: Graphic Packaging Corp 814 Livingston Ct Marietta GA 30067*

HELLSTRÖM, INGEGERD, medical researcher; b. Stockholm; permanent resident, US, 1966, US citizen, 1996; m. Karl Erik Hellström; children: Katarina Elisabet, Per Erik. MD of Medicine, Karolinska Inst. Med. Sch., Stockholm, 1964, PhD of Medicine (Tumor Biology), 1966. Rsch. assoc. (docent), dept. Tumor Biology Karolinska Inst. Med. Sch., Stockholm, 1959-66, asst. prof. dept. tumor biology, 1966; asst. prof. microbiology U. Wash., Seattle, 1966—, rsch. assoc. prof. microbiology, 1969-72, prof. microbiology/immunology, 1972—85, adj. prof. pathology, 1972—85, affiliate prof. pathology, 1985—; mem. and program head, divsn. tumor immunology Fred Hutchinson Cancer Rsch. Ctr., Seattle, 1975—83; sr. scientist Oncogen, Seattle, 1983—85, lab. dir., 1985—86; v.p. Oncogen/Bristol-Myers Squibb, Seattle, 1986-90; v.p. immunological diseases Bristol-Myers Squibb Pharm. Rsch. Inst., Seattle, 1990—97; pron. investigator Pacific Northwest Rsch. Inst., Seattle, 1997—2004. Patents in the field: 17 US patents and 1 UK Patent; mem. editl. adv. bd., Jour. of Nat. Cancer Inst.; assoc. editor, Cancer Research, 1980-87, 1988-93, 1995-; mem. editl. bd., Anticancer Research; mem. gen. assembly, GM Cancer Rsch. Found.; mem. external adv. com, Specialized Ctr. for Cancer Rsch., U. Ill. at Chgo., Coll. Medicine, 1991-; contbr. to 450 sci. publs. Recipient Lucy Wortham James award, Ewing Soc., 1971, Matrix Table award, 1972, Pap award Outstanding Contbn. Cancer Rsch., Papanicolaou Cancer Rsch. Inst., 1973, Am. Cancer Soc. Nat. award 1974, RNO (Knight of Northern Star, First Class Swedish Order of Merit), 1976, Humboldt award to Sr. US Sci., Humbolt Stiftung Bonn, W. Germany, 1980. Mem. AMA, Am. Assn. Immunologists, Am. Fedn. Clin. Rsch., Am. Assn. Cancer Rsch., Soc. Biol. Therapy. Office: Harborview Med Ctr Box 359939 325 Ninth Ave Seattle WA 98104-2499 Home Phone: 206-525-9968; Office Phone: 206-341-5908. Business E-Mail: ihellstr@u.washington.edu.

HELLSTRÖM, KARL ERIK, science educator, researcher; b. Stockholm; permanent resident, US, 1966, US Citizen, 1996; m. Ingegerd Hellström; children: Katarina Elisabet, Per Erik. Candidate of medicine, Karolinska Inst. Med. Sch., Stockholm, 1955, MD, PhD, Karolinska Inst. Med. Sch., Stockholm, 1964. Rsch. fellow, dept. histology Karolinska Inst. Med. Sch., Stockholm, 1953—57, rsch. assoc., dept. histology, 1957, docent in tumor biology, 1958—62, asst. prof., dept. tumor biology, 1962—66; investigator in cell biology funded by Swedish Medical Rsch. Coun, 1964—66; assoc. prof. pathology U. Wash. Sch. Medicine, Seattle, 1966—69, prof. pathology, 1969—83, adj. prof. microbiology and immunology, affiliate prof. pathology, 1984—; prin. investigator Pacific Northwest Rsch. Inst., Seattle, 1997—2004; mem. and head, program of tumor immunology Fred Hutchinson Cancer Rsch Ctr., Seattle, 1975—83; sr. scientist Oncogen, Seattle, 1983—85, lab. dir., 1985—86; v.p. Oncogen/Bristol-Myers, 1986—90; v.p. oncology drug discovery Bristol-Myers Squibb Pharm. Rsch. Inst., 1990—95, v.p. immunotherapeutics drug discovery, 1995—97. Bd. dirs. Seattle Genetics, Inc.; sci. adv. coun. Cancer Rsch. Inst. Inc. Editl. bd.: Cancer Immunology and Immunology; contbr. to 460 sci. publs. Assessor Anti-Cancer Coun., Victoria, BC, Canada; Can. reviewer Netherlands Cancer Found. Recipient Lucy Wortham James award, Ewing Soc., 1971, Parke Davis award in Exptl. Pathology, 1972, Pap award for Outstanding Contbn. in Cancer Rsch., Papanicolaou Cancer Rsch. Inst., Miami, Fla., 1973, Nat. award for Cancer Rsch., Am. Cancer Soc., 1974, RNO (Knight of the Northern Star, 1st Class, Swedish Order of Merit), 1976, Humboldt award to Sr. US Sci., Humboldt Stiftung, Bonn, Germany, 1980. Mem.: Clin. immunology Soc., Am. Assn. for Clin. Rsch., AAAS, Am. Assn. of Immunologists, Am. Assn. Exptl. Pathology, Am. Assn. for Cancer Rsch., NY Acad. Sciences, Sigma XI, The Sci. Rsch. Soc., Alpha Omega Alpha, U. Wash. Chap. Achievements include patents in field. Office: Harborview Med Ctr Box 359939 325 Ninth Ave Seattle WA 98104-2499 Office Phone: 206-341-5907. Business E-Mail: hellsk@u.washington.edu.

HELLWARTH, ROBERT WILLIS, physicist, researcher; b. Ann Arbor, Mich., Dec. 10, 1930; s. Arlen Roosevelt and Sarah Matilda (Townsend) H.; m. Abigail Gurfein, Sept. 20, 1957 (div. 1979); children: Benjamin John, Margaret Eve, Thomas Abraham; m. Theresia deVroom, Dec. 20, 1985; 1 child, William Albert Detroit. BS, Princeton U., NJ, 1952; PhD, St. John's Coll., Oxford U., Eng., 1955. Sr. scientist, mgr. Hughes Research Labs., Malibu, Calif., 1956-70; vis. assoc. prof. elec. engring. and physics U. Ill., Urbana, 1964-65; research assoc., sr. research fellow Calif. Inst. Tech., Pasadena, 1966-70; NSF sr. postdoctoral fellow Clarendon Lab.-St. Peter's Coll., Oxford (Eng.) U., 1970-71; George T. Pfleger prof. elec. engring., prof. physics U. So. Calif., LA, 1970—. Contbr. articles to profl. jours.; assoc. editor: IEEE Jour. Quantum Electronics, 1964—76. Humboldt fellow, Max Planck Inst. Quantenoptik, 1988—89. Fellow IEEE (Quantum Electronics award), Am. Phys. Soc., AAAS, Optical Soc. Am. (Charles Hard Townes award), Am Acad. Arts & Scis.; mem. NAE, NAS. Patentee Q-switched laser, nonlinear optical microscope, phase conjugate mirror. Office: Dept Physics & Astronomy U So Calif Los Angeles CA 90089-0484 E-mail: hellwart@usc.edu.

HELLYAR, MARY JANE, imaging company executive; BA in Chemistry and Math., Coll. St. Catherine, St. Paul; MSChemE, MIT, Cambridge, PhD in Chem. Engring., MBA in Mgmt. of Tech. Rsch. scientist Kodak Rsch. Labs. Eastman Kodak Co., Rochester, NY, 1982, various positions in R & D, film mfg. and chem. process devel., with consumer imaging in strategic planning function, 1994, dir. Color Product Platform, 1995, gen. mgr. Consumer Film Bus., Consumer Imaging, v.p., 1999, pres. Display and Components Group, 2004, sr. v.p., 2005—, pres. Film & Photofinishing Systems Group, 2005—07, pres. Film Products Group, 2007—. Office: Eastman Kodak Co 343 State St Rochester NY 14650 Office Phone: 585-724-4000.*

HELLYER, CONSTANCE ANNE (CONNIE ANNE CONWAY), writer, musician, educator; b. Puyallup, Wash., Apr. 22, 1937; d. David Tirrell and Constance (Hopkins) H.; m. Peter A. Corning, Dec. 30, 1963 (div. 1977); children: Anne Arundel, Stephanie Deak Cunningham; m. Don W. Conway, Oct. 12, 1980 (dec. 2005). BA with honors, Mills Coll., 1959. Grader, rschr. Harvard U., Cambridge, Mass., 1959-60; rschr. Newsweek mag., NYC, 1960-63; author's asst. Theodore H. White and others, NYC, 1964-69; freelance writer, editor Colo., Calif., 1970-75; writer, editor Stanford U. Med. Ctr., 1975-79; comm. dir. No. Calif. Cancer Program, Palo Alto, 1979-82, Stanford Law Sch., Palo Alto, 1982-97; vocalist String of Pearls Band, 1991—, co-leader China tours, 1999, 2001, 2002; percussionist North Coast Symphonic Band, North Oreg. Coast Symphony, 2005—; instr. Osher Lifelong Learning Inst., U. Wash., 2007—. Bd. dirs. North Coast Symphonic Bd., 2006—, Cannon Beach Arts Assn., 2007—. Founding editor (newsletters) Insight, 1978-80, Synergy, 1980-82, Stanford Law Alum, 1992-95; editor (mag.) Stanford Lawyer, 1982-98; contbr. articles to profl. jours. and mags. Recipient silver medal Coun. for Advancement and Support Edn., 1985, 89, award of distinction dist. VII, 1994. Mem. Nat. Assn. Sci. Writers, Phi Beta Kappa. Democrat. Home: PO Box 828 Cannon Beach OR 97110 Personal E-mail: conniepearl@yahoo.com.

HELLYER, TIMOTHY MICHAEL, protective services officer; b. Chgo., Nov. 30, 1954; s. William Al and Dotha Helen (Bucknum) H.; m. Nancy Ruth O'Donnell, Nov. 29, 1986; children: Jennifer Lynn, Allyson Jean. Student, So. Ill. U., 1985-86; BA, Nat. Louis U., 2002; MA, Aurora U., 2003. Cert. firefighter III; cert. paramedic. Firefighter, paramedic Palatine (Ill.) Fire Dept., 1980—2000; ret., 2000; program chair paramedic scis. Ivy Tech. State Coll., South Bend, Ind., 2005—. Instr. CPR, Chgo. Heart Assn., 1976—; pres. N.W. Assn. Provider Emergency Med. Svcs. Sys., 1989-92; mem. No. Ill. Critical Stress Debriefing Team. Deacon Palatine Presbyn. Ch., 1989-92; mem. comm. coun. Sch. Dist. 300, 1993-2003, mem. Year Round Sch. com., 1998-99; mem. improvement team Westfield Cmty. Sch., 1993-2004. Named Firefighter of the Yr., Jaycees of Palatine, 1987. Mem. Prehosp. Care Providers Ill. (bd. dirs. 1990), St. Francis Hook and Ladder Soc., Ill. Profl. Firefighters Assn., Smithsonian Instn., Nat. Trust Historic Preservation, Nat. Geographic Soc., U.S. Naval Inst., Nat. Space Soc. Republican. Presbyterian. Avocations: collecting disney memorabilia, gardening, model railroading. Office: Ivy Tech State College 220 Dean Johnson Blvd South Bend IN 46601 Home: 51288 Harbor Ridge Dr Granger IN 46530-4840 Office Phone: 574-289-7001 6344. Personal E-mail: hellyer4@aol.com. E-mail: thellyer@ivytech.edu.

HELM, DEWITT FREDERICK, JR., professional society administrator, consultant; b. Charlotte, NC, Apr. 24, 1933; s. DeWitt Frederick Sr. and Blanche Buchanan (DeBusk) H.; divorced; children: DeWitt Frederick III, Mary McNair Helm Bishop; m. Anne M. Valle, Mar. 1, 2002. BS in History, Davidson Coll., NC, 1956. Mgr. advt. Vick Chem. Co., NYC, 1956-63; mgr. consumer products Pfizer, Inc., NYC, 1963-66; mgr. consumer product acquisition and devel. A.H. Robins Co., Richmond, Va., 1966-69; exec. v.p. Miller Morton Co., Richmond, 1969-72, pres., 1972-81, Miller Morton of Can. Ltd., 1969-81; sr. v.p. Jack Morton Prodns. Inc., Washington, 1981-84; exec. v.p. Assn. Nat. Advertisers, Inc., NYC, 1984, pres., 1984-93, also bd. dirs.; mng. ptnr. DH Assocs., Palm City, Fla., 1994-97, The Advt. Partnership LLC, Bearfort, SC, 1996—. Deacon, elder Presbyn. Ch., United Meth. Ch., 1990-2003; trustee Christ Ch., NYC, 2000-03; bd. dirs. Nat. Tobacco Festival, Richmond, 1977-81, Traffic Audit

Bur., NYC, 1984-93. With U.S. Army, 1956-58. Mem. Consumer Healthcare Products Assn. (bd. dirs., exec. com. 1972-80, chmn. 1973-75), Coun. Better Bus. Burs. (bd. dirs. 1989-93), Am. Advt. Mus. (founding dir., nat. bd. 1987—), Smithsonian Instn.'s Ctr. for Advt. History (adv. bd. 1989—), Advt. Coun. (bd. dirs., treas. 1984-93, life bd. dirs. 2002—), Advt. Rsch. Found. (bd. dirs. 1984-93), World Fedn. Advertisers (bd. dirs., mgmt. com. 1984-93), Media-Advt. Partnership for Drug-Free Am. (mgmt. bd.), Wintergreen (Va.) Club, Sky Club, Met. Club (N.Y.C.), Harbour Ridge Club (Fla.). Presbyterian. Office Phone: 843-441-0566. Personal E-mail: taphelm@charter.net.

HELM, DONALD CAIRNEY, geologist, engineer, educator; b. Yokohama, Japan, Mar. 26, 1937; s. Nathan Teal and Rebecca Forsyth (Cairney) Helm; m. Usha Monica Sundari Muliyil, Dec. 1961 (div. 1982); m. Karen Emily Reed, Sept. 3, 1982; 1 child, Rebecca Bernice. AB in Math. cum laude, Amherst Coll., Mass., 1959; MDiv in Theology, Hartford Sem. Found., 1962; postgrad., Colo. Sch. Mines, Golden, 1962-63, 64-65; MS in Geol. Engring., U. Calif., Berkeley, 1970, PhD in Civil Engring., 1974. Registered profl. engr., Australia. Vol. in rural devel. Mitraniketan Project, Kerala State, India, 1963-64; hydraulic engr. US Geol. Survey, Portland, Oreg., 1965-68, Berkeley, Calif., 1968-69, research hydrologist Sacramento, 1969-78, Las Vegas, Nev., 1991-93, Carson City, Nev., 1993-96; ret., 1999; rsch. physicist Lawrence Livermore Nat. Lab., U. Calif., 1978-84, ret. 1990, group leader, geohydrology and environ. studies group, 1981-84; prin. research scientist Geomechanics Div. Commonwealth Sci. and Indsl. Research Orgn. (CSIRO), Melbourne, Australia, 1984-92, ret. 1992, hydraulics group leader, 1984-86, chmn. selection com. for hiring research scientists, 1986, rep. to Research Officers Assn., 1986-87, mem. ex-officio divisional staff cons. com., 1986-87; rsch. hydrogeologist Nev. Bur. Mines and Geology U. Nev., Reno, Las Vegas, 1989-98, vis. rsch. scientist Nev. Bur. Mines and Geology Reno, 1989-92; chief Las Vegas Office, 1989-93; prof. geology U. Nev., Reno, 1992-98, adj. prof., 1998—2007; Samuel P. Massie prof. civil engring. Morgan State U., Balt., 1996—. Instr. US Geol. Survey Advanced Groundwater Sch., Denver, 1972—78, UNESCO Internat. Workshop Land Subsidence, Mexico City, 1979, Pacific Sch. Religion, Berkeley, Calif., 1982, Western Australia, 85, US Geol. Survey rsch. hydrologists, Tucson, 1987; advisor, mem. nat. steering com. Geothermal Subsidence Rsch. Program US Dept. Energy, 1976—84; vis. sr. rsch. scientist State Elec. Commn., Victoria, Australia, 1982—83, INTEVEP, Caracas, Venezuela, 1983, US Bur. Reclamation, Phoenix, 1984, Indsl. Tech. Rsch. Inst., Teipei, 1992, Mighty River Power, Hamilton, New Zealand, 2005; internat. exch. scientist Inst. Soil and Rock Mechanics, Chinese Acad. Sci., Wuhan, 1988, U. Colo., Boulder, 1990; grad. faculty joint CSIRO-James Cook U., 1989—90; grad. faculty U. Nev., Reno, 1990—98, grad. faculty hydrology/hydrogeology program, 1991—95, grad. faculty hydrol. scis. program, 1995—98, grad. faculty dept. civil engring., 1994—98, grad. faculty dept. geosci., Las Vegas, 1992—93; coord. multi-agy. rsch. project subsidence of Las Vegas valley, 1989—91; mem. nat. liaison com. between ASCE, Geol. Soc. Am. and Assn. Engring. Geologists, 1997—2000; adj. prof. Royal Melbourne Inst. Tech., 1997—2005, Va. Poly. Inst. and State U., 1999—2005. Contbr. articles to profl. jours., chapters to books. Mem. HS com. Am. Friends Svc. Com., Salem, Oreg., 1966—68; bd. dirs. Montessori Sch. Coun., Melbourne, 1986—87; mem. Md. Tributary Team Protecting the Chesapeake Bay, 1997—2000, Balt. Mayor's Transition Team, 2000; co-chmn. New Eng. Student Christian Movement, 1958—59; bd. dirs. Ctr. Theology and Natural Scis., Grad. Theol. Union, Berkeley, 1981—84. Recipient Bennett-Tyler award in systematic theology, 1962, award for Best Paper of the Yr. Disciplines Environ. and Engring. Geology, Assn. Engring. Geologists, 1994, cert. of Appreciation, Inst. Civil and Hydraulic Engring. Com. Geotech. Engring., 1992, U. Jos, Nigeria, 1998, Fed. U. Tech., Minna, Nigeria, Ahmadu Bello U., Nigeria, 1998. Fellow: Inst. Engrs. Australia (Coll. Civil Engrs.), Geol. Soc. Am.; mem.: ASME, ASCE, NSPE, ASTM (mem. com. solid waste disposal), AAUP, AAAS, Balt. Ethical Soc., Md. Soc. Profl. Engrs. (pres. Balt. chpt., Md. bd. dirs., state v.p.), Nev. Water Resources Assn., Internat. Assn. Hydrological Scientists, Internat. Soc. Rock Mechanics, Internat. Assn. Engring. Geology, Internat. Soil Mechanics and Found. Engring., NY Acad. Scis., Nat. Water Well Assn., Assn. Geoscientists Internat. Devel., Assn. Engring. Geologists, Am. Water Resources Assn., Am. Geophys. Union, Am. Soc. Engring. Edn., Am. Chem. Soc., Am. Inst. Profl. Geologists, Balt. Engrs. Club (bd. dirs.), Outlook Club, Berkeley City Club, SAR (bd. mgrs. John Eager Howard chpt.). Home: 1413 Bolton St Baltimore MD 21217-4202 Business E-Mail: helm@eng.morgan.edu.

HELM, LENORA ZENZALAI, musician, educator; b. Chgo., Ill., Aug. 15, 1961; d. Reginald and Vera H Helm. Studied privately at, Am. Conseratory of Music, 1974—75; BA, Berklee Coll. of Music, 1979—82. Voice and piano instr. Palomba Music, Portchester, NY, 1991—93; voice and drama instr. Dance Cavise, Mammaroneck, NY, 1992—93; vocal and piano instr. Pvt. Instrn., 1991—94; music. dir., theatre arts program Ctr. Sch., NYC, 1992—94; music coord., piano instr. Jacob Riis Settlement, Long Is. City, NY, 1994—97, sr. citizens choir accompanist, 1995—96; tchg. artist and performance artist Young Audiences, NYC, 1999—; LinkUP! tchg. artist Carnegie Hall, NYC, 1999—2003; vocal jazz instr. Nassau BOCES Cultural Arts Ctr., 2000—04; jazz educator, 2000—; tchg. artist Bklyn. Philharm, Shomburg Ctr. for Rsch. in Black Culture, NYC. Co-founder and artistic dir. HARMONY, 2002—; pres., owner, writer, pub. Holly's Hits Music Pub., 1997—; artist mgr. Self Mgr. to Lenora Zenzalai Helm and the Zenzalai Project, 1981—; pres. Internat. Women in Jazz, 1998—2001; dir. youth svcs. Jacob Riis Settlement, Long Island City, 1995—97; adj. prof. jazz vocal studies N.C. Ctrl. U., Durham, 2005—. Musician: (albums) Voice Paintings, 2003, Precipice, 2002 (top 100 jazz CDs in the U.S. by JazzWeek, 2002), Awakenings, 1997, Spirit Child, 1999; mem. vocal quartet Sepia, 1990—, featured guest vocalist Jazzpar 2003 tour in Europe (Chamber Music Am. New Works Creation and Presentation Jazz Composers Commn. award, 2004). Recipient U.S. Jazz Amb., 1998—99, Best New Jazz Artist, Jazz From the City (Internat. Radio Show), 1994, Maj. Young Artist award, Universal Jazz Coalition, 1998, The Dakota award, Dakota Station, 1999, Young Entrepreneur award, Universal Jazz Coalition, 2001, Artist-in-the-Sch. Cmty. award, NY Found. Arts, 2002, New Works Creation and Presentation Jazz Composers Commn. Award, Chamber Music Am., 2004—05, Manhattan Cmty. Arts Fund award, Lower Manhattan Cultural Coun., NYC Dept. Cultural Affairs, 2005. Mem.: SAG, ASCAP, AFTRA, NYC Arts in Edn. Roundtable (bd. dirs.), Grammy in Schs. Com., SESAC, Composer and Publisher, Nat. Acad. of Recording Arts and Sciences, Local 802 Musicians Union, Japan Ctrl. Music Pub. Composer, Internat. Women in Jazz (past pres. 1998—2001, bd. mem.), Internat. Assn. of Jazz Educators, Chamber Music Am. Office: PO Box 20085 New York NY 10014 Office Phone: 212-969-8756. Office Fax: 212-645-1260. E-mail: baoule.music@verizon.net, zenzalai@aol.com.

HELM, LEWIS MARSHALL, communications executive; b. Riverdale, Md., Sept. 9, 1931; s. William P. and Selma S. (Snyder) Helm; m. Alice L. Kupferman, Sept. 12, 1953 (dec.). AA in Comms., Am. U., 1957, MS in Pub. Rels., 1979; grad., U.S. Army War Coll., 1977. Newspaper reporter Wichita (Kans.) Eagle, 1950-51, Washington Times-Herald, 1951-54; press asst. Republican Nat. Com., 1954-55; dir. pub. rels. Plumbing Fixture Mfrs. Assn., Washington, 1956-59, Home Mfrs. Assn., 1961-63; pub. rels. cons., 1959-60, 64-68; info. dir. Citizens for Nixon, 1968; asst. to sec. U.S. Dept. Interior, Washington, 1969, dep. asst. sec. mineral resources, 1969-72; asst. sec. for pub. affairs HEW, Washington, 1973-76; pres. Capital Counselors, Inc., Washington, 1976-86; govt. rels. and mktg. cons., 1987—; commr. Washington Suburban Sanitary Commn., 1991-95, vice-chair, 1992-93, chair, 1993-94. Instr. econs. Cath. U. Am., 1974; assoc. lecturing prof. polit,. sci. George Washington U., 1980; commentator Sta. WAMU-FM, Washington, 1995—2002; adj. prof. Montgomery Coll., 1996—97; adj. instr. Coll. Journalism U. Md., 1998—2002; adj. instr. MBA program and and pub. safety leadership divsn. Johns Hopkins U., 1999—2003. Co-author: Informing the People: A Public Affairs Handbook, 1981; author: Black Horse Cavalry Defend Our Beloved Country, 2004. Exec. dir. Sr. Army Res. Comdrs. Assn., 1985—2004; mem. Soc. of the Cin. in the State of Va.; mem. adv. bd. Vietnam Vets. Inst., 1993—96; bd. dirs. Mid-Atlantic region Audubon Naturalist Soc., 1995—97. Brig. gen. USAR, 1984—88. Decorated Legion of Merit with oak leaf cluster; named Disting. Alumnus, Hargrave Mil. Acad.; named to Hall of Fame, Sr. Army Res. Comdrs. Assn.; recipient Meritorious Svc. medal, Dept. Interior, USPHS, Dept. Army, Spl. Citation for Disting. Svc., Sec. HEW. Personal E-mail: helmsarca@aol.com.

HELM, PEYTON RANDOLPH, academic administrator, history professor; b. Louisville; s. Thomas Kennedy and Nell Hunt (Hoge) H.; m. Patricia Burtow, July, 1980; children: Randolph Burton, Alexander Veasey. BA, Yale U.; PhD, U. Pa.; MA, Colby Coll., 1988. Sr. adminstrv. fellow U. Pa., Phila., 1979-81, corod. coll. house programs, 1981-84, asst. dean advising, 1979-84, assoc. dir. devel., 1984-86, dir. devel., 1986-88; v.p. devel., prof. Colby Coll., Waterville, Maine, 1988—2001, v.p. coll. rels., 2001—03; pres., prof. history Muhlenberg Coll., Allentown, Pa., 2003—. Adj. asst. prof. U. Pa., 1979-88. Contbr. articles to profl. jours. Mem. Am. Philological Assn., Am. Oriental Soc., CASE. Office: Office of President Muhlenberg Coll 2400 Chew St Allentown PA 18104 Office Fax: 484-664-3125, 484-664-3107. E-mail: helm@muhlenberg.edu.*

HELM, STEVEN M, lawyer; b. Monmouth, Ill., Mar. 1, 1948; BA with honors, MacMurray College, U. Ill., 1970; JD, U. Ill., 1973. Corp. counsel, Allied Waste Industries, Scottsdale, Ariz., 1995—2003, corp. sec., v.p.-legal, 1996, gen. counsel, 2003. Mem.: Civil Justice Reform Act Adv. Com. and Rules Com., US Dist. Court, Ctrl. Dist. Ill.; Ill. State Bar Assn. Office Phone: 480-627-2700. Office Fax: 480-627-2728. Business E-Mail: shelm@awin.com.*

HELMAN, ALFRED BLAIR, retired academic administrator, educational consultant; b. Windber, Pa., Dec. 25, 1920; s. Henry E. and Luie (Pritt) H.; m. Patricia Ann Kennedy, June 22, 1947; children: Harriet Ann Helman Hill, Patricia Dawn Helman Magaro. AB magna cum laude, McPherson Coll., 1946, DD, 1956; MA, U. Kans., 1947, postgrad., 1948-51; LLD, Juniata Coll., 1976; LHD, Bridgewater Coll., 1977, Ind. U., 1981, Manchester Coll., 1986. Ordained to ministry Ch. of Brethren, 1942; pastor Newton, Kans., 1944-46, Ottawa, Kans., 1946-54, First Ch. of Brethren, Wichita, Kans., 1954-56; faculty Ottawa U., 1947- 48, 51-54, chmn. div. social scis., 1952-54; faculty U. Kans., 1951-54, Friends U., 1955-56; pres. Manchester (Ind.) Coll., 1956-86, pres. emeritus, 1986—. Chmn. com. on higher edn. Ch. of Brethren, 1965-67, 76-78, nat. moderator, 1975-76, mem. rev. and evaluation com., 1983-85, mem. denominational structure rev. com., 1989-91, mem. pension bd. restructure com., 1986-87; trustee McPherson Coll., 1951-56, chmn., 1955-56; trustee Kans. Found. Pvt. Colls. and Univs., 1955-56; pres. Ind. Conf. Higher Edn., 1960-61; mem. policy bd. dept. higher edn. Nat. Coun. Chs. of Christ Am., 1960-71; mem. pres.'s adv. com. Nat. Assn. Intercollegiate Athletics, 1966-70; mem. exec. com. Ind. Coun. Chs., 1960-62, bd. dirs., 1992-94; bd. dirs. Independent Colls. and Univs. of Ind., 1977-83, 84-86, chmn., 1978-79, 85-86; chmn., interim pres. Coun. Protestant Colls. and Univs., 1967, bd. dirs., 1961-69; bd. dirs. Ctrl. States Coll. Assn., 1965-77, chmn., 1968; pres. Assoc. Colls. of Ind., 1970-72, bd. dirs., 1956-86; mem. commn. on religion in higher edn. Assn. Am. Colls., 1968-71; bd. dirs. CTB, Inc., 1977-92. Author articles on religion and higher edn. Mem. IAUP-UN Commn. on Arms Control Edn., 1991—2002. Named Sagamore of Wabash, Gov. of Ind., 1980, Ky. Col., Gov. of Ky., 1964; recipient Outstanding Local Citizen award, 1972, Sparks-Jones award Associated Colls. Ind., 1977, Legion of Honor award Kiwanis Club North Manchester, 1976, Alumni Honor award, Manchester Coll., 1981, Citation of Merit, McPherson Coll., 2001, Citation for Responsible Philanthropy, Manchester Coll., 2003; elected to Ind. Acad., 1987. Mem. Soc. Historians of Am. Fgn. Rels., Internat. Assn. Univ. Presidents (mem. steering com. N.Am. coun. 1982-84), Ind. Assn. Ch.-Related and Ind. Colls. (pres. 1966-67), Am. Assn. Higher Edn., Am. Acad. Polit. and Social Sci., Nat. Assn. Ind. Colls. and Univs. (bd. dirs. 1983-84), Ind. Acad. Social Scis., Ind. Hist. Assn., Ft. Wayne Rotary (Paul Harris fellow), Quest Club (mem. bd. govs. 1998-90, 92-94, 97-99), Phi Beta Kappa, Phi Alpha Theta, Pi Sigma Alpha, Pi Kappa Delta, Tau Kappa Alpha (hon.).

HELMAN, GERALD BERNARD, diplomat; b. Detroit, Nov. 4, 1932; s. Leo and Ann (Glassman) H.; m. Dolores Hammel, May, 1953; children: Ruth Leea, Deborah Gayle, David Robert. AB, U. Mich., 1953, LLB, 1956. Bar: Mich. 1956. Rsch. asst. U. Mich., 1955; intelligence rsch. specialist Dept. State, 1957, econ. consular officer Milan, 1958, polit. officer Vienna, 1960-62, econ. officer Barbados, 1962-63, fgn. affairs officer Washington, 1963-68; polit. mil. affairs officer, counselor U.S. Mission to NATO, Brussels, 1968-73, dep. dir. NATO-Atlantic polit. mil. affairs Washington, 1974-76, dir. UN polit. affairs, 1976-77; dep. asst. sec. Bur. Internat. Orgn. Affairs, 1977-79; U.S. ambassador to UN Orgns. in Europe, 1979-81; dep. and sr. advisor to undersec. for polit. affairs Dept. State, Washington, 1982-91; v.p. Ellipso, Inc., 1992—. Woodrow Wilson fellow Princeton U., 1973 Jewish. Home: 2900 Maplewood Pl Alexandria VA 22302-2424 Business E-Mail: ghelman@ellipso.com.

HELMAN, ROBERT ALAN, lawyer; b. Chgo., Jan. 27, 1934; s. Nathan W. and Esther (Weiss) H.; m. Janet R. Williams, Sept. 13, 1958; children: Marcus E., Adam J., Sarah E. Student, U. Ill., 1951—53; BSL, Northwestern U., 1954, LLB, 1956. Bar: Ill. 1956. Asso. firm Isham, Lincoln & Beale, Chgo., 1956-64, ptnr., 1965-66; ptnr. firm Mayer, Brown, Rowe & Maw, Chgo., 1967—. Bd. dirs. No. Trust Corp., 1986-2006; lectr. U. Chgo. Law Sch., 1974. Co-author: Commentaries on 1970 Illinois Constitution, 1971; assoc. editor Northwestern U. Law Rev., 1955-56; contbr. articles to profl. jours. Chmn. Citizens' Com. on Juvenile Ct., Cook County, 1969-81; pres. Legal Assistance Found., Chgo., 1973-76; chmn. vis. com. Northwestern U. Law Sch., 1989-92; bd. dirs. United Charities Chgo., 1967-73; emeritus trustee Brookings Instn., trustee Aspen Inst., 1986-92. Mem. ABA, Chgo. Bar Assn., Am. Law Inst., Chgo. Coun. Lawyers, Lawyers Club Chgo., Comml. Club, Chgo. Club, Mid-Day Club, Econ. Club, Order of Coif. Home: 4950 S Chicago Beach Dr Chicago IL 60615-3207 Office: Mayer Brown Rowe & Maw 71 S Wacker Dr Chicago IL 60606 Office Phone: 312-701-7020. Business E-Mail: rhelman@mayerbrown.com.

HELMAN, STEPHEN JODY, lawyer; b. Houston, Dec. 14, 1949; m. Gail Stevenson, 1974; children: Kimberley Brooke, Courtney Elizabeth, Caitlin Rebecca. BA in Spanish and Religion, So. Meth. U., Dallas, 1971; postgrad., Perkins Sch. Theology, 1971—73; JD with honors, U. Tex., 1978. Bar: Tex., 1978; cert. estate planning and probate law, 1987. Assoc. Graves, Dougherty, Hearon & Moody, Austin, Tex., 1978-85, ptnr., shareholder, 1985-93; ptnr. Osborne, Lowe, Helman & Smith, LLP, Austin, 1993-2000, Osborne & Helman, LLP, Austin, 2001—05, Osborne, Helman, Knebel & Deleery, LLP, 2006—. Exam commr. in estate planning and probate law, Tex. Bd. Legal Specialization, 1990-94. Contbr. articles to profl. jours. Fellow Am. Coll. Trust and Estate Counsel (mem. profl. standards com. 1990-93); mem. ABA (mem. real property, probate, and trust law sects.), Coll. of the State Bar of Tex., State Bar Tex. (mem. real property, probate and trust law sects.), Travis County Bar Assn. (mem. probate and estate planning sect., pres. 1991-92, dir. 1989-92, ex-officio dir. 1992-93), Order of Coif. Avocations: nature photography, hiking. Office: Osborne, Helman, Knebel & Deleery LLP 301 Congress Ave Ste 1910 Austin TX 78701-4041 Office Phone: 512-542-2000. Business E-Mail: sjhelman@ohkdlaw.com.

HELMBERGER, DONALD VINCENT, geophysical educator, researcher; b. Perham, Minn., Jan. 23, 1938; s. John David and Mary (Klein) H.; m. Florence Coles; 1 child, Genna; m. Annette Sellon; 1 child, Elliott. B in Geophysics, U. Minn., 1961; MS, U. Calif., San Diego, 1965, PhD, 1967; postdoctoral, MIT, 1968-69. Asst. prof. Princeton (N.J.) U., 1969-70, Calif. Inst. Tech., Pasadena, 1970-74, assoc. prof., 1974-79, prof. geophysics, 1979—, Smits Family prof. geophysics and planetary sci. Recipient medal, Seismological Soc. Am., 2002. Fellow Am. Geophysical Union (Inge Lehmann medalist, 1997); mem. NAS. Office: Calif Inst Tech Dept Geol & Planetary Sci Pasadena CA 91125-0001

HELMER, DAVID ALAN, lawyer; b. Colorado Springs, May 19, 1946; s. Horton James and Alice Ruth (Cooley) H.; m. Jean Marie Lamping, May 23, 1987 (div.). BA, U. Colo., 1968, JD, 1973. Bar: Colo. 1973, U.S. Dist. Ct. Colo. 1973, U.S. Ct. Appeals (10th cir.) 1993, U.S. Ct. Claims 1990, U.S. Supreme Ct. 1991. Assoc. Neil C. King, Boulder, Colo., 1973-76; mgr. labor rels., mine regulations Climax Molybdenum Co., Inc. divsn. AMAX, Inc., Climax, Colo., 1976-83; prin. Helmer & McElyen LLC, Frisco, Colo., 1983—. Sec. Z Comm. Corp., Frisco, 1983-90; cmty. bd. dirs. Wells Fargo Bank, N.A., Frisco Editor U. Colo. Law Rev., 1972-73; contbr. articles to legal jours. Bd. dirs. Summit County Coun. Arts and Humanities, Dillon, Colo., 1980-85; legal counsel Advocates for Victims of Assault, Frisco, 1984—; legal counsel Summit County United Way, 1983-95, v.p., bd. dirs., 1983-88; bd. dirs., legal counsel Summit County Alcohol and Drug Task Force, Inc., Summit Prevention Alliance, 1984—, Pumpkin Bowl Inc./Chldren's Hosp. Burn Ctr., 1989—; chmn. Summit County Reps., 1982-89; chmn. 5th Jud. Dist. (Colo.) Rep. Com., 1982-89; chmn. resolutions com. Colo. Rep. Conv., 1984, del. Rep. Nat. Com., 1984; chmn. reaccreditation com. Colo. Mountain Coll., Breckenridge, 1983, mem. steering com., 1997-99; founder, bd. dirs. Dillon Bus. Assn., 1983-87, Frisco Arts Coun., 1989—; atty. N.W. Colo. Legal Svcs. Project, Summit County, 1983—; mcpl. judge Town of Dillon, 1982—, Town of Silverthorne, Colo., 1982—; bd. dirs. Snake River Water Dist., 1998—, chmn., 2002—. Master Sgt. USAR, 1968-74. Mem. ABA, Colo. Bar Assn., (bd. govs. 1991-93, mem. exec. com. 1995-97), Continental Divide Bar Assn. (prs. 1991-95, v.p. 1995-97), Summit County Bar Assn. (pres. 1990-99), Dillon Corinthian Yacht Club (commodore local club 1987-88, 95-97, vice commodore 1994, club champion 1989-91, 94, 95, 97, 98, 2002, winner Colo. Cup, Colo. State Sailing Championships 1991, Dist. Champion 2000, 02, Champion Dillon Open Regatta 2001), Phi Gamma Delta. Lutheran. Office: PO Box 868 611 Main St Frisco CO 80443-0868 Office Phone: 970-668-0181. Business E-Mail: dave@helmerlaw.com.

HELMER, JAMES JOHN, JR., physician, educator; b. Hollywood, Calif., Sept. 18, 1967; s. James John Helmer, Sr. and Marta Adilia Helmer; m. Stacia Anne Helmer, Aug. 1995; children: Olivia, Cameron. BA Psychology, UCLA, 1991; MA Psychology, Chgo. Med. Sch., 1996, MD, 2000. Resident Family Medicine U. Calif. San Francisco, 2003, asst. clin. prof. Family Medicine, 2004—. Fellow Geriat. Medicine U. Calif. San Francisco, 2004, fellow Faculty Devel., 06; physician VA Palo Alto Healthcare Sys., Monterey, Calif., 2004—. Author (textbook): End of Life Care, 2006. Recipient Tchg. award, U. Calif. San Francisco, 2005. Mem.: Am. Geriat. Soc., Am. Acad. Family Physicians. Avocations: tennis, scuba diving, skiing, camping, woodworking. Home: 951 Hancock St Salinas CA 93906 Office: Univ Calif San Francisco Family Medicine 1441 Constitution Blvd Bld 300 Salinas CA 93906

HELMETAG, CHARLES HUGH, foreign language educator; b. Camden, NJ, Apr. 7, 1935; s. Charles Henry and Agnes Beatrice (Gibb) H.; m. Ruth Judith Crispin, Aug. 22, 1959; children: Steven, Diana. BA, U. Pa., 1957; MA, U. Ky., 1959; PhD, Princeton U., 1968. Instr. German Purdue U., West Lafayette, Ind., 1960-62; asst. prof. German Villanova U., 1964-75, assoc. prof., 1975-80, prof., 1980—, chmn. dept. modern lang. and lit., 1973-88, acting chmn., 2006. Contbg. editor Lit./Film Quar., 2000—; contbr. articles to book chpt., revs., profl. jour. Pres. Rosemont Elem. Sch. PTA, 1973—74, bd. dirs., 1974—75. Fulbright scholar U. Goettingen (Ger.), 1959-60; Germanistic Soc. Am. grantee, 1968; German Acad. Exchange Svc. grantee, 1978 Mem. Am. Assn. Tchr. German, MLA, N.E. MLA (exec. coun. 1991-92), Soc. Exile Studies, AAUP (pres. local chpt. 1972-73), Internat. Brecht Soc., Lit./Film Assn., Internationale Vereinigung für Germanistik, Internat. Soc. for the Study of European Ideas, Phi Kappa Phi (pres. Villanova chpt. 1984). Office: Villanova U Dept Classical &Modern Lang & Lit Villanova PA 19085-1699 Office Phone: 610-519-7794. Business E-Mail: charles.helmetag@villanova.edu.

HELMETAG, DIANA, music educator; b. Bryn Mawr, Pa., 1965; d. Charles and Ruth Helmetag; m. Steven Glanzmann, 1993; children: Amanda, Anna Marie. BS in Music Edn. cum laude, Duquesne U., 1987; MusM, Pa. State U., 1990. Instr. Sch. Music Pa. State U., University Park, 1988, 90, lectr. Delaware County campus Media, 1991-95; music tchr. Radnor (Pa.) Twp. Sch. Dist., 1993-94, 95, 96; piano accompanist Villanova (Pa.) Voices Villanova U., 1995-99; instr. Delaware County C.C., Media, 1996; orch. dir. Upper Merion Area Sch. Dist., King of Prussia, Pa., 1996—, subject area leader, 1997—2001, pit orch. dir., 1997, 1998, 2001—05; dir. orch. and choir, chamber music coach Strings Internat. Music Festival Bryn Mawr Coll., Pa., 2001—. Pianist, violinist Mu Phi Epsilon recitals, Phila., 1991, 92, 94; orch. dir. Schuylkill Valley Area Orch. Festival, Wayne, Pa., 1996—; founding mem. Montgomery County Honors String Orch. Festival, host dir., 2005; music dir. King of Prussia Players, 2000; guest condr. Bucks County String Day, 2003-04. Orch. dir., pianist, violinist Narberth (Pa.) Cmty. Theatre, 1997—. Recipient grad. assistantship Pa. State U., 1987-90. Mem. Am. String Tchrs. Assn. with Nat. Sch. Orch. Assn., Music Educators Nat. Conf., Music Tchrs. Nat. Assn., Coll. Music Soc., Pa. Music Educators Assn. (host. dist. 11 orch. festival 1998, presiding chair in-svc. conf. 2001, host all-state orch. festival 2002, chamber group selected to perform for All-State Conf., 2005), Phi Kappa Phi, Pi Kappa Lambda. Office: Upper Merion Area Sch Dist 435 Crossfield Rd King Of Prussia PA 19406 Business E-Mail: dhelmetag@umasd.org.

HELMHOLZ, R(ICHARD) H(ENRY), law educator; b. Pasadena, Calif., July 1, 1940; s. Lindsay and Alice (Bean) H.; m. Marilyn P. Helmholz. AB, Princeton U., 1962; JD, Harvard U., 1965; PhD, U. Calif., Berkeley, 1970; LLD, Trinity Coll., Dublin, 1992. Bar: Mo. 1965. Asst. prof. history to prof. law & history Washington U., St. Louis, 1970-81; prof. law U. Chgo. Law Sch., 1981—84, Ruth Wyatt Rosenson prof. law, 1984—99, Ruth Wyatt Rosenson disting. svc. prof. law, 2000—. Maitland lectr. Cambridge U., 1987; Goodhart prof. Cambridge U., 2000-01. Author: Marriage Litigation, 1975, Select Cases on Defamation, 1985, Canon Law and the Law of England, 1987, Roman Canon Law in Reformation England, 1990, Spirit of Classical Canon Law, 1996, The Ius Commune in England: Four Studies, 2001, Oxford History of the Laws of England, Vol. 1, 2004. Guggenheim fellow, 1986; recipient Von Humboldt rsch. prize, 1992. Fellow Brit. Acad. (corr.), Am. Acad. Arts and Scis., Am. Law Inst., Medieval Acad. Am.; mem. ABA, Am. Soc. Legal History (pres. 1992-94), Selden Soc. (v.p. 1984-87), Univ. Club, Reform Club. Home: 5757 S Kimbark Ave Chicago IL 60637-1614 Office: U Chgo Law Sch 1111 E 60th St Chicago IL 60637-2776 Office Phone: 773-702-9580. Business E-Mail: dick_helmholz@law.uchicago.edu.

HELMICK, RAYMOND GLEN, priest, educator; b. Arlington, Mass., Sept. 7, 1931; s. Raymond Glen and Alice Cecilia (Clancy) H. BA, Boston Coll., 1956, MA in philosphy, 1957; lic. philosphy, Weston Coll., 1957; lic. theol., Hochschule St. Georgen, Frankfurt, 1964. Joined Jesuit Order, 1949, ordained priest Roman Cath. Ch., 1963. Assoc. dir. Ctr. for Human Rights and Responsibilities, London, 1973-79, Inst. Soc. Rsch., London, 1973-79; found., co-dir. Ctr. of Concern for Human Dignity, London, 1979-81; sr. assoc. Conflict Analysis Ctr., Washington, 1982—; prof. of conflict resolution Boston Coll., 1984—; sr. assoc. Ctr. Strategic and Internat. Studies, Washington, 2000—04. Exec. comm. U.S. Interreligious Comm. for Peace in the Middle East, Seattle, 1987—, adv. bd. Orgn. for Human Rights in Iraq, Boston, 1992—; bd. dirs. Refugee Immigrant Ministry, Boston; v.p. Consent of the Governed, 2005—. Author: (with Richard Hauser) A Social Option, 1975, La Question Libanaise Selon Raymond Edde, 1990; editor: (with Rodney Petersen) Forgiveness and Reconciliation: Religion, Public Policy and Conflict Transformation, 2001, Negotiating Outside the Law: Why Camp David Failed, 2004; video documentaries (with John Michalczyk) Out of the Ashes: Northern Ireland's Fragile Peace, 1998, Prelude to Kosovo: War and Peace in Bosnia and Croatia, 1999, South Africa: Beyond a Miracle, 2000, Unexpected Openings: Northern Ireland's Prisoners, 2001, Different Drummers: Daring to Make Peace in the Middle East, 2003, Killing Silence: Taking on the Mafia in Sicily, 2004; exec. prodr. video documentaries. Mediation No. Irish conflict, 1972-81, 92—, Kurdish conflict, 1973-81, 87—, Lebanese conflict, 1982—, Israeli-Palestinian conflict, 1986—, Balkan conflict, 1995—. Democrat. Roman Catholic. Office: Boston Coll Chestnut Hill MA 02467 Business E-Mail: helmick@bc.edu.

HELMINIAK, DANIEL ALBERT, theologian, counselor; b. Pitts., Nov. 20, 1942; s. Albert Francis and Cecelia (Ziolkowski) H. BA in Philosophy, St. Vincent Coll., 1964; STB, Sacrae Theologiae Licentia, Gregorian U., Rome, 1966-68; PhD in Theology, Boston Coll., Andover Newton Theol. Sch., 1979; MA in Psychology, Boston U., 1983; PhD in Ednl. Psychology, U. Tex. at Austin, 1994. Ordained priest in Roman Cath. Ch., 1967. Assoc. pastor Sts. Simon and Jude Ch., Pitts., 1969-72; candidate Soc. of St. Sulpice, Balt., 1972-78; coord. Paulist Leadership and Renewal Project, Boston, 1978-80; mental health worker McLean Hosp., Belmont, Mass., 1980-81; asst. prof. Oblate Sch. of Theology, San Antonio, 1981-85; dir. for spiritual growth Omega Point Counseling Ctr., Austin, Tex., 1989-91; pastoral counselor Family Counseling Ctr. Episc. Theol. Sem. of S.W., Austin, 1991-93; pvt. practice Med. Arts Sq. Counseling Svcs., Austin, 1993-95. Chaplain Dignity, Boston, 1976-81, San Antonio, 1981-85, Austin, 1985-95; asst. prof. psychology State U. West Ga., Carrollton, 1995-97; psychotherapist and educator Pitts. Pastoral Inst., 1997—. Author: The Same Jesus: A Contemporary Christology, 1986 (hon. mention Cath. Press Assn. 1987), Spiritual Development: An Interdisciplinary Study, 1987, What the Bible Really Says About Homesexuality, 1994, The Human Core of Spirituality: Mind As Psyche and Spirit, 1996, Religion and the Human Sciences: An Approach Via Spirituality, 1998; editl. cons. The Collected Works of Bernard Lonergan, 1986-88; mem. editl. adv. bd. Spirituality Today, 1988-90; contbr. articles to profl. jours. Mem. AIDS task force U. Tex., Austin, 1988-90. Fellow Am. Assn. Pastoral Counselors; mem. APA (assoc.), Am. Acad. Religion, Cath. Theol. Soc. Am., Soc. for Sci. Study of Religion, Soc. for Sci. Study of Sexuality. Office: Pitts Pastoral Inst 6324 Marchand St Pittsburgh PA 15206-4312

HELMKE, PAUL (WALTER PAUL HELMKE JR.), lawyer, former mayor; b. Bloomington, Ind., Nov. 24, 1948; s. Walter P. and Rowene Mary (Crabill) H.; m. Deborah Jane Andrews, Aug. 23, 1969; children: Laura Andrews, Kathryn Elizabeth. BA with highest honors, Ind. U., 1970; JD, Yale U., 1973. Bar: Ind. 1973, Fla. 1982. Atty. Helmke Beams LLP, Ft. Wayne, Ind., 1973-87, 2003—, Barnes & Thornburg LLP, Ft. Wayne, 2000—02; dir. govt. rels. Sentry Points LLP, 2004—06; mayor City of Ft. Wayne, 1988-2000. Asst. county atty. Allen County, Ft. Wayne, 1974-87; pres. Nat. Rep. Mayors and Local Ofcls. Orgn., 1993; pres. US Conf. of Mayors, 1997-98, pres., CEO Brady Campaign to Prevent Gun Violence, 2006- Chmn. Allen-Wells chpt. ARC, Ft. Wayne, 1985-87; candidate for Rep. nomination 4th U.S. Congl. Dist.-Ind., 1980; Rep. nominee for U.S. Senate, Ind., 1998; bd. dirs. Nat. League of Cities, 1995-97, chair pub. safety and crime prevention com., 1995; candidate for Rep. nomination 3d U.S. Congl. Dist. Ind., 2002. Recipient J.C. Gallagher prize Law Sch. Yale U., New Haven, Conn., 1972 Mem. Ind. Assn. Cities and Towns (pres. 1996-97). Republican. Lutheran. Office: Helmke Beams LLP 202 W Berry St Ste 300 Fort Wayne IN 46802-2216 also: Brady Ctr/Campaign to Prevent Gun Violence 1225 Eye St NW Ste 1100 Washington DC 20005 Office Phone: 260-422-7422, 202-289-7319. Personal E-mail: paulhelmke@aol.com. Business E-Mail: paulhelmke@helmkebeams.com, phelmke@bradymail.org.

HELMLY, JAMES R., career military officer; b. Savannah, Ga. married; two children: Lisa, Melanie. BS, SUNY; grad., Army Command Gen. Staff Coll., Armed Forces Staff Coll., U.S. Army War Coll. Enlisted U.S. Army, commd. 2d lt., advanced through grades to lt. gen., 2002; early commd. svc. includes platoon leader 101st airborne divsn., U.S. Army, Ft. Campbell, Ky., and Vietnam; co. comdr. Ft. Benning, Ga.; res. assignments include regimental ops. officer Panama; logistics supply and maintenance officer assignments Ga.; comdr. 352d maintenance bn. Macon, Ga.; dep. chief of staff for tn., dep. chief of staff personnel 449th area support group, Forest Park, Ga.; dep. chief U.S. Army Res., Office to Chief Army Res., Washingtin, 1995—99; comdr. join task force conducting Oper. Provide Refuge, Fort Dix, NJ, 1999—99; military asst., manpower and reserve affairs Office of the Asst., Sec. of the Army, Washington, 1999—2001; commdg. gen. U.S. Army Res.,78th Div., Edison, NJ, 2001—02; comdr. U.S. Army Res. Command, Ft. McPherson, Ga., 2002—; chief U.S. Army Res., 2002—. Office: Office of Chief Army Res 2400 Army Pentagon Washington DC 20310-2400

HELMRICH, JOEL MARC, lawyer; b. Bklyn., Apr. 15, 1953; s. William and Edna (Steigman) H.; m. Barbara Ellen Richter, Sept. 2, 1984; children: Joshua David. BS, Cornell U., 1975, MBA, 1976; JD, Syracuse U., 1979. Bar: Pa. 1979, U.S. Dist. Ct. (we. dist.) Pa. 1979, U.S. Ct. Appeals (3d cir.) 1997. Assoc. Tucker Arensberg, PC, Pitts., 1979-86; shareholder Tucker Arensberg, Pitts., 1986-99; ptnr. Meyer, Unkovic & Scott LLP, Pitts., 1999—. Mem. Pa. Bar Assn., Allegheny County Bar Assn., Comml. Law League Am., Am. Bankruptcy Inst., Cornell Club. Avocations: golf, tennis. Office: Meyer Unkovic & Scott LLP 1300 Oliver Bldg Pittsburgh PA 15222-2304 Office Phone: 412-456-2841. Business E-Mail: jmh@muslaw.com.

HELMS, J. LYNN, retired federal agency administrator; b. DeQueen, Ark., Mar. 1, 1925; s. Frank and Mamie (Johnson) H.; m. Lorraine Bisgard, Mar. 16, 1947; children: Loralyn, Jon, Carole, Zack. Dir. mktg. and sales N. Am. Aviation Co., Columbus, Ohio, 1956-62; group v.p. Bendix Corp., Ann Arbor, Mich., 1962-70; pres. Norden div. United Technologies Corp., Norwalk, Conn., 1970-74, Piper Aircraft Corp., Lock Haven, Pa., 1974-81, chmn. bd., 1978-81; adminstr. FAA, Washington, 1981-83. Dir. Birchminster Industries. Served to lt. col. USMC, 1944-55. Decorated Air medal with oak leaf cluster. Fellow AIAA; mem. Soc. Exptl. Test Pilots.

HELMS, JESSE, retired senator; b. Monroe, NC, Oct. 18, 1921; s. Jesse Alexander and Ethel Mae (Helms) H.; m. Dorothy Jane Coble, Oct. 31, 1942; children: Jane (Mrs. Charles R. Knox), Nancy (Mrs. John C. Stuart), Charles. Student, Wingate Jr. Coll., NC, Wake Forest Coll. City editor Raleigh (N.C.) Times, 1941-42; news and program dir. Sta. WRAL, Raleigh, 1948-51; adminstrv. asst. to U.S. senators Willis Smith and Alton Lennon, 1951-53; exec. dir. N.C. Bankers Assn., 1953-60; exec. v.p., vice chmn. Capitol Broadcasting Co., Raleigh, 1960-72; U.S. senator from N.C., 1973—2002; sr. mem. Com. on Fgn. Relations; mem. Rules & Adminstrn. Com., Republican Policy Com. Chmn. bd. Specialized Agrl. Publs., Inc., Raleigh, 1964-72; mem. Raleigh City Council, 1957-61. Author: Here's Where I Stand, 2005. Bd. dirs. N.C. Cerebral Palsy Hosp., Durham, United Cerebral Palsy N.C., Wake County Cerebral Palsy and Rehab. Center, Raleigh, Camp Willow Run, Littleton, N.C.; former trustee Campbell Coll., Wingate Coll., Meredith Coll., John F. Kennedy Coll. Served with USNR, 1942-45, World War II. Recipient Freedoms Found. award for best TV editorial, 1962, for newspaper article, 1973, So. Bapt. Nat. award for Service to mankind, 1972; Gold medal VFW; Conservative Congressional award, 1976; Liberty award Am. Econ. Council, 1978; Disting. Public Service award Public Service Research Council, 1978; Watchdog of Treasury award; Guardian of Small Bus. award; named Man of Yr. Women for Constl. Govt., 1978; Legislator of Yr. award Nat. Rifle Assn., 1978, Taxpayer's Best Friend award Nat. Taxpayer's Union, 1993; other awards. Mem.: Masons (33d degree), Raleigh Execs. Club (past pres.), Rotary (past pres. Raleigh). Republican. Baptist (Deacon).

HELMS, NEVILLE TROY, manufacturing company administrator; b. Wellington, Kans., Oct. 20, 1960; s. Clifford Wayne and Iva Lynn Helms; m. Lara Kristina Helms, Dec. 31, 1991; children: Joshua, Zachary, Aaron Hemls, Jonathan. BSBA, Kans. State U., Manhattan, 1982; MS in Bus. Adminstrn., Friends U., Wichita, Kans., 1998. Asst. store mgr. Wal-Mart Stores, 1982—85; store mgr. TG&Y Stores, Lubbock, Tex., 1985—89, Hobby Lobby Stores, Aurora, Colo., 1989—92; br. mgr. Hammond Distributors, Wichita, 1992—95; store mgr. Comfort Products Distributors, Wichita, 1995—2000; regional logistics mgr. Wurth Svc. Supply, Wichita, 2000—04; area program mgr. Bruckner Supply Co., Wichita, 2004—. Mem. Nat. Right Life, Washington, 2004—07, Rep. Nat. Com., 2004—07. Mem.: Inst. Supply Mgmt., Mensa. Avocations: coin collecting/numismatics, sports. Home: 1424 Meadow Ridge Ct Derby KS 67037

HELMS, ROBERT BRAKE, economist; b. Mobile, Ala., Jan. 12, 1940; s. Osburn Charles and Julia May (Moore) H.; m. Sharon Gay Schliebe, Aug. 8, 1964; children— Elissa Lynelle, Julianne Nanette BS in Agrl. Adminstrn., Auburn U., 1962; MA in Econs., UCLA, 1966, PhD in Econs., 1973. Asst. prof. Loyola Coll., Balt., 1971-74; dir. health policy studies Am. Enterprise Inst., Washington, 1974-81, resident scholar, dir. health policy studies, 1990; dep. asst. sec. planning and evaluation/health HHS, Washington, 1981-84, acting asst. sec. planning and evaluation, 1984-86, asst. sec. for planning and evaluation, 1986-89; exec. dir. Am. Pharm. Inst., 1989-90. Chmn. Sec.'s Task Force on Hosp. Deregulation, Washington, 1981-83, Sec.'s Task Force on Drug Reimbursement, Washington, 1983-85; mem. White House Working Group on Health Policy and Econs., Washington, 1984-85; steering com. Health Policy Agenda Am. People, Chgo., 1984-88; working party on social policy OECD, Paris, 1984-89; nat. adv. coun. Agy. Health Care Rsch. and Quality, 2005—, mem. HHS Medicaid Commn., 2005-06. Author: Natural Gas Regulation, 1974; editor: Drug Development and Marketing, 1975, The International Supply of Medicines, 1980, Drugs and Health, 1981, American Health Policy: Critical Issues for Reform, 1993, Health Care Policy and Politics: Lessons From Four Countries, 1993, Health Care Reform: Competition and Controls, 1993, Competitive Strategies in the Pharmaceutical Industry, 1996, Medicare in the Twenty-first Century: Seeking Fair and Efficient Reform, 1999. Served to capt. U.S. Army, 1962-64 Republican. Lutheran. Avocations: tennis, travel, internet. Home: 1404 Foggy Glen Ct Silver Spring MD 20906-2092 Office: Am Enterprise Inst 1150 17th St NW Washington DC 20036-4603 Office Phone: 202-862-5877. Personal E-mail: rbhelms@sprintmail.com. Business E-Mail: rhelms@aei.org.

HELMS, ROGER D., lawyer; b. Orlando, June 11, 1953; s. V.S. and Eunice Helms. BS magna cum laude, U. Ctrl. Fla., 1980; JD, U. Fla. Sch. Law, 1982. Fla. Bar: Fla.; bd. cert. Civil Trial Law, Personal Injury, Fla. Bar Assn. Bd. of Legal Specialization & Edn., 1994, 99. From assoc. to ptnr. Troutman, Williams, Irvin, Green, Helms and Polich, Winter Park, Fla., 1983—. Mem. ABA, Acad. Fla. Trial Lawyers. Avocations: offshore fishing, boating. Office: Troutman Williams Irvin Green Helms and Polich 311 W Fairbanks Ave Winter Park FL 32789-5094 Home: 5829 La Belle St Orlando FL 32809-3544 Office Phone: 407-647-2277.

HELMSING, FREDERICK GEORGE, lawyer; b. Mobile, Ala., Dec. 30, 1940; s. Joseph Herman and Mary Gertrude (Zimlich) H.; m. Margaret Sue Oswalt, Mar. 22, 1969; children: Frederick George, Joseph Guy, Margaret Sue. BS in Acctg., Spring Hill Coll., 1963; JD, U. Ala., 1965; LLM in Taxation, NYU, 1967. Bar: Ala. 1965, Fla. 1989. Assoc. Gallalee, Denniston & Edington, Mobile, 1966-76; ptnr. Helmsing, Leach, Herlong, Newman & Rouse, Mobile, 1976—. Instr. U. South Ala., Mobile, 1969-78; instr. law U. Ala., Mobile, 1982 Dem. chmn. 1st Congl. Dist. Campaign, 1976. Fellow: Am. Coll. Trial Lawyers; mem.: ABA (mem. civil and criminal tax penalties com.), Mobile Area C. of C. (mem. taxation and world trade coms.), Mobile Bar Assn., Mobile County Bar Assn. (treas. 1969), Ala. State Bar Assn. (chmn. tax sect. 1979—80), Athelstan Country Club, Mobile County Club. Roman Catholic. Office: Helmsing Leach Herlong Newman & Rouse 200 LaClede Bldg 150 Government St Mobile AL 36602-3114 Home: PO Box 2767 Mobile AL 36652 Office Phone: 251-432-5521. Personal E-mail: FGH@helmsinglaw.com.

HELMS-VANSTONE, MARY WALLACE, anthropology educator; b. Allentown, Pa., Apr. 15, 1938; d. Samuel Leidich and Mary (Wallace) Helms; divorced. BA, Pa. State U., State College, 1960; MA, U. Mich., 1962, PhD, 1967. Instr. Wayne State U., Detroit, 1965-67; asst. prof. Syracuse (N.Y.) U., 1967-68; lectr. Northwestern U., Evanston and Chgo., Ill., 1969-79; prof. U. N.C., Greensboro, 1979—2004, prof. emerita, 2004—, head dept. anthropology Greensboro, 1979-85. Author: Asang: A Miskito Community, 1971, Middle America, 1975, Ancient Panama, 1979, Ulysses' Sail, 1988, Craft and the Kingly Ideal, 1993, Creations of the Rainbow Serpent, 1995, Access to Origins, 1998, The Curassow's Crest, 2000; contbr. articles to profl. jours. Fellow: Am. Anthrop. Assn.; mem.: Medieval Acad. Am., So. Anthrop. Soc. (pres. 1980—81, procs. editor 1982—94), Am. Ethnological Soc., Am. Soc. Ethnohistory (pres. 1976). Avocations: travel, painting, musical activities, crafts. Office: Univ NC Dept Anthropology PO Box 26170 Greensboro NC 27402-6170

HELMUTH, BRIAN, marine biologist, educator; b. Cleve., May 6, 1967; 1 child, Morgan Timmerman-Helmuth. PhD, U. Wash., Seattle, 1997. Assoc. prof. U. SC., Columbia, 1999—. Office: Univ SC Department of Biological Sciences Columbia SC 29208

HELOISE, columnist, writer; b. Waco, Tex., Apr. 15, 1951; d. Marshal H. and Heloise K. (Bowles) Cruse; m. David L. Evans, Feb. 13, 1981. BS in Math. and Bus, S.W. Tex. State U., 1974. Owner, pres. Heloise, Inc. Asst. to columnist mother, Heloise, 1974-77, upon her death took over internationally syndicated column, 1977; author: Hints from Heloise, 1980, Help from Heloise, 1981, Heloise's Beauty Book, 1985, All-New Hints from Heloise, 1989, Heloise: Hints for a Healthy Planet, 1990, Heloise from A to Z, 1992, Household Hints for Singles, 1993, Hints for All Occasions, 1995, In The Kitchen With Heloise, 2000, Heloise Conquers Stinks & Stains, 2002, Get Organized with Heloise, 2004; contbg. editor Good Housekeeping mag., 1983, Speaker for the House; co-founder, 1st co-pilot Mile Pie in the Sky Balloon Club. Mem. Good Neighbor Coun. Tex.-Mex.; sponsor Nat. Smile Week. Recipient Mental Health Mission award Nat. Mental Health Assn., 1990, The Carnegians Good Human Rels. award, 1994. Mem. AFTRA, SAG, Women in Comm. (Headliner 1994), Tex. Press Women, Internat. Women's Forum, Women in Radio and TV, Confrerie de la Chaine des Rotisseurs (bailli San Antonio chpt.), Ordre Mondial des Gourmets De'Gustateurd de U.S.A., Death Valley Yacht and Racket Club, Zonta. Home: PO Box 795000 San Antonio TX 78279-5000

HELOU, GEORGE, science administrator, educator; BS in Physics with High Distinction, tchg. diploma in sci. edn., Am. Univ. Beirut, 1975; MSc, Cornell U., 1977, PhD in Astrophysics and Radio Sci., 1980. With Cornell U., Arcetri Astrophysical Observatory; mem. faculty in Physics, Math and Astronomy Divsn. Calif. Inst. Tech., Pasadena, Calif., exec. dir., Infrared Processing and Analysis Ctr., with, 1983—; dir. NASA Herschel Sci. Ctr.; dep. dir. Spitzer Sci. Ctr. Lectr. in field; visiting positions at several European Universities, including Paris, Leiden and Florence; associated with Infrared Astronomical Satellite, 1983, Infrared Space Observatory, 1995—98, Spitzer Space Telescope, 2003. Contbr. articles to profl. jours. Recipient Philip K. prize for Academic Excellence, 1975, Arcetri Internat. Fellowship, 1980, Dudley award, 1982, NASA Exceptional Svc. medal, 1992, NASA Exceptional Achievement medal, 2001, NASA Pub. Svc. medal, 2004. Mem.: Internat. Astronomical Union, Am. Astronomical Soc. Office: Infrared Processing and Analysis Ctr Calif Inst Tech Mail Code 100-22 770 S Wilson Ave Pasadena CA 91125 Office Phone: 626-395-1919. Office Fax: 626-397-7018.

HELPER, DEBRA J., gastroenterologist; BA in Bioloigy, Ind. U., Bloomington, 1977; MD, Northwestern U., Chgo., 1981. Asst. prof. clin. medicine Ind. U. Sch. Medicine, Indpls., 1988—97, assoc. prof. clin. medicine, 1997—, med. dir. Inflamatory Bowel Disease Ctr., 1995—. Mem. Ind. chpt. Crohn's and Colitis Found., 1992—2005. Named Physician of Yr., Ind. chpt. Crohn's and Colitis Found., 2001; recipient Torch of Friendshipaward, 1995, Excellence in Tchg. award, Ind. U. Sch. Medicine, 2000, 2006. Mem.: AMA, ACP, Am. Soc. Gastrointestinal Endoscopy, Am. Gastroent. Assn. Office: Indiana University School of Medicine 550 N University Blvd #4100 Indianapolis IN 46202 Office Phone: 317-274-3565. Office Fax: 317-278-7057. Business E-Mail: dhelper@iupui.edu.

HELPERN, JOAN (JOAN MARSHALL), fashion designer, entrepreneur; b. NYC, Oct. 10, 1926; d. Edward and Ethel (Tilzer) Marshall; m. David Helpern, Aug. 14, 1960; 1 child, Elizabeth Joan. BA, Hunter Coll., NYC, 1947; MA, Columbia U., 1948; PhD, Harvard U., 1967. Psychologist, author, educator, lectr., 1948-68; dir. child guidance N.Y.C. Bd. Edn., Lexington, Mass.; founder, CEO, designer Joan and David (footwear, sportswear, accessory design/mfg.), NYC, 1968-2000; pres. Joan Helpern Designs, NYC; exec.-in-residence, adj. prof. Columbia U. Sch. Internat. and Pub. Affairs, 2002—. Lectr., US, London, South Africa and China, 1965—, 2001—07. Recipient Coty award Am. Design, 1978, FFANY Footwear Designer award, 1992, Fairchild Footwear Designer award, 1992, Fairchild Hall of Fame award, 1993, Michelangelo Footwear Design award, 1993, Female Bus. Owners award, 1993-94, Athena award Hunter Coll., 1996; Columbia U. grantee, 1947-48; named one of 50 Leading Female Entrepreneurs of World, 1998, 50 Leading Bus. Women of World, Working Woman, 1995, 96, 97, 98. Mem. Com. of 200 (founding mem.).

HELPRIN, MARK, author; b. NYC, June 28, 1947; s. Morris A. and Eleanor (Lynn) H.; m. Lisa Kennedy, June 28, 1980; children: Alexandra Morris, Olivia Kennedy. AB, Harvard U., 1969, AM, 1972; postgrad., Magdalen Coll., Oxford U., Eng., 1976-77. Sr. fellow Claremont Inst. Study of Statesmanship and Polit. Philosophy. Aaron and Helen L. De Roy disting. vis. fellow Hillsdale Coll. Author: A Dove of the East and Other Stories, 1975, Refiner's Fire, 1977, Ellis Island and Other Stories, 1981, Winter's Tale, 1983, Swan Lake, 1989, A Soldier of the Great War, 1991, Memoir from Antproof Case, 1995, A City in Winter, 1996, The Veil of Snows, 1997, The Pacific and Other Stories, 2004, Freddy and Fredericka, 2005. Mem. Coun. on Fgn. Rels.; adviser in def. and fgn. rels. Rep. presdl. nominee Robert Dole. Served with Israeli Army and Air Force, 1972-73. Recipient Prix de Rome, Am. Acad. and Inst. Arts and Letters, 1982, Nat. Jewish Book award, 1982, Helmerich Disting. Author's award, 2006. Fellow Am. Acad. in Rome.

HELSENE, AMY L., lawyer; b. Austin, Minn., June 21, 1973; BA cum laude, U. Minn., Mpls., 1995; JD, U. Minn. Law Sch., Mpls., 1998. Bar: Minn. 1998. Clk. to Hon. James T. Swenson Hennepin County Dist. Ct.; assoc. Larkin, Hoffman, Daly & Lindgren, Ltd., Mpls. Contbr. articles to profl. jours. Named a Rising Star, Minn. Super Lawyers mag., 2006. Mem.: Vol. Lawyers Network, Douglas K. Amdahl Inns of Ct., Minn. Women Lawyers, ABA, Minn. State Bar Assn., Hennepin County Bar Assn., Phi Beta Kappa. Office: Larkin Hoffman Daly & Lindgren Ltd 1500 Wells Fargo Plz 7900 Xerxes Ave S Minneapolis MN 55431 Office Phone: 952-896-3326. E-mail: ahelsene@larkinhoffman.com.*

HELSLEY, ALEXIA JONES, archivist; b. Louisville, Ky., Sept. 9, 1945; d. George Alexander and Evelyn (Masden) J.; m. Terry Lynn Helsley, Oct. 11, 1969; children: Cassandra Keiser Paschal, Jacob Henry. BA in History, Furman U., Greenville, SC, 1967; MA in History, U. SC, 1974; cert., Modern Archives Inst., Washington, 1978, SC Exec. Inst., Columbia, 1995. Archival asst. SC Dept. Archives and History, Columbia, 1968-69, archivist I, 1969-72, asst. reference archivist, 1972-76, supr. reference and rsch., 1976-88, dir. pub. programs divsn., 1988-96, dir. edn., 1996-99; dir. spl. projects, editor Biograph. Directory SC House of Reps., 1999—. Historian Am. Lodging Resources, Inc.; rsch. fellow Inst. So. Studies, U. SC, 2001-02; adj. faculty Midlands Tech. Coll., 2001-02, U. SC, Aiken, 2002—. Author: Harbison: an Historical Sketch, 1986, First Baptist Church of Irmo: Historical Overview, 1992, Researching Family History: A Workbook, 1992, 96, The 1840 Revolutionary Pensioners of Henderson County, North Carolina, 1996, Unsung Heroines of the Carolina Frontier, 1997, Silent Cities: Cemeteries and Classrooms, 1997, South Carolina's African American Confederate Pensioners, 1923-1925, 1998, South Carolinians in the War for American Independence, 2000, The Map of South Carolina, 2003, Beaufort, South Carolina a History, 2005, (TV series) Branches, 2005, Guide to Historic Beaufort, 2006; co-author: SC Court Records, 1993, The Changing Face of SC Politics, 1993, African American Genealogical Research, 1997, The Many Faces of Slavery, 1999, Guide to Historic Henderson County, NC, 2007; contbr. articles to profl. jours. Chair social and recreation com. Harbison Cmty. Assn., Columbia, SC, 1984-89; trustee SC Hall of Fame, Myrtle Beach, 1988-96; vice-chair Columbia Quincentennial Commn. SC, 1989-93; pres. Richland Sertoma, Columbia, 1998-99; bd. vis. Presbyn. Coll., 2001-2003. Recipient Willie Parker Peace History Book award, 1997, Lifetime Achievement award, SC Archival Assn., 2002, Archives award Gov. SC, 2006, Part-Time Tchg. award USCA, 2007; named to Hon. Order of Ky. Cols., 2006, Richland Sertoman of Yr., 2000. Mem.: So. Hist. Assn., SC Hist. Assn., Soc. Am. Archivists (chair reference, access, outreach sect. 1981—83), Joseph McDowell Nat. Soc. DAR, Pace Soc. Am. (trustee), Henderson County Geneal. and Hist. Soc. (v.p. 1998—2007, charter), SC Archival Assn. (pres. 2005). Baptist. Home: 1 Northpine Ct Columbia SC 29212-2911 Office: SC Dept Archives History 8301 Parklane Rd Columbia SC 29223-4905 Personal E-mail: alexiahelsley@yahoo.com. Business E-Mail: helsley@scdah.state.sc.us.

HELSON, HENRY BERGE, publisher, educator, retired mathematician; b. Lawrence, Kan., June 2, 1927; s. Harry and Lida G. (Anderson) H.; m. Ravenna W. Mathews, June 12, 1954; children— David M., Ravenna A., Harold E. AB, Harvard U., 1947, PhD, 1950. Lectr. U. Uppsala, Sweden, 1950-51; instr., then asst. prof. math. Yale, 1951-55; mem. faculty U. Calif. at Berkeley, 1955—, prof. math.; retired, 1993. Vis. prof. Swedish univs., spring 1962, U. Paris, Orsay, France, 1966-67, U. Sci. and Tech., Kumasi, Ghana, spring 1969, U. du Languedoc, Montpellier, France, 1971-72, Marseille, France, fall 1976; vis. prof. Indian Statis. Inst., Calcutta, spring 1980; lectr. St. Mary's Coll. of Calif., 2001-02. Author: Invariant Subspaces, 1964, Harmonic Analysis, 1983, The Spectral Theorem, 1986, Linear Algebra, 1990, Honors Calculus, 1992, Calculus and Probability, 1998, Dirichlet Series, 2005. Mem. Soc. Friends; treas. Friends Com. on Legis. Calif., 1989-95. Sheldon Traveling fellow, Warsaw and Wroclaw, Poland, 1947—48. Home: 15 The Crescent Berkeley CA 94708-1701 E-mail: hhelson@aol.com.

HELSTEIN, IVY RAE, communications executive, psychotherapist, writer; d. Harold and Celia Weintraub Markowitz; children: Hilary, Eden, Flyn. BA, Queens Coll., 1958; MA in Human Behavior, Goddard Coll., Plainfield, Vt., 1979. Founder, pres. Comm. Dynamics, Great Neck, NY, 1973—. Creator Practical Spiritualism; instr., lectr. classroom mgmt. skills various sch. dists., N.Y., 1976; instr. assertiveness tng., conflict mgmt., adult continuing edn. Hofstra U., Hempstead, N.Y., 1976, C.W. Post U., Brookville, N.Y., 1979; adj. faculty Nassau C.C., Garden City, 1977—. Author: Great Persuaders: Sales Training, 1984, Great Communicators II, 1987, Infinite Abilities: Living Your Life on Purpose, 1999. Trainer N.Y. State Child Protective Svcs., 1995—, Suffolk County (N.Y.) Dept. Labor, 1997. Mem. Nat. Spkr. Assn. (profl., past pres., Chpt. Mem. of the Yr. award 1986), Tri-State Nat. Spkrs. Assn. (pres. 1985-86), Authors Guild, Inc. Avocation: world travel. Home and Office: 27 Georgian Ln Great Neck NY 11024-1615 Personal E-mail: IHelstein@aol.com.

HELTNE, PAUL GREGORY, researcher, museum director; b. Lake Mills, Iowa, July 4, 1941; s. Palmer Tilford and Grace Katherine (Hanson) H.; children— Lisa, Christian. BA, Luther Coll., Decorah, Iowa, 1962; PhD, U. Chgo., 1970. Asst. prof. Johns Hopkins U. Sch. Medicine, Balt., 1970-82; dir. Chgo. Acad. Scis., 1982-91, pres., 1991—99, pres. emeritus, 1999—; co-dir. Nature Polis and Ethics Project, 1994—2002; dir. Ctr. for Humans and Nature, 2003—. Cons. WHO, Am. Petroleum Inst. Author, editor: Neotropical Primates: Status and Conservation, 1976, Lion-Tailed Macaque, 1985, Science Learning in the Informal Setting, 1988, Understanding Chimpanzees, 1989, Chimpanzee Cultures, 1994. Trustee Balt. Zool. Soc., 1972-82. Mem. Am. Assn. Mus. (edn. task force, accreditation site visitor), Assn. Sci. Mus. Dirs. (sec.-treas. 1986-96), Internat. Primatology Soc., Soc. Integrative and Comparative Biology, Soc. for Study Evolution, Systematic Zoology Soc. Office: Ctr for Humans and Nature 2430 N Cannon Dr Chicago IL 60614 Office Phone: 773-404-8276. Business E-Mail: paulheltne@humansandnature.org.

HELTON, KATHLEEN JACOBSON, neuroradiologist; d. Gerald Jacobson and Mary Margaret Fitzgerald; m. Stephen Lane Helton, June 7, 1981. MSN, U. of Tenn. Coll. of Nursing, 1979—80; MD, U. of Tenn. Coll. of Medicine, 1986—91. Radiologist Am. Bd. of Radiology, 1996. Resident in radiology Vanderbilt U. Med. Ctr., Memphis, 1992—96, neuroradiology fellow, 1996—98, clin. instr., neuroradiology, 1998; neuroradiologist St Jude Children's Rsch. Hosp., Memphis, 1999—. Reviewer of prof. jours.; cons. in field. Contbr. chapters to books, articles to profl. jours. Recipient Achievement Citation for Scholastic Achievement, Janet M. Glasgow Meml. Fund, 1991; Josephine Cir. scholarship, U. of Tenn. Sch. of Nursing, 1975—77. Mem.: AMA, Am. Soc. of Pediatric Neuroradiology (assoc.), Southeastern Neuroradiological Soc. (assoc.), Am. Coll. Radiology (assoc.), Am. Soc. Neuroradiology (sr.), Alpha Omega Alpha (assoc.). Avocations: swimming, travel, music. Office: St Jude Children's Rsch Hosp 332 N Lauderdale St Memphis TN 38105 Office Phone: 901-495-2412. Business E-Mail: kathleen.helton@stjude.org.

HELTON, TODD, professional baseball player; b. Knoxville, Tenn., Aug. 20, 1973; m. Kristi Helton, Jan. 29. Student, U. Tenn. Player Colo. Rockies, 1997—. Named to Nat. League All-Star Team, 2000—04; recipient Nat. League Gold Glove Award, 2001, 2002, 2004. Achievements include led Nat. League in Hits (216), RBI's (147), and Batting Avg. (.372), 2000. Office: Colo Rockies 2001 Blake St Denver CO 80205-2008*

HELVEY, EDWARD DOUGLAS, lawyer; b. West Palm Beach, Fla., Apr. 26, 1956; s. Wilfred Douglass and Alice Garr (Campbell) Helvey; m. Mary Patricia McGraw, Oct. 26, 1985; children: Megan Anne, Andrew Douglas. BA, Ohio State U., 1978; JD, Cleve. State U., 1981. Bar: Ohio 1982, U.S. Dist. Ct. (no. and so. dists.) Ohio 1982, U.S. Supreme Ct. 1993. Asst. atty. gen. Office Ohio Atty. Gen., Columbus, 1981-84, spl. counsel, 1987-94; staff atty. ITT Consumer Fin. Corp., Columbus, 1984-85, reg. adminstr. govtl. affairs, 1985-88; legis. agt. Ohio Edn. Assn., Columbus, 1988-97, labor. rels. cons., 1997—. Mem. exec. com. Profl. Staff Union Ohio, 1988—, v.p., 1995—98, treas., 2000—06. Bd. dirs. N.W. Civic Assn., Columbus, 1984; alt. del. Nat. Dem. Conv., 1996; mem. Delaware County Dem. Ctrl. Com., 1996—; vice chair Delaware County Dem. Party, 2004—05, chair, 2005—; mem. Delaware County Bd. Elections, 2007—; mem. coun. St. Anthony Parish, 1997—99. Mem.: Ohio Soc. Assn. Execs., Nat. Assn. Legis. and Polit. Specialists Edn., Nat. Staff Orgn. (del. 1994—98, 2000—, bd. dirs. 2003—06), Internat. Found. Employee Benefits, Md. Fin. Svcs. Assn. (bd. dirs. 2003—), Va. Consumer Fin. Assn. (bd. dirs. 1985—88), Pa. Fin. Svcs. Assn. (bd. dirs. 1985—88), Ohio Consumer Fin. Assn. (bd. dirs. 1985—88), Richland County Bar Assn., Columbus Bar Assn., Ohio Bar Assn. Democrat. Roman Catholic. Home: 410 Ashford Dr Westerville OH 43082-7446 Office Phone: 614-895-1041. Personal E-mail: ehelvey@aol.com. Business E-Mail: helveyed@ohea.org.

HELVEY, WILLIAM CHARLES, JR., communications specialist; b. Springfield, Mo., Sept. 4, 1942; s. William C. Sr. and Alice (Essary) H.; m. Julia Faye Howard, June 16, 1962; children: Howard, Harold. BS in Art Edn., S.W. Mo. State U., 1965; MA in Art, U. Mo., 1970. Tchr. art Marshfield (Mo.) H.S., 1965-67; med. illustrator, program emphasis mgr. Mo. Regional Med. Program, Columbia, 1968-80; dir. instrl. media Ctrl. Meth. Coll., Fayette, Mo.; comm. cons., Columbia, 1981-83; state comm. sys. specialist Univ. Ext., Lincoln U., Jefferson City, Mo., 1983—2005; ind. film prodr. Helvey Prodns. Profl. artist, photographer, presenter in field; juror for art and photography; adj. prof. art Stephens Coll. One-man shows (83), in art and photography, group shows (over 100) in arts, including, Arts Ctr. of the Ozarks, Boone County Hist. Mus., Columbia, Mo., Arrow Rock State Hist. Site, Rozier Gallery, Jefferson City, Mo., Columbia Art League, U.S. Social Security Adminstrn., Nat. 4-H Ctr., Silver Springs, Md.; contbr. numerous articles to profl. jours. Project leader Boone County 4-H Clubs, Columbia, 1977-2002. Recipient Unsung Hero award U.S. Dept. Agr., 1988, Mo. Specialist award Mo. State Extension, 1990, 93, numerous awards in art, photography, film and video prodn. Mem.: Columbia Art League (chmn. Boone County art show 1975—, Lifetime Achievement award in art), Aircraft Owners and Pilots Assn. Avocations: nature, aviation, screenplay writing, fine art photography. Home: 908 Shepard Ct Columbia MO 65201-6135 E-mail: bhelvey@aol.com.

HELWICK, CHRISTINE, lawyer; b. Orange, Calif., Jan. 6, 1947; d. Edward Everett and Ruth Evelyn (Seymour) Hailwood; children: Ted C., Dana J. BA, Stanford U., 1968; MA, Northwestern U., 1969; JD, U. Calif., San Francisco, 1973. Bar: Calif., U.S. Supreme Ct. U. S. Ct. Appeals (9th cir.), U.S. Dist. Ct. (no., ctrl., so. and ea. dist.) Calif. Tchr. history New Trier Twp. High Sch., Winnetka, Ill., 1968-69; sec. to the producer Flip Wilson Show, Burbank, Calif., 1970; assoc. Crosby, Heafey, Roach & May, Oakland, Calif., 1973-78; asst. counsel litigation U. Calif., Oakland, 1978-84, mng. univ. counsel, 1984-94, counsel Berkeley campus, 1989-94; gen. counsel, chief exec. systemwide legal office, and sec. for the institution Calif. State U. Sys., 1994—. Lectr. in field. Mem. instnl. rev. bd. Devel. Studies Ctr., Oakland, 1990—; mem. Alameda County Fee Arbitration Panel. Mem. Nat. Assn. Coll. and Univ. Attys. (bd. dirs. 1995-98, 2000-2004, pres. 2002-03), Nat. Assn. Coll. and Univ. Bus. Officers (bd. dirs. 2002—), State Bar Calif. (exec. com. 1980-83, Leadership Calif. 1998), dirs. 1977), Alameda County Bar Found. (adv. trustee 1988-90, bd. dirs. 1991), Order of Coif. Episcopalian. Office: Calif State U 401 Golden Shore 4th Fl Long Beach CA 90802-4275

HELWIG, ARTHUR WOODS, retired chemical company executive; b. St. Louis, Feb. 1, 1929; s. Gunther Albert and Emma (Schumacher) H.; m. Evelyn Morgan, July 10, 1954; children: Paul, Katherine, Elizabeth, Mary. BSChemE, U. Mo.-Rolla, 1950, ChemE (hon.), 1966; MSChemE, U. Ill., 1952. Process engr. Ethyl Corp., Baton Rouge, 1952-53, econs. engr., 1953-56, supr., 1956-59, gen. supt., 1959-64, dir. planning Baton Rouge and Richmond, Va., 1964-74, v.p. planning Richmond, 1974—94; ret., 1994. Bd. dirs. Solite Corp., Richmond, Albemarle Corp. Trustee Sci. Mus. Va., Richmond, 1987-99, chmn., 1992, pres. Found., 1984-87. Mem. Va. Inst. Marine Sci. (marine scis. devel. coun. 1994-99), Met. Richmond C. of C. (bd. dirs. 1986), Engrs. Club Richmond (v.p. 1987—, pres. 1988-89). Methodist. Home: 8911 Highfield Rd Richmond VA 23229-7756 Personal E-mail: helwig1@comcast.net.

HELWIG, DAVID S., healthcare insurance company executive; BA in Math., North Pk. U., Ill. Actuarial positions Integon Life Ins. Co., NC, Mutual of Omaha; chief actuary, assoc. actuary Blue Cross and Blue Shield of Va., 1983—88; v.p., chief actuary Blue Cross of Calif., 1988, sr. v.p., chief actuary, CFO, treas., sr. v.p. consumer svcs. CaliforniaCare Health Plans, sr. v.p., individual and small grp. divsn., pres., CEO, 2001—04; sr. v.p., chief actuary WellPoint Health Networks, Inc., sr. v.p. large grp. divsn. western region, grp. pres. large grp. divsn.; pres., CEO West Region SBU WellPoint, Inc. Fellow: Soc. Actuaries; mem.: Am. Acad. Actuaries. Office: Blue Cross of Calif Large Grp 21555 Oxnard St Woodland Hills CA 91365

HELZ, GEORGE RUDOLPH, chemistry professor; b. Silver Spring, Md., Mar. 4, 1942; married, 1970; 1 child. AB, Princeton U., 1964; PhD in Geochemistry, Pa. State U., 1971. From asst. prof. to assoc. prof. U. Md., College Park, 1970-84, prof. chemistry, 1984—; dir. Md. Water Resources Rsch. Ctr., 1990—2001. Mem. disinfectants chem. subcom. NAS-NRC, 1978; vis. prof. Stanford U., 1983-84, Cox vis. prof., 1998-99; sr. vis. fellow Manchester (Eng.) U., 1989-90. AAAS Environ. fellow, 1988. Mem. Am. Chem. Soc. (chmn. geochem. divsn. 1985), Am. Geophys. Union, Geochem. Soc. (treas. 1975-78), Geol. Soc. Am., Geol. Soc. Washington (pres. 1996). Achievements include research in aqueous geochemistry; geochemistry of mineral deposits; environmental chemistry; fate of pollutants in estuaries. Office: 3101 Chemistry Bldg 091 College Park MD 20742-0001 Office Phone: 301-405-1797.

HELZER, JAMES DENNIS, retired health facility administrator; b. Fresno, Calif., Apr. 27, 1938; s. Alexander and Katherine (Scheidt) H.; m. Joan Elaine Alinder, Feb. 25, 1967; children: Amy, Rebecca. BS, Fresno State Coll., 1960; M.Hosp. Adminstrn., U. Iowa, 1965. Adminstrv. asst. Twilight Haven, Fresno, Calif., 1960-61, adminstr. resident, 1964-65; asst. adminstr. U. Calif. Hosps. and Clinics, San Francisco, 1965-68, Fresno Community Hosp., 1968-71, exec. adminstr., 1971-82, pres., chief exec. officer, 1982-91, Community Hosps. Cen. Calif., 1982-91, cons., 1991-95; adminstr. Veterans Home of Calif., Yountville, Calif., 1995-99; ret., 1999. Served with U.S. Army, 1961-63. Fellow Am. Coll. Hosp. Adminstrs.; mem. Am., Calif. hosp. assns. Clubs: Rotary. Presbyterian. Home: 1164 Secret Lake Loop Lincoln CA 95648-8404

HEMANN, RAYMOND GLENN, research company executive; b. Cleve., Jan. 24, 1933; s. Walter Harold and Marsha Mae (Colbert) H.; m. Lucile Tinnin Turnage, Feb. 1, 1958; children: James Edward, Carolyn Frances; m. Pamela Schaap Lehr, Dec. 18, 1987. BS, Fla. State U., 1957; postgrad., U.S. Naval Postgrad. Sch., 1963-64, U. Calif., LA, 1960—62; MS in Systems Engring., Calif. State U., Fullerton, 1970, MA in Econs., 1972; cert. in tech. mgmt., Calif. Inst. Tech., Pasadena, 1990. Comml., glider and pvt. pilot. Aero. engring. aide U.S. Navy, David Taylor Model Basin, Carderock, Md., 1956; analyst Fairchild Aerial Surveys, Tallahassee, 1957; research analyst Fla. Rd. Dept., Tallahassee, 1957-59; chief Autonetics divsn. N.Am. Aviation, Inc., Anaheim, Calif., 1959-69; v.p., dir. R.E. Manns Co., Wilmington, Calif., 1969-70; mgr. Avionics Design and Analysis Dept. Lockheed-Calif. Co., Burbank, 1970-72, mgr. Advanced Concepts divsn., 1976-82; gen. mgr. Western divsn. Arinc Research Corp., Santa Ana, 1972-76; dir. Future Requirements Rockwell Internat., 1982-85, dir. Threat Analysis, Corp. Offices, 1985-89; pres., CEO Advanced Systems Rsch., Inc., 1989—. Adj. sr. fellow Ctr. Strategic and Internat. Studies, Washington, 1987—; bd. dirs., mem. exec. com. Fla. State U. Rsch. Found., 1995-2003; bd. dirs. Assn. Mgmt. Svc. Inc., Numedeon, Inc., Am. Heart Assn., Pasadena Civic Auditorium Found. Inc., 2000-02; chmn. adv. coun. Coll. Engring. Fla. State U./Fla. A&M U., 1995—; cons. to dir. Ctrl. Intelligence, Nat. Intelligence Coun., Nat. Air Intelligence Ctr., Inst. Def. Analyses, Battelle Meml. Inst., Ctr. Strategic and Internat. Studies; sec., bd. dirs. Calif State U., Fullerton, Econs. Found.; mem. naval studies bd. panels, 1985—, chmn. indsl. panel Nat. Labs. Infrastructure Study, Office Sec. Def., 1995; chmn. indsl. panel Future Dirs. Mil. Aeronautics Study, 1996; asst. prof. ops. analysis dept. U.S. Naval Postgrad. Sch., Monterey, Calif., 1963-64, Monterey Peninsula Coll., 1963; instr. ops. analysis Calif. State U., Fullerton, 1964-67, instr. quantitative methods, 1969-72; program developer, instr. systems engring. indsl. rels. ctr. Calif. Inst. Tech., 1992-96; lectr. Brazilian Navy, 1980, U. Calif., Santa Barbara, 1980, Yale U., 1985, Princeton U., 1986, U.S. Naval Postgrad. Sch., 1986, Ministry of Def., Taiwan, Republic of China, 1990; Calif. Inst. Tech. Assocs., 1992—; mem. exec. forum Calif. Inst. Tech., 1991—. Contbr articles to profl. jours. and new media. Chmn. comdr.'s adv. bd. CAP, Calif. Wing; reader Recording for the Blind, 1989—; bd. dirs. Pasadena Civic Auditorium Found., 2000-02, Boy Scouts Am., 2971-79; bd. dirs., sec.-treas. Jr. All-Am. Football; trustee Art Ctr. Coll. Design, Pasadena, Calif., 2003—; chmn. mech. engring. adv. coun. Fla. A&M U./Fla. State U. Coll. Engring, Tallahassee; mem. dean's adv. coun. Coll. Engring. and Computers Scis. Calif. State U., Fullerton. Syde P. Deeb scholar, 1956; recipient honor awards Nat. Assn. Remotely Piloted Vehicles, 1975, 76, Grad Made Good award Fla. State U., 2005; named to Hon. Order Ky. Cols., 1985; named One of Top 100 Grads, Calif. State U., Fullerton, 2007. Fellow AAAS, AIAA (assoc.); mem. IEEE (life), Ops. Rsch. Soc. Am., Air Force Assn., US Marines Meml. Club (life), N.Y. Acad. Scis., Assn. Old Crows., L.A. World Affairs Coun., Phi Kappa Tau (past pres.). Episcopalian.

HEMBREE, JAMES D., retired chemical company executive; b. Morris, Okla., Feb. 27, 1929; s. James D. and Mary Eleanor H.; m. Joyce Pickrell, Aug. 25, 1951; children: Victoria Lee Krivacs, Alex James, Kent Douglas. BSCh.E., Okla. State U., 1951; MSCh.E., U. Mich., 1952. Dir. mktg. inorganic chems. Dow Chem U.S.A., Midland, Mich., 1968-78, gen. mgr. designed products dept., 1976-78, v.p., 1978-80, group v.p., 1980-83; pres., chief exec. officer Dow Chem. Can., Sarnia, Ont., 1983-86; ret., 1986. Home and Office: 4620 Jupiter Dr Salt Lake City UT 84124-3900 Personal E-mail: jandj_84124@yahoo.com.

HEMBY, JAMES BENJAMIN, JR., college president; b. Ayden, NC, Mar. 1, 1934; m. Joan Edwards Hemby; children: James B. III, Scott Edwards, Thomas Simmen. BA, Barton Coll., 1955; BD, Vanderbilt U., 1958; MA, Tex. Christian U., 1964, PhD, 1965. Grad. teaching fellow Tex. Christian U., Ft. Worth, 1962-64; instr. Memphis State U., 1964-65; dir. admissions Barton Coll., Wilson, NC, 1959-62, assoc. prof. English, 1965-68, prof., 1968-73, chmn. English dept., 1973-79, Am. Coun. Edn. fellow in acad. adminstrn., 1979-80, provost, 1980-83, pres., 1983—2003, pres. emeritus, 2003. Dir. NC Writing Project, 1980-85; pres. NC Lit. and Hist. Assn., 1983-84; chmn. NC Writer's Conf., 1982-85; pres. Carolinas Intercollegiate Athletic Conf., 1989-91, NC Assn. Colls. and Univs., 1993-94, pres. NC Assn. Ind. Colls. and Univs., 1995-99; sr. ptnr. Adminstrv. Cons., 2004-; chmn. compentency testing commn. NC, 1982-85. Editor: Crucible, 1973-83. Bd. dirs. Wilson County chpt. ARC, 1985-96, Flynn Home, 1998-02, Budget & Comm. United Way, 1997-02; mem. Wilson County Bd. Edn., 1974-86, NC Humanities Coun., 1988-91; exec. com. Triangle East, 1985-91, Meth. Home for Children, 2005—; bd. dirs. Lost Colony, 1998-00, exec. com., 2005—, Meth. Home for Children, 2004—, Triangle Radio Reading Svc., 2004—. Lilly Found. vis. scholar, Duke U., 1977; Fulbright grantee, 1990; recipient Disting. Svc. award NC HS Athletic Assn., 1993, Svc. to Mankind award Wilson NC Sertoma Club, 2001; named Citizen of Yr. NC Civitan Club Wilson, 2001. Mem. MLA, Am. Coun. Edn., Nat. Assn. Ind. Colls. and Univs. (bd. dirs. 2000-02, pres. NC chpt. 1995-99), NC Assn. Colls. and Univs. (pres. 1993-94), Internat. Assn. Univ. Pres., Coun. Ind. Colls., Am. Assn. Higher Edn., Nat. Assn. Intercollegiate Athletics (coun. pres. 1991-93), Roanoke Island Hist. Assn. (bd. dirs. 2007—), Rotary (Harris fellow 2002), Wilson C. of C. (bd. dirs.), Traemoor Village Home Owners Assn. (bd. dirs. 2005—). Democrat. Avocations: tennis, bicycling, chess, creative writing. Personal E-mail: jhembyjr@nc.rr.com.

HEMBY-GRUBB, VIRGINIA, education educator, consultant; b. Brookhaven, Miss., Mar. 8, 1960; d. James Ray and Fannie Mae Hemby; m. Robert E Grubb; 1 child, Matthew Winston Jackson. BS, U. So. Miss., 1988—91, MEd, 1991—92, PhD, 1992—95. Assoc. prof. Ind. U. of Pa., Indiana, Pa., 1995—2004, Mid. Tenn. State U., Murfreesboro, Tenn., 2004—. Co-author: Effective Communication Skills for Criminal Justice Professionals, Instructor's Manual and Test Bank for Law Enforcement in the 21st Century; contbr. articles to profl. jours. Recipient Post-Secondary Educator award, Pa. Bus. Edn. Assn., 2002, Golden Pen award, Miss. Bus. Edn. Assn., 1996. Mem.: ASTD (assoc.), Tenn. Bus. Edn. Assn. (assoc.), Assn. Career and Tech. Edn. (assoc.; editor Bus. Edn. Digest 2004), Assn. Bus. Comm. (assoc.), Nat. Bus. Edn. Assn. (assoc.; comm. sect. editor Bus. Edn. Forum 2002—05), Orgnl. Systems Rsch. Assn. (assoc.; exec. v.p. 2004—05, pres. 2005—), So. Bus. Edn. Assn. (assoc.; chair tour com. 2005), Ea. Bus. Edn. Assn. (assoc.; sec. 2002—03), Nat. Assn. Tchr. Educators in Bus. Edn. (assoc.; sec. 2001—03), Beta Gamma Sigma (assoc.), Pi Omega Pi (assoc.), Golden Key (assoc.), Phi Kappa Phi (assoc.), Epsilon Pi Tau (assoc.), Delta Pi Epsilon (assoc.; chair nat. membership com. 2003—05, nat. v.p. 2006—). Avocations: reading, travel, public speaking. Office: Middle Tenn State Univ BMOM Dept Box 40 Murfreesboro TN 37132 Home Phone: 615-904-7954; Office Phone: 615-898-2369. Office Fax: 615-898-5438. E-mail: kvhemby@mtsu.edu, drhembygrubb@comcast.net.

HEMENWAY, ROBERT E., academic administrator, language educator; b. Sioux City, Iowa, Aug. 10, 1941; s. Myrle Emery and Katharine Leone (Cook) H.; m. Marilyn Wickstrom, June 16, 1962 (div. 1970); children: Gina, Jeremy; m. Mattie Fenter, May 12, 1972 (div. 1980); children: Robin, Karintha, Matthew, Langston; m. Leah Renee Hattemer, Dec. 19, 1981; children: Zachary, Arna. BA, U. Nebr., Omaha, 1963; PhD, Kent State U., Ohio, 1966. Asst. prof. English U. Ky., Lexington, 1966-68; assoc. prof. Am. studies U. Wyo., Laramie, 1968-73; prof. U. Ky., Lexington, 1973-86; dean arts and scis. U. Okla., Norman, 1986-89; chancellor U. Ky., Lexington, 1989-95, U. Kans., Lawrence, 1995—. Dean Gov.'s Scholar's Program, Ky., 1984-86; bd. dir., Am. Coun. on Edn. Author: Zora Neale Hurston, 1977 (Best Biography of 1977 award Soc. Midland Authors 1978, Rembert Patrick prize Fla. Hist. Soc. 1978). Mem. Gov.'s Task Force on Literacy, Okla., 1987-89; bd. dirs. Okla. HS Sci. and Math., Oklahoma City, 1985-86, Coun. Colls. Arts and Scis., 1987-89. NEH fellow, 1974-75. Mem. MLA, Am. Studies Assn. (nat. coun.), South Atlantic Assn. Depts. English (pres. 1984-85). Lutheran. Avocation: bridge. Office: Univ Kansas Office of the Chancellor 230 Strong Hall Lawrence KS 66045-7501 Office Phone: 785-864-3131. Office Fax: 785-864-4120. E-mail: chancellor@ku.edu.*

HEMINGER, GARY R., oil industry executive; B acctg., Tiffin Univ., 1976; MBA, Univ. Dayton, 1982. Mgmt. positions Marathon Oil Corp., Houston, 1976—91, v.p. we. div. Speedway SuperAm., 1991—95, mgr. bus. develop & joint interest, 1996—98; v.p. bus. develop. Marathon Ashland Petroleum LLC, 1998—99, sr. v.p. bus. develop., 1999—2001, exec. v.p. supply trans. & mktg., 2001; pres. Marathon Petroleum Co. LLC, 2001—; exec. v.p. Marathon Oil Corp., 2001—. Bd. dir. Fifth Third Bancorp.; mem. Oxford Inst. Energy Studies; chmn. downstream com. Am. Petroleum Inst. Chmn. bd. trustees Tiffin Univ. Office: Marathon Oil Corp 5555 San Felipe Rd Houston TX 77056*

HEMINGWAY, GEORGE THOMSON, marine biologist, educator, priest; b. Corvallis, Oreg., Aug. 23, 1940; s. George Danforth and Margaret Roberta Chadwick Purcell (Hardman) H.; m. Jean Ann Potym, May 25, 1968; 1 child, Gillian Christian Allison. BS, San Diego State U., 1966, MS, 1973; diploma in Theology, Episc. Sch. Theology, 1983. Ordained priest Episc. Ch., 1985. With Scripps Inst. Oceanography div. U. Calif. San Diego, La Jolla, Calif., 1966—, coord. Interaméricas program, 1977—, asst. to dir. marine life research group, 1983-93; prof. and chmn. biology dept. U. Autonoma de Baja Calif., Ensenada, Mex., 1973-74, adj. prof. biology, 1974—; coordinator Calif. Coop. Oceanic Fisheries Investigations, 1979-81, 1985—. Contbr. articles to profl. jours. Active Commn. Ministry, Episc. Diocese San Diego, 1980-84, chmn. Hispanic Com., 1985—; mem. citizen's adv. panel Tecolote Canyon, San Diego, 1980-83; mem. sch. closure panel San Diego Unified Sch. Dist., 1983-85. Recipient Honoris Causa award Univ. Autonoma de Baja Calif., 1974, Commendation, mayor and coun. City of San Diego, 1984, Commendation gov. Calif., 1990; grantee NOAA 1978-83, Tinker Found. 1982-85. Mem. Am. Zool. Soc., Western Soc. Naturalists, AAAS, Am. Inst. Biol. Scis., Hastings Inst. Soc., Ethics and Life Scis. (assoc.), Nat. Assn. Self-supporting Active Ministry, Ctr. Theology and Natural Scis., Nat. Commn. Hispanic Ministries, San Diego Zool. Soc., Phi Beta Delta. Republican. Avocations: horticulture, carpentry, fishing, hiking. Home: 5025 Georgetown Ave San Diego CA 92110-1347 Office: U Calif San Diego Scripps Inst Oceanogra # A-02 La Jolla CA 92093

HEMINGWAY, RICHARD WILLIAM, law educator; b. Detroit, Nov. 24, 1927; s. William Oswald and Iva Catherine (Wildfang) H.; m. Vera Cecilia Eck, Sept. 12, 1947; children: Margaret Catherine, Carol Elizabeth, Richard Albert. BS in Bus, U. Colo., 1950; JD magna cum laude (J. Woodall Rogers Sr. Gold medal 1955), So. Meth. U., 1955; LL.M. (William S. Cook fellow 1968), U. Mich., 1969. Bar: Tex. 1955, Okla. 1981. Assoc. Fulbright, Crooker, Freeman, Bates & Jaworski, Houston, 1955-60; lectr. Bates Sch. Law, U. Houston, 1960; assoc. prof. law Baylor U. Law Sch., Waco, Tex., 1960-65; vis. assoc. prof. So. Meth. U. Law Sch., 1965-68; prof. law Tex. Tech U. Law Sch., Lubbock, 1968-71, Paul W. Horn prof., 1972-81, acting dean, 1974-75, dean ad interim, 1980-81; prof. law U. Okla., Norman, 1981-83, Eugene Kuntz prof. oil, gas and natural resources law, 1983-92, Eugne Kuntz prof. emeritus oil, gas & natural resources law, 1992—. Author: The Law of Oil and Gas, 1971, 2d edit., 1983, lawyer's edit., 1983, 3d edit., 1991, West's Texas Forms (Mines and Minerals), 1977, 2d edit., 1991; contbg. editor various law reports, cases and materials. Served with USAAF, 1945-47. Mem. Tex. Bar Assn., Scribes, Order of Coif (faculty), Beta Gamma Sigma. Lutheran. Avocation: amateur radio. Personal E-mail: rheming1@sbcglobal.net.

HEMINGWAY, THOMAS L., career military officer, lawyer; b. Evanston, Ill., Feb. 7, 1940; m. Judith Casey. BA in Sociology, Willamette U., 1962, JD, 1965. Bar: Oreg., U.S. Ct. Fed. Claims, U.S. Ct. Appeals Fed. cir. Commd. 2d lt. USAF, 1965, advanced through grades to brig. gen., 1992, chief civil law Davis-Monthan AFB, Ariz., 1965-69, chief mil. justice, provincial liaison Udorn Royal Thai AFB, Thailand, 1969-70, chief mil.

justice 15th Air Force March AFB, Calif., 1970-71; assoc. prof. law USAF Acad., Colorado Springs, Colo., 1971-75; staff judge adv. USAF, McChord AFB, Wash., 1975-79, Rhein-Main Air Base, West Germany, 1979-82, sr. judge ct. mil. rev. hdqs. Washington, 1982-83, chief mil. justice divsn. office of judge adv. gen., 1983-85, staff judge adv. 17th Air Force Sembach Air Base, West Germany, 1985-88, staff judge adv. Europe Ramstein Air Base, Germany, 1988-90, dir. judiciary, vice comdr. Air Force legal svcs. ctr. Washington, 1990-91, chief counsel U.S. transp. command, staff judge adv. hdqs. mil. airlift command Scott AFB, Ill., 1991-92, chief counsel U.S. transp. command, staff judge adv. air mobility command, 1992—96; legal adv. US Office Mil. Commn. for mil. tribunals at Guantanamo Bay, Cuba, Washington, 2003—. Chmn. Joint Svc. Com. Mil. Justice; chmn. Mil. Justice Act of 1983 adv. commn. Dept. Def. Decorated Legion of Merit with oak leaf cluster, Bronze Star medal, Air Force Commendation medal, Mil. Achievement medal (Fed. Republic of Germany); recipient Justice Tom C. Clark award DC chpt. Fed. Bar Assn., 1985; recipient Disting. Alumni citation, Willamette Univ. 2002. Mem.: Judge Adv. Assn. (pres. 2005). Office: Office of Military Commissions The Pentagon Washington DC 20301*

HEMKE, FREDERICK L., academic administrator; b. July 11, 1935; s. Fred L. and May H. (Rowell) H.; m. Junita Borg, Dec. 26, 1959; children: Elizabeth Hemke Shapiro, Frederic John Borg. Premiere prix, Cons. Nat. de Musique, Paris, 1956; BS in Music Edn., U. Wis., Milw., 1958; MusM in Music Edn., Eastman Sch. of Music, Rochester, NY, 1962; DMA in Musical Arts, U. Wis., 1975. Chmn. dept. preparatory wind and percussion Sch. of Music Northwestern U., Evanston, Ill., 1962-75, chmn. dept. music performance and studies, 1962-94, prof. of music (saxophone), 1963—, sr. assoc. dean, 1994—2003, acting dean, 2002, Louis and Elsie Snydacker Eckstein prof. music, 2003—, Charles Deering McCormick prof. tchg. exellence, 2004—. Faculty athletics rep. Northwestern U., Big 10 Conf., NCAA 1982-2003; cons. La Voz Corp., Sun Valley, Calif., Frederick Hemke Saxophone Reeds, So. Music Co., San Antonio, Hemke Saxophone Series, The Selmer Co., Elkhart, Ind. Instrumental soloist (recordings) The American Saxophone, Music for Tenor Saxophone, Allan Pettersson, Symphony No. 15 (with Stockholm Philharmonic); Quintet for String Quarter & Saxo-Warren Benson, Concerto-Ross Lee Finney, Simple Gifts for saxophone and organ; author: The Early History of the Saxophone, Hemke Saxophone Series, So. Music Co. Recipient Excellence in Teaching award Northwestern U. Alumni Assn., Music Alumni Achievement award, U. Wis., Milw.; grantee: Nat. Endowment for the Arts. Mem. Ill. Music Educators Assn., Pi Kappa Lambda, Kappa Kappa Psi, Phi Mu Alpha Sinfonia (past province gov.) Office: Northwestern U Sch of Music 1965 S Campus Dr Evanston IL 60208-0874 Business E-Mail: f-hemke@northwestern.edu.

HEMLEY, RUSSELL J., geophysicist; b. Berkeley, Calif., Oct. 26, 1954; BA in Chemistry, Wesleyan U., 1977; MA in Chemistry, Harvard U., 1980, PhD in Phys. Chemistry, 1983. Postdoctoral fellow theoretical chemistry Harvard U., 1983—84; Carnegie fellow Carnegie Instn. Geophys. Lab., Washington, 1984—86, staff scientist, 1987—2007, dir., 2007—. Vis. prof. Johns Hopkins U., Balt., 1991—92, Ecole Normale Supérieure, Lyon, France, 1996. Contbr. articles to sci. jours. Recipient Hillebrand medal, Am. Chem. Soc., 2003, Balzan prize in Mineral Physics, 2005. Fellow: Mineral. Soc. Am. (Mineral. Soc. Am. award 1990), Am. Phys. Soc., Am. Geophys. Union; mem.: Am. Acad. Arts & Scis., NAS. Achievements include patents in field. Office: Geophys Lab Carnegie Instn Washington 5251 Broad Branch Rd NW Washington DC 20015 Office Phone: 202-478-8951. Office Fax: 202-478-8464. E-mail: r.hemley@gl.ciw.edu.*

HEMLOCK, ROBERTA LEIGH, veterinary technician; b. Chgo., Aug. 24, 1946; d. John Nolan and Gertrude Mathilda (Lahti) Hemlock. AA, Chgo. City Coll., 1966; BFA, Art Inst. Chgo., 1970; AAS, Bel-Rea Inst., Denver, 2001. Intelligence analyst State Dept., England, 1972—73; pres. Hemlock, Hemlock & Others, Chgo., 1973—80, design dir., 1973—80; prof. Colo. Inst. Art, Denver, 1980—93; v.p. ops. and design Design Prodns., Inc., Denver, 1993—94; v.p. ops., editor Syber Media Group, Denver, 1994—96; pvt. practice tech. grantwriter Denver, 1996—2000; vet. technician Huron Animal Hosp., Denver, 2001—03; vet. technician/surgery Erie Animal Hosp., Colo., 2003—04, Church Ranch Vet. Wellness Ctr., Denver, 2004—06, practice mgr., 2005—06; supr. surg. svcs. Alameda East Animal Hosp., 2006—. Mem. adv. bd. CCD of Denver, 2001—. Founding exec. dir. Le Musée du Renaissance Mus. of Print Art, 2006. Recipient Honoree Wall of Tolerance, Nat. Civil Rights Meml., Montgomery Ala., 2005. Mem.: AAUW (cons. 2001—), NAVTA, Colo. Assn. Cert. Vet. Technicians (state pub. rels. dir. 2001—04, cert.), Internat. Assn. U. Women (cons. 2001—), Denver Gardens. Avocations: photography, conceptual writing, publishing, collecting early Renaissance art. Home: 10648 Huron St #1505 Northglenn CO 80234-4022 Personal E-mail: rhemlock@excite.com.

HEMMASI, HARRIETTE ANN, university librarian; b. Sherman, Tex., July 10, 1947; d. John Melvin and Evelyn Mae (Walden) Hall; 1 child, Farzaneh. MusB, Baylor U., 1965; MusM, Ind. U., 1971; M Libr Info Sci, U. Calif., Berkeley, 1989. Instr. music Shiraz U., Iran, 1972-80; libr. asst. Humboldt State U., Arcata, Calif., 1984-87; libr. asst. music libr. U. Calif., Berkeley, 1988-89; head tech. svcs. music libr. Rutgers U., New Brunswick, NJ, 1989—98, interim assoc. univ. libr. tech. and automated svcs., 1998—2000; dean of libraries Ind. U., Bloomington, 2003—05; Joukowsky Family univ. libr. Brown U., Providence, 2005—. Adj. instr. Rutgers U., New Brunswick, 1991-92; dir. Music Thesaurus Project at Rutgers U., New Brunswick, 1991—. Contbr. articles to profl. jours., chpt. to book. Vol. Am. Diabetes Assn., Highland Park, N.J., 1993; mem. Cantabile Chorus, Bound Brook, N.J., 1992. Recipient State Merit award State of Calif., 1987. Coop. Rsch. Grant Coun. Libr. Resources, 1991-92. Mem. ALA (subcom. on Music Thesaurus Project 1993—), Music Libr. Assn. (chair subject access subcom. 1988-93, Gerboth award 1993). Avocations: singing, piano playing, walking, reading. Office: Brown U Univ Libr Providence RI 02912 Office Phone: 401-863-2162. E-mail: Harriette_Hemmasi@brown.edu.*

HEMMER, J. MICHAEL, lawyer, rail transportation executive; b. Stillwater, Okla., May 28, 1949; BA with honors, Stanford U., Calif., 1971; JD with honors, U. Calif., Berkeley, 1976. Atty. Covington & Burling, Washington, 1976—2002, ptnr., 1984—2002; v.p. law Union Pacific RR Union Pacific Corp., Omaha, 2002—04, sr. v.p. law, gen. counsel, 2004—. Office: Union Pacific Corp 1400 Douglas St Omaha NE 68179 Office Phone: 402-544-5000.*

HEMMERDINGER, H. DALE, real estate executive; b. Washington, Oct. 31, 1944; s. Monroe Elliott Hemmerdinger and Carol Phyllis (Weil) Haussamen; m. Elizabeth Gould, June 25, 1969; children: Damon John, Katherine Molly. BA, NYU, 1967, postgrad., 1967-68. Cert. real estate broker, N.Y. Pres., chief exec. officer The Hemmerdinger Corp., NYC, 1968—, Atco Properties & Mgmt., Inc., NYC, 1968—. Bd. dirs. Realty Found. of N.Y., N.Y.C.; trustee mem. ex-com. fin. com. NYU, 1994—; chmn. citizens budget commn., N.Y.C., 1995—; spkr., author articles on real estate and economy Bank Credit Analyst and Grant's Interest Rate Observer publs. Commr. conciliation and appeals bd. City of N.Y., 1978-84; mem. Dem. County Com., N.Y.C., 1978—, N.Y. State Senate Adv. Com., 1980-93, N.Y. State Fin. Control Bd., 1990—; mem. N.Y. State Senate Adv. Coun. on State Productivity, 1990-94; gov. Citizens Housing and Planning Coun., N.Y.C., 1982—; mem. exec. com. Assn. for Better N.Y., N.Y.C., 1984—; trustee, mem. exec. com. Nightingale Bamford Sch., N.Y.C., 1985-93; trustee, vice chmn., mem. exec. com. Police Found., 1986—; trustee NYU, 1993—. Mem. Real Estate Bd. N.Y., Manhattan C. of C., Queens C. of C., Harmonie Club (pres. 1985-86), Sky Club, Univ. Club, Commanderie de Bordeaux, N.Y. Yacht Club, Century Club, Princeton Club. Avocations: sailing, sculling. Office: Atco Properties & Mgmt Inc 555 5th Ave Fl 16L New York NY 10017-2416

HEMMING, VAL G., retired dean, educator; b. Rexburg, Idaho, July 9, 1937; m. Alice Bell Hemming; children: Heidi, Julie, Jill, Patrick. BA in Entomology, U. Utah, 1962; MD, U. Utah Coll. Medicine, 1966. Diplomate Am. Bd. Pediatrics, Nat. Bd. Med. Examiners. Commd. 2d lt. USAF, 1965, advanced through grades to col.; pediatric intern U. Utah Affiliated Hosps., 1966—67; resident physician in pediatrics Wilford Hall USAF Med. Ctr., Lackland AFB, Tex., 1968—70; staff pediatrician USAF Hosp., Wiesbaden, Germany, 1970—74; chmn., dir. pediatric residency tng. David Grant USAF Med. ctr., Travis AFB, Calif., 1976—80; assoc. prof. dept. pediatrics Uniformed Svcs. U. Health Scis., Bethesda, Md., 1980—84, prof. dept. pediatrics, 1984—87, prof., chmn. dept. pediatrics, 1987—95, from interim dean to dean F. Edward Hebert Sch. Medicine, 1995—2002, prof. emeritus in pediats., 2002—; splty. cons. in pediatrics to Air Force Surgeon Gen., 1983—90; ret., 1990. Cons. in pediatrics to the asst. sec. for health affairs Dept. of Def., 1988-91; adv. coun. Nat. Inst. of Child Health and Human Devel. Contbr. numerous articles to profl. jours. Mem. Am. Acad. Pediatrics, Am. Pediatric Soc., Infectious Disease Soc. of Am., Western Soc. for Pediatric Rsch., Pediatric Infectious Disease Soc., Lancefield Soc., Internat. AIDS Soc., Am. Soc. for Microbiology. Office: Uniformed Svcs U Health Scis 4301 Jones Bridge Rd Bethesda MD 20814-4712 Home Phone: 301-942-5566; Office Phone: 301-295-3742. Business E-Mail: vhemming@usuhs.mil.

HEMMING, WALTER WILLIAM, retired financial consultant; b. Vineland, NJ, Oct. 2, 1939; s. Percy A. and Marguerite E. (Smith) H.; m. Shirley L. Derocher, June 10, 1961; children: Cynthia, Catherine, Walter Jr. BS, Syracuse U., 1961. CPA, NY, NH. Prin. Arthur Young & Co., Stamford, Conn., 1961-72; contr. Coca-Cola Bottling Co. NY, Hackensack, NJ, 1972-78; exec. v.p., chief oper. officer KW Inc., Manchester, NH, 1978-81; exec. v.p. fin. and adminstrn., chief fin. officer Coca-Cola Bottling Co. NY, Greenwich, Conn., 1981-86, Coca-Cola Bottling Plants of Maine, South Portland, 1987-88; gen. ptnr. Pleasant Ave. Assoc., 1988—2001, H&H Assoc., 1989-99; v.p. bus devel. Coca-Cola Bottling Co. No. New Eng., Bedford, NH, 1989; prin. Hemming Assoc., 1989—; treas., bd. dirs. Island Approaches, Sunset, Maine, 1991—2005. Mem. fin. rev. com. Coca-Cola Bottlers Assn., Atlanta, 1985-89; treas. NH Soft Drink Assn., Manchester, 1979-81; bd. dirs. Centerpoint Bank, 1990-96, mem. exec. com., chmn. audit com., chmn. exec. com., 1995-96; bd. dir. Cmty. Bankshares, Inc., mem. audit com., 1996-97; bd. dirs. Centrix Bank & Trust, mem. exec. com., audit com., loan com., chmn. audit com., 1999-2000, chmn. exec. com., 2001-03, 05, 07. Treas. Clinton (Conn.) United Meth. Ch., 1969-72, Jesse Lee Meth. Ch., Ridgefield, Conn., 1974-77; treas. Hollis (NH) Congl. Ch., 1981, 92-95, asst. treas., 1982-92, deacon, 1988-92, 04-, trustee, 1997-02. Mem. AICPA, NH Soc. CPAs, NY Soc. CPAs. Republican. Avocations: fishing, gardening, woodworking. Home: PO Box 610 Brookline NH 03033-0610 Office: Hemming Assocs 74 Northeastern Blvd Unit 11 Nashua NH 03062-3192 Office Phone: 603-883-6466.

HEMMINGHAUS, ROGER ROY, energy company executive, chemical engineer; b. St. Louis, Aug. 27, 1936; s. Roy Geroge and Henrietta E.M. (Knacht) H.; children: Sheryl Ann, Susan Lynn, Sally Ann; m. Dorotyh O'Kelly, Aug. 18, 1979; children: R. Patrick, Kelley Elizabeth, Roger Christian. Student, Purdue U., 1954-56; BS in Chem. Engring., Auburn U., 1958; grad. cert., Bettis Reactor Engring., Pitts., 1959; postgrad., La. State U., 1963-66. Various tech. and mgmt. positions Exxon Co. U.S.A., Baton Rouge, 1962-66, Benicia, Calif., 1967-70, Houston, 1970-76; refinery gen. mgr. C.F. Industries, East Chicago, Ind., 1976-77; pres. Petro United Inc., Houston, 1977-80; v.p. planning United Gas Pipe Line, Houston, 1980-82, United Energy Resources, Houston, 1982-84; v.p. corp. planning and devel. Diamond Shamrock Corp. (name changed to Maxus Energy Corp., 1987), Dallas, 1984-85, past exec. v.p.; pres. Diamond Shamrock Refining & Mktg., San Antonio, 1985-99; chmn., dir., former CEO UltraMar Diamond Shamrock, Inc., San Antonio, until 1999; chmn., fed. res. agt. Fed. Res. Bank of Dallas, 1999-2000; dir. Luby's Inc., San Antonio, 2001—04. Dir. InterFirst Bank, San Antonio Adviser Jr. Achievement, Baton Rouge, 1956-66; pres. congregation Lutheran Ch., Baton Rouge, 1965, Moraga, Calif., 1969; chmn. indsl. div. United Crusade, Solano County, Calif., 1970; assoc. gen. chmn. United Way, Tex. Gulf Coast, 1983-84. Served to lt. USN, 1958-62. Mem. Am. Chem. Soc., Am. Inst. Chem. Engrs., Naval Architects and Marine Engrs., Am. Petroleum Inst., San Antonio C. of C. (dir.), Tau Beta Pi, Phi Lambda Upsilon, Phi Kappa Phi, Kappa Alpha Clubs: Fair Oaks Country; Plaza, Petroleum (San Antonio). Office: Luby's Inc 13111 Northwest Fwy Ste 600 Houston TX 77040-6392

HEMMINGS, MADELEINE BLANCHET, not-for-profit administrator, grant writer, media consultant; b. Bryn Mawr, Pa., Aug. 14, 1942; d. Wilfred Loyola and Feroline (Sissenere) Blanchet; m. Richard B. Hemmings, Mar. 14, 1970; 1 child, Laurie Cornwall Hemmings Stull. Cert. in lang. and linguistics, U. Fribourg, Switzerland, 1961; BS in Indsl. and Labor Rels., Cornell U., 1976. Owner Hallmark Pers. of Pa., Harrisburg, Pa., 1964-70; assoc. dir. human resources Cornell U., Ithaca, NY, 1972-77; policy dir. employee benefits NAM, Washington, 1977-79; policy dir. edn., employment and tng. C. of C. U.S., Washington, 1979-83; v.p. policy Nat. Alliance Bus., Washington, 1983-85; pres. W.Va. Roundtable, Charleston, 1985—96; exec. dir. Nat. Assn. State Dirs. Careers Tech. Edn., Washington, 1987-96; mng. dir. Nat. Telelearning Network, Inc., Washington, 1996-98; pres. Hemmings Assocs., Inc., 1998—2002; grants coord. Wayne-Finger Lakes Bd. of Coop. Edn. Svcs., Newark, NY, 2002—. Select adv. com. to asst. sec. edn., 1989—93; pres. adv. com. Fed. Office Vocat. Edn. Performance Stds., 1992—95; adv. bd. Ctr. Edn. and Work, U. Wis., 1992—96, Nat. Ctr. Rsch. Vocat. Edn., Berkeley, Calif., 1993—96. Author: (book) The New Job Training Partnership Act, 1982, Economic Development Plan, State of West Virginia, 1987, Education for a Working America, 1994, (newsletter) The Techocrat, 1988—95. Exec. dir. Nat. Vocat. Tech. Edn. Found., 1987—96; campaign mgr. Connie Cook for Congress, Ithaca, 1984; sponsor U.S. Pony Club, Olney, Md., 1987—96. Recipient Individual Contbn. award, Wayne-Finger Lakes Bd. Coop. Svcs., 2006. Mem.: Upstate NY Grant Writers Assn. (bd. dir.), Greater Washington Soc. Assn. Execs. (chief exec. coun. 1989—98), US C. of C. (edn. com. 1987—96), Cornell Pres.' Club. Democrat. Roman Catholic. Achievements include helped raise $16 million for Wayne-Finger Lakes Bd. Coop. Ednl. Svcs. Avocations: thoroughbred breeding and racing, combined training, oil painting. Office: Wayne-FInger Lakes BOCES 131 Drumlin Ct Newark NY 14513 Home: 18 Ryans Way Ithaca NY 14850 Office Phone: 315-332-7379. Office Fax: 315-332-7392. Business E-Mail: mhemmings@wflboces.org.

HEMMINGSEN, BARBARA BRUFF, retired microbiologist; b. Whittier, Calif., Mar. 25, 1941; d. Stephen Cartland and Susanna Jane Bruff; m. Edvard Alfred Hemmingsen, Aug. 5, 1967; 1 child, Grete. BA, U. Calif., Berkeley, 1962, MA, 1964; PhD, U. Calif., San Diego, 1971. Lectr. San Diego State U., 1973-77, asst. prof., 1977-81, assoc. prof., 1981-88, prof., 1988—2004; ret., 2004. Vis. asst. prof. Aarhus U., Denmark, 1971—72; cons. AMBIS, Inc., San Diego, 1984—85, Woodward-Clyde Cons., 1985, 1987—91, Novatron, Inc., 2000—06. Author (with others): (book) Microbial Ecology, 1972; contbr. articles to profl. jours. Mem. Planned Parenthood, San Diego. Mem.: AAAS, San Diego Assn. Rational Inquiry (sec. 1998—2001, treas. 2002—), Am. Women Sci., Am. Soc. Microbiology, Daus. of Union Vets. of Civil War (patriotic instr. Calif.-Nev. dept. 2007), Brit. Isles Geneal. Rsch. Assn. (sec. San Diego chpt. 2006—), Phi Beta Kappa (corr. sec. Nu chpt. Calif. 1994—2002, historian 2003—, past pres.), Sigma Xi. Democrat.

HEMON, ALEKSANDER, writer; b. Sarajevo, Bosnia, 1964; arrived in U.S., 1992; BA, U. Sarajevo, 1990; MA, Northwestern U., 1995. Former journalist. Part-time tchr. Northwestern U. Author: (novels) The Question of Bruno, 2000 (named Best Book LA Times, NY Times Notable), Nowhere Man, 2002, numerous short stories in various publications including Esquire and The New Yorker. Named MacArthur Fellow, John D. and Catherine T. MacArthur Found., 2004.

HEMPE, A. HENRY, labor relations specialist, labor arbitrator, lawyer; b. Milw., Mar. 16, 1938; s. Arnold Herman and Marcia Fleer Hempe; m. Cornelia Macy Gordon, June 26, 1965; children: Andrew, Amy. BS, U. Wis., 1962, JD, 1965. Bar: Wis. 1965, U.S. Dist. Ct. (we. dist.) Wis. 1966. Asst. dist. atty. Rock County, Janesville, Wis., 1965-67, county corp. counsel, 1967-72; ptnr. Hempe & Daniel, Janesville, 1972-76; shareholder, pres. Hempe, Hunsader & Schulz, S.C., Janesville, 1975-86; dep. sec. Wis. Dept. Employment Rels., Madison, 1987-88; commr. Wis. Employment Rels. Commn., Madison, 1987—2003, chair, commr., 1989-97; pres. Midwest Employment Rels. Cons., LLC, Madison, 2003—. Author: Labor-Management Relations in the Public Sector, 2000, Labor-Management Cooperation: A New Way to Do Business. Mem., pres., v.p. Beloit (Wis.) Sch. Bd., 1980-86. bd. dirs. Sinnissipi Coun. Boy Scouts Am., Janesville, 1985-90, Rock County Humane Soc., Janesville, 1978-83, Assn. Labor Rels Agys. USA and Can., Washington, 1991-94; chair Human Rels. Commn., Beloit, 1972-76, Bd. Rev., Beloit. With USMCR, 1960—66, also res. Mem.: Wis. Bar Assn. Avocations: fishing, hunting, softball, jogging, dog training. Home: 5413 Trempealeau Trail Madison WI 53705 Office: MER Consultants PO Box 5344 Madison WI 53705-0344

HEMPEL, JOHN P., mathematics professor; b. Salt Lake City, Oct. 14, 1935; s. Edgar W. and Emma B. (Johnson) H.; m. Edith Froese-Gertzen, Sept. 1, 1965; 1 child, Kristian J. BS, U. Utah, 1957; MS, U. Wis., 1959, PhD, 1962. Asst. prof. Fla. State U., 1962-63, Rice U., Houston, 1964-69, assoc. prof., 1969-76, prof., 1976—. With Inst. Advanced Study, 1971-72; vis. assoc. prof. U. Utah, 1976; vis. prof. U. Mich. 1980-81, U. B.C., 1987-88. Postdoctoral fellow Inst. Advance Study, 1963-64. Mem. Math. Sci. Rsch. Inst. Office: Rice University Dept Math PO Box 1982 6100 South Main Houston TX 77251 Office Phone: 713-348-5126. Business E-Mail: hempel@rice.edu.

HEMPFLING, LINDA LEE, nurse; b. Indpls., July 28, 1947; d. Paul Roy and Myrtle Pearl (Ward) H. Diploma, Meth. Hosp. Ind. Sch. Nursing, 1968; postgrad., St. Joseph's Coll. Cert. med. audit specialist, 2000. Charge nurse Meth. Hosp., Indpls., 1968; staff nurse operating rm. Silver Cross Hosp., Joliet, Ill., 1969; charge nurse oper. rm. Huntington (NY) Hosp., 1969-73; night supr. oper. rm., post anesthesia care unit Hermann Hosp., Houston, 1973-76, unit mgr., purchasing coord. oper. rms., 1976-83; RN med. auditor, quality improvement, tng. coord. Nat. Healthcare Rev., Inc., Houston, 1984—98; RN med. auditor McKesson, 1999—. Future Nurses Am. scholar, 1965, Nat. Merit scholar, 1965. Mem.: Am. Assn. Med. Audit Specialists, Tex. Med. Auditors Assn., Assn. PeriOperative Registered Nurses. Office: 9401 SW Freeway # 631B Houston TX 77074 Home Phone: 713-729-7303.

HEMPHILL, CLARA JACOBS, advocate; d. George and Margaret Allison Hemphill; m. Robert William Snyder, June 9, 1991. Grad., U. Chgo. Editl. writer & reporter NY Newsday; sr. rsch. fellow Pub. Edn. Assn.; founder, project dir. InsideSchools.org, NYC. Author: New York City's Best Public Elementary Schools: a Parent's Guide, Public Middle Schools: New York City's Best, New York City's Best Public High Schools. Co-recipient Pulitzer Prize for Local Reporting, 1991; named one of NY Influentials, NY Mag., 2006; Alfred P. Sloan Found. fellow, Princeton U. Office: c/o Advocates for Children of NY 5th Fl 151 W 30th St New York NY 10001 Office Phone: 212-947-9779. Office Fax: 212-947-9790.

HEMPHILL, JAMES S., investment management executive, financial advisor; b. Richmond, Va., Sept. 13, 1956; s. John Mickle and Marie Jeanne (de Kiewiet) H.; m. Amy Guise, Oct. 16, 1993; children: John Reagan, Katharine Guise, Alexander Dallett. BA with high honors, Swarthmore Coll., 1978. CFP, CLU, ChFC, CIMA. Stockbroker, 2d v.p. Shearson/Am. Express, Media, Pa., 1978-84; asst. v.p. Merrill Lynch, Media, 1984-90; pres. TGS Fin. Advisors, Media, 1990—. Bd. dirs. Suburban Music Sch., Media, 1993-2000, pres., 1997-99; founder Third Thursday Wine Club, Media, 1993—; mem. vestry Holy Trinity Episc. Ch., 2001-03, 04-07, sr. warden, 2006-07. Mem. Fin. Planning Assn., Investment Mgmt. Cons. Assn. Republican. Avocations: travel, wine appreciation, soccer. Office: TGS Financial Advisors 170 N Radnor Chester Rd Ste 110 Radnor PA 19087 Home Phone: 610-399-9255; Office Phone: 610-892-9900. Business E-Mail: jim.hemphill@tgsfinancial.com.

HEMPHILL, JOHN LINDSAY, III, administrative assistant; b. Phila., Nov. 13, 1971; s. John L. and Elsie Hemphill. Student, C.C. Phila., 2004. Cook Phila. Naval Yard, 1994; with Health Dept., Phila., 1995, Phila. Libr., 1996; with revenue and acctg. dept. City of Phila., 2004—. Author: Genesis, Human History in the Eyes of God, 2003, Abraham, Man With Uncommon Faith, 2004, (songs) Private Show for Two, 2003. Missionary Immigration Mission, Sharon Bapt. Ch., Phila. & Arab World Ministries, London, 2003—04. 1st airman USAF, 1990—93, Gulf War. Avocations: calligraphy, art, rollerblading, walking, exercise. Office: City of Phila 1401 John F Kennedy Blvd Philadelphia PA 19102-1663 Personal E-mail: hemphillj1@yahoo.com.

HEMRY, LARRY HAROLD, former federal agency official, writer, inventor; b. Seattle, Jan. 4, 1941; s. Harold Bernard and Florence Usborne (Achilles) H.; m. Nancy Kay Ballantyne, July 10, 1964 (div. Apr. 1976); children: Rachel Dalayne, Aaron Harold, Andrew LeRoy. BA, Seattle Pacific Coll., 1963; postgrad., Western Evang. Sem., Portland, Oreg., 1969-70. Ordained to ministry Free Meth. Ch., 1968. Clergyman Free Meth. Ch., Vancouver, B.C., Can., 1963-64, Mt. Vernon, Wash., 1968-69, Colton (Oreg.) Community Ch., 1969-71; edit clk. Moody Bible Inst., Chgo., 1964-66; pres., founder Bethel Enterprises, Colton, 1969-71; immigration insp. U.S. Immigration and Naturalization Svc., Sumas, Wash., 1972-96. Author, historian: Some Northwest Pioneer Families, 1969, The Hemry Family History Book, 1985; author: An Earnest Plea to Earnest Christians, 1969; contbr. articles to profl. publs.; patentee mech. nut cracker. Chmn. com. to establish and endow the James A. Hemry meml. scholarship fund Seattle Pacific U., 1975. Fellow Seattle Pacific U. (Centurians Club); mem. The Nature Conservancy, The Sierra Club, The Audubon Soc. Avocations: camping, nature study, woodcarving. Home: PO Box 532 Sumas WA 98295-0532

HEMSLEY, STEPHEN J., healthcare company executive; BS, Fordham U., 1974. Mng. ptnr. strategy and planning Arthur Andersen and Co.; sr. exec. v.p. UnitedHealth Group, Detroit, 1997-99, COO, 1998—2006, pres., 1999—, bd. dir., 2000—, CEO, 2006—. Trustee Minn. Pub. Radio, 2002—. Office: UnitedHealth Grp PO Box 1459 Minneapolis MN 55440-1459*

HENARD, ELIZABETH ANN, controller; b. Providence, Oct. 9, 1947; d. Anthony Joseph and Grace Johanna (Lokay) Zorbach; m. Patrick Edward Mann, Dec. 18, 1970 (div. July 1972); m. John Bruce Henard Jr., Oct. 19, 1974; children: Scott Michael, Christopher Andrew. Student, Jacksonville U., Fla., 1966. Sec. So. Bell Tel. & Tel., Jacksonville, 1964-69; office mgr. Gunther F. Reis Assocs., Tampa, Fla., 1969-71; exec. sec. Ernst & Ernst, Tampa, 1971-72; exec. sec. to pres. Lamalie Assocs., Tampa, 1972-74; exec. sec. Arthur Young & Co., Chgo., 1975; adminstrv. asst. Irving J. Markin, Chgo., 1975; contr., v.p., corp. sec. Henard Assocs., Inc., Dallas, 1983-92; realtor Coldwell Banker Residential Real Estate, Tampa, 1999—; contr. Meridian Ptnrs., Tampa, 2003—. Mem. Dallas Investors Group (treas. 1986-91), Tampa Palms Country Club. Republican. Roman Catholic. Avocations: photography, crafts, golf, reading. Home: 5014 Wesley Dr Tampa FL 33647-1375 E-mail: eahenard@aol.com.

HENCE, JANE KNIGHT, interior designer; b. Pitts., June 27, 1937; d. Luther and Doris (Ayers) Knight; m. Carleton Campbell Hence, May 12, 1962 (div. 1975); children: Kyle Fitz-Randolph Hence, Maxson Bentley Hence, Juliellen Hence Casey. Grad., Emma Willard Sch., Troy, NY, 1955; student, Skidmore Coll., Saratoga Springs, NY, 1955—58; Grad., Traphagen Sch. of Design, NYC, 1960; student, Yale U., 1986—90, R.I. Sch. of Design, 1988—90. Owner various bus. ventures including Bed and Breakfast, catering bus., free-lance interior design, 1982—; owner, prin. JKH Design, 1989—; consulting assoc. and designer Michael McKinley & Assocs., Stonington, Conn., 1993—2001. Mem. Westerly Sch. Facilities Com., Westerly, R.I., 1993-96, Westerly Sch. Bldg. Com., 1992-93; mem. Bd. S.E. Mus., Brewster, N.Y., 1970-74; photographer, interviewer Green Light, Newport Designer over 50 bldgs., renovations and additions in New Eng.; co-designer overn 40 bldgs. in R.I. and Conn.; interior designer, 1998—; painter various media in collections in Midwest, South, N.Y. and New Eng.; photographer, interviewer Green Light Quar. bulletin, Newport. Alt. Westerly Zoning Bd., RI, 2000—02. Avocations: travel, reading, opera, theater. Home and Office: 73 Washington St Newport RI 02840-1533 Home Phone: 401-855-3101; Office Phone: 401-847-3767. Personal E-mail: rockbound@earthlink.net.

HENDEE, WILLIAM RICHARD, medical physics educator, academic administrator, radiologist; b. Owosso, Mich., Jan. 1, 1938; s. C.L. and Alvina M. H.; m. Jeannie Wesley, June 16, 1960; children: Mikal, Shonn, Eric, Gareth and Gregory (twins), Lara and Karel (twins). BS, Millsaps Coll., Jackson, Miss., 1959; PhD, U. Tex., 1962; DSc (hon.), Millsaps Coll., Jackson, Miss., 1988. Diplomate Am. Bd. Radiology, Am. Bd. Health Physics. AEC fellow Nat. Reactor Testing Sta., Idaho Falls, Idaho, 1960; asst. prof., then assoc. prof. physics Millsaps Coll., 1962-65, chmn. dept., 1964-65; instr. Miss. State U. (extension), 1963; asst. prof., then assoc. prof. radiology (med. physics) U. Colo. Med. Center, 1965-73, prof., 1974-85, chmn. dept., 1978-85; mem. staff VA Hosp., Denver, 1970-85, Mercy Hosp., 1971-85, Denver Gen. Hosp., 1971-85, Beth Israel Hosp., 1974-85; v.p. sci. and tech. AMA, Chgo., 1985-1991; prof. radiology, biophysics, radiation oncology, bioethics Med. Coll. Wis., Milw., 1991—2006, clin. prof. radiology and biophysics, 1985-91, sr. assoc. dean, v.p., 1991—2005, dean grad. sch., 1995—2006, pres. rsch. found., 2005—06, disting. prof. radiation oncology, biophysics, cmty. and public health, 2006—. Prof. bioengring. Marquette U., 1993—; vis. lectr. Oak Ridge Assoc. Univs., 1964; adj. prof. radiology Northwestern U. Sch. Medicine, 1986-91; adj. prof. elec. engring. U. Wis.-Milw., 2003-. Editor Med. Phys., 2005—; contbr. 375 articles to profl. jours., author/editor 24 books. Served with USMC, 1957-62. Recipient Disting. Alumnus award Millsaps Coll., 1967, Disting. Svc. award Nat. Wildlife Fedn., 1990, Wright Langham Meml. award U. Ky., 1991, Gold medal Am. Roentgen Ray Soc., 2005, Med. Coll. Sic. Disting. Svc. award, 2005; Gilbert X-ray fellow, 1960-62, summer fellow NSF, AEC; campus assoc. Danforth Found., gold medal Am. Roentgen Ray Soc., 2005; Disting. Svc. award, Med. Coll. Wis., 2005. Fellow Am. Coll. Radiology, Am. Inst. Med. and Biol. Engring. (pres. 1998-99); mem. AAAS, Health Physics Soc. (chmn. coms., Elda E. Anderson award 1972), Am. Assn. Physicists in Medicine (pres. 1976-77, Robert S. Landauer Meml. award 1977, William D. Coolidge award 1989), Nat. Wildlife Fedn. (Disting. Svc. award 1990), Soc. Biomed. Engring., (sr. mem.), Soc. Nuclear Medicine (pres. 1980-81, Benedict Cassen Meml. award 1984), Am. Acad. Home Care Physicians (Disting. Svc. award 1991), Am. Bd. Radiology (trustee 1995-05, pres. 2002-04), Omicron Delta Kappa, Theta Nu Sigma. Office: PO Box 170970 Whitefish Bay WI 53217-8087 Office Phone: 414-351-6527. Business E-Mail: whendee@mcw.edu.

HENDERSHOTT, ANNA LORRAINE, educational director; d. Luis Aguirre Cordova and Hortensia Petra Warner, William Alfred Warner (Stepfather); m. David Anthony Hendershott, May 12, 1979; children: David William, Jeffrey Alexander, Julie Anna. BS in Elem. Edn. and Spanish, Grand Canyon U., 1979; MA in Ednl. Leadership, No. Ariz. U., 1997. Tchg. cert. Ariz. Dept. Edn., supervisor cert. Ariz. Dept. Edn., adminstrv. cert. Ariz. Dept. Edn. Bilingual and ESL tchr. Peoria (Ariz.) Unified Sch. Dist., 1980—96, staff devel. specialist, 1994—96, instrnl. program specialist, 1996—98; lang. acquisition dir. Paradise Valley Unified Sch. Dist., Phoenix, 1998—, title VII project devel. and implementation grant dir., 1999—2002. Refugee grant dir. Paradise Valley Unified Sch. Dist., Phoenix, 1999—, grant dir. Indian edn., 2000—; Peoria power play writing and drama project Peoria Unified Sch. Dist., 1995—98; mem. adj. faculty grad. edn. in tchr. edn. Ariz. State U. West, Phoenix, 1997—98; mem. adj. factulty grad. edn. in gifted edn. Ottawa U., Phoenix, 1999—2000; mem. adj. faculty grad. edn. in ESL, gifted edn. and math. Chapman U., Phoenix, 2002—04. Recipient Pride of Peoria Outstanding Employee of Yr. award, Peoria Unified Sch. Dist., 1996; grantee, U.S. Dept. Edn., 1999—2002, 2000—03, 2001—04, 2001—04; scholar, Grand Canyon U., 1975—79, Concordia U., Lang. Villages Tchr. Seminar, Peoria Unified Sch. Dist., 1998. Mem.: Ctrl. Ariz. Bilingual Consortium (pres. elect 2001—02), Ariz. Assn. for Gifted and Talented (bd. dirs. 1998—2005, conf. chair 2001—03, pres. elect 2003—03, pres. 2004—04), Nat. Assn. for Gifted Child, Nat. Staff Devel. Coun., Assn. for Supervision and Curriculum Devel., Ariz. Dept. Edn. Structured English Immersion Task Force (rep. 2003—04), Ctrl. Ariz. Bilingual Consortium (pres. 2003—04), ELL Connections (founding mem. 2004—05), Learning Connections Consortium, Interclub Coun. Ariz. (del. 1989—96), Delta Kappa Gamma (parliamentarian 1989—91, pres. 1992—94, v.p. 1987—89). Republican. Roman Catholic. Avocations: ballet folklorico, painting, crafts, sewing, reading. Home Phone: 623-322-4615.

HENDERSON, ALBERT KOSSACK, publishing and food products executive, consultant; b. Phila., July 9, 1938; s. Harry Brinton, Jr. and Beatrice (Conford) H.; m. Tamara Ann McCormick, Feb. 14, 1968; children: Christopher Findley, Theodore Leon. Mus.B., Ithaca Coll., 1960; postgrad., NYU. Editorial asst. Hearst Headline, 1960-62; asst. sales mgr. Royal McBee, 1960-64; editor Johnson Reprint Corp., 1964-69; gen. mgr., v.p., treas. Brit. Book Centre, Inc., NYC, 1969-77; dir. Pergamon Press, Inc., v.p., treas., 1971-77; exec. v.p., dir. Newman Grove Creamery Co., Nebr., 1977-81; dir. publs. Am. Solar Energy Soc., NYC, 1981-83; pres. Henderson Assoc. Cons., Bridgeport, Conn., 1980—, Chess Combination, Inc., Bridgeport, 1984—; editor Pub. Rsch. Quar., 1994-2000. Mem. Soc. Scholarly Publs., Coun. Sci. Editors. Home: 655 West Ave Milford CT 06461-3003 E-mail: ah@edmonialewis.com.

HENDERSON, ARNOLD GLENN, architect, educator; b. Shawnee, Okla., Nov. 10, 1934; s. Henry Glenn and Pearlalee H.; m. Beatriz Eugenia Chavez Escandon; children: Eric Neal, Alex Jon. B.Arch., U. Okla., 1961, BS in Archtl. Engring, 1961; MS in Architecture, Columbia U., 1964. Asst. prof. architecture U. Ill., Urbana, 1964-68; assoc. prof. U. Okla., 1968-73, prof., 1973—2002, prof. emeritus, 2002—, disting. lectr. Norman, 1984, 88; pvt. practice architecture Norman, Okla., 1975—. Author: Document for an Anonymous Indian, 1974, The Surgeon General's Collection, 1976, (with others) Architecture in Oklahoma, 1978, (with others) The Point Riders Great Plains Poetry Anthology, 1982; co-editor: (with others) Point Riders Press, 1974-; painting exhbns. in Ind., Ill., Okla., La., Wyo., Ark., Kans., Ala., Colo., Tex. and London; author of poetry. Chmn. Norman Housing Authority, 1972-77; mem. Hist. Preservation and Landmark Commn., Guthrie, Okla., 1979-81; chmn. Okla. Hist. Preservation Rev. Com., 2004—. Served with U.S. Army, 1953-55. Grantee NSF, Nat. Endowment Arts, AIA, Okla. Arts Coun., Okla. Humanities Com., Graham Found. for Advanced Studies in the Fine Arts. Fellow AIA (award of excellence 1976); mem. Vernacular Architecture Forum, Nat. Trust Hist. Preservation, Okla. Hist. Soc. (Shirk Meml. award 1991), Soc. Archtl. Historians, Sigma Tau. Democrat. Roman Catholic. Home: 1208 Barkley Ave Norman OK 73071-4812 Office: U Okla Coll Arch Norman OK 73019-0001 Office Phone: 405-325-3868. Business E-Mail: ahenderson@ou.edu.

HENDERSON, BRIAN EDMOND, dean, physician, educator; b. San Francisco, June 27, 1937; s. Edward O'Brien and Antoinette (Amstutz) H.; m. Judith Anne McDermott, Sept. 3, 1960; children: Sean, Maire, Sarah, Brian John, Michael. BA, U. Calif.-Berkeley, 1958; MD, U. Chgo., 1962. Resident Mass. Gen. Hosp., Boston, 1962-64; chief arbovirology Ctr. Disease Control, Atlanta, 1969-70; assoc. prof. pathology U. So. Calif., LA, 1970-74, prof. pathology, 1974-78, prof. preventive medicine, dept. chmn., 1978-88, dir. Kenneth Norris Jr. Comprehensive Cancer Ctr., 1983—93, rschr., 1994—96, prof. dept. preventative medicine, Kenneth T. Norris Chair in Cancer Prevention, 1996—, dir. Zilkha Neurogenetic Inst., 2002—, dean Keck Sch. Medicine, 2004—; pres. Salk Inst. Biol. Studies, La Jolla, Calif., 1993—94. Established LA Cancer Surveillance Program, U. So. Calif., 1972, Hawaii-LA Multiethnic Cohort, 1993; cons. WHO, South Pacific Commn., U.S.-Japan-Hawaii Cancer Program; mem. Charles S. Mott selection com. Gen. Motors Cancer Research Found., 1982-88; bd. councillors Nat. Cancer Inst., 1979-82; mem. sci. council Internat. Agy. for Rsch. on Cancer, 1982-86 Contbr. articles to profl. jours., chpts. to books; mem. editorial bd. Jour. Clin. Oncology; assoc. editor: Cancer Research. Served to lt. col. USPHS, 1964-69 Nat. Acad. Sci. disting. scholar to China, 1982; recipient Richard & Hinda Rosenthal Found. award, Am. Assn. Cancer Research, 1987, Rsch. Excellence in Cancer Epidemiology and Prevention Award, Am. Acad. Cancer Rsch., U. Chgo. Disting. Svc. Award, Presdl. Medallion., U. So. Calif., 1999. Fellow Los Angeles Acad. Medicine; mem. AAAS, NAS, Inst. Medicine, Infectious Disease Soc. Am., Am. Epidemiol. Soc., Alpha Omega Alpha. Democrat. Roman Catholic. Office: Keck School Medicine Comprehensive Cancer Ctr 1441 Eastlake Ave # 44 Los Angeles CA 90089-0112

HENDERSON, CHARLES BROOKE, research and development company executive; b. Washington, Mar. 13, 1929; s. Robert Neel and Dorothy (Brooke) H.; m. Elizabeth Ann Carter, June 6, 1954; children: Katherine, Roger, Sally. BS, Purdue U., 1950; SM in Chem. Engring, MIT, 1952. With Atlantic Research Corp., Alexandria, Va., 1954-88, dir. research and tech., 1971-76, v.p., 1976-80, sr. v.p., 1980-88, also dir. Chmn. bd. dirs. Arctech Inc., 1988-92. Patentee in field. Active Boy Scouts Am., 1965-69, Girl Scouts U.S.A., 1969-71; treas. Loudoun Symphony, 1993-97, bd. dirs., 1993-2001; bd. dirs. Loudoun Arts Coun., 1997-99. Named Nat. Capital Outstanding Young Engr., 1961, One of Maj. Innovators, Tech. Mag., 1981. Fellow: AIAA (assoc.); mem.: Sigma Xi.

HENDERSON, CONNIE CHORLTON, retired city planner, artist, writer; b. Cedar Rapids, Iowa, July 16, 1944; d. Robert Brown and Lorraine Madeline (Marquardt) Chorlton; m. Dwight Franklin Henderson, Dec. 24, 1966; 1 child, Patricia BA, Anderson U., 1966; MA Edn., St. Francis Coll., Ft. Wayne, Ind., 1972; MPA, U. Tex. San Antonio, 1987. Art coord. Ft. Wayne Cmty. Schs., 1966—67; tchr. art East Allen County Schs., New Haven, Ind., 1968—71, 1974—79; instr. Manchester Coll., North Manchester, Ind., 1971—72; rsch. assoc. Tremar Real Estate Rsch., San Antonio, 1983—84; vol. planning asst. City of San Antonio, 1985—88, planner I, 1988—89, project mgmt. specialist, 1990, coord. conservation edn., 1990—91; planner II San Antonio Water Sys., 1991—96, 2003—, coord. water edn., 1996—97, coord. spl. events., 1998—2002; youth edn. specialist, 2003—05; coord. spl. events, 2006; ret., 2006. Docent (vol.) San Antonio Mus. Assn.; rsch. mgr. N. San Antonio C. of C., 1988 Artist: numerous paintings and fiber sculptures in juried and invitational shows, 1966-80; poetess: (2d prize Iowa Poetry Day Assn., 1961) Bd. dirs. Tex. Soc. to Prevent Blindness, San Antonio, 1981-83; v.p. U. Tex. at San Antonio Women's Club, 1981-82, pres. 1983-84; mem. San Antonio Conservation Soc., 1985—, mem. Assistance League of San Antonio, 1988—, liason Thrift House, San Antonio, 1995-96; co-pres. River Gardens Family and Friends, 1993-94, sec., 1995-96; sec. Rebuilding Together San Antonio, 2005-2006 Mem. Am. Planning Assn. (cert. planner, asst. dir. San Antonio sect. 1990, dir., 1991-93), U. Tex. San Antonio Alumni Assn Avocations: travel, reading, landscape design, swimming, music. Home: 18222 Redriver Sky San Antonio TX 78259 Home Phone: 210-496-5934.

HENDERSON, CYNTHIA, medical librarian; d. Donald and Frances Henderson. BS in Ednl. Psychology cum laude, Alcorn State U., 1987; MS in Info. and Libr. Sci., U. Mich., 1991. Asst. prof. Iowa State U., Ames, 1991—92; asst. dir. libr. svcs. Charles R. Drew U. Medicine and Sci., LA, 1992—95; asst. prof. U. Ill., Chgo., 1995—97; dir. John A. Graziano Meml. Libr. Samuel Merritt Coll., Oakland, Calif., 1997—2000; asst. prof. health and human sciences program Samuel Merritt Coll., 1997—2000; dep. dir. multi-media ctr. academic med. libr. Morehouse Sch. Medicine, Atlanta, 2000—04, dir. multi-media ctr. academic med. libr., 2004—. Spl. collections and collections devel. libr. Iowa State U., Ames, 1991—92; health sciences libr. U. Ill., Urbana, 1995—97; reviewer Jour. AMA. Contbr. articles to Bull. Med. Libr. Assn. Mem.: Med. Libr. Assn. Mem. Ame Ch. Avocations: reading, writing, cooking, dancing, sewing.

HENDERSON, DONALD AINSLIE, public health service officer; b. Lakewood, Ohio, Sept. 7, 1928; s. David Alexander and Grace Eleanor (McMillan) Henderson; m. Nana Irene Bragg, Sept. 1, 1951; children: Leigh Ainslie, David Alexander, Douglas Bruce. BA, Oberlin Coll., Ohio, 1950; MD, U. Rochester, 1954; MPH, Johns Hopkins U., 1960; LDS (hon.), U. Rochester, 1977, Oberlin Coll., Ohio, 1978, U. Ill., 1979, U. Md., 1980, Yale U., 1986, Albany Med. Coll., 1989, Lafayette Coll., 1991, U. Mo., 1992, Clarkson U., 2006; LLD (hon.), Marietta Coll., Ohio, 1978; MD (hon.), U. Geneva, 1977; LHD (hon.), SUNY, 1981, Johns Hopkins U., 1994, Towson State U., 1994; LLD (hon.), U. Minn., 2003, U. S.C., 2004, U. Medicine and Dentistry N.J., 2004; DS (hon.), Clarkson U., 2006. Diplomate Am. Bd. Preventive Medicine. Intern, then resident Mary Imogene Bassett Hosp., Cooperstown, NY, 1954-55, 57-59; chief epidemic intelligence service Center Disease Control, USPHS, Atlanta, 1955-57, chief surveillance sect., 1960-66; chief med. officer smallpox eradication WHO, Geneva, 1966-77; dean Johns Hopkins U. Sch. Hygiene and Pub. Health, 1977-90; assoc. dir. Office Sci. and Tech. Policy, Exec. Office Pres. of U.S., Washington, 1991-93; dep. asst. sec., sr. sci. advisor HHS, Washington, 1993—95; prof. Johns Hopkins U. Sch. Pub. Health, Balt., 1977—; dir. Hopkins Ctr. Civilian Biodefense Strategies, 1998—2001; dir., prin. advisor Office of Pub. Health Emergency Preparedness Dept. Health and Human Svcs., 2001—03; resident scholar Ctr. for Biosecurity U. Pitts. Med. Ctr., 2003—; prof. medicine and pub. health U. Pitts. Sch. Medicine, 2003—. Vis. prof. Mayo Clinic, 2006. Contbr. articles to profl. jours. Decorated knight Grand Cross Order of Direkgunabhorn; named Burroughs Wellcome Vis. Prof., Royal Soc. Medicine, 1996, Internat. Hero of Pub. Health, U. Calif., Berkley, 2007; recipient Ernest Jung Found. prize, 1976, Govt. India-Indian Soc. Malaria and Other Communicable Diseases award, 1975, Rosenhaus Internat. award for excellence, 1975, George MacDonald medal, London Sch. Hygiene and Tropical Medicine, Royal Soc. Tropical Medicine and Hygiene, 1976, Health medal, Govt. Afghanistan, 1976, Spl. Albert Lasker Pub. Health Svc. award, WHO, 1976, Health for All medal, 1990, Joseph C. Wilson award in internat. affairs, 1978, James D. Bruce Meml. award, 1978, Outstanding Alumnus award, Delta Omega, 1980, Disting. Alumnus award, Johns Hopkins U., 1982, Dean's medal, 2002, Internat. Merit award, Gairdner Found., 1983, Albert Schweitzer Internat. prize for medicine, 1985, Nat. Medal Sci., 1986, Richard T. Hewitt award, Royal Soc. Medicine, 1986, Edward Jenner medal, 1996, Charles Dana Found. award for pioneering achievement in health, 1986, Japan prize in preventative medicine, 1988, Health medal 1st Grade, People's Republic China, 1988, Medal of Abnegation Uruguay, 1988, Honor award, Pan Am. Health Orgn., 1990, Abraham Lilienfeld award, Am. Coll. Epidemiology, 1991, Award of Excellence, Ronald McDonald Children's Charities, 1992, Surgeon Gen.'s medallion, USPHS, 1992, City of Medicine award, 1993, Waltor Reed medal, Am. Soc. Tropical Medicine and Hygiene, 1993, Merit award, Nat. Coun. Internat. Health, 1993, Gold medal, Albert B. Sabin Found., 1994, Oswaldo Cruz Gold medal of merit, Govt. of Brazil, 1995, Soc. citation, Infectious Diseases Soc. Am., 1996, L. Frank Calderone prize, Columbia U. Sch. Public Health, 1999, Takeru Higuchi Meml. award, U. Kans., 1999, Presdl. Medal Freedom, 2002, Joseph Smadel Medal, Infectious Diseases Soc. Am., 2002, Arthur Kornberg Rsch. award, U. Rochester, 2002, Disting. Alumnus award, 2003, Silver medal, Govt. Italy Ministero Della Salute, 2004, Hutchinson Medal for Disting. Pub. Svc., U. Rochester, 2005; fellow Paul Harris fellow, Rotary Internat., 1993. Fellow: Nat. Acad. Arts and Scis., Nat. Acad. Medcine Mex. (hon.), N.Y. Acad. Medicine (hon. John Stearns award 1995, Annapolis Ctr. Sci. award 2000, Silvia and Herbert Berger award 2001), London Sch. Tropical Medicine and Hygiene (hon.), Am. Acad. Pediat. (hon.), Royal Coll. Physicians (hon.); mem.: APHA, Indian Soc. Malaria and Other Communicable Diseases, Royal Soc. Tropical Medicine and Hygiene, Royal Coll. Physicians Edinburgh (Eng.), Internat. Epidemiol. Assn., Inst. Medicine NAS (Pub. Welfare medal 1978). Home: 3802 Greenway Baltimore MD 21218-1825 Office: U Pitts Med Ctr Ctr for Biosecurity The Pier IV Bldg Ste 210 Baltimore MD 21202 Office Phone: 443-573-3323. E-mail: dahzero@aol.com.

HENDERSON, DONALD BERNARD, JR., lawyer; b. Birmingham, Ala., June 27, 1949; s. Donald B. and Pauline V. (Szulinski) H.; m. Ruth Ann Jeffers, Sept. 12, 1981. BS, U. Ala., 1971, JD, 1974; LLM in Taxation, NYU, 1976. Bar: Ala. 1974, N.Y. 1983. Ptnr. Sirote & Permutt, Birmingham, 1976—83, Kroll & Tract, NYC, 1985-88, LeBoeuf, Lamb, Greene & MacRae, L.L.P., NYC, 1988—; sr. assoc. Mound, Cotton, Wollan and Greengrass, NYC, 1983—85. Lectr. Birmingham chpt. Am. Coll., Bryn Mawr, Pa., 1977-82; bd. dirs. Jackson Nat. Life Ins. Co. NY, SunLife Assurance Co. NY; counsel Bronxville Planning Bd., 1994-2001. Contbr. articles to profl. jours. Pres. Lenox Hill Dem. Club, N.Y.C., 1989-90; mem. Ala. State Dem. Com., 1978-83, N.Y.C. Cmty. Bd. Number 8, 1987-88, Republican Club of Bronxville; mem., chair Bronxville Planning Bd., 2001—. Mem. ABA, N.Y. Bar Assn., Ala. Bar Assn. (sec. tax sect. 1982-83). Home: 108 Midland Ave Bronxville NY 10708-3206 Office: LeBouf Lamb Greene & MacRae LLP 125 E 55th St New York NY 10022-3502 Home Phone: 914-961-7112; Office Phone: 212-424-8694. Business E-Mail: dhenderson@llgm.com.

HENDERSON, DOUGLAS BOYD, lawyer; b. Pitts., Sept. 21, 1935; s. Arthur G. and Mildred E. (Rickenbach) H.; m. Olivia Lauer, July 6, 1957; children: Scotland Weaver, Keith Arthur, Heather Alice Atkinson. BS in Indsl. Engring., Pa. State U., 1957; JD with honors, George Washington U., 1963. Bar: Va. 1962, DC 1963. Mfrs. agt. firm Arthur G. Henderson & Assocs., Pitts., 1957-59; patent agt. Swift & Co., Washington, 1959-62; law clk. to Hon. Donald E. Lane US Ct. Claims, Washington, 1962-63; assoc. Irons, Birch, Swindler & McKie, 1963—65; founding ptnr. Finnegan, Henderson, Farabow, Garrett and Dunner LLP, 1965—. Adv. coun. US Ct. Fed. Claims, 1982-2006; legal adv. bd. Martindale-Hubbell/LEXIS NEXIS, 1996—. Author: Third Party Practice in the United States Court of Claims or Two's Company, Three's A Crowd, 1976; contbr. articles to profl. jours. Bd. advisors George Washington U. Law Sch., 1991-97. Named one of Best Lawyers in Am., 1995—; recipient Golden Eagle award, US Fed. Ct. Claims, 2006; fellow, Pa. State Alumni, 2007—. Fellow: Am. Bar Found. (life); mem.: ABA (ho. of dels. 1999—2005, adv. panel 2006—), CPR Inst. for Dispute Resolution, Assn. Conflict Resolution, Am. Arbitration Assn. (panel of neutrals, nat. patent adv. coun.), US Ct. Fed. Claims Bar Assn. (bd. dirs. 1987—90, founder), Supreme Ct. Hist. Soc., Intellectual Property Owners Assn., Internat. Trademark Assn., Am. Intellectual Property Law Assn., US C. of C. (chmn. patent, trademark and copyright coun. 1980—82), ITC Trial Lawyers Assn. (founder), Bar Assn. DC (chmn. Ct. Claims com. 1973—74, chmn. patent, trademark and copyright law sect. 1974—75, bd. dirs. 1975—76, trustee rsch. found. 1980—81, chmn. Ct. Appeals for Fed. Cir. Com. 1982—83), Fed. Cir. Bar Assn. (founder 1985, bd. dirs. 1985—86, mem. jud. selection com. 1990—, bd. dirs. 1996—99), DC Bar Assn., Va. State Bar, Va. Bar Assn., Internat. Bar Assn., Capital Soc. of Clubs, Tournament Players Club at Avenel, Congl. Country Club, City Club of Washington (bd. govs. 1990—95), Burning Tree Club, Univ. Club, Delta Theta Phi, Phi Gamma Delta. Office: Finnegan Henderson Farabow Garrett & Dunner LLP 901 New York Ave NW Washington DC 20001-4413 Office Phone: 202-408-4001. Office Fax: 202-408-4400.

HENDERSON, DOUGLAS JAMES, physicist, chemist, educator, researcher; b. Calgary, Alberta, Canada, July 28, 1934; arrived in U.S., 1956; s. Donald Ross and Evelyn Louise (Scott) Henderson; m. Rose-Marie Steen-Nielssen, Jan. 21, 1960; children: Barbara, Dianne, Sharon. BA in Math., U. B.C., Vancouver, 1956; PhD in Physics, U. Utah, 1961. Instr. dept. math. U. Utah, Salt Lake City, 1960-61; asst. prof. physics U. Idaho, Moscow, 1961-62, Ariz. State U., Tempe, 1962-64, assoc. prof., 1964-67, prof. physics, 1967-69; assoc. prof. physics U. Waterloo, Can., 1964-67, prof. applied math. and physics, 1967-69; rsch. sci. IBM Almaden Rsch. Ctr., San Jose, Calif., 1969-90, IBM Corp., Salt Lake City, 1990-92, Utah Supercomputing Inst., U. Utah, Salt Lake City, 1990-95; Manuel Sandoval Vallarta prof. physics U. Autonoma Metropolitana, Mexico, 1985—86, Juan de Oyarzabal prof. physics, 1993—95; prof. chemistry Brigham Young U., Provo, Utah, 1995—. Vis. sci. CSIRO Chem. Rsch. Labs., Melbourne, Australia, 1966—67, Inst. Phys. Chemistry, Polish Acad. Scis., 1973, Korea Advanced Inst. Sci., Seoul, 1974, Inst. Theoretical Physics, Ukranian Acad. Scis., 1989; vis. prof. physics Nat. U. La Plata, Argentina, 1973; sabbatical visitor IBM Watson Rsch. Ctr., Yorktown Heights, NY, 1973—74; mem. evaluation panel Commn. Human Resources, NRC, 1976; vis. prof. chemistry U. Utah, 1976, adj. prof. chemistry and math, 1990—, Henry Eyring lectr., 1994; Manuel Sandoval Vallarta Disting. vis. prof. physics U. Autonoma Met., Mexico, 1985, 88, Juan de Oyarzabal prof. physics, Mexico, 1993—95; vis. prof. chem. physics U. Pisa, Italy, 1989; vis. prof. Scoula Normale Superiore, Pisa, Italy, 1989; adj. prof. applied math. and physics U. Waterloo, 1969—85; mem. adv. bd. Chem. Abstracts Svc., 1981—83; vis. prof. chemistry, math, and physics U. Guelph, Canada, 1991; adj. prof. physics Utah State U., 1990—93; hon. prof. chemistry and math. U. Hong Kong, 1992—; hon. prof. molecular biophysics Rush Med. Sch., 2003—. Author: (book) Statistical Mechanics and Dynamics, 1964, Statistical Mechanics and Dynamics, 2d rev. edit., 1982, Stochastic Differential Equations in Science and Engineering, 2006; editor: Physical Chemistry - An Advanced Treatise, Vols. 1-15, 1966—75, Theoretical Chemistry-Advances and Perspectives, Vols. 1-5, 1975—81, Fundamentals of Inhomogeneous Fluids, 1992; editor: (assoc. editor) Jour.

Chem. Physics, 1974—76; mem. editl. bd.:, 1990—92, bd. editors: Ultitas Mathematica, 1971—87, Jour. Phys. Chemistry, 1984—89, Jour. Chem. Phys., 1990—92, assoc. editor: Electrochimica Acta, 1991—99, Condensed Matter Physics, 2005—; contbr. articles to profl. jours. Vol. Loma Prieta Vol. Fire Dept., Los Gatos, Calif., 1983—89; missionary Ch. Jesus Christ Latter Day Saints, Africa, 1957—59. Recipient Johnathan Rodgers award, 1954, Bursary award, NRC of Can., 1956, Outstanding Rsch. Contbn. award, IBM, 1973, Outstanding Innovation award, 1987, Catedra Patrimoniales de Excelencia, Mex., 1993—95; fellow, Corning Glass Found., 1959, Alfred P. Sloan Found., 1964, 1966, Ian Potter Found., 1966, CSIRO Rsch., 1966, Guggenheim Found., 1997; scholar Univ. Great War, 1953, Daniel Buchanan, 1955, Burbridge, 1955. Fellow: Am. Inst. Chemists, Am. Phys. Soc., Inst. Physics; mem.: N.Y. Acad. Scis., Mex. Nat. Acad. Sci. (corr.), Math. Assn. Am., Am. Chem. Soc. (Joel Henry Hildebrand award 1999, Utah award 2005), Can. Assn. Physicists, Sigma Pi Sigma, Sigma Xi, Phi Kappa Phi. Democrat. Member Lds Ch. Achievements include statistical mechanics of liquids; co-developer first successful perturbation theory of liquids; statis. mechanics of surfaces and solid-fluid and liquid-vapor interfaces; structure and electronic properties of amorphous solids; theory of electric double layer; theory of selectivity and transport of ions in biological membranes. Office: Brigham Young U Dept Chemistry Provo UT 84602 Office Phone: 801-422-5934. Business E-Mail: doug@chem.byu.edu.

HENDERSON, DWIGHT FRANKLIN, dean, educator; b. Austin, Tex., Aug. 14, 1937; s. Ottis Franklin and Leona (Bady) H.; m. Connie Chorlton, Dec. 24, 1966; 1 dau., Patricia Ross. BA, U. Tex., 1959, MA, 1961, PhD, 1966. Assoc. prof. Ind. U., Ft. Wayne, 1966-68, chmn. dept. history, 1968-71, assoc. prof. history, 1971-80, chmn. arts and scis., 1971-76, dean arts and letters, 1976-80, acting chancellor, 1978-79; prof. history, dean Coll. Social and Behavioral Scis. U. Tex., San Antonio, 1980-2000, acting v.p. acad. affairs, 1986-87, interim dean Coll. Engring., 2000-2001; Fulbright lectr. East China Normal U., Shanghai, 2002; dir. Freshman Initiative, 2003—05. Author: Private Journals of Georgiana Gholson Walker, 1963, Courts for a New Nation, 1971, Congress, Courts, and Criminals, 1985. Bd. dirs. Ft. Wayne Philharm. Orch., 1973-74, Pub. Transp. Corp., Ft. Wayne, 1975-77, Vis. Nurse Assn., San Antonio, 1989-94, 95-96, Vis. Nurse Assn. Hospice South Tex., 1996-2002, Employment Network, 1990-96,; pres. Mitchell Lake Wetlands Soc., 2004—; docent Mitchell Lake Audubon Ctr., 2004-, mem. stewardship bd., 2006-. With AUS, 1962-64. Tex. Soc. Colonial Dames fellow, 1964-65, 65-66; Ind. U. fellow, 1968, 70, 71; Fulbright U.S.-German Internat. Edn. Adminstrs. Program, 1993. Mem.: Tex. Assn. Deans of Liberal Arts and Scis. (bd. dirs. 1992—98, v.p. 1994, pres. 1995—97), So. Hist. Assn., Assn. Am. Historians, Phi Alpha Theta, Delta Sigma Rho. Home: 18222 Redriver Sky San Antonio TX 78259 Office: U Tex Dept History 6900 N Loop 1604 W San Antonio TX 78249

HENDERSON, EDWARD DREWRY, JR., finance company executive; b. Rochester, Minn., May 13, 1945; s. Edward D. Henderson and Betty Lou Lycan; m. Tricia Peake Henderson, Jan. 14, 1979; children: Jennifer Leigh Davis, Amanda Brooks, Jessica Ann Mandia, Christopher Edward, Elissa Drewry. AB, Dartmouth Coll., 1967; MBA, Columbia U., 1969. Sr. vp Chase Manhatten Bank, NYC, 1969—90; exec. vp First Union Bankcorp, Newark, 1990—98; mng. dir. Sumitomo Mitsui Bankcorp, NYC, 1998—2006; with Moody's Investors Svc., NYC, 2006—. Chmn. Cpc Found., Middletown, NJ, 1991—2006. Recipient Man of Yr., Cpc Behavioral Healthcare, 1999. Mem.: Navesink Country Club, Dragon Soc., Sigma Nu Delta. Episcopalian. Avocations: golf, hunting, fishing, tennis, travel. Home: 15 Deep Hollow Dr Rumson NJ 07760 Office: Moodys Investors Svc 99 Church St New York NY 10007 Home Phone: 908-610-1536; Office Phone: 212-553-1429. Business E-Mail: edward.henderson@moodys.com.

HENDERSON, ERNEST, III, healthcare executive; b. Boston, Oct. 25, 1924; s. Ernest and Mary G. (Stephens) H.; m. Mary Louise Campbell, Dec. 31, 1953; children: Ernest Flagg IV, Roberta Campbell. S.B., Harvard, 1944, MBA, 1949; L.H.D. (hon.), Bard Coll., 1976; DPS, Northeastern U., 1992. With Sheraton Corp. Am., 1946-69, dir., 1953-69, treas., 1956-63, pres., 1963-69, chief exec. officer, 1967-69; pres. Henderson Houses Am., Inc. (and affiliates), 1969-89, chmn., 1989—; pres. Fidelity Products Corp., 1985-89. Bd. dirs. Boston Biotech. Corp. Mem. permanent com. Harvard Class, 1946; permanent sec. Harvard U. Bus. Sch. Class, 1952-2002; Mass. Republican jr. nat. committeeman, 1956-57; mem. Wellesley Town Meeting, 1970-89; grand marshal Wellesley Vets. Day Parade, 1978; vice chmn. emeritus bd. trustees Northeastern U.; trustee Henderson Found., George B. Henderson Found., Cape Cod Symphony, Bard Coll.; trustee Boston Biomed. Rsch. Inst.; bd. dirs. Wellesley Cmty. Ctr. Inc., Robin Moore Entertainment, Inc.; vice chmn. Nat. Ctr. for Family Homelessness. Lt. (j.g.) USNR, World War II. Named hon. Big Chief Many Tepees and blood brother Creek Indian Nation. Mem. Chief Exec.'s Orgn. Marlowe-Shakespeare Soc. (dir.), Mensa. Clubs: Harvard Business School Assn. (Boston) (past pres.), Travelers Century Club; Circumnavigators. Home: 171 Edmunds Rd Wellesley Hills MA 02481-1331 Office: Henderson Houses Am Inc PO Box 420 Sudbury MA 01776-0420

HENDERSON, FLORENCE, actress, singer; b. Dale, Ind., Feb. 14, 1934; d. Joseph and Elizabeth Elder H.; m. Ira Bernstein, Jan. 9, 1956 (div.); children: Barbara, Joey, Robert Norman, Elizabeth; m. John Kappas, Aug. 4, 1987. Attended, St. Francis Acad., Owensboro, Ky; studied at, Am. Acad. Dramatic Arts. Broadway and stage debut in Wish You Were Here, 1952; on tour in Oklahoma!, 1952-53, at N.Y.C. Ctr., 1953, Fanny, 1954, The Sound of Music, 1961, in revival of Annie Get Your Gun, 1974; appeared in The Great Waltz, Los Angeles Civic Light Opera Assn., 1953, on Broadway in The Girl Who Came to Supper, 1963, in revival of South Pacific, 1967, in revival The Sound of Music, Los Angeles Civic Light Opera Assn., 1978, Bells are Ringing, Los Angeles Civic Light Opera Assn., 1979; appeared in Oldsmobile indsl. shows, 1958-61; actress: (movies) Song of Norway, 1970, Shakes The Clown, 1991, Naked Gun 33 1/2: The Final Insult, 1994, The Brady Bunch Movie, 1995, Holy Man, 1998, Get Bruce, 1999, Venus & Vegas, 2007; appeared on TV in Sing Along, 1958, The Today Show, 1959-60, The Brady Bunch, 1969-74, The Brady Bunch Hour, 1977, The Brady Girls Get Married, 1981, A Very Brady Christmas, 1988, The Bradys, 1990, Fudge-A-Mania, 1995, (host) Bradymania, 1993; numerous other TV appearances include The Love Boat, 1976, 83, The Brady Brides, 1981, Hart to Hart, 1981, Fantasy Island, 1981, 83, Alice, 1983, Murder She Wrote, Dean Martin TV Series; hostess Country Kitchen; appeared in TV spl. Just a Regular Kid; guest appearances It's Garry Shandling's Show, Wil Shriner Show, Jay Leno Family Spl.; first female host of The Tonight Show; co-host: Later Today, 1999-2000; writings, A Little Cooking, A Little Talking, and A Whole Lotta Fun; films include: Speaking of Women's Health, Lifetime. Recipient Sarah Siddons award

HENDERSON, FRANCES J., lawyer; b. Glasgow, Scotland, Feb. 17, 1957; LLB with honors, U. Glasgow, Scotland, 1978; LLM, U. Va., 1979; JD, U. Minn., 1984. Bar: DC 1985. Of counsel Graham & James, Washington; ptnr. Sonnenschein Nath & Rosenthal, Washington, 1998—. Office: Sonnenschein Nath & Rosenthal LLP Ste 600, E Tower 1301 K St NW Washington DC 20005 Office Phone: 202-408-6357. Office Fax: 202-408-6399. Business E-Mail: fhenderson@sonnenschein.com.

HENDERSON, FREDA LAVERNE, elementary school educator; b. Parker County, Tex., June 18, 1939; d. Johnnie C. and Golda Arlene (Porter) Holbrooks; m. Ronald S. Henderson, Apr. 12, 1958; children: Ronald Kevin, Kelly Doyle, Chetley Brian, Terry Dean. AA, Am. Inst. Art, 1960; BEd, U. Colo., 1991; MEd, Lesley Coll., Cambridge, Mass., 1997. Pvt. art tchr. for all ages, Colo., 1980—86; elem. tchr. art Ellicott Schs., Colo., 1986—90, tchr. chpt. I, 1991—96, classroom tchr., 1996—2005, Title I reading tchr. Colo., 2005—. Sec. Ellicott Sch. PTA; chmn. High Sch. Booster Club, 1979-80; active vol. activities, 1964-79. Named Walmart Tchr. of Yr., 2002. Home: 1975 Buck Rd Calhan CO 80808-8515 Office: Ellicott Schs # 22 399 S Ellicott Hwy Calhan CO 80808-8963 Personal E-mail: freda_henderson@msn.com.

HENDERSON, FREDERICK A. (FRITZ), automotive executive; b. Nov. 29, 1958; m. Karen Henderson; 2 children. BBA with high distinction, U. Mich., 1980; MBA with high distinction, Harvard U., 1984. From sr. analyst to dir. GM Corp., NY, 1984—87; from dir. to v.p. mortgage banking GMAC, 1987—90, from v.p. fin. to group v.p. fin. Detroit, 1991—92; exec. in charge of ops. automotive compontents group GM Corp., Pontiac, Mich., 1993, v.p., gen. mgr. Delphi Saginaw steering sys. Saginaw, Mich., 1996, v.p., mng. dir. Brazil Sao Paulo, Brazil, 1997—2000, group v.p., 2000—; pres. Latin Am., Africa and Middle East region GM Corp, 2000—02; pres. GM Asia Pacific GM Corp., 2002—04, chmn. GM Europe, 2004—05, vice chmn., CFO, 2006—. Mem. GM Automotive Strategy Bd. GM Corp.; chmn. bd. dirs. Shanghai GM Co., Ltd., 2002; vice-chmn., bd. dirs. Pan Asia Tech. Automotive Ctr.; bd. dirs. Fuji Heavy Industries Ltd.; chmn. bd. dirs. GM Daewoo Auto & Tech. Co. George F. Baker scholar, 1984. Mem.: Conf. Bd. Fin. Execs. Internat., Japan Automobile Mfrs. Assn. (bd. dirs. 2002). Office: GM Corp PO Box 300 300 Renaissance Ctr Detroit MI 48265-3000*

HENDERSON, GENE M., marketing professional; BA, Coe Coll.; MBA, U. Chgo. Former sr. cons. Stuart Weiner and Assocs., Chgo.; former exec. v.p. strategic devel., pres. fund raising and membership svcs., COO Epsilon, Boston; pres., CEO, bd. dirs. DIMAC Mktg. Corp., 1997-98, Transmedia Network, Miami, 1998—. Mem. Direct Mktg. Assn. (ethical bus. practices com., operating com. non profit coun., spkr. ann. conf.). Office: Transmedia Network 11900 Biscayne Blvd Miami FL 33181-2743

HENDERSON, GEORGE, educational sociologist, educator; b. Hurtsboro, Ala., June 18, 1932; s. Kidd Large and Lula Mae (Crawford) H.; m. Barbara Ann Beard, Aug. 9, 1952; children: George, Michele, Faith, Lea, Joy, Lisa, Dawn. Student, Mich. State U., 1950-52; BA, Wayne State U., 1957, MA, 1959, PhD in Ednl. Sociology, 1965. Caseworker Ch. Youth Service, Detroit, 1957-59; social economist Detroit Housing Commn., 1960-61; dir. cmty. svcs. Detroit Urban League, 1961-63; program dir. Mayor's Com. for Detroit Youth, 1963-64; asst. dir. delinquency control tng. center Wayne State U., 1964-65; asst. dir. intercultural rels. Detroit Pub. Schs., 1965-66, asst. to supt., 1966-67; assoc. prof. sociology and edn. U. Okla., 1967-69, Sylvan N. Goldman prof. human rels., 1969—2006, prof. edn., assoc. prof. sociology, 1969—2006, David Ross Boyd prof. human rels., 1985—2006, Regents' prof. human rels., 1989—2006, Kerr-McGee Presdl. prof., 2001—05; dean U. Okla. Coll. Liberal Studies, 1996-2000; dir. human rels. U. Okla., 2000—06. Chmn. dept. human rels. U. Okla., 1969-95; vis. prof. sociology Langston U., 1969-70; disting. vis. prof. U.S. Air Force Acad., 1980-81; cons. in field. Author: Foundations of American Education, 1970, Teachers Should Care, 1970, America's Other Children, 1971, To Live in Freedom, 1972, Education for Peace, 1973, Human Relations, 1974, Human Relations in the Military, 1975, A Religious Foundation of Human Relations, 1977, Introduction to American Education, 1978, Understanding and Counseling Ethnic Minorities, 1979, Police Human Relations, 1981, Transcultural Health Care, 1981, Physician-Patient Communication, 1981, The Human Rights of Professional Helpers, 1983, The State of Black Oklahoma, 1984, Psychosocial Aspects of Disability, 1984, 2004, Mending Broken Children, 1984, College Survival for Student Athletes, 1985, International Business and Cultures, 1987, Understanding Indigeneous and Foreign Cultures, 1989, 2006, Values in Health Care, 1991, Social Work Interventions, 1994, Cultural Diversity in the Workplace, 1994, Migrants, Immigrants and Slaves, 1995, Human Relations Issues in Management, 1996, Our Souls to Keep, 1999, Rethinking Ethnicity and Health Care, 1999, Ethnicity and Substance Abuse, 2002, Excellence in College Teaching and Learning, 2007. Recipient Outstanding Achievement award Human Rels. Assn., 1975, Human Rels. award Met. Human Rels. Commn. Nashville, 1979, Okla. Dept. of Mental Health award, 1996, Okla. Found. for Excellence medal for outstanding coll./univ. tchr., 2000; named to Okla. Higher Edn. Hall Fame, 2003, Okla. Hall Fame, 2003. Mem. AAUP, ACD, Am. Sociol. Assn., Nat. Assn. Human Rights Works, Assn. Black Sociologists, Inter-Univ. Seminar on Armed Forces and Soc., Internat. Soc. Law Enforcement and Criminal Justice Instrs., Am. Assn. High Edn. (Black Caucus award for Ednl. Svc. 1993), Golden Key, Omicron Delta Kappa, Delta Tau Kappa, Phi Kappa Phi, Kappa Alpha Psi. Democrat. Home: 2616 Osborne Dr Norman OK 73069-5031 Office: 601 Elm Ave Norman OK 73019-3100 Business E-Mail: clsdean@ou.edu.

HENDERSON, GEORGE ERVIN, lawyer; b. Pampa, Tex., June 7, 1947; s. Ervin L. and Elizabeth (Yoe) Henderson; m. Linda L. Dalrymple, Aug. 22, 1970; children: Andrew, Elizabeth. BA, Tex. Christian U., 1969; JD, Yale U., 1972. Bar: Tex. 1972, U.S. Dist. Ct. (so. dist.) Tex. 1974, U.S. Dist. Ct. (we. dist.) Tex. 1978. Assoc. Fulbright & Jaworski, Houston, Austin, Tex., 1972-79, ptnr. Austin, 1983—, Sneed & Vine, Austin, 1979-82. Adj. instr. law U. Tex., Austin, 1983—85. Contbr. articles to profl. jours. Mem. rules com. S. Tex. Youth Soccer Assn., 1993—; mem. Greater Austin Soccer Coalition, Austin, 1995—98; elder Univ. Presbyn. Ch., Austin, 2001—04. Capt. USAR, 1972—78. Mem.: ABA, Am. Bankruptcy Inst., Turnaround Mgmt. Assn., San Antonio Bankruptcy Bar Assn., Tex. Bar Found., Travis County Bar Assn. (chmn. 1988—89, vice-chmn. 1997—98, mem. bankruptcy law sect.), Tex. Assn. Bank Counsel (pres. 1985—86), State Bar Tex. (mem. articles 2 and 2A revision subcom. 2005—, chmn. corp. banking and bus. law sect. 1983, mem. coun. corp. banking and bus. law sect. 1985—88), Capital Soccer Club (pres. 1993—95), Austin Yacht Club. Office: Fulbright and Jaworski 600 Congress Ave Ste 2400 Austin TX 78701-3271 Office Phone: 512-536-4524.

HENDERSON, HARRIET, librarian, director; b. Pampa, Tex., Nov. 19, 1949; d. Ervin Leon and Hannah Elizabeth (Yoe) H. AB, Baker U., 1971; MLS, U. Tex., 1973. Sch. libr. Pub. Sch. Sys., Pampa, 1971-72; city libr. City of Tyler, Tex., 1973-80, City of Newport News, Va., 1980-84, dir. librs. and info. svcs. Va., 1984-90; dir. Louisville Free Pub. Libr., 1990-97, Montgomery County (Md.) Pub. Librs., 1997—2005, Richmond Pub. Libr., Va., 2005—. Del. White House Conf. Librs. and Info. Svcs., 1991; mem. Leadership Louisville, 1991—97, Alliant Health Sys. Adult Oper. Bd., 1991—97; mem. adv. com. dept. edn. Spalding U., 1991—95; mem. Md. Adv. Coun. on Librs., 2001—05; diaconate Hiddenwood Presbyn. Ch., Newport News, 1983—85; bd. dirs. Tex. Libr. Sys. Act adv. bd., 1979—80, Peninsula Women's Network, Newport News, 1983—85. Recipient Tribute to Women in Bus. and Industry, Peninsula YWCA, Newport News, 1984. Mem.: ALA (councillor 2001—05), Pub. Libr. Assn. (v.p. 1998, pres. 1999), Va. Libr. Assn. (chmn. legis. com. 1981—84, v.p. 1985, pres. 1986), Ky. Libr. Assn. (chair pub. libr. sect. 1995, Outstanding Pub. Libr. Svc. award 1997). Office: Richmond Pub Libr 101 E Franklin St Richmond VA 23219

HENDERSON, HAZEL, economist, writer; b. Bristol, Somerset, Eng., Mar. 27, 1933; arrived in US, 1957, naturalized, 1962; d. Kenneth and Dorothy May (Jesseman) Mustard; m. Carter Henderson (div. 1981); 1 child, Alexandra Leslie Camille Henderson Cassidy; m. Alan F. Kay, 1996 Baccalaureate, Clifton Sch., Bristol, UK, 1950; ScD hon., Worcester Poly. Inst., Mass., 1975; ScD (hon.), Soka U., Tokyo, 2000, U. San Francisco, 2001. Freelance writer, various locations, 1967—. Vis. regent's lectr. U. Calif., Santa Barbara, 1979, Horace Albright chair dept. forestry, Berkeley, 82; advisor Calvert Social Investment Funds, 1982—2005; pnr. Calvert-Henderson Quality of Life Indicators, 2000—; internat. adv. bd. Inst. Ethos, São Paulo, Brazil; dir. Worldwatch Inst., 1975—2001; guest Today Show, AM Am., Bill Moyers's Jour.; prodr. Sunrise Semester series, CBS, 1977, 78, informative series, PBS, 1984; founder Ethical Markets Media LLC; mem. adv. bd., organizing com. Beyond GDP conf. European Commn., 2007; cons., lectr., presenter in field. Author: Creating Alternative Futures: The End of Economics, 1978, The Politics of the Solar Age: Alternatives to Economics, 1981, 1988, Paradigms in Progress, 1991, 1995, Building a Win-Win World, 1996, Beyond Globalization, 1999; co-author: Planetary Citizenship, 2004, Ethical Markets Growing the Green Economy, 2006, The Power of Yin, 2007; editor: The United Nations: Policy and Financing Alternatives, 1996; syndicated columnist InterPress Svc., LA Times-Mirror Syndicate; contbr. articles to Christian Sci. Monitor, US News and World Report, Time, NY Times, InterPress Svc., to anthologies; mem. editl. bd. Futures U.K., Foresight U.K., Futures Rsch. Quar., Future Survey, Resurgence; prodr.: informative series, PBS, 1984, co-exec. prodr.: PBS series Ethical Markets, 2005—06. Adv. coun. US Congress Office Tech. Assessment, Washington, 1974-80; adv. Com. on Future Fla. State Legislature, Tallahassee, 1984-86; internat. adv. bd. Forum 2000, Prague, 1995-2000; Rsch. Applied to Nat. Needs com. NSF, 1975-78; Pub. Engring. Policy com. Nat. Acad. Engring., 1976-79. Named Citizen of Yr. NY Med. Soc., 1967; awardee UN Environ. Program; co-winner Global Citizen award, 1996 Fellow: Findhorn Found., World Futures Study Fedn., World Bus. Acad., World Wisdom Coun., Club of Rome (hon.), Club Budapest (hon.). Avocations: bicycling, gardening, swimming. Office: PO Box 5190 Saint Augustine FL 32085-5190 Office Phone: 904-826-1381. Business E-Mail: admin@hazelhenderson.com.

HENDERSON, HORACE EDWARD, World War II historian, peace advocate; b. Henderson, NC, July 30, 1917; s. T. Brantley and Maude (Duke) H.; m. Vera S. Schubert; children by previous marriage: Terri Kelley, Elizabeth Smith. Student, Coll. William and Mary, 1934—37, Yale U., 1941—42. Owner Henderson Real Estate & Ins., Williamsburg, Va., 1947—52; coord. Nat. Automobile Dealers Assn., Washington, 1954—56; dir. gen. World Peace Through Law Center, Geneva, 1964—69; chmn. bd. Henderson Real Estate, McLean, Va., 1964—66; exec. dir. World Assn. Judges, 1968—69; pres. Cmty. Methods, Inc., 1969—76; chmn. Congress Reform Com., Washington, 1976; exec. v.p. Am. Lawmakers Assn., Washington, 1977; pres. Williamsburg Vacations, Inc., 1969—84. Chmn., pres. Nat. Assn. for Free Trade, San Francisco, 1986-87; mem. adv. bd. Mut. Security Agy., 1952-53; mem. Pres.'s Conf. on Indsl. Safety, 1952-53; exec. com. U.S. Com. for UN, 1954; dir. Nat. Citizens Com. for Hoover Report, 1954; indsl. adv. com. Fed. Civil Def. Adminstrn., 1952-53; cons. to dir. ICA, 1956; dir. spl. liaison, spl. asst. to dep. under sec. state, Washington, 1958, dep. asst. sec. state internat. orgn. affairs, Washington, 1959-60; dir. Exile Orgns. Free Europe Com., 1962; U.S. del. to ILO, UNESCO, FAO, WHO, ECOSOC, UN. Author: The Greatest Blunders of World War II, 2002, The Scots of Virginia--America's Greatest Patriots, 2001, The Final Word on War and Peace, 2004. Local, state and Nat. pres. US Jaycees, 1947-53; chmn. Va. Rep. party, 1962-64, Americans for Asian Security and Freedom, 1961; campaign dir. Am. Nationalities for Nixon-Lodge, 1960, Rep. candidate for Congress, 1956, for lt. gov. Va., 1957; permanent chmn. Va. Rep. Conv., 1957; asst. nat. dir. Rockefeller for Pres. campaign, 1964, Scranton for Pres. Campaign, 1964; ind. Candidate for U.S. Senator, 1972; mem. Williamsburg (Va.) City Coun., 1948-50; chmn. Com. Against Recognition Red Hungary, 1963; World vice chmn. Operation Brotherhood, 1954-55; owner Powhatan Hist. Corp., Williamsburg, Va., 1957; chmn. World Campaign Conv. for Peaceful Settlement Internat. Disputes, 1975-95, Assn. for Devel. Edn., Washington, 1978-80, World Peace Treaty Campaign, 1997-05; chmn. Coalition World Union Fedn., 2006; pres. Internat. Domestic Devel. Corp., 1975; trustee Valley Forge Found., 1952-55, Jr. C. of C. War Meml. Hdqrs.; elder, deacon Presbyn. Ch. Capt., C.E. AUS, 1942-46. Nominee Nobel Peacce prize, 2007; Recipient spl. citizenship award Am. Heritage Found., 1953; named Outstanding Jaycee of World, 1954. Mem. US C. of C. (dir. 1954), Yale Club, St. Andrew's Soc., Sigma Alpha Epsilon. Visited 47 countries organizing young men's civic groups, 1953-54. Home: Apt 822 1925 Burnt Bridge Rd Lynchburg VA 24503-2246 Personal E-mail: hDukeHen@aol.com. *As my father always told me, "Life is not getting what you want, but making the best of what you get.".*

HENDERSON, ISAAC CRAIG, oncologist, researcher; b. Paullina, Iowa, Aug. 10, 1941; s. Isaac C. and Ora E. (Tjossem) H.; m. Mary Turner Henderson, June 11, 1966; children: Isaac Craig, Amy Hudson. AB, Grinnell Coll., Iowa, 1963; MD, Columbia U., 1970. Cert. internal medicine, 1977, med. oncology, 1979. Intern Presbyn. Hosp., NYC, 1970-71; resident, 1971-72; rsch. assoc. NIH, 1972-74; instr. medicine Harvard U. Med. Sch., Boston, 1975-76; asst. prof., 1976-84; assoc. prof., 1984-92; dir. Breast Evaln. Ctr. Dana Farber Cancer Inst., 1980-92; dir. clin. cancer program U. Calif., San Francisco, 1992-95; chmn., CEO Sequus Pharm., Inc., Menlo Park, Calif., 1995—99; sr. med. advisor and mem. bd. of dir. Alza Corp., Mountain View, Calif., 1999—2002; CEO Access Oncology, NY, 2001—04; pres. Keryx Biopharmaceuticals, Inc., San Francisco, 2004—. Adj. prof., U. Calif., San Francisco, 1995—. Contbr. articles to profl. jours. Served with USPHS, 1972-74. Fulbright Rsch. scholar, 1964-65; Merck, Sharp & Dohme Internat. fellow, 1966; recipient Columbia Presbyn. Med. soc. rsch. prize, 1970. Fellow ACP; mem. Am. Soc. Clin. Oncology, Am. Assn. Cancer Rsch., Soc. Friends. Achievements include research on clin. protocols evaluating new treatment of breast cancer. Office: Keryx Biopharmaceuticals Inc 1373 Bay St San Francisco CA 94123-2201 Office Phone: 415-674-5148. E-mail: ichenderson@hotmail.com.

HENDERSON, JANET E. E., lawyer; b. 1956; BA, U. Okla., 1978; JD, Columbia U., 1982. Bar: Okla. 1982, U.S. Dist. Ct. (no. dist.) Okla. 1982, Ill. 1986, U.S. Dist. Ct. (no. dist.) Ill. 1986. With Sidley & Austin, Chgo., 1985—, ptnr., 1990—. Lectr. on lender liability issues and bankruptcy to legal orgns., including Midwest Assn. Secured Lenders. Harlan Fiske Stone scholar Columbia U., 1982. Mem. ABA, Chgo. Bar Assn., Am. Bankruptcy Inst., Phi Beta Kappa. Office: Sidley & Austin Bank One Plz 10 S Dearborn St Chicago IL 60603 Fax: 312-853-7036.

HENDERSON, JASON CRAIG, financial advisor; b. Des Moines, May 21, 1968; s. Larry Craig Henderson and Royann Thompson, Gene Scott Thompson (Stepfather) and Melody Henderson (Stepmother); m. Carrie Kaye Holmes, May 6, 1994; children: Zoe, Fischer. BA in Bus. Adminstrn., Grand View Coll., Des Moines, 1993. Lic. Ins. Agent Iowa, 1993. Fin. advisor Morgan Stanley Dean Witter, West Des Moines, Iowa, 1993—97; dir. instl. mktg. ING, Des Moines, 1997—98; regional v.p. Sun Life of Can. (U.S.), Boston, 1998—2000, N.Y. Life Ins. Co., NYC, 2000—01, Lincoln Benefit Life (Allstate), Lincoln, 2001—02, Pacific Life Ins. Co., Newport Beach, Calif., 2002—04; fin. advisor, retirement planning specialist Morgan Stanley, West Des Moines, Iowa, 2004—. Bd. mem. Walnut Creek Little League, Waukee, Iowa, 2005—06. Avocations: golf, little league baseball coach. Office: Morgan Stanley 4949 Westown Pkwy Ste 110 West Des Moines IA 50266 Office Phone: 515-224-5523. Business E-Mail: jason.henderson@morganstanley.com.

HENDERSON, JEFF, chef; b. 1965; married. Dishwasher Gadsby's; chef L'Escale and the Dining Room, Ritz Carlton Hotel, Marina del Ray, Calif.; sous chef Hotel Bel-Air, LA, L'Ermitage Hotel, Beverly Hills; chef de cuisine Caesars Palace, Las Vegas; exec. chef Bellagio Café, Las Vegas, 2004—; pres., CEO Urban Ednl. Consulting, Las Vegas. Author: Cooked: From the Streets to the Stove, From Cocaine to Foie Gras; guest appearances include (TV Shows) Oprah Winfrey Show, Good Morning America, Montel Williams Show, The Big Idea with Donny Deutsch, Mike and Juliet in the Morning, (Radio Shows) All Things Considered, Nat. Pub. Radio, The Wendy Williams Show, The Gayle King Show, featured in People mag., USA Today, Newsweek, NY Post, Ebony mag., Essence, Black Enterprise. Named Las Vegas Chef of Yr.; recipient Culinary award of Excellence. Achievements include becoming first African-Am. named to exec. chef position at Caesars Palace. Office: Cafe Bellagio Bellagio Hotel 3600 S Las Vegas Blvd Las Vegas NV 89109*

HENDERSON, JEFFREY W., health products executive; BSEE, Kettering U., Flint, Mich.; MBA, Harvard Grad. Sch. Bus. Adminstrn. With GM; v.p., corp. treas. Eli Lilly & Co., 1998, v.p., corp. contr.; pres., gen. mgr. Eli Lilly Can., Inc.; exec. v.p., CFO Cardinal Health Inc., Dublin, Ohio, 2005—. Office: Cardinal Health Inc 7000 Cardinal Pl Dublin OH 43017*

HENDERSON, JESSICA, science educator; PhD, Oreg. State U. Rsch. analyst Oreg. Med. Assistance Program, Salem, 2001—03; assoc. prof. We. Oreg. U., Monmouth, 2003—. Office: We Oregon Univ 345 N Monmouth Ave Monmouth OR 97361 Home Phone: 541-754-6479. Office Fax: 503-838-8370.

HENDERSON, JOHN DREWS, architect; b. St. Louis, July 30, 1933; s. Russell Dewey and Hazel Agnes (Drews) H.; m. Barbara Lee Beckman, June 25, 1955; children: Susan Lee, John Beckman. BArch, U. Ill., 1956. Registered architect, Calif. With Delawie, Macy & Henderson, San Diego, Calif., 1966-77, Macy, Henderson & Cole, AIA, San Diego, 1977-86; pres. John D. Henderson, FAIA, 1986—. Mem. San Diego Hist. Sites Bd., 1972-78, Gaslamp Quarter Task Force, 1976-78, Gaslamp Quarter Coun., 1984-86; mem. City Mgr.'s Com. for Seismic Retrofit for Older Bldgs., 1986-92; mem. Hist. Am. Bldg. Survey, 1972078, chair, 1976-78; bd. dirs. Hist. Am. Bldgs. Survey Found., 1984-86; Calif. Hist. Bldgs. Code Safety Bd., 1976-96; apptd. by Gov. of Calif. to State Hist. Resources Commn., 1990-02, reapptd., 1994-98, 98-02, chmn. 1992-93, 2000-01, chmn. Calif. Heritage Fund com. 1993—2001; Calif. advisor Nat. Trust Hist. Preservation, 1975-78; bd. dirs. Gaslamp Quarter Found., 1984-86. Lt. USNR, 1956-59. With USN, 1956—59, with USNR, 1959—64. Recipient Hist. Preservation awards from City San Diego, San Diego Hist. Soc., San Diego chpt. and Calif. Coun. AIA, La Jolla Women's Club, Am. Assn. State and Local History, Am. Inst. Planners, Save Our Heritage Orgn., Rancho Santa Fe Assn., Calif. Preservation Found., Ctrl. City Assn., Gaslmp Quarter Assn. Fellow AIA (officer, dir. local chpt. 1969-73, chpt. pres. 1972, editor guidebooks 1970, 76, state bd. dirs. 1971-73, nat. hist. resources com. 1974-76, 78—, emeritus 2002, regional rep. 1976-78, mem. guidebook com., 2002); mem. San Diego Archtl. Found. (bd. dirs. 1984-86, 89-91, mid. 20th century modern com. 2004—), San Diego Hist. Soc. (officer, bd. dirs. 1975, pres. 1975), San Diego Geneal. Soc., San Diego History Campaign (exec. com. 1981-86), Clan Henderson Soc. Republican. Presbyterian. Office Phone: 858-272-0434. E-mail: jhende33@sbcglobal.net.

HENDERSON, JOSEPH RALSTON, educator; b. Elders Ridge, Pa., May 9, 1915; s. John Gordon and Sara Kathryn (Holstein) H.; B.S., Indiana U. of Pa., 1939; M.A., N.Y.U., 1944, Ed.D., 1954; m. Elizabeth Elder, July 23, 1941; children— Kathryn Henderson Anderson, Paul, John, Nancy Henderson Pihlblad. Tchr., prin. Young Twp. (Pa.) Schs., 1935-40, Ezel (Ky.) High Sch., 1941-42; dir. Annville (Ky.) Inst., 1945-48; chmn. div. social scis. Union Coll., Barbourville, Ky., 1948-56; prof., chmn. dept. edn., dir. Grad. Sch., Westminster Coll., New Wilmington, Pa., 1956-82, prof. emeritus, 1982—; acad. visitor in philosophy of edn. Oxford (Eng.) U., 1975; cons. Shutz Sch., Alexandria, Egypt, 1970-84. Mem. bd. edn. Wilmington (Pa.) Area Schs., 1960-63; pres. bd. dirs. Shenango United Presbyn. Home, New Wilmington, Pa., 1982-85. Served with U.S. Army, 1942-45. Recipient Brother Azarias Meml. award, 1978; Outstanding Alumnus award Indiana U. of Pa. Fellow Philosophy of Edn. Soc.; mem. Pa. Assn. Liberal Arts Colls. (pres. 1967-68), Comparative and Internat. Edn. Soc., Phi Delta Kappa (Distinguished Service award 1974, Educator of Yr. 1979), S.A.R. Kappa Delta Pi (Honor Key 1976), Psi Chi, Pi Gamma Mu. Republican. Presbyterian. Club: Rotary (pres. club 1976-77) (New Wilmington). Home: 925 MRG Willow Valley Lakes Dr Apt 205 Meadow Ridge Willow Street PA 17584

HENDERSON, KAREN LECRAFT, federal judge; b. Oberlin, Ohio, 1944; BA, Duke U., 1966; JD, U. N.C., 1969. Ptnr. Wright & Henderson, Chapel Hill, NC, 1969—70, Sinkler, Gibbs & Simons, P.A., Columbia, SC, 1983—86; asst. atty. gen. Columbia, 1973—78; sr. asst. atty. gen., dir. of spl. litigation sect., 1978—82; deputy atty. gen., dir. of criminal div., 1982; judge US Dist. Ct. SC, Columbia, 1986—90, US Ct. Appeals (DC cir.), Washington, 1990—. Apptd. Dist. Ct. Adv. Com. Mem.: ABA (litigation sect. and urban, state and local government law sect.), Am. Law Inst., Supreme Ct. Hist. Soc., Fed. Judges Assn., Fed. Am. Inn of Ct., Am. Judicature Soc., SC Bar Assn. (government law sect., trial and appellate practice sect., fed. judges assn.), NC Bar Assn. Office: US Ct Appeals 333 Constitution Ave NW Washington DC 20001-2802*

HENDERSON, KATHLEEN DENISE ROSS, medical/surgical nurse, educator; b. Camden, NJ, Feb. 4, 1954; r. Andrew Jr. and S. Roberta Richardson (Johnson) R.; 1 child, Thelbert (Jay) Cornish Jr. BSN, Seton Hall. U., 1978; MS, St. Joseph's U., Phila., 1990. Cert. critical care nurse, ACLS, BCLS. Staff nurse Harris Hosp., Ft. Worth, 1980-81, John Peter Smith Hosp., Ft. Worth, 1984; staff nurse, relief charge nurse Med. Plaza Hosp., Ft. Worth, 1983-84; staff nurse, med. ICU-CCU Deborah Heart and Lung Ctr., Browns Mills, N.J., 1984-88, 92—, staff devel. instr., 1988-92. Vol. AIDS Coalition So. N.J., 1993-96. Capt. USAF, 1979-83. Mem. AANC, ANA, N.J.Nurses Assn., Sigma Theta Tau. Home: PO Box 4036 Mount Holly NJ 08060-4036 Office: Deborah Heart and Lung Ctr 200 Trenton Rd Browns Mills NJ 08015-1799

HENDERSON, MADELINE MARY (BERRY), chemist, researcher, consultant; b. Merrimac, Mass., Sept. 3, 1922; d. Burton B. and Irene R. (Murphy) Berry; m. Richard S. Henderson, Nov. 5, 1957; children: Anne M., Matthew R., Katherine M., Laura J. AB in Chemistry, Emmanuel Coll., Boston, 1944; MPA, Am. U., Washington, 1977. Chemist E.I. DuPont, Gibbstown, NJ, 1944—45, MIT, Cambridge, Mass., 1946—52; info. specialist Battelle Meml. Inst., Columbus, Ohio, 1953—55; rsch. assoc. NSF, Washington, 1956—62; computer specialist Nat. Bur. Standards, Washington, 1964—79; cons. Bethesda, 1980—. Chmn. Gordon Rsch. Conf. on Sci. Info. Problems, 1972. Author, co-author, editor books on info. sci.; co-author, author papers, articles on info. sci., standards, and libr. automation. Dept. of Commerce Sci.-Tech. fellow, 1971-72; Am. U. Key Exec. scholar, 1975-77. Fellow AAAS (sec. sect. info. scis. 1978-85); mem. Am. Chem. Soc., Am. Soc. Info. Sci. & Tech. (mem. publs. com. 1983-87, chmn. pub. affairs com. 1987-89, Watson Davis award 1989), Pi Alpha Alpha (nat. honor soc. pub. adminstr.). Office: 7401 Willow Rd #425 Frederick MD 21702-2500

HENDERSON, MAUREEN MCGRATH, medical educator; b. Tynemouth, Eng., May 11, 1926; arrived in U.S., 1960; d. Leo E. and Helen McGrath Henderson. MB BS, U. Durham, Eng., 1949, DPH, 1956. Prof. preventive medicine U. Md. Med. Sch., 1968—75, chmn. dept. social and preventive medicine, 1971—75; assoc. epidemiology Johns Hopkins U. Sch. Hygiene and Pub. Health, 1960—75; prof. epidemiology and medicine U. Wash. Med. Sch., 1975—96, prof. emeritus epidemiology and medicine, 1996—, asst. v.p. and assoc. v.p. health scis., 1975—81, head cancer prevention rsch. program Fred Hutchinson Cancer Rsch. Ctr., 1983—94; mem. Nat. Inst. Environ. Health Scis. Adv. Coun., 1994—97. Chmn. epidemiology and disease control study sect. Nih, 1969—82; chmn. clin. trial rev. com. Nat. Heart Lung and Blood Inst., 1975—79; mem. Nat. Cancer Adv. Bd., 1979—84; mem. bd. Robert Wood Johnson Health Policy Fellowship, 1989—93; bd. radiation effects rsch. NRC, 1991—97. Assoc. editor Hour. Cancer Rsch., 1984—88, mem. editl. bd. Jour. Nat. Cancer Inst., 1988—, mem. editl. adv. bd. Cancer Detection and Prevention, 1992—. Decorated Order of Brit. Empire; recipient John Snow award, Am. Pub. Health Assn., 1990; scholar Luke-Armstrong, 1956—57, John and Mary Markle, Acad. Medicine, 1963—68. Mem.: NAS, Inst. Medicine, Nat. Rsch. Coun. (report rev. com. 1996—2002, mem. com. rsch. priorities for airborne particulate matters 1998—2000), Am. Epidemiol. Soc. (pres. 1990—91), Internat. Coun. Cancer Rsch. (sci. adv. bd. 1989—92), Soc. Epidemiol. Rsch. (chmn. 1969—70), Assn. Tchrs. Preventive Medicine (pres. 1972—73), Am. Coll. Epidemiology. Home: 5309 NE 85th St Seattle WA 98115-3915 E-mail: mhenders@w-link.net.

HENDERSON, MELFORD J., epidemiologist, molecular biologist, chemist; b. Birmingham, Ala., Dec. 28, 1950; s. Robert Burton and Rena Henderson; 1 child, Erica. BS, Bishop Coll., Dallas, 1972; MA, Johns Hopkins U., 1976; student, NYU Dental Sch., 1977—79; MPH, Yale U., 1984. Ordained min. Rsch. assoc. Bishop Coll., 1972-73; rsch. assoc. Sch. of Pharmacy U. Md., Balt., 1976-77; microbiologist Torigian Labs., Queens, NY, 1979-81; pub. health analyst internat. program cardiovasc. diseases NIH, Bethesda, Md., 1984; epidemiologist, analyst Task Force on Black and Minority Health, Bethesda, 1985—. Epidemiologist DC Govt., DC Health Dept., 1985-88, U.S. Govt., Agy. for Health Care Policy and Rsch., 1990; epidemiologist, sr. rsch. assoc. Prospect Assocs., 1989; epidemiologist, program ofcl. U.S. Dept. HHS; program ofcl. Mayor's Health Policy Coun. DC Govt. Author 7 scholarly sci. publs. Recipient numerous awards in chemistry and pub. health; NIH fellow, 1973-76, USPHS fellow, 1982-84, rsch. fellow Assn. Black Cardiologists, 1984-85. Mem. APHA, Md. Pub. Health Assn., Blacks in Govt., Soc. for Epidemiol. Rsch., Assn. Black Cardiologists, Beta Kappa Chi. Business E-Mail: mhenders@ahrq.gov.

HENDERSON, MILTON ARNOLD, professional society administrator; b. Chattanooga, June 22, 1922; s. Milton Arnold and Margaret (Rawlings) H.; m. Joyce Crowder (dec. Nov. 13, 1977); children: George, Linda, Philip.; m. Betty Ann Harnage, Aug. 20, 1982. BS, Northwestern U., 1948. Asst. sales mgr. Coca-Cola Bottling Co., Savannah and Macon, Ga., 1948—54; with Gideons Internat., Chgo., 1954-63, field rep., 1954-55, promotion mgr., 1955-56, with Nashville, 1964—, exec. dir., 1956-87, exec. dir. emeritus, 1987—. Editor The Gideon Mag., Gideon Info. Bull., Gideon News Brief, 1956-87; author: Sowers of the Word, a 95-Year History of The Gideons International, 1899-1994, 1995; attended Gideon convs. and meetings in 74 countries, 1956—. 1st lt. USAAF, 1942-46; capt. USAF, 1951-52. Recipient Community Leader of Am. award, 1969, Personalities of the South award, 1975, Disting. Alumnus award Howe Mil. Sch., Ind., 1985. Mem. Am. Mgmt. Assn., Nashville City Club. Republican. Presbyterian. Home: 2524 Stones River Ct Nashville TN 37214-1425

HENDERSON, RALPH HALE, physician; b. NYC, Mar. 5, 1937; s. Ralph Ernest and Clifford West (Sellers) H.; m. Ilze Sarma, May 21, 1966. AB, Harvard U., 1959, MD, 1963, MPH, 1970, M.Pub. Policy, 1972. Intern, then resident in internal medicine Boston City Hosp., 1963-65; joined USPHS, 1965, capt., 1973-81, asst. surgeon gen., 1981-90, svc. in U.S. and West Africa, 1965-69. Asst. chief venereal disease br., state and cmty. svcs. divsn. Ctrs. Disease Control, Atlanta, 1972-73; dir. venereal disease control divsn. Bur. State Svcs., 1973-76; program mgr. expanded program on immunization WHO, Geneva, 1977-78, dir. expanded program immunization, 1979-89, asst. dir. gen., 1990-98, spl. advisor to dir. gen., 1998-99; Lilly lectr. Royal Coll. Physicians, 1989; lectr. disting. lecture series Baylor Coll. Medicine, 1995. Contbr. to med. publs. Trustee Dermatology Found., 1975-77. Recipient Commendation medal USPHS, 1969, Meritorius Svc. medal, 1984, Disting. Svc. medal, 1990, Donald MacKay Meml. medal Royal Soc. Tropical Medicine and Hygiene, 1990, Internat. Child Survival award U.S. Com. UNICEF and the Task Force for Child Survival and Devel., 1992, Ann. Pub. Health Forum award London Sch. of Hygiene and Tropical Medicine, 1994. Mem. Am. Coll. Preventive Medicine. Home: 1098 Mcconnell Dr Decatur GA 30033-3402

HENDERSON, RICKEY HENLEY, professional baseball coach, retired professional baseball player; b. Chgo., Dec. 25, 1958; Draft pick Oakland Athletics, 1976, outfielder, 1979—84, 1989—93, 1993—95, 1998, NY Yankees, 1984—89, Toronto Blue Jays, 1993, San Diego Padres, 1995—97, 2001, Anaheim Angels, 1997, NY Mets, 1998—2000, spl. instr., 2007, hitting coach, 2007—; outfielder Seattle Mariners, 2000, Boston Red Sox, 2002, LA Dodgers, 2003. Named Am. League Championship Series MVP, 1989, Am. League MVP, 1990; named to Am. League All-Star Team, 1980, 1982—88, 1990—91, Sporting News, 1981, 1985, 1990, Am. League Silver Slugger Team, 1981, 1985, 1990; recipient Golden Glove award, Am. League, 1981, Silver Shoe award, Sporting News, 1982, Golden Shoe award, 1983. Achievements include holding a major league record for stolen bases in one season (130), 1982, and for an entire career (1406); led the Am. League in stolen bases, 1980-86, 88-91, 98. Office: NY Mets Shea Stadium 123-01 Roosevelt Ave Flushing NY 11368-1699*

HENDERSON, RITA ELIZABETH, literary agent, journalist; b. Bitburg, German, Mar. 7, 1964; came to U.S., 1964; d. Walter Wanzley and Lola Bell (Boles) H.; adopted children: Christopher Allan Jackson, Kayla Elizabeth Octavia Davis. AAS, Camden County Coll., Blackwood, NJ, 1984; BS, Glassboro Coll., NJ, 1987. Owner Henderson Lit. Representation, Sicklerville, N.J., 1994—; real estate agt. Weichert Realtors, Medford, N.J., 1998—. Author: The Boyz II Men Success Story: Defying the Odds, 1995; entertainment writer The N.Y. Amsterdam News, 1991-95, The Phila. Tribune, 1993-95. Democrat. Roman Catholic. Avocations: music, archery, antiques, baseball, computers. Office: Weichert Realtors 107 Taunton Blvd Medford NJ 08055-3400

HENDERSON, ROGENE FAULKNER, toxicologist, researcher; b. Breckenridge, Tex., July 13, 1933; d. Philander Molden and Lenoma (Rogers) F.; m. Thomas Richard Henderson II, May 30, 1957; children: Thomas Richard III, Edith Jeanette, Laura Lee. BSBA, Tex. Christian U., 1955; PhD, U. Tex., 1960. Diplomate Am. Bd. Toxicology. Research assoc. U. Ark. Sch. Med., Little Rock, 1960-67; from scientist to sr. scientist and group supr. chemistry and toxicology Lovelace Inhalation Toxicology Research Inst., Albuquerque, 1967—; deputy dir. Nat. Environ. Respiratory Ctr. Lovelace Respiratory Rsch. Inst., Albuquerque, 1998—. Mem. adv. com. Burroughs Wellcome Toxicology Scholar award, 1987-89, NIH toxicology study sect., 1982-86, Nat. Inst. Environ. Health Scis. adv. coun., 1992-95, EPA scientific adv. bd. environ. health commn., 1991-95; mem. bd. sci. counselors EPA, 2002—; mem. Com to Assess the Sci. Base for Tobacco Harm Reduction, adv. group Am. Cancer Soc.on Cancer and the Environment, 1999—, Health Effects Inst. Rsch. Com., 1997—; vice chmn. US Environ. protection Agy. Bd. of Sci. Counselors, 2001—; chmn. clean air sci. adv. com. U.S. EPA, 2004—. Assoc. editor Toxicology Applied Pharmacology, 1989-95, Jour. Exposure Analysis and Environ. Epidemiology, 1991-95; contbr. articles to profl. jours. Named Woman on the Move YWCA, Albuquerque, 1985; grantee NIH, 1958-60, 1960-62, 1986—. Mem. AAAS, NAS (com. toxicology 1985-98, chair 1992-98, 2005-2006, com. epidemiology of air pollution 1983-85, com. biol. markers 1986—, com. on risk assessment methodology 1989-92, bd. environ. studies and toxicology 1998-2004, com. health effects of trichlosoethylene), Am. Chem. Soc. (chmn. ctrl. N.Mex. sect. 1981), Soc. Toxicology (pres. Mountain-West Regional chpt. 1985-86, pres. inhalation specialty sect. 1989—), N.Y. Acad. Scis., Nat. Acad. (nat. assoc.) Presbyterian. Home: 5609 Don Felipe Ct SW Albuquerque NM 87105-6765 Office: Lovelace Respiratory Rsch Inst 2425 Ridgecrest Ave SE Albuquerque NM 87108 Office Phone: 505-348-9464. Business E-Mail: rhenders@lrri.org.

HENDERSON, STANLEY DALE, lawyer, educator, arbitrator; b. Monona, Iowa, June 17, 1935; s. Leon Gilbert and Iva Elizabeth H.; m. DeArliss Garretson, June 15, 1957; children: Lesli Kara, Heidi Elizabeth, Holly Ann. AB, Coe Coll., 1957; postgrad. (Woodrow Wilson fellow), Cornell U., 1957-58; postgrad., U. Chgo. Law Sch., 1958-59; JD, U. Colo., 1961. Bar: Colo. 1961, Va. 1973. Law clk. U.S. Dist. Ct., Denver, 1961-62; mem. firm Williams and Zook, Boulder, Colo., 1962-64; mem. faculty U. Wyo. Coll. Law, 1964-69; prof. law U. Va. Law Sch., Charlottesville, 1970—2004, F.D.G. Ribble prof. law, 1976—2004, prof. emeritus, 2004. Vis. prof. law Ind. U., 1974, Harvard Law Sch., 1978-79, Pepperdine U., 1992-93; arbitrator AAA and FMCS, 1970—. Author: Labor Law; author: (with Dawson and Harvey) Contracts; author: (with Meltzer) Labor Law; contbr. articles to profl. jours. Mem. Va. State Bar, Am. Law Inst., Am. Arbitration Assn., Order of Coif, Phi Beta Kappa, Phi Kappa Phi. Democrat. Presbyterian. Home: 1615 King Mountain Rd Charlottesville VA 22901-3003 Office: U Va Sch Law Charlottesville VA 22901 Office Phone: 434-924-3522. Business E-Mail: sdh6k@virginia.edu.

HENDERSON, STANLEY ELWOOD, academic administrator, consultant; b. Peoria, Ill., Jan. 13, 1947; s. Francis Wilford and Evelyn Mae Henderson; m. Diane Denise Matthews, Apr. 4, 1970; children: Derek Eaton, Duncan Timothy, Daniel Reining. BA with high honor, Mich. State U., 1969; MA, Cornell U., 1971. Admissions counselor Mich. State U., East Lansing, 1970—71; dir. admissions Wichita State U., Kans., 1971—84; dir. enrollment mgmt. and admissions Western Mich. U., Kalamazoo, 1984—95; assoc. v.p. enrollment mgmt. U. Cin., 1995—2003; assoc. provost enrollment mgmt. U. Ill., Urbana, 2003—05; vice chancellor enrollment mgmt. and student life U. Mich., Dearborn, Mich., 2005—. Enrollment mgmt. cons. Bell-Trice Enterprises, Washington, 2003—05; admissions cons. Michael Dolence Assocs., Claremont, Calif., 1993—95; enrollment mgmt. cons. pvt. practice, Canton, 1990—; sr. cons. AACRAO Consulting Svcs., Canton, Mich., 2005—; keynote and plenary spkr.; presenter in field. Co-author: ACT/APP and Other Admissions Uses of the ACT Assessment Program, Good Users of ACT Data and Services; editor: The Admissions Profession: A Guide to Staff Development and Program Management; co-editor: Handbook for the College Admissions Profession; contbr. articles to profl. jours., chapters to books. Vice chair Minorities Math., Sci., and Engring., Cin., 2001—03; academic resource coord. Gates Millenium Scholarship Program, Washington, 2000—03; developer and presenter of college-planning seminars for students and parents Personal Profl. Activity (gratis), 1995—2003, developer and presenter of coll. planning seminars for students and parents Kalamazoo, developer and presenter of coll. planning seminars for parents and students Wichita, Kans., 1974—84. Recipient Leadership Kans., Kans. C. of C., 1985; fellow, U. Ill., Urbana-Champaign, 1976—77; grantee, Cornell U., 1969—70; scholar, Nat. Merit Scholarship Corp., 1965. Mem.: Coll. Bd. (instl. rep. 1984—2003), Nat. Assn. Coll. Admission Counseling, Am. Assn. Collegiate Registrars and Admissions Officers (v.p. enrollment mgmt., admissions, and fin. 1990—93, pres. elect 1994—95, pres. 1995—96, past pres. 1996—97), Phi Beta Kappa, Omicron Delta Kappa, Kappa Delta Pi, Phi Delta Kappa, Phi Kappa Phi. Achievements include co-creation of national enrollment management conference now in its 17th year. Avocation: U.S. Presidents. Office: U Mich Dearborn 4901 Evergreen Rd 1060 AB Dearborn MI 48128-1491 Office Phone: 313-593-5151.

HENDERSON, THELTON EUGENE, federal judge; b. Shreveport, La., Nov. 28, 1933; s. Eugene M. and Wanzie (Roberts) H.; 1 son, Geoffrey A. BA, U. Calif.-, Berkeley, 1956, JD, 1962. Bar: Calif. 1962. Social case worker County of Los Angeles, 1958; jr. rsch. scientist Sys. Devel. Corp., Santa Monica, Calif., 1958—59; atty. U.S. Dept. Justice, 1962-63; assoc. firm FitzSimmons & Petris, 1964, assoc., 1964-66; directing atty. San Mateo County (Calif.) Legal Aid Soc., 1966-69; asst. dean Stanford (Calif.) U. Law Sch., 1968-76; ptnr. firm Rosen, Remcho & Henderson, San Francisco, 1977-80; judge U.S. Dist. Ct. (no. dist.) Calif., San Francisco, 1980-90, 98—, chief judge, 1990-97. Asso. prof. Sch. Law, Golden Gate U., San Francisco, 1978-80 Bd. mem. Rosenberg Found. Served with U.S. Army, 1956-58. Recipient Bernard Witkin Medal, State Bar of Calif., 2004, Pearlstein Civil Rights award, Anti-Defamation League. Bd. mem. Am. Inns of Ct. (Professionalism award, 9th cir., mem. exec. com. Edward J. McFetridge Inn of Ct.); mem. ABA, Am. Law Inst., Fed. Judges Assn., Nat. Bar Assn. (Disting. Svc. award), Charles Houston Law Assn. Office: US Dist Ct US Courthouse PO Box 36060 San Francisco CA 94102

HENDERSON, THOMAS HENRY, JR., lawyer, former legal association executive; b. Birmingham, Ala., Feb. 4, 1939; s. Thomas Henry and Edna (Green) H.; m. Elaine Dauphin (div. 1983); children: Ashley, Michelle; m. Paulette Maehara, June 1988. BSBA, Auburn U., 1961; JD, U. Ala., 1966; LLM, Nat. Law Ctr., George Washington U., 1987. Bar: D.C. 1970, Ala. 1966. Trial atty. organized crime and racketeering sect. U.S. Dept. Justice, Washington, 1966-70, dep. sect. chief mgmt. labor sect., 1970-73; dep. chief counsel, subcom. on adminstrn. practice and procedure U.S. Senate, Washington, 1973-74; dep. sect. chief mgmt. and labor sect. Dept. Justice, Washington, 1974-76, chief pub. integrity sect., 1976-80, sr. counsel criminal divsn., 1980-83; bar counsel D.C. Ct. Appeals, Washington, 1983-87; CEO ATLA, Washington, 1988—2005, ret., 2005—. Columnist Bar Counsels Page, Washington Lawyer mag., bi-monthly, 1983-87. Pres. Christmas in April, Washington, 1986-87. Named Disting. Practitioner of Law, U. Ala. Law Sch., 2004; recipient Justice Howell Heflin award, ATLA, 2004. Mem. Am. Soc. Assn. Execs. (bd. dirs. 1994-97, vice chair 1997-98, Key award 2003), Omicron Delta Kappa. Avocations: golf, skiing, exercise, outdoor adventure.

HENDERSON, VICTOR WARREN, behavioral and geriatric neurologist, epidemiologist, researcher, educator; s. Philip and Jean (Edsel) H.; m. Barbara Curtiss; children: Gregory, Geoffrey, Stephanie, Nicole. BS, U. Ga., 1972; MD, Johns Hopkins U., 1976; MS, U. Wash., 1996. Diplomate Am. Bd. Psychiatry and Neurology, United Coun. Neurologic Subspecialties, 2006. Intern Duke U., Durham, NC, 1976—77; resident Washington U., St. Louis, 1977—80; fellow Boston U., 1980—81; asst. prof. neurology U. So. Calif., LA, 1981—86, assoc. prof. neurology, gerontology and psychology, 1986—93, prof. neurology, gerontology and psychology, 1993—2001, chief divsn. cognitive neurosci. & neurogerontology, 1989—2001, Kenneth and Bette Volk prof. neurology, 1999—2001; prof. geriat., neurology, pharmacology and epidemiology U. Ark. Med. Scis., Little Rock, 2001—04, vice chair dept. geriat., 2001—04; prof. health rsch. and policy and neurology and neurological scis. Stanford U., 2004—, dir. grad. program in epidemiology, 2004—. Dir. NIH Alzheimer's Disease Rsch. Ctr. Clin. Core, 1985—2001, Rural Aging and Memory Study, 2001—04; dir. neurobehavior Clinic/Bowles Ctr. for Alzheimer's and Related Diseases, 1988—2001; chair neurology dept. Los Angeles County/U. So. Calif. Med. Ctr., 1992—97; vis. scientist MIT, 1988—89; vis. prof. U. Melbourne, 2002; co-dir. State of Calif. Alzheimer's Disease Rsch. Ctr. U. So. Calif., 1999—2001, NIH Alzheimer's Disease Ctr., 2001—03; Kearney vis. prof. Mental Health Rsch. Inst. Victoria, Australia, 2002; prof. fellow dept. psychiatry U. Melbourne, 2003—; assoc. chief of staff geriat. and extended care Ctrl. Ark. Vets. Healthcare Sys., 2003—04; lectr. and spkr. in field. Author: (with others) Principles of Neurologic Diagnosis, 1985, Hormone Therapy and the Brain, 2000; mem. editl. bd. profl. jours.; contbr. articles to profl. jours. Recipient Simons Lecture, Alzheimer's Assn. (Boston chpt.), 1995, Solvay Lecture, British Menopause Soc., 1997, Rsch. award, Alzheimer's Assn. (LA chpt.), 1998, Faculty Recognition award, Phi Kappa Phi, 2001, Vis. Rsch. Scholars award, U. Melbourne Collaborative Research Program, 2002; grantee, Alzheimer's Assn., Calif. Dept. Health Svcs., Adminstrn. on Aging, NIH, French Found., 1984—. Fellow: Am. Acad. Neurology (Lawrence McHenry award 2007); mem.: Internat. Soc. for History of Neuroscis., N.Am. Menopause Soc. (trustee 2002—, pres.-elect 2006—), French Found. Alzheimer Rsch., Nat. Aphasia Assn., Internat. Menopause Soc., Internat. Neuropsychol. Soc., Soc. for Behavioral and Cognitive Neurology, Gerontol. Soc. Am., Acad. Aphasia, Am. Neurol. Assn. Office: Stanford U Sch Medicine 259 Campus Dr HRP Redwood Bldg Stanford CA 94305-5405

HENDERSON, WADE J., civil rights advocate, law educator; b. 1948; BA, Howard U.; JD, Rutgers U., Newark. Bar: DC, NJ, US Supreme Ct. Asst. dean & dir. minority affairs Rutgers Univ. Sch. Law; exec. dir. Council on Legal Edn. Opportunity; assoc. dir. nat. office ACLU, Washington; dir. Washington Bureau NAACP; exec. dir. & counsel to Edn. Fund Leadership Conf. on Civil Rights, Washington; Joseph L. Rauh Jr. Prof. Pub. Interest Law David A. Clarke Sch. Law, Univ. of DC, 1999—. Recipient Civil Rights Leadership award, Israeli Embassy & Religious Action Ctr Reform Judaism, 1999, Everett C. Parker award, United Church of Christ, William J. Brennan award, DC Bar, 2002, Cong. Black Caucus Chair award, 2003. Office: Leadership Conference on Civil Rights 10th Fl 1629 K St NW Washington DC 20006 Office Phone: 202-466-3311.

HENDERSON, WILLIAM CHARLES, editor; b. Phila., Apr. 5, 1941; s. Francis Louis and Dorothy Price (Galloway) H. BA, Hamilton Coll., 1963; postgrad., Harvard U., 1963, U. Pa., 1965-66. Assoc. editor Doubleday & Co., NYC, 1972-73; pub. Pushcart Press, Wainscott, NY, 1972—; sr. editor Coward, McCann & Geohagan, Inc., NYC, 1973-75; cons. editor Harper & Row Inc., 1976—. Guest lectr. Harvard U., 1974, Sarah Lawrence Coll., U. Rochester, 1978, 87; lectr. Columbia U., 1978-80, Princeton U., 1984, 86-87, Johns Hopkins U., 1989, Radcliffe Pub. Course, 1989; nat. adv. bd. Ctr. for the Book Library of Congress, 1979; pres. Pushcart Found.; fiction judge Nat. Book Award, 2001. Author: His Son: A Child of the Fifties, 1981, The Kid That Could, 1990, Her Father, 1995, Tower, 2000, Simple Gifts, 2006; editor, pub.: The Publish It Yourself Handbook, 1973, The Pushcart Prize: Best of the Small Presses, 1976—, The Pushcart Book of Short Stories, 2002; editor: Rotten Reviews, 1986, Minutes of the Lead Pencil Club, 1996. Recipient Author award NJ English Tchrs. Assn., 1972, Newsboy award Horatio Alger Soc., 1973, Carey-Thomas award Publishers Weekly, 1978, Poor Richard award, 2001, Ivan Sandrof Lifetime Achievement award Nat. Book Critics Cir., 2006, Writers for Writers award Poets and Writerse/Barnes and Noble, 2006. Mem. P.E.N., The Lead Pencil Club (founder). Home and Office: Pushcart Press PO Box 380 Wainscott NY 11975-0380 Office Phone: 631-324-9300.

HENDIN, DAVID BRUCE, literary agent, writer, numismatist, educator; b. St. Louis, Dec. 16, 1945; s. Aaron and Lillian (Karsh) H.; m. Jeannie Luciano, Oct. 4, 1985; children: Sarah Tsvia, Benjamin Judah, Alexander Jacob. BS in Biology Edn, U. Mo., 1967, MA in Journalism, 1970. Sr. v.p., editorial dir., pub. United Feature Syndicate, Inc., NYC, 1970—93; clin. prof. off campus U. Mo. Sch. Journalism, 1971-86; pres. Pharos Books, 1992-3, DH Literary, Inc., Nyack, NY, 1993—. Adj. lectr. Columbia U. Sch. Journalism, 1974-76; numismatist Joint Sepphoris Excavation, 1985-88. Author: Everything You Need to Know About Abortion, 1971, The Doctor's Save-Your-Heart Diet, 1972, Death As a Fact of Life, 1973, 1984, Save Your Child's Life, 1973, 1986, The Life Givers, 1975, Guide to Ancient Jewish Coins, 1975, The World Almanac Whole Health Guide, 1977, The Genetic Connection, 1978, Collecting Coins, 1979, Guide to Biblical Coins, 1987, 1996, 2000, Not Kosher: Forgeries of Ancient Jewish and Biblical Coins, 2004, Ancient Scale Weights, 2007; mem. editl. bd. Israel Numismatic Jour., 1992—96, Publs. Bd. Union Am. Hebrew Congregations, 1993. Bd. dir. Holyland Conservation Fund, 1973-83; v.p. Council Advancement Sci. Writing, 1975-84; trustee Scripps-Howard Found., 1978-87, Kinsey Inst., 1985-92, Mus. Cartoon Art, 1986-92; chmn. numis. com. The Jewish Mus., 1980-85; mem. adv. com. Sch. Journalims, U. Fla., 1991-97. Recipient award merit Am. Assn. Blood Banks, 1972, Claude Bernard Sci. Journalism award, 1972, cert. commendation Am. Acad. Family Physicians, 1973, Med. Journalism award AMA, 1973, Blakeslee award Am. Heart Assn., 1973, Book of Yr. award Am. Med. Writers Assn., 1977, Best Column award Numismatic Literary Guild, 1993, 2000, Ben Odesser Judaic Literary award 1997, Disting. Alumni award Ladue H.S., 2002, Pres. award Am. Numismatic Assn., 2003. Fellow: Am. Numismatic Soc. (life); mem.: Coun. for Advancement Sci. Writing, Ancient Coin Collectors Guild (treas. 2003—), Am.-Israel Numismatic Assn. (v.p. 1979—85), Sigma Alpha Mu, Kappa Tau Alpha. Office: PO Box 805 Nyack NY 10960-0990 Personal E-mail: dhendin@aol.com.

HENDIN, JOSEPHINE GATTUSO, language educator, writer; m. Herbert Hendin, June 7, 1968; children: Neil, Erik. BA, CCNY, 1960—64; MA, Columbia U., 1964—65, PhD, 1964—68. Asst. prof. Yale U., New Haven, 1968—69; adj. prof. New Sch. Social Rsch., New York, 1969—79; prof. NYU, 1979—, tiro a segno prof. italian am. studies, 2001—. Author: The Right Thing to Do (Am. Book award, 1989), Vulnerable People: A View of American Fiction Since 1945, 1978 (Notable Book Yr., 1978), Heartbreakers: Women and Violence in Contemporary Culture and Literature, 2004, The World of Flannery O'Connor, 1970; contbr. The Bostonians, articles to profl. jours.; editor: Concise Companion to Postwar American Literature and Culture, 2004. Dir., expository writing program NYU, 1983, chair, English dept., 1995—99. Recipient Elena Lucrezia Cornaro award, Nat. Order Sons and Daughters Columbus, 1983-1984, Am. Book Award, Before Columbus Found., 1989; fellow Woodrow Wilson Fellowship, Woodrow Wilson Found., 1964-1966, Vera B. David Fellowship, Columbia U., 1965-1966, President's Fellowship, 1967-1968, John Simon Guggenheim Fellowship, John Simon Guggenheim Found., 1975-1976. Mem.: MLA, Nat. Book Critics Cir., Am. Italian Hist. Assn. (mem. exec. bd. 2001), Nat. Italian Am. Found. Avocations: speedwalking, travel, reading. Office: NYU English Dept 19 University Pl New York NY 10003 Personal E-mail: josephine.hendin@nyu.edu.

HENDLER, JAMES ALEXANDER, computer science educator, consultant; b. NYC, Apr. 2, 1957; s. Samuel I. and Marjorie J. (Rosenblum) H.; m. Terry Spring Horowit, June 16, 1985; 1 child, Sharone Horowit-Hendler. BS in Computer Sci., Yale U., 1978; MS in Psychology, So. Meth. U., 1982; ScM in Computer Sci., Brown U., 1983, PhD in Computer Sci., 1986. Instr. dept. computer sci. Wellesley (Mass.) Coll., 1983, 84; lectr. dept. psychology Brown U., Providence, 1984; asst. prof. computer sci. U. Md., College Park, 1986-92, with Inst. Sys. Rsch., 1988—, with Inst. Advanced Computer Studies, 1988—, head Parallel Understanding Sys. Lab., 1989—2005, dir. Joint Inst. for Knowledge Discovery, 2005—, assoc. prof. computer sci., 1992—99, prof. computer sci., 1999—, head, founder Autonomous Mobile Robotics Lab., 1993—2002; dir. semantic web tech. Md. Info. and Network Dynamics Lab., 2001—, dir., 2004—07; Tetherless World Constellation prof., endowed chair Renssalaer Polytech. Inst., Troy, NY, 2007—. Vis. scientist Internat. Computer Sci. Inst., Berkeley, Calif., 1989, Australian AI Inst., Melbourne, 1991; vis. rschr. NEC Corp., Miyazaki-dia, Japan, 1992; vis. prof. Bar-Ilan U., Ramat Gan, Israel, 1994, Hebrew U., Jerusalem, 1995-96, U. Edinburgh, Scotland, 2006; cons. Pfizer Pharmaceuticals, Sandwich, Eng., 1984—, Gould Corp., 1984-85, Symbolics, Inc., 1984, Dept. Energy, 1988, Traisys Inc., 1989—, others; guest lectr. IBM, 1991; program mgr. Def. Advanced Rsch. Project Agy., 1999-2001; chief sci., 2000-01; chief scientist Info. Sys. office Def. Advanced Rsch. Project Agy., 2000—, Data Grid Corp., 2007-; co-founder Semantic Web. Author: Integrating Marker-passing and Problem Solving: A spreading activation approach to improved choice in planning, 1987; editor: Expert Systems: The User Interface, 1987, Artificial Intelligence Planning Systems: Procs. of First International Conference, 1992, Massively Parallel Artificial Intelligence, 1994, Robots for Kids, 2000, Spinning the Semantic Web, 2003; editor-in-chief IEEE Intelligent Systems, 2005-; bd. rev. editors Sci., 2005-; co-editor: Readings in Planning, 1990, Semantic Web Technology, 2001; contbr. numerous articles to profl. jours., chpts. to books. Bd. dirs. Beth Tikva Synagogue, Rockville, Md., 1990, v.p. 1998—; v.p. Tikvat Israel Congregation, 1999-2005; mem. Inst. for Def. Analysis Def. Sci. Study Group, 1996-97; mem. sci. adv. bd. USAF, 1999-2003, 2007; pres. Tikvat Israel Congregation, 2006. Fulbright fellow Ctr. Internat. Exch. Scholars, 1995, founding Rsch. fellow Kiss Inst. Practical Robotics, 1994; decorated Exceptional Civilian Svc. Medal, USAF, 2002; named hon. fellow U. Edinburgh, Scotland, 2006. Fellow Am. Assn. Artificial Intelligence (chair symposium com. 1993-94, workshop program 1992, conf. com. 2001-05, Robert Engelmore Meml. Lecture prize 2005). Democrat. Jewish. Avocations: scuba diving, travel. Office: RPI Dept Computer Sci 110 8th St Troy NY 12180 Home Phone: 301-871-2210; Office Phone: 301-405-2662.

HENDLER, NELSON HOWARD, physician, health facility administrator, director; b. NYC, Aug. 15, 1944; s. Albert and Winifred (Siff) H.; m. Lee Meyerhoff, Oct. 20, 1974 (div. Nov. 2005); children: Lee Samuel, Alexander, Lindsay, Josepha. BA, Princeton U., 1966; MD, U. Md., 1972, MS, 1974. Diplomate Am. Bd. Psychiatry and Neurology. Resident in psychiatry Johns Hopkins Hosp., Balt., 1975; asst. prof. neurosurgery sch. medicine Johns Hopkins U., 1975—2006; owner, clin. dir. Mensana Clinic, Stevenson, Md., 1978—2006; assoc. prof. physiology sch. dental surgery U. Md., 1986—2006; CEO, Mensana Clinic Diagnostics, 2006. Pres. Reflex Sympathetic Dystrophy Syndrome of Am., 1995-97. Author: Diagnosis and Non-Surgical Management of Chronic Pain, 1981; (with others) Coping with Chronic Pain, 1979; editor Diagnosis and Treatment of Chronic Pain, 1982; contbr. articles to profl. jours., chpts. to books; co-patentee direct current motor protector. Bd. dirs. Md. Mental Health Assn., Balt., 1976-78, Balt. Zool. Soc., 1978-85; bd. dirs. Am. Orgn. Rehab. through Tng., 1983—, pres. Balt. chpt.; bd. dirs. Am. Technion Soc., 1980-92, pres. Balt. chpt. Recipient Janet Travell award Am. Acad. Pain Mgmt.; Falk fellow Am. Psychiat. Assn., 1975. Fellow Acad. Psychosomatic Medicine, Am. Psychiatric Assn.; mem. Am. Inst. Stress (v.p. 1978-89), Internat. Soc. Study of Pain, Am. Acad. Pain Mgmt. (bd. dirs. 2002—, pres. 2006), Am. Pain Found. (bd. dirs. 1997-01), Israeli Pain Soc. (hon.), Princeton U. Alumni Assn. Md. (bd. dirs., pres.), Princeton Club NYC, Safari Internat. Club, Loch Raven Skeet and Trap Club. Republican. Jewish. Avocations: bird hunting, skeet and trap shooting, fishing, record big game hunter. Office: Mensana Clinic 1718 Greenspring Valley Rd Stevenson MD 21153-0642 Office Phone: 410-653-2403. Personal E-mail: docmelse@aol.com.

HENDLEY, DAN LUNSFORD, retired finance company executive; b. Nashville, Apr. 26, 1938; s. Frank E. and Mattie (Lunsford) H.; m. Patricia Fariss, June 18, 1960; children: Dan Lunsford, Laura Kathleen. BA, Vanderbilt U., 1960; grad., Rutgers U., 1969; postgrad., Program Mgmt. Devel., Harvard, 1972. With Fed. Res. Bank Atlanta, 1962-73, v.p., officer in charge Birmingham br., 1969-73; v.p., exec. v.p. AmSouth Bancorp, 1973-77; exec. v.p. First Nat. Bank Birmingham, 1976-77, pres., 1977-79, chmn. bd., chief exec. officer, 1979-83; pres., chief operating officer, bd. dirs. Am South Bank, N.A., 1983-90; v.p. bus. affairs Samford U., Birmingham, Ala., 1991-94; ret., 1994. Trustee Children's Hosp., Samford U. With Tenn. Air N.G., 1961-67. Mem. Kiwanis, Mountain Brook Club, Shoal Creek Club, The Club. Baptist. Home: 3258 Dell Rd Birmingham AL 35223-1318 Personal E-mail: danandpet@charter.net.

HENDRA, BARBARA JANE, public relations executive; b. Watertown, NY; d. Frederick R. and Irene J. H. BA, Vassar Coll., 1960. Dir. publicity Fawcett World Libr., NYC, 1961—69; v.p., dir. publicity and pub. rels. Pocket Books-Simon & Schuster, NYC, 1969—77; corp. dir. publicity and pub. rels. Putnam Pub. Group, NYC, 1977—79; pres. Barbara J. Hendra Assocs., Inc., NYC, 1979—91, The Hendra Agy. Inc, Bklyn., 1991—. Adj. prof. NYU, 1981. Contbg. author: Trade Book Marketing, 1983, The Encyclopedia of Publishing, 1995. Mem. Pubs. Publicity Assn. (bd. dirs. 1977-81, pres. 1979-81), Publicity Club N.Y., Soc. Profl. Journalists, Women's Media Group, Nat. Book Critics Cir., Vassar Club, Regency Whist Club. Home: 140 Sterling Pl Brooklyn NY 11217-3307 Office: The Hendra Agy Inc 142 Sterling Pl Brooklyn NY 11217-3307 Home Phone: 778-789-6032; Office Phone: 718-622-3232.

HENDREN, ROBERT LEE, JR., academic administrator; b. Reno, Oct. 10, 1925; s. Robert Lee and Aleen (Hill) H.; m. Merlyn Churchill, June 14, 1947; children: Robert Lee IV, Anne Aleen. BA magna cum laude, Coll. Idaho, LLD (hon.); postgrad., Army Univ. Ctr., Oahu, Hawaii. Owner, pres. Hendren's Inc., 1947—; pres. Albertson Coll. Idaho, Caldwell, 1987—. Bd. dirs. 1st Interstate Bank Idaho. Trustee Boise (Idaho) Ind. Sch. Dist., chmn. bd. trustees, 1966; chmn. bd. trustees Coll. Idaho, 1980-84; bd. dirs. Mountain View coun. Boy Scouts Am., Boise Retail Merchants, Boise Valley Indsl. Found., Boise Redevel. Agy., Ada County Marriage Counseling, Ada County Planning and Zoning Com.; chmn. bd. Blue Cross Idaho. Recipient Silver and Gold award U. Idaho, Nat. award Sigma Chi. Mem. Boise C. of C. (pres., bd. dirs.), Idaho Sch. Trustees Assn., Masons, KT, Shriners, Rotary (Paul Harris fellow). Home: 3504 Hillcrest Dr Boise ID 83705-4503 Office: Albertson Coll Idaho 2112 Cleveland Blvd Caldwell ID 83605-4432

HENDREN, WILLIAM HARDY, III, surgeon; b. Feb. 7, 1926; BA, Dartmouth Coll., Hanover, New Hampshire, 1948; MD, Harvard Med. Sch., Boston, 1952; D in Med. Sci. honoris causa, U. d'Aix Marseille, France, 1983, Drexel U., Phila., 2004. Cert. gen. surgery Am. Bd. Surgery, thoracic surgery Am. Bd. Surgery, pediat. surgery Am. Bd. Surgery. Chief pediat. surgery Mass. Gen. Hosp., Boston, 1960—82; chief surgery Children's Hosp., Boston, 1982—98, chief emeritus surgery, 1998—; honorary surgeon Mass. Gen., 2004—. Editor: (book) Biography: The Work of Human Hands, 1993; contbr. chapters to books. Hon. Fellow, Royal Coll. Surgeons (Ireland), Royal Coll. Surgeons (Eng.), Royal Coll. Surgeons (Glasgow). Fellow: ACS (v.p. 1998); mem.: Am. Acad. Pediatricians (chmn. surgery sect. 1978), Brit. Assn. Pedit. Surgeons, Am. Urol. Assn., Am. Surg. Soc., Am. Pediat. Surg. Assn. (pres. 1981—83), New Eng. Surg. Soc. (pres. 1992), Boston Surg. Soc. (pres. 1998). Home: 247 King Ceasar Rd Duxbury MA 02332 Office: Childrens Hosp 300 Longwood Ave Boston MA 02115

HENDRICK, BENARD CALVIN, VII, lawyer; b. Odessa, Tex., Oct. 7, 1964; s. Benard Calvin VI and Marita Hendrick; m. Amy Camille Weatherby, Nov. 17, 1990; children: Benard Calvin VIII, Kaitlin Camille. BBA summa cum laude, Angelo State U., San Angelo, Tex., 1987; JD, U. Tex., 1990. Bar: Tex. 1990, U.S. Dist. Ct. (ea., we. and no. dists.) Tex. 1991, U.S. Ct. Appeals (5th cir.) 1995. Assoc. Shafer, Davis, Ashley, O'Leary & Stoker, Odessa, 1990-92, ptnr., 1992—. Ct. apptd. spl. advocate CASA, 2006—. Bd. dirs. Permian Basin Rehab. Ctr., Odessa, 1992-97, Crystal Ball Found., Odessa, 1993-96, Parker House Ranching Mus., 2002—, Black River-A Ctr. for Learning, 1998-2004, Jim Parker Little League Baseball, 2000—; sec. Odessa Youth Baseball Assn., 2004—, bd. mem., 2004-; elder First Christian Ch., Odessa, 1995-98, 2000-2003, trustee, 2006—. Fellow Tex. Bar Found.; mem. Tex. Assn. Def. Counsel (young lawyers com. 1998-2000), State Bar Tex., Ector County Bar Assn. (pres. 1998-99), Ector County Young Lawyers Assn. (pres. 1995), Def. Rsch. Inst. Republican. Mem. Christian Ch. Avocations: hunting, fishing, tae kwon do (3d degree). Home: 2301 La Due Ln Odessa TX 79762 Office: Shafer Davis Ashley O'Leary & Stoker 700 N Grant Ave Ste 201 Odessa TX 79761-4576 Home Phone: 432-550-9889; Office Phone: 432-332-0893. Business E-Mail: chendrick@shaferfirm.com.

HENDRICK, GEORGE, retired English language educator; b. Stephenville, Tex., Mar. 30, 1929; s. Hoyt and Bessie Lea (Sears) H.; m. Willene Lowery, Jan. 21, 1955; 1 dau., Sarah. BA, Tex. Christian U., 1948, MA, 1950; PhD, U. Tex., 1954. Mem. English faculty S.W. Tex. State U., 1954-56, U. Colo., 1956-60; prof. Am. studies J.W. Goethe U., Frankfurt, Germany, 1960-65; prof. U. Ill., Chgo., 1965-67, Urbana, 1967-99, spl. curator Univ. Libr., 1994-97. Author: Katherine Anne Porter, 1965, Henry Salt: Humanitarian Reformer and Man of Letters, 1977, Remembrances of Concord and the Thoreaus, 1977, (with Fritz Oehlschlaeger) Toward the Making of Thoreau's Modern Reputation, 1980, (with Willene Hendrick) On the Frontier: Dr. Hiram Rutherford, 1981, Thoreau Amongst Friends and Philistines, 1982, (with Margaret Sandburg) Ever the Winds of Chance, 1983, the Selected Letters of Mark Van Doren, 1987; (with Willene Hendrick) Katherine Anne Porter, rev. edit., 1988, Fables, Foibles, and Foobles, 1988, (with Willene Hendrick) The Savour of Salt: A Henry Salt Anthology, 1989, To Reach Eternity: The Letters of James Jones, 1989, (with Willene Hendrick) Ham Jones, Antebellum Southern Humorist: An Anthology, 1990, (with Willene Hendrick and Fritz Oehlschlaeger) Salt's Life of Thoreau, 1993, More Rootabagas, 1993, (with Willene Hendrick) Billy Sunday and Other Poems, 1993 (with Nancy Romero) Literary Treasures of the University Library, 1995, (with Willene Hendrick) Selected Poems of Carl Sandburg, 1996, (with Nancy Romero and Maarten van de Guchte) Alvin Langdon Coburn and H.G. Wells: The Photographer and the Novelist, 1997, (with Willene Hendrick) Incidents in the Life of A Slave Girl and A True Tale of Slavery, 1999, (with Barbara Jones and Jean Geil) Learning About Lincoln at the University of Illinois at Urbana-Champaign, 1999, (with Willene Hendrick) Two Slave Rebellions at Sea: The Heroic Slave by Frederick Douglass and Benito Cereno by Herman Melville, 2000, (with Howe and Sackrider) James Jones and the Handy Writers' Colony, 2001, (with Howe and Sackrider) Writings from the Handy Colony, 2001, (with Willene Hendrick) The Creole Mutiny: A Tale of Revolt Aboard A Slave Ship, 2003, (with Willene Hendrick) Fleeing for Freedom: Stories of the Underground Railroad, 2004, (with Willene Hendrick) Why Not Every Man? African Americans and Civil Disobedience and the Quest for the Dream, 2005. Grantee Am. Coun. Learned Socs., Ford Found., NEH. Mem. MLA, James Jones Soc. (pres. 1991-92). Home: 502 W Main St Apt 122 Urbana IL 61801-2537

HENDRICK, HAL WILMANS, human factors educator; b. Dallas, Mar. 11, 1933; s. Harold Eugene and Audrey Sarah (Wilmans) H.; m. Mary Francis Boyle; children: Hal L., David A., John A. (dec.), Jennifer G. BA, Ohio Wesleyan U., 1955; MS, Purdue U., 1961, PhD, 1966. Cert. profl. ergonomist; bd. cert. forensic examiner. Asst. prof. U. So. Calif., LA, assoc. prof., 1979-86; exec. dir. Inst. of Safety and Systems Mgmt., U. So. Calif., LA, 1986-87; prof., dean Coll. of System Sci., U. Denver, 1987-90; prof. U. So. Calif., 1986-95, prof. emeritus LA, 1995—; prin. Hendrick and Assocs., Greenwood Village, Colo., 1996—2004; pres. Found. for Profl. Ergonomics, Highlands Ranch, Colo., 2004—07. Pres. Bd. Cert. in Profl. Ergonomics, 1992-94. Author: Behavioral Research and Analysis, 1980, 2d edit., 1989, 3rd edit., 1990, Good Ergonomics is Good Economics, 1996, Macroergonomics: An Introduction to Work System Design, 2001, Human Factors Issues in Handgun Safety and Forensics, 2007; editor 11 books; contbr. articles to profl. jours. Lt. col. USAF, 1956-76. Fellow APA, Am. Psychol. Soc., Human Factors Ergonomics Soc. (pres. L.A. chpt. 1986-87, 95-96, pres. Rocky Mountain chpt. 1989-90, pres. 1995-96), Internat. Ergonomics Assn. (pres. Geneva 1990-94, sec. gen. 1987-89, exec. com. 1984—2000, U.S. rep. 1981-87); mem. Ergonomics Soc. (U.K.), Soc. for Indsl. and Orgnl. Psychology. Democrat. Avocations: travel, camping, hiking, reading, fishing. Home and Office: 2901 Fairway View Ct Castle Rock CO 80108 Office Phone: 303-843-6325. Personal E-mail: hhendrick@aol.com.

HENDRICK, JAMES T., lawyer; b. Fostoria, Ohio, Mar. 21, 1942; BA with honors and distinction in econs., U. Ill., 1963; JD, Harvard U., 1967. Bar: Ill. 1967, Calif. 1970. Ptnr. Thelen, Reid & Priest (formerly known as Thelen, Marrin, Johnson & Bridges), San Francisco, 1978—. Lt. USN JAG, 1968-71. Mem. ABA. Office: Thelen Reid & Priest 101 2nd St Ste 1800 San Francisco CA 94105-3659 Office Phone: 415-371-1200.

HENDRICK, JOSEPH RIDDICK, III, (RICK), race team owner; b. Warrenton, NC, July 12, 1949; m. Linda Hendrick. Co-founder Hendrick Automotive Group, NC; founder Hendrick Motorsports (formerly All-Star Racing), NC, 1984, now chmn., CEO NC. Technical advisor Days of Thunder, 1990. Founder Hendrick Found. for Children; founder, bd. mem. Hendrick Marrow Program, 1997—. Decorated Order of the Long Leaf Pine; co-recipient Leadership for Life Award, Marrow Found., 1999; recipient Horatio Alger Award, 2006. Mem.: NC Motorsports Assn. (vice chmn.). Achievements include being the car owner for six NEXTEL Cup championships, one Busch Series championship and three Craftsman Truck Series championships. Office: Hendrick Motor Sports Ltd 5315 Stowe Lane Harrisburg NC 28075*

HENDRICKS, DAVID WESLEY, engineering executive; b. Dallas, Feb. 4, 1962; s. Ed Jerald and Susan Meredith Hendricks; m. Catherine Band, Dec. 12, 1992; children: Benjamin W., Laura A. BS in Math. & Computer Scis., Stanford, Calif., 1980—84; MS in Computer Sci., Stanford U., Calif., 1984—86. Mem. of tech. staff Sun Microsys., Mt. View, Calif., 1986—90, staff engr., engrng. mgr. Grenoble, France, 1990—99, sr. engrng. mgr. Menlo Park, Calif., 1999—2004, dir., software engrng., 2004—05; sr. dir. software engrng. Precision I/O, Palo Alto, Calif., 2005; vp software engrng. Kestrel Wireless, Emeryville, Calif., 2006—. Contbr. articles to profl. jours. Mem.: IEEE (assoc.). Achievements include patents for method and apparatus for translucent file system. Avocations: bicycling, exercise. Home Phone: 650-251-9171. Personal E-mail: dave.hendricks@yahoo.com.

HENDRICKS, J(AMES) EDWIN, historian, educator, consultant, author; b. Pickens, SC, Oct. 19, 1935; s. J.E. and Cassie (Looper) H.; m. Sue James, June 28, 1958; children— James, Christopher, Lee BA, Furman U., 1957; MA, U. Va., 1959, PhD, 1961. Vis. prof. history U. Va., Charlottesville, summer 1961; asst. prof. history Wake Forest U., Winston-Salem, NC, 1961-66, assoc. prof., 1966-75, prof., 1975—, chmn. dept. history, 1995-99, dir. Hist. Preservation Program, 1973—. Vis. prof. history U. Tex.-El Paso, summer 1965; preservation cons.; vis. dir. Mus. Albermarle, Elizabeth City, N.C., summer 1975; dir. Preservation Field Sch., summers 1983-86, 88-90, 92-95. Author: (with others) Liquor and Anti-Liquor in Virginia, 1619-1919, 1967; Charles Thomson and the Making of a Nation, 1729-1824, 1979; editor, contbg. author: Forsyth, The History of a County on the March, 1976; author: Wake Forest University School of Law; One Hundred Years of Legal Education, 1994, Seeking Liberty and Justice: A History of the North Carolina Bar Association, 1999. Pres. Hist. Winston, 1979—; chmn. Winston-Salem/Forsyth County Hist. Dists. Commn., 1978-79; pres. Wachovia Hist. Soc., 1983-87. Served with U.S. Army, 1958-59. Recipient R.J. Reynolds rsch. leave, 1973, 87, 2001, 07; Am. Philos. Soc. rsch. grantee, 1969, 70. Mem. N.C. Lit. and Hist. Assn. (pres. 1980-81), Hist. Soc. N.C., So. Hist. Assn., Nat. Trust Hist. Preservation, others Lodges: Kiwanis (pres. 1987-88), Torch (pres. Winston-Salem 1987-88). Democrat. Baptist. Office: Wake Forest U Dept History PO Box 7806 Winston Salem NC 27109-7806 Office Phone: 336-758-5550.

HENDRICKS, JAMES POWELL, artist; b. Little Rock, Aug. 7, 1938; s. Leland Fuller and Christia Beatrice (Powell) H.; m. Betty Jean Fleming,

Nov. 6, 1960 (div. 1977); children: Elizabeth Jane, Valerie Lee; m. Marcia Reed-Hendricks, 1978 (div.); m. Leslie Jill Cernak, 1999. BA, U. Ark., 1962; M.F.A., U. Iowa, 1964. Instr. art State U. Iowa, 1962-64, Mt. Holyoke Coll., 1964-65; mem. faculty U. Mass., Amherst, 1965—, prof. art, 1977—, dir. undergrad. programs in art, 1968-71, dir. grad. programs art, 1974-77, prof. emeritus, 2004. Vis. artist Seoul Inst. of the Arts, Korea, 1986, Portland Sch. Arts, Maine, 1985, San Diego State U., 1986, Internat. Artist Colony, Ctr. Contemporary Visual Arts, Prilep, Macedonia, 1994. One-man shows include Nat. Air and Space Mus., Smithsonian Instn., fall 1969, Hudson River Mus., Yonkers, NY, 1970, U. Mass., Amherst, 1971-78, French and Co. Gallery, NYC, 1972, Warren Benedek Gallery, NYC, 1974, Helen Shlien Gallery, Boston, 1980, 82, 84, Smith Coll., Northampton, Mass., 1983, 84, SUNY, Oswego, 1983, Deerfield Acad., Mass., 1984, Portland Sch. Art, 1985, Space Art Gallery, Seoul, 1986, Mus. Fine Arts, Springfield, Mass., 1986, Slater-Price Fine Arts Gallery, NYC, 1989-90, Ark. Arts Ctr., Little Rock, 1993, Anderson Gallery, 1993, Art Gallery at Macedonia, Skopje, 1994, Westwood Gallery, Inc., NYC, 1996, 2001-02, 07, Hart Gallery, Northampton, Mass., 1996; group exhbns. include, Nat. Gallery Art, 1970, Nat. Air and Space Mus., 1976, 4th Internat. Biennial, Medellín, Colombia, 1981, Seoul Inst. Arts, Korea, in conjunction with World Olympics Arts Festival, 1988, Joy Moos Gallery, Miami, Fla., 1991, Ark. Arts Ctr., Little Rock, 1993, Vesti-dane Gallery, Scottsdale, Ariz., 1997; comms. include: Nat. Gallery Art, NASA, cover for Time mag., 1971, 2 album covers for Neuma Records, Fall 1991; cover commn. for The Mass. Rev., Vol. XXXVII, No. 4, Winter, 1997. Named Ark. Traveler, 1971

HENDRICKS, JOHN S., broadcast executive; b. 1952; BA magna cum laude, U. Ala., Huntsville, 1973, PhD (hon.), 1991. Gov. rels. dir. U. Ala., Huntsville, 1972—73; corp. rels. dir. U. Md., College Park, 1973—78; chmn., CEO The Disney Channel Discovery Comm., Inc., Bethesda, Md., 1982—. Bd. dirs. US Olympic Com., Am. Film Inst., James Madison Coun., Libr. of Congress; adv. bd. Lowell Observatory; bd. trustees U. Md. Coll. Park Found. Mem.: Nat. Cable TV Assn. (bd. mem.), Am. Assn. Univ. Cons. (founder). Office: Discovery Comm, Inc 1 Discovery Place Silver Spring MD 20910*

HENDRICKS, KENNETH, wholesale distribution executive; b. Sept. 8, 1941; m. Dianne Hendricks; 7 children. Founder, CEO, chmn. ABC Supply, Beloit, Wis., 1982—. Owner AmCraft Bldg. Products, Mulehide Products, Hendricks Devel. Group, Corporate Contractors, Inc., Cay Home Furnishing, Fed. Heath Sign Co., Pur Pac, Stratford Simmons. Named Entrepreneur of Yr., Inc. Mag., 2006; named one of Richest People in Am., Forbes mag., 2004—, World's Richest People, 2006—. Achievements include the use of eco-friendly roofing materials. Office: ABC Supply One ABC Pkwy Beloit WI 53511-4466 Office Phone: 608-362-7777. Office Fax: 608-362-2717.*

HENDRICKS, STANLEY MARSHALL, II, executive recruiter, consultant; b. Richmond, Ky., Nov. 15, 1952; s. Stanley Marshall and Margaret Cathleen (Cox) H.; m. Sara Jane Sargent, Aug. 9, 1975; children: Stanley M. III, Elizabeth Jean. BS, Ind. State U., 1976; post baccalaureate degree, Ind. U. Northwest, 1984. Cert. personnel cons. Assoc. A.R. Massena & Assocs., Merrillville, Ind., 1976-77; co-founder, owner Nat. Recruiting Svc., Dyer, Ind., 1977—. Mem. coun. Ind. State U., Terre Haute, 1983-88; pres. Ind. State U. Alumni Coun.; elder, trustee Immanuel Presbyn. Ch., Schererville, Ind., 1978—; bd. dirs., sec. Dollars for Scholars. Mem. Assn. Iron and Steel Engrs., Nat. Assn. Pers. Cons., Fabricating Mfrs. Assn., Iron and Steel Soc., Ind. Soc. Chgo., Am. Tube Assn., Internat. Tube Assn., Ind. State U. Alumni Assn. (v.p., coun. pres.), Order of Omega (hon.), Ky. Cols. (hon.), Rotary (pres., bd. dirs., Paul Harris fellow, asst. dist. gov.), Sycamore Club N.W. Ind. (bd. dirs. 1984-88), Tri-Town Optimist Club (charter). Avocations: flying, woodworking, scuba diving, swimming. Home: 1742 Silver Hawk Dr Crown Point IN 46307 E-mail: stanhen@jorsm.com.

HENDRICKSON, ANITA ELIZABETH, biology professor; b. LaCross, Wis., Feb. 20, 1936; d. Walter V. and Alno (Larkin) Schnell; m. Morris N. Hendrickson, June 8, 1957; children: Lisa, Karin, Gordon. BA, Pacific Luth. Coll., 1957; PhD, U. Wash., Seattle, 1964. Instr. anatomy Northwestern Med. Sch., Chgo., 1964-65; rsch. assoc. Children's Meml. Hosp., Chgo., 1964-65; rsch. instr. dept. biol. structure U. Wash., Seattle, 1965-67, instr. dept. ophthalmology, 1967-69, asst. prof. dept. ophthalmology, 1969-73; affiliate/assoc. prof. dept. ophthalmology Reg. Primate Ctr./U. Wash., 1972—, 1973-81; affiliate Child Devel. & Mental Retardation Ctr., U. Wash., 1975; prof. dept. opthalmology U. Wash., 1981-97, prof. dept. biol. structure, 1984—, chair dept. biol. structure, 1994—, adj. prof. ophthalmology, 1997—. Vis. assoc. prof. neuropathology Harvard Med. Sch., Boston, 1975-76; adj. assoc. prof. dept. psychology U. Wash., 1975-78; mem. NIH VisB study section, 1976-80. Editorial bd. Jour. of Neurosci., 1982-88, Investigative Ophthalmology, 1977-82, Vision Research, 1990-95; contbr. articles to profl. jours. Dolly Green rsch. grantee, 1981; named Alumnus of the Yr., Pacific Luth. U., 1982. Mem. AAAS, Am. Assn. Anatomists, Soc. for Neurosci. (mem. nat. coun. 1982-86), Internat. Soc. for Eye Rsch., Assn. for Rsch. in Vision and Ophthalmology (prog. chmn. 1983-84, trustee 1993—), Cajal Club. Home: 1029C NE 120th St Seattle WA 98125-5003 Office: U Washington Dept Biol Structure Box 357420 Seattle WA 98195-7420

HENDRICKSON, BRUCE CARL, life insurance company executive; b. Holdrege, Nebr., Apr. 4, 1930; s. Carl R. and Ruth E. (Bosserman) H.; m. Carol Schepman, June 12, 1952; children: Julie, Mark Bruce. BA, U. Nebr., 1952. C.L.U., chartered fin. cons. Sr. agt. Prin. Life Ins. Co., Holdrege, 1950—. Bd. govs. Central Nebr. Tech. C.C.; mem. Nebr. Edn. Commn. of States, Nat. Hwy. Safety Advisors Com.; elder First Presbyterian Ch., Holdrege; pres. Holdrege City Council, 1979-86; pres. Phelps County Cmty. Found.; trustee U. Nebr. Found.; moderator Cen. Nebr. Presbytery, Presbyn. Ch. USA, 1986-88, Gen. Assembly Coun., 1998-2004; dir. Mus. Nebr. Art, 1996-2002; mem. pres. club U. Nebr., mem. chancellors club. Served with USNR, 1953-56. Bruce Hendrickson Week declared by Gov. of Nebr., 1975; recipient Distinguished Alumni Achievement award U. Nebr., 1977, Disting. Svc. award Nebr. State Assn. Life Underwriters, 1998. Mem. Nat. Assn. Life Underwriters (pres. 1975-76), Assn. Advanced Life Underwriting, Am. Soc. C.L.U.s., Life Underwriters Polit. Action Com. (chmn. 1989), Life Underwriters Tng. Coun. (trustee 1979-82), Million Dollar Round Table, Phi Kappa Psi. Clubs: Rotary (pres. 1960-61), Holdrege Country (Holdrege); Am. Legion, Elks. Republican. Office: Prin Fin Group PO Box 765 Holdrege NE 68949-0765

HENDRICKSON, CHRIS THOMPSON, civil and environmental engineering educator, researcher; b. Oakland, Calif., Mar. 31, 1950; s. Harold Thompson and E. Jean (Loomis) H.; m. Kathleen Devine, May 28, 1977; children: Andrew, Thomas, Peter. BS, MS, Stanford U., 1973; PhB, Oxford U., 1975; PhD, MIT, 1978. Asst. prof. Carnegie-Mellon U., Pitts., 1978-83, assoc. prof., 1983-87, prof., 1987—; assoc. dean Carnegie Inst. Tech., 1991-96, Duquesne Light Co. prof. engring., 1996—, head dept., 1996—2006. Author: (with others) Transportation Investment and Pricing Principles, 1984, Project Management for Construction, 1989, Knowledge-based Process Planning for Construction and Manufacturing, 1989, Computer Integrated Building Design, 1993, Evironmental Life Cycle Assessment of Goods and Services, 2005; editor Jour. Transp. Engring.; contbr. articles to profl. publs. Bd. mem. St. Edmund's Acad., Pitts., 2000-05. Recipient C.E. Ladd Rsch. award Carnegie Inst. Tech., 1979; Rhodes scholar, 1973. Fellow: AAAS; mem.: ASCE (hon.; com. chmn. 1983—2006, chmn. urban transp. divsn. 1989—90, dept. heads exec. com. 2000—02, Huber Rsch. award 1989, Masters Transp. Engring. award 1994, Fenves Systems award 2002, Turner Lecture award 2002), Transp. Rsch. Bd. (com. chmn. 1989—96), Am. Econ. Assn., Tau Beta Pi, Phi Beta Kappa. Home: 6933 Rosewood St Pittsburgh PA 15208-2638 Office: Carnegie Mellon U Pittsburgh PA 15213-3890 Office Phone: 412-268-2941.

HENDRICKSON, DAVID NORMAN, chemistry professor; b. Mpls., Jan. 1, 1943; s. Henry N. and Lorraine M. Hendrickson; m. Sherry J. Hendrickson, June 19, 1966; children: Shelley A. Radziminski, Susanne M. Desai. BS, UCLA, 1966; PhD, U. Calif., Berkeley, 1969; postgrad., Calif. Tech. U., 1970. From asst. prof. to assoc. prof. U. Ill., Urbana, 1970-78, prof., 1979-88, U. Calif., San Diego, 1989—. Fgn. expert Nanjing U. as part of World Bank Program for Refurbishing Univs. of China, 1984; vis. prof. Tokyo Met. U., 1986, U. Colo., Boulder, 1988, U. Sydney, Australia, 1990, Osaka (Japan) U., 1991; assoc. Ctr. Advanced Study, U. Ill., 1988. Contbr. numerous articles to rsch. jours. Councilor Am. Chem. Soc., Washington, 1986-88. Recipient Humboldt Found. Rsch. prize for sr. U.S. scientists, 1993; DuPont Young Faculty fellow, 1973, U. Ill. Ctr. for Advanced Study fellow, 1975, Camille and Henry Dreyfuss Tchr.-Scholar fellow, 1972-77, A. P. Sloan Found. fellow, 1976-78, Japan Soc. for Promotion of Sci. Sr. Faculty fellow, 1986; Brown & Williamson vis. scholar U. Louisville, 1992. Achievements include research on electron transfer in mixed-valence compounds and properties of single-molecule magnets. Office: U Calif Dept Chemistry and Biochem 9500 Gilman Dr Dept 358 La Jolla CA 92093-0358 Business E-Mail: dhendrickson@ucsd.edu.

HENDRICKSON, PAUL JOSEPH, journalist, writer, educator; b. Fresno, Calif., Apr. 29, 1944; s. Joseph Paul and Rita Bernice Hendrickson; m. Sunday Hendrickson, Sept. 10, 1969 (div. Feb. 1974); m. Cecilia Regina Hendrickson, Mar. 10, 1979; children: Matthew, John. Classical AB in English, St. Louis U., 1967; MA, Pa. State U., 1968. Writer, prodr., publicist WPSX-TV, University Park, Pa., 1969-71; writer Holiday Mag., Indpls., 1971-72; reporter Detroit Free Press, 1972-74, The Nat. Observer, Washington, 1974-77, The Washington Post, 1977-2001; lectr. in creative writing U. Pa., Phila., 1998—. Author: Seminary: A Search, 1983, Looking for the Light, 1992, The Living and the Dead, 1996, Sons of Mississippi, 2003 (Nat. Book Critics Circle award for nonfiction, 2004). Fellow, Alicia Patterson Found., 1980, Lyndhurst fellow, 1985—87, Guggenheim fellow, 1999; grantee, Nat. Endowment for the Arts, 2002. Rman Catholic. Avocation: fly fishing. Home: 30 Colfax Rd Havertown PA 19083 E-mail: phendric@english.upenn.edu.

HENDRICKSON, WAYNE A(RTHUR), biochemist, educator; b. Spring Valley, Wis., Apr. 25, 1941; s. Olaf and Margaret (Oare) H.; children: Helen Margaret, Inga Marie. BA, U. Wis., River Falls, 1963; PhD in Biophysics, Johns Hopkins U., 1968; PhD (hon.), Uppsala U., 1995. Rsch. assoc. Johns Hopkins U., Balt., 1968-69; postdoctoral rsch. assoc. Naval Rsch. Lab., 1969-71, rsch. biophysicist, 1971-84; prof. biochemistry and molecular biophysics Columbia U. Coll. Physicians and Surgeons, NYC, 1984—; investigator Howard Hughes Med. Inst., 1986—. Sci. adv. bd. mem. Progenics Pharms., 1987—; sci. adv. bd. mem., Kinetix Pharms., 1997—; sci. policy com. Stanford Linear Accelerator Ctr., 1992-94; program evaluation bd. Advanced Photon Source, 1988—; biomed. adv. com. for Pitts. Supercomputing Ctr., 1987-92; DOE Synchrotron Rev. Com., 1987-88; proposal rev. panel Cornell High Energy Synchrotron Source, 1987—; mem. NSF Molecular Adv. Panel, 1980-83, NIH Biophys. Chemistry Study Sct., 1986-89; mem. sci. adv. bd. Burnham Inst., 1995—; mem. nat. adv. Gdn. Med. Scis. Coun., 1997—; mem. sci. adv. vom. European Synchrotam Radiation Facility, 1997—, Rutgers Ctr. Advanced Biotech. & Medicine, 1998—; investigator, Howard Hughes Med. Inst. Mem. editl. bd. Jour. Biomolecular Structure and Dynamics, 1986-91; assoc. editor Jour. Molecular Biology, 1987-93; editor Current Opinion in Structural Biology, 1989—, Macromolecular Structures, 1990—, Structure, 1993—; contbr. numerous articles to profl. jours. Recipient Biol. Scis. award Washington Acad. Scis., 1976, Meritorious Civilian Svc. award U.S. Navy, 1978, Arthur S. Flemming award Outstanding Young Fed. Employees, 1979, Aminoff prize Royal Swedish Acad. Scis., 1997, Anfinsen award Protein Soc., 1997, Arthur H. Compton award, Advanced Photon Source, 2001, Gairdner award, Gairdner Found., 2003. Fellow AAAS, Am. Acad. Arts and Scis; mem. NAS (Alexander Hollaender award 1998), Am. Crystallographic Assn. (chmn. biol. macromolecules group 1980, A.L. Patterson award 1981, Fankuchen award com. 1982), Am. Soc. Biochemistry and Molecular Biology (mem. pubs. com. 1997—, Fritz Lipmann award 1991), Biophys. Soc. (coun. mem. 1987-90, mem. publs. com. 1989—), Internat. Union Crystallography (commn. on biol. macromolecules 1981-87, commn. on crystallographic computing 1984-87, commn. on synchrotron radiation, 1990-93). Achievements include rsch. in macromolecular structure and function, in principles of protein structure, dynamics and assembly, in properties of specific proteins, in diffraction methods, in crystallographic computing, and in synchrotron radiation. Office: Columbia U Dept Biochem & Molecular Biophys 650 W 168th St Black Bldg 203 New York NY 10032-3795 Office Phone: 212-305-3456. Office Fax: 212-305-7379. Business E-Mail: wayne@convex.hhmi.columbia.edu.

HENDRIE, JANICE ELLEN, language educator; b. Detroit, Apr. 13, 1946; d. Julius William Semetko and Estelle Alice Justes Semetko; m. Michael VanDyke Hendrie, Aug. 5, 1972; children: Michael Jr., Andrew. BA, Nazareth Coll., Kalamazoo, Mich., 1968; MA, Ea. Mich. U., Ypsilanti, 1973. Spanish and English tchr. Martin Jr. and Sr. HS, Mich., 1967—70; Spanish tchr. Lincoln Jr. HS, Wyandotte, Mich., 1970—72, Grosse Pointe Pub. Schs., Mich., 1972—2006; Spanish tchr., chmn. modern and classical langs. Grosse Pointe South HS, 2001—06. Co-author: Pre-AP Resource Book, 2006. Coord. student vol. activities Casa Maria, Detroit, 1995—2006. King Juan Carlos fellow, Fundacion Ortega y Gassett, U. Minn., 1991. Mem.: Am. Assn. Tchrs. Spanish and Portuguese (state coord. nat. Spanish exam 1994—95), Jr. League Detroit. Avocations: travel, reading. Home: 184 Vendome Grosse Pointe MI 48236

HENDRIE, JOSEPH MALLAM, physicist, nuclear engineer; b. Janesville, Wis., Mar. 18, 1925; s. Joseph Munier and Margaret Prudence (Hocking) H.; m. Elaine Kostell, July 9, 1949; children: Susan Debra, Barbara Ellen. BS, Case Inst. Tech., 1950; PhD, Columbia U., 1957. Registered profl. engr., NY, Calif. Asst. physicist Brookhaven Nat. Lab., Upton, NY, 1955-57, assoc. physicist, 1957-60, physicist, 1960-71, sr. physicist, 1971-97, chmn. steering com., project chief engr. high flux beam reactor design and constrn., 1958-65, acting head exptl. reactor physics divsn., 1965-66, project mgr. pulsed fast reactor project, 1967-70, assoc. head engring. divsn., dept. applied sci., 1967-71, head, 1971-72, chmn. dept. applied sci., 1975-77, spl. asst. to dir., 1981-96; dir. Entergy Ops., Inc., 1987-95; ret. Dir. Houston Industries, Inc., Houston Lighting & Power Co., 1985-96; dep. dir. licensing for tech. rev. U.S. AEC, 1972-74; chmn. U.S. Nuc. Regulatory Commn., Washington, 1977-79, 81, commr., 1980, mem. adv. com. on enforcement policy, 1984-85; lectr. nuc. power plant safety MIT, Ga. Inst. Tech., Northwestern U., summers 1970-77; cons. radiation safety com. Columbia U., 1964-72; mem. adv. com. reactor safeguards AEC, 1966-72, chmn., 1970; U.S. mem. sr. adv. group on reactor safety stds. IAEA, 1974-78; mem. nat. rsch. coun. com. Internat. Cooperation in Magnetic Fusion, 1983-85; cons. AEC, Nuc. Regulatory Commn., 1974-75, GAO, 1975-77, Electric Power Rsch. Inst., 1982, various nuc. utilities, 1981—. Mem. editl. adv. bd. Nuc. Tech., 1967-77. Served with AUS, 1943-45. Recipient E.O. Lawrence award, 1970, George C. Laurence Pioneeering award Am. Nuc. Soc., 1998, Henry DeWolf Smyth Nuc. Statesman award, 2004; decorated comdr. Order of Leopold II (Belgium), 1982. Fellow Am. Nuc. Soc. (dir. 1976-77, v.p. 1983-84, pres. 1984-85), ASME; mem. IEEE, NAE, Am. Phys. Soc., ASTM (com. on rsch. and tech. planning 1985-90), Am. Concrete Inst., Inst. Nuc. Power Operation (adv. coun. 1984-90), NSPE, Sigma Xi, Tau Beta Pi. Achievements include research and publications on physics nuclear reactors, nuclear power plant safety, engineering design reactors, electrical power transmission, chem. physics nitrogen dissociation process, structure oxygen molecule. Office: Brookhaven Nat Lab Upton NY 11973 Home Phone: 631-286-8664; Office Phone: 631-286-8664. Personal E-mail: joehendrie@optonline.net.

HENDRIKSEN, NEIL EVAN, music educator; b. Salt Lake City, Sept. 27, 1955; s. Oscar James and Dorothy Hendriksen; m. Marie Updegraff, Oct. 20, 1977; children: Jacob Thomas, Daren Bradford, Nathan Edward, Douglas Neil, Lauren Clarice. MusB, U. Utah, 1985. Cert. Secondary Tchr. State of Utah, 1985. Dir. choral activities Woods Cross HS, Utah, 1986—; adj. faculty mem. U. Utah, Salt Lake City, 1989—. Clinician, adjudicator Heritage Festivals, Salt Lake City, 1990—, Utah HS Activities Assn., Midvale, 1987—; trombonist, bass trombonist Ballet West/Utah Chamber Orch., Salt Lake City, 1989—; aux. trombonist Utah Symphony Orch., Salt Lake City, 1982—89; trombonist, bass trombonist Pioneer Theatre Co. Orch., Salt Lake City, 1983—89. Musician: numerous symphonic studio performances; singer: numerous soundtracks and studio recordings; musician: numerous studio, movies, advertising and tv appearances; singer: numerous live vocal solo and ensemble performances. Zone commr. Boy Scouts Am., Salt Lake City, 1990—97. Named Secondary Tchr. of Yr., Davis Sch. Dist., 1996, Tchr. of Yr., Woods Cross HS, 1996; recipient Golden Apple award, Utah PTA, 1996. Mem.: Davis Educators Assn. (assoc.), Utah Educators Assn. (assoc.), NEA (assoc.), Utah Music Educators Assn. (assoc.; vice president.choral 2000—02, pres.-elect 2007, Superior Accomplishment award 2006), Am. Choral Dirs. Assn. (life; Utah repertoire/standards chair h.s. 1987—96, dir. choir at nat. conv. 2004—05). Avocations: hiking, target shooting, knife collecting, sight-seeing/travel, camping. Office: Woods Cross HS 600 West 2200 South Woods Cross UT 84087 Business E-Mail: nhendriksen@dsdmail.net.

HENDRIX, ALBERT RANDEL, social services administrator; b. Batesville, Miss., Aug. 17; s. Howard Roy Sr. and Marjorie Corine (Oliphant) H.; m. Sandra June Reynolds, July 15, 1973; children: Jo Ellen, Sarah Elizabeth, Albert Randel Jr., Sandra Louise. BA, U. Miss., 1968, MEd, 1971; PhD, U. So. Miss., 1979. Grants coord. Ellisville (Miss.) State Sch., 1971-75; dir. North Miss. Retardation Ctr., Oxford, 1975-86; exec. dir. Miss. Dept. Mental Health, Jackson, 1986—. Adj. instr. health care adminstrn. U. Miss. Pharmacy Sch., 1977—, acting asst. prof. spl. edn., dept. of curriculum and instrn. Sch. Edn., 1979-87; instr. human svcs. technician program Itawamba Jr. Coll., Fulton, 1981-83; dir. div. of mental retardation, dept. mental health, Jackson, Miss., 1981-82; adv. bd. Congress of Advocates for the Retarded, 1978—. Exec. dir. Miss. Arts Fair for the Handicapped, 1980—; adv. bd. U. Miss. Sch. Edn. (bd. dirs. 1989—), Jackson State U. Sch. Liberal Arts, 1986—; bd. dirs., adv. bd. Jackson State U. Sch. Social Work, 1990—; social work adv. bd. U. So. Miss., 1987-90; v.p. U. Miss. Health Coun., 1986-89; adv. coun. Foster Grandparent Program, Oxford, Miss., 1975-89; mem. Govs. Coun. on Aging, 1976-80. With U.S. Army, 1968-70. Mem. Phi Theta Kappa, Phi Kappa Phi, Phi Delta Kappa. Office: Miss Dept Mental Health Robert E Lee Bldg 239 N Lamar St Ste 1101 Jackson MS 39201-1325

HENDRIX, JANE GALLOWAY, art educator; d. James Caswell and Mary Hulet Galloway; m. David Edwin Hendrix, June 5, 1995; 1 child, James Travis Griffin. MusB, Converse Coll., Spartanburg, SC, 1974; MusM, Winthrop U., Rock Hill, SC, 1977. Tchr. Dunwoody Sch. Arts, Ga., 1982—, dir., 1993—; trainer Kindermusik Internat., Greensboro, NC, 1999—. Chmn. Partnership Kindermusik Educators, 2001—, liaison, 2005, bd. dirs. Singer: (opera and musical theater) various prodns. Mem.: Nat. Assn. Tchrs. Singing, Kindermusik Educators Assn. (assoc.; v.p. 2001—05). Libertarian. Methodist. Avocations: singing, gardening, reading. Office: Dunwoody School for the Arts 1445 Mount Vernon Rd Dunwoody GA 30338 Home Phone: 770-280-1215; Office Phone: 770-280-1215. Office Fax: 770-280-1216; Home Fax: 770-280-1216. E-mail: jhendrix@dbc.org.

HENDRIX, JOHN SHANNON, architecture educator; b. Ithaca, NY, Apr. 27, 1959; s. John David and Margaret Shannon Hendrix. BFA, Art Inst., Chgo., 1983; MA, RI Sch. Design, Providence, 1984; MArch., U. Ill., Chgo., 1993; PhD in Architecture, Cornell U., Ithaca, NY, 2001. Adj. prof. art and archtl. history Roger Williams U./RI. Sch. Design, Bristol, RI, 2000—. Author: The Relation Between Architectural Forms and Philosophical Structures in the Work of Francesco Borromini in Seventeenth-Century Rome, 2002, Architectural Forms and Philosophical Structures, 2003, History and Culture in Italy, 2003, Platonic Architectonics: Platonic Philosophies and the Visual Arts, 2004, Aesthetics and the Philosophy of Spirit, 2005, Architecture and Psychoanalysis, 2006. Home: 212 Hope St Bristol RI 02809 Office: Roger Williams Univ One Old Ferry Rd Bristol RI 02809

HENDRIX, JON RICHARD, biology professor; b. Passaic, NJ, May 4, 1938; s. William Louis and Velma Lucile (Coleman) H.; m. Janis Ruth Rouhselange, Nov. 24, 1962; children— Margaret Susan, Joann Ruth, Amy Therese BS, Ind. State U., 1960, MS, 1963; Ed.D., Ball State U., Muncie, Ind., 1974. Sci. supr. Sch. Town of Highland, Ind., 1960-71; instr. Ind. U., Gary, 1968-69; assoc. prof. biology Ball State U., Muncie, 1972-80, prof., 1980-98, prof. emeritus, 1998—. Cons. Ind. Dept. Pub. Instrn., 1967-71, Ctr. for Values and Meaning, 1971—; mem. Ind. Sci. Edn. Adv. Bd., Dept. Pub. Instrn., 1967-71 Author: The Wonder of Somehow, 1974, The Wonder of Someplace, 1974, The Wonder of Sometime, 1974, Becomings: A Parent Guidebook for In-Home Experiences with Nine to Eleven Year Olds, 1974, Becomings: A Clergy Guidebook for Experiences with Nine to Eleven Year Olds and Their Parents, 1974; contbr. articles to profl. jours. Recipient Outstanding Young Educator award Highland Jr. C. of C., 1968, Outstanding Faculty award in edn. Ind. U. N.W. Campus, 1970, Outstanding Teaching Faculty award Ball State U., 1982, Ball State U. fellowship, 1971-73, Hon. Mem. award Nat. Assn. Biology Tchrs., 1992, Outstanding Undergrad. Sci. Tchr. in Nation, Soc. of Coll. Sci. Tchrs./Kendall Mgmt., 1997; named Ind. Prof. of Yr., Coun. for Advancement and Support of Edn./Carneige, 1997. Fellow Ind. Acad. Sci.; mem. Nat. Sci. Suprs. Assn. (dir. 1969-71), Ind. Sci. Suprs. Assn. (pres. 1968-69), AAUP, Assn. Suprs. and Curriculum Devel., Nat. Biology Tchrs. Assn. (bd. dirs. 1986, 91—), Nat. Sci. Tchrs. Assn. (life), Nat. Soc. Coll. Sci. Tchrs. (undergrad. tchg. award 1997), Central Assn. Coll. Biology Tchrs., Hoosier Assn. Sci. Tchrs. Inc. (bd. dirs. 1968-71, Disting. Svc. award 1997), Ind. Assn. Tchr. Educators, Ind. Assn. Suprs. and Curriculum Devel., Ind. Biology Tchrs. Assn., Kappa Delta Pi, Phi Delta Kappa, Sigma Xi. Home: 8800 W Eucalyptus Ave Muncie IN 47304-9365 Personal E-mail: jonh49@comcast.net.

HENDRIX, LYNN PARKER, lawyer; b. McCook, Nebr., Apr. 24, 1951; s. Jack Hall and Betty Lee (Parker) H.; m. Theresa Louise Zabawa, June 19, 1976; children: Paige Ashley, Parker Jerome, Pierce Reid. BSEE, U. Nebr., 1973, JD with distinction, 1978. Bar: Nebr. 1978, U.S. Dist. Ct. Nebr. 1978, Colo. 1979, U.S. Dist. Ct. Colo. 1979, U.S. Ct. Appeals (10th cir.) 1993, Wyo. 1993, Mont. 1995, N.Y., 2000, U.S. Patent Office, 1994, U.S. Supreme Ct. 2004. Surveyor Nebr. Dept. Roads, McCook, 1973; constrn. adminstr. Commonwealth Electric Co., Lincoln, Nebr., 1974, cons. engr., 1975; instr. U. Nebr., Lincoln, 1974-75; law clk. Nebr. Atty.-Gen., Lincoln, 1976-77; assoc. Holme Roberts & Owen, LLP, Denver, 1978-83, ptnr., 1984—. Trustee, treas., v.p. Rocky Mountain Min. Law Found., pres., 2006—. Editor-in-chief Nebr. Law Rev., 1977-78, exec. editor, 1976-77; contbr. articles to profl. jours. Sec., bd. dirs. Girls Club Denver, 1984-90,

Girls Inc. Metro Denver, 1992—, Remember Found., 2004 Named Adm., Nebr. Navy. Mem. ABA, Colo. Bar Assn., Mont. Bar Assn., Nebr. Bar Assn., Wyo. Bar Assn., N.Y. Bar Assn., S.E. Law Club (pres. 1990-91), Meridian Golf Club, Sigma Alpha Epsilon, Tau Beta Pi, Sigma Tau (pres.), Eta Kappa Nu. Home: 8125 S Glencoe Ct Centennial CO 80122-3876 Office: Holme Roberts & Owen LLP 1700 Lincoln St Ste 4100 Denver CO 80203-4541*

HENDRIX, MARY ELIZABETH, language educator, researcher; b. Tuscaloosa, Ala., Mar. 17, 1973; d. Lawrence Thomson and Evelyn Jacobs Hendrix. BA in English & Dance cum laude, U. Ala., Tuscaloosa, 1998, MA in Secondary Edn., 2000, PhD, 2007. Coord. Am. reads program U. Ala., Tuscaloosa, 1999—2000; tchr. English Meadow Creek High Sch., Lawrenceville, Ga., 2000—01, The Capitol Sch., Tuscaloosa, 2001—02, Shelton State C.C., 2001—04; rsch. asst. U. Ala., 2003—; English tchr. Mem. adv. bd. cmty. svc. & vol. U. Ala., 1999—2000. Mem. Ala. Citizens Constl. Reform, Tuscaloosa, 2004—, Ala. Arise, Birmingham, 2005—06; ctrl. region coord. Constl. Reform Edn. Campaign Greater Birmingham Ministries. Recipient Eddy Fulks award, The Elliott Soc., U. Ala., 1997; scholar, U. Ala., 2005. Mem.: AAUW (pub. policy chair Ala. 2006—07, co-dir. Ready to Run grant 2007—), Southeast Philosophy Edn. Soc., Nat. Coun. Tchrs. English, Am. Ednl. Studies Assn., Am. Ednl. Rsch. Assn., The Blackburn Inst., Alpha Epsilon Lambda, Sigma Tau Delta, Kappa Delta Pi, Phi Delta Kappa. Democrat. Achievements include patents in field. Avocations: writing, dance, exercise, reading, theater. Home: 2706 31st Ave Way Northport AL 35476-3610 Office: U Ala Coll Edn 210 Wilson Hall Box 870302 Tuscaloosa AL 35487 Office Phone: 205-826-5549. Personal E-mail: ehendrix1105@bellsouth.net.

HENDRIX, SCOTT NORTON, history professor; s. Phil Stephenson Hendrix and Sandra Jean Norton. PhD in History, U. Pitts., 2006. Adj. instr. history Cleve. State U., Cuyahoga C.C., Cleve., 2006—. List editor H-War/H-Net for the Humanities, 2006—; presenter in field. Contbr. collection of essays. Sgt. US Army Nat. Guard, 1982—2000. Mem.: Soc. for Mil. History. Home Phone: 216-941-9374.

HENDRIX, SHERMAN SAMUEL, biology professor, researcher; b. Bridgeport, Conn., June 1, 1939; m. Carol Ann Seibel, June 10, 1961; children: Marc, Robin. BA in Biology, Gettysburg Coll., 1961; MS in Zoology, Fla. State U., 1964; PhD in Zoology, U. Md., 1972. Instr. biology Gettysburg (Pa.) Coll., 1964-70, asst. prof., 1970-77, assoc. prof., 1977-90, prof., 1990—, chmn. dept., 1985—90, 1997—2001, coll. marshal, 2000—. Contbr. articles to profl. jours. Bd. dirs. United Way Adams County, Gettysburg, 1983-86; trustee Brayton H. Ransom Meml. Trust Fund, 2004—. Interam. fellow in tropical medicine NIH, 1973. Mem. Am. Soc. Parasitologists (mentor com. 2003-06, chair 2004-06), Helminthological Soc. Washington (pres. 1984, v.p. 2002-04, corr. sec.-treas. 2005—, editl. bd. 1985-2002, editor jours. 1993-98, Anniversary award 1998), Pa. Acad. Sci. (treas. 1986-90, pres. 1990-92, mem. editl. bd. 2006—, Lifetime Achievement award 1998), Wildlife Diseases Assn., Am. Malacological Soc. Lutheran. Achievements include research on aquatic animal parasites. Office: Gettysburg Coll Dept Biology Gettysburg PA 17325

HENDRIX, STEPHEN C., financial executive, consultant; s. Houston W. and Helen Hendrix; children: Kimberly, Jeffrey, Julie. BA, Tex. Christian U., 1964; M in Internat. Svc., Am. U., 1966; MBA, Ohio State U., 1972. CPA, cert. fin. analyst. Jr. officer U.S. Dept. State, AID, Washington, 1967-68; mgr. mktg. adminstrn. Amecom divsn. Litton Industries, College Park, Md., 1968-70; mgr. fin. and planning internat. divsn. Anchor Hocking Corp., Lancaster, Ohio, 1970-73; bank rels. mgr. E.I. Dupont de Nemours & Co., Wilmington, Del., 1973-78; corp. treas. mgr. SmithKline Beckman Corp., Phila., 1978-79, asst. treas. domestic, 1979-82, asst. treas. internat., 1982-87, v.p., asst. treas. internat., 1987-89; v.p., treas. SmithKline Beecham Corp. (formerly SmithKline Beckman Corp.), Phila., 1989-91; treas. Armstrong World Industries, Lancaster, Pa., 1993-96; cons. Astra-Zeneca, Wayne, Pa., 1997-99, LifeSensors Inc., Wayne, 2000—01, fin. cons., 2002—. Contbr. articles to profl. jours. Mem. CFA Inst., Nat. Assn. Corp. Treas. Personal E-mail: stevehendrix@yahoo.com.

HENDRIXSON, PETER S., lawyer; b. Wilmington, Del., Apr. 9, 1947; s. Philip Roe and Betty Jane (Schillo) H.; m. Carolyn Hodge Ford, June 14, 1969; children: Julie Elise, Bradley Scott. BA, Northwestern U., 1969; JD magna cum laude, Harvard U., 1972. Bar: Minn. 1973, U.S. Dist. Ct. Minn. 1973, U.S. Supreme Ct. 1978. Law clerk U.S. Ct. Appeals, Boston, 1972-73; assoc., ptnr. trial dept. Dorsey & Whitney, Mpls., 1973—, chair trial dept., 1989-93, chair trial and adminstrv. group, 1994—, mng. ptnr., 2000—. Editor, officer Harvard Law Review, 1970-72. Treas. Fraser for Mayor Com., Mpls., 1983-95; bd. govs. Children's Theatre, Mpls., 1987-92; various positions Mayflower Congl. Ch.; bd. dirs. La Creche Early Childhood Ctrs., Mpls., 1990-98, Children's Home Soc., St. Paul, 1990—, Guthrie Theater, 1995-00; pres. Children's Law Ctr.; memb. bd. Walker Art Ctr. Mem. Minn State Bar (chair anti-trust law sect. 1992-93), Phi Beta Kappa. Democrat. Congregationalist. Office: Dorsey & Whitney LLP 50 S 6th St Ste 1500 Minneapolis MN 55402 Office Phone: 612-340-2917. Office Fax: 612-340-2868. Business E-Mail: hendrixson.peter@dorsey.com.

HENDRY, ANDREW DELANEY, lawyer, consumer products company executive; b. NYC, Aug. 9, 1947; s. Andrew Joseph and Virginia (Delaney) H.; 1 child, Robert. AB in Econs., Georgetown U., 1969; JD, NYU, 1972. Bar: NY 1973. Va. 1981, Mich. 1984, Pa. 1987. Assoc. Battle and Fowler, NYC, 1972-79; sr. corp. and fin. atty. Reynolds Metals Co., Richmond, Va., 1979-82; sr. staff counsel Burroughs Corp., Detroit, 1982-83, assoc. gen. coun., 1983-86, dep. gen. counsel, 1986-87; v.p. legal affairs Unisys Corp., Blue Bell, Pa., 1987-88, v.p., gen. counsel, 1988-91; sr. v.p., gen. counsel, sec. Colgate-Palmolive Co., NYC, 1991—. Mem. adv. bd. Georgetown U. Law Ctr. Corp. Counsel Inst., 1999—; bd. editors The M&A Lawyer, 1996—, The Met. Corp. Counsel, 1993—. Trustee The O'Neal Sch., 2001—; mem. Georgetown Coll. Adv. Bd., 2002—; bd. dirs., chmn., corp. adv. bd. Nat. Legal Aid and Def., Washington, 1992—99; bd. dirs. Lawyers Alliance for NY, 2000—06, Lawyers Com. for Civil Rights Under Law, 2004—. With JAGC USAF, 1973. Fellow: Am. Bar Found.; mem.: ABA (com. on corp. laws, standing com. on substance abuse), Ctrl. European and Eurasian Law Inst. (bd. dirs. 2002—04), NY State Bar Assn. (steering com. on commerce and industry 1997—), Am. Corp. Counsel Assn. (pres. Mich. chpt. 1985, chmn. nat. pro bono com. 1985—88, bd. dirs. emeritus NY chpt.), Am. Law Inst., NY Athletic Club. Office: Colgate Palmolive Co 300 Park Ave New York NY 10022-7499 Office Phone: 212-310-2239. E-mail: andrew_hendry@colpal.com.*

HENDRY, JEAN SHARON, psychopharmacologist; d. Clarence Richard and Frances Lee (Manger) Shaver; 1 child, Robert Andrew. BA, Hunter Coll., NY, 1976; MA in Psychology, Princeton U., NJ, 1978, PhD in Psychology, 1980. Rsch. asst. Hunter Coll., NYC, 1974-75; asst. instr. Princeton U., Princeton, NJ, 1976—79; postdoctoral fellow in pharm. Med. Coll. Va., Richmond, 1979—82; psychology instr. U. Richmond, 1985-86, Pa. State U., Media, Pa., 1987-88. Guest reviewer various psychological and pharmacological jours. Contbr. numerous articles to profl. jours. Active Arts Coun. of Moore County, World Wildlife Assn.; v.p. Women of Weymouth Ctr. Arts and Humanities. Mem.: APA, Assn. Psychol. Sci., Assn. Princeton Grad. Alumni (elected to bd. 2006), Nature Conservancy, Nat. Audubon Soc., Nat. Wildlife Fedn., Carolina Triangle Club of Princeton (co-chair 2007), Sigma Xi, Phi Beta Kappa (v.p.). Avocations: tennis, exercise, reading, gardening, gourmet cooking. Business E-Mail: jhendry@alumni.princeton.edu.

HENDRY, JOHN V., retired state supreme court justice; b. Omaha, Aug. 23, 1948; BS, U. Nebr., 1970, JD, 1974. Pvt. practice, Licoln, 1974-1995; county ct. judge 3d Jud. Dist., 1995-98; chief justice Nebr. Supreme Ct., 1998—2006. Fellow: Nebr. State Bar Found.; mem.: Nebr. State Bar Assn. Office: Nebr Supreme Ct Rm 2214 State Capitol Lincoln NE 68509

HENDRY, ROBERT RYON, lawyer; b. Jacksonville, Fla., Apr. 23, 1936; s. Warren Candler and Evalyn Marguerite (Ryon) H.; children by previous marriage: Lorraine Evalyn, Lynette Comstock, Krista Ryon; m. Janet LaCoste. BA in Polit. Sci., U. Fla., 1958, JD, 1963. Bar: Fla. 1963; bd. cert. in internat. law. Assoc. Harrell, Caro, Middlebrooks & Whiltshire, Pensacola, Fla., 1963-66, Hewlliwell, Melrose & DeWolf, Orlando, Fla., 1966-67, ptnr., 1967-69; ptnr., pres. Hoffman, Hendry, Parker & Smith and predecessor Hoffman, Hendry & Parker, Orlando, Fla., 1969-77, Hoffman, Hendry & Stoner and predecessor, Orlando, Fla., 1977-82, Hendry, Stoner, Sims & Sawicki, Orlando, Fla., 1982-88, Hendry, Stoner, Townsend Sawicki & Brown, Orlando, Fla., 1988-92, Hendry, Stoner, Sawicki & Brown, Orlando, Fla., 1992—2002, Hendry, Stoner, DeLancett & Brown, Orlando, Fla., 2002—05, Hendry, Stoner & Brown, Orlando, Fla., 2005, Hendry, Stoner, Calandrino & Brown, PA, Orlando, Fla., 2005—. Author: U.S. Real Estate and the Foreign Investor, 1983; contbr. articles to profl. jours. Mem. Dist. Export Coun., 1977-91, vice chmn., 1981, chair, 1995-2006, chair emeritus, 2007—, mem. nat. steering com., 1997-06, trade issues com., 2007—; bd. dirs. World Trade Ctr. and predecessor, Orlando, 1979-89, pres., 1980-82, 84; chmn. Fla. Gov.'s Conf. on World Trade, 1983; chmn. Fla. coun. on internat. edn., 1993-96; mem. internat. fin. and mktg. adv. bd. U. Miami Sch. Bus., Fla., 1979-90, Commn. on Internat. Edn., 1986-88; bd. dirs. Econ. Devel. Commn. of Mid-Fla., 2001-03, Metro Orlando Econ. Devel. Commn., 2000—, bd. dirs., Caribbean Cmty. Found., Inc., 2003—; mem. Metro Orlando Internat. Bus. Coun., 1994-96, Metro Orlando Internat. Affairs Commn., 1995—, Fla. Econ. Summit, 1996-00; mem. internat. trade and econ. devel. bd. and audit com. Enterprise, Fla., 1997-00; chmn. Fla. Trade Grant Review Panel, 1998-01; mem. adv. com. Enterprise Fla. Internat. Bus. Devel., 2000—; bd. dirs. Gulf of Mexico States Partnership, Inc., 2001—, Enterprise Fla. Stakeholders Coun., 2005—, Golden Rule Found., 2000—; co-chair Gulf of Mex. Accord Com. on Legal Infrastructure, 2002—; bd. advisors Fla. Free Trade Area of the Ams., 2001-03; mem. steering com. Orlando Area Com. on Fgn. Affairs, 2002—; mem. internat. programs adv. com. U. Fla. Levin Coll. of Law, 2000—. Lt. U.S. Army, 1958-60, capt. Army N.G., 1960-70. Mem. Fla. Coun. Internat. Devel. (bd. dirs. 1972-85, chmn. 1977-79, adv. bd. 1985-95, chmn. emeritus, 1991—, vice chair 1995-96, chair 1996-98), Fla. Bar (bd. cert. internat. lawyer 1999—, vice chmn. internat. law com. 1974-75, chmn. com. 1976-77, mem. exec. coun. internat. law sect. 1982—, original internat. law certification com. 1998—, chmn. 2001—), Fla. Assn. Voluntary Agys. for Caribbean Action (bd. dirs. 1987—, pres. 1989-91, past pres. 1991-92), Orange County Bar Assn. (treas. 1971-74), Scottish Exec. (founding mem. 2002-), Soc. Internat. Bus. Fellows, Brit.-Am. C. of C. (bd. dirs. 2000-04, sec. 1984-85), Swiss Am. C. of C. (sec. Fla. chpt. 1996—), German Am. Bus. Chamber of Fla.

HENEGAN, JOHN C(LARK), lawyer; b. Mobile, Ala., Oct. 14, 1950; s. Virgil Baker and Marie (Fife) Gunter; m. Morella Lloyd Kuykendall, Aug. 5, 1972; children: Clark, Jim. BA in English and Philosophy, U. Miss., 1972, JD with honors, 1976. Bar: Miss. 1976, US Dist. Ct. (no. dist.) Miss. 1976, NY 1978, US Dist. Ct. (so. dist.) NY 1979, US Ct. Appeals (5th and 11th cirs.) 1982, US Ct. Appeals (2nd cir.) 1984, US Dist. Ct. (so. dist.) Miss. 1984, US Ct. Appeals (fed. cir.) 1995, US Supreme Ct. 1995. Law clk. to judge U.S. Ct. Appeals (5th cir.), 1976-77; atty. Dewey, Ballantine, Bushby, Palmer & Wood, NYC and Washington, 1977-81; exec. asst., chief of staff to Gov. William Winter Jackson, Miss., 1981-84; mem. Butler, Snow, O'Mara, Stevens & Cannada, PLLC, Jackson, 1984—. Lectr. U. Miss. Ctr. for Continuing Legal Edn., 1985, 87, Miss. Jud. Coll., Oxford, 1982; mem. lawyers adv. com. U.S. Ct. Appeals for 5th Cir. Jud. Conf., 1991-93. Editor-in-chief Miss. Law Jour., 1976; editor Miss. Lawyer, 1985; contbr. articles to legal jours. Bd. dirs. Mississippians for Ednl. Broadcasting, Jackson, 1983-90, North Jackson Youth Baseball, Inc., 1991-97, Ctr. and Ctrl. S.W. Miss. Legal Svcs., 1997-04; co-pres. Chastain Mid. Sch. Parent Tchrs. Students Assn., 1995-96; mem. Miss. Ethics Commn., Jackson, 1984-87, chair resonaces bd., mem. exec. com., 2007—; mem. adv. bd. William Winter Inst. Racial Reconciliation, 2004—; del. Hinds County Dem. Conv., 1988; mem. Miss. Dem. Fin. Coun., 1988, Hinds County Dem. Exec. Com., 1989-92; Sunday sch. supt. Covenant Presbyn. Ch., 1989-90, deacon, 1991-96, moderator of diaconate, 1993-94, elder, 1996-02, 04-06, 07—. Recipient Cmty. Svc. award Hinds County Bar Assn., 1998. Fellow Miss. Bar Found.; mem. ABA, FBA, Miss. Bar Assn. (chmn. Law Day USA 1983), Miss. Def. Lawyers Assn., Miss. Law Jour. Alumni Assn. (bd. dirs. 1985-88), 5th Cir. Bar Assn., Fed. Circuit Bar Assn., inds County Bar Assn. (bd. dir. 2002-04, sec., treas. 2004-05, v.p. 2005-06, pres. 2006-07), Jackson C. of C., Am. Inns of Ct. (barrister Charles Clark chpt. 1991-93, assoc. 2004—), Phi Kappa Phi, Phi Delta Phi, Omicron Delta Kappa. Avocation: reading. Home: 2441 Eastover Dr Jackson MS 39211-6727 Office: 210 E Capitol St Fl 17 Jackson MS 39201-2306 Office Phone: 601-985-4530. E-mail: john.henegan@butlersnow.com.

HENEL, CAROLYN E., lawyer; BA, Yale U., 1992; JD, U. Va., 1996. Bar: Calif. 1996, cert.: State Bar Calif. Bd. Legal Specialization (estate planning, trust and probate law). Assoc. Crosby, Heafey, Roach & May, 1996—2002; ptnr. Roisman Henel, LLP, Oakland, Calif., 2002—. Mem. profl. adv. com. East Bay Cmty. Found. Named a No. Calif. Super Lawyer, Law & Politics and San Francisco Mag., 2004, 2005, 2006; named one of Top 100 Attys., Worth mag., 2006. Mem.: ABA, East Bay Tax Club, Estate Planning Coun. East Bay, Alameda County Bar Assn. (chair estate planning com. 2005, 2006), East Bay Regional Pks. Found. (v.p. bd. dirs. 2006). Office: Roisman Henel LLP 1999 Harrison St Ste 1400 Oakland CA 94612 Office Phone: 510-466-6000. Office Fax: 510-466-6040. E-mail: chenel@roismanhenel.com.

HENEMAN, ROBERT LLOYD, management educator; b. Mpls., Jan. 17, 1955; s. Herbert G. Jr. and Jane R. Heneman; m. Renee Brausch, Sept. 9, 1989. BA, Lake Forest Coll., 1977; MA, U. Ill., 1979; PhD, Mich. State U., 1984. Personnel specialist Pacific Gas & Electric Co., San Francisco, 1979-80; assoc. prof. Mgmt. Ohio State U., Columbus, 1984—, dir. grad. programs in labor and human resources. Author: Merit Pay, 1992, Staffing Organizations, 1994, 3d edit., 2000, Business-Driven Compensation Policies, 2000, Strategic Reward Management, 2001. Mem. ch. coun. Holy Trinity Luth. Ch., Columbus. Mem. Acad. of Mgmt. (exec. com. human resource divsn. 1988-93, program chair 1992-93, divsn. chair 1994-95), Am. Compensation Assn. (rsch. com. 1992-93, edn. com. 1993-94, acad. ptnr. network, 1997—, cert. program fac., 1992—), Phi Kappa Phi, Sigma Iota Epsilon, Psi Chi. Home: 333 Old Spring Ct Dublin OH 43017-1114

HENES, DONNA, artist, writer; b. Cleve., Sept. 19, 1945; d. Nathan and Adelaide (Ross) Trugman. Student, Ohio State U., 1963-66; BS, CCNY, 1971, MS in Art Edn., 1972. Prodr. series pub. participatory celebratory events in parks, museums and univs., 100 cities in 9 countries, 1970—. Designer Olympic Medalist Tickertape Parade, N.Y.C., 1984; ednl. cons. New Wilderness Foundation, N.Y.C., 1985; judge Jane Addams Peace Assn. Children's Book Award, N.Y.C., 1983-89; ritual cons. Mama Donna's Tea Garden. Author, designer Dressing Our Wounds in Warm Clothes, 1982, Noting the Process of Noting the Process, 1977, Celestially Auspicious Occasions, 1996, The Moon Watcher's Companion, 2004, The Queen of My Self, 2005, author, performer (CD) Reverence to Her: Part I Mythology, the Matriarchy & Me, 1998, pub., editor quar. Always in Season: Living in Sync with the Cycles, columnist United Press Internat. Religion & Spirituality Forum; editor: Celebration News, 1986—92; internationally syndicated columnist; contbr. numerous articles to profl. jours. Co-founder, pres. STAND (Stand Together Affirmative Neighborhood Devel.), N.Y.C.; composer Chants for Peace/Chance for Peace, Sta. WNYC, first peace message in space, 1982. Fellow Nat. Endowment for Arts, 1982, interarts, 1983, N.Y. Found. for Arts, 1986, 90; grantee N.Y. State Coun. on Arts, N.Y.C. State Bicentennial Commn., Com. for Visual Arts, Money for Women, Beard's Fund, Jerome Found., Ctr. for the Media Arts; recipient Citation award Mayor of N.Y.C. David Dinkins. Mem. Internat. Ctr. for Celebration (bd. dirs., co-founder). Avocations: dance, travel, reading, walking, swimming. Office Phone: 718-857-1343. Personal E-mail: cityshaman@aol.com.

HENES, SAMUEL ERNST, lawyer; b. Oberlin, Ohio, Jan. 28, 1937; s. Ernst Louis and Martha Hannah (Artz) H. AB with honors, Cornell U., 1959; LL.B., Harvard U., 1962. Bar: Ohio, 1962. Assoc. Arter & Hadden, Cleve., 1962-70, ptnr., 1971-89. Trustee Musart Soc., Cleve., 1980— , pres. 1985-94; trustee Young Audiences Greater Cleve., Inc., 1982-85, George P. Bickford Found., 1981-90; hon. trustee So. Lorain County Hist. Soc., Wellington, Ohio, 1988—. Served to 1st lt. U.S. Army, 1963-65 Mem. ABA, Cleve. Bar Assn., Ohio State Bar Assn. Clubs: Rowfant (Cleve.) (sec. 1985-89). Republican. Methodist. Avocations: book collecting, amateur harpsichordist, swimming, travel. Home: 13605 Shaker Blvd Apt 2B Cleveland OH 44120-1503 Office Phone: 216-991-3574. Personal E-mail: shenes@msn.com.

HENEVELD-STORY, CHRISTY JEAN, educational researcher; b. San Jose, Calif., June 30, 1967; d. Sally Jean Dudley and Robert Michael Heneveld, Charles Gustav Sieloff (Stepfather) and Barbara Leech Heneveld (Stepmother); m. Robert David Duis, July 22, 1992; children: James Michael Story, Charles David Story, Christopher Robert Story. PhD, U. Calif., 1998. Lectr. U. Calif., Santa Cruz, 1999—2000; rschr. Ctr. for Study of Law and Soc. - UC Berkeley, 2000—02; tchr. Castilleja Sch., Palo Alto, Calif., 2002—. Internship coord. Castilleja Sch., Palo Alto, Calif., 2002—04. Sec. Ladera Cmty. Assn., unincorporated San Mateo County, Calif., 1999—2002; tutor Los Lomitas Sch. Dist., Atherton, Calif., 2001—04. Fellow, UC Regents, 1991-1992; Post Doctoral fellow, Ctr. for Study of Law and Soc., 2001-2002, Rsch. fellow, Ctr. for Study of Russia and Soviet Union, Moscow, Russia, 1996. Mem.: Western Assn. Women Historians, Am. Assn. Women in Slavic Studies, Am. Hist. Assn. D-Liberal. Avocations: scuba diving, travel, cooking. Home: 170 Pecora Way Portola Valley CA 94028 Office: Castilleja Sch 1310 Bryant St Palo Alto CA 94301 Home Phone: 650-561-9832'; Office Phone: 650-328-3160. Personal E-mail: story@alum.vassar.edu.

HENG, DONALD JAMES, JR., lawyer; b. Mpls., July 12, 1944; s. Donald James and Catharine Amelia (Strom) H.; m. Kathleen Ann Bailey, Sept. 2, 1967; 1 child, Francesca Remy BA cum laude, Yale U., 1967; JD magna cum laude, Minn., 1971. Bar: Calif. 1971, U.S. Dist. Ct. (no. dist.) Calif. 1971, U.S. Ct. Appeals (9th cir.) 1971. Assoc. Brobeck, Phleger & Harrison, San Francisco, 1971-73, ptnr., 1978-90; atty.-adviser Office Internat. Tax Counsel, Dept. Treasury, Washington, 1973-75; pvt. practice law San Francisco, 1990—. Lectr., writer on tax-related subjects Note and comment editor Minn. Law Rev., 1970-71 Co-recipient award for outstanding performance Am. Lawyer Mag., 1981; Fulbright scholar, Italy, 1967-68 Mem. ABA, Calif. Bar Assn., Oakland Mus. Assn. (pres. 1985-87, bd. dirs. 1983-89), Mus. Soc. San Francisco, Fine Arts Mus. (bd. dirs. 1989-90), Order Coif. Republican. Congregationalist.

HENG, GERALD C.W., lawyer; b. London, Mar. 6, 1941; arrived in U.S., 1964; s. Chong-Kwai and York-Choo (Eng); m. Eileen B-Y Tang; 1 child, Sharmaine. BS with honors, Harvard U., Cambridge, Mass., 1967; LLB, London U., 1973; JD, Suffolk U., Boston, 1983; LLM in Taxation, Boston U., 1985. Tchr. Malay and English langs. Ministry of Edn., Malaysia and Singapore, 1959-60; adminstr. hosp. and health Ministry of Health, Malaysia and Singapore, 1960-64; Fulbright fellow, scholar Inst. Internat. Edn., NYC, 1964-69; atty. Heng Assocs., London, 1973-83, ptnr. Brookline, Mass., 1983—. Contbr. articles to newspapers including Boston Globe, Singapore Mirror, Boston Mag. and community newspapers. Mem. ABA, ATLA, Asian-Am. Lawyers Assn., Internat. Assn. Asian Ams. (pres. Boston chpt. 1981—), Boston Bar Assn. (gen. law practice and coms.), Mass. Acad. Trial Attys. Home and Office: 19 Lillian Rd Framingham MA 01701-4820 Office Phone: 508-872-1380. Personal E-mail: gerryheng@gmail.com.

HENGST, HERBERT RANDALL, retired adult education educator; b. Grand Rapids, Mich., May 22, 1924; s. Marion Cecil and L. Elnora H.; m. Georgina Jane, Apr. 1, 1950; children H. Randall II, Julie Ann. AB, Albion Coll., 1948; MS in Edn., Bowling Green State U., 1949; PhD, Mich. State U., 1960. Tchr. Lake Orion (Mich.) H.S., 1949-51; prin. Ortonville (Mich.) H.S., 1951-53, Barnum Jr. H.S., Birmingham, Mich., 1953-58; instr., asst. prof. Mich. State U., East Lansing, 1958-61; dir. higher edn. Mich. Edn. Assn., Lansing, 1961-64; from assoc. prof. to prof. emeritus U. Okla., Norman, 1964—88, asst. dean edn., 1968—71, dir. ctr. studies higher edn., 1971-88, interim dean edn., 1973-74, prof. emeritus, 1988—. Cons. Ministry Edn. Riyadh, Saudi Arabia, 1972-79, Arab Bur. Edn. Gulf States, Riyadh, 1979-87; vis. prof. King Saud U., Riyadh, 1974-75; lectr. in field. Co-author: Contemporary Educational Administration, 1982; co-author, editor: The Geo Lynn Cross Chrestomathy, 1998; editor: Planning & Utilization of Instructional Space, 1960, An Institutional Profile, 1972. Pastor Emanuel, Meth. Charge Gunnisonville, Lansing, 1958-60; co-founder Okla. Inst. Viable Future, Norman, 1975—; bd. dirs., tchr., conf. del. McFarlin Meth. Ch., 1998-99. Recipient Disting. Flying Cross, USAF, 1945; vis. scholar, Harvard U., 1986. Mem. Canterbury Choral Soc. (life), Omicron Delta Kappa, Alpha Tau Omega. Democrat. Avocations: reading, gardening, poetry, singing. Home: 5846 Jenny Ln Bettendorf IA 52722

HENGST, LINDA RUTH, library director; b. Altoona, Pa., Oct. 29, 1946; d. J. Russell and Helen L. Hengst. BS in Social and Behavioral Sci., Ohio State U., 1970. Youth dir. YWCA of Licking County, Newark, Ohio, 1972, asst. exec. dir., exec. dir., 1982-86; asst. regional dir. CARE, Columbus, Ohio, 1986-87; exec. dir. Ohioana Libr. Assn., Columbus, 1988—. Pres. Coun. of Ohio YWCA's, 1992-98, v.p., 2005—; nat. nominating com. YWCA of U.S.A., N.Y.C., 1996-98, nat. strategic planning co., 1994-98; pres. Ohio Womens Inc., Columbus, 1986-88. Avocations: drawing, reading, boating. Home: POB 921 114 Dockside Dr Buckeye Lake OH 43008 Office: Ohioana Libr Assn 274 E 1st Ave Columbus OH 43201 Home Phone: 740-928-2703; Office Phone: 614-466-3831. Personal E-mail: lrhengst@hotmail.com.

HENGSTLER, GARY ARDELL, publisher, editor, lawyer; b. Wapakoneta, Ohio, Mar. 23, 1947; s. Luther C. and N. Delphine (Sims) H.; m. Linda K. Spreen, Mar. 8, 1969 (div. Aug. 1986); children: Dylan A., Joel S.; m. Laura M. Williams, Dec. 15, 1986. BS, Ball State U., 1969; JD, Cleve. State U., 1983. Bar: Ohio 1984, U.S. Dist. Ct. (no. dist.) Ohio 1984, Nev. 2005. Assoc. Blaszak, Schilling, Coey & Bennett, Elyria, Ohio, 1984-85; editor The Tex. Lawyer, Austin, 1985-86; news editor ABA Jour., Chgo., 1986-89, editor, pub., 1989-2000; dir. Donald W. Reynolds Nat. Ctr. Cts. & Media, Reno, 2000—. Contbr. articles to profl. jours. Home: 5055 Carnoustie Dr Reno NV 89502-9724 Office: Donald W Reynolds Nat Ctr Cts & Media U Nev Jud Coll Bldg 358 Reno NV 89557-0001 Home Phone: 775-856-3532; Office Phone: 775-327-8270. Office Fax: 775-327-2160. Business E-Mail: hengstler@judges.org.

HENIKOFF, LEO M., JR., academic administrator, medical educator; b. Chgo., May 9, 1939; m. Carole A. Travis; children from previous marriage: Leo M. III, Jamie Sue. MD with highest honors, U. Ill., Chgo., 1963. Diplomate Am. Bd. Pediat., Am. Bd. Pediat. Cardiology. Intern Presbyn.-St. Luke's Hosp., Chgo., 1963-64, resident, 1964-66, fellow in pediatric cardiology, 1968-69; clin. instr. U. Ill. Coll. Medicine, Chgo., 1964-66; clin. instr. pediatrics Georgetown U. Med. Sch., Washington, 1966-68, clin. asst. prof., 1968; asst. prof. U. Ill. Coll. Medicine, Chgo., 1968-71; asst. prof. pediat. Rush Med. Coll., Chgo., 1971-74, assoc. prof., 1974-79, asst. dean admissions, 1971-74, assoc. dean student affairs, 1974-76, assoc. dean med. scis. and svcs., 1976-79, acting dean v.p. med. affairs, 1976-78, prof. pediatrics, prof. medicine, 1984—; v.p. inter-instl. affairs Rush-Presbyn.-St. Luke's Med. Ctr., Chgo., 1978-79, pres., 1984—2002; pres., CEO; trustee Rush-Presbyn.-St. Luke's Med. Ctr., Chgo., 1984—; dean and v.p. med. affairs Temple U. Sch. Medicine, Phila., 1979-84, prof. pediat. and medicine, 1979-84; pres. Rush U., Chgo., 1984—2002. Adj. attending Presbyn.-St. Luke's Hosp., 1969, asst., 1970-72, assoc., 1973-76, sr. attending, 1977-79, 84—; staff Temple U. Hosp., 1979-84; assoc. staff St. Christopher's Hosp. for Children, 1979-84; mem. Ill. Coun. of Deans, 1977-79; vice chmn. Chgo. Tech. Pk., 1984-85, 86-87, chmn., 1985-86, 87-88; chmn. bd. dirs. Mid-Am. Health Programs, Inc., 1985—, Rush North Shore Health Svcs., 1988-2002, Rush/Copley Health Care Sys. Inc., 1988-2002; bd. dirs. Harris Trust and Savs. Bank, Harris Bankcorp. Inc., Harris Fin. Corp., 1986—, Option Care, Inc., 2002—. Contbr. chpts. to books, articles to profl. jours. Bd. dirs. Fishbein Found., 1975-79, Chgo. Regional Blood Program, 1977-79, Sch. Dist. 69, 1974-75, Johnston R. Bowman Health Ctr. for Elderly, 1984-2002, Chgo. Chamber Musicians, 1998—; bd. mgrs. St. Christopher's Hosp. for Children, 1979-84; bd. govs. Temple U. Hosp., 1979-84, Heart Assn. S.E. Pa., 1979-84; trustee Episc. Hosp., 1983-84, Otho S.A. Sprague Meml. Inst., 1984-2002; adv. bd. Univ. Village Assn., 1984-2002; exec. com. Gov.'s Build Ill. Com., 1985-2002. Lt. comdr. USPHS, 1964-68, Res. 1968—. Recipient Roche Med. award, 1962, Mosby award, 1963, Raymond B. Allen Instructorship award U. Ill. Coll. Medicine, 1966, also Med. Alumni award, 1988, Phoenix award Rush Med. Coll., 1977. Fellow Am. Acad. Pediat., Inst. Medicine Chgo., Coll. Physicians Phila., Am. Coll. Physicians Execs.; mem. Assn. Am. Med. Colls. (chmn. nominating com. 1980, mem. coun. deans 1977-84, mem. audit com. 1984), Coun. Tchg. Hosps. (adminstrv. bd. 1987-90), Pa. Med. Sch. Deans Com., AMA (mem. coun. on ethical and jud. affairs 1984-88), Pa. Med. Soc., Philadelphia County Med. Soc., Assn. Acad. Health Ctrs. (bd. dirs. 1988-94, chmn.-elect 1991-92, chmn. 1992-93), Alpha Omega Alpha (chmn. nat. nominating com. 1981-90, nat. dir. 1979-90, pres. 1989-90), Omega Beta Pi, Phi Eta Sigma, Phi Kappa Phi.

HENIKOFF, STEVEN, research scientist, educator; BS in Chemistry, U. Chgo.; PhD in Biochemistry and Molecular Biology, Harvard U., 1977. Post-doctoral rschr. U. Washington, affiliate assoc. prof. genome sciences, 1985—; mem. basic sciences divsn. Fred Hutchinson Cancer Rsch. Ctr., Seattle, 1988—, Howard Hughes investigator, 1990—. Mem.: NAS. Office: Fred Hutchinson Cancer Rsch Ctr 1100 Fairview Ave N Seattle WA 98109-1024 Office Phone: 206-667-4515. Office Fax: 206-667-5889. E-mail: steveh@fhcrc.org.

HENINGER, GEORGE ROBERT, psychology professor, researcher; b. LA, Nov. 15, 1934; s. Owen P. and Rachel (Cannon) H.; m. Julie Hawkes, June 27, 1957; children: Steven, Catharine, Karen, Brian. BS, U. Utah, 1957, MD, 1960. Diplomate Am. Bd. Psychiatry and Neurology. Intern Boston City Hosp., 1960-61; resident in psychiatry Mass. Mental Health Ctr., 1961-63, chief resident, 1963-64; clin. assoc., clin. neuropharmacology rsch. ctr. St. Elizabeth's Hosp. NIMH, Washington, 1964-65, program specialist, office of dir. Bethesda, Md., 1965-66; asst. prof. psychiatry, assoc. chief rsch. ward Yale U., New Haven, 1966-71, assoc. prof., 1971-76, chief rsch. ward, 1971-78, prof. clin. psychiatry, 1976-78, prof. psychiatry, dir. Abraham Ribicoff Rsch. Facilities, 1978-93, assoc. chmn. rsch. dept. psychiatry, 1988-93, dir. lab. clin. and molecular neurobiology, 1993—. Cons. NIMH, 1975-86, 88-94, NIH, 1987, McGill U., 1989, VA, 1990-94, Nat. Rsch. Coun. Can., 1991-93, Nat. Inst. Aging, 1992-93, Wellcome Trust, 1992-94, Pfizer Inc., Merck, Sharp & Dohme, Inc., The Upjohn Co., Hoffman La Roche, Inc., Burroughs Wellcome Co., Bristol-Meyers Co., Squibb Corp., Kali DuPhar, Inc.; bd. sci. advisors, Neurogen Corp. REviewer manuscripts Archives Gen. Psychiatry, Am. Jour. Psychiatry, Psychiatry Rsch., Biol. Psychiatry, Jour. Affective Disorders, Jour. Clin. Psychopharmacology, Life Scis., Neurochemistry Internat., Psychiatry, Schizophrenia Bull., Psychoneuroendocrinology, Jour. AMA. Sr. asst. surgeon USPHS, 1964-66. Recipient Rsch. Sci. Devel. award Type II, NIMH, 1971, 1st prize Anna Monika Found., 1995; grantee NIMH, 1971, 74, 77, 82, 85, 89, 91. Fellow Am. Coll. Neuropsychopharmacology, Am. Psychiat. Assn.; mem. AAAS, Am. Psychopath. Assn., Soc. Neurosci., Soc. Biol. Psychiatry, Psychiat. Rsch. Soc., N.Y. Acad. Scis., Conn. Psychiat. Soc., Sigma Xi, Phi Kappa Phi, Alpha Omega Alpha. Avocation: running. Office: Yale U 34 Park St New Haven CT 06511

HENINGER, SIMEON KAHN, JR., language educator; b. Monroe, La., Oct. 27, 1922; s. Simeon Kahn and Elsye (Lieber) H.; m. Irene Callen, July 16, 1957; children— Dale Callen, Kathryn Leigh, Philip Ward, Polly Elizabeth, Simeon Kahn III; m. Dorothy Cooper Langston, May 30, 1971 BS, Tulane U., 1944, BA, 1947, MA, 1949; B.Litt. (Fulbright scholar), Oxford U., Eng., 1952; PhD, Johns Hopkins U., 1955. Instr. Duke U., Durham, NC, 1955-57, asst. prof., 1957-62, assoc. prof., 1962-65, prof., 1965-67; prof. English U. Wis.-Madison, 1967-71; chmn. dept. U. Wis., Madison, 1968-70; prof. English U. B.C., Vancouver, Canada, 1971-82; disting. prof. English and comparative lit. U. N.C., Chapel Hill, 1982—. Author: A Handbook of Renaissance Meteorology, 1960, Touches of Sweet Harmony, 1974, The Cosmographical Glass, 1977, Sidney and Spenser: The Poet as Maker, 1989, Proportion Poetical: The Subtext of form in the English Renaissance, 1994; editor: Thomas Watson, The Hekatompathia, 1964, Edmund Spenser, Poetry, 1970, Edmund Spenser, Shepheardes Calender, 1979, Kalendar of Sheepehards, 1979, Framing Fact and Fiction: Perspective in Early Modern England, 1992; asst. editor Modern Language Notes, 1953-55; mem. editorial bd. Duquesne Studies in Lang. and Lit., 1976-93, Renaissance and Reformation, 1976-93, Spenser Studies, 1977-93, Studies in English Lit., 1978-93, John Donne Jour., 1982-93, Huntington Libr. Quar., 1982-86, Spenser Newsletter, 1986-92, Studies in Philology, 1987-93, ANQ: A Quarterly Jour., 1988-93; contbr. articles to profl. jours. Exec. sec.-treas. Southeastern Renaissance Conf., 1958-67; mem. Nat. Shakespeare Anniversary Com., 1963-64; mem. ctrl. exec. com. Folger Inst. Renaissance and 18th Century Studies, 1982-92. Capt. USAAF, 1943-46. Folger Library fellow, 1961, Guggenheim fellow, 1962-63, Southeastern Inst. Medieval and Renaissance Studies fellow, 1967, Huntington Library fellow, 1970-71, 81, Killam Sr. fellow, 1975-76, Folger Inst. fellow, 1984, Ariz. Ctr. for Medieval and Renaissance Studies fellow, 1990. Mem. MLA, ACLU, Renaissance Soc. Am. (adv. coun. 1958-68, 75-80), Spenser Soc. (adv. coun. 1977-80, 86-90, pres. 1988-89), Milton Soc. (adv. coun. 1980-83), Medieval Acad. Am., Phi Beta Kappa Home: 750 Weaver Dairy Rd #247 Chapel Hill NC 27514-1493 E-mail: timdothening@mindspring.com.

HENINGTON, DAVID MEAD, retired library director; b. El Dorado, Ark., Aug. 16, 1929; s. Bud Henry and Lucile Check (Scranton) H.; m. Barbara Jean Gibson, June 2, 1956; children— Mark David, Gibson Mead, Paul Billins. BA, U. Houston, 1951; MS in L.S., Columbia U., 1956. Young adult libr. Bklyn. Pub. Libr., 1956-58; head lit. and history dept. Dallas Pub. Libr., 1958, asst. dir., 1962-67; dir. Waco (Tex.) Pub. Libr., 1958-62, Houston Pub. Libr., 1967-95; ret., 1995. Served with USAF, 1951-55. Council on Library Resources fellow, 1970-71; recipient Liberty Bell award Houston Bar Assn., 1976 Mem. ALA, AIA (hon. mem. Tex. chpt.), Am. Mgmt. Assn., Tex. Libr. Assn. (Libr. of Yr. 1976, Disting. Svc. award 1993), Philos. Soc. Methodist. Home: 6225 San Felipe St Houston TX 77057-2809 Office Phone: 713-780-3798. Personal E-mail: dmhenington@houston.rr.com.

HENISZ, WITOLD JERZY, social sciences educator; b. Warsaw, Aug. 16, 1968; s. Jerzy and Anna Henisz; m. Marcia West, July 13, 1996; children: Sophie, Katrine. BA in Econs., Pol. Sci., Stanford U., 1991; MA in Internat. Relations, Johns Hopkins Sch. Advanced Internat. Studies, Washington, DC, 1993; PhD in Bus., U. Calif., Berkeley, 1998. Asst. prof. mgmt. The Wharton Sch., Phila., 1998—2004, assoc. prof. mgmt., 2004—. Prin. Prima LLC, Phila. Contbr. articles to profl. jours. Mem.: Acad. Mgmt., Acad. Internat. Bus. Avocations: bicycling, hiking, travel, cooking, baseball. Office: The Wharton School 3115 SH-DH 3620 Locust Walk Philadelphia PA 19104-6370 Office Phone: 215-898-0788. Business E-Mail: henisz@wharton.upenn.edu.

HENKE, MICHAEL JOHN, lawyer, educator; b. Evansville, Ind., Aug. 3, 1940; s. Emerson Overbeck and Beatrice (Arney) H.; m. Leni Edith Anderson, Mar. 20, 1966; children: Blake, Paige, Britt. BA summa cum laude, Baylor U., 1962, LLB, 1965; LLM, NYU, 1966. Bar: Tex. 1965, D.C. 1967, Va. 2005. Assoc. Covington & Burling, Washington, 1966-73, Vinson & Elkins, Washington, 1974—75, ptnr., 1976—2004; sec., gen. counsel Space Adventures, Ltd., 2005—. Adj. prof. U. Va. Law Sch., 1988-94, 96—; chmn. pro bono adv. com. Legal Aid Soc., D.C., 1990-96, trustee, 1992-06, chmn. ways & means com., 1997-2000, v.p., 2000—02, pres., 2002-04; Washington adv. coun. Baylor Washington Program, 1989-92; sesquicentennial coun. of 150 Baylor U., 1993-95. Author: (with others) Petroleum Regulation Handbook, 1980, Natural Gas Yearbook, 1995; mem. editl. bd. Nat. Gas Mag., 1992-97, Best Lawyers in America, 1989—, Best Lawyers in Washington, 1997, Worlds Leading Competition and Antitrust Lawyers, 1997—, World's Leading Litigation Lawyers, 1997—; contbr. articles to profl. jours. Founder, chmn. Old Presbyn. Meeting House Day Care Ctr., Alexandria, Va., 1970-74; trustee Alexandria Country Day Sch., 2000-03. Recipient Gladys award La. State U. Sch. Law, 2003; Kenneson fellow. Mem. ABA (chmn. energy antitrust subcom. litigation sect. 1987-88, vice chmn. energy litigation com. 1988-89, chmn. 1989-92, chmn. ann. fall meeting 1993, divsn. dir. 1993-95, co-chmn. audiotaping and videotaping com. 1995-96, co-chmn. ins. coverage litigation com. 1996-98, coun. 1998-2001, co-chair task force on judiciary 2001-03, Pres.'s Commn. on 21st Century Judiciary 2002-03), D.C. Bar Assn., Tex. Bar Assn., Va. State Bar (corp. counsel), Baylor U. Alumni Assn. (bd. dirs. 1994-98, mem. sesquicentennial coun. 2006-), Met. Club, Belle Haven Country Club, Farmington Country Club (Charlottesville). Democrat. Avocations: skiing, fly fishing, tennis, backpacking. Home: 310 Charles Alexander Ct Alexandria VA 22301-1500 Office: Vinson & Elkins 1455 Pennsylvania Ave NW Ste 600 Washington DC 20004-1013 Business E-Mail: mhenke@velaw.com.

HENKE, ROBERT JOSEPH, federal agency administrator; BA, Notre Dame U.; MPA, Syracuse U. Presdl. intern office of asst. sec. for fin. mgmt. and comptroller U.S. Dept. Navy; profl. staff mem. subcom. on def., com. on appropriations U.S. Senate; navy officer Operation Enduring Freedom, Operation Desert Shield, Operation Desert Storm U.S. Naval Reserve; prin. dep. under sec. and comptroller U.S. Dept. Def.; asst. sec. veterans affairs for mgmt. US Dept. Veterans Affairs, 2005—.

HENKE, TRACY ANN, federal official; b. Moscow Mills, Mo., 1969; BA in Polit. Sci., U. Mo., Columbia, 1991. Sr. policy adv. to Senator Christopher S. Bond from Mo. US Senate, Washington; prin. dep. asst. atty. gen., Office Justice Programs US Dept. Justice, Washington, 2001—03, acting asst. atty. gen. Office Justice Programs, dep. assoc. atty. gen., 2003—05; asst. sec., office grants & tng. US Dept. Homeland Security, Washington, 2006, exec. dir. office state and local govt. coord., preparedness, 2006—.

HENKEL, HERBERT LUDWIG, diversified industrial products company executive; b. Reid, Austria, Apr. 22, 1948; m. Gloria Henkel; 2 children. BS in Aerospace Engring. and Applied, Poly. U., MS in Mech. Engring.; MBA, Pace U. Mem. tech. staff Bell Labs.; design engr. Grumman Aerospace; v.p. sales and mktg. Chgo. Pneumatic Tool Co., Hilti, Inc.; pres., COO Southern Fastening Sys. and Unifast Industries, Inc.; pres. Greenlee Textron, Rockford, Ill., 1987-93; pres. indsl. products segments Textron, Inc., 1993-98, exec. v.p., 1998-99, COO, 1998-2000, pres., 1999-2000; chmn., CEO, pres. Ingersoll-Rand Co. Ltd., Montvale, NJ, 2000—. Bd. dirs. C.R. Bard Corp., 3M Corp. Avocations: woodworking, golf, tennis. Office: Ingersoll-Rand Co Ltd 155 Chestnut Ridge Rd Montvale NJ 07645

HENKEL, KATHRYN GUNDY, lawyer; b. West Columbia, Tex., Oct. 16, 1952; d. Louis Ory Jr. and Patricia Dolores (Fields) Gundy. BA cum laude, Rice U., 1973; JD cum laude, Harvard U., 1976. Bar: Tex. 1976, US Dist. Ct. (no. dist. Tex.) 1982, US Ct. Appeals (5th cir.) 1994, US Tax Ct. 1981, US Supreme Ct. 1983; bd. cert. estate planning and probate law, Tex. Bd. Legal Specialization. Ptnr. Hughes & Luce, LLP, Dallas, 1982—. Author: Estate Planning and Wealth Preservation: Strategies and Solutions, 1997. Mem. adv. coun. Cmtys. Found. Tex. Inc., 1982—; mem. planned giving adv. com. Children's Med. Ctr., Dallas; trustee Dallas Opera. Fellow Am. Coll. Trust and Estate Counsel; mem. ABA (vice chair sect. real property, probate and trusts com. on generation-skipping transfers 1992-95, chair sect. of taxation com. on estate and gift taxes 1993-95, coun. dir. sect. taxation 1996-99, co-chair sect. real property, probate and trust law estate planning study com. on law reform), State Bar Tex. (chair sect. taxation 1992-93), Dallas Bar Assn. (past chair sect. taxation), Tex. Bar Found. Roman Catholic. Avocations: reading, travel. Office: Hughes & Luce LLP 1717 Main St Ste 2800 Dallas TX 75201-7342 Office Phone: 214-939-5475. Office Fax: 214-939-5849. E-mail: kathryn.henkel@hughesluce.com.*

HENKEL, KATHY, composer; b. LA, Nov. 20, 1942; d. Norman Nicholas and Lila Rhea (Lee) Henkel; m. Michael Eric Manes (div.). BA in hist., UCLA, 1965; BM in music, Calif. State U., Northridge, 1976, MA in music, 1982. Music rschr. Paramount Pictures, LA, 1978—81; music reviewer L.A. Times, 1979; scriptwriter, prod. KUSC-FM, LA, 1984—89; program annotation, edn. cons. Chamber Music/LA, 1987—95; program annotation L.A. Chamber Orch., 1988—98, edn. cons., 1998—; liner note writer Pro Piano Records, NYC, 1994—2003; composer, owner Sign of the Silver Birch Music, LA, 2004—. Adv. bd. Los Angeles City Coll. Music Dept., 1994—. Composer various chamber music, song cycles. Recipient Commn. for Music award, State of Alaska, 1994. Mem.: Nat. Acad. Rec. Arts and Scis., Profl. Musicians Local 47, Phi Beta Kappa Alumni, Phi Beta Women's Profl. Fraternity. Avocation: hiking Cornwall coastal path. Home: 2367 Creston Dr Los Angeles CA 90068

HENKEN, BERNARD SAMUEL, clinical psychologist, speech pathologist; b. Everett, Mass., May 30, 1919; s. Issac Edward and Sarah B. (Shatzman) H.; m. Charlotte Popovsky, Dec. 20, 1953; children: Karen Beth, Donna Michele. Student, Boston Coll., 1938-41; BS, Harvard U., 1947; MS, Purdue U., 1950; DSc in Psychology, Calvin Coolidge Coll., 1955. Lic. psychologist, rehab. counselor; cert. sch. psychologist, cert. speech and language pathologist, Mass.; diplomate Am. Assn. Clin. Counselors; nat. cert. in speech lang. pathology. Psychologist Carney Hosp., Boston, 1950-51; dir. speech pathology, psychologist Audiology Ctr., Lynn, Mass., 1951-56; psychologist, chief clin. counseling svcs. Brusch Med. Ctr., Cambridge, Mass., 1956-80; speech pathologist Mass. Gen. Hosp., Boston, 1951-52; speech pathologist, sch. psychologist Everett Pub. Schs., 1955-85; psychologist Rescue Inc., 1959-71, v.p., 1972-74; psychologist, clin. counselor North Shore Children's Hosp., Salem, Mass., 1966-74; psychologist Medford (Mass.) Pediatric Assocs., 1974-94. Prof. psychology Calvin Coolidge Coll., Boston, 1958-69; lectr. psychology Lawrence Meml. Hosp., Medford, Mass., 1975-77, univ. extension courses Harvard U., 1960-68; psychologist Alfano Med. Inst., Melrose, Mass., 1956-64; guest lectr. Duke U. Med. Ctr., 1965, 72; co-chair symposium on clin. counseling and medicine Tufts U., 1974. Contbr. articles to profl. jours.; creator Henken Operator Safety Evaluation Technique; editor Clin. Counseling Bulletin, 1970-84. Cpl. M.C., U.S. Army, 1942-45, PTO. Recipient Lifetime Achievement award Mass. Sch. Psychology, 2001, Marie Curie medal of honor, Cambridge, Eng., 2006. Mem. APA (charter mem. divsn. psychotherapy), Am. Coll. Counselors (cert. forensic psychology), Am. Coll. Counselors, Mass. Speech and Hearing Assn. (treas. 1957-59), Am. Assn. Clin. Counselors (pres. 1959-63), Mass. Sch. Psychologists Assn. (pres. 1972-74). Republican. Jewish. Avocations: sports, music. Home and Office: 118 Waverly Ave Melrose MA 02176-4217 Office Phone: 781-665-0408.

HENKIN, ROBERT ELLIOTT, nuclear medicine physician; b. Pitts., June 7, 1942; s. Hyman and Nettie (Jaffee) H.; m. Denise Dulberg, June 26, 1966 (dec. 1985); children: Gregory, Joshua, Steven; m. Renae Marley, Nov. 27, 1988 (dec. Nov. 2006). Student, Cornell U., 1960-62; BA, NYU, 1965, MD, 1969. Diplomate Am. Bd. Nuclear Medicine, Nat. Bd. Med. Examiners. Internship gen. surgery Bellevue Med. Ctr., NYU, NYC, 1969—70; resident in diagnostic radiology Northwestern U., Chgo., 1970—72, resident in nuc. medicine, 1972—74, asst. prof. radiology, 1974—76; from asst. prof. to assoc. prof. radiology Loyola U., Maywood, Ill., 1976—80, dir. nuc. medicine, 1976—98, prof. radiology, 1980—2005, acting chair dept. radiology, 2000—02, dir. nuc. medicine, 2002—05, vice chair dept. radiology, 2002—05, prof. emeritus radiology, 2006—. Fellow Am. Coll. Radiology, Am. Coll. Nuc. Physicians (pres. 1990); mem. AMA, Am. Coll. Physician Execs., Soc. Nuc. Medicine (bd. dirs., trustee 1983-89, 2000-04, v.p. 1995-96, ho. dels. 1998-2004). Home: 875 E 22d St Ste 202 Lombard IL 60148-5025 Home Phone: 630-627-0072. Personal E-mail: unm@mindspring.com.

HENKIN, ROBERT IRWIN, neuroscientist, internist, nuclear medicine physician, medical products executive; b. LA, Oct. 5, 1930; s. William and Ida Mildred (Scher) H.; m. Marsha Lynn Jacobs, May 15, 1964 (div. Jan. 1982); children: Amanda Joan, Michael Jonathan, David Gorman, Joshua Adam, Elizabeth Madeline, Hannah Deborah; m. Jane Pettit, 2007; stepchildren: William Christopher Pettit, Sara Jane Pettit, Andrew Scott Pettit. AB cum laude, U. So. Calif., 1951; MA, UCLA, 1953, PhD, 1956, MD, 1959. Intern in medicine U. Calif. Hosp., LA, 1959-60; resident in medicine Jackson Meml. Hosp., U. Miami (Fla.), 1960-61; commd. officer USPHS, 1961, advanced through grades to sr. surgeon, resigned, 1975; rsch. assoc. Nat. Inst. Mental Health, NIH, Bethesda, Md., 1961-63, sr. investigator, 1963-69; chief sect. on neuroendocrinology Nat. Heart and Lung Inst., NIH, Bethesda, 1969-75; dir. Ctr. Molecular Nutrition and Sensory Disorders Georgetown U. Med. Ctr., Washington, 1975-85, assoc. prof. pediat. and neurology, 1975-82, prof., 1982—, dir. Taste and Smell Clinic, 1985—. Pres., CEO Sialon Corp., Washington, 1987—; cons. Campbell Soup Co., 1969-74, USDA/NIH, 1975—, Hooker Chem. Co., Buffalo, 1976-77, Washington Conf. for Zinc, 1985—, Florasynth, NYC, 1986-91, Squibb Pharm. Co., NYC, 1986-87, Blue Cross/Blue Shield, 2003—, Quigley Pharma, 2004-06, Becton-Dickson, 2006—; guest worker NIH, Bethesda, Md., 2005-. Author: Zinc, 1975; editor Biol. Element Rsch., Nutrition; contbr. articles to profl. jours.; patentee saliva, taste diagnostics, wound healing protein, drugs to treat taste/smell disorders. Recipient Vicennial medal Georgetown U., 1984; Atwater Kent fellow UCLA, 1957; grantee Dept. Def., USDA, NIH, 1969—. Fellow Am. Coll. Nutrition; mem. Biophys. Soc. (charter), Am. Physiol. Soc., Am. Soc. Nutrition, Am. Fedn. Med. Rsch., Am. Soc. Clin. Investigation, Composers Guild Am., Cosmos Club, Phi Beta Kappa, Sigma Xi (nat. lectr. 1984-87, Giovanni di Chiro Sci. award 1998). Avocations: tennis, running, skiing. Home: 6601 Broxburn Dr Bethesda MD 20817-4709 Office: Ctr Mol Nutrn/Sensory Disorders Taste and Smell Clin 5125 MacArthur Blvd NW Ste 20 Washington DC 20016-3300 Home Phone: 301-229-0388; Office Phone: 202-364-4180. Office Fax: 202-364-9727. Business E-Mail: doc@tasteandsmell.com.

HENKIN, TINA M., science educator, researcher; BA in Biology, Swarthmore Coll., 1977; PhD in Genetics, U. Wis., 1984. Joined Ohio State U., 1995—, prof. dept microbiology. Spkr. in field. Contbr. articles to profl. jours. Recipient Award in Molecular Biology, NAS, 2006, Disting. Scholar award, Ohio State U., 2004. Fellow: AAAS, Am. Acad. Microbiology; mem.: RNA Soc., Am. Soc. Microbiology. Office: Ohio State U Dept Microbiology 484 W 12th Ave Columbus OH 43210-1292 Office Phone: 614-688-3831. Office Fax: 614-292-8120. Business E-Mail: henkin.3@osu.edu.

HENLEY, ARTHUR, writer, editor; b. Rockaway Beach, NY, Sept. 9, 1921; s. Nathan Siegel and Theresa (Hohauser) H.; m. Janet Radskin, June 3, 1950; children: Eric, Kenneth. Engr. Assoc., Pratt Inst., 1944; BA, CCNY, 1969. Tech. writer Fairchild Camera Co., 1944-45; TV program cons., 1960—; mem. faculty NYU, 1969-70. Mental health cons., Nat. Assn. Mental Health Keynoter, coll. lectr. Radio writer, producer shows Bob & Ray, Make Up Your Mind, 13 by Henley; others; also writer advt. jingles; TV producer Kate Smith Show, Make Up Your Mind, Broadway Open House; TV writer, producer, also indsl. films, others; mag. contbr. Ladies Home Jour., McCalls, Family Health, Public Affairs Com., N.Y. Times, Sat. Eve Post, others, 1961—; author: The Mathematics of Humor, 1948, Demon In My View, 1966, Make Up Your Mind, 1967, Yes Power, 1969, The Right to Lie, 1970, Schizophrenia, 1971, revised edit. 1987, What Other Child-Care Books Don't Tell You, 1972, The Complete Alibi Handbook, 1972, The Difficult Child, 1973, How to Be a Perfect Liar, 1978, Don't Be Afraid of Cataracts, 1978, Don't be Afraid of Cataracts, rev. edit., 1983, Phobias The Crippling Fears, 1987, paperback edit., 1988, Lily & Joel: A Novel of Life, Love and Audio Tapes, 1992, Talking Book and Braille edit., 1994; contbr. to anthologies How to Write for Pleasure and Profit, You and Your Mind, Treasury of Tips for Writers, How to Write Television Comedy, Tools of the Writer's Trade; editor: Interdisciplinary Communications Program, Smithsonian Inst., 1975. Cons. med. editor: Globe Communications, 1976-79; columnist Brides Mag, 1970. Recipient Russell Sage Found. award., TV-Radio Mirror Gold medals (2).; work included in U. Wyo. Am. Heritage Ctr. Mem. Am. Soc. Journalists and Authors, Nat. Assn. Sci. Writers, PEN, AFTRA. Clubs: Nat. Press. Home and Office: 73-37 Austin St Forest Hills NY 11375-6219 E-mail: ah55@webtv.net. *If I have learned anything from living it is that a static life is no life at all while a life of change without direction is only half a life.*

HENLEY, DON, singer, drummer, songwriter; b. Linden, Tex., July 22, 1947; m. Sharon Summerall, May 20, 1995. Drummer with band Eagles, L.A.; performer: (albums) The Eagle, 1972, Desperado, 1973, On the Border, 1974, One These Nights, 1975, Hotel California, 1976, The Long Run, 1979, Hell Freezes Over, 1994; performer: (solo, singer, composer) I Can't Stand Still, 1982, Building the Perfect Beast, 1985 (Grammy award for song The Boys of Summer), The End of Innocence, 1989, Actual Miles: Henley's Greatest Hits, 1995, Inside Job, 2000, (songs) Dirty Laundry, 1982, Long Way Home, I Will Not Go Quietly, New York Minute, If Dirt Were Dollars, Little Tin God, The Heart of the Matter. Mem. Active So.

Poverty Law Ctr., Walden Woods Project. Named MusiCares Person of Yr., 2007; named to Songwriters' Hall of Fame, 2000. Office: c/o Warner Bros Records Inc 3300 Warner Blvd Burbank CA 91505

HENLEY, DOUGLAS E., medical association administrator; b. Hope Mills, NC, Jan. 1, 1951; m. Mary Henley. MD, U. NC Sch. Medicine, Chapel Hill, 1977. Diplomate Am. Bd. Family Practice. Resident NC Memorial Hospital, Chapel Hill, NC, 1977—80; pvt. practice Hope Mills, NC; exec. v.p. Am. Acad. Family Physicians; assoc. clinical instructor U. NC Sch. of Medicine. Mem. editl. bd. Family Practice News, Jour. Family Practice. Mem. N.C. Cervical Cancer Task Force, U.S. Congress' Office of Tech. Assessment Adv. Panel; bd. dirs. Am. Acad. Family Physicians Found. Office: Am Acad Family Physicians PO Box 11210 Shawnee Mission KS 66207-1210

HENLEY, ERNEST JUSTUS, retired chemical engineering professor; b. Sept. 30, 1926; BS, U. Del., 1950; D Engring. Sci., Columbia U., 1953. Asst. prof. nuc. and chem. engring. Columbia U., NYC, 1953-59; prof. chemistry and chem. engring. Stevens Inst. Tech., Hoboken, NJ, 1959-64; chief of party AID Mission, Rio de Janeiro, 1964-66; prof. chem. engring. U. Houston, 1964—. Founder, bd. dirs. Maxxim Med., St. Petersburg, Fla.; bd. dirs. Circon Corp., St. Petersburg, Fla., Serve Houston, Main St. Theater, Houston, Procedyne Corp., New Brunswick, NJ; tech. cons.; founding dir. RAI Rsch., 1953-82, Henley Healthcare, 1984-2000. Pres. The Henley Found. Office: U Houston Dept Chemical Engineering Houston TX 77204-0001 Home Phone: 713-621-4254; Office Phone: 713-743-4326. Personal E-mail: henleyej@aol.com.

HENLEY, ERNEST MARK, physics professor, retired dean; b. Frankfurt, Germany, June 10, 1924; came to U.S., 1939, naturalized, 1944; s. Fred S. and Josy (Dreyfuss) H.; m. Elaine Dimitman, Aug. 21, 1948; children: M. Bradford, Karen M. BEE, CCNY, 1944; PhD, U. Calif., Berkeley, 1952; DSc (hon.), Ohio State U., 2004, Justus Liebig U., Germany, 2005. Physicist Lawrence Radiation Lab., 1950-51; research assoc. physics dept. Stanford U., 1951-52; lectr. physics Columbia U., 1952-54; mem. faculty U. Wash., Seattle, 1954—, prof. physics, 1961-95; prof. emeritus, 1995—; chmn. dept. U. Wash., 1973-76, dean Coll. Arts and Scis., 1979-87, dir. Inst. for Nuclear Theory, 1990-91; assoc. dir. Inst. for Nuclear Theory U. Wash., 1991—2006. Chmn. Nuclear Sci. Adv. Com., 1986-89. Author: (with W. Thirring) Elementary Quantum Field Theory, 1962, (with H. Frauenfelder) Subatomic Physics, 1974, 2nd edit. 1991, Nuclear and Particle Physics, 1975; mng. editor Internat. Jour. Modern Physics, 1992-; contbr. articles to profl. jours. Bd. dirs. Pacific Sci. Ctr., 1984-87, Wash. Tech. Ctr., 1983-87; trustee Associated Univs., Inc., 1989—, chmn. bd., 1993-96. Recipient Sr. Alexander von Humboldt award, 1984, T.W. Bonner prize Am. Physics Soc., 1989, Townsend Harris medal CCNY, 1989; F.B. Jewett fellow, 1952-53, Sr. fellow NSF, 1958-59, Guggenheim fellow, 1967-68, Sr. fellow NATO, 1976-77. Fellow AAAS (chmn. physics sect. 1989-90), Am. Phys. Soc. (chmn. divsn. nuclear physics 1979-80, pres. 1992, sec. treas. NW sect. 1999-2005, chair NW sect. 2007-, Disting. Svc. award 2004), Am. Acad. Arts and Scis.; mem. NAS (chmn. physics sect. 1998-2001), Sigma Xi. Achievements include research in symmetries, nuclear reactions, weak interactions and high energy particle interactions. Office: Univ Wash Physics Dept PO Box 351560 Seattle WA 98195-1560 Office Phone: 206-543-2896. Business E-Mail: henley@phys.washington.edu.

HENLEY, JACK CARSON, retired military officer; b. W.Va., Oct. 6, 1924; d. Daniel L. and Laura Virginia Henley; BA, Art Inst. Pitts., 1993. Commd. 2d. lt. U.S. Army, 1943, advanced through grades to col., 2005, ret. Pres., chmn. Rama Rama, Miami Beach, Fla., 1960—61. Campaign mgr. Joseph F. Whelan for Senate. Decorated Silver star medal, Two Bronze Star medals with first oak leaf cluster and v. device for valor, Combat Inf. badge, Two Purple Hearts, Commendation medal with two oak leaf clusters, Good Conduct medal with three knots, S. Pacific WWII medal with arrow head, Two bronze battle stars, Presdl. Unit citation with first bronze oak leaf cluster Navy, Meritorious Unit emblem, Am. Def. Svc. medal, The Am. Campaign medal, Asiatic Pacific Campaign medal with two bronze svc. stars and one bronze arrowhead, World War II Victory medal, Army Occupation medal with German and Japan clasp, Nat. Def. Svc. medal, Combat Infantryman badge, Ranger Parachute emblem, Armed Forces Res. medal, Army Res. Components Achievement medal, Armed Forces Expeditionary medal, Philippine Liberation medal with bronze svc. star and bronze arrowhead, Philippine Independence medal with one bronze svc. star, Belgian Fourragere, Solomon Islands Victory medal, Hon. Svc. lapel button World War II. Mem.: DAV, VFW. Home: 713 N 2d St Hamilton MT 59840

HENLEY, JEFFREY O., computer software company executive; b. Phoenix, Nov. 6, 1948; s. Justin Oniel and Jane Ellen (Rice) H.; children: Amy, Julie, Todd. BA in Econs., U. Calif., Santa Barbara, 1966; MBA in Fin., UCLA, 1967. Cost acctg. supr. Hughes Aircraft Co., Culver City, Calif., 1967-70; divsn. contr. Tridair Industries, Redondo Beach, Calif., 1970-72; divsn. contr. internat. ops. Fairchild Camera & Instrument, Mountain View, Calif., 1972-75; dir. fin. Memorex Corp., Santa Clara, Calif., 1975-79; v.p., contr. Saga Corp, Menlo Park, Calif., 1979-86, exec. v.p., CFO, 1986-91, Pacific Holding Co., Menlo Park, Calif., 1986—91, Oracle Corp., Redwood City, Calif., 1991—2004, bd. dirs., 1995—, chmn., 2004—, mem. exec. mgmt. com. Bd. dirs. CallWave, Inc. Bd. dirs. Herbert Hoover Boys' & Girls' Club, Menlo Park, Calif., 1983, pres., 1984; chmn. Mid-Pacific Region Trustees for Boys & Girls Club of Am. Mem. Fin. Exec. Inst., Sigma Phi Epsilon. Republican. Presbyterian. Avocations: golf, running. Office: Oracle Corp 500 Oracle Pky Redwood City CA 94065-1675*

HENLEY, JOSEPH OLIVER, manufacturing executive; b. Sikeston, Mo., June 25, 1949; s. Fred Louis and Bernice (Chilton) H. m. Jane Ann Rhodes, Aug. 21, 1971 BSBA, U. Mo., 1972; MBA, Mich. State U., 1973. Ops. analyst Midland-Ross, Inc., Cleve., 1974, prodn. control mgr., 1974—75; engring. sys. mgr. Cameron-Waldron divsn., Somerset, NJ, 1989—95, prodn. control mgr., 1976—77; prodn. planning and mfg. sys. mgr. ICM divsn. Massey Ferguson, Inc., Akron, Ohio, 1977—78; sr. audit specialist mfg. United Techs. Corp., Hartford, 1978—82, mfg. control sys. mgr. Diesel Sys. divsn., 1983—84, materials mgr. Diesel Sys. divsn., 1983—84, internal cons. Diesel Sys. divsn., 1984—86; inventory mgr. Aircraft divsn. Pratt & Whitney, Hartford, 1986—89, mgr. synchronous mfg. Aircraft divsn., 1989—95; dir. mfg. Case Corp., Racine, Wis., 1996—2000; mfg. exec. cons., 2000—. With Army N.G., 1970-72 Mem. Nat. Assn. Purchasing Mgmt., Am. Prodn. and Inventory Control Soc., Assn. for Mfg. Excellence (N.E. region bd. dirs.), Beta Gamma Sigma, Sigma Iota Epsilon, Omicron Delta Epsilon. Presbyterian. Home and Office: 320 NW Rockwood Ct Lees Summit MO 64081

HENLEY, PATRICIA JOAN, consultant, former superintendent; b. Harrison, Ark., Dec. 30, 1944; d. Durward Milford and Nola V. (Foresee) Ellis; m. Robert Lee Henley; children: Robert, Kevin, Laura. BA, Wichita State U., 1968; MS, Pitts. State U., Kans., 1973, EdS, 1976; PhD, Kans. State U., 1980. Tchr. Wichita (Kans.) Pub. Schs., 1968-70; tchr. Oswego (Kans.) Pub. Schs., 1970-73; elem. prin. Aurora (Mo.) Schs., 1973-77; grad. teaching asst. Kans. State U., Manhattan, 1977-78; asst. supt. Turner Unified Sch. Dist. #202, Kansas City, Kans., 1978-82; supt. Platte County Schs., Platte City, Mo., 1982-89; dep. supt. Kansas City (Mo.) Schs., 1989-91; founding dir. Mo. Ctr. for Safe Schs., 1995—2000; elem. prin. Ft. Osage Schs., Independence, Mo., 1991—95; supt. Univ. Acad., 2000—06; cons., 2006—. Asst. rsch. prof. grad. courses U. Mo. Kansas City; assessor, supt. mem. Mo. Dept. Elem. and Secondary Edn. Spl. Edn. Panel; founding dir. Mo. Ctr. Safe Schs., 1995-2000; prin., CEO U. Acad., 2000—. Recipient Outstanding Leadership award Jackson County Inter-Agy. Coun., 1995, Heroes in Edn. award Reader's Digest, 1995; named Bus. Woman Yr. Townsend Publs., 1989. Mem. Nat. Assn. Elem. Sch. Prins. (Nat. Disting. prin. 1994), Mo. Assn. Elem. Sch. Prins., Kansas City Suburban Assn. Elem. Sch. Prins., Rotary. E-mail: henleyp@sbcglobal.net.

HENLEY, PAUL THOMAS, music educator, researcher; b. Aberdeen, SD, Dec. 2, 1966; s. Gerald Dennis and Nadene Audrey Henley; m. DeAnn Francis Lybeck, Aug. 4, 1990; children: Victoria Ann, Micah Gerald, Katrina Louis. MusB, U. of SD, 1985—89; MA in edn., fine arts and humanities, Chadron State Coll., 1990—95; PhD in music edn., La. State U. and A&M Coll., 1996—99. Dir. of bands Belle Fourche Ind. Sch. Dist., SD, 1989—91, Chadron City Schools, Nebr., 1991—94, Wahlert H.S., Dubuque, Iowa, 1994—96; asst. prof. music U. of Montana-Western, 1999—2000; asst. prof. of music SW Mo. State U., 2000—03; tchg. and learning specialist Tex. State Tchrs. Assn. NEA, 2003—. Chair Mo. Soc. of Music Tchr. Edn., 2000—; membership coord. MayDay Group, 2001—; advisor Student Mo. NEA, 2002—03; mem. dist. academic adv. com. Pflugerville Ind. Sch. Dist., Tex., mem. profl. devel. com., mem. calendar com. Author: (book reviews) Choral Journal; mem. editl. com. Missouri Journal of Research in Music Education, 2002—; contbr. articles to profl. jours. Mem. PTA; mem. academic adv. com. Pflugerville Ind. Sch. Dist.; mem. youth com. Immanuel Lutheran Ch., Pilvergville, Tex.; choir condr. St. Richard's Episc. Ch. U. fellowship, La. State U. and A&M Coll., 1996—99, Funding for Results award, SW Mo. State U., 2001, Music Educators Scholarship Found., 1990, scholar, Blue Cross/Blue Shield of Nebr., 1992. Mem.: Nat. Staff Orgn., Profl. Staff Assn., Tex. State Tchrs. Assn., Assn. of Supervision of Curriculum Devel., MayDay Group (membership coord. 2001—02), NEA, Am. Choral Directors Assn., Music Educators Nat. Conf., Pi Kappa Lambda. Episcopalian. Office: Tex State Tchrs Assn 316 W 12th St Austin TX 78701 Office Phone: 512-476-5355. E-mail: paulh@tsta.org.

HENLEY, RICHARD JAMES, health facility administrator; b. Wroclaw, Poland, May 31, 1956; came to US, 1959; s. Henry and Lidia (Alper) Horczak. BA and MA summa cum laude, CCNY, 1978. Asst. v.p. fin. Mt. Sinai Med. Ctr., NYC, 1978-80, dir. fin. planning, 1980-81, assoc. dir. fin., 1982-84, dir. fin. profl. svcs., 1984-85; v.p. fin., treas. Vassar Bros. Med. Ctr., Poughkeepsie, NY, 1985-92, sr. v.p. for adminstrn., treas., 1992-97, exec. v.p., treas., 1997—2005; exec. v.p., COO, CFO Health Quest, Poughkeepsie, 1999—2005; pres. and CEO Pocono Health Sys., East Stroudsburg, Pa., 2005—, Pocono Med. Ctr., Pa., 2005—. Treas. VBH Corp., Poughkeepsie, 1986-99, Found. Vassar Bros. Med. Ctr., 1986-2003, VBH Ins. Co., Ltd., 1988-2005, pres., 1991—2005, Riverside Diversified Svc., Inc., 1986-92, pres., 1992—2005, Riverside Mgmt. Svc., Inc., 1986-92, pres., 1992—2005, Alamo Amulance Svc., 1986-92, pres., 1992-2005; pres. Hudson Valley Home Care, Inc.; pres. HealthServe, LLC; bus. adv. coun. SUNY, New Paltz, 1999—2005; bd. dir. Dutchess County Econ. Devel. Corp., chmn., 2003-05. Contbr. articles to profl. jours. Treas. Bardavon 1869 Opera House, Poughkeepsie, 1986-91, Family Svcs. Dutchess County, Poughkeepsie, 1987-88, Samuel F. B. Morse Hist. Site, 1998-99; pres. Hudson Terr. Owners' Corp., Poughkeepsie, 1987-88. Fellow Healthcare Fin. Mgmt. Assn. (nat. dir. 1994-96, nat. sec. 1996-97, nat. treas. 1997-98, nat. chmn. elect 1998-99, nat. chmn. 1999-2000, cost effectiveness award 1979-80, William G. Follmer Merit award 1986, Robert H. Reeves Merit award 1989, Fredric T. Muncie Mert award 1991, Medal of Honor award 1994, Stephen A. Ryan Meml. award 2003), Am. Heart Assn. (bd. dirs.), Am. Coll. Health Exec. (regent Hudson Valley Adirondack 2002-06, bd. govs. 2006—), Pocono Mountains C. of C. (dir. 2006—). Office: Pocono Health Sys 206 E Brown St East Stroudsburg PA 18301 Office Phone: 570-476-3348. Business E-Mail: rhenley@pmchealthsystem.org.

HENLEY, ROBERT LEE, school system administrator; b. Aug. 7, 1934; m. Patricia J. Ellis; 3 children. BA, Washington U., St. Louis, 1957, MEd, 1958; EdD, U. Mo., 1967. Tchr., counselor, pers. office, bus. mgr., asst. supt. Mehlville Sch. Dist., St. Louis, 1958-75; supt. schs. Independence (Mo.) Pub. Schs., 1975-93; asst. prof. U. Mo., Kansas City, 1991—. Cons. in field; instr. various colls. & univs., St. Louis and Columbia, 1975—. Trustee Andrew Drumm Inst., Independence, 1980—; bd. dirs. Am. Cancer Soc., Independence, 1978—; adv. com. Kansas City Arts Ptnrs. Program, 1990—. Recipient Community Leader award Comprehensive Mental health Svcs., Jackson County, Mo., 1983, Disting. Svc. award Mo. chpt. Am. Assn. on Mental Deficiency, 1983, Outstanding Educator award State of Mo., 1985, Innovation in Edn. award Nat. Ctr. for Ednl. Computing, 1985-86, Exec. Educator 100 award Exec. Educator Mag., 1987, Sch. Adminstr. award Kennedy Ctr./Alliance for Arts Edn., Washington, 1988, Disting. Svc. award Am. Assn. Sch. Adminstrs., 1993; named Mo. Supt. of Yr., 1992. Mem. Am. Assn. Sch. Adminstrs., Mo. Assn. Sch. Adminstrs. (exec. com. 1988—, Robert L. Pearce award 1991, Disting. Svc. award 1993), Jackson County Sch. Adminstrs. Assn. (pres. 1981), Mid-Am. Assn. Sch. Supts., Met. Sch. Study Group (pres. 1985-86), Independence C. of C.

HENMAN, TIM, professional tennis player; b. Oxford, England, Sept. 6, 1974; m. Ivy Henman (div.); m. Lucy Henman, Dec. 11, 1999; 1 child, Rose Elizabeth. Profl. tennis player, 1993—; mem. Davis Cup squad, 1994. Mem. player coun. ATP, 1997—98, charities chmn., 2000. Recipient Silver medal at Olympics with Neil Broad, 1996; winner Syndney Task Kent, 1997; winner Under 18 singles and doubles Nat. Titles, 1992; winner doubles title Guardian Direct Cup, 1999; winner 11 singles titles, 4 doubles titles. 430-219 career singles record; winner, 11 singles titles ATP. Office: Internat Mgmt Group 1 Erieview Plz Ste 1300 Cleveland OH 44114-1715*

HENNAH, VIVIAN LISA, school system administrator; b. New Haven, Conn. d. George Albert and Bernaddette Keen; m. Allen Harold Stanley, Nov. 20, 1996; children: Harold Beid, Stanley Rudloph; 1 child, Allen Jr. Pub. sch., New Haven. Writer Gifted and Talented, New Haven, 1975—78. Contbr. poet: poetry book Young Words and Vision, Whisper, Giggles Laugh, Patterns of Life, 2003, Best Poets and Poems of 2003. Recipient Editor's Choice award, Poetry.com, Internat. Libr. Poetry, 2005. Home: 151 Cedar St New Haven CT 06519

HENNE, PRESTON A., engineering executive; m. Connie Henne; children: Matthew, Lauren, Alexis. BS in Aero. and Astronautical Engring. with honors, U. Ill., 1969; MS in Engring., Calif. State U., Long Beach, 1974, postgrad. in Bus. Adminstrn. Project aerodynamicist McDonnell Douglas Corp., 1969-94, sect. chief aerodynamics tech. programs, br. chief aerodynamics configuaration design and devel., mgr. advanced program aerodynamics and acoustics, chief design engr. MD-80 program, v.p., gen. mgr. MD-90 program; sr. v.p. GV program Gulfstream Aerospace Corp., Savannah, Ga., 1994—. Spkr. in field. Editor Applied Computational Aerodynamics, 1990; contbr. articles to profl. jours. Recipient Outstanding Recent Alumnus award U. Ill., 1982, Mgmt. award NASA, 1984, Outstanding Alumnus award U. Ill., 1989. Fellow AIAA (applied aerodynamics tech. com., Engr. of Yr. 1996); mem. NAE, Sigma Gamma Tau, Phi Kappa Phi, Sigma Tau, Tau Beta Pi. Avocations: skiing, golf, mountain biking. Home: 1 Belfair Ct Hilton Head Island SC 29928-3343 Office: Gulfstream Aerospace Corp PO Box 2206 Savannah GA 31402-2206

HENNEKE, BEN GRAF, retired humanities educator; b. St. Louis, Mo., May 20, 1914; s. Francis Joseph and Ruby O. (Graff) Henneke; m. Ellen Eaves Henneke, Dec. 26, 1940 (dec.); children: Hilary Carlson, Ben G. Jr. BA in English, U. Tulsa, Okla., 1935; MA in Theatre, U. Iowa, Iowa City, 1940; PHD in Speech, U. Ill., Urbana, 1956; LHD (hon.), U. Tulsa, Okla., 1967. Asst. prof. speech U. Tulsa, 1936—42, assoc. prof. speech, 1942—48, prof. speech, radio, and theatre, 1948—52, acad. v.p., 1952—58, pres., 1958—67, prof. humanities, 1967—79, pres. emeritus, 1982. Cons. Amco Petroeum Co., Am. Petroleum Inst., 1948—58; ednl. advisor Assoc. of Episc. Coll., 1967. Author: Reading Aloud Effectively, 1954, Laura Keene: Actress, Innovation, and Impressario, 1990, Writing with a Quill Pen, 2005. Named to Okla. Hall of Fame, 1962; recipient Silver Anvil award, Pub. Relations Soc. Am., 1945, 1952, 1954. Mem.: Phi Beta Kappa (hon.). Episc. Avocation: book collecting. Home: 3701 N Cin Tulsa OK 74106 Office: U Tulsa 600 S Coll Tulsa OK 74104

HENNELL, ROBERT WILLIAM, III, secondary school educator; b. Mount Vernon, Ohio, Sept. 9, 1952; s. Robert William Hennell, Jr. and Emily Gloria (Catrino) Hennell; m. Elizabeth Ellen Jameson, July 7, 1984; children: Joseph Robert, Jaclyn Grace. MusB in Music Edn. magna cum laude, Bowling Green State U., Ohio, 1974, MusM in Conducting, 1977. Cert. tchr. Ohio, 1974, music educator Music Educator's Nat. Conf., 1991. Dir. of bands Antwerp (Ohio) Local Schs., 1974—75; grad. asst. Bowling Green (Ohio) State U., 1975—77; dir. of bands Antwerp (Ohio) Local Schs., 1977—80; project coord. - LPGA pro-am golf tournament The J.M. Smucker Co., Orrville, Ohio, 1991—92; asst. golf coach Orrville (Ohio) HS, 2001—; dir. of bands Orrville (Ohio) City Schs., 1980—. Cons. Capital U. Complete Band Dir. Workshop, Columbus, Ohio, 1990; guest condr. Firelands Conf. Honor Band, Greenwich, Ohio, 2000. Condr. Orrville (Ohio) Cmty. Band, 1981—90; mem. Orrville Exch. Club, Ohio, 1982—, chmn. youth of month project, 1989—90; civilian participant US Army War Coll., Carlisle Barracks, Pa., 1991; coach Orrville (Ohio) Youth Baseball League, 1993—96. Recipient Golden Apple Achiever award, Ashland Oil Co., 1995. Mem.: Am. Sch. Band Dirs. Assn. (state chair 1986—88, state band clinic chair 1987, all-state band chair 1987), Ohio Music Edn. Assn. (adjudicated event chair 1984—86, band affairs chair 1989—91, dist. pres. 1991—93, adjudicator 1980—99), Music Educator's Nat. Conf. (profl. certification steering com. 1993—94), Ohio HS Golf Coach's Assn., Phi Kappa Phi, Phi Beta Mu. Avocations: reading, book collecting, travel, golf, baseball. Home: 1331 Independence Drive Orrville OH 44667 Office: Orrville City Schools 841 North Ella Street Orrville OH 44667 Office Phone: 330-682-4448. E-mail: orvl_hennell@tcom.net.

HENNEMAN, RICHARD BRUCE, counselor, pastor; b. Latrobe, Pa., Nov. 15, 1954; s. George Henry and Doris Mary Henneman; m. Tammy Sue Nailor, July 16, 1977; children: Janelle Leigh Allen, Michelle Lynn Komora. AA, Shippensburg U., Shippensburg, Pa., 1986; MA in Divinity, Winebrenner Seminary, Findlay, Ohio, 1989, D (hon.) in Life Experience, 1986; ArtsD in Divinity, Rochville U., Wilmington, Del., 2005. Quality control inspector Reeves Hoffman, Carlisle, Pa., 1974—77; 911 comm. operater Cumberland County, 1977—86, deputy coroner, 1981—86; deputy waterways patrolman Commonwealth Pa., Harrisburg, 1981—86; pastor Chs. of God Gen. Conf., Findlay, 1989—; supr., counselor Cornell Abraxas, South Mountain, Pa., 2006—. Asst. chief Friendship Hose Co. #1, Newville, Pa., 1979—86, EMT, 1974—86; dir. Doubling Gap Corp., Newville, 1989—. Republican. Avocations: hunting, fishing, birdwatching.

HENNEMAN, STEPHEN CHARLES, psychotherapist; b. Chgo., June 17, 1949; s. Charles Philip Jr. and Marion Louise (Eichberger) Henneman; m. Patricia Anne York, Feb. 14, 1975 (div. Sept. 1980); 1 child, Charles Philip III; m. Marion Jean McDermand, Oct. 4, 1980; stepchildren: Ervin F. Jr. Schrock, Lisa Ann Schrock, Thomas M. Schrock. BA in Journalism, Colo. State U., 1971; MA in Counseling, U. N.D., 1987. Cert. profl. counselor, Am. Counseling Assn. Commd. 2d lt. USAF, 1971, advanced through grades to maj., 1984; missile launch officer 570th Strategic Missile Squadron, Davis Monthan AFB, Ariz., 1972-76; info. officer 321st Strategic Missile Wing, Grand Forks AFB, ND, 1976-79; missile combat crew flight comdr. 446th Strategic Missile Squadron, Grand Forks AFB, 1980-82; missile combat crew comdr. evaluator 321st Strategic Missile Wing, Grand Forks AFB, 1982, wing nuclear surety officer, 1982-83, chief weapon safety branch, 1983-85; asst. ops. officer 320th Strategic Missile Squadron, F E Warren AFB, Wyo., 1985-86; dep. wing inspector 90th Strategic Missile Wing, F E Warren AFB, 1986-88; ops. officer 319th Strategic Missile Squadron, F E Warren AFB, 1988-89; dep. chief war res. materiel div. Hdqrs. U.S. Air Forces in Europe, Ramstein Air Base, Fed. Republic Germany, 1989-92; vol. and outreach coord. Safe House/Sexual Assault Svcs., Inc., Cheyenne, Wyo., 1992-93; quality control investigator Dept. Employment State of Wyoming, Cheyenne, 1993-95; counselor Wyo. State Penitentiary, Rawlins, 1995-96, counseling team leader, 1996-97; residential counselor Aurora (Colo.) Cmty. Mental Health Ctr., 1997-99, mental health clinician, 1999-2001, profl. counselor, 2001—. Advocate, counselor Safehouse/Sexual Assault Svcs., Inc., Cheyenne, 1985-89; sec., bd. dirs. Carbon County Citizens Organized to See Violence Ended, 1996-97. Mem. ACA, Am. Mental Health Counselors Assn., Colo. Counselors Assn., Nat. Cert. Counselors. Avocations: photography, popular music recordings collecting, reading. Office Phone: 303-617-2756. Business E-Mail: schenneman@comcast.net.

HENNENHOEFER, JAMES A., lawyer; b. St. Louis, July 19, 1941; BS, U. Mo., 1963; JD, Western State U., San Diego, 1970. Bar: Calif. 1971, US Dist. Ct. (so. dist. Calif.) 1971, US Supreme Ct. 1974. Atty. James A. Hennenhoefer, Inc., Vista, Calif., 1971—. Lectr. family law Calif. Continuing Edn. of the Bar, 1978—; judge pro tempore San Diego County Superior Ct., 1975—. Trustee San Diego County Law Libr., 1999—2002. Comdr. USNR. Recipient Norby Judiciary award, Best Family Law Atty., San Diego County, 1999. Mem.: Inns of Ct. (master 1998—2003), Am. Coll. Family Trial Lawyers, Internat. Acad. Matrimonial Lawyers (bd. govs. 1995—98, 2002—06), San Diego County Assn. Cert. Specialists, Am. Acad. Matrimonial Lawyers (chmn. mktg. com. 1990—98, pres. so. Calif. chpt. 1993—94, pres.-elect 2001—03, pres. 2003—05, So. Calif. Family Law Person of Yr. 1998), State Bar Calif. (chmn. exec. com. in family law sect. 1994—95, family law edn. chair 1991—93, chmn. coun. sect. chairs 1997), ABA (chmn. pub. rels. com. in family law sect. 1993—94), North San Diego County Bar Assn. (dir. 1984—87). Office: James A Hennenhoefer PC 316 S Melrose Dr Ste 200 Vista CA 92083-6618 Office Phone: 760-941-2260. Office Fax: 760-945-1805. E-mail: jahesq@aol.com.*

HENNES, ROBERT TAFT, former management consultant, investment executive; b. Jamestown, NY, Mar. 8, 1930; s. Theodore Preston and Lucille (Kane) H.; m. Frances Walker Pratt, May 9, 1953 (div. 1962); children: Robert Taft, Duncan Pratt, Margaret Nickerson, Theodore Preston II; m. Grace Margaret Bruton, Oct. 9, 1971. AB, Harvard U., 1951; MBA, U. Pa., 1952. With Lummus Co., NYC, 1952-62; exec. v.p., dir. Conahay & Lyon, Inc. (advt.), NYC, 1962-70; sr. v.p. Cole & Assos., Boston, 1970-72; chmn., dir. Hennes & Cox Inc., NYC, 1972-77; sr. dir. Spencer Stuart & Assos., NYC, 1977-88. Dir. Oldwyck Industries, Inc., N.Y.C. Mem. Kennett Square Golf and Country Club, Harvard Club of N.Y. Home: PO Box 728 Kennett Square PA 19348-0728

HENNESSEE, E. LEE, securities trade executive, financial consultant; b. Raleigh, NC, Sept. 1, 1953; d. William Edward Hennessee and Mary F. Dillon; m. Charles J. Gradante, Oct. 31, 1992. BA, Randolph Macon Coll., 1975. V.p. Thomson McKinnon Securities, NYC, 1987-87; E.F. Hutton & Co., Inc., NYC, 1987-92, Shearson-Lehman, NYC, 1992-97; chmn., mng. prin., founder WPG Hennessee Hedge Fund Adv. Group, NYC, 1994—. Personal and corp. investor Hedge Fund Cons.; advisor to bd. trustees Randolph Macon W.C., 1981-85. Co-host Squawk Box (monthly) CNBC, N.Y.C. Founder Campership Funds Ann. Charity Girl Scouts of Greater N.Y.; co-founder N.Y.C. Relief to the Homeless. Mem. Jr. League of

N.Y.C., N.Y.C. Women's Christian Fellowship. Home: 45 Sutton Pl S Apt Ph New York NY 10022-2444 Office: Hennessee Hedge Adv Group Fund Advisors 500 5th Ave Fl 47 New York NY 10110-0002*

HENNESSEY, AUDREY KATHLEEN, computer researcher, educator; b. Fairbanks, Apr. 4, 1936; d. Lawrence Christopher and Olga Virginia (Strandberg) Doheny; m. Gerard Hennessey, Mar. 10, 1963; children: Brian, Kate. BA, Stanford U., 1957; HSA, U. Toronto, Ont., Can., 1968; PhD, U. Lancaster, Eng., 1982. Asst. dir. European sales U. Soc., Heidelberg, Germany, 1959—61; landman's asst. Union Oil Co. Calif., Anchorage, 1962; sys. analyst No. Telephones, New Liskeard, Canada, 1962—63; adminstr. group pension Mfgs. Life Ins., Toronto, 1963—65; instr. office sys. Adult Edn. Ctr., Toronto, 1965—68; lectr. office sys. Salford Coll. Tech., Lancashire, England, 1968—70; sr. lectr. data processing Manchester Met. U., England, 1970—79; lectr. computation U. Manchester Inst. Sci. and Tech., 1979—82; assoc. prof. computer sci. Tex. Tech. U., Lubbock, 1982—86, assoc. prof. info. sys., 1987—94, prof. info. sys., 1994—2001; pres., CEO ISOA Inc., 1994—2002; dir. Internat. Ctr. Informatics Rsch., 1996—2000; v.p., gen. mgr. YMG/Rudolph Tech. Inc., 2002—03; pres., CEO Internat. Ctr. Informatics Rsch. Inc., Colleyville, Tex., 2002—; mng. dir. Konsult Europe Ltd./ICIR, 2002—; pres. Hennessey Mgmt. LLC, 2002—. Dir. Inst. for Studies of Orgn. Automation/Tex. Tech. U., Lubbock, 1987-95; vis. instr. Fed. Law Enforcement Tng. Ctr., Glynco, Ga., 1984-88; adj. prof. West Tex. A&M U., Canyon, 1994-95, U. Alaska, Anchorage, 1995, U. Tex., Dallas, 1995-98; mem. NATO panel of experts on visualization of massive data sets, 1996-98. Author: Computer Applications Project, 1982; contbg. author: Semiconductor International, 1998, 2002; editor (procs.) Office Document Architecture Internat. Symposium, English version, 1991; contbr. articles to profl. jours. Organizer Explorer Scouts Computer Applications, Lubbock, 1983-85; treas. Tivoli Wines LLC, 2006—. Recipient various awards, Tex. Instruments, 1982—86, 1994, Xerox Corp., 1985, Halliburton, 1986, Sys. Exploration, 1987, State of Tex., 1988—93, 1996—99, Knowledge-based Image Analysis award, USN Tencap, 1991—96, Immunization Tracking Sys. award, Robert Wood Johnson Found., 1993, Sematech S77 award, 1994, award, Leica GmbH, 1994—2001. Mem.: IEEE (contbg. author Systems Man Cybernetics 1984), Assn. Info. Tech. Profls. (chpt. pres. 1989, Disting. Info Sci. award 1992), Assn. Computing Machinery, Soc. Mfg. Engrs., Spl. Interest Group for Artificial Intelligence (JEDEC working group ISO semiconductor defect data stds. 1999—2002), Sigma Xi Rsch. Soc. (chpt. pres. 1996—97). Achievements include 18 patents in field. Office: Konsult Europe/Internat Ctr Informatics Rsch 1205 Hall Johnson Rd Colleyville TX 76034 Office Phone: 817-479-0565. Personal E-mail: icirinc@aol.com.

HENNESSEY, JOHN WILLIAM, JR., academic administrator, educator; b. Danville, Pa., Mar. 25, 1925; s. John William and Martha Scott (Braun) H.; m. Jean Marie Lande, June 26, 1948 (dec. June 2004); children: John William III, Martha Scott; m. Madeleine May Kunin, Feb. 12, 2006. AB, Princeton U., 1948; MBA, Harvard U., 1950; PhD, U. Wash., 1956; MA (hon.), Dartmouth Coll., 1959; LHD (hon.), York Coll. of Pa., 1978, U. N.H., 1981. From instr. to assoc. prof. orgn. and adminstrn. Coll. Bus. Adminstrn., U. Wash., 1950-57; prof. Amos Tuck Sch. Bus. Adminstrn., Dartmouth Coll., 1957-87, assoc. dean, 1962-68, dean, 1968-76, Charles H. Jones 3d Century prof. mgmt., 1976-87, now emeritus; provost U. Vt., Burlington, 1987-89, interim pres., 1990. Prof. Inst. pour l'Etude des Methodes de Direction de l'Enterprise, Lausanne, Switzerland, 1959; trustee NH Cmty. Loan Fund, 2005—. Author: (with Austin Grimshaw) Organizational Behavior, 1960, (with others) Hospital Policy Decisions, 1966. Trustee Mary Hitchcock Meml. Hosp., Hanover, 1963-86, chmn. bd. 1977-83; trustee Ednl. Testing Svc. 1975-80, 81-85, chmn. bd. 1978-80, 84-85; chmn. governing coun. Dartmouth Hitchcock Med. Ctr., 1977-83, trustee, 1983-86, 91—, chmn. bd. trustees, 1992-95; bd. visitors Grad. Sch. Bus., U. Pitts., 1970-76, 79-88; mem. Pres.'s Coun. on Bus. Sch., U. Vt., 1982-87; dir. Milbank Meml. Fund, 1982-87; trustee U. Vt., 1985-87, Med. Ctr. Hosp. Vt., 1988-90, Vt. Law Sch., 1999—; bd. dirs. Kendal at Hanover, 1995-01, chmn., 1998-2001; bd. dirs. Ams. for Campaign Reform, 2003—, New Hampshire Cmty. Loan Fund, 2005-; mem. Citizens' Commn. NH Ct. Sys., 2005-. 1st lt. U.S. Army, 1943-46. Mem. Am. Assembly Collegiate Schs. Bus. (dir. 1970-77, pres. 1975-76), Phi Beta Kappa. Home: 9 Harbor Watch Rd Burlington VT 05401-5269 Business E-Mail: john.hennessey@dartmouth.edu.

HENNESSEY, PATRICK DANIEL, musician, educator, musicologist; b. New Orleans, La., Sept. 30, 1952; m. Heidi Rebecca Burgo, June 27, 1981. MusB (performance), Calif. State U., Long Beach, 1979; MA in Music Edn., U.Hawaii, Honolulu, 1995. Prin. trombone Royal Hawaiian Band, Honolulu, 1983—; dir. jazz ensembles U. of Hawaii, Honolulu, 1983—. Adj. faculty Chaminade U., Honolulu, 2000—. Musician: (freelance musician) Live and Recorded Performances with numerous nationally recognized artists.; contbr. articles on Royal Hawiian Band to popular publs. Clinician; guest performer Numerous Schools throughout the state of Hawaii, Hawaii, 1983—2003. Petty officer second class USN, 1970—74, Vietnam; Long Beach. Recipient Outstanding Achievement award Musicology, U. Hawaii Dept. Music, 1996, 1997, 1999, Donald Matsumori Rsch. award, 1992, Humanities in the Arts Founder's Award, 2002; grantee, Grad. Student Orgn., 1999. Mem.: Musicians Assn. of Hawaii, Internat. Assn. for Jazz Edn., Hawaiian Hist. Soc., Coll. Music Soc., Soc. for Am. Music, Internat. Trombone Assn., Mortar Board.

HENNESSEY, ROBERT JOHN, pharmaceutical company executive; b. Danbury, Conn., Dec. 5, 1941; s. James P. and Helen H.; m. Carol Stankwitz, Feb. 8, 1964; children: Jil, Christopher, Michele, Matthew. AB, U. Conn., 1963, MA in Internat. Affairs, 1967. Mgmt. intern Sec. of Commerce, Washington, 1967-69; assoc. dir. market planning MSD Internat., Rahway, NJ, 1969-71, dir. strategic planning, 1971-74; dir. corp. strategy devel. SmithKline, Rixensart, Belgium, 1974-76, regional dir. biols. Europe, 1976-79; dir. internat. bus. devel. Abbott Labs., North Chgo., Ill., 1979-82; dir. corp. planning Sterling Drug Inc., NYC, 1980-82, v.p. corp. planning, 1982-86, v.p. corp. devel., 1986-90; pres. Hennessey & Assoc., Ltd., pharm. cons., Westport, Conn., 1990-93; pres., CEO Genome Therapeutics Corp. (former Collaborative Rsch., Inc. now Oscient Pharmaceuticals), Waltham, Mass., 1993—2000; chmn. Oscient Pharmaceuticals, 1993—2003; CEO Penwest Pharmaceuticals, 2005. Bd. dirs. Maggioni-Winthrop, Milan, Steinberg & Lyman Health Care Ventures, NYC, Penwest Pharmaceuticals, 1997-, Oscient Pharmaceuticals. Mem. Fayerweather Yacht Club (Black Rock, Conn.).

HENNESSEY, WILLIAM JOSEPH, physician; b. Troy, NY, Mar. 8, 1947; BS, Rensselaer Poly. Inst., 1969; MD, Albany Med. Coll., 1973. Resident in ob-gyn Albany (N.Y.) Med. Ctr. Hosp., 1973—76; pvt. practice specializing in gynecology Green Island, NY, 1976—. Office Phone: 518-272-9140. E-mail: whennessey@aol.com.

HENNESSY, DANIEL KRAFT, lawyer; b. Summit, NJ, Jan. 4, 1941; s. Robert Emmett and Agnes Lyons (Lindle) H.; m. Susan Elizabeth (Bettina) Ware, June 17, 1972; children— Mary Elise, Daniel Joseph, Michael Ware, Catherine Anne. BS with highest honors, U.S. Naval Acad., 1963; JD cum laude, Harvard U., 1970. Bar: Tex. 1970. Ptnr. Hughes & Luce (formerly Hughes & Hill), Dallas, 1973—2006, Garfield Traub Devel. LLC, Dallas, 2007—, gen. counsel, 2007—. Bd. regents Ave Maria U., 2005—06. Editor: Harvard Law Rev, 1969-70. Mem. bd. advisers Jesuit Coll. Prep. Sch., Dallas, 1975-88; bd. dirs. Dallas-North Tex. region NCCJ, 1976-83, Catholics United for Faith, Inc., 1982-99 , Greater Dallas Right to Life Ednl. Found., 1974-86, The Highlands Sch., 1986—, Cath. Pro-life Com. of North Tex., 2001—, Legatus Internat., Dallas chpt., 2003—, Lumen Inst., 2007—. Lt. USN, 1963—67, Vietnam. Decorated knight grand cross Equestrian Order of Holy Sepulchre of Jerusalem, Knight of Malta. Mem. Dallas Bar Assn., State Bar of Tex., Legatus Internat. Roman Catholic. Home: 4405 Beverly Dr Dallas TX 75205-3001 Office Phone: 972-716-3848. Personal E-mail: hennesdk@yahoo.com.

HENNESSY, DEAN MCDONALD, lawyer, municipal official, director; b. McPherson, Kans., June 13, 1923; s. Ernest Weston and Beulah A. (Dunn) H.; m. Marguerite Sundheim, Sept. 6, 1946 (div. Sept. 1979); children: Joan Hennessy Wright, John D., Robert D. (dec.), Scott D. (dec.); m. Darlene MacLean, Apr. 4, 1981. AB cum laude, Harvard U., Cambridge, Mass., 1947, LLB, 1950; MBA, U. Chgo., 1959. Bar: Ill. 1951. Assoc. Carney, Crowell & Leibman, Chgo., 1950-53; atty. Borg-Warner Corp., Chgo., 1953-62; with Emhart Corp., Farmington, Conn., 1962-88, asst. sec., 1964-67, sec., gen. counsel, 1967-74, v.p., sec., gen. counsel, 1974-76, v.p., gen. counsel, 1976-86, sr. v.p., gen. counsel, 1986-88, ret., 1988. Incorporator Ill. Citizens for Eisenhower, 1952; chmn. Citizens Activities, Ill. Citizens for Eisenhower, 1952, 56; Justice of the peace, mem. bd. suprs. Proviso Twp., Ill., 1952-56; vice chmn. Jr. Achievement Chgo., 1959; program chmn. trade and industries divsn. United Rep. Fund Ill., 1961; trustee West Hartford Bicentennial Trust, Inc., 1976-77, Friends and Trustees of Bushnell Meml., Hartford, 1978-84; bd. dirs. Royal Homestead Condominium Assn., Juno Beach, Fla., 1990-93. Served to lt. (j.g.) USNR, 1943-46. Sheldon fellow Harvard U., 1947. Mem. ABA, Mfrs. Alliance for Productivity and Innovation (vice chmn. law coun. 1984-87, chmn. 1987, 88), John Harvard Soc., Oliver Wendell Holmes Soc. Republican. Presbyterian.

HENNESSY, ELLEN ANNE, lawyer, financial consultant, educator; b. Auburn, NY, Mar. 3, 1949; d. Charles Francis and Mary Anne (Roan) H.; m. Frank Daspit, Aug. 27, 1974. BA, Mich. State U., 1971; JD, Cath. U., 1978; LLM in Taxation, Georgetown U., 1984. Bar: D.C. 1978, U.S. Ct. Appeals (D.C. cir.) 1978, U.S. Supreme Ct. 1984. Various positions NEH, Washington, 1971-74; atty. office chief counsel IRS, Washington, 1978-80; atty.-advisor Pension Benefit Guaranty Corp., Washington, 1980-82; assoc. Stroock & Stroock & Lavan, Washington, 1982-85, Willkie Farr & Gallager, 1985-86, ptnr. Washington, 1987-93; dep. exec. dir. and chief negotiator Pension Benefit Guaranty Corp., Washington, 1993—98; sr. v.p. and dir. Actuarial Sci. Assoc. Holdings Inc., 1998—2000; sr. v.p. Aon Cons. Inc., Washington, 2000—03; pres. Fiduciary Counselors, Inc., 1999—. Adj. prof. law Georgetown U., Washington, 1985—; mem. com. on continuing profl. edn. Am. Law Inst./ABA, 1994—97; dir. Women's Inst. for a Secure Retirement, Nat. Women's Law Ctr. Mem. ABA (supervising editor taxation sect. newsletter 1984-87, mem. standing com. on continuing edn. 1990-94, chair joint com. on employee benefits 1991-92, mem. standing com. on tech. and info. sys. 2002—06, mem. task force on corp. responsiblity, 2002-03), Worldwide Employee Benefits Network (pres. 1987-88), DC Bar Assn. (mem. steering com. tax sect. 1988-93, chair continuing legal edn. com. 1993-95), Am. Coll. Employee Benefits Counsel (bd. govs. 2000-03). Democrat. Avocation: whitewater canoeing. Home: 1926 Lawrence St NE Washington DC 20018-2734 Office: Ste 700 700 12th St NW Washington DC 20005-3949 Home Phone: 202-526-0157; Office Phone: 202-558-5141. Business E-Mail: nell.hennessy@fiduciarycounselors.com.

HENNESSY, JOHN L., academic administrator; b. NYC, Sept. 22, 1952; m. Andrea Hennessy; children: Thomas, Christopher. B in Engring. in Elec. Engring., Villanova U., 1973; MS in Computer Sci., SUNY, Stony Brook, 1975, PhD in Computer Sci., 1977, DSc (hon.), 2001; DHL (hon.), Villanova U., 2001; doctorate (hon.), Universitat Politecnica de Catalunya, 2002, Ecole Polytechnique Federale de Lausanne, 2003. Asst. prof. elec. engring. Stanford U., Calif., 1977—83, assoc. prof. elec. engring., 1983—86, dir., computer rsch. lab., 1983—93, prof. elec. engring. and computer sci., 1986—, Willard and Inez Kerr Bell Endowed Prof. Elec. Engring. and Computer Sci., 1987—2001, chmn. dept. computer sci., 1994—96, dean Sch. Engring., 1996—99, provost, 1999—2000, pres., 2000—. Founder, chief scientist MIPS Computer Sys., 1984—92; chief arch. Silicon Graphics Computer Sys., 1992—98; founder MIPS Techs. (formerly MIPS Computer Sys.), 1998—; chmn. bd. dirs. T-span; mem. com. study internat. devels. in computer sci. and tech. NRC, 1988, mem. computer sci. and tech. bd., 1989—94, mem. com. study acad. careers for exptl. computer scientists, 1992—93, mem. status and direction of high performance computing and comm. initiative, 1995, mem. commn. phys. scis., math. and applications, 1998—99; mem. adv. com. computer and info. sci. and engring. NSF, 1992—96, chair oversight rev. of computer and info. sci. and engring. instnl. infrastructure program, 1992, mem. task force on future supercomputer ctrs. program, 95; tech. adv. bd. Microsoft Corp., 1992—96, Virtual Machine Works, 1995—96, Tensilica, 1998—99; strategic adv. bd. NetPower, 1992—95; mem. fellowship sel. com. Sloan Found., 1993—96; chmn. info. sci. and tech. Def. Advances Rsch. Projects Found., 1993—96, chair, 1994—95; mem. com. study investment strategy DARPA Def. Sci. Bd., 1998—99; mem. various conf. coms.; spkr. in field; bd. dirs. Alantec Corp., 1995—96, Cisco Systems, 2002—; chmn., bd. dirs. Atheros, 1998—. Co-author (with D.A. Patterson): Computer Organization and Design: The Hardware/Software Interface, 1993, Computer Organization and Design: The Hardware/Software Interface, 2d edit., 1998; co-author: Computer Architecture: A Quantitative Approach, 1990; contbr. articles to profl. jours. Named Profl. Young Investigator, NSF, 1984; recipient Disting. Alumnus award, SUNY, Stony Brook, 1991, John J. Gallen Memorial award, Villanova U., 1983, J. Stanley Morehouse Meml. award, 1997, Benjamin Garver Lamme medal, Am. Soc. Engring. Edn., 2000, Eckert-Mauchly award, ACM and IEEE Computer Soc., 2001, Seymour Cray Award, 2001. Fellow: IEEE (Emmanuel R. Piore award 1994, John Von Neumann medal 2000), Am. Acad. Arts and Scis., Assn. Computing Machinery; mem.: NAS, Royal Acad. Engring. Spain (corr.), Nat. Acad. Engring. (peer selection com. computer sci. and engring. 1996—99, chair 2000), Pi Mu Epsilon, Eta Kappa Nu, Tau Beta Pi. Office: Stanford U Office of the Provost Bldg 10 Stanford CA 94305-2061 Fax: 650-724-4062. E-mail: hennessy@stanford.edu.*

HENNESSY, SEAN P., corporate financial executive; From mem. staff to sr. v.p. fin., CFO Sherwin-Williams, Cleve., 1984—2001, sr. v.p., CFO, 2001—. Office: Sherwin Williams 101 Prospect Ave NW Cleveland OH 44115-1075*

HENNESSY, THOMAS CHRISTOPHER, priest, educator, retired dean; b. NYC, Nov. 3, 1916; s. Thomas C. and Anna E. (Regan) H. AB, Georgetown Coll., 1940; MA in Latin and Greek Classics, Fordham U., 1947, MS in Edn., 1957, PhD, 1962. Joined S.J., 1934, ordained priest Roman Cath. Ch., 1947. Tchr. Fordham Prep. Sch., NYC, 1941-44, 49-52, high sch. counselor, 1952-61; counselor educator Fordham U. at Lincoln Ctr., NYC, 1961-81; dean, prof. counselor edn. Sch. Edn. Marquette U., Milw., 1981-85. Editor: The Inner Crusade: The Closed Retreat in the US, 1965, The High School Counselor Today, 1966, The Interdisciplinary Roots of Guidance, 1966, Values and Moral Development, 1976, Value-Moral Education: The Schools and the Teachers, 1979, Fordham: The Early Years, 1998; How the Jesuits Settled in NY, A Documentary Account, 2003; cons. editor: Pers. and Guidance Jour., 1978-81; contbr. numerous articles to profl. jour. Mem. APA. Office: Fordham U Loyola Hall Bronx NY 10458

HENNESSY, WILLIAM JOSEPH, prosecutor; b. St. Paul, May 18, 1942; s. William E. and Julia R. (Luger) H.; m. Sandra Hennessy, July 3, 1965 (div. Jan. 7, 1977); m. Sally Ann Kroiss, Dec. 31, 1996; 1 child, Patricia Lee. BA, St. Thomas U., 1964; LLB, JD, William Mitchell U., 1968. Bar: Minn. 1968, U.S. Supreme Ct. 1975. Sr. ptnr. Hennessy & Richardson, St. Paul, 1970—93; chief prosecutor Cook County, Grand Marais, Minn., 1995—. Mem. adv. com. on the Criminal Rules, Minn. Supreme Ct., 1997-99. Mem. Minn. County Attys. Assn. (bd. dirs. 1996-2001). Avocation: commercial and instrument airplane pilot. Office: Cook County 411 W 2nd St Grand Marais MN 55604-2307 Office Phone: 218-387-3670. Business E-Mail: county.attorney@co.cook.mn.us.

HENNESY, GERALD CRAFT, artist; b. Washington, June 11, 1921; s. Gerald Craft and Frances Lee (Moore) H.; m. Elizabeth Ann Lovering, Mar. 4, 1950; children: Kathleen, Paul, Brian, Shawn, Hugh, Craig. *Son Paul K. Hennesy is a fine art painter and partner in the Studio of Hennesy in Clifton, Virginia. Son Shawn Hennesy is a fine art painter living in Ashburn, Virginia. Gerald and sons Paul and Shawn jointly publish a line of limited edition prints of their paintings. Grandmother Leoda Hennesy, father Gerald Hennesy, and sister Shirley Hennesy have all been artists. Uncle Hugh Hennesy was an art director with the Walt Disney Studio in California, and cousin Dale Hennesy was an Oscar-winning movie art director.* Student, Corcoran Sch. Art, 1939, George Washington U., 1940; BS, U. Md., 1948. Enlisted U.S. Navy, 1942, advanced through grades to comdr., 1956; mgmt. analyst U.S. Air Force Hdqrs., Pentagon, Washington, 1948-52, 53-56; asst dir. for orgn. and mgmt. AEC, 1956-72; artist, dir. Studio of Hennesy, Clifton, Va., 1972—. One man shows include PLA Gallery, McLean, Va., 1967, Tolley Galleries, Washington, 1983, Venable Neslage Galleries, Washington, 1993, Marin-Price Galleries, Chevy Chase Md., 1995-96, 98, 2000, 02, 04, 05, 06, Prince Royal Gallery, Alexandria, Va., 1999, 2003, 05; exhibited works at Corcoran Gallery Art, Washington, 1957, 59, 67, Smithsonian Inst., Washington, 1962, 64, Allied Artists of Am., N.Y.C., 1974, 75; represented in permanent collections at U.S. Ho. of Reps., Washington, Md. State Exec. Mansion, Annapolis, Nat. Hdqrs. Am. Legion, Washington, Nat. Hdqrs. DAR, Washington, Hdqrs. FDIC, Washington, others. Decorated Air medal with one star. Republican. Home and Office: 6811 White Rock Rd Clifton VA 20124-1434

HENNEY, CHRISTOPHER SCOT, immunologist; b. Sutton-Coldfield, Eng., Feb. 4, 1941; s. William Scot and Rhoda Agnes (Bateman) Henney; m. Janet Barnsley, June 20, 1964; children: James Scot, Samantha Jane. BS with honors, U. Birmingham, Eng., 1962, PhD in Exptl. Pathology, 1965, DSc. in Research Immunology (hon.), 1973. Immunologist WHO, Lausanne, Switzerland; assoc. prof. medicine and microbiology med. sch. Johns Hopkins U., Balt., 1978; prof. microbiology and immunology U. Wash., Seattle, 1978-81; head. basic immunology Fred Hutchinson Cancer Research Ctr., Seattle, 1978-81; co-founder, sci. dir., vice chmn. Immunex Corp., Seattle, 1981-89; co-founder, sci. dir., exec. v.p. ICOS Corp., Seattle, 1989—2000; CEO Dendreon Corp., Seattle, 1995—2003, chmn., 1995—2004, Structural Genomix Inc., Xcyte Therapier, Inc. Mem. Am. Assn. Immunology (sect. editor 1972-73), Reticuloendothelial Soc. (sect. editor 1978-79), Am. Cancer Soc. (chmn. immunology rev. com. 1982-83), NIH (mem. pathology study sect. 1978-82). Personal E-mail: chenney@comcast.net.

HENNEY, JANE ELLEN, health facility administrator, educator, oncologist; b. Kendallville, Ind., Mar. 26, 1947; d. Harry H. and Jeanette (Park) H.; m. J. Robert Graham, June 6, 1975. BS, Manchester Coll., North Manchester, Ind., 1969; MD, Ind. U.-Indpls., 1973. Intern St. Vincent's Hosp., Indpls., 1973-74; with Nat. Cancer Inst., Bethesda, Md., 1976—85, dep. dir., 1980—85; assoc. prof. medicine U. Kans. Med. Ctr., Kansas City, Kans., 1985—92, assoc. vice chancellor, acting dir. Mid Am. Cancer Ctr., 1985—92; prof. medicine, v.p. for health svcs. U. N.Mex., 1994—98; dep. commr. for ops. FDA, Rockville, Md., 1992—94, commr., 1998—2001; sr. v.p, provost for health affairs U. Cin., 2003—. Scholar in residence Assoc. Acad. Health Ctrs., 2001—03; bd. dirs. CIGNA Corp., Phila., 2004—, Amerisource Bergen Corp., Chesterbrook, Pa., The Commonwealth Fund, NYC. Served with USPHS, 1976-86. Recipient commendation USPHS, 1979, 81, Sec.'s Recognition award HHS, 1985, Excellence in Women's Health award, Jacobs Inst., Pub. Health Leadership award, Nat. Org. Rare Disorders. Mem.: Inst. Medicine. Avocation: fly fishing. Office: U Cincinnati 2600 Clifton Ave Cincinnati OH 45221 E-mail: jane.henney@uc.edu.

HENNIGAR, DAVID JOHN, portfolio manager, director; b. Windsor, NS, Can., July 5, 1939; s. Dean S. and Jean B. (Jodrey) H.; m. Carolyn Hiltz, June 8, 1964; children: Brian, Jan, Alison. B of Commerce, Mt. Allison U., 1960; MBA, Queen's U., 1962. Investment analyst Burns Fry Ltd. and predecessor co., Toronto, Ont., Canada, 1963-66, br. mgr. Halifax, N.S., Canada, 1966-71, Atlantic regional dir., 1971-93. Chmn. bd. dirs. Annapolis Group Inc., Assisted Living Concepts Inc., Acadian Securities Inc., Aquarius Coatings Inc., High Liner Foods, Inc., VR Interactive Inc.; bd. dirs. Minas Basin Pulp & Power Co. Ltd., Scotia Investment Ltd., Crombie Real Estate Investment Trust, Maritime Paper Products Ltd., Sentex Systems Ltd., KLJ Field Svcs., Inc., Solutioninc Ltd.; chmn. bd. dirs., CEO Landmark Global Fin. Inc. Bd. dirs., treas. Izaak Walton Killam Hosp. for Children, Halifax, 1976-82; bd. dirs. Inst. for Rsch. on Pub. Policy, 1983-89; active Trilateral Commn., 1988-94; bd. govs. Dalhousie U., 1983-90, Internat. Oceans Inst. Can., 2000-04; mem. adv. bd. Hope Air Inc. Mem. Investment Dealers Assn. Can. (nat. bd. dirs. 1985-87), Halifax Club. Home: 51 Forest Ln Bedford NS Canada B4A 1H8 Office: 3 Bedford Hills Rd Bedford NS Canada B4A 1J5 Office Phone: 902-832-2513.

HENNING, GEORGE THOMAS, JR., retired steel company executive; b. West Reading, Pa., Sept. 26, 1941; s. George Thomas and Helen Virginia (Spangler) H.; m. Susan Young, July 21, 1962; children: George Thomas III, Michael Kevin. Mgr. econ. analysis Eastern Gas & Fuel, Boston, 1967; mgr. gen. acctg. Ohio River Co., Cin., 1968; asst. to contr. Eastern Gas & Fuel Assos., Boston, 1969; dir. corp. planning Boston Gas Co., 1970; contr. Eastern Assoc. Coal Corp., Pitts., 1971-74; v.p., contr. Lykes Resources, Inc., 1974-78; asst. contr. Jones & Laughlin Steel Corp., 1979-85; gen. mgr. coal mine ops. and raw materials sales LTV Steel Co., Cleve., 1986, gen. mgr. asset mgmt., 1986-89; v.p., chief fin. officer Pioneer Chlor Alkali Co., Inc., Houston, 1988-95; v.p., CFO Pioneer Cos., Inc., 1995; v.p., contr. The LTV Corp., Cleve., 1995-99, v.p., CFO, 1999—2001, ret., 2001; bus. cons., 2002—. Mem. planning commn. Ferguson Twp., Pa.; trustee Mt. Nittany Conservancy; bd. dirs., v.p. Schlow Ctr. Region Libr.; bd. trustees Pa. State U., University Park. Mem. Pa. State Alumni Assn. (bd. dirs. Centre County chpt.), Lion's Paw Alumni Assn. (bd. dirs.), Omicron Delta Kappa. Methodist. Business E-Mail: ghenning63@psualum.com.

HENNING, JOEL FRANK, lawyer, writer; b. Chgo., Sept. 15, 1939; s. Alexander M. and Henrietta (Frank) H.; m. Grace Weiner, May 24, 1964 (div. July 1987); children: Justine, Sarah-Anne, Dara; m. Rosemary Nadolsky, June 21, 1992 (div. July 2007); 1 child, Alexandra. AB, Harvard U., 1961, JD, 1964. Bar: Ill. 1965. Assoc. Sonnenschein, Levinson, Carlin, Nath & Rosenthal, Chgo., 1965-70; fellow, dir. program Adlai Stevenson Inst. Internat. Affairs, Chgo., 1970-73; nat. dir. Youth Edn. for Citizenship, 1972-75; dir. profl. edn. Am. Bar Assn., Chgo., 1975-78; asst. exec. dir. comm. and edn. ABA, 1978-80; ptnr. Joel Henning & Assocs., 1980-87; sr. v.p., gen. counsel, mem. exec. com. Hildebrandt, Internat., Inc., 1987—; pres., pub. LawLetters, Inc., 1980-89; pub. Lawyer Hiring and Tng. Report, 1980-89; Chgo. theater critic Wall St. Jour., 1989—; pub. Almanac of Fed. Judiciary, 1984-89; editor Bus. Lawyer Update, 1980-87. Mem. faculty Inst. on Law and Ethics, Council Philos. Studies; chmn. Fund for Justice, Chgo., 1979-85 Author: Law-Related Education in America: Guidelines for the Future, 1975, Holistic Running: Beyond the Threshhold of Fitness, 1978, Mandate for Change: The Impact of Law on Educational Innovation, 1979, Improving Lawyer Productivity: How to Train, Manage and Supervise Your Lawyers, 1985, Law Practice and Management Desk Book, 1987, Lawyers Guide to Managing and Training Lawyers, 1988, Maximizing Law Firm Profitability: Hiring, Training and Developing Productive Lawyers, 1991-98, also articles. Chmn. Gov.'s Commn. on Financing Arts in Ill., 1970-71; bd. dirs. Ill. Arts Council, 1971-81, Columbia Coll., Chgo.; bd. dirs., v.p., pub. edn. exec. com. ACLU of Ill.; trustee S.E. Chgo. Commn.; mem. Joseph Jefferson Theatrical Awards Com. Fellow Am. Bar Found. (life); mem. Am. Law Inst., ABA (ho. of dels.), Chgo. Bar Assn., Chgo. Council Lawyers (co-founder), Social Sci. Edn. Consortium. Office: 150 N Michigan Ave Ste 3600 Chicago IL 60601-7572 Home Phone: 312-335-9915; Office Phone: 312-578-0663. E-mail: jfhenning@rcn.com, jfhenning@hildebrandt.com. *The hardest question for me to answer is, "What do you do?" I do a lot. Some of it returns money and satisfaction. Some returns more of one than the other. And, I do some things that make me feel fit. The best of what I do helps integrate my various selves and improves my relations with the world. But I have no facile way to say all of this at cocktail parties when, invariably, that question is popped.*

HENNINGS, DOROTHY GRANT, education educator; b. Paterson, NJ, Mar. 15, 1935; d. William Albert and Ethel Barbara (Moll) Grant; m. George Hennings, June 15, 1968. AB, Barnard Coll., 1956; EdM, U. Va., 1959; EdD, Columbia U., 1965. Tchr. Pierrepont Elem. Sch., Rutherford, NJ, 1956-58, Thomas Jefferson Jr. H.S., Fair Lawn, NJ, 1959-64; prof. edn. Kean U. of N.J., Union, 1965-99, disting. prof. edn., 1999—2002, disting. prof. emeritus, 2002—. Author citation N.J. Inst. Tech., Divsn. Continuing Edn., 1982; author: (with B. Grant) Teacher Moves, 1971; Content and Craft: Written Expression in the Elementary School, 1973; Smiles, Nods and Pauses: Activities to Enrich Children's Communication Skills, 1974; Mastering Classroom Communication: What Interaction Analysis Tells the Teacher, 1975; (with G. Hennings) Keep Earth Clean, Blue and Green: Environmental Activities for Young People, 1976; Words, Sounds, and Thoughts: More Activities to Enrich Children's Communication Skills, 1977; Communication in Action: Teaching the Language Arts, 1978, 8th edit. 2002; (with D. Russell) Listening Aids Through the Grades, 1979; (with G. Hennings) Today's Elementary Social Studies, 1980, 2d edit., 1989; Written Expression in the Language Arts, 1981; Teaching Communication and Reading Skills in the Content Areas, 1982; (with L. Fay) Star Show, 1989, Grand Tour, 1989, Previews, 1989; Reading with Meaning: Strategies for College Reading, 1990, 6th rev. edit., 2004, Poets Journal, 1991, Beyond the Read Aloud: Learning to Read Through Listening to and Reflecting on Literature, 1992, Vocabulary Growth: Strategies for College Word Study, 2001, Words Are Wonderful: An Interactive Approach to Vocabulary, books 1 and 2, 2003, book 3, 2004, book 4, 2005; contbr. articles to Edn., The Record, Lang. Arts, Sci. Tchr., The Reading Tchr., Jour. of Adolescent & Adult Lit., Jour. of Reading, Tchr. to Tchrs., Sci. and Children, Early Years, Reading Rsch. and Instrn., New Eng. Jour. of History, Jour. Reading Edn., others. Mem. Unitarian Ch., Summit, NJ; trustee Kean U. Found., 2005—. Recipient Edn. Press award, 1974, Outstanding Article award, 1999, Bldg. named in her honor, Kean U., 2005; NSF Acad. Yr. Inst. grantee, 1959, Field Enterprise grantee, Columbia U., 1965. Mem. Nat. Coun. Tchrs. English, N.J. Reading Assn. (Disting. Svc. to Reading award 1993), Internat. Reading Assn. (Outstanding Tchr. Educator in Reading award 1992), Suburban Reading Coun., Phi Beta Kappa, Phi Delta Kappa, Phi Kappa Phi, Kappa Delta Pi. Home: 21 Flintlock Dr Warren NJ 07059-5014 Personal E-mail: 2xprofs@optonline.net.

HENNINGSEN, PETER, JR., manufacturing executive; b. Mpls., Oct. 6, 1926; s. Peter and Anna O. (Kjelstrup) H.; m. Donna J. Buresh, June 19, 1948; children— Deborah, Pamela, James. BBA, U. Minn., Mpls., 1950. Packaging engr. govt. and aero. products div. Honeywell, Inc., Mpls., 1950-72; mgr. packaging Internat. Tel. & Tel., NYC, 1972-80; v.p. Raymond Eisenhardt & Son, Inc., 1980-90; pvt. practice Eden Prairie, Minn., 1990—. Sr. assoc. Adalis Corp., 2004—; cons. in field. With USNR, 1944-46. Elected to Packaging Hall of Fame, Packaging Edn. Forum, 1995. Fellow Inst. Packaging Profls. (pres., 1970-71, chmn. bd., 1972-73, named Man of Yr., 1968); mem. ASTM, Aerospace Industries Assn. (chmn. packaging com. 1967), Masons, Shriners Methodist. Home and Office: 7610 Smetana Ln # 211 Eden Prairie MN 55344 Business E-Mail: peterhen@comcast.net.

HENNION, CAROLYN LAIRD (LYN), investment executive; b. Orange, Calif., July 27, 1943; d. George James and Jane (Porter) Laird; m. Reeve L. Hennion, Sept. 12, 1964; children: Jeffrey Reeve, Douglas Laird. BA, Stanford U., Calif., 1965; grad. in Securities Industry Inst., Wharton Sch., U. Pa., Phila., 1992. CFP, fund specialist; lic. ins. agt.; registered gen. securities prin. Portfolio analyst Schwabacher & Co., San Francisco, 1965-66; adminstrv. coord. Bicentennial Commn., San Mateo County, Calif., 1972-73; dir. devel. Crystal Springs Uplands Sch., Hillsborough, Calif., 1973-84; tax preparer Household Fin. Corp., Foster City, Calif., 1982; freelance, 1983-87; sales promotion mgr. Franklin Distbrs., Inc., San Mateo, 1984-86, v.p. and regional sales mgr. of N.W., 1986-91, sr. v.p. Mid-Atlantic, 1991-94; v.p. Viatech, Inc., 1986-92; propr. Buncom Ranch, 1990—; v.p. Keypoint Svcs. Internat., 1992—2002; pres. Brock Rd. Corp., 1993—; v.p. Strand, Atkinson, Williams & York, Medford, Oreg., 1994—2004, sr. v.p., 2004—; asst. treas. Allamar Techs., Inc., 2004—. Editor: Lest We Forget, 1975. Pres. South Hillsborough Sch. Parents' Group, 1974—75; sec. Vol. Bur. San Mateo County, Burlingame, Calif., 1975; chmn. Cmty. Info. Com., Town of Hillsborough, 1984—86, mem., subcom. chmn. fin. adv. com., 1984—86; mem. adv. com. Rogue Valley Internat. Airport, 1996—2003, chair, 2001—03; mem. coun. Town of Buncom, Oreg., 1990—; chmn. Jackson County Applegate Trail Sesquicentennial Celebration, 1995—97; founding dir. So. Oreg. Hist. Soc. Found., 1995—2005, sec., 1995—98, pres., 1998—2001; sec., treas. Oreg. Shakespeare Festival Endowment Fund, 1997—98, pres., 1998—2000; dir. Rogue Valley Manor Cmty. Svcs., 1996—, vice-chair, 1997—2006, chair, 2006—; dir. Craterian Performances Co., 1997—2004, pres., 2001—03; dir. So. Oreg. Estate Planning Coun., 1997—2003, pres., 1998—99; dir. Oreg. Cmty. Found., 2002—, chair grants com., 2007—; chmn. Oreg. Cmty. Found. So. Oreg. Leadership Coun., 2002—; dir. Applegate Valley Rural Fire Protection Dist. #9, 2004—, sec./treas., 2004—; bd. dirs. Pacific N.W. Mus. Natural History, 1995—96, Providence Cmty. Health Found., 1996—2003, sec., 1998—2000, v.p., 2000—01, pres., 2001—02; bd. dirs. Pacific Retirement Svcs., 2006—, Chamber of Medford, Jackson Co., 1997—2000, v.p., 1999—2000; bd. dirs. OR529 Coll. Savs. Network, 2005—. Recipient Coun. for Advancement and Support of Edn. award, 1981, Exemplary Direct Mail Appeals Fund Raising Inst. award, 1982, Golden Mic award Frederic Gilbert Assocs., 1993, White Rose award March of Dimes, 2004, Heritage award, So. Oreg. Hist. Soc., 2004; named Wholesaler of Yr., Shearson Lehman Hutton N.W. Region, 1989, one of Top 300 Fin. Advisors, Worth Mag., 1998, Top 250 Fin. Advisors, 1999, 2001, one of 10 Outstanding Brokers Registered Rep. Mag., 2000, named to Am. Best Fin. Planners Consumers Rsch. Coun., 2005-07. Mem. So. Oreg. Estate Planning Coun., Buncom Hist. Soc., Oreg. Shakespeare Festival (bd. dirs. 2002—), Britt Festivals, So. Oreg. Hist. Soc., Jr. League, Medford Rogue Rotary, Craterian Performances Co. Republican. Home: 3232 Little Applegate Rd Jacksonville OR 97530-9303 Office: Strand Atkinson Williams & York 2495 E Barnett Ste A Medford OR 97504 Business E-Mail: lhennion@strandatkinson.com.

HENNION, REEVE LAWRENCE, communications executive; b. Ventura, Calif., Dec. 7, 1941; s. Tom Reeve and Evelyn Edna (Henry) H.; m. Carolyn Laird, Sept. 12, 1964; children: Jeffrey Reeve, Douglas Laird. BA, Stanford U., 1963, MA, 1965. Reporter Tulare (Calif.) Advance-Register, 1960-62; reporter UPI, San Francisco, 1963-66, mgr. Fresno, Calif., 1966-68, regional exec. Los Angeles, 1968-69, mgr. Honolulu, 1969-72, San Francisco, 1972-75, Calif. editor, 1975-77, gen. news editor, 1977-81, bus. mgr., 1981-83, v.p., gen. mgr. Pacific div., 1983-85; v.p., gen. mgr. Calif.-Oreg. Broadcasting, Inc., 1985-86; pres. Viatech Inc., 1986-92; propr. Buncom Ranch; pres. Keypoint Svcs. Internat., Inc., Medford, Oreg., 1992—2002; interim exec. dir. Rogue Valley Coun. of Govts., 1998. Editor: The Modoc Country, 1971, Buncom: Crossroads Station, 1995. Chmn. Calif. Freedom of Info. Com., 1983-84; chair Jackson County Planning Commn., Jackson County Roads Com.; mayor of Buncom, Oreg.; pres. Buncom Hist. Soc.; active Rogue C.C. Found. Bd. Mem. Am. Planning Assn., Delta Kappa Epsilon. Home: 3232 Little Applegate Rd Jacksonville OR 97530-9303

HENRETTA, DEBORAH A., consumer products company executive; b. Rochester, NY, May 1, 1961; m. Sean Murray; 3 children. Grad., St. Bonaventure U., 1983; MA, Syracuse U. Brand asst., BOLD laundry detergent Procter & Gamble, Cin., 1985—86, asst. brand mgr., BOLD/Dawn laundry detergents, 1986—88, brand mgr., Cheer laundry detergent, 1988—91, assoc. advt. mgr., Tide laundry detergent, 1991—93, mktg. dir., laundry products, N. Am., 1993—96, gen. mgr., fabric conditioners, N. Am., 1996—98, gen. mgr., fabric conditioners and bleach, worldwide, 1998—99, v.p., fabric conditioners and bleach, worldwide, 1999, v.p., N. Am. baby care, 1999—2001, pres. global baby care, 2001—04, pres., global baby care/toddler & adult care, 2004—05, pres. ASEAN, Australasia & India, 2005—07, group pres. Asia, 2007—. Bd. dirs. Sprint Corp., 2004—. Mem. adv. com. Newhouse Sch. Pub. Comm., Syracuse U. Named one of 50 Most Powerful Women in Bus., Fortune, 2002, Top 10 Who Made Their Mark on Mktg., Advt. Age., 2004, 50 Women to Watch, Wall St. Jour., 2006, Next 20 Female CEOs, Pink Mag. & Forté Found., 2006. Office: Procter & Gamble Asia Pte Ltd 238 AThomson Rd Novena Sq Twr A 21-01/10 306874 Singapore*

HENRICK, MICHAEL FRANCIS, lawyer; b. Chgo., Feb. 29, 1948; s. John L. and A. Madeline (Hafner) H.; m. Cissi F. Henrick, Aug. 9, 1980; children: Michael Francis Jr., Derry Patricia. BA, Loyola U., 1971; JD with honors, John Marshall Law Sch., 1974. Bar: Ill. 1974, U.S. Dist. Ct. (no. dist.) Ill. 1974, U.S. Supreme Ct. 1979, Wis. 1985, U.S. Dist. Ct. (ea. dist.) Wis. 1985. Ptnr. Hinshaw & Culbertson, Chgo., Waukegan, Ill., 1974—. Named Ill. Super Lawyer Chgo. Mag.; recipient Corpus Juris Secundum award West Publ. Co., 1974. Fellow Am. Coll. Trial Lawyers; mem. ABA, Def. Rsch. Inst., Ill. Bar Assn., Lake County Bar Assn., Ill. Hosp. Attys. Assn., Internat. Assn. of Def. Counsel, Ill. Def. Attys. Assn., Soc. Trial Lawyers Def. Rsch. Inst., Am. Inns of Ct. Office: Hinshaw & Culbertson 110 N West St Waukegan IL 60085-4330 Business E-Mail: mhenrick@hinshawlaw.com.

HENRIKSEN, EVA HANSINE, retired anesthesiology educator; b. Petaluma, Calif., Jan. 1, 1929; d. Peder Henrik Boas and Karen (Nielsen) Henriksen; m. Daniel Edward MacLean, Aug. 25, 1957 (dec. Dec. 1981); children: Elizabeth, Mary Ann. AA, U. Calif., Berkeley, 1948, BA, 1950; MD, Yale U., 1954. Diplomate Am. Bd. Anesthesiology. Intern, resident Los Angeles County Hosp., LA, 1954-57; from instr. to asst. prof. anesthesia Loma Linda U. (formerly Coll. Med. Evangelists), LA, 1957-68; from instr. to assoc. prof. surgery anesthesiology Sch. Medicine U. So. Calif., LA, 1957-94, assoc. prof. anesthesiology emeritus, 1994—. Anesthesia cons. L.A. Coroner's Office, 1992—. Governing coun. Angelica Luth. Ch., 1992—2000, 2002—07. Democrat. Avocation: patchwork quilt making. Home: 957 Arapahoe St Los Angeles CA 90006-5703

HENRIKSEN, MELVIN, mathematician, educator; b. NYC, Feb. 23, 1927; s. Kaj and Helen (Kahn) Henriksen; m. Lillian Viola Hill, July 23, 1946 (div. 1964); children: Susan, Richard, Thomas; m. Louise Levitas, June 12, 1964 (dec. Oct. 1997). BS, Coll. City N.Y., 1948; MS, U. Wis., 1949, PhD in Math, 1951. Asst. math., then instr. extension div. U. Wis., 1948-51; asst. prof. U. Ala., 1951-52; from instr. to prof. math. Purdue U., 1952-65; prof. math., head dept. Case Inst. Tech., 1965-68; research assoc. U. Calif. at Berkeley, 1968-69; prof., chmn. math. dept. Harvey Mudd Coll., 1969-72, prof., 1972-97, prof. emeritus, 1997—. Mem. Inst. Advanced Study, Princeton, 1956-57, 63-64; vis. prof. Wayne State U., 1960-61; rsch. assoc. U. Man., Winnipeg, Can., 1975-76; vis. prof. Wesleyan U., Middletown, Conn., 1978-79, 82-83, 86-87, 93-94. Author: (with Milton Lees) Single Variable Calculus, 1970; assoc. editor: Algebra Universalis, 1993—, Topology Atlas, 1996-2002, Topological Commentary, 1996-2002; mem. editl. bd. Functiones et Approximatio Commentario Mathematici, 2001-06; author articles on algebra, rings of functions, gen. topology. Sloan fellow, 1956—58. Mem. Am. Math. Soc., Math. Assn. Am. (assoc. editor Am. Math. monthly 1988-91, assoc. editor Algebra Universalis 1993—). Office: Harvey Mudd Coll Math Dept Claremont CA 91711 Office Phone: 909-626-3676. Business E-Mail: henriksen@hmc.edu.

HENRIKSEN, THOMAS HOLLINGER, researcher; b. Detroit, Nov. 16, 1939; s. Paul and Irene (Hollinger) H.; m. Margaret Mary Mueller, Sept. 9, 1968; children— Heather Anne, Damien Paul Hollinger BA, Va. Mil. Inst., 1962; MA, Mich. State U., 1966, PhD, 1969. Asst. prof. SUNY, Plattsburgh, 1969-73, assoc. prof., 1973-79, prof., 1979-80; Peace fellow Hoover Instn. on War, Revolution and Peace Stanford (Calif.) U., 1979-80, research fellow, 1980-82, sr. research fellow, 1982-86, sr. fellow, 1986—, assoc. dir., 1983—2003, exec. sec. nat. fellows program, 1984—2003, mem. Pres.'s Commn. on White House fellows, 1987-93. Mem. U.S. Army Sci. Bd., 1984-90. Author: Mozambique: A History, 1978, Revolutiona and Counterrevolution: Mozambique's War of Independence, 1964-74, 1983, The New World Order: War, Peace and Military Preparedness, 1992, Clinton's Foreign Policy in Somalia, Bosnia, Haiti, and North Korea, 1996, Using Power and Diplomacy to Deal With Rogue States, 1999; co-author: The Struggle for Zimbabwe: Battle in the Bush, 1981, American Power After The Berlin Wall, 2007; contbg. author, editor: Soviet and Chinese Aid to African Nations, 1980; Communist Powers in Sub-Saharan Africa, 1981; assoc. editor Yearbook on Internat. Communist Affairs, 1982-91; contbg. author, editor: One Korea? Challenges and Prospects for Reunification, 1994. Trustee George C. Marshall Found., 1993—. Served to lt. U.S. Army, 1963-65 Home: 177 Lundy Ln Palo Alto CA 94306-4563 Office: Stanford U Hoover Instn Stanford CA 94305 Office Phone: 650-723-4255.

HENRIKSON, ARTHUR ALLEN, political cartoonist, educator; b. Oak Park, Ill., June 1, 1921; s. Allen Bernhardt and Florence Ella (Dixon) H.; m. Lois Elizabeth Wessling, July 3, 1943; children: Diane Elizabeth Russell, Janet Christine, Michele Charlene Smetana. Student, Austin Acad. Fine Arts, Chgo., Chgo. Acad. Fine Arts, 1936-37; BS, Northwestern U., 1946, postgrad., 1946-51. With advt. dept. Snips Mag., Chgo., 1947-56; advt. and layout Des Plaines (Ill.) Jour., 1956; with Wessling Svcs., Des Moines. Illustrator: Living the Good Life Microwave Recipebook, 1990, PMS-Solving the Puzzle, 1995; editl. polit. cartoonist for The Daily Herald, Paddock Pubs., Arlington Heights, Ill., 1955-2001, Des Plaines Jour., 1956-69, Rockford Newspapers, Inc., 1959-73, Reporter/Progress, Downers Grove, Ill., 1959-2001, The Doings, Hinsdale, Ill., 1960-73, Ill. Cartoon Svc., 1961-81, Ind. Register, Libertyville, Ill., 1961-75, Suburban Life, Berwyn, Ill., Harvey (Ill.) Tribune, 1962-73, St. Petersburg Times/Brandon Times, Fla., 2003—, others; cartoons to Modern Medicine, Esquire, Nat. Enquirer, AMA, Christian Sci. Monitor; cartoons reprinted in Today's Cartoon, 1962, Best Gag Cartoons of the Year, 1964, Best Editorial Cartoons of the Year, 1972-2002, also in Chgo. Sun Times, Chgo. Daily News, Chgo. Tribune, L.A. Times, Sacramento Bee, San Diego Union, U.S. News and World Report, numerous others; cartoons exhibited at Columbia U., 1960, Art Inst. Chgo., 1962, White House, Washington, 1963, LWV, Washington, 1963, others; promotional cartoons for NBC-TV, for Motorola; cartoons in permanent collections at Libr. of Congress, Lyndon Baines Johnson Libr., Mus. of Cartoon Art, State Hist. Soc. Mo., others. Mem. bd. deacons First Congl. Ch., United Ch. of Christ, Des Plaines, 1970-74, chmn., 1972, 74, moderator, 1976, also mem. mission bd. and music bd.; bd. dirs. Northwest Cmty. coun. Girls Scouts U.S., 1972-79; mem. Sch. Bd. Caucus, Des Plaines, 1968-72, pres., 1970. Lt. USAF, 1942—46, capt. Med. Adminstrv. Corps USAF, 1946. Recipient numerous awards for cartoons including Sigma Delta Chi Peter Lisagor award, George Washington Honor medal Freedoms Found., 1962, 63, 64, 65, 66, 69. Mem.: Assn. Am. Editl. Cartoonists, Ret. Officers Assn. Avocations: music, theater, art, travel. Home and Office: 27 N Meyer Ct Des Plaines IL 60016-2243 Office Phone: 847-296-1309. E-mail: lahenrkson@aol.com.

HENRIKSON, C. ROBERT, insurance company executive; BA, U. Pa.; JD, Emory U.; grad., Wharton U. Pension sales rep. MetLife Inc., 1972—79, nat. dir. NYC, 1979—81, asst. v.p., 1981—83, v.p. group pensions, 1983—91, sr. v.p. pensions dept., 1983—95, exec. v.p., 1995—96, instl. bus., 1996—97, sr. exec. v.p., 1997—99, 1999—2002, pres. U.S. instl. and fin. svcs., 2002—, pres., COO, 2004—06, chmn., pres., CEO, 2006—. Bd. mem. emeritus Am. Benefits Coun.; bd. mem. NY Botanical Garden, NY Philharm., Wharton Sch. S.S. Huebner Found. Ins. Edn., chmn. bd.; mem. commn. on global aging CSIS; trustee Am. Mus. Natural History. Alumni trustee Emory U., Atlanta. Office: Metlife Inc 27-01 Queens Plaza N Long Island City NY 11101 Business E-Mail: rhenrikson@metlife.com.

HENRIKSON, DONALD MERLE, forensic pathologist; b. Walla Walla, Wash., May 2, 1947; s. James Christan and Carol Jean (DuBois) H.; m. Eileen Ruth Mikita, Oct. 12, 1980. BA, Harvard U., 1969; MD, U. Calif., Davis, 1981. Diplomate Am. Bd. Pathology. Assoc. pathologist Lab. Medicine Cons., Inc., Auburn, Calif., 1986-87, FPMG, Inc., 1987-88; owner, pathologist FFPMG, 1989-94; assoc. pathologist NCFP, Inc., Sacramento, 1994—2002; pathologist Placer County Coroner's Office, Auburn, 2002—. Mem. med. staff Sierra Valley Dist. Hosp., Loyalton, Calif., 1992-95, Oroville Hosp. and Med. Ctr., 1986-95, Sierra Nev. Meml. Hosp., Grass Valley, Calif., 1986—, Sutter Auburn Faith Hosp., 1986—; asst. clin. prof. U. Calif. Sch. of Medicine, Davis, 1994-2002. Mem. Placer County Child Death Rev. Team, Auburn, 1990—; mem., former chair Sacramento County Child Death Rev. Team, Sacramento, 1994-2001; mem. Nevada County Child Death Rev. Team, Nevada City, 1996—. Sgt. U.S. Army, 1969-71. Fellow Coll. of Am. Pathologists; mem. AMA, AAAS, Am. Acad. Forensic Scis., Am. Soc. for Clin. Pathology. Avocations: hiking, golf, piano. Office: Placer County Coroner Auburn Justice Ctr 2929 Richardson Dr Auburn CA 95603 Office Phone: 530-889-7807. Business E-Mail: dhenriks@placer.ca.gov.

HENRIKSON, MARY IDA, artist, educator; BA, Ctrl. Wash. U., Ellensburg, 1968; MFA, Claremont U., Calif., 1971. One-woman shows include Tongass Hist. Mus., Ketchikan, 1991, Ariel Gallery, NYC, 1992, Soho Coho Gallery, Ketchikan, 1994, 1997, 1999, 2002, 2004, Main St. Gallery, 1995, 2000, Resurrection Art Gallery, Seward, Alaska, 1998, exhibited in group shows at Anchorage Mus. History and Art, 1976, 1994, 2002, 2004, Visual Arts Ctr., Anchorage, 1990, Grace Cathedral, San Francisco, 1990. Named Artist in Residence, Sitka Fine Arts Camp, 1978; recipient award, Ketchikan H.S., 1993, Thorne Bay Sch. Dist., 1995, Alaska State Ferry, Aurora, 1997, Alaska State Ferry, LeConte, 1999, Craig Alaska Sch. Dist., 2000, Alaska Geog. Vol. 27 no. 3, 2000, Rasmunson Found., 2003; Travel grantee, Alaska State Coun. on the Arts, 1989.

HENRION, ROSEMARY PROVENZA, psychotherapist, educator; b. Greenville, Miss., Oct. 2, 1929; d. Vincent and Camille (Portera) Provenza; m. Albert Joseph Henrion, Sept. 8, 1956 (dec.); 1 child, Albert Joseph Jr. BSN, U. Tex., Galveston, 1963; MSN in Psychiat./Mental Health Nursing, Vanderbilt U., 1972; MEd in Secondary Edn., U. So. Miss., 1974. RN Tex.; cert. logotherapist. Psychotherapist St. Mary's Hosp., Galveston, Tex., 1951—52, office and pvt. duty surg. nurse, 1952—53; supr. ob-gyn. nursing Greenville Gen. Hosp., 1954—56, head nurse, ob-gyn. and med.-surg. nursing, 1953—54; instr. nursing Providence Hosp. Sch. Nursing, Waco, Tex., 1957—59; dir. inservice edn., asst. dir. nursing svc. Meml. Hosp., Gulfport, Miss., 1966—67, dir. nursing svc., 1967—68; psychiat. clin. nurse specialist Biloxi VA Med. Ctr., Miss., 1972—89, in-house cons., 1975—92, assoc. chief nursing svc., 1989—92; clin. nurse specialist VA Outpatient Ctr., Pensacola, Fla., 1992—98; adj. clin. prof., psychiat.-mental health nursing La. State U., New Orleans, 1975—76; adj. clin. prof. grad. nursing program U. So. Miss., Hattiesburg, 1983—92; faculty V.F. Inst. Logotherapy, Berkeley and San Jose, Calif., 1983—92, Abilene, Tex., 1993—; clin. instr. grad. nursing program U. So. Ala., 1998—99. Internat. bd. dirs. V. F. Inst. of Logotherapy, 1992—; guest lectr. internat. program on logotherapy U. South Africa, Pretoria, 2005; co-founder The Inst. Meaningful Living, 2003—. Co-author: The Power of Meaningful Intimacy: Key to Successful Relationships, 2004; contbg. author: International Forum for Logotherapy, 1983—2006, Favorite Counseling and Therapy Techniques, 1997, Favorite Counseling and Therapy-Homework Assignments, 2000; contbr. articles to profl. jours. Mem. Pope John Paul II Cultural Ctr. Mem.: AAUW, Menninger Soc., Nat. Women's History Mus. (charter 2004), Women's Mus., Miss. Bd. Nursing (pres. 1977—79), Smithsonian Instn., Vanderbilt Alumni Assn., The Wilson Assocs. (assoc.), Sigma Theta Tau Internat. (Iota chpt. 1972—). Home and Office: 19 Wenmar Ave Pass Christian MS 39571-3144 Office Phone: 228-860-4570, 228-860-4570.

HENRIQUES, DIANA BLACKMON, journalist; b. Bryan, Tex., Dec. 17, 1948; d. Lawrence Ernest and Pauline (Webb) Blackmon; m. Laurence Barlow Henriques, Jr., June 7, 1969. BA with distinction, George Washington U., 1969. Editor Lawrence Ledger, Lawrenceville, NJ, 1969-71; reporter Asbury Park Press, NJ, 1971-74; copy editor Palo Alto Times, Calif., 1974-76; investigative reporter Trenton Times, NJ, 1976-82; bus. writer The Phila. Inquirer, 1982-86; writer Barron's Fin. Weekly, NYC, 1986-89; investigative reporter NY Times, 1989—. Vis. fellow, cons. Woodrow Wilson Sch., Princeton U., NJ, 1981-82, Guggenheim Found., NY, NJ, 1981-82. Author: (books) The Machinery of Greed, 1986, Fidelity's World, 1995, The White Sharks of Wall Street, 2000; contbr. articles to profl. jours. Mem. internat. coun. Elliott Sch. Internat. Affairs George Washington U. Recipient Bell Prize N.J. Press Assn., 1977, Investigative Reporting prize Deadline Club, 1997, George B. Polk award for military reporting, 2005; co-recipient Loeb award Deadline Reporting, 1999. Mem. NY Fin. Writers Assn., Phi Beta Kappa, Lectr. Am. Press Inst. Avocations: walking, reading. Office: The New York Times 229 W 43rd St New York NY 10036-3959

HENRIQUES, SEAN PAUL See SEAN PAUL

HENRIQUEZ, ALLEN, artist; b. NYC, June 4, 1953; s. Charles Leo and Rosetta (Martin) Henriquez; m. Regina Millicent Thomas; children: Shad Alan Bert, Sean Allen. Radiology, Cmty. Coll. Air Force, 1978; Fire Safety, John Jay Coll., 1989. Artist, writer The 7th Renaissance, NYC, 2004, 3 on a Rock, 1995—2004. Writer: numerous screenplays, manuscripts, novels, plays. Sgt. USAF, 1974—78. Recipient Drawing award, The Sch. Art League, 1972, NAACP (Jamaica Branch), 1972. Mem.: Ward Nasse Gallery, Long Island Black Artist Assn. Avocations: bongo, trumpet. Office: The 7th Renaissance PO Box 53 Lawrence NY 11559 Home: 120 Beach 19th St Apt 21D Far Rockaway NY 11691-3714 Office Phone: 917-327-2336. Business E-Mail: the7thR@aol.com. E-mail: geanate@aol.com.

HENRY, BARBARA ANN, publishing executive; b. Oshkosh, Wis., July 23, 1952; d. Robert Edward and Barbara Frances (Aylesworth) Henry BJ, U. Nev., 1974. With Gannett Co., 1974—; reporter Reno Gazette-Jour., 1974—78, city editor, 1978-80, mng. editor, 1980-82; asst. nat. editor USA Today, Washington, 1982-83; exec. editor Reno Gazette-Jour., 1981-86; editor, dir. Rochester (NY) Dem. & Chronicle and Times-Union, 1986—91; pub. Great Falls (Mont.) Tribune, 1992-96; pres., pub. Des

Moines Register, 1996—2000, The Indianapolis Star, 2000—; pres. Ind. Newspaper Group, 2002—; sr. group pres. Interstate Newspaper Group, 2005—. Recipient Publisher of the Year, Gannett Newspaper Group, 2001, Touchstone award, Girls Inc. of Indpls., 2007. Mem. Soc. Profl. Journalists, Associated Press Mng. Editors, Am. Soc. Newspaper Editors Avocation: skiing. Mailing: Indianapolis Star PO Box 145 Indianapolis IN 46206-0145 Office Phone: 317-444-8131. E-mail: barbara.henry@indystar.com.*

HENRY, BRAD (C. BRAD HENRY), governor; b. Shawnee, Okla., June 10, 1963; m. Kimberley Blain; children: Leah, Laynie. BA, Okla. U., 1985, JD, 1988. Bar: Okla. 1988, U.S. Ct. Appeals (10th cir.), U.S. Dist. Ct. (we. dist.) Okla. Staff researcher Okla. State Senate, Oklahoma City, summer 1984, mem.; econs. tchg. asst. U. Okla., Norman, 1983-85; legal asst. Henry Henry & Henry, Shawnee, summer 1985; law clk. Andrews Davis Legg Bixler Milsten & Murrah, Oklahoma City, summer 1987; pres. Brad Henry Oil Co., Inc., Shawnee, 1987-89; legal intern Cleveland County Legal Aid Office, Norman, 1987-88; assoc. atty. Andrews Davis Legg Bixler Milsten & Price, Oklahoma City, 1988-89; atty. City of Shawnee, 1989—2002, state senator, 1989—2002; assoc. Charles T. Henry, Inc. & Assocs., Shawnee, 1989—; gov. State of Okla., Oklahoma City, 2003—. Mng. editor Okla. Law Rev., 1988. Trustee St. Gregory's Coll.; bd. dirs. Gateway to Prevention and Recovery, Inc.; mem. Okla. Acad. for State Goals, First Bapt. Ch., Shawnee; active Muscular Dystrophy Assn.; commr. U. Okla. Election Commn., 1987-88; bd. govs. U. Okla., 1982-84; Okla. and Cleveland County coord. Robert Henry for Atty. Gen. Campaign, 1986. Mem. ABA, ATLA, Okla. Bar Assn., Am. Inn of Ct., Pottawatomie County Bar Assn. (pres. 1991), Shawnee C. of C. (amb.), Lions, Jaycees, Delta Tau Delta (pres. 1984), Phi Delta Phi. Democrat. Baptist. Office: Office of Gov State Capitol Bldg Ste 212 Oklahoma City OK 73105 Office Phone: 405-521-2342. Office Fax: 405-521-3354.*

HENRY, BRIAN THOMAS, lawyer; b. Chgo., Dec. 25, 1954; s. Thomas Joseph and Shirley Grace (Pfaff) H.; m. Mary Elizabeth Collins, Sept. 17, 1983; children: Kyle Justin, Erin Maureen, Colin Thomas. BA Honors in History magna cum laude, Loyola U., Chgo., 1977; JD, U. Ill., 1980. Bar: Ill. 1980, U.S. Dist. Ct. (no. dist.) Ill. 1980. Ptnr. Pretzel & Stouffe Chtd., Chgo., 1980—; fellow Am. Coll. of Trial Lawyers. Faculty instr. Ill. Assn. of Def. Trial Counsel Trial Acads., 1990-2007; seminar speaker Chgo. Bar Assn. Comparative Negligence Seminar, 1990, 91; cons. health care com. Inst. of Medicine of Chgo.; frequent lectr. med. groups. Editor-in-chief Recent Decisions Sect. of Ill. Bar Jour. Fellow Am. Coll. Trial Lawyers; mem. ASTL, ABA, Ill. Assn. Hosp. Attys., Ill. Assn. Def. Trial Counsel, Internat. Assn. Def. Counsel (faculty instr. trial acad. 2001), Ill. Bar Assn., Phi Alpha Theta, Phi Alpha Delta. Office: Pretzel & Stouffer Chtd 1 S Wacker Dr Ste 2500 Chicago IL 60606-4614 Office Phone: 312-578-7408. Business E-Mail: bhenry@pretzel-stouffer.com.

HENRY, CARL NOLAN, lawyer; b. Washington, Sept. 30, 1965; s. Robert Benjamin Covington III and Inola Francis Henry. BA in Polit. Sci., U. Calif., Berkeley, 1987, JD, 1993. Bar: Calif. 1993, U.S. Supreme Ct. 1997, U.S. Ct. Appeal (9th cir.) 1993, U.S. Dist. Ct. (no., ctrl. dists.) Calif. 1993. Dep. atty. gen. Calif. Dept. Justice, LA, 1994-99, 99—; staff atty. to Hon. Janice Rogers Brown Calif. Supreme Ct., San Francisco, 1999. Career Awareness Acad. scholar Home Savings Am., 1983; Liberal Arts award Bank Am., 1983. Mem. L.A. Angel City Links Assn. (O. J. Simpson Acad. scholar 1983), L.A. Ephebian Honor Soc. Democrat. Methodist. Avocations: sports, politics, music, history, education. Office: Calif Dept Justice 300 S Spring St Ste 5000 Los Angeles CA 90013-1230

HENRY, CHARLES JAY, library and information scientist; b. Washington, June 17, 1950; s. Charles J. and June (Statz) H.; m. Nancy C. Todd, Oct. 4, 1986. BA, Northwest Mo., 1972; MA, Columbia U., 1977, MPhil, 1980, PhD, 1987. Instr. Columbia U., NYC, 1981-82; asst. to dean Columbia Coll., NYC, 1982-85; asst. dir., divsn. humanities, hist. Columbia Libr., NYC, 1985-91; dir. libr. Vassar Coll., Poughkeepsie, N.Y., 1991-96; dir. Am. Arts and Letters Network, 1995-96; vice-provost Rice U., Houston, 1996—2007; pres. Coun. on Libr. and Info. Resources, 2007—. Internat. rsch. fellow London Guildhall U., 1995—; chair nat. steering com. for computer scis. and humanities, 1998—; sr. advisor Internat. U., Bremen, Germany. Co-author: Computing and Humanities: New Dir., 1990; contbr. articles to profl. jours; panel mem., speaker in field. Lectrs., symposia peace edn. UN, Peace Edn. Columbia U.; pres. Nat. Initiative for a Networked Cultural Heritage, 2002-03. Fulbright scholar Vienna, 1980-81; Lilian Becker scholar Middlebury Coll., 1977; MacArthur Found. grantee, 1984-87; Presidents fellow Columbia U. 1978-79, 79-80; recipient Best Paper award humanities architecture divsn. Conf. Cybernetics and Systems Rsch., Vienna, 1992, All Conf. award, 1996; Fulbright fellow New Zealand, 2003, China, 2007. Mem. AAAS, ALA, Assn. Computers and Humanities (exec. coun. 1994-96), Am. Soc. for Info. Sci., N.Y. Acad. Sci., Coalition for Networked Info. (project leader 1991—), Bd. of Governors, TX Digital Libr. Alliance, Cosmos Club. Democrat. Achievements include rsch. in cybernetics and systems rsch. Office: Coun on Libr and Info Resources 1755 Massachusetts Ave, NW Ste 500 Washington DC 20036 Office Phone: 202-939-4752. Office Fax: 202-939-4765. Business E-Mail: chenry@clir.org.

HENRY, DALE, artist; b. Anniston, Ala., Feb. 8, 1931; s. Elbert Postell and Vivian Penn (Dunlap) Henry. Various part time and civil svc. jobs; tchr. Sch. of Visual Arts, NYC, 1970—86; ret. One-man shows include Gallery Nine, Berkeley, Calif., 1961, Calif. Palace of Legion of Honor, San Francisco, 1964, Esther Robles Gallery, L.A., 1965, Mills Coll. Art Gallery, Oakland, Calif., 1968, Fischbach Gallery, 1971, Galleria Toselli, Milan, 1972, John Weber Gallery, NYC, 1972—73, 1976—77, 1979, The Clocktower, 1975, Hal Bromm Gallery, 1978, William Paterson Coll., Ben Shahn Gallery, Wayne, N.J., 1980, Sarah Lawrence Coll., Yonkers, N.Y., 1985, exhibitions include Witte Meml. Mus. Ann., San Antonio, 1952, Dallas Mus. for Contemporary Art, 1960, Legion of Honor Mus., 1960—65, Poindexter Gallery, N.Y.C., 1962, Va. Mus. Fine Arts, Richmond, 1962, John Weber Gallery, 1971—80, Gallery of Loretta Hilton Ctr., Webster Coll., St. Louis, 1976, Inst. for Art and Urban Resources, Long Island City, 1976, G.M. Vieville and S.P. Najar Gallery, Paris, 1977, Moore Coll of Art, Pa., 1977, USIA World Traveling Exhbn., 1977—80, Munson-Williams-Proctor Gallery, Utica, N.Y., 1981, Bard Coll., 1981; works featured in publs. including: San Francisco Chronicle, Art in Am., N.Y. Times, Village Voice; works feature ArtForum, Flash Art; collections, Estate of Marconi, Milan, Hamburg & Family, Tang, L.I., Estate of John Reeves White, N.Y., Mills Coll., Oakland, Calif., Adirondack Planning Commission, Bickford, Nathaniel & Family, Legion of Honor, Estate Vera List, N.Y.C.; contbr. articles in field. Recipient Creative Pub. Svc. award, State of N.Y., 1981, Bd. Trustees' Calif. Legion of Honor, 1962; grantee, NEA, 1982.

HENRY, DANIEL T., diversified financial services company executive; Grad., Iona Coll., New Rochelle, NY; MBA, Hofstra U., Hempstead, NY. Ptnr. Ernst & Young; comptr. Am. Express, 1990, exec. v.p., CFO US Consumer, Small Bus. and Mcht. Svcs., exec. v.p., acting CFO, 2007—. Office: Am Express 200 Vesey St New York NY 10285 Office Phone: 212-640-5028. Office Fax: 212-640-9662.*

HENRY, DEWITT PAWLING, II, literature educator, art association administrator, writer; b. Wayne, Pa., June 30, 1941; s. John and Kathryn (Thralls) Henry; m. Constance Joy Sherbill, Aug. 25, 1973; children—Ruth Kathryn, David Jung Min. AB, Amherst Coll., 1963; A.M., Harvard U., 1965, PhD, 1971; postgrad., U. Iowa-Iowa City, 1964-66. Editor Ploughshares, dir. Ploughshares, Inc., Watertown, Mass., 1971-89, exec. dir., 1989-95, interim dir., editor-in-chief, 2007—; dir. Book Affairs, Inc., Watertown, 1975—85. Adj. prof. Emerson Coll., Boston, 1982-83, asst. prof. creative writing and lit., 1983-89, assoc. prof., 1989-2006, prof., 2006—, acting chair div. writing, pub. and lit., 1987-88, chair, 1989-93; mem. adv. panel Mass. Coun. on the Arts, Boston, 1981-83; literature panelist Nat. Endowment for the Arts, Washington, 1982-85, 92-93; mem. adv. bd. New England Found. for Arts, 1983-85; mem. Watertown Arts Lottery coun., 1987-92; bd. dirs., treas. Associated Writing Programs, 1988-90, pres., 1990-91. Author: The Ploughshares Reader, New Fiction for the 80s, 1985, Other Sides of Silence, New Fiction from Ploughshares, 1993, Fathering Daughters, 1998, Breaking Into Print, 2000, Sorrow's Company: Writers on Loss and Grief, 2001, The Marriage of Anne Maye Potts, 2001; columnist Wilson Libr. Bull., 1979-81; staff editor The Pushcart Prize, 1978—. Fellow Woodrow Wilson found., 1963; fellow Coordinating Council of Literary Mags., 1979, Nat. Endowment for Arts, 1979 Mem. Associated Writing Programs, Phi Beta Kappa Presbyterian. Home: 33 Buick St Watertown MA 02472-2176 Office: Emerson Coll Writing Lit Pub Divsn 120 Boylston St Boston MA 02116-4624 Home Phone: 617-926-4174; Office Phone: 617-824-8241. Personal E-mail: dewitt_henry@emerson.edu.

HENRY, DINAH D., science educator; d. Donald and Ruth Kretzer; m. John Aldrich Henry, Oct. 21, 1978; children: Shannon, David. BS, Bowling Green State U., Ohio, 1977; MA, Coll. Mt. St. Joseph, Ohio, 1989. English tchr. Paulding H.S., Ohio, 1977—81; substitute tchr., tutor Paulding Exempted Villiage Schs., Ohio, 1988—94; adj. faculty N.W. State C.C., Archbold, Ohio, 1991—, life scis. lab. coord., 1997—2001, life scis. tutor, 2003—. Yearbook advisor Paulding Schs., 1978—80; sci. fair judge Paulding Schs. and NW Ohio Dist., 1981—2004. Blood donor ARC, Ohio, 1974—; mem. adminstrv. coun. Evansport United Meth. Ch., Ohio, 2002—. Avocations: reading, travel. Office: NW State CC 22600 St Rt 34 Archbold OH 43502

HENRY, ED, news correspondent; 1 child, Patrick. BA in English, Siena Coll., Loudonville, NY. Investigative reporter with columnist Jack Anderson; sr. editor, columnist Roll Call, Washington, 1992—2004; Capitol Hill corr. CNN, Washington, 2004—06, White House corr., 2006—. Polit. analyst C-SPAN, WUSA-CBS affiliate; chief polit. analyst WMAL-ABC Radio. Recipient Dirksen award for disting. reporting in Congress, Nat. Press Found., 2006. Office: CNN 1620 I St NW Washington DC 20006 Office Phone: 202-777-7266.

HENRY, EDWARD FRANK, retired data processing executive; b. East Cleveland, Ohio, Mar. 18, 1923; s. Edward Emerson and Mildred Adelia (Kulow) H.; m. Nicole Annette Peth, June 18, 1977. BBA, Dyke Coll., 1948; postgrad., Case Western Reserve U., 1949, Cleve. Inst. Music, 1972. Internal auditor E.F. Hauserman Co., 1948-51; sales and radio announcer Sta. WSRS, 1951; office mgr. Frank C. Grismer Co., 1951-52, Broadway Buick Co., 1952-55; sec., treas. Commerce Ford Sales Co., 1955-65; nat. mgr. Auto Acctg. divsn. United Data Processing Co., Cin., 1966-68; v.p. Auto Data Sys. Co., Cleve., 1968-70; pres. Profl. Mgmt. Computer Sys., Inc., Cleve., 1970—2003, Profl. Mgmt. Computer Sys. Became Internat., 1999—2003, ComputerEASE, Small Bus. Computer Ctrs. divsn. Profl. Mgmt. Computer Sys., Inc., 1985—2003, VideoEASE CompuAIDE Computerized Video Rental Sys. divsn. Profl. Mgmt. Computer Systems, Inc., 1987-89; pres. CompuPRINT divsn. Profl. Mgmt. Computer Sys., Inc., 1995—2003, pres. TravelEASE divsn., 1996—2002; ret., 2007. Drum maj., musician Wurlitzer Marching Band, Cleve., 1939—42, The Ed Henry Dance Band, 1939—42; with USAF Marching Band, Kearns, Utah, 1943; dramatic dir., actor Euclid Little Theatres, Jewish Cmty. Ctr.; actor Cleve. Playhouse, 1961—63; dramatic dir., actor various other theatres; exec. artistic dir. NorthCoast Cultural Ctr., 1989—. Contbr. photography, Travel Agents Internat. mag., 1990 (hon. mention, 1990); prodr., dir. (Jesters) (plays) National Book of the Play Acapulco, Mexico, 1985, nat. prodr., dir. (Jesters) Nat. Book of the Play Reno, 1988—, Bally's Celebrity Rm., Las Vegas, 1989—96, Hyatt Regency O'Hare, 1998, Millennium, 2000, Nat. Book of the Play Bally's Las Vegas. Charter pres. No. Ohio Coun. Little Theatre, 1954—56; founder, artistic and mng. dir. Exptl. Theatre, Cleve., 1959—63; bd. dirs. Cleve. Philharm. Orch., 1972—74, Cleve. Jazz Orch., 1991—2006, Cleve. Opera League, Back on Board, 2002. 1st lt. USAF, 1943—46, PTO, capt. USAF, 1946—58, capt. USAFR, 1995. Decorated Bronze Star with 3 oak leaf clusters; named and featured in publ. book Showtime in Cleveland: The Rise of A Regional Theater Center (John Vacha). Mem.: APA, Res. Officers Assn., Internat. Soc. Photographers (Silver award bowl 2006, Bronze Commemorative award 2006), Associated Photographers Internat., Internat. Platform Assn., Am. Soc. Profl. Cons., Nat. Assn. Profl. Cons., Data Processing Mgmt. Assn., Mil. Order World Wars (comdr. Cleve. chpt. 1994—95, dept. comdr. State of Ohio 2001—, adjutant 2001—, nat. staff mem. 2003—), Inst. Mgmt. Accts., Am. Mgmt. Assn., Air Force Assn. (life), Art Inst. Chgo., Cleve. Mus. Art, Nat. Assn. Met. Mus. Art of N.Y., Mayfield Area C. of C., Ky. Cols., Rotary, Univ. Club, Acacia Country Club, Hermit Club, Cleve. Grays Club, Deep Springs Trout Club, Jesters (dramatic dir. 1971—, dir. 1981, impresario 1984—99, impresario emertus 2000, Cleve. Ct. # 14, SOBIB, Kachina, dir. emeritus 2007), Grotto, Scottish Rite (dramatic dir. 1967—, thrice potent master 1982—84, class named in his hon. 1994), DeMolay (master Cleve. chpt. 1942, Legion of Honor 1970), Sojourners (Nat. President's cert. 1977—78, pres. Cleve. chpt. #23 1978), Masons (60 yr. honor 2004, hon. 33d degree), Am. Legion, VFW, KT, Heroes of '76 (comdr. Cleve. 1977), Cuyahoga County Meml. Lodge (worshipful master 1993—94), Shriners (dramatic dir. 1968—88), Phi Kappa Gamma (charter pres., past nat. pres.). Republican. Presbyterian. Home: 666 Echo Dr Gates Mills OH 44040-9606 Office: Profl Mgmt Computer Systems Inc 19701 S Miles Rd Cleveland OH 44128-4257

HENRY, EMIL WILLIAM, JR., diversified financial services company executive, former federal agency administrator; b. Dec. 28, 1960; s. Emil William and Sherrye (Patton) Henry; m. Jody Cregan Sollers, June 14, 1986; 3 children. BA cum laude, Yale U., 1983; MBA, Harvard U., 1987. With merchant banking dept. Morgan Stanley; chmn. asset mgmt. Gleacher Ptnrs., mng. dir., sr. ptnr., chmn. Gleacher Fund Advisors; asst. sec. for fin. institutions US Dept. Treasury, Washington, 2005—07; mng. dir. pvt. equity Lehman Brothers, NYC, 2007—. Recipient Alexander Hamilton award, US Dept. Treasury, 2007. Office: Lehman Bros Inc 745 7th Ave 30th Fl New York NY 10019*

HENRY, FRANCES ANN, retired journalist, educator; b. Denver, July 23, 1939; d. Lewis Byford and Betsy Mae (Lancaster) Patten; m. Charles Larry, June 28, 1963 (div. May 1981); children: Charles Kevin, Tracy Diane. BA in English, Carleton Coll., 1960; MA in Social Sci., U. Colo., Denver, 1988; MA in Journalism, Memphis State U., 1989. Cert. tchr. Lang. arts tchr. Rolla (Mo.) Pub. Schs., 1963-66; journalism/English tchr. Douglas County Pub. Schs., Castle Rock, Colo., 1976-99, retired, 1999, chmn. English dept., 1992-98; asst. prof. Memphis State U., 1991-92; mng. editor Douglas County News-Press, Castle Rock, 1986-87; editor Fourth World Bulletin, 1988; exec. editor Daily Helmsman Memphis State U., 1988-89, gen. mgr. Daily Helmsman, 1991-92; sole proprietor The Editor's Desk, 1997—. Contbr. articles to profl. jours. Recipient Gov.'s Excellence in Edn. award Colo. Endowment for Humanities, 1997, Lifetime Achievement award Journalism Edn. Assn., 2006. Mem. ACLU, Colo. HS Press Assn. (sec. 1981-83, pres. 1983-91, Colo. Journalism Tchr. of Yr. 1985), Mensa, Kappa Tau Alpha. Democrat. Episcopalian. Personal E-mail: fhenry1@comcast.net.

HENRY, FREDERICK B., foundation administrator; Pres. Bohen Found., 1984—. Bd. mem. Am. Ctr., Paris, 1991; chmn. Am. Ctr. Found.; bd. dir. Georges Pompidou Art & Culture Found., Paris & Houston, Aspen Valley Cmty. Found., Aspen, Colo., Bklyn. Acad. Music, Des Moines Art Ctr., Iowa, Dia Ctr. for Arts, NYC, Public Agenda Found., NYC, Whitney Mus. Am. Art, NYC; bd. trustee Solomon R. Guggenheim Mus., NYC, 2002—. Office: Bohen Foundation 415 W 13th St New York NY 10014 Office Phone: 212-414-4575.

HENRY, J. MYRLE, pharmacist; b. Jacksonville, Fla., Aug. 30, 1938; s. Joseph Mason and Ovieda Ida (Dossey) H.; m. Tommie Claire Williams, Aug. 28, 1959; children: Cheri Kim, Kathy Lynn. BSP, U. Fla., 1961. Registered pharmacist Fla. Pharmacist Barwick Drugs, Plant City, Fla., 1961, Magnolia Pharmacy, Plant City, 1962-66, pharmacist, co-owner, 1966-80; co-owner H&R Drug Ctr., Plant City, 1973-85, owner, 1985-93, Herring Drug, Plant City, 1977-86; pharmacist, owner Magnolia Pharmacy, 1980-2000; pharmacist Kash n Karry Pharmacy, Plant City, 2000—. Past mem. Hillsborough County Citizens Adv. Com.; pres. The Fla. Opry; past pres. East Hillsboro Hist. Soc.; Plant City Down Town Bus. and Merchants Assn.; founder, past pres. Bapt. Towers Plant City, Inc.; deacon 1st Bapt. Ch.; past pres. Christian Living Ctr., Inc.; trustee So. Fla. Bapt. Hosp.; past bd. dirs. Hillsborough County unit Am. Cancer Soc., past chmn. Plant City br.; founder, past chmn. Strawberry Classic Car Show. Named Plant City's Citizen Yr., group of 10 clubs Kiwanis, Civitan, Rotary, C. of C., Pilot, Optimist, Lions, Womans, Jr. Womans and Rotary Daybreak, 2001; recipient Wyeth Bowl of Hygeia Cmty. Svc. award for Fla., 2007. Mem.: East Hillsborough C. of C. (past bd. dirs., past treas.), Fla. State Pharm. Assn., Am. Pharm. Assn., Hillsborough County Pharmacy Assn. (past pres.), Plant City Lions Club (past pres.), Kappa Psi. Avocations: swimming, tennis, gardening. Office: Kash n Karry Pharmacy Wheeler St Plant City FL 33566 Home: PO Box RR Plant City FL 33564-9038

HENRY, JED WILLIAM, urologist; b. Wilmington, Ohio, July 4, 1977; s. John William and Judy Ann Henry; m. Darci Leigh Gray, June 23, 2001. BA (hon.), Kenyon Coll., Gambier, Ohio, 2000; MD, Ohio State U., Columbus, 2004. Urology resident coll. medicine NE Ohio U., Akron, Ohio, 2004—. Fellow, Ohio Bd. Regeants, 2000; Howard Hughes Med. Inst. fellowship, Howard Hughes, 1999. Mem.: Endourologic Soc. (assoc.), Am. Assn. Clin. Urologists (assoc.), Ohio Urol. Soc. (assoc.), Am. Urol. Assn. (assoc.), Phi Beta Kappa. Achievements include research in genital edemo in Crohn's disease. Home: 1690 Wiltshire Rd Akron OH 44313 Home Phone: 330-836-3295.

HENRY, JOHN COOPER, journalist; b. San Antonio, Sept. 18, 1948; s. Deck Houston and Ruth Brophy (Cooper) H.; m. Patricia Mayer, Oct. 3, 1981. BS in History, Miss. State U., 1975. Photographer Starkville (Miss.) Daily News, 1975; politics and govt. reporter Delta Dem. Times, Greenville, Miss., 1975-79; reporter, editor Austin Am.-Statesman, 1979-85; asst. state editor Austin (Tex.) Am.-Statesman, 1985-86, state capitol bur. chief, 1986-88, asst. bus. editor, 1989-90; asst. city editor Houston Chronicle, 1990-93, night city editor, 1993-95, polit. editor, 1995—97, Washington bur. reporter Washington, 1997—99, asst. Washington bur. chief, 1999—2000, Washington bur. chief, 2000—05; news editor AP, Washington, 2005—. Mem. steering com., reporters com. Freedom of the Press, Washington, 1985—; mem. steering com. Tex. Media: A First Amendment and Freedom of Info. Coalition, Austin, 1986-95. Asst. comm. dir. Gil Carmichael for Gov. campaign, Meridian, Miss., 1975. Staff Sgt. USAF, 1967-71. John S. Knight Journalism fellow, Stanford (Calif.) U., 1988-89. Mem. Soc. Profl. Journalists, Freedom of Info. Found. Tex. (bd. dirs. 1990-96), U.S. Golf Assn. Presbyterian. Avocations: golf, hiking, fly fishing. Office: Associated Press 2021 K St NW Washington DC 20006

HENRY, JOHN W., professional sports team executive; b. Quincy, Ill., 1949; m. Peggy Henry; 1 child. Founder, chmn. John W. Henry & Co., Inc., Boca Raton, Fla., 1981—, Westport, Conn., 1981—; chmn., majority owner Class AAA Tucson Toros, Pacific Coast League, 1989-97; co-owner W. Palm Beach Tropics, Sr. Baseball League, 1989—; limited ptnr. N.Y. Yankees, 1992; chmn. Fla. Marlins Baseball Club, Miami, 1999—2002; majority owner Boston Red Sox, 2002—. Mem. Nat. Assn. Futures Trading Advisors (bd. dirs.), Managed Futures Trade Assn. (bd. dirs.), Nat. Futures Assn. (mem. nominating com.), Futures Industry Assn. (bd. dirs.). Office: Boston Red Sox 4 Yawkey Way Boston MA 02215-3496*

HENRY, JOSEPH DEAN, music educator, director; b. Augusta, Maine, Aug. 5, 1954; s. George A. and Jacqueline Henry; m. Kimberly G. Gowen, June 27, 1987; children: Kaelen E., Kelsey L. BS, U. So. Maine, Gorham, 1976; MusM, U. Maine, 1985; D in Musical Arts, U. Mo., Kansas City, 1991. Dir. choral activities Eureka Coll., Ill., 1991—; artistic dir., condr. Peoria Area Civic Chorale, Ill., 1994—2006. Recipient Hall of Fame, Peoria Symphony Orch., 2006. Mem.: Am. Choral Dirs. Assn. (assoc.), Music Educators Nat. Conf. (assoc.). Office: Eureka Coll 300 College Ave Eureka IL 61530 Business E-Mail: jdhenry@eureka.edu.

HENRY, JOSEPH PATRICK, chemicals executive; b. Mansfield, Ohio, Mar. 3, 1925; s. Harold H. and Louise A. (Droxler) Henry; m. Jeanette E. Russell, Oct. 26, 1957; 1 child, Jeanette Louise. Attended, Bowling Green State U., 1943—44; BS, Ohio State U., 1949. Ohio sales mgr. NaChurs Plant Food Co., Marion, 1949—55; organizer, pres. Growers Chem. Corp., Milan, 1955—, Sandusky Imported Motors, Inc., Ohio, 1958—78; pres. Homestead Motors, Inc., 1978—83. Co-owner Homestead Inn Restaurant, Homestead Farms; v.p. South Avery Corp. Motels, 1961, Homestead Inn, Inc. Motels, 1963—; dir. Erie County Bank, Vermilion, Ohio, Soc. Bank of Firelands. Mem. Milan C. of C. With USMCR, 1943—46, PTO. Named to Lakewood (Ohio) HS Athletic Hall of Fame, 1997; recipient Bus. Adv. Coun. Gold Medal, Rep. Congressional Com., 2003, Businessman of Yr., Rep. Congl. Com., 1999. Mem. Nat. Fedn. Ind. Bus. (nat. adv. coun.), AAAS, Ohio Farm Bur. Fedn., Aircraft Owners and Pilots Assn., Internat. Flying Farmers, Ohio Restaurant Assn., Ohio Motel-Hotel Assn., Ohio Licensed Beverage Assn., Am. Horse Show Assn., Nat. Trust for Hist. Preservation, N.A.M., Internat. Platform Assn., Huron County Hist. Soc., Ohio Farm Bur. (pres.), Ohio, Internat. (dir. 1978-84), Arabian Horse Assns., Antique Auto. Club Am., Sports Car Am., N. Am. Yacht Racing Union, Sandusky Yacht Club, Sandusky Sailing Club, Catawba Island Club. Achievements include developing (with V.A. Tiedjens) foliage fertilization and direct to seed fertilization of commercial field crops. Home: 128 Center St Milan OH 44846-9757 Office: Growers Chem Corp PO Box 1750 Milan OH 44846-1750 also: Homestead Farms RR 1 Milan OH 44846-1700 Office Phone: 419-499-2508.

HENRY, KATHLEEN MARIE, marketing executive; b. Stillwater, Okla., Sept. 24, 1950; d. Irl Wayne and Hulda Mary Henry. BS, U. Ctrl. Okla., Edmond, 1972. Community relations dir./account exec. Lowe Runkle Advt., Oklahoma City, 1972-74, account coordinator, 1975; sales promotion cons. McDonald's Corp., Houston, 1974, regional advt. supr. Southfield, Mich., 1975, regional advt. mgr., 1976-78, local store mktg. mgr. Oak Brook, Ill., 1978-80, staff dir., store mktg./sales promotion, 1980-82, home office dir. store mktg./sales promotion, 1982-83, dir. nat. sales promotion, 1983-84, internat. mktg. dir., 1984-85; mktg. dir. McDonald's System France, 1985-86, McDonald's System Europe, 1985-88, v.p. mktg., 1988-97; pres. Henry Jamieson Assocs., Tulsa, Okla., 1997—; pres., COO Zepper Entertainment, Tulsa, 2004—. Publicity chmn. Keep Okla. Beautiful, 1973-74; publicity chmn. Muscular Dystrophy Assn. Am., Okla. chpt., 1973-74; bd. dirs. Southfield Arts Coun., Mich., 1976-78; commr. Lake Keystone Planning and Zoning Commn., 1999—; bd. dirs. Perry H.S. Alumni Assn., 1999—; bd. dirs. sec. Keystone Peninsula Property Owners Assn., 1998—; commr. State of Okla. Film and Music Commn., 2005—; mem. adv. bd. Tulsa Symphony Orch., 2007—. Recipient Chgo. YWCA Leadership award, 1978, Disting. Former Student award U. Ctrl. Okla., 1979, Bronco award U. Ctrl. Okla. Centennial, 1991; named Outstanding Sr. Woman U. Ctrl. Okla., 1972, Outstanding Greek Woman,

1972. Mem. U. Ctrl. Okla. Alumni Assn. (dir. 1974, 1998-2002, found. bd. dirs. 1999—), U. Ctrl. Okla. Centennial Commn., Sigma Kappa. Office: Henry Jamieson Assocs Rte 3 Box 150A Cleveland OK 74020

HENRY, LAURIN LUTHER, public affairs educator; b. Kankakee, Ill., May 23, 1921; s. Laurimer Luther and Jeanette Belle (Wagner) H.; m. Kathleen Jane Stephan, May 18, 1946; children— Stephanie Jane, Robin Leigh. BA, DePauw U., 1942; MA, U. Chgo., 1948, PhD, 1960. Staff asst. Public Adminstrn. Clearing House, Chgo. and Washington, 1950-55; research asso., sr. staff mem. Brookings Instn., Washington, 1955-64; prof. govt. and fgn. affairs U. Va., 1964-78; dean Sch. Community and Public Affairs, Va. Commonwealth U., Richmond, 1978-86, prof., 1986-87, prof. emeritus, 1987—. Guest scholar U. Va., 1988-95; vis. prof. Johns Hopkins U.; cons. to govt. Author: Presidential Transitions, 1960, The NASA-University Memorandum of Understanding, 1967; co-author: Presidential Election and Transition of 1960-61, 1961; contbr. articles profl. publns. Served with USNR, 1942-46. Recipient L.D. White prize Am. Polit. Sci. Assn., 1961. Fellow Nat. Acad. Pub. Adminstrn. (sr.); mem. Nat. Assn. Schs. Public Affairs and Adminstrn. (pres. 1971-72), Am. Soc. Pub. Adminstrn., Phi Beta Kappa, Phi Kappa Phi. Home: 500 Crestwood Dr Apt 1204 Charlottesville VA 22903-4853

HENRY, LAWRENCE C. (LONNY HENRY), investment banker; Mng. dir. Goldman Sachs, NYC; now sr. mng. dir. Bear, Stearns & Co., Inc., NYC. Named a Top Dealmaker, Dealmaker mag., 2006; recipient Jack A. Shaffer Fin. Adv. award, Am. Hotel & Lodging Assn., 2005. Office: Bear Stearns & Co Inc 383 Madison Ave New York NY 10179 Office Phone: 212-272-2000. Office Fax: 212-272-7047.*

HENRY, MARTIN DANIEL, military academy vice president; b. Pitts., Dec. 13, 1940; s. Martin A. and Margaret (Fisher) H.; m. Aimee Monteverde, Nov. 21, 1973; children: Donna, Nicholas, Bryan. BA, St. Vincent Coll., 1962; MEd, Duquesne U., 1965; MBA, Barry U., 1973; PhD, U. Pitts., 1979; JD, U. Dayton, 1984. Bar: Ohio, 1984. Tchr. South Hills Cath. High Sch., Pitts., 1963-65; adminstr. U. Pitts., 1966-71; dean LaRoche Coll., Pitts., 1971-74; v.p. acad. affairs Barry U., Miami, Fla., 1974-79; v.p. adminstrn. U. Dayton, Ohio, 1979-85; pres. St. Leo (Fla.) Coll., 1985-87, Gannon U., Erie, Pa., 1987-91. Speaker numerous univs., seminars, confs. Author: The Practice of Management, 1980; author invited and juried papers. Recipient Disting. Alumnus award St. Vincent Coll., Latrobe, Pa., 1985, Bicentennial Medallion of Distinction U. Pitts, 1987. Mem. Ohio State Bar Assn. Roman Catholic. Avocations: racquet sports, spectator sports, movies, travel. Personal E-mail: drdanhenry@yahoo.com.

HENRY, NICHOLAS LLEWELLYN, public administration educator; b. Seattle, May 22, 1943; s. Samuel Houston and Ann (Connor) H.; m. Muriel Bunney; children: Adrienne Richardson, Miles Houston. BA, Centre Coll. Ky., 1965; MA, Pa. State U., 1967; MPA, Ind. U., 1970, PhD, 1971. Asst. to dean Coll. Arts and Scis.; instr. Ind. State U., 1967-69; vis. asst. prof. U. N.Mex., 1971-72; asst. prof. polit. sci. U. Ga., 1972-75, assoc. prof., 1975-78, prof., 1978-87, dir. Ctr. Pub. Affairs, 1975-80, dean Coll. Pub. Programs, 1980-87; prof., pres. Ga. So. U., Statesboro, 1987-98, prof. polit. sci., 1998—. Author or editor 12 books; contbr. numerous articles to profl. jours. Recipient Author of Yr. award Assn. Sci. Jours., Laverne Burchfield award ASPA, 2002; named One of 100 Most Influential People in Ga., Ga. Trend, 1994. Fellow Nat. Acad. Pub. Adminstrn.; mem. Cosmos Club (Washington). Office: Ga So U PO Box 8009 Statesboro GA 30460-1000 Home Phone: 912-790-8093. Business E-Mail: nic_henry@georgiasouthern.edu.

HENRY, PETER YORK, lawyer, mediator; b. Washington, Apr. 28, 1951; s. David Howe III and Margaret (Beard) Henry; m. Deidra B. Hagdorn, May 1995; 1 child, Chance Hagdorn stepchildren: Nathan Hebert, Christpher Hebert;children from previous marriage: Ryan York, Zachary Price. BBA, Ohio U., 1973; JD, St. Mary's U., San Antonio, 1976. Bar: Tex. 1976. Sole practice, San Antonio, 1976—. Mem.: ATLA, San Antonio Bar Assn., San Antonio Trial Lawyers Assn. (bd. dirs. 1989—90), Tex. Trial Lawyers Assn., Tex. Bar Assn., Phi Delta Phi. Home: 7642 Bluesage Cove San Antonio TX 78249-2541 Office Phone: 210-223-9244. Personal E-mail: lawofpyh@aol.com.

HENRY, PHILIP LAWRENCE, marketing professional; b. LA, Dec. 1, 1940; s. Lawrence Langworthy and Ella Hanna (Martens) H.; m. Claudia Antonia Huff, Aug. 9, 1965 (div. 1980); children: Carolyn Marie, Susan Michelle; m. Carrie Katherine Hoover, Aug. 23, 1985. BS in Marine Engring., Calif. Maritime Acad., 1961. Design engr. Pacific Telephone Co., San Diego, 1963-73; svc. engr. Worthington Svc. Corp., San Diego, 1973-78; pres. Realmart Corp., San Diego, 1978-81; dir. mktg. Orbit Inn Hotel and Casino, Las Vegas, 1981-84; pres. Comml. Consultants, Las Vegas, 1984—2002, Gray Electronics Co., Las Vegas, 1986—. Chmn. bd. dirs. Las Vegas Accomodations Unltd., 1997-2000; mng. mem. G/Tracker Techs., LLC, 1998, Strobe Detector Techs., LLC, 1998; bd. dirs. Silver State Classic Challenge, Inc. Inventor electronic detection devices, 1986—. Served to lt. (j.g.) USNR, 1961-67. Republican. Avocations: amateur radio, open road auto racing, storm chasing. Home Phone: 775-289-6254; Office Phone: 775-289-6254. Personal E-mail: mail@philhenry.com.

HENRY, RENE ARTHUR, writer, consultant; b. Charleston, W.Va., June 13, 1933; s. Rene A. and Lillian E. H.; children: Deborah Marie, Bruce Rexford. AB in Econ., Coll. William and Mary, Williamsburg, Va., 1954; postgrad. in Mktg., W.Va. U., 1954—56. Cert. in Conflict Resolution Harvard Law Sch., Boston, 1999. Account exec. Flournoy & Gibbs, Toledo, 1956-59; publicity dir. Lennen & Newell, Inc., San Francisco, 1959-67; sr. v.p., dir. Daniel J. Edelman, Inc., LA, 1967-70; pres. Rene A. Henry, Jr., Inc., 1970-74; ptnr. Allen, Ingersoll, Segal & Henry, Inc., 1974-75; prin. ICPR, 1975-81; pvt. practice mgmt. and sports mktg. cons., 1981-86, 90-91; pres., CEO Nat. Inst. Bldg. Scis., Washington, 1986-88; cons., designate asst. adminstr. AID, Dept. State, 1989-90; spl. asst. to dir. Fed. Contract Compliance Programs office US Dept. Labor, Washington, 1991; exec. dir. univ. rels. Tex. A&M U., College Station, 1991-96; dir. Office of Comm. and Govt. Rels. US EPA, Phila., 2003—06; v.p. pub. rels. St. Croix USVI, Innovative Comm. Corp., West Palm Beach, Fla., 2003—06, counselor to chmn., pres. and CEO, 2006—. Exec. sec. to bd. dirs. Coun. Housing Prodrs., 1968-75; spl. advisor The Pres.'s Coun. on Phys. Fitness and Sports, 1981-89; spl. cons. Nat. Fitness Found., 1981-89. Author: How to Profitably Buy and Sell Land, 1977, Marketing Public Relations, 1995, You'd Better Have a Hose If You Want to Put Out the Fire: The Complete Guide to Crisis and Risk Communications, 1999, Offsides!: Fred Wyant's Provocative Look Inside the National Football League, 2001; co-author: MIUS and You--The Developer Takes a Look at a New Utility Concept, 1980, Bears Handbook, 1996. Mem. adv. bd. Internat. Children's Mus., 2003—07; asst. to pres., media coms. internat. rels., pub. rels., long range strategic planning task force U.S. Olympic Com., 1984—89; campaign dir. for athletes and entertainers Bush for Pres. and Bush/Quayle '88 presdl. election campaigns; adv. bd. Ctr. Crisis Pub. Rels. and Litigation Lehigh U. With US Army, 1956—58. Decorated Knight of Honor, The Sovereign Order of St. John Jerusalem, Knights Hospitaller, promoted to Knight of Grace 2006; named San Francisco Bay Area Pub. Relations Man of Year, 1963; recipient Clarion award Women in Comm., 1980, Alumni Svc. award Coll. William and Mary, 2003; named to Granby HS Hall of Fame, Norfolk, Va., 2001. Mem.: Acad. Motion Picture Arts and Scis., Pub. Rels. Soc. Am. (chmn. Coll. Fellows 2001, Disting. Citizen award L.A. chpt. 1979, Paul M. Lund award for Public Svc. 2005, 3 Silver Anvils), Acad. TV Arts and Scis. (past chair bld. com.), Sigma Nu. Episcopalian.

HENRY, ROBERT HARLAN, federal judge, former attorney general; b. Shawnee, Okla., Apr. 3, 1953; BA, U. Okla., 1974, JD, 1976. Bar: Okla. 1976. Atty. Henry, West, Still & Combs, Shawnee, Okla., 1977—83, Henry, Henry & Henry, Shawnee, 1983—87; mem. Okla. Ho. of Reps., 1976—86; atty. gen. State of Okla., Oklahoma City, 1987—91; dean, prof. Okla. City U. Law Sch., 1993—94; judge US Ct. Appeals (10th cir.), Oklahoma City, 1994—. Mem. Nat. Conf. Commrs. on Uniform State Law. Fellow: Am. Bar Found.; mem.: William J. Holloway, Jr. Am. Inn of Ct., ABA, Okla. City Bar Assn., Nat. Assn. Attys. Gen. (chmn. state constl. law adv. com., vice-chmn. civil rights com.), Am. Coun. Young Polit. Leaders, Okla. Bar Assn. Office: US Ct Appeals 10th Cir 200 NW 4th St Rm 2421 Oklahoma City OK 73102-3026 also: Byron White US Cthse 1823 Stout St Denver CO 80257*

HENRY, ROBERT JOHN, lawyer; b. Chgo., Aug. 1, 1950; s. John P. and Margaret P. (Froelich) Henry; m. Sara Mikuta; children: Cherylyn, Deanna, Laurin, Joseph Mikuta, Nicholas Mikuta. BA cum laude, Loyola U., Chgo., 1973, JD cum laude, 1975. Bar: Ill 1975, U.S. Dist. Ct. (no. dist.) Ill. 1975. Atty. Continental Ill. Nat. Bank, Chgo., 1975-77, Allied Van Lines, Inc., Chgo., 1977-81, assoc. gen. counsel, 1981-88, gen. counsel, 1988-90, v.p. adminstrn., gen. counsel, 1990-93, v.p. gen. counsel, 1993-99; v.p., assoc. gen. counsel SIRVA, Inc., Chgo., 1999—2005; ptnr. Scopelitis, Garvin, Light & Hanson, Chgo., 2005—. Gen. counsel NFC N.Am., 1996-99. Bd. dirs. Naperville C. of C., 1999—2002. Alt. scholar Weymouth Kirkland Found., 1971. Mem. Chgo. Bar Assn. Office Phone: 312-422-1200. Business E-Mail: rhenry@scopelitis.com.

HENRY, RONALD JAMES WHYTE, academic administrator, physicist, educator; b. Belfast, No. Ireland, Feb. 5, 1940; came to U.S., 1965; s. William James Louis and Mary Ann (Whyte) H.; children: Norah Lynn, Andrea Marie. BSc, Queen's U., Belfast, 1961, PhD, 1964. Asst. lectr. Queen's U., 1964-65; rsch. assoc. Goddard Space Flight Ctr., Greenbelt, Md., 1965-66; asst. physicist Kitt Peak Nat. Obs., Tucson, 1966-69; assoc. prof. La. State U., Baton Rouge, 1969-73, prof., 1973-89, chmn. dept. physics and astronomy, 1976-82, dean basic scis., 1982-89; v.p. acad. affairs Auburn (Ala.) U., 1989-91; provost, exec. v.p. for acad. affairs Miami U., Oxford, Ohio, 1991-94; provost, v.p. acad. affairs Ga. State U., Atlanta, 1994—. Com. on undergrad. sci. edn. Nat. Rsch. Coun., 1998-2004; bd. trustees CAEL, 2005-. Fellow Am. Physics Soc. Republican. Avocation: golf. Office: Ga State U Atlanta GA 30302-3999 Office Phone: 404-413-2574. E-mail: rhenry@gsu.edu.

HENRY, RONALD KENNETH, lawyer; b. Detroit, Jan. 12, 1951; s. Charles G. and Barbara J. (Retz) H.; m. Constance Burner Henry, Apr. 23, 1983; children: Laura, Rebecca, Kristin. BA, U. Mich., 1973, JD, 1976. Bar: DC 1976; US Supreme Ct. 1982. Ptnr. Dickstein, Shapiro & Morin, Washington, DC; ptnr. litig., chair Govt. Contracts Dept. Kaye Scholer LLP, Washington, DC. Lectr. govt. contracts law, 1978—; counsel Children's Rights Coun., Washington, 1987—, Men's Health Network. Mem. ABA, DC Bar Assn., Am. Law Inst. Avocations: tennis, racquetball, chess. Office: Kaye Scholer LLP McPherson Bldg 901 Fifteenth Street, NW, Ste 1000 Washington DC 20005 Office Phone: 202-682-3590. E-mail: rhenry@kayescholer.com.

HENRY, SALLY MCDONALD, lawyer; b. Durham, NC, Aug. 1, 1948; d. John Frederick and Mary Frances (McDonald) Henry. BA, Duke U., 1970; MA in Anthropology, SUNY, Binghamton, 1973; JD, NYU, 1982. Bar: U.S. dist. ct. (ea. dist.) N.Y. Tchr. Endicott (N.Y.) Pub. Schs., 1971-75, Monticello (N.Y.) Pub. Schs., 1975-79; clk. U.S. Bankruptcy Ct., Bklyn., 1982-83; assoc. Skadden, Arps, Slate, Meagher & Flom L.L.P., NYC, 1983-91, ptnr., 1991—, skadden., NYC. Author: Ordin on Contesting Confirmation, 1998; editor articles Rev. Law and Social Change, 1981-83; editor Portable Bankruptcy Code and Rules, ABA, contbr. numerous articles to profl. jours. Mem. rules com. Ea. dist. N.Y. bar, Bklyn, 1984. Mem.: NY Bar Assn. Home: 395 Riverside Dr Apt 6A New York NY 10025-1843 Office: skadden 4 Times Sq New York NY 10036 Office Phone: 212-735-2560.

HENRY, SARAH M., museum staff member, historian; b. NYC, May 30, 1961; d. Robert Henry and Selina Trieff; m. Michael Gorin, July 23, 1958; children: Emma May Gorin, Molly Rose Gorin. BA, Yale U., 1983; PhD, Columbia U., 1995. Asst. prof. Union Coll., Schenectady, NY, 1996—2001; dep. dir. Mus. of City of N.Y., 2001—. Office: Mus of City of NY 1220 Fifth Ave New York NY 10029 Home Phone: 212-242-7131; Office Phone: 212-534-1672.

HENRY, SHERRYE P., political advisor, radio personality; b. Memphis, July 13, 1935; Grad. magna cum laude, Vanderbilt U.; MBA, Fordham U. Asst. adminstr. Office Women's Bus. Ownership SBA; sr. advisor to Congresswoman Louise M. Slaughter, 2000—. Vice-chair interagy. com. on women's bus. enterprise. Author of 2 books including The Deep Divide: Why American Women Resist Equality; contbr. numerous articles to nat. mags.; creator, host Woman! program on Sta. WCBS-TV, N.Y.C.; ind. prodr., broadcaster Sherrye Henry Program WOR Radio, N.Y.C. Active Group for the South Fork, eastern end of L.I., N.Y., Fedn. Protestant Welfare Agys. N.Y., The Retreat, East Hampton, N.Y. Mem. Women's Forum N.Y. (founding mem.).

HENRY, STEPHEN LEWIS, retired lieutenant governor, orthopedic surgeon, educator; b. Owensboro, Ky., Oct. 8, 1953; s. Virgil Lewis and Wanda (Harper) Henry; m. Heather Reneé French, Oct. 27, 2000. BS, We. Ky. U., 1976; MD, U. Louisville, 1981. Diplomate Am. Bd. Orthopaedic Surgery. Intern gen. surgery U. Louisville Med. Ctr., 1981-82, resident, 1982-86, instr. orthopedic surgery, 1986—; lt. gov. Commonwealth of Ky., 1995—2003. Clin. investigator Richards Med. Co., Memphis, 1986—; athletic physician football teams U. Louisville, 1987—, Seneca High Sch., 1987—, Ky. State Football Championships, 1986—; commr. "A" dist. Jefferson County, 1992-95. Editor: Sports Medicine; contbr. abstracts and articles to profl. jours., chpts. to books. Treas. Louisville Tyler Park Neighborhood Assn., 1983-88, pres., 1988-89 Recipient best paper award So. Med. Assn., 1985, best clin. rsch. award U. Cin., 1986, outstanding resident rsch. award U. Louisville, 1988, Edwin G. Bovill rsch. award Orthopaedic Trauma Assn., 1989, Bell award for outstanding vol., Louisville, 1989, Presdl. recognition Nat. Vol. Week, The White House, 1989; named Outstanding Young Leader in Ky., 1988, One of 10 Outstanding Young Ams., U.S. Jaycees, 1989, Bell award, 1989, Jefferson award, 1989, Owensboro award for excellence, 1990, Lawrence-Grever award, 1990; grantee Richards Med. Co., 1986, Dept. Navy, 1989. Mem. Jefferson County Med. Soc., So. Orthopedic Assn., Ky. Med. Assn., U. Louisville House Staff Assn. (com. on health, phys. edn. and med. aspects of sports 1987—). Democrat. Office Phone: 502-464-0955.

HENRY, SUE, retired social worker, educator; b. Marion, Ind., Aug. 25, 1934; d. William Floyd and Mildred Ethel (Schwark) H. AB, Earlham Coll., Richmond, Ind., 1956; MSc in Social Adminstrn., Western Res. U., Cleve., 1964; DSW, U. Denver, 1972. Teenage program dir. YWCA, Lima, Ohio, 1956-62; br. exec. YWCA Met. Cleve., 1964-67; spl. svcs. dir. YWCA Met. Denver, 1967-70; asst. prof. U. Pa., Phila., 1972-76; assoc. prof. U. Denver, 1976-82; faculty fellow Colo. Divsn. Mental Health, Denver, 1984-85; adj. faculty Met. State Coll., Denver, 1985-89; prof. U. Denver, 1982-99, prof. emerita, 2000—. Cons. Denver Internat. Program, 1977—; rsch. assoc. Applied Social Sci. Cons., Denver, 1982-87. Author: Group Skills in Social Work, 1981, revised edit., 1992; sr. editor: Social Work with Groups Mining the Gold, 2002; mem. editl. bd. Social Work with Groups, 1981—; contbr. articles to profl. jours. Com. chair Am. Friends Svc. Com., Phila., 1972-76; mem. Planning Commn., Gilpin County, Colo., 1985-88, chair Citizen Adv. Bd. Health and Human Svcs., 1997-2002; bd. pres. Columbine Family Health Ctr., 1988-92. W.T. Grant fellow YWCA of USA, NYC, 1962-64, doctoral tng. grantee Children's Bur., US Govt., 1970-72; recipient Contbn. to Profl. Lit. award Assn. Social Group Workers, 1986, Contbn. to Prof. Lifetime Achievement award Assn. Social Group Workers, 2001. Mem. AARP (mem. nat. legis. coun. 2002-04), Coun. Social Work Edn. (ho. of dels. 1981-83), Assn. for Advancement Social Work with Groups. Democrat. Avocations: international cuisine cooking, travel, weaving. E-mail: shenry@du.edu.

HENRY, SUSAN ARMSTRONG, biology professor, dean; b. Alexandria, Va., June 27, 1946; d. Frederic Sylvester and Frederica Ann (Thompson) A.; m. Peter Edward Henry, July 20, 1968; children: Rebecca Alice, Joshua Armstrong. BS in Zoology, U. Md., College Park, 1968; PhD in Genetics, U. Calif., Berkeley, 1971. Postdoctoral fellow Brandeis U., Waltham, Mass., 1971-72; asst. prof. genetics, molecular biology Albert Einstein Coll. Medicine, Bronx, NY, 1972-77, assoc. prof. genetics and molecular biology, 1972-82, prof., 1972-87, dir. Sue Golding grad. div., 1983-87; prof. biol. scis. Carnegie Mellon U., Pitts., 1987-2000, head dept. biol. scis., 1987-91, program dir. undergrad. biol. scis. edn. initiative, Howard Hughes Med. Inst., 1989-2000, dean Mellon Coll. Sci., 1991-2000; dean Coll. of Agrl. and Life Sci. Cornell U., Ithaca, NY, 2000—. Mem. nat. adv. gen. med. scis. coun. NIH, 1995-98, adv. com. rsch. on minority health, 1998-00, chmn., 1999-00; co-dir. W.M. Keck Ctr. Advanced Tng. Computational Biology, 1992-97; bd. dirs. Agrium, Inc. Contbr. over 100 articles to profl. jours. Mem. N.Y. Farm Bur. Recipient Merit award NIH, 1991, 95, Career Devel. award, 1975-80, Irma T. Hirschl Faculty award Hirschl Found., 1980-85; rsch. grantee NIH, 1972—. Fellow AAAS (mem. com. coun. affairs 2004—, sect. biol. scis. coun. del. 2004—); mem. Genetics Soc. Am., Am. Soc. Biol. Chemists, Am. Soc. Microbiologists (grad. microbiology tchg. award nominating com. 2003-), Nat. Acads. (nat. rsch. coun. com. sci. and tech. to support health care, sustainability, and other aspects of devel. assistance 2004-05). Office: Office of the Dean CALS Cornell U 260 Roberts Hall Ithaca NY 14853-5905 Home Phone: 607-277-8476; Office Phone: 607-255-2241. E-mail: sah42@cornell.edu.

HENRY, THOMAS REID, education educator, researcher; s. Kenneth George and Doris Anne Henry; m. Michelle Madeline Lavelle, June 10, 1988; children: Kenneth William, Katharine Anne. MD, Johns Hopkins U., Balt., 1980. Cert. Neurology Am. Bd. Psychiatry & Neurology, 1988. Asst. prof. neurology U. Mich., Ann Arbor, 1988—94; prof. neurology Emory U., Atlanta, 1994—. Sec. prof adv. bd. Epilepsy Found. of Am., Landover, Md., 2004—. Author (editor): (book) Functional Neuroimaging in Epilepsy. Mem. Ga. Epilepsy Found., Atlanta, 1995—2006. Grantee Epilepsy Rsch. award, NIH, 2002—06. Fellow: Am Clin. Neurophysiology Soc. (councilor 1999—2002). Presbyterian. Achievements include research in Limbic system mapping in epilepsy. Avocations: running, backpacking, tennis, reading, classical music. Office: Emory Univ Sch of Medicine 101 Woodruff Cir WMRB-6000 Atlanta GA 30322 Office Phone: 404-778-5943.

HENRY, THORNTON MONTAGU, lawyer; b. Bermuda, May 8, 1943; s. Otis R. and Barbara M. Henry; m. Ann Portlock, Aug. 28, 1971; children: Ruth Montagu, Thornton Bradshaw, John Gordon. BA, Washington and Lee U., 1966, LLB, 1969; LLM in Taxation, Georgetown U., 1974. Bar: Fla. 1972, US Dist. Ct. (so. dist. Fla.), US Tax Ct. 1973, US Ct. Claims 1974, US Ct. Appeals (11th cir.) 1982; cert. in taxation, Fla. Tax law specialist IRS, Washington, 1972-74; chmn., pvt. client svcs. grp. Jones, Foster, Johnston & Stubbs, P.A., West Palm Beach, Fla., 1974—. Counsel, bd. profl. adv. Cmty. Found. for Palm Beach and Martin Counties; bd. dirs. Integrity Bank Fla. Author: On This Rock: A Photographic Essay on the Churches of Bermuda, Rockbridge Heritage: A Photographic Essay on Rockbridge County, Va. Pres., elder Meml. Presbyn. Ch.; bd. dirs., past pres. Rehab. Ctr. Children and Adults, Inc.; past pres. planned giving coun. Palm Beach County; mem. adv. com. Habitat for Humanity; mem. planned giving com. Norton Mus. Art; bd. dirs. Palm Beach Roundtable; chmn. planned giving com. Pl. of Hope. Capt. US Army, 1970—72. Named one of Top 100 Attys., Worth mag., 2005. Mem. ABA (tax com.), Fla. Bar Assn., Fla. Bar (tax sect.), Palm Beach County Bar Assn. (chmn. probate and guardianship practice com. 1984-2002), East Coast Estate Planning Coun. (past pres.), Palm Beach Tax Inst., Kiwanis (past pres.). Order St. John of Jerusalem (trustee, comdr., knight). Republican. Avocations: jogging, furniture restoration, reading, photography, missionary work. Office: Jones Foster Johnston & Stubbs 505 S Flagler Dr Ste 1100 West Palm Beach FL 33401-5923 Office Phone: 561-659-3000. Office Fax: 561-650-0465. Business E-Mail: thenry@jones-foster.com.

HENRY, VIC HOUSTON, lawyer; b. Big Spring, Tex., 1958; s. Don Vernor and Patricia Jean H.; m. Candace Lee McComb, Dec. 27, 1980; children: Taylor McComb, Lee Houston. BA with highest honors, U. Tex., Austin, 1980; JD cum laude, Georgetown U., Washington, 1983. Bar: Tex. 1983, U.S. Ct. Appeals (5th, 8th, 10th and D.C. cirs.) 1985, U.S. Ct. Appeals (fed. cir.) 1987, U.S. Dist. Ct. (no. dist.) Tex. 1983, U.S. Dist. Ct. (ea. and we. dists.) Tex. 1985, U.S. Dist. Ct. (ea. and we. dists.) Okla. 1985, U.S. Dist. Ct. (ea. and we. dists.) Ark. 1985, U.S. Dist. Ct. (no. dist.) Ala. 1985, U.S. Claims Ct. 1986, U.S. Supreme Ct. 1985. Law clk. to presiding justice U.S. Dist. Ct., Dallas, 1983—84; assoc. Storey Armstrong Steger & Martin, Dallas, 1984—88, ptnr., 1989—97, Henry Oddo Austin & Fletcher, P.C., Dallas, 1997—. Mem. faculty U. Tex. Arlington Asbestos Abatement, 1987; mem. adv. group Civil Justice Reform, U.S. Dist. Ct. (no. dist.) Tex., 1990; speaker seminars including Am. Corp. Counsel Assn., 1987, Notre Dame U. Sch. of Law, 2000-02, Georgetown U. Law Ctr., 2001. Adminstrv. asst. Tex. Senate, Austin, 1976-78, Tex. Ho. of Reps., Austin, 1979-80, U.S. Ho. of Reps., Washington, 1980-82; chmn. deacons Gaston Ave. Baptist Ch., Dallas, 1988, 2002-04; bd. dirs. United Cerebral Palsy of Dallas, 2004-. Mem. ABA (chmn. litig. subcom. firms 5-15 lawyers), Tex. State Bar, Conf. Freight Counsel, Transp. Lawyers Assn., Dallas Inn Ct. (barrister 1988-91). Avocations: basketball, travel, fly fishing. Office: Henry Oddo Austin & Fletcher PC 1700 Pacific Ave Ste 2700 Dallas TX 75201-7353 Office Phone: 214-658-1900.

HENRY, WILLIAM RAY, business administration educator; b. Russellville, Ark., Dec. 30, 1925; s. Mace Leon and Violet May (Shinn) H.; m. Norma Talmadge Wright, Nov. 27, 1954; children— William Ray, Lisa Carolyn, Linda Carol, Lara Carlene. BS, U. Ark., 1948, MS, 1953; PhD, N.C. State U., 1957. Asst. prof., then asso. prof., prof. N.C. State U., Raleigh, 1956-70; prof. bus. adminstrn. Ga. State U., Atlanta, 1970—, prof. emeritus fin., 1993—. Author: (with others) Managerial Economics, 1978; contbr. (with others) articles to profl. jours. Served with USAAF, 1944-45. Recipient award of merit Am. Agrl. Econs. Assn., 1957, 61

HENSARLING, JEB, congressman; b. Stephenville, Tex., May 29, 1957; m. Melissa Fore; children: Claire, Travis. BA magna cum laude in Econs., Tex. A&M U., 1979; JD, U. Tex., 1982. Mem. Staff of US Senator Phil Gramm of Tex., 1985—89; atty. Oppenheimer, Harrison, Blend and Tate, San Antonio; v.p. Maverick Capital, Dallas; prin.-owner F-H and Assocs., Dallas; mem. US Congress from 5th Tex. dist., 2003—, mem. budget com., mem. fin. svcs. com., chmn. budget and appropriations task force Rep. Study Com. Bd. dirs. IMCO Recycling Inc. Co-founder Family Support Assurance Corpn.; mem. adv. bd. Children's Edn. Fund; exec. dir. Nat. Rep. Senatorial Com., 1991—93; chair re-election campaign US Senator Phil Gramm of Tex., 1990; bd. dirs. Am. Cancer Soc.-Dallas Metro Area, Tex. Pub. Policy Found. Recipient Spirit of Enterprise award, Small Bus.

Adv. award, Hero of the Taxpayer award, Fighter for Free Enterprise award, True Blue award, Family Rsch. Coun. Republican. Episcopalian. Office: US Ho Reps 132 Cannon Ho Office Bldg Washington DC 20515 Office Phone: 202-225-3484.*

HENSEL, KATHERINE RUTH, portfolio manager, investment advisor; b. Summit, NJ, Nov. 24, 1959; d. John Charles and Carolyn (Bahle) Hensel; m. Jean-Paul Fouillade, Sept. 24, 1994 (div. Dec. 2001);. AB, Harvard U., 1981, MBA, 1985. Securities analyst Donaldson Lufkin & Jenrette, NYC, 1981-83; investment banker Paine Webber, NYC, 1985, Shearson Lehman Bros., NYC, 1986, sr. v.p., securities analyst, 1987-91; mng. dir. Lehman Bros., NYC, 1992, chief investment strategist, 1993-95; sr. equity rsch. analyst Chancellor Capital Mgmt., NYC, 1996—97; mng. dir., dir. rsch. Chancellor LGT, NYC, 1997—98; mng. ptnr. Sage Asset Mgmt., NYC, 1999—. Contbr. articles to profl. jours. Named Instl. Investor All Am. Rsch. Team, 1989-93. Office: Ste 930 500 Fifth Ave New York NY 10110 E-mail: Khensel@sageasset.com.

HENSELMANN, CASPAR GUSTAV FIDELIS, sculptor; b. Mannheim, Germany, Mar. 13, 1933; came to U.S., 1950; s. Albert Edward and Lore Elfriede (Feist) Henselmann; m. Evangeline Karantzaki, Dec. 30, 1961; children: Xavier, Samuel. Student, Northwestern U., 1950-52; diploma in med. art, U. Ill. Coll. Medicine, 1955; BFA, Art Inst., Chgo., 1956; postgrad. studies, Wayne State U., Columbia U., 1958-61. Fellow W. B. Saunders Pub. Co., Phila., 1956; med. illustrator pvt. practice, NYC, 1968—; art dir. Aron & Falcone Advtg., Chatham, N.J., 1972-73; assoc. prof. sculpture CW Post Ctr. Long Island (N.Y.) Univ., 1976-77, Hofstra Univ., Hempstead, N.Y., 1987-88; prof. LI U., Bklyn., 1996—. Vis. artist St. Cloud (Minn.) State Coll., 1975, Ox-Bow Sch. of Painting, Sugatuck, Mich., 1976, Memphis Acad. Fine Arts, 1982, Md. Art Inst., 1982, Univ. N.C., Chapel Hill, 1983; lectr. and critic Grad. Sch. of Architecture, U. Pa., Phila., 1993, Grad. Sch. Architecture, Columbia U., N.Y.C., 1994; mem. Berlin-Spandau Internat. City Planning Project Team, Columbia U., 1993. One-man shows include Rice Gallery, N.Y.C., 1961, 63, Kern County Mus., Bakersfield, Calif., 1965, Stable Gallery, 1968, 55 Mercer Gallery, 1972, 74, 75, 76, 77, Sculpture Now, NYC, 1979, Fredericsburg (Va.) Ctr. for Creative Arts, 1979, Walter Bischoff Gallery, Chgo., 1986, Drothea Van Der Koelen, Mainz, Germany, 1989, Walter Bischoff, Stuttgart, Berlin, Germany, 1990, 94, 97, Kunstverein Bielefeld Mus. in Waldhof, Germany, 1991, Bill Bace Gallery, N.Y.C., 1992, 95, Stadt Gallery, Lahr, Germany, 1993, Offenberg Mus., Germany, 1994, View Pardo Gallery, N.Y.C., 1996, Kingsborough C.C., Bklyn., 1997, Lindenau Mus., Altenburg, Germany, 1991, Rosenberg & Kaufman Gall., NYC, 1995, Villa Haiss Mus., Altenburg, Neuberger Mus., Purchase, N.Y., 1999, Robert Pardo Gallery, 1999, Forum Munich, 2003, Artefact, Zurich, Wooster Artspace, NY, 2004, 07; exhibited in group shows Am. Painting and Sculpture Annual, Phila., 1964, Nat. Design Ctr., Chgo., 1964, New Eng. Artists Annual, Silvermine, Conn., 1964, Arts Coun. of Great Britain, Whitechapel Gallery, London, 1970, Marika Malacorda Gallery, Geneva, 1976, Memphis (Tenn.) Acad. Fine Arts, 1982, Nina Owen Gallery, Chgo., 1987, U. Mass., Amherst, 1989, Bischoff Gallery, 1998, U. L.I., 1998, Pardo Gallery, 1999-2002, Chelsea Studio Gallery, N.Y.C., 2002, Berlin, 2002, Wooster Artspace, 2003, Robert Pardo, 2003, Milano Artefact, 2005, Haverstraw, NY, 2007, Bau Inst., Hudson, NY, 2007; represented in collections in Marshall-Isley Bank Lobby, Milw., 1971, Mannesmann Internat. Hdqrs., Dusseldorf, Germany, 1985, Deutsche Bank, N.Y.C., 1990, Julius Baer Bank, N.Y.C., 1992, Kunsthalle, Bremen Germany, 1993, Collection Hurrle, Durbach, Germany, 1994, Lindenau Mus., Villa Haiss Mus., Neuberger Mus., Swiss Paraplegic Ctr., Nottwil, Switzerland, 2005, Kresge Mus., Lansing, Mich., 2006. Commr. City of Denver, 2004—05. Home: 21 Bond St New York NY 10012-2451 E-mail: chenselmann@earthlink.net.

HENSELMEIER, SANDRA NADINE, retired training services executive; b. Indpls., Nov. 20, 1937; d. Frederick Rost Henselmeier and Beatrice Nadine (Barnes) Henselmeier Enright; m. David Albert Funk, Oct. 2, 1976; children: William H. Stolz Jr., Harry Phillip Stolz II, Sandra Ann Stolz. AB, Purdue U., 1971; MAT, Ind. U., 1975. Exec. sec. to dean Ind. U. Sch. Law, Indpls., 1977—78; adminstrv. asst. Ind. U.-Purdue U., Indpls., 1978—80, assoc. archivist, 1980—81; program and comm. coord. Midwest Alliance in Nursing, Indpls., 1981—82; tng. coord. Coll./Univ. Cos., Indpls., 1982—83; pres. Better Bus. Comms., Indpls., 1983—96; ret., 1996. Adj. lectr./lectr. U. Indpls. Ctr. Continuing Mgmt. Devel. and Edn., Indpls., 1984—94. Author: Successful Customer Service Writing, Winning with Effective Business Grammar, Successful Telephone Communication and Etiquette, Management Writing; contbr. articles to profl. jours. Mem.: Econ. Club of Indpls. Republican. Presbyterian. Avocations: travel, walking, reading, learning new ideas. Personal E-mail: shenselmeier@iquest.net.

HENSGEN, HERBERT THOMAS, medical technologist; b. Cin., May 28, 1947; s. Herbert and Carolyn Elizabeth (Stites) H. BS, U. Cin., 1973, MS, 1978; AAS, Cin. State Tech. and C.C., 1981. Reg. med. technologist. Grad. tchg. asst. U. Cin., 1976-77; lectr. Xavier U. (formerly Edgecliff Coll.), Cin., 1977-78; tech. Our Lady of Mercy Hosp. (now Mercy Hosp. Anderson), Cin., 1979-81, med. lab. tech., 1981—84, med. technologist, 1984—86; rsch. asst. Cin. Children's Hosp. Med. Ctr., 1986—. Instr. Cin. State Tech. and C.C., 1984-85. Contbr. article to Gen. and Comparative Endocrinology; co-author abstracts for Soc. for Pediat. Rsch., Endocrine Soc. Deacon Madisonville Bapt. Ch., 1977. Mem. Am. Soc. Clin. Pathologists, Triple Nine Soc., Am. Mensa Ltd. Achievements include production of data suggesting lack of insulin-like growth factor-1 (IGF-I) may mediate growth retardation in the neonatal rat; discovery of evidence that IGF-I may be one of several growth factors regulating differentiation of the fetal brain; demonstration that the antigonadal effect of prolactin in the lizard Anolis carolinensis is directed toward the smaller ovarian follicles; research on effects of IGF-I and its binding proteins on fetal and neonatal development. Home: 7420 Drake Rd Cincinnati OH 45243-1422 Office: Cin Children's Hosp Med Ctr Dept Endocrinology 3333 Burnet Ave Cincinnati OH 45229-3026

HENSHAW, GUY RUNALS, management consultant; b. Moscow, Idaho, Sept. 27, 1946; s. Paul C. and Helen E. Henshaw; m. Susan S. Seigel, Dec. 29, 1968; children: Christine, Victoria. BA, Ripon Coll., Wis., 1968; MBA, U. Pa., Phila., 1970. V.p. Security Nat. Bank, Walnut Creek, Calif., 1970-80, Bank Am., San Francisco, 1980-84; pres., dir. CivicBan Corp., Oakland, Calif., 1984-93; chmn. Payday, Payroll Co., San Francisco, 1993-96; mng. dir. Henshaw/Vierra, LLC, Walnut Creek, Calif., 1996—. Dir. Fair Isaac Corp., Mpls., Minn., I Sys. LLC, Burlington, Vt.; v.p., Eubel Brady & Suttman Asset Mgmt., Dayton, 2000. Chmn. bd. trustees Head Royce Sch., Oakland, 1982-90; trustee Ripon Coll., 1994—; dir. John Muir Health Sys., Walnut Creek, 1999—. Lt. col. U.S. Army, 1968-96. Mem.: Penn Club NY, Skyline Country Club, Diablo Country Club, Pacific Union Club. Episcopalian. Avocations: tennis, travel. Office: Henshaw/Vierra LLC 1460 Maria Ln Ste 290 Walnut Creek CA 94596 Office Phone: 510-749-3225. Business E-Mail: guy@henshawvierra.com.

HENSHAW, JONATHAN COOK, retired manufacturing executive; b. Dobbs Ferry, NY, Jan. 29, 1922; s. Elmer Ellsworth and Leonora Agnes (Scott) H.; m. Martha Emily Stock, July 14, 1948; children: William (dec.), Jane, Mary, Thomas, Daniel, Anne. BS, Fordham U., Bronx, NY, 1950; MBA, NYU, 1952; AA in Real Estate, Bucks County C.C., Pa., 1988. CPA NY. Staff acct. Coopers & Lybrand, NYC, 1951-55, 68-69; v.p., treas. J.A. Ewing & McDonald, Inc., NYC, 1955-62; asst. treas. Block Drug Co., Jersey City, 1962-64; contr., asst. treas. Turner Jones Co., Inc., NYC, 1964-68; treas. Visual Electronics, NYC, 1969—, Crane Co., NYC, 1970-80; assoc. broker Fox & Lazo Realtors, 1980-83, John T. Henderson, Inc., 1983-87, Richard A. Weidel Corp., Newtown, Pa., 1987—2002; ret., 2002. Served as sgt. AUS, 1943-46. Decorated Purple Heart. Roman Catholic. Home: 48 Falcon Rd Levittown PA 19056-1906

HENSLEE, GREGORY L., automotive executive; Mgmt. positions through dist. mgr. & computer ops. mgr. O'Reilly Automotive Inc., Springfield, Mo., 1984—95, v.p. store ops., 1995—99, co-pres., 1999—, CEO, 2005—. Office: O'Reilly Automotive Inc 233 S Paterson Springfield MO 65802*

HENSLEIGH, HOWARD EDGAR, lawyer; b. Blanchard, Iowa, Oct. 29, 1920; s. Albert Dales and Eula Fern (Bair) H.; m. Janice Lee Pedersen, Aug. 15, 1948; children: Susan Lee Hensleigh Harvey, Nancy Ann Hensleigh-Quinn, Jonathan Blair. BA, Iowa U., 1943, JD, 1947; postgrad., Columbia U., 1954-55. Bar: Iowa 1947, N.Y. 1955, Mass. 1968. Commd. U.S. Army, 1943, advanced through grades to col., 1965, ret., 1973; legal adviser U.S. Mission to NATO, Paris, 1958-60; dep. asst. gen. counsel office of Sec. Def. U.S. Govt., Washington, 1960-67, dep. asst. to sec. treas., 1967-68; asst. gen. counsel Raytheon Co., Bedford, Mass., 1968-91, ret., 1991; pvt. practice Carlisle, Mass., 1991—2004. Participated in U.S. Italy Internat. Ct. Justice, The Hague, 1989. Chmn. town com. Carlisle Reps., 1972-80; sch. com. Carlisle, 1973-75, bd. selectmen, 1977-80; pres. 517th Parachute Regimental Combat Team Assn. Inc., 2003-05. Mem.: ABA, Am. Soc. Internat. Law, Fed. Bar Assn. Office Phone: 650-493-5000 ext 23214. Personal E-mail: hhensleigh@earthlink.net.

HENSLER, DAVID J., lawyer; b. Alexandria, Va., June 9, 1943; AB cum laude, St. Louis U., 1965, JD cum laude, 1967. Bar: Mo. 1967, D.C. 1969; U.S. Supreme Ct. 1971. Atty., gen. counsel's office Securities and Exchange Commn., 1967-68; ptnr. Hogan & Hartson, Washington, dir. litig. practice group. Adj. prof. Georgetown U. Law Ctr., 1978-86; mem. exec. com. Council for Ct. Excellence, 1986-90. Notes and Comments Editor: St. Louis U. Law Jour., 1966-67. Mem. ABA (litigation sect.), D.C. Bar Assn., Mo. Bar Assn., Fed. Bar Assn., Defense Rsch. Inst. Office: Hogan & Hartson LLP Columbia Square 555 13th St NW Ste 800E Washington DC 20004-1161 Office Phone: 202-637-5600. Office Fax: 202-637-5910. Business E-Mail: djhensler@hhlaw.com.

HENSLEY, ELIZABETH CATHERINE, nutritionist, educator; b. Mpls., Feb. 27, 1921; d. Erich Christian and Lulu Mabel (Elliott) Selke; m. Eugene B. Hensley, June 10, 1954 (dec. 1992). BS in Edn., U. N.D., 1942; MS, Cornell U., 1944, postgrad., 1950-51. Instr. food and nutrition U. Del., 1944-47; asst. prof. Okla. A&M U., 1947-50; mem. faculty U. Mo., Columbia, 1951—, prof. food and nutrition, 1954-84, prof. emeritus, 1984—, chmn. dept. home econs., 1954-55, head dept. food and nutrition, 1955-65, co-chmn. dept. human nutrition, 1973-76. Author: Basic Concepts of World Nutrition, 1981. Mem. Am. Home Econs. Assn., Nutrition Today Soc., Mo. Home Econs. Assn., Boone County Hist. Soc., PEO, Pi Lambda Theta, Omicron Nu, Phi Upsilon Omicron, Gamma Sigma Delta, Kappa Alpha Theta Mem. Christian Ch. (Disciples Of Christ). Home: 802 Greenwood Ct Columbia MO 65203-2841

HENSLEY, MARY LYNNE FLOYD, academic medical center administrator; b. Covington, Ky., June 6, 1952; d. Robert Forsythe and Maysie McDowell (Williams) Floyd; m. Carl Evans Hensley II, Apr. 15, 1972; children: Carl Evans III, John Thomas, James Michael. Student, Am. U., DC, 1970-71; AS, U. State of N.Y., Albany, 1983; BBA with high distinction, U. Iowa, 1985; cert., U. Iowa Advanced Mgmt. Inst., 1990; cert. exec. program in healthcare mgmt., Ohio State U., 1993; M Accountancy, U. Iowa, 1998. Acctg. technician R&D VA Med. Ctr., Iowa City, 1982-86; adminstr. dept. neurology U. Iowa, Iowa City, 1986-98, interim assoc. dir. faculty practice plan Coll. Medicine, 1994—95, asst. to head dept. radiology, 1998-99, asst. to head dept. neurology and Inst. Neurol. Diseases, 1999—2006; adminstrv. ctr. dir. depts. psychiatry, neurology, neurosurgery and otolaryngology Clin. Neurosci. Ctr. Med. Sch. U. Minn., Mpls., 2006—. Adj. lectr. dept. health mgmt. and policy Coll. Pub. Health U. Iowa, 1999—, grad. program in hosp. and health adminstrn., 1994-99, tchg. asst. dept. acctg., 1997-98; mem. EEG adv. com. Kirkwood Community Coll., Cedar Rapids, Iowa, 1986-98; internship preceptor, project preceptor, mentor grad. program in hosp. and health adminstrn. U. Iowa, 1992—; coop. edn. preceptor Coll. Bus. Adminstrn., U. Iowa, 1989, 93-98. Mem. PTA, Iowa City, 1982—98; pack com. chmn. Boy Scouts Am., 1987—88, pack treas., 1988—89, den leader, 1986—89, troop merit badge instr., 1989—98; past mem. Iowa Med. Group Mgmt. Assn. Am. U. scholar, 1970-71, E. Lester Williams scholar, U. Iowa, 1984-85, Ponder Fund scholar U. Iowa, 1985, Am. Coll. Med. Practice Execs. scholar, 1997; recipient Fedn. of Schs. of Accy. award U. Iowa, 1997, Healthcare Fin. Mgmt. High Scorer award, 1998. Fellow: Accrediting Commn. Edn. Health Svcs. Adminstrn., Healthcare Fin. Mgmt. Assn. (bd. examiners 1999—2002, leader splty. group on fin. mgmt. of physician pratices 2001—02, cert., Follmer Bronze Merit award 2001, Silver Reeves award 2005), Am. Coll. Healthcare Execs. (diplomate 1996, bd. cert.), Am. Coll. Med. Practice Execs. (cert.); mem.: ANA (pres. Acad. Neurology Adminstrs., with Assn. Univ. Profs. Neurology 2000—01), Med. Group Mgmt. Assn. (pres.-elect Neurosci. Adminstrn. Assembly 2001—02, pres. 2002—03, past pres. 2003—05), Inst. Mgmt. Accts., Phi Eta Sigma, Beta Gamma Sigma, Alpha Sigma Lambda, Beta Alpha Psi, Omicron Delta Kappa, Mortar Bd. Republican. Methodist. Avocations: hiking, history, art, music, travel. Office: U Minn Med Sch Rm 12-114 PWB MMC 295 420 Delaware St SE Minneapolis MN 55455 Office Phone: 612-625-8681. Office Fax: 612-625-7950. Business E-Mail: hensley@umn.edu.

HENSLEY, NOEL M. B., lawyer; b. LA, Dec. 25, 1944; BS magna cum laude, North Tex. State U., 1975; JD cum laude, So. Meth. U., 1978. Bar: Tex. 1978. Law clk. to Hon. Robert W. Porter US Dist. Ct. (No. Dist.) Tex., 1978-80; mem. Haynes & Boone LLP, Dallas, 1980—, ptnr., Bus. Litig. Arbitrator Nat. Assn. Securities Dealer, 1986—; instr. Nat. Inst. Trial Advocacy, 1989—, So. Meth. U. Sch. Law, 1990—92. Editor: Southwestern Law Jour., 1977—78. Rsch. fellow, Southwestern Legal Found. Fellow: Tex. Bar Found., Dallas Bar Found.; mem.: Am. Law Inst., State Bar Tex. (Litig. Sect.), ABA (Litig. Sect.), Order of Coif. Office: Haynes & Boone LLP 3100 NationsBank Plz 901 Main St Ste 3100 Dallas TX 75202-3789 Office Phone: 214-651-5631. Office Fax: 214-200-0470. Business E-Mail: noel.hensley@haynesboone.com.

HENSLEY, PATRICIA DRAKE, principal; BLS in Liberal studies, St. Louis U., Mo., MA in Edn., PhD in Edn. Adminstrn. Cert. use of tech. in sch. setting Tech. Leadership Acad. Tchr. grades 7 and 8 math. and sci., 1976—82; prin. St. Mary Magdalen, St. Louis, 1982—86; vice-prin. St. Elizabeth Acad., St. Louis, 1986—91; prin. St. Francis of Assisi, St. Louis, 1991—95; acad. adviser grad. programs Webster U., St. Louis, 1990—2002; prin. Ursuline Acad., St. Louis, 1995—. Adj. instr. math. and computer sci. Webster U., St. Louis, 1986—; nat. media cons. FM radio stas.; fellow St. Louis Prin. Acad., 1994; state prin. assessor NASSP, 1994; grant reviewer U.S. Dept. Edn., 2002. Mem. Archdiocesan Com. for Rev. of H.S. Admissions, 1997—99; bd. dirs., co-chair ednl. policies com. DeSmet Jesuit H.S., 1998—; bd. dirs. Vianney H.S., 1999—. Office Phone: 314-966-4556 ext. 212. Personal E-mail: pdrakehensley@hotmail.com.

HENSLEY, RALPH HENRY, III, federal management analyst; b. Balt., June 8, 1967; s. Charles, Jr. (Stepfather) and Donna Rae Turner. Assoc. in Gen. Studies, Piedmont Va. C.C., Charlottesville, 1996; diploma in internat. hotel and restaurant mgmt., ATI Career Inst., Falls Church, Va., 1996. Edn. analyst Chief of Naval Ops., Washington, 1993—95; mgmt. analyst, family svcs. Bur. of Naval Pers., Washington, 1996; lead, manpower analyst Field Support Activity, Washington, 1996—99; sr. program analyst EER Systems Inc., Chantilly, Va., 1999—2002; exec. asst. to dep. for resource mgmt. Missile Def. Agy., Washington, 2002—04, chief staff officer, resource mgmt., 2004—05, asst. chief infrastructure planning & policy, 2005—. Sr. chief petty officer USNR, 1985—, mobilized command sr. enlisted adv., Navy Mobilization Processing Site, Norfolk, Va. Decorated Meritorious Svc. Medal Comdt., Naval Dist. Wash., Joint Svc. Achievement Medal Joint Task Force Armed Forces Inaugural Com., Navy Commendation Medal (Gold Star in lieu of Second Award) Chief of Naval Ops., Joint Svc. Commendation Medal (2nd Award) U.S. European Command, Navy Achievement Medal Commdg. Officer, Naval Air Facility Wash. DC, Navy Commendation Medal Chief of Naval Ops.; recipient Distinct Svc. medal, Piedmont Va. CC, 1991-1993. Mem.: VFW (life), Navy Reserve Assn. (life), Reserve Enlisted Assn. (life), Nat. Assn. Uniformed Svcs. (life), Am. Legion (life). Democrat. Methodist. Avocations: cycling, reading, volunteering. Home Phone: 540-722-9796. Personal E-mail: ralphhensley2003@yahoo.com.

HENSLEY, WILLIAM MICHAEL, lawyer; b. Fresno, Calif., Apr. 25, 1954; s. Goldie Reeves and Allene (Watson) H.; m. Mari Bordona Calabrese, May 1981 (div. Jan. 1984); 1 child, Gilliann Mar; m. Anne Fields, Nov. 20, 1988. BA in Speech Comm., U. So. Calif., 1976; JD, Rutgers U., Camden, NJ, 1979. Bar: Calif. 1979, U.S. Ct. Appeals (9th cir.) 1981, U.S. Dist. Ct. (ctrl. dist.) Calif. 1981, U.S. Dist. Ct. (no. dist.) Calif. 1983, U.S. Dist. Ct. (ea. dist.) Calif. 1986, U.S. Dist. Ct. (so. dist.) Calif. 1993, U.S. Supreme Ct. 1998. Law clk. to Hon. Zenovich Calif. Ct. Appeals, 5th Appellate Dist., Fresno, 1979-81; assoc. Kadison, Pfaelzer, Woodard, Quinn & Rossi, LA, 1981-87, Irell & Manella, LA, 1987-92, Menke, Fahrney & Carroll, Costa Mesa, Calif., 1992-95; atty. Jackson, DeMarco, Tidus & Peckenpaugh, Irvine, Calif., 1995—. Mem. editl. bd. Matthew Bender Calif. Real Estate Reporter, 1993—; contbr. articles to profl. jours. Mem.: Orange County Bar Assn. Democrat. Mem. Ch. of Christ. Avocations: gardening, walking, hiking, cooking. Home: 25 Pacific Crst Laguna Niguel CA 92677-5314 Office: Jackson DeMarco Tidus & Peckenpaugh 2030 Main St Ste 1200 Irvine CA 92614 Home Phone: 949-493-4560; Office Phone: 949-752-8585, 949-851-7425. Business E-Mail: mhensley@jdtplaw.com.

HENSON, C. WARD, mathematician, educator; b. Worcester, Mass., Sept. 25, 1940; s. Charles W. and Daryl May (Hoyt) H.; m. Faith deMena Travis, August 31, 1963; children: Julia Rebecca, Suzanne Amy, Claire Victoria. AB, Harvard U., 1962; PhD, MIT, 1967. Asst. prof. Duke U., Durham, NC, 1967-74, N.Mex. State U., Las Cruces, 1974-75, U. Ill., Urbana, 1975-77, assoc. prof., 1977-81, prof., 1981—, chmn. dept. math., 1988-92. Vis. assoc. prof. U. Wis., Madison, 1979-80; vis. prof. RWTH Aachen, Fed. Republic Germany, 1985-86, Univ. Tübingen, Fed. Republic Germany, 1992-93. Mem. Assn. for Symbolic Logic (sec.-treas. 1982-2000, pub. 1999-2004), Am. Math. Soc. Office: U Ill Dept Math 1409 W Green St Urbana IL 61801-2943 Office Phone: 217-333-2768. E-mail: henson@math.uiuc.edu.

HENSON, DANIEL S., marketing executive; married; 2 children. Grad., George Washington Univ., 1984. District mktg. mgr. & other mgmt. positions G.E. Co., 1987—95, gen. mgr. European equip. fin. London, 1995; chief quality officer GE Capital, 1998—99, pres., gen. mgr., auto fin. svc., 1999—2001; pres., CEO GE Capital Fleet Svcs., 2001—02, GE Vendor Fin. Svcs., 2002—05; chief comml. officer GE Comml. Fin., 2005—06; v.p., chief mktg. officer G.E. Co., 2006—. Office: General Electric 3135 Easton Turnpike Fairfield CT 06828*

HENSON, GLENDA MARIA, newswriter; b. Marion, NC, June 17, 1960; d. Douglas Bradley and Glenda June (Crouch) H. BA in English cum laude, Wake Forest U., 1982. Reporter Ark. Dem., Little Rock, 1982-84; bur. reporter Tampa Tribune, Crystal River, Fla., 1984; statehouse reporter Ark. Gazette, Little Rock, 1984-87, bur. chief Washington, 1987-89; editl. writer Lexington (Ky.) Herald-Leader, 1989-94; editl. writer, columnist The Charlotte (N.C.) Observer, 1994-98; dep. editl. page editor Austin (Tex.) American-Statesman, 1998-2001, asst. mng. editor enterprise, 2001—04; dep. editl. page editor Sacramento Bee, Calif., 2004—. Lectr. journalism, Indonesia, 2001; juror Nat. Headliner Awards, 2002—04, ASNE Writing Awards, 2001—03, Nieman Fellowship Selection Com., 2004. Editor: Pulitzer Prize Series, 2005, Jefferson Fellowship of the East-West Center, 2007. Mem. Wake Forest Presdl. Scholarship Com., Ky., 1992, Wake Forest Bd. Visitors, 1995-99; Pulitzer Prize juror, 1994, 95, 99, 2000. Nieman fellow Harvard U., 1993-94, Found. Am. Comm. Econs. fellow, 1997; recipient Pulitzer prize, 1992, Walker Stone award Scripps Howard Found., 1992, Ky. Press Assn. award, 1992, N.C. Press Assn. award, 1995-96, Leadership award Duke U., 1995, Nat. Headliner award, 1996, Mary Morgan Hewitt award, 2007; named Wake Forest Woman of Yr., 1992 Mem. Soc. Profl. Journalists (Sigma Delta Chi award 1991, Green Eyeshade award Atlanta chpt. 1992), Nat. Conf. Editorial Writers, Investigative Reporters & Editors Assn., Am. Soc. Newspaper Editors, Omicron Delta Kappa. Avocations: skiing, bicycling, swimming, travel, rafting. Office: Sacramento Bee 2100 Q St Sacramento CA 95816 Home Phone: 916-254-7370; Office Phone: 916-321-1907. Business E-Mail: mhenson@sacbee.com.

HENSON, JANE ELIZABETH, information management professional, adult education educator; b. Ft. Wayne, Ind., Dec. 1, 1946; d. Robert Eugene and Lucile Catherine (Feeney) Tucker; m. Phillip Likins Henson, Aug. 23, 1971; 1 child, Robert Likins. BS in Edn., Ind. U., 1970, MS in Edn., 1973, MLS, 1976. Tchr. pub. schs., Ft. Wayne, 1970-71, Nevada, Mo., 1971-72; libr., cataloger Ctrl. Conn. State U., New Britain, 1976-77; libr. numeric data U. Wis., Madison, 1978-80; adj. prof. libr. Navy Safety Sch. Ind. U., Bloomington, 1981-83, reference libr. Vocat. Edn. Project, 1984-86; asst. dir. ERIC Clearinghouse, Bloomington, 1988-95, assoc. dir., 1995-98, co-dir., 1999—2003; assoc. dir. Ctr. for Social Studies and Internat. Edn., Bloomington, 2004—. Co-author: Rising Expectations: A Framework for ERIC's Future in the National Library of Education, 1997; editor: Libraries Link to Learning: Final Report on the Indiana Governor's Conference on Libraries and Information Services, 1990. Chair ERIC tech. com. U.S. Dept. Edn. ERIC Program, Washington, 1990-2003, mem. ERIC exec. com., 1990-2003 Mem. Am. Soc. Info. Sci. (dept. dir. SIG cabinet 1993, chair behavioral and social sci. SIG 1994, cert. of appreciation 1993). Roman Catholic. Avocations: reading, travel. Office: Ctr for Social Studies and Internat Edn 2805 E 10th St Ste 140 Bloomington IN 47408-2698 Home Phone: 812-336-8288; Office Phone: 812-855-3838. Business E-Mail: henson@indiana.edu.

HENSON, O'DELL WILLIAMS, JR., retired anatomy educator; b. Kansas City, Mo., Jan. 11, 1934; s. O'Dell Williams and Natalie (Smith) H.; m. Miriam Morgan, Aug. 1, 1964; 1 child, Phillip William. BA, U. Kans., 1957, MA, 1960; PhD, Yale U., 1964. From instr. to assoc. prof. dept anatomy Yale U., New Haven, 1964-74; prof. dept cell biology and anatomy U. N.C., Chapel Hill, NC, 1974—2004, ret., 2004. Chmn. Commn. Anatomy, N.C., 1982-2003. Recipient Phi Sigma award 1960, Alexander Von Humbolt award 1982, Cen. Carolina Bank Excellence in Tchg. award 1982, NIH-Nat. Inst. Deafness and Other Communicative Disorders Claude Pepper award, 1989. Fellow AAAS. Home: 317 Reade Rd Chapel Hill NC 27516-1509 E-mail: owh@med.unc.edu.

HENSON, RAY DAVID, law educator, consultant; b. Johnston City, Ill., July 24, 1924; s. Ray David and Lucile (Bell) Henson. BS, U. Ill., 1947, JD, 1949. Bar: Ill. 1950, U.S. Supreme Ct. 1960. Assoc. CNA Fin. Corp., Chgo., 1952-70; prof. law Wayne State U., 1970-75, Hastings Sch. Law, U. Calif., San Francisco, 1975—95, prof. emeritus, 1995—. Author: Landmarks of Law, 1960, Secured Transactions, 1973, 2d edit., 1979, Documents of Title, 1983, 2d edit., 1990, The Law of Sales, 1985, others; editor: The Business Lawyer, 1967-68; contbr. numerous articles to law revs. Mem. legal adv. com. N.Y. Stock Exch., 1971-75. Served with USAAC, 1943-46. Mem. Am. Law Inst. (life), ABA (chmn. bus. law sect. 1969-70, adv. bd. jour. 1974-80, chmn. uniform comml. code com.), Ill. Bar Assn. (chmn. corp. banking and bus. law sect. 1963-65, chmn. uniform comml. code com.), Chgo. Bar Assn. (chmn. uniform comml. code com.). Home: 1400 Geary Blvd San Francisco CA 94109-6561 Office: U Calif Hastings Sch Law 200 Mcallister St San Francisco CA 94102-4707

HENSON, ROBERT FRANK, retired lawyer; b. Jenny Lind, Ark., Apr. 10, 1925; s. Newton and Nell Edith (Kessinger) H.; m. Jean Peterson Henson, Sept. 14, 1946 (dec. Apr. 8, 2006); children: Robert F., Sandra Henson Curfman, Laura, Thomas, David, Steven. BS, U. Minn., Mpls., 1948, JD, 1950. Bar: Minn. 1950, U.S. Supreme Ct. 1972. Atty. Soo Line R.R., 1950-52; ptnr. Cant, Haverstock, Beardsley, Gray & Plant, Mpls., 1952-66; sr. ptnr. Henson & Efron, Mpls., 1966-94, of counsel, 1995—2004; ret., 2004. Chmn. Minn. Lawyers Profl. Responsibility Bd., 1981-86; co-chmn. Supreme Ct. Study Com. on Lawyer Discipline, 1992-94. Trustee Mpls. Found., 1974-85, Emma Howe Found, 1986-90; chmn. Hennepin County Mental Health and Mental Retardation Bd., 1968-70. Served with USN, 1943-46. Fellow Am. Bar Found.; mem. ABA, Hennepin County Bar Assn. (pres. 1968-69), Minn. Bar Assn., Order of Coif. Unitarian Universalist. Personal E-mail: rhenson41025@comcast.net.

HENTERLY, MARY B., biology educator; b. Detroit, Jan. 22, 1954; d. John R. and Mary Barbara (Plageman) Henterly; m. Douglas W. Vanscoy, Sept. 26, 1982; children: Alexis Yan Yang, Kai Ethan. BS in Environ. Interpretation, Ohio State U., Columbus, 1982; cert edn., U. Puget Sound, Tacoma, 1988; MS in Sci. Edn., U. Wash., Seattle, 1999. RN Ohio. Interpretive pk. ranger Mt. Rainier Nat. Pk., Wash., 1985—90; emergency nurse Tacoma Gen. Hosp., 1985—90; tchr. sci. Curtis Sr. H.S., University Place, Wash., 1990—. Mem.: NSTA, NEA, Gamma Sigma Delta. Avocations: gardening, quilting, hiking. Office: Curtis Sr HS 8425 40th St W University Place WA 98466-2099

HENTGES, DAVID JOHN, microbiology educator; b. LeMars, Iowa, Sept. 18, 1928; s. Romaine Francis and Geneva Mae (Kruger) Hentges; m. Kathleen Edwina Mullan, Dec. 28, 1957; children: Stephen Edward, Kathleen Marie, Margaret Ann. BS, U. Notre Dame, 1953; MS, Loyola U., Chgo., 1958, PhD, 1961. Asst. prof. Creighton U. Sch. Medicine, Omaha, 1964-67, assoc. prof., 1967-68, U. of Mo. Sch. of Medicine, Columbia, 1968-72, prof., 1972-81, interim chmn., 1976-79; prof., chmn. Tex. Tech. U. Sch. Medicine, Lubbock, 1981-96, vice provost for rsch., dean grad. sch. biomed. scis., 1996-98, assoc. dean basic scis., 1996-98, dean emeritus, 1998—. Editor: Human Intestinal Microflora, 1983, Medical Microbiology, 1986, Microbiology and Immunology, 2d edit., 1995; regional editor Microbial Ecology in Health and Disease, 1987-96; mem. editl. bd. Infection and Immunity, 1983-92, Anaerobe, 1998-2004; contbr. chpts. to books and articles to profl. jours. Lay gen. chmn. Diocesan Cath. Appeal, Lubbock, 1989, 1997; co-exec. dir. Cath. Found. Diocese of Lubbock, 1998—2002. Decorated knight grand cross Order of the Holy Sepulchre, knight of merit with star Constantinian Order of St. George. Fellow Am. Acad. Microbiology (emeritus); mem. Cath. Acad. Scis., Soc. for Microbial Ecology and Disease (pres. 1987-89), Rotary Club, Sigma Xi. Roman Catholic. Avocations: gardening, fly fishing. Home: 4601 88th St Lubbock TX 79424-4107 Personal E-mail: djh18micro@hotmail.com.

HENZE, WILLIAM F., II, lawyer; b. Cleve., Apr. 20, 1949; m. Nancy A. Harmel, Oct. 3, 1980. BA, Ohio Wesleyan U., 1971; JD, U. Ariz., 1974; LLM, NYU, 1976. Bar: Ariz. 1974, N.Y. 1977, Tex. 1984. Ptnr. Jones Day, NYC. Instr. in law NYU, 1974-76. Trustee Phoenix Country Day Sch., 1997—. Mem. Phi Beta Kappa. Office: Jones Day 222 E 41st St New York NY 10017-6702

HENZLIK, RAYMOND EUGENE, zoophysiologist, educator; b. Casper, Wyo., Dec. 26, 1926; s. William H. Henzlik and Adeline Adele (Brown) Wolff; m. Wilma Louise Bartels, Oct. 1, 1950; children: Randall Eugene, Nancy Jo. BS, U. Nebr., Lincoln, 1948, MS, 1952, PhD, 1960; postgrad., Cornell U., Ithaca, NY, 1961-62. Tchr. biology and chemistry York (Nebr.) High Sch., 1948-50; sci. edn. supr. Tchrs. Coll., U. Nebr., Lincoln, 1951-53; tchr. biology Omaha North High Sch., 1953-56; instr. biology Nebr. Wesleyan U., Lincoln, 1957-59; asst. prof. zoology and biology U. Nebr., Lincoln, 1959-61; asst. prof. biology Ball State U., Muncie, Ind., 1962-67, assoc. prof. physiology, 1967-69, prof. physiology, 1970—. Adj. vis. prof. vet. physiology Tex. A&M U., College Station, 1984-85; anatomy cons. Nat. Prescription Footwear Applicators Assn., Muncie, 1962—; lectr. Pedorthics Tech. Program, Muncie, 1977—; cons. ednl. affairs Argonne (Ill.) Nat. Lab., 1970-76; dir. ednl. program Am. Diabetes Assn., Muncie, 1979-83; vis. prof. health sci. USAF European Ctr., Ramstein and Rhein Main, Germany, 1977-78; lectr. Ind. Health Care Assn., 1985-91. Author: Human Physiology Lab Manual, 1976-92; contbr. articles to profl. jours. Pres. Muncie Tech. Soc., 1975—80; mem. bd. Am. Diabetes Assn. Delaware County, Muncie, 1979—85. Radiation biology fellow NSF/AEC, U. Mich., 1960, Radiobiology fellow AEC/NSF, Cornell U., 1961-62, Radiation Biology Rsch. fellow U.S. Radiobiology Lab N.C. State U., 1965, P.R. Nuclear Ctr., 1967. Mem. AAAS, Nutrition Today Soc., Ind. Acad. Sci., Muncie Tech. Soc., Mensa, Sigma Xi, Phi Delta Kappa. Avocations: reading, book collecting. Home: 5009 N Somerset Dr Muncie IN 47304-6501

HEPFER, CHERYL LYNN, lawyer; b. McKeesport, Pa., Nov. 19, 1946; d. Robert and Ruth June (Mendlowitz) Palkovitz; m. Kenneth C. Hepfer, May 24, 1968; children: Lisa Beth, Michael, Dara. BS, Carnegie-Mellon U., 1968; postgrad., U. Pitts., 1968-69; JD, Am. U., 1972. Bar: Md. 1972, Pa. 1972, D.C. 1974, U.S. Ct. Mil. Appeals 1974, U.S. Supreme Ct. 1975, U.S. Ct. Claims 1978, U.S. Dist. Ct. Md. and D.C., U. S. Ct. Appeals (4th cir.). Assoc. Law Offices of Arthur V. Butler, Wheaton, Md., 1973-74; pvt. practice Oxon Hill, Md., 1974-75; ptnr. Bury, Meehan, Kovach & Hepfer, Oxon Hill, 1975-76, Meehan, Kovach & Hepfer, Upper Marlboro, Md., 1976-88; pvt. practice Upper Marlboro, 1988—. Lectr. Prince George's County Continuing Legal Edn. Bd. dirs., v.p. Shaare Tikvah Congregation, 1986-88; v.p. Shaare Tikvah Sisterhood, 1984-86, co-pres., 1986-88; mem. Prince George's County Lawyer's div. United Jewish Appeal, 1985—, chmn., 1985-88, mem. profl. div. Washington area, 1987—. Fellow Am. Acad. Matrimonial Lawyers (membership chair 1991—, sec. Md. chpt.), Internat. Acad. Matrimonial Lawyers; mem. ABA, Md. State Bar Assn. (coun. family-juvenile law sect.), Prince George's County Bar Assn. (family law chair 1990), Assn. Trial Lawyers Am., Md. Trial Lawyers Assn. Avocations: flying, cooking, reading, swimming. Office: The Law Offices of Cheryl Lynn Hepfer 220 N Adams St Rockville MD 20850-1829 E-mail: Law@Hepfer.com.*

HEPNER, JON R., investment company executive; b. Freeport, Ill., June 10, 1942; s. John and Sara Jane Hepner; m. Gail K. Hepner; children: Lisa L., E. Elizabeth. BBS in Bus. Adminstrn., Northwestern U., 1964. V.p. La Salle Nat. Bank, Chgo., 1965—75, Hibernia Bank, New Orleans, 1975—77, Corpus Christi (Tex.) Bank and Trust, 1977—81; investment cons. Merrill Lynch, 1981—86; sr. v.p. investment A.G. Edwards & Sons, Corpus Christi, 1986—. Dir. Karen Henry Found., 1996—2000, Padre Isles Property Owners Assn., Corpus Christi, 1998—; trustee Corpus Christi Fire Fighters Pension Fund, 2001—. Mem.: Corpus Christi Execs. Assn. (pres. 1991), Corpus Christi Rotary Club (treas. 1987). Office: A G Edwards and Sons 409 S Carancahua Corpus Christi TX 78401 Office Phone: 361-882-1600.

HEPP, JOHN HENRY, IV, historian, lawyer; b. West Chester, Pa., Oct. 21, 1959; s. John Henry Hepp, III and Rose Hunt Hepp; m. Julie Kay Benigni, Dec. 29, 1984; 1 child, John Henry V. BA, Temple U., 1982; JD, U. of Pa., 1986; PhD in History, U. of NC, 1997. Bar: Pa. 1986. Atty. Dechert Price and Rhoads, Phila., 1986—91; lectr. U. of NC, Chapel Hill, NC, 1998—99; asst. prof. Wilkes U., Wilkes-Barre, Pa., 1999—2005, assoc. prof., 2005—. Author: The Middle-Class City: Transforming Space and Time in Philadelphia, 1876-1926, 2003. Mem.: Hist. Soc. Pa. (editl. bd. 2007—), Pa. Hist. Assn. (mem. coun. 2007—, editl. bd. 2005—), Soc. for Historians of the Gilded Age and Prog. Era (mem. H-SHGAPE editl. bd. 1997—2000), Am. Studies Assn., Am. Hist. Assn., Athenaeum of Phila., Order of the Coif. Office: Wilkes U Dept History Wilkes Barre PA 18766 Home: 112 LLanfair Rd Bala Cynwyd PA 19004 Office Phone: 570-408-4225. E-mail: john.hepp@wilkes.edu.

HEPPA, DOUGLAS VAN, computer specialist; b. Bklyn., May 26, 1945; s. Joseph Charles and Antoinette Palmer (Vanasco) H.; m. Barbara Zanlunghi. BS in Social Sci., Poly. Inst. N.Y., 1968, BS in Math., 1971, MS Insl. & Applied Math., 1973, postgrad., 1983—. Assoc. engr. Raytheon Co., Portsmouth, RI, 1968-70; systems engr. PRD Electronics, Syosset, NY, 1970-71; mathematician USN, New London, Conn., 1971; asst. computer engr. George Sharp, NYC, 1972-73; programmer N.Y.C. Dept. Social Svcs., 1975; quantitative analyst N.Y.C. Fire Dept., 1976-80, assoc. staff analyst, 1980-81, computer specialist, 1991—99; with Algorithm Devel. Co., Maspeth, NY, 1999—. Pres. Algorithm Devel. Co., Queens, NY, 1985—. Mem. Math. Assn. Am., Am. Mgmt. Assn., Soc. for Indsl. & Applied Math., Assn. for Computing Machinery, IEEE, Am. Math. Soc. Avocations: fishing, swimming, boating, amateur radio, astronomy. Home: 64-08 60 th Rd Maspeth NY 11378 Office: Algorithm Devel Co 64-08 60th Rd Maspeth NY 11378-3433

HEPPELL, JACQUES PHILIPPE, surgeon, educator; m. Odette Lise Chamberland, Oct. 9, 1952; children: Patrick Jacques, Catherine Anne, Simon Pierre. MD, U. Montreal, 1974. Prof. surgery Mayo Clinic Coll. Medicine, Scottsdale, Ariz., 2000—. Office: Mayo Clinic 5777 E Mayo Blvd Phoenix AZ 85054 Office Phone: 480-342-2697.

HEPPER, CAROL, artist, educator; b. McLaughlin, SD, Oct. 23, 1953; d. Adolph and Lavern Hepper. BS, S.D. State U., 1975. Instr. drawing Standing Rock C.C., Ft. Yates, ND, 1980-82, Sch. Visual Arts, NYC, 1984. Vis. lectr. RISD, Providence, 1986-88, SUNY, Purchase, 1989, Princeton (NJ), 1989, 2005, Harvard U., Cambridge, Mass., 1999. One-woman shows include Inst. for Art and Urban Resources, Queens, NY, 1982, Rosa Esman Gallery, NYC, 1988-89, 91, Worcester (Mass.) Art Mus., 1992, Miss. Mus. Art, Jackson, 1995, Orlando (Fla.) Art Mus., 1995, Portland Inst. for Contemporary Art, 1996, Hopkins Ctr. Dartmouth Coll., Hanover, NH, 2000, Md. Inst. Coll. Art, Balt., 2002, Burapha U., Chonburi, Thailand, 2003, others; exhibited in group shows at Contemporary Art Ctr., Cin., 1987, Sculpture Ctr., NYC, 1987, Art Gallery Western Australia, Perth, 1986, Art Gallery NSW, Sidney, 1986, Guggenheim Mus., NYC, 1987, Aldrich Mus. Art, Ridgefield, Conn., 1988, Walker Art Ctr., Mpls., 1989, Phillips Collection, Washington, 1992, Portland Art Mus., 1993, Decordova Mus., and Sculpture Park, Lincoln, Mass., 1993-94, Laumeier Sculpture Park, St. Louis, 1995—, White House Sculpture Garden, Washington, 1995, Neuberger Mus. Art, Purchase, NY, 1997, Mead Art Mus., Amherst Coll., Mass., 2006; represented in permanent collections Walker Art Ctr., Minn., Guggenheim Mus., NYC, Mus. Contemporary Art, Chgo., Mus. Modern Art, N.Y.C., SD Meml. Art Ctr., New Sch. Social Rsch., NYC, Met. Mus., NYC, NY Pub. Libr., Hood Mus., Hanover, N.H., New Sch. for Social Rsch., NYC, ND Mus. Art, Grand Forks, Newark Mus., Portland Art Mus., Detroit Inst. Arts, Orlando (Fla.) Art Mus., NY Pub. Libr., Am. Telephone and Telegraph, NY, Phoenix Art Mus., Champion Paper, Stanford Conn., Aterrana Found., Vaduz, Leichtenstein. Betty Brazil meml. sculpture grantee, 1981, Louis Comfort Tiffany Found. sculpture grantee, 1984, Pollock-Krasner Found. sculpture grantee, 1986, N.Y. Found. for Arts sculpture grantee, 1989, Nat. Endowment for Arts grantee, 1990. Office Phone: 212-619-8108. Personal E-mail: carolhepper@hvc.rr.com. E-mail: carolhepper@yahoo.com.

HEPPERLY, PAUL REED, plant pathologist; b. Elmhurst, Ill., Jan. 4, 1952; s. John Thrane Sr. and Marian (Urban) H.; m. Julia Silvina Mignucci, June 25, 1974; 1 child, Reed Paul. BS in Psychology, U. Ill., 1973, PhD in Plant Pathology, 1979. Asst. prof. plant pathology, dir. internat. soybean program U. P.R., Mayaguez, 1979-82, assoc. prof. plant pathology, 1983-85; rsch. plant pathologist tropical agrl. rsch. sta. USDA-Agrl. Rsch. Svc., Mayaguez, 1985-91. Cons. in soybean pathology and breeding Inst. Colombian Agr., Palmira, 1980-81, Inst. Ecuadorean Agr., Pichilingue, 1982. Contbr. articles to profl. publs. Mem. Am. Phytopathological Soc., Am. Soc. Horticultural Sci., Mycol. Soc. Am., Citizens for Healthy Environment, Sigma Xi, Gamma Sigma Delta, Phi Kappa Phi, Phi Eta Sigma. Achievements include discovery of novel seed treatment and separation techniques to improve seed quality of soybean, sorghum and other corps, and new sources of disease resistance in papaya. Home: 558 Calle Las Caiseas Bo Algarrobo Mayaguez PR 00682-5967

HEPPNER, DONALD GRAY, JR., immunology research physician, army officer; b. Lynchburg, Va., Jan. 17, 1956; s. Donald Gray Sr. and Nathalie (Ward) H.; m. Mary Virginia Leach, June 12, 1983; children: Charlotte Nathalie, Virginia Dearing, William Lynch. BA in Biochemistry/German Lit., U. Va., 1978, MD, 1983. Diplomate Am. Bd. Internal Medicine, 1986, Am. Bd. Infectious Diseases, 1990, 2003, Gen. Staff Coll, Ft. Leavenworth, Tex., 1993. Commd. capt. U.S. Army, 1987, advanced through grades to col., 2002; intern in internal medicine U. Minn. Hosps. and Clinics, Mpls., 1983-84, resident in internal medicine, 1984-86; rsch. assoc. Dight Lab., U. Minn., Mpls., 1987; with emergency medicine dept. Abbot North Western Hosp., Mpls., 1986-88; fellow infectious diseases U. Md., Balt., 1988-90; infectious disease officer Dept. Immunology, Walter Reed Army Inst. of Rsch., Washington, 1990-93; asst. chief dept. immunology Armed Forces Rsch. Inst. Med. Scis., 1993-94, chief dept. immunology and medicine Bangkok, 1994-97; overseas malaria vaccine trial coord. dept. immunology Walter Reed Army Inst. Rsch., Forest Glen, Md., 1997-99, chief dept. immunology, 1999—2006; dir. U.S. Army Malaria Vaccine Program, 2001—, acting dir. divsn. communicable diseases and immunology, 2006, dir. divsn. of malaria vaccine devel., 2006—. Attending physician Walter Reed Army Med. Ctr., Washington, 1991-93, 2003-06; advisor NRC, 1995-97; mem. Fed. Malaria Vaccine Coord. Com. Contbr. more than 80 articles to profl. jours. Mem. Com. on Fgn. Rels., Charlottesville, Va., 1983—. Fellow: ACP, Royal Asiatic Soc., Royal Geog. Soc.; mem.: VFW (life), Am. Soc. Tropical Medicine and Hygiene, Armed Forces Infectious Disease Soc. (life), Va. Soc. Sons of Am. Revolution, U. Va. Alumni Assn. (life), Soc. War 1812, Philos. Soc. Washington, Order Mil. Med. Merit, Am. Legion, Mil. Order Fgn. Wars. Achievements include development and testing of malaria vaccines for military and public health benefit. Office: Walter Reed Army Inst Rsch Divsn Malaria Vaccine Devel 503 Robert Grant Ave Silver Spring MD 20910 Office Phone: 301-319-9414. E-mail: donald.heppner@na.amedd.army.mil.

HEPTINSTALL, ROBERT HODGSON, physician; b. Keswick, Eng., July 22, 1920; s. James A. and Mabel (Sanders) H.; m. Ann Enraght Porter, Jan. 25, 1950; children: Bridget, Gillian, Jonathan, James, Caroline, Christopher. MB, BS, London U., 1944, MD, 1948. Intern, house surgeon Charing Cross Hosp., London, 1944; jr. lectr. pathology St. Mary's Hosp., London, 1947-50, sr. lectr. pathology, 1950-60; vis. prof. pathology Washington U., St. Louis, 1960-62; assoc. prof. pathology Johns Hopkins Med. Sch., Balt., 1962-67, prof. pathology, 1967-69, 88—, Baxley prof. pathology, dir. dept., 1969-88; pathologist in chief Johns Hopkins Hosp., 1969-88; disting. svc. prof. pathology, 1992—. Pathology study sect. NIH, 1963-67, pathology tng. com., 1967-71; sci. adv. bd. Nat. Kidney Found., 1969-73. Author: Pathology of the Kidney, 1966, 6th edit., 2007; editor Lab. Invest, 1976-81; mem. editl. bd. Kidney Internat., Lab Investigation. With M.C., Royal Army, 1944-47. Recipient gold medal Danish Surg. Soc., 1984, David M. Hume Meml. award Nat. Kidney Found., 1986. Mem.: Renal Pathology Soc. (pres. 1980—83), Internat. Soc. Nephrology (v.p. 1981—84, Jean Hamburger award 1999), Am. Soc. Nephrology (pres. 1972—73, John P. Peters award 1993), Internat. Acad. Pathology (Maude Abbott lectr. 1983, Disting. Pathologist award 2002), Danish Soc. Nephrology (hon.), Alpha Omega Alpha.

HEPWORTH, JOHN LEONARD, chemist, researcher; b. Salt Lake City, Nov. 2, 1927; s. Peter Leonard and Flora Victoria (Burningham) H.; m. Caryl Peterson, Mar. 19, 1951; children: Dale, Diana, Vicki, Joseph, James, John T. BS, U. Utah, 1952; MS, U. Idaho, 1958. Chemist GE Co., Richland, Wash., 1953-57, Am. Potash and Chem. Corp., Henderson, Nev., 1957-58; sr. chemist Thiokol Corp., Brigham City, Utah, 1958-90, supr. propellant devel. sect., 1960, sr. scientist, 1967, dept. mgr. asst., 1970. Instr. propellant chemistry Utah State U., Logan, 1962; cons. Battelle Inst., Hanford, Wash., 1965-68, McGraw-Hill, Inc., 1968-90; vol. substitute tchr. math., chemistry, physics, religion Box Elder H.S., Brigham City, Utah, 1998—; vol. tchr. for young adults with spl. needs, 1999—. Author: A Review of Hydrazinium Diperchlorate, 1967; contbr. articles to profl. publs. Missionary LDS Ch., 1948-50, 90-93; instr. Early Morning Seminary, 1954-57; officer PTA, 1960-62; coach Little League Sports, 1964-75; H.S. athletic officiator, 1972-92. With USN, 1946-48. Republican. Achievements include patents for development of separation process of Uranium and Plutonium from fission products, separation of radioactive Cesium from fission products, development of first stage propellant for Minuteman, C-4 and C-5 Trident, and Peacekeeper missiles, supervision of space shuttle development, development of delayed quick-cure catalyst employed in all three stages of Trident missiles; effect of di-n-butyl phosphate on the partition of zirconum between aqueous solutions and 2.2.4, trimethylpentane. Home: 560 Holiday Dr Brigham City UT 84302-2387 Personal E-mail: jhepworth@besstek.net.

HERALD, J. PATRICK, lawyer; b. Latrobe, Pa., Sept. 27, 1947; s. John P. and Doris Faye (Galvin) H.; m. Bridget Grace Tobin, Aug. 17, 1973; children: Brian Michael, Matthew Patrick, Molly Bridget, John Francis. AB in History, John Carroll U., 1969; JD, U. Notre Dame Law Sch., 1972. Bar: Ill. 1972, U.S. Dist. Ct. (no. dist.) Ill. 1972, U.S. Ct. Appeals (7th cir.) 1975, U.S. Supreme Ct. 1978. Assoc. Baker & McKenzie, Chgo., 1972-79, ptnr., 1979—. Fellow Am. Coll. Trial Lawyers, Internat. Acad. Trial Lawyers; mem. ABA, Ill. Bar Assn., Chgo. Bar Assn., 7th Cir. Bar Assn., Soc. Trial Lawyers (bd. dirs. 1987-89), Internat. Assn. Def. Counsel, Chgo. Trial Lawyers Club (pres. 1982-83). Roman Catholic. Office: Baker & McKenzie 1 Prudential Plz 130 E Randolph St Fl 3500 Chicago IL 60601-6213 Home: 14 Sheffield Ln Oak Brook IL 60523 Office Phone: 312-861-2830. Business E-Mail: j.patrick.herald@bakernet.com.

HERB, FRANK STEVEN, lawyer; b. Cin., Nov. 9, 1949; s. Frank X. and Jean M. (Zurcher) H.; m. Jean L. Jeffers, June 21, 1971; children: Tracy Lynn, Jacquelyn Anne. BS, Bowling Green U., 1971; JD, U. Cin., 1974. Bar: Ohio 1974, Fla. 1978, U.S. Dist. Ct. (no., mid., and so. dists.) Fla., U.S. Ct. Appeals (11th cir.); cert. county and cir. ct. mediator, Fla. Supreme Ct. Assoc. Connaughton Law Offices, Hamilton, Ohio, 1974; jud. advocate gen., chief of civil law USAF, Tyndall AFB, Fla., 1975—78; ptnr. Nelson Hesse, Sarasota, Fla., 1979—. Author: (with others) Bennedicts on Admiralty, 1996, 97, 98; contbr. chpts. to books. Bd. dirs. Brock Wilson Found., Sarasota, 1983-92; pres. Riegels Landing Assn., Sarasota, 1986-90, 98-2000; dir., chmn. Siesta Key Utilities Assn., 1994-2006, Am. Boat and Yacht Council, 2005-; mem. govt. rels. com. Nat. Marine Mfrs. Assn. Capt. JAGC USAF, 1975—78. Decorated USAF Meritorious Svc. medal. Mem. Ohio Bar Assn., Fla. Bar Assn. (chmn. 12th Jud. cir. unauthorized practice of law com. 1986-93, fee arbitration com. 12th jud. cir. 1996-2002), Sarasota Bar Assn., Def. Rsch. Inst., Maritime Law Assn., Am. Boat and Yacht Counsel (dir.), Nat. Marine Mfrs. Assn. (govt. rels. com.), The Field Club (commodore, dir. exec. com.). Republican. Roman Catholic. Avocations: boating, woodworking, skiing, tennis, golf. Office: Nelson Hesse 2070 Ringling Blvd Sarasota FL 34237-7002 Office Phone: 941-366-7550. Business E-Mail: sherb@nelsonhesse.com.

HERB, MARVIN J., food products executive; b. 1937; BS, U. Buffalo, 1959; MBA, U. Toledo, 1964. Mgmt. trainee Kroger Co., Toledo, 1960-65; with Pepsi-Cola Co., Inc., 1965-72; various positions including pres. Pepsi-Cola Bottling Co. Indpls, Inc.; with Borden, Inc., NYC, 1972-76, v.p. dairy and svc. divsn., 1976-77, pres. dairy and svc. divsn., 1977-78, corp. v.p., pres. dairy and svc. divsn., 1978-81; chmn. bd. Hondo, Inc., Niles, Ill., 1981—. Trustee Loyola U., Chgo. Named one of Forbes' Richest Americans, 2006. Office: Hondo Inc 7400 N Oak Park Ave Niles IL 60714-3818

HERBERMAN, RONALD BRUCE, medical association administrator, immunologist; b. Bklyn., Feb. 26, 1940; married, 1963; children: Steve, Holly. BA, NYU, 1960, MD, 1964; MD (hon.), U. Rome, 1986. Intern, asst. resident medicine Mass. Gen. Hosp., 1964-66; clin. assoc. immunologist USPHS, 1966-68; sr. investigator immunology br. Nat. Cancer Inst. NIH, Bethesda, Md., 1968-71, head cellular and tumor immunology sect. Lab. Cell Biology, 1971-74, chief Lab. Immunodiag., 1975-81, chief biol. therapeutic br., 1981-85; dir. U. Pitts. Cancer Inst., 1985—; prof. medicine and pathology Sch. Medicine U. Pitts., 1985—. Acting assoc. dir. biol. response program Nat. Cancer Inst., NIH, 1981-85, dir. immunodiag. contract program, 1972-76; mem. FDA rev. panel diagnostic tests, 1979-83; mem. AIDS clin. drug devel. com. Nat. Inst. Allergy and Infectious Disease, 1986—. Sect. editor: Jour. Immunology, 1974-77; assoc. editor Cancer Rsch., 1975-80, Clin. Immunoology and Immunopathology, 1978-85, Jour. Immunol. Methods and Clin. Immunol. Therapy, 1980-90, Jour. Clin. Immunology, 1981—, Jour. Nat. Cancer Inst., 1972-80. Fellow Am. Acad. Microbiology, Clin. Immunol. Soc., Soc. Biol. Therapy (pres. 1996-98), Am. Soc. Clin. Oncology; mem. Soc. Leukocyte Biology (pres. 1984), Am. Soc. Clin. Investigation, Am. Assn. Immunologists, Am. Assn. Cancer Rsch., Internat. Soc. Interferon Rsch. Achievements include research in cancer immunology and immunotherapy; immunodiagnstic tests for cancer; natural killer cells characterization and in vivo role in resistance to cancer and AIDS. Office: Univ Pitt Cancer Inst 5150 Centre Ave Ste 500 Pittsburgh PA 15232 Home Phone: 412-963-0846; Office Phone: 412-623-3205. Business E-Mail: herbermanrb@upmc.edu.

HERBERS, TOD ARTHUR, publisher; b. Cin., Sept. 11, 1948; s. Walter Fred and Jeanette Ruth (Dalton) H.; m. Suzanne Jeannine Daly, Sept. 7, 1974. BA, Cath. U. Am., 1970. With Nation's Bus. mag., Washington, 1972-75, promotion dir., 1974-75, Washingtonian mag., Washington, 1975-76, circulation and promotion dir., assoc. pub., 1976-77; pub. Am. Film mag., Washington, 1977-82; mng. pub. Science 86 Mag., Washington, 1982-86; pub. Sci. Illustrated Mag., Washington, 1987-89; pres. Jour. NIH Rsch., Washington, 1989-94; pub. On Target Media, Inc., Washington, 1994—2003; pub., pres. Home & Design Mag., Homestyles Media Inc.,

Silver Spring, Md., 2002—. Home: 8428 Holly Leaf Dr Mc Lean VA 22102-2224 Office: Homestyles Media Inc Ste 150 12501 Prosperity Dr Silver Spring MD 20904 Office Phone: 301-622-0040. Business E-Mail: therbers@homeanddesign.com.

HERBERT, ADAM WILLIAM, JR., former academic administrator, educator; b. Muskogee, Okla., Dec. 1, 1943; s. Addie Herbert; m. Karen Y. Lofty, Apr. 1980. BA, U. So. Calif., 1966, MPA, 1967; PhD, U. Pitts., 1971. Instr., asst. prof., coord. acad. programs Ctr. Urban Affairs Sch. Pub. Adminstrn., U. So. Calif., LA, 1969-72; assoc. prof., chmn. urban affairs program div. environ. and urban systems Va. Poly. Inst. State U., Blacksburg, 1972-75, prof., dir. North Va. programs, Ctr. for Pub. Adminstrn. and Policy, 1978-79; White House fellow, spl. asst. sec. HEW, Washington, 1974-75; spl. asst. to under sec. HUD, Washington, 1975-77; prof., dean Fla. Internat. U., Miami, 1979-87, assoc. v.p. for acad. affairs, chief acad. officer North Miami campus, 1985-88, v.p., chief adminstrv. officer, 1987-88; pres. U. North Fla., Jacksonville, 1989—98; chancellor State Univ. Sys. of Fla., 1998—2001; Regents prof., exec. dir. Fla. Ctr. for Pub. Policy and Leadership U. North Fla., Jacksonville, Fla.; pres. Ind. Univ. Sys., Bloomington, 2003—07.*

HERBERT, ALBERT EDWARD, JR., interior and industrial designer; b. Detroit, June 12, 1928; s. Albert Edward and Gladys Mae (Speechley) H. Student, Pratt Inst., 1947-50. Owner, operator Albert Herbert Designs, 1957—; designer for V'Soske, Inc. Baker Furniture. Author: (with Roger P. Myers) The Last Survivor, 1976, Killer Pack, 1976, The Skytower Disaster, 2000; contbr. articles to mags. Served with USAF, 1952-56. Fellow Am. Soc. Interior Designers (life). Home: Fords Colony 104 Baltusrol Williamsburg VA 23188 Business E-Mail: mrdesign28@cox.net.

HERBERT, BOB, columnist; b. Mar. 7, 1945; m. Suzanne. BS, Empire State Coll., SUNY, 1989. Reporter, night city editor Star-Ledger, Newark, 1970-76; reporter Daily News, NYC, 1976-81, city hall bur. chief, 1981-83, city editor, 1983-85, columnist, 1985-93; panelist Sunday Edition talk show WCBS-TV, NYC, 1990-91; host Hotlines issues show WNYC-TV, NYC, 1990-91; nat corr NBC News, 1991—93; op-ed columnist N.Y. Times, NYC, 1993—. Taught journalism Bklyn Coll, Columbia Univ. Author: Promises Betrayed: Waking Up from the American Dream, 2005. Avocations: reading, tennis, rotisserie baseball. Office: New York Times 229 W 43rd St New York NY 10036-3959

HERBERT, GARY RICHARD, lieutenant governor; b. American Fork, Utah, May 7, 1947; s. Duane and Carol Herbert; m. Jeanette Snelson; children: Nathan, Daniel, Bradley, Kimberli, Shannon, Heather. Lic. real estate broker 1969. Pres. Herbert & Associates Inc., Orem, Utah; county commr. State of UT, Salt Lake City, 1990—2004, lt. gov., 2005—. Pres. Utah State Assn. County Commrs. and Couns., 2000; chmn. Mountainland Assn. Govts., Utah County Coun. Govts., Utah Adv. Coun. on Intergovernmental Relations. Bd. dirs. Provo/Orem C. of C. Mem.: Utah Assn. Counties (v.p. 2002, pres. 2003), Utah Assn. Counties Insurance Mutal (past pres.), Utah Assn. Realtors (past pres.), Nat. Assn. Realtors (chmn. Local Fiscal Affairs Com. 1999). Republican. Avocations: golf, tennis. Office: Utah State Capitol Ste 325 PO Box 142325 Salt Lake City UT 84114 Office Phone: 801-538-1041. Office Fax: 801-538-1133. Business E-Mail: gherbert@utah.gov.

HERBERT, GAVIN SHEARER, health care products company executive; b. LA, Mar. 26, 1932; s. Gavin and Josephine (D'Vitha) H.; children by previous marriage Cynthia, Lauri, Gavin, Pam; 2d. m. Ninetta Flanagan, Sept. 6, 1986. BS, U. So. Calif., 1954. With Allergan, Inc., Irvine, Calif., 1950—, v.p., 1956-61, exec. v.p., pres., 1961-77, chmn. bd., CEO, 1977-91, chmn. bd., 1992-95, chmn. emeritus; pres. Eye and Skin Care Products Group Smith Kline Beckman Corp., 1981-89. Exec. v.p. Smith Kline Beckman Corp., 1986-89; bd. dirs. Allergan, Inc. Mem. adv. bd. Am. Acad. Ophthalmology Found. Mem. Rsch. to Prevent Blindness (bd. dirs.), Big Canyon Country Club, Newport Harbor Yacht Club, Pacific Club, Beta Theta Pi. Republican.

HERBERT, JAMES ALAN, writer; b. Burlington, Vt., July 29, 1945; s. Alan Wells and R. Marion Moren; m. Martha Lebedzinski, 1976 (div. 1983); children: Denise M., Jeni Ayn; m. Margaret Beyer, 1992; 1 child: Alicia Ayn Student, Wittenberg U., Springfield, Ohio, 1963—65; BS in Econs., SUNY, Buffalo, 2000. With McLean Trucking Co., 1969-86. Author: The Tenth Millennium, 1988, Rock and Roll Politics, 1992, Economics, 1996, 2d edit., 2000, Vietnam Memoir, 2000, Redesigning Social Security, 2004 Committeeman Conservative Party, N.Y., 1971. Served to cpl. USMC, 1966-69, Vietnam Recipient Conspicuous Svc. award State of N.Y., 1991. Mem. Toastmasters Internat. (treas. Buffalo chpt. 1988-90), U.S. Masters Swimming, Buffalo Transp. Club Avocations: boating, golf, gardening. Personal E-mail: jalanherbert@yahoo.com.

HERBERT, JAMES ARTHUR, retired art educator, artist, filmmaker; b. Boston, Feb. 13, 1938; s. James Arthur and Bernice Frances (Burns) H. AB magna cum laude, Dartmouth Coll., 1960; M.F.A., U. Colo., 1962. Instr. U. Colo., 1962; artist-in-residence Yale Summer Sch. Art and Music, 1965; mem. faculty dept. art U. Ga., Athens, 1962—, prof., 1973—, rsch. prof., 1992—, disting. rsch. prof. art, 1999—2006, disting. rsch. prof. emeritus, 2006—. One-man shows include Babcock Galleries, NYC, 1967 , U. Colo., Boulder, 1972 , Poindexter Gallery, NYC, 1972 , 1973 , 1974 , 1976 , Mus. Modern Art, 1970 , 1972 , 1974 , 1977 , 1981 , 1988 , 1994 , 1998 , 1999 , 2005 , Walker Art Ctr., Mpls., 1973 , 1982 , Harvard U., 1973 , High Mus. Art, Atlanta, 1979 , Kennedy Ctr., Washington, 1981 , Libr. of Congress, 1983— , Museu Tropical, Lisbon, Lisbon, Portugal, 1993 , Art Gallery Toronto Can., 1994 , Oberhausen Internat. Film Festival, Germany, 1999 , Brit. Coun., Cologne, Germany, 1999 , Film Mus. Munich, 1999 , Atl. Contemporary Art Ctr., 2000 , Mus. Modern Art, NYC, 2005 , exhibited in group shows at Krannert Art Mus., Urbana, Ill., 1974 , New Orleans Mus. Art, 1975 , 1980 , 1989 , Whitney Mus. Am. Art, 1969 , 1973 , 1974 , 1983 , Westdeutsche Kurzfilmtage, Oberhausen, W. Ger., 1970 , 1972 , 1989 , 1992 , 2001 , La Cinémathèque Royale de Belgique, Knokke-Heist, Belgium, 1974—75 , Mus. Modern Art, NYC, 1979 , P.S. 1, 1979 , Stedelijk Mus., Amsterdam, 1982 , Kennedy Ctr., Washington, 1983 , Monique Knowlton Gallery, NYC, 1983 , IRCAM, Pompidou Ctr., Beaubourg, France, 1984 , Cinémateque Française, Beaubourg, 1985 , Bibliotheque Nat., Avignon, France, 1985 , Mus. Modern Art, NYC, 1986 , 1991 , LA County Mus. Art, 1988 , Carnegie-Mellon U. Art Gallery, Pitts., 1988 , Va. Mus. Fine Art, Richmond, Va., 1988 , Southeastern Ctr. for Contemporary Art, Winston-Salem, N.C., 1988 , Corcoran Gallery of Art, Washington, 1989 , Kuznetsky Most Exhbn. Hall, Moscow, 1989 , Art Gallery of Ont., 1989 , Long Beach Mus. Art, Calif., 1989 , 1991 , Norton Galley Art, Palm Beach, 1989 , Sheridan Opera House, Telluride, Colo., 1989 , 1991 , 1993 , Mus. Fine Arts, Boston, 1990 , Art Inst., Chgo., 1990 , Pacific Film Archive, Berkeley, Calif., 1991 , Walker Art Ctr., Mpls., 1991 , Sundance Theatre, Park City, Utah, 1992 , Melbourne Internat. Film Theatre, Australia, 1992 , European Media Art Theatre, Osnabrück, Germany, 1992 , Toronto Film Festival Theatre, Can., 1992 , NY Film Festival at Lincoln Ctr., 1992 , Inst. de Estadios Norteamericanos, Barcelona, Spain, 1992 , Melbourne Internat. Film Mus., Australia, 1992 , Eldorado Theatre, Royal Palace, Antwerp, Belgium, 1993 , Odense Internat. Film Theater, Denmark, 1993 , Fifth Media Festival Theatre, Hertogenbosch, The Netherlands, 1993 , Vienna Shortfilm Mus., Antwerp (Belgium) Sinema festival Theatre, 1993 , Rio Internat. Festival Hall, Rio de Janeiro, Brazil, 1993 , Sydney Internat. Film Mus., Australia, 1994 , Vherskě Hradiště, Czech Republic, 1994 , Kunstencentrum, Leuveen, Netherlands, Gaumont Marignan Theater, Paris, 1995 , Toronto Internat. Film Festival, 1997 , 1999 , Sundance Film Festival Theater, Park City, Utah, 1998 , 1999 , Rotterdam Internat. Film Festival, The Netherlands, 1998 , 1999 , 2000 , Edinburgh Internat. Film Festival, Scotland, 1999 , Rio Internat. Film Festival, Brazil, 1999 , Sao Paulo Internat. Film Festival, 1999 , Film Theatre Brit. Coun., Cologne, Germany, 1999 , Staatliche Galerie Moritzburg, Halle, Germany, 1999 , Mus. Nat. Ctr. de Arte Reina Sofia, Madrid, Spain , Regensburger Kurzfilmwoche, Germany, 2003 , Metropolis Kino Hamburg, 2003 , Oberhausen Internat. Film Festival, 2004 , London Film Festival, 2005 , No. Ireland Internat. Film Festival, Belfast, 2006 , Buenos Aires Internat. Festival of Ind. Cinema, 2006 , The Era of New Horizons Internat. Film Festival, Wroctaw, Poland, 2006 , Represented in permanent collections NYU , exhibited in group shows at Rotterdam Internat. Film Festival, 2007 , Represented in permanent collections Am. Fedn. Arts , Royal Film Archives Belgium , Centre Beaubourg, Paris , Mus. Modern Art, NYC , Whitney Mus. Am. Art , Cornell U. , Am. Film Inst. , Chase Manhattan Bank , Coca Cola USA , Herbert F. Johnson Mus. Art at Cornell U. , Walker Art Ctr., Mpls. , Anthology Film Archives, NYC; author: Stills: Photographs by James Herbert, 1992. Recipient Awards in the Visual Arts, Rockefeller Found., 1987; Woodrow Wilson fellow, 1960-62, Guggenheim Found. fellow, 1971-72, 89-90; grantee Am. Film Inst., 1969, Nat. Endowment Arts, 1975, 78, 81, 82, Louis Comfort Tiffany Found., 1980, Rockefeller Found., 1993; comm. Libr. of Congress, 1983, Adolph and Esther Gottlieb Found., 1991. Office: U Ga Sch Art Athens GA 30602

HERBERT, JAMES CHARLES, academic administrator; b. Dayton, Ohio, Nov. 22, 1941; s. Charles August and Helen Louise (Korte) H.; m. Sandra Lynn Swanson, June 4, 1966; children: Kristen, Sonja. BA, U. Dayton, 1963; MA, Brandeis U., 1965, PhD in History of Ideas, 1970. Instr. history Cath. U. Am., Washington, 1967-69; asst. prof. history and philosophy U. D.C., Washington, 1971-73; asst. prof. gen. honors program U. Md., College Park, 1973-79; Am. Coun. on Edn. fellow U.S. Dept. Edn., Washington, 1979-80; dir. governance study Carnegie Found. for Advancement Teaching, Washington, 1980-82; dir. acad. rels. Coll. Bd., NYC, 1982-84, exec. dir. acad. affairs, 1984-89; dir. edn. programs NEH, Washington, 1989-95, dir. rsch. and edn. programs, 1995-99, dir. rsch. programs, 1999—2004. Mem. Nat. Performance Review, Office of V.P. of U.S., 1993; vis. rsch. scholar Inst. for Philosophy and Pub. Policy, U. Md., 1998-99; acting chmn. NEH, 2001; sr. adv. NSF/NEH, 2003-2005. Gen. editor Academic Preparation Series, 6 vols., 1985-86; editor, writer: Academic Preparation for College, 1983; writer: Control of the Campus, 1982. GM scholar, 1959-63, NDEA fellow, 1963-66, Folger Shakespeare Libr. fellow, 1971, Am. Coun. on Edn. fellow, 1979-80, Cambridge U. fellow, 2005. Mem. Am. Philos. Assn., AAUP, Nat. Collegiate Honors Coun. (exec. com. 1978-80, 81-84, pres. N.E. region 1978-79), D.C. Edn. Licensure Commn. Avocations: writing, swimming, travel, gardening. Home Phone: 202-547-8478. Business E-Mail: agoraassociates@att.net.

HERBERT, JEFF, insurance company executive; BBA, U. Tex., Austin; MBA, U. Houston. Exec. mktg. position Kraft Gen. Foods; v.p. Sauces Group - Meal Enhancement Divsn. Campbell Soup Co.; exec. mktg. position Zyman Group, Atlanta; v.p. mktg. and innovation Coca-Cola Co., pres. Ams. Beverage Ptnrs. Worldwide, sr. v.p. mktg.; sr. v.p., chief mktg. officer AFLAC Inc., Columbus, Ga., 2006—. Office: AFLAC Inc 1932 Wynnton Rd Columbus GA 31999 Office Phone: 706-323-3431.*

HERBERT, KATHY J., retail executive; MBA, Lake Forest Grad. Sch. Mgmt., 1985. Dir. personnel tng. Jewel-Osco divsn. Am. Stores Co., 1996—98, v.p. human resources, 1998—2001; exec. v.p. human resources Albertson's, Inc., Boise, 2001—. Bd. dirs. TYCO Healthcare, 2007—. Chair Jewel-Osco United Way Campaign; bd. dirs. Chgo. Sinfonietta, Kohl's Childrens Mus. Office: Albertsons Inc 250 Parkcenter Blvd PO Box 20 Boise ID 83706 Office Phone: 208-395-6200. Office Fax: 208-395-6349.

HERBERT, KEVIN BARRY JOHN, classics educator; b. Chgo., Nov. 18, 1921; s. William Patrick and Margaret (Lomasney) H.; m. Margaret Frances Lambin, Dec. 28, 1946; children: John Barry (dec.), Catherine Ann (Mrs. John Reilly). BA, Loyola U., Chgo., 1946; MA, Harvard U., Cambridge, Mass., 1949, PhD, 1954. Instr. classics Marquette U., Milw., 1948—52; instr. Ind. U., Bloomington, 1952—54; master St. Paul's Sch., Concord, NH, 1954—55; asst. prof. Bowdoin Coll., Brunswick, Maine, 1955—62; asso. prof., prof. Washington U., St. Louis, 1962—92, chmn. dept., 1982—92, prof. emeritus, 1992—, curator emeritus, 1994—; reader Advanced Placement Latin, 1962—68, chief reader, 1969—73; mem. Latin test com. Coll. Entrance Exam. Bd., 1968—73; dir. tours to Europe and Mid. East, 1973—96; referee Am. Coun. Learned Socs., 1990—94; mem. editorial and adv. bd. Internat. Jour. Classical Tradition, 1993—. Curator John Max Wulfing Coin Collection, 1966—94. Author: Hugh of St. Victor: Soliloquy on the Earnest Money of the Soul, 1956, Ancient Art in Bowdoin College, 1964, Greek and Latin Inscriptions in the Brooklyn Museum, 1972; co-editor: Ancient Collections in Washington University, 1973; contbr. to: Great Events from History, 2 vols., 1972, Greek Coins in the Wulfing Collection of Washington University, 1979, Maximum Effort The B-29s Against Japan, 1983, Roman Republican Coins in the Wulfing Collection of Washington University, 1987, Roman Imperial Coins in the Wulfing Collection of Washington U.: 31BC-AD180, 1996; prodr. exhbns. and descriptive catalogs Washington U. Gallery of Art: Greek Coins, Fall term, 1989, Roman Republican Coins, Fall term, 1990, Goddesses, Queens and Women of Achievement: 550 B.C.-A.D. 1979, Spring Term, 1993; guest editor Classical Bull., 1998, 99; translator (Greek and Latin commentaries) St. Paul Epistle to the Romans, 1999-2000, (Latin texts) On the Inconstancy of Witches, 2006; contbr. articles to profl. jours. With USAAF, 1942—45. Decorated DFC, Air medal with two silver oak leaf clusters; Wilbour fellow Bklyn. Mus., 1967. Fellow Am. Numis. Soc.; mem. Am. Philol. Assn., Classical Assn. Middle West and South. Home: 1124 Basswood Ln Saint Louis MO 63132-3008 Office Phone: 314-935-5123. Business E-Mail: kherbert@wustl.edu.

HERBERT, LEROY JAMES, retired accounting firm executive; b. Long Branch, NJ, Aug. 3, 1923; s. LeRoy J. and Edna Hazel (Keller) H. BS, U. Md., 1950. CPA, N.J., N.Y., Ohio, Tenn., La., N.C., Va.; chartered acct. South Africa. Profl. staff mem. Ernst & Ernst, Balt., 1950-58, asst. mgr., 1958-60, mgr. internat. ops. NYC, 1960-63, ptnr., 1963-67; sr. U.S. ptnr. Whinney Murray Ernst & Ernst, London and Paris, 1967-70; ptnr. in charge internat. ops. NYC, 1970-78; internat. exec. ptnr. Ernst & Whinney Internat., NYC, 1979-83; ret., 1983. Bd. dirs., past chmn. Monmouth Med. Ctr., Long Branch; bd. dirs. Brookdale CC Found., U. Md. Found., St. Barnabas Health Care Sys., Ronald McDonald House, Long Branch, N.J., Monmouth Med. Ctr. Found. With U.S. Army, 1942-46. Recipient Disting. Alumnus award U. Md. Coll. Bus. and Mgmt., 1980, Disting. Acctg. Alumnus award, 1991; named to Long Branch H.S. Disting. Alumni Hall of Fame, 1996. Mem. AICPA, N.Y. Assn. CPAs, Ohio Assn. CPAs, Md. Assn. CPAs, Transvaal Soc. Accts. (South Africa), Deal Country Club, Harpoon and Needle Club, Pres.'s Club (U. Md.), Beta Alpha Psi Episcopalian. Home: 1 Channel Dr Apt 1111 Monmouth Beach NJ 07750

HERBERT, MARILYNNE, public relations executive, freelance photographer; b. Columbus, Ga., Aug. 12, 1944; d. Herbert Paul and Victoria (Raskin) Gruber; m. Victor Daniel Herbert, June 23, 1968 (div. 1990), remarried Oct. 6, 2002; children: Alissa, Laura. BA, Colo. Woman's Coll., 1966. Adminstrv. asst. pub. rels. dept. Mt. Sinai Med. Ctr., NYC, 1966-68; freelance photographer NYC, 1977—; sr. account exec. Ruder-Finn, Inc., NYC, 1986-93; dir. pub. rels. Iona Coll., New Rochelle, NY, 1993-94; sr. account exec. Coll. Connections Inc., NYC, 1994-96; sr. mgr. media rels. Halstead Comm., NYC, 1997—2002, exec. v.p., 2002—; cmty. rels. coord. Osborn Retirement Cmty., 1995—2003. Bd. dirs. Women of Westchester, White Plains, NY, 1977-79, Byrdcliffe Performing Arts Orgn., New Rochelle, 1987-91, Nat. Women's Polit. Caucus, Westchester County, 1988-90, Sr. Pers. Placement Bur., Inc., 1989-92, Dystonia Med. Rsch. Found., 2007—; bd. dirs., sec. New Rochelle Cmty. Fund, 1986-91. Recipient Spl. Recognition award Nat. Women's Polit. Caucus, 1989, Clarion award Assn. Women in Comm., 2001. Mem. Am. Soc. Mag. Photographers, Assn. for Women in Comm., Lake Katonah Club (bd. govs. 1995-98, 2006—) Jewish. Home: 77 Upper Lake Shore Dr Katonah NY 10536-2646 Office: Halstead Comm 329 E 82d St New York NY 10028 E-mail: halstead@halsteadpr.com.

HERBERT, WILLIAM CARLISLE, lawyer; b. Gainesville, Fla., Aug. 25, 1947; s. Thomas Walter and Jean Elizabeth (Linton) H.; m. Mary Lee Dedinsky. AB, Princeton U., 1969; MSJ, Northwestern U., 1970, JD cum laude, 1976. Bar: Ill. 1976, US Ct. Appeals (7th cir.) 1977, Fla. 1978, US Dist. Ct. (no. dist.) Ill. 1978, US Supreme Ct. 1980, US Tax Ct. 1982. Law clk. to Hon. Latham Castle US Ct. Appeals (7th cir.), 1976-77; ptnr. Foley & Lardner, Chgo. Exec. editor Northwestern U. Law Rev., 1976. Mem. ABA, Ill. State Bar Assn., Fla. Bar, Chgo. Bar Assn., Legal Club Chgo., U. Club Chgo. Presbyterian. Office: Foley and Lardner 321 N Clark St 270o Chicago IL 60610 Home Phone: 773-327-1092; Office Phone: 312-832-4551. E-mail: wcherbert@aol.com.

HERBIG, JOAN E., information technology executive; BA in French, U. Louisville; MS in Computer Sci., U. Ky. Customer support IBM Corp.; sr. product line mgr. Digital Comm. Assoc., 1987—95; with XcelleNet, 1995—2005, CEO, Cambia, 2005—. Bd. dirs. AeA, Tech. Assn. Ga.; bd. adv. Atlanta CEO Coun. Recipient Woman of Yr. Tech., (WIT) Women in Tech., 2001. Mem.: Women in Tech. Internat. (Women Forging the Future award 2001), Ga. 100 Mentoring Program, Ga. Exec. Women's Network. Office: Cambia Ste 675 11675 Rainwater Dr Alpharetta GA 30004

HERBOLD, PATRICIA LOUISE, ambassador; BA, Edgecliff Coll.; JD, No. Ky. Mayor, Montgomery, Ohio; v.p., gen. counsel Bank One; mem. Taft, Stettinius & Hollister; commr. Wash. State Gambling Commn., 1997—2000; chmn. Rep. party King County, Wash.; U.S. amb. to Singapore US Dept. State, 2005—. Bd. dirs. Wash. Policy Ctr. Office: US Embassy 27 Napier Rd Singapore 258588 Singapore Office Phone: 65 6476 9167.

HERBST, ABBE ILENE, lawyer; b. NYC, June 19, 1955; d. Seymour and Charlotte Herbst. BA summa cum laude, Fordham U., 1976, JD, 1979. Bar: N.Y. 1980, N.J. 1980, U.S. Dist. Ct. (so. dist.) N.Y. 2002, U.S. Supreme Ct. 1986. Law clk. Keenan, Powers & Andrews, NYC, 1978-79, assoc., 1980-83, DeForest & Duer, NYC, 1983-90, ptnr., 1991—2001; shareholder Anderson Kill & Olick, PC, NYC, 2002—. Editor: Fordham Urban Law Jour., 1978—79, AKO Estate Planning & Tax Advisor, 2002—. Recipient Outstanding Presentation award, Cmty. Svc. Soc., 1986. Mem. ABA, N.Y. State Bar Assn., N.J. State Bar Assn., N.Y. County Lawyers Assn., Fin. Women's Assn. N.Y., Riverdale Mental Health Assn., Phi Beta Kappa. Avocations: travel, collecting miniature cat figurines. Office: Anderson Kill & Olick PC 1251 Ave of the Americas New York NY 10020 Home Phone: 718-884-4700; Office Phone: 212-278-1781. Business E-Mail: aherbst@andersonkill.com.

HERBST, ARTHUR LEE, obstetrician, gynecologist; b. NYC, Sept. 14, 1931; s. Jerome Richard and Blanche (Vatz) H.; m. Lee Ginsburg, Aug. 10, 1958. AB magna cum laude, Harvard Coll., 1953, MD cum laude, 1959; DSc (hon.), N.E. Ohio U., 2001. Diplomate Am. Bd. Ob-gyn. (bd. dirs. 1985-93, dir. div. gynecol. oncology 1989-91). Intern Mass. Gen. Hosp., Boston, 1959—60, resident, 1960—62; resident in ob-gyn. Boston Hosp. for Women, 1962—65; instr., assoc. prof. ob-gyn. Mass. Gen. Hosp. and Harvard U. Med. Sch., Boston, 1965—76; Joseph B. DeLee prof. ob-gyn. U. Chgo., 1976—84, Joseph B. DeLee Disting. Service prof., 1984—2005, disting. prof. emeritus, 2005—; chmn. dept. ob-gyn. Chgo. Lying In Hosp., 1976—2001; chmn. exec. com. U. Chgo. Hosps. and Clinics, 1980. Chmn. dean's adv. bd. U. Ariz. Coll. Sci., 2006—. Contbr. articles to profl. jours. Nat. adv. coun. Wis. Alumni Rsch. Found., 2007—. Fellow Royal Coll. Obstetricians and Gynecologists (hon.), Inst. Med., Nat. Acad. Scis.; mem. AMA, ACS, ACOG, Am. Gynecol. and Obstet. Soc. (pres. 1997-98), Am. Assn. Profs. Ob-Gyn., Ctrl. Assn. Obstetricians and Gynecologists, Chgo. Gynecologic Soc., Soc. Pelvic Surgeons, Endocrine Soc., Infertility Soc., Soc. Gynecologic Oncologists. Home: 1234 N State Pkwy Chicago IL 60610-2219 Office: U Chgo Med Ctr 5841 S Maryland Ave MC2050 Chicago IL 60637-1463 Office Phone: 773-702-6671.

HERBST, ERIC, physicist, astronomer, chemist; b. NYC, Jan. 15, 1946; s. Stuart Karl and Dorothy (Polakoff) H.; m. Judith Strassman, Oct. 15, 1972; children: Elisabeth, Andrea, Seth. AB, U. Rochester, 1966; MA, Harvard U., 1969, PhD, 1972. Asst. prof. chemistry Coll. of William and Mary, Williamsburg, Va., 1974-79, assoc. prof.chemistry, 1979-80; assoc. prof. physics Duke U., Durham, NC, 1980-86, prof. physics, 1986-91, Univ. zu Köln, Cologne, Germany, 1988-89, Ohio State U., Columbus, 1991—, prof. astronomy, 1992—, prof. chemistry, 2003—. Cons. NASA, Washington, 1985-90, NSF, Washington, 1989-92. Contbr. over 280 articles and 25 revs. to profl. jours. Recipient Humboldt award Humboldt Found., 1988, Max Planck prize Max Planck Soc., 1993. Fellow Am. Phys. Soc., Royal Soc. Chem. (Centenary medal 2004); mem. Am. Astron. Soc., Am. Chem. Soc., Inst. Physics, Internat. Astron. Union. Achievements include theory of how organic molecules are formed in space; theory of floppy molecules. Office: Ohio State U Dept Physics 191 W Woodruff Ave Columbus OH 43210-1106 Home Phone: 614-292-6951; Office Phone: 614-292-6951. Business E-Mail: herbst@mps.ohio-state.edu.

HERBST, JAN FRANCIS, physicist, researcher; b. Tucson, May 1, 1947; s. Alva and Frances Theresa (Feler) H.; m. Margaret Mae Priest, July 24, 1982; children: Helen, John, Mary. BA in Physics, U. Pa., 1968, MS, 1968; PhD, Cornell U., 1974. Postdoctoral rsch. assoc. Nat. Bur. Standards, Gaithersburg, Md., 1974-76; asst. physicist Brookhaven Nat. Lab., Upton, NY, 1976-77; assoc. sr. rsch. physicist GM Rsch. Labs., Warren, Mich., 1977-81, staff rsch. scientist, 1981-85, mgr. magnetic materials sect., 1984—2002, sr. staff rsch. scientist, 1985-93, prin. rsch. scientist, 1993—, mgr. solid state materials for energy storage and conversion group, 2002—. Mem. basic energy scis. adv. com. Dept. Energy, 1996-2000, panel chair workshop on devel. of secure energy future, 2002; mem. panel for physics Nat. Rsch. Coun. bd. assessment NIST Programs, 2000—03. Contbr. articles over 100 to profl. jours. Recipient Campbell award GM Rsch. Labs., 1983, McCuen award GM Rsch. Labs., 1987, Kettering award GM Corp., 1987. Fellow Am. Phys. Soc. (sec.-treas. div. condensed matter physics 1985-90, nominating com. 1996-98, Internat. prize for new materials 1986). Achievements include patents in field. Avocations: reading, numismatics. Office: GM R&D Ctr MC 480-106-224 30500 Mound Rd Warren MI 48090-9055 Business E-Mail: jan.f.herbst@gm.com.

HERBST, JANE ELIZABETH, school librarian; b. NYC, Sept. 14, 1950; d. John Joseph Abritis and Helen Elizabeth Heath; m. Mitchell J. Maushay, Aug. 30, 1986 (dec. Aug. 14, 1990); m. Thomas Michael Herbst, June 26, 1993; children: Elizabeth Channan, Daniel Baoanthi. BA in Humanities, Dowling Coll., Oakdale, NY, 1972; MS in Libr. and Info. Sci., LI U., Greenvale, NY, 1986. Chief copy editor Phys. Rev. D, Am. Inst. Physics, Upton, NY, 1973—76; tech. editor Data Comm., Melville, 1976—80; publications mgr. Inst. Advanced Studies World Religions, Stony Brook, 1980—86; children's libr. Sachem Pub. Libr., Holbrook, 1984—2000; instr. Palmer Sch. Libr. and Info. Sci., LI U., Greenvale, 1986—88; sch. libr. media specialist Silas Wood Early Childhood Ctr., South Huntington,

1988—92, Babylon Junior-Senior H.S., Babylon, 1992—. Instr. NY State United Tchrs., Effective Tchg. Program, Albany, 2001—. Author (editor): (poetry anthology) Peel Me a Banana, Baby, I'll Be Home By Twelve. Warden St. Mary's Episcopal Ch., Ronkonkoma, NY, 1990—93; policy bd. mem. Suffolk's Edge Tchr. Ctr., Wheatly Heights, 1992—. Recipient Outstanding Contbn. Sch. Libr. Media Profession, Suffolk Sch. Libr. Media Assn., 2006; grantee, NEH, 2005. Mem.: ASCD, ALA, Am. Assn. Sch. Librs., NY Libr. Assn., Suffolk Sch. Libr. Media Assn. (past pres. 2005—), Beta Phi Mu. Episcopalian. Avocations: acting, singing, travel. Office: Babylon Junior-Senior High School 50 Railroad Avenue Babylon NY 11702 Home Phone: 631-981-6113; Office Phone: 631-893-7910. E-mail: jherbst@babylonusfd.org.

HERBST, JOHN EDWARD, federal agency administrator, former ambassador; b. Rockville Center, NY, Aug. 12, 1952; s. Christopher and Mary Rose (Vaccheli) H.; m. Nadezda Christoff, May 22, 1977; children: Maria, Ksenia, Aleksandra, Nicholas, John. BSFS, Georgetown U., 1974; MA, Tufts U., 1978; MALD, Fletcher Sch., Medford, Mass., 1979. Staff asst. Am. Embassy, Jidda, Saudia Arabia, 1980-82, polit. officer Moscow, 1985-87, Office of Israel, Arab-Israeli Affairs, 1982-84; dir. policy devel. NSC, Washington, 1977-88; dep. dir. econs. Office Soviet Affairs, U.S. State Dept., Washington, 1988-97; consul gen. Am. Consulate, Jerusalem, 1997-2000; US amb. to Republic of Uzbekistan US Dept. State, Tashkent, 2000—03, US amb. to Ukraine Kiev, 2003—06; coord. Office Reconstruction & Stabilization US Dept State, 2006—. Contbr. articles to profl. publs. Recipient Presdl. Disting. Svc. award, Disting. Honor award, US Dept. State. Mem. Phi Beta Kappa, Phi Alpha Theta. Avocations: reading, sports. Office: Office Coord Reconstruction & Stabilization US Dept State 2201 C St NW Washington DC 20520

HERBST, JURGEN, historian, educator; b. Braunschweig, Germany, Feb. 22, 1928; arrived in U.S., 1954, naturalized, 1957; s. Hermann and Annemarie Herbst; m. Susan Lou Allen, Sept. 16, 1951; children: Christian, Annemarie, Stephanie. Student, U. Gottingen, 1947-48; BA, U. Nebr., 1950; MA, U. Minn., 1952; PhD, Harvard U., 1958. Instr. edn. and history Wesleyan U., Middletown, Conn., 1958-59, asst. prof., 1959-65, asso. prof., 1965-66; assoc. prof. ednl. policy studies and history U. Wis., 1966-69, prof., 1969-94, prof. emeritus, 1994—; profl. assoc. Ft. Lewis Coll., Durango, Colo., 1999—. Author: The German Historical School in American Scholarship, 1965, The History of American Education, 1973, From Crisis to Crisis: American College Government, 1636-1819, 1982, And Sadly Teach: Teacher Education and Professionalization in American Culture, 1989, The Once and Future School: 350 Years of American Secondary Education, 1996, Requiem for a German Past: A Boyhood among the Nazis, 1999, School Choice and School Government: A Historical Study of the United States and Germany, 2006; editor: Our Country, 1963, History of Elementary School Teaching Curriculum, 1990, Aspects of Antiquity in the History of Education, 1992, German Influences on Education in the United States to 1917, 1995, Mutual Influences on Education: Germany and the United States in the Twentieth Century, 1997. Am. Coun. Learned Socs. grantee, 1960; Fulbright Commn. grantee, 1963, 81; Nat. Endowment for Humanities grantee, 1972-73; Nat. Inst. Edn. grantee, 1973-76; Internat. Research and Exchanges Bd. grantee, 1977; Guggenheim Found. grantee, 1978-79; Wis. Inst. Rsch. in Humanities grantee, 1978-79; Spencer Found. grantee, 1986, 99. Mem. Nat. Acad. Edn., Am. Hist. Assn., Orgn. Am. Historians, History of Edn. Soc. (pres. 1978-79), Internat. Standing Conf. for the History of Edn. (mem. exec. com., pres. 1988-91). Democrat. E-mail: jherbst@animas.net.

HERBST, ROBERT LEROY, organization executive; b. Mpls., Oct. 5, 1935; s. Walter Peter and Bernice Mickey (Mikkelson) H.; m. Evelyn Clarice Elford, Sept. 22, 1956; children— Eric Elford, Peter Robert, Amy Jo. BS in Forest Mgmt, U. Minn., St. Paul, 1957. Dep. commnr. Minn. Conservation Dept., 1966-69; nat. exec. dir. Izaak Walton League Am., 1969-70; commr. natural resources State of Minn., 1971-77; asst. sec. fish, wildlife and parks Dept. Interior, Washington, 1977-81, sec., Jan. 20-26, 1981; exec. dir. Trout Unltd., 1981-90; pres. Lake Superior Ctr., Washington, 1990-92, A-S5 Energy Co., Reno, Nev., 1997-98; Washington rep. TVA, Washington, 1992-96; CEO, chmn. bd. dirs. Global Environment & Tech. Found., Annandale, Va., 1996—. Instr. U. Minn., 1954; mem. adv. faculty N. Am. Sch. Conservation, 1969-77; chmn. Gt. Lakes Fisheries Commn., 1978-80, steering com. Nat. Fishing Week, 1991; mem. U.S. Commn. UNESCO, 1978-79, Pres. Carter's Interagency Coun., 1978-80; co-chmn. Nat. Adv. Coun. Environ. Edn., 1989, chmn., 1990-92; mem. U.S. bd. Environ. Ctr. for Ctrl. and Ea. Europe, 1997—, chmn. bd. dirs.; chmn. bd. dirs. Nat. Wildlife Refuge Assocs., 1998-2001. Author: Careers in Environment, 1973; contbr. articles to profl. jours. Mem. nat. bd. Boy Scouts Am., 1969—77; exec. bd. Viking Coun., 1975—76; bd. govs. African Inst. Econs. Edn. and Devel., 1980; pres. Nat. Watershed Protection Ctr., 1994; U.S. rep. Regional Environ. Ctr. for Ctrl. and Ea. Europe, chair bd. dirs.; chmn. bd. Nat. Reach Coun.; mem. Annandale United Meth. Ch., 1969—77. Recipient Nat. Svc. award Izaak Walton League Am., 1971; Silver Beaver award Boy Scouts Am., 1977; Disting. Svc. award U. Minn., 1969, 2003, Washington Acad. Sci. award, 2001, Outstanding Achievement award U. Minn., 2003; named Pub. Adminstr. of Yr. in Minn. Am. Soc. Pub. Adminstrn., 1976; named to Nat. Fresh Water Fishing Hall Fame, 2003, Wall-Outstanding Alumni, U. Minn., 2005. Mem. Natural Resource Coun. Am. (chmn. 1989-91, Honor award 1994), Land Between Lakes Assn.(chmn. 1982-91, trustee 1981-91). Democrat. Office: Global Environment Technol 2900 S Quincy St Ste 410 Arlington VA 22206-2281 Business E-Mail: bherbs@getf.org.

HERBST, STEVEN, sports association executive; b. Peekskill, NY; s. Adolph and Rose Herbst; m. Beth Helen Bevitt, June 27, 1996; 1 child, Sam. BA in Sports Mgmt., U. Mass. Prodn. asst., game logger NBA Entertainment, 1989, sr. dir. prodn., 1995—99, v.p. series programming and NBA TV; assoc. prodr. NBA Inside Stuff, 1990—93; sr. v.p. broadcasting, gen. mgr. NBA TV NBA, 2006—. Office: NBA Olympic Tower 645 5th Ave Fl 10 New York NY 10022-5986*

HERBST, TODD L., lawyer; b. NYC, July 15, 1952; s. Seymour and Charlotte (Wolper) H.; m. Robyn Beth Kellman, June 3, 1979; children: Scott Marshall, Carly Nicole. BA, CUNY, 1974; JD, John Marshall Law Sch., 1977. Bar: NY 1978. Assoc. Max E. Greenberg, Cantor & Reiss, NYC, 1977—83, mng. ptnr., 1984—87; sr. ptnr. Greenberg, Trager & Herbst LLP, NYC, 1988—. Bus. cons. Shimizu Corp., U.S., 1983—, Dillingham Constrn. Holdings, Inc., San Francisco, 1987—2001, Jolly Hotels, Italy, 1993—, NTT Internat. Corp., Japan and U.S., 1996—, Legal Commentary UPN News, NYC, Extell Devel. Corp., Bronfman Haymes Real Estate Ptnrs., S.J.P. Properties, Inc., Durst Orgn., Rose Assocs., Inc., Stillman Devel. Internat., Kreisler Borg Florman Gen. Constrn. Co., Inc., Madison Equities, LLC, Bayrock Real Estate, LLC, Moinian Group, Monmouth U.; lectr. Nat. Assn. Corp. Real Estate Execs. Exec. editor: John Marshall Law Rev. Mem.: ABA (A/V rated), AIA, NY State Bar Assn., N.Y. County Lawyers Assn. Home: 7 Brookwood Ln New City NY 10956-2203 Office: Greenberg Trager & Herbst LLP 12th Fl 767 Third Ave New York NY 10017-2023 Home Phone: 845-634-6939; Office Phone: 212-688-1900. Business E-Mail: therbst@gthny.com.

HERCH, FRANK ALAN, law librarian, lawyer; b. Chgo., May 5, 1949; s. Robert Gilbert and Shirley (Berman) H.; m. Ruth Blackwell, Dec. 29, 1971; children: Nathaniel, Rachmiel. BA in Sociology and History, U. Calif., Davis, 1971; MLS, U. Calif., Berkeley, 1972; JD, U. Calif., Davis, 1975. Bar: Calif. 1981, U.S. Dist. Ct. (no. dist.) Calif. 1981. Reference libr. Alameda County Law Libr., Oakland, Calif., 1975-78; asst. law libr. Georgetown U. Law Ctr., Washington, 1978-81; atty. Blackwell, Herch & Herch, Oakland, 1981-87; libr. Cityline Info. Svc. Oakland Pub. Libr., 1984-87; dir. Clark County Law Libr., Las Vegas, Nev., 1987—97; assoc. dir. pub svc. San Diego County Pub. Law Libr., San Diego, 1998—99; project mgr. and law libr. U.S. Dept. Interior Libr., Wash., 2000—02; dep. project mgr. collection bldg. and tech. svs. NASA Goddard Space Flight Ctr. Libr. , Greenbelt, Md., 2002—. Lectr. John F. Kennedy U. Sch. of Law, 1977-78, St. Mary's Coll. Paralegal Program, Moraga, Calif., 1981-87; law libr. and rsch. cons. Nev. Civil Jury Instructions Com. Monterey Coll. of Law, Alameda County Bar Assn., Oakland, 1981-87; lectr. Legal Method and Process criminal justice dept. U. Nevada, Las Vegas, 1997, computer apllications parallel program U. San Diego, 1999, govt. info. sources San Jose State U. M.L.S. program Govt. Info. Sources, 2000; dir. Fed. Communicative Commn. Libr., 2002-05; libr. mgr. Fed. Energy Regulatory Commn. Libr., 2005-07. Editor U. Calif. Davis Law Rev., 1974-75, writer, 1973-74; editor Jazz Rag mag., 1975-85, book revs. Legal Pub. Rev., Legal Information Alert, Business Information Alert, 1989—. Steering com. Second Start: Adult Literacy Program, Oakland, 1984-87; mem. exec. bd. East Bay Info. and Referral Network, Berkeley, 1984-87; mem. Clark County Merit Ins. Task Force, 1992. Recipient Cert. of Leadership Nat. U., Oakland, 1987, Leadership award City of Oakland, 1987, Pro Bono Svc. award Nev. State Bar Assn., 1997. Mem. Am. Assn. Law Librs. (cert. 1978, v.p. West Pacific chpt. 1991-92, pres. 1992-93, sec. and treas. state, city and county law librs. spl. interest sect. 1989-92, chmn. regional meeting com., key issues forums, gov.'s conf. on future of librs. 1990, v.p., pres. elect, 1994—, legal info to the pub. special interest sect.), Nev. Libr. Assn. (chmn., bd. rep. so. dist. 1989). Avocations: jazz performances, acting. *I have been asked repeatedly how I can maintain my optimism and motivation when things appear to have gone wrong. I respond by insisting that even the most adverse events in our economy, the environment and our lives will bring lessons to be embraced and circumstances than can be turned into more positive results, Tolerance, flexibility and adaptability have been my watchwords.*

HERCULES, DAVID MICHAEL, chemistry professor, consultant; b. Somerset, Pa., Aug. 10, 1932; s. Michael George and Kathryn (Saylor) H.; m. Nancy Catherine Miller, Sept. 23, 1957 (div. 1968); 1 dau., Kimberly Ann; m. Shirley Ann Hoover, Dec. 14, 1970; children: Sherri Kathryn, Kevin Michael. BS, Juniata Coll., 1954; PhD, MIT, 1957. Asst. prof. Lehigh U., 1957-60; assoc. prof. Juniata Coll., Huntington, Pa., 1960-63; asst. prof. MIT, 1963-68, assoc. prof., 1968-69, U. Ga., Athens, 1969-74, prof., 1974-76; prof. dept. chemistry U. Pitts., 1976-94, chmn., 1980-89, Miles prof., 1990-94; Centennial prof. Vanderbilt U., Nashville, 1995—2007, Centennial prof. emeritus, 2007—, chmn. dept., 1995—2003. Mem. vis. com. for chemistry Lehigh U., 1980-84; vis. prof. Mich. State U., 1972; chmn. Gordon Research Conf. on Electron Spectroscopy, 1974, Gordon Research Conf. on Analytical Chemistry, 1966; co-chmn. Internat. Conf. Chemiluminescence, 1972; univ. rep. Council on Chem. Research, 1980-88; mem. program com. Pitts. Conf. on Analytical Chemistry and Applied Spectroscopy, 1977-94; mem. vis. scientist program NSF, 1964-76 Mem. editorial bds.: Applied Spectroscopy, 1963-65, Analytical Chemistry, 1964-67, Jour. Electron Spectroscopy, 1971-77, Environ. Analytical Chemistry, 1973—, Spectrochimica Acta, 1973-83, Talanta, 1974-80, Spectroscopy Letters, 1975—, The Scis., 1979-84, Trends in Analytical Chemistry, 1980-88, Jour. Trace and Microprobe Techniques, 1980-93, Fresenius Zeitschrift für Analytische Chemie, 1987-; patentee (in field). Recipient Benedetti-Pichler award Am. Microchem. Soc., 1987, Achievement in Analytical Chemistry award Ea. Analytical Symposium, 1988, prize Alexander von Humboldt Found., 1984, Disting. Alumnus award Juniata Coll., 1989, Pres.'s Disting. Rsch. award U. Pitts., 1990; John Simon Guggenheim Meml. fellow, 1973. Mem. Am. Chem. Soc. (Petroleum Research Fund adv. bd. 1978-80, chmn. div. analytical chemistry 1977-78, analytical chemistry award 1986, Arthur W. Adamson award disting. svc. in advancement of surface chemistry 1993, Pitts. sect. award 1997), Soc. Applied Spectroscopy (Lester W. Strock medal New Eng. sect. 1981, Pitts. Spectroscopy award 1996), Am. Vacuum Soc., Photoelectric Spectrometry Group, Pa. Acad. Scis., Spectroscopy Soc. Pitts. (award 1996), Soc. Analytical Chemists Pitts., Sigma Xi Home: 200 Olive Branch Rd Nashville TN 37205-3220 Office: Vanderbilt U Dept Chemistry Box 1822, Sta B Nashville TN 37235 E-mail: david.m.hercules@vanderbilt.edu.

HERDEG, HOWARD BRIAN, retired physician; b. Buffalo, Oct. 14, 1929; s. Howard Bryan and Martha Jean (Williams) H.; m. Beryl Ann Fredricks, July 21, 1955; children: Howard Brian III, Erin Ann Kociela. Student, Paul Smith's Coll., 1947-48, U. Buffalo, 1948-50, Canisius Coll., 1949; DO, Phila. Coll. Osteo. Medicine, 1954; MD, U. Calif., Irvine, 1962. Diplomate Am. Acad. Pain Mgmt. Intern Burbank (Calif.) Hosp., 1954-55; practice medicine specializing in gen. medicine, surgery and pain mgmt., Woodland Hills, Calif., 1956—; ret., 2004. Chief med. staff West Park Hosp., Canoga Park, Calif., 1971-72, trustee, 1971-73; chief family practice dept. West Hills Hosp. and Med. Center (formerly Humana Hosp. West Hills, 1982-85, 88-89), exec. com., 1984-85, 88-89. Mem. Hidden Hills (Calif.) Pub. Safety Commn., 1978-82; bd. dirs. Hidden Hills Cmty. Assn., 1971-73, pres. 1972; bd. dirs. Hidden Hills Homeowners Assn., 1973-75, pres. 1976-77; bd. dirs. Woodland Hills Freedom Season, 1961-67, pres. 1962; mem. Hidden Hills City coun., 1984-2001, mayor pro tem, 1987-90, mayor, 1990-92. Recipient Disting. Svc. award Woodland Hills Jr. C. of C., 1966. Mem. Woodland Hills C. of C. (dir. 1959-68, pres. 1967), Calabasas C. of C., Tustin C. of C., Tustin Hist. Soc., Tustin Santa Ana Rotary Club, Rotary (pres. elect 2005-06, pres. 2006—, dir. 2007-), Theta Chi, Gamma Pi. Republican. Home: 13368 Savanna Tustin CA 92782-9143 Personal E-mail: docherdeg@cox.net.

HERDEG, JOHN ANDREW, lawyer; b. Buffalo, Sept. 15, 1937; s. Franklin Leland and Susannah Estelle (Clark) H.; m. Judith Coolidge Carpenter, June 24, 1961; children: Judith Leland Herdeg Wilson, Andrew Carpenter Herdeg, Fell Coolidge Herdeg. BA, Princeton U., 1959; LLB, U. Pa., 1962. Bar: Conn. 1963, Del. 1964. Atty. Wilmington Trust Co., Del., 1963-75, sr. v.p. in charge of trust dept., 1975-85, bd. dirs., chmn. trust com., corp. sec., 1977-85; pres. Herdeg & Assocs., Wilmington, 1986-98; ptnr. Herdeg, duPont & Dalle Pazze, LLP, Wilmington, 1999—. Co-founder, chmn. bd. dirs. Christiana Bank & Trust Co., Greenville, Del., 1992—. Co-author: Delaware Total Return Unitrust Statute, 2001. Bd. trustees Henry Francis duPont Winterthur (Del.) Mus., 1970—, chmn., 1977—86; bd. trustees Historic Deerfield, Inc., 2004—; supr. Pennsbury Twp., Chester County, Pa., 1968—74. Mem.: Walpole Soc., Conferie des Chevalier du Tastevin, Soc. Colonial Wars (gov. 2005—07, Del. 2005—07), West Chop Club, Mill Reef Club, Vicmead Hunt Club (bd. govs. 1977—84), Wilmington Club (bd. govs. 1997—2007, pres. 2005—07). Avocations: tennis, photography, decorative arts. Home: PO Box 614 Mendenhall PA 19357-0614 Office: Herdeg DuPont & Dalle Pazze LLP 12th & Orange St Ste 500 Wilmington DE 19801-1140 Office Phone: 302-655-6500. E-mail: jherdeg@dellaw.com.

HERDMAN-FISHER, CAROLYN A., music educator; b. Johnstown, Pa., Mar. 30, 1980; d. Francis Paul and Barbara Ann Herdman; m. Thomas P. Fisher, June 19, 2004. BS Music Edn., Clarion U. Pa., Clarion, Pa., 2002; postgrad. in instrnl. tech., U. Md. U. Coll., Coll. Park. Cert. Md.Tchg.(Music K-12) Md., 2002, Pa. Tchg.(Music K-12) Pa., 2002, Kindermusik Kindermusik Internat., 2003. Musician The Mountain Playhouse, Jennerstown, Pa., 1998—; choral dir. Charles County Pub. Schs., Waldorf, Md., 2002—. Pvt. music instr., Waldorf, Md., 2002—; adjudicator Md. All-State Band and Chorus, 2002—; clinician (woodwind), Pa., 2002—, Md., 2002—; summer reading tchr. Charles County Pub. Schs., Reading Acad., Bryons Road, Md., 2003—; musician St. Ignatius Cath. Ch., Port Tobacco, Md., 2004—. Mem.: NEA, Md. Music Educators Assn., So. Md. Music Educators, Edn. Assn. of Charles County, Am. Fedn. of Musicians, Music Educators Nat. Conf., Order of Ea. Star. Roman Cath. Avocations: jogging, travel. Home: 5028 Skylark Dr La Plata MD 20646 Office Phone: 301-535-5949. Personal E-mail: tomcarolynfisher@comcast.net.

HEREMANS, JOSEPH PIERRE, physicist; b. Leuven, Belgium, Jan. 8, 1953; came to U.S., 1984; s. Joseph Felix Heremans and Marie Therese Bracke; m. Claire Pierre Mali, July 1, 1978; children: Hilde Anne, Joseph Paul. Elec. Engr., U. Louvain, Belgium, 1975, PhD in Applied Physics, 1978. Aspirant Belgium Nat. Sci. Found., Louvain, 1978-80, charge de recherche, 1980-83; rsch. scientist GM Rsch. and Devel. Ctr., Warren, Mich., 1984-85; from group leader to sect. mgr. GM Rsch., Warren, 1985—99; rsch. fellow Delphi Rsch. Labs., Shelby Township, 1999—2005; prof. mech. engring. and physics Ohio State U., Columbus, 2005—. Invited prof. U. Louvain, 1989; vis. scientist U. Tokyo, 1982, MIT, Cambridge, 1980-81. Editor: Growth, Characterization and Properties of Ultrathin Magnetic Films and Multilayers, 1989, Survey of Semiconductor Physics, 2002; contbr. articles to profl. jours. Fellow Am. Phys. Soc.; mem. AAAS, Materials Rsch. Soc. Achievements include patents in field. Office: Ohio State Univ Dept Mech Engineering E443 Scott Lab 201 W 19th Ave Columbus OH 43210-1142 Office Phone: 614-247-8869. Business E-Mail: heremans.1@osu.edu.

HERENTON, WILLIE W., mayor; b. Memphis, Apr. 23, 1943; divorced; children: Errol, Rodney, Andrea. BS, LeMoyne-Owen Coll., 1963; MA, Memphis State U., 1966; PhD, So. Ill. U., 1971; PhD (hon.), Rhodes Coll., Christian Brother's Coll. Elem. sch. tchr. Memphis City Sch. System, 1963-67, elem. sch. prin., 1967-73; dept. supt. Memphis City Schs., 1974-78, supt. of schs., 1979-91; mayor Memphis, 1991—. Bd. dirs. Nat. Urban League Edn. Adv. Coun., 1978, Nat. Jr. Achievement, Jr. Achievement of Memphis 1979—, United Way Greater Memphis, 1979-, Promous Cos., Inc., First Tenn. Nat. Corp.; mem. Nat. Alliance of Black Educators, 1974—, Am. Assn. Sch. Adminstrs., Am. Mgmt. Assn.; mem. exec. bd. Nat. Conf. Christians and Jews.; served March of Dimes, United Way, Rotary Club, Boy Scouts of Am., Econ. Club Memphis. Named one of Top 100 Sch. Adminstrs. in U.S. and Can., Exec. Educator Jour., 1980, 84, Municipal Leader of Yr., American City & County Mag., 2002, named one of 100 Most Influential Black Americans, Ebony mag., 2006; Fellow Rockefeller Found., 1973; recipient Horatio Alger award, 1988. Mem.: Am. Mgmt. Assn., Am. Assn. of Sch. Adminstrn. Baptist. Office: Office of Mayor 125 N Main St Ste 700 Memphis TN 38103-2017 Office Phone: 901-576-6010, 901-576-6007. Office Fax: 901-576-6023. Business E-Mail: mayor@cityofmemphis.org.*

HERESI, GUSTAVO A., physician; b. Arequipa, Peru, May 12, 1975; arrived in US, 2002; MD with honors, Nat. U. San Augustin, Peru, 2000. Diplomate internal medicine Am. Bd. Internal Medicine, 2005. Attending physician Hosp. Civico-Policial, Arequipa, 2000—01; intern U. Miami Jackson Meml. Med. Ctr., Fla., 2002—03, resident, 2003—05; fellow Cleve. Clinic Found., 2005—. Contbr. articles to profl. jours. Recipient Disting. Med. Residentaward, Dept. Medicine, U. Miami, 2005. Mem.: Am. Thoracic Soc., Am. Coll. Chest Physicians. Office: Cleveland Clinic 9500 Euclid Ave A90 Cleveland OH 44195 Home Phone: 216-513-4855; Office Phone: 216-444-4707. Office Fax: 216-445-8160. Business E-Mail: heresig@ccf.org.

HERESNIAK, MARTY, music educator, actor; b. Poughkeepsie, NY, Jan. 10, 1953; life ptnr. Augustine Zagari (dec.). MusB, Ithaca Coll., NY, 1974; MusM, Ithaca Coll., 1977. Cert. tchr. K-12 music NY. Pvt. studio tchr., 1973—. Presenter in field. Contbr. articles to profl. jours. Mem.: Nat. Assn. Tchrs. Singing (papers selection com. 2004), Germania Singing Soc. (musik dir. 1984—88), Pi Kappa Lambda, Phi Mu Alpha.

HERGE, HENRY CURTIS, JR., information technology executive, consultant; b. Hartford, Conn., Sept. 13, 1950; s. Henry Curtis and Josephine (Breen) Herge; m. Donna Gay Takeda, Dec. 20, 1974 (div. Dec. 1982); m. Madge Lynn Henley, Feb. 19, 1983; children: H. Curtis III, Erika Ainsley, Alyssa Taylor, Whitney Meghan. BSME, BA, Rutgers U., 1972. Prodn. splst. GE, Columbia, Md., 1972—73, engring. foreman med. sys. divsn. Milw., 1973—74, buyer internat. sales divsn. NYC, 1974—76; sr. sys. analyst Arthur Andersen & Co. (now Accenture), NYC, 1976—78; cons. mgr. Accenture, Stamford, Conn., 1978—85, ptnr., 1985—, practice dir. cons. divsn. Rochester, NY, 1987—92. Sr. v.p. Tech. Solutions Co., 1992—94; ptnr. Diamond Tech. Ptnrs., Chgo., 1994—95; prin. A. T. Kearney divsn. Electronic Data Sy., Plano, Tex., 1995—, global contracts mgr., 1997—, svc. delivery quality, 1998—; cons. strategic devel. mgr. Electronic Data Sys., 2002—, strategic devel. mgr. solutions cons. N.E. USA; bd. dirs. Value-2-Xerox Corp. Elder First Presbyn. Ch. Pitts., 2006—, chair adult edn. program; bd. dirs. Jamaican Advantages thru Sports for Youth, 2006—. Mem.: Am. Prodn. and Inventory Soc. (v.p. 1985). Avocations: mission work, skiing, travel, canoeing, kites. Home: 16 Lancashire Way Pittsford NY 14534-9786 Office Phone: 585-242-6163. Business E-Mail: curt.herge@eds.com.

HERGE, J. CURTIS, lawyer; b. Flushing, NY, June 14, 1938; s. Henry Curtis and Josephine E. (Breen) H.; m. Joyce Dorean Humbert, Aug. 20, 1960 (div. 1988); children: Cynthia Lynda, Christopher Curtis; m. Shirley Brooks Labonte, Dec. 22, 1989. Student, Cornell U., 1956-58; BA, Rutgers U., 1961, JD, 1963. Bar: N.Y. 1964, U.S. Supreme Ct. 1970, U.S. Ct. Claims 1974, D.C. 1974, Va. 1976. Assoc. Mudge Rose Guthrie & Alexander, NYC, 1963-71; spl. asst. to atty. gen. U.S. Dept. Justice, Washington, 1973; assoc. solicitor conservation and wildlife U.S. Dept. Interior, Washington, 1973-74, asst. to sec. and chief staff, 1974-76; ptnr. Sedam & Herge, McLean, Va., 1976-85, Herge, Sparks & Christopher LLP, McLean, Va., 1985—. Bd. dirs. Diversified Labs., Inc., Ann E.W. Stone & Assocs., Inc., Palmer Tech. Svcs., Inc., Eaton Design Group, Inc., George Washington Banking Corp., Eaton Purchase Mgmt., Inc., George Washington Nat. Bank, Congl. Inst. Inc., Citizens United for Am., Am. Def. Lobby, Coun. Nat. Def., Renascence Found., The Am. Lobby Econ. Recovery Taskforce, Nat. Bank No. Va., Am. Freedom Found., Creative Response Concepts Inc., Congl. Inst., Inc.; spkr. in field. Adv. bd. Washington Legal Found., Nat. Taxpayers Legal Fund; Va. Commonwealth escheator Loudoun County and City of Fairfax, 1979-83; co-dir. spokesmen resources Com. for Re-election of Pres., 1971-72; mem. No. Va. Estate Planning Council; mem. natural resources coun. Rep. Nat. Com.; mem. Fairfax County Rep. Com., Conservative Rep. Com.; mem. Office Pres.-Elect Fed. Election Commn. Transition Team, 1980; co-chmn. N.Y. Honor Am. Day, 1970; expert witness, charitable fund-raising, U.S. Tax Ct. Sebastian Gaeta scholar Rutgers U., 1963. Mem. ABA, N.Y. State Bar Assn., Va. Bar Assn., D.C. Bar Assn., Capital Hill Club, Phi Kappa Sigma. Clubs: Capitol Hill. Office: Herge Sparks & Christopher LLP 6862 Elm St Ste 360 Mc Lean VA 22101-3867 Home: 4976 Championship Cup Ln Spring Hill FL 34609-0355

HERGER, WALTER WILLIAM, congressman; b. Yuba City, Calif., May 20, 1945; m. Pamela Sargent; 8 children. Grad., Calif. State U. Sacramento, 1969. Mem. Calif. State Assembly, 1980—86, US Congress from 2nd Calif. dist., 1987—; mem. ways and means com.; chair human resources subcom., mem. trade subcom.; owner Herger Gas, Inc. Recipient Outstanding Young Man of Am. award, US Jaycees, 1979, Spirit of Am. award, US C. of C., 2000. Mem.: NRA, Nat. Fedn. Ind. Businessmen, Calif. C. of C., Calif. Cattleman's Assn., S. Yuba Rotary Club. Republican. Mem. Lds Ch. Office: US Ho Reps 2268 Rayburn Ho Office Bldg Washington DC 20515-0502 Office Phone: 202-225-3076. Office Fax: 202-225-0852.*

HERGERT, HERBERT LAWRENCE, retired consultant; b. Portland, Oreg., Feb. 20, 1927; s. John Edward and Elizabeth (Blahm) Hergert; m. Lois Marion Lilly, Dec. 20, 1949 (dec. Mar. 2, 2007); children: Lawrence A., Gregory K., David E., Daniel W. BA, Reed Coll., 1948; MS, Oreg. State U., 1951, PhD, 1954. Asst. prof. Oreg. State U., Corvallis, 1952-54; rsch. chemist Rayonier Inc., Shelton, Wash., 1954-70; asst. dir. R&D ITT Rayonier Inc., NYC, 1970-72, v.p., dir. R&D, 1972-80, dir. quality, 1971-79, v.p., dir. tech. mktg., 1980-87; sr. scientist Repap Techs. Inc., Valley Forge, Pa., 1987-97. Trustee Textile Rsch. Inst., Princeton, N.J., 1976-82, Tech. Assn. Pulp & Paper Industries, Atlanta, 1980-83; forest products con., Pottstown, Pa., 1987-97; adj. prof. N.C. State U., 1998—. Contbr. over 90 papers to profl. jours. and 7 chpts. to books. Chmn., bd. dirs. Shelton (Wash.) Gen. Hosp., 1962-66, Shelton Sch. Dirs., 1966-70; adv. bd. Cons. Bapt. Theol. Seminary, Denver, 1968-79. Corp. USAAF, 1945-46. Fellow Internat. Acad. Wood Sci.; mem. Internat. Paleobotanical Soc., Soc. Wood Sci. and Tech., Am. Chem. Soc., Tech. Assn. Pulp and Paper Industry. Republican. Baptist. Achievements include 6 U.S. patents and 36 foreign patents. Home and Office: 901 Burdan Dr Pottstown PA 19464-4475

HERGUTH, ROBERT JOHN, retired columnist; b. Chgo., Apr. 4, 1926; s. Harry Conrad Herguth and Loretta (Oberreither) Herguth-Slimmer; m. Margaret Ann Silsbee, Apr. 16, 1966; children: Amy Rene, Robert Charles, Mary Jennifer BA in Journalism, U. Mo., 1948. Copy editor, reporter Peoria Star, Ill., 1948-54; reporter, feature writer, columnist Chgo. Daily News, 1954-78; columnist Chgo. Sun Times, 1978-97, freelance weekly columnist, 1997-2001. Chmn. Chgo. Journalism Hall of Fame Com., 2005. Mem. editl. bd. Chgo. Sun Times., 1985-86. With U.S. Army, 1950-52. Inducted into Chgo. Journalism Hall of Fame, 1996. Mem. Chgo. Newspaper Guild (Page One award 1973), Chgo. Press Club (v.p. 1984-87, pres. 1987). Democrat. Roman Catholic.

HERING, DORIS MINNIE, dance critic; b. NYC, Apr. 11, 1920; d. Harry and Anna Elizabeth (Schwenk) H. BA cum laude, Hunter Coll., 1941; MA, Fordham U., 1985. Freelance dance writer, 1946-52; assoc. editor, prin. critic Dance mag., NYC, 1952-72; exec. dir. Nat. Assn. for Regional Ballet, NYC, 1972-87; adj. assoc. prof. dance history NYU, 1968-78; freelance dance writer, lectr., cons., 1987—. Dance panel NEA, 1972-75, cons., 1991—; dance panel NY State Coun. Arts, 1992-96, program auditor, 1997—; bd. dirs. Walnut Hill Sch., 1975—, Internat. Ballet Competition, 1981—; hon. bd. dirs. Phila. Dance Alliance, 1980—; cons. Regional Dance Am.; adj. assoc. prof. dance history NYU Grad. Sch. Edn. Author: 25 Years of American Dance, 1950, Dance in America, 1951, Wild Grass, 1965, Giselle and Albrecht, 1981; sr. editor Dance mag., 1989—. Howard D. Rothschild Rsch. fellow Harvard U., 1991-93; recipient 33d ann. Capezio Dance Found. award for lifetime svc., 1985, Award of Distinction Dance mag., 1987, Sage Cowles Land Grant chair in dance U. Minn., 1993, Sr. Critics tribute Dance Critics Assn., 2002, Annual award, Martha Hill Dance Fund, 2002; named to Hunter Coll. Alumni Hall of Fame, 1986. Mem. Dance Critics Assn., Assn. Dance History Scholars, Phi Beta Kappa, Chi Tau Epsilon (hon.). Office Phone: 212-787-3834.

HERKENHOFF, KENNETH EDWARD, geologist, researcher; s. Edward John and Louise Bernice Herkenhoff; m. Lottie Diane Soll, Dec. 18, 1983; children: Lee James, Sean Arthur, Bryce Edward. AB, U. Calif., Berkeley, 1981; PhD, Calif. Inst. Tech., Pasadena, 1989. NRC postdoctoral fellow Jet Propulsion Lab., Pasadena, 1989—91, mem. tech. staff, 1991—98; rsch. geologist US Geol. Survey, Flagstaff, Ariz., 1998—. Achievements include cameras on Mars exploration rovers. Office: US Geol Survey 2255 N Gemini Dr Flagstaff AZ 86001 Home Phone: 928-213-8711; Office Phone: 928-556-7205.

HERKERT, CRAIG R., retail executive; BS in Mktg., St. Francis Coll.; Master's, No. Ill. U. With Albertson's, Inc., Boise, Idaho; sr. v.p. fresh food mktg. Acme Supermarkets, 1998—99, pres. ea. region Malvern, Pa., 1999—2000; exec. v.p. and COO internat. div. Wal-Mart Stores, Inc., 2000—04, exec. v.p., pres., CEO Americas, 2004—. Office: Wal-Mart Stores Inc 702 SW Eighth St Bentonville AR 72716

HERLANDS, E. WARD, poet, printmaker; b. NYC, Mar. 31, 1925; d. Max and Rose (Polaner) Schenker; m. Robert E. Herlands; children: Wendy, Nancy. BS, Pratt Inst., NYC, 1946. Instr. U. Conn., Sterling Barn Theatre; fashion designer. Permanent judge Poetry Prize, Pratt U. and Coll. Acad. Am. Poets. Contbr. chapters to books, articles to profl. jour. Recipient Graphics award, Soc. of Old Greenwich, Highest Honors award, Pratt Inst., Augustus St. Gauden's medal; grantee, Ctr. for Independent Study, New Haven, Conn. Mem. Poets and Writers, Poetry Soc. Am., Acad. Am. Poets, Conn. Poetry Soc., Stamford Art Assn., Pratt Inst. Alumni Assn. Avocations: visual arts, verbal arts. Home: 179 Fox Ridge Rd Stamford CT 06903-2216 Office Phone: 203-322-3811. Personal E-mail: herlands18@optonline.net.

HERLEY, DAVEEN DOROTHY, artist, educator; arrived in U.S., 1965; d. Stewart Barker and Elizabeth Gladys Hodges; m. Patrick James Herley (dec.). BA, Rhodes U., 1955, edn. diploma, 1956; BEd with distinction, Rhodes U., Grahamstown, South Africa, 1959; Masters Degree, Adelphi U., 1975. Cert. elem. edn. and art edn. N.Y. Lectr. art, prof. edn. Grahamstown (South Africa) Tng. Coll., 1957—60; H.S. art tchr. Woodbury Down Comprehensive, London, 1961—64; elem. tchr. South Haven (N.Y.) Sch. Dist., 1972—89, South Country Sch. Dist., East Patchogue, NY, 1989—2002; adj. prof. Suffolk County C.C., Selden, NY, 1972—. Chair ednl. problems com. Bellport Tchrs. Assn., East Patchogue, NY, 1990—93; workshop leader in field. Author: Art Through Your Child's Eyes, 1975; exhibitions include, Brookhaven, Smithtown and East Hampton, N.Y., St. James Bellport, 1972—, Crazy Monkey Gallery, 2007—. Mem. Smithtown Arts Coun., East End Arts Coun., South Bay Art Assn.; atendee Oxford Round Table, 2007. Recipient Recognition award, Bellport Tchrs. Assn., 1990, 1991, 1992, 1993, Cert. Spl. Recognition, South Country Sch. Dist., 2001, 2002. Mem.: SAEYC (pres. 1975—77), NAEYC, South Bay Art Assn., Internat. Dyslexia Soc., Movable Book Soc. Avocations: collecting movable books, gardening, golf, antiques. Personal E-mail: herley67@aol.com.

HERLIHY, EDWARD D., lawyer; b. Glens Falls, NY, May 4, 1947; BA, Hobart Coll., 1969; JD, George Washington U., 1972. Bar: N.Y. 1973, D.C. 1973. Ptnr. Wachtell, Lipton, Rosen & Katz, NYC, 1984—. Contbr. articles to profl. jours. Named one of 100 Most Influential Lawyers, Nat. Law Jour., 2006. Office: Wachtell Lipton Rosen & Katz 51 W 52nd St Fl 29 New York NY 10019-6150 Office Phone: 212-403-1207. E-mail: edherlihy@wlrk.com.*

HERLIHY, SCOTT C., lawyer; BBA, Coll. of William & Mary, 1985; JD, Univ. Notre Dame, 1991. CPA; bar: Va. 1991, DC 1992. Litig. cons. Peterson & Co., 1985—88; mng. ptnr., No. Va. office Latham & Watkins LLP, Reston, Va., now ptnr., corp. dept. Washington. Mem.: ABA. Office: Latham & Watkins LLP Ste1000 555 Eleventh St NW Washington DC 20004-1304 Business E-Mail: scott.herlihy@lw.com.

HERLIHY-CHEVALIER, BARBARA DOYLE, retired mental health nurse; b. Cambridge, Mass., June 28, 1935; d. William A. and Aloyse V. (Mahoney) Doyle; m. Timothy J. Herlihy, Aug. 20, 1955 (dec. Oct. 1983); children: Michael, Ann-Marie, Sharon, Ellen, Stephen, Kathleen, James; m. Robert J. Chevalier, May 28, 1994 (dec. Oct. 1995); 1 stepchild, Ron. RN, Mass. Gen. Hosp., 1956; BS in Human Svcs., N.H. Coll./So. N.H. U., 1983; MS in Nursing, Anna Maria Coll., 1987. Nat. cert. instr. and coord. remotivation therapy. Pvt. duty nurse N.E. Bapt. Hosp., MGH, Boston, 1956, St. John's Hosp., Lowell, Mass., 1966—70; charge nurse Tewksbury Hosp. Mass. Dept. Pub. Health, Mass., 1970—76; coord. remotivation therapy Danvers State Hosp., Mass., 1976—79; registered cmty. mental health nurse Mass. Dept. Mental Health, Lawrence, 1979—91; ret., 1991. Mental health nurse Lowell Adult Day Treatment, Mass., 1991—94. Fellow Nat. Remotivation Therapy Orgn. (nat. instr., coord., Dorothy Hoskins Smith honorarium 2001); mem. Internat. Adv. Coun. Remotivation Therapy, Nat. Remotivation Therapy Orgn., Inc., Bay State Remotivation Coun. Home: 142 Trull Rd Tewksbury MA 01876-1705 Personal E-mail: barbhc851@verizon.net.

HERLIK, ED, military officer, pilot, small business owner, entrepreneur; (parents Am. citizens); s. Querin Herlik; m. Cindy Strong-Herlik, Aug. 1982. BS in Engring. and Internat. Affairs, Air Force Acad., Colo. Springs, Colo., 1980; MA in Nat. Security Studies, Calif. State U., San Bernardino, 1986; degree, Air War Coll., 2006. Lic. airline transport pilot FAA, 1993. Commd. lt. USAF, 1980, advanced through grades to lt. col., 2001; pilot USAF Res., Colo. Springs, 1990—; prin., owner Innovate Ltd., Colo. Springs, 1992—. Cons. in field. Author: Separated by War, An Oral History by Desert Storm Fliers and Their Families. Intern Chmn. Senate Armed Svcs. Com., Washington, 1979; vol. various presdl. and congl. campaigns, Colo. Springs, 2000—06; co-founder, CEO The Patriot's Fund, Colo. Springs, 2002—06. Decorated Co. Grade Officer of Yr. USAF Res. Assn., Wing Jr. Officer of Yr. USAF. Mem.: AIAA, Air Force Acad. Assn. Graduates, Mensa, Phi Kappa Phi. Achievements include patents for innovative airtankers and innovative methods for aerial fire fighting; method and system to measure dynamic loads or stresses in aircaft, machines, and structures; patents pending for stratospheric indefinate-endurance airships; hybrid engine for vehicles. Avocations: flying, scuba diving, exercise, hunting, travel. Home Phone: 719-590-1518; Office Phone: 719-440-4423. Personal E-mail: innovateltd@aol.com.

HERLING, IRVING MARC, internal medicine educator, cardiologist; b. NYC, Jan. 7, 1949; MD, U. Pa., 1974. Diplomate Am. Bd. Internal Medicine, Am. Bd. Cardiovasc. Disease. Intern Hosp. of U. Pa., Phila., 1974-75, resident in internal medicine, 1975-77, fellow in cardiology, 1977; mem. faculty U. Pa. Sch. Medicine, 1977—, assoc. prof. medicine. Fellow ACP, Am. Coll. Cardiology; mem. Am. Heart Assn. (fellow coun. clin. cardiology). Office: U Pa Med Ctr Penn Tower #800 3400 Spruce St Ste 907 Philadelphia PA 19104-4206 also: 250 King of Prussia Rd Radnor PA 19087 Office Phone: 215-662-6020, 610-902-2273.*

HERLONG, HENRY MICHAEL, JR., federal judge; b. Washington, June 1, 1944; s. Henry Michael Sr. and Josie Payne (Blocker) H.; m. Frances Elizabeth Thompson, Dec. 30, 1983; children: Faris Elizabeth, Henry Michael III. BA, Clemson U., 1967; JD, U. S.C., 1970. Bar: S.C. 1970, U.S. Ct. Appeals (4th cir.) 1972, U.S. Dist. Ct. S.C. 1972. Legis. asst. U.S. Senator Strom Thurmond, Washington, 1970-72; asst. U.S. atty. Dept. Justice, Greenville, S.C., 1972-76, Columbia, S.C., 1983-86; U.S. Magistrate judge U.S. Dist. Ct., Columbia, S.C., 1986-91, U.S. Dist. judge Greenville, S.C., 1991—; prin. Coleman & Herlong, Edgefield, S.C., 1976-83. Dir. Edgefield (S.C.) Devel. Bd., 1978-83, S.C. Assn. of Counties, 1980-83; active S.C. Rural Devel. Bd., 1980-83, Edgefield County Coun., 1979-83. Capt. USAR, 1970-75. Mem. S.C. Bar, Edgefield County Bar, Lions Club, Sertoma Club. Republican. United Methodist. Avocations: hunting, fishing, gardening. Office: US Dist Courts PO Box 10469 300 E Washington St Greenville SC 29603-1000

HERMAN, ALEXIS M., retired labor union administrator; b. Mobile, Ala., July 16, 1947; Student, Edgewood Coll. Sacred Heart, 1966—67; BA, Xavier U., New Orleans, 1969; Ph.D (hon.), Lesley Coll. Community worker Interfaith, Inc., Mobile, Ala., 1969; social worker Catholic Social Svc., Mobile, Ala., 1969—72; consult., supr. Recruitment & Training Program Inc., NYC, 1973—74; nat. dir. Minority Women's Employment Program, Washington, 1974—77; dir., founder, Women's Bur. US Dept. Labor, Washington, 1977-81; v.p., co-founder Green, Herman & Associates, 1981—85; founder, pres., CEO A.M. Herman & Assocs., Washington, 1985—93; chief staff, then dep. chair Dem. Nat. Conv. Com., Washington, 1989—91, CEO, 1991-92; dep. dir. Clinton-Gore Presdl. Transition Office, Washington, 1992-93; asst. to Pres. , pub. liaison dir. The White House, Washington, 1993-96; sec. U.S. Dept. Labor, Washington, 1997-2001; chmn., CEO New Ventures, Inc., Washington, 2001—; chairperson Coca-Cola Human Resources Diversity Task Force, Ga., 2001—; chmn. Toyota N Am. Diversity Bd., 2002—. Mem. bd. dirs. Entergy Corp., 2003—, Cummins Inc., President Life Insurance Co., MGM Mirage. Recipient Outstanding Young Person in Atlanta award, 1974, Atlanta's First Woman award, 1976, Dorothy I. Height Leadership award, Ctrl State U., Sara Lee Front Runner award, 1999. Mem. Atlanta Black Woman's Coalition, Am. Soc. Bus. & Profl. Women, Diocesan Commn. Social Justice, Internat. Personnel Mgmt. Assn., Nat. Coun. Negro Women, Delta Sigma Theta. Democrat.

HERMAN, ANDREA MAXINE, newspaper editor; b. Chgo., Oct. 22, 1938; d. Maurice H. and Mae (Baron) H.; m. Joseph Schmidt, Oct. 28, 1962. BJ, U. Mo., 1960. Feature writer Chgo.'s Am., 1960-63; daily columnist News Am., Balt., 1963-67; feature writer Mainichi Daily News, Tokyo, 1967-69; columnist Iowa City Press-Citizen, 1969-76; music and dance critic San Diego Tribune, 1976-84; asst. mng. editor features UPI, Washington, 1984-86, asst. mng. editor news devel., 1986-87; mng. editor features L.A. Herald Examiner, 1987-91; editor/culture We/Mbl Newspaper, Washington, 1991—. Recipient 1st and 2d prizes for features in arts James S. Copley Ring of Truth Awards, 1982, 1st prize for journalism Press Club San Diego, 1983. Mem. Soc. Profl. Journalists, Am. Soc. Newspaper Editors, AP Mng. Editors, Women in Communications. Avocations: music, art.

HERMAN, DARREN, entrepreneur, marketing executive; b. 1982; BS, Skidmore Coll., 2004. Founder & pres. Dynamify Prodns., NYC, 2001—04; founder & CEO InGame Advt. (IGA) Inc., NYC, 2004; chief comml. officer IGA Partners N.Am., NYC, 2005—06; sr. dir. bus. devel. IGA Worldwide Inc., NYC, 2006—. Named one of Best Entrepreneurs Under 25, Bus. Week, 2006. Office: IGA Worldwide Inc Ste 602 111 Broadway New York NY 10006 Office Phone: 212-381-0950. Office Fax: 212-240-9055. Personal E-mail: dherman@igaww.com.

HERMAN, DAVID J., infectious diseases physician; b. St. Louis, Nov. 19, 1958; MD, U. Mo., 1985. Diplomate Am. Bd. Internal Medicine, Am. Bd. Infectious Disease. Resident in internal medicine Northwestern U., Chgo., 1985—88; fellow in infectious disease U. Minn., Mpls., 1988—91; physician Somerset Med. Ctr., 1991—, Med. Ctr. Princeton, NJ, 1991—, R.W. Johnson Univ. Hosp., 1991—, St. Peter's Univ. Hosp., 1996—. Named one of Top Drs. in NY Metro area, Castle Connolly, 1999—2005, Top Drs. 2003, N.J. Monthly Mag. Office: 411 Courtyard Dr Hillsborough NJ 08844 also: 11 State Rd Ste 200 Princeton NJ 08540-1318 also: 81 Veronica Ave Somerset NJ 08873 Office Phone: 908-725-2522. E-mail: dherman@idcare.com.

HERMAN, DAVID JAY, orthodontist; b. Rome, NY, Oct. 4, 1954; s. Maurice Joseph and Bettina S. (Stiener) H.; m. Mary Beth Appleberry, Apr. 11, 1976; children: Jeremiah D., Kellin A. BA in Biology, San Jose State U., 1976; DDS, Emory U., 1981; MS in Orthodontics, U. N.C., 1992, MPH, 1992. Comdr. USPHS, 1981-97; advanced gen. practice resident Gallup (N. Mex.) Indian Med. Ctr., 1983-84; Navajo area dental br. chief Window Rock, Ariz., 1986-89; mem. grad. residency com. U. N.C., Chapel Hill, 1990-91; Navajo area orthodontic specialist Shiprock, N.Mex., 1992-97; clin. dir. Nizhoni Smiles Inc., 1997-99; pvt. practice Farmington, N.Mex., 1998—; pres. Four Corners Orthodontics, Inc., 1998—. Mem. health adv. bd. Navajo Reservation Headstart, 1986—89; health promotion/disease prevention cons. USPHS/Indian Health Svc. Navajo Area, Window Rock, 1986—89; cons. Ariz. IHS Periodontal Health Task Force, 1986—90. Asst. wrestling coach Winslow (Ariz.) H.S., 1984-86, Gallup High Sch., 1987-89, Chapel Hill H.S., 1991-92, Farmington H.S., 1992—, Aztec H.S., 1998-2000; mem. H.S. Youth Wrestling Program, 1992-2000; mem. corp. bd. San Juan Reg. Med. Ctr., 1996—. Recipient Healthy Mothers/Healthy Babies Disease Prevention award, 1988, USPHS Achievement medal, 1985, Headstart Achievement award, 1989, Ariz. Pub. Health Assn. Hon. award, 1989; Nat. Health Svc. Corp. scholar Emory U., 1977-81. Mem. ADA, Am. Assn. Orthodontists, Rocky Mountain Soc. Orthodontists, N.Mex. Soc. Orthodontists (pres. 1998-99), Northwestern N.Mex. Sco. Orthodontists (pres. 1999-00), Navajo Area Dental Soc. (pres. 1985), Am. Assn. Mil. Orthodontists (sec.reas. 1992, v.p. 1993-94, pres. 1995-97). Avocations: wrestling, weightlifting, jogging, skiing, backpacking. Office Phone: 505-564-9000. Personal E-mail: farmngnm@orthodon.com.

HERMAN, DOROTHY, real estate broker; b. Bklyn., May 10, 1953; d. Joseph Edward and Louise (Dicerbo) D'Ambrosio; m. Jay Herman; 1 child, Christine. BA, Adelphia U., 1983. Cert. fin. planner. Mgr. Merrill Lynch Realty, LI, NY, 1982-84, regional v.p., 1985-87, pres. L.I., 1988-90; co-owner, pres. Prudential L.I. Realty (aquired Douglas Elliman), 1990—2003; co-owner, pres., CEO Prudential Douglas Elliman Real Estate, NYC, 2003—. Mem. faculty N.Y. Inst. Tech., 1988— Contbr. weekly article to Newsday, 1990. Mem. Internat. Assn. of Fin. Planners (cert. fin. planner), L.I. Bd. Realtors, Columbia Soc. Real Estate Appraisers. Avocation: racquetball. Office: Prudential Douglas Elliman 575 Madison Ave 4th Fl New York NY 10022 also: 110 Walt Whitman Rd Ste 106 Huntington Station NY 11746 Office Phone: 212-891-7695.

HERMAN, EDITH CAROL, journalist; b. Edgewood, Md., July 1, 1944; d. Herbert R. and Thirza E. (Simmons); m. Leonard Wiener. BA, Purdue U., 1966. Reporter Hollister Newspaper Chain, Wilmette, Ill., 1966-68, Chgo. Tribune Newspaper, 1968-79, edn. editor, 1971-74, feature writer, 1976-79; sr. editor TV Digest Inc., 1980-83; pub. rels. mgr. AT&T, 1983-90; pub. rels. cons. Bethesda, 1990—93, Warren Comm., 1994—, assoc. mng. editor, 2001—. Bd. dirs. Sigma Delta Chi Found. of Washington, 1990—92. Recipient Journalism award Ill. Edn. Assn., 1969-70; Editorial award Ill. Automatic Merchandising Council, 1977 Mem.: Soc. Profl. Journalists. Home: 5501 Burling Ct Bethesda MD 20817-6309 E-mail: eherman@warren-news.com.

HERMAN, ELLEN ROMBS, retired literature and language educator, painter; d. Vincent Joseph and Ruth (Burns) Rombs; m. James Paul Herman, June 24, 1967; children: Laura Brooks, Julia. BA, Marquette U., Milw., 1966, MEd, 1995. Cert. reading specialist pre-k-12, elem. tchr. Tchr. grades 3 and 5 Holy Family Sch., St. Louis Park, Minn., 1967—70; tchr. grade 2 Greendale (Wis.) Sch. Dist., 1970—71; tchr. grade 5 art St. Mary Parish Sch., Hales Corners, 1982—83, tchr. and reading tutor, 1990—94; tchr. reading and lang. arts grade 8 Holy Angels Sch., West Bend, 1994—98; tchr. art grades 6-8 St. Mary Parish Sch., Hales Corners, 1998—99, tchr. reading and lang. arts grades 6 and 7, 1999—2006; ret., 2006; docent Haggerty Mus. Art, Marquette U., Milw., 2007—. Sec. Friends of Hales Corners Libr., 1990—92, pres., 1992—95. Mem.: Wis. State Reading Assn., Nat. Coun. Tchrs. English, Pi Lambda Theta. Avocations: painting, reading, boating, skiing, hiking.

HERMAN, GEORGE ADAM, writer, literature educator; b. Norfolk, Va., Apr. 12, 1928; s. George Adam and Minerva Nevada (Thompson) H.; m. Patricia Lee Glazer, May 26, 1955 (div. 1989); children: Kurt, Erik, Karl, Lisa, Katherine, Christopher, Jena, Amanda; m. Patricia Jane Piper Dubay, Aug. 25, 1989; children: Lizette, Paul, Kirk, Victoria. PhB, Loyola Coll., 1950; MFA, Cath. U., 1954; cert. of fine arts, Boston Coll., 1953. Asst. prof. Clarke Coll., Dubuque, Iowa, 1955-60, Villanova (Pa.) U., 1960-63; asst. prof., playwright in residence Coll. St. Benedict, St. Joseph, Minn., 1963-65; chmn. theatre dept. Coll. Great Falls, Mont., 1965-67; media specialist Hawaii State Dept. Edn., Honolulu, 1967-75, staff specialist, 1975-83; sr. drama critic Honolulu Advertiser, 1975-80; artistic dir. Commedia Repertory Theatre, Honolulu, 1978-80; freelance writer, lectr., composer Portland, Oreg., 1983—. Author: (plays) Company of Wayward Saints, 1963 (McKnight Humanities award 1964), Mr. Highpockets, 1968, A Stone for Either Hand, 1969, Tenebrae, 1984, Nine Dragons, The Hidden Place, 2003, (novels) Carnival of Saints, 1994 (finalist Oreg. Book Awards 1994), A Comedy of Murders, 1994, Tears of the Madonna, 1995, The Florentine Mourners, 1999, The Toys of War, 2002, Little Rome, Iowa, 2003, Nine Dragons, 2003, Necromancer, 2003, The Arno Serpent, 2007; composer (ballets) The Dancing Princesses, Fraidy Cat. Pres. local chpt. Nat. Sch. Pub. Rels. Assn., Honolulu, 1981-83; bd. dirs. Honolulu Community Theatre, 1981-82, Hawaii State Theatre Coun., Honolulu, 1981. With U.S. Army, 1950-52. Recipient Hartke Playwrighting award Cath. U., 1954, Humanities award McKnight Found., 1963, Excellence award Am. Security Coun., 1967. Avocations: directing theatre, lecturing. Office Phone: 503-452-3701. Personal E-mail: gadamo@aol.com.

HERMAN, HANK, writer; b. NYC, Nov. 13, 1949; s. Philip and Stella (Rubenfeld) H.; m. Carol K. Korngut, Dec. 30, 1972; children: Matt, Greg, Robby. BA, U. Pa., 1971. Advt. copywriter Prentice-Hall, Englewood Cliffs, NJ, 1972-73; assoc. editor Travel Mgmt. Daily, NYC, 1973-74; mng. editor TravelScene, NYC, 1975-77, Health Mag., NYC, 1978-79, editor in chief, 1980-88; freelance writer, 1989—. Health reporter Sta. WINS-Radio, N.Y.C., 1987-90. Award-winning columnist Westport News, 1993—; author numerous mag. articles and youth sports fiction books, 1973—. Avocations: running, tennis, skiing, coaching youth sports.

HERMAN, JOAN ELIZABETH, health insurance company executive; b. NYC, June 2, 1953; d. Roland Barry and Grace Gales (Goldstein) Herman; m. Richard M. Rasiej, July 16, 1977. AB, Barnard Coll., 1975; MS, Yale U., New Haven, 1977. Actuarial student Met. Life Ins. Co., NYC, 1978-82; asst. actuary Phoenix Mut. Life Ins. Co., Hartford, Conn., 1982-83, assoc. actuary, dir. underwriting rsch., 1983-84, 2nd v.p., 1984-85, v.p., 1985-89, sr. v.p., 1989-98; pres. splty. bus. WellPoint Health Networks, Woodland Hills, Calif., 1998, grp. pres., 1999—2001, pres. splty., sr. and state sponsored progs. divsn., 2002—04; pres., CEO, splty. sr. and state sponsored bus. divsn. WellPoint, Inc., Indpls., 2004—. Bd. dirs. PM Holdings, Inc., Phoenix Grp. Holdings, Inc., Phoenix Am. Life Ins. Co., Emprendimiento Compartido, S.A.; v.p. BC Life & Health Co., Profl. Claims Svcs. Inc., Proserv., MEDIX. Contbr. articles to profl. jours. Bd. dirs. Health Ins. Assn. Am., 2002—03; capt. fundraising team Greater Hartford Arts Coun., Hartford, 1986; bd. dirs. Children's Fund Conn., 1992—98, My Sister's Pl. Shelter, Hartford, 1989—94, Western Mass. Regional Nat. Conf. Conn., 1995—98, Greater Hartford Arts Coun., 1997—98, Hartford Ballet, 1989—95, corporator, 1995—98; bd. dirs. Leadership Greater Hartford, 1989—94, chmn. bd. dirs., 1993—94; bd. dirs. So. Calif. Leadership Network, 2003—; mem. bd. founders Am. Leadership Forum Hartford, 1991—98; corporator Hartford Sem., 1994—98; bd. dirs. Hadassah, Glastonbury, Conn., Temple Beth Hillel, South Windsor, Conn., 1983—84. Fellow: Soc. Actuaries (chair health sect. coun. 1994—95); mem.: Am. Leadership Forum, Am. Acad. Actuaries (bd. dirs. 1994—97). Jewish. Avocations: reading, swimming, bicycling, jogging, aerobic dancing, hiking. Office: WellPoint Inc 1 Wellpoint Way Thousand Oaks CA 91362-3893 Home Phone: 310-454-5716. Business E-Mail: joan.herman@wellpoint.com.

HERMAN, JOHN C., lawyer; b. Wilmington, Del., Aug. 31, 1967; s. John T. and Lynn J. Herman; m. Lisa Vash Herman, Apr. 5, 1997; children: John C. Jr., Henry J. BS in Biochemistry summa cum laude, Marquette U., 1988; JD, Vanderbilt U., 1992. Bar: Ga. 1992. Assoc. King & Spalding, Atlanta, 1992—2001, ptnr., 2001—02, Duane Morris LLP, Atlanta, 2002—, chair Atlanta litig. dept. Mem. adv. bd. Strobel Group, Nashville, 2003—; mem. lawyers adv. panel Ga. Biomed. Partnership, Atlanta, 2004. Editor-in-chief Vanderbilt Jour. Transnational Law, 1991—92; contbr. articles to profl. jours. Pro bono vol. 1000 Lawyers for Justice, Atlanta, 1992—93; alumni coun. Vanderbilt U. Sch. Law, Nashville, 1998—; ann. fund agt. Atlanta Legal Aid Soc., 2001—; mem. adv. bd. Sci-Trek Mus., Atlanta, 2002—04. Named Ga. Super Lawyer, Legal Trends/Atlanta Mag., 2005; John Wade Scholar, Vanderbilt U., 1989—92. Mem.: ABA, U.S. Supreme Ct. Bar, Ga. Bar Assn. (intellectual property sect.). Avocations: sports, travel, music. Office: Duane Morris LLP 1180 W Peachtree St Atlanta GA 30309 Office Phone: 404-253-6900. Office Fax: 404-253-6901. Business E-Mail: jcherman@duanemorris.com.

HERMAN, JOHN HUGHES, lawyer; b. Akron, Ohio, Sept. 29, 1945; s. George K. and Imogene (Hughes) H.; m. Elizabeth R. Allis, May 30, 1970 (div. 1975); 1 child, Nicholas; m. Diane L. Seeley, Aug. 25, 1979; children: Dustan Hendrickson, Margot. BA in econs. cum laude, Yale U., 1967; JD, Harvard U., 1970. Bar: U.S. Dist. Ct. Minn. 1971, Minn. 1972, U.S. Ct. Appeals (8th cir.) 1975. Atty. Minn. Pub. Interest Rsch. Group, Mpls., 1971-73; ptnr. Pepin, Dayton, Herman & Graham, Mpls., 1973-88, Leonard, Street & Deinard P.A., Mpls., 1988—, Faegre & Benson LLP, Mpls. Adj. prof. environ. law Hamline Law Sch., 1978, U. Minn. Law Sch., 1980; adj. prof. legis. advocacy William Mitchell Coll. Law, 1999—2001. Contbr. articles to profl. jours. Bd. dirs. Jungle Theater, Minn. chpt. Nature Conservancy, otehrs; chair lakes water quality task force Mpls. Park Bd., 1993, U. Minn., Coll. Architecture and Landscape Architecture (adv. bd.) 1995-, Met. Region (transp. adv. bd.) 1999-2003, Trust for Pub. Land (adv. bd.) Minn. 2001-, Citizen's Commn. Minn. Resources (commr.) 2006-. Named Environmentalist of Decade, Sierra Club, Mpls., 1979, Best Lawyers in Am., 2007, Am.'s Leading Lawyers for Bus., Chambers USA, Super Lawyer, Minn. Law & Politics, Best Lawyers in MN Govt. Affairs, Best Author's award Law Article. Office: Faegre & Benson LLP 90 S 7th St 2200 Wells Fargo Center Minneapolis MN 55402 Office Phone: 612-766-8908. Office Fax: 612-766-1600. Business E-Mail: jherman@faegre.com.

HERMAN, KENNETH BEAUMONT, lawyer; b. Medford, Mass., Jan. 23, 1944; s. Beaumont Alexander and Winifred (Small) H.; m. Agnes Anne Burch, Sept. 18, 1976; children: Alexander Beaumont, Juliana Burch. AB, Harvard U., 1966; JD, Harvard Law Sch., 1969. Bar: N.Y. 1971. Tchr. St. Dominic Savio High Sch., East Boston, Mass., 1969-70; assoc., then ptnr. Fish & Neave, NYC, 1970—2004; ptnr. Ropes & Gray LLP, NYC, 2005—. Mem. Larchmont (N.Y.) Recreation Com., 1983-94, trustee Larchmont Hist. Soc., 1987-88. Mem. ABA, N.Y. State Bar Assn., N.Y. Intellectual Property Law Assn. (chmn. com. on incentives for innovation 1987-88), Fed. Cir. Bar Assn., Am. Intellectual Property Law Assn., Assn. Bar of City of N.Y., Am. Arbitration Assn. (panel arbitrators). Avocations: sailing, skiing, kayaking, reading. Home: 810 Pirates Cv Mamaroneck NY 10543-4717 Office: Fish & Neave IP Group Ropes & Gray LLP 1211 Avenue of the Americas New York NY 10036-8704 Office Phone: 212-596-9020. Business E-Mail: kenneth.herman@ropesgray.com.

HERMAN, LYNN BRIGGS, state legislator; b. Philipsburg, Pa., Oct. 30, 1956; s. Frederick Jr. and Barbara Ann (Briggs) H. BA, U. Pitts., Johnstown, 1978; MPA, U. Pitts., 1980. Adminstrv. asst. Pa. Dept. Edn., Harrisburg, 1980-81; adminstrv. analyst Pa. Dept. Transp., Harrisburg, 1981-82; mem. Pa. Ho. of Reps., Harrisburg, 1982—. Chmn. local govt. com. Pa. Ho. of Reps., 1997—, chmn. legis. data processing com., 1994—, co-chmn. house history caucus; founder, co-chmn. Penn State Forum. Capitol Centennial Commn., 2004—. Elected pres. Centre County's 148th Pa. Vol. Inf. Regiment Civil War reenactment group, 1998-2003. Named Outstanding Legislator, Pa. Rifle and Pistol Assn., 1987, State Ofcl. of Yr., Nat. Assn. Home Builders, 2004; named to Outstanding Young Men of Am.; recipient Presdl. Recognition award Moshannon Valley Econ. Devel. Partnership, 1990, Champion of Good Govt. award Common Cause of Pa., 1999, Disting. Svc. award Pa. Mcpl. Authorities Assn., 2002. Mem. Pa. Assn. State Retirees (Legislator award 2003), Frat. Order Police, Pa. State Alumni Assn., Ctrl. Pa. Civil War Round Table (pres. 2004—), Centre County Hist. Soc., Centre County Geneaol. Soc., Pa. SAR, Philipsburg Hist. Found. (hon. trustee), Sons Union Vets. Civil War, Penn State Quarterback Club, Grange, Elks, Kiwanis, Masons. Republican. Home Phone: 814-342-1484; Office Phone: 717-787-8594. Business E-Mail: lherman@pahousegop.com.

HERMAN, MARTIN NEAL, neurologist, educator; b. Washington, July 19, 1939; m. Sydney Beryl Epstein, July 1, 1962; children: Kenneth Dayan, Heidi Felice. AA, George Washington U., 1960; BS, Northwestern U., 1961, MD, 1964. Diplomate Am. Bd. Electroencephalography, Am. Bd. Psychiatry and Neurology, Nat. Bd. Med. Examiners; lic. N.J. Intern Georgetown U./D.C. Gen. Hosp., Washington, 1964; resident psychiatry U. Rochester (N.Y.)/Strong Meml. Hosp., 1964; resident neurology U. Va., Charlottesville, 1967-70; rsch. fellow clin. neurophysiology NIH, Bethesda, Md., 1970-71; asst. prof., dir. electroencephalography N.J. Coll. Medicine and Dentistry, Newark, 1971-74; dir. neurology Monmouth Med. Ctr., Long Branch, N.J., 1974—. Asst. clin. prof. Hahnemann Med. Coll. and Hosp., 1974-91; clin. assoc. prof. Pa. U., Drexel U. Coll. Medicine, 1991—; attending physician Martland Hosp., Newark, 1971-74, East Orange (N.J.) VA Hosp., 1971-74, Riverview Med. Ctr., Red Bank, N.J., 1983—. Contbr. chpts. to books and articles to profl. jours. Mem. AMA, Am. Acad. Neurology, Am. Med. Electroencephalographic Soc., Am. Clin. Neurophysiology Soc., N.J. Med. Soc., N.J. Acad. Medicine, Ea. Assn. Electroencephalographers, Phi Eta Sigma. Home Phone: 732-229-7833; Office Phone: 732-935-1850. Personal E-mail: mnhermes1@comcast.net.

HERMAN, MARY MARGARET, neuropathologist; b. Plymouth, Wis., July 26, 1935; d. Elmer Fredolein and Esther Lydia (Bross) H.; m. Lucien Jules Rubinstein, Jan. 31, 1969. BS in Med. Sci., U. Wis., 1957, MD, 1960. Diplomate Nat. Bd. Med. Examiners, Am. Bd. Anatomic Pathology, Am. Bd. Neuropathology. Intern Mary Hitchcock Meml. Hosp., Hanover, NH, 1960-61; resident in neurology U. Wis. Hosps., 1961-62; intern in pathology Yale U., New Haven, 1962-63, asst. resident in pathology, 1963-64, fellow in neuropathology, 1964-65, rsch. assoc. pathology, 1967-68; fellow in neuropathology Stanford U., Palo Alto, Calif., 1965-66, fellow, acting instr. neuropathology, 1966-67, asst. prof. pathology, 1967-74, assoc. prof., 1974-81; prof., co-dir. divsn. neuropathology U. Va. Sch. Medicine, Charlottesville, 1981-91, prof. clin. pathology, 1991-92; spl. expert neuropathology in clin. brain disorders br. NIMH, Washington, 1991-96, sr. staff scientist, 1996—; neuropathologist NIMH Brain Collection, 1992—, Stanley Fund Brain Collection, 1992—2002. Vis. asst. prof. Albert Einstein Coll. Medicine, Bronx, NY, 1971—72; mem. program project rev. com. Nat. Inst. Neurol. and Communicative Diseases NIH, 1973—77; cons. lab. svc. VA Hosp., Salem, Va., Ctrl. Va. Tng. Ctr., Lynchburg, 1982—92, ad hoc mem. pathology A study sect., 1986—91; cons. neuropathologist DC Med. Examiner's Office, Washington, 1992—, Med. Examiner's Office, No. Va. Dist., Fairfax, 2000—, DC Gen. Hosp., 1992—2002; mentor scientist NIH Intramural Rsch. Tng. award, Fogarty Fellows, Howard Hughes Med. Inst./MCPS/NIH student and tchr. internships program, Stanley Found. scholar's program. Mem. editl. bd.: Jour. Neuropathology and Exptl. Neurology, 1989—93, 2001—; contbr. over 200 articles to profl. jours. Recipient Rsch. Career Devel. award, NIH, 1967—72, Staff Recognition award, 2000—06, Faculty Devel. award, Merck Found., 1969. Mem.: AAAS, AMA, Am. Assn. Anatomists, Soc. Biol. Psychiatry, Am. Assn. Neuropathologists (Weil award 1974), Am. Soc. for Investigative Pathology, Soc. for Devel. Biology, Internat. Soc. Neuropathology, Am. Soc. Cell Biology (rsch. fellowship program, mentor scientist summer tchr. 1994), Internat. Acad. Pathology, Soc. In Vitro Biology, Soc. Neurosci. Achievements include research in neuropathology of major mental disorders, neurodegeneration and aluminum neurotoxicity, and embryonal tumors of the CNS. Avocations: tennis, gardening, music. Home: 10008 Stedwick Rd Apt 304 Montgomery Village MD 20886-3718 Office: NIMH NIH 49 Convent Dr Rm BIB80 MSC 4425 Bethesda MD 20892-4425 Office Phone: 301-480-0042. Office Fax: 301-480-0023. Business E-Mail: mh230t@nih.gov.

HERMAN, MICHELLE, writer; b. Bklyn., Mar. 9, 1955; d. Morton and Sheila Marcia (Weiss) Herman. BS, Bklyn. Coll., 1976; MFA in English, U. Iowa, 1986. Manuscript editor Van Nostrand Reinhold Co., NYC, 1976; reporter Assoc. Press, City Desk, NYC, 1977; freelance editor various pubs., NYC, 1977-84; instr. U. of Iowa, Iowa City, 1984-86; prof. English Ohio State U., Columbus, 1988—. Author: (novel) Missing, 1990 (Harold U. Ribdow award Hadassah 1990), (stories) A New and Glorious Life, 1998, Dog, 2005, (novel) The Middle of Everything: Memoirs of Motherhood, 2005; short stories; playwright: Tyler and Althea, 1980; editor (lit. mag.) The Journal. NEA fellow, 1986; recipient Tchg.-Writing award U. Iowa, 1985, 86, James Michener award 1987, Ohio Arts Coun. awards, 1989, 99, 2004. Democrat. Jewish. Office Phone: 614-292-5767.

HERMAN, PETER WINDLEY, lawyer; b. NYC, 1944; AB, Columbia U., 1965, JD cum laude, 1970. Bar: N.Y. 1971. Ptnr. & head, Real Estate Dept. Milbank, Tweed, Hadley & McCloy, NYC. Contbr. columns in newspapers. Chmn. Regional Plan Assn., NY; sec. Downtown Lower Manhattan Assn. Mem. ABA, N.Y. State Bar Assn. (mem. environ. law com.), Assn. Bar City N.Y. (chmn. transp. com. 1979-82), Urban Land Inst. Office: Milbank Tweed Hadley & McCloy 1 Chase Manhattan Plz Fl 47 New York NY 10005-1413 Office Phone: 212-530-5742. Office Fax: 212-530-5219. Business E-Mail: pherman@milbank.com.

HERMAN, RAYNA S., pharmaceutical consultant; BA in Chemistry, Ind. U., 1991; MBA, Washington U., 1996. Sales/mktg. staff Merck & Co., Inc., West Point, Pa., 1991-99; prin., owner Health Strategies Group, Lambertville, N.J., 1999—. Bd. dirs. Big Bros. Big Sisters, Montgomery County, 1999-2001; collegiate advisor Sigma Sigma Sigma, 2002-03; active Jr. League, 2002—. Mem.: Healthcare Bus. Women's Assn.

HERMAN, RICHARD GERALD, research chemist, consultant, educator; b. Springville, NY, Mar. 11, 1944; s. Richard Arthur and Mary Ann (Hoffman) H.; m. Helen Lynn Ramer; children: Richard David, Sarah Louise, Jonathan Garett. BS, SUNY, Fredonia, 1966; PhD, Ohio U., 1972. Cert. secondary edn. tchr., N.Y. Postdoctoral fellow Lund (Sweden) U., 1972-73, Tex. A&M U., College Station, 1973-75; rsch. scientist I Lehigh U., Bethlehem, Pa., 1975-82, rsch. scientist II, 1982-89, prin. rsch. scientist, 1989—, interim dir. Zettlemoyer Ctr. for Surface Studies, 1989; exec. dir. Zettlemoyer Ctr. for Surface Studies, Bethlehem, Pa., 1995-2001. Adj. assoc. prof. dept. chemistry Lehigh U., 1980—81, adj. prof. dept. chem. engring., 2002—07, adj. prof. dept. chemistry, 2007—. Editor: Catalytic Conversions of Synthesis Gas and Alcohols to Chemicals, 1984, Advances in Clean Fuel Technology and Control of Atmospheric Emissions, 2000, Catalytic Surface Centers and Mechanisms, 2002; contbg. author: New Trends in CO Activation, 1991, also others; contbr. over 120 articles to Catalysis, Chem. Engring. Sci., Inorganic Chemistry, Chem. Comm., also others. Tchr. Bible class Christ Evang. Luth. Ch., Schoenersville, Pa., 1981—, youth retreat asst., 1987-90; asst. coach Tri-Boro Youth Soccer, Whitehall, Pa., 1987-92, Lehigh Valley United Sr. Soccer Team, 1998-2005. Recipient Outstanding Achievement award SUNY, Fredonia, 1991, Disting. Svc. award Tri-Boro Youth Soccer, 1995. Mem.: Catalysis Soc. N.Am., Am. Chem. Soc. (chmn. Lehigh Valley chpt. 1989). Republican. Achievements include 5 patents for methanol synthesis, amine synthesis and water gas shift; development of new process for obtaining high cetane liquid fuels from alcohols; development of new catalytic process for low temperature abatement of NOx emissions. Office: Lehigh U Dept of Chemistry 6 E Packer Ave Bethlehem PA 18015-3102 Home Phone: 610-776-0704; Office Phone: 610-758-3486. E-mail: rgh1@lehigh.edu.

HERMAN, RICHARD H., academic administrator; m. Susan Herman. BA cum laude, Stevens Inst. Tech., 1963; PhD in Math., U. Md. Various positions UCLA, 1968—72, Pa. State U., 1972—90; dean Coll. Computer, Math. and Phys. Scis. U. Md., College Park, 1990—98; provost, vice chancellor acad. affairs U. Ill., Urbana-Champaign, 1998—, interim chancellor, 2004—05, chancellor, 2005—. Chmn. adv. com. for directorate math. and phys. sci. NSF; chair Joint Policy Bd. for Math.; mem. adv. bd. Mellon Coll. Sci. Contbr. articles to profl. jours. Bd. dirs. United Way, Champaign County C. of C. Fellow, Alexander von Humboldt Found. Mem.: Assn. Univs. for Rsch. in Astronomy, Inc. (mem. obs. coun.), Sigma Xi, Tau Beta Pi. Office: Office of Chancellor 204 Swanlund Adminstrn Bldg 601 E John St Champaign IL 61820*

HERMAN, ROBERT LEWIS, cork company executive; b. NYC, July 16, 1927; s. Nat W. and Ruth (Stockton) H.; m. Susan Marie Volper, Dec. 10, 1966; children: Candia Ruth, William Neal. AB, Columbia U., NYC, 1948, BS, 1949. V.p. Joseph Samuels & Sons, Inc., Whippany, NJ, 1953-62; pres. Dependable Cork Co., Inc., Morristown, NJ, 1962—. Sr. chmn. Amorim Indsl. Solutions, Inc., Trevor, Wis., 1999—; bd. dirs. Concorco LDA, Lisbon, Portugal, Oporto, Portugal, Amorim Indsl. Solutions, LDA, Oporto, Portugal. Inventor Corticiera natural cork wallcovering. Comdr. C.E. Corps, USNR, 1949-53. Mem. NJ Mfrs. Assn., Naval Res. Assn., US C. of C., Navy League Club, Columbia U. Club, Princeton Club (NYC). Home Phone: 516-585-1550. Personal E-mail: rlhcork@aol.com.

HERMAN, RUSS MICHEL, lawyer; b. New Orleans, Apr. 26, 1942; s. Harry and Reba Nell (Hoffman) Herman; m. Barbara Ann Kline, July 5, 1965; children: Stephen Jay, Penny Lynn, Elizabeth Rose. BA, Tulane U., 1963; LLB, Tulane U., 1966. Bar: La. 1966, U.S. Dist. Ct. La. 1966, U.S. Ct. Appeals (5th cir. and 11th cir) 1970, U.S. Supreme Ct. 1972, diplomate: Am. Bd. Profl. Liability Attys., Nat. Coll. Advocacy. Law clk. La. Ct. Appeals, 4th Cir., New Orleans, 1965—66; with Herman, Hermann, Katz & Cotlar (formerly Herman & Herman), New Orleans, 1966—, ptnr., sr. ptnr.; ptnr. Herman Mathis Casey Kitchens and Gerel. Lectr. in field; faculty Practicing Law Inst., Nat. Coll. Trial Advocacy; lectr. Tulane U., La. State U., Loyola U., New Orleans, Georgetown U.; guest TV programs including Good Morning Am., Today Show, CNN Newsline, others; mem. ethics panel U.ist. Ct., Ea. Dist. of La. Contbr. over 100 articles to profl. jours.; contbg. editor: Expert Witness Reporter, Trial Diplomacy Jour.; author (performer): (video) Trial Practice series, Courtroom Persuasion: Art, Drama and Science; author: Louisiana Personal Injury, 2 vols.; contbr. Louisian Bench Book for District Court Judges on Complex Litigation: Ethics and Discovery. Pres. Civil Justice Found., 1987—88, Roscoe Pound Found., 1991—93; adv. coun. Nat. Jud. Coll. With USAF. Named one of Louisiana's Top Ten Litigators, Nat. Law Jour. Fellow: Internat. Barristers, Internat. Acad. Trial Lawyers (dir.); mem.: ATLA (pres. 1989—90, chair r.r. hwy. crossing accident litigation group, co-chair Rezulin litigation group, Joe Tonahill award 1998, Lifetime Achievement award 1999, Leonard M. Champion of Justice award 2001), Am. Bd. Trial Advocates, Am. Coll. Barristers (barrister), La. Trial Lawyers Assn. (pres. 1980—81, Outstanding Trial Lawyer 1977). Office: Herman Herman Katz & Cotlar 820 Okeefe Ave New Orleans LA 70113-1116 Home: 1050 Highway 98 E Unit 1401e Destin FL 32541-7906 Office Phone: 504-581-4892. Business E-Mail: rherman@hhkc.com.

HERMAN, RUSSELL LELAND, mathematics, physics professor; b. Manchester, NH, Apr. 23, 1951; m. Ann Diggs, Dec. 14, 2004; children: EliJacob Weinstock-Herman, Arianna Zimmerman, Nathan Moshe Weinstock-Herman, Shoshana Joele Weinstock-Herman, Avi Micah Weinstock-Herman. BS in Math., Empire State Coll., SUNY, 1981; MA in Physics, Temple U., 1982; PhD in Physics, Clarkson U., Potsdam, NY, 1988, MS in Math., 1986. Math. and physics prof. U. NC, Wilmington, 1990—. Vis. asst. prof. St. Lawrence U., Canton, 1988—90. Recipient Disting. Tchg. professorship, U. NC Wilmington, 2005, Chancellor's Tchg. Excellence award, 2005, Bd. Gov.'s award for Tchg. Excellence, U. NC, 2006; numerous grants in ednl. rsch., NSF and U. N.C. Wilmington, 1991—2005. Mem.: Am. Assn. Physics Tchrs., Soc. for Indsl. and Applied Math., Am. Math. Soc., Math. Assn. of Am., Am. Phys. Soc. Office: U NC Wilmington 601 S College Rd Wilmington NC 28403 Home Phone: 910-763-4372; Office Phone: 910-962-3722. Business E-Mail: hermanr@uncw.edu.

HERMAN, SARAH ANDREWS, lawyer; b. Fargo, ND, June 20, 1952; BA magna cum laude, U. N.D., 1974; JD, U. Mich., 1977. Bar: N.D. 1977, U.S. Dist. Ct. N.D. 1978. With Nilles, Hansen & Davies, Ltd., Fargo, ND, 1977—94, bd. dirs.; ptnr., trial and labor and employment practice groups Dorsey & Whitney LLP, ptnr. in charge Fargo office, 1997—, co-head labor employment group, 1996—2000, mgmt. com. mem., group head for firm-wide regulatory group: Labor and Employment, Energy, Environ., Legislative, Indian, and Gaming, 2000—05. Mem. Fed. Practice Com., 8th Cir. Gender Task Force. Co-chair N.D. Gender Fairness, 1993-94. Mem. ND State Bar Assn. (pres. 2000), Cass County Bar Assn. Office: Dorsey & Whitney LLP Ste 402 Dakota Ctr 51 N Broadway Fargo ND 58102 Office Phone: 701-235-6000. Office Fax: 701-235-9969. Business E-Mail: herman.sarah@dorsey.com.

HERMAN, SIDNEY N., lawyer; b. Chgo., May 14, 1953; s. Leonard M. and Suzanne (Nierman) H.; m. Meg Dobies. BA, Haverford Coll., 1975; JD, Northwestern U., 1978. Bar: Ill. 1978, U.S. Dist. Ct. (no. dist.) Ill. 1978, U.S. Ct. Appeals (7th cir.) 1982, U.S. Supreme Ct. 1983. Assoc. Kirkland & Ellis, Chgo., 1978-84, equity ptnr., 1984-93; founding ptnr. Bartlit Beck Herman Palenchar & Scott, Chgo., 1993—. Bd. dirs. Todd Shipyards Corp., Sigmatron, Inc., Chgo., Global Material Techs., Chgo. Lawyers' Com. for Civil Rights Under Law, Inc.; mem. law bd. Northwestern U. Sch. Law. Articles editor Northwestern U. Law Rev. Trustee Francis W. Parker Sch.; bd. mem. Chgo. Lawyers' com. for Civil Rights Under Law. Mem. ABA, Ill. Bar Assn. Jewish. Office: Bartlit Beck Et Al Courthouse Pl 54 W Hubbard St Ste 300 Chicago IL 60610-4668 Office Phone: 312-494-4400. Business E-Mail: skip.herman@bartlit-beck.com.

HERMAN, STAN, fashion designer; b. NJ; Grad., U. Cin. Designer Jr. Forum, Mr. Mort, QVC, 1993—. Dir. 7th on Sixth fashion shows, 7th on Sale benefit; lectr. design schools around the world. Singer: (Operas) La Boheme, Die Fledermaus; performer: (Broadway plays) La Plume de ma Tante'; designer (uniforms) FedEx, McDonald's, Le Parker Meridien Hotel, MGM Grand, Monte Carlo, TWA Airlines, United Airlines, Amtrack Acela bullet trains. Recipient Coty Young Designer award, 1965, Coty Fashion award, 1969, 1975. Mem.: Gay Men's Health Classic (bd. mem.), Fashion Bid (bd. mem.), Bryant Park Restoration (bd. mem.), Midtown Manhattan Cmty. (bd. mem.), Richard Tucker Found. (bd. mem.), Coun. of Fashion Designers of Am. (pres. 1991—2006, Lifetime Achievement award 2006). Office: Council of Fashion Designers of America 80 W 40th St New York NY 10018 Office Phone: 212-840-3405.*

HERMAN, STEPHEN CHARLES, lawyer; b. Johnson City, NY, Apr. 28, 1951; s. William Herman and Myrtle Stella (Clark) Keithline; m. Jeanne Ellen Nelson, Sept. 9, 1972; children: Neelie Kristine, Stefanie Anne, Christopher William. Student, Cedarville Coll., 1969-72; BA, Wright State U., 1973; JD, Ohio No. U., 1976. Bar: Mo. 1977, Ill. 1977, Tex. 2004; U.S. Dist. Ct. (ea. dist.) Mo. 1978, U.S. Dist. Ct. (no. dist.) Ill. 1979, U.S. Dist. Ct. (ea. dist) Mich. 1988, U.S. Dist. Ct. (so. dist.) Tex. 1997; U.S. Ct. Appeals (D.C. cir.) 1979, U.S. Ct. Appeals (7th cir.) 1979, U.S. Ct. Appeals (5th cir.) 1980, U.S. Ct. Appeals (10th cir.) 1992; U.S. Supreme Ct. 1986, U.S. Ct. Internat. Trade, 1998. Atty. Mo. Pacific Railroad Co., St. Louis, 1977-78; assoc. Belnap, McCarthy, Spencer, Sweeney & Harkaway, Chgo., 1978-82; ptnr. Belnap, Spencer & McFarland, Chgo., 1982-83, Belnap, Spencer, McFarland & Emrich, Chgo., 1983-84, Belnap, Spencer, McFarland, Emrich & Herman, Chgo., 1984-89, Belnap, Spencer, McFarland, Herman, 1990-96, McFarland & Herman, 1996-01; atty. Stephen C. Herman, P.C., Chgo., 2001—03, Waco, Tex., 2003—06, LA, 2006—. Mem. Mo. Bar Assn., Ill. State Bar Assn., Chgo. Bar Assn., Tex. Bar Assn., Assn. Transp. Law Profls., Transp. Lawyers Assn. Office: 10850 Wilshire Blvd Ste 402 Los Angeles CA 90024 Home Phone: 310-470-4426; Office Phone: 310-470-8454. Personal E-mail: schrmn@aol.com.

HERMAN, WILLIAM ARTHUR, engineering and physics laboratory director; b. Washington, Mar. 9, 1947; s. William Jackson and Alma Rebecca (Wattwood) H. BSEE, George Washington U., 1968. Chief microwave sect. Southeastern Radiol. Health Lab., Montgomery, Ala., 1968-70; chief microwave measurements unit FDA, Rockville, Md., 1970-73, dep. chief. electromagnetics br., 1973-74, sr. engr. electromagnetics br., 1974-79, assoc. dir. divsn. electronic products, 1979-83, dir. divsn. phys. scis., 1983—2004; dep. dir. Office Sci. and Engring. Labs. CDRH/FDA, 2004—. Mem. Interagy. Group on Sci. Performance Measures, Rockville, 1994—96; staff mem. blue ribbon panel FDA, Washington, 1990; FDA coord. scholar-in-residence program NSF/FDA, 2003—; expert panelist NAS Symposium on Video Display Terminals and Vision, 1981, NIH Bioengring. Symposium: Bldg. the Future of Biology and Medicine, Instruments and Devices Panel, 1998; expert bioengring. panelist NSF, 1999—; mem. planning com. White House Conf. on emerging tech. for Am. with Disabilities, 2004. Contbr. articles to profl. jours.; patentee in field. With USPHS, 1968-74. Mem. IEEE (sr.), World Future soc., Mensa, Tau Beta Pi, Amnesty Internat., Cosmos Club, Sigma Tau, Omicron Delta Kappa, Phi Eta Sigma, Alpha Theta Nu.

HERMAN, WILLIAM CHARLES, lawyer; b. NYC, Nov. 6, 1935; s. Milton and Hortense (Rosenthal) H.; m. Elizabeth Leitner; children: Howard, Sarah Jane (dec.). BA, CCNY, 1958; LLB, Columbia U., 1959. Bar: N.Y. 1960, U.S. Dist. Ct. (so. and ea. dists.) 1964, U.S. Ct. Appeals (2d cir.) 1964, U.S. Supreme Ct. 1964. Assoc. Howard H. Spellman, NYC, 1960-61; pvt. practice law NYC, 1962-65; assoc. Gilbert S. Rosenthal, NYC, 1965-70; ptnr. Rosenthal & Herman, NYC, 1970-82, Rosenthal, Herman & Mantel, P.C., NYC, 1982-94, Rosenthal & Herman, P.C., NYC, 1994—2002, Herman Sloan Robarge & Sullivan, LLP, NYC, 2002—06, Rosenthal & Herman PC, NYC, 2007—. Bd. dirs., Camphill Spl. Schs., Inc., Glenmoore, Pa., 1980—; bd. dirs. Camphill Found., Kimberton, Pa., 1987—; trustee Camphill Assn., N.Am., Copake, N.Y., 1982—. With U.S. Army, 1959-60. Fellow Am. Acad. Matrimonial Lawyers; mem. ABA, N.Y. State Bar Assn., N.Y. County Lawyers Assn. (bd. dirs. 1979-85, chmn. matrimonial law com. 1982-84), Am. Coll. Family Trial Lawyers (diplomate). Avocations: charitable activities, fishing, platform tennis. Home: 95 Lord Kitchner Rd New Rochelle NY 10804-2230 Office Phone: 212-370-4900. E-mail: wch@randhpc.com.

HERMAN, WILLIAM GEORGE, municipal official; b. West Chester, Pa., Sept. 2, 1956; s. Albert William Jr. and Beverly Lou (Marshall) H.; m. Mary Jo Batchelder, July 7, 1983; children: Brian William, Andrew Albert. Grad. H.S., Weare, NH, 1974. Cert. pub. mgr. Reporter, photographer Union Leader Corp., Manchester, NH, 1973—80; prin., owner Herman Assocs. P.R., Manchester, 1980—82; press sec. Gov. John H: Sununu, Concord, NH, 1982—83; programs info. officer N.H. Divsn. Human Svcs., Concord, 1984—86, Divsn. Econ. Devel., Concord, 1986—92; pub. info. officer Fed. Emergency Mgmt., Boston, 1992—; town adminstr. Town of Milton, NH, 1993—95, Town of New Durham, NH, 1995—2005, Town of Auburn, NH, 2005—. Affiliate, cons. Mcpl. Resources, Inc., Meredith, 1995—; bd. dirs. N.H. Sch. Health Care Coalition, treas., 2002-2003, chmn. 2003-2005, NH Pub. Works Mut. Aid Program, 1999—, sec., treas. 2003-06, N.H. Pub. Works Stds. and Tng. Coun., 2000—, vice-chmn., 2000-03, chmn., 2003-06; mem. U.S. Selective Svc. #4, Merrimack County, 1999-2004. Vice chmn. US Selective Svc. # 10, Hillsborough County, 1982—98; chmn. Bd. Selectmen, Weare, NH, 1984—96; commr., officer So. NH Planning Commn., Manchester, 1984—96, 2007—; chmn. Concord Regional SW/RRC, 1987—; dir. Greater Manchester ARC, 1988—94; trustee YMCA Camp Coniston, Grantham, NH, 1989—93; dir. ARC Blood Svc., Dedham, Mass., 1989—98; dir., treas. New Durham Food Pantry, 2005—. Recipient George Washington honor medal Freedom Found., Valley Forge, Pa., 1973, Svc. award Town of Weare, 1996, Grassroots govt. leadership award Nat. Assn. Towns & Twps., Washington, 1991. Mem. Am. Acad. Cert. Pub. Mgrs. (ho. of dels. 2000—, chmn. integrated mktg. com. 2001-04, bylaws com. 2001-02, bd. dirs. mem.-at-large 2002-04, pres-elect 2005, pres., 2006, past pres. 2007), Internat. City/County Mgmt. Assn. (small cmtys. task force 1999-2001), N.H. Assn. Cert. Pub. Mgrs. (officer, sec. 1999-2001, treas. 2001-04), N.H. Mcpl. Mgmt. Assn. Republican. Avocations: reading, travel, computers. Home: 203 Loudon Rd Unit 721 Concord NH 03301 Office: Town of Auburn PO Box 309 Auburn NH 03032-0309

HERMAN, archbishop, head of Orthodox Church in America; b. Briarford, Pa., Feb. 1, 1932; Degree in bus. admin. and secretarial sci. with honors, Robert Morris Coll., Pitts.; grad., Saint Tikhon Seminary, South Canaan, Pa., 1963. Rector Saint John the Baptist Ch., Dundaff, Pa., Saints Peter and Paul Church, Uniondale, Pa.; tonsured to monastic rank Orthodox Ch. in Am., 1970, dep. abbot Saint Tikhon Monastery, 1971, ordained Holy Diaconate and Holy Priesthood, 1964, bishop of Wilkes-Barre, 1973—81, rector Saint Tikhon Monastery, 1981—, bishop of Phila., 1981—2002; elevated to archbishop, 1994—; archbishop of Washington, metropolitan of Am., Canada Orthodox Ch. in Am., 2002—. Adjutant Gen. Corps US Army, Labrador. Office: Orthodox Church in Am Saint Tikhon's Monastery South Canaan PA 18459

HERMANCE, FRANK S., electronics executive; b. Dec. 29, 1948; BSEE, Rochester Inst. Tech., 1971, MSEE, 1973. Sr. v.p. ops. Taylor Instrument Co., Rochester, NY; gen. mgr. waveform measurement div. Tektronix; group v.p. precision instruments div. Ametek Inc., Paoli, Pa., 1990—94, pres. electronic instruments group, 1994—96, exec. v.p., COO, 1996, pres., COO, 1996—99, pres., CEO, 1999—2000, chmn., CEO, 2001—. Bd. dir. IDEX Corp. Bd. mem. Portland Cmty. Coll. Fellow: Am. Soc. Mech. Engineers Internat.; mem.: Engring. Soc. for Advanced Mobility Land Sea Air Internat., IEEE, Mfr. Alliance for Productivity & Innovation, World Affairs Council Phila. (vice-chmn.). Office: Ametek Inc Bldg 4 37 N Valley Rd Paoli PA 19301*

HERMANCE, MYRON E., JR., conductor, educator; b. Hudson, NY, May 7, 1928; s. Myron Erastus and Thelma (Miller) Hermance; m. Alicia Van Zoeren Hermance, June 21, 1952; children: Susan Adella, Dirk Edward, Melanie Jo, Peter Alan, Gay Marie, Rhonda Kay, Philip Jon. MusM, Ind. U., 1956; BA, Hope Coll., 1950. Cert. Secondary Teaching Mich., 1950, Music Education NY State, 1961. Profl. vocalist chs., colls. and theater, Western Mich. and Ea. NY, 1952—; pvt. voice educator NY, 1952—; vocal and instrumental educator Fremont HS, Mich., 1952—57; music supr. Holton Pub. Schs., Mich., 1957—60; vocal music educator Schenectady City Schools, NY, 1960—87; cellist Music Co. Orch., Burnt Hills, NY, 2003. Orchestral condr. Albany and Schenectady Sr. Ctrs., 1994—2006; ch. music ministry Ref. Chs., Schenectady and Albany, NY, Congl. Ch., Fremont, Mich., 1952—60. Chaplain US Power Squadron, 1996—2007; commd. preacher Reformed Ch. Am., 2001—07. Recipient Teacher's Performance Inst., Rockefeller Found., Oberlin Coll., 1968. Mem.: NY State Sch. Music Assn. (all-state voice judge 1997—2006), Music Educators Nat. Conf., Nat. Assn. Tchrs. of Singing (life). Democrat. Avocations: civil war historian, genealogy, theology, art, boating. Home and Studio: 25 Alvey St Schenectady NY 12304 E-mail: mehermance@aol.com.

HERMANCE, RONALD E., JR., bank executive; CFO Southold Savs. Bank, NY; bd. mgrs. Hudson City Savs. Bank, 1988, sr. exec. v-p., COO, 1988—97, pres., COO, 1997—2002, Hudson City Bancorp, Inc., 1999—2002; pres., CEO Hudson City Bancorp, Inc. and Hudson City Savs. Bank, 2002—, chmn., 2005—. Bd. dirs. Fed. Home Loan Bank NY, 2004—. Office: Hudson City Bancorp Inc West 80 Century Rd Paramus NJ 07652 Office Phone: 201-967-1900.*

HERMAN-GIDDENS, GREGORY, lawyer; BA, U. NC, 1984; JD, Tulane U., 1988; LLM in Estate Planning, U. Miami, 1993; grad., Leadership Chapel Hill, Carrboro, 2006. Bar: NC 1988, US Dist. Ct. (mid. dist.) NC 1988, Fla. 1992, US Tax Ct. 2001, US Supreme Ct. 1998, US Tax Ct. 2001, Tenn. 2004; CFP; cert. specialist in estate planning and probate law, NC State Bar Bd. Legal Specialization; grad. leadership triangle program 1996; cert. fin. planner Bd. Stds., Inc., 2007. Assoc. N. Joanne Foil, Atty. at Law, Durham, N.C., 1988-92, Catalano, Fisher, Gregory & Crown, Chartered, Naples, Fla., 1993, Northen, Blue, Rooks, Thibaut, Anderson & Woods, L.L.P., Chapel Hill, N.C., 1994-96; pvt. practice Chapel Hill, 1996—. Profl. adv. com. Triangle Cmty. Found., 1999—; lectr. in field. Mem. Chapel Hill Bd. Adjustment, 1989—92; bd. dirs. Friends of Chapel Hill Sr.Ctr., 1994—97; mem. Orange County Adv. Bd. on Aging, 1994—97, vice chair, 1996—97; treas., bd. dirs. Orange County Literacy Coun., Carrboro, NC, 1994—98. Named one of NC Legal Elite in Tax and Estate Planning, 2007, NC Super Lawyer in Estate Planning and Probate Law, 2007. Mem.: ABA (probate and trust sect. 1996—, coms. on stds. of tax practice and tax practice mgmt. of tax sect., coms. on lifetime and testamentary charitable gift planning, com. on planning for execs. and profls. of real property), Durham/Orange Estate Planning Coun., Nat. Acad. Elder Law Attys., NC Bar Assn. (career devel. com. young lawyers divsn. 1990—91, law and aging com. young lawyers divsn. 1994—98, dir. young lawyers divsn. 1997—98, endowment com. 1997—, elder law sect. coun. 1998—2001, newsletter editor 2001—03), Psi Chi, Phi Beta Kappa. Office: 205 Providence Rd Chapel Hill NC 27514 Office Phone: 919-493-6351. Business E-Mail: ghgiddens@trustcounselpa.com.

HERMANIES, JOHN HANS, retired lawyer; b. Aug. 19, 1922; s. John and Lucia (Eckstein) H.; m. Dorothy Jean Steinbrecher, Jan. 3, 1953. AB, Pa. State U., 1944; JD, U. Cin., 1948, D of Law (hon.), 1992. Bar: Ohio 1948. Atty. Indsl. Commn. Ohio, 1948-50; asst. atty. gen. State of Ohio, 1951-57, asst. to gov., 1957-59; ptnr. Hermanies & Major (formerly Beall, Hermanies, Bortz & Major), Cin., 1958-99; mem. bd. grievances and discipline Supreme Ct. Ohio, 1976-82; ret., 1999. Mem. Ohio Bd. Bar Examiners, 1963—68. Mem. Southwest Ohio Regional Transit Authority, 1973-76; trustee U. Cin, 1977-92, Found. Bd., 1992-99, trustee emeritus, 1999—; mem. bd. elections Hamilton County, Ohio, 1984-88; chmn. exec. com. Hamilton County Rep. Party, 1974-88. With USMC, WWII. Mem. ABA, Ohio Bar Assn., Cin. Bar Assn., Queen City Club, Hyde Park Golf and Country Club. Home: 1201 Edgecliff Pl Cincinnati OH 45206-2847

HERMANN, ALLEN MAX, physics professor; b. New Orleans, July 17, 1938; s. Edward Frederick and Miriam (Davidson) H.; m. Leonora Christopher, May 19, 1979; children: Miriam, Mary, Neil, Scott. BS with honors in Physics, Loyola U., New Orleans, 1960; MS in Physics, U. Notre Dame, 1962; PhD in Physics, Tex. A&M U., 1965. Sr. rsch. scientist Jet Propulsion Lab., Pasadena, Calif., 1965—67, tech. mgr., 1985—86; asst. prof. physics Tulane U., New Orleans, 1967—70, assoc. prof. physics, 1970—75, prof. physics, 1975—81; task mgr. Solar Energy Rsch. Inst., Golden, Colo., 1980—85; prof., chmn. dept. physics U. Ark., Fayetteville, 1986—89, Disting. prof., 1989; prof. dept. physics U. Colo., Boulder, 1990—2005; vis. prof. dept. elec. and computer engring. U. Ky., Lexington, 2005—07; dir. Ctr. Nanoscale Sci. and Engring. U Ky., 2005—07. Cons. Jet Propulsion Lab., 1978-81, 86-87, NASA-Lewis Rsch. Ctr., Cleve., 1978-80, Cardiac Pacemakers Inc., Mpls., 1976-79, Radiation Monitoring Devices, Newton, Mass., 1990-93, Superconducting Core Techs., Denver, 1989-95, Sumitomo Electric Industries, Osaka, Japan, 1991-98, MV Sys., Inc., Golden, 1999—. Founding co-editor Applied Physics Communication; editor: Applied Physics Book Series; contbr. numerous articles to profl. jours. Bd. dirs. Colo. Assn. Retarded Citizens, Denver, 1983-85. Recipient NASA Outstanding Achievement award 1970, 72, Disting. Scientist award Am. Assn. Physics Tchrs., 1987; named Hero, State of Ark., Ark. Times mag.; named Person of the Yr., Superconductivity Week, 1989; elected to Acad. Disting. Grads., Coll. Sci., Tex. A&M U., 1999. Fellow Am. Phys. Soc.; mem. IEEE (sr.). Home: 2704 Lookout View Dr Golden CO 80401-2520 Office: U Colo PO Box 390 Boulder CO 80309-0390 Business E-Mail: allen.hermann@colorado.edu.

HERMANN, DONALD HAROLD JAMES, law educator; b. Southgate, Ky., Apr. 6, 1943; s. Albert Joseph and Helen Marie (Snow) H. AB (George E. Gamble Honors scholar), Stanford U., 1965; JD, Columbia U., 1968; LLM, Harvard U., 1974; MA, Northwestern U., 1979, PhD, 1981; MA in Art History, Sch. Art Inst. Chgo., 1993; MLA, U. Chgo., 2001. Bar: Ariz. 1968, Wash. 1969, Ky. 1971, Ill. 1972, U.S. Supreme Ct. 1974. Mem. staff, directorate devel. plans U.S. Dept. Def., 1964-65; With Legis. Drafting Research Fund, Columbia U., 1966-68; asst. dean Columbia Coll., 1967-68; mem. faculty U. Wash., Seattle, 1968-71, U. Ky., Lexington, 1971-72, DePaul U., 1972—, prof. law and philosophy, 1978—, dir. acad. programs and interdisciplinary study, 1975-76, assoc. dean, 1975-78, dir. Health Law Inst., 1985—2000; lectr. dept. philosophy Northwestern U., 1979-81; counsel DeWolfe, Poynton & Stevens, 1984-89. Vis. prof. Washington U., St. Louis, 1974, U. Brazilia, 1976, U. P.R. Sch. Law, 1993; lectr. law Am. Soc. Found., 1975-78, Sch. Edn. Northwestern U., 1974-76, Christ Coll. Cambridge (Eng.) U., 1977, U. Athens, 1980; vis. scholar U. N.D., 1983; mem. NEH seminar on property and rights Stanford U., 1981; participant law and econs. program U. Rochester, 1974; mem. faculty summer seminar in law and humanities UCLA, 1978; Bicentennial Fellow of U.S. Constitution Claremont Coll., 1986; Law and Medicine fellow Cleve. Clinic., 1990; bd. dirs. Coun. Legal Edn. Opportunity, Ohio Valley Consortium, 1972, Ill. Bar Automated Rsch. Corp., 1975-81, Criminal Law Consortium Cook County, Ill., 1977-80; cons. Adminstrv. Office Ill. Cts., 1975-90; reporter cons. Ill. Jud. Conf., 1972-90; mem. Ctr. for Law Focused Edn., Chgo., 1977-81; faculty Instituto Superiore Internazionale Di Science Criminali, Siracusa, Italy, 1978-82; cons. Commerce Fedn., State of São Paulo, Brazil, 1975; residential scholar Christ Ch., Oxford, 1999. Editor: Jour. of Health and Hosp. Law, 1986-96, DePaul Jour. Healthcare Law, 1996—, AIDS Monograph Series, 1987—. Mem. Cook County States Atty. Task Force on Gay and Lesbian Issues, 1990—, Contemporary Arts Coun. Chgo., 1999—; bd. dirs. Ctr. Ch.-State Studies, 1982—, Horizons Cmty. Svcs., 1985—88, Chgo. Area AIDS Task Force, 1987—90, Howard Brown Health Ctr., 1994—; v.p. Inst. Genetics, Law and Ethics, Ill. Masonic Hosp., 1993—2000; trustee 860 N. Lakeshore Trust, Chgo., 1993—95; bd. visitors Oriental Inst. U. Chgo., 1995—; co-chair parity and inclusion com. Ill. HIV Prevention Cmty. Group Ill. Dept. Pub. Health; dir. Inst. Genetics, Law and Ethics, Ill. Masonic Hosp., 1993—2000; bd. dirs. Gerber-Hart Libr. and Archives, Mostly Music of Chgo., 1998—2001; mem. scholars' group ethics and med. rsch. NIH/U. Ill. Med. Sch. John Noble fellow Columbia U., 1968, Internat. fellow, NEH fellow, Law and Humanities fellow U. Chgo, 1975-76, Law and Humanities fellow Harvard U., 1973-74, Northwestern U., 1978-82, Criticism and Theory fellow Stanford U. 1981, NEH fellow Cornell U., 1982, Judicial fellow U.S. Supreme Ct., 1983-84, U. Ill. fellow med. ethids rsch. group; Dean's scholar Columbia U., 1968, Univ. scholar Northwestern U., 1979. Mem.: ABA, Am. Inn of Ct. (Abraham Lincoln Marowitz chpt.), Chgo. Coun. Fgn. Rels., Ill. Assn. Hosp. Attys., Am. Acad. Healthcare Attys., Am. Assn. Law Schs. (del., sect. chmn., chmn. sect. on jurisprudence), Soc. Am. Law Tchrs., Internat. Penal Law Soc., Soc. Writers on Legal Subjects, Soc. Phenomenology and Existential Philosophy, Soc. Bus. Ethics, Am. Philos. Assn., Am. Judicature Soc., Nat. Health Lawyers Assn., Internat. Assn. Philosophy of Law and Soc., Am. Soc. Polit. and Legal Philosophy, Am. Soc. Law, Medicine and Ethics, Am. Law Inst., Am. Acad. Polit. and Social Sic., Chgo. Bar Assn., Ill. Bar Assn., Soc. Contemporary Art Art Inst. Chgo., Evanston Hist. Soc., Northwestern U. Alumni Assn., Chgo. Literary Soc., Quadrangle Players, Renaissance Soc. (bd. dirs. 1995—), Lawyers Club Chgo., Arts Club Chgo., Cliff Dwellers Club, Tavern Club, Quadrangle Club, University Club, Hasty Pudding Club, Signet Club Harvard. Episcopalian.

HERMANN, JANIE, librarian; MLIS, U. Western Ont., 1996. Middle sch. tchr., Kingston, Ont.; rsch. asst. U. Western Ont.; children's literature libr. Nat. Libr. Can.; reference & interlibr. loan libr. Hobart & William Smith Colls., Geneva, NY; tech. training libr. Princeton Pub. Libr., NJ, founder Tuesday Tech. Talks@PPL. Named one of the Movers & Shakers, Libr. Jour., 2007. Office: Princeton Pub Libr 65 Witherspoon St Princeton NJ 08542 Office Phone: 609-924-9529. E-mail: JHermann@princetonlibrary.org.

HERMANN, KELLY A., music educator; b. Sacramento, Apr. 5, 1982; d. Mark A. and Donna J. Hermann. MusB, Evangel U., Springfield, Mo., 2004; MusM, Mo. State U., Springfield, 2007. Undergrad. tchg. asst. Evangel U., Springfield, Mo., 2002—04; office asst. Ctrl. Assembly God, Springfield, 2004—06; grad. tchg. asst. Mo. State U., Springfield, 2006—. Music theory tutor Mo. State U., 2005—07. Ch. choir mem. Ctrl. Assembly God, 2003—07. Mem.: Mo. Music Educators Assn., Mu Phi Epsilon (rec. sec. 2006—07, Disting. Svc. award 2005), Concert Chorale (treas. 2006—07), Pi Kappa Lambda, Alpha Chi.

HERMANN, ROBERT BELL, physical chemist, consultant; b. Bellevue, Pa., Dec. 12, 1930; s. Gustave Adolph and Alida Hermann; m. Phyllis Ann Halley, Aug. 7, 1958 (div. Feb. 1982); children: Deborah, David, Stephen; m. Carol Sue Lester, June 12, 1985. BS in Chemistry, U. Mich., 1953; MS, Wayne State U., 1960, PhD, 1962. Organic chemist Parke-Davis & Co., Detroit, 1953-58; NSF postdoctoral fellow U. Wis., Madison, 1962-63; postdoctoral fellow Ill. Inst. Tech., Chgo., 1963-64; computational chemist Eli Lilly & Co., Indpls., 1964-93. Vis. prof. Ind. U.-Purdue U. Ind., Indpls., 1994—; cons. Eli Lilly & Co., 1994—. Contbr. articles to profl. jours. Presbyterian. Achievements include research of relationship between molecular surface area and solubility especially with regard to hyrdophobic interactions; patent for inhibitors of phospholipase A2. Office Phone: 317-277-8608. Personal E-mail: robeherma@aol.com.

HERMANN, ROBERT CHARLES, JR., neurologist, educator; b. Temple, Tex., Aug. 1, 1944; s. Robert Charles and Jewel Irene Hermann; m. Mary Frances Goggans; children: Robert Charles III, Randall Scott. MD, U. Tex., Galveston, 1965—69. Cert. neurologist Am. Bd. Neurology/Psychiatry, 1979, in electromyography Am. Assn. Electrodiagnostic Medicine, 1988, clinical neurophysiologist Am. Bd. Neurology/Psychiatry, 1996. Med. internship U. Tex. Med. Br., 1969—70, assoc. prof., 2002—03; neurology resident Mayo Clinic, Rochester, Minn., 1970—75, cons. neurology, asst. prof, 1975—88, 1990—2002, cons. neurology Scottsdale, Ariz., 1988—90, emeritus prof. Rochester, 2002—06; clin. prof. neurology/medicine U. Tex. Health Sci. Ctr., San Antonio, 2003—. Dir. electromyography lab. U. Tex. Med. Br., 2002—03; emg lab. dir. UTHSCSA, San Antonio, 2003—. Contbr. articles to profl. jours., chapters to books. Maj. USAF, 1971—73, Lackland AFB. Recipient Woltman award for outstanding resident in neurology, Mayo Clinic, 1975, Tchr. of Yr. award, Mayo Med. Fellows Assn., 1982, 1984, 1991, 1997, Outstanding Tchr. award in basic scis., Mayo Med. Sch., 1985, Tchg. Hall of Fame, Mayo Med. Fellows Assn., 1997, Spl. Recognition award for tchg. in clin. neurophysiology, Mayo Clinic, 2002, Hall of Fame, Taylor HS, 2003, Taylor Legends award, 2006. Fellow: Am. Acad. Neurology. Office: Univ Tex Health Sci Ctr SA 4647 Medical Dr San Antonio TX 78229 Home Phone: 830-755-6064. Business E-Mail: hermannr@uthscsa.edu.

HERMANN, ROBERT EWALD, retired surgeon; b. Highland, Ill., Jan. 28, 1929; s. Ewald E. and Erna (Pabst) H.; m. Barbara Bower, Aug. 23, 1952 (dec. Aug. 1980); m. Polly Dreher, Mar. 8, 1986; childrn: Robert Jr., Barry, Monty. AB cum laude, Harvard U., 1950; MD, Washington U., St. Louis, 1954. Diplomate Am. Bd. Surgery. Intern, resident Univ. Hosps., Cleve., 1954-61; chmn. gen. surgery Cleve. Clinic, 1969—94, emeritus cons. dept. gen. surgery, 1994—96; clin. prof. surgery Case Western Res. Sch. Medicine, Cleve., 1970—96. Dir. Am. Bd. Surgery, Phila., 1975-81; mem. Residency Rev. Com., Chgo., 1975-81. Author: Surgery of Gallbladder, Bile Ducts, Pancreas, 1979, Surgical Practice of Cleveland Clinic, 1985; contbr. over 180 articles to med. jours., 53 chpts. to books. Trustee Cleve. Clinic Found., 1976-77. Capt. M.C. U.S. Army, 1956-57. Recipient Roswell Park Gold medal Buffalo Surg. Soc., 1993. Mem. ACS (gov. 1981-87, v.p. 1996-97, Disting. Svc. award 1994), Am. Surg. Soc., German Surg. Soc. (hon.), Internat. Surg. Soc., Internat. Coll. Surgeons (hon.), Soc. Surg. Oncology, Soc. Surgery Alimenatary Tract (pres. 1988-89), Assn. Program Dirs. Surgery (pres. 1979-81), Ea. Surg. Soc. (pres. 1985-86), Pan-Pacific Surg. Assn. (v.p. 1991-93), Joint Commn. on Accreditation of Healthcare Orgns. (bd. commrs. 1997-2002). Republican. Avocations: tennis, golf, sailing, music. Home: 1 Bratenahl Pl Apt 1403 Bratenahl OH 44108-1156 Office: Cleve Clinic A-80 9500 Euclid Ave Cleveland OH 44195-0001 Personal E-mail: rhermannmd@aol.com.

HERMANN, ROBERT JAY, former manufacturing executive, consultant; b. Sheldahl, Iowa, Apr. 6, 1933; s. John and Ellen Melinda (Ericson) H.; m. Darlene Velda Lowman, Mar. 20, 1954; children: Scott Alan, Sherie Lynn. BSEE, Iowa State U., 1954, MSEE, 1959, PhD, 1963. Dep. dir. research and engring. Nat. Security Agy., Ft. Meade, Md., 1973-75; spl. asst. to supreme allied comr. Europe SHAPE, Casteau, Belgium, 1975-77; dep. under sec. of def. for research and engring. Dept. Def., Washington, 1977-79, asst. sec. of Air Force for research, devel. and logistics, 1979-81; dir. Nat. Reconnaissance, 1979-81; spl. asst. for intelligence to under sec. of def. for research engring. Dept. Def., Washington, 1981-82; v.p. systems tech. and analysis United Techs., Hartford, Conn., 1982-84, v.p. advanced systems def. and space group, 1984-87, v.p. sci. and tech., 1987-92, sr. v.p. sci. and tech., 1992-98; sr. ptnr. Global Tech. Partners, LLC, 1998—. Cons. Def. Sci. Bd., 1985-; mem. vis. com. advanced tech. Nat. Inst. Stds. and Tech., 1992-97; mem. Pres. Fgn. Intelligence Adv. Bd., 1993-01; mem. commn. on phys. scis., math. and applications NRC, 1993-98; bd. dirs. Draper Labs., 1992-01, Am. Nat. Stds. Inst., 1994-02. 1st lt. USAF, 1955-57. Recipient Arthur Fleming Washington Jaycees, 1972; recipient Nat. Capital Nat. Capital Area Architects and Engrs., Washington, 1967, Air Force Disting. Service medal USAF, Washington, 1980, Disting. Grad. award Iowa State U., 1995. Mem. NAE, AIAA, Armed Forces Comms. and Electronics Assn. (bd. dirs. 1979-83), Security Affairs Support Assn. (pres. 1983-86, award 1994), Navy League (chmn. indsl. exec. bd. 1989, Dept. Def. Fubini award 2004). Home: 1 Carnoustie Cir Bloomfield CT 06002 Office Phone: 860-216-5531. Personal E-mail: rjhinct@aol.com.

HERMANN, THOMAS C., chemistry professor; b. Wertingen, Bavaria, Germany, Sept. 30, 1966; MS, U. Ulm, 1986—92; PhD, Ludwig-Maximilians U., Munich, 1992—96. Post-doctoral fellow Institut de Biologie Moléculaire et Cellulaire, CNRS, Strasbourg, France, 1996—98; rsch. assoc. Meml. Sloan-Kettering Cancer Ctr., NYC, 1999—2001; sr. scientist Anadys Pharmaceuticals, Inc., San Diego, Calif., 2001—02, prin. scientist, 2002—05; asst. prof. U. Calif. San Diego, La Jolla, 2005—. Recipient Otto-Hahn medal, Max-Planck Soc., 1996; fellow, Studienstiftung des Deutschen Volkes, 1988—91; grantee PhD fellowship, 1993—96, Long-Term fellowship, European Molecular Biology Orgn., 1996—98. Mem.: Am. Chem. Soc. Office: Univ Calif San Diego 9500 Gilman Dr La Jolla CA 92093-0358 Office Fax: 858-534-0202. Business E-Mail: tch@ucsd.edu.

HERMANSEN, JOHN CHRISTIAN, application developer, linguist, consultant; b. Athens, Greece, Oct. 21, 1949; s. John Theodore and Lois Ann Hermansen; m. Sharyl Lynn Miner (div. 1994); children: John Theodore, Janet Lois. BA in Speech, Linguistics, Pa. State U., 1975; PhD in Computational Linguistics, Georgetown U., 1985. Cert. knowledge engr., 1992. Propr. CompAssociates, Inc., Washington, 1974-78; lectr., univ. fellow computational linguistics Georgetown U., Washington, 1980-83, dir. Lang. Processing Ctr., Sch. Langs. and Linguistics, 1982-85; artificial intelligence rsch. scientist Planning Rsch. Corp., McLean, Va., 1985-88, computational linguistics cons., 1988-90; cons. knowledge engring. Sterling Software, Inc., McLean, 1991-95; lead scientist linguistics analysis team State Dept. CLASS Project, Lang. Analysis Systems, Inc., Herndon, Va., 1986—2002; computational linguistics cons. Ctr. for Applied Linguistics, Washington, 1985-94; CEO Lang. Analysis Systems, Inc., Herndon, 1991—2006; CTO IBM Global Name Recognition, Va., 2006—. Instr. effects of Asian organized crime on U.S., Fla. NG, 2000; spkr. in field Co-author: Southeast Asia Refugee Testing Report, Vols. I and II, 1985, Report on the Evaluation of Kenya Radio Language Arts Project, 1985, PAKTUS Version 1 User's Guide, 1986, Building NLU Systems in the PAKTUS Environment: Developer's Introduction, 1987, Message Processing Systems: Evaluation Factors, 1987, Meronomy, Word Experts and Prepositional Phrase Attachment in PAKTUS, 1989, Techniques in Multilingual Name Searching, 1989, The Automated Templating System for Database Update from Unformatted Message Traffic, 1995, The On-Line Name Reference Library Project, 1999, Combatting Asian Organized Crime, 2001, Advanced Name Matching for Enhanced Airline Security, 2002, Predictive Technology and Border Security, 2002, Name Recognition Tech., 2003, Names Have Currency, Technology for Finance, 2003, Asian Name Tracing, Interpol, 2005, Tracking Terrorists, 2005, Metadata about Names, 2005, Global Security: The Asian Perspective, Singapore, 2005, Interpol Complex Crime Symposium, 2006; contbr. articles to profl. jours.; patentee in field. Recipient Fast 50 Champion CEO, Fast Co. mag., 2003, Fed. Computer Week "Fed. 100" award, 2004. Mem. IEEE, Assn. for Computational Linguistics, Internat. Assn. Knowledge Engrs., Data Adminstrn. Mgmt. Assn. Home: 12012 Robin Dr Catharpin VA 20143-1307 Office: IBM Global Name Recognition 2214 Rock Hill Rd Herndon VA 20170-4214 Office Phone: 703-435-0378. E-mail: jhermansen@us.ibm.com.

HERMANSEN, MARCUS C., pediatrics professor, director; b. Rensselaer, Ind., Sept. 14, 1952; s. Henry J. and P. Elaine Hermansen; m. Mary Goetz Hermansen, Jan. 2, 1997; children: Sloan Baloga, R. Ian Wilson,

Vanessa Wilson, Lauren Wilson, Caitlin Barnhart. BS, Purdue U., West Lafayette, Ind., 1974; MD, Ind. U., Indpls., 1977. Diplomate Am. Bd. Pediat., 1982, Am. Bd. of Pediat., Sub-Bd. Neonatal-Perinatal Medicine, 1983. Neonatologist U. Ky., Lexington, 1982—86; dir. neonatology Allegheny Gen. Hosp., Pitts., 1986—95, Riverside Regional Med. Ctr., Newport News, Va., 1994—97, So. NH. Med. Ctr., Nashua, 1997—; assoc. prof. pediat. Dartmouth Med. Sch., Hanover, NH, 1997—. Author: Perinatal Causes of Cerebral Palsy, 2006, Risk Management in Neonatal-Perinatal Medicine, 2005. Vol. mediator City Nashua, 1997—. Recipient Kenney Rsch. award, Midwest Soc. Pediat. Rsch., 1982, Physician Champion, So. NH. Health Sys., 2006. Fellow: Am. Acad. Pediat. Home: 14 Gregg Rd Nashua NH 03062 Office: So NH Med Ctr 8 Prospect St Nashua NH 03061-2014 Home Phone: 606-883-8243; Office Phone: 603-883-5955. Office Fax: 603-883-5951. Personal E-mail: doublethis@gmail.com. E-mail: marcus.hermansen@snhmc.org.

HERMELING, CAROLINE L., lawyer; b. St. Louis, 1961; BA in Econs., U. Notre Dame, 1983; JD cum laude, St. Louis U., 1986. Bar: Mo. 1986, Ill. 1987, US Dist. Ct. (ea. dist. Mo.). CEO, mem. exec. com. Husch & Eppenberger, LLC, St. Louis, 2007—. Recipient Vol. Lawyer award, Legal Svcs. of Ea. Mo. Vol. Lawyers Prog., 2001, Justice award, St. Louis Daily Record, 2007. Mem.: Ill. State Bar Assn., Comml. Real Estate Women. Office: Husch & Eppenberger LLC Ste 600 190 Carondelet Plz Saint Louis MO 63105-3441 Office Phone: 314-480-1922. Office Fax: 314-480-1505. E-mail: carrie.l.hermeling@husch.com.

HERMINGHOUSE, PATRICIA ANNE, foreign language educator; b. Melrose Park, Ill., Mar. 13, 1940; m. 1964; 2 children. BA, Knox Coll., 1962; MA, Washington U., 1965, PhD in German, 1968. Asst. prof. German U. Mo.-St. Louis, 1966-67, vis. lectr., 1968-69; asst. prof. Washington U., St. Louis, 1967-78, assoc. prof. German, 1978-83; Fuchs prof. German studies U. Rochester, NY, 1983—, chmn. dept. fgn. langs., lits. and linguistics NY, 1983—89. Lectr. German, Fontbonne Coll., 1965-66. Internat. Research & Exchanges Bd. ad hoc grantee, 1976. Editor or co-editor: Literatur der DDR in den siebziger Jahren, 1983, Literatur und Literaturtheorie in der DDR, 1976, Frauen im Mittelpunkt, 1987, Gender and Germaness, 1997, Ingeborg Bachmann and Christa Wolf, 1998, German Feminist Writings, 2000; editor GDR Bull., Newsletter Lit. and Culture in German Dem. Republic, 1975-83; co-editor: Women in German Yearbook, 1994-2002. Recipient Susan B. Anthony Lifetime Achievement award, 2003; grantee Fulbright German Studies Summer Seminar, 2005; sr. fellow, NEH, 1991. Mem. MLA, Am. Assn. Tchrs. German (exec. coun. 1979-81), German Studies Assn. (exec. com., v.p./pres. 2001-02, pres. 2003-04), Coalition Women German (coord. 1974-75, nat. steering. com. 1976-79, 94-2002), Assn. Depts. Fgn. Langs. (exec. com.). Address: U Rochester Dept Modern Lang and Cultures Box 270082 Rochester NY 14627-0082 Business E-Mail: pahe@troi.cc.rochester.edu.

HERMSEN, JAMES R., lawyer; b. Orange, Calif., Oct. 2, 1945; BA, U. Wash., 1967, JD, 1970. Bar: Wash. 1971, Oreg. 2004. Mem. Bogle & Gates, PLLC, Seattle, Dorsey & Whitney, Seattle, 2000—, ptnr., trial, regulatory, tech. group. Mem. Bur. of Competition Fed. Trade Commn., 1971-73. Mem. Seattle-King County Bar Assn., Wash. State Bar Assn., Phi Beta Kappa, Omicron Delta Epsilon, Phi Delta Phi. Office: Dorsey & Whitney 1420 5th Ave Ste 3400 Seattle WA 98101-4010 Office Phone: 206-903-8852. Office Fax: 206-903-8820. E-mail: hermsen.james@dorsey.com.

HERMSEN, KENNETH PAUL, dental educator, forensic odontologist; b. Omaha, Nebr., June 7, 1948; s. Kenneth Leo and Lois Elaine Hermsen; m. Linda Kay Wilson, June 26, 1970; children: Kevin Patrick, Michael Scott. BS, U. Nebr., Lincoln, 1971; DDS, U. Nebr. Med. Ctr., Lincoln, 1975; MS, U. Nebr., Lincoln, 1980. Cert. endodontics U. Nebr. Med. Ctr. Coll. of Dentistry. Endodontist Heartland Endodontic Specialists, Omaha, 1990—2006; assoc. prof. endodontics Creighton U. Sch. of Dentistry, Omaha, 1977—90, 2006—. Forensic dental cons. Douglas County Coroner's Office, Omaha, 1991—; forensic odontologist region 7 Disaster Mortuary Operational Response Team, Nebr., 1996—; leader Nebr. Forensic Dental Identification Team, Omaha, 2002—; co-chairperson Mass Fatality Response Subcom., Omaha Metro Med. Response Sys., 2003—; forensic dental cons. Eppley Airport Fire and Rescue, Omaha, 2004—; dental dir. Hope Med. Outreach Coalition, Omaha, 2005—. Founding com. mem. Nebr. Wind Symphony, Omaha, 1975—76; dental rep. Omaha Oral Health Collaborative, 1997—; participating dentist Hope Med. Outreach Coalition, Omaha, 1998—2005. Recipient Champion of Hope award, Hope Med. Outreach Coalition, 2002, Outstanding Tchr. award, Creighton U. Sch. of Dentistry Graduating Class, 1979, 1980, 1983, 1984. Fellow: Am. Coll. Dentists; mem.: ADA, Am. Soc. of Forensic Odontology, Am. Acad. of Forensic Sciences, Nebr. Assn. of Endodontists (pres. 1991—92), Am. Assn. of Endodontists, Nebr. Dental Assn. (trustee 1997—2000), Omaha Dist. Dental Soc. (pres. 1996—97), Pierre Fauchard Acad., Omicron Kappa Upsilon. Office: Creighton U Sch Dentistry 2500 California Plz Omaha NE 68178 Home Phone: 402-493-3907; Office Phone: 402-280-4574. Personal E-mail: kenher8630@aol.com. Business E-Mail: kennethhermsen@creighton.edu.

HERNANDEZ, ANTONIA, foundation administrator, lawyer; b. Torreon, Coahuila, Mexico, May 30, 1948; came to U.S., 1956; d. Manuel and Nicolasa (Martinez) H.; m. Michael Stern, Oct. 8, 1977; children: Benjamin, Marisa, Michael. BA, UCLA, 1971, JD, 1974. Bar: Calif. 1974, D.C. 1979. Staff atty. Los Angeles Ctr. Law and Justice, 1974-77; directing atty. Legal Aid Found., Lincoln Heights, Calif., 1977-78; staff counsel U.S. Senate Com. on the Judiciary, Washington, 1979-80; assoc. counsel Mexican Am. Legal Def. Edn. Fund, Washington, 1981-83, employment program dir., 1983-84, exec. v.p., dep. gen. counsel Los Angeles, 1984-85, pres., gen. counsel, 1985—2004; pres., CEO Calif. Community Found., 2004—. Bd. dirs. Golden West Financial Corp., Automobile Club of So. Calif., Am. Charities. Contbr. articles to profl. jours. Active Inter-Am. Dialogue Aspen Inst., Nat. Com. Innovations in State and Local Govt., Nat. Endowment for Democracy, Pres.'s Commn. White House Fellowships; trustee Rockefeller Found. AAUW fellow, 1973-74. Mem. ABA, State Bar Calif., Washington D.C. Bar Assn., Mexican-Am. Roman Catholic. Avocations: gardening, outdoor sports. Office: Calif Community Found 445 S Figueroa St Los Angeles CA 90071

HERNANDEZ, CARLOS I., historian, educator; b. Mayaguez, PR, Aug. 2, 1965; s. Americo and Armida Hernandez; m. Xenia I. Medina, July 4, 1993; children: Diego, Rocio I. BA, U. P.R., Mayaguez, 1990; PhD in History, U. P.R., Rio Piedras, 2005; MA in History, Ctr. Advanced Studies P.R.and the Caribbean, San Juan, PR, 1996. Instr. U. P.R., Aguadilla, 1997—99, Ponce, 1999—2002, Utuado, 2002—02, Río Piedras. Coord. com. for the autonomy U. P.R., Aguadilla, 1997—99. Contbr. articles to profl. jours. Rschr. Atlantea Project U. P.R., Rio Piedras, 1997—2005. Decanato de Estudios Graduados e Investigacion grantee, U. P.R., 2003—04. Mem.: Ramey AFB Hist. Assn. (assoc.), Internat. Assn. Oral History (assoc.), Puerto Rican Assn. Historians (assoc.). Avocations: surfing, chess. Home: Urb Constancia LafayetteSt #3264 Ponce PR 00717 Home Phone: 787-812-0769. Home Fax: 787-848-6539. Personal E-mail: caivhernandez@yahoo.com.

HERNANDEZ, DAVID N(ICHOLAS), lawyer; b. Albuquerque, Nov. 5, 1954; s. B.C. and Evangeline (C De Baca) H.; m. Alice A. McLish, June 7, 1975. BA, U. N.Mex., 1975, MBA, 1978, JD, 1979. Bar: N.Mex. 1979, U.S. Dist. Ct. N.Mex. 1979. Law clk. to presiding justice N.Mex. Supreme Ct., Santa Fe, 1979-80; assoc. Knight, Custer & Duncan, Albuquerque, 1980-82; sole practice David N. Hernandez & Assoc., Albuquerque, 1982—; of counsel Western Glass & Panels, Albuquerque. Mem. com. rules appellate ct. procedure N.Mex. Supreme Ct., 1984—; bd. dirs. Delta Dental N.Mex., Albuquerque. Mem. Environ. Planning Commn., Albuquerque, 1984-86, PHS assocs. Presbyn. Healthcare Found., 1985—. Named one of Outstanding Young Men Am., 1980. Mem. ABA, N.Mex. Bar Assn. (pres. 2000-01), Albuquerque Bar Assn., Am. Judicatur Soc., Greater Albuquerque C. of C. (bd. dirs. 1982-86, polit. action com. 1983-85). Avocations: tennis, golf, reading, fishing, politics.

HERNANDEZ, ENRIQUE, JR., (RICK HERNANDEZ), security firm executive; b. LA, Nov. 2, 1955; m. Megan Beth McLeod, June 12, 1982; 5 children. AB cum laude, Harvard U., 1977, JD, 1980. Litigation atty. Brobeck, Phleger & Harrison, LA; chmn., CEO Inter-Con Security Systems Inc., 1984—; co-founder, principal ptnr. Interspan Communications. Bd. dir. McDonalds Corp., 1996—, Nordstrom Inc., 1997—, non-exec. chmn.; bd. dir. Tribune Co., 2001—, Wells Fargo & Co., 2003—; mem. US Nat. Infrastructure Advisory Com., 2002—. Mem., pres. Bd. LA Police Commn., 1993—95; chmn. bd. regents Loyola High Sch., LA; vice chmn., bd. dir. Children's Hosp., LA; bd. trustees U. Notre Dame, LA County Mus. Art; com. mem. Harvard Coll. Visiting Com., Harvard U. Resources Com. Office: Inter-con Security Systems Inc 210 South De Lacey Ave Pasadena CA 91105*

HERNANDEZ, FELIX ABRAHAM, professional baseball player; b. Valencia, Venezuela, Apr. 8, 1986; 1 child. Pitcher Seattle Mariners, 2005—. Achievements include being the youngest pitcher to appear in the major leagues since Jose Rijo in 1984; being the youngest Opening Day starting pitcher for the Seattle Mariner's since Dwight Gooden in 1985. Office: Safeco Field PO Box 4100 Seattle WA 98104 Office Phone: 206-346-4000.*

HERNÁNDEZ, FERNANDO VARGAS, lawyer; b. Irapuato, Mex., Sept. 8, 1939; came to U.S., 1942, naturalized, 1957; s. José Espinosa and Ana Maria (Vargas) H.; m. Bonnie Corrie, Jan. 8, 1966 (div. Feb. 1991); children: Michael David, Alexandra Rae, Marcel Paul; m. Tetiana Vanganen, Dec. 13, 2006. BS, U. Santa Clara, 1961; MBA, 1962; JD, U. Calif., Berkeley, 1966. Bar: Calif. 1967, U.S. Dist. Ct. (no. dist.) Calif. 1967. Sole practice law, San Jose, Calif., 1967—. Lectr. law Lincoln U.; lectr. bus. U. Santa Clara. Mem. San Jose Housing Bd., 1970-73; arbitrator Santa Clara County Superior Cts., 1979-2005, judge pro tem, 1979—. Contbg. editor to legal pleadings books. Active San Jose Civic Light Opera, 1981-83. With AUS, 1962-63. Mem. Calif. State Bar Assn., Santa Clara County Bar Assn. (chmn. torts sect. 1977-78, features editor In Brief mag. 1990-93), Calif. Trial Lawyers Assn. (bd. govs. 1979-82), Santa Clara County Trial Lawyers Assn., La Raza Lawyers Assn., Tapestry in Talent (bd. dirs. 2000-04), Greater San Jose Hispanic C. of C. (founder, corp. counsel, bd. dirs. 2003-04). Roman Catholic. Office: 46 S 1st St San Jose CA 95113-2406 Office Phone: 408-280-5000. Business E-Mail: fernandolaw@pacbell.net.

HERNANDEZ, GARY A., lawyer; b. Merced, Calif., Feb. 15, 1959; s. Rosendo and Margaret (Salazar) Hernandez; m. Teri L. Bond, Sept. 9, 1989. AB, U. Calif., Berkeley, 1981; JD, U. Calif., Davis, 1984. Bar: Calif. 1985, DC 2006. Dep. city atty. City and County of San Francisco, 1988-90; dep. ins. commr. Calif. Dept. Ins., San Francisco, 1991—95; ptnr. Long & Levit, San Francisco, 1995-97, Sonnenschein Nath & Rosenthal, LLP, San Francisco, 1997—. Bd. dirs. Iteris Inc., 1999—. Co-author eBusiness and Insurance: A Legal Guide To Transacting Insurance and Other Business on the Internet, 2001; editor (newspaper) Perspectiva, 1984-88; mem. editl. bd. Calif. Ins. Law & Regulation Reporter, 1998—. Bd. dirs. Ins. Regulators Examiners' Soc. Found.; bd. trustees U. Calif. Merced Found.; mem. Calif. adv. bd. Trust for Pub. Lands. Mem. Internat. Assn. Ins. Receivers, City Club of San Francisco, Club Mercedes. Democrat. Roman Catholic. Office: Sonnenschein Nath & Rosenthal LLP 26th Fl 525 Market St San Francisco CA 94105 Home Phone: 415-819-4845; Office Phone: 415-882-2466.

HERNANDEZ, GILBERTO JUAN, accountant, auditor, management consultant; b. Havana, Cuba, July 12, 1943; came to U.S., 1960; s. Gilberto E. and Zoila M. (Mendez) H.; m. Maria-Elena Diaz Lugo, Jan. 19, 1968 (div. 1971); 1 child, A. Patrick; m. Maria-Carmen Marcet, Dec. 23, 1972; children: Martin J., David J., Thomas J. BBA, Pace U., 1968. CPA, N.Y., Fla. Auditor sr. Arthur Andersen & Co., NYC, Tampa, 1968—73; v.p., treas. Coaxial Comms., Inc., Sarasota, Fla., 1973—81; tax mgr. Laventhol & Horwath, Tampa, Fla., 1981—83; mem. firm ValienteHernandez P.A., CPAs, Auditors and Consultants, Mems. Polaris Internat., Tampa, 1983—. Chmn. N.Am. region Polaris Internat., 2002-04 Commr. City of Tampa Housing Authority, 1981-93; treas., bd. dirs. Ybor City Devel. Corp., Tampa, 1988—; past chmn. Tampa Bay Econ. Devel. Corp. Mem. AICPA, N.Y. State Soc. CPA, Fla. Inst. CPA (bd. dirs., pres. West Coast chpt., past chmn. com. on unauthorized practice of pub. accountancy 1993-94, Outstanding Chmn. of Yr. 1994), Nat. Assn. Housing and Redevel. Ofcls. (bd. govs. 1988-94), Govt. Fin. Officers Assn., Fla. Assn. Govt. Fin. Officers, Ybor City C. of C. (chmn. 1997-98, chmn. 1998-99), Ybor City Rotary Club (pres. 1990-91). Avocations: geography, travel, hiking. Office: ValienteHernandez PA 1715 N Westshore Blvd Ste 950 Tampa FL 33607-3920 Office Phone: 813-933-3943. Business E-Mail: ghernandez@vhcpa.com.

HERNANDEZ, HEATHER MARIE, organist, music director; b. Kenosha, Wis., Apr. 16, 1975; d. Thomas Anthony and Shelia Kay Harrington; m. Robert Lewis Hernandez, Aug. 4, 2001. BA in Music, Bethany Coll., Lindsborg, Kans., 1997; MusM, U. Nebr., Lincoln, 1999, D in Musical Arts, 2005. Organist Grace Episcopal Ch., Muskogee, Okla., 1990—93, First Presbyn. Ch., McPherson, Kans., 1996—97; grad. tchg. asst. U. Nebr., Lincoln, 1997—99; asst. organist St. George's Anglican Ch., Paris, 2000—01; cathedral organ scholar St. Cecilia Cathedral, Omaha, 2001—04; dir. parish music Luth. Ch. the Master, Phoenix, 2004—; accompanist Phoenix Girls Chorus, 2005—. Counselor, choral music liaison Okla. Summer Arts Inst., Tahlequah, 1997; participant Internat. Organ and Clavichord Acad., Smarano, Italy, 1998; competitor Mikael Tariverdiev Internat. Organ Competition, Kaliningrad, Russia, 2003. Recipient 3d prize, 6e Concours Internat. d'Orgue de Lorraine, 2000, 1st prize, 71e Concours Internat. d'Orgue de l'U.F.A.M., 2001; fellow Eva Christensen Fellowship, U. Nebr., 2004; grantee Verna Ross Orndorff Career Performance Grant, Sigma Alpha Iota, 2002. Mem.: Am. Guild Organists (sec. 2004), Pi Kappa Lamba Nat. Music Honor Soc., Sigma Alpha Iota Internat. Music Frat. (mem. at large 2006, sec. 2007). Episcopalian. Home: 22218 N 32d Ave Phoenix AZ 85027 Office: Lutheran Ch the Master 2340 W Cactus Phoenix AZ 85029 Home Phone: 623-582-3441. Personal E-mail: hmharrington@hotmail.com. Business E-Mail: mastermusic@cox.net.

HERNANDEZ, H(ERMES) MANUEL, lawyer; b. Bronx, NY, Mar. 16, 1955; s. Manuel and Aurora O'Neill H.; m. Hortensia Beatriz Carrasquillo, Aug. 28, 1980; children: Antonio, Victoria, Stephanie. BS in Criminal Justice magna cum laude, Met. State Coll. Denver, 1976; JD, U. Denver, Denver, 1979. Bar: Colo. 1979, NY 1986, DC 1986, Fla. 1988; cert. trial adv Nat. Bd. Trial Advocacy; cert. criminal trial specialist and criminal appellate specialist Fla. Bar 1993. Trial atty. criminal div. US Dept. Justice, Washington, 1979-80; asst. U.S. atty. criminal and civil div. US Dept. Justice (Colo., Puerto Rico, Fla. mid. dist.), 1980-89; pvt. practice Orlando, Fla., 1989—. Chmn. civilian rev. bd. Seminole County Sheriff's Office, Orlando, 1992-93. Mem. Nat. Criminal Def. Lawyers Assn., Fla. Fed. Bar Assn. (Orlando chpt., v.p. 1988-89, pres. 1989-90, 90-91, 1999-2001, nat. del. 1991, 92, 93, 2001), Fla. Bar, Fla. Assn.(chair criminal law sect., 2002-2003) Criminal Def. Lawyers, Hispanic Bar Assn. (charter mem. Orlando chpt.), Ctrl. Fla. Criminal Trial Lawyers Assn. Republican. Roman Catholic. Avocations: music, history. Office: PO Box 916692 Longwood FL 32791 Office Phone: 407-682-5553.

HERNANDEZ, ISRAEL, federal agency administrator; b. 1969; BA, U. Tex., 1992; MPA, Tex. A&M U., 1999. Dep. asst. to Pres. George W. Bush The White House, dep. to sr. advisor Karl Rove; dir. voter outreach office of strategy Bush-Cheney campaign, 2000; liaison Bush-Cheney re-election campaign, 2004; sr. advisor to sec. of commerce and acting under sec. for internat. trade US Dept. Commerce, asst. sec. trade promotion, dir-gen. U.S. and fgn. comml. svc., 2005—. Office: Internat Trade Adminstrn US Dept Commerce 1401 Constitution Ave NW Washington DC 20230 Office Phone: 202-482-5777. Office Fax: 202-482-5013.

HERNANDEZ, JO FARB, museum director, consultant; b. Chgo., Nov. 20, 1952; BA in Polit. Sci. & French with honors, U. Wis., 1974; MA in Folklore and mythology, UCLA, 1975; postgrad., U. Calif., Davis, 1978, U. Calif., Berkeley, 1978-79, 81. Registration Mus. Cultural History UCLA, 1974-75; Rockefeller fellow Dallas Mus. Fine Arts, 1976-77; asst. to dir. Triton Mus. Art, Santa Clara, Calif., 1977-78, dir., 1978-85; adj. prof. mus. studies John F. Kennedy U., San Francisco, 1978; grad. advisor arts adminstrn. San Jose (Calif.) State U., 1979-80; dir. Monterey (Calif.) Peninsula Mus. Art, 1985-93, cons. curator, 1994—2000; prin. Curatorial and Mus. Mgmt. Svcs., Watsonville, Calif., 1993—2000; dir. Natalie and James Thompson Art Gallery, San Jose State U., Calif., 2000—, Saving and Preserving Arts and Cultural Environ., 2006—. Panelist Creative Works Fund, 2001, 04; adj. prof. gallery mgmt. art dept. U. Calif., Santa Cruz, 1999—2000; dir. Thompson Gallery, San Jose State U., 2000—; lectr., panelist, juror, panelist in field USIA, Calif. Arts Coun., Calif. Confedn. for Arts, Am. Assn. Mus., Western Mus. Assn., Am. Folklore Soc., Calif. Folklore Soc., Internat. Coun. on Mus., others; vis. lectr. U. Wis., 1980, U. Chgo., 1981, Northwestern U., 1981, San Jose State U., 1985, UCLA, 1986, Am. Cultural Ctr., Jerusalem, 1989, Tel Aviv, 89, Binational Ctr., Lima, Peru, 1988, Daytona Beach Mus. Art, 1983, UCLA, 1986, Israel Mus., 1989, Mont. State U., 1991, Oakland Mus., 1996, High Mus. Art, Atlanta, 1997, Mus. Am. Folk Art, NY, 1998, San Francisco Mus. Modern Art, 1998, U. Calif., 1998, Grinnell Coll., Iowa, 1999, Arts Coun. Silicon Valley, 2000, U. Calif., Santa Cruz, 2000, ICOM, Barcelona, 2001, Intuit Gallery, Chgo., 2004, Chgo., 07; guest curator San Diego Mus. Art, 1995—98; bd. dirs. Saving and Preserving Art and Cultural Environ.; cons. in field. Author: (mus. catalogs) The Day of the Dead: Tradition and Change in Contemporary Mexico, 1979, Three from the Northern Island: Contemporary Sculpture from Hokkaido, 1984, Crime and Punishment: Reflections of Violence in Contemporary Art, 1984, The Quiet Eye: Pottery of Shoji Hamada and Bernard Leach, 1990, Alan Shepp: The Language of Stone, 1991, Wonderful Colors: The Paintings of August Francois Gay, 1993, Jeannette Maxfield Lewis: A Centennial Celebration, 1994, Armin Hansen, 1994, Jeremy Anderson: The Critical Link/A Quiet Revolution, 1995, A.G. Rizzoli: Architect of Magnificent Visions, 1997 (one of 10 Best Books in field Amazon.com), Misch Kohn: Beyond the Tradition, 1998, Fire and Flux: An Undaunted Vision/The Art of Charles Strong, 1998, Mel Ramos: The Galatea Series, 2000, Holly Lane: Small Miracles, 2001, Irvin Tepper: When Cups Speak/Life with the Cup, 2002, Marc D'Estout: Domestic Objects, 2003, Peter Shire: Go Beyond the Ordinary, 2004, Forms of Tradition in Contemporary Spain, 2005, Gerald Walburg, 2007; co-author: Sam Richardson: Color in Space, 2002; mem. editl. bd. Raw Vision Mag., 2001-; contbr. articles to profl. jours. Bd. dirs. Bobbie Wynn and Co. of San Jose, 1981-85, Santa Clara Arts and Hist. Consortium, 1985, Non-Profit Gallery Assn., 1979-83, v.p., 1979-80; mem. nat. adv. bd. The Fund for Folk Culture, Santa Fe, 1995-98; mem. founding and exec. bd. Alliance for Calif. Traditional Arts, 2002—; mem. founding internat. adv. bd. Friends of Fred Smith, 2002—. Recipient Golden Eagle award, Coun. Internat. Non-theatrical Events, 1992, Leader of Decade award, Arts Leadership Monterey Peninsula, 1992, merit award, N.Y. Book Show, 1997, Chgo. Folklore prize, U. Chgo./Am. Folklore Soc., 2006; Rsch. grantee, Calif. State U., 2001—03, Dean's grantee, 2001, 2005, Lottery Fund grantee, 2000, 2004, Sr. Fulbright Scholar, 2007—. Mem.: Nat. Coun. for Edn. in Ceramic Arts, Western Mus. Conf. (bd. dir., exec. com. 1989—91, program chair 1990), Am. Folklore Soc., Art Table, Calif. Assn. Mus. (bd. dirs. 1985—94, v.p. 1987—91, chair nominating com. 1988, chair ann. meeting 1990, chair nominating com. 1990, pres. 1991—92, chair nominating com. 1993), Am. Assn. Mus. (lectr. 1986, mus. assessment program surveyor 1990, nat. program com. 1992—93, mus. assessment program surveyor 1994), Phi Beta Kappa. Office: School Art and Design San Jose State U One Washington Square San Jose CA 95192-0089 Office Phone: 408-924-4328, 408-924-4328.

HERNANDEZ, JOSE YOLANDO BALAGTAS, surgeon; b. Manila, Philippines, Dec. 30, 1938; came to U.S., 1964; s. Pablo Manio and Leoncia (Balagtas) Hernandez; m. Minerva Cuadrante, Dec. 17, 1966; children: Jay, Myra, Maureen. MD, U. St. Thomas, Manila, Philippines, 1962. Diplomate Am. Bd. Surgery, Am. Bd. Colon-Rectal Surgery, Internat. Bd. Proctology. Fellow: Soc. Philippine Surgeons in Am., Southeastern Surgical Congress, Internat. Acad. Proctology, InterAm. Coll. Physicians and Surgeons, Internat. Coll. Surgeons, Am. Soc. Colon Rectal Surgeons, Am. Soc. Abdominal Surgeons; mem.: AMA, Coll. Internat. Chirurgiae Digestiva, Endoscopic Surgeons, Am. Gastroent. Roman Catholic, Avocations: ballroom dancing, golf, music. Home and Office: 3053 Carlow Cir Tallahassee FL 32309-3302

HERNANDEZ, KEITH, retired professional baseball player; b. San Francisco, Oct. 20, 1953; s. John and Jackie H.; m. Sue Broeker, Jan. 28, 1978 (div. 1986); children: Jessica, Melissa, Mary Elise Student, Coll. San Mateo. Player St. Louis Cardinals, 1974-83, N.Y. Mets, 1983-89, Cleve. Indians, 1989. Mem. Nat. League All-Star Team, 1979, 80, 84, 86, 87; baseball announcer Sports New York(SNY), 2006- Named to Sporting News Nat. League All-Star Fielding Team, 1978-87; named co-Most Valuable Player Nat. League, Baseball Writers Assn. of Am., 1979; established major league record for game-winning RBIs (24), 1985; Nat. League record for lifetime game-winning RBIs (94); mem. Nat. League All-Star Team, 1979-80, 84, 86-87, World Series Championship Team, 1982, 86. Home: SportsNet New York 75 Rockefeller Plz New York NY 10019

HERNANDEZ, LAZARO, apparel designer; b. Miami, Fla. Attended, U. Miami; BA, Parsons Sch. of Design, 2002. Former intern Michael Kors; designer, co-founder, co-owner (with Jack McCollough) Proenza Schouler, 2003—. Work featured in Women's Wear Daily, People, Town & Country and New York mag. Named Designers of the Yr. (with Jack McCollough), Parsons Benefit and Fashion Show; recipient Womenswear Designer of Yr. award (with Jack McCollough), Coun. Fashion Designers Am., 2007. Office: c/o PR Consulting 42 Bond St 6 Fl New York NY 10012*

HERNANDEZ, LIVAN EISLER, professional baseball player; b. Villa Clara, Cuba, Feb. 20, 1975; Pitcher Fla. Marlins, 1996-99, San Francisco Giants, 1999—2002, Montreal Expos, 2003—04, Wash. Nationals, 2005—. Office: RFK Stadium 2400 E Capitol St SE Washington DC 20003

HERNANDEZ, MACK RAY, lawyer; b. Austin, Tex., Sept. 8, 1944; s. Mack and Mary (Prado) Hernandez; m. Jayne Webb Barrett, Aug. 2, 2001; 1 child, John Christopher. BA, U. Tex., 1967, JD, 1970. Bar: Tex. 1970, U.S. Dist. Ct. (we. dist.) Tex. 1972. Pvt. practice, Austin, 1971—. Adv. bd. Laredo Nat. Bank, Tex., 2006, Treaty Oak Bank, Austin, 2006; Keeton fellow U. Tex. Law Sch.; mem. adv. coun. Coll. Fine Arts U. Tex. Bd. dir. Austin C. of C., 1983-86, Meals on Wheels, Austin, 1972-76; trustee Austin

C.C., 1988—; vice-chair, 1990-92, chair, 1992-94; chmn. bd. dir. Am. Cancer Soc., Austin, 1988-95; trustee Austin Mus. Art, 2000—. Mem.: Tex. Bar Found., Coll. of State Bar, Travis County Bar Assn., Tex. Bar Assn., Am. Inns. Ct. (master, Robert C. Calvert chpt.). Avocations: travel, jogging, hiking, backpacking. Office: 919 Congress Ave Ste 900 Austin TX 78701 Office Phone: 512-477-9433. Business E-Mail: MackRay@Hernandez.com.

HERNANDEZ, MICHELLE A., lawyer; d. Stella V. Martinez; m. Jon J Hernandez, Aug. 4, 2000; 1 child, Mia Estella. BA magna cum laude in Polit. Sci., U. N.Mex, Albuquerque, 1993; JD, UCLA, 1997. Bar: N.Mex 1997, US Ct. Appeals (10th cir.) 1999, US Dist. Ct. N.Mex 2000. Jud. law clk. N.Mex Supreme Ct., Sr. Justice Joseph F. Baca, Santa Fe, 1997—99; shareholder Modrall Sperling Law Firm, Albuquerque, 1999—. Bd. dirs. Defense Lawyers Assn., Internat. Assn. Defense Counsel, Litigation Counsel of Am. Co-author: (insurance article) Def. Lawyers Assn. Mem. Verne Payne Inns of Ct., Albuquerque, 1999—2002, Leardership Albuquerque, 2004—; local advance team Clinton/Gore, Albuquerque; bd. mem., exec. comittee mem., treas. U. N.Mex Alumni Assn., 1999—2007; founding mem. U. N.M. Young Alumni Assn., 1999—2000; bd. dirs. Greater Albuquerque C. of C., chair leadership conf., 2006—07; bd. dirs. Albuquerque Alumni Assn., 2006—07. Lubric Pioneering Women in Law Scholarship, 1997. Fellow: N. Mex. Emerge; mem.: Hispanic Bar Assn., N.Mex Bar Assn., UCLA La Raza Law Students Assn., Phi Beta Kappa. Home Phone: 505-848-1800; Office Phone: 505-848-1800. Office Fax: 505-848-1889.

HERNANDEZ, MINERVA CUADRANTE, physician, consultant; d. Arsenio Francisco Cuadrante and Mercedes Rontas Relunia; m. Jose Yolando Balagtas Hernandez, Dec. 17, 1966; children: Jay, Myra, Maureen. MD, U. St. Tomas, Manila, 1962. Intern St. Clare's Hosp., Schenectady, NY, 1964—65; jr. resident Springfield Hosp., Mass., 1965—66; pediatric resident Trumbull Meml. Hosp., Warren, Ohio, 1966—69; resident, gen. pathology Allentown Hosp., Pa., 1969—70; staff physician Fla. State Hosp., Chattahoochee, 1974—78, Southwestern State Hosp., Thomasville, Ga., 1980—85; physician advisor Profl. Found. for Health Care, Tampa, Fla., 1985—89; staff physician Tricare Clinic, Atlantic Beach, Fla., 1993—97; med. dir. Spectrum Health Care Partnership, Cecil Field, Fla., 1995—96; physician Fla. State U., Thagard Student Clinic, Tallahassee, 1997—2004. Mem. Springtime Tallahassee, 1983. Fellow: Am. Bd. Disability (analyst), Am. Coll. Utilization Rev. Physicians; mem.: Panhandle Med. Soc., Assn. Am. Philippine Physicians, Am. Acad. Family Physicians. Avocations: ballroom dancing, creative writing, reading. Home: 3053 Carlow Cir Tallahassee FL 32309 Office: Fla State Univ Thagard Student Health Ctr Tallahassee FL 32309

HERNANDEZ, RAMON ROBERT, retired minister, school librarian; b. Chgo., Feb. 23, 1936; s. Eleazar Dario and Marie Helen Hernandez; m. Fern Ellen Muschinske, Aug. 11, 1962; children: Robert Frank, Maria Marta. BA, Elmhurst Coll., Ill., 1957; BD, Eden Theol. Sem., St. Louis, 1962; MA, U. Wis., 1970. Co-pastor St. Stephen United Ch. Christ, Merrill, Wis., 1960-64; dir. youth work Wis. Conf. United Ch. Christ, Madison, 1964-70; dir. T.B. Scott Free Library, Merrill, 1970-75, McMillan Meml. Library, Wisconsin Rapids, Wis., 1975-83, Ann Arbor (Mich.) Pub. Library, 1983-94; pastor Comty. Congl. Ch., Pinckney, Mich., 1994-98. Seminar leader on pub. libr. long-range planning, budgeting and handling problem patrons. Editl. com. mem. Songs of Many Nations Songbook, 1970; contbr. articles to profl. jours. Ann Arbor Homeless Coalition, 1985-88; bd. dirs., sec., v.p. Riverview Hosp. Assn., Wisconsin Rapids, 1977-83; bd. dirs. Hist. Soc. Mich., 1988-90, Ind. Living, Inc., Dame County, Wis., 2001-03; trustee Madison Pub. Libr, Wis., 2000-06 Mem. ALA, Wis. Libr. Assn. (Leadership award 1980, pres. 1980), Rotary (pres. Merrill chpt. 1974-75, Community Svc. award 1975, pres. Ann Arbor chpt. 1990-91, Paul Harris fellow 1994).

HERNANDEZ, WILLIAM H., chemical company executive; BS, Wharton Sch. Bus. Univ. Pa.; MBA, Harvard Univ. CMA. Fin. analyst Ford Motor Co.; fin. mgmt. positions through v.p. fin. & CFO automotive Borg-Warner Corp., 1974—90; corp. controller PPG Industries, Inc., Pitts., 1990—94, v.p., controller, 1994, sr. v.p. fin., treas., CFO, 1995—. Bd. dir. Pentair Inc., 2001—03, Eastman Kodak. Office: PPG Industries Inc One PPG Pl Pittsburgh PA 15272*

HERNÁNDEZ DENTON, FEDERICO, judge; b. Santurce, PR, Apr. 12, 1944; s. Federico and Teresa (Denton) Hernandez-Morales; m. Isabel Pico, 1966. BA, Harvard U., 1966, JD, 1969. Bar: PR 1971. Dir. Consumer Rsch. Ctr. and Bus. Adminstrn. Rsch. Ctr. U. PR, 1970-72; dir. PR Consumer Svc. Adminstrn., 1973; sec. PR Dept. Consumer Affairs, 1973-76; asst. prof. Law Sch. Interam. U., PR, 1977-84, dean PR, 1984-85; justice Supreme Ct. PR, San Juan, 1985—2004; pres. PR Bd. of Bar Examiners, 1987—2004; chief justice PR Supreme Ct., San Juan, 2004—. Pres. PR Bd. Bar Examiners, 1987—2004; chairperson Jud. Code Comm., 2003—05. Mem. ABA, Am. Law Inst., PR Bar Assn. Office: Supreme Ct of PR PO Box 9022392 San Juan PR 00902-2392 Office Phone: 787-724-3535. Business E-Mail: FedericoH@tribunales.gobierno.pr.

HERNANDEZ-FALLOUS, JACQUELINE, marketing executive; b. NYC, Jan. 10, 1966; d. Diego and Mercedes (Zubiaurre) H. BA cum laude, Tufts U., 1988; postgrad., CUNY, 1994—. Advt.-classified sales rep. Boston Globe, 1988-90; telemarketing sales mgr. Village Voice, NYC, 1990-92, inside sales mgr., 1992-93, target mktg. and corp. mktg. mgr., 1993; dir. Time Inc. Internat.; dir. interactive sale Turner Broadcasting, 2000, v.p. integrated sales; v.p. global account devel. Turner Internat.; pub. People en Español, 2004—. First v.p. Internat. Advt. Assn. Named a Woman to Watch, Advt. Age, 2007; recipient President's Award, Time Inc., Exec. of the Year, Mktg. y Medios, 2006. Mem. NAFE, Women in Comms. (vol. career devel. com. 1993-94). Office: Time Inc Rockefeller Ctr New York NY 10020 Office Phone: 212-522-7004. E-mail: jackie_hernandez-fallous@peoplemag.com.*

HERNDON, ALICE PATTERSON LATHAM, public health nurse; b. Macon, Ga., Dec. 18, 1916; d. Frank Waters and Ruby (Dews) Patterson; m. William Joseph Latham, July 21, 1940 (dec. Apr. 1981); children: Jo Alice Latham Miller, Marynette Latham Herndon, Lauruby Latham Herndon; 1 adopted child, Courtney Marie Herndon; m. Sidney Dumas Herndon, Apr. 26, 1985. Diploma, Charity Hosp. Sch. Nursing, New Orleans, 1937; student, George Peabody Tchrs. Coll., 1938-39; BS in Pub. Health Nursing, U. N.C., 1954; MPH, Johns Hopkins U., 1966. Staff pub. health nurse assigned spl. venereal disease study USPHS, Darien, Ga., 1939—40; county pub. health nurse Bacon County, Alma, Ga., 1940—41; USPHS spl. venereal disease project Glynn County, Brunswick, 1943—47, county pub. health nurse, 1949—51, Ware County, Waycross, 1951—52; pub. health nurse surp. Wayne-Long-Brantley-Liberty Counties, Jesup, 1954—56; dist. dir. pub. health nursing Wayne-Long-Appling-Bacon-Pierce Counties, Jesup, 1956—70; dist. chief nursing S.E. Ga. Health Dist., 1970—79, organizer mobile health svcs., 1973—. Founder, exec. dir. Wayne County Home Health Agy., 1968—80; exec. dir. Ware County Home Health Agy., 1970—79, mem. exec. com., 1978—85; mem. governing bd. S.E. Ga. Health Sys. Agy., 1975—82; organized and mem. governing bd. Health Dept. Home Health Agy., 1978—, also author numerous grant proposals; governing bd. Brunswick Civic Orch., 1993—97. Contbr. to state nursing manuals. Mem. adv. coun. Ware Meml. Hosp. Sch. Practical Nursing, Waycross, Ga., 1958; mem. Altar Guild St. Paul's Episc. Ch., 1979—86, vestrywoman, 1981—82; mem. Altar Guild St. Marks Episcopal Ch., Brunswick, Ga., 1994—2001; bd. dirs. Wayne County Mental Health Assn., 1959—61, 1981—82, Wayne County Tb Assn., 1958—62, a non-alcoholic organizer Jesup group Alcoholics Anonymous, 1962—63. Recipient recognition Gen. Svc. Bd., Alcoholics Anonymous, Inc. Fellow APHA; mem. ANA, 8th Dist. (pres. 1954-58, sec. 1958-60, dir. 1960-62, 1st v.p. 1962), Ga. Nurses Assn. (exec. bd. 1954-58, program rev. continuing edn. com. 1980-86, Dist. 21 Excellence in Nursing award 1994), Ga. Pub. Health Assn. (chmn. nursing sect. 1956-57), Ga. Assn. Dist. Chiefs Nursing (pres. 1976). Home: PO Box 859 Brunswick GA 31521-0859

HERNDON, JAMES HENRY, orthopedic surgeon, educator; b. LA, Oct. 31, 1938; s. James Greene and Kathleen Theresa (Murphy) H.; m. Geraldine Grace Armiger, Feb. 26, 1971; chidlren: Jennifer, Jonathan. BS, Loyola U., LA, 1961; MD, UCLA, 1965; MA, Brown U., 1979; MBA, Boston U., 1990; MA (hon.), Harvard U., 1999; DHL (hon.), Loyola-Marymount U., 2004. Diplomate Am. Bd. Orthopaedic Surgery (bd. dirs., pres. 1991-92). Intern Hosp. of U. Pa., Phila., 1965-66, resident in surgery, 1966-67; resident in orthopaedics Mass. Gen. Hosp., Boston, 1970, chief resident in orthopaedics, 1967-70; asst. clin. prof. orthopaedic surgery Mich. State U., Grand Rapids, 1974-77, assoc. clin. prof., 1977-78; prof., chmn. dept. orthopaedics Brown U., Providence, 1979-88; surgeon-in-chief dept. orthopaedic surgery R.I. Hosp., Providence, 1979-88; Silver prof., chmn. dept. orthopaedic surgery U. Pitts., Pitts., chief orthopaedics, 1988-98; chief dept. orthopeadics and rehab. Presbyn. U. Hosp., Pitts., 1988-98; assoc. sr. vice chancellor Health Svcs. U. Pitts. Med. Ctr., 1995-98, v.p. med. svcs., 1995-98; chmn. ptnrs. dept. orthopaedic surgery Mass. Gen. Hosp., 1998—2004, Brigham and Women's Hosp., 1998—2004. Examiner Am. Bd. Orthopaedic Surgery, Chgo., 1977—2004, pres., 1990-91; William H. and Johanna A. Harris prof. Harvard Med. Sch., 1998—. Reviewer Jour. Bone and Joint Surgery, 1975—, bd. trustees, 2005-, treas., 2007—; contbr. articles to profl. jours., chpts. to books; author books in field. Trustee Meeting St. Sch., Providence, 1984-88, Harmarville Rehab. Hosp., Pitts., 1989-95; mem. bd. govs. Arthritis Found., Providence, 1984-88, Pitts., 1989—98, Boston, 1998-2004; bd. dirs. Make A Wish Found., chmn., 1998-99. Recipient Edith and Carl Lasky Meml. award UCLA Med. Sch., 1965, Bronze award Am. Congress Rehab. Medicine, 1972, Clin. Rsch. award N.Y. Med. Soc., 1974. Fellow ACS, Am. Acad. Orthopaedic Surgeons (treas. 1994-97, pres. 2003—04); mem. Am. Orthopaedic Assn. (pres. 1999-00), Orthop. Rsch. Soc., Residence Rev. Com. Orthopaedic Surgery (past chmn.), Am. Soc. Surgery of Hand, Internat. Soc. for Quality in Health Care. Office: Massachusetts Gen Hosp Gray 624 55 Fruit St Boston MA 02114-2696

HERNDON, JOHN LAIRD, accounting firm executive; b. Shreveport, La., 1958; s. Jack and Irene Herndon. BS Econs., Millsaps Coll., Jackson, Miss., 1981; MBA, U. Miss., Oxford, 1997. Cons., Jackson, Miss., 1981-84; fin. analyst Coldwell Banker, LA, 1984-86; sr. fin. analyst Kenneth Leventhal & Co., LA, 1986-87; asst. contr. E&Y Real Estate Group, LA, 1987-89, contr., 1989-95; dir. Ernst & Young LLP, NYC, 1996—. Developer multiple e-bus. applications; author numerous articles; speaker in field. John Palmer scholar U. Miss., Oxford, 1996-97. Mem. Mensa Internat., Urban Land Inst. Episcopalian. Avocations: tennis, golf. Office: Ernst & Young LLP 125 Chubb Ave Lyndhurst NJ 07071-3504 E-mail: jlherndon@yahoo.com.

HERNDON, ROBERT MCCULLOCH, neurologist, researcher; b. Richmond, Va., May 29, 1935; s. Lee Roy and Lois Ruth (McCulloch) H.; m. Kathryn Lucille Stearns, June 11, 1955; children: Robert McCulloch, William, Cynthia. BA, U. Chgo., 1955; MD, U. Tenn., 1958. Diplomate Am. Bd. Psychiatry and Neurology. Intern, then resident in neurology Wayne State U. Hosp., Detroit, 1959-61; fellow in neuropathology Montreal (Que., Can.) Neurol. Inst., 1962-63; fellow in anatomy Harvard U. Med. Sch., 1965-66; asst. prof. neurology Stanford U. Med. Sch., 1966-69; neurologist, then chief neurology Palo Alto (Calif.) VA Hosp., 1966-69; assoc. prof. Johns Hopkins U. Med. Sch., 1969-77; prof. neurology Ctr. Brain Rsch., U. Rochester (N.Y.) Med. Ctr., 1977-88, chmn., 1977-87; chief neurology Good Samaritan Hosp., Portland, Oreg., 1988-94; prof. neurology Oreg. Health Scis. U., Portland, 1988-96; chief, chairperson neurol. svcs. dept. Legacy Portland Hosps., 1993-94; prof. U. Miss., Jackson, 1996—; staff neurologist VA Med. Ctr., Jackson, Miss., 1996—2000, U. Miss. Med. Ctr., 2000—. Dir. Multiple Sclerosis Soc. Clinic, Rochester, 1978-88; mem. med. adv. bd. Multiple Sclerosis Soc. U.S., Internat. Fedn. Multiple Sclerosis Socs.; editor Internat. Jour. MS Care, 1999—. Pres. Consortium of Multiple Sclerosis Ctrs., 1993-94. With USAF, 1963-65. Fellow Am. Acad. Neurology; mem. Am. Neurol. Assn., Am. Acad. Sci., Am. Assn. Neuropathologists (Arthur Weil award 1969, 72, Moore award 1983), Soc. Exptl. Neuropathology (pres. 1988-91), Alpha Omega Alpha. Office: Univ Miss Med Ctr 2500 N State St Jackson MS 39216 Office Phone: 601-984-5500. Business E-Mail: rherndon@umsmed.edu. E-mail: r_herndo@bellsouth.net.

HERNDON, ROY CLIFFORD, physicist; b. Washington, Sept. 25, 1934; BS, Washington and Lee U., 1955; PhD, Fla. State U., 1962. Staff physicist Lawrence Livermore (Calif.) Lab., 1962—67; prof. Nova U., Ft. Lauderdale, 1967—75; dir. CBTR Ctr. for Biomed. & Toxicol. Rsch., Fla. State U., Tallahassee, 1983—. Dir. Inst. Internat. Coop. Environ. Rsch.; exec. dir. Fla. Hazardous Waste Adv. Coun., Tallahassee, 1980-82; mem. adv. bd. Fla. State U. System, Tallahassee, 1988—; hon. prof. Tech. U. Budapest, 1992. Author: (with others) Methods of Computational Physics, 1966, Land Use: A Spatial Approach, 1980, Theories of Electrons in Disordered Systems, 1982; contbr. over 100 articles to profl. jours. Mem. AAAS, Am. Phys. Soc., Phi Beta Kappa, Sigma Xi. Office: CBTR Fla State U 226 Morgan Bldg 2035 E Paul Dirac Dr Tallahassee FL 32310-3713

HERNQUIST, LARS ERIC, astronomer, educator; b. Princeton, NJ, Dec. 14, 1954; s. Karl Gerhard and Thyra Hildegard (Josefson) H.; m. Dale Marie Clarke, Aug. 28, 1982; 1 child, Kirsten Marie. BA, Cornell U., 1977; PhD, Calif. Inst. Tech., 1985. Rsch. fellow U. Calif., Berkeley, 1985-87, Inst. for Advanced Study, Princeton, NJ, 1987-90, Princeton U., 1990-91; asst. prof. of astronomy Lick Obs. U. Calif., Santa Cruz, 1991—98; prof. astronomy Harvard-Smithsonian Ctr. Astrophysics, 1998—. Contbr. articles to profl. publs. Fellow NSF, 1979, Sloan Found., 1991. Fellow Am. Acad. Arts & Scis.; mem. Am. Astron. Soc., Am. Phys. Soc., Internat. Astron. Union, Phi Beta Kappa, Phi Kappa Phi. Office: Harvard-Smithsonian Ctr Astrophysics P-222--MS 51 60 Garden St Cambridge MA 02138 Office Phone: 617-496-4180. Business E-Mail: lhernquist@cfa.harvard.edu.*

HERNSTADT, JUDITH FILENBAUM, city planner, real estate and broadcast executive; b. NYC, Nov. 18, 1942; d. Alex and Ruth Selena (Silberman) Filenbaum. BA, NYU, 1964, M Urban and Regional Planning, 1966; cert. smaller co. mgmt. program, Harvard Bus. Sch., 1977. With Office Planning Coordination, State of N.Y., 1966-68; ptnr. Devel. Planning Assocs., NYC, 1967-68; with engring. scis. dept. Svc. Bur. Corp., NYC, 1968-69; planning cons. Llewelyn-Davies Assocs., NYC, 1969-71, Arlen Realty & Devel. Corp., NYC, 1971-73; ptnr. Planning & Devel. Team, NYC and Las Vegas, 1974—; v.p. Sta. KVVU-TV Nev. Ind. Broadcasting Corp., Las Vegas, 1974-75, pres., 1976-77, Hernstadt Broadcasting Corp., 1978-81. Chmn. adv. bd. Internat. Film and TV Exch., Inc., 1996—2000; mem. coun. Rockefeller U., 1998—. Condr. TV interview programs. Bd. dirs. Nat. Com. on Am. Fgn. Plicy, Decorative Arts Trust, 1980—98, Eastside Internat. Cmty. Ctr., 1988—96; bd. advisors ACORN Found.; mem. fine arts com. U.S. Dept. State, 1976—; del. Fine Arts Fedn. N.Y., 1970—90; mem. Hudson Inst., 1980—92. Mem.: Nat. Inst. Social Scis., Women's Fgn. Policy Group, Hadji Baba Soc., Harvard Club (N.Y.C.), Lotos Club, Explorers Club. Home: 927 5th Ave New York NY 10021-2650

HEROD, CHARLES CARTERET, retired Afro-American studies educator; b. Florence County, S.C., Nov. 18, 1924; s. George William and Essie Lee (Johnson) H.; m. Agustina Benedicto; children: Charles-Francis, Ilona-Nora, Olivia Maria. A.B. in History and English magna cum laude, Rutgers U., 1964, A.M. in History, 1968, Ph.D. in History, 1973. Lic. tchr. N.J. Tchr. dept. social studies East Orange High Sch., N.J., 1964-66; instr. dept. history Rutgers U., New Brunswick, N.J., 1966-73; prof. Afro-Am. studies, SUNY-Plattsburgh, 1974—05; ret.; lectr. in field. Author: The Nation in the History of Marxian Thought, 1976; Afro-American Nationalism, 1986. Mem. editorial bd. Can. Rev. Studies in Nationalism, P.E.I. U., Can. Contbr. revs., articles to profl. jours. Named Hon. Squadron Comdr. 380th Bomb Wing, Plattsburgh AFB, 1978; grantee NDEA, 1966, U. Vienna, 1970-73, Ctr. for East Asian Studies, 1975; recipient Special Diplome, French Guerelme; honored prof. Coll. Coun., Interim Pres. SUNY-Plattsburgh, 2003. Mem. Am. Assn. for Advancement of Slavic Studies, N.Y. State Assn. European Historians, Royal Archaeol. Inst. Great Britain and Ireland, N.Y. African Studies Assn., Univ. Coll. Honor Soc. of Rutgers U., Habsburg Discussion Group, Pi Sigma Alpha. E-mail: herodcc@plattsburg.edu.

HEROLD, JEFFREY ROY MARTIN, retired library director; b. Chgo., Aug. 9, 1941; s. Roy George and Anne (Polacek) H.; m. Carol Ann Courtial, June 20, 1964; children: Kristin Ann, Timothy Scott. MEd, SUNY, Buffalo, 1966; PhD, Ohio State U., 1969; MLS, Kent State U., 1986. Teaching assoc. Ohio State U., Columbus, 1965-69; asst. prof. edn. SUNY, Cortland, 1969-74, Ind. U. Pa., 1974—75; lectr. in edn. Kelvin Grove Coll., Brisbane, Australia, 1976—78; assoc. dir. office continuing edn. Ohio State U., Columbus, 1978—84; extension libr. Columbus Pub. Libr., 1985—87; dir. Bucyrus Pub. Libr., 1987—2000, Bucyrus Libr. Consortium, Ohio, 1989—2000; ret., 2000. Book reviewer: Libr. Jour., 1988-97. Founder and pres. SUNY Founds. of Edn. Assn., 1971—72; chair McGovern for Pres. Com. Cortland County, NY, 1972; mem. leadership bd. Nat. Multiple Sclerosis Soc., Idaho, 2002—06. Grantee Timken Found., 1989, 1996, Ohio Humanities Coun., 1994, 1995, 1997, Libr. Svcs. and Tech. Act, 1998, Leidy Found., 2002, 2003, Kissler Family Found., 2003, Morrison Found., 2003, Idaho Cmty. Found., 2004. Avocations: reading, walking.

HEROLD, KARL GUENTER, lawyer; b. Munich, Feb. 3, 1947; came to U.S., 1963; s. Guenter K.B. and Eleonore E.E. H.; children: Deanna, Donna, Nicole, Jessica, Christine, Karl-Matthäus. BS, Bowling Green State U., 1969; JD, Case Western Res. U., 1972. Bar: Ohio 1972, N.Y. 1985; avocat, France, 1992; mem. Anwaltskamer, Frankfurt, Germany. Ptnr.-in-charge, European bus. practice coord. Jones Day, Frankfurt, Germany, 1972—2004. Trustee Internat. and Comparative Law Ctr. Southwest Legal Found., Dallas, 1983; bd. dir. Didier Taylor Refractories Corp., Cin., Redland Corp., San Antonio, v.p., Redland Credit Corp., San Antonio, v.p., Redland Fin. Inc., San Antonio, v.p., 1979-86, Zircoa Inc., Solon, Ohio, 1988-92. Contbr. articles to profl. jours. Trustee Cleve. Internat. Program, 1982-88; bd. dir., v.p. Spl. Olympics Deutschland, 2005-, bd. trustees, 2005-; chmn. bd. dir. Frankfurt Internat. Sch., 1991-93; adv. com. Am. Coun. on Germany, 1995—, Atlantik Bruecke, Berlin, 1992—; donors bd. Inst. Law and Fin., Frankfurt, 2003—. Exec. mem. Am. C. of C., mem. ABA, Internat. Bar Assn., Order of Coif, Omicron Delta Kappa. Office: Jones Day 222 E 41st St New York NY 10017 also: Jones Day Hochhaus am Park Grueneburg Weg 60323 Frankfurt Germany Office Phone: + 496997263939. E-mail: KGHerold@JonesDay.com.

HEROLD, ROCHELLE SNYDER, early childhood educator; b. Bklyn., Oct. 6, 1941; d. Abe and Anna (Chazen) Snyder; m. Frederick S. Herold, May 7, 1966; children: David Marc, Caryn Michele. BA, Bklyn. Coll., 1963; MS, CCNY, 1968. Cert. tchr., N.Y.; cert. child-care provider, Fla. Tchr. N.Y.C. Pub. Schs., 1963-68; tchr., adminstr. Chanute AFB Pvt. Sch., Rantoul, Ill., 1970-72; dir. early childhood edn. Temple Solel, Hollywood, Fla., 1974-99, dir. social and ednl. programs for young couples, families and singles, 1995-99. Cons. bd. dirs. Temple Solel, 1982-99; nursery sch. com. PTO, 1982-89; lectr., coord. at tchr. seminars, parenting lecture series; freelance writer parenting mags. Author, illustrator: A Family Seder Through a Child's Eyes, 1984, Celebrating Shabbat in the Home, 1992, Perfect Parenting, 1994, Choosing Cheesie, 2000, Baby Bear Learns to Share, 2001, A Bear in the Brook, 2001, Seven Secrets of P-E-R-F-E-C-T Parenting, 2004. Mem. AMA Aux., Fla. Med. Assn. Aux., Soc. Children's Book Writers and Illustators, Temple Solel Sisterhood. Avocations: ventriloquism, arts and crafts, interior design, directing children's musical productions. Home Phone: 954-966-4678. Personal E-mail: rsherold@aol.com, perfectparenting@aol.com.

HERON, DAVID WINSTON, librarian; b. Los Angeles, Mar. 29, 1920; s. Charles Morton and Elizabeth (Atsatt) H.; m. Winifred Ann Wright, Aug. 24, 1946; children— Holly Winston, James, Charles. AB, Pomona Coll., 1942; BLS, U. Calif., Berkeley, 1948; MA, UCLA, 1951. Reference asst. UCLA Library, 1948-52; librarian Am. embassy, Tokyo, 1952-53; staff asst. to librarian Grad. Reading Room UCLA, 1953-55; asst. to dir. Stanford Libraries, 1955-57, asst. dir., 1959-61; asst. librarian Hoover Instn., Stanford, 1957-59; dir. libraries U. Nev., Reno, 1961-68, U. Kans., Lawrence, 1968-74; univ. librarian U. Calif. at Santa Cruz, 1974-78, emeritus librarian, 1979—; sr. lectr. Sch. Library and Info. Studies, 1978-79; head reader services Hoover Instn., 1980-86. Library adviser U. Ryukyus, Naha, Okinawa, 1960-61; mem. Kans. Library Adv. Commn., 1973-74 Author: Forever Facing South, 1991, Night Landing, 1999; editor: A Unifying Influence, 1981; mem. editorial bd. Coll. and Rsch. Librs.; contbr. articles to gen. and profl. jours. Served as 1st lt. AUS, 1942-46, ETO. Mem. ALA (exec. bd.), Kans. Library Assn., Nev. Library Assn. (pres. 1963-65), Assn. Research Libraries (bd. dirs. 1974), ACLU, Assn. Coll. and Research Libraries (editor monographs; chmn. U. libraries sect. 1970-71). Democrat. Home: 120 Las Lomas Dr Aptos CA 95003-3221

HERON, EARL D., communications executive; b. Kingston, St. Andrew, Jamaica, Dec. 24, 1934; s. Thomas Alexander Heron and Evelyn Theodora (Williams) HEron; m. Catherine Evangeline Hall, Aug. 24, 1961; 1 child, Ian. Diploma, ICS, London, 1972; degree in psychology, Fordham U., NYC, 1983. Asst. clk., acting dep. clk. cts. Jamaica Civil Svc., Kingston, 1958—65; tech., sec. Transplant Glass Coatings Co., Kingston, 1966—77, asst. mgr., 1972—77; varius positions AT&T Security, NYC, 1978—91. Author of poems. Founder, mem. Ronald Reagan Rep. Ctr., Washington, 1991, George Washington Edn. Ctr., Mt. Vernon, Va., 2004, Martin Luther King Meml., Washington, 2004, Rosa Parks Wall Tolerance, Montgomery, Ala., 2004, Pacific Aviation Mus., Montgomery, 2006, Disabled Vets. Meml., Washington, 2006; mem. Rep. Senatorial Inner Cir., 1993—, Woodrow Wilson Internat. Acad. Scholars, Washington, 1995—. Avocations: classical music, poetry, gardening. Home: 410 Sterling Pl Brooklyn NY 11238

HERON, JULIAN BRISCOE, JR., lawyer; b. Washington, Dec. 17, 1939; s. Julian B. Sr. and Doris S. (Strange) H.; m. Kathleen Ann Sweeney, Aug. 13, 1983; children: Kimberle, Melissa, Julian III, Kevin, Kathleen. BS, U. Ky., 1962, LLB, 1965. Bar: Ky. 1965, D.C. 1966, U.S. Dist. Ct. D.C. 1966, Md. 1968, U.S. Ct. Appeals (D.C. cir.) 1968, U.S. Supreme Ct. 1968. Ptnr. Pope, Ballard & Loos, Washington, 1968-81, Heron, Burchette, Ruckert & Rothwell, Washington, 1981-90, Tuttle, Taylor & Heron, Washington, 1990—. Chmn. U.S. Agrl Export Devel. Coun., 1983—85. Mem. Dominican 3rd Order Preachers; bd. of overseers Pontifical Faculty of Theology of the Immaculate Conception of the Dominican House of Studies; pres. Washington Internat. Horse Show, 1984, 1985, Nat. Horse Show, 1994—96. Fellow: ABA (chmn. agr. com. adminstrv. law sect.); mem.: Bar Assn. D.C., Md. Bar Assn., Ky. Bar Assn., D.C. Bar Assn.

(chmn. ethics com.), Va. Angus Assn. (bd. dirs., treas. 2000—04), Barristers, Legatus, Knight of the Equestrian Order of the Holy Sepulchre of Jerusalem Legatus, KC, The Golf Club Va. Republican. Roman Catholic. Office: Tuttle Taylor & Heron 1015 15th St NW Ste 1200 Washington DC 20005 Office Phone: 202-289-3388.

HEROS, ROBERTO COSME C., neurosurgeon; b. Havana, Cuba, Sept. 27, 1942; m. Deborah O.; children: Elsa, Rob, Carlos. MD, U. Tenn., Memphis, 1968. Diplomate Am. Bd. Neurol. Surgery. Intern in surgery Mass. Gen. Hosp., Boston, 1968-69; asst. resident gen. surgery, 1969-70; resident in neurosurgery, 1972-77; asst. in neurosurgery, 1976-77; attending neurosurgeon Presbyn. U. Hosp., Pitts., 1977-79; assoc. chief neurosurgery, 1979-80; asst. prof. neurosurgery U. Pitts., 1977-80, dir. neurosurgery residents ednl. program, 1979-80; asst. prof. surgery Harvard Med. Sch., Boston, 1980-83; assoc. prof. surgery, 1983-89; prof. surgery, 1989-90; Lyle A. French prof., chmn. dept. neurosurgery U. Minn., 1990-95; prof., chair dept. neurol. surgery U. Miami, 1995—. Dir. U. Miami Internat. Health Ctr. Chmn. editl. bd. Neurosurgery, 1988; contbr. articles to profl. jours. Chmn. Brain Attack Nat. Coalition, neurovasc. com. World Fedn. Neurosurg. Soc. Maj. USAF, 1970—72. Recipient Medal of Surgery U. Tenn., 1968, Dean's medal, 1968. Fellow: ACS; mem.: Congress Nuerol. Surgeons (v.p. 1986—87), Neurosurg. Soc. Am., Am. Acad. Neurol. Surgeons (pres. 2001), Am. Assn. Neurol. Surgeons (pres. 2002), Alpha Omega. Office: U Miami Med Sch 1095 NW 14th Terr Miami FL 33136-1407 Office Phone: 305-243-4572. E-mail: rheros@med.miami.edu.

HERPEL, LAURA BOGAN, pulmonologist, researcher; b. July 8, 1972; BA in Biology with distinction, Hendrix Coll., Conway, Ark., 1994; MD, U. SC Sch. Medicine, Columbia, 1999. Cert. in internal medicine Am. Bd. Internal Medicine, in pulmonary medicine Am. Bd. Internal Medicine. Intern then resident Johns Hopkins U. Sch. Medicine, Balt., 1999—2002, pulmonary, critical care, sleep fellow, 2002—. Contbr. articles to profl. jours. Grantee, NIH, 2004, 2005, Nat. Heart Lung and Blood Inst. NIH, 2005. Mem.: Am. Thoracic Soc., Am. Coll. Chest Physicians (mem. in tng., CHEST Found. Clin. Trainee award 2006). Office: Johns Hopkins Sch Medicine 5501 Hopkins Bayview Cir Baltimore MD 21224 Office Phone: 410-550-2233.

HERPST, ROBERT DIX, lawyer, optical materials company executive; b. Teaneck, NJ, Jan. 23, 1947; s. Harold Dix and Anita Augusta (Adams) H.; children: Katherine Elizabeth, Lauren Gabrielle, Sarah Elizabeth; m. Theresa M. Jacobini, Oct. 24, 1987. BS, NYU, 1969; JD, Rutgers U., 1972. Bar: NJ 1972, US Supreme Ct. 1979. Assoc. Pitney, Hardin & Kipp, Morristown, NJ, 1972-77, BOC Group, Inc., Montvale, NJ, 1977-89, div. counsel, 1978-82, corp. counsel, asst. sec., 1982-88. Pres. Internat. Crystal Labs., Garfield, NJ, 1982—88, mng. dir., chmn. bd. dirs., 1988—; bd. suprs. Solaris Optics, S.A., Warsaw, 2003—04. Achievements include patents in field. Avocations: golf, politics, stock market, graphic arts. Office: Internat Crystal Labs 11 Erie St Garfield NJ 07026-2307 Business E-Mail: rherpst@internationalcrystal.net.

HERR, BRUCE, lawyer; b. Chgo., Aug. 12, 1943; s. Ross and Emilie (Robert) H.; m. Ellen Epstein, Feb. 22, 1968; children: Sarah, Rachel. BA cum laude, Harvard U., 1965, JD, 1968. Bar: N. Mex. 1969, Ill. 1970, U.S. Dist. Ct. N. Mex. 1969, U.S. Ct. Appeals (10th cir.) 1969, U.S. Supreme Ct. 1973. Staff atty. DNA Legal Svcs., Shiprock, N. Mex., 1969-70, Appellate Defender Project, Springfield, Ill., 1970-73; legal dir. Office of Ill. Appellate Defender, Springfield, 1973; appellate defender N. Mex. Pub. Defender Dept., Santa Fe, 1973-76; assoc., shareholder Montgomery & Andrews, PA, Santa Fe, 1976-99, of counsel, 1999-2000; with Office Lab. Counsel, Los Alamos Nat. Lab., 2000—. Mem. N. Mex. Supreme Ct. Com. on Civil Procedure Rules, 1983-98, chair, 1996-98, chair task force on electronic filing, 1994-96, mem. disciplinary bd., 2003—; mem. ethics adv. com. N. Mex. State Bar, 1985-88, 96-2002, chair employment and labor law sect., 1994-95; mem. legal com. Santa Fe Cmty. Fdn., 2002—. Pres. Friends of Santa Fe Pub. Libr., 1997-98; tutor Literacy Vols. Santa Fe, 1996-2001; bd. dirs. Santa Fe Bus. Incubator, Inc., 1995-96; v.p. Santa Fe Econ. Devel., Inc., 1999-2000. Lifetime hon. bd. mem. Santa Fe Bus. Incubator, Inc., 1996. Mem. ABA, First Jud. Dist. Bar Assn., Oliver Seth Am. Inn of Ct., Santa Fe County C. of C. (dir. 1992-96, chair 1995-96, Bd. Mem. of Yr. 1993-94). Avocations: running, hiking, reading, community activities. Home: 148 Encina St # A Santa Fe NM 87501-6528 Office: Los Alamos Nat Lab PO Box 1663 MS A-187 Los Alamos NM 87545-0001 E-mail: herr@lanl.gov.

HERR, DAVID FULTON, lawyer, educator; b. St. Paul, July 13, 1950; s. Robert and Janet H.; m. Mary Kay Strand, Oct. 25, 1986; children: Ehrland A. Truitt, Alec F. BA, U. Colo., 1972, MBA, 1977; JD cum laude, William Mitchell Coll. Law, 1978. Bar: Minn. 1978, U.S. Dist. Ct. Minn. 1978, U.S. Ct. Appeals (8th cir.) 1978, U.S. Ct. Appeals (3rd cir.) 1983, U.S. Claims Ct. 1986, U.S. Supreme Ct., 1989. Assoc. Robins, Davis & Lyons, Mpls., 1978-81; from assoc. to ptnr., applleate litig. Maslon Edelman Borman & Brand, Mpls., 1981—. Adj. prof. William Mitchell Coll. Law, St. Paul, 1978—. Author: Multidistrict Litigation, 1986, (with others) Motion Practice, 1986, 3d edit., 1998, Discovery Practice, 1982, 4th edit., 2005, Minnesota Practice, 1986, 4th edit., 2005, Annotated Manual for Complex Litig. Manual, 2005, Multidistrict Litig., 2005, and other works. Fellow Am. Acad. Appellate Lawyers (pres. 2004-05); mem. Am. Law Inst., Minn. State Bar (chmn. litigation sect. 1985-86, task force on complex litigation 1990—, Advocate's award 1999), Hennepin County Bar Assn., Ramsey County Bar Assn., Lawyers-Pilots Bar Assn. Office: Maslon Edelman Borman & Brand LLP 3300 Wells Fargo Ctr 90 S 7th St Minneapolis MN 55402 Office Phone: 612-672-8350. Office Fax: 612-642-8350. Business E-Mail: david.herr@maslon.com.

HERR, DWIGHT L., lawyer; b. Twin Falls, Idaho, Dec. 4, 1940; s. Julius E. and Amelia C. Herr; m. Laureen S. Chun, Dec. 16, 1967; children: Roger, Leilani. BA, U. Oreg., Eugene, 1963; LLB, U. Calif., Berkeley, 1966. Pvt. atty. Law Offices Paul Fulfer, Modesto, Calif., 1966—68; asst. county coun. County Santa Cruz, Calif., 1968—75, chief dep. county coun., 1975—84, county coun., 1984—2000; pvt. atty, Scotts Valley, Calif., 2000—. Cons. County Santa Cruz, 2000—; ct. mediator Superior Ct. Santa Cruz, 2001—03; presenter in field. Co-author: (book) The Legal History of Santa Cruz County, 2006. Mem. Cabrillo Coll. Cmty. Chorus, Aptos, Calif., 2004—; gov. bd. High St. Cmty. Ch., Santa Cruz, 2003—06. Mem.: Estate Planning Coun., Calif. Stat Bar Assn., County Couns. Assn. Calif. (pres. 1995—96). Avocations: singing, golf.

HERR, HARRY WALLACE, medical researcher, educator, surgeon, urologist; b. St. Louis, Oct. 1, 1943; s. Harry M. and Harriet Wallace Herr; m. Sheri Machele Herr, Oct. 23, 1999; children: Julie Christine Rozell, Nicole Alison, Annek Lynn Smith, John William. BA, U. Calif., Davis, 1965; MD, U. Calif., Irvine, 1969; student, Columbia U., 2004—. Diplomate Am. Bd. Urology, 1976. Intern U. So. Calif. Med. Ctr., LA, 1969—70; urology resident U. Calif., Irvine, 1970—74; immunology, urologic oncology fellow Cornell Grad. Sch. Med. Scis./Meml. Sloan-Kettering Cancer Ctr., NYC, 1974—76; attending surgeon Meml. Sloan-Kettering Cancer Ctr., NYC, 1979—. Prof. urology Meml. Sloan-Kettering/Cornell U. Med. Coll., NYC, 1997—. Contbr. papers, book chpts., revs. in field. Recipient FC Valentine award, NY Acad. Medicine, 1976, Jane Ewing award, Soc. Surg. Oncology, 1980; fellow, ACS, 1978. Fellow: Am. Assn. Genito-Urinary Surgeons; mem.: Am. Assn. Cancer Rsch., Am. Soc. Clin. Oncology, Am. Urologic Assn. Office: Memorial Sloan Kettering Cancer Ctr 1275 York Ave New York NY 10021 Business E-Mail: herrh@mskcc.org.

HERR, HUGH MILLER, biomechatronics researcher, educator; b. Oct. 25, 1964; BA in Physics, Millersville U. Pa., 1990; MS in Mech. Engring., MIT, 1993; PhD in Biophysics, Harvard U., 1998. Postdoctoral fellow MIT, 1998—99; instructor Harvard Med. Sch., 1999—2003, asst. prof., 2003—04; instructor MIT-Harvard Divsn. Health Sciences and Tech., Cambridge, Mass., 1999—2003, asst. prof., 2003—04; asst. prof., media arts and scis. MIT, Cambridge, Mass., assoc. prof., media arts and scis., dir., biomechatronics group. Founder, dir. Herr Inst. for Human Rehabilitation, Artificial Intelligence Lab., MIT, Cambridge, Mass.; cons. Flex-Foot, Inc., 2001—02, Össur, Inc., 2002—03; mem., Native Am. Student program Harvard Med. Sch., 2002—03; mem., BioMatrix Mentoring program MIT-Harvard Divsn. Health Sciences and Tech., 2002—; mem., elec. engring. and computer sci. Women's Tech. program MIT, 2003—; mem. scientific merit review bd. for rehabilitation ctr. grants Nat. Inst. on Disability and Rehabilitation Rsch., 2000—01; mem. scientific merit review bd. for small bus. innovation rsch. program NIH, 2002; mem. scientific merit review bd. for rehabilitation R&D svc. Dept. Veterans Affairs, 2002—05; spkr. in field. Work featured by various nat. and internat. media including Scientific American Frontiers, Technology Review, National Geographic, History Channel and Discovery Channel, editl. bd. ad hoc reviewer Biologically Inspired Intelligent Robots, 2002, Proceedings of the Royal Soc.: Biol. Sciences, 2003—, IEEE Transactions on Biomedical Engring., 2003—, Internat. Jour. Robotics Rsch., 2003—, Machines Called Robots, 2003, Jour. Exptl. Biology, 2003—, assoc. editor Jour. NeuroEngring. and Rehabilitation, 2003—. Named Office of Navel Rsch. Fellow, 1992, Howard R. Thranhardt Lecture Honorarium, 2001; named to Sports Hall of Fame, 1989, US Coll. Academic Team, 1990; recipient Young Am. award, 1990. Mem.: IEEE, Am. Acad. Orthotists and Prothetists, Soc. Exptl. Biologists. Achievements include co-inventor of Inflatable Limb Prosthesis with Preformed Inner Surface, 1990; co-inventor of Shoe and Foot Prosthesis with a Coupled Spring System, 1994; inventor of Crutch with Elbow and Shank Springs, 1995; co-inventor Shoe and Foot Prosthesis with Bending Beam Spring Structures, 1997 and 2000; co-inventor of Electronically Controlled Prosthetic Knee, 2001; co-inventor of a swimming robot actuated by living muscle tissue, 2002; co-inventor of a variable-impedance Ankle-Foot Orthosis to Assist Drop Foot Gait, 2003; co-inventor of an apparatus for generalized characterization and control of muscle, 2003; co-inventor of a dynamic bioreactor for the characterization and control of Tissue-Actuated Swimming Robots, 2003; co-inventor of a low-cost, body oreientation sensor, 2004; patents pending in field; several projects underway; Variable-Damper Knee Prosthesis is commercialized by Ossur, Inc., this is a benefit to transfemoral amputees throughout the world; Active Ankle-Foot Orthosis is in process of being commercialized and has the potential for improving the life of millions of stroke patients in the US. Office: MIT Media Lab Rm E15-419 20 Ames St Cambridge MA 02139 Office Phone: 617-258-6574. Office Fax: 617-253-8542. Business E-Mail: hherr@media.mit.edu.*

HERR, PETER HELMUT FRIEDERICH, sales executive; b. Hamburg, Germany, Apr. 23, 1951; came to U.S., 1978; s. Helmut and Ellen (Schmidt) H.; m. Kim Lovett, Sept. 29, 1984 (div. Nov. 1991); 1 child, Andrew; m. Monika Berns, Nov. 19, 1991; children, Jan, Maximilian. BS in Mech. Engring., U. Braunschweig, 1974, MS in Aero. Engring., 1978. Aero. engr. R & D Beech Aircraft Corp., Wichita, Kans., 1978-81, regional mgr., 1981-86, sr. regional mgr., 1987-92, dir. internat. market devel., 1992-93, regional dir. western Europe and Africa, 1993-94; v.p. internat. sales for Europe, Africa Mid. East Raytheon Aircraft, Wichita, Kans., 1994—. Sec., treas. Euroflight, Inc., Wichita, 1985—. Cpl. German Air Force, 1970-72. Lutheran. Avocations: flying, golf, boating. Home: 15229 E Zimmerly Ct Wichita KS 67230-9244 Office: Beechcraft Corp 10511 E Central Ave Wichita KS 67206-2557 also: Hawker Beechcraft Germany Ungersborn 7 D35756 Mittenaar 1 Germany

HERR, RICHARD, history professor; b. Guanajuato, Mexico, Apr. 7, 1922; s. Irving and Luella (Winship) H.; m. Elena Fernandez Mel, Mar. 2, 1946 (div. 1967); children: Charles Fernandez, Winship Richard; m. Valerie J. Jackson, Aug. 29, 1968; children: Sarah, Jane. AB, Harvard U., 1943; PhD, U. Chgo., 1954; Doctorate (hon.), U. Alcalá de Henares, Spain, 2001. Instr. Yale U., 1952-57, asst. prof., 1957-59; assoc. prof. U. Calif., Berkeley, 1960-63, prof. history, 1963-91, prof. emeritus, 1991—, chancellor's fellow, 1987-90. Directeur d'études associé, sixième sect. Ecole Pratique des Hautes Etudes, Paris, 1973; dir. Madrid Study Ctr., U. Calif., 1975-77; chair Portuguese Studies Program, U. Calif., Berkeley, 1994-98, chair Spanish Studies Program, U. Calif. Berkeley, 2002-04; vis. life mem. Clare Hall, Cambridge, Eng., 1985—; vis. prof. U. Alcalá. Henares, Spain, 1991; bd. dirs. Internat. Inst. Found. in Spain, Boston, 1997-2000; fellow Ctr. for History of Freedom, Washington U., St. Louis, 1994. Author: The Eighteenth Century Revolution in Spain, 1958, Tocqueville and the Old Regime, 1962, An Historical Essay on Modern Spain, 1974, Rural Change and Royal Finances in Spain at the End of the Old Regime, 1989 (Leo Gershoy award Am. Hist. Assn. 1990); co-author: An American Family in the Mexican Revolution, 1999; editor: Memorias del cura liberal don Juan Antonio Posse, 1984; co-editor, contbr.: Ideas in History, 1965, Iberian Identity, 1989; editor, contbr.: The New Portugal: Democracy and Europe, 1993, Themes in Rural History of the Western World, 1993; asst. editor: Jour. Modern History, 1949-50; mem. editl. bd. French Historical Studies, 1966-69, Revista de Historia Economica, 1983-91. With AUS, 1943-45. Decorated Comendador of the Orden de Isabel la Católica (Spain); recipient Bronze medal Collège de France, Paris, The Berkeley citation U. Calif., 1991; Social Sci. Rsch. Coun. grantee, 1963-64; Guggenheim fellow, 1959-60, 84-85; NEH sr. fellow, 1968-69. Fellow Am. Acad. Arts and Scis.; mem. Am. Philos. Soc., Real Academia de la Historia Madrid (corr.), Soc. for Spanish and Portuguese Hist. Studies. Office: U Calif Dept History Berkeley CA 94720-2550 E-mail: rherr@berkeley.edu.

HERREGAT, GUY-GEORGES JACQUES, retired banker; b. Oostende, West Flanders, Belgium, July 22, 1939; came to US, 1966; s. Georges-Albert Maurice and Marie-Gerard S. (Elleboudt) H. Licence en philosophie, U. Louvain, 1961, licence en philosophie et lettres, 1964; postgrad., Yale U., New Haven, Conn., 1966-67, PhD in Econs., 1972. Rsch. asst. U. Louvain (Belgium), 1964-66; rsch. assoc. Nat. Bur. Econ. Rsch., NYC, 1967-72; internat. economist Brown Bros. Harriman & Co., NYC, 1973-74; asst. v.p. Chem. Bank, NYC, 1974-76; dep. chief economist European Am. Bank, NYC, 1977-80; sr. advisor, sr. v.p. Societe Generale de Banque, NYC, 1980-85; mgr. Banque Worms, NYC, 1985-86; sr. v.p., dep. gen. mgr. Credit du Nord, NYC, 1986-93; sr. v.p. Banque Paribas, NYC, 1993-2000; mgr. dir. risk mgmt. BNP-Paribas, NYC, 2000—04, ret. Cons. Am. Bankers Assn., NYC, 1971, SEIDEIS-Futuribles, Paris, 1967-80, Ford Found., NYC, 1972-73. Author: Managerial Profiles and Investment Patterns, 1972, (with others) The Diffusion of New Industrial Processes, 1974, The Finances of the Performing Arts, 1974; contbr. articles to profl. jours. Yale U. fellow, 1966-67, Nat. Bur. Econ. Rsch. fellow, 1971-72; named Aspirant de Recherches Fonds Nat. Belge de la Rsch. Scientifique, 1967-72. Mem. Am. Econ. Assn., Acad. Polit. Sci., Yale Alumni Assn., Japan Soc., Inst. Internat. Bankers, Belgian-Am. C. of C. (bd. dirs. 1986—). Home: 30 E 81st St New York NY 10028-0222 also: 253 Atlantic Fire Island Pines NY 11782 also: 800 West Ave Miami Beach FL 33139-5542

HERREMANS, PAUL WILLIAM, mathematics educator; b. Conklin, Mich., Apr. 13, 1952; s. Albert August and Eleanor Herremans; m. Marilee Ellen Turcotte, June 9, 1978; children: John, Scott, Todd. BE in Physical Edn. and Psychology, Olivet Coll., Mich., 1974. Coach football, basketball, baseball and track Mich. HS, Ravenna; advisor Mid. Sch. Student Coun., Ravenna, 1974—92; coach Odyssey the Mind, Ravenna, 1986—94. Mem.: Nat. Coun. Tchrs. Math. Independent. Roman Catholic. Avocations: travel, woodworking, gardening, golf. Home: 3510 Truman Rd Ravenna MI 49451

HERRERA, ARTURO, artist; b. Caracas, Venezuela, 1959; BFA, U. Tulsa, 1982; MFA, U. Ill., Chgo., 1992. Resident ArtPace, San Antonio, 1999—. One-man shows include MWMWM Gallery, Chgo., 1993, 1994, Ctr. Contemporary Arts, Santa Fe, 1993, Randolph St. Gallery, Chgo., 1995, Hermetic Gallery, Milw., 1995, Mus. Contemporary Arts, Chgo., 1995, Revolution Gallery, Ferndale, Mich., 1996, Univ. Club., Chgo., 1996, Gahlberg Gallery Coll. DuPage, Glen Ellyn, 1996, Brent Sikkema/Wooster Garden, NYC, 1998, Renaissance Soc. U. Chgo., 1998, Worcester Art Mus., Mass., 1998, Art Inst. Chgo., 1998, Dia Ctr. Arts, 1998, exhibited in group shows at Gallery 400, Chgo., 1992, Nomadic Site, L.A., 1992, MWMWM Gallery, Chgo., 1993, Klein Art Works, 1993, Sch. Art and Design U. Chgo., 1994, Sotheby's Inc., Chgo., 1994, Drawing Ctr., NYC, 1994, Layton Gallery Milw. Inst. Art and Design, 1994, Feature, NYC, 1994, 1995, PS 122, 1994, Ten in One Gallery, Chgo., 1994, LACE, L.A., 1995, 213 Inst. Pl., Chgo., 1995, TBA Exhbn. Space, 1995, Chgo. Cultural Ctr., 1996, NIU Gallery, Chgo., 1996, Randolph St. Gallery, 1996, Thread Waxing Space, NY, 1996, Gallery 312, Chgo., 1996, Gallery 16, San Francisco, 1997, Real Art Ways, Hartford, Conn., 1997, Stephen Friedman Gallery, London, 1998, Brent Sikkema, NYC, 1999, Whitney Biennial, 2002, Perforations, McKenzie Fine Art Inc., NYC, 2003, MoMa at El Museo, El Museo del Barrio, NYC, 2004. Recipient award, Art Matters, Inc., 1995, Marie Walsh Sharpe Art Found., 1997, Louis Comfort Tiffany Found., 1997, Pollock-Krasner Found., 1998; grantee YADDO fellowship, Saratoga Springs, NY, 2002, DAAD fellowship, Berlin, 2003; CAAP grantee, Dept. Cultural Affairs, Chgo., 1995, SA grantee, Ill. Arts Coun., Chgo., 1995, visual arts fellow, 1996. Office: c/o Sikkema, Jenkins & Co 530 W 22nd St New York NY 10011-1108

HERRERA, CAROLINA, fashion designer; b. Caracas, Venezuela, Jan. 8, 1939; d. Guillermo and Maria Cristina Pacanina; m. Reinaldo Herrera, 1968; children: Mercedes, Ana Luisa, Carolina Adriana, Patricia. Founder, head designer Carolina Herrera, 1981—, launched bridal collection, 1987; opened Carolina Herrera / New York boutique, NYC, 2000. Released fragrance Carolina Herrera, 1988, Carolina Herrera for Men, 1991, Aqua Flore, 1995, 212 Carolina Herrera, 2003, 212 Men, 2004. Recipient Red Cross, 1979, Best Design Hall of Fame, 1980, Latin Am. Designer "Fashion award", 1987, Pratt Inst., 1990, Mary Ann Magnin awards, 1994, Special Distinction to a Career in the World of Design, Internat. Fashion Ctr. de New York, 1995, Reward to an enterprising spirit, Women's Div., Albert Einstein Coll. of Med. of Yeshiva U., 1996, Women with Heart award, Am. Aevet Assn., 2001, Womenswear Designer of Yr. award, Coun. Fashion Designers Am., 2004, Golden Plate award, Acad. Achievement, 2005. Office: 501 7th Ave Fl 17 New York NY 10018-5903 Office Phone: 212-944-5757. Office Fax: 212-944-7996.*

HERRERA, DENNIS J., lawyer; b. Bay Shore, NY, Nov. 6, 1962; m. Anne Herrera; 1 child, Declan. BA, Villanova U.; JD, George Washington U. Bar: Calif. 1989. City. atty. City of San Francisco, 2002—; ptnr. Kelly, Gill, Sherburne & Herrera, San Francisco; chief staff U.S. Maritime Adminstrn., Washington; pres. San Francisco Police Commn.; with San Francisco Pub. Transp. Commn. Chmn. San Francisco Ethics Commn. Office: City Hall Rm 234 1 Doctor Carlton B Goodlett Pl San Francisco CA 94102 Office Phone: 415-554-4748. Business E-Mail: cityattorney@ci.sf.ca.us.*

HERRERA, GUILLERMO ANTONIO, pathologist, educator, researcher; b. Havana, Cuba, Mar. 16, 1952; came to U.S., 1967; s. Guillermo S. and Olga (Del Castillo) H.; m. Elba A. Turbat, Dec. 23, 1972; 1 child, Marlene F. Student, U. Miami, 1970; MD cum laude, U. P.R., 1975. Diplomate Am. Bd. Pathology, Am. Bd. Anat. and Clin. Pathology; cytopathology added qualification bd.; lic. physician Fla., N.Mex., Ala., Miss., La., Mo. Intern categorical pathology Brooke Army Med. Ctr., Ft. Sam Houston, Tex., 1975-76, resident pathology, anatomic and clin., 1975-79, chief resident, 1978-79; asst. prof. dept. pathology Sch. Medicine and Dentistry U. Ala., Birmingham, 1982-87, scientist II Nephrology Rsch. and Tchr. Ctr. Sch. Medicine, 1982-88, dir. nephropathology Schs. Medicine and Dentistry, 1987-88, assoc. prof. dept. pathology, 1987-88, prof. pathology, head surg. pathology, 1991-95, sr. scientist Comprehensive Cancer Ctr., 1991-95, acting med. dir. Sch. Cytotech., 1991-93, faculty mem. Grad. Sch., 1991-95; assoc. prof., head surg. pathology U. Miss. Med. Ctr., 1989-91; head surg. pathology, attending pathologist VA Hosp., Birmingham, 1991-95; sr. scientist, co-dir. EM Core Facility Comprehensive Cancer Ctr. Ala., 1991-95; prof. pathology, medicine, cell biology La. State U., Shreveport, 1996—2006, chmn. dept. pathology, 1996—2006; prof. St. Louis (Mo.) U., 2006—, chmn. dept. pathology, 2006—. Assoc. pathologist Palm Beach Pathology, Good Samaritan Hosp., West Palm Beach, Fla., 1988-89; faculty Grad. Sch. U. Miss., 1989-91; cons. pathologist VA Hosp., Jackson, 1990-91; attending pathologist, head surg. pathology VA Hosp., Birmingham, 1991-95; acting med. dir. Sch. Cytotech., U. Ala., Birmingham, 1991-93, acting head cytopathology, 1991-93, faculty mem. Grad Sch., 1991-95; sr. scientist Comprehensive Cancer Ctr. Ala., co-dir. EM Core facility, 1991-95; cons. Overton Brooks VA Hosp., Shreveport, La. Mem. editl. bd.: Ultrastructural Pathology and Pathology Case Revs., 1995—, Human Pathology and Applied Immunohistochemistry and Molecular Morphology, 2001—, manuscript reviewer: Applied Pathology, Diagnostic Cytopathology, Am. Jour Medicine, Am. Jour. Kidney Diseases, Archives of Pathology and Laboratory Medicine, 2005, Ultrastructural Pathology, Stain Tech. and Histochemistry, Am. Jour. Clin. Pathology, Pathobiology, Human Pathology, Cancer, Kidney Internat., Pathology Rsch., Practice and Annals of Saudi Medicine, Am. Jour. Pathology, mem.: NIH rev. panel, assoc. editor: Ultrastructural Pathology Jour., 2004—; contbr. articles to profl. jours., chpts. to books. Maj. M.C., U.S. Army, 1974-82, col. USAR, 1988-96, ret. Grantee U. P.R., 1972-75, Brooke Army Med. Ctr., Ft. Sam Houston, 1978-79, U. Ala., Birmingham, 1983-86, 87-88, Universita Degli Studi di Milano, 1984, VA, 1986—, Nat. Cancer Inst., 1991—, NIH, 1992—, Ala. Kidney Found., 1992-93, Leukemia Soc. Am., 1997-99. Mem.: N.Y. Acad. Scis., Birmingham Soc. Pathologists (v.p. 1987—88), Tex. Electron Microscopy Soc., Internat. Acad. Pathology, Arthur Purdy Stout Soc. Surg. Pathologists, Am. Soc. Nephrology, Rsch. Soc., Soc. Advancement Sci., Renal Pathology Soc. (chmn. tng. com. 1996—98, sec.-treas. 1999—2005), Soc. Ultrastructural Pathology (sec.-treas. 1988—91, treas. 1991—99), Electron Microscopy Soc. Am., Armed Forces Soc. Lab. Scientists, Am. Soc. Clin. Pathology, Alpha Omega Alpha. Roman Catholic. Office Phone: 314-577-8475. Business E-Mail: gherrer1@slu.edu.

HERRERA, LUIS, library director; m. Nancy C. Herrera. BS, U. Tex., El Paso; MLS, U. Ariz.; MPA, Calif. State U., Long Beach. Mid. sch. libr.; assoc. dir. Long Beach Pub. Libr., 1983—89; dep. dir. San Diego Pub. Libr., 1989—95; dir. info. svcs. City of Pasadena, Calif., 1995—2005; city libr. San Francisco Pub. Libr., 2005—. Chair ptnrs. in edn. adv. bd. Pasadena Unified Sch. Dist.; bd. dirs. El Centro de Acción Social; bd. mem. Pacific Oaks Coll., Pasadena, Bill and Melinda Gates Libr. Found. Recipient Future Urban Adminstr. award, Calif. State U., Long Beach. Mem.: ALA, REFORMA (Libr. of Yr. 1993), Calif. Libr. Assn. (pres. 1982—83), Pub. Libr. Assn. (pres. 2003—04). Office: San Francisco Pub Libr 100 Larkin St San Francisco CA 94102 Office Phone: 415-577-4236. Personal E-mail: lherrerasfpl@yahoo.com. Business E-Mail: citylibrarian@sfpl.org.

HERRERA, MARY E., state official; b. Aug. 27, 1956; children: Nathan, Monique. BBA, Coll. Santa Fe, 1996, MBA, 1999; cert. in Prog. Adminstrn. for Sr. Execs., Harvard U. John F. Kennedy Sch. Govt.; certs. in Labor, Employment and Benefits Law, Inst. Applied Mgmt. Clk. typist Bernalillo County, N.Mex., 1974, asst. comptr., 1989—95, dir. human resources, 1996—2000, county clk., 2001—06; sec. state State of N.Mex., Santa Fe, 2007—. Voting mem. N.Mex. Election Reform Task Force; chair State Dem. Women N.Mex. Mem.: Nat. Assn. Hispanic Ofcls. (treas.), Nat. Assn. Counties, Nat. Assn. Latino Elected and Appointed Ofcls. (bd. mem.). Democrat. Office: Office Sec State State Capitol North Annex Ste 300 Santa Fe NM 87503*

HERRERA, PALOMA, dancer; b. Buenos Aires, Dec. 21, 1975; d. Alberto Oscar and Diana Lia (Rube) H. Attended, Olga Ferri Studio, 1982, Ballet Sch. of Minsk, 1987, English Nat. Ballet, London, 1990, Sch. Am. Ballet, NYC, 1991; diploma, Inst. Superior Art at The Colon Theatre, Buenos Aires, 1991. Soloist Am. Ballet Theatre, NYC, 1992-95, prin. dancer, 1995—. Dancer (ballets) Don Quixote, 1987, 88, soloist La Bayadere, The Sleeping Beauty, Don Quixote, Met. Opera, N.Y.C., 1992, Etudes, The Sleeping Beauty, Swan Lake, Symphonie Concertante, Voluntaries, 1993, prin. Symphonic Concertatne, Symphonic Variations, 1993; prin. Peasant Pas de Deux in Giselle, Colon Theatre, Buenos Aires, 1992, La Bayadere, 1993; prin. Don Quixote, soloist Etudes, Voluntaries, Theme and Variations, Kennedy Ctr., Washington, 1993; prin. The Nutcracker, Dorothy Chandler Pavilion, L.A., 1993, Palace Theatre, Stamford, Conn., 1993; repertoire Met. Opera House Symphonic Variations, Theme and Variations, The Nutcracker, Cruel World, Symphonie Concertante, Gala Performance, 1994, La Bayadera, Don Quixote, Paquite, How Near Heaven, Les Sylphides, Cruel World , Tchaikovsky Pas de Deux, Romeo and Juliet, 1995; guest artist Ballet Gala, Toronto, 1993, Colon Theatre, Buenos Aires, 1993, Gala Ballet of Aix-En-Provence, France, 1993, New Generation Ballet, Moscow, Gala Tribute to Nureyev, Toronto, Le Gala des Etoiles, Montreal, Internat. Evenings of Dance, Vail, Colo., Don Quixote, Kremlin Palace, Moscow, 1995. Recipient First prize Latino Am. Ballet Contest, Lima, Peru, 1985, Coca-Cola Contest of Arts and Scis., 1986, Finalist diploma XIV Varna (Bulgaria) Internat. Competition of Ballet, 1990; scholar Colon Theatre Found., 1989; Dance scholar Antorchas Found., 1991. Home: One Lincoln Plz 20 W 64th St Apt F New York NY 10023-7129 also: Billinghurst 2553 10 Piso Dto CP 1425 Buenos Aires Argentina Office: American Ballet Theatre 890 Broadway Fl 3 New York NY 10003-1278

HERRERA-LASSO, MIGUEL, manufacturing executive; Pres. European ops. Lear Corp., Southfield, Mich., sr. v.p., pres. elec. and electronic systems, 2005—. Office: Lear Corp 21557 Telegraph Rd PO Box 5008 Southfield MI 48086 Office Phone: 248-447-1500. Office Fax: 248-447-1722.*

HERRERA-LLERANDI, RODOLFO EDUARDO, surgeon, educator; b. Guatemala City, Guatemala, Aug. 6, 1915; s. Carlos and Chusita (Llerandi) H.; m. Odette Lefebre, June, 1954 (div. 1961); m. Evelina Gonzalez, 2003. BA, Paris U., 1932, BA, BPh, 1934; BS, MIT, 1938; MD, Harvard U., 1942; D (hon.), Francisco Marroquin U., Guatemala, 1995. Diplomate Am. Bd. Surgery. Resident and fellow in surgery Mass. Gen. Hosp., Boston, 1942-47; instr. in surgery Harvard Med. Sch., Boston, 1945-47; chief of surgery Hosp. San Vincente, Guatemala City, Guatemala, 1948-58; hon. prof. surgery U. De San Carlos, Guatemala City, 1955-67, Hosp. Mil., Guatemala City, 1955-67; dean and prof. surgery U Francisco Marroquin Sch. of Medicine, Guatemala City, 1978—; surgeon in chief U. Hosp. Esperanza, 1963—. Pres. Nat. Congress Medicine, 1956-57, Nat. Anti-TB Assn., Guatemala, 1960-62, Fund. Chusita Llerandi de Herrera, Guatemala, 1972—. Contbr. articles to profl. jours, sci. mags. Cons. Nat. Anti-TB Assn., Guatemala, Child Welfare Assn., Guatemala. Capt. Guatemalan Army. Decorated comdr. Legion of Honor France, chevalier Order St. Fortunat, Order Rodolfo Robles, Order Elisa Molina de Stahl Guatemala; recipient Orden del Quetzal, Gold medal, Mass. Gen. Hosp., 1961, U. San Carlos, 1967, Disting. Citizen diploma, Municipality de Guate, Guatemala, 1980, Banco Indsl., S.A., 1989, Rotary Club Guatemala, 1989. Mem. Internat. Soc. Surgery (nat. del. 1977-91), Am. Assn. Thoracic Surgeons (hon.), Coll. of Physicians and Surgeons of Guatemala. Avocations: helicopter pilot, collector mayan relics, Russian icons. Office: F Marroquin U Med Sch Med 6a Ave 7-55 Zona 10 01010 Guatemala City Guatemala Home Phone: (502) 3310922; Office Phone: 502 3393244. Business E-Mail: llerandi@ufm.edu.gt.

HERRERO RODRIGUEZ DE MIÑON, MIGUEL, lawyer, legislator, consultant; b. Madrid, June 18, 1940; s. Miguel Herrero and Carmen Rodriguez de Miñon; m. Cristina de Jauregui Segurola, Nov. 6, 1975; children: Miguel, Cristina, Amaya. Student, U. Oxford, England, 1958, U. Luxembourg, 1962, U. Geneva, 1964; LLD, U. Madrid, 1965; BA, Licentiate Philosphy, U. Louvain, Belgium, 1966-68; Licentiate Literature, U. Madrid, 1969. Sr. legal advisor Spanish Adminstrn. (Conejo de Estado), Madrid, 1966—; gen. sec. Ministry of Justice, Madrid, 1976-77; mem. parliament, 1977—93; leader parliamentary majority, 1980-81; leader opposition parliamentary group, 1982-87; spokesman fgn. affairs opposition parliamentary group, 1987—91. Drafter Spanish Constitution, 1977—78; mem. Trilateral Commn., 1982—2004, Real Acad. Ciencias Morales y Politicas, 1991—, Constitutional Ct., Andorra, 2001—. Author: numerous books on constitutional law; contbr. articles to profl. jours. Decorated Gran Collar Merito Civil, Gran Cruz San Raimundo de Peñafort, Gran Cruz Isabel La Catolica, Orden del Merito Constitucional (Spain); Order of Merit (Italy). Mem. Bar Assn. Madrid, Nuevo Club, Gran Peña, Madrid Club de Campo. Roman Catholic. Avocations: hunting, collecting antique books. Office: Mayor 70, bajo izq 28013 Madrid Spain Office Phone: 34 915595405.

HERRETT, RICHARD ALLISON, agricultural research institute administrator; b. Buffalo, Aug. 4, 1932; s. Wilbert Atherton and Loys (Richards) H.; m. Virginia Walker, July 28, 1958 (div. July 1978); children: Steven Jay, Jeffrey James, William Allan; m. Joan Hanhauser Maurer, Aug. 26, 1978; 1 child, Maxwell. BS in Agrl. Rsch., Rutgers U., 1954; MS in Agronomy/Organic Chemistry, U. Minn., 1956, PhD in Plant Biochemistry/Organic Chemistry, 1959; postgrad., George Washington U., U. Calif., Berkeley. Leader rsch. team Boyce Thompson Inst., Yonkers, N.Y., 1959-61, Union Carbide Corp., Clayton, N.C., 1961-70; tech. mgr. ICI Ams. Inc., Wilmington, Del., 1970-75, dir. rsch. and devel., 1975-87, mem. govt. rels., sci. liaison, 1987-92; pres., cons. EnvirAg Assocs., Bethesda, Md., 1992-94; exec. dir. Agrl. Rsch. Inst., Bethesda, 1995—2002; ind. contractor, 2002—. Bd. dirs., treas., trustee N.C. Biotech Ctr., Research Triangle Park; bd. dirs. Agrl. Rsch. Inst./Bio, Washington; treas. C.V. Riley Found., Washington, 1988-92; vice chmn. exec. bd. Bus. Coun. on Indoor Air; appointee N.C. Bd. Sci. and Tech.; presenter in field. Contbr. chpts. to books, articles to profl. jours.; patentee in field. Upton Meml. scholar Rutgers U. Mem. AAAS, Internat. Union of Pure and Applied Chemists (fin. chmn.), Nat. Agrl. Chems. Assn. (chmn., mem. rsch. dirs. com.), Am. Chem. Soc., Weed Sci. Soc. Am., Sigma Xi, Inst. Food Technologists. Avocations: racquetball, skiing. Home: 23 Sonneborn Ln Severna Park MD 21146-4803 Office: Nat Assn State Depts Agr 1156 15th St NW Ste1020 Washington DC 20005 Office Phone: 202-296-9680. Personal E-mail: ariherrett@aol.com.

HERRICK, GREGORY EVANS, computer company executive; b. Ottumwa, Iowa, Nov. 23, 1951; s. Walter Edward and Doris Ann (Evans) H. BS, U. Iowa, 1974. Gen. mgr. retail stores Amana (Iowa) Soc., 1975; mktg. mgr. Meredith Corp., Des Moines, 1977—80; mktg. devel. mgr. Fingerhut Corp., Minnetonka, Minn., 1980—82; founder, pres., chief exec. officer, chmn. Zeos Internat., Mpls., 1982—95; CEO Yellowstone Aviation, Inc., Jackson, Wyo., 1996—; founder, mgr. Golden Wings Flying Mus., Mpls., 1998—; pres. Sky Media Historic Aviation and Flying Books, 1999—; founder, chmn. Aviation Found. Am., 2002—. Organizer Nat. Air Tour, 2003; founder Aircraft Owner mag., 2004. Editor: Complete Desk Reference, 1973; founder, pub. Aircraft Owner mag., 2005—; patentee and inventor electronics equipment. Mem.: Inst. Am. Entrepreneurs (Minn. Entrepreneur of Yr. 1991). Republican. Roman Catholic. Avocations: flying, skiing, sailing. Address: PO Box 6291 Jackson WY 83002-6291

HERRICK, JOHN DENNIS, financial planner, consultant, retired food products executive; b. St. Paul, Oct. 8, 1932; s. Willard R. and Gertrude (O'Connor) H. BA, U. St. Thomas, 1954; MBA (hon.), U. Laval, 1969. Field auditor Gen. Mills, Inc., Mpls., 1954-59, acctg. supr. Kankakee, Ill., 1959-61, adminstrv. mgr. Chgo., 1961-62, mgr. auditing Mpls., 1962-65, mgr. new bus. devel., 1965-66, dir. adminstrn. and controller Smiths Food Group (subs.) London, 1966-68; pres. Gen. Mills Cereals Ltd., Toronto, Ont., Canada, 1969-71; chmn. bd., pres., chief exec. officer Gen. Mills Canada, Inc., Toronto, Ont., Canada, 1971-86; chief operating officer Borden & Elliot, Toronto, 1986-89; cons. Palm Beach Gardens, Fla., 1989—; pres. J.D. Herrick Found. Past chmn. Grocery Products Mfrs. of Can., Toronto; dir. CP Express & Transport, Toronto; adv. bd. American Coll. Louvain, Belgium. Past pres. Jr. Achievement Can., Toronto, 1970-71, Am. Club; past chmn. Toronto Area Inds. Devel. Bd., Emmanuel Convalescent Found., Toronto, Toronto Harbour Commn.; past pres., mem. coun. Bd. Trade Met. Toronto; past vice-chmn. Nat. Theater Sch. Can., Montreal; bd. dirs., past pres. Cath. Charities Palm Beach; mem. pres.'s coun. U. St. Thomas; chmn.'s adv. bd. Rep. Nat. Com., pres. Roundtable NRSC; mem., treas. Rep Exec. Com., Palm Beach County; bd. past pres. DePorres P.L.A.C.E.; bd. dirs. Liberty Ednl. Forum; bd. govs. U. St. Thomas Law Sch.; rector's coun. St. Vincent de Paul Seminary. Capt. USAF, 1954-57. Decorated knight grand cross Knights of Holy Sepulchre, Order of St. John, knight comdr. Order of Polonia Restituta; recipient Queen's Silver Jubilee medal, 1978, Queen's Golden Jubilee medal, 2003, Bishop Cretin award, 2004; named Disting. Alumnus, U. St. Thomas, 1984. Mem.: Can. C. of C. (past chmn., gov.), Palm Beach Yacht Club, Capital Hill Club (Washington), KC, Accademia Italiana Della Cucuna Club, Hot Stove Club, NY Athletic Club, Gov. Club, Lambton Golf and Country Club, Royal Can. Yacht Club, Empire Club, Beefeater Club. Roman Catholic. Home: 529 S Flagler Dr 2 H West Palm Beach FL 33401-5933

HERRICK, TODD W., manufacturing executive; b. Tecumseh, Mich., 1942; Grad., U. Notre Dame, 1967. Dir. Tecumseh (Mich.) Products Co., 1973—, pres., COO, 1984—, CEO, 1987—2007, chmn. bd., 2003—07; chmn. emeritus Tecumseh (Mich.) Products Ct., 2007. Bd. trustees Howe Mil. Sch. Bd. mem. US C. of C. Capt. US Army. Office: Tecumseh Products Co 100 E Patterson St Tecumseh MI 49286-2087 Office Fax: 517-423-8760.

HERRICK, TRACY GRANT, fiduciary; b. Cleve., Dec. 30, 1933; s. Stanford Avery and Elizabeth Grant (Smith) Herrick; m. Maie Kaarsoo, Oct. 12, 1963; children: Sylvi Anne, Alan Kalev. BA, Columbia U., 1956, MA, 1958; postgrad., Yale U., 1957; MA, Oxford U., England, 1960. Economist Fed. Res. Bank, Cleve., 1960-70; sr. economist Stanford Rsch. Inst., Menlo Park, Calif., 1970-73; v.p., sr. analyst Shuman, Agnew & Co., Inc., San Francisco, 1973-75; v.p. Bank of Am., San Francisco, 1975-81; pres. Tracy G. Herrick, Inc., 1981—. Lectr. Stonier Grad. Sch. Banking Am. Bankers Assn., 1967—76; commencement spkr. Memphis Banking Sch., 1974; bd. dirs. Jefferies Group, Inc., chmn. bd. audit com., 1989—96, chmn. bd. compensation com., 1991—96, dir., 1983—99; bd. dirs. Jefferies & Co., Inc.; dir. Com. Monetary Rsch. and Edn., Inc.; chief economist, bd. dirs. Pvt. Bank of the Peninsula, Palo Alto, Calif., 2003—. Author: Bank Analyst's Handbook, 1978, Timing, 1981, Power and Wealth, 1988; contbr. Mem. adv. bd. Kara Found., Palo Alto, Calif. Fellow: Fin. Analysts Fedn.; mem.: San Francisco Soc. Security Analysts, Assn. Investment Mgmt. Rsch. Republican. Congregationalist. Home: 1150 University Ave Palo Alto CA 94301-2238 Office Phone: 650-321-4540.

HERRIDGE, ELIZABETH, museum director; Mng. dir. Guggenheim Hermitage Mus., Las Vegas, 2003—. Office: Guggenheim Hermitage Mus 3355 Las Vegas Blvd S Las Vegas NV 89109 Office Phone: 702-414-2002. E-mail: eherridge@guggenheim.org.

HERRIFORD, ROBERT LEVI, SR., retired military officer; b. Lewistown, Ill., May 4, 1931; s. John and Lola (Braden) H.; m. Muriel Jean Davis, July 10, 1949; children: Robert Levi, Thomas Merle, David William, Deborah S., Traci Ann. BS, U. Ariz., 1966, MBA, 1968. Enlisted U.S. Army, 1948, commd. 2d lt., 1952, advanced through grades to maj. gen., 1979; service in Vietnam, 1966-67; comdr. 269th Ordnance Group Ft. Bragg, NC, 1969-71; chief spl. items mgmt. Tank Automotive Command Detroit, 1971-72; comdr. Korean Procurement Agy. Seoul, 1973-74; dir. procurement Armaments Command Rock Island, Ill., 1974-76; comdr. Def. Contracts Region NY, 1976-78; asst. dep. chief of staff logistics Pentagon, 1978-80; dir. procurement and prodn. Devel. and Readiness Command Alexandria, Va., 1980-83; assoc. chief ops. officer, dir. support svcs. Argonne Nat. Lab., Ill., 1983—95; ret., 1995. Chmn. Minority Bus. Opportunity Council, N.Y.C., 1976-78. Decorated Legion of Merit, D.S.M., Def. Superior Service medal, Bronze Star, Airmedal, numerous others. Mem. Am. Def. Preparedness Assn., Assn. U.S. Army, Am. Legion, Nat. Contracts Mgmt. Assn. (chpt. pres. 1975-76) Office Phone: 217-793-1049. Personal E-mail: RobLHerr@insightbb.com. *There is no substitute in any career, but particularly in an Army officer's career, for hard work, dedication and absolute integrity. Subordinates, peers, and superiors can sense it in training, in garrison, and in battle. Many people, in all pursuits and professions, are created equal in talent. Only a very few are willing to give to that talent all the care and dedication that is required to bring it to the top of their chosen field. It is often easier to explain why you didn't make it than to devote all that is required to develop this talent.*

HERRIMAN, DARLEEN ANN, music educator; b. LA, Aug. 19, 1951; d. Manuel Bibbins and Mathilda B. (Miljak) Diaz; m. Raymond James Herriman, Jan. 12, 1973; children: James, Rachel, Joseph, Michael, Matthew. AA, Palomar Coll., 1998; music cert., Biola U., 1999. Music specialist San Diego Schs., 1995—2000; choral dir. San Diego Childrens Choir, 2001—03; choral dir., music specialist Francisc Parker Sch., San Diego, 2003—. Youth choral dir. St. Michael Cath. Ch., Poway, Calif., 1993—; founder, dir. North County Interfaith Childrens Choir, Escondido, Calif., 2003—. Mem.: Am. Choral Dirs. Assn. Republican. Roman Catholic. Avocations: harp, piano, writing, attending concerts and musical theater. Office: Francis Parker Sch 4201 Randolph St San Diego CA 92103

HERRING, CHARLES DAVID, lawyer, educator; b. Muncie, Ind., Mar. 18, 1943; s. Morris and Margaret Helen Herring; children: David, Margaret, Christopher. BA, Ind. U., 1965, JD cum laude, 1968. Bar: Ind. 1968, US Dist. Ct. (so. dist.) Ind. 1971, Calif. 1971, US Dist. Ct. (so. dist.) Calif. 1971, US Ct. Appeals (9th cir.) 1984. Rsch. assoc. Ind. U., 1965—68; intern Office of Pros. Atty., Monroe County, Ind., 1967—68; ptnr. Herring & Stubel, San Diego, Herring, Stubel & Lehr, San Diego, Herring & Loftus, San Diego, 1972—2002; shareholder Herring & Herring, 2002—; pvt. practice San Diego, 1972—. Prof. law Western State U., 1972—91; judge pro tem San Diego Probate Ct., San Diego Superior Ct., mediator; spkr. in field. Author: (with Jim Wade) California Cases on Professional Responsibility, 1976. Vice chmn. Valle de Oro Planning Com., Spring Valley, Calif., 1972-75; chmn. Valle de Oro Citizens Exec. Com. for Cmty. Planning, Spring Valley, 1975-78; mem. Coronado Cays Architecture Com.; chmn. bd. Operation Interdependence, 2007-. Served with US Army, 1965—72, served with USAR, 1972—80. Mem.: ABA (Best Brief award 1968), Conf. Spl. Ct. Judges, San Diego County Bar Assn., Calif. Bar Assn., Ind. Bar Assn., San Diego Lions Club (past pres., chmn. bd. 1989—2006), Order of Coif. Republican. Avocations: computers, boating, swimming, golf. Home: 4 Gingertree Ln Coronado CA 92118 Office: Herring & Herring, APC 1001 B Ave Ste 215 Coronado CA 92118 Office Phone: 619-437-9175. Business E-Mail: dherring@herringlaw.net.

HERRING, (WILLIAM) CONYERS, retired physicist, educator; b. Scotia, NY, Nov. 15, 1914; s. William Conyers and Mary (Joy) H.; m. Louise C. Preusch, Nov. 30, 1946; children— Lois Mary, Alan John, Brian Charles, Gordon Robert. AB, U. Kans., 1933; PhD, Princeton, 1937. NRC fellow Mass. Inst. Tech., 1937-39; instr. Princeton, 1939-40, U. Mo., 1940-41; mem. sci. staff Div. War Research, Columbia, 1941-45; prof. applied math. U. Tex., 1946; research physicist Bell Telephone Labs., Murray Hill, NJ, 1946-78; prof. applied physics Stanford (Calif.) U., 1978-81, prof. emeritus, 1981—. Mem. Inst. Advanced Study, 1952-53 Recipient Army-Navy Cert. of Appreciation, 1947; Distinguished Service citation U. Kans., 1973; J. Murray Luck award for excellence in sci. reviewing Nat. Acad. Scis., 1980; von Hippel award Materials Rsch. Soc., 1980, Wolf prize in physics, Wolf Found., Israel, 1985. Fellow Am. Phys. Soc. (Oliver E. Buckley solid state physics prize 1959), Am. Acad. Arts and Scis.; mem. AAAS, NAS, Am. Soc. Info. Scis. Home: 3945 Nelson Dr Palo Alto CA 94306-4524 Office Phone: 650-723-0686. Business E-Mail: conyers@stanford.edu.

HERRING, DAVID JOHN, dean, law educator; b. Detroit, July 9, 1958; s. John Edward and Hermia Rowena (Schellenberg) H.; m. Lu-in Wang, May 17, 1986; children: An-Li Wang Herring, Maia Tao Herring. BBA, U. Mich., 1980, JD, 1985. Bar: Mich. 1985, Ill. 1987, Pa. 1991. Jud. law clk. Mich. Ct. Appeals, Southfield, 1985-86; Bigelow fellow, instr. law U. Chgo. Sch. Law, 1986-87; asst. clin. prof. law U. Mich. Law Sch., Ann Arbor, 1987-90; dir. Legal Clinics U. Pitts. Sch. Law, 1990—98, assoc. dean for academic affairs, 1990—98, interim dean, 1998, dean, 1998—. Mem. Pa. Legal/Med. Adv. Bd. Child Abuse, Harrisburg, 1990—; mem., cons. Child Devel. Office, U. Pitts., 1990—. Author: (atty. tng. manual) Agency Attorney in Child Abuse Cases, 1990; contbr. articles to profl. jours. Grantee HHS, 1988, Legal Svcs. Corp., Pitts., 1990—. Mem. ABA, Mich. Bar Assn., Pa. Bar Assn. Avocation: running. Office: U Pitts Sch of Law 3900 Forbes Ave Pittsburgh PA 15213

HERRING, HUBERT B., editor; Bus. editor NY Times, NYC. Office: Bus Desk NY Times 229 W 43rd St New York NY 10036 Office Phone: 212-556-7395. Office Fax: 212-556-1967.

HERRING, JERONE CARSON, retired lawyer, bank executive; b. Kinston, NC, Sept. 27, 1938; s. James and Isabel (Knight) H.; m. Patricia Ann Hardy, Aug. 6, 1961; children: Bradley Jerone, Ansley Carole. AB, Davidson Coll., 1960; LL.B., Duke U., 1963. Bar: N.C. 1963. Assoc. McElwee & Hall, North Wilkesboro, N.C., 1965-69; ptnr. McElwee, Hall & Herring, North Wilkesboro, 1969-71; exec. v.p., sec., gen. counsel Br. Banking & Trust Co., Winston-Salem, NC, 1971—2003, BB&T Corp., Winston-Salem, 1995—2003. Mem. bd. adv. U. N.C. Ctr. Banking and Fin.; mem. bd. visitors Davidson Coll. Bd. dirs. Montreat Conf. Ctr. Devel. Found., Black Mountain Cmty. Devel. Fund; mem. Town of Montreat Planning and Zoning Commn.; Served to capt. U.S. Army, 1963-65. Mem. NC Bar Assn. Presbyterian. Personal E-mail: jherring123@charter.net.

HERRING, JOAN SANDERS, secondary school educator; b. St. Louis, Dec. 19, 1941; d. Eugene William Sanders and Ruth Chestine (Bailey) Williford; m. Whitley S. Ward, June 30, 1961 (div. 1987); children: Todd Ward, Susan Ward Wright; m. Charles E. Herring, May 19, 1990. BA in Chemistry, Emory U., 1963. Rsch. chemist Armour Agrl. Chem. Co., Atlanta, 1963-65; tchr. Alameda (Calif.) Unified Sch. Dist., 1966, 67, Naples (Fla.) Christian Acad., 1987—89. Mem. hosp. svc. league, Naples Cmty. Hosp., 1969-71; tchr. Sunday sch., First Presbyn. Ch., Naples, 1973, 74, 76, vacation Bible sch., 1975; treas. Mothers Club, Naples Christian Acad., 1981-82. Mem. Phi Beta Kappa, Sigma Pi. Republican. Avocations: tennis, competitive ballroom dancing.

HERRING, KATHERINE L., historian; d. Raymond R. Jr. and Shirley M. Orben; m. Daniel A. Herring, Sept. 2, 2000; 1 child, Daniel Quintin. BA in History, Adrian Coll., Mich., 2000; MA in Hist. Adminstrn., Ea. Ill. U., Charleston, 2004. Admissions counselor U. Findlay, Ohio, 2000—01; historic sites intern Macon County Conservation Dist., Decatur, Ill., 2003—04, vol. coord., 2004; hist. interpreter Toledo Area Metroparks, 2005—. Mem.-at-large Hist. Adminstrn. Program Alumni, Charleston, 2005—; mem. coord. coun. Midwest Outdoor Mus.; chmn. daycare bd. 1st United Meth. Ch., Bellevue, Ohio, 2006—, mem. staff parish com., 2006. Mem.: Assn. State and Local History, Order Ea. Star. Republican. Office: Toledo Area Metroparks 5100 W Central Ave Toledo OH 43615

HERRING, OLIVER, artist; b. Heidelberg, Germany, 1964; BFA, U. Oxford Ruskin Sch. Drawing and Fine Art, Eng., 1988; MFA, Hunter Coll., NY, 1991. One-man shows include work Space Gallery, New Mus. Contemporary Art, NYC, 1993, Mannheimer Kunstverein, Mannheim, 1993, Max Protetch Gallery, NYC, 1994, 1996, 1997, 1998, Space Untitled, NY, 1994, Bernard Toale Gallery, Boston, 1994, Solomon R. Guggenheim Mus., NY, 1996, Mus. Modern Art, NYC, 1996, Manfred Baumgartner Gallery, Washington, 1996, Newlyn Art Gallery, Penzance, Eng., 1997, Camden Art Ctr., London, 1997, Ace Galleries, LA, 1999, Exit, Inst. Visual Arts, Milw., 2001, Concealed Mystery Sonata, Paris, 2002, exhibited in group shows at List Art Ctr., Brown U., Providence, 1995, Queens Libr. Gallery, NY, 1996, New Mus. Contemporary Art, 1996, Randolph St. Gallery, Chgo., 1996, Contemporary Mus., Honolulu, 1996, Max Protetch Gallery, NYC, 1997, Galerie Thaddaeus Ropac, Paris, 1997, Alterations, James Grayham and Sons, NYC, 2001, Officina Americana, Galleria d'Arte Moderna, Bologna, Italy, 2002. Grantee, Mass. Arts Lottery, 1989, NY Found. Arts, 1995, Joan Mitchell Foundation, 1999. Office: c/o Max Protetch Gallery 511 W 22d St New York NY 10011

HERRING, REBECCA ROYCE, music educator, consultant; b. Charlotte, NC, Mar. 16, 1954; d. Earle Allen Royce and Edna Linder; m. Kenny Herring, Feb. 11, 2000; children: Elizabeth Danielle, Michael Alexander. BA, U. N.C., 1973; B in Theatre, U. N.C., 1974; MA in End., Johnson State Coll., 1998; specialist in supervision and tng., Coll. State Joseph, 1999; cert. in advanced grad. studies in edn., Boston U., 2005. Dir. vocal music West Mecklenburg H.S., Charlotte, NC, 1999—2003; chairperson dept. fine and performing arts E. E. Waddell H.S., Charlotte, 2003—. Dir. ADEPT Ednl. Cons., Charlotte, 2000—. Singer: Singers of Renaissance; contbr. articles to profl. jours. Mem.: MENC (assoc.), Am. Choral Dir.'s Assn. (assoc.). Office: E E Waddell High Sch 7030 Nations Ford Rd Charlotte NC 28217 Home Phone: 704-537-2580; Office Phone: 980-343-6769. Office Fax: 980-343-6771. Personal E-mail: rebeccaherring@bellsouth.net. Business E-Mail: rebeccak.herring@cms.k12.nc.us.

HERRINGER, FRANK CASPER, diversified financial services company executive; b. NYC, Nov. 12, 1942; s. Casper Frank and Alice Virginia (McMullen) H.; m. Maryellen B. Cattani; children: William, Sarah, Julia. AB magna cum laude, Dartmouth Coll., Hanover, NH, 1964, MBA with highest distinction, 1965. Prin. Cresap, McCormick & Paget, Inc., NYC, 1965-71; staff asst. to Pres. of US, Washington, 1971-73; adminstr. U.S. Urban Mass Transp. Adminstrn., Washington, 1973-75; gen. mgr. San Francisco Bay Area Rapid Transit Dist., 1975-78; exec. v.p. Transam.

Corp., San Francisco, 1979-86, pres., dir., 1986-99, CEO, 1991-99, chmn., 1996—; mem. exec. bd. AEGON N.V., 1999-2000; chmn. AEGON USA, 1999-2000. Bd. dirs. Amgen Corp., Charles Schwab & Co., Mirapoint, Inc., Aegon USA, Calif. Pacific Med. Ctr., Cardax Pharmaceuticals, Inc. Mem. Cypress Point Club, San Francisco Golf Club, Nanea Golf Club, Olympic Club, Claremont Country Club, Pacific Union Club, Stock Farm Club, Phi Beta Kappa. Office: Transam Corp 600 Montgomery St San Francisco CA 94111-2702

HERRINGER, MARYELLEN CATTANI, lawyer; b. Bakersfield, Calif., Dec. 1, 1943; d. Arnold Theodore and Corinne Marilyn (Kovacevich) C.; m. Frank C. Herringer; children: Sarah, Julia. AB, Vassar Coll., Poughkeepsie, NY, 1965; JD, U. Calif., Boalt Hill, 1968; Exec. Program, Stanford Grad. Sch. Bus., 1994. Assoc. Davis Polk & Wardwell, NYC, 1968-69, Orrick, Herrington & Sutcliffe, San Francisco, 1970-74, ptnr., 1975-81; v.p., gen. counsel Transamerica Corp., San Francisco, 1981-83, sr. v.p., gen. counsel, 1983-89; ptnr. Morrison & Foerster, San Francisco, 1989-91; sr. v.p. gen. counsel APL Ltd., Oakland, Calif., 1991-95, exec. v.p., gen. counsel, 1995-97; gen. counsel allied bus. Littler & Mendelson, San Francisco, 2000. Bd. dirs. ABM Industries Inc., PG&E Corp., Pacific Gas and Electric Co., Wachovia Corp. Author: Calif. Corp. Practice Guide, 1977, Corp. Counselors, 1982. Regent St. Mary's Coll., Moraga, Calif., 1986-, pres., 1990-92, trustee, 1990-99, chmn., 1993-95; trustee Vassar Coll., 1985-93, The Head-Royce Sch., 1993-02, Mills Coll., 1999-, The Benilde Religious & Charitable Trust, 1999-, Alameda County Med. Ctr. Hosp. Authority, 1998-02, U. Calif. Berkeley Art Mus., 2001-; bd. dirs. The Exploratorium, 1988-93. Mem. ABA, State Bar Calif. (chmn. bus. law sect. 1980-81), Bar Assn. San Francisco (co-chair com. on women 1989-91), Calif. Women Lawyers, San Francisco C. of C. (bd. dirs. 1987-91, gen. counsel 1990-91), Am. Corp. Counsel Assn. (bd. dirs. 1982-87), Women's Forum West (bd. dirs. 1984-87). Democrat. Roman Catholic. Personal E-mail: mherringer@aol.com.

HERRINGTON, DAVID MCLEOD, cardiologist, educator; b. Seattle, Feb. 15, 1957; s. Robert and Margaret (McLeod) H.; m. Deirdre Achtellik, Nov. 26, 1983; children: Daniel, Kristen. BS in Math., Davidson Coll., NC, 1979; MD, U. N.C., 1983; MHS in Epidemiology, Johns Hopkins U., 1989. Lic. physician, N.C., Md. Intern Johns Hopkins Hosp., Balt., 1983-84, resident, 1984-86, fellow various divsns., 1986-90; asst. prof. cardiology Bowman Gray Sch. Medicine, Wake Forest Univ., Winston-Salem, NC, 1990-95, assoc. prof., 1995—, and assoc., pub. health sci. Dir. SHAC Clinic, U. N.C. Sch. Medicine, Chapel Hill, 1980-81, dir. CROP Lunch, 1980-81; mem. FDA adv. com. on use of QCA in Angiography, Bethesda, Md., 1991, NIA adv. com. on Conf. on DHEA and Aging, 1992; chmn. cardiovascular endpoints com. Asymptomatic Carotid Atherosclerosis Study, 1993—; rapporteur cardiovascular working group NIH Workshop on Menopause, Bethesda, 1993; mem. NIA ad hoc rev. com., 1994, sci. adv. cardiovascular disease, Kronos Longevity Rsch. Inst. Editl. cons. Am. Jour. Medicine, Am. Jour. Cardiology, Am. Jour. Epidemiology and Prevention, Arteriosclerosis and Thrombosis, Catheterization and Cardiovascular Diagnosis, Controlled Clin. Trials, Circulation, Exptl. Gerontology, IEEE Transactions on Biomed. Engring., New Eng. Jour. Medicine, Transactions on Med. Imaging, Williams and Wilkins; contbr. articles to profl. jours., chpts. to books. Bd. dirs. Sem. Ridge Neighborhood Assn., Lutherville, Md., 1988-90; mem. Leadership Circle, United Way, Winston-Salem, N.C., 1991—. Recipient Andrew W. Mellon Found. fellowship award in clin. epidemiology, 1986-88, Hartford Geriatric Acad. Initiative fellowship award, 1992; grantee Nat. Rsch. Svc., 1986-88, Nat. Am. Heart Assn., 1991-94, Wyeth-Ayerst, 1992-99, NIH, 1994-99. Fellow Am. Coll. Cardiology; mem. Am. Heart Assn. (fellow coun. on epidemiology and prevention 1995), Am. Fedn. Clin. Rsch. (young faculty award So. sect. 1991), N.Y. Acad. Scis. Avocation: astronomy. Office: Cardiology Wake Forest Sch Medicine Med Ctr Blvd Winston Salem NC 27157-0001*

HERRINGTON, E. PAUL, III, lawyer; BA in English, Bucknell Univ., Lewisburg, Pa., 1977; JD, Univ. Louisville, 1982. Bar: Ky. 1982. Assoc. to ptnr. Barnett & Alagia, 1982—89; sr. ins. counsel Humana Inc., Louisville, 1989—. Pres. Ky. Shakespeare Festival. Mem.: Louisville Bar Assn., Ky. Bar Assn., ABA (ho. dels. 1998—, bd. govs. 2006—, founding mem. Health Law sect. 1996—97). Office: Humana Inc Fl 7 500 W Main St Louisville KY 40202 Office Phone: 502-580-3716. Office Fax: 502-580-4831.

HERRINGTON, HOWARD RAY, artist; b. Pitts., June 22, 1925; s. Lee Roy and Orlie Eleanor (Bowie) Herrington; m. Evelyn Amelia Swienski, Sept. 7, 1957 (dec. May 1966); children: Linda Lee, Debra Lynn, Cathy Ann. Diploma, Simboli Art Acad., 1951; cert., Carnegia Mellon U., 1985, U. Pitts., 1987. Ordained deacon Eastminster Presbyn. Ch., Pitts., 1972. Artist Advertizers Assn., Pitts., 1951—53; supr. artist Pitts. Area Transp. Study, 1960—66; supr. mapping dept. Pitts. Regional Planning, 1966; supr. Southwestern Pa. Regional Planning Commn., Pitts., 1966—69; supr. cartography Dept. City Planning, Pitts., 1969—91. Bd. deacons Eastminster Presbyn. Ch., Pitts., 1972—84. Pvt. 1st class USMC, 1943—45, PTO-Okinawa. Mem.: R-E Club, Order Eagles, VFW, Am. Legion. Democrat. Presbyterian. Avocations: drawing, painting, reading, movies, music. Home: 630 N Aiken Ave Pittsburgh PA 15206

HERRINGTON, JOHN DAVID, III, retired lawyer, director; b. Warren, Ohio, Nov. 19, 1934; s. John David Jr and Gertrude Francis (Herlinger) Herrington; m. Phoebe Jane Henderson, Mar. 16, 1957; children: Gay Annette, Joy Ann, Jennifer John. BSBA, Ohio State U., 1956. CPA Pa. With Price Waterhouse & Co., Pitts., 1956-63; asst. to sec.-treas. Fisher Sci. Co., Pitts., 1963-65, controller, 1965-71, v.p. fin., treas., 1971-78, sr. v.p. fin., treas., 1979-82; exec. dir. Reed Smith Shaw & McClay, Pitts., 1982-86; ret., 1986. Bd. dirs. Hi Pure, Inc, Rochester Sci., Pfeiffer Glass, E & A Bldg. Corp., F. S. de Mex., Conco Inc. Bd. dirs. Family and Children Svcs. Pitts. With AUS, 1957—58. Mem.: AICPA, Assn. Legal Adminstrs., Pa. Soc. CPAs, Planning Execs. Inst., Tax Execs. Inst., Fin. Execs. Inst. Home: 9402 Babcock Blvd Allison Park PA 15101-2011 also: 9721 S Old Oregon Inlet Rd Nags Head NC 27959-9376

HERRINGTON, PATSY JEAN STARK, music educator; d. Orlin Ray and Madeline Whiteley Stark; m. Sterling Ross Herrington; children: Bobby Max Ham, Kimberly Jean Ham Eudy, Lex S., Lisa P. Herrington Welborn. Student, Wayland Bapt. U., Plainfield, Tex., 1965—70; BA, North Tex. U., Denton. Cert. Am. Coll. Musicians. Piano/organ tchr., Quitaque; organist 1st Bapt. Ch., Quitaque; adjucator Am. Coll. Musicians, Austin, Tex. Mem.: Nat. Guild Piano Tchrs. (tchr. divsn.), We the Women (pres. 2002—). Home: 217 Morris Quitaque TX 79255

HERRLING, CHRISTOPHER J., lawyer; BA, Univ. Rochester, 1976; JD, Catholic Univ., Washington, 1980. Bar: DC 1981, NY 1981. Staff atty. Legal Aid Soc., Washington, 1984—94, exec. dir., 1994—97; pro bono counsel Wilmer Cutler Pickering Hale & Dorr, Washington, 1997—. Mem. ABA AIDS Coord. Com., 2003—03. Recipient Pub. Svc. award, Bar Assn. DC, 1997. Office: Wilmer Cutler Pickering Hale & Dorr 2445 M St NW Washington DC 20037 Office Phone: 202-663-6780. Office Fax: 202-663-6363. Business E-Mail: christopher.herrling@wilmerhale.com.

HERRMAN, ERNIE, retail executive; Buyer TJX Cos., Inc., Framingham, Mass., 1989, v.p., sr. mdse. mgr., 1995—96, v.p., gen. mdse. mgr., 1996—98, sr. v.p. merchandising, 1998—2001, exec. v.p. merchandising Marmaxx Group, 2001—04, exec. v.p., COO Marmaxx Group, 2004—05, exec. v.p., pres. Marmaxx Group, 2005—07, sr. exec. v.p., pres. Marmaxx Group, 2007—. Office: TJX Cos Inc 770 Cochituate Rd Framingham MA 01701 Office Phone: 508-390-1000.*

HERRMANN, BENJAMIN EDWARD, former insurance executive; b. Bensonhurst, NY, May 9, 1919; s. Benjamin Edward and Ethel (Cuff) H.; m. Jean Clare Yancey, Oct. 19, 1946 (dec. Mar. 1, 1994); children: Benjamin E., Elizabeth M.; m. Mary Anne O'Connor, Oct. 20, 1995. BS, Columbia, 1941. C.L.U. With Home Life Ins. Co. N.Y., NYC, 1941-68; regional v.p. Northeastern U.S., P.R., 1960-68; agy. v.p. Acacia Mut. Life Ins. Co., Washington, 1968-75; exec. com., dir. Acacia Nat. Life Ins. Co.; Acacia Equity Sales Corp. regional v.p. Met. N.Y., Home Life Ins. Co., NYC, 1975-78, v.p. sales adminstrn., 1978-80, v.p. mktg., 1980-84; pres. Nat. Benefit Plans Inc., Norfolk, Va., 1986-93. Mem. Planning Bd., Madison, N.J., 1963-68, chmn., 1967-68; mem. Zoning Bd. Adjustment, 1964-68, chmn., 1966. Served to 1st lt. USAAF, 1943-46, PTO. Fellow Life Mgmt. Inst.; mem. Life Ins. Mgmt. and Rsch. Assn. (exec. devel. com., chmn. agy. officers roundtable com. 1968-76, chmn. 1976, chmn. tng. dirs. subcom. 1974-76, grad. sch. agy. mgmt., agy. officer sch., sr. mktg. officers' seminar), Soc. CLUs, Golden Key Soc., U.S. Squash Racquets Assn. (bd. dirs. 1986-95), Va. Squash Racquets Assn. Inc. (pres. 1986-91, chmn. 1991-95), Intertel, Mensa, Kingsmill Golf Club, The Jesters Club, Nat. Eagle Scout Assn. Republican. Presbyterian. Home: 105 Elizabeth Page Williamsburg VA 23185-5108 E-mail: ben.herrmann@cox.net.

HERRMANN, DEBRA MCGUIRE, chemist, educator; b. Ft. Benning, Ga., Dec. 28, 1955; d. Delbert Wayne and Twyla Pauline (Moran) McGuire; m. David Read Hermann, Aug. 2, 1980; children: Adam James Hermann, Jesse Read Hermann, Aaron Matthew Hermann. BS in Chemistry, U. Tex., 1979, U. Ark., 1989. Rsch. chemist Dow Chem., Oyster Creek, Freeport, Tex., 1980-84; chemist Aluminum Co. Am., Bauxite, Ark., 1984-87; tchr. Little Rock Sch. Dist., 1987-90; tchr. chemistry and integrated physics and chemistry Carroll Ind. Sch. Dist., Southlake, Tex., 2002—04; tchr. advanced placement and pre advanced placement chemistry Keller Ind. Sch. Dist., Tex., 2004—. Pres., bd. dirs. Little Peoples Acad. Sch. Montessori, Ottumwa, Iowa, 1990—93; den leader Cub Scouts. Mem.: PEO, Phi Beta Kappa. Democrat. Presbyterian. Avocations: walking, sailing, gardening, painting. Home: 1100 Harbor Haven St Southlake TX 76092-2811

HERRMANN, EDWARD KIRK, actor; b. Washington, July 21, 1943; s. John Anthony and Jean Eleanor (O'Connor) H; m. Leigh Curran, Sept. 9, 1978 (div.). BA, Bucknell U., 1965; postgrad. (Fulbright scholar), London Acad. Music and Dramatic Art, 1968-69. With Dallas Theater Center, 4 years. Appeared in numerous plays including Moonchildren, Mrs. Warren's Profession (Tony award for Best Supporting actor 1976), Journey's End, 1978, The Beach House, 1979-80, Hedda Gabler, The Front Page, 1981, Plenty, 1982 (Theater Guild medal), Uncle Vanya, 1984, Tom and Viv, 1985, Not About Heroes, 1985, Julius Caesar, 1988, A Walk in the Woods (London), 1988-89, Harvey, 1990, Candy is Dandy: An Evening with Odgen Nash, 1993, Life Sentences, 1993; films include The Paper Chase, 1972, The Great Gatsby, 1973, Day of the Dolphin, 1973, The Great Waldo Pepper, 1974, The Betsy, 1977, The North Avenue Irregulars, 1977, The Brass Target, 1978, Take Down, 1978, Harry's War, 1979, Reds, 1981, Death Valley, 1982, A Little Sex, 1982, Annie, 1982, Mrs. Soffell, 1984, The Purple Rose of Cairo, 1985, The Man with One Red Shoe, 1985, Compromising Positions, 1985, The Lost Boys, 1987, Overboard, 1987, Big Business, 1988, Hero, 1992, Born Yesterday, 1993, My Boyfriend's Back, 1993, The Foreign Student, 1994, Richie Rich, 1994, Nixon, 1995, Critical Care, 1997, Better Living, 1998, Walking Across Egypt, 1999, Double Take, 2001, Down, 2001, The Cat's Meow, 2001, The Emperor's Club, 2002, Intolerable Cruelty, 2003, Welcome to Mooseport, 2004, The Aviator, 2004, Relative Strangers, 2006, The Pleasure of Your Company, 2006, Factory Girl, 2006, I Think I love My Wife, 2007; TV films include Eleanor and Franklin: The White House Years (TV Critics Circle award as Best Actor 1977), A Love Affair: The Eleanor and Lou Gehrig Story, 1978, Freedom Road, 1978, Portrait of a Stripper, 1979, Sorrows of Gin, 1979, M.A.S.H, 1979, The Private History of a Campaign that Failed, 1980, Dear Liar, 1981, The Electric Grandmother, 1982, The Gift of Life, 1982, Concealed Enemies, 1984, (BBC) A Foreign Field, 1992, Don't Drink the Water, 1994, The Face on the Milk Carton, 1995, Here Come the Munsters, 1995, Soul of the Game, 1996, A Season in Purgatory, 1996, What Love Sees, 1996, Pandora's Clock, 1996, Saint Maybe, 1998, Atomic Train, 1999, Vendetta, 1999, James Dean, 2001, (voice) Isaac's Storm, 2003, Bereft, 2004, (narrator) Eighty Acres of Hell, 2006, Violent Earth: New England's Killer Hurricane 2006; TV series: Gilmore Girls, 2000-; (host, cable TV) Our Century. Office: Ames Cushing William Morris Agy 151 S El Camino Dr Beverly Hills CA 90212-2704*

HERRMANN, JEFFREY W., lawyer; b. Bklyn., Nov. 10, 1952; s. Siegfried and Ann Herrmann; m. Linda J. Lowenstein, Sept. 12, 1976; children: Suzanne J., Neil L. BA in History, Columbia U., NYC, 1973, JD, 1976. Sr. ptnr. Cohn Lifland Pearlman Herrmann & Knopf LLP, Saddle Brook, NJ, 1976—. Pres. B'nai Brith Lodge, Fair Lawn, NJ, 1986—87, Fair Lawn Jewish Ctr., Fair Lawn, NJ, 2001—03. Mem.: ABA, Bergen County Bar Assn., NJ State Bar Assn. (chmn. securities litig. com.). Democrat. Jewish. Avocations: baseball, astronomy, Shakespeare. Office: Cohn Lifland Pearlman Herrmann & Knopf Park 80 Plz West One Saddle Brook NJ 07663 Home Phone: 201-791-5640; Office Phone: 201-845-9600. Office Fax: 201-845-9423. E-mail: jwh@njlawfirm.com.

HERRMANN, JEFFREY WILLIAM, engineering educator; s. Joseph William and Cecelia Herrmann; m. Laureen Garrity, July 9, 1995; 1 child, Colleen Rose. BS, Ga. Inst. Tech., Atlanta, 1990; PhD, U. Fla., Gainesville, 1993. Asst. prof. U. Md., College Park, 1995—2001, assoc. prof., 2001—, acting dir. Computer Integrated Mfg. Lab., 1996, assoc. dir. Computer Integrated Mfg. Lab., 1998—99, dir. Computer Integrated Mfg. Lab., 1999—. Presenter, cons. in field. Co-author: Product Engineering and Manufacturing, 1998, 2d edit., 2002; editor: Handbook of Production Scheduling, 2006; assoc. editor: IIE Trans. on Scheduling and Logistics, ASME Jour. Mech. Design, mem. editl. bd.: IIE Trans., 1996—98, 2001—02, Prodn. and Ops. Mgmt., 1999; contbr. articles to profl. jours., chapters to books. Recipient Jiri Tlusty Outstanding Young Mfg. Engr. award, Soc. Mfg. Engrs., 2003; grad. rsch. fellow, NSF, 1990—93, Presdl. scholar, Ga. Inst. Tech., 1985—90. Mem.: ASME, Am. Assn. Engring. Edn., Inst. Ops. Rsch. and Mgmt. Scis. Roman Catholic. Achievements include research in production scheduling; manufacturing system design; decision-making in product development. Office Phone: 301-405-5433.

HERRMANN, LACY BUNNELL, investment company executive, entrepreneur, venture capitalist; b. New Haven, May 12, 1929; s. James Joseph and Helen Georgia (Bunnell) H.; m. Elizabeth Ocumpaugh Beadle, May 23, 1953; children: Diana Parsons, Conrad Beadle. AB, Brown U., 1950; postgrad., London Sch. Econs., 1953-54; MBA, Harvard U., 1956. Asst. to purchasing mgr. and buyer Westinghouse Elec. Corp., Metuchen, NJ, 1956-60; asst. v.p. Douglas T. Johnston & Co., Inc., NYC, 1960-66; v.p. Johnston Mut. Fund, Inc., NYC, 1964-66; gen. ptnr. Tamarack Assocs., NYC, 1966-84; chmn. bd., pres. Family Home Products, Inc., NYC, 1972-84, Buxton's Country Shops, Jamesburg, NJ, 1973-86. Founder, pres. STCM Corp., moneymarket fund, NYC, 1974-76; vice chmn. bd. trustees, v.p. Centennial Capital Cash Mgmt. Trust, NYC successor to STCM Corp., 1976-81; chmn. bd. trustees, pres. successor fund Capital Cash Mgmt. Trust, 1981—; founder, chmn. bd. trustees, pres. Trinity Liquid Assets Trust, 1982-85, Oxford Cash Mgmt. Fund, 1982-88, Prime Cash Fund, 1982—; chmn., CEO, Aquila Mgmt. Corp., 1983—; founder, sponsor, mgr. Pacific Capital Cash Assets Trusts, 1984—, Hawaiian Tax-Free Trust, 1985—, Churchill Cash Reserves Trust, 1985—, Tax-Free Trust Ariz., 1986—, Tax-Free Trust Oreg., 1986—, Tax-Free Fund Colo., 1987—, Churchill Tax-Free Fund of Ky., 1987—, Pacific Capital Tax-Free Cash Assets Trusts, 1988—, Pacific Capital U.S. Govt. Securities Cash Assets Trust, 1988—, Narragansett Insured Tax-Free Income Fund, 1992—, Tax-Free Fund for Utah, 1992—, Aquila Rocky Mountain Equity Fund, 1994—, Aquila Cascadia Equity Fund, 1996-02, Aquila Three Peaks High Income Fund, 2006—, VP Aquila Distributors, Inc.; bd. dirs. Quest for Value Fund Investment Trust, Quest for Value Accumulation Trust, Quest Cash Res., Inc.; trustee Oppenheimer/Quest group funds global Value Fund, 1994—, Oppenneimer Rochester Funds; founding dir. mgmt. cons. firm merged with Towers, Perrin, Forster & Crosby; instr. Rutgers U., 1958-59; chmn., pres. bd. dirs. In-Cap Mgmt. Corp, 1984-98; spkr. in field. Contbr. articles to profl. jours. Organizer, trustee endowed award Internat. div. Grad. Sch. Journalism, Columbia U., 1962—; trustee Meml. and Endowment Trust of St. Paul's Ch., Westfield, N.J., 1968-96; mem. capital devel. com. St. Luke's Ch., Darien, Conn., 1978-85, mem. coll. scholarship fund com., 1976-85; trustee Brown U., 1990-96, trustee emeritus, 1996—, Hopkins Sch., New Haven, 1993-2003. Lt. (j.g.) USN, 1951-54, Korea; lt. USNR ret. Mem. N.Y. Soc. Security Analysts, Harvard Bus. Sch. Club N.Y. (bd. dirs., officer, 1958-71), Assoc. Alumni Brown U. (bd. dirs. 1978-87, exec. com. 1980-85, pres. 1983-85), Harvard Club, N.Y. Athletic Club, Brown U. Club, Brown U. of Fairfield Country Club (pres. 1977-82, bd. dirs. 1977—), Univ. Club (R.I.), Faculty Club Brown U., Stratton Mountain Country Club, Orleans Yacht Club, Ariz. Club, Eastward Ho, Chatham Mass., Outrigger Canoe Club (Honolulu), Lahaina Yacht Club (Maui). Republican. Episcopalian. Office: 380 Madison Ave New York NY 10017-2513 Home: 3310 Kendal Way Sleepy Hollow NY 10591 Office Phone: 212-697-6666. Personal E-mail: lherrmann@aquilafunds.com.

HERRMANN, PAUL C., physician, chemist; b. Radford, Va., Oct. 7, 1968; s. E. Clifford and Marilyn H.; m. Sarah E. Herrmann, July 7, 1996. BS in Chemistry, Andrews U., 1991; PhD in Chemistry, Stanford U., 1996; MD, Loma Linda U., 2000. Printer's apprentice Quick Print, Loma Linda, Calif., 1983-87; waste water lab. analyst Andrews U., Berrien Springs, Mich., 1987-89, boiler rm. water analyst, 1987-89; rschr. indsl. coop. LECO Corp., St. Joseph, Mich., 1989; sci. and engring. rsch. participant Oak Ridge (Tenn.) Nat. Lab., 1990; tchg. and rsch. asst. Stanford (Calif.) U., 1991-96, rsch. assoc., 1997; clin. fellow NIH, Bethesda, Md., 2000—. Contbr. articles to profl. jours.; lectr. in field. Mem. AMA, NY Acad. Scis., Phi Kappa Phi, Phi Lambda Epsilon, Pi Mu Epsilon, Sigma Xi. Avocations: archery, history, literature, hiking. Home: PO Box 437 Loma Linda CA 92354-0437 Business E-Mail: pherrmann@llu.edu.

HERRMANN, ROBERT LAWRENCE, biochemist, educator; b. NYC, July 17, 1928; s. Philip Charles and Florence Gertrude (Benn) Herrmann; m. Elizabeth Ann Cook, Aug. 12, 1950; children: Stephen, Karen, Holly, Anders. BS in Chemistry, Purdue U., 1951; PhD in Biochemistry, Mich. State U., 1956. Postdoctoral fellow MIT, 1956-59; from asst. prof. to assoc. prof. biochemistry Boston U. Sch. Medicine, 1959-76; prof., chmn. dept. biochemistry Oral Roberts U. Sch. Medicine and Dentistry, Tulsa, 1976-81, assoc. dean biomed. sci., 1978-79; lectr. chemistry Gordon Coll., Wenham, Mass., 1981, adj. prof., 1982-97; exec. dir. Am. Sci. Affiliation, 1981-93; program dir. John Templeton Found., 1992—2002. Judge Templeton Prize Progress in Religion, 1999—2001. Editor: Prog. in Theology newsletter of John Templeton Found., 1992—2000; contbr. chapters to books, articles to profl. jours. Mem. Bd. Health, Bedford, Mass., 1975—76; trustee Christian Med. Soc., 1976—79, Barrington Coll., 1975—78, Templeton Found., 1987—95, 1996—2002, Southeastern Mass. U., 1988—91. With USN, 1946—48, with USN, 1951—52. Fellow: AAAS, Gerontol. Soc.; mem.: Am. Sci. Affiliation, European Soc. Study Sci. and Theology, Sci. and Religion Forum, Am. Soc. Biochem. and Molecular Biology. Evangelical Christian. Home and Office: 12 Spillers Ln Ipswich MA 01938-2430

HERRMANN, THOMAS FRANCIS, systems administrator; b. Kenosha, Wis., Sept. 28, 1951; s. Matthias Bernard and Sebastiana J. (Placente) H.; m. Gail Ann Sipsma, Oct. 25, 1975; children: Aaron Matthew, Joel Michael, Andrew Jacob, Justin Thomas. Student, Gateway Tech. Inst., 1969, U. Wis., Kenosha, 1973, Kennedy-We. U., 1995—97; BA magna cum laude, Shefferton U., 2001. Programmer Snap-On Tools Corp., Kenosha, 1975—79; project leader Jacobsen Mfg. Co., Racine, Wis., 1979—80; database analyst Jupiter Transp. Co., Kenosha, 1980—82; sys. programmer Citibank S.D., Sioux Falls, 1982—85; database adminstr. Sandoz Crop Protection, Chgo., 1985—86; cons. data processing Applied Info. Devel., Inc., Oak Brook, Ill., 1986—89, Trilogy Cons. Corp., Waukegan, Ill., 1989; database adminstr. Waste Mgmt., Inc., 1989—93; mgr. database Newark Electronics, Inc., 1993—97, ADP/Adminstrv. Solutions Group, 1997—2000; mgr. change control, customer svc. delivery team Washington Mut., 2000—. Pres. Software AG User Group, Chgo., 1991-95, v.p. midwest region; pres. CD Cleavers, 1995-99 Editor newsletter Open Channel, 1985-92 Candidate Common Coun., Kenosha; dir./sec. Vernon Hills Youth Baseball/Softball Assn.; youth and young adult sports coach, 1970—. Mem. Data Processing Mgmt. Assn. (reporter newsletter 1981-82), Nat. Youth Sports Coach Assn. (life, cert.), Chgo. Indsl. Chess League, USS Halsey Club (Sioux Falls), USS Voyager Club (Vernon Hills, Ill.) Roman Catholic. Avocations: sports, music, books. E-mail: tfhermann@yahoo.com, thomas_f_herrmann@hotmail.com.

HERRNKIND, HILDA MARIE, writer, military volunteer; b. Miami, Fla., Jan. 6, 1974; d. Jeanette Marie Herrnkind. A of Bus Admin. (hon.), Mt. Wachusett C.C., 1999. Cert. computer asst. acctg., Mt. Wachusett C.C., 1999; small bus. mgmt. Mt Wachusett C.C., 2000. Sales and svc. assoc. Bankboston, Gardner, Mass., 1996—99; writer Ind., 1999—. Coord. first investment seminar for customers Bankboston, Gardener, Mass., 1998, coord. first how-to banking program for H.S. students, 98. Contbr. (photos) A Moment in Time, In Enduring Textures, 2000, At the End of a Rainbow, In Chasing Dreams, 2000, Internat. Libr. Photography. Vol. USNG, Gardner, Mass., 2001; founder, pres. Make a Difference Found. in Memory of Jeanette Marie Herrnkind, 2004—; asst. to commdg. officer USNG, Gardner, Mass., 2001—02, asst. for N.Y. relief drive, 2001, mng. unit raffle, 2001—02. Decorated Unit Coin Vol. Svcs. USNG; named to Wall of Tolerance New Civil Right Meml. Ctr., Montgomery, Ala., 2004; recipient Svc. Stars for Intergrity and Teamwork, Bankboston, 1997—98. Mem.: USNG (hon.; auxliary mem. 2001), Alpha Beta Gamma (life Nat. Bus. Honor Soc. Cert. 1994). Avocations: reading, singing, travel, sports.

HERRNSTADT, RICHARD LAWRENCE, American literature educator; b. NYC, Nov. 4, 1926; s. Oscar Edward and Helen (Lidz) H.; m. Helen Lea Appel, June 18, 1950; children— Steven, Ellen Sara, Owen BS, U. Wis., 1948, MS, 1950; PhD, U. Md., 1960. Instr. English Iowa State U., Ames, 1954-58, asst. prof., 1958-61, assoc. prof., 1961-65, prof., 1965-92, prof. emeritus, 1992—. Editor: The Letters of A. Bronson Alcott, 1969; contbr. articles to profl. jours. Bd. dirs. Ames Cmty. Sch. Dist., 1967—74, Iowa Humanities Programs, 1973—79, v.p., 1978—79; bd. dirs. Area Edn. Agy. 11, Johnston, Iowa, 1977—91, v.p., 1980—84, pres., 1984—87; bd. dirs. Youth and Shelter Svcs., Ames, 1980—91, v.p., 1984—85, pres., 1985—87; bd. dirs. Joint Action in Cmty. Svc., 1994—2006. Served with USN, 1945—46. Recipient faculty citation Iowa State U. Alumni Assn., 1983 Mem. MLA, Am. Studies Assn. (exec. council 1969-76), Thoreau Soc., Mid-Am. Am. Studies Assn. (v.p. 1961-62, pres. 1962-63), AAUP. Democrat. Jewish. Home: 5320 N Via Sempreverde Tucson AZ 85750-5970

HERROD, HENRY GRADY, III, pediatrics professor, allergist, immunologist; b. Oakland, Calif., Apr. 30, 1945; MD, U. Ala., 1972. Cert. allergy and immunology; cert. pediats. Intern U. Wash., Seattle, 1972-73, resident in pediats., 1973-74; resident rsch. assoc. in allergy and immunology NIH, Bethesda, Md., 1974-76; fellow in allergy and immunology Duke U., Durham, 1976-78; physician Le Bonheur Childrens Med. Ctr., Memphis; prof. U. Tenn., Memphis, dean, 1998—2005; fellow Urban Child Inst., Memphis, 2005—. Mem. AAAI, AAI, AAP, APS. Office: Urban Child Inst 600 Jefferson # 221 Memphis TN 38105 Home Phone: 901-685-6016; Office Phone: 901-576-3155. Business E-Mail: hherrod@utmem.edu.

HERRON, BONNIE L., management consulting company executive; BA in Edn., U. Toronto, BA in Phys. Edn.; MBA, Mercer U. Dir. athletics, Ontario, Canada; gen. mgr. Datavue Corp.; dir. planning Quadram Corp., Intelligent Systems Corp., CFO, v.p. and corp. sec.; exec. dir. Gwinnett Innovation Pk. Chair Growth Capital SIG, Entrepreneurial SIG; adv. coun. Intellectual Capital Partnership Prog., Ga.; bd. dirs. Tech. Assn. Ga.; bd. dirs. southeast chpt. Am. Electronics Assn.; mem. steering com. Gwinnett Tech. Forum; bd. dirs., former chair Nat. Bus. Incubation Assn.; bd. dirs. Atlanta Venture Forum. Named Woman of Yr. Tech. (small/medium bus.), (WIT) Women in Tech., 2005. Office: Intelligent Systsems Corp 4355 Shackleford Rd Norcross GA 30093 Office Phone: 770-381-2900. Office Fax: 770-381-2808. E-mail: bherron@intelsys.com.

HERRON, CINDY, actress, vocalist; b. San Francisco, Sept. 26, 1965; m. Glenn Braggs; 1 child, Donovan Andrew. Vocalist En Vogue, Atco/Eastwest Records, NYC. Albums include Born to Sing (Platinum 1990), Funky Divas, Remix to Sing, Runaway Love, The Best of En Vogue, 1999; actress (motion picture) Juice, 1992. Recipient Soul Train Music award, 1991; nominated Grammy award, 1990. Office: care En Vogue Atco Eastwest Records 75 Rockefeller Plz New York NY 10019-6908

HERRON, DAVID A., stock exchange executive; Grad., U. Calif., Berkeley, 1976. Floor reporter Pacific Stock Exch., mem. and specialist, Boston Stock Exch., 1982—84; various positions Fidelity Investments, 1984—98; v.p. listed equities Charles Schwab & Co., Inc., 1998; CEO Chgo. Stock Exch. (CHX), 2002—, CHX Holdings, Inc. Gov. Boston Stock Exch., 1991; trustee Cin. Stock Exch., 1996—2001; ofcl. Am. Stock Exch. Bd. mem. Ill. Coun. Edn., Midwest Regional Bd. of Operation Hope. Mem.: Security Traders Assn. Chgo. (bd. mem.). Office: Chgo Stock Exch One Financial Pl 440 S LaSalle St Chicago IL 60605*

HERRON, EDWIN HUNTER, JR., energy consultant; b. Shreveport, La., June 7, 1938; s. Edwin Hunter and Helen Virginia (Russell) H.; m. Frances Irvine Hunter, June 27, 1959; children: Edwin, David, Ashley. BS in Chem. Engring., Tulane U., 1959, MS, 1963, PhD (NSF fellow 1963-64), 1964. Rsch. engr. Exxon Rsch. & Engring. Co., Linden, N.J., 1959-61; sr. rsch. egnr. Exxon Prodn. Rsch. Co., Houston, 1964-66; corp. planning advisor Esso Europe, London, Eng., 1966-74; fin. analyst Exxon Corp., NYC, 1974-78; v.p. Gruy Petroleum Tech., Inc., McLean, Va., 1978-84; pres. Petro-Analysis, Inc. (named changed to Hunter Trading Co. Inc.), 1984—, Petroleum Equities, Inc., 1987—; dir. petroleum projects CORE Internat., Inc., 1989—; pres. Petroleum Holdings, Inc., 1993—; dir. World Energy Sys. Inc., 1999—2005. Contbr. articles to profl. publs. Recipient Levey award Tulane U., 1970. Mem. Soc. Petroleum Engrs., Am. Inst. Chem. Engrs., Sci. Rsch. Soc., Soc. Tulane Engrs., Tau Beta Pi. Home Phone: 703-356-9878; Office Phone: 703-734-0253. Business E-Mail: hunter.herron@petroleumequities.com.

HERRON, HARRIETTE A., retired occupational health nurse; b. Barberton, Ohio, Dec. 25, 1940; d. Edward Francis Hone and Monica Beatrice Lustig; m. Richard Hagen (div.); children: John Hagen, Robin Hagen, David Hagen, Denise Hagen. RN, Akron Gen. Hosp., 1961; BS in healthcare, U. St. Francis, 1985; degree in cons. nurse paralegal, Nat. Inst. for Paralegal Arts and Sci., 1999. Cert. occupational health nurse Calif., 1985; CPR First Aid Am. Red Cross, 1992. RN, charge nurse Akron Children's Hosp., Ohio, 1968—70; first aid attendent, RN Motion Picture Industry, Calif., 1970—76; dept. head Walt Disney Prodn., Burbank, Calif., 1976—86; med. supr. UPS, LA, 1986—93; med. svcs. and health safety UPS Corp. Office, Atllanta, 1993—2000, mgr. region occupl. health Laguna Hills, Calif., 2000—03; ret., 2003. Pres., dir. Southern Calif. Assn. Occupational Health Nurses, Los Angeles, Calif., 1986—88. Contbr. articles various profl. jours. Presenter, clin. session Annual Am. Assn. of Occupational Health Conf., 1985, 1986, Am. Soc. of Safety Engrs Nat. Conf., 1985, Calif. State Conf. Occupational Health Nurses, 1985; review com. NY libr. , McNeil Consumer Products Co. "Worksite Wellsite", 1988; presenter US Dept. of Health and Human Svcs. "Health Objectives for the Nation", 1988; co-chair Calif. State Occupational Health Nurses Conf., 1988; presenter Annual Mtg. AHA, Savannah, Ga., 1995. Recipient Outstanding Vol. of Yr., YWCA, 1974. Mem.: Am. Heart Assn. Avocations: travel, dance. Home: 135 Hillside Ln Roswell GA 30076 Personal E-mail: haherron@bellsouth.net.

HERRON, J. JAY, lawyer; b. Lake City, Minn., 1954; Student, Calif. State U., Fullerton; BS, U. Calif., Berkeley, 1977; JD, Stanford U., 1980. Bar: Calif. 1980, US Dist. Ct. (ctrl. dist.) Calif. 1980. Ptnr. O'Melveny & Myers LLP, Newport Beach, Calif., 1990—. Lectr. Calif. Continuing Edn. of the Bar, 1990—. Mem.: Order of the Coif, Beta Alpha Psi, Phi Beta Kappa. Office: O'Melveny & Myers LLP 610 Newport Ctr Dr 17th Flr Newport Beach CA 92660 Office Phone: 949-823-6922. Office Fax: 949-823-6994. Business E-Mail: jherron@omm.com.

HERRON, ORLEY R., college president; b. Olive Hill, Ky., Nov. 16, 1933; s. Orley R. and Hyllie W. (Weaver) H.; m. Donna Jean Morgan, Aug. 24, 1956; children: Jill Donette, Morgan Niles, Mark Weaver. BA, Wheaton Coll., 1955; MA, Mich. State U., 1959, PhD, 1965; LittD (hon.), Houghton Coll., 1972; LHD (hon.), Lesley Coll., 1983. Dean of students Westmont Coll., Santa Barbara, Calif., 1961-67; dir. doctoral program/student pers. U. Miss., 1967-68; asst. to pres. Ind. State U., 1968-70; pres. Greenville (Ill.) Coll., 1970-77, Nat Louis U. (formerly Nat. Coll. Edn.), Evanston, Ill., 1977-97; chmn., pres. ORH group eBooks Interactive, 1998—; founder AutoeDirect.com, Inc., 2000—; chmn., CEO Herron Multimedia, 2001—, BOT-Best of Thrift Travel, 2003—; chmn. Significant Living, 2003—; chmn., CEO Premier Entertainment, 2005—. Mem. Ill. Commn. for Improvement Elem. and Secondary Edn., 1983-1985; chmn. bd. Harris Bank, Wilmette, Ill., 1991—, also bd. dirs.; bd. dirs. Corp. Cmty. Schs. Am., 1989—. Author: Role of the Trustee, 1969, Input-Output, 1970, New Dimensions in Stude Personnel Administration, 1970, A Christian Executive in a Secular World, 1979, Who Controls Your Child?, 1980, Words to Live By, 1997, Notes for the New Millennium, 2000, Song of Blessing, 2004; (cassette) Governing Higher Education in the 70's, 1970; exec. prodr., composer, songwriter (CD) I Love You My Dearest Darling, 2001, (featuring Orley Herron and The Crew Cuts) Until We Meet Again, 2005. Rep. of Pres. U.S. 25th Anniversary UNESCO, 1971; adv. bd. Expt. on Internat. Living, Santa Barbara, 1961-67; mem. Gov.'s Task Force on Encouraging Citizen Involvement in Edn., 1986-87; nat. dir. educators for reelection of Pres., 1972; bd. dirs. Ch. Centered Evangelism; mem. Chgo. Sun. Evening Club, 1987-97; founder Santa Barbara Industries. Lt. comdr. U.S. Naval Res., 1973-77. Recipient Crusader Christian Contbn. award Wheaton Coll., 1955, 74, Outstanding Citizen award Greenville Jaycees, 1971, Outstanding Educator award Religious Heritage of Am., 1987, Disting. Alumnus award Wheaton Coll., Outstanding Alumnus award New Philadelphia H.S., Amicus Polonae award, 1996. Mem. AAUP, SAG, Am. Assn. Higher Edn., Coun. Interinstnl. Cooperation (pres.), Coun. Advancement Small Colls. (sec.), Christian Coll. Consortium (exec. com.), Fedn. Ind. Ill. Colls. (exec. bd. 1971-97), Assn. Free Meth. Ednl. Instns. (pres. 1973-75), Rotary, Kiwanis. Office Phone: 847-295-4221.

HERSBERGER, RODNEY M., library association executive, school librarian; BA in Acctg., Ind. U., MLS; MBA, Northern Ill. U. With Northern Ill. U.; asst. to dean adminstrv. services U. Okla., acting asst. dir. tech. services; with Calif. State U. Bakersfield, 1984—, dean U. Libr.; founder LibrariesByDesign, LLC, 2001—. Mem.: ALA-AIA (juror libr. buildings award com. 1997, 1999), Libr. Adminstrn. Mgmt. Assn. (chair fin. mgmt. com. 1982—84, rep. to ALA Coun. 1989—93), ALA (mem. budget analysis and review com. 2005—, treas. 2007—). Office: Walter W Stiern Libr Calif State U-Bakersfield 9001 Stockdale Hwy Bakersfield CA 93311-1022 Office Phone: 661-654-3042. Office Fax: 661-654-3238. Business E-Mail: rhersberger@csub.edu.*

HERSCH, DENNIS STEVEN, bank executive, lawyer; b. Bklyn., Mar. 20, 1947; s. Alfred and Florence (Flom) H.; m. Huguette Marcelle Lefebvre, June 20, 1976; children: Gregory Alain, Jeremy Lawrence. AB cum laude, Bklyn. Coll., 1967; JD cum laude, NYU, 1970. Bar: N.Y. 1971, U.S. Dist. Ct. (so. dist.) N.Y. 1972, U.S. Ct. Appeals (2nd cir.) 1975. Assoc. Davis Polk & Wardwell, NYC, 1970-78, ptnr., 1978—2005, co-head mergers & acquisitions practice group; global chmn. mergers & acquisition J.P. Morgan Chase & Co., NYC, 2006—. Bd. dirs. Limited Brands, Inc. Contbr. articles to profl. jours. Recipient Judge Learned Hand Award, Am. Jewish Com., 2003. Mem. ABA, N.Y. State Bar Assn, Lawyer's Com N.Y. Pub. Library, Horiticultural Soc. N.Y. (chmn. & dir.). Jewish. Office: JP Morgan & Chase Co 277 Park Ave New York NY 10017 Home Phone: 212-288-4033; Office Phone: 212-622-1751. Business E-Mail: dennis.s.hersch@jpmorgan.com.

HERSCHBACH, DUDLEY ROBERT, chemistry professor; b. San Jose, Calif., June 18, 1932; s. Robert Dudley and Dorothy Edith (Beer) Herschbach; m. Georgene Lee Botyos, Dec. 26, 1964; children: Lisa Marie, Brenda Michele. BS in Math., Stanford U., 1954, MS in Chemistry, 1955; AM in Physics, Harvard U., 1956, PhD in Chem. Physics, 1958; DSc (hon.), U. Toronto, 1977, Cornell Coll., 1988, Framingham State Coll., 1989, Adelphi U., 1990, Dartmouth Coll., 1992, Charles U., Prague, 1993, U. Ill., Chgo., 1994, Wheaton Coll., 1995, Franklin & Marshall Coll., 1998. Asst. prof. U. Calif., Berkeley, 1959—62, assoc. prof., 1961—63; jr. fellow Harvard U., Cambridge, Mass., 1957—59, prof. chemistry, 1963—76, Frank B. Baird prof. sci., 1976—2002, mem. faculty coun., 1980—83, master Currier House, 1981—86, rsch. prof., 2002—. Cons. editor W.H. Freeman lectr. Haverford Coll., 1962; Falk-Plaut lectr. Columbia U., 1963; vis. prof. Göttingen (Germany) U., 1963, U. Calif., Santa Cruz, 1972; Harvard lectr. Yale U., 1964; Debye lectr. Cornell U., 1966; Rollefson lectr. U. Calif., Berkeley, 1969; Reilly lectr. U. Notre Dame, 1979; Phillips lectr. U. Pitts., 1971; disting. vis. prof. U. Ariz., 1971, U. Tex., 1977, U. Utah, 1978; Gordon lectr. U. Toronto, 1971; Clark lectr. San Jose State U., 1979; Hill lectr. Duke U., 1988; Priestly lectr. Pa. State U., 1990; Kaufman lectr. U. Pa., 1990; Polanyi lectr. U. N.C., 1991; Dreyfus lectr. Dartmouth Coll., 1992; Pauling lectr. Calif. Inst. Tech., 1993; Bernstein lectr. UCLA, 1994; Brown lectr. Rutgers U., 1995; chair bd. trustees Sci. Service. Assoc. editor Jour. Phys. Chemistry, 1980—88, pub. over 400 rsch. papers. Named to Calif. Pub. Edn. Hall of Fame, 1987; recipient pure chemistry award, Am. Chem. Soc., 1965, Centenary medal, 1977, Pauling medal, 1978, Spiers medal, Faraday Soc., 1976, Polanyi medal, 1981, Langmuir prize, 1983, Nobel Prize in chemistry, 1986, Nat. Medal of Sci., NSF, 1991, Heyrovsky medal, 1992, Sierra Nevada Disting. Chemist award, 1993, Kosolapoff medal, 1994, William Walker prize, 1994, Council of Scientific Society President's award for support of science, 1999; fellow Guggenheim fellow, U. Freiburg, Germany, 1968, vis. fellow, Joint Inst. for Lab. Astrophysics, U. Colo., 1969, Sloan fellow, 1959—63, Exxon Faculty fellow, 1980—96, Miller fellow, U. Calif. Berkeley, 1997; scholar Fairchild Disting. scholar, Calif. Inst. Tech., 1976. Fellow: Am. Acad. Arts and Scis., Am. Phys. Soc. (chmn. chem. physics divsn. 1971—72), N.Y. Acad. Sci. (hon.; life); mem.: Am. Philos. Soc., NAS, Royal Soc. Chemistry (fgn.) (hon.), Am. Chem. Soc., AAAS, Sigma Xi, Phi Beta Kappa (orator Harvard U. 1992). Office: Harvard U Dept Chemistry Mallickrodt Lab 035 12 Oxford St Cambridge MA 02138-2902

HERSCHER, URI DAVID, academic administrator, history educator, rabbi; b. Tel Aviv, Mar. 14, 1941; s. Joseph and Lucy (Nee Strauss) H.; m. Eleanor Grant, June 15, 1969 (div. 1983); children: Joshua, Gideon; m. Myna Meshul, Oct. 14, 1990; children: Adam, Aron. BA, U. Calif., Berkeley, 1964; MA in Hebrew Lit., Hebrew Union Coll., 1970, PhD in Am. Jewish History, 1973. Dean admissions Hebrew Union Coll., Cin., 1970-72, asst. to pres., 1972-75, exec. v.p., prof. Am. Jewish history Cin., NYC, LA and Jerusalem, 1975—95; founding pres., CEO, bd. mem. Skirball Cultural Ctr., LA, 1995—. Author: Jewish Agricultural Utopias in America, 1981; co-author: On Jews, America and Immigration, 1982; editor: Queen City Refuge, 1989; contbr. articles to profl. jours. Mem. ethics com. City of LA, 2001—06. Named one of Top 5 Rabbis in Am., Newsweek Mag., 2007. Mem. Cen. Conf. Am. Rabbis, Am. Jewish Com. Achievements include the Skirball Cultural Center being the largest nondenominational Jewish cultural center in the world. Office: Skirball Cultural Ctr 2701 N Sepulveda Blvd Los Angeles CA 90049 Office Phone: 310-440-4541.

HERSCHLEIN, JAMES D., lawyer; AB magna cum laude, Boston Coll., 1982; JD, St. John's U., 1985. Bar: NY 1986, DC. Ptnr. litig. dept., mem exec. com. Kaye Scholer LLP, NYC. Named one of Fifteen Lawyers 40 and Under Shaping the Law for the 21st Century, NY Lawyer, 2001; recipient Thurgood Marshall award, 1988, Legal Aid Pro Bono Publico award for affirmative litigation, 2001. Mem.: ABA (mem. product lability ltigation com., mem. pharma. & med. devices subcom.), Fed. Bar Coun., Assn. Bar of City NY (chair young lawyers com. 1991—93, sec. 2000—03). Office: Kaye Scholer LLP 425 Park Ave New York NY 10022 Office Phone: 212-836-8655. E-mail: jherschlein@kayescholer.com.

HERSEE, STEPHEN DEREK, science educator; b. Hastings, Eng., Mar. 20, 1950; arrived in U.S., 1986; s. Douglas Haig and Muriel (Miles) H.; m. Kirsty Jane Mills, May 18, 1991; children: Louise, Matthew. BSc, Brighton Poly., Sussex, Eng., 1972, PhD, 1975. Prin. scientist Plessey Rsch. Ltd., Caswell, Eng., 1975-80; engr. Thomson CSF, Orsay, France, 1980-86; sr. engr. Gen. Electric Co., Syracuse, N.Y., 1986-91; prof. U. N.Mex., Albuquerque, 1991-96, 1996—. Permanent mem. nat. organizing com. OMVPE Workshop, 1995—; presenter in field. Contbr. articles to profl. jours. Mem. IEEE (sr.), Am. Assn. Crystal Growth. Achievements include patents in semiconductor laser structure, epitaxial growth equipment; pioneering research in MOCVD growth of quantum well semiconductor lasers; demonstrated record power output from advanced semiconductor lasers. Office: U NMex Ctr High Tech Materials Albuquerque NM 87131-0001

HERSEY, GEORGE LEONARD, retired art historian; b. Cambridge, Mass., Aug. 30, 1927; s. Milton Leonard and Katharine (Page) H.; m. Jane Maddox Lancefield, Sept. 2, 1953; children: Donald, James. BA, Harvard U., 1951; MFA, Yale U., 1954, MA, 1961, PhD, 1964. Instr. art Bucknell U., Lewisburg, Pa., 1954-55, asst. prof., 1955-59, acting chmn., 1958-59; instr. Yale U., New Haven, 1963-65, asst. prof., 1965-68, assoc. prof., 1968-74, prof., 1974-98, ret., 1998. Mem. adv. bd. Conn. Preservation Trust, 1977-79; mem. Conn. State Commn. Capitol Restoration, 1977-79; lectr. Princeton U., Columbia U., other univs., orgns. Author (some books have been translated into German, Italian, Japanes, Turkish, and Russian): Alfonso II and the Artistic Renewal of Naples, 1969, The Aragonese Arch at Naples, 1443-1475, 1973; High Victorian Gothic: A Study in Associationism, 1972, Pythagorean Palaces: Magic and Architecture in the Italian Renaissance, 1975, Architecture, Poetry and Number in the Royal Palace at Caserta, 1983, The Lost Meaning of Classical Architecture, 1988, (with R. Freedman) Possible Palladian Villas, 1992, High Renaissance Art in St. Peter's and the Vatican, 1993, The Evolution of Allure, Sexual Selection from the Medici Venus to the Incredible Hulk, 1996, The Monumental Impulse: Architecture's Biological Roots, 1999, Architecture and Geometry in the Age of the Baroque, 2001, Falling in Love with Statues: Artificial Humans from Pygmalion to Present, 2006; also numerous articles and revs.; co-editor: Architectura, 1971—; editor: Yale Publ. in History of Art, 1974-90; art exhbn. co-organizer The Taste of Angels: Neapolitan Paintings in North America, 1650-1750, Yale Univ. Art Gallery and other museums, 1987-88. With U.S. Mcht. Marine, 1945-46, U.S. Army, 1946-47. Recipient Monticello prize, 1961; Fulbright scholar, Italy, 1962; Morse fellow, London, 1966, Schepp fellow, Florence, Italy, 1972; resident Am. Acad. Rome, 1994. Mem.: Soc. Archtl. Historians (bd. dirs. 1971—73), Dunky Club (hon.). Democrat. Home: 167 Linden St New Haven CT 06511-2407 E-mail: g.hersey@comcast.net.

HERSH, IRA PAUL, tax specialist, financial consultant; b. Bklyn., July 14, 1948; s. Saul and Mildred (Leibowitz) Hershkowitz; m. Jan Bennett; children: Marcy Fay, Gregory Alexander, Carrie Elizabeth. Tax mgr. Wiss and Co., NYC, 1970—77; contr. Assets Adminstrn. and Mgmt., Stamford, Conn., 1978—79; tax mgr. Exec. Monetary Mgmt., Inc., NYC, 1980—84; pvt. practice Wilton, Conn., 1985—. Pres. MacArthur Equities Ltd., 1985—. Mem. Rolling Hills Country Club. Home and Office: 20 Branch Brook Rd Wilton CT 06897-1520 E-mail: taxplan@optonline.net.

HERSH, NEAL RAYMOND, lawyer; b. LA, July 12, 1951; BA, UCLA, 1973; JD, Southwestern U., 1976. Bar: Calif. 1976, US Dist. Ct. (Ctrl. Dist. Calif.) 1977, US Supreme Ct. 1982. Pres., bd. dir. Levitt & Quinn Family Law Center, Inc., LA; prin. atty. Am. Assn. Mediate Divorce; ptnr. Hersh, Mannis & Bogen, LLP, Beverly Hills, Calif. Spkr. in field; commentator AM LA KABC news radio, Hard Copy, Entertainment Tonight, Celebrity Justice, Burden of Proof, CNN, 2001, CNBC, 2001, Court TV, 2001. Contbr. articles to numerous profl. jours. Named a Super Lawyer, LA mag., 2003, 2004. Fellow: Internat. Acad. Matrimonial Lawyers, Am. Acad. Matrimonial Lawyers; mem.: State Bar Calif. (mem. family law sect.), ABA (mem. family law sect.), LA County Bar Assn. (mem. family law sect.), Beverly Hills Bar Assn. (chmn. 2001—02, mem. family law sect., mem. exec. com. family law sect. 1997—). Office: Hersh Mannis & Bogen LLP Ste 209 9150 Wilshire Blvd Beverly Hills CA 90212 Office Phone: 310-786-1910. Office Fax: 310-786-1917. E-mail: nhersh@hershmannis.com.

HERSH, SEYMOUR MYRON, journalist, writer; b. Chgo., Apr. 8, 1937; s. Isadore and Dorothy (Margolis) H.; m. Elizabeth Sarah Klein, May 30, 1964; children: Matthew, Melissa, Joshua. BA in History, U. Chgo., 1958. Police reporter City News Bur., 1959-60; UPI Corr. Pierre, SD, 1962-63; AP corr. Chgo. and Washington, 1963-67; with staff NY Times, Washington, DC, 1972-75, 1979, NYC, 1975-78; nat. corr. Atlantic Monthly, 1983-86; corr. New Yorker Mag., 1992—. Press sec. Senator Eugene J. McCarthy of Minn. (in NH primary), 1968 Offered stories on the My Lai Massacre through Dispatch News Service., reports on US military actions in Afghanistan, 2001, breaking stories on Iraqi prisoner abuse in Abu Ghraib prison, May 2004; author: Chemical and Biological Warfare: America's Hidden Arsenal, 1968, My Lai 4: A Report on the Massacre and Its Aftermath, 1970, Cover-Up: The Army's Secret Investigation of the Massacre of My Lai 4, 1972, The Price of Power: Kissinger in the Nixon White House, 1983 (Los Angeles Times Book prize, 1983, Nat. Book Critics Circle award, 1983, Investigative Reporters amd Editors prize, 1983), The Target Is Destroyed, What Really Happened to Flight 007 and What America Knew About It, 1986, The Samson Option: Israel's Nuclear Arsenal and America's Foreign Policy, 1991 (Investigative Reporters and Editors prize, 1992), The Dark Side of Camelot, 1997, Chain of Command: The Road From 9/11 to Abu Ghraib, 2004; contbr. articles to magazines. Recipient Worth Bingham prize, Sigma Delta Chi Disting. Service award, Pulitzer prize for internat. reporting, 1970; George Polk award, 1970; Scripps-Howard Pub. Service award and 2nd Polk award for stories on B-52 bombing in Cambodia, 1973; Sidney Hillman and 3rd Polk awards for stories on domestic CIA spying, 1974; John Peter Zenger Freedom of The Press award, 1975; Drew Pearson prize for stories on CIA involvement in Chile.; 2nd Sigma Delta Chi Disting. Service award, 1981 and 4th Polk award, 1981, for articles on CIA involvement in Libya, 5th Polk award, 2004, for reports on torture of Iraqis at Abu Ghraib prison; Nat. Mag. Award for pub. interest for 3 articles on US intelligence used to justify the war in Iraq, 2004. Office: The New Yorker 4 Times Sq New York NY 10036

HERSH, STEPHEN PETER, psychiatrist, psycho-oncologist, chronic pain expert, educator; b. NYC, Aug. 11, 1940; s. Joseph Harrison and Lillian (Berk) H.; m. Jean Ann Lehrke, Apr. 10, 1969; children: Damon, Katharine, Justin, Tessa. BA, Amherst Coll., 1962; MD, NYU, 1967. Diplomate Am. Bd. Psychiatry and Neurology. Pediatric intern NYU-Bellevue Med. Ctr., NYC, 1967-68, fellow in child psychiatry, 1970-72; resident in psychiatry U. Pa., Phila., 1968-70; chief Ctr. for Studies in Child and Family Mental Health, NIMH, Rockville, Md., 1972-73, spl. asst. to dir., 1973-74, asst. dir., 1975-79; dir. div. children and youth St. Elizabeths Hosp., Washington, 1981; co-founder, co-dir., chmn. bd. Med. Illness Counseling Ctr., Chevy Chase, Md., 1982-94, exec. med. dir., 1995—, pres., 2002—; behavioral health and medicine cons. Marriott Internat., 1996—99. Clin. prof. psychiatry and pediat. George Washington U. Med. Ctr., Washington, 1989—; cons. pediat. br. Nat. Cancer Inst., Bethesda, Md., 1972-99; nat. adv. coun. Nat. Anthrop. Film Ctr., Smithsonian Instn., Washington, 1979-81; chmn. sci. adv. bd. St. Jude Children's Rsch. Hosp., Memphis, 1980-82; attending physician, 1993—; dir., prin. investigator HIV Neuropsychology R&D project Nat. Cancer Inst., 1988—; med. staff clin. ctr., NIH, 1992-99; dir. rsch. grant J.W. and Alice S. Marriott Found., 2002—; cons. Edison Pharma, 2007—. Author: The Executive Parent, 1979, The Physician and the Mental Health of the Child, 1981, Beyond Miracles, 2000; contbg. editor Journeys, 1994-96; contbr. articles to profl. jours., chpts. to books. Svcs. com. Am. Cancer Soc., Washington, 1974-79; mem. com. on traffic Somerset (Md.) Town Coun., 1975-78; bd. dirs. Barker Found., Washington, 1984-87; mem. med. bd. Lupus Found. Greater Washington, 1988—, My Image After Breast Cancer, 1995—; bd. med. advisors Multimedia Med. Sys., 1997; vol. emergency response physician Md. Dept. Health and Mental Hygiene, 2003—; alumni bd. govs. NYU Sch. Medicine, 2004—; profl. adv. bd. Wellness Cmty., Washington, 2005—. Recipient spl. award Nat. Consortium for Child Mental Health Svcs., 1979, Alumni Leadership award NYU Sch. Medicine, 2005. Fellow, Am. Psychiat. Assn. (disting. life, Significant Achievement award 1993); mem. AAAS, APA, Am. Pain Soc., Internat. Assn. Study Pain. Democrat. Achievements include research in mitochondrial disorders; development of pain curriculum at NYU School of Medicine. Home: 421 Kent Square Rd Gaithersburg MD 20878-5711 Office: Med Illness Counseling Ctr 2 Wisconsin Cir Chevy Chase MD 20815-7003 Office Phone: 301-654-3638 ext. 203. Personal E-mail: sphersh@covad.net. *We all should engage in healing. Healing involves helping ourselves or another gain an improved sense of well-being and control. Joyful moments then become more available, involvement with others through love more possible, and life itself more a celebration.*

HERSHATTER, RICHARD LAWRENCE, lawyer, writer; b. New Haven, Sept. 20, 1923; s. Alexander Charles and Belle (Blenner) Hershatter; m. Mary Jane McNulty, Aug. 16, 1980; 1 stepchild, Kimberly Ann Matlock Kleiman;children from previous marriage: Gail Brook, Nancy Jill, Bruce Warren. BA, Yale U., New Haven, Conn., 1948; JD, U. Mich., 1951. Bar: Conn 1951, Mich 1951, US Supreme Ct. 1959. Pvt. practice, New Haven, 1951—85, Clinton, Conn., 1985—99; state trial referee, 1984—. Author: The Spy Who Hated Licorice, 1966, The Spy Who Hated Caramel,

1968, The Spy Who Hated Fudge, 1970;: 2d edit., 2001, Hung Jury, 2001, The Spy Who Hated Taffy, 2001; columnist Longboat Key News; columnist: Manatee River News. Mem. Branford Bd. Edn., Conn., 1963—71, Clinton Rep. Town Com., Conn., 1982—2000, chmn. Conn., 1984—88. With Air Corps US Army, 1942—44, With U.S. Inf., 1944—46. Mem.: Mystery Writers Am, Middlesex County Bar Asn, Conn. Sch. Attys. Coun. (pres. 1977), Banyan Bay Club (v.p., bd dirs 1988—), Masons. Personal E-mail: hershatter@aol.com.

HERSHBERGER, ROBERT GLEN, architect, educator; b. Pocatello, Idaho, Apr. 4, 1936; s. Vernon Elver and Edna Syvilla (Kinsley) H.; m. Deanna Marlene Van Dyke, Mar. 25, 1961; children: Vernon, Andrew. AB, Stanford U., 1958; BArch, U. Utah, 1959; MArch, U. Pa., 1961, PhD, 1969. Registered architect, Idaho, Ariz. Project architect Spencer & Lee, Architects, San Francisco, 1961-63; project designer GBQC Architects, Phila., 1967-69; asst. prof. Idaho State U., Pocatello, 1963-65; adj. asst. prof. Drexel U., Phila., 1967-69; practicing architect Archtl. & Planning Cons., Tempe, Ariz., 1969-87; prof. Sch. of Architecture Ariz. State U., Tempe, 1969-87, acting dir. Sch. Architecture, 1986-87, assoc. dean. Coll. of Architecture and Environ. Design, 1987; prof. U. Ariz. Coll. Arch., Tucson, 1988—2001, dean, 1988-96; ptnr. Hershberger and Nickels Archs./Planners, 1998—; prin. Hershberger Arch. and Planner, Payson, Ariz., 2002—. Chmn. Environ. Design Rsch. Assoc., Washington, 1976-79, chair Archs. in Edn. Com. AIA, Washington, 1983-85; v.p. Arch. Rsch. Ctrs. Consortium, 1994-96. Prin. works include Covenant Bapt. Ch. (AIA Excellence award), Urban Renewal Plan Downtown Tempe (AIA Citation), Hershberger residence (AIA honor 1990); author: Architectural Programming and Predesign Manager, 1999; Archtl. Programming in Architect's Handbook of Professional Practice, 2001, Handbook of Environmental Psychology, 2002. Bd. dirs. Rio Salado Found.; mem. Tempe Design Rev. Com., 1985-87, Tempe Elec. Adv. Com., 1982-85, Pocatello Planning Commn., 1962-65; mem. Tucson Planning Commn., 2000-02; mem. pub. arts com. U. Ariz., 1988-96, chmn., 1994-96, mem. campus design rev. adv. com., 1990-96, chmn., 1990-93; chair staff parish com. Catalina United Meth. Ch., 1995; bd. dirs. Catalina Day Care Ctr., 1990-93, So. Ariz. chpt. Make-A-Wish Found., 1995-96; mem. fin. com. Christ Ch. United Meth., 2000-01; mem. Payson Hist. Preservation Conservation Commn., 2003-2006; archtl. rev. com. Portal 4, Pine, Ariz., 2003-2006; chair Payson Design Rev., 2003-2006; chair staff parish rels. com. Payson United Meth. Ch., 2004-2006. Recipient Crescordia Environ. Excellence award Valley Forward Assn., 1986, Hon. Mention award Ariz. Hist. Mus. competition, 1985. Fellow AIA (pres. Rio Salado chpt. 1981, 74-88, bd. dirs. So. Ariz. chpt. 1988-96, pres., 1993, Gold medal adv. bd. 1992-95). Democrat. Methodist. Avocations: fly fishing, skiing, hunting, tennis, golf, photography. Office: PO Box 2266 Payson AZ 85547 Home: 204 N Forest Park Dr Payson AZ 85541 Office Phone: 928-970-9280. E-mail: hershberger@npgcable.com.

HERSHCOPF, GERALD THEA, retired lawyer; b. Feb. 8, 1922; s. Paul and Rose (Thea) Hershcopf; m. Elaine Yeckes, June 10, 1950; 1 child, Jane. AB, Columbia U., 1943; cert. in French Civilization, U. Paris, 1945; JD, Harvard U., 1949. Bar: N.Y. 1949, U.S. Dist. Ct. (so. dist.) N.Y. 1960, U.S. Supreme Ct. 1981. Assoc. Marshall, Bratter, Greene, Allison & Tucker, NYC, 1949—54; ptnr. Starr & Hershcopf, NYC, 1954—56, Hershcopf, Stevenson, Tannenbaum, San Filippo, Donovan & Korn, 1956—91, Eisen, Hershcopf & Schulman, 1991—2006; ret., 2006. Gen. ptnr. Norfolk Realty Corp., NYC, 1961—86; chmn. bd. N.Am. Planning Corp., NYC, 1968—71; pres. Consortium Met. Law Schs., NYC, 1983—. B. dirs. N.Y. divsn. Am. Cancer Soc., 1997—98. With US Army, 1943—46, ETO. Mem.: VFW, Real Estate Bd. N.Y., Judge Advs. Assn., N.Y. State Bar Assn. (gen. practice sect.), Assn. Bar City N.Y., Am. Legion, Doubles Club (N.Y.C.), French-Am. C. of C., Harvard Club, N.Y. Athletic Club, Columbia U. Tennis Club, Beta Sigma Rho. Home: 737 Park Ave New York NY 10021-4256

HERSHENHORN, ROBERT GENE, bank executive; b. St. Louis, Nov. 2, 1943; s. Isadore and Dorothy Hershenhorn; m. Dittany R. Felker, June 11, 1963 (div. Feb. 1975); children: Lindsay, Alexis; m. Judith Marie Holmberg, Aug. 5, 1995; 1 child, Sarah. BA, Washington U., 1965; JD, Chgo.-Kent Coll. of Law, 1968. Chmn. of the bd. First Bank of Ill., 1976—. Owner Hershenhorn Bancorp. holding co.; past chmn. bd. dirs. Chgo. Econometrics & Forecasting Assocs.; past chmn. bd., prin. Petroco, Sierra Hotel, Conoco. Bd. dirs. Joffrey Ballet, Chgo., 1996-97, Lincoln Park Zoo, Chgo., 1998-2003; founding mem. fin. com. Peter Fitzgerald for U.S. Senate, 1998; past trustee Barat Coll., Lake Forest, Ill., Chgo. Acad. of Sci. and Mus.; past bd. dirs. Little City, Devel. Office of Chgo. Province of the Soc. of Jesus, Chgo. Hearing Soc., Chgo. Internat. Film Festival, U. Chgo. Cancer Rsch. Found., Lake Forest Symphony, United Way, Northlight Theater, Touchstone Theater, Drexel Hom for the Aged, others; mem. vis. com. U. Chgo. Divsn. Biol. Scis., 2001-, Pritzker Sch. Medicine, 2001-. Mem. ABA, Ill. Bar Assn., Chgo. Bar Assn., Ind. Bankers of Am., Am. Bankers Assn., Banker's Club of Chgo. Avocations: travel, tennis, biking. Office: First Bank & Trust Co of Ill 300 E Northwest Hwy Palatine IL 60067-8133

HERSHENOV, BERNARD ZION, research and development company executive; b. NYC, Sept. 22, 1927; s. Joseph and Rebecca (Landes) H.; m. Miriam Leah Gold, Oct. 27, 1950 (dec. July 27, 2000); 1 child, Ruth Lois; m. Harriet S. Indik, Sept. 10, 2006. BS, U. Mich., 1950, MS, 1952, PhD, 1959. Asso. research engr. U. Mich., Ann Arbor, 1951-59; devel. engr. Gen. Electric Co., Schenectady, 1959-60; mem. tech. staff, head microwave integrated circuits RCA Research Labs., Princeton, N.J., 1960-72; dir. Research Labs., Tokyo, 1972-75, head energy systems Princeton, 1976-79, dir. Solid State Devices Lab., 1979-83, dir. Optical Systems and Display Materials Lab., 1983-84, dir. Optoelectronics Research Lab., 1984-87; dir. mktg. coordination David Sarnoff Research Ctr. (subs. of SRI Internat.), Princeton, 1987-88; dir. internat. bus. devel., 1989-93; sr. advisor Sarnoff Research Ctr. (subs. of SRI Internat.), Princeton, 1994-95; cons., 1993-95. Contbr. articles in field. V.p. Jewish Community Center, Princeton, 1970-71, pres., 1971-72, trustee, 1977-79; mem. physics adv. com. U. Mich., 1988—. Served with USN, 1946-47. Recipient RCA Outstanding Achievement awards, 1963, 66, Microwave Application award Microwave Theory and Techniques Soc. of IEEE, 1992. Fellow IEEE; mem. Sigma Xi, Phi Kappa Phi. Jewish. Home and Office: 22 Raleigh Rd Kendall Park NJ 08824-1007 Office Phone: 732-297-5298.

HERSHENSON, MARTHA BRADFORD, history educator; b. Chgo., June 20, 1944; d. William Stephen Bradford and Barbara Hearn Kennedy; m. Loren Victor Hershenson, Sept. 4, 1988; 1 child, Holly Ann Boes. BA in History, Lake Forest Coll., 1966; M in Edn., Nat. Lewis U., 1971. Cert. K-8 edn. Ill., 6-12 edn. Ill. 6th grade educator Deerfield (Ill.) Grammar Sch., 1966—68, Woodland Intermediate Sch., Gages Lake, Ill., 1968—70; 4th-6th grade educator North Shore Sch. Dist., Highland Park, Ill., 1970—. Suicide phone worker Reed Zone Ctr., Chgo., 1973; supr. for student tchrs. North Shore Sch. Dist. 112, Highland Park, Ill., 1978—2002; mentor Lake Forest Coll.; 6th grade team leader Edgewood Mid. Sch., Highland Park, 2003—04. Bd. dirs. Highland Park Cmty. Orgn., 1995—97; mem. alumni bd. Lake Forest Coll., 1996—2000; mem. Youth, Edn. and Arts, Highland Park, 1998; sponsor trip to Ireland with h.s. students Rotary Internat. Project- Towards a Better Understanding (TABU), Highland Park, 1997; coll. scholarship sponsor Highland Park C. of C., 1992—2005. Named Best Tchr. on North Shore, Pioneer Press Survey of 17 Counties, 1994. Mem.: DAR (life), Ill. Fedn. Tchrs. (various edn. orgns. 1974—75), Maine Hist. Soc. (life), Descendants of Mayflower Soc. (life; bd. assts. for Ill. 2002—05), John Butler Civil War Soc. for Ill. (life), Highland Pk. Rotary Internat. (life). Avocation: genealogy. Home: 600 Beverly Pl Lake Forest IL 60045 Office: Edgewood Mid Sch 929 Edgewood Rd Highland Park IL 60035 Home Phone: 847-295-0366.

HERSHENSON, MIRIAM HANNAH RATNER, librarian; b. Springfield, Mass., July 23, 1944; d. David and Thelma (Wasserman) Ratner; children: Trent M., Scott D. AB, Syracuse U., 1966; MS, Simmons Coll., 1967; postgrad., Nova U., 1987-89. Cert. tchr./librarian, Mass. Media specialist Quincy (Mass.) Pub. Schs., 1967-71, Virginia Beach (Va.) Pub. Schs., 1982-84, Portsmouth Pub. Schs., Va., 1984; regional children's coord. Broward County Libr., Ft. Lauderdale, Fla., 1985-88, br. liaison, 1988-89, br. librarian, 1989-93, regional br. supr., 1993-2001; head pub. svc. Nova Southeastern U./ Broward County Libr., 2001—03; pub. svc. adminstr. Broward County Libr., Ft. Lauderdale, 2003—07; regional libr. mgr. Northwest Regional Libr., Coral Springs, 2007—. Mem. ALA, Pub. Libr. Assn., Fla. Libr. Assn. (caucus chair 1990-91), Broward County Libr. Assn. (pres. 1994-95), Hadassah (life, chpt. pres. 1983-84), Nat. Coun. Jewish Women (life), Jewish Women Internat. (life), Brandeis Univ. Women (life). Office: NW Regional Libr 3151 University Dr Coral Springs FL 33065 Home Phone: 954-564-2199; Office Phone: 954-341-3965 247. Business E-Mail: mhershen@browardlibrary.org.

HERSHEY, BARBARA (BARBARA HERZSTEIN), actress; b. Hollywood, Calif., Feb. 5, 1948; d. William H. Herzstein; 1 child, Tom; m. Stephen Douglas, Aug. 8, 1992 (div. 1995). Student public schs., Hollywood. Appearences include (TV series) The Monroes, 1966-67, From Here to Eternity, 1979, (mini-series) A Man Called Intrepid, 1979, Return to Lonesome Dove, 1993, Abraham, 1994; other TV appearances include Gidget, 1965, The Invaders, 1967, Daniel Boone, 1967, Love Story, 1973, Bob Hope Chrysler Theatre, 1967, High Chaparral, 1967, Kung Fu, 1973, CBS Playhouse, 1967, (TV movies) Flood, 1976, In the Glitter Palace, 1977, Just a Little Inconvenience, 1977, Sunshine Christmas, 1977, Angel on My Shoulder, 1980, The Nightingale, 1985, My Wicked, Wicked Ways. The Legend of Errol Flynn, 1985, Passion Flower, 1986, Killing in a Small Town, 1990 (Emmy award 1990, Golden Globe award 1991), Paris Trout, 1991 (Emmy award nomination), Stay the Night, 1992, Abraham, 1994, (films) With Six You Get Egg Roll, 1968, Last Summer, 1969, Heaven with a Gun, 1969, The Liberation of L.B. Jones, 1970, The Baby Maker, 1970, The Pursuit of Happiness, 1971, Dealing, 1971, Boxcar Bertha, 1972, Angela (Love Comes Quietly), 1974, The Crazy World of Julius Vrooder, 1974, Diamonds, 1975, You and Me, 1975, Dirty Night's Work, 1976, The Stunt Man, 1980, Take This Job and Shove It, 1981, The Entity, 1982, The Right Stuff, 1983, Americana, 1983, The Natural, 1984, Hoosiers, 1986, Hannah and Her Sisters, 1986, Tin Men, 1987, Shy People, 1987 (Best Actress Cannes Film Festival, 1987), A World Apart, 1988 (Best Actress Cannes Film Festival, 1988), The Last Temptation of Christ, 1988, Beaches, 1988, Tune in Tomorrow, 1989, Defenseless, 1991, The Public Eye, 1992, Falling Down, 1993, Swing Kids, 1993, Splitting Heirs, 1993, A Dangerous Woman, 1993, Last of the Dogmen, 1995, Portrait of a Lady, 1996 (nominated Golden Globe Best Supporting Actress, nominated Academy award Best Supporting Actress), The Pallbearer, 1996, A Soldier's Daughter Never Cries, 1998, Frogs for Snakes, 1998, The Staircase, 1998, Breakfast of Champions, 1999, Passion, 1999, Lantana, 2001, 11:14, 2003, Riding the Bullet, 2004; (theatre, Broadway) Einstein and the Polar Bear, 1981. Recipient Golden Palm award for best actress Cannes Film Festival, 1987, 1988. also: Bymel O'Neill Mgmt care Suzan Bymel N Vista Los Angeles CA 90046

HERSHEY, DALE, lawyer, educator; b. Pitts., Mar. 24, 1941; s. Henry E. and Elizabeth (Loeffler) H.; m. Susanne Jarrett Wilson, July 8, 1967; children: Lauren Dixon, Justin Alexander. BA, Yale U., 1963; LLB, Harvard U., 1966. Bar: Pa. 1966, U.S. Dist. Ct. (we. dist.) Pa. 1966, U.S. Ct. Appeals (3d cir.) 1971, U.S. Tax Ct. 1978, U.S. Supreme Ct. 1979, Ct. Internat. Trade 1999. With Eckert Seamans Cherin & Mellott, LLC, Pitts., 1966—. Sr. lectr. law Tepper Sch. of Bus. Carnegie Mellon U., 2001—, lectr. Acad. for Lifelong Learning; pres. Charleston Trust/U.S.A.; vis. prof. E.M. Lyon, Ecully, France, 2003, 05. Bd. dirs. Legal Aid Soc. Pitts., pres., 1983-89; hon. pres. Gateway to the Arts, Inc.; bd. dirs. Friends of Carnegie Libr., Pitts. Chamber Music Soc., pres., 1992-94; active Leadership Pitts., 1989-90. Mem. ABA, Internat. Bar Assn., Pa. Bar Assn. (Pro Bono award 1988), Allegheny County Bar Assn. (bd. dirs. Bar Found., 2001-04, mem. judiciary com. 1997-2000), Am. Law Inst., Harvard Law Sch. Assn. Western Pa. (pres. 1985-86), Harvard-Yale-Princeton Club, Yale Club (Pitts.) (pres. 1987-89). Unitarian Universalist. Home: 311 Dorseyville Rd Pittsburgh PA 15215-1022 Office: Eckert Seamans Cherin & Mellott LLC 600 Grant St Ste 4400 Pittsburgh PA 15219-2702 Office Phone: 412-566-6058. Business E-Mail: dhershey@eckertseamans.com.

HERSHEY, MARK A., lawyer; B in Fin., Pa. State U.; JD, Villanova U. Assoc. Corp. Dept. Stradley Ronon Stevens & Young, LLP, Phila.; v.p. transactional law IKON Office Solutions Inc., Malvern, Pa., sr. v.p., gen. counsel, sec., 2005—. Office: IKON Office Solutions 70 Valley Stream Pky Malvern PA 19355 Office Fax: 610-296-8000.

HERSHEY, NATHAN, lawyer, educator; b. NYC, Apr. 28, 1930; s. Harry and Hannah (Horwitz) Hershey; m. Carol Fine, July 13, 1958; children: Suzanne, Madeleine. AB, NYU, 1950; LLB, Harvard U., 1953. Bar: D.C. 1953, Pa. 1977. Individual practice law, NYC, 1955—56; rsch. assoc. in health law U. Pitts., 1956—58, asst. prof., 1958—63, assoc. prof., 1963—68, prof., 1968—; mem. Pa. Bd. Med. Edn., 1974—80; of counsel Markel, Schafer, and Goldman P.C., Pitts., 1977—, Post & Schell, Phila., 1984—94. Cons. Pa. State Com. on Pub. Health and Welfare, 1973—80; v.p. U. Pitts. Senate, 1995—98, pres., 1998—2001. Author (with others): Hospital Law Manual, 1959; author: (with Robert D. Miller) Human Experimentation and the Law, 1976; author: Hospital-Physician Relations, 1982; editor: Hosp. Law Newsletter; contbr. articles to profl. jours. Bd. dirs. Women's Health Svcs., 1976—91, bd. v.p., 1982—91; bd. dirs. Hill House Assn., Pitts., 1964—71. With US Army, 1953—55. Mem.: Am. Pub. Health Assn., Soc. Hosp. Attys. Western Pa. (dir. 1974—85, past pres.), Am. Soc. Hosp. Attys. (past pres.), Inst. Medicine of NAS. Democrat. Jewish. Home: 5423 Northumberland St Pittsburgh PA 15217-1128 Office: 2200 Lawyers Bldg Pittsburgh PA 15219

HERSHEY, NONA, artist, printmaker, educator; b. NYC, Oct. 31, 1946; d. Don and Rita (Meyrson) H.; m. Richard Akre Trythall, Jan. 19, 1972; (div. 1992). BFA, Temple U., 1967; MFA, Temple U., Rome, 1969; studied lithography, Istituto Statale d'Arte, Urbino, Italy, 1979-80; studied woodcut and printing, Yoshida Hanga Acad., Tokyo, 1990-91. Asst. prof. drawing and printmaking Daeman Coll., Buffalo, 1972-73; mem. faculty studio art St. Stephen's Sch., Rome, 1973-79; lectr. studio art John Cabot Coll., Rome, 1979; asst. prof. printmaking Temple Abroad, Tyler Sch. of Art, Rome, 1979-90; vis. assoc. prof. drawing and printmaking Study Abroad Program, Temple U., Tokyo, 1990-91; vis. assoc. prof. printmaking Wesleyan U., Middletown, Conn., 1991-92; vis. assoc. prof. drawing and painting U. Iowa, Iowa City, 1992; assoc. prof. printmaking Mass. Coll. Art, Boston, 1993—. Vis. artist-critic Calcografica Nazionale, Rome, 1986, Istituto la Grafica, Latina, Italy, 1987, RI Sch. Design, Rome, 1987, 89, 90, 93, U. Conn., Storrs, 1992, 98, RI Sch. Design, Providence, 1998, 01, SUNY, Albany, 1993, Syracuse (NY) U., 1993, NY Grad. Sch. Figurative Art, NYC, 1993, Union Coll., Schenectady, NYC, 1994, U. Iowa, 1995, Cornell U., Ithaca, NY, 1997, Harvard U., Cambridge, Mass., 2003, Hartford Art Sch., Conn., 2005; artist-in-residence The MacDowell Colony, Peterborough, NH, 1989, 93, Ucross Found., Clearmont, Wyo., 1992, The Ballinglen Arts Found., County Mayo, Ireland, 2001, Asillah Forum Found., Morocco, 2002. One-woman shows include Jane Haslem Gallery, Washington, 1976, Laboratorio Artvisive, Foggia, Italy, 1979, 86, Villa Schifanoia Gallery, Florence, Italy, 1980, Il Patio Gallery, Ravenna, Italy, 1982, Galleria Il Ponte, Rome, 1985, 90, Mary Ryan Gallery, N.Y.C., 1983, 87, Dolan/Maxwell Gallery, Phila., 1987, Palazzo Sormani, Milan, 1993, RI Sch. Design, 1994, Miller/Block Gallery, Boston, 1995, 99, 02, 04, Robert Lehman Art Ctr., AIA, 2001, Soprafina Gallery, Mass., 2002, St. Botolph Club, Boston, 2003; group exhbns. include Smithsonian Inst., Washington, 1973, Honolulu Acad. Arts, 1973, USIS, Rome, 1973, Jane Haslem Gallery, 1974, 75, Mus. Fine Arts, Boston, 1975, Garden Gallery Modern Art, Raleigh, N.C., 1975, Met. Mus., Fla., 1977, USIS, Bucharest, Hungary, 1978, Am. Acad., Rome, 1978, Laboratorio Artivisive, 1981, 92, Rassegna di Grafica Contemporanea, Casalpusterlungo, Italy, 1982, Clark Gallery, Lincoln, Mass., 1983, Mary Ryan Gallery, 1983, 84, 85, 86, 88, 91, 92, Noyes Mus., N.J., 1984, Galleria Il Ponte, 1984, Dolan/Maxwell Gallery, 1985, Calcografia Nazionale, Rome, 1986, Palazzo Ducale, Pesaro, Italy, 1986, Bklyn. Mus., 1986, Walker Art Ctr., Mpls., 1986, Garton & Cooke Gallery, London, 1987, Istituto per la Grafica, Latina, Italy, 1987, Premio Sassoferrato, Italy, 1987, Premio Internazionale Biella per l'Incisione, Italy, 1987, Pa. Acad. Fine Arts, Phila., 1987, Premio Internazionale d'Arte Contemporanea, Campobello di Mazara, Italy, 1988, Greenville Mus. Fine Arts, N.C., Taipei Fine Art Mus., 1988, Dedalos Gallery, San Severo, Italy, 1990, Gallery Kabutoya, Tokyo, 1991, Art Multiple, Dusseldorf, Germany, 1992, G.W. Einstein Gallery, N.Y.C., 1993, Meml. Hall Ctr. for Arts, Vt., 1999, Atrium Mus., St. Louis, 1999, Rose Art Mus., Mass., 2000, ARTcetera, BCA, Boston, 2000, Hess Gallery, Mass., 2000, Corcoran Gallery of Art, Washington, DC, 2001, Nat. Acad. Design, NYC, 2001, John Elder Gallery, N.Y.C., Plum Gallery, Mass, 2002, Parchman Stremmel Gallery, San Antonio, 2002, Kochi Triennial Exhbn., Japan, 2002, Andersen Fine Art, Mass., 2003, Newton Art Ctr., Boston, 2003, Mass. Coll. Art, Boston, 2003, Emmerson Coll., Boston, 2004, Zimerli Art Mus., New Brunswick, NJ, 2005, Simmons Coll. Boston, 2006, Birckbottom Gallery, Soherville, Mass., 2006, The Schoolhouse Gallery, 2006, Danforth Mus. Art, 2006, Tufts U. Art Gallery, Mass., 2006; public collections include Met. Mus. Art, N.Y.C., Minn. Mus. Art, St. Paul, Pa. Acad. Fine Arts, Mint Mus., N.C., Nat. Print Cabinet, Rome, Civic Mus., Piacenza, Italy, Mcpl. Mus. Graphic Art, Caracas, Venezuela, Crakow Nat. Mus., Poland, Skopje Mus. Contemporary Art, Yugoslavia, Yale U. Art Gallery, S-E Banken, Stockholm, Mus. Fine Arts, Boston, Boston Pub. Library, Corcoran Mus. Art, Washington DC, Davison Art Ctr., NC, Wesleyan, U. Middletown, Conn., Fogg Art Mus., Mass., Free Library of Phila., Georgetown U., Washington DC, Haper Coll., Ill., Harvard U. Law Sch., Hunterdon Art Ctr., NJ, Library of Congress, Washington DC., Duke Mus. Art, NC, Georgetown U., Wash., Meml. Art Gallery, Rochester, NY, Decordoua Mus., Lincoln, Mass., Hartford Art Sch., Conn. Mass. Cultural Coun. grantee, 2004. Democrat. Office: Mass Coll Art 621 Huntington Ave Boston MA 02115-5801

HERSHEY, PAUL CHRISTIAN, engineer; b. Washington, Jan. 18, 1958; s. John Franklin and Doris Gonso Hershey; m. Cheryl Lynn Poole, May 31, 1980; children: Peter Christian, Stephen Paul, Jeffrey Franklin. AB in Math., Coll. William and Mary, Williamsburg, Virginia, 1980; MSEE, U. Md., College Park, 1984, PhD in Elec. Engring., 1994. Systems engr. BDM Corp., McLean, Va., 1980—82; assoc. engr. Fairchild Comm. Co., Germantown, Md., 1982—85; sr. engr. IBM, Manassas, Va., 1985—94; sr. tech. staff Brit. Telecom., Reston, Va., 1994—96; dir. engring. Tellabs, Inc., Ashburn, Va., 1996—2000; v.p. engring. Hyperchip, Montreal, 2000—04; chief sr. scientist HAI, A Raytheon Co., Arlington, Va., 2005—. Adj. prof. George Washington U., Ashburn, 1997—; rsch. visionary bd. mem. Motorola, Inc., Schaumburg, Ill., 2006—. Baseball mgr. and coach Little League, Babe Ruth, AAU, Ashburn, 1992—2007; choir mem. United Meth. Ch., Ashburn, 1980—2007. Recipient 1st-5th Plateau Patent awards, IBM Corp., 1995—98, Dir. Recognition award, Tellabs, Inc., 1999, Outstanding Tech. Achievement award, HAI, A Raytheon Co., 2005; fellow, Fairchild Industries, 1982—84, IBM Corp., 1991. Mem.: IEEE. Achievements include patents for system and associated method for the synchronization and control of multiplexed payloads over a telecommunications network; dynamic real-time routing in a data communications network; system and method for ring latency measurement and correction; event driven interface having a dynamically, reconfigurable counter for monitoring a high speed data network according to changing traffic events; real-time addressing for high speed serial bit stream; system and method for adaptive, active, monitoring of a serial data stream having a characteristic pattern; system and method for workstation monitoring and control of multiple networks having different protocols; system and method for adaptive active monitoring of high speed data streams using finite state machines; high availability data processing system and method using finite state machines; dynamic switching system for switching between event driven interfaces in response to switching bit pattern including in data frame in a data communications network; real-time high speed data capture in response to an event; intelligent real-time monitoring of data traffic; real-time event classification for a data communications network; inband directed routing for load balancing and load distribution in a data communication network; system for configuring an event driven interface including control blocks defining good loop locations in a memory which represent detection of a characteristic pattern; automated benchmarking with self customization; network security system and method using a parallel finite state machine adaptive active monitor and responder; information collection architecture and method for a data communications network; telecommunications netowrk management observation and response system; event driven interface for a system for monitoring and controlling a data communications network; system and method for response time measurement in high speed data transmission networks; system for transmitting information over a data communications network; monitoring a synchronous digital hierarchy transmission path; system and method for response time monitor in high speed data transmission networks; apparatus and method for using finite state machines to monitor a serial data stream for characteristic patterns; enhanced real-time topology analysis method for high speed networks; system for processing data from scanned documents. Avocations: singing, coaching baseball, softball. Home: 43761 Woodworth Ct Ashburn VA 20147 Home Phone: 703-858-0012. Personal E-mail: cphershey@aol.com.

HERSHEY, ROBERT LEWIS, mechanical engineer, management consultant; b. Chgo., Dec. 18, 1941; s. Maurice and Rose Beverly (Barrish) H. BSME summa cum laude, Tufts U., 1963; MSME, MIT, 1964; PhD in Engring., Cath. U. Am., 1973. Registered profl. engr.; cert. mfg. engr. Engr. Bell Telephone Labs., Whippany, NJ, 1963-67; acoustics mgr. Weston Instruments, Inc., Poughkeepsie, NY, 1967-68; sr. scientist Bolt Beranek & Newman, Washington, 1968-71; acoustics program mgr. Booz Allen & Hamilton, Bethesda, Md., 1971-79; program v.p. Sci. Mgmt. Corp., Washington, 1979-80, divsn. v.p., 1980-88; exec. engr. O'Donnell Cons. Engrs., Inc., Washington, 1988—. Sec. Engring. Registration Bd., D.C., 1987-98, D.C. Profl. Coun., Washington, 1974; mem. coordinating com. on productivity Am. Assn. Engring. Socs., Washington, 1984-88. Author: How to Think With Numbers, 1982, All the Math You Need to Get Rich, 2001. Sci. policy analyst George H.W. Bush Presdl. Campaign, Washington, 1988, 92, Bob Dole Presdl. Campaign, Washington, 1996, George W. Bush Presdl. Campaign, Washington, 2000, 04; pres. Hamilton House Assn. Resident Tenants, Washington, 1987-88, 90—; mem. Joint Bd. on Sci. Engring. Edn., Washington, 1972-78 Recipient Design award Machinery Mag., 1963. Fellow ASME (chmn. Washington chpt. 1978-79, Dedicated Svc. award 2001), NSPE (sec. profl. engrs. in industry 1973-75); mem. AAAS, DC Sci. Writers Assn., Philos. Soc. Washington (pres. 2004-05), Capital PC User Group, Acoustical Soc. Am. (chmn. Washington chpt. 1982-83), D.C. Soc. Profl. Engrs. (pres. 1975-76, 2002-03, 06-07, nat. dir. 1980-86, Young Engr. of Yr. 1974), D.C. Coun. Engring. and Archtl. Socs.

(del. 1969—, pres. 1978-79, Pres.'s award 1989, Nat. Capital award 1974), Soc. Mfg. Engrs. (chmn. Washington Robotics Internat. chpt. 1986-87), Mensa, Washington Coal Club, MIT Club of Washington (pres. 1979-80), Cosmos Club, Washington Tufts Alliance (v.p. 1970-71, steering com. 1999—), Tau Beta Pi (pres. Tufts student chpt. 1962-63, v.p. Washington alumni chpt. 1988-89), Sigma Xi. Republican. Avocations: chess, tennis, sports cars, golf. Home: Apt 1033 1255 New Hampshire Ave NW Washington DC 20036-2328 Business E-Mail: hershey@cpcug.org.

HERSHMAN, ELLIOTT B., orthopedist, surgeon; b. 1953; MD, U. Rochester, 1979. Diplomate Am. Bd. Orthop. Surgery. Vice chmn. Dept. Orthop. Surgery Lenox Hill Hosp., NYC; dir. orthop. surgery Pro-HEALTH; orthopaedic surgeon Manhattan Orthopaedics, NYC. Mem. medical staff NY Jets, 1987—91, team orthopaedic surgeon, 1991—, NY Islanders, Westchester Wildfire Basketball Club; orthopaedic cons. surgeon Hunter Coll. Athletic Program, NY Dragons Arena Football Team; lectr. in field. Contbr. articles to med. jours. Mem.: Academic Orthopaedic Soc., NY Soc. Orthopaedic Surgeons, Am. Acad. Pain Medicine, Am. Acad. Sports Medicine, Eastern Orthopaedics Assn., NFL Physicians Soc., Greater Met. Sports Medicine Soc., Am. Med. Assn., NY County Med. Soc., NY State Med. Soc., Am. Coll. Sports Medicine, Am. Acad. Orthopaedic Surgery. Office: Manhattan Orthopaedics 130 E 77th St New York NY 10021 also: NY Jets 1000 Fulton Ave Hempstead NY 11550 Office Phone: 212-744-8114. Office Fax: 212-472-5624.*

HERSHNER, ROBERT FRANKLIN, JR., judge; b. Sumter, SC, Jan. 21, 1944; s. Robert Franklin and Druie (Goodman) H.; m. Sally Sinclair, May 19, 1990; children: Bryan, Andrew. AB, Mercer U., 1966, JD, 1969. Bar: Ga. 1971, U.S. Dist. Ct. (mid. dist.) Ga. 1971, U.S. Dist. Ct. (so. dist.) Ga. 1979, U.S. Ct. Appeals (11th cir.) 1981, U.S. Supreme Ct. 1978. Atty. Ga. Legal Svcs. Corp., Macon, 1972; assoc. Adams, O'Neal, Hemingway & Kaplan, Macon, 1972-76; ptnr. Kaplan & Hershner, P.A., Macon, 1976-80; judge U.S. Bankruptcy Ct. for Mid. Dist. Ga., Macon, 1980—, chief bankruptcy judge, 1986—. Active Fed. Jud. Ctr. Com. on Bankruptcy Edn., 1990—99, chmn., 1994—99; elected mem. bd. Fed. Jud. Ctr., 2001—. Contbr. Georgia Lawyers Basic Practice Handbook, 2d edit., Post-Judgment Procedures, 1979; cons. Norton Bankruptcy Law and Practice. V.p. Macon Heritage Found., 1977-78. Capt. U.S. Army, 1970-75. Mem. Ga. Bar Assn., Macon Bar Assn., Nat. Conf. Bankruptcy Judges (gov., v.p. 1996-97, pres. 1997-98), Blue Key, Phi Eta Sigma. Methodist. Office: US Bankruptcy Ct PO Box 86 Macon GA 31202-0086

HERSLEY, DENNIS CHARLES, environmentalist, software systems consultant; b. Idaho Falls, Idaho, July 11, 1947; s. Cyril R. and Bardella (Webb) H.; m. Jane Anne Lilly, Jan. 16, 1993; children: Cary Connolly, Laura Lilly, Claire Lilly Morrow. Student, U. So. Calif., 1964-65; electronics tech. cert., Idaho State U., 1970; postgrad., U. Santa Clara, 1979. Cert. FCC 1st class radio engr. with TV and radar endorsements. Ptnr. Intensive Care Tech. Svcs., Pocatello, Idaho, 1972-74; test engrng. mgr. Nat. Semiconductor, Sunnyvale, Calif., 1975-76; test ops. mgr. Amdahl Ireland, Ltd., Dublin, 1978; engr., planner, analyst Amdahl Corp., Sunnyvale, 1979-85; CFO, chmn. Provista Software Internat., San Jose, Calif., 1985-86; pres. Almaden Consulting, Santa Cruz, Calif., 1985—; co-founder, pres., dir. non profit sci. rsch. Citizens United for Responsible Environmentalism, Inc., Santa Cruz, Calif., 1994—; CFO Rsch. Consultation, Inc., Santa Cruz, Calif., 1998—. Planner, sponsor Fusewest Regional Tech. Conf., Scottsdale, Ariz., 1988-89; tech. curriculum advisor Idaho State U., 1970-75; featured on KKUP radio talk show "Mold Can Make You Sick," 2001; participant 3d Internat. Conf. on bioaerosols, Fungi and Mycotoxins, 1998. Inventor calculator design, 1975, featured on BBC documentary, 1998. Recipient Outstanding Alumnus award Idaho State U., 1975, Honored Donor award Monterey Bay Aquarium, 1996. Mem. Calif. Assn. Non-Profits, No. Calif. Focus Users Group (asst. editor 1988-90), Santa Cruz Tech. Alliance. Office: CURE 2375 Benson Ave Santa Cruz CA 95065-1674

HERSMAN, DEBORAH A. P., federal agency administrator; BA, Virginia Tech. U., 1992; MS, George Mason U., 1999. Staff dir., sr. legis. aide to senator of W. Va. US Senate, Washington, 1992—99, sr. profl. staff mem., Com. on Commerce, Sci. & Transp., 1999—2004; mem. Nat. Transp. Safety Bd. (NTSB), Washington, 2004—. Office: National Transportation Safety Board Rm 4401 490 L'Enfant Plaza East SW Washington DC 20594 Office Phone: 202-314-6662.

HERSON, ARLENE, television producer, journalist, television personality, radio commentator; b. NYC; d. Sam and Mollie (Friedman) Hornreich; m. Milton Herson, June 16, 1963; children: Michael, Karen. Student, Queens Coll., 1957, New Sch. for Social Rsch., NYC, 1960. Exec. sec. Tex McCrary, Inc., NYC, 1958—60; asst. to William L. Safire, Safire Pub. Rels., NYC, 1960—62; columnist Advisor, Inc., Middletown, NJ, 1974—78; prodr., host Arlene Herson Show, NYC, 1978—, Manhattan Cable TV, 1980—. Syndicated on Tempo TV, 1988, Channel Am., 1989-93, Boca Raton Ednl. TV, 2006-; spokesperson Storer Cable TV, Monmouth County, 1989-91, Nutri/Sys., Monmouth and Ocean Counties, 1989-90; news anchor Nostalgia Cable TV Network at Rep. Nat. Conv., 1993; cons., talent coord. Super Annuities, 1993-94; moderator debate on capital punishment, 1998; moderator panel on assisted suicide, 1999; panelist radio program Fla. Forum NPR, 2004—; panelist, interviewer The Am. Sr. Side-WXEL-Nat. Pub. Radio, 1999-04; co-host radio sta. WJNA, Lunch Bunch; entertainment chmn. Polo Club, 2001—; master of ceremonies Calvacade of Stars, 2004—, Wings of Memory Soc., 2005; mem. grievance com. Fla. Bar, 2003-06; presdl. appointee US Holocaust Meml. Coun., 2004-, mem. com. on conscience, 2006; mem. Fla. Film and Entertainment Adv. Coun., 2005—, vice chmn. membership, 2006-; lectr., spkr. in field. Contbg. writer The Washington/Hampton Connection Dan's Papers, 1993-98, The Hill Newspaper, 1994-98; exec. prodr. The Magic Flute, conductor Victor Borge, DAR Constitution Hall, Washington, 1995, 1776, 1997; exec. prodr., casting dir. (musical) 1776, DAR Constitution Hall, Washington, 1996, encore prodn., 1998; prodr. 1776 (featuring current mems. of Congress), 1998; interviewer Steven Spielberg's Shoah Found., 1997-99; host WXEL-TV Pledge Drive, 2000. 92d St. Y benefit com. Variety-The Children's Charity; active Women's Project and Prodns., 1992; com. mem. Children's Psychiat. Ctr., 1971-90, Monmouth Park Charity Fund, 1980-90; corp. exec. bd. Family and Childrens Svcs., 1985—90; life mem. N.Y. chpt. Brandeis U. Libr. Fund; dir.'s resource coun. Nat. Women's Econ. Alliance; social com. Westbridge Condominium; fin. chmn. Mike Herson for Congress, 1994, fin.com. March of Dimes, 1995; profl. women's coun. Nat. Mus. of Women in the Arts, 1994; com. mem. Vicent T. Lombardi Cancer Rsch. Ctr., 1994-98, Parkinson's Action Network, 1996; publicity chmn.exhbn. for Israel Tennis Ctrs. Excalibur Soc. of Lyn U., 1996—; adv. coun. to co-chmn. Rep. Nat. Com., 1997—2000; active Power of Women Effecting Renewal, 1997; 2d decade coun. Am. Film Inst., 1998; bd. dirs. A Healing Among Nations, 1999; active Soc. of 100, Fla. Philharm. Orch., 1999; benefit com. Caldwell Theatre, 1999; bd. dirs. Miami City Ballet; founder Israel Children's Ctrs., 2000; bd. dirs. Fla. Film and Entertainment Adv. Coun., 2001—; mem. com. Shaare Zedek Med. Ctr., 2001; honors bd. dirs. Miami City Ballet, 2000—05; com. mem. Ctr. for the Arts, 2001—03, Palm Beach Cultural Coun., 2001—03; corp. exec. com. Ctrl. Park Conservancy, Women of Washington; corp. exec. com. mentor program Women's Econ. Devel. Coun.; bd. dirs. Miami City Ballet Sch., 2001—03; exec. com. Cmty. Rels. Coun., 2001—03; leadership coun., exec. com. Rep. Jewish Coalition, 2002—; mem. Garnet Soc. PBS, Nat. Pub. Radio, 2004—; life mem. Boca Raton cancer unit Papanicolau Corps for Cancer Rsch., 2002—; mem. Boca Raton Mus. Art, 2002—, coun. trustees, 2001—03; apptd. by Gov. Jeb Bush Fla. Film Entertainment Coun., 2004—; founder Lippy Leadership Soc., 2005; mem. com. on conscience U.S. Holocaust Mus., 2006; vice chmn. membership Fla. Film and Entertainment Adv. Coun., 2006—; adv. coun., presdl. appointment Take Pride in Am., 1993; bd. dirs. women's activities campaign Sen. Jacob J. Javits, NYC, 1968, Monmouth Mus., 1982—86, Will Rogers Inst., 1992—, Washington Symphony Orch., 1994—98, v.p., 1994; bd. dirs. Boca Raton Ednl. TV, 2001—, Palm Beach Internat. Film Festival, 2005—, Together Against Gangs, 2006; mem. Legacy Light Soc., 2007—. Recipient CAPE award for best talk show on Cable TV Network, 1984-93, Best Single Program with Suzanne Sommers, 1988, Woman of Achievement in Comm. award Adv. Commn. on Status of Women, 1986, Pub. and Leased Access (PAL) award for best talk show Paragon Cable TV, N.Y.C., 1988, spl. resolution N.J. Assembly, 1988, Willie award for outstanding svc. Will Rogers Inst., 1992; named Disting. Alumni mem. Waldorf Astoria, 1998; nominated Cable Ace award Best Talk Show nationwide The Arlene Herson Show, 1987, 89. Mem. NAFE, NATAS, Nat. Acad. Cable Programming, Nat. Assn. Profl. Women, Women in Comm., Women in Cable, Women in Film and Video, Am. Women in Radio and TV, Power Women Effecting Renewal, Internat. Radio and TV Soc., Internat. Newswoman's Assn., Rep. Gov's. Assn., Nat. Press Club, Friends for Life, Friars Club (house com. 1993, admissions com. 1994—), Bethesda Country Club, Lotos Club, East River Tennis Club, Excalibur Soc. of Lynn U., Seagate Beach Club, Boca Raton Rep. Club, Polo Club (cmty. rels. com. 1998-99, social com. 2000-, entertainment chmn. 2001-05), Palm Beach Rep. Club, Profl. Bus. Forum, Boca Raton Roundtable, Hadassah (life). Avocations: tennis, swimming, reading. Fax: 561-998-4776. E-mail: aherson123@aol.com.

HERSTAND, THEODORE, retired theatre artist, educator; b. NYC, May 14, 1930; s. Max Arthur and Rose (Shyatt) H.; m. Jo Ellen Gillette, Aug. 23, 1957; children: Sarah Ellen, Michael Simpson. Cert. Advanced Studies, U. Birmingham, Eng., 1951; BA, U. Iowa, 1953, MA, 1957; PhD, U. Ill., 1963. Instr. theatre Parsons Coll., Fairfield, Iowa, 1953-54, Eastern Ill. U., Charleston, 1957-59; asst. prof. SUNY, Plattsburgh, 1960-64, asso. prof., 1963-64; asst. prof. U. Ill., 1964-66; asso. prof. U. Minn., Mpls., 1966-70; prof., chmn. dept. theatre, drama and dance Case Western Res. U., Cleve., 1970-77, chmn. faculty senate, 1975-76; dir. Sch. Drama, U. Okla., Norman, 1977-79, prof., 1979-92; prof. emeritus U. Okla., Norman, 1992—; artistic dir., actor Okla. Profl. Theatre, 1978; ret., 1992. Vis. prof. Mpls. Coll. Art and Design, 1969; vis. dir. Colo. Shakespeare Festival, Boulder, 1968, 82; theatre bldg. cons. Eastern Ill. U., Charleston, Ill. State U., Bloomington, Jewish Community Center Theater, Mpls.; ednl. cons. in arts; spl. contbr. Silver Burdett Music Series. Profl. actor, dir. over 70 plays; author: (plays) Sugar and Lemon, 1968; new version Oedipus, 1978, Dov, 1982, The Emigration of Adam Kurtzik, 1985, 89, It Should Be So, 1989, The Minor Matter of Cynthia Smith, 1990, Bittersweet, 1996, It Should Be, 2003; assoc. editor: Drama Survey, 1967-70; contbr. revs., articles to profl. jours.; founder Klein Nat. Playwriting award, 1974, Bliss Nat. Playwriting award, 1980. Bd. dirs. Theater-in-the-Round, Mpls., 1968, v.p., 1969; bd. dirs. Gt. Lakes Shakespeare Festival, 1970-71, Okla. Arts Inst., mem. theatre panel, 1991-2003, chair 1994-2003; chmn. bd. dirs. Okla. Hillel Found., 1981-82; trustee Karamu House, 1975-77, Temple B'nai Israel, Oklahoma City, 1989-92, 1999-2002; chmn. new plays program S.W. Theatre Assn., 1985-89; bd. dirs. Okla. Israel Exch., 2003-06, v.p., 2004-07. Fellow, Coll. Fellows of Am. Theatre, 2004—. Mem.: Jewish Theatre Assn., Nat. Theatre Conf., Dramatists Guild, Omicron Delta Kappa. Personal E-mail: herstand@comcast.net.

HERSTEIN, GARY L., philosophy professor, researcher; b. Lancaster, Calif., Feb. 6, 1957; s. Galen Lansford Herstein and Donna Millicent Frankenburger. BA in Philosophy, Occidental Coll., LA, 1983; MA in Interdisciplinary Studies, DePaul U., Chgo., 1992; PhD in Philosophy, SIU Carbondale, Ill., 2005. Rsch. asst. Ctr. Dewey Studies, Carbodale, Ill., 2001—04; adj. instr. Cardean Learning Group, Chgo., 2005—. Author: (book) Whitehead and the Measurement Problem of Cosmology. Sp4 US Army, 1975—78, Wildflecken, Germany. Grantee Dissertation Rsch. award, SIU Carbondale, 2004 - 2005. Mem.: Assn. Symbolic Logic, Philosophy Sci. Assn., Soc. Advancement Am. Philosophy, Am. Philos. Assn. Democrat-Npl. Agnostic. Avocations: equestrian, fencing. Office: Marrimack Coll Dept Philosophy Mail Drop 57 North Andover MA 01845 Home Phone: 978-685-5435. Personal E-mail: gherstein@netzero.net.

HERSZENHORN, DAVID, journalist; m. Christina Pan Marshall; 2 children. BA, Dartmouth Coll., 1994. Met. staff reporter New York Times, 1991—, NYC schools reporter. Mem.: Townsend Harris High School Alumnia Assn. (pres., 2001-2004, chmn. bd. dir., 2004-). Office: New York Times 229 W 43rd St New York NY 10036 Office Phone: 212-556-1866. E-mail: dahers@nytimes.com.

HERT, THERESA M., mathematics educator; m. Paul Hert, May 31, 1986. M in Math., Calif. State U., San Bernardino, 1993. Math. tchr. Norte Vista High, Riverside, Calif., 1987—94, Banning High, Calif., 1994—99; math. instr. Mt. San Jacinto Coll., Calif., 1999—. Deacon Idyllwild Cmty. Presbyn. Ch., Calif., 2002—. Mem.: Delta Kappa Gamma (assoc.; treas. 2002—06). Office: Mt San Jacinto Coll 1499 N State St San Jacinto CA 92583 Office Phone: 951-487-3751. Business E-Mail: thert@msjc.edu.

HERTEL, SUZANNE MARIE, musician; b. Hastings, Neb., Aug. 8, 1937; d. Louis C. Hertel and W. Lenore (Cross) Budd. BA, Doane Coll., Crete, Nebr., 1959; MSM, Union Theol. Sem., 1961; postgrad., U. Hartford, 1966, U. Conn., 1975; MA, Merrill Palmer Inst., 1977; EdD, Boston U., 1982. Tchr. music Pub. Sch., Wethersfield, Conn., 1962—63; libr. serials Hartford Sem. Found., 1963—64; tchr. elem. Pub. Sch., Glastonbury, Conn., 1965—79; asst. prof. U. No. Iowa, Cedar Falls, 1979—81; tng. mgr. Focus Rsch. Sys. Inc., W. Hartford, Conn., 1982—89; pers. adminstr. City of Hartford, 1989—99; cons., 1999—2002. Mem. leadership educators program John F. Kennedy Sch. Govt., Harvard U., 1999; mem. Human Resource Mgmt. Del., Russia and Estonia, 1992, Initiative Edn., Sci. and Tech., South Africa, 1995. Recipient Maria Miller Stewart award, 1992. Mem.: Am. Guild Organists. Democrat. Home Phone: 860-561-0670. Personal E-mail: smher82@aol.com.

HERTELENDY, PAUL, critic, writer, poet; b. Budapest, Hungary, June 10, 1932; arrived in U.S., 1940; s. Andor and Elizabeth (Hitt) Hertelendy; children: Glen, Ann, Ralph. BSE, Princeton U., NJ, 1953; MSE, Stanford U., Calif., 1957; PhD, U.Calif., Berkeley, 1965. Rsch. engr. Nat. Bur. of Standards, Washington, 1958—64; music and dance critic Oakland (Calif.) Tribune, 1964—79, San Jose (Calif.) Mercury News, 1979—99; webmaster, CEO artssf.com, Berkeley, Calif., 1999—; poet laureate Smithsonian Instn. Nat. Bd., Washington, 2000—. Nat. bd. mem. Smithsonian Instn., Washington, 1995—2001; chair of adv. coun. Lawrence Hall of Sci., Berkeley, Calif., 1999—2003; mem., bd. dirs. SAM Tech., San Francisco, 1997—; bd. mem.; bd. chair Chinese Culture Ctr., San Francisco, 1980—93. Author: (books of poetry) The Very Slender Volume, 1999, Vietnam, Venice, Varied Vales, 2000, Poetrose in the 'Oughties, 2001, Glaciers and Butterflies, 2002, Too good to Last, 2004; contbr. articles to Performing Arts, Dance Mags, Contra Costa Times, others. Trustee Coll. Prep. Sch., Oakland, 2001—03. Ensign US Coast and Geod. Survey, 1953—56, Washington, DC. Mem.: U. of Calif. (Berkeley) Alumni Assn. (life). Roman Catholic. Avocations: hiking, tennis, travel, language study, soccer refereeing. Office: Artssf.com Box 1290 Berkeley CA 94701 Home Phone: 510-652-9482; Office Phone: 510-652-9482.

HERTWECK, E. ROMAYNE, psychology professor; b. July 24, 1928; s. Garnett Perry and Nova Gladys (Chowning) H.; m. Alma Louise Street, Dec. 16, 1955; 1 child, William Scott. BA, Augustana Coll., 1962; MA, Pepperdine U., 1963; EdD, Ariz. State U., 1966; PhD, U.S. Internat. U., 1978. Cert. sch. psychologist, Calif. Night editor Rock Island (Ill.) Argus Newspaper, 1961; grad. asst. psychology dept. Pepperdine Coll., LA, 1962; counselor VA Ariz. State U., Tempe, 1963; assoc. dir. Conciliation Ct., Phoenix, 1964; prof. Phoenix Coll., Phoenix, 1965, Mira Costa Coll., Oceanside, Calif., 1966—2003, ret., 2003. Mem. senate coun. Mira Costa Coll., 1968-70, 85-87, 89-91, chmn. psychology-counseling dept., 1973-75, chmn. dept. behavioral sci., 1976-82, 87-88, 90-91; part-time lectr. dept. bus. adminstrn. San Diego State U., 1980-84, Sch. Human Behavior U.S. Internat. U., 1984-89; prof. psychology Chapman Coll. Mem. World Campus Afloat, 1970; pres. El Camino Preschs., Inc., Oceanside, Calif., 1985—2005; CEO Nutri-Cal, Inc., Oceanside, Calif., 1996-2003. Bd. dirs. Lifeline, 1969, Christian Counseling Center, Oceanside, 1970-82; mem. City of Oceanside Childcare Task Force, 1991—2001; mem. City of Oceanside Community Rels. Commn., 1991-96, vice chair, 1994; mem. steering com. Healthy Cities Project City of Oceanside, Calif., 1993-95. Mem. Am. Western, North San Diego County (v.p. 1974-75) psychol. assns., Am. Assn. for Counseling and Devel., Nat. Educators Fellowship (v.p. El Camino chpt. 1976-77), Am. Coll. Personnel Assn., Phi Delta Kappa, Kappa Delta Pi, Psi Chi, Kiwanis (charter mem. Carlsbad club, dir. 1975-77). Home: 2024 Oceanview Rd Oceanside CA 92056-3104 Personal E-mail: rhertweck@cox.net.

HERTZ, ARTHUR HERMAN, communications executive; b. Bklyn., Sept. 10, 1933; s. Edwin Carl and Blanche H.; Stephen R., Andrew P. BBA, U. Miami, Fla., 1955, postgrad., 1955-56. Acct. Aetna Mortgage Co., Miami, Fla., 1955, Wometco Enterprises, Inc., Miami, 1955-60, contr., v.p., 1960-64, sr. v.p., 1964-71, exec. v.p., treas., CFO, 1971-81, COO, 1981-84, chmn., CEO, 1985—; exec. v.p., COO WEI Enterprises Corp., Miami, 1984-85; exec. v.p. Wometco Broadcasting Co., Inc., Miami, 1984-85. Past pres. Orange Bowl Com.; past chair City of Miami Off St. Parking Authority; past chair Pub. Health Trust, Miami Dade County; past chmn. audit com. bd. trustees U. Miami. Mem. AICPA, Fla. Inst. CPAs, Greater Miami C. of C. (gov. 1975-78), Iron Arrow, Phi Kappa Phi, Omicron Delta Kappa, Phi Eta Sigma. Home: 610 Fluvia Ave Coral Gables FL 33134-7016 Office: Wometco Enterp PO Box 149019 Coral Gables FL 33114-9019 Office Phone: 305-529-1403. Business E-Mail: Arth@wometcoent.com.

HERTZ, DANIEL LEROY, JR., entrepreneur; b. Montclair, NJ, Feb. 27, 1930; s. Daniel Leroy and Elizabeth Nielsen (Beet) H.; m. Valerie A. Smith, Mar. 15, 1956 (div. 1962); m. Isabel Waud Hurd, Apr. 18, 1970; children: Valerie H. Boyle, Suzanne E., Daniel L. III, Seana L. Burdge. Degree in mech. engring., Stevens Inst. Tech., 1952, M Engring. (hon.), 1982. Sales engr. C.E. Conover & Co., Fairfield, NJ, 1953-58; founder, pres. Seals Eastern, Red Bank, NJ, 1958—. Adv. bd. polymer tech. cons. Tex. A&M U., College Station, 1990-94, CHEMTECH, Washington, 1983-91, Elastomerics, Atlanta, 1984-92. Contbr. chpts. to Intermediate Rubber Technology, 1983, Handbook of Elastomers, 1988, 2d edit., 2000, Vanderbilt Handbook, 1990, 14th edit., 2000, Engineering with Rubber, 1992, 2d edit., 2000, Rubber Products Manufacturing Technology, 1993, Rubber Technology, 2001, Elastomer Technology- Special Topics, 2003; contbr. articles to profl. jours. Vis. com. mech. engring. dept. Stevens Inst. Tech., 1992-96; sec. Riverside Dr. Assn., Red Bank, 1980-85; mem. vestry, treas. All Saints Meml. Ch. Cpl. U.S. Army, 1950-51, Korea Mem. Am. Chem. Soc. (treas. rubber divsn. 1988-90, chmn. 1996, Disting. Svc. award 2000, Melvin Mooney Disting. Tech. award 2007), N.Y. Rubber Group (chmn. 1983), Rumson Country Club, Nassau Club, Seabright Tennis Club, Church Club (NY). Republican. Episcopalian. Achievements include 5 U.S. patents. Home: 8 Hasler Ln Little Silver NJ 07739-1650 Office: 134 Pearl St Red Bank NJ 07701-1525 Office Phone: 732-747-9200. Business E-Mail: dhertz@sealseastern.com.

HERTZ, HARRY STEVEN, government official; b. NYC, Feb. 25, 1947; s. Marcus and Alice (Oppenheimer) H.; m. Francine Turkowitz, June 21, 1969; children: Matthew Adam, Joshua Lee BS in Chemistry, Poly. Inst. Bklyn., 1967; PhD in Organic Chemistry, MIT, 1971. Alexander von Humboldt fellow U. Munich, Fed. Republic Germany, 1971-73; research chemist Nat. Bur. Standards (now Nat. Inst. Standards and Tech.), Gaithersburg, Md., 1973-78, chief organic analytical rsch. div., 1978-83; dir. Ctr. for Analytical Chemistry Nat. Bur. Standards, Gaithersburg, Md., 1983-91, acting dir. Nat. Measurement Lab., 1989, dir Chem. Sci. and Tech. Lab., 1991-92, dep. dir. Office Quality Programs and Malcolm Baldrige Nat. Quality Award, 1992-96; dir. Baldrige Nat. Quality Program and Malcolm Baldrige Nat. Quality award, 1996—. Health environ. rsch. adv. com. Dept. Energy, Washington, 1984-89, good mfg. practices adv. com. FDA, 1988-90; steering com. conf. bd. Global Ctr. Performance Excellence, 1996—2000; nat. quality com. United Way Am., 1997—2000; operating com. Juran Ctr. for Leadership in Quality, 2000-. Co-editor: Trace Organic Analysis, 1979; mem. editl. bd. Analytical Chemistry, 1984-86, Chem. and Engring. News, 1990-92; contbr. articles to profl. jours. Recipient Bronze medal Dept. Commerce, 1981, Arthur S. Flemming award for Outstanding Fed. Service, 1985, Silver medal Dept. Commerce, 1986, Gold medal Dept. Commerce, 1998. Fellow AAAS, mem. Am. Soc. for Mass Spectroscopy (sec. 1983-85), Am. Chem. Soc., Nat. Com. for Clin. Lab. Standards (pres. 1986-88), Sigma Xi. Avocations: racquetball, hiking. Office: Nat Inst Standard & Tech A600 Adminstrn Bldg Gaithersburg MD 20899-1020 Home Phone: 301-540-3032. Business E-Mail: hertz@nist.gov.

HERTZ, KENNETH THEODORE, healthcare executive; b. Jackson Heights, NY, Aug. 19, 1951; s. Irwin R. and Dorothy S. H.; m. Debra Pitre, July 12, 1997. BA in Spl. Studies, SUNY, Fredonia, 1974; cert. med. and dental practice mgmt., Loyola U., 1992. Cert. med. practice exec. Gen. mgr. Cape Cod Symphony, West Barnstable, Mass., 1974-75; mng. dir. Tulsa Philharm., 1975-78; pres., gen. mgr. Atlanta Ballet, 1979-89; instr. continuing edn. Oglethorpe U.; dir. Atlanta Great Artists Series, 1989-90, Atlanta Arts Devel. Svcs., 1989-90; exec. dir. New Orleans Symphony, 1990-91; adminstr. M.D. Care, Inc., New Orleans, 1991-95; dir. acquisitions and network devel. Tenet Healthcare, New Orleans, 1995-96, area mgr. practice ops., 1996-97; adminstr. MacArthur Surg. Clinic, Alexandria, La., 1977—2002, KTH Cons. LLC, 2003—05; sr. cons. MGMA Health Care Cons. Group, 2005—. Mem. dance panel City of Atlanta, 1983-89, Ga. Coun. for Arts, 1984-88, NEA, 1985-87; dir. Dance/USA, 1985-89; mem. adv. bd. cert. program in med./dental practice mgmt. Loyola U., 1993—; mem. Pres.'s Adv. Coun., De La Salle H.S., 1993-2000. Chmn. Atlanta C. of C. Cultural Programming Task Force, 1987—89, Atlanta C. of C. "Arts Alive", art celebration, 1986, Ga. Profl. Arts Caucus, 1983—85; bd. dirs. Big Bros./Big Sisters, 1988—89, Arts Festival Atlanta, BVA, 1986—90, Bus. Vols. for Arts, New Orleans Ballet Assn., 1996—98, Rapides Symphony Orch., 1998—2000, Ballet Alexandria, 2000—, Am. Jewish Com., Atlanta, 1967. Mem. Midtown Bus. Assn. (dir. 1984-89), Ga. Citizens for Arts, Am. Symphony Orch. League, La. Med. Group Mgmt. Assn. (bd. dirs. 2001—, sec. 2003—, v.p., 2004-05), Ctrl. La. Med. Group Mgmt. Assn. (v.p. 2001-02, pres. 2002—), Alpha Phi Omega

HERTZ, LEON, publishing executive; b. Perth, Australia, Aug. 1, 1938; came to US, 1975; s. A. and Rose (Traub) H.; m. Linda Paula Cooper, June 1, 1980; 1 child, Monique. Dir. Mirror Newspapers News Ltd., Sydney, Australia, 1967-75; gen. mgr., dir. Australian Nationwide News, Sydney, Australia, 1969-75; v.p., gen. mgr. Express News Corp. Am., San Antonio, 1975-80; v.p., assoc. pub., gen. mgr. NY Post Am., NYC, 1980-86; gen. mgr., dir. News Internat., London, 1986-87; exec. v.p. charge global mktg. News Corp. Ltd., NYC, 1987; exec. v.p. News Am., NYC, 1987—. Bd. dirs. Media Council of Australia, Sydney, 1970-75; chmn. Australian Newspaper Council, Sydney, 1973-75. Named Officer, Order of Australia, 2006. Mem. Am.-Scandinavian Fedn. (trustee), Am. Australian Assn. (dir., mem. adv. coun.). Clubs: Cruising Yacht (Sydney); Friars (NYC), Metro. Club (NYC). Avocation: sailing. Home: 4 E 88th St New York NY 10128-0509 Office: News America Inc 1211 Avenue Of The Americas New York NY 10036-8701 Office Phone: 212-852-7009. E-mail: lhertz@newscorp.com.

HERTZ, MICHAEL K., lawyer; b. Indpls. BS, Georgetown U., 1982; MA, U. Chgo., 1984; JD, Columbia U., 1988. Bar: NY 1989. Ptnr. (currently on indefinite leave of absence) Latham & Watkins LLP, NY, 1988—98; co-founder, exec. dir. and pres. Probono.net, 1998—. Bd. dir. NPower. Office: Pro Bono Net 151 West 30th St 10th Floor New York NY 10001 Office Phone: 212-760-2554 x479. Business E-Mail: mhertz@probono.net.

HERTZ, PAUL LOUIS, astrophysicist; b. Eglin AFB, Fla., Sept. 15, 1955; s. Louis Oppenheimer Hertz and Paulette (May) Meddin; m. Ninamarie Maragioglio, June 24, 1979; children: Joia Maragioglio, Kellen Maragioglio, Brielle Maragioglio. SB in Math., MIT, 1977, SB in Physics, 1977; AM in Astronomy, Harvard U., 1978, PhD of Astronomy, 1983. Rsch. assoc. NRC, Washington, 1983—85; astrophysicist US Naval Rsch. Lab., Washington, 1985—2000; sr. scientist Office of Space Sci. NASA, Washington, 2000—07, acting Discovery prog. scientist, 2000, dir. Sci. Policy, Process and Ethics Office, 2007—. Sr. contract assoc. prof. George Mason U., Fairfax, Va., 1993—; lectr. No. Va. CC, Annandale, 1990-92, Prince Georges CC, Largo, Md., 1991. Contbr. numerous articles to profl. jours. Recipient Robert Trumpler award, Astron. Soc. Pacific, 1985, Meritorious Presdl. Rank award. Mem. Internat. Astron. Union, Am. Astron. Soc. Office: Sci Policy Process and Ethics Office NASA 300 E St SW Washington DC 20546-0001 E-mail: Paul.Hertz@hq.nasa.gov.*

HERTZBERG, DAVID GORDON, retired lawyer; b. Detroit, Feb. 21, 1918; s. Harry Aaron and Sarah Silk Hertzberg; m. Millicent Brower, Aug. 28, 1942 (dec. Oct. 2000); children: Richard York, Jane Elyse Litin. BBA, U. Mich., 1939; LLB, JD, Harvard Law Sch., 1942. Bar: Mich. 1946, US Supreme Ct. 1958. Estate tax agt. US IRS, Detroit, 1946; tax atty. Hertzberg & Noveck, Detroit, 1947—88; ret., 1989. Trustee, v.p. Sigmund and Sophie Rohlik Found., Southfield, Mich., 1990—2007. Sr. lt. USN, 1942—46. Mem.: Masons (32 degree), Phi Beta Kappa. Avocations: sailing, skiing, running. Home: 22855 Shagbark Beverly Hills MI 48025-4771

HERTZBERG, HENRY, retired radiologist; b. Bklyn., Oct. 21, 1933; s. Louis and Bessie (Eisman) H.; m. Dori Balter, June 10, 1962; children: Richard, Lisa. BS, CCNY, 1955; MD, SUNY, Bklyn., 1959. Diplomate Am. Bd. Radiology. Intern Kings County Med. Ctr., Bklyn., 1959-60; resident Roosevelt Hosp., NYC, 1960-63; dir. radiology Fort Gordon (Ga.) Army Hosp., 1963-65; pvt. practice Green Brook, N.J.; assoc. dir. dept. radiology Somerset Med. Ctr., Somerville, N.J., 1975-85; dir. dept. radiology Muhlenberg Med. Ctr., Plainfield, NJ, 1985-92, attending radiologist, 1992—2002. Clin. asst. prof. radiology Rutgers U. Med. Ctr., 1985—. Capt. M.C., U.S. Army, 1963-65. Mem. AMA. Avocation: travel. Home: 182 Deer Run Watchung NJ 07069-6222 Office: Assoc Radiologists PA 239 Us Highway 22 Green Brook NJ 08812-1916

HERTZIG, MARGARET E., psychiatrist; b. NYC, Feb. 9, 1935; d. Morris and Grace Koenig Hertzig; m. Herbert George Birch, Dec. 11, 1961 (dec. Feb. 5, 1973); children: Sarah Ellen Birch, Martin Lawrence Birch. AB, Vassar Coll., 1956; MD, NYU, 1960. Diplomate psychiatry Am. Bd. Psychiatry and Neurology, 1968, child psychiatry Am. Bd. Psychiatry and Neurology, 1977. Rotating intern Jewish Hosp. Bklyn., 1960—61, pediat. resident, 1961—62; psychiatric resident Bellevue Psychiat. Hosp., 1962—64; rsch. fellow NYU Sch. Medicine, 1964—66; assoc. prof. psychiatry Cornell U. Med. Coll., NYC, 1977—95; assoc. attending psychiatrist N.Y. Hosp.-Cornell Med. Ctr., NYC, 1977—95; dir. child and adolescent outpatient dept. Payne Whitney Clinic-N.Y. Presbyn. Hosp., NYC, 1977—; prof. psychiatry Weill Med. Coll. Cornell U., NYC, 1995—, interim vice-chair child and adolescent psychiatry, 2002—; attending psychiatrist N.Y. Presbyn. Hosp., Weill Cornell Med. Ctr., NYC, 1995—. Cons. Spl. Citizens Inc., NYC, 1980—. Fellow, NYU Sch. Medicine, 1964—66. Fellow: Am. Acad. Child and Adolescent Psychiatry. Office: Weill Med Coll Cornell Univ 525 East 68th St New York NY 10021 Office Phone: 212-746-5712. Business E-Mail: mehertzi@med.cornell.edu.

HERTZOG, NOEL KENT, retired elementary school educator; b. Reading, Pa., Aug. 16, 1944; s. Norman and Mae Rebecca Hertzog; m. Wendy Denise Wenrich, June 29, 1974; children: Kent Matthew, Ashley Noelle. BS, Pa. State U., 1970. Tchr. Eastern Lebanon County Schs., Myerstown, Pa., 1970—2005; head tchr. Millbach Elem. Sch., Pa., 1970—71; pilot program for open space edn. Newmanstown Elem. Sch., Pa., 1971—72; intermediate level tchr. Ft. Zeller Elem. Sch., Richland, Pa., 1972—97; primary level tchr. Schaefferstown Elem. Sch., Pa., 1997—2005; ret., 2005. Pres. Millcreek Recreation Bd., Newmanstown, Pa., 1971—96; head coach Newmanstown Maroons Baseball, 1980—95, Elco Jaycee Baseball, Myerstown, Pa., 1984—89; donor Millcreek Cmty. Ctr., Newmanstown, 1996—2005; vice chmn. Millcreek Twp. Suprs., Newmanstown, 2000—06; donor Ch. Christian Outreach, Newmanstown, 1999—2006, Sunday sch. tchr., 1999—2006. Mem.: Ctrl. Pa. Charter Sports Hall of Fame, Lebanon County Assn. Ret. Tchrs. (life), Lodge 62 Free and Accepted Masons. Democrat. Avocations: hunting, football, travel, sports. Home: 33 W Park St Box 365 Newmanstown PA 17073

HERVIEUX-PAYETTE, CÉLINE, Canadian senator; b. L'Assomption, Quebec, Can., Apr. 22, 1941; JD, U. Montreal, 1973. Cert.: Can. Investment Dealers Assn. Parlimentary sec. Solicitor Gen. Can., Min. State for Fitness and Amateur Sports, Min. State for Youth, 1979—85; senator The Senate of Can., Ottawa, 1995—. Dir. projects Premier Bourassa's Cabinet, 1973—78; dir. pub. rels. Steinberg Inc., 1978—79; v.p. bus. ventures SNC Group, 1985—89; exec. v.p., assoc. Donancy Ltd., 1990; v.p. pub. affairs Medycis, 1991; v.p. regulatory and legal affairs Fonorola Inc., 1991—95; counsellor Fasken, Martineau, Dumoulin, Montreal, 1995—. With Commonwealth Parliamentary Assn., 2001; pres. Can. Club Montreal, 2001, Can.-Mex. Friendship Group, 1996—. Named Woman of Yr., 1984; recipient Commemorative medal, Confederation of Can., 1993. Mem.: Interparliamentary Forum of the Ams. (pres. 2001—), FWA Que., Que. Bar Assn., Can. Bar Assn. Liberal. Office: The Senate of Canada 361-E Centre Block Ottawa ON Canada K1A 0A4

HERWIG, NELSON GENE, retired curator, retired counselor; b. Johnson City, Tex., May 24, 1939; s. Walter Nelson Herwig and Valentine Sophie Fuchs; m. Kathleen Rose Blount, July 28, 1968; children: Penny Jo Reilly, Kurtis Vaughn, Walter Eugene, Fritz. Degree, Del Mar Coll., Corpus Christi, Texas, 1960—64; degree in chem. abuse counseling, U. Houston, 1989—92; attended, Sch. Tradional Chinese Medicine & Acupuncture, Houston, 1991—93. Cert. suicide counselor Am. Assn. Suicidology, 1991, lic. chemical abuse counselor Tex. Alcohol & Drug Commn., 1993. Geophysicist Humble Oil & Refining Co. (now Exxon), Houston, 1965—68; aquarium supr. San Antonio Zoo & Aquarium, 1969—78; pub. aquarium curator Houston Zoo & Aquarium, 1978—2003; ret., 2003. Author: Handbook of Drugs & Chemicals Used in the Treatment of Fish Diseases; photographer (numerous mag. & univ. tchg. aides), author, cons. editor Freshwater & Marine Aquarium Mag., Calif. Mem.: Internat. Remote Viewing Assn. (corr.), Assn. Rsch. & Enlightenment (assoc.), Am. Mensa (life). Independent. Luth. Home Phone: 713-723-6139. Personal E-mail: nherwig@aol.com.

HERZ, ANDREW LEE, lawyer; b. NYC, Nov. 12, 1946; s. John W. and Elise J. H.; children: Adam, Matthew, Daniel, Michael. BA, Columbia U., 1968, JD, 1971. Bar: NY 1972. Assoc. Milbank, Tweed, Hadley & McCloy, NYC, 1971-75, Nickerson, Kramer, Lowenstein, Nessen, Kamin & Soll, NYC, 1975-76, Marshall, Bratter, Greene, Allison & Tucker, NYC, 1977-80; gen. counsel N.Y. State Mortgage Loan Enforcement and Adminstrn. Corp., NYC, 1980—81; ptnr. Richards & O'Neil, LLP, NYC, 1981-2001, Bingham McCutchen LLP, NYC, 2001—04, Patterson Belknap Webb & Tyler LLP, NYC, 2004—. Lectr. Real Estate Inst., NYU, 1988-93; cons. NY Real Property Svcs., 1987. Author: Office Lease Operating Expense Clauses-Definitional Problems, 1986, Renegotiating Commercial Leases, 1993, Liability Risks for Ducking Loan Commitments, 1995; co-author: Japanese Yen Financing of U.S. Real Estate, 1989, Real Estate Management Agreements, 1990, Subleases: The Same Thing as Leases, Only Different, 2000; contbr. articles to profl. jours. Chmn. zoning bd. appeals Village of Ossining, NY, 1980-88; bd. dirs. Planned Parenthood NYC, 1987-94, 2006-, AIDS Resource Ctr., 1991-94, Comml Real Estate Law Advisor, Realcomm, 2001-02; adv. bd., mem. Georgetown U. Continuing Legal Edn. Advanced Comml. Leasing Inst., 2004-. Harlan Fiske Stone Scholar, 1971. Mem.: ABA (vice chmn. 1988—90, chair real estate mgmt. com. 1990—91, co-chair real estate asset mgmt. com. 1992—94, chair real estate asset mgmt. com. 1994—95, lending and financing subcom. 1997—99, comml. office leasing com. 1999—2001, co-chair comml. leasing com. 1999—2001, real property divsn.), Urban Land Inst. (dir.), Real Estate Bd. NY, Assn. Bar City NY, NY State Bar Assn. (co-chmn. comml. leasing com. 1991—96, exec. com. 1991—96, editor NY Real Property Jour. 1996—97, real property sect.), Am. Coll. Real Estate Lawyers (vice chair office leasing com. 1997—98, chair office leasing com. 1999—2001), Columbia Law Sch. Alumni Assn. (dir. 1999—2003). Democrat. Office: Patterson Belknap Webb & Tyler LLP 1133 Ave of the Americas New York NY 10036 Home: 33 Cushman Rd White Plains NY 10606 Office Phone: 212-336-2910. Business E-Mail: alherz@pbwt.com.

HERZ, IRENE LAUREL, web site design company executive, librarian; b. Bklyn., Apr. 26, 1948; d. Emanuel Albert Herz and Florence Jeanette Hirschberg; m. Duane Edward Tiemann, Oct. 5, 1985. BA, Barnard Coll., 1968; M in Libr. and Info. Sci., Pratt Inst., 1975. Sys. analyst Blue Cross/Blue Shield Conn., North Haven, 1985—88; sr. tech. project analyst Prodigy Svcs. Co., White Plains, NY, 1989—96; mgr., internet/intranet devel. ITT Industries, Upper Saddle River, NJ, 1996—2001; freelance Web designer Ossining, NY, 2001—04; pres. Aunt Reenee's Websites, Ossining, NY, 2004—. Co-founder Conn. RAMIS Users' Group, North Haven, 1986—88; chair ITT Web Devel. Ctr. Excellence, Upper Saddle River, NJ, 1997—2000. Author: Hey! Don't Do That!, 1978. V.p. voter svcs. LWV, Briarcliff, Ossining, Croton, Cortlandt, NY, 1993—95, membership dir., 1998—99; vol. database adminstr. Ossining Food Pantry, 2004—05; dist. leader Ossining Dem. Party, 2004—05; trustee Ossining Pub. Libr., 1995—2002. Mem.: Greater Ossining C. of C. (coord. village fair 2005, dir. comms. 2006), Rotary (bd. dirs. Ossining chpt. 2005—06, v.p. Ossining chpt. 2006—, pres. Ossining chpt. 2007—). Democrat. Jewish. Avocation: gardening. Home Phone: 914-941-7284; Office Phone: 914-941-7284. Business E-Mail: ireneherz@auntreeneeswebsites.com.

HERZ, MARVIN IRA, psychiatrist, researcher; b. NYC, Dec. 24, 1927; s. Jules Edward and Vivian M. (Becker) Herz; m. Beatrice Leslie Mittelman, Sept. 13, 1952; 3 children. BA, U. Mich., 1949; MS in Psychology, Yale U., 1950; MD, Chgo. Med. Sch., 1955; cert. in Psychoanalysis, Columbia U., 1968. Diplomate Am. Bd. Psychiatry and Neurology (sr. examiner). Intern U. Ill. Rsch. and Ednl. Hosps., 1955-56; resident in psychiatry Michael Reese Hosp., Chgo., 1956-59; dir. inpatient svc. divsn. psychiatry Montefiore Hosp., NYC, 1961-63; dir. Westchester Sq. Day Hosps., NYC, 1963-65; asst. prof. psychiatry Albert Einstein Coll. Medicine, NYC, 1963-65; assoc. in psychiatry Columbia U., 1965-68, asst. prof., 1968-72, assoc. prof., 1972-77; ward adminstr. Washington Heights Cmty. Svc., N.Y. State Psychiat. Inst., 1965-68, dir., 1968-72; asst. attending psychiatrist Vanderbilt Clinic, Presbyn. Hosp., NYC, 1965-68; dir. cmty. svcs. N.Y. State Psychiat. Inst., 1972-77, acting clin. dir., 1975-76; med. dir. Ga. Mental Health Inst., Atlanta, 1977-78, dir. ops. rsch., 1977-78; prof. Emory U., 1977-78; prof., chmn. dept. psychiatry SUNY Sch. Medicine, Buffalo, 1978-91; dir. psychiatry Erie County Med. Ctr., Buffalo, 1978-91; head dept. psychiatry Buffalo Gen. Hosp., 1978-91; prof., dir. Mental Health Svcs. Rsch. U. Rochester, NY, 1991—2002, prof. emeritus, 2002; vol. prof. U. Miami, Fla., 2003; attending psychiatrist Jackson Meml. Hosp. Cons. Task Panel Pres.'s Commn. Rsch. Mental Illness, 1977, Robert Wood Johnson Found., 1992, Nat. Heart and Lung Inst.; cons. psychiatry VA Hosp., Buffalo, 1978—91; sr. sci. advisor to dir. NIMH, 1989—91; cons. psychiatry edn. br., 1978; chmn. psychiat. adv. com. N.Y. State Office Mental Health, 1980—87. Contbr. articles to med. jours. Served to lt. comdr. USNR, 1959—61. Recipient award for outcomes rsch., World Assn. Psychosocial Rehab., U.S. Br., 1994, Heinz Lehmann Rsch. award, N.Y. State Office Mental Health, 1994, award for svcs. rsch., 2002. Fellow: Am. Coll. Psychoanalysts (treas. 1991—95, v.p. 1996—97, pres. elect 1997—98, pres. 1998—99), Am. Coll. Psychiatrists (bd. regents 1990—93, 2d v.p. 1994—95, v.p. 1995—96, pres. elect 1996—97, pres. 1997—98, Dean award 1993, Bowis award 2006), Am. Psychiat. Assn. (chmn. com. to develop practice guidelines schizophrenia 1992—97, chair rsch. prize com. 1996—2000, chair commn. on quality indicators 2006—, disting. life fellow, Hosp. Psychiatry Rsch. prize 1988, Alexander Gralnick award 2003); mem.: Am. Psychoanalytic Assn., Assn. Psychoanalytic Medicine (chmn. com. comm. psychiatry 1975—76), Assn. Clin. Psychosocial Rsch. (pres. 1993—95), Alpha Omega Alpha. Office: Mental Health Hosp Ctr 1695 NW 9th Ave #2101 Miami FL 33136 Personal E-mail: marvles@aol.com. Business E-Mail: mherz@med.miami.edu.

HERZBERG, DOROTHY CREWS, retired secondary school educator; b. NYC, July 8, 1935; d. Floyd Houston and Julia (Lesser) Crews; m. Hershel Zelig Herzberg, May 22, 1962 (div. Apr. 1988); children: Samuel Floyd, Laura Jill, Daniel Crews. AB, Brown U., Providence, RI, 1957; MA, Stanford U., Calif., 1964; JD, San Francisco Law Sch., 1976. Legal sec. various law firms, San Francisco, 1976-78; tchr. Mission Adult Sch., San Francisco, 1965-66; tchr. secondary and univ. levels Peace Corps, Nigeria, 1961-63; investigator Office of Dist. Atty., San Francisco, 1978-80; sr. adminstr. Dean Witter Reynolds Co., San Francisco, 1980-83; registered rep. Waddell and Reed, 1983-84; tax preparer H&R Block, 1987; revenue officer IRS, 1987-89; tchr. ESL West Contra Costa Sch. Dist., Richmond, Calif., 1991—2005; ret., 2005. Sponsor debate team, Richmond H.S., 2001-03, Close UP, 2001-. Editor: (newsletters) Coop. Nursery Sch. Council, 1969-71, Miraloma Life, 1976-82. Bd. dir. LWV, San Francisco, 1967-69, mem. speakers bur., 1967-70; pres. Council Coop. Nursery Schs., San Francisco, 1969-71; bd. dirs. Miraloma (Calif.) Improvement Club, 1977-88, pres., 1980-81; alt. supr. San Francisco Mayor's Commn. on Criminal Justice, 1978; chairperson social justice coun. Unitarian Universalist Ch. Berkeley, 1997-2005; bd. dir. Greater Richmond Interfaith Programs, 2004—. Recipient Schweitzer award, Unitarian Universalist Ch. of Berkeley, 2006. Democrat. Home: 1006 Richmond St El Cerrito CA 94530-2616 Personal E-mail: dorothycherzberg@gmail.com.

HERZBERG, PETER JAY, lawyer; b. Newark, Feb. 3, 1950; s. Arno and Annelle (Baruch) Herzberg; m. Lisa F. Chrystal, Mar. 13, 1982. BA, Haverford Coll., 1972; JD, U. Pa., 1975. Dep. atty. gen. N.J. Dept. Law and Pub. Safety, Trenton, 1975-78, 80, 82-83; staff atty. Sierra Club Legal Def. Fund, Washington, 1978-80; acting asst. counsel to gov. of N.J. Trenton, 1981; John F. Baker scholar, 1971; atty. Pitney Hardin, Morristown, NJ. Mem. Phi Beta Kappa. Office: Pitney Hardin PO Box 1945 Morristown NJ 07962-1945 Office Phone: 973-966-8058. Business E-Mail: pherzberg@pitneyhardin.com.

HERZBERG, THOMAS, artist, educator, illustrator; b. Chgo., Feb. 3, 1954; s. Carroll Alexander and Victoria Herzberg; m. Rosemary Ann Morrissey, Aug. 11, 1979; 1 child, Kyli Rose. BA, Northeastern U., 1975; MFA, No. Ill. U., 1979. Instr. Am. Acad. Art, Chgo., 2000—, fine art dept. chair, 2005—. Illustrations appeared in Chgo. mag., Advertising Age, Playboy mag., World Book, Chgo. Tribune, Washington Post, Art Inst. Chgo., Goodman Theatre, Chg. Exhibited Art Inst. Chgo., 1978, 84, De Cordova Mus., Lincoln., Mass., 1978-79, 83, Silvermine Guild Artists, New Canaan, Conn., 1980, Met. Mus. and Art Ctr., Coral Gables, Fla., 1980, 82, Hunterdon Art Ctr., Clinton, NJ, 1982, U. Dallas, 1983, 10th, 12th and 13th Ann. Soc. Newspaper Design, Am. Soc. Illustrators 28th, 39th and 41st Ann. Exhbns.; represented in permanent collections USAF, De Cordova Mus., Terrance Gallery, Palenville, NY, Met. Mus. and Art Ctr., Silvermine Guild Artists, Carnegie Inst., Art Inst. Chgo., Lincoln Park Zoo, Chgo. Symphony Orch.; over 1900 illustrations in newspapers, mags., books, mus. graphics, 1981—. Mem. Air Force Art Program, 1998—, governing bd., 2004. Named Best of Show 3 Ann. Ill. Regional Print Show, 1980; recipient Award of Excellence New Horizons in Art North Shore Art League, 1980-82, Weston Press and Gallery award 8th Internat. Miniature Print Exhbn. Pratt Graphic Ctr., 1981, Cert. of Design Excellence Print's Regional Design Ann., 1994-97, also numerous awards Art Direction mag. creativity show, 1992-93, Soc. Newspaper Design, Cert. of Merit Soc. Illustrators. Office Phone: 312-461-0600. Personal E-mail: therzb@earthlink.net.

HERZECA, LOIS FRIEDMAN, lawyer; b. July 7, 1954; d. Martin and Elaine Shirley (Rapoport) Friedman; m. Christian S. Herzeca, Aug. 15, 1980; children: Jane Leslie, Nicholas Cameron. BA with honors, SUNY-Binghamton, 1976; JD cum laude, Boston U., 1979. Bar: NY 1980, US Dist. Ct. (so. dist.) NY 1980, US Dist. Ct. (ea. dist.) NY 1980. Atty. antitrust div. U.S. Dept. Justice, Washington, 1979-80; assoc. Fried, Frank, Harris, Shriver & Jacobson LLP, NY, 1980-86, ptnr. NY, 1986—. Editor Am. Jour. Law & Medicine, 1978—79. Dir. Volunteers of Legal Svc., Children for Children Found. Mem.: Legal Aid Soc. (Cmty. Devel. Adv. Com.), Assn. Bar City NY, ABA. Office: Fried Frank Harris Shriver & Jacobson LLP 1 New York Plz Fl 22 New York NY 10004-1980 Office Phone: 212-859-8076. Office Fax: 212-859-4000. Business E-Mail: lois.herzeca@friedfrank.com.

HERZENBERG, ARVID, physicist, researcher; b. Vienna, Apr. 16, 1925; m. Marjorie Swift, Nov. 30, 1949; children: Catherine, Anne, Stephen. BS, U. Manchester, Eng., 1949, DSc, 1964. Mem. faculty U. Manchester, 1952-69; prof. applied physics Yale U., 1969—, emeritus prof. physics & applied physics, 1995—. Contbr. articles to profl. jours. Fellow Brit. Physics Soc., Am. Physics Soc. Achievements include research in geomagnetism, electron-molecule collisions, x-ray analysis of macromolecules. Home: 6 LeGrand Rd North Haven CT 06473-1013 Business E-Mail: arvid.herzenberg@yale.edu.

HERZENBERG, CAROLINE STUART LITTLEJOHN, physicist; b. East Orange, NJ, Mar. 25, 1932; d. Charles Frederick and Caroline Dorothea (Schulze) Littlejohn; m. Leonardo Herzenberg, July 29, 1961; children: Karen Ann, Catherine Stuart. SB, MIT, 1953; SM, U. Chgo., 1955, PhD, 1958; DSc (hon.), SUNY, Plattsburgh, 1991. Asst. prof. Ill. Inst. Tech., Chgo., 1961-66, research physicist ITT Research Inst., 1967-70, sr. physicist, 1970-71; lectr. Calif. State U., Fresno, 1975-76; physicist Argonne (Ill.) Nat. Lab., Ill., 1977-2001. Prin. investigator NASA Apollo Returned Lunar Sample Analysis Program, 1967—71; disting. vis. prof. SUNY, Plattsburgh, 1991; mem. final selection com. Bower award and prize for Achievement in Sci., 1993—94, bd. adv.; mem. nat. panel advisors PBS TV Bill Nye the Sci. Guy, 1991—95; mem. steering com. Midwest Consortium Internat. Security Studies, 1994—95. Prodr., host (TV series) Camera on Science; author: Women Scientists from Antiquity to the Present: An Index, 1986; author: (with R. H. Howes) Their Day in the Sun: Women of the Manhattan Project, 1999; contbr. articles to profl. jours. Past chmn. NOW chpt., Freeport, Ill.; candidate for alderman Freeport, 1975. Finalist Am. Phys. Soc. Congl. Scientist Fellowship, 1976—77; recipient award in sci., Chgo. Women's Hall of Fame, 1989. Fellow: AAAS, Assnq. Women in Sci. (nat. sec. 1982—84, pres. 1988—90), Am. Phys. Soc. (past chmn. com., past sec.-treas. Forum Physics and Soc., chair elect, past exec. bd. Forum History Physics, mem. panel pub. affairs); mem.: Sigma Xi. Home and Office: 1700 E 56th St Apt 2707 Chicago IL 60637-5092 E-mail: carol@herzenberg.net.

HERZER, MARIAN DAY, not-for-profit developer, educator; b. Williston, ND, July 1, 1933; d. Joseph Rollin and Catherine Elizabeth (Bissett) Day; m. Kaye H. Herzer, June 12, 1954; children: Scott Kaye, Kent Day, Brett Herbert. BS in Music, Drama, Business, U. N.D., 1955; AA in real estate, Whatcom Cmty. Coll., 1979. Cert. mgmt. tng. Spokane (Wash.) Leadership Inst., 1975, lic. real estate Wash., 1976, real estate instr. Wash., 1977. Program dir. YWCA, Grand Forks, ND, 1955—56; tchr. secondary edn. Montgomery, Ala., Schertz, Tex., Redondo Beach, Calif., 1957—67; exec. dir. Sinto Ctr., Project JOY, Spokane, Wash., 1969—75; realtor Arnasons & Century 21, Seattle and Bellingham, Wash., 1976—85; corp. sales mgr. Fairwood Village, Spokane, 1985—87; devel. dir., vol. mgr. Hospice of North Idaho, Coeur d'Alene, Idaho, 1987—89; vol. mgr. Wash. County, Hillsboro, Oreg., 1989—95; retired, 1995. Pres. Prevention, Edn. and Devel., Spokane, 2000—03; sec. N.W. Regional Mental Health Bd., Bellingham, Wash., 1978—82, Whatcom County Bd. of Realtors, Bellingham, 1976—82; generalist com. Health Improvement Partnership, Spokane, 1997—99. Editor: Living, Loving, Letting Go, 2002; author: Six Scripts for Seniors, 1988. Sec. No. Va. Action Com., Washington, 1967; mem. So. Poverty Law Ctr., Montgomery, 1993—2002, Poor People's Campaign; bd. dirs. Citizens League, Spokane, 1997—2001. Named Outstanding Vol., Inland N.W. Sr. Wellness Conf., 2005; recipient Disting. Svc. award, ACTION - Region X, 1993, Marian Herzer award, Spokane Parks & Recreation, 1985, Outstanding Vol. Mgr. award, Retired and Sr. Vol. Program, 1998, Ethel Percy Andrus Award for Cmty. Svc., Wash. State, 2002, Spokane Woman of Achievement award for Comty. Svc., YWCA, 2002, Outstanding Vol. award, Retirement and Sr. Vol. Program, 2002. Mem.: DAR (Outsting Cmty. Svc. award 2003, Oustanding Vol. award 2003, LaVina Hensky Excellence award 2005), AARP, Sr. Svc. of Wash. Avocations: music, reading, travel, art collecting, writing. Home: 8230 No Pamela St Spokane WA 99208 Office: Prevention Education and Devel Inc 315 W Mission Ste 22 Spokane WA 99201 Office Phone: 509-326-1471. Personal E-mail: dayher2@msn.com.

HERZFELD, CHARLES MARIA, physicist, educator; b. Vienna, June 29, 1925; came to U.S., 1942, naturalized, 1949; s. August Alfred and Frieda Auguste (Poehlman) H.; children: Charles Christopher, Thomas Augustine, Paul Vincent; m. Shannon Stock Shuman, June 9, 1990. BS in Chem. Engring. cum laude, Cath. U. Am., 1945; PhD (Carnegie Found. fellow), U. Chgo., 1951. Lectr. chemistry Cath. U. Am., 1946; lectr. gen. sci. Coll. U. Chgo., 1946-47; lectr. physics DePaul U., Chgo., 1948-50; physicist Ballistic Research Lab., Aberdeen, Md., 1951-53, Naval Research Lab., Washington, 1953-55; lectr. physics U. Md., 1953-57, prof. physics, 1957-61; cons. chief heat and power div. Nat. Bur. Standards, 1955-56, acting asst. chief, 1956-57, chief heat div., 1957-61, asso. dir. bur., 1961; asst. dir. Advanced Research Project Agy., Dept. Def., 1961-63, dir. ballistic missile def., 1963; dep. dir. Advanced Research Projects Agy., 1963-65, dir., 1965-67; tech. dir. def. space group ITT, Nutley, NJ,

1967-74, tech. dir. aerospace-electronics-components-energy group, 1974-76, tech. dir. telecommunications and electronics group N.Am., 1978-79; v.p., dir. research ITT Corp., 1979-83, v.p., dir. research and tech., 1983-85; vice chmn. Aetna, Jacobs and Ramo, NYC, 1985-90; dir. def. rsch. and engring. Dept. Def., Washington, 1990-91; cons. to Office Sci. and Tech. Policy, Exec. Office Pres. of U.S., Washington, 1991. Chmn. bd. Westronix Co., Midvale, Utah, 1985-88; mem. Def. Sci. bd., 1968-83, Def. Policy Bd., 1985-90, Nat. Commn. on Space, 1985-86; cons. in field; fellow Hudson Inst., 1970-90; mem. Brookings Inst. 5th Conf. for Career Execs. in Fed. Govt., 1958, mem. chief of Naval Ops. exec. panel, 1970-2000; mem. Tech. Review Bd. Hong Kong, 1993-94, Nat. Security Advisory Bd., Los Alamos Nat. Lab.; adj. fellow Ctr. Strategic and Internat. Studies, Washington, 1995—; mem. bd. regents, sr. fellow Potomac Inst. for Policy Studies. Editor: Temperature, Its Control in Science and Industry, vol. III, 1962; contbr. articles to profl. jours. Recipient Flemming award, 1963; Meritorious Civilian Service medal Dept. Def., 1967 Fellow AAAS, Am. Phys. Soc., Conf. on Sci., Philosophy and Religion, Coun. Fgn. Rels., Ctr. for Strategic and Internat. Studies (Washington); mem. Explorers Club, Inst. for Strategic Studies (London), Cath. Assn. Internat. Peace (pres. 1959-61), Cosmos Club (Washington).

HERZFELD, SIEGFRIED, manufacturing executive, consultant; arrived in U.S., 1938, naturalized, 1946; s. William and Irma (Rapp) Herzfeld; m. Bruna Leoni, June 16, 1960; children: William, Oliver, Doris. B in Engring., City U., NYC, 1945; M in Engring., Polytech. Inst., 1948; postgrad., Columbia U., 1948—53. Founder, pres. Internat. Machine Co., NYC, 1947—89; dir. purchasing Stark Carpet Inc., NYC, 1989—. Founder, pres. Internat. Rug Co., NYC, 1947—89, Internat. Rare Book Co., NYC, 1960—95; cons. Tech. Adv. Svc. for Attys., Blue Bell, Pa., 1990—. Editor: (book) The Setting Sun, 1985; author: How Even A Bungler Can Make A Fortune, 2004. Treas. West Side Block Assn., NYC, 1997—. Avocations: calligraphy, Ju Jitsu, philology, Italian incunabula.

HERZIG, DAVID JACOB, retired pharmaceutical company executive, consultant; b. Cleve., Dec. 13, 1936; s. Marvin Laurence and Lillian Gertrude (Blaine) H.; m. Phyllis Glicksberg, Sept. 2, 1962; children: Michael, Pamela, Roberta, Karen. BA, Oberlin Coll., 1958; PhD in Chemistry, U. Cin., 1963. Vis. scientist NIH, Bethesda, Md., 1963-65, staff fellow, 1965-67; sr. rsch. assoc. NYU Sch. Medicine, NYC, 1967-68, Warner Lambert, Parke-Davis Co., Ann Arbor, Mich., 1968-77, dir. immunopharmacology, 1977-81, dir. sci. devel., 1981—91, v.p. drug devel. and sci. devel., 1991—99. Contbr. articles to profl. jours. Bd. dirs. Mich. Ctr. High Tech., 1992-95. Fellow Damon Runyon Meml. Fund. Mem. Licensing Exec. Soc., Mich. Biotech. Assn. (bd. dirs. 1993-96, pres. 1994-96), N.Y. Acad. Scis., N.Y. Fencers Club (bd. dirs. 1970-77), Sigma Xi. Avocations: squash, fencing, furniture building. Home and Office: 3540 Windemere Dr Ann Arbor MI 48105-2842 E-mail: davidjhherzig@world.oberlin.edu, dherzig01@yahoo.com.

HERZLICH, HAROLD J., chemical engineer; b. Bklyn. m. Carol Ast; children: Amy, Adam. BSChemE, NYU, 1956; student, So. Conn. Coll., Quinnipiac Coll. Mem. prodn. squadron Goodyear Tire & Rubber Co., Akron, Ohio, 1956-57, mem. process devel., 1957-58; prodn. compounder Armstrong Rubber Co., New Haven, 1958-61, sr. compounder, 1961-62, divsn. compounder, 1962-65, mgr. pass tire comp. devel., 1965-66, mgr. auto tire comp. devel., 1966-68, mgr. pass car tire comp. devel., 1968-70, sr. rsch. chemist, 1970-73, mgr. compound rsch., 1973-75, mgr. compound devel., 1975-85, dir. tire engring., legal matters and product reliability, 1985-88, Pirelli Armstrong Tire Co., New Haven, 1988-90; consulting tire engr. Tire Engring., Chemistry and Safety, Las Vegas, 1990—. Pres. Elasphalt Corp.; chmn. Internat. Tire Conf.; speaker in field. Tech. editor Rubber and Plastics News. With USCG. Mem. ASTM (mem. E-40), Am. Chem. Soc. (chmn. rubber divsn. 1982—, chmn.-elect 1981, mem. membership com., mem. edn. com., mem. budget and fin. com., treas. rubber divsn. 1978-81, bus. mgr. rubber chemistry and tech., mem. divsn. chemistry and law, hon. life), Soc. Automotive Engrs., Acad. Forensics Sci. (engring. divsn.), Tire Soc., Conn. Rubber Group (edn. chmn., vice chmn., chmn. 1966, hon. life). Avocations: sports, travel. Home and Office: Tire Engring Chemistry & Safety 8908 Desert Mound Dr Las Vegas NV 89134-8801 E-mail: harherz@juno.com.

HERZLINGER, REGINA, economist, educator, writer; m. George Herzlinger. BS, MIT; Doctorate, Harvard Bus. Sch. Economist, Washington; v.p. Various Cons. Firms, Cambridge; asst. sec. Gov. Commonwealth Mass.; prof. Harvard Bus. Sch., Boston, 1971—. Pub. bd. dirs. 13 cos. Author: (books) Market-Driven Health Care, 2000, Consumer-Driven Health Care, 2004, 4 other books. Avocations: art, gardening, aerobics. Office: Harvard Bus Sch Soldier's Field Boston MA 02163 Business E-Mail: rherzlinger@hbs.edu.

HERZOG, ARTHUR, III, author; b. NYC, Apr. 6, 1927; s. Arthur Jr. and Elizabeth Lindsay (Dayton) H.; 1 son by previous marriage, Matthew Lennox. Student, U. Ariz., 1945-46; BA, Stanford U., 1950; MA, Columbia U., 1956. Editor Fawcett Publs., 1957-59. Cons. Peace Corps, 1967-68; polit. cons., 1969-71; bd. dirs. Leslie Mandel Enterprises, Mandel Airplane Funding and Leasing Co. Author: (with others) Smoking and the Public Interest, 1963, The War-Peace Establishment, 1965, The Church Trap, 1968, McCarthy for President, 1969, The B.S. Factor, 1973, The Swarm, 1974, Earthsound, 1975, Orca, 1977, Heat, 1977, rev. edit., 1989, IQ 83, 1978, Make Us Happy, 1978, Glad to be Here, 1979, Aries Rising, 1981, The Craving, 1982, L.S.I.T.T., 1983, Vesco-From Wall Street to Castro's Cuba, The Rise, Fall and Exile of the King of White Collar Crime, 1987, Takeover, 1987 (formerly L.S.I.T.T.), The Woodchipper Murder, 1989, Seventeen Days: The Katie Beers Story, 1993, How to Write Almost Anything Better and Faster, 1995, Body Parts, 2001, Imortalon, 2003, The Village Buyers, 2003, Icetopia, 2004, The Town That Moved to Mexico, 2004, Murder in Our Town, 2007, (almost all works transl. and published in Hungary); contbr. articles profl. jours. Campaign mgr. Oreg., nat. pub. rels. dir. Eugene McCarthy Presdl. Campaign, 1968; founder New Democratic Coalition, N.Y. and nationally, 1968-69, Lexington Dem. Club, 1974. With USNR, 1944-45. Mem.: PEN, Authors League, Authors Guild, Pigeon Point Club Tobago. Address: PO Box 294 Wainscott NY 11975-0294 Home Phone: 631-373-3068; Office Phone: 212-879-3089. E-mail: artherzog@aol.com. *I do not believe that money and success should figure as strongly as it does in our estimate of what is a good life. Since it often does, though, I would point to perseverance as a major element of success. Another, mostly overlooked, is a lack of dogmatism and a belief in skepticism and personal happiness as ends in themselves.*

HERZOG, BRIGITTE, lawyer; b. St. Sauveur, France, Jan. 11, 1943; arrived in U.S., 1970, naturalized, 1976; d. Roger and Berthe (Niobey) Ecolivet; m. Peter E. Herzog, June 29, 1970; children: Paul Roger, Elizabeth Ann. Licence en Droit, Law Sch. Pantheon, Paris, 1967; diploma d'Etudes Superieures in internat. and criminal law, Law Sch. Pantheon, 1968; diploma, Acad. Internat. Law, The Hague, Netherlands, 1969; JD, Syracuse Coll. Law, NY, 1975. Bar: Paris 1968, NY 1976. Assoc. Chardenon Law Firm, Paris, 1968-70, Cleary, Gottlieb et al, Paris, 1976-77; staff atty. Carrier Corp., Syracuse, 1977-83, sr. atty., 1983-84, asst. gen. counsel, 1984-86, counsel European and Transcontinental Ops. Surrey, England, 1986-89, assoc. gen. counsel Syracuse, 1990; dir. legal affairs Otis, Paris, 1990-92; v.p. legal affairs European and Transcontinental Ops. Otis Internat., Inc., 1992-97; dep. gen. counsel Otis Elevator Co.-Europe; v.p. legal affairs Otis Elevator North European Area, 1998—2001; dep. gen. counsel Otis World Hdqrs., Farmington, Conn., 2002—05; dir. bus. practices United Tech. Corp., 2005—. Contbr. to Harmonization of Laws in EEC Fifth Sokol Colloquium, 1983; contbr. articles on French and internat. law to profl. jours. Bd. dirs. Syracuse Stage Guild, 1974-77; chair legal com. European Elevator Assn. Mem. ABA, Am. Fgn. Law Assn. Roman Catholic. Home: 42 Jillian Cir West Hartford CT 06107 Office: United Technologies Corp One Financial Plaza Hartford CT 06101 Home Phone: 860-521-0681; Office Phone: 860-728-7837. Business E-Mail: brigitte.herzog@utc.com.

HERZOG, JENNIFER A., biology professor; b. Buffalo, Jan. 21, 1975; MS, MPhil, Yale U., 2000. Asst. prof. biology Herkimer (N.Y.) County C.C., 2001—. Mem. Utica Coll. Regional Sci. Fair Com., 2001—; co-chair Am. Soc. Microbiology Conf. Undergraduate Educators, 2007. Recipient 40 Under 40 award, 2004. Mem.: Am. Soc. Microbiology. Office Phone: 315-866-0300.

HERZOG, JOHN E., numismatist; b. NYC, Mar. 18, 1936; s. Robert I. and Norma (Englander) H.; m. Diana E. Rigby; children: Mary, Sarah. BA, Cornell U., 1957; postgrad., N.Y. Inst. Fin., 1958; MBA, NYU, 1970. With Eastman Dillon (Paine Weber), Phila., 1957-59; chmn. Herzog, Heine, Geduld, NYC, 1959—2002, R.M. Smythe & Co. Inc., 1996—. Charter mem. regulatory policy adv. com. N.Y. Stock Exch., 1981—, mem. regional firms adv. com. Bd. dirs. Resources for Children with Spl. Needs, N.Y.C.; trustee The Knox Sch., 1986-91, Randolph Macon Woman's Coll., Securities Industry Inst.; bd. regents L.I. Coll. Hosp., Bklyn.; founder, chair Mus. Am. Fin.; mem. adv. coun. Cornell Libr.; mem. bd. overseers NYU Stern Sch. Bus. Mem.: Smithsonian Instn. (nat. bd. dirs.), Securities Industry Assn. (chmn. N.Y. Area firms com., econ. edn. com. N.Y.dist.). Office: R M Smthye & Co Inc 2 Rector St New York NY 10006-1844 Office Phone: 212-312-6333.

HERZOG, LESTER BARRY, lawyer; b. Presov, Slovakia, July 3, 1953; came to U.S., 1965; s. Alexander and Flora (Braun) H.; m. Terry Lynn Hochhauser, Feb. 6, 1979; children: Simcha, Sarah, Chaim, Judah, Leah. BA, Rabbinical Sem. Belz, Bklyn., 1974; MBA with distinction, L.I. U., 1977; JD cum laude, Bklyn. Law Sch., 1983. Bar: N.Y. 1984, U.S. Dist. Ct. (ea. and so. dists.) N.Y. 1984; CPA, N.Y. Sr. auditor Seidman & Seidman, NYC, 1977-83; sr. trial atty. Office Corp. Counsel N.Y.C. Law Dept., Bklyn., 1983-89; pvt. practice NYC, 1989—. Adj. assoc. prof. law and acctg. L.I. U., Bklyn., 1985—. Contbr. articles to profl. jours. Mem. ABA, AICPA (exam grader 1981-83), N.Y. State Bar Assn. Democrat. Jewish. Avocations: chess, fishing, gardening. Home and Office: 1729 E 15th St Brooklyn NY 11229-2084 Office Phone: 718-376-7635.

HERZOG, PETER EMILIUS, retired legal educator; b. Vienna, Dec. 25, 1925; came to U.S., 1950, naturalized, 1955; s. Paul and Leopodine (Mannhart) H.; m. Brigitte Ecolivet, June 29, 1970; children: Paul, Elizabeth Ann. Student, U. Vienna, 1949-50; BA, Hobart Coll., 1952; LLB summa cum laude, Syracuse U., 1955; LLM, Columbia U., 1956. Bar: N.Y. 1957. Dep. asst. atty. gen. N.Y. State Dept. Law, Albany, 1955-57, asst. atty. gen., 1957-58; asst. prof. law Syracuse U. Coll. Law, 1958-62, assoc. prof., 1962-66, prof., 1966-83, Crandall Melvin prof., 1983-94, Crandall Melvin prof. emeritus, 1995—, law librarian, 1960-68; staff mem. Columbia U. Project on Inter Procedure, 1960-63; assoc. dir. Project on European Legal Instns., 1968-73; ret. Staff mem. UN Commn. on Internat. Trade Law, 1968-69; rsch. fellow Procedural Aspects Internat. Law Inst., 1968-71; lectr. Hague (Netherlands) Acad. Internat. Law, 1992; cons. N.Y. State Eminent Domain Commn., 1971; vis. prof. U. Paris, 1976-77, U. Dijon, France, 1987, U. Fribourg, Switzerland, 1987. Author: (with Martha Weser) Civil Procedure in France, 1967, (with Ivan Head and Frank Dawson) International Law, National Tribunals and the Rights of Aliens, 1971, (with Hans Smit) The Law of the European Economic Community, A Commentary, 1976, 2d edit., 2006, (with Schlesinger, Baade and Wise) Comparative Law, 6th edit., 1998; contbr. articles to legal publs. Jervey fellow Columbia U., 1956. Mem. Am. Soc. Internat. Law, Soc. de Législation Comparée, Internat. Law Assn., Internat. Acad. Comparative Law (assoc.), Order of Coif, Phi Beta Kappa. Roman Catholic.

HERZOG, ROLAND W., medical educator; PhD, Auburn U., Ala., 1996. Asst. prof. pediat. U. Pa., Phila., 2000—05; assoc. prof. pediat. U. Fla., Gainesville, 2005—. Recipient Career Devel. award, Nat. Hemophilia Found., 2000—03. Mem.: Am. Soc. Gene Therapy (Young Investigator award 2003). Achievements include patents for gene therapy for hemophilia. Office: U Fla 1376 Mowry Rd Rm 203 Gainesville FL 32610 Home Phone: 352-331-9937; Office Phone: 352-273-8113.

HERZOG, THOMAS, obstetrician, gynecologist, gynecological oncologist and surgeon, educator; b. Dec. 7, 1959; BA in Zoology, Miami Univ., Oxford, Ohio, 1982; MD, U. Cinn., 1986. Cert. Obstetrics & Gynecology, Gynecologic Oncology. Intern, obstetrics & gynecology Univ. Cin., 1986—87, resident, gynecological oncology, 1987—90; fellow Wash. Univ., St. Louis, 1990—93, instr., gynecological oncology, 1990—95, asst. prof., gynecological oncology, 1995—2001, fellow program dir., gynecological oncology, 1998—2004, assoc. prof., obstetrics & gynecology, 2001—04; prof. obstetrics and gynecology Columbia Univ. Coll. Physician and Surgeons, 2004—; dir., divsn. gynecologic oncology, dept. obstetrics and gynecology NY-Presbyn. Hosp./Columbia Univ. Med. Ctr., 2004—; staff mem., clin. obstetrics and gynecology Columbia Univ. Herbert Irving Comprehensive Cancer Ctr., NYC, 2004; prof. clin. obstetrics and gynecology Columbia U. Med. Ctr., 2005—. Office: Columbia Univ Coll Physicians and Surgeons Irving Pavilion Rm 8th Fl 161 Fort Washington Ave New York NY 10032 Office Phone: 212-305-3410. Office Fax: 212-305-3412.*

HERZOG, WERNER (WERNER STIPETIC), film director; b. Munich, Sept. 5, 1942; m. Marthe Grohmann, 1967 (div. 1987); 3 children; m. Lena Herzog; attended U. Munich, Duquesne U. Dir., prodr., writer: (films) Signs of Life, 1968, Even Dwarfs Started Small, 1970, Fata Morgana, 1971, The Land of Silence and Darkness, 1971, Aguirre, Wrath of God, 1972, The Enigma of Kaspar Hauser, 1974 (Cannes Internat. Film Festival Grand Prize), The Great Ecstasy of Woodcutter Steiner, 1974, Heart of Glass, 1976, Stroszek, 1977, Nosferatu, 1979, Woyzeck, 1979, Le pays du silence et de l'obscurité, 1980, Fitzcarraldo, 1982 (Best Dir., Cannes Internat. Film Festival), Where the Green Ants Dream, (also author screenplay), 1984, Echoes from a Somber Empire, 1990, Schrei Aus Stein, 1991, Lessons of Darkness, 1992, Bells from the Deep: Faith and Superstition in Russia, 1993, Little Dieter Needs to Fly, 1997, My Best Friend, 1999, Pilgramage, 2001, Invincible, 2001, Wheel of Time, 2003, The White Diamond, 2004, Grizzly Man, 2005 (honored for best non-fiction film, NY Film Critics Circle, 2005, Directors' Guild Am. award for Outstanding Directorial Achievement in Documentary, 2005), The Wild Blue Yonder, 2005 (honored for best non-fiction film, NY Film Critics Circle, 2005, World's First Undersea Outer-Space Sci-Fi Documentary), Rescue Dawn, 2006; (TV films) Huie's Sermon, 1980, God's Angry Man, 1980, Glaube und Wahrung, 1980, Ballad of the Little Soldier, 1984, Herdsmen of the Sun, 1989, Giovanna d'Arco, 1989; co-dir. Les Francais Vus Par, 1993, The Transformation of the World into Music, 1994, Death for Five Voices, 1995, Wings of Hope, 2000, others; appeared in films Man of Flowers, 1984, Tokyo-Ga, 1985; named 35th Greatest Director of All Time, Entertainment Weekly. Office: New Yorker Films 85 5th Ave Fl 11 New York NY 10003-3019*

HERZSTEIN, BARBARA See **HERSHEY, BARBARA**

HERZSTEIN, ROBERT ERWIN, lawyer; b. Denver, Feb. 26, 1931; s. Sigmund Edwards and Estelle Ruth (Borwick) H.; m. Priscilla Holmes, July 11, 1956; children: Jessica Anne, Emily Holmes, Robert Holmes. AB, Harvard U., 1952, LLB, 1955. Bar: Colo. 1956, D.C. 1959, U.S. Supreme Ct. 1962. Sr. ptnr., other positions Arnold & Porter, Washington, 1958-80, sr. ptnr., 1981-89; undersec. for Internat. Trade U.S. Dept. Commerce, Washington, 1980-81; ptnr. Shearman & Sterling, Washington, 1989-95, counsel, 1995-99; mem. Miller & Chevalier, Washington, 1999—2004, of counsel, 2004—. Contbr. articles to profl. jours. Trustee Internat. Law Inst., Washington, 1974—; chmn Ptnrs. for Dem. Change; bd. dirs. Appleseed Found., Washington, Coun. of Ams., NY, 1990—2004; bd. dirs., mem. faculty Salzburg Seminar in Am. Studies, 1986—93. Mem. ABA, Am. Soc. Internat. Law, Coun. on Fgn. Rels. Home: 4710 Woodway Ln NW Washington DC 20016-3241 Office: 655 15th St NW Ste 900 Washington DC 20005-5701 Office Phone: 202-626-5983. Business E-Mail: rherzstein@milchev.com.

HESCHEL, MICHAEL SHANE, retail food products executive; b. June 18, 1941; m. Judi Heschel; 2 children. BS in Indsl. Engring., Ohio State U., 1964, MBA, 1965, MS in Indsl. Engring., 1967; PhD in Indsl. Engring., Ariz. State U., 1970. Former sr. mgmt. systems analyst Boeing Aircraft Co.; former corp. mgr. ops. rsch. FMC Corp.; former corp. v.p. info. svcs. Am. Hosp. Supply Corp.; former corp. v.p. info. resources Baxter Internat. Inc.; former chmn., CEO Security Pacific Automation Co.; group v.p. info. systems The Kroger Co., Cin., 1991-94, sr. v.p., 1994-95, exec. v.p., chief info. officer, 1995—. Office: The Kroger Co 1014 Vine St Cincinnati OH 45202-1100 Home Phone: 513-233-9490; Office Phone: 513-762-4374.

HESER, CHERYL J., library director; b. Iowa City, Mar. 14, 1948; d. Eugene W. and Myrtle A. Elliott; m. Douglas C. Heser, June 8, 1974; children: Clinton D., Anne J. Heser Robinson, Joshua R. BA, Ea. Mont. Coll., 1970, tchg. cert., 1972; postgrad., Western Mont. Coll., 1995. Tchr. Rosebud (Mont.) Schs., 1986—91, tchr., sch. libr., 1993—98; advt. mgr. Ind. Enterprise, Forsyth, Mont., 1991—93; dir. Rosebud County Libr., Forsyth, 1997—. Presenter in field. Author: Lewis & Clark Activity Book, 2003, Look to the Mountains: A Lewis & Clark Cantata with Narration, 2004, Living History Presenter: Tea with Dolly Madison, 2005. Judge speech and drama meets, Forsyth, 1997—; spkr. Mont. Com. for the Humanities Spkrs. Bur., 2005—; mem. Immaculate Conception Ch., Forsyth, 1986—. Mem.: Mont. Libr. Assn. (dir. at large 1997—99, chair Lewis & Clark task force 1999—2003, Mountain Plains Libr. Assn. rep. 2000—03, Media award 2002). Roman Catholic. Avocations: writing, music. Office: Rosebud County Libr 201 N Ninth Ave Forsyth MT 59327 Home Phone: 406-356-4372; Office Phone: 406-346-7561. Personal E-mail: cheser@rosebudcountmt.com.

HESHMAT, HOOSHANG, manufacturing executive; b. Tabriz, Iran, Aug. 20, 1950; BS, Pa. State U., 1977; MS, Rensselaer Poly. Inst., 1979, PhD in Mech. Engring., 1988. With Reliance Electric Co.; co-founder, pres., CEO, tech. dir. Mohawk Innovative Tech., Inc. Co-author: (chpt.) Compressor Handbook; contbr. over 146 articles to profl. jours.; Patentee in field. Recipient Tech. Creativity award Mech. Tech. Inc., 1990; Thomas A. Edison Patent award, 2002. Fellow Soc. Tribologists and Lubrication Engrs., ASME (chmn. internat. joint conf. 1994, vice chmn. rsch. com. tribology, tribology divsn. exec. com., Wilbur Deutsch Meml. award 1983, Burt L. Newkirk award 1985, Capt. Alfred E. Hunt award 1993, Creative Rsch. award 1995, Al Sonntag award 1996, Thomas A. Edison Patent award 2002, Frank P. Bussick award 2003, Microturbine and Small Turbomachinery Com. Best Paper award 2005, Mayo D. Hersey award 2007). Office: Mohawk Innovative Tech Inc 1037 Watervliet Shaker Rd Albany NY 12205-2033

HESS, ADAM R., lawyer; b. Reading, Pa., Apr. 22, 1965; BS Chem. Engring., Lehigh Univ., 1987; JD, George Washington Univ., 1992. Bar: Pa. 1992, DC 1994, Va. 2002, US Dist. Ct. (DC, ea., we. dist. Mich., ea. dist. Va.), US Ct. Appeals (Fed. cir.) 1994, US Ct. Appeals (DC cir.) 1997, US Supreme Ct. 2001. Ptnr., leader No. Va. IP Litigation group Pillsbury Winthrop Shaw Pittman, McLean, Va. Mem.: ABA, Bar Assn. DC, Fed. Cir. Bar Assn., Am. Intellectual Property Law Assn., Am. Inst. Chem. Engineers, Giles Sutherland Rich Am. Inns of Ct. Office: Pillsbury Winthrop Shaw Pittman 1600 Tysons Blvd Mc Lean VA 22102 Office Phone: 703-905-2089. Office Fax: 703-905-2500. Business E-Mail: adam.hess@pillsburylaw.com.

HESS, ASHLEY W., lawyer; b. May 25, 1973; BA, U. Va., 1995; JD, Washington and Lee U. Sch. of Law, 1998. Bar: Ky. 1998, Ohio 2003. Staffwriter Environ. Law Digest, 1996—97. Named one of 40 Under 40, Cin. Bus. Courier, 2005, Ohio's Rising Stars, Super Lawyers, 2005, 2006. Mem.: Young Professionals Assn. Louisville (founding mem. 1999, bd. dir. 1999—2001, chmn., workforce devel. com. 1999—2001), Bacchanalian Soc., Inc. (founding mem. 2002—), Ky. Bar Assn., Ohio State Bar Assn., ABA, U. Va. Alumni Assn., Lee Alumni Assn., Assn. for Corp. Growth, Cin. Bar Assn. (co-chair, Bus. Law Sect. 2003—06), U. Club Cin. (membership com. 2003—05, house & fin. com. 2004—). Office: Greenebaum Doll & McDonald PLLC 2800 Chemed Ctr 255 E 5th St Cincinnati OH 45202-4728 Office Phone: 513-455-7600. Office Fax: 513-455-8500.

HESS, CHARLES EDWARD, environmental horticulture educator; b. Paterson, NJ, Dec. 20, 1931; s. Cornelius W. M. and Alice (Debruyn) H.; children: Mary, Carol, Nancy, John, Peter; m. Eva G. Carroad, Feb. 14, 1981. BS, Rutgers U., 1953; MS, Cornell U., 1954, PhD, 1957; DAgr (hon.), Purdue U., 1983; DSc (hon.), Delaware Valley Coll., Doylestown, Pa., 1992. From asst. prof. to prof. Purdue U., West Lafayette, Ind., 1958-65; rsch. prof., dept. chmn. Rutgers U., New Brunswick, NJ, 1966, assoc. dean, dir. NJ Agrl. Exptl. Sta., 1970, acting dean Coll. Agrl. and Environ. Sci., 1971, dean Cook Coll., 1972-75; assoc. dir. Calif. Agrl. Exptl. Sta., 1975-89; asst. sec. sci. and edn. USDA, Washington, 1989-91; dean Coll. Agrl. and Environ. Scis. U. Calif., Davis, 1975-89, prof. dept. environ. horticulture, 1975-94, prof. emeritus, 1994—, dir. internat. programs Coll. Agrl. and Environ. Scis., 1992-98, spl. asst. to provost, 1994—2003, spl. asst. to chancellor, 2003—04. Cons. U.S. AID, 1965, Office Tech. Assessment, U.S. Congress, 1976-77, Nat. Rsch. Coun., 2005—; chmn. study team world food and nutrition study NAS, 1976; mem. Calif. State Bd. Food and Agr., 1984-89; mem. Nat. Sci. Bd., 1982-88, 92-98, vice-chmn., 1984-88; co-chmn. Joint Coun. USDA, 1987-91; mem. external adv. com. Western Ctr. for Agrl. Health and Safety, 2005—. Mem. West Lafayette Sch. Bd., 1963-65, sec., 1963, pres., 1964; mem. Gov.'s Commn. Blueprint for Agr., 1971-73; bd. dirs. Davis Sci. Ctr., 1992-94; trustee Internat. Svc. for Nat. Agrl. Rsch., The Hague, Netherlands, 1992-98, bd. chmn., 1995-96; chair adv. com. U. Calif. Davis Retiree Ctr., 2005—. Mem. U.S. EPA (mem. biotech. sci. adv. com. 1992-96), AAAS (chmn. agriculture sect. 1989-90), Am. Soc. Hort. Sci. (pres. 1973), Internat. Plant Propagators Soc. (pres. 1973), Agrl. Rsch. Inst., U. Calif. Davis Emerti Assn. (pres. 2004-06), Phi Beta Kappa, Sigma Xi, Alpha Zeta, Phi Kappa Phi, Gamma Sigma Delta (Disting. Achievement in Agr. award 2004). Office: U Calif Coll Agrl Environ Scis Dept Environ Horticulture Davis CA 95616 Office Phone: 530-758-0671, 530-752-8117. Business E-Mail: cehess@ucdavis.edu.

HESS, DARLA BAKERSMITH, cardiologist, educator; b. Valparaiso, Fla., June 4, 1953; d. James Barry and Irma Marie (Baker) Bakersmith; m. Leonard Wayne Hess, July 20, 1988; 1 child, Ever Marie. BS, Birmingham So. Coll., 1975; MD, Tulane U., New Orleans, 1979. Diplomate Am. Bd. Internal Medicine, Am. Bd. Cardiovascular Disease. Commd. ensign USNR, 1979, advanced through grades to lt. comdr., 1988; resident in internal medicine Portsmouth Naval Hosp., Va., 1979-82, cardiologist, head non-invasive cardiology Va., 1986-88; fellow in cardiology San Diego Naval Hosp., 1982-84; cardiologist, head med. officer in charge ICU Camp

Lejeune Naval Hosp., N.C., 1984-85; dir. noninvasive sect. cardiology, dir. fetal echocardiography U. Mo., Columbia, 1991—99; asst. prof. medicine U. Miss. Med. Ctr., Jackson, 1988-91, asst. prof. ob/gyn., 1990-91; co-dir. fetal echocardiography U. Mo., Columbia, 1991—99, co-dir. Adult Congenital Heart Disease Clinic, 1991—99, assoc. prof. medicine, assoc. prof. ob/gyn., 1998—2001; cardiologist Lehigh Valley Heart Specialists, Pa., 2006—07. Clin. assoc. prof. Pa. State U., 2006—07. Author: (with others) Obstetrics and Gynecology Clinics, 1992, Clinical Problems in Obstetrics & Gynecology, 1993, General Medical Disorders During, 1991; co-editor: Fetal Echocardiography, 1999; contbr. articles to So. Med. Jour., Ob/Gyn. Clinics N.Am., Soc. Perinatal Obs., Jour. Reproductive Medicine, others. Fellow Am. Coll. Cardiology, Fellow Am. Heart Assn. (fellow stroke coun.), Fellow Am. Soc. Echocardiography; mem. Am. Assn. Nuclear Cardiology, Phi Beta Kappa, Alpha Omega Alpha. Republican. Anglican. Home: 7945 Springhouse Rd New Tripoli PA 18066 Office Phone: 610-217-5753. E-mail: darlahess@aol.com.

HESS, DENNIS WILLIAM, chemical engineering educator; b. Reading, Pa., Mar. 1, 1947; s. John William and Dorothy E. (Miller) H.; m. Patricia Ruth Weidner, June 1, 1968; children: Amy R., Sarah E. BS in Chemistry, Albright Coll., 1968; MS in Phys. Chemistry, Lehigh U., 1970, PhD in Phys. Chemistry, 1973. Staff researcher Fairchild Semiconductor, Palo Alto, Calif., 1973-77; from asst. prof. to prof. chem. engring. U. Calif., Berkeley, 1977-91; prin. investigator Materials and Molecular Research div. Lawrence Berkeley Lab., 1978-84, Ctr. for Adv. Materials, Lawrence Berkeley Lab., 1983-85; asst. dean Coll. Chemistry U. Calif., Berkeley, 1982-87; vice chmn. dept. chem. engring U. Calif., Berkeley, 1988-91; chmn. dept. chem. engring. Lehigh U., Bethlehem, Pa., 1991-96; William W. LaRoche Jr. prof. chem. and biomolecular engring. Ga. Inst. Tech., Atlanta, 1996—. Editor Electrochem. and Solid State Letters, 2004—; contbr. articles to profl. jours. Fellow AAAS, AIChE (Charles M.A. Stine award 1999), The Electrochem. Soc. (pres. 1996-97, Thomas D. Callinan award 1993, Solid State Sci. and Tech. award 2005); mem. Am. Chem. Soc., Am. Inst. Physics, Materials Rsch. Soc., Sigma Xi, Tau Beta Pi. Office: Ga Tech Sch Chem and Biomolecular Engring 311 Ferst Dr Atlanta GA 30332-0100 Office Phone: 404-894-5922. E-mail: dennis.hess@chbe.gatech.edu.

HESS, DONALD MARC, diversified financial services company executive; b. Bern, Switzerland, Aug. 3, 1936; s. Hector Albert and Louise (McNeir) Hess; divorced; 1 child, Alexandra. Ecole Superieure De Commerce, Neuchatel U.; brewmaster, Doemens, Munich, 1957. Pres. Steinholzli Brewery, Bern, 1957-68; chmn. Hess Holding, Bern, 1968—. Chmn. Valser Mineral Water, Ltd., Vals, Switzerland, Hess Ltd., Bern, Blue Lake, Ltd., Blausee, Switzerland, Hess Internat., V.V., Rotterdam, Netherlands; CEO The Hess Collection Winery, Napa, Calif.; bd. dirs. Kambly Bisquits, Ltd., Trubschachen, Switzerland, 1988—. Hess Art Collection Ltd., Bern, 1998—; founder Hess Collection Contemporary Art Mus., Napa, Calif., 1989—, Hess Collection Art Exbhn. Space at Vinopolis-City of Wine, 1 Bank End, London, 1999—. Editor: Hess Collection, 1989 (named one of best books in Switzerland 1989), Hess Collection New Works, 1998, Franz Gertsch, Hess Collection, 1999. Co-founder Kunst Heute Found., Bern, 1982; pres., mem exec. com. Internat. Green Cross Switzerland, 1994-96. Named one of Top 200 Collectors, ARTnews Mag., 2004, 2006; recipient, 2005. Avocation: Collector Contemporary Art. Mailing: Hess Collection 4411 Redwood Rd Napa CA 94558

HESS, EVELYN VICTORINE, medical educator; b. Dublin, Nov. 8, 1926; arrived in U.S., 1960, naturalized, 1965; d. Ernest Joseph and Mary (Hawkins) H.; m. Michael Howett, Apr. 27, 1954. MB, B.Ch, BAO, U. Coll., Dublin, 1949; MD, Univ. Coll., Dublin, 1980. Intern West Middlesex Hosp., London, Eng., 1950; resident Clare Hall Hosp., London, 1951-53, Royal Free Hosp. and Med. Sch., London, 1954-57; rsch. fellow in epidemiology of Tb Royal Free Med. Sch., London, 1955; fellow U. Tex. Southwestern Med. Sch., Dallas, 1958—59, asst. prof. internal medicine, 1960-64; assoc. prof. dept. medicine U. Cin. Coll. Medicine, 1964-69, McDonald prof. medicine, 1969—, dir. div. immunology, 1964-95. Sr. investigator Arthritis and Rheumatism Found., 1963-68; attending physician Univ. Hosp., VA Hosp.; cons. Children's Hosp., Cin., 1967—, Jewish Hosp., Cin., 1968—; mem. various coms., mem. nat. adv. coun. NIH; mem. various coms. FDA, Cin. Bd. Health. Contbr. articles to profl. jours., chapters to books. Active Nat. Pks. Assn., Smithsonian Instn., others. Recipient award Arthritis Found., 1973, 78, 83, Am. Lupus Soc., 1979, Am. Acad. Family Practice, 1980, State of Ohio, 1989, Spirit of Am. Women, 1989, Daniel Drake medal U. Cin., 2001, Gold medal Lupus Found., 2004, Lifetime Hess Rsch. award Lupus Found., 2005; fellow Royal Free Med. Sch., Scandinavia, 1956; Empire Rheumatism Coun. travelling fellow, 1958-59. Master ACP (gov. Ohio chpt. 1999-2003, Master Tchr. award 1995); fellow AAAS, Am. Acad. Allergy, Royal Soc. Medicine, ACR (master, Disting. Rheumatologist award 1996); mem. Heberden Soc., Am. Coll. Rheumatology, Pan-Am. League Assns. for Rheumatology (Gold medal 2003), Ctrl. Soc. Clin. Rsch., Am. Fedn. Clin. Rsch., Am. Assn. Immunologists, Am. Soc. Nephrology, Am. Med. Womens Assn. (Local Hero award 2004), Am. Soc. Clin. Pharmacology and Therapeutics, N.Y. Acad. Scis., Soc. Exptl. Biology and Medicine, Rheumatological Soc. Colombia (hon.), Rheumatological Soc. Peru (hon.), Rheumatological Soc. Italy (hon.), Clin. Immunol. Soc. Japan (hon.), Cuban Soc. Rheumatology (hon.), Alpha Omega Alpha. Achievements include research in immunology, rheumatic diseases. Home: 2916 Grandin Rd Cincinnati OH 45208-3418 Office: U Cin Med Ctr ML 563 ML 563 MSB Cincinnati OH 45267-0001 Office Phone: 513-558-4701. Business E-Mail: hessev@email.uc.edu.

HESS, FREDERICK J., lawyer; b. Highland, Ill., Sept. 22, 1941; s. Fred and Matilda (Maiden) H.; m. Mary V. Menkhus, Nov. 13, 1976; children: Frederick, M. Elizabeth. BS in Polit. Sci. and History, St. Louis U., 1963; JD, Washburn Sch. Law, Topeka, 1971. Bar: Kans. 1971, Ill. 1975, U.S. Supreme Ct. 1975, D.C. 1977, U.S. Tax Ct. 1977. Asst. U.S. atty. Dept. Justice, East St. Louis, Ill., 1971-73, 1st asst. U.S. atty., 1973-76; ct. appt. U.S. Atty. E. Dist. of Ill., 1977; ptnr. Stiehl & Hess, Belleville, Ill., 1977-82; U.S. atty. U.S. Dist. Ct. (so. dist.) Ill., East St. Louis, 1982-93; pvt. practice Lewis Rice & Fingersh, Belleville, 1993—. Bd. dirs., past pres. Nat. Assn. Former U.S. Attys., 1996; judge Ill. Ct. of Claims, 1997-2003; commr. Ill. Exec. Ethics Commn., 2004—. Served to capt. USAF, 1964-68. Fellow ABA Found., ISBA Found., Ill. Bar Assn.; mem. Kans. Bar Assn., D.C. Bar Assn., Tamarack Golf Club, Stone Wolf Golf Club. Republican. Office: Lewis Rice & Fingersh 325 S High St Belleville IL 62220-2116 Office Phone: 618-234-8636.

HESS, GEORGE FRANKLIN, II, lawyer; b. Oak Park, Ill., May 13, 1939; s. Franklin Edward and Carol (Hackman) H.; m. Diane Ricci, Aug. 9, 1974; 1 child, Franklin Edward. BS in Bus., Colo. State U., 1962; JD, Suffolk U., 1970; LLM, Boston U., 1973. Bar: Pa. 1971, Fla. 1973, U.S. Tax Ct. 1974, U.S. Dist. Ct. (so. dist.) Fla. 1975. Assoc. Hart, Childs, Hepburn, Ross & Putnam, Phila., 1970-72; instr. Suffolk U. Law Sch., Boston, 1973-74; ptnr. Henry, Hess & Hoines, Ft. Lauderdale, Fla., 1974-79, Mousaw, Vigdor, Reeves & Hess, Ft. Lauderdale, Fla., 1979-94; pvt. practice Ft. Lauderdale, Fla., 1995—. Bd. dirs. Childrens Home Soc., Ft. Lauderdale, 1985-89, Nadeau Charitable Found., 1985-2000; trustee endowment fund All Sts. Ch., 1995—. Lt. USNR, 1963-66. Mem. ABA, SAR, Fla. Bar Assn., Broward County Bar Assn., Lauderdale Yacht Club, USN League, Phi Alpha Delta. Episcopalian. Home: 2524 Castilla Is Fort Lauderdale FL 33301-1505 Office: 333 N New River Dr E Fort Lauderdale FL 33301-2241 Office Phone: 954-764-2068. Personal E-mail: gfhess2@aol.com.

HESS, GEORGE PAUL, biochemist, educator; b. Vienna; came to U.S., 1938; s. Henry Steven Hess and Edith Muller; children: Alvis, Peter, Richard, Paul, David. AB, U. Calif., Berkeley, 1951, PhD, 1953. Postdoctoral fellow MIT, 1953—55, Nat. Infantile Paralysis, 1953-55; instr. Cornell Med. Sch., 1955—56; asst. prof. biochemistry Cornell U., Ithaca, NY, 1956-60, assoc. prof., 1960-64, prof., 1964—. Vis. fellow chemistry Yale U., 1960, U.S. Dept. State Cultural Exchange prof. to Europe, 1963, 70; vis. prof. biophysics U. Pa., Phila., 1964-65, biochemistry U. Hawaii, Honolulu, Jan. 1966, chemistry U. Ariz., Tucson, Feb. 1968, biology MIT, 1990; lectr. Naito Found., Japan, 1988. Mem. editl. bd. Biochemistry; adv. bd. Ctr. Molecular and Behavioral Neuroscis., Universidad del Caribe Ctr. With US Army, 1945—47. Recipient Alexander von Humboldt Sr. Scientist award U. Konstanz, 1982, Outstanding Educator Recognition award Cornell Merrill Presdl. scholar, 1994, 97, Wellcome vis. professorship, 1998; Guggenheim fellow, sr. Fulbright grantee Max-Planck-Inst. fur physikalische Chemie, 1962-63; spl. NIH fellow Med. Rsch. Coun. Lab Molecular Biology, 1969-70; Churchill Coll. U. Cambridge vis. fellow 1969-70; NIH Nat. Inst. of Neurol. Diseases and Stroke Fogarty scholar, 1999-2000; postdoctoral fellow Infantile Paralysis, MIT, 1953-1955. Fellow AAAS, Am. Acad. Microbiology, Biophys. Soc.; elected mem. NAS, mem. Am. Soc. Cell Biol.; Am. Chem. Soc., Fedn. Am. Soc. of Exptl. Biologists, N.Y. Acad. Scis., Soc. Neurosci., Protein Soc. Home: 123 Heights Ct Ithaca NY 14850-2450 Office: Cornell Univ 216 Biotechnology Bldg Ithaca NY 14853-2703 Office Phone: 607-255-4809. Business E-Mail: gph2@cornell.edu.

HESS, JOHN B., oil industry executive; s. Leon Hess. BA, Harvard Univ., 1975, MBA, 1977. With Amerada Hess Corp., 1980—, chmn., CEO NYC, 1995—. Mem.: Nat. Petroleum Coun. Office: Amerada Hess Corp 1185 Avenue Of The Americas New York NY 10036-2601*

HESS, JOHN WARREN, professional society administrator; b. Lancaster, Pa., May 6, 1947; s. John Warren and Barbara Kathryn (Spencer) H.; m. Letitia Jean Schrantz, Mar. 20, 1971; children: Nathan James, Joshua Kyle. BS in Geol. Scis., Pa. State U., 1969, PhD in Geology, 1974. Asst. rsch. prof. water resources ctr. Desert Rsch. Inst., Las Vegas, Nev., 1974-78, assoc. rsch. prof., 1978-86, rsch. prof., 1985—2001, dir. environ. isotope lab., 1981-87, dep. dir., 1987-89, exec. dir., 1989-2000, interim v.p. rsch., 1994-95, v.p. acad. affairs, 1995—2001, congrl. fellow, 2000—01; exec. dir. Geol. Soc. Am., Boulder, Colo., 2001—. Chmn. bd. dirs. Karst Waters Inst., Charlestown, W.Va. Contbr. over 85 articles to profl. jours. Adult leader Boy Scouts Am., Las Vegas, 1978—2001, Boulder, Colo., 2002—. Recipient Alumni Achievewment award Coll. Earth and Mineral Scis., Pa. State U., 2004; Hon. Rsch. fellow U. Glasgow, Scotland, 1980-81; Centennial fellow Coll. Earth and Mineral Scis., Pa. State U. Fellow Geol. Soc. Am. (chair hydrogeology divsn., 1995-96), Nat. Speleological Soc.; mem. AAAS, Am. Geophys. Union, Internat. Assn. Hydrogeologists, Geochem. Soc. Office: Geol Soc Am 3300 Penrose Pl Boulder CO 80301 Home Phone: 303-666-8615; Office Phone: 303-357-1039. Business E-Mail: jhess@geosociety.org.

HESS, KARL, engineering educator, science educator; b. Trumau, Austria, June 20, 1945; arrived in US, 1977, naturalized, 1988; s. Karl Joseph and Gertrude (Resch) Hess; m. Sylvia Horvath, Sept. 1967; children: Ursula, Karl. PhD, U. Vienna, Austria, 1970; DSc (hon.), ETH, Zurich, Switzerland, 2003. Rsch. asst. U. Vienna, 1969-71, asst. prof., 1971-77, lectr., 1977; vis. assoc. prof. U. Ill., Urbana, 1977-80, prof. elec. and computer engring., 1988—, adj. prof. supercomputing applications, 1990—, Swanlund Endowed chair, 1996—, prof. physics. Contbr. articles to profl. jours. Scholar, U. Ill., 1982—83; Fulbright scholar, 1973—74. Fellow: NAE, NAS, AAAS, IEEE (J. J. Ebers award 1994, David Sarnoff Field award 1995, H. Welker Meml. medal 2001), Nat. Sci. Bd., Am. Acad. Arts and Scis., Am. Phys. Soc. Achievements include patents in field. Avocations: classical music, chess. Office: U Ill Beckman Inst 405 N Mathews Ave Urbana IL 61801-2325 Home: 75348 Melelina Pl Kailua Kona HI 96740 Office Phone: 217-333-6362. Business E-Mail: k-hess@uiuc.edu.

HESS, MICHAEL DAVID, lawyer; b. NYC, Nov. 8, 1940; s. Jacques J. and Lee B. (Berman) H.; m. Lynn Carol Levine, June 16, 1963; children: Laurie R., Geoffrey N. AB, Yale Coll., 1962; JD, Harvard U., 1965. Bar: N.Y. Chief civil divsn. Office of U.S. Atty., NYC, 1966-73; ptnr. Weil Gotshal, NYC, 1973-83; sr. ptnr. Gelberg & Abrams, NYC, 1983-86, White & Case, NYC, 1986-93, Chadbourne & Parke, NYC, 1993-98; corp. counsel, law dept. head City of N.Y., 1998—2001; ptnr., sr. mng. dir. Giuliani Partners LLC, NYC, 2002—. Chmn., bd. trustees Horace Mann Sch., Bronx, N.Y., 1994-2001. Mem. ABA, N.Y. State Bar Assn., N.Y.C. Bar Assn., Phi Beta Kappa. Office: Giuliani Partners LLC 5 Times Sq New York NY 10036 Office Phone: 212-931-7396. Business E-Mail: michael.hess@giulianipartners.com.

HESS, MICHAEL EDWARD, federal agency administrator; m. Teresa Crawford; children: Ken, James, Corinne, Henry. B in Engring., U.S. Mil. Acad., 1971; M in European History, Columbia U.; MBA, NYU; grad. Nat. Strategic Studies Program, Army War Coll. Liaison office chief, Kosovo Forces Hdqs. Dept. Army, US Dept. Def., spl. asst. to chief of staff, Office of High Rep. Bosnia-Herzegovina, dep. chief of staff, Coalition Provisional Authority, humanitarian coord. Office Reconstruction. and Humanitarian Assistance; v.p. banking Citigroup, Inc., v.p. audit and risk review; asst. adminstr. Bur. Democracy Conflict and Humanitarian Assistance US Agy. Internat. Devel., Washington, 2005—. Office: US Agy Internat Devel Ronald Reagan Bldg 1300 Pennsylvania Ave NW Rm 806-084 Washington DC 20523-6100 Office Phone: 202-712-0100.

HESS, PATRICK HENRY, chemist, researcher; b. Albia, Iowa, Aug. 6, 1931; s. John Henry and Mary Ellen (Judge) H.; m. Ann Marie Malone, June 6, 1959; children: Michelle, Maria, Margaret, Catherine, John. BS in Chemistry, U. Iowa, 1953; MS in Organic Chemistry, U. Nebr., 1958, PhD in Organic Chemistry, 1960. Chemist Iowa State Hygienic Labs., 1953-54; teaching asst. U. Nebr., 1956-57, rsch. asst., 1957-58, rsch. fellow, 1958-60; rsch. chemist Chevron Research Co., Richmond, Calif., 1960-64, Chevron Oil Field Rsch. Co., La Habra, Calif., 1964-65; sr. rsch. chemist Chevron Oil Field Research Co., La Habra, Calif., 1965-69, sr. rsch. assoc., 1969-92; ret., 1992. Rsch. group supr. Chevron Corp. Contbr. articles to profl. jours.; patentee crude oil recovery. Active youth sports PTA. Served with USAF, 1954-55. Rsch. fellow 3-M, 1958-59, Monsanto, 1959-60. Mem. Am. Chem. Soc., Soc. Petroleum Engrs., Sigma Xi, Alpha Chi Sigma, Alpha Tau Omega Republican. Roman Catholic. Home: 12463 Jeremiah Dr Auburn CA 95603-9051 E-mail: pathess@inreach.com. *Retirement is great - so long as one doesn't become too retired.*

HESS, SIDNEY J., JR., lawyer; b. Chgo., June 26, 1910; s. Sidney J. and Alma (Katz) Hess; m. Jacqueline Engelhardt, Aug. 28, 1948; children: Karen E. Hess Freeman, Lori Hess Pleiss. PhB, U. Chgo., 1930, JD, 1932. Bar: Ill. 1932. Practiced in, Chgo., 1932—; mem. firm Aaron, Aaron, Schimberg & Hess, 1933—84, D'Ancona & Pflaum, 1985—2003, Seyarth Shaw L.L.P., 2003—. Bd. dirs., legal counsel Jewish Fedn. of Met. Chgo., 1968-75, v.p., 1972-74, pres., 1974-76; dir., legal counsel Jewish United Fund Met. Chgo., 1971-75, pres., 1974-76; legal counsel Jewish Welfare Fund Met. Chgo., 1969-73; bd. dirs. S. Silberman & Sons, Chgo. Metallic Products, Inc., Vienna Sausage Mfg. Co. Mem. exec. com. Anti-Defamation League, 1954-57, HIAS, 1974-90; mem. nat. devel. coun., aims com., citizens bd. U. Chgo.; bd. dirs. Schwab Rehab. Hosp., 1957-65, pres., 1959-64; trustee Michael Reese Health Trust, 1991—, vice-chair, 2006—. Recipient Judge Learned Hand Human Rels. award Am. Jewish Com., 1979, Julius Rosenwald Meml. award Jewish Fedn. Met. Chgo., 1994, Army Commendation Medal (USAF); elected to Jewish Cmty. Ctrs. Hall of Fame, 1985, City of Chgo. Sr. Citizens Hall of Fame, 1987. Fellow Ill. Bar Found. (charter mem.); mem. ABA, Ill. State Bar Assn., Chgo. Bar Assn., Am. Judicature Soc., U. Chgo. Law Sch. Assn. (dir.), Standard Club (past pres., dir.), Mid-Day Club (Chgo.), Northmoor Country Club (Highland Park, Ill.), Tamarisk Country Club (Rancho Mirage, Calif.), Phi Beta Kappa, Pi Lambda Phi. Home: 1040 N Lake Shore Dr Chicago IL 60611-1165 Office: Ste 2400 131 S Dearborn St Chicago IL 60603-5577 Office Phone: 312-460-5624. Office Fax: 312-460-7624. Business E-Mail: shess@seyfarth.com. *In my judgment the principles and standard of conduct which one must observe in daily life include a clear recognition of the rights and privileges of others, coupled with a desire to provide assistance to those who are less fortunate and unable to provide for themselves. No conduct of one's affairs can be adequate and fulfilling without recognition and observance of relationships with family. In all dealings, one must act with the highest degree of integrity and conscientious application.*

HESS, STANLEY O., retired art educator; b. Weatherford, Okla., July 8, 1923; s. Otto Mathias Hess and Julia Telford Claunch; m. Mildred Ann Elmenhorst, Jan. 26, 1948 (dec. Apr. 1991); children: Patricia, Catherine, Thomas, Rebecca, Mary, Michael; m. Joanne Lenore Gravelin, June 6, 1992. BFA in Art, U. Okla., 1948, MFA in Art, 1950. Spl. instr. art U. Okla., Norman, 1948—50; instr. art William Woods Coll., Fulton, Mo., 1951; prof. art Drake U., Des Moines, 1951—85. Supt. Iowa State Fair Art Salon, 1952—70. One-man shows include U. Okla., 1950, 1956, Sioux City Art Ctr., 1958, Des Moines Art Ctr., 1958, Mabee-Gerrer Mus. Art, St. Gregory's U., Shawnee, Okla., 1994, exhibited in group shows at Renwick Gallery, Washington, 1978, Okla. Arts Workshop, Tulsa, 1993—95, Tulsa Mayfest Gallery, 1994—2000, Leslie Powell Found., Lawton, Okla., 1995, Holliman Gallery, Tulsa, 1996, Mabee-Gerrer Mus. Art, 1997, Anderson Gallery, DesMoines, 1997, Okla. Artists Painting Biennial, 1997, Okla. Forestry Mus., Idabel, 1998, Okla. City Art Ctr., 1999, Drake U. Beinnial Faculty Exhbn., Butler Inst. Am. Art, others; contbr. articles to profl. jours. 1st lt. US Army, 1942—45, PTO. Avocations: reading, bridge. Home: 5412 S 76th East Ave Tulsa OK 74145-7819 E-mail: stanleyohess@mailstation.com.

HESS, STEPHEN, political scientist, writer; b. NYC, Apr. 20, 1933; s. Charles and Florence (Morse) Hess; m. Elena Shayne, Aug. 23, 1959 (div. 1979); children: Charles P., James R.; m. Beth Amster, Aug. 22, 1982. Student, U. Chgo., Ill., 1950-52; BA, Johns Hopkins U., 1953. Jr. instr. polit. sci. Johns Hopkins U., 1953-55; staff asst. to US Pres., 1959-61; asst. to minority whip US Senate, 1961; assoc. fellow Inst. for Policy Studies, 1964-65; fellow Inst. Politics J.F. Kennedy Sch. Govt., Harvard, 1967-68; dep. asst. to US Pres. for urban affairs, 1969; nat. chmn. White House Conf. on Children and Youth, 1969-71; sr. fellow Brookings Inst., Washington, 1972—2004, sr. fellow emeritus, 2004—. Mem. Washington regional selection panel Pres.'s Commn. White Ho. Fellows, 1973; cons. Ford Found., 1974—76; mem. DC Bd. Higher Edn., 1973—76; chmn. DC Coun. Home Rule Transition Commn., 1974; US alt. rep. UNESCO Gen. Conf., 1974; mem. Alumni fellows adv. com. Inst. Politics, J. F. Kennedy Sch. Govt., Harvard U., 1974—; mem. 20th Century Fund Task Forces, 1975, 78, US Nat. Commn. UNESCO, 1975—77; editor-in-chief Nat. Rep. Platform, 1976; mem. adv. coun. gen. govt. Rep. Nat. Com., 1978—81; U.S. alt. rep. UN Gen. Assembly, 1976; cons. USIA, 1976, US Office Mgmt. and Budget, 1977; mem. vis. com. Gerald R. Ford Inst. Pub. Svc., Albion Coll., 1979—82; fellow faculty govt. Harvard U., 1979—82; mem. adv. com. Fund Investigative Journalism, 1981—; mem. sr. adv. bd. ctr. for press, politics and pub. policy John F. Kennedy Sch. Govt., Harvard U., 1987—; vis. prof. Johns Hopkins U., 1990, UCLA, Washington Program, 1990; disting. rsch. prof. media and pub. affairs The George Washington U., Washington, 2004—. Author (with Malcolm Moos): Hats in the Ring: The Making of Presidential Candidates, 1960, America's Political Dynasties, 1966, America's Political Dynasties, rev. edit., 1996; author: (with David S. Broder) The Republican Establishment, 1967; author: (with Milton Kaplan) The Ungentlemanly Art: A History of American Political Cartoons, 1968; author: (with Earl Mazo) Nixon: A Political Portrait, 1968, Nixon: A Political Portrait, rev. edit., 1969, The Presidential Campaign, 1974, The Presidential Campaign, rev. edit., 1987; author: (with Milton Kaplan) The Ungentlemanly Art: A History of American Political Cartoons, rev. edit., 1975; author: Organizing the Presidency, 1976, The Washington Reporters, 1981, The Government/Press Connection: Press Officers and Their Offices, 1984, The Ultimate Insiders: U.S. Senators in the National Media, 1986, Live from Capitol Hill! Studies on Congress and the Media, 1991, International News & Foreign Correspondents, 1995, International News & Foreign Correspondents, rev. edit., 1997, Presidents & The Presidency, 1995, News & Newsmaking, 1995; author: (with Sandy Northrop) Drawn & Quartered, 1996; author: The Little Book of Campaign Etiquette, 1998, The Little Book of Campaign Etiquette, rev. edit., 2000, Organizing the Presidency, rev. edit., 2002, Through Their Eyes: Foreign Correspondents in the United States, 2005; editor (with Marvin Kalb): The Media and the War on Terrorism, 2003. With AUS, 1956—58. Fellow: Nat. Acad. Pub. Adminstrn. Home: 2801 New Mexico Ave NW Apt 1417 Washington DC 20007 Office: Brookings Instn 1775 Massachusetts Ave NW Washington DC 20036-2103 Home Phone: 202-333-4432; Office Phone: 202-797-6078. E-mail: shess@Brookings.edu.

HESS, STEVEN CHARLES, lawyer; b. Lansing, Mich., Sept. 20, 1948; s. C.J. and Dorothy (Dalton) H.; m. Karen Lucy Tracz, Oct. 12, 1973; children: Margaret, Andrew, Benjamin, Daniel. BA, Mich. State U., 1970; JD, Harvard U., 1973. Bar: Mich. 1973, US Dist. Ct. (we. and ea. dists.) Mich., US Ct. Appeals (6th cir.). Ptnr. Doyle, Carruthers & Hess, P.C., Lansing, 1973-81, Warren, Carruthers & Hess, P.C., Lansing, 1982; asst. gen. counsel Blue Cross & Blue Shield of Mich., Lansing, 1983-88, sr. v.p., gen. counsel Detroit, 1988; exec. v.p. & gen. counsel Accident Fund Ins. Co. of Am., Lansing, Mich., 2003—. Office: Accident Fund Ins Co of Am 232 S Capitol Ave PO Box 40790 Lansing MI 48901 Office Phone: 517-367-1766. Office Fax: 517-316-2778. Business E-Mail: stevenh@accidentfund.com.

HESS, TERRY LEE, writer, educator, logistician; b. Balt., July 22, 1954; d. Lee Hess Ray and Ruth Carol Smith, Iva Estelle Teague (Stepmother). MA in English Creative Writing Nonfiction, U. Ctrl. Fla., 2002, postgrad. Program mgr., logistic engr. TRW Aerospace, Redondo Beach, Calif., 1982—89; sr. logisitics engr. Boeing/McDonnell Douglas, Kennedy Space Ctr., Cape Canaveral, Fla., 1990—97; mng. editor Fla. Rev., Orlando, 1999—2002, non-fiction editor, 2001—02; sr. proposal specialist Johnson Controls, Inc., Cape Canaveral, 2003, proposal mgr., 2003—06; ops., planning mgr. IAP World-Wide Svcs., Cape Canaveral, Fla., 2006—07; proposal mgr. PAE Lockheed Martin, Cape Canaveral, Fla., 2007—. Instr. U. Ctrl. Fla., 2001—03. Author: (Memoir) Bellingham Review, 2002 (AWP Intro Award for Creative Nonfiction, 2001), Cypress Dome, 2000, 4th edit., 2003. Fin. advisor 53rd Assembly Dist., 27th Congl. Dist., Rep. Party, LA, 1985—87. With USAF, 1972—76, with USMC, 1978—82. Recipient United Arts Emerging Writers award, First Place Nonfiction and Second Place Fiction, United Arts, Orlando, Fla., 1999. Office: IAP World Wide Svcs 7315 N Atlantic Ave Cape Canaveral FL 32926 Home: 4830 Doreen Rd Cocoa FL 32927-8360 Office Phone: 321-302-9106. Personal E-mail: hes1of6@bellsouth.net.

HESS, WENDI ELIZABETH, secondary school educator; b. Sheboygan, Wis. d. Ervin George and Marjorie Margarite Gutschenritter; m. A. Dean Hess, July 21, 1973. BS in Upper Elem. Edn., U. Wis., Oshkosh, 1973, MS in Edn. Reading, 1977, postgrad. Tchr. Peace Corps, Sierra Leone, 1973—74, Howard-Suamico Sch. Dist., Green Bay, Wis., 1974—. Cheerleading coach Howard-Suamico Sch. Dist., Green Bay, 2001—04, lang.

arts com. sec., 1978—88, mem. social studies com., 1984—99, mem. cmty. linkage com., 2006. Bd. dirs. Brown County chpt. Izaak Walton League Am., Green Bay, 1990—2001; mem. decoration com. Village Ashwaubenan, Wis., 1998—. Recipient Robert Sanderson award, Izaak Walton League, 2000. Mem.: Howard-Suamico Edn. Assn., United N.E. Educators, Wis. Edn. Assn., Wis. State Reading Assn., U. Wis. Oshkosh Alumni Assn., Kappa Delta Pi.

HESSE, GREGORY GETTY, lawyer; b. Rossville, Kans., Oct. 24, 1963; s. Frederick Burns and Hazel Elizabeth (Getty) H.; m. Patricia Anne Strecker, Oct. 27, 1990. BBA, So. Meth. U., 1986; JD, U. Tex., 1988. Bar: Tex. 1989, U.S. Dist. Ct. (no., ea., so. and we. dists.) Tex. 1989, U.S. Ct. Appeals (5th cir.) 1992. Assoc. Jenkens & Gilchrist PC, Dallas, 1989—96, shareholder, Bankruptcy and Reorganization practice group, 1997—2007; ptnr. Hunton & Williams LLP, Dallas, 2007—. Mem. ABA, Tex. Bar Assn., Dallas Bar Assn., Am. Bankruptcy Inst. (contbg. ed. Am. Bankruptcy Inst. Journal) Office: Hunton & Williams LLP Energy Plaza 30th Fl 1601 Bryan St Dallas TX 75201-3402

HESSE, KAREN (KAREN SUE HESSE), writer, educator; b. Balt., Aug. 29, 1952; d. Alvin Donald and Frances Broth Levin; m. Randy Hesse; children: Kate, Rachel. BA, U. Md., 1975. Reference libr. U. Md., 1973-75, leave benefit coord., 1975-76; advt. sec. Country Journal mag., 1976-77, typesetter, proofreader, 1978-88; mental health care provider, 1989-91; children's lit. reviewer, 1993-94. Author: (children's books) Wish on a Unicorn, 1991 (Hungry Mind Rev. Children's Book of Distinction 1992), Letters From Rifka, 1992 (Nat. Jewish Book award 1993, IRA Children's Book award 1993, Christopher award 1992, Sydney Taylor Book award 1992, ALA Notable Book 1992, ALA Best Book for Young Adults 1992, Sch. Libr. Jour. Best Book of Yr. 1992, Horn Book Outstanding Book of Yr. 1992, Booklist Editors' Choice 1992, NY Pub. Libr. 100 Titles for Reading and Sharing 1992), Poppy's Chair, 1993 (Am. Booksellers Assn. Pick of List 1993), Lester's Dog, 1993 (Best Book of Yr. Sch. Libr. Jour. 1993, Notable Children's Trade Book in Field of Social Studies 1993), Lavender, 1993, Sable, 1994 (Sch. Libr. Jour. Best Book of Yr. 1994, NY Pub. Libr. 100 Titles for Reading and Sharing 1994, Boston Globe 10 Best Trade Books 1994, Parenting Mag. 40 Outstanding Children's Books 1994), Phoenix Rising, 1994 (Sch. Libr. Jour. Best Book of Yr. 1994, IRA Tchr.'s Choice 1995, NY Pub. Libr. Books for the Teenage 1995, Best Book for Young Adults ALA 1995, Notable Book, 1995, Wilson Libr. Bull. 33 Favorite Reads 1994 (S.C. Jr. Book award, 1996, others), A Time of Angels, 1995 (IRA Tchr's Choice 1996, IRA Young Adults' Choice, 1997, NY Pub. Libr. Books for the Teenager 1995), The Music of Dolphins, 1996 (Pub.'s Weekly Best Book of Yr. 1996, Best Book of Yr. Sch. Libr. Jour. 1996, Book Links, 100 Titles for Reading and Sharing NY Pub. Libr. Children's Book 1996, Best Books for Young Adults ALA, 1997, Golden Kite Honor Book, 1997), Out of the Dust, 1997 (Newbery medal 1998, Scott O'Dell award 1998), Just Juice, 1998 (100 Titles for Reading and Sharing NY Pub. Libr. 1998, Notable Children's Trade Book in the Field of Social Studies 1998), Come On, Rain!, 1999 (BCCB Blue Ribbon Book, NYPL 100 Books for Reading & Sharing, Jr. Library Guild selection, Book of the Month Club selection, Hon. Mention award, Columbus Internat. Film Fest., ALA Notable Video, 2004); contbr. When I Was Your Age, Vol. II, 1999 (2000 Books for the Teen Age), A Light in the Storm, 1999 (Notable Children's Trade Book in the Field of Social Studies 1999, Kennedy Ctr. Stage Adaptation, 2001), Stowaway, 2000 (SLJ Book of Yr., 2001, Capitol Choice Noteworthy Books for Children (10-14), 100 Titles for Reading and Sharing NY Pub. Libr., 2000, Jr. Libr. Guild Selection), Witness, 2001 (NY Pub. Libr. 100 Books for Reading and Sharing, ALA Notable Children's book, LA 100 Best Books 2001, 2002 IRA Notable 2002, CBC Choice 2002, Myers Award 2002, NCTE Notable 2002, Christopher award 2002, Parents Guide to Children's Media award); Aleutian Sparrow, 2003 (Jr. Libr. Guild selection 100 Titles for Reading and Sharing), The Stone Lamp, 2003 (NY Pub. Libr. 100 Titles, Assn. Jewish Librs. Notable), The Cats in Krasinski Square, 2004 (PW Best Book award 2004, Bologna Ragazzi Honorable Mention, Kirkus Editor's Choice 2004, N.Y. Pub. Libr. 100 Titles for Reading and Sharing, Parent Choice Gold award, Book Sense Children's Picks List for Winter 2004-05, ALA Notable, Koret Jewish Book award), The Young Hans Christian Andersen, 2005 (Notable Children's Trade Book in Field of Social Studies); contbr. articles to profl. jours. Chmn. Sch. Bd., 1989; sec. bd. dirs. Moore Free Libr., 1989-91; active Hospice, 1988—. MacArthur fellow, 2003—. Mem. Soc. Children's Book Writers and Illustrators, So. Vt. Soc. Children's Book Writers (leader 1985-92), Ctr. for Children's Environ. Lit., Author's Guild. Avocations: reading, hiking, cultivating friendships, music. Office: Scholastic 557 Broadway New York NY 10012-3919

HESSE, MARTHA O., gas industry executive; b. Hattiesburg, Miss., Aug. 14, 1942; d. John William and Geraldine Elaine (Ossian) H. BS, U. Iowa, 1964; postgrad., Northwestern U., 1972-76; MBA, U. Chgo., 1979. Rsch. analyst Blue Shield, 1964-66; dir. div. data mgmt. Am. Hosp. Assn., 1966-69; dir., COO SEI Info. Tech., Chgo., 1969-80; assoc. dep. sec. Dept. of Commerce, Washington, 1981-82; exec. dir. Pres.' Task Force on Mgmt. Reform, 1982; asst. sec. mgmt. and adminstrn. Dept. of Energy, Washington, 1982-86; chmn. FERC, Washington, 1986-89; sr. v.p. 1st Chgo. Corp., 1990; CEO Hesse Gas Co., Houston, 1990—2003. Bd. dirs. Mut. Trust Life, AMEC plc, Terra Industries, Enbridge Energy Prnrs., chmn. bd., 2007—. Home: 4171 Autumn Hills Dr Winnemucca NV 89445

HESSELBEIN, FRANCES RICHARDS, foundation administrator, writer, editor; b. South Fork, Pa.; d. Burgess Harmon and Anne Luke (Wicks) Richards; widowed, 1978; 1 child, John Richards. DHL (hon.), Buena Vista Coll., 1987, Juniata Coll., 1990, Hood Coll., 1991; D Mgmt. (hon.), GM Inst., 1990; LLD (hon.), Wilson Coll., 1991, Moravian Coll., 2000, U. St. Thomas, 2006; LHD (hon.), Marymount-Tarrytown Coll., 1993; DHL (hon.), Boston Coll., 1994, U. Nebr., Kearney, 1994, Lafayette Coll., 1995, Carroll Coll., 1996, Fairleigh Dickinson U., 1996, Muhlenburg Coll., 1996; D in Pub. and Internat. Affairs, U. Pitts., 2001; DHL (hon.), Mt. Mary Coll., 2002, Union Inst. and Univ., 2003, U. Cin., 2003, CUNY, Staten Island, 2007. CEO Talus Rock Girl Scout Coun., Johnstown, 1970-74, Penn Laurel Girl Scout Coun., York, Pa., 1974-76, Girl Scouts U.S., NYC, 1976-90; pres., CEO Peter F. Drucker Found. Nonprofit Mgmt., NYC, 1990-99, chmn., 1999—2003; chmn., founding pres. Leader To Leader Inst., NYC, 2003—06. Chmn. Nat. Bd. Vols. Am., 2003-06; bd. dirs. Mut. of Am. Ins. Co., NYC; nat. bd. visitors Peter F. Drucker Grad. Mgmt. Sch. Claremont (Calif.) Grad. Sch., 1987—; chmn. bd. govs. Josephson Ethics Inst., 1989-99; adv. com. to bd. dirs. N.Y. Stock Exch., 1988-91; bd. govs. Ctr. for Creative Leadership, Greensboro, N.C., 1992-98; adv. bd. Harvard Bus. Sch.'s Initiative on Social Enterprise, Harvard's Kennedy Sch. Hauser Ctr. Nonprofit Policy and Leadership Program, Randall L. Tobias Ctr. Leadership Excellence Indiana U., 2005; chmn. Vols. Am., 2002-06, Leader to Leader Inst., 2003-. Editor-in-chief Leader to Leader; co-editor The Leader of the Future, The Organization of the Future, The Community of the Future, Drucker Found. Future Series, Leader to Leader Book, 1999, Leading Beyond the Walls, 1999, Leader of the Future 2, 2006, Be-Know-Do, 2004; author: Hesselbein on Leadership, 2002. Trustee Juniata Coll., Huntingdon, Pa., 1988—, Allentown (Pa.) Coll., 1988-97; mem. Pres.'s Adv. Com. on Points of Light Initiative Found., 1989; bd. dirs. Nat. Exec. Svc. Corps., N.Y., Commn. on Nat. and Cmty. Svc., 1991-94; adv. bd. The Leadership Inst., U. So. Calif., 1991, Harvard U.'s John F. Kennedy Sch. Govt. Nonprofit Policy and Leadership Program. Recipient Outstanding Achievement award Inter-Svc. Club Coun., Johnstown, 1976, Entrepreneurial Woman award Women Bus. Owners of NY, 1984, Nat. Leadership award United Way of Am., Washington, 1985, Disting. Cmty. Svc. award Mut. Am. Ins. Co., 1985, Dir.'s Choice-award Nat. Women's Econ. Alliance, 1989, Pa. Soc. Disting. Citizen award, 1991, Wilbur M. McFeeley award, U. Pitts. Legacy Laureate award, 2000, Internat. Leadership award Athena Found., 2001, Henry Russo award Ind. U. Ctr., 2001, Dwight D. Eisenhower Series Nat. Security award, 2002, Leadership Devel. award, Boston U., 2003, Juliette award Girl Scouts USA, 2004, Visionary award Am Soc. Assn. Execs., 2004; named to Bus. Hall of Fame, Johnstown, 1995; named Outstanding Exec., Savvy Mag., 1985, Disting. Alumni Fellow U. Pitts., 1999, Disting. Dau. of Pa., Gov. Ridge, 1999, Woman of Yr., Boy Scouts Greater NY; on cover BusinessWeek, 1990, Presdl. Medal of Freedom, 1998; featured in Chief Exec. mag., 1995, Fortune, 1995-96, Chapel of Four Chaplains Gold Legion of Hon. medal, 1999, Athena Found.-Internat. Leadership award, 2001, Henry Rosso award Ind. U. Ctr., 2001-02, Marion Gisalon award Boston U., 2003, Visionary award A.S.A.E., 2004, Disting. Svc. award Columbia U. Tchrs. Coll., 2006, Disting. Leadership award Miss Hall's Sch., 2006, Frances Hesselbein Student Leadership Program award Mil. Child Edn. Coalition, 2006; established Frances Hesselbein How To Be Leadership award for Ethical Leadership at Jr. Achievement, 2003; New Zealand Fulbright John F. Kennedy fellow, 2007. Mem. Pa. Soc., Cosmos Club (Washington). Office: Leader to Leader Inst 320 Park Ave 3d Fl New York NY 10022-6815 Office Phone: 212-224-1154. Office Fax: 212-224-2508. Business E-Mail: frances@leadertoleader.org.

HESSELINK, LAMBERTUS, electrical engineering and physics educator; b. Enschede, The Netherlands, Dec. 4, 1948; came to U.S., 1971; s. Lambertus and Wilhelmina (ten Tye) H. BSME, Twente Inst. Tech., Enschede, 1970, BS in Applied Physics, 1971, postgrad., 1974; MSME, Calif. Inst. Tech., 1972, PhD in Applied Mechs., Physics, 1977. Rsch. fellow Calif. Inst. Tech., Pasadena, 1977-78, instr. applied physics, 1978-80, sr. rsch. fellow fluid mechs., 1979-80; asst. prof. aeros. and astronautics Stanford (Calif.) U., 1980-85, asst. prof., 1985—, assoc. prof. elec. engring., 1980-85, asst. prof., 1985-90, prof. electrical engring. and aeronautics/astonautics, 1990—. Cons. Hughes Aircraft Corp., Culver City, Calif., 1978-79, MCC Corp., 1986-92; invited scientist mem. image processing work group for Hubble Space Telescope, 1990; assoc. editor Jour. Applied Sci. and Applied Optics, 1990; founder Siros Technologies, Inc.; cons. to industry and govt.; mem. scientific adv. bd. USAF, 1995—; founder Senvid, Inc. Patentee in field. Recipient Stheeman prize Twente Inst. Tech., 1970; Fulbright fellow 1971-74; Josephine de Karman fellow, 1974-75. Fellow SPIE, Optical Soc. Am.; mem. AIAA (Engr. of Yr. 1982), Soc. Photo-Optical Instrumentation Engrs. Optical Soc. Am., Am. Phys. Soc., Royal Dutch Acad. Arts and Scis. (corr.), Sigma Xi. Office: Stanford U Mail Code 4075 CISX Bldg Rm 325 Stanford CA 94305-4075 E-mail: bert@kaos.stanford.edu.

HESSER, AMANDA LEA, journalist, chef; b. Doylestown, Pa., Sept. 8, 1971; d. Thomas Dean and Judith Ann Hesser; m. Tad Friend. BS in Economics and Fin., Bentley Coll., 1993; Graduate Diplome, Ecole de Cuisine LaVarenna, Villecien, France, 1995. Apprentice under Chef Jean-Michel Bouvier L'Essentiel in the Haute Savoie, France; apprentice Château du Fey, Burgundy, France; freelance writer Washington Post, 1996, Scranton Times, Seventeen mag., Country Home mag.; jr. reporter NY Times, NYC, 1997; columnist, Food Diary (biweekly) NY Times mag., NYC; food writer NY Times, NYC, editor, T Living. Author: The Cook and the Gardener, 1999 (IACP/Gourmet Mag. Literary Food Writing award, 2000, named Best Book in France by a Non-French Writer, Versailles Cookbook Fair), Cooking for Mr. Latte: A Food Lover's Courtship, with Recipes, 2003. Office: NY Times 229 West 43rd St New York NY 10036 E-mail: amandah@nytimes.com.

HESSER, ELISE L., retired elementary school educator; b. Douglas, Ariz., Dec. 24, 1950; d. Norman Merritt Littrell and Marjorie Theodora Lammers; m. Jessie Toles Jr.; m. John W. Hesser III (dec.); 1 child, Norman Christoher. BA in Elem. Edn., U. Ariz., Tucson, 1975, M in Edn. Adminstrn., 1975. Cert. tchr. Ariz. Tchr. grades K-6 Sahuarita Sch. Dist., Ariz., 1972—2005; ret. V.p. Sahuarita Edn Assn., 1988—95; pres. Sahuarita TEam Officer Prevention Drug Awareness Group, Suhuarita, 1992; wrestling coach K-8 after sch. program Suhuarita Sch. Dist., 1980—90. Author of poems. Democrat. Avocations: bridge, reading, swimming.

HESSLER, DAVID WILLIAM, information and multimedia systems educator; b. Oak Park, Ill., May 9, 1932; s. William Wigney and Gwendolyn Eileen (Butler) H.; m. Helen Montgomery, Aug. 27, 1955; children: Leslie Susan McCormick, Laura Lynne. BA, U. Mich., 1955, MA, 1961; PhD, Mich. State U., 1972. Comml. photographer Oscar & Assocs., Chgo., 1950; equipment engr. Western Electric Co., Chgo., 1958-59; dir. librs. and media Ann Arbor (Mich.) Pub. Schs., 1966-67; asst. prof. edn. Western Mich. U., 1967-72, assoc. prof., 1974-77; dir. instrnl. svcs., dir. broadcasting, prof. edn. U. S.C., 1973-74; cons., asst. dir. Audio-Visual Edn. Ctr. U. Mich., Ann Arbor, 1960-66, prof. Sch. Info., 1977-98, prof. emeritus, 1998—, dir. instrnl. strategy svcs. for schs. of edn., libr. sci., 1979-81, pres. Ann Arbor sys. and tech., 1987—, exec. dir. for info. svcs. Info-Span, 1991-92; exec. v.p. Infotronix, Ann Arbor, 1993-97. Cons. Presdl. Commn. on World Hunger; cons. media and tech.; instrnl. designer and evaluator; bd. dirs. Kirsch Techs.; vis. prof., cons. dept. biblioteconomia U. Brazil, 1981. Author: (with J. Smith) Student Production Guide, 1975, Technology for Communication and Instruction, 1983; producer/dir. numerous films, filmstrips, TV programs and sound/slide programs for various ednl. levels. Lt. USAF, 1955-58; capt. Res. ret. Decorated Air Force Commendation medal; named Mich. Most Valuable Tchr. Chrysler Corp., 1965; Ednl. Profl. Devel. Act fellow, 1968-69. Mem. ALA, ASTD, Assn. Image and Info. Mgmt., M Club, Phi Kappa Phi. Home: 24 Southwick Ct Ann Arbor MI 48105-1410 Office: U Mich Sch Info West Hall 550 E University Ave Ann Arbor MI 48109-1092 Business E-Mail: dwh@umich.edu.

HESTER, DOUGLAS BENJAMIN, lawyer; b. McKenzie, Ala., Sept. 18, 1927; s. Mack Ellis and Carrie Lottie (Taylor) H.; m. Melissa Hood Fuller, Apr. 16, 1960; children: Carlotta Marie, Benjamin Alexander. BS, U. Ala., 1950, LL.B., 1952. Bar: Ala. 1952, D.C. 1960, U.S. Supreme Ct. Law asst. Office Legis. Counsel-U.S. Senate, Washington, 1952-54, asst. counsel, 1954-69, sr. counsel, 1969-80; legis. counsel U.S. Senate, 1980-91; mem., liaison between Ala. and U.S. Congress Svc. Corps. of Retired Execs., 1992-93. Trustee Centro Anglo-Espanol, Washington, 1990. Served with AUS, 1945-47. Mem. ABA, D.C. Bar Assn., Ala. Bar Assn., Farah Order of Jurisprudence, Pi Alpha Delta, Omicron Delta Kappa, Sigma Delta Pi, Pi Kappa Phi. Home: 2171 Vaughn Ln Montgomery AL 36106-3252

HESTER, FRANCIS BARTOW, III, (FRANK HESTER), lawyer; b. Interlachen, Fla., Oct. 13, 1920; s. Francis Bartow Jr. and Flora McRae H.; m. Joyce Slate, Dec. 21, 1946; children: Susan Hester Elmore, Blanche Hester Wolfson, F. Bartow Hester Jr. Student, Ga. Inst. Tech., 1938-42, U. Ga., 1946; LLB, Emory U., 1948. Bar: Ga. 1952, U.S. Dist. Ct. (no. dist.) Ga. 1952, U.S. Ct. Appeals (4th cir.) 1990, U.S. Ct. Appeals (5th cir.) 1955, U.S. Ct. Appeals (6th cir.) 1967, U.S. Ct. Appeals (7th cir.) 1994, U.S. Ct. Appeals (11th cir.) 1981, Ga. Supreme Ct. 1952, Ga. Ct. Appeals 1952, U.S. Bd. Immigration Appeals 1985, U.S. Supreme Ct. 1960. Spl. agt. FBI, Cleve., Phila., Atlanta, 1948-51; criminal case trial lawyer Hester & Hester, 1952-99. Spl. investigator of fraud in Ga. State Govt., 1958-59. With Air Corp., U.S. Army, 1942-45. Recipient Commendation, Ga. Ho. of Reps., 1997. Mem. Ga. Bar Assn., Ga. Assn. Criminal Def. Lawyers, Former Spl. Agts. of FBI Assn., Inc., Atlanta Bar Assn., Mason (32d degree), 6th Bomb Group Assn. (Tinian 1945), Cherokee Town & Country Club, Shriner (Yaarab temple), Sigma Alpha Epsilon. Democrat. Avocation: boating. Home: 4704 Polo Ln Se Atlanta GA 30339-5328

HESTER, JAMES MCNAUGHTON, retired foundation administrator, artist; b. Chester, Pa., Apr. 19, 1924; s. James Montgomery and Margaret (McNaughton) H.; m. Janet Rodes, May 23, 1953; children: Janet McN., Margaret, Martha. BA, Princeton U., 1945, LL.D. (honoris causa), 1962; BA (Rhodes scholar 1947-50), Oxford U., Eng., 1950, D.Phil., 1955; LL.D., Lafayette Coll., 1964, Morehouse Coll., 1967; L.H.D., Hartwick Coll., 1964; LHD (hon.), Pace U., 1971, U. Pitts., 1971, Colgate U., 1974; L.H.D., N.Y. U., 1977; DCL, Alfred U., 1965; LLD (hon.), Hofstra U., 1967, Hahnemann Med. Coll., 1967, Fordham U., 1971, Amherst Coll., 1975, New Sch. for Social Rsch., 1975, Union Coll., 1983. Civil information officer Fukuoka Mil. Govt. Team, Japan, 1946-47; asst. to Am. sec. to Rhodes Trustees, 1950; asst. to pres. Handy Assocs., Inc. (mgmt. cons.), NYC, 1953-54; account supr. Gallup and Robinson, Inc., Princeton, NJ, 1954-57; provost Bklyn. center L.I. U., 1957-60, v.p., 1958-60; prof. history, exec. dean arts and sci., dean Grad. Sch. Arts and Sci. N.Y.U., 1960-61, pres., 1962-75; rector UN U., Tokyo, 1975-80; pres. N.Y. Bot. Garden, 1980-89, The Harry Frank Guggenheim Found., NYC, 1989—2004, also bd. dirs.; ret., 2004. Trustee Lehman Found. Served with USMCR, 1943-46, 51-52. Mem. Assn. Am. Rhodes Scholars Clubs: Century Assn., University, Pretty Brook Tennis.

HESTER, LINDA HUNT, dean, retired sociology and physical education professor; b. Winston-Salem, NC, June 16, 1938; d. Hanselle Lindsay and Jennie Sarepta (Hunt) H. BS with honors, U. Wis., 1960, MS, 1964; PhD, Mich. State U., East Lansing, 1971. Lic. ednl. counselor, Wis. Instr. health and phys. edn. for women U. Tex., Austin, 1960—62; asst. dean women U. Ill., Urbana, 1964—66; dean of women, asst. prof. sociology and phys. edn. Tex. Woman's U., Denton, 1971—73; ret., 1973. Rsch. assoc. bur. higher edn. Mich. Dept. Edn., Lansing, 1969-70; vol. counselor Dallas Challenge and Dallas Ind. Sch. Dist., 1989-90. Friend of Kimbell Art Mus. com. of 1000 Philharmonic Ctr. for Arts, Naples, Fla.; mem. and donor Naples Mus. Art; founder Women's Mus., Dallas; founding mem. Dallas Ctr. Performing Arts, Winspear Opera Hall, Dallas; assoc. mem. Dallas Mus. Art, 1991—; Stradivarious mem. Dallas Symphony, 1991—; mem. Nat. Women's History Mus., Washington; bd. dirs. Dallas Opera, 1986—; mem. Friends Art Alliance, Dallas; mem. governing bd. The Arts Cmty. Alliance, 2005—. Named to Distinguished Svc. Registry in Counseling and Devel.; fellow, Coll. Edn. Mich. State U., 1968. Mem. ACA, Am. Coll. Pers. Assn., Nat. Assn. Women in Edn., Brookhaven Country Club, Wyndemere Country Club, Delta Kappa Gamma, Alpha Lambda Delta. Republican. Presbyterian. Avocations: golf, sailing, cooking, music, reading. Home: 7606 Wellcrest Dr Dallas TX 75230-4857

HESTER, NANCY ELIZABETH, county government official; b. Miami, Fla., Jan. 20, 1950; d. George Temple and Lorraine Patricia (Cluney) Hester. BA, Bucknell U., 1972; MIA, Columbia U., 1974; MBA, Fla. Internat. U., 1979; postgrad. Fla. Atlantic U., 2000—. Treasury rep. Westinghouse Electric Co., NYC, 1974—76; adminstrv. officer serving in bldg. and zoning, gen. svcs. and corrections and rehab. depts. Metro Dade County, Fla., 1979—2000, bur. comdr. corrections and rehab. dept., 1990—2000. Adj. prof. Fla. Internat. U., Miami, 1980-83. Bd. dirs. YWCA Greater Miami, 1988-92, LWV Dade County, 1993-98; pres. bd. dirs., pres. bd. trustees edn. fund, 1994-96; mem. adv. bd. SafeSpace, 1995-2001, v.p. adv. bd., 2000. Mem.: DAR.

HESTER, NORMAN ERIC, chemical company technical executive, chemist; b. Niangua, Mo., Dec. 16, 1946; s Eric Ira and Norma Josephine (Wright) H.; m. Sylvie Jean Hunt, June 16, 1973; children: Jenay Aimee, Yvette Joy, Trinity Marie. AA, El Camino Coll., 1966; BS, Calif. State U., Long Beach, 1968; MS, U. Calif., Riverside, 1971, PhD, 1972. Postdoctoral rsch. chemist U. Calif. Air Pollution Ctr., Riverside, 1972-74; air quality chemist EPA, Las Vegas, Nev., 1974-77; program mgr. Rockwell Internat., Newbury Park, Calif., 1977-80; group head Occidental Petroleum Rsch. Ctr., Irvine, Calif., 1980-83; tech. dir. Truesdail Labs. Inc., Tustin, Calif., 1983—. Pvt. environ. cons., Mission Viejo, Calif., 1983. Contbr. articles to profl. jours. Mem. Am. Chem. Soc., Assn. Ofcl. Racing Chemists. Republican. Avocations: growing hybrid roses, hiking, travel. Office: Truesdail Labs Inc 14201 Franklin Ave Tustin CA 92780-7008 Home Phone: 949-581-7620; Office Phone: 714-730-6239. E-mail: norman@truesdail.com, normanhester@netscape.net.

HESTER, SEAN W., lawyer; b. May 19, 1968; married; 2 children. BBA with high honors, U. Okla., 1989; JD, Baylor U., 1992. Cert.: Tex. Bd. Legal Specialization (personal injury trial law), bar: Tex. 1992, US Dist. Ct. (ea. and no. dists. Tex.), US Ct. Appeals (5th cir.). Pvt. practice atty.; ptnr. Roberts & Roberts, Tyler, Tex. Named a Rising Star, Tex. Super Lawyers mag., 2006. Mem.: Tex. Trial Lawyers Assn., Smith County Bar Assn., Phi Delta Phi. Office: Roberts & Roberts 118 W 4th St Tyler TX 75701 Office Phone: 903-597-6000. E-mail: sean@robertslawfirm.com.*

HESTER, THOMAS PATRICK, lawyer; b. Tulsa, Okla., Nov. 20, 1937; s. E.P. and Mary J. (Layton) H; m. Nancy B. Scofield, Aug. 20, 1960; children: Thomas P. Jr., Ann S., John L. BA, Okla. U., 1961, LLB, 1963. Bar: Okla. 1963, Mo. 1967, N.Y. 1970, D.C. 1973, Ill. 1975. Atty. McAfee & Taft, Okla. City, 1963-66, Southwestern Bell Telephone Co., Okla. City, St. Louis, 1966-72, AT&T, NYC, Washington, 1972-75; gen. atty. Ill. Bell Telephone Co., Springfield, 1975-77, gen. solicitor Chgo., 1977-83, v.p., gen. counsel, 1983-87; sr. v.p., gen. counsel Ameritech, Chgo., 1987-91, exec. v.p., gen. counsel, 1991-97; ptnr. Mayer, Brown & Platt, Chgo., 1997—; sr. v.p., gen. counsel, sec. Sears, Roebuck and Co., 1998-99, FMC Corp., 2000. Corp. counsel ctr. adv. bd. Northwestern U., 1987-97. Mem. Taxpayers Fedn. Ill., Springfield, 1987-97, chmn. bd. trustees 1987-88; mem. adv. bd. Ill. Dept. Natural Resources, 1991-2000—, chmn., 1993-98; trustee Art Inst. Chgo., 1995-2000. Fellow Am. Bar Found.; mem. Am. Law Inst.

HESTER, THOMAS RODERICK, JR., plastic surgeon, educator; b. Cairo, Ga., Mar. 24, 1942; Grad., Emory U., Atlanta, 1963, MD, 1967. Cert. Am. Bd. Surgery, 1973, Am. Bd. Plastic Surgery, 1980. Intern surgery Grady Meml. Hosp., Atlanta, 1967—68; resident plastic reconstructive surgery Emory Affiliated Hosps., 1968—72; chief surgery Colquitt County Meml. Hosp., Moultrie, Ga., 1972—76; chief resident plastic surgery Emory U., 1976—78; assoc. prof. plastic and reconstructive surgery Emory U. Sch. Medicine, 1980—93, program dir. divsn. plastic surgery, 2001; asst. prof. plastic and reconstructive surgery Emory U., 2001—, chief divsn. plastic surgery, 2001—, William G. Hamm chair plastic surgery, 2005—; founder Paces Plastic Surgery, 1993—. Contbr. articles to med. jours., chapters to books. Maj. USAR, 1973—76. Recipient Best Jour. Article, Aesthetic Soc. Ednl. Rsch. Found., 1997. Fellow: Am. Coll. Surgeons; mem.: AMA, Southeastern Surg. Soc., So. Med. Assn., Med. Assn. Atlanta, Jurkiewicz Soc., James C. Thoroughman Surg. Soc., Ga. Med. Assn., Ga. Soc. Plastic Surgeons, Southeastern Soc. Plastic and Reconstructive Surgeons, Am. Assn. Plastic Surgeons, Am. Soc. Aesthetic Plastic Surgery (Simon Fredericks award 1992), Internat. Soc. Aesthetic Plastic Surgeons, Am. Soc. Plastic Surgeons, Alpha Omega Alpha Honor Med. Soc. Office: Paces Plastic Surgery 3200 Downwood Cir Ste 640A Atlanta GA 30327 Office Phone: 404-351-0051. Office Fax: 404-351-0632.

HESTER, THOMAS ROY, anthropologist, educator; b. Crystal City, Tex., Apr. 28, 1946; s. Jim Tom and Mattie Laura (Umphres) H.; m. Lynda Sue Broadway, July 2, 1966; children: Lesley Elise, Amy Lynne. BA with honors, U. Tex., Austin, 1969; PhD, U. Calif., Berkeley, 1972. Acting asst. prof. anthropology U. Calif., Berkeley, 1972-73; asst. prof. anthropology U. Tex., San Antonio, 1973-75, assoc. prof., 1975-77, prof., 1977-87, prof. anthropology Austin, 1987—2003, prof. emeritus, 2003—; dir. Ctr. for Archaeol. Research, 1974-87, Tex. Archeol. Rsch. Lab., 1987—2000. Vis.

assoc. prof. U. Calif., Berkeley, 1976. Author: (with R. Heizer and J. Graham) Field Methods in Archaeology, 1975, Digging into South Texas Prehistory, 1980, (with R. Heizer and C. Graves) Archaeology: A Bibliographical Guide to the Basic Literature, 1980, (with G. Ligabue, S. Salvatori, M. Sartor) Colha e I Maya Dei Bassipiani, 1983, (with E.S. Turner) A Field Guide to the Stone Artifacts of Texas Indians, 1985, 2d edit., 1993, (with G. Ligabue) Robert F. Heizer's Age of Giants, 1990, (with H.J. Shafer) Maya Stone Tools, 1991; Ethnology of Texas Indians, 1991, (with H.J. Shafer and K.F. Feder) Field Methods in Archaeology, 7th edit., 1997; editl. bd. numerous jours.; contbr. articles to profl. jours. Woodrow Wilson fellow, 1969-70 Fellow Tex. Archeol. Soc. (pres. 1993); mem. Soc. Am. Archaeology (exec. com. 1984-86, award 2000), Assn. Field Archaeology (exec. com. 1979-82), Soc. Archaeol. Sci., Accademia Nazionale dei Lincei (fgn.), Sigma Xi (pres. Alamo chpt. 1979). Democrat. Methodist. Office: U Tex Archeol Rsch Lab Austin TX 78712-1100 Home: PO Box 625 Utopia TX 78884-0625 E-mail: secocreek@swtexas.net.

HESTERBERG, EARL J., automotive executive; BA, Davidson Coll.; MBA, Xavier Univ. With Nissan Motor Corp., 1982—98, v.p., gen. mgr. Nissan div., 1991—95, v.p. sales Nissan Europe, 1996—98; pres., CEO Gulf States Toyota, 1998—99; v.p., mktg.,sales & svc. Europe Ford Motor Corp., 1999—2004, v.p. No. Am. mktg., 2004—05; pres., CEO Group 1 Automotive Inc., Miami, Fla., 2005—. Office: Group 1 Automotive Ste 100 950 Echo Ln Houston TX 77024*

HESTERBERG, LARRY ALLEN, aerospace engineer; b. Springfield, Ill., June 20, 1964; s. Harold August Walter and Ruth Helen Folkerts Hesterberg, Jo Ashbaugh (Stepmother). BS Aerospace Studies, minors: Space Studies, Computer Sci., Humanities, Embry-Riddle Aero. U., Daytona Beach, FL, 1998. Cert. pvt. pilot Daytona Beach CC, Fla., 1992, cooperative edn., aircraft maintenance Capitol Area Vocational Ctr., Ill., 1982. Computer operator Direct Mail Express, Daytona Beach, Fla., 1993—95; sr. database specialist Mktg. Gen., Inc., Alexandria, Va., 1996—98; satellite systems engr. Lockheed Martin Tech. Support Group, Springfield, Va., 1998—2000; command & control subsytem engr. ASRC Aerospace, Greenbelt, Md., 2000—01; sr. systems engr. AERA, Inc., Alexandria, Va., 2001—03, Lockheed Martin Mgmt. and Data Sys., Gaithersburg, Md., 2003—04; sr. network data comm. analyst Lockheed Martin Info. and Tech. Svc., Fredericksburg, Va., 2004—06, Fallujah, Iraq, 2004—06; commn. mgr. DynCorp. Internat., Nairobi, Kenya, 2006—07, Juba, Sudan, 2006—07. Vol. Smithsonian Inst. Nat. Air and Space Mus., 1996; commn. mem. City of Alexandria, VA, Pub. Records Adv. Commn., Alexandria, Va., 1997—99. Recipient Honor Roll, Embry-Riddle Aero. U., Spring 1993, Dean's List, Daytona Beach C.C., 1990 & 1992. Mem.: Soc. Satellite Profls. Internat., Nat. Aeronautic Assn., AIAA, Mensa, Aircraft Owners and Pilots Assn., Aero Club of Wash., DC, Fla. State Soc., Ill. State Soc., Sigma Chi (Outstanding Alumni Rels. Award 1992, Cert. of Appreciation 1996, Life Loyal Sig 2005), Eta Iota Ho. Corp. (corp. sec. 1991—92, trustee 1995—96). Home: 3310 Wyndham Cir Unit 310 Alexandria VA 22302 Home Phone: 517-217-6837. Personal E-mail: larry.hesterberg@att.net.

HESTERMAN, PHILLIP KARL, music educator; b. Sheboygan, Wis., Nov. 3, 1961; s. Marvin Henry Hesterman and Karilyn Marie Heermann, June Carole Kastens (Stepmother); m. Rebecca Lynn Metzger; children: Micah, Andrea, Bryce. BS in Edn., Concordia Teachers Coll., 1984; MA in Ch. Music, Concordia U., 1994; MA in Tchg., Hastings Coll., 2000. Tchr. Trinity Luth. Sch., Janesville, Minn., 1984—85; tchr. and music dir. St. John Luth. Ch. and Sch., Chaska, Minn., 1985—89; music dir. and tchr. Trinity Luth. Ch. and Sch., Sheboygan, 1989—95; asst. prof. of music Concordia U., Austin, 1995—97; choral dir. Bastrop H.S., Tex., 1997—98; min. of music Trinity Luth. Ch. and Sch., Grand Island, Nebr., 1998—. Dir. Austin Children's Choir, 1995—96; asst. dir. South Ctrl. Nebr. Children's Chorale, Hastings, 1999—; adj. instr. in music Hastings Coll., 1999—. Composer: (partita for organ) Partita on "Good Christian Friends, Rejoice and Sing", 1996. Mem.: Music Educators Nat. Conf., Nebr. Music Educators Assn., Am. Choral Dirs. Assn., Nebr. Choral Dirs. Assn. (chmn. children's choirs repertoire and stds. 2003), Choristers Guild. Lutheran. Avocation: travel, reading, computers. Office: Trinity Luth Ch and Scl 212 W 12th St Grand Island NE 68801 Office Phone: 308-382-0753. Personal E-mail: philhest@kdsi.net.

HESTON, CHARLTON (JOHN CHARLTON CARTER), actor; b. Evanston, Ill., Oct. 4, 1924; s. Russell Whitford and Lilla (Charlton) Carter; m. Lydia Marie Clarke, Mar. 17, 1944; children— Fraser Clarke, Holly Ann. Student, Northwestern U., 1941-43. Mem. Nat. Council on the Arts, 1967-72 Author: The Actor's Life, 1979, In the Arena, 1995; performances include: (stage) Antony and Cleopatra, 1947, Leaf and Bough, 1948, Design for a Stained Glass Window, 1949, The Tumbler, 1960; (TV appearances) Wuthering Heights, Macbeth, Taming of the Shrew, Of Human Bondage, Jane Eyre, The Nairobi Affair, 1984, The Proud Men, 1987, TNT, 1988, 90, 91, A Man For All Seasons (also dir.), 1988, Original Sin, 1989, Treasure Island, 1990, The Little Kidnappers, 1990, The Crucifer of Blood, Crash Landing: The Rescue of Flight 232, 1992, The Avenging Angel, 1995; (TV series) The Colbys, 1985-87, Chiefs (miniseries), 1983, (also writer) Charleton Heston Presents the Bible, 1993; (films) Dark City, Greatest Show on Earth, 1952, The Savage, 1952, Ruby Gentry, 1952, The President's Lady, 1952, Pony Express, 1983, Arrowhead, 1953, Bad for Each Other, 1954, Naked Jungle, 1954, The Secret of the Incas, 1954, The Far Horizons, 1955, Lucy Gallant, 1955, Private War of Major Benson, 1955, The Ten Commandments, 1956, Three Violent People, 1956, Touch of Evil, 1958, The Big Country, 1958, Ben Hur, 1959 (Acad. award for best actor), The Wreck of Mary Deare, 1959, El Cid, 1961, The Pigeon That Took Rome, 1962, 55 Days of Peking, 1963, Diamond Head, 1963, The Agony and The Ecstasy, 1963, The War Lord, 1965, The Greatest Story Ever Told, 1965, Khartoum, 1966, Planet of the Apes, 1967, Will Penny, 1968, Number One, 1969, Beneath The Planet of the Apes, 1969, Julius Caesar, 1970, The Hawaiians, 1970, The Omega Man, 1971, Antony and Cleopatra (also dir.), 1971, Skyjacked, 1972, Call of the Wild, 1972, Soylent Green, 1973, The Three Musketeers, 1973, Airport, 1974, The Four Musketeers, 1974, Earthquake, 1974, Midway, 1976, Two-Minute Warning, 1976, The Last Hard Men, 1976, The Prince and the Pauper, 1977, Gray Lady Down, 1977, Mountain Men, 1980, The Awakening, 1980, Mother Lode (also dir.), 1982, Solar Crisis, 1989, Almost An Angel, 1990 (cameo), Wayne's World 2 (cameo), Tombstone, 1993, True Lies, 1994, In the Mouth of Madness, 1995, Hamlet, 1996, Alaska, 1996, Ben Johnson: Third Cowboy On The Right, 1996, Hercules (voice), 1997, Illusion Infinity, 1998, Gideon's Webb, 1998, Armageddon (voice), 1998, Toscano, 1999, Any Given Sunday, 1999, Town & Country, 1999; TV movie Avenging Angel, 1995, I Am Your Child, 1997; dir. The Caine Mutiny Court-Martial (Beijing), 1988. Trustee Los Angeles Center Theatre Group, Am. Film Inst., 1971— , chmn., 1973; head President's Task Force on Arts and Humanities, 1981—; led the Pledge of Allegiance at the Republican Conv., New Orleans, 1988. Served in USAAF, World War II. Recipient Jean Hersholt award as Humanitarian of Yr. Am. Acad. Motion Picture Arts and Scis., 1978, Citizenship medal VFW, 1982, Golden medal City of Vienna, 1995. Mem. Screen Actors Guild (pres. 1966-71), NRA (pres. 1998-2003) Office: care Jack Gilardi ICM 8942 Wilshire Blvd Beverly Hills CA 90211-1934

HESTON, THOMAS J., historian, educator; b. Bethesda, Md., Nov. 2, 1945; s. Walter Enoch and Vivian Janney Heston; m. Susan Luella De Vore, Oct. 1969; 1 child, Timothy Michael. AB, Gettysburg Coll., 1967; MA, Case Western Res., 1972, PhD, 1975. Grad. fellow Case Western Res., 1970—74; veterans benefits counselor VA, Cleve., 1974—75; asst. prof. West Chester State Coll., Pa., 1975—81; assoc. prof. West Chester U., Pa., 1981—86, prof., 1986—. Acting asst. dean Coll. of Arts & Sci., West Chester U., 1986—87, dept. chair, 1990—92; cons. Sta. WPHL-TV, 1995, Phila. Inquirer, Pa. Vets. Mus., 2003—04. Author: (book) Sweet Subsidy, 1987; contbr. articles to profl. jours. and encys. With US Army, 1968—70. Grantee Bernadette E. Schmitt fellowship, Case Western Res. U., 1973. Mem.: Soc. of Mil. History, US Naval Inst., Soc. of Historians of Am. Fgn. Rels., Orgn. of Am. Historians. Office: Dept of History West Chester U West Chester PA 19383 Home Phone: 610-269-4231; Office Phone: 610-436-2972. Business E-Mail: theston@wcupa.edu.

HETE, JOSEPH C., air transportation executive; Mgmt. positions ABX Air Inc., Wilmington, Ohio, 1980—86, v.p. adminstrn., 1986—91, bd. dir., 1988—, sr. v.p. adminstrn., 1991—97, sr. v.p., COO, 1997—2000, pres., COO, 2000—03, pres., CEO, 2003—. Office: ABX Air Inc 145 Hunter Dr Wilmington OH 45177

HETFIELD, JAMES, singer; b. LA, Aug. 3, 1963; Former co-founder, singer Phantom Lord; former co-founder, lead singer, songwriter & rhythm guitarist Leather Charm; co-founder, lead singer, songwriter & rhythm guitarist Metallica, 1981—. Albums include Kill 'em All, 1983, Ride the Lightning, 1984, Master of Puppets, 1986, ...And Justice for All, 1988, Metallica, 1991, Live Sh*t: Binge and Purge, 1993, Kill 'Em All, 1995, Load, 1996, Reload, 1997, Garage Inc., 1998 (Grammy award), S & M, 1999, St. Anger, 2003 (Grammy award best metal performance, 2003); played on compilation albums including Metal Massacre, 1982, The Good, The Bad and The Live, 1990, Rubaiyant: Elektra's 30th Anniversary, 1990, For Those About To Rock: Moscow, 1992, Woodstock '94, 1994, Spawn: The Album, 1997, Woodstock '99, 2000, WCW: Mayhem The Music, 1999, M:I-2, 2000, NASCAR: Full Throttle, 2001, Swizz Beatz Presents G.H.E.T.T.O. Stories, 2002, Biker Boyz Soundtrack, 2003, We're A Happy Family: Tribute to the Ramones, 2003, I've Always Been Crazy: Tribute to Waylon Jennings, 2003. Recipient Grammy award, 1990, 91. Office: c/o Metallica Elektra Records 75 Rockefeller Plz New York NY 10019-6908

HETHERINGTON, JOHN JOSEPH, lawyer; b. Phila., Jan. 22, 1947; s. Jack Joseph and Josephine J. (Krawiec) H.; children: Wendy Lynn, John Joseph, Patrick John. BA, U. Pa., 1974; JD, Gonzaga U., 1977. Bar: Pa. 1977, U.S. Dist. Ct. (ea. dist.) Pa. 1979, U.S. Ct. Appeals (3d cir.) 1983; cert. elder lawyer Nat. Elder Law Found., 1993, cert. 2000. Staff atty. Legal Services Northeast Pa., Wilkes-Barre, 1977-79; sole practice Chalfont, Pa., 1979-82, Hilltown, Pa., 1986—2000; assoc. Toll, Hetherington & Ghen, Doylestown, Pa., 1982-86; ptnr. Corr, Stevens & Fenningham, 2000—04; pvt. practice Pa., 2005—. Cons., lectr. pre-retirement workshops, Devon, Pa., 1984—; lectr. programs on elder law and social security claims CLE, 1981-99; mem. adj. faculty Bucks County C.C., 2002—. With USAF, 1966-69. Mem.: Nat. Orgn. Social Security Claimants Reps., Nat. Acad. Elder Law Attys., Bucks County Bar Assn., Pa. Bar Assn. Republican. Roman Catholic. Avocations: horticulture, collecting contemporary music, sailing. Office: 43 N Main St Chalfont PA 18914 Office Phone: 215-822-0115. E-mail: jjhelderlaw@comcast.net.

HETHERWICK, GILBERT LEWIS, lawyer; b. Winnsboro, La., Oct. 30, 1920; s. Septimus and Addie Louise (Gilbert) H.; m. Joan Friend Gibbons, May 31, 1946 (dec. Aug. 1964); children: Janet Hetherwick Pumphrey, Ann Hetherwick Lyons Winegeart, Gilbert, Carol Hetherwick Sutton, Katherine Hetherwick Hummell; m. Mertis Elizabeth Cook, June 7, 1967 (dec. May 2003). BA summa cum laude, Centenary Coll., 1942; JD, Tulane U., 1949. Bar: La. 1949. With legal dept. NorAm Energy Corp., Shreveport, La., 1949-53; dir. Blanchard, Walker, O'Quin and Roberts, PLC, Shreveport, 1953-99, of counsel, 2000—. Mem. Shreveport City Charter Revision Com., 1955; mem. Shreveport Mcpl. Fire and Police Civil Svc. Bd., 1956-92, vice chmn., 1957-78, chmn., 1978-88. Served with AUS, 1942-46. Recipient Tulane U. Law Faculty medal, 1949. Mem. ABA, La. Bar Assn., Shreveport Bar Assn. (pres. 1987), Energy Bar Assn., Order of Coif, Phi Delta Phi, Omicron Delta Kappa. Episcopalian. Home: 4604 Fairfield Ave Shreveport LA 71106-1432 Office: Bank One Tower Shreveport LA 71101

HETLAND, JAMES LYMAN, JR., banker, lawyer, educator; b. Mpls., June 9, 1925; s. James L. and Evelyn E. (Lundgren) H.; m. Barbara Anne Taylor, Sept. 10, 1949; children: Janice E., James E., Nancy L., Steven T. BSL., U. Minn., 1948, JD, 1950. Bar: Minn. 1950. Law clk. Minn. Supreme Ct., 1949—50; assoc. firm Mackall, Crounse, Moore, Helmey & Palmer, Mpls., 1950—56; prof. U. Minn. Coll. Law, 1956—71; v.p. urban devel. First Nat. Bank Mpls., 1971—75, sr. v.p. law and urban devel., 1975—82, sr. v.p., gen. counsel, sec., 1982—88; sr. v.p. First Bank Sys., 1987—88; counsel to bd. and sec. First Bank, N.A., 1986—90; of counsel Rasmussen & Assocs., Ltd., 1990—99, Leighton, Hetland & Stein, PLLP, Mpls., 2002—. Adj. prof. Hubert Humphrey Inst., U. Minn., 1976—90, regents adv. com., 1982—90; adj. prof. Bus. Coll. ext., 1975—81, Coll. Law, 1980—90; labor arbitrator, 1967—; chmn. Minn. Citizens Coun. Crime and Delinquency, 1978—83; chmn. adv. coms. Minn. Supreme Ct., 1958—90; chmn. Telecommuters, Inc., 1992—96. Co-author: Minnesota Jury Instruction Guides, 1963, 2d edit., 1974, Minnesota Practice, 3 vols., 1970. Chmn. Met. Coun. Twin Cities, St. Paul, 1967-71, Mpls. Charter Commn., 1963-70; chmn. Mpls. Citizens League, 1963-64, bd. dirs., 1953-67; bd. dirs. Mpls. Downtown Coun., 1971—, vice chmn., 1978-82, chmn., 1982-83; chmn. bd. Minn. Zool. Garden, 1978-83; nat. v.p., exec. com. Nat. Mcpl. League, 1979-82, pres., 1982-85, chmn. bd., 1985-87; vice chmn. Minn. Press Coun., 1973-81; vice chmn. bd. Minn. Health Care Cost Coalition, 1980; bd. dirs. Interstudy, 1972-79, chmn., 1974; mem. Bus. Urban Issues Coun., Conf. Bd., 1980-89; bd. dirs. Freshwater Biol. Rsch. Found., 1971-85, adv. bd., 1985—; bd. dirs. Mpls. Community Coll. Found., 1978-83, Minn. Exptl. City, 1972-75, Minn. Campfire Girls, 1974-79, Mpls. YMCA, 1957-76; bd. dirs. Health Central, Inc., 1973-87, exec. com., 1977-87; bd. dirs. Citizen Coun. on Crime and Justice, 1977—, chmn., 1979-82; bd. dirs. Ctr. for Policy Studies, 1983—, Twin Cities Habitat for Humanity, 1988-95; mem. exec. com. Partnership Dataline U.S.A., 1983; bd. dirs., exec. com. Health One, 1987-93; trustee Metro State U., 1989-98, Mpls. United Way, 1988-99; chmn. Mpls. Urban Tennis, 1987-94. With AUS, 1943-46. Mem.: ABA, Hennepin County Bar Assn., Minn. Bar Assn., Rotary. Republican. Lutheran. Personal E-mail: jbh@mninter.net. *Seeking to improve services for urban citizens through new public and private service delivery systems has been a keystone for setting involvement priorities. Effective service delivery systems are essential if an urban society is to preserve a free public-private economic democracy. Involvement and change in the private sector is as important as in the public sector.*

HETLAND, JOHN ROBERT, law educator; b. Mpls., Mar. 12, 1930; s. James L. and Evelyn (Lundgren) H.; m. Mildred Woodruff, Dec. 1951 (div.); children: Lynda Lee Catlin, Robert John, Debra Ann Allen; m. Anne Kneeland, Dec. 1972; children: Robin T. Willcox, Elizabeth J. Pickett. BSL., U. Minn., 1952, JD, 1956. Bar: Minn. 1956, Calif. 1962, U.S. Supreme Ct, 1981. Practice law, Mpls., 1956-59; prof. law U. Calif., Berkeley, 1959-91; prof. emeritus, 1991—; prin. Hetland & Kneeland, PC, Berkeley, 1959—. Vis. prof. law Stanford U., 1971, 80, U. Singapore, 1972, U. Cologne, Fed. Republic Germany, 1988. Author: California Real Property Secured Transactions, 1970, Commercial Real Estate Transactions, 1972, Secured Real Estate Transactions, 1974, 1977; co-author: California Cases on Security Transactions in Land, 2d edit., 1975, 3d edit., 1984, 4th edit., 1992; contbr. articles to legal, real estate and fin. jours. Served to lt. comdr. USNR, 1953-55. Fellow Am. Coll. Real Estate Lawyers, Am. Coll. Mortgage Attys., Am. Bar Found.; mem. ABA, State Bar Calif., State Bar Minn., Order of Coif, Phi Delta Phi. Home and Office: 20 Red Coach Ln Orinda CA 94563-1112 Office Phone: 925-254-4755. E-mail: johnhetland@comcast.net.

HETTCHE, L. RAYMOND, engineering educator, retired research scientist; b. Balt., Mar. 24, 1938; s. Leroy and Dorothy (Curtain) H.; m. Patricia Durkan, July 1965; children: Lisa, Kathleen, Matthew, Craig. BSCE, AB in Math., Bucknell U., 1961; MSCE, Carnegie-Mellon U., 1961, PhD in CE, 1965. Asst. prof. Rutgers U., New Brunswick, N.J., 1964-66; resident rsch. assoc. Nat. Bur. Standards, Washington, 1966-68; structural engr. metallurgy div. Naval Rsch. Lab., Washington, 1968-71, head thermomech. effect sect., 1971-73, head mech. br. metallurgy div., 1973-75, supt. materials sci. div., 1975-81; now, dir. Applied Rsch. Lab. Pa. State U., State College, 1981—2002, prof. engrng. rsch., 2002—, prof. engrng. rsch. emeritus. Navy rep. Tech. Working Group Export Control, Washington, 1979-81; navy rep. subgroup P materials panel for metals Tech. Cooperation Program, Washington, 1977-81; session chmn. Submarine Tech. Symposium, Columbia, Md., 1990. Contbr. numerous articles to profl. jours. Tau Beta Pi Nat. fellow, 1961-63; NSF fellow, 1963; recipient Outstanding Achievement award Am. Def. Preparedness Assn., 1986. Office: Pa State U Applied Rsch Lab PO Box 30 State College PA 16804-0030 Business E-Mail: lrh3@psu.edu.

HETTIARACHCHI, CHAMIL HIROSHAN, civil engineer, educator; arrived in US, 2001; s. Dayananda Hettiarachchi and Sisilin De Livera Kulatunga; m. Vijayamala Chandrakanthi Hettiarachchi, 2002. BCE, U. Moratuwa, Sri Lanka, 1998; M in Engrng., Asian Inst. Tech., Thailand, 2001; PhD, NJ Inst. Tech., Newark, 2005. Tchg. asst. U. Moratuwa, 1998; rsch. engr. Lanka Hydraulic Inst., Moratuwa, 1998—99; tchg. asst. Thammasat U., Pathumthani, Thailand, 2000; rsch. asst. NJ Inst. Tech., 2001, grad. tchg. asst., 2002—05; geotechnical engr. Matrix New World Engrng., East Hanover, NJ, 2005, Langan Engrng. & Environ. Svcs., Elmwood Park, NJ, 2005; asst. prof. civil engrng. Lawrence Technol. U., Southfield, Mich., 2006—. Vis. rschr. U. Calgary, Alt., Canada, 2002—06. Contbr. articles to profl. jours. Grantee, Mich. Dept. Transp., 2007—; scholar, The Govt. Norway, 1999—2001, NJ Inst. Tech., 2001—05. Fellow: ASCE (assoc.); mem.: Tau Beta Pi. Achievements include development of a mathematical model to investigate the settlement behavior of Bioreactor Landfills. Bioreactor landfills are a sustainable waste management technology; research in evaluation of the correlation of surface texture and segregation, with the measurement of air voids of asphalt pavements; investigation of the scouring at bridge piers in the State of Michigan; investigation of the potential use of thermal characteristics of the groundwater flow as a natural tracer to understand the flow pattern. Office: Lawrence Technol Univ 21000 West Ten Mile Rd Southfield MI 48075 Office Phone: 248-204-2538. Business E-Mail: hiroshan@ltu.edu.

HETTINGER, MICHAEL EUGENE, corneal surgeon; b. Memphis, Sept. 20, 1946; s. Elmer Eugene and Jeanette M. Hettinger; m. Terry Carmack Hettinger, Oct. 9, 1976; children: Christian Andrew, Michael Eugene Jr., Rachel Elise. BA in Biology, Rhodes Coll., Memphis, 1968; MS in Pathology, U. Tenn., Memphis, 1971. Toxicologist City of Memphis Hosps., 1970—75, acting dir. toxicology lab., 1971—72, med. technologist clin. chemistry lab., 1972—75; intern Regional Med. Ctr. Memphis, 1975—76; resident in ophthalmology U. Ala., Birmingham, 1976—79; fellow anterior segment surgery Mass. Eye and Ear Infirmary, Boston, 1979—81; dir. corneal and external disease svc. Kans. U. Med. Ctr., 1981—84; med. dir. Kans. Eye Bank, 1981—89; ptnr. Kansas City Eye Clinic, Overland Park, Kans., 1983—; co-med. dir. Midwest Transplant Network Eye Bank, 1994—2006. Clin. fellow ophthalmology Harvard Med. Sch., Boston, 1979—81; asst. prof. ophthalmology Kansas City U. Med. Ctr., 1981—84, clin. asst. prof. ophthalmology, 1984—96; vis. grand rounds prof. dept. ophthalmology U. Tenn., 1983; vis. lectr. dept. microbiology U. Health Svcs., 1983; lectr. in field; fellow staff Mass. Eye and Ear Infirmary, Boston, 1979—81; mem. provisional staff New Eng. Bapt. Hosp., Boston, 1980—81; mem. med. staff VA Hosp., Kansas City, Mo., 1981—84; mem. staff dept. ophthalmology Kans. U. Med. Ctr., 1981—96; mem. staff Shawnee Mission Med. Ctr., Kans., 1983—, Children's Mercy Hosp., Kansas City, Mo., 1985—93, Miami County Hosp., Paola, Kans., 1990—. Contbr. articles to profl. jours. Bd. dirs. Midwest Transplant Network, Kansas City. Recipient Spl. Achievement award, U. Tenn. Ctr. Health Scis., 1975, Fellowship award, Bausch and Lomb, 1979—80; grantee, USPHS, 1969—71, Nat. Soc. to Prevent Blindness, 1980—81; scholar, Omicron Delta Kappa, 1966—68. Fellow: ACS; mem.: Internat. Soc. Refractive Surgery, Cornea Soc., Am. Soc. Cataract and Refractive Surgery, Kansas City Soc. Ophthalmology and Otolaryngology, Kans. Med. Soc., Midwest Corneal Assn., Med. Soc. Johnson and Wyandotte Counties (treas. 2003, sec. 2004, pres-elect 2005, pres. 2006), Midwest Transplant Network (bd. dir. 2000—), Am. Acad. Ophthalmology (mem. coun. 2002—06), Eye Bank Assn. Am. (chmn. grievance com. 1981, mem. accreditation com. 1982—87, Paton Soc. 1982—, med. adv. bd. 1983—, fin. com. 1985—, bd. dirs. 1987—90, treas. 1990—98, bd. dirs. 1991—, exec. com. 1991—, legis. and regulatory affairs com. 1998—2002, chmn.-elect. bd. dirs. 2000—02, chmn. bd. dirs. 2002—04, R. Townley Paton award 2006), Kansas City Ind. Physicians Assn. (treas. 2004—06, bd. dirs.). Methodist. Avocations: golf, reading. Office: Kansas City Eye Clinic 7504 Antioch Overland Park KS 66204 Office Phone: 913-341-3100. Business E-Mail: mgalloway@kceyeclinic.com.

HETTRICK, GEORGE HARRISON, lawyer; b. Piney River, Va., Aug. 15, 1940; s. Ames Bartlett and Frances Caryl (O'Brian) H.; m. Lee Ann Hettrick; children: Heather White Hettrick Brugh, Edward Lord. BA, Cornell U., 1962; JD, Harvard U., 1965. Bar: Va. 1965. Assoc. Hunton & Williams LLP, Richmond, Va., 1965-73; spl. counsel Gov. of Va., 1970—71; ptnr., bus. practice group Hunton & Williams LLP, Richmond, Va., 1973—, and chmn., cmty. svc. com. Managing ptnr. Hunton & Williams Church Hill Neighborhood Pro Bono Law Office, Richmond, Virginia, 1990-, Hunton & Williams U. Va. Law Sch. Pro Bono Partnership Office, Charlottesville, Virginia, 2003-; chmn. Community Svc. com. Contbr. articles to profl. jours. Pres. bd. trustees Va. Episcopal Sch., Lynchburg, 1978—81; spl. counsel Gov. of Va., Richmond, 1971—72; vice-chmn. bd. dirs. Va. Port Authority, Norfolk, 1970—75, former commr., vice-chmn.; Va. State adv. com. Neighborhood Assistance Program; past dir., chmn. Peter Paul Devel. Ctr., Inc.; bd. dirs. Lawyers Helping Lawyers, 1992—, St. Mary's Hosp., 1996—2005, St. Francis Hosp., Regional Meml. Med. Ctr, Greater Richmond Bar Found., 1999—, pres., 2003—05; mem. Henrico County Cmty. Svcs. Bd., Va., 1997—2005, chmn., 2002—03; bd. dirs. Chesterfield/Colonial Heights Drug Ct. Found., 2002—; bd. dirs., vice chair Va. Network Nonprofit Orgns., 2000—05; bd. mem. Partnership for Nonprofit Excellence, 2007—. Capt. US Army, 1966—68. Fellow Va. Law Found.; mem. ABA, Va. Bar Assn. (chmn. substance abuse com. 1995-96), Va. State Bar, Richmond Bar Assn. (chmn. pro bono com. 1998-2001). Republican. Episcopalian. Office: Hunton & Williams LLP Riverfront Plz East Tower 951 E Byrd St Richmond VA 23219-4074 Home Phone: 804-364-5612; Office Phone: 804-788-8324. Office Fax: 804-788-8218. Business E-Mail: ghettrick@hunton.com.

HETZER, G. SCOTT, energy executive; BBA, U. Richmond, Va., 1978; MBA, U. Va., 1984. Mng. dir. Wheat First Butcher Singer; v.p., treas. Dominion, Richmond, 1997—99, sr. v.p., treas., 1999—, sr. v.p., treas. Va. Power and Consol. Natural Gas Co., 2000—, pres. Dominion Capital. Office: Dominion PO Box 26532 Richmond VA 23261-6532 Office Phone: 804-819-2000. Office Fax: 804-819-2214.*

HETZLER, SUSAN ELIZABETH SAVAGE, educational administrator; b. Monticello, Iowa, Mar. 18, 1947; d. Robert Engelbert and Josephine May (Ricklefs) Savage; children: Stephanine, Michael. BS in Edn., Rockford Coll., Ill., 1971; 2MS in Edn., No. Ill. U., 1978, cert. advanced study, 1984; PhD, Walden U., Mpls., 1989. Cert. elem. tchr., adminstr., Ill., Iowa; supr., sociology tchr., Ill. Elem. tchr. Freeport (Ill.) Sch. Dist., 1971-86; prof. elem. edn. Iowa State U., Ames, 1986-90; dir. tchr. edn. and devel. Iowa Dept. Edn., Des Moines, 1990-96; prof. edn., dean sch. edn. Buena Vista U., Storm Lake, Iowa, 1996-99; program admin. for educator preparation Tex. State Bd. for Educator Certification, Austin, 1999—2001; dir. tchr. edn. Tex. Higher Edn. Coord. Bd., Austin, 2001—. Curriculum cons. Ames Sch. Dist., 1985-90, Des Moines Sch. Dist., 1985-90; mem. ISU adv. bd., Ames, 1991—. Author: Elementary Education Practicum Teaching, 1988, Learning Centers, 1989. Comsnr. Drug and Alcohol Prevention Project, Freeport, 1976-85; chairperson Stephenson County (Ill.) Cancer Soc., 1976-78, small bus. dvsn. United Way, Freeport, 1980-85; vol. BSA and GSA, Freeport, 1974-85. Recipient Excellence in Teaching award Iowa State U., 1989-90, Outstanding Elem. Tchrs. Am. Ill., 1974, 81. Mem. AAUP, ASCD, NEA, Iowa ASCD, Am. Assn. Colls. of Tchr. Edn., Iowa Assn. Colls. of Tchr. Edn., Iowa Ednl. Rsch. and Eval. Assn., Assn. Tchr. Educators, Tex. Tchr. Educators, Tex. Coun. Women Sch. Execs., Exec. Women in Tex. Govt., Delta Kappa Gamma, Phi Delta Kappa, Rotary, Kiwanis. Presbyterian. Avocations: reading, skiing, tennis, piano, antiques, golf. Home: 511 Mandarin Flyway Cedar Park TX 78613 Office: Tex Higher Edn Coord Bd 1200 E Anderson Ln PO Box 12788 Austin TX 78711 Office Phone: 512-427-6220. Business E-Mail: susan.hetzler@thecb.state.tx.us.

HEUER, ALAN J., finance company executive; BA, Colgate Univ.; MBA, Univ. Rochester. Positions through chief banking officer Marine Midland Bank; exec. v.p. retail banking Bank of NY; exec. v.p., pres. U.S. region MasterCard Worldwide, Purchase, NY, 1995—99, head customer group, 1999—2004, COO, 2004—. Office: MasterCard Worldwide 2000 Purchase St Purchase NY 10577*

HEUER, GERALD ARTHUR, mathematician, educator; b. Bertha, Minn., Aug. 31, 1930; s. William C. F. and Selma C. (Rosenberg) Heuer; m. Jeanette Mary Knedel, Sept. 5, 1954; children: Paul, Karl, Ruth, Otto. BA, Concordia Coll., 1951; MA, U. Nebr., 1953; PhD, U. Minn., 1958. Math. instr. Hamline U., 1955-56, Concordia Coll., Moorhead, Minn., 1956-57, asst. prof., 1957-58, assoc. prof., 1958-62, prof., 1962-95, Sigurd and Pauline Prestegaard Mundhjeld prof., 1988-95, chmn. dept., 1963-70, research prof., 1970-71, prof. emeritus, mathematician-in-residence, 1995—; mathematician Remington Rand Univac, summer 1958. Vis. prof. U. Nebr., Lincoln, 1960—61, Wash. State U., Pullman, 1980—81; mathematician Control Data Corp., 1960—62, cons., 1960—63; vis. lectr. Math. Assn. Am., 1964—66; cons. NSF-AID, India, 1968—69; guest spkr. Minn. sect. Math. Assn. Am., 1956, Nebr. sect. Math. Assn. Am., 1961, No. Ctrl. sect. Math. Assn. Am., 1974; vis. prof., scholar Math. Inst. Cologne (Germany) U., 1973—74; vis. prof., scholar Inst. Stats., Econs. and Ops. Rsch. Graz U., Austria, 1987—88, rsch. prof., Austria, 1990, vis. prof., Austria, 94, Austria, 97; dir. U.S. Math. Olympiad Tng. Session; leader U.S. team Internat. Math. Olympiad, 1988—90; invited plenary spkr. Internat. Symposium Ops. Rsch., Passau, Germany, 1995. Author (with Ulrike Leopold-Wildburger): (book) Balanced Silverman Games on General Discrete Sets, 1991, Silverman's Game, 1995; contbr. articles to profl. jours.; reviewer: Zentralblatt für Mathematik, 1967—, Math. Revs., 1978—. Grantee Rsch., NSF, 1963, 1964, 1966; scholar Bush Rsch., Concordia Coll., 1983—84, Centennial Rsch., 1992, 1993, 1994, 1995; Faculty fellow, NSF, Univ. Calif. Berkeley, 1966—67. Mem.: Österreichische Math. Gesellschaft (Vienna), Deutsche Math.-Vereinigung e.v. (Berlin), Nat. Geographic Soc., Am. Math. Soc., Math. Assn. Am. (pres. Minn. sect. 1959—60, nat. bd. govs. 1971—73, com. Putnam prize 1987—90, com. Am. math. competitions 1988—, problem books editl. bd. 1999—, cert. meritorious svc. 1994), Sigma Xi. Lutheran. Home: 1216 Elm St S Moorhead MN 56560-4049 Office: Concordia Coll Dept Math Moorhead MN 56562-0001 Office Phone: 218-299-3348. Business E-Mail: heuer@cord.edu.

HEUER, MARTIN, retired human resources specialist; b. Algoma, Wis., Oct. 16, 1934; s. Orland Fred and Gertrude Mayme (Zimmerman) Heuer; m. Rita Mae Prokash, Oct. 27, 1954; children: Martin Joseph, Ronald James. AA, SUNY, 1973, AS, 1975. Commd. 2d lt. C.E. U.S. Army, 1954, advanced through grades to lt. col., 1968; flight comdr., adminstrv. and maintenance officer 1st Aviation Co., Ft. Riley, 1958-61; with 937th Engr. Aviation Co. Panama and Lima, Peru, 1961-65; maintenance officer 174th Aviation Co., Vietnam, 1966; adj. 14th Combat Aviation Bn., 1966-67; dir. sys., curriculum and spl. projects divsn. Army Primary Helicopter Sch., Ft. Wolters, Tex., 1967-69; aviation advisor Wis. Army N.G., West Bend, 1969-70; airfield comdr. Cu Chi Army Airfield, Vietnam, 1970-71; airfield comdr., adj. 165th Combat Aviation Group, Vietnam; engr. advisor Wis. N.G., Eau Claire, 1971-73; mgr., area mgr. Manpower Temp. Svcs., 1973-76; exec. v.p. Aide Svcs. Inc. and KARI Svcs. Inc., Tampa, Fla., 1976-80, pres., chmn., 1980—2002, ret., 2002. Pres. Seminole HS Band Boosters, 1974—79; v.p. Pinellas County Band Boosters, 1977—78; v.p. and bd. dir. Vietnam Helicopter Air Crew Mus., Tampa, 1999—2002; bd. dir. Seminole HS Booster Assn., 1975—79, pres., 1978—79. Decorated Legion of Merit with 1 oak leaf cluster, Bronze Star with 3 oak leaf clusters, Air medal with 3 oak leaf clusters; recipient First Band Booster Pres. award, Seminole HS, 1979, Svc. to Mankind award, Sertoma, 1980. Mem.: Nat. Assn. Temp. Svcs. (treas./sec. Fla. chpt. 1991—94), Soc. Am. Mil. Engrs., Assn. Manpower Franchise Owners (dir. 1980—82, treas. 1981—82, dir. 1983—86, chmn. 1984—86), Vietnam Helicopter Pilots Assn. (bd. dir. Fla. chpt. 1993—2002, v.p. 1996—98, pres. 1998—2000, chmn. bd. dir. 2000—02), Future Farmers Am. Alumni Assn., Ret. Officers Assn., Res. Officers Assn., Air Force Assn., Army Aviation Assn. Am., Assn. U.S. Army (chmn. bd. govs. 1981—82, asst. state v.p. Suncoast chpt. and Fla. 1981—82, state v.p. 1982—84, chmn. chpt. comms. nat. adv. bd. 1982—86, mem. corp. adv. coun. 1985—90, FLA exec. coun. 1985—90, bd. dir. Sun Coast chpt. 1994—2002), Assault Helicopter Co. Assn. (pres. 174th chpt. 2006). Republican. Personal E-mail: martyheuer@aol.com.

HEUER, ROBERT MAYNARD, II, opera company executive; b. Detroit, Nov. 27, 1944; s. Robert Maynard and May Elizabeth (Quinn) H. Student, Capital U., 1963-64; BA, Wayne State U., 1976. Youth dir. Grace Luth. Ch., Detroit, 1964-66; costume designer, prodn. mgr. U. Windsor, Ont., Canada, 1967-69; program coord. Detroit Youtheatre, Detroit Inst. Arts, 1970-71; mng. dir. Mich. Opera Theatre, Detroit, 1971-79; prodn. dir. Fla. Grand Opera (formerly Greater Miami Opera), 1979-83, asst. gen. mgr., 1984-85, gen. mgr., CEO, 1986-97, gen. dir., CEO, 1997—. Mem. Performing Arts Ctr. Found. Greater Miami. Recipient Narot Humanitarian award, 2001. Mem.: Opera Am., Greater Miami C. of C. Home: 547 Navarre Ave Coral Gables FL 33134-4231 Office: Fla Grand Opera 1200 Coral Way Miami FL 33145-2927 Office Phone: 305-444-8668 ext. 202. Personal E-mail: rmheuer@fgo.org.*

HEUERMANN-NOWIK, PATRICIA CALHOUN, theater director; d. William Royal Calhoun and Nancy Lee Griffitts; m. Eric Heuermann (div.); children: Beryl Lee, William Whitney, Lana Amanda, Linda Dilwara; m. Vete Nowik, Mar. 29, 1985. Grad., Curtis Inst. Music, 1951—55. Dir. opera theatre Emory U., Atlanta, 1968—75, Clark Coll., 1972—75; founder, artistic music dir. Atlanta Opera, 1975—80; mng. dir., touring ednl. program N.C. Opera, Charlotte, 1980—82; founder, artistic dir. Singers Theatre N.Y., NYC, 1983—92; instr. stage artistry Am. Inst. Musical Studies, Graz, Austria, 1994—2001; dir. opera theatre Hofstra U., Hempstead, NY, 2000—06. Chair internat. opera singers competition Ctr. Contemporary Opera, 1990—94, chair artistic adv. bd., 1990—96. Mem.: Opera for Youth (bd. dirs. 2000—02, program chair nat. conf. 1995), N.Y. Singing Tchrs. Assn. (bd. dirs. 1998—99), Opera Am., Nat. Opera Assn. (N.E. regional gov. 1991—94, bd. dirs. 1991—95, v.p. resources 1995—98, v.p. programs 1998—2000, pres. 2000—02). Democrat. Avocations: cooking, reading, travel. Home: 20-49 48th St Astoria NY 11105 Office: Hofstra U Music Dept 112 Hofstra Univ Hempstead NY 11549-1120 Personal E-mail: patruschka@mindspring.com.

HEUISLER, CHARLES WILLIAM, lawyer; b. Phila., May 24, 1941; s. Isaac Kilner and Mary Gertrude (Smith) H.; m. Judith Ann Hargadon, June 26, 1965; children: Karen L. Heuisler Murphy, Susan M. Heuisler McCabe, Charles W. Jr. BA in Modern Lang., Coll. of Holy Cross, 1963; JD, Villanova U., 1966. Bar: NJ 1966, US Dist. Ct. NJ 1966, US Ct. Appeals (3d cir.) 1970, US Supreme Ct. 1972; cert. civil trial atty. Am. Bd. Trial Advs. Law clk. to Hon. John B. Wick, Superior Ct. of NJ, Chancery Divsn., Camden, 1966-67; shareholder Archer & Greiner, Haddonfield, NJ, 1972—. Counsel, mem. adv. bd. Haddonfield Symphony Soc., 1980—. Mem. FBA, NJ Bar Assn. (trustee from Camden County 1989-93), Camden County Bar Assn. (pres. 1985-86, Peter J. Devine award 1991), Rotary (pres. Camden chpt. 1987-88). Avocations: tennis, sailing. Home: 1236 Folkestone Way Cherry Hill NJ 08034-3021 Office: Archer & Greiner PC One Centennial Sq Haddonfield NJ 08033 Home Phone: 856-429-4473; Office Phone: 856-354-3081. Business E-Mail: cheuisler@archerlaw.com.

HEUMAN, DONNA, lawyer; b. Seattle, May 27, 1949; d. Russell George and Edna Inez (Armstrong) H. BA in Psychology, UCLA, 1972; JD, U. Calif., San Francisco, 1985. Cert. shorthand reporter Calif. Owner Heuman & Assocs., San Francisco, 1978-86; lic. real estate broker Calif., 1990—2002; owner Heuman Law Office, 2002—07; co-founder, chair, CEO Atherton Park Foods, Inc., Menlo Park, Calif., 1996—. Mem. Hastings Internat. and Comparative Law Rev., 1984-85; bd. dirs. Saddleback, 1987-89. Jessup Internat. Moot Ct. Competition, 1985; mem. North Fair Oaks Adv. Coun., vice chair, sec. 1993-95. Mem. ABA, NAFE, ATLA, AOPA, Nat. Shorthand Reporters Assn., Women Entrepreneurs, Mensa, Calif. State Bar Assn., Nat. Mus. of Women in the Arts, Calif. Lawyers for the Arts, San Francisco Bar Assn., Commonwealth Club, World Affairs Coun., Zonta (bd. dirs.). Office: 750 18th Ave Menlo Park CA 94025-2018 Home Phone: 650-326-4990; Office Phone: 650-326-4500. Business E-Mail: drh@heuman.org. E-mail: athpark@aol.com.

HEUSCHELE, SHARON JO, dean; b. Toldeo, Ohio, July 12, 1936; BE, U. Toledo, 1965, MEd, 1969, PhD, 1973. Cert. elem., secondary tchr., Ohio. Asst. prof. Ohio Dominican Coll., Columbus, 1970-73, St. Cloud (Minn.) U., 1973-74; assoc. prof. Ohio State U., Columbus, 1974-79; dean instl. planning Lourdes Coll., Sylvania, Ohio, 1980—; chmn. sociology, econs. and polit. sci. dept. Cons. U. Hawaii, 1979, others. Bd. dirs. Trinity-St. Paul Inner City Program, Toledo, 1968; cons. Ohio Civil Rights Commn., 1972; active Dem. campaigns. U. Toledo fellow, 1967-69; recipient citation U. Toledo, 1979, Journalistic Excellence award Columbia Press Assn., N.Y.C., 1954. Mem. Am. Coun. Edn., Ohio Conf. Coll. and Univ. Planning, Soc. Coll. and Univ. Planning (com. 1984-85), Phi Theta Kappa, Phi Kappa Phi (citation 1973), U. Toledo Alumni Assn., USCG Aux. Roman Catholic. Avocations: fossil and mineral collecting, poetry, novel writing, horseback riding. Office: Lourdes Coll 6832 Convent Blvd Sylvania OH 43560-2891

HEUSER, MARK CHARLES, military officer, educator; s. Howard William Heuser and Sherril Christine Hamlin; m. Donna Marie Cowan; 1 child, Megan Elaine Hanson. Cert. naval sci. instr. USN, Fla., 1996. Commd. lt. USN, 1972, advanced through grades to master chief petty officer, 1990—, instr. naval sci. jr. ROTC Houston, 1995—. Decorated Several awards USN. Mem.: Fleet Res. Assn (assoc.). Republican. Office: Spring Branch Navy JROTC 10660 Hammerly Blvd Houston TX 77043 Home Phone: 281-238-8133. Business E-Mail: mark.heuser@springbranchisd.com.

HEVEL, GARY FRANCIS, public information officer, consultant; b. Salida, Colo., Nov. 30, 1941; s. Francis Marion and Doris Hevel; m. Julie Ann Fortin, July 18, 1980; 1 child, Amanda Simone; m. Susan Platkin, June 30, 1970 (div. 1980); 1 child, Derek Forrest. BS, Pittsburg State U., 1969. Mus. specialist Dept. Entomology, Washington, 1969—73, collections mgr., 1973—95, pub. info. officer, 1995—. Cons. US Mil., 1969—70, Dorling Kindersley, NYC, 2000—01, Fish & Wildlife Dept., Cabin John, Md., 2000—02, Orkin Exterminating Co., 2001, USA Weekend Mag., Arlington, Va., 2003, IMAX Co., 2003, Andrew Stewart Pub., NYC, 2005—06. Editor: (prodn. of U.S. stamps) Insects and Spiders; co-editor: Animal; co-creator (species biodiversity inventory) Bio-Blitz, co-developer (exhibition) BugFest; contbr. articles to profl. jours. Mem.: Coleopterists Soc., N.Y. Entomol. Soc., Entomol. Soc. Wash., Entomol. Soc. Am., Kans. Entomol. Soc. Achievements include discovery of some 200 new insect species; World record for kinds of insects collected at residence; Published photo in book, Magnificent Foragers; Tarantula wrangler for National Geographic Explorer; Collected insects in 24 countries and territories; Featured in Washington Post, USA Today and other newspapers; Interviewed by BBC, CBS, CNN, Nat. Pub. Radio, Spanish television, Chinese television, Wisconsin Public Radio. Avocations: collecting postcards & stamps, bird watching, photography. Home: 15410 Johnson Rd Silver Spring MD 20905 Office: Smithsonian Institution PO Box 37012 10th Street & Constitution Avenue NW Washington DC 20013-7012 Office Phone: 202-633-1016. Personal E-mail: hevels@comcast.net. E-mail: hevelg@si.edu.

HEWES, LAURENCE ILSLEY, III, lawyer, management consultant; b. Palo Alto, Calif., Sept. 18, 1933; s. Laurence Ilsley, Jr. and Patricia Esther (Jackson) H.; m. Mary Clarke Darling, Oct. 1, 1960; children: Laurence Ilsley IV, Henry Patrick Darling, Mary Clarke Danforth. AB, Yale U., 1956, LLB, 1959. Bar: D.C. 1961, U.S. Dist. Ct. D.C., 1961, U.S. Ct. Appeals (D.C. cir.) 1961, U.S. Supreme Ct. 1966. Assoc. counsel U.S. Senate Comm. Labor and Human Resources, Washington, 1961; assoc. counsel Econ. Devel. Adminstrn. U.S. Dept. Commerce, Washington, 1961-62; staff dir., counsel Pres.'s Com. on Equal Opportunity in Armed Forces, Washington, 1962-63; assoc. then ptnr. Hydeman & Mason and successor firms, Washington, 1963-72; ptnr. Boasberg & Hewes (and successor firms), Washington, 1972-80, Wald Harkader & Ross, Washington, 1980-85; exec. dir., gen. counsel The Support Ctr., 1985-88; pres., chief exec. officer, gen. counsel Corp. Against Drug Abuse, 1989-93; legal, devel. and mgmt. cons. Washington, 1994—. Bd. dirs., Officer Taft Corp., Washington and N.Y.C., 1967-72; bd. dirs., mgr. Grants Mgmt. Adv. Svc., Inc., 1975-80; lectr. non-profit orgn. field. Contbr. articles to profl. jours., chpts. to books. Bd. trustees, Wooster Sch., Danbury Conn., 1981-89, Friends of Superior Ct. of D.C., 1973-87. Served with USAFR, 1959-66. Mem. ABA, D.C. Bar Assn., Cosmos Club, Yale Club (N.Y.C.), Mountain View Country Club. Democrat. Avocations: music, reading, walking, fly fishing, tennis. Home: Lawrence I & Mary D Hewes III 4944 Western Ave Bethesda MD 20816-1714 Home Phone: 301-320-4944; Office Phone: 301-320-4944. Personal E-mail: lhewes@starpower.net.

HEWES, ROBERT CHARLES, radiologist; b. Balt., Feb. 14, 1953; s. Gordon Cecil and Gladys Dorothy (Barringham) H.; m. Judith Renee Lacy, Mar. 23, 1975; children: Christy, Amy, Jeremy. Student, Columbia Union Coll., 1973, Kettering Coll. of Med. Arts, 1971; BS, Loma Linda U., 1976, MD. Diplomate Am. Bd. Med. Examiners, Am. Bd. Radiology, Am. Bd. Vascular and Interventional Radiology. Resident in radiology Loma Linda U., Calif., 1978-81, asst. prof. radiology, 1983-84, pres. house staff assn., 1980; fellow in orthopedic radiology Hosp. for Spl. Surgery Cornell U. Med. Ctr., NYC, 1981-82; fellow in interventional radiology Johns Hopkins U. Hosp., Balt., 1982-83; assoc. prof. Wright State U.; mem. staff Kettering (Ohio) Med. Ctr., 1984—2002, vice chmn. dept. radiology, 1985-87, chmn., 1988-95; pres. Patient First Imaging Network, 1994-95, med. dir., 1996-98; radiologist, mem. med. staff Hilton Head Regional Med. Ctr., 1999—, med. dir. dept. radiology, 2007—. Pres. Kettering Radiologists, Inc., 1987-95, 97-99, Alumni Assn. Spring Valley Acad., 1987-89, Housestaff Assn. Loma Linda Univ., 1980-81; bd. dirs. Spring Valley Acad., chmn. fin. mgmt. com., 1998-99; vol. radiology edn. program Micronesia, 1998-2004; med. dir. Carolina Conf. Seventh Day Adventist, 2006—. Contbr. articles on radiology to profl. jours. Bd. dirs. Seventh Day Adventist Ch., Kettering, Ohio, Hilton Head Island, SC. Recipient Philip Wilson award Hosp. Spl. Surgery, 1982, Cert. of merit Am. Roentgen Ray Soc., 1983, Disting. Alumnus award Kettering Coll. Med. Arts, 1990; named Physician of Yr., Hilton Head Regional Med. Ctr., 2006. Mem.: Beufort County Med. Soc., Miami Valley Radiol. Soc. (pres. 1994), Soc. of Interventional Radiology, Radiol. Soc. N.Am., AMA, Alpha Omega Alpha (award). Republican. Adventist. Avocations: golf, travel, watersports. Office: Hilton Head Hosp Dept Radiology PO Box 22886 Hilton Head Island SC 29925-2886 Office Phone: 843-689-8442. Personal E-mail: bobhewes@aol.com.

HEWITSON, WILLIAM CRAIG, physician, career officer; b. Park City, Utah, July 4, 1961; s. William Glenn and Darlene Marie Hewitson; m. children: William Brent, Staci Anne, Andrew Craig. BA with honors, U. Utah, 1986; MD, USUHS, 1991; MPH, Johns Hopkins U., 1995; BS, U. NY, 1995; MHA, Baylor U., 2006. Diplomate Am. Bd. Preventive Medicine. Officer U.S. Army, advanced through grades to lt. col., 1986; transitional intern Fitzsimons Army Med. Ctr., Aurora, Colo., 1991—92; 2d brigade surgeon 7th Inf. Divsn., Ft. Ord, Calif., 1992—93, divsn. surgeon Ft. Lewis, Wash., 1993—94; resident in general preventive medicine Walter Reed Army Inst. Rsch., Washington, 1994—96; chief injuries and occupation illnesses U.S. Army Ctr. for Health Promotion and Preventive Medicine, Aberdeen Proving Grounds, Md., 1996—98; chief preventive medicine divsn. Gen. Leonard Wood Army Cmty. Hosp., Ft. Leonard Wood, Mo., 1998—2000; healthcare adminstrv. fellow Baylor U., Ft. Sam Houston, Tex., 2000—02; chief epidemiology and disease surveillance Brooke Army Med. Ctr., Ft. Sam Houston, Tex., 2002—03; chief cmty. health practices br. Army Med. Dept. Ctr. and Sch., Ft. Sam Houston, Tex., 2003—06; cons. to surgeon gen. for nuclear, biol. and chem. surety medicine U.S. Army Med. Command, Ft. Sam Houston, Tex., 2006—. Dir. The Preventive Health Care Mgmt. Group, Salt Lake City, 1996-97; cons. Med. Adv. Sys., Owings, Md., 1995-98. Contbr. articles to profl. jours. Advancement chmn. Big Piney dist., Boy Scouts Am., Waynesville, Mo., 1999, Four Rivers dist. health and safety com., 1998, Pack com. chmn., Ft. George G. Meade, 1995-97, health and safety com. Eagle dist., 2001-02; missionary, Argentina, 1980-82; mem. St. Thomas Episcopal Ch., San Antonio, Tex. Fellow Am. Coll. Preventive Medicine; mem. AMA (Physician Recognition award 1997, 2000, 03, 06), Assn. Mil. Surgeons U.S., Masons. Avocations: running, exercise, flying, golf, tennis. Office: 2250 Stanley Rd #574 Fort Sam Houston TX 78234-2641 Business E-Mail: nbcdoc@satx.rr.com.

HEWITT, CONRAD W., former commissioner, accountant; b. Sheffield, Ill. BS in Finance, U. of Ill. at Urbana-Champaign, 1958. CPA. Joined Comml. Nation Bank, Peoria, Ill., 1958, Ernst & Ernst (now Ernst & Young), LA, 1962; mng. ptnr. Ernst & Young, Hawaii, 1972, mng. ptnr. Northwest, 1979, mng. ptnr. No. Calif. San Francisco, 1986—95; supt. of banks State of Calif., 1995—97; state commr. Calif. State Dept. Financial Inst., 1997—98. Bd. dir. N. Bay Bancorp, 1999—, Point W. Capital Corp., San Francisco, 2000, Varian Inc., 2003—, Spectrum Organic Prod., Inc., 2002—. Past pres. No. Calif. Boy Scouts Am.; mem. bus. advisory coun. U. of Ill. at Urbana-Champaign. Joined USAF, 1958—62. Mem.: Nat. Assn. Corp. Directors (founder, past pres.), AICPA. Republican. Office: Point West Capital Corporation 800 Powell St San Francisco CA 94108-2006

HEWITT, DENNIS EDWIN, financial executive; b. LA, Apr. 9, 1944; s. Robert Sherwood and Anna Marie (Linge) H.; m. Kathryn Dale Lefler, June 11, 1966; children— Denise, Dawn BS, UCLA, 1966; MBA, U. So. Calif., 1968. Fin. analyst Rockwell Internat., LA, 1967-72; div. contr. Arcata Co., NYC, 1972-76; v.p., contr. Weeden Co., NYC, 1976-78; sr. v.p., treas. Young & Rubicam Inc., NYC, 1979-88; treas. Omnicom Group Inc., NYC, 1988—; pres., CEO Omnicom Capital Inc., NYC, 2000—. Republican. Avocations: golf, tennis. Home: 1 Richmond Dr Old Greenwich CT 06870-1413 Office: Omnicom Capital Inc 1 E Weaver St Greenwich CT 06831-5146 Office Phone: 203-625-3010. Business E-Mail: dennis.hewitt@oci-ct.com.

HEWITT, DON S., television news producer; b. NYC, Dec. 14, 1922; s. Ely S. and Frieda (Pike) H.; children: Jeffrey, Steven, Jill, Lisa; m. Marilyn Berger, Apr. 14, 1979. Student, NYU, 1941; degree (hon.), Brandeis U., 1990; DFA (hon.), Am. Film Inst., 1993. War corr., World War II; prodr. 1st Kennedy-Nixon TV debate, 1960; exec. prodr. CBS Evening News with Walter Cronkite, 1960-65, 60 Minutes, 1968—2004, CBS News, 2004—. Delivered 1st ann. William S. Paley lectr. Mus. of TV and Radio, 1993. Recipient Paul White award Radio and TV News Dirs. Assn., 1987; Gold medal Internat. Radio and TV Soc., 1987, Broadcaster of Yr. award, 1980; Gold Baton award Columbia DuPont, 1988, Peabody award, 1989, Lowell Thomas Centennial award, 1992, 1st ann. Goldsmith award for Investigative Reporting, John F. Kennedy Sch. Govt. Harvard U., 1992, Lifetime award Prodrs. Guild Am., 1993, Founders award Internat. Coun. of TV Acad. Arts and Scis., 1995, Com. to Protect Journalists 9th Ann. Burton Benjamin Meml. award Internat. Press Freedom, 1999; named to Hall of Fame, NATAS, 1990. *Sometimes I think I am not sure of what I absolutely know is so.*

HEWITT, EMILY CLARK, federal judge, minister; b. Balt., May 26, 1944; d. John Frank and Margaret Genevieve (Gray) H. AB, Cornell U., 1966; MPhil, Union Theol. Sem., 1975; JD, Harvard U., 1978. Bar: Mass. 1978, US Dist. Ct. Mass. 1979, US Ct. Appeals (1st cir.) 1984, US Ct. Appeals (fed. cir.) 1999, US Supreme Ct. 2003; ordained priest Protestant Episcopal Ch. 1974. Adminstr. Upward Bound Progs. Cornell and Hofstra U., NYC, 1967-69; asst. min. St. Mary's Episcopal Ch., Manhattanville, NY, 1972-73; lectr. Union Theol. Sem., NYC, 1972-73, 74-75; asst. prof. Andover Newton Theol. Sch., Newton Centre, Mass., 1973-75; assoc. Hill & Barlow, Boston, 1978-85, ptnr., 1985-93; gen. counsel GSA, 1993-98; judge US Ct. Fed. Claims, Washington, 1998—. Co-author: Women Priests: Yes or No?, 1973; contbr. works in field. Bd. dirs. Mass. Found. for Humanities and Pub. Policy, South Hadley, 1983-89. Mem.: US Jud. Conf. (com. on fin. disclosure 2006—), Mass. Conveyancers Assn. (exec. com. 1990—93), New Eng. Women in Real Estate (dir. 1985—89), ABA (vice chair Bid Protest com. sect. pub. contract law 2000—02). Office: US Ct Fed Claims 717 Madison Pl NW Washington DC 20005

HEWITT, JACQUELINE N., astronomy educator; AB in Econs., Bryn Mawr Coll., 1980; PhD in Physics, MIT, 1986. Prof. physics MIT, 1989—; dir. MIT Kavli Inst. for Astrophysics and Space Rsch., 2002—. Recipient Annie Jump Cannon award in Astronomy, 1989; David and Lucille Packard fellow, 1990; Henry G. Booker prize award, 1993; Maria Goeppart-Mayer award Am. Phys. Soc., 1995; Alfred P. Sloan rsch. fellow, 1990. Fellow: Am. Phys. Soc. Office: MIT Dept Physics Room 37-241 Cambridge MA 02139 Business E-Mail: jhewitt@mit.edu.

HEWITT, JENNIFER LOVE, actress, singer; b. Waco, Tex., Feb. 21, 1979; d. Danny and Pat. Actor: (films) Munchie, 1992, Little Miss

Millions, 1993, Sister Act 2: Back in the Habit, 1993, Little Miss Millions, 1993, House Arrest, 1996, Trojan War, 1997, I Know What You Did Last Summer, 1997, Can't Hardly Wait, 1998, Telling You, 1998, Zoomates (voice), 1998, I Still Know What You Did Last Summer, 1998, The Suburbans, 1999, Heartbreakers, 2001, The Devil and Daniel Webster, 2001, The Tuxedo, 2002, Garfield: The Movie, 2004, Garfield: A Tale of Two Kitties, 2006, (TV series) Kids Inc., 1989-91, Shaky Ground, 1992, The Byrds of Paradise, 1994, McKenna, 1994-95, Party of Five, 1995-99, Ghost Whisperer, 2005-, (TV films) The Audrey Hepburn Story, 2000, 100 Greatest Love Songs, 2002, A Christmas Carol, 2004; actor, prodr.: (films) If Only, 2004, (TV series) Time of Your Life, 1999-2000; actor, co-exec. prodr.: (TV movies) The Audrey Hepburn Story, 2000, In the Game, 2004, A Christmas Carol, 2004, (voice) The Magic 7, 2006. Prodr. (films) One Night, 2002. Singer: (albums) Let's Go Bang, 1995, Jennifer Love Hewitt, 1996, Love Songs, 1998, BareNaked, 2002. Office: William Morris Agy 151 S El Camino Dr Beverly Hills CA 90212-2775

HEWITT, JOHN R., lawyer; b. Pitts., July 13, 1944; BA, John Carroll Univ., 1966; JD, Cleve. State Univ., 1974; LLM, Georgetown Univ., 1987. Bar: Ohio 1974, DC 1981, US Dist. Ct. (so. dist) Ohio 1982, US Dist. Ct. DC 1982. Trial atty. Ohio Ct. of Claims Def. Sect., 1975—77; asst. atty. gen. State of Ohio, Columbus, 1975—80; chief trial atty. Ohio Divsn. Securities, 1977—80; and gen. counsel Ohio Pub. Employees Retirement Sys., 1977—80; staff atty., trading, mkts. br., SEC, divsn. enforcement, Washington, 1980—82, sr. counsel, change of corp. ownership br., 1982—86; atty. Tyler Cooper & Alcorn, New Haven, 1986—89; v.p., assoc. gen. counsel Shearson Lehman Brothers, NYC, 1989—91, 1st v.p., assoc. gen. counsel, 1991—93; sr. v.p., assoc. gen. counsel Lehman Brothers, NYC, 1993—95; counsel Mayer, Brown, Rowe & Maw LLP, NYC, 1995—2006; ptnr. McCarter & English LLP, NYC, 2006—. Contbr. articles to profl. journals. Recipient Fin. Netnews Internet Compliance Person of the Yr. award, 1998. Office: McCarter & English LLP 245 Park Ave 27th Fl New York NY 10167 E-mail: jhewitt@mccarter.com.

HEWITT, KAREN PECKHAM, prosecutor; b. 1964; Grad., U. Calif. Berkeley, 1986; JD, U. San Diego Sch. Law, 1989. Lawyer McInnis, Fitzgerald, Rees, Sharkey, and McIntyre, San Diego, 1989—92; trial atty., litig. team leader, Constl. Spl. Torts Sect., Civil Divsn. US Dept. Justice, 1992—2000, asst. US atty. (so. dist) Calif., 2000—03, dep. chief civil divsn. (so. dist.) Calif, 2003—06, exec. asst. US atty. (so. dist.) Calif., 2006—07, interim US atty. (so. dist.) Calif. San Diego, 2007—. Office: US Atty's Office 880 Front St Rm 6293 San Diego CA 92101 Office Phone: 619-557-5610. Office Fax: 619-557-5782. E-mail: karen.hewitt@usdoj.gov.*

HEWITT, LESTER L., lawyer; b. Houston, Mar. 11, 1942; BSME, U. Houston, 1965, LLB cum laude, 1968. Bar: Tex. 1968. Examiner U.S. Patent Office, 1968-69; atty. Pravel, Hewitt, Kimball & Krieger, Houston, 1971-98; ptnr., co-head intellectual property practice nationally Akin Gump, Strauss, Hauer & Feld LLP, Houston. Assoc. prof. engring. law U. Houston, 1973-80. Mem. Am. Intellectual Property Law Assn. (treas. 1985-88), Houston Intellectual Property Law Assn. (pres. 1991-92), Order of the Barons, Phi Delta Phi, Pi Tau Sigma, Tau Beta Pi, Omicron Delta Kappa. Office: Akin Gump Strauss Hauer & Feld LLP 44th fl 1111 Louisiana St Houston TX 77002 Office Phone: 713-220-5851. Business E-Mail: lhewitt@akingump.com.

HEWITT, LLEYTON GLYNN, professional tennis player; b. Adelaide, Australia, Feb. 24, 1981; s. Glynn and Cherilyn; m. Bec Cartwright, July 21, 2005; 1 child, Mia Rebecca. Profl. tennis player (ATP), 1998—. Mem. Australian Davis Cup Team, 1999—. Global amb. Special Olympics, 2002—. Named Most Popular South Australian Athlete, 2001—03, Male Athlete of the Yr., Australian Sports Awards, 2002, Sportsman of the Yr., GQ (Australia), 2003, Young Australian of Yr., 2003. Achievements include winning US Open, 2001, Wimbledon, 2002; winning doubles (with Max Mirnyi), US Open, 2000; winner of 26 career singles titles, 2 doubles titles, ATP Tour; being a member of Australian Davis Cup Championship Team, 1999. Avocations: golf, Australian Rules Football. Office: Octagon 1751 Pinnacle Dr Ste 1500 Mc Lean VA 22102*

HEWITT, PAUL BUCK, lawyer; b. St. Louis, July 27, 1949; s. John York and Kathryn Louise (Buck) H.; m. Marla Ivy Zimmers, Feb. 17, 1985; children: Anna Ruth, Rachel Elizabeth. BA in Econs., Northwestern U., 1971; JD cum laude, U. Wis., 1974. Bar: D.C. 1979, Wis. 1974. Law clk. to chief justice Wis. Supreme Ct., Madison, 1974-75; atty. Bureau of Competition FTC, Washington, 1975-78; assoc. Akin Gump Strauss Hauer and Feld, Washington, 1978-82, ptnr., 1983—. Articles editor Wis. Law Rev., 1973—74. Mem. ABA, D.C. Bar, Wis. Bar Assn. Office: Akin Gump Strauss Hauer and Feld LLP 1333 New Hampshire Ave NW Washington DC 20036-1564 Office Phone: 202-887-4120. Business E-Mail: phewitt@akingump.com.

HEWITT, RUTH PRICE, retired librarian, elementary school educator; b. Washington, May 17, 1948; d. Irby Lee Price and June Helen (Garrison) Price Kurze; m. Stephen Allen Hewitt, Oct. 17, 1981. BA in Elem. Edn., Newberry Coll., SC, 1970; MLS, U. SC, Columbia, 1987; postgrad., Clemson U., SC, 1972, postgrad., 1976, LaVerne Coll., Calif., 1971, Furman U., Greenville, SC, 1978. Tchr. Laurel Creek Elem. Sch., Mauldin, SC, 1970—71, Sue Cleveland Elem. Sch., Piedmont, SC, 1971, Alexander Elem. Sch., Greenville, SC, 1971—73, Haynsworth Pvt. Sch., Greenville, 1974—77; sub. tchr. Prince Georges Co. Schs., Upper Marlboro, Md., 1973—74; sub. tchr. Trinity Luth. sch. Greenville Co. Pub. Sch., 1977—80; libr., media specialist Ambler Elem. Sch., Pickens, SC, 1980—83; ret., 1983. Sch. rep. Assn. Classroom Tchrs., 1972—73. Author parent enrichment program for SC pub. schs. Chmn. tenant adv. com. Breckinridge Apts., 1976; vol. Alexander Elem., 2002—07, Laurel Creek Elem. Sch., 2001; sec. sch. bd. Our Saviour Luth. Ch., Greenville, 1982—85. Pres. scholar, Newberry Coll., 1967—68. Mem.: Kappa Delta (chaplain 1968—69). Republican.

HEWITT, SARAH NICHOLE, educational consultant, researcher; b. Monroe, Wis., Nov. 20, 1980; d. James Daryl and Marsha Elaine Hewitt. BS in Biology, U. Miami, 2003, MS in Edn., 2005. With Sunshine Ace Hardware, Dunedin, Fla., 1999—2002; asst. to CEO Kane's Ace Hardware, Homosassa Springs, 2001—04; intern Helen Ellis Meml. Hosp. Emergency Rm., Tarpon Springs, 2002; rsch. asst. dept. pediatrics U. Miami, Coral Gables, 2002—03; intern Orthop. Specialists, Palm Harbor, 2000; rsch. asst. office spl. edn. U. Miami, 2000—05; tchr. Chgo. Pub. Schs., 2005—. Rsch. cons. office spl. edn. U. Miami, 2000—05; cons. Kane's Ace Hardware, Homosassa Springs, 2001—. Site leader Habitat for Humanity, Miami, 1999—2001; vol. Helen Ellis Meml. Hosp., Tarpon Springs, 2002—02; mem. v.p. adv. com. U. Miami, 2002—03; mem., vol. Miami Children's Hosp., 1999—2003; co-chair FunDay U. Miami, 1999—2003. Mem.: Coun. Exceptional Children, Pi Lambda Theta. Roman Catholic. Avocations: soccer, community service, travel, hiking, camping. Office: 1949 Spanish Oaks DR N Palm Harbor FL 34683 Office Phone: 727-560-3087. Personal E-mail: sarahnhewitt@gmail.com.

HEWITT, THOMAS FRANCIS, hotel executive; b. Marblehead, Mass., Dec. 7, 1943; s. Ralph Augustine and Shirley Elizabeth (Morris) H.; m. Sharyn Ann Holleran, June 11, 1968; 1 son, Sean Thomas. BBA, Bryant Coll., 1967; D (hon.), Johnson and Wales U. Gen. mgr. Sheraton LaGuardia, NYC, 1973-74; gen. mgr. Sheraton Heights Hotel, Hasbrouck Heights, N.J., 1974-75, Sheraton Plaza Hotel, Chgo., 1975-78; v.p., gen. mgr., area mgr. The Sheraton-Boston Hotel (The Sheraton Corp.), Boston, 1978-81; v.p., gen. mgr. Sheraton New Orleans Hotel, 1981, sr. v.p., gen. mgr., area mgr., 1983—; pres. Sheraton Corp. N.Am., 1983-85; exec. v.p. through pres., COO The Continental Cos., 1985—98; chmn., CEO Interstate Hotels Inc., 1999—2002; dir. Interstate Hotels & Resorts, 2002—05, CEO, 2005—. Chmn. Interstate Hotels Corp., Pitts., 1999. Mem. aviation com. New Orleans C. of C.; mem. Coconut Grove C. of C., Dade County's Beacon Coun. Recipient Lawson A. Odde award, Am. Hotel and Lodging Assn., 2001. Mem. Hotel Sales Mgrs. Assn., Greater New Orleans Hotel-Motel Assn. (dir.), Am. Hotel and Motel Assn. (vice chmn. internat. travel com.). Roman Catholic. Office: Interstate Hotels & Resorts 4501 N Fairfax Dr Arlington VA 22203

HEWITT, VIVIAN ANN DAVIDSON (MRS. JOHN HAMILTON HEWITT JR.), retired librarian; b. New Castle, Pa., Feb. 17, 1920; d. Arthur Robert and Lela Luvada (Mauney) Davidson; m. John Hamilton Hewitt, Jr., Dec. 26, 1949; 1 son, John Hamilton III. AB with honors, Geneva Coll., 1943, LHD, 1978; BSLS, Carnegie Mellon U., 1944; postgrad., U. Pitts., 1947-48. Sr. asst. libr. Carnegie Libr., Pitts., 1944-49; instr., libr. Sch. Libr. Sci. Atlanta U., Atlanta U., 1949-52; with Readers Reference Svc., Crowell-Collier Pub. Co., NYC, 1953-55; libr. Rockefeller Found., NYC, 1955-63; librarian Carnegie Endowment Internat. Peace, NYC, 1963-83; librarian Mexican Agrl. Program, Rockefeller Found., summer 1958; dir. libr. and info. svcs. Katherine Gibbs Sch., NYC, 1984-86; reference asst. Coun. on Fgn. Rels., 1986-89. Lectr. spl. librarianship at grad. schs. of L.S. and info. throughout U.S. and Can., 1968-88; condr. profl. seminars Am. Mgmt. Assn., 1968-69, UN Inst. Tng. and Rsch., 1973, 74, Grad. Sci. Libr. and Info. Sci., Rutgers U., 1986; mem. faculty Grad. Sch. Libr. and Info. Sci., U. Tex., Austin, summer 1985; SLA rep. to Internat. Fedn. Libr. Assns., 1970-73, 73-75, 75-77; mem. nat. adv. com. Ctr. for the Book, Libr. of Congress, 1979-84; mem. adv. bd. Who's Who Among African Ams., 1975—. Contbr. chpt. to: The Black Librarian in America, 1970, What Black Librarians Are Saying, 1972, New Dimensions for Academic Library Service, 1975, A Century of Service, 1976, Handbook of Black Librarianship, 1977, 2d edit., 2000, The Black Librarian in America Revisited, 1994, Notable Black American Men, 1999. Nat. historian Northeasterners, Inc., 1996—; docent Cathedral of St. John the Divine, 1983—; bd. dirs. Graham-Windham, 1967, sec., 1980—87; bd. dirs. Laymen's Club, Cathedral Ch. of St.John the Divine, 1975—82, sec., 1986—93. Recipient Outstanding Cmty. Svc. awards, United Fund N.Y., 1965—77, Disting. Alumna award, U. Pitts.-Carnegie Mellon U. Alumni Assn., 1978, Merit award, Carnegie Mellon U. Alumni Assn., 1979, Leadership award, Carnegie Mellon U. Black Alumni, 2001. Mem.: ALA (Disting. Svc. to Librarianship award Black Caucus 1978, Leadership in Profession award Black Caucus 1992, Spirit Ctr. award 2005), Jack and Jill Am., Inc. (ea. regional dir. 1967—69), Spl. Librs. Assn. (rep. to Pacem in Terris Convocation 1965, rep. to White House Conf. Internat. Coop. Yr. 1965, pres. N.Y. chpt. 1970—71, nat. pres. 1978—79, Hall of Fame 1984, Leadership award 2001), Am. Soc. Order of St. John, Pierians, Inc. (hon.), Alpha Kappa Alpha, Tower Soc. Geneva Coll. Democrat. Episcopalian. Home: 862 West End Ave New York NY 10025-4959 Personal E-mail: jhh2nyc@aol.com.

HEWLETT, JAMIE, graphics designer, animator, cartoonist; b. England, Apr. 3, 1968; Illustrator Atomtan, Deadline mag., 1988—96; co-founder & animator Gorillaz, 1998—. Co-creator & artist (comics) Tank Girl, 1988—96, artist 2000 AD, 1990—91; co-author: (films) Tank Girl, 1995; dir.: (films) Gorillaz Phase One: Celebrity Take Down, 2002, Gorillaz Phase Two: Slowboat to Hades, 2006; with Gorillaz (albums) Gorillaz, 2001, Laika Come Home, 2002, Demon Days, 2005 (Billboard Top Electronic Album, 2005), (songs) Clint Eastwood, 2001 (2 MTV Europe awards for Best Dance Act & Best Song, 2001), El Manana, 2005 (mtvU Woodie award for Best Animated Video, 2006), Feel Good Inc., 2005 (2 MTV Video Music awards for Best Spl. Effects & Breakthrough Video, 2005, Grammy award for Best Pop Collaboration with Vocals, 2006), Dare, 2005. Co-recipient Best Group award, MTV Europe Awards, 2005, Ivor Novello Songwriter of Yr. award (with Damon Albarn), Brit. Acad. Songwriters & Composers, 2006; named Top Electronic Artist, Billboard, 2005; recipient Designer of Yr. award, Brit. Design Mus., 2006.*

HEWLETT, JOYCELYN JANICE, lawyer; b. Basseterre, Saint Christopher-Nevis, July 2, 1964; d. James Stanley and Sarah H.; 1 child: Nyah. BA, U. V.I., Charlotte Amalie, 1986; JD, Howard U., 1992. Bar: Md. 1992, D.C. 1993, Virgin Islands 1995, U.S. Dist. Ct. (D.C. dist.) 1993, U.S. Dist. Ct. (Virgin Islands) 1995. News reporter intern Ft. Myers (Fla.) News-Press, 1984; news reporter, features editor V.I. Daily News, St. Thomas, 1985-89; law clk. Dudley Topper Feuerzeig, St. Thomas, 1990; legal intern D.C. Superior Ct., 1990-91; assoc. Bryan Cave, Washington, 1992-94; law clk. V.I. Territorial Ct., St. Thomas, 1994-96; atty. U.S. Atty, St. Thomas, V.I. Dept. Justice. Mordecai Wyatt Johnson Meml. Scholar Howard U., 1991. Mem. ABA, Nat. Bar Assn. (Greater Washington Area chpt.), V.I. Bar Assn (pres.-elect 2006-07). Office: Virgin Island Dept Justice 6040 Castle Coakley Christiansted VI 00820-5203

HEWLETT, RICHARD GREENING, historian; b. Toledo, Feb. 12, 1923; s. Timothy Younglove and Gertrude Josephine (Greening) H.; m. Marilyn Eloise Nesper, Sept. 6, 1946. Student, Dartmouth, 1941-43, Bowdoin Coll., 1943-44; MA, U. Chgo., 1948, PhD, 1952. Intelligence specialist USAF Hdqrs., Washington, 1951-52; reports analyst AEC, Washington, 1952-57, chief historian, 1957-75, ERDA, Washington, 1975-77, U.S. Dept. Energy, 1977-80; sr. assoc., sr. v.p., chmn. bd. History Assoc., Inc., Rockville, Md., 1980—. Regents' lectr. U. Calif., 1982; historiographer Episcopal Diocese of Washington, 1978-2005, also Washington Cathedral, 1978—, honorary canon, 2003-; chmn. fed. govt. resource group Nat. Coordinating Com. for Promotion of History, 1977-81; mem. U.S. Del. 2d UN Internat. Conf. on Peaceful Uses Atomic Energy, 1958. Author: Jessie Ball du Pont, 1992, The Foundation Stone: Henry Yates Satterlee and the Creation of Washington National Cathedral, 2007; co-author: The New World, 1939-46, 1962, Atomic Shield, 1947-52, 1969, Nuclear Navy, 1946-52, 1974, Atoms for Peace and War, 1953-61, 1989. Served with USAAF, 1943-46. Recipient David D. Lloyd prize Harry S. Truman Libr. Found., 1970; Distinguished Service award AEC, 1973. Mem. Am. Hist. Assn., Orgn. Am. Historians (Richard W. Leopold prize 1970), Soc. History Tech., Hist. Soc. Episc. Ch., Nat. Coun. Pub. History, Soc. for History in Fed. Govt. (v.p. 1983-85, Henry Adams prize 1990, Franklin D. Roosevelt award 1994), Cosmos Club. Episcopalian. Office: History Assocs Inc 300 N Stonestreet Ave Rockville MD 20850 Home Phone: 301-530-3359. E-mail: rhewlett6@cs.com.

HEWLETT, WALTER B., application developer; b. Washington, June 23, 1944; s. William Hewlett. BA in Physics, Harvard U., 1966; MA in Engring., Stanford U., 1968, MA in Ops. Rsch., 1973, PhD in Music, 1980. Founder, dir. Ctr. for Computer Assisted Rsch. in Humanities, Stanford U., 1984—; mem. Humanities and Sci. Council Stanford U., 1990—, adv. bd. mem. Inst. for Econ. Policy Rsch., 1990—, mem. Libraries and Academic Info. Resources Adv. Council, 1992—2000, former adv. bd. mem. Ctr. for Study of Language and Info., hon. co-chair Think Again fundraising tour, 2000—01, consulting prof., music dept. Bd. dirs. Hewlett-Packard, 1987—2002, Agilent, 1999—; chmn. bd. dirs. Vermont Telephone. Trustee, now chmn. William & Flora Hewlett Found., 1966—; trustee Stanford U., 2003—, William R. Hewlett Revocable Trust, Packard Humanities Inst., Stanford Theatre Found.; mem. bd. of overseers Harvard U., 1997—2003; bd. dirs. Public Policy Inst. of Calif., 1998—, Flora Family Found., 2005—. Office: William and Flora Hewlett Found 2121 Sand Hill Rd Menlo Park CA 94025

HEWLETT-KIERSTEAD, NANCY CARRICK, psychologist, educator; b. Schenectady, Feb. 19, 1927; d. Clarence Wilson and Mary Stephens (Carrick) Hewlett; m. Andrzej T. Romer, June 19, 1952 (div. 1969); children: Jan Edward, Anna Louise, Mary Helena; m. Henry A. Kierstead, July 26, 1981 (dec. Feb. 1990). BFA, Cornell U., 1949; MA (univ. fellow), U. Mich., 1952; PhD (univ. fellow), U. Conn., 1972. Registered clin. psychologist. Tchr. art Thomaston (Conn.) H.S., 1960-63; freelance artist, potter, 1962-67; assoc. prof. psychology Eastern Conn. State U., Willimantic, 1969-84, ret., 1984; clin. psychologist Effective Coping Strategies, Ill., Conn., 1982-91; writer, 1987—. Author: The Green Ribbon, 1997. Asst. clk. Storrs (Conn.) monthly meeting Soc. of Friends, 1978-80, clk., 1980. Mem. ACLU, ADL, Hemlock Soc., Choice in Dying, Framingham (Mass.) Friends Mtg. Home: PO Box 185 Waban MA 02468-0002

HEWSON, PAUL DAVID See BONO

HEXTALL, RON, professional sports team executive, former professional hockey player; b. Winnipeg, Man., May 3, 1964; m. Diane H.; children: Kristen, Bretton. Goalie Phila. Flyers, 1986—89, 1994—99, Quebec Nordiques, 1992-93; with NY Islanders, 1993—94; dir. player pers. Phila. Flyers; asst. gen. mgr. LA Kings, 2006—; gen. mgr. Manchester Monarchs, 2006—. Mem. AHL All-Star team, 1985-86, NHL All-Star first team, 1986-87, NHL All-Rookie team, 1986-87; player NHL All-Star game, 1988. Recipient Vezina Trophy (NHL top goaltender), 1987, Conn Smythe Trophy (Stanley Cup Playoff Most Valuable Player), 1987, Dudley (Red) Garrett Meml. trophy, 1985-86; named Rookie of the Year Sporting News, 1986-87. Office: LA Kings Ste 3100 1111 S Figueroa St Los Angeles CA 90015

HEXTER, RALPH J., academic administrator, literature educator; AB, Harvard U.; BA, MA, Corpus Christi Coll., U. Oxford; PhD, MPhil, Yale U. Prof. classics and comparative lit., dir. grad. program in comparative lit. U. Colo., Boulder; prof. Classics Dept. Yale U., New Haven; prof. classics and comparative lit. U. Calif., Berkeley, 1995—2005, dean Coll. Arts and Humanities, exec. dean Coll. Letters and Sci.; pres. Hampshire Coll., Amherst, Mass., 2005—. Vis. lectr. Folger Inst., Washington; fellow Villa I Tatti, Harvard Ctr. for Studies in Italian Renaissance, Florence, Italy. Author: Equivocal Oaths and Ordeals in Medieval Literature, 1975, Ovid and Medieval Schooling: Studies in Medieval School Commentaries on Ovid's Ars Amatoria, Epistulae ex Ponto and Epistulae Heroidum, 1986, A Guide to the Odyssey: A Commentary on the English Translation of Robert Fitzgerald, 1993; co-author (with Daniel Selden): Innovations of Antiquity; contbr. articles to profl. jours. Office: Office of Pres First Fl Rm 110, The Charles W Co 893 West Street Amherst MA 01002 Office Phone: 413-559-2251. Office Fax: 413-559-5584.*

HEY, NANCY HENSON, retired educational administrator; b. Cleve., Apr. 1, 1935; d. Henry Brumback Henson and Isabelle (Smock) Selverstone; m. Robert Pierpont Hey, July 4, 1959; 1 child, Julie Dean. AB, Bates Coll., 1957; MS in Edn., Bank Street Coll. Edn., 1961. Cert. advanced profl. in early childhood nursery thru grade 3 Md. Primary tchr. Concord Pub. Sch., Mass., 1958-59; tchr. The Potomac Sch., McLean, Va., 1959-60, Galloway Sch., Atlanta, 1968-69; head tchr. Beauvoir Sch. Nursery Dept., Washington, 1969-70; supr. student tchr. U. Md. Coll. Edn., Coll. Pk., Md., 1973-76, Tufts U., Medford, Mass., 1978-79; head tchr. Newton Ctr. Day Care Ctr., 1980-81, Cmty. Child Devel. Ctr., Peabody, Mass., 1981-82; dir. Greater Lawrence YWCA Children's Ctr., Mass., 1982-86; tchr. Prince George's County Pub. Sch., Md., 1986-88; dir. Child Devel. Ctr., FTC, Washington, 1988-92; dir. Chevy Chase Plz. Children's Ctr., Washington, 1992-93; assoc. dir. Ctr. for Young Children, U. Md., Md., 1994—2007; ret., 2007. Supr. student tchrs. Simmons Coll., Boston, 1965-67; teaching asst. to head of lower sch.Shady Hill Sch., Cambridge, Mass., 1960-61; mem. task force com. Region III Dept. of Social Svcs., Middleton, Mass., 1984-86; bd. dirs. Greater Lawrence Coun. for Children, 1984-86. Mem.: Nat. Coalition for Campus Children's Ctrs. (pres. DC Metro chpt. 2004—06), Dirs. Exch., Congressional and Fed. Child Care Dir. Assn. (sec. 1990—92), Nat. Assn. Edn. of Young Children. Home: 10908 Candlelight Ln Potomac MD 20854-2756 Personal E-mail: nhey@umd.edu.

HEY, RICHARD NOBLE, marine geophysicist; b. Lebanon, Tenn., June 2, 1947; s. Richard and Miriam (Jennings) Hey; m. Donna Dale, 2003; 1 child, Dylan. BS, Calif. Inst. Tech., Pasadena, 1969; PhD, Princeton U., NJ, 1975. Rsch. assoc. U. Tex., Galveston, 1974-75; from asst. to geophysicist Hawaii Inst. Geophysics, Honolulu, 1975-80; from asst. to assoc. rsch. geophysicist Scripps Inst. Oceanography, La Jolla, Calif., 1981-86; prof. U. Hawaii, Honolulu, 1986—. Adj. lectr. Scripps Inst. Oceanography, La Jolla, 1983—90. Fellow: Am. Geophys. Union, Geol. Soc. Am.; mem.: AAAS. Office: U Hawaii at Manoa Inst Geophysics Planetology Honolulu HI 96822 Office Phone: 808-956-8972. Business E-Mail: hey@soest.hawaii.edu.

HEY, ROBERT PIERPONT, retired editor; b. East Providence, RI, Jan. 24, 1935; s. Daniel Chase and Grace (Pierpont) H.; m. Nancy Henson, July 4, 1959; 1 dau., Julie. AB, Harvard U., 1955. Gen. assignment reporter, local edn. reporter Christian Sci. Monitor, Boston, 1960-64, asst. to Am. news editor, then asst. Am. news editor, 1964-67, S.E. U.S. corr., then Washington corr., 1967-76, asst. mng. editor, 1976-79, mng. editor features Boston, 1979-83, editorial writer, 1983-86, Washington Corr., 1986-91; mng. editor AARP Bull., 1991-2000; purchasing agt. Arkell Safety Bag Co., NYC, 1956-58; with public relations dept. U. Pitts., 1964. Served with AUS, 1958-60.

HEYBURN, JOHN GILPIN, II, federal judge; b. Boston, 1948; m. Martha Keeney, 1976. BA, Harvard U., 1970; JD, U. Ky., 1976. Ptnr. Brown, Todd & Heyburn, Louisville, 1976-92; judge US Dist. Ct. (we. dist.), Louisville, 1992—, chief judge, 2001—. Chmn. US Jud. Panel on Multidistrict Litig., 2007—. Mem. Budget Com. Jud. Conf.of US, 1994-04, chmn. 1997-04; chair Jefferson County Crime Commn.; mem. vis. com. U. Ky., 1980; active Leadership Louisville Found. With USAR, 1970-76. Mem. ABA, Ky. Bar Assn., Louisville Bar Assn., U. Ky. Coll. Law Alumni Assn. Office: US Dist Ct Gene Snyder US Courthouse 601 W Broadway Ste 239 Louisville KY 40202-2227

HEYDE, MARTHA BENNETT, psychologist; b. New Bern, NC, Jan. 31, 1920; d. George Spotswood and Katherine (McIntosh) Bennett; m. Ernest R. Heyde, Aug. 17, 1946. AB, Columbia U., 1941, MA, 1949, PhD, 1959. Instr. psychol. founds and svcs. Tchrs. Coll., Columbia U., NYC, 1957-59, rsch. assoc., 1960-70, cons., 1970-73. Contbg. author: (rsch. monograph) The Vocational Maturity of Ningh Grade Boys, 1960, Floundering and Trial After High Sch., 1967; co-author: Vocational Maturity During the High School Years, 1979. Mem. Barnard Coll. alumnae coun. Columbia U., 1956-61, 69—, pres. class, 1956-61, trustee, 1974-79, hon. vice chmn. Barnard Coll. Centennial, 1987-89. Mem. APA, Sigma Xi, Kappa Delta Pi, Pi Lambda Theta. Home: 530 E 23rd St Apt 8E New York NY 10010-5030

HEYDERMAN, ARTHUR JEROME, engineer, civilian military employee; b. Bklyn., Jan. 1, 1946; s. Herbert Robert and Sally (Baron) H.; m. Renee Linda Pearlman, July 4, 1967; children: Brian Douglas, Deborah Ann, Cathy Ruth. BS in Applied Math., Poly. Inst. Bklyn., 1966, MS in Applied Math., 1973; postgrad., Stevens Inst. Tech., 1982, Brookings Inst., 1992, Wharton Sch. Bus., U. Pa., 1993. Nuclear weapons engr. U.S. Army Armaments R&D Ctr., Picatinny Arsenal, N.J., 1971-83, asst. tech. dir., 1983-84, chief prodn. program planning, 1984, assoc. tech. dir., 1984-86; armaments rsch. and devel. prog. mgr. U.S. Army Armaments Munitions and Chem. Command, Rock Island, Ill., 1986-93, chief of rsch. devel., test and evaluation integration, 1993-94; chief improved armor engring. U.S. Army Armaments Rsch., Devel. and Engring. Ctr., Rock Island, Ill., 1994-96; chief armor engring. U.S. Armaments Rsch. Devel. & Engring. Ctr., Rock Island, Ill., 1996-98, chief arty. sys. & armor divsn., 1998—99; chief prodn. and logistics engring. support U.S. Armaments Rsch. Devel. and Engring. Ctr., Rock Island, Ill., 1999—2003; enterprise mgr. U.S. Army Armaments Rsch., Devel. and Engring. Ctr., Rock Island, 2003—04, assoc. dir. sys. engring., analysis and configuration mgmt., 2004—06, Rock Island site mgr., 2006—07. Bd. dirs., sec./treas., pres. Iowa-Ill. chpt. Am. Def. Preparedness Assn., Rock Island; lt. col. nuclear weapons officer USAR, Ft. Sheridan, Ill., 1989-93; pres. OPICON, Bettendorf, Iowa, 1989—; nat. coun. Am. Def. Preparedness Assn.; coun. mem. Quad-Cities Engring. and Sci. Coun.; adj. faculty U.S. Army Command and Gen. Staff Coll., Ft. Leavenworth, Kans., 1981-89, Scott C.C., 1997. Contbr. column to Rock Island Argus/Moline Dispatch; guest editor Quad Cities Times; contbr. tech. papers on weapons and weaponry assessment to profl. meetings. Pres., bd. dirs. Sussex County Jewish Ctr., Newton, N.J., 1979-86; fundraiser United Jewish Fedn., Davenport, Iowa, 1986-99; mem. Rock Island Arsenal Com. for Disabled, 1987-93, Quad Cities Coalition for Choice; dir. intake Quad City chpt. ACLU; mem. platform com. Scott County Dem. Ctrl. Com., 1994—; mem. 1st dist. Iowa Dem. Ctrl. Com., 1994—2003, 07—; mem. platform com. Iowa State Dem. Party; chmn. Quad Cities WWII Commemoration Com., 1995, Quad Cities Vietnam Wall Com., 1997, Quad Cities Korean War Commemoration Com., 2003; mem. Iowa Sesquecentennial Commemoration Com., 1995, Rock Island County, Ill. C. of C. Spkrs. Bur., 1996; bd. dirs. Jewish Fedn. of Quad Cities, 1996-99; funds distbn. panelist United Way of Quad Cities, 1999-2000, 07—; bd. dirs. Iowa Civil Liberties Union, 1997—2003, 07—, sec.-treas., 2004—05; bd. dirs. Iowa Civil Liberties Found., 1997—2005; mem. Scott County Foster Care Citizens Rev. Bd., 2000-01. Capt. U.S. Army, 1968-71, Vietnam; maj./lt. col. USAR, 1971-93. Decorated Bronze Star; Cross of Gallantry (Vietnam); named to Hon. Order St. Barbara, U.S. Army Field Arty. Assn.; recipient Civilian of Yr. award Fifth Region Assn. of the U.S. Army, 1998; recipient Nat. President's award, Women in Def., 2003. Mem. VFW, ACLU (nat. bd. dirs. 1998—), NAACP (bd. dirs. Quad Cities chpt. 1996-2001), U.S. Army Acquisitions Corps, U.S. Army Engr. Assn., Assn. U.S. Army (v.p. Ft. Armstrong chpt. 1993—, acting pres. chpt. 1996-97), Soc. Am. Mil. Engrs. (scholar 1966), Soc. Am. Mil. Comptrs., Federally Employed Women, Planned Parenthood (mem. cmty. coun.), Nat. Soc. Scabbard and Blade (chpt. v.p. 1965-66), Nat. Def. Indsl. Assn. (pres. Iowa Ill. chpt., Nat. Gold medal 2005, award for lifetime contbns. 2005, LTG Lawrence Skibble award for lifetime contbn. to nat. def. 2005), Res. Officers Assn., Women in Def., Poly. Alumni Assn. (pres. Quad City chpt. 1989—), Nat. Assn. Ret. Fed. Employees, Mensa, Intertel, Vietnam Vets. Jewish. Avocations: horticulture, art, bonsai, cooking, photography. Home: 1430 Grappler Ct Bettendorf IA 52722-1847 Business E-Mail: heydermana@mchsi.com.

HEYDON, PETER NORTHRUP, farmer, educator, philanthropist; b. Hackensack, NJ, Nov. 25, 1940; s. Clark A. and Elizabeth VanFleet (Northrup) H.; m. Henrietta M. Heydon, Aug. 24, 1968. BA, Princeton U., NJ, 1962; MA, U. Mich., Ann Arbor, 1963, PhD, 1970. Lectr. in humanities & English U. Mich., Ann Arbor, 1963-80, adj. prof., 1980-86. Chmn. Clements Library Assocs., Ann Arbor, 1970-2005; trustee Folger Shakespeare Libr., Washington D.C., 1986-99, Nat. Pub. Radio Found., 1994—; dir. Farrar, Straus & Giroux, NYC, 1970-94; pres. Browning Inst., NYC, 1971-85, Firenze, 1971-85; pres. Beacon Theatre Assocs., NYC, 1990-2006. Founder, bd. dirs. The Mosaic Found., 1989—. Mem. The Lotos Club, The Grolier Club, The Century Assn., Maitre, Commanderie de Bordeaux á Detroit, Commandeur Chevaliers du Tastevin. Avocations: restoration of classic and special interest automobiles, preservation of national register historic buildings, wine fraternities, horse breeding. Office: Heydon Washington St Prop 324 E Washington St PO Box 7801 Ann Arbor MI 48107-7801 Office Phone: 734-747-7070.

HEYDRICK, LINDA CAROL, consulting company executive, editor; b. Pomona, Calif., July 25, 1947; d. Robert Bruce and Wanda Georgine (Wellman) Middough; m. Stephen R. Bova, Jan. 20, 1968 (div. May 1981); children: Karen E., Lori L.; m. Allen L. Heydrick, Mar. 15, 1995. Student, El Camino Coll., Gardena, Calif., 1965-66. Sec. TRW, Inc., Manhattan Beach, Calif., 1967-68, USAF NCO Clubs, Mildenhall, England, 1968-70; adminstrv. asst. Prudential-Bache Securities, NYC, 1970-73, Tex. Instruments, Inc., Dallas, 1980-83; asst. to pres. Acclivus Corp., Dallas, 1983-85, mgr. design and prodn., 1985-88, mgr. ops., 1988-89, v.p. ops., 1989—. Cons. Digital Equipment Corp., Boston, 1984-89, coord. internat. translations of books, audiotapes and videotapes, 1993—. Editor: (books and videotapes) BASE for Sales Performance, 1984, Acclivus Sales Negotiation, 1985, The New BASE for Sales Excellence, 1989, Major Account Planning and Strategy, 1993, rev., 1996, Building on the BASE (award for best new tng. products Human Resource Exec.), 1993, R3 Service, (award for best new tng. product Human Resource Exec. 1998), 1997, Creating R3 Value, 2002; editor, pub. Denton Bible Ch., The Titus 2 Woman, More of Christ, 1993-. Mem.: ASTD, Instrnl. Sys. Assn. Republican. Avocations: christian studies, fine arts, design, performing arts. Office: Acclivus Corp 14500 Midway Rd Dallas TX 75244-3109

HEYER, JOHN HENRY, II, lawyer; b. Rochester, NY, May 4, 1946; s. Joseph Lester and Margaret Mary (Darcy) H.; m. Charla Ann Prewitt (dec.); children: Thomas, William, John III, Richard, Mary; m. Alenka Marija Lavrencic, 2004. BA, U. Colo., 1969; JD, U. Denver, 1972. Bar: Colo. 1973, U.S. Dist. Ct. Colo. 1973, N.Y. 1976, Pa. 1979, U.S. Dist. Ct. (we. dist.) N.Y. 1980, U.S. Supreme Ct. 1982; solicitor Law Soc. Eng. and Wales 2003. Atty. Texaco, Inc., Denver, 1973-75; sole practice Olean, NY, 1975—; agt. Commonwealth Land Title Inst. Co., 1982—. Pres. Northeastern Land Svcs., Inc., Olean, NY, 1982—; agt. Commonwealth Land Title Ins. Co., 1982—; v.p. Vector Capital Corp., Rochester, NY, 1985-87; chpt. 7 trustee we. dist. US Bankruptcy Ct., NY, 1986—. Editor: New York Oil and Gas Statutes, 1985, 2d edit. 2006. Asst. dist. atty. Cattaraugus County, Olean, 1978-81; bd. dirs. Olean YMCA, 1989-99, v.p. 1993-94, pres., 1994-99, pres. bd. trustees, 1999—; bd. dirs. Buffalo Philharm. Symphony Cir., v.p., 1993, pres., 1994-95; bd. dirs. Friends of Good Music, pres. 1994-95. Mem.: SAR, Ind. Oil and Gas Assn. NY (bd. dirs. 1986—, sec. 1986—87, v.p. 1988—), Energy and Mineral Law Found. (trustee 1984—, exec. com. 1994—95), Cattaraugus County Bar Assn. (sec.-treas. 1997, v.p. 1998, pres. 1999), Erie County Bar Assn., NY State Bar Assn. (real property sect., real property devel. com.), Selden Soc. Roman Catholic. Office: PO Box 588 201 N Union St Olean NY 14760-2738

HEYER, STEPHANIE, science educator; b. Phoenix, Nov. 16, 1968; adopted d. John Edward and Marietta Pace Heyer; life ptnr. Stephanie Gonzales, Mar. 27, 1999. BS in Ecology and Evolutionary Biology, U. Ariz., 1991; MA in Secondary Edn., Calif. State U., 2005. Cert. sci. tchr. Calif. Commn. Tchr. Credentialling, 1996. Naturalist intern Clemmie Gill Sch. Sci. and Conservation, Springville, Calif., 1991—93; sci. club presenter Sci. Adventures, Huntington Beach, Calif., 1993—94; mid. sch. sci. tchr. Long Beach Unified Sch. Dist., Calif., 1996—, beginning tchr. support and assessment program mentor tchr., 2001—03, 2005—06; gifted and talented edn. dept. head Stanford Mid. Sch., Long Beach, 2003—06; summer enrichment program tchr. Long Beach Unified Sch. Dist., 2003—; mentor tchr. for student tchr. Calif. State U., 2003—. Curriculum cons. and workshop presenter Long Beach Unifed Sch. Dist., 1998—; workshop presenter Calif. Assn. for the Gifted, 2003—04, Calif. Sci. Tchrs. Assn., 2004, Nat. Assn. for the Gifted, Utah, 2004, Greater L.A. Tchrs. of Sci. Assn., 2005, Nat. Sci. Tchr. Assn., 2006. Mem. Human Rights Campaign, 2003—05, Equality Calif., 2002—05. Mem.: Nat. Assn. for Gifted Children, Calif. Assn. for the Gifted, Nat. Sci. Tchr. Assn., Phi Kappa Phi Honor Soc. (recipeint chpt. scholarship 2004), Pi Lambda Theta Internat. Honor Soc. Christian. Avocations: reading, music, camping, travel, movies. Home Phone: 562-429-0611. Personal E-mail: scienceeduc8r@hotmail.com.

HEYER, STEVEN J., former hotel and beverage company executive; b. June 13, 1952; Former sr. v.p., mng. ptnr. Booz Allen & Hamilton, NYC; former pres., COO Young & Rubicam Advt. Worldwide; former pres., COO Turner Broadcasting Sys., Inc. subs. AOL Time Warner; former pres., COO Coca-Cola Ventures; pres., COO The Coca-Cola Co., Atlanta, 2002—04; CEO Starwood Hotels & Resorts Worldwide, Inc., White Plains, NY, 2004—07. Bd. dirs. Equifax Inc., Coca-Cola Enterprises, Inc., Coca-Cola FEMSA, Lazard Ltd., Internet Security Systems Inc., 2004—. Bd. advisors Amos Tuck Sch., Dartmouth Coll.; bd. dirs. Piedmont Hosp., Atlanta, Trinity Sch., Atlanta; bd. visitors Emory U., Atlanta; ret. chmn. bd. dirs. Cable Advt. Bur.; bd. dirs. Ad Coun.

HEYL, ALLEN VAN, JR., geologist; b. Allentown, Pa., Apr. 10, 1918; s. Allen Van and Emma (Kleppinger) H.; m. Maxine LaVon Hawke, July 12, 1945; children: Nancy Caroline, Allen David Van. BS in Geology, Pa. State U., 1941; PhD in Geology, Princeton U., 1950. Field asst. major regional exploration, govt. geologist Nfld. Geol. Survey, summers 1937-40, 42; jr. geologist U.S. Geol. Survey, Wis., 1943-45, asst. geologist Wis., 1945-47, assoc. geologist Wis., 1947-50, geologist Washington and Beltsville, Md., 1950-67, staff geologist Denver, 1968-90; cons. geologist, 1990—91. Disting. lectr. grad. coll. Beijing, China and Nat. Acad. Sci., 1988; disting. invited lectr. Internat. Assn. Genesis Ore Deposits 9th Symposium, Beijing, 1994; chmn. Internat. Commn. Tectonics of Ore Deposits. Contbr. numerous articles to profl. jours., chpts. to books and books. Fellow Instn. Minin and Metallurgy (Gt. Britain), Geol. Soc. Am., Am. Mineral Soc., Soc. Econ. Geologists, Inst. Genesis of Ore Deposits (hon., life), Geol. Soc. Wash., Colo. Sci. Soc., Rocky Mountain geol. Soc., Friends of Mineralogy (hon., life), Evergreen Naturalist Audubon Soc., Sigma Xi, Alpha Chi Sigma. Lutheran. Home: PO Box 1052 Evergreen CO 80437-1052

HEYLER, GROVER ROSS, retired lawyer; b. Manila, June 24, 1926; s. Grover Edwin and Esther Viola (Ross) H.; m. Caroline Yarbrough, Aug. 10, 1949; children: Richard Ross, Sue Louise, Randall Arthur BA, UCLA, 1949; LLB, U. Calif., Berkeley, 1952. Bar: Calif. 1953. Atty. Latham & Watkins, LA, 1952—93, chmn., corp. securities dept., 1967-89. Chmn. Nat. Alliance for Rsch. into Schizophrenia and Depression, NYC, 2002—04. Mem. Calif. Bar Assn. (com. on drafting Calif. corps. code 1971-75), Order of Coif, UCLA ALumni Assn. (bd. dirs. 1966-70, 1988-90), L.A. Country Club. Home: 491 Homewood Rd Los Angeles CA 90049-2713

HEYMAN, IRA MICHAEL, federal agency administrator, law educator, museum executive; b. NYC, May 30, 1930; s. Harold Albert and Judith (Sobel) H.; m. Therese Helene Thau, Dec. 17, 1950 (dec.); children: Stephen Thomas (dec.), James Nathaniel; m. Elizabeth Diringer Nelson, July 17, 2005. AB in Govt., Dartmouth Coll., 1951; JD, Yale U., 1956; LLD (hon.), U. Pacific, 1981, Hebrew Union Coll., 1984, U. Md., 1986, SUNY, Buffalo, 1990, Dartmouth Coll., 2001. Bar: NY 1956, Calif. 1961. Legis. asst. to U.S. Senator Ives, 1950-51; assoc. Carter, Ledyard & Milburn, NYC, 1956-57; law clk. to presiding justice U.S. Ct. Appeals (2d cir.), New Haven, 1957-58; chief law clk. to Supreme Ct. Justice Earl Warren, 1958-59; acting assoc. prof. law U. Calif., Berkeley, 1959-61, prof. law, 1961—93, prof. city and regional planning, 1966-93, prof. emeritus, 1993—, vice chancellor, 1974-80, chancellor, 1980-90, chancellor emeritus, 1990—; counselor to Sec. of Interior Dept. Interior, Washington, 1993-94; sec. Smithsonian Inst., Washington, 1994-99, sec. emeritus, 2000—; mem. Citizens' Stamp Adv. Com., 2000—. Vis. prof. Yale Law Sch., 1963—64, Stanford Law Sch., 1971—72; bd. dirs. Presidio Trust. Editor Yale Law Jour.; contbr. articles to profl. jours. Sec. Calif. adv. com. U.S. Commn. Civil Rights, 1962-67; trustee Dartmouth Coll., 1982-93, chmn., 1991-93, Smith Coll., 2004—; mem. Lawyers' Com. for Civil Rights under Law, 1977-95, Citizens Stamp Advisory Com., USPS, 2000-; chmn. exec. com. Nat. Assn. State Univs. and Land Grant Colls., 1986; bd. regents Smithsonian Instn., 1990-94; bd. dirs. Presidio Trust, 2000-04. 1st lt. USMC, 1951-53, capt. Res. ret Decorated chevalier Legion of Honor (France). Mem. Am. Acad. Arts and Sci. Office Phone: 510-642-1731. Business E-Mail: mheyman@law.berkeley.edu.

HEYMAN, JOSEPH MARTIN, gynecologist; b. Bklyn., May 21, 1942; s. Ezekiel and Elaine Olga (Adelman) H.; m. Laurel Ann Taylor, June 10, 1967; children: Eve Renata, Todd Sanford. BS, CCNY, 1963; MD, SUNY, Bklyn., 1967. Diplomate, Am. Bd. Ob.-Gyn. Intern USPHS Marine Hosp., Staten Island, NY, 1967-68; chief outpatient dept., venereal disease control officer USPHS Northern Navajo Indian Hosp., Shiprock, N.Mex., 1968-70; resident in ob.-gyn. Sinai Hosp., Balt., 1970-73; staff ob.-gyn. Women's Health Care, West Newbury, Mass., 1973—, former pres.; pres. med. staff Anna Jaques Hosp., Newburyport, Mass., 1990-92; ob.-gyn. private practice. Bd. dirs. Tufts Associated HMO, Waltham, Mass., 1986-96; exec. com. bd. trustees Anna Jaques Hosp., 1995-99; pres. Healthy Women and Babies, L.L.C.; mem. Health and Human Svcs. Practicing Physics Adv. Coun., 1999-2003; dir. Lower Merrimac Valley Physician Hosp. Orgn., 2001—; mem. steering com. Connecting for Health, 2003—; mem. bd. commrs. Joint Commn. on Accreditation Health Care Orgns., 2003—; dir. Joint Commn. Resources, 2006—. Contbr. articles to profl. pubs. Pres., West Newbury PTA, 1978; mem. adv. com. Physician Edn. Ctr. Found., 1996—. Fellow ACOG; mem. AMA (coun. on med. scis. 1996-2002, chair 2000-01, ho. dels. 1986—, accreditation program governing body 1997-2000, trustee 2002—, sec. 2005-06, chair-elect, 2007—), Mass. Med. Soc. (exec. bd. 1983—2004, spkr. ho. dels. 1992-94, v.p. 1994-95, pres.-elect 1995-96, pres. 1996-97), Whittier Ind. Practice Assn. (pres. 1985-95, exec. bd. 1985—). Democrat. Avocations: computers, reading, music, politics. Office: 24 Morrill Pl Amesbury MA 01913 Office Phone: 978-388-1259.

HEYMAN, LAWRENCE MURRAY, printmaker, painter; b. Washington, June 30, 1932; s. Philip I. and Gertrude B. H. BFA, Tyler Sch. Fine Arts, Temple U., 1954, BS in Edn., 1955; MFA, Am. U., 1972. Instr. fine arts in printmaking R.I. Sch. Design, 1967-69, asst. prof. fine arts and printmaking, 1972-79, dir. printmaking program, 1976-79; lectr. Am. U., 1971-72. Exhibited in one-man shows, Mickelson Gallery, Washington, 1966, 77, R.I. Sch. Design, 1969, 79, St. John's U., St. Paul, 1980, Mus. City of N.Y., 1984, Starr Gallery, Newton, Mass., 1985, Plum Gallery, Kensington, Md., 1986, 88, NIH, Bethesda, Md., 1990, Vets.' Meml. Auditorium, Providence, 1991; group shows including, Providence Art Club, (prize 1974, 76), Bibliotheque Nationale, Paris, 1977 (purchase honor 79), San Francisco Art Mus., 1977, Plum Gallery, Kensington, Md., 1985, 86, 89, Starr Gallery, Newton, Mass., 1991, Galerie Foret-Verte, Paris, 2004; represented in permanent collections Bibliotheque Nationale, Paris, Bklyn. Mus., Brooks Meml. Mus., Tenn., Mus. City of N.Y., Portland (Oreg.) Art Mus.; U.S. rep. Art in Embassies program exhbn., Istanbul, Turkey, 1976; Commd.: print edits. for Associated Am. Artists, N.Y.C., 1964, 68, 69, Antares Editions d'Art, Paris, 1970, 71, 72, Judith Selkowitz Fine Arts, N.Y.C., 1978; featured in book Painting the Town, 2000. Served with U.S. Army, 1955-57. Nominee and finalist for Nat. Arts medal Nat. Endowment for Arts, 1987; finalist 1989 Portrait Painting Competition Artist's Mag. Mem. Whitegate Features Syndicate Fine Arts. Office: 71 Faunce Dr Providence RI 02906-4805 Home Phone: 401-837-2151; Office Phone: 401-274-2149. Business E-Mail: staff@whitegatefeatures.com.

HEYMAN, MELVIN BERNARD, pediatric gastroenterologist; b. San Francisco, Mar. 24, 1950; s. Vernon Otto and Eve Elsie Heyman; m. Jody Ellen Switky, May 8, 1988. BA in Econs., U. Calif., Berkeley, 1972; MD, UCLA, 1976, MPH in Nutrition, 1981. Diplomate in pediatrics and pediatric gastroenterology Am. Bd. Pediatrics. Intern, resident L.A. County-U. So. Calif. Med. Ctr., 1976-79; fellow UCLA, 1979-81; asst. prof. U. Calif., San Francisco, 1981-88, assoc. prof., 1988-94, prof., 1994—, chief pediatric gastroenterology, hepatology and nutrition, 1990—, dir. tng. program i pediatric gastroenterology and nutrition, 1997—, Anita Ow Wing endowed chair, 2006—. Mem. cons. staff San Francisco Gen. Hosp., Scenic Gen. Hosp., Modesto, Calif.; assoc. dir. Pediatric IBD Consortium 2000—. Contbr. articles to profl. jours. Chmn. sci. adv. com. San Francisco chpt. Crohn's and Colitis Found. Am., 1987-94, bd. dirs., 1986-03; mem. City and County San Francisco Task Force on Nutrition and Phys. Activity for Children, 2003-04; bd. dirs. Nat. PTA, 2005-; chmn. bd. Inflammatory Bowel Diseas Summer Camp Found., 2005-. Recipient Investigator award, NIH-NIDDK, 2002—; rsch. grantee, Children's Liver Found., 1984—85, John Tung grantee, Am. Cancer Soc., 1985—89, NIH-NIDDK grantee, 1998—, UC Mexus project grantee. Mem.: Am. Bd. Pediatric Gastroenterology (chair sub-bd. 2000—01), Am. Gastroenterol. Assn., Am. Inst. Nutrition, Am. Acad. Pediat. (com. on nutrition 1999—2006, exec. com. sect. on pediat. gastroenterology and nutrition 1999—, chair 2005—), N.Am. Soc. Pediat. Gastro Nutrition (chair patient care com. 1997—2000). Avocations: skiing, swimming, hiking, tennis, biking. Office: U Calif Dept Pediat PO Box 0136 San Francisco CA 94143-0136 Office Phone: 415-476-5892. Business E-Mail: mheyman@peds.ucsf.edu.

HEYMAN, RALPH EDMOND, lawyer; b. Cin., Mar. 14, 1931; s. Ralph and Florence (Kahn) H.; m. Sylvia Lee Schottenstein, Jan. 2, 1984; children: Michael Cary, Cynthia Ann Heyman Eeg, Ginger Florence. AB magna cum laude (Rufus Choat scholar), Dartmouth Coll., 1953; LLB cum laude, Harvard U., 1956; LLM, U. Cin., 1957. Bar: Ohio 1956, Ill. 1957. Pvt. practice, Cin., 1956-58, Dayton, 1958—; assoc. Freiden & Wolf, 1956-58; from assoc. to ptnr. Smith & Schnacke, 1958-88; ptnr. Chernesky, Heyman & Kress, Dayton, Ohio, 1988—. Lectr. estate planning U. Cin., 1958-61; lectr. participant Southwestern Ohio Tax Inst., 1957-65; lectr., moderator Dayton Bar Assn. Tax Insts., 1975-79, 94; lectr. continuing edn. program U. Dayton, 1989; lectr. estate planning Dayton Area Tax Profls., 1993; lectr. on venture capital Miami Valley Venture Assn., 1998; dir., gen. counsel Towne Properties, Ltd., Hills Developers LLC, Aristocrat Products, Inc., K.K. Motorcycle Supply, Inc. Mem. Bd. Rural Zoning Commn. Montgomery County, 1969-71; bd. dirs., pres. Jewish Fedn. Dayton, 1993-97; nat. trustee NCCJ; past pres. Temple Israel; pres. Temple Israel Found., 1999-2001; bd. dirs. United Way Greater Dayton Area, 1999-2002. Recipient Humanitarian award NCCJ, 1997, Robert A. Shapiro Vol. award Jewish Fedn., 1998; named Ohio Super Lawyer, Law and Politics Mag., Cin. Mem. ABA, Ohio Bar Assn., Dayton Bar Assn. (past chmn. tax com.), Cin. Bar Assn., Lawyers Club, Bicycle Club, Meadowbrook Country Club, Dayton City Club (past pres.), B'nai Brith, Phi Beta Kappa Office: Chernesky Heyman & Kress PLL PO Box 3808 1100 Courthouse Plz SW Dayton OH 45401-3808 Office Phone: 937-449-2820. E-mail: reh@chklaw.com.

HEYMAN, RONNIE FEUERSTEIN, lawyer; b. NYC, 1948; m. Samuel J. Heyman, Nov. 1970; children: Lazarus, Eleanor, Jennifer, Elizabeth. BA magna cum laude, Harvard U. Radcliffe Coll., 1969; JD, Yale U., 1973. Bar: Conn. 1973. Ptnr. Heyman & Heyman; atty., prin. Heyman Properties, Westport, Conn. Pres. women's divsn. Albert Einstein Coll. Medicine, 1985—87, hon. pres. women's divsn.; dir. Ctr. Jewish Life Duke U. Established The Heyman Chair in Legal Ethics Yale Law Sch.; The Samuel and Ronnie Heyman Ctr. for Ethics, Pub. Policy and the Professions Duke U.; The Samuel & Ronnie Heyman Ctr. on Corp. Governance Yeshiva U., bd. trustees, bd. dirs. Benjamin N. Cardozo Sch. Law; trustee Barnard Coll.; exec. com. internat. directors' coun. Guggenheim Mus.; collectors' com. Nat. Gallery, Washington. Named one of Top 200 Collectors, ARTnews mag., 2000—06. Mem.: Yale Law Sch. Assn. Avocation: Collector modern and contemporary art, especially Miró, Léger, Gorky, Giacometti, and Dubuffet. Office: Heyman Properties 333 Post Rd W Westport CT 06880

HEYMAN, SAMUEL J., chemical manufacturing company executive; b. NYC, Mar. 1, 1939; s. Lazarus S. and Annette (Silverman) Heyman; m. Ronnie Feuerstein, Nov. 1970; children: Lazarus, Eleanor, Jennifer, Elizabeth BS magna cum laude, Yale Coll., 1960; LLB, Harvard U., 1963. Bar: Conn. 1963. Atty. US Dept. Justice, Washington, 1963-64; asst. US atty. Dist. Conn., New Haven, 1964-67, chief asst. US atty., 1967-68; CEO Heyman Properties, Westport, Conn., 1968—; chmn. G-I Holdings Inc. (formerly GAF Corp.), Wayne, NJ, 1983—, Internat. Specialty Products Inc., Wayne, NJ, 1991—, CEO, 1991—99. Hon. dir. Benjamin N. Cardozo Sch. Law Yeshiva U., established The Samuel & Ronnie Heyman Ctr. on Corp. Governance; bd. visitors Terry Sanford Inst. Pub. Policy Duke U., established The Samuel and Ronnie Heyman Ctr. for Ethics, Pub. Policy and the Professions; dean's adv. bd. Harvard Law; established The Heyman Chair in Legal Ethics Yale Law Sch.; founder & chmn. Partnership for Pub. Svc., Washington, 2001—. Named one of Top 200 Collectors, ARTnews mag., 2000—06. Avocation: Collector modern and contemporary art, especially Miró, Léger, Gorky, Giacometti, and Dubuffet. Office: Internat Specialty Products Inc 1361 Alps Rd Wayne NJ 07470

HEYMAN, WILLIAM HERBERT, financial services executive; b. NYC, Apr. 20, 1948; s. George Harrison and Edythe Jane (Forman) H., Jr.; m. Katherine Elizabeth Dietze, May 7, 2007. AB magna cum laude, Princeton U., 1970; JD cum laude, Harvard U., 1973. Bar: NY 1974, DC 1991. Assoc. Cravath, Swaine & Moore, NYC, 1975-78, White & Case, NYC, 1973-75, Stroock & Stroock & Lavan, NYC, 1978-79; gen. ptnr., COO Mercury Securities, NYC, 1979-88; mng. dir. Smith Barney, Harris Upham & Co., Inc., NYC, 1989-91; dir. divsn. market regulation SEC, Washington, 1991-93; mng. dir. Salomon Bros. Inc., Washington, 1993-95; exec. v.p. Citigroup Investments, Inc., NYC, 1995—2000, chmn., 2001—02; CEO Tribecca Investments LLC, NYC, 1996—2002; exec. v.p., chief investment officer Travelers Cos., 2002—, vice chmn., 2005—. Bd. dirs. Max Re Capital Holdings Ltd., Max Re Ltd.; bd. govs. Nat. Assn. Securities Dealers. Trustee Mt. Sinai-NYU Med. Ctr., 1994-99, Hosp. for Joint Diseases, 1994-98; mem. NY area firms adv. com. NY Stock Exch., 1996-2002; mem. adv. bd. fin. math. Courant Inst. Math. Scis. NYU; bd. dirs. Student/Sponsor Partnership of NY, 1989-91, 93-2003, mem. adv. bd., 2004-; bd. dirs. 92d St. YM&YWHA, NYC, 1979-90, hon. bd. dirs., 1991-; coun. overseers United Jewish Appeal-Fedn. NY, 1986-88; mem. fin. com. NY State Reps., 1986-90, v.p. NY County Reps. Com., 1987-90; mem. nat. fin. com. George Bush for Pres., 1987-88; hon. chmn. Bicentennial Presdl. Inaugural, 1989; pub. mem. Adminstrv. Conf. of the U.S., 1989-90; mem. NY regional panel for selection of White House Fellows, 1989, 2002-05; mem. fin. products adv. com. Commodity Futures Trading Commn., 1992-93. Mem. Securities Industry Assn. (chmn. adv. coun.), Coun. on Fgn. Rels., Harvard Law Sch. Assn. (nat. coun. 1986-90), Econ. Club NY, Century Country Club (Purchase, NY), Army and Navy Club (Washington), Univ. Club (NY), Nassau Club (Princeton, NJ), Mid Ocean Club (Bermuda), Doonbeg Golf Club (County Clare, Ireland), Phi Beta Kappa. Jewish. Office: St Paul Travelers Cos 385 Washington St Saint Paul MN 55102-1396 Home Phone: 212-517-4084. Business E-Mail: william.h.heyman@travelers.com.

HEYMANN, C(LEMENS) DAVID, author; b. NYC, Jan. 14, 1945; s. Ernest Frederick and Renee K. (Vago) H.; m. Jeanne Ann Lunin, Nov. 10, 1974 (div. 1995); children: Chloe Colette, Paris Kent Fineberg-Heymann; m. Rebecca Ellen Coughlan, 1995 (div. 1996). BS, Cornell U., 1966; MFA, U. Mass., 1969. Lectr. English lit. SUNY-Stony Brook, 1969-74, Antioch Coll., NYC campus, 1975. Mem. judges panel Am. Book Awards, 1979-80,

Nat. Book Critics Circle, 1978-79 Author: (poetry) The Quiet Hours, 1969; Ezra Pound: The Last Rower, 1976, American Aristocracy: The Lives and Time of James Russell, Amy and Robert Lowell, 1980, Poor Little Rich Girl: The Life and Legend of Barbara Hutton, 1983, A Woman Named Jackie: An Intimate Biography of Jacqueline Bouvier Kennedy Onassis, 1989, Liz: An Intimate Biography of Elizabeth Taylor, 1995, RFK: A Candid Biography of Robert F. Kennedy, 1998, The Georgetown Ladies' Social Club: Power, Passion, and Politics in the Nation's Capital, 2003 American Legacy: The Story of John and Caroline Kennedy, 2007; also book revs. and articles for nat. mags. and newspapers. Israeli govt. writer's grantee, 1984-85 Address: William Morris Agy 1325 Avenue Of The Americas New York NY 10019-6026

HEYMANN, DAVID L., public health service officer; b. Pa., 1946; married; 3 children. BA, Pa. State U.; MD, Wake Forest U. Sch. Medicine; diploma in tropical medicine & hygiene, London Sch. Hygiene & Tropical Medicine. Gen. med. officer USPHS, 1971—74; med. officer WHO Smallpox Eradication Program, India, 1974—76; med. epidemiologist in sub-Saharan Africa US CDC, 1976—89; chief of rsch. activities, global program on AIDS WHO, dir. program on emerging & other communicable diseases, exec. dir. communicable diseases, 1998—2003, dir.-gen.'s spl. rep. for polio eradication, 2003—. Mem.: Inst. Medicine. Office: WHO Avenue Appia 20 1211 Geneva Switzerland Office Phone: 41 22 791 2111. Office Fax: 41 22 791 3111.

HEYMANN, PHILIP BENJAMIN, law educator; b. Pitts., Oct. 30, 1932; m. Ann Ross Heymann; 2 children. AB in Philosophy, Yale U., 1954; grad. studies, U. Sorbonne, Paris, 1954—55; JD, Harvard U., 1960. Bar: DC 1960, Mass. 1970. Law clk. to Justice John Harlan US Supreme Ct., Washington, 1960—61; asst. to Solicitor Gen. US Dept. Justice, Washington, 1961-65; acting adminstr. bur. security & consular affairs US Dept. State, Washington, 1966—67, dep. asst. sec. state for bur. internat organizations, 1967, exec. asst. to Under Sec. of State, 1967-69; asst. atty. gen. criminal divsn US Dept. Justice, Washington, 1978-81, dep. atty. gen., 1993-94; lectr. law Harvard Law Sch., Cambridge, Mass., 1969—71, prof. law, 1971—, James Barr Ames prof. law, 1989—, named dir. Ctr. Criminal Justice, 1981, assoc. dean, 1985—87. Assoc. prosecutor and cons. to Watergate Spl. Prosecution Force, summers 1973-75 Author: The Politics of Public Management, 1987, Towards Peaceful Protest in South Africa, 1992, Terrorism and America: A Commonsense Strategy for a Democratic Society, 2000, Terrorism, Freedom, and Security, 2003; co-author (with William N. Brownsberger): Drug Addiction and Drug Policy: The Struggle to Control Dependence, 2001; editor: South Africa: Policing the Conflict, 1993. Served with USAF, 1955-57. Office Phone: 617-495-3137. Office Fax: 617-496-4913. Business E-Mail: heymann@law.harvard.edu.

HEYMANN, S. RICHARD, lawyer; b. Chgo., Sept. 18, 1944; s. Samuel R. and Ann (Menning) H.; m. Jane Ann Gebhart, June 14, 1980; children: Elizabeth Jane, Catherine Claire. BS, U. Wis., 1966; JD, U. Mich., 1969. Bar: Mo. 1969, Wis. 1988. Law clk. Minn. Supreme Ct., St. Paul, 1970-72; assoc. Bryan, Cave, McPheeters & McRoberts, St. Louis, 1972-79, ptnr., 1980-87, Foley & Lardner, Madison, Wis., 1987-99; dir. Inst. for Environ. Studies U. Wis., Madison, 1996—. Adj. prof. U. Wis. Law Sch.; fellow U. Wis. Bus. Ctr.Urban Land Econs. Rsch. Fellow, Ctr. for Urban Land Econs. Mem. U. Wis. Found., Wis. Alumni Assn. (bd. dirs. 1985-87), Madison Club, Maple Bluff Country Club. Office: U Wis Law Sch 801 Magdeline Rd Madison WI 53704 E-mail: srheymann@wisc.edu.

HEYNEMAN, DONALD, parasitology and tropical medicine educator; b. San Francisco, Feb. 18, 1925; s. Paul and Amy Josephine (KLauber) H.; m. Louise Davidson Ross, June 18, 1971; children: Amy J., Lucy A., Andrew P., Jennifer K., Claudia G. AB magna cum laude, Harvard U., 1950; MA, Rice U., 1952, PhD, 1954. Instr. zoology UCLA, 1954-56, asst. prof., 1956-60; head dept. parasitology U.S. Navy Med. Research unit, Cairo, also co-dir. Malakal, Sudan, 1960-62; assoc. research parasitologist Hooper Found. U. Calif., San Francisco, 1962-64, assoc. prof., 1966-68, prof., 1968-91, prof. emeritus, 1991—, asst. dir. Hooper found., 1970-74, acting chmn. dept. internat. health, 1976-78, assoc. dean Sch. Pub. Health Berkeley and San Francisco, 1987-91, assoc. dean emeritus, 1991—, chmn. joint med. program, 1987-91, chmn. emeritus, 1991—. Research coordinator U. Calif. Internat. Ctr. Med. Research and Tng., Kuala Lumpur, Malaysia, 1964-66; cons. physiol. processes sect. NSF, 1966-91; environ. biology div. NIH, 1968-91; mem. tropical medicine and parasitology study sect. NIAID-NIH, 1973-76; mem. adv. sci. bd. Gorgas Meml. Inst., 1967-90; cons. WHO, 1967, mem. sci. tech. rev. com. on Leishmaniases, 1984; cons. UN Devel. Program, 1978-91, US-AID, others; panel reviewer Internat. Nomenclature of Diseases, 1984—; Am. cons. and U.S. prin. investigator U. Linkage Project, Egypt-U.S., 1984—; mem. Calif. Health Adv. Com., 1983—. Author: (with R. Boolootian) An Illustrated Laboratory Text in Zoology, 1962, An Illustrated Laboratory Text in Zoology, A Brief Version, 1977, International Dictionary Medicine and Biology, (with R. Goldsmith) Textbook of Tropical Medicine and Parasitology, 1989;coauthor, contbg. editor Phytolacca dodecandra: Endod, 1984, Endod II, 1987; contbr. articles to jours., chpts. to books.; editorial cons. Am. Jour. Tropical Medicine and Hygiene, Jour. Parasitology, Jour. Exptl. Parasitology, Sci., 1968—, other jours. Served with AUS, 1943-46. NIH grantee, 1966-85. Mem. Am. Soc. Parasitologists (council 1970-74, pres. 1982-83), Am. Micros. Soc. (exec. com. 1971-75), Am. Soc. Tropical Medicine and Hygiene (councilor 1981-84), So. Calif. Parasitol. Soc. (pres. 1957-58), No. Calif. Parasitologists (sec.- treas. 1969-72, pres. 1977-78), Phi Beta Kappa. Home: 1400 Lake St San Francisco CA 94118-1036 Personal E-mail: dheyneman@attglobal.net.

HEYRMAN, LAURA GARDNER, art historian, educator; b. Feb. 22, 1958; BA, Oberlin Coll., Ohio, 1980; MA, Johns Hopkins U., Balt., 1981; PhD, U. Minn., Mpls., 1994. Adj. instr. Bluegrass Cmty. and Tech. Coll. (formerly Lexington CC), Lexington, Ky., 1990—.

HEYSTEE, SUSAN, information technology executive; Degree in math. with dual concentration in computer sci. and bus. adminstrn. (with honors), U. Waterloo. Sr. positions with SSA Global; v.p. consulting practice Baan Americas, 1997, v.p., svcs., sr. v.p. field ops., pres., 2001—02, exec. v.p. worldwide solutions sales and delivery, 2002—04; v.p., area gen. mgr., Midwest area Novell, Inc., 2004—05, pres. Americas, 2005—, also mem. worldwide mgmt. com. Office: Novell Inc 404 Wyman Ste 500 Waltham MA 02451

HEYVAERT, ALAN, environmental scientist, educator; s. John and Ruth Heyvaert; m. Ellen Levy. BA, U. Colo., Boulder, 1982; PhD, U. Calif., Davis, 1998. Staff rsch. assoc. U. Calif., Davis, 2001—05; asst. rsch. prof. Desert Rsch. Inst., Reno, 2005—. Contbr. articles to profl. publs. Mem.: North Am. Lake Mgmt. Soc., Am. Water Resources Assn., Societas Internationalis Limnologiae Theoreticae et Applicatae, Am. Soc. Limnology and Oceanography. Achievements include research in watershed management and paleolimnology. Office: Desert Rsch Inst 2215 Raggio Pkwy Reno NV 89512 Office Phone: 775-673-7322.

HEYWANG-KOEBRUNNER, SYLVIA H., radiologist, educator; b. Karlsruhe, Germany, July 31, 1956; d. Walter and Ditha (Bierwag) H.; m. Gerhard Köbrunner, Mar. 11, 1989; children: Sandra, Petra. MD, Ludwig-Maximilians U., Munich, Germany, 1981, Dr. med. habil, 1992. Bd. cert. physician, 1982, radiologist, 1990. Resident radiology Ludwig-Maximilians U., Munich, 1983-90, mem. staff, 1990-92, asst. prof., 1991-92, U. Leipzig, Germany, 1993; asst. prof., vice dir. diagnostic radiology U. Halle, Germany, 1994-96; assoc. prof., vice dir. diagnostic radiology Martin Luther U., Halle, Germany, 1996—2003; assoc. prof., head dept. breast imaging and intervention Tech. U., Munich, 2003—07; head Nat. Reference Ctr. Mammography, 2007—. Author: Contrast-enhanced MRI of the breast, 1990, 2d edit., 1996, Breast Imaging, 1996, 2d edit. in English, 2001, in German 2003, Handbook Diagnostic Radiology - Breast, 2004; mem. editl. bd. European Radiology, Diagnostic Imaging, Roentgenpraxis; reviewer Radiology, Jour. Computer Assisted Tomography, JMRI, European Jour. Radiology, Jour. Magnetic Resonance Imaging, Investig Radiology, European Radiology, Acta Radiologica, Roe Fo.; contbr. articles to profl. jours. Scholar breast imaging German Cancer Assn., 1982; recipient MR prize Internat. MR-Symposium, 1991, Holthusen Ring, German Roentgen Soc., 1992, European Yvette Mayent-Curie prize, 1999. Mem. German Radiol. Soc. (mem. breast imaging com., Holthusenring award 1992), German Senology Soc. (bd. mem. 1995—), Radiol. Soc. N.Am., European Assn. Radiology, European Soc. Magnetic Resonance Medicine, European Congress Radiology (head breast com. 2000—), N.Y. Acad. Sci. Achievements include inauguration of contrast enhanced breast MRI; introduction vacuum-assisted breast biopsy in Europe; patents for breast biopsy coil; substance for interstitial marker solution; minimal invasive breast biopsy using fluorescence marker; first MR-guided vacuum breast biopsy; fixation device for MRI of the breast; development of web-based data base and reporting system for documentation and reporting of breast screening (with KV Bavern); research in image-based clinical studies. Avocations: music, science. Office: Nat Reference Ctr Mammography Munich Einsteinstr 3 81675 Munich Germany Business E-Mail: heywangkoe@referenzzentrum-muenchen.de.

HEYWARD, ANDREW JOHN, former broadcast executive; b. Roslyn, NY, Oct. 29, 1950; s. E.J.R. and Elisabeth Heyward; m. Jody Gaylin Heyward, May 23, 1976; children: David, Emily, Sarah. BA, Harvard U., 1972. Producer Sta. WNEW-TV News, NYC, 1974-76, Sta. WCBS-TV News, NYC, 1976-78, exec. producer, 1978-81; producer CBS Evening News CBS News, NYC, 1981-84, sr. producer, 1984-87; exec. producer 48 Hours, NYC, 1987-93, Eye to Eye, 1993-94; v.p. CBS News, 1994-96; exec. producer CBS Evening News, 1994-96; pres. CBS News, 1996—2005. Mem. NATAS (Emmy award 1977-78, 84, 88-93, 95). Business E-Mail: andrew.heyward@gmail.com.

HEYWARD, PETER E., lawyer; b. NYC, June 23, 1953; BA, Wesleyan U., 1974; JD, Columbia U., 1979. Bar: NY 1980, DC 1991. Law clerk to Judge John R. Bartels US Dist. Ct., NY, 1979—81; sr. atty. Federal Reserve Bd., 1986—89; of counsel Jones Day Reavis & Pogue, Washington; ptnr., banking and fin. svcs. Venable LLP, Washington, 2001—. Mem.: ABA (mem. banking law com. 1990—, vice chair internat. banking subcom. 1998—2000, chair fin. holding co. subcom. 2000—), Federal Bar Assn. (mem. banking law com. 2003—, mem. exec. council), NYC Bar Assn. (mem. banking law com. 1999—2001, mem. insurance law com. 2001—03, mem. banking law com. 2003—). Office: Venable LLP 575 7th St NW Washington DC 20004 Office Phone: 202-344-4616. Office Fax: 202-344-8300. Business E-Mail: peheyward@venable.com.

HEYWARD, WILLIE BRUCE, lawyer, advocate; b. Charleston, SC, Mar. 12, 1946; s. Willie B. and Albertha Gantt Heyward; 1 child, Dominique Ajené. BA, UCLA, 1977; JD, U. Calif., San Francisco, 1980. Bar: SC 1997. Staff atty. Neighborhood Legal Assistance, Inc., Charleston, 1997—2002, SC Ctrs. for Equal Justice, Inc, North Charleston, 2002—04; mng. atty. Ctr. for Heirs' Property Preservation, North Charleston, 2004—06; dir. Heirs' Property Law Ctr., LLC, North Charleston, 2006—. Econ. devel. Charleston Empowerment Corp, 2000—07. With US Army, 1964—73. Named Ellen Hines Smith Legal Services Lawyer of Yr., SC Bar Assn., 2004. Independent. Episcopalian. Avocations: walking, chess, reading. Home: 265 St Margaret St Charleston SC 29403 Office: Heirs' Property Law Center LLC 2148 Dorchester Rd North Charleston SC 29405 Home Phone: 843-744-6272; Office Phone: 843-225-8754. Office Fax: 843-225-8765. Personal E-mail: heywarddwighth@msn.com. Business E-Mail: willie@heirspropertylawcenter.org.

HEYWOOD, GAIL ANNE, musician, educator; b. Hartford, Conn., July 25, 1958; d. Laurier Joseph and Shirley Lucille Alix; m. Neil Chaplain Heywood, June 29, 1991; m. Steven James Barber, Sept. 5, 1981 (div. Nov. 29, 1990); children: Katelyn Rose, Kimberly Anne Barber, Daniel Steven Barber. AA in Liberal Studies, Bay Path Jr. Coll., 1976—78; BA in Music, Ctrl. Conn. State Coll., 1981. Cert. in religious edn. Diocese of LaCrosse, Wis., 1995. Nurses aid Prospect Hill Rehab. Ctr., East Windsor, Conn., 1976—78; music instr. Inst. of Living, Hartford, Conn., 1980—86; music min./cantor St. Philip the Apostle Ch., Rudolph, Wis., 1992—; gen. music tchr., k-8 St. Philip Sch., Rudolph, Wis., 1994—97; music instr./sole operator Heywood Music Studios, Rudolph, Wis., 1986—; webmaster Wis. Music Tchrs. Assn., Racine, Wis.; accompanist/musician St. Vincent de Paul Parish, Wisconsin Rapids, Wis., 2002—. Clinician, adjudicator Wis. Music Tchrs. Assn., Racine, Wis., 1998—2004; childrens choir dir. St. Stanislaus Parish, Stevens Point, Wis., 1991; substitute accompanist St. Stanislaus Ch., Stevens Point, Wis., 2003—; chair, north ctrl. divsn. badger keyboard competition Wis. Music Teachers Assn., Stevens Point, Wis., 1997—97, North Ctrl. divsn. badger keyboard competition chair, 2001—01; employee adv. group Inst. of Living, Hartford, Conn., 1984—86. Musician: (featured soloist) Womens Composer Concert, (solo performance) Charity Auction, Sam Kimble Band, 1980—84; actor: Guys & Dolls, 1979. Mem. St. Francis Group, PCCW, Rudolph, Wis., 1991—2004; litury comm. St. Philip the Apostle Parish, Rudolph, Wis., 1991—, music minister, 2006; mem. Greater Hartford Youth Chorale, 1974—75; treas. St. Philip Home and Sch. Assn., Rudolph, Wis., 1994—97; com. mem. Boy Scout Troop 114, Rudolph, Wis., 1995—2004. Recipient Outstanding Music Dept. Mem., Granby Meml. H.S., 1973—75, Excellence in Tchg. award, 2004; grantee, Music Teachers Nat. Assn., 1999, 2006. Mem.: Wis. Music Teachers Assn. (assoc.; pres. 2003—, membership sec. 1998—2003, Excellence in Tchg. award 1995, 1997, Member of the Yr. for Stevens Point ares 1999, Outstanding Svc. award 2000, Excellence in Tchg. award 2001, 2004). Avocations: travel, gardening, crafts. Home: 1531 Main St Rudolph WI 54475 Office: Heywood Music Studios 1531 Main St Rudolph WI 54475 E-mail: heywood@tznet.com.

HEYWOOD, HARRIETT, lawyer, consultant; b. Durham, NC; d. Chester; m. James N. Washington, Sept. 1985; 1 child, James. BA, Johnson C. Smith U., 1969; JD, Howard U., 1972. Bar: NJ 1972, DC 1986. Office gen. counsel US Dept. Vet. Affairs, Washington, 1972—77, sr. atty., 1977—98, sr. atty., office discrimination complaints adjudication, 1998—2001, assoc. dir., ctr. women vets., 2001—04, coord. debt collection program, 1981—83, mgr., fed. womens program, 1996—97; atty., pvt. practice Silver Spring, Md., 2004—. Dist. ethics com. mem. Essex County Bar Assn., 1979—81; def. adv. com. women in svcs. mem. Dept. of Def., Pentagon, Arlington, Va., 2000—01. Vice chair, dist. 14 Montgomery county Dem. Club, Silver Sping, 2004—; bible study tchr. Peoples Cmty. Bapt. Ch., Silver Spring, 2000—. Named one of 25 Influential Black Women for 2003, The Network Jour. Mem.: Nat. Coun. Negro Women (Potomac Valley chpt.), DC Bar Assn., Delta Sigma Theta (chaplain 1995—, historian 2003—, Women with a Purpose award 2001). Baptist. Avocations: piano, reading, tennis.

HEYWOOD, JOHN BENJAMIN, mechanical engineering educator; b. Sidcup, Kent, Eng., Jan. 11, 1938; s. Harold and Frances Dora (Weaver) H.; m. Marguerite Gilkerson, Dec. 28, 1961; children: James, Stephen, Benjamin. BA, Cambridge U., 1960, DSc, 1984; MS, MIT, 1962, PhD, 1965; DTech (hon.), Chalmers U. Tech., 1999; DSc (hon.), City U., London. Lectr. Northeastern U., Boston, 1963-65; rsch. officer Cen. Electricity Generating Bd., Leatherhead, 1965-67, group leader, 1967-68; rsch. assoc. mech. engring. dept. MIT, Cambridge, 1964-65, asst. prof. mech. enginrg., 1968-70, assoc. prof., 1970-76, prof., 1976-92, dir. Sloan Automotive Lab., 1972—, co-dir. leaders for mfg. program, 1991-93; Sun Jae prof. mech. engring., 1992—; dir. Ctr. for 21st Century Energy, 2002—; co-dir. Ford-MIT Alliance, 2003—. Author, editor: (with others) Open-Cycle MHD Power Generation, 1969; author: (with others) The Automobile and the Regulation of its Impact on the Environment, 1975, Internal Engine Combustion Fundamentals, 1988, (with E. Sher) The Two-Stroke Engine, 1999; contbr. Ency. Britannica, chpts. to books, numerous articles, papers to profl. jours., confs., symposia U.S.A, Eng., Europe. Recipient Ayerton Premium Inst. Elec. Engrs., U.K., 1969; Fulbright travel scholar, 1960; Richard C. Mellon Overseas fellow Churchill Coll., Cambridge, Eng., 1976-77; recipient Nat. award for Advancement of Motor Vehicle R&D, US DOT, 1996. Fellow U.K. Instn. Mech. Engrs. (George Stephenson Internat. Lectr. 1997); mem. Soc. Automotive Engrs. (Ralph R. Teeter Outstanding Young Engr. award 1971, Arch T. Colwell Merit award 1973, 81, 89, Outstanding Oral Presentation award 1980, 2001, Horning Meml. Best Paper award 1984, Rsch. on Automotive Lubricants award 2001), ASME (Freeman scholar 1986, Honda lectr. 1990, Honda medal 1999), Nat. Acad. Engring., Am. Acad. Arts and Scis. Achievements include rsch. interests in thermodynamics, combustion, energy, power and propulsion, performance, efficiency and emissions of spark-ignition and diesel engines, control of air pollution, engine design and manufacture. Office: MIT Dept Mech Engring 77 Mass Ave # 3-340 Cambridge MA 02139-4307 Office Phone: 617-253-2243.

HEZIR, JOSEPH S., energy and environmental executive; b. Pitts., Pa., Aug. 27, 1950; s. Joseph F. and Elizabeth G. F.; m. Joyce Ann Martincic, May 12, 1979; children: Alexandra M., Damjan S. BS, Carnegie-Mellon U., 1972, MS, 1974. Rsch. engr. St. Joe Minerals Corp., Monaca, Pa., 1971, Carnegie-Mellon U., Pitts., 1972; planning analyst City of N.Y., 1973; budget examiner U.S. Office Mgmt. and Budget, Washington, 1974-82, dep. assoc. dir., 1986-92; sr. corp. analyst Exxon Rsch. and Engring. Corp., Florham Park, NJ, 1982; mng. ptnr. The EOP Group, Inc., Washington, 1992—. Mem. adv. bd. Competitiveness Policy Coun., Washington, 1992-94, NASA Adv. Coun., Washington, 1992-93. Dir. nat. capital chpt. ARC, Washington, 1987-90. Fellow Coun. Excellence in Govt.; mem. NAS (mem. study bds.), Croatian Fraternal Union Am. Roman Catholic. Home: 1509 Pennycress Ln Vienna VA 22182-1473 Office: EOP Group Inc 819 7th St NW Washington DC 20001-3762 Home Phone: 703-759-2138; Office Phone: 202-833-8940. E-mail: jshezir@819eagle.com.

HIAASEN, CARL, writer, reporter; b. 1953; Attended, Emory U.; BA in Journalism, U. Florida, 1974. Gen. assignment reporter then investigative reporter The Miami Herald, Miami, Fla., 1976. Co-author: (novels) (with Bill Montalbano) Powder Burn, 1981, Trap Line, 1982, A Death in China, 1984; author Tourist Season, 1986, Double Whammy, 1987, Skin Tight, 1989, Native Tongue, 1991, Strip Tease, 1993, Stormy Weather, 1993, Lucky You, 1997, Team Rodent, 1998, Sick Puppy, 2000, Basket Case, 2002, Hoot, 2002, Skinny Dip, 2004 (Publishers Weekly Bestseller, 2005), (collection of columns) Kick Ass, 1999, Paradise Screwed, 2001. Office: c/o Esther Newberg Internat Creative Mgmt 40 W 57th St New York NY 10019

HIATT, ARNOLD, apparel and retail executive; b. May 26, 1927; s. Alexander and Dorothy H.; m. Anne Wechsler (dec.). BA, Harvard U., 1948. Pres., founder Blue Star Shoe Co., Lawrence, Mass., 1952-69; pres., chief exec. officer Stride Rite Corp., Boston, 1969-89, chmn. bd., 1982-92; chmn. Stride Rite Found., Boston, 1982—. Bd. dirs. Dreyfus Fund. Former mem. bd. regents of higher edn. Commonwealth of Mass.; mem. bd. trustees Isabela Stewart Gardner Mus., The John Merck Found.; former mem. vis. com. Boston U. Sch. Medicine; bd. overseers Harvard U., 1984-90; former chair Bus. for Social Responsibility. Mem. Am. Footwear Industries Assn. (dir., chmn. 1980).

HIATT, FLORENCE ELLEN, musician; b. Elwood, Ind. d. Merrill Paul and Mildred Lenore (Knotts) H.; m. Frank Alvin Robertson, Sept. 1, 1948 (div. 1963); children: Lana Glynn, Bradley Reid. Attended, Cin. Conservatory Music, 1945—49; diploma, Ecoles d'Art et Musique, Fontainebleau, France, 1961; MusB, Auburn U., Ala., 1964; MusM, Ind. U., Bloomington, Ind., 1972; postgrad., Fla. State U., Tallahassee, 1984—85. Mem. faculty piano and organ Auburn U., 1964-65; asst. mus. dir. then mus. dir. Lakewood Mus. Playhouse, Barnesville, Pa., 1971-72; mus. dir. Clinton Mus. Theatre, Conn., 1974-75; organist, choirmaster St. Thomas Episcopal Ch., Columbus, 1960—70; mus. dir. Springer Opera House, Springer Theatre, Springer Ballet and Sch. Theatre Arts, Columbus, 1971—84. Music dir. Temple Israel, Columbus, 1970—; mem. organ and harpsichord faculty Columbus Coll., 1982—86; keybd. specialist Columbus Symphony Orchestra, 1967—91; organist St. Luke United Meth. Ch., Columbus, 1984—99; archael. rschr. Budapest, Hungary, 1994. Author, composer choral, organ and vocal music. Wessex Theol. Coll. hon. fellow, Eng. Mem. Royal Coll. Organists, Am. Guild Organists (cert., past dean), Guild of Temple Musicians, Alliance Francaise, Mortar Bd. Soc. Home: 2801 Gardenia St Columbus GA 31906-2130 Personal E-mail: piperflo@charter.net.

HIATT, FRED, journalist; b. Washington, Apr. 30, 1955; m. Margaret Shapiro; 3 children. BA in History, Harvard U., 1977. City Hall reporter Atlanta Jour.-Constitution, 1979—80; reporter The Washington Star, 1981; Va. reporter The Washington Post, 1981—83, Pentagon reporter, 1983—86, Northeast Asia co-bur. chief, 1987—90, Moscow co-bur. chief, 1991—95, editl. page editor & editl. writer, 2000—. Author: (novels) The Secret Sun, 1992, (children's book) If I Were Queen of the World, 1997, Baby Talk, 1999. Office: The Washington Post 1150 15th St NW Washington DC 20071-0001 Business E-Mail: fredhiatt@washpost.com.

HIATT, HOWARD H., internist, educator; b. Patchogue, NY, July 22, 1925; s. Alexander and Dorothy (Askinas) Hiatt; m. Doris Bieringer, Nov. 29, 1947; children: Jonathan, Deborah, Frederick. MD, Harvard U., 1948. From intern to resident in medicine Beth Israel Hosp., Boston, 1948—50; rsch. fellow Cornell U. Med. Coll., 1950—53; clin. investigator USPHS, 1953—55; mem. faculty Med. Sch., Harvard U., 1955—, H.L. Blumgart prof. medicine, 1963—72, prof. medicine, 1972—, prof. medicine Sch. Pub. Health, 1984—92, dean Sch. Pub. Health, 1972—84; physician-in-chief Beth Israel Hosp., 1963—72; sr. physician Brigham Women's Hosp., Boston, 1984—, co-chief divsn social medicine and health inequalities, 2003—. Mem.: NAS Inst. Medicine, Partners in Health, Bd. Physicians for Human Rights (bd. dirs. 1996—2002), Am. Acad. Arts and Scis. (sec. 1992—97, dir. Initiatives for Children 1992—2002), Assn. Am. Physicians, Am. Soc. Clin. Investigation, Alpha Omega Alpha. Home: 130 Mt Auburn St Cambridge MA 02138-5757 Office: Brigham and Women's Hosp Boston MA 02115 Business E-Mail: HHiatt@partners.org.

HIATT, JONATHAN PAUL, lawyer, labor union administrator; b. 1949; married; 3 children. BA, Harvard U.; JD, U. Calif., Berkeley, 1974. Bar: Calif. 1975. Ptnr. Angoff, Goldman, Manning, Pyle, Wagner & Hiatt, Boston, 1974—95; gen. counsel Svc. Employees Internat. Union, 1988—95, AFL-CIO, Washington, 1995—. Exec. dir. lawyers coordinating com. AFL-CIO, Washington; practitioner-in-residence Ctr. for Social Justice Boalt Hall Sch. Law., U. Calif., Berkeley. Bd. dirs. Nat. Employment Law Project, NYC, Appleseed Found., Washington; adv. bd. Peggy Browning Fund, Phila.; bd. advs. DC Employment Justice Ctr.; adv. bd.

ex-officio NYU Ctr. for Labor and Employment Law. Mem.: Am. Arbitration Assn. (bd. dirs. 2002—). Office: Gen Counsel AFL CIO 815 16th St NW Washington DC 20006 Office Phone: 202-637-5155. E-mail: jhiatt@aflcio.org.*

HIATT, PETER, retired library and information scientist; b. NYC, Oct. 19, 1930; s. Amos and Elizabeth Hope (Derry) H.; m. Linda Rae Smith, Aug. 16, 1968; 1 child, Holly Virginia. BA, Colgate U., 1952; MLS, Rutgers U., 1957, PhD, 1963. Libr. intern Elizabeth (N.J.) Pub. Libr., 1955-57; head Elmora Br. Libr., Elizabeth, 1957-59; instr. Grad. Sch. Libr. Svc., Rutgers U., 1960-62; libr. cons. Ind. State Libr., Indpls., 1963-70; asst. prof. Grad. Libr. Sch., Ind. U., 1963-66, assoc. prof., 1966-70; dir. Ind. Libr. Studies, Bloomington, 1967-70; dir. continuing edn. program for libr. pers. Western Interstate Commn. for Higher Edn., Boulder, Colo., 1970-74; dir. Grad. Sch. Libr. and Info. Sci., U. Wash., Seattle, 1974-81, prof., 1974-98; dir. libr. insts. at various colls. and univs.; adv. projects U.S. Office Edn.-ALA, 1977-80; prof. emeritus U. Wash., 1998—. Bd. dir. King County Libr. Sys., 1989-97, pres., 1991, 95, sec., 1993-94; prin. investigator Career Devel. and Assessment Ctrs. for Librs.: Phase I, 1979-83, Phase II, 1990-93. Author: (with Donald Thompson) Monroe County IN Public Library: Planning for the Future, 1966, The Public Library Needs of Delaware County, 1967, (with Henry Drennan) Public Library Services for the functionally Illiterate, 1967 (with Robert E. Lee and Lawrence A. Allen) A Plan for Developing a Regional Program of Continuing Education for Library Personnel, 1969, Public Library Branch Services for Adults of Low Education, 1964; dir., gen. editor: The Indiana Library Studies, 1970-74; author: Assessment Centers for Professional Library Leadership, 1993, Fund Raising for Turtle Bluff Orchestra, 2002; mem. editl. bd. Coll. and Rsch. Librs., 1969-73; co-editor Leads: A Continuing Education Newsletter for Library Trustees, 1973-75, Octavio Noda; author chpts., articles on libr. continuing edn., staff devel. and libr. adult svcs. Mem. selection com. Jefferson County Pub. Libr., Washington, 2000—01; bd. dirs., sec., pres. Port Townsend Pub. Libr. Found., 2002—; bd. dirs. Turtle Bluff Chamber Orch., Jefferson County, Wash., 2000—03, mem. soloist competition jury, 2000—03, mem. scholarship com., 2000—04, chair spl. fundraising com., 2002—03, mem. new music group, 2002—; founder, bd. dir. Camerata Olympica, North Olympic Peninsula, 2004—05. Mem. ALA (life mem., officer), Pacific N.W. Libr. Assn., Assn. Libr. and Info. Sci. Educators (officer, Outstanding Svc. award 1979), ACLU. Home: 20 Sequim Pl Port Townsend WA 98368-9414 Personal E-mail: phiatt@cablspeed.com. *I know of no other profession which helps so many people and organizations change and grow--from pre-school years through retirement, as does library and information science. It is a joy to be part of that.*

HIBBARD, JUDITH USHER, obstetrician; b. Chgo. m. Mark C. Hibbard. Studied, Edgewood Coll., Madison, Wis., 1966—68; BS in Secondary Edn., Gen. sci. & History, U. Wis., Madison, 1968—72, MS in sci. Edn., 1968—72; studied, Coll. of DuPage, Glen Ellen, Ill., 1977—78, Ill. Benedictine Coll., Lisle, 1978—79; MD, Loyola U., Maywood, Ill., 1979—82. Diplomate Nat. Bd. Med. Examiners, 1983, Am. Bd. Ob-Gyn., 1990, in Maternal-Fetal Medicine 1991. Sci. tchr. Verona Mid. Sch., Wis., 1970—72, Toledo Jr. H.S., Oreg., 1972—74; sci. and math. tchr. Mesquite H.S., Ridgecrest, Calif., 1975—77; resident, ob-gyn. U. Chgo., 1982—86, fellow, instr., maternal-fetal medicine, 1986—89, asst. prof., maternal-fetal medicine, 1989—96, acting dir., ob-gyn. ultrasound, 1999—2000, assoc. prof., clin. ob-gyn., 1996—2001, fellowship dir., maternal-fetal medicine, 2001—, prof., maternal-fetal medicine, 2001—, sect. chief, maternal-fetal medicine, 2003—. Reviewer for various jours. Recipient Hon. Sci. award, Bausch and Lomb, 1968, Scholastic Achievement award, Am. Med. Women's Assn., 1982, Young Investigator's award, Am. Diabetes Assn., 1988, Faculty Devel. Tng. award, Berlex Found., 1991, Young Investigator's Travel award, NIH, 1994. Mem.: Chgo. Soc. Perinatal Obstetricians, Chgo. Gyn. Soc., Ill. Perinatal Assn., Ctrl. Assn. of Ob-Gyn., Internat. Soc. of Ultrasound in Ob-Gyn., Internat. Soc. for Study of Hypertension in Pregnancy, Nat. Perinatal Assn., Soc. Obstetric Medicine, Soc. Maternal Fetal Medicine, Am. Coll. Ob-Gyn., Pi Lambda Theta, Alpha Omega Alpha. Office: Dept Ob-Gyn U Ill 820 S Wood St MC808 Chicago IL 60612

HIBBARD, WILLIAM LOUIS, computer scientist; b. Mpls., Mar. 18, 1948; s. William Daniel and Anna Stenger Hibbard; m. Alice Jane Snyder, Apr. 9, 1988. BA, U. Wis., Madison, 1970, MS, 1974, PhD, 1995. Sr. scientist U. Wis., Madison, 1978—. Author: (visualization software) Vis5D, 1989, VisAD, 1998, Cave5D, 1994, (book) Super-Intelligent Machines, 2002. Office: U Wis 1225 West Dayton St Madison WI 53706 Home Phone: 608-873-0689; Office Phone: 608-263-4427.

HIBBERT, ROBERT GEORGE, lawyer, food company executive; b. Marlboro, Mass., July 3, 1950; s. Charles Harris and Mary Barbara (Sauage) H.; m. Cynthia Joan Miller, June 12, 1971; children: Lauren, Meg, Robert J. BA, Columbia U., 1972; JD, Am. U., 1975. Bar: Mass. 1975, Md. 1975, DC 1985. Trial atty. office of gen. counsel USDA, Washington, 1975-79, dir. standards and labeling divsn. food safety inspection service, 1980-85; v.p., gen. counsel Am. Meat Inst., Arlington, Va., 1985-88; ptnr. McDermott, Will & Emery, Washington, Kirkpatrick & Lockhart Preston Gates Ellis LLP, Washington, 2006—. Mem. ABA, Mass. Bar Assn., Md. Bar Assn., DC Bar Assn., Am. Agrl. Law Assn., Internat. HACCP Alliance (sec.-treasurer) Office: Kirkpatrick & Lockhart Preston Gates Ellis LLP 1601 K St NW Washington DC 20006-1600 Office Phone: 202-778-9315. Office Fax: 202-778-9100.*

HIBBS, CLAIR M., retired pathologist; b. Lucerne, Mo., Oct. 10, 1923; s. Grover Clarence and Bertha Cassiday H.; m. Ann Elisabeth Robinson, Dec. 26, 1946; children: Drew Robinson, Gerald Wayne. BS in Agr., U. Mo., Columbia, 1949, DVM, 1953; MS in Pathology, Kans. State U., Manhattan, 1962, PhD in Pathology, 1965. Gen. vet. practice Philips Magilton & Hibbs, David City, Nebr., 1953—60; instr. Kans. State U., Manhattan, 1960—65, 1965—68, assoc. prof., 1968—69, U. Nebr., North Platte, 1969—73, prof., 1973—79; dir. N.Mex. Diagnostic Lab N.Mex. State U., Albuquerque, 1979—90. Advisor Norden Labs. (divsn. Smith-Kline), Lincoln, Nebr., 1988—89; cons. Triple J Zahnis Lab., Bellingham, Wash., 2000—; bd. dirs. Nebr. Med. Rsch. Com., 1977; pres. Western Vet. Conf., 1997—98. Contbr. more than 60 articles to profl. publs. Mm3/c USN, 1943—46. Recipient Disting. Svc. award, Nebr. Vet. Med. Assn., 1978—79, N.Mex. Vet. Assn., 1986, N.Mex. Dept. Agr., 1986; fellow kidney rsch. fellow, Mark Morris Found., 1962. Mem.: Western Vet. Med. Assn. (past pres. 1998), Rotary (past pres. 1977, pres. Mt. Baker club 2005—), Am. Legion (comdr. 1958). Home: 1172 Edgewater Ln Lynden WA 98264-1079 Office Phone: 360-354-2113.

HIBBS, ERNEST G., computer scientist, engineering executive; s. James Bennett and Carolyn Hibbs; m. Meridith Murray, Sept. 14, 2001; 1 child, Carolyn. BS in Computer Sci., U. Md., Adelphi, 1994, MS in Software Engrng., 2001. With Dept. Def. Clin. Info. Tech. Program Office, Va., 1999—2004, process improvement cons., 2005—06; requirements mgr. and process improvement cons.; dep. program mgr. Army Knowledge Online, Fort Belvoir, Va., 2004—05; computer scientist Dept. Def. Global Command Control Sys.-Joint Program Mgmt. Office, Def. Info. Sys. Agy., Falls Ch., 2006—. Served with USN, 1979—85, served with USN, 1986—98. Decorated Navy Commendation medal, Navy Achievement medal (3); named Sailor of the Yr., USS Jacksonville, Sub Squadron 8, 1987. Mem.: IEEE, Assn. Computing Machinery. Achievements include research in DNA Synchro; decoding QWERTY symmetric patterns. Home: 7787 Grandwind Dr Lorton VA 22079-4738 Office: Def Info Sys Agy Dept Def Global Command Control Sys Join SKY 7 5275 Leesburg Pike Falls Church VA 22041 Home Phone: 703-339-8995. Personal E-mail: emhibbs1@cox.net.

HIBBS, JOHN DAVID, computer company executive, electrical engineer, small business owner; b. Del Norte, Colo., Jan. 26, 1948; s. Alva Bernard and Frances Ava (Cathcart) Hibbs; m. Ruthanne Johnson, Feb. 28, 1976. BSEE, Denver U., 1970. Elec. engr. Merrick and Co., Denver, 1972-73; lighting engr. Holophane div. Johns Manville, Denver, 1973-79; lighting products mgr. Computer Sharing Svcs., Inc., Denver, 1979-83; pres., owner Computer Aided Lighting Analysis, Boulder, Colo., 1983-86, Hibbs Sci. Software, Boulder, Colo., 1986—; chmn. bd. Sport Sail Inc., 1996-97. Co-founder Sport Sail, Inc. Author: CALA, CALA/Pro, PreCALA. With USNR, 1970—72. Recipient 1st prize, San Luise Valley Sci. Fair, 1963. Mem.: IEEE, Computer Soc. of IEEE (chmn. computer problem set com. 1991—95), Illuminating Engring. Soc. N.Am. (chmn. computer com. 1988—91). Achievements include patents in field. Avocations: woodworking, bicycling, sailing, skiing. Home and Office: PO Box 1920 Boulder CO 80306-1920 E-mail: jdhibbs@ieee.org.

HIBBS, LOYAL ROBERT, lawyer; b. Des Moines, Dec. 24, 1925; s. Loyal B. and Catharine (McClymond) H.; children: Timothy, Theodore, Howard, Dean. BA, U. Iowa, 1950, LLB, JD, 1952. Bar: Iowa 1952, Nev. 1958, U.S. Supreme Ct. 1971. Ptnr. Hibbs Law Offices, Reno, 1972—. Moderator radio, TV Town Hall Coffee Breaks, 1970-72; mem. Nev. State Bicycle Adv. Bd., 1996-2000, Reno Bicycle Com., 1995-99; mem. Reno Parks, Recreation and Cmty. Svc. Commn., 1998—, chmn., 2001—. Fellow Am. Bar Found. (Nev. chmn. 1989-94); mem. ABA (standing com. Lawyer Referral Svc. 1978-79, steering com. state dels. 1979-82, consortium on legal svcs. and the pub. 1979-82, Nev. State Bar del. to Ho. of Dels. 1978-82, 89-90, bd. govs. 1982-85, mem. legal tech. adv. coun. 1985-86, standing com. on nat. conf. groups 1985-91, chmn. sr. lawyers divsn. Nev. 1988—), Nat. Conf. Bar Pres.'s Iowa Bar Assn., Nev. Bar Assn. (bd. govs. 1968-78, pres. 1977-78), Washoe County Bar Assn. (pres. 1966-67), Nat. Jud. Coll. (bd. dirs. 1986-92, sec. 1988-92), Assn. Def. Counsel No. Calif., Assn. Def. Counsel Nev., Assn. Ski Def. Attys., Aircraft Owners and Pilots Assn. (legal svcs. plan 1991—), Washoe County Legal Aid Soc. (co-founder), Lawyer-Pilots Bar Assn. (chmn. Nev.), Greater Reno C. of C. (bd. dirs. 1968-72), Washoe County Golf Task Force, Phi Alpha Delta. Home: 3600 Salerno Dr Reno NV 89509 Office: 421 Court St Ste 100 Reno NV 89501-1793 Office Phone: 775-786-3737. Personal E-mail: loyalhibbs@aol.com.

HICK, KENNETH WILLIAM, marketing executive; b. New Westminster, BC, Can., Oct. 17, 1946; s. Les Walter and Mary Isabelle (Warner) H. BA in Bus., Ea. Wash. State coll., 1971; MBA, U. Wash., 1973, PhD, 1975. Regional sales mgr. Hilti, Inc., San Leandro, Calif., 1976-79; gen. sales mgr. Moore Internat., Inc., Portland, 1979-80; v.p. sales and mktg. Phillips Corp., Anaheim, Calif., 1980-81; owner, pres., CEO K.C. Metals, San Jose, Calif., 1981-87, Losli Internat., Inc., Portland, 1987-89; pres. Resources N.W., Inc., Portland, 1989—. Comms. cons. Asso. Pub. Safety Comm. Officers, Inc., State of Oreg., 1975-93; numerous cons. assignments, also seminars, 1976-2006. Contbr. articles to numerous publs. Mem. Oreg. Gov.'s Tax Bd., 1975-76; pres. Portland chpt. Oreg. Jaycees, 1976; bd. fellows U. Santa Clara, 1983-90. With USAF, 1966-69. Decorated Commendation medal; U. Wash. fellow, 1973. Mem. Am. Mgmt. Assn., Am. Mktg. Assn., Assn. MBA Execs., Assn. Gen. Contractors, Soc. Advancement Mgmt., Home Builders Assn. Roman Catholic. Home: 21462 SW St James Pl West Linn OR 97068 Office: Resources Northwest Inc 8415 SW Seneca # 210 Tualatin OR 97062 Office Phone: 503-612-6628. Personal E-mail: rnwi@integra.net.

HICKCOX, LESLIE KAY, education educator, consultant; b. Berkeley, Calif., May 12, 1951; d. Ralph Thomas and Marilyn Irene (Stump) H. BA, U. Redlands, 1973; MA in Exercise Physiology, U. of the Pacific, 1975; MEd in Curriculum Teaching, Columbia U., 1979; MEd in Health Edn., Oreg. State U., 1987, MEd in Guidance & Counseling, 1988, EdD in Edn., 1991. Cert. Calif. State C.C. instr. (life). Phys. edn. instr., dir. intramurals SUNY, Stony Brook, 1981-83; instr. health edn. Linn-Benton C.C., Oreg., 1985-94; instr. human studies and comm. studies Marylhurst U., Portland, 1987-96, 2002—04; edn. supr., instr. Oreg. State U., Corvallis, 1988-90; instr. health edn., gerontology Portland CC, 1994—95, 2003—; instr. health edn. U. Auckland, New Zealand, 1991; instr., coord. dept. health, phys. edn. and recreation Rogue C.C., Grants Pass, Oreg., 1995-97; assoc. prof., coord. health and phys. edn. Western Mont. Coll., Dillon, Mont., 1997-99; asst. prof. health edn. Northeastern Ill. U., Chgo., 1999—2002; assoc. prof. health edn. West Liberty State Coll., W.Va., 2005—. Founder Experiential Learning Inst., 1992—, found., Lilly N.W. High Edn. Tchg. Conf., 1996; founding v.p. Home Health Diagnostics, Portland, Oreg., 1996, dir. health info., 1996-2003. Contbr. articles to profl. jours. Mem. Assn. Tchr. Educators, Soc. Pub. Health Educators, Am. Assn. Health Edn., Higher Edn. R&D Soc. Australasia, Coun. for Adult and Experiential Learning, Adult Higher Edn. Alliance, Kappa Delta Phi, Phi Delta Kappa. Home: 700 Northwood Ct Apt 102 Wheeling WV 26003-2683 Office Phone: 304-336-8132. Personal E-mail: lesliekayh@msn.com.

HICKEL, WALTER JOSEPH, investment company executive, government agency administrator; b. Claflin, Kans., Aug. 18, 1919; s. Robert A. and Emma (Zecha) H.; m. Janice Cannon, Sept. 22, 1941 (dec. Aug. 1943); 1 child, Theodore; m. Ermalee Strutz, Nov. 22, 1945; children: Robert, Walter Jr., Jack, Joseph, Karl. DEng (hon.), Stevens Inst. Tech., 1970, Mich. Tech. U., 1973; LLD (hon.), St. Mary of Plains Coll., 1970, St. Martin's Coll., 1971, U. Md., Adelphi U., 1971, U. San Diego, 1972, Rensselaer Poly. Inst., 1973, U. Alaska, 1976, Alaska Pacific U., 1991, Benedictine Coll., Kans., 2003; D in Pub. Adminstrn. (hon.), Willamette U., 1971. Founder Hickel Investment Co., Anchorage, 1947—2007; gov. State of Alaska, Alaska, 1966—68, 1990—94; sec. U.S. Dept. Interior, 1969-70; founder Inst. of the North, 1995—; sec. gen. The No. Forum with Arctic and Sub-Arctic Regional Govts., 1994—. Nominated for pres. at Rep. Nat. Convention, 1968; founder Commonwealth North, 1979—; co-founder Yukon Pacific Corp. Author: Who Own's America?, 1971, Crisis in the Commons--The Alaska Solution, 2002; contbr. articles to newspapers. Mem. Rep. Nat. Com., 1954-64; bd. dirs. Salk Inst., 1972-79, NASA Adv. Coun. Exploration Task Force, 1989-91; USAR amb. representing Alaska. Named Alaskan of Year, 1969, Man of Yr. Ripon Soc., 1970; recipient DeSmet medal Gonzaga U., 1969, Horatio Alger award, 1972, Grand Cordon of the Order of Sacred Treasure award His Imperial Majesty the Emperor of Japan, 1988. Mem. Pioneers of Alaska, Equestrian Order Holy Sepulchre, KC. Home: 1905 Loussac Dr Anchorage AK 99517-1225 Office: PO Box 101700 Anchorage AK 99510-1700 Personal E-mail: wjhickel@gci.net. *We shall never understand peace, justice and the living of life until we recognize that all people are human and that humans are the most precious things on earth.*

HICKEN, JEFFREY PRICE, lawyer; b. Macomb, Ill., Oct. 25, 1947; s. Victor and Mary Patricia (O'Connell) H.; m. Mary Sarah Schmidt, Aug. 23, 1969; children: Andrew, Molly, Elizabeth. BA, Cornell Coll., 1969; JD, U. Ill., 1972. Bar: Minn. 1972, U.S. Dist. Ct. Minn. 1980, U.S. Ct. Appeals (8th cir.). Assoc. Weaver, Talle & Herrick, Anoka, Minn., 1972-77; sr. ptnr. Hicken, Scott & Howard, P.A., Anoka, 1977-00, 1998—. Mem. Minn. Family Law Certification Commn., 1999. Bd. dirs. Anoka Lyric Arts; precinct chair Dem. Farmer-Labor Party, Anoka, 1976—. Capt. U.S. Army, 1969-77. Recipient J. Franklin Littel scholarship Cornell Coll., Mt. Vernon, Iowa, 1969 Fellow Am. Acad. Matrimonial Lawyers (cert. arbitrator, bd. mgrs. 1992--); mem. Minn. State Bar Assn., Anoka County Bar Assn. (pres. 1990-91). City of Anoka Charter Commn. (chmn. 1978—). Democrat. Avocations: running, violin. Office: Hicken Scott & Howard PA 2150 3rd Ave Ste 300 Anoka MN 55303-2200 Home: 3145 Dean Ct # 802 Minneapolis MN 55412 Personal E-mail: legaljay@aol.com.

HICKENLOOPER, JOHN W., mayor; b. Feb. 7, 1952; m. Helen Thorpe; 1 child, Teddy. BA in English, Wesleyan U., 1974, MS in Geology, 1980. Exploration geologist Buckhorn Petroleum, Denver, 1981—86; founder The Wynkoop Brewing Co., 1988—98; mayor City and County of Denver, 2003—. Co-founder CultureHaus, Chinook Fund; bd. dirs. Colo. Bus. Com. for the Arts, Denver Metro Conv. and Visitors Bur., Denver Art Mus., Denver Civic Ventures, Volunteers for Outdoor Colo. Office: Denver City and County Bldg 1437 Bannock St Ste 350 Denver CO 80202 Office Phone: 720-865-9000. Office Fax: 720-865-8787. Business E-Mail: MileHighMayor@ci.denver.co.us.*

HICKERSON, GLENN LINDSEY, leasing company executive; b. Burbank, Calif., Aug. 22, 1937; s. Ralph M. and Sarah Lawson (Lindsey) H.; m. Jane Fortune Arthur, Feb. 24, 1973 BA in Bus. Adminstrn., Claremont McKenna Coll., Calif., 1959; MBA, NYU, 1960. Exec. asst. Douglas Aircraft Co., Santa Monica, Calif., 1963; sec., treas. Douglas Fin. Corp., Long Beach, Calif., 1964—67, regional mgr. customer financing, 1967; exec. asst. to pres. Universal Airlines, Inc., Detroit, 1967—68, v.p., treas., asst. sec., 1968—69, pres., 1969-72; v.p., treas., asst. sec. Universal Aircraft Svc., Inc., Detroit, 1968-69, chmn. bd., 1969—72; v.p., treas. Universal Airlines Co., Detroit, 1968—69, pres., 1969—72; group v.p. Marriott Hotels, Inc., Washington, 1972—76; dir. sales Far East and Australia Lockheed Calif. Co., 1976—78, dir. mktg. Americas, 1978—79, dir. mktg. Internat., 1979—81, v.p., internat. sales, 1981—83; v.p. comml. mktg. internat. Douglas Aircraft Co., McDonnell Douglas Corp., 1983—89; mng. dir. GPA Asia Pacific, El Segundo, Calif., 1989—90; exec. v.p. GATX Air Group, San Francisco, 1990—95, pres., 1995—98, chmn. adv. bd., 1998—; pres. Hickerson Assocs., 1998—; chmn. JetWorks Leasing, LLC, 2006—. Lt. (j.g.) USCGR, 1960—62. H.B. Earhart Found. fellow, 1962 Mem.: St. Francis Yacht Club, Pacific Union Club. Office Phone: 415-568-4822. Business E-Mail: ghickerson@jetworks.aero.

HICKEY, BOBBY RAY, underwriting assistant; b. Louisville, Apr. 13, 1960; s. Virgle Ray and Doris Jean (Adams) H. Student, U. Louisville, 1990. Various positions Kroger, Louisville, 1980-87; student asst. U. Louisville, 1987-91, libr. asst. I, 1991-95; mail courier Ky. Farm Bur. Ins., Louisville, 1995, underwriting asst., 1995—2001, Adecco, 2001—02, Today's Staffing, 2003—04; dep. clk. Jefferson County Cir. Ct., Clk.'s Office, 2004—. Auto underwriting dept. rep. to safety com. Ky. Farm Bur., 1996. Neighborhood rep. West Jefferson County Cmty. Task Force, Inc., Louisville, 1996—, v.p. 2002-04, pres. 2004-05; neighborhood rep. Family Health Ctrs., Louisville, 1986—, vice chmn., 1991-03, chmn., 2003-06, chmn. nominating com., 1994-03, mem. mktg. com., 1997; mem. Friends of Marine Hosp., 2004—; mem. bd. Portland NOW, 2006—, exec. com., 2007-. Recipient Barney H. Kroger Cert. Merit Cmty. Svc., 1982, William O. Cowger award Jefferson County Rep. Com., Louisville, 1986, Mayor's citation City of Louisville, 1990, 96, cert. of recognition Jefferson County Commr., 1996. Mem. Toastmasters (v.p. pub. rels. Ky. Farm Bur. chpt. 1996). Roman Catholic. Avocations: theater, reading, community service, theater, travel, music. Office: 700 W Jefferson St Louisville KY 40202 Home: 3031 Portland Ave Louisville KY 40212 Personal E-mail: bobby.hickey@insightbb.com.

HICKEY, CATHERINE JOSEPHINE, school system administrator; b. NYC, Mar. 14, 1936; d. John James and Delia Bridget (Finnegan) Tighe; m. Stephen M. Hickey, Mar. 30, 1959; children: Catherine, Marie, Joanne, Clare, Geraldine, Margaret. BS, Fordham U., 1958, PhD, 1983; MS, CUNY, 1974; LHD (hon.), Mercy Coll., 1990, Iona Coll., Kings Coll., Wilkes-Barre, Pa. Prin. Sacred Heart Sch., Dobbs Ferry, N.Y., 1977-89; instr., adj. prof. Mercy Coll., Dobbs Ferry, 1983-87, Long Island U., Dobbs Ferry, 1984-87, Fairfield (Conn.) U., 1984-87; supt. schs. Archdiocese of N.Y., NYC, 1989—, sec. of edn., 2000—. Roman Catholic. Home: 415 Marlborough Rd Yonkers NY 10701-6709 Office: Archdiocese NY 1011 1st Ave New York NY 10022-4106

HICKEY, ELIZABETH LOUISE, advertising agency executive; b. NYC, Nov. 6, 1958; d. Louise Anthony and Josephine Morgan (Stancisko) Piccioli; m. Mark Hickey, Oct. 15, 1983; children: Caitlin, John, Alanna, Shannon. BA, U. Rochester, 1979; Cert. in Graphic Design, Mass. Coll. Art, 1984. Art and recreation therapist Fernald State Sch., Waltham, Mass., 1979-82; art dir. Wizard of Adz, Dedham, Mass., 1984-89; graphic designer Imageworks, Waltham, 1984-92; pres., mktg. dir. Limo Dreams, Inc., Waltham, 1985-90; creative dir. Wizard of Adz, Dedham, Mass., 1989; art dir. Emerson Lane Fortuna, Boston, 1989—91. Faculty mem. Mass. Coll. Art, 198799, mem. portfolio rev. com.; faculty mem. Emerson Coll., 2002—; art dir. Arnold Fortuna Lane, Boston, 1991-93; sr. art dir. Hill Holliday, 1993-94; creative dir. Holland Mark Martin, 1994-96, Heater Advt. 1997-98; v.p. assoc. creative dir. Arnold Advt., 1996-97; CEO, creative dir. Velocity Inc., 1999—. Author: Design Secrets Advertising, 2002, Designs that Stand Up, Speak Out, and Can't be Ignored, 2004. Recipient Alcoholism and Communications Mktg. Achievement award, 1986, New Eng. Best of Broadcast award, 1991, 1993, 1997, 1999, Francis J. Hatch award, 1991, 1993, 1994, 1996, 1999, 2000, Cannes Internat. advt. award, 1994, Clio Nat. Advt. award, 1994, MCIcon award, 2001, award, The London Show, 1994. Mem.: Big Idea Group. Democrat. Avocations: skiing, competitive and performance Lindy dancing, stand-up comedy, poetry, swing dancing. Home and Office: 306 Dartmouth St Boston MA 02116 Office Phone: 617-247-1111. E-mail: lisa@velocityadvertising.com.

HICKEY, FRANCIS ROGER, physicist, researcher; b. Troy, NY, June 8, 1942; s. Frank R. and Ann M. (O'Malley) H.; m. Paula Williamson, Aug. 29, 1964; children: Sharon Ann, Kevin Derus (dec.). BS, Siena Coll., 1964; MS, Clarkson U., 1967, PhD, 1970. From asst. to assoc. prof. Physics Hartwick Coll., Oneonta, N.Y., 1969-83, prof. Physics, 1983—. Adv. bd. Sci. Discovery Ctr. of Oneonta, 1989—, Oneonta Newman Found, 1988—; nat. councillor Soc. Physics Students, 1974-75. Contbr. articles to profl. jours. Founding mem. Oneonta region chpt. The Compassionate Friends. Mem. Am. Phys. Soc., Am. Assn. Physics Tchrs. Roman Catholic. Achievements include development of Physics Educational Computer Programs. Home: 117 Glen Dr Oneonta NY 13820-3553 Office: Hartwick Coll Physics Dept Oneonta NY 13820 Home Phone: 607-433-2492; Office Phone: 607-431-4739. Business E-Mail: hickeyr@hartwick.edu.

HICKEY, JEROME EDWARD, investment company executive; b. Chgo., June 25, 1937; s. Matthew Joseph and Naomi (Pope) H.; m. Denise Coakley, May 20, 1967; children: J. Graham, Matthew, Elizabeth, George, Peter. BS in Econs., Coll. of the Holy Cross, 1959; MA in Philosophy, Boston Coll., 1964. Instr. Cranwell Sch., Lenox, Mass., 1964-66; acct. exec. Paine Webber, NYC, 1966-68; v.p. Hickey & Co., Chgo., 1968-72, Ralph W. Davis, Chgo., 1972-75, Weeden & Co., Chgo., 1975-78; founder, pres. Jerome Hickey Assocs., Chgo., 1979-84; pres. No. Trust Brokerage, Chgo., 1984-87; sr. v.p. Stein Roe & Farnham, Chgo., 1988-93; sr. v.p., mng. dir. SEI Corp., Chgo., 1993-96; founder, mng. dir. Dearborn Ptnrs., Chgo., 1997—. Dir. Western Golf Assn., Golf, Ill., 1979—, chmn. exec. com., 1991-96; trustee St. Ignatius Coll. Prep., Chgo., 1988-93, chmn., 1990-93; dir. USO of Ill., Inc., 2002—. Named Outstanding Young Man in Am., 1971. Mem. Knollwood Club (Lake Forest, Ill., dir. 1976-79), Bond Club Chgo. (dir. 1974-75), Econ. Club Chgo., Desert Forest Golf Club, The Boulders, Burning Tree Club. Roman Catholic. Home: 245 Leeds Ct Lake Bluff IL 60044 Office: Dearborn Ptnrs 200 W Madison St Chicago IL 60606-3414 Business E-Mail: jhickey@dearpart.com.

HICKEY, JOHN HEYWARD (JACK), lawyer; b. Miami, Fla., Dec. 18, 1954; s. Weyman Park Hickey and Alice Joan (Heyward) Brown. BA magna cum laude, Fla. State U., 1976; JD, Duke U., 1980. Bars: Fla. 1980, U.S. Dist. Ct. (so. dist) Fla. 1980, U.S. Dist. Ct. (mid. dist.) Fla. 1982, U.S. Ct. Appeals (5th cir.) 1982, U.S. Ct. Appeals (11th cir.) 1983, U.S. Supreme Ct. 1985. Trial lawyer Smathers & Thompson, Miami, 1980-85, Hornsby & Whisenand P.A., Miami, 1985—, ptnr., 1988, Hickey & Jones P.A., Miami, 1988—99, Hickey Law Firm, P.A., Miami, 1999—. Lectr. securities litigation Internat. Assn. Fin. Planners, 1989, 90, Fla. Inst. CPAs, 1990, Flood Ins. Conf., Columbus, Ohio, 1991, Scottsdale, Ariz., 1992, Orlando, Fla., 1993; lectr. admiralty law, Fla. Bar, 1994, 2000; lectr. slip and fall litigation ATLA, Montreal, Can., 2001-02. Contbg. author: Fla. Bar Jour., 1990, Trial mag., 2000, P&I Internat., 1998. Interviewer of prospective undergrads. Duke U. Alumni Adv. Com., 1984—; arbitrator Miami Marine Arbitration Coun. Fellow Fla. Bar Found. (life); mem. ABA (litigation mgmt./econs. com. 1986—, comml. transactions and banking com. 1986—), Fla. Bar (chmn. admiralty law com. 2000-01, chmn. grievance com. 1986-89, vice chmn. 1999—, lectr. Bridge the Gap seminars 1984-85, jud. evaluation com. 1985, chmn. 11th cir. fee arbitration com. 1991—, cert. civil trial lawyer 1990—, lectr. admiralty law 1994, chair admiralty law com. 1997—), Dade County Bar Assn. (bd. dirs. 1996-99, treas. 1999-2000, sec. 2000-01, v.p. 2002-02, pres.-elect 2002-03, pres. 2003-04, bd. dirs. 1998—, chmn. membership com. 1982-83, chmn. cir. ct. com. 1983-84, dir. 1984-86, chmn. young lawyers sect. meetings and programs com. 1985-86, chmn. young lawyers sect. sports com. 1984-85, exec. com. 1985—, chmn. profl. arbitration subcom. 1986—, cert. of merit 1985, 88, 89, 91, 921, 93, bd. dirs. 1990-93, 97—, chmn. banking and corp. litigation com. 1990, 91, 92, chmn. civil litigation com. 1992-93, exec. com. 1992-93), Greater Miami C. of C., Coral Gables C. of C., Propellor Club of U.S. (Miami divsn.), Fla. Coun. Bar Assn. Pres. (life), Assn. Trial Lawyers Am., Southeastern Admiralty Law Inst. (proctor), Maritime Law Assn., Miami Marine Arbitration Coun., Phi Beta Kappa. Office: Hickey Law Firm PA 1401 Brickell Ave Ste 510 Miami FL 33131-3501 Office Phone: 800-215-7117. Business E-Mail: hickey@hickeylawfirm.com.

HICKEY, JOHN KING, lawyer, career officer; b. Mt. Sterling, Ky. s. John Andrew and Anna Christine H.; m. Elizabeth Jane Pattavina, Nov. 23, 1944; children: Roger Dennis, John King, Patricia Elizabeth Corsini. JD, U. Ky., 1948; M in Internat. Affairs, George Washington U., 1974. Bar: Ky. 1949, Colo. 1958, U.S. Ct. Military Appeals 1959, U.S. Supreme Ct. 1959. Commd. 2d. lt. U.S. Army Air Forces, 1942; advanced through grades to col. USAF, 1964, ret., 1970; dir. legal judicial adminstrn. Council State Govts., Lexington, Ky., 1971-73; dir. continuing legal edn. U. Ky. Coll. Law, Lexington, Ky., 1973-86; pvt. practice Lexington, Ky., 1986—. Mem. Nat. Assn. Attorneys Gen. (outstanding contributions award 1973, sec.), U. Ky. Law Alumni Assn. (sec., treas. 1973-76, appreciation award 1976), Ctrl. Ky. Knife Club (plaque 1997). Democrat. Roman Catholic. Avocations: machairologist, reading, walking, swimming. Office: 3340 Nantucket Dr Lexington KY 40502-3205 Personal E-mail: kinghickey@aol.com.

HICKEY, JOHN MILLER, lawyer; b. Cleve., June 4, 1955; s. Lawrence Thomas and Margaret (Miller) H.; m. Sharon Salazar, Aug. 4, 1984; children: Theodore James, John Salazar, Margaret Maureen. Student, U. Wales, UK, 1975-76; BA, Tulane U., 1977; JD cum laude, Calif. We. Sch. Law, 1981; LLM in tax, NYU, 1982. Bar: Calif. 1981, N.Mex. 1983, U.S. Dist. Ct. N.Mex. 1983, U.S. Tax Ct. 1983, U.S. Ct. Appeals (10th cir.) 1983. Prodn. control mgr. Randall-Textron, Inc., Wilmington, Ohio, 1977-78; assoc. Montgomery & Andrews, Santa Fe, 1983-88; shareholder, dir. Compton, Coryell, Hickey & Ives, Santa Fe, 1988-93, Hickey & Ives, Santa Fe, 1993-97, Hickey & Johnson PA, Santa Fe, 1998-99, White, Koch, Kelly & McCarthy, P.A., Santa Fe, 1999—2005, Thompson, Rose & Hickey, PA, Santa Fe, 2006—. Mem. legal com. Santa Fe Cmty. Found., 2000—; mem. adv. bd. Presbyn. Med. Svcs. Found. Fellow: Am. Coll. Trust and Estate Counsel; mem.: State Bar N.Mex. (bd. dirs. taxation sect. 2002—). Republican. Roman Catholic. Avocations: bicycling, squash, reading. Home: 806 Camino Zozobra Santa Fe NM 87505-6101 Office: Thompson Rose & Hickey PA 1751 Old Pecos Tr Ste I Santa Fe NM 87505 Office Phone: 505-988-2900. Business E-Mail: jhickey@trhpa.com.

HICKEY, JOHN THOMAS, retired electronics company executive; b. Chgo., Oct. 28, 1925; s. Matthew J., Jr. and Naomi (Pope) H.; m. Joanne R. Keating, Sept. 17, 1949; children: Kathleen Coakley Barrie, John, Michael, James, Roger. BS in Commerce, Loyola U., Chgo., 1948; MBA, U. Chgo., 1952. With Motorola Inc. (and subs.), 1943—55, gen. mgr. semicondr. div., 1955-58, asst. to pres., 1958-62, dir. long range planning, 1962-65, v.p. planning, 1965-70, v.p. finance, sec., 1970-74, sr. v.p., CFO, dir., 1974—84, exec. v.p., CFO, dir., 1984—86, chmn. fin. com., dir., 1986-96; ret., 1996. Served with AUS, 1944-46. Mem. Skokie Country Club (Glencoe, Ill.), Ocean Forest Golf Club. Home (Summer): 2320 Indigo Ln Glenview IL 60026 Home (Winter): PO Box 31065 Sea Island GA 31561-1065

HICKEY, JOHN THOMAS, JR., lawyer; b. Evanston, Ill., July 9, 1952; s. John Thomas and Joanne (Keating) H.; m. Candis Bailey, July 7, 1979; children: Alison, Jack, Patrick, Claire, Matthew. AB magna cum laude, phi beta kappa, Georgetown U., 1974; JD, U. Chgo., 1977. Bar: Ill. 1977, U.S. Dist. Ct. (no. dist.) Ill. 1977, U.S. Ct. Appeals (7th cir.) 1977, U.S. Ct. Appeals (10th cir.) 1987. Assoc. Kirkland & Ellis, Chgo., 1977-83, ptnr., mem. firm mgmt. com., 1983—. Mem. adv. bd. Leading Lawyers Network. Fellow Am. Coll. Trial Lawyers. Office: Kirkland & Ellis 200 E Randolph St Fl 59 Chicago IL 60601-6609 Office Phone: 312-861-2348. Office Fax: 312-861-2200. Business E-Mail: jhickey@kirkland.com.

HICKEY, JOSEPH MICHAEL, investment banker; b. Greenburgh, Pa., June 6, 1940; s. Joseph Michael and Margaret (Nelson) H.; m. Suzanne Klempay, July 2, 1970. BS, Ind. U. Pa., 1963. Sales rep. 3M Co., St. Paul, 1967-69; acct. exec. Hornblower & Weeks, Helphill, Noyes, Cleve., 1970-75; pres. Prescott, Ball & Turben, Cleve., 1976-88; dist. chmn. Nat. Assn. Security Dealers, Cleve., 1979-81; mem. mktg. com. SIA, NYC, 1982-86, mem. regional firms com., 1989; chmn. bd. Canregie Capital Mgmt. Co., Cleve., 1983-86; pres. J.W. Charles Group, Cleve., 1988-90; chmn. Pierman Golf Co., North Palm Beach, Fla., 1991-92; pres. Greyfriar Capital Corp., North Palm Beach, Fla. S.E. region adv. bd. No. Trust. Capt. US Army, 1963—67. Mem. Kirtland Country Club, Loxahatchee Club, Castle Pines Golf Club, Lost Tree Club, The Bear's Club.

HICKEY, KEVIN FRANCIS, software company executive; b. Bridgeport, Conn., June 20, 1951; s. Herbert Augustine and Anne Therese (Pisani) H.; m. Christine Marie Hackett, June 10, 1973 (div. 1978); m. Eileen Michael O'Gara, July 4, 1981; children: Frances, Augustine. AB, Harvard U., 1973; MHSA, U. Mich., 1976; JD, Loyola U., Chgo., 1984. Bar: Ill. 1984. Dir. Am. Hosp. Assn., Chgo., 1978-83; exec. v.p. First Health Assocs., Chgo., 1983-85; v.p., gen. counsel Metlife Healthcare Mgmt. Corp., St. Louis, 1985-88; sr. v.p. Lincoln Nat. Life Ins. Co., Ft. Wayne, Ind., 1988-92; regional v.p. Aetna Health Plans, Chgo., 1992-94, sr. v.p. ops. Hartford, Conn., 1994-96; pres. Health Plans of Am., Farmington, Conn., 1996-97; exec. v.p. Oxford Health Plans, Norwalk, Conn., 1997-98; chmn., CEO IntelliClaim, Inc., Norwalk, Conn., 1998—2005. Chmn. NEIC, Secaucus, N.J., 1994-95. Contbr. articles to profl. publs. Personal E-mail: khickey@gmail.com.

HICKEY, LEO JOSEPH, museum curator, educator; b. Phila., Apr. 26, 1940; s. James Joseph and Helen Marie (Schwarz) H.; m. Judith McKendry, June 29, 1968; children: Geoffrey Alan, Damian Michael, Jason Alexander. BS, Villanova U., 1962; MA, Princeton U., 1964; postgrad., Rutgers U., 1963-65; PhD, Princeton U., 1967; MA (privatim), Yale U., 1983. Postdoctoral fellow NRC-Smithsonian Inst., Washington, 1966-69, assoc. curator, 1969-80; chmn. exhibits com. Natural History Mus., Smithsonian, 1973-75, curator, 1980-82; prof. geology Yale U., New Haven, 1982—; dir. Peabody Mus., Yale U., 1982-87; prof. biology Yale U., 1982-97, chair dept. geology and geophysics, 2003—; curator of paleobotany Peabody Mus. Nat. History, 1982—. Adj. prof. botany U. Md., College Park, 1981-85; adj. prof. geology U. Pa., Phila., 1982-, chmn. dept. geology and geophysics, 2003-; past pres., pres., v.p. Yellowstone-Bighorn Rsch. Assn., Red Lodge, Mont., 1979-86; dir. Mus. of Am. Theatre, New Haven, 1983-87; mem. Mars Lander Sci. Team, 1999—. Author: Stratigraphy and Paleobotany of Golden Valley Formation, 1977, On Wood and the Forest Primeval: The Geological History of Wood, 2003; co-author: The Great Dinosaur Mural, 1990; editor: (with D.W. Taylor) Origin, Early Evolution, and Phylogeny of the Flowering Plants, 1996. Recipient H.A. Gleason award NY Bot. Gardens, 1977, Best Paper award Geol. Soc. Washington, 1981, Disting. Alumnus award Villanova U., 1982, Ann. Book award Dinosaur Soc., 1992; grantee Smithsonian Rsch. Found., 1972-76, Nat. Geog. Soc., 1979, 84-85, NSF, 1984, 90, 92, 2000, 03, Bay Found., 1995-96, 2000, Nason Found., 2002. Fellow Geol. Soc. Am.; mem. AAAS, Bot. Soc. Am., Paleontol. Soc. Democrat. Roman Catholic. Office: Peabody Mus Natural History PO Box 208118 170 Whitney Ave New Haven CT 06520-8118 also: Yale Geology Dept PO Box 208109 New Haven CT 06520-8109 Home Phone: 203-785-8668; Office Phone: 203-432-5006. Business E-Mail: leo.hickey@yale.edu.

HICKEY, PAUL ROBERT, anesthesiologist, educator; b. Corinth, NY; s. William Joseph Hickey; m. Ann Marie Murphy, Oct. 9, 1956; children: Julia, Brendan, Claire, Connor, Meghan. BA cum laude, Yale U., 1966; MD, Columbia U., 1970; MA (hon.), Harvard U., 1996. Diplomate Am. Bd. Anesthesiology, Nat. Bd. Med. Examiners; lic. physician, N.Y., Mass., Ohio. Surg. intern Columbia Presbyn. Med. Ctr., NYC, 1970-71, asst. resident, 1971-72; resident anesthesia Mass. Gen. Hosp., Boston, 1978-80, fellow cardiac anesthesia svc., 1980-81; clin. and rsch. assoc. in surgery Nat. Heart and Lung Inst., NIH, Bethesda, Md., 1972-74; clin. fellow anesthesia Harvard Med. Sch., 1978-80, rsch. fellow anesthesia, 1980-81, instr. anesthesia, 1981-83, asst. prof., 1983-86, assoc. prof., 1986-96, prof. anaesthesia, 1996—, chair exec. com. dept. anesthesia, 1997—. Staff physician emergency rm. St. Anne's Hosp., Fall River, Mass., 1974-78, Falmouth (Mass.) Hosp., 1974-78; asst. in anesthesia Children's Hosp. Med. Ctr., Boston, 1981-83; clin. assoc. in anesthesia, Mass. Gen. Hosp., 1981—; cons. in anesthesia Brigham and Women's Hosp., Boston, 1982—; assoc. in anesthesia The Children's Hosp., 1984-86, sr. assoc. in anesthesia, 1986-92, anesthesiologist-in-chief, 1992—, chmn. physican orgn., 1998—; cons. cardiac anesthesia Project Hosp., Washington, 1984—; vis. prof. various univs., 1983—; chmn. anesthesia/intensive care subcom. Project Hope steering com. for Sino-Am. Children's Med. Ctr., 1990-93; assoc. examiner Am. Bd. Anesthesiology, 1988—, assoc. oral examiner, 1991—; lectr. various orgns., univs., hosps. Cons., editl. bd. Anesthesiology, 1981-91, Jour. Thoracic and Cardiovascular Surgery, 1984—, New Eng. Jour. Medicine, 1992—, Pediatric Rsch., 1994—; editl. bd. Jour. Cardiothoracic Anesthesia, 1986-92, Anesthesia and Analgesia, 1987-97; contbr. articles to profl. jours., chpts. to books. Grantee Janssen Pharmecutica, Inc., 1982-83, 85-88, NIH, 1985—, Mass. Humane Soc., 1982-83, Medasonics, 1990-91. Fellow Am. Acad. Pediatrics; mem. AAAS, Andrew G. Morrow Surg. Soc., Am. Soc. Anesthesiologists (com. on circulation 1983-85, com. on pediatric anesthesia 1992-94), Internat. Anesthesia Rsch. Soc., Soc. Cardiovascular Anesthesiologists (internat. affairs com. 1987—), Assn. Univ. Anesthetists, Soc. Pediatric Anesthesia, Soc. Acad. Anesthesia Chmn., Mass. Med. Soc. Office: Children's Hosp Anesthesia Dept 300 Longwood Ave Boston MA 02115-5724

HICKEY, ROBERT JOSEPH, research scientist, educator; s. John and Stella Teresa Hickey; m. Linda Helen Malkas, Feb. 14, 1981. PhD in Biochemistry, CUNY, 1979. Assoc. prof. pharmacology Ind. U. Sch. Medicine, 1989—2001, assoc. prof. medicine and pharmacology Indpls., 2002—07. Founder CS-Keys Inc., Indpls., 2006—07, sci. advisor, 2006—07. Contbr. scientific papers. Mem.: Am. Assn. Cancer Rsch. (corr.). Independent. Achievements include discovery of identification of a unique molecular signature for cancer. Avocations: flying, swimming, gardening, woodworking. Home Phone: 317-852-9361; Office Phone: 317-278-4298. Office Fax: 317-274-8046.

HICKEY, WILLIAM V., manufacturing executive; b. 1945; BS U.S. Naval Acad, MBA Harvard U. With W.R. Grace & Co.; joined Sealed Air Corp., Saddle Brook, NJ, 1980, exec. v.p., 1994—96, pres., COO, 1996—2000, pres., CEO, 2000—. Bd. dirs. Universal Foods Corp. Office: Sealed Air Park 80 East Saddle Brook NJ 07663*

HICKEY, WIN E(SPY), former state legislator, social worker; b. Rawlins, Wyo. d. David P. and Eugenia (Blake) Espy; children: John David, Paul Joseph. BA, Loretto Heights Coll., 1933; postgrad., U. Utah, 1934, Sch. Social Svc., U. Chgo., 1936; LLD (hon.), U. Wyo., 1991. Dir. Carbon County Welfare Dept., 1935—36; field rep. Wyo. Dept. Welfare, 1937—38; dir. Red Cross Club, Europe, 1942—45; commr. Laramie County, Wyo., 1973—80; mem. Wyo. Senate, 1980—90; dir. United Savs. & Loan, Cheyenne; active Joint Powers Bd. Laramie County and City of Cheyenne. Pub. Where the Deer and the Antelope Play, 1967; pres. Meml. Hosp. of Laramie County, 1986—88, Wyo. Transp. Mus., 1990—92; pres. county and state mental health assn., 1959—63; trustee U. Wyo., 1967—71; active Gov. Residence Found., 1991—93, Wyo. Transp. Mus., 1993—; trustee St. Mary's Cathedral, 1986—; active Nat. Coun. Cath. Women; pres., bd. dirs. U. Wyo. Found., 1986—87; chmn. adv. coun. div. cmty. programs Wyo. Dept. Health and Social Svcs.; chair Am. Heritage Assocs. of U. Wyo., 1992—96. Named Outstanding Alumna, Loretto Heights Coll., 1959, Woman of Yr., Commn. for Women, 1988, United Med. Ctr., Cheyenne, 1998, Legislator of Yr., Wyo. Psychologists Assn., 1988, Family of the Yr., U. Wyo., 1995, Person of Yr., United Med. Ctr., Cheyenne, Wyo., 1998. Mem.: Altrusa Club (Cheyenne).

HICKMAN, BERT GEORGE, JR., economist, educator; b. LA, Oct. 6, 1924; s. Bert George and Caroline E. (Douglas) H.; m. Edythe Anne Warshauer, Feb. 9, 1947; children: Wendy Elizabeth, Paul Lawrence, Alison Diane. BS, U. Calif.-Berkeley, 1947, PhD, 1951. Instr. Stanford U., 1949-51; research asso. Nat. Bur. Econ. Research, 1951-52; asst. prof. Northwestern, 1952-54; mem. sr. staff Council Econ. Advisers, 1954-56; research assoc. Brookings Instn., 1956-58, mem. sr. staff, 1958-66; prof. Stanford U., 1966-95, prof. emeritus, 1996—. Vis. prof. U. Calif. at Berkeley, 1960, London Grad. Sch. Bus Studies, 1972-73, , Inst. Advanced Studies, Vienna, Austria, 1974, 1975, Kyoto U., 1977; NSF fellow Netherlands Econometric Inst., Rotterdam, 1964-65; Ford Found. Faculty research fellow, 1968-69; mem. com. econ. stability Social Sci. Research Council, 1959-61, chmn., 1962-95; chmn. exec. com. Project Link, 1969—; chmn. Energy Modeling Forum working group on macroecon. impacts of energy shocks Stanford U., 1982-83; Am. coord. US-USSR program on econ.-math. macromodeling Am. Coun. Learned Socs., 1988-90. Author: Growth and Stability of the Postwar Economy, 1960, Investment Demand and U.S. Economic Growth, 1965, (with Robert M. Coen) An Annual Growth Model of the U.S. Economy, 1976; Editor: Quantitative Planning of Economic Policy, 1965, Econometric Models of Cyclical Behavior, 1972, Global International Economic Models, 1983, International Monetary Stabilization and the Foreign Debt Problem, 1984, International Productivity and Competitiveness, 1992; co-editor: Global Econometrics, 1983, Macroeconomic Impacts of Energy Shocks, 1987, Link Proceedings, 1991, 92, Studies in Applied Economics, Vol. 1, 1997; contbr. articles to profl. jours. Served with USNR, 1943-46. Vis. fellow Internat. Inst. Applied Systems Analysis, 1979, 80; resident fellow Rockefeller Found., 1989; named Hon. Prof. U. Vienna, Austria, 1985. Fellow Econometric Soc.; mem. Am. Econ. Assn. (chmn. census adv. com. 1968-71, tech. subcom. to rev. bus. cycle devels. 1962-68, nominating com. 1978-79, chmn. seminar on global modeling, conf. on econometrics and math. econs. 1975-83), Phi Beta Kappa, Phi Eta Sigma. Home: 620 Sand Hill Rd Apt 312G Palo Alto CA 94304 Office: Stanford U Dept Econs Stanford CA 94305 Business E-Mail: bhickman@stanford.edu.

HICKMAN, ELIZABETH PODESTA, retired counselor; b. Livingston, Ill., Sept. 30, 1922; d. Louis and Della (Martin) Podesta; m. Franklin Jay Hickman, Mar. 17, 1944 (dec.); children: Virginia Hickman Hellstern, Franklin. BE summa cum laude, Ea. Ill. State U.; MA, George Washington U., 1966, EdD (Exxon Found.-Raskob Found. grantee), 1979; postgrad., U. Chgo., 1945, U. Va., 1964-66; postgrad. (fellow), Northeastern U., 1967-68. Lic. counselor, Va. Tchr. pub. schs., Ill., Ohio, Va., Naples, Italy, 1944-64; dir. coll. transfer guidance Maymount Coll. Va., Arlington, 1964-67, dir. Counceling Ctr., 1974-81, assoc. dean counseling and residence life, 1981-84; cmty. counselor Divsn. Mass. Employment Security, Newton, 1968-69; tchr. English conversation, Fuchu, Japan, 1969-73; placement dir., career counselor Coll. of Gt. Falls, Mont., 1973-74; assoc. rschr. George Washington U., Washington, 1986. Lectr. Far East divsn. U. Md., Fuchu, 1971-73; spl. advisor Internat. Ranger Camps, Denmark and Switzerland, 1974-81; spl. cons. Internat. Quaker Sch., Werkhoven, The Netherlands, 1959-63; mem. steering com. Pres.'s Com. on Employment of Handicapped, 1974-95. Vol., ARC, 1967-68, Family Svcs., 1954-75, White House Agy. Liaison, 1986—, Kennedy Ctr. Adminstrn., Washington, 1984—, Arlington Free Clinic, 2000-02. With WAVES, 1943-44. Recipient Disting. Alumnus award Ea. Ill. U., 1984. Mem. Brent Soc., Rose Soc., Potomac (Ill) Soc., Italian Am. Soc., Marymount U. Angels Soc., Women's Com. Nat. Symphony Orch., Washington Opera Guild, Delta Epsilon Sigma, Pi Lambda Theta. Roman Catholic. Home: 4708 38th Pl N Arlington VA 22207-2915

HICKMAN, FREDERIC W., retired lawyer; b. Sioux City, Iowa, June 30, 1927; s. Simeon M. and Esther (Nixon) Hickman; m. Katherine Heald, July 15, 1964; children: Mary Sanders, Sara Ridder. AB, Harvard U., 1948, LLB magna cum laude, 1951. Bar: Ill. 1951. Assoc. Sidley & Austin, Chgo., 1951-55; ptnr. Hopkins & Sutter, Chgo., 1956-71, 75-92, sr. counsel, 1993-2001. Asst. sec. tax policy Dept. Treasury, Washington, 1972—75; draftsman Ill. Income Tax, 1969; author, lectr. taxation. Pres. Nat. Tax Assn., 1989—90; mem. Ill. Humanities Coun., 1977—82, Citizens Commn. Pub. Sch. Fin., 1977—78; chmn. bd. trustees Am. Conservatory Music, 1980—90. With USN, 1945—46. Mem.: ABA, Am. Coll. Tax Counsel (regent 1989—92), Internat. Fiscal Assn. (dir. 1973—77), Chikaming Country Club (Lakeside, Mich.), Legal Club (pres. Chgo. 1980—81), Mid-Day Club (Chgo.), Union League Club (Chgo.), Comm. Club (Chgo.). Republican. Methodist. Home: 360 Green Bay Rd # 4E Winnetka IL 60093-4032

HICKMAN, LUCILLE, physical therapist; b. Chgo., July 21, 1949; d. Louis Melvin and Edna (Edwards) H. BA in Sociology, Lake Forest Coll., 1972; BS in Physical Therapy, Chgo. Med. Sch., 1975; MS in Health Sci., Gov.'s State U., 1985. Staff phys. therapist Michael Reese Hosp., Chgo., 1975-79; dir. phys. therapy Provident Med. Ctr., Chgo., 1979-83; instr. phys. therapy Chgo. State U., 1983-87; pres. adminstrv. dir. R.O.C. Phys. Therapy Svcs., Chgo., 1985—93; founder, pres. PhysioCare Ltd., Chgo., 1988—93. Pvt. practice therapy cons., Chgo., 1983—93. Mem. Am. Phys. Therapy Assn., Nat. Soc. Allied Health. Democrat. Episcopalian. Achievements include patents for exercise machine, 1998. Avocations: piano, composing, cooking, writing.

HICKMAN, R(OBERT) HARRISON, political pollster, strategist; b. Whiteville, NC, Feb. 10, 1953; s. Robert Raymond and Marietta (Harrison) H.; m. Caroline Isabelle Mesrobian, Aug. 15, 1981; 1 child, Ralfe Harrison. AB, Guilford Coll., 1975; MA, U. Nebr., 1977; postgrad., Tulane U., 1980, U. Mich., 1979. V.p. Hamilton & Staff, Inc., Chevy Chase, Md., 1980-84; ptnr. Hickman-Brown Rsch., Inc., Washington, 1984—2003, Global Strategy Group, LLC, 2003—; adj. prof. George Washington U., Washington, 1993—. Election cons. CBS News, N.Y.C., 1982—. Disting. Alumni lectr. Guildford Coll., Greensboro, N.C., 1987; named most valuable pollster 1986 elections, U.S. News & Report, 1986; recipient Good Guy award Nat. Women's Polit. Caucus, 1987, Alumni Excellence award Guilford Coll., 1991; named Best in the Bus., Cable News Network Inside Politics, 1988. Mem. Am. Assn. Polit. Cons., Am. Assn. Pub. Opinion Rsch., Am. Polit. Sci. Assn., Kenwood Country Club (Bethesda, Md.). Democrat. Methodist. Avocations: golf, reading. Home: 3828 Gramercy St NW Washington DC 20016-4226 Office: 4445 Willard Ave Ste 1040 Chevy Chase MD 20815-3694

HICKMAN, RONALD LEE, media broker, broadcast executive; b. Belmar, NJ, Sept. 23, 1932; s. Charles Alfred and Thelma Hefter Hickman; m. Barbara Alice Sanders; children: Ronald Hickman, II, David, Todd. Student, Pikeville Coll., 1953—55. Announcer, sportscaster, salesman WPKE-AM, Pikeville, Ky., 1952—55; salesman, news dir., gen. mgr. WNNJ-AM & FM, Newton, NJ, 1955—63; gen. mgr., part-owner WKER-AM, Pompton Lakes, NJ, 1963—69; pres., gen. mgr. WKFD-AM, Wickford, RI, 1969—78; founder, gen. mgr., pres. WOTB-FM, Middletown/Newport, RI, 1978—83; media broker Hickman Assocs. Author: Touching the Stars, 1986, The Media Brokers, 2000. Pres. Newton Country Club, 1995—97; founder Newton (N.J.) Jaycee Chpt., 1959—60; pres. N.J. Broadcasters Assn., 1964; bd. dirs. People's Credit Union, Middletown, RI, 1982—86. Pvt. USAF, 1951—51. Recipient Best News Story, AP to WOTB-FM, 1982. Mem.: Men's Golf Assn. (pres. 1998—2000), Tiger Point Golf and Country Club. Episcopalian. Avocations: golf, music, photography. Home and Office: 48 Timberton Dr Hattiesburg MS 39401 Office Phone: 601-544-4466. Personal E-mail: ronhickman@bellsouth.net.

HICKMAN, ROSE, lawyer; BA in Philosophy, Coll. William and Mary, Williamsburg, Va., 1997, BS in Physics, 1997; JD, U. So. Calif., LA, 2001. Atmospheric sci. rschr. NASA Langley, Norfolk, Va., 1996—97, Ga. Inst. Tech., Atlanta, 1997—97; programmer/analyst BellSouth Intelliventures, Atlanta, 1997—98; judicial extern, Hon. Mitchell R. Goldberg Riverside, Calif., 1998; law clk. Blakely, Sokoloff, Taylor & Zafman, LA, 1999—2000; summer assoc. Pretty, Schroeder, & Poplawski, LA, 2000; atty. Christie, Parker & Hale, LLP, Pasadena, Calif., 2001—06, Hogan & Hartson, LA, 2006—. Contbr. INTA Bulletin newsletter. Named Rising Star Super Lawyer, Law & Politics Mag., 2004—07, L.A. Mag., 2004—07. Mem.: LA County Bar Assn. IP and Entertainment Law Sect. (exec. com. mem. 2007—), Internat. Trademark Assn. (bull. com. mem. 2006—), LA County Bar Assn. Barristers (exec. com. mem. 2003—, networking com. chair 2003—, v.p. 2006—07), US Patent Bar, Calif. Bar, LA Intellectual Property Law Assn. Achievements include prosecuting patents for the design of the Mars Exploration Rover Athena; worked on the successful Markman brief and summary judgment motion dealing with inoperable claim limitations, affirmed by the Federal Circuit in Chef America, Inc. v. Lamb-Weston. Office: Hogan and Hartson LLP Ste 1400 1999 Ave of the Stars Los Angeles CA 90067 Home Phone: 310-936-2397; Office Phone: 310-785-4600. Business E-Mail: rahickman@hhlaw.com.

HICKMAN, TRAPHENE PARRAMORE, retired library director, consultant; b. Dallas, Jan. 31, 1933; d. Redden Travis and Stella (Moore) P.; m. John Robert Hickman, June 9, 1950; children: Lynn Kleifgen, Laurie Ward AA, Mountain View C.C.; BA, U. Tex-Arlington; MLS, U. North Tex. Cert. libr., Tex. Libr. Cedar Hill (Tex.) Pub. Libr., 1959-77; dir. Dallas County Libr. Sys., Dallas, 1977-93; libr. cons. Dallas County, 1993-95; libr.

High Pointe Elem. Sch. Cedar Hill Ind. Sch. Dist., 2003—. Chair leadership coun. and family ministries FUMC of Cedar Hill. Editor: History and Directory of Cedar Hill, 1976; editor News and Views newsletter Dallas county Employees, 1986-92. Chmn. Bicentennial Com., Cedar Hill, 1976; del. Dem. Nat. Conv. 9th Senate Dist., Tex., 1976; chmn. Sesquicentennial Com., Cedar Hill, 1984-86; Dallas County Dem. Forum; mem. Electoral Coll., 1988; chairperson Women's Bd. Northwood Inst., Cedar Hill; active Dallas County Sesquicentennial Com., 1996-; lay speaker United Methodist Ch., 2004. Recipient Newsmaker of Yr. award Cedar Hill Chronicle, 1976; named Amb. of Goodwill, State of Tex., 1976 Mem. ALA, Tex. Libr. Assn. (legis. com. 1984-95, councillor 1982-83, trustee com. 1987-95, pub. info. com. 1987-95), Pub. Libr. Adminstrs. of North Tex. (sec., v.p., pres. 1980, 87), Dallas County Libr. Assn., N.E. Tex. Libr. Sys. (legis. commn. 1978-95, Libr. of Yr. 1987), U. North Tex. Sch. Libr. and Info. Scis. Alumni Assn. (pres. 1987-88), Cedar Hill C. of C., Cedar Summit Book Club (officer), Dallas Area Storytelling Guild (pres. 1995-99) Democrat. Methodist. Avocations: writing, reading, storytelling, gardening, bridge, travel, square dancing. Home and Office: 421 Lee St Cedar Hill TX 75104-2697

HICKMAN, WALTER DIXON, II, information technology manager; b. Union Springs, Ala., Nov. 23, 1968; s. Walter Dixon and M. Dianne Hickman; 1 child, Kalen Seth. B in Bus. Adminstrn. cum laude, Ga. State U., Atlanta, 1995. Cert. Oracle Profl. Oracle Corp., 2000. Database programmer eTour.com, Atlanta, 2000—01; mgr. data svcs. State Ga. AOC, Atlanta, 2001—. Cons. RACE Inc., Atlanta, 1998—2001. Mem.: Mensa. Home: Prattville AL 36066 Home Phone: 334-391-6334; Office Phone: 404-656-7691. Personal E-mail: whickman44@yahoo.com.

HICKOK, D. ALICIA, lawyer; b. Whittier, Calif., Oct. 19, 1960; d. Gus J. Gerson, Jr. and Diane E. Gerson; m. Peter K. Hickok, Mar. 16, 1985; children: Samuel, Elonnai, Bennet. BA cum laude, Tex. Christian U., 1979; JD cum laude, U. Pa., 2001. Bar: Pa. 2001, N.J. 2001, U.S. Dist. Ct. (ea. dist.) Pa., U.S. Dist. Ct. N.J., U.S. Ct. Appeals (3rd cir.). Law clk. to hon. M.O. Rendell 3d Cir. Ct. Appeals, 2001—02; atty. Drinker, Biddle & Reath, Phila., 2002—. Tchg. asst. U. Pa., 1999; coach mem. Jessup Internat. Moot Ct. Team, 1999—2000, 2000—01. Assoc. editor: U. Pa. Law Rev., 1999—2000, tech. editor:, 2000—01. Mem.: ABA (antitrust, internat. law and lit. sects.). Avocations: bridge, bread baking. Office: Drinker Biddle & Reath One Logan Sq 18th and Cherry Philadelphia PA 19103 Home Phone: 610-328-3729; Office Phone: 215-988-3364. E-mail: alicia.hickok@dbr.com.

HICKOK, EUGENE WELCH, former federal agency administrator; b. Jan. 1, 1950; m. Katharine Pauley; 2 children. BA, Hampden-Sydney Coll., 1972; master's, U. Va., 1978, PhD, 1983. Spl. asst. Office Legal Counsel U.S. Dept. Justice, 1986—87; dir. fin. aid Hampden-Sydney Coll., Va.; assoc. dir. dept. polit. sci. Miss. State U.; instr. polit. sci. Dickinson Coll., Carlisle, Pa., dir. Clarke Ctr. Interdisciplinary Study of Contemporary Issues; sec. edn. Commonwealth of Pa. Dept. Edn., Harrisburg, 1995—2001; under sec. US Dept. Edn., Washington, 2001—04, acting dep. sec., 2003—04, dep. sec., 2004—05. Dir. Clarke Ctr. Interdisciplinary Study of Contemporary Issues. Author books; contbr. articles to profl. jours. Mem. Carlisle Area Sch. Bd. Recipient Ganoe Award for Inspirational Teaching, 1985, 1990, Edward C. First Jr. Faculty Achievemet award, 1995, Dickinson Sch. Law; Adj. scholar Heritage Found.

HICKOK, ROBERT L., lawyer; b. Hanover, NH, Sept. 20, 1952; BA summa cum laude, Lehigh U., 1974; JD magna cum laude, Harvard U., 1978, AM, 1978. Bar: Pa. 1979, D.C. 1981, N.J. 1995, U.S. Dist. Ct. (ea. dist.) Pa. 1979, U.S. Ct. Appeals (3d cir.) 1979. Law clerk to Hon. Leonard Garth U.S. Ct. Appeals 3rd cir., Newark, 1978-79; asst. atty. U.S. Attys. Office, Phila., 1979-83; assoc. Pepper, Hamilton & Scheetz, Phila., 1983-86, ptnr., 1986, Pepper Hamilton LLP, Phila. Lectr. Rutgers U. Camden (N.J.) Law Sch., 1983—. Recipient Sears Prize. Mem. ABA, DC Bar Assn, NJ Bar Assn. Fed. Bar Assn., Pa. Bar Assn., Phila. Bar Assn. (fed. cts. com.), Harvard Law Sch. Greater Phila. (pres. exec. com.). Editor: Harvard Law Review. Office: Pepper Hamilton LLP 18th Arch St Philadelphia PA 19103 Office Phone: 215-981-4583. Office Fax: 215-981-4750. E-mail: hickokr@pepperlaw.com.

HICKS, ALLEN MORLEY, retired hospital administrator; b. Toronto, Iowa, May 11, 1928; s. Perle and Grace (Mowry) H.; m. Sue Hicks; children by previous ma rriage: David, Dennis, Wendy, Patricia. Student, Long Beach City Coll., 1949-50; BS, U. Iowa, 1952, MS, 1954. Adminstrv. resident St. Lukes Hosp., Davenport, Iowa, 1953-54; adminstr. Schmitt Meml. Hosp., Beardstown, Ill., 1954-57, Pekin (Ill.) Meml. Hosp., 1957-63, Ill. Masonic Hosp. and Med. Center, Chgo., 1963-72; pres. Community Hosp., Indpls., 1972-84, Meth. Health Care Systems, Memphis, 1984-85, VHA Enterprises, 1985-90; adminstr. Midwest Med. Ctr., Indpls., 1991-93. Sr. advisor St. Vincent's Hosp. and Health Care Corp.; chmn. bd. Vol. Hosps. Am., 1980-84, Multi-Mut. Ins. Cos. of Bermuda and Cayman Islands; bd. dirs. Am. Coll. Testing, Ind. Blue Cross, Am. Health Capital, Indpls. Conv. Ctr.; preceptor masters degree program in health and hosp. adminstrn. U. Iowa; chmn. com. extended care Coun. on Assn. Svc., 1963; pres. Chgo. Hosp. Coun., 1970-71. Campaign chmn., bd. dirs., chmn. indsl. divsn. United Fund, Pekin, Ill., 1959-64; pres. Tazwell County United Cerebral Palsy, 1960-61; chmn. Cancer Crusade, Pekin, 1960-61; svc. chmn. Tazewell County, 1958-60; chmn. bd. Tomahawk dist. Creve Coeur coun. Boy Scouts Am., 1963-64, bd. dirs. Crossroads council; bd. dirs. Cancer Soc., Hosp. Research and Devel. Inst., Inc.; pres. Meth. Health Sys. Memphis, 1984-85. H. With USNR, 1945- 49, 51-52. Recipient Outstanding Young Man of Year award State Ill., 1960; Distinguished Service award Pekin Jr. C. of C., 1960; Boss of Year award Marquette chpt. Nat. Secs. Assn., 1962 Fellow Am. Coll. Health Adminstrn.; mem. Am. Hosp. Assn. (del. 1971— , chmn. com. community relations), Ill. Hosp.Assn. (trustee, chmn. com. personnel relations), Am. Coll. Hosp. Adminstrs., Am. Assn. Maternal and Infant Health, Ill. Welfare Assn., Ill. C. of C., Am. Legion, Am. Vets., 500 Assn., Beta Gamma Sigma. Presbyterian (elder, trustee). Clubs: Mason, Elks, Kiwanis (bd. dirs. Internat. Found. 1981-85, pres. local chpt. 1983).

HICKS, BETTY HARRIS, real estate broker, company executive; b. Tellico Plains, Tenn., May 5, 1946; d. Ellis Fay Harris and Dellie Elizabeth Lynn; m. Roy Edward Hicks, Oct. 8, 1981. Student, Hiwasse Coll., 1982; cert., Trees Real Estate Sch., 1983. Sewing machine operator Colonial Garments, Tellico Plains, 1965—79; owner, operator Garner's Beauty Salon, 1980—81; sec. Monroe County C. of C., Madisonville, Tenn., 1981—82; salesperson Norman Lee Real Estate, Madisonville, 1982—83, Wattenbarger Real Estate, Loudon, Tenn., 1983—84; broker, owner AApple Realty Co., Loudon, Tenn., 1984—91, Anchor Properties, Loudon, Tenn., 1992—; prin., owner Anchor Mortgage Co., Loudon, 2003—. Tchr. Tenn. Real Estate Sch., Knoxville, 1998; pres. Loudon County Bd. Realtors. Pres. Loudon C. of C., Loudon. Named Realtor of Yr., 1987; recipient Cert. of Appreciation, Loudon C. of C., 1988, City of Loudon, 1988. Mem.: Loudon County C. of C. Republican. Avocations: genealogy, gardening, cooking, reading, bird watching. Office: Anchor Properties 811 Mulberry St Loudon TN 37774 Home Phone: 865-408-0103; Office Phone: 865-408-0802. Personal E-mail: betty127@msn.com.

HICKS, C. FLIPPO, lawyer; b. Fredericksburg, Va., Feb. 24, 1929; s. Robert A. and Nell (Jones) Hicks; m. Patricia DeHardit (dec. 1983); children: Robert, Patricia Shull, J. Flippo(dec.) , Paula Mooradian. BS in Commerce, U. Va., 1950, LLB, 1952. Bar: Va. 1952, U.S. Supreme Ct. 1955. Asst. atty. gen. Commonwealth of Va., Richmond, 1953-59; ptnr. Martin, Hicks, Ingles, Ltd., Gloucester, Va., 1959-91; gen. counsel Va. Assn. Counties, Richmond, 1991—2003; pvt. practice Gloucester, 2003—. Bd. trustees St. Paul's Coll., 2004—; Presdl. elector, 1968, 1976, 1980; pres. exec. coun. Episcopal Diocese of Va., 1970—71, mem. standing com., 1971—74. Fellow: Am. Bar Found.; mem.: ABA (Leader of the Yr. award gen. practice sect., Constbar Leader of the Yr. 1992), Defenders Commn. Va., Nat. Assn. Counties Civil Attys. (pres. 1999—2002, bd. dirs.), Va. State Bar (pres. 1990—91). Democrat. Episcopalian. Avocations: gardening, college sports. Office: PO Box 1300 6517 Main St Gloucester VA 23061 Office Phone: 804-693-6953. E-mail: hicks@3bubbas.com.

HICKS, CAROL ANN, small business owner, educator; b. Danville, Ill., Mar. 14, 1943; d. Hughie Jay Johnson and Doris N. Jean Bostwick; children: Beverly, Bobbi Ann, Sandra, Michael. AS, Danville Area CC, Ill., 1985, AS in Desk Top Publ., 1996; B in Elem. Edn., Ea. Ill. U., 1988. Grain technician Danville Grain Inspection, 1981-91; tchrs. aide reading and phonics Honeywell Sch., Hoopston, Ill., 1985-88; substitute tchr. Hoopeston (Ill.) Area Cmty. Schs., 1988—2000; mgr., asst. mgr. Casey's Gen. Store, Hoopeston, Gifford, Ill., 1994-98; owner, mgr. Carol's Corner and Genealogy Plus, Hoopeston, 1998—, Pape Meml. Home & Gardens, 2001—. Ct. reporter The Neighbor, Attica, Ind., 2001—04. Author: The Presley Family History, 1993, (newsletter) Presley Research Assn., 1993-99; editor: The Chronicle, Hoopeston, Ill., 2004—; contbr. columns to newspapers, 2000-04. Grant Twp. com. chmn. Dem. Party, Hoopeston, 1997—2000; hospice vol. USMC Logan Campus, Danville, 1991-96. Mem. Am. Legion Aux., Barbara Standish NSDAR (historian, regent 1991-95, 2000—), VFW Aux., Kappa Delta Pi (Beta Pi chpt.). Mem. Ch. LDS. Avocations: genealogy, research history, bowling, reading, travel. Home: 326 W Orange St Hoopeston IL 60942-1952 E-mail: chicks@advancenet.net.

HICKS, CHRISTOPHER, music company executive; b. Richmond, Calif. Student, Howard U., 1989—93. Co-founder Ivory Coast Entertainment, 1994—96; founding ptnr. Noontime Entertainment, Atlanta, 1997—; v.p. urban A&R Warner/Chappell Music, Inc., 2004—07, sr. v.p. A&R & head of urban music, 2007—; sr. v.p. urban A&R Atlantic Records, 2007—. Office: Warner/Chappell Music Inc 10585 Santa Monica Blvd Los Angeles CA 90025-4950 also: Atlantic Records Urban A&R 75 Rockefeller Plz 17th Fl New York NY 10019*

HICKS, DAVID ERIC, retired sports association executive; b. Montreal, Quebec, Canada, Dec. 8, 1950; s. Eric Percy Hicks and Ruth Erna Rogers; m. Christine Cary, Apr. 22, 1953. BS, Western Mich. U., 1973. Nat. Coaching dipl. NSCAA, 1984, Nat. Advance Coach dipl. NSCAA, 1985, Nat. Youth Lic. US Soccer, 1998. Dir. soccer programs Kalamazoo Family YMCA, 1976—80; men's head soccer coach Loy Norrix HS, Kalamazoo, 1977—80; soccer dir. Springfield YMCA, Ill., 1980—2006; v.p. Ill. Youth Soccer Assn., Chgo., 1980—; league dir. Ctrl. Ill. Youth Soccer League. Dir. soccer camps YMCA Camp Tecumseh, Brookston, Ind., 1980—86. Recipient Meritorious Svc. award, Ill. Youth Soccer Assn., 2005. Mem.: Nat. Soccer Coaches Assn. Am. (assoc. Long Term Achievement award 2002). Independent. Avocations: travel, gardening, collecting hockey memorabilia, ethnic cooking, photography. Office: Ciysl 2700 West Lawrence Ave Suite Q Springfield IL 62704 Home Phone: 217-546-6584; Office Phone: 217-391-4118. Personal E-mail: dave.hicks@insightbb.com.

HICKS, DONALD ALBERT, economics professor; b. Buffalo, Mar. 31, 1947; s. Donald Eugene Hicks and Jane Marie Cigard; 1 child, Brittany. BA, Ind. U., Bloomington, 1969; PhD, U. NC, Chapel Hill, 1975. Policy analyst Office of Gov., Raleigh, NC, 1973—75; prof. polit. economy, pub. policy U. Tex., Dallas, 1975—, asst. dean grad. studies, 1976—78, spl. asst. office of pres., 2006—; mem. sr. urban police staff Exec. Office of Pres., Washington, 1980—81. Sr. cons. strategic analysis North Tex. Commn., Dallas-Ft. Worth Airport, 1986—89, v.p. regional tech., 1989—91; cons. in field. Author: Advanced Industrial Development, 1985, Automation Technology and Industrial Reference, 1986; editor: Is Technology Enough?, 1988. Lt. USN, 1970—72. Sr. rsch. fellow, IC2 Inst., U. Tex., Austin, 2000. Mem.: Greater Dallas C. of C. (mem. econ. coun. 2004—). Avocation: travel. Home: 5718 Buffridge Tr Dallas TX 75252 Office: U Tex Dallas Box 830688 Richardson TX 75083

HICKS, DREW M., lawyer; b. Dayton, Ohio, Sept. 11, 1976; BA, Duke U., 1999; JD, U. Cin. Coll. Law, 2003. Bar: Ohio 2003. Assoc. Keating, Muething & Klekamp PLL, Cin. Named one of Ohio's Rising Stars, Super Lawyers, 2005, 2006. Mem.: Cin. Bar Assn., Cin. Bar Assn. Office: Keating Muething & Klekamp PLL One E Fourth St Ste 1400 Cincinnati OH 45202 Office Phone: 513-579-6565. Office Fax: 513-579-6457.

HICKS, GARY ELLIS, state supreme court justice; b. Colebrook, NH, Nov. 30, 1953; s. Parker Alba and Janet Louise (Brakel) H.; m. Patricia Susan Garrell, Nov. 29, 1975; children: Rebecca, James. BA, Bucknell U., 1975; JD, Boston U., 1978; BA (hon.), 2000. Bar: N.H. 1978, U.S. Dist. Ct. N.H. 1978. Assoc. Wiggin and Nourie, Manchester, NH, 1978-84, ptnr., 1984—2001; assoc. justice NH Superior Ct., 2001—06, NH Supreme Ct., 2006—. Coun. mem. N.H. Jud. Coun., 1996-2001, vice chairperson, 2000-01. Pres. Manchester Inst. Arts and Sci., 1987-90, chmn. bd. trustees, 1997—; fin. chmn. N.H. Dem. Party, 1987. Mem. ABA, N.H. Bar Assn., Manchester Bar Assn., Lawyers Assistance Com. Democrat. Avocations: reading, golf. Office: NH Supreme Ct One Charles Doe Dr Concord NH 03301 Office Phone: 603-271-2646. Business E-Mail: ghicks@courts.state.nh.us.

HICKS, GREGORY STEVEN, government agency administrator; b. Ft. Wayne, Ind., Dec. 24, 1959; s. Earl Hoyt and Sarah Helen (Bobo) H.; m. Nita Dawn Noblitt, Nov. 9, 1985. BS in Fin., Ind. U., 1983; MBA, U. Indpls., 1995. Asst. v.p. Fidelity Fed. Savs. and Loan, Seymour, Ind., 1983; fin. dir. Devel. Svcs., Columbus, Ind., 1983—85, account coord., 1985—86; exec. dir. Jennings County Econ. Devel., North Vernon, Ind., 1986—88; dir. Columbus Econ. Devel. Bd., 1989—91; mgr. nat. devel. PSI Energy, Plainfield, Ind., 1992—95, acct. mgr. comml. and indsl. sales, 1995—97; strategic mktg. rep. Cinergy Power Mktg. and Trading, Cin., 1997—98, mgr. retail aggregation, 1998; v.p. mktg. and bus. devel. Gaylor, 1998—99; v.p. bus. devel. Home Fed. Savs. Bank, Columbus, 1999—2003; dep. exec. dir. Ind. Dept. Commerce, 2003—04; v.p. bus. banking Fifth Third Bank, Columbus, 2004—06; agt. State Farm Ins., North Vernon, Ind., 2006—. Active Assn. for Retarded Citizens, North Vernon, 1983-86, Jennings County Econ. Devel., 1985-88; head coach Hayden Elem. Girls and Boys Basketball, North Vernon, 1984-86; sec. bd. dirs. Jennings Community Hosp. Found., 1987-88; bd. dirs. Columbus Found. for Youth, 2000-03; mem. fin. com. St. Marys Ch., N. Vernon, Ind., 1997-2002; mem. Columbus Econ. Devel. Bd., 1999-2003. Mem. South Cen. Savs. and Loan League (v.p. 1983), Columbus Area C. of C. (bd. dirs. 2001-03), Rotary (treas. 2000-01), Kiwanis (treas. local chpt. 1985-86, pres. 1987-88, lt. gov. 1991-92), Kappa Delta Rho (bd. dirs. 1984-92). Home: 565 Persimmon Dr North Vernon IN 47265-6730 Office: State Farm Ins 865 N State St North Vernon IN 47265 Office Phone: 812-346-9700. Personal E-mail: greg.hicks@53.com. Business E-Mail: greg.hicckspprm@statefarm.com.

HICKS, HAROLD EUGENE, chemical engineer; b. Mpls., Jan. 20, 1919; s. Julius and Della (Beebe) H.; m. Ruth Esther Nelson, Oct. 4, 1941 (dec. Mar. 1989); children: Barbara H. Young, Charlotte H. Silvia, David H., Douglas E.; m. Virginia C. Hobson, Mar. 31, 1990. B Chem. Engring., U. Minn., 1941; postgrad., U. Del., 1946-47. Chemist Hercules Powder Co., Wilmington, Del., 1941, rsch. chemist, 1941, 46-50, prodn. supr. Hattiesburg, Miss., 1950-64, plant mgr. Chicopee, Mass., 1964-66, Hercules Inc., Franklin, Va., 1966-68, Brunswick, Ga., 1968-76, Louisiana, Mo., 1978-80; tech. advisor Dawood-Hercules, Lahore, Pakistan, 1976-78; vol. exec. Internat. Exec. Svc. Corp., 1986-94; pres. The Book Shop, Inc., Brunswick, 1991—. Bd. dirs. Downtown Devel. Authority, Brunswick. Mem. county cos. Glynn County; dir. St. Mark's Towers, Glynn-Brunswick Navy League of the U.S., Pine Belt Savings & Loan Assn, Hattiesburg, Miss., 1958-64, dir., 1st Nat. Bank of Brunswick, Ga., 1969-76. Maj. U.S. Army, 1941-46, ETO. Mem. AIChE (emeritus), Am. Chem. Soc. (emeritus), Rotary. Episcopalian. Avocations: computers, photography, travel, reading, gardening. Home: 262 Sutherland Bluff Dr Townsend GA 31331-9239

HICKS, JEFF J., advertising executive; BA, Amherst Coll.; MBA, Harvard U., 1997. Branding exec. Leo Burnett, Chgo., v.p., 1994; pres., ptnr. Crispin Porter + Bogusky, Miami, 1997—, CEO, 2004—. Spkr. in field. Office: Crispin Porter + Bogusky 3390 Mary St Ste 300 Miami FL 33133 Office Phone: 305-859-2070.*

HICKS, JOCELYN MURIEL, laboratory medicine specialist; b. Leamington Spa, Warwickshire, Eng., Aug. 17, 1937; arrived in U.S., 1965; d. Harold Archie and Muriel Ellen (Cumberland) Bingley; m. John Geoffrey Hicks, Aug. 15, 1959 (div. Nov. 1965); m. Melvin Blecher, May 1, 1973. BS, U. London, 1959, MSc, 1962; PhD, Georgetown U., 1971. Fellow Georgetown U. Med. Ctr., Washington, 1969-71; dir. clin. chemistry Children's Hosp. Nat. Med. Ctr., Washington, 1971-75, chmn. dept. lab. medicine, 1975-90, chief of lab. medicine and pathology, 1990—2001, dir. clin. support svcs., 1995-99; asst. prof. George Washington U. Med. Ctr., Washington, 1972-74, assoc. prof., 1975-81, prof., 1981—2002, prof. emeritus, 2002—; mem. profl. staff The Hosp. for Sick Children, Washington, 1984—2001; exec. dir. Ctr. Complex Diseases, 1999-2001; exec. dir. emeritus Children's Nat. Med. Ctr., 2002—; COO genetics divsn. Genetics and IVF, Fairfax, Va., 2002—04; pres. JMBH Assocs., Washington, 2004—. Pres. Children's Faculty assocs. Children's Hosp., Washington, 1989—90, chmn. bd. dirs., 1990—93, chmn. exec. com., 1994—95; clin. affiliate Cath. U. Am., Washington, 1982—94; cons. Johnson and Johnson Clin. Diagnostics, Bayer Diagnostics, i-Stat Corp. Author: Selected Analyses of Clinical Chemistry, 1984, Textbook of Clinical Chemistry, 1984, Directory of Rare Analyses, 1986, 1987, 1990, 1992, 1994, 1997, 1998, 2000, 2005, The Neonate, 1974, Pediatric Reference Ranges, 1995, 1997; co-author: Biochemical Basis of Pediatric Disease, 1992, Biochemical Basis of Pediatric Disease, 2d edit., 1995; co-editor: Point-of-Care Testing, 1999, 2004; contbr. articles to profl. jours. Recipient Kone award, Assn. Clin. Biochemists, 1987. Fellow: Internat. Fedn. Clin. Chemistry and Lab. Medicine (treas. 2003—05, pres. 2006—, treas. 2003—05, pres. 2006—, Concustell award 2006), Acad. Clin. Lab. Physicians and Scientists, Royal Coll. Pathologists U.K., Spanish Soc. Clin. and Molecular Pathology (hon.), Portuguese Soc. Clin. Pathologists (hon.), Assn. Clin. Biochemistry (hon.), Am. Assn. Clin. Chemistry (hon.; bd. dirs. 1978—81, pres. 1981—82, chmn. publs. commn. 1982—87, Joseph H. Roe award 1976, Bernard Gerulat Meml. award 1983, Fisher award 1984, Van Slyke award 1988, Miriam Reiner award 1991, Outstanding Contbns. to Clin. Chemistry 1993, Outstanding Spkr. award 2002, Roger Boeckx Meml. lectr. 2002), Israeli Soc. Clin. Biochemistry (hon.), Egyptian Soc. Lab. Medicine (hon.); mem.: Croatian Soc. Med. Biochemistry (hon.), Egyptian Soc. Clin. Chemistry (hon.). Home and Office: JMBH Assocs 4329 Van Ness St NW Washington DC 20016-5625 Home Phone: 202-363-0373.

HICKS, JONATHAN P., journalist; Reporter Ariz. Daily Star; bus. writer Cleveland Plain Dealer, 1982—85, New York Times, 1985—92, polit., metro. reporter, 1992—. Faculty mem. Century Inst., 1999. Author: (articles) Coors Mends Minority Fences, 1985. Mem.: Kappa Alpha Psi Frat. (past editor jour.). Office: The New York Times 229 W 43rd St New York NY 10036

HICKS, LINDA REONA, elementary school educator; b. Taloga, Okla., Oct. 14, 1949; d. Kenneth Merl and Ima Jean (Coyle) Hicks. BA, Southwestern Okla. State U., 1971, EdM, 1975; Reading Recovery cert., West Tex. A & M U., 2002; postgrad., Ft. Hays State U., 2004—05. Cert. reading specialist. Music and English educator Hardesty Pub. Schs., Okla., 1971—74, Tyrone Pub. Schs., Okla., 1974—2000; reading recovery educator Unified Sch. Dist. 480 Lincoln Elem., Liberal, Kans., 2001—05; elem. music educator Unified Sch. Dist. 480 McKinley Elem., Lincoln Elem., MacArthur Elem., 2005—07; music educator Lincoln Elem., MacArthur Elem. Unified Sch. Dist. 480, Liberal, 2007—. Chair Tyrone Tchrs. Inservice Com., 1996—97; mem. North Ctrl. Accreditation Steering Com. for Lincoln Elem., Liberal, Kans., 2001—05. Music dir. First Assembly of God, Liberal, 1988—, sec. bd., 2000—03, 2005—. Named Tchr. of Yr., Tex. County Edn. Assn., 1976, Tyrone Edn. Assn., 1998—99, Tchr. of Today, Masons, 1998—99. Mem.: Music Educators Nat. Conf., Internat. Reading Assn., Reading Recovery Coun. N.Am. (assoc.), Assn. Am. Educators (assoc.), Am. Choral Dirs. Assn. (life), Delta Kappa Gamma. Republican. Avocations: reading, scrapbooks, singing, playing musical instruments. Office: USD480 Liberal KS 67901 Home Phone: 580-854-6583.

HICKS, MARION LAWRENCE, JR., (LARRY HICKS), lawyer; b. Bethlehem, Pa., Sept. 5, 1945; s. Marion Lawrence and Martha (McCracken) H.; m. Beverly Brickman, Nov. 28, 1970; children: Yale McCracken, Hadley Brook, Kelley Hayden. BA History, Duke U., 1967; JD with honors, U. Tex., 1970. Bar: Tex. 1970. Law clk. 9th cir. US Ct. Appeals, LA, 1970-71; assoc. Thompson, Knight, Simmons & Bullion, Dallas, 1971-77; ptnr., head Dallas office Thompson & Knight LLP, 1977—. Spkr. in field. Editor Tex. Law Rev.; contbr. articles to profl. jour. Mem. ABA (real property, trust and probate sects.), Am. Coll. Mortgage Atty. (regent), State Bar Tex., Dallas Bar Assn. (past chmn. real property sect., legal aid and legal svc. com.), Coll. State Bar Tex., Order of Coif, Tower Club (bd. govs.), Phi Delta Phi. Avocations: sports, hunting, fishing. Home: 4310 Throckmorton St Dallas TX 75219-2240 Office: Thompson & Knight LLP 1700 Pacific Ave Ste 3300 Dallas TX 75201-4693 Home Phone: 214-219-4450; Office Phone: 214-969-1627. Business E-Mail: larry.hicks@tklaw.com.

HICKS, PATRICIA J., secondary school educator; b. Harrisburg, Pa., Feb. 21, 1951; d. Joseph and Jean (Snyder) Agosta; m. David Hicks, Sept. 22, 1951; 1 child, Lindy. BA, U. West Fla., 1973, MEd, 1991. Tchr. Sch. Bd. Okaloosa County, Ft. Walton Beach, Fla., 1974—. Dept. chairperson Choctawhatchee HS, Ft. Walton Beach, 1975—. Mem.: Coun. for Exceptional Children (assoc.), Alpha Delta Kappa. Home: 362 Marie Circle Fort Walton Beach FL 32548 Home Phone: 850-243-0147; Office Phone: 850-833-3614. Personal E-mail: pjh47@yahoo.com.

HICKS, PAUL B., psychiatrist, director; MD, PhD, Baylor Coll. Medicine, Houston, 1983. Lic. Psychiatrist Am. Bd. Psychiatry and Neurology, 1990. Sr. staff Scott and White Clinic, Temple, Tex., 1987—2000; psychiatrist Ctrl. Tex. Vets. Health Care Sys., Waco, 2000—03, dep. dir. mental health and behavioral medicine Temple, 2003—. Mem.: Soc. Neuroscience. Achievements include research in behavioral pharmacology. Office Phone: 254-743-1270. Office Fax: 254-743-0304. Business E-Mail: paul.hicks@va.gov.

HICKS, RITCHIE B., physical education educator; b. Tallahassee, Fla. d. Frank Evans and Isabella (Lawrence) Stewart; m. Eddie Jay Hicks; children: Eddie Darrell, Jay Freeman, Michele Dianne. AA, Howard Coll.; BS in Edn., Fla. A & M Univ.; MA in Secondary Sch. Adminstr., N.E. Mo.

State Univ. Cert. health and phys. edn. tchr., secondary sch. adminstr. Phys. edn. tch. Scott Jr. High Sch., Savannah, Ga., Florissant Jr. High Sch., Mo.; head track coach Berkeley Sr. High Sch., Mo.; phys. edn. tchr. Airport Elem. Sch., Berkeley, Mo., Berkeley Jr. High Sch., Mo.; phys. edn. and health tchr. Ferguson Middle Sch., Mo.; basketball, volleyball and track coach McCluer North Sr. High Sch., Florissant, Mo.; chairperson, dept. phys. edn. Cross Keys Middle Sch., Florissant, Mo. Mem. sch. and dist. curriculum and instrn. coms., 1995; mem. Bldg. Improvement Com.; dir. Sch. Intramural Program, 1995. Writer guidelines for Cross Keys Mid. Sch. phys. edn. students. Apptd. to Youth Adv. Commn. City of Florissant, Mo.; coach Mo. State H.S. Basketball, Track and Field Championship Teams; bd. trustees Ward Chapel AME Ch., 1995, dir. Richard and Sarah Allen Summer Acad., 1995; coord. bldg. Ferguson-Florissant Scholarship Run/Walk Program, 1995. Recipient Tchr. of Yr. award State of Mo., 1992, Mid. Sch. Phys. Edn. Tchr. of Yr. Nat. Assn. Sport and Phys. Edn., 1993, Mo. Coach of Yr. for track and field, 1982, Salute to Am. Tchr. Walt Disney, 1993; named to Nat. Women's Hall of Fame. Mem. Nat. Edn. Assn., Am. Assn. Univ. Women, Mo. AAHPERD (middle and secondary sch. phys. educator award of 1993), AAHPERD (middle sch. phys. edn. tchr. award of 1993), Am. Running and Fitness Assn., Phi Delta Kappa. Avocations: fitness walking, reading, weight training, golf, dance.

HICKS, SARAH ELLINGTON, lawyer; b. Lexington, Ky., Oct. 29, 1977; BA, U. Miami, 2000; JD, U. Cin., 2003. Bar: Ohio 2003, US Dist. Ct. Southern Dist. Ohio. Law clerk Wood & Lamping L.L.P., Cin., assoc., 2003—. Named one of Ohio's Rising Stars, Super Lawyers, 2005, 2006. Mem.: Internat. Found. Employee Benefits, Ohio State Bar Assn., Cin. Bar Assn. Office: Wood & Lamping LLP 600 Vine St Ste 2500 Cincinnati OH 45202-2491 Office Phone: 513-852-6000. Office Fax: 513-852-6087.

HICKS, SHERMAN GREGORY, pastor; b. Bklyn., June 22, 1946; s. Charles Sr. and Sarah Mae (Rollins) H.; m. Anna Marie Peck, Sept. 12, 1970 (div.); children: Andrea, Geoffrey, Christopher. BA, Wittenberg U., 1968; MDiv, Hamma Sch. Theology, 1973; DD (hon.), Carthage Coll., 1988, Elmhurst Coll., 1989, Wittenberg U., 1990. Ordained to ministry Luth. Ch., 1973. Pastor Concordia Luth. Ch., Buffalo, 1973-77; co-pastor Holy Trinity Luth. Ch., East Orange, N.J., 1977-79; asst. to bishop Ill. Synod, Luth. Ch. Am., Chgo., 1979-87; bishop Met. Chgo. Synod, Evang. Luth. Ch. in Am., Chgo., 1988-95; sr. pastor First Trinity Luth. Ch., Washington, 1996—2003; mission dir. divsn. outreach Evang. Luth. Ch. Am., 2003—. Pres. of bd. Third World Social Svcs., 1998; bd. dirs. Mission Resource Inst. Pres. Interfaith Coun. for Homeless, Chgo., 1988, AIDS Nat. Interfaith Network, 1991; trustee Carthage Coll., Kenosha, Wis., 1988, Nat. AIDS Fund, 1997; bd. dirs. Luth. Social Svcs. Ill., 1988-95, Bethphage, Omaha; mem. Coun. Religious Leaders, Chgo., 1988-95; bd. dirs. Leadership Coun. for Met. Open Cmty., Luth. Housing Svcs., Luth. Svcs. in Am. Named One of Outstanding Young Men in Am., Jaycees, 1974; recipient Alumni Citation, Wittenberg U., 1993. Office: The Luth Ctr 700 Light St Baltimore MD 21230 Office Phone: 410-230-2878. Personal E-mail: doelca8@aol.com, sgreghicks@aol.com. *In my experiences with life I have discovered that there are three very basic questions that we humans have the need to know answers for: (1) Who am I? (2) For what purpose am I here? (3) What am I going to do? Within the context of our faith we can find the answers.*

HICKS, TAYLOR REUBEN, singer; b. Birmingham, Ala., Oct. 6, 1976; s. Brad and Linda Hicks. Student, Auburn U.; grad., U. Ala., Birmingham. Lead singer Little Memphis Blues Orch., Birmingham, Ala.; signed to 19 Recordings Ltd., 2006—. Singer: (albums) In Your Time, 1997, Under the Radar, 2005, (songs) Do I Make You Proud?, 2006. Achievements include winning 5th season of American Idol, 2006. Office: 19 Entertainment Ltd 33 Ransomes Dock 35-37 Parkgate Rd London SW11 4NP England Office Phone: 20-7801-1919. Office Fax: 20-7801-1920. E-mail: contact@19.co.uk.

HICKS, THOMAS O., professional sports team executive, real estate developer; b. Houston, Feb. 7, 1946; s. John H. Hicks Jr.; m. Cinda Hicks, 1990; 6 children. BBA, U. Tex., 1968; MBA, U. So. Calif., 1970. Investment officer Morgan Guaranty Trust Co., NYC, 1968-74; pres. First Dallas Capital Corp., Dallas, 1974-77; co-mng. ptnr. Summit Ptnrs., Dallas, 1977-83; co-chmn., co-CEO, Hicks & Haas Inc., Dallas, 1983-89; chmn., CEO, Hicks, Muse, Tate & Furst Inc., Dallas, 1989—2004; owner, chmn. Dallas Stars, 1995—, Tex. Rangers, Arlington, 1998—; CEO, chmn. Southwest Sports Group Inc., Hicks Holdings LLC, 2005—. Bd. dirs. MLB Advanced Media; vice chair bd. govs. NHL, 2007—. Contbr. United Way, Goodwill, Dallas Art Mus., Dallas Symphony Orchestra, Sci. Place at Fair Park. Recipient Henry Cohn Humanitarian Award, Anti-Defamation League, 2000, Marshall Trojan Award, U. So. Calif. Marshall Sch. Bus., 2005. Avocation: golf. Office: Southwest Sports Group Inc 260 Ave of the Stars Frisco TX 75034*

HICKS, TYLER GREGORY, publishing company executive, writer; b. NYC, June 21, 1921; s. Ernest Tyler and Mary B. (O'Brien) H.; m. Saretta M. Gratke, Feb. 23, 1946 (dec. Mar. 1974); children: Gregory T., Barbara L., Steven D.; m. Mary T. Shanley, Aug. 29, 1975. B of Mech. Engring., Cooper Union Advancement Sci., 1948. Engr. Merport Realty Co., 1943-46; design engr. Lockwood-Greene Engrs. Inc., 1946-49; editor in chief Profl. and Reference Books div. McGraw-Hill Co., NYC, 1962-85, pres., chmn. bd. dirs. employees fed. credit union, 1970-95, bd. dirs., 1995—. Instr. Cooper Union, N.Y.C.; owner Internat. Engring. Assocs.; pres. Internat. Wealth Success Inc., Rockville Centre, N.Y.; lectr. in field Author: How To Borrow Your Way to a Great Fortune, 1970, Magic Mind Secrets for Building Riches Fast, 1971, How To Make One Million Dollars in Real Estate in Three Years Starting with No Cash, 2000, Tyler Hicks' Encyclopedia of Wealth-Building Secrets, 1980, How to Borrow Your Way to Real Estate Riches, 1987, Business Capital Sources, 1984, Financial Broker, Finder, Business Broker Complete Success Kit, 1988, Real Estate Riches Success Kit, 1988, Complete Business Borrowers Success Kit, 1988, 101 Ways to 100% Financing of Business and Real Estate, 1997, How to Get Rich on Other People's Money, 1988, Standard Handbook of Engineering Calculations, 1995, Handbook of Mechanical Engineering Calculations, 1998; co-author: Handbook of Electric Power Calculations, 1984, Handbook of Chemical Engineering Calculations, 1984; co-editor: Standard Handbook of Consulting Engineering, 1986, How to Get Rich on Other People's Money, 1988, How to Build A Million Dollar Fortune, 1989, Mail Order Success Secrets, 1990, How to Make Big Money in Real Estate, 2000, 199 Greate Home Businesses You Can Start (and Prosper In), for Under $1,000, 1993, How to Start Your Own Business on a Shoestring and Make Up to $500,000 a Year, 1995, 203 Home-Based Businesses, 1999, Handbook of Civil Engineering Calculations, 2007, Civil Engineering Formulas, 2002, Mechanical Engineering Formulas, 2003, 209 Easy Spare-Time Ways to Build Zero Cash Into 7 Figures A Year in Real Estate, 2004, How to Acquire $1 Million in Real Estate in One Year in Your Spare Time, 2006, Handbook of Mechanical Engineering Calculations, 2007. With U.S. Mcht. Marines, 1936-43. Mem. ASME, US Naval Inst., Internat. Oceanographic Found., Rockville Links Golf Club, Huntington Yacht Club. Home: 24 Canterbury Rd Rockville Centre NY 11570-1310 Office: McGraw-Hill 2 Penn Plz Rm 1500 New York NY 10121-1599 Office Phone: 516-766-5850. Personal E-mail: tyghicks@aol.com. Business E-Mail: tyhicks@iwsmoney.com. *The clearest and strongest thought permeating my life is based on my own experience and observation of lives of thousands of people throughout the world. This thought is: Men and women can achieve in life whatever goals they set for themselves if a person combines careful planning and analysis of each objective with mental images of successful achievement. This approach seems to work everywhere— for everyone. Choosing to do what one enjoys also contributes to success because better performance occurs when people like what they're doing. Helping others achieve their goals in life brings great rewards to both the helper and the person assisted.*

HICKS, WALTER JOSEPH, electrical engineer; b. Lawrence, Mass., Mar. 10, 1935; s. Walter Francis and Ethel Mary (Royds) H.; m. Faith Winifred McCrum, Apr. 4, 1959; children: Janet Lee, Walter David, Pamela Jean. BSEE, MSEE, MIT, 1957; PhD in Plasma Physics, N.Mex. State U., 1969. Elec. engr. Raytheon Co., Bedford, Mass., 1957-67, radar system engr., dept. mgr., 1970-74, tech. advisor Lowell, Mass., 1974-84, cons. engr. Bedford, 1984-98; CEO Paradox Sci. of Acton, Mass., 1998—2005, Paradox Sci., Inc., 2005—. Mem. sci. adv. bd. USAF, Washington, 1983. Patentee in field. Elder United Presbyn. Ch., Newton, Mass., 1978-82. Home: 7 Pinewood Rd Acton MA 01720-4409 Office Phone: 978-266-8984. Personal E-mail: peradox.sci@verizon.net.

HICKS, WAYLAND R., rental company executive; b. 1942; BS, Ind. U. With Xerox Corp., London, from v.p. to group v.p., pres. reprographics bus., 1966-86, exec. v.p., pres. bus products and systems group, 1986-89, exec. v.p. mktg. and customer ops. Stamford, Conn., 1989—94; vice-chmn., CEO Nextel Comm. Corp., 1994—95; pres., CEO Indigo NV, 1996—97; vice-chmn., COO United Rentals, Greenwich, Conn., 1997—2003, vice-chmn., CEO, 2003—07, vice-chmn., 2007—. Bd. dir. Perdue Farms Inc. Lt. USAF. Office: Xerox Corp Long Ridge Rd PO Box 1600 Stamford CT 06904-1600*

HICKS, WENDELL, history professor, political scientist, publishing executive; b. Pitts., July 2, 1946; s. John Verris and Juanita H.; m. Patricia Ann Du Hart, Jan. 15, 1976 (div. Jan. 1980); children: Wendell Leon Jr., Gregory Moore. BA, Fayetteville State U., NC, 1971; MA, N.C. Ctrl. U., Durham, 1973. Grad. asst. N.C. Ctrl. U., Durham, 1972; instr. St. Augustine's Coll., Raleigh, NC, 1973—74; grad. asst. U. Toledo, 1974-78; prof. history Bowling Green State U., Ohio, 1978; pub. Azaka Publs., Pitts., 1983—. Author: The Bloody Flux: The World's No. 1 Killing Disease for the Past Six Centures, 1982, The Ku Klux Klan: A Psychoanalytical and Medical Perspective, 1992, A 2001 Historical Update on Black Holes: The Most Contructive and Destructive Objects in the Universe, 2001. Co-chmn. Operation PUSH, Pitts., 1983; active NAACP, Pitts., Vet. Club, Fayetteville, N.C.; mem. Nat. Campaign Tolerance. With USN, 1965-71. Mem.: AAUP, Phi Alpha Theta (v.p. 1976—77, pres. 1977—78), Pi Gamma Mu. Democrat. Methodist. Avocations: football, track and field, swimming, weightlifting, boxing. Home and Office: Azaka Publs 715 Mercer St Apt 711 Pittsburgh PA 15219-4146 Home Phone: 412-904-2411.

HICKS, WILLIAM ALBERT, III, lawyer; b. Welland, Ont., Can., Apr. 6, 1942; s. William Albert and June Gwendolyn (Birrell) H.; m. Bethany G. Galvin, May 21, 1982; children: James Christopher, Scott Kelly, Alexandra Elizabeth, Samantha Katherine. AB, Princeton U., 1964; LLB, Cornell U., 1967. Bar: N.Y. 1967, Ariz. 1972, U.S. Dist. Ct. Ariz. 1972. Assoc. Seward & Kissel, NYC, 1967-68, Snell & Wilmer LLP, Phoenix, 1972-75, ptnr., 1976—2007, Ballard Spahr Andrews & Ingersoll, LLP, Phoenix, 2007—. Instr. Ariz. State U., 1974-75. Mem. U.S. Olympic Fencing Squad, 1964; bd. adv. Casino USA, Inc., 1981-84; bd. dirs. Scottsdale Arts Ctr. Assn., 1984-88, v.p. devel., 1985-87; bd. dirs. Valley Leadership, Inc., 1987-91, sec., 1988-89, sec.-treas., 1989-90; bd. dirs. Scottsdale Cultural Coun., 1988-97, vice chmn., 1992-95, chmn., 1995-96; active The Luke's Men, 1992-2003, bd. dirs., 1993-97, 99-2002, sec., 1993-94, v.p. 1995-96, pres., 1996-97; adv. bd. Scottsdale Arts Ctr., 1988-91, chmn., 1988-90; bd. dirs., vice chmn. Ariz. Coun. on Econ. Edn., 1999-2000, chmn., 2000—. Capt. JAG Corps, USAF, 1968-72. Decorated DSM. Mem. ABA, Ariz. State Bar Assn., N.Y. State Bar Assn., Nat. Assn. Bond Lawyers (vice chmn. com. on fin. health care facilities 1982-83, chmn. com. on fin. health care facilities 1983-86, securities law and disclosure com. 1994-2000), Assn. for Govtl. Leasing and Fin., Princeton U. Alumni Assn. Ariz. (pres. 1978-81, 2003—, sec. 1981—), Paradise Valley (Ariz.) Country Club, Princeton Club N.Y. Office: Ballard Spahr Andrews & Ingersoll LLP 3300 Tower 18th Fl 3300 N Central Ave Phoenix AZ 85012 Office Phone: 602-798-5432. Business E-Mail: hicksw@ballardspahr.com.

HICKSON, ERNEST CHARLES, financial executive; b. LA, July 14, 1931; s. Russell Arthur and Marilyn Louise (Mambert) H.; m. Janice Beleal, Sept. 5, 1959; children: Arthur, Jennifer, Barton. BS, U. So. Calif., 1961; postgrad., UCLA Grad. Sch. of Bus. Admin., 1961-63. Lic. real estate broker Calif., 1956. Credit supr. ARCO (Richfield Oil), LA, 1955-60; asst. v.p. Union Bank L.A., 1960-64; v.p. County Nat. Bank (now Wells Fargo), Orange, Calif., 1964-67; v.p., sr. loan ofcr. City Bank, Honolulu, 1967-70; pres., CEO Shelter Corp. (merged with USF), 1968-72; exec. v.p., dir. U.S. Fin., Inc. NYSE, San Diego, 1970-73, pres., CEO USF Investors, 1971-73; exec. v.p. Sonnenblick Goldman, LA, 1973-76; pres., CEO First Hawaiian Devel., Honolulu, 1976-82; sr. ptnr. TMH Resources and affiliates, Laguna Niguel, Calif., 1982—. Expert witness in fin. Author: The Developers, 1978; editor: (newsletter) Financial Marketing, 1978-83. Staff sgt. USAF, 1951—54. Recipient Exec. award Grad. Sch. of Credit and Fin. Mgmt., Stanford U., 1964, Assocs. award The Nat. Inst. of Credit, UCLA, 1959. Mem. U. So. Calif. Assocs., U. So. Calif. Pres.'s Circle, Urban Land Inst., Town Hall, Salt Creek Club (charter), Pacific Club (Honolulu), Outrigger Canoe Club (Honolulu), Phi Gamma Delta. Avocations: tennis, walking, writing, swimming. Office Phone: 949-495-9400. Fax: 948-495-9458. Personal E-mail: ernesth541@aol.com.

HICKSON, ROBIN JULIAN, mining company executive; b. Irby, Eng., Feb. 27, 1944; s. William Kellett and Doris Matilda (Martin) H.; m. P. Anne Winn, Mar. 28, 1964; children: Richard, Sharon, Nicholas, Steven. BS in Mining Engring. with honors, U. London, 1965; MBA, Tulane U., 1990. Chartered engr., U.K. and Europe. Mining engr. N.J. Zinc Co., Austinville, 1965-70, divisional mgr. Jefferson City, Tenn., 1970-71; spl. project engr. Kerr McGee Corp., Grants, N.Mex., 1971-72; gen. mgr. Asarco, Inc., Vanadium, N.Mex., 1972-78, Gold Fields Mining Corp., Ortiz, N.Mex., 1978-83, Mesquite, Calif., 1982-86; v.p. Freeport Mining Co., New Orleans, 1986-91, Freeport Indonesia Inc., Irian Jaya, 1991-92; pres. Freeport Rsch. and Engring. Co., New Orleans, 1992-93; sr. v.p. Cyprus Climax Metals Co., Tempe, Ariz., 1993-94; pres. Cyprus Amax Engring. and Project Devel. Co., Tempe, 1994-99; exec. officer Cyprus Amax Minerals Co., 1994-99; sr. v.p. engring. and project mgmt. Kvaerner Metals, San Ramon, Calif., 2000—02; pres., COO Gabriel Resources Ltd., Toronto, Ont., Canada, 2002—03; prin., sr. v.p. McIntosh Engring., Tempe, 2003—. Author (with others): Interfacing Technologies in Solution Mining, 1981, Mineral Processing: Plant Design, Control and Practice, 2002. Recipient Robert Earll McConnell award AIME, 1999. Mem. Instn. Mining and Metallurgy, Am. Inst. Mining and Metallurgy, and Metall. Soc., N.Mex. Mining Assn. (bd. dirs. Santa Fe chpt. 1975-83), Calif. Mining Assn. (bd. dirs. Sacramento chpt. 1982-86), Beta Gamma Sigma. Episcopalian. Avocations: ornithology, travel. Home: 12246 S Honah Lee Ct Phoenix AZ 85044-3455 Office: Ste 101 1438 W Broadway Tempe AZ 85282 Home Phone: 480-598-9693; Office Phone: 480-831-0310 215. Business E-Mail: rjhickson@mcintoshengineering.com. E-mail: annerobin@worldnet.att.net.

HIDALGO, ALFREDA EDITH, elementary school educator; b. Phila., Pa., Nov. 15, 1932; d. George Francisco and Esther Jane (Butler) Hidalgo. BS in Edn., Temple U., Phila., 1954, MS in Edn., 1958, postgrad., 1962. Tchr. elem. sch. Phila. Sch. Sys., 1954—62, chmn. mid. sch. reading, 1962—84, counselor, adminstr., 1984—88; ret. Reading vol. Experience Corp., Phila., 1988—2001. Recipient Four Chapelans award for Volunteer Work, Stephen Smith Home for the Aged. Mem.: NAACP, Nat. Tchrs. Assn., Alpha Kappa Alpha (Rose award). Democrat. Baptist. Avocations: art, dance, reading. Home: 100 West Ave 506 W Jenkintown PA 19046

HIDALGO, DAVID ARTHUR, plastic surgeon; b. Hartford, Conn., 1952; BS, BA magna cum laude, Georgetown U., MD cum laude, 1978. Cert. Nat. Bd. Med. Examiners, 1980, Am. Bd. Surgery, 1984, Am. Bd. Plastic Surgery, 1987. Intern in surgery NYU Med. Ctr., NYC, 1978—79, resident in surgery, 1979—83, resident in plastic surgery, 1983—85, fellow in plastic surgery, 1985—86; affiliated with Meml. Sloan-Kettering Cancer Ctr., NYC, 1986—2000, chief plastic surgery, 1992—2000; assoc. attending surgeon Manhattan Eye, Ear & Throat Hosp., 1986—; affiliated with NY-Presbyn. Hosp., 1986—, Southampton Hosp., 2000—; pvt. practice aesthetic plastic surgery NYC, 2000—. Clin. prof. Cornell Med. Ctr., 1999—; lectr., presenter in field; spkr. on panels; vis. prof. Johns Hopkins U., Yale U., U. Pa., U. Chgo., various other coll. and U., Plastic Surgery Ednl. Found., 2002. Contbr. Plastic and Reconstructive Surgery, Annals of Plastic Surgery;, author numerous chpt. in textbooks and other reference publ. in plastic surgery; publr. (videos on plastic surgery technique), guest appearances ABC News, CBS Nes. Named Among Beauty's Best, NY mag., 2003, The Producer, Elle mag., 2004; named one of Best Doctors in Am., Northeast Region, Best Doctors in NY, NY Mag., 1991—; named to The List in plastic surgery, NY Times mag., 2005; recipient First Prize, Plastic Surgery Ednl. Found. Nat. Sr. Resident's Conf., 1985, Best Paper of Yr. award to appear in Plastic and Reconstructive Surgery, Am. Soc. Maxillofacial Surgeons, 1989, 2003, Best Surgical Technique Video awards, 1992, Health and Sci. Network, 1990, James Barrett Brown award for Best Sci. Paper of Yr., Am. Assn. Plastic Surgeons, 1991, Clin. Rsch. award, Plastic Surgery Ednl. Found., 2001. Fellow: Am. Coll. Surgeons; mem.: NY Regional Soc. Plastic and Reconstructive Surgery, NY County Med. Soc., NY State Med. Soc., Am. Soc. Maxillofacial Surgeons (ASMS Award 2003), Am. Assn. Plastic Surgeons, Am. Soc. Aesthetic Plastic Surgery, Am. Soc. Plastic Surgeons, Alpha Omega Alpha Med. Honor Soc. Avocations: art, painting. Office: 655 Park Ave Fl 1 New York NY 10021-5937 Office Fax: 212-517-2527. E-mail: info@drdavidhidalgo.com.*

HIDALGO, ISMAEL J., pharmaceutical scientist; s. Deciderio and Rafaela Hidalgo; m. Margarita Gantes, Aug. 23, 1979; children: Carlos A., Daniel A. BS in Pharmacy, U. Panama, Panama City, 1978; PhD, U. So. Calif., LA, 1986. Lab. asst. U. Panama, 1978—80; postdoctoral fellow U. Kans., Lawrence, 1986—88, asst. rsch. scientist, 1989—90; rsch. investigator SmithKline Beecham, King of Prussia, Pa., 1990—91, sr. rsch. investigator, 1991—92; rsch. fellow Rhone-Poulenc Rorer, Collegeville, Pa., 1993—95, sr. rsch. fellow, 1995—97; co-founder, chief sci. officer Absorption Systems, Exton, Pa., 1997—. Named Entrepreneur of the Yr. in the Life Scis. for the Phila. area, Ernst & Young, 2002; fellow, UpJohn Co., 1986—88; scholar, OAS, 1980—82. Mem.: AAAS (assoc.), Am. Assn. Pharm. Scientists (assoc.), Am. Chem. Soc. (assoc.). Roman Catholic. Achievements include patents for device to measure electrical resistance of cell monolayers in side-by-side diffusion apparatus; first to characterizing a cell culture model (Caco-2) of small intestinal permeability. Avocations: golf, travel, music, reading. Office: Absorption Systems LP Ste 300 440 Creamery Way Exton PA 19341 E-mail: hidalgo@absorption.com.

HIDDEN-DODSON, NANCY, retired psychologist, consultant, educator; b. Everett, Mass., July 24, 1939; d. Frank Foster Thomas and Grace Evelyn Hickey; m. Edward Wesley Dodson, Dec. 21, 1985; m. Edwin William Hidden, Aug. 6, 1960 (div. Jan. 15, 1976); children: William Thomas Hidden, Glen Allen Hidden, Mark Samuel Hidden. BE in Sci. Edn., U. Alaska, 1970, M in Counseling Psychology, 1972; EdD, Seattle U., 1992. Cert. Tchr., Counselor Alaska, 1972, NH, 1974, CC Counselor and Instr. Calif., 1976, Counselor Nat. Bd. Cert. Counselors, 1985, Ednl. Staff Assoc., Counselor Wash., 1987, Ednl. Staff Assoc., Ednl. Psychology Wash., 1992, Ednl. Specialist in Ednl. Psychology Seattle U., 1992, lic. Mental Health Counselor Wash., 2001. Tchr. Tamworth Sch. Dist., NH, 1965—66, State Operated Schs., Northway, Alaska, 1971; sci. tchr. Conway Sch. Dist., 1972—74; instr. psychology Tanana Valley C.C., Fairbanks, 1974—86, counselor, coord. paraprofl. counseling program, 1977—81, student svcs. coord., 1978—81, dir. student svcs., 1981—82, dean students, 1982—85; mental health counselor Ctr. Family Counseling, Fairbanks, 1976—77, Peninsula Psychol. Ctr., Silverdale, 2001—03; ednl. counselor, psychologist Ocosta Sch. Dist., Westport, 1988—92; ednl. psychologist North Kitsap Sch. Dist., Poulsbo, 1992—2001. Dir. upward bound U. Alaska, Fairbanks, 1974—75; cons. Tanana Chiefs Counsel, Fairbanks, 1974—85, Maniilaq Assn., Kotzebue, 1975—85; cons. divsn. social and health svc. Wash., Wash., 1995—2003; dir., founder Interior Alaska Dispute Resolution Svcs., Fairbanks, 1985—86, Alaska Dispute Resolution Ctr., Fairbanks, 1985—87; mental health specialist Pudget Sound Mediation & Evaluation, Westport, Wash., 2000—05. Author: Musings Of A Women, 2004, Dancing with Nature, 2006; contbr. articles in field. Founder deeded land Hidden Hill Friends Ctr., Chena Ridge Friends Meeting, Fairbanks, 1980—2005. Recipient cert. Recognition, Boarding Home Program, Alaska, 1970, Fairbanks Head Start, 1976, Alaska State Police, 1980, Hospice Care, Fairbanks, 1984, Kingston Jr. High, 1993, 1994, 1995; scholarship, Pk. Coll., 1958-1960, Alaska, 1968-1970. Mem.: APA. Peace Party. Society Of Friends. Avocations: bicycling, poetry, crafts, sewing. Home Phone: 360-268-1961; Office Phone: 360-821-9048. Personal E-mail: nedodson@comcast.net.

HIDEN, ROBERT BATTAILE, JR., lawyer; b. Boston, May 8, 1933; s. Robert Battaile Sr. and Clotilda (Waddell) H.; m. Ann Eliza McCracken, Mar. 27, 1956; children: Robert B. III, Elizabeth Patterson, John Hughes. BA, Princeton U., NJ, 1955; LLB, U. Va., Charlottesville, 1960. Bar: NY 1961, US Ct. Appeals (2d cir.) 1974, US Dist. Ct. (so. dist.) NY 1975, US Supreme Ct. 2005. Assoc. Sullivan & Cromwell, NYC, 1960—67, ptnr., 1968—98, of counsel, 1999—2000, sr. counsel, 2001—. Articles editor and contbr. U. Va. Law Rev., 1959-60; contbr., mem. editl. bd. Futures Internat. Law Letter, 1987-92. Trustee Hampton U. and Hampton Inst., Va., 1984—2003; mem. Dillard scholarship com. U. Va. Law Sch., 1984—98, 2001—02; gov. Ramapo Coll. Found., NJ, 2002—; commr. Larchmont Little League, NY, 1964—68; chmn. Larchmont Jr. Sailing Program, 1977—78; vestry, jr. warden St. John's Episc. Ch., 1970—76, 1982—86, 1999—2002. Served to lt. (j.g.) USNR, 1955—57. Mem. ABA, NY State Bar Assn., Assn. of Bar of City of NY, NY County Bar Assn., Am. Judicature Soc., Larchmont U. Club (pres. 1976-77), Larchmont Yacht Club (trustee 1979-85, sec. 1990—), Coral Beach Club (Bermuda), Raven Soc., Order of Coif, Omicron Delta Kappa. Democrat. Avocations: skiing, golf, sailing, tennis. Office: Sullivan & Cromwell 125 Broad St Fl 28 New York NY 10004-2489 Home: 14 Indian Cove Rd Mamaroneck NY 10543 Personal E-mail: rbobhiden@aol.com.

HIDY, GEORGE MARTEL, chemical engineer, engineering executive; b. Kingman, Ariz., Jan. 5, 1935; s. John William and Margaret (Coqueron) H.; m. Dana Sexton Thomas, Oct. 15, 1958; children— Anne, Adrienne, John; m. 2d, Doris A. Wilson, Sept. 28, 1990. AB, Columbia U., NYC, 1956, BS, 1957; MSE., Princeton U., NJ, 1958; D.Eng., Johns Hopkins U., Balt., 1962. Asst. dir. chemistry and microphysics Nat. Ctr. Atmospheric Rsch., Boulder, Colo., 1967-69; group leader chem. physics Rockwell Internat. Sci. Ctr., Thousand Oaks, Calif., 1969-73, assoc. dir., 1973-74; gen. mgr. Environ. Rsch. & Tech., West Lake, Calif., 1974-76, v.p., 1976-84; pres. Desert Rsch. Inst., Reno, 1984-87; v.p. Electric Power Rsch. Inst., Palo Alto, Calif., 1987-94; assoc. dir. coll. engring. Ctr. Environ. Rsch. and Technol. U. Calif., Riverside, 1994-96; prin. Envair/Aerochem Assocs., Riverside, 1995—; via. Indsl. prof. environ. engring. U. Ala., Birmingham, 1996-99; prin. Envair Aerochem, 1999—; interim dir.

N.Mex. State U. Carlsbad Ctr. for Environ. Monitoring/Rsch., 2001—02. Commr., Calif. Youth Soccer Assn., L.A., 1982-84; bd. dirs. El Pueblo Health Ctr., 2003—, chmn., 2004—. Fellow AAAS, Air and Waste Mgmt. Assn.; mem. Am. Meteorol. Soc., Am. Chem. Soc., Am. Geophys. Union. Home: 6 Evergreen Dr Placitas NM 87043-8903 E-mail: dhidy113@comcast.net.

HIEATT, ALLEN KENT, retired language educator; b. Indpls., Jan. 21, 1921; emigrated to Can., 1968, returned to U.S., 1986. s. Allen Andrew and Violet Rose (Kent) H.; m. Constance Bartlett, Oct. 25, 1958; children by previous marriage: Alice Coulombe, Katherine Marsh. AB, U. Louisville, 1943; PhD, Columbia U., 1954. Lectr. Columbia U., NYC, 1944-45, instr., 1945-55, asst. prof., 1956-59, assoc. prof., 1960-69; prof. English U. Western Ont., London, 1969-86, emeritus, 1987—; sr. founding editor Spenser Newsletter, London, Ont., 1970-75; ret., 1987. Mem. editorial bd. Duquesne Studies, Pitts., 1976—, Spenser Studies, 1979—; editorial cons. Spenser Ency., 1990; co-editor: College Anthology of British and American Verse, 1964, Poetry in English: An Anthology, 1987; author: Short Time's Endless Monument, 1960, (with C. Hieatt) The Canterbury Tales of Geoffrey Chaucer, 1964, rev. edit., 1981, Spenser: Selected Poetry, 1970, Chaucer, Spenser, Milton, 1975; translator: (with M. Lorch) Lorenzo Valla, On Pleasure, 1977; co-author: (with C. Hieatt) (children's book) The Canterbury Tales of Geoffrey Chaucer, 1961. Cutting fellow, 1946-47; leave grantee Can. Council, Oxford, Eng., 1977-78; rsch. fellow Social Sci. and Humanities Rsch. Coun. Can., 1981-82 Fellow Royal Soc. Can.; mem. MLA (chmn. div. English lit. Renaissance 1978-79, William Riley Parker Prize, 1984), Spenser Soc. (pres.), Renaissance Soc. Am. (chmn. north central div. 1973-79) Home: 335 Essex Mdws Essex CT 06426-1526 Office Phone: 860-767-9045.

HIEATT, CONSTANCE BARTLETT, English language educator; b. Boston, Feb. 11, 1928; d. Arthur Charles and Eleonora (Very) Bartlett; m. Allen Kent Hieatt, Oct. 25, 1958. Student, Smith Coll., 1945-47; AB, Hunter Coll., 1953, AM, 1957; PhD, Yale U., 1959. Lectr. City Coll., CUNY, 1959-60; from asst. prof. to assoc. prof. English Queensborough C.C., CUNY, 1960-65; from assoc. prof. to prof. St. John's U., Jamaica, NY, 1965-69; prof. English U. Western Ont., London, Canada, 1969-93, prof. emeritus, 1993—. Author: (with A.K. Hieatt) The Canterbury Tales of Geoffrey Chaucer, 1964, rev. edit., 1981, Spenser: Selected Poetry, 1970; The Realism of Dream Visions, 1967, Beowulf and Other Old English Poems, 1967, rev. edit., 1983, Essentials of Old English, 1968, The Miller's Tale By Geoffrey Chaucer, 1970; (with Sharon Butler) Pleyn Delit: Medieval Cookery for Modern Cooks, 1976, rev. edit., 1979; (with Brenda Hosington) rev. 2d edit., 1996, Karlamagnus Saga, Vols. I and II, 1975, Vol. III, 1980; (with Sharon Butler) Curye on Inglysch, 1985; An Ordinance of Pottage, 1988; (with Robin F. Jones) La Novele Cirurgerie, 1990; (with Minnette Gaudet) Guillaume de Machaut's Tale of the Alerion, 1994; (with Brian Shaw and Duncan Macrae-Gibson) Beginning Old English, 1994; (with Rudolf Grewe) Libellus de Arte Coquinaria, 2001, (with Terry Nutter and Johnna H. Holloway) Concordance of English Recipes: Thirteenth Through Fifteenth Centuries, 2006; also children books (with Hieatt) The Canterbury Tales of Geoffrey Chaucer, 1961, Sir Gawain and the Green Knight, 1967, The Knight of the Lion, 1968, The Knight of the Cart, 1969, The Joy of the Court, 1971, The Sword and the Grail, 1972, The Castle of Ladies, 1973, The Minstrel Knight, 1974. Yale U. fellow, and Lewis-Farmington fellow, 1957-59, Vis. fellow Yale U., 1985-86, 89-93; Can. Council and Social Sci. and Humanities Rsch. Coun. grant. Fellow Royal Soc. Can.; mem. MLA, Medieval Acad. Am., Internat. Soc. Anglo-Saxonists, Can Soc. Medievalists. Episcopalian. Home: 335 Essex Mdws Essex CT 06426-1526 Personal E-mail: constance.hieatt@yale.edu.

HIEBERT, RAY ELDON, writer, educator; b. Freeman, SD, May 21, 1932; s. Peter Nicholas and Helen (Kunkel) H.; m. Roselyn Lucille Peyser, Jan. 30, 1955 (div. Apr. 1985); children: David, Steven, Emily, Douglas; m. Sheila Jean Gibbons, Dec. 21, 1985 BA, Stanford U., 1954; MS, Columbia U., 1957; MA, U. Md., 1961, PhD, 1962. Faculty Am. U., 1958- 67, prof. journalism, chmn. dept. journalism, 1962-67; dir. Washington Journalism Center, 1965-68; head dept. journalism U. Md., College Park, 1968-72; dean Coll. Journalism, 1973-79, prof. internat. media sys., 1980-98, prof., dean emeritus, 1998—. Pres. Comm. Rsch. Assocs., 1979—; dir. Am. Journalism Ctr., Budapest, Hungary, 1991-95; acad. adv. U.S. Voice of Am., 1983-91; vice chmn. Montgomery County (Md.) Cable-TV Commn., 1973-77; mem. St. Mary's County Cable-TV Commn., 2001-05; tchr. internat. media sys. seminar; cons. China media project, U. Md., 2002-. Author: more than 20 books; editor. Fulbright fellow to Africa, 1982; recipient U. Md. Landmark award for Internat. Svc., 2000. Mem. Soc. Profl. Journalists (pres. Md. chpt. 1977-78), Cosmos Club (Washington), Kappa Tau Alpha, Phi Kappa Phi, Omicron Delta Kappa. Home: 38091 Beach Rd Coltons Point MD 20626-0180 Office: 1220 Watergate S 700 New Hampshire Ave NW Washington DC 20037 Business E-Mail: hiebert@umd.edu.

HIEKEN, CHARLES, lawyer; b. Granite City, Ill., Aug. 15, 1928; s. Samuel and Margaret (Isaacs) H.; m. Donna Jane Clanin, Jan. 6, 1961; children: Tina Jane, Seth Paul. SBEE, SMEE, MIT, 1952; LLB, Harvard U., 1957. Bar: Ill. 1957, Mass. 1958, U.S. Supreme Ct. 1960, U.S. Ct. Customs and Patent Appeals 1961, U.S. Ct. Claims 1963, U.S. Ct. Appeals (fed. cir.) 1982. Patent asst. Lab. Electronics, Boston, 1954-56, Fish, Richardson & Neave, Boston, 1956-57; assoc. Hill, Sherman, Meroni, Gross & Simpson, Chgo., 1957, Joseph Weingarten, Boston, 1957-58, Wolf, Greenfield & Hieken, Boston, 1958-61, ptnr., 1961-70; prin. Charles Hieken Law Offices, Waltham, Mass., 1970-87; ptnr. Fish & Richardson, Boston, 1987-94, prin., 1995—. Mem. Pres. Carter's adv. com. on indsl. innovation, 1979. Mem. pres.'s adv. coun. Bentley Coll., 1993—; mem. coun. Harvard Law Sch. Assn., 1998-02; mem. Harvard Com. on Univ. Resources, 2005—. Served with U.S. Merchant Marine, 1944-47, U.S. Army, 1952-54. Named Friend of the Arts, Sigma Alpha Iota, 2007; named to Granite City H.S. Wall of Fame, 2006. Mem.: IEEE (sr.; life), Fed. Cir. Hist. Soc. (bd. mem. 2007—), Boston Patent Law Assn. (chmn. pub. rels. com. 1965—66, chmn. antitrust law com. 1966—70, treas. 1970—71, v.p. 1971—72, pres.-elect 1972—73, pres. 1973—74, chmn. antitrust law com. 1978—80), Ill. State Bar Assn. (privileged mem.), Mass. Bar Assn. (chmn. intellectual property com. 1977—80), Boston Bar Assn. (civil procedure com. 1959—), U. Mass. Club (founding bd. govs.), Down Town Club (bd. govs 1988—2003, v.p. gen counsel 2000—03), Tau Beta Pi, Eta Kappa Nu. Office: Fish & Richardson PC 225 Franklin St 31st Fl Boston MA 02110-2804 Business E-Mail: hieken@fr.com.

HIELSCHER, ANDREAS HELMUT, biomedical engineer; b. Bremen, Germany, Feb. 15, 1964; arrived in U.S., 1991; s. Helmut Reinhardt and Inge Hielscher; m. Maria Anagnostopoulou, May 15, 1995; 1 child, Amélie Lukia Inge. BS in Physics, U. Hannover, Germany, 1989; MS in Applied Physics, U. Hannover, 1991; PhD, Rice U., Tex., 1995. Postdoctoral fellow Los Alamos Nat. Lab., N.Mex., 1995—98; asst. prof. SUNY - Downstate Med. Ctr., Bklyn., 1998—2001; adj. prof. Poly. U., 1999—2001; assoc. prof. of biomedical engring. and radiology Columbia U., NYC, 2001—. Contbr. articles to sci. and profl. jours. Recipient Shechao Charles Feng Meml. prize, SPIE Internat. Soc. of Optical Engring., 1997, Young Investigator award, Whitaker Found., 1999; grantee Optical Tomography Diagnosis Joint Diseases, Nat. Inst. Arthritis and Musculoskeletal and Skin Diseases, 1999—, Optical Tomographic Imaging Brain Injuries and Diseases, NYC Coun. Spkrs. Fund Biomed. Rsch., 1999—2003, Model Based Iterative Reconstruction Techniques Optical Tomography, Whitaker Found., 1999—2003, MRI Compatible Diffuse Optical Tomography Sys. for Small Animal Oximetry, Nat. Inst. for Biomedical Imaging and Bioengineering, 2003—; Dirs. Postdoctoral fellow, Los Alamos Nat. Lab., 1995, Dept. Biomed. Engring. and Laser Medicine fellow, Free U. of Berlin, 2003. Mem.: IEEE, SPIE Internat. Soc. of Optical Engring., Optical Soc. of Am. (chair of biomedical optical spectroscopy group 2001—03). Achievements include patents for Characterization of highly scattering media by measurement of diffusely backscattered polarized light, US Patent No. 6, 011, 626; patents pending for Iterative reconstruction scheme for optical tomography based on the equation of radiative transfer; A digital signal processor-based detection system for optical tomography. Office: Columbia Univ 500 W 120th St MC8904 New York NY 10027

HIER, DANIEL BARNET, neurologist; b. Chgo., Mar. 23, 1947; BA, Harvard U., 1969, MD, 1973. Medical intern Bronx Mcpl. Hosp., NYC, 1973-74; neurology resident Mass. Gen. Hosp., Boston, 1974-77, neurology fellow, 1977-79; neurologist Michael Reese Hosp., Chgo., 1979-89, chmn. neurology, 1987-89; head neurology U. Ill., Chgo., 1989—2003, assoc. prof. neurology, 1989-91, prof., 1991—. Fellow Am. Acad. Neurology, Am. Heart Assn. (stroke council). Home: 1206 Manor Dr Wilmette IL 60091-1029 Office Phone: 312-996-1759. E-mail: dbhier@gmail.com.

HIER, MARSHALL DAVID, lawyer; b. Bay City, Mich., Aug. 24, 1945; s. Marshall George and Helen May (Copeland) H.; m. Nancy Speed Brown, June 26, 1970; children: John, Susan, Ann. BA, Mich. State U., 1966; JD, U. Mich., 1969. Bar: Mo. 1969. Assoc. Peper, Martin, Jensen, Maichel and Hetlage, St. Louis, 1969-76, ptnr., 1976-95; prin. Bertram, Peper and Hier, P.C., St. Louis, 1996—. Bd. dirs. Gateway Ctr. Met. St. Louis, Mercantile Libr. Assn., St. Louis Soc. Blind and Visually Impaired. Contbr. articles to profl. jours. Mem. St. Louis Bar Assn. (editor jour. 1988—), St. Louis Civil Round Table (former pres.). Baptist. Home: 17141 Chaise Ridge Rd Chesterfield MO 63005-4457 Office Phone: 314-621-1988. Business E-Mail: hier@bphstl.com.

HIER, MARVIN, rabbi; b. 1939; Ordained Rabbi. Founder, current dean Simon Weisenthal Ctr., 1977—. Co-prodr.: The Long Way Home (two Acad. Awards, 1997), Genocide, Echoes that Remain, (and writer): Liberation. Named one of The Top 50 Rabbis in America, Newsweek Mag., 2007; recipient Chevalier in the Ordre National du Merite, Pres. France. Achievements include meeting with world leaders incl. George Bush, Bill Clinton, George W. Bush, Jimmy Carter, King Hussein of Jordan, Menachem Begin, Shimon Peres, Yitzhak Shamir, Yitzhak Rabin, Pope John Paul II. Office: Simon Weisenthal Ctr 1399 S Roxbury Los Angeles CA 90035*

HIERONYMUS, EDWARD WHITTLESEY, retired lawyer; b. Davenport, Iowa, June 13, 1943; BA cum laude, Knox Coll., 1965; JD with distinction, Duke U., 1968. Bar: Calif. 1969, Iowa 1968. Ptnr. O'Melveny & Myers, LA, 1974—96, of counsel, 1996—99, ret., 1999. Contbr. articles on law to profl. jours. Exec. sec. Los Angeles Com. Fgn. Relations, 1975-86. Served with Judge Adv. Gen. U.S. Army, 1965-74. Mem. ABA (award for profl. merit 1968), Calif. Bar Assn. (founding co-chair natural resources subsect., real property sect. 1986-88), Los Angeles County Bar Assn., Iowa Bar Assn. Office: O'Melveny & Myers 400 S Hope St Los Angeles CA 90071-2899

HIERS, RICHARD HYDE, lawyer, educator, writer; s. Glen and Mildred H.; m. Jane Gale, 1954; children: Peter, Rebecca. BA, Yale U., 1954, BD, 1957, MA, PhD, 1959-61; JD, U. Fla., 1983. Bar: Fla. 1984, US Dist. Ct. (we. dist.) Tex. 1988, US Ct. Appeals (5th cir.) 1988. Instrn. asst. Yale Divinity Sch., 1958—61; asst. prof. Coll. Liberal Arts and Scis., U. Fla., Gainesville, 1961-66, assoc. prof., 1966-72, prof., 1972—2003, prof. emeritus, 2003—, affiliate prof. law Coll. Law, 1994—2003, affiliate prof. law emeritus, 2003—. Pres. Am. Acad. Religion, Southeastern Region, 1969-70; pres. Soc. Biblical Literature, Southeastern Region, 1982-83; jud. law clk. US Ct. Appeals, 5th cir., 1987-88; chmn. adv. com., Jour. Law and Religion, 2006-. Author several books; contbr. numerous articles to profl. jours., chpts. to books. Former pres. Gainesville/Alachua County Citizen's Housing Assn., Gainesville Coun. on Human Relations; former chmn. Citizen's Adv. Com. for a Workable Program, Gainesville, Fla.; former mem. Gainesville Civilian Regional Blood Ctr. Adv. Bd. Recipient Disting. Faculty award, Fla. Blue Key Orgn., 1998. Mem. AAUP (pres. U. Fla. chpt. 1972-74), Fla. Bar Assn., Bar Assn. of 5th Fed. Cir., Soc. Christian Ethics, Yale Whiffenpoofs of 1954, Order of the Coif, Phi Beta Kappa (pres. U. Fla. chpt., 1975-76), Phi Kappa Phi (pres. U Fla chpt., 1995-96), League of Conservation Voters, Save-the-Redwoods League. Democrat. Presbyterian. Avocations: hiking, reading, singing. Office: U Fla 107 Anderson Hall Gainesville FL 32611-7410 Business E-Mail: hiers@law.ufl.edu. *All decisions affecting ourselves, other persons, and other living beings, are basically ethical decisions. And ethical decisions inevitably give expression to our fundamental loyalties and convictions as to the meaning of life that are, ultimately, religious in character.*

HIESTAND, EDGAR LEROY, minister; b. Oak Park, Ill., Jan. 7, 1934; s. Edgar Leroy Hietstand and Alice Lillian Pettey; m. Nancy Ann Innis, Aug. 19, 1955; children: Sarah, John, Amy, Marietta. BA, Northwestern U., Evanston, Ill., 1955; MDiv, Yale Div. Sch., New Haven, 1955; DMin, Garrett Evang. Theol. Sch., Evanston, 1992. Ordained min. United Meth. Ch., 1961. Pastor Aldersgate United Meth. Ch., Wheaton, Ill., 1959—63, Neighborhood United Meth. Ch., Maywood, Ill., 1963—70, West Ridge United Meth. Ch., Chgo., 1970—84, River Forest United Meth. Ch., Ill., 1984—97, Harvard United Meth. Ch., Ill., 1997—99; ecumenical, interreligious officer United Meth. Ch. No. Ill. Conf., Oak Park, 1999—. Chmn. Peace and World Order, United Meth. Ch. No. Ill., 1962—66, registrar bd. ordained ministry, 1980—88, chmn. Commn. on Christian Unity Interreligious Concerns, Ill., 1992—96, sec. India Reconnect Mission, Ill., 2000—, webmaster, editor Commn. on Christian Unity Interreligious Concerns, 2000—. Mem. steering com. Office Econ. Opportunity, Cook County, Ill., 1967—70; chmn., organizer, founder Rogers Pk. Nuc. Freeze Campaign, Chgo., 1982; pres. Ill. Conf. Chs., 1996—99; World Meth. del. Vatical Interreligious Collaboration, 1999; organizer Interfaith Cmty. Congregation, Oak Park; bd. dirs. High Ridge YMCA, Chgo., 1979. Mem.: Belles Lettres Soc. Avocations: photography, singing. Home and Office: 1124 S Clinton Ave Oak Park IL 60304

HIESTAND, SHEILA PATRICIA, lawyer; b. Levittown, Pa., July 10, 1969; d. John Douglas Lloyd and Eileen Ann Cassidy; m. David Michael Hiestand, July 25, 1992; 1 child, Michael David. BA in Spanish and English, Centre Coll., Danville, Ky., 1990; JD, U. Ky., 1993. Bar: Ky. 1993, U.S. Dist. Ct. (ea. and we. dists.) Ky. 1994, U.S. Ct. Appeals (6th cir.) 1997. Assoc. Landrum & Shouse, Lexington, Ky., 1993-98, ptnr., 1999—; atty. Becker Law Office, 2000, Bubalo & Hiestand, 2004—. Bd. dirs., officer Vol. Ctr. of the Bluegrass, 1995-98; girls basketball coach Christ the King Sch., 1993-98. Mem. Fayette County Bar Assn. (Outstanding Young Lawyer 1998, pres. young lawyers sect. 1996-98, bd. dirs. 1996-99), Ky. Bar Assn. (bd. dirs. young lawyers sect., convention CLE com. 1997-98), Chair Ky. Bar Assn. (Young Lawyer Sect.), mem. bd. Governors, named Fayette County Bar Assn. Outstanding Young Lawyer 1998, bd. mem. Alzheimer's Assn. Lexington (Co-Chair annual Memory Walk), bd. mem. Volunteer Ctr. Bluegrass, The Million Dollar Advs. Forum. Roman Catholic. Office: Bubalo & Hiestand PLC Ste 800 401 S 4th St Louisville KY 40202 Office Phone: 502-753-1600. Office Fax: 502-753-1601.

HIETALA, VALERIE GRACE, realtor, environmentalist, educator; d. Douglas Waldie Dill; m. Kaarlo John Hietala, July 27, 1999; children: Rachel, Kaarlo John, Ingrid, Amber, Sasha. BS in Agr., U. Wis., 1973; MS, U. Colo., 1991. Cert. edn. Fla., 1998, Fla. Assn. Realtors, 2002. Environ. educator Cheyenne Mountain Zoo, Colorado Springs, Colo., 1984—90; dir. Blue Belly Lizard, Los Olivos, Calif., 1993—96; environ. educator McIntosh Mid. Sch., Sarasota, Fla., 1996—2000; dir. Lucy Spoons Island Outfitters, Holmes Beach, 1998—2002; realtor, real estate sales Re/Max Gulfstream, 2000—. Environ. educator, cons. Butterfly Assn., Bradenton, Fla., 1999—. Jewelry, Non Titled (Longboat Key Art award, 2004). Edn. com. DAR, Anna Maria, Fla., 2003—04. Scholar, Longboat Key Art Ctr., 2004. Mem.: Selby Bot. (assoc.), Ringling Art Musuem (assoc.), DAR (assoc.). Achievements include research in Geneological research for Daughters of the American Revolution. Avocations: travel, swimming, photography, scuba diving, art. Personal E-mail: wawanuky@runbox.com.

HIGASHIDA, RANDALL TAKEO, radiologist, neurosurgeon, medical educator; b. LA, Oct. 26, 1955; s. Henry and Alice Higashida; m. Jean Kim, May 17, 1986. BS, U. So. Calif., 1976; MD, Tulane U. Diplomate Am. Bd. Radiology. Intern Harbor UCLA Med. Ctr., 1980-81, resident in radiology, 1981-84, fellow in diagnostic/interventional neuroradiology, 1984-85; asst. prof. radiology UCLA Med. Ctr., 1985-86; assoc. prof. radiology U. Calif. San Francisco Med. Ctr., 1986-94, prof. radiology and neurosurgery, 1994—. Cons. Target Therapeutics Corp., Fremont, Calif., 1989-93, Interventional Therapeutics Corp., Fremont, 1986-93, Cordis Corp., Miami Lakes, Fla., 1993-96; mem. exec. com. stroke rsch. grants Abbott Labs., Chgo., 1994-96. Mem. editl. bd. Jour. Endovasc. Surgery, 1994-96, Jour. Minimally Invasive Neurosurgery, 1994-96; manuscript reviewer Am. Jour. Neuroradiology, 1992—. Recipient rsch. award Am. Heart Assn., Dallas, 1978-79. Mem. AMA, Am. Soc. Neuroradiology (sr. mem., exec. coun. joint section of cerebrovascular neurosurgery) , Soc. Cardiovascular and Interventional Radiology, Am. Soc. Interventional and Therapeutic Neuroradiology (exec. com. 1994-96), Internat. Soc. Endovascular Surgery. Republican. Protestant. Avocations: hiking, tennis, biking, photography, travel. Office: UCSF Medical Ctr 505 Parnassus Ave # L352 San Francisco CA 94143-0001

HIGBEE, BETH, communications executive; b. 1971; B in Journalism, Pa. State U., 1992, B in French, 1992. Editor Rodale Press, founding mem., new media divsn.; dir. ops., entertainment websites NBCi, sr. product mgr.; co-founder Snap.com; v.p., new media Scripps Networks Interactive, 2000, sr. v.p. Named one of 40 Executives Under 40, Multichannel News, 2006. Mem.: Step Up Women's Network NY.

HIGBEE, DALE (STROHE), musician, retired psychologist; b. Proctor, Vt., June 14, 1925; s. Paul Wilbur Higbee and Catherine Ann Strohe; 1 child, Catherine Ann Higbee Mize. AB, Harvard, Cambridge, Mass., 1949; PhD, Univ. Tex. at Austin, Austin, Tex., 1954; studied flute with, Georges Laurent, Arthur Lora, Marcel Moyse; studied recorder with, Carl Dolmetsch. Clin. psychologist SC State Hosp., Columbia, SC, 1954—55, VA Med. Ctr., Salisbury, NC, 1955—87; freelance flutist & recorder player NC, 1954—87; music dir. Carolina Baroque, Salisbury, NC, 1988—. Contbr. articles to profl. jour. Gov. Dolmetsch Found., 1963—. Pfc. 314th reg., 79th divsn., 1943—45. Decorated Combat Infantry badge, Purple Heart. Home and Office: Carolina Baroque 412 S Ellis St Salisbury NC 28144

HIGBEE, DONNA GOOD, writer, researcher; b. Cedar Rapids, Iowa, Feb. 28, 1947; d. Richard Vernon and Freda Lee Good; m. William Higbee, Sept. 23, 1989. BA in Dramatic Arts, Pasadena Playhouse Coll. Theatre Arts, Calif., 1967; AA in Psychology, Santa Barbara City Coll., Calif., 1982; BA in religious studies, U. Calif., Santa Barbara, 1985. Cert. clin. hypnotherapist Hypnosis Motivation Inst., 1994. Personal asst. to chancellor U. Calif., Santa Barbara, 1986—90; exec. asst., pub. rels. 2020 Group, Santa Barbara, 1993—94; pres. Daona Promotions, Santa Barbara, 1994—; dir. Contact Encounters Investigation Team, Santa Barbara, 1994—. Freelance writer, lectr., Santa Barbara, 1994—; counselor, lectr. Natural Alternative Medicine, Santa Barbara, 1996—. Actress: (films) The Girl Next Door, 2003; Shop Girl, 2003; Mrs. Harris, 2004; In Her Shoes, 2004; Chumscrubber, 2004; The Wedding Crashers, 2004; Monster-In-Law, 2005; (TV pilot) NYPD 2069, 2003; (TV movie) Turning Homeward, 2003; (TV series) Arrested Development, 2004; Wedding Chapel, 2005; author (children's book): Paula Pelican; contbr. articles to profl. jours. Involved in Katrina relief Am. Red Cross. Mem.: AFTRA, SAG, U. Calif. Alumni Assn., Pasadena Playhouse Alumni & Assocs. Avocations: music, dance.

HIGBY, LAWRENCE M., medical products executive; BS, U. Calif. Exec. v.p. mktg., chmn. Orange County edit. LA Times, Times Mirror Co., 1986—94; group v.p., pres. & COO 76 Products Co. Unocal Corp., 1994—97; pres., COO Apria Healthcare Group, Lake Forest, Calif., 1997—2002, pres., CEO, 2002—. Office: Apria Health 26220 Enterprise Ct Lake Forest CA 92630-8405 Office Phone: 949-639-2000. Office Fax: 949-587-9363.

HIGBY, WAYNE (DONALD), artist, educator; b. Colorado Springs, Colo., May 12, 1943; s. Donald W. and Betty (Bates) H.; m. Donna Claire Bennett, Mar. 12, 1966; children: Austin Myles, Sarah Lark. BFA, U. Colo., 1966; MFA, U. Mich., 1968. Prof. art NY State Coll. Ceramics, Alfred U., 1973—2007, chair divsn. ceramic art, 1983—91, Robert C. Turner chair ceramic art, 2005—, Kruson Disting. prof., 2007—. Panelist Task Force for Individual Artists NY State Coun. Arts, 1980-82, chair, 1978, mem. visual arts panel, 1976, 77; mem. NEA Visual Artists Fellowship/Crafts, 1986, NEA Visual Arts Overview Panel, 1989-90; hon. prof. Shanghai U., 2000, ceramic art Jingdezhen Ceramic Inst, People's Republic of China, 1994; bd. dirs. Intrnat. Acad. Ceramics. One-man shows include Helen Drutt Gallery, 1988, 90, Mus. of Art and Design, Helsinki, Finland, 1999; exhibited in groups shows at Chunichi Internat. Exhbn. Ceramic Art, Nagoya, Japan, 1980, 85, respectively, Everson Mus. Art, Syracuse, NY, 1981, 87, 89, Am. Craft Mus., NYC, 1982, 89, Jacksonville Mus. Art, Fla., 1982, Nelson-Atkins Mus. Art, Kansas City, 1983, Boston Mus. Fine Arts, 1984, Victoria and Albert Mus., London, 1986, Seoul Olympics Arts Festival, 1988, Nat. Mus. Ceramic Art, Balt., 1989, Kanazawa, Ishibkawa Pref, Japan, 1991, Nat. Mus. Modern Art, Tokyo, 1992-93, Met. Mus. Art, NYC, 1999; public collections include Met. Mus. Art, NYC, Mpls. Mus. Art, Phila. Mus. Art, Everson Mus. Art, Joslyn Mus. Art, Omaha, Am. Craft Mus., Victoria and Albert Mus., Boston Mus. Fine Arts, Bklyn. Mus. Art, LA County Mus. Art. Bd. dirs. Haystack Mountain Sch. Crafts, Deer Isle, Maine, 1983—, pres., 1989-92, chmn., 2000—. Howard Found. fellow, 1985-86, 89-90; recipient Master Tchr. award U. Hartford, 1990, Chancellor's award SUNY, 1993, Master of the Media award James Renwick Alliance, 2005, Hon. of Coun. award Nat. Coun. Edn. in Ceramic Art, 2005; named visionary of Am. craft Am. Craft Mus., 1995, Disting. Educator James Renwick Alliance, 2002, 1st Fgn. Citizen of Jingdezhen People's Republic of China, 2004. Mem. Coll. of Fellows Am. Craft Coun. Office: N Y State Coll Ceramics Alfred U Alfred NY 14802-2207 Office Phone: 607-871-2207. Personal E-mail: higbyw@yahoo.com.

HIGDAY, PAUL T., medical products distribution company executive; b. Leawood, Kans. m. Laura Higday. BSE in mgmt., U. Pa., BSE in computer sci. Sr. cons. to Ernst & Young LLP, Signet Bank; joined Owens & Minor, Inc., Glen Allen, Va., 1999, dir. architecture and external systems, now v.p. IT and program devel. Dir. U. Pa. Liberty Bell Classic. Named one of Premier 100 IT Leaders, Computerworld, 2005. Office: Owens & Minor 9120 Lockwood Blvd Mechanicsville VA 23116-2015 Office Phone: 804-747-9794. Office Fax: 804-270-7281.

HIGDON, HAL, sportswriter; m. Rose Higdon. BA in Art, Carleton Coll., Northfield, Minn. Profl. marathoner, 1959; features writer Sports Illustrated, 1963; coulmnist Runner's World, 1966—, now contbg. editor. Consul. Chicago Marathon; co-founder Road Runners Club Am. Author: (35 published books including) The Crime of the Century, The Horse that Played Center Field, Run Fast, Marathon: The Ultimate Training Guide, Boston: A Century of Running, The Runner's World Guide to Masters Running. Recipient Journalism award, RRCA, 1980, Harold Hirsch award, North American Ski Journalists Assn., 1995, Career Achievement award, Am. Soc. of Journalist and Authors, 2003. Achievements include 111 marathons incl. four overall victories, and numerous age-group wins; winner, 3000 meter Steeplechase in Masters Divsn., 1975; world masters title, 1977, 1981, 1991; holder of American Masters Steeplechase Record.*

HIGDON, LEO IGNATIUS, JR., (LEE), academic administrator; b. Chgo., 1946; married; 4 children. BA in History, Georgetown U., 1968; MBA in Fin., U. Chgo., 1972. Vice chmn., mem. exec. com. Salomon Bros., Inc., 1973-93; dean Darden Grad. Sch. Bus. Adminstrn. U. Va., 1993-97; pres. Babson Coll., Wellesley, Mass., 1997—2001, Coll. of Charleston, SC, 2001—06, Conn. Coll., 2006—. Bd. dirs. Crompton Corp., Eaton Vance Corp., Newmont Mining. Contbr. articles to profl. and popular publs. Mem. Peace Corps., Malawi, South Africa. Office: Conn Coll 270 Mohegan Ave New London CT 06320*

HIGDON, PAMELA LEIS, writer; b. San Bernardino, Calif., Sept. 2, 1943; d. Stella Doss and Raymond Ellsworth Leis; m. Sherman Robert Higdon Jr., Aug. 29, 1964 (dec.); 1 child, Mary Katherine Christian. BS Edn., Tex. Technol. U., Lubbock, 1966. Cert. tchr. Tex., 1966. Tchr. elem. sch., sci. coord. for elem. sch., dist. lang. arts com. mem., after sch. computer instr. Arabian Am. Oil Co., Ras Tanura, Ea. Province, Saudi Arabia, 1978—86; editor/writer, Bird Talk Mag. and Birds USA Fancy Publs., Irvine, Calif., 1987—90; writer/editor, product developer, project mgr., acquisitions editor Ednl. Insights, Carson, Calif., 1990—94; freelance writer and editor PLH Writing/Editing, Castroville, Tex., 1994—. Author: (children's ednl. book) Science Notes: How Things Move; author, editor (pet care book) The Essential Cockatiel, The Essential Zebra Finch; editor: (prehospital med. booklet) The Life You Save: Community Defibrillation Programs & the Emergency Care Responder; author: (monthly newsletter Can. Paramedics) Jour. Emergency Med. Svcs.; editor (monthly periodicals) Journal of Emergency Medical Services, Fire Rescue Magazine, Clarity, EMS Insider, EMS M&S, EMS Best Practices, Caring for the Ages-for Long-Term Care Practitioners; author (with Julie Mancini): (bird watching book) Watching Backyard Birds; author: (children's ednl. book) Pattern Blocks (math series); author, project mgr. (computerized ednl. games) Geosafari & Geosafari Jr., assorted; author (with Katherine Christian): (ednl. book) Third Grade Review; writer, Nat. Wildlife Fedn. (interactive, wildlife, ednl.) Insects, Exotic Animals, Sea Life, Wild Animals, Dinosaurs; author (with Dr. David McCluggage): (animal care book) Holistic Care for Birds: A Manual of Wellness and Healing; author: (pet care book) Bird Care and Training, (bird care book) Happy Healthy Pets: The Quaker Parrot; writer, editor (pet care book) The Essential African Grey; copy editor: The Hospitalist. Vol. writer cmty. newsletter Mills Br. Village Bd. Dirs., Kingwood, Tex., 1996—2000; vol. writer, designer, pub. town newsletter Castroville, Tex., 2001—03; exec. bd., rec. sec. Meth. Ch., Castroville, 2003—04; past chair Landmark Hist. Preservation Commn., 2004—05. Recipient Cmty. Svc. award, Mills Br. Village Bd. Dirs., 1997. Mem.: DAR (life), Daus. Confederacy, Daus. Republic Tex. (rec. sec. 2002—04). Democrat. Avocations: mentoring children, quilting, reading, swimming, birdwatching.

HIGGINBOTHAM, EDITH ARLEANE, radiologist, researcher; b. New Orleans, Sept. 14, 1946; d. Luther Aldrich and Ruby (Clark) H.; m. Terry Lawrence Andrews (div. 1979); m. Donald Temple Ford (div. 1989). BS, Howard U., 1967, MS, 1970, MD, 1974. Diplomate Am. Bd. Radiology, Am. Bd. Nuclear Medicine. Intern St. Vincent's Hosp., NYC, 1974-75, resident in diagnostic radiology, 1975-78, resident in nuclear radiology, 1978-79; asst. prof. radiology, chief nuclear medicine Howard U., Howard U. Hosp., Washington, 1979-82; assoc. prof. clin. radiology, dir. nuclear medicine U. Medicine and Dentistry N.J., Newark, 1982-90; locum tenens radiologist Sterling Med., Cin., 1991-94, Med. Nat., San Antonio, 1990-91; diagnostic radiologist Diagnostic Health Imaging Systems, Lanham, Md., 1994-95; locum tenens radiologist, 1995-97; radiologist, dir. radiology N.E. Wash. Med. Group, Colville, Wash., 1997—99; radiologist Mount Carmel Hosp., Colville, 1997-99, Barstow (Calif.) Cmty. Hosp., 1999, Queen of Peace Hosp., Mitchell, SD, 1999—2002, New Ulm Med Ctr., Minn., 2002—03, dir. radiology, 2003; radiologist Naeve Hosp., Albert Lea (Minn.) Med. Ctr., Mayo Health Sys., 2003—. Cons. Biotech. Rsch. Inst., Rockville, Md., 1989-94; profl. assoc. Ctr. for Molecular Medicine and Immunology, Newark, 1984-90; asst. prof. radiology George Washington U., Washington, 1990; counselor Am. Coll. Radiology, SD, 2001; presenter in field. Contbr. articles to profl. jours. Named Outstanding Working Woman, Glamour mag., 1981, Hon. Dep. Atty. Gen., State of La., 1982. Mem.: SD Med. Assn. (continuing med. edn. com. 2001), Freeborn County Med. Soc. (pres. 2005), Minn. Med. Assn. (continuing med. edn. com. 2005), Soc. Nuclear Medicine, Radiol. Soc. N.Am., Am. Coll. Radiology, Phi Delta Epsilon, Sigma Xi. Roman Catholic. Avocations: aerobics, reading, music, travel. E-mail: ehigginbothammd@charter.net.

HIGGINBOTHAM, EVE JULIET, ophthalmologist, educator, dean; b. New Orleans, Nov. 4, 1953; d. Luther Aldrich and Ruby Edith (Clark) H.; m. Frank Christopher Williams, June 7, 1986. BSChE, MS in Engring., MIT, 1975; MD, Harvard U., 1979. Intern Pacific Med. Ctr., San Francisco, 1979-80; resident La. State U. Eye Ctr., 1980-83; fellow Mass. Eye and Ear Infirmary, Boston, 1983-85; asst. prof. U. Ill., Chgo., 1985-90; assoc. prof. U. Mich., Ann Arbor, 1990-94; prof., chair dept. ophthalmology and visual sciences U. Md., Balt., 1994—2005; dean Morehouse Sch. Medicine, Atlanta, 2005—, sr. v.p. acad. affairs, 2005—. Co-editor: Management of Difficult Glaucoma, 1994, Clinician's Guide to Comprehensive Ophthology, 1998; contbr. articles to profl. jours; mem. editl. bd. Jour. of Glaucoma, 1990-93, Archives of Ophthalmology, 1994—; sect. editor: Glaucoma in Principles and Practice of Ophthalmology. Bd. dirs. Prevent Blindness Am., Schaumburg, Ill., 1990-97, chair publs. com., 1990-95, chair scientific adv. com., 1995—. Fellow Am. Acad. Ophthalmology (trustee 1992-95); mem. Women in Ophthalmology (bd. dirs. 1990-99), Assn. Univ. Profs. Ophthalmology, Assn. in Rsch. in Vision and Ophthalmology, Inst. Medicine, Md. Soc. Eye Physicians and Surgeons (v.p. 1997-99, pres. 2000—), Balt. City Med. Soc. (treas. 1999-00, v.p. 2000—). Avocations: golf, piano. Office: Office of Dean Morehouse Sch Medicine 720 Westview Dr SW Atlanta GA 30310-1495

HIGGINBOTHAM, JOAN E., astronaut; b. Chgo., Aug. 03; BSEE, So. Ill. U., 1987; M in Mgmt., Fla. Inst. Tech., 1992, M in Space Sys., 1996. Payload elec. engr. divsn. ele. and telecomm. sys. NASA, Kennedy Space Ctr., Fla., 1987, lead orbiter experiments space shuttle Columbia, 1987, exec. staff asst. to dir. shuttle ops. and mgmt., backup orbiter project engr. space shuttle Atlantis, lead orbiter project engr. space shuttle Columbia; astronaut, mission specialist NASA, Johnson Space Ctr., Houston, 1996—. Assigned tech. duties in Payloads & Habitability branch, Shuttle Avionics & Integration Lab. (SAIL), Kennedy Space Ctr. Ops. Support Branch; worked in the astronaut office CAPCOM branch; assigned to robotics branch; assigned as lead for the Internat. Space Station Systems Crew Interfaces Sect.; crew mem. to operate the Space Station Remote Manipulator System STS-116 Mission (Discovery), 2006. Named Disting. Alumni, Fla. Inst. Tech., 1997, So. Ill. U.; named one of 50 Disting. Scientists and Engineers, Nat. Tech. Assn., Top 50 Women of 2004, Essence Mag.; recipient Key to City of Cocoa, Fla., Key to City of Rockledge, Presdl. Sports award in bicycling and weight training, Outstanding Woman of Yr. award, Exceptional Svc. Medal, NASA. Mem.: Gulf Coast Apollo Chpt. Links, Inc., Bronze Eagles, Delta Sigma Theta. Achievements include actively participating in 53 space shuttle launches at Kennedy Space Center. Avocations: weightlifting, bicycling, music, motivational speaking. Office: Astronaut Office/CB NASA Johnson Space Ctr Houston TX 77058*

HIGGINBOTHAM, JOHN TAYLOR, lawyer; b. St. Louis, Feb. 10, 1947; s. Richard Cann and Jocelyn (Taylor) H.; m. Lauren Flint Totty, Aug. 9, 1975 (div. 1979). BA, UCLA, 1969; JD, Columbia U., 1972. Bar: N.Y. 1975, Calif. 1976. Assoc. Kirlin, Campbell & Keating, NYC, 1972-74; atty. Nat. Bank of N.Am., NYC, 1974-76, Bank of Am., 1977; assoc. Barger & Wolen, LA, 1977-78, Halperin, Shivitz, Scholer, Schneider & Eisenberg, 1978-79; atty., dir. real estate Korvettes, Inc., NYC, 1979-82; assoc. Leon Katz, Bklyn., 1983-84, Finley, Kumble, Wagner, Heine, Underberg, Manley & Casey, NYC, 1984-86; assoc. regional counsel HUD, NYC, 1986-88; assoc. Fink, Weinberger, Fredman, Berman, Lowell & Fensterheim, NYC, 1988—89; atty. First Sterling Capital Resources, Inc., Manhasset, NY, 1989—93; counsel Willkie, Farr & Gallagher, NYC, 1993. Editor: Safe Deposit Decisions and Practice, 1977—. Mem. NARAS, NATAS, Acad. Motion Picture Arts and Scis., League Am. Theatres and Prodrs. Inc.

HIGGINBOTHAM, KENNETH JAMES, finance company executive; b. Phila., Aug. 3, 1942; s. James V. and Elizabeth R. (Roebus) H.; m. Ruth M. Schaffer, Apr. 12, 1969; children: Jennifer K., Scott G. BA, Rutgers U., 1971; MBA, Drexel U., 1973. Cert. sr. advisor. Fin. analyst, discount window Fed. Res. Bank Phila., 1972—77; cons. corp. cash mgmt. First Pa. Bank NA, Phila., 1977—79; cons. EFT Control Data Corp., Mpls., 1979—84; dist. rep. Aid Assn. for Luths., Appleton, Wis., 1984—94; reg. rep. Lincoln Fin. Advisors, Richboro, Pa., 1994—2000; prin. Ind. Retirement Planners LLC, Richboro, 2000—. Adj. faculty LaSalle U., Phila., 1977—. Bd. dirs. Mallard Creek Condominium Assocs., Bucks County Estate Planning Coun. With USN, 1963-67. Mem. AAUP, Fin. Planning Assn., Bucks County Estate Planning Coun. (officer, past pres.), Northampton Twp. Bus. and Profl. Assn. Office: Independent Retirement Planners LLC Mallard Creek Village 130 Almshouse Rd Ste 201 B Richboro PA 18954-1917 Home Phone: 215-357-9024; Office Phone: 215-357-0911. Personal E-mail: plannerken@aol.com.

HIGGINBOTHAM, PATRICK ERROL, federal judge; b. McCalla, Ala., Dec. 16, 1938; Student, U. Ala., 1956, Arlington State Coll., 1957, North Tex. State U., 1958, U. Tex., 1958; BA, U. Ala., 1960, LLB, 1961; LLD (hon.), So. Meth. U., 1989. Bar: Ala. 1961, Tex. 1962, US Supreme Ct. 1962. Assoc. to ptnr. Coke & Coke, Dallas, 1964—75; judge US Dist. Ct. (no. dist.) Tex., Dallas, 1976—82, US Ct. Appeals (5th cir.), Dallas, 1982—2006, sr. judge, 2006—. Adj. prof. So. Meth. U. Law Sch., 1971—, adj. prof. constl. law, 1981—, U. Tex. Sch. Law, 1998; M.D. Anderson pub. svc. prof. in residence Tex. Tech. U. Sch. Law, 1999; John Sparkman jurist-in-residence U. Ala. Sch. Law, 1995, 97, 99; vis. prof. St. Mary's Law Sch., 2006—07; conferee Am. Assembly, 1975, Pound Conf., 1976; bd. suprs. Inst. Civil Justice Rand. Contbr. articles to profl. jours. With JAG USAF, 1961—64. Named Outstanding Alumnus, U. Tex., Arlington, 1978, One of Nation's 100 Most Powerful Persons for the 80's, Next Mag.; recipient Dan Meador award, U. Ala., Samuel E. Gates Litigation award, Am. Coll. Trial Lawyers, 1997, A. Sherman Christensen award, 2002, Judge of Yr. 2006, Tex. Ann. Bd. Trial Advs. Fellow: Am. Bar Found.; mem.: ABA, Ctr. for Am. and Internat. Law (bd. dirs. 1998—, chmn.), Am. Inns of Ct. Found. (pres. 1996—2000), Farrah Law Soc., Patrick E. Higginbotham Inn of Ct., Nat. Jud. Coun. State and Fed. Cts., Am. Judicature Soc., Am. Law Inst., Dallas Bar Found., Dallas Bar Assn., Bench and Bar, Order of Coif (hon.), Omicron Delta Kappa. Office: US Ct Appeals Rm 400 903 San Jacinto Blvd Austin TX 78701*

HIGGINBOTHAM, WENDY JACOBSON, legislative staff member, writer; b. Salt Lake City, Oct. 23, 1947; d. Alfred Thurl and Virginia Lorraine (LaCom) Jacobson; m. Keith Higginbotham, July 12, 1969; children: Ann Elizabeth Morley, Ryan Keith, Laura Carol Hoopes. Student, Occidental Coll., 1965—66, U. Grenoble, France, 1967; BA cum laude with highest honors, Brigham Young U., 1969. Tchg. instr. Brigham Young U., Provo, Utah, 1969-70, editor univ. press, 1970-71; freelance editor Camarillo, Calif., 1971-78; freelance newspaper writer Vienna, Va., 1983-85; mem. profl. staff U.S. Senate Labor Com., Washington, 1985-86; exec. asst. U.S. Senator Orrin G. Hatch, Washington, 1986-88, legis. dir., 1988-91, chief of staff/adminstrv. asst., 1991-94, chief policy adviser, 1994-95; polit. adviser, freelance writer Washington, 1996—. Mem. Profl. Rep. Women, Phi Kappa Phi. Republican. Mem. Lds Ch. Avocations: travel, hiking. Home: 2022 Willow Branch Ct Vienna VA 22181-2972

HIGGINBOTTOM, SAMUEL LOGAN, retired air transportation executive; b. North Lawrence, Ohio, Oct. 5, 1921; s. Samuel Bradlaugh and Vera Abbie (Gutchess) H.; m. Fair Steinschneider, Aug. 30, 1947 (dec. May 1997); children: Samuel Logan, Marie Fair, Michele Rowan Maclaren; m. Janaina Dornelles, Aug. 4, 1998. BS in Civil Engring, Columbia, 1943; grad. Advanced Mgmt. Program, Harvard U. Design engr. Parsons, Brinckerhoff, Hogan & McDonald, NYC, 1945-46; v.p. engring., flight, test and inspection Trans World Airlines, Inc., 1946-64; v.p. engring. and maintenance Eastern Air Lines, Inc., 1964-67, v.p. operations group, 1967-69, sr. v.p., 1969, exec. v.p., 1969-70, pres., chief operating officer, 1970-73; chmn., pres., chief exec. officer Rolls-Royce Inc., NYC, 1974-86. Bd. dirs. Heico Corp. Emeritus chmn. bd. trustees Columbia U.; mem. adv. bd. Taub Inst. Capt. USAAF, WWII, ETO. Decorated hon. comdr. Order Brit. Empire; recipient Egleston medal Columbia U. Engring. Sch., 1977 Fellow AIAA; mem. Soc. Automotive Engrs., Conquistadores del Cielo, Wings Club (pres.1980-81), Deering Bay Yacht and Country Club, Tau Beta Pi, Psi Upsilon, Theta Tau. Roman Catholic.

HIGGINS, BRADFORD R., federal agency administrator; m. Kimberly Rossetter; 1 child, Schuyler. BS, Columbia U., 1974, JD, 1978. Assoc. Simpson Thacher & Bartlett, 1978—80; mng. dir. Bear Sterns Asset Mgmt., 1980—87; CFO Coalition Provisional Authority, Iraq; chief of planning, Iraq reconstruction mgmt. office US Dept. State, CFO, sr. advisor office asst. sec. resource mgmt., sr. advisor to US amb. Iraq, asst. sec. for resource mgmt., CFO, Bur. Resource Mgmt., 2006—. Office: US Dept State Harry S Truman Bldg 2201 C St NW Rm 7427 Washington DC 20520 E-mail: higgnsbr@state.gov.

HIGGINS, BRIAN, congressman; b. Buffalo, Oct. 6, 1959; s. Dan and Mary Higgins; m. Mary Jane Hannon; children: John, Maeve. BS in Polit. Sci., Buffalo State Coll., 1984, MA in Hist., 1985; MA in Pub. Policy and Adminstrn., Harvard U. John F. Kennedy Sch. Govt., 1996. Mem. Buffalo Common Coun., 1987—93; lectr. hist. and econs. Buffalo State Coll.; mem. NY State Assembly from 145th dist., 1998—2004, US Congress from 27th NY dist., 2005—. Mem. transp. and infrastructure com. US Congress, mem. govt. reform com. Recipient Forty Under Forty award, Bus. First newspaper; scholar Judge John D. Hillary Scholarship award; Inaugural Western N.Y. Harvard Grad. Fellowship, 1995. Democrat. Roman Catholic. Office: US House Reps 431 Cannon House Office Bldg Washington DC 20515-3227 Office Phone: 202-225-3306. Office Fax: 202-226-0347.*

HIGGINS, BRIAN ALTON, art gallery owner, artist; b. Brookline, Mass. s. Gerald and Catherine (Walsh) H.; m. Jane Edgington, July 1, 1975; children: Brenda, Belinda, Devon. Ops. mgr. Sta. WMTW-TV, Portland, Maine, 1965-68; v.p., gen. mgr. Sta. WSMW-TV, Worcester, Mass., 1974-84; pres. Brian Edgington Collection Am. Art, 1974—. Exhbns. include Danforth Mus. Art, For Pastels Only, Pastel Soc. Am., Land, Sea, Earth, San Francisco, 1997, Art on Paper, 21st Ann. (Md. Fedn. Art), Pastel Painters' Soc. Cape Cod, Ann. Exhbn. Award, Internat. Assn. Pastel Socs., 1998, Pastel Soc. of the Southwest, 18th Ann., Renaissance in Pastel, Conn. Pastel Soc., 1999, Art of Northeast, 50th Ann. award, Lindenberg Gallery, NYC, Gallery 214, Montclair, NJ, 2000, Conn. Acad. Fine Arts, 2000-03, 05-06 (award), Slater Mus., 2000—, Reading Between the Lines: A National Exhbn., Constn. Sq. Hist. Site, Ky., 2000 (Purchase award), Pastel Painters of Maine, 2000 (Merit award 2000), Nat. Pastel Exhbn., Impact Artists Gallery, Buffalo, NY, 2000 (award 2000), 50th Nat. Exhbn. Contemporary Realism in Art, Acad. Artists Assn., 2000-05, 13th Ann. Exhbn. Pastel Soc., Oreg., 2000, Good and Evil, Fredericksburg Ctr. for Creative Arts, Va. Mus. Fine Arts, 2000, 20th Anniversary Miniature Juried Show, Colorado Springs, 2001, Edward Hopper Ctr., NY, 2001, Pastel Nat., Wichita, Kans., 2002, Mass Gen. Hosp., 2003-04, 2006-07, 68th Exhbn., Cooperstown, NY (Grumbacher Gold medal 2003), San Diego Art Inst., 2004, 07, Butler Inst. Am. Art, 2007. Chmn. bd. Ctrl. Mass. Symphony Orch., 1979—, Ctrl. Mass. chpt. Am. Heart Assn.; bd. dirs. Ctrl. Mass. chpt. ARC; mem. coun. YMCA, Worcester Art Mus.; past vice-chmn. Maine Project Hope. Recipient numerous civic awards. Mem. Degas Pastel Soc., Pastel Soc. Am., Conn. Acad. Fine Arts, United Pastelists Am., Acad. Artists Assn. Home: Ridge Rd West Brookfield MA 01585 Office: PO Box 1011 West Brookfield MA 01585-1011 Personal E-mail: brianhiggins@charter.net, jebahiggins@yahoo.com.

HIGGINS, DANIEL B., lawyer; b. Willcox, Ariz., Oct. 14, 1948; BA with distinction, Stanford U., 1973; JD magna cum laude, U. Santa Clara, 1977. Bar: Calif. 1977. Atty. McCutchen, Doyle, Brown & Enersen, San Francisco; ptnr. Paul, Hastings, Janofsky & Walker LLP, San Francisco, mem. policy com., chmn. healthcare practice group. Comment editor: U. Santa Clara Law Rev., 1976-77; contbr. articles to profl. jours. Mem. ABA (mem. healthcare and antitrust sects.), Am. Acad. Healthcare Attys., Nat. Health Lawyers Assn., Healthcare Fin. Mgmt. Assn., Phi Beta Kappa. Office: Paul Hastings Janofsky & Walker LLP 55 Second St Twenty-Fourth Floor San Francisco CA 94105 Office Phone: 415-856-7052. Office Fax: 415-856-7152. Business E-Mail: danhiggins@paulhastings.com.

HIGGINS, GEORGE EDWARD, sculptor; b. Gaffney, SC, Nov. 13, 1930; BA, U. N.C. Instr. sculpture Parsons Sch. Design, NYC, 1961-62. Vis. prof. Cornell U., 1968, U. Wis., 1968-69, U. Ky., 1969-70, Sch. Visual Arts, N.Y.C., 1964-72 One man shows, Leo Castelli Gallery, N.Y.C., 1960, 63, 66, Richard Feigen Gallery, Chgo., 1964, Mpls. Inst. Art, 1964, exhibited group shows Art, USA, 1959, Detroit Inst. Art, 1959-60, Carnegie Inst., 1961, Mus. Modern Art, N.Y.C., 1961, 63, Martha Jackson Gallery, N.Y.C., 1960, Andrew Dickson White Gallery, 1960, Bernard Gallery, Paris, France, 1960, Whitney Mus., N.Y.C., 1964, 66, Documenta, Kassel, Germany, 1968, Art Inst. Chgo., Brandeis U., Tate Gallery, London, Phila. Mus. Arts, New Sch. Art Center, N.Y.C., Smithsonian Instn., numerous others; represented in permanent collections, Whitney Mus., N.Y.C., Guggenheim Mus., N.Y.C., Albright-Knox Gallery, Buffalo, Houston Mus. Fine Arts, Mus. Modern Art, N.Y.C., Albright Art Gallery, Chase Manhattan Bank, N.Y.C., others. Address: 2655 Henley Rd Sanford NC 27330-7549

HIGGINS, GINA O'CONNELL, psychologist, writer; b. Bklyn. d. Paul Bernard Patrick Joseph and Virginia Payne (Conrad) O'Connell; m. James T. Higgins, Aug. 5, 1972 (div. June 1997); children: Caitlin, Taryn; m. R.D. Norton, June 13, 1998; children: Maya, Elias. BA magna cum laude, Tufts U., 1972, MEd, 1974; EdD, Harvard U., 1985. Lic. psychologist, Mass. Diagnostician, med. edn. and evaluation clinic North Shore Children's Hosp., 1982-87; psychotherapist, intake diagnostician, case cons. Mental Health Ctr., North Shore Children's Hosp., 1982-86; fellow Clin. Devel. Inst., Belmont, Mass., 1990—2002; staff psychologist Mass. Gen. Hosp., Boston, 1993—2001; pvt. practice psychotherapy and psychodiagnosis, Salem, Mass., 1993—2002. Lectr. Middlesex C.C., Bedford, Mass., 1974-75, Eliot Pearson dept. child study Tufts U., 1974-75; lectr. Lesley Grad. Sch., Cambridge, Mass., 1974-76, asst. prof., 1976-81; clin. assoc. Harvard Med. Sch./Mass. Gen. Hosp., Boston, 1994-2002. Author: Resilient Adults: Overcoming a Cruel Past, 1994. Recipient scholarship and fellowships. Mem APA, Mass. Psychol. Assn. Office: One Salem Green Ste 555 Salem MA 01970 Office Phone: 978-741-3459.

HIGGINS, JAMES HENRY, III, marketing executive; b. Providence, May 8, 1940; s. James Henry Jr. and Betty (Hall) H. AB, Brown U., Providence, RI, 1962. Mem. faculty The Gov.'s Acad., Byfield, Mass., 1964-66; rsch. assoc. Entelek Inc., 1966-69; mgr. sch. svc. group Sterling Inst., 1969-72; v.p. Vickerman and Schultz, Inc., Washington, 1985-87; sr. v.p. Complete Comm., Inc., Washington, 1987-90; dir. devel. The Brit. Consortium, Washington, 1990—. Mktg. cons. Time Life Video, NYC, 1972-73, Longman Group Ltd., Eng., 1973-74, McGraw-Hill Publ. Co., NYC, 1975-85. Lectr., contbr. articles to boating publ. Mem. mgmt. com. A.S.K. Brown Mil. Collection, Brown U., 1990-2000; pres. City Tavern-Preservation Found., 2000. Mem. Am. Soc. Assn. Execs., Naval War Coll. Found. (assoc.), Mystic Seaport Mus. (yachting com. 1986-2000), Antique and Classic Boat Soc. (pres., v.p., bd. dirs. 1978-94), Lake Placid Inst. (bd. dirs. 1996-2001, adv. bd. 2002—), Adirondack Archtl. Heritage (bd. dirs. 2000—), City Tavern Club (bd. govs. 1998-2000, sec. 1998-2000), Agawam Hunt Club, Hope Club, St. Regis Yacht Club. Home: 2807 O St NW Washington DC 20007-3130 Office: 1101 30th St NW Ste 500 Washington DC 20007-3708

HIGGINS, JAY F., diversified financial services company executive; b. Gary, Ind., June 25, 1945; s. J. Francis and Veronica (Conroy) H.; m. Gail Marie Joy, Nov. 23, 1979; children: Maura Ellis, Kerry Elizabeth, Erin Leigh, Conor Francis. AB, Princeton U., 1967; MBA, U. Chgo., 1970. With Salomon Bros., NYC, 1970-92, v.p., 1976, gen. ptnr. mergers and acquisitions dept., 1978, head corp. fin. dept., 1986, vice chmn., head global investment banking, 1987-92; mng. ptnr. Cloverleaf Ptnrs., Inc., Greenwich, Conn., 1992—98; chmn. Bengal Partners, LLC, North Palm Beach, Fla., 1998—. With USAR, 1967. Mem. Knights of Malta. Roman Catholic. Office: Bengal Partners LLC 701 US 1 Ste 401 North Palm Beach FL 33408 Home: 2818 Old Cypress North Jupiter FL 33410 Office Phone: 561-844-4000.

HIGGINS, JEAN, television producer; Prodr.: (films) Repossessed, 1990, My Fellow Americans, 1996, Arlington Road, 1999; (TV films) Perfect Harmony, 1991, The Ernest Green Story, 1993, The Four Diamonds, 1995; (TV series) Lost, 2004 (best TV series, drama, Producers Guild Am., 2006). Mailing: c/o Lost ABC Inc 500 South Buena Vista St Burbank CA 91521-4562

HIGGINS, JOHN P., JR., (JACK), federal agency administrator; m. Lucy Higgins. BS in Bus, Bethel Coll., McKenzie, Tenn. Various mgmt. positions US Dept. Health, Edn. & Welfare to US Dept. Edn., Washington, 1970—; chief mgmt improvement team US Dept. Edn., Washington, 1994—96, dep. insp. gen, 1996—2002, insp. gen., 2002—. Recipient Presdl. Rank award, 1999. Office: Office of Inspector Gen US Dept Edn 550 12th St SW Rm 8099 Washington DC 20065 Office Phone: 202-245-6900.*

HIGGINS, JOHN PATRICK, lawyer, mediator, lobbyist, educator; b. Beloit, Wis., Feb. 13, 1952; s. John Eugene and Catherine Marie (Beaudry) H. BA cum laude, St. Norbert Coll., 1973; postgrad., DePaul U. Law Sch., 1974-76; JD, U. Wis., Madison, 1977; MBA, Keller Grad. Sch. Mgmt., Milw., 1986. Bar: Wis. 1977, U.S. Dist. Ct. (ea. and we. dists) Wis., 1977, U.S. Ct. Appeals (7th cir.), 1977, U.S. Supreme Ct., 1983. Assessment technician Kenosha County Assessor, Wis., 1973-75; law clk. various firms, Madison, Wis., 1976-77; claims atty. Employers Ins. of Wausau (Wis.), 1977-80, trial counsel, 1980-99; ptnr. Guttormsen, Hartley, Wilk & Higgins, Kenosha, 2000—; mng. ptnr. Higgins Investment Properties, LLC, 2002—. Part time instr. North Ctrl. Tech. Inst., Wausau, 1980; adj. prof. Marian Coll., Fond du Lac, Wis., 1990-2000, Carthage Coll., Kenosha, Wis., 2000-01, Cardinal Stritch U., 2005—; dir. , v.p. legal John E. Higgins Appraisal Co., Kenosha, 1977-97; lectr., spkr. various profl. and fraternal groups; mem. dist. 1 investigative com. Office of Lawyer Regulation Wis. Supreme Ct., 2001—, chmn., 2006—; bd. dirs. St. Joseph HS, 2002—. Author articles and monographs. Bd. dirs., arbitrator Roman Cath. Archdiocese of Milw., 1983-85; mem. human rels commn. City of Kenosha, 1997-2001, vice chmn., 1999-2001; mem. City of Kenosha Zoning Appeals Bd., 2001—, vice chmn., 2004, chmn., 2004—; bd. dirs. Michael Naidicz Found., 2002—. Fellow Young Lawyers Assn.; mem. State Bar Wis. (bd. govs. 1990-91, bd. dirs. young lawyers divsn. 1978-87, sec. 1979-82, chmn. law reform com. 1984-87, chmn. planning conf. young lawyers divsn. 1986, chmn. gavel awards com. 1985-87, chmn. comm. com. 1984-87, interprofl. com. 1987-89, conv. & entertainment com. 1988-1992, 94-97, chmn., mem. various coms.), Thomas More Soc., State Bar Assn. Wis., Civil Trial Coun. Wis., Kenosha Bar Assn., St. Norbert Coll. Alumni Assn. (exec. bd. dirs. 1979-87, chpt. liaison, editor chpt. newsletter, class devel. agt. 1998-99), Nat. Assn. State Bar Jours. (bd. trustee 1986-89), Am. Corp. Coun. Assn. (bd. dirs. 1989-98, pres. Wis. chpt. 1997-98), Am. Acad. ADR Attorneys, Wis. Assn. Workers' Compensation Attys., Wis. Mediation Assn., Phi Alpha Delta. Office: Guttormsen Hartley Wilk & Higgins LLP 600 52d St Ste 200 Kenosha WI 53140 Home Phone: 262-697-3623; Office Phone: 262-658-4800. Business E-Mail: JPH@kenoshalawyers.com.

HIGGINS, KATHRYN O'LEARY (KITTY), federal agency administrator, former consulting firm executive; b. Sioux City, Iowa, Oct. 11, 1947; d. Paul C. and Mary Kathryn (Callaghan) O'Leary; widowed; children: Liam James, Kevan Paul. BS, U. Nebr., 1969. Manpower specialist US Dept. Labor, Washington, 1969-78; asst. dir. employment policy White House Domestic Policy, Washington, 1978-81; staff dir. minority U.S. Senate Labor & Human Resources Com., Washington, 1981-86; chief of staff U.S. Representative Sander Levin, Washington, 1986-93; chief of staff Sec. Robert Reich US Dept. Labor, Washington, 1993-95; asst. to Pres & sec. to cabinet The White House, Washington, 1995-97; dep. sec. US Dept. Labor, Washington, 1997-99; v.p. pub. policy Nat. Trust for Hist. Preservation, Washington, 1999—2004; pres., CEO TATC Cons. Firm, Washington, 2004—05; mem. Nat. Transp. Safety Bd. (NTSB), Washington, 2006—. Bd. dirs. Ignatian Vol. Corps. Democrat. Roman Catholic. Avocations: cooking, antiques, book club. Office: Nat Transp Safety Bd 490 L Enfant Plz SW Washington DC 20594 Office Phone: 202-314-6145.

HIGGINS, M. EILEEN, management consultant, educator; b. Dayton, Ohio, Apr. 4, 1943; d. Harold Elwood and Esther Marie (Kelly) Benjamin; m. James Edward Higgins (div.); children: Joseph Benjamin, James Timothy; m. Edward William Lavine, Jan. 1, 2000 (dec. Nov. 2006). BA in Psychology, Pa. State U., 1965; MBA, Frostburg State U., 1985; postgrad., U. Md., 2002—. Editl. asst. Signal Mag., Washington, 1965—66; publ. editor Nat. Coun. on Radiation Protection and Measurements, Washington, 1966—67; pvt. practice Montgomery Village, Md., 1967—78; sr. mng. editor Aspen Publ., Rockville, Md., 1978—88; prof. Frostburg (Md.) State U., 1989—. Trainer Georgetown U., Washington, 2000—; cons. in field; deans adv. panel, students adv. bd. U. Md., 2001—03. Editor: Editl. Experts, 1969—78; contbr. articles to profl. jours. Dir. publ. Am. Soc. Parenteral and Enteral Nutrition, Silver Spring, 1990—91. Mem.: Orgnl. Behavior Tchg. Soc., S.E. Decision Sci. Inst., Acad. Mgmt., Internat. Acad. Bus. Disciplines, Mgmt., Spirituality and Religion (sec.-treas. 2003—05), Frederick County C. of C. (spkrs. bur.), Am. News Women's Club. Avocations: reading, travel, yoga, hiking, music. Home: PO Box 383 Libertytown MD 21762 Office: Frostburg State Univ Univ Md System Bldg 32 W Washington St Hagerstown MD 21740 Personal E-mail: eileenbenj@aol.com.

HIGGINS, PAUL JOHN, medical director, career military officer; b. Nov. 13, 1959; BS with honors, Siena Coll., 1980; MD, Georgetown U., 1984; grad. with honors, Air Force Aerospace Medicine primary course, 1994. Advanced through grades to rear admiral USCG, 2004, chief health svcs., head Coast Guard Health Svc. Program, chief operational medicine Washington, dir. Health and Safety, 2004—. Chief resident family medicine U. Va.; pub. health svc. provider, NY. Office: USCG 2100 2nd St SW Washington DC 20593

HIGGINS, ROBERT (WALTER), career officer, physician; b. Uniontown, Wash., Nov. 9, 1934; s. Nelson Leigh and Abbie Elizabeth (Rowe) H.; m. Barbara Jean Wright, Aug. 19, 1956 (dec. Feb. 2002); m. Judith Ellen Glenn, Nov. 15, 2003; children: Fred, Colleen, Jay. BS in Pharmacy, Wash. State U., Pullman, 1957; MD, U. Wash., Seattle, 1965. Pharmacist Wenatchee (Wash.) Thrifty Drugs, 1957-59; owner Higgins Drug Store, Pullman, Wash., 1959-61; intern L.A. County Harbor Gen. Hosp., Torrance, 1965-66; commd. lt. USN, 1966; ships surgeon USS Tutuila, Vietnam, 1966-68; ptnr. Ludwick, Zook & Higgins Family Medicine, Wenatchee, 1968-72; commd. lt. comdr. USN, 1972, advanced through grades to rear adm., 1988; chmn. dept. family medicine Naval Hosp., Charleston, SC, 1972-78, Camp Pendleton, Calif., 1978-80, Bremerton, Wash., 1980-86, comdg. officer Camp Pendleton, 1986-87; med. officer USMC Washington, 1987-89; dep. surgeon gen. USN, 1989-93. Specialty advisor surgeon gen. USN, Washington, 1973-86. Contbg. author: Behavioral Disorders, 1984, 90; contbr. articles to profl. jours. Scoutmaster Boy Scouts Am., Charleston, 1974-78, Camp Pendleton, 1978-80; trustee Family Health Found. Am., Wash. State U. Found., 1992-98; bd. visitors Wash. State U. Coll. Pharmacy, 1998—, pres., 2002-05. Decorated Disting. Svc. medal, Legion of Merit, Meritorious Svc. medal, Navy Commendation medal; recipient Alumni Achievement award Wash. State. U., 1988, Disting. Alumnus award U. Wash. Sch. Medicine, 1996; bd. regents disting. alumnus award, Wash. State U., 2002. Fellow: Am. Acad. Family Physicians (pres. 1984—85, alt. del. to AMA 1985—91, del. 1992—2000, John G. Walsh award 2001), Philippine Acad. Family Physicians (hon.); mem.: World Orgn. Family Medicine (v.p. 1986—95, pres.-elect 1995—98, pres. 1998—2001), Coll. Family Physicians Can. (hon.), Uniformed Svcs. Acad. Family Physicians (pres. 1974—76), Masons. Avocations: birdwatching, fly fishing, model airplanes, stamp collecting/philately, jogging. Home and Office: 2303 Highland Dr Anacortes WA 98221-3143 Personal E-mail: rhigginsmd@aol.com.

HIGGINS, ROBERT ARTHUR, electrical engineer, educator, consultant; b. Watertown, SD, Sept. 5, 1924; s. Arthur C. and Nicoline (Huseth) H.; m. Barbara Jeanne Fagerlie, 1958; children— Patricia Suzanne, Daniel Alfred, Steven Robert BEE with honors, U. Minn., 1948; MSEE, U. Wis., 1964; PhDEE, U. Mo., 1969. Registered profl. engr. Engr. Schlumberger Well Survey Corp., Tex., 1948-57; rsch. technologist Mobil Rsch. and Devel. Corp., Tex., 1958-61; rsch. engr. United Aircraft Rsch. Labs., Conn., 1965; staff specialist Remote Sensing Inst., SD, 1969-71; asst. prof. elec. engring. SD State U., 1969-74, assoc. dir. Engring. Expt. Sta., 1973-77, prof. elec. engring., 1974-79; cons. Mankato State U., 1980; prin. engr. Sperry Univac, 1981-85; prof. elec. engring. St. Cloud (Minn.) State U., 1985-95, prof. emeritus, 1995—. Cons. Control Data Corp., 1977-80, Lawrence Livermore Lab., 1971-73, USAF Office Sci. Rsch., Fla., 1976, NCR-Comten, 1988-90, FMC Corp., 1991-92, Ontrack Computer Sys., 1993-98, Minn. Orchestral Assn., 1996-2006; project dir., cons. NSF, 1973-80, 87-89. Contbr. articles to profl. jours. Bd. dirs. Eden Prairie Bd. Edn., Minn., 1982-85, Nat. Storage Industry Consortium, 1995-98. With CE, AUS, 1943-46. NASA fellow, 1966-68; grantee NSF, 1966, 72, 74, 86, AEC, 1971-73, Office Water Resources Rsch., 1971-74 Mem. IEEE (sr., life), Am. Soc. Engring. Educators, Sigma Xi, Eta Kappa Nu. Home: 11260 Windrow Dr Eden Prairie MN 55344-4055 E-mail: rahiggins@ieee.org.

HIGGINS, ROD (RODERICK DWAYNE HIGGINS), professional sports team executive, retired professional basketball player; b. Monroe, La., Jan. 31, 1960; m. Concetta Higgins; children: Rick, Cory. Student, Calif. State U., Fresno. Profl. basketball player Chgo. Bulls, 1982—85, 1986, Seattle SuperSonics, 1985, San Antonio Spurs, 1985, NJ Nets, 1986, Golden State Warriors, 1986—92, 1994—95, Sacramento Kings, 1992—93, Cleve. Cavaliers, 1993—94; asst. coach Golden State Warriors, 1994—2000; asst. gen. mgr. Washington Wizards, 2000—03; gen. mgr. Golden State Warriors, 2004—07, Charlotte Bobcats, 2007—. Office: Charlotte Bobcats 333 E Trade St Charlotte NC 28202*

HIGGINS, ROLAND LOUIS, history professor; b. Toledo, Oct. 9, 1946; s. Louis Eugene and Marie Styring Higgins; m. Lynn Diane Anthony, Dec. 30, 1968; 1 child, Julian Anthony. BA, Oberlin Coll., 1968; MA, U. Minn., 1976, PhD, 1981. Prof. Keene State Coll., NH, 1982—. Lectr. U. Vt., Burlington, 1982, Dartmouth Coll., Hanover, NH, 1982; semester-at-sea lectr. U. Pitts., 1983; humanities adv. bd. mem. NH Pub. Radio, Concord, 1984—89. China content editor: Edn. About Asia, 1994—2001, book rev. editor: Ming Studies, 1996—98; contbr. articles to profl. jours. and encys. in field. Faculty Rsch. Travel grantee, Keene State Coll., 1991, 2004, Rsch. grantee, NEH, 1992. Mem.: World History Assn., Soc. Qing Studies, Soc. Ming Studies (bd. dirs. 2007—), Am. Hist. Assn., Assn. Asian Studies (Rsch. Travel grantee 1981), Human Rights Watch, Amnesty Internat. Liberal. Avocations: languages, photography. Office: Keene State Coll 229 Main St MS 3400 Keene NH 03435-3400 Home Phone: 603-643-6361. Office Fax: 603-358-2184. Business E-Mail: rhiggins@keene.edu.

HIGGINS, DAME ROSALYN, judge; b. London, June 2, 1937; d. Lewis Cohen and F. Inberg; m. Terence L. Higgins, 1961; 2 children. Student, Cambridge U., Yale U.; D (hon.), Univ. Paris, 1980, Univ. Dundee, 1992, Durham and London Sch. Econ., 1995, London City Univ., 1996. Intern Office Legal Affairs UN, 1958; Commonwealth Fund fellow, 1959; vis. fellow Brookings Inst., Washington, 1960; jr. fellow internat. studies L.S.E., 1961-63, vis. fellow, 1974-78; staff specialist internat. law Royal Inst. Internat. Affairs, 1963-74; prof. internat. law U. Kent, Canterbury, England, 1978-81, L.S.E., 1981-95; judge Internat. Ct. of Justice, The Hague, Netherlands, 1995—2006, pres., 2006—. Mem. com. human rights UN, 1985-95, Queen's Counsel, 1986; vis prof. Stanford U., 1975, Yale U., 1977; chmn. Pub. Insternat. Law adv. bd., Brit. Inst. Internat. Comparative Law, 19922-2005. Author: The Development of International Law through the Political Organs of the United Nations, 1963, Conflict of Interests, 1965, The Administration of the United Kingdom Foreign Policy through the United Nations, 1966, UN Peacekeeping: Documents and Commentary; editor: (with James Fawcett) Law in Movement—Essays in Memory of John McMahon, 1974, Problems & Process, 1994, Terrorism & International Law, 1997; contbr. articles to profl. jours. Recipient Yale Law Sch. Medal of Merit, 1997, Manley O. Hudson Medal, 1998. Mem. Ordre Palmes Academiques. Avocations: sports, cooking. Office: Internat Ct Justice Peace Palace 2517KJ The Hague Netherlands*

HIGGINS, ROXANNE SNELLING, educational consultant; b. Ft. Eustis, Va., Aug. 17, 1954; d. William Rodman and Anne Louise (Kurtz) Snelling; m. Robert K. Higgins, June 16, 2001; m. Vincent James Elliott, Oct. 3, 1983 (div.); children: Brian William Elliott, Lauren Elizabeth Elliott. BA, Denison U., 1976; MBA, Syracuse U., 1978. Intern. loan officer First Pa. Bank, Phila., 1978—82; ins. assoc. Ind. Sch. Mgmt., Wilmington, Del., 1982—83, dir. mgmt. insts., 1983—87, cons., exec. dir. consortium, 1984—, v.p., 1986—90, pres., 1990—. Office: Ind Sch Mgmt 1316 N Union St Wilmington DE 19806-2594

HIGGINS, RYAN K., lawyer; b. El Paso, Tex., Mar. 31, 1971; m. Laura Higgins. BA, Eckerd Coll., 1992; JD, So. Meth. U., 1998. Bar: Tex. 1998, NY 1999, US Dist. Ct. (so. dist. NY), US Dist. Ct. (so. dist. Tex.). Assoc. Boies, Schiller & Flexner LLP, NYC, 1999—2005, Rusty Hardin & Assocs., P.C., Houston, 2005—. Articles editor: So. Meth. U. Internat. Law Rev., 1997—98. Named a Rising Star, Tex. Super Lawyers mag., 2006. Office: Rusty Hardin & Assocs PC 1401 McKinney Ste 2250 Houston TX 77010 Office Phone: 713-652-9000. E-mail: rhiggins@rustyhardin.com.*

HIGGINS, SARAH JEAN, literature and language professor; b. Helena, Ark., Sept. 30, 1970; d. Charlie E. and Wanda J. Webb; m. Michael D. Higgins, July 7, 2003; children: Megan M. Webb, Amber I., Brittney D. BA in English, U. Ark., 1998, MA in Tchg., 1999. Lic. tchr. Ark. Dept. Edn., 1999. Tchr. Van Buren HS, Ark., 1999—2002; instr. N.W. Ark. CC, Bentonville, Ark., 2004—; tchr. Belle Point Ctr, Ft. Smith, Ark., 2005—, Fort Smith Pub. Schs., 2005—. Mem.: Nat. Coun. Tchrs. English, Am. Sch. Counselor Assn., Phi Delta Kappa (Secondary Tchr. of Yr. Western Ark. chpt. 2006), Chi Sigma Iota. Avocations: piano, reading, travel. Home: PO Box 529 West Fork AR 72774 Home Phone: 479-530-3804. Home Fax: 479-839-8293. Personal E-mail: sarah@arkansasusa.com.

HIGGINS, SISTER THERESE, literature educator, former college president; b. Winthrop, Mass., Sept. 29, 1925; d. James C. and Margaret M. (Lennon) Higgins. AB cum laude, Regis Coll., 1947; MA, Boston Coll., 1959, DHL, 1993; PhD, U. Wis., 1963; DHL, Emmanuel Coll., 1977, Lesley Coll., 1991; postgrad. in lit. and theology, Harvard U., 1965-66; LLD (hon.), Northeastern U., 1982, Bentley Coll., 1992, Regis Coll., 1994. Joined Congregation of Sisters of St. Joseph, Roman Cath. Ch., 1947; asst. prof. English, Regis Coll., Weston, Mass., 1963-65, asst. prof., 1965-67, assoc. prof. English lit., 1968—, pres., 1974-92, also trustee, v.p. devel., 2003—05; cons., 1995—. Book reviewer Boston Globe, 1965—. Trustee Waltham (Mass.) Hosp., 1978—85, Cardinal Spellman Philatelic Mus., 1976—92; mem. Mass. Gov.'s Commn. on Status Women, 1977—79. U. Wis. rsch. grantee Eng. Mem. Nat. Cath. Ednl. Assn., AAUW, MLA, AAUP, Assn. Ind. Colls. and Univs. Mass. (exec. com.), New Eng. Colls. Fund, NEASC (commn.). Office: Regis Coll 235 Wellesley St Weston MA 02493-1505 Business E-Mail: therese.higgins@regiscollege.edu.

HIGGINS, WALTER M., III, electric power industry executive; b. 1945; BS in Nuclear Sci., U.S. Naval Acad., 1966; student, U.S. Nuclear Power Tng. Program, 1966-68, U. Idaho, 1979; MBA, George Washington U., 1975-77. Commd. USN, 1966, advanced through grades; nuclear engr. Charleston Navy Shipyard, until 1974; sr. nuclear engr. Bechtel Power Corp., Washington, 1975; with U.S. Nuclear Regulatory Commn., Washington, 1975-77; various mgmt. and exec. positions Portland (Oreg.) Gen. Electric Co., 1977-91; pres., COO Louisville Gas and Electric Co., 1991—93; chmn., pres. CEO Sierra Pacific, 1993—98, AGL Resources Inc., Atlanta, 1998—2000, Sierra Pacific Resources, Las Vegas, 2000—07, chmn., 2007—. Office: Sierra Pacific Resources 6226 W Sahara Ave Las Vegas NV 89146*

HIGGINS, WILLIAM WOODS, painter, art educator; b. St. Paul, Feb. 19, 1947; s. John Russell-William Higgins and Helen Catherine Woods; children: Alexander, Catherine. MA, U. Toledo, 1971. Painter, 1972—; lectr. art, theology, and philosophy Geologengasse, Vienna, 1987—. Exhibits include Longboat Key (Fla.) Art Ctr., 1973, 75, Sarasota (Fla.) Art Ctr., 1977, 79, Whitney Mus., N.Y.C., 1979, Coconut Grove (Fla.) Art Festival, 1987, 88, 89, 92, Coconut Grove Playhouse, 1988, Spoleto Festival, Charleston, S.C., 1991, 92, 97, 98, XIII Internat. Congress of Vedanta, Oxford, Ohio, 2002; author: Karma, Metapsychological Art and Raja Yoga, 2003, Religious and Symbolic Game Theory, 2006, others. Avocations: swimming, chess, writing screenplays. Office: Geologengasse 8/6 A-1030 Vienna Austria Home Phone: 843-835-5342. Personal E-mail: utchateye@lowcountry.com.

HIGGINSON, JOHN, retired career officer; b. St. Louis, Oct. 24, 1932; s. John and Clara Elizabeth (Lindemann) H.; married; children: Robert, Mark, Patrick, Paul. BA, St. Mary's U., 1954; BS, Naval Postgrad. Sch., 1966; MS, George Washington U., 1968. Ensign USN, advanced through grades to Rear Adm., ret.; comdr. Helicopter Anti-submarine Squadron 2, 1973-74, Helicopter Anti-submarine Squadron 10, 1976-78, USS Inchon, 1979-80, Amphibious Squadron 7, 1981-83, Amphibious Group 3, 1985, Naval Surface Group, Long Beach, 1986, ret., 1990-92; pres. Long Beach C. of C. Prof. mgmt. Naval War Coll., Newport, R.I. Co-author: Sea and Air, The Marine Environment, 1968, 2nd. edit., 1973. Bd. dirs. United Way, LA, Long Beach Symphony, Long Beach Youth Activities, DARE, Inc., Leadership Long Beach, St. Mary's Med. Ctr.; trustee Long Beach City Coll. Found.; dir. Internat. City Theater, Arts Coun. for Long Beach; exec. bd. Long Beach coun. Boy Scouts of Am.; trustee The Pacific; exec. coun. Industry-Edn. Coun. Calif.; former chmn. LA Combined Fed. Campaign; pres., CEO Am. Gold Star Manor Charitable Trust, 1993-. Mem. Navy Helicopter Assn. (former pres.), Fed. Exec. Bd. (former chmn.), Rotary (commr. Calif., mem. Vets. Meml. Commn.). Home: 5341 Las Lomas Park Estates Long Beach CA 90815 Office Phone: 562-426-7654.

HIGGS, C. FRED, III, mechanical engineer, educator; BS, Tenn. State U., Nashville, 1995; MS, Rensselaer Poly. Inst., Troy, NY, 1997, PhD, 2001. Postdoctoral rschr. Ga. Inst. Tech., Atlanta; asst. prof. dept. mech. engring. and Inst. Complex Engineered Systems Carnegie Mellon U., Pitts. Faculty mem. Sloan PhD prog. Alfred P. Sloan Found., 2004—. Contbr. articles to sci. jours. Recipient Jr. Faculty Coupon award, GE, 2003, Faculty Early Career Devel. award, NSF, 2007; grantee Struminger Tchg. fellowship, 2007. Mem.: Materials Rsch. Soc., Nat. Soc. Black Engrs., Soc. Tribology and Lubrication Engrs., ASME. Office: Carnegie Mellon U Dept Mech Engring 309 Scaife Hall 5000 Forbes Ave Pittsburgh PA 15213 Office Phone: 412-268-2486. Office Fax: 412-268-3348. E-mail: higgs@andrew.cmu.edu.*

HIGGS, JOHN H., lawyer; b. Balt., Mar. 10, 1934; s. E. Homer and Josephine (Doughty) H.; m. Helen Platt, Aug. 25, 1956; children: Sarah, Anne, Julia, Susan. AB, Dartmouth Coll., 1956; LLB, U. Pa., 1960. Bar: N.Y. 1961. Founder Higgs Pavements Co., Milford, Conn., 1953-56; assoc. Sullivan & Cromwell, NYC, 1960-61, 62-68, Wickes, Riddell, Bloomer, Jacobi & McGuire, NYC, 1968, ptnr., 1969-79, Morgan, Lewis & Bockius, LLP, NYC, 1979-97, ret.; ptnr. Skyport Indsl. Park, Newark. Sec. Ea. States Bankcard Assn., Lake Success, N.Y., 1970-88; bd. dirs. Mizuho Corp. Bank, 1974—, Mizuho Found. Inc., N.Y., 1989—; mem. staff adv. com. on comml. bank supervision State N.Y., 1965-66. Contbr. articles to profl. jours. Mayor Village of Pelham Manor, N.Y., 1979-81. Home: John's Island 45 Wax Myrtle Way Vero Beach FL 32963-3721

HIGH, (MARY) ELIZABETH HILLEY, retired art educator; b. Wilson, NC, Mar. 24, 1920; d. Howard Stevens Hilley and Maggie Tucker; m. Larry Allison High, May 12, 1940; children: Rebecca Elizabeth Tingen, Larry Allison, Robert Marshal, Margaret Almand Nowell. BA magna cum laude, Atlantic Christian Coll., 1939; MEd, East Carolina U., 1972. File clk. U.S. Army Depots, Richmond, Va., 1941—44, chief personnel; tchr. Nash County Schs., Rocky Mount, NC, 1966—82. Pres. Nash County Assn. Classroom Tchrs., Nashville, 1976—77; mem. NC State Sch. Accreditation Bd. Mem. Planning Bd., Nashville, 1964—66; former chmn. NC Assn. Educators, Secondary Divsn.; former pres. NC Art Edn. Assn.; mem. acquisitions com. Nash County Arts Coun., 2001—03. Recipient Painting prize, Rocky Mt. Ann. Art Exhibit. Mem.: NC Mus. Art, Womens' Soc. Christian Svc., Barton Soc., Friends Cooley Libr., Friends Braswell Libr., Kappa Delta Pi, Delta Kappa Gamma. Meth. Home: 213 N Collins St Nashville NC 27856 Home Phone: 252-459-2432. Personal E-mail: lizhigh@embarqmail.com.

HIGH, KEITH B., information scientist; b. Pitts., Oct. 11, 1961; s. Frederick Maurice and Jean Orr High; m. Karen T. Tompkins, Aug. 25, 1984. Student, Gordon-Conwell Theol. Sem., South Hamilton, Mass., 1984—87, Trinity Episcopal Sch. Ministry, Ambridge, Pa., 1985—86; BA, Gordon Coll., Wenham, Mass., 1987; postgrad., Westminster Theol. Sem., Phila., 1987—88, Temple U., 1989—91, U. Md., College Park, 2003—04. Cert. geog. info. sci. profl. GIS Certification Inst., 2004, floodplain mgr. Assn. State Floodplain Mgrs., 2004. Acting geog. info. sci. lab. dir. Temple U., Phila., 1991; geog. info. sci. specialist Nat. Pk. Svc., Bushkill, Pa., 1991—92, geog. info. sci. program dir., 1992—97, geog. info. sci. and IT dir., 1997—2000; sr. geog. info. sci. analyst II PBS&J, Beltsville, Md., 2000—03, sr. project mgr., 2003—04, Pitts., 2004—06; exec. v.p., COO earth loGIStics, LLC, Beaver, Pa., 2006—. Mem. organizing com. 3 Rivers HAZUS Users Group, California, Pa., 2004—06; elder Presbyn. Ch. (USA), Stroudsburg, Pa., 1993—99; mem. com. preparation for ministry Lehigh Presbytery, Presbyn. Ch. (USA), Allentown, Pa., 1992—98, mem. com. ministry, 1999—2000, commr., 1996—98; bd. dirs. Wanashee Conservancy, McDonald, Pa., 2006, ESRI Mid-Atlantic Users Group, Fairfax, Va., 2003—04; mem. oversight com. GIS Certification Inst., Park Ridge, Ill., 2005—06. Dean's scholar, Gordon Coll., 1980—81. Mem.: Geospatial Info. and Tech. Assn., Am. Planning Assn., Geog. and Land Info. Soc., Cartography and Geog. Info. Soc., Am. Soc. Photogrammetry and Remote Sensing (cert. mapping scientist 2004). Republican. Presbyterian. Avocations: baseball, Civil War history, duck pin bowling. Office: earth loGIStics LLC 6052 Tuscarawas Road Beaver PA 15009 Office Phone: 724-495-1130. Business E-Mail: kbhigh@earth-logistics.com.

HIGH, KEMBA M., special education educator; b. White Plains, NY, Jan. 6, 1972; d. Charles Anthony and Hannah Louise High. BS, Lincoln U., Pa., 1994; M in Elem. Edn., Lehman Coll., 2002, M in Spl. Edn., 2005. Spl. edn. tchr. NY City Bd. Edn., Bronx, 1998—2000, Yonkers Bd. Edn., 2000—; after sch. dir. White Plains Youth Bur., 1998—2000; early intervention Tender Care Agencies, Mt. Vernon, NY, 2004—. Democrat. Bapt. Home: 34 S Kensico Ave Apt 18 White Plains NY 10601

HIGH, S. DALE, construction executive; b. Lancaster, Pa., May 2, 1942; s. Sanford H. and Erma (Denlinger) H.; m. Sadie S. Horst; children from previous marriage: Steven D., Gregory A., Suzanne M. BSBA, Elizabethtown Coll., 1963, LDH (hon.), 1993; LDH (hon.), Thaddeus Stevens Coll. Tech., 2002. Exec. v.p. High Steel Structures, Inc., Lancaster, 1963-77; ptnr. High Properties, Lancaster, 1963—; chmn., pres. High Industries, Inc., Lancaster, 1977—2005; chmn. High Cos., 2006—. Bd. dirs. High Investors, Ltd., Lancaster, High Food Svcs., Ltd., Lancaster, High Hotels Ltd., Lancaster, Pa. Chamber, Inc., 1995—, Penn Sq. Gen. Corp., chmn.; chmn. bd. dirs. Sageworth Holdings, Inc., 2000—; mem. panel of judges Ctrl. Pa. Entrepreneur of the Yr. Award Program, 1994—95, chmn., 1996; bd. dirs. Educators Mutal Life Ins. Co., 1979—2002. Trustee The High Found., Lancaster, 1980—, Elizabethtown Coll., Pa., 1974—99, Lancaster Gen. Hosp., 1976—84, Lancaster County Cmty. Found., 1985—2005, chmn., 2004—05; judge Ea./Ctrl. Pa. Entrepreneur of Yr. Program, 2004; mem. coun. Pa. Soc.; mem. Pa. State Rep. com., Harrisburg, 1985; co-chmn. fin. Lancaster County Rep. Com., 1985—88; chmn. Pa. Chamber PAC, 2002; mem. adv. com. Friends of Better Govt. PAC, 2000—, chmn., 2000—02; bd. dirs. United Way Lancaster County, 1975—78, Lancaster County Rev. Commn., 1984—86, Pa. Chamber of Bus. and Industry, Harrisburg, 1991—, vice-chair, 2000—02, chmn., 2003—04; bd. dirs. Modern Transit Partnership, 1998—2002, Team Pa. Found., 2003—. Named Outstanding Young Man, Lancaster Jaycees, 1977, Disting. Pennsylvanian, Phila. C. of C., 1981; recipient Exemplar award Lancaster C. of C. and Industry, 1995, Disting. Bus. Alumni award Elizabethtown Coll., 1995, Jr. Achievement Spirit Achievement award, 1997, Pa. Dutch Coun./BSA Disting. Citizen award, 1999; named Ctrl. Pa. Master Entrepreneur of Yr. Ernst & Young, 1999, Pa. Chamber of Bus. and Industry Outstanding Bus. Leader, 1999, Nat. Entrepreneur of Yr., Real Estate, Ernst and Young, 1999, Centennial medal Elizabethtown Coll., 2000, Cmty. Svc. award Lancaster Rotary Club, 2000, Educate for Svc. award Elizabethtown Coll., 2000, Bus. Achievement award West Shore C. of C., 2001, Family Bus. of Yr. award Wharton Enterprising Families Initiative, 2002, Disting. Alumni award Lampeter Strasburg Sch. Dist., 2003. Mem. World Pres.'s Orgn., Lancaster C. of C. (bd. dirs. 1976-82, chmn. 1981), Newcomen Soc. U.S., Lancaster Country Club Republican. Presbyterian. Avocations: reading, bicycling, hiking, travel. Office: High Cos PO Box 10008 1853 William Penn Way Lancaster PA 17605-0008

HIGH, TIMOTHY GRIFFIN, artist, educator, curator, writer; b. Memphis, Tenn., Mar. 10, 1949; s. Warren Barrett and Jo Ellen (Wise) High; m. Cynthia Spikes, Aug. 10, 1973. BFA, Tex. Tech U., 1973; MA in Printmaking, Art History, U. Wis., Madison, 1975; MFA, U. Wis., 1976. Assoc. prof. U. Tex., Austin, 1976—. Visual artist; freelance writer. One-man shows include: Amarillo Art Mus., Tex., 1993, Martin-Rathburn Gallery, San Antonio, Adair Margo Gallery, 1996, 1997, Tarrytown Gallery, Austin, 2001, Gallery W, Sacramento, 2002, La. State U. Sch. Art Gallery, Baton Rouge, 2005. Group shows 117th Ann. Exhbn. NAD, Mus. Visual Art, NYC, 2002, An Odessey, U.Wis.-Madison, 2006, Passion and Process - Masters of American Printmaking, 2007. Traveling exhibitions include: Texas Prints, 2001, Tex. Xpress-I, 2001, Border Crossings, 2001, Three Aces, 2002, Bread Upon the Water, 2003, Contemporary American Serigraphs, 2004—07, Codex Silver Portfolio, 2004, Catfish Press Portfolio, 2004, Semographics I, U. Wis., Madison, 2006. Represented in permanent collections: Art Inst. Chgo., Bklyn. Mus., Mus. Fine Art, Boston, Met. Mus. Art, NYC, Fogg Mus., Cambrige, Mass., Mus. Fine Art, Houston, Milw. Mus. Art, 21c. Museum, Louisville, KY. Vol. curator VAM Gallery, First Evangelical Free Ch., Austin, 2002—. Recipient Tchg. Excellence award, U. Tex. Austin, Coll. Fine Arts, 2007; Travel fellow, Ford Found., 1978, Indvidual Artist fellow, Nat. Endowments Arts, 1989, curatorial grant, Tex. Comm. Arts, 2001. Mem.: CIVA Printmakers Network (chair 2003), Christians Visual Art, Tex. Fine Arts Assn., Nat. Assn. Scholars (panelist conv. 1993), Mid-Am. Coll. Art Assn. (conf. spkr. 1998), So. Graphics Coun. (conf. coord. 1989, 2001, mem. nominating com. 2005—). Avocations: travel, photography, backpacking, fly fishing, reading. Address: care/Terra Rosa Studio 2308 Lawnmont Ave Austin TX 78756-1915 Office: Univ of Tex Austin Dept Art & Art History Austin TX 78712 Office Phone: 512-971-9478. Business E-Mail: tim.high@mail.utexas.edu.

HIGHAM, ROBIN, historian, editor, publisher; b. London, June 20, 1925; came to US, 1940, naturalized, 1954; s. David and Margaret Anne (Stewart) H.; m. Barbara Davies, Aug. 5, 1950; children: Peter (dec.), Susan Elizabeth (dec.), Martha Anne, Carol Lee. AB cum laude, Harvard U., Cambridge, Mass., 1950, PhD, 1957; MA, Claremont Grad. Sch., Calif., 1953. Instr. Webb Sch. Calif., 1950-52; grad. asst. in oceanic history Harvard U., 1952-54; instr. U. Mass., 1954-57; asst. prof. U. NC, Chapel Hill, 1957-63; assoc. prof. history Kans. State U., 1963-66, prof., 1966—98; historian Brit. Overseas Airways Corp., 1960-66, 76-78; editor Mil. Affairs, 1968-88, emeritus; editor Aerospace Historian, 1970-88, emeritus, 1989—; editor, pub. Jour. of the West, 1977—2004; adv. editor Tech. and Culture, 1967-85; founder, pres. Sunflower Univ. Press, 1977—2004; mil. adv. editor Univ. Press Ky., 1970-75. Cons. Epic of Flight, Time/Life Books, 1980-82; lectr. in field; mem. publs. com. Conf. Brit. Studies, 1965-93; advisor Core Collection for Coll. Librs., 1971-72; pres., cons. com. Revue Internat. d'Histoire Militaire, 1976-85, mem. mil. archives com., 1990—, acting pres., 1996-2000, sec. gen., 2002-2003, 04—; founder, organizer Conf. Historic Aviation Writers, 1982-98. Author: Britain's Imperial Air Routes, 1918-39, 1960, The British Rigid Airship, 1908-31, 1961, Armed Forces in Peacetime: Britain 1918-39, 1963, The Military Intellectuals in Britain: 1918-1939, 1966, (with David H. Zook) A Short History of Warfare, 1966, Hebrew edit., 1970, Chinese edit., 1985, The Compleat Academic (Macmillan Book Club choice), 1975, Air Power: A Concise History (selection Mil. Book Soc., History Book Club, Flying Book Club), 1973, 2d enlarged edit., 1984, 3d enlarged edit., 1988, The Bases of Air Strategy, 1998, (with Mary Cisper & Guy Dresser) A Brief Guide to Scholarly Editing, 1982, Diary of a Disaster: British Aid to Greece, 1940-41, 1986; editor: Bayonets in the Streets, 1969, 89, Civil Wars in the Twentieth Century, 1972, A Guide to the Sources of British Military History, 1971, A Guide to the Sources of U.S. Military History, 1975, (with Donald J. Mrozek) supplements, 1981, 86, 93, 99 (with Carol Brandt) The U.S. Army in Peacetime: Essays in Honor of the Bicentennial, 1975, Intervention or Abstention, 1975, (with Jacob W. Kipp) Soviet Aviation and Air Power, 1977, Garland Military History Bibliographic Series (with Jacob W. Kipp), 1978-92, Flying Combat Aircraft (with A. T. Siddall) vol. 1, 1975, (with Carol Williams) vol. 2, 1978 and vol. 3, 1981; editor (with George E. Ham) The Rise of the Wheat State: a History of Kansas Agriculture, 1861-1986, 87, (with Thanos Veremis) The Metaxas Dictatorship: Aspects of Greece, 1936-1940. (with John T. Greenwood and Von Hardesty) Russian Aviation & Air Power, 1998, A Handbook of Air Ministry Organization, 1998; ed. Writing Official Military History, 1999, Official Military History, 2 vols., 2000, (with Frederick W. Kagan) A Military History of Russia, A Military History of the Soviet Union, 2002, (with David A. Graff) A Military History of China, 2002, Research on World War I: A Handbook, 2003, 100 Years of Air Power and Aviation, 2003 (History Book Club Selection 2003), Flying American Combat Aircraft of World War I, 2004, II, 2005, (with Stephen J. Harris) Why Air Forces Fail, 2006 (Mil. Book Bluc Selection 2006, History Book Club Selection 2006); sr. advisor on Ency. of U.S. Mil. History, Acad. Mil. Scis., Beijing, 1988—; advisory editor Ency. of USAF, 1988-92; mem. aviation editl. adv. bd. Smithsonian Inst. Press, 1989-92; adv. Greenwood Press, 1992—; mem. editl. bd. Defence Analysis, 1984—; cons., contbr.: Dictionary of Business Biography, 1980-86, Encyclopedia of the American Military, 1994; contbr. New Dictionary of Nat. Biography, Oxford, 1994-2002; contbr. articles to profl. jours. Trustee U.S. Commn. on Mil. History, 1993-2000; mem. Kans. State Aviation Adv. Com., 1986-95, sec., 1992-95. Pilot RAFVR, 1943—47. Named Disting. Grad., Faculty Kans. State U., 1971; recipient Victor Gondos award Am. Mil. Inst., 1983, Samuel Eliot Morison award for disting. scholarship Am. Mil. Inst., 1986, Stamey Tchg. award Kans. State U., 1996, Aviation Honors award Gov. Kans., 2000; Social Sci. Rsch. Coun. nat. security policy rsch. fellow, 1960-61. Mem. AIAA (standing com. history 1973—), Soc. History Tech., Am. Aviation Hist. Soc., RAF Hist. Soc., Friends of RAF Mus. (life), Burma Star Assn. (life), Air Force Hist. Found. (trustee 1984-98), Soc. Army Hist. Rsch. (corr. mem. coun. 1980-98), Am. Mil. Inst., WWII Studies Assn. (dir. 1973-75, 79-82, 83-2001, archivist 1977-2003), Am. Aviation Hist. Soc., Am. Air Mus. in Britain (founding), Nat. D-Day Mus (now Nat. WWII Mus.; charter mem.), US Commn. on Mil. History, Riley County Hist. Soc. (past dir., chmn. long-range planning com. 1980-97). Home: 2961 Nevada St Manhattan KS 66502-2355 Personal E-mail: marolyn@flinthills.com.

HIGHBY, DENNIS, retail executive; With Cabela's Inc., Sidney, Nebr., 1976—, v.p., 1996—2003, pres., CEO, 2003—. Bd. dirs. Cabela's Inc., 2003—. Office: Cabela's Inc One Cabela Dr Sidney NE 69160*

HIGHFILL, PHILIP HENRY, JR., retired language educator; b. Petersburg, Va., Aug. 12, 1918; s. Philip Henry and Grace (Jones) H.; m. Annabelle Holloweli (Molly), 1943; children: Mary Hollowell, Philip Henry III. BA, Wake Forest Coll., 1942; postgrad., Middlebury Coll., 1946; MA, U. N.C., 1948, PhD, 1950. Reporter Daily Advance, Elizabeth City, NC, 1942, 46, Shreveport Times, La., 1942; instr. U. Rochester, NY, 1950—53, asst. prof., 1953—55; assoc. prof. George Washington U., Washington, 1955-61, prof., 1961-89, prof. emeritus, 1989. Cons. lit. Folger Shakespeare Library, Washington, 1964-68. Co-author: (with Kalman A. Burnim and Edward A. Langhans) A Biographical Dictionary of Actors, Actresses, Musicians, Dancers, Managers and Other Stage Personnel in London, 1660-1800, 16 vols., 1973-93; (with George Winchester Stone) In Search of Restoration and 18th-Century Theatrical Biography, 1976, (with Kalman A. Burnim) John Bell, Patron of Theatrical Portraiture, 1998; editor: Shakespeare's Craft, 1982; contbr. numerous articles and revs. to scholarly jours. With US Army, 1942—46. Grantee Huntington Library, 1959, NEH, 1967-68, 70-71, 74-76, 84-87; fellow John Simon Guggenheim Found., 1959-60, Folger Shakespeare Library, 1968, Theodore Stewart fellow Nat. Library Scotland, 1975; fellow Washington Evening Star, 1963; recipient George Freedley award Theatre Library Assn., 1980. Mem. MLA, South Atlantic MLA, Soc. for Theatre Rsch. (Eng.), Am. Soc. Theatre Rsch. (spl. award 1994), Am. Soc. for 18th Century Studies, Am. Handel Soc. (bd. dirs. 1986-93), Lit. Soc. Washington (v.p. 1991, pres. 1992-93), Wafflers Club, Cosmos Club (v.p. 1979, pres. 1980, bd. dirs. 1976-81) Avocations: travel, music, cooking. Home: 5105 Westpath Ct Bethesda MD 20816-2319

HIGHMAN, BRUCE JAMES, lawyer; b. LA, Nov. 25, 1956; s. Arthur and Edith Louise (Arkoff) H.; m. BA, U. Calif., Berkeley, 1977; JD, Stanford U., 1981. Bar: Calif. 1981, US Dist. Ct. (no. dist.) Calif. 1983, US Ct. Appeals (9th cir.) 1983, US Dist. Ct. (ea. dist.) Calif. 1987, US Supreme Ct. 1987, US Dist. Ct. (cen. dist.) Calif. 1991. Law clk. to assoc. justice Alaska Supreme Ct., Juneau, 1981-82; pvt. practice law San Francisco, 1982—. Mem. Bar Assn. San Francisco, Nat. Employment Lawyers Assn., Calif. Employment Lawyers Assn. Democrat. Jewish. Office: 870 Market St Ste 467 San Francisco CA 94102-3011 Office Phone: 415-982-5564. Business E-Mail: bruce.highman@highman-ball.com.

HIGHSMITH, SHELBY, federal judge; b. Jacksonville, Fla., Jan. 31, 1929; s. Isaac Shelby and Edna Mae (Phillips) H.; m. Mary Jane Zimmerman, Nov. 25, 1972; children: Holly Law, Shelby. AA, Ga. Mil. Coll., 1948; BA, JD, U. Kansas City, 1958. Bar: Fla. 1958. Trial atty., Kansas City, Mo., 1958-59, Miami, Fla., 1959-70; circuit judge Dade County, Fla., 1970-75; sr. ptnr. Highsmith, Strauss, Glatzer & Deutsch, P.A., Miami, 1975-91; judge US Dist. Ct. (so. dist.) Fla., Miami, 1991—. Chief legal adviser Gov.'s War on Crime Program, 1967-68; spl. counsel Fla. Racing Commn., 1969-70; mem. Inter-Agy. Law Enforcement Planning Coun. Fla., 1969-70. Served to capt. AUS, 1949-55. Decorated Bronze Star; recipient Outstanding Alumni Achievement Law award, U. Mo., 1998, Korean War Svc. medal, Pres. South Korea on 50th Anniversary of Korean War, Disting. Alumnus award, Ga. Mil. Coll., 2002. Fellow Internat. Soc. Barristers; mem. ABA, Dade County Bar Assn., Bench and Robe, Torch and Scroll, Miccosukee Golf and Country Club, Wildcat Cliffs Country Club, (Highlands, N.C.), Omicron Delta, Phi Alpha Delta. Republican. Roman Catholic. Office: Fed Justice Bldg 99 NE 4th St Rm 1027 Miami FL 33132-2138 Home Phone: 305-666-1357; Office Phone: 305-523-5170. Business E-Mail: shelby_highsmith@flsd.uscourts.gov.

HIGHSTEIN, JENE ABEL, sculptor; b. Balt., June 16, 1942; s. Gustav and Ada Abel Highstein; m. Alanna Heiss (div.); 1 child, Lokke Abel; m. Katharine Duane; children: Alex, Jesse. BA, U. Md., 1963; postgrad., U. Chgo., 1963—65, NY Studio Sch., 1966, Royal Acad. Sch., London, 1967—70. Vis. artist Emily Carr Coll. Art, Vancouver, B.C., Can., 1979, Tyler Sch. Art, Phila., 1990, RI Sch. Design, Providence, 1991, Vt. Studio Ctr., Johnsonville, Vt., 1993, Brandeis U., Waltham, 1995; instr. Sch. Visual Arts, NY, 1974, NYU, NYC, 1984-86, Parsons Sch. Design, NY, 1983; vis. prof. UCLA, 1987, Cranbrook Acad. Art, Bloomfield Hills, Mich., 1990; vis. lectr. Harvard U., Cambridge, Mass., 1995-96. One-man shows include Baumgartner Galleries, Washington, 1993, Ace Contemporary Exhbns., LA, 1993, Portland (Oreg.) Art Mus., 1993, St. Gauden's Meml., Cornish, NH, 1993, Secca, Winston-Salem, NC, Ace Gallery NY, Art Space, Seoul, 1996, Stark Gallery, NY, 1997, Hill Gallery, Birmingham, Mich., 1998, 5501 Columbia Arts Ctr., Dallas, 1998, Anders Tornberg Gallery, Sweden, 1998, Todd Gallery, London, 1998, Crosby St. Project Space, 1999, Auchincloss Gallery, 1999, Grant Selwyn Fine Art, 2000, U. Hartford Joseloff Gallery, 2000, Anthony Grant Gallery, 2005, Madison Square Pk., NY, 2005, Baumgartner Gallery, NY, 2006; group shows include Kunstmuseum, Passau, Germany, 1992, Rhona Hoffman Gallery, Chgo., 1992, Anders Tornberg Gallery, Lund, Sweden, 1993, Bklyn. Mus., 1993, Portland Art Mus., 1993, Andre Emmerich Gallery, NYC, 1993, Galerie Art 4, Galerie de l'Esplanade, Paris, 1993, Werkstaat Kollerschlag, Austria, 1993, Kunst Halle Krems, Austria, 1993, Caldas Da Rainha, Portugal, 1993, Drawing Ctr., NYC, 1993, Baumgartner Galleries, Washington, 1994, Neuberger Mus. Art, Purchase, NY, 1994, Michael Klein Gallery, NYC, 1995, Galerij S 65, Aalst, Belgium, 1995, Bilboa Guggenheim, Spain, Snow Show, Rovaniemi, Finland, others; represented in permanent collections at Balt. Mus. Art, Bklyn. Mus., Collection Panza di Biumo, Varese, Italy, Dallas Art Mus., Detroit Inst. Arts, Musee Pleine Aire, Paris, Met. Mus. Art, NYC, Mus. Contemporary Art, NYC, Mus. Modern Art, NYC, New Mus. Contemporary Art, NYC, NY Pub. Libr., Portland Art Mus., Rose Art Mus., Brandeis U., Waltham, Mass., San Diego Mus. Contemporary Art, La Jolla, Calif., David and Alfred Smart Art Mus., Chgo., Solomon R. Guggenheim Mus., NYC, Victoria and Albert Mus., London, LA County Mus., Harvard U. Mus., Yale Art Mus., others Grantee Change Inc., 1974, Creative Artists Pub. Svc., 1975, Theo Doran award Ninth Paris Beinnale, 1975, Nat. Endowment for Arts, 1976, 77, 78, 84, 94, Creative Artists Pub. Svc., 1979; recipient John Simon Guggenheim award, 1980, St. Gauden's Meml. prize, 1992. Office: 515 W 36th St New York NY 10018-1100 Office Phone: 212-594-2479. Personal E-mail: jenehighstein@earthlink.net.

HIGHT, B. BOYD, retired lawyer; b. Lumberton, NC, Feb. 15, 1939; s. B. Boyd and Mary Lou (Lennon) H.; m. Mary Kay Sweeney, Mar. 31, 1962; children: Kathryn, Kevin. BA, Duke U., 1960; LLB, Yale U., 1966; diploma in comparative law, U. Stockholm, 1967. Assoc. O'Melveny & Myers, Los Angeles, 1967-74, ptnr., 1974—79, 1981—84, 1989—2005; dep. asst. sec. trans. and telecommunications U.S. Dept. State, Washington, 1979-81; exec. v.p., gen. counsel Sante Fe Internat. Corp., Alhambra, Calif., 1985—89. Bd. dirs. Planned Parenthood L.A., 1986-95, pres., 1992-94; mem. bd. overseers Rand Ctr. Russian and Eurasian Studies, 1987-2000, chair, 1994-2000; trustee Am. U. Cairo, 1987—, chmn., 2004—, Autry Nat. Ctr., 2002—; bd. dirs. Calif. Supreme Ct. Hist. Soc., 1993-2001; bd. overseers The Huntington, 1996—. Mem. Coun. Fgn. Rels., Pacific Coun. on Internat. Policy, Calif. Club (pres. 2005-07), LA Country Club. Democrat. Office: O'Melveny & Myers 400 S Hope St Los Angeles CA 90071-2899

HIGHT, ORIAN LANGLEY, retired education educator; d. Vernon Arthur Langley and Ida Mae Langley/Fitzgerald; m. Adolph Aubrey Hight, Dec. 14, 1957; children: James Emmett II, Bryan Keith. BS in Chemistry, Hampton U., 1955; MS in Chemistry, Syracuse U., 1959; PhD in Math. Edn., U. Md., 1993. Postgrad. profl. tchrs. cert. Va., cert. tchr. Mass., N.C., advanced profl. tchrs. cert. Md. Middle sch. and H.S. math.-sci. tchr. various pub. sch. systems, 1955—86; math. rsch. asst. U. Md., College Park, 1989—90, math. counseling asst., 1990—93; instr. grad. edn. Trinity Coll., Washington, 1994; asst. prof. Prince George's CC, Largo, Md., 1994—97, assoc. prof., 1997—; ret., 2000. Workshop presenter in field. Compiler: Transparency Masters to Accompany Mary Kay Beaver's Essential Mathematics, 1997. Fund-raising vol. Am. CAncer Soc., New Bedford, Mass., 1964, March of Dimes, Woodbridge, Va., 1973, The Kidney Found., Woodbridge, 1975, March of Dimes, Olney, Md., 1984, Am. Lung Assn., Olney, 1994, Am. Heart Assn., Williamsburg, Va., 1999, 2000. Scholar, Hampton U., 1951—55; GE Chemistry summer fellow, Union Coll., 1956, NSF Summer fellow, Syracuse U., 1957, 1959, NSF fellow, 1958—59, Patricia Roberts Harris fellow, U. Md., 1986—89, Other Race Grant fellow, 1989—90. Mem.: Nat. Sci. Tchrs. Assn., Assn. for Women in Math., Am. Math. Soc., Math. Assn. Am., Nat. Coun. Tchrs. Math., Delta Sigma Theta. Democrat. Baptist. Achievements include wrote proposal, designed, developed and implemented a federally funded grade 9 remedial math program at Gar-Field Senior High School, Woodbridge, Virginia; conducted a survey on the study skill habits of students enrolled in freshman biology and chemistry courses at University Maryland, College Park. Avocations: reading, sewing, gardening, walking. Home: 3484 Frances Berkeley Williamsburg VA 23188

HIGHTOWER, DENNIS FOWLER, retired entertainment company executive, educator; b. Washington, Oct. 28, 1941; s. Marvin William and Virginia (Fowler) H.; m. Denia Stukes, Feb. 2, 1962; children: Dennis Fowler Jr., Dawn Denise. BS, Howard U., 1962, D (hon.), 1996; MBA, Harvard U., 1974. Mgr. Xerox Corp., Rochester, NY, 1970-72; sr. assoc., engagement mgr. McKinsey & Co., Inc., Cleve., 1974-78; v.p., gen. mgr. lighting affiliate GE, Monterrey, Mexico, 1978-81; v.p. corp. planning Mattel, Inc., Hawthorne, Calif., 1981-84; mng. dir., office mgr. Russell Reynolds Assocs., Inc., LA, 1984-87; pres. Disney consumer products for Europe, Mid. East & Africa The Walt Disney Co., Paris, 1987-95, pres. Walt Disney TV & Telecomm., ret. Burbank, Calif., 1995-96; sr. lectr. Bus. Sch. Harvard U., 1996—. Bd. dirs. Domino's Pizza, 1999—, Accenture, Ltd., Northwest Airlines, Inc., The Gillette Co., 1999—2005, The TJX Companies, Inc., PanAmSat Corp.; ptnr. Wash. Baseball Club. Trustee So. Calif. Ctr. for Non-Profit Mgmt., L.A., 1984-87, Howard U., 1996—; mem. steering com. pub. and pvt. partnerships program D.C. Pub. Sch. System, Washington, 1985-87; mem. Harvard overseers' vis. com. Harvard Bus. Sch., 1994—. Maj. U.S. Army, 1962-70. Recipient Disting. Alumni citation Nat. Assn. Equal Opportunity in Higher Edn., 1985, Disting. Postgrad. Achievement in Bus. award Howard U., 1986, Dept. Commerce Pioneer award 1996; named One of 25 Top Black Mgrs. in Am., Black Enterprise mag., 1988. Mem. Harvard Bus. Sch. Alumni (bd. dirs. 1986-89, citation 1989, Achievement award 1992), Harvard Bus. Sch. Assn. So. Calif. (bd. dirs. 1984-86, pres. 1986-87, citation 1987), Howard U. Alumni Assn. (Outstanding Alumni Achievement award 1984), Harvard Club N.Y.C. (Egdes Group Corp. Leadership award 1992), Jonathan Club (L.A.), Cercle Foch (Paris), Calif. (L.A.) Club. Avocations: collecting antique billiard equipment and 18th and 19th century oriental sculpture, photography, travel, scuba diving, swimming. Office: Washington Baseball Club 600 New Hampshire Ave NW Washington DC 20037

HIGHTOWER, JACK ENGLISH, retired judge, former congressman; b. Memphis, Tex., Sept. 6, 1926; s. Walter Thomas and Floy Edna (English) H.; m. Colleen Ward, Aug. 26, 1950; children— Ann, Amy, Alison. BA, Baylor U., 1949; JD, 1951; LLM, Univ. Va., 1992. Bar: Tex. 1951. Since practiced in, Vernon; mem. Tex. Ho. of Reps., 1953-54; dist. atty. 46th Jud. Dist. Tex., 1955-61; mem. Tex. Senate, 1965-75, pro tempore, 1971; mem. 94th-98th Congresses from 13th Tex. Dist., 1975-85; 1st asst. atty. gen. State of Tex., 1985-87; justice Texas Supreme Ct., Austin, 1988-95; ret., 1996. Mem. Tex. Law Enforcement Study Commn., 1957; del. White House Conf. Children and Youth, 1970; alt. del. Dem. Nat. Conv., 1968; bd. regents Midwestern U., Wichita Falls, Tex., 1962-65; trustee Baylor U., 1972-81, acting gov., 1971; trustee Wayland Bapt. U., Plainview, Tex., 1991-2001, Bapt. Children's Home, 1959-62, Tex. Scottish Rite Hosp. Children, 1991—, chmn., 2002—; trustee Human Welfare Commn.; bd. dirs. Bapt. Std., 1959-68; mem. Nat. Commn. on Librs. and Info. Sci., 1999-2005. With USNR, 1944-45. Named Outstanding Dist. Atty, Tex., Tex. Law Enforcement Found., 1959, Disting. Alumnus, Baylor U., 1978; recipient Knapp-Porter award Tex. A&M Univ., 1980. Mem. Tex. Dist. and County Attys. Assn. (pres. 1958-59), Scottish Rite Ednl. Assn. Tex. (exec. com. 1990—), Tex. Supreme Ct. Hist. Soc. (pres. 1991-98), Tex. Bar. Found. (fellow 1992), SAR, U.S. Supreme Ct. Hist. Soc., Tex. State Hist. Assn. (exec. coun. 1998-2002), Masons (grand master Tex. 1972), Lions (pres. Vernon 1961), Scottish Rite Freemasonry (sovereign grand inspector gen. 1992-).

HIGHTOWER, JOHN BRANTLEY, retired museum administrator; b. Atlanta, May 23, 1933; s. Edward A. and Margaret (Kimzey) H.; m. Martha Ruhl, Feb. 25, 1984; children: Amanda, Matthew. BA in English, Yale U., 1955; DFA, Calif. Coll. Arts and Crafts. Asst. to pub. Am. Heritage Pub. Co., Inc., NYC, 1961-63; exec. asst. NY State Coun. Arts, NYC, 1963-64, exec. dir., 1964-70; dir. Mus. Modern Art, NYC, 1970-72; pres. Am. Coun. Arts, NYC, 1972-74, South St. Seaport, 1977-83; dir., vice chmn. So. St. Seaport, 1983-84; exec. dir. Richard Tucker Music Found., 1977-89, Maritime Ctr. at Norwalk, 1984-89; dir. planning and devel. for the arts U. Va., 1989-93; pres., CEO The Mariners' Mus., Newport News, Va., 1993—2006. Exec. com. WHRO, Norfolk, 1996-99; vice chmn., Newport News Pub. Art Found., 2000—; founder, chmn. Adv. for Arts, 1974-77; instr. arts mgmt. Wharton Sch., U. Pa., 1976-77, New Sch., 1976-77; cultural advisor Rockefeller Mission to Latin Am., 1969; vis. critic in arts adminstrn. Grad. Sch. Drama, Yale U., 1972-77; chmn. Planning Corp. for Arts, Urban Arts Corps. Bd. dir. NY State Coun. on Arts, Poets and Writers, Downing Gross Cultural Arts Ctr. Capt. USMCR, 1955-63. Fulbright fellow; recipient NY State award, 1970. Mem. Century Assn. (NYC), 1805 Club (London). Office Phone: 757-591-7700. Business E-Mail: jhightower@mariner.org.

HIGHTOWER, RANDALL DEE, oncologist; b. Russellville, Ark., Jan. 30, 1956; s. Charles Evans and Billie Regina Hightower; m. Amy Burford Hightower, Aug. 12, 1979; children: Nathaniel Wilson, Ashley Kristan, Kelli Page. BS in Chemistry, Ark. Tech. U., Russellville, 1979; MD, U. Ark., Little Rock, 1984. Lic. physician Ark., 1984, diplomate Am. Bd. Ob-GYn., 1990, Am. Bd. Gynecologic Oncology, 2000. Intern, resident in ob-gyn. Portsmouth Naval Hosp., Va., 1984—88; staff physician USN, Portsmouth, 1984—88, 1993—98, Fla., 1989—90, Guantanamo Bay, Cuba, 1988—89; fellow in gynecologic oncology U. Miami/Jackson Meml. Hosp., Fla., 1990—93; dir. gynecologic oncology svcs., dept. ob-gyn. Naval Med. Ctr., Portsmouth, 1996—98; gynecologic oncologist, urogynecologist U. Mo. Hosp., Columbia, 1998—2001, Washington Regional Med. Ctr., Fayetteville, Ark., 2001—. Chmn. ethics com. Naval Med. Ctr., Portsmouth, 1996—98; presenter in field. Contbr. articles to profl. jours. Bd. dirs. Helping Oncology Patients Excel (HOPE), Springdale, Ark., 2003—06. Comdr. USN, 1980—98. Recipient award for outstanding achievement in cancer rsch., Upjohn, Miami, 1991, Excellence in Tchg. award, U. Mo., 2001. Fellow: Am. Coll. Obstetricians and Gynecologist; mem.: AMA, Soc. Gynecologic Oncology (co-chmn. oncology conf. 2001), Alpha Chi. Avocations: tennis, fishing. Home: 88 N Skyview Ln Fayetteville AR 72701 Office: Washington Regional Splty Clinic 82 W Sunbridge Fayetteville AR 72703 Office Phone: 479-575-9000. Fax: 479-251-8188. Business E-Mail: rhightower@wregional.com.

HIGLEY, BRUCE WADSWORTH, orthodontist; b. Iowa City, Dec. 1, 1928; s. Lester Bodine and Harriet (Wadsworth) H.; m. Marta Beatriz Velasco, Sept. 23, 1966. D.D.S., State U. Iowa, 1952, MS, 1953; student, Grinnell Coll., 1946-48, orthodontic certificate, 1953. Diplomate Am. Acad. Pain Mgmt. Research, instr. Iowa Dental U., 1952-53; practice dentistry, specializing in orthodontics South Miami, Fla., 1955—; Owner, chmn. bd. M.B.H. Enterprises, Inc., Miami, Fla., 1960—. Vice chmn. dist. coun. Boy Scouts Am., 1959-62; Mem. Personnel Bd., South Miami, 1959. 1st lt. Dental Corps AUS, 1953-55 Fellow Internat. Coll. Cranio-

Mandibnlar ORthopaedics, World Fedn. Orthodontists; mem. Am. Assn. Orthodontics, Fla. Orthodontic Soc., So., Miami socs. orthodontists, Fla., Am. socs. dentistry for children, Fla., Fla. East Coast, Miami dental socs., Am., S. Dade dental assns., Fedn. Dentaire Internat., English Royal Acad., C. of C. (past dir., sec., treas.), Psi Omega, Omicron Kappa Upsilon. Presbyn. (deacon). Clubs: Rotarian (pres. 1961-62), Elk, Coral Reef Yacht, Coral Gables Country, Royal Palm Tennis; Bankers, Executive (Miami); Army-Navy. Home: 2000 Brickell Ave Miami FL 33129-1721 Office: 7210 S Red Rd Miami FL 33143-5321 Office Phone: 305-666-8781. Personal E-mail: drhigley@higleyorthodonticspecialist.com. E-mail: bligley1@bellsouth.net.

HIJAZI, YAZAN S., research scientist, educator; b. Amman, Jordan, Apr. 1, 1978; s. Said A. Hijazi and Moghraby T. Aida. BSc in Elec. Engring., Fla. Internat. U., Miami, 2000, MSc in Elec. Engring., 2002, PhD, 2006. Grad. rschr. Future Aerospace Sci. and Tech. Ctr. Space Cryoelectronics, Miami, 1998—2004; lab mgr., sr. rschr. Ctr. Nanoscale Info. Devices, Miami, 2004—06. Mem.: IEEE (assoc.), Etta Kappa Nu. Achievements include patents for use of patterned Soft Underlayers (SUL) in 3D magentic devices. Avocations: music writing, guitar, hiking, soccer, languages. Home Phone: 787-218-8055; Office Phone: 787-743-7979 4195.

HILBERN, SANDRA J., library director; b. Vallejo, Calif., July 2, 1945; d. Curtis Tom Sr. and Pauline Stout (Daniels) Hamilton; m. James W. Hilbern Sr., Nov. 27, 1970 (div. Aug. 1993); 1 child, James William Jr. BSE, Northeastern Okla. State U., 1970, MS, 1973; postgrad., U. Tex., Dallas, 1977, So. Ill. U., 1978, Northeastern Okla. State U., 1976-89. Cert. tchr., libr., Okla.; cert. for the blind/visually impaired. Elem. tchr. Okay (Okla.) Pub. Schs., 1970-75; sr. vocat. rehab. counselor State Okla. Dept. Rehab., Muskogee , 1975-98; prof. Connors State Coll., Muskogee, 1989-2000, mem. gerontol. consumer adv. com., 1999-2000; libr. media specialist Okla. Sch. for Blind, Muskogee, 2000—. Unit commr. Boy Scouts Am., Muskogee, 1984-86; coach, team mother Green County Soccer League, Muskogee, 1979-81; publicity dir. single living bd. Christ Ch., Tulsa, 1998—, Phoenix Singles pres., v.p., 1996-99. Sgt. U.S. Army, 1966-69. Recipient Outstanding Recognition award for Outstanding Svc., U.S. Ho. of Reps., 1998, Pres.'s award for Outstanding Svc. Okla. Rehab. Counselors Assn., 1984, Starfish Recognition award Connors State Coll., 2000. Mem. Okla. Rehab. Soc. (sec. 1978-84), Okla. Assn. C.C.'s., Am. Libr. Assn., Okla. Libr. Assn., Assn. Libr. Media Specialists. Democrat. Avocations: silk and dried floral arranging, organizing fine arts and cultural tours. Office: Okla Sch for the Blind 3300 Gibson St Muskogee OK 74403

HILBERT, DAVID R., philosopher, educator; b. Ann Arbor, Apr. 19, 1959; BA, Princeton U., NJ, 1981; PhD, Stanford U., Calif., 1987. Asst. prof. philosophy Calif. Inst. Tech., Pasadena, 1989—96; assoc. prof. philosophy U. Ill., Chgo., 1997—2006. Office: U Ill 601 S Morgan St Chicago IL 60607 Office Phone: 312-996-5490.

HILBERT, RITA L., librarian; b. Orange, NJ, Nov. 1, 1942; d. Ralph P. LaSalle and Arlene (Julian) Strobel; children: Toby Gayle Buchanan, Stacey Giordano, Joseph, Matthew. AA, NYU, 1988, BA, 1990; MLS, Rutgers U., 1992. Merchandising rsch. analyst Burrelle's, Livingston, NJ, 1975-82; teaching asst. Montessori Sch., Millburn, NJ, 1982-84; outreach specialist Rockwood Meml. Libr., Livingston, 1984-90, head spl. svcs., 1990-92; libr. dir. Lincoln Park (N.J.) Pub. Libr., 1992-94, Mount Olive Township Pub. Libr., 1994—. Mem. Adult Sch. Bd., Livingston, 1990—, Lincoln Pk. Bd. of Edn., 1995-98, chair policy com., 1997-98, negotiations com., 1997-98. Member Livingston Adv. Com. for the Handicapped, 1985—, Livingston Coun. for Sr. Citizens, 1985—, Region III Com. for Svcs. to Spl. Populations, sec., 1987-88; elected mem. Lincoln Park Bd. Edn., 1995-98, chair policy and negotiations coms., 1995-98; trustee Lincoln Park Libr., 1997-98. Recipient Founder's Day award NYU, 1990. Mem.: AAUW (scholarship 1987), ALA, Morris Automated Info. Network (sec. 1993—94, v.p. 1995, pres. 1996, rep. planning coun. 2004), NJ Assn. Libr. Assts. (pres. 1989—90, scholarship in her name 1994), NJ Libr. Assn. (scholarship 1990), Mt. Olive C. of C. (rec. sec. 2002—05, bd. dirs. 2005, v.p. 2006, Bus. Person of Yr. 2005), Mt. Olive Twp. Hist. Soc. (founding and charter mem.), Morris County 200 Club, Kiwanis (hon.; bd. dirs. 1999—), Alpha Sigma Lambda. Avocations: walking, painting, travel. Office: 202 Flanders-Drakestown Rd Flanders NJ 07836 Office Phone: 973-691-8686.

HILBERT, ROBERT S(AUL), optical engineer; b. Washington, Apr. 29, 1941; s. Philip G. and Bessie (Friend) H.; m. Angela Cinel Ferreira, June 19, 1966; children: David M., Daniel S. BS in Optics, U. Rochester, 1962, MS in Optics, 1964. Optical design engr. Itek Corp., Lexington, Mass., 1963-65, supr. lens design sect., 1965-67, asst. mgr. optical engr. dept., 1967-69, mgr. optical engring. dept., 1969-74, dir. optics, 1974-75; v.p. engring. Optical Rsch. Assocs., Pasadena, Calif., 1975-84, sr. v.p., 1985-91, pres., COO, 1991-2000, pres., CEO, 2000—, also bd. dirs. Lectr. Northeastern U., Burlington, Mass., 1967-69; mem. trustees vis. com. Sch. Engring. and Applied Sci., U. Rochester, 1995-97. Mem. devel. bd. Coll. Optical Sci., U. Ariz., 2007. Recipient Future Scientist of Am. award, 1957; Am. Optical Co. fellow U. Rochester, 1962. Fellow Soc. Photo-Optical Instrumentation Engrs. (chmn. fellows com. 1998); mem. Optical Soc. Am. (engring. coun. 1990-92, mem. Fraunhofer award com. 1997-98), Lens Design Tech. Group (chmn. 1975-77). Jewish. Achievements include 6 patents in lens systems. Avocations: reading, movies. Home: 863 San Vicente Rd Arcadia CA 91007 Office: Optical Rsch Assocs 3280 E Foothill Blvd Pasadena CA 91107-3103 Home Phone: 626-446-9942; Office Phone: 626-795-9101 306. Business E-Mail: bob@opticalres.com.

HILBORN, MARILYN ANN, educational consultant; b. Baytown, Tex., Sept. 23, 1942; d. Wilburn C. Simpson and Ivy Lorraine Whitworth-Simpson; m. Robert J. Hilborn, July 4, 1968; children: Robert Scott, Kelley Lawrence. BA, U. Houston, 1966, MA, 1985. Cert. tchr. Tex., 1966. Educator, tchr., coord. Houston Ind. Sch. Dist., 1968—2001; pvt. practice edn. cons. Houston, 2001—. Textbook writer, cons. Longman/Pearson, Alloy Multimedia. Author: (novel) Personal Justice, 1981 (West Coast Rev. of Books Porgie award, 1982). Grantee Secondary Educators Summer Study, NEH, 1986, 1995. Mem.: TESOL. Avocations: yoga, travel, bicycling. Office: 1800 Stoney Brook Dr #108 Houston TX 77063 Office Phone: 713-952-5037.

HILBRECHT, NORMAN TY, lawyer; b. San Diego, Feb. 11, 1933; s. Norman Titus and Elizabeth (Lair) H.; m. Mercedes L. Sharratt, Oct. 24, 1980. BA, Northwestern U., 1956; JD, Yale U., 1959. Bar: Nev. 1959, U.S. Supreme Ct. 1963, U.S. Ct. Appeals, (9th dist.), 1986. Assoc. counsel Union Pacific R.R., Las Vegas, 1962; ptnr. Hilbrecht & Jones, Las Vegas, 1962-69; pres. Hilbrecht, Jones, Schreck & Bernhard, 1969-83, Hilbrecht & Assocs, 1983—, Mobil Transport Corp., 1970-72; gen. counsel Bell United Ins. Co., 1986-94; mem. Nev. Assembly, 1966-72, minority leader, 1971-72; mem. Nev. Senate, 1974-78; legis. comm., 1977-78; oper. mem. Corp. Svcs. Group, 1998—; pres. Corp. Svcs. Co., 1998—, Nev. Incorporating Co., 1998—; mng. mem. Amcorp LLC., 1999—. Asst. lectr. bus. law U. Nev., Las Vegas. Author: Nevada Motor Carrier Compendium, 1990, Nevada Corporation Handbook, 1999. Labor mgmt. com. NCCJ, 1963; mem. Clark County Dem. Ctrl. Com., Nev., 1959-80, 1st vice chmn., 1965-66; del. Western Regional Assembly on Ombudsman; chmn. Clark County Dem. Conv., 1966, Nev. Dem. Conv., 1966; pres. Clark County Legal Aid Soc., 1964, Nev. Legal Aid and Defender Assn., 1965-83; assoc. for justice Nat. Jud. Coll., 1993-2006; active United Way Leadership Coun., 1994-2006. Capt. AUS, 1952-67. Named Outstanding State Legislator Eagleton Inst. Politics, Rutgers U., 1969. Mem. ABA, ATLA, Am. Judicature Soc., Am. Acad. Polit. and Social Sci., State Bar Nev. (chmn. adminstrv. law com. 1991-94, chmn. sect. on adminstrv. law 1996), Nev. Trial Lawyers (state v.p. 1966), Supreme Ct. Hist. Soc., Am. Assn. Ret. Persons (state legis. com. 1991-94), Literary Soc. Las Vegas, Las Vegas Social Register, Rotary, Las Vegas Rotary Found. (pres. 2004-05, sr. mem. 2006-), U. Nev.-Las Vegas Found., Elks, Phi Beta Kappa, Delta Phi Epsilon, Theta Chi, Phi Delta Phi. Lutheran. Office: 723 S Casino Ctr Blvd Las Vegas NV 89101-6716 Home Phone: 702-361-6008; Office Phone: 702-384-1036. Business E-Mail: hilbrecht@lvcm.com.

HILCHEY, TIM, editor; BA Journalism, U. New Hampshire, 1984. Writer NY Times, 1992—99; dep. editor NY Times Syndication Sales Corp, 2000—. Office: NY Times Syndication Sales Corp 14th Fl 122 E 42nd St New York NY 10168 Office Phone: 212-499-3530. Office Fax: 212-499-3382. E-mail: hilchey@nytimes.com.

HILDEBRAND, DANIEL WALTER, lawyer; b. Oshkosh, Wis., May 1, 1940; s. Dan M. and Rose Marie (Baranowski) H.; m. Dawn E. Erickson; children: Daniel G., Douglas P., Elizabeth A., Rachel E., Jacob E., Catherine E. BS, U. Wis., 1962, LLB, 1964. Bar: Wis. 1964, US Dist. Ct. (we. dist.) Wis. 1964, NY 1965, US Dist. Ct. (so. and ea. dists.) NY 1967, US Ct. Appeals (2d cir.) 1968, US Dist. Ct. (ea. dist.) Wis. 1970, US Ct. Appeals (7th cir.) 1970, US Supreme Ct. 1970, US Tax Ct. 1986, US Ct. Appeals (8th cir.) 1988, US Ct. Appeals (DC cir.) 1991, US Dist. Ct. (no. dist.) Ill. 2005. Assoc. Willkie, Farr & Gallagher, NYC, 1964-68; from assoc. to ptnr. DeWitt Ross & Stevens S.C., Madison, Wis., 1968—. Lectr. U. Wis. Law Sch., Madison, 1972-2000; mem. Joint Survey Com. on Tax Ememptions Wis; chair Code of Profl. Responsibility Rev. Com., 1985-87, chair Wis. Ethics 2000 Com., 2003-06. Editor: U. Wis. Law Rev., 1963-64. Pres. Wis. Law Foun., 1993-95, Wis. Jud. Commn., 1992-98, chmn., 1997-98. Fellow Am. Bar Found. (life), Wis. Bar Found. (life); mem. ABA (com. pub. fin. judicial campaigns 2001-02, trial practice com. litigation sect., ho. of dels. 1992-2006, standing com. on ethics 1997-03, Wis. state del. 1995-2003, bd. govs. 2003-06, exec. com. 2005-06, Amicus Briefs com., 2006-), Wis. Bar Assn. (bd. govs. 1981-93, exec. com. 1987-93, chmn. 1988-89, pres. 1991-92), Dane County Bar Assn. (pres. 1980-81), 7th Cir. Bar Assn., Am. Law Inst., Am. Acad. Appellate Lawyers, James E. Doyle Inn of Ct. Roman Catholic. Office: 2 E Mifflin St Ste 600 Madison WI 53703-2890 Office Phone: 608-283-5610. Business E-Mail: dwh@dewittross.com.

HILDEBRAND, JEFFREY D., oil industry executive; married; 3 children. B, U. Tex., Austin, M in Petroleum Engring. Petroleum geologist, engr. Dan A. Hughes Co., Beeville, Tex.; with Am. Energy Capital Corp., 1988; geologist Exxon; co-founder Hilcorp Energy Co., 1989, pres., CEO. Named one of 400 Richest Ams., Forbes mag., 2006. Mem.: Tex. Ind. Petroleum Royalty Owners Assn., La. Oil and Gas Assn., Houston Geol. Soc., Soc. Petroleum Engrs., Ind. Petroleum Assn. Am. Office: Hilcorp Energy Co 1201 Louisiana Ste 1400 Houston TX 77002

HILDEBRAND, JOHN FREDERICK, columnist, educator; b. Chgo., Dec. 23, 1940; s. Paul Hedden and Harriet L. (Cummins) H.; m. Vasana Lohitkoopt, June 24, 1972; children: Marisa Cummins, Shana Victoria, Brent Daniel. B Journalism, U. Mo., 1965; MS in Journalism, Columbia U., 1966. Reporter Poplar Bluff (Mo.) Daily Am. Republic, 1963, Joplin (Mo.) Globe, 1964, AP, Jefferson City and Kansas City, Mo., 1965; fgn. svc. officer U.S. Info. Svc., Washington and Bangkok, 1966-70; reporter Newsday, Melville, NY, 1970-74, asst. city editor, 1974-76, edn. writer, 1976—. Adj. prof. journalism Chulalongkorn U., Bangkok, 1967; pres. Lloyd Neck (N.Y.) Holding Corp., 1988-91, bd. dirs., 1986-95. Vestryman St. John's Episcopal Ch., Cold Spring Harbor, N.Y., 1992-98. Recipient citation Adelphi U., Garden City, N.Y., 1987, citation Kappa Delta Pi, Oakdale, N.Y., 1988, citation Phi Delta Kappa Suffolk County Chpt., 1999, Newsday Pub.'s. Spl. Achievement award, 1997, Pub. Svc. award Press Club Long Island, 2007. Mem. Edn. Writers Assn. (1st prize opinion article 1978, 1st prize article series 1982, 97, 1st prize article package 1992), Phi Gamma Delta (sec. Chi Mu chpt. 1964). Home: 23 Target Rock Dr Huntington NY 11743-1464 Office: Newsday Inc 235 Pinelawn Rd Melville NY 11747-4250 Office Phone: 631-843-2956. Business E-Mail: john.hildebrand@newsday.com.

HILDEBRAND, JOHN G(RANT), neuroscientist, educator; b. Boston, Mar. 26, 1942; s. John G. and Helen S. Hildebrand; m. Gail Deerin Burd, July 24, 1982. AB, Harvard U., 1964; PhD, Rockefeller U., 1969; Laurea Honoris Causa, U. Cagliari, Italy, 2000. Instr. neurobiology Harvard U. Med. Sch., Boston, 1970-72, asst. prof., 1972-77, assoc. prof., 1977-80, vis. prof., 1980-81; prof. biol. scis. Columbia U., NYC, 1980-85; prof. neurobiol., biochemistry, molecular biophysics and cellular biology, entomology U. Ariz., Tucson, 1985—, Regents prof., 1989—, dir., Ariz. Rsch. Lab., divsn. neurobiology, 1985—. Assoc. behavioral biology Harvard U. Mus. Comparative Zoology, Cambridge, Mass., 1980-97; trustee Marine Biol. Lab., Woods Hole, Mass., 1981-89, mem. exec. com., 1981-88; Jan de Wilde lectr. U. Wageningen, The Netherlands, 1992; King Solomon lectr. Hebrew U., Jerusalem, 1995; K.D. Roeder lectr. Tufts U., 1995; Felix Santschi lectr. U. Zurich, Switzerland, 1995; Grandpierre Meml. lectr. Columbia U., 2002; Padykula lectr. Wellesley Coll., 2003; Cajal lectr. Cajal Inst., Madrid, 2004; Kravitz lectr. Marine Boil. Lab. Woods Hole, Mass., 2007. Co-editor: Chemistry of Synaptic Transmission, 1974, Receptors for Neurotransmitters, Hormones, and Pheromones in Insects, 1980, Molecular Insect Science, 1990; devel. neurosci. sect. editor Jour. Neurosci., 1983-88; co-editor Jour. Comparative Physiology A, 1990—; mem. editorial bd. various other jours. Trustee Rockefeller U., N.Y.C., 1970-73. Recipient Javits Neurosci. award Nat. Isnt. Neurol. and Communicative Disorders and Stroke, NIH, 1986-94, Merit award Nat. Inst. Allergy and Infections Diseases, NIH, 1986-97, R.H. Wright award Simon Fraser U., B.C., Can., 1990, Max Planck Rsch. award Max Planck Gesellschaft and Alexander von Humboldt-Stiftung of Germany, 1990, Founder's Meml. award Entomol. Soc. Am., 1997, award Humboldt Found., 1997, Manheimer Lectureship award Monell Chem. Senses Ctr., 2005, Henry and Phyllis Koffler prize, 2006, Outstanding Svc. to Biol. Scis. award Am. Inst. Biol. Scis., 2006, Lifetime Achievement award APA Diversity Program Neurosci., 2006; fellow Helen Hay Whitney Found., 1969-72, A.P. Sloan Found., 1973-77. Fellow: AAAS, Royal Entomol. Soc. UK; mem.: NAS, Ariz. Arts, Scis. and Tech. Acad. (chmn. 2005—06, founding fellow), Am. Acad. Arts and Sci., Norwegian Acad. Sci. and Letters, Deutsche Akademie der Naturforscher Leopoldina, Internat. Soc. Chem. Ecology (pres. 1998—99), Soc. Integrative and Comparative Biology, Internat. Soc. Neuroethology (pres. 1995—98, Silver medal 2006), Soc. Neurosci. (treas. 1993—94), Assn. Chemoreception Sci. (pres. 2002—03, IFF Innovative Rsch. award 1997), Am. Soc. Biochemistry and Molecular Biology. Avocations: music, lower brass instruments. Home: 629 N Olsen Ave Tucson AZ 85719-5136 Office: U Ariz ARL Div Neurobiology PO Box 210077 Tucson AZ 85721-0077 Business E-Mail: jgh@neurobio.arizona.edu.*

HILDEBRAND, PHILLIP J., insurance company executive; b. Prineville, Oreg., 1952; Attended, Northern Ariz. U., 1974. Sr. v.p. New York Life Ins. Co., NYC, 1997—2001, exec. v.p., 2001—06, chief dist. officer, life annuity, 2001—06, vice chmn., 2006—. Office: NY Life Ins Co 51 Madison Ave New York NY 10010*

HILDEBRAND, ROGER HENRY, astrophysicist, physicist; b. Berkeley, Calif., May 1, 1922; s. Joel Henry and Emily (Alexander) H.; m. Jane Roby Beedle, May 28, 1944; children: Peter Henry, Alice Louise, Kathryn Jane, Daniel Milton. AB in Chemistry, U. Calif., Berkeley, 1947, PhD in Physics, 1951. Physicist, U. Calif., 1942-51; physicist Tenn. Eastman Corp., Oak Ridge Nat. Lab., 1945; asst. prof. dept. physics Enrico Fermi Inst., U. Chgo., 1952-55, asso. prof., 1955-60, prof., 1960—, prof. dept. astronomy and astrophysics, 1978—, Samuel K. Allison Disting. Service prof., 1985—, chmn. dept. astronomy and astrophysics, 1984-88; dir. Enrico Fermi Inst., 1965-68, dean coll., 1969-73. Assoc. lab. dir. for high energy physics Argonne (Ill.) Nat. Lab., 1958-64; chmn. sci. policy com. Stanford (Calif.) Linear Accelerator Ctr., 1962-66; mem. physics adv. com. Nat. Accelerator Lab., 1967-69; mem. sci. and ednl. adv. com. Lawrence Berkeley Lab., 1972-80; chmn. com. to rev. U.S. medium energy sci. AEC and NSF, 1974; chmn. airborne obs. users group NASA, 1983-84; chmn. sci. cons. group Stratopheric Obs. for Infrared Astronomy (SOFIA), NASA, 1985-89, mem. sci. working group, 1995-97, sci. coun., 1997—; mem. space astronomy and astrophysics Space Sci. Bd., 1987-90; mem. coun. Columbus Project, 1987-88; mem. sci. and tech. adv. panel for the submillimeter array Harvard/Smithsonian Ctr. for Astrophysics, 1989-95; mem. astronomy and astrophysics survey com. NAS Panel for Infrared Astronomy, 1989-90; chmn. Dannie Helneman prize com. Am. Inst. Physics, 1990; mem. sci. and tech. adv. group Large Millimeter Telescope, 1995—; mem. obs. vis. com. Assn. Univs. for Rsch. in Astronomy, 1993-96, chmn. Stratospheric Obs. Infrared Astronomy sci. coun., 1997—; mem. NASA review panel for Small Explorer (SMEX) Proposals, 2000; mem. NASA/JPL bd. for Planck High Frequency Instrument Detectors, 2000-02; mem. faculty Canary Islands Winter Sch. Astrophysics, 2000. Guggenheim fellow, 1968-69, Alfred P. Sloan Found. fellow, 1975. Fellow Am. Phys. Soc., Am. Acad. Arts and Scis.; mem. Am. Astron. Soc., Internat. Astron. Union, Midwestern Univs. Rsch. Assn. (dir. 19956-58, 62-68), Kavli Inst. for Comological Physics (chair adv. com. 2001-2003, assoc. mem. 2003-),Phi beta Kappa, Sigma Xi. Office: U Chgo Enrico Fermi Inst 5640 S Ellis Ave Chicago IL 60637-1433

HILDEBRAND, VERNA LEE, human ecology educator; b. Dodge City, Kans., Aug. 17, 1924; d. Carrell E. and Florence (Smyth) Butcher; m. John R. Hildebrand, June 23, 1946; children: Carol Ann, Steve Allen. BS, Kans. State U., 1945, MS, 1957; PhD, Tex. Women's U., 1970. Tchr. home econs. Dickinson County H.S., Chapman, Kans., 1945-46; tchr. early childhood Albany (Calif.) Pub. Schs., 1946-47; grad. asst. Inst. Child Welfare U. Calif., Berkeley, 1947-48; tchr. kindergarten Albany Pub. Schs., 1948-49; dietitian commons and hosp. U. Chgo., 1952-53; instr. Kans. State U., Manhattan, 1953-54, 59, Okla. State U., Stillwater, 1955-56; asst. prof. Tex. Tech U., Lubbock, 1962-67; from asst. prof. to prof. Mich. State U., East Lansing, 1967-97, prof. emeritus, 1997—. Legis. clk. Kans. Ho. of Reps., Topeka, 1955. Author: Introduction to Early Childhood Education, 1971, 6th edit., 1997, Guiding Young Children, 1975, 7th edit., 2004, Parenting and Teaching Young Children, 1981, 90, Management of Child Development Centers, 1984, 6th edit., 2006, Parenting: Rewards and Responsibilities, 1994, 7th edit., 2004, tchrs. annotated edit., 2003; co-author: China's Families: Experiment in Societal Change, 1985, Knowing and Serving Diverse Families, 1996, 2d edit., 1999. Mem. Nat. Assn. for the Edn. Young Children (task force 1975-77), Am. Home Econs. Assn. (bd. dirs., Leader award 1990), Women in Internat. Devel., Nat. Assn. Early Childhood Tchr. Edn. (award for meritorious and profl. leadership 1995).

HILDEBRANDT, FREDERICK DEAN, JR., management consultant; b. Upper Darby, Pa. m. Marjorie Louise Smith, July 27, 1968; children: Frederick Dean III, Elizabeth Florence. AB magna cum laude, Dartmouth Coll., 1954, MS, 1955. Engr. Eastman Kodak Co., Rochester, N.Y., 1957-60; systems mgr. J.T. Baker Chem. Co., Phillipsburg, N.J., 1960-63; assoc. Booz, Allen & Hamilton Inc., NYC, 1963-72, v.p., 1972-78; sr. v.p. Am. Ins. Assn., NYC, 1978-81; v.p. Travelers Ins. Cos., Hartford, Conn., 1981-89; pres. Dean Hildebrandt & Assocs., Simsbury, Conn., 1989—. Adminstr. Ins. Rsch. Coun., 1979, bd. dirs., 1982-88; vice chmn. bd. dirs. Workers Compensation Rsch. Inst., 1987-88 With U.S. Army, 1955-57. Mem. Inst. Mgmt. Cons. (cert. mgmt. cons.), Phi Beta Kappa.

HILDEBRANDT, GEORGE FREDERICK, lawyer; b. Claverack, NY, Mar. 28, 1959; s. Harry and Sophie Evelyn (Reutenauer) H. BA, Syracuse U., 1981, JD, 1984. Bar: N.Y. 1985, U.S. Dist. Ct. (no. dist.) N.Y. 1986, U.S. Supreme Ct. 1997, U.S. Ct. Appeals (2d cir.) 1998. Atty. Frank H. Hiscock Legal Aid Soc., Syracuse, N.Y., 1985-88; pvt. practice Syracuse, 1988—. Mem. Nat. Assn. Criminal Def. Lawyers, NY State Acad. Trial Lawyers. Office: 300 Crown Bldg 304 S Franklin St Syracuse NY 13202-1233

HILDESTAD, TERRY D., energy executive; m. Katharine Hildestad; 3 children. B, Dickinson State Univ. Mgmt. positions Knife River Corp., 1974—91, pres., 1991—93, pres., CEO, 1993—2005; pres., COO MDU Resources Group, Bismarck, ND, 2005—06, pres., CEO, 2006—. Mem. adv. bd. We. ND U.S. Bank. Bd. mem. Dickinson State Univ. Found. Office: MDU Resources Group 1200 W Century Ave Bismarck ND 58506*

HILDING, JEREL LEE, music and dance educator, retired dancer; b. New Orleans, Sept. 24, 1949; s. Oscar William and Loeta Dana (Boldra) H.; m. Krystyna Zofia Jurkowski, July 1, 1978; children: Dennis Jozef, Kristopher Jay. BA, La. State U., New Orleans, 1971. Prin. dancer Joffrey Ballet, NYC, 1975-89; dir. arts in edn. N.J. Ballet, 1989-90; assoc. prof., dir. dance U. Kans., 1990—. Avocations: piano, sports. Office: U of Kansas Dept Music and Dance 460 Murphy Hall 1530 Naismith Dr Lawrence KS 66045-0001

HILDRETH, EUGENE A., physician, educator; b. St. Paul, Mar. 11, 1924; s. Eugene A. V. and Lila K. (Clator) Hildreth; m. Dorothy Anne Myers, Mar. 23, 1946; children: Jeffrey Reed, William Myers, Anne Sarver, Katherine Clator. BS, Washington Jefferson Coll., 1943; MD, U. Va., 1947. Diplomate Am. Bd. Internal medicine, Am. Bd. Allergy and Immunology. Intern Johns Hopkins, 1947—48; resident in medicine Hosp. U. Pa., 1948—49, USPHS Postdoctoral Research fellow in cardio-vascular disease, 1949—51, chief resident in medicine, 1953—54, fellow in allergy and immunology, 1954—58, faculty, 1954—69, faculty, 1971—; instr. medicine U. Pa., Phila., 1953—54, asso. medicine, 1954—55, asst. prof. medicine, 1955—60, assoc. prof., 1960—69; assoc. dean U. Pa. (Sch. Medicine), 1964—69, prof. clin. medicine, 1971—90, prof. emeritus, 1990—, acting chmn. dept. research medicine, 1960—64. Chmn. dept. medicine Reading (Pa.) Hosp. and Med. Ctr.; cons. project site visits USPHS, 1965—70; cons. VA Hosp. Phila., 1955—; nat. adv. com. Medic Alert Found. Internat., 1964—83; cons. Citizens' Com. to Study Grad. Med. Edn., 1966; Am. Bd. Med. Spltys. rep. of subsplty. Bd. Allergy and Immunology of Am. Bd. Internal Medicine, 1969—72; mem. Am. Bd. Internal Medicine, 1969—72, 1975—82, cons., com. mem., 1972—75, chmn. certifying exam. com., 1978—81, mem. core exam. com., 1986—87, mem. exec. com., 1978—82, chmn., 1981—82; founding com. Am. Bd. Allergy and Immunology, 1970, mem., 1970—72, 1st co-chmn.; mem. rep. Am. Bd. Med. Spltys., 1976—83, chmn. nominating com., 1979—80; mem. med. adv. bd. Lupus Found. Del. Valley, 1979—; chmn. Federated Coun. Internal Medicine; appeals bd. liaison Coun. of Grad. Med. Edn., 1980—. Co-author: Low Fat Diet, 1953; mem. editl. bd.: Annals Internal Medicine, 1960—68, Postgrad. Medicine, 1969—75, Jour. Berks County Med. Soc., 1969—73, Internal Medicine Digest, 1971—75; contbr. chapters to books, articles to profl. jours. With USNR, 1943—45, with USNR, 1951—53. Grantee, USPHS; scholar John and Mary R. Markle scholar in acad. medicine, 1958—63. Master: ACP (mem. bd. regents 1985—92, chmn. bd. regents 1989—91, pres. 1991—92, immediate past pres. 1992—, mem. ethics com. 1986—90, chmn. com. to delineate privileges of med. procedures, mem. nominating 1997—); fellow: Am. Clin. and Climatologic Assn., Acad. Medicine of Singapore (hon.); mem.: ACGME (mem. residency rev. com. internal medicine), AAAS, Working Group on Disability of U.S. Presidents, Royal Soc. Medicine, Federated Coun. Internal Medicine, Am. Acad. Allergy, Inst. Medicine of NAS (mem. nominating com. 1982—84, mem. coun. 1986—90, chmn. nominating com. for coun. memberships 1989—90, mem. fin. com. 1988—90), N.Y. Acad. Scis., Fedn. AM. Socs. for Exptl. Biology, Peripatetic Soc., Phila. Art Mus. Home: 2000 Cambridge Ave Apt 129 Wyomissing PA 19610

HILDRETH, JAMES DAVID, musician, educator; b. Buffalo, June 27, 1958; s. Charles David Hildreth and Charlotte May Matteson. MusB in Organ Performance, U. Cin., 1980; M of Sacred Music, So. Meth. U., Dallas, 1982. Organist Immanuel United Meth. Ch., Lakeside Park, Ky., 1973—80; organist, accompanist First United Meth. Ch., Irving, Tex., 1980—82, dir. music ministries Griffin, Ga., 1982—87; organist Broad St. Presbyn. Ch., Columbus, Ohio, 1987—. Organist Columbus Symphony Orch., 1989—, Pro Musica Chamber Orch., Columbus, 2000—; new organ cons. First Presbyn. Ch., Gallipolis, Ohio, 1992, First Cmty. Ch., Dublin, 1995; adj. prof. organ Capital U., Columbus, 2002—04; music dir. cons. Overbrook Presbyn. Ch., Columbus, 2004; reviewer organ, choral recordings Am. Guild Organists, NYC, 2005—; organ recitalist Fourth Presbyn Ch., Chgo., St. Thomas Ch., NYC, Methuen Meml. Music Hall, Mass., Houghton Coll., NY. Deacon Broad St. Presbyn. Ch., 1994—2002. Named Outstanding Young Men of Am., 1985; recipient Strader full-tuition scholarship, U. Cin. Coll.-Conservatory of Music, 1976—80, Dean's award for Outstanding Achievement, 1980; fellow Pi Kappa Lambda, U. Cin., 1979. Mem.: Organ Hist. Soc. (performer nat. conv. 2003), Am. Guild Organists (dean Columbus, Ohio chpt. 1995—97, performer region V conv. 2007, coord. AGO/Quimby region V competition for young organists 2007), Am. Dove Assn. Christian. Achievements include First American organist to perform in Organ Hall in Dnepropetrovsk, Ukraine, 2004. Avocations: photography, travel, bicycling, hiking. Home: 2651 Sparrow Hill Dr Columbus OH 43219 Office: Broad St Presbyn Church 760 E Broad St Columbus OH 43205 Office Phone: 614-221-6552. Office Fax: 614-221-5722. Personal E-mail: jdhildreth58@worldnet.att.net.

HILDRETH, JAMES ROBERT, retired air force officer; b. Pine Bluff, Ark., May 4, 1927; s. William Wilson and Martha Leah (Chidester) H.; m. Beth Dixon Baker, July 12, 1955; children: John Baker, William Reid, Margaret Leah, Mark Dixon, Amy Beth. BA cum laude, La. Poly. Inst., 1952. Commd. 2d lt. USAF, 1952, advanced through grades to maj. gen., 1976; ret., 1981; comdr. 1st Air Commando Sqdn., 1967, Army War Coll., 1969—70; comdr. 4th Tactical Fighter Wing, 1970—72; dep. dir. ops. Office of Joint Chiefs of Staff, 1972—73; dep. comdr. 13th Air Force, 1973—75; sr. Air Force rep. Weapons Systems Evaluation Group, Office of Sec. Def., 1975—76; comdr. Tactical Fighter Weapons Center, 1976—79; comdr. 13th Air Force, 1979—81. Pres. So. Nev. Fed. Exec. Agy., 1975-76; mem. adv. bd. United Way, Las Vegas, Nev., 1975-79; bd. dirs. Las Vegas C. of C., 1976-79; dist. chmn. Boy Scouts Am., 1979-81. Decorated D.S.M. (2), Silver Star, Def. Superior Svc. medal, Legion of Merit (3), D.F.C. (3), Bronze Star, Air medal (14), Meritorious Svc. Medal, Air Force Commendation medal (3), Purple Heart, Cross of Gallantry (Vietnam), Rep. Phillipines Legion of Honor. Mem. Kappa Sigma, Phi Kappa Phi, Omicron Delta Kappa, Sigma Tau Delta. Clubs: DAV. Methodist. Home: 315 E Branch St PO Box 897 Spring Hope NC 27882-0897 Office: 9070 Edgerton Rd Spring Hope NC 27882-8916 Personal E-mail: cbhild@yahoo.com.

HILDRETH, PETER C., state agency administrator; Mem. NH House Reps.; gen. practice lawyer Winograd P.A., Concord, NH, 1984—88; hearings examiner NH Dept. Safety, 1988—92; dir. securities registration Office of Sec. of State, NH, 1992—2001; commr. NH Banking Dept., Concord, 2001—. Democrat. Office: NH Banking Dept 64 B Old Suncook Rd Concord NH 03301-7317 Office Phone: 603-271-3561. Office Fax: 603-271-1090. E-mail: phildreth@banking.state.nh.us.

HILDRETH, RICHARD G., lawyer, educator; b. 1943; BS, U. Mich., 1965, JD, 1969; diploma in Law, Oxford U., 1969, U. Stockholm, 1973. Bar: Calif. 1969. Atty. Steinhart & Falconer, San Francisco, 1969—78; prof. Univ. Oreg. Sch. Law, 1978—; dir. Environ. & Natural Resources Ctr., Univ. Oreg., Ocean & Coastal Law Ctr, Univ. Oreg. Mem. editl. adv. bd. Coastal Mgmt., Ocean Development & Internat. Law. Co-author: Coastal & Ocean Law: Cases & Materials, Coastal & Ocean Mgmt. Law in a Nutshell, Ocean & Coastal Law. Office: Ocean and Coastal Law Center School of Law 1221 University of Oregon Eugene OR 97403-1221*

HILDRETH, SUSAN, state librarian; Grad., Syracuse U.; MLS, SUNY Albany; MBA, Rutgers U. Libr. Edison Twp. Libr., NJ, Yolo County Libr.; libr. dir. Benicia Pub. Libr.; county libr. Auburn-Placer County Libr.; dep. dir. support services Sacramento Pub. Libr.; planning cons. libr. devel. services bur. Calif. State Libr., state libr., 2004—; dep. city libr. San Francisco; city libr. Mem.: Calif. Libr. Assn. (pres., treas.), ALA (mem. at-large governing coun.), Pub. Libr. Assn. (pres. 2006—07, mem. exec. com.). Office: Stanley Mosk Library and Courts Bldg 914 Capital Mall Rm 220 Sacramento CA 95814 Office Phone: 916-654-0174. Office Fax: 916-654-0064. Business E-Mail: csl-adm@library.ca.gov.*

HILE, MICHELE VERA, middle school educator; b. Bay City, Mich., July 8, 1950; d. Michael Kosa and Irene Mae Keene; m. Thomas Arthur Hile, Dec. 28, 1974; children: John Thomas, Allen Thomas. BSc, Mich. State U., 1972, MA, 1978. Cert. tchr. Mich., 1972. Tchr. Mid. Sch. Caro (Mich.) Cmty. Schs., 1972—. Instr. water aerobics WaterArt, Toronto, 2001—06; pre-need funeral cons. Ransford Funeral Home, Caro, Mich., 2005—. Sec. Thumb Area Ctr. Arts, Caro, 1996—2004; chmn. lumanaria Tuscola County Relay for Life-ACS, Caro, 2002—; min. Universal Brotherhood, Coral Springs, Fla., 2005—; treas. Watrousville United Meth. Ch., Caro, 1989—2005, lay leader, membership sec.; sec. Juniata Township Zoning Bd., Caro, 1972—76. Mem.: NEA, Mich. Edn. Assn., Caro Edn. Assn. (sec. 1996—). Avocations: reading, travel, theater, lawncare. Home: 1726 S Ringle Rd Caro MI 48723 Office: Caro Middle Sch 301 N Hooper St Caro MI 48723-1499 Office Phone: 989-673-3167. Personal E-mail: cen55375@centurytel.net.

HILEMAN, BETTE, journalist; b. Akron, Ohio, Mar. 4, 1937; d. Francis Matthew and Elsie Josephine Buresh; m. Stephen Caswell Clapp, Sept. 25, 2004; m. Samuel Palmer Hileman, June 20, 1963 (div. Mar. 27, 1978); children: Milena Lee, Charles Warren, Frank Stafford. AB, Mt. Holyoke Coll., 1959. H.S. tchg., sci, math. Va., 1974. H.s. tchr. Brimmer and May Sch., Chestnut Hills, Mass., 1960—61, Bath County H.S., Warm Springs, Va., 1972—73, Clifton Forge H.S., Clifton Forge, Va., 1974—75; head of sci. dept. Stuart Hall Sch., Staunton, Va., 1978—81; assoc. editor Environ. Sci. & Tech. , Pub. by Am. Chem. Soc., Washington, 1981—84; sr. editor Chem. & Engring. News, Weekly Newsmagazine of Am. Chem. Soc., 1984—. Contbr. articles to profl. jours. Chair Hist. Dist. Commn., East New Market, Md., 1994—2001. Recipient Phi Beta Kappa, Phi Beta Kappa Soc., 1959. Mem.: New Dominion Chorale. Avocations: singing, swimming, hiking, skiing. Home: 17267 Banbury Ct Jeffersonton VA 22724 Office: Chem & Engring News 1155 16th St NW Washington DC 20036 Office Phone: 202-872-4583. Business E-Mail: b_hileman@acs.org.

HILER, EDWARD ALLAN, agricultural and engineering educator; b. Hamilton, Ohio, May 14, 1939; s. Earl and Thelma (Kolb) H.; m. Patricia Burke; children: Karen, Richard, Scott. BS in Agrl. Engring., MS in Agrl. Engring., Ohio State U., 1963, PhD in Agrl. Engring., 1966. Registered profl. engr., Tex. Asst. prof. Tex. A&M U., College Station, 1966-69, assoc. prof., 1969-73, prof., 1973—, head dept. agrl. engring., 1974-88, dep. chancellor for acad. program planning and rsch., 1989-91, interim chancellor, 1991, exec. dep. chancellor, 1991, dep. chancellor for acad. and rsch. programs, 1991-92; vice chancellor, dean agrl. and life scis., dir. Tex. Agrl. Expt. Sta., 1992—2004; dir. Tex. Coop. Ext., 1998—2002, Ellison chair in internat. floriculture, depts. hort. scis. and biol. and agrl. engring., 2005—. Cons. on water conservation, environ. quality, energy and biol. processes and future agrl. engring. Office Tech. Assessment, U.S. Congress, Office of Water Rsch. and Tech., Dept. Interior, others. Contbr. over 100 articles to profl. jours. Recipient numerous ednl. and rsch. awards. Fellow AAAS, Instn. Agrl. Engrs. Eng., Am. Soc. Engring. Edn., Am. Soc. Agrl. Engrs. (bd. dirs., pres. 1991-92, trustee Found.); mem. NAE. Presbyterian. Avocations: golf, photography, reading. Home Phone: 940-575-9242. Business E-Mail: e-hiler@tamu.edu.

HILES, BRADLEY STEPHEN, lawyer; b. Granite City, Ill., Nov. 11, 1955; s. Joseph J. and Betty Lou (Goodman) H.; m. Toni Jonine Failoni, Aug. 12, 1977; children: Eric Stephen, Nina Catherine, Emily Christine. BA cum laude, Furman U., 1977; JD cum laude, St. Louis U., 1980. Bar: Mo. 1980, U.S. Dist. Ct. (ea. dist.) Mo., 1980, Ill. 1981. From assoc. to ptnr. Blackwell Sanders Peper Martin, St. Louis, 1980—. V.p., sec., gen. counsel Miss. Lime Co., 1992. Editor-in-chief St. Louis Univ. Law Jour., 1979-80; contbr. articles to profl. jours. Mem. Bar Assn. of Met. St. Louis (chmn. environ. and conservation law com. 1993-94). Republican. Baptist. Avocations: gospel singing, bicycling. Home: 34 Meditation Way Ct Florissant MO 63031-6535 Office: Blackwell Sanders Peper Martin 720 Olive St Fl 24 Saint Louis MO 63101-2338 Home Phone: 314-921-1777; Office Phone: 314-345-6489. E-mail: bhiles@blackwellsanders.com.

HILFERTY, BRYAN CAREY, public relations specialist; b. Arlington, Mass., Aug. 10, 1960; s. Walter Gerard and Ruthe (Hughes) H.; m. Shawna LaNaye Patton, Aug. 16, 1990. BA, U. Mass., 1987; MA, Colo. State U., 1996. Commd. 2d lt. U.S. Army, 1984, advanced through grades to lt. col., 2002; asst. prof. English U.S. Mil. Acad., West Point, N.Y., 1996-99; pub. affairs officer U.S. Army, Alaska, 1999—2001, pub. affairs officer 10th Mountain divsn., Afghanistan Ft. Drum, NY, 2001—04; pub. affairs officer Dept. Army, 2004—. Contbr. articles to profl. jours. Decorated Bronze Star medals (3). Mem. Pub. Rels. Soc. Am., Assn. U.S. Army, VFW, Rotary. Roman Catholic. Home: 1910 Rampart Dr Alexandria VA 22308 Office Phone: 703-693-0295. E-mail: bhilferty@cox.net.

HILFIGER, TOMMY (THOMAS JACOB HILFIGER), apparel designer; b. Elmira, New York, Mar. 24, 1951; m. Susie Hilfiger, 1980 (div. 2000); 4 children. Designer, owner People's Place, NY, to 1979; pres. Tommy Hilfiger Corp., 1982—89, head designer now prin. designer, 1984—, dir., 1992—, hon. chmn. bd., 1994—. Host (TV series) the Cut, 2005—; actor: (films) The Intern, 2000, Zoolander, 2001; (TV series) Rich Girls, 2003, (TV) The Beatles Revolution, 2000; voice (TV series) Frasier, 1994, guest appearances (TV) VH1 Fashion Awards, 1997, ESPN Sports Century, 2000; guest appearances Pulse, 2004. Founder Tommy Hilfiger Corp. Found., 1995—; mem. Martin Luther King Jr. Nat. Mem. Project Found., Anti-Defamation League; dir. Fresh Air Fund, Race to Erase MS, 1994—. Recipient From the Catwalk to the Sidewalk award, VH1, 1995, Designer of the Year award, GQ, 1998, Parson's Sch. Design, 1998, International Designer of the Year award, GQ, 2002, Future of Am. award, Drug Abuse Resistance Education (D.A.R.E.), 2002. Mem. Coun. Fashion Designers Am. (Menswear Designer of Yr. 1995). Address: Tommy Hilfiger Corp 25 W 39th St New York NY 10018 Office: Tommy Hilfiger Corp 9 F Novel Industrial Blvd 850-870 Lai Chi Kok Rd Cheung Sha Wan Hong Kong Office Phone: 212-840-8888, 852 2216 0668.*

HILFMAN, DAVID L., air transportation executive; m. Tracey Hilfman; 1 child, Marshall. Grad., U. South Fla. Bus. Sch., Tampa. With Ea. Airlines, 1981—87, campus sales rep. U. South Fla., 1981; with Continental Airlines, Inc., 1987—, regional mgr. field sales NYC, dir. western sales divsn. LA, sr. dir. US field sales Houston, staff v.p. nat. sales, v.p. multinational sales and revenue programs, 2000—01, v.p. sales, 2003, v.p. sales and reservations, 2003—04, sr. v.p. sales, 2004—. Named one of 25 Most Influential Travel Execs., Bus. Travel News, 2001, 2002. Office: Continental Airlines Inc PO Box 4607 Houston TX 77210 Office Phone: 713-324-5000. Office Fax: 713-324-2637.*

HILGENBERG, JOHN CHRISTIAN, corporate financial executive, consultant; b. Balt., Sept. 6, 1941; s. Carl R. and Elizabeth (Rianhard) Hilgenberg; m. Evelyn Brantley Handy, Apr. 1, 1971; children: Rodney, Crady. BA, Yale U., 1963; MBA, U. Va., 1965. With internat. lending divsn. Md. Nat. Bank, Balt., 1970-75; v.p., dir. fin. svcs. S.M. Hyman Co., Balt., 1975-78; v.p. fin. Eastmet Corp., Balt., 1978-85. Trustee Harbor Hosp. Ctr., 1975—2002, Harbor Hosp. Found., 2002—; v.p., treas., dir. Sky Alland Rsch. Corp., 1986, 1989—90; pres., bd. dirs. Ski Tech. Holdings, Inc., 1987—89, CADS USA, Inc., 1987—89; mng. ptnr. Eager St. Group, Inc., Balt., 1991—; cons., investor in early-stage cos.; bd. dirs. Synthecell Corp., pres., 1992—95; bd. dirs. Cyto Pulse Scis., Inc.; bd. dirs., lead dir. Salar, Inc. Lt. USNR, 1965—70. Mem.: Balt. Choral Arts Soc. (dir. 1975—2004), Bachelors Cotillon, Md. Club, Elkridge Club. Republican. Episcopalian. Address: 2705 Greenspring Valley Rd PO Box 338 Stevenson MD 21153 Office Phone: 888-828-1400.

HILGENBRINK, ROBERT J., academic administrator; b. Quincy, Ill., June 6, 1949; s. Joseph H. and Marie D. Hilgenbrink; m. Donna R. Griep, Aug. 22, 1987; children: Laura L Bruzan, Suzanne R. Smith. BA in History, Quincy U., 1971; MA in Econs., Western Ill. U., 1975. Cert. tchg. K-12 Ill., 1974. Dean bus. svcs. and treas. John Wood CC, Quincy, Ill., 1976—91; v.p. bus. svcs. Heartland CC, Normal, Ill., 1991—95; v.p., fin. and treas. Waubonsee CC, Sugar Grove, Ill., 1995—98; v.p. adminstrv. svcs., treas. Southwestern Ill. Coll., Belleville, 1998—. Bd. mem. State Univs. Retirement Sys. of Ill., Champaign, 2005—, treas., 2007—. Contbr.: guide Education Law. Mem. Sister Cities Commn., Quincy, 1989—91, Nat. Ski Patrol Sys., Denver, 1981—, Weimaraner Club Of Am., Wakefield, RI, 1994—. Specialist 4th class US Army, 1971—73. Mem.: Ill. Coun. Econ. Edn. (bd. mem. 1989—91), Ctrl. Assn. Coll. and Univ. Bus. Officers (current issues com. 2002—05, bd. dirs. 2006—), Nat. Assn. Coll. and Univ. Bus. Officers, Ill. Assn. C.C. Chief Fin. Officers (chair 1996—97, 1991—92). Home: 108 Eden Park Blvd Shiloh IL 62269 Office: Southwestern Ill Coll 2500 Carlyle Ave Belleville IL 62221 Home Phone: 618-632-9346; Office Phone: 618-222-5244. Business E-Mail: robert.hilgenbrink@swic.edu.

HILGER, ROBYN, music educator; b. Okla. m. David Hilger. B summa cum laude in Instrumental Music Edn., Okla. City Univ., 1999. Cert. in Early Adolescence/Young Adult Music Nat. Bd. Tchg. Standards. Adj. tchr. Okla. City Pub. Schs., 1999—2000; music tchr. Okla. City Pub. Schs. (Belle Isle Enterprise Sch.), 2000—, and Fine Arts Team Leader and Band and Orchestra Dir. Asst. dir. Okal. All Star Centennial Band. Named Okla. City Pub. Schs. Dist. Tchr. of Yr., 2005, Okla. Tchr. of Yr., 2006. Office: Belle Isle Enterprise Sch 5904 North Villa Ave Oklahoma City OK 73112 E-mail: Robynh@okcentennialband.com.*

HILGERS, JOHN JACK WILLIAM, management and transportation consultant; b. Carmel-by-the-Sea, Calif., Nov. 17, 1934; s. Rudolph Joseph and Eleanor Maude (King) H.; m. Sharon Ann Hilgers, Dec. 15, 1968; children: Jon Marc, John Jack William Jr. BA in Psychology, San Jose State U., 1956; BA in Criminology, U. Calif., Berkeley, 1963; MS in Sys. Mgmt., U. So. Calif., 1984; MS in Urban Studies, Old Dominion U., 1995, PhD in Urban Svcs., 1998. Enlisted USMC, 1957, advanced in grades to col., ret. Norfolk, 1988; rsch. asst. Bur. Rsch. Old Dominion U., Norfolk, 1988-90, program mgr. Coll. Bus. and Pub. Adminstrn., 1991-98, assoc. dir. Internat. Maritime Ports and Logistics Inst., 1993—98; exec. asst. Va. Legislature, 1999—2007. Dir., mem. exec. com. Atlantic Rim Network, Boston, 1995-2001; exec. sec. Maritime Adv. Coun., Norfolk, 1991-2005; mem. tech. com. Met. Planning Orgn., Hampton Roads, Va., 1996-98; internat. maritime com. chmn. Conf. of World Regions, 1997-03. Editor (newsletter) Bullets and Cannonballs, 1993-98, (mag.) Bus. and Econ. Quar., 1992-96. Divsn. dir. United Way, Norfolk, 1996, 97, Virginia Beach Sister City Group, 1995-2000; trustee Old Dominion U., 1998-2002, Old Dominion U. Rsch. Found. Bd., 2001--. Recipient Va. Commerce Builder award, 1999, Va. Patrick Henry award, Commonwealth of Va., 2001. Mem.: ASPA (exec. com. transp. policy and adminstrn. com. 1997—2001), Internat. Bus. Coun., Econs. Club (Hampton Roads), Propeller Club U.S. (dir. Port of Norfolk 1996—2003), Pepper Lovers Club Va. Internat. (dir. 1994—96), Hampton Roads Fgn. Commerce Club (pres. 1996), Rotary (pres. Sunrise Norfolk chpt 1997—98, asst. gov. Dist. 7600 2002—04, Paul Harris fellow 1996, 2002), Phi Alpha Alpha, Phi Kappa Phi. Avocation: antique and classic automobiles. Home and Office: 1309 Lakeview Dr Virginia Beach VA 23454 Personal E-mail: jackhilgers@earthlink.net.

HILGRAVES, REBEKKAH, singer, consultant; d. George Graves and Marthaan Fenton. MusB, No. Ill. U., DeKalb, 1988. Opera singer, 1988—; tech. cons. SheTech and Co., Austin, Tex., 1996—. Singer: (Operas) La Traviata, The Eglantine, Don Carlo, Suor Angelica. Mem.: Nat. Assn. Tchrs. Singing. Achievements include research in psycho-spirituality singing. Office Phone: 800-343-7179.

HILL, ALAN GORDON, sociologist, educator; b. Greenville, SC, Jan. 25, 1945; s. Arthur G. Hill, Bonta Bush Hill; m. Toyo Murono; 1 child, Arthur. M.Phil., MA, Columbia University, New York, NY, 1967—76; BA, Furman University, Greenville, 1963—67. Chair, Dept. of Sociology Delta College, University Center, MI, 1987—2002; Sociology Instructor Furman University, Greenville, SC, 1979—87. Executive Officer Michigan Sociological Association, MI, 2000—02. Author: (Book) Discovering Society, 1999 (Distinguished Contribution to Instruction, Computers and Sociology Section, American Sociological Assn., 2000). Moderator New Hope Baptist Church, Bay City, MI, 2001—02; Vice President Michigan Region of the American Baptist Churches, E. Lansing, MI, 1996—97; President Delta Chapter of AAUP, University Center, MI, 2002—02. Sergeant Army Medical Service Corps, 1969—75, various. Mem.: Michigan Sociological Association (Past President), Michigan Sociological Association (Executive Officer 2000—02), American Sociological Association (Distinguished Contribution to Instruction (listed above) 2000). Baptist. Home: 3637 Monitor Road Bay City MI 48706-9219 Office: Delta College 1961 Delta Road University Center MI 48710 Home Phone: 989-667-0412; Office Phone: 989-686-9369. Business E-Mail: aghill@alpha.delta.edu.

HILL, ALFRED, law educator; b. NYC, Nov. 7, 1917; m. Dorothy Turck, Aug. 12, 1960; 1 dau., Amelia. BS, Coll. City N.Y., 1937; LL.B., Bklyn. Law Sch., 1941, LL.D., 1986; S.J. D., Harvard U., 1957. Bar: N.Y. State bar 1943, Ill 1958. With SEC, 1943-52; prof. law So. Meth. U., 1953-56, Northwestern U., 1956-62, Columbia U., 1962-75, Simon H. Rifkind prof. law, 1975—93, Simon H. Rifkind prof. law emeritus, 1993—. Contbr. articles on torts, conflict of laws, fed. cts. constl. law to legal jours. Mem. Am. Law Inst. Home: 79 Sherwood Rd Tenafly NJ 07670-2734 Office: Columbia Law Sch New York NY 10027 Home Phone: 201-567-7863.

HILL, ALICE LORRAINE, historian, researcher, genealogist; b. Moore, Okla., Jan. 15, 1935; d. Robert Edward and Alma Alice (Fraysher) H.; children: Debra Hrboka, Pamela Spangler (dec.), Eric Shiver, Lorraine Styczinski. BS in Bus. and Acctg., Ctrl. State U., Wilberforce, Ohio, 1977; student, U. Okla., Norman, 1977-78; postgrad., Calif. Luth. U., Thousand Oaks, 1988; student in Edn., UCLA, 1990. Cert. CC life instr. acctg., bus. and indsl. mgmt., computer and related techs., and real estate, Calif.; real estate broker, Wash., Calif. Former model, 1990-95; with L.A. Unified Sch. Dist., 1990-95; real estate broker Shiver Realty, Oxnard, Calif., 2003—; tchr. mentor K-12 Asuza (Calif.) Pacific U., 2005—. Founder Los Artistas for creative activities for young people, 1975. Author: America, We Love You (Congl. Record Poem, made into World's 1st Internat. Patriotic song), 1975, Land of Lands (now world's first internat. patriotic song); author: (lyrics) Come Listen to the Music, 2004, Someday John, 2005 Nominee Legendary Poet Author award; named hon. grad., Patricia Stevens Modeling Sch., Fla.; recipient Hon. recognition, Okla. State Bd. of Regents for Higher Edn., 1977, Presdl. citations for Pres. Ford, 1976, 1975, Admired Woman of the Decade award, 1994, Lifetime Achievement award, 1995, Most Gold Record award, 1995, Woman of Yr. award, 1995, The Alice Lorraine Hill Poet of Yr. medallion, The Famous Poets Soc., 2003, Recognition award, Entertainer Indi Assn., 2007, Key award for rsch.; scholar Leadership Enrichment Program, Okla., 1977. Mem.: Freedom Force Internat., Internat. Poetry Soc. (disting., internat. hall of fame 1996, Best Poets of 20th Century). Office: 3461 Regatta Pl Oxnard CA 93035 Office Phone: 805-816-5314. Personal E-mail: alicehill@losartistas.us.

HILL, ALLEN EDWARD, delivery service executive; b. Decatur, Ala., Sept. 9, 1955; BA, David Lipscomb U., Nashville, 1977; JD, Nashville Sch. Law, 1984. Bar: Tenn. 1984. Joined as package loader and sorter United Parcel Svc. Inc., 1976, joined legal dept., 1988, v.p., dept. mgr. corp. legal group, 1995—2003, sr. v.p. legal and pub. affairs, gen. counsel, corp. sec., 2004—06, sr. v.p. human resources, 2005—. Bd. vis. Ga. State U. Coll. Law. Mem.: ABA, Tenn. Bar Assn., Am. Corp. Counsel Assn. Office: United Parcel Svc Inc 55 Glenlake Pkwy NE Atlanta GA 30328*

HILL, ANITA FAYE, law educator; b. Lone Tree, Okla., July 30, 1956; d. Albert and Erma Hill. BS with honors in Psychology, Okla. State U., 1977; JD, Yale U., 1980; degree (hon.), Simmons Coll., 2001, Dillard U., 2001. Atty. Wald, Harkrader and Ross, Washington, 1980—81; asst. Office of Civil Rights, US Dept. Edn., Washington, 1981-82; mem. legal staff EEOC (reporting to Clarence Thomas), Washington, 1982-83; prof. Oral Roberts U., 1983-88, Coll. Law, U. Okla., Norman, 1986—96; prof. social policy, law, and women's studies Heller Sch. for Social Policy and Mgmt., Brandeis U., Waltham, Mass., 1997—. Spkr., lectr. on sexual harassment for colls. and orgns. Co-editor: Race, Gender and Power in America, 1995; author: Speaking Truth to Power, 1997; contbr. articles to law jours. Named Women of Yr., Glamour Mag., 1991. Baptist. Office: Brandeis U Heller 328 415 South St Waltham MA 02454-9110 Office Phone: 781-736-3896. E-mail: ahill@brandeis.edu.*

HILL, ANTONY J. DEV., headmaster, history educator; BA with honors, Sydney U.; MEd, Boston U. Lawyer, Sydney; tchr. Narrabeen Girls' HS; asst. head of sch. King's Sch., Sydney; head of sch. Christ Church Grammar, Perth, Melbourne Grammar, Australia, St. Mark's Sch., Boston, 1994—2006. Mem. Nat. Bd. Employment, Edn. and Tng., Sch. Coun., Australia. Mem.: AISV, AISWA, NCISA, AHISA, HMC, Australian Coll. Edn., Phi Delta Kappa.

HILL, BARBARA BENTON, healthcare executive; b. Balt., May 28, 1952; d. George Stock and Charlotte (Russ) Benton; m. Charles David Hill, June 4, 1970 (dec. Oct. 1980); children: Gregory George, Douglas Charles; m. Ancelmo E. Lopes, May 9, 1987. BA, John's Hopkins U., 1973, MS, 1976. Counselor Planned Parenthood of Md., Balt., 1975-76, Hillcrest Clinic, Balt., 1977, dir. community rels., 1977-78, adminstr., 1978-80, exec. dir., 1980-83; pres. Hill & Ward Constrn. Co., Balt., 1980-81; exec. dir. East Balt. Med. Plan, Balt., 1983-84; v.p. John's Hopkins Health Plan, Balt., 1984-85, pres., 1985-91, Hopkins Preferred Network, Balt., 1986-91; v.p. mid-atlantic group ops. Prudential Ins. Co., Balt., 1991-93, v.p. health care policy Newark, 1993-94; pres. Aetna Health Plans of Midwest, Chgo., 1994-96, Rush Prudential Health Plans, Chgo., 1996—. Treas. Greater Balt. com., 1993-94, bd. dirs., 1991-94; mem. Mayor's Econ. Adv. Coun., 1993-94. Named Businessperson of the Yr., Balt. Bus. Jour., 1989. Mem.

Ill. Assn. HMOs (v.p. 1994-96, pres. 1996—), Md. C. of C. (bd. dirs. 1993-94), Phi Beta Kappa. Office: Rush Prudential Health Plans 233 S Wacker Dr Ste 3900 Chicago IL 60606-6324

HILL, BARON PAUL, congressman; b. Seymour, Ind., June 23, 1953; s. Edwin Merrill and Edith Goen Hill; m. Betty Jean Schepman, 1972; children: Jennifer, Cara, Elizabeth. BS in History, Furman U., 1975. Fin. analyst Merrill Lynch; mem. Ind. State Ho. Reps, 1982—90, US Congress from 9th Ind. dist., 1999—2005, 2007—, mem. energy & commerce com., sci. & tech. com. Exec. dir. State Student Assistance Commn., 1992; involved with Am.Red Cross, Seymour Chamber Commerce, Seymour Jaycees. Mem.: Elks Club. Democrat. Methodist. Office: 223 Cannon House Office Bldg Washington DC 20515 also: 320 W 8th St Ste 114 Bloomington IN 47404 Office Fax: 812-523-1474.*

HILL, BARRY MORTON, lawyer; b. Wheeling, W.Va., Sept. 13, 1946; m. Jacqueline Sue Jackson, Aug. 12, 1967 (div. Mar. 1988); children: Jackson Duff, Brandy; m. Lisa C. Wien, Jan. 7, 1989; 1 child, Gabriel Hunter. BS in Journalism, W.Va. U., 1968, JD, 1977. Bar: W.Va. 1977, U.S Dist. Ct. (no. and so. dists.) W.Va. 1977, Ohio 1978, U.S. Dist. Ct. (no. dist.) Ohio 1978, U.S. Ct. Appeals (3d, 4th, 6th and D.C. cirs.) 1984, U.S. Supreme Ct. 1984, U.S. Ct. Appeals (2d and 11th cirs.) 1986, Pa. 1986, U.S. Ct. Appeals (5th, 7th and 10th cirs.) 1988; cert. civil trial specialist Nat. Bd. Trial Adv., med. profl. liability trial specialist Am. Bd. Profl. Liability Attys. CEO Hill Williams, Wheeling, W.Va. Spl. asst. atty. gen., State of W.Va., for antitrust and consumer protection litigation; chmn. W.Va. std. med. malpractice jury instrn. com., 2000; adj. prof. Saba U. Sch. of Medicine, 1994-96. Founding sponsor Civil Justice Found. 1st lt. US Army, 1969—71. Mem.: ATLA (chmn. propulsid litigation group 2000—, chmn. Baycol litigation group 2002—04), So. Trial Lawyers Assn. (bd. govs. 1988—2005), W.Va. Trial Lawyers Assn. (pres. 1987—88, ct. apptd. state liaison propulsid multi-dist. litig. US Dist. Ct. 2001—05, Outstanding mem. 1984), Pa. Trial Lawyers Assn., Ohio Acad. Trial Lawyers. Democrat. Avocations: scuba, tennis, travel, writing, golf. Office: Hill Williams 89 12th St Wheeling WV 26003-3266 Office Phone: 304-233-4966. Business E-Mail: bhill@hwlaw.us.

HILL, BECKY (REBECCA BAKER HILL), librarian; b. Niagara County, NY; Attended, Heidelberg Coll., Tiffin, Ohio; MLS, U. Mich. With Tiffin Seneca County Pub. Libr., 1976—84, Rutherford B. Hayes Presdl. Ctr., Fremont, Ohio, 1984—, co-head libr., genealogy expert, head libr., project coord. Fellow: Ohio Genealogical Soc. (former trustee); mem.: Ohio Libr. Coun. (office holder), Sandusky County Genealogical Soc., Wilson, NY Hist. Soc. (life), Seneca County Genealogical Soc. (founding mem.). Office: Rutherford B Hayes Presdl Ctr Spiegal Grove Fremont OH 43420-2796 Office Phone: 419-332-2081. Office Fax: 419-332-4952. Business E-Mail: bhill@rbhayes.org.*

HILL, BOB (ROBERT G. HILL), former professional basketball coach; b. Columbus, Ohio, Nov. 24, 1948; s. Robert Calvin and Kathryn Francis (Near) H.; m. Pamela Jean Postle, Aug. 10, 1974; children: Cameron Sage, Christopher Postle, Casey Tyler. Grad., Bowling Green State U., Ohio. Minor league baseball player San Diego Padres orgn.; asst. coach Bowling Green State U., 1971—75, U. Pitts., 1975—77, U. Kans., 1977—85, NY Knicks, 1985—86, head coach, 1986—87; scout Charlotte Hornets, 1987—88; TV analyst NJ Nets, 1987—88; head coach Virtus Knorr, Bologna, Italy, 1988—89; asst. coach Ind. Pacers, 1990, head coach, 1990—93; asst. coach Orlando Magic, 1993—94; head coach San Antonio Spurs, 1994—96, Fordham U., 1999—2002; asst. coach Seattle SuperSonics, 2005—06, head coach, 2006—07. Author: Coaching for Success and Beyond, 2000.*

HILL, BRIAN A., former professional basketball coach; b. East Orange, NJ, Sept. 19, 1947; m. Kay Hill; children: Kimberly, Christopher. BS in Phys. Edn., Kennedy Coll., 1969. Coach Clifford Scott HS, 1970-72; asst. coach Montclair State U., 1972-74, Lehigh U., 1974, head coach, 1975-83; asst. coach Pa. State U., 1983-86, Atlanta Hawks, 1986-90, Orlando Magic, Fla., 1990-93, head coach, 1993-97, Vancouver Grizzlies, 1997-99; asst. coach New Orleans Hornets, 2001—03, NJ Nets, 2004—05; head coach Orlando Magic, 2005—07. Head coach NBA Ea. Conf. All-Star Team, 1995. Co-host: ESPN NBA Match-Up, 2000—01. Co-recipient Breath of Life award, Nat. Cystic Fibrosis Found., 2003, Jefferson Awards for Pub. Svc., 2006.*

HILL, BRUCE MARVIN, statistician, educator; b. Chgo., Mar. 13, 1935; s. Samuel and Leah (Berman) H.; m. Linda Ladd, June 18, 1958; children— Alec Michael, Russell Andrew, Gregory Bruce; m. Anne Edith Gardiner Bruce, Aug. 5, 1972. BS in Math., U. Chgo., 1956; MS in Stats., Stanford U., 1958, PhD in Stats., 1961. Mem. faculty U. Mich., Ann Arbor, 1960—, assoc. prof. stats. and probability theory, 1964-70, prof., 1970—. Vis. prof. bus. Harvard U., 1964-65; vis. prof. systems engring. U. Lancaster, U.K., 1968-69; vis. prof. stats. U. London, 1976; vis. prof. econs. U. Utah, 1979; vis. prof. math. U. Milan, U. Rome, 1989. Author: Hill Tail index estimator; editor Jour. Am. Statis. Assn., 1977-83, Jour. Bus. and Econ. Stats., 1982—; contbr. articles to profl. jours., chpts. to books on stats, encys. Grantee NSF, 1962-69, 81-86, 89—, USAF, 1971-73, 87-89. Fellow Am. Statis. Assn. (pres. Ann Arbor chpt. 1986-91), Inst. Math. Stats.; mem. AAUP, Am. Math Assn., Rsch. Club U. Mich., Psi Upsilon, Sigma Chi. Office: U Mich Dept Stats Ann Arbor MI 48109-1027 Home: 1645 Polipoli Rd Kula HI 96790-7524 Personal E-mail: bhill@prodigy.net, bbbmhill@earthlink.net.

HILL, CATHARINE BOND (CAPPY), academic administrator, economics professor; b. Feb. 1954; m. Kent Kildahl; children: John, Thomas, Elizabeth. BA, Williams Coll., 1976; BA with 1st class honors, Oxford U., 1978; PhD, Yale U., 1985. With Congl. Budget Office, 1981—82, The World Bank, 1982—87; adv. for fiscal & trade policy, Ministry Fin. Govt. of Zambia, Lusaka, 1994—96; John J. Gibson prof. econ. Williams Coll., Williamstown, Mass., 1985—2006, chair dept. econs. and Ctr. for Devel. Econs., 1997—99, provost, John J. Gibson prof. econs., 1999—2006; pres. Vassar Coll., Poughkeepsie, NY, 2006—. Contbr. articles to profl. jours.; co-editor: Public Expenditure in Africa, 1996. Grantee, NSF, Coun. on Fgn. Rels., Am. Coun. Learned Socs. Avocation: golf. Office: Vassar Coll 124 Raymond Ave Poughkeepsie NY 12604*

HILL, CHARLES GRAHAM, JR., chemical engineering educator; b. Elmira, NY, July 28, 1937; s. Charles Graham and Ethel Mayburn (Pfleegor) H.; m. Katharine Mertice Koon, July 11, 1964; children: Elizabeth, Deborah, Cynthia. BS, MIT, 1959, MS, 1960, ScD, 1964. Asst. prof. MIT, Cambridge, 1964-65, U. Wis., Madison, 1967-71, assoc. prof., 1971-76, prof. chem. engring., 1976—, John T. and Magdalen L. Sobota prof. chem. engring., 1995—, prof. food sci., 1989—, chmn. dept. chem. engring., 1989-92. Cons. A.D. Little, Cambridge, 1964-65, Joseph Schlitz Brewing Co., Milw., 1973-76, Nat. Bur. Stds., 1979-95. Author: Introduction to Chemical Engineering Kinetics and Reactor Design, 1977; contbr. articles to profl. jours. Capt. U.S. Army, 1965-67. Gen. Motors Nat. scholar, 1955-59; NSF fellow, 1959-62, Ford Found. fellow, 1964-65, Fulbright Sr. fellow, 2000. Fellow AIChE; mem. Am. Chem. Soc., Inst. Food Technologists, Am. Oil Chemists Soc., Soc. Biological Engring, Sigma Xi, Tau Beta Pi, Phi Lambda Upsilon. Republican. Presbyterian. Office: U Wis Dept Chem Engring 1415 Engineering Dr Madison WI 53706-1607 Office Phone: 608-263-4593. Business E-Mail: hill@engr.wisc.edu.

HILL, CHRISTOPHER R., federal agency administrator, former ambassador; b. Little Compton, RI; m. Patty Hill; children: Clara, Amy, Nat. BA in Econs., Bowdoin Coll., Brunswick, Maine, 1974; MS, Naval War Coll., 1994. Vol. Peace Corps, Cameroon; contractor USAID; with Sr. Fgn. Svc., Class of Minister-Counselor; sr. country officer for Polish affairs US Dept. State, US amb. to Macedonia Skopje, 1996—99; spl. asst. to the Pres., sr. dir. S.E. European affairs NSC, Washington, 1999—2000; US amb. to Poland US Dept. State, Warsaw, 2000—04, US amb. to Republic of Korea Seoul, 2004—05, asst. sec. for E. Asian & Pacific Affairs Washington, 2005—. Spl. envoy to Kosovo US Dept. State, 1998—99, head, US delegation to Six-Party Talks on North Korean Nuclear Issue, 2005—. Recipient Robert S. Frasure award for Peace Negotiations, US Dept. State, Disting. Svc. award for Bosnian peace negotiations. Office: US Dept State Harry S Truman Bldg 2201 C St NW Rm 6205 Washington DC 20520

HILL, CHRYSTIE R., library and information scientist; b. Mar. 24; BS in Biology and Psychology, Pacific Lutheran U.; MA in History, Sarah Lawrence Coll., 1999; MS in Libr. and Info. Sci., U. Washington, Seattle, 2001. Reference asst. Sarah Lawrence Coll.; reference libr. Seattle Pub. Libr.; founder It Girl Consulting, 2001—; online cmty. mgr. WebJunction, 2003—. Lectr. in field. Contbr. articles to profl. publications. Named one of the Movers & Shakers, Libr. Jour., 2007. Mailing: WebJunction.org 1100 Dexter Ave North Seattle WA 98122 Office Phone: 206-851-5963. Personal E-mail: chrystiehill@gmail.com. Business E-Mail: chrystie@itgirlconsulting.com.

HILL, CLARA EDITH, psychologist, educator; b. Shivers, Miss., Sept. 13, 1948; d. Fletcher Von and Anna (Teich) H.; m. James Gormally, May 25, 1974; children: Kevin, Katherine. BA, So. Ill. U., 1970, MA, 1972, PhD, 1974. Lic. psychologist, Md. Asst. prof. dept. psychology U. Md., College Park, 1974-78, assoc. prof. dept. psychology, 1978-85, prof. dept. psychology, 85—. Author: Therapist Techniques and Client Outcomes, 1989, Working with Dreams in Psychotherapy, 1996, Helping Skills: Facilitating Exploration, Insight and Action 2d edit., 2004, Helping Skills: The Empirical Foundation, 2001, Dream Work in Therapy: Facilitating Exploration, Insight and Action, 2004; co-author (with K.M. O'Brien): Helping Skills: Facilitating Exploration, Insight and Action, 1999; co-author: (with L.G. Castonguay) Insight in Psychotherapy, 2007; editor: Jour. Counseling Psychology, 1994—99, Psychotherapy Rsch., 2004—. Recipient Outstanding Lifetime Achievement award, Soc. for Counseling Psychology, 2005; grantee, NIMH, 1983—92. Fellow APA (Leona Tyler divsn. 17 award 2002, Disting. Psychologist divsn. 29 award 2003); mem. Soc. Psychotherapy Rsch. (pres. N.Am. chpt. 1990, pres. internat. orgn. 1994-95, Disting. Rsch. Career award 2007), Assn. Study of Dreams, Soc. Exploration of Psychotherapy Integration. Avocations: reading, dining out, walking. Office: U Maryland Dept Psychology College Park MD 20742-0001 Business E-Mail: Hill@psyc.umd.edu.

HILL, DAVID, broadcast executive; b. Australia; V.p. of Sports Nine Network, Australia, 1977—88; head Eurosport, England, 1988—91, Sky Sports, England, 1991—93; pres. Fox Sports, Los Angeles, 1993—; CEO Fox Sports Network, 1996—; chmn., CEO Fox TV, 1996—. Office: Fox Sports PO Box 900 Beverly Hills CA 90213-0900 also: 575 Amalfi Dr Pacific Palisades CA 90272-4504

HILL, DAVID ALLAN, electrical engineer; b. Cleve., Apr. 21, 1942; s. Martin D. and Geraldine S. (Yoder) H.; m. Elaine C. Dempsey, July 9, 1971. BSEE, Ohio U., 1964, MSEE, 1966; PhD in Elec. Engring., Ohio State U., 1970. Vis. fellow Coop. Inst. for Rsch. Environ. Sci., Boulder, Colo., 1970-71; rsch engr. Inst. for Telecommunication Scis., Boulder, 1971-82; sr. scientist Nat. Inst. Stds. and Tech., Boulder, 1982—. Adj. prof. U. Colo., Boulder, 1980-. Editor Geosci. and Remote Sensing Jour., 1980-84, Antennas and Propagation Jour., 1986-89; contbr. over 150 articles to profl. jours., chpts. to books. Recipient award for best paper Electromagnetic Compatability Jour., 1987, 2003. Fellow IEEE (chpt. chmn. 1975-76, editor 1986-89); mem. Electromagnetic Soc. (bd. dirs. 1980-86), Internat. Union Radio Sci. (nat. com. 1986-89), Colo. Mountain Club (Boulder), Sierra Club. Office: Nat Inst Stds & Tech 813-02 325 Broadway St Boulder CO 80305-3337 Office Phone: 303-497-3472. Business E-Mail: dhill@boulder.nist.gov.

HILL, DAVID LAWRENCE, research corporation executive; b. Nov. 11, 1919; s. David Alexander and Mabel Clair (Brown) H.; m. Mary M. Shadow, Dec. 31, 1950 (dec. Jan. 1992); children: David A., Mary C., Robert L., John F., Cynthia A., Sandra E., James A. BS, Calif. Inst. Tech., 1942; PhD (Socony Vacuum Co. fellow), Princeton U., 1951. With U. Chgo. Metall. Lab. and Argonne Nat. Lab., 1942-46, assoc. physicist, group leader, 1944-46; assoc. prof. physics Vanderbilt U., Nashville, 1949-52, assoc. prof., 1952-54; staff mem. Los Alamos (N. Mex.) Sci. Lab., 1954-58, group leader theoretical nuclear physics, 1955-58, mgmt. cons., 1958-60; pres. Phys. Sci. Corp., Fairfield, Conn., 1960-62, Nanosecond Systems, Inc., Fairfield, Conn., 1963-72, Particle Measurements, Inc., Southport, Conn., 1965-81, Harbor Rsch. Corp., Southport, Conn., 1978—. Guest scholar Inst. Theoretical Physics, Copenhagen, summer 1950; cons. theoretical physics U, Calif., Los Alamos (N. Mex.) Sci. Lab., 1952-54; chmn. bd. Integrated Total Systems, Inc., Hingham, Mass, 1968-81; pres. Southport Computers, Inc., Conn., 1973-81, Valutron N.V., Netherlands Antilles, 1980—; pres. Patent Enforcement Fund, Inc., Southport, Conn., 1990—, Inventors' Def. Fund, Inc., 1996—; chmn. bd. dirs. Cassar Hill L.L.C., mgr., 1996—, Panatron Inc., Panama, 1999—, Safriton Inc., Panama, 1999—, Diamotron Inc., Panama, 2000—; lectr. in field; sci. adv. to Vice Presdl. nominee, Senator Estes Kefauver, 1956; incorporator, exec. v.p. dir. Los Alamos Investment Corp., 1956-58; cons. physicist in field. Contbr. articles to profl. jours. Adv. com. on sci. and tech. of Adv. Coun. of Dem. Nat. Com., 1959-61. Fellow Am. Phys. Soc., AAAS; mem. IEEE, Fedn. Am. Scientists (nat. chmn. 1953-54), Sigma Xi.

HILL, DAVID LAWRENCE, lawyer; b. Balt., Mar. 21, 1945; s. Albert Lawrence and Thelma Jane (Pierson) H.; m. Carol Lee Cato, Feb. 12, 1966 (div.); children: Dave Jr., Brian L., Martha J.; m. Pamela Ann Haddad, Mar. 02, 2000. AB, W.Va. U., 1969, MA, 1971; JD, Wake Forest U., 1974. Bar: N.C. 1974, U.S. Dist. Ct. (mid. dist.) N.C. 1974, W.Va. 1976, U.S. Dist. Ct. (so. dist.) W.Va. 1976, U.S. Supreme Ct., 2005. Pvt. practice, Winston-Salem, NC, 1974—75; hearing officer N.C. Bd. Alcohol Control, Raleigh, NC, 1975—78; pvt. practice Hurricane, W.Va., 1978—. Mem. mental hygiene com., 1986—; bar US Dist. Ct. (no. dist.) W.Va., 2003, US Supreme Ct., 2005. Mem. B'nai Brith. Mem. Masons, Shriners, Scottish Rite. Home: PO Box 506 Hurricane WV 25526-0506 Office: 210 Midland Trl Hurricane WV 25526 Office Phone: 304-562-2274.

HILL, DAVID R., federal agency administrator, lawyer; b. Mo., 1963; m. Kristina Hill; 3 children. BA with honors, U. Mo., 1985; JD, Northwestern U. Law clk. to Judge James K. Logan U.S. Ct. Appeals (10th cir.); assoc. counsel com. on agriculture U.S. Ho. of Reps., Washington; ptnr. Wiley, Rein, & Fielding, LLP, Washington, Blackwell Sanders Peper Martin, LLP, Kansas City, Mo.; dep. gen. counsel for energy policy US Dept. Energy, Washington, 2002—05, gen. counsel, 2005—. Office: US Dept Energy Forrestal Bldg 1000 Independence Ave SW Rm 6A 245 Washington DC 20585-1000 Office Phone: 202-586-5281. Office Fax: 202-586-1499. E-mail: david.r.hill@hq.doe.gov.

HILL, DAVID WARREN, lawyer; b. Taunton, Mass., May 27, 1946; s. Warren Witherell and Frances Robbins (Allen) H.; m. Jane Leslie Shields, June 14, 1969; children: Trevor Campbell, Ainsley Shields. BS in Engring., U.S. Mil. Acad., 1969; MSBA, Boston U., 1974; JD, George Washington U., 1977, LLM with highest honors, 1981. Bar: D.C. 1977, Va. 2003. Commd. 2d lt. U.S. Army, 1969, advanced through grades to maj., 1976, ret., 1990; tech. advisor U.S. Ct. Customs and Patent Appeals, Washington, 1976-77; assoc. Finnegan, Henderson, Farabow, Garrett & Dunner, Washington, 1977-83, ptnr., 1983—. Chmn. bd. 1st Ch. of Christ Scientist, Alexandria, Va., 1985, McLean, Va., 1993-94, 2d reader, 1998-2001; bd. dirs. Reps. Abroad, Tokyo, 1988; scoutmaster troop 51 Boy Scouts Am., Tokyo, 1988-89. Mem. Am. Intellectual Property Law Assn. (com. chmn. 1980-85, 95-97, 00-02, bd. dirs. 2005-06, treas. 2006-), Internat. Assn. Protection Intellectual Property US (exec. com. 2005-), Licensing Execs. Soc., U.S. Trademark Assn., Bar Assn. D.C. (coun. Patent Trademark Copyright sect. 1985-87), D.C. Bar Assn. (officer intellectual property law sect. 1985-86, 91-97), Va. State Bar (bd. govs. intellectual property sect. 2003—), Am. C. of C. in Japan (com chmn. 1987-89), Army and Navy Club, Tokyo Am. Club. Republican. Office: Finnegan Henderson Farabow Garrett & Dunner Two Freedom Sq 11955 Freedom Dr Reston VA 20190-5675 Home Phone: 703-847-0209; Office Phone: 571-203-2735. Business E-Mail: david.hill@finnegan.com.

HILL, DEBORA ELIZABETH, writer, journalist, screenwriter; b. San Francisco, July 10, 1961; d. Henry Peter and Madge Lillian (Ridgeway-Aarons) H. BA, Sonoma State U., Rohnert Park, Calif., 1983. Talk show host Rock Jour. Viacom, San Francisco, 1980-81; interviewer, biographer Harrap Ltd., London, 1986-87; editor North Bay Mag., Cotati, Calif., 1988; guest feature writer Argus Courier, Petaluma, Calif., 1993-95; concept developer BiblioBytes, Hoboken, NJ, 1994-95; feature writer The Econs. Press, 1996-97. Assoc. prodr. White Tiger Films, 1995—; concept developer Star Trek: Voyager and Star Trek: Deep Space Nine, 1997—98; mem. MedioCom, 2001—03; script cons. Shadowhawk Prodns., Ireland, 2003—06; founder with Jetta Cons. Lost Myth Ink Film Fund, 2007. Author: The San Francisco Rock Experience, 1979, CUTS from a San Francisco Rock Journal, 1982, Punk Retro, 1988, A Ghost Among Us, 2002, A Wizard By Any Other Name, 2004, (sequel) Jerome's Quest, 2003; author: (with Sandra Brandenburg) The Land of the Wand, 2006; author: The Crystal Chalice, 2007, numerous poems, short stories; co-writer, cons. prodr. The Danger Club; contbr.: Unconditional Love: Pet Tales By the Humans Who Love Them, 2004, Celebrations: Love Letters to my Mother, 2004; contbr. articles to profl. jours. Named Best Poet, Internat. Biographical Ctr., Cambridge, 2003. Mem.: FilmTies, ScriptNet, Film Industry Group. Democrat. Avocations: clothing design, cooking, internet, reading, interior decorating. Home and Office: Lost Myths Ink LLC 8312 Windmill Farms Dr Cotati CA 94931-4570 Office Phone: 707-792-7918. Personal E-mail: debhill@att.net.

HILL, DEBRA S., lawyer; b. Dennison, Ohio, Apr. 21, 1957; d. Richard A. and Shirley L. (Delcoma) Hill. BA, Kent State U., 1983, MA, 1986; JD, Case Western Reserve U., 1991. Bar: Ohio 1991, Fla. 1998. Gen. counsel Arthur Treachers, Inc., Jacksonville, 1994—97; vis. asst. prof. Fla. Costal Sch. of Law, Jacksonville, 1997—2001; shareholder Debra S. Hill, PA, Jacksonville, 2000; pres. Saculla Hill & Co., Inc., Jacksonville, 2001—02; mng. ptnr. Smith Hill Law Firm, Jacksonville, 2002—. Office: The Hill Law Firm 8834 Goodby's Executive Dr Jacksonville FL 32217 Office Phone: 904-346-0140. Business E-Mail: dhill@fdn.com.

HILL, DIANE LOUISE, educator; b. Niagara Falls, NY, June 10, 1951; d. Joseph A. and Margaret (Ditchkus) Heiman; m. James D. Hill, Sept. 27, 1975; children: Jennifer, Melanie. BS in Edn., Slippery Rock U., 1973; cert. in Chem. Tech., Brazosport Jr. Coll., 1978. Cert. elem. tchr., Pa., Tex. Spl. educator I Columbia Brazoria Ind. Sch. Dist., Tex., 1973-74; tchr. emotionally disturbed Brazosport Ind. Sch. Dist., Lake Jackson, Tex., 1974-78; dir., tchr. Creative Tchg., Lake Jackson, 1982—; chem. technician Dow Chem., Freeport, Tex., 1978-79; computer tech asst. bereavement program Meth. Hosp. Coordinator computer lab. Ney Elem. Sch., Lake Jackson, 1985-87. Coord. bereavement program Meth. Hosp.; voter registrar Brazoria County. Mem. Tex Computer Edn. Assn., Computer Using Educators, AAUW (dir. Sat. Morning enrichment 1987—, social newsletter 1984-86), Rotary Internat. Republican. Methodist. Home: 57 Oyster Creek Ct Lake Jackson TX 77566-4622

HILL, DONALD DEE, management consultant, educator, writer; b. Moultrie, Ga. s. Thomas Dee and Vivan Mae (Monk) H. BCE, Ga. Tech., Atlanta. Registered profl. engr., Ala., Ga. Structural engr. Patchen & Zimmerman Cons. Engrs., Augusta, Ga.; asst. dir. F.S.D. Am. Plywood Assn., Tacoma; mng. dir., CEO Internat. Gas Turbine Inst. Cons., lectr. to Czech Republic; lectr., Vietnam, 1997, Ctr. for Pvt. Enterprise, US Chamber; lectr. advanced mgmt. course for vis. Asian execs. Kennesaw State U.; lectr. and spkr. in field. Columnist Convene Mag. V.p. Letterman's Club; 1st lt. U.S. Army. Named Eagle of the Acropolis, Palais de Congres, Nice, France; named to Coll. of 17 Gentlemen, Netherlands Congress Bur.; named Ark. Traveler, Gov. of Ark.; recipient R. Tom Sawyer Gas Turbine award ASME, 1996. Mem.: Ga. Tech. Alumni Assn., Meeting Profls. Internat., Am. Soc. Assn. Execs., Kappa Sigma. Avocation: weightlifting. Home and Office: 5108 Parkside Dr Roswell GA 30075-7654

HILL, DONALD S., state commissioner; married; 2 children. BS cum laude, U. N.H., 1971; MBA, Plymouth State Coll., 1983. Acct. I, II, III N.H. Dept. Edn., Concord, 1971-76, bus. adminstr. III, 1976-82, chief of bus. mgmt., 1982-83; sr. bus. supr. N.H. Dept. of Adminstrv. Svcs., 1983-88, asst. commr., budget officer, 1988-96, commr., 1996—. Budget com. Town of Pembroke, N.H., 1981-87, town treas., 1981-84, bd. of selectman, 1972-81. Office: NH Adminstrv Svcs Dept State House Annex - Rm 120 25 Capitol St Concord NH 03301-6312

HILL, DRAPER, editorial cartoonist; b. Boston, July 1, 1935; s. L. Draper and Jean Hutchins (Thompson) H.; m. Sarah Randolph Adams, Apr. 22, 1967; children: Jennifer Randolph, Jonathan Draper. BA magna cum laude, Harvard U., 1957; postgrad, Slade Sch. Fine Arts, Univ. Coll., London, Eng., 1960-63. Reporter and cartoonist Quincy (Mass.) Patriot Ledger, 1957-60; editorial cartoonist Worcester (Mass.) Telegram, 1964-71, Comml. Appeal, Memphis, 1971-76, The Detroit News, 1976-99; contbg. cartoonist Oakland Press, Pontiac, Mich., 2003—04. Dir. Play of Month Guild, N.Y.C., 1958-82; instr. drawing Worcester Art Sch., 1967-71; lectr. Thomas Nast, Garibaldi, Beerbohm, Gillray, and others. Author: Mr. Gillray, The Caricaturist, 1965, Fashionable Contrasts, 1966, (with James Roper) The Decline and Fall of the Gibbon, 1974, The Satirical Etchings of James Gillray, 1976, (essay) Cartoons & Caricatures in Ency. of Collectibles, 1978, Political Asylum: Editorial Cartoons by Draper Hill, 1985; also catalogs; one-person shows include Art Gallery of Windsor (Ont.), 1985-86, Detroit Hist. Mus., 1996, Detroit Artists Market, 2005. Mem. Egyptians, Memphis, 1972—76, Club Odd Vols., Boston, 1965—2000; mem. adv. bd. Swann Found. for Caricature and Cartoon, NYC, 1980—93, 1998—. Winner Thomas Nast prize for editorial cartooning Landau-in-der-Pfalz, Fed. Republic Germany, 1990. Mem.: Witagemote Soc., Assn. Am. Editl. Cartoonists Notebook (2d v.p. 1972—74, 1st v.p. 1974—75, pres. 1975—76, author quar. column History Corner Assn. Notebook 1974—99), Prismatic Club. Home: 368 Washington Rd Grosse Pointe MI 48230-1616

HILL, (KARIM) DULÉ, actor, dancer; b. Orange, NJ, May 3, 1975; m. Nicole Lyn, July 10, 2004. Ed., Seton Hall U. Actor: (films) Sugar Hill, 1994, She's All That, 1999, Men of Honor, 2000, Holes, 2003, Sexual Life, 2005, Edmond, 2005, The Numbers, 2005, The Guardian, 2006; (TV films) The Ditchdigger's Daughters, 1997, Color of Justice, 1997, Love Songs, 1999, 10.5, 2004; (TV series) CityKids, 1993, The West Wing, 1999—2006, Psych, 2006; (Broadway plays) Bring in Da' Noise, Bring in Da' Funk, 1996; (plays, nat. tour) The Tap Dance Kid; (plays) Shenandoah,

Little Rascals, Black & Blue, Dutchman, 2007; guest appearance (TV series) NY Undercover, 1994, Cosby, 1996, Smart Guy, 1997, featured in Ebony Mag., 2007. Avocations: bowling, paint ball, Monopoly, tap dancing.*

HILL, EARL MCCOLL, lawyer; b. Bisbee, Ariz., June 12, 1926; s. Earl George and Jeanette (McColl) H.; m. Bea Dolan, Nov. 22, 1968 (dec. Aug. 1998); children: Arthur Charles, John Earl, Tamara Fegert. BA, U. Wash., 1960, JD, 1961. Bar: Nev. 1962, U.S. Ct. Claims 1978, U.S. Ct. Appeals (9th cir.) 1971, U.S. Supreme Ct. 1978. Law clk. Nev. Supreme Ct., Carson City, 1962; assoc. Gray, Horton & Hill, Reno, 1962-65, ptnr., 1965-73, Marshall Hill Cassas & de Lipkau (and predecessors), Reno, 1974—2005, Sherman & Howard, Denver, 1982-91; of counsel Parsons Behle & Latimer, Reno, 2006—. Judge pro tem Reno mcpl. ct., 1964—70; lectr. continuing legal edn.; mem. Nev. Commn. on Jud. Selection, 1977—84; trustee Rocky Mountain Mineral Law Found., 1976—, sec., 1987—88. Contbr. articles to profl. jours. Mem. ABA, State Bar Nev. (chmn. com on jud. adminstrn. 1971-77), Washoe County Bar Assn., Am. Judicature Soc., Lawyer Pilots Bar Assn., Soc. Mining Law Antiquarians (sec.-treas. 1975-2005), Prospectors Club. Office: 50 W Liberty St Ste 750 Reno NV 89501 Office Phone: 775-323-1601. Business E-Mail: ehill@parsonsbehle.com.

HILL, EDWIN D., trade association administrator; b. Center Township, Pa., Aug. 11, 1937; m. Rosemary Hill; children: Michele Hill , Toni Hill , Edwin Jr. Hill. Apprentice, wireman Local Union 712 Internat. Brotherhood Elec. Workers, Beaver, Pa.; pres., co-founder Internat. Brotherhood Elec. Workers Credit Union, 1964—70, bus. mgr., 1970—82; internat. rep. 3d Dist. Internat. Brotherhood Elec. Workers, 1992—94, v.p. 3d Dist., 1994—97, internat. sec. Washington, 1997, internat. sec.-treas., 1998, pres., 2001—. Treas., v.p., COPE chmn. Beaver County Building Trades Council, 1970—78; v.p., COPE chmn. Beaver County Central Labor Council, 1972—77; pres., Internat. Convention Internat. Brotherhood Electrical Workers, San Francisco, 2001; mem. exec. com. & council Penn. AFL-CIO, 1976—97; v.p., mem. exec. com. AFL-CIO; trustee Nat. Electrical Benefit Fund; sec. Nat. Electrical Annuity Fund. Active with March of Dimes, YMCA, United Way; adv. bd. Pa. State U., Geneva Coll.; dir. Beaver County Med. Ctr. Avocations: golf, skiing.*

HILL, ELIZABETH ANNE, academic administrator, lawyer; b. NYC, Dec. 29, 1942; d. Harry Gerald and Grace Marie (Byrne) H. BA, St. Joseph's Coll., Bklyn., 1964; MA, Columbia U., 1965; JD, St. John's Law Sch., Jamaica, NY, 1978. Bar: N.Y. 1979, U.S. Dist. Ct. (ea. dist.) N.Y. 1979; cert. tchr. English and social studies K-12, N.Y. HS tchr. Acad. St. Joseph, Brentwood, NY, 1967-70, Bishop Kearney HS, Bklyn., 1970-71; co-dir. formation program Sisters of St. Joseph, Brentwood, 1971-76; atty. Cath. Migration Office, Bklyn., 1978-80; exec. asst. to pres. St. Joseph's Coll., Bklyn., 1980-97, pres., 1997—. Mem. bd. dirs. LI Assn., Commn. Independent Colls. and Univs., Myrtle Ave. Revitalization Project, Bklyn. C.of C.; mem. bd. trustees LI Reg. Adv. coun. Higher Edn. Mem. Bishop's Commn. on Pub. Policy, Bklyn., 1978-81; mediator Diocesan Mediation and Arbitration Panel, Bklyn., 1981—; bd. dirs. Independence Cmty. Found., Fort Greene Strategic Neighborhood Action Partnership, Fair Media Coun.; trustee Mary Louis Acad. and Xaverian H.S. Mem. Nat. Assn. Coll. and Univ. Attys. Office: St Joseph's Coll 245 Clinton Ave Brooklyn NY 11205-3602 Business E-Mail: sehill@sjcny.edu.

HILL, EMITA BRADY, academic administrator, consultant; b. Balt., Jan. 31, 1936; d. Leo and Lucy McCormick (Jewett) Brady; children: Julie Beck, Christopher, Madeleine Vedel. BA, Cornell U., 1957; MA, Middlebury Coll., 1958; PhD, Harvard U., 1967. Instr. Harvard U., 1961-63; asst. prof. Western Reserve U., 1967-69; from asst. prof. to v.p. Lehman Coll. CUNY, Bronx, NY, 1970-91; chancellor, grad. faculty Ind. U., Kokomo, Ind., 1991-99, chancellor emerita, 1999—. Vis. advisor Salzburg Seminar Univs. Project; cons. in field. Trustee Am. U. in Central Asia; mem. Women's Forum of NY. Mem.: Internat. Assn. Univ. Pres., Phi Beta Kappa. Avocations: music, scuba diving, tennis.

HILL, FAITH, musician; b. Jackson, Miss., Sept. 21, 1967; d. Ted and Edna Perry; m. Daniel Hill, 1988 (div. 1991); m. Tim McGraw, Oct. 6, 1996; children: Gracie, Maggie, Audrey. Grad., McLaurin H.S. With Warner Bros. Records, 1993—. Musician: (albums) Take Me As I Am, 1993, It Matters To Me, 1995, Faith, 1998, Breathe, 1999 (Billboard Hot 100 Airplay Track of Yr., 2000, Am. Music Awards Favorite Country Album, 2001, Top Selling Album, Can. Country Music Assn., 2001, Grammy award for Best Country Album, 2001), Cry, 2002 (Best Female Country Vocal Performance Grammy, 2003, Hottest Female Video of Yr., Country Music TV Flameworthy Video Music Awards, 2003), Fireflies, 2005, Sunshine & Summertime, 2005, (songs) It's Your Love, 1997 (4 Acad. Country Music awards for Song of Yr., Single of Yr., Video of Yr., Vocal Event of Yr., 1998), This Kiss, 1998 (Video of Yr. award, Country Music Assn., 1998, Acad. Country Music, TNN/Music City News, 1999, Single of Yr., Acad. Country Music, 1999), Just to Hear You Say You Love Me, 1998 (Vocal Event of Yr., Acad. Country Music, Music City News, 1999, Music City News Song of Yr. award, 1999), Breathe, 1998 (Grammy award for Best Country Vocal Performance, 2001), (with Tim McGraw) Let's Make Love, 1998 (Grammy award for Best Country Collaboration with Vocals, 2001), Like We Never Loved at All, 2005 (Grammy award for Best Country Collaboration with Vocals, 2006); performer: (film soundtracks) Practical Magic, 1998, How the Grinch Stole Christmas, 2000, Pearl Harbor, 2001, (TV soundtracks) King of the Hill; actor: (films) The Stepford Wives, 2004. Founder Faith Hill Family Literacy Project, 1996. Recipient New Female Vocalist of Yr., Acad. Country Music, 1993, Female Vocalist of Yr., 1999, 2001, Top Country Female Artist, Billboard, 1994, Hot 100 Singles Female Artist of Yr., 2000, Female Star of Tomorrow, TNN/Music City News, 1995, Female Vocalist of Yr., 2000, TNN/CTM Country Weekly Music Awards, 2001, Female Country Artist of Yr., Country Weekly, 2000, Favorite Female Performer, People's Choice Awards, 2001—03, Favorite Female Country Artist, Am. Music Awards, 2001—03, 2006, Favorite Pop-Rock Female Artist, 2001, 5 Platinum awards, Can. Rec. Industry Assn., 2001, Best CountryVocal Performance, Best Country Album, & Best Country Collaboration with Vocals, Grammy awards, 2001, Best Country Collaboration With Vocals (with Tim McGraw), 2006. Office: c/o Creative Artists Agy 3310 West End Ave 5th Fl Nashville TN 37203

HILL, G. RICHARD, lawyer; b. Chapel Hill, NC, Oct. 22, 1951; BA magna cum laude, U. Minn., 1973, MA, 1975; JD, Yale U., 1978. Bar: Wash. 1978. Atty. McCullough Hill, Seattle. Adj. prof. law U. Wash., 1987-88; co-founder Pacific Real Estate Inst. Editor: Regulatory Taking: The Limits of Land Use Controls. Mem. ABA (mem. urban, state and local govt. law sect., chair 1995-96, mem. exec. com. 1992-95, chmn. land use planning and zoning com. 1990-92, co-chmn. subcom. hazardous waste and mcpl. liability 1984-86, chmn. subcom. on land use litigation and damages 1986-88). Office: McCullough Hill 701 Fifth Ave 7220 Seattle WA 98104 Office Phone: 206-812-3388. Business E-Mail: rich@mhseattle.com.

HILL, GARY D., lawyer; b. Eugene, Oreg., Apr. 7, 1952; s. Virgil R. and Doris C. Hill; m. Patricia L. Hill, July 10, 1976 (dec. Nov. 2002). BA, Linfield Coll., McMinnville, Oreg., 1974; JD, Northwestern Sch. of Law, Portland, 1981. Bar: Oreg. 1982. News anchor Sta.-KPTV, Portland, Oreg., 1976-92; pvt. practice Portland, Oreg., 1981-84, 88-92, Lake Oswego, Oreg., 2005—; atty. Hergert & Assocs., Oregon City, Oreg., 1992—2005. Vol. Oreg. Reps., Portland, 1996, Oreg. Dole-Kemp Presdl. campaign, 1996. Recipient Am. Juris Prudence award, Lawyers Coop. Pub. Co., 1981. Mem.: Oreg. Assn. Family Law Practitioners, Oreg. State Bar Assn. (mc. law related edn. com. 1996—97, chair-elect small firm and sole practitioner sect. 1997—98, chair 1998—99, juvenile and family law sect. 1992—, recognition for participation in CLE 1985, 1991). Avocations: golf, sailing, fishing. Office: 4248 Galewood Lake Oswego OR 97035 Business E-Mail: garydhill@garydhilllaw.com.

HILL, GEORGE JAMES, physician, educator; b. Cedar Rapids, Iowa, Oct. 7, 1932; s. Gerald Leslie and Essie Mae (Thompson) H.; m. Helene (Zimmermann), July 16, 1960; children: James Warren, David Hedgcock, Sarah, and Helena Rundall. BA, Yale U., 1953; MD, Harvard U., 1957; MA, Rutgers U., 1999; DLitt, Drew U., 2005. Intern N.Y. Hosp., 1957-58; fellow and resident in surgery Peter Bent Brigham Hosp. and Harvard Med. Sch., 1958-61, 63-66; clin. assoc. NIH, Bethesda, Md., 1961-63; instr. surgery U. Colo., 1966-67, asst. prof., 1967-72, asso. prof., 1972-73; prof. Washington Univ., 1973-76; prof., chmn. Marshall Univ., 1976-81; prof., dir. surg. oncology U. of Medicine and Dentistry of N.J., N.J. Med. Sch., Newark, 1981-96; adj. prof. surgery Uniformed Svcs. U. of Health Scis., Bethesda, Md., 1989—; Am. Cancer Soc. prof. clin. oncology U. Medicine and Dentistry N.J., N.J. Med. Sch., Newark, 1989-92; pres. faculty N.J. Med. Sch., Newark, 1991-92; interim pres. Sterling Coll., Craftsbury Common, Vt., 1996; prof. emeritus U. of Medicine and Dentistry of N.J. , N.J. Med. Sch., Newark, 1997—; rsch. coord. St. Barnabas Med. Ctr., Livingston, NJ, 1997-99. Adj. prof. history Kean U., Union, N.J., 2000-2001; hon. mem. med. sch. staff St. Barnabas Med. Ctr., 1999—; chmn. clin. cancer edn. com. Nat. Cancer Inst., 1978-80; vis. fellow in molecular biology, Princeton U., 1988; clin. prof. surgery Sch. Medicine Mt. Sinai U., 1999—. Author: Leprosy in Five Young Men, 1970, paperback edit., 1979; Outpatient Surgery, 1973, 3d edit., 1988; Clinical Oncology, 1977, Edison's Environment, 2007; contbg. 150 articles to med. journals. Active Nat. coun. Boy Scouts Am., 1968—2005, chmn. health career exploring com. Nat. coun., 1987—92; nat. dir. at large Am. Cancer Soc., 1989—96, mem. nat. exec. com., 1990—91, hon. life mem., 1996—, pres. W.Va. divsn., 1980—81; mem. NJ State Commn. on Cancer Rsch., 1983—84; pres. Tri State Area coun. Boy Scouts Am., Huntington, W.Va., 1980—82, v.p. Essex coun., 1983—89, commr. No. NJ coun., 1998, v.p. No. NJ coun., 2000—05; trustee Frost Valley YMCA, 1986—, NJ State Opera, 2004—, v.p., 2006—; pres. N.J. divsn. Am. Cancer Soc., 1987—89; pres. Hill Family Trust, 1989—; trustee Sterling Coll., Craftsbury Common, Vt., 1990—2002, sec., 1993—96, interim pres., 1996, emeritus trustee Craftsbury Common, Vt., 2003—; vestry Ch. of the Holy Innocents, 1994—96, 2002—05, warden, 2005—07. Capt. M.C. USNR, active duty USN, 1990—91, ret., 1992. Named Jerseyan of Week, Newark-Star Ledger, 1987, 1993; recipient Damon Runyon fellowship, 1957—58, Lederle Med. Faculty award, 1970, Civic Actions medal, Republic South Vietnam, 1972, Silver Beaver award, Boy Scouts Am., 1981, Nat. William Spurgeon III award, 1994, Silver Antelope award, 1998, Vigil honor, 2005, Disting. Eagle award, 2005, Am. Cancer Soc. Nat. Divisional award, St. George medal, 1992, Gorgas medal, Assn. Mil. Surgeons U.S., 1991, Outstanding Svc. medal, Uniformed Svcs. U. Health Scis., 1992, Meritorious Svc. medal, USN, 1993, N.J. Disting. Svc. medal, 2001. Fellow: Royal Soc. Medicine, Explorers Club; mem.: SAR (pres. N.J. Soc. 2001—02, nat. trustee 2002—03, trustee NJ state soc. 2004—, v.p. gen. 2005—06. Patriot medal 2003), ACS (com. on cancer 1987—93), AAUP (pres. chpt. 1988—89), NJ Med. Club (pres. 1999—2001), Med. Soc. NJ (chmn. com. cancer control 1985—94, sec. 1995—96), Essex County Med. Soc. (pres. 1995—96), Med. History Soc. NJ (v.p. 2000—02), Am. Assn. Cancer Rsch., Oncology Nursing Soc. (hon.), Am. Assn. Cancer Edn. (pres. 1985—86, Edwards medal 1994), Ctrl. Surg. Assn., Soc. Surg. Oncology (exec. coun. 1985—88), Soc. Univ. Surgeons, Acad. Medicine NJ (pres. 1992—93), Colonial Soc. Pa., Descs. of Founders of NJ (dep. gov. gen. 2006—), St. Nicholas Soc. NY, Huguenot Soc. Am., Naval Res. Assn. (v.p. 3d dist. 2004—06), Soc. Mayflower Descs. (gov. NJ state soc. 2007—), Order Founders and Patriots of Am. (gov. NJ state soc. 2005—07), Soc. Colonial Wars (gov. NJ state soc. 2006—), Soc. of the Cin., Soc. War of 1812, Order Crown Charlemagne, Welcome Soc. Pa., Harvard Club (NYC and Boston), Army and Navy Club, Ancient and Hon. Arty. Co. Mass., Alpha Omega Alpha, Sigma Xi (chpt. pres. 1986—87). Republican. Episcopalian. Address: 3 Silver Spring Rd West Orange NJ 07052-4317

HILL, GRANT, professional basketball player; b. Dallas, Oct. 5, 1972; s. Calvin and Janet Hill. BA in History, Duke U., Durham, NC, 1994. Forward Detroit Pistons, 1994—99, Orlando Magic, Fla., 2000—07, Phoenix Suns, 2007—. Mem. US Olympic Team, 1996. Named Co-Rookie of Yr., 1995, Rookie of Yr., The Sporting News, 1995; named to NBA All-Rookie First Team, 1995, Ea. Conf. All-Star Team, 1995—98, 2000—01, 2005, All-NBA First Team, 1997. Achievements include being a member of NCAA Champion Duke Blue Devils, 1991, 92. Avocation: African-Am. art collector. Mailing: Phoenix Suns 201 E Jefferson St Phoenix AZ 85004*

HILL, GREGORY PAUL, oil industry executive; b. Springfield, Ill, Mar. 2, 1961; s. James Isaac and Bonnie Lee (Ball) Hill; m. Sandra Lynne Lozano, May 17, 1986; 1 child, Justin Gregory. BSME, U. Wyo., Laramie, 1983. Divsn. engrng. mgr. Shell Calif. Prodn., Inc., Bakersfield, Calif., 1988-90; strategic planning mgr. Shell Oil Co., Houston, 1991-92; mgr. petroleum engrng. Shell Western E&P, Houston, 1992-93; area mgr. LA Basin Calresources, LLC, Bakersfield, 1994-95, v.p. oper., 1996, Aera Energy, LLC, Bakersfield, 1996—97; v.p. planning exec. strategy/affairs Shell Internat., London, 1998; sr. v.p. innovation and breakthrough performance Aera Energy LLC, Bakersfield, 1999, sr. oper. v.p., 1999—2002; CEO Enterprise/Shell, Shell Internat. E&P, London, 2002—03; v.p. prodn. Europe Shell E&P Internat., 2003—06, exec. v.p. Asia divsn., 2006—. Lobbyist Shell Oil Co., Calif., 1987; chmn. bd. dirs. Terrain Tech., LLC, 1999—2002; chmn. Enterprise Oil PLC, 2002—03. Mem.: Tau Beta Pi (treas. 1982—83), Pi Tau Sigma, Phi Kappa Phi. Republican. Roman Catholic. Avocations: mountain climbing, skiing, fishing, hunting, investing. Home: PO Box 4704 Houston TX 77210 Office: Shell EP Internat 83 Clemenceau Ave Singapore 239920 Office Phone: +65 6215 1240. Personal E-mail: gpslhill@aol.com. Business E-Mail: g.hill@shell.com.

HILL, HAROLD NELSON, JR., lawyer; b. Houston, Apr. 26, 1930; s. Harold Nelson and Emolyn Eloise (Geeslin) H.; m. Betty Jane Fell, Aug. 16, 1952; children: Douglas, Nancy. BS in Commerce, Washington and Lee U., Lexington, Va., 1952; PhD, Washington & Lee U., 1981; LL.B., Emory U., 1957, PhD, 1986. Bar: Ga. 1957. Assoc., then partner firm Gambrell, Harlan, Russell, Moye & Richardson, 1957-66; asst. atty. gen. Ga., 1966-68; exec. asst. atty. gen., 1968-72; partner firm Jones, Bird & Howell, 1972-74; assoc. justice Supreme Ct. Ga., 1975-82, chief justice, 1982-86; ptnr. Hurt, Richardson, Garner, Todd & Cadenhead, Atlanta, 1986-92, Judicial Resolutions Inc., Atlanta, 1993-94; of counsel Long, Aldridge & Norman, Atlanta, 1994-95. Author: History of the Supreme Court of Georgia, 1946-1996, 2005. Served with AUS, 1952-54. Fellow Am. Bar Found.; mem. Am. Law Inst., State Bar Ga., Lawyers Club Atlanta, Old War Horse Lawyers Club. Methodist.

HILL, HARRY HOFFMAN, JR., musician, educator; b. Atlanta, Jan. 11, 1956; s. Harry Hoffman and Pauline (Duncan) Hill; m. Karen Leigh Farah, Mar. 1, 1986; children: Stephen Michael, Gabriel Farah, Nathaniel Hoffman. MusB, Ga. State U., 1979; MusM, U. Mich., 1981; D in Musical Arts, U. S.C., 1999. Prin. clarinetist Asheville (S.C.) Symphony Orch., 1985—; prof. Limeston Coll., Gaffney, SC, 1985—. Mem. bd. overseers Master Works Festival, Winona Lake, Ind., 2000—. Founder, coord., clarinetist: Arbor Wind Trio, 1984—. Mem. exec. bd. Cherokee County/Limestone Coll. Arts Coun., Gaffney, 1995—; mem. Christian Performing Artists' Fellowship, Winona Lake, 1997—, bd. dirs., 2004—. Recipient Fullerton Found. Tchg. award, Fullterton Found./Limestone Coll., 1991, 1995, 1999. Mem.: Coll. Music Soc., Internat. Clarinet Assn. Avocations: bicycling, gardening, cooking, camping. Office: Limestone Coll 1115 College Dr Gaffney SC 29340 Office Phone: 864-488-4507.

HILL, HENRY ALLEN, physicist, researcher; b. Port Arthur, Tex., Nov. 25, 1933; s. Douglas and Florence Hill. BS, U. Houston, 1953; MS, U. Minn., 1956, PhD, 1957; MA (hon.), Wesleyan U., 1966. Research asst. U. Houston, 1952-53; teaching asst. U. Minn., 1953-54, research asst., 1954-57; research assoc. Princeton U., 1957-58, instr., then asst. prof., 1958-64; assoc. prof. Wesleyan U., Middletown, Conn., 1964-66, prof. physics, 1966-74, chmn. dept., 1969-71; prof. physics U. Ariz., Tucson, 1966-95, prof. emeritus, 1995—. Chmn. bd. Zetetic Inst., 1992—; researcher on nuclear physics, relativity, astrophysics, and optics. Contbr. articles to profl. jours. Sloan fellow, 1966-68 Fellow Am. Phys. Soc.; mem. AAAS, SPIE, Am. Astron. Soc., Optical Soc. Am., Am. Geophys. Union. Office: Zetetic Inst 1665 E 18th St Ste 206 Tucson AZ 85719-6809

HILL, HOWARD DARNELL, retired education educator, educational consultant; b. May 4, 1942; s. Howard Jr. and Della Mae (Williams) H.; m. Clemmie Faye Coulter, Dec. 24, 1963; children: Ray Darnell, Edith Renee (dec.). BA in Social Studies, Philander Smith Coll., 1964; MSE in Secondary Sch. Adminstrn., Ark. State U., 1968; PhD in Curriculum and Instrn., Kans. State U., 1973; postdoctoral study in ednl. adminstrn., U. SC, 1983—85. Secondary sch. tchr. Jonesboro Pub. Sch., Ark., 1964—66; supr. instrn. Marion Sch., 1966—69; asst. prin. West Memphis Schs., 1969—70; secondary sch. tchr. Tunica Pub. Sch., Miss., 1970—71; asst. prof. edn. U. Houston, 1973—77; assoc. prof. Miss. Valley State U., Itta Bena, 1977—78; prof., chmn., program coord. dept. edn. SC State U., Orangeburg, 1978—87; dir. chpt. programs Phi Delta Kappa Hdqs., Bloomington, Ind., 1987—97; dean Sch. Grad. Studies SC State U., 1997—98, dir. doctoral program, chair ednl. leadership/counselor edn., 1998—2001; v.p. acad. affairs Claflin U., Orangeburg, SC, 2001—05; pres., CEO, Assocs. in Edn., 2006—; loaned exec. S.C. United Way of the Midlands, 2006—07; vis. prof. edn. SC State U., 2007—. Columnist: newspaper The Times and Democrat; contbr. articles to profl. jours., chapters to books. Chmn. The Regional Med. Ctr. Found. Bush-Hewlett scholar Harvard U., 2002. Mem.: ASCD, SC Assn. Sch. Adminstrs., S.C. Assn. Sch. Adminstrs., S.C. Coun. Social Studies, Nat. Soc. Study of Edn., Nat. Assn. Secondary Sch. Prins., Assn. Tchr. Educators, Nat. Alliance Black Sch. Educators, Nat. Coun. Social Studies, Rotary (scholarship programs com. Dist. 7770 2000—07, pres. Orangeburg-Morning chpt. 2001—02, coord. vocat. awareness 2003—05), Orangeburg C. of C. (bd. dirs. 2000—02, v.p. 2001—02), Phi Delta Kappa. Home: 1186 Pruitt Dr NW Orangeburg SC 29118-4024 Office Phone: 803-534-5568. Business E-Mail: educationconsultant@sc.rr.com.

HILL, J. EDWARD, physician, educator; b. Omaha, Nebr., Feb. 2, 1938; m. Jean Hill; 2 children. MD, U. Miss., 1964. Diplomate Am. Bd. Family Practice. Intern Naval Hosp., 1964-65; assoc. prof. U. Miss. Med. Sch.; rsch. dir. North Miss. Med. Ctr., Tupelo, 1995—2001; pvt. practice. Dir. family practice residency program North Miss. Med. Ctr., med. dir. Pres. Miss. affiliate Am. Heart Assn.; adv. bd. Head Start Program; pres. Sch. Bd.; bd. dirs. local ch. Recipient Miss. Family Dr. of Yr. 1991, runner up Family Dr. of Yr. Good Housekeeping mag. 1977. Mem. AMA (bd. trustees 1996-2007, chair bd. trustees, 2002-2007, pres. bd. trustees 2005-2007, chair bd. com. on membership, fin. com., pres. AMA Found., AMA del. 1984), Miss. State Med. Assn. (former chmn. bd. trustees, pres.), Miss. Acad. of Family Physicians (former pres.), Am. Acad. of Family Physicians (alternate delegate, delegate), So. Med. Assn. (former pres.), World Med. Assn. (chair-elect, 2007, chair 2007-), C. of C. (chair indsl. devel. com.). Office: 1665 S Green St Tupelo MS 38804*

HILL, JAMES CLINKSCALES, federal judge; b. Darlington, SC, Jan. 8, 1924; s. Albert Michael and Alberta (Clinkscales) H.; m. Mary Cornelia Black, June 7, 1946; children: James Clinkscales, Albert Michael. BS in Commerce, U. S.C., 1948; JD, Emory U., 1948. Bar: Ga. 1948, U.S. Supreme Ct. 1969. Assoc. Gambrell, Russell, Killorin & Forbes, Atlanta, 1948—55, ptnr., 1955—63, Hurt, Hill & Richardson, Atlanta, 1963—74; judge US Dist. Ct. (no. dist.) Ga., 1974—76, US Ct. Appeals (5th cir.), Atlanta, 1976—81, US Ct. Appeals (11th cir.), Atlanta, 1981—89, sr. judge, 1989—. Past chmn. com. on appellate ednl. programs Fed. Jud. Ctr.; mem. com. on intercir. assignments Jud. Conf. U.S., 1990—. With USAF, 1943—45. Fellow: ACTL; mem.: ABA, Am. Judicature Soc., Atlanta Bar Assn., State Bar Ga., World Assn. Judges, Am. Law Inst., Am. Bar Found. (life), Old War Horse Lawyers, Lawyers Club Atlanta (life). Republican. Baptist. Office: US Ct Appeals 300 N Hogan St Jacksonville FL 32202-4259 also: Elbert P Tuttle US Ct Appeals Bldg 56 Forsyth St NW Atlanta GA 30303 E-mail: JCHretreat@aol.com.*

HILL, JAMES SCOTT, lawyer; b. Boston, Mar. 21, 1924; s. Benjamin B. and Dorothy (Scott) H.; m. Sally C. Foss, June 28, 1945; children: Richard B., Chessye F., Cynthia C., Michael O. BA magna cum laude, Williams Coll., 1947; JD, Columbia U., 1949. Bar: N.Y. 1949, N.J. 1958. Assoc. Baldwin, Todd & Lefferts, NYC, 1949-50; corp. sec., atty. Johnson & Johnson, NJ, 1950-66; v.p., sec., gen. counsel Celanese Corp., NYC, 1966-74; v.p., gen. counsel, dir. Liggett & Myers, Durham, NC, 1974-76; v.p. law and govt. affairs CBS Inc., NYC, 1976-78; group pres. law and regulatory affairs Am. Hosp. Supply Corp., Evanston, Ill., 1978-81; of counsel Shanley & Fisher, 1981-88, Smith, Stratton, Wise, Heher & Brennan, Princeton, NJ, 1988—. Judge Princeton (N.J.) Twp., 1959-65 Treas. N.J. Republican Fin. com., 1965-70; trustee John Seward Johnson Sr. Charitable Trusts, Princeton Med. Ctr., N.J. State Aquarium, Trinity Counselling Svc., Princeton, N.J.; chmn. Williams Coll. Devel. Coun.; chmn. Boyden Soc.-Deerfield Acad.; bd. dirs. Friends of Channel 13; mem. exec. com. Friends of the Inst. for Advanced Study, Princeton. Served to lt. USAAF, 1943-46. Fellow Am. Coll. Trust and Estate Counsel (mem. charitable planning and exempt orgn. com.); mem. Assn. Gen. Counsel, Met. Club (Washington), Princeton Club (N.Y.C.), Mid-Ocean Club (Bermuda), Bedens Brook Club (bd. govs. 1995—), Springdale Club, Nassau Club (trustee 1993-96), Jasna Polana Golf Club (Princeton), Chi Psi. Republican. Episcopalian (warden). Home: 155 Lambert Dr Princeton NJ 08540-2306 Office: care Smith Stratton 2 Research Way Princeton NJ 08540-6628 Office Phone: 609-987-6670. Office Fax: 609-987-6651. Business E-Mail: jhill@smithstratton.com.

HILL, J(AMES) TOMILSON, investment banker; b. Westbury, NY, May 24, 1948; s. James Tomilson Jr. and Dorothy H. (Kutcher) Hill; m. Janine A. Wolf, Feb. 2, 1980; children: Margot Langdon, Astrid Tomilson. BA, Harvard U., 1970, MBA, 1973. V.p. mergers and acquisitions 1st Boston Corp., NYC, 1973-79; sr. v.p. Smith Barney, Harris Upham & Co. Inc., NYC, 1979-82; mng. dir., dir. mergers and acquisitions, co-head investment banking divsn. Shearson Lehman Bros. Inc., NYC, 1982-90; vice-chmn., co-chief exec. officer Lehman Bros., NYC, 1990-93; bd. dirs. Shearson Lehman Bros. Holdings, Inc., co-pres., co-COO, 1993; co-COO Lehman Bros., 1993; co-CEO Shearson Lehman Bros., 1993, SLB Asset Mgmt., 1993; vice chmn., mem. investment and mgmt. com. Blackstone Grp., NYC, 1993—; pres., CEO Blackstone Alternative Asset Mgmt., 1995—. Bd. dirs. Allied Waste. Contbr. articles to profl. publs. Chmn. Hirshhorn Mus. and Sculpture Garden; vice chmn. Lincoln Ctr. Theater; bd. dirs. Milton Acad., Nightingale-Bamford Sch. Named one of 200 Top Collectors, ARTnews mag., 2003—06. Mem. Coun. Fgn. Rels. (chmn. investment subcom. of fin. and budget com.), Piping Rock Club, Meadow Brook Club, Links Club, River Club, Knickerbocker Club. Avocation:

Collector postwar Am. and European art. Office: Blackstone Group 345 Park Ave Ste New York NY 10154-0004 Home Phone: 212-734-9015; Office Phone: 212-583-5809. Business E-Mail: hill@blackstone.com.

HILL, JANET SWAN, library and information scientist, educator; BA in Geology, magna cum laude, Vassar Coll., 1967; MLS, Devner U., 1970. Intern Libr. of Congress, Washington, 1970—71, cataloger Geography and Map Divsn., 1971—75, head Cataloging Unit, Geography and Map Divsn., 1975—77; head Catalogue Dept. Northwestern U. Libr., Evanston, Ill., 1977—89; asst. dir. tech. services Univ. Libraries U. Colo., Boulder, 1989—90, 1990—. Manuscript cons. ALA Publishing, 1985—89; editl. bd. The Complete Libr. Policy Toolkit, 1995—97; manuscript referee Libr. Resources and Tech. Services, 1986—; adv. editor Libri: Internat. Jour. Libraries and Info. Services, 1995—; vis. lectr. Sch. Info. Studies U. Wis., Milwaukee, 2005. Mem. Joint Steering Com. Revision of Anglo-American Cataloging Rules, 1989—95. Recipient Meritorious Svc. award, Libr. of Congress, 1975, Ralph E. Ellsworth award for excellence in librarianship, U. Colo. Libraries, 1991, Best of CCQ award, Cataloging and Classification Quarterly, 2002. Mem.: Colo. Libr. Assn., Colo. Alliance of Rsch. Libraries, Assn. Libr. and Info. Sci. Edn., Maps and Geography Roundtable, Assn. Libr. Collections and Tech. Services, Allied Profl. Assn., ALA (mem. fin. and audit com. 2004—, mem. exec. bd. 2004—07, mem. strategic plan task force 2005—, hon. mem. task force 2005—, policy monitoring com. 2006, governing coun. 2007—), Beta Phi Mu. Office: Univ Colorado Libraries CB 184 1720 Pleasant St Boulder CO 80309 E-mail: janet.hill@colorado.edu.

HILL, JANINE, think-tank manager; m. J. Tomilson Hill, Feb. 2, 1980; 2 children. Assoc. Sullivan & Cromwell; v.p. corp. fin. dept. Salomon Bros.; asst. treas. Time, Inc.; dep. dir. studies adminstrn. Coun. Fgn. Rels., NYC. Mem. bd. Telluride Mountain Film; bd. advs. Duke U. Nasher Mus. Art; mem. bd. Am. friends Louvre. Named one of Top 200 Collectors, ARTnews mag., 2003—06. Mem.: Colony Club (gov.). Office: Coun Fgn Rels Harold Pratt House 58 E 68th St New York NY 10021 E-mail: jhill@cfr.org.

HILL, JERRY DEAN, secondary school educator; b. Stuart, Va., June 27, 1952; s. Walter Doyle and Doris Gracie Hill. AA in Liberal Arts, Bluefield Coll., 1972; BA in Religious Edn., Gardner-Webb U., 1974; MD in Christian Edn., So. Bapt. Theol. Sem., 1978. Ednl. dir. Martinez Bapt. Ch., Augusta, Ga., 1978—80; farmer Lawsonville, NC, 1980—84; tchr. Martinsville City Schs., Va., 1984—89; music dir. Bethany Christian Ch., Roanoke, Va., 1986—89; fine and performing arts chair Newport Sch., Kensington, Md., 1989—2001; tchr. Arlington (Va.) County Pub. Schs., 2001—04, Prince George's County Pub. Schs., Md., 2004—. Mem. accreditation teams Middle States & Assn. Ind. Md. Schs., 1996—2000; mem. profl. devel. com. Assn. Ind. Md. Schs., Md., 1997—2001; liaison Nat. Assn. Music Educators, Reston, Va., 2000. Avocations: piano, photography, travel. Office Phone: 703-619-0590. Personal E-mail: jdeanhill@aol.com.

HILL, JIMMIE DALE, retired federal agency administrator; b. Fort Worth, Tex., Dec. 28, 1933; s. William Haden and Myrtle Maude H.; m. Martha Lee Hoad, May 26, 1956; children: William, Loretta, Carol, Patricia. Student, DelMar Coll., 1955-57, U. Okla., 1957-58, U. Wichita, 1963-64. Enlisted in U.S. Air Force, 1951, advanced through grades to maj., 1974; comptroller for space systems acquisition Los Angeles, 1963-70; adv. CIA, 1970-73; ret., 1974; spl. asst. to undersec. Air Force, Washington, 1974-78; dir. Office of Space Systems, Dept. Air Force, 1978-82; dep. undersec. Air Force Space Systems, 1982-96; dep. dir. Nat. Reconnaissance Office, 1982-96. Scoutmaster Boy Scouts Am., 1971-76, Decorated Legion of Merit; recipient Disting. Civilian Svc. medal Dept. Def., 1974, 76, 87, 96, Presdl. Rank award of Meritorious Exec., 1980, 88, Presdl. Rank of Disting. Exec., 1981, 91, Air Force sr. exec. award, 1982-87, 89, 90, 92, 93, 94, 95, Air Force Exceptional Civilian Svc. award, 1987, 96, Nat. Intelligence Disting. Svc. medal, Ctrl. Intelligence Agy. Disting. Intelligence medal, Disting. Svc. medal NASA, Goddard Meml. Trophy, Nat. Space Club, 1996, Goddard Astronautics award AIAA, 1998. Mem. Air Force Assn., Am. Inst. Aeronautics and Astronautics. Methodist. Home: 7501 Browns Farm Rd Spotsylvania VA 22553 Personal E-mail: jimmiehill@aol.com. *Choose an occupation or profession because you like it, not for recognition and reward. For if you're happy in your work, with loyalty, dedication and hard work, ample recognition and reward will follow.*

HILL, JOHN ANDREW, protective services official; b. Allentown, Pa., Sept. 24, 1967; adopted s. Dennis McCann and Nancy Lou Hill, s. Theresa Marie Hill (Stepmother); m. Tami Sue Moyer, May 19, 1990; children: Kyle Anthony, Jami Nicole, Laura Beth. Parts counterman Rothrock Motor Sales, Allentown, Pa., 1987—88; sgt. Androscoggin County Sheriff's Office, Auburn, Pa., 1988—93; patrolman Allentown Police, 1993—2001, tactical team mem., sniper, 2001—03, patrol sgt., 2001—, k9 unit supr., handler, 2003—. Cpl. (e-4) USMC, 1990—91, Saudi Arabia, Kuwait. Decorated Combat Action Ribbon USMC, Kuwait Liberation medal Kuwait; recipient Achievement award, City of Allentown, 1996, 1998, Heroism award, 2005. Mem.: Internat. Police Work Dog Assoc., Nat. Tactical Officers Assoc., Pa. Police Work Dog Assoc., North Am. Police Work Dog Assoc., Fraternal Order Police, NRA (life), Am. Veterans, VFW, Marine Corps League. R-Consevative. Catholic. Avocations: boating, fishing, computers, working with dogs. Office: Allentown Police 425 Hamilton St Allentown PA 18101 Home Phone: 610-756-4141; Office Phone: 610-437-7753. Office Fax: 610-437-8721. Business E-Mail: hill@allentowncity.org.

HILL, JOHN H., federal agency administrator; m. Pepper Hill; 2 children. BA, Taylor U., 1973. With Ind. State Police, 1974—2003; comdr. Comml. Vehicle Enforcement Divisn., 1989—94, 2000—03, comdr. logistics divisn., 1988, field enforcement comdr., 1995—99; chief safety officer, asst. adminstr. Fed. Motor Carrier Safety Adminstrn., 2003, adminstr., 2006—. Mem. Comml. Vehicle Info. Sys. com., 1991; mem. various committees Comml. Vehicle Safety Alliance; mem. task force for identification security Am. Assn. Motor Vehicle Adminstrs., 2001—03, chmn. internat. law enforcement com. Office: Fed Motor Carrier Safety Adminstrn 400 7th St NW Washington DC 20590

HILL, JOHN HOWARD, retired lawyer; b. Pitts., Aug. 12, 1940; s. David Garrett and Eleanor Campbell (Musser) H. BA, Yale U., 1962, JD, 1965. Bar: Pa. 1965, US Dist. Ct. (we dist.) Pa. 1965, US Ct. Appeals (3d cir.) 1965, US Supreme Ct. 1982. Assoc. Reed, Smith, Shaw & McClay, Pitts., 1965-75, ptnr., 1975-90; of counsel Jackson Lewis LLP, Pitts., 1991—2004, ret., 2004. Bd. dirs. Travelers Aid Soc., Pitts., 1972-99, treas., 1982-87, pres., 1987-90; bd. dirs. Pitts. Opera, Pitts. Symphony Soc. Mem.: ABA, Allegheny County Bar Assn., Pa. Bar Assn., Pa. Soc., Fox Chapel Golf Club, Duquesne Club, Phi Gamma Delta. Republican. Presbyterian. Office: Jackson Lewis LLP One PPG Pl 28th Fl Pittsburgh PA 15222-5414 Personal E-mail: sedgewycke@aol.com.

HILL, JOHN SYLVESTER, allergist; b. Charleston, W.Va., 1948; MD, U. W.Va., 1974. Diplomate Am. Bd. Allergy and Immunology, Am. Bd. Internal Medicine. Intern Charleston (W.Va.) Area Med. Ctr., resident in internal medicine; fellow in allergy and immunology Virginia Mason Clinic, Seattle; now with St. Joseph Hosp., Lexington, Ky. Mem. Ky. Med. Assn. Office Phone: 606-276-1452.

HILL, JUDITH DEEGAN, retired lawyer; b. Chgo., Dec. 13, 1941; d. William James and Ida May (Scott) Deegan; children: Colette M., Cristina M. BA, Western Mich. U., 1960; cert., U. Paris, Sorbonne, 1962; JD, Marquette U., 1971; postgrad., Harvard U., 1984. Bar: Wis. 1971, Ill. 1973, Nev. 1976, DC 1979. Tchr. Kalamazoo Bd. Edn., Mich., 1960-62, Maple Heights Bd. Edn., Ohio, 1963-64, Shorewood Bd. Edn., Wis., 1964-68; corp. atty. Fort Howard Paper Co., Green Bay, Wis., 1971-72; sr. trust adminstr. Continental Ill. Nat. Bank & Trust, Chgo., 1972-76; atty. Morse, Foley & Wadsworth Law Firm, Las Vegas, 1976-77; dep. dist. atty., criminal prosecutor Clark County Dist. Atty., Las Vegas, 1977-83; atty. civil and criminal law Edward S. Coleman Profl. Law Corp., Las Vegas, 1983-84; pvt. practice law, 1989-99; ret., 1999; dep. city atty. criminal divsn. City of Las Vegas, 1984—89. Bd. dirs. YMCA, Highland Park, 1973-75, Planned Parenthood of So. Nev., 1977-78, Nev. Legal Svcs., Carson City, 1979-87, state chmn., 1984-87; bd. dirs. Clark County Legal Svcs., Las Vegas, 1980-87, St. Jude's Ranch for Children, 1999-2001; mem. Star Aux. for Handicapped Children, Las Vegas, 1986-96, Greater Las Vegas Women's League, 1987-88; jud. candidate Las Vegas Mcpl. Ct., 1987, New Symphony Guild, Variety Club Internat., 1992-93; mem. Nat. Conf. for Cmty. and Justice, So. Nev., 1998-2000; mentor in Clark County Sch., 1999-2005. Auto Splties. scholar, St. Joseph, Mich., 1957-60, St. Thomas More scholar Marquette U. Law Sch., Milw., 1968-69; juvenile law internship grantee Marquette U. Law Sch., 1970; named one of first 100 Women Attys. in the State of Nev., Oct. 1999. Children's Village Club (pres. 1980). Home: 3681 Mountcrest Dr Las Vegas NV 89121-4917 Office Phone: 702-384-2244. Home Fax: 702-384-2244.

HILL, KENNETH, demographer, educator; b. Reading, Eng., Oct. 22, 1945; s. Basil and Betty Hill; m. Althea Gibbins, June 8, 1968 (div. Aug. 15, 1998); children: Katherine Henning, Nicholas, Rosamund; m. Cynthia Stanton, Sept. 8, 2001. BA, Oxford U., Eng., 1967; PhD, London Sch. Hygiene and Tropical Medicine, 1974. Sr. rsch. assoc. NAS, Washington, 1977—86; prof. Johns Hopkins U., Balt., 1986—. Vis. prof. Harvard U., 2005—. Fellow rsch. grantee, NIH, 1988—. Mem.: Population Assn. Am. (bd. dirs. 1993—96). Office: Harvard Ctr for Population and Devel 9 Bow St Cambridge MA 02138 Home Phone: 301-741-5872; Office Phone: 617-496-6708. Office Fax: 617-495-8231. Business E-Mail: kenneth_hill@harvard.edu.

HILL, KENNETH CLYDE, clergyman; b. Kingsport, Tenn., Mar. 22, 1953; s. Hubert Clyde and Erma Lee (Harless) H.; m. Janet Reynolds, Oct. 15, 1976; children: Matthew Joseph, Timothy Aaron, Lydia Rebekah. BS in Speech, History, East Tenn. State U., 1974; MS in Speech, Ind. State U., 1976; BA in Bibl. Studies, Bapt. Christian Coll., 1986; M. Religious Edn., Manahath Sch. Theology, 1989; D in Religious Edn., Andersonville Bapt. Sem., 2001. Ordained to ministry Evang. Meth. Ch., 1982. Pulpit supply various ch. congregations, Ind., 1976—82; pastor Crestwood Bapt. Ch., Ft. Wayne, Ind., 1980-81; pres., CEO Appalachian Ednl. Comm. Corp., Bristol, Tenn., 1981—; deacon Evang. Meth. Ch., Kingsport, Tenn., 1982-86, elder, 1986—; chmn. Publs. Bd. of the Evang. Meth. Ch., Kingsport, 1986—; sec. Gen. Conf. Evang. Meth. Ch., Kingsport, 1990—; gen. dir. Siloam Internat., Inc., 1990—96, 2004—; v.p. Southwest Radio Ch. of the Air, Inc., 1993—; pastor Lakeview Bible Chapel, Kingsport, 1993-96; pres., CEO Info. Comm. Corp., Bristol, 1996—; pastor Morrison City Mission Ch., Kingsport, 1999—2007. Trustee Graham Bible Coll., 1982-85; gen. dir. Mission Field Task Force, Santiago, Chile, 1991, 93, 95-96, 98, 2000, 05; bd. dirs. Bancroft Gospel Ministry, Kingsport, Tenn., v.p. 2006—; bd. dirs. Manahath Sch. Theology, Max Meadows, Va., sec., 2002—; chmn. Servant Ministries, Kingsport, 1990-91; mem. Mission Field Task Force, Blantyre, Malawi, 1989. Author: (with Ronald Cooke) Reconstructionism: Is It Scriptural, 1989; (with Keith Walsworth) What's Next? 1993; (with others) Why I Still Believe We Live in the Last Days—Nuclear Proliferation, 1993; (with Joan B. Collins) Constitution in Crisis, 1994; (with Bill Usselton) Constitution Conspiracy, 1994; (with Jim Nicholls) Reflections on the Fairness Doctrine, 1994; (with Jose Holoway and N.W. Hutchings) International Christian Broadcasting from South America, 1995, Prayers Jabez Did Not Pray, 2002; editor: A Classic Christmas, 1995; prodr. (video) The Temple Mount, 1993, Petra in History and Prophecy, 1993, The Revived Roman Empire, 1993, 25 Messianic Signs, 1993, Prayers Jabez Didn't Pray, 2002, Studies in Jude, 2005; prodr., writer (video) Jude, 2006; contbr. articles to profl. jours. Disaster vol. ARC, 1986-92; bd. dirs. Radio Reading Svcs. Corp., Kingsport, 1989-90; vol. World Reach, Inc., Honduras, 1986-91; vol. task force Honduras, 1991—, radio project Somotillo, Nicaragua, 2002; chmn. Sister Cmty. Project, Blountville, Tenn., 2006—. Mem. Va. Assn. Broadcasters (bd. dirs. 2004—), Delta Sigma Rho, Tau Kappa Alpha. Home: Ste 100 340 Martin Luther King Jr Blvd Bristol TN 37620 Office: Appalachian Ednl Comm Corp PO Box 2061 Bristol TN 37621-2061 Home Phone: 423-292-5880. Business E-Mail: kchill@aecc.org.

HILL, KENT RICHMOND, federal agency administrator; b. Nampa, Idaho, May 24, 1949; s. Double E. and Helen Louise (Robertson) H.; m. Janice Elaine Hurn, June 12, 1972; children: Jennifer Lynn, Jonathan Kent. BA in History, N.W. Nazarene Coll., 1971; diploma for basic Russian lang., Def. Lang. inst., 1972; postgrad., Georgetown U., 1973-74; MA in Russian and East European Studies, U. Wash., 1976, PhD in History, 1980. Tchg. asst. in history N.W. Nazarene Coll., Nampa, Idaho, 1969-71; Russian translator US Army, 1972-74; tchg. asst. in history of Christianity U. Wash., Seattle, 1980, asst. prof. history, 1980-85; assoc. prof. history Seattle Pacific U., 1985-86; pres. Inst. on Religion and Democracy, Washington, 1986-92, Ea. Nazarene Coll., Quincy, Mass., 1992—2001; asst. adminstr. bur. for Europe and Eurasia US Agy. Internat. Devel., Washington, 2001—05, asst. adminstr. for global health, 2005—. Interviews, speaker, presenter in field. Author: The Puzzle of the Soviet Church: An Inside Look at Christianity and Glasnost, 1989, Turbulent Times for the Soviet Church, 1991, The Soviet Union on the Brink, 1991; contbr. articles to profl. publs. Bd. dirs. Peter Deyneka Russian Ministries, 1991-2001, Keston Coll., 1985-2001; mem. nat. exec. bd. World Without War Coun., Berkeley, Calif., 1986-2001; bd. advisors Inst. on Religion and Democracy, 1984-86, bd. dirs., 1993-2001; mem. ch. bd. 1st Ch. of Nazarene, Seattle, 1980-85; bd. trustees Russian-Am. Christian U., Moscow, 1998-2000; bd. dirs. Quincy Hist. Soc., 1997-2000. Named Alumnus of Yr., N.W. Nazarene Coll., 1988, to Presdl. Leadership list John Templeton Found., 1999; presented with Key to City, Mayor of City of Nampa, 1983; named Prof. of Yr. Seattle Pacific U., 1986; grantee Seattle Pacific U., 1981-82, 82-83, 84, 85, U. Wash., 1979-80; Nat. Def. Fgn. Lang. fellowship, 1976-77, Earhart fellow Internat. Rsch. and Exchs. fellow, 1978; recipient Pushkin award for Outstanding Scholarship, Def. Lang. Inst., 1972. Office: US Agy Internat Devel 1300 Pennsylvania Ave NW Rm 306-004 Washington DC 20523 Home Phone: 703-978-5289; Office Phone: 202-712-0790. Business E-Mail: khill@usaid.gov.

HILL, LABAN CARRICK, writer; b. 1960; Tchr. Columbia U., Baruch Coll., St. Michaels' Coll., Vt. Author: Bugged Out!, 1997, Watch Out for Room 13, 1997, The Evil Pen Pal, 1998, Welcome to Horror Hospital, 1998, Xtreme Mystery Series, 1999, A Reader's Companion to Jonathan Franzen's The Corrections, 2002, Contemporary Poetry of New England, 2003, Spy Survival Handbook, 2004, Harlem Stomp! A Cultural History of the Harlem Renaissance, 2004 (Nat. Book Award finalist, 2004), Casa Azul, 2005. Personal E-mail: labanhill@yahoo.com.

HILL, LARKIN PAYNE, jewelry designer, manufacturer; b. Oct. 30, 1954; d. Max Lloyd and Jane Olivia (Evatt) H. Student, Coll. Charleston, SC, 1972—73, U. N.C., Chapel Hill, 1973. Lic. real estate broker, N.C. Sec., property mgr. Max L. Hill Co., Inc., Charleston, S.C., 1973-75, sec., data processor, 1979-82, v.p. adminstrn., 1982—, Mt. Pleasant, SC, 2004—; ops. mgr. Shorline Internat. Real Estate, 2003—04; pres., jewelry designer and mfr. Pearl, LLC, 2004—. Resident mgr. Carolina Apts., Carrboro, N.C., 1975-77; sales assoc., Realtor, Southland Assocs., Chapel Hill, N.C., 1977-78; jewelry designer Pearl, LLC, pres.; cons. specifications com. Charleston Trident Multiple Listing Service, 1985. Bd. dirs. Charleston Area Arts Coun., 1992-93; co-chair Beaux Arts Ball, Sch. Arts. Mem. Royal Oak Found., Scottish Soc. Charleston (bd. dirs. 1989-91), Preservation Soc., Charleston Computer Users Group, N.C. Assn. Realtors, Spoleto Festival USA (chmn. auction catalog com. 1990-92). Republican. Methodist. Avocations: reading, crossword puzzles, American Staffordshire Terriers. Home: 7 Riverside Dr Charleston SC 29403-3217 Office: Max L Hill Co INc 824 Johnnie Dodds Blvd Mount Pleasant SC 29464 also: Pearl LLC PO Box 22813 Charleston SC 29413 Office Phone: 843-853-3947. Business E-Mail: info@pearlllc.com.

HILL, LEWIS REUBEN, horticulturist, nursery owner, writer; b. Greensboro, Vt., July 1, 1924; s. Alvah Aaron and Grace Gibson (Towle) H.; m. Nancy May Davis, May 4, 1969. High sch. grad., Greensboro, Vt. Owner, mgr. Hillcrest Nursery, Greensboro, 1947-82, Vermont Daylilies, Greensboro, 1982-93, Berryhill Nursery, Greensboro, 1993—. Author: Fruits and Berries for the Home Garden, 1977, Pruning Simplified, 1979, Cold Climate Gardening, 1981, Secrets of Plant Propagation, 1985, Yankee Summer, 2000; co-author (with Nancy Hill): Country Living, 1987, Successful Perennial Gardening, 1988, Christmas Trees, 1989, Fetched Up Yankee, 1990, Daylilies, The Perfect Perennial, 1991, Bulbs-Four Seasons of Beautiful Blooms, 1994, Pruning Made Easy, 1997, Lawns, Grasses & Groundcovers, 1995, The Lawn and Garden Owners Manual, 2000, The Flower Gardener's Bible, 2003; (with others) Berries, 1991, Vines, 1992, Wise Garden Encyclopedia, 1997, 1990 edit., Vermont Voices, 1991, others; contbr. articles to popular mags. Del. State Rep. Conv. twice; various town offices and coms. Recipient Disting. Svc. award Vt. Edn. Assn., 1967, Gov's Commn. on Children and Youth, Montpelier, Vt., 1970; 4-H citation Nat. Extension Svc., Washington, 1974; cert. of appreciation Ea. Nurserymen's Assn., Montpelier, 1982; Lit. Excellence award Greensboro Libr., 1990, Vt. Horticulture Achievement award Vt. Profl. Horticulturists, 1993, Quill and Trowel award Garden Writers of Am., 1995. Mem. League Vt. Writers, Vt. Profl. Horticulturists (bd. dirs., pres.),Internat. Ribes Assn. Mem. United Ch. Avocations: photography, skiing, motorcycling, nature. Home and Office: Hillcrest Farm 353 Hillcrest Rd Greensboro VT 05841 Personal E-mail: hillnl@localnet.com. *Nancy and I think having a goal, and always keeping it in mind, is important, whether it is developing a new plant or a book.*

HILL, LLOYD LESTER, food service executive; b. Nacagdoches, Tex., Jan. 8, 1944; s. Lloyd Lester and Ruby (Murchison) Hill; m. Carol Ann London, Dec. 20, 1964; children: Ronald Lloyd, Brandt Lloyd; m. Sue Ann Staggs, June 25, 1978; 1 child, Joshua Lloyd. Student psychology, N. Tex. State U., 1962—65; student, U. Tex., 1965—67, Columbia U., 1980; MBA, Rockhurst Coll., 1985. Dist. sales mgr. Marion Health and Safety div. Marion Labs., Dallas and Los Angeles, 1969—74, regional sales mgr. Chgo., 1974—76, mgr. new bus. devel. Kansas City, 1976—77, dir. sales, 1977—79; regional mgr. Norton SPD, Cranston, RI, 1979—80; sr. v.p. Kimberly Services Inc., Kansas City, 1980—88, dir., 1982—88; exec. v.p., bd. dirs. Kimberly Quality Care, 1988—91, pres., 1991-94; exec. v.p., COO Applebee's Internat. Inc., Overland Pk., Kans., 1994, co-CEO, 1997, CEO, 1998—2006, chmn., 2000—, also bd. dirs., 1989—. Named one of America's Best CEOs, Institutional Investor mag., 2005. Republican. Methodist. Office: Applebees Internat Inc 4551 W 107th St Ste 100 Overland Park KS 66207-4037 Fax: 913-341-1694.

HILL, LORIE ELIZABETH, psychotherapist; b. Buffalo, Oct. 21, 1946; d. Graham and Elizabeth Helen (Salm) H. Student, U. Manchester, Eng., 1966-67; BA, Grinnell Coll., 1968; MA, U. Wis., 1970, Calif. State U., Sonoma, 1974; PhD, Wright Inst., 1980. Instr. English U. Mo., 1970-71; adminstr., supr. Antioch-West and Ctr. for Ind. Living, San Francisco, Berkeley, 1975-77; dir. tng. Ctr. for Edn. and Mental Health, San Francisco, 1977-80, exec. dir., 1980-81; pvt. practice Berkeley and Oakland, Calif., 1976—; instr. master's program in psychology John F. Kennedy U., Orinda, Calif., 1985, 94—. Founder group of psychotherapists against racism; spkr. on cross-cultural psychology; creater Jump Start, a violence prevention and unlearning racism program for youth; trainer for trainers 3rd Internat. Conf. Conflict Resolution, St. Petersburg, Russia; sr. facilitator Color of Fear. Organizer against nuc. war; founding mem. Psychotherapists for Social Responsibility; psychologist Big Bros. and Big Sisters of the East Bay, 1986—88; vol. instr. City of Oakland Youth Skills Devel. Program; founder, dir. Providing Alternatives to Violence; creator Jump-Start program; active Rainbow Coalition for Jesse Jackson's Presdl. Campaign, Ron Dellums Re-election Com.; campaigner for Clinton-Gore; co-founder Wellstone Progressive Dem. Club, 2003, East Bay Votes!. Mem. Calif. Psychol. Assn. (chair pub. interest divsn. 1997, Helen Margulies Mehr Pub. Svc. award 1996, chair social issues 1996—, Silver Psi award 1999), Wellstone Dem. Renewal Club (co-founder), East Bay Votes (co-founder). Democrat-Socialist. Avocations: sports, travel, music, reading. Office: 2955 Shattuck Ave Berkeley CA 94705-1808 Office Phone: 510-644-0922, 510-486-8088. Personal E-mail: loriepav@aol.com.

HILL, LOUIS ALLEN, JR., retired dean, civil engineer, consultant; b. Okemah, Okla., May 18, 1927; s. Louis Allen and Gladys Adelia (Dietrich) Hill Wise; m. Jeanne Rose Murray, June 14, 1951; children: Dawn, David, Dixon. BA, Okla. State U., 1949, BSC.E., 1954, MSC.E., 1955; PhD, Case Inst. Tech., 1965. Registered profl. engr., Okla., Ariz. Engr. Lee Hendricks Engring., Tulsa, 1955-57, Hudgins, Thompson, Ball & Assocs., Oklahoma City, 1957-58; asst. prof. civil engring. Ariz. State U., 1958-66, assoc. prof., 1966-70, prof., 1970-74, chmn. dept. civil engring., 1974-81; dean Coll. Engring. U. Akron, 1981-88, assoc. v.p. rsch. and grad. studies, 1988. Chmn. Ohio Engring. Dean's Council, 1983-85; trustee Engring. Found. of Ohio, 1985-88; staff engr. Salt River Project, Ariz., 1962; cons. in field. Author: Fundamentals of Structures, 1975, Compendium of Structural Aids, 1975, Structured Programming in Fortran, 1981; contbr. numerous articles to profl. jours.; designer numerous bridges, hwys. Ch. leader-tchr. 1st Bapt. Ch., 1971-88, Scottsdale Presbyn. Ch., 1990—. Served to capt. C.E., U.S. Army, 1945-47, 51-53, The Philippines, Japan. Recipient Disting. award Akron Coun. Engring. and Sci. Socs., 1987, commendation Minorities in Mainstream Tech. Com., 1990, Disting. Svc. award U. Akron Coll. Engring., 1994; named Educator of Yr., Inroads N.E. Ohio, Inc., 1986, Sr. Svc. award Presbytery of Grand Canyon, 2001; Louis A. Hill Jr. Ann. Faculty award established and endowed in his honor Qua Tech., 1987, Louis A. Hill Jr. scholarship established in his honor Minorities in Mainstream Tech. Com., 2004, Mayor Plusquellic proclaimed April 23, 1997 as Dr. Louis A. Hill Day in City of Akron; fellow Continental Oil Co., 1955, faculty fellow NSF, 1963. Fellow ASCE (life); mem. NSPE (sec., profl. engr. in edn. 1986-88), Am. Soc. Engring. Edn. (life, Western Electric Fund award 1967), Sigma Xi, Tau Beta Pi, Omicron Delta Kappa. Republican. Home and Office: 3208 N 81st Pl Scottsdale AZ 85251-5800

HILL, LOWELL DEAN, agricultural marketing educator; b. Delta, Iowa, Apr. 27, 1930; s. Frederick Carl and Harriet Jane (Atwood) H.; m. Betty Elaine Carpenter, Dec. 9, 1951; children: Rebecca Elaine, Brent Howard. BS in Agrl. Edn., Iowa State U., 1951; MS in Agrl. Econs., Mich. State U., 1961, PhD in Agrl. Econs., 1963. Asst. prof., then assoc. prof. dept. agrl. econs. U. Ill., Urbana, 1963-72, prof., 1972-77, L.J. Norton prof. agrl. mktg., 1977-98, L.J. Norton prof. emeritus, 1998—. Cons. Office Tech. Assessment, Washington, 1986-88, South Am. and Europe, 1995, FAO, Rome, 1978-80, U.S. AID, 1983, World Bank, Washington, 1989-90, 92-93, Argentina, Colombia, Chile, 1989-94, U.S. Feed Grains Coun., Venezuela, Japan, Korea, 1990-93, USDA, Russia, 1993-96; mem. adv.

com. Fed. Grain Inspection Svc., USDA, 2000-2003. Author: Grain Grades and Standards: Historical Issues, 1990; editor: Role of Government in a Market Economy, 1982, Corn Quality in World Markets, 1985. Cpl. U.S. Army, 1952-54. Fellow East West Ctr.; recipient Quality of Comm. award, 1980, 88, Disting. Policy Contbr. award 1988, Extension Programs award, 1989, Disting. Svc. award USDA, 1989, Internat. Mktg. Support award Am. Soybean Assn., 1989, Faculty award for rsch. excellence, 1991; Univ. scholar, 1992. Fellow: Am. Agrl. Econ. Assn.; mem.: Coun. Agrl. Sci. and Tech. (chmn. 1989—90). Office Phone: 217-328-2361. E-mail: l-hill3@uiuc.edu.

HILL, LUTHER LYONS, JR., lawyer; b. Des Moines, Aug. 21, 1922; s. Luther Lyons and Mary (Hippee) H.; m. Sara S. Carpenter, Aug. 12, 1950; children— Luther Lyons III, Mark Lyons. BA, Williams Coll., 1947; LLB, Harvard U., 1950; LLD (hon.), Simpson Coll., 1979. Bar: Iowa 1951. Law clk. to Justice Hugo L. Black U.S. Supreme Ct., 1950-51; assoc., ptnr. Henry & Henry, Des Moines, 1951-69; mem. legal staff Equitable Life Ins. Co. of Iowa, 1952-87, exec. v.p., 1969-87, gen. counsel, 1970-87; of counsel Nyemaster, Goode, McLaughlin, Voigts, Wiest, Hansell O'Brien, Des Moines, 1992—. Counsel, adminstr. Iowa Life and Health Ins. Guaranty Assn. Bd. dirs., past pres. United Cmty. Svcs. Greater Des Moines; past trustee, past chmn. Simpson Coll., Indianola, Iowa. Capt. M.I., AUS, WWII, ETO. Mem. ABA, Iowa Bar Assn., Polk County Bar Assn., Assn. Life Ins. Counsel, Des Moines Club, Wakonda Club. Republican. Avocation: mountain climbing. Office: Ste 1600 700 Walnut St Des Moines IA 50309-3800

HILL, MARK C., lawyer; b. Marshall, Tex., Aug. 25, 1951; s. James E. and Gussie L. (Chastain) H.; m. Kathryn Jane Kilgore, June 14, 1975; children: James K., Elizabeth W., John T. BBA, Tex. Christian U., 1973; JD, U. Tex., 1976. Bar: Tex. 1976, U.S. Dist. Ct. (no., ea. and we. dists.) Tex., U.S. Dist. Ct. (ea. dist.) Okla., U.S. Dist. Ct. Nebr., U.S. Ct. Appeals (5th, 10th and 14th cirs.), Temporary Emergency Ct. Appeals, U.S. Tax Ct., U.S. Supreme Ct. Atty., ptnr. Cantey & Hanger, Ft. Worth, 1976-84; ptnr. in charge Haynes & Boone, Ft. Worth, 1984-97, mem. mgmt. com., 1984-92; sr. v.p., corp. sec., gen. counsel Tandy Corp. (now RadioShack), Ft. Worth, 1997—98; gen. coun., corp. sec., RadioShack Corp., 1997—2006, sr. v.p., 1998—2006, chief adminstrv. officer, 2003—06, chief corp. devel. officer, 2005—06. Chmn. Tarrant County CSC, Ft. Worth, 1988-90. Named Outstanding Young Leader Ft. Worth C. of C., 1986; recipient Honarary State FFA Degree Tex. Future Farmers Am., 1987. Fellow Tex. Bar Found.; mem. ABA, Tarrant County Bar Assn. (dir. 1986-88), Internat. Assn. Def. Counsel, Am. Soc. Corp. Secs., Am. Corp. Counsel Assn., Sigma Alpha Epsilon. Presbyterian.

HILL, MARTHA N., dean, community health nurse; b. Boston, July 14, 1943; d. Paul Lawrence Norton and Margaret M. Hagerty; m. Gary S. Hill, June 18, 1966; children: Paul, Justin. Diploma, Johns Hopkins Hosp., Balt., 1964; BSN, The Johns Hopkins U., 1966, PhD, 1987; MSN, U. Pa., 1977. From instr. to assoc. prof. Johns Hopkins Hosp. Sch. Nursing, Balt.; nurse specialist in hypertension Hosp. of U. Pa., Phila.; dean Johns Hopkins Univ. Sch. of Nursing, Balt., 2002—. Contbr. articles to profl. jours. Recipient Malcolm Alderfer Schweiker award, 1985, Ruth B. Freeman award 1987; fellow Am. Acad. Nursing, 1989. Mem. ANA (rep. to NIH high blood press coord. com.), Am. Heart Assn. (vice chmn. coun. cardiovasc. nursing 1989-91, pres. 1997-98), Inst. of Medicine.

HILL, MARY C., hydrologist; b. Balt., Aug. 18, 1955; d. William E. and Ruth Jane Hill; m. J. Dungan Smith, Mar. 17, 1990; stepchildren: Wray C. Smith, Kirsten R. Smith, Martha H. Smith. AB, Hope Coll., 1976; MSE, Princeton U., 1979, PhD, 1985. Lectr. Rutgers U., New Brunswick, N.J., 1981, U. Colo., Boulder, 2000; rsch. asst. Princeton U., 1977-81; hydrologist opers. profl. U.S. Geol. Survey, Trenton, N.J., 1981-87, rsch. hydrologist Lakewood, Colo., 1987-97, Boulder, Colo., 1997—. Adj. faculty Colo. Sch. of Mines, Golden, 1989—, U. Colo., Boulder, 1994—; coord./tchr. Internat. Groundwater Modeling Assn., U.S. Geol. Survey, 1983—. Author: (computer program) MODFLOWP, 1992, UCODE, 1998, 2005, MODFLOW, 2000, 2005, (book) Effective Groundwater Model Calibration, 2006; contbr. articles to profl. jours. Grantee Yucca Mountain Project, U.S. Geol. Survey, DOE, 1995—, Superior Svc. award, 1997, Meritorious Svc. award, 2006. Fellow Geol. Soc. Am.; mem. ASCE (Walter L. Huber rsch. prize 2000), Am. Geophys. Union, Nat. Ground Water Assn. (Darcy lectr. 2001, M. King Hubbert award, 2005), Internat. Assn. Hydrological Sci. (pres. internat. commn. groundwater, 2005-). Achievements include rsch. in the use of numerical models and data in the simulation of groundwater systems. Office: US Geol Survey 3215 Marine St Boulder CO 80303-1066 Business E-Mail: mchill@usgs.gov.

HILL, MELVIN JAMES, retired oil industry executive; b. Santa Ana, Calif., May 19, 1919; s. Albert Frederick and Alice Lucile (Moody) H.; m. Daphne G. Langston, Mar. 1, 1947; children: Patricia Michalek, Candace A. AB, U. Calif., Berkeley, 1941. With Western Gulf Oil Co., Calif., 1941-56, Gulf Rsch. & Devel. Co., Harmarville, Pa., 1956-63, Gulf Oil Corp., Pitts., 1963-75, v.p., 1971-74, sr. v.p., 1974-75, exec. v.p., 1981-84; ret., 1984; pres. Gulf Energy and Minerals Co.-Internat., Houston, 1975-78, Gulf Exploration & Prodn. Co., Pa., 1978-81. Mem. Am. Petroleum Inst., Am. Assn. Petroleum Geologists, Am. Inst. Profl. Geologists, Geol. Soc. Am., Soc. Exploration Geophysicists, Am. Geophys. Union. Home: 970 Aurora Ave Apt F201 Boulder CO 80302 E-mail: hill.melvin@comcast.net.

HILL, MILLICENT E., English educator; b. Nashville, Mar. 23, 1940; d. Jeremiah W. and Mildred Moore; m. Ezekiel H. Hill Jr. (div.); children: Caroll E. Hill-Goldsmith, David E. BA, Fisk U., 1962; postgrad., U. So. Calif., 1990. Cert. tchr. Calif. Englisht chr. L.A. Unified Sch. Dist., 1966—99; dir. edn. Huio St. Enterprises Inc., LA, 1999—2000; acad. advisor Unity T.W.O. Satellite House, LA, 1999—. Author: (anthology) Timothy & Friends, 1999, Love Letters in Silence, 2000. Founder Martin Luther King Jr. Mus., LA, 1986—99. Named one of Tchrs. Who Make A Difference, John Walsh Show, 2002; recipient Tchr. of Yr. award, NAACP, 1989, Outstanding Svc. award, Mayor Richard Riordan, 1999, Congresswoman Maxine Waters, 1999, Proven Achievers award, Channel 5 News, KJLH, 2003. Avocations: singing, piano, poetry, reading. Home: 755 E 92d St Los Angeles CA 90002 Office: Mama Hill's Help Inc 755 E 92d St Los Angeles CA 90002 Office Phone: 323-969-6910. Office Fax: 323-305-1661. E-mail: hllmllcnt@aol.com.

HILL, MILTON KING, JR., retired lawyer; b. Balt., Nov. 29, 1926; s. Milton King and Mary Fusselbaugh (Hall) H.; m. Agnes Ciotti, June 11, 1949; children: Thomas Michael, Milton King, III, Susan Hill. BS in Bus. and Pub. Adminstrn., U. Md., 1950, JD, 1952. Bar: Md. 1952, U.S. Dist. Ct. Md. 1952, U.S. Ct. Appeals (4th cir.) 1952. Assoc. Smith, Somerville & Case, Balt., 1952-55, ptnr., 1955-90; ret. Mem. faculty Md. Hosp. Ednl. Inst. Served with USAF, 1944-46. Fellow Am. Coll. Trial Lawyers, Internat. Soc. Barristers; mem. Md. State Bar Assn., Md. Bar Assn., Nat. Conf. Commrs. Uniform State Laws (pres. 1981-83, chmn. model punitive damages act drafting com.), Assn. Def. Trial Counsel (pres. 1964-65), Internat. Assn. Ins. Counsel, ABA (ho. of dels. 1981-83), Md. Bar Found., Am. Acad. Hosp. Attys. Clubs: Potapskut Sailing Assn., Wednesday Law. Home: 8810 Walther Blvd Apt 2329 Parkville MD 21234-5762 E-mail: khill2329@comcast.net.

HILL, NED CROMAR, dean, finance educator, consultant; b. Salt Lake City, Dec. 18, 1945; s. Richard G. Sharp and Bettie (Cromar) Hill; m. Claralyn Martin, Nov. 26, 1968; children: Evan M., Jonathan C., Aaron R., Joseph B., Alison. Student, Brigham Young U., 1967; BS in chemistry, U. Utah, 1969; MS in chemistry, Cornell U., Ithaca, NY, 1971, PhD in fin., 1976. Cert. cash mgr. Asst. prof. fin. Cornell U., 1976-77, Ind. U., Bloomington, 1977-81, assoc. prof. fin., 1981-87; Joel C. Peterson prof. fin. Brigham Young U., Provo, Utah, 1987-96, asst. to pres., 1996-98, dean, Marriot Chair Bus. Mgmt., Marriott Sch. Mgmt., 1998—. Cons. Hill Fin. Assocs., Bloomington, 1978—; bd. dirs. Beneficial Life Ins. Co., Morgan Stanley Bank, Pete Suazo Bus. Ctr. Author: Essentials in Cash Management, 1984, Short-Term Financial Management, 1987; co-founder Jour. Cash Mgmt., 1981, EDI Forum: Jour. Electronic Commerce, 1987. Mem. Utah Info. Tech. Commn., 1993-97; stake pres. Ch. Jesus Christ of the Latter Day Saints, 1982-87, 2000—05; fin. v.p. Boy Scouts Hoosier Trails Council, Bloomington, 1980-86. With US Army, 1971—72. Named Outstanding Faculty Mem., Marriott Sch. Mgmt., Brigham Young U., 1992. Mem. Fin. Mgmt. Assn. (bd. dirs. 1986-88), Phi Beta Kappa, Phi Kappa Phi. Republican. Avocations: vocal music, birding. Office: Brigham Young U Marriott Sch of Mgmt 730 TNRB Provo UT 84602 Home Phone: 801-375-2417; Office Phone: 801-422-4122. Business E-Mail: ned_hill@byu.edu.*

HILL, NICHOLAS S., physician, researcher; b. Troy, NY, Dec. 27, 1949; s. Nicholas Snowden Hill, IV and Barbara Charlotte (Seim) Hill; m. Sophia P. Paraskos, Aug. 16, 1975; children: Kyra A., Alyssa N. AB, Harvard U., Cambridge, Mass., 1967—71; MD, Dartmouth Med. U., Hanover, NH, 1971—75. Diplomate in internal medicine, pulmonary and critical care Am. Bd. Internal Medicine. Resident in internal medicine Tufts-New Eng. Med. Ctr., Boston, 1975—77; sr. med. resident Boston VA Hosp., 1978; fellow in cardiovasc. medicine U. Mass. Med. Ctr., Worcester, 1979; fellow in pulmonary medicine Boston U., 1979—82; staff physician divsn. pulmonary critical care and sleep medicine RI Hosp., Providence, 1987—2002; chief divsn. pulmonary, critical care and sleep medicine Tufts-New Eng. Med. Ctr., Boston, 2002—. Author: (books) Pulmonary Hypertension Therapy, 2006; editor: Long-term Mechanical Ventilation, 2001, Ventilator Strategies in Critical Care, 2001, Noninvasive Ventilation, Principles and Practice; mem. editl. bd.: Am. Jour. Respiratory Critical Care Medicine, 1994—97, 2000—06, assoc. editor: Chest, 2005—. Recipient Henry Chadwick medal, Mass. Thoracic Soc., 2006, Disting. Scholar in Critical Care Medicine, Am. Coll. Chest Physicians, 2002; Parker B. Francis Fellow award, PFB Found., 1983. Fellow: Am. Coll. Chest Physicians (chair home care network 2002—04); mem.: Am. Physiology Soc., Mass. Thoracic Soc. (councilor Boston chpt. 1983—87), Am. Thoracic Soc. (mem. planning com. 2002—06). Achievements include research in evaluating clinical applcations of noninvasive ventilation; clinical applications of pulmonary hypertension therapies. Avocation: triathlons. Home: 120 Farm Rd Sherborn MA 01770 Office: Tufts-New England Med Ctr 750 Washington St #257 Boston MA 02111 Home Phone: 508-655-0484; Office Phone: 617-636-4288. Office Fax: 617-636-5953. Business E-Mail: nhill@tufts-nemc.org.

HILL, PATRICIA FRANCINE, information technology executive, educator; b. Buffalo, Jan. 9, 1955; d. Walter W. and M. Phyllis (Jones) H. BA in Math., Swarthmore Coll., 1977, BS in Engring., 1977; MS in Computer Engring., U. Mich., 1980; MBA, Harvard U., 1990. Tech. staff AT&T Bells Labs., Middletown, NJ, 1980-86; sr. systems analyst Internat. MarketNet (IMNET), NYC, 1986, Marine Midland Bank, NYC, 1987-88; sr. bus. cons. Kraft Gen. Foods, Skokie, Ill., 1990—92; dir. support svcs. Hyatt Hotel Corp., Chgo., 1993-94; mng. prin. Oracle Corp., 1995-96; cons. Ameritech, Chgo., 1996—2003; analyst Motorola Corp., Ill., 2003—04, Talk Am., 2004—. Cons. McDonald's Corp., Oakbrook, Ill., 1992-93; lectr. in field. Active various charitable orgns. Mem. Nat. Assn. Negro Bus. and Profl. Women, Nat. Tech. Assn. Democrat. Mem. Ch. of Christ. Avocation: athletics.

HILL, PHILIP BONNER, lawyer; b. Charleston, W.Va., May 1, 1931; AB, Princeton U., 1952; LLB, W.Va. U., 1957. Bar: W.Va. 1957, Iowa 1965. Assoc. Dayton, Campbell & Love, Charleston, 1957—61; ptnr. Porter, Hill, Thomas, Williams & Hubbard, Charleston, 1961—65; v.p. Thomas & Hill, Charleston, 1961—65; assoc. counsel Equitable Life Ins. Co. of Iowa, Des Moines, 1965—68, counsel, 1968—75; ptnr. Riemenschneider, Hanes & Hill, Des Moines, 1975—79, Austin & Gaudineer, Des Moines, 1979—82, Snyder & Hassig, Sistersville and New Martinsville, W.Va., 1982—96, of counsel, 1997—99, Bowles Rice McDavid Graff & Love, LLP, Martinsburg, W.Va., 2000—. Mem. staff W.Va. Law Rev., 1955-57; contbr. articles to profl. jours. Lt. USNR, 1952—54. Fellow W.Va. Bar Found.; mem. ABA (exec. coun. young lawyers sect. 1966-67), W.Va. State Bar (chmn. jr. bar sect. 1961-62, bd. govs. 1989-92), W.Va. Bar Assn. (pres. 1998-99), Iowa State Bar Assn., Assn. Life Ins. Counsel, Am. Judicature Soc., Phi Delta Phi. Office: Bowles Rice McDavid Graff & Love LLP PO Drawer 1419 101 S Queen St Martinsburg WV 25402-1419 Home Phone: 304-876-6227; Office Phone: 304-263-0836. Business E-Mail: phill@bowlesrice.com.

HILL, RAYMOND JOSEPH, packaging company executive; b. Chanute, Kans., May 4, 1935; s. Raymond Joseph and Emma Leona (Arthurs) Hill; m. Bettie Anne Handshumaker, Mar. 2, 1957; children: David, Dianne, Todd, Scott, Jennifer. A in Engring., Coffeyville Coll., Kans., 1955; MBA, U. Denver, 1977. Field engr. Phillips Petroleum Co., Bartlesville, Okla., 1957—59; design engr. Thiokol Chem. Corp., Brigham City, Utah, 1959—60; tech. supr. Hercules Chem. Corp., Salt Lake City, 1960—68; project mgr. aerospace div. Ball Corp., Boulder, Colo., 1968—70, plant mgr. and v.p. mfg. metal container div. Findlay, Ohio and Denver, Colo., 1970—78, pres. agrl. systems div. Westminster, Colo., 1978—85, 1990—93; exec. v.p. food plastics N.Am.; pres. Chesnee Assocs., Inc., Internat. Cons., 1993—97; exec. v.p. The PopStraw Co., also bd. dirs.; bd. dirs. Navaho Agrl. Products Industries, United Energy Devel., Packaging Adv. Coun., Flex Packing Assn., The Hallmark Group, Packaging Ptnrs., Classic Signatures, Inc., PopStraw Co.; mem. policy adv. com. to Office of U.S. Trade Rep., 1980—. Mem.: Irrigation Assn., Soc. Tool Engrs., Nat. Food Processors Assn., Am. Ordnance Assn., Rotary. Republican. Episcopalian. Home: 889 Turnbridge Cir Naperville IL 60540-8342 Office: Chesnee Assocs Inc 2010 E Algonquin Rd Ste 210 Schaumburg IL 60173-4168

HILL, RICHARD (RICK) ALLAN, former congressman; b. Grand Rapids, Minn., Dec. 30, 1946; m. Betti Christie, June 10, 1983; children: Todd, Corey, Mike. BA in Econs. and Polit. Sci., St. Cloud State U., 1968; JD, Concord U. Sch. Law, 2005. Surety bonding businessman, owner InsureWest, 1968-90; real estate and investment ptnr., 1983—; committeeman State Rep. Party, 1990-94; legis. liaison to Gov. Marc Racicot, Mont., 1993; mem. 105th-106th Congress from Mont. dist. U.S. Ho. Reps., Washington, 1997-2001, mem. banking and fin. svcs. com., mem. resources com., mem. small bus. com. Fin. chair State Rep. Party, 1989-91, state chair, 1991-92. Bd. dirs. Mont. Sci. and Tech. Alliance, 1992, Blue Cross Blue Shield Mont., 2003-. Republican. Home: PO Box 4717 Helena MT 59604-4717

HILL, RICHARD DEVEREUX, retired banker; b. Salem, Mass., Nov. 6, 1919; s. Robert W. and Grace (Dennis) H.; m. Polly Bergstedt, Sept. 13, 1947; children: Steven D., Johanna Hill Simpson, Richard Devereux. AB, Dartmouth Coll., Hanover, NH, 1941; MCS, Amos Tuck Sch. Adminstrn. and Finance, Hanover, NH, 1942; postgrad. in banking, Rutgers U., New Brunswick, NJ, 1951; LLD (hon.), Babson Coll., Babson Park, Mass., Northeastern U., Boston, Salem State Coll., Mass.; D in Bus. Adminstrn. (hon.), Boston Coll., Tufts U., Medford, Mass. With The First Nat. Bank of Boston, 1946-84, loan officer, 1948-51, asst. v.p., 1951-55, v.p., 1955-65, exec. v.p., 1965-66, pres., 1966-71, chmn. bd., chief exec., 1971-83, chmn. exec. com., 1983-84, chmn. bd., chief exec. officer, 1971-83, Bank of Boston Corp., 1971-83, chmn. exec. com., 1983-84. Pres. fed. adv. coun. Fed. Res. System, 1977; chmn. Inst. Internat. Fin. Inc., 1983-86. Former chmn. transp. com. New Eng. Coun.; mem. vis. com. Sloan Sch. Mgmt., MIT, 1967-70; mem. Greater Boston adv. bd. Salvation Army; mem. bd. visitors Fletcher Sch. Internat. Law and Diplomacy, 1980—2002; trustee Dartmouth Coll., 1973-83, chmn. trustees 1981-83, trustee emeritus, former mem. investment com.; pres. emeritus, hon. trustee Mus. Fine Arts, Boston; former trustee Boston Urban Found.; hon. mem. Corp. Woods Hole Oceanographic Instn.; former overseer Crotched Mountain Found.; former chmn. Bus. Coun. for Internat. Understanding. Advanced through ranks to lt. comdr. USNR, 1942—48. Named New Englander of Yr. New England Coun., 2007; recipient Acad. Disting. Bostonians award Greater Boston C. of C., Christian A. Herter award World Affairs Coun., Lifetime Achievement award Boston Coll., 2005; received letter of commendation from Bureau of Ordnance. Mem. Internat. Monetary Conf. (hon.; past pres.), Transp. Assn. Am. (bd. dirs., past chmn. investor panel), Assn. Res. City Bankers (hon.; past pres.), Am. Inst. Banking (adv. com. Boston chpt. 1967-82), Dartmouth Alumni Assn. Boston (past v.p.), New Eng. Exeter Alumni Assn. (past pres.), Mass. Hist. Soc., Masons, Comml. Club (Boston), Eastern Yacht Club (Marblehead), Royal Bermuda Yacht Club, Riddell's Bay Golf and Country Club (Bermuda), Coral Beach and Tennis Club (Bermuda), Sigma Nu. Republican. Congregationalist. Home: Sargent Rd Marblehead MA 01945 Office: 100 Federal St Boston MA 02110-1802 Address: Fox Hill Village Westwood MA 02090 Office Phone: 617-434-2180. Personal E-mail: rdhill00@comcast.net.

HILL, RICHARD EARL, academic administrator; b. Clintonville, Wis., Mar. 30, 1929; s. Lyle Earl and Gladness Josephine (Love) H.; m. Marilyn Jean Thompson, June 5, 1951; children: Mark R., Kenneth L., Richard Earl, Joy A., Sarah J. BA, Carroll Coll., Waukesha, Wis., 1951, L.H.D., 1974; M.Div., McCormick Theol. Sem., 1956. Ordained to ministry Presbyterian Ch., 1956; pastor chs. in Wis., 1955-62; pastor Frame Meml. Presbyn. Ch., Stevens Point, Wis.; also univ. pastor U. Wis., Stevens Point, 1962-69; asst. to pres. Carroll Coll., 1969-74; pres. Huron (S.D.) Coll., 1974-77, Lakeland Coll., Sheboygan, Wis., 1977-89, pres. emeritus, 1991—, chancellor, 1989-91. Pres. S.D. Fedn. Pvt. Colls., 1977; exec. com. Colls. Mid-Am., 1975-77; mem. 6th Congl. Dist. Acad. Selection Com., 1978-89; v.p. Wis. Found. Ind. Colls., 1983-85, pres., 1985-86. Mem. Am. Assn. Colls., Council Advancement and Support Small Colls., Council Advancement and Support Edn., Wis. Assn. Ind. Colls. and Univs. (pres. 1980-83), Am. Mgmt. Assn., Sheboygan Econ. Club (pres. 1985), Pi Kappa Delta, Pi Gamma Mu. Clubs: Rotary. Address: 23033 Westchester Blvd Apt C-404 Port Charlotte FL 33980 Home Phone: 941-624-6452.

HILL, RICHARD LEE, lawyer; b. Spanish Fork, Utah, May 17, 1951; s. Von and Maxine (Chambers) H.; m. Kathryn Smith, July 10, 1980; children: Natalie Kathryn, Nicole Charlene, Kristina Michelle, Kara Alexandra, Alexis Marie. BS cum laude, Brigham Young U., Hawaii, 1976; JD, Brigham Young U., 1979. Bar: Utah 1979, U.S. Dist. Ct. (cen. dist.) Utah 1979, U.S. Supreme Ct. 1979. Ptnr. Parker, McKeown, McConkie, Salt Lake City, 1979-82, Hill, Johnson, Schmutz, Provo, Utah, 1982—. Mem. Utah Arts Coun., 1994—97; bd. dirs. Provo Theatre Co., 1987—. Mem. Utah Bar Assn., Riverside Country Club. Mem. Lds Ch. Avocation: acting. Office: Hill Johnson & Schmutz 4844 N 300 W Provo UT 84604 Home Phone: 801-224-1122; Office Phone: 801-375-6600. Business E-Mail: rlhill@hjslaw.com.

HILL, RICHARD S., manufacturing executive; BSE, U. Ill., 1974; MBA, Syracuse U., 1981. With GE, Motorola, Hughes Aircraft; v.p., gen. mgr. oscilloscope group Tektronix, Inc., 1990—91, pres., test & measurement group, 1991—93; CEO Novellus Systems, Inc., San Jose, Calif., 1993—, chmn., 1996—. Mem.: bd. dirs., Novellus Systems, Inc., 2003-. Office: Novellus Systems Inc 4000 N First St San Jose CA 95134*

HILL, RONALD CHARLES, surgeon, educator; b. Parkersburg, W.Va., Sept. 4, 1948; s. Lloyd E. and Margaret (Pepper) H.; m. Lenora Jane Rexrode, June 12, 1971; children: Jeffrey, Mandy. BA with honors, W.Va. U., 1970, MD, 1974. Diplomate Am. Bd. Surgery, Am. Bd. Thoracic Surgery. Surg. intern Duke U. Med. Ctr., Durham, NC, 1974—75; resident in surgery Duke U., Durham, NC, 1974—85, rsch. assoc., 1976—79, tchg. scholar, 1984—85; asst. prof. surgery W.Va. U., Morgantown, 1985—90, assoc. prof., 1990—96, prof. surgery, 1996—2007, clin. prof. surgery Sch. Osteopathic Medicine, 1999—2007. Cons. VA Med. Ctr., Clarksburg, W.Va., 1985—2007; dir. surg. rsch. dept. surgery W.Va. U., 1986—88, student coord. dept. surgery, 1986—97; mem. adh hoc com. merit rev. bd. for cardiovasc. studies VA, Washington, 1988—90; mem. Surg. Edn. and Self-Assessment Programs; chmn. instnl. rev. bd. Protection Human Subjects, 1994—2004, program dir. dept. surgery, 1998—2003, dir., thoracic surgery program, 2005—07. Contbr., co-contbr. numerous book chpts. and articles to profl. publs. Mem.-at-large adminstrv. bd. Drummond Chapel United Meth. Ch., Morgantown, 1987—89, 1993—95, fin. com., 1994—96, lay del. to ann. conf., 1995—97, chmn. coun. on evangelism, 1999—2001. Named Outstanding Attending Surgeon, 1998—99; recipient Lange Med. Book award, 1971, 1973, 1974, Roche Med. award, 1972, Merck Med. Book award, 1974, Sowers award, Founders Soc. Duke U., 1992, Disting. Svc. award, 2005. Fellow ACS (coun. W.Va. chpt. 1999-2001, sec.-treas. 2001-2002, 2d v.p. 2002-2003, 1st v.p. 2003-2004, pres. 2004-05, chmn. com. on applicants dist. 1 W.Va.), Southeastern Surg. Congress, Assn. Acad. Surgery, Sabiston Soc., Am. Coll. Cardiology, Am. Coll. Chest Physicians, So. Thoracic Surg. Assn. (program chmn. 1995-96, coun. 1999-2000), Soc. Thoracic Surgeons; mem. Am. Heart Assn., (v.p., pres. elect, pres. W. Va. affiliate 1994-96), Soc. Univ. Surgeons, Am. Assn. Thoracic Surgery, Internat. Surg. Soc., Assn. Programs Dirs. in Surgery, Assn. Surg. Edn., So. Surg. Assn., W.Va. Med. Assn., Monongalia County Med. Assn. (v.p. 2007-),Mended Hearts, Lakeview Country Club, Pines Country Club, Phi Beta Kappa, Alpha Omega Alpha, Alpha Epsilon Delta, Profl. Assn. Diving Instrs. Soc. (cert. master scuba diver). Republican. Avocations: fishing, photography, scuba diving, shell collecting. Office: VA Med Ctr Fletcher NC 28732 Home Phone: 828-687-6507; Office Phone: 828-298-7911 x15113.

HILL, SHEPARD W., air transportation executive; b. Freeport, NY, 1952; married; 2 children. BA, Stetson Univ., 1975; grad., Naval War Coll., Annapolis, Md., 1984; grad., program sr. execs. nat. and internat. securtiy, Harvard Univ. John F. Kennedy Sch. Govt. Chief staff, legis. dir. Congressman Bill Chappell, 1987; former v.p., aerospace govt. affairs mktg. Rockwell Aerospace and Defense; v.p., space sys. Boeing Co., Chgo., v.p., space and communications, govt. rels., currently sr. v.p., bus. strategy devel. Office: Boeing Co 100 N Riverside Plz Chicago IL 60606-1596

HILL, STEPHEN S., lawyer; b. Washington, Oct. 27, 1951; AB magna cum laude, Harvard U., 1973, JD, 1976. Bar: Mass. 1977, DC 1977, US Dist. Ct. (DC dist.) 1977, Supreme Jud. Ct. Mass. 1977, US Ct. Appeals (DC cir.) 1977, US Supreme Ct. 1983, US Ct. Appeals (6th cir.) 1985. Ptnr. Sidley & Austin, Washington, Howrey LLP, Wash., 2002—. Mem. bd. trustees Legal Aid Soc. DC, 1983—2002, sec., 1993—95, v.p., 1995—98, pres., 1998—2000, mem. exec. com., 1993—2002. Fellow: Am. Bar Found. 1998; mem.: ABA (antitrust, litig. sect. 1978), Assn. Trial Lawyers Am. 1997. Office: Howrey LLP 1299 Pennsylvania Ave NW Washington DC 20004 Office Phone: 202-383-6967. Office Fax: 202-383-6610. E-mail: hillstephen@howrey.com.

HILL, SUSAN BEASLEY, recreational therapist; b. Hattiesburg, Miss., June 16, 1944; d. William Lee Beasley, Jr. and Alice Odelle (Taylor) Beasley; 1 child, Susannah Odelle. BA in English, Speech and DRama,

Greensboro Coll., 1966; MSW, U. N.C., 1982. Tchr., prin. John Umstead Hosp., Butner, NC, 1967—70; crisis counselor, co-founder Dial Help, Salisburg, NC, 1970—71; social worker Rowan County Dept. Social Svc., Salisburg, 1970—71; sales mgr./pub. rels. Beasley Lumber Co., Scotland Neck, NC, 1971—80; bus. owner, mgr. Repeat Performances, Raleigh, 1976—78; co-dir., counselor, tchr. Project Redirection Wake County Pub. Schs., Raleigh, 1978—79; clin. social worker, therapist Orange-Person-Chatham Mental Health Ctr., Chapel Hill, NC, 1980—81; clin. social worker, therapist Adult Outpatient Group Clinic N.C. Meml. Hosp., Chapel Hill, 1981—82; clin. social worker/family advisor Divsn. for Disorders of Devel. and Learning U. N.C., Chapel Hill, 1982; pvt. counselor, ednl. tchr. Harnett County, NC, 1982—; dir. Learning Ctr. Acads. Plus, Dunn, NC, 1993—95; activity profl. Dunn (N.C.) Rehab. and Nursing Ctr., 1998—. Shut-in and nursing home ministry Gospel Tabernacle Ch., Dunn, 1982—90. Author: (newspaper series) Aegism: A Six Party Study, 1981. Mem. women's bd. Gospel Tabernacle Ch., 1987, active, 1988—. Republican. Avocations: cooking, painting, politics, cats. Office: Dunn Nursing and Rehab Ctr 711 Susan Tart Rd Dunn NC 28334

HILL, TERRELL LESLIE, chemist, researcher, biophysicist; b. Oakland, Calif., Dec. 19, 1917; s. George Leslie and Ollie (Moreland) H.; m. Laura Etta Gano, Sept. 23, 1942; children: Julie Lisbeth Eden, Carolyn Jo (Mrs. Gary Lineburg), Ernest Evan. AB, U. Calif., Berkeley, 1939, PhD, 1942; postgrad., Harvard U., 1940. Instr. chemistry Western Res. U., 1942-44; rsch. assoc. radiation lab. U. Calif. at Berkeley, 1944-45; rsch. assoc. chemistry, then asst. prof. chemistry U. Rochester, 1945-49; chemist U.S. Naval Med. Rsch. Inst., 1949-57; prof. chemistry U. Oreg., 1957-67, U. Calif. at Santa Cruz, 1967-71, adj. prof., 1977-89, prof. emeritus, 1989—, vice chancellor for scis., div. natural scis., 1968-69; research chemist NIH, Bethesda, Md., 1971-88, scientist emeritus, 1988—. Mem. biophysics study sect. USPHS, 1954-57; chemistry panel NSF, 1961-64 Author: Statistical Mechanics, 1956, 87, Statistical Thermodynamics, 1960, 86, Thermodynamics of Small Systems, vol. I, 1963, 94, 2002, vol. II, 1964, 94, 2002, Matter and Equilibrium, 1965, Thermodynamics for Chemists and Biologists, 1968, Free Energy Transduction in Biology, 1977, Cooperativity Theory in Biochemistry, 1985, Linear Aggregation Theory in Cell Biology, 1987, Free Energy Transduction and Biochemical Cycle Kinetics, 1989, 2005, also rsch. papers. Guggenheim fellow Yale, 1952-53; recipient Arthur S. Flemming award U.S. Govt., 1954; Distinguished Civilian Service award U.S. Navy, 1955; award Washington Acad. Scis., 1956; Disting. Service award USPHS, 1981; Disting. Service award U. Oreg., 1983; Sloan Found. fellow, 1958-62 Mem Nat. Acad. Scis., Am. Chem. Soc. (Kendall award 1969), Biophys. Soc., NAACP, ACLU, Phi Beta Kappa. Home: 3400 Paul Sweet Rd Apt C220 Santa Cruz CA 95065

HILL, THOMAS ALLEN, lawyer; b. Salem, Ohio, Mar. 29, 1958; s. Charles Spencer and Dorothy Jane (Allen) H. BA magna cum laude, Hiram Coll., 1980; JD, George Washington U., 1984. Bar: Ohio 1984, Pa. 1987, D.C. 1988, U.S. Supreme Ct. 1989, Tex. 1990, Okla. 1991, U.S. Dist. Ct. (no. dist.) Ohio, 2004. Legis. intern Office of Hon. John Conyers, Jr., Washington, 1979; asst. to dean campus Life for Housing, conf. dir. Hiram (Ohio) Coll., 1980-81; corp. counsel Capitol Oil & Gas Inc., Austintown, Ohio, 1984-93; gen. counsel, sec. North Coast Energy, Inc., Cleve., 1987-2001, Trinity Oil & Gas, Inc. subs. North Coast Energy Inc., Warren, Ohio, 1990-93; gen. counsel Eric Petroleum Corp., Austintown, Ohio, 2001—. Mem. mini-task force on notices of violation Ohio Div. Oil and Gas, Columbus, 1988-90; part-time fin. analyst Primerica Fin. Svcs., Inc., 1997-2000; corp. sec. Peake Energy, Inc., Ravenswood, W.Va., 2000-01. Mem. ABA, Ohio Bar Assn., Mahoning County Bar Assn., Pa. Bar Assn., Okla. Bar Assn., D.C. Bar Assn., State Bar Tex., Trumbull County Bar Assn., Ohio Oil and Gas Assn., Christian Legal Soc., Energy Bar Assn., Ohio Land Title Assn., Ohio Geneal. Soc., Mahoning Valley Hist. Soc., Austintown Hist. Soc., Gen. Soc., War of 1812, SAR, Order of Arrow, Kappa Delta Pi, Pi Gamma Mu. Republican. Avocations: local history, study of amaranth. Home: 4841 Westchester Dr Apt 102 Youngstown OH 44515-2548 Office: Eric Petroleum Corp 6075 Silica Rd Ste A Austintown OH 44515 Office Phone: 330-533-1828. *Motto: I Peter 1: 23-25.*

HILL, THOMAS WILLIAM, JR., lawyer, educator; b. NYC, Dec. 25, 1924; s. Thomas William Sr. and Marion (Bond) H.; m. Elizabeth Rowe, June 18, 1949; children: Gretchen P., Catharine B., Thomas William III. BS, U. Pa., 1948; MBA, NYU, 1950; JD, Columbia U., 1953. Bar: N.Y. 1953, D.C. 1954, U.S. Supreme Ct. 1958, Fla. 1989; CPA N.Y. Sr. tax acct. Hurdman & Cranstoun, 1949-50; asst. U.S. atty. So. Dist. N.Y., 1953-54; assoc. Cahill, Gordon, Reindel & Ohl, 1954-58; sr. ptnr. Spear & Hill, 1958-75; ptnr. Sidley & Austin, 1981-86; pres. Belco Petroleum Co., NYC, 1962-63; legal adviser Sultanate of Oman, 1972-76. Adj. prof. law U. Miami, 1986-97. Contbr. articles to profl. jours. Vice chmn., pres., trustee Internat. Coll., Beirut, Lebanon, 1978-91. 1st lt. AUS, 1943-46. Decorated Bronze Star, Purple Heart, Medal of Oman (Sultanate of Oman), Order of Homayun (Iran). Mem. ABA, Assn. of Bar of City of N.Y., IBA, Racquet and Tennis Club (N.Y.C.), Mayacoo Golf Club, Taconic Golf Club, Phi Delta Phi, Kappa Sigma. Home: 1967 Breakers Pointe Way West Palm Beach FL 33411-5119 Office Phone: 561-793-4031. Personal E-mail: twhilljr@adelphia.net.

HILL, VICTOR ERNST, IV, retired mathematics professor, musician; b. Pitts., Nov. 3, 1939; s. Victor Ernst III and Lois Kathryn (Rahenkamp) H.; m. Christi Deanne Adams, Aug. 12, 1967 (div. 1981); children: Victoria Christina Hill Resnick, Christopher Andrew Michael. BS, Carnegie-Mellon U., 1961; MA, U. Wis.-Madison, 1962; PhD, U. Oreg., 1966, performer's cert. in harpsichord, 1966. Asst. prof. math. Williams Coll., Williamstown, Mass., 1966-72, assoc. prof, 1972-78, prof., 1978-89, Thomas T. Read prof. math., 1989—2006; ret., 2006. Instr. music Carnegie-Mellon U., 1960-61; vis. prof. math. Ga. Inst. Tech., 1987-88, 91-92, artist-in-residence, 1987-88; vis. prof. music U. Oreg., 1967; concert organist, harpsichordist, 1964—; editor Tudor Choral Works Broude Bros. Author: Groups, Representations, and Characters, 1975, Groups and Characters, 2000; composer organ and choral works. Reader Rec. for Blind and Dyslexic, Inc., Williamstown, 1971—, bd. trustees Berkshire unit, 1996-99; organist-choirmaster St. John's Episcopal Ch., Williamstown, 1972-96. Mem. Assn. Anglican Musicians (archivist 1982—, editl. bd. 1996—, bd. review 1998—), Am. Guild Organists (dean Berkshire chpt. 1982-84, exec. bd. 1995-98), Assn. Christians in Math. Scis., Nat. Assn. Scholars, Soc. of St. Margaret (assoc.), Charles Williams Soc., Richard III Soc. Home: PO Box 11 Williamstown MA 01267-0011 Personal E-mail: vhill@williams.edu.

HILL, VICTORIA RUTH, librarian; b. NYC, Dec. 4, 1960; d. Arthur Burit and Patricia Smith Hill. BA, U. Pa., 1983; MS in Libr. Sci., Pratt Inst., Bklyn., 1989. Cert. profl. libr. N.Y. Mgr. of libr. svcs. Bklyn. Pub. Libr., 1984—, children's cluster specialist, 2001—. Recent grad. trustee Pratt Inst., 1990—92, mem. dean search com. Sch. Info. and Libr. Sci., 1991—92, 1999. Amb. People to People Amb. Tour, Rio de Janeiro and Manaus, Brazil, 2004; mem. vestry St. John's Episcopal Ch., Bklyn., 1984—97, past mem. spl. events com. Named one of Outstanding Young Women of Am., 1986; fellow Internat. Youth Libr., Munich, 1995, Libr.'s Study Tour of Germany, SUNY, Goethe Inst., 1992. Mem.: ALA, Assn. Libr. Svc. to Children (Robert F. Sibert Award com. 2002—03), N.Y. Black Libr.'s Caucus. Avocations: travel, public speaking. Home: 36 Saint John's Pl Aptt # 2 Brooklyn NY 11217-3206 Office: Bklyn Pub Libr Canarsie Br 1580 Rockaway Pky Brooklyn NY 11236 Home Phone: 718-622-8924; Office Phone: 917-309-6621. Office Fax: 718-257-6557; Home Fax: 718-257-6557. Personal E-mail: vickyhill@yahoo.com. E-mail: v.hill@brooklynpubliclibrary.org.

HILL, VIRGIL LUSK, JR., academic administrator, military officer; b. Shelby, NC, Apr. 2, 1938; s. Virgil Lusk and Ellen (Dilling) H.; m. Mary Kimberly Jordan, Jan. 11, 1964; children: James S., Katherine E. BS in Naval Sci., U.S. Naval Acad., 1961. Commd. ensign USN, 1961, advanced through grades to rear adm. (upper half), 1989; served on USS Thomas Jefferson, Groton, Conn., 1968-70; material officer COMSUBRON 18, Charleston, SC, 1970-73; exec. officer USS L. Mendel Rivers, Charleston, 1973-75; comdg. officer USS Hammerhead, Norfolk, Va., 1976-80; dir. spl. projects Office Chief Naval Ops., Washington, 1980-83; comdr. Submarine Devel. Squadron 12, Groton, 1983-85; dir. attack submarine divsn. Office of Chief Naval Ops., Washington, 1985-87; comdr. Submarine Group 5, San Diego, 1987-88; supt. U.S. Naval Acad., Annapolis, Md., 1988-91; comdr. operational test and evaluation forces USN, Norfolk, 1991-93; pres. Valley Forge (Pa.) Mil. Acad. and Coll., 1993-2000; sr. fellow Villanova U., 2002—. Bd. dirs. Greater Main Line br. ARC, Southeastern Pa. chpt. Decorated Distinguished Svc. medal with gold star, Legion of Merit with 3 gold stars, Meritorious Service medal with 3 gold stars, Navy Commendation medal with 1 gold star; recipient Admiral David Glasgow Farragut award Naval Order of U.S. 1996, Robert Morris award Boy Scouts Am., 1996, Order of Magna Charta, 1996. Mem. Assn. Mil. Colls. and Schs. of the U.S. (former pres.), United Svcs. Orgn. of Phila. (bd. dirs.), Assn. Ind. Colls. and Univs. Pa. (bd. dirs.), Nat. Assn. Ind. Colls. and Univs. (pub. rels. commn.), Pa. Assn. Colls. and Univs., Pa. Assn. Ind. Schs., Nat. Assn. Ind. Schs., U.S. Naval Inst., Naval Order of the U.S., Mil. Order of Fgn. Wars, U.S. Navy League, Naval Submarine League, World Affairs Coun. of Phila., Sunday Breakfast Club of Phila., Penn Club of Phila., Union League of Phila. (bd. dirs.), St. David's Golf Club (Wayne, Pa.), others. Personal E-mail: virgilhill@aol.com.

HILL, WILLIAM U., state supreme court justice, former state attorney general; b. Montgomery, Ala., 1948; BA, U. Wyo., 1970, JD, 1974. Bar: Wyo. 1974. Asst. atty. gen. State of Wyo., Cheyenne, Wyo., 1974—77; atty. priv. practice, Riverton, Wyo., 1977—80, Seattle, 1977—80; chief of staff, chief counsel Sen. Malcolm Wallop, Wash., DC, 1980—89; atty. priv. practice, Cheyenne, Wyo., 1989—91; asst. U.S. atty., 1991—95; atty. gen. State of Wyo., Cheyenne, Wyo., 1995—98; justice Wyo. Supreme Ct., Cheyenne, 1998—, chief justice, 2002—06. Mem.: Wyo. State Bar Assn. Office: Wyoming Supreme Court 2301 Capitol Ave Cheyenne WY 82001-3656*

HILLABRANDT, LARRY LEE, service industry executive; b. Apr. 5, 1947; s. Ronald Edward and Marion Alice (Smith) H.; m. Beverly Ann Johnson, Jan. 25, 1969; 1 son, Larry Lee. BS, Purdue U., 1969, MS, 1971; PhD in Bus. Adminstrn., Belford U., 2006. With Mobil Chem. Co., various locations, 1971-84, fin. analyst Jacksonville, Ill., 1973, sr. systems analyst Macedon, N.Y., 1973-74, fin. analyst, 1974, plant controller Frankfort, Ill., 1974-77, distbn. supt. NE region, 1979-80; div. gen. mgr. Belleville, Ont., Can., 1980-84; bus./fin. mgr. George Heisel Corp., Rochester, N.Y., 1984-85; pres. ZIP, Inc., Rochester, N.Y., 1985-97, prin., owner, 1997—; CFO Expedite Ventures Inc., Rochester, 2005—. Mem. Purdue Alumni Assn., Krannert Grad. Sch. Alumni Assn., Lima Gun Club, Farview Golf and Country Club, Zeta Psi Alumni Assn. Home: 53 Stoney Lonesome Rd Honeoye Falls NY 14472 Office Phone: 585-454-6950 ext. 110. Personal E-mail: tiny2too@frontiernet.net. Business E-Mail: csscorp@frontiernet.net.

HILLARD, JAMES RANDOLPH, psychiatry educator; b. Ft. Smith, Ark., Mar. 15, 1951; s. James Milton and Louise (Winzenried) H.; m. Aingeal Grehan, Sept. 18, 2001; children by previous marriage: Miriam Elena, Ian James Adams, Nathaniel Kenneth. BA, U. N.C., 1973; MD, Stanford U., Palo Alto, Calif., 1977. Diplomate Am. Bd. Psychiatry and Neurology; lic. psychiatrist, N.C., Va., Ohio. Intern Duke U. Med. Ctr., Durham, N.C., 1977-79, resident, 1979-81; psychiatrist dept. student health U. Va., 1981, asst. prof. dept. behavioral medicine and psychiatry, 1981-84; dir. psychiat. emergency svc. dept. psychiatry U. Cin., 1984-89, prof., chmn. dept. psychiatry, 1989—2006. Pres. U. Cin. Med. Assocs., 1993—, assoc. dean for clin. affairs, 1997—.; assoc. provost human health affairs Mich State U., 2007—. Editor Current Psychiatry, 2002-2006 contbr. articles to profl. jours., chpts. to books. Home: 3046 Ononta Ave Cincinnati OH 45226-2015 Office: 222 Piedmont Ave Cincinnati OH 45219 Office Phone: 513-475-8015. Business E-Mail: Hillarjr@ucphysicians.com.

HILL-COOK, PATRICIA ANN, social services administrator; b. Cinn., Oct. 12, 1953; d. Clinton Hill, Willie Bell and Terrell Lewis (Stepfather); 1 child, Nathan G. Cook. A in Social Svc. Tech., U. Cinn., 1986, BS in Social Sci, 1997. Housing coord./case mgr. Welcome House Ky., Covington, 1993—95; outreach and recruitment specialist U. Cinn., 1995—97; workforce devel. specialist Work Resource Ctr., Cinn., 1997—. Spkr. in field. Author: Personally Speaking, 2001. Youth leader Golden Leaf Bapt. Ch., Cinn., 1997, pres. women's missionary group, 2001. Recipient Activist award, Voices in Action, Cinn., 2002; Martin Luther King Jr. scholar, U. Cinn., 1996. Democrat. Baptist. Office: Work Resource Ctr 2901 Gilbert Cincinnati OH 45207 Office Phone: 513-281-2316. Business E-Mail: pcook@workrc.org.

HILLE, BERTIL, physiology educator; b. New Haven, Oct. 10, 1940; s. C. Einar and Kirsti (Ore) H.; m. Merrill Burr, Nov. 21, 1964; children: Erik D., J. Trygve. BS, Yale U., 1962; PhD, Rockefeller U., 1967. H.H. Whitney fellow Cambridge U., 1967-68; asst. prof. U. Wash., Seattle, 1968-71, assoc. prof., 1971-74, prof. physiology, 1974—. Vis. prof. U. Saarland, Hamburg, Germany, 1975-76. Author: Ion Channels of Excitable Membranes, 3d edit., 2001; mem. edit. bd.: Jour. Gen. Physiology, 1971—, Am. Jour. Physiology, 1984—87, Jour. Neurosci., 1984—87, Neuron, 1987—, Curr. Opinion Neurobiol., 1990—99, Procs. of NAS, 1996—99; contbr. articles to profl. jours. Recipient Alexander von Humboldt Sr. Scientist award, 1975, Bristol-Myers Squibb award, 1990, (with Dr. Clay Armstrong) Louisa Gross Horowitz prize for biology or biochemistry Columbia U., 1996, (with Drs. Clay Armstrong and Roderick MacKinnon) Albert Lasker Basic Med. Rsch. award, 1999, Gairdner Found. Internat. award, 2001. Mem. NAS, Biophys. Soc. (K.S. Cole award 1975), Am. Acad. Arts and Sci., Inst. of Medicine, Soc. Neurosci. Home: 10630 Lakeside Ave NE Seattle WA 98125-6934 Office: U Wash Physiology & Biophysics Dept 1959 NE Pacific St HSB Rm G424 Box 357290 Seattle WA 98195-7290 E-mail: hille@u.washington.edu.

HILLEARY, VAN (WILLIAM VANDERPOOL HILLEARY), former congressman, lawyer; b. Rhea County, Tenn., June 20, 1959; s. Bill and Evelyon Hilleary; m. Meredith Brown, June 3, 2000. BS in Bus. Adminstrn., U. Tenn., 1981; JD, Samford U., 1990. Bar: Tenn. With SSM Industries, Inc., Spring City, Tenn., 1984—86, dir. planning and bus. devel., 1992—94; mem. US Congress from 4th Tenn. dist., 1995—2003; mem. fin. services com.; mem. edn. and the workforce com.; of counsel, pub. law & policy strategies group Sonnenschein Nath & Rosenthal LLP, Washington, 2003—. Served USAF, 1981-1982, USAFR, 1982—; served in Persian Gulf. Decorated 2 US Air Medals, Nat. Svc. medal, Kuwaiti Liberation Medal. Mem. Am. Legion, Sigma Chi. Republican. Presbyterian. Office: Sonnenschein Nath & Rosenthal LLP Ste 600, E Tower 1301 K St NW Washington DC 20015 Office Phone: 202-408-9182. Office Fax: 202-408-6399. Business E-Mail: vhilleary@sonnenschein.com.

HILLEN, JOHN FRANCIS, think-tank executive, former federal agency administrator; BA, Duke U.; MA, King's Coll.; MBA, Cornell U.; doctorate, Oxford U. COO Island ECN; head def. and intelligence practice Am. Mgmt. Sys. Inc.; def. policy adv. & speechwriter to Pres. The White House, Washington, 2000; asst. sec. for polit. military affairs US Dept. State, Washington, 2005—07. Cons. ABC News; trustee Internat. Inst. Strategic Studies, London; trustee, dir. program on nat. security Fgn. Policy Rsch. Inst.; trustee Phila. U.; spkr. in field. Contbg. editor: Nat. Law Review; co-editor: (book) Future Visions for U.S. Defense Policy, 1999; author: Blue Helmets: The Strategy of UN Military Operations, 1997; contbr. articles to profl. jours. and newspapers. Reconnaissance and spl. ops officer US Army, 1988—2000. Mem.: Veterans of Fgn. Wars (life), Coun. Fgn. Rels. (life). Office: Fgn Policy Rsch Inst 1528 Waltnut St Ste 610 Philadelphia PA 19102

HILLENBRAND, DAVID M., museum administrator; s. Martin J. Hillenbrand; m. Georgianna Hillenbrand; children: Stuart, Joseph. With Mobay Chem., 1980—88; sr. v.p., gen. site mgr. Miles Inc., Elkhart, 1991—94; pres., CEO Canadian Ops. Bayer Inc., 1994—2002; exec. v.p Bayer Polymers, 2002—03; pres. Carnegie Museums of Pitts., 2005—. Dir. Koppers, 1999—. Office: Carnegie Museums 4400 Forbes Ave Pittsburgh PA 15213-4080 Office Phone: 412-622-3333.

HILLENBRAND, LAURA, writer; b. Fairfax, Va., 1967; Student, Kenyon Coll. Contbg. writer editor: Equus Mag., 1989—; contbr. articles (Nat. Mag. award, 2003); author: Seabiscuit: An American Legend, 2001 (finalist Nat. Book Critics Cir. award, BookSense Nonfiction book award year, William Hill Sportsbook Year award Great Britain, 2001); cons.: (films) Seabiscuit. Spokesperson, advocate Chronic Fatigue Symdrome. Recipient Two time winner Eclipse award, Highest honor in thoroughbred racing journalism. Office: Ballantine Books Random House 1745 Broadway New York NY 10019*

HILLENBRAND, SHEA MATTHEW, professional baseball player; b. Mesa, Ariz., July 27, 1975; Attended, Mesa C.C., 1994—96. Profl. baseball player Boston Red Sox, 2001—03, Ariz. Diamondbacks, 2003—04, Toronto Blue Jays, 2005—06, LA Angels, 2006—07. Lectr. Polaroid Clinic, Fenway Park. Avocation: weightlifting.*

HILLENBURG, STEPHEN, writer, television producer, animator; b. Fort Sill, Okla., Aug. 21, 1961; m. Karen Hillenburg; 1 child. BS in Marine Biology, Humboldt State U., 1984; MFA in Experimental Animation, Calif. Inst. of Arts, 1992. Marine sci. instructor Orange County Ocean Inst., Dana Point, Calif., 1985—87. Creator, writer, prodr., dir. & storyboard artist (TV series) Rocko's Modern Life, 1993—96, creator, writer, exec. prodr. SpongeBob SquarePants, 1999—2004 (Emmy nom. for outstanding children's program, 2002, Emmy nom. for outstanding animated program, 2003, 2004), creator, animator (films) The Green Beret and Wormholes, dir., prodr., writer, actor, composer & storyboard artist The SpongeBob SquarePants Movie, 2004 (Annie award nom. for dir., 2005). Recipient Princess Grace award in film, 1992, Walk the Talk award, Heal the Bay, 2001, Princess Grace Statue award, 2002.

HILLENMEYER, HENRY REILING, JR., restaurant company executive; b. Temple, Tex., Nov. 13, 1943; s. Henry Reiling and Lucy Carolyn (Taylor) H.; m. Sallie Long Sigler, Oct. 30, 1976; children: Henry Reiling, Edward Ferriday, Taylor Jennings, Morgan Andrew, Hunter Taverner. BA, Yale U., 1965. Trainee Kanawha Valley Bank, Charleston, W.Va., 1965-67, asst. sec., 1967-68; v.p. CBM, Inc., Cleve., 1968-70, pres., 1970-72, chmn., dir., 1972-74; pres., dir. Ireland's Restaurants, Inc., Nashville, 1974-78; exec. v.p. Womco, Inc., Nashville, 1978-82; pres., dir. So. Hospitality Corp., Nashville, 1983-89, chmn., pres., dir., 1989-94; chmn., CEO, dir. Skillsearch Corp., Nashville, 1995-99, Cooker Restaurant Corp., 1999—2004; cons., 2004—. Bd. dirs. Jr. Achievement, Nashville, 1985—, chmn., 1991-92, 97-99; bd. dirs. Tenn. Spl. Olympics, Nashville, 1986-90; trustee Harding Acad., Nashville, 1985-90; nat. assoc. Boys Clubs of Am., N.Y.C., 1986-90. Mem. World Pres. Orgn., Belle Meade Country Club, Scroll and Key Soc., Fence Club, Yale Club of Middle Tenn. (pres. 1983-88). Republican. Episcopalian. Home and Office: 8 Foxhall Close Nashville TN 37215-1808 Home Phone: 615-383-7144; Office Phone: 615-292-4687. Personal E-mail: hilly615@bellsouth.net.

HILLER, DAVID DEAN, publishing executive; b. Chgo., June 12, 1953; AB, Harvard U., 1975, JD, 1978. Bar: Ill. 1981. Law clk. to Hon. Judge Malcolm Wilkey US Ct. Appeals DC Cir., 1978-79; law clk. to Hon. Justice Potter Stewart US Supreme Ct., 1979-80; spl. asst. to Atty. Gen. William French Smith US Dept. Justice, 1981—82, assoc. dep. atty. gen., 1982—83; assoc. Sidley & Austin, Chgo., 1983—86, ptnr., 1986; v.p., gen. counsel Tribune Co., Chgo., 1988—93, sr. v.p., gen. counsel, 1993, sr. v.p. devel., 1993—2000, pres. interactive, 2000—04, sr. v.p. pub., 2003—04; pres., pub. Chgo. Tribune, 2004—06; pub., pres., CEO LA Times, 2006—. Bd. dirs. CareerBuilder, Classified Ventures, CrossMedia Services. Editor Harvard Law Rev., 1977-78. Bd. trustees Roosevelt U., Chgo. Hist. Soc.; bd. dirs. Chgo. Tribune Found., McCormick Tribune Found. Mem. ABA, Chgo. Coun. Fgn. Rels, Econ. Club Chgo. (bd. dirs.). Office: LA Times 202 W 1st St Los Angeles CA 90012*

HILLERMAN, TONY, writer, journalist, educator; b. Sacred Heart, Okla., May 27, 1925; s. August Alfred and Lucy Mary (Grove) Hillerman; m. Marie Elizabeth Unzner, Aug. 16, 1948; children: Anne, Janet Hillerman Grado, Anthony Jr., Monica Hillerman Atwell, Steven, Daniel. Student, Okla. State U., 1942-43; BA, U. Okla., 1948; MA in English, U. N.Mex., 1965, LittD (hon.), 1990, Ariz. State U., 1991. Police reporter Borger (Tex.) News-Herald, 1948; reporter, city editor constn. Morning Press, Lawton, Okla., 1949-50; polit. reporter UP, Oklahoma City, 1950-52, bur. mgr. Santa Fe, 1952-54; reporter, then city editor and editor The New Mexican, Santa Fe, 1954-62; prof. journalism U. N.Mex., Albuquerque, 1965-87, asst. to pres., 1963-65, 81-84. Author: (novels) The Blessing Way, 1970, The Fly on the Wall, 1971, The Boy Who Made Dragonfly, 1972, Dance Hall of the Dead, 1973 (Edgar Allen Poe award, 1973), Listening Woman, 1986, People of Darkness, 1986, The Dark Wind, 1986, The Ghostway, 1986, Skinwalkers, 1986 (Anthony award, 1987), A Thief of Time, 1988 (Macavity award Mystery Readers Internat., 1988, Dept. Interior award, 1990), Talking God, 1988 (Media award Am. Anthrop. Assn., 1990), The Joe Leaphorn Mysteries, Coyote Waits, 1990, Sacred Clowns, 1993, Finding Moon, 1995, The Fallen Man, 1996, The First Eagle, 1998, Hunting Badger, 1998, The Wailing Wind, 2002, Sinister Pig, 2003, Skeleton Man, 2004, (non-fiction) The Great Taos Bank Robbery, 1996, New Mexico, 1996, Rio Grande, 1996, The Spell of New Mexico, 1996, Indian Country, 1996, The Best of the West, 1996, The Oxford Book of American Detective Stories, 1996, Seldom Disappointed, 2001, Kilroy Was There, 2005; contbr. articles, audio recs.; editor: The Mysterious West, 1994. With inf. US Army, 1943—45, ETO. Decorated Bronze Star, Silver Star, Purple Heart; recipient Golden Spur award, Western Writers Am., 1987, Spl. Friend of Dineh award, Navajo Tribal Coun., 1987, Grand Prix de Littérature Policière award, France, 1992, Amb. award, Ctr. for the Indian, 1992. Mem.: Internat. Crime Writers Assn., Mystery Writers Am. (pres. 1988, Grand Master award 1991, Robert Keroch Lifetime Achievement award 2005). Democrat. Roman Catholic. Avocation: trout fishing.

HILLERY, THOMAS HUNGIVILLE, journalist, financial consultant; b. Boston, Dec. 15, 1962; BA, Clark U., 1985; Magistri in Artibus Liberalibus, Harvard U., 1997. Accredited assessor #666 Mass. Mem. promotions dept. Sta. WCRB-FM, Waltham, Mass., 1990-92; journalist Dorchester News, Boston, 1992—. Author: (screenplay) Project Solitude. Bd. assessors Town of Sudbury, 1987—96; trustee Hillery Charitable Trust; mem. Boston Com. Fgn. Rels., Freedom's Found. Valley Forge. Thomas H. Hillery fellow, Hillery pedigree registered, Coll. Arms London, armorial bearing granted. Mem.: Jonas Clark Fellows, Mass. Assn. Assessing Officers, Internat. Assn. Assessing Officers, New Eng. Hist. Geneaol. Soc., Internat. Platform Assn., Harvard Investment Assn., Clark U. Alumni

Coun., U.S. Libr. Congress, Clark Legacy Soc., Nat. Trust Hist. Preservation, Nat. Press Club, Harvard Club Boston, Ancient and Honorable Arty. Co. (sgt. of arty., color guard), Sons Am. Legion Post 191 (chaplain), Mil. Order Royal Legion U.S., Shriners, Order Eastern Star, Scottish Rite, Masons (mem. Grand Royal Arch chpt. exemplification degree team 1992—93, dist. dep. grand treas. 1992—93, past master Charles A. Welch Lodge, past high priest Houghton Royal Arch), KC, Sons Union Vets. Civil War. Home: 66 Willow Rd Sudbury MA 01776-2663 Office: 299 Savin Hill Ave Ste 1 Boston MA 02125-1055 Personal E-mail: tomhillery02125@cs.com.

HILLESTAD, CHARLES ANDREW, lawyer; b. McCurtain, Okla., Aug. 30, 1945; s. Carl Oliver and Aileen Hanna (Sweeney) H.; m. Ann Ramsey Robertson, Oct. 13, 1973. BS, U. Oreg., 1967; JD, U. Mich., 1972. Bar: Colo. 1972, U.S. Dist. Ct. Colo. 1972, U.S. Ct. Appeals (10th cir.) 1972, Oreg. 1993; lic. real estate broker, Colo. Law clk. to presiding justice Colo. Supreme Ct., Denver, 1972-73; ptnr. DeMuth & Kemp, Denver, 1973-83, Cornwell & Blakey, Denver, 1983-90, Scheid & Horlbeck, Denver, 1990-93, Gablehouse & Epel, Denver, 1993-94; pvt. practice Cannon Beach, Oreg., 1994—. Co-developer award winning Queen Anne Inn, Capitol Hill Mansion and Cheyenne Canyon Inn Hotels (4-diamond award AAA); mem. ad hoc com. Denver Real Estate Atty. Specialists. Author: Preventive Law for Innkeepers; co-author: Annual Surveys of Real Estate Law for Colorado Bar Association, Absolutely Every B&B in Colorado; contbr. articles to profl. jours.; assoc. editor Inn Times. Past coun. mem. Denver Art Mus.; past chmn. Rocky Mountain chpt. Sierra Club; past v.p., bd. dirs. Seaside C. of C.; past bd. dirs. Hist. Denver, Inc. Staff sgt. U.S. Army, 1968-70. Recipient Colo. Co. of Yr. award Colo. Bus. Mag., Award of Honor Denver Ptnrship., Newsmaker of Yr. and Outstanding Achievement awards Am. Assn. Hist. Inns, Tourism Person of Yr. award Denver Conv. and Visitor's Bur., Rocky Mountain Spectacular Inn award B&B Rocky Mountains Assn., Best Inns of Yr. awards County Inns Mag. and Adventure Rd. Mag., Best of Denver award Westward newspaper. Mem. Colo. Bar Assn., Oreg. Bar Assn., Denver Bar Assn., Colo. Lawyers for the Arts, POETS, Astoria C. of C., Seaside C. of C., Cannon Beach C. of C. Avocations: photography, art collecting, historic and environmental preservation, history and architecture reading, rafting. Office: PO Box 1065 1347 S Hemlock Cannon Beach OR 97110 Office Phone: 503-436-1314.

HILLEY, MARY KAY, music educator; b. Ft. Valley, Ga., Oct. 31, 1963; d. John Dunham and G. Joan (Baker) Warner; m. Harry Quinton Dunlap (div.); 1 child, John Quinton Dunlap; m. Daniel Grover Hilley, Sept. 15, 2001. AA in Music, Darton Coll., 1996; BS in Music Edn., Ga. Southwestern State U., 1999. Tchr. Wheeler Piano Studio, Americus, Ga., 1997—2000; pvt. piano tchr. Leesburg, Ga., 1999—. Organist 1st Presbyn. Ch., Albany, Ga., 1998—2000; pianist, choir dir. Northgate Presbyn. Ch., Albany, 2000—. Mem.: Nat. Guild Piano Tchrs. Avocations: reading, bicycling, sewing, camping. Home and Studio: 129 Lee Dr Leesburg GA 31763 Home Phone: 229-446-6179.

HILLIARD, CAROL, nurse, educator, consultant, researcher; d. Elias and Eula Mae (Holt) Hilliard. AAS, Bronx CC, 1971; BSN, Hunter-Bellevue Sch. Nursing, 1981, MSN, 1983. Staff nurse Fordham Hosp., NYC, 1971—73; per diem work in ER, ICU and post anesthesia care unit Columbia Presbyn. Hosp., 1973—90; per diem work in ER, ICU & PACU Lincoln Hosp., 1991—95, Bellevue Hosp., 1990, Lenox Hill Hosp., 1973—2003; from staff nurse to operating room instr. NY Med. Coll., NYC, 1974—78; from staff nurse to nurse edn. instr. ER, ICU, PACU Harlem Hosp., NYC, 1978—90; asst. prof. nursing Hostos CC, NYC, 1990—95; coord., nurse cons. The Exhale Nurse Cons., NYC, 1996—, The Exhale Nursing Review, 1998—. Tchr. state bd. review classes Megan Evers Coll., Bklyn., 1996—98. Instr. CPR & basic life support for health care profls. Am. Red Cross, 1980—. Mem.: NY Assn. Black Nurses, Critical Care Nurses Assn., NY State Nurses Assn., Emergency Dept. Nursing Assn., Am. Nursing Assn. Democrat. Baptist. Avocations: sewing, decorating, dance, jazz, computers. Home and Office: The Exhale Nurse Cons 1295 Grand Concourse Rm 3C Bronx NY 10452 Personal E-mail: budstallion@verizon.net.

HILLIARD, DAVID CRAIG, lawyer, educator; b. Framingham, Mass., May 22, 1937; s. Walter David and Dorothy (Shortiss) H.; m. Celia Schmid, Feb. 16, 1974. BS, Tufts U., 1959; JD, U. Chgo., 1962. Bar: Ill. 1962, U.S. Supreme Ct. 1966. Mng. ptnr. Pattishall, McAuliffe, Newbury, Hilliard & Geraldson, Chgo., 1983—2002, sr. ptnr., 2003—. Adj. prof. law Northwestern U., 1971—, chmn. Symposium Intellectual Property Law and the Corp. Client, 1986-2005; lectr. in advanced trademark law and info. regulation U. Chgo. Law Sch., 1999—. Author: Unfair Competition and Unfair Trade Practices, 1985, Trademarks, 1987, Trademarks and Unfair Competition, 1994, 6th edit., 2005, Trademarks and Unfair Competition Treatise, 3d edit., 2007, online edit., 2007; editor-in-chief Chgo. Bar Record, 1978-81. Trustee Art Inst. Chgo., 1980—, vice-chmn., 1998-2000, exec. com., 1994-2000, chmn. sustaining fellows, 1981-85, chmn. adv. com. dept. architecture, 1981—, pres. aux. bd., 1977-79, chmn. exhbns. com., 1993-2006, chmn. bd. govs. of the sch., 1997-2000; trustee Newberry Libr., 1983—, exec. com., 1987—, vice-chmn., 2006-; trustee Robert Allerton Trust, 2002-; pres. Lawyers Trust Fund Ill., 1985-88; vis. com. DePaul U. Law Sch., U. Chgo. Sch. of Law, chmn., 1987-88, Northwestern U. Assocs., 1985—; profl. adv. bd. Atty. Gen. Ill., 1982-84; mem. Ill. Commn. on Rights of Women, 1983-85; bd. dirs. Ill. Inst. Continuing Legal Edn., 1980-82; pres. Planned Parenthood Assn. Chgo., 1975-77. Lt. JAGC, USN, 1962-66. Recipient Maurice Weigle award, 1974, Chgo. Coun. Lawyers award for jud. reform, 1983. Fellow Am. Coll. Trial Lawyers (chmn. courageous adv. com. 1995-97); mem. ABA (chmn. trademark divsn. 1986-87, mem. coun. 1991-95, intellectual property law sect.), Ill. Bar Assn., Chgo. Bar Assn. (pres. 1982-83, founding chmn. young lawyers sect. 1971-72), Internat. Trademark Assn. (bd. dirs. 1989-91, CPR disting. panel of neutrals 1994—), Arts Club, Chgo. Club, Econ. Club, Grolier Club, Lawyers Club, Legal Club (pres. 1989-90), Univ. Club, Casino, Wayfarers Club (pres. 1994-95). Home: 1320 N State Pky Chicago IL 60610-2118 Office: Pattishall McAuliffe Newbury Hilliard & Geraldson 311 S Wacker Dr Ste 5000 Chicago IL 60606-6631 Office Phone: 312-554-8000. Business E-Mail: dhilliard@pattishall.com.

HILLIARD, EARL FREDERICK, congressman, lawyer; b. Apr. 9, 1942; s. Mary Franklin Hilliard; m. Iola H. Hilliard, June 9, 1967; children: Alesia, Earl F. BA, Morehouse Coll., 1964; JD, Howard U., 1967; MBA, Atlanta U., 1970; LHD (hon.), Talladega Coll., 2000. Rsch. asst. Howard U., 1965-67; instr. Miles Coll., 1967-68; asst. to pres. Ala. State U., 1968-70; ptnr. Hilliard, Jackson, Little & Stansel, Birmingham, 1974-78; pvt. practice Birmingham; pres. Am. Trust Life Ins. Co.; mem. Ala. Ho. of Reps., 1974-80, chmn. Black legis. caucus, 1975; mem. Ala. Senate, 1980-93, U.S. Congress from 7th Ala. dist., 1993—2002; ptnr. Hillard, Smith & Hunt, Birmingham, 2003—. Appointed amb. peace Universal Peace Fedn., 2007. Reginald Herber Smith Comty. Lawyer fellow, 1970-71. Mem. NAACP (life), Nat. Bar Assn. (life), Ala. Black Lawyers Assn., Morehouse Coll. Alumni Assn. (life), Alpha Phi Alpha (life). Democrat. Baptist. Home: 1625 Castleberry Way Birmingham AL 35214-4867 Office: Hilliard Smith & Hunt PO Box 12445 Birmingham AL 35202-2445 Home Phone: 205-798-7352; Office Phone: 205-326-8844. E-mail: earlhilliard@bellsouth.net.

HILLIARD, ROBERT GLENN, insurance company executive, lawyer; b. Anderson, SC, Jan. 18, 1943; s. Baz Robert and Louise (Holcombe) H.; m. Heather Ann Prevost, Apr. 1, 1966; children: Kathryn Louise Stuart, Nancy Ann, Mary Elizabeth Glenn. BA, Clemson U., 1965; JD, George Washington U., 1968. Bar: S.C. 1969. Gen. counsel Liberty Life Ins. Co., Greenville, SC, 1965-82, 1975-82; v.p., gen. counsel, sec. Liberty Life Ins. Co., Greenville, SC, 1975-82; pres., chief exec. officer Liberty Life; pres. Liberty Life Ins. Co., Greenville, SC, 1982-88, chmn. bd., 1988-89; dir. Liberty Corp., 1982-89; pres., CEO, Security Life of Denver ING Americas, Atlanta, 1989—92, pres., CEO ING America Life, 1992—93, CEO, pres., chmn., 1993—2003; non-exec. chmn. Conseco, Carmel, Ind., 2003—04, chmn., 2004—. Bd. dirs. Carolina First Corp., Security Life; founder, chmn. emeritus Foothills Trail Conf.; chmn. Netherlands Ins. Co., ING Can., N.Am. Investment Centre, NN Fin. Bd. dir. Piedmont Hosp., Atlanta; vice chmn., fin., High Mus.; chmn. investment com., Clemson Univ. Found.; former chmn. bd. dirs. S.C. Gov.'s Sch. for Arts, Perception, Inc. Recipient Jim Kern award Am. Hiking Soc. Mem. ABA, S.C. Bar Assn., Am. Coun. Life Ins., Assn. Life Ins. Counsel, INternat. Ins. Soc., Org. for Internat. Investment, Internat. Bus. Fellows, Bare Minimum Track Club (co-founder, bd. dirs.), Greenville Country Club, Poinsett Club (S.C.), Colo. Concern, Colo. Forum, Denver Athletic Club, Univ. Club. Presbyterian. Office: Conseco 1355 Peachtree St Ste 640 Atlanta GA 30309 Office Phone: 404-745-9770. E-mail: rglennhilliard@aol.com.*

HILLIARD, SAM BOWERS, geography educator; b. Hart County, Ga., Dec. 21, 1930; s. Asa Farris and Flora Elizabeth (Bowers) H.; m. Joyce Collier, June 4, 1955; children— Steven Glen, Anita Joy. AB, U. Ga., 1960, MA, 1962; MS, U. Wis., 1963, PhD, 1966. Electrician Savannal River Valley plant Dupont Co., Aiken, SC, 1954-59; teaching asst. U. Wis., 1961-65, instr. Milw., 1965-67; asst. prof. geography So. Ill. U., 1967-71; prof. La. State U., Baton Rouge, 1971-82, alumni prof., ret., 1983-93, chmn. dept. geography, 1976-79, 85-86, dir. Sch. Geosci., 1977-79. Columnist The Hartwell Sun newspaper; historian Hart County. Author: Hog Meat and Hoecake: Food Supply in the Old South, 1972, An Atlas of Antebellum Southern Agriculture, 1984; co-author: Louisiana: Its Land and People, rev. edit., 1987, The South Revisited: Forty Years of Change, 1992, Vignettes of Hart, vol. 1, 2001, vol. 2, 2002, A Century of Rural Education: Hart County, 1860-1960, A Calling of Churches: Sketches of Hart County Churches, 2003; contbr. articles to profl. jours. County historian, 1998. Served with U.S. Navy, 1950-54. Mem. Nat. Geog. Soc., Agrl. History Assn.

HILLIER, J(AMES) ROBERT, architect; b. Toronto, Ont., Can., July 24, 1937; came to US, 1941, naturalized, 1961; s. James and Florence (Bell) H.; m. Barbara Ann Weinstein, Apr. 7, 1986; 1 child, Jordan Rebecca Hillier; children by previous marriage: Kimberly (dec.), James Baldwin. BA, Princeton U., 1959, MFA, 1961; MBA (hon.), Bryant Coll., 1992. Project designer J. Labatut, Princeton, NJ, 1961-62; project mgr. Fulmer & Bowers, Princeton, 1961-66; prin. J. Robert Hillier, Princeton, 1966-72; pres. The Hillier Group, Princeton, 1972-87, chmn. bd., 1987—2000, Hillier Architecture, 2000—07; prin, dep. chmn. RMJM Hillier, 2007—; pres. Hillier Properties, LLC. Adj. faculty Sch. Arch. Princeton U. Prin. works include Bryant Coll. campus, Smithfield, RI, 1969, Peddie Campus Bldgs., 1970—, Rutgers U. Athletic Center, Piscataway, NJ, 1977, Butler Hosp, Providence, 1978, NJ State Justice Complex, Trenton, 1985, Harbor Island Design, Tampa, Fla., 1981, Beneficial Corp. Complex, 1982, Merritt Tower, 1985, Wharton Sch. Exec. Ctr., 1986, NJ Aquarium, 1991, Am. Home Products Corp. Hdqrs., 1992, Sprint World Hqrs., 1997, Glaxo Smith Kline Hdqrs., 1998, Capital One Corp. Hdqrs., 2002, Restoration Supreme Ct. Bldg., Washington, 2003, Princeton Pub. Libr., 2004, Va. State Capital restoration and preservation, 2004, The Waxwood, Princeton, 2005, Natirar, Spa and Hotel, Peapack, NJ, 2005, U. Med. Ctr. at Princeton, 2006, Los Colinas Live Master Plan, 2007. Trustee Peddie Sch., Hightstown, NJ, 1981—, McCarter Theatre, Princeton, 1983-89, Bryant Coll., Smithfield, RI, 1993-96, Edison Coll. Found., Milton Hershey Sch., 1997-2002; bd. overseers NJ Inst. Tech. Recipient over 300 design awards from archtl. assns., 1966—; Architect of Yr. award NJ Contractors Assn., 1976, 87, 92, 97, Disting. Svc. award Internat. Assn. Conf. Ctrs., 1988, Award of Excellence NJ Bus. and Industry Assn., 1988, NJ Entrepreneur of Yr., 1989, Cmty. Svc. Human Rels. award, 1992, Da Vinci award Profl. Svc. Mgmt. Assn., 2002, Master of Infrastructure medal Perjendel Coun., 2005; named Innovator of the Yr., Princeton C. of C., 2006. Fellow AIA (v.p. NJ chpt. 1974); mem. Nat. Coun. Archtl. Registration Bds., Princeton Quadrangle Club, Nassau Club, Princeton Club, Lookaway Golf Club. Avocations: running, swimming, golf. Home: 2846 River Rd New Hope PA 18938-9527 Office: RMJM HIllier 500 Alexander Rd Princeton NJ 08540-6002 Office Phone: 609-452-8888. Business E-Mail: jrhilier@rmjmhillier.com.

HILLIKER, DONALD BECKSTETT, lawyer; b. Dixon, Ill., Jan. 6, 1944; s. Donald Herschel and Bernadette (Welch) H.; m. Carolyn Ann Beckstett, Dec. 16, 1972; children: Carrie Ford, Sarah Dillon. BS, Loyola U., Chgo., 1966; JD, Northwestern U., 1969. Bar: Ill. 1969, U.S. Dist. Ct. (no. dist.) Ill. 1969, U.S. Ct. Appeals (7th cir.) 1971, U.S. Ct. Appeals (6th cir.) 1988, U.S. Supreme Ct. 1989. Lawyer, legal aid bur. United Charities Chgo., 1969—70; assoc. Isham, Lincoln & Beale, Chgo., 1970—74, ptnr., 1976—79, Coin, Crowley, Nord & Hilliker, Chgo., 1979—81, Phelan, Pope & John, Ltd., Chgo., 1981—90, Pope & John, Ltd., Chgo., 1990—95; ptnr., chmn. pro bono com. McDermott, Will & Emery, Chgo., 1995—. Vis. asst. prof. law, asst. dean Sch. Law, Northwestern U., Chgo., 1975-76; mem. com. on profl. responsibility Ill. Supreme Ct., 1978-95; bd. dirs. Legal Assistance Found., pres., 2002-2004; adj. prof. law Northwestern U., Chgo., 1993—. Co-author: Law Journal Seminars Press, 1980, 84; contbr. articles to numerous legal jours.; editorial bd. Northwestern U. Law Rev., 1969-70. Pres. sch. bd. St. Clement Sch., Chgo., 1984-87; nat. chmn. ann. fund drive Northwestern U. Sch. Law, 1986-88, mem. visitors com., 1988-94. Reginald Heber Smith fellow, 1969-70. Fellow Am. Bar Found.; mem. ABA (co-chair ethics beyond the rules task force 1994-98, co-chair comml. and banking litig. com. 1997-98, standing com. ethics and profl. responsibility 1997-03, chair 2001-03, chair coord. coun. Ctr. Profl. Responsibility 2005—, litig. sect. coun. 1998-01, chair sect./divsn. com. on ethics and professionalism, co-chair pro bono and pub. interest com. 2003-06, commn. to evaluate model code jud. conduct 2003—07), Chgo. Bar Assn. (chair large law firm com. 1998-2000, profl. responsibility com.), Chgo. Coun. Lawyers (legal counsel 1981-83), Am. Law Inst., Ctr. Ethics and Corp. Policy (bd. dirs. 1991-94), Order of Coif. Democrat. Roman Catholic. Office: McDermott Will & Emery LLP 227 W Monroe St Ste 5200 Chicago IL 60606-5096 Office Phone: 312-984-7610. Office Fax: 312-984-7700. Business E-Mail: dhilliker@mwe.com.

HILLINGER, CHARLES, journalist, writer; b. Evanston, Ill., Apr. 1, 1926; s. William Agidious H. and Caroline Bruning; m. Arliene Otis, June 22, 1948; children: Brad, Tori. BS in Polit. Sci., UCLA, 1951; degree (hon.), Marymount Coll., Rancho Palos Verdes, Calif., 1997. Circulation mgr., columnist Park Ridge Advocate, Ill., 1938-41; copy boy, libr., feature writer Chgo. Tribune, 1941-43; reporter, feature writer, syndicated columnist LA Times, 1946-92, ret., 1992. Author: California Islands, 1957, Bel-Air Country Club, A Living Legend, 1993, Charles Hillinger's America, 1996, Charles Hillinger's Channel Islands, 1998, Hillinger's California, 1997, California Characters, 2002, (audiobooks) Charles Hillinger's America, 1999, California Characters, 2001, California, 2003. Mem. adv. bd. Santa Cruz Is. Found., Santa Barbara, Calif., 1992—; treas. 8-Ball Welfare Found., 1992-. With USN, 1943-46. Mem. Greater LA Press Club (sec. 1978-88, v.p. 1988-90, pres. 1990-92), Dutch Treat Club W. Avocations: tennis, golf, hearts. Home: 3131 Dianora Dr Rancho Palos Verdes CA 90275 Home Phone: 310-377-6472. Personal E-mail: chxlat@aol.com.

HILLION, PIERRE THÉODORE MARIE, mathematical physicist; b. Saint-Brieuc, France, Jan. 31, 1926; s. Pierre Auguste Alexandre and Olive Jane (Marion) H.; m. Jane Garde, July 9, 1955 (dec.); children: Catherine, Pierre, Joëlle, Hervé. Licencie es Scis., Engr. Ecole, 1950; Docteur es Sciences, 1957. Engr. Le Matèriel Electrique Schneider-Westinghouse, 1950-55; math. physicist Sect. Technique de L'Armèe, 1955-64; head math. phys. dept. Laboratoire Ctrl. de L'Armement, 1964-83; sci. cons. Ctr. D'Analyse de Dèfense, 1983-91; maitre de confs. Ecole Nationale Supérieure des Techniques Avancèes, 1976-88; mem. Electromagnetic Acad. MIT. Contbr. articles on high energy physics, math. physics and numerical analysis to profl. jours. Mem. du bur. Assn. de Parents d'Elèves, 1965-76. With French Army, 1950. Recipient Mèrite pour la Recherche et l'Invention, 1965, Palmes Acadèmiques, 1970, Ordre Nat. pour le Mèrite, 1978, Legion d'Honneur, 1988. Mem. Societé Mathèmatique de France, Société Française de Radioprotection, Syndicat de la Presse Scientifique, Internat. Assn. Math. Physics. Roman Catholic. Home: 86 bis Rt de Croissy 78110 Le Vesinet Yvelines France Personal E-mail: pierre.hillion@wanadoo.fr.

HILLIS, JOHN DAVID, broadcast executive, television producer, newswriter; b. Washington, Dec. 28, 1952; s. Willard E. and Holly M. Hillis; m. Catherine H. McQuaig, Nov. 21, 1975; children: Faith Courteney, David Esten, Elizabeth Nicole. BA in Journalism, cum laude, U. Ga., 1975. Film editor Sta. WSB-TV, Atlanta, 1973-74, asst. producer, 1974-76, news producer, 1976; exec. news producer Sta. KOTV-TV, Tulsa, 1976-79; news producer Sta. WRAL-TV, Raleigh, N.C., 1979-80, Cable News Network, Inc., Atlanta, 1980-81, exec. producer, Newswatch, 1981-83, exec. producer, 1983-84, spl. events producer, 1984; news dir. Cablevision Systems Corp., Woodbury, N.Y., 1984-86; gen. mgr. Rainbow News 12 Co., Woodbury, 1986-89; pres., CEO Allnewsco, Inc., Washington, 1989—2002, Newschannel 8 Cable Svc., Springfield, Va., 1991—2002; pres., prin. Equinox Media Internat., LLC, Fairfax, Va., 2002—. Contbr. articles to profl. jours. Mem. strategic com. Greater Washington Bd. of Trade; bd. dirs. Va. Cmty. Found. Recipient Radio Newscast award Ga. AP Broadcasters, 1973, TV Newscast award Okla. AP Broadcasters, 1978, TV Series award News Acad. Cable Programming, 1985, Washington Region Emmy award, 1997, Cable Ace awards, 1996, 97, 98, Cmty. Spirit award NCTA, 1999, Scripps-Howard award, 1999. Mem. NATAS (Bd. of Govs. award Washington chpt.), Soc. Profl. Journalists (disting. svc. award 1998), Radio TV News Dirs. Assn., Nat. Press Club, Assn. Regional News Channels (founder, chmn. 1993), Nat. Cable TV Assn. (satellite network com.). Methodist. Office: Equinox Media Internat LLC PO Box 41 Round Hill VA 20142-0041 Business E-Mail: mail@equinox-media.com.

HILLIS, WILLIAM DANIEL, biology professor; b. Paris, Ark., June 12, 1933; s. Charles Raymond Hillis and Carra Elizabeth (Daniel) Coffee; m. Argye Idell Briggs, Dec. 23, 1952; children: William Daniel Jr., David Mark, Argye Elizabeth Trupe. BS, Baylor U., 1953; MD, Johns Hopkins U., 1957. Lic. in medicine and surgery Md., Tex. Asst. prof. pathobiology Johns Hopkins U. and Sch. Hygiene and Pub. Health, Balt., 1965-68, assoc. prof., 1968-72; asst. prof. Johns Hopkins U. Sch. Medicine, Balt., 1972-76, assoc. prof., 1976-82; prof., chmn. dept. biology Baylor U., Waco, Tex., 1982-85, Cornelia Marshall Smith prof. biology, 1985-98, disting. prof. biology, 1995—, exec. v.p., 1985-89, v.p. student affairs, 1989-98. Cons. Nat. Cancer Inst., Bethesda, Md., 1965-68, Nat. Heart and Lung Inst., Bethesda, 1977-82; dir. Health Professions Rsch. Tng. Program, Balt., 1979-82, Out-Patient Clin. Rsch. Ctr., Balt., 1975-82. Contbr. articles to profl. jours. Pres. Bapt. Home Md., Balt., 1972-81; Md. rep. exec. com. So. Bapt. Conv., NAshville, 1977-82; bd. dirs. Food for Hungry, Glendale, Calif., 1972-82, Caritas, Waco, Tex., chair, 1989-95. Col. USAF, 1960-65, USAFR, 1965-85. Named Outstanding Prof., Baylor U., 1985; recipient Louis Livingston Seaman award, Assn. Mil. Surgeons U.S., 1978, Disting. Alumnus award, Baylor U., 1998. Mem. Am. Assn. Immunologists, Soc. for Exptl. Biology and Medicine, Am. Soc. for Microbiology, N.Y. Acad. Sci., McLennan County Med. Soc., Waco C. of C. (bd. dirs. 1987), Johns Hopkins Soc. of Scholars, Mortar Bd., Phi Beta Kappa, Alpha Omega Alpha, Omicron Delta Kappa. Clubs: Brazos (Waco); Johns Hopkins (Balt.). Democrat. Avocations: vocal music, drama, gardening, carpentry, stamp collecting/philately. Office Phone: 254-710-2091. Personal E-mail: wm.hillis@att.net.

HILLMAN, HENRY LEA, investment company executive; b. Pitts., Dec. 25, 1918; s. J.H. (Jr.) and Juliet Cummins (Lea) H.; m. Elsie Mead Hilliard, May 12, 1945; children: Lea, Audrey, Henry, William. AB, Princeton U., 1941. Chmn. exec. com. Hillman Co. Emeritus mem. exec. com. Allegheny Conf. on Cmty. Devel.; chmn. Hillman Found., Inc., Henry L. Hillman Found.; trustee emeritus Carnegie Inst. Lt. USNR, 1942—45. Named one of Forbes' Richest Americans, 1999—, World's Richest People, Forbes mag., 2001—. Mem.: Duquesne (Pitts.), Pitts. Golf, Fox Chapel Golf, Rolling Rock (Ligionier, Pa.) (hon. gov.), Laurel Valley Golf (Ligionier, Pa.), Links (NYC). Home: Morewood Heights Pittsburgh PA 15213 Office: Hillman Co 330 Grant St Pittsburgh PA 15219-2202

HILLMAN, JENNIFER ANNE, federal official; b. Toledo, Jan. 29, 1957; d. Charles Winchell and Anne Sylvia (Mossberg) H.; m. Mitchell Rand Berger, Oct. 20, 1990; children: Benjamin Stanley Berger, Daniel Charles Berger. BA, Duke U., 1978, MEd, 1979; JD, Harvard U., 1983. Bar: DC, US Ct. Internat., US Mil. Appeals. Asst. to chancellor Duke U., Durham, NC, 1979-80; freshman Proctor Harvard U., Cambridge, Mass., 1981-83; assoc. Patton, Boggs & Blow, Washington, 1983—; legis. asst. Senator Terry Sanford, Washington, 1987-88, legis. dir., 1988-92; dep. cluster coord. for fin. instns. US Presdl. and Vice Presdl. Transition Team, Washington, 1992-93; ambassador, chief textile negotiator Office of US Trade Rep., Exec. Office of Pres., Washington, 1993-95; gen. counsel Office of the US Trade Rep., 1995-97; commr. US Internat. Trade Commn., Washington, 1998—, vice-chmn., 2002—04. Trustee Duke U., 1977-80; adj. prof. Sch. Law Georgetown U., 2005—. Adviser Terry Sanford for Senate Campaign, 1986, 1992; Trinity Coll. bd. visitors Duke U., 1999—; commr. Stoddert Youth Soccer, 2000—; mem. Selection Panel on Truman Scholars, 2000—; pres. Trade Policy Forum, 2001—04; mem. N.C. Dems., Raleigh, 1986—, Georgetown Presbyn. Ch., 1988—; tchr. adult learning Sacred Heart, Washington, 1983—92. Mem. Coun. on Women's Studies Duke U., Phi Beta Kappa. Avocations: running, scuba diving, travel, reading. Office: Internat Trade Commn 500 E St SW Washington DC 20436-0003

HILLMAN, NOEL L., federal judge, former prosecutor; b. Red Bank, NJ, Dec. 22, 1956; BA cum laude, Monmouth Coll., 1981; JD cum laude, Seton Hall U., 1985; LLM, NYU, 1998. Judicial law clk. to Hon. Maryanne Trump Barry US Dist. Ct., NJ, 1986—88; assoc. Lord Day & Lord, Barrett Smith, NYC, 1988—92; asst. US atty. Dist. NJ US Dept. Justice, Newark, 1992—2001, trial atty. Campaign Fin. Task Force Washington, 1999—2000, dep. chief criminal divsn., 2000—01, prin. dep. chief Office Pub. Integrity, 2001—02, acting chief, 2002—03, chief, 2003—06; judge US Dist. Ct. NJ, Camden, 2006—. US delegate to Global Forums III and IV, UN Convention Against Corruption, Merida, Mexico, Vienna. Avocations: reading, politics, surfing, bicycling, kayaking, skiing. Office: Mitchell H Cohen Fed Bldg & US Courthouse 1 John F Gerry Plz Camden NJ 08101

HILLMAN, PETER N., lawyer; b. NYC, Mar. 19, 1953; BA magna cum laude, with highest honors, Williams Coll., 1975; JD, Columbia U., 1978. Bar: NY 1979, US Dist. Ct. (So. Dist.) NY 1979, US Dist. Ct. (DC) 1979, US Ct. Appeals (11th Cir.) 1981, US Supreme Ct. 1982, US Ct. Appeals (6th Cir.) 1982, US Ct. Appeals (9th Cir.) 1984, US Dist. Ct. (Ea. Dist.) NY 1986, US Dist. Ct. (Conn.) 1989, US Ct. Appeals (2nd Cir.) 1992, US Dist. Ct. (No. Dist.) NY 1998. Mem. Chadbourne & Parke LLP, NYC, 1978—, ptnr., 1986—, chmn., Employment Law. Contbr. articles to profl. jour.; lectr. in field. Harlan Fiske Stone Scholar. Mem.: ABA (Tort & Ins. Practice

Sect., Labor & Employment Law Sect.), NY State Bar Assn., Phi Beta Kappa. Office: Chadbourne & Parke LLP 30 Rockefeller Plz New York NY 10112 Office Phone: 212-408-1010. Office Fax: 212-541-5369. Business E-Mail: phillman@chadbourne.com.

HILLMAN, ROBERT ANDREW, lawyer, educator; b. NYC, Dec. 23, 1946; s. Herman D. and Edith N. (Geilich) H.; m. Elizabeth Hall Kafka, Aug. 24, 1969; children: Jessica H., Heather D. BA, U. Rochester, 1969; JD, Cornell U., 1972. Bar: N.Y. 1973, Iowa 1976. Law clk. to judge U.S. Dist. Ct., NYC, 1972-73; assoc. Debevoise & Plimpton, NYC, 1973-74; prof. law U. Iowa, Iowa City, 1975-82, Cornell U., Ithaca, NY, 1982—, assoc. dean, 1990-97, Edwin Woodruff prof. law. Author or co-author: Common Law and Equity Under the UCC, 1985, Law: Its Nature, Functions, and Limits, 1986, Contract and Related Obligation: Theory, Doctrine, and Practice, 1987, 5th edit., 2006, The Richness of Contract Law, 1997, Modern American Contract Law, 2000, Principles of Contract Law, 2004; reporter Am. Law Inst. Prins. of The Law of Software Contracts; contbr. articles to profl. jours. Mem. Am. Law Inst. Avocations: tennis, bicycling. Office: Cornell U Law Sch Myron Taylor Hall Ithaca NY 14853 E-mail: rah16@cornell.edu.

HILLMER, MARGARET PATRICIA, library director; b. Cirencester, Gloucestershire, Eng., Mar. 17, 1936; came to U.S., 1960; naturalized, 1973; d. John Albert and Margaret Evelyn (Richardson) Hall; m. Max Lorraine Hillmer, Mar. 24, 1962; children: Felicity Margaret, Jennifer Anne. ALAM, London Acad. Music Dram. Art, London, 1955; AB magna cum laude, Heidelberg Coll., 1976; AM in Libr. Sci., U. Mich., 1977. Cert. libr. Ohio. Speech and ballet tchr., Cirencester, 1955-58; governess NSW, Australia, 1959—60; ballet instr., choreographer Heidelberg Coll., Tiffin, Ohio, 1969-73, adminstrv. asst. pub. rels. Water Quality Lab., 1978-79; head reference dept. Tiffin-Seneca Pub. Libr., 1979-80, libr. dir., 1980—. Contbr. articles to profl. publs. Chair Take Our Daughters to Work Day, 1993-2000; bd. dirs. Tiffin-Seneca Teen Ctr., 1992—; mem. Tiffin City Schs. Bd. Edn., 1991-2003, pres., 1995-96; mem. Seneca County Dept. Human Svcs. Bd., 1984-91, pres., 1987-89. Recipient Liberty Bell award Seneca County Bar Assn., 1990, People's Law Sch. award Ohio Acad. Trial Lawyers, 1993, Athena award Tiffin Area C. of C., 1999; named Ohio Libr. of Yr., 2004. Mem. ALA, AAUW, LWV (pres. Tiffin chpt. 1980-82, chair internat. rels. Ohio 1975-76), Ohio Libr. Assn. (legislation com. 1985-89, chair legis. network 1989-93, chair awards and honors com. 1995-96, seminar spkr. 1985—), Pub. Libr. Assn., Freedom to Read Assn., Tiffin Rotary Club (pres. 2001-02), Beta Phi Mu. Democrat. Episcopalian. Avocations: reading, theater, classical music. Home: 25 Southview Pl Tiffin OH 44883-3312 Office: Tiffin-Seneca Pub Libr 77 Jefferson St Tiffin OH 44883-2339 Home Phone: 419-447-7080; Office Phone: 419-447-3751. Business E-Mail: hillmepa@oplin.org.

HILLOCKS, GEORGE, JR., language educator, researcher; b. Cleve., June 15, 1934; s. George and Ina Ternan Hillocks; m. Jo Anne Bruce, 1957 (div. 1998); children: Marjorie Anne, George McInnes. BA, Coll. Wooster, Ohio, 1956; MA, Case Western Res. U., Cleve., 1958, PhD, 1970; diploma in English Studies, U. Edinburgh, 1959. English tchr. Euclid Pub. Schs., Ohio, 1956-58, 59-65; English instr. Bowling Green State U., Ohio, 1965-70, asst. prof. English Ohio, 1970-71; asst. prof. Edn. U. Chgo., 1971-75, assoc. prof. Edn., 1975-85, prof. Edn. and English, 1985—2003. Dir. MA program in tchg. English U. Chgo., 1971-2002; vis. Thomas R. Watson disting. prof. U. Louisville, 2000. Author: Research on Written Composition: New Directions for Teaching, 1986, Teaching Writing as Reflective Practice, 1995 (David H. Russel award 1997), Ways of Thinking, Ways of Teaching, 1999, The Testing Trap: How Statewide Writing Assessments Control Learning, Choice: Outstanding Academic Work, 2002, Narrative Writing: Learning a New Model for Teaching, 2006; co-author: The Dynamics of English Instruction, 1971. Fellowship Ctr. for Advanced Study in Behavioral Scis., 2000—01. Fellow Nat. Conf. Rsch. Lang. and Literacy (pres. 2000-01); mem. Nat. Acad. Edn., Nat. Coun. Tchrs. English (chair Assembly for Rsch. 1986, Disting. Svc. award, 2004), Am. Ednl. Rsch. Assn. Avocations: reading, writing, bagpipes. Home: 2012 W 110th St Chicago IL 60643 Office Phone: 773-429-0119. Business E-Mail: ghillock@uchicago.edu.

HILL ROTMAN, CARLOTTA H., physician; b. Chgo., Apr. 8, 1958; d. Clarence Kenneth and Vlasta (Cizek) Hayes; m. Chester James Hill III, June 10, 1967 (div. 1974); m. Carlos A. Rotman, July 31, 1980; children: Robin Mercedes. BA magna cum laude, Knox Coll., 1969; MD with honors, U. Ill., 1973. Diplomate Nat. Bd. Med. Examiners, Am. Bd. Dermatology. Intern Mayo Sch. Medicine, Rochester, Minn., 1973-74; resident U. Ill., Chgo., 1975-78, asst. prof. clin. dermatology Coll. Medicine, 1978-93, assoc. prof. clin. dermatology Coll. Medicine, 1993—. Mem. U. Ill. Senate, Chgo., 1986-91, 99-2002; councilor Chgo. Med. Soc., 1990-96, 1999-2006. Contbr. articles to profl. jours. Bd. dirs. Summerfest St. James Cathedral, Chgo., 1986-91, YWCA, Lake Forest, Ill., 1995-, pres., 1998-2000; master gardner Chgo. Bot. Garden, Glencoe, Ill., 1994-98; bd. dirs. Lake Bluff Open Lands Assn., 1997-2006, Friends of Ryerson Woods, 2005—, Lake Forest/Lake Bluff Hist. Soc., 2006—; mem. Lake Bluff Libr. Bd., 2001-05. Recipient Janet Glascow award Am. Women's Med. Assn., 1973. Mem. Am. Acad. Dermatology, Herb Soc. Am. (ways and means No. Ill. unit 1992-94, treas. N. Ill. unit 1996-00, vice chair 2000-02, chair 2002-04, ctrl. dist. steering com. 2004-06, nat. herb garden com. 2006—), Chgo. Dermatol. Care Soc., Ill. Dermatologic Soc., Phi Beta Kappa, Alpha Omega Alpha. Avocations: travel, cooking, gardening, reading. Office: Dept Dermatology 808 S Wood St Chicago IL 60612-7300 Office Phone: 312-996-6966. Business E-Mail: chhill@uic.edu.

HILLS, AUSTIN EDWARD, vineyard executive; b. San Francisco, Oct. 13, 1934; s. Leslie William and Ethel (Lee) H.; m. Erika Michaela Brunar, May 20, 1978; children: Austin, Justin. AB, Stanford U., 1957; MBA, Columbia U., 1959. Chmn. bd. dirs. Hills Bros. Coffee, Inc., San Francisco, 1976, Grgich Hills Cellar, Rutherford, Calif., 1977—. Pres. Hills Vineyards, Inc., Rutherford, 1975-97; pres. Pacific Coast Coffee Assn., San Francisco, 1975-76, Hills Vineyard, Inc., 1999—. Pres. San Francisco Soc. for Prevention of Cruelty to Animals, 1972-78, No. Calif. Soc. for Prevention of Cruelty to Animals, 1972-78. With Air N.G. Mem. Am. Soc. Enologists. Libertarian. Office: 490 Post St Ste 1049 San Francisco CA 94102-1301 Personal E-mail: hillsa@pacbell.net.

HILLS, CARLA ANDERSON, lawyer, former secretary of housing and urban development; b. LA, Jan. 3, 1934; d. Carl H. and Edith (Hume) Anderson; m. Roderick Maltman Hills, Sept. 27, 1958; children: Laura Hume, Roderick Maltman, Megan Elizabeth, Alison Macbeth. AB cum laude, Stanford U., 1955; student, Oxford U., Eng., 1954; LLB (hon.), Yale U., 1958; degree (hon.), Pepperdine U., 1975, Washington U., 1977, Mills Coll., 1977, Lake Forest Coll., 1978, Williams Coll., 1981, Notre Dame U., 1993, Wabash Coll., 1997. Bar: Calif. 1959, DC 1974, US Supreme Ct. 1965. Asst. US atty. civil divsn. US Dept. Justice, LA, 1958-61; ptnr. Munger, Tolles, Hills & Rickershauser, LA, 1962-74; asst. atty. gen. civil divsn. US Dept. Justice, Washington, 1974-75; sec. US Dept. Housing & Urban Devel., Washington, 1975-77; ptnr. Latham, Watkins & Hills, Washington, 1978-86, Weil, Gotshal & Manges, Washington, 1986-88; US Trade Rep. Exec. Office of the Pres., Washington, 1989-93; chmn., CEO Hills & Co. Internat. Cons., 1993—. Chair Nat. Com. for US-China Rels.; bd. dir. Inst. Internat. Econ.; bd. dirs. CSIS; mem. adv. bd. Calif. Coun. on Criminal Justice, 1969—71; bd. dirs. Chevron Corp., 1977—88, 1993—2006, TCW Group, Inc., 1993—, Am. Internat. Group, 1993—2006, Time Warner, 1993—2001, Time Warner Inc. (formerly AOL/Time Warner), 2001—06, Lucent Tech., Inc., 1996—2006; bd. dirs Gilead Sciences, Inc., 2007—; adj. prof. Sch. Law UCLA, 1972; mem. corrections task force LA County Sub-Regional; mem. standing com. discipline US Dist. Ct. for Ctrl. Calif., 1970—73; mem. Adminstrv. Conf. US, 1972—74; bd. councillors U. So. Calif. Law Ctr., 1972—74; mem. at large exec. com. Yale Law Sch., 1973—78; mem. exec. com. law and free soc. State Bar Calif., 1973; trustee Pomona Coll., 1974—79; mem. com. on Law Sch. Yale U. Coun.; mem. Sloan Commn. on Govt. and Higher Edn., 1977—79, Internat. Found. for Cultural Cooperation and Devel., 1977—89, Am. Com. on East-West Accord, 1977—79, Trilateral Commn., 1977—82; mem. adv. com. Princeton U., Woodrow Wilson Sch. of Pub. and Internat. Affairs, 1977—80; mem. Fed. Acctg. Std. Adv. Coun., 1978—80; Gordon Grand fellow Yale U., 1978; trustee Brookings Instn., 1985, Am. Productivity and Quality Ctr., 1988; mem. Calif. Gov. Coun. Econ. Policy Adv., 1993—98; coun. mem. Coun. Fgn. Rels., 1993—; mem. Trilateral Commn., 1993—; chair bd. dir. Inter-Am. Dialogue, 1999—; vice chair Coun. Fgn. Rels., 2001—. Co-author: Federal Civil Practice, 1961; co-author, editor: Antitrust Adviser, 1971, 3d edit., 1985; contbg. editor: Legal Times, 1978-88; mem. editorial bd. Nat. Law Jour., 1978-88. Trustee U. So. Calif., 1977-79, Norton Simon Mus. Art, Pasadena, Calif., 1976-80; trustee Urban Inst., 1978-89, chmn., 1983-89; co-chmn. Alliance to Save Energy, 1977-89; vice chmn. adv. coun. on legal policy Am. Enterprise Inst., 1977-84; bd. visitors, exec. com. Stanford U. Law Sch., 1978-81; bd. dir. Am. Coun. for Capital Formation, 1978-82; mem. exec. com. Inst. for Internat. Econ., 1993—; mem. adv. com. MIT-Harvard U. Joint Ctr. for Urban Studies, 1978-82. Fellow Am. Bar Found.; mem. Am.'s Soc. (bd. dir.), LA Women Lawyers Assn. (pres. 1964), ABA (chair publ. com. antitrust sect. 1972-74, council 1974, 77-84, chair 1982-83), Fed. Bar Assn. (pres. LA chpt. 1963), LA County Bar Assn. (fed. rules and practice com. 1963-72, chair issues and survey 1963-72, chair sub-com. revision local rules for fed. cts. 1966-72, jud. qualifications com. 1971-72), Am. Law Inst., Am.-China Soc. (bd. dir. 1995-), Am. Soc. (bd. trustees 1996-2002), Asia Soc. (bd. trustees 1996-2002); Clubs: Yale of So. Calif. (dir. 1972-74); Yale (Washington). Office: Hills & Co 1120 20th St NW Ste 200N Washington DC 20036 Home Phone: 202-966-2065; Office Phone: 202-822-4700.

HILLS, JOHN MERRILL, educational association administrator, consultant, public relations executive, researcher; b. Wethersfield, Conn., May 6, 1944; s. Merrill Clarke and Elizabeth (Tarrant) H.; m. Irene Jeanne Lavallee, Oct. 7, 1974 (div.); children: John M. Jr., Sara Clarke. Student, U. Hartford, 1963; BBA, Nichols Coll., 1969; postgrad., U. Md., 1976. Salesman Peter A Frasse and Co., Inc., Hartford, Conn., 1963-64; dir. alumni relations, asst. dir. admissions Nichols Coll., Dudley, Mass., 1969-72; regional dir. Georgetown U., Washington, 1972-74; dir. devel. cen. adminstrn. U. Md., College Park, 1974-77; v.p. Roanoke Coll., Salem, Va., 1977-86, The Brookings Instn., Washington, 1986-98; pres. JMH Assocs., 1998—. Pres. J.M.H. Assocs., Washington, 1979—; cons. Am. Assn. Univ. Cons., Inc., Washington, 1975-77; mgmt., pub. relations and fund raising cons. Trustee, mem. exec. com. Nichols Coll., Dudley, Mass., 1993-2000, Higher Edn. Roundtable, Lamplighters; judge U.S. Steel Alumni Award, Pitts., 1979-86; bd. dirs. Mill Mountain Theater, Roanoke, 1983-86, Roanoke ARC, 1984-86, Roanoke Valley C. of C., 1983-86; mem. adv. bd. Phoenix Soc. Georgetown U. Sch. Law.; nat. bd. equality forum, 2007-; mem. Little Theater of Alexandria. With U.S. Army, 1965-67, N.G. Recipient Alumni Achievement award Nichols Coll., 1991; named one of Outstanding Young Men Am., U.S. Jaycees, 1980, Outstanding Nat. Advisor, Pi Lambda Phi, Conn., 1983, 86. Mem. Nat. Soc. Fund Raiser Execs., Coun. for Advancement and Support of Edn. (faculty chmn.), Alexandria Sportsman's Club (mem. exec. com.), Hunting Hills Club, Jefferson Club (Roanoke), Met. Club Washington, Paul Hill Choral Soc. (mem. corp. bd.). Roman Catholic. Avocations: sailing, jogging. Home (Summer): 17 Josephine St Rehoboth Beach DE 19971-2017 Office: JMH Assocs 5801 Bayview Dr Fort Lauderdale FL 33308 also: JMH Assocs 429 R St NW Washington DC 20001 Office Phone: 954-267-9155. Personal E-mail: jackhills@jackhills.com.

HILLS, KENDELL LENAR, music educator; b. Savannah, Ga., Dec. 14, 1977; s. Kathryn Silas; m. Jennifer Chisholm, May 13, 2004; 1 child, Kennedy Kathryn. BA in Music cum laude, Savannah State U., 2005. Chem. ops. specialist US Army, Ft. Stewart, Ga., 1997—2005; music tchr. Chatham County Pub. Schs., Savannah, 2006—. Mem.: Ga. Music Educators Assn., Music Educators Nat. Conf., Masons (sec. local lodge 2001—). Avocation: music arrangement and composition. Personal E-mail: abraham906@aol.com. Business E-Mail: hillsk0@savstate.edu.

HILLS, PATRICIA GORTON SCHULZE, curator, art historian; b. Baraboo, Wis., Jan. 31, 1936; d. Hartwin A. Schulze and Glennie Gorton Baker; m. Frederic W. Hills, Jan. 17, 1958 (div. Feb. 1974); children: Christina, Bradford; m. Guy Kevin Whitfield, Jan. 3, 1976; 1 child, Andrew. BA, Stanford U., 1957; MA, Hunter Coll., 1968; PhD, NYU, 1973. Curatorial asst. Mus. Modern Art, NYC, 1960-62; guest curator Whitney Mus. Am. Art, 1971-72, assoc. curator 18th and 19th Century art, 1972-74; vis. asst. prof. art dept. Hunter Coll., 1973; adj. assoc. prof. fine arts Inst. Fine Arts NYU, 1973-74; assoc. prof. fine arts and performing arts York Coll. CUNY, 1974-78; assoc. prof. dept. art history Boston U., 1978-88, prof., 1988—, chmn. dept., 1995-97. Adj. assoc. prof. Grad. Sch. Arts and Scis., Columbia U., 1974—75; adj. curator Whitney Mus. Am. Art, 1974—87. Author: Eastman Johnson, 1972, The American Frontier: Images and Myths, 1973, The Painters' America: Rural and Urban Life, 1810-1910, 1974, Turn-of-Century America: Paintings, Graphics, Photographs, 1890-1910, 1977, Alice Neel, 1983, Social Concern and Urban Realism: American Painting of the 1930s, 1983, John Singer Sargent, 1986, Stuart Davis, 1996, Modern Art in the USA: Issues and Controversies of the 20th Century, 2001, May Stevens, 2005; co-author: The Figurative Tradition and the Whitney Mus. Am. Art, 1980, Jacob Lawrence: Thirty Years of Prints: 1963-2000, 2001, Eastman Johnson: Painting America, 1999, Syncopated Rhythms: 20th-Century African American Art from the George and Joyce Wein Collection, 2005. Fellow: Danforth Found. Grad. Women, 1968-72, John Simon Guggenheim Meml. Found., 1982-83, Charles Warren Ctr. Studies in Am. History, 1982-83, W.E.B. DuBois Inst. Afro-Am. Rsch., Harvard U., 1991-92, 2006-07, NEH, 1995, Gilder Lehrman Inst. of Am. History, 2005, Smithsonian Am. Art Mus., 2005-06, Georgia O'Keeffe Mus. Rsch. Ctr., 2006. Mem. Coll. Art Assn., Women's Caucus for Arts, Am. Studies Assn., Am. Assn. Mus. Home: 238 Putnam Ave Cambridge MA 02139-3767 Office: Boston U Dept Art History Boston MA 02215 Office Phone: 617-353-2520. Business E-Mail: pathills@bu.edu.

HILLS, REGINA J., journalist; b. Sault Sainte Marie, Mich., Dec. 24, 1953; d. Marvin Dan and Ardithanne (Tilly) H.; m. Vincent C. Stricherz, Feb. 25, 1984. BA, U. Nebr., 1976. Reporter UPI, Lincoln, Nebr., 1976-80, state editor, bur. mgr., 1981-82, New Orleans, 1982-84, Indpls., 1985-87; asst. city editor Seattle Post-Intelligencer, 1987-99, online prodr., 1999—2001, mng. prodr., 2001—06; web editor U. Wash., Seattle, 2006—. Panelist TV interview show Face Nebr., 1978-81; vis. lectr. U. Nebr., Lincoln, 1978, 79, 80; columnist weekly feature Capitol News, Nebr. Press Assn., 1981-82. Mem.: U. Nebr. Alumni Assn., Zeta Tau Alpha. Office: Univ Wash Box 351210 Seattle WA 98195-1210 Home Phone: 206-935-7430; Office Phone: 206-543-2560. E-mail: ghills@u.washington.edu.

HILLS, RODERICK M., lawyer, former government official; b. Seattle, Mar. 9, 1931; s. Kenneth Maltman and Sarah B. (Love) H.; m. Carla Helen Anderson, Sept. 27, 1958; children: Laura, Roderick Jr., Megan, Allison. BA in History, Stanford U., 1952, LLB, 1955. Bar: Calif. 1957, U.S. Supreme Ct. 1960, D.C. 1977. Law clk. to Justice Stanley F. Reed U.S. Supreme Ct., 1955-57; assoc. Musick, Peeler & Garrett, LA, 1957-62; ptnr. Munger, Tolles & Hills, LA, 1962-75; chmn. Republic Corp., LA, 1971-75; counsel to Pres. U.S., 1975; chmn. SEC, 1975-77; chmn., CEO Peabody Coal Co., St. Louis and Washington, 1977-79; ptnr. Latham, Watkins & Hills, Washington, 1978-82; chmn. Sears World Trade, Inc., Washington, 1982-84; chmn., mng. dir. The Manchester Group, Ltd. (renamed Hills Enterprises, Ltd.), Washington, 1984—; mng. ptnr. Donovan, Leisure, Rogovin, Huge & Schiller, Washington, 1989-92; chmn. internat. practice group Shea & Gould, Washington, 1992-94; ptnr. Mudge Rose Guthrie Alexander & Ferdon, Washington, 1994-95, Hills Stern & Morley, Washington, 1995—. Vis. prof. law Harvard U., 1969—70; lectr. law Stanford U., 1960—69; disting. faculty fellow in internat. fin. Yale U. Sch. Mgmt., 1986—89; vice chmn. bd. dirs. Oak Industries, 1990—2000, Feg. Mogul Corp., 1977—2003, chmn., 1996; bd. dirs. Regional Market Makers, Chiquita Brands Internat., 2002—07; chmn. Hills Governance Program, CSIS, 2001—. Bd. editors, comment editor: Stanford Law Rev, 1953-55. Trustee Com. Econ. Devel., 1978—, co-chair, 2005—; dir. U.S.-ASEAN Bus. Coun., Inc., 1982—, chmn., 1986-90, vice chmn., 1990—. Fellow Am. Bar Found.; mem. ABA, U.S. Supreme Ct. Bar Assn., L.A. County Bar Assn., State Bar Calif., Order of Coif, Chancery Club, Chevy Chase Club, Phi Delta Phi. Republican. Episcopalian. Avocations: tennis, golf, history. Home: 3125 Chain Bridge Rd NW Washington DC 20016-3411 Office: Hills Stern & Morley 901 15th St NW Washington DC 20005 Office Phone: 202-822-1611. E-mail: rmhills@hillsandstern.com.

HILLS, STEPHEN P., publishing executive; s. Oscar and Carol Hills; m. Joslyn Hills; 2 children. Grad., Yale U., 1981; MBA, Harvard Bus. Sch., 1987. Dir. advt. and mktg. ITB, Inc., Emeryville, Calif., 1981—82; co-founder The Bay City Bus. Jour., Emeryville, 1982; bus. intern The Washington Post, 1986—87, advt. sales rep., 1987, various positions in advt. and mktg., 1987—93, named v.p. advt., 1993, v.p. sales & mktg., 2001—02, pres. & gen. mgr., 2002—. Dir. Greater Washington Bd. Trade; mem. sales adv. com. Nat. Newspaper Network. Office: The Washington Post 1150 15th St NW Washington DC 20071*

HILLSMAN, JOAN RUCKER, music educator; b. Anderson, SC, Mar. 25, 1943; d. William Isaiah and Elizabeth Gilliard Rucker; m. Horace Jerome Hillsman (dec. Mar. 2002); 1 child, Quentin Jerome. B in Music Edn., Howard U., 1964, M in Music Edn., 1969; PhD in Musicology, Union Inst., 1978. Music tchr. St. Mary's County Pub. Schs., Leonardtown, Md., 1964—67, D.C. Pub. Schs., Washington, 1967—88, supr. music, 1988—96; prof. music Bowie (Md.) State U., 1996—. Owner, music cons., talent promoter Joan Hillsmans Music Network, Suitland, Md., 1996—; adj. music prof. Union Inst., Cin., Shenandoah Conservatory and Union Inst. Cmty. and Civic awards; organizer nation's Capitol 1st Gospel Homeless Choir. Author: Gospel: An African American Art Form, 1990, 1992, numerous poems. Vol. music for the elder various nursing homes, 2000—; vol. Prince George County Dems., 2002. Recipient Key to City of Detroit; Joan Hillsman's Day in the Nation's Capital named in her honor. Mem.: Gospel Music Workshop Am. (scholarship chair), Coll./Univ. Assn., Music Educators Nat. Conf. (D.C. pres. 1996—2000, Outstanding Educator award 1996), Nat. Coun. Univ. Women, Black Urban League, Top Ladies Orgn., Sigma Alpha Iota, Phi Delta Kappa, Alpha Kappa Alpha. Baptist. Avocations: music, poetry, bowling, research. Home: 3706 Stoneclift Rd Suitland MD 20746 Office: Bowie State Univ Fine and Performing Arts 14000 Jericho Park Rd Bowie MD Office Fax: 301-736-2838. Personal E-mail: joanhillsman@comcast.net.

HILLSMAN, SALLY T., sociologist; b. Teaneck, NJ, Aug. 28, 1941; d. Robert Bryan and Mary Andrew Hillsman. AB, Mt. Holyoke Coll., 1963; PhD, Columbia U., 1970. Asst. prof. sociology Queens Coll., CUNY, NYC, 1971—76; project dir. Vera Inst. of Justice, NYC, 1976—79, asst. dir., 1978—79, dir. rsch., 1979—91, assoc. dir., 1989—91; v.p. rsch. Nat. Ctr. for State Courts, Williamsburg, Va., 1991—96; dep. dir. Nat. Inst. Justice USDOJ, Washington, 1996—2002; exec. officer Am. Sociol. Assn., Washington, 2002—. Trustee Vera Inst. of Justice, NYC, 2003—; mem. sec. adv. bd. Dept. U.S. Commerce, 2002—; exec. com. Consortium Social Scis. Assns., 2002—. Contbr. articles pub. to profl. jour. V.p. Soc. for the Study of Social Problems, 1982—83; com. of profl. ethics Am. Sociol. Assn., 2001—03. Fellow: Nat. Acad. of Pub. Adminstrn.; mem.: Am. Soc. of Criminologists, Am. Acad. for the Advancement of Sci., Phi Beta Kappa. Office: Am Sociol Assn 1307 NY Ave Ste 700 Washington DC 20005 Office Phone: 202-383-9005. Business E-Mail: hillsman@asanet.org.

HILLSTROM, THOMAS PETER, engineering executive; s. Harry Edward and Mary Pauline Hillstrom; m. Jean Elizabeth Greenfield; children: Edward, Mary. BS in Mech. Engring., Northwestern U., Evanston, 1966; MBA, Northwestern U., Chgo., 1977. Design engr. Internat. Harvester, Hinsdale, Ill., 1966-74, project engr., 1974-78, product safety engr., 1978-82; mgr. engring. Fire Apparatus Div., FMC, Tipton, Ind., 1982-85; mgr. contract engring. FMC Naval Systems Div., Mpls., 1985-87, program mgr., 1987-90, mgr. splty. engring., 1990-91; program mgr. BAE Sys., Mpls., 1985—. Patentee in field. Mem. Soc. Automotive Engrs., Am. Soc. Agrl. Engrs., System Safety Soc., Boy Scouts Am. Order of the Arrow. Republican. Office: BAE Systems 4800 E River Rd Minneapolis MN 55421-1402 Home: 4340 Hackley Pt Ln Muskegon MI 49441

HILLYARD, IRA WILLIAM, retired pharmacologist, educator; b. Richmond, Utah, Mar. 23, 1924; s. Neal Jacobsen and Lucille (Duce) H.; m. Venice Lenore Williams, July 10, 1945 (dec.); children: Christine, Kevin, Eric; m. Norma Larsen, May 1, 1970. BS, Idaho State U., 1949; MS, U. Nebr., 1951; PhD, St. Louis U., 1957. Pharmacologist Mead Johnson Co., Evansville, Ind., 1957-59; sr. pharmacologist, sect. leader Warner-Lambert Research Inst., Morris Plains, NJ, 1959-69; assoc. prof. pharmacology Idaho State U. Coll. Pharmacy, Pocatello, 1969-73, 77-79, dean, 1979-87, prof. pharmacology, 1979-91, prof. emeritus, 1991—; ret., 1991. Dir. pharmacology and toxicology ICN Pharms., Irvine, Calif., 1973-77, cons., 1977-80; cons. Pennwalt Pharm. Co., Rochester, N.Y., 1978-83 Contbr. articles to profl. jours. Served with USN, 1943-45, 51-53. Decorated Purple Heart. Fellow Am. Found. Pharm. Edn.; mem. Western Pharmacology Soc., Am. Assn. Colls. Pharmacy, Am. Soc. Pharmacology and Exptl. Therapeutics, N.Y. Acad. Scis., Sigma Xi, Rho Chi, Phi Delta Chi. Lodges: Rotary. Home: 594 S 800 W Mapleton UT 84664-4313 E-mail: ihnh@aol.com. *I firmly believe that we make individual contributions to the welfare and progress of mankind only if every action is based on truth. If we remain honest and open-minded in our approach, truth will always be recognized and those challenging decisions which must precede every action, will be correctly made even though each decision may not always be agreeable to us or to others. In the end, however, if truth prevails, progress will be made because we will all recognize the correctness of what is said or done.*

HILPERT, EDWARD THEODORE, JR., retired lawyer; b. Frazee, Minn., Apr. 29, 1928; s. Edward Theodore Sr. and Hulda Gertrude (Wilder) H.; m. Susan Hazelton, May 5, 1973. AB, U. Wash., Seattle, 1954, JD, 1956. Bar: Wash. 1956, US Dist. Ct. (we. dist.) Wash. 1956, US Tax Ct. 1959, US Ct. Appeals (9th cir.) 1959, US Supreme Ct. 1970. Law clk. to Hon. George H. Boldt U.S. Dist. Ct. (we. dist.) Wash., Tacoma, 1956—58; assoc. Ferguson & Burdell, Seattle, 1958—63, ptnr., 1963—91; sr. ptnr. Schwabe, Williamson, Ferguson & Burdell, Seattle, 1992—2003, ret., 2004. Exec. com. 9th cir. Jud. Conf., San Francisco, 1987—90. Judge pro tem Seattle Mcpl. Ct., 1971-80. Capt. USAR, 1946-49, 50-52, Korea. Mem.: ABA, Mensa, The Rainer Club, Seattle Tennis Club, Broadmoor Golf Club, Sea Pines Country Club. Republican. Lutheran. Office: Schwabe Williamson Ferguson & Burdell US Bank Ctr 1420 5th Ave Ste 3010 Seattle WA 98101-2393 Home: 26 Twin Pines Rd Hilton Head Island SC 29928 Personal E-mail: sshathhi@aol.com.

HILSMAN, ROGER, political scientist, educator; b. Waco, Tex., Nov. 23, 1919; s. Roger and Emma (Prendergast) H.; m. Eleanor Willis Hoyt, June 22, 1946; children— Hoyt R., Amy, Ashby, Sarah. BS, U.S. Mil. Acad., 1943; MA, Yale U., 1950, PhD, 1951. Commd. 2d lt. U.S. Army, 1943, advanced through grades to maj., 1951; with (Merrill's Marauders), Burma, 1944; comdg. officer (OSS guerrilla group in), Burma, 1944-45; asst. chief Far East intelligence operations, Hdqrs. OSS, Washington, 1945-46; spl. asst. to exec. officer CIA, 1946-47; planning officer NATO affairs, Joint Am. Mil. Adv. Group, London, Eng., 1950-52; internat. politics br. Hdqrs. U.S. European Command, 1952-53; resigned, 1953; research fellow Center Internat. Studies, Princeton, 1953-54, research asst., 1954-55; research assoc., lectr. Woodrow Wilson Sch.; lectr. internat. relations Columbia, 1958; research asso. Washington Center Fgn. Policy Research, lectr. internat. affairs Sch. Advanced Internat. Studies, Johns Hopkins, 1957-61. Chief fgn. affairs div., legislative reference service Library Congress, 1956-58, dep. dir. for research, 1958-61; dir. bur. intelligence and research State Dept., 1961-63; asst. sec. state Far Eastern affairs, 1963-64; prof. govt. Columbia U., 1964-89, prof. emeritus, 1990—; lectr. Nat. War Coll., Air U., Army War Coll., Indsl. Coll. Armed Forces.; Fulbright Disting. lectr., India, 1985; USMC Found. chair mil. affairs, 1991. Author: Strategic Intelligence and National Decisions, 1956, To Move a Nation, 1967, The Politics of Policy Making in Defense and Foreign Affairs, 1971, The Crouching Future: International Politics and U.S. Foreign Policy— A Forecast, 1975, To Govern America, 1979, The Politics of Governing America, 1985, The Politics of Policy Making: Conceptual Models and Bureaucratic Politics, 1987, 90, 92, American Guerrilla: My War Behind Japanese Lines, 1990, George Bush vs Saddam Hussein: Military Success! Political Failure?, 1992, The Cuban Missle Crisis, The Struggle Over Policy, 1996, From Nuclear Military Strategy to a World Without War, A History and Proposal, 1999; co-author: Military Policy and National Security, 1956, Alliance Policy in the Cold War, 1959, NATO and American Security, 1959, Foreign Policy in the Sixties, 1965, The Superpowers and Revolution, 1986, Nuclear Strategy and Arms Control, 1986, A Layman's Guide to the Universe, the Earth, Life on Earth, and the Migrations of Mankind, 2003. Rockefeller fellow, 1958. Home: 317 W Main St #2105 Chester CT 06412-1057

HILST, GLENN RUDOLPH, environmental sciences administrator, researcher; b. May 1, 1923; s. William Frederick and Lola Katherine (Cordes) H.; m. Lorraine Virginia Pilke, June 2, 1949 (div. 1976); children: Randolph Glenn, Elizabeth Ann, Katherine Louise; m. Zenobia R. Scoggins, June 21, 1986. SB, MIT, 1948, SM, 1949; PhD, U. Chgo., 1957. Rsch. assoc. Argonne Nat. Labs. Chgo., 1952-54; mgr. atmospheric physics GE Co., Richland, Wash., 1954-60; exec. v.p. Travelers Rsch. Corp., Hartford, Conn., 1960-70, 74-76; v.p. Aero Rsch. Assocs. of Princeton, Inc., NJ, 1970-74; sr. program mgr. Electric Power Rsch. Inst., Palo Alto, Calif., 1977-87; ret., 1987. Cons., 1976-77; sr. sci. advisor Battelle N.W. labs., 1988-93; mem. com. NAS, NAE. Author: Air Pollution, 1968, Toward a National Urban Policy, 1971, Encyclopedia of Physical Science and Technology, 1987; contbr. articles to profl. jours. Task force mem. State of Conn., 1967; commr. Conn. Air Pollution Control Commn., 1968. With USAF, 1941-46. Fellow AAAS (sec. 1979-82), Am. Meteorol. Soc. (councilor 1967-70, Charles F. Brooks award 1973, Cleveland Abbe award 1995), Explorers Club; mem. Nassau Club (Princeton), Sigma Xi Home: 22975 SE Black Nugget Rd Apt 247 Issaquah WA 98029 Personal E-mail: ghilst@aol.com.

HILT, THOMAS HARRY, minister; b. Phila., May 19, 1947; s. Francis Joseph and Alice Elizabeth (Flanagan) H.; m. Carolyn Louise Poulsen, Aug. 23, 1969; 1 child, Tamara Leah. BA, Tusculum Coll., Greeneville, Tenn., 1969; grad., Missionary Tng. Sch., Long Beach, Calif., 1974; M Ministry, Internat. Sem., Plymouth, Fla., 1983, D Ministry, 1984; PhD, Carolina U. of Theology, 1992. Ordained min. of Gospel, Okinawa, Japan, 1979. Mem. staff Christians in Action, Long Beach, 1974-77, missionary Okinawa, Japan, 1977-79; founder Christians in Action Evang. Ch., Guam, 1979-81; founder, dir. Micronesian Evang. Mission, Barrigada, 1981—; founder, adminstr. Evang. Christian Acad., Chalan Pago, Guam, 1982—2003; sr. pastor Ch. of the Cross, Sarasota, Fla., 2001—02; pres. SonHaven Ministries Internat., Sarasota, 2001—; founder, adminstr. SonHaven Prep. Acad., Sarasota, 2002—. Founder, dir. Family Counseling Ministries, 1990-2001; mem. Nat. Bible Week-Guam Com., 1988-92; advisor Guam chpt. Women's Aglow Fellowship Internat., 1987-90; chaplain Guam Fire Dept., 1992-2000; chmn. bd. Guam Critical Incident Stress Mgmt. team, 1997-2000. Mem. Guam Gov.'s Social Svcs. Adv. Bd., 1981-83; mem. standards of licensing com. child welfare task force Guam Dept. Pub. Health and Social Svcs., 1982-83; mem. Blue Ribbon Commn. on Edn., 1991-93; minister Cmty. Care Faith Presbyterian Ch., Sarasota, Fla., 2005—. With U.S. Army, 1970-73. Recipient award Ancient Order of Chamorri, 1983, 1st place award Guam Press Club, 1985. Fellow Am. Acad. Experts in Traumatic Stress; mem. Am. Acad. Experts in Traumatic Stress, Guam Ministerial Assn. (sec.-treas. 1980-81, pres. 1983-84, 86-88, v.p. 1991-92), Bible Soc. Micronesia (pres. bd. dirs. 1989-90, v.p. bd. 1991-92, 99-2000). Home: 5351 Avant Ave Sarasota FL 34235 Office: Po Box 50517 Sarasota FL 34232-0304 Home Phone: 941-355-2276; Office Phone: 941-360-2000. Personal E-mail: rancom95@earthlink.net. *It has been my experience that God does not grant us special favors, but rather special grace.*

HILTON, ANDREW CARSON, investment company and retired manufacturing executive, management consultant; b. D'Lo, Miss., Nov. 20, 1928; s. A.C. and Pearl (Walters) H. BA, U. Md., 1952; MA, George Washington U., 1953; PhD, Western Res. U., 1956. Former research asso. Personnel Research Inst., Western Res. U.; cons. Psychol. Corp., NYC; dir. personnel relations Raytheon Co.; then dir. personnel Internat. Tel.& Tel. Corp.; sr. v.p. adminstrn. Coltec Industries Inc., NYC, 1963-83, exec. v.p., 1983-91, vice chmn., 1991-94, also bd. dirs., vice chmn., 1991-94; proprietor Hilton Mgmt. Enterprises Inc., 1994—. Contbr. articles to profl. jours. Mem. APS, N.Y. Acad. Scis. Clubs: University (N.Y.C.), Aspetuck Valley Country Club, Weston, Conn.

HILTON, (WILLIAM) BARRON, hotel executive; b. Dallas, Oct. 23, 1927; s. Conrad Hilton; 8 children. DHL, U. Houston, 1986. Founder, pres. San Diego Chargers, 1960—66; pres. Am. Football League; v.p. Hilton Hotels Corp., Beverly Hills, Calif., 1954, pres., CEO, 1966—96, chmn., 1979—2004, co-chmn., 2004—; chmn. Hilton Equipment Corp., Beverly Hills, Calif. Mem. gen. adminstrv. bd. Mfrs. Hanover Trust Co., NYC; bd. dirs. Conrad N. Hilton Found., So. Calif. Visitors Coun. and Exec. Coun. on Fgn. Diplomats. Named one of 400 Richest Ams., Forbes mag., 2006; named to, Culinary Inst. Am. Hall of Fame, 1986; recipient Am. Spirit award, Nat. Bus. Aircraft Assn., 1995, Chevalier of Confrerie de la Chaine Des Rotisseurs, Magestrial Knight, Sovereign Mil. Order Malta. Mem.: Peace Found. Coun., Conouistadares del Cielo. Office: Hilton Hotels Corp 9336 Civic Center Dr Beverly Hills CA 90210-3604*

HILTON, CLAUDE MEREDITH, federal judge; b. Scott County, Va., Dec. 8, 1940; s. Claude Swanson and Edna (Fletcher) H.; m. Joretta Cabaniss, June 16, 1963; children: John, Rachel. BS, Ohio State U., 1963; JD, Am. Univ., 1966. Bar: Va. 1966, US Ct. Appeals (4th cir.) 1967, US Supreme Ct. 1981. Dep. clk. of cts. Arlington County, Va., 1964-66, asst. commonwealth atty. Va., 1967-68, commonwealth atty. Va., 1974; sole practice Arlington, 1967-85; judge US Dist. Ct. (ea. dist.) Va., Alexandria, 1985—, now chief judge; judge Fgn. Intelligence Surveillance Ct., 2000—. Asst. commonwealth atty., Arlington, 1967-68, commonwealth atty., 1974; dep. clk. ct., Arlington, 1964-66; commr. in chancery U.S. Ct. Appeals (4th cir.), 1976-85; bd. govs. criminal law sect. Va. State Bar, 1979-84, chmn., 1982-83, mem. ins. com., 1981-85. Mem. ABA, Va. Bar Assn., Arlington County Bar Assn. Lodges: Masons, Alexandria Lodge of Perfection, Kena Temple. Republican. Methodist. Home: 3912 N Upland St Arlington VA 22207-4642 Office: US Courthouse 401 Courthouse Sq Alexandria VA 22314-5704*

HILTON, JAMES L., university librarian; m. Molly Hilton; children: Michael, Meghan. BA in psychology, Univ. Tex., 1981; MA in psychology, Princeton Univ., 1983, PhD in social psychology, 1985. With U. Mich. Ann Arbor, 1985—2006, Arthur F. Thurnau prof. psychology, 1997—2000, assoc. provost for Academic, Info., and Instrnl. Tech., interim univ. libr., 2005; v.p., chief info. officer U. Va., Charlottesville, 2006—. Fellow, Sweetland Writing Ctr., CIC Academic Leadership Program. Office: Libr Adminstrn U Mich 818 Hatcher S Ann Arbor MI 48109-1205 Office Phone: 734-764-9356. Fax: 734-763-5080.

HILTON, LINDA D., academic administrator; d. Charles W. and Delores R. Neary; m. Richard D. Hilton, Nov. 23, 1973; children: Guinevere Boston, Julia. BA, Villanova Univ., Villanova, Pa., 1985—87; MS, Drexel Univ., Phila., Pa., 1987—90. Libr. The Hill Sch., Pottstown, Pa., 1985—90; dean of adminstrn. The Haverford Sch., Haverford, Pa., 1990—98; chief tech. officer Lyndon State Coll., Lyndonville, Vt., 1999—2003; chief info. officer Vt. State Coll., Waterbury, Vt., 2003—. Recipient David H. Clift Scholarship, Am. Libr. Assn., 1997. Mem.: Datatel User Group Governing Bd. (bd. mem. 2003—06). Office: Vermont State Collegtes POBox 359 Waterbury VT 05676

HILTON, MICHAEL E., lawyer; m. Theresa D. Rabe, Apr. 26, 1983; children: Stephen, Brian, Katherine. BS in Civil Engring., U. Tex. at Arlington, 1985; JD, St. Mary's U., San Antonio, Tex., 1988. Bar: Ohio Supreme Ct. 1989, U.S. Patent and Trademark Office 1989, cert.: U.S. Ct. of Appeals, Fed. Circuit 1990, bar: Mich. Supreme Ct. 1993. Sr. counsel Procter & Gamble Co., Cin., 1988—95, assoc. gen. counsel global beauty care, 1999—2001; assoc. gen. counsel Procter & Gamble, Far East, Kobe, Japan, 1995—99; prin. Harness, Dickey & Pierce, PLC, Troy, Mich., 2001—. Mem.: ABA, Mich. Intellectual Property Assn., Am. Intellectual Property Assn. Achievements include enforcing patents in Asia, thereby obtaining recoveries consistent with corresponding enforcement activities in the U.S. Avocations: pottery, travel. Office: Harness Dickey & Pierce PLC 5445 Corporate Dr Troy MI 48098 Home Phone: 248-373-7354; Office Phone: 248-641-1600. E-mail: mhilton@hdp.com.

HILTON, NICKY (NICHOLAI OLIVIA HILTON), apparel designer; b. Oct. 5, 1983; d. Rick and Kathy Hilton; m. Todd Andrew Meister, Aug. 15, 2004 (annulled Nov. 9, 2004). Designer Samantha Thavasa, Tokyo, 2001—. Actor: (films) Wishman, 1991. Contbr. Free Arts for Abused Children Found. Achievements include appeared on cover of numerous mag. including Maxim, GQ, FHM, Vanity Fair, others; heiress and great-grand daughter of Conrad Hilton, founder of Hilton Hotel Chains; modeled for Anand Jon.

HILTON, PARIS, actress; b. NYC, Feb. 17, 1981; d. Rick and Kathy (Richards) Hilton. Designer Samantha Thavasa, Tokyo, 2001—. Founder Heiress Records, 2004—, Club Paris, Orlando, Fla., 2005—, Jacksonville, Fla., 2006—. Actor: (films) Wishman, 1991, Sweetie Pie, 2000, Zoolander, 2001, QIK2JDG, 2002, Nine Lives, 2002, Wonderland, 2003, The Cat in the Hat, 2003, L.A. Knights, 2003, Raising Helen, 2004, The Hillz, 2004, House of Wax, 2005, Bottoms Up, 2006, Pledge This!, 2006; co-star: (TV series) The Simple Life, 2003; The Simple Life 2: Road Trip, 2004; The Simple Life 3: Interns, 2005; The Simple Life 4: 'Til Death Do Us Part, 2006; The Simple Life 5: Goes to Camp, 2007; actor(guest appearances): Saturday Night Live, 2003, Las Vegas, 2003, The O.C., 2003, Veronica Mars, 2004, American Dreams, 2005; author: (novels) Confessions of an Heiress: A Tongue-in-Chic Peek Behind the Pose, 2004 (Publishers Weekly Bestseller list, 2004); singer: (albums) Paris, 2006, (songs) Stars Are Blind, 2006. Contbr. Toys for Tots. Achievements include appeared on cover of numerous mag. including Maxim, GQ, FHM, Vanity Fair, others; heiress and great-grand daughter of Conrad Hilton, founder of Hilton Hotel Chains; modeled for designers March Bouwer and Catherine Malandrino; worked on ad campaign for Italian label Iceberg.

HILTON, PEREZ (MARIO ARMANDO LAVANDEIRA JR.), celebrity gossip blogger; b. Miami, Mar. 23, 1978; s. Mario and Teresita L. BFA, NYU, 2000. Media rels. asst. GLAAD; mng. editor Instinct mag.; blog host PageSixSixSix.com, PerezHilton.com. Actor: (TV miniseries) What Perez Said, 2007. Named one of Top 10 Entertainment News Sites, ComScore Media Metrix, Top 25 Web Celebs, Forbes mag., 2007. Mailing: 8174 Sunset Blvd. #993 Los Angeles CA 90046 Business E-Mail: Perez@PerezHilton.com.*

HILTON, PETER JOHN, mathematician, educator; b. London, Apr. 7, 1923; s. Mortimer and Elizabeth (Freedman) H.; m. Margaret Mostyn, Sept. 14, 1949; children: Nicholas, Timothy. MA, Oxford U., Eng., 1948, PhD, 1950, Cambridge U., 1952; HHD (hon.), No. Mich. U., Marquette, 1977; DSc (hon.), Meml. U. Nfld., Can., 1983, U. Autonoma Barcelona, Spain, 1989. Lectr. Manchester U., Eng., 1948-52, sr. lectr., 1956-58; lectr. Cambridge U., 1952-55; Mason prof. pure math. Birmingham U., Eng., 1958-62; prof. math. Cornell U., 1962-71, U. Wash., 1971-73; Beaumont prof. Case Western Res. U., 1973-82; disting. prof. SUNY, Binghamton, 1982-93, emeritus, 1993—; disting. prof. U. Ctrl. Fla., Orlando, 1993—2004. Guest prof. Swiss Fed. Inst. Tech., Zurich, 1966—67, Zurich, 1981—82, Zurich, 1988—89, Courant Inst. Math. Scis., NYU, 1967—68, Ohio State U., 1977, U. Autonoma, Barcelona, 1989, U. Lausanne, 1996; Erskine fellow U. Canterbury, 2001, 02; Mahler lectr. Australian Math. Soc., 1997; vis. fellow Battelle Seattle Rsch. Ctr., 1970—71, fellow, 1971—; co-chmn. Cambridge Conf. on Sch. Math., 1965; chmn. com. applied math. tng. NRC, 1977—; chmn. U.S. Commn. on Math. Instrn., 1979—80; sec. Internat. Commn. Math. Instrn., 1979—82. Author: Homotopy Theory, 1953, (with S. Wylie) Homology Theory, 1960, Homotopy Theory and Duality, 1966, (with H.B. Griffiths) Classical Mathematics, 1970, General Cohomology Theory and K-Theory, 1971, (with U. Stammbach) Course in Homological Algebra, 1971, 2d edit., 1997, Le Langage des Categories, 1973, (with Y.C. Wu) Course in Modern Algebra, 1974, (with G. Mislin and J. Roitberg) Localization of Nilpotent Groups and Spaces, 1975 (with J. Pedersen) Fear No More, 1982, Nilpotente Gruppen und Nilpotente Räume, 1984, (with J. Pedersen) Build Your Own Polyhedra, 1987, (with J. Pedersen) College Preparatory Mathematics, 1992, (with D. Holton and J. Pedersen) Mathematical Reflections, 1997, 2d edit., 2001, (with D. Holton and J. Pedersen) Mathematical Vistas, 2002; editor: Ergebnisse der Mathematik, 1964—, Ill. Jour. Math., 1962-68, Jour. Pure and Applied Algebra, 1970-75, Topics in Modern Topology, 1968, Miscellanea Mathematica, 1991; contbr. articles to profl. jours. Recipient Silver medal U. Helsinki, Finland, 1975, Centenary medal John Carroll U., 1985. Mem. Am. Math. Soc., Math. Assn. Am. (1st v.p. 1978-80), Can. Math. Soc., Math Soc. Belgium (hon.), London Math. Soc., Cambridge Philos. Soc., Brazilian Acad. Scis. (hon.). Home: 29 Murray St Binghamton NY 13905-4504 Office: SUNY Dept Math Scis Binghamton NY 13902-6000 Office Phone: 607-777-4867. Business E-Mail: megwelsh2@aol.com.

HILTON, STANLEY GOUMAS, lawyer, educator, writer; b. San Francisco, June 16, 1949; s. Lukas Stylianos and Effie (Glafkides) Goumas; m. Raquel Estrella Villalba, Feb. 25, 1996 (div.); children: Loucas, Angelika, Karmen (triplets). BA with honors, U. Chgo., 1971; JD, Duke U., 1975; MBA, Harvard U., 1979. Bar: Calif. 1975, U.S. Dist. Ct. Calif. 1975, U.S. Ct. Appeals (9th cir.) 1983, U.S. Supreme Ct. 1985. Libr. asst. Duke U. Libr., Durham, NC, 1972-75, Harvard U. Libr., Cambridge, Mass., 1977-79; minority counsel US Senator Bob Dole, Washington, 1979-80; adminstrv. asst. Calif. State Senate, Sacramento, 1980-81; pvt. practice San Francisco, 1981—. Tutor Harvard U., 1978—79; adj. assoc. prof. Golden Gate U., San Francisco, 1991—; CEO Froggg, Inc., 1999—, San Francisco Landlords Union, 1999—, Taxpayers US, 2001—, Russo-Am. Joint Econ. Venture, 2006—; pres. Fair Play In the Middle East Com., 2002—; chair Vegetarians World Unite, 2001—, 911 Victims Fund, 2004—; founder, pres. Cicero-Aristotle Sch. Rhetoric, 2004—; profl. spkr.; polit. writer. Author: Bob Dole: American Political Phoenix, 1988, Senator for Sale, 1995, Glass Houses, 1998 (Best writer 1998), To Pay or Not to Pay, 2003. Pres. Com. to Stick With Candlestick Park, San Francisco, 1992-96, Value Added Tax Now, San Francisco, 1994—, Save the 4th Amendment, San Francisco, 1995—, 911 Truth Movement, 2001—; pres., CEO Animalism, Inc., San Francisco Landlord's Union, 2001—; chmn. Hillsborough, Richest City in the World, 2001—; pres. Save the Cows, 2004; CEO Fountain of Youth; alt. mem. San Mateo County Dem. Ctrl. Com., 2002—; Dem. candidate for Gov. Calif. spl. recall election, 2003; governing bd. Hillsborough Governing Bd., 2005—; founder, pres. Frogs United; chair ImpeachBush.com., 2004. Mem. Calif. State Bar, Abolish the Fed. Res. Bank Assn. (pres. 1999—), Hellenic Law Soc., Bechtel Toastmasters Club (pres.), Rhinoceros Toastmasters Club, San Francisco Toastmasters Club, Ams. For Better Congress (pres. 2003—), Debtors United (chmn. 2004—), Dems. for a New Am. (pres. 2003—). Avocations: stamp collecting/philately, photography, classical music, ancient greek and roman history. Office: 580 California St Ste 500 San Francisco CA 94104-1000 Home Phone: 415-902-2360; Office Phone: 415-786-4821. Personal E-mail: loucasloukas@yahoo.com, 456141r@gmail.com.

HILTON, STEVEN J., real estate executive; Project mgr. Premier Cmty. Homes; co-founder Monterey Homes (merger Homeplex Mortgage Investment Co.), 1985, treas., sec., 1985-96; pres., co-CEO, Meritage Corp., Plano, Tex., 1996-98, co-chmn, co-CEO, 1998—2006, chmn., CEO, 2006—. Mem. Nat. Homebuilders' Assn., Nat. Bd. Realtors, Ctrl. Ariz. Homebuilders' Assn., Scottsdale Bd. Realtors. Office: Meritage Corp 4050 W Park Blvd Plano TX 75093-3839*

HILTON, THEODORE CRAIG, computer scientist, Internet company executive; b. Oakland, Calif., June 14, 1949; s. Theodore Caldwell and Maxine (Donnelly) Hilton; m. Peggy Estes, May 21, 1990; children: Christopher, Kelly, Clark, Lisa, Trey, Veronique. BS in internat. rels., Occidental Coll., 1972; BS, Calif. Inst. Tech., 1972; MS in Computer Sci., N.Y. Inst. Tech., 1980; DSc in Computer Studies (hon.), U. London, 1995. Ptnr., founder Ctrl. Data Corp., LA, 1971—, CEO, 1972—73; prof. Lake (Fla.) Coll., 1981-85, dept. chmn., 1983-85; prin. rsch. invest. U.S. Dept. Def., LA, 1985-88; chmn. Global Scholar LLC, 1996—. Creator computer sys. E-City, 1956, Broadcast Mgmt. Sys., 1972, ICSS, 1974, EBook, 1993, Quality Assurance Sys., 1994, Nat. Curriculum Clearinghouse Sys., 2002; adv. bd. Accurate Rsch. Corp., 2000; bd. dirs. TBS S.A., Carolina Access LLC, S.E. Data Comms., Nat. Scholar Corp., LW Industries. Author: (book) Web Databases & PHP3, 1999, Web Databases & PHP3, Japanese edit., 2000, Web Databases & PHP3, Polish/Russian edits., 2002, Data-Base Development, 1999, Web Databse, 2000; contbr. articles to profl. jours. Named SC Bus. Man of Yr., 1999, Wall St. Businessman of Yr., 2000, 2004, N.C. Businessman of Yr., 2001—02; recipient Congl. medal Distinction, 2001. Mem.: IEEE, N.Y. Acad. Scis., Data Processing Mgmt. Assn., Logistics Engrs. Soc., Am. Mgmt. Assn., IEEE Computer Soc., Rotary (Paul Harris fellow). Achievements include patents for ultra-wide band voting system; autonomous network smart labels; filterable digital advertising; internet database management system; image system and public network exchange system; medical measurement devices; patents in field; patents for multi-dimensional learning matrix; learning management process. Office: Cen Data Corp 145 N Church St Ste 418 Spartanburg SC 29306-5163 E-mail: tcraig@www-data.com.

HILTS, EARL T., lawyer, government official, educator; b. Ilion, NY, Mar. 31, 1946; stepson Leon Thomas and Gertrude Annette (Daly) Butler; m. Mae Hwa Kim, Apr. 13, 1973; children: Troy Alan, Kimberly Michelle. BS, St. Lawrence U., 1967; JD, Albany Law Sch., 1970. Bar: NY 1972. Gen. atty.-advisor Dept. Army Watervliet Arsenal, N.Y., 1978-80, supervisory atty.-advisor N.Y., 1980-99; ret., 1999; pvt. practice, 1999—. Adj. prof. Schnectady C.C., 1985—, St. Rose Coll., 1999—. Catechism instr. St. Mary's Ch., 1990-92; pee wee football coach, wrestling coach Shenendehowa Sch., 1983-87; little league coach West Crescent Halfmoon Baseball League, 1980-90. Capt. JAGC, U.S. Army, 1972-76. Scholar St. Lawrence U., 1963-67, Albany Law Sch., 1967-70. Mem. N.Y. State Bar Assn., Am. Legion, Pi Mu Epsilon. Republican. Roman Catholic. Home and Office: 28 Oakwood Blvd Clifton Park NY 12065-7413 Home Phone: 518-383-1292; Office Phone: 518-383-1292.

HILTY, JAMES WALTER, historian, educator, media consultant; b. Columbus, Ohio, May 22, 1939; s. Robert Burns and Henrietta Isabel Hilty; m. Shirley Brown, Jan. 1963 (dissolved June 1975); children: Carolyn Marland, Robert; m. Kathleen Griffin Hilty, Oct. 19, 1979; 1 child, Maura. BS, Ohio State U., 1965, MA in Edn., 1966, MA in History, 1967; PhD in History, U. Mo., 1973. Prof. history Temple U., Phila., 1970—, assoc. dean Grad. Sch., 1978—80, acting dean Grad. Sch., 1980—81, asst. v.p. acad. affairs, 1982—82, dir. planning, 1982—85, asst. to pres., 1985—88, chair dept. history, 1988—94, dean Ambler Coll., 2005—. Trustee Atwater Kent Mus., Phila., 1985—2002; cons. NBC News, NYC, 1993, A&E Biography, NYC, 2002. Author: JFK: Idealist Without Illusions, 1976, Robert Kennedy: Brother Protector, 1998; contbr. articles to profl. jours. Pres. Ogontz Vol. Fire Co., Montgomery County, 1980—85; bd. mem. Fire Adv. Bd., Montgomery County, Pa., 1979—94, ARC, Phila., 1985—95. With USMC, 1958—62, PTO. Recipient Disting. Tchg. award, Lindback Found., 2001. Mem.: Orgn. Am. Historians. Democrat. Avocations: golf, gardening. Office: Temple Univ Ambler Coll Ambler PA 19002 Home Phone: 610-277-6847. Business E-Mail: james.hilty@temple.edu.

HILTZ, ARNOLD AUBREY, retired chemist; b. Can., July 31, 1924; arrived in U.S., 1953; s. Aubrey Claremont and Fannie Mae (Bryanton) H.; m. Margery Jane (Beer), July 17, 1946; children: Sharon Lynne Romino, Deborah Jane. BS in Chemistry, Acadia U., Wolfville, NS, Can., 1947; PhD in Phys. Chemistry, McGill U., Montreal, Que., Can., 1952; LLD (hon.), U. Prince Edward Island, 2004. Ordained deacon and priest Episc. Ch., 1976. Rsch. sci. officer Def. Rsch. Bd. Can., Quebec City, 1951—53; rsch. chemist Am. Viscose Corp., Phila., 1953—59, group leader, 1959—60, Avisun Corp., Phila., 1960—65; rsch. chemist Borden Chem. Co., Phila., 1965—66; sr. scientist GE, Phila., 1966—79, mgr. materials applications, 1979—91. Tutor math. and sci. Rose Tree Media, Pa. Sch. Dist., 1958-74. Contbr. articles to profl. journals; patentee in field. Docent Phila. Mus. Art, 1988—2003; sch. dir. Rose Tree Media Pa. Sch. Dist., 1969—74, tutor math. and sci. Rose Tree Media, 1958—74; bd. dirs., treas. Middletown Free Libr., Pa., 1964—69; vol. gallery guide Art Gallery N.S., 2004—06; treas. Halifax County Condo. Corp., 2004—06; hon. asst. to dean All Saints Cathedral, Halifax, 2003—; bd. dirs. Sheepscot Island Co., MacMahan Island, Maine, 1983—85. Recipient Silver medal Gov. Gen. Can. 1942, Can. Def. medal, Can. Vol. Svc. medal, Claspto CVSM, War medal 1939-45, Gen. Svc. badge, Can. Overseas medal 1945, Frank J. Sensebrenner fellow McGill U., 1949-51. Mem.: Am. Chem. Soc. (chem. abstractor 1958—79, sci. lectr. 1958—2003), Halifax County Condominium Assn. (treas. 2004—06), Hebrides Home Owners Assn. (pres., bd. dir. 1999—2001, treas. 2002—05). Republican. Episcopalian. Avocations: art, music, reading, gardening, golf. Home: 40 Regency Pk Dr # 607 B3S 1L4 Halifax NS Canada Personal E-mail: aandmhiltz@aol.com.

HILTZ, KENNETH A., corporate financial executive; BBA, Xavier Univ.; MBA, Univ. Detroit. CPA, cert. mgmt. acct. Mng. dir. AlixPartners LLC; sr. v.p., CFO Harnischfeger Ind. (now Joy Global Inc.), 1999—2001; CFO, chief restructuring officer Hayes Lemmerz Internat. Inc., 2001—03; CFO Foster Wheeler Ltd., 2003—04, Dana Corp., Toledo, 2006—. Mem. adv. bd. Sch. Bus. Adminstrn., Oakland Univ. Office: Dana Corp 4500 Dorr St Toledo OH 43615*

HILTZ, STARR ROXANNE, sociologist, educator, writer, consultant, computer scientist; b. Little Rock, Sept. 7, 1942; d. John Donald and Mildred V. Smyers; m. Murray Turoff, 1985; children: Jonathan David, Katherine Amanda. AB, Vassar Coll., Poughkeepsie, NY, 1963; MA, Columbia U., NYC, 1964, PhD, 1969. Prof. sociology Upsala Coll., East Orange, NJ, 1969—85; info. sys. N.J. Inst. Tech., Newark, 1985—93, disting. prof. info. sys., 1993—. Cons. social impacts of computer systems. Author: Creating Community Services for Widows, 1976, (with M. Turoff) The Network Nation, 1978, 2d edit., 1993, (with E. Kerr) Computer-Mediated Communication, 1982, Online Communities, 1984, The Virtual Classroom, 1994, (with L. Harasim, L. Teles and M. Turoff) Learning Networks, 1995, (with Ricki Goldman) Learning Together Online, 2004. Recipient N.J. Woman of the Millennium for Ednl. Tech., 2000. Mem.: Assn. for Info. Sys., Assn. Computing Machinery. Unitarian Universalist. Home: 19 Meadowbrook Rd Randolph NJ 07869-3808 Office: NJ Inst Tech Info Systems Newark NJ 07102

HILTZIK, MICHAEL, journalist; b. NYC, Nov. 9, 1952; s. Harold & Bernice (Rothman) Hiltzik; m. Deborah Ibert, 2 children, Andrew, David. BA English, Colgate U., 1973; MS Journalism, Columbia U. Grad Sch Journalism, 1974. Journalist Buffalo Courier-Express, Buffalo, 1974-78, bureau chief, 1976-78; staff writer Providence Journal-Bulletin, Providence, 1979-81; finan. writer L.A. Times, 1981-83, N.Y. fin. corr. NYC, 1982-88, Nairobi bur. chief Nairobi, Kenya, 1988-93, Moscow corr. Moscow, 1993-94, fin. staff writer/editor, columnist LA, 1994—2006. Author, non-fiction: A Death in Kenya, 1991, Dealers of Lightning: Xerox PARC and the Dawn of the Computer Age, 1999, The Plot Against Social Security: How the Bush Plan is Endangering Our Financial Future, 2005. Co-recipient Pulitzer prize for Beat Reporting, 1999, recipient, ABA Silver Gavel award, Overseas Press Club citation for coverage of E. Africa.

HILYARD, NANN BLAINE, librarian; married. Page Northbrook Pub. Libr., 1969; head libr. Nancy Carol Roberts Meml. Libr., Brenham, Tex., 1975; dir. Fargo Pub. Libr., ND, Lake Villa Dist. Libr., Ill., Zion-Benton Pub. Libr., Zion, Ill. Co-editor, Perspectives Pub. Libr. Jour.; audiobooks reviewer Libr. Jour. Mem.: ALA (councilor Maine chpt. 1987—90, councilor at large 1998—2001, 2001—04, mem. exec. bd. 2004—07), Pub. Libr. Assn. (mem. small and medium-sized libr. sect. com.). Avocations: quilting, gardening, travel. Office: Zion-Benton Public Library 2400 Gabriel Ave Zion IL 60099 Office Phone: 847-872-4680 ext. 110. Office Fax: 847-872-4942. E-mail: mgonzalez@greenwichlibrary.org.

HILZINGER, KURT JOHN, health products executive; b. Royal Oak, Mich., May 4, 1960; s. Franklin D. and Colleen M. (Sullivan) Hilzinger; m. Deborah A. Gill, July 5, 1985; children: John K., Grant F., Bradley D. BBA, U. Mich., 1983. CPA. Staff acct. Price Waterhouse, NYC, 1983-86; v.p. Citicorp, NYC, 1986-91; v.p., CFO, treas. AmeriSource Health Corp., Malvern, Pa., 1991-99, COO, 1999—2001; exec. v.p., COO Amerisource-Bergen Corp., 2001—02, pres., COO, 2002—. Chmn. bd. Healthcare Distbn. Mgmt. Assn.; bd. dir. Humana, Inc.; mem. Phila. CFO Forum, 1993, Del. Valley Venture Group, 1993. Mem.: Assn. for Corp. Growth, AICPA. Office: Amerisource Bergen Corp 1300 Morris Dr Ste 100 Chesterbrook PA 19087*

HIMBURG, SUSAN PHILLIPS, dietician, educator; b. Norfolk, Va., May 17, 1946; d. Claude Ralph Jr. and Sarah Ann (Gilbert) Phillips; m. James Donald Himburg, Feb. 9, 1968; 1 child, Karlene Susan. BS in Food and Nutrition, Fla. State U., 1968; M in Dietetics, Emory U., 1972; PhD in Edn., U. Miami, Fla., 1979. Dietetic intern Emory U., Atlanta, 1971; clin. dietitian Emory U. Hosp., Atlanta, 1972-73; from instr. to prof. Fla. Internat. U., Miami, 1973—, dir. coordinated program in dietetics, 1979-99, dir. health scis. recruitment and retention program, 1985—2007, chmn. dietetics and nutrition, 1992—97, SACS self-study dir., 1997—2000, SACS dir., 2006—. Grant reviewer disadvantaged assistance program HHS, Rockville, Md., 1989—; site visitor So. Assn. Colls. and Schs., Atlanta, 1987—. Author: (tng. manual) ADA Self-Study, 1988, 91, 95; contbr. articles to profl. jours. Recipient Univ. Svc. Medallion, Fla. Internat. U., 2000. Fellow Am. Dietetic Assn. (site visitor 1985-2006, chairperson commn. on accreditation 1992-93, medallion 1996); mem. Soc. Nutrition Edn., Fla. Dietetic Assn. (del. 1990-2000, Disting. Dietitian 1995), Miami Dietetic Assn. (mem. nominating com. 1989, Disting. Dietitian 1994), Phi Kappa Phi, Kappa Omicron Nu. Office: Fla Internat Univ Dietetics & Nutrition Miami FL 33199-0001 Home: P O Box 560847 Miami FL 33256-0847 E-mail: himburgs@fiu.edu.

HIMELFARB, RICHARD JAY, investment company executive; b. Balt., Feb. 3, 1942; s. Jacob and Jennie (Willen) H.; m. Margaret Conn, Sept. 7, 1969; children: Elizabeth Jayne, Michael Ross. BA, Johns Hopkins U., 1962; LLB, Yale U., 1965. Bar: Md., 1965. Assoc., then ptnr. Weinberg & Green (now Saul Ewing LLC), Balt., 1967-83; exec. v.p. Legg Mason, Inc., Balt., 1983—2005, also bd. dirs., 1983—2005; sr. v.p. Stifel Fin. Corp., 2005—, exec. v.p., 2005—. Bd. dirs. Center Stage, Inc., Balt., 1984-2002, Balt. Goodwill Industries, 1984-93, Kennedy Krieger Inst., 1993—, Bryn Mawr Sch., 1991-94; mem. bd. visitors U. Md., Balt., 1990-96, chmn., 1996-2000; chmn. U. Md. Balt. Found., 2000—; bd. visitors Inst. of Human Virology, 1997—; bd. dirs. Balt. Devel. Corp., 1997-2003, UMB Rsch. Park Corp., 2003—. Capt. US Army, 1965—67. Mem.: Phi Beta Kappa. Home: 116 Taplow Rd Baltimore MD 21212-3312 Office: Stifel Nicolaus & Co Inc 100 Light St Baltimore MD 21202-1099

HIMELFARB, STEPHEN ROY, lawyer; b. Washington, Feb. 19, 1954; s. Jordan Sheldon and Marion (Soloman) H.; m. Anne Patricia Spille, June 26, 1983; children: Kara Michelle, Bradley Richard. BSBA, Am. U., 1976; JD, George Mason U., 1980. Bar: D.C. 1982, Md. 1982, Va. 1988, U.S. Dist. Ct. D.C. 1982, U.S. Dist. Ct. Md. 1982, U.S. Ct. Appeals (D.C. and 4th cirs.) 1982, U.S. Dist. Ct. (ea. dist.) Va. 1988, U.S. Tax Ct. 1990, U.S. Bankruptcy Ct. (ea. div.) Va. 1988, U.S. Supreme Ct. 1985. From v.p. to pres. ECA Bus. Comm. Network, Washington, 1982-85; ptnr. Himelfarb & Podryhula, Washington, 1984-93, Speights & Micheel, Washington, 1986-88, Sheeskin, Hillman & Lazar, PC, Rockville, Md., 1989-90, Ahmad & Himelfarb, PC, Rockville, Md., 1993-95; pvt. practice Bethesda, Md., 1995—. V.p. Video Shack Inc., Woodbridge, Va., 1984-95; mng. mem. Anne's Properties, LLC, 2003— Mem. ABA, Md. State Bar Assn., Va. Bar Assn., Assn. Trial Lawyers Am., Phi Delta Phi. Democrat. Jewish. Avocations: electronics, coin-op/americana collecting, model trains, radio control models. Home: 1214 Winter Hunt Rd Mc Lean VA 22102-2434 Office: 4701 Sangamore Rd Ste S-225 Bethesda MD 20816-2508 Office Phone: 301-229-7900.

HIMES, DIANE ADELE, buyer, fundraiser, actress, lobbyist; b. San Francisco, Aug. 11, 1942; d. L. John and Mary Louise (Young) H. BA, San Francisco State U., 1964. Founding mem., actress South Coast Repertory Co., 1964—66; rep. west coast home furnishings Allied Stores, nationwide; gift buyer Jordan Marsh, Miami; buyer The Broadway Stores; west coast sales mgr. Xmas divsn. Vincent Lippe Corp., LA; midwest sales mgr. Vincent-Lippe Chgo. Actress Nine 'O Clock Players, 1995, short film The Traveling Companion, 1998. Statewide co-chair Californians Initiative No On #102, 1988; founding co-chair Life AIDS Lobby, 1985—88; mem. Beverly Hills rent control bd., 1984; co-chair Californians Against Proposition #64, 1986; co-chmn. Mcpl. Elections Com., LA; bd. dirs. L.A. Women's Shakespeare Group, 1992—94. Named Woman of Yr. of L.A., ACLU, 1987, Christopher Street West, 1988. Avocation: acting.

HIMES, JAMES ALBERT, retired veterinary medicine educator; b. Lucas, Ohio, Aug. 12, 1919; s. Albert Merle and Nina Grace (Galleher) H.; m. Ruth Naomi Banks, Apr. 26, 1958 (div. 1973); children: Leslie Jo, Jillyn Alicia; m. Genia Lee, May 10, 1973 (div. 2000). BS, Muskingum Coll., 1941; postgrad., U. Nebr., 1941-42, 46; VMD, U. Penn., 1950; PhD, Cornell U., 1965. Veterinarian, Tenn., Va., Fla., 1950-62; rsch. asst. Cornell U., Ithaca, NY, 1962-65; from asst. prof. to assoc. prof. U. Fla., Gainesville, 1965-76, dir. vet. medicine edn., 1975-77, prof., 1976-90; from asst. dean to assoc. dean U. Fla. Coll. Vet. Medicine, Gainesville, 1977-90; prof. emeritus U. Fla., Gainesville, 1990—. Editor: Part X, Spontaneous Animal Models of Human Disease, 1979. Sgt. U.S. Army, 1942-45. Mem. AVMA, Fla. Vet. Med. Assn. (Vet. of Yr. 1987, Exec. Disting. Svc. award 1992), Alachua Vet. Med. Assn. (sec.-treas. 1973-74, pres. 1995), Marion County Vet. Assn. Avocations: reading, music, walking, jogging, cooking. Home: 2841 SW 37th Pl Apt 59F Gainesville FL 32608-3122 Business E-Mail: himesJ@vetmed.ufl.edu.

HIMES, JOHN HARTER, medical researcher, educator; b. Salt Lake City, July 25, 1947; s. Ellvert Hiram and Mildred Anna (Harter) H.; children: Rachel Anne, Matthew Hiram, Sarah Elizabeth; m. LaVell Gold. BS, Ariz. State U., 1971; PhD, U. Tex., 1975; MPH, Harvard U., 1982. Rsch., sr. scientist Fels Rsch. Inst., Yellow Springs, Ohio, 1976-79; Fels asst. prof. Wright State U. Sch. Medicine, Dayton, Ohio, 1977-79; sr. analyst, project dir. Abt Assocs., Cambridge, Mass., 1979-82; assoc. prof. CUNY, Bklyn., 1982-87; from assoc. prof. to prof. U. Minn. Sch. Pub. Health, Mpls., 1992—, dir. nutrition coord. ctr., 1995—. Expert com physical status WHO, Geneva, Switzerland, 1991-94, expert adv. panel nutrition, 1994—; mem. tech. working groups Ctrs. for Disease Control, Washington and Atlanta, 1988-97. Author: Parent-specific Adjustment for Assessment of Recumbent Length & Stature, 1981, Anthropometric Assessment of Nutritional Status, 1991; contbr. articles to profl. jours. Recipient Nathalie Masse Meml. prize Internat. Children's Ctr., Paris, 1979. Fellow Human Biology Coun.; mem. APHA, N.Am. Assn. Study Obesity, Internat. Assn. Human Auxology, Pan Am. Health Orgn. (tech. adv. nutrition 1994—2000, Nat. Ctr. Health Stats. (tech. working group 1994-97), Am. Soc. Nutritional Scis., Soc. for Study Human Biology, Sigma Xi, Phi Kappa Phi, Delta Omega. Home Phone: 952-920-1075. Business E-Mail: himes@epi.umn.edu.

HIMLER, THOMAS CHARLES, psychologist; b. Cleve., June 30, 1942; s. Norbert and Grace Himler; m. Myra Stull (div.); 1 child, Tara. BS, Ohio State U., 1965; MA, John Carroll U., 1971; PhD, U. Akron, 1983. Nat. cert. sch. psychologist. Tchr. St. Barnabas Sch., Northfield, Ohio, 1965—68, Broadway Sch., Maple Heights, Ohio, 1968—69; sch. psychologist Lorain County, Elyria, Ohio, 1971—79, PSI Assocs., Cleve., 1980—82; asst. prof., adj. SD State U., Sioux Falls, 1985—87; sch. psychologist Sioux Falls Sch. Dist., 1982—; pvt. practice Sioux Falls, 1983—. Mem. biomed. ethics com. Children's Care Hosp. and Sch., Sioux Falls, 1995—97; chmn. Sioux Falls Sch. Dist. Sch. Psychology Sect., 1995—97; chmn. psychology consulting staff Avera-McKennan Hosp., Sioux Falls, 1995—99, mem. med. exec. com, 1998—99. Mem.: APA, Internat. Assn. Sch. Psychologists, Nat. Assn. Sch. Psychologists, Mensa. Avocations: sailing, scuba diving, skiing, travel. Office: Sioux Falls Sch Dist 201 E 38th St Sioux Falls SD 57105 Office Phone: 605-367-7924.

HIMMA, KENNETH EINAR, philosophy educator; BA, U. Ill., Chgo., 1985; MA, UCLA, 1987; JD, U. Wash., 1990, PhD, 2001. Bar: Wash. 1992, Calif. 1990. Lectr. philosophy, info. scis. and law U. Wash., Seattle, 2001—04; assoc. prof. philosophy Seattle Pacific U., 2004—. Contbr. more than 100 articles to profl. jours. Mem. steering com. Jubilee NW, Seattle, 2004—05. Mem.: Golden Key Nat. Honor Soc., Phi Kappa Phi, Phi Beta Kappa. Office: Seattle Pacific U 3307 Third Ave West Seattle WA 98119 Office Phone: 206-281-2038. Office Fax: 206-281-2335. E-mail: himma@spu.edu.

HIMMELBERG, CHARLES JOHN, III, mathematics professor, researcher; b. North Kansas City, Mo., Nov. 12, 1931; s. Charles John and Magdalene Caroline (Batliner) H.; m. Mary Patricia Hennessy, Jan. 27, 1962; children: Charles, Ann, Mary, Joseph, Patrick. BS, Rockhurst Coll., 1952; MS, U. Notre Dame, 1954, PhD, 1957. Assoc. analyst Midwest Rsch. Inst., Kansas City, Mo., 1957-59; asst. prof. math. U. Kans., Lawrence, 1959-65, assoc. prof., 1965-68, prof., 1968—2005, emeritus prof., 2005—, chmn. dept. math., 1978-99. Mem. editorial bd. Rocky Mountain Jour. Math, 1972-88; contbr. articles to profl. jours. Mem. Am. Math. Soc., Math. Assn. Am. Roman Catholic. Office: U Kans Dept Math Lawrence KS 66045-7523 Business E-Mail: himmelberg@ku.edu.

HIMMELBLAU, DAVID MAUTNER, chemical engineer; b. Chgo., Aug. 29, 1923; s. David and Roda (Mautner) H.; m. Betty H. Hartman, Sept. 1, 1948; children: Andrew, Margaret Ann. BS, MIT, Cambridge, 1947; MBA, Northwestern U., Evanston, Ill., 1950; PhD, U. Wash., Seattle, 1957. Cost engr. Internat. Harvester Co., Chgo., 1946-47; cost analyst Simpson Logging Co., Seattle, 1952-53; mgr. Excel Battery Co., Seattle, 1953-54; tchg. asst., instr. U. Wash., Seattle, 1955-57; successively asst. prof., asso. prof., prof. chem. engring. U. Tex., Austin, 1957—, chmn. dept., 1973-77. Pres. RAMAD Corp.; Univ. Fed. Credit Union, 1964-68; exec officer CACHE Corp. of Mass., 1984-2000. Author: Basic Principles and Calculations in Chemical Engineering, 1962, 7th edit., 2004, Process Analysis and Simulation, 1968, Process Analysis by Statistical Methods, 1970, Applied Nonlinear Programming, 1974, 2d edit., 1999, Optimization of Chemical Processes, 1989, 2d edit., 2000; contbr. articles to profl. jours. Served with US Army, 1943-46, 51-52. Grantee, NSF, 1953—94, NATO Sci. Com., 1969. Mem. Am. Inst. Chem. Engrs. (dir. 1973-76), Am. Chem. Soc., Am. Math. Soc., Ops. Rsch. Soc. Am., Soc. Indsl. and Applied Math., Sigma Xi, Delta Mu Delta. Clubs: Headliners (Austin). Home: 4609 Ridge Oak Dr Austin TX 78731-5211 Office: Univ Texas Coll Engring Austin TX 78712 Office Phone: 512-471-7445. Business E-Mail: himmelblau1@che.utexas.edu.

HIMMELFARB, GERTRUDE, writer, educator; b. NYC, Aug. 8, 1922; d. Max and Bertha (Lerner) H.; m. Irving Kristol, Jan. 18, 1942; children—William, Elizabeth. BA, Bklyn. Coll., 1942; MA, U. Chgo., 1944, PhD, 1950; L.H.D. (hon.), R.I. Coll., 1976, Kenyon Coll., 1985, Adelphi U., 1989, Boston U., 1987, Yale U., 1990; Litt. D. (hon.), Smith Coll., 1977, Lafayette Coll., 1978, Jewish Theol. Sem., 1978, Williams Coll., 1989; LLD (hon.), Union Coll., 1989. Distinguished prof. history Grad. Sch., CUNY, 1965-88, prof. emeritus, 1988—. Author: Lord Acton: A Study in Conscience and Politics, 1952, Darwin and the Darwinian Revolution, 1959, Victorian Minds, 1968, On Liberty and Liberalism— The Case of John Stuart Mill, 1975, The Idea of Poverty, 1984, Marriage and Morals Among the Victorians, 1986, The New History and the Old, 1987, Poverty and Compassion: The Moral Imagination of the Late Victorians, 1991, Untimely Thoughts on Culture and Society, 1994, The De-Moralization of Society: From Victorian Virutes to Modern Values, 1995, One Nation, Two Cultures, 1999, The Road to Modernity: The British, French, and American Enlightenment, 2004, The Moral Imagination, 2006; editorial bd.: Am. Scholar, First Things. Trustee Nat. Humanities Ctr.; bd. Woodrow Wilson Internat. Ctr., Brit. Inst. of U.S., Inst. Contemporary Studies; mem. coun. scholars Libr. of Congress; mem. council acad. advisors Am. Enterprise Inst. Recipient Rockefeller Found. award, 1962-63, 63-64, 80-81, Nat. Humanities Presdl. medal, 2004; Guggenheim fellow, 1955-56, 57-58; sr. fellow NEH, 1968-69; Am. Council Learned Socs. fellow, 1972-73; Phi Beta Kappa vis. scholar, 1972-73; Woodrow Wilson Ctr. fellow, 1976-77 Fellow British Acad., Am. Philos. Soc., Royal Hist. Soc., Am. Acad. Arts and Scis., Soc. Am. Historians; mem. Am. Hist. Assn., Conf. on Brit. Studies.

HIMMELFARB, JOHN DAVID, artist; b. Chgo., June 3, 1946; s. Samuel and Eleanor (Gorecki) Himmelfarb; m. Mary Louise Day. AB, Harvard U., 1968; MA, Grad. Sch. Edn., 1970. One-man shows include Ill. Arts Coun., Chgo., 1974, Graphics I&II, Boston, 1974, Ill. Ctr., Chgo., 1975, U. Nebr., Omaha, 1976, Dorothy Rosenthal Gallery, Chgo., 1976, Ill. State Mus., Springfield, 1978, Albrecht Mus. Art, St. Joseph, Mo., 1978, Ball State U., 1978, 89, Sheldon Meml. Art Gallery, 1978, Ill. Wesleyan U., 1979, Terry Dintenfass Inc., NYC, 1979, 83, 86, 89, 91, Gallery 72, Omaha, 1979, 83, 85, 87, 90, 92, 94, 96, 99, 2001, 03, 05, Fountain Gallery, Portland, Oreg., 1980, Hull Gallery, Washington, 1980, Barbara Balkin Gallery, Chgo., 1982, Area X Gallery, NYC, 1985, Brody's Gallery, Washington, 1985, 90, Sioux City Art Ctr., 1985, 2000, Davenport Mus., 1986, John Nichols, NYC, 1986, Blanden Art Mus., 1987, Evanston Art Ctr., 1987, 96, Fundacio Josep Artigas, Barcelona, Spain, 1989, Kalamazoo Inst. Arts, 1989, Miami U. Art Mus., 1990, Ark. Art Ctr., 1990, Madison Art Ctr., 1990, Huntington Mus. Art, 1990, Cissie Peltz Gallery, 1991, Anchor Graphics, 1992, U. No. Iowa, 1993, Gallery 1756, Chgo., 1995, Chgo. Cultural Ctr., 1995, Spaightwood Gallery, Madison, Wis., 1996, 99, Jean Albano Gallery, Chgo. 1996, 98, 2000, 2002, 2005, William Havu Gallery, Denver, 2002, 04, Ind. U. N.W., 2002, Ctr. for Contemp. Art, Christchurch, New Zealand, 2001, 03, Coll. Lake County, Grays Lake, Ill., 2005, Phyliss Stigliano Gallery, Bklyn., 2005, Salena Gallery, L.I. U., Bklyn., 2005, Bklyn. Publ Libr., 2006, Wise Ross Gallery, NYC, 2007, others; exhibited in group shows at Minn. Mus. Art, Total Mus. Contemporary Art, Seoul, Korea, Bklyn. Mus., Indpls. Mus. Art, Art Inst. Chgo., Walker Art Ctr., Nat. Mus. Am. Art, Mus. Nat. de la Estampa, Gilcrease Mus., Flatfile Galleries; represented in permanent collections: Art Inst. Chgo., Nat. Mus. Am. Art, Fogg Mus. Art, Cleve. Mus. Art, Mpls. Inst. Art, Mus. Modern Art, NYC, Bklyn. Mus., Balt. Mus. Art, Des Moines Art Ctr., High Mus. Art, Atlanta, Toledo Mus. Art, Univs. Wis., Minn., Oreg., Iowa, Total Mus. Contemporary Art, Seoul, Korea, Brit. Mus., others. NEA fellow in painting, 1982, in drawing, 1985, Ill. Arts Council fellow, 1986, 02, Pollock-Krasner fellow, 2002. Studio: 2400 S Oakley Ave Chicago IL 60608-4902 Office Phone: 733-376-0366. Business E-Mail: johnhimmelfarb@mac.com.

HIMMELREICH, DAVID BAKER, lawyer; b. Reading, Pa., Feb. 11, 1954; s. Lester Leon and Jane (Baker) H. AB in Econs., Lafayette U., 1976; JD, U. Pitts., 1979. Bar: Pa. 1980, U.S. Tax Ct. 1980. Sr. atty. Ayco Corp., Albany (NY) and Stamford (Conn.), 1979-84; sr. cons. Peat Marwick Main & Co., NYC, 1984-86; ptnr. Hynes, Himmelreich, Glennon & Co., Stamford, 1986—. Mem. Conn. State Treasurers Adv. Coun., 2004—. Bd. dirs. Project Return, Westport, Conn., 1986—; dir. Alcohol and Drug Dependency Coun. of Conn., Westport. Independent. Lutheran. Home: 190 Gregory Blvd Norwalk CT 06855-2620 Office: Hynes Himmelreich Box 4004 Darien CT 06820-4004 Address: 30 Old Kings Highway South Darien CT 06820 Office Phone: 203-656-5500. Business E-Mail: duke@hhg.net.

HIMMLER, BRUNO JON, physician, military officer; b. Sioux City, Iowa, Jan. 30, 1967; s. Victor W. and Charlotte M. Himmler; m. Mary M. Nelson, May 15, 1993; 1 child, William R. MD, U. SD, Vermillion, 1993. GMO USN, Norfolk, Va., 1994—97; clin. dir. Siouxland CHC, Sioux City, 2000—04, Ft. Hall IHS, Idaho, 2005—. Lt. comdr. USPHS, 2005—. Decorated Navy Commendation two medals USN. Fellow: Am. Acad. Family Physicians. Home: 5295 W Buckskin Rd Pocatello ID 83201 Office: Fort Hall Service Unit PO Box 717 Mission Rd Fort Hall ID 83203 Home Phone: 208-540-0577; Office Phone: 208-238-5427. Personal E-mail: bruno.himmler@ihs.gov.

HIMPSEL, FRANZ JOSEF, physicist, researcher; b. Rosenheim, Germany, 1949; arrived in US, 1977; Diploma in Physics, U. Munich, 1973, PhD in Physics, 1977. With IBM Rsch., Yorktown Heights, NY, 1977-95, 1st level mgr., 1982-85, 2nd level mgr., 1985-95; prof. physics U. Wis., Madison, 1995—, co-dir. sci. Synchrotron Radiation Ctr., 1997—2002, Ednor M. Rowe prof. physics, 2000—. Contbr. articles to sci. jours. Recipient Humboldt Rsch. Prize, 2005. Fellow: Am. Vacuum Soc. (Peter Mark award 1985), Am. Phys. Soc. (Davisson-Germer prize in Atomic or Surface Physics 2007); mem.: German Phys. Soc., NY Acad. Sciences. Office: U Wis Dept Physics 1150 University Ave Madison WI 53706-1390 Office Fax: 608-265-2334. E-mail: fhimpsel@wisc.edu.*

HINCHEY, JOHN WILLIAM, lawyer; b. Knoxville, Tenn., June 18, 1941; s. Roy William and Ruth (Ownby) H.; m. Sherie Paulette Archer, May 12, 1968; children: Paul William, Meredith Marie, John Oliver. AB, Emory U., 1964, LLB, 1965; LLM, Harvard U., 1966; MLitt., Oxford U., 1980. Bar: Ga. 1965, U.S. Dist. Ct. (no., mid. and so. dists.) Ga. 1968, U.S. Ct. Appeals (11th cir.) 1968, U.S. Supreme Ct. 1970. Asst. atty. gen. State of Ga., Atlanta, 1968-72; ptnr. McConaughey & Hinchey, Decatur, Ga., 1972-76, Phillips & Mozley, Atlanta, 1976-84, Phillips, Hinchey & Reid, Atlanta, 1984-92, King and Spalding, Atlanta, 1992—. Contbr. articles to profl. jours. Mem.: ABA (chair Forum on Constrn. Industry), Am. Arbitration Assn. (constrn. arbitration master panel 2004—), CPR Inst., Alternative Dispute Resolution Counsel, Chartered Inst. Arbitrators, London Ct. Internat. Arbitration, Atlanta Bar Assn. (chair constrn. law sect. 1999—2000), Ga. Bar Assn., Am. Coll. Constrn. Lawyers (bd. govs. 2001—04, sec. 2005—, pres.-elect 2007—), Druid Hills Golf Club. Republican. Methodist. Office: King & Spalding LLP 1180 Peachtree St NE Atlanta GA 30309-3521 Office Phone: 404-572-4922. Business E-Mail: jhinchey@kslaw.com.

HINCHEY, MAURICE D., congressman; b. NYC, Oct. 27, 1938; s. Maurice D. and Rose (Bonack) Hinchey; children: Maurice Scott, Josef L., Michelle R. BS in Polit. Sci. and English, SUNY, New Paltz, 1968, MA in English, 1970; grad. student in Pub. Adminstrn. and Econs., SUNY, Albany. Mem. NY State Assembly, 1975—93, US Congress from 22nd NY dist., 1993—, mem. banking and fin. svcs. com., 1993—98, mem. natural resources com., mem. appropriations com., 1998—, mem. joint econ. com. Chmn. NY Urban Cultural Pks. Adv. Coun. Co-author: Organized Crime and the Solid Waste Industry, 1986, NY City Water Supply, A Hist., 1988. Hudson River Greenway Coun.; bd. dirs. Children's Rehab. Ctr., WAMC Nat. Pub. Radio; bd. visitors US Mil. Acad. at West Point. Served in 7th Fleet USN, 1956—59. Named a Champion of Sci., Sci. Coalition, 2002; recipient Legislator of Yr. award, Environ. Planning Lobby, 1975, 1979, NY State Bar Assn. Environ. award, 1989, William Hoyt Environ. award, Audubon NY and Audubon Coun. NY, 1990, Edgar Wayburn award, Sierra Club, 2000, Celebrating a Greener NY award, NY League Conservation Voters, 2000, Nelson A. Rockefeller award, NY Water Environment Assn., 2001. Mem. Saugerties Dem. Club (founding mem.), NY State Dem. Commn. (vice-chmn.). Democrat. Roman Catholic. Office: US House Reps 2431 Rayburn House Office Bldg Washington DC 20515-3222 Office Phone: 202-225-6335. Office Fax: 202-226-0774.*

HINCHEY, TIM, professional sports team executive; m. Mia Hinchey; children: Alexandria, Madison, Gabriella, Aidan, Brendan. With NHL LA Kings, 1991; v.p. mktg. and corp. sales ECHL Utah Grizzlies and the E Ctr.; sr. v.p. bus. devel. ECHL Long Beach Ice Dogs; dir. strategic alliances Maloof Sports & Entertainment; v.p. brand devel. No. Calif. Krispy Kreme Doughnuts; alliance mktg. dir. Runyon, Saltzman & Einhorn; sr. v.p. corp. devel., chief mktg. officer NBA New Orleans/Okla. City Hornets; exec. v.p.

bus. ops. NBA Charlotte Bobcats and WNBA Charlotte Sting, 2006—. Office: Charlotte Bobcats 333 E Trade St Charlotte NC 28202*

HINCHIE, WILLIAM JULES, nuclear engineer, director; b. Apg, Md., June 24, 1961; s. John Charles and Marie Antonette Hinchie; m. Carol Ann Schneider, June 9, 1990; children: Joshua Daniel, Angela Marie, Mary Monica, Joseph Thomas, Tesera Marie. BS nuc. engring., Kans. State U., Manhattan, Kansas, 1984. Emergency preparedness engr. Callaway Nuc. Plant - Union Electric, Fulton, Mo., 1985—86, material engr. to lab supr., 1986—, comml. grade lab supr., 1999—. Liturgist, musician Jefferson City Diocese, 1985—; sr. cons. materials engr., 2003—; bus. owner Legacy Bus. Group, 2004—. Liturgist and musician Jefferson City Diocese, Fulton, Mo., 1985—2004. Captian US Army Res., 1981—94, Missouri. Decorated Army Achievement Medal US Army. Mem.: KC (grand knight 1990—95). Home: 710 Collier Lane Fulton MO 65251-1346 Office: Nuclear Engineering PO Box 620 Fulton MO 65251-0620 Home Phone: 573-642-1218; Office Phone: 573-676-8176. Office Fax: 573-676-8971. Personal E-mail: hinchie@swbell.net. E-mail: wjhinchie@cal.ameren.com.

HINCKLEY, GORDON B., religious organization administrator; b. Salt Lake City, June 23, 1910; s. Bryant S. and Ada (Bitner) H.; m. Marjorie Pay, Apr. 29, 1937 (dec. Apr. 6, 2004); children: Kathleen Hinckley Barnes Walker, Richard G., Virginia Hinckley Pearce, Clark B., Cynthia Jane Hinckley Dudley. Ordained 15th pres., prophet LDS Ch., 1995. Asst. Coun. of Twelve Apostles Ch. of Jesus Christ of Latter-day Saints, Salt Lake City, 1958-61, mem. Coun., 1961-81, mem. Quorum Twelve Apostles, 1961—95, counselor in 1st presidency, 1981-81, 2nd counselor in 1st presidency, 1982-85, 1st counselor in 1st presidency, 1985-95, pres., 1995—. Proselyting mission Brit. Isles LDS Ch. Named one of most admired men in world 2nd consecutive yr., Ann. Survey Ams., 2001. Mem. Lds Ch. Address: Ch of Jesus Christ of Latter-day Saints 47 E South Temple St Salt Lake City UT 84150

HINCKLEY, GREGORY KEITH, software industry executive; b. San Francisco, Oct. 3, 1946; s. Homer Clair and Josephine F. (Gerrick) H. BS in Math. and Physics, Claremont Men's Coll., 1968; MS in Applied Physics, U. Calif., San Diego, 1970; MBA, Harvard U., 1972. CPA, Ill. Second v.p. Continental Bank, Chgo., 1972—78; dir. fin ITEL Corp., San Francisco, 1978—79; group contr. Raychem Corp., Menlo Park, Calif., 1979—83; v.p. fin., CFO Bio-Rad Labs., Richmond, Calif., 1983—89; sr. v.p. fin., CFO Crowley Maritime Corp., San Francisco, 1989—91; sr. v.p., CFO VLSI Tech. Inc., 1992—97; pres. Mentor Graphics Corp., Wilsonville, Oreg., 1997—, also bd. dirs. Bd. dirs. Amkor Tech., Chandler, Ariz., Oreg. Mus. Sci. and Industry, Portland, Arcsoft, Inc., Fremont, Calif., Intermec, Inc., Everett, Wash. Bd. dirs. Portland Opera. Fulbright fellow, Eng., 1968. Mem. AICPAs. Home: 2417 SW 16th Ave Portland OR 97201-2308

HINCKS, MARCIA LOCKWOOD, retired insurance company executive; b. NYC, July 3, 1935; d. John Salem and Dorothy Elinor (Tufts) Lockwood; m. John Winslow Hincks, June 14, 1958; children: Rebecca Towne, Jennifer Winslow, John Morris, Benjamin Lockwood. BA, Bryn Mawr Coll., 1956; LLB, Yale U., 1959. Bar: Conn. 1960. Atty. Aetna Life & Casualty, Hartford, Conn., 1961—64, 1967—70, counsel, 1970—81, v.p., ins. counsel, 1981—91, sr. counsel litigation, 1991—93. Chmn. United Way Capital Area, Hartford, 1984—85; trustee Hotchkiss Sch., Lakeville, Conn., 1973—78, Hartford Coll. Women, 1978—2006; bd. dirs. Hartford Hosp., 1983—, chmn., 1998—2002; bd. dirs. Conn. Water Co., Clinton, 1983—. Recipient Cmty. Svc. award United Way Capital Area, 1982, Alexis de Tocqueville award United Way of Am., 1987. Mem.: Assn. Life Ins. Counsel, Conn. Bar Assn., ABA, Hartford Golf. Democrat. Conglist.

HIND, HARRY WILLIAM, pharmaceutical company executive; b. Berkeley, Calif., June 2, 1915; s. Harry Wyndham and B.J. (O'Connor) H.; m. Diana Vernon Miesse, Dec. 12, 1940; children: Leslie Vernon Hind Daniels, Gregory William. BS, U. Calif., Berkeley, 1939, LLD, 1968; DSc (hon.), U. Scis. Phila., 1982. Founder Barnes-Hind Pharms., Inc., Sunnyvale, Calif., 1939—. Pres. Hind Health Care, Inc. Contbr. articles to profl. jours.; designer ph meter and developer of ophthalmic solutions. Recipient Ebert award for pharm. rsch., 1948, Eye Rsch. Found. award, 1958, Helmholtz Ophthalmology award for rsch., 1968, Carbert award for sight conservation, 1973, Alumnus of Yr. award U. Calif. Sch. Pharmacy, 1965, Disting. Svc. award U. Calif. Proctor Found., 1985, Commendation by Resolution State of Calif., 1987, Pharmaceutical Achievements commendation State of Calif. Assembly, Hon. Recognition award Contact Lens Mfrs. Assn., 1990. Fellow AAAS; mem. Am. Pharm. Assn., Am. Optometric Assn. (Man of Yr. award Pharmacist's Planning Svc. 1987), Contact Lens Soc. Am. (Hall of Fame 1989), Am. Assn. Pharm. Scientists, Am. Chem. Soc., Calif. Pharm. Assn., NY Acad. Scis., Los Altos Country Club, Sigma Xi, Rho Chi, Phi Delta Chi.

HINDELANG, THOMAS JOSEPH, finance educator, dean; b. Detroit, Mar. 27, 1943; s. John Louis, Jr. and Louise Mary H.; m. Christine Kydd, July 19, 1980; children: Meredith J., Stephen T. BS, U. Detroit, 1965; MBA, U. Mich., 1966; MS, Stanford U., 1969; D in Bus. Administrn., Ind. U., 1973. CPA, Ind.; cert. data processor Data Processing Mgmt. Assn. From asst. prof. to prof. fin. Drexel U., Phila., 1973—80, prof. of fin., 1980—, asst. dean of grad. schl., 1979-81, asst. dean of COBA, 1981-83, pres. of faculty senate, 1989-91, head dept. fin., 1983-94, George B. Francis prof., 1992—, assoc. dean, 1994-95, acting v.p. acad. affairs, 1995-96, exec. asst. to pres., 1995-97, sr. adv. COBA accreditation, assoc. dean grad. programs, 1997-2000, sr. assoc. dean for grad. and profl. programs, 2000—04, vice dean, 2004—. Exec. dir. LeBow Coll. Ctr. for Tchg. Excellence, 2003—; pres. N.E. Decision Scis. Inst., 1978-79; acad. liason com. Fin. Execs. Inst., Phila., 1991-94 Author: The Strategic Evaluation & Management of Capital Expenditures, 1987, Financial Analysis Software to Accompany Capital Budgeting, 1990, Capital Budgeting, 1992; twelve books and software packages; Created 4 online MBA courses in Drexel's Nat. Raked Online Techno MBA Program. Mem. Ea. Fin. Assn. (pres. 1995-96, chair bd. trustees 1996-97), Fin. Mgmt. Assn., Fin. Execs. Inst., Decision Scis. Inst. Avocations: tennis, gardening, investing. Office: Drexel U 3141 Chestnut St Philadelphia PA 19104-2875 Office Phone: 215-895-2111. Business E-Mail: Thomas.Hindelang@drexel.edu.

HINDEN, STANLEY JAY, newspaper editor; b. NYC, Jan. 27, 1927; s. Edward I. and Rose (Kroshinsky) H.; m. Sara Leopold, May 24, 1953; children: Alan, Lawrence, Pamela. BA, Syracuse U., 1950. Reporter, polit. editor, editor editl. pages, nat. corr. Washington Newsday, Garden City, NY, 1952-71; exec. editor, editor Nat. Jour., Washington, 1971-73; editl. page features editor, editor Dist., Md. and Va. weekly sects., fin. reporter, columnist Washington Post, 1973-96, fin. writer column Washington Investing. Author: How to Retire Happy, 2001; contbr. polit. column Inside Politics, Newsday, 1955-65, Retirement Jour. column Washington Post, 1996-2003. Served with AUS, 1945-46. Home: Apt 630 3310 N Leisure World Blvd Silver Spring MD 20906-5664 Office: 1150 15th St NW Washington DC 20071-0001 Personal E-mail: stanjh@aol.com.

HINDERAKER, IVAN, retired political science professor; b. Hendricks, Minn., Apr. 29, 1916; s. Theodore and Clara (Hanson) H.; m. Evelyn Birkholz, June 7, 1941 (dec. June 17, 2004); 1 child, Mark (dec. Feb. 23, 2004). BA, St. Olaf Coll., 1938; MA, U. Minn., 1942, PhD, 1949. Mem. faculty UCLA, 1948—, prof. polit. sci., 1956—, chmn. dept., 1960-62; vice chancellor acad. affairs U. Calif.-Irvine, 1962-64; chancellor U. Calif.-Riverside, 1964-79, chancellor emeritus, 1979—; ret., 1979. Mem. Minn. Ho. of Reps., 1941-43; mem. Calif. Transp. Commn., 1978-84, chmn., 1982. Served to 1st lt. USAAF, 1943-46. Home: 19191 Harvard Ave #919 Irvine CA 92612

HINDERAKER, JOHN HADLEY, lawyer, political blogger; b. Watertown, SD, Sept. 19, 1950; s. Irving Alden and Eula Mae (Jertson) H.; m. Shannon Faye Smith, Jan. 3, 1981 (div. 1993); children: Eric, Laura, Alison, Kathryn; m. Loree Kay Miner, June 4, 1994. AB magna cum laude, Dartmouth Coll., 1971; JD cum laude, Harvard U., 1974. Bar: Minn. 1974; admitted to practice US Ct. of Appeals, 8th Cir., 9th Cir., US Dist. Ct. Dist. Minn. Assoc. Faegre & Benson LLP, Mpls., 1974-81, ptnr., 1981—. Chmn. practice standards com., Faegre & Benson, 1986; fellow Claremont Inst.; lectr. in field. Contbr. articles to profl. jours. including Nat. Rev., Am. Enterprise, Am. Experiment Quarterly and newspapers from Fla. to Calif.; guest appearances Fox News; author (blog website) powerlineblog.com 2002-. Bd. dirs. Ctr. of the Am. Experiment, 1996. Named Super Lawyer of the Yr., Jour. Law and Politics, 2005; named one of Minn. Top Commercial Litigators, Minn. Jour. of Law and Politics, Top 25 Web Celebs, Forbes mag., 2007. Fellow Claremont Inst.; mem. ABA, Minn. State Bar Assn. (mem. ethics com. 1979-85), Hennepin County Bar Assn. Republican. Lutheran. Avocations: authoring commentaries on polit. and econ. issues, weightlifting. Office: Faegre & Benson 2200 Wells Fargo Ctr 90 S 7th St Minneapolis MN 55402-3901 Office Phone: 612-766-8430. Office Fax: 612-766-1600. Business E-Mail: JHinderaker@faegre.com. E-mail: powerlinefeedback@gmail.com.*

HINDERLITER, RICHARD GLENN, electrical engineer; b. Tulsa, Apr. 9, 1936; s. Robert Verl and Aileen (Burton) H.; m. Leila Ratzlaff, June 8, 1958; children: Daniel Scott, Susan Paige, Alison Ann, Matthew Glenn. BSEE with honors, U. Kans., 1958; MSEE, NYU, 1960, PhD in Ops. Rsch., 1973. Staff mem. Bell Labs. , Murray Hill, NJ, 1958-62; dept. head Bell Labs., Holmdel, NJ, 1962-72, Whippany, NJ, 1972-82; divsn. mgr. AT&T, NYC, 1982-83, Bellcore, Morristown, NJ, 1984-91. Contbr. articles to Internat. Conf. on Communications, Computer Mag., Internat. Symposium on Subscriber Loops, Internat. Teletraffic Conf. Chmn. Zoning Bd. of Adjustment, Chatham Twp., N.J., 1992-99; scoutmaster Boy Scouts Am., Kansas City, Mo., Chatham Twp., Red Bank, N.J., Wichita, Kans., 1956—; v.p. Stonebrooke Estates Howeowners Assn.; treas. Kansas City Northland Art League, 2004— Recipient Silver Beaver award Morris-Sussex coun. Boy Scouts Am., 1988, Eagle Scout Hall of Fame, 1998, Outstanding Vol. award with spl. recognition Vols. of Morris County; James E. West fellow Boy Scouts Am. Fellow AAAS; mem. IEEE (sr.), N.Y. Acad. Scis., Inst. for Ops. Rsch. and the Mgmt. Scis., Meth. Friday Niters Fellowship Soc. (pres.), Methodist Inquirers Fellowship (pres.), Kiwanis (treas. Chatham, pres. North Kansas City, Mo. chpt., George F. Hixson fellow), Tau Beta Pi, Sigma Tau (v.p.), Theta Tau (vice regent), Eta Kappa Nu (pres.), Alpha Phi Omega, Pi Mu Epsilon, Sigma Pi Sigma. Methodist. Achievements include application of ops. rsch. techniques to large software systems. Personal E-mail: hondolite@prodigy.net.

HINDERY, LEO JOSEPH, JR., communications executive; b. Springfield, Ill., Oct. 31, 1947; s. Leo Joseph and E. Marie (Whitener) H.; m. Deborah Diane Sale, Feb. 20, 1980; 1 child, Robin Cook. BA, Seattle U., 1969; MBA, Stanford U., 1971. Asst. treas. Utah Internat., San Francisco, 1971-80; treas. Natomas Co., San Francisco, 1980-82; exec. v.p. fin. Jefferies & Co., LA, 1982-83; CFO A.G. Becker Paribas, NYC, 1983-85; chief officer planning and fin. Chronicle Pub. Co., San Francisco, 1985-88; mng. gen. ptnr. InterMedia Ptnrs. (merged with ATT Broadband/Internet Svcs.), San Francisco, 1988-97; pres. Tele-Communications, Inc., 1997—99; pres., CEO AT&T Broadband and Internet Services, 1999; chmn., CEO GlobalCenter Global Crossing Ltd., 1999—2000, chmn., CEO, 2000, YES Network, 2001—04; supporter John Kerry presdl. campaign, 2004; mng. ptnr. InterMedia Partners VII, LLP, 2004—; chmn. HL Capital, Inc. Bd. dirs. GT Group Telecom Inc., Tanning Tech. Corp., TD Waterhouse Group Inc., VerticalNet, Inc. Mem. adv. coun. Stanford Bus. Sch.; bd. trustees Hampton U.; bd. dirs. Daniels Fund; vice chmn. Mus. of TV and Radio. With US Army, 1968—70. Avocation: golf.

HINDI, RIYADH, engineering educator, researcher; b. Mosul, Nainava, Iraq, Aug. 7, 1966; s. Nafea Hindi and Monera Naoom; m. Luma Kutaimi, Dec. 3, 1975; children: Lourdes S., Noah B. BSc in Civil Engring., U. Baghdad, 1988, MSc in Structural Engring., 1992; PhD in Structures, U. B.C., 2001. Registered profl. engr., Assn. Profl. Engrs. and Geoscientists, B.C. Structural designer Hindi Engring., Victoria, B.C., Canada, 1995—97; rsch. asst. U. B.C., Vancouver, 1997—2001; bridge designer McElhanney Engring., Surrey, 1999—2001; asst. prof. Bradley U., Peoria, Ill., 2001—. Faculty advisor Bradley U., Peoria, Ill., 2001—, dir. structural lab., 2001—. Contbr. articles to profl. jours. Recipient Outstanding faculty award, Bradley U., 2004, Faculty award for Excellence in Rsch. and scholarship, Coll. Engring. Bradley U., 2006. Mem.: ASCE (assoc.), Earthquake Engring. Rsch. Inst. (assoc.), Am. Concrete Inst. (assoc.), St. Sharbel Ch. (assoc.), St. Vincent de Paul Ch. (assoc.). Roman Catholic. Achievements include patents for Using opposing spirals to confine reinforced concrete members to enhance strength and ductility. Home: 1118 W Pembrook Dr Peoria IL 61614 Office: Bradley U 1501 W Bradley Ave Peoria IL 61625 Home Phone: 309-692-0538; Office Phone: 309-677-2945. Office Fax: 309-677-2867. Personal E-mail: rhindi@hotmail.com. E-mail: hindi@bradley.edu.

HINDMAN, CRAIG A., engineering executive; BA in Liberal Arts, Colgate U., Hamilton, NY, 1976; M in Mgmt., Northwestern U., 1987. Sales trainee Buildex divsn. Ill. Tool Works (ITW), Glenview, 1976, various sales, sales mgmt. and mktg. mgmt. positions, gen. mgr. Buildex divsn., 1993, v.p., gen. mgr. Paslode divsn., 1997—99, v.p., gen. mgr. Duo-Fast, 1999—2002, pres. Finishing Group, 2002, exec. v.p., 2004—. Office: Ill Tool Works 3600 W Lake Ave Glenview IL 60026-1215 Office Phone: 847-724-7500. Office Fax: 847-657-4572.*

HINDMAN, LARRIE C., lawyer; b. Meservey, Iowa, Mar. 30, 1937; s. Marvin C. and Fredona E. (Lemke) H.; m. Jeannie Carol Richey, June 18, 1961; children: Bryant C., Derek Cory. BS, Iowa State U., 1959; JD, U. Iowa, 1962. Bar: Mo. 1963, Kans. 1975. Ptnr. Stinson Morrison & Hecker LLP, Kansas City, Mo., 1962-2000. Contbr. legal articles to profl. jours. Mem.: Am. Land Title Assn. (lender counsel), Am. Coll. Real Estate Lawyers, Club at Porto Cima. Office: Stinson Morrison & Hecker LLP 1201 Walnut Ste 2800 Kansas City MO 64106-2150 Home: 1186 Grand Cove Rd Sunrise Beach MO 65079 Office Phone: 816-842-8600.

HINDO, WALID AFRAM, radiology educator, researcher; b. Baghdad, Iraq, Oct. 4, 1940; arrived in U.S., 1966, naturalized, 1976; s. Afram Paul and Laila Farid (Meshaka) H.; m. Fawzia Hanna Batti, Apr. 20, 1965; children: Happy, Rana, Patricia, Heather, Brian MB, ChB, Baghdad U., 1964. Diplomate Am. Bd. Radiology. Instr. radiology Rush Med. Coll, Chgo., 1971-72; asst. prof. Northwestern U., Chgo., 1972-75; assoc. prof. medicine and radiology Chgo. Med. Sch., 1975-80, prof., chmn. dept. radiology, 1980-90, prof. dept. radiology, 1990—, dir. radiology rsch. program, 1990-94; cons. UtiliMed, Northbrook, Ill., 1994—96; pres. Northbrook Inst. for Rsch. and Devel., 1992—. Dir. radiology rsch. program VA Med. Ctr., North Chicago, Ill., 1990-94; cons. Ill. Cancer Coun. Contbr. articles on cancer treatment, imaging and managed care to profl. jours. Bd. dirs. Lake County div. Am. Cancer Soc., Ill., 1975-80. Served to lt. M.C., Iraq; Army, 1965-66 Recipient Golden Apple award, The Chgo. Med. Sch., 1994; named Prof. of Yr., Chgo. Med. Sch., 1981, 82, 83, 85, 86. Mem. Radiology Soc. North Am., Am. Soc. Acad. Radiologists. Republican. Roman Catholic. Office: Northbrook Inst for R&D Ste 119 1955 Raymond Dr Northbrook IL 60062-6732 Home Phone: 847-204-0988; Office Phone: 847-753-9149.

HINDS, EDWARD DEE, insurance and investment professional, financial planner; b. Madera, Calif., May 13, 1949; s. Edward Dee Jr. and Donna (Parker) H.; m. Olga P. Hinds; children: Sarah, Stephen, Rebekah. Grad., Life Underwriting Tng. Coun., 2002. CLU; ChFC; CFP; registered fin. cons.; fellow Life Underwriter Tng. Coun.; accredited estate planner; chartered advisor for sr. living. Sr. acct. agt. Allstate, Lemoore, Calif., 1983—90; gen. agt. various cos. Paso Robles, Calif., 1990—; gen. ptnr. Edward D. Hinds, Ins. and Fortress Fin. Strategies, Paso Robles, 1990—97, Edward D. Hinds, Ins., 1995—; founder, gen. ptnr. Fortress Fin. Strategies, A Registered Investment Adviser, 1995—97; founder, gen. mgr. Hinds Fin. Group, LLC, 1998—; founder, CFO Acorn Fin. Advisors, Inc., 2007—. Benefits cons. U-Haul Dealers, Ctrl. Calif., 1992—, KOA, Calif., 1997. Mem.: Nat. Assn. Alternative Benefit Cons., Nat. Assn. Health Underwriters, Million Dollar Roundtable, Nat. Assn. Estate Planners and Couns., Nat. Assn. Ins. and Fin. Advisors, Soc. Fin. Profls. Office Phone: 805-239-7443. Business E-Mail: dhinds@hindsfinancial.com.

HINDS, SARA FEAGAN, elementary school educator; b. Elizabethtown, Ky., Sept. 25, 1978; d. Harry Lee and Elizabeth Parker Feagan; m. Shawn Timothy Hinds, Nov. 11, 2000; 1 child, Caitlin Michelle. BA in French & Internat. Rels., Roanoke Coll., Salem, Va., 1996—2000; MA in French Lang. & Lit., U. Ky., Lexington, 2000—02; MEd, Georgetown Coll., Ky., 2004—06. Tchg. asst. U. Ky., 2000—02; mid. sch. French & social studies tchr. Lexington Sch., 2002—. Mem.: Nat. Coun. Social Studies, Am. Coun. Tchg. Fgn. Lang., Am. Assn. Tchrs. French, Alpha Phi Omega (v.p. 1999—2000). R-Liberal. Luth. Office: Lexington Sch 1050 Lane Allen Rd Lexington KY 40504 Home Phone: 859-433-5420. Business E-Mail: shinds@thelexingtonschool.org.

HINE, DARLENE CLARK, history educator, administrator; b. Morley, Mo., Feb. 7, 1947; d. Levester and Lottie May (Thompson) Clark; m. William C. Hine, Aug. 21, 1970 (div. 1975); m. Johnny Earl Brown, July 25, 1981 (div. Aug. 1986); 1 child, Robbie Davine. BA in Am. History, Roosevelt U., 1968; MA, Kent State U., 1970, PhD in Afro-Am. History, 1975, Hon. LHD, U. Mass, 1998, hon. LittD, Purdue U., 2002, SUNY hon. LHD, Buffalo State Coll., 2002. Teaching asst. Kent State U., Ohio, 1968-71; asst. prof. history, coordinator Black studies, SC State Coll., Orangeburg, 1972-74; asst. prof. Purdue U., West Lafayette, Ind., 1974-79, assoc. prof. history, 1979-85, interim dir. African Studies and Research Ctr., 1978-79, vice provost, 1981-86, prof. history, 1985-87; John A. Hannah Disting. prof. Am. History, Mich. State U., East Lansing, 1987-2004, adj. John A. Hannah Disting. prof. Am. History, 2004-; bd. trustee prof. of African Am. Studies, prof. history, Northwestern U., Evanston, Ill., 2004-; mem. Ind. Com. for Humanities, 1983-85; vis. disting. prof. history, Ariz. State U., 1985; vis. disting. prof. of women's studies, U. Delaware, 1989-90; Robert E. McNair vis. prof. So. Studies, U. SC, 1996; Harold Washington vis. prof., Roosevelt U, Chgo. Ill., 1996; Avalon Disting. vis. prof., Northwestern U., 1997; mem. adv. bd. ProQuest Women's History, 2001-02; inaugural dir. Ctr. for African Am. History, 2003-; mem. exec. com. Nat. Acad. for Critical Studies, 1996-; invited lectr. colls. and univs. including Harvard U., 1975, U. Ill., Chgo., 1981, Ind. U., 1982, U. Tex., Austin, 1983, So. Meth. U., 1983, Duke U., 1990, U. NC, Chapel Hill, 1992, Emory U., 1994; grant rev. panelist NEH, 1979-80, Ford Found., NRC, 1980, 81, 82. Fellow Ctr. for the Study of Behavioral Sciences, Stanford, CA, 2000-01; adv. bd. mem. Ctr. for New Deal Studies, Roosevelt U., 1997-, Jour. African American Men and Boys, The U. Kansas, Ctr. for Multicultural Leadership, 1999-, William J. Clinton Oral History Project, 2001 and several others; mem. adv. com. The Nat. Women's History Project, 1984-; mem. So. Historical Assn. Com. on Sexual Harassment, 2000-; bd. overseers, Wellesley Ctr. for Women, 2002-; mem. coun. scholars, Am. Slavery Meml. Mus., 2002-; mem. Bd. Scholars Consultants for the HistoryMakers, 2003-. Author: Black Victory: The Rise and Fall of the White Primary in Texas, 1979, new edit. 2003, When the Truth is Told: A History of Black Women's Culture and Community in Indiana, 1875-1950, 1981, Black Women in White: Racial Conflict and Cooperation in the Nursing Profession 1890-1950, 1989, Hine Sight: Black Women and the Re-Construction of American History, 1994, Speak Truth to Power: Black Professional Class in United States History, 1996; co-author A Shining Thread of Hope: The History of Balck Women in America, 1998, The African-American Odyssey, 2nd edit., 2002, African Americans: A Concise History, Combined Vol., 2003, The African-American Odyssey, 3rd edit., 2005, African-American History, 2006; edited books Black Women in the Nursing Profession: An Anthology of Historical Sources, 1985, The State of Afro-American History, Past, Present, and Future, 1986, Black Women in the United States 1619-1989, 1990, Black Women in America, 2nd edit., 2005; co-editor of several book; contbr. chpts. to books, articles to publs., book revs. to jours.; editl. adv. bd. Jour. Women's History, 1987-96, The Frederick Douglass Papers Project, 1988-, Martin Luther King Jr. Papers Project, 1987-, Black American and Diasporic Studies Series, 2001, African Am. Studies Ctr., 2005 and several others; mem. editl. bd. Dictionary of American Nurses, 1985, Jour. Negro History, 1979-87, Encyclopedia of the Harlem Renaissance, 2000, Encyclopedia of the Midwest, 2000 and several others; mem. editl. com. African American Research Library, 1996-; assoc. editor The Historian, 1995-; contbg. editor Souls: A Critical Journal of the Black Politics, Culture and Society, 1998-; NEH advisor, Remembering Jim Crow, American Radio Works, 1999-; mem adv. panel, Homer G. Philips Hosp. Project, 2000-; mem. adv. bd. Percy Julian Biography Project WGBH-NOVA, 2002-; guest appearance WGN-9 News, Black Women in America: An Historical Encyclopedia, Chgo., Ill., 2005, Power Point Radio, African American Historians and the History of Black Women in America, WCLK 91.9 FM, Atlanta, Ga., 2005. Alumni fellow Kent State U., 1971-72,Nat. Humanities Ctr. fellow, 1986, Am. Council Learned Socs. fellow, 1986; faculty devel. grantee Purdue U., 1978-79; research awardee Rockefeller Archive Ctr., 1978; Rockefeller Found. fellow for minority group scholars, 1980; research grantee Eleanor Roosevelt Inst., 1980-81; project grantee Fund for Improvement of Post-Secondary Edn., 1980-82; NEH grantee, 1982-83, Am. Coun. of Learned Societies Fellow, 1986-87, Nat. Humanities Ctr. Fellow, 1986-87, Emeline Bigelow Conland Fellow, Radcliffe Inst. for Advanced Study, Harvard U., 2003-04; recipient Women's Honors in Pub. Svc., Minority Fellowship programs and Cabinet on Human Rights, Am. Nurses Assn., 1988, Disting. Alumni award Roosevelt U., 1988, Lavina L. Dock Book award, Am. Assn. for the History of Nursing, 1990, Spl. Achievement award, Kent State U. Alumni Assn., 1991, Anna Julia Cooper award for Disting. Scholarship, Sage Women's Edl. Press, 1993, LeSteffin award, Steffin Found. Inc., 1994, Dartmouth award, ALA, 1994, Zora Neal Hurston-Paul Robeson award, Nat. Coun. for Black Studies, Inc., 1995, Avery Citizenship award, Avery Rsch.Ctr., Coll. Charleston, 1997, Disting. Black Women award, Black Women in Sisterhood for Action, Washington, DC, 1999, Carter G. Woodson medallion, ASALH, Washington, DC, 2001, Michiganian of Yr. award, Detroit News, Bingham Farms, Mich., 2002; Mem. Assn. for Study of Negro Life and History (exec. council 1979-84, 2nd v.p. 1985-88, program com. ann. mtg. 1982, 1997, 1999), Orgn. Am. Historians (mem. program com. 1981-87, co-chair 1998, nominating com. mem. 1983-85, pres. 2001-02), So. Hist. Assn. (mem. exec. coun., 1990-92, program com. mem. 1983, 1986, chair, 1989, nominating com. mem., 1995, pres-elect, v.p. 2001-02, pres. 2002-03), So. Assn. Women Historians (v.p. 1983-84, pres. 1984-85), Am. Hist. Assn.(mem. nominating com. 1987-88 chair 1988-89), Assn. Black Women Historians (v.p. 1981-82, Letitia Woods Brown Book award, 1990, Letitia Woods Brown Meml. Anthology prize, 1993,1995), Phi Alpha Theta. (hon.), Phi Beta Kappa (hon.), Delta Sigma Theta Sorority (hon.);Fellow Am. Acad. Arts & Sciences Democrat. Baptist. Home: 2357 Burcham Dr East Lansing MI

48823-7241 Address: African American Studies Dept 2-320 Kresge Hall 1880 S Campus Dr Evanston IL 60208-2209 Office Phone: 517-355-3418, 847-467-0269. Office Fax: 517-432-6268, 847-467-0271. Business E-Mail: hined@msu.edu, d-hine@northwestern.edu.

HINE, JONATHAN TRUMBULL, JR., translator, educator; b. Norfolk, Va., Aug. 3, 1947; s. Jonathan Trumbull Hine and Carrie Louise Curtis; m. Carol Ann Snyder, Dec. 29, 1970; 1 child, Daniel Edward. BS in Italian, U.S. Naval Acad., Annapolis, Md., 1969; MPA, U. Okla., 1982; PhD, U. Va., 2000. Cert. rsch. adminstr. Commd. ensign USN, 1965, advanced through grades to lt. comdr., 1976, ret., 1989; profl. translator, 1961—; rsch. analyst U.S. Naval War Coll., Newport, R.I., 1988-89; adminstr. physics dept. U. Va., Charlottesville, 1989-95, assoc. dir. housing, 1995-2000. Owner Scriptor Svcs. LLC, Charlottesville, 1984—. Translator: Fundamentals of Naval Strategy, 1990; contbr. articles and book revs. to mags. and profl. jours. Vet. scouter Boy Scouts Am., Italy, R.I., Va., 1986—. Decorated Navy Commendation medal, 1982, 86, 89; recipient Cross of St. George, Episcopal Ch., 1988. Mem.: Am. Translation Studies Assn., U.S. Naval Inst., Soc. Tech. Comm., Am. Evaluation Assn., Soc. Rsch. Adminstrs., Am. Translators Assn. (accreditation). Episcopalian. Avocations: choral singing, bicycling. Office: Scriptor Svcs LLC PO Box 4623 Charlottesville VA 22905-4623 Business E-Mail: hine@scriptorservices.com.

HINE, ROBERT VAN NORDEN, JR., historian, educator; b. LA, Apr. 26, 1921; s. Robert Van Norden and Elizabeth (Bates) H.; m. Shirley M. McChord, June 24, 1949; 1 child, Allison. BA, Pomona Coll., Claremont, Calif., 1948; MA, Yale U., New Haven, Conn., 1949, PhD, 1952. From instr. history to prof. emeritus U. Calif., Riverside, 1954—90, prof. emeritus, 1990—, prof. recalled Irvine, 1990—. Author: California's Utopian Colonies, 1953, California's Utopian Colonies, rev. edit., 1983, Edward Kern and American Expansion, 1962, rev. edit., In the Shadow of Fremont, 1982, Bartlett's West: Drawing the Mexican Boundary, 1968, The American Frontier: Readings and Documents, 1972, The American West: An Interpretive History, 1973; author: (with John Mack Faragher) The American West: A New Interpretive History, 3d edit., 2000 (Wrangler award Cowboy and Western Heritage Mus., Caughey award, Western Hist. Assn.); author: Community on the American Frontier: Separate But Not Alone, 1980, California Utopianism: Contemplations of Eden, 1981; editor: William Andrew Spalding, Los Angeles Newspaperman, 1961, Soldier in the West: Letters of Theodore Talbot, 1972, Josiah Royce: West As Community in Writing Western History, 1991, Josiah Royce: From Grass Valley to Harvard, 1992 (Commonwealth Club award, 1992), Second Sight, 1993 (N.Y. Times Notable Book of 1993), Broken Glass: A Family's Journey through Mental Illness, 2006; editor: (with John Mack Faragher) Frontiers: A Short History of the American West, 2007; contbr. articles to profl. jours. Recipient Harbison award for disting. teaching Danforth Found., 1968, Wagner Meml. award Calif. Hist. Soc., 1986; Huntington Libr. fellow, 1953, 60, Guggenheim fellow, 1958, 68, Nat. Endowment Humanities sr. fellow, 1977, Calif. Coun. Promotion of History award, 1994. Mem.: Western History Assn. (life hon. 1990, Award of Merit 1996), Book Club of Calif. (Lifetime Achievement award 2006), Phi Beta Kappa. Home: 19191 Harvard Ave # 233 Irvine CA 92612-4670 E-mail: rvhine@uci.edu.

HINEGARDNER, LAURA A., lawyer; BA, U. Ky., 1993; JD, U. Cin., 1996. Bar: Ky. 1996, Ohio 1997. Atty. Katz, Teller, Brant & Hild, Cin. Former mem. Class VIII, Cin. Acad. Leadership for Lawyers; bd. mem. Fort Thomas Edn. Found. Mem. Charities Guild of Northern Ky. Named one of Ohio's Rising Stars, Super Lawyers, 2006. Avocations: sports, pilates. Office: Katz Teller Brant & Hild 255 E 5th St Ste 2400 Cincinnati OH 45202-4724 Office Phone: 513-977-3484. Office Fax: 513-762-0084.

HINELINE, CURT ROY, lawyer; b. 1959; BS in Bus. Adminstrn., Univ. Neb., Lincoln, 1982; JD magna cum laude, Univ. Puget Sound, 1986. Bar: Wash. 1986, US Ct. Appeals (9th, 8th cir.) 1988, US Dist. Ct., Oreg. Dist. 1991. Mem. Bogle & Gates PLLC, Seattle; ptnr., trial, regulatory, tech. practice group Dorsey & Whitney LLP, Seattle, 1999—, and co-chair, securities, fin. inst. litig. practice group. Named a Super Lawyer, Wash. Law and Politics, 2003. Mem.: ABA, Wash. State Bar Assn., Oreg. State Bar Assn., Phi Delta Phi. Office: Dorsey & Whitney LLP Ste 3400 US Bank Ctr 1420 Fifth Ave Seattle WA 98101-4010 Office Phone: 206-903-8853. Office Fax: 206-903-8820. Business E-Mail: hineline.curt@dorsey.com.

HINER, JOHN PATRICK, newspaper editor; b. Dearborn, Mich., July 18, 1960; s. John Henry and Rose Mary (Nagy) H.; m. Cheryl Ann Zarosley, Aug. 24, 1985 (div. May 1997); 1 child, Alexander Cassidy; m. Kathleen Marie Shannon, July 3, 1999. BA, Adrian Coll., Mich., 1982. Reporter Daily Telegram, Adrian, 1982-84, news editor, 1984-86; reporter Citizen-Patriot, Jackson, Mich., 1986-89, asst. metro editor, 1989-94; metro editor Bay City (Mich.) Times, 1994—2006, editor, 2006—. Chmn. bus. wire story com. AP Mich., Detroit, 1996, chmn. spot news wire story com., 1999. Author: The Pocket Pro, 1994. Chmn. devel. com. Leadership Bay County, Bay City, 1994-2000; bd. dirs. Bay Area Family Y, Bay City, 1997-99. Newswriting award AP, 1983, 87, 88, 90, 91, 90, 88, UPI, 1990; Sch. Bell award Mich. Edn. Assn., 1988. Mem. Rotary (bd trustee 1995-98). Avocations: writing, reading, tennis, golf, travel. Office: Bay City Times 311 5th St Bay City MI 48708-5853 Office Phone: 989-894-9632. E-mail: jhiner@bc-times.com, wordherder@hotmail.com.

HINER, LESLIE DAVIS, lawyer, consultant; b. Canton, Ohio, Sept. 30, 1957; d. Wendell Hughes and Margaret Alvina Davis; m. Ward Christopher Hiner, July 23, 1983; children: Elaine Margaret, Travis Davis. BA, Coll. Wooster, 1980; JD, U. Akron, 1985. Bar: Ind. 1985. Intern Legis. Svcs. Agy., Indpls., 1984; assoc. Ecklund, Frutkin & Grant, Indpls., 1985-87; co-owner, v.p., gen. counsel Hiner Van & Storage, Kokomo, Ind., 1987-91; assoc. Russell McIntrye Jessup Hilligoss & Raquet, Kokomo, Ind., 1991-91; Ind. senate majority atty., 1993-94; pvt. practice, 1994-95; gen. counsel, elections dep. Ind. Sec. of State, 1995-97; pvt. practice, session atty. Rep. caucus Ind. Ho. of Reps., Indpls., 1997-2000, policy dir., caucus atty. Rep. caucus, 2000—03, chief of staff to Rep. leader, 2003—04, chief of staff to Spkr. of House, 2004—. Mem. adj. faculty U. Indpls., 1986—87, 1992—93. Bd. dirs. Montessori Children's Home, 1989—90, cmty. affairs com. chmn., 1990; mem. Altrusa Cmty. Affairs Com., 1989—91; mem. sch. bd. Irvington Cmty. Sch. (Pub. Charter Sch.), 2002—; chair Irvington Cmty. Sch. (Pub. Charter Sch.), 2003—; campaign chair Johnson for State Senate Re-election Com., 1990; campaign mgr. Kenley for State Senate, 1992; precinct committeeman Lawrence Township, 1995—2006, vice ward chmn., 2006—; mem. fin. com. Howard County Reps., 1991; mem. bd. dirs. Irvington Cmty. Charter Sch., 2002—; mem. devel. adv. com. Ctr. on Philanrophy I.U. Charter Sch. Bd., 2003—; chair Irvington Cmty. Charter Sch., 2003—; bd. dirs. United Way, Howard County, 1990, exec. com., 1990, allocations coun., 1987—91, vice chmn., 1989, chmn., 1990, past chmn., 1991, campaign vol., 1988, 1989; atty. Legal Aid, Kokomo, 1987—91; vol. Bona Vista Rehab. Ctr., Capital Campaign Col., 1991; mem. Indpls. Symphonic Choir. Named Howard County Woman of the Yr. in Bus. Industry, 1991. Mem.: Federalist Soc. (pres. bd. dirs. lawyers divsn., Indpls. chpt. 2004—), Indpls. Bar Assn. (women in law divsn., govt. practice divsn.), Federalist Soc. (bd. dirs. lawyers divsn. Indpls. chpt. 1994—), Ind. State Bar Assn. (women in law com. 2003—, improvements in the judicial system com. 2003—), Brebeuf Jesuit Mother's Assn., Richard D. Lugar Excellence Pub. Svc. Series Alumna, U. Akron Sch. Law Alumni Assn. (life), Greater Indpls. Rep. Women's Club (life). Lutheran. Avocations: piano, reading, needlepoint, tennis, singing. Office: Ind Ho of Reps Statehouse 200 W Washington St Indianapolis IN 46204 Office Phone: 317-232-9640. E-mail: lhiner@iga.state.in.us.

HINERFELD, NORMAN MARTIN, manufacturing executive; b. NYC, May 17, 1929; s. Benjamin B. and Anne (Blitz) H.; m. Ruth Jean Gordon, Dec. 25, 1952; children— Lee Ann, Thomas Benjamin, Joshua Gordon. AB, Harvard U., 1951, MBA, 1953. Security underwriter, underwriting dept. Goldman Sachs & Co., 1953; asst. to pres. Julius Kayser & Co., 1955-56, Catalina, Inc., 1956-57, v.p. mfg., 1957-64, sr. v.p., 1964-67; v.p. Kayser-Roth Corp., 1967—74, exec. v.p., 1967-74, mem. exec. com., 1972—85, pres., COO, 1974-76, dir., 1958-85, chmn. exec. com., 1976-85; chmn., CEO Wingspread Corp., 1985—88; chmn. Pandora Industries, Inc., NYC, 1988—, Tica Industries, Inc., NYC, 1990—; chmn., CEO The Delta Group, 1993—; cons. to non-profit orgns., 2004—. Sec.-treas. Thermacon Industries Inc., New Hyde Park, N.Y., 1989—2003; chmn. Care Anyware LLC, 1999—; bd. dirs. Supermarkets Gen. Corp.; chmn. coun. Ctr. for Study Democratic Instns.; mem. U.S.A.-BIAC to OECD, 1978—; mem. exec. com. Dist. Export-Coun. U.S. Dept. Commerce, 1978—; mem. adv. coun. on Japan-U.S. Econ. Rels., 1980—; adjucator Mass Tort Life Ins. Settlement, 1999-2001; vol. cons. Nat. Exec. Svc. Corps, 2004—. Author: (with D. Moross) Automation-Challenge to Management, 1953; patentee self-programmed automatic machinery. Bd. overseers NYU Sch. Bus., 1984-88; chmn. Metro N.Y.-Bus. Execs. for Nat. Security, 1990—, mem. exec. com., 1992—; chmn. fin. com. Animal Med. Ctr., N.Y.C., 1999—. 1st lt. U.S. Army, 1953-55. Mem. Am. Arbitration Assn. (chmn. bd. 1984-90, exec. com., bd. dirs. 1969—), Am. Apparel Mfrs. Assn. (bd. dirs., past pres., mem. exec. com.), Internat. Apparel Fedn. (past pres.), Nat. Knitted Sportswear Assn. (exec. com., bd. dirs.), U.S. C. of C. (chmn. export policy com. 1979-89). Home: 11 Oak Ln Larchmont NY 10538-3917 Office Phone: 914-834-7799. Personal E-mail: Norcomp@aol.com.

HINERFELD, ROBERT ELLIOT, lawyer; b. NYC, May 29, 1934; s. Benjamin B. and Anne (Blitz) H.; m. Susan Hope Slocum, June 27, 1957; children: Daniel Slocum, Matthew Ben. AB, Harvard U., 1956, JD, 1959. Bar: Calif. 1960. Asst. U.S. atty So. Dist. Calif., 1960-62; assoc. Leonard Horwin, Beverly Hills, Calif., 1962-66; mem. Simon, Sheridan, Murphy, Thornton & Hinerfeld, LA, 1967-74, Murphy, Thornton, Hinerfeld & Cahill, 1975-83, Murphy, Thornton, Hinerfeld & Elson, 1983-85, Manatt, Phelps & Phillips LLP, 1985-2000, sr. of counsel, 2000—05; pvt. practice, 2005—; arbitrator bus. panel L.A. Superior Ct., 1979-82; assoc. ind. counsel (diGenova), 1993-95. Judge pro tempore Beverly Hills Mcpl. Ct., 1967-74; clin. lectr. U. So. Calif. Law Ctr., 1980-81, guest lectr., 1993-96; expert witness, 1988—, legal affairs on-air guest spkr. sta. KCRW-FM, Santa Monica, Calif., 1998-99. Contbr. articles to profl. jours. Trustee Westland Sch., LA, 1970—75, Pacific Hills Sch., 1971—72. Fellow: Am. Bar Found. (life); mem.: ABA (mem. Ctr. for Profl. Responsibility), Calif. Acad. Appellate Lawyers (membership com. 1983—88, 2d v.p. 1985—87, 1st v.p. 1987—88, pres. 1988—89), Am. Arbitration Assn. (arbitrator comml. panel 1966—, mem. large complex case panel 2003—), State Bar Calif. (mem. disciplinary investigation panel dist. 7 1977—80, hearing referee State Bar Ct. 1981—83, exec. com. litig. sect. 1983—85, referee rev. dept. 1984—87, civil litig. adv. group 1985—88, mem. Jud. Nominees Evaluation Commn. 2000—04, mem. com. on criminal law and procedure, chmn. spl. com. revision fed. criminal code), L.A. County Bar Assn. (spl. com. jud. evaluation 1978—82, arbitration com. 1981—83, spl. com. on appellate elections evaluation 1996—2000, settlement officer 2d appellate dist. appellate case project 1996—2005), Assn. Profl. Responsibility Lawyers, Harvard Club So. Calif. (dir. 1974—83, sec. 1978—80, mem. prize book com. 1992—94). Home and Office: 371 24th St Santa Monica CA 90402-2517 Home Phone: 310-394-4261; Office Phone: 310-394-4902. Personal E-mail: rhinerfeld@mac.com.

HINERFELD, RUTH G., civic organization executive; b. Boston, Sept. 18, 1930; m. Norman Hinerfeld, children: Lee, Thomas, Joshua. AB, Vassar Coll., 1951; grad. Program in Bus. Adminstrn., Harvard-Radcliffe Coll., 1952. With LWV, 1954—, UN observer, 1969-72, chairperson internat. rels. com., 1972-76, 1st v.p. in charge legis. activities, 1976-78, pres., 1978-82. Dir. LWV Overseas Edn. Fund, 1975-76, trustee, 1975-86; chair LWV Edn. Fund, 1978-82; mem. White House Adv. Com. Trade Negotiations, 1975-82; sec. UN Assn. US, 1975-78, bd. govs., 1975-2007, vice chmn., 1983-2007, mem. econ. policy coun., 1976-93; bd. dirs. Overseas Devel. Coun. 1974-00; trustee, vice chair Inst. of Internat. Edn., 1997—; mem. U.S. del. auspices of Nat. Com. on U.S.-China Rels. and Chinese People's Inst. Fgn. Affairs, 1978. Mem. coun. Nat. Mcpl. League, 1977-80, 83-86; del.-at-large Internat. Women's Yr. Conf., Houston, 1977; mem. exec. com. Leadership Conf. on Civil Rights, 1978-82; trustee Citizens Rsch. Found., 1978-2000; mem. Nat. Petroleum Coun., 1979-82; mem. U.S. del. to World Conf. on UN Decade for Women, 1980; mem. adv. com. Nat. Inst. for Citizen Edn. in the Law, 1981-91; mem. North South Roundtable, 1978-88; mem. nat. gov. bd. Common Cause, 1984-90; vice chmn. U.S. com. UNICEF, 1986-90, treas., 1990-91; mem. vis. com. Harvard U. Bus. Sch., 1984-90; bd. dirs. Com. for Modern Cts., 1993-96. Recipient Disting. Citizen award Nat. Mcpl. League, 1978; Outstanding Mother award Nat. Mother's Day Com., 1981; Aspen Inst. Presdl. fellow, 1981. Mem. Coun. on Fgn. Rels., Phi Beta Kappa. Office: 11 Oak Ln Larchmont NY 10538-3917

HINES, ANDREW HAMPTON, JR., utilities executive; b. Lake City, Fla., Jan. 28, 1923; s. Andrew Hampton and Louise Dixie (Howland) H.; m. Ann Groover, June 28, 1947' children: Andrew Hampton III, Elizabeth Renee, John Bradford, Daniel Howland. BME with high honors, U. Fla., 1947; degree (hon.), Stetson U., 1987, U. South Fla., 1989, Rollins Coll., 1989, Fla. So. Coll., 1994. Registered profl. engr., Fla. With R&D depts. GE, 1947-51; pres. Fla. Power Corp., 1972-82; chmn. bd. Fla. Progress Corp., St. Petersburg, 1982-91, Precise Power Corp., Bradenton, Fla., 1990-97. Cons. Triangle Cons. Group; past chmn. N.Am. Electric Reliability Coun.; exec.-in-residence Eckerd Coll., 1990-2001. Life trustee Asbury Theol. Sem.; bd. dirs. U. Fla. Found., Sunday sch. tchr. Christian Missionary Alliance Ch.; chmn. Pinellas County Cmty. Reuse Orgn., 1994-97; chmn. No Casinos in Fla., Inc., 1994-1998. 2d lt. USAAF, 1943-45. Decorated Air medal, Prisoner of War medal. Fellow ASME; mem. U.S. Energy Assn., Blue Key, St. Petersburg Yacht Club, Sigma Tau, Phi Kappa Phi, Tau Beta Pi, Beta Gamma Sigma. Personal E-mail: ahh@tampabay.rr.com. *You cannot out give God. If you cast your bread upon the waters it will come back buttered.*

HINES, ANGUS IRVING, JR., petroleum marketing executive; b. Suffolk, Va., Aug. 7, 1923; s. Angus Irving and Lois E. (Howell) H.; m. Genevieve Hopkins McCollum, Nov. 24, 1949 (div. 1977); children: Ann Russell Hines Mauer, Marilyn N. Hines Stulb, A. McCollum, Angus Irving III. Pres. Angus I. Hines, Inc., Suffolk, 1945—; Angus Hines, Inc., Svc. Gas Co., Inc. Served with U.S. Maritime Service, 1943-45; ETO. Mem. Va. Petroleum Jobbers Assn. (past pres.), Rotary (past pres.), Quiet Birdmen. Methodist. Office: Angus I Hines Inc PO Box 1080 1426 Holland Rd Suffolk VA 23439-1080 Home Phone: 757-627-4488; Office Phone: 757-539-0832. Personal E-mail: angushines@aol.com.

HINES, CHERYL, actress; b. Miami Beach, Sept. 21, 1965; m. Paul Young, Dec. 30, 2002; 1 child, Catherine Rose. Attended, W. Va. U., Fla. State U.; BA in radio and TV, U. Cent. Fla. Mem. The Groundlings Theater, star Cheryl Hines' One Woman Show; actor: (TV series) Curb Your Enthusiasm, 2000—05 (Emmy nomination best supporting actress, 2003), (voice) Father of the Pride, 2004—05,; (TV films) Double Bill, 2003; (films) Cheap Curry and Calculus, 1996, Along Came Polly, 2004, Our Very Own, 2005, Lucky 13, 2005, Herbie: Fully Loaded, 2005, RV, 2006, Keeping Up with the Steins, 2006, Waitress, 2007, (guest appearances): (TV series) Unsolved Mysteries, 1997, Suddenly Susan, 1998, Wayans Brothers, 1998, Friends, 2000, Everybody Loves Raymond, 2002, Reno 911, 2003; exec. prodr.: Campus Ladies, 2006.*

HINES, COLLEEN M., clinical nurse specialist; d. David Walter Mullis and Jo Wilma Clary; m. Thomas E. Hines, Aug. 2, 1969. BS, Tex. Women's U., 1966, MS, 1979. RN Tex., cert. diabetes educator, childbirth educator. Staff nurse Parkland Hosp., Dallas, 1966—67, head nurse, 1967—75, nursing care supr., 1975—80, clin. nurse specialist, 1980—2003; program coord. Region 10 Edn. Svc. Ctr., Richardson, Tex., 2004—. Past mem. breastfeeding task force State of Tex. Dept. Health, Austin. Contbr. articles to profl. jours. Named Employee of Yr., Parkland Hosp., 1989. Mem.: Am. Assn. Diabetes Educators (past pres. local chpt., diabetes in pregnancy interest group), Tex. Nurses. Assn. (bd. dirs. 2005—), Am. Nurses Assn. (bd. dirs. 2000—03, 2005—), Sigma Theta Tau (past pres. Tex. Women's U. chpt.). Baptist. Avocations: reading, travel. E-mail: cmhteh@sbcglobal.net.

HINES, ELIZABETH, geographer, educator; b. Greensboro, NC, Feb. 5, 1951; d. James Emmett and Genevieve Givler Hines; m. Michael Wolfe, June 14, 1987; 1 child, Ginger Leonard. BA, U. NC, Greensboro, 1981; MA, U. Kans., Lawrence, 1984; PhD, La. State U., Baton Rouge, 1992. Lectr. geography La. State U., Baton Rouge, 1985—92, La. Tech, Ruston, 1990—91; assoc. prof. geography U. NC, Wilmington, 1992—. Editor: The NC Geographer; contbr. articles to profl. jours. Bd. dirs. Wilmington Food Bank, NC, 2006—, African Am. Heritage Found. Wilmington, Inc., 2004—, chmn. program com., 2004—. Recipient Pres.'s award, African Am. Heritage Found. Wilmington, Inc., 2006. Mem.: NAACP, NC Geog. Soc., SEDAAG, Assn. Am. Geographers (assoc.). Home: 801 Jennings Dr Wilmington NC 28403 Home Phone: 910-962-3012; Office Phone: 910-962-3012. Business E-Mail: hinese@uncw.edu.

HINES, NORMAN WILLIAM, law educator, retired dean; b. 1936; AB, Baker U., 1958; LLB, U. Kans., 1961; LLD, Baker U., 1999. Bar: Kans. 1961, Iowa 1965. Law clk. US Ct. Appeals 10th cir., 1961-62; tchg. fellow Harvard U., 1961-62; asst. prof. law U. Iowa, 1962-65, assoc. prof., 1965-67, prof., 1967-73, J.F. Rosenfield disting. prof., 1973—, dean, 1976—2004, dean emeritus, Joseph F. Rosenfield Prof., 2004—. Vis. prof. Stanford U., 1974—75. Editor (notes and comments): Kans. Law Rev. Founder, pres. Johnson County Heritage Trust. Fellow, Harvard U., 1961—62. Fellow: Am. Law Inst., Iowa State Bar Found., ABA Found.; mem.: Assn. Am. Law Schs. (exec. com. 2004—, pres. 2005), Order of Coif, Environ. Law Inst. (assoc.). Office: U Iowa Coll Law Iowa City IA 52242-0001 Office Phone: 319-335-9236. Business E-Mail: n-hines@uiowa.edu.

HINES, PRESTON HARRIS, state supreme court justice; b. Atlanta, Sept. 6, 1943; s. James Reuben and Edith (Hawkins) Hines; m. Helen Holmes Hill; children: Mary Margaret, James Harris. AB in Polit. Sci., Emory U., 1965, JD, 1968. Bar: Ga. 1968, U.S. Dist. Ct. Ga. 1973. Law clk. Civil Ct. Fulton County, 1968-69; pvt. practice Marietta, Ga., 1969-74; judge State Ct. of Cobb County, 1974-82, Superior Ct. of Ga., 1982—95; justice Ga. Supreme Ct., 1995—. Chmn. attys. divsn. Cobb County United Appeal, 1972; participant Leadership Ga., 1975, Leadership Atlanta, 1978-79; pres. YMCA Cobb County, 1976; co-treas. Cobb Landmarks Soc., 1976-77; former bd. dirs. Cobb County Emergency Aid Assn., Cobb-Marietta Girls Club, Ga. chpt. Leukemia Soc. Am., Cobb County Children's Ctr., Met. Atlanta Red Cross, First Presbyn. Day Kindergarten; mem. cmty. adv. com. Marietta-Cobb County LWV; bd. dirs. Kennesaw Coll. Found.; trustee Cobb Cmty. Symphony. Named Outstanding Young Man of Yr., Ga. Jaycees, 1975, Boss of Yr., Cobb County Legal Secs. Assn., 1975-76, 83-84. Mem. ABA, State Bar Ga. (chmn. Law Day com. 1975, mem. exec. com. younger lawyers sec. 1974-76), Cobb Jud. Cir. (sec. 1972-73, chmn. Law Day com. 1972), Joseph Henry Lumpkin Inn of Ct. Ga., Atlanta Lawyers Club, Kiwanis (bd. dirs. Marietta chpt., chmn. Key Club com., past chmn. spiritual aims com., past pres.), Cobb County C. of C., Sigma Alpha Epsilon (Atlanta and Marietta chpts.). Office: Supreme Court 244 Washington St Atlanta GA 30334*

HINES, THOMAS SPIGHT, historian, educator, architecture critic; b. Oxford, Miss., Oct. 28, 1936; s. Thomas S. and Polly M. Hines; children: Tracy Odessa, Taylor Spight. BA, U. Miss., 1958; PhD, U. Wis., 1971. Prof. history and architecture UCLA, 1968—; Ruth Carter Stevenson prof. U. Tex., 2003—04. Vis. prof. Sch. Architecture and Am. studies program U. Tex., Austin, 1974-75; Fulbright prof. Am. studies U. Exeter, Eng., 1984-85; vis. prof. Sch. Arch. Columbia U., 2004. Author: Burnham of Chicago: Architect and Planner, 1974, Richard Neutra and the Search for Modern Architecture: A Biography and History, 1982, The Architecture of Richard Neutra: From International Style to California Modern, 1982, William Faulkner and the Tangible Past: The Architecture of Yoknapatawpha, 1996, Irving Gill and the Architecture of Reform, 2000; hist. advisor, co-author film Frank Lloyd Wright, 1985; hist. advisor Robert Moses: Urban Planner for WGBH, 1988; contbr. chpts. to books, articles to profl. jours. 1st lt. US Army, 1960—63. Recipient John H. Dunning prize Am. Hist. Assn., 1976, Honor award, AIA, 2007, Collaborative Achievement award AIA, 2007; NEH fellow, 1978-79; Fulbright fellow, 1984-85; Guggenheim fellow, 1987-88; Getty scholar, 1996-97. Mem.: Am. Acad. Arts and Scis. Democrat. Episcopalian. Office: UCLA Dept Architecture Perloff Hall 405 Hilgard Ave Los Angeles CA 90095-9000 Business E-Mail: hines@history.ucla.edu.

HINES, WALTER JAMES, stock exchange executive; b. Providence, Nov. 14, 1947; s. Walter Joseph and Marguerite Ann (Adams) H.; m. Karen Janice Ness, June 27, 1970. BA in Modern Langs., Providence Coll., 1969. With GE, Plainville, Conn., 1973-77; controller GE Precision Protective Devices Inc., Palmer, 1977-79, GE Midwest Electric Products Inc., Makato, Minn., 1979-83; corp. controller Modular Computer Systems Inc., Ft. Lauderdale, Fla., 1983-87; corp. v.p. fin. and adminstrn. AEG Corp., Somerville, NJ, 1987-88; sr. v.p. fin. and adminstrn. Coffee, Sugar and Cocoa Exch. Inc., NYC, 1989; now sr. v.p., CFO NY Bd. Trade. CFO NY Exchs. Hdqrs. Project, NYC, 1991; treas. Commodities Exch. Ctr., NYC, 1992. 1st lt. U.S. Army, 1969-72. Avocations: running, landscaping. Office: NY Bd Trade World Fin Ctr One North End Ave 13th Fl New York NY 10282*

HINES, WILLIAM EUGENE, banker; b. NYC, July 5, 1914; s. William J. and Alice M. (Callahan) H.; m. Dorothy H. Moore, June 4, 1949; children: Alice M., Dorothy H., Margaret M., William J., Elizabeth A., Robert J. Student, Columbia U.; grad., Rutgers U., 1948. With Bankers Trust Co., NYC, 1950—, asst. v.p., 1958-63, v.p., 1963—. Instr. Am. Inst. Banking, 1948—64, Am. Youth Hostels, 1954—65, former chmn., now dir. Chmn. planning bd. Village of Quogue, NY, 1991-2003, bd. trustees, 2005—; trustee Quogue Libr., 1993-2000, treas., 2001—; fin. com. Immaculate Conception Ch., 2007—. Mem. N.Y. Soc. Security Analysts, Accts. Club N.Y.C., Nat. Assn. Mental Health (nat. treas., dir. 1966, nat. trustee, adminstrv. com.), Quogue Assn. (pres. 1994-96, trustee 1992-2000), Shinnecock Yacht Club (commodore 1974-76, treas. 1980-94). Office: PO Box 5035 21 Quaquanantuck Ln Quogue NY 11959

HINGLE, PAT, actor; b. Miami, Fla., July 19, 1924; s. Clarence M. and Marvin (Patterson) H.; m. Julia Wright, Oct. 25, 1979; children— Jody, Billy, Molly. BFA, U. Tex., Austin, 1949; PhD (hon.), Otterbein Coll., Westerville, Ohio, 1974. Numerous acting roles on stage, screen and TV, including End as a Man, 1953, On the Waterfront, 1953, The Long Grey

Line, 1954, Festival, 1954, Cat on a Hot Tin Roof, 1955, 83, 93, Girls of Summer, 1956, The Strange One, 1956, Dakr at the Top of the Stairs, 1957, No Down Pavement, 1957, J.B., 1958, The Deadly Game, 1960, Macbeth, 1961, Troilus and Cressida, 1961, Strange Interlude, 1963, Blues for Mr. Charlie, 1964, A Girl Could Get Lucky, 1964, Invitation to a Gunfighter, 1964, The Glass Menagerie, 1965, The Odd Couple, 1966, Nevada Smith, 1966, Johnny No-Trump, 1967, Hang 'Em High, 1968, The Price, 1968, Bloody Mama, 1969, Child's Play, 1970, Norwood, 1970, Wusa, 1970, The Selling of the President, 1972, That Championship Season, 1973, Super Cops, 1973, Hazel's People, 1973, Running Wild, 1973, The Lady from the Sea, 1976, Independence, 1976, The Gauntlet, 1977, Norma Rae, 1979, When You Comin' Back, Red Ryder, 1979, Thomas A. Edison, Reflections of a Genius, 1978, A Life, 1980, Running Brave, 1982, Sudden Impact, 1983, Falcon and the Snowman, 1984, Brewster's Millions, 1985, Blue Skies, 1988, Rescue of Jessica McClure, 1989, Batman, 1989, The Kennedys of Massachusetts, 1989, The Grifters, 1990, Moon for the Misbegotten, 1990, The Habitation of Dragons, 1991, Gunsmoke III, 1991, Batman Returns, 1992, Citizen Cohn, 1992, Simple Justice, 1992, Will and Bart Show, 1992, Cheers, 1993, In the Heat of the Night, 1993, Lightnin' Jack, 1994, The Quick and the Dead, 1994, Friendly Suit, 1994, One Christmas, 1994, Batman Forever, 1995, Truman, 1995, Wings, 1996, Larger Than Life, 1996, Bastard Out of Carolina, 1996, A Thousand Acres, 1996, Batman and Robin, 1997, The Shining, 1997, 1776, 1997-98, Touched By an Angel, 1999, Morning, 2000, The Angel Doll, 2000, Road to Redemption, 2000, The Runaway, 2000, Our Town, 2002, Goodbye to Eddie Hart, 2003, Laughing Clown, The List, 2005, Talladega Nights, 2007; command performances at White House, 1965, Libr. of Congress, 1984. Served with USNR, 1942-46, 51-52.

HINGSON, RALPH W., medical educator; b. July 21, 1948; BA in Internat. Rels., Johns Hopkins U., 1969, ScD, 1974; MPH, U. Pitts., 1970. Prof. dept. social behavior sci. Boston U. Sch. Pub. Health, 1986—2007; dir. divsn. prevention and epidemiology Nat. Inst. on Alcohol Abuse and Alcoholism. Cons., Nat. Ctr. for Substance Abuse Prevention, Nat. Trans. Rsch. Bd., others; nat. bd. advs. MADD,; former v.p. Pub. Policy; pres. Internat. Coun. Alcohol Drugs and Traffic Safety. Contbr. numerous articles to profl. jours. Named one of America's 10 Outstanding Young Men, U.S. Jaycees, 1984; recipient Hero award, MADD, 1995, Innovators Combating Substance Abuse award, Robert Wood Johnson Found., 2001, Widmark award, Internat. Coun. Alcohol Drugs and Traffic Safety, 2002, Ralph W. Hingson Rsch. in Practice Presdl. award, MADD, 2003. Home: 4 Louisburg Sq Boston MA 02108-1203 Office: Nat Inst Alcohol Abuse and Alcoholism Rm 2077 5635 Fishers Ln Bethesda MD 20892-1706 Office Phone: 301-443-1274. Business E-Mail: rhingson@mail.nih.gov.

HINKEL, DANIEL FARRIS, lawyer, writer, investment company executive; b. Olney, Ill., Sept. 25, 1948; s. William Woodrow Hinkel and Martha Lucille Farris; m. Mary Torrence Sneed, Feb. 9, 1980; 1 child, John Henry. BS, Ea. Ill. U., Charleston, 1969; JD, U. Ill., Champaign, 1972. Bar: Ga. 1974, Ind. 1972. Atty. Am. Fletcher Bank, Indpls., 1972—74, Powell Goldstein, Atlanta, 1974—77, Life Ins. Co. Ga., Atlanta, 1977—80; ptnr. Harman Asbill, Atlanta, 1980—84, Hurt Richardson, Atlanta, 1984—92, Vamer Stephens, Atlanta, 1992—96; v.p. ING Investment Mgmt., Atlanta, 1996—. Author: Practical Real Estate Law, 1990, 5th edit., 2007, Georgia Real Estate Law and Procedures, 1996, 6th edit., 2007, Georgia Construction Mechanics and Materialmen's Liens, 1978, 3d edit., 2007. Mem.: ABA (chair standing com. legal assts. 1992—98), Ind. Bar Assn., State Bar Ga. (mem. exec. com. real property sect. 2004—). Home: 1718 Mason Mill Rd NE Atlanta GA 30329

HINKELMAN, RUTH AMIDON, insurance company executive; b. Streator, Ill., June 4, 1949; d. Olin Arthur and Marjorie Annabeth (Wright) Amidon; m. Allen Joseph Hinkelman, Jr., Oct. 28, 1972; children: Anne Elizabeth, Allen Joseph III. AB in Econs., U. Ill., 1971. Underwriter Kemper Ins. Group, Chgo., 1971-75; acct. exec. Near North Ins. Agy., Chgo., 1975-76; underwriter Gen. Reinsurance Corp., Chgo., 1976-78, asst. sec., 1978-79, asst. v.p., 1979-83, 2nd v.p., 1983-87, v.p., 1987—. Home: 133 Linden Ave Wilmette IL 60091-2838 Office: Gen Reinsurance Corp 1 N Wacker Dr Ste 1700 Chicago IL 60606 Office Phone: 312-207-5332. Business E-Mail: rhinkelm@genre.com.

HINKLE, BARTON LESLIE, retired electronics company executive; b. Miami Beach, Fla., Nov. 2, 1925; s. Frank Leslie and Kathryn Barton (Paddock) H.; m. Christine Smith, Aug. 22, 1949 (dec. Aug. 1955); m. Sabrena Sanford, Apr. 4, 1959; children— Karen, Douglas, Jean, Maria, Elizabeth. BS in Chem. Engring, Purdue U., 1949; MS, Inst. Textile Tech., 1951; PhD, Ga. Inst. Tech., 1953. Research asst. Ga. Inst. Tech. Exptl. Sta., Atlanta, 1951-53; research engr. E.I. duPont de Nemours & Co., Inc., Richmond, Va., 1953-55, research supr., 1955-57, tech. supt., 1957-61, mfg. supt., 1961-62, asst. plant mgr., 1962-64, plant supt. Clinton, Iowa, 1964-69, product mgr. Wilmington, Del., 1969-71, lab. mgr., 1971-75, adminstrv. and planning asst., 1976-77, personnel mgr., 1977-84; v.p. human resources Electromagnetic Scis., Inc., Norcross, Ga., 1984-87, cons. human resources, 1987—. Patentee in field aerosol electrification, viscous polymers, cellophane. Sr. warden, vestryman St. Davids Episcopal Ch., 1975-78. Served with AUS, 1944-46, ETO. Republican. Home: 9399 Colvincrest Dr Mechanicsville VA 23116-2909 E-mail: blhink@comcast.net.

HINKLE, BETTY RUTH, retired academic administrator; b. Atchison, Kans., Mar. 18, 1930; d. Arch W. and Ruth (Baker) Hunt; m. Charles L. Hinkle, Dec. 25, 1950 (div.); children: Karl, Eric. BA, U. Corpus Christi, Tex., 1950; MS, Baylor U., Waco, Tex., 1956; MA, U. North Colo., Greeley, Colo., 1972, EdD, 1979. Cert. tchr., Tex., Mass., Colo.; cert. adminstr., Colo. Tchr. Alice (Tex.) Ind. Sch. Dist., 1950, Waco (Tex.) Ind. Sch. Dist., 1951-52, 53-58, Hawaii Pub. Schs., Oahu, 1952-53, Newton Pub. Schs., Newtonville, Mass., 1962-63, Colorado Springs (Colo.) Pub. Schs., 1966—75; cons., exec. dir. spl. project unit Colo. State Dept. Edn., Denver, 1975—95, asst. commr., 1995, ret., 1995, rep. fed. rels. Office Commr. Edn., 1995-96, ret., 1996. Pvt. cons., 1997-2001; pres. BH Cons., Colorado Springs, 1997-2001; mem. cabinet Colo. Dept. Edn., mem. Quality Coun., fed. liaison rep. to chief state sch. officers, Washington, chmn. 1996; alt. foreman Denver Grand Jury, 1983; mem. state exec. fellowship program Instn. Ednl. Leadership, Coun. Chief STate Sch. Officers and U.S. Dept. Edn., 1985. Vol. for Colo. Mountain Reclamation Projects, 2001—. Recipient Dept. Edn. Specialists award Colo. Assn. Sch. Execs., 1979, Employee Yr. award Colo. Dept. Edn., 1986, Fed. Ednl. Program Adminstrv. Coun. ann. award for Distinctive Svc. to Colo. Children, 1988; named an Outstanding Secondary Educator of Am., 1974. Mem. Am. Assn. Sch. Adminstrs., Colo. Assn. Sch. Execs. (coord. coun. 1976-79, v.p. dept. edn. specialists 1974-75, pres. 1975-76), Colo. Assn. Sch. Execs., Phi Delta Kappa. Home: 1011 N 18th St Colorado Springs CO 80904-2852 Personal E-mail: b3h@comcast.net.

HINKLE, CHARLES FREDERICK, lawyer, educator; b. Oregon City, Oreg., July 6, 1942; s. William Ralph and Ruth Barbara (Holcomb) H. BA, Stanford U., 1964; MDiv, Union Theol. Sem., NYC, 1968; JD, Yale U., 1971. Bar: Oreg. 1971; ordained to ministry United Ch. of Christ, 1974. Instr. English, Morehouse Coll., Atlanta, 1966-67; assoc. Stoel Rives LLP, Portland, Oreg., 1971-77, ptnr., 1977—. Adj. prof. Lewis and Clark Law Sch., Portland, 1978-2001; bd. govs. Oreg. State Bar, 1992-95. Oreg. pres. ACLU, Portland, 1976-80, nat. bd. dirs., 1979-85; bd. dirs. Kendall Cmty. Ctr., 1987-93, Youth Progress Assn., 1994-98, Portland Baroque Orch., 1999-2000; mem. pub. affairs com. Am. Cancer Soc., 1994-99; mem. Oreg. Gov.'s Task Force on Youth Suicide, 1996. Recipient Elliott Human Rights award Oreg. Edn. Assn., 1984, E.B. MacNaughton award ACLU Oreg., 1987, Wayne Morse award Dem. Com. Oreg., 1994, Tom McCall Freedom of Info. award Women in Comm., 1996, Civil Rights award Met. Human Rights Commn., 1996, Pub. Svc. award Oreg. State Bar, 1997. Fellow Am. Bar Found.; mem. ABA (ho. of dels. 1998-2000), FBA, Multnomah County Bar Assn., Am. Constn. Soc. (bd. dirs. 2005—),City Club Portland (pres. 1987-88). Democrat. Home: 14079 SE Fairoaks Way Milwaukie OR 97267-1017 Office: Stoel Rives 900 SW 5th Ave Ste 2600 Portland OR 97204-1268 Office Phone: 503-294-9266. Business E-Mail: cfhinkle@stoel.com.

HINKLE, DOUGLAS PADDOCK, retired languages educator; b. Stamford, Conn., June 9, 1923; s. Frank Leslie and Kathryn B. Paddock Hinkle; m. Rose-Marie Hecker, Apr. 14, 1966; children: Anthony Barton, Monica Kathryn. BA, U. Va., Charlottesville, 1952, MA, 1954. Lic. law enforcement officer, Ohio. Tchr. English Va. Pub. Schs., Nelson County, 1948-49; dir. binat. ctr. US Info. Svc., La Paz, Bolivia, 1955-57, Caracas, Venezuela, 1958; asst. prof. Spanish and French Sweet Briar Coll., Amherst, Va., 1958-62, Southwestern U., Memphis, 1962-63; coll. editor modern langs. D.C. Heath & Co., Boston, 1963-65; assoc. prof. modern langs. Ea. Ky. U., Richmond, 1965-67; sr. lectr. modern langs. Ohio U., Athens, 1967-93, prof. emeritus modern langs., 1994—; forensic artist LETN-TV, Dallas, 1990-91. Program evaluator NEH, Washington, 1975-78. Author: (books) Faces of Crime, 1989, Mug Shots, 1990, (book of poetry) Poetry Is You, 1977, (slideshow/video program) Remembering Faces, 1990; mem. editl. bd. NAMES, 1968-74; contbr. numerous articles to profl. jours. Chmn. drug abuse com. Kiwanis Club, Athens, Ohio, 1983-87; cert. aux. Athens Police Dept., 1982-87, forensic artist, 1981-87; bd. dirs. Cen. Va. Crime Clinic, Richmond, 1994-97. Cpl. US Army, 1943-46. Recipient Caballero, Order of Condor award Republic of Bolivia, 1957, Citizenship award Athens Bar Assn., 1983. Mem. Portrait Soc. Am., Am. Soc. Marine Artists, Ctrl. Va. Crime Clinic (bd. dirs. 1995-98), Va. Mus. Fine Arts, Fraternal Order of Police (hon. permanent mem.), Raven Soc., Va. Hist. Soc., Phi Beta Kappa. Republican. Roman Catholic. Avocations: painting, writing, historical linguistics, marksmanship. Home: 6413 Poplar Rd Quinton VA 23141 Personal E-mail: rmhdph@peoplepc.com.

HINKLE, JANET, financial analyst; b. Groton, Conn., Mar. 26, 1958; d. David Randall and Muriel (Nelson) Hinkle; m. Richard Alden Wilcox, Oct. 1, 1983 (div. Mar. 1991); 1 child, Lillian Marie. AA in Fashion Design cum laude, Endicott Jr. Coll. Women, Beverly, Mass., 1978; BA in Psychology, Conn. Coll., 1981; MBA, Rensselaer Poly. Inst., 2004. Sr. analyst Sonalysts, Inc., Waterford, Conn., 1983—. Coporator Lawrence and Meml. Hosp., New London, Conn., 1995—, mem. planned giving com., 1998—99; mem. gift com. adv. Cmty. Found., New London, 1998—; mem. curriculum com. planned sci. and tech. Magnet HS, 2003—; bd. dirs. United Way SECT. Named to Outstanding Young Women of Am., 1997. Mem.: Thames Club. Republican. Avocations: training horses, ballet, tennis, skiing, painting. Home: 221 Elm St Stonington CT 06378-1165 Office: Sonalysts Inc 215 Parkway N Waterford CT 06385-1209

HINKLE, MURIEL RUTH NELSON, naval warfare analysis company executive; b. Bayonne, NJ, Mar. 17, 1929; d. Andrew and Florence Martha Ida (Nuber) Nelson; m. David Randall Hinkle, June 5, 1954; children: Valerie Nelson, Janet Lee, Sally Ann. Student, Md. Coll. for Women, 1947-49; BA, U. Md., 1951. Mgr. Wildacres Thoroughbred Horse Farm, Waterford, Conn., 1960-70; illustrator naval warfare predictions/computer simulated naval engagements Analysis & Tech., Inc., North Stonington, Conn., 1970-73; pres. Sonalysts, Inc., Waterford, Conn., 1973-88, 94-98, CEO, 1973-2001, pres., CEO emerita, 2001—; also founder, past dir. Command Engring. & Tech. Svcs. Co.; pres., CEO, chmn. Stonington Farms Inc. (now Mystic Valley Hunt Club), 1983. Adv. bd. Conn. Nat. Bank, 1988-92; chmn., CEO Angiers Assocs., 1989-96, S.I. Devel. Corp., 1989-2001; cons. Def. Nuclear Agy. for Tactical Nuclear Effects in anti-submarine warfare, 1974-75; spl. edn. substitute tchr. Waterford Pub. Schs., 1968-74; bd. dirs. Sonalysts, Inc. Co-author: Scope of Acoustic Communications Systems in Naval Tactical Warfare, 1974, Non-Acoustic Anti Submarine Warfare, 1974, Nuclear Weapons Effects in Anti Submarine Warfare, 1974, Measures of Effectiveness, Naval Tactical Communications, 1975, Destroyer ASW Barrier, 1977. Bd. trustees Thames Sci. Ctr., 1979-82. Recipient commendation for svcs. to submarine force Comdr. Submarine Squadron Ten, 1973, SBA New Eng. Contractor of Yr. award, 1986, SBA Adminstr.'s award for excellence, 1985, 86, bus. assoc. of yr. award Naval Inst., 1999, Disting. Cmty. Svc. award Mitchell Coll., 2001, William Crawford Disting. Svc. award C. of C., 2002. Mem. Am. Horse Shows Assn., Nat. Audubon Soc., Submarine Devel. Group Two Wives Club (pres. 1968), Sigma Kappa (pres. Senesk chpt. 1987-89), Navy Wives Club. Republican. Baptist. Home: 9 Cove Rd Stonington CT 06378-2304 Office: Sonalysts Inc PO Box 280 215 Parkway N Waterford CT 06385-1209 Office Phone: 860-326-3670.

HINKLE, WILLIAM PAUL, mechanical and electrical engineer, consultant; b. Thomasville, NC, Sept. 24, 1921; s. William Alphus and Julia Ida (Snider) H.; m. Dora Nell Workman, July 15, 1950; children: Paula Yvonne, William Lynn. BS in mech. engring., N.C. State U., 1943; postgrad., Citadel Coll., Charleston, SC, 1944-45; postgrad. engring. cert., Western Electric Grad. Sch., Princeton, NJ, 1967-69. Registered profl. engr., N.C.; land surveyor, N.C.; pesticide applicator, N.C. Naval architect Charleston Navy Yard, 1943-46; mech. planning engr. AT&T Techs., Greensboro, N.C., 1946-75; profl. engr., cons. Thomasville (N.C.) Svc., 1976—; pres. Thomasville Golf Course, 1976—. Autor: "G" Factor Designs, 1960, Electical Shielding, 1963; inventor: magnetic trim strips, cabinet mounting frames. Instr. pub. speaking Boy Scouts Am., Winston-Salem, N.C., 1973. With USN, 1943-46. Mem. IEEE (sr. life mem., del. 1966-67, publicity chmn. 1965-70, Exec. Com. award 1968), ASME (life, Carolina chmn. 1971-72, Dist. Chmn. award 1972, Ann. Handbook award 1943), NSPE (exec. com. 1964-67, Exec. Com. award 1967), Am. Congress Surveying and Mapping, Nat. Soc. Profl. Surveyors, Toastmasters Internat. (disting., club pres. 1965, 73, dist. area gov. 1967-68, Disting. Toastmaster award 1969, Gov. of Yr. 1968, Hall of Fame award 1968). Methodist. Avocations: collecting antique artware, stock car engine development, carpentry designs, golf, photography. Home: 1524 Lexington Ave Thomasville NC 27360-3329 Office: Thomasville Golf Course 1515 Lexington Ave Thomasville NC 27360-3328

HINMAN, ALAN RICHARD, public health physician, epidemiologist; b. New Orleans, Mar. 23, 1937; s. E. Harold and Katharine Ellen (Fradenburgh) H.; m. Donna Virgene Graham, Dec. 21, 1959 (div. 1962); m. Lucy Winkler Householder, May 30, 1965; children: Johanna Mary, Katharine Emily. BA, Cornell U., 1957; MD, Western Res. U., 1961; MPH, Harvard U., 1969. Intern Cleve. Met. Hosp., 1961—62, resident in internal medicine, 1962—64, chief resident, 1964-65; with USPHS, 1965-70, 77-96; advanced through grades to asst. surgeon gen., 1988; epidemic intelligence svc. officer Ctr. for Disease Control, Calif. State Dept. Health, 1965-66; regional evaluation officer malaria eradication program Ctrs. for Disease Control, Atlanta, 1966-67, San Salvador, El Salvador, 1967-68, asst. chief viral diseases br. epidemiology program Atlanta, 1969-70; dir. Bur. Epidemiology, N.Y. State Dept. Health, Albany, 1970-71, asst. commr. epidemiology and preventive health svcs., 1971-75; asst. commr., dir. Bur. Preventive and Med. Svcs., Tenn. Dept. Pub. Health, Nashville, 1975-77; dir. divsn. immunization Ctr. for Prevention Svcs., Ctrs. for Disease Control, Atlanta, 1977-88; coord. nat. vaccine program Office of Asst. Sec. for Health, 1987-90; asst. surgeon gen. USPHS, 1988-96; dir. Nat. Ctr. for Prevention Svcs. Ctrs. for Disease Control, 1988-95; sr. advisor to dir. Ctrs. for Disease Control and Prevention, 1995-96; coord. CDC World Bank collaboration on immunizations Task Force Child Survival and Devel., Atlanta, 1996-2000, sr. pub. health scientist, 1996—; prin. investigator All Kids Count, 2000—04; coord. PARTNERS TB ctrl. program, 2001—02. Adj. asst. prof. preventive and cmty. medicine Albany Med. Coll., Union U., 1970-75; adj. asst. prof. pub. health Rensselaer Poly Inst., 1971-75; assoc. clin. prof. dept. preventive medicine Vanderbilt U., 1975-77; clin. asst. prof. dept. cmty. medicine Divsn. Healthcare Svcs., U. Tenn., 1975-77; clin. asst. prof. dept. family and cmty. health Meharry Med. Coll., 1975-77; clin. assoc. prof. dept. preventive medicine-cmty. health Emory U. Sch. Medicine, Atlanta, 1978-90; vis. prof. Case Western Res. U. Sch. Medicine, 1984; adj. prof. Emory U. Sch. Pub. Health, 1990—; vis. lectr. Shanghai 1st Med. Coll., 1981; sr. pub. health scientist The Task Force for Child Survival and Devel., 1996—. Contbr. over 300 articles to profl. jours. Decorated D.S.M.; recipient Indian Health Svc. Dir. Spl. Excellence award, 1992. Fellow ACP, APHA (mem. gov. coun. 1975-77, mem. program devel. bd. 1984-86, mem. nominating com. 1984-86, chair 1985-86, chair-elect epidemiology sect. 1985-87, chair sect. 1987-89, past chair 1989-91, mem. exec. bd. 1991-95, spkr. governing coun. 1995—), Am. Acad. Pediat., Am. Coll. Epidemiology (mem. exec. bd. 1990-94, v.p. 1991-92, pres. 1992-93), Am. Coll. Preventive Medicine (regent 1974-75, 77-81, v.p. for pub. health 1975-76); mem. AMA, Am. Epidemiol. Soc., Am. Soc. Tropical Medicine and Hygiene, Am. Venereal Disease Assn. (bd. dirs. 1972-75, sec.-treas. 1975-77), Assn. Tchrs. Preventive Medicine, Infectious Diseases Soc. Am., Internat. Epidemiol. Assn., Physicians for Social Responsibility, Soc. Epidemiol. Rsch., Soc. Med. Decision Making. Home: 2194 Creek Park Rd Decatur GA 30033-2714 Office Phone: 404-687-5636. Business E-Mail: ahinman@taskforce.org.

HINMAN, GEORGE WHEELER, physics professor; b. Evanston, Ill., Nov. 7, 1927; s. Norman Seymour and Bess H.; m. Mary Louise Cauffield, June 19, 1952; children: Norman Field, Lydia Seymour, Nancy Wheeler. BS in Physics and Math., Carnegie Mellon U., Pitts., 1947, MS in Physics, 1950, DSc in Physics, 1952. Asst. prof., then assoc. prof. physics Carnegie Mellon U., Pitts., 1952-63; chmn. physics Gen. Atomic Co. subs. Gulf Oil Corp., San Diego, 1963-69; prof. physics, dir. Applied Energy Studies Wash. State U., Pullman, 1969—97; dir. N.Mex. Energy Research & Devel. Inst., Santa Fe, 1982-83; chair environ. sci. & regional planning, 1989-97. Cons. Los Alamos (N.Mex.) Nat. Lab., 1976-90, GAO, 1977—, Nat. Nuclear Accreditation Bd., 1992-98. Author: Dictionary of Energy, 1983, Nuclear Power at the Crossroads, 1994; contbr. articles to profl. jours. Grantee NSF, others. Fellow Am. Phys. Soc.; mem. Am. Nuclear Soc., AAAS, Am. Soc. Engring. Edn. Democrat. Avocation: fly fishing. Home: 925 SW Fountain St Pullman WA 99163-2132 Office: Wash State U Troy Hl Rm 305 Pullman WA 99164-4430 Office Phone: 509-335-8689. Personal E-mail: ghinman@insightful.net. Business E-Mail: ghinman@wsu.edu.

HINMAN, HARVEY DEFOREST, lawyer; b. May 7, 1940; s. George Lyon and Barbara H.; m. Margaret (Snyder), June 23, 1962; children: George, Sarah, Marguerite. BA, Brown U., 1962; JD, Cornell U., 1965. Bar: Calif., 1966. Assoc. Pillsbury, Madison, and Sutro, San Francisco, 1965—72, ptnr., 1973—93; v.p., gen. counsel Chevron Corp., San Francisco, 1993—2002; of counsel Pillsbury, Winthrop, Shaw, Pittman LLP, San Francisco, 2003—. Bd. dirs. Big Sur Environ. Inst., 2004—, pres., 2004. Bd. dirs., sec. Holbrook Palmer Park Found., 1977—86; trustee Castillija Sch., 1988—89; bd. govs. Filoli Ctr., 1988—2006, pres., 1994—95; bd. dirs. Phillips Brooks Sch., 1978—84, pres., 1983—84. Fellow: Am. Bar Found.; mem.: Legal Aid Soc. (bd. dirs. 2004—). Office: 50 Fremont St San Francisco CA 94105

HINNERS, STACY CHUBAK, lawyer; b. Huron, Ohio, Aug. 25, 1978; d. James and Francine Chubak; m. Jason Hinners, Aug. 17, 2002; 1 child. BA, Ohio Wesleyan U., Delaware, 2000; JD, U. Dayton, Ohio, 2003. Bar: Ohio 2003, US Dist. Ct. (so. dist.) Ohio 2003, US Ct. Appeals (6th cir.) 2006, US Supreme Ct. 2007, US Ct. Appeals (7th cir.) 2007. Staff atty. Judge John W. Kessler, Montgomery County Ct. of Common Pleas, Dayton, Ohio, 2003—04; atty. Mezibov & Jenkins Co. LPA, Cin., 2004—. Mem.: Nat. Employment Lawyers Assn., Cin. Bar Assn., Omicron Delta Kappa. Independent. Roman Catholic. Office: Mezibov & Jenkins Co LPA 401 E Court St Ste 600 Cincinnati OH 45202 Office Phone: 513-723-1600. Office Fax: 513-723-1620. Business E-Mail: shinners@mezibovjenkins.com.

HINNRICHS-DAHMS, HOLLY BETH, elementary school educator; b. Milw., Oct. 31, 1945; d. Helmut Ferdinand and Rae W. (Beebe) Hinnrichs; m. Raymond H. Dahms, June 11, 1983 (dec. Oct. 1983). Student, U. Wis., Milw., 1964, student, 1966, student, 1979—, Chapman Coll., Orange, Calif., 1965—67, Internat. Coll. Copenhagen, 1968, Temple U., Phila., 1970, BA, Alverno Coll., Milw., 1971; postgrad., Marylhurst Coll., 1972, Chapman Coll., 1973—74, Inst. Shipboard Edn., 1978—79, postgrad., 1994, postgrad., 2005. V.p. Hinnrichs Inc., Germantown, Wis., 1964-72; tchr. Germantown Recreation Dept., 1965; coach Milw. Recreation Dept., 1966-67; rep. for wis. Chapman Coll., Orange, Calif., 1967; clk. Stein Drug Co., Menomonee Falls, Wis., 1967-72; tchr. Milwa. Area Cath. Sch., 1967-72, 83, 90-91, 96—, Germantown Schs., St. Lawrence Sch., 1991-92; asst. mgr. Original Cookie Co. (Mother Hubbard's) Cookie Store, Northridge Mall, Milw., 1977-84, Sav-U Warehouse Deli, 1984-85, mgr. office, 1985-90; with Pilgrim Message Ctr., 1987—. Substitute tchr. Cath. schs. Milw. area, 1975-80, 83-89, 90, 92—, St. Rose Sch., 1989-90; tchr. Indian Cmty. Sch., Milw., 1971-72, 88, 94-2000, Martin Luther King Sch., 1973-74, Crossroads Acad., Milw., 1974-75, Harambee Cmty. Sch., 1980-83; tutor Brookfield Learning Ctr., Wis., 1986-87; Midwest rep. World Explorer Cruises, 1978-82; security guard Indian Summer Festival, Milw., 1989—; mem. replacement crew Hallmark Cards, 1997-98; with US Census, 2000. Mem Wis. Math. Coun., Nat. Coun. Tchrs. Math., Internat. Inst. Milw. Friends of Mus., US Lighthouse Soc., Great Lakes Lighthouse Soc., Miniss Kitigan Drum (Milw. chpt.), Golden Rule, Order Eastern Star, Hostelling Internat., Alpha Theta Epsilon. Christian Scientist. Home: N88w15041 Cleveland Ave # 3 Menomonee Falls WI 53051-2239 Office Phone: 262-253-2150. Personal E-mail: hhinnrichsdahms@yahoo.com.

HINOJOSA, FEDERICO GUSTAVO, JR., retired judge; b. Edinburg, Tex., Apr. 16, 1947; s. Federico Gustavo and Zulema (Trevino) H.; m. Yolanda Silva, 1970 (div. 1977); children: Cynthia, Zelda Cassandra; m. Magdalena Garza, Oct. 30, 1992. BA, Pan Am. U., 1969; JD, U. Houston, 1977. Bar: Tex. 1977, U.S. Dist. Ct. (so. dist.) Tex. 1977, U.S. Ct. Appeals (5th cir.) 1980, U.S. Supreme Ct. 1980. Assoc. Clark, Lowes & Carrithers, Houston, 1977-79; ptnr. Clark & Hinojosa, Houston, 1979-81; child support atty. Tex. Dept. Human Resources, McAllen, 1981-83; asst. dist. atty. Hidalgo County, Edinburg, 1983-84; assoc. Atlas & Hall, McAllen, 1984-87; ptnr. Lewis, Pettitt & Hinojosa, McAllen, 1987-91; justice Tex. Ct. Appeals for 13th Dist., Corpus Christi, 1991—2006, ret., 2006. Sgt. USAF, 1970—74. Fellow Tex. Bar. Found. (life); mem. State Bar Tex., Mexican-Am. Bar Tex., Mexican-Am. Bar Assn. Coastal Bend (dir. 1993-94), Hidalgo County Bar Assn. (dir. 1986-90). Democrat. Office: 710 Laurel Ave Mcallen TX 78501 Office Phone: 956-687-8203. Personal E-mail: judgehinojosa@gmail.com.

HINOJOSA, RICARDO H., federal judge; b. Rio Grande City, Tex., 1950; BA, U. Tex., 1972; JD, Harvard U., 1975. Law clk. Tex. Supreme Ct., 1975-76; assoc. Ewers & Toothaker, McAllen, Tex., 1976-79, ptnr., 1979-83; judge US Dist. Ct. (so. dist.) Tex., McAllen, 1983—. Mem. Pan Am. U. Bd. Regents, 1979—83, chmn., 1981—83; mem. US Sentencing Commn., 2003—, chmn., 2004—; adj. prof. U. Tex. Sch. Law. Recipient Disting. Svc. award, Pan-Am. U. Alumni Assn., 1986, Disting. Alumnus award, U. Tex. Ex-Students Assn., 2001. Office: US Dist Ct So Dist Tex 1701 W Bus Hwy 83 Ste 1028 Mcallen TX 78501 Office Phone: 956-618-8100.*

HINOJOSA, RUBÉN, congressman; b. Edcouch, Tex., Aug. 20, 1940; m. Martha Lopez; 5 children. BBA, U. Tex., Austin, 1962; MBA, U. Tex.-Pan Am., Edinburg, 1980. Mem. Tex. State Bd. Edn., 1974—84; pres., CFO H & H Foods; mem. US Congress from 15th Tex. dist., 1997—, mem. edn. and the workforce com., ranking mem. select edn. subcommittee, mem. fin. svcs. com., founder Rural Housing Caucus, co-founder, co-chair Fin. and Econ. Literacy Caucus. Founding chmn. bd. trustees South Tex. Cmty. Coll., 1993—96. Named Hispanic Man of Yr. Rio Grande Valley, 1994; recipient Lifetime Achievement award Hispanic Bus. Mag. Democrat. Office: US Ho Reps 2463 Rayburn Ho Office Bldg Washington DC 20515-4315 Office Phone: 202-225-2531.*

HINOJOSA-SMITH, ROLAND, language educator, writer; b. Mercedes, Tex., Jan. 21, 1929; s. Manuel Guzman and Carrie Effie (Smith) H.; children: Clarissa Elizabeth, Karen Louise, Robert Huddleston. BS, U. Tex., 1953; AM, N.Mex. Highlands U., 1963; PhD, U. Ill., 1969. Chmn. dept. modern langs. Tex. A&I U., Kingsville, 1970-74, dean Coll. Arts and Scis., 1974-76, v.p. acad. affairs, 1976-77; prof. English U. Minn., Mpls., 1977-81; Ellen Clayton Garwood prof. English U. Tex., Austin, 1985—, Mari Sabusawa Michener chair, 1989-93, dir. Tex. Ctr. for Writers, 1989-93, prof. dept. Spanish and Portuguese, 1993—. Juror Pulitzer Prize Novel, 1994; USIA cons., Panama, Mexico, Iraq, France; judge Pulitzer Prize, 2003—04; lectr. in field. Author: Estampas del Valle, 1973 (Quinto Sol 1973), Klail City, 1976 (Casa de las Americas 1976), Korean Love Songs, 1978, The Valley, 1983, Dear Rafe, 1985, Partners in Crime, 1985, Fair Gentlemen of Belken County, 1986, Klail City, 1987, Becky and Her Friends, 1990, Los Amigos de Becky, 1991, Korea Liebes Lieder, 1992, The Useless Servants, 1993, Ask a Policeman, 1998, My Dear Rafe/Mi Querido Rafa, 2005, We Happy Few, 2006; guest editor Am. Short Fiction, 1993-94. Illini (U. Ill.) Comback Guest, 1996. Named Disting. Alumnus, U. Ill., 1998, U. Tex.-Brownsville, 1998, Celebrity Author, Scott Foresman, 1999—2001, Disting. Vis. Prof., U. Kans., summer, 1994, Marshal, U. Tex., 1995—2001; recipient Outstanding Latino faculty mem., Hispanic Caucus Am. Assn. Higher Edn., Disting. Achievement award, U. Ill., 1998; fellow, Ford Found., 1979. Fellow Soc. Spanish and Spanish Am. Studies, The Hispanic Soc. (assoc.); mem. MLA, Academia Real de la Lengua. Democrat. Roman Catholic. Office: U Tex Dept English Austin TX 78712 Office Phone: 512-471-8796. Business E-Mail: rorro@mail.utexas.edu.

HINRICHS, CHARLES A., paper company executive; b. St. Louis, Dec. 3, 1953; s. John H. and Anne B. (Beasley) Hinrichs; m. Linda J. Miller, Aug. 6, 1977; children: Christopher J., Jonathan C. BS in Acctg., U. Mo., 1976; MBA, St. Louis U., 1981. Asst. treas. United Mo. Bank of Kirkwood, St. Louis, 1976-79; asst. v.p. Commerce Bank of St. Louis, 1979-81; sr. v.p. Boatmen's Nat. Bank of St. Louis, 1981—; v.p. & treas. Smurfit-Stone Container Corp., 1998—2002, sr. v.p. & CFO, 2002—05, sr. v.p. & CFO, 2005—. Bd. dir., mem. exec. com. Downtown St. Louis, Inc., 1990. Mem.: Forest Hills Country Club, Mo. Athletic Club. Office: Smurfit-Stone Container Corp 150 N Michigan Ave Chicago IL 60601*

HINSHAW, ADA SUE, nursing educator, former dean; b. Arkansas City, Kans., May 20, 1939; d. Oscar A. and Georgia Ruth (Tucker) Cox; children: Cynthia Lynn, Scott Allen Lewis. BS, U. Kans., 1961; MSN, Yale U., 1963; MA, U. Ariz., 1973, PhD, 1975; DSc (hon.), U. Md., 1988, Med. Coll. of Ohio, 1988, Marquette U., 1990, U. Nebr., 1992, Mount Sinai Med. Ctr., NY, 1993, U. Medicine and Dentistry N.J., 1995, Grand Valley State U., 1995, U. Toronto, Can., 1996, St. Louis U., 1996, Georgetown U., 1998. Instr. Sch. Nursing U. Kans., 1963-66; asst. prof. U. Calif., San Francisco, 1966-71; prof. U. Ariz., Tucson, 1975-87; dir. nursing rsch. U. Med. Ctr., Tucson, 1975-87; dir. Nat. Inst. Nursing Rsch. Pub. Health Svc., Dept. Health and Human Svcs., NIH, Washington, 1987—94; prof. U. Mich. Sch. Nursing, Ann Arbor, 1994—, dean, 1994—2006, dean emeritus, 2006—. Contbd. articles to profl. jours. Recipient Kay Schilter award U. Kans., 1961, Lucille Petry Leone award Nat. League for Nursing, 1971, Wolanin Geriatric Nursing Rsch. award U. Ariz., 1978, Alumni of the Yr award Sch. Nursing U. Kans., 1981, Disting. Alumni award Sch. Nursing Yale U., 1981, Alumni Achievement award U. Ariz., 1990, Disting. citation Kans. Alumni Assn., 1992, Health Leader of the Yr. award Pub. Health Svc., 1993, Centennial award Columbia Sch. Nursing, 1993, Presdl. Meritorious Exec. Rank award, 1994. Mem. ANA (Nurse Scientist of Yr. Award 1985, Salute to Nurses award 1994), Coun. Nurse Rschrs. (Nurse Scientist of Yr. Award 1985), Md. Nurses Assn., Western Soc. for Rsch. in Nursing, Am. Acad. Nursing, Inst. Medicine (mem. 1989-, coun. mem. 1999-04, mem. com. 1995-99, Walsh McDermott medal, 2005), Sigma Xi, Sigma Theta Tau (Beta Mu Chpt. award of Excellence in Nursing Edn., 1980, Elizabeth McWilliams Miller Excellence in Rsch. Award, 1987), Alpha Chi Omega. Avocations: hiking, camping, bicycling. Office: U Mich Sch Nursing 400 N Ingalls St Rm 4221 Ann Arbor MI 48109-2003 E-mail: ahinshaw@umich.edu.

HINSHAW, CARROLL ELTON, economics professor; b. Texarkana, Ark., Aug. 2, 1936; s. Curtis Tillman and Loma Dean (Roberts) H.; m. Jane A. Simpson, Aug. 11, 1957; children: Stephen, Rebecca, Carroll. BBA, Baylor U., 1958; PhD, Vanderbilt U., 1966. Assoc. prof. La. Coll., 1962-64; from asst. prof. econs. to prof. emeritus Vanderbilt U., Nashville, 1966—2000, prof. emeritus, 2000—, asst. dean Coll. Arts and Sci., 1970-72, assoc. dean, 1972-74. Vis. asst. prof. Getulio Vargas Found., Rio de Janeiro, Brazil, 1967-69; CEO Shiloh Paper, Inc.; CFO Farmhouse Foods, Inc.; cons. in field. Author: Forecasting and Recognizing Business Cycle Turning Points, 1968; Contbr. articles to profl. jours. H.B. Earhart fellow, 1965-66 Mem. Am. Econ. Assn. (sec. 1976-93, treas. 1988-96, sec., treas. emeritus, 2000), Beta Alpha Psi, Omicron Delta Epsilon. Baptist. Office: Am Econ Assn 2014 Broadway Ste 305 Nashville TN 37203-2425 also: Dept Econs Vanderbilt Univ Nashville TN 37232-0001 Home: 814 Huntington Cir Nashville TN 37215

HINSHAW, CHESTER JOHN, lawyer; b. Sacramento, Mar. 10, 1941; s. Chester Edward and Gertrude Lorraine (Miller) H.; m. Karen Forbes Breakey, Feb. 19, 1977. AB, Stanford U., 1963; JD, U. Calif., Berkeley, 1966. Bar: Calif. 1966, U.S. Dist. Ct. (no. dist.) Calif. 1967, U.S. Ct. Appeals (9th cir.) 1967, N.Y. 1968, U.S. Dist. Ct. (so. dist.) N.Y. 1972, U.S. Dist. Ct. (ea. dist.) N.Y. 1974, U.S. Ct. Appeals (2d cir.) 1974, U.S. Dist. Ct. (no. dist.) N.Y. 1980, U.S. Dist. Ct. (ea. dist.) Mich. 1982, U.S. Dist. Ct. (no. dist.) Tex. 1983, Tex. 1984, U.S. Ct. Appeals (5th cir.) 1984, U.S Supreme Ct. 1991. Assoc. Chadbourne & Parke, NYC, 1967-74, ptnr., 1974-83, Jones Day, Dallas, 1983-99. Lectr. U. Calif., Berkeley, 1966. Mem. ABA, Tex. Bar Assn., Calif. Bar Assn. Home: 5510 Park Ln Dallas TX 75220-2158 Office Phone: 214-368-4332. Personal E-mail: chet.hinshaw@earthlink.net.

HINSHAW, EDWARD BANKS, retired broadcast executive; b. Aurora, Ill., Feb. 27, 1940; s. Lorenzo M. and Emily (Roach) H.; m. Victoria Leone Biggers, Jan. 16, 1965; children: Eric, Brian. Student, Harvard Coll., 1958-59, U. Minn., 1959-62. Announcer Sta. KSTP-Radio-TV, Mpls., 1959-64; announcer Voice of America, Washington, 1964-65; reporter, anchorman Jour. Broadcast Group, Inc. (formerly Sta. WTMJ, Inc.), Milw., 1965-70, editorialist, 1970-74, editorial dir., 1974—, mgr. public affairs, 1979-90, mgr. pers. and editorial affairs, 1990-94, v.p. human resources, 1994—2002. Instr. broadcast journalism U. Wis., Whitewater, 1976, 79, 86. Trustee Nat. First Amendment Congress, 1980-83; chair Wis First Amendment Congress, 1985; bd. chair Milw. Urban League, 1987; bd. dirs. Children's Outing Assn., 1987-90, Ko-Thi Dance Co., 1992-99, pres., 1994-96; bd. dirs. Richard and Ethel Herzfeld Found., 1997—, Pabst Theater, 2002—, Riverworks Devel. Corp., Milw. Ctr. for Independence, 2004—, Lionel's House, 2003—, Donors Fourm of Wis., 2004—, Regency House Condo. Assn., 2005—. Recipient DuPont-Columbia Citation in Broadcast Journalism, 1978; Abe Lincoln Merit award So. Baptist Radio-TV Commn., 1978; NCCJ Gold Media Medallion, 1977; named to Wis. Broadcasters Hall of Fame, 2002. Mem.: Milw. Press Club (bd. dirs. 1990—95, pres.-elect 1992, pres. 1993, Knight of the Golden Quill, Hall of Fame 2002), Wis. Broadcasters Assn. Found. (treas. 2000—), Nat. Broadcast Editl. Assn. (pres. 1980—81), Nat. Conf. Editl. Writers (life), Sigma Delta Chi (Disting. Svc. award 1977, Excellence in Journalism award 1988, Freedom of Info. award 1994). Business E-Mail: ehinshaw@wi.rr.com.

HINSHAW, ERNEST THEODORE, JR., private investor, retired Olympic team official, retired finance company executive; b. San Rafael, Calif., Aug. 26, 1928; s. Ernest Theodore and Ina (Johnson) H.; m. Nell Marie Schildmeyer, June 24, 1952; children: Marc Christopher, Lisa Anne, Jennifer, Amy Lynn. AB, Stanford U., 1951, MBA, 1957. Staff asst. to pres. Capital Research and Mgmt. Co., Los Angeles, 1957-58, dir. planning, 1967-68; fin. analyst Capital Research Co., Los Angeles, NYC, 1958-68, v.p., 1962-71, mgr. N.Y.C. office, 1962-66; dir., exec. v.p. Am. Funds Service Co., Los Angeles, 1968-69, pres., 1969-72, chmn. bd., 1972-82; dir. pres. Capital Data Systems, Inc., Los Angeles, 1971-73, chmn., 1973-79; v.p. Capital Group, Inc., Los Angeles, 1973-83; sr. v.p. Growth Fund Am., 1973-74, pres., 1974-76, chmn. bd., 1976-82, dir., 1974-96; sr. v.p. Income Fund Am., 1973-74, pres., dir., 1974-76, chmn. bd., 1976-82, dir., 1974-96; commr. yachting 1984 Olympic games Los Angeles Olympic Organizing Com., 1980-84. Dir. Capital Research & Mgmt. Co., 1972-83; mem. guest faculty Northwestern U. Transp. Center, 1965-66; mem. ops. com. Investment Co. Inst., 1970-74 Bd. dirs. Newport Harbor Nautical Mus., 1989-92, Girl Scout Coun. Orange County, 1993—2002, chair fin. com., 1996-97, treas., 1998-01; trustee Friends of Girl Scouts Trust; mem. investment com. Hoag Hosp. Found., 1992-97. Served to 1st lt. USMC, 1951-53. Mem. Soc. Airline Analysts (sec. 1965-66), Nat. Kite Class (pres. 1968-69), Lido 14 Internat. Class Assn. (pres. 1978-79), Assn. Orange Coast Yacht Clubs (commodore 1976), So. Calif. Yachting Assn. (commodore 1979), B.O.A.T., Inc. (dir. 1977-81), Pacific Coast Yachting Assn. (dir. 1979-80), U.S. Yacht Racing Union (dir. 1980-81), U.S. Sailing Ctr. Long Beach, Calif. (adv. coun. mem.). Clubs: Lido Isle Yacht (Newport Beach, Calif.) (commodore 1973), Stanford U. Sailing (trustee 1984-96), St. Francis Yacht (San Francisco), Ft. Worth Boat Democrat.

HINSHAW, MARK LARSON, architect, urban planner; b. Glendale, Calif., Aug. 17, 1947; s. Lerner Brady and Alice Elaine (Larson) H.; m. Caryl Ann Kunsemuller, Dec. 21, 1968 (div. 1982); 1 child, Erica; m. Marilyn Kay Smith, June 18, 1983 (div. 1997); children: Lindsay, Christopher. BArch magna cum laude, U. Okla., 1970; M in Urban Planning, CUNY, 1972. Registered arch., Wash. Sr. planner Planning Dept., Anchorage, 1976-77; project planner TRA, Seattle, 1977-82; urban designer City of Bellevue, Wash., 1982-90; ind. cons., 1991-97; dir. urban design LMN Archs., Seattle, 1997—. Arch.-in-the-sch. Seattle Sch. Dist., 1979. Columnist on architecture, urban design: Seattle Times, 1993—2004; author: Citistate Seattle: Shaping a Modern Metropolis, 1999—; contbg. editor: Landscape Architecture Mag.; contbr. articles to profl. jours. and books. Mem. Urban Beautification Commn., Anchorage, 1975, Design Jury, Hemet (Calif.) Civic Ctr. Competition, Seattle Design Commn., 1990-91; mem. Downtown Seattle Design Rev. Bd., 1996-. 1st lt. USAF, 1972-76. NEA grantee, 1975; recipient merit award for Hist. Preservation, City of Seattle, 1983. Fellow AIA (pres. Seattle chpt. 1992-93), Am. Inst. Cert. Planners (mem. nat. bd. 1994-98); mem. Am. Planning Assn. (sec. Wash. chpt. 1982, v.p. 1983-85, pres. 1987-89).

HINSHAW, VIRGINIA, academic administrator; BA in Lab. Tech., Auburn U., 1967, MS in Microbiology, 1967, PhD in Microbiology, 1972. Clin. and rsch. microbiologist Med. Coll. Va., 1967—68; rsch. virologist U. Calif., Berkeley, 1974, St. Jude Children's Rsch. Hosp., 1975—85; assoc. prof. virology dept. patho-biol. scis. U. Wis., Madison, 1985—88, prof., 1988—92, interim assoc. dean for rsch. and grad. studies Sch. Vet. Medicine, 1992—93, assoc. vice-chancellor, 1994—95, vice chancellor for rsch., dean Grad. Sch., 1995—2001; provost, exec. vice chancellor U. Calif., Davis, 2001—. Office: Univ Calif Davis One Shields Ave Davis CA 95616

HINSON, BOBBY D., lawyer; b. Lancaster, SC, Mar. 14, 1962; AB magna cum laude in Economics and Polit. Sci., Duke U., 1984; JD, U. Va., 1987. Bar: NC 1987, SC 1989, US Ct. Appeals 4th Cir. Assoc. Kennedy Covington Lobdell & Hickman LLP, Charlotte, NC, 1987—94; mem. Womble Carlyle Sandridge & Rice PLLC, Charlotte, NC, 1994—, leader real estate develop. practice group. Bd. dirs. Habitat for Humanity, Charlotte, NC, Jackson Park Ministries. Mem.: SC Bar Assn. (real property sect.), NC Bar Assn. (real property sect.), Mecklenburg County Bar Assn. Office: Womble Carlyle Sandridge & Rice PLLC One Wachovia Ctr Ste 3500 301 S College St Charlotte NC 28202-6037 Office Phone: 704-331-4918. Office Fax: 704-338-7803. Business E-Mail: bhinson@wcsr.com.

HINSON, DUANE KEITH, minister, counselor; b. Winterhaven, Fla., June 15, 1949; adopted s. William Jesse and s. Faith Donella Hinson; m. Dema Geneva Kinnie, Sept. 5, 1970; children: Darcy Amity Ogle, Eryn Bethany Erickson, Ashley Jannah, Matthew Kent. BS, U. Calif., Irvine, 1971; MDiv, Princeton Theol. Sem., NJ, 1974. Ordained minister Christian & Missionary Alliance, 2002. Asst. pastor youth First Presbyn. Ch., San Mateo, Calif., 1974—75; owner Hinson's Construction, Anaheim, Calif., 1977—83, Hinson's Washer and Dryer Svc., Anaheim, 1983—90, Palo Cedro Laundry and Cleaners, Calif., 1991—99; sales rep. PWS, S. San Francisco, 1991—93; asst. pastor counseling and recovery Risen King Cmty. Ch., Redding, Calif., 1993—2002; pastoral counselor Don Ostendorf Ctr. Counseling, Redding, 2002—06, Christian Counseling Ctr., Fremont, Calif., 2005—, Hayward, Calif., 2005—. Mem.: Am. Assn. Pastoral Counselors, Am. Assn. Christian Counselors. Avocations: woodworking, writing. Office: Christian Counseling Center 1357 Mowry Ave Fremont CA 94538 Home Phone: 408-225-8606; Office Phone: 510-794-8581.

HINSON, H. DOUGLAS, lawyer; b. Staunton, Va., June 27, 1960; s. Harold D. and Betty M. (Morris) H.; m. Michelle R. Olsen, Aug. 9, 1986. BA magna cum laude, Emory U., 1982; JD cum laude, Georgetown U., 1986. Bar: Ala. 1986, Ga. 1989, U.S. Dist. Ct. (no. and so. dists.) Ala. 1986, U.S. Ct. Appeals (11th cir.) 1987, U.S. Dist. Ct. (no. dist.) Ga. 1989. Assoc. Bradley, Arant, Rose & White, Birmingham, Ala., 1986-88; assoc. Alston & Bird, Atlanta, 1988-94, ptnr., litig., 1994—. Active Salvation Army. Mem. Phi Beta Kappa. Avocations: golf, travel. Office: Alston & Bird 1 Atlantic Ctr 1201 W Peachtree St NW Atlanta GA 30309-3424 Office Phone: 404-881-7590. Office Fax: 404-881-7777. Business E-Mail: doug.hinson@alston.com.

HINSON, JACK ALLSBROOK, research toxicologist, educator; b. Mullins, SC, Aug. 18, 1944; s. Layton Liston and Will (Allsbrook) H.; m. Joanne Edwards Kidd; children: Edward Thomas, Richard William. BS, Coll. of Charleston, 1966; MS, U. S.C., 1968; PhD, Vanderbilt U., 1972. Postdoctoral fellow Nat. Inst. of Health, Bethesda, Md., 1972-75, sr. staff fellow, 1975-80; rsch. toxicologist Nat. Ctr. Toxicological Rsch., Jefferson, Ark., 1980-90, chief biochem. mechanisms br., 1989-90; adj. prof. U. Ark. Med. Sci., Little Rock, 1980-90, prof., dir. div. toxicology. Dir. interdisciplinary toxicology program U. Ark. Med. Sci., 1990—; chmn. Ark. Toxicology Symposium, 1992-99; adj. assoc. prof. U. Tenn. Ctr. for Health Scis., Memphis, 1982-90; vis. fellow Middlesex Hops. Med. Sch., London, 1982; vis. prof. U. Leiden, The Netherlands, 1986. Editor Drug Metabolism Revs., 1997—, mem. editl. bd., 1995-97; mem. editl. bd. Toxicology and Applied Pharmacology, 1980-89, 96—, Jour. Toxicology and Environ. Health, 1991—; contbr. chpts. to books and articles to profl. jours. Mem. Soc. Toxicology (pres. South Ctrl. chpt. 1990-92), Am. Soc. Pharmacology and Exptl. Therapeutics, Internat. Soc. for Study of Xenobiotics. Episcopalian. Home: 8 Piedmont Ln Little Rock AR 72223-2232 Office: U Ark Med Sci Divsn Toxicology 4301 W Markham St # 638 Little Rock AR 72205-7101 Home Phone: 501-225-5671. Business E-Mail: HinsonJackA@uams.edu.

HINSON, ROBERT WILLIAM, advertising executive, consultant; b. Neptune, NJ, Nov. 30, 1944; s. Herbert William and Bernice (Stadelhofer) H. AB in Econs. and Sociology, Boston Coll., 1966. Media planner Benton & Bowles, Inc., NYC, 1968—70; v.p., assoc. media dir. SSC&B: Lintas Worldwide, NYC, 1970—74, sr. v.p., dir. media ops., 1976—80; v.p., assoc. media dir. Foote Cone & Belding, Inc., LA, 1974—76; exec. v.p., chmn. mgmt. com., chmn. ops. com., dir. media svcs. Rosenfeld, Sirowitz & Lawson, Inc., NYC, 1980—85, exec. v.p., dir. mktg. and media svcs., chief adminstrv. officer, 1986—87; pres., CEO Hinson and Assocs., Inc., NYC, 1987—91. Cons. in field, 1991—. Author: Media Leverage, 1985. Media dir. Tuesday Team, Reagan-Bush '84 campaign, 1984; sustaining mem. Rep. Nat. Com.; mem. Ronald Reagan Presdl. Libr. Found., Monmouth County (N.J.) Rep. Orgn.; bd. dirs. Monmouth Symphony Orch.; mem. nat. campaign com. Boston Coll. Mem. NATAS, Nat. Assn. TV, Arts and Scis., Internat. Radio and TV Soc., Media Dirs. Industry Coun., Am. Assn. Advt. Agys. (media policy com. 1980-87), Am. Rsch. Found. (media com. coun. 1983-86), Boston Coll. Alumni Assn., Wagner Soc. N.Y., Monmouth County Hist. Soc., Alliance Francaise of Monmouth County, Alliance Francaise of Ft. Lauderdale, Nature Conservancy, Nat. Trust for Hist. Preservation, Vieux Carre Property Owners Assn., N.Y. Athletic Club, Deal (N.J.) Golf and Country Club, Allenhurst (N.J.) Beach Club, Coral Ridge (Fla.) Country Club Roman Catholic. Home: #609 133 N Pompano Beach Blvd Pompano Beach FL 33062-5728 also: 921 Chartres St New Orleans LA 70116-3227

HINTIKKA, JAAKKO, philosopher, educator; b. Helsingin Pitäjä, Finland, Jan. 12, 1929; s. Toivo Juho and Lempi J. (Salmi) H.; m. Merrill Bristow Provence, Feb. 11, 1978 (dec.); m. Ghita Holmström, Dec. 19, 1987. Grad. in Philosophy, U. Helsinki, Finland, 1952, PhD, 1956; postgrad., Harvard U., 1954; Doctorate (hon.), U. Liège, 1984, Jagiellonian U., 1995, Uppsala U., 2000, U. Oulu, 2001, U. Turku, 2003. Jr. fellow Soc. Fellows, Harvard U., 1956-59; prof. philosophy U. Helsinki, 1959-70; rsch. prof. Acad. Finland, 1970-81; prof. philosophy Fla. State U., Tallahassee, 1978-90, McKenzie prof., 1986-90, also prof. computer sci., 1986-90; prof. Boston U., 1990—. Vis. prof. Brown U., 1962, U. Calif., Berkeley, 1963, Hebrew U. Jerusalem, 1974; part-time prof. philosophy Stanford U., 1964-82, Immanuel Kant lectr., 1985; John Locke lectr. Oxford (Eng.) U., 1964; fellow Ctr. for Advanced Study in Behavioral Scis., 1970-71; Hägerström lectr. U. Uppsala, 1983; co-chair Am. organizing com. Twentieth World Congress Philos., 1998. Author: Knowledge and Belief, 1962, 2d edit., 2005, Models for Modalities, 1969, Tieto on valtaa, 1969, Logic, Language-Games and Information, 1973, Time and Necessity, 1973, Knowledge and the Known, 1974, (with U. Remes) The Method of Analysis, 1974, The Intentions of Intentionality, 1975, The Semantics of Questions and the Questions of Semantics, 1976, Aristotle on Modality and Determinism, 1977, The Game of Language, 1983, (with J. Kulas) Anaphora and Definite Descriptions, 1985, (with Merrill B. Hintikka) Investigating Wittgenstein, 1986, (with Martin Kusch) Kieli ja maailma, 1988, (with Merrill B. Hintikka) The Logic of Epistemology, 1989, Intentionnalite et mondes possibles, 1989, (with James Bachman) What If? Toward Excellence in Reasoning, 1990, (with Gabriel Sandu) On the Methodology of Linguistics, 1991, Eseje Logiczno-Filozoficzne, 1992, Fondements d'une theorie du langage, 1994, The Principles of Mathematics Revisited, 1996, Ludwig Wittgenstein: Half-truths and One-and-a-Half Truths, 1996, Lingua Universalis vs. Calculus Ratiocinator, 1996, Language, Truth and Logic in Mathematics, 1997, Paradigms for Language Theory, 1997, El Viaje Filosófico más Largo, 1998, Inquiry as Inquiry, 1999, On Goedel, 2000, On Wittgenstein, 2000, Filosofian Köyhyys ja Rikkaus, 2001, Aspects of Aristotle, 2004, Socratic Epistemology, 2007; contbr. over 300 articles to profl. jours.; editor-in-chief: Internat. Jour. Synthese, 1965-76, 82-02; editor: Synthese Libr., 1965-2002 Acta Philosophica Fennica, 1973-79, Synthese Lang. Libr., 1976-84, (with Patrick Suppes) Aspects of Inductive Logic, 1966, Philosophy of Mathematics, 1969, (with Donald Davidson) Words and Objections, 1969, (with Patrick Suppes) Information and Inference, 1970, (with others) Approaches to Natural Language, 1973, Rudolf Carnap, Logical Empiricist, 1976, (with others) Essays on Wittgenstein in Honor of G.H. von Wright, 1976, (with Robert Butts) Procs. 5th Internat. Congress Logic, Methodology and Philosophy of Science (4 vols.), 1977, (with Lucia Vaina) Cognitive Constraints on Communication, 1984, (with S. Knuuttila) The Logic of Being, 1986, (with Leila Haaparanta) Frege Synthesized, 1987, Aspects of Metaphor, 1994, From Dedekind to Gödel, 1995. Decorated comdr. Order of the Lion of Finland, 1st class, 1987; recipient Wihuri Internat. prize, 1976, E.J. Nyström prize Soc. Scientiarum Fennica, 1988, Suomen Kulttuurirahasto grand prize, 1989, Rolf Schock prize, Royal Swedish Acad. Sciences, 2005; Guggenheim fellow, 1979-80. Mem. Assn. Symbolic Logic (v.p. 1968-70), Internat. Inst. Philosophy (v.p. 1993-96, pres. 1999-2002), Internat. Union History and Philosophy Sci. (v.p. 1971-75, pres. 1975), Finnish Acad. Sci. and Letters (hon.; coun. 1972-79), Philosophy of Sci. Assn. (governing bd. 1970-72), Societas Scientiarum Fennica, Internat. Fedn. Philos. Socs. (governing bd. 1978-88, 93-98, v.p. 1993-98), Am. Philos. Assn. (v.p. Pacific divsn. 1974-75, pres. 1975-76), Am. Acad. Arts and Scis., Norwegian Acad. Sci., C.S. Peirce Soc. (pres. 1997), Russian Acad. Scis. (fgn. mem.), Hungarian Acad. Scis., Phi Beta Kappa (hon.). Home: 38 Flint Dr Marlborough MA 01752-6701 Office: Boston U Dept Philosophy Boston MA 02215-1401 also: U Helsinki Inst Philosophy PO Box 9 FIN 00014 Helsinki Finland Business E-Mail: hintikka@bu.edu.

HINTON, JAMES FORREST, JR., lawyer; b. Gadsden, Ala., Nov. 19, 1951; s. James Forrest Sr. and Juanita Grey (Weems) H. BA, Vanderbilt U., 1974; JD, U. Ala., 1977. Bar: Ala. 1977, D.C. 1979, U.S. Dist. Ct. (so. dist.) Ala. 1979, U.S. Ct. Appeals (5th cir.) 1980, U.S. Ct. Appeals (11th cir.) 1981, La. 1982, U.S. Dist. Ct. (ea. and mid. dists.) La. 1982, U.S. Dist. Ct. (no. dist.) Ala 1982, U.S. Supreme Ct. 1982, U.S. Dist. Ct. (we. dist.) La. 1983, U.S. Dist. Ct. (no. dist.) Ohio 1983, U.S. Ct. Appeals (D.C. cir.) 1984, U.S. Ct. Appeals (fed. cir.) 1985, U.S. Dist. Ct. (so. dist.) Tex. 1987, U.S. Dist. Ct. (no. dist.) Tex. 1991, Tex. 1992, Tenn. 1992, U.S. Dist. Ct. (ea. and we. dists.) Ark. 1992, U.S. Ct. Appeals (6th and 8th cirs.) 1992, U.S. Dist. Ct. (ea. and we. dists.) Tex. 1993, U.S. Dist. Ct. (mid. dist.) Ala. 1993, U.S. Dist. Ct. (ea. and mid. dist.) Tenn. 1994, U.S. Dist. Ct., Colo. 2000. Law clk. to chief judge U.S. Dist. Ct. (so. dist.) Ala., Mobile, 1977-79; ptnr. Darby, Myrick & Hinton, Mobile, 1979-82; dir. McGlinchey Stafford Lang, New Orleans, 1982-93; ptnr. Adams & Reese, New Orleans, 1993-97; shareholder Berkowitz, Lefkovits, Isom & Kushner, Birmingham, 1997—2003, Baker, Donelson, Bearman, Caldwell & Berkowitz, 2003—. Contbr. articles to profl. jours. Mem. ABA (antitrust, intellectual property, litigation sects.), FBA, La. Assn. Def. Counsel, Order of Coif, Phi Beta Kappa. Office: Baker Donelson Bearman Caldwell & Berkowitz PC Wachovia Tower Ste 1600 420 20th St N Birmingham AL 35203-5200 Home Phone: 205-298-1899; Office Phone: 205-250-8332. Business E-Mail: fhinton@bakerdonelson.com.

HINTON, PAULA WEEMS, lawyer; b. Gadsden, Ala., Dec. 5, 1954; d. James Forrest and Juanita (Weems) H.; m. Steven D. Lawrence, Mar. 31, 1984; 1 child, David Hinton Lawrence. BA in Polit. Sci. magna cum laude, U. Ala., 1976, MPA, JD, U. Ala., 1979. Bar: Ala. 1979, U.S. Dist. Ct. (so. dist.) Ala. 1980, U.S. Dist. Ct. (so. dist.) Tex. 1981, U.S. Ct. Appeals (5th and 11th cirs.) 1981, Tex. 1982, U.S. Dist. Ct. (no. dist.) Tex. 1988, U.S. Dist. Ct. (ea. and we. dists.) Tex. 1989, U.S. Dist. Ct. (no. and mid. dists.) Ala. 1993, U.S. Supreme Ct. 1998. Law clk. to magistrate U.S. Dist. Ct. Ala., Mobile, 1979-80; assoc. Vinson & Elkins, LLP, Houston, 1981-88; ptnr. Akin Gump Strauss Hauer & Feld, L.L.P., Houston, 1989—2001, Vinson & Elkins, Houston, 2001—. Panel arbitrators Am. Arbitration Assn., 1989—97; mem. Supreme Ct. Gender Bias Reform Implementation Com., 1998—, co-chair, 2000—, chair, 2002—; mem. faculty Tex. Coll. Judicial Studies, 2004; mem. adv. bd. U. Houston Sch. Law Found.; bd. dirs. U. Ala. Law Sch. Found; spkr. in field. Contbr. articles to profl. jours. Mem. women's initiative cabinet United Way Tex. Gulf Coast; chair women initiative com. United Way Great Houston; bd. dirs. Planned Parenthood Houston, 2000—03, SE Tex., Inc., 2000—03. Named a Tex. Super Lawyer, Tex. Monthly and Law and Politics, 2003, 2004; Rotary fellow, U. Sevilla, Spain, 1980—81. Fellow: Am. Bar Found., Tex. Bar Found. (co-chmn. nominating com. 2002—03, chair new fellows com. 2003, liaison to bd. 2003—05), Houston Bar Found. (life; bd. dirs. 1994—96, chmn. 1996—97, bd. dirs. 2002—); mem.: ATLA, ABA (mem. litigation sect., internat. law and practice sect., women's adv. com. on corp. counsel, women and the law sect., commn. on women's Margaret Brent League, bus. law sect., mem. Ctr. Profl. Responsibility), Tex. Supreme Ct. Gender Bias Task Force Implementation Com. (chair 2006—), Am. Law Inst., Am. Inns of Ct., Tex. Assn. Def. Counsel, Coll. State Bar Tex., Tex. Assn. Def. Counsel, Internat. Assn. Def. Counsel, Am. Law Inst., Tex. Ctr. for Legal Ethics and Professionalism, Tex. Exec. Women, London Ct. of Internat. Arbitration, Internat. Bar Assn. Section on Bus. Law (sect. bus. law, barristers & advocates forum), Houston Bar Assn. (minority opportunities in legal profession com. 1997, civil justice ctr. com. 1997—98, litig. sect.), Greater Houston Partnerships, Exec. Women's Partnership (steering com. 2002—03), U. Houston Law Found. (adv. bd), State Bar Tex. (chair women in the profession com. 1996—98, ad hoc com. to select minority dirs. 1997, local grievance com. 1998, mem. disciplinary rules of profl. conduct com. 2000—01,04-05, chair Tex. Supreme Ct. gender bias task force com. 2000—, bd. dirs. 2002—05, vice chair spl. pattern jury charge oversight com. 2003, exec. com. 2003—04, coun. litig. sect. 2005, mem. litigation sect., women and law sect., internat. law sect., antitrust and bus. litigation sect., co-chair adminstrn. com., co-chair sect. coord. com., discipline and client atty. asst. com., pub. svc. and edn. com., women and the sect. Ma'at Justice award 2003, Woman on Move award 2004), Alexis de Tocqueville Soc., Supreme Ct. Hist. Soc., Am. Inns of Ct., Phi Delta Phi, Omicron Delta Kappa, Pi Sigma Alpha. Office: Vinson and Elkins LLP First City Tower 1001 Fannin St Ste 2500 Houston TX 77002-6760 Business E-Mail: phinton@velaw.com.

HINTON, THOMAS ALLEN, government agency administrator; b. Anderson, Ind., June 27, 1954; s. N. Keith and Reba Lucille Hinton; m. Mary Anne Hoerner, July 26, 1975; children: Gregory Neal children: Jarod Thomas, Matthew Allen, Laura Elizabeth, Kristen Rebecca, Katherine JoAnn, Caleb Timothy, Nasia Anne, Truman David, Hannah Suzanne. BS, Ind. Wesleyan U., Marion, 1978. V.p. govt. rels.-cmty. devel Marion-Grant County C. of C., 1987—89; dir. customer rels. Wesley Press Pub. Co., Indpls., 1989—91; sr. v.p. T-3/Family Co., Gas City, Ind., 1991—99; dir. state rels. The Heritage Found., Washington, 1999—2004; sr. state liaison Office Under Sec. of Def., Arlington, Va., 2004—. Adminstrv. dir. US Fireworks Safety Coun., Washington, 1992—99; mem. adv. group Educating Mil. Children Interstate Compact, Lexington, Ky., 2006—. Musical rec., He's Alive, 1979; contbg. author: The Teen Sex Survival Manual: How to Cope in an R-rated World, 1987. Mem. Pub. Safety and Civil Justice Task Force Coun. State Govts., Lexington, Ky., 2001—04; pres. Grant County Right to Life, Ind., 1982—87; v.p. Ind. Fedn. for Life, Indpls., 1986—88; chmn. Grant County Hwy. Study Commn., Marion, 1988—89; v.p. Grant Cunty. Crime Stoppers, 1988—89; state conv. del. Rep. Party, 1986—88, ward chmn., 1986—89, precinct committeeman, 1986—99; cons. candidates for state rep., Marion, 1986—2006; bd. advisors Fairmount Twp., Ind., 1994—99; founder Christian Awareness Inst., Marion, 1984—86; bd. advisors Fairmount Wesleyan Ch., 1992—99. Named col., adc, Gov. N.Mex, 2002; named to Hon. Order Ky. Cols., 1994; recipient Small Bus. Builder's award, Ind. C. of C., 1990, award for outstanding achievement in polit. sci., Ind. Wesleyan U., 2001, Orator's award, Debater's award, Buckley Sch. Pub. Speaking, 2002. Mem.: Acad. Polit. Sci. Avocations: family activities, natural health research, home business development, singing, writing. Office: Office of Under Sec Def 1525 Wilson Blvd Ste 225 Arlington VA 22209 Home Phone: 540-374-1078; Office Phone: 703-588-0948. Personal E-mail: thomasahinton1954@yahoo.com.

HINTON, VELECIA ANN, academic administrator; b. St. Louis, Nov. 12, 1957; d. Grady, Sr. and Clara B. (Gardner) Blunt; m. Rodney B. Patterson, Mar. 8, 1980 (div. May 1991); children: Islandia E. McIntyre, Amber T. Patterson-Fuller, Osha L. Patterson; m. Elbert J. Hinton, Aug. 21, 1994. AA in Biblical Theology, Internat. Bible Coll. and Seminar, 1987; BA in Social Svcs., Lael Coll. & Grad. Sch., 1992; MMin in Christian Counseling, Christian Bible Coll. & Seminary, 2000; DMin in Christian Edn., Patriot U., 2004. Cert. Christian counseling therapist Christian Bible Coll. and Sem., 2000. Child care adminstr. St. Louis Pub. Schs., 1989—99; pastor Footsteps of Jesus Christ Apostles' Doctrine Ch., Inc., St. Louis, 1994—; adminstr. Footsteps of Jesus Christ Coll., St. Louis, 2003—. Adv. bd. mem. Black African-Am. Christian Counselors, Detroit, 2000—04. Author: Preach the Word, 7 vol. set, 1999—2004, Bishop and Pastor, A Love Story, 2005. Dist. sec. Full Gospel Assembly Ch., Pine Lawn, Mo., 1993—. Avocations: bowling, writing, singing, teaching, preaching. Home: 9916 Castle Dr Saint Louis MO 63136 Home Phone: 314-388-4747; Office Phone: 314-369-1200. Personal E-mail: fojccollege@aol.com.

HINTZ, CHAD JASON, lawyer; b. Minot, ND, July 3, 1974; m. Michelle Hintz. BA in Architecture, U. Minn., 1996; JD, William Mitchell Coll. Law, 2001. Bar: Minn. 2001, US Dist. Ct. (dist. Minn.) 2004, US Ct. Appeals (8th cir.) 2004. Assoc. Burke & Thomas, P.L.L.P., St. Paul, 2002—. Adj. prof. appellate advocacy William Mitchell Coll. Law, 2005. Contbr. articles to profl. publs. Named a Rising Star, Minn. Super Lawyers mag., 2006. Mem.: Def. Rsch. Inst., Minn. Def. Lawyers Assn., Minn. State Bar Assn. (mem. professionalism com. 2004—05), Ramsey County Bar Assn. Office: Burke & Thomas PLLP 3900 Northwoods Dr Ste 200 Saint Paul MN 55112 Office Phone: 651-490-1808. E-mail: hintz@burkeandthomas.com.*

HINTZ, PAM K., secondary school and science educator; b. Drayton, ND, Feb. 21, 1960; d. Edward and Lois Ososki; m. Kenneth D. Hintz, Dec. 28, 1983; children: Robert K., Steven D.; 1 child, Shanna M. Shanahan. BS, U. Mary, Bismarck, ND, 1982. Tchr. secondary sci. Grant County H.S., Elgin, ND, 1982—. Edn. liaison Am. Legion Aux., Elgin, ND, 1990—2006; musician St. John's Cath. Ch., New Leipzig, 1982—2006; nd sci. fair dir. ND Sci. and Engring. Fair, Fargo, 2005—06; dir./facilitator ND State Water Commn. - Divsn. Edn., Bismarck, 1994—2006. Recipient ND Environ. Educator Yr., ND Forestry Divsn., 2002; grantee, Mont.-Dakota Utilities, 2004, ND Game and Fish, 2004, U. ND, 2004. Mem.: ND State Sci. Tchrs. Assn. (assoc.), Nat. Sci. Tchr. Assn. (assoc.). Roman Catholic. Avocations: camping, fishing. Home: 301 2nd Ave NW Elgin ND 58533 Office: Grant County High Sch 110 N West St Elgin ND 58533 Home Phone: 701 584 2357; Office Phone: 701 584-2374. Personal E-mail: kdhintz@westriv.com.

HINTZ, SCOTT RAYMOND, investor, financial consultant; s. Jack Raymond Hintz and Bobbie Jo Wagner-McElroy; m. Andrea Jean Vaughn-Hintz (div.); children: Hayden, Logan. BA in Bus. Adminstrn., Calif. State U., Fullerton, 1992; LLB, West Coast Sch. Law, Downey, Calif., 2006. Lic. N.A.S.D. Series 7 & 63, Ga. Life and Annuity Ins. Mktg. asst. Merrill Lynch, LA, 1990—92, registered rep. NYC, 1992, Bear Stearns, Atlanta, 1993; fin. cons. Merrill Lynch, Atlanta, 1993—94; investment exec. Paine Webber, Atlanta, 1994—98; self-employed investor Atlanta, 1993—. Pres. Falcon Mgmt. Group, Atlanta, 1997—; mng. mem. Hintz Properties, Atlanta, 1999—. Vol. Vets. Hosp., Calif. and Ga., 1987—, U.S. Ho. of Reps., Calif., 1985—88. Group exec. officer USAF, 1988, Colo. Finalist Jr. Achievement, Calif.; named to Honor Rolls, Nat. and Golden Key Honor Socs., Calif., Commandant's and Deans' Honor Rolls, USAF and Prep Sch., Colo. Mem.: Mensa. Avocations: boxing, flying, golf, skiing, tennis. E-mail: scott_r_hintz@yahoo.com.

HINZ, CARL FREDERICK, JR., immunologist, educator; b. Cleve., Apr. 9, 1927; s. Carl Frederick and Marie (Jones) H.; m. Joan Herndon, June 5, 1953; children— Elizabeth, Richard, Catherine, Gretchen. BS, Western Res. U., 1948, MD, 1951. Faculty dept. medicine Western Res. U. Sch. Medicine, Cleve., 1953-67, asst. prof., 1961-67, research asso. div. research in med. edn., 1964-67; prof., asso. dean U. Conn. Sch. Medicine, 1967-92, acting head dept. medicine, 1979-80, emeritus, 1992—. Mem. Conn. Med. Exam. Bd., 1976-80 Chmn. bd. dirs. blood svcs. Conn. region ARC, 1993-95, chair coun. of chairs North Atlantic area, 1995-98. Markle scholar, 1959-64; scholar-in-residence Inst. Medicine, Nat. Acad. Sci., 1987-88. Fellow ACP; mem. Am. Soc. Clin. Investigation, Am. Assn. Immunologists, Am. Soc. Hematology, Central Soc. Clin. Research, Am. Fedn. Clin. Research, Conn. Med. Soc., Hartford County Med. Assn. (dir. 1976-92, pres. 1986-87), Conn. Lung Assn. (pres. 1979-81) Home: 11 Highwood Dr Avon CT 06001-2411

HINZ, THEODORE VINCENT, architect; b. June 5, 1933; s. Theodore V. and Lillian (Adolph) H.; m. Louise R. Symmons; 1 child, Linda. BArch, Pratt Inst., 1956. Registered arch., NY, NJ, Va., Md., Conn., Ill. Draftsman, designer Muller & Ash Archs., NYC, 1956-59; designer Urban, Brayton & Burrows, NYC, 1959; designer, project arch. Goldstone & Dearborn, NYC, 1959-66, assoc., 1966-70; ptnr. Goldstone, Dearborn & Hinz, NYC, 1970-73, Goldstone & Hinz, NYC, 1973—. Capt. C.E., U.S. Army, 1956-57. Recipient cert. Merit for Excellence in Design for Greenacre Park, 1972, Good Neighbor award Volvo Hdqs. N.J. Mfg. Assn., 1973, Bus. Friend of Arts award, 1988, Lumen citation Illumination Engring. Soc., 1990, Spl. Recognition award Concrete Industry Bd., 1993, Build N.Y. award Gen. Bldg. Contractors of N.Y., 1993. Mem. AIA, N.Y. Soc. Archs., N.Y. State Assn. Archs., Constrn. Specifications Inst., Bayside Hist. Soc. (trustee 1975-77, 81-83, v.p. 1977-79, pres. 1979-81), Queens Hist. Soc. (trustee 1980-87). Office: Goldstone & Hinz Architects PC 104 E 40th St Rm 803 New York NY 10016-1838 Office Phone: 212-986-7855.

HINZ, WILLIAM MAX, retired pediatrician, military officer; b. Grafton, Wis., May 28, 1935; s. William Herman Hinz and Ilma Louise Weipking Hinz; m. Eleanor Marie Ryan, June 13, 1964; children: Eleanor, Nancy, William, Margaret. BS, U. Wis., Madison, 1961; MD, George Wash. U., Washington, 1964; Navy Flight Surgeon, Naval Aerospace Med. Inst., Penscola, Fla., 1979. Cert. Am. Bd. Pediat., NC. Gen. med. officer, Vietnam, 1967—68; pediatrician USNH, Bremerton, Wash., West Side Clin., Green Bay, Wis.; flight surgeon NAS Agana, Guam, 1979—81; dir. clin. svcs. Naval Hosp., LeMoore, Calif., 1981—83; pediatrician pvt. practice, Kingsford, Mich., 1983—97; chief of staff Dickinson County Meml. Hosp., 1995—97; ret., 2005. Contbr. articles to profl. jour. Sgt. USMC, 1954—57, capt. USN, 1963—95, comdg. officer USNR, 1993—95. Decorated Nat. Defense Svc. medal (3), Vietnam Svc. medal, Vietnam Campaign medal, Legion Merit, Navy Commeddation medal (2); recipient Vietnam Cross Gallantry, Presdl. Unit Citation. Mem.: AMA, Assn. Mil. Surgeons U.S., Am. Acad. Pediat. Independent. Luthern. Avocations: reading, sports. Office Phone: 262-692-9350.

HIPFEL, STEVEN J., lawyer; Grad., U.S. Army Command and Gen. Staff Coll., 1998; LLM in Environ. Law, George Washington U., 2000. Head internat. environ. law br. Internat. and Operational Law Divsn. Office of Judge Advocate Gen. of Navy, Pentagon, 1997—99; acting ocean affairs asst. Under Sec. of Def. for Policy, Pentagon, 1998; environ. counsel to commdr. Navy Region S.W., 2000—03, chief naval ops. environ. coun., 2003—. Contbr. articles to profl. jours.; article submissions editor: Environ. Lawyer, 1999—2000, bd. editors: Free Speech Yearbook, 1997—2000. Address: 6035 Wilmington Dr Burke VA 22015 Office Phone: 703-602-6843. E-mail: shipfel@aol.com.

HIPP, WILLIAM HAYNE, broadcast executive; b. Greenville, SC, Mar. 11, 1940; s. Francis Moffett and Mary Matilda (Looper) H.; m. Anna Kate Reid, June 14, 1963; children: Mary Hengian, Francis Reid, Anna Hayne. BA, Washington and Lee U., 1962; MBA, U. Pa., 1965. With Met. Life Ins. Co., 1965-69; v.p. Liberty Life Ins. Co., Greenville, SC, 1969-74, exec. v.p., 1977-79, chmn. bd. dirs., 1979—; chief exec. officer Liberty Corp., Greenville, 1979—, also bd. dirs. Bd. dirs. Wachovia Corp., SCANA Corp., S.C. Rsch. Authority, Trustee, vice-chmn. Nat. Urban League, 1979-89; trustee Com. Econ. Devel., N.Y., 1988—, Episcopal H.S., Alexandria, Va., 1982-88; chmn. Greenville Urban League, 1978, Greenville YMCA, 1979; trustee Greenville County Sch. Sys., 1975-76, Washington and Lee U., Lexington, Va., 1985-95, Greenville C. of C., 1985; trustee, chmn. Alliance for Quality Edn., 1986—, Greenville Hosp. Sys., 1989-95; bd. dirs. Am. Coun. Life Ins., 1995—, S.C. State Devel. Bd., 1980-85, and others. Mem. Greenville C. of C. (chmn. 1985). Office: Liberty Corp PO Box 789 2000 Wade Hampton Blvd Greenville SC 29615-1037

HIPPEAU, ERIC, book publishing executive; b. Paris, Aug. 16, 1951; came to U.S., 1986; Student, Sorbonne Univ., Paris. V.p. computer publs. IDG, NYC; pub. IDG Info World; pub. Computer World Ziff-Davis, NYC, 1989—90, exec. v.p., 1990—91, pres., COO, 1991, chmn., CEO, 1991—93, Ziff Comms. Co., NYC, 1993—2000; pres., exec. mng. dir. Softbank Intl. Ventures, 2000—. Dir. Yahoo!, Inc., 1996—. Office: Ziff-Davis Inc 28 E 28th St New York NY 10016-7900

HIPPENSTEELE, DAVID SIMON, engineer; b. Ft. Wayne, Ind., Feb. 14, 1977; s. Michael Dale and Donna Kay Hippensteele; m. Krista Eileen Bubb, Aug. 28, 2004. BME, Purdue U., Ft. Wayne, 2002; MBA, Ind. U., Ft. Wayne, 2006. EIT Ind., 2002. Engr. McCoy Bolt Works, Inc, Ft. Wayne, 1999—2002; devel. engr. McCoy Bolt Works, Inc., Ft. Wayne, 2003—; process engr. Millennium Industries, Ligonier, Ind., 2002—03. Mem.: Soc. Automotive Engrs., Mensa. Achievements include patents pending for load detection nut. Home: 6011 Allendale Ct Fort Wayne IN 46809 Office: McCoy Bolt Works Inc 2811 Congressional Pkwy Fort Wayne IN 46808 Home Phone: 260-747-6194; Office Phone: 260-482-4476. Office Fax: 260-483-6775. Business E-Mail: daveh@mccoybolt.com.

HIPPLE, WALTER JOHN, language educator; b. Chgo., Mar. 14, 1921; s. Walter John and Emilie (Scheu) H.; m. Anne Ruth Poier, Nov. 27, 1962; children: Heidi Kristina, Ethan John; m. Kay F. Moomaw. BA, U. Chgo., 1947, MA, 1948, PhD, 1954; postdoctoral, U. London, 1957, Cambridge U., Eng., 1961-62; LittD, Shimer Coll., 1977. Lectr. Roosevelt U., Chgo., 1948; instr. U. Chgo., 1948-50, U. Ark., 1951-52; asst. prof. U. Fla., Gainesville, 1952-56; assoc. prof. Cornell Coll., Mt. Vernon, Iowa, 1957-61; prof. U. Pacific, Calif., 1962, Idaho State U., 1963, U. So. Calif., 1963; prof., chmn. dept. humanities Ind. State U., Terre Haute, 1963-72; dean Shimer Coll., Mt. Carroll, Ill., 1972-76; acad. v.p. West Chester (Pa.) State Coll., 1976-77; prof. philosophy West Chester (Pa.) U., 1977-91, assoc. to pres., 1977-79, dir. honors, 1979-91, prof. emeritus, 1991; prof. English Heilongjiang (People's Republic of China) U., Harbin, 1991-92. Chmn. Com. on Humanities in Secondary Schs. Ind., 1965-69; prof. univs. and insts. in Peoples Republic of China, 1986-92; guest prof. U. Autonomous Region Caribbean Coast Nicaragua, 1997, U. Guyana, 2001, Ginling Coll., Nanjing Normal U., Peoples Republic of China, 2004-05. Author: The Beautiful, the Sublime and the Picturesque in Eighteenth Century British Aesthetic Theory, 1957; editor, author introduction: Alexander Gerard, An Essay on Taste, 1963; contbr. articles to profl. jours. With U.S. Army, 1943-45. Guggenheim fellow, 1961-62. Home: 328 S Darlington St West Chester PA 19382-3341 Business E-Mail: whipple@wcupa.edu.

HIPWELL, ARTHUR P., lawyer, managed health care company executive; b. 1949; BBA, U. Notre Dame; JD, U. Louisville. Bar: 1976. Tax counsel Humana, Inc., 1979—90, v.p., assoc. gen. counsel, 1990—92, sr. v.p., gen. counsel, 1992—93, 1994—99, 1999—, Galen Health Care, Inc., 1993—94. Office: Humana Inc 500 W Main St Louisville KY 40202*

HIRABAYASHI, LANE RYO, political science professor; b. Seattle; BA with honors, Sonoma State Coll., 1974; MA in Anthropology, U. Calif., Berkeley, 1976, PhD, 1981. Vis. lectr. U. Calif., Santa Barbara, 1982, Calif. State U., Long Beach, 1982, UCLA, 1983, San Francisco State U., 1983, assoc. prof., 1984; prof. Asian Am. and Ethnic Studies U. Colo., Boulder; prof. ethnic studies U. Calif., Riverside; George and Sakaye Aratani prof. Japanese Am. internment, redress, and cmty. Dept. Asian Am. Studies., UCLA, 2006—. Cons. Japanese Am. Nat. Mus., Los Angeles, 1985—. Contbr. articles to profl. jours. Mem. Ctr. Japanese Am. Studies, San Francisco, 1975; bd. dirs. Japanese Community Youth Council, San Francisco, 1983—. Doctoral fellow Inter-Am. Found., 1977-79; post-doctoral fellow UCLA, 1981. Mem. Am. Anthropol. Assn., Assn. for Asian Am. Studies. Office: UCLA Asian Am Studies Dept BOX 957225 3336 Rolfe Hall Los Angeles CA 90095 Office Phone: 310-267-5592. Office Fax: 310-267-5590. E-mail: hirabaya@ucla.edu.

HIRAHARA, PATTI, public relations executive; b. Lynwood, Calif., May 10, 1955; d. Frank C. and Mary K. Hirahara; m. Terry K. Takeda, Sept. 1995. AA, Cypress Coll., 1975; BA, Calif. State U., Fullerton, 1977. Pub. affairs dir. United TV, LA, 1977-80; v.p. Asian Internat. Broadcasting Co., LA, 1980-81; mktg. cons. Disneyland, Anaheim, Calif., 1982; pub. rels. agt. Japan External Trade Orgn., LA, 1982-86, 87-92; owner, pres. Prodns. By Hirahara, Anaheim, 1982—. Comml. photographer Hirahara Photography, Anaheim, 1977-83; publicist Tokyo Met. Govt., 1981, World Trade Week So. Calif., 1997, 98, 99; advisor State Colo. Trade Mission to Japan, 1986, State Ariz. Trade/Investment Mission to Japan, 1987, County Riverside, Calif. for Japanese trade, investment, tourism, 1986-88; coord. JETRO's Bus. Study Series, L.A., 1988; advisor Japan External Trade Orgn., 1987-88, TV Prodr./Host: Images, 1980, Expressions, 1994; reader panel Callaway Mag., 2005. Mem. reader panel Golf for Women Mag., Callaway Golf Mag., 2005. Bd. dirs. Nisei Week Japanese Festival, L.A., 1980-81; mem. Anaheim H.S. 20 Yr. Reunion Com., 1993. Nat. scholar Seventeen Mag. Youth Adv. Coun., 1973; named Orange County Nisei Queen, Suburban Optimist Club, Buena Park, Calif., 1974, nat. semi-finalist Outstanding Working Women Competition Glamour Mag., 1975; recipient svc. award Suburban Optimist Club of Buena Park, 1975. Mem. NAFE, Soc. Profl. Journalists (bd. dirs. 1980-81), World Trade Ctr. Assn. Orange County, Japanese Am. Citizens League, Am. Women in Radio and TV (bd. dirs. So. Calif. chpt. 1980-82, vice-chair western conf. 1981), So. Calif. Golf Assn., Pub. Rels. Soc. Am. (Orange County chpt. 1990), Adelaide Price Elem. Sch. (30 yr. reunion chair 1997), Suburban Optimist Club of Buena Park (bd. dirs. 1993-96, chairperson 30th Anniversary Celebration 1996, Optimist of Yr. 1995-96), Anaheim (Calif.) Hills Women's Golf Club (v.p., bd. dirs. 2005), Alpha Gamma Sigma.

HIRAI, CRAIG KAZUO, accountant; b. Honolulu, Jan. 3, 1949; s. Ralph and Tamie (Matsuo) H.; m. Linda Kuulei Goto, Oct. 12, 1980; children: Susan, Midori. BS, U. So. Calif., 1970; MS, MBA, U. Pa., 1971-72; JD, U. Calif., Hastings, 1978; LLM in Taxation, NYU, 1979. Bar: Hawaii 1978, U.S. Dist. Ct. Hawaii, 1978, U.S. Tax Ct. 1979, U.S. Ct. Appeals (9th cir.) 1982; CPA, Hawaii, lic. real estate broker, Hawaii. Assoc. Fong & Miho, Honolulu, 1980-82; from assoc. to dir. Torkildson, Katz, Fonseca, Jaffe, Moore & Hetherington, Honolulu, 1982—2004; dir. Bowen Hunsaker Hirai, CPAs, APC, Honolulu, 2004—. Mem. 1st taxation dist. Hawaii Bd. of Taxation Rev., 1988-92; chmn., vice chmn. Hawaii Rental Housing Trust Fund Commn., 1992-98. Deacon Ctrl. Union Ch., Honolulu, 1988-92, trustee, 1992-95; chmn. Hawaii Rental Housing Trust Fund Adv. Commn., 1998-2000, Hawaii Tax Rev. Commn., 2001-03; dir. Housing and Cmty. Devel. Corp. Hawaii, 1998-2000, Hawaii Cmty. Reinvestment Corp., 2004—. Mem. ABA, AICPA, Hawaii Bar Assn., Hawaii Soc. CPAs (chmn. tax com. 1986-87, vice chmn., then chmn. ethics com. 1994-95, 99—), Hawaii Assn. Realtors (chmn. taxation/fin. subcom. 1988-2001, vice-chmn. legis. com. 1992-93, 96-99, 2004-05) Democrat. Home: 802 Puuikena Dr Honolulu HI 96821-2500 Office: Bowen Hunsaker Hirai CPAs APC 733 Bishop St Ste 2020 Honolulu HI 96813 Home Phone: 808-373-9909; Office Phone: 808-526-2020. E-mail: craig@bhhcpa.net.

HIRAI, DENITSU, surgeon; b. Yokkaichi, Mie, Japan, July 27, 1943; came to U.S. 1969; s. Denyomu and Shizuo (Tanaka) H.; m. Fumiko Hada, June 14, 1969; 1 child, R. Lisa. MD, U. Tokyo, 1968; MBA, U. So. Calif., 2003. Diplomate Am. Bd. Surgery, Am. Bd. Quality Assurance and Utilization Rev. Physicians, Am. Bd. Surg. Critical Care; cert. nutrition support physician; cert. wound care specialist. Intern and residency Waterbury (Conn.) Hosp., 1969-74; fellow Mt. Sinai Hosp., 1974-75; asst. chief surgery VA Med. Ctr., Lincoln, Nebr., 1975-80, chief surgery, 1981-2000; asst. clin. prof. surgery Creighton U., Omaha, 1982-84, asst. prof. surgery, 1984-2000; clin. instr. U. Nebr., Omaha, 1986-88, clin. asst. prof. surgery, 1988-2000; assoc. prof. clin. surgery, mem. surgery staff Sch. Medicine U. So. Calif., LA, 2000—. Author: Brain Ticklers (Japanese), 1983. Fellow ACS, Am. Coll. Critical Care Medicine; mem. AAAS, AMA, ACS, Am. Soc. Parenteral and Enteral Nutrition, Soc. Am. Gastrointestinal Endoscopic Surgeons, Southwestern Surg. Congress, Soc. Critical Care Medicine, Assn. VA Surgeons. Avocations: photography, braille transcription, karate. Office: LAOPC 351 E Temple St Los Angeles CA 90012 Personal E-mail: dhirai@usc.edu.

HIRAI, KAZUO (KAZ), electronics executive; b. Tokyo, 1964; B in Liberal Arts, Internat. Christian Univ., Tokyo, 1984. With CBS/Sony Inc. (now Sony Music Entertainment Japan), 1984, Sony Music Japan, NYC; joined Sony Computer Entertainment Am., Inc., Foster City, Calif., 1995—, pres., 1996—2006, CEO, 2003—06, chmn., 2006—07; v.p. corp. exec. group Sony Computer Entertainment, Inc., Tokyo, 2006—07, pres., 2006—07, group COO, 2006—07, chmn., group chief exec., 2007—. Named Mogul in the Running, "New Establishment List", Vanity Fair, 2004; named one of Most Powerful Executives in the Business, Entertainment Weekly. Office: Sony Corp 7-35 Kitashinagawa 6-chome Tokyo 141-0001 Japan Office Phone: 650-655-8000.*

HIRANANDANI, MANISH ASHOK, electrical engineer; arrived in US, 2002; s. Ashok and Hema Hiranandani; m. Neha Hiranandani. BS in Electronics and Comm. Engring. with honors, Jawaharlal Nehru Technol. U., Hyderabad, India, 2002; MSEE, U. Miss., Oxford, 2005. Rsch. asst. Ctr. Applied Electromagnetics Sys. Rsch., Oxford, Miss., 2002—05; radio frequency hardware engr. Intel Corp., Hillsboro, Oreg., 2005—. Recipient Grad. Senator Svc. award, Grad. Student Coun., U. Miss., 2004—05, Best Grad. Student Presentation award, Miss. Acad. Scis., 2005; Grad. Rsch. grant, Grad. Rsch. Coun., U. Miss., 2004—05. Mem.: IEEE, Microwave Theory and Techniques Soc., Antenna Propagation Soc., Toastmasters Club. Home: 2613 NW Overlook Dr Apt 925 Hillsboro OR 97124 Office:

Intel Corp 5200 Elam Young Pky Mail Stop HF1-1-06 Hillsboro OR 97124 Office Phone: 503-696-9605. Personal E-mail: manish.hiranandani@gmail.com. Business E-Mail: manish.a.hiranandani@intel.com.

HIRANO, ASAO, neuropathologist, educator; b. Tomioka, Gunma, Japan, Nov. 26, 1926; s. Yoshiro and Miyoe Hirano; m. Keiko Okubo, May 23, 1959; children: Michio, Ikuo, Yoko, Shigeo MD, Kyoto U., 1952. Chief resident neurology Montefiore Hosp., Bronx, 1957-58; vis. scientist NIH, 1959-65; head div. neuropathology Montefiore Med. Ctr., Bronx, 1965—95, Harry M. Zimmerman prof. neuropathology, 1995—; prof. pathology Albert Einstein Coll. Medicine, 1971—, prof. neurosci., 1974—. Vis. prof. Kansai Med. U., Osaka, Japan, 1985, Nippon Med. Sch., Tokyo, 1993. Author: Atlas of Neuropathology, 2d rev. edit., 1974, A Guide to Neuropathology, 1976, 2d edit., 1986, 3d edit., 1992, 4th edit., 2003, English edit., 1981, German edit., 1983, Metastatic Tumors of the Nervous Systems, 1982, Color Atlas of Neuropathology, 1980, 3d edit., 2006, English 1st edit., 1988, French edit., 1981; editor: Neuropsychiatric Disorders in the Elderly, 1983, Patholoy of the Myelinated Axon, 1985, Amyotrophic Lateral Sclerosis, Progress and Perspectives in Basic Research and Clinical Application, 1995; mem. internat. editl. bd. Sec. 5 Excerpta Medica, 1976-; mem. editl. com. Neurol. Medicine, 1978-; mem. adv. bd. Jour. Neuropathology and Exptl. Neurology, 1971-81, mem. editl. bd., 1981-84; mem. editl. bd. Progress in Computerized Tomography, 1978-, Annals of Neurology, 1983-89, Acta Neuropathologica, 1991-2004, Amyotrophic Lateral Sclerosis and Other Motor Neuron Disorders, 1999-2004; mem. cons. editor Human Cell; mem. adv. bd. Clin. Neuropathology, 1982—. Neuropathology and Applied Neurobiology, 1983—2000; hon. editor Brain Tumor Pathology, 1993—, Neuropathology, 1994-2003; mem., neuropathology cons. Surg. Neurology, 1996—2004; mem. internat. adv. bd. Med. Electron Microscopy, 1997-; mem., cons. editor Human Cell. Recipient Billings Silver medal AMA, 1959, Key to Osaka City, Japan, 1977, Royal Coll. Lectr. award Can. Assn. Neuropathologists, Royal Coll. Physicians and Surgeons Can., 1980, 1st Jack Prichard Meml. Lectr. award Queen's U., Belfast, 1981, 1st Endowment Lectr. of Neuropathology in memory of Mrs. Rajan Bharati and 150th Yr. Celebration of Madras Med. Coll., 1984, Commendation award Hon. Ben Blaz, 1992, Plaque, U.S. Ho. Reps., 1992, Order of Rising Sun, Gold Rays with Rosette, Govt. of Japan, 2001. Mem.: World Fedn. Neurology (rsch. com. 1978), Brit. Neuropathol. Soc. (assoc. 1982—2000), Am. Soc. Cell Biology, Am. Assn. Neuropathologists (pres. 1977—78, Weil award 1968, award for meritorious contbn. to neuropathology 1995), Australian and New Zealand Soc. Neuropathology (hon.), Western Pacific Neurol. Soc. (hon.), Japanese Soc. Neuropathology (hon.), Internat. Soc. Neuropathology (hon.), Am. Neurol. Assn. (hon.), Japanese Soc. Neurosurgery (sr.), Am. Acad. Neurology (sr.), Assn. for Rsch. in Nervous and Mental Diseases (sr.). Office: Montefiore Med Ctr 111 E 210th St Bronx NY 10467-2401 Office Phone: 718-920-4447. Business E-Mail: ahirano@montefiore.org.

HIRANO, IRENE ANN YASUTAKE, museum director; b. LA, Oct. 7, 1948; d. Michael S. and Jean F. (Ogino) Yasutake; 1 child, Jennifer. BS in Pub. Adminstrn., U. So. Calif., 1970, MPA, 1972. Project adminstr. U. So. Calif., 1970-72; assoc. dir. Asian Women's Ctr., 1972-73; nat. project coord., Japanese site supr. Nat. Asian Am. Field Study, LA, 1973-75; cons. U.S. Dept. Health, Edn. and Welfare, Adminstn. on Aging, San Francisco, 1975; exec. dir. T.H.E. Clinic for Women, Inc., LA, 1975-88; exec. dir., pres. Japanese Am. Nat. Mus., LA, 1988—. Pres., CEO Nat. Ctr. for Preservation of Democracy, 2000-; lectr., spkr. in field. Mem. L.A. Ednl. Alliance for Restructuring Now, 1993—, Pres's. Com. on Arts & Humanities, 1994—, Commn. on Future of Smithsonian Inst., 1993—, L.A. Coalition, 1993—, accreditation commn., Am. Assn. Mus.; trustee Marlborough Sch., 1993—; co-founder Leadership Edn. for Asian Pacifics, 1983, pres. 1983-86, v.p. 1986-90; pres., bd. dirs. Asian Pacific Am. Support Group, U. So. Calif., 1984-88; bd. dirs. Liberty Hill Found., 1984-88, community funding bd., 1981-84; trustee, chair Kresge Found., Troy, Mich.; chairperson Calif. Commn. on the Status of Women, 1981-82, commn. mem., 1976-83; adv. bd. on North Am. Diversity, Toyota; nat. bd. mem. Smithsonian Inst.; bd. mem. and sec.-treas. LA, Inc. Convention and Visitors Bur.; vice-chair Calif. Japanese Am. Cmty. Leadership Coun. Recipient Nat. Outstanding Asian/Pacific Islander award NEA, 1983, Outstanding Women of the '90's, Robinson's Corp., 1992, Outstanding Svc. award Nat. Women's Polit. Caucus, 1986, Nat. Inst. Women of Color, 1984, Outstanding Alumni award U. So. Calif., 1994, So. Calif. Hist. Soc. Cmty. award, 1995. Office: Japanese Am Nat Mus 369 E First St Los Angeles CA 90012-3901*

HIRAYAMA, EIJI, psychologist, educator; b. Tokyo, Sept. 13, 1955; s. Gosai Hirayama and Shizuko Lee; m. Atsuko Hanaoka; three children. BA, Aoyamagakuin U., Tokyo, 1979, Rikkyo U., 1981; MA, Kyushu U., Fukuoka, Japan, 1986, PhD, 1996. Cert. clin. psychologist. Chief Psychol. Clinic, Kyushu U., Fukuoka, 1989-90; counselor Student Counseling Ctr., Fukuoka U., 1990-96; assoc. prof. Matsuyama (Japan) Shinonome Coll., 1996-99, Aoyama Gakuin U., Tokyo, 1999—; vis. scholar UCLA, 2004—06. Author: Clinical Psychology Today: On Mental Health, 1994, Encounter Group and the Process of Personal Growth, 1998, Group Approach in Psychotherapy, 2004; contbr. articles to profl. jours. Mem. APA, Japan Psychoanalytical Assn., Assn. Japanese Clin. Psychology (The Most Disting. Sci. award 1999). Home: 2-4-12 Nishi-Ohi Shinagawa-ku Tokyo 140-0015 Japan Office: Aoyama Gakuin U Dept Psychology 4-4-25 Shibuya Shibuya-ku Tokyo 150-8366 Japan Office Phone: 81-3-3409-7665. Business E-Mail: ehirayama1@yahoo.co.jp.

HIRES, WILLIAM LELAND, psychologist, consultant; b. South Orange, NJ, July 5, 1918; s. Harrison Streeter and Christine B. (Leland) H.; m. Karen Reynolds Perrott, July 12, 1975; 1 child, Jennifer Leland. BS, Haverford Coll., 1949; PhD, U. Pa., 1972. Asst. to dean of admissions, asst. dir of scholarships U. Pa., 1952-55; supr. psychol. svcs., spl. classes, asst. supt. Office Supt. Chester County (Pa.) Schs., 1956-59; assoc. prof. West Chester Coll., 1960-61; adminstrv. asst. Office of Pres., asst. to sec. U. Pa., 1961-64; assoc. Edward N. Hay & Assocs., 1964-65; asst. supt. pub. schs. Chester County, 1966-68, pvt. cons., 1968-75; dir. diagnostic and consultative svc. Chester County Intermediate Unit, 1975-76, pvt. practice psychology, 1976-78; dir. pupil svcs. Upper Darby (Pa.) Sch. Dist., 1978-81; dean acad. studies Curtis Inst. Music, Phila., 1981-86; ptnr. Hires Assocs., Phila., 1987—. With USMC, 1942—46, with US Army, 1941—42, with US Army, 1950—52, lt. col. AUS, 1978—, col. hon. Pa. Army N.G. ret. Mem. AAAS, APA, Soc. of Cin., Welcome Soc., Hist. Soc. Pa., 1st Troop Phila. City Cavalry (hon.), Soc. Colonial Wars Pa. (hon. gov.), Phila. Club, Franklin Inn Club, Merion Cricket Club, Harvard-Radcliffe Club of Phila., The Rabbit, Aztec Club of 1847. Personal E-mail: whires@comcast.net.

HIRJI, RAFIK F., water resources expert; b. Lindi, Tanzania, July 22, 1956; arrived in U.S., 1983; s. Fatehali H. and Sakar H. Sunderji; 1 child, Zahra R. BSCE, U. of Dar es Salaam, Tanzania, 1981; MSc in Environ. Engring. and Sci., Stanford U., Calif., 1984, PhD in Water Resources Planning, 1990. Registered profl. civil engr., Calif. Design engr. Gauff Engrs., Gmbh, Dar es Salaam, 1981—83; sr. water resources engr. Montgomery Watson Engrs., Sacramento, 1989—93; sr. water resources specialist World Bank, Washington, 1994—. Editor: World Bank Water Resources and Environment Technical Note Series (14); author: Climate Variability and Water Resources Degradation in Kenya; editor: Defining and Mainstreaming Environmental Sustainability in Water Resources Management in Southern Africa; contbr. articles to profl. jours. Mem.: ASCE. Achievements include pioneering work on environmental aspects of water resources management and development; development of Leading Global Program on Lake Basin Management; Leading Global Effort on Environmental Flow Analysis. Office: World Bank 1818 H St NW Washington DC 20433 Home Phone: 301-656-4982.

HIRNING, FREDRIC CARL, pharmacist; b. Lodi, Calif., Aug. 20, 1947; s. Clarence Christian Reuben and Gertrude (Hoff) H.; m. Marilyn Kay Truitt, Aug. 31, 1968; children: Lindsay Ann, Katherine Erin, John Michael. BS in Pharmacy cum laude, U. of Pacific, 1970, PharmD cum laude, 1972. Cert. in pharmacy mgmt. U. NC, 1989, health care mgmt. U. Southern Calif., 1991, diabetes case mgmt. Am. Pharm. Assn. From pharmacist to dir. pharmacy Mercy Hosp., Sacramento, 1970-76; dir. pharmacy St. Joseph's Med. Ctr., Stockton, 1976-80, pharmacist, 1980-82, Relief Pharmacy Svc., Stockton, 1985-87; dir. pharmacy svcs. Sutter Davis Hosp., Calif., 1983-85, Drs. Hosp. Manteca, Calif., 1987—2003, clin. coord. pharmacy svcs., 1998—2003; con. pharmacist Omnicare Pharmacy, Stockton, Calif., 2003—05; staff pharmacist, diabetes case mgr. Raleys Pharmacy, Oakley, Calif., 2006—. Adj. prof. U. of the Pacific Sch. Pharmacy, Stockton, 1987-89, new dean search com., 1994-95; instr. chemical dependency studies Calif. State U., Sacramento, 1991-95; instr. drug & alcohol counselor cert. program U. of the Pacific, Stockton, 1993-95, bd. dirs. pharmacy assoc., 1990-97; field monitor Occupl. Healthcare Svcs., Larkspur, Calif., 1988-93; chmn. Calif. Vet. Diversion Com., 1993-95; vice-chmn. Calif. Nursing Diversion Com., 1992-94; cons. and presenter in field. Co-author: Purchasing and Inventory Control, 1992, Points of Light, A Guide for Helping., 1996; contbr. articles to profl. jours. Active Bishops Adv. Com. on Drug and Alcohol, Fresno, 1987—, Partners in Prevention/Parents Who Care, Stockton, 1987-95, Pharmacists Against Drug Abuse, 1986—, Calaveras County Drug Abuse Task Force, San Andreas, Calif., 1986-87, Leadership, Manteca, 1989-90; asst. scoutmaster Boy Scouts Am., Stockton, 1991-97; bd. dirs. PALS-Drug Treatment Program, Stockton, 1993-95; coun. mem. Lincoln H.S., Stockton, 1991-93. Recipient Geigy Leadership award Sacramento Valley Soc. Hosp. Pharmacists, 1976, Commendation award San Joaquin County Sheriff, 1982, Appreciation award Boy Scouts Am., 1990, Nat. Cmty. Svc. award U.S. Pharmacist jour., 1993; named Disting. Pharmacist, Roerig Pharmaceuticals, 1989, Disting. Alumni, U. of the Pacific Alumni Assn., 1997; named to Lodi Sports Hall of Fame, 1994. Fellow Am. Pharm. Assn. (del. 1990-95); mem. Internat. Pharmacy Fedn., Acad. Pharmacy and Practice & Mgmt. of Am. Pharm. Assn. (edn. standing com. 1993-94, vice-chmn. awards standing com., sect. chmn. 1994-95, Merit award 1999), Am. Soc. Health-Sys. Pharmacists, Calif. Pharmacists Assn. (editl. rev. com. 1993-99, ednl. found. adv. com. 1997-99, Bowl of Hygeia award 1991), Am. Inst. for the History of Pharmacy, Christian Pharmacists Fellowship Internat., Internat. Pharmacists Anonymous, Am. Pharm. Assn. Found., Am. Soc. Health-Sys. Pharmacists Found., Internat. Coalition Addiction Studies Educators, Acad. Hosp. Pharmacists (bd. dirs. 1994-96, Quality Commitment award 1995), San Joaquin Pharmacists Assn. (bd. dirs. 1989-94, pres. 1993), Cen. Valley Soc. Hosp. Pharmacists (bd. dirs. 1988-93, pres. 1992, Pharmacist of Yr. 1992), San Francisco Zool. Soc., U.S. Holocaust Meml. Mus. Assn., Nat. Eagle Scout Assn., Rho Chi. Republican. Episcopalian. Avocation: travel. Office: Raleys Pharmacy 2075 Main St Oakley CA 94561 Office Phone: 209-327-7156.

HIROKAMI, JUNICHI, conductor, music director; b. Tokyo, 1958; Grad., Tokyo Coll. Music, Japan, 1983. Asst. condr. to Yuzo Toyama Nagoya (Japan) Philharmonic Orch., 1983—84; prin. guest condr. Norrkoping Symphony Orch., Sweden, 1988—90, chief condr., 1990—95; guest condr. Royal Philharm., 1992—; permanent guest condr. Japan Philharmonic Orch., 1995—2006; chief condr. Limburg Orch., Maastricht, Netherlands, 1997—2002; prin. guest condr. Royal Liverpool Philharmonic, 1997—2000; music dir. Columbus Symphony Orch., 2006—. Concert condr. NHK Symphony Orch., Japan, 1985, Yomiuri Nippon Symphony Orch., Tokyo Met. Symphony Orch.; condr. concert tour Concertgebouw Orch. Condr.: Operas debut in Un Ballo in Maschera with Australian Opera, with Royal Philharmonic.; recording Norrkoping Orch.; guest appearances (TV series) Midnight Concerts, Nihon TV. Recipient winner, Kondrashin Internat. Conducting Competition, Amsterdam, 1984. Office: Columbus Symphony Orchestra 55 E State St Columbus OH 43215*

HIRONAKA, HEISUKE, mathematics professor, academic administrator; b. Yamaguchi-ken, Japan, Apr. 9, 1931; DPhil, Kyoto U., 1963; PhD, Harvard U., 1960. Prof. math. Harvard U., prof. emeritus; prof. Kyoto U., prof. emeritus; resident Yamaguchi U., Yamaguchi, Japan, 1996—2001; academic dir. U. Creation, Takasaki, Japan. Dir. Inamori Found.; faculty appointments Brandeis U., Columbia U.; hon. prof. Shang Dong U., China; mem. selection com. for math. sciences Shaw Prize, 2006. Recipient Fields medal Internat. Congress Nice, 1970, Order of Culture, Japan, 1975, Order Nat. de la Legion d'Honneur, 2004. Mem.: fgn. mem of the Academies of France, Russia, Korea and Spain, Am. Acad. Arts and Sciences, Japan Acad., Japan Assn. for Math. Sciences (now called Internat. Soc. for Math. Sciences) (pres.). Achievements include proof of the theorem concerning the resolution of singularities on an algebraic variety for all dimensions. Office: U Creation Art Music and Social Work Yachiyo Campus 2-3-6 Yachiyo-machi Takasaki-shi Gunma 370-0861 Japan Address: Internat Soc for Math Sciences 2-1-18 Minami Hanadaguchi-cho Sakai Osaka 590-0075 Japan E-mail: hironaka@math.harvard.edu.

HIRONO, MAZIE KEIKO, congresswoman, former lieutenant governor; b. Fukushima, Japan, Nov. 3, 1947; arrived in U.S., 1955, naturalized, 1959; m. Leighton Kim Oshima. BA, U. Hawaii, 1970; JD, Georgetown U., 1978. Dep. atty. gen., Honolulu, 1978-80; Shim, Tam, Kirimitsu & Naito, 1984-88; mem. Hawaii Ho. of Reps., Honolulu, 1980-94; lt. gov. State of Hawaii, 1994—2002; mem. US Congress from 2nd Hawaiian dist., 2007—. Bd. dirs. Nat. Asian Pacific Am. Bar Assn.; chair Hawaii Policy Group, Nat. Commn. on Tchg. and Ams. Future, Govs. Task Force on Sci. and Tech. Dep. chair Dem. Nat. Com., 1997; bd. dirs. Nuuanu YMCA, Honolulu, 1982—2004, Moiliili Cmty. Ctr., Honolulu, 1984—, Blood Bank of Hawaii. Mem. U.S. Supreme Ct. Bar, Hawaii Bar Assn., Phi Beta Kappa. Democrat. Office: 5104 Prince Kuhio Fed Bldg Honolulu HI 96850 also: 1229 Longworth House Office Bldg Washington DC 20515 E-mail: hirono@hawaii.rr.com.*

HIROSE, TERUO TERRY, surgeon, educator; b. Tokyo, Jan. 20, 1926; arrived in U.S., 1959; s. Yohei and Seiko (Ogushi) H.; m. Tomiko Kodama, June 1, 1976; 1 son, George Philamore. BS, Tokyo Coll., Japan, 1944; MD, Chiba U., Japan, 1948, PhD, 1958. Diplomate Am. Bd. Surgery, Am. Bd. Thoracic Surgery. Intern Chiba U. Hosp., Japan, 1948-49, resident in surgery, 1949-52; practice medicine specializing in surgery Chiba, Japan, 1952-53; resident in surgery Am. Hosp., Chgo., 1954; resident in thoracic surgery Hahnemann Med. Coll., Phila., 1955-56; chief of surgery Tsushimi Hosp., Hagi, Japan, 1958-59; tchg. fellow surgery NY Med. Coll., NYC, 1959-60; rsch. fellow advanced cardiovasc. surgery Hahnemann Hosp., Phila., 1959; asst. prof. surgery Chiba U., Japan, 1959; instr. NY Med. Coll., NYC, 1961-62, resident in thoracic surgery, 1961-62; sr. attending surgeon St. Barnabas Hosp., NYC, 1965-81; pvt. practice NYC, 1965-89, NJ, 1965-89; chief vascular surgery Union Hosp., Bronx, NY, 1966-67; attending surgeon Flower and Fifth Ave Hosp., NYC, 1973-80; clin. prof. surgery NY Med. Coll., NY, 1974-89; dir. cardiovasc. lab. St. Barnabas Hosp., NYC, 1975-84; attending surgeon Jewish Hosp. Med. Center, Bklyn., 1976-80, St. Vincent Hosp., NYC, 1976-88, Mamonides Hosp., Bklyn., 1976-78, Passaic Gen. Hosp., 1977-88, Westchester County Hosp., NY, 1977-78, Yonkers Profl. Hosp., NY, 1978-79, Westchester Sq. Hosp., 1978-84, Yonkers Gen. Hosp., Yonkers, NY, 1980-89, St. Joseph Hosp., Yonkers, NY, 1980-89; dir. KPMG Health Care, Japan, 1997—2001; chmn., prof. dept. head and health care admin. Shumei U., Tokyo, 1999—2006, prof. emeritus, 2006—, dean Premedical Tokyo, 2006—. Author: (in Japanese) A Chaos of American Medicine, 1987, Japanese Doctor, 1987, Where American Medicine Is Going, 1988, Major Surgery Without Blood Transfusion, 1990, Problems and Solutions of American Medicine, 1991, Warning for Modern Medical Science (New Medical Ethics), 1992, Comparative Studies of Medical System in the World, 1992, The Changing Face of Geriatrics, 1994, Monologue of Japanese American Physician, 1995, Environmental Medicine, 1998, Japan! Do Not Follow American Health Care System, 1998, Quality of Life in Modern Medicine, 1998, Medicine About Life and Death, 1998, 99, Why AIDS Can Not Be Conquered, 1999, Mechanism of Human Body, 2000, Comparison of Healthcare Systems Between U.S.A. and Japan, 2000, Medicine of Death, 2000, Lifestyle Related Medicine and Cutting Edge Technique, 2001, Alternative Medicine, 2001, Thanatology, 2000, Protect Japanese Health Care System By Health Care Reform, 2002, Basic and Practice of Health Care Administration, 2002, Better Understanding of Physician and Hospital, 2003, What Can We Learn from Medical Education System in USA, 2003, How Should We Take Care of Aged Population, 2004, Japanese Medicine in the 21st Century, 2005; editor Japanese Med. Planner Ltd.; contbr. moe than 900 articles to profl. jours. Recipient Hektoen Bronze medal, AMA, 1965, Gold medal, 1971. Fellow: NY Acad. Medicine, Internat. Coll. Surgeons, Am. Coll. Cardiology, Am. Coll. Chest Physicians, Am. Coll. Angiology; mem.: Soc. Vascular Surgery, Japanese Assn. Health Care Adminstrs. (chmn., pres. 1999—2006), Am. Writers Assn., Am. Fedn. Clin. Rsch., Am. Geriatric Soc., Internat. Cardiovasc. Soc., Pan Pacific Surg. Assn., NY Soc. Thoracic Surgery, Am. Assn. Thoracic Surgery, Japan PEN Club. Achievements include invention of single pass low prime oxygenator; pioneer aortocoronary direct bypass surgery, open heart surgery without blood transfusion. Office Phone: 718-884-1370. Personal E-mail: coronarybypass@earthlink.net. *One should respect another's religion or creed and offer assistance regardless of whether or not one is in agreement with the other's belief, provided that belief harms no other.*

HIRREL, LEO P., historian, retired military officer; b. Alexandria, Va., Dec. 31, 1952; s. Michael A. and Evelyn L. Hirrel. BA, Loyola Coll., Balt., 1974; MA, Univ. Va., Charlottesville, Va., 1981, PhD in History, 1989; MLS, Cath. Univ. of Am., Washington, 2000. Hist. cons., Gaithersburg, Md., 1995—98; libr. asst. Cath. Univ. of Am., Washington, 1998—99; hist. US Army Ctr. & Mil. History, Washington, 1999—2002, US Joint Forces Command, Norfolk, Va., 2002—. Project dir. Am. Religious Experience, Morgantown, W.Va., 1998—. Author: Children of Wrath: New School Calvinism and Antebellum Reform, 1998, Response to Terrorism: US Joint Forces Command of 11 September, 2003. Lt. col. USAR, 1974—2002. Mem.: Soc. Hist. Am. Republic. Home: 5020 Cypress Point Cir Virginia Beach VA 23455 Office: US Joint Forces Command 1562 Mitscher Ave #200 Norfolk VA 23551 Office Phone: 757-836-6369. Personal E-mail: leohirrel@aol.com.

HIRSCH, ANTHONY TERRY, physician; b. NYC, Jan. 29, 1940; s. Robert S. and Minna Hirsch; m. Barbara Hershan, July 8, 1961; children: Deborah, Kenneth, Steven. BS cum laude, Tufts U., 1961, MD, 1965. Diplomate Am. Bd. Pediatrics, Am. Bd. Allergy-Immunology. Pvt. practice pediatrics Children's Med. Group, LA, 1973-84; chair dept. pediatrics, dir. residency tng. program in pediatrics White Meml. Med. Ctr., LA, 1984—. Capt. USAF, 1969-71. Fellow Am. Acad. Pediatrics (chair access task force Calif. br., mem. nat. access task force, chair coun. on pediatric practice), Am. Acad. Allergy-Immunology. Avocation: sailing. Office: White Meml Med Ctr Dept Pediat 1701 Cesar Chavez Ave # 456 Los Angeles CA 90033-2410

HIRSCH, BETTE G(ROSS), academic administrator, language educator; b. NYC, May 5, 1942; d. Alfred E. and Gladys (Netburn) Gross; m. Edward Raden Silverblatt, Aug. 16, 1964 (div. Feb. 1975); children: Julia Nadine Silverblatt Young, Adam Edward Silverblatt; m. Joseph Ira Hirsch, Jan. 21, 1978; stepchildren: Hillary, Michelle, Michael. BA with honors, U. Rochester, 1964; MA, Case Western Res. U., 1967, PhD, 1971. Instr. and head French dept. Cabrillo Coll., Aptos, Calif., 1973-90, 2003—04, divsn. chair fgn. langs. and comms. divsn., 1990-95, interim dir. student devel., 1995-96, dean of instrn., transfer and distance edn., 1996—2003, emerita and adj. instr. French, 2004—. Mem. steering com. Santa Cruz County Fgn. Lang. Educators Assn., 1981-86; mem. liaison com. fgn. langs. Articulation Coun. Calif., 1982-84, sec., 1983-84, chmn., 1984-85; workshop presenter, 1982—; vis. prof. French Mills Coll., Oakland, Calif., 1983; mem. fgn. lang. model curriculum stds. adv. com. State Calif., 1984; instr. San Jose (Calif.) State U., summers 1984, 85; reader Ednl. Testing Svc. Advanced Placement French Examination, 1988, 89; peer reviewer for div. edn. programs, NEH, Washington, 1990, 91, 93; grant evaluator, NEH, 1995; mem. fgn. lang. adv. bd. The Coll. Bd., N.Y.C., 1986-91. Author: The Maxims in the Novels of Duclos, 1973; co-author (with Chantal Thompson) Ensuite, 1989, 93, 98, 2003, 05, Moments Litteraires, 1992, 2006, (with Chantal Thompson and Elaine Phillips) Mais Oui! workbook, lab. manual, video manual, 1996, 2000, 04; contbr. revs. and articles to profl. jours. Pres. Loma Vista Elem. Sch. PTA, Palo Alto, Calif., 1978-79; bd. dirs. United Way Stanford, Palo Alto, 1985-90, mem. allocations com., 1988, bd. dirs. Cabrillo Music Festival, 1996-2003, sec., 1998, v.p., 2000-2002; bd. dirs. Cmty. TV of Santa Cruz County, 1997-99, vice chair, 1997-98. Grantee NEH, 1980-81, USIA, 1992; Govt. of France scholar, 1982, 2003. Mem.: MLA (mem. adv. com. on fgn. langs. and lits. 1995—2000, chair 1999—2000, com. on info. tech. 2001—, chair 2003—, mem. com. on cmty. colls. 2004—, ad hoc com. on the structure of the ann. conv. 2006—), Am. Assn. Tchrs. of French, Assn. Depts. Fgn. Langs. (exec. com. 1985—88, pres. 1988), Assn. Calif. C.C. Adminstrs. Democrat. Jewish. Avocations: travel, reading, gourmet cooking, antiques. Home: 4149 Georgia Ave Palo Alto CA 94306-3813 Office: Cabrillo College 6500 Soquel Dr Aptos CA 95003-3194 Business E-Mail: behirsch@cabrillo.edu. *Treat life like a work of art in progress. Strive for the creative, the exceptional. Do it all with style.*

HIRSCH, CHARLES S., city health department administrator; b. Chgo., 1937; m. Claude Hirsch; 1 child, Sophie. BS, U. Ill., Urbana, 1958; MD, U. Ill., Chgo., 1962. Internist U. Hosp., Cleve., 1962—63; resident, pathology Case Western Reserve U. Inst. Pathology, Cleve., 1963—65; resident, neurol. pathology Md. State Med. Examiner's Office, Balt., 1965—66, resident, forensic pathology, 1966—67; dep. coroner Cayuga Co., Ohio, 1976—79; dir., forensic pathology Hamilton Co., Ohio, 1979—85; prof., forensic pathology SUNY Med. Sch., Stony Brook; med. examiner Suffolk Co., NY, 1985—89; prof., forensic medicine and pathology, chmn. NYU Sch. Medicine, NYC; chief med. examiner N.Y.C. Dept. Health and Mental Hygiene, 1989—. Recipient Disting. Alumnus award, U. Ill., Chgo., 2003. Office: Office of the Chief Medical Examiner 520 First Ave New York NY 10016

HIRSCH, DAVID L., lawyer; BA, Pomona Coll., 1959; JD, U. Calif., Berkeley, 1962. Bar: Calif. 1963. Dir. real estate, constrn. and property mgmt. svcs. and risk mgmt. coun. Metaldyne/NI Industries, Inc., Taylor, Mich., 1966—; pres. NI Industries, Inc., Taylor, Mich., 2004—. V.p. mem. commn. on Govt. Procurement for U.S. Congress, 1971. Mem. editl. bd. Bur. Nat. Affairs' Fed. Contracts Report. Fellow Am. Bar Found.; mem. ABA (life fellow of fellows, chair emerging issues com. sect. pub. contract law, sec. pub. contract law sect. 1977-78, mem. council 1978-80, chmn. 1981-82), Calif. Bar (bd. advisors pub. law sect.), Los Angeles County Bar Assn., Fed. Bar Assn., Nat. Contract Mgmt. Assn. (nat. bd. advisors), Fin. Exec. Inst. (legal advisor com. on govt. bus.). Office: Masco Tech Corp/NI Industries Inc 21001 Van Born Rd Taylor MI 48180-1340

HIRSCH, EDWARD MARK, language educator, poet; b. Chgo, Jan. 20, 1950; s. Kurt and Irma (Ginsburg) H.; m. Janet Landay, May 29, 1977. BA, Grinnell Coll., 1972; PhD, U. Pa., 1978. Asst. prof. Wayne State U., Detroit, 1978-82, assoc. prof., 1982-85, U. Houston, 1985-87, prof. English, 1987—; pres. John Simon Guggenheim Meml. Found., 2003—. Author: (poems) For the Sleepwalkers, 1981 (Lavan Younger Poets award 1985), Wild Gratitude, 1986 (Nat. Book Critics Cir. award), The Night Parade, 1989, Earthly Measures, 1994, On Love, 1998, Lay Back the Darkness, 2003; (prose) How to Read a Poem and Fall in Love with Poetry, 1999, Responsive Reading, 1999, The Demon and the Angel: Searching for the Source of Artistic Inspiration, 2002, Poet's Choice, 2006; editor: Transforming Vision: Writers on Art, 1994; co-editor: A William Maxwell Portrait, 2004, Theodore Roetlke: Selected Poems, 2005. Nat. Endowments for Arts Creative Writing fellow, 1982, Guggenheim fellow, 1985; recipient Tex. Inst. of Arts and Letters award, 1987, Lit. award Am. Acad. Arts Letters, 1998; recipient Prix de Rome, 1988, Lyndhurst prize, 1994-96; MacArthur fellow, 1998. Office: John Simon Guggenhaim Meml Found 90 Park Ave New York NY 10016 Office Phone: 212-687-4470.

HIRSCH, ERIC DONALD, JR., language educator; b. Memphis, Mar. 22, 1928; s. Eric Donald and Leah (Aschaffenburg) H.; m. Mary Monteith Pope, June 15, 1958; children: Eric, John, Frederick, Elizabeth. BA, Cornell U., 1950; MA, Yale U., 1955, PhD (Fulbright fellow), 1957; LittD (hon.), Williams Coll., 1989, Rhodes Coll., 1993, Rollins Coll., 1994, Marietta Coll., 1997. Instr. Yale, 1956-61, asst. prof. English, 1961-64, assoc. prof., 1964-66; prof. U. Va., Charlottesville, 1966—, chmn. dept. English, 1968-71, 81-83, dir. composition, 1971—, Kenan prof. English, 1973—, Linden Kent prof. English Charlottesville, 1989-94, Univ. prof. edn. and humanities, 1994; founder, chmn. Core Knowledge Found., Charlottesville, 1986—. Bd. dirs. U. Press; lectr. in field; supervising com. English Inst., 1972-74; mem. nat. adv. coun. N.Y. Regent's Competency Tests in Writing, 1979; advisor Nat. Coun. Ednl. Rsch., 1983; bd. dirs. Founds. Literacy Project, 1985—; pres. Cultural Literacy Found., 1987, Core Knowledge Found., 1990; dir. Albert Shanker Inst., 1997—. Author: Wordsworth and Schelling: A Typological Study of Romanticism, 1960, Innocence and Experience: An Introduction to Blake, 1964 (Explicator award), Validity in Interpretation, 1967, The Aims of Interpretation, 1976, The Philosophy of Composition, 1977, Cultural Literacy: What Every American Needs to Know, 1987; co-author: A Dictionary of Cultural Literacy, 1993, 2002; editor: A First Dictionary of Cultural Literacy, 1989, 2004, The Core Knowledge Series, Book I: What First Graders Need to Know, 1991, Book II: What Second Graders Need to Know, 1991, Book III: What Third Graders Need to Know, 1992, Book IV: What Fourth Graders Need to Know, 1992, Book V: What Fifth Graders Need to Know, 1993, Book VI: What Sixth Graders Need to Know, 1993, The Schools We Need and Why We Don't Have Them, 1996, The Knowledge Deficit, 2006; mem. adv. bd. Jour. Basic Writing, Blake Studies, Critical Inquiry, Genre New Lit. History, Lit. in Performance; contbr. articles to profl. jours. Pres. Coalition for Core Curriculum, 1989—, 1989—. With USNR, 1950—52. Recipient Fordham award 2003; Morse fellow, 1961-62, Guggenheim fellow, 1964-65, sr. fellow NEH, 1971, 80-81, fellow Center for Humanities Wesleyan U., 1973, fellow Council Humanities Princeton U., 1976, fellow Center for Advanced Study in Behavioral Scis., 1980-81, fellow Humanities Research Ctr., Australian Nat. U., 1982; Bateson lectr. Oxford U., 1983 Fellow: Internat. Acad. Edn. in Royal Acad. Sci. Lit. and Arts (Brussels); mem.: MLA, Am. Fedn. Tchrs. (Biennial Quest award 1997), Am. Acad. Arts and Scis. (supervisory com. 1981—86), Byron Soc. Home: 2006 Pine Top Rd Charlottesville VA 22903-1233 Personal E-mail: edh9k@aol.com. Business E-Mail: edh9k@virginia.edu.

HIRSCH, GEORGE AARON, publishing executive; b. NYC, June 21, 1934; s. George J. and Sylvia (Epstein) H.; m. Shay Yandell Scrivner; children: David Aaron, William George; stepchildren: Ian Gregory Scrivner, Sean Gabriel Scrivner. AB magna cum laude, Princeton U., 1956; MBA, Harvard U., 1962. With Time-Life Internat., 1962-67; founding pub., pres. New York Mag., NYC, 1967-71; chmn., pres., CEO New Times Comm. Corp., NYC, 1973-79; founding pub. New Times mag., NYC, 1973-79, The Runner Mag., NYC, 1978-87; v.p., pub. Runner's World Mag., 1987—2000, worldwide pub., 2000—02, worldwide pub. emeritus, 2003—04; group pub. Rodale Active Network, 1987—97; pub. dir. Men's Health mag., 1987—2002; dir. internat. mags. Rodale Press, 1995—2002. Host "The Runner's Corner", ESPN Sports Ctr., 1983—84; TV sports commentator Olympic Games, 1984, 88, 92; bd. dirs. Salon Media Group Inc.; chmn. bd. dirs. NY Roadrunners, Quadratown Pub. USA, La Cucina, Italy. A founder NYC Marathon, 1976; Dem. candidate for 15th Congl. Dist., NY, 1986; del. Dem. Nat. Conv., 1988. With USNR, 1957-60. Mem. Mag. Pubs. Assn. (chmn. internat. com. 2000-04), Century Assn. Club. Personal E-mail: georgehirsch1@hotmail.com.

HIRSCH, GILAH YELIN, artist, writer; b. Montreal, Que., Can., Aug. 24, 1944; came to U.S., 1963; d. Ezra and Shulamis (Borodensky) Y. BA, U. Calif., Berkeley, 1967; MFA, UCLA, 1970. Prof. art Calif. State U., Dominguez Hills, L.A., 1973—. Adj. prof. Internat. Coll., Guild Tutors, L.A., 1980-87, Union Grad. Sch., Cin., 1990 50 solo exhbns., mus. collections, 15 pubs. Founding mem. Santa Monica Art Bank, Calif., 1983-85; bd. dir. Dorland Mountain Colony, Temecula, Calif., 1984-88 Named artist-in-residence, RIM Inst., Payson, Ariz., 1989—90, Tamarind Inst. Lithography, Albuquerque, 1973, Rockefeller Bellagio Ctr., Italy, 1992, Tyrone Guthrie Ctr. for Arts, Annamahkerrig, Ireland, 1993, Internat. Sympat., Slovakia, 2004, 2005; recipient Disting. Artist award, Calif. State U., 1985, Found. Rsch. award, 1988—89, 1997—98, Creative Rsch. award, Sally Canova Rsch. Scholarship and Creative Activities awards program, 1997—99, 2003; grantee, Nat. Endowment Arts, 1985, Class Found., 2003, Calif. State U., Dominguez Hills, 2005, Panavision grantee, Panavision Films, Inc., L.A., 2005; Dorland Mountain Colony fellow, 1981—84, 1983, 1984, 1992, 1995, 2003, fellow, Banff Ctr. for Arts Can., 1985, MacDowell Colony fellow, N.H., 1987. Office: Calif State Univ Dominguez Hills 1000 E Victoria St Carson CA 90747-0001 Personal E-mail: gilah@linkline.com.

HIRSCH, HARVEY STUART, psychiatrist; b. NYC, Nov. 3, 1950; s. Leoanrd Samuel and Roberta Joan (Dreyer) H.; m. Linda Karen Green, Sept. 27, 1981; children: Daniel, Carly. BA, Columbia U., 1972; MD, Mt. Sinai Med. Sch., NYC, 1976. Diplomate Am. Bd. Psychiatry and Neurology, Nat. Bd. Med. Examiners, 1976. Intern Mt. Sinai Hosp., NYC, 1976, attending physician, 1979—; clin. instr. Mt. Sinai Med. Sch., NYC, 1979—; resident Mt. Sinai Hosp., NYC, 1977-79, chief resident, 1979—. Recipient Ams. Top Psychiatrists, Consumers Rsch. Coun. of Am., Wash., D.C., 2003. Mem. Am. Psychiat. Assn., Cum Laude Soc., Le Club (N.Y.C.), Phi Beta Kappa. Avocations: tennis champion, swimming champion. Office: 880 Fifth Ave New York NY 10021 Office Phone: 212-828-2213. Personal E-mail: hirschharvey@yahoo.com.

HIRSCH, HORST EBERHARD, metal products executive, consultant; b. Woelsendorf, Fed. Republic Germany, July 26, 1933; came to U.S., 1984; s. Albert and Emilie (Eberhardt) H.; m. Helga G. Gruber, May 2, 1961; children: Manon K., Fabiane M., Erin A. Diploma in chemistry, Tech. U. Karlsruhe, Fed. Republic Germany, 1959, D in Chem. Tech., 1961. Postdoctoral fellow NRC of Can., 1961-62; R & D engr., mgr. Cominco Ltd., Trail, B.C., Canada, 1962-84; pres., CEO Cominco Electronic Materials Inc., Spokane, Wash., 1984-88; pres. Johnson Matthey Electronics N.Am., Spokane, 1989-91, MSM (Metals and Semiconductor Materials), 1991—; vis. exec. IESC (Internat. Exec. Svc. Corps), 1992, field assoc., 1993—; co-founder, CM, HT Metals LLC, 2001—. Mem. bd. mgmt. B.C. Rsch. Coun., Vancouver, 1980-84; senate U. B.C., Vancouver, 1981-85; mem. adv. com. Wash. Tech. Ctr., 1992-94. Contbr. articles on chemistry and metallurgy to profl. publs., chpts. to books; patentee in field. Recipient Excellence in Innovation award Fed. Govt. Can., 1985. Mem. Soc. German Mining and Metall. Engrs. Lutheran. Avocations: reading, skiing, swimming, golf. Home Phone: 509-448-3577. Personal E-mail: zollegeg@aol.com.

HIRSCH, IRVING B., lawyer; b. NYC, Mar. 15, 1954; BA, CUNY, 1975; JD, Bklyn. Law Sch., 1978. Bar: NY 1979. Joined Manhattan dist. atty.'s office, NYC, 1978, asst. dist. atty., dep. bur. chief trial bur., chief spl. projects bur., chief narcotics eviction program; ptnr. Wilson, Elser, Moskowitz, Edelman & Dicker LLP, NYC. Mem.: NY County Lawyers Assn., NY State Bar Assn. Office: Wilson Elser Moskowitz Edelman & Dicker LLP 23rd Fl 150 E 42nd St New York NY 10017-5639 Office Phone: 212-490-3000 ext. 2411. Office Fax: 212-490-3038. Business E-Mail: hirschi@wemed.com.

HIRSCH, JEFFREY ALLAN, lawyer; b. Chgo., June 14, 1950; m. Lennie Sue Henderson, June 16, 1979; children: Lea, Ashley. BSBA, U. Fla., 1972, JD with honors, 1975. Bar: Fla. 1975, U.S. Dist. Ct. (so. and mid. dists.) Fla. 1975. Assoc. Swann & Glass, Coral Gables, Fla., 1975-76, Glass, Schultz, Weinstein & Moss, Coral Gables, 1976-80; ptnr. Holland & Knight, Ft. Lauderdale, Fla., 1980-93; prin. shareholder Greenberg, Traurig, P.A., Ft. Lauderdale, Fla., 1993—. Exec. dir. Govtl. Research Ctr., Gainesville, Fla., 1975. Active Leadership Broward, Ft. Lauderdale, 1986—, Leadership Fla., 1994—. Mem. ABA, Fla. Bar Assn., Broward County Bar Assn. Avocations: reading, travel. Office: Greenberg Traurig PA 401 E Las Olas Blvd Ste 2000 Fort Lauderdale FL 33301-2278 Office Phone: 954-765-0500. E-mail: hirschj@gtlaw.com.

HIRSCH, JEROME S., lawyer; BA in Econs., SUNY, Binghamton, 1970; JD, Fordham U., 1974. Bar: N.Y. Ptnr. Skadden, Arps, Slate, Meagher & Flom, NYC, 1982—. Mem. ABA, N.Y. State Bar Assn., Assn. Bar City of N.Y. Office: Skadden Arps Slate Meagher & Flom 4 Times Sq New York NY 10036-6595

HIRSCH, JUDD, actor; b. NYC, Mar. 15, 1935; s. Joseph Sidney and Sally (Kitzis) H. BS in Physics, CCNY, 1960. Broadway appearances in Barefoot in the Park, 1966, Knock Knock, 1976 (Drama Desk award for best featured actor), Chapter Two, 1977-78, Talley's Folly, 1980 (Tony nomination), I'm Not Rappaport, 1985-86, (Tony award for best actor in play 1986, Outer Critics Circle award, 1986), Conversations with My Father, 1992 (Tony award for best actor in play 1992, Outer Critics Circle award, 1992), A Thousand Clowns, 1996, Art, 1998, I'm Not Rappaport, 2002, Sixteen Wounded, 2004; off-Broadway appearances in On the Necessity of Being Polygamous, 1963, Scuba Duba, 1967-69, King of the United States, 1972, Mystery Play, 1972, Hot L Baltimore, 1973, Prodigal, 1973, Knock Knock, 1975, Talley's Folly, 1979 (Obie award), The Seagull, 1983, I'm Not Rappaport, 1985, Below the Belt, 1996; regional appearances include Theater for Living Arts, Phila., Line of Least Existence, Harry Noon and Night, The Recruiting Officer, 1969-70, Annenberg Ctr., Phila., Hough in Blazes, 1971, Seattle Repertory, Conversations with My Father, 1991, Scarborough, Eng., 1994, London, 1995, Chapel Hill, NC, Death of a Salesman, 1994, Long Wharf Theater Robbers, 1995, Manitoba Theatre Ctr., Winnipeg and Royal Alexandra Theatre, Toronto, Death of A Salesman, 1997, Art, London, 1999, 2001; stock and tours A Thousand Clowns, Threepenny Opera, Fantastiks, Woodstock, NY, 1964, Peterpat, Houston and Ft. Worth, 1970, Harvey, Chgo., 1971, And Miss Reardon Drinks a Little, Palm Beach, Fla., 1972, I'm Not Rappaport, nat. tour, 1986-87, Conversations With My Father, Doolittle Theatre, LA, 1993, Art, nat. tour, 1999-2000; TV series include Delvecchio, 1976-77, Rhoda, 1977, Taxi, 1978-83 (Emmy award for best actor in a comedy series, 1981, 1983), Dear John (Golden Globe award 1988), 1988-92, George and Leo, 1997, Regular Joe, 2003, Numbers, 2004-05; TV movies include The Law, 1974, Fear on Trial, 1975, The Legend of Valentino, 1975, The Halloween That Almost Wasn't, 1979, Sooner or Later, 1979, Marriage Is Alive and Well, 1980, First Steps, 1985, Brotherly Love, 1985, The Great Escape-Untold Story, 1988, She Said No, 1990, Betrayal of Trust, 1993, Color of Justice, 1997, Rocky Marciano, 1999; films include King of the Gypsies, 1978, Ordinary People (nominated Acad. Award), 1980, Without a Trace, 1983, Teachers, 1984, The Goodbye People, 1984, Running on Empty, 1988, Independence Day, 1996, Man On the Moon, 1999, A Beautiful Mind, 2001, Zeyda and the Hitman, 2004; dir. Squaring the Circle, 1962, Not Enough Rope, 1973, Talley's Folly, 1981, Art, 2000-01. Mem. Acad. Motion Picture Arts and Scis., Acad. TV Arts and Scis., Actors Equity Assn., SAG, AFTRA, SSDC.

HIRSCH, JULES, physician, researcher; b. NYC, Apr. 6, 1927; Student, Rutgers U., 1943—45; MD, U. Tex., 1948; DSc (hon.), SUNY, 1988. Intern pathology and medicine Duke Hosp., NC, 1948—50; from asst. resident to resident coll. medicine SUNY, Syracuse, 1950—52; asst. prof., assoc. physician Rockefeller U., NYC, 1954—60, assoc. prof., physician, 1960—67, prof., sr. physician, 1967—98. Sherman Fairchild prof. Rockefeller U., 1988—98, emeritus, 1998—; sr. physician Rockefeller U. Hosp., 1967—, physician-in-chief, 1992—96, emeritus, 1996—. Recipient Robert H. Herman award, 1994, McCollum award, 1984. Fellow: ACP, Royal Coll. Physicians Edinburgh; mem.: Harvey Soc., Am. Fedn. Clin. Rsch., Assn. Am. Physicians, Am. Soc. Clin. Nutrition, Am. Soc. Clin. Investigation, Inst. of Medicine of NAS, AAAS, Assn. for Patient Oriented Rsch. (founding mem.). Achievements include research in obesity, human behavior, internal medicine, biochemistry and physiology of lipids, lipid metabolism and nutrition. Office: Rockefeller U 1230 York Ave New York NY 10021-6399 Business E-Mail: hirsch@mail.rockefeller.edu.

HIRSCH, LARRY JOSEPH, retired retail executive, lawyer; b. Boston, July 1, 1938; s. Samuel and Anne (Rossman) Hirsch; m. Kay Pollock, Mar. 15, 1974. BA, Syracuse U., 1962; JD, Suffolk U., Boston, 1968; grad. gemologist, Gem Inst. Am., Los Angeles, 1981. Bar: Mass. 1968, R.I. 1968, Fla. 1970. Mgr. Vality Dept. Store, Groton, Conn., 1962—63; asst. area dir. Am. Jewish Com., Miami, 1968—69; asst. city atty. City of Miami, 1969—71; atty. Feuer and Feuer, Miami, 1971—74, Turano and Turano, Westerly, RI, 1974—78; asst. town solicitor Town of Westerly, RI, 1975—76; pres. Westerly Jewelry Co. Inc., RI, 1978—2000; ret. RI, 2000—; atty. RI, 1974—. Adv. bd. Fleet Bank, Westerly, 1984-90; chmn. adv. group Westerly Edn. Endowment Fund, 2000-01, dir., 2001, 02; bd. dir. Washington Trust Bancorp, Inc., 1994-; pres. Local Devel. Co., Westerly, 2000-04, dir., 2000—. Pres. Chariho Westerly Animal Rescue League, 1976—2003, trustee, 1976—, Ctr. for the Arts, Westerly, RI, 1984, Westerly Hosp., RI, 1984—94, mem. human resources com., 1998—2000; mem. fin. com. Cmty. Hosp. of Westerly, 1984—2001, incorporator, 1985—, bd. gov., 1995—2002, v.p., 1999—2002, Westerly Heart Assn., 1986; incorporator Westerly Pub. Libr., RI, 1997—; pres. Local Devel. Corp., 1998—2006, dir., 1998—; mem. site planning group West HS, RI, 1998—2000, mem. student handbook com., 1999—2000; mem. Dante Italian Heritage Soc., 2004—, treas., 2004—05; dir. Chariho Westerly Animal Rescue League, RI, 2001—; v.p. Congregation Sharon Zedek, 2000—05; dir. Stand Up for Animals, Key West, Fla., 2004—; bd. dir. Chariho Westerly Animal Rescue League, 1976—, Joint Devel. Task Force, Westerly, RI, 1988—2005, v.p., 1994—99, dir., 2001—, pres., 1999—2000; mem. Charter Revision Com. Westerly, RI, 1985—89; bd. dir. Animal Rescue League of So. R.I., 1988—94; mem. adv. coun. Westerly Integrated Social Svc. Program, 1996, chmn., 1997—2000; bd. dir. Am. Heart Assn., Westerly, RI, 1986—93; mem. salary rev. and benefits com. Westerly Fire Dist., RI, 1996—2002; v.p. Stand Up for Animals, 2005—. Served in US Army, 1958—60. Larry Hirsch Day named in his honor, Town of Westerly, 1980; recipient Someone Spl. Award, Channel 26 WTWS TV, New London, Conn., 1987, Sam Walton Bus. Leadership Award Westerly Pawcatuck C. of C., 2000; named Columbus Citizen of Yr., Golden Key Club, Westerly, 1989, Citizen of Yr., Westerly Pawcatuck C. of C., 2000. Mem.: Gemological Inst. Am., Am. Gem Soc. (cert. gemologist), New Eng. Appraiser Assn., Nat. Assn. Jewelry Appraisers, Fraternal Order of Police (assoc.; scholar com.), Westerly Track Club (pres. 1976, bd. dir. 1976—95), Elks (Larry Hirsch Run 1980—95). Avocations: long distance running, humane treatment of animals. Personal E-mail: larryjhirsch@cox.net.

HIRSCH, LAURENCE ELIOT, construction executive, investment banker; b. NYC, Dec. 19, 1945; s. S. Richard and Lillian (Avenet) H.; m. Susan Judith Creskoff, Dec. 23, 1967; children: Daria Lee, Bradford Richard. BS in Econs., U. Pa., 1968; JD cum laude, Villanova U., 1971; MS in Internat. Pub. Policy, Johns Hopkins Sch. Internat. Studies, 2005. Bar: Pa. 1972, Tex. 1973. Assoc. Wolf, Block, Schorr & Solis Cohen, Phila., 1971-73, Bracewell & Patterson, Houston, 1973-76, ptnr., 1976-78; pres. Southdown, Inc., Houston, 1977-85, CEO, 1984-85; pres. Centex Corp., Dallas, 1985-88, CEO, 1988—2004, also chmn. bd. dirs., 1991—2004; chmn. Eagle Materials, Inc., Dallas, 1994, Ctr. European Policy Analysis, 2005—. Bd. dirs. Belo Corp.; chmn. Highlander Ptnrs., L.P., 2006. Mem. bd. cons. Villanova U. Law Sch. With USAR, 1968—75. Office: Highlander Ptnrs 3811 Turtle Creek Blvd Ste 250 Dallas TX 75219 Office Phone: 214-245-5000. Business E-Mail: lhirsch@eaglematerials.com, lhirsch@highlander-partners.com.

HIRSCH, LAWRENCE LEONARD, physician, retired educator; b. Chgo., Aug. 20, 1922; m. Donna Lee Sturm; children: Robert, Edward, Sharon. BS, U. Ill., 1943; MD, U. Ill., Chgo., 1950. Diplomate: Am. Bd. Family Medicine. Intern. Ill. Masonic Med. Ctr., Chgo., 1950-51; practice medicine specializing in family medicine Chgo., 1951-70; dir. ambulatory care Ill. Masonic Med. Ctr., Chgo., 1970-71, dir. family practice residency program, 1971-75; prof., chmn. dept. family medicine Chgo. Med. Sch., 1975-89, prof. emeritus, 1989—. Mem. med. licensing bd. State of Ill., 1982-94, chmn., 1988-94, hosp. licensing bd., 1994-2004; bd. dirs. Ill. Coun. for continuing Med. Edn., 1981-85, pres., 1986-87; cons. recombinant DNA Abbott Labs., 1980-87; lectr. in field; staff pres. Ill. Masonic Med. Ctr., 1970. Book rev. editor: Soc. of Tchrs. Family Medicine, 1979-89; book reviewer: Jour. AMA, 1969-; contbr. articles to profl. jours. Bd. dirs. Mid-Am. chpt. ARC, Chgo., 1978-88; nat. pres. Alpha Phi Omega, Kansas City, Mo., 1974-78; exec. com. Chgo. Found. Med. Care and PSRO, 1977-84, Ill. State Inter-Ins. Exchange, 1975-2006; bd. dirs. Crescent Counties Found. for Med. Care, 1985-91; commr. Northbrook (Ill.) Park Dist., 1987-91, pres., 1990—; mem. Village of Northbrook Planning Commn., 1987-89. With US Army, 1943—46. Recipient Silver Beaver award Boy Scouts Am., 1963; recipient Silver Antelope award Boy Scouts Am., 1967, Disting. Eagle award Boy Scouts Am., 1969, Brotherhood award Lakeview Interfaith Council, 1968, Physician Speaker award AMA, 1981; inducted into City of Chgo. Sr. Citizens Hall of Fame, 1991. Fellow AAAS, Am. Acad. Family Physicians (mem. congress of dels.); mem. Chgo. Med. Soc. (pres. 1979, Pub. Svc. award 1990), Ill. Acad. Family Physicians (pres. 1977), Assn. Depts. Family Medicine (exec. com.), Masons, Shriners, Kiwanis (dir. local club). Democrat. Unitarian Universalist.

HIRSCH, MARTIN, dentist; m. Noreen Hirsch; 2 children. BS, CUNY, 1968; DMD, U. Pa., 1972; splty. prosthondontics, U. Iowa, 1975; splty. maxillofacial prosthetics, U. Chgo., 1976. Dental extern Coatsville Hosp., Pa., 1971—72; dental intern Mt. Sinai Hosp., NYC, 1972—73; resident VA Hosp., Iowa City, 1973—75, U. Chgo. Hosp. and Clinics, 1975—76; asst. prof. dept. otolaryngology Abraham Lincoln Sch. Medicine U. Ill. Med. Ctr., Chgo., 1976—77, dir. maxillofacial prosthetics clinic Craniofacial Anamolies Ctr., 1976—77; asst. prof. U. Ill. Coll. Dentistry, Chgo., 1977—93; staff dept. dentistry U. Ill. Hosp. Med. Ctr., Chgo., 1979—83; staff dept. surgery dental sect. Cuneo Hosp., Chgo., 1979—87; staff dept. surgery dental section Cabrini Hosp., Chgo., 1979—92; staff dept. dentistry Ill. Masonic Med. Ctr., Chgo., 1979—, mem. head and neck treatment ctr., 1981—; sr. staff dept. dental surgery Columbus Hosp., Chgo., 1979—98; pvt. practice gen., cosmetic and prosthetic dentistry Chgo., 1979—; attending Cath. Health Ptnrs., Chgo., 1998—2001, Resurrection Health Care St. Joseph's Hosp., 2001—. Adj. instr. U. Chgo. Hosps. and Clinics, 1975—76; spkr., presenter in field. Spkr. Am. Cancer Soc., Chgo., 1981—87, chmn. profl. edn. com., 1981—85, mem. oral cancer com., 1982—86. Mem.: ADA, Chgo. Dental Soc., Ill. Dental Soc. Avocations: swimming, reading. Office: 2800 N Sheridan Rd Chicago IL 60657-6156 Office Phone: 773-248-6140. Personal E-mail: drmartinhirsch@aol.com.

HIRSCH, MARTIN STANLEY, internist, epidemiologist, researcher; b. Cortland, NY, Apr. 16, 1939; s. Hans and Grete (Lipper) H.; m. Corinne Becker, Oct. 18, 1964; children: Tera Gretchen, Michael Edward. AB, Hamilton Coll., 1960; MD, Johns Hopkins U., 1964; MA, Harvard U., 1990. Diplomate Am. Bd. Internal Medicine, Am. Bd. Internal Medicine and Infectious Diseases. Intern in medicine U. Chgo. Clinics and Hosp., 1964-65, resident in medicine, 1965-66; fellow in virology Ctr. for Disease Control, Atlanta, 1966-68; fellow Nat. Inst. for Med. Rsch., London, 1968-69; fellow in infectious diseases Harvard U., Boston, 1969-71, asst. prof., 1971-76, assoc. prof., 1976-88, prof. medicine, 1988—; assoc. physician MGH, Boston, 1981-87; physician Mass. Gen. Hosp., Boston, 1988—. Mem. sci. adv. bd. AM Found. for AIDS Rsch., 1987—; chmn. AIDS program adv. com. NIH, Bethesda, Md., 1989-92. Editor-in-chief: Jour. of Infectious Diseases, 2002—; contbr. 150 chpts. to books, more than 240 articles to profl. jours. Surgeon USPHS, 1966-68. Fellow Infectious Disease Soc. Am.; mem. Am. Soc. Clin. Investigation, Am. Soc. Virology, Assn. Am. Physicians, Phi Beta Kappa, Alpha Omega Alpha. Achievements include first isolation of HIV-1 from genital secretions, central nervous system and blood monocytes; pioneering treatment of human Herpes virus and HIV infections with agents used singly or in combination. Office: Mass Gen Hosp Infectious Disease Unit 65 Landsdowne St Cambridge MA 02139

HIRSCH, MAXINE K., special education educator, councilman; b. Bklyn., July 31, 1932; d. Charles and Mary Kunitz; m. Stuart M. Hirsch, June 20, 1954 (dec. Nov. 2, 2000); children: Charles L., Robin F. Student, Bard Coll., 1950—51; BA, Bklyn. Coll., 1954; student, Rutgers U., 1956—58; MA, Kean Coll., 1982. Cert. tchr. N.J., supr. N.J., tchr. handicapped N.J. Tchr. Oak Tree Sch., Edison, NJ, 1955—56; realtor Stuart Hirsch Agy., Plainfield, NJ, 1966—68; tchr. Cook Sch., Plainfield, 1969—73; tutor Adolescent and Drug Abuse Unit Fair Oaks Hosp., Summit, NJ, 1974—78; tchr. Summit Jr. H.S., 1977—89; councilwoman Borough New Providence, NJ, 1984—2004. Mem. bd. trustees New Providence Cmty. Pool, 1980—83; trustee ch. coalition New Providence Affordable Housing, 1996—; mem. bd. trustees New Providence Sr. Citizens, 2005—, pres. bd. trustees, 2006, 2007; chmn. bd. New Providence Affordable Housing, 1989—; bd. dirs. New Providence Parent Tchr. Student Assn., 1972—76; mem. Union County Cmty. Devel. Bd., NJ, 1996—99, NJ, 2002—; mem. open space com. Borough New Providence, New Providence, 2004—06. Named to Hall Fame, N.J. League Municipalities, 2005. Mem.: N.J. Assn. Elected Women Ofcls. (bd. dirs., pres. 1990—91). Republican. Jewish. Avocations: reading, politics, investments, movies. Home: 11 Colonial Way New Providence NJ 07974 Personal E-mail: maxinehirsch@comcast.net.

HIRSCH, PAUL J., orthopedist, surgeon, health facility administrator, medical educator; b. Bklyn., Oct. 12, 1937; s. Morris M. and Dorothy (Woltizer) H.; 1 child, Jeremy S. BA in English, Roanoke Coll., 1957; MD, U. Va., 1961. Diplomate Am. Bd. Orthopedic Surgery. Intern NYU-Bellevue Med. Ctr., NYC, 1961-62, resident, 1964-68; chief orthop.

surgery Raritan Valley Hosp., Green Brook, NJ, 1969-71; pvt. practice orthop. surgery Bridgewater, NJ, 1971—; clin. prof. orthop. surgery Seton Hall Sch. Grad. Med. Edn. Vice chmn., bd. dirs. MIIX Group, Inc.; pres., med. dir. InterMedix, Lawrenceville, N.J.; emeritus staff, orthop. svc. Somerset (N.J.) Med. Ctr.; courtesy staff Robert Wood Johnson U. Hosp., New Brunswick, N.J.; clin. asst. prof. orthop surgery Rutgers Med. Sch., 1971-79; clin. instr. orthop. surgery NYU-Bellevue Med. Ctr., 1969-79; clin. assoc. prof. orthop. surgery N.J. Med. Sch., 1980—; clin. prof. orthop. surgery Seton Hall Sch. Postgrad. Medicine; chmn., bd. trustees Jour. Bone and Joint Surgery, 1999; mem. practicing physicians adv. group Nat. Com. Quality Assurance, 1996-98. Chmn. publs. com. Jour. Med. Soc. N.J., 1980-85; contbr. articles, editor profl. jours.,; mem. editl. bd. N.J. Medicine; editor-in-chief N.J. Medicine. Chmn. N.J. Com. for Quality Orthop. Care; trustee Rutgers Prep. Sch., pres. bd. trustees, 1983—86; trustee Raritan Valley C.C., 1986—; bd. dirs. N.J. Med. Polit. Action Com., 1983—; bd. trustees Orthop. Rsch. and Edn. Found., 1989—94. Mem.: N.J. State Med. Underwriters, Inc (bd. dirs. 1990—99, vice chmn. bd. dirs. 1991—99), Med. Inter-Ins. Exch. N.J. (bd. govs. 1987—90), Ind. Sch. Chmn. Assn., N.J. Assn. Med. Splty. Socs. (pres. 1979—80, dir. 1981—85), N.J. Hosp. Assn. (trustee 1986—89), N.J. Health Scis. Group (treas. 1982—83), Internat. Soc. Orthop. Surgery and Traumatology, Am. Trauma Soc. (pres. ctrl. Jersey unit 1977—81), Acad. Medicine of N.J. (chmn. orthop. sect. 1975—78, trustee 1978—91, pres.-elect 1982—83, pres. 1983—84), Somerset County Med. Soc. (bd. trustees), Med. Soc. N.J. (chmn. orthop. sect. 1977—78, ho. of dels. 1976—, treas. 1982—86, 2d v.p. 1986—87, 1st v.p. 1987—88, pres.-elect 1988—89, pres. 1989—90, trustee 1982—91), N.J. Orthop. Soc. (pres. 1979—80), Ea. Orthop. Assn. (trustee 1981—84), Am. Coll. Physician Execs., Am. Acad. Orthop. Surgeons (bd. councilors 1982—88), Am. Orthop. Assn., AMA, ACS. Office: Green Knoll Profl Park #720 US Hwy 202-206 Bridgewater NJ 08807-1746

HIRSCH, RAYMOND ROBERT, chemicals executive, lawyer; b. St. Louis, Mar. 20, 1936; s. Raymond Winton and Olive Frances (Gordon) H.; m. Joanne Therese Dennis, Jan. 30, 1960; children: Amy Elizabeth, Thomas Christopher, Timothy Joseph, Mary Patricia. LL.B., St. Louis U., 1959. Bar: Mo. 1959. With Treasury Dept., 1960-62, Petrolite Corp., St. Louis, 1962—, sec., 1971—, v.p., gen. counsel, 1973-82, sr. v.p., gen. counsel, 1982-92; of counsel Guilfoil, Petzall & Shoemake, St. Louis, 1992-2000. Mem. Pub. Defender Commn., Mo. Mcpl. judge City of Bridgeton, Mo., 1970-73; mem. City of Des Peres Planning and Zoning Commn., 1974-78; mem. bd. edn. Spl. Sch. Dist. St. Louis County, 1981-83; mem. Mo. Air N.G., 1959-60; trustee Childhaven. Mem. ABA, Am. Soc. Corp. Secs., Mo. Bar Assn., Bar Assn. St. Louis, Mo. Athletic Club. Roman Catholic. Office: Guilfoil Petzall & Shoemake 100 S 4th St Saint Louis MO 63102-1800 Home: 119 Thorncliff Ln Saint Louis MO 63122-5206 Office Phone: 314-241-6890. E-mail: rrhirsch@charter.net.

HIRSCH, (WILLIAM) REECE, lawyer; b. Dallas, Jan. 4, 1960; BS, Northwestern U., Evanston, Ill., 1982; JD, U. So. Calif., 1990. Bar: Calif. 1990. Assoc. Davis Wright Tremaine LLP, San Francisco, 1994—98, ptnr., 1998—2002, Sonnenschein Nath & Rosenthal LLP, San Francisco, 2002—. Mem. editl. adv. bd. BNA's Health Law Reporter, Healthcare Informatics, TIPS on Managed Care. Mem.: ABA (mem. health law sect.), Healthcare Fin. Mgmt. Assn., Am. Health Lawyers Assn., Calif. Soc. Healthcare Attorneys. Office: Sonnenschein Nath & Rosenthal 525 Market St, 26th Fl San Francisco CA 94105 Office Phone: 415-882-0300. Office Fax: 415-543-5472. Business E-Mail: rhirsch@sonnenschein.com.

HIRSCH, RICHARD GARY, lawyer; b. LA, June 15, 1940; s. Charles and Sylvia (Leopold) H.; m. Claire Renee Recsei, Mar. 25, 1967; 1 child, Nicole Denise. BA, UCLA, 1961; JD, U. Calif., Berkeley, 1965. Bar: Calif. 1967, U.S. Dist. Ct. (ctrl. dist.) Calif. 1967, U.S. Supreme Ct. 1972, U.S. Ct. Appeals (9th cir.) 1989, U.S. Dist. Ct. (ea. dist.) Calif. 1991. Dep. dist. atty. L.A. Dist. Atty.'s Office, 1967-71; ptnr. Nasatir, Hirsch, Podberesky & Genego, Santa Monica, Calif., 1971—. Commr. Calif. Coun. Criminal Justice, 1977-81; mem. Spl. Com. on Cts. in the Media/Judicial Coun. Calif., 1979. Co-author: California Criminal Law Proceedings/Practice, 5 edits. Pres. bd. trustees Santa Monica Mus. Art, 1984-91; chmn. Greek Theatre Adv. Com., L.A., 1976-79; mem. L.A. Olympic Organizing Com., 1981-84; bd. dirs. Ocean Park Cmty. Ctr., 1995—, bd. chair, 1997-2001. Recipient Spl. Merit Resolution, LA City Coun., 1984, Criminal Def. Atty. of Yr. award, Century City Bar Assn., 1996, Lifetime Achievement award, Criminal Cts. Bar Assn., 2003. Fellow Am. Bd. Criminal Lawyers (bd. dirs., v.p. 1998-2000, pres.-elect 2001, pres. 2002); mem. Calif. Attys. Criminal Justice (pres. 1987, bd. trustees), Criminal Cts. Bar Assn. (pres. 1981, Spl. Merit award 1988), L.A. County Bar Assn. (Criminal Def. Atty. of Yr. 1999), Santa Monica C. of C. (bd. dirs. 1995-97). Avocations: cooking, reading, community service. Office: Nasatir Hirsch Podberesky & Genego 2115 Main St Santa Monica CA 90405-2215 Office Phone: 310-399-3259. Personal E-mail: richardghirsch@aol.com.

HIRSCH, ROBERT LOUIS, energy analyst, consultant; b. Evanston, Ill., Mar. 6, 1935; s. Louis Aaron and Dorothy Jean (Block) H.; m. Evelyn Podhouser, Feb. 1, 1959 (div. 2000); children: Allen, Lauri, Scott. BS, U. Ill., Champaign-Urbana, 1958, PhD, 1964; MS, U. Mich., Ann Arbor, 1959. Rsch. engr. Atomics Internat., 1959-60; physicist, later dir. ITT Indsl. Labs., Fort Wayne, Ind., 1964-68; sr. physicist controlled thermonuclear rsch. AEC (now Dept. Energy), Washington, 1968-72, divsn. dir., 1972—76; asst. adminstr. solar, geothermal and advanced energy sys. ERDA (presdl. appointment), 1976-77; dep. mgr. sci. and tech. dept. Exxon Corp., 1977; gen. mgr. exploratory petroleum rsch. Exxon Rsch. and Engring. Co., 1977-80, mgr. Synthetic Fuels Rsch. Lab. Baytown, Tex., 1980-83; v.p., mgr. rsch. and tech. svcs. dept. Arco Oil and Gas Co., Dallas, 1983-91; CEO ARCO Power Techs., Inc., 1986-91; v.p. Washington office Electric Power Rsch. Ins., 1991-94; cons. in tech. and mgmt., 1994—; exec. advisor Advanced Power Technologies, Washington, 1997—2001; pres. The Energy Tech. Collaborative, Inc., 1995-97; sr. energy analyst Rand, 2001—02; chmn. bd. on energy and environ. sys. NRC, 1996—2003; sr. energy program advisor SAIC, 2003—. Mem. bds. Annapolis Ctr. and Fusion Power Assocs.; participant in Atlantic Coun. Studies; mem. LDRD Bd. Lawrence Livermore Nat. Lab., 1993-95; mem. U.S.-USSR Joint Commn. on Peaceful Uses of Atomic Energy, 1970s; chmn. US del. US-USSR Joint Fusion Power Coord. Com., 1970s; mem. Internat. Fusion Rsch. Coun., 1970s, Dept. Energy Rsch. adv. bd., 1980s; vice chmn. com. on sci., engring. and tech. Fed. Coord. Coun. for Sci. Engring. and Tech., 1976; adv. bd. Princeton Plasma Physics Lab., 1980s, Oak Ridge Nat. Lab., 1993-97; rsch. coord. coun. Gas Rsch. Inst., 1980s. Contbr. articles to profl. jours; patentee in field. Elected nat. assoc. Nat. Acads., 2001. Recipient Meritorious award William Jump Found., 1971, Disting. Svc. award AEC, 1974, spl. achievement award Fusion Power Assocs., 1982, spl. Achievement award ERDA, 1976, 77, commendation NASA, 1982, merit award U. Mich. Engring. Alumni Soc., 1997; AEC Spl. fellow, 1960-63. Fellow AAAS; mem. Am. Nuc. Soc. (chmn. fusion tech. group, dir. 1975-76, 78-79, outstanding tech. achievement award 1983), Tau Beta Pi (U. Ill. Alumni Honor award), Phi Epsilon Pi. Home and Office: 723 Fords Landing Way Alexandria VA 22314 Personal E-mail: rlhirsch@comcast.net.

HIRSCH, ROBERT MAURICE, hydrologist; s. James C. and Constance (Klauber) H.; children: Jacob R., Benjamin A. BA, Earlham Coll., 1971; MS, U. Wash., 1972; PhD, Johns Hopkins U., 1976. Hydrologist U.S. Geol. Survey, Reston, Va., 1976-88, asst. chief hydrologist, 1988-93, acting dir., 1993-94, chief hydrologist, 1994—. Author: Statistical Methods in Water Resources, 1992. Recipient Meritorious Svc. award U.S. Dept. Interior, Washington, 1988, Disting. Svc. award, 1994, Water Mgmt. Achievement award Interstate Coun. Water Policy, Washington, 1996. Fellow AAAS; mem. ASCE, Am. Goephys. Union, Am. Water Resources Assn. Office: USGS 409 Nat Ctr Reston VA 20192-0001 Home Phone: 703-994-5205. Business E-Mail: rhirsch@usgs.gov.

HIRSCH, ROSEANN CONTE, publisher; b. NYC, Feb. 5, 1941; d. Frank and Anna (Burzycki) Conte; m. Barry Jay Hirsch, Oct. 1, 1967; children: Brian Christopher, Nicholas Benjamin, Jonathan Alexander. Student, Boston U., 1958-61; BA, Columbia U., 2004. Editorial asst. Grolier, Inc., 1962-64; editor Ideal Pub. Corp., NYC, 1968-74; editorial dir. Sterling's Mags., Inc., NYC, 1975-78, Hearst Spl. Publs., Hearst Corp., NYC, 1978-84; v.p. Ultra Communications, Inc., NYC, 1984-89; pub., pres. Dream Guys, Inc., NYC, 1986-93; pres. Lamppost Press, Inc., NYC, 1989—. Author: Super Working Mom's Handbook, 1986; editor: Young & Married Mag., 1976-77, 100 Greatest American Women, Good Housekeeping's Moms Who Work; contbr. articles to various mags. Home and Office: Lamppost Press Inc 870 United Nations Plaza 10E New York NY 10017 Home Phone: 212-750-0706; Office Phone: 212-750-0706.

HIRSCHBERG, JOSEPH GUSTAV, physicist, educator; b. Chgo., Apr. 13, 1921; s. Joseph Gustav and Lillian Hirschberg; m. Delores Dietrich, Jan. 1944 (div. Apr. 1946); m. Ginette Henriette Tetard, Apr. 26, 1947 (dec. Aug. 1992); children: Dorothy Jean Pixomatis, Joseph Gerald, Anne Marie Tumarkin, Lynn Susan Sontag; m. Judith Klausner Mintz, Apr. 2, 1996. AB, Dartmouth Coll., 1943; MS, U. Wis., 1951, PhD, 1952. Rsch. assoc. U. Wis., 1953—57; head optical group, rsch. physicist Plasma Physics Lab., Princeton, 1958—65; prof. d'Echange U. Paris, 1963; prof. physics U. Miami, Fla., 1965—85, chmn. dept., 1965—72, dir. optical physics lab., 1968—, prof. emeritus physics, 1986—. Pres. Fed. Engring. Corp., 1953—58; contractor Langley Rsch. Ctr., NASA, 1966—69; vis. rsch. faculty Oak Ridge Nat. Lab., Tenn., 1966; vis. rsch. physicist Princeton U., NJ, 1976, sr. rsch. faculty, 1986—89; leader solar eclipse expdns., Mexico, 1970, Canada, 72, Kenya, 73; vis. astronomer Sacramento Peak Obs., 1977; vis. scientist Inst. de Pathologie Cellulaire, Paris, 1980, Chercheur d'Echange, Mus. d'Histoire Naturel, Paris, 1983, Chercher d'Echange, Hosp. Henri Mondor, Creteil, France, 1985; vis. sr. scientist Max Planck Inst. Biophys. Chemistry, Göttingen, Germany, 1996, Göttingen, 97, Göttingen, 2002. Co-author: Spectroscopic Measurements, 1962; author: Physics of Music, 1974; co-author: Cell Structure and Function by Microspectrofluorometry, 1989, Photobiology, 1995; contbr. articles to sci. jours.; author: Physics for the Arts, 2001; co-editor: Fluorescent Probes in Oncology, 2002. Served to capt. USAAF, 1943—47. Fellow: Papanicolaou Cancer Rsch. Inst., European Acad. Scis., Arts and Letters, Optical Soc. Am., Am. Phys. Soc.; mem.: AAAS, Fla. Acad. Scis., Am. Soc. Photobiology, Sigma Xi, Phi Beta Kappa, Omega Delta Kappa, Sigma Pi Sigma. Achievements include co-discoverer of telluric sodium absorption in solar radiation; invention of optical spectroscopic devices; infrared turbidity meter; Brillouin laser ocean probe; non-linear optical interference microscope; microfluorospectrometers; x-ray microscopy; solar and tidal energy systems; compact triangular interferometer; hydrogen economy devices; photoacoustic microscope; combination fluorescene and phase microscope with large working space. Home: 1046 Alfonso Ave Coral Gables FL 33146-3302 Office Phone: 305-284-2323. E-mail: jhirshberg@aol.com.

HIRSCHEY, MARK, finance educator, investment advisor; b. Mpls., Oct. 13, 1951; s. Kenneth Alfred and Elizabeth Marie (Boulger) H.; married; children: Nicholas, Jessica, Sarah. BA, St. John's U., Collegeville, Minn., 1973; MA, U. Wis., 1974, PhD, 1977. Asst. prof. U. Wis., Madison, 1977-84; assoc. prof. U. Colo., Denver, 1984-86, Rice U., Houston, 1986-88; prof. U. Kans., Lawrence, 1988—2005, Anderson W. Chandler prof. bus., 2005—. Founding pres. Assn. of Financial Economists; vis. prof. Consortium Internat. U, Asolo, Italy, 2000, Asolo, 02. Author more than 85 academic rsch. articles, scholarly books and scholarly textbooks, co-editor Advances in Financial Economics; co-editor: (adv. editor) Fin. Review, Journ. of Bus. Fin. & Acctng. (London) and Managerial & Decision Econ. Stockton Rsch. fellow U. Kans., 1993. Mem. Assn. Fin. Economists (pres. 1983—). Republican. Avocation: waterfowl and upland bird hunting. Office: U Kans Sch Bus 345-D Summerfield Hall 1300 Sunnyside Ave Lawrence KS 66045-0001 Office Phone: 785-864-7563 (785) 864-7563. E-mail: mhirschey@ku.edu.*

HIRSCHFELD, LOUISE See KERZ, LOUISE

HIRSCHFELD, MICHAEL, lawyer; b. Bronx, July 4, 1950; s. Lawrence John and Ida (Miller) H.; m. Heidi P. Greenspan, June 17, 1973; children: Adam Lawrence, Philip Richard. BEE summa cum laude, CCNY, 1972; JD cum laude, U. Pa., 1975; LLM in Taxation, NYU, 1980. Bar: N.Y. 1976, U.S. Dist. Ct. (so. and ea. dists.) N.Y. 1976, U.S. Tax Ct. 1978. Assoc. Shearman and Sterling, NYC, 1975-80, Roberts and Holland, NYC, 1980-83, Carro, Spanbock, Kaster and Cuiffo, NYC, 1983-85, ptnr., 1985-88, Winstown & Strawn, NYC, 1988-98, Dechert LLP, NYC, 1998—. Lectr. NYU, Assn. of Bar of City of New York, Fundamentals of Internat. Taxables, 2001-03, ABA, ALI-ABA, PLI, Syracuse U., U. Tex., Tulane U., Georgetown U.; chmn. NYU Inst. Real Estate Taxation; co-chmn. 49th, 50th, 52d, 53d and 54th ann. Fed. Income Taxation Confs.; 11th-23d ann. NYU Confs. on Fed. Taxation of Real Estate Taxations: mem. nat. edn. bd., Business Entities (RIA publ.) Real Estate Tax Digest, Jour. of Internat. Tax, Tax. Mgmt. Real Estate Jour.; mem. adv. bd. Tax Mgmt. Real Estate, Inst. Fed. Tax. Co-author: Real Estate Limited Partnerships, 3rd edit., 1991; bd. editors Real Estate Tax Digest, BNA Tax Mgmt.; editl. adv. bd. NYU Real Estate Adv. Bd. Mem.: Am. Tax Policy Inst. (treas. 2005—), Am. Coll. Tax Counsel, Internat. Tax Assn., Assn. of Bar of City of N.Y. (mem. com. on taxation of bus. entities), N.Y. State Bar Assn. (exec. com. 1987—97, lectr., co-chmn. coms. on income from real property tax sect. 1988—91, co-chmn. com. on preferences and minimum tax 1991—92, co-chmn. com. on individuals 1992—93, co-chmn. com. U.S. activities of fgn. taxpayers 1993—96, co-chmn. com. on real property 1996—98, co-chmn. tax accts. 1997—98, com. on internat. mems.), Am. Law Inst. (lectr.), ABA (tax sect. vice chmn. ACRS depreciation recapture subcom. 1983—85, task force pres.'s tax reform proposals minimum tax subcom. 1985—86, chmn. syndications subcom. 1985—87, chmn. real estate tax problems com. 1989—91, co-chmn. govt. subcom. 1992—94, vice chmn. gov. submission com. 1992—95, chmn. govt. subcom. 1994—97, coun. 1997—2000, coun. dir. tax sect. internat. com. 1997—2000, vice chmn. individual income taxpayers com. 2000—02, vice chair com. ops. 2001—04, lectr. taxaction sect., chair 911 task force, co-chair Katrina task force). Avocation: music (drum). Office: Dechert LLP 30 Rockefeller Plz Fl 22 New York NY 10112-2200 Office Phone: 212-698-3635. Fax: 212-698-3599. Business E-Mail: michael.hirschfeld@dechert.com.

HIRSCHFIELD, ALAN JAMES, entrepreneur; BS, U. Okla.; MBA, Harvard U. V.p. Allen & Co., Inc., 1959-67; v.p. fin., dir. Warner Bros. Seven Arts, Inc., 1967-68; with Am. Diversified Enterprises, Inc., 1968-73; pres., CEO Columbia Pictures Industries, NYC, 1973-78; vice chmn., COO 20th Century-Fox Film Corp., LA, 1979-81, chmn. bd., CEO, 1981-85; cons., investor entertainment industries, LA, 1985-89; mng. dir. Wertheim Schroder & Co., LA, 1990-92. Co-CEO, co-chair Data Broadcasting Corp., 1990-2000; bd. dirs. Cantel Med. Corp., Carmike Cinemas, Inc., Leucadia Nat. Corp. Bd. dirs. Cmty. Found. Jackson Hole; trustee Dana Farber Cancer Inst, 2002. Office: PO Box 7443 Jackson WY 83002-7443

HIRSCHFIELD, BRADLEY, rabbi; BA, U. Chgo.; MA, MPhil, Jewish Theological Seminary. Cert. ordained Rabbi Metivta. V.p. Nat. Jewish Ctr. for Learning and Leadership (CLAL). Former prof. Dept. Talmud and Rabbinics Metivta; cons. communal inst. and found.; spkr. in field of religion and philosophy Aspen Inst., Wash. Nat. Cathedral; key panelist Parliament of the World's Religions, Barcelona, 2004. Author: (religion books) Embracing Life and Facing Death: A Jewish Guide to Palliative Care, 2003; Appeared in Documentary: Freaks Like Me; co-prodr.: (films) When Good Gods Go Bad, 2007; Radio and TV appearances incl. ABC-Nightline UpClose (the only rabbi ever featured), CNN, CBS, PBS-Frontline: Faith and Doubt at Ground Zero & Religion & Ethics Newsweekly, NPR, commentator WWSB-TV, Sarasota, Fla.; contbr. articles. Named one of The Top 50 Rabbis in America, Newsweek Mag., 2007. Jewish. Office: c/o CLAL 440 Park Ave S New York NY 10016-8012 Office Phone: 212-779-3300. Office Fax: 212-779-1009.*

HIRSCHHORN, BERNARD, educator, historian, researcher, writer; b. NYC, Aug. 23, 1922; s. Benjamin and Pauline (Schechner) H. BSS cum laude, City Coll. N.Y., 1943; MA in History, Columbia U., 1944, MPhil in History, 1978, PhD in History, 1981. Lic. tchr., N.Y. High sch. social studies tchr. Bd. Edn., NYC, 1952-65, high sch. chmn., 1965-91; rschr., writer NYC, 1991—. Adj. asst. prof. history Bd. Higher Edn., N.Y.C., 1947-76; dir. N.Y.C. Coun. on Econ. Edn., 1980's; asst. examiner Bd. Examiners of City of N.Y., 1965-1980s; assoc. Seminar on The City, Columbia U., 1976—. Author: The Perilous Presidency, 1979, Words and Issues: From 'Slivers' to Missiles (N.Y. Times paperback), 1985, Democracy Reformed: Richard Spencer Childs and His Fight For Better Government, 1997; co-author: The Encyclopedia of New York City, 1995, Dictionary of American Biography, 1995, Walt Whitman: An Encyclopedia, 1998, A Global Encyclopedia of Historical Writing, 1998, Scribner's Encyclopedia of American Lives, 1999, American National Biography, 1999, Encyclopedia of the American Civil War, 2000, Historical Dictionary of the Gilded Age, 2003, Encyclopedia-USA, vol. 29, 2003, The Encyclopedia of New York State, 2005, The Encyclopedia of the Gilded Age and Progressive Era, 2005, Historical Dictionary of the 1940s, 2006, Encyclopedia of American Urban History, 2006; bibliographer Richard Spencer Childs, The Urban History Newsletter, 1996, 1997; editor (guest): Urban History (Mag. History issue), 1990; reviewer Social Education, The New American Poverty, 1985, Boston's Wayward Children: Social Services for Homeless Children, 1830-1930 (Mag. History issue), 1990, Good-Bye Machiavelli: Government and American Life (History issue), 1998, The History Teacher, The Great Depression, 1999, The History Teacher, The House of Rothschild: Money's Prophet 1798-1848, 2000, White House Studies, FDR and His Enemies, 2002, White House Studies, The Kennedy's and Cuba: The Declassified Documentary History, 2004; contbr. articles to profl. jours. and newspapers. Pvt. U.S. Army, 1946-47. Recipient NEH award, Harvard U., 1983, Tufts U., 1984, Brandeis U., 1985, Brown U., 1986, Princeton U., 1987, St. Andrews (Scotland) U., 1987; Fulbright scholar, Institut d'Etudes Politiques, Paris, 1963, English-Speaking Union scholar, Oxford (Eng.) U., 1982. Mem.: Henry George Sch. Social Sci., Pen Am. Ctr., New Eng. Historical Assn., Nat. Civic League, Soc. Historians of the Gilded Age and Progressive Era, Urban History Assn., Org. Am. Historians, Nat. Coun. History Edn. Democrat. Jewish. Avocations: attending cultural events (including films), nature walks, beach walking, swimming. Home: 301 E 21st St New York NY 10010-6534

HIRSCHHORN, ERIC LEONARD, lawyer; b. NYC, Apr. 28, 1946; m. Leah Wortham, Oct. 31, 1981; children: Alexander, Elizabeth, Anne. BA, U. Chgo., 1965; JD, Columbia U., 1968. Bar: N.Y. 1968, U.S. Supreme Ct. 1972, D.C. 1973. Reginald Heber Smith Community Lawyer fellow MFY Legal Svcs., NYC, 1968-71; counsel Dem. Study Group N.Y. State Assembly, Albany, 1971; legis asst. to Rep. Bella Abzug, U.S. Ho. of Reps., Washington, 1971-73; assoc. Cadwalader, Wickersham & Taft, NYC, 1973-75; chief counsel subcom. on govt. info. and individual rights U.S. Ho. of Reps., Washington, 1975-77; dep. assoc. dir. internat. affairs & trade U.S. Office Mgmt. & Budget, Washington, 1977-80; dep. asst. sec. export adminstrn. U.S. Dept. Commerce, Washington, 1980—81; ptnr. Winston & Strawn LLP (formerly Bishop, Cook, Purcell & Reynolds), Washington, 1981—. Exec. sec. Industry Coalition on Tech. Transfer, Washington, 1986—. Author: The Export Control and Embargo Handbook, 2000, 2d edit., 2005; contbr. articles to profl. jours. Mem. Assn. Bar City N.Y., Thurgood Marshall Am. Inn of Ct., D.C. Bar (legal ethics com. 1997-98, 99-2005, vice-chmn. 2001-03, chmn. 2003-05, rules of profl. conduct rev. com. 2004-, vice-chmn. 2006-). Office: Winston & Strawn LLP 1700 K St NW Washington DC 20006 Office Phone: 202-282-5706.

HIRSCHHORN, JOEL, lawyer; b. Bklyn., Mar. 13, 1943; s. Leo S. and Thelma (Bassin) H.; m. Evelyn Ruth Finkelstein, Jan. 29, 1966; children: Bennett K., Douglas K. BA, U. Conn., 1964; JD, U. Wis., 1967. Bar: Fla. 1967, Wis. 1967, U.S. Ct. Appeals (1st, 2d, 3d, 4th, 5th, 6th, 7th, 8th, 9th, 10th and 11th cirs.), U.S. Tax Ct., U.S. Supreme Ct. Pvt. practice, Miami, Fla., 1967—69; assoc. Wilson, Abramson & Rosenthal, Miami, 1970—72; pvt. practice Miami, 1972—89; sr. ptnr., head litig. dept. Broad & Cassel, Miami, 1989—90; pvt. practice Miami, 1990—99; ptnr. Hirschhorn & Bieber, PA, Coral Gables, Fla., 2000—. Lectr. in field. Mem. bd. dir. Hope Ctr., Miami, 1974-82, bd. trustees, 1982-84, hon. trustee, 1984-2001; exec. bd. mem. Greater Miami chpt. Am. Jewish Com., 1986-76, v.p., 1972-76, chmn. nat. legal com., 1989-90; chmn. Dade County Alliance for Safer Cities, 1972-73; former bd. dir., sec. Concern Unltd., Inc.; former bd. dir., v.p. Advocate Program, Inc.; mem. Dade County Cmty. Rels. Bd., 1978-81; bd. trustees Freedom to Read Found., 1997-2001, 2002-06, treas., 1999-2005. Fellow Am. Bd. Criminal Lawyers (pres. 2003), Internat. Acad. Trial Lawyers; mem. ABA, Nat. Assn. Criminal Def. Lawyers (bd. dir 1979-86, chmn. Fair Trial/Free Press and Televised Criminal Trials com. 1977-79, cert. appreciation work in criminal def. 1979, work regarding opposition to cameras in courtrooms 1980), First Amendment Lawyers. Assn. (pres. 1974-75), Fla. Bar Assn. (chmn. fed. practice com. 1983, ethics com. criminal law sect. 1986-87), State Bar Wis. (past pres., non resident lawyers divsn. 2005, bd. govs. 2004-07), Dade County Bar Assn. (cert. of appreciation 1975), Fla. Criminal Def. Lawyers Assn., Acad. Fla. Trial Lawyers, Wis. Law Found. Democrat. Jewish. Office: 550 Biltmore Way Penthouse Three A Coral Gables FL 33134 Office Phone: 305-445-5320. E-mail: jhirschhorn@aquitall.com.

HIRSCHHORN, KURT, pediatrics educator; b. Vienna, May 18, 1926; arrived in U.S., 1940, naturalized, 1945; s. Emanuel and Helen (Mayberger) Hirschhorn; m. Rochelle Reibman, Dec. 20, 1952; children: Melanie D., Lisa R., Joel N. Student, U. Pitts., 1944; BA, NYU, 1950, MD, 1954, MS, 1958. Intern Bellevue Hosp., NYC, 1954—55, resident, 1955—56; fellow NYU, 1956—57, U. Uppsala, Sweden, 1957—58; instr. NYU Sch. Medicine, 1956—58, asst. prof., 1958—63, assoc. prof., 1963—66; Arthur J. and Nellie Z. Cohen prof. genetics and pediat. Mt. Sinai Sch. Medicine, CUNY, 1966—76, Herbert H. Lehman prof., chmn. pediat., 1977—95, prof. pediat., human genetics and medicine, 1995—. Adj. prof. biology NYU, 1966—74; established investigator Am. Heart Assn., 1960—65; career scientist N.Y.C. Health Rsch. Coun., 1965—75. Author numerous sci. publs.; editor (with Harry Harris): Advances in Human Genetics, 1969—95; mem. editl. bd.: 16 sci. jours. Mem. coun. Village Cmty. Sch., 1968—73, chmn., 1972—73. With US Army, 1944—47. Recipient Rudolph Virchow medal, 1974, Alumni Achievement award, NYU Sch. Medicine, 1982, Jacobi medal, Mt. Sinai Med. Ctr., 1993, William Allan award, Am. Soc. Human Genetics, 1995, J. Lester Gabrilove award for significant contbns. to medicine, Mt. Sinai Sch. Medicine, 2001, The Col. Harland Sanders Genetics Lifetime Achievement award, The March of Dimes, 2006; Bergquist fellow, NYU, 1958. Fellow: AAAS, N.Y. Acad. Medicine, Am. Acad. Pediat.; mem.: Am. Cancer Soc. (coun. 1989—92), Am. Soc. Pediatric Chmn. (coun. 1983—86), Environ. Mutagen Soc. (coun. 1969—76), Genetics Soc. Am., Harvey Soc. (v.p. 1979—80, pres. 1980—81, coun. 1981—84), Am. Assn. Immunologists, Am. Soc. Human Genetics (pres. 1969, dir. 1964—65, 1968—71, Human

Genetics Edn. Excellence award 2002), Am. Pediatric Soc. (Howland award for disting. svc. to pediatrics 2006), Am. Assn. Physicians, Am. Soc. Clin. Investigation, Am. Coll. Med. Genetics, Inst. Medicine of NAS, Pediatric Travel Club, Alpha Omega Alpha, Sigma Xi, Phi Beta Kappa. Home: 29 Washington Sq W New York NY 10011-9180 Office: Mt Sinai Sch Medicine 1 Gustave L Levy Pl New York NY 10029-6500 Office Phone: 212-241-4305. Business E-Mail: kurt.hirschhorn@mssm.edu.

HIRSCHHORN, ROBERT B., lawyer; BA in Govt. and Internat. Rels. cum laude, Clark U., 1978; JD, St. Mary's U., 1981. Assoc. Goldstein, Goldstein & Hilley, San Antonio, 1981—84, Cathy E. Bennett & Assocs., Lewisville, Tex., 1984—. Co-author: Blue's Guide to Jury Selection. Office: Cathy E Bennett & Assocs Ste 203 217 S Stemmons Lewisville TX 75067 Office Phone: 972-434-5879. Office Fax: 972-434-0176. E-mail: rbh@cebjury.com.*

HIRSCHHORN, ROCHELLE, genetics educator; b. Bklyn., Mar. 19, 1932; d. Hyman and Anna Reibman; m. Kurt Hirschhorn; children: Melanie D., Lisa R., Joel N. BA, Barnard Coll., 1953; MD, NYU, 1957. Intern NYU-Bellevue Med. Divsn., NYC, 1958—59; rsch. fellow, tchg. asst. NYU Sch. Medicine, NYC, 1963—65, assoc. rsch. scientist, 1965—66, instr. medicine, 1966—69, asst. prof. medicine, 1969—74, assoc. prof. medicine, 1974—79, prof. medicine, 1975—, head divsn. med. genetics, 1984—, prof. medicine and cell biology, 1996—. Hon. fellow Galton Lab. Human Genetics & Biometry Univ. Coll., London, 1971—72; assoc. attending physician in medicine Bellevue Hosp., NYC, 1969—80, Univ. Hosp., NYU Sch. Medicine, 1974—81; attending physician Bellevue Hosp., 1980—, Univ. Hosp., 1981—; com. mem., study sect. NIH, 1973—; vis. prof. Harvard U., 1995, U. Calif., San Francisco, 1995; mem. scientific search com. Barnard Coll., 2003—; internat. adv. bd. Peking U. Ctr. Med. Genetics, 2005—07. Trustee AIDS Med. Found./AMFAR; judge Westinghouse Nat. Sci. Talent Search; founding mem. Village Cmty. Sch.; senator NYU Senate, mem. pediatrics search com., 1987—89, human subjects instl. rev. bd., 1989—94, co-dir. second year med. genetics course, 1989—93, NYU appts. and promotions com., 1995—2002; adv. bd. mem. Genzyme Corp., Pompe, 2002—. Named Disting. Alumna, Barnard Coll., Hero of the Arthritis Found.; recipient Alumni Berson award, NYU Sch. Medicine, Lifetime Achievement award, Jeffrey Modell Found. Master: Am. Coll. Rheumatology; fellow: AAAS, Hero Arthritis Found., Am. Coll. Med. Genetics (founding fellow); mem.: Inst. of Medicine of NAS, Am. Assn. Physicians, Nat. Acad. Sci. Inst. Medicine, Harvey Soc. (coun. 1989—92), Soc. for Inherited Metabolic Diseases, Peripatetic Soc., Interurban Clin. Club (pres. 1987—88), Am. Soc. Human Genetics (cert. 1987), Am. Assn. Immunologists, Assn. Am. Physicians, Am. Soc. for Clin. Investigation, Harvey Soc. (councilor 1989), Alpha Omega Alpha (councillor Delta of N.Y. 1982—2002). Achievements include elucidation of pathophysiologic mechanisms, delineation of molecular and biochemical defects of genetic disorders including adenosine deaminase and glycogen storage disease type II; providing proof of principle of therapeutic options and cloning of the therapeutic molecule; identification of somatic mosaicism due to reversion to normal of inherited mutations and of increasing incidence and significance for gene therapy. Office: NYU Med Ctr 550 1st Ave CD612 New York NY 10016-6402 Home Phone: 212-982-0861; Office Phone: 212-263-6276. Business E-Mail: hirscr01@med.nyu.edu.

HIRSCHKOP, PHILIP JAY, lawyer, educator; b. Bklyn., May 14, 1936; s. Abraham and Frances H.; children: Jacqueline, Jon David, Adam Abraham. AB, Columbia Coll., 1960; BS in Engring., Columbia U., 1961; JD, Georgetown U., 1964. Bar: Va. 1964, D.C. 1964, U.S. Dist. Ct. (ea. and we. dists.) Va. 1964, U.S. Dist. Ct. D.C. 1964, U.S. Ct. Mil. Appeals 1964, U.S. Ct. Appeals (4th and D.C. cirs.) 1965, U.S. Supreme 1967, U.S. Ct. Claims 1969, U.S. Dist. Ct. (no. dist.) Tex. 1973, U.S. Ct. Appeals (5th cir.) 1973, U.S. Tax Ct. 1974, U.S. Ct. Appeals (11th cir.), 1981, N.Y., 1982, U.S. Dist. Ct. (ea. dist.) N.C., U.S. Dist. Ct. D.C. Patent examiner U.S. Patent Office, Washington, 1961-63; legis. asst. congressman Richard Ichord, Washington, 1964; pvt. practice Alexandria, Va., 1964—. Adj. prof. law Georgetown U., Washington, 1969-75; profl. law lectr. George Washington U., 2001; chair steering com. Nat. Prison Project, Washington, 1975—; spkr. in field. Contbr. articles to profl. jours. Nat. bd. dirs. ACLU, N.Y.C., 1966-86. With Spl. Forces, U.S. Army, 1954-56. Recipient Disting. Svc. award, Va. Trial Lawyers Assn., 1999, War Horse award, So. Trial Lawyers Assn., 2000. Fellow Va. Law Found.; mem. ATLA (state committeman), PETA (gen. counsel), NCIA (dir., counsel), Va. Bar Assn., Alexandria Bar Assn., Trial Lawyers for Pub. Justice (bd dirs., founder 1986-96), Law Students Civil Rights Rsch. Coun. Office: Hirschkop & Assocs PC 908 King St Ste 200 Alexandria VA 22314

HIRSCHMAN, BARRY H., human resources specialist; b. Perth Amboy, NJ, Dec. 21, 1972; s. Monroe and Susan Hirschman (Stepmother); m. Randi Joy Lipkin, Aug. 31, 2003. BA, Bowling Green State U., 1994; postgrad., Rutgers U., 2004—. Cert. human resources profl. Sr. recruiter, acct. mgr., Princeton, NJ; group human resources mgr. Mistras Holdings Group, Princeton Junction, NJ, 1999—. Bd. dirs. Princeton East Condo. Assn., East Windsor, NJ. Sgt. US Army. Mem.: Soc. Human Resources. Office: Mistras Holdings Group 195 Clarksville Rd Princeton Junction NJ 08550 E-mail: bhirschman@pacndt.com.

HIRSCHMAN, CHARLES, JR., sociologist, educator; b. Atlanta, Nov. 29, 1943; s. Charles Sr. and Mary Gertrude (Mullee) H.; m. Josephine Knight, Jan. 29, 1968; children: Andrew Charles, Sarah Lynn. BA, Miami U., Oxford, Ohio, 1965; MS, U. Wis., 1969, PhD, 1972. Vol. Peace Corps, Malaysia, 1965-67; prof. Duke U., Durham, NC, 1972-81, Cornell U., Ithaca, NY, 1981-87, U. Wash., Seattle, 1987—, chair dept. sociology, 1995-98, Boeing internat. prof., 1999—. Cons. Ford Found., Malaysia, 1974-75; chair social scis. and population study sect. NIH, Washington, 1987-91; vis. scholar Russell Sage Found., 1998-99. Author: Ethnic and Social Stratification in Peninsula Malaysia, 1975; editor: The Handbook of International Migration: The American Experience, 1999; contbr. articles to profl. jours. Fellow Ctr. Advanced Study in the Bahavioral Scis., Stanford, Calif., 1993-94. Fellow AAAS (chair sect. K on social, econs. and polit. scis. 2004-), Am. Acad. Arts and Scis.; mem. Assn. for Asian Studies (bd. dirs. 1987-90), Population Assn Am. (bd. dirs. 1992-94, v.p. 1997, pres. 2005). Office: U Wash Dept Sociology PO Box 353340 Seattle WA 98195-3340 Home Phone: 206-525-5324; Office Phone: 206-543-5035. Business E-Mail: charles@u.washington.edu.

HIRSCHMAN, KAREN L., lawyer; b. York, Pa., Dec. 15, 1952; BA, U. Del., 1973; MA, U. Tex., 1980, JD with honors, 1983. Bar: Tex. 1983, DC 2002, NY 2003. Ptnr., co-head Litig. Sect. Vinson & Elkins LLP, Dallas. Fellow: Tex. Bar Found.; mem.: ABA, Am. Law Inst. Office: Vinson & Elkins LLP Trammell Crow Ctr 2001 Ross Ave, Ste 3700 Dallas TX 75201 Office Phone: 214-220-7795. Business E-Mail: khirschman@velaw.com.

HIRSCHMANN, FRANZ GOTTFRIED, aerospace executive; b. Kempten, Germany, Oct. 4, 1945; came to U.S., 1973; s. Kurt Rudolf G. and Linda (Krieger) H.; m. Cindy Villarica, Nov. 27, 1992; children: Dillon G., Michael A. BS, FWG Coll., Cologne, Germany, 1965; MA, U. Bonn, Germany, 1973; MBA, Pepperdine U., 1981. Mktg. mgr. Western US and S. Am. regions United Techs./Ambac, LA, 1978-80; mktg. mgr. Western U.S. and Pacific regions Buehler Inc., LA and NC, 1981-83; mgr. internat. mktg. Gen. Dynamics, Pomona, Calif., 1983-84, mgr. info. svcs., 1984-88, mgr. spl. projects, 1988-89; mgr. bus. devel. and market rsch. Hughes Aircraft Co., Canoga park, Calif., 1989-93, mgr. strategic planning, 1993-98; mgr. bus. analysis Boeing, Anaheim, Calif., 1999—2001, mgr. all Boeing space patents, 2001—04; mgr. bus. devel., intellectual property Boeing Math. & Computing Techs., Seattle, 2004—. Owner Hirschmann Industries (Entertainment Co.), 1992—; confiscator, team leader E.I.A. 10 year Forecast, 1989-2001. Author: Mandaic Inscription, 1970; inventor deciphering lang. computer. Vol. Lincoln Club, LA, 1981; co-founder Retinitis Pigmentosa Found.; chmn. North Orange County Cub Scouts, 2000-04, comm. mem Boy Scout Troop #553; co-lead multiple environ. campaigns, 1996-; fund raiser Sierra Club, 1996—. Mem. Nat. Mgmt. Assn., Pepperdine U. Alumni Assn. (exec. bd.), Sierra Club (leader, vice chmn. coun. 1990-93), No. Orange County Cub Scouts (chmn. 2000-, co-lead multiple environ. campings). Democrat. Lutheran. Avocations: photography, hiking, sailing, yoga, ancient languages. Home: 14222 110 Ave Ct E Puyallup WA 98374 Office: Phantom Worka/M&CT PO Box 3707 Seattle WA 98124 Home Phone: 253-840-0422; Office Phone: 425-865-4329. Personal E-mail: fghirschman@aol.com.

HIRSCHMANN, JAMES WILLIAM, III, diversified financial services company executive; b. Phila., Oct. 10, 1960; s. James William Jr. and Elizabeth Jane (Murray) H.; m. Laura Anne Gumina, May 16, 1986; children: James William IV, Samantha Anne. BSBA, Widener U., Chester, Pa., 1982. Internal auditor Western Savs. Bank, Phila., 1981-82; cost analyst Berkey Film Processing (name now Qualex), Bensalem, Pa., 1982-83; account mgr. U.S. Lines, Cranford, N.J., 1983-84, dist. sales mgr., 1984-85, regional sales mgr., 1985-86; v.p. Atalanta/Sosnoff Capital, NYC, 1986-88; v.p., dir. mktg. Fin. Trust Co., Denver, 1988-89; with Western Asset Mgmt. Co., Pasadena, Calif., 1989—, pres., CEO, 1999—; pres., COO Legg Mason, Inc., Balt., 2006—07. Patentee recycling trash receptacle. Trustee Widener U. Mem. Assn. Investment Mgmt. Sales Execs., Investment Mgmt. Inst., Fellowship Christian Athletes, Manhattan Country Club. Republican. Roman Catholic. Avocations: basketball, running, tennis, travel, collectables. Office: Western Asset Mgmt Co 385 E Colorado Blvd Pasadena CA 91101*

HIRSCHMANN, PETER, video game company executive; b. Aug. 24, 1971; married. With Amblin Entertainment; prodr. LucasArts, San Francisco, 2002—04, v.p. product devel., 2004—. Prodr.: (video games) The Lost World: Jurassic Park, 1997, Medal of Honor, 1999, Medal of Honor: Underground, 2000, Medal of Honor: Frontline, 2002, Medal of Honor: Allied Assault, 2002, Star Wars: Galaxies - An Empire Divided, 2003, Secret Weapons Over Normandy, 2003, Star Wars: Knights of the Old Republic II - The Sith Lords, 2004, Star Wars: Galaxies - Jump to Light Speed, 2004, Star Wars: Battlefront, 2004, Star Wars: Republic Commando, 2005, Star Wars: Galaxies - The Total Experience, 2005, Star Wars: Episode III - Revenge of the Sith, 2005, Star Wars: Battlefront II, 2005, LEGO Star Wars: The Video Game, 2005, Star Wars: Empire at War - Forces of Corruption, 2006, Star Wars: Empire at War, 2006, LEGO Star Wars II: The Original Trilogy, 2006; exec. prodr.: (video games) Mercenaries: Playground of Destruction, 2005. Office: LucasArts PO Box 29908 San Francisco CA 94129-0908*

HIRSCHMANN, RALPH FRANZ, chemist; b. Fuerth, Bavaria, Germany, May 6, 1922; came to U.S., 1937; s. Carl and Alice (Buchenbacher) H.; m. Lucy Marguerite Aliminosa, Mar. 9, 1951; children— Ralph F., Carla M. Hirschmann Hummel AB, Oberlin Coll., 1943, D.Sc. (hon.), 1969; MA, U. Wis., 1948, PhD, 1950, DSc (hon.), 1996. Asst. dir. Merck Sharp & Dohme Research Labs., Rahway, N.J., 1964-68, dir., 1968-71, sr. dir. West Point, Pa., 1972-74, exec. dir., 1974-76, v.p. Rahway, 1976-78, sr. v.p., 1978-87; rsch. prof. chemistry U. Pa., Phila, 1987—2006, Makineni prof. bioorganic chemistry Phila., 1994—2006, emeritus prof., 2006—; prof. biomed. research Med. U. S.C., Charleston, 1987-97. Mem. N.J. Gov.'s Commn. on Sci. and Tech., 1984; mem. adv. com. NSF, 1985; mem. com. to survey opportunities in chem. scis. NRC, 1982; Romanes lectr. U. Edinburgh, Eng., 1985; Charles D. Hurd lectr. Northwestern U., 1985; Shell Disting. lectr., 1994, Monsanto lectr. Purdue U., 1996; mem. com. on chem. and pub. affairs Am. Chem. Soc. Contbr. numerous articles to profl. jours.; patentee in field Trustee Oberline Coll., 1986-93. Served with U.S. Army, 1943-46, PTO. Recipient Nichols medal, 1988, Chem. Pioneer award Am. Inst. Chemists, 1992, Gold medal Max Bergman Kreis, 1993, Alfred Burger award Am. Chem. Soc., 1994, Padmavathy and Noth Guthikonda Meml. award, 1996, Dr. Josef Rudinger award European Peptide Soc., 1996, Rsch. Achievement award in medicinal and natural products chemistry Am. Assn. Pharm. Scientists, 1996, Nat'l Acad. Sci. award for Industrial Application of Science, 1999, Arthur C. Cope Medal, 1999, Ed Smissman Bristol-Meyers Squibb award, 1999, Nat'l Medal of Science, 2000, Williard Gibbs Medal, 2002. Fellow AAAS, ACS (Medicinal Chemistry award 1986, Carothers award Del. sect. 1994); mem. Am. Acad. Arts and Scis., Am. Soc. Biol. Chemists, NAS; sr. fellow, Institutes of Medicine. Home: Meadowood 711 Radcliff Ct Lansdale PA 19446 Office: U Pa Dept Chemistry 231 S 34th St Philadelphia PA 19104-3803 Home Phone: 484-991-1107; Office Phone: 215-898-7398. Personal E-mail: thehirschmanns@aol.com.

HIRSCHOWITZ, BASIL ISAAC, physician; b. Bethal, South Africa, May 29, 1925; came to U.S., 1953, naturalized, 1961; s. Morris and Dorothy (Drieband) H.; m. Barbara L. Burns, July 6, 1958; children: David E., Karen, Edward A., Vanessa. BSc, Witwatersrand U., Johannesburg, 1943, MB, BChir, 1947, MD, 1954; MD (hon.), U. Gothenburg, Sweden, 2004. Intern, resident Johannesburg Gen. Hosp., 1948-50; house physician Postgrad. Med. Sch., London, Eng., 1950; registrar Central Middlesex Hosp., London, 1951-53; instr., asst. prof. U. Mich., 1953-56; asst. prof. Temple U., 1957-59; dir. divsn. gastroenterology U. Ala. Hosp. and Clinics, 1959—87; assoc. prof. medicine U. Ala. Med. Ctr., Birmingham, 1959—64, prof. medicine, 1964-95, emeritus prof., 1995, prof. physiology, 1970—, Reynolds lectr., 2007; chmn. faculty coun. U. Ala. Sch. Medicine, 1989-90; chmn. exec. com. U. Ala. Hosp., 1986-88. Disting. faculty lectr. U. Ala., 1988, Reynolds lectr., 2007. Named U. chair in honor, 1997; named to, Ala. Acad. Honor, 1991, Ala. Health Care Hall of Fame, 2002; recipient Charles F. Kettering prize, GM Cancer Found., 1987, Seale Harris award, So. Med. Assn., 1992, Markowitz award, Am. Soc. Surg. Rsch., 1999, Pioneer in Endoscopy award, Soc. Am. Gastrointestinal Surgeons, 2003, Brohee medal, World Congress Gastroenterology, 2006. Master ACP (Laureate award 1989); fellow AAAS, Am. Gastroent. Assn. (Friedenwald medal 1992), Assn. Am. Physicians, Royal Coll. Physicians (Edinburgh), Royal Coll. Physicians (London), Royal Soc. Medicine (hon.), Royal Philatelic Soc., (London); mem. AMA, South African, Brit., Ala. Med. Assns., Med. Rsch. Soc. Gt. Britain, Am. Fedn. Clin. Rsch., So. Soc. Clin. Investigation, Am. Physiol. Soc., Biophys. Soc., Am. Soc. Gastro-Intestinal Endoscopy (Schindler medal 1974, Disting. lectr. 1994, Spl. Recognition award 2006), Am. Coll. Gastroenterology (Disting. Sci. Achievement award 1982), Brit. Soc. Gastro-Intestinal Endoscopy (hon.), Brit. Soc. Gastroenterology (Hurst lectr. 1966, Found. lectr. 1988, Astra internat. lectr. 1997), Italian Soc. Gastroenterology corr.), William Beaumont Soc. (Eddy Palmer award for contbns. to endoscopy 1976), Soc. Exptl. Biology and Medicine, Sigma Xi, Alpha Omega Alpha. Office: U Ala Med Ctr Birmingham AL 35294-0001 Business E-Mail: bih@uab.edu.

HIRSCHSON, LINDA BENJAMIN, lawyer; b. NYC, Jan. 21, 1941; d. Philip David and Ruth (Levy) Benjamin; m. Albert M. Hirschson, Dec. 22, 1963; children: Jay Philip, Pamela Ellen. AB, Barnard Coll., 1962; LLB cum laude, Columbia U., 1965; LLM in Taxation, NYU, 1973. Bar: NY 1965, US Tax Ct. 1975, US Dist. Ct. (so. and ea. dists. NY) 1976. Assoc. Kaye, Scholer et. al., NYC, 1965-70; tchg. fellow NYU Law Sch., NYC, 1970-73; assoc. prof. Hofstra Law Sch., Hempstead, NY, 1974-77; assoc. Gilbert, Segall & Young, NYC, 1977-79, ptnr., 1979-93, Katten, Muchin & Zavis, NYC, 1994-96, Parson & Brown, NYC, 1996-98; shareholder Greenberg Traurig, LLP, NYC, 1998—. Contbg. editor: Rev. Taxation/Individual Jour., 1982—89, editor-in-chief: Estate and Gift Tax After ERTA, 1982; co-author (with Arthur M. Sherwood): Changes in the New York Definition of Trust Accounting Principal and Income, 2002. Trustee Calhoun Sch., NYC, 1986—92; treas. Friend Joffrey Ballet NY chpt., 1988—91; treas., bd. dirs. Barnard Bus. and Profl. Women, NYC, 1982—86; mem. EPTL Adv. Com. to NY State Legislature, 1990—94, 1997—, advisor, 1997. Named Outstanding Alumna The Calhoun Sch., 1985; named one of Top 100 Attys. Worth mag., 2006. Fellow: Am. Coll. Trust and Estate Counsel (chmn. transfer tax com. 1998—2001, regent 2003—, state chair 2006—); mem.: ABA (chmn. martial deduction com. real property, probate and trust sect. 1996—, supervisory coun. real property probate and trust sect. 2001—07), Assn. Bar City NY (estate and gift tax com. 1989—92, chmn. Mortimer Hess lectr. com. 1992—94, com. trusts, estates and surrogate's ct. 2001—04), NY State Bar Assn. (chmn. taxation com. tax sect. 1986—89, chair trusts and estates law sect. 1996), United Jewish Appeal Fedn. (honoree trusts and estates group). Avocations: skiing, tennis, jogging. Office: Greenberg Traurig MetLife Bldg 200 Park Ave Fl 14 New York NY 10166-1400 Office Phone: 212-801-9342. E-mail: hirschsonl@gtlaw.com.

HIRSH, ALLAN THURMAN, JR., publishing executive; b. Cumberland, Md., Aug. 19, 1920; s. Allan Thurman and Ellinor Goldsmith (Ottenheimer) H.; m. Eleanor R. Rosenthal, June 17, 1944; children: Helene, Allan III, Eleanor. BS in Econs., Johns Hopkins U., 1941. CPA, Md. Acct. Burke Landsberg Gerber, Balt., 1941-42; pres. Ottenheimer Pubs., Inc, Balt., 1946-89, chmn. bd., 1989—; v.p. Allan Pubs., Inc., Balt., 1980—2003, Creative Horizons (formerly Ottenheimer Creations Inc.), Balt., 1994—2003, Thurman House, Hong Kong, 1994—2003; ptnr. Ottenheimer Properties LLC, 2003—. Bd. dirs. Balt. Hebrew Congregation, 1960-63, 83-86, 11 Slade Apt. Corp., 1985-88, 98-2003, pres., 1987-88, treas., 1998-2002, Lincoln Towers, West Palm Beach, Fla., 2005—; assoc. Jewish Charities, Balt., 1972-79; pres. Forest Park H.S. PTA, 1968, Balt. City Coll. PTA, 1971; bd. dirs. Hebrew Burial and Social Service Soc., 1946, pres. 1972-79; mem. adv. coun. on aging Johns Hopkins, 2004—. With USN, 1942-46. Mem.: Suburban (Balt.) (dir. 1974-79, v.p. 1976-79); Presidents (West Palm Beach, Fla.). Democrat. Jewish. Home: Apt 710 11 Slade Ave Baltimore MD 21208 Personal E-mail: allanhirsh@aol.com.

HIRSH, ANNETTE MARIE, artist; b. Milw., Oct. 20, 1921; d. Isidor and Ruby Zolin; children: Jay, T. Robin. Student, Milw. State Tchrs. Coll., 1939—41, Layton Sch. Art, Milw., 1968, Shorewood Opportunity Sch., 1956—58. Advt. artist Gimbels, Milw., 1941—42, Boston Store, Milw., 1942—44; fashion artist Goldblatt's Dept. Store, Chgo., 1944—46; docent Milw. Art Ctr., 1960—66; tchr. art Shorewood Opportunity Sch., 1966—72; tchr. watercolor Milw. Area Tech. Coll., 1972—2001; curator Baron Mus. Judaica, Milw., 1970—; silversmith pvt. practice, Milw., 1953—. Historian Wis. Designer Crafts Coun., 1991—2006. Avocations: genealogy, painting, walking. Home: 4124 N Ardmore Ave Milwaukee WI 53211

HIRSH, BERNARD, supply company executive, consultant; b. Seguin, Tex., July 18, 1916; s. Samuel and Sarah (Marks) H.; m. Johanna Charlotte Cristol, Feb. 14, 1941 (dec. Jan. 1977); children: Richard, Robert, Terry, Cristy; m. Beatrice Castelle, Feb. 11, 1978. BA, LLB, JD, U. Tex., 1939. Bar: Tex. 1939. Claims rep. Globe, Eagle & Royal Ins. Cos., 1939, R.A. Handley Claim Svc., Dallas, 1940—41; spl. agt. War Food Adminstrn., U.S. Govt., Dallas, 1941-44; pres. Milliners Supply Co., Dallas, 1945-82, chmn. bd., 1982—2000. Dir. Forestwood Nat. Bank, 1980—86. Pres. Temple Emanu-El Brotherhood, Dallas, 1960-62, Temple Emanu-El, Dallas, 1970-72, Nat. Fedn. Temple Brotherhoods, N.Y.C., 1974-76; chancellor Jewish Chautauqua Soc., N.Y., 1970-72; mgr. freshman football team U. Tex., Austin, Tex., 1933; mem. Tex. Defense Guard, 1941-42. Mem. Dallas Bar Assn., State Bar Tex. Avocations: travel, reading.

HIRSH, CRISTY J., principal; b. Dallas, Oct. 3, 1952; d. Bernard and Johanna (Cristol) Hirsh. BS in Early Childhood and Elem. Edn., Boston U., Mass., 1974; MS in Spl. Edn., U. Tex., Dallas, 1978; MEd in Counseling and Student Svcs., U. North Tex., Denton, 1991. Cert. counselor, sch. counselor; lic. profl. counselor, Tex.; cert. tchr., Tex., Mass.; cert. prin., Tex. Dir., learning specialist Specialized Learning, Dallas, 1981—93; counselor, mem. adj. faculty Eastfield Coll., Mesquite, Tex., 1992—95; counselor Grapevine-Colleyville Ind. Sch. Dist., Tex., 1995—2000, alternative sch. prin., 2000—. Mem. adj. faculty Richland Coll., Dallas, 1991—92. Mem. ACA, ASCD, Am. Sch. Counselor Assn., Coun. for Exceptional Children, Coun. for Children with Behavior Disorders, Tex. Assn. for Alternative Edn., Pi Lambda Theta, Phi Delta Kappa. Avocations: travel, theater, films, cooking, reading. Office: VISTA Alternative Campus 3051 Ira E Woods Ave Grapevine TX 76051-3817

HIRSH, JACK, medical researcher; b. Melbourne, Australia, Jan. 5, 1935; Grad., U. Melborne Med. Sch.; DSc (hon.), McMaster U., 1999. Expanded knowledge of hematology at Washington U., St. Louis, London Postgraduate Med. Sch., U. Toronto; joined faculty of medicine McMaster U., Hamilton, Canada, 1973, prof. emeritus of medicine, chmn., dept. medicine; dir. Henderson Rsch. Ctr., Hamilton, Canada. V.p., med. Ontario Heart Found. Named to Canadian Hall of Fame, 2000; recipient Disting. Rsch. Professorship award, Heart and Stroke Found. Ontario, Trillium Clin. Scientist award, Ontario Ministry Health, Ham-Wasserman Lectureship, Am. Soc. Hematology, 1996, Editl. Excellence award, Am. Coll. Chest Physicians, 1996, Prix Galien award, 1999, Gairdner Found. Internat. award, 2000. Fellow: Royal Soc. Can.; mem.: Med. Rsch. Coun. Can. (coun. mem.), Internat. Soc. on Thrombosis and Haemostasis (chmn.), Order of Can. Office: Henderson Rsch Ctr McMaster U 711 Concession St Hamilton ON L8V 1C3 Canada Office Phone: 905-527-2299 42600. Office Fax: 905-575-2646. Business E-Mail: jhirsh@thrombosis.hhscr.org.

HIRSH, SHARON LATCHAW, academic administrator, art history educator; b. Mt. Lebanon, Pa., Apr. 19, 1948; d. Raymond J. and Mary Cassel (Hudock) Latchaw; m. Neil Hirsh (dec.); 1 child, Michael. BA, Rosemont Coll., 1970; MA, U. Pitts., 1971, PhD, 1974. From asst. prof. to prof. Dickinson Coll., Carlisle, Pa., 1974—2005, Charles A. Dana prof. art history; acting pres. Rosemont Coll., Bryn Mawr, Pa., 2005—06, pres., 2006—. Vis. curator Montreal Mus. Fine Arts, 1989, Schweizerisch Institute für Kunstwissenschaft in Zurich; dir. Trout Gallery, Carlisle, Pa., 1992; vis. sr. fellow Ctr. for Advanced Studies in Visual Arts, Nat. Gallery, 1998; vis. scholar Art Inst. Chgo. Co-curator Ferdinand Hodler: Views and Visions exhibit, Cin. Mus. Art, Nat. Acad. Design, Ontario Art Gallery, Wadsworth Atheneum Mus.; author: Ferdinand Hodler, 1981, Hodler's Symbolist Themes, 1983, Fine Art of the Gesture, 1989, Symbolism and Modern Urban Soc., 2004; co-editor: Art, Culture, and National Identity in Fin-de-Siecle Europe, 2003; contbr. articles to profl. jours. Recipient Ganoe award for Inspiration Teaching, 1981, Lindback award for Disting. Teaching, 1991; Andrew Mellon grantee, 1972, 1973. Mem.: Interdisciplinary Nineteenth Century Studies Assn., Coll. Art Assn. Office: Rosemont Coll Office of Pres 1400 Montgomery Ave Bryn Mawr PA 19010 Office Phone: 610-527-0200.

HIRSHFIELD, STUART, lawyer; b. NYC, Dec. 31, 1941; s. William Louis and Anne H.; m. Susanne Drucker, Jan. 22, 1967; children: Matthew S., Edward R. BA, Syracuse U., 1963, JD, 1966. Bar: NY 1966, US Dist. Ct. (so. and ea. dists.) NY 1968, US Ct. Appeals (2nd cir.) 1968. Assoc. Krauss & Krauss, NYC, 1966-67; atty. NY Cen. RR, NYC, 1967-69; assoc. Blum, Haimoff, Gersen, Lipson & Szabad, NYC, 1969; atty. CIT Fin., NYC, 1970-72; assoc. Shea & Gould, NYC, 1972-77, ptnr., 1977-88; ptnr., chmn. bankruptcy practice group Dewey Ballantine, NYC, 1988—2003; ptnr., co-head bankruptcy and bus. reorgn. dept. Ropes & Gray LLP, NYC, 2003—. Bd. dirs. 565 Tenants Corp. Contbr. Asset Based Financing--A Transactional Guide, 1985. Assn. atty. Allenwood Civic Assn., Great Neck,

NY, 1984; bd. advisors Syracuse U. Coll. Law, 1990—2006, exec. com., 1991—96; trustee The Colonial Theatre, 2004—. With USAR, 1966—72. Fellow Am. Coll. Bankruptcy (2d cir. admissions coun. 1994-2001, chair 1998-2001, bd. regents 1998-2001, bd. dirs. 2001-07), Am Coll. Bankruptcy Found. (bd dirs. 2002-), Am Bar Found.; mem. ABA (com. on bankruptcy 1983—), NY Bar Assn., Assn. Bar City NY (corp. reogn. com. 1975-78, 82-85), Assn. Comml. Fin. Attys. (dir. 1980-93), Country Club Pittsfield, Rockefeller Ctr. Club, Phi Delta Phi. Office: Ropes & Gray LLP 1211 Ave Americas New York NY 10036 Home Phone: 212-688-1148; Office Phone: 212-841-0682. Office Fax: 646-728-1599. Business E-Mail: stuart.hirshfield@ropesgray.com.

HIRSHON, ROBERT EDWARD, lawyer; b. Portland, Maine, Apr. 2, 1948; s. Selvin and Gladys (Wein) H.; m. Roberta Lynn Miller, Aug. 16, 1969; children: Todd, Sara, Jason, Miriam. BA, U. Mich., 1970, JD, 1973. Bar: Maine 1973, U.S. Dist. Ct. Maine 1973, U.S. Ct. Appeals (1st cir.) 1977, U.S. Supreme Ct. 2000. Shareholder Drummond, Woodsum & MacMahon P.A., Portland, Maine, 1973—2003; CEO Tonkon Torp LLP, Portland, 2003—. Adj. prof. law U. Maine Law Sch. Contbr. articles to profl. jours. Chairperson Breakwater Sch Bd., Portland, 1978-85; mem. Zoning Bd. Appeals, Cape Elizabeth, Maine, 1983-90. Mem. ABA (mem. Ho. of Dels. 1992—, chair standing com. lawyers pub. svc. responsibility 1990-93, chair steering com. pro bono ctr. 1991-96, chair torts and ins. practice sect. 1996-97, chair standing com. on membership 1997-2000, pres. 2001-02), Maine Bar Assn. (pres. 1986, chair continuing legal edn. com. 1975-83), Cumberland County Bar Assn., Maine Bar Found. (pres. 1990), Multromah Bar Assn. Avocations: reading, tennis, skiing. Home: 3 Oakhurst Rd Cape Elizabeth ME 04107 Office: Tonkon Torp LLP 1600 Pioneer Tower 888 SW Fifth Ave Portland OR 97204 Business E-Mail: bobh@tonkon.com.

HIRSHON, SHELDON IRA, lawyer; b. Bklyn., Mar. 27, 1947; s. Jay and Jeanne (Benk) H.; m. Claudia Glenn Barasch; children: Ariel, Yaniv, Jessica. BS, NYU, 1968, JD, 1972, LLM, 1978. Bar: N.Y. 1972. Assoc. Graubard, Moskovitz, McGoldrick, Dannett & Horowitz, NYC, 1972-76, Windels, Marx, Davies & Ives, NYC, 1976-78, Krause, Hirsch & Gross, NYC, 1978-80; assoc., ptnr. Stroock & Stroock & Lavan, NYC, 1980-87; ptnr. Proskauer, Rose LLP, NYC, 1987—. Mem. ABA, N.Y. Bar Assn., Assn. Bar City N.Y. Office: Proskauer Rose LLP 1585 Broadway Fl 27 New York NY 10036-8299 Office Phone: 212-969-3270. Business E-Mail: shirshon@proskauer.com.

HIRSHOWITZ, MELVIN STEPHEN, lawyer; b. NYC, Dec. 11, 1938; s. Samuel Albert and Lillian Rose (Minkow) H.; m. Susan Bonnie Brezel, June 19, 1983; children: Lauren Allison, Emily Sara. BA with hons., Cornell U., 1960; LLB cum laude, Harvard U., 1963; MA in Biology, CUNY, 1977. Bar: N.Y. 1963, N.J. 1987, U.S. Dist. Ct. (so. dist.) N.Y. 1969, (ea. dist.) N.Y. 1977, N.J. 1993, U.S. Ct. Appeals (2d cir.) 1978, U.S. Supreme Ct. 1994. Assoc. atty. SEC, NYC, 1963-65; sole practitioner Melvin Hirshowitz Law Office, NYC, 1968-76, 87--; of counsel Hyman Bravin Law Offices, NYC, 1976-87. Author: (manual) Proof of an Over the Counter Manipulation, 1964. Vice chmn. N.Y. Libertarian Party, 1970-72, candidate for surrogate ct. judge and ct. of appeals judge. Mem. N.Y. County Lawyers Assn. (com. on profl. ethics 1986-92, com. fed. legislation 1986-88), Assn. of Bar of City of N.Y. (com. on the civil ct. 1986-89), N.Y. State Bar Assn., Harvard Club of N.Y.C., Phi Beta Kappa, Pi Delta Epsilon. Republican. Jewish. Avocations: bird watching, art, tennis. Office: 630 3rd Ave New York NY 10017-6705 Home Phone: 914-636-6747; Office Phone: 212-867-9595. Personal E-mail: mshlawoffices@aol.com.

HIRT, F. WILLIAM, insurance company executive; BA, Wittenberg Univ., 1947. CPCU. With Erie Indemnity Co. (Erie Ins. Group), Erie, Pa., 1947—, v.p., 1967—76, pres., 1976—81, CEO, 1981—90, chmn., 1981—. Co-trustee H.O. Hirt Trusts. Office: Erie Indemnity Co 100 Erie Insurance Place PO Box 1699 Erie PA 16530*

HIRT, JANE, editor; B in Journalism, U. Nebr., Lincoln. With Chgo. Tribune, 1990—2002, sports copy editor, fgn. and nat. desk copy editor, fgn. and nat. news editor; founding co-editor RedEye, 2002—05, editor, 2005—. Named one of Top 40 Under 40, Crain's Chgo. Bus., 2006. Office: RedEye Tribune Tower 435 N Michigan Ave Chicago IL 60611 E-mail: jhirt@tribune.com.*

HIRT, JOAN B., education educator; b. Huntington, NY, Feb. 20, 1951; d. Warren G. and Ruth T. Hirt. BA in Russian Studies, Bucknell U., 1972; MAEd, U. Md., 1979; PhD, U. Ariz., 1992. Assoc. dir. housing and dining svcs. Humboldt State U., Arcata, Calif., 1979-88; assoc. dean students U. Ariz., Tucson, 1988-92; assoc. prof. higher edn. and student affairs Va. Tech. U., Blacksburg, 1994—. Cons. in edn.; corp. cons. Contbr. chpts. to books, articles to profl. jours. Mem. Am. Coll. Pers. Assn. (bd. dirs. CxII 1996-99), Assn. for Study of Higher Edn., Nat. Assn. Student Pers., Am. Coll. Pers. Assn. Office: ELPS 0302-Va Tech U 307 W Eggleston Hall Blacksburg VA 24061 Office Phone: 540-231-9700.

HIRTH, JOHN PRICE, metallurgical engineering educator; b. Cin., Dec. 16, 1930; s. John Willard and Betty Ann (Price) H.; m. Martha Joan Davis, Nov. 28, 1953; children: John Marcus, Laura Ellen, James Gregory, Christina Louise. B. Metall. Engring., Ohio State U., 1953; MS, Carnegie-Mellon U., 1953, PhD, 1957; DSc (hon.), Ohio State U., 1995. Asst. prof. metall. engring. Carnegie-Mellon U., Pitts., 1958-61; Mershon prof. Ohio State U., 1961-67; vis. prof. Stanford, 1967-68; prof. Ohio State U., Columbus, 1967-88, Wash. State U., Pullman, 1988—. Aizen vis. prof. Nat. U. Mex., Mexico City, 1976; cons. in field; bd. overseers Acad. for Contemporary Problems, 1971-76. Author: Condensation and Evaporation, 1964, Theory of Dislocations, 1968, 82; editor: Scripta Metallurgica, 1974-94. Served with USAF, 1953-55. Fulbright fellow Bristol U., Eng., 1957-58 Fellow AAAS, TMS (Hardy medal 1960, Mehl medal 1980, Mathewson medal 1982), Am. Soc. Engring. Edn. (McGraw award 1967), Am. Soc. Metals (Stoughton award 1964, Campbell lectr. 1972, White award 1989, Gold medal 1994, Sauveur Achievement award 1998); mem. NAS, NAE, ASME (Nadai medal 1999), Norwegian Acad. Scis. and Letters, AIME (hon.), Sigma Xi. Home: 114 E Ramsey Canyon Rd Hereford AZ 85615-9614 Personal E-mail: jphmdh1@cox.net.

HIRUKI, CHUJI, plant pathologist, educator; b. Fukue, Nagasaki, Japan, June 16, 1931; arrived in Can., 1966; s. Chuichi and Mitsu (Kawamuko) H.; m. Yasuko Hijikata, Dec. 26, 1961; children: Tadaaki, Lisa. BSc, Kyushu U., Fukuoka, 1954, PhD, 1963. Plant pathologist Hatano Tobacco Expt. Sta., Hatano, Japan, 1954-65; asst. prof. U. Alberta, Edmonton, Can., 1966-70, assoc. prof., 1970-76, prof., 1976-91, univ. prof., 1991-96, univ. prof. emeritus, 1996—. Vis. plant pathologist, U. Calif., Berkeley, 1963-64; vis. scientist INRA, Versailles, France, 1972; vis. prof. Agrl. U., Wageningen, The Netherlands, 1973; CSFP vis. prof. U. Queensland, Brisbane, Australia, 1984-85; hon. disting. scientist China Paulownia Rsch. Ctr., 1993-95; internat. cons. forest pathology FAO UN, 1993-95; hon. disting. prof. Yunnan Biotech. Rsch. Inst., Kunming, China, 2000-, hon. dist. prof. Life Sci., Zhejiang U., China, 2002-; chmn. Internat. Working Group Plant Viruses with Fungal Vectors, 1988-93, IUFRO Working Party on Virus and Mycoplasma Diseases, 1982—, Internet Orgn. of Mycoplasmology Subsect. on Phytoplasmas, 1992—. Editor: Tree Mycoplasmas and Mycoplasma Diseases, 1988; over 200 scientific rsch. papers, 300 rsch. paper presentations. Fellow U. Wis., 1964-66, The Netherlands Internat. Ctr., 1973; recipient rsch. award Disting. Fgn. Specialist Govt. Japan, 1991, J. Gordin Kaplan award U. Alberta, 1993; named Nat. Sci. Coun. lectr. Govt. Republic China, 1989. Fellow Royal Soc. Can., Am. Phytopathological Soc. (Pacific divsn., Lifetime Achievement award 1993), Can. Phytopathological Soc. (pres. 1990-91, award for outstanding rsch. 1996); mem. Internat. Soc. Plant Pathology (treas. 1998—), NY Acad. Scis., Phytopathological Soc. Japan (award excellence in rsch. 1990), Goto Camellia Soc. (pres. 2002-), Internat. Orgn. Mycoplasmology (Mycoplasma Recognition award 1998). Avocations: reading, classical music, swimming. Home: 152 Windermere Cres Edmonton AB Canada T6R 2H6 Office: U Alta Dept Agr Food and Nutrition Edmonton AB Canada T6G 2P5 Business E-Mail: chiruki@ualberta.ca.

HISCOCK, RICHARD CARSON, legislative staff member; b. Washington, Dec. 18, 1944; s. Earle Francis and Alice Morgan (Carson) H.; m. Nancy Lynn Schafer, Oct. 12, 1968 (div. Jan. 1986); m. Virginia Murray Brierley, July 6, 1996. Student, Am. U., 1964-66. Fisherman F/V Benjo, Chatham, Mass., 1977-78; asst. harbormaster Town of Chatham, 1977—87; exec. dir. US Lifesaving Mfrs. Assn., North Chatham, Mass., 1984-86; investigator Marine Safety Cons., Fairhaven, Mass., 1987-91; pres. ERE Assoc. Ltd., 1991—2002; mem. sr. profl. staff, subcom. on Coast Guard and Marine Transp. Com. on Transp. and Infrastructure, US House of Reps., Washington, 2007—. Instr. hypothermia, cold water survival, emergency rescue equipment and fishing vessel safety, 1979—; mem. Comm. Fishing Industry Vessel Adv. Com., 1991-98; mem. Cape Cod Coastal Zone Mgmt. Adv. Com., 1977-92, chmn., 1986-91; mem. Barnstable County Coastal Resources Com., 1992-93; mem., chmn. Chatham Waterways Adv. Com., 1983-87; founder, bd. dirs. Marine Safety Found., Inc., Mass., 1993, v.p., 1999—; mem. Chatham Fin. Com., 1993-95; mem. Chatham Bylaw Rev. Com., 1995-97; industry advisor USCG Fishing Vessel Casualty Task Force, 1999. Contbr. articles to profl. jours. Mem. planning commn., Waitsfield, Vt., 2003—05. Recipient Pub. Svc. Commendation, USCG, 1984, Cert. of Merit, USCG, 1998, Meritorious Team Commendation, USCG, 1999, Plimsoll award, Editors of Profl. Mariner, 2006. Mem. Soc. Naval Architects and Marine Engrs., U.S. Marines Safety Assn., Mass. and Vt. Soc. Mayflower Descs., Mad River Path Assn. (bd. dirs. 2003-05, v.p. 2003-04, pres. 2004—05). Achievements include drafting a bill to establish crew licensing, inspection and additional safety requirements of certain fishing industry vessels; rsch. on comml. fishing, uninspected vessel safety, fishing vessel safety and hypothermia. Office: US House of Reps Subcom on Coast Guard 507 Ford House Office Bldg Washington DC 20515 Home: 3016 Hightower Place 115 Fairfax VA 22031 E-mail: richard@offsoundings.com, rch@gmavt.net.

HISCOX, FRANK S., lawyer; b. 1952; BA in English with honors, U. Calif., Santa Barbara, 1974; MA in English with honors, U. Calif., 1977; student, U. Tex., Austin; JD with honors, U. San Francisco, 1982. Bar: Calif. 1982. Ptnr., intellectual property and trademark, copyright, and brand mgmt. practice groups Dorsey & Whitney LLP, Palo Alto, Calif. Named one of Best Lawyers in Silicon Valley, 2000—02. Mem.: Santa Clara County Bar Assn., Silicon Valley Intellectual Property Assn., Internat. Trademark Assn. Office: Dorsey & Whitney LLP Ste 200 850 Hansen Way Palo Alto CA 94304-1017 Office Phone: 650-494-8700. Office Fax: 650-494-8771. Business E-Mail: hiscox.frank@dorsey.com.

HISE, MARK ALLEN, dentist; b. Chgo., Jan. 17, 1950; s. Clyde and Rose T. (Partipilo) Hise. AA, Mt. San Antonio Coll., Walnut, Calif., 1972; BA with highest honors, U. Calif., Riverside, 1974; MS, U. Utah, 1978; DDS, UCLA, 1983. Instr. sci. NW Acad., Houston, 1978-79; chmn. curriculum med. coll. prep program UCLA, 1980-85; instr. dentistry Coll. of Redwoods, Eureka, Calif., 1983—2007; pvt. practice Arcata, Calif., 1983—2001, Scotia, Calif., 2002—, Eureka, Calif., 2006—. Numerous radio and TV appearances; spkr. in field. Editor: Preparing for the MCAT, 1983—85; contbr. articles to profl. jours. Named Best Dentist on North Coast, Times-Std. Newspaper, 2002, 2006, 2007; recipient awards for underwater photography; fellow, NIH, 1975—79; Henry Carter scholar, U. Calif., 1973, Regents scholar, 1973, Calif. State scholar, 1973—74. Mem.: ADA, AAAS, Calif. Dental Assn. Roman Catholic. Avocation: underwater photography. Office: 1600 Myrtle Ave Eureka CA 95501 Personal E-mail: mhise@aol.com.

HISE, RICHARD TODD, marketing professional, educator, consultant; b. Washington, July 10, 1937; s. Theodore Richard and Lenor Mary (Parry) H.; m. Carol Lee Zeigler, Dec. 20, 1964; children: Richard William (dec.), Amy Caroline, Emily Carol. BA, Gettysburg Coll., 1959; MBA, U. Md., 1961, DBA, 1970. Instr. Elizabethtown (Pa.) Coll., 1962-64, Mich. State U., East Lansing, 1964-65, U. Md., College Park, 1965-70; assoc. prof., prof., head bus. adminstrn. Shippensburg (Pa.) State Coll., 1970-74; assoc. prof., dir. MBA program Va. Commonwealth U., Richmond, 1974-77; prof., holder Foley's professorship in retailing and mktg. Tex. A&M U., College Station, 1977—. Cons. IBM, Color Tile, Harley Davidson, Hotel Sofitel, Rosewood Properties, Mary Kay Cosmetics, Fleetwood Enterprises, OI Corp. Author: Quantitative Techniques for Marketing Decisions, 1973, Product/Service Strategy, 1977, Basic Marketing: Concepts and Decisions, 1979, Effective Salesmanship, 1980, Cases in Marketing Strategy, 1984, Basic Marketing: Concepts, Decisions, and Strategies, 1986, Millennial Marketing: Strategies for Success in the 21st Century and Beyond, 2001; contbr. more than 75 articles to profl. jours. including Jour. Mktg., Jour. Advt., Jour. Advt. Rsch., Jour. Global Mktg., Jour. Product Innovation Mgmt., Jour. Tchg. Internat. Bus., Mgmt. Acctg., Jour. Retailing, Jour. Acad. Mktg. Sci., among others. Sustaining mem. Rep. Nat. Com., 2001. Mem. Am. Mktg. Assn., Acad. Internat. Bus., Internat. Mgmt. Devel. Assn., Am. Legion, Pi Lambda Sigma, Beta Gamma Sigma, Phi Kappa Phi. Republican. Baptist. Avocations: international travel, impressionism art. Home: 1107 Merry Oaks Dr College Station TX 77840 Office: Tex A&M U Dept Mktg College Station TX 77843 E-mail: dick-hise@tamu.edu.

HISERT, GEORGE ARTHUR, lawyer; b. Schenectady, NY, Sept. 18, 1944; BS summa cum laude, Brown U., 1966, MS, 1966; JD cum laude, U. Chgo., 1970. Bar: Calif. 1971. Law clk. to Hon. Sterry R. Waterman U.S. Ct. Appeals (2d cir.), 1970—71; ptnr. McCutchen, Doyle, Brown & Enersen, San Francisco, 1977—93, Brobeck, Phleger & Harrison, San Francisco, 1993—2003, Bingham McCutchen LLP, 2003—. Mem. editl. bd. Chgo. Law Rev., 1969-70. Mem. ABA (subcom. letter of credit, vice chair 2003-06, chair 2006—, subcom. secured trans. of uniform comml. code com. bus. law sect., subcom. on syndications and loan participations of comml fin. svc. com., liaison bus. law sect. to uniform comml. code permanent editl. bd. 1993-05), Internat. Bar Assn. (banking law com., bus. law sect.), State Bar Calif. (uniform comml. code com. bus. law sect., vice-chair 1992-93, chair 1993-94), Am. Coll. Comml. Fin. Lawyers, Order of Coif, Sigma Xi. Office: Bingham McCutchen LLP Three Embarcadero Ctr San Francisco CA 94111 Office Phone: 415-393-2577. Business E-Mail: george.hisert@bingham.com.

HISKES, DOLORES G., language educator; b. Chgo. d. Leslie R. and Dagmar (Brown) Grant; m. John R. Hiskes; children: Robin Caproni, Grant. Student, U. Ill., Chgo. Tutoring programs cons.; presenter in field. Author, illustrator: Phonics Pathways, Reading Pathways. Recipient 6 nat. awards for Best Phonics Program in U.S. Mem. Internat. Reading Assn., Assn. Am. Educators, Assn. Ednl. Therapists, Calif. Assn. of Res. Specialists, Orton Dyslexia Soc., Learning Disabilities Assn., Nat. Right to Read Found., The Calif. Reading Assn., Pubs. Mktg. Assn., Calif. Watercolor Soc., Commonwealth Club of Calif., Bay Area Ind. Pubs. Assn. Achievements include development of ednl. games The Train Game, Blendit!, Wordworks, The Shor-Vowel Dictionary. Avocations: watercolors, travel, reading, exercise. Office: Dorbooks PO Box 2588 Livermore CA 94551-2588 Office Phone: 925-449-6983. Business E-Mail: dor@dorbooks.com.

HISS, SHEILA MARY, librarian; b. Evanston, Ill., May 7, 1949; d. Bernard F. and Mary Cecelia (Schubert) H.; m. John D. Hales Jr., Oct. 16, 1976; children: Christina Marie, John Daniel III. BA in History, Mundelein Coll., 1971; MLS, Ind. U., 1973; postgrad., Florence U., Italy, 1986, Fla. State U. Libr. art and music dept. Jacksonville (Fla.) Pub. Libr., 1974-76; asst. libr. North Fla. Jr. Coll., Madison, 1977-91; dir. libr. svcs. North Fla. C.C., Madison, 1991—. Mem. adv. bd. Coll. Ctr. for Libr. Automation, Tallahassee, Fla., 1991—, mem. exec. com., 1994-96, 98-2004, 2006—, chmn. exec. com. 2000-01, state joint selection com., 2001-02 Contbr. articles to profl. jours. Mem.: ALA, Beta Phi Mu. Roman Catholic. Avocations: weaving, basketry. Home: 13337 County Road 136 Live Oak FL 32060-6366 Office: North Fla Cmty Coll 325 NW Turner Davis Dr Madison FL 32340-1602 Office Phone: 850-973-1625.

HITCHCOCK, BION EARL, lawyer; b. Muscatine, Iowa, Oct. 9, 1942; s. Stewart Edward and Arlene Ruth (Eichelberger) H. BSEE, Iowa State U., 1965; JD, U. Iowa, 1968. Bar: Iowa 1968, Okla. 1968, U.S. Ct. Customs and Patent Appeals 1973, U.S. Ct. Appeals (fed. cir.) 1982. Atty. Phillips Petroleum Co., Bartlesville, Okla., 1968-69, 73-76; mgr. licensing Phillips Petroleum Co. Europe-Africa, Brussels, 1977-80; sr. patent counsel Phillips Petroleum Co., Bartlesville, 1980-84, assoc. gen. patent counsel, 1984-2000; asst. gen. counsel intellectual property Chevron Phillips Chem. Co., LP, Houston, 2000—02; pvt. practice Sugar Land, Tex., 2002—. Bd. dirs. Bartlesville Symphony Orch., 1973-77, 80-91, pres., 1975-77, 82-84; bd. dirs. Bartlesville Allied Arts and Humanities Coun., 1976-77, 80-86, 1st v.p., 1982-83; mem. Govt. and Fin. Goals for Bartlesville Com., 1974-75; bd. dirs. Bartlesville Cmty. Concert Assn., 1982-90, Okla. Assn. Symphony Orchs., 1983-88. Lt. JAGC, USN, 1969-73. Mem. ABA, Okla. Bar Assn. (dir. patent trademark and copyright sect. 1980-86, sec. 1982-83, vice chmn. 1983-84, chmn. 1984-85), Iowa Bar Assn., Washington County Bar Assn. (pres. 1981-82), Am. Intellectual Property Law Assn., Am. Judicature Soc., Fed. Cir. Bar Assn., Licensing Execs. Soc., Eta Kappa Nu. Home: 1227 Misty Lake Ct Sugar Land TX 77478-5613

HITCHCOCK, FREDERICK E., JR., (FRITZ), automotive company executive; CEO, owner Hitchcock Automotive Resources, City of Industry, Calif., 1980—. Recipient All Star Dealer Award, Sports Illus., 1988, 1995, Quality Dealer Award, Time Mag., 1993. Mem.: State of Calif. New Motor Vechicle Bd. (pres.), NADFC (ambassador), NADA (chmn. Gov. Rel. Com.). Office: Hitchcock Automotive Resoure 17340 Gale Ave La Puente CA 91748-1512

HITCHCOCK, JANE STANTON, playwright, novelist; b. NYC, Nov. 24, 1946; d. Robert Tinkham Crowley and Joan (Alexander) Stanton; m. William Mellon Hitchcock, Oct. 10, 1975 (div. Jan. 1991); m. Jim Hoagland, July 14, 1995. BA, Sarah Lawrence Coll., Bronxville, 1964-68. Author: Grace, 1982, Trick of the Eye, 1992 (Edgar award nominee, Hammett prize nominee), The Witches' Hammer, 1994, Social Crimes, 2002, One Dangerous Lady, 2005; screenwriter Our Time, 1974, First Love, 1976; producer Stalking Immortality (documentary) 1978; playwright Grace, 1981, Bhutan or Black Tie in the Himalayas, 1983, The Custom of the Country, 1986, Vanilla, 1990. Mem. PEN, The Dramatists' Guild, The Writers' Guild. Avocations: weightlifter, medieval literature, book collecting.

HITCHCOCK, JOANNA, publisher; b. London; BA, Oxford U., Eng., 1960, MA in Modern History, 1965. Asst. publicity dept. Oxford U. Press, London, 1962-66; asst. promotion mgr. Princeton (N.J.) Univ. Press, 1966-68, advt. and exhibits mgr., 1968-69, staff editor, 1970-72, mng. editor, 1972-80, exec. editor, 1980-84, asst. dir., 1985-87, exec. editor for humanities, 1988-92; dir. U. of Tex. Press, Austin, 1992—. Mem. Princeton U. Libr. Coun., 1986-95; adv. com. Tex. Book Festival, 1996-. Mem. Am. Assn. Univ. Presses (bd. dirs. 1984-87, chair equal opportunities com. 1985-86, ann. program planning com. 1986-87, pres. 1997-98, past pres. 1998-99). Home: 1507 Preston Ave Austin TX 78703-1903 Office: Univ of Texas Press PO Box 7819 Austin TX 78713-7819

HITCHCOCK, JOHN C., communications media executive; Mng. ed. AP-Dow Jones News Services, 1995—98; sr. ed. Americas Dow Jones Newswires Dow Jones & Co., mgr. dir. L.Am. Jersey City, 1999—, mng. dir. Energy, 2002; v.p. sales, mktg. OsterDowJones Commodity News, 2003—. Office: Dow Jones & Co Harborside Fin Ctr 800 Plaza Two Jersey City NJ 07311-1199

HITCHCOCK, KEN, professional hockey coach; b. Edmonton, Alta., Can., Dec. 17, 1951; m. Nancy; children: Emily, Alex, Noah. Student, U. Alta., Edmonton, Can. Head coach Kamloops Blazers, 1984-90; asst. coach Phila. Flyers, 1990-93; head coach Kalamazoo Wings, 1993-94; coach All-Star Games IHL, 1993-94, 94-95; head coach Dallas Stars, 1996—2002, Phila. Flyers, 2002—06, pro scout, 2006; head coach Columbus Blue Jackets, 2006—. Named Coach of Yr. Minor Hockey, 1982-83, Alta. Minor Hockey Assn., 1983-84, WHL, 1986-87, 89-90, top coach Canadian Major Jr. Hockey, 1989-90. Achievements include being the head coach of Stanley Cup Champion Dallas Stars, 1999. Office: Columbus Blue Jackets Nationwide Arena 200 W Nationwide Blvd, Ste Level Columbus OH 43215*

HITCHCOCK, WALTER ANSON, retired educational consultant; b. Shelton, Wash., Dec. 9, 1918; s. Paul H. and Hazel (Boyington) H.; m. Helen Nadine Rainbolt, Mar. 13, 1944; children: Paul H., Walter Anson, Larry W. BABA, Wash. State U., Pullman, 1940, BEd, 1941, MA in Edn., 1948, EdD, 1966; postgrad., U. Okla., Norman, 1943-44, summer 1946. Tchr. bus. subjects Omak Sr. H.S., Wash., 1941-42; counselor Weatherwax Sr. H.S., Aberdeen, Wash., 1946-47; prin. Wilbur H.S., Wash., 1947-49; supt. schs. Nespelem, Wash., 1949-50, Wilbur, 1950-55, Moxee, Wash., 1955-59, West Valley schs., Spokane, 1959-66, Kennewick schs., 1966-69; dep. supt. Spokane city schs., 1969-72, supt., 1972-80; assoc. Interpacific Investors Services, 1980-85; pres. Skookum Investments, 2004—05. Mem. adv. com. on tchr. edn. Ea. Wash. State U., 1959-63, ednl. imperatives com., 1984-86; adminstrv. adv. com. State Sch. Supt., mem. spl. edn. com., 1976-79; mem. Wash. State Ednl. TV Adv. Com., 1972-74; mem. spl. edn. adv. com. Cen. Wash. State U., 1975-79. Mem. Tri-Cities United Cmty. Svcs., 1967-69, v.p., 1968; active Benton-Franklin Govtl. Conf., 1968-69; bd. dirs. Expo 74, 1972-75, United Way, Spokane County, 1972-79, Inland Empire Red Cross, Inland Empire Coun. Boy Scouts Am., Spokane Area Youth Com., OK Boys Ranch sponsored by Olympia Kiwanis, 1993-94; panel mem. Eastern Wash. Area Agy. on Aging, 1984-85. Served with AUS, 1942-45. Mem. Am. Assn. Sch. Adminstrs. (mem. SASA-AASA rels. com. 1971-74), NEA, Wash. Edn. Assn. (bd. dirs. dept. adminstrn. and supervision 1968-69), Inland Empire Edn. Assn. (pres. 1972-73), N.W. Regional Sch. Adminstrs. (chmn.), Yakima Valley Sch. Adminstrs. (chmn.), Spokane Area Supts. Assn. (pres.), Lincoln-Adams Bi-County Activities Assn. (pres.), Wash. Assn. Sch. Adminstrs. (pres. 1969-70, mem. exec. com.), Wash. State Sch. Retirees Assn. (del. 1986-99, 2001—, mem. fin. com. 1994—, chmn. 1996-97, 99—, actuarial study com. 1998-2000, facility need com. 1999-2000), Thurston County Sch. Retirees Assn. (bd. dirs. 1986-95, 97, 99-2002, found. com. 1996-2002), Phi Kappa Phi, Alpha Kappa Psi, Phi Delta Kappa, Sigma Phi Epsilon. Presbyterian. (trustee 1957-59, ruling elder). Clubs: Lion, Wilbur Commercial (pres. 1952-54), Kiwanis (trustee 1961-63, 67-69, 72-76). Personal E-mail: whitchcock@juno.com.

HITCHENS, CHRISTOPHER ERIC, columnist, writer; b. Portsmouth, Eng., Apr. 13, 1949; naturalized, US, 1981; s. Eric Ernest and Yvonne Jean (Hickman) Hitchens; m. Eleni Meleagrou, 1981 (div.); children: Alexander,

Sophia; m. Carol Blue, 1991; 1 child, Antonia. BA in Philosophy, Politics, Econs., Oxford U., Eng., 1970. Social sci. corr. The Times Higher Edn. Supplement, London, 1971—73; writer, asst. editor New Statesman, London, 1973—81; rschr., reporter Weekend World (London TV), 1974-80; fgn. corr. Daily Express, London, 1974-80; Washington columnist The Spectator, 1981-86; "Am. Notes" columnist Times Lit. Supplement, London, 1982—; columnist, "Minority Report" The Nation, NYC, 1982—2002; columnist, contributing editor Vanity Fair mag., 1992—; columnist Atlantic Monthly, 2002—. Vis. prof. U. Calif., Berkeley, U. Pitts., 1997, New Sch. Social Rsch., 2002—. Author: Karl Marx and the Paris Commune, 1971, Hostage to History: Cyprus from the Ottomans to Kissinger, 1984, Imperial Spoils: The Curious Case of the Elgin Marbles, 1986, Prepared for the Worst: Selected Essays, 1989, Blood Class and Nostalgia: Anglo American Ironies, 1990, For the Sake of Argument: Essays and Minority Reports, 1993, When the Borders Bleed: The Struggle of the Kurds, 1994, The Missionary Position: Mother Teresa in Theory and Practice, 1995, No One Left to Lie To: The Triangulations of William Jefferson Clinton 1999, Unacknowledged Legislation: Writers in the Public Sphere, 2001, The Trials of Henry Kissinger, 2001, Letters to a Young Contrarian: The Art of Mentoring, 2001, Why Orwell Matters, 2002, The Long Short War: The Postponed Liberation of Iraq, 2003, Blood Class and Empire: The Enduring Anglo-American Relationship, 2004, Thomas Jefferson: Author of America, 2005, Love, Poverty and War: Journeys and Essays, 2005, Thomas Paine's "Rights of Man": A Biography, 2006, God Is Not Great: How Religion Poisons Everything, 2007; co-author: (with Pete Kellner) Callaghan: The Road to Number 10, 1976; co-editor: Blaming the Victims: Spurious Scholarship and the Palestinian Question, 1988; writer, narrator: (films) The God That Fled: Bhagwan Rajneesh, 1980, The Enchanted Glass: Britain and Its Monarchy, 1988, Cyprus: An Island Stranded in Time, 1989, Come Home, America, Why Bill Clinton Will be President, 1992, Hell's Angel: Mother Teresa, 1996, All the Rage: The Death Penalty in America, 1997, The Failure of Spike Lee, 1997, Princess Diana: The Mourning After, 1998, The Trials of Henry Kissinger, 2002, Lone Star: Deep in the Mind of Texas, 2004 Office: 2022 Columia Rd NW Washington DC 20009*

HITCHENS, WILLIAM RANDOLPH (RANDY), healthcare executive; b. Logansport, Ind. s. William T. and Alberta J. Hitchens; m. Katherine J. Hitchens, Oct. 8, 1977; children: Cyrena, Chase, Carin. BS in Pharmacy, Purdue U., 1976; MBA, Ind. U., 1983. Pharmacist, mgr. Revco Drug, Ft. Wayne, Ind., 1977—83; assoc. product mgr. Boehringer Mannheim, Indpls., 1983, account mgr., 1984, product mgr., 1984—87, group mktg. mgr., 1987—90, sr. group product mgr., 1990—92, regional bus. mgr., 1992—94, nat. accounts managed care, 1994—97, dir. corp. partnership, 1997—98; corp. accts. dir. Roche, Indpls., 1998, nat. dir. corp. accounts, 1998—2004, dir. sales and mktg., 2004—05, area bus. dir., 2005—. Ofcl. U.S. Swimming, 1996-2004. Mem. Acad. Managed Care Pharmacists (legis. com. 1997-98, strategic mtkg. com. 1999). Presbyterian. Avocations: running, travel. Office: Roche 9115 Hague Rd Indianapolis IN 46256-1045 Office Phone: 317-521-3760.

HITCHINGHAM, EILEEN, librarian, dean; BS, Chestnut Hill Coll.; MLS, Western Mich. U.; PhD in Edn., Wayne State U. Libr. Countway Libr. Medicine, Harvard U., 1967—68; sci. and engring. libr., head of reference, acting assoc. dean pub. svcs., automation coord. Oakland U., 1968—87; dean libr. svcs. U. Idaho, 1987—90; dean libr. svcs., assoc. prof. Coll. Info. Studies Drexel U.; dean univ. librs. Va. Tech. U., Blacksburg, 1995—. Cons. Mich. Libr. Consortium, Nat. Librs. Assn., GM. Office: Univ Librs Va Tech PO Box 90001 Blacksburg VA 24062-9001 Office Phone: 540-231-5593. E-mail: hitch@vt.edu.*

HITE, DAVID L., lawyer; b. Thornville, Ohio, Apr. 30, 1916; s. Frank C. Hite and Mary Pannabaker; m. Maxine Witherbee, July 15, 1943; 1 child, Diane. BS, Kent Sate U., 1938; JD, Capital U., 1946. Neuropsychiat. fellow Psychology Ct. Neuropsychiat. Inst., Hartford, Conn., 1939; pvt. practice Utica and Newark, Ohio, 1946—. Capt. OSS, 1942-46. Mem. ABA (pub. utilities sect., small trusts and estate com., adminstrn. and distbrn. of estates com.), Ohio Bar Ass., Cleve. Bar Assn., Licking Bar Assn. Office: Hite & Hite 964 N 21st St Ste D Newark OH 43055-7230 E-mail: hite@nextek.net.

HITE, JANET SUE, elementary school educator; b. Logansport, Ind., Feb. 22, 1948; d. Joseph William and Ruth Elizabeth (McVay) H. AA, Palomar Coll, San Marcos, Calif., 1968; BA in English, Pepperdine U., LA, 1970; MA in Edn., Pepperdine U., Malibu, Calif., 1980. Cert. tchr. Calif., profl. adminstrv. svcs. Calif. Tchr. Graham Elem. Sch., LA, 1971-75, 76-82, Uniontown (Ky.) Pub. Sch., 1975-76, Paseo del Rey Fundamental Magnet Sch., Playa del Rey, Calif., 1982-90, magnet sch. coord., 1990-94, magnet coord. Natural Sci. Magnet Sch., 1994-97; asst. prin. 186th St. Sch., Gardena, Calif., 1997—2001; prin. Chapman Elem. Sch., Gardena, 2001—. Master tchr. Pepperdine U., L.A., 1979-90; adj. prof. Loyola Marymount U., Westchester, Calif., 1993-2003; cons. program quality rev. team L.A. Unified Sch. Dist., 1993-95. Editor: Creative Writings, 1980. Co-founder, co-dir. Cultural and Urban Environ. Studies Inc., L.A., 1979-84; active San Dieguito United Meth. Ch. Grantee L.A. Ednl. Partnerships, 1983, 90, L.A. Unified Sch. Dist., 1984, City of Gardena, 2001, L.A. Unified Sch. Dist., 2001; recipient Red Apple award Tchr. Remembrance Day Found., 1972, Outstanding Tchr. of Yr. award Westchester C. of C., 1990, Calif. State Title I Achieving Schs. award, 2003, Calif. Disting. Sch. award, 2006. Mem. ASCD, Phi Delta Kappa (charter, Pepperdine chpt., newsletter editor 1979-80, treas. 1980-81, 3d v.p. 1981-82, 1st v.p. 1982-83, pres. 1983-84, advisor 1985-95), Loyola Marymount U. chpt. Kappa Delta Pi (charter). Republican. Methodist. Avocations: collecting knives, travel, camping, reading. Home: 7740 Redlands St Apt M3073 Playa Del Rey CA 90293-8452 Office: Chapman Elem Sch 1947 Marine St Gardena CA 90249

HITE, WILLIAM P., labor union administrator; Apprentice United Assn. of Journeymen & Apprentices of Plumbing & Pipe Fitting Industry of US and Can., 1968—72, journeyman, 1972, del. to Chgo. Fedn. of Labor, 1983, bus. agt. Local 597, 1986, asst. bus. mgr., 1993, fin. sec.-treas. Local 597, internat. rep., 1996, adminstrv. asst. to gen. pres., 1999—2001, asst. gen. pres., 2001—04, gen. pres. Washington, 2005—. Office: United Assn Bldg 901 Massachusetts Ave NW Washington DC 20001-4397*

HITES, RONALD ATLEE, chemist, educator; b. Jackson, Mich., Sept. 19, 1942; s. Wilbert T. and Evelyn J.H.; m. Bonnie Rae Carlson, Dec. 26, 1964; children: Veronica, Karin, David. BA in Chemistry, Oakland U., Rochester, Mich., 1964; PhD in Analytical Chemistry, MIT, Cambridge, Mass., 1968. NAS fellow Agrl. Rsch., Peoria, Ill., 1968-69; mem. rsch. staff, dept. chemistry MIT, Cambridge, 1969-72, asst. prof. chem. engring., 1972-76, assoc. prof., 1976-79; prof. Ind. U., Bloomington, 1979-89, Disting. prof. pub. and environ. affairs and chemistry, 1989—, dir. Environ. Sci. Rsch. Ctr., 2001—. Cons. EPA, 1974—. Assoc. editor Environ. Sci. Tech., 1990—; mem. editorial bd. Chemosphere, 1979-99; contbr. articles to prof. jours. Grantee NSF, 1974—, EPA, 1974—, Dept. Energy, 1977-95. Fellow AAAS; mem. Am. Chem. Soc. (award in environ. sci. 1991), Am. Soc. for Mass Spectrometry (pres. 1988-90, mem. editl. bd. 1990-96), Soc. Environ. Toxicol. Chemistry (bd. dirs. 1997-2000, Founders award 1993), Internat. Assn. Great Lakes Rsch. (bd. dirs. 2006—), Sigma Xi. Office: Ind U Sch Pub and Environ Affairs 410H Bloomington IN 47405 Office Phone: 812-855-0193. Business E-Mail: hitesr@indiana.edu.

HITLIN, DAVID GEORGE, physicist, researcher; b. Bklyn., Apr. 15, 1942; s. Maxwell and Martha (Lipetz) H.; m. Joan R. Abramowitz, 1966 (div. 1981); m. Abigail R. Gumbiner, 1982 (div. 1998); m. Martha Mann Slagerman, 2000. BA, Columbia U., 1963, MA, 1965, PhD, 1968. Instr. Columbia U., NYC, 1967-69; rsch. assoc. Stanford (Calif.) Linear Accelerator Ctr., 1969-72, asst. prof., 1975-79, mem. program com., 1980-82; asst. prof. Stanford U., 1972-75; assoc. prof. physics Calif. Inst. Tech., Pasadena, 1979-85, prof., 1985—. Mem. adv. panel U.S. Dept. Energy Univ. Programs, 1983; mem. program com. Fermi Nat. Accelerator Lab., Batavia, Ill., 1983—87, Newman Lab., Cornell U., Ithaca, NY, 1986—88; mem. rev. com. U. Chgo., Argonne Nat. Lab., 1985—87; chmn. Stanford Linear Accelerator Ctr. Users Orgn., 1990—93; mem. program com. Brookhaven Nat. Lab., Upton, NY, 1992—95; spokesman BABAR Collaboration, 1994—2000; mem. high energy physics adv. panel DOE/NSF, 2001—04; mem. Univs. Rsch. Assn. Fermilab Bd. Overseers, 2003—06; mem. bd. Fermi Rsch. Alliance. Contbr. numerous articles to profl. jours. Fellow Am. Phys. Soc. Achievements include research in elementary particle physics. Office: Calif Inst Tech Dept Physics 356-48 Lauritsen Pasadena CA 91125-0001 Home Phone: 310-472-0700; Office Phone: 626-395-6694. Business E-Mail: hitlin@hep.caltech.edu.

HITT, DAVID HAMILTON, SR., retired health facility administrator; b. Tuscaloosa, Ala., May 14, 1925; m. Lola McKinney, Mar. 12, 1999 (dec.); m. Frances Ford, Aug. 12, 1949 (dec.); children: David Hamilton, Kathryn Ann; m. Mary Chesser, July 10, 2004. BS, MS in Commerce and Bus. Adminstrn, U. Ala.; MHA, U. Minn., 1952. Hosp. adminstr. U. Ala. Hosp., 1947-50; various positions, including chief exec. officer Baylor U. Med. Center, 1952-79; sr. v.p. James A. Hamilton Assocs. (hosp. consultants), Dallas, 1979-84; pres., chief exec. officer Meth. Hosps. of Dallas, 1984-96, also bd. dirs., pres. emeritus; chmn. bd. dirs. Am. Rubber Tech. Inc., Jacksonville, Fla. Dir. emeritus Bapt. Med. Ctr., Jacksonville, Fla., Dallas Meth. Hosps. Found.; pres. Dallas Hosp. Coun., 1959; mem. adminstrv. bd. Con. Tchg. Hosps. of Assn. Am. Med. Colls., 1972-79; assoc. clin. prof. Washington U., St. Louis, 1961-96; adj. assoc. prof. Trinity U., San Antonio, 1964-96. Contbr. numerous articles to profl. jours. Mem. exec. bd. council Boy Scouts Am.; v.p. Community Council Greater Dallas. Recipient Earl M. Collier award Distinguished Hosp. Adminstrn. Tex., 1973, Dean Conley award, Silver Beaver award Boy Scouts. Fellow Am. Coll. Healthcare Execs. (Gold medal award for excellence in healthcare mgmt. 1990, past regent, editl. bd. Frontiers Health Svcs. Mgmt. 1991-93); mem. Am. Hosp. Assn. (life, Citation for Meritorious Svc. 1987, Disting. Svc. award 1992, trustee, past chmn. coun. financing), Tex. Hosp. Assn. (trustee, treas., v.p., pres., chmn. ho. of dels. 1967), Am. Protestant Hosp. Assn. (past trustee), Alumni Assn. U. Minn. Program Hosp. Adminstrn. (past pres.), Marine Corps Assn., Exch. Club East Dallas (pres. 1957), Rotary (Dallas) (bd. dirs., dist. Ethics Bus. award 1993). Home: 6255 W Northwest Hwy # 209 Dallas TX 75255 Personal E-mail: twintree75@yahoo.com.

HITT, JOHN CHARLES, academic administrator; b. Houston, Dec. 7, 1940; s. John Charles and Mary W. (Green) H.; m. Martha Ann Halsted, Dec. 23, 1961; children: John Charles, Sharon Aileen. AB cum laude, Austin Coll., 1962; MS (Danforth fellow, NSF fellow), Tulane U., 1964, PhD (Danforth fellow, NSF fellow), 1966. Cert. psychologist, Tex. Asst. prof. psychology Tulane U., 1966-69; assoc. prof. psychology Tex. Christian U., Ft. Worth, 1969-77, assoc. dean of univ., 1972-77; v.p. Tex. Christian U. Research Found., 1974-77; dean Grad Sch. Tex. Christian U., 1975-77; v.p. acad. affairs Bradley U., Peoria, Ill., 1977-87, provost, 1981-87; v.p. acad. affairs, prof. psychology U. Maine, Orono, 1987-92, interim pres., 1991-92; pres. U. Ctrl. Fla., Orlando, 1992—. Bd. dirs. Space Coast Devel. Commn., Orlando Regional Health Care Sys.; bd. trustees EDUCOM, 1993—; adv. bd. World Trade Ctr., 1993-94, Orlando Sci. Ctr., 1992—; bd. dirs. Seminar on Acad. Computing, 1984-88, chmn. bd. dirs., 1986-87; chair task force distance learning State U. Sys. of Fla., 1993; pres.'s commn. NCAA, 1993—; nat. adv. bd. Ctr. for the Study of Sports in Soc., 1994—. Mem. bd. co-editors Psychological Research, 1973-77; editl. bd. TQM in Edn., 1993—; editl. adv. bd. Met. Univs., 1993—; contbr. articles in psychology and neurosci. to profl. jours. Chmn. com. on social scis. Austin Coll. 125th Anniversary Commn., 1973-77; charter mem. Austin Coll. Bd. Edn. Visitors, 1976-80; Tex. Christian U. rep. Leadership Ft. Worth, 1973-74; program chmn. Forum Ft. Worth, 1976-77; mem. Tarrant County United Way Budget Com., 1975-77, Forward Ft. Worth, 1976-77, Econ. Devel. Commn. Mid-Fla., Found. Orange County Pub. Schs., Fla Info. Resource Network; chmn. loaned exec. program Heart of Ill. United Way, 1979, chmn. edn. unit, 1980, bd. dirs. 1983-87; bd. dirs. Greater Peoria YMCA, 1980-84, SunBank, 1992—, mem. community adv. council St. Francis Med. Ctr., Peoria, 1984-87; bd. dirs. Inst. Phys. Medicine and Rehab., Peoria, 1981-87, pres. bd. dirs., 1986-87, Heart of Fla. United Way, 1993—; v.p. Penobscot Valley United Way, Bangor, Maine, 1989-92; trustee Bangor YWCA, 1991-92; vestry St. John's Episcopal Ch., Bangor, 1990-91. Recipient John Young Award, Orlando Regional C. of C., 1998, Jack Holloway Star of Gratitude Award, United Cerebral Palsy, 1998, Tree of Life Award, Jewish Nat. Fund, 1999, James B. Green Award, Metro Orlando Econ. Devel. Commn., 2002. Mem. APA, AAAS, Psychonomic Soc., Soc. for Neurosci., Am. Assn. Higher Edn., Peoria Area C. of C. (bd. dirs. 1986-87), Greater Orlando C. of C., Winter Park C. of C., Fla. Assn. of Colls. and Univs. (bd. dirs.), Sigma Xi, Alpha Chi, Psi Chi, Phi Kappa Phi, Beta Gamma Sigma, Omicron Delta Kappa. Home: 1000 Central Florida Blvd Orlando FL 32826-2404 Office: Office of Pres Millican Hall 308 PO Box 160002 Orlando FL 32816-0002*

HITT, LEO N., lawyer, educator; b. Pitts., Oct. 20, 1955; s. Joe Stephen and Laurene (Lally) H.; m. Mary Elizabeth Wolf, Jan. 26, 1985; children: Nancy Anne, Elizabeth Lea. BA summa cum laude, U. Pitts., 1977, JD cum laude, 1980; LLM in Taxation, N.Y.U., 1983. Bar: Pa. 1980, U.S. Dist. Ct. (we. dist.) Pa. 1983, U.S. Tax Ct. 1981, U.S. Ct. Fed. Claims, 1997. Atty., tax sr. Kenneth Leventhal & Co., NYC, 1980-81; atty., tax counsel Touche Ross & Co., Pitts., 1981-83; assoc. Reed Smith LLP, Pitts., 1983-88, ptnr., 1989—, mem. tax, benefits and wealth planning group. Adj. prof. tax grad. sch., law sch. Duquesne U., Pitts., 1987—, sch. law U. Pitts., 1988—; seminar speaker various profl. orgns., Pitts., 1983—. Comments editor: U. Pitts. Law Review, 1979-80. Mem. Allegheny County Bar Assn., Pitts. Internat. Tax Soc., Allegheny Tax Soc., Pitts. Tax Club. Roman Catholic. Avocations: skiing, opera, gourmet cooking. Office: Reed Smith LLP 435 6th Ave Pittsburgh PA 15219-1886 Home Phone: 724-327-8881; Office Phone: 412-288-3298. Office Fax: 412-288-3063. Business E-Mail: lhitt@reedsmith.com.

HITTINGER, WILLIAM CHARLES, electronics company executive; b. Bethlehem, Pa., Nov. 10, 1922; s. John Tilghman and Pearl (Heimbach) H.; m. Elizabeth Herman, July 9, 1944; children— Patricia, William, David, Nancy. BS with honors in Metall. Engring, Lehigh U., 1944, D.Engring. (hon.), 1973. Engr. Western Electric Co., 1946-52; prodn. mgr. Semiconductor div. Nat. Union Radio Corp., 1952-54; exec. dir. Bell Telephone Labs., 1954-66; pres. Bellcomm Inc., Washington, 1966-68, Gen. Instrument Corp., NYC, 1968-70; v.p., gen. mgr. RCA Corp., Somerville, NJ., 1970-72, exec. v.p. NYC, 1972-86. Bd. dirs. UNC Inc., Annapolis, Md., Stabler Cos., Inc., Harrisburg, Pa., Biotechnica Internat. Inc., RCA Corp., Thomas & Betts, Recognition Equipment, Allen Bradley, Am. Fletcher Corp., Bethlehem Steel. Bd. dirs. Bethlehem Fgn. Policy Assn., 1960-62, Nat. Action Council for Minorities in Engring., Inc.; trustee, interim pres. Lehigh U., 1997. Served to capt. AUS, 1943-46. Named hon. citizen Bethlehem, 1966 Fellow IEEE, Royal Acad. Arts; mem. Nat. Acad. Engring., Omicron Delta Kappa, Phi Gamma Delta, Sigma Xi, Tau Beta Pi. Home and Office: PO Box 1979 Bethlehem PA 18016-1979 Office Phone: 610-625-4021. E-mail: wchitt@aol.com.

HITTLE, RICHARD HOWARD, gas and oil industry executive, consultant; b. Columbus, Nebr., Apr. 30, 1923; s. Arthur Howard and Frieda Margaret (Poppe) H.; m. Catherine Louise Dethlefsen, May 11, 1951; children: Ann-Louise, Thomas Woodford, Bradley Arthur. Student, Cambridge U., Eng., 1945; BS, U. Denver, 1950, LLB, 1951; MBA, Harvard U., 1955. With Conoco Inc., 1955-87, mgr. internat. acquisitions, 1964-75; pres. Continental Overseas Oil Co., NYC also Stamford, Conn., 1969-75; gen. mgr., v.p. internat. govt. affairs Conoco, Inc., Stamford, 1975-83, Wilmington, Del., 1983-87. Bd. advisors Merck Forest and Farmland Ctr., Rupert, Vt. Served with AUS, 1943-46, Europe, USAF, 1951-53. Mem. Dorset Nursing Assn. (bd. trustees), Harvard Club (N.Y.C.), Stanwich Club, Dorset Field Club (Vt.), Met. Club (Washington), Dorset Field Club, Merck Forest and Farmland Ctr. (bd. advisors). Clubs: Harvard (N.Y.C.); Stanwich (Greenwich, Conn.); Dorset Field. (Vt.); Metropolitan (Washington). Republican. Congregationalist. Home and Office: PO Box 325 Dorset VT 05251-0325 Personal E-mail: rhkh@comcast.net.

HITTNER, DAVID, federal judge; b. Schenectady, NY, July 10, 1939; s. George and Sophie (Moskowitz) H.; children: Miriam, Susan, George. BS, NYU, 1961, JD, 1964. Bar: N.Y. 1964, Tex. 1967. Pvt. practice, Houston, 1967-78; judge Tex. 133d Dist. Ct., Houston, 1978-86, U.S. Dist. Ct. (so. dist.) Tex., Houston, 1986—2004, sr. judge, 2004—. Author 2 books; contbr. articles to profl. jours. Mem. Nat. coun. Boy Scouts Am. Capt. inf., paratrooper U.S. Army, 1965-66. Recipient Silver Beaver award Boy Scouts Am., 1974, Silver Antelope award Boy Scouts Am., 1988, Samuel E. Gates award Am. Coll. Trial Lawyers. Mem. ABA (Merit award), State Bar Tex. (Outstanding Lawyer in Tex. award), Houston Bar Assn. (Pres.'s and Dirs.' award), Am. Law Inst., Masons (33d degree), Order of Coif (hon.). Office: US Courthouse 515 Rusk St Ste 8509 Houston TX 77002-2603 Office Phone: 713-250-5711.

HITTNER, GEORGE J., lawyer; b. Houston, Oct. 29, 1978; s. David and Helen Mintz Hittner. AA, Wentworth Mil. Acad., Lexington, Mo., 1997; BS, Tex. A&M U., College Station, 1999; JD, MPA, U. Tex., Austin, 2002. Bar: Tex. 2003. Law clk. to Hon. Jane Bland 281st Dist. Ct., Houston, 2000; statewide campaign mgr. Chief Justice Tom Phillips re-election campaign, Austin, Tex., 2002; policy analyst, asst. staff counsel 78th Tex. Legislature, Austin, 2003; atty. Haynes and Boone, L.L.P., Houston, 2003—06; sr. adv. Employment Standards Adminstrn. US Dept. Labor, Washington, 2006—07, spl. asst. to asst. sect., Office Adminstrn. and Mgmt., 2007—. Mem. Nat. Jewish Com. on Scouting, 2000—, Greater Houston Partnership Local Rels. Com., 2006; mem. bd. visitors Wentworth Mil. Acad., 2005—, mem. alumni coun., 1997—; founder Fire Fighter Found. Houston; adv. com. mem. John Ben Shepperd Ann. Leadership Forum, Austin, 2004—06. Named Tex. Rising Star, Tex. Monthly Mag., 2006. Mem.: Houston Young Lawyers Assn., Boy Scouts Am., Houston Realty Breakfast Club, Masons (life). Jewish. Office: U S Labor Dept 200 Constitution Ave Ste S2203 Washington DC 20210 Home Phone: 713-824-1270; Office Phone: 202-693-4040. Office Fax: 202-693-4055. Personal E-mail: hittnerg@gmail.com. Business E-Mail: hittner.george@dol.gov.

HITZ, FREDERICK PORTER, public and international affairs educator; b. Washington, Oct. 14, 1939; s. Frederick Porter and Elizabeth (Hume) H.; m. Mary Buford Bocock, Sept. 7, 1963; 1 child, Eliza. AB, Princeton U., 1961; JD, Harvard U., 1964. Bar: Mass. 1965, Va. 1966, D.C. 1976, U.S. Supreme Ct. 1988. Asst. lectr., law dept. U. IFE, Ibadan, Nigeria, 1964-65; fgn. svc. officer US Dept. State, Abidjan, Cote d'Ivoire, 1963—73, congl. rels. officer Washington, 1974-75, dep. asst. sec. legis. affairs, 1975-77; mem. energy policy and planning staff Exec. Office of Pres., Washington, 1977; dir. congl. affairs U.S. Dept. Energy, Washington, 1977-78; legis. counsel CIA, Washington, 1978-81; ptnr. Schwabe, Williamson & Wyatt, Washington, 1982-90; inspector gen. CIA, Washington, 1990-98; lectr. in pub. and internat. affairs Princeton U. Woodrow Wilson Sch., NJ, 1998—2006, Weinberg prof. of pub. policy, 1999—2006; sr. fellow Princeton U. Butler Coll., 2000—; lectr. U. Va. Sch. Law, Charlottesville, Va., 2004—; lectr. Woodrow Wilson dept. politics U. Va., Charlottesville, 2004—. Mem. Coun. Fgn. Rels., 2003—. Author: The Great Game: The Myth and Reality of Espionage, 2004. Trustee Potomac Sch., McLean, Va., 1989-95, chmn. bd. trustees, 1992-94; vestry St. Paul's Ch., Alexandria. Mem. ABA, Wash. Nat. Cathedral, Protestant Episcopal Cathedral Found., Deer Isle Yacht Club (Maine), Met. Club (Washington, bd. govs. 1994-99, sec. 1995-96, pres. 1998-99), Ivy Club (Princeton, N.J., grad. bd. 2001-). Democrat. Episcopalian. Avocations: sailing, skiing, squash. Personal E-mail: fphitz@aol.com. E-mail: fhitz@princeton.edu.

HITZMAN, DONALD OLIVER, microbiologist; b. Milw., Dec. 2, 1926; s. Walter John and Irene (Smith) H.; m. Mary Elizabeth Neumann, Aug. 20, 1952; children: Murray W., Daniel C. AB, Carleton Coll., Northfield, Minn., 1948; MS, U. Ill., 1950, PhD, 1954. Resident microbiologist Texaco Co., Long Beach, Calif., 1951; sr. rsch. assoc. Phillips Petroleum Co., Bartlesville, Okla., 1954-85; v.p. rsch. Geo-Microbial Tech., Inc., Ochelata, Okla., 1985—. Contbr. articles to sci. publs. With USAAF, 1944-45. Fulbright scholar, Australia, 1951. Mem. Soc. Microbiology, Soc. Indsl. Microbiology, Am. Chem. Soc. Republican. Episcopalian. Achievements include over 60 patents; numerous fgn. patents. Office: Geo-Microbial Tech East Main St Ochelata OK 74051 Home Phone: 918-333-1717; Office Phone: 918-535-2281. E-mail: gmtgeochem@aol.com.

HIXON, CARL KILMER, retired advertising executive, writer; b. Chgo., Nov. 9, 1924; s. Carl Kilmer and Anne Alfield (Olson) Hixon; divorced; children: Todd, Carol, Carl Jr.; 1 child, Joseph. BA, DePauw U., Greencastle, Ind., 1949. Lic. pilot, racing driver Sports Car Club Am., cert. scuba advanced open water diver, blue water sailor. V.p. creative Kerker, Peterson, Hixon, Hayes, Inc., Mpls., 1952—59; assoc. creative dir., v.p., bd. dir. Leo Burnett Co., Inc., Chgo., 1959—70, vice chmn., creative dir. Western Europe and South Africa London, 1970—76, exec. v.p. Chgo., 1976—80, cons., 1980—86, Crain Comm., Chgo., 1980—86; freelance writer, 1980—. Corr. Crain Comm., Chgo., 1980—82. Author: (column) Hixon at Large, Advertising Age, 1980—86; contbr. articles to profl. pubs.; author: Guadalcanal: an American Story, 1999, (TV series) Stalin, Discovery Channel. With US Merchant Marine, 1943—44, PTO, with USMC, 1944—46. Mem.: Guadalcanal Campaign Veterans Assn. (hon.), Anglesy Shooting Club. Home: Apt 1 481 Homestead Rd La Grange Park IL 60526-1991

HIXON, JAMES A., lawyer, rail transportation executive; Asst. tax counsel Norfolk So. Corp., Va., 1985, gen. tax atty., asst. v.p., tax counsel, v.p. taxation, 1993—99, sr. v.p. employee rels., 1999, sr. v.p. adminstrn., sr. v.p. legal and govt. affairs, 2003, exec. v.p. law and corp. rels., 2005—. Office: Norfolk So Corp Three Commercial Pl Norfolk VA 23510-2191 Office Phone: 757-629-2680.*

HIXSON, ELMER L., retired engineering educator; Prof. emeritus dept. elec. engring. U. Tex., Austin. Recipient Fellow Mems. award Am. Soc. Engring. Educators, 1992. Fellow Acoustical Soc. Am.; mem. IEEE (life), Inst. for Noise Control Engring. (founding mem.). Office: U Tex Dept Elec & Computer Engring Austin TX 78712 E-mail: ehixson@mail.utexas.edu.

HIXSON, HARRY F., JR., health products executive; BSChemE, Purdue U.; MBA, U. Chgo.; PhD in Phys. Biochemistry, Purdue U. Pres., COO Amgen, Inc., 1985—91; pres., CEO GeneSys Therapeutics, Inc., 1991—92; CEO, chmn. bd. , pres. Elitra Pharms., Inc., San Diego, 1998—. Dir. Signal Pharms., Inc.

HJERPE, CARL WILLIAM, retired mechanical engineer, banker; b. New Britain, Conn., Sept. 24, 1915; s. Carl Albin Hjerpe and Hannah Caroline Johnson; m. Phyllis Anne Fredeen; children: Kari, Anne. BS in Mech. Engring., Rensselaer Poly., Troy, NY, 1939; M of Engring., Rensellaer Poly., Troy, NY. Sales and svc. person Thrush Co., Boston, 1939—40; piping engr. Sanderson and Porter Co., NYC, 1945—50; constrn. supr. A. J. Eckert Co., Albany, NY, 1950—55, C.A. Hjerpe Co., New Britain, 1955—60; pres., treas. C.W. Hjerpe, Inc., New Britain, 1961—87; ret. Pres. Conn. Mech. Contracators Assn., Conn., 1977; dir. Fed. Savings Bank, New Britain, 1970—92. Dir. YMCA, New Britain, 1970—80, New Britain Gen. Hosp., 1975—85; moderator South Congl. Ch., 1970—71. Lt. col. USMC Res. arty. USMC, 1941—45, PTO. Mem.: ARC (pres. local chpt.), Shuttle Meadow Country Club, Mason's Island Yacht Club (commodore), Rotary Club (pres. 1975). Republican. Avocations: golf, reading, music, sailing.

HJERPE, EDWARD ALFRED, III, finance and banking executive; b. Worcester, Mass., Jan. 25, 1959; s. Edward Alfred Jr. and Nancy Ann (O'Connor) H.; m. Macrina Goody, Aug. 17, 1985; children: Christine G., Edward A. IV, Catherine Ann. BA in Econs. and Bus., St. Anselm Coll., 1981; MA in Econs., U. Notre Dame, 1984, PhD in Econs., 1985. Industry economist Commodity Futures Trading Commn., Washington, 1985-86; fin. economist Fed. Home Loan Bank Bd., Washington, 1986-88; v.p., chief economist Fed. Home Loan Bank, Boston, 1988-89, sr. v.p., 1989-92, exec. v.p., CFO, 1992-97; sr. v.p., treas., CFO First Fed. Am. Bancorp, Inc., Fall River, Mass., 1997—98, exec. v.p., COO, CFO Swansea, Mass., 1998—2004; pres., COO Mass./RI region Webster Bank, 2004—. Bd. dirs. Dentaquest Ventures, 2003—. Contbr. articles to profl. jours. Bd. trustees St. Anselm Coll., 1992—, chmn. fin. com., mem. exec. com.; chmn. fin. com. Medway Town, 1995-98; bd. trustees Roger Williams Med. Ctr., Providence, 2000—, chmn., 2004—; bd. dirs. United Way Fall River, Mass, 2001—. Recipient A. Schmitt Dissertation fellowship. Mem. Am. Econ. Assn., Omicron Delta Epsilon, Delta Epsilon Sigma, Pi Gamma Mu. Roman Catholic. Home: One Great Rd Barrington RI 02806-1579

HJORT, HOWARD WARREN, economist, consultant; b. Plentywood, Mont., Dec. 20, 1931; BS, Mont. State U., 1958, MS, 1959; postgrad., N.C. State U. Staff economist Office of Sec. Agr., Washington, 1963-65, spl. asst. to under sec., 1965; dir. staff for program planning and analysis Office of Sec., 1965-69; planning and mgmt. adviser with Ford Found., India, 1969-72; dir. Office of Econs., Policy Analysis and Budget, 1977-81; co-founder Schnittker Assocs. (agrl. cons.), Washington, 1972-77; ptnr. EPI (McLean), Va., 1981-84; dir. policy analysis div. FAO, Rome, 1984-90, dir. liaison office for N.Am. Washington, 1990-91, dep. dir. gen. Rome, 1992-97; cons., 1998—.

HJORTSBERG, WILLIAM REINHOLD, writer; b. NYC, Feb. 23, 1941; s. Helge Reinhold and Anna Ida (Welti) H.; m. Marian Souidee Renken, June 2, 1962 (div. 1982); children: Lorca Isabel, Max William.; m. Sharon Leroy, July 21, 1982 (div. 1985); m. Janie Camp, Jan. 27, 2007. BA, Dartmouth Coll., 1962; postgrad., Yale U., 1962-63, Stanford U., 1967-68. Ind. author, screenwriter, 1969—. Adj. prof. media and theatre arts Mont. State U., 1991—. Author: Alp, 1969, Gray Matters, 1971, Symbiography, 1973, Toro! Toro! Toro!, 1974, Falling Angel, 1978, Tales & Fables, 1985, Nevermore, 1994, Odd Corners, 2004, (films): Thunder and Lightning, 1977, Legend, 1986, Angel Heart, 1987; co-author TV film: Georgia Peaches, 1980; contbg. editor Rocky Mountain Mag., 1979; contbr. fiction to Realist, Playboy, Cornell Rev., Penthouse, Oui, Sports Illustrated; contbr. criticism to N.Y. Times Book Rev. Recipient Playboy Editorial award, 1971, 78; Wallace Stegner fellow, 1967-68; Nat. Endowment Arts grantee, 1976. Mem. Authors Guild, Writers Guild Am. Avocations: fly fishing, gardening, collecting modern first editions, art, antique toys. Home: 2586 Boulder Rd Mc Leod MT 59052 Office: care Harold Matson Co Ste 714 276 Fifth Ave New York NY 10001 Office Phone: 212-679-4490.

HLATKY, MARK ANDREW, cardiologist, researcher; b. Windber, Pa., June 4, 1950; s. George Andrew and Rose Annette (Gonnella) H.; m. Donna Marie Alvarado, May 12, 1984; 1 child, Nicholas Michael. BS, MIT, 1972; MD, U. Pa., 1976. Diplomate Am. Bd. Internal Medicine, Am. Bd. Cardiovasc. Disease; lic. physician, Calif. Intern, resident U. Ariz., Tucson, 1976-79; Robert Wood Johnson clin. scholar U. Calif., San Francisco, 1979-81; fellow in cardiology Duke U., Durham, NC, 1981-83, asst. prof. medicine, 1983-89; assoc. prof. health rsch. and policy, assoc. prof. medicine Stanford (Calif.) U., 1989-96, prof. health rsch. and policy, prof. medicine, 1996—. Attending physician, cardiovasc. medicine svc. Stanford U. Med. Ctr., 1989—; mem. Health Care Tech. Study sect. NIH, Rockville, Md., 1992-96. Contbr. articles to profl. jours. Sloan scholar, 1972. Fellow Am. Coll. Cardiology; mem. Am. Heart Assn. (fellow coun. on clin. cardiology), Phi Beta Kappa. Achievements include research in outcomes after coronary surgery, coronary angioplasty, acute myocardial infarction, and cardiac arrhythmias. Home: 168 Rinconada Ave Palo Alto CA 94301-3725 Office: Stanford U Sch Medicine HRP Redwood Bldg Rm 150 Stanford CA 94305 Office Phone: 650-723-6426. E-mail: hlatky@stanford.edu.

HLAVACEK, ROY GEORGE, publishing executive; b. Chgo., Sept. 17, 1937; s. George Louis and Lillian Barbara H.; m. Nancy Elaine Wroblaski, Aug. 3, 1963; children: Carrie Lee Felix, Alexander Michael BS, U. Ill., 1960; MBA, U. Chgo., 1969. Project engr. R&D Ctr., Swift & Co., Chgo., 1960-65; v.p., editor, pub. Food Processing mag., Foods of Tomorrow mag. Food Publs. div. Putman Pub. Co., Chgo., 1965-92; v.p., group pub. Food Group, Delta Comms. Inc., Chgo., 1992-2001; v.p. comms. Inst. Food Technologists, 2001—. Adv. com. dept. food sci. U. Ill., Urbana-Champaign, 1988-93 Patentee in field Commr. Oak Park (Ill.) Landmarks Commn., 1972-79, chmn., 1976-79; treas. Oak Park Bicentennial Commn., 1973-76, Ernest Hemingway Found. of Oak Park, 1983-2000 Mem. ASME, Food Processing Machinery and Supplies Assn. (dir. 1987-91), Inst. Food Technologists (councilor 1975-81, chmn. Chgo. sect.), Pi Tau Sigma, Sigma Tau Home: 904 Forest Ave Oak Park IL 60302-1310 Office: Inst Food Technologists 525 W Van Buren Chicago IL 60607 Business E-Mail: rghlavacek@ift.org.

HLAVAY, JAY ALAN, financial analyst; b. Pitts., Sept. 30, 1956; s. Joseph and Margaret Marie (Danjou) H.; m. Cayce Avril Martin, Sept. 26, 1992; children: Joseph Martin, Christopher Jay. Student, Rutgers U., 1979; BS in Geology magna cum laude, U. Pitts., 1983, MBA, 1989. Geologist RSC Energy Corp., New Philadelphia, Ohio, 1983-85; dist. geologist Carless Resources Inc., New Philadelphia, 1985-89; gen. mgr. What on Earth, Pitts., 1989-90; prin. OPUS Energy Cons. Svcs., Coraopolis, Pa., 1990-92; exploration fin. analyst Union Pacific Resources, Ft. Worth, 1991-92, Austin chalk analyst, 1992-93, contr. Gulf of Mexico/Other Profit Ctr., 1993-95, contr. Gulf Coast Profit Ctr., 1996, project mgr. fin. ops., 1996-97, mgr. compensation, people dept., 1997-98, fin. advisor, 1998—2000; mgr. strategic and bus. analysis Food Lion, LLC, Salisbury, NC, 2000—03; dir. fin. and acctg. Sweetbay Supermarkets, Tampa, Fla., 2003—. Navy ROTC scholar, 1974; recipient Appreciation award Tuscarawas Valley Desk and Derrick Club, 1985, 86, 87; recipient West Allegheny Sch. Dist. Disting. Alumni award, 1988. Mem. Am. Assn. Petroleum Geologists (co-chmn. fin. com. S.W. sect. ann. conv. 1993), Sigma Gamma Epsilon. Office: Sweetbay/Kash n' Karry Supermarkets 3801 Sugar Palm Dr Tampa FL 33619 Office Phone: 813-620-1139 ext. 444. Business E-Mail: jhlavay@kashnkarry.com.

HLAVINKA, PAUL THOMAS, lawyer; b. East Bernard, Tex., Mar. 19, 1950; s. William Joseph and Mary Jo (Novosad) Hlavinka; m. Kimberly Hlavinka. BA in Polit. Sci., Rice U., Houston, 1973; MA in Journalism, U. Tex., Austin, 1977, JD, 1977. Bar: Tex. 1977. Reporter, adminstrv. asst. Houston Post Co., 1972-73; tchr. journalism U. Tex., Austin, 1974-77; researcher, assoc. law Atchley & Russell, Texarkana, Tex., 1975-78; ptnr. Morris & Hlavinka, Houston, 1982-94; owner Hlavinka & Assocs., Attys., Houston, 1994—; of counsel Barron & Newburger, Austin, 2005—. Rep. office Czech Invest, the Czech Republic Agy. for Fgn. Investment, 1995—; v.p., bd. dirs. Hlavinka Equipment Co., East Bernard; editor, publ. The Rice Football Webletter, 1998—. Assoc. vestry St. John the Divine Episcopal Ch., Houston, 1989-90. Sgt. USAFR, 1970-76. Mem. State Bar of Tex. (dist. admissions com. 1982-95), Rice U. Alumni Assn. (bd. dirs. 1988-91), Exec. bd. 1989-91), Friends of the Fondren Libr. (sec., bd. dirs. 1990-91), Czechoslovak Nat. Coun. Am., Internat. Inst. of Edn., Houston Fgn. Affairs Coun., Rice Athletic Fund/Owl Club (bd. dir. 2006-), Czech Ednl. Found. of Tex. (bd. dir. 1995-, sec. 1997-), Tex. Czech Heritage and Cultural Ctr. (bd. dir. 2006-). Avocations: book and antique collecting, travel. Office: Hlavinka & Assocs 2044 Bissonnet St Houston TX 77005-1647 Home: 2325 Glen Haven Blvd Houston TX 77030-3607 Office Phone: 713-521-1335.

HLOBIK, LAWRENCE S., agricultural products executive; With fertilizer, chem., and agribus. industries, 27 yrs.; CEO Terra Nitrogen, Tulsa; sr. v.p. Terra Industries, Tulsa; pres. AgriBusiness Group J.R. Simplot Co., Boise, 1998—2002, CEO, dir. bd., 2002—. Vice-chmn. Fertilizer Inst., 2002—04, bd. chmn., 2004—; bd. dir. Phosphate and Potash Inst. Office: JR Simplot Co PO Box 27 Boise ID 83707 also: JR Simplot Co 999 Main St Ste 1300 Boise ID 83702 Office Phone: 208-336-2110. Office Fax: 208-389-7515.

HO, BETTY JUENYÜ YÜLIN, retired musician, physiologist, educator; b. Nanking, China, Nov. 20, 1930; came to U.S., 1947; d. William Tien-Hu and Gwei-Hsin (Wang) Ho; m. Lajos Rudolf Elkan, Feb. 27, 1958 (div. Aug. 1967); children: Amanda, Anita, Julien (dec.), Raoul. Student, We. Coll., Oxford, Ohio, 1947—48; BS, Columbia U., 1952; postgrad., Lausanne U., Switzerland, 1955—56, piano studies with Maurice Perrin, Lausanne, 1956—58, CCNY, 1966—67, postgrad., 1972—74. Lab. technician Columbia U., NYC, 1953—54; ct. report typist Palais de Justice, Lausanne, 1956—57; pianist, accompanist Ecole de Ballet Mara Dousse, Lausanne, 1958—60; tchr. English Montcalme Inst., Lausanne, 1960—61; tchr. piano Le Manoir Inst., Lausanne, 1960—61, NYC, 1964—65. Rsch. dir. Juvenescent Rsch. Corp., N.Y.C., 1963— Author: The Living Function of Sleep, Life & Aging, 1967, The Origin of Variation of Races of Mankind & The Cause of Evolution, 1969, A Scientific Guide to Peaceful Living, 1972, A Chinese and Western Guide to Better Health and Longer Life, 1974, How to Stay Healthy A Lifetime Without Medicines, 1979, A Chinese & Western Daily Practical Health Guide, 1982, Immediate Hints to Health Problems, 1991, 101 Ways to Live 150 Years Young and Healthy, 1993, A Unique Guide for Health, Youth, and Longevity, 1993, A Unique Health Guide for Young People, 1994, How To Live a Long Life, 2004. Named Citizen of Yr. Principality Hutt River Province, Queensland, Australia, 1994, Royal Patronage Status for Life, 1995. Achievements include patents for infant feeding method. Home and Office: Juvenescent Research Corp 807 Riverside Dr Apt 1F New York NY 10032-7352 Office Phone: 212-795-2292.

HO, CHIH-MING, physicist, researcher; b. Chung King, China, Aug. 16, 1945; arrived in U.S., 1968; s. Shao-Nan and I-Chu Ho; m. Shirley T.S. Ho, Mar. 4, 1972; 1 child, Dean. BSME, Nat. Taiwan U., 1967; PhD, Johns Hopkins U., 1974. Assoc. rsch. scientist Johns Hopkins U., Balt., 1974-75; asst. prof. U. So. Calif., LA, 1976-81, assoc. prof., 1981-85, prof., 1985-91; assoc. vice-chancellor for rsch. UCLA, 2001—05, prof., 1991—, Ben Rich-Lockheed Martin prof., 1996—, dir. Ctr. for Cell Control, 2006—. Dir. Ctr. for Micro Sys., 1993—2000; cons. Flow Industries, Kent, 1982, Dynamics Tech., Torrance, Calif., 1977—87, Rockwell Internat., Canoga Park, Calif., 1980—83; dir. Inst. for Cell Mimetic Space Exploration, 2002—, Ctr. for Cell Control, 2006—; sci. advisor LNM, Inst. Mechanics, China; K.T. Lee hon. chair prof. Nat. Cheng Jung U.; Kuo-Nien hon. chair prof. Nat. Tsinghua U.; hon. prof. Inst. Mechanics, Chin. Acad. Scies., Nanjing U. Aeronautics and Astronautics, China. Contbr. articles to profl. jours.; patentee in field. Fellow AIAA, Am. Phys. Soc.; mem. Nat. Acad. Engring., Academia Sinica, Phi Beta Kappa, Tau Beta Pi, Sigma Xi, Phi Tau Phi. Achievements include research in micro-electro-mechanical systems, biomedical engineering, turbulence, aerodynamics, noise. Business E-Mail: chihming@ucla.edu.

HO, DAVID D. (DA-I HO), research physician, virologist, scientific organization director; b. Taichung, Taiwan, Nov. 3, 1952; arrived in U.S., 1964; s. Paul and Sonia Ho; m. Susan Kuo Ho; children: Kathryn, Jonathan, Jaclyn. Student, MIT, 1970—71; BS summa cum laude, Calif. Inst. Tech., 1974; MD, Harvard, 1978; DSc (hon.), Bard Coll., 1997, Grad. Sch. CUNY, 1998, Swarthmore Coll., 1998, Tufts U., 1999, SUNY, Inst. Tech., 2000, Columbia U., 2000. Clin. tng. resident and chief resident internal medicine and infectious diseases Cedars-Sinai Med. Ctr., UCLA Sch. Medicine, 1978—82; clin. and rsch. fellow Infectious Disease Unit Mass. Gen. Hosp., 1982—85; rsch. fellow medicine Harvard Med. Sch., 1982—85; instructor in medicine Mass. Gen. Hosp. and Harvard Med. Sch., 1985—86; physician, rsch. scientist divsn. infectious diseases, dept. medicine Cedars-Sinai Med. Ctr., 1986—90; asst. prof. medicine in residence UCLA Sch. Medicine, 1986—89, assoc. prof. medicine in residence, 1989—90; prof. medicine and microbiology, co-dir. Ctr. for AIDS Rsch. NYU Sch. Medicine, 1990—96, dir., 1994—96; founding scientific dir., CEO Aaron Diamond AIDS Rsch. Ctr., NYC, 1990—, also bd. dir., 1998—; Irene Diamond prof., physician Rockefeller U., 1996—. Hon. prof. Peking Union Med. Coll., 1997, Chinese Acad. Med. Sciences, 1997, Wuhan U., 2002, Chinese Acad. Sciences, 2003, Fudan U., 2003; bd. dir. MIT Corp., 2003—. Contbr. articles to profl. jours. Bd. trustee Calif. Inst. Tech., 1997—; bd. overseers Harvard U., 1998—2004. Named Man of Yr., Time Mag., 1996; recipient Ernst Jung-Preis Fur Medizin (Germany), 1991, Mayor's award (N.Y.C.) for Excellence in Sci. and Tech., 1993, Squibb award, Infectious Disease Soc. Am., 1996, Bernard Field Meml. award, 1997, Scientific Honoree, NY Acad. Medicine, 1998, Golden Plate award, Am. Acad. Achievement, 1998, Hoechst Marion Roussel award, 1999, Presdl. Citizens medal, 2001, Friendship award, State Coun. People's Republic of China, 2003, Sydney Rubbo award, Australia Soc. Microbiology, 2003, Edward Ahrens award in Clin. Investigation, 2003, Lewis and Jack Rudin NY prize for Med. Rsch., 2003, Inspiration award, Asian Excellence award, 2006. Fellow: AAAS (Ernst Jung prize in medicine), Am. Acad. Microbiology, Am. Acad. Arts and Sciences; mem.: Chinese Acad. Engring. (fgn. mem. 2003—), Academia Sinica (Republic of China), NAS, IOM, NIH vaccine working group, Chinese Am. Leadership Orgn. (Chinese Am. leadership orgn., com. of 100 1990—), AmFAR (bd. dirs. sci. bd.). Office: Aaron Diamond AIDS Rsch Ctr 455 1st Ave 7th Fl New York NY 10016-9121 Address: Rockefeller U 1230 York Ave New York NY 10021 Office Phone: 212-448-5000. Office Fax: 212-725-1126. Business E-Mail: dho@rockefeller.edu.

HO, ERIC CALEB, lawyer; s. Joseph and Grace W. Ho; m. Cindy Feng, Oct. 10, 1992; children: Paul, Mary, Hannah. BS in Elec. Engring. and Computer Sci., Univ. of Calif. at Berkeley, 1990; JD, U. of So. Calif., 1994. Elec. engr. Hughes Aircraft EDSG, El Segundo, Calif., 1990—91; law assoc., corp. law dept. Union Pacific RR, City of Commerce, Calif., 1991—93, Litton Industries, Beverly Hills, 1992—94; patent atty. Blakely, Sokoloff, Taylor & Zafman, West Los Angeles, 1994—98, Sun & Ho, Assn. of Law Practices, Santa Monica, 1998—99; pvt. practice Northridge, 1999—2006; patent counsel Qualcomm, Inc., San Diego, 2006—. Alumni scholarship, UCLA, 1990, Hon. scholarship, UC Berkeley, 1990, Regents scholarship, UCLA, 1990. Mem.: ABA (assoc.), U.S. Patent and Trademark Office Soc. (assoc.), Am. Intellectual Property Law Assn. (assoc.), U.C. Berkeley Alumni Assn. (assoc.). Achievements include drafting for inventors at Fortune 100 companies. Business E-Mail: ericho@qualcomm.com.

HO, REGINALD CHI SHING, medical educator; b. Hong Kong, Mar. 30, 1932; came to U.S., 1940; s. Chow and Elizabeth (Wong) Ho; m. Sharilyn Dang , Nov. 14, 1964; children: Mark, Reginald, Gianna Masca, Timothy. Student, St. Louis U., 1954, MD, 1959. Diplomate Nat. Bd. Med. Examiners, Am. Bd. Internal Medicine. Rotating intern U. Cin. Hosps., 1959-60, resident in internal medicine, 1960-62; fellow in hematology and oncology Barnes Hosp./Washington U., St. Louis, 1962-63; assoc. clin. prof. medicine JAB Sch. Medicine U. Hawaii, Honolulu, 1972-77, clin. prof. medicine, 1977—; attending physician dept. hematology and oncology Straub Clinic and Hosp., Honolulu, 1973—. Prin. investigator Hawaii Cmty. Clin. Oncology Program, Honolulu, 1983-86; adj. prof. clin. sci. Cancer Rsch. Ctr. Hawaii, 1989—, mem. various coms. Contbr. articles to med. jours. Bd. dirs. Cath. Svcs. for Families, 1987-91. Mem. AMA, ACP, Am. Cancer Soc. (divsn. del. 1982-93, del. dir. 1983-92, exec. com. 1989-94, chair med. and sci. exec. com. 1991-92, v.p. 1991-92, pres. 1992-93, immediate past pres. 1993-94, bd. dirs. Hawaii divsn. 1968—, pres. 1976-77, chmn. bd. dirs. 1977-78, hon. life mem. 1989—, bd. dirs.), Hawaii Med. Assn. (Hawaii cancer commn. 1980-85, chair cancer com. 1981-90), Honolulu County Med. Assn. (del. to Hawaii Med. Assn. 1969-72), Exptl. Med. Care Rev. Orgn. (exec. com., chair ambulatory care edn. audit com. 1972), Alpha Omega Alpha. Roman Catholic. Avocation: tennis. Office: Straub Clinic Hosp 888 S King St Honolulu HI 96813-3083 Home Phone: 808-247-0638.

HO, ROBERT EN MING, neurosurgeon, educator; b. Honolulu, Nov. 13, 1942; s. Donald Tet En Ho and Violette (Weeks) Gould; m. Edie Olsen, June 27, 1964; children: Lisa, Amy. BS cum laude, Mich. State. U., 1964; MD, Wayne State U., 1968. Diplomate Am. Bd. Neurol. Surgery. Surg. intern Detroit Gen. Hosp., 1968-69, surg. resident, 1969-70, neurosurg. resident, 1972-76; microsurg. fellow Neurochirurgische Universtatskilinik, Zurich, Switzerland, 1976; instr. dept. neurosurgery Wayne State U., Detroit, 1977-79; dir. dept. neurosurgery Gertrude Levin Pain Clinic, 1977-80; asst. prof., 1979-84; chief neurosurg. svcs. Health Care Inst., 1979-84; clin. asst. prof., 1984—. Founder, dir. Microneurosurg. Lab., 1977-89, dir. spine and spine reconstruction dept. neurosurgery med. sch., 1992-97; dir. neuroscis. intensive care unit Harper Hosp., Detroit, 1980-84, spine and spine reconstruction fellowship Wayne State Med. Sch., 1992-97; mem. audit com. Detroit Gen. Hosp., 1977-80, mem. med. device com., 1977-80, mem. credentials com, 1978-84; sec., treas. Detroit Neurosurg. Acad. Program Com., 1978-84; mem. emergency room com. Harper Hosp., 1980-84, neuroscis. intensive care unit com., 1980-84; dir. Oakland-Macomb PPO; chief neurol. sect. William Beaumont Hosp., Troy, Mich., mem. adv. bd., 1986-90; chmn. adv. com. traumatic brain injury/spinal cord injury, State Mich., 1993-96; presenter of numerous exhibits, profl. papers; organizer numerous med. meetings; lectr. in field. Contbr. articles to profl. jours. Served with U.S. Army, 1970-72, Vietnam. Recipient Intern of Yr. award Detroit Gen. Hosp., 1969. Mem. AMA, ACS, Congress Neurol. Surgeons, Detroit Neurosurg. Acad., Mich. Assn. Neurol. Surgeons (sec.-treas. 1979-82, v.p. 1982-84, pres. 1984-86, bd. dirs. 1986-90), Mich. State Med. Soc., Oakland County Med. Soc., Wayne County Med. Soc., Internat. Coll. Surgeons (U.S. sect.), Am. Assn. Neurol Surgeons (spinal disorders sec. 1981-2002, cerebrovascular surgery sect.). Office: 43650 Garfield Rd Clinton Township MI 48038 Office Phone: 586-263-0820.

HO, YIK HONG, colon and rectal surgeon; b. Singapore, Apr. 21, 1956; s. Peng Yoke Ho and Mei Yiu (Lucy) Fung; m. Chui Wah Ludmilla Tung, Sept. 13, 1984; 1 child, Elaine Jo-Lan. MBBS with honors, U. Queensland, 1980, MD, 2001. Intern Princess Alexandra Hosp., Brisbane, Australia, 1980-81, resident, 1981-82; med. officer Sai Ying Pun Hosp./Tang Shiu Kin Hosp., Hong Kong, 1982-83; registrar U. Surg. Unit Queen Mary Hosp., Tung Wah Hosp., Hong Kong, 1983-89; sr. registrar Singapore Gen. Hosp., 1989-93, cons., 1993-98, dir. Pelvic Floor Lab., 1996—2002, sr. cons., 1998—2002; vis. staff sr. cons. surg. oncology Nat. Cancer Centre, 1999—2002; clin. sr. lectr. Nat. U. Singapore, 2001—02; prof., head dept. surgery James Cook U. Sch. Medicine, 2002—; coord. North Queensland Ctr. for Cancer Rsch., Australian Inst. Tropical Medicine, 2004—; dep. dean Sch. of Med. James Cook U., 2006—. Rsch. fellow U. Hosp U. Nottingham, England, 1989; part-time clin. lectr. Nat. U. Singapore, 1990—2001; dep. chmn. Electronics Med. Records Workgroup Singapore Gen. Hosp., 1994—2002; head North Queensland Ctr. Cancer Rsch., Australian Inst. Tropical Medicine. Mem. editl. rev. com. Annals of Acad. of Medicine, 1994-2002, mem. editl. com., 2000-2002; mem. editl. com. Singapore Gen. Hosp. Procs., 1995-99, assoc. editor, 1995-98, editor, 1999-2002; mem. editl. bd. Internat. Surgery, 2002—, World Gastroenterology Jour.; contbr. articles to profl. jours. Scholarship Australian Kidney Found., 1977. Fellow Royal Australasian Coll. Surgeons, Royal Coll. Surgeons (Edinburgh), Royal Coll Physicians and Surgeons (Glasgow), Internat. Coll. Surgeons (Singapore sect. com. mem. 1994-96, 98-99, treas. 97-99, sec. 1999, pres. 2000-02, world additional gov. 1999-2000, additional v.p. 2001—), Australian Coll. Tropical Medicine; mem. Singapore Soc. Continence (v.p. 1993-2002), Biomed. Rsch. and Exptl. Therapeutics Soc. Singapore (hon. sec. 1993-95, pres. 1995-97), Internat. Soc. Surgery (nat. rep. 1999-2002), Am. Soc. Colon-Rectal Surgeons (mem. internat. adv. com. 2000). Avocations: exercise, computer, photography, swimming, tai-chi. Office: James Cook U Dept Surgery Sch Medicine Queensland 4811 Australia Office Phone: 617-47961417. Personal E-mail: yik-hong.ho@bigpond.com. Business E-Mail: yikhong.ho@jcu.edu.au.

HOAG, DAVID GARRATT, retired aerospace engineer; b. Boston, Oct. 11, 1925; s. Alden Bomer and Helen Lucy (Garratt) H.; m. Grace Edward Griffith, May 10, 1952; children— Rebecca Wilder, Peter Griffith, Jeffrey Taber, Nicholas Alden, Lucy Seymour. BS, MIT, 1946, MS, 1950. Staff engr. instrumentation lab. MIT, Cambridge, 1946-57; tech. dir. Polaris Missile Guidance, 1957-61; tech. dir., program mgr. Apollo Spacecraft Guidance, 1961-72; advanced system dept. head C.S. Draper Lab., Inc., Cambridge, 1972-86; ret., 1990. Recipient Pub. Svc. award NASA, 1969, Spl. award Royal Inst. Navigation, Britain, 1970, Laurels, Aviation Week, 1970. Fellow AIAA (Louis W. Hill Space Transp. award 1972); mem. Nat. Acad. Engring., Inst. Navigation (Thurlow award 1969, pres. 1978-79), Internat. Acad. Astronautics (assoc. editor ACTA Astronautica 1979-79). Home: 116 Winthrop St Medway MA 02053-2310

HOAGLAND, ALBERT SMILEY, electrical engineer, researcher; b. Berkeley, Calif., Sept. 13, 1926; s. Dennis Robert and Jessie Agnes (Smiley) H.; m. Janine Maryse Simart, May 23, 1950; children: Catherine, Nicole, Richard. BS, U. Calif.-Berkeley, 1947, MS, 1948, PhD, 1954. Registered profl. engr., Calif. Asst. prof. elec. engring. U. Calif.-Berkeley, 1954-56; sr. engr. IBM, San Jose, Calif., 1956-59; mgr. engring sci. San Jose Research Lab., 1959-62; sr. tech. cons. IBM World Trade, The Hague, Holland, 1962-64; mgr. engring. sci. IBM Research Ctr., NYC, 1964-68, dir. tech. planning Research Div., 1968-71; corporate program coordinator IBM, Boulder, Colo., 1971-76; mgr. exploratory magnetic rec. San Jose Research Lab., 1976-82; tech. adv. Gen. Products Div., 1982-84; acting dir. Ctr. for Magnetic Recording Research, U. Calif. San Diego, 1983-84; prof. elec. engring., dir. Inst. Info. Storage Tech. Santa Clara U., Calif., 1984—2005; exec. dir. Magnetic Disk Heritage Ctr., 2005—. Lectr. computer design U. Calif. Berkeley, 1948-54, 56-62; adj. prof. U. Calif. San Diego, 1986; cons. State Calif., 1955-56, IBM, 1954-56, also numerous cons. in data storage industry, 1984—; chmn. Nat. Computer Conf. Bd., 1976-78; adj. prof. Harvey Mudd Coll. Author: Digital Magnetic

Recording, 1963; co-author 2d edit., 1991, reprinted, 1998; contbr. articles on magnetic rec. and info. storage tech. to profl. publs.; patentee in field Chmn. adv. com. The Magnetic Rec. Conf., 1993—97; trustee Charles Babbage Inst.; regent Inst. Info. Mgmt., 1985—92; exec. dir. Magnetic Disk Heritage Ctr. at Santa Clara U., 2001—05. With USNR, 1943—46. Recipient outstanding paper award IEEE, 1965 Fellow IEEE (dir. 1974-77, Centennial medal 1984, 3d Millenium medal 2000), Am. Fedn. Info. Processing Socs. (dir. 1969-78, pres. 1978-80); mem. IEEE Computer Soc. (pres. 1971-73), Rsch. Soc. Am. (pres. Sequoia chpt. 1962-63), Phi Beta Kappa, Sigma Xi, Eta Kappa Nu, Tau Beta Pi. Clubs: Golden Bear. Home: 13834 Upper Hill Dr Saratoga CA 95070-5334 Office: care Computer History Mus 1401 N Shoreline Blvd Mountain View CA 94043 Personal E-mail: ahoagland@gmail.com. Business E-Mail: ahoagland@magneticdiskheritagecenter.org.

HOAGLAND, CHRISTINA GAIL, occupational therapist, industrial drafter; b. Long Beach, Calif., July 18, 1954; d. Joseph Richard and Dorothy Marian (Bell) H. BS in Occupl. Therapy, Loma Linda U., 1975; AS in Indsl. Drafting Tech., Mt. San Antonio Coll., 1985. Registered occupl. therapist; cert. brain injury specialist Am. Acad. for the Cert. Brain Injury Specialists. Occupl. therapist Yuka Mission Hosp., Zambia, Africa, 1976-77; staff occupl. therapist Glendale (Calif.) Adventist Med. Ctr., 1978-79; indsl. drafter Amerex Co., Riverside, Calif., 1985-88; re-entry occupl. therapist Rancho Los Amigos, Downey, Calif., 1989-90; staff occupl. therapist Corona (Calif.) Cmty. Hosp., 1990-92; occupl. therapist Linda R. Brown, Visalia, Calif., 1992; floating staff occupl. therapist Hilltop Rehab. Hosp., Grand Junction, Colo., 1992—95, St. Mary's Rehab. Ctr., Grand Junction, 1995—97; OTR, ind. living skills trainer supr. Interim Home Health Care, 1998—; floating staff occupl. therapist Grand Junction Cmty. Hosp., 2000—; staff occupl. therapist Hinsdale Sanitarium and Hosp., 1977—78. Bd. mem. Brain Injury Trust Fund. Bd. dirs. LWV, Mesa County, Colo. Mem. Am. Occupl. Therapy Assn., Occupl. Therapy Assn. Colo. Nat. Mus. Women in Arts. Western Colo. Ctr. for the Arts. Democratic Socialist. Seventh-Day Adventist. Home: 578 N 26th St Grand Junction CO 81501-7961 Office Phone: 970-241-3166.

HOAGLAND, DONALD WRIGHT, lawyer; b. NYC, Aug. 16, 1921; s. Webster Comley and Irene (Wright) H.; m. Mary Tiedeman, May 14, 1949; children: Peter M., Mary C., Sara H., Ann W. BA, Yale U., 1942; LLB, Columbia U., 1948. Bar: N.Y. 1948, Colo. 1951. Assoc. firm Winthrop, Stimson, Putnam & Roberts, NYC, 1948-51; ptnr. Davis, Graham & Stubbs, Denver, 1951-63, 66-87, of counsel, 1987—; with AID, 1964-66, asst. adminstr. devel. finance and pvt. enterprise, 1965-66, cons. Indonesia, 1967-75. Lectr. U. Denver Sch. Law, 1971-75; chmn. bd. Bi-Nat. Devel. Corp., 1968-70; dir. Centennial Fund, Inc., 2d Centennial Fund, Inc., Gryphon Fund, Inc., 1959-63; mem. Colo. Supreme Ct. Grievance Com., 1992-98. Mem. Denver Planning Bd., 1955-61, 67-70, chmn., 1959-61; bd. dirs., v.p. Denver Art Mus., 1959-63, 72-76, 79-82; bd. dirs. Colo. Urban League, 1960-63, 66-72, chmn. bd., 1968-72; adv. bd. Vols. Tech. Assistance vice-chmn. bd. Denver chpt. ARC, 1959-61; bd. dirs. Legal Aid Soc. Colo., 1972-84, pres., 1975-79; trustee Phillips Exeter Acad., 1960-67, Colo. Rocky Mountain Sch., 1981-84, Am. U., Washington, 1982-85; chmn. bd. dirs. Legal Aid Found., Colo., 1983-87; bd. dirs. Colo. Bus. Coalition for Health, 1988-89, Colo. Found. for Ednl. Excellence, 1998-2004; exec. dir. Ctr. for Health Ethics and Policy U. Colo., Denver, 1987-91; chmn. Colo. Health Data Commn., 1986-88, Gov. Romer's panel health advisors, 1992-94, Social Sci. Found. Denver U., 1975-2007; active Caring for Colo. Found., 1999-2002, chmn., program com., 2003—; chmn. Colo. Pub. Health Edn. and Rsch. Adv. Com., 2002—; pres. Colo. Found. Pub. Health and Environment, 1995-98, bd. dirs., 1995-2005; ethics com. Nat. Jewish Med. and Rsch. Ctr., 1993-2005. With USNR, 1943-45. Decorated Air medal with oak leaf cluster. Mem. ABA, Colo. Bar Assn., Denver Bar Assn. Home: 355 Garfield St Denver CO 80206-4509 Office: Davis Graham & Stubbs 1550 17th St Ste 500 Denver CO 80202

HOAGLAND, JIMMIE LEE, newspaper editor; b. Rock Hill, SC, Jan. 22, 1940; s. Lee Roy and Edith Irene (Sullivan) H.; m. Jane Stanton Hitchcock, July 14, 1995; children: Laura Lee (dec.), Lily Hue, Lee Clayton. AB in Journalism, U. S.C., 1961; student, U. Aix-en-Provence, France, 1961-62, Columbia U., 1968-69. Reporter Evening Herald, Rock Hill, 1960; copy editor N.Y. Times Internat. Edit., Paris, France, 1964-66; reporter Washington Post, 1966-69, Africa corr., 1969-72, Middle East corr., 1972-75, Paris corr., 1975-77, fgn. editor, 1979-81, asst. mng. editor, 1981-86, assoc. editor, chief fgn. corr., 1986—. Author: South Africa: Civilizations in Conflict, 1972. Ford Found. fellow Columbia U., 1968-69; recipient Pulitzer prize internat. report, 1970; Overseas Press Club award internat. reporting, 1977; Pulitzer prize for commentary, 1991; Eugene Meyer Career Achievement award, 1994. Mem. Coun. on Fgn. Rels., Phi Beta Kappa, Pi Kappa Alpha. Office: Washington Post 1150 15th St NW Washington DC 20071-0002 Business E-Mail: jimhoagland@washpost.com.

HOAGLAND, KARL KING, JR., lawyer; b. St. Louis, Aug. 21, 1933; s. Karl King and Mary Edna (Parsons) H.; m. Sylvia Anne Naranick, July 13, 1957; children: Elisabeth Parsons, Sarah Stewart, Karl King III, Alison T. BS in Econs., U. Pa., 1955; LLB, U. Ill., 1958. Bar: Ill. 1958, U.S. Dist. Ct. (so. dist.) Ill. 1958. V.p., gen. counsel, sec. Jefferson Smurfit Corp., St. Louis, 1960-92, Container Corp. Am., St. Louis, 1986-92; of counsel Hoagland, Fitzgerald, Smith & Pranaitis, Alton, Ill., 1987—. Chmn. bd. dirs. Millers' Mut. Ins. Assn. Ill., 1989-92. Asst. editor: U. Ill. Law Forum, 1957-58. Trustee, treas. Monticello Coll. Found., 1965—. 1st lt. USAF, 1958-60. Mem. Ill. Bar Assn., Madison County Bar Assn., Alton-Wood River Bar Assn., Lockhaven Country Club, Mo. Athletic Club, Crystal Lake Club, Orcas Tennis Club, Order of the Coif, Beta Gamma Sigma. Episcopalian. Avocations: tennis, skiing, hunting, fishing, golf. Home (Summer): PO Box 1454 Eastsound WA 98245 Home (Winter): PO Box 130 Alton IL 62002

HOAGLAND, MAHLON, biochemist, educator; b. Boston, Oct. 5, 1921; s. Hudson and Anna (Plummer) H.; m. Olley Virginia Jones, Jan. 10, 1961; children from previous marriage: Judith, Mahlon, Robin. Student, Williams Coll., 1940—41, Harvard U., 1941—43, MD, 1948; ScD (hon.), Worcester Poly. Inst., 1973, U. Mass., 1984. From rsch. fellow to asst. prof. medicine Med. Sch. Harvard U. at Mass. Gen. Hosp., 1948-60; assoc. prof. bacteriology and immunology Med. Sch. Harvard U., 1960-67; prof. biochemistry, chmn. dept. Med. Sch. Dartmouth, 1967-70; pres., sci. dir. Worcester Found. for Biomed. Rsch., Shrewsbury, Mass., 1970-85, pres. emeritus, 1985—. Rsch. assoc. Carlsberg Labs., Copenhagen, 1951-52, Cavendish Labs., Cambridge, Eng., 1957-58; cancer rsch. scholar Am. Cancer Soc., 1953-58; founder, spokesman Del. for Basic Biomed. Rsch., 1978-85. Author: 6 Books; contbr. over 68 articles to profl. jours. Recipient Franklin medal, 1976; 2 book awards Am. Med. Writers Assn., 1982, 96. Fellow Am. Acad. Arts and Scis.; mem. NAS. Achievements include discovery of mechanism of amino acid activation and (with P.C. Zamecnik) transfer ribonucleic acid. Home: PO Box 183 Academy Rd Thetford VT 05074-0183 Office Phone: 802-785-2233.

HOAGLAND, SAMUEL ALBERT, lawyer, pharmacist; b. Mt. Home, Idaho, Aug. 19, 1953; s. Charles Leroy and Glenna Lorraine (Gridley) H.; m. Karen Ann Mengel, Nov. 20, 1976; children: Hiliary Anne, Heidi Lynne, Holly Kaye. BS in Pharmacy, Idaho State U., 1976; JD, U. Idaho, 1982. Bar: Idaho 1982, U.S. Dist. Ct. Idaho 1982, U.S. CT. Appeals (9th cir.) 1984. Lectr. clin. pharmacy Idaho State U., Pocatello, 1976-78, lectr. pharmacy law, 1985-86, dean's adv. council Coll. Pharmacy, 1987-92; hosp. pharmacist Mercy Med. Ctr., Nampa, Idaho, 1978-79; retail pharmacist Thrifty Corp., Moscow, Idaho, 1980-82; assoc. Dial, Looze & May, Pocatello, 1982-89, Prescott & Foster, Boise, Idaho, 1989-90; gen. counsel Design Innovations and Rsch. Corp., 1991-95; pvt. practice, 1990—2001, 2006—; with Hoagland, Dominick & Hicks, PLLC, 2001—06. Chmn. malpractice panel Idaho Bd. Medicine, Boise, 1983-92, adminstrv. hearing officer, 1989-92; adj. prof. pharmacy law Idaho State U., 2001—; pres. The Pharmacy Doctors, Inc., 2005—. Contbr. to law publs. Bd. dirs. Cathedral Pines Camp, Ketchum, Idaho. Mem. Idaho State Bar Assn., Idaho Trial Lawyers Assn., Boise Bar Assn., Capital Pharm. Assn., Am. Pharm. Assn., Idaho Soc. Hosp. Pharmacists (bd. dirs., pres.-elect 2005-06, pres. 2006—), Am. Soc. Pharmacy Law, Flying Doctors Am. (Atlanta) (bd. dirs.). Home: 11901 W Mesquite Dr Boise ID 83713-0813 Office: 1471 Shoreline Dr Ste 100 Boise ID 83702-9104 Office Phone: 208-386-9292.

HOAGLIN, THOMAS E., savings and loan association executive; b. Charleston, W.Va., May 4, 1949; BA in Econs., Denison U., 1971; MBA, Stanford U., 1973. Chmn., CEO Banc One Services Corp., 1997—98; exec. v.p., pvt. banking Bank One Corp., 1998—99; vice chmn. AmSouth Bancorporation, 2000; chmn., pres., CEO Huntington Bancshares Inc., Columbus, Ohio, 2001—07, chmn., CEO, 2007—. Pres., chmn., CEO Huntington Nat. Bank, Columbus; bd. dirs. Denison U., The Columbus (Ohio) Partnership, Columbus (Ohio) Downtown Devel. Corp., Columbus (Ohio) Coll. Art and Design, Ohio Ctr. Sci. and Industry; bd. dir. Capital South Corp., The Gorman-Rupp Co., Mansfield, Ohio; bd. trustees Ohio Health. Bd. dir. Greater Columbus (Ohio) C. of C., Ohio Bus. Roundtable. Mem.: The Fin. Svcs. Roundtable, World Pres. Org. Office: Huntington Bancshares Inc Huntington Ctr 41 South High St Columbus OH 43287*

HOAK, JONATHAN S., SR., lawyer; b. Eugene, Oreg., July 1949; BA, U. Colo., 1971; postgrad., Exeter U., Eng.; JD, Drake U., 1977. With Heritage Comms., Des Moines, 1971-74; assoc. Sidley & Austin, 1979-85, ptnr., 1985-90; gen. atty. fed. sys. divsn. AT&T, 1990-93; sr. v.p., gen. counsel NCR Corp., Dayton, Ohio, 1993—2006; v.p., chief ethics and compliance officer Hewlett-Packard Co., Palo Alto, Calif., 2006—. Bd. counselors Drake U. Law Sch., U. Dayton Sch. Law Adv. Coun. Mem. ABA, Fed. Cir. Bar Assn., Ohio Bar Assn. Office: HP 3000 Hanover St Palo Alto CA 94304-1185*

HOANG, DUC VAN, pathologist, educator; b. Hanoi, Vietnam, Feb. 17, 1926; came to U.S. 1975, naturalized 1981; s. Duoc Van and Nguyen Thi (Tham) H.; m. Mau-Ngo Thi Vu, 7 children. MD, Hanoi U. Sch. Medicine, Vietnam, 1952; DSc, Open Internat. U., Sri Lanka, 1989. Dean Sch. Medicine Army of the Republic of Vietnam, Saigon, 1959-63; dean Minh-Duc U. Sch. Medicine, Saigon, 1970-71; clin. prof. theoretical pathology U. So. Calif. Sch. Medicine, LA, 1978—. Adj. prof. Emperor's Coll. Traditional Oriental Medicine, Santa Monica, Calif., 1988-91; initiator of attitudinal immunology. Author: Towards an Integrated Humanization of Medicine, 1957; The Man Who Weights the Soul, 1959; Eastern Medicine, A New Direction?, 1970; also short stories; author introdn. to work of Marie Noël, Vietnamese transl. of La Rose Rouge; translator: Pestis, introduction to the work of Albert Camus, Vietnamese translation of La Peste; editor: The East (co-founder); jour. Les Cahiers de l'Asie du Sud-Est. Founder, past pres. Movement for Fedn. Countries S.E. Asia; co-founder, past v.p. Movement for Restoration Cultures and Religions of Orient; mem. The Noetic Inst., 1988—, Internat. Found. for Homeopathy, 1987; founder, pres. Intercontinental Found. for Electro-Magnetic Resonance Rsch., 1989—; coord. Unity and Diversity World Health Coun., 1992—. Named hon. dean, The Open Internat. U. of Complementary Medicines, Sri Lanka, 1989; Unity-and-Diversity World Coun. fellow, 1990—. Mem. AAUP, Assn. Clin. Scientists, Am. Com. for Integration Eastern and Western Medicine (founder), Assn. Unitive Medicine (founder, pres.), U. So. Calif. Faculty Member Club (L.A.). Roman Catholic. Home: 3630 Barry Ave Los Angeles CA 90066-3202 E-mail: hoangvduc@yahoo.com.

HOAR, SAMUEL NEIL, JR., lawyer; b. Boston, June 9, 1955; m. Eve Hoar; children: Sam, Bailey. AB, Dartmouth Coll., 1980; JD magna cum laude, Boston U., 1985. Bar: Mass. 1985, Vt. 1987, NY 1999. Law clk. to Hon. Bailey Aldrich US Ct. Appeals (1st Cir.), 1985—86; atty. Dinse Knapp & McAndrew, 1987—92, dir. and ptnr. Litig. Practice Group, 1992—, hiring ptnr., mem. mgmt. com., ptnr.-in-charge Plattsburgh NY Office, leader Ins. Practice Group. Law lectr. Boston U. Sch. Law, 1986; mem. adv. com. on civil rules Vt. Supreme Ct., 2000, mem. jury policy com., 2001—03. Founding pres. South Burlington Youth Soccer Assn.; youth soccer coach South Burlington; mem. bd. dirs., pres. Allenbrook Homes for Youth; town agent and grand juror Town of Hinesburg, Vt., delinquent tax collector Vt. Mem.: New England Bar Assn. (bd. dirs.), Vt. Bar Found. (bd. dirs. 2000—, pres. 2002), Def. Rsch. Inst., Fedn. Def. and Corp. Counsel, ABA, Vt. Bar Assn. (bd. managers 2000—, pres. 2006—07), Chittenden County Bar Assn., Burlington Tennis Club (past pres.). Office: Denise Knapp & McAndrew PC PO Box 988 Burlington VT 05402 Office Phone: 802-864-5751. Office Fax: 802-862-6409. E-mail: shoar@dinse.com.

HOARE-TEMPLE, PIERS HOWARD, building maintenance executive; b. London, Mar. 5, 1946; s. Euan Temple and Margot Carol Blaut Temple Hoare; m. Jane Evelyn Montague Browne, Aug. 19, 1978; 1 child, Guy Arthur Anthony. Salesman Va. Oak Tannery, Luray, 1965-67; barrister The English Bar, London, 1972-87; chmn. bd., majority shareholder Blaut Verwaltung & Grundstücks GmbH & Co., Neu Isenburg, Germany, 1987—, Heritage Restoration Ltd., Jersey, Channel Islands, 1991—, Heritage Restoration GmbH, Dusseldorf, Germany, 1992—2003; owner Reisebüro Engels, Friedberg, Germany, 1987—94. Cons. Riverside (Great Stour Ltd.), Canterbury, Eng., 1994, dir. Canterbury Leisure Devel. Ltd., 1993—2006. Mem. mgmt. com., trustee Hearing Rsch. Trust, London, 1988—; chmn. Richmond Legal Advice Svc., London, 1973—. Lt. comdr. Naval Res. Decorated Reserve Decoration, Her Majesty the Queen, 1985. Mem. Criminal Bar Assn., Conservative Lawyers Assn., Pres.'s Res. Officers' Assn. (com. mem.), Royal Naval Res. Officer Dining Club (v.p.), Naval Club London (counselor bd.), Old Pauline Club (com. mem.). Ch. of Eng. Avocations: travel, wining and dining, swimming, socializing. Office: Blaut Verwaltung und Grundstucks GMBh & Co Dornhofstrasse 89 Neu Isenburg 63263 Germany Home Phone: 0044-207-834 8724; Office Phone: 0049 6102 25265. E-mail: pierstemple@googlemail.com.

HOBART, BILLIE, education educator, consultant; b. Pitts., Apr. 19, 1935; d. Harold James Billingsley and Rose Stephanie (Sladack) Green; m. W.C.H. Hobart, July 20, 1957 (div. 1967); 1 child, Rawson W. BA in English, U. Calif., Berkeley, 1967, EdD, 1992; MA in Psychology, Sonoma State U., Rohnert Park, Calif., 1972. Cert. tchr. Calif., Irlen screener 2003. Asst. prof. Coll. Marin, Kentfield, Calif., 1969-78; freelance cons., writer, 1969—; asst. prof. Contra Costa Coll., San Pablo, Calif., 1986-99, Santa Rosa Jr. Coll., Calif., 1999—. Author: (cookbook) Natural Sweet Tooth, 1974, (non-fiction) Expansion, 1972, Purposeful Self: Coherent Self, 1979, 2002, (non-fiction) Talking to Dead People, 1996, On the Subject of Prayer, 2000, SpaceFlight, 2006, (biography) Captain Granville Perry Swift, California Pioneer and Sonoma Bear, 1999, (fiction) Last Days of Gifted Light, 2000, Timethinner, 2001, Getting to Start, 2001, Clearing to Core, 2002, The Lori Stories, 2006; contbr. articles to profl. jours. Served with WAC, 1953-55. Mem. No. Calif. Coll. Reading Tchrs. Assn. (pres. 1996-98), Mensa, Commonwealth Club San Francisco, Phi Delta Kappa. Home and Office: PO Box 1542 Sonoma CA 95476-1542

HOBART, REBECCA WESTON, retired elementary school educator; b. Edmunds, Maine, Mar. 20, 1921; d. Ralph Chandler Hobart and Edith Avis MacRae. BA, Gorham Tchrs. Coll., Maine, 1950. Tchr. Town of Lubec, Maine, 1941—81; ret., 1981. Libr. Lincoln Meml. Libr., Dennysville, Maine, 1988—2004. Author: Dennysville 1786-1986 and Edmunds, Too, 1986. Sec. Dennysville River Hist. Soc., 1988—2003, newsletter editor, 1988—2007; treas. Dennysville Congl. Ch., 1956—99. Republican. Avocation: genealogy. Home: 46 The Lane Dennysville ME 04628

HOBART, THOMAS D., lawyer; b. Lake City, Iowa, Jan. 1, 1947; s. Francis W. and Blanche E. Hobart; m. Jeri W. Hobart, July 17, 1971; children: Thomas Wilson, Jaye States. BA in Polit. Scis. and Psychology, U. Iowa, 1969, JD, 1974. Bar: Iowa 1974, U.S. Dist. Ct. (no. and so. dists.) Iowa 1974. Assoc. atty. Meardon, Sueppel & Downer, Iowa City, 1974-77, mem., 1978—. Bd. dirs., v.p. Sys. Unlimited, Iowa City, 1994—98. Named one of Best Lawyers in Am., Bus. Litig. and Personal Injury. Fellow: Iowa Acad. Trial Lawyers; mem.: Order of Coif, Johnson County Bar Assn. (pres. 1993—94). Democrat. Home: 1205 Seymour Ave Iowa City IA 52240 Office: Meardon Sueppel and Downer 122 S Linn St Iowa City IA 52240 Home Phone: 319-338-8016; Office Phone: 319-338-9222. Business E-Mail: TomH@meardonlaw.com.

HOBAUGH, CHARLES O., astronaut; b. Bar Harbor, Maine, Nov. 5, 1961; s. Jimmie and Virginia Hobaugh; m. Corinna Lynn Leaman; 4 children. BSc in Aerospace Engring., U.S. Naval Acad., 1984. Commd. 2d lt. USN, 1984; advanced through grades to maj. USMC, various assignments, 1984—87, with marine attack squadron, 1987—91; project officer, 1992—94; student Naval Test Pilot Sch., 1991—92, instr., 1994—96; astronaut NASA, Houston, 1996—. Pilot STS-104 mission to Internat. Space Station, 2001, STS-118 Mission (Endeavour) to Internat. Space Station, 2007. Decorated Strike/Flight Air medal USN, Combat Action ribbon. Mem.: U.S. Naval Acad. Alumni Assn. Achievements include logging over 3,000 flight hours in more than 40 different aircraft and has over 200 V/STOL shipboard landings. Avocations: weightlifting, volleyball, boating, water-skiing, snow skiing, soccer, bicycling, running, triathlons. Office: Astronaut Office CB NASA Johnson Space Center Houston TX 77058*

HOBBS, ANN S., lawyer; b. Washington, Nov. 20, 1945; BS, U. Md., Coll. Park, 1968; PhD in Biophysics, U. Md., Balt., 1973; JD with honors, U. Md. Sch. Law, 1991. Bar: Md. 1991, US Ct. of Appeals, Federal Circuit 1992, DC 1993, US Patent and Trademark Office. Former rsch. scientist NIH, Md.; former faculty mem. U. Md. Sch. of Medicine; former patent advisor/atty. Office of Tech. Transfer, NIH; atty. priv. practice; ptnr., patent prosecution & intellectual property litigation Venable LLP, Washington, 2005—. Mem.: ABA, DC Bar Assn., Am. Soc. for Biochemistry and Molecular Biology, NY Acad. of Sci. Office: Venable LLP 575 7th St NW Washington DC 20004 Office Phone: 202-344-4651. Office Fax: 202-344-8300. Business E-Mail: ashobbs@venable.com.

HOBBS, C. FREDRIC, artist, filmmaker, writer; b. Phila., Dec. 30, 1931; s. Robert Frederic and Gertrude (Madison) H.; children: Leslie Newbold, Mary Alison. Grad., Menlo Sch.; BA, Cornell U., Ithaca, NY, 1953; grad., Academia de San Fernando de Bellas Artes, Madrid, 1955-56. Pres. Fredric Hobbs Films, Inc., 1975; chmn., chief exec. officer Virginia City Restoration Corp., Nev., 1978-85. Writer, dir., producer 4 feature films, (TV series) Taiwan, The Other China, 1988-90, (TV/multimedia series) Fastfuture, 2000—; author: The Richest Place on Earth, 1978, Eat Your House: Art Eco Guide to Self Sufficiency, 1980, The Spirit of the Monterey Coast, 1990, (book chpt.) Nightmare, USA, 2007, and others; also articles; one-man shows include, Calif. Palace Legion of Honor, San Francisco, 1958, Mus. Sci. and Industry, Los Angeles, 1976, San Francisco Mus. Modern Art, 1980-81, Sierra Nevada Mus. Art, 1984; maj. mus. exhbns. include Concurso Internat. Palacio de la Virreina, Barcelona, Spain (17 countries), Art USA, Madison Sq. Garden, N.Y., Pa. Acad. Fine Arts., Phila, Internat. Drawing Competition II, Nat. Fine Arts Collection, Smithsonian Inst., Washington, Drawings USA 63" II Biennial, St. Paul Art Ctr., Minn., Ann. Sculpture-Painting Exhbns., SFAI, San Francisco Mus. Art, III and V Invitationals, Finch Coll. Mus. Art., N.Y.C., Gallery Modern Art., N.Y.C., Nat. Gallery Art, Washington, Reed Coll., Portland, Oreg., U. Pacific, Stockton, Calif., San Diego Mus. Art., Mills Coll., Oakland, Calif., Touring Am. Mus., Ebert Gallery, 1994, 95, 97, others; permanent collections include Mus. Modern Art, N.Y.C., Met. Mus. Art, N.Y.C., Spencer Meml. Ch., N.Y.C., Calif. Palace Legion of Honor, Finch Coll. Mus. Art, St. Paul Art Gallery, San Francisco Mus. Modern Art, Fine Arts Mus. San Francisco, Sierra Nevada Mus. Art, Reno, Stanford (Calif.) U. Mus. Art., San Francisco State Coll., U. Calif. Media Ctr., San Jose (Calif.) Mus. Art., Oakland (Calif.) Mus. Art., Johnson Mus., Cornell U., Penn Treaty Pk. Pl., Phila., Pa., others; galleries include Twentieth Century West Galleries, N.Y.C., Braunstein Gallery, San Francisco, Heritage Gallery, L.A., Ebert Gallery, San Francisco, others. 1st lt. USAF, 1953—55. Mem. Film Arts Found. Democrat. Episcopalian. Home and Office: The Madison Hobbs Studio PO Box 223759 Carmel CA 93922 *To create a work of art is an act of faith in the human spirit and in God. Art must always transcend materialist values and monuments to success. It is often the work of fools and children yet it is the ultimate reality.*

HOBBS, CHRISTOPHER ROLLIN, botanist, writer; b. Douglas, Ariz., Nov. 6, 1944; s. Kenneth Rollin Hobbs and Elinor Osgood Spencer; 1 child, Ken Hoshi. BA, Calif. State U., Sacramento, 2006; student, U. Calif., Berkeley, 2006—. Lic. acupuncturist Calif. Acupuncture Bd., 1995. Formulator, designer herbal and nutritional products Rainbow Light Nutritional Sys., Santa Cruz, Calif., 1984—. Spkr. in field; cons. in field. Author: (books) Medicinal Mushrooms, 1995, Herbal Remedies for Dummies, 1998, (book) Peterson's Field Guide to Medicinal Plants of the Western U.S., 2002, (books) 20 other books. Named Clinician of Yr., Natural Foods Merchandiser, 1997, Herbal Educator of Yr., Internat. Herb Growers and Marketers, 2004; named one of Most Influential People in Natural Products Industry, Nat. Nutritional Foods Assn., 2006. Mem.: Am. Herbalists Guild (mem. profl. rev. com. 1989—2007, founding mem.), Soc. for Ethnobiology, Soc. Econ. Botany, HerbalGram (mem. adv. bd. 1995—2007). Avocations: hiking, dance, classical music, guitar, singing. Home: 2640 Portage Bay East 7 Davis CA 95616 Office: Univ Calif Berkeley 3060 Valley Life Scis Bldg 3140 Berkeley CA 94720 Office Phone: 530-750-3371. Personal E-mail: business@christopherhobbs.com.

HOBBS, DAVID ELLIS, mechanical engineer; BA in Engring. Sci., Dartmouth Coll., 1963; BSME, Case Inst. Tech., 1964; MSME, Rensselaer Poly. Inst., 1967, PhD in Mech. Engring., 1983. With turbine component design group Pratt & Whitney, East Hartford, Conn., 1964-67, with turbine analysis and tech. devel. group, 1967-77, with compressor analysis and tech. devel. group, 1977-94; gas turbine design sys. cons. FTS Cons., Inc., East Hartford, Conn., 1995-2000, TurboVision Cons. Group, Miami, Fla., 1995—. Contbr. articles to profl. jours. Recipient Horner citation United Technologies Corp., 1993. Fellow AIAA (assoc., chmn. Conn. sect. 2001-06); mem. ASME (gas turbine turbomachinery com., axial compressor panel, Gas Turbine award 1988). Home: 20 Bayberry Trl South Windsor CT 06074-3809 E-mail: dehobbs@cox.net.

HOBBS, FRANKLIN DEAN, III, lawyer; b. Huntington Park, Calif., May 30, 1952; s. Frank Dean II and Bette J. (Little) H.; m. Victoria Shevlin, Mar. 6, 1987; children; Rebecca Ellen, Franklin Dean IV; stepchildren: Matthew Martin Howley, Lauren Ann Howley. BA, Claremont McKenna Coll., 1974; JD, UCLA, 1977. Bar: Calif. 1977, U.S. Supreme Ct. 1983. Assoc. Rutter, Ebbert & O'Sullivan, LA, 1977-82; mem. Rutter, O'Sullivan, Greene & Hobbs, Inc., LA, 1983-95, Rutter, Greene & Hobbs, LA, 1996, Rutter Hobbs & Davidoff Inc., LA, 1997—. Pres. Music Ctr. in the Wings, LA, 1986-87; bd. dirs. LA-Nagoya Sister City, 1984-87, Dream St. Found., 1989-98. Fellow Am. Acad. Trial Counsel; mem. Assn. Bus. Trial Lawyers, LA Country Club, Calif. Club. Republican. Episcopalian.

Office: Rutter Hobbs Davidoff Inc 1901 Avenue Of The Stars Los Angeles CA 90067-6001 Office Phone: 310-286-1700. Business E-Mail: fhobbs@rutterhobbs.com.

HOBBS, GERALD S. (JERRY), private equity firm executive; Attended, NYU, Am. Inst. Banking. Various positions Procter & Gamble, 1966—69; joined Billboard Publications, Inc. (BPI), 1969, led mgmt. buyout, 1984, headed sale to Affiliated Publications, 1987; led the acquisition BPI Communications, L.P., 1992, brokered sale to VNU NV, 1994; CEO VNU USA, Inc. (now VNU Inc.), 1994; joined mgmt. bd. VNU N.V., Netherlands, 1998—2003, vice chmn. mgmt. bd., 2001—03; mng. dir., operating ptnr. Boston Ventures Mgmt., Inc., 2005—. Bd. dir. BNA, Inc., 2003, New Track Media, Medley Global Advisors Holdings LLC; mem. supervisory bd. Nielsen (formerly VNU, N.V.), 2003—. Mem.: Am. Bus. Press (vice chmn. 1990). Office: Boston Ventures Mgmt Inc 125 High St 17th Fl Boston MA 02110-2003 Office Phone: 617-350-1500. Office Fax: 617-350-1509.*

HOBBS, GREGORY JAMES, JR., state supreme court justice; b. Gainesville, Fla., Dec. 15, 1944; s. Gregory J. Hobbs and Mary Ann (Rhodes) Frakes; m. Barbara Louise Hay, June 17, 1967; children: Daniel Gregory, Emily Mary Hobbs Wright. BA, U. Notre Dame, 1966; JD, U. Calif., Berkeley, 1971. Bar: Colo. 1971, Calif. 1972. Law clk. to Judge William E. Doyle 10th U.S. Cir. Ct. Appeals, Denver, 1971-72; assoc. Cooper, White & Cooper, San Francisco, 1972-73; enforcement atty. U.S. EPA, Denver, 1973-75; asst. atty. gen. State of Colo. Atty. Gen.'s Office, Denver, 1975-79; ptnr. Davis, Graham & Stubbs, Denver, 1979-92; shareholder Hobbs, Trout & Raley, P.C., Denver, 1992-96; justice Colo. Supreme Ct., Denver, 1996—. Counsel No. Colo. Water Conservancy, Loveland, Colo., 1979-96. Contbr. articles to profl. jours. Vol. Peace Corps-S.Am., Colombia, 1967-68; vice chair Colo. Air Quality Control Com., Denver, 1982-87; mem. ranch com. Philmont Scout Ranch, Boy Scouts Am., Cimarron, N.Mex., 1988-98; co-chair Eating Disorder Family Support Group, Denver, 1992—. Recipient award of merit Denver Area Coun. Boy Scouts, 1993, Pres. award Nat. Water Resources Assn., Washington, 1995. Fellow Am. Bar Found.; mem. ABA, Colo. Bar Assn., Denver Bar Assn. Avocations: backpacking, fishing, poetry. Office: Colo Supreme Ct 2 E 14th Ave Denver CO 80203-2115*

HOBBS, GUY STEPHEN, financial executive; b. Lynwood, Calif., Feb. 23, 1955; s. Franklin Dean and Bette Jane (Little) H.; m. Laura Elena Lopez, Jan. 6, 1984; 1 child, Mariah Amanda. BA, U. Calif., Santa Barbara, 1976; MBA, U. Nev., 1978. Sr. rsch. assoc. Ctr. for Bus. and Econ. Rsch., Las Vegas, Nev., 1978-80; pvt. practice mgmt. cons. Las Vegas, 1979-82; mgmt. analyst Clark County, Las Vegas, 1980-81, sr. mgmt. analyst, 1981-82, dir. budget and fin. planning, 1982-84, comptroller, dir. fin., chief fin. officer, 1984-96; pres. Hobbs, Ong & Assocs., Inc., 1996—. Lectr. in mgmt. Coll. Bus. and Econs., U. Nev., Las Vegas, 1977-88; pres. Pacific Blue Ent., 1991—; mem. Interim Legis. Com. Infrastructure Fin., 1993-94; mem. Interim Legis. Com. Studying Laws Relating to the Distbn. of Taxes in Nev., 1995-96, 97—; mem. fiscal rev. com. Henderson State Coll., 2001, County Mgrs.'s orgnl. rev. com., 2001; chmn. Gov.'s Task Force on Tax Policy in Nev., 2001-02; mem. exec. adv. bd. Dept. Econs. U. Nev., Las Vegas, 2004—; mem. growth task force Clark County, 2004—; prodr. game day U. Nev., Las Vegas, 2004; mem. Supreme Ct. Funding Commn., 2006. Author pubs. in field. Instr. Las Vegas Baseball Acad., 1998—2001; mem. exec. bd. Miss Nev. USA and Miss Nev. Teen USA, 1996—2002; head coach Silver State Girls Soccer League, 1998—2001; pres. U.S. Youth Soccer-Nev., 2003—; exec. prodr. WUSA exhbn. game between San Diego Spirit and San Jose Cyber Rays, 2002, WUSA exhbn. game between Boston Breakers and San Jose Cyber Rays, 2003; exec. producer Las Vegas Soccer spectacular; gen. mgr. Las Vegas Tabagators of Women's Premier Soccer League, 2004—. Mem. Am. Soc. Pub. Adminstrn. (Pub. Adminstr. of Yr. 1987), Govt. Fin. Officers Assn. (Fin. Reporting Achievement award 1984-95, Disting. Budget Presentation, award 1993-96), Nev. Taxpayers Assn. Republican. Avocations: sports, photography, travel. Office: Hobbs Ong & Assocs Inc 3900 Paradise Rd Ste 152 Las Vegas NV 89169 Office Phone: 702-733-7223.

HOBBS, HELEN HASKELL, medical geneticist; BA in Human Biology, Stanford U., 1974; MD, Case Western Reserve U., 1979. Cert. Am. Bd. Internal Medicine, 1983, Endocrinology & Metabolism, 1986. Intern, internal medicine Columbia-Presbyn. Med. Ctr., NYC, 1979—80; resident, internal medicine Parkland Meml. Hosp., Dallas, 1980—82; chief resident, internal medicine U. Tex. Southwestern, 1982—83, postdoctoral fellow in endocrinology & molecular genetics, 1983—87, asst. prof., 1987—90, assoc. prof., 1991—94, prof. internal medicine & molecular genetics, 1995—; chief med. genetics divsn. U. Tex. Southwestern Med. Ctr., Dallas, 1995—, dir. McDermott Ctr. Human Growth & Devel., 2000—; investigator Howard Hughes Med. Inst., 2002—. Consulting editor Circulation, 2002—. Recipient Heinrich Wieland prize, 2005. Fellow: Am. Acad. Arts & Sciences; mem.: NAS, Am. Soc. Human Genetics, Am. Heart Assn. (est. investigator 1990—95), Am. Soc. Clin. Investigation (nat. coun. 1992—94, v.p. 1996—97), Assn. Am. Physicians, Inst. Medicine. Office: UT Southwestern Med Ctr at Dallas 6000 Harry Hines Blvd Dallas TX 75390-9046 Office Phone: 214-648-6724. Office Fax: 214-648-7539. E-mail: helen.hobbs@utsouthwestern.edu.*

HOBBS, JAMES BEVERLY, business administration educator, writer, academic administrator; b. Topeka, Sept. 9, 1930; s. Kenneth Beverly and Ida (Burkholder) H.; m. Peggy Genevieve Whitney, Nov. 2, 1957; children: David Beverly, Nancy Ruth. AB, Harvard U., 1952; MBA, U. Kans., 1957; DBA, Ind. U., 1962. Fin. analyst Hotpoint divsn. GE, Chgo., 1957-60; asst. prof. mgmt. and acctg. Kans. State U., 1962-66, assoc. dean, 1964-66; assoc. prof. mgmt. and acctg. Lehigh U., 1966-70, prof., 1970-79, Frank L. Magee Disting. prof. bus. adminstrn., 1979-91, Frank L. Magee Disting. prof. bus. adminstrn. emeritus, 1991—, chmn. dept. mgmt., fin., mktg. and law, 1970-75, chmn. dept. mgmt., fin. and mktg., 1982-83, dir. MBA program, 1986-89, co-chmn. mgmt. dept., 1989-90, assoc. dean Coll. Bus. and Econ., 1993, assoc. dean Coll. Arts and Scis., 1993-95, chmn. art and architecture dept., 1996, assoc. dean emeritus Coll. Arts & Scis., 1999—. Vis. prof. acctg. U. Canterbury, New Zealand, 1976, Mich. Technol. U., 1975; vis. prof. mgmt. U. Edinburgh, Scotland, 1984, Ecole Superieure Commerce de Poitiers, France, 1990, Acad. Ednl. Devel., Bishkek, Kyrghystan, 1999; participant mission to Ulan Bator, Mongolia, UN Devel. Program, 1992; participant missions to Ternopil, Ukraine, Vladivostok, Russia, Bratislava, Slovak Republic and Kishnev, Moldova, Internat. Exec. Svc. Corps, 1993, 95, 97, 98, mission to Skopje, Macedonia, U.S. Energy Assn., 1997; acad. cons. Author: Financial Accounting, 1984, Corp. Staying Power, 1987, Homophones & Homographs, 2006. Served as naval aviation cadet USN, 1952, as regtl. sgt. maj. U.S. Army, 1952-54, Korea. Recipient Silver Palm award, Boys Scouts Am., 1946. Mem. Mensa, Phi Beta Kappa, Phi Kappa Phi, Beta Gamma Sigma, Beta Alpha Psi, Sigma Iota Epsilon, Omicron Delta Epsilon, Omicron Delta Kappa, Delta Mu Delta, Phi Beta Delta. Unitarian Universalist. Home: 1915 Black River Rd Bethlehem PA 18015-8920 Office Phone: 610-758-3439. E-mail: jbh1@lehigh.edu.

HOBBS, LEWIS MANKIN, astronomer; b. Upper Darby, Pa., May 16, 1937; s. Lewis Samuel and Evangeline Elizabeth (Goss) H.; m. Jo Ann Faith Hagele, June 16, 1962; children: John, Michael, Dara. B of Engring. Physics, Cornell U., 1960; MS, U. Wis., 1962, PhD in Physics, 1966. Jr. astronomer Lick Obs., U. Calif., Santa Cruz, 1965-66; faculty U. Chgo., 1966—, prof. astronomy and astrophysics, 1976—2003, prof. emeritus, 2003; dir. Yerkes Obs. Williams Bay, Wis., 1974-82. Bd. dirs. Assn. Univs. for Rsch. in Astronomy, Washington, 1974-85; mem. Space Telescope Inst. Coun., 1982-87; astronomy com. of bd. trustees Univs. Rsch. Assn., Inc., Washington, 1979-83, chmn., 1979-81; bd. govs. Astrophys. Rsch. Consortium, Inc., Seattle, 1984-91; mem. Users Com. for Hubble Space Telescope, NASA, 1990-94; mem. telescope allocation com. Nat. Optical Astronomy Obs., 1998-2000. Contbr. articles to profl. jours. Bd. dirs. Mil. Symphony Assn. of Walworth County, 1972-88. Alfred P. Sloan scholar, 1955-60. Mem.: Internat. Astron. Union, Am. Phys. Soc., Am. Astron. Soc. Office: U Chgo Yerkes Observatory Williams Bay WI 53191 Office Phone: 262-245-5555.

HOBBS, MICHAEL EDWIN, broadcast executive; b. Washington, Nov. 26, 1940; s. Robert Boyd and Barbara Alberta (Davis) H.; m. Ann Reed, Sept. 16, 1989. AB cum laude, Dartmouth Coll., 1962; JD, Harvard U., 1965. Bar: Mass. 1966. Staff counsel, asst. to gen. mgr. Sta. WGBH Ednl. Found., Boston, 1966-67; exec. asst. ednl. TV stas. Nat. Assn. Ednl. Broadcasters, Washington, 1967-70; sec. PBS, Washington, 1970-87, gen. counsel, 1970-71, dir. adminstrn., 1970-73, v.p., 1973-76, sr. v.p., 1976-87, sr. v.p. for policy and planning, 1987-91; sr. fellow Hartford Gunn Inst., Alexandria, Va., 1991—. Active Alexandria Rep. City Com., 1997—, chmn. 1998-2000; bd. dirs. Old Town Civic Assn., 2001—, pres., 2004-06; bd. dirs. Agenda: Alexandria, 2005—, treas., 2006—; co-chair Alexandria Fedn. Civic Assns., 2006—. Mem.: ABA, Nat. Acad. TV Arts and Scis., Mass. Bar Assn., George Town Club, Phi Beta Kappa. Home and Office: Hartford Gunn Inst 419 Cameron St Alexandria VA 22314-3221 Personal E-mail: mhobbs27@comcast.net.

HOBBS, PATRICK ESMOND, dean, law educator; m. Joanne Hobbs; children: Patrick, John, Alexandra. BS magna cum laude, Seton Hall U., 1982; JD, U. NC, Chapel Hill, 1985; LLM in Taxation, NYU Sch. Law, 1988. Assoc. Hannoch Weisman, P.C., Roseland, NJ, 1985—87, Shanley & Fisher, P.C., Morristown, 1987—90; asst. prof. law Seton Hall U. Sch. Law, 1990—93, assoc. prof., 1993—97, prof., 1997—, assoc. dean fin., 1995—99, dean, 1999—. Contbr. articles to law jours. Mem. Legal Edn. Task Force, 1996; project dir. Newark in 21st Century Commn., 1997; mem. N.J. Commn. on Professionalism, 2000—; bd. mem. N.J. Inst. Continuing Legal Edn., 2000—, Beth Israel Med. Ctr., 2002—; mem. Newark Arena Commn., 2002—. Mem.: ABA, Essex County Bar Assn., N.J. State Bar Assn., Am. Bar Fellows. Office: Seton Hall U Sch Law One Newark Ctr Newark NJ 07102 E-mail: hobbspat@shu.edu.

HOBBS, TRUMAN MCGILL, federal judge; b. Selma, Ala., Feb. 8, 1921; s. Sam F. and Sarah Ellen (Greene) H.; m. Joyce Cummings, July 9, 1949; children— Emilie C. Reid, Frances John Rose, Dexter Cummings, Truman McGill. AB, U. N.C., 1942; LL.B., Yale U., 1948. Bar: Ala. 1948. Practiced in, Montgomery, 1951-80; law clk. U.S. Supreme Ct., 1948-49; ptnr. Hobbs, Copeland, Franco & Screws, 1951-80; U.S. dist. judge Montgomery, 1980—; now sr. judge. Chmn. Ala. Unemployment Appeal Bd., 1952-58 Pres. United Appeal Montgomery; pres. Montgomery County Tb Assn.; v.p. Ala. Com. for Better Schs.; Chmn. Montgomery County Exec. Democratic Com., 1970. Served to lt. USNR, 1942-46, ETO, PTO. Decorated Bronze Star medal. Fellow Am. Coll. Trial Lawyers; mem. Internat. Acad. Trial Lawyers, Ala. Plaintiffs Lawyers Assn. (past pres.), Ala. Bar Assn. (pres. 1970-71), Montgomery County Bar Assn. (past pres.) Home: 2301 Fernway Dr Montgomery AL 36111-1603

HOBBY, SCOTT M., lawyer; b. Phila., Mar. 24, 1945; BA, Emory U., 1967; JD cum laude, U. Ga., 1973. Bar: Ga. 1973. Mem. Powell, Goldstein, Frazer & Murphy, Atlanta; ptnr. Outsourcing and Sys. Integration Practice Hunton & Williams, Atlanta, Sutherland Asbill & Brennan, Atlanta, 2007—. Mem. editorial bd. Ga. Law Review, 1968-69, 72-73 Lt. (j.g.) USN, 1969-72. Mem. ABA, State Bar Ga., Atlanta Bar Assn., Phi Sigma Alpha, Phi Kappa Phi, Phi Delta Phi. Office: Sutherland Asbill & Brennan 999 Peachtree St NE Atlanta GA 30309-3996 Office Phone: 404-853-8051. Business E-Mail: scott.hobby@sablaw.com.

HOBBY, WILLIAM PETTUS, retired broadcast executive; b. Houston, Jan. 19, 1932; s. William Pettus and Oveta (Culp) H.; m. Diana Poteat Stallings, Sept. 11, 1954; children: Laura Poteat Beckworth, Paul William, Andrew Purefoy, Katherine Pettus Gibson. BA, Rice U., 1953. Pres. H & C Communications, Inc., 1979-83, chmn. bd., chief exec. officer, 1983-96; lt. gov. Tex., 1973-91; chancellor Univ. of Houston Sys., 1995-97. Sid Richardson prof. Lyndon B. Johnson Sch. Pub. Affairs, U. Tex., Austin, 1990-97; Radoslav Tsanoff prof. Rice U., Houston, 1991—. Served to lt. (j.g.) USNR, 1953-57. Office: Hobby Comm LLC 2131 San Felipe Houston TX 77019-5620 Office Phone: 713-521-0960.

HOBERMAN, MARY ANN, author; b. Stamford, Conn., Aug. 12, 1930; d. Milton and Dorothy (Miller) Freedman; m. Norman Hoberman, Feb. 4, 1951; children: Diane, Perry, Charles, Meg. BA, Smith Coll., 1951; MA, Yale U., 1984. With advt. dept. Gimbel's Dept. Store, NYC, 1951-52; newspaper reporter Harrisburg, Pa., 1952; editor N.Y. Graphic Soc., Greenwich, Conn., 1963-64. Poetry cons.; lectr. in field; program coord. C.G. Jung Ctr., N.Y.C., 1981; adj. prof. Fairfield (Conn.) U., 1980-83; instr. Yale U., New Haven, 1989; founder, mem. The Pocket People, 1968-75; founder, performer Women's Voices, 1983-93. Author: All My Shoes Come in Two's, 1957, How Do I Go?, 1958, Hello and Good-by, 1959, What Jim Knew, 1963, Not Enough Beds for the Babies, 1965, A Little Book of Little Beasts, The Raucous Auk, 1973, The Looking Book, 1973, Nuts to You and Nuts to Me, 1974, I Like Old Clothes, 1976, Bugs, 1976, A House Is a House for Me, 1978, Yellow Butter, Purple Jelly, Red Jam, Black Bread, 1981, The Cozy Book, 1982, Mr. and Mrs. Muddle, 1988, A Fine Fat Pig and Other Animal Poems, 1991, Fathers, Mothers, Sisters, Brothers, 1991; editor: My Song is Beautiful, 1994, The Cozy Book, 1995, The Seven Silly Eaters, 1997, One of Each, 1997, Miss Mary Mack, 1998, The Llama Who Had No Pajama, 1998, And to Think that We Thought We Would Never Be Friends, 1999, The Cozy Book, 1999, The Eensy Weensy Spider, 2000, the Two Sillies, 2000, Michael Finnegan, 2001, It's Simple, Said Simon, 2001, You Read to Me, 2001, The Looking Book, 2002, The Marvelous Mouse Man, 2002, Right Outside My Window, 2002, Bill Grogan's Goat, 2002, Mary Had a Little Lamb, 2003, You Read to Me, I'll Read to You II, 2003, Whose Garden Is It?, 2003, Yankee Doodle, 2003, You Read to Me, I'll Read to You III, 2005, You Read to Me, I'll Read to You IV, 2007, I'm Going to Grandma's, 2007, Mrs. O'Leary's Cow, 2007. Bd. dirs. Greenwich Libr., 1988-91, Literacy Vols., 1997-2003, Conn. Ctr. for the Book, 2003—. Recipient Nat. Book award, 1984, Poetry for Children award Nat. Coun. Tchrs. English, 2003, medal Smith Coll., 2007. Mem. Authors Guild. Avocations: dance, gardening, hiking, tennis. Home: 98 Hunting Ridge Rd Greenwich CT 06831-3134

HOBERMAN, STUART A., lawyer; b. NYC, Nov. 21, 1946; BBA, Baruch Coll., NYC, 1969; JD, Bklyn. Law Sch., 1972; LLM, N.Y. Univ., 1973. Bar: NY 1973, NJ 1977, Pa. 1979, U.S. Supreme Ct. 1976. Assoc. Windels and Marx, NYC, 1973-77, Wilentz, Goldman, and Spitzer, Woodbridge, NJ, 1977-80, ptnr., 1980—. Trustee Emmanuel Cancer Found., Kenilworth, NJ, 1983—90, Cancer Care of NJ, 1999—. Mem.: N.J. State Bar Assn. (bank law sect. chmn. 1986—87, corp. and bus. law sect. chmn. 1988—90, chmn. exec. com. of gen. coun. 1990—92, trustee 1990—94, trustee N.J. State Bar Found. 1992—, treas. 1995—96, trustee 1997—2001, pres. 1999—2001, first v.p. 2003—, pres.-elect 2004, pres. 2005). Office: Wilentz Goldman & Spitzer Ste 900 Box 10 90 Woodbridge Ctr Dr Woodbridge NJ 07095-1142 Office Phone: 732-855-6052. Office Fax: 732-726-6518. Business E-Mail: shoberman@wilentz.com.

HOBGOOD, W. SANDS, systems engineer; b. Feb. 4, 1945; AB, MS, U. NC, Chapel Hill. Sr. sys. engr. IBM, NYC, 1969—99. Contbr. articles to profl. jours.; composer: numerous liturgical works and arrangements, 2000—06. Organist, choirmaster Aldersgate United Meth. Ch., Chapel Hill, 1998—2002; assoc. music dir. Univ. United Meth. Ch., Chapel Hill, 2002—06. Recipient Outstanding Contbn. award, IBM, 1970. Mem.: Am. Guild Organists, Condrs. Guild Am. Home: 303 Ridgecrest Dr Chapel Hill NC 27514-2105

HOBLIT, GREGORY, film director, television executive; b. Abilene, Tex., Nov. 27, 1944; m. Debrah Farentino, Sept. 10, 1994; 1 child, Sophie. Bachelors, Masters, UCLA. Dir. (TV series): Hill Street Blues, 1981 (Emmy awards Outstanding Drama Series, 1981, 82, 83, 84, nominated 1985, 86), L.A. Law, 1986 (nominated Emmy award Outstanding Drama Series, 1986), NYPD Blue, 1993 (DGA award Outstanding Directorial Achievement in Dramatic Shows-Night, pilot episode, 1993, TV Prodr. of Yr. award 1994, Emmy award Outstanding Drama Series, 1995); dir.: (TV films) Roe vs. Wade (Emmy award, 1994), 1989, (films) Primal Fear, 1996, Fallen, 1998, Frequency, 2000, Hart's War, 2002, Fracture, 2007; assoc. prodr. (TV) Dr. Strange, 1978, Bay City Blues, (exec.) 1983, Hooperman (Emmy award, outstanding directing in a comedy series 1988), 1987, Cop Rock (co-exec.), 1990, Civil Wars, 1991; supervising prodr. (TV series) Paris, 1979; prodr. (TV films): Vampire, 1979. Office: c/o DGA 7920 W Sunset Blvd Los Angeles CA 90046-3300 and: Abilene Pictures 335 N Maple Dr Beverly Hills CA 90210-3857 Office: c/o David Wirtschafter William Morris Agy 151 El Camino Dr Beverly Hills CA 90212*

HOBSON, BURTON HAROLD, publishing executive; b. Galesburg, Ill., Apr. 16, 1933; s. Burt and Geneva (Sornberger) H.; m. Maxine C. Meyer, Aug. 9, 1953; children: Alice L., Andrew J., Mark R. BA, U. Chgo., 1953; LHD (hon.), Johnson Wales U., 2002. Mgr. collector's coin dept. Marshall Field & Co., Chgo., 1953-61; sales mgr. Sterling Pub. Co., Inc., NYC, 1961-66, v.p. sales, 1966-72, exec. v.p., 1972-79, pres., 1979-95, chmn., 1995—2003, dir., 1966—2003; pres. Pub. Adv. Svc., 2003—. Author: (with Fred Reinfeld) Manual for Coin Collectors and Investors, 1963, Picture Book of Ancient Coins, 1963, U.S. Commemorative Coins and Stamps, 1964, Catalogue of the World's Most Popular Coins, 1965, What You Should Know about Coins and Coin Collecting, 1965, Hidden Values in Coins, 1965, International Guide to Coin Collecting, 1966, Coins You Can Collect, 1966, Coin Identifier, 1966, Coin Collecting As a Hobby, 1967, (with Robert Obojski) Illustrated Encyclopedia of World Coins, 1970, Catalogue of Scandinavian Coins, 1970, Historic Gold Coins of the World, 1971, Coin Collecting for Beginners, 1970, Stamp Collecting for Beginners, 1970, Coins and Coin Collecting, 1971; editor: Benenson Restaurant Guide, 1985; pub.: Gastronome mag., 1993—2002. Recipient Robert Friedberg award for numismatic lit., 1972 Mem. Am. Numismatic Soc., Confrérie des Chevaliers du Tastevin, Confrérie de la Chaine des Rotisseurs (nat. pres.), Culinary Inst. Am. (trustee), Wildlife Trust (trustee), Am. Acad. Chefs (hon. trustee), Univ. Club NY, Delta Upsilon. Home and Office: 600 Harbor Blvd Unit 833 Weehawken NJ 07086-6748 Personal E-mail: burtonhh@msn.com.

HOBSON, DAVID LEE, congressman, lawyer; b. Cin., Oct. 17, 1936; m. Carolyn Alexander; children: Susan Marie, Lynn Martha, Douglas Lee. BA, Ohio Wesleyan U., 1958; JD, Ohio State U. Coll. Law, 1963; degree (hon.), Ctrl. State U., Wittenberg U. Resident counsel Kissell Co., Springfield, Ohio; atty. Union Ctrl. Life Ins. Co., Cin.; mem. Ohio State Senate, 1982-90, majority whip, 1986-88, pres. pro tem, 1988-90; mem. US Congress from 7th Ohio dist., 1991—, mem. appropriations com., ranking mem. energy and water devel. subcommittee. Trustee Ohio Wesleyan U. Mem. 121st TAC Fighter Wing Ohio Air Nat. Guard, 1958—63. Named Pub. Ofcl. of Yr., Dayton Chpt. NASW, 1991; recipient Nathan Davis award, AMA, 1990, Spirit of Enterprise award, US C. of C., 1992, Ground Water Protector award, Nat. Ground Water Assn., 2001, Healthcare Leadership award, Am. Assn Nurse Anesthetists, 2002, Pub. Svc. award, AIAA, 2007. Mem. ABA, AMVETS, Ky. Bar Assn., Ohio Bar Assn., Springfield Bd. Realtors, Springfield Area C. of C., Non-Commissioned Officers Assn., Masons (32 degrees), Am. Legion, VFW, Moose, Elks, Rotary, Shrine Club. Republican. Methodist. Office: PO Box 269 Springfield OH 45501-0269 also: US Ho Reps 2346 Rayburn Ho Office Bldg Washington DC 20515-3507 Office Phone: 202-225-4324, 937-325-0474. Office Fax: 937-325-9188.*

HOBSON, GEORGE DONALD, retired geophysicist; b. Hamilton, Ont., Can., Jan. 8, 1923; s. Robert Charles and Agnes Hamilton (Mathieson) H.; m. Arletta Louise Russell, May 21, 1948; children: Robert, Linda, Douglas, Donna. BA, McMaster U., 1946, DSc (hon.), 1991; MA, Toronto U., 1948. Registered profl. geophysicist, Can. Party chief, ptnr. Heiland Exploration Can. Ltd., Calgary, Alta., 1948-55; geophysicist Can. Fina Oil Co., Calgary, 1955-56; chief geophysicist Merrill Petroleums Ltd., Calgary, 1956-57; geophysicist Pacific Petroleums Ltd., Calgary, 1957-58; chief seismic sect. Geol. Survey Can., Ottawa, Ont., 1958-69, chief geophysics div., 1969-71; dir. Polar Shelf Project, Ottawa, 1972-88, sr. advisor, 1988-90; rsch. assoc. Nunavut Rsch. Inst., Iqaluit, NWT, Canada, 1997—. Author or co-author over 200 articles in field. Recipient No. Sci. award and Centennial medal Dept. Indian and No. Affairs, Can., 1991, Ind. Achievement award Am. Soc. Mech. Engrs., Massey Medal, 1991, Royal Can. Geog. Soc., Queen Elizabeth Goldn Jubilee medal 2002. Fellow Exploration Geophysicists India, Royal Can. Geog. Soc. (bd. govs. 1987-94, Massey medal 1991, Camsell award 1998, The Queen's Golden Jubilee Medal), Arctic Inst. N.Am. (bd. govs. 1984-91); mem. Sci. Inst. N.W. Territory (bd. govs. 1990-93), Soc. Exploration Geophysicists (v.p. 1968), Assn. Profl. Engrs., Geologists, Geophysicists Alta., Can. Soc. Exploration Geophysicists. Mem. United Ch. Can. Avocations: genealogy, barbershop singing. Home: PO Box 161 5428 Long Island Rd Manotick ON Canada K4M 1A3

HOBSON, JADE, journalist, consultant; b. NYC, Mar. 12, 1945; d. John Louis and Elizabeth Anne (Stanton) Campo; m. David Alan Hobson, Dec. 30 (div. Mar. 1972); m. Martin Charnin, Dec. 18, 1984 (div. Mar. 2007). BA, NYU, 1967. Asst. editor Glamour mag., NYC, 1970; accessory editor Vogue mag., NYC, 1970-78, fashion editor, 1978-81, fashion dir., 1981-86, creative dir. fashion, 1987-88; v.p., dir. creative svcs for fashion and design group Revlon Inc., 1988; exec. creative dir. Mirabella Mag., 1988-94; fashion dir. N.Y. Mag., 1994-98; freelance journalist, 1999—. Pres., landscape designer Growing Things, Inc., Wilton, Conn., 2002—; cons. editor Self mag., NYC, 1979—81. Costume coord.: (plays) Upstairs at Oneals, 1981; Laughing Matters, 1989; Martin Charnin, the Hits and the M.S.'s, 1990. Mem.: ASPCA, Am. Assn. Landscape Archs., Hort. Soc. NY, Am. Hort. Soc., Assn. Profl. Landscape Designers, Humane Soc. NY (bd. dirs., sr. v.p.), Wilton Garden Club (bd. dirs.). Avocations: opera, ballet, theater, skiing, travel. Personal E-mail: jadehobson@aol.com.

HOBSON, JAMES RICHMOND, lawyer; b. Atlanta, Sept. 13, 1937; s. Richmond Pearson and Alice Chambers (Carey) H.; m. Nancy Hulbert Saussy, Nov. 29, 1963; children: Kathleen Hunter, Caroline Richmond, Susan Saussy. BA in English, Cornell U., 1959; MA in Govt., Georgetown U., 1963; JD, U. San Francisco, 1971. Bar: Calif. 1972, U.S. Ct. Appeals (9th cir.) 1972, U.S. Dist. Ct. (no. dist.) Calif. 1972, D.C. 1973, U.S. Ct. Appeals (D.C. cir.) 1973, U.S. Dist. Ct. D.C. 1973. Staff writer Charlotte (N.C.) Observer, 1963; rschr., writer Rep. Nat. Com., Washington, 1964-65; Washington editor Med. Econs. Mag., 1965; info. officer Hoover Instn., Stanford, Calif., 1966-72; atty., mgr. FCC, Washington, 1972-78; asst. v.p. GTE Svc. Corp., Washington, 1978-81; Washington counsel GTE Corp., Washington, 1982-91; v.p. Donelan, Cleary, Wood & Maser, PC, Washington, 1991-95, prin., 1995—, pres., 2000—; of counsel Miller & Van Eaton, PLLC, 2000—. Co-editor: The Communications Act: A Legislative

History of the Major Amendments, 1935-1996, 1999. Bd. dirs. Mid-Peninsula Citizens for Fair Housing, Palo Alto, Calif., 1971-72; sr. warden Immanuel Ch. on the Hill, Alexandria, Va., 1977, 90, jr. warden, 1976, 88; traffic and parking bd. City Alexandria, 1980-82; mem. Alexandria Libr. Co., 1991—, pres., 1995-96; mem. panel arbitrators Am. Arbitration Assn., 1994-97; adv. bd. Inst. for Conflict Analysis and Resolution, George Mason U., 1989—, chmn., 1995-98, 2004-05; bd. trustees Goodwin House, Inc., 1996-2001, exec. com., 1998-2001. Mem. ABA, Fed. Comm. Bar Assn. (exec. com. 1984-87, 94-96), Met. Club. Washington, Sigma Alpha Epsilon. Episcopalian. Home: 3613 Trinity Dr Alexandria VA 22304-1840 Home Phone: 703-370-1134; Office Phone: 202-785-0600. E-mail: jhobson@millervaneaton.com.

HOBSON, MELLODY, investment company executive; b. Chgo., Apr. 3, 1969; BA, Woodrow Wilson Sch. Internat. Rels., Princeton U., 1991. Joined mktg. team Ariel Capital Mgmt., Inc., 1991—94, sr. v.p., dir. mktg., 1994—2000, pres., 2000—. Bd. mem. Tellabs, Inc., 2002—; fin. corr. ABC's Good Morning Am. Bd. dir. Chgo. Pub. Edn. Fund, Chgo. Pub. Libr., Field Mus.; bd. trustees Princeton U. Named a Global Leader Tomorrow, World Econ. Forum, Davos, Switzerland, 2001; named one of 30 Leaders of Future, Ebony, 40 under 40, Crain's Chgo. Bus. Office: Ariel Capital Mgmt LLC 200 E Randolph Dr Ste 2900 Chicago IL 60601 Office Phone: 312-726-0140. Office Fax: 312-612-2702.*

HOBSON, STEPHEN GILBERT, conductor, music educator; b. Mason City, Iowa, Jan. 18, 1946; s. Stephen and Lee Hobson; m. Sharon Lee Williams, June 15, 1968; children: Lisa Hobson-McMahon, Stephen. BS in Edn., Ctrl. Mich. U., Mount Pleasant, Mich., 1970; MusM in Conducting, Mich. State U., East Lansing, Mich., 1980. Dir. orch. Traverse City Jr. High, Traverse City, Mich., 1970—74, Traverse City H.S., Traverse City, Mich., 1974—83; music dir. and condr. Omaha Area Youth Orch., Omaha, 1983—93; orch. condr. & string dept. chairperson U. Nebr., Omaha, 1983—86; dir. orch. Evanston Twp. H.S., Evanston, Ill., 1993—2001, Highland Pk. H.S., Highland Pk., Ill., 2001—. Mem., bd. dirs. and u.s. rep. World Fedn. of Amateur Orch., Toyohashi, Japan, 1998—2005; advisor, minority recruitment com. Chgo. Civic Orch., Chgo., 1998—98; guest lectr. Northwestern U., Evanston, Ill., 1998—99; orch. condr. Music Inst. of Chgo., Winnetka, Ill., 1994—98. Contbr. articles pub. to profl. jour. Nominee Tchr. of the Yr., Mich. Sch. Band & Orch. Assn., 1982, 1983. Mem.: Ill. Music Educators Assn. (pres., dist. vii orch. directors 1998—2000), Music Educators Nat. Conf., Am. String Teachers Assn. (nebr. state pres. 1988—90). Achievements include Guest Conductor, Blue Lake Internat. Orch. 1982, 1983; Guest Conductor for Orch. Festivals throughout the U.S; Conducted orch. on concert tours in Norway, Sweden, Denmark, Netherlands, Germany, Austria, China, Mexico, England, Canada; Conducted Carnegie Hall concerts in 1990, 2001; Conducted Omaha Youth Orch. at Midwest Internat. Band & Orch. Clinic, 1988; Guest Conductor, Blue Lake Fine Arts Camp, 1976-1983. Office: Highland Pk H S 433 Vine Ave Highland Park IL 60035 Home Phone: 847-548-6443; Office Phone: 224-765-2166. Business E-Mail: shobson@dist113.org.

HOBSON, SUELLEN ANN WEBER, retired elementary school educator; b. Houston, Apr. 25, 1947; d. Marvin Ernst Herman Weber and Anita Clair Perkins; children: Eric Austin Williamson, Jerod Michael Williamson. BS in Elem. Edn., N.Mex. State U., 1976. Tchr. Alamogordo Pub. Schools, N.Mex., 1977—2006. Educator mentor/workshop facilitator Alamogordo Pub. Sch., 1996—2004. Mem.: N. Mex.'s Classroom Tchr.'s Assn. (assoc.). Mem. Christian Ch. Avocation: floral design. Home: 2500 First St Alamogordo NM 88310 Home Phone: 505-437-4613. E-mail: suellen@barricklow.com.

HOBURG, JAMES FREDERICK, electrical engineering educator; b. Pitts., Dec. 30, 1946; s. William Lawrence and Virginia (Stewart) H.; m. Margaret Jean Ryan, Mar. 4, 1978 BS, Drexel U., 1969; SM, MIT, 1971, PhD in Elec. Engring., 1975. Instr. MIT, Cambridge, Mass., 1973-75; asst. prof. elec. engring. Carnegie-Mellon U., Pitts., 1975-80, assoc. prof. elec. engring., 1980-84, prof. elec., computer engring., 1984—, assoc. head, dept. elec., computer engring., 1985-91. Cons. rsch. devel. orgns. Contbr. articles to profl. jours. Fellow IEEE; mem. Electrostatics Soc. Am., Am. Soc. Engr. Edn., Sigma Xi, Tau Beta Pi, Eta Kappa Nu Avocations: long distance running, walking, mountain climbing. Home: 1000 Oak Creek Ln Baden PA 15005-2856 Office: Carnegie-Mellon U Dept Elec and Computer Engring Schenley Park Pittsburgh PA 15213-3830

HOCH, BENJAMIN, lawyer; b. NYC, June 6, 1963; BS, Bklyn. Coll., 1985; JD, Harvard Univ., 1988. Bar: N.Y. 1989, US Dist. Ct. (so. N.Y.). Ptnr. & co-chmn. corp. reorganization & bankruptcy group Dewey Ballantine LLP, NYC. Mem.: ABA, N.Y. State Bar Assn., Am. Bankruptcy Inst., Turnaround Mgmt. Assn. Office: Dewey Ballantine LLP 1301 Ave of the Americas New York NY 10019-6092 Office Fax: 212-259-6928, 212-259-6333. Business E-Mail: bhoch@dbllp.com.

HOCH, DAVID ALLEN, athletic director; b. Northampton, Pa., July 26, 1946; s. Sterling Palmer and Evelyn Mae (McCallister) H.; m. Diane Duffy, June 18, 1977; children: Matthew David, Jennifer Lynn. AB in German, Grove City Coll., Pa., 1968; MEd in Phys. Edn., The Coll. N.J., 1972; EdD in Phys. Edn., Temple U., 1989. Tchr., coach Washington Twp. H.S., Sewell, N.J., 1968-71, Upper Dublin H.S., Ft. Washington, Pa., 1972-78, Ramsey (N.J.) H.S., 1978-79, Germantown Acad., Ft. Washington, 1981-89; instr., coach Pa. State U., Altoona, 1979-80; instr. phys. edn., basketball coach U. Pitts., Bradford, 1989-93; athletic dir. Eastern Tech. H.S., Balt. County, 1994—2003, Loch Raven H.S., Balt. County, 2003—. Presenter in field. Mem. editl. adv. bd. Athletic Bus. mag., 1999-, pub. com. NFHS Coaches Quar., 2002—; contbr. articles to profl. jours., chpts. in books. Mem. AAHPERD, NEA, Nat. H.S. Athletic Coaches Assn. (Regional Athletic Dir. of Yr. award 1999), Nat. Interscholastic Athletic Adminstrs. Assn. (state award of merit for Md. 2002, Nat. Dist. Svc. award, 2004), Nat. Fedn. Coaches Assn. (Md. state dir. 2000—), Md. State Athletic Dirs. Assn. (v.p. 1999-2003, pres. 2003-2005, Athletic Dir. of Yr. 2000), Md. Assn. for Health, Phys. Edn., Recreation and Dance (v.p. athletics, 2000-01), Md. State Coaches Assn. (pres. 2002-03, newsletter editor and membership dir. 2001—), Nat. Assn. Sports Pub. Address Announcers (Md. state rep. 2004—). Presbyterian. Avocations: running, marathons, gardening, photography. Home: 1207 Peachtree Rd Fallston MD 21047-1804 Office: Loch Raven HS 1212 Cowpens Ave Towson MD 21286 Business E-Mail: dhoch@bcps.org.

HOCH, EDWARD DENTINGER, writer; b. Rochester, NY, Feb. 22, 1930; s. Earl George and Alice Mary (Dentinger) Hoch; m. Patricia Ann McMahon, June 5, 1957. Student, U. Rochester, 1947-49. Rsch. asst. Rochester (N.Y.) Pub. Libr., 1949-50; circulation asst. Pocket Books, NYC, 1952-54; pub. rels. writer Hutchins Advt. Co., Rochester, 1954-68. Author: (novels) The Shattered Raven, 1969, The Judges of Hades, 1971, The Transvection Machine, 1971, The Spy and the Thief, 1972, City of Brass, 1972, Fellowship of the Hand, 1973, The Frankenstein Factory, 1975, The Thefts of Nick Velvet, 1978, The Monkey's clue and the Stolen Sapphire, 1978, The Quests of Simon Ark, 1984, Leopold's Way, 1985, The Night My Friend, 1991, Diagnosis: Impossible, 1996, The Ripper of Storyville, 1997, The Velvet Touch, 2000, The Night People, 2001, The Old Spies Club, 2001, The Iron Angel, 2003, More Things Impossible, 2006; editor Dear Dead Days, 1972, All But Impossible, 1981, Murder Most Sacred, 1989, (book) The Best Detective Stories of the Year, 1976—81, Year's Best Mystery and Suspense Stories, 1982—95, Twelve American Detective Stories, 1997. Trustee Rochester Pub. Libr., 1981—98. With US Army, 1950—52. Mem.: Internat. Assn. Crime Writers, Crime Writers of Can., Crime Writers Assn. (Eng.), Authors Guild, Sci. Fiction Writers Am., Mystery Writers Am., Inc. (dir., pres. 1982, Edgar award 1967, Edgar scroll 1980, Grand Master 2001). Roman Catholic. Home and Office: 2941 Lake Ave Rochester NY 14612-5529 Home Phone: 585-865-1179; Office Phone: 585-865-1179. Personal E-mail: edhoch@frontiernet.net. *After publishing over 900 short stories and 50 books, I have to admit that I write primarily to entertain. But I've yet to decide whether it's more to entertain the reader or myself.*

HOCH, PAUL FREDERICK, JR., history educator; b. Raleigh, NC, Sept. 13, 1946; s. Paul Frederick and Sarah Locke (Hardison) Hoch; m. Frances Joan Shamberg, June 12, 1977. BA, U. of the South, Sewanee, Tenn., 1968; MA, U. NC, Chapel Hill, 1975. Resident asst. NC Sch. Arts, Winston-Salem, 1974—75; rsch. asst. City of Raleigh, 1975—79, Ctr. Urban Affairs, Raleigh, 1979—80; sec.-treas. Smith-Hardison Investment Co., 1984—99, v.p., 1998—99, pres., 1999—2006, also bd. dirs.; instr. history Wake Tech. C.C., Raleigh, 1992—. Advisor History Club Wake Tech. C.C., Raleigh, 2004—. Drug awareness chair N.C. Dist. East Civitan, 1990—93, dist. bd. dirs., 1992—96, chair rsch./planning com., 1993—94, gov. elect, 1993—94, dist. gov., 1994—95, editor dist. newspaper, 1995—96; mem. South Raleigh Civitan Club, 1984—99, pres., 1989—90; bd. dirs. Spl. Olympics NC, 1996—99; world team mem., site coord. World Games-Spl. Olympics, 1998—99; mem. Wake County Co-Ordinated Transp. Bd., 1987—93, chmn., 1988—91; citizen patrol officer Raleigh Police Dept., 1988—95, vol. rsch./planning, 1988—92, squad leader, 1989—95; active Internat. Visitors' Coun.; ative Sister Cities Assn. Raleigh; mem. internat. students host com. NC State U.; chalicist, lay reader Ch. Good Shepherd, Raleigh, NC, 1984—. Named one of Outstanding Young Men Am., 1981; recipient Civitan Dist. Honour Key, N.C. Order of the Long Leaf Pine, Gov. N.C., 1980, Outstanding Achievement award, Office Gov./Crime Control, 1992. Mem.: Constnl. Monarchy Assn. (life), NC Mus. Natural Scis. Friends (bd. dirs. 1989—95), NC Mus. Art Soc., NC History Mus. Assocs., Hot Stove League Raleigh (bd. dirs. 1998—), Clan Lindsay Assn. (newspaper editor 1993—95), Order First Families N.C., Wake County Hist. Soc., St. Andrew Soc. NC, English Speaking Union, 200 Club Wake County, Capital City Civitan Club (pres.-elect 2006—07, pres. 2007—). Democrat. Episcopalian. Avocations: baseball, baseball memorabilia collecting. Home: 4113 Oak Park Rd Raleigh NC 27612 Office: Wake Tech CC 9101 Fayetteville Rd Raleigh NC 27603

HOCHBERG, BAYARD ZABDIAL, retired lawyer; b. NYC, May 16, 1932; s. Abraham and Sonia (Pincus) Hochberg; m. Arlene Beethoven, Feb. 15, 1953; children: Ronny Mark, Randy Jean, Elizabeth Joyce. BA, CCNY, 1953; LLB, U. Va., 1958, JD, 1958. Bar: Md. 1958, Va. 1958. Law bailiff to Hon. Joseph Allen Supreme Bench Balt., 1958-59; asso. law office Paul Berman, Esq., Balt., 1959-68; ptnr. Levin, Hochberg & Chiarello, Balt., 1968-82; sr. ptnr. Hochberg, Chiarello & Costello, Balt., 1983-2000, Hochberg, Costello & Baron, Balt., 2001—02, of counsel, 2002—. Mem. editl. bd. Va. Law Rev., 1956—58; editor: Law Weekly DICTA. Nat. pres. Cavalier Health Found. Served to maj. USAR, 1953—75. Fellow: Md. Bar Found. (emeritus fellow), Am. Coll. Trial Lawyers; mem.: ATLA, ABA (Md. del. standing com. state legis. 1970—73, mem. tort and ins. practice sect. 1979—2002), Md. Trial Lawyers Assn. (co-chmn. com. legis. 1970—72, bd. govs. 1970—76, v.p. Balt. 1975, mem. Amicus brief com. 1979—81), Balt. County Bar Assn. (mem. family law com.), Balt. Bar Assn. (chmn. legis. com. 1968—69, bd. govs. 1969—70, mem. jud. adminstrn. com. 1980—86, mem. family law com. 1985—88), Md. Bar Assn. (chmn. ins., negligence and workmens compensation section 1973, mem. exec. bd., mem. state-city medicolegal com. 1979—91, chmn. 1983—86, mem. ct. appeals rules com. 1993—2002), Cavalier King Charles Spaniel Club (bd. dirs. 1993—2001, v.p. 1998—2001, chair ethics com. 1993—2002), Order of Coif. Home: 1978 Shadybrook Trail Charlottesville VA 22911 Office Phone: 410-823-2922. Personal E-mail: arlbob@earthlink.net.

HOCHBERG, FAITH S., US district court judge; BA summa cum laude, Tufts U., 1972; JD magna cum laude, Harvard U., 1975. Law clk. to Hon. Spottswood W. Robinson III U.S. Ct. Appeals (D.C. cir.), 1975-76; pvt. practice Washington, Boston, Roseland, N.J., 1977-83; asst. U.S. atty. Dist. N.J., Newark, 1983-87; ptnr. Cole, Schotz, Bernstein, Meisel & Forman, Hackensack, NJ, 1987-90; sr. dep. chief counsel Office Thrift Supervision, U.S. Treasury Dept., Jersey City; dep. asst. sec. law enforcement U.S. Treasury Dept., Washington; U.S. Atty. Dist. of N.J., 1994-99; judge U.S. Dist. Ct., 1999—. Office: US Courthouse and PO Bldg Newark NJ 07102

HOCHBERG, LOIS J., school psychologist; b. Bklyn., Dec. 22, 1942; d. Helen and George Robins; m. Martin N Hochberg, Mar. 5, 1967; children: Leigh Robert, Lauren Kim Benthien. EdM, Teachers Coll., Columbia U., 1974—77. School Psychologist State of NJ. Dept. of Edn., 1981, Learning Disabilities- Teacher Consultant NJ. Dept. of Edn., 1977, Teacher of the Handicapped NJ. Dept. of Edn., 1977, Kindergarten and Common Branch Teacher NY Dept. of Edn., 1964. Elem. sch. tchr. Lynbrook Pub. Schools, Hewlett, NY, 1964—68; ednl. coord. Young World Day Sch., Mahwah, NJ, 1971—75; sch. psychologist Valley Hosp., Ridgewood, NJ, 2001—. Sch. psychologist Woodcliff Lake and Maywood Schools, NJ, 1981—83; sch. psychologist St. Joseph's Hosp. and Med. Ctr., Paterson, NJ, 1982—2001. Mem. and pres. Bd. of Edn., Wyckoff, NJ, 1974—84; founding adv. bd. Wyckoff Cmty. Learning Ctr., NJ, 1976—86. Mem.: NJ. Assn. of Sch. Psychologists, Nat. Assn. Sch. Psychologists, Pi Lambda Theta. Achievements include research in developmental outcome of high-risk premature infants. Home: 344 West Shore Dr Wyckoff NJ 07481 Office: Valley Home Care 15 Essex Rd Ste 9 Paramus NJ 07652-1412 Home Phone: 201-891-9222; Office Phone: 201-447-8151. E-mail: lhochbe@valleyhealth.com.

HOCHBERG, RONALD MARK, lawyer; b. Bklyn., Apr. 3, 1955; s. Fred S. and Adele (Gunsberg) H.; m. Sharon A. Berg, Aug. 11, 1985; children: Rachel, Sarah. BA, Rutgers U., 1977; JD, Bklyn. Law Sch., 1980; LLM, U. Miami, 1982. Assoc. Klatsky & Klatsky, Red Bank, NJ, 1980-81, Fuerst, Singer & Yusem, Somerville, NJ, 1982-83, Law Offices of Steven Schanker, Melville, NY, 1983-86; ptnr. Schanker & Hochberg, Attys., Huntington, NY, 1986—. Frequent lectr. on estate planning; instr. Adelphi U., 1984-93. Columnist Financial World Mag., 1993-97; contbr. articles to profl. publs. Mem. ABA, N.Y. State Bar Assn., Estate and Tax Planning Coun. Avocations: skiing, sailing. Office: Schanker & Hochberg 27 W Neck Rd PO Box 1905 Huntington NY 11743-2618 Office Phone: 631-424-5400. Business E-Mail: mark@schankerhochberg.com.

HOCHEDLINGER, KONRAD, biology professor, biomedical researcher; b. Austria; PhD, U. of Vienna, 2003. Rschr. Inst. for Molecular Pathology, Whitehead Inst., 1999—2005; asst. prof. of Medicine Mass. Gen. Hosp. Center for Regenerative Medicine Laboratories, 2005—. Rschr. Harvard Stem Cell Inst., 2005—. Contbr. Grantee Genzyme Postdoctoral Fellowship, Whitehead Inst., 2004. Office: Cancer Ctr and Ctr for Regenerative Medicine Mass Gen Hosp Richard B Simches Bldg CPZN 4242 185 Cambridge St Boston MA 02114 Office Phone: 617-643-2075. Office Fax: 617-724-2662. E-mail: khochedlinger@helix.mgh.harvard.edu.*

HOCHFELDER, SCOTT Z., toy company executive, lawyer; b. Chgo., June 10, 1964; s. Allen R. and Carol (Greenwald) H.; m. Jean Sacon, childre: Noah, Alexandra, Ely AB, Brown U., 1986; MPP, U. Mich., 1990; JD, Northwestern U., 1993. Mem., assoc. editor Northwestern Law Review, 1991—93; assoc. Wildman, Harrold, Allen & Dixon, Chgo., 1993—97; assoc. gen. counsel Levy Restaurants, Chgo., 1997—2001; assoc. gen. counsel, asst. sec. KB Toys Inc., Pittsfield, Mass., 2002—05, gen. counsel, sec., 2005—. Rsch. assoc. & community rels. specialist ICF Tech., Fairfax, Va., 1987—88. Area chair Brown U., Chgo., 1994—; bd. mem. Carol Gollob Found., Chgo., 1995—. Mem.: Am. Corp. Counsel Assn., Chgo. Bar Assn., ABA. Office: KB Toys Inc 100 W St Pittsfield MA 01201

HOCHGREBE, NOLAN ROBARDS, secondary school educator; b. St. Louis, Oct. 10, 1980; s. William Erwin and Susan Marie Hochgrebe; m. Carrie Beth Migneco, Aug. 10, 1981. BS in Edn. (cum laude), U. Mo., Columbia, 2001—03, M in Curriculum & Instrn., 2003—04. Secondary Social Studies (9th-12th) tchr. Mo. Bd. Edn., 2003, Mid. Sch. Social Studies (5th-9th) tchr. Mo. Bd. Edn., 2004, cert. phys. edn. grades K-12 2007. 9th grade geography tchr. Blue Springs Freshman Ctr., Mo., 2003—04; 7th grade history tchr. Sunny Vale Mid. Sch., Blue Springs, 2004—. Asst. football coach (varsity level) Luth. HS S.uu, St. Louis, 2000—02; asst. basketball coach (8th grade) Sunny Vale Mid. Sch., 2004—, asst. football coach (8th grade), 2005—. Sponsor Fellowship of Christian Athletes, Mo., 1999. Mem.: Nat. Coun. Social Studies (assoc.), Mo. State Tchrs. Assn. (assoc.). Home: 1915 NW Elmwood Dr Grain Valley MO 64029 Office: Blue Springs Sch Dist 1801 NW Vesper Blue Springs MO 64015

HOCHHALTER, GORDON RAY, advertising communications executive; b. Jerome, Idaho, Oct. 3, 1946; s. Ralph R. and Evelyn (McClellan) H. BA, Brigham Young U., 1972. Asst. promotion supr. Armstrong World Industries, Lancaster, Pa., 1972-74, promotion supr., 1974-76, sr. promotion supr., 1976; asst. advt. mgr. R.R. Donnelley & Sons Co., Chgo., 1976-79, asst. mgr. advt., sales promotion, 1979-81, advt. mgr., 1981-84, group mgr. mktg. com., creative devel., 1984-86, dir. mktg. com., creative dir., 1986-91; v.p., gen. mgr., creative dir. Mobium Corp. Design & Comm., Chgo., 1991-96, v.p., creative dir. design and conceptual devel., 1996-97; chief creative officer Mobium Creative Group, Chgo., 1998-99, mng. ptnr. creativity, strategy, technology, 2000—04; mng. ptnr. creativity strategy connectivity Mobium Creative Group/MDC Ptnrs., 2004—. V.p., creative cons. Caviale Fashions, NYC, 1987—; mem. internet adv. bd. B2B Works, bd. dirs., Design Industry Found. Fighting Aids (Chgo.), 2003-, Literacy Chgo. Bd. Dirs., 2000-02; spkr. in field. Author: Strategies for a New Age of Bus. Comm., 1998, New Media in a New Age of Bus. Comm., 1998, Creative Leverage in a New Age of Bus. Comm., 1999, Hugging Your Customers in the Face of Bus. Comm. Change, 2002, Leveraging the Paradigm Shifts that are Changing Bus. Comm., 2001, Increasing Your Brandwidth in the Face of Bus. Comm. Change, 2002, Interactivating Your Messages in the Face of Bus. Comm. Change, 2002, others; monthly columnist Integrated Mktg. and Promotion Mag.; contbr. to profl. jour. and Libr. of Congress. Recipient London Internat. Advt. awards, 1987, One Show, Type Dirs. Club, Clio awrds, Art Dirs. Club awards, Andy awards, Addy awards, Internat. Advt. Festival AIGA awards, ProCom awards, Ace awards, Chgo. Tower awards, 1987-2006, Am. Bus. Media CEBA awards, 2002-03, Am. Bus. Press Objective and Results award, 1992, Cresta Internat. Advt. award, 1993, Sawyer award Bus. Mktg. Mag., 1993, Marcom High-Tech. Advt. award, 1994-96, Pinnacle award, 1994, Icon award Bus. Week Mag., 1994-95, 98-2000, Creativity, 2000. Mem. Am. Ctr. for Design, Am. Advt. Fedn., Chgo. Advt. Fedn., Bus. Mktg. Assn.(bd. dir. Chgo. chpt. 1998-2000), TansWorld Advertising Agency Network, Assn. Am. Advertising Agencies, NY Art Dir. Club. Business E-Mail: ghochhalter@mobium.com.

HOCHHAUSER, RICHARD MICHAEL, marketing professional; b. NYC, Aug. 25, 1944; s. Stanley and Rita (Weingarten) H.; m. Carole Beth Wasserstein, Sept. 6, 1969; children: Jonathan, Jennifer. BS, Carnegie Mellon U., 1966; MBA, Columbia U., 1968. Systems engr. U.S. Dept. of Navy, Washington, 1968-70; v.p. market research Quayle Plesser & Co., NYC, 1970-75; pres. research RMH Research, Inc. subs. Harte-Hanks Communications, Fort Lee, NJ, 1975-80; pres. mktg. services Harte Hanks Inc., Fairlawn, NJ, 1980-84, pres. direct mktg. NYC, 1984-95, exec. v.p., 1996—, COO, 1998—2002, pres., 1999—2002, pres., CEO, 2002—07, CEO, 2007—. Faculty NYU. Mem. Direct Mktg. Assn. (exec. com., bd. dirs., chmn.). Avocations: horticulture, antique watches. Home: 1025 5th Ave # 9dn New York NY 10028-0134 Office: Harte Hanks Inc 55 Fifth Ave New York NY 10003 E-mail: rmh@hartehanks.com.*

HOCHHEIMER, FRANK LEO, brokerage and financial industry executive; s. Arthur A. and Alice Hochheimer; m. Beverly Widman; 1 child, Martin. BA in Math., Queens Coll., 1965; MA in Math., Hofstra U., 1966; MA in Econometrics, New Sch. Social Rsch., 1973. Instr., chmn. math dept. N.Y. Inst. Tech., 1966—74; mgr. S. Bauer & Sons, NYC, 1974—75; analyst Merrill Lynch, NYC, 1974—75, computer specialist, commodity divsn., 1976—78, mgr., tech. analysis, 1978—79, v.p., dir. rsch., 1980—83; v.p., dir. Futures Info. Svcs., NYC, 1983—85, v.p., mgr. global securities data and pricing svc., 1985—90; v.p., mgr. CMO dept. Merrill Lynch Mortgage Capital, NYC, 1990—95; v.p., mgr. Merrill Lynch Ops. Sys. and Telecomm., NYC, 1995—2001; dir., dept. mgr. Merrill Lynch Global Markets and Investment Banking Divsn., NYC, 2001—03; mgr. reference and vendor data Enteprise Risk Mgmt. Group Am. Internat. Group, NYC, 2003—. Contrbr. articles to profl. jours. Mem. Am Econs. Assn., Nat. Assn. Bus. Economists, Market Technicians Assn., Futures Industry Assn. (former dir., teas. rsch. div.), Securities Industry Assn. (data mgmt. divsn.).

HOCHLERIN, DIANE, pediatrician, educator; b. NYC, Feb. 4, 1942; d. William J. and Bertha Hochlerin. BS, U. City of N.Y., 1958; MD, Med. Coll. Pa., 1966. Diplomate Am. Bd. Pediats. Intern Albert Einstein Hosp., Phila., 1966-67; resident Phila. Gen. Hosp., 1967-69; attending pediatrician St. Luke's Roosevelt Hosp., NYC, 1969—; now sr. attending physician St. Luke's Roosevelt Hosp, NYC; clin. assoc. prof. pediats. Columbia U., NYC, 1969—; asst. attending physician Cath. Med. Ctr., NYC, 1993-99. Faculty advisor Adelphi U., N.Y.C., 1994. Fellow Am. Acad. Pediats.; mem. N.Y. State Med. Soc., County Med. Soc. Home: 305 E 86th St New York NY 10028 Office: 241 Central Park West New York NY 10024

HOCHMAN, JUDITH SHERYL, cardiologist, researcher; b. NY, Feb. 20, 1951; m. Richard Fuchs, June 28, 1981; children: Michael, Daniel, Benjamin. BA magna cum laude, Brandeis Univ., 1972; MA in Cellular and Develop. Biology, Harvard Univ., 1974; MD, Harvard Med. Sch., 1977. Resident, internal medicine Peter Bent Brigham Hosp.; chief med. resident Univ. Mass. Med. Ctr.; fellow, cardiovascular medicine John Hopkins Univ. Med. Ctr.; dir. cardiac care unit St. Lukes Roosevelt Hosp. Ctr., NYC, 1983—2003, dir. cardiac stepdown, 1992—2003, dir. cardiac rsch., 1997—2003, sr. attending in medicine, 1997—2003; assoc. prof. medicine Columbia Univ., NYC, 1996—2003; Harold Snyder Family Prof., Cardiology, dir., cardiovascular clin. rsch., clin. chief Leon H. Charney Divsn. Cardiology NYU Med. Ctr., NYU Sch. Medicine, NYC, 2003—. Com mem. Program Project Review Com., Bethesda, 1996—; adv. bd. Cardio Tech., Pine Brook, N.Y., 1997-; chair, NIH Women's Health Initiative Adv. Com.; study chair, Occluded Artery and SHOCK Trials. Co-author: (chpt. in book) Textbook of Cardiovascular Medicine, 1998, Atlas of Heart Disease, 1996; mem. editl. bds. Circulation, American Heart Journal, Critical Pathways in Cardiology, Acute Cardiac Care; contbr. articles to profl. jours. Fellow Am. Coll. Cardiology, AHA (chair acute cardiac care ctr.); mem. Am. Fedn. Clinical Rsch. (chair), N.Y. Heart Assn., Am. Assn. Advancement of Sci., AMA, Phi Beta Kappa. Avocations: skiing, tennis, sailing. Office: NYU Med Ctr Schwartz Health Care Ctr 11 1173 530 First Ave New York NY 10016 Office Fax: 212-263-6927.*

HOCHMAN, KENNETH GEORGE, lawyer; b. Mt. Vernon, NY, Nov. 12, 1947; s. Benjamin S. and Lillian (Gilbert) H.; m. Carol K. Hochman, Apr. 8, 1979; children: Brian Paul, Lisa Erin. BA, SUNY, Buffalo, 1969;

JD, Columbia U., 1972. Bar: Ohio 1973, Fla. 1977, N.Y. 1979. Assoc. Jones Day, Cleve., 1972-79, ptnr., 1980—, chmn. wealth mgmt., 1989—, ptnr. adminstn. Cleve. office, 2000—. Trustee Katharine Kenyon Lippitt Found., Cleve., 1988, Kenridge Fund, Cleve., 1989, Bolton Found., Cleve., 1990, Elisha-Bolton Found., Cleve., 1993, Montefiore Found., Cleve., 2005. Trustee United Way of Cleve., 2002—; pres. Temple Tifereth-Israel, 2006—. Harlan Fiske Stone scholar Columbia U., 1971, 72. Fellow Am. Coll. Trusts and Estate Counsel; mem. Phi Beta Kappa. Office: Jones Day North Point 901 Lakeside Ave E Cleveland OH 44114-1190 Business E-Mail: kghochman@jonesday.com.

HOCHMAN, RICHARD H., investment company executive; b. Bklyn., Oct. 15, 1945; s. Albert A. and Francis Roth Hochman; m. Carol J. Hochman, Oct. 15, 1980; children: Nathaniel H., Jason H. BA with honors, Johns Hopkins U., 1967; MBA, Harvard U., 1969. With Corp. Fin. Dept. E.F. Hutton, NYC, 1969—84, sr. v.p., 1979—84, mem. Corp. Fin. Mgmt. Com., Underwriting Commitment Com., and Tax Shelter Underwriting Com.; mng. dir. Drexel Burnham Lambert, Inc., NYC, 1984—90; mng. dir. Investment Banking Group, mem. Dept and Equity Commitment Coms. PaineWebber, Inc., NYC, 1990—95; founder, chmn. Regent Capital Mgmt. Corp., NYC, 1995—. Bd. dirs. Cablevision Sys. Corp., R.A.B. Holdings, Santa Monica Amusements; bd. advisors Caymus Ptnrs. Bd. trustees Johns Hopkins U., Balt., 1995—; trustee Brooklyn Mus. Art. Mem.: Phi Beta Kappa. Home: 1100 Park Ave New York NY 10128 Office: Regent Capital Mgmt Corp Ste 1700 505 Park Ave New York NY 10022 Office Phone: 212-735-9900. Office Fax: 212-732-9908. E-mail: rhochman@regentcapitalpartners.com.*

HOCHMUTH, GEORGE J., horticultural educator; b. Balt., Mar. 31, 1953; married; 2 children. BS in Horticulture, U. Md., 1975; PhD in Plant Breeding and Plant Genetics, U. Wis., 1980. Staff Hochmuth Farms, Mardela Springs, Md., 1974; entomology technician U. Md. Vegetable Rsch. Farm, Salisbury, Md., 1972, summer vegetable rsch crew leader, 1973, 74; with USDA Vegetable Rsch. Lab., Beltsville, Md., 1974, 75; rsch. asst. dept. horticulture U. Wis., 1975-80; asst. prof. plant and soil scis. U. Mass., Amherst, 1980-84; asst. prof. and extension vegetable specialist, Vegetable Crops Dept. U. Fla., Gainesville, 1984-88, assoc. prof. and extension vegetable specialist, Horticultural Scis. Dept., 1988-93, prof. and extension vegetable specialist, Horticultural Scis. Dept., 1993—. Contbr. over 350 articles to scientific jours. Recipient Extension Publ. award So. Region Am. Soc. for Hort. Sci., 1989, 1994, Extension Edn. Aids award Am. Soc. for Hort. Sci., 1994, Extension Divsn. Excellence award, 1994, Outstanding Extension Educator award, 1995. Fellow: Am. Soc. Hort. Sci. Office: U Fla Rsch Adminstrn 1022 McCarty Hall PO Box 110200 Gainesville FL 32611 Office Phone: 850-875-7116. E-mail: gjh@ifas.ufl.edu.

HOCHREITER, JOSEPH CHRISTIAN, JR., engineering company executive; b. Bristol, Pa., Jan. 29, 1955; s. Joseph Christian and Mary Claire (Boyer) H.; m. Eileen Grace Wachtman, Aug. 31, 1984; children: Erich, Kristen. BA, Temple U., 1978; postgrad., Drexel U., 1983-85. Cert. ground water prof. Hydrologic tech. U.S. Geological Survey, Trenton, N.J., 1973-78, hydrologist, 1979-87; hydrologic mgr. Environ. Resources Mgt., Inc., Princeton, N.J., 1987-90, br. mgr., 1990-92, principal, 1991-92; v.p. Blasland, Bouck & Lee, Cranbury, NJ, 1992—2005; pres. Sr. Environ. Consulting, LLC, 2005—. Lectr. Pa. State U., Trevose, Pa., 1980-84. Mem. editl. bd Jour. Ground Water, Columbus, Ohio, 1989-93; contbr. articles to profl. jours. Founder Bucks County Homeless Shelter, Levittown, Pa., 1985; bd. dirs. ARC, Langhorne, Pa., 1985-91, Human Growth Ctr., Holland, Pa., 1987-92, 96-2000, pres. bd. dirs., 2001—; fin. com. LBCCC Welcoming the Strangr program, 2001-02; recording engr. Youth Orch. of Bucks County, 1999—, chmn. bd., 2006—; adv. bd. ARC Homeless Shelter, Levittown, 2005—. Recipient Adult Vol. award Bucks County Courier Times, 1987. Mem. Urban Land Inst. NJ, Nat. Ground Water Assn. (fellowship com. 1995), Assn. Ground Water Scientists and Engrs., NJ Acad. Sci., Geol. Assn. NJ. Home: 252 Hollow Branch Ln Yardley PA 19067-5791 Office: Senior Environmental Consulting LLC 252 Hollow Branch Ln Yardley PA 19067 Office Phone: 215-493-0343. E-mail: jhochreiter@verizon.net.

HOCHSCHILD, ADAM, journalist; b. NYC, Oct. 5, 1942; s. Harold K. and Mary (Marquand) H.; m. Arlie Russell, June 26, 1965; children: David, Gabriel. AB cum laude (hon. nat. scholar 1960-61), Harvard U., 1963. Reporter San Francisco Chronicle, 1965-66; writer, editor Ramparts mag., 1967-68, 73-74; commentator Nat. Pub. Radio, 1982-83. Regents lectr. U. Calif.-Santa Cruz, 1987; lectr. Grad. Sch. Journalism U. Calif., Berkeley, 1992—; Fulbright lectr., India, 1997-98. Author: Half the Way Home: A Memoir of Father and Son, 1986 (Notable Book of Yr. ALA and N.Y. Times Book Rev.), The Mirror at Midnight: A South African Journey, 1990, The Unquiet Ghost: Russians Remember Stalin, 1994 (Notable Book of Yr. N.Y. Times Book Rev. and Libr. Jour., Madeline Dane Ross award Overseas Press Club Am., Gold medal Soc. Am. Travel Writers), Finding the Trapdoor: Essays, Portraits, Travels, 1997 (PEN/Spielvogel-Diamonstein award for the Art of the Essay), King Leopold's Ghost: A Story of Greed, Terror and Heroism in Colonial Africa, 1998 (Mark Lynton History prize, Gold medal Calif. Book awards, Lionel Gelber prize, Duff Cooper prize), Bury the Chains: Prophets and Rebels in the Fight to Free an Empire's Slaves, 2005 (Gold medal Calif. Book awards, Lionel Gelber prize, LA Times Book prize, PEN USA Lit. award); co-founder, editor: Mother Jones mag., 1974—81, commentator: Pub. Interest Radio, 1987—88; contbr. articles to mags. Recipient Cert. of Excellence, Overseas Press Club, NYC, 1981, Spann prize Eugene V. Debs Found., 1984, Thomas Storke Internat. Journalism award World Affairs Coun. No. Calif., 1987, award for mag. reporting Soc. Profl. Journalists, 1999, Lannan Lit. award Lannan Found., 2005. Mem. PEN, Nat. Writers Union, Nat. Book Critics Circle.

HOCHSCHILD, ROGER C., finance company executive; BA, Georgetown U.; MBA, Amos Tuck Sch. Bus. Sr. exec. MBNA Am. Bank, 1994—98; exec. v.p. diversified fin. services Morgan Stanley, 1988—2001, exec. v.p., chief adminstrv. officer, chief strategic officer, 2001—04, pres., COO, Discover Financial Services, 2004—. Office: Morgan Stanley 2500 Lake Cook Rd Riverwoods IL 60015 Office Phone: 224-405-0900. Office Fax: 224-405-2009.*

HOCHSCHWENDER, KARL ALBERT, international trade and government relations consultant; b. Mannheim, Germany, Feb. 1, 1927; came to U.S., 1931, naturalized, 1938; s. Karl Georg and Maria Irma (Recken) H.; m. Lilli Gettinger, July 4, 1964 (dec. 1999). BA, Yale U., New Haven, Conn., 1947, MA, 1949, PhD, 1962. Instr. polit. sci. Fla. State U., Tallahassee, 1949-51; assoc. Mott of Washington & Assocs., Washington, 1954-58; rsch. analyst U.S. Govt., Washington, 1959-60; asst. to mgmt. Am. Hoechst Corp., Bridgewater, NJ, 1961-63, mgr. govt. rels., 1963-68, dir. pub. rels., 1968-72, dir. pub. affairs, 1972-83; prin. Palatine Assocs., Princeton, NJ, 1983—. Mem. roster of tech. specialists Office of Spl. Rep. for Trade Negotiations, Exec. Office Pres., 1964-67. Trustee United Fund Somerset Valley, N.J., 1969-75; mem. Princeton Site Plan Rev. Adv. Bd., 1992-99, vice chmn., 1994-99. Recipient Leonard D. White Meml. award Am. Polit. Sci. Assn., 1963; fellow Yale U., 1952-54. Mem. Am. Assn. Exporters and Importers (bd. dirs. 1963-2000, v.p. 1967-83, pres. 1983, chmn. 1983-85), Chem. Comm. Assn. (bd. dirs. 1976-80), Soc. Plastics Industry (chmn. food, drug and cosmetics packaging material com. 1972-76), Yale Club N.Y.C. Office: Palatine Assocs PO Box 1466 Princeton NJ 08542-1466

HOCHSTEIN, LEONARD MARK, plastic surgeon; b. Moscow, June 18, 1966; Grad., La. State U., 1986; MD, La. State U. Med. Ctr., 1990. Cert. Plastic Surgery, Am. Bd. Med. Specialties, Miami Soc. Plastic Surgeons, Am. Soc. Plastic and Reconstructive Surgeons, Millard Soc. Residency tng. U. Tex. Med. Ctr., Southwestern Parkland Meml. Hosp., Dallas, 1991—95; fellowship, Hand Surgery U. Miami Jackson Meml. Hosp., 1995, fellowship, Plastic Surgery, 1996, 1996—98; pvt. practice Aventura, Fla. Recipient Academic award in Plastic Surgery, 1997. Achievements include fluency in Russian and Spanish. Office: 19495 Biscayne Blvd Ste 204 Miami FL 33180 Office Phone: 305-931-3338. Office Fax: 305-931-3324.*

HOCHSTETTLER, THOMAS JOHN, academic administrator, historian; b. Bryan, Ohio, July 23, 1947; s. Hugh Donavon and Martha Lucille Taylor Hochstettler; m. Marcia Della Glas, Jan. 4, 1975; children: William Cameron Glas-Hochstetler, Taylor David Glas-Hochstettler, Benjamin Joseph Glas-Hochstettler. BA, Earlham Coll., 1969; MA, U. Mich., 1970, PhD, 1978. From lectr. history to sr. planning assoc. Stanford (Calif.) U., 1978—86, sr. planning assoc. and staff economist, 1986—87; lectr. history Bowdoin Coll., Brunswick, Maine, 1987—92, dean planning and gen. adminstrn., 1987—92, acting treas., 1990—92; dir. planning U. Houston Sys., 1992—96; assoc. provost Rice U., Houston, 1996—2002, adj. asst. prof. history, 1998—2000; vis. prof. history Internat. U. Bremen, Freie Hansestadt Bremen, Germany, 1999—2002, v.p. academic affairs, 1999—2004; pres. Lewis & Clark Coll., Portland, Oreg., 2004—. Mem. bd. trustees New Eng. Regional Computing Consortium, 1987—92; bd. dir. Oreg. Ind. Colls. Found. Moderator First Congl. Ch., Houston, 1992—94; bd. dirs. Midcoast Maine Red Cross, Brunswick, Maine, 1987—91, United Way of Midcoast Maine, Brunswick, 1987—92, World Affairs Coun. Oreg. Fellow, Woodrow Wilson Found., 1969—70, Horace H. Rackham Doctoral fellowship, U. Mich., 1973—74, Stanford U. Dept. of History, 1978—80; grantee, Deutsche Akademische Austauschdienst, 1975—76. Mem.: Rotary Club of Bremen Germany (youth svc. officer. mem., exec. com. 2000—04), Rotary Club Houston. Achievements include founding of International University Bremen, the first comprehensive private research university to be established on the European Continent following World War II. Office: Lewis & Clark College 0615 SW Palatine Hill Road Portland OR 97219-7899 Home Phone: 503-635-7788; Office Phone: 503-768-7680. Business E-Mail: pres@lclark.edu.

HOCHSTRASSER, DONALD LEE, cultural anthropologist, community health and public administration educator; b. Taylorsville, Ky., June 10, 1927; s. Emil John and Mary E. (Schad) H.; m. Marie Emlen, Apr. 9, 1960; 1 child, Letitia Cope; stepchildren: Eloise Q. Hatch, Laura A. Hatch. BA, U. Ky., 1952, MA, 1955; postgrad. (univ. fellow) Northwestern U., 1955-56; PhD in Anthropology, U. Oreg., 1963; MPH, U. Calif.-Berkeley, 1969. Rsch. asst. dept. rural sociology U. Ky., Lexington, 1954-55, instr. dept. anthropology, 1956-57, 1959-60, instr. dept. cmty. medicine, 1961-63, asst. prof., 1963-66, assoc. prof., 1966-73, prof., 1973-80, assoc. dir. Ctr. Devel. Change, 1970-73, prof. cmty. health Coll. Allied Health, prof. anthropology Coll. of Arts and Scis., prof. pub. adminstrn. Grad. Ctr. Pub. Adminstrn., 1980-93, prof. emeritus dept. health svcs., 1993—; tchg. fellow dept. anthropology U. Oreg., Eugene, 1957-58, instr., 1958-59, NSF rsch. fellow, 1960-61; USPHS spl. rsch. fellow Sch. Pub. Health, U. Calif.-Berkeley, 1968-69; chmn. state family planning rev. com. Ky. State Comprehensive Health Planning Coun., 1972-74; mem. state family planning task force Coun. Health Svcs., Ky. State Dept. Human Resources, 1974-78; cons., adv. numerous orgns.; vis. scholar dept. adminstrv. and social health scis. Sch. Pub. Health, U. Calif.-Berkeley, 1979; dir. Bluegrass Regional Birth Planning Coun., Inc., Lexington, 1978-81, Lexington Planned Parenthood, Inc., 1982-89; mem. adv. coun. Ctr. of Creative Living/Adult Care Program of Lexington-Fayette County Health Dept., 1989. Mem. Union of Concerned Scientists, Am. Farmland Trust, Wilderness Soc. Served with USN, 1946-47. Grantee pub. health, family planning, sickle cell anemia, Tb control and occupl. health-risk factors. Fellow Am. Anthrop. Assn., Soc. Applied Anthropology; mem. Soc. Med. Anthropology (founding), Am. Pub. Health Assn. (founding mem. population sect.), Assn. Tchrs. Preventive Medicine, AAAS, AAUP, Phi Beta Kappa, Sigma Xi, Alpha Kappa Delta, Delta Omega. Democrat. Clubs: Univ. Faculty, Alumni. Contbr. numerous articles to profl. publs. Home: 953 Holly Springs Dr Lexington KY 40504-3119 Office: Univ Ky Med Ctr 208A Annex 2 Lexington KY 40536-0001

HOCHSTRASSER, ROBIN M., chemist, educator; b. Edinburgh, Jan. 4, 1931; U.S. citizen; married; 2 children. BSc in Applied Chemistry, Heriot-Watt U., Scotland, 1952, DSc honoris causa, 1984; PhD in Pure Chemistry, U. Edinburgh, 1955. Instructor dept. chemistry U. BC, Canada, 1957—60, asst. prof., 1961—63; rsch. fellow NRC, Canada, 1960; rsch. assoc. Fla. State U., 1960—61; assoc. prof. chemistry U. Pa., Phila., 1963—67, prof. chemistry, 1967—68, Blanchard prof. chemistry, 1968—83, Doonner prof. phys. sciences, dept. chemistry, 1983—, dir. Regional Laser and Biomedical Tech. Lab., 1978—. Vis. prof., fellow Clare Coll., Cambridge U., Eng. 1972; vis. prof. Australian Nat. U., Canberra, 1973, U. Grenoble, France, 1974, 1989, Calif. Inst. Tech., 1975, U. Paris, 1987, Universitat Munchen, 1980; dir. NIH Laser Rsch. Resource, 1981-; Hinshelwood Lectr., Oxford U., 1982; invited lectr. in field. Contbr. articles to profl. jours.; mem. editl. bd. Chemical Physics Letters 1969-; editor Chemical Physics, 1975-. Chair John Scott Adv. Panel, City Phila., 1985—. Pilot Officer Royal Air Force, Edn. Branch, 1955—57. Recipient Bourke medal Faraday Soc., 1980, Internat. Soc. Optical Engring. Spl. President's award, 1986, NIH MERIT award, 1990-2000, LICOR award, U. Nebr., 1996, E. Bright Wilson award in Spectroscopy, 1998, Centenary Sliver medal, Royal Soc. Chemistry, 2000, Benjamin Franklin Medal in Chemistry, 2003, Albert F. Cotton award in Chemistry, 2005; Courtald scholar, 1952-55, Alfred P. Sloan Found. fellow, 1963-67, John Simon Guggenheim fellow, 1972, Alexander von Humboldt sr. fellow, 1978, Christianson Fellow, Oxford U., 1982. Fellow Am. Acad. Arts and Sciences, Am. Phys. Soc.(chair, chem. physics divsn, 1998), Optical Soc. Am. (Ellis R. Lippincott award 1997); mem. AAAS, AAUP, Am. Chem. Soc. (chair, divsn. biophysical chemistry, 1998, Phila. Sect. award 1990, Peter Debye award 1997, Ahmed Zewail award in Ultrafast Sci. and Tech., 2007), Royal Inst. Chemistry, Am. Inst. Physics, Biophys. Soc., NAS. Office: U Pa Dept Chemistry Office 258 N 231 S 34th St Philadelphia PA 19104-6323 Office Phone: 215-898-8410. Business E-Mail: hochstra@sas.upenn.edu.*

HOCHULI, EDWARD G., lawyer; b. Milw., Dec. 25, 1950; BA with honors, U. Tex., El Paso, 1972; JD with distinction, U. Ariz., 1976. Bar: Ariz. 1976, U.S. Dist. Ct. Ariz. 1977, U.S. Ct. Appeals (9th cir.) 1981. Law clerk to Hon. C.A. Muecke U.S. Dist. Ct. Ariz., Phoenix, 1976-78; mem. Jones, Teilborg, Sanders, Haga & Parks P.C., 1978-83; spl. asst. atty. gen. State of Ariz., 1979; ptnr. Jones, Skelton & Hochuli, Phoenix, 1983—; referee NFL, 1990—92, head referee, 1992—. Mem. ABA, Assn. Trial Lawyers Am., Ariz. Trial Lawyers Assn., State Bar Ariz., Ariz. Assn. Def. Counsel (bd. dirs. 1982—), Maricopa County Bar Assn., Def. Rsch. and Trial Lawyers Assn., NFL Referee Assn.(bd. dirs., 1995-, pres., 1999-2001) Achievements include referee, Super Bowl XXXII, XXXVIII. Office: Jones Skelton & Hochuli 2901 N Central Ave Ste 800 Phoenix AZ 85012-2798 E-mail: ehochuli@jshfirm.com.

HOCK, FREDERICK WYETH, retired lawyer; b. Newark, July 10, 1924; s. Herbert Hummel and Carol (Wyeth) H.; m. Alfheld Catherine Larsen, Mar. 4, 1945; children: Carolyn, Sandra, Rhonda; m. Ellen Barbara Weidner, June 28, 1975. AA, Princeton U., 1944; BA, Rutgers U., 1948, LLB, 1950, JD, 1968. Bar: NJ 1949. Assoc. Stevenson, Willette & McDermott, 1949-51; pvt. practice, 1951-65; ptnr. Hock & Sharkey, East Orange, NJ, 1965-79; sr. ptnr. Hock Silverlieb & Kramer, Livingston, NJ, 1979-93, Gulkin, Hock & Lehr, 1994-2000, Hock Graziano & Koprowski, 2000—05; ret., 2006. Acting judge East Orange Mcpl. Ct., 1954—57. Office Phone: 732-571-8720.

HOCKEIMER, HENRY ERIC, engineering executive; b. Winzig, Germany, Apr. 3, 1920; came to U.S., 1946, naturalized, 1951; s. Erich and Gertrude (Masur) H.; m. Margaret Feeny, May 26, 1956; children: Ellen Patricia, Henry Eric. Student, RCA Insts., 1946—47; electronics and bus. mgmt., NYU, 1948—51. With Philco-Ford Corp., Phila., 1947—, gen. mgr. communications and tech. services div., 1962-63, corp. v.p., 1963-72; v.p., gen. mgr. refrigeration products div. Connorsville, Ind., 1972-75; pres. Ford Aerospace & Communications Corp., Dearborn, Mich., 1975-85; v.p. Ford Motor Co., 1981-85; cons. USIA, Washington, 1985, dep. dir. TV and film service, 1986-87, asst. dir., 1987-88, assoc. dir. for mgmt., 1988-91, cons., 1991—; commr. RIAS, 1991—. Mem. Engring. Soc. Detroit, Smithsonian, Univ. Club Washington, Washington Arts Soc. Personal E-mail: hhockeimer@aol.com.

HOCKENBERG, HARLAN DAVID, lawyer; b. Des Moines, July 1, 1927; s. Leonard C. and Estyre M. (Zalk) H.; m. Dorothy A. Arkin, June 3, 1953; children: Marni Lynn, Thomas Leonard, Edward Arkin. BA, U. Iowa, 1949, JD, 1952. Bar: Iowa 1952. Assoc. Abramson & Myers, Des Moines, 1952-58, Abramson, Myers & Hockenberg, Des Moines, 1958-64; sr. ptnr. Davis, Hockenberg, Wine, Brown, Koehn & Shors, Des Moines, 1964-95; shareholder, dir. Sullivan & Ward, P.C., Des Moines, 1995—2007, Coppola, McConville, Coppola, Hockenberg & Scalise, PC, 2007—. Bd. dirs. West Des Moines State Bank, Rep. Jewish Coalition, Smoother Sailing Found. Mem. bd. editors U. Iowa Law Review. Mem. Citizens Ind. Cts., Internat. Rels. and Nat. Security Adv. Coun., Rep. Nat. Com., 1978; chmn. Coun. Jewish Fedns., Small Cities Com., 1970-71; mem. exec. com. Am. Israel Pub. Affairs Com.; pres. Wilkie House, Inc., Des Moines, 1965-66, Des Moines Jewish Welfare Fedn., 1973-74; mem. Presdl. Commn. on White House Fellowships, 1988-92; mem. Holocaust Meml. Coun., 2003-06. With USNR, 1945-46. Mem. Iowa State Bar Assn. (past chair professionalism com.), Des Moines C. of C. (pres. 1986, chmn. bur. econ. devel. 1979, 80, bd. dirs. 1986), Des Moines Club, Pioneer Club, Delta Sigma Rho, Omicron Delta Kappa, Phi Epsilon Pi Office: Coppola McConville Coppola et al 2100 Westown Pkwy Ste 210 West Des Moines IA 50265 Office Phone: 515-453-1055. Business E-Mail: hdhockenberg@cmcslaw.com.

HOCKENBERRY, E'RENA, music educator; b. Tilden, Ill., Oct. 28, 1927; d. Clarence and Frances Terry, adopted d. Emil B. and Mrs. Hatch; m. Charles E. Hockenberry, Mar. 17, 1946; children: Coreen Hockenberry Grogan, Ted D. BS, cert., Colo. State Coll., 1946; MA, U. No. Colo., 1972. Elem. educator Greeley (Colo.) Pub. Sch.; music educator Jeff County Pub. Sch., Colo. Mem.: Colo. Music Educators (past historian, past pres.). Democrat. Avocation: golf. Home: 6527 W 34th Ave Wheat Ridge CO 80033

HOCKEY, CHRISTOPHER LAWRENCE, academic administrator; b. Syracuse, NY, May 7, 1979; s. Sharlene Marie and Dennis Charles Spina (Stepfather); m. Melissa L. Hockey. BSc, SUNY, Oswego, NY, 2002; MSc, Syracuse U., NY, 2005. V.p. Student Assn. SUNY, Oswego, 2001—02, transfer coord., 2006—; assoc. mgr. Discovery Channel Stores, Victor, NY, 2002; resident dir. Utica Coll., NY, 2002—06, instr., 2004—06, coord. orientation staff, 2002—04. Adv. Alpha Omega Phi, Utica, 2004—06, Tau Sigma, Oswego, NY, 2006—; presenter in field. Named Senator of the Yr., SUNY Oswego Student Assn., 2002; Teachers and Adminstr. scholarship, Baldwinsville Ctrl. Sch. Dist., 1997. Mem.: Nat. Orientation Dirs. Assn., Am. Coll. Pers. Assn., NY State Transfer Articulation Assn., Omicron Delta Kappa. Democrat. Methodist. Avocations: reading, camping, weight-lifting. Office: SUNY Oswego 611 Culkin Hall Oswego NY 13126 Home Phone: 315-402-2746. Business E-Mail: chockey@oswego.edu.

HOCKFIELD, SUSAN, academic administrator, medical educator; m. Thomas Byrne; 1 child, Elizabeth Hockfield Byrne. BA in Biology, U Rochester, 1973; PhD in Anatomy & Neuroscience, Georgetown U, 1979; MA (hon.), Yale U, 1994; D (hon.), Brown U., Providence, 2006. NIH Post-Doc Fellow Dept. of Anatomy and Neuroscience Program, U of Calif., San Francisco, 1979—80; jr. staff investigator Cold Spring Harbor Lab, Cold Spring Harbor, NY, 1980—82, sr. staff investigator, 1982—85; asst. prof. Sect. of Neurobiology Yale U Sch. of Med., New Haven, 1985—89, assoc. prof., 1989—91, 1991—94, prof. Dept. of Neurobiology, 1994—2004; dean, Grad. Sch. of Arts and Sci. Yale U., 1998—2002, provost, 2003—04; pres. and prof. neurosci. MIT, Cambridge, 2004—. Mem. Nat. Adv. Neurol. Disorders and Stroke Coun. NIH, 2002—04; mem. at large AAAS, Sect. on Neuroscience, 2000—04; bd. trustees Cold Spring Harbor Lab., NY, 1998—2004; Brain Cancer Adv. Panel James S. McDonnell Found., 1997—2002; bd. dir. Haskins Lab., 1988—2002; U Adv. Council Yale-New Haven Tchrs. Inst., 1998—2002; elected mem. of the bd. Council of Grad. Sch., 2002; neuroscience adv. bd. Astra Pharmaceuticals, 1997—99; program dir. Summer Neurobiology Program Cold Spring Harbor Lab., Cold Spring Harbor, NY, 1985—97; councilor Soc. for Neuroscience, 1992—96; sci. adv. bd. Hereditary Disease Found., 1991—95, 1996—2000; mem. NIH Study Section (Visual Sci. B), 1988—92; chair Gordon Conf. on Neural Plasticity, 1997; participant, mem. of bd. several orgns., studies and soc.; bd. dirs. Gen. Electric Co., 2006—; class B dir. Nat. Math and Sci. Initiative; mem. Woods Hole Oceanographic Inst. Co-author (with S.Carlson,P.Levitt,E.Evans,L.Silberstien & J. Pintar) Molecular Probes of the Nervous System: Selected Methods for Antibodies and Nucleai Acid Probes; contbr. chapters to books, opinion pieces, articles to profl. jours. Bd. mem. WGBH Ednl. Found., Inc., 2004—, Boston Symphony Orchestra; bd. overseers Carnegie Corp. NY; bd. trustees Lord Found. Mass. Recipient PHS Post-doctoral Rsch. Award, NIH, 1980, Grass Traveling Sci. Award, Soc. for Neuroscience, 1987, Charles Judson Herrick Award, Am. Assn. Anatomists, 1987, William Edward Gilbert Prof. of Neurobiology, Yale U., 2001, Wilbur Lucius Cross medal, 2004, Golden Plate award, 2005, Meliors citation for Sheffield medal, U. Rochester, 2004, Amelia Earhart award, Women's Union, 2005, hons., Tsinghua U., 2005, Cold Spring Harbor Labor Honors, 2006; grantee Esther A. and Joseph Klingenstein fellowship, NSF, NIH, 1985. Fellow: AAAS (mem.-at-large, Section on Neuroscience 2000—), American Acad. Arts & Scis. (fell. 2004); mem.: Soc. Neuroscience. Achievements include three patents in field of neuroscience. Office: Off of Pres Rm 3-208 MIT 77 Massachusetts Ave Cambridge MA 02139-4307 Office Phone: 617-253-0148. Office Fax: 617-253-3124.

HOCKLESS, MARY FONTENOT, educational consultant; b. New Iberia, La., July 23, 1954; d. Gill B. and Thelma Fontenot; m. Joseph W. Hockless; children: Kellie, Amie, Marcus. BA in Speech Pathology, U. La., 1978, EdM, 1984, postgrad., 2003—. Cert. speech pathology, early intervention guidance & counseling K-12, family svc. coord. Speech therapist Iberia Sch. Dist., New Iberia, La., 1977, presch. tchr., early interventionist; coord. La. Dept. Edn., 1992, regional coord., 1992—2000; rsch. U. Ark., Little Rock, 2000—03; pvt. practice First Steps Referral and Cons. LLC, New Iberia, 2003—. Contbr. articles to profl. jours.; author: (manual) Challenging Behavior Support, 2002, Perfect Rhythm, 2003. Named Tchr. of Yr., Jaycees, New Iberia, 1985, Outstanding Alumni, U. Southwestern La., 2003. Home: PO Box 12213 New Iberia LA 70562 Office: First Steps Refferal Consulting 134 E Main St Ste 4 New Iberia LA 70560-3798

HOCKNEY, DAVID, artist; b. Bradford, Yorkshire, Eng., July 9, 1937; s. Kenneth and Laura Hockney. Student, Bradford Coll. Art, 1953—57, Royal

Coll. Art, London, 1959—62, degree (hon.), 1992, U. Aberdeen, 1988. Lectr. U. Iowa, 1964, U. Colo., 1965, U. Calif., Berkeley, 1967, UCLA, 1966, hon. chair of drawing, 1980. One-man shows include Kasmin Gallery, 1963-89, Mus. Modern Art, N.Y.C., 1964, 68, Stedelijk Mus., Amsterdam, Netherlands, 1966, Whitechapel Gallery, London, 1970, Andre Emmerich Gallery, N.Y.C., 1972-96, Musee des Arts Decoratifs, Paris, 1974, Museo Tamayo, Mexico City, 1984, LA Louver, Calif., 1986, 89, 95, 98, 05, 07, Nishimura Gallery, Tokyo, 1986, 89, 90, 94, Met. Mus. Art, 1988, L.A. County Mus. Art, 1988, 96, 2006, Tate Gallery, London, 1988, 92, 2007, Royal Acad. Arts, London, 1995, 99, Hamburger Kunsthalle, 1995, Nat. Mus. Am. Art, Washington, 1997, 98, Mus. Ludwig, Cologne, 1997, MFA, Boston, 1998, 2006, Centre Georges Pompidou, Paris, 1999, Musee Picasso, Paris, 1999, Mus. Contemparty Art, L.A., 2001, Kunst-Und Ausstellung Halle, Bonn, 2001, La. Mus Mod. Art, Copenhagen, 2001, Annely Juda Fine Art, London, 1997, 99, 2003, 06, Richard Gray Gallery, NY, 1992, 99, 02, 04, Nat. Portrait Gallery, London, 2003, 06, Whitney Biennial, NY, 2004, others; designer: Rake's Progress, Glyndebourne, Eng., 1975; sets for Magic Flute, Glyndebourne, 1978, Parade Triple Bill, Stravinsky Triple Bill, Met. Opera House, 1980-81, Tristan und Isolde, Los Angeles Music Ctr. Opera, 1987; Turandot, Lyric Opera, Chgo., 1992—, San Francisco Opera, 1993, Die Frau Ohne Schatten, Covent Garden, London, 1992, L.A. Music Ctr.Opera, 1993; author: David Hockney by David Hockney, 1976, David Hockney: Travels with Pen, Pencil and Ink, 1978, Paper Pools, 1980, David Hockney Photographs, 1982, Cameraworks, 1983, David Hockney: A Retrospective, 1988, Hockney Paints the Stage, 1983, That's the Way I See It, 1993, David Hockney's Dog Days, 1998, Hockney on Art, 1999, Secret Knowledge: Rediscovering the Lost Techniques of the Old Masters, 2001, Hockney's Portraits and People, 2003, Hockney's Pictures, 2004, David Hockney: Portraits, 2006; illustrator: Six Fairy Tales of the Brothers Grimm, 1969, The Blue Guitar, 1977, Hockney's Alphabet, 1991. Recipient Guinness award and 1st prize for etching, 1961, Gold medal Royal Coll. Art, 1962, Graphic prize Paris Biennale, 1963, 1st prize 8th Internat. Exhbn. Drawings Lugano, Italy, 1964, 1st prize John Moores Exhbn. Liverpool, Eng., 1967, German award of Excellence 1983, 1st prize Internat. Ctr. of Photography, N.Y., 1985, Kodak photography book award for Cameraworks, 1984, Praemium Imperiale Japan Art Assn., 1989, 5th Ann. Gov. Calif. Visual Arts award, 1994, Charles Wollaston award Royal Acad. Arts London, 1999; named Companion of Honour, Her Majesty, the Queen of Eng., 1997. Office: 7508 Santa Monica Blvd Los Angeles CA 90046-6407

HOCTOR, JAMES JOSEPH, lawyer; b. Biddeford, Maine, Dec. 4, 1963; s. Michael James and Lorraine Belair Hoctor; m. Lynn Marie Hoctor, May 3, 1997; children: Michael James, James Lawrence. BS in Acctg., U. Fla., Gainesville, 1985, MA in Acctg., 1986; JD, Duke U., NC, 1990. CPA Fla., 1987; bar: Fla. 1990. Acct. Ernst & Whinny, Orlando, Fla., 1986—87; lawyer Lowndes Drosdick Doster, Orlando, 1990—. Bd. dirs. Friends Marcella Mus., Orlando, 2002—. Home: 1891 Winchester Dr Winter Park FL 32789 Office: Lowndes Drosdick Doster 215 N Eola Dr Orlando FL 32801 Office Phone: 407-418-6254, 407-843-4444. Business E-Mail: jim.hoctor@lowndes-law.com.

HOCUTT, MAX OLIVER, retired philosophy educator; b. Berry, Ala., July 3, 1936; s. Harry Juell and Edith Pauline (Skelton) H.; m. Dorothy Lois Etheredge, Nov. 22, 1957; children: James Max, Cassandra Diane. BA in Philosophy with honors, Tulane U., 1957, MA, 1958; PhD, Yale U., 1960. Instr. U. South Fla., Tampa, 1960-62, asst. prof., chmn. dept. philosophy, 1962-65; assoc. prof. U. Ala., 1965-70, prof., 1970—2001, chmn. dept., 1978-91; ret., 2001. Vis. fellow, Oxford U., 1971, Princeton U., 1979, St. Andrews U., 1987; bd. dirs. ACLU, University, 1969. Author: The Elements of Logical Analysis and Inference, 1979, First Philosophy, 1980, Grounded Ethics, 2000; editor: Behavior and Philosophy, 1992-96; contbr. articles to profl. jours. Honors scholar, Tulane U., 1957, So. Fellowships Career Tchg. fellow, Yale U., 1958—60. Mem. Ala. Philos. Soc. (pres. 1967), So. Soc. Philosophy and Psychology, Am. Philos. Assn., Phi Beta Kappa. Home: 5510 Golden Pond Ave Northport AL 35473-1529 Office: U Ala Dept Philosophy Tuscaloosa AL 35487-0001

HODAPP, HEIDI FRANCINE, middle school educator; b. Ventura, Calif., Dec. 12, 1975; d. Howard Leroy and Jo-Anne Frances Hodapp. BS in Interdisciplinary Studies, Old Dominion U., Norfolk, Va., 1998, MS in Edn., 1999. Tchr., chair sci. Bayside Mid. Sch., Virginia Beach, Va., 1999—. Mem. prins. adv. com. Bayside Mid. Sch., 2005—, mem. sch. planning coun., 2005—; mentor, 2004—. Mem.: Va. Edn. Assn., Nat. Sci. Tchrs. Assn., Va. Mid. Sch. Assn. Roman Catholic. Home: 604 Glengarry Ct Virginia Beach VA 23451 Office: Bayside Mid Sch 965 Newtown Rd Virginia Beach VA 23462 Business E-Mail: heidi.hodapp@vbschools.com.

HODEL, MARY ANNE, library director; b. St. Louis, Aug. 12; d. William George and Florence Marie (Betz) H.; children: Courtney Hodel Denham, Christian Hodel Denham. BA, U. Wis., 1972; MLS, Cath. U., 1973. Project libr. TRACOR-JITCO, Rockville, Md., 1973—74; project mgr. to database mgr. Nat. Resources Libr. US Dept. Interior, Washington, 1974—77; cataloger USAF Base Libr., Ramstein, Germany, 1977—79; project libr. to automation libr. Law Libr. Georgetown U., Washington, 1984—85, automation libr. Law Libr., 1985—91; chief state libr. resource ctr. Enoch Pratt Free Libr., Balt., 1991—95; dir. Ann Arbor Dist. Libr., Mich., 1995—2001; dir., CEO Orange County Libr. Sys., Orlando, Fla., 2002—. Network coord. Coun. Md. Librs., 1991-95; mem. Sailor Implementation group, 1992-95, grants and devel. task force liaison, 1993-95; v.p. Mich. Libr. Consortium, 1998-99, bd. pres., 1999-2000, bd. dirs.; spkr. in field Mem. exec. com. Ann Arbor Hands On Mus., 1998—2001. Recipient Libr. of Yr. award Libr. Jour., 1997-98. Mem.: ILAMA, ALA (local arrangements chmn. ann. conf. Orlando 2004, Libr. of Yr. award 1997—98), Law Librs. Soc. Washington (pres. acad. spl. interest sect. 1988—89, prog. coord. 1989, chair innovative interfaces users workshop 1989, rec. sec. 1989—91, prog. coord. 1990), Md. Libr. Assn. (del. to ALA legis. day 1992, conf. planning com. 1993—94, co-chair tech. interest group 1994, prog. coord. 1994), Md. Assn. Profl. Libr. Adminstrs., Pub. Libr. Assn. (sys. sect. v.p./pres.-elect 1994—95, pres. 1995—, chair Leonard Wertheimer award com. 2000—01), Mich. Libr. Consortium (v.p. 1999, pres. 1999—2000), Am. Assn. Law Librs. (prog. coord. ann. meeting 1987, chair innovative interfaces users com. 1988—89, editor innovative interfaces users com. 1989), Mich. Libr. Assn. (chair pub. libr. divsn. 2001—). Avocations: travel, photography. Office: Orlando Pub Libr 101 E Central Blvd Orlando FL 32801 Office Phone: 407-835-7601. E-mail: hodel.maryanne@ocls.info.

HODES, PAUL WILLIAM, II, congressman, lawyer; b. NYC, Mar. 21, 1951; s. Robert Bernard and Florence (Rosenberg) H.; m. Margaret (Peggo) Ann Horstmann; children: Maxwell, Ariana. BA cum laude, Dartmouth Coll., Hanover, NH, 1972; JD cum laude, Boston Coll., 1978. Bar: NH 1978, Mass. 1980. Asst. atty. gen. State of NH, Concord, 1978-82, spl. prosecutor, 1982—83; co-founder, ptnr. Roussos, Hage, & Hodes, Concord, NH, 1984—89, shareholder, 1989—96; ptnr. Shaheen & Gordon, 1996—2006; mem. US Congress from 2nd NH Dist., 2007—, mem. fin. svcs. com., oversight & govt. reform com. Ptnr. Big Round Music LLC, 1998—. Lyricist The People's House, 2001, mem. (6 recs.) Peggosus. Bd. dirs. Capital Ctr. Arts, 1990-97, 02-, chair 1990-96; bd. dirs. Tricinium Ltd., 2001—; mem. NH State Coun. on Arts, 2001-06. Recipient hon. award Parents Choice Found., 1987, 96. Mem. NARAS, ASCAP. Democrat. Jewish. Office: 506 Cannon House Office Bldg Washington DC 20515 also: 114 N Main St 2nd Fl Concord NH 03303 Office Phone: 202-225-5206, 603-223-9814.*

HODES, RICHARD J., federal agency administrator, immunologist, researcher; b. NYC, Dec. 31, 1943; BA, Yale U., 1965; MD, Harvard U., 1971. Diplomate Am. Bd. Internal Medicine. Clin. investigator Nat. Cancer Inst. NIH, Bethesda, Md., dep. chief, acting chief immunology br. Nat. Cancer Inst., dir. Nat. Inst. Aging, 1993—. Program coord. US-Japan Coop. Cancer Rsch. Program, 1982—; mem. sci. adv. bd. Cancer Research Inst., 1992—; mem. The Dana Alliance for Brain Initiatives, 1995—. Fellow: AAAS; mem.: Inst. Medicine. Office: Nat Inst on Aging Bldg 31C 31 Center Dr Bethesda MD 20892 Office Phone: 301-496-9265. Office Fax: 301-496-2525. E-mail: hodesr@31.nia.nih.gov.*

HODES, ROBERT BERNARD, lawyer; b. Bklyn., Aug. 25, 1925; s. James and Florence (Cohen) H.; m. Florence R. Rosenberg, Dec. 22, 1946 (div. Nov. 1984); 1 child, Paul; m. Cecilia Mendez, Dec. 18, 1984; children: James, Maria Paz. AB, Dartmouth Coll., 1946; LLB, Harvard U., 1949. Bar: N.Y. Supreme Ct. 1950, U.S. Dist. Ct. (so. dist.) N.Y. 1951, U.S. Tax Ct. 1955, U.S. Claims Ct. 1957, U.S. Ct. Appeals (2d cir.) 1959. Assoc. Willkie Farr & Gallagher, NYC, 1949-56, ptnr., 1956-95, co-chmn., 1982-95, counsel, 1995—. Bd. dirs. Mueller Industries, Inc. Active Beaver Dam Sanctuary, Inc., Nat. Philanthropic Trust. Home: 860 United Nations Plz New York NY 10017-1810 Office: Willkie Farr & Gallagher 787 7th Ave New York NY 10019-6099 Home Phone: 212-759-1657; Office Phone: 212-728-8538. Business E-Mail: rhodes@willkie.com.

HODES, SCOTT, lawyer; b. Chgo., Aug. 14, 1937; s. Barnet and Eleanor (Cramer) H.; m. Maria Bechily, 1982; children— Brian Kenneth, Valery Jane, Anthony Scott. AB, U. Chgo., 1956; JD, U. Mich., 1959; LLM, Northwestern U., 1962. Bar: Ill. 1959, D.C. 1962, N.Y. 1981. Assoc. Arvey, Hodes, Costello & Burman, Chgo., 1959-61, ptnr., 1965-91, Ross & Hardies, Chgo., 1992—2003, Bryan Cave LLP, Chgo., 2004—. Bd. dirs. First Investors Life Ins. Co. NY, Richardson Electronics, Ltd.; dir. State Ill. Savs. and Loan Bd. Author: The Law of Art and Antiques, 1966, What Every Artist and Collector Should Know About the Law, 1974; Assoc. news editor: Fed. Bar News, 1963-70; co-editor: Conf. Mut. Funds, 1966, Legal Rights in the Art and Collectors' World, 1986; Contbr. articles to profl. jours. Chmn. Philippine Exch. Nurses award com., 1966; nat. chmn. Lawbooks USA, 1962-73; chmn. Mut. Funds and Investment Mgmt. Conf., 1966-75; co-chmn. Chgo. World Friendship Day, 1967; mem. Ill. Arts Coun., 1973-75; Committeeman Ill. 9th Dist. Dem. Com., 1970-82; bd. dirs. Michael Reese Hosp. Rsch. Inst., 1965-73, United Cerebral Palsy Chgo., 1976-84; governing bd. Chgo. Symphony Soc., 1978-1999; governing mem. Art Inst. Chgo., 1980—; com. on internat. investment and tech. Dept. State, 1980-83; bd. dirs. Chgo. Neighborhood Theatre Found., 1980-92, Harold Washington Found., 1988-2000; exec. com. Anti Defamation League, 1990-98; chmn. Mayor's Task Force on Neighborhood Land Use, 1986-88; chmn. Navy Pier Devel. Authority, 1988-89; mem. Ill. Atty. Gen. adv. com., 1991-95; spl. counsel Art in Embassies Program, Dept. State, 1992-94; co-chmn. Private Enterprise Rev. and Adv. Bd., Ill., 1992-94; pres. Lawyers Creative Arts, 2000-04; mem. exec. com. Mex. Fine Arts Ctr. Mus., 2003—. Capt. JAGC, AUS, 1962-64. Decorated Army Commendation medal; named one of Chicago's ten outstanding young men Jr. Assn. Commerce and Industry, 1968, Chgo. Artist's award for Support of Visual Arts, 1996, Disting. Svc. award Lawyer's Creative Arts, 1997, also Leavens award, 2006, Civic award Weizmann Inst. Sci., 2005. Mem. FBA. (chmn. coun. financing 1966-71, chmn. younger lawyers div. 1963-64, nat. coun. 1965—, hon. trustee found. 1994—, Disting. Svc. award 1971, 75, 86, Earl Kintner Outstanding Svc. award, 1998), Ill. Bar Assn., Chgo. Bar Assn., Chgo. Bar Found. (dir. 2007—), Chgo. Art Inst. (life), Chgo. Hist. Soc. (life), Judge Adv. Gens. Assn. (life), Masons (32 deg.), Chicagoland C. of C. (dir. 2006—), Standard Club, Mid-Day Club, Econ. Club Chgo., Zeta Beta Tau, Tau Epsilon Rho. Jewish. Home: 1540 N Lake Shore Dr Chicago IL 60610-6684 Office: Bryan Cave 161 N Clark St Ste 4300 Chicago IL 60601-7567 Business E-Mail: scott.hodes@bryancave.com.

HODESS, ARTHUR BART, cardiologist; b. NYC, Jan. 15, 1950; s. Samuel and Dora (Rosenkrantz) H.; m. Carol Yasuna, Aug. 31, 1969 (div. May 1985); children: Joshua David, Jeremy Scott; m. S. Christina Ellsworth, Dec. 23, 1987; children: Jonathan Ellsworth, Jason Dorian, Jordan Gottier. BA, Boston U., 1970; MD, Columbia U., 1974. Intern Hosp. of U. Pa., Phila., 1974-75, resident in medicine, 1975-77, fellow in cardiology, 1977-79; asst. instr. dept. medicine Hosp. U. of Pa., Phila., 1974-79; instr. physiology, dept. animal biology U. Pa., Sch. Veterinary Medicine, Phila., 1977-78; clin. assoc. dept. medicine U. Pa., Phila., 1979-81; attending cardiologist Brandywine Hosp., Coatesville, Pa., 1979—, dir. critical care, 1989—, chief of cardiology, 1990—, chmn. dept. medicine, 1991-95; pres. Brandywine Valley Cardiovascular Assocs., Thorndale, Pa., 1991—. Contbr. articles to profl. jours. V.p. Chestnut Hollow Homeowners Assn., West Chester, Pa., 1990-94, bd. dirs. 1995; bd. dirs. Beth Israel Congregation, Chester County, 1991-96. Fellow Clin. Coun. Cardiology Am. Heart Assn. Fellow: ACP, Am. Soc. Angiology, Am. Coll. Chest Physicians, Am. Coll. Cardiology; mem.: Soc. Cardiovasc. Computed Tomography, Soc. Critical Care Medicine, Cardiac Electrophysiology Soc., Am. Soc. Echocardiography. Office: Brandywine Valley Cardio 3025 Zinn Rd Thorndale PA 19372-1131 Office Phone: 610-384-2211.

HODGE, BOBBY LYNN, mechanical engineer, manufacturing executive; b. Yadkinville, NC, Oct. 14, 1956; s. Robert Henry and Betty Jean (Martin) H.; m. Robin Mayhue Renegar, June 8, 1979; children: Andrew, Adam. AAS with honors, Forsyth Tech. Inst., Winston-Salem, NC, 1976; BS in Engring. Tech., U. NC, Charlotte, 1978. Design engr. Clark/Gravely Corp., Clemmons, NC, 1978-79, project engr., 1979-80; design engr. Ingersoll-Rand, Davidson, NC, 1980-83, devel. engr., 1983-85; sr. applications engr. INA Bearing Co., Ft. Mill, SC, 1985-87, mgr. automotive driveline engring. group, 1987-88, mgr. automotive applications engring., 1988-89, dir. automotive applications engring., 1989-96, dir. automotive engring., 1996-99; v.p. engring./product devel. The Setco Group, Cin., 1999—2002, v.p. engring/quality, 2002—. Internat. spkr. on design and application of rolling element bearings and machine tool spindles. Contbr. articles to profl. jours. Mem. adv. coun. U. NC-Charlotte Coll. Engring. Mem. ASME, SAE, Soc. Mfg. Engrs., Soc. Tribologists and Lubrication Engrs., Am. Soc. Metals. Republican. Baptist. Achievements include 10 patents in field. Avocations: golf, hunting, woodworking. Home: 1518 Jolee Dr Hebron KY 41048-9514 Office: The Setco Group 5880 Hillside Ave Cincinnati OH 45233-1599 Home Phone: 859-689-2642. Personal E-mail: hodge1518@aol.com. Business E-Mail: bhodge@setcousa.com. *One of the most important tasks anyone can undertake is to establish a vision for their life. Without a vision there can not be direction. Without direction, any success or achievement comes merely by accident.*

HODGE, GAMEEL BYRON, surgeon; b. Spartanburg, SC, Sept. 16, 1917; s. Charles B. and Mary (Bargoot) H.; m. Katie Adams, Sept. 22, 1943; children: Susan, Byron, John Adams. BS, Wofford Coll., 1938; MD, Vanderbilt U., 1942, D Pub. Service (hon.), U. SC, 1982; DSc (hon.) Wofford Coll., 2003. Diplomate Am. Bd. Surgery. Intern Duke U. Med. Sch. and Hosp., Durham, NC, 1942-43, asst. resident, 1943-47, chief resident surgeon, 1947-48; attending surgeon Spartanburg Gen. Hosp.; cons. surgeon St. Luke's Hosp., Tryon, NC, 1948-58, Cherokee County (SC) Meml. Hosp., 1948-74; thoracic surgeon Spartanburg County Tb Hosp., 1948-69; chief surgery Mary Black Meml. Hosp., 1969-72; assoc. clin. prof. surgery Med. U. SC, Spartanburg, 1970-2003, ret., 2003. Author Reflections on Building an Institution, 2006; contbr. articles to profl. jours. Chmn. Spartanburg County Commn. for Higher Edn., 1967—; trustee Spartanburg Day Sch., 1958—. With M.C., USAR, 1942-53. Recipient Disting. Svc. award U. SC Ednl. Found., 1991. Fellow Am. Coll. Chest Physicians, Internat. Acad. Proctology, NY Acad. Sci., Am. Fedn. Clin. Rsch., Indsl. Medicine Assn.; mem. Am. Heart Assn., SC Med. Assn., SC Surg. Soc., SC Vascular Surg. Soc., AMA, Spartanburg Med. Soc., Am. Geriatrics Soc., Deryl Hart Surg. Soc., Duke U. Med. Alumni Assn. (past pres.), Spartanburg Area C. of C. (past pres., Neville Holcombe Disting. Service award 1988), Kiwanis (Citizenship of Yr. award 1969), Omicron Delta Kappa, Order of Palmetto, Phi Beta Kappa, Phi Beta Pi. Episcopalian. Clubs: Piedmont, Carolina Country. Home: 2500 Old Knox Rd Spartanburg SC 29302-3427 Personal E-mail: daffodilkatie@msn.com, gbhodge@msn.com.

HODGE, JAMES LEE, German language educator; b. Harrisburg, Pa., Sept. 18, 1935; s. Earl Henry and Catherine Margaret (Ferber) M.; m. Janice Ellen Dunn, June 21, 1958; children: Geoffrey Lee, Stephen Charles. AB, Tufts U., 1957; A.M., Pa. State U., 1960, PhD, 1961. Grad. asst. Pa. State U., 1957-60; instr. German Bowdoin Coll., Brunswick, Maine, 1961-63, asst. prof., 1963-68, assoc. prof., 1968-74, prof., 1974—2004, prof. emeritus, 2004—, George Taylor Files prof. modern langs., 1977, chmn. dept. German, 1974—93, 1999—2002. Mem. IIE Fulbright Screening Com., 1973, 91. Author: Portable German Tutor, 1970; editor: (with Buehne and Pinto) Helen Adolf Festschrift, 1968; editor: (with T. Beebee and S. Cerf) The Speech of Richard von Weizsacker on May 8, 1985; editorial staff German Quar, 1976-83; contbr. articles to profl. jours. and reference works. Cubmaster Pine Tree council Boy Scouts Am., Brunswick, 1974. NDEA grantee, 1966-67; Bowdoin Mellon grantee, 1977, 84 Mem. AAUP, Am. Assn. Tchrs. German, MLA. Independent. Home: 37 Meadowbrook Rd Brunswick ME 04011-3421 Office: Bowdoin Coll Dept German Brunswick ME 04011 E-mail: jhodge@bowdoin.edu.

HODGE, LINDA M., former educational association administrator; m. Bob Hodge; 3 children. Pres. Hawaii State PTA; chair Resource Develop., Bylaws, Tech./Safety, and Membership coms. Nat. PTA, region 7 dir. Alaska, Hawaii, Idaho, Mont., Oreg., Wash., Wyo., v.p. programs, 1999—2001, pres. elect, 2001—03, pres., 2003—05. Former mem. Exec., Budget, Elections, Leadership, and Nominating Coms., IOD Cultural Arts Subcommittee; com. mem. Nat. Rsch. Coun., NAS; nat. adv. bd. mem. Neag Sch. Edn., U. Conn. Recipient Hon. Svc. Award, Calif. PTA, Continuing Svc. Award, Vallejo Sch. Dist. Award. Office: Nat PTA Ste 1300 541 N Fairbanks Ct Chicago IL 60611-3396 also: 1090 Vermont Ave NW, Ste 1200 Washington DC 20005-4905 Office Phone: 312-670-6782, 202-289-6790. Office Fax: 312-670-6783, 202-289-6791.

HODGE, PHILIP GIBSON, JR., mechanical and aerospace engineering educator; b. New Haven, Nov. 9, 1920; s. Philip Gibson and Muriel (Miller) Hodge; m. Thea Drell, Jan. 3, 1943; children: Susan E., Philip T., Elizabeth M. AB, Antioch Coll., Yellow Springs, Ohio, 1943; PhD, Brown U., Providence, 1949. Rsch. asst. Brown U., 1947-49, asso., 1949; asst. prof. math. UCLA, 1949-53; assoc. prof. applied mechanics Poly. Inst. Bklyn., 1953-56, prof., 1956-57; prof. mechanics Ill. Inst. Tech., 1957-71, U. Minn., Mpls., 1971-91, prof. emeritus, 1991—. Russell Severance Springer vis. prof. U. Calif., 1976; vis. prof. emeritus Stanford U., 1993—; sec. U.S. nat. com. Theoretical and Applied Mechanics, 1982-2000. Author: 5 books, the most recent being Limit Analysis of Rotationally Symmetric Plates and Shells, 1963, Continuum Mechanics, 1971; also numerous rsch. articles in profl. jour.; tech. editor Jour. Applied Mechanics, 1971-76. Recipient Disting. Service award Am. Acad. Mechanics, 1984; Karman medal ASCE, 1985. NSF sr. postdoctoral fellow, 1963 Mem. NAE, ASME (hon., Worcester Reed Warner medal 1975, ASME medal 1987, Daniel C. Drucker medal 2000), Internat. Union Theoretical and Applied Mechanics (del. 1982-2000, asst. treas. 1984-92, mem. at large 2000—). Home: 580 Arastradero Rd Apt 701 Palo Alto CA 94306-3948 E-mail: philip@kellys.org.

HODGE, ROBERT JOSEPH, retail executive; b. St. Louis, July 5, 1937; s. Joseph Edward and Alberta Marie (Oehler) H.; m. Carmen Maria Villalobos, Sept. 1, 1960; children: Ralph, Robert, Carmen. BS in Indsl. Relations, St. Louis U., 1959. Meat dept. merchandiser Kroger Co., Cleve., 1972-74, corp. v.p. deli/bakery Cin., 1981-83, v.p. Atlanta div., 1983-85, meat merchandiser St. Louis, 1977-80, v.p. gateway region, 1985-87; v.p. meat ops. Ralph's Grocery Co., Los Angeles, 1974-77; gen. mgr. Super X Drug, Melbourne, Fla., 1980-81; sr. v.p. Dillon Co., Hutchinson, Kans., 1987-89; sr. v.p. merchandising, manufacturing Kroger Co., Cin., 1989-92, pres. Cin./Dayton mktg. area, 1992—. Sgt. U.S. Army, res., 1959-66. Avocations: golf, skiing. Home: 614 Watchcove Ct Cincinnati OH 45230-3777 Office: Kroger Co 150 Tri County Pkwy Cincinnati OH 45246-3246

HODGE, ROGER D., editor; b. Del Rio, Tex., Aug. 12, 1967; m. Deborah A. Hodge; 2 children. Joined Harper's Mag., NYC, 1996, sr. editor, author, Weekly Rev., 2000—04, dep. editor, 2004—06, editor, 2006—. Office: Harper's 11th fl 666 Broadway New York NY 10012 Office Phone: 212-420-5720. Office Fax: 212-228-5889.

HODGE, SHAWNA MARIE, nutritionist, consultant, researcher; b. Oshkosh, Wis., July 1, 1973; d. Robert Thomas and Georgia Faye (Walker) Sutton; m. Sean Paul Hodge, Mar. 15, 1999; children: Marcus William, Caitlin Lynne, Ellen Anne. BS in Exercise Physiology, Concordia U., Mequon, Wis., 1995; MS in Nutritional Studies, U. Wis., Stout, 1997; D in Physiology, Mich. State U., East Lansing, 2001. Cons. Total Health Concepts, East Lansing, Mich., 1997—2001; nutritionist U. Detroit Mercy, 2001—05, Meriks Better Health Clinic, Columbus, Ohio, 2005—07, head nutritionist, 2007—. Rschr. U. Detroit, 2000—05; cons., spkr. in field. Vol. Habitat for Humanity, Ohio, 2005—. Republican. Protestant. Avocations: travel, exercise, photography, backpacking.

HODGE, TIMOTHY, performing company executive, actor; b. Newark, Jan. 11, 1982; s. Romaine Hodge. BA, Garamond Coll., NY, 2004. CEO, COO Musician Artist Agy., Hawthorne, NY, 2002—; CEO, chmn. Hodge Music Group, Beverly Hills, Calif., 2004—07. Mem.: Am. Talent Assn., Nat. Assn. Promotional Mgmt. Office: Musician Artist Agy 306 Memorial Dr Hawthorne NY 10532 Office Phone: 347-307-5857. Personal E-mail: tr0167@yahoo.com. Business E-Mail: musicianartistagency@musician.org.

HODGE, VERNE ANTONIO, judge; b. St. Thomas, VI, Nov. 16, 1933; s. John Wesley Hodge and Idalia Victoria Stout; children: Verne Jr., Bridget, Teresa. BS magna cum laude, Hampton U., 1956; JD cum laude, Howard U., 1969. Bar: VI 1969, D.C. 1969, U.S. Ct. Appeals (3d cir.) 1970, U.S. Supreme Ct. 1973. Internal auditor, internal revenue agt. VI Govt., 1958-61; pub. accountant, comptroller Mannassah Busline, Inc., St. Thomas, 1961-65; bus. mgr., personnel dir. VI Dept. Pub. Works, 1965-66; private practice law VI, 1969-73; atty. gen., 1973-76; chief judge VI Territorial Ct., St. Thomas, 1976-99, ret., 1999; designated justice VI Supreme Ct., St. Thomas, 2007. Past chmn. Eastern region Nat. Assn. Attys. Gen.; mem. VI Indsl. Incentive Bd., 1963-64, VI Bd. Elections, 1964-66. Author: The Need for Constitutional Courts in U.S. Territories, 1968, The Mirror Theory and Its Effects, 1969. Served to 1st lt., inf. U.S. Army, 1956-58. Recipient Am. Jurisprudence awards in state, local and fed. taxation, 1968-69, certificate in advanced income tax law Internal Revenue Service, 1960, award of merit 9th Inf. Div. U.S. Army, 1958 Mem. Am. Judges Assn., Am., Nat., VI bar assns. Democrat. Lutheran. *Nothing is so complicated that it cannot be simplified by hard work.*

HODGEN, MAURICE DENZIL, retired history professor, writer; b. Timaru, New Zealand, Aug. 7, 1929; s. William Arnold and Lindsey Frances (Neill) H.; m. Rhona Brandstater, June 20, 1951; children: Philip

Denzil, Victoria Anne. Student, Avondale Coll., Cooranbong, Australia, 1948-50; MA, Columbia U., 1956, Ed.D., 1958. Asst. prof. La Sierra Coll., Riverside, Calif., 1958-64; lectr. Solusi Coll., Bulawayo, Zimbabwe, 1964-66; dir. tchr. edn. Helderberg Coll., Somerset W., S. Africa, 1966-68; assoc. prof. Sch. Edn., Loma Linda U., Calif., 1968—72, prof., 1972—84, dean Grad. Sch., 1978—87, coop. faculty, 1985—88; devel. officer Claremont (Calif.) Grad. U., 1987-93; mgmt. cons., 1999—. Exec. dir. Cmty. Found. of Riverside County, 1993-99. Served with U.S. Army, 1953-55.

HODGES, ADELE E., career military officer; b. Bridgeport, Conn., 1955; Grad., So. Conn. State Coll., 1977; MBA, M in Military Art and Sci.; M, Strategic Military Studies. Advanced through grades to col. USMC, 2002; with 3d supply battalion Support Activity Supply Sys. Mgmt. Unit, Okinawa, Japan, 1981—83, Marine Forces Pacific Hdqs., Hawaii, 1983—86; ground supply Marine Corps Property Purchasing and Contracting SASSY Mgmt. Officer 4th Marine Aircraft Wing, New Orleans, 1986—90; battalion supply officer Hdqs. Battalion 2d Marine Divisn, 1990; deployed with 2d marine divsn. Operation Dessert Storm, 1991—93; asst. base supply officer Marine Corps Air Ground Combat Ctr., 1993—97; project mgr. combined arms exercise program and enhanced equipment allowance pool Marine Corps Combat Devel. Command, Quantico, Va., 1997—2000; exec. officer brigade svc. support one, comdr. 1st maintenence batallion 1st Force Svce. Support Group, Camp Pendleton, Calif., 2000—02; stationed at NATO Joint Warfare Ctr., Stavanger, Norway, 2003—05; comdr. Camp Lejeune, NC, 2006—. Decorated Meritorious Svc. Medal, Navy Commendation Medal with 3 start, Navy Achievement Medal.

HODGES, ANN, retired television editor, columnist; b. McCamey, Tex., Sept. 7, 1928; d. Ernest Cornelius and Margaret Isabel (Wood) Haynes; m. Cecil Ray Hodges, July 2, 1954 (div. Nov. 1974); children: Craig McNeley, Elizabeth Ann. BJ, U. Tex., 1948. Reporter Houston Chronicle, 1948-51; soc. editor The News, Mexico City, 1951-52, TV editor, columnist, TV critic, 1962—2003; ret., 2003. Mem. adv. bd. U. Miami TV Ctr. for Advancement of Modern Media, 1994—; U.S. juror Banff TV Festival, 1995. Mem.: Houston Press Club (pres. 1967), TV Critics Assn. (founder, exec. bd., v.p., pres.), Critics Consensus (dir. 1965—75). Personal E-mail: ahodges@comcast.net.

HODGES, ANN, actress, singer, dancer; b. Elizabethtown, Ky., June 24; d. Henry Lavely and Margaret Rhodes (Lewis) H.; m. Richard Angleine; 1 child, Michael Christian Angeline; m. Barry C. Tuttle, Sept. 16, 1969 (div. 1972). Cert., registered yoga alliance tchr.; ordained min. Congl. Ch. Practical Theology. Yoga instr., Tampa, St. Petersburg, Safety Harbor, Clearwater, Fla., Under the Live Oak, Casa Bella Vista. Pvt. instr. Yoga, Fla. Appeared in (Broadway shows) No Strings, The Rothchilds, Heathen, (off-Broadway shows) The Boys From Syracuse, There Goes The Old Ballgame, Bella, (TV shows) The Jackie Gleason Show, The Steve Allen Show, The Ed Sullivan Show, Bell Telephone Hour, Ellery Queen, Omnibus, The Vic Damone Show, The Big Record, (TV spls.) Once Upon A Mattress, The G.M. Spectacular, The Esso Spectacular, (motion pictures) The Cardinal, The New Life Style, Oldsmobile, (plays) Applause, The Best Little Whorehouse in Texas, Gypsy,(leading roles in plays) Hello Dolly!, Sugar Babies, Chicago, Can Can, Sweet Charity, Mame, Damn Yankees, See How They Run, Catch Me If You Can., Legends!, I Ought to Be in Pictures, How the Other Half Loves, Pajama Tops, The Last of the Red Hot Lovers, Pal Joey, Cole Porter Reveiw, Gone with the Wind (role of Belle Watling in American Premiere Production), The Greenwich Village Scandals of 1923; also many commls., voice overs and indsls.; performer numerous charities including Am. Cancer Soc., Am. Heart Assn., Handicapped, Abused Wives and Children; star performer Gasparilla Coronation, 1991, guest performer Fla. Orch. at Clearwater Jazz Festival. Yoga instr. Safety Harbor Spa, Don CeSar, Harbour Island Athletic Club, Casa Bella Vista. Named the Queen of Mus. Theatre by the Press, one of Tampa Bay's top achievers. Mem.: Suncoast Yoga Tchrs. Assn. (past pres., bd. dirs.). Avocations: yoga, swimming, horse back riding, piano playing, embroidery.

HODGES, DEWEY HARPER, aerospace engineer, educator; b. Clarksville, Tenn., May 18, 1948; s. Plummer Maxwell Sr. and Etha Maude (Harper) H.; m. Margaret Elin Jones, Aug. 14, 1971; children: Timothy, Jonathan, David, Philip, Benjamin. BS in Aerospace Engring., U. Tenn., 1969; MS in Aero. and Astro. Engring., Stanford U., 1970, PhD in Aero. and Astro. Engring., 1973. Rsch. scientist U.S. Army Aeroflight Dynamics Directorate, Ames Rsch. Ctr., Moffett Field, Calif., 1970-80, sr. rsch. scientist, theoretical group leader, 1980-86; prof. aerospace engring. Ga. Inst. Tech., Atlanta, 1986—. Instr. No. Calif. Bible Coll., San Jose, 1974-86; lectr. Stanford U., 1980-86; guest rsch. scientist DLR Inst. Structural Mechanics, Braunschweig, Fed. Republic of Germany, 1984. Author: Nonlinear Composite Beam Theory, 2006; co-author (with G. Alvin Pierce): Introduction to Structural Dynamics and Aeroelasticity, 2002; co-author: (with George J. Simitses) Fundamentals of Structural Stability, 2006; contbr. 275 articles to profl. jours. and conf. procs., chapters to books. Elder Christian Comty. Ch., San Jose, 1980-86, Mt. Paran Ch., Atlanta, 1992-94, Chalcedon Presbyn. Ch., Cumming, Ga., 2003-. Capt. US Army, 1973—77. Fellow AIAA, Am. Helicopter Soc., Am. Acad. Mechanics; mem. ASME, Tau Beta Pi, Pi Tau Sigma. Republican. Presbyterian. Achievements include patents for hingeless helicopter rotor with improved stability; real-time missile guidance system. Avocations: piano, singing, squash, theology. Home: 1172 Branch Water Ct Atlanta GA 30338-4026 Office: Ga Inst Tech Sch Aerospace Engring Atlanta GA 30332-0150 Office Phone: 404-894-8201. Business E-Mail: dhodges@gatech.edu. *We know about the wise men who sought the Lord Jesus at His birth. I believe that wise men still seek Him and that His promise of abundant life to those who follow Him is still being fulfilled today.*

HODGES, HEATHER M., ambassador; BA, Coll. St. Catherine; MA, NYU. Joined Fgn. Svc., US Dept. State, 1980; chief non-immigrant visa sect. US Embassy, Caracas, Venezuela, dep. chief of consular sect. Guatemala, 1983—85, Peru desk officer Washington, 1985—87, prin. officer US Consulate Bilbao, Spain, 1989—91, dep. dir. Office of Cuban Affairs Washington, 1991—93, dep. chief of mission Managua, Nicaragua, 1993—96, Lima, Peru, 1997—2000, Madrid, 2000—03; US amb. to Moldova US Dept. State, Chisinau, 2003—06; counsel Senate Sub-com. on Immigration and Refugee Affairs US Congress, 1987—89.

HODGES, JOSEPH GILLULY, JR., lawyer; b. Denver, Dec. 7, 1942; s. Joseph Gilluly Sr. and Elaine (Chanute) H.; m. Jean Todd Creamer, Aug. 7, 1971; children: Ashley E., Wendy C., Elaine V. BA, Lake Forest Coll., 1965; JD, U. Colo., 1968. Bar: Colo. 1968, U.S. Dist. Ct. Colo. 1969, U.S. Ct. Mil. Appeals 1969. Assoc. Hodges, Kerwin, Otten & Weeks, Denver, 1969-73, Davis, Graham & Stubbs, Denver, 1973-76, ptnr., 1976-86; pvt. practice, Denver, 1986—. Bd. dirs. Arapahoe Colo. Nat. Bank, Littleton, Colo., 1971-90, Cherry Creek Improvement Assn., Denver, 1979-91; bd. trustees Lake Forest (Ill.) Coll., 1977-87; pres. Colo. Arlberg Club, Winter Park, Colo., 1984-85; treas. St. Johns Episcopal Cathedral, Denver, 1981-96; chmn. bd. Spalding Cmty. Found., 1995—. Capt. USAR, 1969-74. Named Best Lawyers in Am., Woodward/White, N.Y.C., 1994-95. Fellow Am. Coll. Trust and Estate Counsel (state chmn. 1991-96); mem. ABA (chmn. probate divsn. G-2 Tech. 1990-95, coun. mem. real property, probate and trust law sect. 1996—), Am. Judicature Soc., Colo. Bar Assn. (chair probate coun. 1981-82), Denver Bar Assn., Denver Estate Planning Coun., Colo. Planned Giving Roundtable (bd. 1991-94), Rotary Club Denver, Kappa Sigma, Phi Alpha Delta. Republican. Avocations: skiing, hiking, fishing, photography, computers. Office: 3300 E 1st Ave Ste 600 Denver CO 80206-5809 Home: 2552 E Alameda Ave Unit 5 Denver CO 80209-3324

HODGES, JOT HOLIVER, JR., retired lawyer, corporate financial executive; b. Archer City, Tex., Nov. 16, 1932; s. Jot Holiver and Lola Mae (Hurd) H.; m. Virginia Cordray Pardue, June 11, 1955; children: Deborah, Jot, Darlene. BS, BBA, Sam Houston State U., 1954; JD, U. Tex., 1957. Bar: Tex. 1958, U.S. Dist. Ct. (so. dist.) Tex. 1958, U.S. Ct. Appeals (5th cir.) 1958. Asst. atty. gen. State of Tex., Austin, 1958—60; chmn. bd. Presidio Devel. Corp., Missouri City, Tex., 1971. Organizer, founder 3 banks, several corps. and ltd. partnerships; residential and comml. real estate developer. Contbr. articles to profl. jours. Capt. US Army. Mem.: Quail Valley Country Club, Houston Club. Home: 3527 Thunderbird St Missouri City TX 77459-2445

HODGES, MARLANE FAIRLEIGH, retired management educator; b. Three Rivers, Mich., Feb. 28, 1939; d. Ronald Edward and Evelyn May (Roth) Paxson; m. James Parkinson Fairleigh, June 25, 1960 (dec.); children: William Paxson, Karen Hofferber; m. Bob Shiver Hodges, Sept. 17, 2006. MusB, U. Mich., 1960; MBA, Jacksonville State U., 1986. Cert. econ. devel. fin. profl. Nat. Devel. Coun., 1989. Mem. adj. faculty Providence Coll., 1976-80, R.I. Coll., Providence, 1978-80; grad. asst. news bur. and info. ctr. Jacksonville (Ala.) State U., 1983-84, grad. asst. Coll. Commerce, 1984-85; bus. cons. Jacksonville State U. Small Bus. Devel. Ctr., 1985-96. Presenter in field. Contbr. articles to profl. jours.; soprano soloist (songs) Coll. Music Soc. Internat. Conf., Berlin, Germany, 1995, Vienna, Austria, 1997, (chamber music recitals) Auburn U., Jacksonville State U., 1998, Gadsden, Ala., 2001, lectr.-recitalist (songs) U. Ala., Tuscaloosa, 1997, U. Ctrl. Fla., Orlando, 1999, Jacksonville State U., 1999, State U. West Ga., 1998, Valdosta State U., 2001, U. South Fla., Tampa, 2003, recitalist (chamber music) Colonial Dames Am., Gadsden, Ala., 2001, Gadsden Music Club, 2001. Chair Jacksonville State U. campus United Way Calhoun County, 1986-87. Mem. Coll. Music Soc., Sigma Beta Delta. Avocations: vocal performing, water-skiing, swimming, hiking. Home: 13116 Janda Rd Seneca SC 29672

HODGES, MICHELE, chamber of commerce executive; b. 1967; 2 children. Pres. Troy Chamber of Commerce, Oakland Chamber Network, Mich. Named one of 40 Under 40, Crain's Detroit Bus., 2006. Office: Troy Chamber of Commerce 4555 Investment Dr 3rd Fl Ste 300 Troy MI 48098 Office Phone: 248-641-0197.

HODGES, RICHARD DEAN, instrument and electrical technician; b. Overton, Tex., Jan. 3, 1960; s. Donald Gene and Patricia Ann Hodges; m. Lisa Inez Ramos, Dec. 31, 2000; children: Richard Dean Jr., Jacob Quincy, Sara Lynn. AAS, Coll. Mainland, Texas City, Tex., 1999; BS, Hamilton U., 2004. Cert. journeyman, instrument/elec. technician 1983; indsl. firefighter, substation maintenance technician, marine firefighter. Flight ops. coord. U.S. Army, Ft. Hood, Tex., 1988—92; process technician Valero Refining, Texas City, Tex., 1993—95, maintenance planner, 1995—98, instrument, elec. technician, 1998—2002; utilities technician U. Tex. Med. Br., Galveston, 2002—04; maintenance supr. Tex. Dept. Criminal Justice, Darrington Maximum Security Unit, Rosharon, 2004—05; instrument and elec. technician Monsanto Electronic Material Corp., Pasadena, Tex., 2005—. Specialist US Army, 1988—92, Iraq. Decorated Army Commendation medal with Oak Leaf Cluster US Army, Army Achievement medal with 3 Oak Leaf Clusters, Good Conduct medal, Nat. Def. Svc. medal, Kuwait Liberation medal, Southwest Asia Svc. medal with 2 Bronze Stars, Army Svc. ribbon, Enlisted Air Crew badge, Driver badge with Bar, Expert badge Rifle, Expert badge Grenade, Lifesaver award, Combat Lifesaver award, Desert Storm; recipient Top Gun Pistol, Tex. Dept. Criminal Justice, Top Gun Rifle, Dr. Beto Academic Excellence award. Mem.: Internat. Brotherhood Elec. Workers Local 527, Intertel, Am. Mensa. Independent. Lutheran. Avocations: martial arts, firearms, camping, hiking, movies. Home and Office: 1925 26th Ave N Texas City TX 77590 Office Phone: 409-771-9077. E-mail: lihodges@utmb.edu.

HODGES, ROBERT H., JR., federal judge; b. Columbia, SC, Sept. 11, 1944; BS, U. SC, 1966, JD, 1969. Legis. aide to Senator Strom Thurmond US Senate, Washington, 1969-71; legis. aide to Congressman Floyd Spence US Ho. Reps, Washington, 1971-77; v.p., gen. counsel First Nat. Bank of SC, Columbia, 1977-85; exec. v.p., gen. counsel SC Bankers Assn., Columbia, 1985-86; with Quinn, Arndt & Manning, Columbia, 1986-90; judge US Ct. Fed. Claims, Washington, 1990—, now sr. judge. With Air Force Guard USAF Guard Res., 1963-69. Mem. ABA, SC Bar, So. Assn. Bank Counsel, Richland County Bar Assn. Office: US Ct Fed Claims 717 Madison Pl NW Rm 605 Washington DC 20439-0002*

HODGES, VERNON WRAY, mechanical engineer; b. Roanoke, Va., Dec. 26, 1929; s. Charlie Wayne and Kathleen Mae (Williams) Hodges; m. Lorraine Patricia Smart, Apr. 1, 1955 (div. 1966); children: Vernon Wray Jr.(dec.) , Gregory Elmer, Michelle Lynn; m. Linda Lou Wall, Feb. 3, 1967 (dec. Apr. 1997); children: Kenneth Wray, Kelly Diane; m. Emily Louise Tinsley, Aug. 19, 2000; children: John Keith Tinsley, Karen Denise Tinsley. BS in Mech. Engring., Va. Poly. Inst. and State U., Blacksburg, 1951; MS in Systems Mgmt., U. So. Calif., LA, 1978. Registered profl. engr., Kans., Wash., Calif. Commd. 2d lt. USAF, 1951, advanced through grades to major, 1964, ret., 1965; flight test engr. Boeing Co., Wichita, Kans., 1966-71, sr. engr. Seattle, 1971-76; systems test engr. Rockwell Internat., Edwards AFB, Calif., 1976-77, sr. engr. El Segundo, Calif., 1981—84, Palmdale, Calif., 1984—90, Hughes Helicopters, Inc., Culver City, Calif., 1977-81, Computer Scis. Corp., Edwards AFB, 1990-93. Comml. pilot, 1953—; asst. prof. air sci. Boston U., 1958—61. Active Rep. Party, Sacramento, 1977—, Rep. Nat. Com., Washington, 1977—; elder, deacon Presbyn. Ch. USA, Lancaster, 1981—. Recipient Letters of Commendation, USAF. Mem. ASME, NSPE (sec. 1972-75), Air Force Assn., Masons (50 yr. mem.), Shriners, Elks. Home: 2915 W Ave J-4 Lancaster CA 93536 E-mail: vwhodges0819@verizon.net.

HODGES, WILLIAM TERRELL, federal judge; b. Lake Wales, Fla., Apr. 28, 1934; s. Haywood and Clara Lucy (Murphy) H.; m. Peggy Jean Woods, June 8, 1958; children: Judson, Daniel, Clay. BSBA, U. Fla., 1956, JD, 1958, LLD (hon.). Bar: Fla. 1959. Mem. firm Macfarlane, Ferguson, Allison & Kelly, Tampa, 1958-71; instr. bus. law U. South Fla., Tampa, 1961-66; judge US Dist. Ct. (mid. dist.) Fla., Tampa, 1971—82, 1989—99, chief judge, 1982—89, sr. judge, 1999—. Mem. com. on ops. jury system Jud. Conf., 1982-87, cir. coun., 11th cir., 1981-86; mem., adv. com. on criminal rules procedure and evidence Jud. Conf., 1987-93, chmn., 1990-93; ad hoc com. on habeas corpus reform; chmn., bench book com. Fed. Jud. Ctr., 1987-93; chmn., Ad Hoc Com. of the Jud. Conf. to study relations within the Fed. Jud. Ctr., 1997-98; chmn., US Jud. Panel on Multidistrict Litig., 2000-07. Exec. editor, U. Fla. Law Rev., 1957-58. Mem. Am., Tampa-Hillsborough County bar assns., Fla. Bar (chmn. grievance com. 1967-70, chmn. uniform comml. code com. 1970-71), Dist. Judges Assn. 5th Circuit (co-chmn. com. on pattern jury instrn. 1977-81), Dist. Judges Assn. 11th Circuit (chmn. jury instrns. com. 1982— , pres. 1981-82) Am. Judicature Soc. Office: US Dist Ct 207 NW 2nd St Rm 337 Ocala FL 34475-6666*

HODGESS, ERIN MARIE, statistics educator; b. Pitts., Nov. 12, 1960; d. Edwin E. and Justine J. (Plazak) H. BS in Econs., U. Dayton, 1981; MA in Econs., U. Pitts., 1987; MS in Stats., Temple U., 1989, PhD in Stats., 1995. Econ. rsch. analyst Mellon Bank, NA, Pitts., 1981-85; programmer Techalloy Co., Inc., Rahns, Pa., 1985-86; programmer analyst The Linpro Co., Berwyn, Pa., 1986-87, Jones Apparel Group, Bristol, Pa., 1987-88; programming cons. various cos., Phila., 1988-89; teaching asst. Temple U., Phila., 1990-92, adj. instr., 1992-94, group leader grad. asst. tng. workshop, 1992; asst. prof. U. Houston-Downtown, 1994—2000, assoc. prof., 2000—. Spkr. Temple U.-Rutgers U. Stats. Day, Brunswick, N.J., 1988; presenter Statis. Sci. Conf., Rider U. Lawrenceville, N.J., 1995. Contbr. articles to profl. jours., including Jour. Statis. Sci., Linear Algebra and Its Applications. Fellow Temple U., 1988-90, grantee, 1994. Mem. Am. Statis. Assn. (presenter winter meeting Raleigh, N.C. 1995), Soc. Indsl. and Applied Math., Inst. Math. Stats. (presenter 4th matrix workshop McGill U., Montreal Que., Can. 1995), Intertel Internat., Mensa. Democrat. Roman Catholic. Avocations: golf, swimming, cycling. Office: U Houston-Downtown One Main St Houston TX 77002 Home: Apt 279 2475 Underwood St Houston TX 77030-3535 Home Phone: 713-666-8527; Office Phone: 713-226-5242. Business E-Mail: hodgess@uhd.edu.

HODGMAN, DAVID RENWICK, lawyer; b. Boston, Sept. 22, 1947; s. Donald Renwick and Naomi (Meyer) H.; m. Liane Mary Blum, July 23, 1977; children: Daniel, Thomas, Jessica. BA, Grinnell Coll., 1969; JD, Yale U., 1974. Bar: Ill. 1974, US Tax Ct. 1981, US Dist. Ct. (no. dist. Ill.) 1975, US Ct. Appeals (7th cir.) 1987. Assoc. D'Ancona & Pflaum, Chgo., 1974-79, Schiff, Hardin & Waite, Chgo., 1979-82, ptnr., 1992; ptnr., mem. exec. com. Schiff Hardin, LLP, Chgo. Contbr. articles to profl. law jours. Named a Leading Lawyer, Ill. Leading Lawyer Network; named an Ill. Super Lawyer; named one of Top 100 Attys., Worth mag., 2006, Best Lawyers In Am. Fellow Am. Coll. Trust & Estate Counsel; mem. ABA, Ill. Bar Assn., Chgo. Bar Assn. (chair probate practice com. 1990-91), Chgo. Estate Planning Coun. Avocations: sports, family and minor home repairs. Office: Schiff Hardin 6600 Sears Tower Chicago IL 60606-6473 Office Phone: 312-258-5500. Office Fax: 312-258-5600. E-mail: dhodgman@schiffhardin.com.*

HODGSON, ERNEST, toxicologist, educator; b. Durham, Eng., July 26, 1932; arrived in U.S., 1955; s. Ernest Victor and Emily (Moses) Hodgson; m. Mary Kathleen Devlin, Dec. 21, 1957 (dec.); children: Mary Elizabeth, Audrey Catherine, Patricia Emily Devlin, Ernest Victor Felix. BSc with honors, Kings Coll. U., Durham, Eng., 1955; PhD, Oreg. State U., 1959. Rsch. fellow Oreg. State U., Corvallis, 1955-59, U. Wis., Madison, 1959-61; asst. prof. N.C. State U., Raleigh, 1961-63, assoc. prof., 1963-65, prof. toxicology, 1965—, William Neal Reynolds prof., 1977—, chmn. toxicology dept., 1982-97, Disting. Alumni Rsch. prof., 1987-90. Mem. adv. panel U.S. EPA, Washington, 1982—85; mem. toxicology study sect. NIH, Washington, 1985—89; mem. study sect. NIEHS, 1992—96, chmn., 1994—96; pres. Toxicology Comm., Raleigh, 1982—; vis. scientist U. Wash., Seattle, 1975. Author, editor: Introduction to Biochemical Toxicology, 1980, 3d edit., 2000, Modern Toxicology, 1987, 3d edit., 2004, Dictionary of Toxicology; editor: Revs. Biochemical Toxicology, 1979—, Revs. Environ. Toxicology, 1984—, Jour. Biochemical and Molecular Toxicology; mem. edit. bd. Chemico-Biol. Interactions; contbr. articles to profl. jours. Chmn. policy rev. com. Gov.'s Waste Mgmt. Bd., Raleigh, 1984. Grantee, NIH, 1962—, U.S. Army, 2000—. Mem.: AAAS, Internat. Soc. Study Xenobiotics (mem. coun. 1986—89, sec.-elect 1990—92, sec. 1992—94, pres.-elect 1996—97, pres. 1998—99, Disting. Svc. award 2004), Am. Chem. Soc. (Sterling Hendricks award USDA 1997, Burdick and Jackson Internat. award in pesticide chemistry), Am. Soc. Pharmacology (mem. drug metabolism com. 1981—84), Soc. Toxicology (pres. N.C. chpt. 1984—85, mem. edn. com. 1984—, pres. mechanisms sect. 1991—92, Edn. award 1984, Merit award 1994), Sigma Xi (chpt. pres. 1974). Democrat. Avocations: history, writing, travel. Office: NC State U Dept Toxicology PO Box 7633 Raleigh NC 27695-0001 Office Phone: 919-515-5295. Business E-Mail: ernest_hodgson@ncsu.edu.

HODGSON, JOSEPH, education educator; b. Houston, Tex., Aug. 18, 1941; s. Joseph Hodgson, Jr. and Frances R. Hodgson; m. Endang T. Triwati, Nov. 9, 1992. MA, Colgate U., Hamilton, NY, 1965. Cert. in edn. Pa. Dept. Edn., 1981. Sales mgr. Homestar Industries, Newtown Square, Pa., 1995—98; adj. faculty Bucks County C.C., Newtown, Pa., 2004—. Interpreter Nat. Constn. Ctr., Phila., 2006—07. Mem. soccer rules com. Nat. HS Activities Assn., Kans. City, Mo., 1976—81; pres. NC Soccer Assn., Chapel Hill, 1978—80. Named Nat. So. Soccer Coach of Yr., Nat. HS Athletic Coaches Assn., 1976, 1980, Nat. So. Soccer Coach of Yr., Nat. Soccer Coaches Assn. Am., 1979; fellow, U. NC, Chapel Hill, 1970—72. Mem.: Pa. Edn. Assn. Home Phone: 213-760-2510.

HODGSON, PAUL EDMUND, surgeon, department chairman; b. Milw., Dec. 14, 1921; s. Howard Edmund and Ethel Marie (Niemi) H.; m. Barbara Jean Osborne, Apr. 22, 1945; children: Ann, Paul. BS summa cum laude, Beloit Coll., 1943; MD cum laude, U. Mich., 1945. Diplomate: Am. Bd. Surgery. Intern U. Mich. Hosp., 1945-46, resident in surgery, 1948-52; mem. faculty dept. surgery U. Mich., 1952-62, assoc. prof., 1956-62; prof. surgery U. Nebr. Coll. Medicine, Omaha, 1962-88, prof. emeritus, 1988—, asst. dean for curriculum, 1966-72, chmn. dept. surgery, 1972-84. Trustee Beloit Coll., 1977-80 Served to capt. M.C. U.S. Army, 1946-48. Mem. A.C.S., Frederick A. Coller Surg. Soc., Soc. Univ. Surgeons, Central Surg. Assn., Soc. Surgery Alimentary Tract, Am. Assn. Surgery Trauma, Western Surg. Assn., Am. Surg. Assn. Presbyterian. Office: Dept Surgery Med Ctr 983280 Nebraska Medical Center Omaha NE 68198-3280

HODGSON, W(ALTER) JOHN (BARRY HODGSON), surgeon; b. Middlesborough, Eng., Sept. 17, 1939; came to U.S., 1975; s. Walter Aggett and Constance Lillian (Nelson) H.; m. Jean C. Morgan, Apr. 20, 1967; children: Sean, Russell, Miranda. MB, BS, Charing Cross Med. Sch., London, 1964; M of Surgery, London U., 1976. Rotating intern, resident London U., 1964-75; surgeon Bronx (NY) VA Med. Ctr., 1975-78, asst. chief surg. svc., 1977-82; pvt. practice specializing in surgery Mt. Sinai Hosp., NYC, 1978-81; chief gastrointestinal surgery Westchester Med. Ctr., Valhalla, NY, 1981-94; dept. surg. Montefiore Med. Ctr. and Einstein Hosp., Bronx, 1997—; prof. surgery NY Med. Coll., Valhalla, 1987-98, course organizer for laparoscopic surgery, 1990-92, prof. cell biology and anatomy, 1993—; clin. prof. surgery NYU, 1995—; prof. surgery Albert Einstein Coll. Medicine, 1998—. Contbr. articles to profl. jours.; editor: Liver Tumors: Multidisciplinary Management, 1987; inventor cavitron surg. technique for livor tumor surgery. Organizer, coach Larchmont (NY) Jr. Soccer League, 1977; mem. Larchmont Rep. Com., 1985. Cavitron Co. grantee, 1978, Cavitron Lasersonics grantee, 1987, Ethicon grantee, 1999. Fellow ACS, Am. Coll. Gastroenterology; mem. NY Surg. Soc. for Acad. Surgery, Am. Assn. Clin. Anatomists, Am. Soc. Colon & Rectal Surgery, Soc. Am. Gastroendoscopic Surgery, Larchmont Yacht Club. Episcopalian. Avocations: sailing, hill walking, skiing. Office: Montefiore Med Park Dept Surgery 1575 Blondell Ave Dept Surgery Bronx NY 10461-2660 Office Phone: 718-405-8239. E-mail: wjbhodgson@optonline.net.

HODIS, HOWARD NEIL, medical educator; b. LA, Jan. 21, 1958; BS, U. So. Calif., LA, 1980, MD, 1984. Intern, internal medicine LA County/U. So. Calif. Med. Ctr., 1984—85, resident, internal medicine, 1985—87, chief resident, 1987—88; fellow U. So. Calif. Sch. Medicine, 1988—90; asst. prof. U. So. Calif., Keck Sch. Medicine, LA, 1990-96, asst. prof. molecular pharmacology and toxicology, 1996, assoc. prof. medicine and preventive medicine, 1996, prof. medicine and preventative medicine, prof. molecular pharmacology and toxicology, sch. pharmacy, Henry J. Bauer and Dorothy Bauer Rawlins prof. cardiology, 2004—, dir., atherosclerosis rsch. unit. Office: U So Calif Divsn Cardiology 2250 Alcazar St CSC 132 9067 Los Angeles CA 90033-1004 Office Phone: 323-442-1478. Office Fax: 323-442-2685. Business E-Mail: athero@usc.edu.*

HODKINSON, SYDNEY PHILLIP, composer, educator, musician, conductor; b. Winnipeg, Man., Can., Jan. 17, 1934; s. Ernest and Irene (Pilgrim) H.; m. Elizabeth Jane Deischer, July 22, 1955; children: Mark, Scott, Grant. MusB, U. Rochester, 1957, MusM, 1958; D of Mus. Arts, U. Mich., 1968. Mem. faculty U. Va., 1958-63, Ohio U., Athens, 1963-66, U. Mich., Ann Arbor, 1968-73; prof. composition, chair conducting and ensembles Eastman Sch. Music, Rochester, NY, 1973—99. Artist-in-residence, Mpls.-St.Paul, 1970-72; Meadows chair composition So. Meth. U., Dallas, 1984-86; vis. prof. composition U. Western Ont., London, Can., 1990, Aspen Music Festival, 1998—, Ind. U., 2002, Duke U., 2003; Almand chair composition Stetson U., 2004—. Composer numerous works for brass, woodwinds, strings and percussion, 1954—, also for orch., chorus, stage, opera, wind and chamber ensembles; artist various recs. Guggenheim fellow, 1978-79; grantee U. Va., 1961, Ohio U., 1964, Can. Coun., 1966, 69, 77-78, Danforth Found., 1966-68, U. Mich., 1969, 70-73, Ford Found., 1976, Nat. Endowment for Arts, 1975-76, 78, 83-84, 90-91, Martha Baird Rockefeller Found., 1976. Mem. Am. Inst. Arts and Letters, Broadcast Music Inc., Am. Composers Alliance, Am. Music Ctr., Phi Mu Alpha Sinfonia. Home: 2589 John Anderson Dr Ormond Beach FL 32176-2417 Home Phone: 386-441-1719; Office Phone: 386-822-8988. E-mail: shodkinson@cfl.rr.com.

HODNIK, DAVID F., retail company executive; b. 1947; Grad., Western Ill. U., 1970. Sr. auditor Paul Pettengill & Co., 1969-72; with Ace Hardware Corp., Hinsdale, Ill., 1972—, acct., 1972-74, mgr. acctg., 1974-76, controller, 1976-80, v.p., treas., 1980-82; v.p. fin., treas. ACE Hardware Corp., Oak Brook, Ill., 1982-88, sr. v.p., 1988-90, exec. v.p., 1990-93, exec. v.p., COO, 1993-95, pres., COO, 1995-96, pres., CEO, 1996—. Office: ACE Hardware Corp 2200 Kensington Ct Oak Brook IL 60523-2100 E-mail: hodnik@acehardware.com.

HODOSH, RICHARD M., neurosurgeon; b. Providence, 1946; BS, Brown U.; MD, U. Cin. Diplomate Am. Bd. Neurol. Surgery. Intern Parkland Meml. Hosp.-U. Tex. Health Scis. Ctr., Dallas, 1972—73; resident in neurol. surgery U. Tex. Health Scis. Ctr., Dallas, 1973—78; fellow in neurol. radiology Nat. Hosp. Neurol. Diseases, Queen Sq., London, 1975; fellow in cerebrovascular surgery Kantonsspital, U. Zurich, Switzerland; attending physician Overlook Hosp., Summit, 1980—, Morristown (N.J.) Meml. Hosp., 1980—; founding med. dir. Atlantic Health Sys. Neuroscience Ctr., Overlook Hosp., Summit, NJ; dir., cerebrovascular surgery Atlantic Health Sys., Summit. Dir. neuroscis. Atlantic Health Sys., Summit; clin. prof. neurosurgery U. Medicine and Dentistry N.J. Med. Sch., Newark. Named one of Top Drs. in N.Y. Metro Area, Castle Connolly, 2003—07, Top Drs., N.J. Monthly Mag., 2004—07; recipient, N.Y. Mag., 2004—07. Fellow: ACS; mem.: Am. Schizophrenia Assn., Am. Heart Assn. (former pres. Heritage Affiliate, mem. adv. bd., pres. NYC chpt. 2007—), Acoustic Neuroma Assn. Office: Atlantic Brain and Spine Inst 99 Beauvoir Ave Summit NJ 07901 Office Phone: 908-522-4979. Office Fax: 908-522-5377. E-mail: rhodosh@heart.org.

HODOUS, ROBERT POWER, lawyer; b. Zanesville, Ohio, July 29, 1945; s. Robert Frank and Nancy Aurelia (Power) H.; m. Susan Cottrell Birkhead, Feb. 1, 1969; children: Robert Everett, Shannon Alycia. BA, Miami U., Oxford, Ohio, 1967; JD, U. Va., Charlottesville, 1970. Bar: Va. 1970. Assoc. firm McGuire, Woods & Battle, Charlottesville, 1970-71; asst. trust officer Nat. Bank & Trust Co., Charlottesville, 1971-72, trust officer, 1972-75, sec., 1975-79, Jefferson Bankshares, Inc. (formerly NB Corp.), Charlottesville, 1979-91, v.p., sec., 1985-91, sr. v.p., sec., 1987-91; asst. to pres. Jefferson Nat. Bank, Charlottesville, 1987-91; pvt. practice law Charlottesville, 1991-92; mem. firm Payne & Hodous, L.L.P., Charlottesville, 1992—. Author: Let's Really Change Taxes, 1998. Chmn. profl. div. Thomas Jefferson Area United Way, 1973, vice-chmn., 1978-79, campaign chmn., 1979-80, v.p. planning, 1981, pres., 1983; bd. dirs. Central Va. chpt. ARC, 1972-78, treas., 1972-75, chmn., 1975-77; commr. Charlottesville Redevel. and Housing Authority, 1974-78; mem. Region X Cmty. Mental Health and Retardation Svcs. Bd., 1973-79, chmn., 1974-76, mem. exec. com., 1976-78; v.p. Soccer Orgn. of Charlottesville-Albemarle, 1985-86, pres., 1986-88; co-pres. Greenbier Sch. PTA, 1985-86; chmn. recreation precinct Charlottesville City Dem. Com., 1971, Rep. com., 1992—; chmn. City Rep. Com., 2000-06; bd. dirs. Charlottesville-Albemarle Cmty. Found., 1987-2000, chmn. devel. com., 1991-93, mem. exec. and fin. coms., 1991-2000, chmn. fin. com., 1997-2000; bd. dirs. Free Enterprise Forum, 2002-. Mem.: Charlottesville C. of C. (govt. affairs com. 1996—, co-chair 2002—04), Computer Law Assn., Va. Bankers Assn. (com. drafted Va. Trust Subs. Act 1973, trust com. 1974—77, legal affairs com. 1986—91, large bank legis. coord. 1987—91), Va. State Bar, Charlottesville-Albemarle Bar Assn., Va. Bar Assn., Fairview Club (Charlottesville) (pres. 1974—75). Roman Catholic. Home: 1309 Lester Dr Charlottesville VA 22901-3143 Office: 412 E Jefferson St Charlottesville VA 22902-5109 *To me success is indicated by feelings of personal peace and satisfaction, not by external possessions. My goals are to do my best in contributing to the success of endeavors in which I become involved and to remember that the people involved in activities are the most important part of the activities. I feel my family is my most important endeavor. I hope never to become so involved in activities that I cannot enjoy my family, my surroundings and people I meet, or that I cannot spend the time necessary to do well those activities in which I am involved.*

HODSOLL, FRANCIS SAMUEL MONAISE, government official; b. LA, May 1, 1938; s. Frank and Adelaide (Monaise) H.; m. Margaret Mimi McEwen, Aug. 18, 1963; children— Lisa-Monaise, Francis Hamill McEwen BA, Yale U., 1959; MA, LLB, Cambridge U., 1963; JD, Stanford U., 1964; Fgn. Svcs. econ. course, Washington, 1972; DFA (hon.), Pratt Inst., 1983, U. Mass., 1986. Assoc. Sullivan & Cromwell, NYC, 1965-66; fgn. service officer Adminstrv. Office Am. embassy, Belgium, 1966-68; asst. polit. advisor SHAPE, Belgium, 1968-69; controlling dir. Warner, Barnes & Co., Manila, 1964-71; oceans policy officer State Dept., Washington, 1969-71; spl. asst. chmn. Council on Environ. Quality, Washington, 1972-73; spl. asst. adminstr. EPA, Washington, 1973-74; dir. energy conservation div. Commerce Dept., Washington, 1974, staff dir. cabinet work edn. task force, 1974, exec. asst. to undersec., 1974-76, dept. asst. sec. commerce for energy and strategic resources, 1976-77; dir. Office of Law of Sea Negotiation State Dept., Washington, 1977, dep. U.S. spl. rep. for nonproliferation, 1978-80; mem. White House transition team Exec. Office Pres., Washington, 1980-81; dep. asst. to Pres. and dep. to chief of staff White House, Washington, 1981; chmn. Nat. Endowment for Arts, Washington, 1981-89; exec. assoc. dir., CFO U.S. Govt. Office Mgmt. and Budget, Exec. Office of Pres., Washington, 1989-91; dep. dir. for mgmt. Office Mgmt. and Budget, Exec. Office of Pres., Washington, 1991-93. Chair, bd. dirs. Ctr. for Arts & Culture, Washington, 2001—06; sr. cons. Logistics Mgmt. Inst., 2001—, Gene Rouleau & Assocs., 2002—03; co-chmn. Sally Mae Edn. Svcs. Coun., 1995—96, Am. Assembly Arts and the Pub. Purpose, 1996—97; co-chair, CEO Southwest Colo. Data Ctr., 1994—97; CEAR reviewer Assn. Govt. Accts., 2003—; mem. performance consortium oversight com. Nat. Acad. Pub. Adminstrn., 2003—05; cons. in field; mem. U.S. Nat. Commn. for UNESCO, 2004—, vice coord. culture com., chair world heritage sub-com., 2005—; mem. GAO Panel Inspectors Gen., 2006—, Preserve Am. Summit Global Preservation Cmty. Panel; prodr. pres.'s com. on arts and humanities Symposium on Film, TV, Digital Media and Popular Culture, 2006; evaluator AFI project 20/20 Film Exchange, 2006—. Chmn. bd., commissioners Ouray County, 2000—01; vice chair Nat. Assn. Counties Geospatial Data com., 1998—99; review com. New Century Colo., 1999—2000, com. mem., 1999—2000; mem. Nat. Assn. Counties Rural Leadership Caucus and Chair Rural Telecom. Task Force, 1999—2001; vice chair steering com. Nat. Assn. Counties Telecom and Tech., 2000—01; co. chmn. Am. Assembly Arts, Tech. and Intellectual Property, 1999—2002; chmn. bd. dirs. Ctr. for Arts and Culture, 2001—05; prin. coun. Excellence in Govt., 1993—; chmn. Ouray County (Colo.) Rep. com., 1995—96; commr. Ouray County, 1997—2001; mem. Gen. Govt. Transition Team Colo. Gov. elect Bill Owens, 1998—99; dir. Colo. River Water Conservation Dist., 1997—2001. Fellow Nat. Acad. Pub. Adminstrn.; mem. Nat. Assn. Counties (presdl. transition team), NY State Bar Assn., Stanford U. Alumni Assn., Yale Club, Met. Club, Zeta Psi. Republican. Episcopalian. Personal E-mail: fhodsoll@cox.net.

HODSON, ROY GOODE, JR., retired logistician; b. Enon, Ala., July 22, 1927; s. Roy Goode and Ilda Fern (Jinks) H.; m. Mildred Bernice Parlier, Dec. 3, 1966 (dec. July 1992); children: Joan Hodson Bash, Scott Daniel, Jayne Clymer. Student, San Diego Jr. Coll., 1947-49, San Diego Vocational, 1947-49, San Diego State Coll., 1949-50. Security officer US Naval CB Ctr. (Civil Service), Port Hueneme, Calif., 1950-52; logistician Gen. Dynamics, San Diego, 1952-64, GTE Govt. Systems, Inc., Mt. View, Calif., 1964-89. Bd. dirs. San Jose Civic Light Opera Assn., 1988-95; advisor San Jose Children's Musical Theater, 1995-2002; mem. Boys and Girls Club; hon. dep. sheriff Limeston County, Ala.; With U.S. Army, 1945-47. Recipient Bravo award Silhoutte mag., 1988, Ginny award, 1989. Mem.: Yuma C. of C., Internat. Platform Assn., Internat. Freelance Photographers Orgn., Ariz. County Attys. and Sheriffs Assn., Muscular Dystrophy Assn. (rsch. leaders), Wildlife Land Trust, Nat. Audubon Soc., Ind. Sheriffs Assn., Spiceland Hist. and Tourism Soc., Am. Film Inst., Humane Soc. U.S., Nat. Arbor Day Found., Easter Seals Found., Nat. Svc. Found., Nature Conservancy, Nat. Pks. and Conservation Assn., Nat. Humane Edn. Soc., Archaeol. Inst. Am., Cornell Lab. of Ornithology, Am. Birding Assn., Am. Philatelic Soc., Am. Image Press Club, Am. Legion, Am. Assn. Ret. Persons, AMVETS. Democrat. Mem. Church of Christ. Avocations: photography, genealogy, music. Home: 11373 E 39th Ln Yuma AZ 85367-7651

HODSON, SARA SUZANNE, manuscripts curator; b. Whittier, Calif., June 3, 1949; d. C. Hartley and Elizabeth M. H.; m. Peter J. Blodgett, Mar. 26, 1988. BA with honors, Whittier Coll., Calif., 1971, MA in English, 1977; MLS, UCLA, 1979. Libr. asst. The Huntington Libr., San Marino, Calif., 1973-77, curator of lit. manuscripts, 1979—. Adv. bd. DuPlessis Archives, Fuller Sem., Pasadena, Calif., 1994-95; adj. instr. Claremont Grad. Sch., Calif., 1994; mem. faculty Western Archives Inst., Pomona, Calif., 1994, Pasadena, 1995, 96, 2000-02, 06. Contbr. essays to Conrad Aiken: A Priest of Consciousness, 1989, Dictionary of Literary Biography Yearbook, 1992, Pre-Raphaelites in Context, 1992; editor: Guide to Literary Manuscripts, 1979, (with Jeanne Campbell Reesman) Jack London: One Hundred Years a Writer, 2002; contbr. articles to profl. jours. Recipient scholarship Calif. Scholarship Fedn., 1967. Fellow Soc. Am. Archivists (chair manuscripts repositories sect. 1994-95, vice chair/chair elect privacy and confidentiality roundtable, 1994-95, chair 1996-97, Calvin Pease award com. 1998, publs. bd. 1998-2004); mem. ALA, Soc. Calif. Archivists (treas. 1986-88, v.p. 1990-91, pres. 1991-92, Lifetime Achievement award 1996), Jack London Soc. (adv. bd. 1996—, pres. 2004-06), Renaissance Conf. of So. Calif., Whittier Coll. Alumni Assn. (bd. dirs. 1998-2000). Avocations: free-lance percussion, reading.

HODSON, WILLIAM DAVID, elementary school educator, consultant; b. La Jolla, Calif., Apr. 16, 1947; s. Richard B. and Ruth C. Hodson; m. Keri Kathleen Gould (div.); m. Charlene Teller, June 11, 1998. EdB, No. Ariz. U., Flagstaff, 1969, MEd, 1980; EdD in Leadership, U. Nev., Reno, 1993. Cert. tchr. math. 7-19 Ariz. Tchr. math. Payson HS, Ariz., 1969—72; tchr. Chinle Jr. HS, Ariz., 1972—2006, tchr. sci., 2006—. Curriculum sec. Chinle Unified Schs.; sch. improvement chair Chinle Jr. HS, 1994—2003. With US Army, 1970. Mem.: ASCD. Democrat. Home: PO Box 87 Chinle AZ 86503 Office: Chinle Jr HS PO Box 587 Chinle AZ 86503

HOE, RICHARD MARCH, insurance and securities consultant, writer; b. Plainfield, NJ, June 16, 1939; s. Arthur James Hoe and Marjorie (Vandergrift) Beeson; m. Lynne Hovell, Sept. 26, 1964; children: Joshua Blake, Susan Brooke, Seth Jamieson. Student, Pace U., 1964-67, U. Tenn., 1976. CLU. Asst. to controller, fleet mgr., asst. purchasing agt. Hoe & Co. Inc., Bronx, NY, 1964—66; pres. OJS Mfg. Co., Bklyn., 1966-68, Fresh Impressions Inc., NYC, 1968; agt. Fidelity Mut. Life, NYC, 1968—72; asst. mgr. Fin. Life, NYC, 1972—73; brokerage mgr. Am. Life N.Y., NYC, 1973—75; exec. Provident Life & Accident Ins. Co., Chattanooga, 1975—78; mgr. Jefferson Standard, Tulsa, Okla., 1978—81; pres. Hoe & Co. Inc., Tulsa, 1981—93; fin. planner, designer, cons. Tulsa, 1978—99; specialist Am. Citizens Fin. Svcs., Tulsa, 1989—99; exec. v.p. Summit Fin. Group, Tulsa, 2000—05; fin. planner Richard Hoe Investments, LLC, 2005—. Lectr. project bus. Tulsa Pub. Schs., 1983, 85, cons., 1984-86; mem. exec. faculty, Calif. Inst. Fin., Calif. Luth. U. Grad. Sch., Thousand Oaks, Calif., 2007—; lectr. in field; founder employee and exec. benefit plans, residual split-dollar, money purchase flexible spending plans, pvt. sector social security alternative portable plans, satellite split-dollar, satellite supplemental pensions, lifetime income nontaxable retirement plans, balanced funding plans. Author: Love in Pasadena, 1996; columnist (monthly) Broker World, 1985-86, 87-88, Probe, Life Assn. News, Life Insurance Selling, 2000—; contbr. articles to profl. jours., novelist. Chmn. fund raising Grimes Elem. Sch., Tulsa Pub. Schs., 1984-87; mem. gifted and talented com. Tulsa Pub. Schs., 1982; bd. dirs. Nat. ALS Found., N.Y.C., 1971-82. Fellow: Life Underwriter Tng. Coun. (moderator 1979—86); mem.: Tulsa Estate Planning Forum (treas. 2005—), Okla. Planned Giving Coun., Reach Across Divisions, Nat. Okla. Multiple Sclerosis Soc. Republican. Episcopalian. Avocations: writing, chess, bicycling, jazz. Home: 5843 E 50th St Tulsa OK 74135-6885 Office: Richard Hoe Investments LLC 7134 S Yale Ave Ste 560 Tulsa OK 74136-6352 Office Phone: 918-398-7200. E-mail: richardhoe@richardhoe.com.

HOEBEL, BARTLEY GORE, psychologist, educator; b. NYC, May 29, 1935; s. Edward Adamson and Frances (Gore) H.; m. Cynthia A. Eney, June 22, 1962; children— Valerie, Carolyn, Brett. AB, Harvard, 1957; PhD, U. Pa., 1962; PhD (hon.), U. Cath. Louvain, 1991. Mem. faculty psychology dept. Princeton, 1962—, prof, 1970—. Founder, pres. Delaware River Steamboat Floating Classroom, Inc., 2000—. Contbg. author: Handbook of Psychopharmacology, 1977, S.S. Stevens Handbook of Experimental Psychology, 1988, Handbook of Obesity, 1997, 2004; contbr. articles to tech. jours. and books. Fellow AAAS, APA (pres. physiol. and comparative psychol. divsn. 1994), Am. Psychol. Soc.; mem. Soc. Neurosci., Soc. Study Ingestive Behavior (pres. 1995), Ea. Psychol. Assn. (pres. 1997). Unitarian Universalist. Home: 207 Hartley Ave Princeton NJ 08540-5615 Office: Dept Psychology Princeton Univ Princeton NJ 08544 Office Phone: 609-258-4463. Business E-Mail: hoebel@princeton.edu.

HOEBEN, BARBARA J., pharmacist; d. Theodore L. and Maureen A. Hoeben; m. John F. Landolt III. BA in Music, Drake U., Des Moines, 1995, PharmD, 1997; M of Pharmacy, U. Tex., San Antonio, 2005. Chief pharmacy svcs. 48th Med. Group, RAF Lakenheath, England, 1999—2003; clin. pharmacy flight comdr. 59 MDW Wilford Hall, Lackland AFB, Tex., 2005—. Clin. asst. prof. U. Tex., San Antonio, 2003—. Maj. USAF, 1997. Mem.: Soc. Air Force Pharmacists, Assn. Mil. Surgeons US, Am. Pharmacists Assn., Am. Coll. Clin. Pharmacy.

HOECKER, THOMAS RALPH, lawyer; b. Chicago Heights, Ill., Dec. 14, 1950; s. William H. and Norma M. (Wynkoop) H.; m. V. Sue Thornton, Aug. 28, 1971; children: Elizabeth T., Ellen T. BS, No. Ill. U., 1972; JD, U. Ill., 1975. Bar: Ill. 1975, Ariz. 1985. Assoc. Davis and Morgan, Peoria, Ill., 1975-80, ptnr., 1980-84; assoc. Snell and Wilmer, Phoenix, 1984-86, ptnr., 1987—. Mem. steering com. Western Pension Conf., Phoenix, 1986-92, pres., 1991-92. Fellow Am. Coll. Employee Benefits Coun. (charter), Ariz. Bar Found.; mem. ABA (chair tax sect. employee benefits com. 2002-03, co-chair legis. and adminstrv. subcom. of labor sect. employee benefits com. 1994-96), Ariz. Bar Assn., Ill. Bar Assn., Marciopa County Bar Assn., (mem. investment com. 1988-94). Avocation: fly fishing. Office: Snell Wilmer 1 Arizona Ctr Phoenix AZ 85004 Office Phone: 602-382-6361. Business E-Mail: thoecker@swlaw.com.

HOEFER, RICHARD A., social work educator, non-profit management consultant; BSW, U. Kans., Lawrence, 1974; MSW, U. Kans., 1981; MA, U. Mich., Ann Arbor, 1989; PhD, U. Mich., 1989. Asst. prof. No. Ill. U., DeKalb, 1989—92; prof. social work U. Tex., Arlington, 1992—. Cons. in field. Author: Advocacy Practice for Social Justice, 2006; editor: Cutting Edge Social Policy, Welfare to Work: An International Response, 2006, The Social Policy Jour./Jour. Policy Practice. Bd. dirs. Fencing Inst. of Tex., Farmer's Branch, 2005—. Named Social Worker of Yr., Tarrant County, Tex., 1999; recipient Torgerson Tchg. award, U. Tex. at Arlington Sch. Social Work, 1998; Fulbright scholar, 1996. Mem.: NASW, Assn. Cmty. Orgn. and Social Adminstrn. (bd. dirs. 2004—), Assn. Rsch. Nonprofit Orgns. and Voluntary Actions, Tex. Polit. Action Candidate Election (pres. 1994—98). Avocation: fencing. Office: Dept Social Work U Tex at Arlington PO Box 19129 Arlington TX 76019 Office Phone: 817-272-3947. Office Fax: 817-272-2046.

HOEFFLIN, RICHARD MICHAEL, lawyer, judicial administrator; BS in Acctg., Calif. State U., Northridge, 1971; JD, Loyola U., LA, 1974. Bar: Calif. 1974, U.S. Dist. Ct. (cen. dist.) Calif. 1974, U.S. Tax Ct. 1976, U.S. Dist. Ct. (no. and so. dists.) Calif. 1976, U.S. Supreme Ct. 1982, cert.: (mediator). With Lewitt, Hackman, Hoefflin, Shapiro, Marshall, 1974—2000, ptnr., 1977—2000; prin. Hoefflin & Assocs., ALC, 2000—. Judge pro tem L.A. Superior Ct., 1982—, Ventura County Superior Ct., 1991—, Fee Dispute Resolution Svcs. for L.A. County Bar. Co-founder Ventura County Homeowners for Equal Taxation, Westlake Village, Calif., 1978—79; pres., gen. counsel Westlake Hills Homeowners Assn., 1975—77; chmn. Celebrity Love Match Tennis Tour for John McEnroe United Cerebral Palsy/Spastic Children Found., 1990—96; bd. dirs. Michael Hoefflin Found., 1996—, No. Ranch Country Club, 2000—03, Alliance for Arts, 2000—06, chmn. bd., 2005—06. Mem.: ABA, Westlake Hills Owners Assn. (pres. 1977—78), San Fernando Valley Bar Assn. (co-chair bus. and real estate sect. 1995—97), Ventura County Bar Assn., L.A. Bar Assn., Sherwood Country Club, North Ranch Country Club (pres. tennis assn. 1984—85, golf bd. mem., sec. 2000—03). Office: 2659 Townsgate Rd #232 Westlake Village CA 91361 Office Phone: 805-497-8605. Business E-Mail: rmhoefflin@hoefflinlaw.com.

HOEFFLIN, STEVEN M., plastic surgeon; b. Seattle, Feb. 7, 1946; m. Linda Manus (div. 1976); 2 children; m. Pamela Wilson. BA in Biology, Calif. St. U., in Northridge, 1968; MD with honors, UCLA, 1972. Intern UCLA Med. Ctr., 1972—73, resident, 1973—77; asst. clinical prof. Divsn. of Plastic Surgery at UCLA Med. Ctr., 1979—89; chief of plastic surgery Brotman Med. Ctr., 1980—85, UCLA-Santa Monica Hosp. Med. Ctr., 1982—89; plastic surgeon Santa Monica (Calif.) Hosp.; assoc. clin. prof. UCLA; visiting prof. Internat. School of Aesthetic Plastic Surgery. Co-author: Ethnic Rhinoplasty, 1998; author: (Medical, nonfiction) The Beautiful Face: The First Mathematical Definition, Classification, and Creation of True Facial Beauty, 2000. Recipient Joel McCrea Achievement award, Am. Cinema awards, 1994, Golden Star Halo award, So. Calif. Motion Picture Coun. for outstanding achievement as a plastic surgeon and contribution in the entertainment industry, 1994, Michael Bolton Humanitarian award, 1995. Fellow: The Internat. Coll. Surgeons, Am.Coll. Surgeons; mem.: Am. Assn. Hand Surgery, Am. Burn Assn., LA County Med. Assn., Royal Soc. Medicine, Rhinoplasty Soc., Plastic Surgery Edn. Found., Bay Surg. Soc., Lipoplasty Soc., Am. Soc. Aesthetic Plastic Surgery, Am. Soc. Plastic Surgeons, LA Soc. Plastic Surgeons (pres.), Am. Bd. Plastic Surgery (diplomat), Alpha Omega Alpha. Achievements include being Michael Jackson's former plastic surgeon. Office: 1530 Arizona Ave Santa Monica CA 90404-1208*

HOEFLE, H. FREDERICK, lawyer; b. Cin., Apr. 7, 1938; s. Henry Alfred and Norma (Lambeck) H.; m. Joyce Ann Dreier, Aug. 21, 1965 (dec. Jan. 19, 1996); children: Jennifer, Meredith. AB with high honors, U. Cin., 1960; JD, Chase Coll. Law, Cin., 1965. Bar: Ohio 1965, U.S. Supreme Ct. 1971, U.S. Ct. Appeals (D.C., 5th and 6th cirs.), U.S. Dist. Ct. (so. dist.) Ohio, U.S. Dist. Ct. (ea. dist.) Ky. Assoc. Shea & McKay, Norwood, Ohio, 1966-71; asst. atty. gen. State of Ohio, Cin., 1971-79; pvt. practice, Cin., 1971—; sr. trial counsel Hamilton County Pub. Defender, Cin., 1979-90. Mem. death penalty task force U.S. Ct. Appeals (6th cir.). Contbg. author: Ohio Death Penalty Manual, 1981; Ohio Appellate Manual, 1983. Mem. Ohio Death Penalty Task Force, Columbus, 1981—. Mem. Cin. Bar Assn. (exec. com. 1976, spl. award of merit 1978), Ohio State Bar Assn., Stewart Inn of Ct. (Courageous Advocate award), Cin. Criminal Def. Lawyers Assn. (Pres.'s award 1996), Order of Curia, Phi Beta Kappa, Phi Delta Theta. Democrat. Unitarian. Home: 4532 Runningfawn Dr Cincinnati OH 45247-7530 Office: 810 Sycamore St Cincinnati OH 45202-2156 Office Phone: 513-579-8700.

HOEFLICH, CHARLES HITSCHLER, banker; b. Phila., Apr. 4, 1914; s. Llewellyn Ashbridge and Mary Ann (Osterheldt) H. BS in Econs., U. Pa., 1936; cert. in banking, Rutgers U., 1949; cert. in bank mktg., Northwestern U., 1955; LLD, Okla. Christian U., 1972. V.p. Phila. Nat. Bank, 1951-62; pres. Union Nat. Bank & Trust Co., Souderton, Pa., 1962-76, chmn. bd. dirs., 1976-84, chmn. exec. com., 1984-86; chmn. Univest Corp. Pa., Souderton, 1973-86, chmn. emeritus, 1986—. Sec.-treas. Intercollegiate Studies Inst., Wilmington, Del., 1955—; trustee Okla. Christian U., Oklahoma City, 1974—; founder Penn Found. for Mental Health, 1955—, now dir. emeritus, Adult Care Total Svcs., now-dir. emeritus; bd. dirs. The Lamb Found., Eisenhower Commn., 2002, Human Rels. Found.; life mem. Rep. presdl. task force, 1981-92, 2000—; chmn. Bedminster Zoning Bd. Recipient Presdl. citation USAAF, 1946, Citizen of Yr. award Fed. Bar Assn., 1960, Lifetime Achievement award Intercoll. Studies Inst., 2000. Mem. Bank Mktg. Assn. (pres. 1964-65), Am. Bankers Assn., Union League Club (Phila.), Indian Valley Country Club (Telford, Pa.), The Exec. Com. (assoc.), Heritage Found., Intercollegiate Studies Inst. Republican. Avocations: collecting americana antiques and art, painting, horticulture. Office: Univest Corp Pa Main And Broad St Souderton PA 18964 Office Phone: 215-721-2400. Office Fax: 215-721-2433.

HOEFLIN, RONALD KENT, philosopher, writer; b. Richmond Heights, Mo., Feb. 23, 1944; s. William Eugene and Mary Elizabeth (Dell) Hoeflin. Student, Calif. Inst. Tech., 1962-63, U. Calif., Berkeley, 1966-67, U. N.C., 1970-71; BA, U. Minn., 1968, Shimer Coll., 1974; MLS, Ind. U., 1970; MA, New Sch. Social Rsch., 1979, PhD, 1987. With various librs., 1969-85; publisher, editor Triple Nine Soc., NYC, 1979-81, 85-89; publisher, editor, founder Top One Percent Soc., NYC, 1989—, One-in-a-Thousand Soc., NYC, 1992—. Designer Mega Test, 1985, Titan Test, 1990, Ultra Test, 1995, Hoeflin Power Test, 1996; author: The Encyclopedia of Categories: A Theory of Categories and Unifying Paradigm for Philosophy, 2 vols., 2005. Mem.: Am. Philos. Assn. (Fifth Ann. Rockefeller prize 1988), Prometheus Soc. (founder 1982), Mega Soc. (founder 1982), Mensa. Office: PO Box 539 New York NY 10101-0539 Personal E-mail: hoeflin@aol.com.

HOEFT, ROBERT GENE, agricultural studies educator; b. David City, Nebr., May 21, 1944; s. Otto O. Hoeft and Lula (Barlean) Pleskac; m. Nancy A. Bussen, Sept. 1, 1990; children: Jeffrey, Angela. BS, U. Nebr., 1965, MS, 1967; PhD, U. Wis., 1972. Asst. prof. S.D. State U., Rapid City, 1972-73, U. Ill., Urbana, 1973-77, assoc. prof., 1977-81, prof., 1981—, head dept. crop scis., 2005—. Author: Modern Corn Production, 1986, Modern Corn & Soybean Production, 2000; editor Jour. Prodn. Agr., 1986-92. Recipient Funk award U. Ill., 1990, Robert E. Wagner award Potash and Phosphate Inst., 1998. Fellow Soil Sci. Soc. Am., Am. Soc. Agronomy (pres. 2002-03, CIBA-Geigy award 1978, Agronomic Extension award, grantee 1988, Agronomic Achievement award-soils 1995, Werner Nelson award for diagnosis of yield limiting factors 1996); mem. Coun. for Sci. and Tech. Office: U Ill 1102 S Goodwin Ave Urbana IL 61801-4730 Business E-Mail: rhoeft@uiuc.edu.

HOEG, DONALD FRANCIS, chemist, consultant, research and development company executive; b. Bklyn., Aug. 2, 1931; s. Harry Herman and Charlotte (Bourke) H.; m. Patricia Catherine Fogarty, Aug. 30, 1952; children— Thomas Edward, Robert Francis, Donald John, Mary Beth, Susan Catherine. BS in Chemistry summa cum laude, St. John's U., NYC, 1953; PhD in Chemistry, Ill. Inst. Tech., 1957. Fellow in chemistry and chem. engring. Armour Research Found., 1953-54; grad. research asst. Ill. Inst. Tech., 1954-56; research chemist W.R. Grace & Co., 1956-58, sr. research chemist, 1958-61; group leader addition polymer chemistry Roy C. Ingersoll Research Center, Borg-Warner Corp., Des Plaines, Ill., 1961-64, mgr. polymer chemistry, 1964-66, assoc. dir., head chem. research dept., 1966-75, dir., 1975-88; pres. DFH Assocs., 1988—. Former mem. solid state scis. adv. bd. NAS; bd. overseers Lewis Coll. Scis. and Letters of Ill. Inst. Tech., 1980-91; bd. dirs. Ill. Inst. Tech. Alumni, 1979-82, Mt. Prospect Combined Appeal, 1963-65 Bd. editors: Research Mgmt. Mag, 1979-82; contbr. numerous articles tech. publs., chpts. in books; patentee in field. TaPing Lin scholar, 1955-56; AEC asst., 1954; Armour Research Found. fellow, 1953-54; Ill. Inst. Tech. Achievement award, 1983 Mem. Am. Chem. Soc., AAAS, N.Y. Acad. Scis., Dirs. Indsl. Research, Am. Mgmt. Assn. (v.p. council 1984-88), Research Dirs. Assn. Chgo. (pres. 1977-78), Indsl. Research Inst. (bd. dirs. 1986-88), Sigma Xi. Office Phone: 847-577-5951. Personal E-mail: dfh1931@aol.com. *I've counseled myself that all ideas and concepts, no matter how seemingly difficult, are products of man's mind, and, therefore fundamentally understandable.*

HOEG, MATTHEW, lawyer; b. Oceanside, NY, 1960; AB with honors, Coll. William & Mary, 1982; JD, U. Houston, 1985. Bar: Tex. 1985. Ptnr., Labor/Employment Sect. Andrews Kurth LLP, Houston, mem. mgmt. com. Editor: Houston Law Rev., 1983—85. Mem.: ABA, State Bar Tex., Houston Young Lawyers Assn., Houston Bar Assn., Order of Barons. Office: Andrews Kurth LLP 600 Travis St Ste 4200 Houston TX 77002 Office Phone: 713-220-4012. Office Fax: 713-238-7328. Business E-Mail: matthewhoeg@andrewskurth.com.

HOEHN, ELMER LOUIS, lawyer, state and federal agency administrator, educator, consultant; b. Memphis, Ind., Dec. 19, 1915; s. Louis and Agnes (Goss) H.; m. Frances Cory, June 10, 1943; children: Kathleen Gillmore, G. Patrick. BS, Canterbury Coll., 1936, Northwestern U., 1937; JD, U. Louisville, 1940. Bar: Ky. 1940, D.C. 1969, U.S. Supreme Ct. 1969, U.S. Ct. Appeals 1970, Ind. 1981. Prof. bus. and law Jeffersonville High Sch., Ind., 1937-41, IUS, 1940-41; with legal and personnel div. Am. Barge Lines, 1942-44; realtor Ind., 1949—; apptd. dir. by Gov. Ind. Oil and Gas, 1949-53; apptd. adminstr. by Pres. U.S. Oil Import Adminstrn., Nat. Security Agy., Crude Oil, Petroleum Products & Petrochem. Feedstocks, 1965-69; sec.-treas. Am. Assn. Oil Well Drilling Contractors, 1956-60; exec. sec. Ind. Oil Producers and Land Owners Assn., 1953-64; pvt. practice law Washington, 1969-91, Indiana, 1981—. ADR civil mediator, Ind., 1993; gov.'s rep. Interstate Oil & Gas Compact Commn., 1949—53, 1961—65; apptd. commr. by gov. Ohio River Greenway Devel. Commn., 1994; cons. petroleum, natural resources, energy and environment; chmn. Clark County Redevel. Commn., 1996—, Charlestown Ammo INAAP Reuse Authority, 1997—. Mem. Ind. Gen. Assembly, 1945- 49, minority floor leader, 1947, chief clk., 1949, Democratic chmn., Clark County, Ind., 1945-52; Ind. del. Dem. Nat. Conv., 1964, chmn. 8th Congl. Dist., 1952-58; mem. Ind. Dem. Exec. Com., 1952-58, Ind. and Midwest campaign mgr., LBJ campaign for president, 1960. Named Hon. Citizen, Ind. and Ky., Citoyen Honneur, Soufflenheim, France, Ambassador, Clark County, Ind., Disting. Benefactor, Clark Meml. Hosp. Interfaith Ctr.; recipient Humanitarian award, ARC, 2003, Chancellor's Medallion award, IUS, 2003, Helping Hand award, Haven House Svcs., Lewis & Clark Bicentennial Commemoration, Falls of the Ohio, Ea. Legacy, 2003—. Mem. ABA, Fed. Bar Assn., Ky. Bar Assn. (Disting. sr. counselor 1990), D.C. Bar Assn., Ind. Bar Assn. (Disting. Sr. Counselor 1990), Coop. Oil and Gas Assns. (liason com. Washington 1969-91), Am. Inn of Ct., Univ. Club (Louisville), Sigma Delta Kappa. Clubs: Nat. Lawyers, Nat. Press (Washington); Ind. Legislators (Indpls.); Filson (Louisville), Elks Country (Jeffersonville). Roman Catholic. Home: 2105 Utica Pike Jeffersonville IN 47130-5005 Personal E-mail: ehoehn@watertowersquare.com.

HOEHN-SARIC, R. CHRISTOPHER, educational organization executive; Co-founder Health Mgmt. Corp., LifeCard Internat., Sterling Capital, Ltd., prin., 1983—; co-CEO, chmn. of bd. Sylvan Learning Systems, Inc.; gen. ptnr. Sterling Venture Partners, Sterling Capital Partners; chmn, CEO Sylvan Ventures, Educate, Inc., Balt. Bd. mem. Laureate Edn., Inc., The Becker Grp., Fla. Coastal Sch. Law, Meritas LLC, Safety Systems Corp., CA Holding I, Inc., CA Holding II, Inc.; adv. coun. mem. Sheridan Libraries, Johns Hopkins U. Office: Educate Inc 1001 Fleet St Baltimore MD 21202 Office Phone: 410-843-8000. Office Fax: 410-843-8441.*

HOEKSTRA, EDWARD JOHN, foundation administrator; b. London, Apr. 7, 1950; s. Eduard Karel Hoekstra and Pauline Anita Hoekstra-Batt; m. Susan Louise Guastaferri, May 18, 1990; 1 child, Paula Elizabeth. MD, Amsterdam U., 1975; MPH, Sch. Pub. Health Utrecht, Utrecht, The Netherlands, 1983; MPH in Occupl. Health, U. Amsterdam, 1986; MS in Epidemiology, Sch. Pub. Health Leiden, Leiden, The Netherlands, 1993. Med. officer WHO, Beijing, 1998—2000; sr. health advisor UNICEF, NYC, 2000—. Mem. disaster assessment, coord. UN Office Coordination Humanitarian Affairs, Geneva, 1998—; acting chief health svc. rsch. and evaluation br. CDC, Atlanta, 1992—98; med. chief dept. of occupl. health Ministry Health Aruba, Oranjestad, Netherlands Antilles, 1990—92; chief occupl. physician Mercedes Benz Netherlands Occupl. Health Ctr. Utrecht, Utrecht, 1983—90; health ins. physician Dutch Social Security Health Dept., Utrecht, 1996—2003. Recipient Spl. Act or Svc. award, CDC, 1994, Commd. Corps award, 1996, Secretary's award Disting. Svc., 1998, Taskforce Immunization Africa award, WHO, 2002, Best Achievements award, ARC, 2002. Mem.: Internat. Commn. Occupl. Health (assoc.), Can. Pub. Health Assn. (assoc.). Office: Unicef 3 UN Plz New York NY 10017 Home Phone: 212-951-7282; Office Phone: 212-326-7555. E-mail: ehoekstra.

HOEKSTRA, MARK RAINS, information technology executive, consultant; s. Bernard and Mildred Hoekstra; m. Susan Lynelle Wilkins, June 19, 1981; children: Andrew Mark, Christina Lynelle, Matthew David. AA, Grand Rapids Jr. Coll., 1972; BBA, Western Mich. U., Kalamazoo, 1974; M Mgmt., Aquinas Coll., Grand Rapids, 1992. Cert. cons. SAP Toronto, Can., 1998; pedorthist Pedorthic Mgmt., 1978. Retail footware buyer, planner Hoekstra Shoes, Grand Rapids, 1975—81; mfg. sys. assoc. Beta Cons., Grand Rapids, 1981—83; cons. Computer Alliance, Grand Rapids, 1983—84; prodn. and material planner Rowe Internat., Grand Rapids, 1984; prodn. mgr. Ctr. Mfg., Byron Center, Mich., 1984—86; mfg. systems cons. Computer Strategies, Grand Rapids, 1987—89; ptnr. SilverLake Resources, Grand Rapids, 1991—2004; owner, ptnr. i3 Bus. Solutions, Grand Rapids, 2004—. Cons. enterprise resource planning implementation Douglas AutoTech, Bronson, Mich., 1988—89. Contbr. articles to profl. publs. Treas. Calvin Christian Refromed Ch., Grand Rapids, 1993—94; deacon, mem. coun. Calvin Christian Ref. Ch., Grand Rapids, 2005—07; bd. dirs. Big Star Lake Owners Assn., Baldwin, Mich., 2001—07; bd. dirs., econ. adv. bd. Goodwill Industries, Grand Rapids, 2002—03. Mem.: APICS (pres. Grand Rapids chpt. 1998—99, Platinum award, cert. enterprise concepts and fundamentals, cert. identifying and creating demand, cert. delivering products and svcs., cert. designing products and processes), Grand Rapids C. of C., Sigma Chi (life; grand praetor 2004—06, award of favor and distinction 2004). Achievements include design of shop floor data collection applications. Home: 2148 Edgewood SE Grand Rapids MI 49546 Office: i3 Business Solutions LLC 5005 Cascade Rd SE Grand Rapids MI 49546 Home Phone: 616-949-0998; Office Phone: 616-956-6888. Business E-Mail: mhoekstra@i3bus.com.

HOEKSTRA, PETER, congressman, manufacturing executive; b. Groningen, The Netherlands, Oct. 30, 1953; arrived in US, 1957; m. Diane M. Johnson; children: Erin, Allison, Bryan. BA in Polit. Sci., Hope Coll., 1975; MBA, U. Mich., 1977. Furniture exec. Herman Miller, Inc., 1977-92, project mgr., product mgr., dir. product mgmt., dir. dealer mktg., v.p. dealer mktg., 1988-92, v.p. product mgmt., 1992-93; mem. US Congress from 2d Mich. dist., 1993—, chmn. select edn. subcom. edn. and the workforce com., 2001, mem. com. on transp. and infrastructure, mem. permanent select com. on intelligence, 2001—, chmn., 2004—07. Contbr. to project devel. Equa Chair, recognized as outstanding product of 1980s by Time Mag. Recipient Deficit Hawk award, Concord Coalition, 1996, Disting. Alumni award, Hope Coll. Alumni Assn., 2001, Pub. Policy award, Volunteer Ctr. Nat. Network Coun., 2003, Pub. Svc. award, Friends of Libraries USA and American Libraries Assn., 2003, Hero of Taxpayer, Americans for Tax Reform, 2004, Navigator award, Potomac Inst. Policy Studies, 2005. Republican. Christian Reformed Ch. Office: US Ho Reps 2234 Rayburn House Office Bldg Washington DC 20515-2202 E-mail: tellhoek@mail.house.gov.*

HOEL, DAVID GERHARD, statistician, science educator; b. LA, Nov. 18, 1939; s. Paul Gerhard and Hazel Bessie (Helvig) H.; m. Nancy Carolyn Keller, Sept. 3, 1961; children: Erik Gerhard, Brian David, Christian Paul. AB, U. Calif., Berkeley, 1961; PhD, U. N.C., Chapel Hill, 1966. Postdoctoral fellow Stanford U., Calif., 1966-67; sr. mathematician Westinghouse Rsch. Labs., Pitts., 1967-68; statistician Oak Ridge (Tenn.) Nat. Lab., 1968-70; adj. prof. dept. biostats. U. N.C., Chapel Hill, 1970—. Math. statistician Nat. Inst. Environ. Health Scis., Research Triangle Park, N.C., 1970-73, chief biometry br., 1973-81, acting sci. dir., 1977-79, dir. div. biometry and risk assessment, 1981-93; prof., chair Med. U. S.C., Dept. Biometry and Epidemiology, 1993-97, disting. univ. prof., 1997—; mem. coun. fellows Collegium Ramazzini, 1987; vis. scientist Radiation Effects Rsch. Found., Hiroshima, Japan, 1979-80, dir., 1984-86; mem. NAS sci. bd. on toxicity and environ. health hazards, Washington, 1981-85, NAS com. on biol. effects of ionizing radiation, 1986-89, NAS com. to provide interim oversight of Dept. Energy nuclear weapons complex, 1988-90, NAS com. on environ. epidemiology, 1990, NAS com. on epidemiology and vets. affairs, 1990-2002, NAS com. on applied and theoretical stats, 1991-94, NAS com. on the health effect of mustart gas, 1991-92, NAS com. on radiol. safety in the Marshall Islands, 1992—, chmn. NAS com. to study the mortality of mil. pers. present at atmospheric tests of nuc. weapons, 1993-94; chmn. NCRP sci. com. on extrapolation of risks from non-human exptl. systems to man; mem. sci. adv. bd. Nat. Ctr. for Toxicological Rsch., 1977-80, EPA Radiation Com., 1993-94, Environ. Health Found., 1994—. Contbr., co-contbr. articles to profl. publs.; co-editor workshop, conf. proceedings. Recipient NIH Dir. award, 1977, Mortimer Spiegelman Gold medal award APHA, 1977; Pub. Health Svc. Supr. Svc. award USPHS, 1980, Disting. Scientist award S.C. U. Rsch. and Edn. Found., 1993, Ramazzini award Collegium Ramazzini and the Town of Carpi, 1994; named Sr. Exec. Svc., Bonus Nat. Inst. Environ. Health Scis., 1983, 87-91. Fellow AAAS, Am. Statis. Assn. (sec. biometrics sect. 1979); mem. NAS Inst. Medicine, Internat. Statis. Inst., Royal Statis. Soc., Radiation Rsch. Soc., Health Physics Soc., Biometric Soc., Soc. for Risk Analysis (coun. mem. 1982-85). Home: 36 S Battery St Charleston SC 29401-2327 Office: 135 Cannon St Ste 302 PO Box 250835 Charleston SC 29425-0551

HOEL, LESTER A., civil engineering educator, department chairman; b. Bklyn., Feb. 26, 1935; s. Johannes and Julia (Michelsen) Hoel; m. Unni Sonja Blegen, Jan. 24, 1959; children: Julie Britt Bryan, Sonja Leslie, Lisa Hoel Rafael. BCE, CCNY, 1957; MS in Civil Engring, Bklyn. Poly. Inst., 1960; DEng, U. Calif., Berkeley, 1963. Registered profl engr, Calif, Pa, Va. Asst. prof. engring. San Diego State Coll., 1962-64; Fulbright research scholar Inst. Transport Economy, Oslo, 1964-65; prin. engr. Wilbur Smith & Assoc., San Francisco, 1965-66; faculty Carnegie-Mellon U., Pitts., 1966-74, prof. civil engring., 1970-74; assoc. dir. Transp. Research Inst., 1966-74; Hamilton prof. dept. civil engring. U. Va., 1974-99, chmn. dept., 1974-89, L.A. Lacy Disting. prof., 1999—; dir. Ctr. Transportation Stud., 2002—. Author: (book) Traffic and Highway Engineering, 3d edit., 2002; editor: Public Transportation, 1979, Public Transportation, rev 2d ed, 1992, Transportation Infrastructure Engineering: A Multi-Modal Integration, 2007; mem. editl. bd.: transp. jours.; contbr. technical papers, books and articles. Recipient Alumni Award in Civil Eng, Col City NY, 1957, Stanley W Gustafson Leadership Award, Hwy Users Fedn, 1989, S S Steinberg Educ Award, Am Rd and Transp Builders, 1991, Disting. Faculty award, Coun. Univ. Transp. Ctrs., 2002, Jack H. Dillard Best Paper award, Va. Transp. Rsch. Coun., 2003; grantee Fulbright Travel, 1964—65. Fellow: ASCE (Huber Research Prize 1976, Frank Masters Award 1990, James Laurie Prize 1999), Inst Transp Engrs (Wilbur S Smith Dinsting Educator Award 2001), Nat Acad Eng; mem.: Am Soc Eng Educ, Transp Research Bd (chmn exec comt 1986, chmn comt tranps profl needs, truck weight study, Pyke Johnson Award 1977), Tau Beta Pi, Chi Epsilon, Sigma Xi. Home: 1340 Sunset Cir Charlottesville VA 22901 Business E-Mail: LAH@virginia.edu.

HOELSCHER, ROBERT JAMES, lawyer; b. Cleve., July 5, 1952; s. Max W. and Lorraine A. (Bass) H.; m. Constance J. Fiske, Sept. 20, 1986; children: Ann, Carol. BA, Pa. State U., 1974; JD, Harvard U., 1977. Bar: Pa. 1977, N.J. 1992, U.S. Dist. Ct. (ea. dist.) Pa. 1978, U.S. Ct. Appeals (3d. cir.) 1983, U.S. Dist. Ct. N.J. 1992. Law clk. Supreme Ct. Pa., Pitts., 1977—78; assoc. Drinker Biddle & Reath, Phila., 1978—86; ptnr. Drinker, Biddle & Reath, Phila., 1986—97; counsel CoreStates Fin. Corp. (now Wachovia Corp.), Phila., 1997—. Articles editor Harvard Jour. on Legislation, 1977. Trustee Old Pine St. Ch., Phila., 1984-87, sec. bd. trustees, 1990-93; trustee Friends of Old Pine St., 1999—; elder First Presbyn. Ch., Ardmore, Pa., 1995-2001, 03—. Mem. Phi Beta Kappa. Presbyterian. Office: Wachovia Corp Legal Divsn PA4840 123 S Broad St Philadelphia PA 19109 Office Phone: 215-670-6877.

HOELZLER, MICHAEL GEBHARD, veterinarian, surgeon; b. Williams Lake, Can., Oct. 19, 1973; arrived in US, 2000; s. Gebhard and Eva Elizabeth Hoelzler. BS, U. BC, Vancouver, Can., 1995; DVM, We. Coll. Vet. Medicine, Saskatoon, Can., 1999. Diplomate Am. Coll. Vet. Surgeons, 2005. Intern Ont. Vet. Coll., Guelph, Ont., Canada, 1999—2000; surg. intern Affiliated Vet. Specialists, Jacksonville, Fla., 2000—01; resident surgery U. Tenn., Knoxville, Tenn., 2001—04; staff surgeon Garden State Vet. Specialists, Tinton Falls, NJ, 2004—. Contbr. chapters to books, articles to profl. jours. Mem.: N.J. Vet. Med. Assn., Am. Coll. Vet. Surgeons, Am. Vet. Med. Assn., Phi Zeta (Clin. Rsch. award 2004). Roman Catholic. Avocations: physical fitness, travel. Office: Garden State Veterinary Specialists One Pine Street Tinton Falls NJ 07753 Office Phone: 732-922-0011. Office Fax: 732-922-0991. Business E-Mail: hoelzler@yahoo.ca.

HOENIG, STEVEN LAWRENCE, chemist; b. Queens, NY, June 18, 1957; s. William Frederick and Emily Alice (Montag) H. BS, Polytechnic Inst. N.Y., 1985; MS, L.I. U., 1985. Chemist U.S. Customs Svc., NYC, 1986-91, electronic specialist, 1988-91; forensic chemist DEA, NYC, 1991—98; forensic cons. Claudian Rsch. Group, Queens, NY, 1998—2003; instr. chemistry Keiser U., Ft. Lauderdale, Fla., 2003—05; sr. chemist Fla. Dept. Health, Miami, 2004—. Mem. ASTM, Am. Chem. Soc., N.Y. Acad. Scis.

HOENIG, THOMAS M., bank executive; b. Ft. Madison, Iowa, Sept. 6, 1946; BA in Econs., St. Benedict's Coll., 1968; MA, PhD, Iowa State U. of Sci. & Tech., Ames, 1974. Economist banking supervision area Fed. Res. Bank Kans. City, 1973—81, v.p., 1981—86, sr. v.p., 1986—91, pres., CEO, 1991—. Mem. Free Open Market Com.; bd. dirs., mem. banking adv. bd. U. Mo., Kansas City; mem. banking adv. bd. U. Mo., Columbia. Trustee Benedictine Coll., Atchison, Kans., Midwest Rsch. Inst. Office: Fed Res Bank of Kans City 925 Grand Blvd Kansas City MO 64198 Office Phone: 816-881-2874.*

HOENS, HELEN E., state supreme court justice; b. Elizabeth, NJ, July 31, 1954; m. Robert W. Schwaneberg; 1 child, Charles. BA with high honors, Coll. of William and Mary, 1976; JD cum laude, Georgetown U., 1979. Bar: NJ 1979, DC 1979, NY 1981, US Ct. Appeals (2nd cir.) 1985, US Ct. Appeals (3rd cir.) 1989, US Dist. Ct., NJ 1979, US Dist. Ct., DC 1979, US Dist. Ct., So. Dist. NY 1981. Law clk. to Hon. John Gibbons US Ct. Appeals (3rd cir.), 1979—80; assoc. Dewey Ballentine, NY, 1980—83, Law Offices of Russel H. Beatie, Jr., 1983—85, Pitney Hardin Kipp & Szuch, Morristown, NJ, 1985—88, Lum Hoens Conant Danzis & Kleinberg, Roseland, 1988, ptnr., 1989—94; judge NJ Superior Ct., Morristown, 1994—2002, appellate judge, 2002—06; assoc. justice NJ Supreme Ct., Trenton, 2006—. Contbr. articles to law jours. Recipient Spl. Recognition Award, Autism Soc. Am., 1993. Mem.: Essex County Bar Assn. (chair Rights and Persons with Disabilities). Office: NJ Supreme Ct PO Box 970 25 Market St Trenton NJ 08625*

HOEPFNER, MARK THOMAS, surgeon; s. John J. and Phyllis A. Hoepfner; m. Kristina Sue Holman, Oct. 8, 1983; children: Matthew, Alicia. BS in Chemistry cum laude, Seattle U., 1977; BS in Biochemistry, U. Wash., Seattle, 1978, MD, 1982. Resident in gen. surgery Mayo Clinic, Rochester, Minn., 1982—88, fellow in gastroenterology, 1985—86; ptnr. Berliner, Rayfield, Hoepfner, Las Vegas, 1988—97; pres. Surgeons Chartered, Las Vegas, 1997—. Dir. med. adv. bd. Nev. Early Breast and Cervical Cancer Detection Program, Las Vegas, 1997—99; chief dept. gen. surgery Sunrise Hosp., Las Vegas, 1999—2005. Contbr. articles to profl. jours. Mem. Women's Health Connection, Las Vegas, 1997—2006; med. advisor Susan G. Komen Found., Las Vegas, 1998—2006. Named one of Our Best Doctors, Las Vegas Life Mag., 2004, Am.'s Top Surgeons, Consumers Rsch. Coun. Am., 2002—07; recipient Physician's Recognition award, AMA, 1999—. Fellow: ACS (licentiate; cancer liaison physician 1993—), Southwestern Surg. Congress (licentiate); mem.: Am. Bd. Surgery (licentiate; diplomate), Priestly Soc. Mayo Clinic (licentiate). Avocations: reading, languages, food and wine. Office: Surgeons Chtd 700 Shadow Ln Ste 335 Las Vegas NV 89106 Office Phone: 702-382-6591. E-mail: mhoepfner@aol.com.

HOEPNER, THEODORE JOHN, banker; b. Redwood Falls, Minn., June 28, 1941; s. John W. and Lenore Theodora (Gandrud) H.; m. Barbara Jo Vierling, Dec. 26, 1964; children: Theodore J. Jr., Jennifer. BA, Carleton Coll., Northfield, Minn., 1963; AMP, Harvard U., 1983. Asst. sec. Irving Trust Co., NYC, 1963-68; exec. v.p. Flagship Nat. Bank of Miami Beach, Fla., 1968-77; chmn., pres., chief exec. officer Flagship Nat. Bank of Jacksonville, Fla., 1977-83; chmn., chief exec. officer Sun Bank (merger), Miami, 1983-90; chmn., pres., CEO Sun Bank, N.A., Orlando, Fla., 1990-95, SunTrust Banks of FL Inc., 1995—. Dir. Poe and Brown, Inc., 1994. Founding co-chmn. Beacon Coun., Miami, 1985; trustee U. Miami, 1987-90; chmn. United Way, Orlando, 1993, campaign chair, 1992; trustee Rollins Coll., 1993—. Named Bus. Leader of Yr., Miami News, 1987. Mem. Young Pres. Orgn., Greater Miami C. of C. (chmn. 1988—, Forty-Niners, Country Club Orlando. Republican. Presbyterian. Avocations: hunting, fishing. Office: SunTrust Bank of FL Inc 200 S Orange Ave Orlando FL 32801-3410

HOEPPNER, DAVID WILLIAM, mechanical engineering educator; b. Waukesha, Wis., Dec. 17, 1935; s. William Frank and Lillian Hulda (Rosche) H.; m. Sue Ellen McFarlane, June 13, 1959; children: Laura Anne, Lynne Susan, Amy McFarlane. BME, Marquette U., 1958; MS, PhD, U. Wis., 1963. Asst. prof. metall. engring. U. Wis., Madison, 1963-64; rsch. metallurgist Battelle Meml. Inst., Columbus, 1964-69; group leader Lockheed Calif. Co., Burbank, 1969-74; prof. U. Mo., Columbia, 1974-78; Cockburn prof. U. Toronto, Ont., Canada, 1978-85; prof., chmn. dept. mech. engring. U. Utah, Salt Lake City, 1985-92, prof. mech. engring., 1992—. Cons. Rolls Royce, Derby, Eng., 1973-95, Pratt and Whitney of Can., Longueuil, Que., 1978-2003, Lockheed Aircraft (1976, 1985-2003), Boeing, 1992-95; pres. Faside Internat. Inc., Salt Lake City, 1978—. Author: (with Wallace) Case Studies in Aircraft Corrosion, 1986; editor: Effect of Environment and Complex Load History on Fatigue, 1970, Fracture Prevention, 1974, Fatigue of Weldments, 1977; co-editor: Fretting Fatigue, Current Technology and Practice, 2000, Fretting Fatigue, Advances in Basic Understanding and Applications, 2003. Internat. senator Jaycees, Santa Paula, Calif., 1973; mem. city planning commn., Santa Paula, 1972-74. Named to Wall Fame, Waukesha South H.S., 2006; recipient Outstanding Sci. and Tech. Achievement medal, Gov. Utah, 2005. Mem. AIAA, ASME, ASTM (chmn. subcom. 1969-79, co-editor fretting fatigue, 1999, 2003), Am. Soc. Metals, Am. Soc. Engring. Edn., Soc. Automotive Engrs., Sigma Xi. Avocations: gardening, reading, skiing, hiking. Office Phone: 801-581-3851.

HOERDER, DIRK, history educator; b. Eutin, Germany, May 15, 1943; s. Rolf and Johanna I. M. (Koch) H.; m. Christiane Harzig, July 30, 1993; 1 child, Anna. MA, U. Minn., 1968; PhD, Free U. Berlin, 1971. Asst. prof. Free U. Berlin, 1969-75; prof. U. Bremen, Germany, 1997—2005, State U. Ariz., Tempe, 2006—. Guest prof. Duke U., Durham, N.C., 1995, U. Toronto, 1996-97, York U., North York, Ont., Can., 1991-92, U. Paris-St. Denis, 2002, 2005-06; fellow Harvard U., Cambridge, Mass., 1973-75. Editor: Struggle a Hard Battle: Essays on Working-Class Immigrants, 1986; co-editor (with Christiane Harzig) The Immigrant Labor Press in North America (3 vols.), 1987, (with Leslie Page Moch) European Migrants: Global and Local Perspectives, 1995, Creating Societies. Immigrant Lives in Canada, 1999, Cultures in Contact: World Migrations in the Second Millenium, 2002. Mem. Orgn. Am. Historians, Am. Hist. Assn., Can. Ethnic Studies Assn., Can. Studies Assn. in German-Speaking Countries (v.p. 2001-03, pres. 2003-05).

HOERNER, ROBERT JACK, lawyer; b. Fairfield, Iowa, Oct. 12, 1931; s. John Andrew and Margaret Louise (Simmons) Hoerner; m. Judith Chandler, Apr. 21, 1954 (div. Feb. 1975); children: John Andrew II, Timothy Chandler, Blayne Marie Hoerner Murray, Michelle Margaret Hoerner Smith; m. Mary Paolano, June 3, 1989. BA, Cornell Coll., 1953; JD, U. Mich., 1958. Bar: Ohio 1960, US Supreme Ct 1964, US Ct Appeals (6th cir) 1972, US Ct Appeals (fed cir) 1990. Law clk. to hon. Chief Justice Earl Warren US Supreme Ct., Washington, 1958-59; assoc. Jones Day, Cleve., 1959-63, 65-66; chief evaluation sect. antitrust divsn. Dept. Justice, Washington, 1963-65; ptnr. Jones, Day, Reavis & Pogue, Cleve., 1967-93. Contbr. articles to profl jours; editor (editor-in-chief): (journal) Mich Law Rev. Trustee New Orgn Visual Arts, Cleveland, Ohio, 1976—80, 1987—90. With Counter Intelligence Corps US Army, 1953—55. Mem.:

ABA (antitrust sect, patent sect), Fed. Bar Assn., Cleve. Intellectual Property Law Assn., Greater Cleve. Bar Assn., Ohio Bar Assn., Leland Mich. Country Club, Order of Coif, Phi Beta Kappa. Democrat. Home: 360 Darbys Run Bay Village OH 44140-2968 Office: Jones Day 901 Lakeside Ave E Ste N-335 Cleveland OH 44114-1190 Office Phone: 440-356-3723. Business E-Mail: rjhoerner@jonesday.com.

HOESLI, HANNA, dentist; BS in Biology, UCLA, 1978; DDS, U. So. Calif, 1982. Pvt. practive, LA, 1982—; clin. prof. U. So. Calif Sch. Dentistry. Recipient Am. Assn. Dental Anesthesiology Sr. Recognition award. Mem.: Am. Dental Assn., Calif. Dental Soc., LA Dental Soc., U. So. Calif. Dental Sch. Alumni Assn., Acad. Gen. Dentistry, Phi Betta Kappa Alumni. Office: 7060 Hollywood Blvd #400 Hollywood CA 90028 also: U So Calif Sch Dentistry 925 W 34th St DEN 235 Los Angeles CA 90089 E-mail: drhanna@flash.net.

HOEVEN, JOHN, governor; b. Bismarck, ND, Mar. 13, 1957; m. Mical (Mikey); children: Marcela, Jack. B in history and econ., Dartmouth Coll., 1979; MBA, J.L. Kelloge Grad. Sch. Mngmt., Northwestern U., 1981. Exec. v.p. First Western Bank, Minot, N.D., 1986-93; pres., CEO Bank of ND (BND), 1993-2000; gov. State of ND, Bismarck, 2000—. Econ. adv. N.D. Univ.; trustee Bismarck State Coll.; regent Minot State U., chmn, Midwestern Gov. Conf. Cmty. chair Mo. Slope Areawide Campaign, 1998; chair Minot Chamber Commerce AFB Retention com., Minot Area Devel. Corp.; dir. Minot Kiwanis Club, Souris Valley Humane Soc, State Fair Adv. com.; mem. bd. dirs. First Western Bank and Trust, N.D. Bankers Assn., State Bank Bd., N.D. Small Bus. Investment Co., Prairie Pub. Broadcasting, N.D. Econ. Devel. Assn., Bismarck YMCA, Harold Schafer Leadership Ctr. Republican. Roman Catholic. Office: Gov Office Dept 101 600 E Blvd Ave Bismarck ND 58505-0001 Office Phone: 701-328-2200. Office Fax: 701-328-2205.*

HOFACKET, JEAN, library director; M in Libr. and Info. Sci., Emporia State U., Kans. Dir. info. svcs. AIDS Info. Network, Phila.; dir. Found. Ctr., San Francisco; dep. county libr. Alameda County Libr., Fremont, Calif., 2000—05, interim county libr., 2005, county libr., 2005—. Contbr. articles to profl. jours. Office: Alameda County Libr 2450 Stevenson Blvd Fremont CA 94538 Office Phone: 510-745-1510. E-mail: jhofacket@aclibrary.org.

HOFER, ROY ELLIS, lawyer; b. Cin., Oct. 10, 1935; s. Eric Walter and Elsie Katherine (Ellis) H.; m. Suzanne Elizabeth Sturtz, June 6, 1956 (div. 1974); m. Cynthia Ann Corson, June 5, 1981; children: Kimberly, Tracy, Eric. BChemE, Purdue U., 1957; JD, Georgetown U., Washington, DC, 1961. Patent examiner US Patent & Trademark Office, Washington, 1957-59; patent agt. Exxon Corp., Washington, 1959-61; ptnr. Brinks Hofer Gilson & Lione, Chgo., 1961—, pres., 1995-99. Adv. com. No. Dist. Ill., 1991-95. Contbr. articles to profl. jours. Bd. dirs. Chgo. Lung Assn., 1982-83, Ctr. for Conflict Resolution, 1983-88, 90-91, pres., 1991-97; bd. dirs. Union League Club Chgo., 1984-88, Boys and Girls Club, Chgo., 1985-89, Ill. Inst. CLE, Chgo., 1986-88, Ill. chpt. Crohn's and Colitis Found. Am., 2001-06. Mem. ABA (dir. litigation sect. 1982-87), Fed. Cir. Bar Assn. (pres. 1993-94), Chgo. Bar Assn. (pres. 1988-89), Intellectual Property Law Assn. Chgo., Am. Intellectual Property Law Assn., Legal Club Chgo., Phi Eta Sigma, Tau Beta Pi, Omega Chi Epsilon. Republican. Office: Brinks Hofer Gilson & Lione Ste 3600 455 N Cityfront Plaza Dr Chicago IL 60611-5599 Office Phone: 312-321-4204. Business E-Mail: rhofer@usebrinks.com.

HOFER, STEPHEN ROBERT, lawyer; b. Anderson, Ind., July 25, 1950; s. Robert E. and Maxine (Hert) H.; m. Cheryl A. Stiles, Aug. 27, 1994; children: Victoria Sloane, Morgan BrynRose. AB, Ind. U., 1976; JD, Northwestern U., 1980. Bar: Calif. 1980, U.S. Dist. Ct. (ctrl. dist.) Calif. 1980, U.S. Ct. Appeals (9th cir.) 1980, U.S. Dist. Ct. (ea., no., and so. dists.) Calif. 1982, U.S. Supreme Ct. 1995. Mng. editor Daily Herald-Tel., Bloomington, Ind., 1972-74; asst. city editor Miami Herald, Ft. Lauderdale, Fla., 1976-77; atty. Gibson Dunn & Crutcher, LA, 1980-84; venue press chief L.A. Olympic Organizing Com., 1983-84; v.p., gen. counsel Am. Golf Corp., Santa Monica, Calif., 1984-92; of counsel Bailey & Marzano, Santa Monica, 1992-98; ptnr., chair corp. and transactional dept. Bailey & Ptnrs., Santa Monica, 1998—2005; pres. Aerlex Law Group, Santa Monica, 2006—. Instr. law U. So. Calif., L.A., 1983-84, lectr. aviation law Calif. State U., L.A. Sec., bd. dirs. Mus. of Flying, Santa Monica, 1986-89; bd. dirs. L.A. Philharmonic Assn., 1992-95, Santa Monica Symphony Assn., 1999-2000; pres. L.A. Philharmonic Bus. and Profl. Assn., 1992-95. Mem.: SAR, Soc. Ind. Pioneers, Order of Descendants of Ancient Planters, Soc. of War of 1812, Sons of Union Vets. of Civil War, Jamestowne Soc. Democrat. Avocations: symphonic music and jazz, mountain climbing, travel, genealogy, photography. Business E-Mail: shofer@aerlex.com.

HOFERER, PAUL R., lawyer, rail transportation executive; BA, Ctrl. Mo. State U., Warrensburg, 1972; JD, Washburn U. Sch. Law, Topeka, 1975. Mem. law dept. Burlington No. Santa Fe Corp., Ft. Worth, 1975—89, gen. atty., 1989—94, asst. gen. counsel, 1994, asst. v.p., 1995—98, gen. counsel, 1999—2002, v.p., gen. counsel, 2002—. Bd. govs. Washburn U. Sch. Law. Mem.: Nat. Assn. RR Trial Counsel (pres.). Office: Burlington No Santa Fe Corp PO Box 961056 Fort Worth TX 76161-0056 Office Phone: 817-352-2332, 817-352-2332. E-mail: paul.hoferer@bnsf.com.

HOFF, BENJAMIN LLOYD, writer, scriptwriter; b. Portland, Oreg., Nov. 27, 1946; s. Lloyd Henry and Clementine Catlin (Elmer) Hoff; m. Deborah Alysoun Pratt, May 1, 1993; 1 stepchild, Joel Orion Newman. BA in Asian Art, Evergreen State Coll., 1973. Author: The Tao of Pooh, 1982 (NY Times Bestselling Paperback Authors, 1994), The Singing Creek Where the Willows Grow: the Rediscovered Diary of Opal Whiteley, 1986 (Am. Book award), The Te of Piglet, 1992, N.Y. Times Bestselling Paperback Authors, 1994, The Singing Creek Where the Willows Grow: the Mystical Nature Diary of Opal Whiteley, 1995. Avocations: landscape photography, classical guitar, fine pruning, tennis.

HOFF, CHARLES WORTHINGTON, III, retired banker; b. Balt., Mar. 1, 1934; s. Charles Worthington Jr and Sarah Durant (Yearley) Hoff; m. Margaret Elizabeth Ober, Sept. 7, 1967; children: Zoe Carey, Alexandra Yearley, Juliana Macgill, Margaret Frazier, Charles Worthington IV. BS in Bus., Johns Hopkins U., 1961; postgrad., Stonier Sch. Banking, 1964-66. With First Nat. Bank Md., Balt., 1955-77, div. v.p., 1968-77; exec. v.p. Farmers & Mechanics Nat. Bank, Frederick, 1977-81, pres., 1981-93, chmn., 1993—2001, also bd. dirs.; ret., 2001. Bd dirs F & M Bancorp, pres, 1983—93, chmn., 1993—2001, chmn. emeritus, 1991—. Bd dirs Children's Aid and Family Serv Soc Baltimore, 1972—77, mem exec comt, fin comt, 1974—76; pres Oriole Advs, Inc, 1963, treas, 1964—65; mem exec comt, mem fin comt, trustee Hood Col, 1985—97, chmn fin comts, trustee emeritus, 1997—; trustee Frederick Mem Hosp, 1983—89, Community Found Frederick County Md, 1987—92. Mem.: Frederick County CofC (bd dirs 1980—82), Md Bankers Asn (bd dirs 1988—90, vpres 1992—93, pres-elect 1993—94, pres 1994—95), Am Inst Banking, Am Bankers Asn (coun, vpres Md 1983, educ, policy and develop coun 1990—93, bd dirs 1995—98), Club 18, Frederick Cotillion Club, Dataw (SC) Island Club, Cap and Gown Club (Princeton, NJ), Holly Hills Country Club, Rotary. Democrat. Methodist. Personal E-mail: mrchair@aol.com.

HOFF, GERHARDT MICHAEL, lawyer, insurance company executive; b. Vienna, June 12, 1930; came to U.S., 1951, naturalized, 1955; s. Erich Theodor and Vilma (Frank) Klockenhoff; m. Lisa Decristoforo, June 1, 1970; children: Michael, Elisabeth, Anne-Christine. Student, U. Munich Law Sch., Germany, 1948-51, Columbia U., 1951-52; LL.B., NYU, 1958; LL.M. in Taxation, Emory U., 1982; C.L.U., 1961. Bar: Mass. 1959, D.C. 1968, Ga. 1984. With Mass. Mut. Life Ins. Co. and Variable Annuity Life Ins. Co., 1958-67; v.p. Variable Annuity Life Ins. Co. Am., Washington, 1967-68; mem. staff fin. services group ITT Corp., 1968-69; pres. ITT Hamilton Life Ins. Co., also ITT Variable Annuity Ins. Co., St. Louis, 1970-72, Sun Life Ins. Co. Am., Balt., 1972-78, 81-83, chief exec. officer, 1972-83; pres. Sun Life Group Am., Inc., Atlanta, 1978-83. Chmn. law practice Bus. Planning Corp. Am., Atlanta, 1983—; founder (with Lisa Hoff) Cities in Color, Inc., 1985—. Served with AUS, 1955-57. Decorated Commendation ribbon with pendant. Mem. Am. Soc. C.L.U.'s, ABA Clubs: Capital City (Atlanta). Presbyterian. Office: 12 Braemore Dr NW Atlanta GA 30328-4845 Office Phone: 404-255-1185. E-mail: gmhoff2@aol.com. *We'll get along better with others if we recognize their right to be hard or easy on themselves, depending on their own choice of priorities.*

HOFF, JOHN SCOTT, lawyer; b. Des Moines, Jan. 2, 1946; s. John Richard and Valetta R. (Scott) H.; m. Susan Murial Felver, June 21, 1972 (div. 1975); m. Shirley Jo Ward, June 21, 1975 (separated 1996); children: Jennifer Jo, John Baron. BSBA, Drake U., 1967; MBA, Calif. State U., Fullerton, 1971; postgrad., Oxford U., Eng., 1973; JD, Southwestern U., LA, 1975; MA in Mil. History, Am. Mil. U., 1995. Bar: Iowa 1976, Ill. 1977, Calif. 1980, Nebr. 1983, D.C. 1983, Wis. 1984, N.Y. 1995, Minn. 1996, U.S. Ct. Claims 1976, U.S. Ct. Customs and Patent Appeals 1976, U.S. Ct. Mil. Appeals 1976, U.S. Dist. Ct. (no. dist.) Ill. 1977, U.S. Ct. Appeals (7th cir.) 1979, U.S. Supreme Ct. 1982, U.S. Dist. Ct. (so. dist.) Iowa 1987, U.S. Ct. Appeals (9th and 10th cirs.) 1988, U.S. Dist. Ct. Ariz. 1990, U.S. Ct. Appeals (6th cir.) 1990, Mich. 1991, U.S. Ct. Appeals (8th cir.) 1991, U.S. Dist. Ct. (cen. dist.) Ill. 1996; CPCU; chartered cost analyst; FAA comml. pilot; cert. flight instr., instrument and mult-erg ratings. Staff atty. FAA Hdqrs., Washington, 1975-76; assoc. Lord, Bissell & Brook, Chgo., 1976-81; ptnr. Lapin, Hoff, Slaw & Laffey, Chgo., 1981-92, John Scott Hoff & Assocs., P.C., Chgo., 1992—; adj. prof. aviation law John Marshall Law Sch., Chgo., 1993—. Real estate broker Ill. Dept. Profl. Regulation, Springfield, 1980— Contbr. articles to profl. jours. Bd. dirs. USO of Ill., 1996—. Col. USAF, 1967—98. Decorated Legion of Merit. Mem. ABA, Aviation Ins. Assn. (dir. 1988-1990, v.p. 1990-92, pres. 1992-94), Air Force Assn. (v.p., pres. 1980-93), Internat. Soc. Air Safety Investigation (v.p.), Nat. Aero. Assn., Gen. Aviation Pilots' Assn., Res. Officers Assn., Mil. Officers Assn., Chgo. Bar Assn., Lawyers-Pilots Bar Assn., NTSB Bar Assn., Aircraft Owners and Pilots Assn., Exptl. Aircraft Assn., Nat. Assn. Flight Instrs., Aero. Club Chgo. Republican. Presbyterian. Avocations: flying, military history. Office: Hoff & Collins 20 S Clark St Ste 2210 Chicago IL 60603-1816 Office Phone: 312-346-8111. Business E-Mail: jsh@aviationattorney.com.

HOFF, JONATHAN M(ORIND), lawyer; b. Chgo., July 4, 1955; s. Irwin S. and Ida (Indritz) H. AB, U. Calif., Berkeley, 1978; JD, UCLA, 1981. Bar: Calif. 1981, U.S. Dist. Ct. (no. and cen. dists.) Calif. 1981, N.Y. 1982, U.S. Dist. Ct. (so. dist.) N.Y. 1982, U.S. Ct. Appeals (4th, 5th, 7th, 8th, 9th, 10th cirs.) 1982. Ptnr. Weil, Gotshal & Manges, NYC, 1981-98, Cadwalader, Wickersham & Taft, NYC, 1998—. Comment editor UCLA Law Rev., 1980-81; contbr. articles to law jours. Mem.: ABA, Calif. Bar Assn. Office: Cadwalader Wickersham & Taft LLP One World Fin Ctr New York NY 10281 Office Phone: 212-504-6000.

HOFF, JULIAN THEODORE, neurosurgeon, educator; b. Boise, Idaho, Sept. 22, 1936; s. Harvey Orval and Helen Marie (Boraas) H.; m. Diane Shanks, June 3, 1962; children— Paul, Allison, Julia. BA, Stanford U., Calif., 1958; MD, Cornell U., NYC, 1962. Diplomate Am. Bd. Neurol. Surgery. Intern N.Y. Hosp., NYC, 1962-63, resident in surgery, 1963-64, resident in neurosurgery, 1966-70; asst. prof. neurosurgery U. Calif., San Francisco, assoc. prof. neurosurgery, 1974-78, prof. neurosurgery, 1978-81, U. Mich., Ann Arbor, 1981—, head sect. neurosurgery, 1981—90, chair dept. neurosurgery, 1990—96. Sec. Am. Bd. Neurol-Surgery, 1987-91, chmn., 1991-92; mem. bd. sci. councillors Nat. Inst. Neurol. Diseases and Stroke-NIH, 1993-97, nat. adv. coun., 1999—. Editor: Practice of Neurosurgery, 1979-85; Current Surgical Management of Neurological Diseases, 1980; Neurosurgery: Diagnostic and Management Principles, 1992, Mild to Moderate Head Injury, 1989; co-editor: Neurosurgery: Scientific Basis of Clinical Practice, 1985, 3rd edit., 1999; contbr. articles to profl. jours. Served to capt. US Army, 1964-66. Recipient Tchr.-Investigator award, NIH, 1972—77, Javits Neurosci. Investigator award, 1985—99, Macy Faculty scholar, London, 1979. Fellow: ACS (2d v.p.-elect 1998—99); mem.: Soc. Neurol. Surgeons (pres. 1999—2000, Grass prize 2001), Cen. Neurosurg. Soc. (pres. 1985—86), Am. Acad. Neurosurgeons (treas. 1989—92, sec. 1992—, pres. 1996—), Congress Neurol. Surgeons (v.p. 1982—83, Honored Guest 2003), Am. Surg. Assn., Am. Assn. Neurol. Surgeons (v.p. 1991—93, pres. 1993—94, Cushing medal 2001), Inst. Medicine NAS. Republican. Presbyterian. Home: 2120 Wallingford Rd Ann Arbor MI 48104-4563 Office: U Mich Hosp TC 3893 Ann Arbor MI 48109 Office Phone: 734-936-5020. Business E-Mail: jhoff@umich.edu.

HOFF, PETER SLOAT, academic administrator, educator; m. Dianne L. Balzer; children: Marc, Jay, Lara. BA in English with honors, U. Wis., 1966; MA in English, Stanford U., 1968, PhD in English and Humanities, 1970. Prof., faculty devel. leader U. Wis., 1970—87, adminstr.; acad. vice chancellor Ind. U. S.E., 1987—90, Univ. Sys. of Ga., 1990—93, Calif. State U., 1993—97; pres. U. Maine, Orono, 1997—2004, univ. sys. prof., 2004—. Contbr. articles on nineteenth and twentieth century Brit. fiction. Player French horn in orchs. Mich., Wis., Ind., Ga., Calif., Maine. Mem. Phi Kappa Phi, Phi Beta Kappa. Office Phone: 207-581-2722. E-mail: peterhoff@umaine.edu.

HOFFA, JAMES PHILLIP, labor union administrator; b. Detroit, May 19, 1941; s. James R. and Josephine Hoffa; m. Virginia Harris; children: David, Geoffrey. BS in Economics, Mich. State U., 1963; LLB, U. Mich., 1966. Laborer Internat. Brotherhood Teamsters, Detroit and, Alaska, 1960—68, atty., 1968-93, exec. asst. to pres. Mich. Joint Coun. 43, 1993-98, gen. pres., 1999—. Mem. Pres. Council on the 21st Century Workforce, 2002, Secretary of Energy Adv. Bd., 2002. Named Man of Yr., Bay Area Union Labor Party, 2001, Friends of Ireland, 2004; recipient Labor Initiative award, Ctr. for Disabled, 2001, honoree, Irish-Am. Labor Coalition, 2001, Govt., Labor, Mgmt. Good Scout award, Nat. Capital Area Coun. Boy Scouts of Am., 2003; grantee Ford Found. fellowship, 1967. Mem.: Alpha Tau Omega. Avocations: fishing, hunting, golf. Office: Internat Brotherhood Teamsters Office of the Gen Pres 25 Louisiana Ave NW Washington DC 20001-2130*

HOFFENBERG, MARVIN, retired political science professor; b. Buffalo, July 7, 1914; s. Harry and Jennie Pearl (Weiss) H.; m. Betty Eising Stern, July 20, 1947; children: David A., Peter H. Student, St. Bonaventure Coll., 1934—35; BSc, Ohio State U., 1939, MA, 1940, postgrad., 1941. Asst. chief divsn. interindustry econs. Bur. Labor Statistics, Dept. Labor, 1941-52; cons. U.S. Mut. Security Agy., Europe, 1952, Statistik Sentralbyra, Govt. Norway, Oslo, 1954; economist RAND Corp., 1952—56; dir. rsch., econ. cons. dept. deVegh & Co., 1956—58; staff economist Com. Econ. Devel., 1958-60; project chmn. Rsch. Analysis Corp. (formerly Johns Hopkins U. Ops. Rsch.), 1960-63; dir. cost analysis dept. Aerospace Corp., 1963-65; rsch. economist Inst. Govt. and Pub. Affairs, UCLA, 1965-67, prof.-in-residence polit. sci., 1967-85, prof. emeritus, 1985—; dir. M.P.A. program, co-chmn. Interdepartmental Program in Comprehensive Health Planning UCLA, 1974-76. Author: (with Kenneth J. Arrow) A Time Series Analysis of Inter-Industry Demand, 1959; editor: (with Levine, Hardt and Kaplan) Mathematics and Computers in Soviet Economics, 1967; contbr. articles to profl. jours., chpts. to books. Mem. bd. advisers Sidney Stern Meml. Trust; bd. dirs. L.A. chpt. Am. Jewish Com.; foreman L.A. County Grand Jury, 1990-91; commr. L.A. County Economy and Efficiency Commn., 1991-92. C.C. Stillman scholar Ohio State U., 1940, U. fellow, 1941; Littauer fellow Harvard U., 1946; recipient Disting. Svc. award Coll. Adminstrv. Scis., Ohio State U., 1971. Mem.: AAAS (life fellow 1957), Am. Jewish Com. (bd. mem. LA chpt.). Jewish. Home: 1365 Marinette Rd Pacific Palisades CA 90272 Home Phone: 310-454-4403. Business E-Mail: hoffen@ucla.edu.

HOFFER, JOHN LEE, health facility administrator, medical educator; BS, LeTourneau U., 1955; PhD in Biomed. Engring., U. N.C., Chapel Hill; MD, U. N.C., 1976. Diplomate Am. Bd. Anesthesiology, Am. Bd. Quality Assurance and Utilization Rev. Physicians. Resident anesthesiology U. N.C. Hosps.; assoc. prof. anesthesiology Ohio State U., 1979—83, assoc. prof. biomed. engring., 1979—83; assoc. prof. anesthesiology and physiology Northeastern Ohio U. Coll. Medicine, 1984—92; prof. engring. Tex. A&M U., 1992—; prof. anesthesiology Tex. A&M U. Health Sci. Ctr., Sch. Medicine, 1992—. Chmn. libr. com., Scott & White Regional Clinics, mem. quality assurance com., coord. CPI, mem. instnl. rev. bd., mem. tenure and faculty promotion com. Fellow, NIH. Office: Dept Anesthesiology 2401 S 31st St Temple TX 76508

HOFFERT, BARBARA, editor; Book reviewer Libr. Jour., NYC, 1986—92, book review editor, 1992—. Bd. mem., past pres. Nat. Book Critics Circle; past chair materials selection com., Reference & User Services Assn., div of ALA. Recipient Louis Shores-Greenwood Pub. Group award, ALA, 2006. Office: Library Journal 360 Park Ave S New York NY 10010 Office Phone: 646-746-6806. Business E-Mail: hoffer@reedbusiness.com.

HOFFERT, ERIC MICHAEL, application developer, information technology executive; b. Bklyn., Oct. 7, 1962; s. Martin I. Hoffert and Linda Moses; m. Sara A. Topitzer, Aug. 12, 1989; 1 child, Maya Leah Hoffert Topitzer. BS in Computer Sci., NYU, 1985; BSME, Cooper Union, 1985; MSc in Math. Scis., NYU, 1988. Sr. rsch. scientist AT&T Bell Labs., Holmdel, NJ, 1985—89; mgr. multimedia comm. Apple Computer, Inc., Cupertino, Calif., 1989—96; chief tech. officer Magnifi, Inc., Los Gatos, Calif., 1996—2002; CEO Versatility Software, Inc., South Orange, NJ, 2002—, Cons. Stanford U., Palo Alto, Calif., 2002—05, Carnegie Mellon U., Pitts., 2003—04, Campbells Soup, Camden, NJ, 2003, Scripps Networks, Knoxville, Tenn., 2005—06. Author: Frontiers of Scientific Visualization, 1994, (book chapter) Scientific Visualization, 1994, (songs) The Speedies - Soundtrack for HP Global Advertising Campaign, 2005; mem. editl. bd.: Jour. Digital Asset Mgmt., 2004—06; contbr. articles to profl. jours. Recipient CEO Tech. award, Apple, 1995, Honors award, Computerworld, 2001, Wiz Kids award, Customer Relationship Mgmt., 2006; scholar, Cooper Union, 1981—85, AT&T Bell Labs., 1985—88. Democrat. Jewish. Achievements include twelve patents; development of Apple QuickTime; patents pending for DIVER technology development; development of multimedia search engine. Avocations: jogging, hiking, reading, space technology research, victorian architecture and renovation. Home and Office: Versatility Software Inc 349 Montrose Avenue South Orange NJ 07079 Home Phone: 973-762-9293; Office Phone: 973-762-9323. Business E-Mail: eric@versatility-inc.com.

HOFFERT, MARTIN IRVING, aerospace scientist, educator; b. Bklyn., July 1, 1938; s. Solomon and Ceil (Hyman) H.; m. Linda Epstein, Sept. 4, 1960; 1 child, Eric; m. 2d, Iris E. Fierst, Jan. 29, 1965. BS in Aero. Engring., U. Mich., 1960, MS in Astronautics, 1964; PhD in Astronautics, Poly. Inst. Bklyn., 1967; MA in Liberal Studies, New Sch. for Social Research, 1969. Sr. scientist Gen. Applied Sci. Labs., Westbury, NY, 1962-67; research scientist NYU, 1967-68; sr. research scientist Advanced Tech. Labs., Westbury, 1968-69; mem. research staff Riverside Research Inst., NYC, 1969-72; sr. research assoc. Goodard Inst. for Space Studies NASA, NYC, 1972-74; sr. research scientist NYU, 1974-76, assoc. prof. applied sci., 1976-83, prof. applied sci., 1983-94, chmn. applied sci., 1984-91, prof. physics, 1995—2005, prof. emeritus, 2005—. Mgmt. ops. working group in planetary atmosphere NASA, Washington, 1986-90; bilateral coop. working group VIII U.S. Del. Joint U.S.-USSR Commn., 1986-92; cons. Exxon Rsch. & Engring., Annandale, N.J., 1986-95, Lawrence Livermore Nat. Lab., 1990—. Contbr. over 65 articles to profl. jour. and chpts. to books. Fellow AAAS; mem. AAIA, Am. Geophys. Union, Am. Metereol. Soc., Aspen Global Change Inst. (adv. bd.). Democrat. Jewish. Avocations: bicycling, hiking, boating. Home: 12 Oak Dr Great Neck NY 11021 Office: NYU Dept Physics New York NY 10003 Office Phone: 212-998-3747. E-mail: marty.hoffert@nyu.edu.

HOFFHEIMER, DANIEL JOSEPH, lawyer; b. Cin., Dec. 28, 1950; s. Harry Max and Charlotte (O'Brien) Hoffheimer; m. Elizabeth Lee Hoffheimer; children: Rebecca, Rachel, Leah. Grad., Phillips Exeter Acad., 1969; AB cum laude, Harvard Coll., Cambridge, Mass., 1973; JD, U. Va., Charlottesville, 1976. Bar: Ohio 1976, US Dist. Ct. (so. dist.) Ohio 1976, US Ct. Appeals (6th cir.) 1977, US Ct. Appeals (DC and fed. cir.) 1986, US Ct. Internat. Trade 1986, US Tax Ct. 1992, US Supreme Ct. 1980, US Ct. Military Justice 2007, cert.: (Specialist Estate Planning Trust and Probate Law). Assoc. Taft, Stettinius & Hollister, Cin., 1976-84, ptnr., 1984—. Lectr. law Coll. Law, U. Cin., 1981-83; trustee Judges Hogan & Porter Meml. Trust; mem. adv. bd. Ohio Dist. Ct. Rev.; state counsel Ohio, John Kerry for Pres. Com., 2004; legal counsel Greater Cin. Found., 2006—; faculty Xavier U. Pvt. Bus. Inst., 2007—. Editor-in-chief U. Va. Jour. Internat. Law, 1975-76; co-author: Practitioners' Handbook Ohio First District Court Appeals, 1984, 2d edit., 1991, Federal Practice Manual, U.S. 6th Circuit Court of Appeals, 1999, Manual on Labor Law, 1988; mem. editl. bd. Probate Law Jour. Ohio, 2000—; contbr. articles to profl. jours. Mem. Cin. Symphony Bus. Rels. Com., 1977-86, Cin. Composers Guild, 1988-93, Ohio Supreme Ct. Com. Racial Fairness, 1993-00; trustee Underground R.R. Freedom Ctr., 1995—, presiding co-chair, 2004-06; adv. bd. Consumer Protection, Cin., 1978-80, Hoxworth Blood Ctr. U. Cin. Hosp., 1994-99; bd. dirs. Hebrew Union Coll. Jewish Inst. Religion, 1994—, WGUC-FM Pub. Radio, 1988—, vice chmn., 1993-96, chmn., 1996-98, Greater Cin. Chinese Music Soc., 2003-06; trustee Cin. Chamber Orch., 1977-80, Seven Hills Sch., Cin., 1980-86, Internat. Visitors Ctr., Cin., 1980-84, Friends Coll. Conservatory of Music, Cin., 1985-86, Cin. Symphony Orch., 1988-94, 96-05, sec., 1996-99, vice chair 1999-00, chair, 2001-04, Children's Psychiat. Ctr., Cin., 1986-89, treas., 1987-89; vice chmn. Jewish Hosp., Cin., 1989-92; Leadership Cin., 1989-90; sec., trustee Cin. Symphony Musicians Pension Fund, 1989-99, Jewish Cmty. Rels. Coun., 1990-98, v.p., 1996-98; sec. Nat. Conf. Commn. Justice, 1992-99, treas. 1999-00, trustee emeritus, 2000—; counsel Cin. AIDS Commn., 1991—, Cin. Inst. Fine Arts Govt. Affairs Com., 1993-94, B'nai B'rith Nat. Coun. Legacy Devel., 1996-97; legal counsel Greater Cin. Found., 2006-; state legal counsel Kerry-Edwards 2004, Inc., 2004-06. Named Outstanding Young Man, US Jaycees, 1984, 98; recipient Leadership Cin. C. of C. Disting. Leadership Alumni award, 2005. Life fellow Am. Bar Found.; fellow Ohio Bar Found., Am. Coll. Trust and Estate Counsel; mem. ABA, Internat. Bar Assn., Internat. Trade Bar Assn., Internat. Arbitration Assn. (comml. arbitrator 1991-95), Fed. Bar Assn. (treas. 1984, sec. 1985, v.p. 1986-87, pres. 1987-88), Ohio State Bar Assn. (bd. govs. Est. Pl. Trust and Probate Law sect. 1996—), Cin. Bar Assn. (trustee 1988-93, v.p. 1990-91, pres. 1992-93, chair Cin. Acad. Leadership for Lawyers 1998-2000), Harvard Club of Cin. (bd. dirs. 1980-88, v.p. 1983-86, pres. 1986-87). Democrat. Jewish. Avocations: music, opera, art, judaica. Home: 1 Forest Hill Dr Cincinnati OH 45208-1953 Office: 425 Walnut St Ste 1800 Cincinnati OH 45202-3957 Office Phone: 513-381-2838. Business E-Mail: hoffheimer@taftlaw.com. *The elusive meaning and joy of life is really at our fingertips: to make life better for others.*

HOFFHEIMER, MICHAEL HARRY, law educator; b. Cin., Dec. 21, 1954; s. Harry Max and Charlotte (O'Brien) H.; m. Luanne Buchanan; children: Joseph Allen, Jean Sarah. BA with gen. honors, Johns Hopkins U., 1977; MA, U. Chgo., 1978, PhD in History, 1981; JD cum laude, U. Mich., 1984. Bar: Ohio 1984, U.S. Dist. Ct. (ea. dist.) Ky. 1984, U.S. Ct. Appeals (6th cir.) 1984, U.S. Dist. Ct. (so. dist.) Ohio 1985, D. C. Ct. Appeals 1985, U.S. Supreme Ct. 1987, U.S. Ct. Appeals (5th cir.) 1987. Intern Office of State Appellate Defender, Ottawa, Ill., summer-fall 1982; summer assoc. Frost & Jacobs, Cin., 1983, assoc., 1984-87; asst. prof. law U. Miss., Oxford, 1987-90, assoc. prof. law, 1990-97, prof. law, 1997—, Miss. Def. Lawyers Assn. Disting. lectr., 1998—. Adj. faculty U. Cin. Coll. Law, 1985-87; panel mem. Hamilton County Pub. Defender, Cin., 1985-87. Author: Justice Holmes and the Natural Law, 1992, Eduard Gans and the Hegelian Philosophy of Law, 1995, Directory of Law Reviews, 6th edit., 2005, Fiddling for Viola, 2000; articles editor U. Mich. Jour. Law Reform, 1983; contbr. articles to profl. jours. Kunstader fellow, U. Chgo., 1978—79.

HOFFHEIMER, MINETTE GOLDSMITH, community service volunteer; b. Cin., May 1, 1927; d. Philip Hess and Cecile (Crager) Goldsmith; m. Arthur Hoffheimer Jr., June 16, 1948; children: Craig R., Roger Steven, James Martin, Mark Todd. Student, Conn. Coll. for Women, New London, 1945-48. Editor, prodr. (book in braille) Lilias Yoga and You, 1974, (poems) Marjorie's Book, 1974; editor: Lilias Yoga and Your Life, 1981; contbr. short story: (anthology) Cincinnati Short Story Winners, 1985. Trustee, sec. Cin. chpt. Nat. Coun. Jewish Women, 1966-73, chmn. and developer Large Type Program of Aid to Visually Handicapped, 1964-75, chmn. Angel Ball, 1968, on Angel Ball com. 1964-69, treas. thrift shop, 1965-67, auditor, mem. budget, ways and means, survey and evaluation coms., 1971; trustee Clovernook Home and Sch. for Blind, Cin., 1980-87; founder, 1st pres. Clovernook Assocs., Cin., 1981-85; chmn. edn. com., Boca Raton Mus. Art, 1996-2006, bd. trustee, 1996-2006; program developer, tchr. of Yoga to Blind, Cin., 1973-87; initiated Artful Memories art program Memory and Wellness Ctr. Coll. Nursing, Fla. Atlantic U., Boca Raton, Fla., 2004—. Named Vol. of Yr. Clovernook Home and Sch. for Blind, 1976, Woman of Yr. Cin. Enquirer, 1983. Mem. Brandeis, Nat. Braille Assn. (After 4000 hours svc. award 1971, 35 yr. cert. 2006), Cin. Yoga Tchrs. Assn., Life Long Learning Soc. Fla. Atlantic U., Friends of Boca Raton Mus. Art., others. E-mail: mghno1@aol.com.

HOFFINGER, ADAM STEVEN, lawyer; b. NYC, Oct. 22, 1956; s. Jack S. and Bernice Claire (Green) Hoffinger; m. Elizabeth Katherine Ramage, Aug. 4, 1985; children: Katherine, William, Margaret. BA, Trinity Coll., Hartford, Conn., 1978; JD, Fordham U., 1982. Bar: NY 1983, DC 1992, admitted to practice: US Supreme Ct. 1992, US Dist. Ct. (So. Dist.) NY 1983, US Dist. Ct. (Ea. Dist.) NY 1983, US Ct. Appeals (2nd Cir.) 1986, US Ct. Appeals (DC Cir.) 1990, US Dist. Ct. Md. 1996. Assoc. Anderson, Russell, Kill & Olick, NYC, 1982-85; asst. U.S. Atty. So. Dist. N.Y., NYC, 1985-90; prin. Schwalb, Donnenfeld, Bray & Silbert, Washington, 1990—98; ptnr. DLA Piper Rudnick Gray Cary, Washington, 1998—, head DC litigation, 1998—2006, chmn. White Collar practice group; ptnr. Morrison and Foerster, Washington, 2006—. Instr. Georgetown Univ. Law Ctr., George Mason Univ. Law Sch., Fed. Judicial Ctr. Editor: Fordham Urban Law Jour.; contbr. articles to profl. jour. Bd. dir. NY Ave. Found., Washington, 1993—. Named one of Top Lawyers in Washington, Legal Times, Best Lawyers in Am., 2001—, 75 Best Lawyers in Washington, Washingtonian mag., 2002, Greater Washington Legal Elite, Smart CEO Mag., 2005. Mem.: DC Bar, Assn. Bar City NY, ABA (white collar crime com.). Democrat. Jewish. Office: Morrison and Foerster 2000 Pennsylvania Ave NW Washington DC 20006-1888 Office Phone: 202-887-6924. Office Fax: 202-887-0763. Business E-Mail: ahoffinger@mofo.com.

HOFFINGER, SCOTT A., pediatric orthopaedic surgeon; b. Bronx, Sept. 17, 1959; s. Murray and Arline Hoffinger; m. Eileen Ryan Hoffinger, Oct. 10, 1987; children: Laura, Erin, Patrick, Kevin. AB, U. Mich., 1980, MD, 1983. Cert. Am. Bd. Orthopaedic Surgeons, lic. Calif. Asst. prof. U. Wash., Seattle, 1989—93; chief orthopaedics Children's Hosp. Oakland, 1994—. Bd. dirs. Med. Ins. Exch. Calif., Oakland; presenter in field. Contbr. articles to med. jours. and chpts. to books. Mem.: Am. Acad. for Cerebral Palsy and Devel. Medicine (treas. 1995—), Am. Acad. Orthopaedic Surgeons, Pediat. Orthopaedic Soc. Office: Children's Hosp Oakland 747 52d St Oakland CA 94609

HOFFLUND, MARK, theater director; AB in English, Princeton U.; MFA Profl. Theatre Training Program, U. Calif. San Diego. Actor, asst. dir., and dramaturgical assoc. Old Globe Theatre, San Diego; mng. dir. Idaho Shakespeare Festival. Bd. dir. San Diego Performing Arts League, Shakespeare Theatre Assn. of Am., Boise City Arts Commn., Boise Convention and Visitors Bur.; chmn. Idaho Commn. on the Arts, 2001—. Mem. Nat. Coun. on Arts Nat. Endowment for Arts, 2005—. Mailing: Idaho Shakespeare Festival PO Box 9365 Boise ID 83707 also: NEA 1100 Pennsylvania Ave NW Washington DC 20506

HOFFLUND, PAUL, lawyer; b. San Diego, Mar. 27, 1928; s. John Leslie and Ethel Frances (Cline) H.; m. Anne Marie Thalman, Feb. 15, 1958; children: Mark, Sylvia. BA, Princeton U., NJ, 1950; JD, George Washington U., 1956. Bar: D.C. 1956, U.S. Dist. Ct. D.C. 1956, U.S. Ct. Appeals (D.C. cir.) 1956, Calif. 1957, U.S. Dist. Ct. (so. dist.) Calif. 1957, U.S. Ct. Mil. Appeals 1957, U.S. Ct. Claims 1958, U.S. Ct. Appeals (9th cir.) 1960, U.S. Supreme Ct. 1964, U.S. Tax Ct. 1989. Assoc. Wencke, Carlson & Kuykendall, San Diego, 1961-62; ptnr. Carlson, Kuykendall & Hofflund, San Diego, 1963-65, Carlson & Hofflund, San Diego, 1965-72; Christian Sci. practitioner San Diego, 1972-84; arbitrator Mcpl. Cts. and Superior Ct. of Calif., San Diego, 1984-99; pvt. practice San Diego, 1985—. Adj. prof. law Nat. U. Sch. Law, San Diego, 1985-94; judge pro tem Mcpl. Ct. South Bay Jud. Dist., 1990-99; disciplinary counsel to U.S. Tax Ct., 1989-2003; asst. U.S. atty. U.S. Dept. of Justice, L.A., 1959-60, asst. U.S. atty. in charge, San Diego, 1960-61, spl. hearing officer, San Diego, 1962-68; asst. corp. counsel Govt. of D.C., 1957-59. Author: (chpt. in book) Handbook on Criminal Procedure in the U.S. District Court, 1967; contbr. articles to profl. jours. Treas. Princeton Club of San Diego; v.p. Community Concert Assn., San Diego; pres. Sunland Home Found., San Diego, Trust for Christian Sci. Orgn., San Diego; chmn. bd. 8th Ch. of Christ, Scientist, San Diego; chmn. Christian Sci. Com. on Instnl. Work in Calif., 2004—. With USN, 1950-53, comdr. JAGC, USNR, 1953-72, ret. Mem. ABA, San Diego County Bar Assn. Phi Delta Phi. Democrat. Avocations: theater, classical music, bridge, fine art, biblical study. Home and Office: 6146 Syracuse Ln San Diego CA 92122-3301 *Decisions should be based on divine direction rather than human determination. Pray first; then act. A life devoid of spirituality lacks dimension. The steps of a good man are ordered by the lord: And he delighteth in his way.*

HOFFMAN, ALAN CRAIG, lawyer, consultant; b. Chgo., Oct. 1, 1944; s. Morris Joseph and Marie E. Hoffman; m. Pamela Hoffman. BA, Carthage Coll., Kenosha, Wis., 1968; JD, John Marshall Law Sch., 1973. Bar: Fla. 1973, Ill. 1973, U.S. Dist. Ct. (no. dist.) Ill. 1974, U.S. Dist. Ct. (mid. dist.) Fla. 1981, U.S. Ct. Appeals (7th cir.) 1975, U.S. Ct. Appeals (5th and 11th cirs.) 1981, U.S. Supreme Ct. 1977. Staff atty. Cook County Legal Assistance Found., Brookfield, Ill., 1973-74, Patient Legal Svcs., Chgo., 1974; pvt. practice law Chgo., 1973—, River Grove, Ill., 1973-86, Oak Brook, Ill., 1980-87, Hinsdale, Ill., 1987-93; with assocs., 1980—. Spl. asst. atty. gen. Ill. Criminal Justice Divsn., Chgo., 1977—79, Ill. Condemnation Divsn., Chgo., 1980—87; pres. Almar, Ltd., 1986—91; v.p. Marach, Ltd., 1986—89, Hoffman Realty, 1978—; pres., dir. North Shore Greenview Bldg. Corp., 1978—2002; asst. prof. Lewis U., 1974—79; vis. profl. Coll. Law Paraprofl. Ctr., 1974—76, adj. prof., 1979—80; adj. prof. law Health Law Inst. Loyola U., Chgo., 2000—; assoc. prof. No. Ill. U., 1979—80; v.p. Adv. Svc., Inc.; cons. Med-Legal Cases, 1982—; moderator seminar Am. Coll. Legal Medicine, 2006; mem. legal com. C. of C. Barrington Hills, 2006—. Author (with F. Lane and D. Birnbaum): Lane's Medical Litigation Guide, 1981; mem. editl. bd.: Jour. Legal Medicine, 1980—, Med. Malpractice Prevention, 1986—96, Med. Malpractice Prevention Ob-Gyn, 1987—96, contbg. author: Legal Medicine: Legal Dynamics of Medical Encounters, 1988, Legal Medicine: Legal Dynamics of Medical Encounters, 3d edit., 1995, Legal Medicine: Legal Dynamics of Medical Encounters, supplements.; contbr. Med. Trial Technique Quar. Mem. Oak Park Twp. (Ill.) Mental Health Bd., 1975—80, v.p., 1975, chmn. program com., 1975—77, pres., 1978; mem. governing bd. Women In Need Growing Stronger, 1993—96; bd. govs. Jewish Fedn. Chgo., Coun. for Elderly, 1995—98; co-chair Rainbow House Bread and Roses Ann. Fundraiser, 1997—98; mem. bd. Cary Pk. Found., 2000—07; bd. dirs. Cary Pk. Dist. Found., 2004—. Fellow: Am. Coll. Legal Medicine (editl. bd. med. and legal textbook com. 1987—, textbook update com. 1988, program com. 1988—, legal com. 1988—, profl. devel. com. 1990—98, moot ct. competition com. 1992—98, student awards com. 1992—, chmn. 1992—, co-chair com. violence and abuse in the family 1993); mem.: ATLA, ABA (civil procedure and evidence com. 1993—, comml. tort com. 1993—), Chgo. Bar Assn., Ill. State Bar Assn. (vice chmn. standing com. on mentally disabled 1975—77, chmn. 1977—78), Fla. Bar Assn. (health law com. 1983—84, out-of-state practitioner com. 1988—91), Ill. Trial Lawyers Assn. (profl. negligence com. 1982), Mensa, Phi Alpha Delta. Office Phone: 312-855-0000. Personal E-mail: achassoc@aol.com. Business E-Mail: alan@alan-c-hoffman.com.

HOFFMAN, ALAN JAY, lawyer; b. Phila., Aug. 31, 1948; s. Heinz Julius and Sylvia (Wise) H.; m. Julie Goldman; children: Jennifer, Lauren, Allison. BBA, Temple U., 1970; JD, Villanova U., 1973. Bar: Pa. 1973, U.S. Dist. Ct. (ea. dist.) Pa. 1973, U.S. Dist. Ct. Del. 1973, U.S. Ct. Appeals (3rd cir.) 1973, Del. 1977, U.S. Supreme Ct. 1984, D.C. 1990. Asst. U.S. atty. U.S. Dept. Justice, Wilimington, Del., 1973-78; ptnr. Dilworth, Paxson, Kalish & Kauffman, Phila., 1979-92, mem. exec. mgmt. com., 1989-90, chmn. new bus. com., 1990-91; ptnr. Blank Rome LLP (formerly Blank, Rome, Comisky and McCauley), Phila., 1992—, adminstrv. ptnr. in charge Wilmington, Del., 1996—2002, chmn. litigation and dispute resolution dept., 1996—, mem. exec. mgmt. com. Phila., 1998—, co-chmn. atty. recruiting com., 1998—. Lectr. Widener Del. Law Sch., Wilmington, 1974, Mealy's Conf. on Toxic Torts, 1999—, Mealy's Conf. on MTBE pollution, 2000. Contbg. co-editor Villanova Law Rev., 1972-73; contbr. articles to profl. jours. Bd. dirs. Men's Club Temple Adath Israel, Merion, Pa., 1993-94; pres. Villanova Law Sch. Inn of Ct., 1999—. Recipient Atty. Gen.'s Spl. Commendation U.S. Dept. Justice, Washington, 1977. Fellow Am. Bar Found.; mem. ATLA, ABA, Pa. Bar Assn., Fed. Bar Assn., Phila. Bar Assn., Del. Bar Assn., Del. Trial Lawyers Assn., Pa. Trial Lawyers Assn., White Manor Country Club (pres. 1993—, 1st v.p. 1990-93, bd. dirs. 1988-90, admissions chmn. 1989—), J. Willard O'Brien Villanova Law Sch. Inn of Ct. (pres. 1999—). Avocation: golf. Office: Blank Rome LLP One Logan Sq Philadelphia PA 19103-6998 Office Phone: 215-569-5500. Business E-Mail: hoffman@blankrome.com.

HOFFMAN, ALAN JEROME, mathematician, educator; b. NYC, May 30, 1924; s. Jesse and Muriel (Schrager) H.; m. Esther Atkins Walker, May 30, 1947 (dec. July 1988); children: Eleanor, Elizabeth Hoffman Perry; m. Elinor Klausner Hershaft, Sept. 2, 1990. AB, Columbia U., 1947, PhD, 1950; DSc (hon.), Technion U., 1986. Mem. Inst. Advanced Study, Princeton, NJ, 1950-51; mathematician Nat. Bur. Standards, Washington, 1951-56; sci. liaison officer Office Naval Research, London, 1956-57; cons. Gen. Electric Co., NYC, 1957-61; rsch. staff mem. IBM Rsch. Ctr., Yorktown Heights, NY, 1961—2002, fellow, 1978—2002, fellow emeritus, 2002—. Vis. prof. Technion, Haifa, Israel, 1965, Stanford U., 1980-91, Rutgers U., 1990-96, Ga. Inst. Tech., 1992-93; adj. prof. CUNY, 1965-76, Yale U., 1976-85; Phi Beta Kappa lectr., 1989-90. With U.S. Army, 1943-46, ETO, PTO. Recipient von Neumann prize Ops. Rsch. Soc. and Inst. Mgmt. Sci., 1992, Founder's award Math. Programming Soc., 2000. Fellow Inst. for Ops. Rsch. and Mgmt. Sci., N.Y. Acad. Sci., Am. Acad. Arts and Scis.; mem. NAS, Am. Math. Soc. (coun. 1982-84). Office: IBM TJ Watson Rsch Ctr PO Box 218 Yorktown Heights NY 10598-0218 Office Phone: 914-945-2270.

HOFFMAN, ALFRED, JR., ambassador, real estate developer; married; 5 children. BS, US Military Acad., West Point; MBA, Harvard Univ. Pvt. developer, Tampa Bay, 1975—85; CEO, chmn. Fla. Design Communities, 1985—89, 1993—94; CEO, dir. Watermark Communities LP, 1995—2005, chmn., 2005; CEO, chmn. Courtyards at Sun City Ctr., Inc. and Sun City Ctr. Office Plz. Inc.; US amb. to Portugal US Dept. State, Lisbon, 2005—. Bd. dir. Aston Care Sys. Inc. Fighter pilot USAF. Office: Am Embassy 5320 Lisbon Pl Washington DC 20521

HOFFMAN, ALICE, writer; b. NYC, Mar. 16, 1952; m. Tom Martin; children: Jake, Zack. BA, Adelphi U., 1973; MA, Stanford U., 1975. Author: Property of, 1977, The Drowning Season, 1979, Angel Landing, 1980, White Horses, 1982, Fortune's Daughter, 1985, Illumination Night, 1987, At Risk, 1988, Seventh Heaven, 1990, Turtle Moon, 1992, Second Nature, 1994, Practical Magic, 1995, Local Girls, 1999, Fireflies: A Winter Tale, 1999, Horsefly, 2000, The River King, 2000, Blue Diary, 2001, Aquamarine, 2001, Indigo, 2002, Green Angel, 2003, The Probable Future, 2003, Blackbird House, 2004, The Ice Queen, 2005, (screenplay) Independence Day, 1983. Mirelles fellow Stanford U., 1975, Breadloaf fellow, 1976. Office: c/o Putnam Berkley 200 Madison Ave New York NY 10016-3903

HOFFMAN, ALICIA CORO, retired federal executive; b. Havana, Cuba, Mar. 28, 1937; d. Daniel P. and Alicia G. (Mignagaray) Camacho; m. Carlos J. Coro, May 1958 (dec. 1983); children: Alicia Biciocchi, Carlos M. Coro, Christina Kunowsky; m. Kenneth M. Hoffman, Mar. 1997. Tchg. diploma, U. Havana, 1961; MEd, U. Md., 1972. Tchr., supr. Montgomery County Pub. Schs., Rockville, Md., 1966-71; edn. spcialist U.S. Dept. Edn., Washington, 1971-80, dir. Horace Mann Learning Ctr., 1980-85, dep. asst. sec., acting asst. sec., Office for Civil Rights, 1985-87, dir. bilingual edn., 1987-88, dir. sch. improvement, 1988-96, sr. advisor, 1996-97; ret., 1997. Bd. dirs. Montgomery Pub. TV, 1984-94, Md. Higher Edn. Commn., 2004-05; bd. regents U. Sys. Md., 2005-. Recipient Presdl. Meritorious Rank award, U.S. Sr. Exec. Svc., 1992, Hispanic Achievement award in Edn., Hispanic Orgns., 1992, named Hispanic Woman of Yr., 1986. Mem. Nat. Asns. Cuban Am. Educators (bd. dirs. 1992-98), Nat. Assn. Cuban Am. Women (advisor 1980-88). Roman Catholic. Home: 909 Parsons Dr Madison MD 21648-1103

HOFFMAN, ALLAN SACHS, chemical engineer, educator; b. Chgo., Oct. 27, 1932; s. Saul A. and Frances E. (Sachs) H.; m. Susan Carol Freeman, July 29, 1962; children: David, Lisa. BSChemE, MIT, 1953, MSChemE, 1955, ScDChemE, 1957. Instr. chem. engring. MIT, Cambridge, 1954-56, asst. prof., 1958-60, assoc. prof., 1965-70; research engr. Calif. Research Corp., Richmond, 1960-63; asso. dir. research Amicon Corp., Cambridge, 1963-65; prof. bioengring. and chem. engring. U. Wash., Seattle, 1970—; asst. dir. Center for Bioengring., 1973-83. Cons. to various govtl., indsl. and acad. orgns., 1958—; UN adviser to Mexican govt., 1973-74. Author: (with W. Burlant) Block and Graft Copolymers, 1960; author numerous articles and book chpts. on chem. engring. and biomaterials; patentee in field Kimberly Clark fellow, 1954-55, Visking fellow, 1955-56, Fulbright fellow, 1957-58, Battelle fellow, 1970-72; Festschrift in honor of 60th birthday 8 issues of Jour. Biomaterials Sci., Polymer Edn., 1993. 94; recipient Founders award Controlled Release Soc., 2004. Mem. AIChE, NAE (elected mem. 2005), Am. Chem. Soc., Am. Soc. Artificial Internal Organs, Internat. Soc. Artificial Internal Organs (trustee, bd. dirs. 1987-90), Soc. Biomaterials (pres. 1983-84, Clemson award biomaterial sci. lit., 1985, Founder's award, 2000), Controlled Release Soc. (Excellence in Guiding Grad. Rsch. award 1989, 98, Founders award 2007), Japan Biomaterials Soc. (Biomaterials Sci. prize 1990, Symposium in honor of 70th birthday 2002), Soc. Polymer Sci. Japan (Internat. award 2006). Office: U Wash Mail Box 355061 Seattle WA 98195-5061 Business E-Mail: hoffman@u.washington.edu.

HOFFMAN, ANN FLEISHER, labor lawyer, educator, consultant; b. Phila., June 1, 1942; d. Willis Jr. and Mary (Leffler) Fleisher; m. Charles Stuart Hoffman Jr., June 7, 1964 (div. 1979); m. Arnold Perry Rubin, Jan. 1, 1985 (div. 1993). BA, Barnard Coll., 1964; JD, U. Md., 1972. Bar: Md., 1972, N.Y., 1978. Reporter, producer Sta. WBAL-TV, Balt., 1965-68; assignment editor, producer Sta. WJZ-TV, Balt., 1968-69; assoc. Edelman, Levy and Rubenstein, Balt., 1972-77; assoc. gen. counsel Internat. Ladies' Garment Workers Union, NYC, 1977-79, dir. Profl. And Clerical Employees div., 1987-91, asst. dir. legis. dept. Washington, 1991-94, assoc. dir., 1994-95; exec. asst. to Atty Gen. U.S. Dept. Justice, Washington, 1979-81; counsel Dist. 1 Communications Workers Am., NYC, 1981-85, adminstrv. asst. to v.p. NYC and Cranford, N.J., 1985-87; assoc. legis. dir. Union of Needletrades, Indsl. and Textile Employees, 1995-96, legis. dir., 1997—2001. Lectr. U. Md. Sch. of Law, Balt., 1972-77; adj. faculty Cornell U. Trade Union Women's Studies Program, N.Y.C., 1979-85; trustee Botto House Am. Labor Mus., Haledon, N.J., 1986-89; pub. mem. pub. employee rels. bd., D.C., 2004— Author: (with others) Legal Status of Homemakers in Maryland, 1978, Bargaining for Child Care, 1985, 2d edit., 1991. Founding mem. Women's Law Ctr., Balt., 1971-77; mem. Balt. City Charter Review Commn., 1973-76; bd. dirs. ACLU Md. Chpt., Balt., 1975-77, Campfire Girls Chesapeake Council, Balt., 1976-77; co-chair Sachs for Atty. Gen., Md., 1976-77; pub. mem. N.Y. State Banking Bd., N.Y.C., 1984-85. Mem. Coalition of Labor Union Women (treas. N.Y.C. chpt. 1981-83), Nat. Network of Women Union Lawyers (founder), Lawyers and Legal Workers for Working Women (founder), Nat. Writers Union (DC chpt. treas. 2005—), Cornell U. Adj. Faculty Fedn., Friends of Earth (bd. dirs. 1996-2006), Ams. for Democratic Action (bd. dirs. 2003—), Order of Coif. Home: 2810 Mckinley St NW Washington DC 20015-1216

HOFFMAN, BARRY PAUL, lawyer; b. Phila., May 29, 1941; s. Samuel and Hilda (Cohn) H.; m. Mary Ann Schrock, May 18, 1978; children: Elizabeth Barron, Hayley Rebecca. BA, Pa. State U., 1963; JD, George Washington U., 1968. Bar: Pa. 1972, Mich. 1983. Asst. U.S. Senator Wayne Morse, Oreg., Washington; spl. agt. FBI, Washington; asst. dist. atty. Phila. Dist. Atty.'s Office; exec. v.p., gen. counsel Valassis Communications, Inc., Livonia, Mich., also bd. dirs. 1st lt. U.S. Army, 1963-65, Korea. Home: 49933 Standish Ct Plymouth MI 48170-2882 Office: Valassis Communications Inc 19975 Victor Pkwy Livonia MI 48152-7001 E-mail: hoffmanb@valassis.com.

HOFFMAN, BASIL, actor, educator; b. Houston, Jan. 18, 1941; s. David and Beulah (Novoselsky) H.; m. Christine Elizabeth Reed, June 3, 1988. BBA, Tulane U., 1960; grad., Am. Acad. Dramatic Arts, NYC, 1962. Made profl. acting debut White Barn Theatre, Irwin, Pa., 1963; film appearances include Lady Liberty, 1972, At Long Last Love, 1975, Lucky Lady, 1975, All the President's Men, 1976, Close Encounters of the Third Kind, 1977, Comes a Horseman, 1978, The Electric Horseman, 1979, Ordinary People, 1980, Night Shift, 1982, My Favorite Year, 1982, All of Me, 1984, Kidco, 1984, The Milagro Beanfield War, 1988, Communion, 1989, Lambada, 1990, Switch, 1991, The Ice Runner, 1993, The Double O Kid, 1993, Pontiac Moon, 1994, Down with Love, 2003; TV films include Cage Without a Key, The Moneychangers, Jennifer: A Woman's Story, Games Mother Never Taught You, Columbo: the Bye-Bye Sky High I.Q. Murder Case, Love's Dark Ride, Kindred: The Embraced, The Ratings Game, The Great Ice Rip-off, Scout's Honor, Outlaws, Ellery Queen: Too Many Suspects, Hefner: The Unauthorized Biography; regular TV appearances on Square Pegs, 1982-83, others; author: Cold Reading and How to Be Good at It, 1999, Acting and How To Be Good At It, 2007. Guest lectr. Am. Acad. Dramatic Arts, N.Y.C., Hollywood, Calif., U. S.C., UCLA, Tulane U., Calif. State U., Northridge, Am. Film Inst., LA, Acad. Libanaise Beaux-Arts, Beirut; trustee Am. Acad. Dramatic Arts, N.Y.C. and Hollywood, 1995—. Mem. SAG (bd. dirs. 1991), AFTRA, Am. Entertainment Assn., Acad. Motion Picture Arts and Scis. (fgn. lang. award nominating com. 1981-2007, makeup award nominating com. 1990-97).

HOFFMAN, BRENDA JOYCE, gastroenterology educator; b. Madisonville, Ky., Sept. 4, 1957; d. John Willis and Lavada Fae (Baxter) H. BS, Murray State U., 1979; MD, U. Ky., 1983. Diplomate Am. Soc. Gastroenterology and Internal Medicine. Resident Med. U. S.C., Charleston, 1983-86, chief med. resident, 1986-87, gastroent./internal medicine fellow, 1987-89, therapeutic fellow, 1989-90, clin. instr. medicine, 1990-91, asst. prof. medicine, 1991-95, assoc. prof. medicine, 1995-2000, prof. medicine, 2001—, chief endosonography, clin. dir., 1993—. Contbr. articles to profl. jours. Fellow ACP, Am. Coll. Gastroenterology; mem. Am. Gastroent. Assn., Am. Soc. Gastrointestinal Endoscopy. Avocations: soccer, sailing, reading. Office: Med U SC 171 Ashley Ave Charleston SC 29425-0001

HOFFMAN, BRIAN M., chemistry professor; b. Chgo., Aug. 7, 1941; BS, U. Chgo., 1962; PhD, Calif. Inst. Tech., 1966; postdoctoral study, MIT, 1966—67. Asst. prof. dept. chemistry Northwestern U., Evanston, Ill., 1967—71, prof., 1974—. Vis. prof. Wichita State U., Kans., 1981; FMC lectr. Princeton U., 1988; Dow rsch. prof. chemistry, 1990-92; mem. local com. XIII Internat. Conf. on Magnetic Resonance in Biol. Sys., 1988; vice-chmn. Metals in Biology Gordon Rsch. Conf., 1987, chmn., 1988; mem. Nat. Biomed. ESR Ctr. Adv. Com. US/USSR Acad. Seminar on Environmentally-Related Catalysis, 1985, Nat. Com. Internat. Conf. on Bioinorganic Chemistry, 1989; mem. BMT study sect., NIH, 1988-92, chmn., 1990-92; mem. Ark.EPSCoR Nat. Rev. Bd., 1990; mem. Coun. Gordon Rsch. Confs., 1991-94; mem. NSF Biophysics Rev. Panel, 1994—97; lectr. in field. Bd. editors Inorganic Chemistry, 1984-89; mem. editl. bd. various jours. Recipient Nat. Merit Scholarship, 1959-62, NSF predoctoral fellowship, 1962-66, AFOSR-NRC postdoctoral rsch. fellowship, 1966-67, Alfred P. Sloan fellowship, 1971-73, NIH career devel. award, 1972-77, Bruker prize for ESR, Royal Soc. Chemistry, 1997, Gold medal Internat. EPR Soc., 1999. Fellow AAAS; mem. NAS, Am. Chem. Soc. (alternate councilor inorganic divsn. 1986-89, chmn. bioinorganic subdivsn. 1991-93), Am. Assn. Biol. Chemists, Biophys. Soc., Phi Beta Kappa. Achievements include research in electron paramagnetic resonance and electron-nuclear double resonance of metalloenzymes; long-range electron transfer within protein complexes; magnetism and metallic conductivity in molecular crystals. Office: Dept of Chemistry Northwestern University 2145 Sheridan Rd Evanston IL 60208-3113

HOFFMAN, BRIDGET C., lawyer; b. Cin., Feb. 22, 1977; BA in Polit. Sci., Xavier U., 1998; JD, U. Cin., 2002. Bar: Ohio 2002. Assoc. Taft, Stettinius & Hollister LLP, Cin., mem., Women's Resource Grp. Named one of Ohio's Rising Stars, Super Lawyers, 2005, 2006. Office: Taft Stettinius & Hollister LLP 425 Walnut St Ste 1800 Cincinnati OH 45202-1800 Office Phone: 513-381-2838. Office Fax: 513-381-0205.

HOFFMAN, CARL H., lawyer; b. St. Louis, May 28, 1936; s. Carl Henry and Anna Marie (Remlinger) H.; m. Pamela L. Polk, May 8, 1971 (div. Novl 1982); children: Kurt M., Jennifer K. BS, St. Louis U., 1958; postgrad., U. Mex., Mexico City, 1958, U. Nev., 1960—61, Tex. Technol. Coll., 1961—62; JD, Washington U., St. Louis, 1966. Bar: Mo. 1966, Fla.

1969, U.S. Supreme Ct. 1970; cert. civil trial adv. Nat. Bd. Trial Advocacy. Pilot Eastern Airlines, Inc., Miami, Fla.; assoc. Spencer & Taylor, Miami, Fla., 1969—70; pvt. practice Miami, 1970—80; ptnr. Hoffman & Hertzig, P.A., Coral Gables, Fla., 1980—. Capt. USAF, 1958-63. Mem. AIAA, ABA, ATLA, SAE Internat., Fla. Bar (cert. civil trial lawyer, cert. bus. litigation lawyer, chmn. aviation law com. 1997-98), Fla. Acad. Trial Lawyers, Am. Jurisprudence Soc., Greater Miami C. of C. (trustee). Office: Hoffman & Hertzig PA 901 Ponce De Leon Blvd Ste 500 Coral Gables FL 33134-3073 Home Phone: 305-447-4670; Office Phone: 305-445-3100 ext. 104. Business E-Mail: chh@hoffhertz.com.

HOFFMAN, CHARLES LOUIS, physician; b. Dayton, Ohio, May 10, 1925; s. Hugh Holland and Ruth Louise (Thiele) H.; m. Nancy Adele Fahrendorf, June 14, 1947; children: Thomas C., Mary Lynne Hoffman Lamb, Lori Hoffman Brustkern, William Edward. Student, U. Dayton, 1943; AB, Oberlin Coll., Ohio, 1945; MD, St. Louis U., 1949. Med. intern US Marine Hosp., Balt., 1949-50, chief op. dept. Kirkwood, Mo., 1950-51; chief med. officer 2nd Coast Guard Dist., St. Louis, 1951; resident internal medicine US Marine Hosp., San Francisco, 1951-53, chief resident internal medicine, 1953-54, asst. chief internal medicine, 1954-55; pvt. practice internal medicine Marin County, Calif., 1955-92; cons. internal medicine and pulmonology Neumiller Hosp., Tamal, Calif., 1957-83; active staff Marin Gen. Hosp., 1955—92; chief of med. staff Ross Gen. Hosp., Calif., 1969. Exec. com. Ross Gen. Hosp., 1968-71, 82-88; med. dir. Rafael Convalescent Hosp., 1987—; med. coord. Regional Cancer Found., San Francisco, 1992-2004; co-founder Med. Ins. Exch. Calif., 1975. Knighted, Sovereign Mil. Order of St. John of Jerusalem, 1992. Fellow AMA, Calif. Med. Assn.; mem. Calif. Soc. Internal Medicine (bd. dirs. 1976-79), Marin Med. Soc. (pres. 1975-76, bd. dirs. 1966-69, 74-77, 88—), Calif. Acad. Medicine, Serra Club of Marin (pres. 1961), Gen. Soc. Mayflower Descendants, Calif. Soc. Mayflower Descendants, Internat. Med. Assn. Lourdes, Elks (Man of Yr. in the Healing Arts 1976). Republican. Roman Catholic. Avocations: swimming, scuba diving, bridge, backgammon. Home: 48 Junipero Serra Ave San Rafael CA 94901-2320

HOFFMAN, DANIEL (GERARD), literature educator, poet; b. NYC, Apr. 3, 1923; s. Daniel and Frances (Beck) H.; m. Elizabeth McFarland, May 22, 1948; children: Kate, MacFarlane. BA, Columbia U., 1947, MA, 1949, PhD, 1956; DHL, Swarthmore Coll., 2005. Instr. English Columbia U., 1952-56; vis. prof. Am. Lit. Faculté des Lettres, Dijon, France, 1956-57; asst. prof. to prof. English Swarthmore Coll., 1957-66; prof. English U. Pa., 1966-83, poet-in-residence, 1978-93, Felix E. Schelling prof. English lit., 1983-93, prof. emeritus, 1993—. Fellow Ind. U. Sch. Letters, 1959; George Elliston lectr. poetry U. Cin., 1964; lectr. 6th Internat. Sch. Yeats Studies, Sligo, Ireland, 1965; poetry cons. Libr. of Congress, 1973-74, hon. cons. in Am. letters, 1974-77; poet-in-residence Cathedral Ch. of St. John the Divine, 1988-99; vis. prof. English, King's Coll. London, 1991-92. Author: (poetry) An Armada of Thirty Whales, 1954, A Little Geste and Other Poems, 1960, The City of Satisfactions, 1963, Striking the Stones, 1968, Broken Laws, 1970, The Center of Attention, 1974, Able Was I Ere I Saw Elba, 1977, Brotherly Love, 1981, Hang-Gliding from Helicon, 1988, Middens of the Tribe, 1995, Darkening Water, 2002, Beyond Silence: Selected Shorter Poems, 2003, Makes You Stop and Think: Sonnets, 2005; (poetry transl.) A Play of Mirrors by Ruth Domino, 2002; (criticism) Paul Bunyan: Last of the Frontier Demigods, 1952, The Poetry of Stephen Crane, 1957, Form and Fable in American Fiction, 1961, Barbarous Knowledge, 1967, Poe Poe Poe Poe Poe Poe Poe, 1972, Faulkner's Country Matters, 1989, Words to Create a World, 1993; (memoir) Zone of the Interior, 2000; editor: The Red Badge of Courage, 1957, American Poetry and Poetics, 1962, Ezra Pound and William Carlos Williams, 1983; editor, contbr.: (criticism) Harvard Guide to Contemporary American Writing, 1979 Served to 1st lt. USAAF, 1943—46. Decorated Legion of Merit; recipient U. Chgo. Folklore prize, 1949, Poetry Center Introductions prize, 1951, Yale Series of Younger Poets award, 1954, Ansley prize, 1956, Lit. award Athenaeum of Phila., 1963, 83, medal for excellence Columbia U., 1964, Nat. Inst. Arts and Letters award in poetry, 1967, meml. medal Hungarian PEN, 1980, Hazlett Meml. award for lit., 1984, Paterson Poetry prize, 1989, Aiken Taylor award for Modern Am. Poetry, 2003, Arthur Rense Poetry prize, 2005; poetry grantee Ingram Merrill Found., 1971-72; fellow Am. Council Learned Socs., 1961-62, 66-67, NEH, 1975-76, Guggenheim Meml. Found., 1983-84. Mem. MLA, Assn. Literary Scholars and Critics, Acad. Am. Poets (chancellor 1973-97, chancellor emeritus 1997—), Authors Guild (council). Clubs: Century (N.Y.C.); Franklin Inn (Phila.).

HOFFMAN, DARLEANE CHRISTIAN, chemistry professor; b. Terril, Iowa, Nov. 8, 1926; d. Carl Benjamin and Elverna (Kuhlman) Christian; m. Marvin Morrison Hoffman, Dec. 26, 1951; children: Maureane R., Daryl K. BS in Chemistry, Iowa State U., 1948, PhD in Nuclear Chemistry, 1951; Doctorate (hon.), Clark U., 2000, U. Bern, Switzerland, 2001. Chemist Oak Ridge Nat. Lab., Tenn., 1952—53; staff radiochemistry group Los Alamos Sci. Lab., N.Mex., 1953—71, assoc. leader chemistry-nuclear group, 1971—79, leader chem.-nuclear divsn., 1979—82, leader isotope and nuclear chem. divsn., 1982-84; prof. chemistry U. Calif., Berkeley, 1984—91, prof. emeritus, 1991—93, prof. grad. sch., 1993—; faculty sr. scientist Lawrence Berkeley Nat. Lab., 1984—; dir.'s fellow Los Alamos Nat. Lab., 1990—; dir. G.T. Seaborg Inst. Transactinium Sci. Lawrence Livermore Nat. Lab., 1991—96. Panel leader, spkr. women in sci. confs. NAS-NRC, 1975, 79, 83, 97, 2003, subcom. nuc. and radiochemistry, 1978—81, chmn. subcom. nuclear and radiochemistry, 1982—84, bd. radioactive waste mgmt., 1994—99; titular mem. commn. on radiochem. and nuc. techniques Internat. Union of Pure and Applied Chem., 1983—87, sec., 1985—87, chmn., 1987—91, assoc., 1991—93; energy rsch. adv. bd. cold fusion panel Dept. Energy, 1989—90, nuc. energy rsch. adv. com, 2000—01; conf. lectr. Welch Fedn., 1991, 97, lect. tour Tex. univs., 2000; separations subpanel separations tech. and transmutation systems panel NAS, 1992—94; steering com. Accel. Transmutation Waste Roadmapping Study, 1999; ANTT subcom. NERAC, 2002—07; mem. commn. on endpoints spent nuc. fuel and hi-level radioactive waste NAS-NRC Bd. Radioactive Waste Mgmt., 1994—99, NAS-NRC BRWM Joint US/Russian Commn., 2001—02; mem. US-Russian Joint Commn. Collaboration to Prevent Radiol. Terrorism, 2004—06; presenter, spkr., lectr. in field. Author: The Transuranium People, 2000; contbr. articles to profl. jours. Named Japan Soc. Promotion Sci. lectr., 1987, Disting. Lectr., Inst. Phys. Rsch. and Tech., Ames Lab., 1998; named to Women in Tech. Internat. Hall of Fame, 2000; recipient Alumni Citation of Merit, Coll. Scis. and Humanities, Iowa State U., 1978, Disting. Achievement award, Iowa State U., 1986, Berkeley Citation, U. Calif., 1996, US Nat. Medal Sci., 1997, Leonard A. Ford Lectureship, Mankato State U., 1998, Frontiers Sci. award, Soc. Cosmetic Chemists, 1998, John V. Atanasoff Rsch. and Discovery award, Iowa State U. Coll. Liberal Arts and Sci., 2007; fellow, Guggenheim Found., Berkeley, 1978—79; Sr. Postdoc. fellow, NSF, Norway, 1964—65. Fellow: AAAS (coun. mem. 1995—97), Norwegian Acad. Sci. and Letters, Am. Acad. Arts and Scis., Am. Phys. Soc., Am. Inst. Chemists (pres. N.Mex. chpt. 1976—78); mem.: Radiochem. Soc. (Lifetime Achievement award 2003), Am. Chem. Soc. (John Dustin Clark award 1976, Nuc. Chemistry award 1983, Francis P. Garvan-John M. Olin medal 1990, Priestley medal 2000, Mosher award 2001), Japan Soc. Nuc. and Radiochems. (hon.; internat. mem. 2004), Sigma Xi (Procter prize for sci. achievement 2003), Alpha Chi Sigma (Hall of Fame 2002), Sigma Delta Epsilon, Pi Mu Epsilon, Iota Sigma Pi (nat. hon. mem. 1993), Phi Kappa Phi. Office: Lawrence Berkeley Nat Lab MS70R0319 NSD Berkeley CA 94720 Business E-Mail: dchoffman@lbl.gov.

HOFFMAN, DARNAY ROBERT, management consultant; b. NYC, Nov. 25, 1947; s. Bill and Toni (Darnay) H.; m. Jennifer Lea Sheppard, Aug. 20, 1984; children by previous marriage: Brandon, Brett; m. Sydney Biddle Barrows, May 14, 1994. BA, SUNY, 1977; MBA, CUNY, 1980; JD, Yeshiva U., 1982. Bar: N.Y. 1995, U.S. Dist. Ct. (so., ea., we. and no. dists.) N.Y. 1995, U.S. Ct. Appeals (fed. cir.) 1995, U.S. Tax Ct. 1995, U.S. Ct. Internat. Trade 1995, U.S. Dist. Ct. Colo. 2000, U.S. Dist. Ct. (no. dist.) Ga. 2000, U.S. Ct. Appeals (fed. cir.). Pres., mgmt. cons. Darnay Hoffman Assocs., Inc., 1969—; mgmt. cons. Hoffman Rsch. Group Inc., NYC, 1977—; rsch. assoc. Baruch Coll., 1977-79. Bd. dirs. Hobton Realty Corp.; dir. Nat. Conf. Law Historians Am., 1987—. Author: Murder in the Wilderness, 1989, Allen Contact, 1989, (pamphlet) Products in Decline, 1980. Mem. ABA, ATLA, Am. Mgmt. Assn., Am. Mktg. Assn., Acad. Mgmt. Scis., Nat. Assn. Criminal Def. Attys., N.Y. State Bar Assn., N.Y. County Lawyers Assn., Assn. Bar of City of N.Y., N.Y. State Trial Lawyers Assn., Player's, Beta Gamma Sigma, Alpha Delta Sigma. Office Phone: 212-712-2766. Personal E-mail: darnayh@aol.com.

HOFFMAN, DAVID H., city manager; BA, Yale U.; LLD, U. Chgo., 2005. Clk. to Supreme Ct. Justice Rehnquist; asst. US atty. US Atty.'s Office, Chgo., 1998—2005, dep. chief Narcotics & Gangs sect., 2002—05; inspector gen. City Hall, Chgo., 2005—. Dir. Project Safe Neighborhoods, Chgo., 2003—. Named one of 40 Under 40, Crain's Chgo. Bus., 2006. Office: Office of Inspector Gen City of Chgo PO Box 2996 Chicago IL 60654-2996 Office Phone: 773-478-7799. Office Fax: 773-478-3949.

HOFFMAN, DAVID JOHN, physiologist, ecotoxicologist; b. New London, Conn., Sept. 22, 1944; s. John Leslie and Margaret Amy (Stokes) H.; m. Suzanne Elizabeth O'Clair, Aug. 20, 1966; children: Michael David, James Stephen. BS, McGill U., 1966; PhD, U. Md., 1971. Instr. in genetics, embryology U. Md., College Park, 1968-71; postdoctoral fellow/NIH Oak Ridge Nat. Lab., Oak Ridge, Tenn., 1971-73; faculty, biology dept. Boston Coll., Newton, Mass., 1973-74; sr. staff physiologist Health Effects Rsch. Lab/U.S. EPA, Cin., 1974-76; rsch. physiologist Patuxent Wildlife Rsch. Ctr./USDI, Laurel, Md., 1976—. Adj. prof. U. Md., 1992—. Mem. editl. bd. Archives of Environ. Contamination and Toxicology Jour., 1986—, Jour. Toxicology and Environ. Health, 1989-96, Environ. Toxicology and Chemistry, 1990-92, Oecologia Montana, 1992—, Current Topics in Ecotoxicology and Environ. Chemistry, 1995—, Current Topics in Toxicology, 1996—; editor: Handbook of Ecotoxicology, 1995, 2d edit., 2003; contbr. over 200 chpts. to books, articles to profl. jours. and symposia. Recipient dissertation fellowship U. Md., College Park, 1970, spl. achievement award USDI, 1990, 94, 96, 2003, Honor award, 1995. Mem. AAAS, Teratology Soc., Soc. Environ. Chemistry and Toxicology (editoral bd. 1990—), Soc. Exptl. Biology and Medicine, Soc. Toxicology, Nature Conservancy, Nat. Audubon Soc., Phi Sigma Soc. Avocations: distance swimming, adult fitness swimming, fishing, boating, birdwatching. Office: Patuxent Wildlife Rsch Ctr USDI Laurel MD 20708 Address: PO Box 3117 Crofton MD 21114 Office Phone: 301-497-5712. Business E-Mail: david_hoffman@usgs.gov.

HOFFMAN, DONALD ALFRED, lawyer; b. Milw., May 4, 1936; s. Harry Gustav and Emily Frances (Schwartz) H.; m. Louise Hardie Chapman, June 8, 1963; children: Donald Hardie, Richard Rainey. BBA, U. Wis., 1958, JD, 1968. Bar: La. 1969, US Supreme Ct. 1972, US Ct. Appeals (5th cir.) 1973, US Dist. Ct. (ea., mid. and we. dists.) La. Assoc. Lemle & Kelleher, New Orleans, 1968-73; ptnr. Lemle, Kelleher, Kohlmeyer, Matthews & Schumacher, New Orleans, 1973-75, McGlinchey, Stafford, Mintz & Hoffman, New Orleans, 1975-78; city atty. City of New Orleans, 1978-79; dir. Carmouche, Gray & Hoffman, New Orleans, 1979-82; sr. dir. Hoffman, Siegel, Seydel, Bienvenu & Centola, New Orleans, 1982—2000, Hoffman Seydel LLC, New Orleans, 2004. Recipient Chevelier of the Order of Merit, French govt. Fellow Am. Bar Found., La. Bar Found.; mem. Am. Bd. Trial Advocates, French-Am. C. of C. Presbyterian. Home: 1524 4th St New Orleans LA 70130-5918 Office: Hoffman Seydel LLC Ste 3770 701 Poydras St New Orleans LA 70139 Office Phone: 504-587-0900 ext. 102. Business E-Mail: dhoffman@hoffmanseydel.com.

HOFFMAN, DONALD CLINTON, physicist, researcher; b. San Francisco, June 23, 1948; s. William Walter and Myrah Ione (Johnston) H. BS in Physics, U. Hawaii, 1980, MS in Physics, 1983, PhD in Physics, 1985. Enlisted man USN, 1967-78, ret., 1978; rsch. asst. U. Hawaii, Honolulu, 1980-85; scientist Lockheed Co., Sunnyvale, Calif., 1985-90, Applied Tech. Assocs., Mt. View, Calif., 1990—. Mem. Am. Phys. Soc., Mensa. Republican. Avocation: microcomputers. Office: Applied Tech Assocs Inc Space Divsn 1320 Villa St Mountain View CA 94041-1126

HOFFMAN, DONALD DAVID, cognitive and computer science educator; b. San Antonio, Dec. 29, 1955; s. David Pollock and Loretta Virginia (Shoemaker) H.; m. Geralyn Mary Souza, Dec. 13, 1986; 1 child from previous marriage, Melissa Louise. BA, UCLA, 1978; PhD, MIT. MTS and project engr. Hughes Aircraft Co., El Segundo, Calif., 1978-83; rsch. scientist MIT Artificial Intelligence Lab, Cambridge, Mass., 1983; asst. prof. U. Calif., Irvine, 1983-86, assoc. prof., 1986-90, prof., 1990—. Cons. Fairchild Lab. for Artificial Intelligence, Palo Alto, Calif., 1984; panelist MIT Corp. vis. com., Cambridge, 1985, NSF, Washington, 1988; conf. host IEEE Conf. on Visual Motion, Irvine, 1989, Office of Naval Rsch. Conf. on Vision, Laguna Beach, Calif., 1992; vis. prof. Zentrum für Interdisziplinäre Forschung, Bielefeld, Germany, 1995-96, cons. Sextant Tech. Inc., Irvine, Calif., 2000-05. Author: Visual Intelligence, 1998; co-author: Observer Mechanics, 1989, Automotive Lighting and Human Vision, 2007; mem. editl. bd. Cognition, 1991-2002, Psychol. Rev., 1995-96; contbr. articles to profl. jours. Vol. tchr. Turtle Rock Elem. Sch., Irvine, 1988-90. Recipient Distinguished Scientific award, Am. Psychol. Assn., 1989, Troland Rsch. award US Nat. Acad. Scis., 1994; grantee NSF, 1984, 87, 2001. Mem.: Am. Psychol. Soc., Assn. for Sci. Study of Consciousness, Assn. Sci. Study Consciousness. Avocations: running, swimming, racket sports, ice skating. Office: U Calif Dept Cognitive Sci Irvine CA 92697-0001 Office Phone: 949-824-6795. Business E-Mail: ddhoff@uci.edu.

HOFFMAN, DONALD M., lawyer; BS, UCLA, 1957, LL.B., 1960. Bar: Calif. 1961. Pvt. practice, L.A. County, 1961—; ptnr. firm Greenwald, Hoffman, Meyer & Montes, 1964—. Pres. L.A. Estate Planning Council. Served to 2d lt. U.S. Army. Mem. Am., Los Angeles County bar assns., Phi Alpha Delta, Beta Gamma Sigma. Office: 500 N Brand Blvd Ste 920 Glendale CA 91203-1923 Office Phone: 818-507-8100. Business E-Mail: dmhoffman@ghmmlaw.com.

HOFFMAN, DUSTIN LEE, actor; b. LA, Aug. 8, 1937; s. Harry and Lillian Hoffman; m. Anne Byrne, May 4, 1969 (div. Oct. 6, 1980); children: Karina, Jenna; m. Lisa Gottsegen, Oct. 21, 1980; children: Jacob, Rebecca, Max, Alexandra. Student, Santa Monica City Coll., Pasadena Playhouse; studied with, Barney Brown, Lonny Chapman & Lee Strasberg. Stage debut: Sarah Lawrence Coll. prodn. of Yes Is for a Very Young Man; Broadway debut: A Cook for Mr. General, 1961; appeared in Endgame, The Quare Fellow, In The Jungle of Cities, A Country Scandal, The Dumbwaiter, The Room, Waiting for Godot, Picnic on the Battlefield, Dirty Hands, The Cocktail Party, All Theatre Company of Boston, Three Men on a Horse, 1964, Harry, Noon and Night, 1965, The Journey of the Fifth Horse (Obie award 1966), 1966, Fragments, 1966, Eh? (Drama Desk award 1967, Verna Rice award 1967, Theatre World award 1967), 1966, Jimmy Shine, 1968, Death of a Salesman, 1984, The Merchant of Venice, 1989; recorded: Death of a Salesman on Caedmon Records (Drama Desk award 1984); appeared in films: The Tiger Makes Out, 1967, The Graduate, 1967 (Acad. award nom. best actor 1968, BAFTA award best actor 1969, Golden Globe award most promising newcomer 1968), El Millón de Madigan, 1969, Sunday Father, 1969, Midnight Cowboy, 1969 (Acad. award nom. best actor 1970, BAFTA award best actor 1970), John and Mary, 1969 (BAFTA award best actor 1970), Little Big Man, 1970 (BAFTA award nom. best actor 1972), Who Is Harry Kellerman and Why Is He Saying Those Terrible Things About Me?, 1971, Straw Dogs, 1971, Alfredo, Alfredo, 1972, Papillon, 1973, Lenny, 1974 (Acad. award nom. best actor 1975, BAFTA award nom. best actor 1976), All the President's Men, 1976 (BAFTA award nom. best actor 1977), Marathon Man, 1976 (BAFTA award nom. best actor 1977), Straight Time, 1978, Agatha, 1979, Kramer vs. Kramer, 1979 (Acad. award best actor, 1980, BAFTA award nom. best actor 1981, Golden Globe award best actor 1980), Tootsie, 1982 (Acad. award nom. best actor 1983, Golden Globe award best actor 1983, BAFTA award best actor 1984), Ishtar, 1987, Rain Man, 1988 (Acad. award best actor 1989, BAFTA award nom. best actor 1990, Golden Globe award best actor 1989), Family Business, 1989, Dick Tracy, 1990, Billy Bathgate, 1991, Hook, 1991, Hero, 1992, Outbreak, 1995, American Buffalo, 1996, Sleepers, 1996, Mad City, 1997, Wag the Dog, 1997 (Acad. award nom. best actor 1998), Sphere, 1998, Messenger: The Story of Joan of Arc, 1999, Tuesday (voice), 2001, Moonlight Mile, 2002, Confidence, 2003, Runaway Jury, 2003, I Heart Huckabees, 2004, Finding Neverland, 2004, Meet the Fockers, 2004, Lemony Snicket's A Series of Unfortunate Events, 2004, (voice) Racing Stripes, 2005, The Lost City, 2005, Perfume: The Story of a Murderer, 2006, Stranger Than Fiction, 2006; appeared in TV movies: Journey of the Fifth Horse, 1966, The Star Wagon, 1967, The Point (voice), 1971, Death of a Salesman, 1985 (Emmy award best actor 1986, Golden Globe award best actor 1986), A Wish for Wings That Work, 1991; TV series: Liberty's Kids (voice), 2002; prodr. films: Straight Time, 1978, A Walk on the Moon, 1999, The Furies, 1999; exec. prodr. TV movie: The Devil's Arithmetic, 1999. Decorated officer Order of Arts and Letters (France), 1995, Golden Globe lifetime achievement award, 1997, AFI Life Achievement award, 1999. Office: Creative Artists Agy 9830 Wilshire Blvd Beverly Hills CA 90212*

HOFFMAN, E. LESLIE, lawyer; b. Charleston, W. Va., Aug. 8, 1947; s. E. Leslie and Mary Jane (Lively) H.; m. Susan Sandy, Sept. 9, 1967 (div. 1983); children: Melissa North, Marc Clayton. BA Polit. Sci., West Va. U., 1969, JD, 1972. Bar: W.Va. 1972, U.S. Dist. Ct. (no. and so. dists.) W.Va. 1972, U.S. Ct. Appeals (4th crct.) 1973, U.S. Ct. Appeals (9th crct.) 1984. Asst. atty. gen. State W. Va., Charleston, 1972-76; asst. U.S. Atty. so. dist. W. Va., Charleston, 1976-81; asst. dir. atty. gen's. advocacy inst. U.S. Dept. Justice, Washington, 1982, trial atty. fraud sect., 1983-86; dep. sect. chief fraud sect. U.S Dept. Justice, Washington, 1987-88; counsel Pettit & Martin, Washington, 1988-90, ptnr., 1991-95, Piper Marbury Rudnick & Wolfe, Washington, 1995—2002, Jackson & Kelly PLLC, Washington, 2002—. Mem. ABA. Democrat. Episcopalian. Office: Jackson & Kelly PLLC 2401 Pennsylvania Ave NW Washington DC 20037 E-mail: phoffman@jacksonkelly.com.

HOFFMAN, EDWARD TED CHARLES, III, director, educator; b. New Orleans, Oct. 16, 1979; s. Edward Charles Hoffman, II and Jan S. Hoffman, Linda F. Hoffman (Stepmother); m. Deanne Nicole Miller, Mar. 12, 2005. MusB in Edn., So. Miss., Hattiesburg, 2002; MEd, Auburn U., Ala., 2005; postgrad., U. Nebr., Lincoln, 2007—. Lic. music tchr. Dept. of Edn., 2002, history tchr. Dept. of Edn., 2002. Asst. to the dean, academic advisor U. So. Miss., Hattiesburg, 1998—2002; tchr. Jones County Schs., Laurel, Miss., 2002—03; dir. music, chmn. arts North Forrest Bands, Hattiesburg, 2003—06; band dir. Madison Ctrl. Bands, Miss., 2006—. Disaster relief vol. ARC, Hattiesburg, 1997—2007; capt. CAP, Jackson, Miss., 2007. Named Bandsmen of Yr., U. So. Miss., 1999, Oustanding Am. Tchr., NHR, 2005, Band Dir. of Yr., SEMBDA, 2005; named to The Chancellors List, NHR, 2005. Fellow: Ronald E McNair Scholar Program; mem.: Miss. HS Activities Assn., Tubists Universal Brotherhood Assn., Coll. Music Soc., Music Educators Nat. Conf., SE Miss. Band Dirs. Assn. (v.p. 2005—06), Ctrl. Miss. Band Dirs. Assn. (chmn. 2007—07), Coll. Band Dirs. Assn., Nat. Fedn. HS, Miss. Music Tchrs. Assn., Nat. Band Assn., Auburn Alumni Assn., U. So. Miss. Alumni Assn., Ctrl. Miss. Alumni Assn., Tau Beta Sigma, Omicron Delta Kappa, Gamma Beta Phi (treas.), Kappa Delta Pi, Golden Key Honors Soc., Phi Kappa Phi, Delta Tau Delta (v.p., asst. chpt. advisor 1999—2005, Mr. Delta Tau Delta). Avocations: scuba diving, coin collecting/numismatics, water sports, gardening, running. Home Phone: 601-896-2901.

HOFFMAN, ELIZABETH, academic administrator, economics professor; BA in History, Smith Coll., 1968; MA in History, U. Pa., 1969, PhD in History, 1972; PhD in Econs., Calif. Inst. Tech., 1979. Academic and adminstrv. positions U. Fla., Northwestern U., Purdue U., U. Wyo., U. Ariz., Iowa State U.; prof. econs., history, polit. sci., psychology U. Ill., Chgo., 1997—2000, prof. Inst. of Govt. and Pub. Affairs, 1997—2000, provost and vice chancellor, 1997—2000; pres. U. Colo. Sys., Boulder, Colo., 2000—05; prof. Grad. Sch. Pub. Affairs U. Colo., Denver, 2005—06; exec. v.p., provost Iowa State U., 2007—. Mem. bd. dir. Nat. Sci. Bd., 2002—. Author books; contbr. articles to profl. jours. Named one of 100 women making a difference, Today's Chgo. Woman, 1999, 25 Most Powerful People, Colo. Biz Mag., 2004; recipient Ronald H. Coase prize, Electronic Intelligence citation, ANBAR. Office: Iowa State U Provost Office 1550 Bdshr Ames IA 50011-2021*

HOFFMAN, FAITH LOUISE, social worker; b. Buffalo, June 7, 1944; d. William George Hoffman, Louise Caroline Hoffman; children: Donald Louis, Louis William, Christopher Robert. BS magna cum laude, Medaille Coll., 1983—87; MSW, SUNY, Buffalo, 1991—93. LCSW 1993. Case mgr. N.Y. Crime Victim's Assistance Program, Buffalo, 1987—88; dir. domestic violence program YWCA of Tonawanda's, 1988—90; dir. family support program Concerned Ecumenical Ministry, Buffalo, 1990—92; social worker Dept. Veteran's Affairs Med. Ctr., Buffalo, 1993—95, women veteran's program mgr., 1995—. Adj. prof. U. Buffalo Grad. Sch. Social Work, 2004—; dir., founder Hopegivers, Buffalo, 1991—; dir. VA Domestic Violence Program, Buffalo, 1995—; field faculty SUNY, Buffalo, 1996—; domestic violence cons. Erie County Dept. Health, Buffalo, 2000—02; spkr. in field. Named cmty. hero, torchbearer Western N.Y. Olympic Torch Relay, Atlanta Olympic Com., 1996—96; recipient Svc. to Mankind award, Sertoma Greater Buffalo, 1998—98, ann. leadership award, YWCA Western N.Y., 2001—01, Joan A. Levine award, Woman Focus, 2002, Fed. Woman of Yr. award, Buffalo (N.Y.) Fed. Exec. Bd., 2003, Person of Yr. award, Jewish War Vets. Am.-Buffalo Frontier Post 25, 2004. Office: VA Western NY Healthcare Sys 3495 Bailey Ave Buffalo NY 14215 Home Phone: 716-837-0540; Office Phone: 716-862-8675. Business E-Mail: faithhoffman@va.gov.

HOFFMAN, FRANKLIN THOMAS, artist, printmaker, retired army officer; b. El Paso, Sept. 10, 1953; s. Franklin A. and Evelyn M. (Parker) H. BA in Art cum laude, U. Alaska, 1982. Enlisted U.S. Army, 1972, commd. 2d lt., 1982, advanced through grades to capt., 1985; comdr. HHB 1st Cavalry, Ft. Hood, Tex., 1988-90; asst. prof. mil. sci. Mont. State U., Bozeman, 1990-95; founder Bozeman Pass Printmakers, 1996. Designer-craftsman U.S. Army Europe, Germany, 1984. Decorated Meritorious Svc. medal. Mem. Soc. N.Am. Goldsmiths, Am. Legion. E-mail: fhprintmkr@cs.com.

HOFFMAN, FRED L., human resources specialist; b. Wauseon, Ohio, Mar. 13, 1953; s. Lowell Max and Annabell (Whitmire) Hoffman; m. Diane Patricia Pope, Sept. 19, 1975; 1 child, Brandon C. BSBA, Bowling Green U., 1975. Asst. mgr. indsl. rels. Colonial Press div. Sheller-Globe Corp., Clinton, Mass., 1975-76, dir. human resources Leece-Neville div. Gainesville, Ga., 1976-88; v.p. human resources, staff ops. Golder Assocs.,

Atlanta, 1988—, also bd. dirs. Bd. dirs. Hoffman-Rettig Foods, Inc., Maquoketa, Iowa. Guest columnist: BG News, 1971—75. Lt. col. aide-de-camp gov.'s staff Gov. Joe Frank Harris, Atlanta, 1983—91; state dir. pub. rels. Ohio League Coll. Reps., Columbus, 1974, 1975. Recipient Disting. Svc. award, Bowling Green State U., 1975. Mem.: Soc. Human Resources Mgmt., Antaen Soc. (pres. 1974—75), Atlanta C. of C., Atlanta Athletic Club, Pres.'s Club Bowling Green State U., Phi Delta Theta, Omicron Delta Kappa. Home: 235 Parian Run Duluth GA 30097-2418 Office: Golder Assocs Corp 3730 Chamblee Tucker Rd Atlanta GA 30341-4414 Personal E-mail: hoffmandp@yahoo.com. Business E-Mail: fhoffman@gdder.com.

HOFFMAN, GILBERT L., information technology executive; Sr. v.p. & chief info. officer Maritz, Inc., St. Louis. Named a Premier 100 IT Leader, Computerworld mag., 2001. Office: SVP & CIO Maritz Inc 1375 N Hwy Dr Fenton MO 63099

HOFFMAN, IRA ELIOT, lawyer; b. Highland Park, Mich., Jan. 3, 1952; s. Maxwell Mordecai and Leah (Silverman) Hoffman; m. Ruth Felsen, Aug. 19, 1975 (div. 1981); 1 child, Daniel Gideon; m. Meredith Lippman, Dec. 17, 1988 (div. 2004); 1 child, Lauren Samantha. BA, U. Mich., 1973; MSc in Econs., London Sch. Econs., 1975; JD cum laude, U. Miami, 1983. Bar: Fla. 1983, U.S. Ct. Appeals (D.C. cir.) 1984, D.C. 1985, Md. 1991, U.S. Ct. Appeals (10th and 4th cirs.) 1992, U.S. Dist. Ct. D.C. 1992, U.S. Dist. Ct. Md. 1992, U.S. Ct. Appeals (fed. cir.) 1994, U.S. Ct. Fed. Claims 1998, U.S. Ct. Appeals (11th cir.) 2001, U.S. Dist. Ct. (so. dist.) Fla. 2001. Tchr. London Sch. Econs., 1975-77; rsch. assoc. Shiloah Ctr. Mid. East Studies, Tel Aviv U., 1978-80; staff atty. FTC, Washington, 1983; law clk. U.S. Ct. Appeals (D.C. cir.), Washington, 1983-84; assoc. Fried, Frank, Harris, Shriver & Jacobson, Washington, 1984-86, 87-88; counsel Ministry of Def. Mission to the U.S., Govt. of Israel, NYC, 1986-87; counsel to vice chmn. U.S. Internat. Trade Commn., Washington, 1988-89; assoc. Howrey & Simon, Washington, 1989-91; pres. Israel Housing Investors, Inc., Rockville, Md., 1990-92; v.p. H.P.F. Prefab Constrn., Ltd., Givatayim, Israel, 1991-92; of counsel Savage & Schwartzman, Balt., 1992-94, McAleese & Assocs., P.C., McLean, Va., 1995-98, Grayson & Kubli, P.C., McLean, 1998—2001; pres. Smart Planet, LLC, Rockville, Md., 1998—2000; v.p. Grayson, Kubli & Hoffman, P.C., McLean, 2002—04; ptnr. The Goldstein LawGroup, Washington, 2004—05; prin. Hoffman & Assocs. PC, Bethesda, 2005—. Adj. prof. George Mason U. Sch. Law, 2006—. Translator: The Emergence of Pan-Arabism in Egypt, 1980; contbr. articles to profl. jours. Spl. counsel Nat. Sudden Infant Death Syndrome Found., Landover, Md., 1984—86; hon. counsel to chmn. Nat. Holocaust Meml. Coun., Washington, 1985. Mem.: ABA. Jewish. Avocations: travel, sports, history. Office: 6701 Democracy Blvd Ste 300 Bethesda MD 20817 Office Phone: 301-571-2440. Business E-Mail: hoffman@hoffman-law.net.

HOFFMAN, IRWIN, orchestra conductor; b. NYC, Nov. 26, 1924; s. Harry and Augusta (Cohen) H.; m. Esther Glazer, Feb. 21, 1946 (div. 1990); children: Joel H., Gary, Toby, Deborah; m. Maria Lourdes Lobo, 1990. Student, Juilliard Sch. Music, 1942-43, 45-48; MusD (hon.), U. Tampa, 1984. Dir. music Orquesta Sinfonica de Chile, 1994-97. Condr. Phila. Orch. at Robin Hood Dell, summer 1942, Bronx (N.Y.) Symphony, 1948-52, Yonkers (N.Y.) Philharm., 1950-52, Westchester (N.Y.) Chamber Orch., 1950-52, for Martha Graham Dance Co., 1949-50; condr., mus. dir. Vancouver (B.C., Can.) Symphony Orch., 1952-64; assoc. condr. Chgo. Symphony Orch., 1964-68, acting music dir., 1968-69, condr., 1969-70, prin. condr. Grant Park, Chgo., 1965-73; permanent condr. Belgian Radio and TV Symphony Orch., 1973-76; music dir. Fla. Orch., 1968-87, music dir. laureate, 1987-95; music dir. Flagstaff (Ariz.) Festival of Arts, 1983-95; condr. St. Louis Little Symphony, summers 1959-64, lectr., condr., U. B.C., State Coll. Wash., 1958, guest condr. Toronto, Vancouver, Chgo., Israel Philharm., 1960, Dallas Symphony, 1962, Brazil, 1962, 78, St. Louis Symphony Orch., 1963, Miami and Tampa symphonies, 1967, protege of Serge Koussevitzky, Tanglewood, 1948-50, guest condr. BBC Symphony, Manchester, Eng., 1968, Brussels (Belgium) Radio Orch., 1968, Strasbourg (France) Radio Orch., 1968, BBC Welsh, 1969-82, BBC Scottish, 1971-82, BBC No. Orch., 1971-82, Orch. Nat., France, 1970, Orch. Philharmonique, France, 1970, Orch. Nat., Peru, 1970, Philharmonia Orch., Eng., 1971, Chgo., Vancouver symphonies, 1971, N.J., Denver, Costa Rica, 1977-78, Chgo., 1977, Montevideo (Uruguay) Nat., 1979, Buffalo symphonies, 1980-81, New Orleans Philharm., 1981, Winnipeg Symphony, 1985, Pitts. Symphony, 1986, Colorado Springs Symphony, 1989, Kitchener-Waterloo Symphony, 1989, music dir. Nat. Symphony Orch. of Costa Rica, 1987-2001; guest condr. Israel Chamber Orch., 1990, Jalapa Symphony, Mex., 1990, Phoenix Symphony, 1991, UNAM Mex., 1991, Orch. Symphonique Francaise, 1991, Orquesta Sinfonica, Caracas, 1992, 93, 94, Orquesta Sinfonica De Chile, 1992, 93, 94, music dir. 1995-97; guest condr. Orquesta Sinfonica de San Luis, Argentina, 1994, Orquesta de Sodre, Montevideo, Uruguay, 1994, Orquesta de Concepcion, Chile, 1995, Orquesta Sinfonica de Buenos Aires, 1996, 98, Taipei Symphony Orch., 1997, 98, 99, 2000, Orquesta Sinfonica de Bogotá, 1998, 99, Fla. Orch., 1999, Nat. Symphony Guatemala, 1998, Orquestra Sintonica Panama, 1999; music dir. Orquesia Sinfonica-De Bogota, Colombia, 2000-03, Filarmonica Orq de Bogota, 2004—, Beijing Symphony Orch., 2004-05, Cali Symphony Orch., 2005, Taipei Nat. Orch., 2005, Budapest Concert Orch., 2005, ORQ, Sinfonica de Venezuela, 2005; composer two string quartets, violin sonata, Orquesta Filarmónica of Bogotá, Columbia, 1997, 98, others; collector autography music manuscripts, mus. memorabilia. Served with AUS, 1943-45. Juilliard fellow, 1948. Home and Office: Apdo 818-1260 Plaza Colonial Escazu San José Costa Rica

HOFFMAN, JAMES PAUL, lawyer; b. Waterloo, Iowa, Sept. 7, 1943; s. James A. and Luella M. (Prokosch) Hoffman; 1 child, Tiffany K. BA, U. No. Iowa, 1965; JD, U. Iowa, 1967. Bar: Iowa 1967, U.S. Dist. Ct. (no. dist.) Iowa 1981, U.S. Dist. Ct. (so. dist.) Iowa 1968, U.S. Dist. Ct. (so. dist.) Ill. 1971, U.S. Tax Ct. 1971, U.S. Ct. Appeals (8th cir.) 1970, U.S. Supreme Ct. 1974. Sr. mem. James P. Hoffman, Law Offices, Keokuk, Iowa, 1967—. Author: The Iowa Trial Lawyers and the Use of Hypnosis, 1980. Chmn. bd. Iowa Inst. Hypnosis. Fellow: Am. Inst. Hypnosis; mem.: ATLA, ABA, Lee County Bar Assn., Iowa Trial Lawyers Assn., Ill. Trial Lawyers Assn., Iowa Bar Assn. Democrat. Roman Catholic. Home and Office: Middle Rd PO Box 1087 Keokuk IA 52632-1087 Office Phone: 319-524-4441.

HOFFMAN, JERRY IRWIN, retired dental educator; b. Chgo., Nov. 20, 1935; s. Irwin and Luba Hoffman; m. Sharon Lynn Seaman, Aug. 25, 1963; children: Steven Abram, Rachel Irene. Student, DePaul U., 1953-56; BS in Biology and Chemistry, Roosevelt U., 1956; DDS, Loyola U., Chgo., 1960; M of Health Care Adminstrn., Baylor U., 1972. Certificate, General Practice Residency, U.S. Army, 1978. Commd. officer U.S. Army, 1960 (served to 1962, returned 1964), advanced through grades to col., 1978, hdqrs. rep. local dental tng. confs. Europe Garmisch, Fed. Republic Germany, 1965-67; cons. to Comdg. Gen. U.S. Army Med. Research and Devel. Command, Washington, 1972-76; cons. Office of Surgeon Gen. U.S. Army, Washington, 1972-76, liaison rep. to Nat. Adv. Council and Oral Biology and Medicine Study Sessions of the Nat. Inst. Dental Research and NIH, 1973-76, resident in Gen. Practice Residency, 1976-78; comdg. officer U.S. Army Dental Activity, Fort Monmouth, NJ, 1979-82; ret., 1982; pvt. practice dentistry Chgo., 1962-64; assoc. prof. operative dentistry Loyola U. Sch. Dentistry, Maywood, Ill., 1982-93, dir. gen. practice residency, 1982-85, coordinator extramural dental resources, 1983-85, assoc. dean for clin. affairs, 1985-93; dir. sci. programs Chgo. Dental Soc., 1993—2002, ret., 2002. Staff dentist Silas B. Hayes Army Hosp., Fort Ord, Calif., 1976-79, Patterson Army Hosp., Ft. Monmouth, 1979-82; lectr., presenter seminars in field. Contbr. articles to profl. jours. Decorated Legion of Merit, Meritorious Svc. Medal with oak leaf cluster. Fellow: Am. Coll. Dentists, Internat. Coll. Dentists, Odontographic Soc.; master: Acad. Gen. Dentistry; mem. ADA, Ill. Dental Soc., Chgo. Dental Soc., Am. Assn. Dental Schs., Am. Soc. Assn. Execs., Assn. Healthcare Execs., Profl. Conv. Mgmt. Assn., Omicron Kappa Upsilon. Personal E-mail: ddscds@aol.com.

HOFFMAN, JILL M., neuroscientist, researcher; b. Nashua, NH, Dec. 21, 1978; d. Frederick Ray Hoffman and Cynthia Ann Twombly. BS, U. New Eng., Maine, 2003. Rsch. asst. dept. physiology med. sch. Dartmouth U., Lebanon, NH, 2003—05; rsch. study coord. Children's Hosp. Boston, 2005—06; grad. tchg. asst. neuroscience program coll. medicine U. Vt., Burlington, 2006—. Recipient Best Basic Sci. Rsch. award, New Eng. Perinatal Soc., 2004. Mem.: Am. Soc. Pharmacology and Exptl. Therapeutics (mem. student chpt. exec. com. 2003—05, Exptl. Biology award 2002, fellow 2002), Soc. Neuroscience. Roman Catholic.

HOFFMAN, JOEL ELIHU, lawyer; b. NYC, Sept. 23, 1937; s. Samuel S. and Flora (Pasachoff) H.; m. Sandra Joyce Stone, June 3, 1962 (div. June 1985); children: Susanna Beth, Alexander Laurence, Jeremy Andrew; m. Katherine Louise Joss, Feb. 15, 1986. BA, NYU, 1957; LLB, Yale U., 1960. Bar: N.Y. 1960, D.C. 1963. Trial atty. antitrust div. U.S. Dept. Justice, Washington, 1960-63; assoc. Wald, Harkrader and Ross, Washington, 1963-68, ptnr., 1968-85, Sutherland, Asbill and Brennan, Washington, 1985-99, of counsel, 1999—. Adj. prof. law Franklin Pierce Law Sch., 1997-2003, Law Sch. George Mason U., 1998—. Mem. editorial adv. bd. Food Drug and Cosmetic Law Jour., 1981-89; contbr. articles to profl. jours. Mem. ABA (chmn. food and drug com. adminstrv. law sect. 1976-82, 95-99, vice chmn. consumer product regulation com. 1976-2000, coun. mem. 1973-76). Office: Sutherland Asbill & Brennan 1275 Pennsylvania Ave NW Washington DC 20004-2415 Office Phone: 202-383-0100.

HOFFMAN, JOHN FLETCHER, retired lawyer; b. NYC, May 22, 1946; s. George Fletcher and Helen (Gilbert) H.; m. Coralie Tallman, June 29, 1969; children: Julie Gilbert, William Delano. BS, St. Lawrence U., 1969; JD, Washington and Lee U., 1975. Bar: N.Y. 1976, U.S. Dist. Ct. (so. dist.) N.Y. 1976, U.S. Dist. Ct. (ea. dist.) N.Y. 1978, U.S. Supreme Ct. 1980, U.S. Ct. Appeals (2d cir.) 1982, U.S. Dist. Ct. (no. dist.) Tex. 1988, U.S. Ct. Appeals (11th cir.) 1991, U.S. Ct. Appeals (fed. cir.) 1999. Assoc. Cadwalader, Wickersham & Taft, NYC, 1975-83, ptnr., 1983-94; v.p., assoc. gen. counsel Schering-Plough Corp., Kenilworth, NJ, 1995—2005; ret. Trustee First Unitarian Congl. Soc. Bklyn., 1980-83; v.p. fin. Unitarian Universalist Congregation of Monmouth County, 2002-04, sr. v.p., 2004-06, pres., 2006—; trustee, treas. Bklyn. Children's Mus., 1985-95. Mem.: ABA, Order of Coif, Omicron Delta Kappa.

HOFFMAN, JOHN RAYMOND, lawyer; b. Rochester, NY, July 24, 1945; s. Raymond Edward and Ruth Emily (Karnes) H.; m. Linda Lee Moore, Aug. 22, 1970; 1 child, Heather Anne. BA, Washburn U., 1967; JD, U. Mo.-Kansas City, 1971. Bar: Mo. 1972, Tenn. 1976, Kans. 1980, U.S. Supreme Ct. 1975. Law clk. United Telecom, Kansas City, Mo., 1967-70, gen. atty., 1970-75; gen. counsel, sec. United Telephone Sys.-S.E. Group, Bristol, Tenn., 1975-80; v.p., gen. counsel United Telephone Sys. Inc., Kansas City, Mo., 1980-84; sr. v.p. legal, dir. US Telecom, Inc., Kansas City, Mo., 1984-86; sr. v.p. external affairs Sprint Corp., Kansas City, Mo., 1986-99, ret., 2000; chmn. FCC N.Am. Numbering Coun., 1999—2000. Bd. dirs. United Telephone Co. of N.W., 1990-98. Author: That Was a Pin? The History of Sprint Corp., 2000. Bd. dirs. Ctr. Pub. Utilities, N.Mex. State U., 1989—90, Kansas City Area Econ. Devel. Coun., 1988—89, Trinity Luth. Hosp., Kansas City, 1984—89, Bishop Miege H.S. Found., 1990—92, 1999—2001, Health Initiatives, Inc., Kansas City, 1985—89, pres., 1986—89; bd. dirs. Kansas City Young Audiences, 1981—85, Johnson County Fire Dist., Prairie Village, Kans., 1982—86, Kansas City/Coro Found., 1983—84, Friends of the Zoo, Kansas City, 2000—01. Mem. ABA, Mo. Bar Assn., Tenn. Bar Assn., Kans. Bar Assn., Kansas City Bar Assn., Competitive Telecommunications Assn. (chmn. 1986-88), Ind. Telephone Pioneers Assn., Phi Delta Phi. Club: Optimist.

HOFFMAN, JONATHAN FREDERICK, military officer; b. Omaha, Sept. 24, 1963; s. Alice Carol Hoffman; m. Mary Elizabeth Sinkhorn, Apr. 7, 1993. With US Army, 1981—94, Germany, 1981—94; recruiter US Army Nashville Recruiting Bn., Paducah, Ky., 1994—96; various assignments US Army, 1981—94, Germany, 1981—94. Environ. compliance officer US Army, Ft. Knox, 2003—. Decorated 6 Good Conduct medals US Army, Meritorious Svc. medal, Gold Recruiters Badge. Mem.: Nat. Assn. Safety Profls., World Safety Orgn. Avocations: gardening, weightlifting.

HOFFMAN, JUDY GREENBLATT, preschool director; b. Chgo., June 12, 1932; d. Edward Abraham and Clara (Morrill) Greenblatt; m. Morton Hoffman, Mar. 16, 1950 (div. Jan. 1983); children: Michael, Alan, Clare. BA summa cum laude, Met. State Coll., Denver, 1972; MA, U. No. Colo., 1976, MA in Spl. Edn. Moderate Needs, 1996. Cert. tchr. Colo. Pre-sch. dir. B.M.H. Synagogue, Denver, 1968-70, Temple Emanuel, Denver, 1970-85, Congregation Rodef Shalom, Denver, 1985-88; tchr. Denver Pub. Schs., 1988—. Bilingual tchr. adults in amnesty edn. Denver Pub. Schs., 1989-90. Author: I Live in Israel, 1979, Joseph and Me, 1980 (Gamoran award), (with others) American Spectrum Single Volume Encyclopedia, 1991. Coord. Douglas Mountain Therapeutic Riding Ctr. for Handicapped, Golden, Colo., 1985—; dir. Mountain Ranch Summer Day Camp for Denver Pub. Schs., 1989-91. Mem. Nat. Assn. Temple Educators. Democrat. Avocations: riding, writing, music. Personal E-mail: jhoff3@earthlink.net.

HOFFMAN, JULIEN IVOR ELLIS, pediatrician, cardiologist, educator; b. Salisbury, So. Rhodesia, July 26, 1925; arrived in U.S., 1957, naturalized, 1967; s. Bernard Isaac and Minrose (Bermant) H.; m. Kathleen (Lewis), 1986; children: Anna, Daniel. BS, U. Witwatersrand, Johannesburg, South Africa, 1944, BSc (hon.), 1945, MB, BCh, 1949, MD, 1970. Intern, resident internal medicine, South Africa, 1950-56; rsch. asst., postgrad. Med. Sch., London, 1956-57; fellow pediatric cardiology Boston Children's Hosp., 1957-59; fellow Cardiovasc. Rsch. Inst., San Francisco, 1959-60; asst. prof. pediat., internal medicine Albert Einstein Coll., NYC, 1962-66; assoc. prof. pediat. U. Calif., San Francisco, 1966-70, prof., 1970-94, prof. physiology, 1981-88, prof. emeritus, 1994—. Sr. mem. Cardiovasc. Rsch. Inst. U. Calif., San Francisco, 1966—; mem. bd. examiners, sub-bd. pediat. cardiology Am. Bd. Pediat., 1973—78, sub-bd. pediat. intensive care, 1985—87; chmn. Louis Katz Award Com., Basic Sci. Coun., Am. Heart Assn., 1973—74, George Brown Meml. lectr., 1977; George Alexander Gibson Meml. lectr. Royal Coll. Physicians (Edinburgh), 1978; Lilly lectr. Royal Coll. Physicians (London), 1981; Isaac Starr lectr. Cardiac Systems Dynamics Soc., England, 1982, John Keith lectr., 85; Disting. Physiology lectr. Am. Coll. Chest Physicians, 1985; Nadas lectr. Am. Heart Assn., 1987; 1st Donald C. Fyler lectr. Children's Hosp., Boston, 1990; 1st MacDonald Dick lectr. U. Mich., Ann Arbor; Kreidberg lectr. Med. Sch. Tufts U., 2004; Tabatznik lectr. Mt. Sinai Hosp., Balt., 2005. Co-editor: Rudolph's Pediatrics, 1982—96, Coronary Circulation, 1990, Recent Advances in the Coronary Circulation, 1993, Pediatric Cardiovascular Medicine, 2000. Recipient Bayer Cardiovasc. Mentor award, 1989. Fellow Royal Coll. Physicians; mem. World Congress Pediat. Cardiology and Cardiac Surgery (hon. joint pres. Paris 1993), Am. Physiol. Soc., Am. Pediatric Soc., Soc. Pediatric Rsch. Achievements include extensive research into congenital heart disease and coronary blood flow. Home: 925 Tiburon Blvd Belvedere Tiburon CA 94920-1525 Home Phone: 415-435-6941. Business E-Mail: julien.hoffman@ucsf.edu.

HOFFMAN, KARLA LEIGH, mathematician, educator; b. Paterson, NJ, Feb. 14, 1948; d. Abe and Bertha (Guthaim) Rakoff; m. Allan Stuart Hoffman, Dec. 26, 1971; 1 child, Matthew Douglas. BA, Rutgers U., 1969; MBA, George Wash. U., Washington, DC, 1971, DSc in Ops. Rsch., 1975. Ops. rsch. analyst IRS, Washington, 1970-72; rsch. asst. George Washington U., 1972-75, assoc. profl. lectr., 1978-85; NSF postdoctoral rsch. fellow NAS, Washington, 1975-76; assoc. prof. sys. engring. dept. George Mason U., Fairfax, Va., 1985-86, assoc. prof. ops. rsch. and applied stats., 1986-89, prof. ops. rsch., 1990—, disting. prof., 1989, interim dept. chmn., 1996-97, chmn., 1997-98, chmn. sys. engring. and ops. rsch., 1998—2000. Mathematician Nat. Bur. Stds., Washington, 1976—84; vis. assoc. prof. ops. rsch. U. Md., 1982; mng. ptnr. Optimization Software Assocs.; cons. Govt. Agys., Airline, Telecom. and Def. Industries; bd. dirs. Parkinsons Found. Nat. Capital Area, 2006. Assoc. editor Internat. abstracts of Ops. Rsch., 1991—96, The Math. Programming Jour., Series B, 1987—, The Ops. Rsch. Soc. Jour. on Computing, 1991—96, Jour. Computational Optimization and Applications, 1992—98, mem. editl. bd. Annals of Ops. Rsch., 2000—; contbr. articles to profl. jours. Bd. dirs. Nat. Capital Region Parkinsons Found., 2006. Recipient Applied Rsch. award, Nat. Inst. Stds. and Tech., 1984, Silver medal, U.S. Dept. Commerce, 1984, Disting. Prof. award, 1989, Kimball medal, Inst. Ops. Rsch. & Mgmt. Svc., 2005. Fellow: Inst. Ops. Rsch. and Mgmt. Sci. (treas. 1995—96, exec. com. 1995—99, pres. 1998, Kimball medal 2005); mem.: Math. Programming Soc. (editor newsletter 1979—82, chmn. com. algorithms 1982—85, coun. 1985—88, exec. com., chmn. membership com. 1988—89), Ops. Rsch. Soc. Am. (sec.-treas. Computer Sci. Tech. sect. 1979—80, vis. profl. lectr. 1980—, vice chmn. sect. 1981, chmn. sect. 1982, chmn. tech. sect. com. 1983—86, coun. 1985—88, chmn. Lanchester Prize com. 1989, treas. 1993—94). Home: 6921 Clifton Rd Clifton VA 20124-1525 Office Phone: 703-993-1679. Business E-Mail: khoffman@gmu.edu.

HOFFMAN, KENNETH CARY, lawyer; b. Miami, Fla., Oct. 17, 1958; s. Larry J. and Deborah (Alexander) H.; m. Hillary Hoffman, Sept. 21, 1958; children: Julian, Andrew, Kevin, Gregory. BA, Tulane U., 1980; JD, U. Miami Law Sch., 1983. Shareholder, group head aviation practice group Greenberg Traurig LLP, Miami. Dir. Venture Coun. Forum, Miami, Fla., 1989-91. Dir. Bakehouse Art Complex, Miami, Fla., 1988-91. Office: Greenberg Traurig LLP 1221 Brickell Ave Miami FL 33131-3224 Office Phone: 305-579-0809. Office Fax: 305-579-0717. Business E-Mail: hoffmank@gtlaw.com.

HOFFMAN, KENNETH MYRON, mathematician, educator; b. Long Beach, Calif., Nov. 30, 1930; s. Myron Grant and Madge (Harrison) H.; children: Donna, Laura, Robert; m. Alicia C. Coro, Mar. 1997. AA, John Muir Coll., 1950; AB, Occidental Coll., 1952; MA, UCLA, 1954, PhD, 1956. Instr. math. MIT, Cambridge, 1956-59, asst. prof., 1959-61, assoc. prof., 1961-63, prof., 1963-96, prof. emeritus, 1996—, chmn. pure math., 1968-69; chmn. Commn. on Edn., 1969-71, head dept. math., 1971-79; exec. dir. Commn. on Resources for Math. Sci., NRC, 1981-85, Math. Scis. Edn. Bd. NRC, Washington, 1989-91; assoc. exec. officer for edn. NRC, Washington, 1991-94; pres. MSTE.NET, Madison, Md., 1996—. Chmn. adv. com. NSF Sci. and Engring. Edn. Directorate, 1984-85; cons. Math. Scis. Edn. Bd. NRC, 1985-89; head, Office Govtl. and Pub. Affairs, Joint Policy Bd. for Math., 1984-89; chmn. Md. Math. & Sci. Coalition, 1996—; pres. Nat. Alliance State Sci. and Math. Coalitions, 1997-2002, sr. counsel, 2002—; chair Govs. Adv. Com. on STEM Edn., 2005-06. Author: (with Ray Kunze) Linear Algebra, 1961, Fundamentals of Banach Algebras, 1962, Banach Spaces of Analytic Functions, 1962, Analysis in Euclidean Space, 1975; Contbr. (with Ray Kunze) articles to profl. jours. Mailing. Fellow Alfred P. Sloan Found., 1964-66. Fellow AAAS (coun.); mem. Am. Math. Soc. (past mem. coun.), Math. Assn. Am., Nat. Coun. Tchrs. Math., Phi Beta Kappa. Office: MSTE net 909 Parsons Dr Madison MD 21648 E-mail: ken@mste.net.

HOFFMAN, KENNETH R., lawyer; b. Washington, Aug. 1, 1952; BS, Frostburg State Coll., 1974; JD, U. Md. Sch. of Law, 1977. Bar: Md. 1977, DC 1998. Law clerk to Judge C. Awdry Thompson Ct. of Special Appeals, Md., 1977—78; ptnr., employee benefits & taxation Venable LLP, Washington. Mem. Comptroller's Task Force on Tax Reform, 1985—86; pres. Pro Bono Resource Center of Md., Inc., 1997—99; adjunct prof. U. Balt.; mem., tax advisory com. Congressman Benjamin Cardin. Sec. & trustee Nat. Aquarium in Balt. Found., Inc; bd. dirs & past pres. CollegeBound Found., Inc.; bd. dirs. Nat. Aquarium Inst. Mem.: ABA (mem. employee benefits com.), DC Bar Assn., Md. Bar Assn. (chair taxation section 1991—92, mem. special pro bono com. 1995—97). Office: Venable LLP 575 7th St NW Washington DC 20004 Office Phone: 202-344-4810. Office Fax: 202-344-8300. Business E-Mail: krhoffman@venable.com.

HOFFMAN, LARRY J., lawyer; b. NYC, Aug. 20, 1930; s. Max and Pauline (Epstein) H.; m. Deborah E. Alexander, Oct. 2, 1954; children: Lisa, Ken, Heidi, Mark. AA, U. Fla., Gainesville; JD, U. Miami. Bar: Fla. 1954. Chmn. Greenberg, Traurig, PA, Miami, 1968—. Mem. ABA, Fla. Bar Assn., Dade County Bar Assn. Avocations: art, computers, photography, golf. Office: Greenberg Traurig LLP 1221 Brickell Ave Miami FL 33131-3224 Business E-Mail: hoffmanl@gtlaw.com.

HOFFMAN, LAWRENCE A., rabbi; PhD, Hebrew Union Coll.-Jewish Inst. Religion, 1972. Cert. ordained Rabbi 1969. Co-founder, dir. Synagogue 2000; Barbara and Stephen Friedman Chair in Liturgy, Worship, and Ritual Hebrew Union Coll.-Jewish Inst. Religion, 2006—. Editor: Minhag Ami: My People's Prayer Book; co-editor: Two Liturgical Traditions; author (religion books): What is a Jew?, Israel: A Spiritual Travel Guide. Named one of The Top 50 Rabbis in America, Newsweek Mag., 2007. Office: Hebrew Union Coll-Jewis Inst Religion 3101 Clifton Avenue Cincinnati OH 45220-2448*

HOFFMAN, LINDA M., chemist, educator; b. NYC, Dec. 18, 1939; d. Theodore and Esther Weiss; m. Robert G. Hoffman, Feb. 2, 1958; 1 child, Samuel A. BS in Chemistry, Queens Coll., 1959; MS, NYU, 1967, PhD in Organic Chemistry, 1970. Rsch. assoc. Kingsbrook Jewish Med. Ctr., NYC, 1973-77; asst. prof. Baruch Coll., CUNY, NYC, 1977-79, assoc. prof., 1979-82, prof., 1982—, chair dept. natural scis., 1995-98. Reviewer grant proposals NIH. Contbr. articles on Tay-Sachs disease and on glycosphingolipids as markers for cancer to profl. jours. Mem. edn. com. UN Internat. Sch., N.Y.C., 1981-84; bd. dirs. Forest Hills Gardens Corp., 1993-2000. Recipient Moore award Am. Soc. Neuropathologists, 1981, 84, Founders Day award NYU, 1971, 112th Precinct Cmty. Coun. award, 1993; postdoctoral fellow Sloan Kettering Inst. Cancer Rsch., N.Y.C., 1972-73. Mem. AAAS, Am. Chem. Soc., Sigma Xi. Office: Baruch Coll Dept Natural Scis One Bernard Baruch Way New York NY 10010-5518 Business E-Mail: linda_hoffman@baruch.cuny.edu.

HOFFMAN, LINDA R., social services administrator; b. New Haven, July 23, 1940; d. Bernard Harry and Sylvia (Paul) Rosenfield; m. Peter A. Hoffman, Sept. 25, 1965; 1 child, Tracie Hoffman Cohen. BA, Russell Sage Coll., Troy, NY, 1962; MSW, Columbia U., NYC, 1968. Cert. social worker NY. Case worker Conn. Dept. Welfare, New Haven, 1962-63, NYC Bur. Child Welfare, NYC, 1963-65, supr., 1965-66; asst. to commr. program planning NYC Dept. Social Svcs., NYC, 1968-70; spl. asst. to commr. NYC Spl. Svc. for Children, NYC, 1972-79; pres. NY Found. Sr. Citizens, NYC, 1979—. Cons. USIA, Teheran, Iran, 1975; adj. prof. Columbia Sch. Social Work, chmn. dean's adv. coun. Bd. dirs. Grosvenor Neighborhood House, 2002, West Side YMCA, 2004—. Recipient Presdl. Recognition award for Cmty. Svc., 1983, East Manhattan C. of C., award for Disting. Civic Svc., 1990, The Mcpl. Art Soc. NY award, 1997; named to Columbia U. Sch. Social Work Hall of Fame, 2000. Mem. NASW (cert.),

Women's City Club of NY, YWCA NYC Acad. Women Achievers, Women's Forum. Avocations: boating, fishing, thoroughbred race horses. Office: NY Found Sr Citizens 11 Park Pl Ste 1416 New York NY 10007-2801

HOFFMAN, LLOYD ALAN, plastic surgeon; b. NYC, Apr. 16, 1952; MD, Northwestern U., Evanston, Ill., 1978. Diplomate Am. Bd. Plastic Surgery with subspecialty in hand surgery, Am. Bd. Surgery. Intern N.Y. Hosp., NYC, resident in gen. surgery; resident in microsurgery NYU, NYC, resident in plastic surgery, fellow in hand surgery; chief divsn. plastic surgery N.Y. Hosp./Cornell U., NYC, 1987—98; chief combined plastic surgery program Cornell and Columbia Univs., NYC, 1998—, assoc. prof. plastic surgery. Named one of Top Doctors in NY, NY mag. Achievements include targeting the interface between a limb allograft and the recipient immune system, the effect of cyclosporin A on the migration and distribution of dendritic cells in the transplanted rat limb and experiments on craniofacial synostosis. Office: NY Hosp-Cornell U Med Ctr Box 115 525 E 68th St New York NY 10021-4873 also: 12 E 68th St New York NY 10021 Office Phone: 212-861-1640. Fax: 212-452-5125.*

HOFFMAN, MARGUERITE STEED, former art gallery director; m. Robert Kenneth Hoffman; 1 child, Katherine. Positions with Dallas Mus. Art; former dir. Gerald Peters Gallery. Bd. trustees Dallas Mus. Art, 1999—, chmn. bd.; bd. dirs. Tex. Freedom Network; mem. coun. Dallas Women's Found.; donated contemporary art collection and a $20 million endowment Dallas Mus. Art, 2005. Named one of Top 200 Collectors, ARTnews mag., 2003—06. Avocation: Collector postwar Am. and European art, Chinese monochromes. Office: Dallas Mus Art 1717 N Harwood Dallas TX 75201

HOFFMAN, MARIAN RUTH, singer, voice educator; m. Warren Marlyn Hoffman, Aug. 13, 1955; children: Mark Edward, Paul Stephen, Jeffrey Brian, Thomas Warren. MusB, U. Dubuque, Iowa, 1955; MFA, U. Minn., Mpls., 1973. Tchr. music Darlington Pub. Schools, Wis., 1955—58; instr. voice Inver Hills C.C., Minn., 1973—75, Home Studio, St. Paul, 1973—; profl. soloist Westminster Presbyn. Ch., Mpls., 1974—2004; instr. voice Normandale C.C., Bloomington, 1974—86, Bethel U., St. Paul, 1981—91. Pres., , v.p., editor Thursday Musical, Mpls., 1974—; bd. mem. Schuessler Vocal Arts Ctr., 1990—; v.p. Young People's Symphony Concert Assn., 2005—. Singer: (recitals and concerts) 10-15 Appearances Yearly; singer: (various roles) (operas) Rape of Lucretia, Madame Butterfly, Savitri, Riders of the Sea, Tender Land, Wise Women; singer: (anna, mother superior, singer) (musical theater) King and I, Sound of Music, West Side Story, Oliver. Parish leader Westminster Presbyn. Ch., Mpls., 1990, elder, 2005—. Recipient Alumni Notable Achievement award, U. Minn., 2004. Mem.: Am. Guild Organists (sec. 1967—68), Nat. Assn. Tchrs. Singing (sec. 1978—80, emeritus 2002), Sigma Alpha Iota (life; v.p. 2000—05, Sword Honor, Alumni Distinction 2000, 2003). Avocations: travel, walking, knitting, gardening. Home Phone: 651-484-3940. Personal E-mail: marianhoffman@comcast.net.

HOFFMAN, MARK, broadcast executive; b. LA; married; 3 children. BA, U. Calif. Berkeley; MA in Journalism, U. Mo. News assoc. KNX Radio, LA, 1981—82; prodr. KMGH-TV, Denver, WNEV-TV, Boston; exec. prodr. to mng. editor WLS-TV, Chgo.; asst. news dir. WABC-TV, NYC; news dir. WAGA-TV, Atlanta, WBBM-TV, Chgo.; v.p., news KNBC-TV, LA, 1993; v.p., gen. mgr. KDNL-TV, St. Louis; exec. prodr./develop. WarnerBrothers/Telepictures; exec. prodr. CNBC, LA, 1997—98, v.p./mng. editor, 1999—2000, v.p./mng. editor, bus. develop., 2001; interim pres. CNBC Europe, 2000—01; pres. CNBC, 2005—; pres., gen. mgr. WVIT-NBC, Hartford, Conn., 2001—05. Bd. dirs. MetroHartford C. of C., Greater Hartford Econ. Devel. Coun., Urban League of Greater Hartford, Sci. Ctr. Conn., Jr. Achievement S.W. New England. Office: CNBC 900 Sylvan Ave Englewood Cliffs NJ 07632 Office Phone: 201-735-2622.*

HOFFMAN, MARY CATHERINE, retired nurse, anesthetist; b. Winamac, Ind., July 14, 1923; d. Harmon William Whitney and Dessie Maude (Neely) Hoffman. RN, Meth. Hosp., Indpls., 1945; cert. obstet. analgesia and anesthesia, Johns Hopkins Hosp., 1949; grad., Cleve. Sch. Anesthesia, 1952. Staff nurse Meth. Hosp., 1945-49; rsch. asst., then staff anesthetist Johns Hopkins Hosp., 1949-62; staff anesthetist Meth. Hosp., 1962-64, U. Chgo. Hosps., 1964-66; chief nurse anesthetist Paris (Ill.) Cmty. Hosp., 1966-80; staff anesthetist Hendricks County Hosp., Danville, Ind., Ball Meml. Hosp., Muncie, Ind., 1981-86; ret. Mem. Am. Assn. Nurse Anesthetists, Am. Heart Assn., Ind. Fedn. Bus. and Profl. Women's Clubs (Ill. dist. chmn. 1977-78, state found. chmn. 1978-79, Found. award 1979). Republican. Presbyterian. Home: 1700 N Maddox Dr Muncie IN 47304-2674

HOFFMAN, MATHEW, lawyer; b. Bklyn., Mar. 9, 1954; s. S. David and Naomi B. (Brosterman) H.; m. Bracha Hoffman; children: Ari, Gavriel, Shelhevet, Miri, Shira, Tova, Elisheva, Adina. BA, U. Mich., 1974; JD, Columbia U., 1977. Bar: N.Y. 1978, U.S. Dist. Ct. (so. and ea. dists.) N.Y. 1978, U.S. Ct. Appeals (2d and 7th cirs.) 1980, U.S. Dist. Ct. (we. dist.) Mich., 2003; ordained rabbi, 1988. Atty. Proskauer, Rose, NYC, 1978-80, Gordon, Hurwitz, NYC, 1980-85; ptnr. Koether, Harris & Hoffman, NYC, 1985-89, Keck Mahin & Cate, NYC, 1989-94, Rosen & Reade, NYC, 1994-96; ptnr., head of litigation Todtman, Nachamie, Spizz & Johns, P.C., NYC, 1997—. Arbitrator Wuhan Arbitation Commn., 2004—. Contbr. articles to profl. jours. Mem. Jewish Flame (trustee 1979—). Home: 62 Rosehill Ave New Rochelle NY 10804-3615 Office: Todtman Nachamie Spizz & Johns PC 425 Park Ave New York NY 10022-3506 Office Phone: 212-754-9400. Business E-Mail: mhoffman@tnsj-law.com.

HOFFMAN, MICHAEL J., manufacturing executive; BA in Mktg. Mgmt., U. St. Thomas, St. Paul; MBA, U. Minn. Sales, svc., mktg. positions Toro Co., Mpls., 1977—89, various mgmt. positions, 1989—97, v.p., gen. mgr., comml. bus., 1997—2000, v.p., gen. mgr. consumer bus., 2000—01, group v.p., consumer and landscape contractor bus.; 2001—02, group v.p., consumer, landscape contractor, internat. businesses, 2002—04, COO, 2004—05, pres., 2004—, CEO, 2005—, chmn. bd., 2006—. Office: Toro Co 8111 Lyndale Ave S Minneapolis MN 55420 Office Phone: 952-888-8801.*

HOFFMAN, MICHAEL JEROME, humanities educator; b. Phila., Mar. 13, 1939; s. Nathan P. and Sara (Perlman) H.; m. Margaret Boegeman, Dec. 27, 1988; children by previous marriage: Cynthia, Matthew. BA, U. Pa., 1959, MA, 1960, PhD, 1963. Instr. Washington Coll., Chestertown, Md., 1962-64; asst. prof. U. Pa., Phila., 1964-67; from asst. prof. to prof. U. Calif., Davis, 1967—2001, asst. vice chancellor acad. affairs, 1976-83, chmn. English dept., 1984-89, dir. Davis Humanities Inst., 1987-91, coord. writing programs, 1991-94, undergrad. coord., 1994-95, grad. advisor, 1995-98, dir. honors program, 1992-99. Chmn. joint projects steering com. U. Calif.-Calif. State U., 1976-87; chmn. adv. bd. Calif. Acad. Partnership Program, 1985-87; dir. Calif. Humanities Project, 1985-91. Author: The Development of Abstractionism in the Writings of Gertrude Stein, 1965, The Buddy System, 1971, The Subversive Vision, 1972, Gertrude Stein, 1976, Critical Essays on Gertrude Stein, 1986, Essentials of the Theory of Fiction, 1988, 2d rev. edit., 2005, Critical Essays on American Modernism, 1992. With USAR, 1957-61. Nat. Def. Edn. Act fellow U.S. Govt., 1959-62. Mem. Modern Lang. Assn. (Am. lit. group). Democrat. Jewish. Avocation: tennis. Home: 4417 San Marino Dr Davis CA 95618-5012 Office: Univ Calif Dept English Davis CA 95618 Business E-Mail: mjhoffman@ucdavis.edu.

HOFFMAN, MICHAEL WILLIAM, lawyer, accountant; b. Bowling Green, Ohio, Feb. 5, 1955; s. Oscar William and Marie Louise Hoffman; m. Lynne Ellen Steele, Aug. 31, 1975; children: Megan, Jessica, Kristine, Robert. BA in Acctg. summa cum laude, Bowling Green State U., 1976; JD, U. Toledo, 1981. Bar: Ohio 1981, Ga. 1983; CPA, Ga., Ohio. Acct. Ernst & Whinney, Toledo, 1976—81; acct., ptnr. Touche Ross & Co., Atlanta, 1981—86; v.p. Profl. Svcs. Network Inc., Atlanta, 1986; assoc. Chamberlain, Hrdlicka, White, Johnson & Williams, Atlanta, 1986—89; ptnr. Somers & Altenbach, Atlanta, 1989—91; chmn., CEO Hoffman & Assocs., Attys. at Law, LLC, Atlanta, 1991—. Organizing dir. Paces Bank & Trust Co., Atlanta; spkr. in field. Author: RIA's U.S.A. News for the Inbound Investor, 1983. Treas. Friendship Force Internat., 1984; Eagle scout Boy Scouts Am.; mem. parish coun. Holy Family Ch., 2004—, coach youth basketball and baseball. Recipient Leadership award Boy Scouts Am., 1986. Mem.: AICPA, ABA, Estate Planning Coun. of North Ga., Ga. Soc. CPAs (chmn. Tax Forum Com. 1990—92, chmn. Estate Gift & Trust Sect. 1997—2000, Disting. Chair award 1998—99, v.p. mgmt. com. 2000—01, bd. dirs. 2000—01), Am. Assn. Atty.-CPA, State Bar Ga. (fiduciary law sect., tax sect.), Bowling Green State U.-Atlanta Alumni Assn. (parents adv. coun. 1999—2000), Atlanta Country Club (bd. dirs. 1998—2001). Republican. Avocations: golf, tennis, hiking, reading, fishing. Home: 535 Willow Knoll Dr Marietta GA 30067-4647 Office: # 300 6100 Lake Forrest Dr NW Atlanta GA 30328-3845 Office Phone: 404-255-7400. Business E-Mail: mike@hoffmanandassoc.net.

HOFFMAN, NANCY, art gallery director; b. NYC, 1944;, Wellesley Coll., 1964, Columbia U., 1966. Asst. registrar Asia House Gallery, NYC, 1964-69; dir. Contemporary Gallery French & Co., NYC, 1969-72; owner, pres. Nancy Hoffman Gallery, NYC, 1972—. Lectr., jury exhibitor throughout U.S. Contbr. chpt. to text. Office: Nancy Hoffman Gallery 429 W Broadway New York NY 10012-3799 Office Phone: 212-966-6676. Business E-Mail: nancyhoffmangallery@hotmail.com.

HOFFMAN, NANCY M., painter; b. Boston, June 24, 1949; d. Theodore Fiske Hoffman and Margaret Louise Shepphard. BFA, Sch. Art Inst., Chgo., 1972, MFA, 1974. Instr. art U. RI, Kingston, 1973—74; asst. prof. art U. Hartford, Conn., 1974—80. Exhibitions include The Susan Caldwell Gallery, NY, 1980, 1981, The Trompe L'oeil Gallery, 1982, 1983, The Fun Gallery, 1984, The Barbara Braathen Gallery, 1985, They Maryanne MCcarthy Gallery, 1985, Castell Gallery, 1987, Antoine Candau Installation, Paris, 1988, Hokin Gallery, Palm Beach, Fla., 1989, Fiac Art Fair, Paris, 1992. Mem.: Coll. Arts Assn. Avocations: bicycling, dance, singing. Home and Studio: 1 Central Sq Apt 102 Keene NH 03431

HOFFMAN, NATHANIEL A., lawyer; b. Cin., Mar. 4, 1949; s. Ralph H. and Betty (Goldfarb) H.; m. Sara Naomi Fishman, Aug. 3, 1980; children: Joshua, Rebecca, Esther, David. BA, Yale U., 1971; JD, U. Mich., 1975. Bar: Calif. 1975, Wis. 1983. Assoc. McDonough, Holland & Allen, Sacramento, 1975—78, Herz, Levin, Teper, Sumner & Croysdale, Milw., 1982—85; ptnr. Michael, Best & Friedrich, Milw., 1985—2004, Whyte Hirschboeck Dudek SC, Milw., 2005—. Atty. N.Y.C. Pub. Devel. Corp., 1980-82. Mem. ABA, State Bar Wis., Milw. Bar Assn., State Bar Calif. Home: 3258 N 51st Blvd Milwaukee WI 53216-3236 Office: Whyte Hirschboeck Dudek SC 555 E Wells St Ste 1900 Milwaukee WI 53202 Home Phone: 414-444-5733; Office Phone: 414-978-5634. Business E-Mail: nhoffman@whdlaw.com.

HOFFMAN, PAUL FELIX, geologist, educator; b. Toronto, Ont., Can., Mar. 21, 1941; s. Samuel and Dorothy Grace (Medhurst) Hoffman; m. Erica Jean Westbrook, Dec. 4, 1976; 1 child, Guy Samson. BS, McMaster U., 1964; MA, Johns Hopkins U., 1965, PhD, 1970. Lectr. Franklin & Marshall Coll., Lancaster, Pa., 1968-69; rsch. scientist Geol. Survey Can., Ottawa, Canada, 1969-92; prof. U. Victoria, BC, Canada, 1992-94; Sturgis Hooper prof. geology Harvard U., Cambridge, Mass., 1994—. Lectr. U. Calif., Santa Barbara, 1971—72; mem. Internat. Union Geol. Scis., Commn. Precambrian Stratigraphy, 1976; vis. prof. U. Tex., Dallas, 1978; vis. prof., Lamont-Doherty Earth Observatory Columbia U., 1990; dir. lectr. Am. Assn. Petroleum Geologists, 1979—80; adj. prof. Carleton U., 1989—92; associated with Earth System Evolution Program Can. Inst. Advanced Rsch., 1994—; associated with NASA Astrobiology Inst., 1999—, Tectonics Spl. Rsch. Ctr., U. Western Australia, 2002—; mem. vis. com., dept. earth, atmospheric and planetary sciences MIT, 1996—. Assoc. and N.Am. editor Tectonics, 1982—92, assoc. editor Geology, 1982—84, Astrobiology, 2001—. Recipient Bownocker medal, Ohio State U., 1989, Henno Martin medal, Geol. Soc. Namibia, 2000, Alfred Wegener medal, European Union Geosciences, 2001; Sherman Fairfield Disting. Scholar, Calif. Inst. Tech., 1974—77. Fellow: AAAS, Geol. Soc. Am., Royal Soc. Can. (Willet G. Miller medal 1997), Geol. Assn. Can. (Past Pres.' medal 1976, Logan medal 1992); mem.: NAS (fgn. assoc.), Soc. for Sedimentary Geology, Am. Acad. Arts and Sci. (fgn. hon.), Can. Soc. Petroleum Geologists (R. J. W. Douglas Meml. medal 1991), Am. Geophys. Union. Home: 1 Waterhouse St Apt 45 Cambridge MA 02138-3610 Office: Harvard U Geological Mus Rm 203D Dept Earth/Planetary Sci 20 Oxford St Cambridge MA 02138-2902 Office Phone: 617-495-3636. E-mail: hoffman@eps.harvard.edu.

HOFFMAN, PAUL JEROME, psychologist, statistician; b. San Francisco, June 25, 1923; s. Louis and Bessie (Brodofsky) H.; m. Elaine Stroll, Mar. 18, 1944; children: Valerie, Elizabeth, Jonathan. BA in Exptl. Psychology, Stanford U., 1949, PhD in Psychology and Statistics, 1954. Diplomate Am. Coll. Forensic Examiners, Am. Bd. Psychol. Specialties; lic. psychologist, Oreg., Calif. Asst. prof. Wash. State U., Pullman, 1953-57, U. Oreg., Eugene, 1957-60, adj. prof., 1967-76; prin. Paul J. Hoffman Assocs., San Carlos, Calif., 1985—; pres. Magic7 Software Co., Los Altos, Calif., 1985-98, Paul J. Hoffman Psychometrics, Inc., Los Altos, Calif., 1978-83. Cons. Am. Airlines, Dallas, 1990, 91, Nat. Heart, Lung and Blood Inst. NIH, Bethesda, Md., 1978, Am. Assn. State Psychol. Bds. Nat. Exam. Com., N.Y.C., 1972-78; prof. dept. adminstrv. sci. U.S. Naval Postgrad. Sch., Monterey, Calif., 1981-84; consulting psychologist Hewlett Packard Co., Palo Alto, Calif., 1981-83; vis. disting. prof. psychology U. Hawaii, Honolulu, 1978; testing cons. Nat. Bd. Med. Examiners and Am. Bd. Internal Medicine, Phila., 1971-72; pres., founder Oreg. Rsch. Inst., Eugene, 1960-77. Author: (with others) Decision Processes, 1954, Formal Representation of Human Judgement, 1968, Computer Aided Decision Analysis, 1993, Expert Evidence: A Practitioner's Guide to Law, Science and the FJC Manual, 1997; contbr. 53 articles to profl. jours. Chair fgn. policy Dem. Ctrl. Com., Oreg., 1960-72; advisor Sen. Wayne Morse, Oreg., 1964-70; chmn. Bob Straub for Gov. Com., Oreg., 1974. Lt. USAF, 1942-46. Grantee NIH, 1958-77, NSF, 1961-63. Fellow AAAS, APA, Psychonomic Soc., Psychometric Soc., Human Factors Soc.; mem. Am. Statis. Assn., Oreg. Psychol. Assn. (pres. 1962-63), Oreg. Inventors Coun., Am. Coll. Forensic Examiners. Achievements include copyrights for expert systems software, consensus building software. Home: 1120 Royal Ln San Carlos CA 94070-4277 E-mail: paul.hoffman@mindspring.com.

HOFFMAN, PAUL SHAFER, lawyer; b. Harrisburg, Pa., Dec. 12, 1933; s. Paul and Lucy Rose (Shafer) H.; m. Patricia Ann Rudisill, 1958; children: Eric, Kathryn, Julia, Margot. AB in Physics, Gettysburg Coll., 1957; JD, Harvard U., 1962. Bar: N.Y. 1963, U.S. Patent Office 1963, U.S. Dist. Ct. (so. dist.) N.Y. 1977, U.S. Ct. Appeals (2d cir.) 1977, U.S. Supreme Ct. 1977. Assoc. Kenyon & Kenyon, NYC, 1962-63; application analyst IBM-ASDD, Yorktown, NY, 1963-66; dir. tech. research Matthew Bender Co., NYC, 1966-68; v.p. Bowne and Co., Inc., NYC, 1968-77; sole practice Croton-on-Hudson, NY, 1977—. Mem. Croton Sch. Bd., 1972-75, pres., 1974-75; trustee Village Croton-on-Hudson, 1977-81, acting village justice, 1991—; bd. dirs. Croton Caring Com., Inc., 1982—. Served to cpl. U.S. Army, 1952-54. Mem. N.Y. State Bar Assn. (assoc. editor-in-chief N.Y. State Bar jour. 1991-98), Westchester County Bar Assn., Computer Law Assn. (bd. dirs. 1984-94, 96-2001). Clubs: Harvard (N.Y.C.). Lodges: Masons. Republican. Lutheran. Office: 139 Grand St Croton On Hudson NY 10520-2306

HOFFMAN, PAUL STOKES, microbiologist, researcher; b. Newport News, Va., Jan. 24, 1950; s. Ira Stokes and Emily VanArsdale Hoffman; m. Laura Francis Ricketts, June 2, 1973. BS, Va. Tech, Blacksburg, 1972; MSc, Iowa State U., Ames, 1974; PhD, Va. Tech, Blacksburg, 1977. Post doctoral fellow, biochemistry U. Ga., 1977—79, vis. prof., microbiology, 1981—82; asst. prof. U. Memphis, 1979—83, U. Tenn, Memphis, 1983—90; prof., microbiol & medicine Dalhousie U., Halifax, Nova Scotia, Canada, 1990—2004; prof. medicine & microbiology U. Va., Charlottesville, Va., 2004—; asst. dir. anti infectives GlaxoSmithKline, Collegeville, Pa., 1999—2000. Ceo HoffGen, Halifax, 2000—05. Editor: (scientific specialty books) Helicobacter Infection and Immun. Recipient Tchg. award, U. Tenn. Med. Sch., 1983—84, Rsch. award, Dept. Medicine, Dalhousie U., 2002; Rsch. grant, NIH, 1982—90, 2006—, Oper. grants, Can. Inst. Health Rsch., 1991—2006. Mem.: Am. Soc. Microbiology (regional pres. 1985—86). Non-Partisan. Achievements include patents pending for vaccine targets and drug discovery. Office: U Va 409 Lane Rd Bldg MR4 Rm 2146 Charlottesville VA 22908 Home Phone: 434-971-1233. Business E-Mail: psh2n@virginia.edu.

HOFFMAN, PHILIP EDWARD, legislative consultant; b. Jackson, Mich., Nov. 10, 1951; s. Ralph Jacob Jr. and Nancy Joan (Vanantwerp) H.; m. Dennise Fitzgerald, Jan. 29, 1977; children: R. Jacob, Benjamin, Philip. BS, Ferris State U., 1974; postgrad. in edn., Mich. State U., 1975. Undercover narcotics investigator Region II Metro Squad, 1974-77; deputy sheriff Jackson County Sheriff's Dept., Jackson, 1974-82; mem. Mich. Ho. of Reps., Lansing, 1982-93, Mich. Senate from 19th dist., Lansing, 1993—2002; v.p. pro tempore Mich. Senate, Lansing; founder, prin. Hoffman Legis. Cons. LLC, 2003—. Treas., bd. dirs. Am. 1st Fed. Credit Union, Jackson, Mich., 1996—; treas., bd. trustees Jackson CC, 2004—. Pres. Great Sauk Trail coun. Boy Scouts Am., 1995-96, v.p. 1992-95; past pres. Land O'Lakes Coun., 1992-94; bd. dir. Port St. James, Beaver, Mich., 2002-, Beaver Island Boat Co., Mich., 2006-. Named Outstanding Legislator of Yr., Mich. Assn. Chiefs Police, 1993, Legis. Conservationist of Yr., Mich. United Conservation Clubs, 1994, Guardian of Small Bus., Nat. Fedn. Ind. Bus., 1996, Legis. of Yr., Mich. Sheriff's Assn., 1997; Federalism Summit, 1995; Toll fellow, 1995; Fleming fellow, 1994, 95, fellow Coun. State Govts., Ctr. for Policy Alternatives; recipient Silver Beaver award Boy Scouts Am., 1997, Advocate of Yr. award Mich. Mfrs. Assn., 1998, Flame Leadership award Ferris State U., 1998, Star award Dep. Sheriff's Assn. Mich., 1999, Legis. Leadership award Mich. Soft Drink Assn., 1999, Disting. Svc. award Ind. Colls. and Univs. of Mich. Assn., 2000; Am. Legion Legislative award, 2000, Disting. Svc. medal Mich Dept. Mil. and Vets Affairs, 2001, Legis. Leadership award Internat. Brotherhood Elec. Workers and Mich. Chpt. Nat. Elec. Contractors Assn., 2001, Disting. Citizen of Yr. award, Boy Scouts Am., 2001, Legislator of Yr. award, Police Officers Assn. Mich., 2001, Adjutant Gen. Patriot award Mich. Dept. Mil. and Vets. Affairs, 2001, Presdl. Citation award Mich. Sheriff's Assn., 2002, others. Mem. NAACP (life), Am. Legis. Exch. Coun. (Outstanding Legis. Mem. of Yr. 1992, chmn. telecom. task force, 1992-95, bd. dirs. 1996), Jackson C.C. Alumni Assn. (Disting. Svc. award 1987), Ferris State U. Alumni Assn. (Disting. Alumnus 1990), Mich. Jaycees (1 of 10 Outstanding Young People in Mich. 1985). Republican. Roman Catholic. Office: 721 N Capitol Ave Ste 3 Lansing MI 48906 Home Phone: 517-688-4580; Office Phone: 517-371-3333. Office Fax: 517-487-3505.

HOFFMAN, PHILIP GUTHRIE, former university president; b. Kobe, Japan, Aug. 6, 1915; s. Benjamin Philip and Florence (Guthrie) H. (Am. citizens); m. Mary Elizabeth Harding, Aug. 31, 1939; children: Philip Guthrie, Mary Victoria Hoffman Cobb, Ruth Ann Hoffman Cabler, Jeanne Hoffman Camp. Student, George Washington U., 1936-37; AB, Pacific Union Coll., 1938; MA, U. So. Calif., 1942; PhD, Ohio State U., 1948; H.H.D. (hon.), Jacksonville U.; LL.D. (hon.), U. Americas, U. Akron; L.H.D. (hon.), Pikeville Coll., Marshall U., U. Houston, 1987; D.L. (hon.), Kyung Hee U., Korea; D.H.C. (hon.), Autonomous U., Guadalajara (Mex.); Litt.D. (hon.), U. St. Thomas, 1979. Credit mgr. Harding Sanitarium, Worthington, Ohio, 1938-40; instr. history Ohio State U. Columbus, 1946-49; asst. prof. history U. Ala., Tuscaloosa, 1949-51, assoc. prof., 1951-53, dir. arts and scis. extension services, 1949-53; dean, assoc. prof. history gen. extension div. Oreg. System Higher Edn., Portland, 1953-55; prof. history Portland State Coll., Oreg., 1955-57, dean faculty Oreg., 1955-57; v.p., dean faculties, prof. history U. Houston, 1957-61, pres., 1961-79, pres. emeritus, 1979—. Cons. Mitchell Energy and Devel. Corp., Houston, 1980-81; pres. Tex. Med. Ctr. Inc., Houston, 1981-85; dir. Fed. Res. Bank Dallas Mem. Nat. Commn. on Accrediting; mem. Am. Council on Edn., Coll. Entrance Exam. Bd. Lt. (j.g.) USNR, 1943-45. Recipient Centennial Achievement award Ohio State U., 1970, Merit award U. So. Calif., 1975. Mem. Tex. Hist. Assn., Gulf Hist. Assn., Am. Hist. Assn., Assn. Tex. Coll. and Univs. (pres.), Assn. Urban Univs. (pres. 1965-66), Nat. Assn. State Univs. and Land-Grant Colls. (dir. 1971-75), So. Univ. Conf. (pres. 1976-77), Phi Kappa Phi, Phi Alpha Theta (nat. pres. 1952-54), Omicron Delta Kappa Clubs: Petroleum (Houston), Torch (Houston); Houston; River Oaks (Houston). Lodges: Rotary. Home: 2929 Buffalo Speedway Unit 2208 Houston TX 77098-1711

HOFFMAN, PHILIP SEYMOUR, actor; b. Fairport, NY, July 23, 1967; 1 child. Grad., NYU, Tisch Sch. Drama. Co-artistic dir. LAByrinth Theater Co.; co-founder Cooper's Town Productions. Actor: (TV films) The Yearling, 1994; (TV miniseries) Empire Falls, 2005; (films) Triple Bogey on a Par Five Hole, 1991, My New Gun, 1992, Leap of Faith, 1992, Scent of a Woman, 1992, Szuler, 1992, My Boyfriend's Back, 1993, Money for Nothing, 1993, Joey Breaker, 1993, The Getaway, 1994, When a Man Loves a Woman, 1994, Nobody's Fool, 1994, The Fifteen Minute Hamlet, 1995, Hard Eight, 1997, Twister, 1996, Boogie Nights, 1997, Montana, 1998, Next Stop Wonderland, 1998, The Big Lebowski, 1998, Happiness, 1998, Patch Adams, 1998, Culture, 1998, Flawless, 1999, Magnolia, 1999, The Talented Mr. Ripley, 1999, State and Main, 2000, Almost Famous, 2000, Forest Hills Bob, 2001, Love Liza, 2002, Punch-Drunk Love, 2002, Red Dragon, 2002, 25th Hour, 2002, Owning Mahowny, 2003, Cold Mountain, 2003, Along Came Polly, 2004, Capote, 2005 (Best Actor, Nat. Bd. Review, 2005, Best Actor, Broadcast Film Critics Assn., 2005, Best Actor, Critics Choice award, 2005, Best Performance by an Actor in a Motion Picture-Drama, Hollywood Fgn. Press Assn. (Golden Globe award), 2006, Best Actor, Nat. Soc. Film Critics award, 2006, Outstanding Performance by a Male Actor in a Leading Role, Screen Actors Guild award, 2006, Actor in a Leading Role, British Acad. Film and TV Arts, 2006, Performance by an Actor in a Leading Role, Acad. Motion Picture Arts & Sciences, 2006, Best Male Lead, Independent Spirit award, 2006), Mission: Impossible III, 2006; dir.: (plays) The Last Days of Judas Iscariot, 2005; actor: Jack Goes Boating, 2007. Named one of 100 Most Influential People, Time Mag., 2006; recipient Best Actor, Boston Soc. of Film Critics award, 2005. Office: Paradigm Talent Agy # 2500 10100 Santa Monica Los Angeles CA 90067-4003*

HOFFMAN, REID, Internet company executive; b. Aug. 5, 1967; BS with Distinction in Symbolic Systems, Stanford Univ., 1990; M in Phil., Oxford Univ., London, 1993. Prin. investor Nanosolar, Inc.; angel investor Friendster, Inc., Aufklarung LLC, 2001—; with divsn. human interface design Apple Computers, Inc.; founder SocialNet; exec. v.p. PayPal Inc. (sold to eBay), 2001—02; founding CEO LinkedIn Corp., Mountain View, Calif., 2003—07, chmn. & pres., products, 2007—. Bd. dir. Jumpstart

Tech., LLC, Six Apart, 2003—, Grassroots Enterprises, 2003—, Vendio, 2003—, Mozilla Corp., 2005—, Tagged, 2005—, Kiva.org, 2006—; mem. advisory bd. EZCab, WeAttract.com, Lulan LLC, 2003—, Ctr. for Citizen Media, 2006—. Mem. provost coun. Coll. Eight, U. Calif., San Francisco, 2006—. Named one of 50 Who Matter Now, CNNMoney.com Bus. 2.0, 2006. Office: LinkedIn Corp 2029 Stierlin Ct Mountain View CA 94043*

HOFFMAN, RICHARD BRUCE, lawyer; b. Columbus, Ohio, June 8, 1947; s. Marion Keith and Ruth Eileen (McLear) Hoffman; m. Sandra Kay Schenkel, July 26, 1975; children: Kipp Hunter, Tyler Blake. BS in Gen. Engring., U. Ill., 1970; JD, DePaul U., 1973; LLM, John Marshall Sch. of Law, 1981. Bar: Ill. 1973, U.S. Dist. Ct. (no. dist.) Ill. 1973, U.S. Patent and Trademark Office 1973, U.S. Ct. Appeals (7th cir.) 1979, U.S. Ct. Appeals (fed. and 9th cirs.) 1982. Assoc. McCaleb, Lucas & Brugman, Chgo., 1973-76, ptnr., 1976-84, Tilton, Fallon, Lungmus & Chestnut, Chgo., 1984-2001, Marshall, Gerstein & Borun LLP, Chgo., 2001—. Mem.: ABA, Intellectual Property Law Assn. Chgo., Internat. Trademark Assn., Am. Intellectual Property Law Assn., Chgo. Bar Assn., Ill. Bar Assn., Union League Club of Chgo., Lawyers Club Chgo. Office: Marshall Gerstein & Borun LLP 6300 Sears Tower 233 S Wacker Dr Chicago IL 60606-6357 Office Phone: 312-474-6300. Business E-Mail: rhoffman@marshallip.com.

HOFFMAN, RICHARD M., lawyer; b. NYC, Oct. 22, 1942; s. Simon and Pearl (Lancet) H.; children: Mark, Michael Grad., CCNY, 1964; LL.B., Bklyn. Law Sch., 1967. Bar: NY 1968. Law clk. to US Dist. Judge US Dist. Ct. (ea. dist.) NY, NYC, 1967-69; assoc. Kramer, Lowenstein, Nessen & Kamin, NYC, 1969-73; various positions legal dept. Gen. Instrument Corp., NYC, 1973-81, v.p., gen. counsel, 1981-86, v.p. gen. counsel, sec., 1986-91; pvt. practice, NYC, 1991-94; sr. v.p., gen. counsel Coltec Industries Inc., NYC, 1994-95; of counsel Rubin, Baum, Levin, Constant & Friedman, NYC, 1995-99; ptnr. Friedman Kaplan Seiler & Adelman and predecessor firm, NYC, 1999—. Mem.: ABA. Home: 60 Brite Ave Scarsdale NY 10583-2328 Office Phone: 212-833-1116. Business E-Mail: rhoffman@fklaw.com.

HOFFMAN, RICHARD W., automotive executive; BS in fin. and mgmt. sci., Calif. State U., Northridge. Programmer DePaul U., Chgo.; IT positions with Embassy Entertainment, Digital Equipment Corp., Cummins Inc., Dole Foods Inc., Yamaha Motor USA; dir. IT Hyundai Motor Am./Hyundai Motor Fin. Co.; now pres., CEO Hyundai Info. Systems N.Am., 2005—. Vice chair bd. UCLA Anderson Sch. Mgmt. IS Associates. Named one of Premier 100 IT Leaders, Computerworld, 2005. Office: Hyundai Info Systems NAm 10550 Talbert Ave Fountain Valley CA 92728-0850

HOFFMAN, RICHARD WILLIAM, retired banker; b. Rice Lake, Wis., Feb. 8, 1918; s. William A. and Anna (Amundson) H.; m. June M. Weink, June 27, 1948; children: William H., Stephen C. BA, U. Wis., 1939; MBA, 1954; postgrad., Grad. Sch. Banking, U. Wis., 1952, BAI Sch. for Bank Auditors and Comptrollers, 1957; grad. certificate, Am. Inst. Banking, 1960. With First Wis. Nat. Bank Milw., 1939-83, asst. v.p., asst. comptroller, 1959-63, v.p., comptroller, 1963-70, 1st v.p., 1970-83; v.p. First Wis. Corp., 1965-83; instr. Duke U., 1943-45, Army Finance Sch., Ft. Benjamin Harrison, 1945, Am. Inst. Banking, 1946-62, U. Wis., 1946-62, BAI Sch. Bank Adminstrn., 1956-77. Mem. Polit. Edn. and Action League, 1962-68; adv. com. Pub. Expenditure Survey Wis., 1963-83; asso. div. chmn. Milw. County United Fund, 1960-63; mem. Milw. Am. Revolution Bicentennial Commn., 1975-76; exec. v.p. army fin. K.I.T., 1979—. Served to maj., Finance Corps AUS, 1941-46, sevred to lt. col. USAR, 1946-84 Mem. Am. Inst. C.P.A.s, Am. Legion, Fin. Execs. Inst., Nat. Alumni Assn. Bank Adminstrn. Inst., Res. Officers Assn., Wis. Econ. Devel. Assn., Soc. Ret. U.S. Army Fin. Officers, Ala. Soc. CPA's, Beta Alpha Psi, Beta Gamma Sigma. Clubs: Wisconsin Alumni. Home: 3801 Oak Grove Dr Apt 107 Montgomery AL 36116-1169

HOFFMAN, RONALD, historian, educator; b. Balt., Feb. 10, 1941; s. Emanuel and Ethel (Lubin) H.; m. Sandra Zalma Rudman, Aug. 28, 1965; children: Maia, Barak. AA, Balt. C.C., 1963; BA, George Peabody Coll., 1964; MA, U. Wis., 1965, PhD, 1969. Asst. prof. history U. Md., College Park, 1969—74, assoc. prof., 1974—92, prof., 1992—95; dir. Omohundro Inst. Early Am. History and Culture, Williamsburg, Va., 1992—; prof. Coll. William and Mary, Williamsburg, 1993—. Cons. Office Sec. Def., Washington, 1975—; symposia dir. U.S. Capitol Hist. Soc., Washington, 1977-93. Author: A Spirit of Dissension, 1973, Princes of Ireland, Planters of Maryland: A Carroll Saga, 1500-1782, 2000, (Libr. Va. Book Literary award non-fiction, So. Hist. Assn. Frank L. and Harriet C. Owsley award, Md. Hist. Soc. book prize 2002); co-author: The Pursuit of Liberty: A History of the American People, 1983; editor: Dear Papa, Dear Charley: The Papers of Charles Carroll of Carrollton, 3 vols. (J. Franklin Jameson award Am. Hist. Assn.); co-editor: Diplomacy and Revolution, 1971, Sovereign States in an Age of Uncertainty, 1982, Slavery and Freedom in the Age of the American Revolution, 1983, Arms and Independence: The Military Character of the American Revolution, 1983, An Uncivil War: The Southern Backcountry during the American Revolution, 1985, Peace and Peacemakers: The Treaty of 1783, 1985, The Economy of Early America: The Revolutionary Period, 1763-1790, 1989, We Shall Overcome: Martin Luther King, Jr., and the Black Freedom Struggle, 1990, To Form a More Perfect Union: The Critical Ideas of the Constitution, 1992, Religion in a Revolutionary Age, 1994, Of Consuming Interests: The Style of Life in the Eighteenth Century, 1994, The Transforming Hand of Revolution, 1996, Launching the Extended Republic: The Federalist Era, 1996, The Bill of Rights: Government Proscribed, 1997, Native Americans and the New Republic, 1999; contbr. articles to profl. jours. 3d class petty officer USNR, 1959-61. Fellow Ford Found., 1967, Eleutherian Mills-Hagley Found., 1978; grantee NEH, 1977, 2004, Nat. Hist. Publs. and Records Commn., 1979-. Mem. Am. Hist. Assn., Orgn. Am. Historians, Assn. Documentary Editing, So. Hist. Assn., Va. Hist. Soc., Md. Hist. Soc. Democrat. Jewish. Office: Omohundro Inst Early Am History and Culture PO Box 8781 Williamsburg VA 23187-8781 Home: 430D E Duke Of Gloucester St Williamsburg VA 23185-4250 Home Phone: 757-253-1668. Business E-Mail: ieahc1@wm.edu.

HOFFMAN, RONALD BRUCE, biophysicist, consultant, life scientist; b. Balt., Mar. 29, 1939; s. Marvin Lionel and Edna Mildred (Fillman) H.; m. Carolyn Jean Phillips, July 6, 1969; children: Christine B., David A., Matthew T. BS in Physics, U. Md., 1962; MA in Psychology, U. Houston, 1971, PhD in Biophys. Sci., 1974. Cert. human factors engring. profl. Assoc. engr. Douglas Aircraft Co., Inc., Santa Monica, Calif., 1962-64; aerospace engr. NASA Johnson Space Ctr., Houston, 1964-67, 68; sr. rsch. analyst Northrop Svcs., Inc., Houston, 1974; NRC-NASA rsch. assoc. NRC, Washington, 1975-77; rsch. scientist, mgr. life scis. GE/MATSCO, Houston and Moffett Field, Calif., 1977-80; site mgr. Tech. Inc., Washington, 1980-82; sr. project mgr. GE, Washington, 1982-85; mgr. biotech. Advanced Tech. Inc., Reston, Va., 1985-87; lead scientist MITRE Corp., McLean, Va., 1987-95, sr. human factors engr., 1995-96; lead human factors engr. Mitretek Systems (formerly with MITRE Corp.), McLean, 1996—2001; sr. rsch. psychologist Sci. Applications Internat. Corp., McLean, 2001—04; discipline scientist neuroscis. Wyle Lab., 2004—05; human factors engr. MEI Techs., 2005—. Co-investigator Apollo-Soyuz Test Project exptl. team NASA, Houston, 1974-75; mem. govt. industry adv. group for man systems integrated standards, Houston, 1988; life sci. cons. Mitsui and Co., Ltd., Biosystems Internat., Tokyo, 1985-86. Fellow AIAA (assoc., USAF space ops. workshop Colorado Springs, Colo. 1984-85, chmn. life scis. and sys. tech. com. 1989-91, chmn. human factors engring. working group 1991-96, dep. group dir. space and missiles group 1993-96), Aerospace Med. Assn., Aerospace Human Factors Assn. (pres. 2007); mem. Soc. for Neurosci., Human Factors and Ergonomics Soc. (pres. Potomac chpt. 1997), Southwestern Psychology Assn., Am. Soc. Gravitational and Space Biology, Sigma Xi (rsch. fellow 1974), Phi Kappa Phi. Avocations: photography, scuba diving. Office: MEI Techs 2525 Bay Area Blvd Ste 300 Houston TX Home Phone: 281-486-1984; Office Phone: 281-483-6269. Business E-Mail: ronald.b.hoffman-1@nasa.gov.

HOFFMAN, RONALD L., manufacturing executive; m. Cynthia Hoffman. BS, Okla. State U. With Allis Chalmers, 1970—72, Vickers, 1972—85; pres. Tulsa Winch, Okla., 1985—96; joined Dover (acquired Tulsa Winch), NYC, 1996—; exec. v.p. Dover Resources, Inc., 2000—02, pres., 2002—03, Dover Corp., NYC, 2003—05, COO, 2003—05, pres., CEO, 2005—. Lifetime mem. Collinsville Edn. Found. Office: Dover Corp 280 Park Ave New York NY 10017-1292*

HOFFMAN, S. DAVID, lawyer, engineer, military officer, educator; b. NYC, June 16, 1922; s. Joseph and Ida Hoffman; m. Naomi Barbara Brosterman, June 30, 1946; children: Mathew E., Robert Adam. BE in Elec. Engring., Yale U., 1945; JD, St. John's U., NYC, 1955; postgrad., Sch. Naval Justice, Newport, RI, 1950. Bar: N.Y. 1955, U.S. Supreme Ct. 1960, U.S. Ct. Mil. Appeals 1961, U.S. Patent Office 1964, Ill. 1981. Engr. Western Electric Co., NYC, Newark, 1946-49; head elec. engring. Am. Nat. Stds. Inst., NYC, 1949-66, resident legal counsel, 1955-66, dir. contracts and cert., 1955-66; v.p., gen. counsel Underwriters Labs. Inc., Northbrook, Ill., 1966-88, cons. counsel to the pres., 1988-90; arbitrator Lake and Cook County (Ill.) Cts., 1989—. Sec. US nat. com. Internat. Electrotech. Commn., 1955—66; vol., cons. multimedia resource, visual arts asst. Highland Park HS, Ill., 1989—; adj. prof. divsn. indsl. and systems engring. dept. mech. engring. U. Ill., Chgo., 1974—92; vol. internet tutor Highland Park Libr., 1996—; US Presdl. Exec. Interchange program mgr. tech. activities Nat. Bur. Stds. for US Consumer Products Safety Commn., 1970—71. Contbr. numerous articles to profl. jours. Mem. indsl. adv. bd. U. Ill., Chgo., 1974-95; commr. City of Highland Park (Ill.) Telecomms. Commn., 1998-2000; on-line instr. Sr. Net, 1998—; lic. amatuer radio operator, 1981—; mem. U.S. Navy-Marine Military Affiliate Radio Svc., 1991—. With USNR, 1942-46, 50-52, ret. comdr. JAG Corp. Recipient Achievement award U.S. Pres. Commn. on Exec. Interchange, 1973-74, Merit awards (2) Am. Nat. Stds. Inst., Joint award ASTM-Stds. Engring. Soc., Robert J. Painter Meml. award, 1977, Stds. Engring. Soc. Leo B. Moore medal 1980, Margaret Dana award ASTM, 1989. Fellow: IEEE (life), Stds. Engring. Soc. (life).

HOFFMAN, SHARON LYNN, adult education educator; b. Chgo. d. David P. and Florence Seaman; m. Jerry Irwin Hoffman, Aug. 25, 1963; children: Steven Abram, Rachel Irene. BA, Ind. U., 1961; M Adult Edn., Nat.-Louis Univ., 1992. High sch. English tchr. Chgo. Pub. Schs., 1961-64; tchr. Dept. of Def. Schs., Braconne, France, 1964-66; tchr. ESL Russian Inst., Garmisch, Fed. Republic Germany, 1966, 67; tchr. adult edn. Monterey Peninsula Unified Schs., Ft. Ord, Calif., 1977-79; tchr. ESL MAECOM, Monmouth County, NJ, 1979-80; lectr., tchr. adult edn. Truman Coll./Temple Shalom, Chgo.; tchr. homebound Fairfax County Pub. Schs., Fairfax, Va., 1976; entry operator Standard Rate & Data, Wilmette, Ill., 1986-87; rsch. editor, spl. projects editor Marquis Who's Who, Wilmette, 1987-92; mem. adj. faculty Nat.-Louis U., Evanston and Wheeling, Ill., 1993-99, tutor coord., then coord. learning specialist, 1993-99; pres. Cultural Transitions, Pebble Beach, Calif., 1992—. Mem.: TESOL, ASTD, Nat. Coun. Tchrs. English. Personal E-mail: culturaltrans1@aol.com.

HOFFMAN, SHARONA, law educator; b. San Rafael, Calif., July 23, 1964; d. Morton and Aviva Hoffman; m. Andy Podgurski, July 10, 2005. BA, Wellesley Coll., 1985; JD, Harvard Law Sch., 1988; LLM in Health Law, U. Houston, 1999. Jud. law clk. Hon. Douglas W. Hillman, U.S. Dist. Judge, Grand Rapids, Mich., 1988—89; atty. O'Melveny & Myers, LA, 1989—92; sr. trial atty. EEOC, Houston, 1992—98; asst. prof. law and bioethics Case Western Res. U. Sch. Law, Cleve., 1999—2003, assoc. prof., 2003—05, co-dir. Law-Medicine Ctr., prof., 2005—, assoc. dean academic affairs, 2006—. Mem. MetroHealth Hosp. IRB, Cleve., 2000—; mem. ethics com. U. Hosps., 2003—. Contbr. articles to acadamic jours. Mem. Anti-Defamation League, Cleve., 1996—. Grantee, NEH, 2002; scholar, Case Western Res. U., 2005; Glennan fellow, 2000—01. Mem.: ABA, Assn. Am. Law Schs. (exec. com. mem. 2003—, employment discrimination sect.), Am. Soc. Law, Medicine & Ethics. Avocations: travel, exercise, reading. Office: Case Western Reserve U Sch Law 11075 East Blvd Cleveland OH 44106 Office Phone: 216-368-3860. Office Fax: 216-368-2086. E-mail: sharona.hoffman@case.edu.

HOFFMAN, STANLEY MARC, composer, editor; b. Cleve., 1959; BMus in Music Composition cum laude, Boston Conservatory of Music, 1981; MMus in Music Composition, New Eng. Conservatory of Music, 1984; PhD in Music Composition/Theory, Brandeis U., 1993. Engraver Scores Internat., Boston, 1990-98; chief editor ECS Pub., Boston, 1998—. Vocalist Temple B'nai Torah High Holiday Choir, 1997—, condr.; condr. Temple Israel High Holidays Choir, Swampscott, Mass., 1988-96, Temple Emmanuel Choir, Newton, Mass., winter 1983. Composer: There Is a Flower (oboe and piano), 1980, rev., 2000, Three Short Piano Pieces, 1980, Two-part Invention (piano), 1980, The Man in the Street (cello), 1981, Romance for Orchestra (in C minor), 1982, Rondino (wind quintet), 1983, Little Sea Nocturne (orch.), 1982, String Sextet (2 violins, 2 violas, 2 cellos), 1984, rev. 2000, Cycles (piano), 1985, Thirteen Ways of Looking at a Blackbird (BMI award 1984-85, mezzo soprano, string quartet), 1984, rev., 1993, Of All the Souls that Stand Create (baritone, piano), 1985, rev., 1993, Anim Zemiros (acapella choir), 1985, rev., 1993, String Quartet, 1987, rev., 1993, Poem and Lamentations (violin, piano), 1987, Piano Piece, 1986, Hymn of Glory (violas, cellos), 1988, rev., 1994, Rain (a cappella choir), 1988, rev., 1993, Nocturne for Nine Players (2 flutes, oboe, clarinet, bassoon, 2 horns, harp, percussion), 1992, Veshameru (cantor, choir, organ), 1993, Moulded Clay-Chiselled Rock (instrument in C, piano), 1994, Bagatelle (bassoon or bass trombone), 1994, A Song Without Words (horn), 1994, A Psalm Beyond the Silences (choir, piano), 1994, Lord of the World (a cappella choir, 1994, A Pacific Prelude (brass quintet), 1995; There Is a Name (children's choir, guitar) 1995, Trio in One Movement (clarinet, viola, cello), 1995, Psalm 23 (a cappella choir), 1998, Psalm 1 (a cappella choir), 1998, Psalm 121 (a cappella choir), 1998, The Writing of Autumn (choir, piano), 1999, Psalm 130 (a cappella choir), 1999, Psalm 146 (a cappella choir), 1999, Three Miniatures (a cappella treble choir), 1999, Intermezzo, Organ, 1999, Psalm 67 (choir, organ), 1999, She Gave Him All Her Heart, 2000, Psalm 117 (a cappella male, treble or mixed choir), 2000, A Lovely Summer Night (alto saxophone and piano), 2000, Behold, God Is My Salvation (choir, organ), 2001, Yih'yu l'ratzon (May the words of the mouth) (a cappella), 2001, A Prayer for Chanukah, (choir, piano), 2001, Grant Us Peace (a cappella choir), 2002, FantasyPiece (cello, bass), 2001, Land of Crystal Dreams (choir), 2002, Yism'chu (soprano, choir), 2003, A Prayer for the World (choir), 2003, Mi y'maleil (Who Can Recount) (choir, piano), 2005, Interlude for Orchestra, 2005, Psalm (By the Rivers of Water), 2006, An Easy Decision (choir or voice, piano), 2006, Variation on Pankleidir, Herr (organ or piano manuals), 2006, others. Office: ECS Pub Co 138 Ipswich St Boston MA 02215-3534

HOFFMAN, STEPHEN LEV, physician; b. Long Branch, NJ, July 31, 1948; s. Julian and Betty Louise (Spiegal) H.; m. Kim Lee Sim, Oct. 16, 1988; children: Alexander Dov, Seth Ari Sim-Son, Benjamin Uri Sim-Mun. BA, U. Penn, 1970; MD, Cornell U., 1975; DTMH, U. London, 1978. Resident family medicine U. Calif. Med. Ctr., San Diego, 1975-78, dir. tropical diseases and travelers clinic, 1979-80, clin. instr. family and community medicine, 1979-80; commd. officer USNR, advanced through grades from 1st rank lt. to capt., 1980-92; head dept. clin. investigation and epidemiology U.S. Naval Med. Rsch. Unit 2 Jakarta Detachment, Indonesia, 1980-84; head divsn. clin. investigation and epidemiology, Infectious Diseases Program Ctr. Naval Med. Rsch. Inst., Bethesda, Md., 1985-87, dir. malaria program, 1987—2001; adj. assoc. prof. Uniformed Svcs. Univ. Health Scis., Bethesda, 1985-91, prof., 1991—2001; rsch. physician dept. immunology div. communicable diseases Divsn. Communicable Diseases Walter Reed Army Inst. Rsch., Washington, 1985-88; attending staff Dept. Medicine Divsn. Infectious Diseases Nat. Naval Med. Ctr., Bethesda, 1989—2001; mem. attending staff emergency medicine dept. Providence Hosp., Washington, 1985—; sr. v.p. biologics Celera Genomics, Rockville, Md., 2001—02; founder, chief exec., scientific officer Sanaria Inc., Rockville, Md., 2002—. Vis. prof. Manidol U., Bangkok, Thailand, 1996—; pres. Am. Com. on Clin. Tropical Medicine and Traveler's Health, 1996—. Mem.: Inst. Medicine, Am. Soc. Tropical Medicine & Hygiene (former pres.), Am. Soc. Clin. Investigation. Office: Sanaria Inc Ste L 12115 Parklawn Dr Rockville MD 20852 Office Phone: 301-770-3222. Office Fax: 301-770-5554.

HOFFMAN, THOMAS EDWARD, dermatologist; b. LA, Oct. 14, 1944; s. David Maurice and Ann (Corday) H.; m. Donna Madsen, 1973 (div. 1977); m. Linda L., Feb. 20, 1979; children: David, Jay. AB, U. So. Calif., 1966; MD, Tulane U., 1970. Intern U. So. Calif. USC Med. Ctr., 1970-71; residency dermatology Stanford (Calif.) U., 1973-76, fellow dermatopathology, 1973-74; dermatologist pvt. practice, Menlo Park, Calif., 1976—. Clin. assoc. prof. Stanford (Calif.) U., 1981-97, clin. prof. dermatology, 1997. With USPHS, 1971-73. Recipient Achievement award Tulane U., 1970. Fellow Am. Coll. Physicians, Am. Acad. Dermatology, Am. Soc. Dermatopathology, Am. Soc. Dermatologic Surgery, Am. Soc. Laser Medicine & Surgery, San Francisco Dermatologic Soc. (pres. 2000-01). Avocations: tennis, skiing. Office: Menlo Dermatology Med Group 888 Oak Grove Ave Menlo Park CA 94025-4432 Office Phone: 650-325-1511. Business E-Mail: mdmg@mdmg.com.

HOFFMAN, TREVOR WILLIAM, professional baseball player; b. Bellflower, Calif., Oct. 13, 1967; Student, U. Ariz. Draft pick Cin. Reds, 1989; pitcher Fla. Marlins, 1993, San Diego Padres, 1993—. Founder Trevor's Kidney Kids. Named Fireman of Yr., The Sporting News, 1996, 1998, Rolaids Relief Man of Yr., 1998; named to Nat. League All-Star Team, Maj. League Baseball, 1998—2000, 2002, 2006—07; recipient Hutch award, 2004, Lou Gehrig Meml. award, 2006. Achievements include becoming Maj. League Baseball's all-time career saves leader, 2006; first to reach 500 career saves, June 6, 2007 against the Los Angeles Dodgers; led Nat. League in saves, 1998 (53), 2006 (46). Office: San Diego Padres PO Box 122000 San Diego CA 92112-2000*

HOFFMAN, VALERIE JANE, lawyer; b. Lowville, NY, Oct. 27, 1953; d. Russell Francis and Jane Marie (Fowler) H. Student, U. Edinburgh, Scotland, 1973-74; BA summa cum laude, Union Coll., 1975; JD, Boston Coll., 1978. Bar: Ill. 1978, US Dist. Ct. (no. dist.) Ill. 1978, US Ct. Appeals (3rd cir.) 1981, US Ct. Appeals (7th cir.) 1983. Assoc. Seyfarth Shaw LLP, Chgo., 1978—87, ptnr., 1987—. Adj. prof. Columbia Coll., 1985. Contbr. articles to legal publs. Dir. Remains Theatre, Chgo., 1981-95, pres., 1991-93, v.p., 1993-95; dir. The Nat. Conf. for Cmty. and Justice, Chgo. Region, 1993-2004, nat. trustee, 1995-2004; trustee bd. advisors Union Coll., 1996-99, trustee, 1999—, trustee and sec., Grad. Coll. Union U., 2003-2007; dir. AIDS Found. of Chgo., 1997-2004, exec. com., 1999-2003. Mem. ABA, Univ. Club Chgo. (bd. dirs. 1984-87), Phi Beta Kappa. Office: Seyfarth Shaw LLP 2029 Century Park East Ste 3300 Los Angeles CA 90067

HOFFMAN, WAYNE MELVIN, retired airline official; b. Chgo., Mar. 9, 1923; s. Carl A. and Martha (Tamillo) H.; m. Laura Majewski, Jan. 26, 1946; children— Philip, Karen, Kristin. BA cum laude, U. Ill., 1943, JD with high honors, 1947. Bar: Ill. bar 1947, N.Y. bar 1958. Atty. I.C. R.R., 1948-52; with N.Y.C. R.R. Co., 1952-57, exec. asst. to pres., 1958-60, v.p. freight sales, 1960-61, v.p. sales, 1961-62, exec. v.p., 1962-67; chmn. bd. N.Y. Central Trans. Co., 1960-67, Flying Tiger Line, Inc. and Tiger Internat., Inc., 1967-86. Trustee McCallum Theatre, Palm Desert, Calif., Eisenhower Med. Ctr., Rancho Mirage, Calif. Served to capt. inf. AUS, World War II. Decorated Silver Star, Bronze Star with oak leaf cluster, Purple Heart with oak leaf cluster; Fourragere (Belgium). Mem. Bohemian Club (San Francisco), Vintage Club (Indian Wells), Phi Beta Kappa. Home: 74-435 Palo Verde Dr Indian Wells CA 92210-7367 Office: 2450 Montecito Rd Ramona CA 92065-1644

HOFFMAN, WILLIAM, writer; b. Charleston, W.Va., May 16, 1925; s. Henry William and Margaret Julia (Beckley) H.; m. Alice Richardson, Nov. 13, 1924; children: Ruth Beckley, Margaret Kay. BA, Hampden-Sydney Coll., 1949, DLitt (hon.), 1980; postgrad., Washington and Lee U., 1949-50, DLitt (hon.), 1995; postgrad., State U. Iowa, 1950-51; DLitt (hon.), Sewanee, U. of South, 1999—. Prof. English lit. Hampden-Sydney (Va.) Coll., 1952-59, writer-in-residence, 1964-71. Bd. dirs. The Kay Co., Charleston. Author: The Trumpet Unblown, 1955, Days in the Yellow Leaf, 1958, A Place for My Head, 1960, The Dark Mountains, 1963, Yancey's War, 1966, A Walk to the River, 1970, A Death of Dreams, 1973, The Land That Drank the Rain, 1982, Godfires, 1985, Furors Die, 1990, Tidewater Blood, 1998, Blood and Guile, 2000, Wild Thorn, 2002, Lies, 2005, (short stories) Virginia Reels, 1978, By Land, by Sea, 1988, Follow Me Home, 1994, Best American Short Stories: Prize Stories The O. Henry Awards, Doors, 1999 With U.S. Army, 1943-46, ETO. Recipient Emily Clark Balch prize Va. Quar. Rev., 1988, Andrew Lytle prize The Sewanee Rev., 1989, Goodheart prize The Arthur and Margaret Glasgow Endowment Com., Washington and Lee U., 1989, Dos Passos prize, 1993, Hillsdale prize for fiction Fellowship So. Writers, 1995, Hammett award Internat. Assn. Crime Writers, 1998; named Cultural Laureate, State of Va., 1986; NEA fellow, 1976 Mem. Authors Guild, Fellowship of So. Writers. Republican. Presbyterian.

HOFFMAN, WILLIAM YANES, plastic surgeon; b. Rochester, NY., 1952; MD, U. Rochester, 1977. Plastic surgeon U. Calif. San Francisco Med. Ctr.; also prof. plastic surgery U. Calif., San Francisco. Office: UC San Francisco Plastic Surgery 350 Parnassus Ave Ste 509 San Francisco CA 94117-3608 also: Prof & Chief Plastic Surgery Univ Calif San Francisco Box 0932 San Francisco CA 94143-0932 Office Phone: 415-353-4287. Business E-Mail: hoffmanw@surgery.ucsf.edu.

HOFFMANN, CARL KONRAD, lawyer; b. Plant City, Fla., Mar. 10, 1929; s. Virginia Pauline (Randolph) H.; m. Patricia Ray Shepard, Mar. 18, 1961; children: Debra, Sandra, David, William. BS, Northwestern U., 1951; JD, Yale U., 1957. Bar: Fla., Va., D.C. Ptnr. Kimbrell & Hamann PA, Miami, Fla., 1970—93, mng. dir., 1990—94. Adj. prof. bus. law U. North Fla., Jacksonville, 1994—98. Elder Presbyn. Ch. Lt. USN, 1951-54, Korea. Mem. Nat. Soc. SAR (pres. gen. 1997-98, sec. gen.1996-97). Avocations: stamp collecting/philately, historical research, travel. Home: PO Box 4332 Anna Maria FL 34216-4332

HOFFMANN, CHRISTOPH LUDWIG, lawyer; b. Elsterwerda, Germany, Oct. 9, 1944; came to U.S., 1965; s. Gunther and Ruth (Hornschuh) H.; m. Susan Magnuson, June 18, 1983. Student, Freie U. Berlin, 1964-65; BA, U. Wis., 1966; JD, Harvard U., 1969. Bar: Mass. 1969, R.I. 1977. Assoc. Bingham, Dana & Gould, Boston, 1969-76; asst. gen. counsel Textron Inc., Providence, 1976-83; v.p., gen. counsel, sec. Pneumo Corp., Boston, 1983-85; sr. v.p., gen. counsel, sec. Pneumo Abex Corp., Boston,

1985-91; v.p., sec., gen. counsel Raytheon Co., Lexington, Mass., 1991-94, sr. v.p. law, human resources and corp. adminstrn., sec., 1994-95, exec. v.p. law and corp. adminstrn., sec., 1995-98; ltd. ptnr. Carlisle 1999, L.P., 1998—. Bd. dirs. Med. Web Techs., Inc., Info. Mng., Inc., Red Lodge Ales Brewing Co.; chmn., trustee Beth Israel Deaconess Hosp., Needham, 1994—; mem. adv. bd. eLaw Forum Corp., 1999—. Mem. ABA, Mass. Bar Assn., R.I. Bar Assn., Assn. Gen. Counsel.

HOFFMANN, DONALD, architectural historian; b. Springfield, Ill., June 24, 1933; s. George C. and Ines (Catron) H.; m. Theresa Cecelia McGrath, Apr. 12, 1958; children— George, Alan, Eric, Michael, Valerie. Student, U. Chgo., 1949-53, U. Kansas City, Mo., 1958. Mem. staff Kansas City (Mo.) Star, 1956-90, art critic, 1965-90. Mem. journalism adv. com. Fulbright Scholarship Program, 1968-70. Editor: The Meanings of Architecture-Buildings and Writings by John Wellborn Root, 1967; author: The Architecture of John Wellborn Root, 1973, Frank Lloyd Wright's Fallingwater, 1978, 2d rev. edit., 1993, Frank Lloyd Wright's Robie House, 1984, Frank Lloyd Wright: Architecture and Nature, 1986, Frank Lloyd Wright's Hollyhock House, 1992, Understanding Frank Lloyd Wright's Architecture, 1995, Frank Lloyd Wright's Dana House, 1996, Frank Lloyd Wright, Louis Sullivan and the Skyscraper, 1998, Frank Lloyd Wright's House on Kentuck Knob, 2000, Mark Twain in Paradise: His Voyages to Bermuda, 2006; asst. editor Jour. Soc. Archtl. Historians, 1970-72; contbr. articles to profl. jours. Younger Humanist fellow NEH, 1970-71; Art Critic's fellow-grantee Nat. Endowment for Arts, 1974. Mem. Soc. Archtl. Historians (bd. dirs. 1968-70), Art Inst. Chgo. (life) Home: 6441 Holmes St Kansas City MO 64131-1110 Office Phone: 816-333-0355. E-mail: donaldhffmnn@yahoo.com.

HOFFMANN, FRANCES PORTER, librarian; b. Louisville, Dec. 27, 1927; d. Robert Hugh and Frances (Pfeffer) Porter; m. John F. Hoffmann, Sept. 14, 1948; children: Frances H. Stains, Amy H. Veeneman BA in History, Trinity U., San Antonio, 1949; MSLS, Our Lady of the Lake U., San Antonio, 1978. Office mgr. acad. libr. St. Mary's U., San Antonio, 1975-77, libr. assoc., 1977-79, tech. svcs. libr., asst. prof., 1979-84; coord. tech. svcs. and automated systems Palo Alto Coll., San Antonio, 1986-90, spl. project libr., asst. prof., 1990-95; devel. coord. I Care San Antonio, 1995—. 1st v.p. Nueces County Pharm. Assn. Auxiliary, Corpus Christi, Tex., 1965; chaplain Tom Brown Middle Sch. PTA, Corpus Christi, 1966; troop leader Girl Scouts of Am., Corpus Christi, 1960-65; docent San Antonio Mus. Assn., 1968-69; v.p. Tech. Svcs. Int. Group, 1992-93; pres. Coun. Rsch. Acad. Librs., 1993-94; devel. coord. I Care San Antonio, 1998. Mem. ALA, Nat. Soc. Daughters of the Am. Revolution Presbyterian. Avocations: genealogy, collecting pre-1950 fashion jewelry, needlecrafts, travel.

HOFFMANN, INGE SCHNEIER, psychologist, educator; b. Vienna, Jan. 16, 1929; came to U.S., 1940; d. Josef Michael Schneier and Szerena Susan Löffelholz; m. Stanley Harry Hoffmann, Oct. 6, 1963. BA, Bard Coll., Annandale-on-Hudson, NY, 1950; MA, Harvard U., Cambridge, Mass., 1953. Lic. clin. psychologist, Mass. Lectr., asst. to dir. Social Sci. Found. U. Denver, 1953-54; rsch. assoc., assoc. dir. rsch. AIR, Inc., 1954-56; rsch. assoc. Ctr. for Internat. Studies, MIT, 1956-59; lectr. Harvard Coll., 1970-76; lectr. psychology, dept. psychiatry Harvard U. Med. Sch., Cambridge Hosp., 1976—. Faculty assoc. Currier House, Harvard U., 1970—, mem. group on study of violence Med. Sch., 2004—; affiliate Ctr. for European Studies, Harvard U., 1994—. Co-author: Coercive Persuasion, 1961, DeGaulle, Artiste de la Politique, 1973; contbr. articles to profl. jours.; patentee design of art fabrics. Active in mediating Palestinian-Israeli conflict, 1976—; mem. Lifton Study Group on Mass Violence, 2004—. Recipient painting awards Mus. of Modern Art, others; Bard scholar Schepp Found., N.Y., 1947, 48, 49, 50; Radcliffe Inst. scholar Harvard U., 1970, 71, 72. Mem. Cambridge Art Assn., Harvard U. Shop Club, Boston Psychoanalytic Inst. (friend, collaborator 1972-89), Internat. Soc. Polit. Psychology (founding mem. 1987—). Avocations: lieder singing, painting. Office: 91 Washington Ave Cambridge MA 02140-2716

HOFFMANN, INGRID, chef, television personality; Owner Capricieuse, Miami, Rocca restuarant, Miami. Host (TV series) cooking and style show, Despierta Am., Delicioso, DirecTv, 2005—06, Galavision, 2006—, Simply Delicioso, Food Network; contbr. BuenHogar, columns in newspapers. Office: Food Network 75 9th Ave New York NY 10011

HOFFMANN, JOAN CAROL, retired academic dean; b. Cedarburg, Wis., Feb. 20, 1934; d. Frank Ernst and Althea Wilhelmina (Behm) H. Nursing diploma, Michael Reese Hosp., 1955; BS in Zoology, U. Wis., Madison, 1959; PhD in Physiology, U. Ill., Chgo., 1965. RN, Wis., Ariz. Sci. instr. Michael Reese Hosp., Chgo., 1959-62; USPHS trainee U. Ill., Chgo., 1962-64; NSF postdoctoral fellow Coll. de France, Paris, 1964-65; asst. prof. U. Rochester, NY, 1965-70; assoc. prof., prof. U. Hawaii, Honolulu, 1970-83; dean of students U. Mass. Med. Sch., Worcester, 1983-94; ret., 1994. Chmn. anatomy U. Hawaii, 1973-80. Contbr. articles to sci. jours. NIH rsch. grantee, 1966-75. Mem. Endocrine Soc., Soc. for Study of Reprodn., Am. Assn. Anatomists, Women in Endocrinology (sec. 1978-79, pres. 1987-88), Am. Coun. Edn. (bd. dirs., Mass. chpt., network identification program 1993-94), Phi Beta Kappa, Sigma Xi. Avocations: gardening, needlecrafts, wood turning, reading. Home: 3525 Cass Ct #416 Oak Brook IL 60523-3707 Personal E-mail: jchamc@comcast.net.

HOFFMANN, KATHRYN ANN, humanities educator; b. Rockville Centre, NY, Oct. 26, 1954; d. Manfred and Catherine (Nanko) H.; m. Brook Ellis, Nov. 25, 1987. BA summa cum laude, SUNY, Buffalo, 1975; MA, Johns Hopkins U., 1979, PhD, 1981. Asst. prof. French lit. and lang. U. Wis., Madison, 1981-88, U. Hawaii-Manoa, Honolulu, 1992-97, assoc. prof., 1997—2001, prof., 2001—; mng. ptnr. Yuval Design Partnership, Chgo., 1988-92. Assoc. editor: Substance, 1982-87; author: Society of Pleasures: Interdisciplinary Readings in Pleasure and Power during the Reign of Louis XIV, 1997 (Aldo and Jeanne Scaglione prize for French and Francophone Studies 1998); translator: Masturbation: The History of a Great Terror, 2001; contbg. author: Ascending Chaos: The Art of Masami Teraoka, 2007; contbr. articles to profl. jours.; designer clothing accessories. Recipient Regents' medal for excellence in tchg., 1998; fellow, Inst. Rsch. in Humanities, 1984—85, Am. Coun. Learned Socs., 1984—85, Camargo Found., 1998; grantee, NEH Endowment Fund, 1993, 1995. Mem.: MLA (Aldo and Jeanne Scaglione prize for French and Francophone studies 1998), History of Sci. Soc., Soc. for Interdisciplinary Study Social Imagery, Soc. for Interdisciplinary French 17th Century Studies (exec. com. 1994—96), N.Am. Soc. for 17th Century French Lit., Am. Soc. for 18th Century Studies, Internat. Soc. for the Study of European Ideas, Phi Beta Kappa. Home: Apt M12 217 Prospect St Honolulu HI 96813-1778 Office: U Hawaii Manoa Langs & Lits Europe Ams 1890 East West Rd Rm 483 Honolulu HI 96822-2318 Office Phone: 808-956-4170. E-mail: hoffmann@hawaii.edu.

HOFFMANN, LOUIS GERHARD, immunologist, educator; b. Bloemendaal, Netherlands, July 12, 1932; arrived in U.S., 1950; s. Gerhard Hendrik and Louise Gertrude (Tobi) Hoffmann; m. Georgianna Grace Stracke, Nov. 4, 1955; children: Julianna Tobi, Eugenie Claire. BA with honors, distinction, Wesleyan U., 1953; MSc in Hygiene, Johns Hopkins U., 1958, ScD, 1960. Diplomate Am. Bd. Sexology. NSF postdoctoral fellow U. Calif., Berkeley, 1960-62; from instr. to asst. prof. microbiology Johns Hopkins U., Balt., 1962-64; asst. prof. U. Iowa, Iowa City, 1964-67, assoc. prof., 1967-74, prof., 1974-96; ret., 1997; pvt. practice sex therapy team, 1978—. Contbr. articles to profl. jours. Mem. Dem. Ctrl. Com., Johnson County, Iowa, 1966—76. Fellow, NIH, 1962—63; grantee, 1964—67, 1980—83, NSF, 1968—74, Iowa Heart Assn., 1969—72, 1977—79, Damon Runyon Meml. Fund, 1972—74. Home: 4 Timberwick Rd Santa Fe NM 87508

HOFFMANN, MANFRED WALTER, consulting company executive; b. Bklyn., Apr. 21, 1938; s. Hermann Karl and Emilie (Talmon) H.; m. Barbara Ann Kenvin, Aug. 5, 1961; children: Lisa Joy, Lauren Kimberly, Kurt William. BS, Cornell U., Ithaca, 1960; MEd, Temple U., Phila., 1972, PhD, 1977. With Sun Oil Co., 1967-71, mgr. mktg. devel. Rosemont, Pa., 1971-72, mgr. tng., 1973-77, dir. orgn. and mgmt. devel., 1977-79; dir. human resources and adminstrn. Sun Prodn. Co., Dallas, 1979-83; dir. world wide human resources Sun Exploration & Prodn. Co., 1983-90; pres. Gyroscopic Mgmt. Inc., 1989—. Lectr. Grad. Sch., U. Tex., Dallas, 1979-2000. Pres. PTA, bd. mem. Beechwood Sch., 1975-77; cons. exec. com. Orgns. Industrialization Congress Am., 1975-79; bd. dirs. Job Opportunity for Youth, 1980-81; bd. dirs. Dallas SER, 1986—. Served with USMCR, 1956-62. Mem. Am. Soc. Tng. and Devel., Am. Soc. Pers. Adminstrn., Dallas C. of C., Tex. Assn. Bus. Republican. Episcopalian. Home: PO Box 2040 Anacortes WA 98221-7040

HOFFMANN, MARK R., physical chemist, educator; b. St. Paul, Minn., Oct. 3, 1958; s. Gerhard R. and Heidi B. Hoffmann; m. Cathy Hacking, June 22, 1993. BA, Northwestern U., Evanston, Ill., 1980; PhD, U. Calif., Berkeley, 1984. Post doctoral rsch. assoc. U. Chgo., 1985—86; postdoctoral rsch. assoc. U. Utah, Salt Lake City, 1986—88; asst. prof. U. ND, Grand Forks, 1988—94, assoc. prof., 1994—2000, prof., 2000—06, Chester Fritz disting. prof., 2006—, chmn. dept. chemistry, 2003—. Author: Low-lying Potential Energy Surfaces, 2002; contbr. scientific papers. Grantee, Am. Chem. Soc., 1992, Office of Naval Rsch., 1996-1999, NSF, 1999-2003, 2003—, DOE, 2004—. Mem.: Am. Phys. Soc., Am. Chem. Soc. Achievements include research in new methods of molecular electronic structure theory. Avocation: photography. Office: Univ ND Dept Chemistry 151 Cornell St Stop 9024 Grand Forks ND 58202-9024 Office Phone: 701-777-2742. E-mail: mhoffmann@chem.und.edu.

HOFFMANN, MARTIN RICHARD, lawyer; b. Stockbridge, Mass., Apr. 20, 1932; m. Margaret Ann McCabe; children: Heidi H. Slye, William, Bern. AB, Princeton U., NJ, 1954; LLB, U. Va., Charlottesville, 1961. Bar: DC 1961. Law clk. US Ct. Appeals (4th cir.), 1961-62; asst. U.S. atty. Washington, 1962-65; minority counsel com. on judiciary Ho. of Reps., Washington, 1965-67; legal counsel to Senator C. Percy, US Senate, Washington, 1967-69; asst. gen. counsel Univ. Computing Co., Dallas, 1969-71; gen. counsel AEC, Washington, 1971-73; spl. asst. to sec. and dep. sec. def. Washington, 1973-74; gen. counsel Dept. Def., Washington, 1974-75; sec. Dept. Army, Washington, 1975-77; mng. ptnr. Gardner, Carton & Douglas, Washington, 1977—89; v.p., gen. counsel, sec. Digital Equipment Corp., Maynard, Mass., 1989-93; sr. vis. fellow Ctr. for Policy, Tech. and Indsl. Devel., MIT, Cambridge, 1993—95; of counsel Skadden, Arps, Slate, Meagher & Flom, Washington, 1996-2000. Bd. dirs. Castle Energy, Phila., Sea Change Corp., Maynard, Mass. Maj. USAR, 1954-73. Mem. Met. Club. Home: 2700 Calvert St NW 217 Washington DC 20008 Personal E-mail: mrhoffmann101@aol.com.

HOFFMANN, MARY JUKICH, voice educator; b. Funter Bay, Alaska, Feb. 17, 1926; d. Nick and Smiljena Jukich; Diploma, Juneau Alaka HS. Dir. mus. U. C.C., Waterloo, Ill., 1945—2004; pvt. voice, piano, organ tchr. Waterloo, 1956—. Vocal soloist various chs., lodges, weddings, funerals. Mem.: V.F.W. Serbian Orthodox. Home: 1225 Lakeview Dr Waterloo IL 62298-2731

HOFFMANN, MICHEAL JOSEPH, theater director; s. Norman Edward and Carmelita Elaine Hoffmann; m. Melissa Ann Lynch, Nov. 22, 1997; children: Christian Nathaniel, Michaela Marie. Asst. to QC and shipping Hollingsworth & Vose Co., West Groton, Mass., 1992—96; artistic dir. Up Stage Right, Fitchburg, 1994—2003; circulation mgr. Nashoba Pub., Ayer, Mass., 2000—01; theatre dept. dir. St. Bernard's Ctrl. Cath. HS, Fitchburg, 2001—03; CEO, dir. programming The Four Guys Orgn. Inc., Fitchburg, 2002—05; dir. theatre Bigelow Mid. Sch., Newton, Mass., 2004—; ops. mgr. Commonwealth Ballet Co., Acton, Mass., 2005—06; adminstr. Wooden Kiwi Prodn., Somerville, Mass., 2006—; dir. music, organist Pilgrim Ch., Nashua, NH, 2006—. Chmn. The Four Guys Orgn. Inc., Groton, 2002—. Named Youngest Profl. Organist in NE, State NH, 1989. Mem.: Am. Guild Organists (assoc.). Liberal. Roman Catholic. Avocations: piano, theater. Home: PO Box 1143 Shirley MA 01464 Home Phone: 978-502-4426; Office Phone: 617-625-9663. Personal E-mail: mikejosephh@aol.com.

HOFFMANN, RICHARD JOHN, biology professor, dean; s. Edward J. and Dorothy L. Hoffmann; m. Vicki Wetherington; children: Erin, Christopher. BS, Coll. William & Mary, Williamsburg, Va., 1969; MA, PhD, Stanford U., Calif., 1974. Asst. prof. biol. scis. U. Pitts., 1975—79; prof. zoology and genetics Iowa State U., Ames, Iowa, 1980—98, assoc. dean liberal arts and scis., 1993—97, interim dean liberal arts and scis., 1997—98; dean arts and scis. SUNY, Albany, NY, 1998—2001, U. Nebr., Lincoln, Nebr., 2001—. Contbr. articles to profl. jours. Mem. Mt. Desert Island Biol. Lab., Salsbury Cove, Maine, 1987—90. First lt. USAR, 1970—77. Recipient Boss of Yr., U. Nebr., 2006; grantee, NSF, 1978—95, NIH, 1979—82; Woodrow Wilson fellow, 1969—70. Fellow: AAAS; mem.: Coun. Colls. Arts and Scis., Soc. Study of Evolution, Sigma Xi, Phi Beta Kappa. Achievements include research in biology of adaptation. Avocation: photography. Office: University of Nebraska-Lincoln 1223 Oldfather Hall Lincoln NE 68588

HOFFMANN, ROALD, chemist, educator; b. Zloczow, Poland, July 18, 1937; arrived in U.S., 1949, naturalized, 1955; s. Hillel and Clara (Rosen) Safran, Paul Hoffmann (Stepfather); m. Eva Börjesson, Apr. 30, 1960; children: Hillel Jan, Ingrid Helena. BA, Columbia U., 1958; MA, Harvard U., 1960, PhD, 1962; D Tech. (hon.), Royal Inst. Tech., Stockholm, 1977; D.Sc. (hon.), Yale U., 1980, Columbia U., 1982, Hartford U., 1982, CUNY, 1983, U. P.R., 1983, U. Uruguay, 1984, U. La Plata, 1984, SUNY, Binghamton, 1985, Colgate U., 1985, Lehigh U., 1989, Carleton Coll., 1989, Ben Gurion U. of the Negev, 1989, U. Md., 1990, U. Athens, 1991, U. Thessaloniki, Greece, 1991, U. Ariz., 1991, U. Cen. Fla., 1991, Bar Ilan U., 1991, U. St. Petersburg, Russia, 1991, U. Barcelona, 1992, Ohio State U., 1993; D.Sc., Northwestern U., 1996, The Technion, 1996, Brandeis U., 1997, Georgetown U., 2000, Durham U., 2000, Luther Coll., 2001. Jr. fellow Soc. Fellows Harvard U., 1962—65; assoc. prof. Cornell U., Ithaca, NY, 1965—68, prof., 1968—74, John A. Newman prof. phys. sci., 1974—96, Frank T. Rhodes prof. humane letters, 1996—. Tage Erlander prof. Swedish Rsch. Coun. Author (with R.B. Woodward): Conservation of Orbital Symmetry, 1970; author: Solids and Surfaces, 1988; author: (with V. Torrence) Chemistry Imagined, 1993; author: (poetry) The Metamict State, 1987, Gaps and Verges, 1990, (non-fiction) Soliton, 2002, (poetry) Memory Effects, 1999, The Same and Not the Same, 1995; author: (with S. Leibowitz Schmidt) Old Wine, New Flasks, 1997; author: (drama, with C. Djerassi) Oxygen, 2000; author: Soliton, 2002, Catalista, 2002. Recipient award in pure chemistry, Am. Chem. Soc., 1969, Arthur C. Cope award, 1973, Fresenius award, Phi Lambda Upsilon, 1969, Harrison Howe award, Rochester sect. Am. Chem. Soc., 1970, ann. award, Internat. Acad. Quantum Molecular Scis., 1970, Guggenheim Fellowship, 1978, Pauling award, 1974, Nobel prize in Chemistry, 1981, inorganic chemistry award, Am. Chem. Soc., 1982, Nat. medal of Sci., 1983, Priestley medal, 1990, Centennial medal, Harvard U., 1994, Jawarharlal Nehru Birth Centenary award, 1998, Pergamon Press Fellowship in Lit., 1988. Mem.: NAS (award in chem. scis. 1986), Finnish Acad. Arts and Letters, Royal Swedish Acad. Scis., Indian Nat. Sci. Acad., Royal Soc. (fgn. mem.), Internat. Acad. Quantum Molecular Scis., Russian Acad. Scis. (N.N. Semenov Gold medal), Am. Acad. Arts and Scis. Avocation: poetry. Office: Dept Chemistry and Chem Biology 222A Baker Laboratory Cornell Univ Ithaca NY 14853-1301 Office Fax: 607-255-4137. Business E-Mail: rh34@cornell.edu.

HOFFMANN, THOMAS RUSSELL, business management educator; b. Milw., Sept. 10, 1933; s. Alfred C. and Florence M. (Morlock) H.; m. Lorna G. Gruenzel, Aug. 31, 1957; 1 child, Timothy Jay. BS, U. Wis., 1955, MS, 1956, PhD, 1959. Cert. in prodn. and inventory mgmt., 1976, in integrated resource mgmt., Am. Prodn. and Inventory Control Soc., 1982. Engring. trainee Allis-Chalmers Mfg. Co., 1956-59; asst. prof. U. Wis. Sch. Commerce, 1959-63; mem. faculty U. Minn. Sch. Mgmt., Mpls., 1963-99, prof., 1965-99, chmn. dept. mgmt. scis., 1969-78; dir. West Bank Computer Center, 1971-87. Cons. to industry. Author: Production Management and Manufacturing Systems, 2 edit., 1967-71, (with others) Fortran 77: A Structured, Disciplined Style, 1978, 83, 88, Production and Inventory Management, 1983, 2d edit., 1991, Production and Operations Management, 1989; editor-in-chief Jour. Ops. Mgmt., 1993-95; contbr. articles to profl. jours. Chmn. long range planning com. Luth. Ch., 1971, pres., 1974, 89, treas., 1977-82, 93-98; pres. Ctrl. Lutheran Ch. Found., 1996. Mem. Am. Prodn. and Inventory Control Soc. (pres. Twin Cities chpt., 1970-71, internat. pres. 1998). Home: 4501 Sedum Ln Edina MN 55435-4051 Office: U Minn Carlson Sch Mgmt Minneapolis MN 55455 Business E-Mail: thoffmann@csom.umn.edu.

HOFFMEYER, WILLIAM FREDERICK, lawyer, educator; b. York, Pa., Dec. 20, 1936; s. Frederick W. and Mary B. (Stremmel) Hoffmeyer. AB, Franklin and Marshall Coll., 1958; JD, Dickinson Sch. Law, 1961. Bar: Pa. 1962, U.S. Dist. Ct. (mid. dist.) Pa. 1981, U.S. Supreme Ct. 1983. Pvt. practice law, 1962-81; sr. ptnr. Hoffmeyer & Semmelman, 1982—. Adj. prof. real estate law, paralegal program Pa. State U., 1978—2000; adj. prof. real estate law York Coll., 1980—92; author, lectr., moderator, course planner CLE program Pa. Bar Inst., Nat. Bus. Inst.; author, lectr., moderator, course planner CLE program and other CLE providers Sterling Ednl. Svcs., 1/2 Moon Ednl. Svcs. Author: Abstractor's Bible, 1981, Pennsylvania Real Estate Installment Sales Contract Manual, 1981, Real Estate Settlement Procedures, 1982, Contracts of Sale, 1984, How to Plot a Deed Description, 1985. Recipient Disting. Svc. award, Gen. Alumni Assn. Dickinson Sch. Law, 1993. Mem.: ABA, Am. Coll. Real Estate Lawyers, York County Bar Assn. (chmn. continuing legal edn. com. 1992—96), Pa. Bar Assn. (co-chmn. unauthorized practice law com., medal 1997), York C. of C. (chair small bus. support network 1997—99), Shriners (past pres. York County), Masons, Lions (past pres. East York club). Address: 30 N George St York PA 17401-1214 Office Phone: 717-846-8846.

HOFFNER, MARILYN, university administrator; b. NYC, Nov. 16, 1929; d. Daniel and Elsie (Schulz) H.; m. Albert Greenberg, May 29, 1949; children: Doren Roe, Peter Cooper. BFA, Cooper Union. Art dir. Printers' Ink mag., NYC, 1953-63, Print Mag., NYC, 1960-62; corp. art dir. Vision, Inc., L.Am., 1963-75, 92-95; dir. alumni rels. and devel. Cooper Union, 1974-96, exec. dir. instnl. advancement, 1996-99, cons., 1999-2001; pres. Alumni Assn., 1999-2001. Project dir. Nat. Graphic Design Archives, 1990-97; bd. dirs. Art Dirs. Club N.Y., 1973-75, 79-82, exec. sec., 1973-75, exec. treas., 1979-82. Contbg. editor Print mag., Art Direction, Graphis mag.; designer mags., advt., books and exhbns. Mem. Citizens Adv. Cultural Arts Com. Dutchess County, 1978-80. Recipient Gold medal Art Dirs. Club, 1979, N.Y. State Coun. of the Arts award, 1995; named Alumnus of the Yr., Cooper Union, 1968. Mem. Cooper Union Alumni Assn. (editor-in-chief 1971-74, 1st v.p. 1974-75), Coun. Advancement and Support of Edn., Type Dirs. Club (numerous awards), Nat. Arts Club (Exhbn. com.). Home: 51 5th Ave New York NY 10003-4320 Home Phone: 212-675-1958. E-mail: cu1948@aol.com.

HOFFSCHNEIDER, GERTRUDE DELORES, pre-school educator; d. Gustoph Henry Steffen and Anne Ida Ebert; m. Dale Wilbur Hoffschneider, July 15, 1956; children: Fred Philip, Charles William, Joel Thomas, Jonathan Andrew. BS, Concordia U., 1957; MA, NYU, 1969. Educator various elem. schs., Calif., 1953—64, Ill., 1953—64, Ind., 1953—64, Mich., 1953—64, NYC Bd. Edn., Bklyn., 1970—73; educator early childhood Ironwood Area Schs., Mich., 1973—90; site mgr. L.A. County Head Start, Maywood, 1991—93; substitute tchr. L.A. Unified Sch. Dist., 1993—96, Oxnard Sch. Dist., 1996—2000, Ft. Wayne Cmty. Schs., Ind., 2000—05. Fellow, NYU, 1969—70. Mem.: Am. Orff. Schulwerk Assn., Orgn. Am. Koda'ly Educators, Am. Guild Organists (mem.-at-large 2004—). Democrat. Lutheran. Avocations: music, reading, piano, gardening.

HOFFSETTE, LEON MERLE, security specialist, retired military officer; b. Kansas City, Mo., May 29, 1953; s. Merle Smedley Hoffsette and Marjorie Fern Roe; m. Dianna Lea Huls, Sept. 22, 1979; children: Adam Merle, Amanda Noel. BA, U. Mo., Columbia, 1975; MA, Calif. State U., Sacramento, 1985. Commd. officer USAF, 1976, advanced through grades to col., 1998, ret., 2006, USAF liaison officer to the US Congress, sec. of the Air Force of Legis. Liaison The Pentagon Washington, 1989—92, KC-135 squadron comdr. 909th Air Refueling Squadron Okinawa, Japan, 1995—96, USAF diplomatic officer US Embassy Copenhagen, 1997—2001, dean students, prof. strategy and internat. security Air War Coll. Montgomery, Ala., 2001—03; dept. chmn., prof. aerospace studies U. Mo., Columbia, 2003—06, facility security officer, 2007—. Pres. The Pines Homeowners Assn., Columbia, 2005—07. Decorated Legion of Merit USAF; named Comdr. of the Order of the Dannebrog, Queen Margrethe II of Denmark, 2001. Master: Ancient Free and Accepted Masons; mem.: Air Force Assn., Mil. Officers Assn. Am., Daedalians, Mark Twain Lake Sailing Assn., Rotary South, Sigma Phi Epsilon (faculty counselor 2004—06). Republican. Methodist. Avocations: travel, sailing, flying (aircraft & hot air balloons), fitness, snow skiing. Home: 2501 Woodberry Ct Columbia MO 65203 Office: Office of Research 310 Jesse Hall Columbia MO 65211 Home Phone: 573-445-8788; Office Phone: 573-882-2791. Personal E-mail: hoffsette@earthlink.net. Business E-Mail: hoffsettel@missouri.edu.

HOFKIN, GERALD ALAN, gastroenterologist; b. Balt., July 4, 1936; AB, MA, Johns Hopkins U., 1957; MD, U. Md., 1961; MBA, Johns Hopkins U., 2003. Diplomate Am. Bd. Internal Medicine, Am. Bd. Gastroenterology. Intern U. Md. Hosp., Balt., 1961, resident in medicine, 1962-63, 64-65, Sinai Hosp., Balt., 1963-64, 65-66; resident in gastroenterology Letterman Hosp., San Francisco, 1966-67; pvt. practice Balt., 1969-91, Woodholme Gastroenterology Assocs., Balt., 1999—; staff Sinai Hosp., Balt., 1991-99, Chmn. med. exec. com. Sinai Hosp. Med. Staff, Balt., 1989, pres., 1992-93. Contbr. articles to profl. jours. Maj. US Army, 1966—69. Decorated Army Commendation medal. Fellow ACP, Am. Coll. Gastroenterology; mem. Am. Soc. Gastroenterol. Endoscopy , Md. Soc. Gastrointesinal Endoscopy (pres. 1995-97), Balt. Amateur Radio Club (v.p. 1978-79), Balt. Radio Amateur TV Soc., Alpha Omega Alpha. Avocations: amateur radio, computers, bridge. Office: Woodholme Gastroenterology Assoc 2411 W Belvedere Ave Baltimore MD 21215-5229 Home: 2811 D Damascus Ct Baltimore MD 21209-3037 Office Phone: 410-367-9600. Personal E-mail: ghofkin@pol.net.

HOFMAN, ELIZABETH ELVERETTA, retired mathematics educator, guidance counselor, dean; b. South Bend, Ind., Feb. 27, 1917; d. Curtis Hamilton and Ossie Marie (Meissner) Vernon; m. Raphael B. Hofman, June 10, 1942 (dec.). Diploma, Mich. County Normal Tng. Sch., Alpena,

1936—37; attended, Huntington Coll., Ind., 1941—42; BS, Western Res. U., Cleve., 1947, MA in Edn., 1948. Cert. HS math. tchr. Western Res. U., 1947, in pupil personnel svcs. Western Res. U., 1964. Tchr. grades K-8 Alpena County Schs., 1937—41; math. tchr. grades 4-8 Warrensville Heights Jr. HS, Ohio, 1945—63, math. tchr. jr. and sr. HS, advisor math., 1963—72, part time guidance counselor, 1960—64, 1963—72, tchr. math. grades 11 and 12, 1960—64, dean of girls, 1968—72, ret., 1972. Mem.: NEA, Ohio Ret. Tchrs. Assn., Nat. Ret. Tchrs. Assn. Home: 700 Brittany O Delray Beach FL 33446-1073

HOFMANN, ALAN FREDERICK, biomedical researcher, educator; b. Balt., May 17, 1931; s. Joseph Enoch and Nelda Rosina (Durr) Hofmann; m. Marta Gertrud Pettersson, Aug. 15, 1959 (div. 1976); children: Anthea Karin, Cecilia Rae; m. Helga Katharina Aicher, Nov. 3, 1978. BA with honors, Johns Hopkins U., 1951, MD with honors, 1955; MD, U. Lund, Sweden, 1965; MD (hon.), U. Bologna, Italy, 1988. Intern, resident dept. medicine Columbia Presbyn. Med. Ctr., NYC, 1955-57; clin. assoc. clin. ctr. Nat. Heart Inst., NIH, Bethesda, Md., 1957-59; postdoctoral fellow, dept. physiol. chemistry U. Lund, Sweden, 1959-62; asst. physician Hosp. Rockefeller U., NYC, 1962-64, assoc. physician, 1964-66; outpatient physician N.Y. Hosp., NYC, 1963-64; cons. in medicine, assoc. dir. gastroenterology unit Mayo Clinic, Rochester, Minn., 1966-77; prof. medicine, attending physician Med. Ctr. U. Calif., San Diego, 1977-98, emeritus prof., 1998—. Asst. prof. dept. medicine Rockefeller U., NYC, 1964—66; assoc. prof. medicine and biochemistry U. Minn. Mayo Grad. Sch., 1966—69, assoc. prof. medicine and physiology, 1969—70, prof., 1970—73, Mayo Med. Sch., 1973—77; cons. physiology Mayo Clinic, Rochester, 1975—77; adj. prof. pharmacy U. Calif., San Francisco, 1986—94; vis. prof. U. Mich., Ann Arbor, 1980—85. Contbr. articles to profl. jours., chapters to books. Co-recipient Eppinger prize, Falk Found., 1976; recipient Travel award, Wellcome Trust, 1961—63, NSF, 1964, Sr. Scientist award, Humboldt Found., Fed. Rep. Germany, 1976, 1991, Disting. Achievement award, Modern Medicine mag., 1978, Chancellor's Rsch. Excellence award, U. Calif., 1986, Disting. Alumnus award, Mayo Found., 2001, Disting. Mentor award, Found. Digestive Health Nutrition, 2004; Sr. fellow, NIH, 1986. Fellow: AAAS, Royal Soc. Medicine, Royal Coll. Physicians (hon.); mem.: Am. Gastroent. Assn. (Disting. Achievement award 1970, co-winner Beaumont prize 1979, Friedenwald medal 1994), Am. Physiol. Soc. (Horace Davenport medal 1996), Am. Liver Found., Serbian Soc. Medicine (hon.), Royal Flemish Acad. Medicine (hon.; fgn. corr. mem.), Chilean Soc. Gastroenterology (hon.), Soc. Gastrointestinal Radiology (hon.), Swedish Soc. Gastroenterology (hon.), Gastroent. Soc. Australia (hon.), Brit. Soc. Gastroenterology (hon.), German Soc. Digestive and Metabolic Disease (hon. Siegfried Thannhauser medal 1996), Assn. Am. Physicians, Am. Soc. Clin. Investigation, Am. Assn. Study Liver Disease (Disting. Achievement award 1997), Sigma Xi, Phi Beta Kappa, Omicron Delta Kappa, Alpha Omega Alpha. Achievements include description and modelling of the enterohepatic circulation of bile acids; clarification of the multiple physiological roles of bile acids; conjugated bile acid replacement therapy for bile acid deficiency in short bowel syndrome; discovery of new vertebrate bile acids; structure-function relationships of bile acids; therapeutic uses of bile acids in liver, biliary and intestinal disease. Home: 5870 Cactus Way La Jolla CA 92037-7069 Personal E-mail: hofmannaf@cs.com. Business E-Mail: ahofmann@ucsd.edu.

HOFMANN, ANDREAS G., engineer, researcher; b. Wiesbaden, Germany, June 6, 1961; BSEE, MIT, Cambridge, Mass., 1982; M of Mech. Engring., Rensselaer Poly. Inst., Troy, NY, 1985; PhD, MIT, 2005. Edison program engr. GE, Pittsfield, Mass., 1982—85; sr. software engr. Lisp Machine INc., Cambridge, 1985—86; dir. application products Gensym Corp., Cambridge, 1986—95; sr. cons. Monitor Co., Cambridge, 1995—97; dir. expert sys. devel. Pegasystems Inc., Cambridge, 1997—99; post-doctoral assoc. MIT, 2005—. Sr. cons. Pegasystems Inc., Cambridge, 2000—03. Chmn. MIT Alumni Assn., Cambridge, 1998—99. Mem.: Sigma Xi. Achievements include patents pending for a method of balance control for humanoid robots that exploits angular momentum. Home Phone: 617-797-6659.

HOFMANN, HERBERT C., diversified holding company executive; BA, Cornell U., Ithaca, NY; grad. mgmt. devel. program, Harvard U. Various mgmt. positions with subs. Loews Corp., 1966—81, v.p. ops. planning, 1976—92, sr. v.p., 1992—; COO Bulova Corp., 1981—89, pres., CEO, 1989—. Office: Bulova Corp One Bulova Ave Woodside NY 11377 Office Phone: 718-204-3600.*

HOFMANN, IRENE E., art museum director; b. NY; B in Art Hist., Wash. U., St. Louis, 1991; M in Modern Art Hist., Sch. of the Art Inst., Chicago, 1993. Exhbn. curator Cranbrook Art Mus., Bloomfield Hills, Mich.; curator Orange County Mus. of Arts, Baltimore, 2001; exec. dir. Contemporary Mus., Baltimore, 2006—. Co-curator (exhibitions) Calif. Biennial, Orange County Mus. of Art, Baltimore, 2002, curator Poetic Engineering, 2005, co-curator Girls Night Out, 2005. Office: Contemporary Museum 100 W Centre St Baltimore MD 21201 Office Phone: 410-783-5720 ext. 102. E-mail: ihofmann@contemporary.org.

HOFMANN, JOHN RICHARD, JR., retired lawyer; b. Oakland, Calif., June 24, 1922; s. John Richard and Esther (Starkweather) H.; m. Mary Macdonough, Feb. 6, 1954; children: John Richard III, Gretchen Hofmann, Sarah Worthington Hack, Joan Macdonough Alexander. AB, U. Calif., Berkeley, 1943; JD, Harvard U., 1949. Bar: Calif. 1950. Assoc. Pillsbury, Madison & Sutro, San Francisco, 1949-58, ptnr., 1959-92, of counsel, 1992-96, ret., 1996—; exec. v.p. MPC Ins., Ltd., 1988-96. City atty. City of Belvedere, Calif., 1958. Mem. County of Marin (Calif.) Aviation Commn., 2001—05, chmn., 2003—05. Office: Pillsbury Winthrop Shaw Pittman LLP PO Box 7880 San Francisco CA 94120-7880 Office Phone: 415-983-1522.

HOFMANN, PAUL BERNARD, healthcare consultant; b. Portland, Oreg., July 6, 1941; s. Max and Consuelo Theresa (Bley) H.; m. Lois Bernstein, June 28, 1969; children: Julie, Jason. BS, U. Calif., Berkeley, 1963, MPH, 1965, DPH, 1994. Research assoc. in hosp. adminstrn. Lab. of Computer Sci., Mass. Gen. Hosp., Boston, 1966-68, asst. dir., 1968-69; asst. adminstr. San Antonio Community Hosp., Upland, Calif., 1969-70, assoc. adminstr., 1970-72; dep. dir. Stanford (Calif.) U. Hosp., 1972-74, dir., 1974-77; exec. dir. Emory U. Hosp., Atlanta, 1978-87; exec. v.p., chief ops. officer Alta Bates Corp., Emeryville, Calif., 1987-91, cons., 1991-92, Alexander & Alexander, San Francisco, 1992-94; disting. vis. scholar Stanford (Calif.) U. Ctr. for Biomed. Ethics, 1993-97; sr. fellow Stanford (Calif.) U. Hosp., 1993-94; sr. cons. strategic healthcare practice Alexander & Alexander Cons. Group, San Francisco, 1994-97; sr. v.p. strategic healthcare practice Aon Cons., San Francisco, 1997-99; pres. The Hofmann Healthcare Group, San Francisco, 2000-01; with Provenance Health Ptnrs., Moraga, Calif., 2001—05; pres. The Hofmann Healthcare Group, Moraga, Calif., 2005—. Instr. computer applications Harvard U., 1968-69; lectr. hosp. adminstrn. UCLA, 1970-72, Stanford U. Med. Sch., 1972-77; assoc. prof. Emory U. Sch. Medicine, Atlanta, 1978-87. Author: The Development and Application of Ethical Criteria for Use in Making Programmatic Resource Allocation Decisions in Hospitals, 1994; co-editor: Managing Ethically: A Guide for Executives, 2001, Mistakes in Healthcare Management: Identification, Prevention and Correction, 2005; contbr. articles to profl. jours Served with U.S. Army, 1959. Fellow Am. Coll. Hosp. Adminstrs. (recipient Robert S. Hudgens meml. award 1976); mem. Am. Hosp. Assn., U. Calif. Grad. Program in Health Mgmt. Alumni Assn. (Disting. Leadership award 2004). Office Phone: 925-247-9700. Business E-Mail: hofmann@hofmannhealthcare.com.

HOFMANN, THEO, biochemist, educator; b. Zurich, Switzerland, Feb. 20, 1924; emigrated to Can., 1964, naturalized, 1969; s. Edwin and Hedwig (Moos) H.; m. Doris Topham Forbes, July 15, 1953; children: Martin Ian, Tony David, Peter Adrian. Diploma chem. engring., Swiss Fed. Inst. Tech., Zurich, 1947, Dr. Sc. Tech. in Pharmacy, 1950. Research asst. U. Aberdeen, Scotland, 1950-52; sci. officer Hannah Dairy Rsch. Inst., Ayr, Scotland, 1952-56; lectr. Sheffield U., England, 1956-64; prof. biochemistry U. Toronto, Ont., Can., 1964-89, emeritus prof. biochemistry, 1989—. Vis. assoc. prof. U. Wash., 1962-63; vis. scientist Commonwealth Sci. and Indsl. Rsch. Orgn., Sydney, Australia, 1971-72; vis. prof. divsn. natural scis. U. Calif.-Santa Cruz, 1981; vis. prof. physical chemistry, U. Lund, Sweden, 1987. Assoc. editor: Can. Jour. Biochemistry, 1968-71; Contbr. numerous articles to profl. jours. Med. Rsch. Coun. grantee, Can., 1964-94. Mem. Can. Soc. Biochemistry and Molecular and Cellular Biology, Am. Soc. Biochemistry and Molecular Biology, Biochem. Soc. Green Party. Achievements include rsch. in function and evolution of enzymes. Home: 199 Arnold Ave Thornhill ON Canada L4J 1C1 Office: U Toronto Dept Biochemistry Toronto ON Canada M5S 1A8 Home Phone: 905-889-1554; Office Phone: 416-978-6457. Business E-Mail: theo@hera.med.utoronto.ca.

HOFMANN, THOMAS W., oil industry executive; BS, U. Del., 1973; MS, Villanova U., 1994. With Coopers & Lybrand, Sun Co. Inc. (now Sunoco, Inc.), Phila., 1977—; comptroller Sun Co. Inc., Phila., 1990-91, dir. tax adminstrn., 1991-94, dir. performance analysis, 1994-95, comptroller, 1995-98, v.p., CFO, 1998—2002, sr. v.p., CFO, 2002—, also bd. dir. V.p. fin. Helios Capital Corp. subs. Sun Co. Inc., 1987. Office: Sunoco Inc 10 Penn Ctr 1801 Market St Philadelphia PA 19103-1699*

HOFRICHTER, DAVID ALAN, management consultant; b. Lakewood, Ohio, July 10, 1948; s. David Christian and Virginia Amelia (Rickley) H.; m. Carol Ann Rybak, May 15, 1971; children: Kristin Ann., Matthew David. BA, Baldwin-Wallace Coll., 1970; MA, Duquesne U., 1972, PhD, 1976. Assoc. Hay Group, Inc., Pitts., 1977—78, prin., 1978—80, dir. orgn. and manpower svc., 1980—81, gen. mgr. Cin., 1981—89, ptnr., gen. mgr., 1983—85, v.p., gen. mgr., 1985—86, sr. v.p., gen. mgr. Chgo., 1986—89, v.p., regional mgr., 1989—90, v.p., mng. dir., 1990—94, v.p., mng. dir. global account mgmt. and midwest ops., 1994-98; sr. v.p., mng. dir. U.S. Bus. Devel., 1998—99, global mng. dir. e-bus., 1999; ptnr. in charge midwest consulting Pricewaterhouse Coopers, Chgo., 1999—2001, ptnr., nat. practice dir., 2001—02; nat. practice dir., prin. Buck Cons. (a Mellon Cons. Co.), Chgo., 2002—03; mng. dir. Mellon Fin. Corp., Chgo., 2003—05; exec. mgmt. team Mellon HR & IS, Chgo., 2003—; global mng. dir. Buck Consultants ACS, Inc., Chgo., 2005—07; prin., coop. leader Hewitt Assocs., Chgo., 2007—. Ptnrs. mgmt. com. Hay Group, Inc., 1990, bd. dirs., Nat. Health Care Practice, Chgo., Vinings, Inc.; mem. adv. bd. exec. rewards bd. World at Work, 2006—; lectr. Hay Compensation Confs.; spkr. Conf. Bd. Fortune Mag. Conf., 1996. Author: Executive Compensation in Health Care, 1986, Selecting People Who Can Implement Strategy, 1989, Reinforcing Organizational and Individual Competencies Through Compensation, 1992, Broad Banding: Fit or Fad, 1993, The Changing Nature of Work and Organization, 1993, People, Performance, and Pay, 1996, Secrets of the Rich and Famous, 1999, How to Survive the Invasion of the E-People, 2000, People, Competencies and Performance, 2001, Dreaming About Performance, 2001, Managing Compensation in Uncertain Times: A Total Performance System, 2002, Effective Executive Compensation Governance, 2006 Named Top 25 Cons. in World, Consuting Mag., 2003. Mem. Am. Psychol. Assn., Am. Soc. Cons. Mgmt. Engrs., Fin. Planning Assn. for City Chgo., Pa. Psychol. Assn., Nat. Register Health Svc. Providers in Psychology, Chgo. Exec. Club, Ruth Lake Country Club (Hindsdale, Ill., v.p.), Oak Brook (Ill.) Polo Club. Republican. Roman Catholic. Avocations: golf, swimming, flying, tennis, shooting. Home: 60 Derby Ct Oak Brook IL 60523-2650 Office: Buck Cons One N Dearborn St Chicago IL 60602 Office Phone: 312-846-3400. Personal E-mail: david.hofrichter@hotmail.com.

HOFSOMMER, DONOVAN LOWELL, history professor; b. Ft. Dodge, Iowa, Apr. 10, 1938; s. Vernie George and Helma J. (Schager) H.; m. Sandra Louise Rusch, June 13, 1965; children: Kathryn Anne, Kristine Beret, Knute Lars. BA, U. Northern Iowa, 1960, MA, 1966; PhD, Okla. State U., 1973. Tchr. Fairfield (Iowa) High Sch., 1961-65; instr. U. Northern Iowa, Cedar Falls, 1965-66, Lea Coll., Albert Lea, Minn., 1966-70; teaching asst. Okla. State U., Stillwater, 1970-73; assoc. prof. and dept. head Wayland Coll., Plainview, Tex., 1973-81; corp. historian So. Pacific Co., San Francisco, 1981-85; hist. cons. Burlington No. Inc., Seattle, 1985-87; vis. prof. U. Mont., Missula, 1986-87; exec. dir. ctr. Western studies Augustana Coll., Sioux Falls, SD, 1987-89; prof. history St. Cloud (Minn.) State U., 1989—. Cons. Dyanelectron and Dynarail, Pueblo, Colo., 1979-81, Grand Trunk Corp., Detroit, 1988-95; mem. editl. bd. annals of Iowa, Iowa City, 1975-94, R.R. history, Akron, Ohio, 1975—. Author: Prairie Oasis, 1975, Katy Northwest, 1976, Southern Pacific 1901-1985, 1986; co-author: History of Great Northern Railway, 1988, Quanah Route, 1991, Grand Trunk Corp., 1995, The Tootin' Louie, 2004, History of Minneapolis & Saint Louis, 2004, Steel Trails of Hawkeye Land, 2005, Minneapolis and the Age of Railways, 2005, HIstory of Iowa Central Railway, 2005; editor: Lexington Group Transport History, 1975—; mem. editl. bd. Annals of Iowa, Iowa City, 1975-92, R.R. History, Akron, Ohio, 1975—. With U.S. Army, 1960-66. Mem. Okla. Hist. Soc. (Wright Heritage award 1979), Ry. and Locomotive Hist. Soc. (Book award 1988, Sr. Achievement award 1995), Western History Assn., Orgn. Am. Historians, State Hist. Soc. Iowa, Am. Assn. for State and Local History (Leadership History award 2006). Episcopalian. Home: 1803 13th Ave SE Saint Cloud MN 56304-2231 Office: St Cloud State U Dept History Saint Cloud MN 56301 Office Phone: 320-308-4906.

HOFSTETTER, JANE ROBINSON, artist, educator; b. Oakland, Calif., Feb. 23, 1936; d. Thomas O. and Fern (Worstell) Robinson; m. William R. Hofstetter, Aug. 3, 1958; children: David, Glen. Student, U. Calif., Berkeley, San Francisco Sch. of Design, Chouinard Art Inst., LA. Lectr. in field. Represented in permanent collections Triton Mus. Art, Santa Clara, Calif., State of Calif. Collection, Asilomar, San Ramon and Santa Clara City Halls, Kayser Hosp., Calif., IBM Hdqs. and Gen. Facilities, Gould Inc., No. Calif. Savings and Loan, Systems Control Inc., Zerox Corp., Finance Am.; author Seven Keys To Great Paintings, 2005. Recipient Triton Art Mus. award and numerous others. Mem. Nat. Watercolor Soc., Watercolor West Soc., Nat. Transparent Watercolor Soc. Am., Soc. Western Artists. Studio: 308 Dawson Dr Santa Clara CA 95051-5806 Office Phone: 408-248-4425. E-mail: jrhofstetter@comcast.net.

HOGAN, ADEN ELLSWORTH, JR., city government administrator; b. Fredonia, Kans., July 31, 1951; s. Aden Ellsworth Sr. and Maxine Ruth (Buchanan) H.; m. Debra Ann Ford, July 26, 1969 (div. Apr. 1982); 1 child, Michael Troy; m. Denna Marie Moore, Dec. 9, 1982 (div. Dec. 1999); m. Anne M. Rohach, Jan. 1, 2000. AA with honors, Mesa State Coll., 1985, BBA cum laude, 1987; MPA, U. Colo., 1992. Credentialed mgr. 2003. Engring. technician Dept. Engring. City of Dodge, Kans., 1970—77; prodn. mgr. Gingery Assn. Inc., Engrs., Grand Junction, Colo., 1978—84; planner Mesa County Govt., Grand Junction, 0984—1985, dir. risk and fleet mgmt. divsn., 1985—92; dir. risk mgmt. City of Oklahoma City, 1992—95, asst. to city mgr., 1995-96; town adminstr. Town of Parker, Colo., 1996—2005; asst. town mgr. Town of Lochbuie, Colo., 2005—. Regional rep. N.W. Colo. Transp. Task Force, Glenwood Springs, 1988-91; mem. Gov.'s Round Table for Local Transp. Needs, Denver, 1989-92; bd. dirs. Colo. Club Classics, Ltd., Grand Junction; mem. response team for Oklahoma City bombing, 1995; mem. Kans. Hunter Safety Inst. Author: (manual) Fleet Policies and Procedures, 1989, Safety Manual, 1989, A View From the Top-Management Perspectives of Risk Management, 1995, (book) The Public Officials' Guide to Infrastructure Security Planning, 2004; co-author: Disaster Medicine, 2002. Spkr. Grand Junction Helicopter Ops. Task Force, 1986; instr. Kans. Hunter Safety Program, Dodge City, 1974-77; chmn. S.W. Kans. Ducks Unltd., Dodge City, 1974-77, Grand Junction Bd. Adjustment and Appeals, 1986-90. Named to Hon. Order of Buffalo, Kans. Fish and Game Hunter Soc., 1976; Colo. Gen. Assembly scholar, 1986-88. Mem. USTA (life), Pub. Risk Mgrs. Assn. (seminar presenter 1993-94), Internat. City Mgrs. Assn., Ducks Unltd. (chmn. 1975-78), Horizon Tennis Club (bd. dirs., pres. Grand Junction chpt. 1989-91). Republican. Avocations: tennis, fishing, stamp collector, reading. Home: 10631 Tucson Way Commerce City CO Home Phone: 720-840-5526; Office Phone: 303-437-0438. Personal E-mail: aehogan@comcast.net. E-mail: aden@peakprofesionalsolutions.com.

HOGAN, BRIAN JOSEPH, editor; b. Aberdeen, SD, Apr. 11, 1943; s. Arthur James and Magdalena (Frison) H.; m. Jamie Isabelle Schwingel, June 21, 1987. BS in Aerospace and Mech. Engring., U. Ariz., 1965, BS in Geophysics-Geochemistry, 1968; MS in Journalism, U. Utah, 1972. Rsch. asst. U. Va. Rsch. Labs for Engring. Scis., Charlottesville, 1965-66; exploration geophysicist Anaconda Co., Tucson, 1968-71; assoc. editor Benwill Pub. Co., Brookline, Mass., 1973-74; asst. editor Design News, Boston, 1974-75, midwest editor Chgo., 1975-87, sr. editor Newton, Mass., 1987-89, mng. editor, 1989-97; chief editor Mfg. Engring.-Soc. Mfg. Engrs., Dearborn, Mich. Author stage plays The Young O'Neil, 1983, Awakening, 1984. Precinct worker Cook County Rep. Com., Oak Park, Ill., 1986-87; interpreter Frank Lloyd Wright Home and Studio Found., Oak Park, 1981-87. Recipient numerous awards Am. Soc. Bus. Press Editors, Soc. Tech. Communication, Aviation Space Writers Assn. Mem. Am. Hist. Print Collectors Soc. Republican. Roman Catholic. Avocations: photography, print collecting, bicycling, hiking. Office: Mfg Engring 1 SME Dr PO Box 930 Dearborn MI 48121-0930 Office Phone: 313-425-3252. Business E-Mail: bhogan@sme.org.

HOGAN, BRIGID L.M., molecular biologist; b. England, Aug. 28, 1943; BA, U. Cambridge, 1964, PhD, 1968. NATO rsch. fellow dept. biology MIT, 1968-70; lectr. biochemistry U. Sussex, England, 1970-74; sci. staff Imperial Cancer Rsch. Fund, Mill Hill, England, 1974-84; head lab. molecular embryology Nat. Inst. Med. Rsch., Mill Hill, England, 1985-88; prof. cell biology Vanderbilt Med. Sch., Nashville, 1988—2002; prof. and chair dept. cell biology Duke U. Med. Ctr., 2002—. Hortense B. Ingram chair molecular oncology Howard Hughes Med. Inst., 1993-2002; vice chair Basement Membrane Gordon Conf., 1994, chair, 1996; co-chair sci. human embryo rsch. panel NIH, 1994; Jenkinson meml. lectr. U. Oxford, 1995; Margaret Pittman lectr. NIH, 1996. Mem. Br. Soc. Cell Biology (com. 1982-86), Br. Soc. Devel. Biology (com. 1984-88), NAS Inst. Medicine ((in conjunction with NRC) mem. adv. com. Human Embryonic Stem Cell Rsch., 2006-), European Molecular Biology Orgn. Office: Duke U Med Ctr 388 Nanaline Duke Bldg Box 3709 Durham NC 27710 Office Phone: 919-684-8085. Office Fax: 919-685-8592. E-mail: B.Hogan@cellbio.duke.edu.

HOGAN, CLARENCE LESTER, retired electronics executive; b. Great Falls, Mont., Feb. 8, 1920; s. Clarence Lester and Bessie Hogan; m. Audrey Biery Peters, Oct. 13, 1946; 1 child, Cheryl Lea. BSChemE, Mont. State U., 1942, Dr. Engring. (hon.), 1967; MS in Physics, Lehigh U., 1947, PhD in Physics, 1950, D in Engring. (hon.), 1971; AM (hon.), Harvard U., 1954; Doctorate (hon.), Mont. State U., 1968; D in Sci. (hon.), Worcester Poly. U., 1969. Rsch. chem. engr. Anaconda Copper Mining Co., 1942-43; instr. physics Lehigh U., 1946-50; mem. tech. staff Bell Labs., Murray Hill, NJ, 1950-51, sub-dept. head, 1951-53; assoc. prof. Harvard U., Cambridge, Mass., 1953-57, Gordon McKay prof., 1957-58; gen. mgr. semi-conductor products divsn. Motorola, Inc., Phoenix, 1958-60, v.p., 1960-66, exec. v.p., dir., 1966-68; pres., CEO Fairchild Semicondr. (formerly Fairchild Instruments), Mt. View, Calif., 1968—74, vice chmn. bd. dirs., 1974-85. Gen. chmn. Internat. Conf. on Magnetism and Magnetic Materials, 1959, 60; mem. materials adv. bd. Dept. Def., 1957-59; mem. adv. coun. dept. electrical engring. Princeton U.; mem. adv. bd. sch. engring. U. Calif., Berkeley, 1974—, adv. bd. dept. chem. engring. Mont. State U., 1988—; mem. nat. adv. bd. Desert Rsch. Inst., 1976-80; mem. vis. com. dept. electric engring. and computer sci. MIT, 1975-85; mem. adv. coun. div. electrical engring. Stanford U., 1976-86; mem. sci. and edni. adv. com. Lawrence Berkeley Lab., 1978-84; mem. Pres.'s Export Coun., 1976-80; mem. adv. panel to tech. adv. bd. U.S. Congress, 1976-80. Chmn. Silicon Valley Cmty. Found., Calif., 1983—85; mem. vis. com. Lehigh U., 1966—71, trustee, 1971—80, also life trustee; trustee Western Electronic Edn. Fund; dir. Computer History Mus., 1982—86; mem. governing bd. Maricopa County Jr. Coll.; bd. regents U. Santa Clara. Lt. (j.g.) USNR, 1942—46. Recipient Community Svc. award NCCJ, 1978, Medal of Merit Am. Electronics Assn., 1978, Berkeley Citation U. Calif., 1980; named Bay Area Bus. Man of Yr. San Jose State U., 1978, One of 10 Greatest Innovators in Past 50 Yrs. Electronics Mag., 1980, chair (hon.) Computer Sci. and Engring. U.C. Berkeley, 1997. Fellow AAAS, IEEE (Frederick Philips Gold medal 1976, Edison Silver medal Cleve. Soc. 1978, Pioneering medal for microwave theory and tech. 1993), Inst. Elec. Engrs. (hon.); mem. NAE, Am. Phys. Soc., Masons, Sigma Xi, Tau Beta Pi, Phi Kappa Phi, Eta Kappa Nu, Kappa Sigma. Democrat. Baptist. Achievements include patentee in field; inventor microwave gyrator, circulator, isolator. Avocations: woodworking, computer programming. Home: 36 Barry Ln Atherton CA 94027-4023

HOGAN, CURTIS JULE, labor union administrator, industrial relations specialist, consultant; b. Greeley, Kans., July 25, 1926; s. Charles Leo and Anna Malene (Rousselo) H.; m. Lois Jean Ecord, Apr. 23, 1955; children: Christopher James, Michael Sean, Patrick Marshall, Kathleen Marie, Kerry Joseph. BS in Indsl. Rels., Rockhurst Coll., 1950; postgrad., Georgetown U., 1955, U. Tehran, Iran, 1955-57. With Gt. Lakes Pipeline Co., Kansas City, Mo., 1950-55; with Internat. Fedn. Petroleum and Chem. Workers, Denver, 1955-85, gen. sec., 1973-85; pres. Internat. Labor Rels. Svcs., Inc., 1976—. Cons. in field; lectr. Rockhurst Coll., Kansas City, 1951-52. Contbr. articles to profl. publs. Served with U.S. Army, 1945-46. Mem. Internat. Indsl. Rels. Assn., Indsl. Rels. Rsch. Assn., Oil Chem. and Atomic Workers Internat. Union. Office: Internat Fed Petroleum Chem Workers 435 S Newport Way Denver CO 80224-1321

HOGAN, EDWARD ROBERT, financial services executive; b. Yonkers, NY, Mar. 21, 1939; s. John J. and Blanche (Corradi) H.; m. Linda Carroll, Sept. 25, 1959 (div. Oct. 1975); children: Linda Hogan Benya, Edward R. Jr., Barbara Hogan Comblo; m. Sandra Lesperance, Sept. 17, 1993. Dist. mgr. New Eng. Life, Thornwood, N.Y., 1962-64; pres. Profl. Employment Svcs., Scarsdale, N.Y., 1964-66, Royal Transport & Distbn. Inc., Yonkers, N.Y., 1966-71; v.p. Fin. Ins. Group, NYC, 1971—74, Franklin United Life Ins. Co., Garden City, N.Y., 1974-79; sr. v.p. Adv. Svcs. Corp., White Plains, N.Y., 1979-83; pres. Faculty Svcs. Corp., Wappingers Falls, N.Y., 1983—, FSC Adminstrv. Svcs. Corp., Wappingers Falls, N.Y., 1986—. Registered prin. Cadaret, Grant & Co., Inc., Syracuse, N.Y., 1989—. Pres. Yonkers Young Rep. Orgn., 1960-64; v.p. Westchester County Young Reps., White Plains, 1961-63; candidate 1st Assembly Dist. State Assembly, Yonkers, 1962; Westchester County campaign dir. U.S. Sen. James L. Buckley, 1968. With USN, 1957-59. Mem. Nat. Tax Shelter Annuity Assn. Avocations: boating, flying, skiing. Office: Faculty Svcs Corp PO Box 1635 Wappingers Falls NY 12590-8635 Office Phone: 845-297-0300. Personal E-mail: facultysc@optonline.net.

HOGAN, ERNESTINE DEARING, retired mathematics educator, retired school system administrator; b. Cleveland, Ga., Oct. 3, 1946; d. Columbus and Amanda Mae Dearing; m. Marshall Hogan, May 12, 1979. BA in Math., Spelman Coll., Atlanta, 1968; MEd in Math. Edn., Ga. State U., Atlanta, 1975; EdD in Ednl. Leadership, Clark Atlanta U., 2003. Cert. tchr. Ga. Math. tchr. Atlanta Pub. Schs., 1968—2000, model teache leader, 2000—06; adminstr. Sci. and Math. Summer Enrichment Acad. Atlanta Pub. Schs. and Spelman Coll., 2000—06; ret., 2006. Math/sci. cons. Atlanta Pub. Schs., 2007. Author: Insights for Life, 2007. Contact person March of Dimes, College Park, Ga., 2006; vol., contbr. YMCA, Atlanta, 2006—07. Named Oustanding Young Woman of Am., 1974, 1978, Star Tchr., Ga. C. of C., 1994, 1997, 1999; recipient Area Tchr. of the Yr., Atlanta Bd. Edn., 1978, 1989. Mem.: Nat. Coun. Tchrs. Math., Spelman Coll. Alumni Assn. Avocations: walking, travel, reading, movies. Home: 5035 Green Tree Trail College Park GA 30349

HOGAN, FELICITY, artist; b. England; m. Michael Clark, Dec. 1995. Co-dir. Mus. Contemporary Art, Washington, 1996—. Exhibitions include Clark & Hogan: Paintings & Collaborations, Barry Gallery, 2002—03, Mus. Contemporary Art, 1997—, Clark in Context: Day of the Revolutionary, 2003. Office: Mus Contemporary Art 1054 31st St Washington DC 20007 E-mail: felicityhogan@aol.com.

HOGAN, FRANK W., III, lawyer, manufacturing executive; b. Lowell, Mass., July 16, 1960; BA, Boston U., 1982, JD, 1987. Assoc. Winthrop, Stimson, Putnam & Roberts (now Pillsbury Winthrop LLP), 1988—95, ptnr., 1995—97; v.p., gen. counsel, sec. Silgan Holdings, Stamford, Conn., 1997—2002, sr. v.p., 2002—, gen. counsel, 2002—, sec., 2002—. Mem.: ABA. Office: Silgan Holdings Ste 400 4 Landmark Sq Stamford CT 06901

HOGAN, HARLAN ROBERT, voice-over actor; b. Chgo., Sept. 30, 1946; s. Harlan Vincent and Marjorie Catherine (Thurber) H.; children: Jameson, Graham; m. Lesley Ann Schwartz, July 29, 1989. BFA, Ill. Wesleyan U., 1968. Announcer Sta. WHUT-radio, Anderson, Ind., 1968-69, Sta. WCLR-radio, Skokie, Ill., 1969-71; advt. mgr. Advanced Systems, Elk Grove, Ill., 1971-74; pres., voice over actor Wordsworth, Inc., Chgo., 1974—. Author: VO: Tales and Techniques of a Voice-Over Actor, 2002; co-author: The Voice Actor's Guide to Home Recordings, 2005. Recipient Golden Trumpet award Chgo. Pub. Relations Club, 1976, Best Commls. award Worlds Best Commls., 1985; NY Film Festival Silver Medal, Author and Narrator, 1999, Bronze Medal, 2000. Mem. AFTRA (rec. sec. 1995-96), SAG (v.p. Chgo. 1983-84), Internat. Brotherhood of Magicians, Magic Castle. Avocations: motorcycling, sailing, magic, bicycling. Home: 110 Arboretum Dr North Barrington IL 60010-6591 Business E-Mail: harlan@harlanhogan.com.

HOGAN, ILONA MODLY, lawyer; b. Erlangen, Fed. Republic of Germany, Nov. 23, 1947; arrived in U.S., 1951, naturalized, 1960; d. Stephen Bela and Gunda Pauline (Gastiger) Modly; m. Lawrence J. Hogan, Mar. 16, 1974; children: Matthew Lawrence, Michael Alexander, Patrick Nicholas, Timothy Stefan. Student, Marymount Coll., 1965-67; AB in Internat. Affairs, George Washington U., 1969; JD, Georgetown U., 1974. Bar: D.C. 1975, Md. 1975. Intern and clk. AID, 1965-69; adminstrv. and legis. asst. to mem. Ho. of Reps., 1969-72; editor Legis. Digest, Ho. of Reps., Washington, 1972-73; asso. and law clk. firm Trammell, Rand, Nathan and Lincoln, Washington, 1972-74; mng. ptnr. firm Hogan and Hogan, Washington and Md., 1974-93; of counsel Venable, Baetjer, Howard & Civiletti, Washington, 1989-91; pres. Amcom Inc., 1978—; of counsel Salisbury & McLister, Frederick, Md., 1993-2001; global mgr. Bechtel Telecom., 2001—. Mem. Prince George's Bd. Libr. Trustees, Md., 1976—78, Prince George's County Econ. Devel. Adv. Com., 1979—82; v.p. St. John's Sch. Bd., 1987—88, pres., 1989; treas. U. Md. Bd. Regents, 1988—95; trustee St. James Sch., 1989—90; mem. Lawyers Steering com. for Reagan-Bush, 1980; nat. vice-chmn. Assn. Execs. for Reagan-Bush, 1984; mem. bus. and industry adv. com. 50th Am. Presdl. Inaugural, 1985; mem. Md. steering com. Bush for Pres., 1988; mem. Presdl. Personnel Adv. Com., 1989, Gov.'s Higher Edn. Transition Team, 1988; elected mem. County Commrs. Frederick County, 1994—2001; Frederick County co-chair Bush-Cheney Campaign, 2000; bd. advisors Frostburg State U., 2001—03; trustee Frederick C.C. Found., 2001—03, Md. Higher Edn. Commn., 2003—. Mem.: ABA, D.C. Bar, Md. Bar Assn. Republican. Roman Catholic. Home: 5614 New Design Rd Frederick MD 21703-8306 Office: 5275 Westview Dr Frederick MD 21703-8306 E-mail: imhogan@bechtel.com.

HOGAN, JOHN DONALD, retired college dean, finance educator; b. Binghamton, NY, July 16, 1927; s. John D. and Edith J. (Hennessy) H.; m. Anna Craig, Nov. 26, 1976; children: Thomas P., James E. AB, Syracuse U., 1949, MA, 1950, PhD, 1952. Registered prin. Nat. Assn. Securities Dealers. Prof. econs., chmn. dept. Bates Coll., Lewiston, Maine, 1953-58; dir. edn. fin. research State of N.Y., 1959, chief mcpl. fin., 1960; staff economist, dir. research Northwestern Mut. Life Ins. Co., Milw., 1960-68; v.p. Nationwide Ins. Cos., Columbus, Ohio, 1968-76; dean Sch. Bus. Adminstrn. Central Mich. U., Mt. Pleasant, 1976-79; v.p. Am. Productivity Ctr., Houston, 1979-80; pres., chmn., chief exec. officer Variable Annuity Life Ins. Co., Houston, 1980-83; sr. v.p. Am. Gen. Corp., Houston, 1983-86; dean, prof. fin. Coll. Commerce U. Ill., Champaign, 1986-91; dean, prof. fin. and econs. Coll. Bus. Adminstrn. Ga. State U., Atlanta, 1991-97, prof. fin. and econs., 1998—2001, dean and prof. emeritus, 2002—. Bd. dirs. Sinfonia da Camera, Champaign, Ga. Coun. on Econ. Edn., Pvt. Industry Coun., World Trade Ctr., Atlanta; vis. prof. fin. Poznan (Poland) U. Econs., Caucasus Sch. Bus., Tbilisi, Georgia; cons. in field. Author: American Social Legislation, 1965, U.S. Balance of Payments and Capital Flows, 1967, School Revenue Studies, 1959, Fiscal Capacity of the State of Maine, 1958, American Social Legislation, 1973; editor: Dimensions of Productivity Research (2 vols.), 1981; contbr. articles to jours., abstracts to profl. meetings. Bd. dirs. Goodwill Industries, Columbus, 1972-76, chmn. capital fund drive, 1974-75; mem. Houston Com. on Fgn. Rels., 1980—, Chgo. Coun. on Fgn. Rels., 1986—, Chgo. com., 1987—; mem. dean's coun. Maxwell Grad. Sch., Syracuse U., 2003—. Served with U.S. Army, 1944-46, ETO; capt. (ret.) USAR. Maxwell fellow Syracuse U., 1950-52; recipient Best Article award Jur. Risk and Ins., Alumni Appreciation award U. Ill., 1991, 1964, Medal of Merit Poznan U., Poland, 1999; Maxwell Centennial lectr. Maxwell Grad. Sch., Syracuse U., 1970. Mem.: Inst. Rsch. in Econs. of Taxation (dir. 1984—), Nat. Tax Assn. (dir. 1981—85, treas., exec. com. 1988—2001), Nat. Assn. Bus. Economists, Inst. Mgmt. Scis., Am. Econ. Assn., Acad. Mgmt., Columbus C. of C. (chmn. econ. policy com. 1972—76), World Trade Club (Atlanta, bd. dirs. 1993—99), Columbus Athletic Club, Heritage Club (Houston), Commerce Club (Atlanta), Lincolnshire Fields Country Club (Champaign), Univ. Club (Chgo.), Beta Gamma Sigma, Phi Kappa Phi. Office: Ga State U Coll Bus Adminstrn Univ Plaza Atlanta GA 30303-3083 also: 3892 Byrnwyck Pl NE Atlanta GA 30319-1654

HOGAN, JOHN PAUL, chemistry researcher, consultant; b. Lowes, Kentucky, Aug. 7, 1919; s. Charles F. and Alma (Wyman) H.; m. Glenda M. (Moultrie), 1943; children: E. Fay, Hogan Sweney, Kenneth B., Susan G., Hogan Lair. Attended, U. Redlands, 1940-41; BS in Chemistry and physics, Murray State U., 1942, ScD (hon.), 1971. Tchr. Mayfield High Sch., Ky., 1942-43; physics instr. Okla. State U., Stillwater, 1943-44; rsch. chemist Phillips Petroleum Co., Bartlesville, Okla., 1944-48, group leader, 1948-60, polymer sci. sect. mgr., 1960-77, polymer sci. sr. research assoc., 1977-85, cons., 1985-86, Bartlesville, Okla., 1986—. Chmn. N.E. Okla. sect. Am. Chem. Soc., 1970. Patentee in field; contbg. chapters to books. Recipient Creative Invention Award, Am. Chem. Soc., 1969; Pioneer Chemists Award, 1972; Perkin medal, Soc. Chem. Industry, 1987; Heros in Chemistry Award Am. Chem. Soc., 1998; named Disting. Alumnus, Murray State U., 1972; Inventor of Yr., Okla. Bar Assn. Copyright and Patent Sect., 1976; Polymeric Materials Man of Yr., Soc. Plastics Engr., 1981; Paul Harris fellow Rotary Found., 2000; named to Hon. Order of Ky. Col., 1972; inductee Nat. Inventor Hall of Fame, 2001, Okla. Inventors Hall of Fame, 2002. Fellow Am. Inst. Chemists. Republican. Baptist. Avocations: Ch. work, fly fishing, chess, gardening. Home: 1049 S E Greystone Ave Bartlesville OK 74006-5010

HOGAN, JOHN W., JR., lawyer; b. New Haven, Feb. 22, 1939; BA, Coll. Holy Cross, 1961; JD, Conn. U., 1964. Bar: Conn. 1964, US Dist. Ct. (Dist. Conn.) 1965, US Tax Ct. 1969. Sr. prin. Hogan & Rini, PC, New Haven; of counsel Berchem Moses & Devlin PC, Conn. Mem. Nahley Mediation Panel, 1989—90; mng. trustee The David T. Langrock Found. Class gifts and bequests chair Coll. of the Holy Cross; chair New Haven Devel. Commn.; dir. The New Haven Regional Leadership Coun.; trustee Hosp. St. Raphael; dir., sec. and counsel The Found. of the Greater New Haven C. of C. and The Greater New Haven C. of C.; dir. Friends of Legal Svcs., New Haven; dir., sec. Shubert Performing Arts Ctr.; dir. The New Haven Land Trust; pres., dir. Vis. Nurse Assn. Greater New Haven. Recipient Citizen of Yr. award, Conn. Cts. of Probate, 1989. Mem.: ABA (mem. house of delegates 2002—), Conn. Bar Assn. (clients' security fund 1973—91, ho. dels. 1978—83, exec. com. banking law sect. 1981—98, chair clients' security fund 1985—91, chair awards com. 1996—2000, v.p. 2001—02, pres.-elect 2002—03, pres. 2004, John Eldred Shields Meml. Disting. Profl. Svc. award 1995). Office: Berchem Moses & Devlin PC 75 Broad St Milford CT 06460 Office Phone: 203-783-1200. Office Fax: 203-873-2235. Business E-Mail: jhogan@bmd-law.com.

HOGAN, JOSEPH M., health products executive; b. Mar. 7, 1957; m. Lisa Hogan; children: Tyler, Jason, Nicolas. BS in Bus. Adminstrn., Geneva Coll.; MBA, Robert Morris U., 1984. Sales, mktg. in plastics G.E., 1985—98; pres., CEO G.E. Fanuc Automation N. Am., 1998—2000; exec. v.p., COO G.E. Med. Sys., 2000; pres., CEO G.E. Healthcare Technologies, 2000—05; sr. v.p. G.E., 2005—; pres., CEO G.E. Healthcare, 2005—. Bd. mem. NY Acad. Med., Multiple Myeloma Rsch. Found.; mem. adv. bd. Ctr. Disease Control. Office: GE Healthcare 3000 N Grandview Blvd Waukesha WI 53188*

HOGAN, KURT AVERY, music educator; s. Robert Clement and Arlene Edith Hogan; m. Jena Lynn Reidt, July 19, 1986; children: Jared R., Korey R. BS in Edn., S.E. Mo. State U., Cape Girardeau, 1981; MS in Edn., S.W. Bapt. U., Bolivar, Mo., 1999, MS in Edn. Adminstrn., 2003. Lifetime cert. K-12 vocal and instrumental music Mo., cert. elem. prin. grades K-8 Mo. Supr. Six Flags Over Mid-Am., Eureka, Mo., 1974—81; gen. mgr. Magic Castle Pizza, Chesterfield, Mo., 1981—83; claims specialist State Farm Fire and Casualty, Ellisville, Mo., 1984—95; elem. music tchr. Meramec Valley R-III Sch. Dist., Pacific, Mo., 1995—. Asst. summer band camp Pacific HS Marching Band, 2003—; chmn. curriculum revision elem. art, music and phys. edn. Meramec Valley R-III, Pacific, 2006—07. Active mission trip basketball camp First Bapt. Ch. Villa Ridge, Gunnison, Colo., 2005; active basketball camp Crosspoint Christian Sch., Union, Mo., 2005; active mission trip sports camp First Bapt. Ch. Villa Ridge, Dauphin Island, Ala., 2006; elder chmn. First Evangelical Free Ch., Villa Ridge, 2001—02, mem. pers. com., 2002—06. Mem.: ASCD, Mo. Music Educators Assn., Nat. Assn. for Music Edn. Avocations: writing music, coaching baseball and basketball, trombone, float trips, singing. Home: 105 Valley Side Ln Labadie MO 63055 Office: Meramec Valley R-III Sch Dist 126 N Payne St Pacific MO 63069

HOGAN, MARY BETH, lawyer; b. 1963; AB, Princeton U., 1985; JD, Rutgers, 1990. Bar: NJ 1990, NY 1992. Clerk Supreme Ct. NJ, 1990—91; ptnr. Debevoise & Plimton LLP, NYC. Bd. dirs. Catalyst; v.p., bd. dirs. Nazareth Housing. Named one of Litigation's Rising Stars, The Am. Lawyer, 2007. Mem.: Assn. of Bar of City of NY, ABA. Office: Debevoise & Plimpton LLP 919 Third Ave New York NY 10022 Office Phone: 212-909-6996. Office Fax: 212-909-6836.*

HOGAN, MICHAEL J., academic administrator; m. Virginia Hogan; children: Christopher, David, Joe, AnnElizabeth. BA, U. No. Iowa; MA, U. Iowa, PhD in History. Vis. prof. SUNY, Stony Brook, 1974—75, U. Tex., Austin, 1976—77; from asst. prof. to assoc. prof. to prof. Miami U., Oxford, Ohio, 1977—86; prof. Ohio State U., 1986—2004, univ. disting. scholar, 1990—2004, chair dept. history, 1993—99, dean Coll. Humanities, 1999—2003, exec. dean Colls. Arts and Scis., 2001—04; exec. v.p., provost U. Iowa, Iowa City, 2004—07, Wendell Miller prof. history, 2004—06; pres. U. Conn., Storrs, 2007—. Louis Martin Sears disting. prof. history Purdue U.; cons. in field. Author: Informal Entente: The Private Structure of Cooperation in Anglo-America Economic Diplomacy, 1918-1928, 1977, The Marshall Plan: America, Britain, and the Reconstruction of Western Europe, 1947-1952, 1987 (Stuart L. Bernath Book Award, Soc. Historians of Am. Fgn. Rels., George Louis Beer Prize, Am. Hist. Assn., Quincy Wright Prize, Internat. Studies Assn.), A Cross of Iron: Harry S. Truman and the Origins of the National Security State, 1945-1954, 1998; editor: Paths to Power: The Historiography of American Foreign Relations to 1941, 2000; contbr. articles to profl. jours. Recipient Bernath Lecture prize, Soc. Historians of Am. Fgn. Rels., 1984; fellow, Harry S. Truman Libr. Inst., Woodrow Wilson Internat. Ctr. for Scholars. Mem.: Soc. Historians of Am. Fgn. Rels. (v.p. 2002, pres. 2003). Office: U Conn Office of Pres 352 Mansfield Rd, Unit 2048 Storrs Mansfield CT 06269-2048 Office Fax: 860-486-2048. E-mail: president@uconn.edu, mike.hogan@uconn.edu.*

HOGAN, NEVILLE JOHN, mechanical engineering educator, consultant; b. Dublin, Feb. 11, 1949; came to U.S., 1970; s. Walter Henry and Edna Constance (Liller) H.; m. Sara Jane Seiden; children: Alexandra, Brian, Amanda, Victoria. Diploma in engring. with honors, Coll. Tech., Dublin, 1970; MS in Mech. Engring., MIT, 1973, mech. engring. degree, 1976, PhD in Mech. Engring., 1977; D (hon.), Tech. U. Delft, 1997, Dublin Inst. Tech., 2004. Product devel. and design engr. Donnelly Mirrors Ltd., Nass, Ireland, 1977-78; prof. MIT, Cambridge, 1978—; dir. Newman Lab., 1992—. Cons. in phys. systems modeling, design and control and in biomed. engring. Contbr. numerous articles to profl. jours. TRW Found. fellow, Whitaker Health Scis. Fund fellow; recipient Silver medal Royal Acad. Medicine, Ireland, 2004. Mem.: ASME, AAAS, Neural Control of Movement Soc., Soc. Neuroscience, Sigma Xi.

HOGAN, RANDALL J., manufacturing and electronics executive; BS in Civil Engring., MIT; MBA, U. Tex. Cons. McKinsey & Co.; with Gen. Electric; with Pratt & Whitney divsn. United Techs., pres. carrier transicold divsn.; exec. v.p. and pres. of elec. and elec. enclosures group Pentair, Inc., Golden Valley, Minn., 1998—99, pres. and COO, 1999—2000, pres. and CEO, 2001—02, chmn. and CEO, 2002—. Office: Pentair Inc Ste 800 5500 Wayzata Blvd Golden Valley MN 55416*

HOGAN, ROBERT HENRY, trust company executive; b. NYC, Apr. 12, 1926; s. Frederick Avertus and Carrie (Cronhardt) H.; m. Katherine Ann Wilkes, Feb. 9, 1957; children: Robert Wilkes, Mary Katherine, Margaret Ann, John William. Student, CCNY, 1943-44. Field rep. Moral Re-Armament, Inc., various locations, 1947-65, dir. NYC, 1965-68; portfolio mgr. U.S. Trust Co., NYC, 1969-72, asst. sec., 1972-78, asst. v.p., 1978-82, v.p., 1982-85, sr. v.p., 1985-2000. Mem. advisory bd. Uncommon Friends Found., Ft. Myers, Fla. M/sgt. U.S. Army, 1944-46, ETO. Mem. CFA Inst. (formerly Assn. Investment Mgmt. and Rsch.), N.Y. Soc. Security Analysts. Republican. Episcopalian. Avocations: stamp collecting/philately, antiquarian books, fishing.

HOGAN, STEVEN L., lawyer; b. LA, Aug. 31, 1953; s. Kenneth Carlton Hogan and Ninon Michelle Kingsley; m. Debra Karen Garshfield, June 27, 1975; children: Rebecca Sarah, Cheryl Lee. AB magna cum laude, UCLA, 1975; JD, U. So. Calif., 1978. Bar: Calif. 1978, U.S. Ct. Appeals (9th cir.) 1979,U.S. Dist. Ct. (cen. dist.) Calif. 1979, U.S. Supreme Ct. 2000, U.S. Ct. Appeals (3d cir.) 2002, U.S. Dist. Ct. (so. dist., ea. dist., no. dist.) Calif. 1985. Assoc. Anderson, McPharlin & Conners, LA, 1978-80; ptnr. Bryan Cave, LA, 1980-95; shareholder Lurie, Zepeda, Schmalz & Hogan, Beverly Hills, Calif., 1995—. Mem. Beverly Hills Estate Planning Coun. Named a Super Lawyer of So. Calif.; recipient Am. Jurisprudence award in bus. organs. and advanced constl. law. Mem. LA County Bar Assn., Order of Coif, Phi Beta Kappa, Phi Gamma Mu, Water Buffalo Club. Office: Lurie Zepeda Schmalz & Hogan 9107 Wilshire Blvd Ste 800 Beverly Hills CA 90210-5533 Office Phone: 310-274-8700. Business E-Mail: shogan@lurie-zepeda.com.

HOGAN, TERRENCE JAMES, academic administrator, consultant; b. Cleve., May 22, 1955; s. Joseph Patrick and Mary Catherine Hogan; m. Deborah Susan Haas, Feb. 18, 1955; children: Connor O'Rourke, Olivia Haas. BSc in Radio/TV, Ohio U., 1977, MA in Orgnl. Comm., 1983, PhD in Higher Edn., 1992. Dean of students Ohio U., Athens, 1998—2004, sr. assoc. v.p., dean of students, 2004—. Bd. dirs. N.Am. Interfraternal Found., Indpls. Exec. officer, mem. Athens Civitan Club, 1986—95; chair, vol. O'Bleness Hosp. Fund Dr., Athens, 2001—04; mem. Team Athens County, 1999; exec. officer, mem. HAVAR, Inc., Athens, 1985—2001, Athens Youth Hockey Assn., 1995—2001. Named Disting. Pres., Civitan Internat., 1992; grantee Internat. Student Vol. Program, Nat. Assoc for Fgn. Student Affairs, 1990, Appalachian Access, Corp. for Nat. and Cmty. Svc., 1993—96, Integrating Service-Learning, Ohio U. Found. 1804 Fund, 1993, Ohio AppalCorps AmeriCorps Program, Corp. for Nat. Svc., 1996—99, Monday Creek Restoration Project, Ohio Campus Compact, 1996, Health-Corps, Corp. for Nat. Svc., 1996, Learn and Serve Ohio U., 1997—99. Mem.: Am. Coun. on Edn., Am. Assn. for Higher Edn., Am. Coll. Pers. Assn., Nat. Assn. Student Pers. Administrators (nat. chair fraternity/sorority affairs knowledge cmty. 2002—04). Avocations: golf, basketball, youth sports. Home: 30 Elmwood Pl Athens OH 45701 Office: Ohio University 202 Baker Univ Center Athens OH 45701 Home Phone: 740-592-3582; Office Phone: 740-593-1800. Office Fax: 740-593-0223. Personal E-mail: hogan@ohio.edu.

HOGAN, THOMAS FRANCIS, federal judge; b. Washington, May 31, 1938; s. Bartholomew W. and Grace (Gloninger) H.; m. Martha Lou Wyrick, July 16, 1966; 1 son, Thomas Garth. AB, Georgetown U., 1960, JD, 1966; postgrad., George Washington U., 1960-62. Bar: Md. 1966, U.S. Dist. Ct. D.C. 1967, D.C. 1967, U.S. Ct. Appeals (D.C. cir.) 1972, U.S. Dist. Ct. Md. 1973, U.S. Supreme Ct. 1973. Law clk. to presiding judge US Dist. Ct. DC, 1966-67; counsel Nat. Commn. on Reform of Fed. Criminal Laws, Washington, 1967-68; ptnr. McCarthy & Wharton, Rockville, Md., 1968-75, Kenary, Tietz & Hogan, Rockville, 1975-81, Furey, Doolan, Abell & Hogan, Chevy Chase, Md., 1981-82; judge US Dist. Ct. DC, Washington, 1982—2001, chief judge, 2001—. Asst. prof. Potomac Sch. Law, Washington, 1977-79; adj. prof. law Georgetown Law Ctr., 1985—; mem. U.S. Jud. Conf., 2001—, mem. specialties com., 2001—. Pub. mem. Officer Evaluation Bd. U.S. Fgn. Service, 1973; chmn. Christ Child Inst. for Disturbed Children, 1975; bd. dirs. Providence Hosp., Washington, 1984-86. Recipient cert. recognition and appreciation for vol. services Montgomery County Govt., 1976; recipient cert. appreciation Christ Child Soc., 1976; St. Thomas More fellow Georgetown U. Law Ctr., 1965-66 Mem. ABA (Md. chmn. Drug Abuse Edn. Program, Young Lawyers sect. 1970-73, mem. Litigation sect.), Bar Assn. D.C. (mem. com. on D.C. cts.), Md. State Bar Assn. (Litigatin sect.), Montgomery County Bar Assn. (chmn. legal ethics com. 1973-74, lawyer referral service com. 1974-75, adminstrn. justice com. 1979-82, bd. govs. 1977-78), Nat. Inst. for Trial Advocacy Assocs., Def. Research Inst., Md. Assn. Def. Trial Counsel, Md. Trial Lawyers Assn., Georgetown U. Alumni Assn., Smithsonian Assocs., John Carroll Soc., Knights of Malta. Clubs: Barristers, Chevy Chase, Lawyers. Office Phone: 202-354-3420.

HOGAN, WILLIAM T., retired academic administrator; b. Lowell, Mass., Feb. 4, 1933; married, 1959; 3 children. BS, Northeastern U., 1955; MS, MIT, 1959; PhD in M.E., Northeastern U., 1965. Mech. engr. Gen. Electric, 1955-56; mech. design engr. Redstone Arsenal, Ala., 1956-58; sr. scientist Avco Corp., 1961-63, Lowell Technol. Inst. (now U. Lowell (Mass.), 1963—91, assoc. prof. mech. engring. to prof. and head dept. to dean engring., pres., 1981—91; chancellor U. Mass., Lowell, 1991—2006.

HOGANS, MACK L., paper company executive; BS in Forestry, U. Mich.; MS in Forest Resources, U. Wash. Forester, govt. affairs mgr. Weyerhaeuser Co., Tacoma, Wash., 1979-90, v.p. govt. affairs, 1990-95, sr. v.p. corp. affairs, 1995—. Chair Weyerhaeuser Co. Found.; bd. dirs. Wash. Coun. Internat. Trade. Bd. dirs. U. Puget Sound, Zion Preparatory Acad., Pub. Affairs Coun., Discovery Inst., Nature Conservancy. Office: Weyerhaeuser Co PO Box 9777 Federal Way WA 98063-9777

HOGE, FRANZ JOSEPH, accounting firm executive; b. NYC, Apr. 2, 1944; s. Albert and Sophie (Hutter) H.; m. Margaret Ann Hoefling, Oct. 11, 1969; children: Joanne Curoe, Susan Glennon, Daniel. BBA, CCNY, 1966. CPA, N.Y., Ohio. Staff acct. Coopers and Lybrand, NYC, 1968-70, in-charge acct., 1970-73, mgr., 1973-77, ptnr., 1977-80, mng. ptnr. Dayton, Ohio, 1980-97, Ohio unit leader, 1993-97, mid. market industry leader, 1993-97; ret., 1997. Chmn. bus. adv. bd. Wright State U., 1986-2001; chmn. bd. The Fund for Dayton Urban Children and Schs., 1997-2003; bd. dirs. Nat. Ctr. Indsl. Competitiveness, Premier Health Ptnrs., Athenaeum of Ohio; chmn. bd. Good Samaritan Hosp., 1989-99, chmn. Montgomery County Human Svc. Levy Coun., 2001—; mem. Montgomery County Homeless Solutions Policy Bd., 2006—. Co-author two audit and acctg. guides, 1978, 79. Bd. dirs. Dayton Mus. Natural History, pres. 1983-90, Dayton Opera Assn., pres. 1983-92, Maria Joseph Living Care Ctr., chmn. 1984-95; chmn. bd. dirs. NCCJ, 1999-2002, chmn., Kettering Children's Choir, 1992-2006; v.p. Assn. for Corp. Growth, Hipple Cancer Rsch. Ctr., Dayton, 1981-87, Big Bros./Big Sisters Found., Dayton, 1983-87, Dayton Performing Arts Fund, 1983-87; bd. dirs. Wright State U. Found., 1996-2001. Named Montgomery County Citizen of the Yr, 2003. Mem. Moraine Country Club. Republican. Roman Catholic. Home: 939 Laurelwood Rd Dayton OH 45419-1228 Personal E-mail: hoge939@msn.com.

HOGE, WARREN M., editor; b. NYC, Apr. 13, 1941; s. James F. Hoge and Virginia (McClamroch) Barber; m. Olivia Larisch, Nov. 21, 1981; 1 child, Nicholas; stepchildren: Christina, Tatjana. BA, Yale U., 1963; postgrad., George Washington U., 1964-65. Reporter Washington Star, 1964-66; bur. chief N.Y. Post, Washington, 1966-69, city editor, asst. mng. editor NYC, 1970-75; dep. met. editor N.Y. Times, NYC, 1976-78, fgn. corr. Rio de Janeiro, 1979-83, fgn. editor NYC, 1984-87, asst. mng. editor, 1987-90; asst. mng. editor and editor N.Y. Times Mag., NYC, 1991-92, asst. mng. editor for culture, style, book rev., and recruitment of writers, 1993-96; chief London Bur., N.Y. Times, 1996—2003; fgn. affairs corr. UN, NYC, 2004—. Baptist. Home: 325 East 57 New York NY 10022 Office: NY Times Fgn Desk 229 W 43rd New York NY 10036

HOGENSEN, MARGARET HINER, retired librarian; b. Ottawa, Kans., Oct. 11, 1920; d. Hebron Henry and Nellie Evelyn (Godard) Hiner; widowed. BA, U. Wichita, 1942; BS in Libr. Sci., U. Denver, 1945. Circulation librarian Boise Pub. Library, Idaho, 1945-49, Pomona Pub. Library, Calif., 1950-51; reference librarian WFIL-TV, Phila., 1963-69; rsch. dir. Concept Films, Washington, 1969-72; ind. researcher, cons. Greenbelt, Md., 1973-80; ret., 1996. Bd. dirs. Greenbelt Homes, Inc., 1977-93, 1998-2000, 2003-2004, pres., 1983-88, treas. 1998-2000; past bd. dirs. Greenbelt Consumer Coop., Nat. Coop. Bus. Assn.; pres. Ea. Coop. Housing Orgn., 1992-95. Mem.: Nat. Assn. Housing Coops (bd. dirs. 1986—87, 1990—94). Democrat. Christian Scientist. Home: 17769 Village Rd Springdale AR 72764

HOGG, DAVID CLARENCE, physicist; b. Vanguard, Sask., Can., Sept. 5, 1921; came to U.S., 1953, naturalized, 1964; s. Francis Sandison and Frances Katherine (Gadsby) H.; m. Jean E. MacMillan, Feb. 15, 1947; children— David Randal, Rebecca Jean. BSc, U. We. Ont., 1949; MSc, McGill U., 1951, PhD, 1953. With Bell Telephone Labs., 1953—77, head atmospheric physics rsch., 1966—72, head antenna and propagation rsch. Holmdel, NJ, 1972—77; chief environ. radiometry wave propagation lab. Environ. Rsch. Lab., NOAA, Boulder, Colo., 1977—83, chief radio meteorology wave propagation lab., 1983—86; lectr., adj. prof. U. Colo., 1984—, lectr. ECE dept, 1989—; sr. scientist Colo. Inst. Rsch. Environ. Scis., U. Colo., 1986—89. Research, numerous publs. on microwaves, optics, satellite communications and remote sensing; patentee microwave antennas; composer vocal, choral, strings and piano classical music. Served with Can. Army, 1940-45. Recipient Silver medal U.S. Dept. Commerce, 1983, Composer's award Colo. Music Educators Assn., 1992. Fellow IEEE (founder Jersey Coast sect., Disting. Achievement award 1984); mem. NAE, Union Radio Scientifique Internat., Am. Music Ctr. Episcopalian. Home: 4978 Carter Ct Boulder CO 80301-3895

HOGG, JAMES HENRY, JR., retired education educator; b. Pleasantville, Pa., Aug. 15, 1926; s. James Henry and Carrie Ethel (Swan) H.; m. Elizabeth Beatrice George, Sept. 8, 1945 (dec. Feb. 1988); children: Carolyn Elizabeth, James Henry III; m. Reva Rowene Heffernan, Jan. 1, 1992. BA, Houghton Coll., 1951; MA, Allegheny Coll., 1961; EdD, Pa. State U., 1971. Cert. secondary tchr., Pa. Tchr. English and social studies Meadville (Pa.) Sr. H.S., 1962-67; instr. in secondary edn. Pa. State U., University Park, 1968-71, asst. prof., 1971-77, assoc. prof., 1977-91; ret., 1991. Trustee Houghton Coll., 1964-67; Pa. State Adv. Bd., Mid. States Assn. Colls. and Schs., 1984-91 (chmn. evaluation teams, 1983-91). Contbr. articles to profl. jours. Councilman Cooperstown Borough, 1993-98, 2000—. With U.S. Army, 1944-46, ETO. Named participant in 2d Inst. Am History Pa. State U., 1966, Assn. Tchr. Educators LaureATE, 1989; recipient cert. of appreciation U.S. House Reps. Page Sch., 1985. Mem. Nat. Assn. Tchr. Educators, Pa. Assn. Tchr. Educators, Phi Delta Kappa, Alpha Tau. Republican. Methodist. Avocations: hunting, fishing, bowling, chess. Home: 148 Lakeview Dr Cooperstown PA 16317 E-mail: jameshg@csonline.net.

HOGG, JAMES STUART, lawyer; b. NYC, Aug. 5, 1952; s. John S. and Rosalie (Smith) H.; m. Kathleen Anne Rhoades, May 20, 1978; children: John S., Robert W., Elizabeth A. BA, Kalamazoo Coll., 1974; JD, U. Mich., 1977. Bar: N.Y. 1978, Ohio 1985. Assoc. Brown, Wood, Ivey, Mitchell & Petty, NYC, 1977-80, Carter, Ledyard & Milburn, NYC, 1980-83; sr. counsel The Standard Oil Co., Cleve., 1983-87; asst. gen. counsel GenCorp Inc., Fairlawn, Ohio, 1987-88; v.p. law GenCorp Automotive, Akron, Ohio, 1989-93; of counsel Ulmer & Berne, LLP, Cleve., 1994-96; prin. Cowden, Humphrey, Nagorney & Lovett Co., L.P.A., Cleve., 1996—. Bd. trustees Applewood Ctrs. Inc., exec. com., program planning com. chair. Mem. ABA, Cleve. Bar Assn., Ohio Bar Assn. Republican. Episcopalian. Avocations: golf, tennis. Office: Cowden Humphrey Nagorney & Lovett Co LPA 1414 Terminal Tower Cleveland OH 44113 Office Phone: 216-241-2880. E-mail: jamie@cowdenlaw.com.

HOGG, ROBERT VINCENT, JR., mathematical statistician, educator; b. Hannibal, Mo., Nov. 8, 1924; s. Robert Vincent and Isabelle Frances (Storrs) H.; m. Carolyn Joan Ladd, June 23, 1956 (dec. June 1990); children: Mary Carolyn, Barbara Jean, Allen Ladd, Robert Mason; m. Ann Burke, Oct. 15, 1994. BA, U. Ill., 1947; MS, U. Iowa, 1948, PhD, 1950. Asst. prof. math. U. Iowa, Iowa City, 1950-56, assoc. prof., 1956-62, prof., 1962-65, chmn. dept. stats., prof. stats., 1965-83, 92-93, Hanson prof. mfg. productivity, 1993-95, prof. emeritus, 2001—. Co-author: Introduction to Mathematical Statistics, 1959, 6th edit., 2005, Finite Mathematics and Calculus, 1974, Probability and Statistical Inference, 1977, 7th edit., 2005, Applied Statistics for Engineers and Physical Scientists, 1987, 2d edit., 1992, A Brief Course in Mathematical Statistics, 2007; assoc. editor Am. Stats., 1971-74; contbr. articles to profl. jours. Vestryman local Episc. ch., 1958-60, 66-68, 91-92, 2001-03. With USNR, 1943-46. Grantee NIH, 1966-68, 75-78, NSF, 1969-74; Disting. Alumni Award, U. Iowa, 2003. Fellow Inst. Math. Stats. (program sec., bd. 1968-74, Carver medal 2006), Am. Statis. Assn. (pres. Iowa sect. 1962-63, coun. 1965-66, 73-74, vis. lectr. 1965-68, 77-85, chmn. tng. sect. 1973, assoc. editor jour. 1978-80, pres.-elect 1987, pres. 1988, past pres. 1989, Founders award 1991, Noether award 2001); mem. Math. Assn. Am. (pres. Iowa sect. 1964-65, 95-96, bd. govs. 1971-74, visa. lectr. 1976-81, Outstanding Tchg. award 1993), Internat. Statis. Inst., Rotary (pres. Iowa City 1984-85), Sigma Xi (pres. Iowa dist. chpt. 1970-71), Pi Kappa Alpha. Home: 30130 Trails End Buena Vista CO 81211 Office: U Iowa Dept Statis Acturial Sci Iowa City IA 52242 E-mail: bhogg@mccoymail.net.

HOGG, VIRGINIA LEE, retired medical educator; b. Marblehead, Mass., July 30, 1938; d. Richard Caldwell and Leola Mary Jewett; m. Ronald James Hogg, July 13, 1964; children: Scott Jameson, Carol Lee. BS, Bridgewater State Coll., Mass., 1960, MEd, 1965; EdD, Boston U., Mass., 1980. Cert. health edn. specialist Nat. Commn. Health Edn. Credentialing, Inc., Pa., 1989. Tchr. Stoughton Pub. Schs., Stoughton, Mass., 1961—67; full prof. Bridgewater State Coll., 1968—97; ret., 1997. Cons. self-employed (Platinum Resources), Naples, Fla., 1999—2003. Legal advocacy chair AAUW, Naples, 2004—06. Recipient Honor award, Mass. Assn. Health, Phys. Edn. and Recreation, 1982, Profl. Merit award, Ea. Dist. Assn. Health, Phys. Edn. and Recreation, 1985, Franklin D. Roosevelt award, March of Dimes, 1992, Profl. Leadership award, Bridgewater State Coll., 1994; Fulbright scholar-Peoples Republic China, U.S. Govt., 1990. Mem.: Am. AAHPERD, Am. Coll. Health Assn., Am. Assn. U. Women (v.p. membership 2000—02). Avocations: tennis, mentoring, event planning, travel, cooking. Home Phone: 239-642-9304.

HOGLE, ANN MEILSTRUP, painter, art educator; b. San Francisco, Sept. 23, 1927; d. Carlton Fredrick Meilstrup and Lillian (Hackney) Meilstrup Willer; m. Richard Raymond (div.); children— Timothy, Megan, Catherine; m. George H. Hogle, Aug. 29, 1966. Student U. Oreg., 1945-47, Marylhurst Coll., 1949-50; B.F.A., Calif. Coll. of Arts and Crafts, 1976, M.F.A., 1978. One-person shows include Stanford U., Calif., 1966, Palo Alto Cultural Ctr., Calif., 1976, William Sawyer Gallery, San Francisco, Butters Gallery, Portland, 1993, Menlo Pk. Libr., Menlo Pk., Calif., 1994, Smith Andersen Gallery, Palo Alto Calif., 1995, Bolinas Gallery, Bolinas, Calif., 1995, de Saisset Mus., Santa Clara, Calif., 1998, Fresno Art Mus., Fresno, Calif., 1998, Vorpal Gallery, San Francisco, 1999, Commonweal, Bolinas, Calif., 1999, John Natsoulas Gallery, Davis, Calif., 2001, guest artist Marin Agricultural Land Trust, Point Reyes Sta., Calif., 2003; exhibited in group shows at Portland Art Mus., Janus Gallery, Los Angeles, Richmond Art Ctr., William Sawyer Gallery, San Francisco, 84, Purdue U., Ind., Penninsula Mus., Monterey, Calif., 1993; represented in permanent collections Kemper Ins. Cos., St. Francis Meml. Hosp., Dysan Corp., First Interstate Bank. Portland Mus. Recipient Phelan awards exhibit Legion of Honor, 1965. Personal E-mail: ghogle711@earthlink.net. Business E-Mail: hogle@artistforum.com.

HOGLUND, FORREST EUGENE, retired petroleum company executive; b. Lawrence, Kans., July 1, 1933; s. Roy A. and Edna M. (McMichael) H.; m. Sally Sue Roney, June 19, 1956; children: Kelly M., Shelly L., Kristan K. BS in Mech. Engring, U. Kans., 1956. Registered profl. engr., Tex. With Exxon Corp., 1957-1977; v.p. ops. Exxon Corp. (Middle East), NYC, 1973-75, v.p. gas, 1976-77; pres., COO Tex. Oil and Gas, Dallas, 1977-83, pres., CEO, 1983-87; dir. USX Corp., Pitts., 1986-87; chmn., CEO EOG Resources, Houston, 1987—99, Arctic Resources, Houston, 1999—2004, SeaOne Maritime Corp., Dallas, 2004—. Former chmn. bd. visitors Univ. Cancer Found.--M.D. Anderson; former chmn. Houston Mus. Natural Sci. With C.E., U.S. Army, 1957-58. Mem. Am. Petroleum Inst., AIME, Soc. Petroleum Engrs., Ind. Petroleum Assn. Am., Tex. Ind. Producers and Royalty Assn., Petroleum Club, Dallas Country Club, River Oaks Country Club, Tau Beta Pi, Pi Tau Sigma, Sigma Tau, Omicron Delta Kappa. Office: Hoglund Interests 5910 N Central Expressway Ste 250 Dallas TX 75206 Office Phone: 214-987-4924.

HOGLUND, HEATH, lawyer; b. St. Cloud, Minn., Oct. 13, 1969; s. Wayne L. and Elizabeth M. Hoglund; m. Mercedes M. Kearns, Aug. 18, 2002. BS, U. Minn., 1992, MS, JD, U. Minn., 1997. Assoc. atty. Limbach & Limbach, L.L.P., San Francisco, 1997—99; ptnr. Hoglund & Pamias, P.S.C., San Juan, 2000—. Adj. prof. Interamerican U. Sch. Law, San Juan, 2001, Vytatus Magnus Sch. Law, Kaunas, Lithuania, 2002—05, U. PR, 2006. Recipient Outstanding Vol. Pub. Svc. award, Bar Assn. San Francisco, 1998, Wiley W. Manuel award for Pro Bono Legal Svcs., Bd. Govs. State Bar Calif., 1999. Mem.: ABA (assoc.; chair spl. com. diversion patent fees 2003—05), Assn. Puertorican Intellectual Property Profls. (pres. 2006). Office: Hoglund & Pamias PSC 256 Eleanor Roosevelt St San Juan PR 00918 Office Phone: 787-772-9200. Office Fax: 787-772-9533. Business E-Mail: heath@hhoglund.com.

HOGLUND, ROBERT N., utilities executive; BA with high honors, Univ. Va., MBA, JD, Univ. Va. Fin. mgmt. positions Merrill Lynch, Barr Devlin, Morgan Stanley; mng. dir. M&A Citigroup, NYC, 1997—2004; sr. v.p. fin. Consolidated Edison Inc., NYC, 2004—05; sr. v.p., CFO Consolidated Edison Co. of NY; CFO, controller Orange & Rockland Utilities; sr. v.p., CFO Consolidated Edison Inc., NYC, 2005—. Office: Consolidated Edison Inc 4 Irving Pl New York NY 10003*

HOGUE, TERRY GLYNN, lawyer; b. Merced, Calif., Sept. 23, 1944; s. Glynn Dale and Lillian LaVonne (Carter) H.; m. Joanne Laura Sharples, Oct. 3, 1969; children: Morgan Taylor, Whitney Shannon. BA, U. Calif., Fresno, 1966, postgrad., 1967; JD, U. Calif., San Francisco, 1972. Bar: Calif. 1972, Idaho 1975, US Dist. Ct. (ctrl. dist.) Calif. 1973, US Dist. Ct. Idaho 1975, US Supreme Ct. 1976. Assoc. Reid, Babbage & Coil, Riverside, Calif., 1972-75; pvt. practice, Hailey, Idaho, 1975-77; ptnr. Campion & Hogue, Hailey, 1977-80, Hogue & Speck, Hailey and Ketchum, Idaho, 1980-82, Hogue, Speck & Aanestad, Hailey and Ketchum, 1982-97, Hogue & Dunlap, LLP, Hailey and Ketchum, 1998—. Bd. dirs. Blaine County Med. Ctr., Hailey, 1975-91. Sgt. US Army, 1969-71. Mem. ABA, Calif. Bar Assn., Idaho Bar Assn. (hearing panel of profl. conduct bd. 1991-97, chmn. profl. conduct bd. 1994-95), 5th Jud. Dist. Bar Assn. (magistrate com. 1991-93, ethics com. 1991-93), Idaho Trial Lawyers Assn. (bd. dirs. 1982-93, treas. 1985-86, sec. 1986-87, v.p. 1988-89, pres. 1989-90), Assn. Trial Lawyers Am. (sec. coun. of pres. 1989-90, Atla Weideman Wisocki award 1990), Am. Inns. of Ct. (charter Master Bench chpt.), Hailey C. of C. (bd. dirs. 1975-83), Rotary. Home: PO Box 1259 500 Onyx Dr Ketchum ID 83340-1259 Office: Hogue & Dunlap LLP PO Box 460 Hailey ID 83333-0460 also: PO Box 538 Ketchum ID 83340-0538 Office Phone: 208-788-3567.

HOGUET, KAREN M., retail executive; m. David Hoguet; 2 children. Grad., Brown U.; MBA, Harvard U., 1980. With Boston Cons. Group, Chgo.; sr. cons. mktg. and long-range planning Macy's Inc. (formerly Federated Dept. Stores, Inc.), Cin., 1982-85; dir. capital and bus. planning Macy's Inc., Cin., 1985-87, operating v.p. planning and fin. analysis, 1987-88, corp. v.p., 1988-91, sr. v.p. planning, 1991—97, treas., 1992—97, sr. v.p., CFO, 1997—2005, exec. v.p., CFO, 2005—. Mem.: Phi Beta Kappa. Office: Macy's Inc 7 W 7th St Cincinnati OH 45202-2424 Fax: 513-579-7555.*

HOGWOOD, CHRISTOPHER JARVIS HALEY, music educator; b. Nottingham, Eng., Sept. 10, 1941; s. Haley Evelyn and Marion Constance (Higgott) Hogwood. BA, Cambridge U., Eng., 1964, MA, 1969; postgrad., Charles U., Prague, Czechoslovakia, 1964-65; DMus (hon.), Keele U., Eng., 1991. Founding mem. Early Music Consort London, 1965—76; dir. The Acad. Ancient Music, London, 1973—; music faculty Cambridge U., 1975—, hon. prof. music, 2002—. Artistic dir. Handel & Haydn Soc., Boston, 1986—2001, condr. laureate, 2001—; hon. prof. music Keele U., 1986—90; dir. music St. Paul Chamber Orch., 1987—92, prin. guest condr., 1992—98; internat. prof. early music performance Royal Acad. Music, London, 1992—; vis. prof. dept. music King's Coll., London, 1992—96; artistic dir. Summer Mozart Festival Nat. Symphony Orch. USA, 1993—2001; assoc. dir. Beethoven Academie, Antwerp, 1998—2002; prin. guest condr. Kammerorchester Basel, 2000—06, Orquesta Ciudad de Granada, 2001—04, Orch. Sinfonica di Milano Giuseppe Verdi, 2003—06. Author: (book) Music at Court, 1977, The Trio Sonata, 1979, Haydn's Visits to England, 1980, Handel, 1984; editor: Music in Eighteenth Century England, 1983, Holmes' Life of Mozart, 1991, The Keyboard in Baroque Europe, 2003. Decorated Comdr. of the Brit. Empire; named Freeman, Worshipful Co. Musicians, London, 1989, Chistopher Hogwood Historically Informed Performance Fellowship in his honor, Handel & Hadyn Soc.; recipient Wilson Cobbett medal, Worshipful Co. Musicians, London, 1986, Disting. Musician award, Inc. Soc. Musicians, 1997, Martinu medal, Bohuslav Martinu Found., Prague, 1999; Hon. fellow, Jesus Coll., Cambridge, 1989—, Pembroke Coll., Cambridge, 1992—. Home and Office: 10 Brookside Cambridge CB2 1JE England

HOHENBERGER, PATRICIA JULIE, fine arts and antique appraiser, consultant; b. Holyoke, Mass. d. Ambrose Harrington and Irene Leo (Ducharme) Reynolds; m. John H. Hohenberger, June 27, 1953; children: Lisa Maria, Julie Suzanne, John Henry, James Reynolds, Patricia Antonia. BA in English, Coll. New Rochelle, NY, 1950; MA in Folk Art Studies, NYU, 1983. Cert. elem. edn. tchr., Mass. Tchr. Hadley (Mass.) Pub. Schs., 1950-52, Springfield (Mass.) Pub. Schs., 1952-54; owner, dir. The Brown House Nursery Sch., Williamstown, Mass., 1962-64; tchr. Coindra Hall, Huntington, N.Y., 1970-71, St. Edward the Confessor, Syosset, N.Y., 1971-81; pres. Patricia Reynolds Hohenberger Appraisals, Northport, N.Y., 1983—. Cons. O'Toole-Edwald Art Assn., Inc., N.Y., 1984-91, Alexander-Benwood Co., Inc., Huntington, N.Y., 1991—; lectr. Symposium-Gen. Accident Ins., N.Y., 1994. Author: (monograph) Gentle Reminders of the Past, 1984. Recipient Recognition for Achievement award Alexander-Benwood Co., Inc., Huntington, N.Y., 1995. Mem. Nat. Trust for Historic Preservation, Nat. Mus. Women in the Arts (charter), New England Appraisers Assn. Roman Catholic. Avocations: collecting American decorative arts and antiques, photography. Home: 72 Burt Ave Northport NY 11768-2046 E-mail: prhohen@aol.com.

HOHENDAHL, PETER UWE, German language and literature educator; b. Hamburg, Germany, Mar. 17, 1936; came to U.S., 1964; s. Wilhelm and Emilie (Uelschen) H.; m. Iky Maria Zoetelief, July 2, 1965; children: Deborah, Gwendolyn. Student, U. Bern, Switzerland, 1955, U. Hamburg, 1955-57, 59-63, PhD, 1964; postgrad., U. Goettingen, Fed. Republic Germany, 1958. Asst. prof. Pa. State U., 1965-68; assoc. prof. Washington U., St. Louis, 1968-69, prof., 1970-77, head dept., 1972-77; prof. comparative and German lit. Cornell U., Ithaca, NY, 1977—, chmn. dept. German, 1981-86, Schurman prof. German and Comparative lit., 1985—, dir. Inst. for German Cultural Studies, 1992—2007. Merton vis. prof. Berlin U., 1976; disting. vis. prof. Ohio State U., 1987; supr. Studien zur Literatur des 19, Jahrhunderts, 1993, sr. fellow Am. Inst. Contemporary German Studies, Washington, 2000, corr. fellow Inst. Germanic Studies, U. London-Sch. Advanced Study, London, 2001-; Passagen, Festschrift fuer Peter Uwe Hohendahl zum 65. Geburtstag, Weidler Buchverlag, Berlin, Germany, 2001, Am. Acad. Arts and Scis., 2003. Author: Literaturkritik und Oeffentlichkeit, 1974, Der Europaeische Roman der Empfindsamkeit, 1977, The Institution of Criticism, 1982, Literarische Kultur im Zeitalter des Liberalismus, 1985, A History of German Literary Criticism, 1988, Building a National Literature, 1989, Reappraisals: Shifting Alignments in Postwar Critical Theory, 1991, Heinrich Heine and the Occident: Multiple Identities, Multiple Receptions, 1991, Geschichte, Opposition, Subversion, Studien zur Literatur des 19, Jahrhunderts, 1993, Prismatic Thought: Theodor W. Adorno, 1995, (with R.A. Berman, K. Kenkel and A. Strum) Oeffentlichkeit: Geschichte eines kritischen Begriffs, 2000, others; mem. editl. bd. Studies in 20th Century Lit., 1979—, German Quar., 1983-88. Recipient Humboldt Rsch. prize for fgn. humanists, 2005; fellow Harvard U., 1964-65, fellow Ctr. for Interdisciplinary Rsch., Bielefeld, 1981, 87, Guggenheim Found., 1983-84. Mem. MLA, Am. Assn. Tchrs. German, N.Am. Heine Soc. (exec. coun. 1982—, pres. 1986-90), Zeitschrift fuer Germanistik (bd. dir. 1990-2001). Home: 81 Genung Rd Ithaca NY 14850-9602 Office: Cornell U Dept of German Studies Ithaca NY 14853 E-mail: puh1@cornell.edu.

HOHLT, RICHARD FREDERICK, lobbyist; b. Indpls., Dec. 4, 1947; s. Edgar F. and Mabel F. Hohlt; m. Deborah Lee Messick, Sept. 25, 1993. BS, Milliken U., 1970. Internal auditor, systems analyst, Indpls.; asst. to treasurer Marion County, Indpls.; asst. to Mayor Richard G. Lugar City of Indpls., 1975—76; dep. campaign mgr. Richard Lugar for Senate Com., 1976—77; exec. asst. to US Senator Richard G. Lugar US Senate, 1977—80; asst. v.p., govt. affairs US League Savings Institutions, 1980—82, v.p., govt. affairs, 1982—84, sr. v.p., govt. affairs; pres. Hohlt & Co. Served in USAF Res., 1970—76. Mem.: Off The Record Club.*

HOHMANN, JAMES E., insurance company executive; b. Jan. 3, 1956; BA, Northwestern Univ.; MBA, Univ. Chgo. Mng. ptnr. Tillinghast life ins. practice Towers Perrin, Chgo.; pres. fin. institutions Zurich Kemper Life; pres., CEO XL Life & Annuity, 2001—04; exec. v.p., chief adminstrv. officer Conseco Inc., Carmel, Ind., 2004—06, interim CEO, 2006, pres., COO, 2006; pres. Allstate Fin. Allstate Corp., Northbrook, Ill., 2007—. Fellow: Soc. Actuaries; mem.: Am. Acad. Actuaries. Office: Allstate Corp 2775 Sanders Rd Northbrook IL 60062*

HOHN, ARNO R., pediatric cardiologist; b. Paterson, NJ, Aug. 4, 1931; MD, NY Med. Coll., 1956. Cert. Am. Bd. Pediatrics, Am. Bd. Pediatrics, Pediatric Cardiology. Intern, pediatric cardiology Roosevelt Hosp., NYC, 1956—57; resident, pediatric cardiology Children's Hosp., Buffalo, 1957—58, fellow, pediatric cardiology, 1958—59, 1962—63, asst. chief resident, pediatric cardiology Phila., 1961—62; past head, divsn. pediatric cardiology Med. U. SC; cardiologist, clin. affiliate Children's Hosp., LA, former head, divsn. cardiology; clin. affiliate LA County and U. So. Calif. Med. Ctr.; prof. pediatrics U. So. Calif. Sch. Medicine. Mem.: Calif. Soc. Pediatric Cardiology, Southwestern Pediatric Soc., Am. Pediatric Soc., Am. Coll. Cardiology, Am. Heart Assn., Am. Acad. Pediatrics. Office: Childrens Hosp LA Divsn Cardiology 4650 Sunset Blvd M/S #34 Los Angeles CA 90027 Office Phone: 323-669-2535. Office Fax: 323-671-1513. Business E-Mail: ahohn@chla.usc.edu.*

HOHN, DAVID, physician; b. Tucson, 1942; BS cum laude, U. Ill., 1964, MD, 1970. Intern Rush-Presbyn. St. Luke's Hosp., Chgo., 1970—71; resident in gen. surgery U. Calif., San Francisco, 1971—78, asst. prof. surgery, 1978—84, assoc. prof. surgery, 1984—87, U. Tex. Med. Sch., M.D. Anderson Cancer Ctr., 1987—90; prof. surgery U. Tex. Med. Sch., 1990—97; v.p. patient care M.D. Anderson Cancer Ctr.-U. Tex., Houston, 1993—97; pres., CEO Roswell Park Cancer Inst., 1997—. Deans coun. Univ. Buffalo Sch. Med. Mem.: Soc. of Surg. Oncology, Surg. Infection Soc., Surg. Infection Soc., Am. Assn. for Cancer Rsch., Am. Soc. for Clin. Oncology, Am. Fedn. for Clin. Rsch., Am. Coll. Physician Execs., Assn. for Acad. Surgery. Office: Roswell Park Cancer Inst Elm And Carlton St Buffalo NY 14263-0001

HOHN, HARRY GEORGE, retired insurance company executive, lawyer; b. NYC, Mar. 1, 1932; s. Harry George and Violia (Meehan) H.; m. Janet Jean LaRosa, June 19, 1954; children: Cynthia, Jennifer, Nancy, Patricia. BS, NYU, 1953, LLM, 1959; JD, Fordham U., 1956. Bar: N.Y. 1956, U.S. Supreme Ct. 1976. With N.Y. Life Ins. Co., NYC, 1956-2000, sr. v.p., gen. counsel, 1977-82, exec. v.p., gen. counsel, 1982-83, exec. v.p., 1983-86, CEO, 1990-97, also chmn. bd. dirs., past vice chmn. bd. dirs., 1997—, ret. chmn., CEO, 1997. Bd. dirs. Life and Health Ins. Med. Rsch. Fund, Million Dollar Roundtable Found.; chmn. bd. dirs. Life Ins. Coun. N.Y.; past chmn. Am. Coun. Life Ins.; mem. internat. adv. bd. Credit Comml. de France; trustee Mainstay Funds. Editor: Fordham Law Rev, 1955-56. Trustee Am. Coll., Com. Econ. Devel.; trustee emeritus Found. Ind. Higher Edn.; chmn., bd. trustees Nat. AIDS Fund; bd. govs. United Way of Tri-State; mem. adv. bd. North Fork Environ. Coun., Bowery Mission; chmn. bd. advisors Resurrection Sch. in Harlem, N.Y.C. Fellow Am. Bar Found. (life); mem. Assn. Life Ins. Counsel (bd. govs.), Bus. Roundtable. Republican. Roman Catholic. Office: NY Life Ins Co 51 Madison Ave New York NY 10010-5077 Office Phone: 212-576-5077. Personal E-mail: hghnf@aol.com.

HOHNER, KENNETH DWAYNE, retired fodder company executive; b. St. John, Kans., June 24, 1934; s. Courtney Clinton and Mildred Lucile (Forrester) H.; m. Sherry Eloi Anice Edens, Feb. 14, 1961; children: Katrina, Melissa, Steven, Michael. BS in Geol. Engring., U. Kans., 1957. Geophysicist Mobil Oil Corp., New Orleans, Anchorage, Denver, 1957-72; sr. geophysicist Amerada Hess Corp., Houston, 1972-75, ARAMCO, London, 1975-79; far east area geophysicist Hamilton Bros., Denver, 1979-83; owner Hohner Poultry Farm, Erie, Colo., 1979-94; pres. Hohner Custom Feed, Inc., Erie, Colo., 1982-94, ret., 1994. Fin. sec., mem. ch. bd. Valley Heights Christian Ch., Thornton, Colo., 2003—05. Mem.: Soc. Exploration Geophysicists. Home: 1201 W Thornton Pkwy Lot 390 Denver CO 80260-5424 Personal E-mail: kenho@usa.com.

HOHNHORST, JOHN CHARLES, judge; b. Jerome, Idaho, Dec. 25, 1952; m. Raelene Casper; children: Jennifer, Rachel, John. BS in Polit. Sci./Pub. Adminstrn., U. Idaho, 1975, JD cum laude, 1978. Bar: Idaho 1978, U.S. Dist. Ct. Idaho 1978, U.S. Ct. Appeals (9th cir.) 1980, U.S. Ct. Claims 1983, U.S. Supreme Ct. 1987. Adminstrv. asst. to Sen. John M. Barker Idaho State Senate, 1975; ptnr. Hepworth, Lezamiz & Hohnhorst, Twin Falls, Idaho, 1978—2001; dist. judge 5th Jud. Dist. Ct., Twin Falls County, Idaho, 2001—. Contbr. articles to profl. jours. Mem. planning & zoning comm. City of Twin Falls, 1987-90. Mem. ABA, ATLA, Idaho State Bar (commr. 1990-93, pres. 1993), Am. Coll. Trial Lawyers, Idaho Trial Lawyers Assn. (regional dir. 1985-86), 5th Dist. Bar Assn. (treas. 1987-88, v.p. 1988-89, pres. 1989-90), Am. Acad. Appellate Lawyers,

Greater Twin Falls C. of C. (chmn. magic valley leadership program 1988-89, bd. dirs. 1989-92), Phi Kappa Tau (Beta Gamma chpt., Phi award 1988). Office: Theron Ward Jud Bldg 427 Shoshone St N PO Box 126 427 Twin Falls ID 83303-0126 Office Phone: 208-736-4047.

HOI, SAMUEL CHUEN-TSUNG, academic administrator; b. Hong Kong, Mar. 25, 1958; came to U.S., 1975; JD, Columbia U. Bar: N.Y. 1983. Dir.-Paris Campus Parsons Sch. Design, 1988—91; dean Corcoran Coll. Art & Design, Washington, 1991—2000; pres. Otis Coll. Art & Design, LA, 2000—. Mem., bd. dirs. Leadership Washington, 1996. Mem. Assn. Ind. Colls. of Art and Design, Nat. Assn. Schs. Art and Design (bd. dirs.). Office: Office of the President Otis Coll Art & Design 9045 Lincoln Blvd Los Angeles CA 90045*

HOIBY, LEE, composer, concert pianist; b. Madison, Wis., Feb. 17, 1926; s. Henry Bjorn and Violet Ethel (Smith) H. MusB, U. Wis., 1947; MA, Mills Coll., Oakland, Calif., 1952; cert., Curtis Inst., Phila., 1952; DFA (hon.), Simpson Coll., Indianola, Iowa, 1985. Composer (operas) The Scarf, 1955, Piano Concerto 1, 1957, A Month in the Country, 1964, Summer and Smoke, 1970, Something New for the Zoo, 1979, The Italian Lesson, 1980, The Tempest, 1985, This Is the Rill Speaking, 1992, (ballet) After Eden, 1967, (cantatas) Hymn of the Nativity, 1960, For You O Democracy, 1993, (oratorio) Galileo Galilei, 1975, Piano Concerto 2, 1979, (baritone and orch.) The Tides of Sleep, 1960, I Have A Dream, 1988, Serenade for Violin and Orch., 1987, Flute Concerto, 1994, (opera) Romeo and Juliet, 2003, (organ and chorus) Song of Songs, 2004, also chamber, choral, vocal, theatre music. Recipient Am. Acad. Arts and Letters award, 1957; fellow Fulbright Found., 1952, Guggenheim Found., 1958, Nat. Endowment for the Arts, 1980, Rockefeller Found. grantee, 1979. Mem. ASCAP, Am. Guild Organists (hon.) Home: 9807 County Hwy 28 Long Eddy NY 12760 Office Phone: 845-887-4321. E-mail: aquarius@pronetisp.net.

HOIDAL, DAVID, health facility administrator; B in Psychology, U. Nebr.; M in Health Adminstrn., U. Mo., Columbia. With HCA Penninsula Hosp., Hampton, Va., 1985, CEO, 1989—93, HCA DePaul Hosp., New Orleans, 1993—97; sr. v.p. COO Tulane U. Hosp. and Clinic, New Orleans, 1997—2000; exec. dir. The Kirklin Clinic UAB, Birmingham, Ala., 2000—02; pres. Callahan Eye Found. Hosp. UAB Health Sys., Birmingham, 2002; CEO U. Ala. Hosp. UAB Health Sys., 2004—. Office: Univ Ala Hosp at Birmingham 619 19th St S Birmingham AL 35249

HOIE, ERIC B., pharmacist, educator; b. Davenport, Iowa, Oct. 23, 1957; s. John M. and Leocadia S. Hoie; m. Anisa J. Lerum, May 13, 1987. BS in Biology, Creighton U., Omaha, 1980; Pharm.D, U. Nebr., Omaha, 1987. Asst. prof. pharmacy practice U. Nebr. Med. Ctr., Omaha, 1990—2003; assoc. prof. Creighton U., Omaha, 2003—. V.p. Childrens' Cancer Camps Nebr., Omaha, 1996. Office: Creighton U 2500 California Plz Omaha NE 68178 Office Phone: 402-280-3795. Business E-Mail: ehoie@creighton.edu.

HOINES, DAVID ALAN, lawyer; b. St. Paul, Oct. 18, 1946; s. Arnold H. and Patricia (Olson) H.; m. Bonnie K. Smith, June 4, 1983. BA, Calif. State U., San Jose, 1969; JD, Santa Clara U., 1972; LLM in Taxation, Boston U., 1973. Bar: Fla. 1975, Calif. 1975, NY 1999, U.S. Dist. Ct. (so. dist.) Fla. 1975, U.S. Dist. Ct. (no. dist.) Calif. 1980, U.S. Dist. Ct. (mid. dist.) Fla. 1984, U.S. Dist. Ct. (ctrl. dist.) Calif. 1990, U.S. Ct. Claims 1980, U.S. Tax Ct. 1975, U.S. Ct. Appeals (fed. cir.) 1990, U.S. Ct. Appeals (4th cir.) 1985, U.S. Ct. Appeals (5th cir.) 1978, U.S. Ct. Appeals (9th cir.) 1980, U.S. Ct. Appeals (11th cir.) 1981, U.S. Supreme Ct. 1980; cert. specialist civil trial lawyer Fla. Bar, 1991. Pvt. practice, Ft. Lauderdale, Fla., 1975—. Adj. instr. Nova U. Ctr. for Study of Law, 1977. Author: Taxman and the Textbook, The Ripon Forum, 1972. Mem. ABA, ATLA., Broward County Bar Assn., State Bar Fla., State Bar Calif., State Bar of N.Y., Hundred Club of Broward County, Tau Delta Phi. Avocations: ocean diving (free and scuba), snowskiing, boating, reading. Office: 3081 E Commercial Blvd 200A Fort Lauderdale FL 33308 Office Phone: 954-772-2444. Personal E-mail: dahfl@aol.com.

HOISINGTON, STEVEN H., industrial engineer; b. Aberdeen, Md., Dec. 3, 1953; s. Beverly Ann and James Ellis Hoisington; 1 child, Lenny James. AA in Mech. Engrng. Tech., Rochester C.C., 1976; BS in Indsl. Engrng., U. Wis., Menomonie, 1978; MBA, Winona State U., 1984. Cert. mech. engrng. tech., Minn., Six Sigma Black Belt, Wis. From engr. to dir. quality and customer satisfaction IBM, Rochester, Minn., 1979—99; v.p. quality Johnson Controls, Inc., Milw., 1999—2005; sr. v.p. ops. Exel, Bracknell, England, 2005—06; v.p. quality and reliability Electro-Motive Diesels, Inc., LaGrange, Ill., 2006—. Co-author: Six Sigma in Corporate Real Estate, 2003, Six Sigma in Healthcare, 2003, Learn to Talk Money - The Economic Case for Quality, 2005, Loyalty Elephant, Customer Center Six Sigma: Linking Customers, Process Improvement, and Financial Results, 2001, China, 2003, Russia, 2004, Implementing Strategic Change: Tools to Transform an Organization, 2005 (India), 2006 (US); contbr. chapters to books, articles to profl. jours. Malcolm Baldrige Nat. Quality award examiner US Dept. Commerce, Nat. Inst. Sci. and Tech., Gaithersburg, Md., 1993—; chmn. bd. dirs. Wis. Forward (Quality) Award, Madison, 1999—. Mem.: Inst. Indsl. Engrs. (v.p.), Am. Soc. for Quality (cert. mgr.), Am. Legion, VFW (life; chaplain). Achievements include patents for minimum contamination during mfr. of disk drives. Office: Electro-Motive Diesels Inc 9301 W 55th St La Grange IL 60525 Business E-Mail: steve.hoisington@emdiesels.com.

HOIVIK, THOMAS HARRY, military educator, international consultant; b. Mpls., June 6, 1941; s. Tony Horace and Helen Lenea (Carlsen) H.; m. Judith Lisa Kohn; children: Todd, Gregory. BA, U. Minn., 1963; grad. with distinction, Naval Test Pilot Sch., 1969; MS with distinction, Naval Postgrad. Sch., 1973; grad. with distinction, Naval War Coll., 1976; MA, Salve Regina U., 1988. Cert. exptl. test pilot, air transport pilot, jet aircraft, helicopter, glider single and multi-engine. Commd. ensign USN, 1963, advanced through grades to capt., 1963-91; test pilot Naval Air Test Ctr., Patuxent River, Md., 1968-71; program mgr. H-53 aircraft Naval Air Systems Command, Washington, 1976-78; comdg. officer Helicopter Mine Countermeasure Squadron 14, Norfolk, Va., 1978-80; dir. U.S. Naval Test Pilot Sch., Patuxent River, 1980-82; fed. exec. fellow Ctr. for Strategic and Internat. Studies, Washington, 1982-83; chair tactical analysis Naval Postgrad. Sch., Monterey, Calif., 1983-85; comdg. officer Naval Air Sta., Willow Grove, Pa., 1985-87; chair applied systems analysis Naval Postgrad. Sch., Monterey, 1987-91, prof. acquisition mgmt. and ops. rsch., 1991—; ret. capt. USN, 1991; dir. test and evaluation sr. level curriculum Defense Acquisition U., 1993—. Mem. U.S. Congrl. Study Group on Nat. Strategy, Washington, 1982-83, World Economy, 1982-83; cons. U.S., Internat. Govt. Orgns., 1990—; founder, pres. Lysonics Rsch. Internat., 1993, Inst. for In-Flight Rsch., 1996; flight demonstration pilot Paris Internat. Air Show, 1967 Contbr. articles to profl. jours. Bd. dirs. Vocat. Edn. Bd., Montgomery County, Pa., 1985-87, Congrl. Svc. Acad. Appointment Bd., Phila., 1985-87; youth leader, counselor YMCA, St. Paul, 1955-61. Recipient Legion of Merit Pres. of U.S., 1987, Outstanding Youth Leadership award YMCA, 1960; established U.S. Helicopter Speed Record, 1966. Mem. AIAA, Soc. of Exptl. Test Pilots, Internat. Test and Evaluation Assn. (Internat. Test and Evaluation Cross award 1997), Nat. Contract Mgmt. Assn., Ops. Rsch. Soc. Am., Mil. Ops. Rsch. Soc., U. Minn. "M" Club, Disable Am. Vets, Sigma Alpha Epsilon. Avocations: tennis, music composition. Office: Naval Postgrad Sch Monterey CA 93943

HOJAHMAT, MARHABA, research scientist; b. 1966; d. Hojahmat Yusup and Rehima Yusup; 1 child, Yifutehaer Nijiati. M in engrng., Tokyo U. Sci., 1997, PhD, 2000. Post-doctoral rschr. U. Ky., Lexington, 2000—02, rsch. assoc., 2002; rsch. scientist Yaupon Therapeutics Inc., Lexington, 2002—. Contbr. articles to profl. jours. Japanese Govt. scholarship, Ministry of Edn., Sci. and Culture of Japan, 1996—2000, ITOCHU award, ITOCHU Co., Japan, 1995, STTR, NIH, 2002. Mem.: Soc. Silicon Chemistry, Japan, Chem. Soc. Japan, Am. Chem. Soc., Am. Assn. Pharm. Scientists. Home: 175 Malabu Dr Apt 33 Lexington KY 40503 Office: Yaupon Therapeutics Inc Univ Ky A169 ASTeCC Bldg Lexington KY 40506 Office Phone: 859-257-2300. Office Fax: 859-257-2489. E-mail: mhoja2@uky.edu.

HOJNOWSKI, JULES AUSTIN, entrepreneur; b. Elmira, NY, Nov. 3, 1959; m. Michael Q. Hojnowski, Sept. 4, 1994. BS, Elmira Coll., 1985, MS, 2001. Profl. spinner of exotic fibers, 2000—. Author: Mark Twain's Three Medieval Books Made into Curriculums with the Use of Multiple Intelligences and Activities, 2005; contbr. articles to profl. jours. Mem.: So. Atlantic MLA (corr.; spkr. 2002, 2006), Elmira, Mark Twain Soc. (assoc.; student asst. 1982—2000), Mark Twain Boyhood Assn. (assoc.), Mark Twain Forum (corr.), Mark Twain Club (assoc.; pres. 1976—77). Home: 1690 Trumansburg Rd Ithaca NY 14850-9213 Personal E-mail: jah@twcny.rr.com.

HOKBORG, SVEN-OLOF, military officer; b. Karlstad, Sweden, May 24, 1941; came to U.S., 1969; m. Ingalill Hokborg. M Aero. Engrng., Royal Inst. Tech., Stockholm, 1965; MBA, U. Stockholm, 1969; M Sys. Mgmt., U. So. Calif., 1972. Commd. lt. Swedish Air Force, 1965, advanced through grades to maj. gen., 1988, lectr. aeronautics Air Force Acad. Uppsala, Sweden, 1965, vice tech. dir. fighter wing F12 Kalmar, Sweden, 1965-69; with sys. planning divsn. Air Materiel Dept., Stockholm, 1969; asst. air attaché Royal Swedish Embassy, Washington, 1970-73; chief flight safety materiel sect. Air Materiel Dept., Stockholm, 1973-74, dir. planning directorate, 1979-80, comdr. Air Force Material Command, 1989-93; chief project mgmt. group New Attack A/C for Air Force, 1974-79; dir. Aircraft Directorate, 1980-89; def. and air attaché Def. Coop. Sweden-US Embassy, Sweden, 1994-98; chmn. SAAB Nyge Aero Corp, 2000—03, chmn., CEO, 2003—, SAAB Techs., Inc., 2003—. Expert Def. Dept. Commn. for Accident Investigations. Author tech. textbooks in field; contbr. articles to profl. jours. Bd. dirs. Swedish Aviation History; chmn. Swedish-Am. C. of C., Washington, DC. Hon. fellow Am.-Scandinavian Found., NY, 1969-70; recipient Thulin Gold medal for Aero. Achievement, 1995, Program Mgr. of Yr., Swedish Acad. Projects, 1998, Legion of Merit, 1999. Mem. Royal Acad. Mil. Scis., Aero. Rsch. Inst. Sweden (former vice chmn. bd. dirs.), Swedish Soc. Aero. and Astronautics (pres. 1983-86). Office: Saab Techs Inc One Crystal Pk 2011 Crystal Dr Ste 903 Arlington VA 22202 Office Fax: 703-302-5630. Business E-Mail: svenolof.hokborg@saabtechnologiesinc.com.

HOKE, SHEILA WILDER, retired librarian; b. Greensboro, NC; d. Herbert Bruce Wilder and Virginia Dare (Caylor) Wilder-Dell; m. Robert Edward Hoke, Nov. 22, 1958 (dec.); children: Raymond Fellow, Philip Wilder. Student, Montclair Coll., 1948; BA in History, U. Kans., 1950, postgrad., 1951, BS in Edn., 1952; postgrad., John Hopkins U., 1955; MLS, U. Wis., 1955; MS in Edn., Southwestern Okla. State U., 1977; postgrad., Johns Hopkins U., Montclair State Coll. Tchr. history Fredonia (Kans.) High Sch., 1952-54; student asst. U. Wis., Madison, 1954-55; children's libr. BR Enoch Pratt Libr., Balt., 1955-58; libr. dir. U.S. Army Spl. Svcs., Bavaria, Fed. Republic Germany, 1958-59; libr. U.S. Army Dependent Schs., Straubing, Fed. Republic Germany, 1959-60; cataloger Southwestern Okla. State U. Libr., Weatherford, 1963-69, libr. dir., 1969-93; ret., 1993. Mem. spl. projects com. Okla. Dept. Edn., 1974, adv. com. Okla. State Regents Libr., 1975-77. Mem. Okla. State Regents for Higher Edn. Libr. Networking, 1989-93; mem. sr. citizens choir 1st Bapt. Ch., Weatherford; vol. with children Agape Med. Clinic; reading tutor to 1st grade student Weatherford Pub. Schs.; vol. helper for home-bound; active sr. citizens groups. Mem. AAUW (pres., state bd. dirs. 1980, Weatherford br. 1981-83), Nat. Assn. Ret. Fed. Employees, Okla. Libr. Assn. (chmn. tech. svcs. divsn. 1969-70, chmn. coll. and univ. divsn. 1972-73, chmn. adminstrs. workshop 1973, chmn. libr. edn. divsn. 1975-76, chmn. recruitment com. 1978, archives com. 1980), Okla. Ret. Tchrs. Assn., Weatherford C. of C. (edn. com. 1974-75, cert. meritorious achievement from Gov. Nigh 1985), Custer County Hist. Soc., western Okla. Hist. Soc., Higher Edn. Alumni Coun. Okla., Delta Kappa Gamma (pres. Lambda chpt. 1980-82), Phi Alpha theta, Kappa Kappa Iota (pres. Lambda chpt. 1984-85, 2005-06). Republican. Baptist. Avocation: travel. E-mail: shoke@itlnet.net.

HOKENSTAD, MERL CLIFFORD, JR., social work educator; b. Norfolk, Nebr., July 21, 1936; s. Merl Clifford and Flora Diane (Christian) H.; m. Dorothy Jean Tarrell, June 24, 1962; children: Alene Ann, Laura Rae, Marta Lynn. BA summa cum laude, Augustana Coll., 1958; Rotary Found. fellow, Durham U., Eng., 1958-59; MSW., Columbia U., 1962; PhD, Brandeis U., 1969, Inst. Ednl. Mgmt., Harvard U., 1977. With Lower East Side Neighborhood Assn., NYC, 1962-64; community planning assoc. United Community Services, Sioux Falls, SD, 1964-66; instr. Augustana Coll., Sioux Falls, 1964-66; research assoc. Ford Found. Project on Community Planning for Elderly, Brandeis U., Waltham, Mass., 1966-67; prof., dir. Sch. Social Work, Western Mich. U., Kalamazoo, 1968-74; prof., dean Sch. Applied Social Scis., Case Western Res. U., Cleve., 1974-83, Ralph and Dorothy Schmitt prof., 1983—, chmn. PhD program, 1990-94; prof. internat. health Sch. of Medicine, 1994—. Vis. prof. Inst. Sociology, Stockholm U., 1978, Fulbright lectr., 1980; vis. prof. Nat. Inst. Social Work, London, 1981, Sch. Social Work, Stockholm U., 1982-86, Eotvos Lorand U., Budapest, Hungary, 1992, 95, 96, London Sch. Econs., 1994; Fulbright rsch. scholar Inst. Applied Social Rsch., Oslo, 1989; fellow U. Canterbury, Christchurch, New Zealand, 1994; mem. UN tech. com. World Assembly on Aging, 2000-02; mem. U.S. delegation UN World Assembly on Aging, 2002. Author: Participation in Teaching and Learning: An Idea Book for Social Work Educators; editor: Meeting Human Needs: An International Annual, Vol. V, Linking Health Care and Social Services: International Perspectives; editor-in-chief Internat. Social Work Jour., 1985-87; co-editor: Profiles in Internat. Social Work, 1992, Issues in International Social Work, 1997, Models of International Exchange, 2003, Lessons from Abroad: International Social Welfare Innovations, 2004; (internat. issue) Jour. Gerontol. Social Work, 1988, Jour. Sociology and Social Welfare, 1990, Jour. Social Policy and Administration, 1993, Jour. Aging Internat., 1994, Jour. Applied Social Scis., 1996; contbr. articles to profl. jours., chpts. to books. Mem. alcohol tng. rev. com. Nat. Inst. Alcoholism and Alcohol Abuse, 1974-78; workshop leader Am. Assn. State Colls. and Univs., 1974; chmn. U.S. com. XVIII Internat. Congress Schs. Social Work, 1976; chmn. Kalamazoo County Cmty. Mental Health Svcs. Bd., 1971, vice chmn., 1972; mem. edn. and tng. task force Mich. Office Drug Abuse and Alcoholism, 1972-73; mem. Mich. Assn. Mental Health Bds., 1972; bd. dirs. Cleve. United Way Svcs., 1982-84, del. assembly, 1974-82, mem. periodic rev. oversight com., 1982, mem. leadership devel. com., 1978, cmty. resources com., 1988—; bd. dirs. Kalamazoo United Way, 1968-72; trustee Cleve. Internat. Program for Youth Workers and Social Workers, chmn. program com., 1985-87; mem. program devel. com. Cleve. Center on Alcoholism, 1976; trustee Alcoholism Services Cleve., Inc., 1977-86, v.p., 1982-85; trustee Cmty. Info./Vol. Action Ctr., 1982-88, chmn. leadership devel. com., 1984-86, chmn. unmet needs com., 1986-88, exec. com., 1985-88, v.p., 1986-88; exec. com. Western Reserve Geriatric Edn. Ctr., 1995-2006; mem. adv. com. Coun. for Internat. Exch. Scholars, 1991-93, Ctr. for Cmty. Solutions Coun. on Older Persons, 1991—, vice chmn., 2005-06, chmn. 2006—, chmn. caregiver support program initiative, 1995-96; mem. adv. coun. Cuyahoga County Dept. Sr. and Adult Svcs., 1998—2003, chair, 2001—03; bd. dirs. Western Res. Area Agy. on Aging, 2004—; mem. task force of social transition in Soviet Union, US State Dept. Bur. Human Rights and Humanitarian Affairs; mem. UN NGO Com. on Aging, 1996—; co-chmn. US Com. for Internat. Yr. of Older Persons, 1999. Named Outstanding Alumnus, Augustana Coll., 1980, Ohio Soc. Worker of the Yr., 1992, Columbia U. Sch. Social Work Hall of Fame, 2006; Fulbright Research fellow; NIMH trainee, 1960-62; Vocat. Rehab. trainee, 1966; Gerontology trainee, 1967; Rotary Found. fellow, 1958-59; recipient Golden Achievement Award, Golden Age Ctr., 2003. Mem. NASW (internat. com. 1989-93, chmn. 1992-93, found. pioneer 2003—, Internat. Rhoda G. Sarnat award 2006), Acad. Cert. Social Workers, Internat. Assn. Schs. Social Work (exec. bd. 1978-92, 98—, treas. 1978-86, v.p. N.Am. 1988-92, membership sec. 1996-00, Katherine Kendall award 2004), Internat. Coun. on Social Welfare (dir. U.S. com. 1982-92), Coun. on Social Work Edn. (del. 1972-75, 77-83, chmn. ann. program meeting 1973, chmn. com. on nat. legis. and adminstrv. policy 1975-79, nominating com. 1978-81, internat. com. 1980-86, 96-2006, chmn. com. 1982-84, dir. 1979-82, exec. com. 1986-89, pres. 1986-89, Lifetime Achievement award 2002), Nat. Conf. on Social Welfare (bd. dirs. 1978-80, chmn. sect. V program com. 1977-78), World Future Soc. (area coord. 1972-74), Fulbright Assn. (v.p. N.E. Ohio chpt. 1990-91), Nat. Coun. on Aging (bd. dirs. 1991-97, internat. com. 1991-97, pub. policy com. 1992-97). Democrat. Episcopalian. Home: 2917 Weymouth Rd Cleveland OH 44120-2234 Office: Case Western Res U 10900 Euclid Ave Cleveland OH 44106-1764 Office Phone: 216-368-2323. Business E-Mail: mch2@cwru.edu.

HOKE-SCEDROV, BONNIE CAROL, music educator, soprano; d. John Lindsay and Sylvia Hyde Hoke; m. Andre Scedrov, July 23, 1983; 1 child, Kyrill Andre Scedrov. MusB in Vocal Performance, Oberlin Coll., Ohio, 1980, BA in English, 1980; MusM in Performance, Fla. State U., Tallahassee, 1983. Tchr. voice Gwynedd Mercy Acad., Phila., 1997—. Tchr. masterclass voice Ga. State U., Atlanta, 1998, Ferris Women's Coll., Yokohama, Japan, 1999, Ferris Women's Coll., Yokohama, Japan, 2000; adj. prof. Rowan U., Glassboro, NJ, 2001—02; sr. fellow music U. Pa., Phila., 2001—; lectr. Keio U., Tokyo, 1997, Tokyo, 2004. Singer: (albums) A Lover's Promise: Songs of Johannes Brahms, 2002, (Operas) Vienna Chamber Opera, 1992, Pensacola Opera, 1998, Gulf Coast Opera, 1998, Natchez Opera, 1992, Ash Lawn-Highland Opera, 1994, Aspen Opera Theater, 1990, Bravo!Colorado Festival, 1990, Syracuse Symphony, 1990, various recitals in Washington, Princeton, NY, and Tokyo; contbr. chapters to books. Soprano soloist Child Awareness Program Poland, Washington, 1999; mem. Song as Second Lang. Ednl. Programs, Phila., 2004—. Recipient Top prize, Fifth Internat. Mozart Competition, Salzburg, Austria, 1991, Second prize, Opera Columbus Competition, Columbus, Ohio, 1991; fellow, Aspen Opera Theater, Colo., 1990, Académie Musicale de Villecroze, Provence, France, 1999. Mem.: Nat. Assn. Tchrs. Singing. Office: The Univ Pa Dept Music 201 South 34th St Philadelphia PA 19104-6313 Home Phone: 215-545-5443; Office Phone: 215-898-7544.

HOKIN, LOWELL EDWARD, biochemist, educator; b. Chgo., Sept. 20, 1924; s. Oscar E. and Helen (Manfield) H.; m. Mabel Neaverson, Dec. 1, 1952 (dec. Aug. 2003); children: Linda Ann, Catherine Esther (dec.), Samuel Arthur; m. Barbara M. Gallagher, Mar. 23, 1978 (div. July 1998); 1 child, Ian Oscar; m. Vivian Littlefield-Moore, Aug. 6, 2006. Student, U. Chgo., 1942-43, Dartmouth Coll., 1943-44, U. Louisville Sch. Medicine, 1944-46, U. Ill. Sch. Medicine, 1946-47; MD, U. Louisville, 1948; PhD, U. Sheffield, Eng., 1952. Postdoctoral fellow dept. biochemistry McGill U., 1952-54, faculty, 1954-57, asst. prof., 1955-57; mem. faculty U. Wis., Madison, 1957—, prof. physiol. chemistry, 1961-68, prof. pharmacology, 1968-99, prof., chmn. pharmacology, 1968-93, prof. emeritus, 1999—. Contbr. numerous articles to tech. jours., chpts. to numerous books on phosphoinositides, biol. transport, the pancreas, the brain and lithium in manic-depression. With USNR, 1943—45. Mem.: AAAS, N.Y. Acad. Scis., Am. Soc. Pharmacology and Exptl. Therapeutics, Biochem. Soc. (U.K.), Am. Soc. Biochemistry and Molecular Biology. Achievements include discovery of phosphoinositide signaling system. Home: 4021C Monona Dr Monona WI 53716 Office: U Wis Med Sch Dept Pharm 1300 University Ave Madison WI 53706-1510 Office Phone: 608-224-2190. Business E-Mail: lehokin@wisc.edu.

HOLABIRD, JOHN AUGUR, JR., retired architect; b. Chgo., May 9, 1920; s. John Augur and Dorothy (Hackett) H.; m. Donna Katharine Smith, Nov. 25, 1942 (div. 1969); children: Jean, Katharine, Polly, Lisa (dec.); m. Marcia Stefanie Fergestad, June 28, 1969 (dec. Mar. 1994); children: Ann, Lynn; m. Janet Nothhelfer Connor, May 7, 1996. BA, Harvard U., 1942, MArch, 1948. Archtl. designer Holabird & Root, Chgo., 1948-49, 55-64, assoc. firm, 1964-70, ptnr., 1970-87. Tchr. drama Francis Parker Sch., Chgo., 1949-55; stage designer NBC-TV, 1955 Major: archtl. works include Francis Parker Sch, Chgo., Ravinia Stage and Restaurant, Highland Park, Ill., 1970, Bell Telephone Labs, Naperville, Ill., 1975, Canal Bldg, Chgo., 1974. Pres. Park West Community Assn., 1962; dir. Lincoln Park Conservation Assn., 1960-64, Corlands, 1979-85; mem. Chgo. Commn. on Historic and Archtl. Landmarks, 1981-85; bd. dirs. Lincoln Park Community Conservation, 1964; trustee Francis Parker Sch., Ravinia Festival Assn., Ill. Inst. Tech., 1980-86. Served with U.S. Army, 1942-45. Decorated Silver Star, Bronze Star; Fourragère (Belgium); Order of William (The Netherlands). Fellow AIA (pres. Chgo. chpt. 1977-78); mem. Tavern Club, Harvard Club (dir. 1974-78), Phi Beta Kappa. Democrat. Home: 200 E Pearson St Apt 3W Chicago IL 60611-2352 Office: Holabird & Root 300 W Adams St Chicago IL 60606-5101

HOLBA PUACZ, JEANNE, librarian, educator; b. Chgo., Ill., Sept. 5, 1970; d. Michele Campbell Roedel and Edward Holba; m. Christopher Puacz, Apr. 20, 1996; children: Zofia Puacz, Declan Puacz, Phoebe Puacz. BA, U. Ill., 1991, MLS, 1992; BS, Ind. State U., 1998. Libr. U. Ill., Urbana-Champaign, 1992—95; sch. media specialist Josephinum H.S., Chgo., 1995—96; document control specialist Toyota Motor Mfg. N.Am., Princeton, Ind., 1996—98; reference and sys. libr. Vigo County Pub. Libr., Terre Haute, Ind., 1998—2005; faculty Ind. U. Sch. Libr. and Info. Sci., Bloomington, Ind., 2001—04, U. Ill. Grad. Sch. Libr. and Info. Sci., Urbana-Champaign, 2004—. Cons., Naperville, 2004—. Contbr. chapters to books. Recipient Mover & Shaker award, Libr. Jour., 2003; Inst. Mus. and Libr. Svcs. Doctoral fellow, U. N.Tex., 2005—. Mem.: Libr. Instrn. Roundtable (adult learners com.), Assn. Libr. and Info. Sci. Edn., Am. Soc. Info. Sci. and Tech., ALA. Home: 5335 Wirestem Ct Naperville IL 60564 Home Phone: 630-544-6267. Personal E-mail: jpuacz@uiuc.edu.

HOLBEN, DAVID, chef; Grad., Culinary Inst. Am., Hyde Park, NY, 1980. Opening chef Cafe Royal, Plz. of Americas Hotel, Dallas; cook Roger Verge's Le, Loulin de Mougins, France, L'ecole de L'Amandier, Paul Bocuse, Lyon, L'Hotel George V, Paris; exec. chef Riviera Restaurant, Dallas; co-ptnr. Meditteraneo, 1993, Toscana, 1994; co-founder FoodStar Restaurant Grp., Inc., 1997—; corp. exec. chef, v.p. Wynnwood, Dallas, 1999; mgr. culinary ops. Bistral, Seventeen Seventeen Restaurant, Atrium Cafe; corp. exec. chef Shoreline Restaurant Corp.; exec. chef Culpepper Steak House, Del Frisco's Double Eagle Steak House, Dallas, 2005—. Guest chef Celebrity Chef Tour, 2006. Named one of America's Best New Chefs, Food and Wine Mag., 1990. Achievements include cooking for Pres. Jimmy Carter and Pres. George Bush. Office: Del Frisco's Double Eagle Steak House 5251 Spring Valley Rd Dallas TX 75240 Office Phone: 972-490-9000.*

HOLBEN, SHARIE CECILIA, small business owner; b. Grand Rapids, Mich., Sept. 12, 1961; d. Erwin Francis and Ardis Jean (Gilbert) Schmuker; m. Thomas William Jordan, Dec. 4, 1982 (div. July 2001); m. Ronald

James Holben, May 5, 2003. Registered well drilling contractor Mich. Fashion cons. Mullberry Bush, Houghton Lake, Mich., 1982-84; freelance artist Houghton Lake, 1984-90; owner Jordan Illustration and Design, Houghton Lake, 1991-96; co-owner Jordan Well Drilling, Houghton Lake, 1994—2001; svc. tech. Hart Well Drilling, 2002—. Cons. Buyers Guide Weekly, Houghton, 1988—90. Founding chmn. Ann. Meml. Day Parade, Houghton Lake, 1992—99. Recipient Emily Hilton-Janice Reeney Art award, Kenowa Hills, 1979. Mem.: Mich. Environ. Health Assn., Mich. Ground Water Assn., Eagles Aux. (chaplain, activity chmn. 1991—92, trustee, v.p. 1992—94, Mrs. Eagle award 1991—92, Outstanding Vol. Work and Svc. award 1991—92). Avocations: boating, horticulture, music.

HOLBERT, KELLY MCKAY, exhibition coordinator, art historian; b. Wash., Feb. 27, 1967; d. John McKay and Sara (Hedekin) Holbert. BA in History of Art cum laude, Princeton U., NJ, 1989; MA, Yale U., New Haven, Conn., 1991, MPhil, 1993, PhD, 1995. Carol Bates grad. fellow Walters Art Gallery, Balt., 1995—96, rsch. assoc. medieval art, 1996—98; asst. curator medieval art Walters Art Mus. (formerly known as Walters Art Gallery), Balt., 1998—2002; exhbn. coord. Smith Coll. Mus. Art, Northampton, Mass., 2002—. Lectr. in field. Contbr. articles to profl. jours., chapters to books; contbg. author Medieval Art, 1997, Manuscripts and Rare Books, 1997, volume editor (collection catalogue) Ethiopian Art: The Walters Art Museum, 2001. Sumner McK. Crosby grant, 1992, 1993—94, Andrew W. Mellon Dissertation fellowship, 1994—95. Mem.: Medieval Acad. Am., Internat. Ctr. Medieval Art, Coll. Art Assn., Am. Assn. Museums. Office: Smith Coll Mus Art Elm St at Bedford Ter Northampton MA 01063 Business E-Mail: kholbert@smith.edu.

HOLBERTON, PHILIP VAUGHAN, entrepreneur, educator; b. NYC, Sept. 29, 1942; s. Robert Maynard and Charlotte Metcalf (Stone) H.; m. Gale Russell, May 16, 1970 (div. 1980); children: Matthew Russell, Alexandra; m. Anne Meigs Blodget, June 6, 1987; 1 child, Philip Vaughan Jr., Tod. AB in Acctg., Franklin and Marshall Coll., Lancaster, Pa., 1964. CPA, N.Y. Auditor Hurdman and Cranstoun CPAs, NYC, 1964-72; mgr. audit svcs. Peat Marwick CPAs, NYC, 1975-79; investment profl. McDonald & Co., NYC, 1972-75; asst. contr. Becton Dickinson & Co., Franklin Lakes, NJ, 1979-81, group contr. Paramus, NJ, 1981-85; v.p. fin. Gen. Cinema Theatres, Chestnut Hill, Mass., 1985-91; v.p. fin. and adminstrn., CFO, Cambridge, Neuroscience, Inc., Cambridge, Mass., 1991-95; founder Holberton Group, Inc., Lincoln, Mass., 1995—2005; founder, chief bus. officer Maxthera, Inc., Lincoln, 2005—07. Outside dir. Mgmt. Decision Lab., NYU, 1981-84; adj. faculty Northeastern U., Brandeis U., Babson Coll.; bd. dirs. Barbour Stockwell, Inc. Chmn. strategic planning panel United Way of Bergen County, Paramus, 1983-85; dir. Poppenhusen Inst., College Point, N.Y., 1981-83; sr. warden St. Anne's in the Fields, Lincoln, Mass., 1994-96. Mem. AICPA, Fin. Execs. Inst. (pres. bd. dirs. Boston chpt. 1995-96), Nat. Spkrs. Assn., New Eng. Spkrs. Assn. (bd. dirs. 1998-2002). Office: Holberton Group Inc PO Box 254 Lincoln MA 01773-0254 Home Phone: 781-259-9122. Business E-Mail: pholberton@holberton.com.

HOLBIK, KAREL, economics professor; b. Czech Republic, Sept. 9, 1920; came to U.S., 1948, naturalized, 1952; s. Karel and Catherine (Krouzel) H.; m. Olga Rehackova, Sept. 10, 1956; 1 son, Thomas. JD, Charles U., Prague, 1947; MBA, U. Detroit, 1949; PhD, U. Wis., 1956. Researcher Bank of Am., San Francisco, 1951-53; teaching asst. in banking U. Wis., 1953-55; asst. prof. econs. Lafayette Coll., Easton, Pa., 1955-58; prof. econs. Boston U., 1958-86, prof. econs. emeritus, 1986—. Cons. U.S. Naval War Coll., Newport, R.I., 1963-64, lectr., 1964-73; vis. prof. U. Brussels, 1969-70; vis. faculty Harvard U., 1981-98; chief sect. for devel. fin. instns. UN, 1976-80; Fulbright sr. scholar U. Tunis, 1983-84; internat. fin. cons., 1986—. Author: Italy in International Cooperation, 1959, Postwar Trade in Divided Germany, 1964, The United States, The Soviet Union and the Third World, 1968, West German Foreign Aid 1956-1966, 1968, American-East European Trade, 1969, Contemporary American Economic Problems, 1970, Trade and Industrialization in the Central American Common Market, 1972, Monetary Policy in Twelve Industrial Countries, 1973, Industrialization and Employment in Puerto Rico, 1975; others. Mem. Am. Econ. Assn., Am. Fin. Assn. Home: 313 Country Club Rd Newton MA 02459-3148 *It appears that America, more than any other country, challenges human capabilities and permits individual dreams to come true.*

HOLBROOK, HAL (HAROLD ROWE HOLBROOK JR.), actor; b. Cleve., Feb. 17, 1925; s. Harold Rowe and Aileen (Davenport) H.; m. Ruby Elaine Johnston, Sept. 22, 1945 (div.); children: Victoria, David; m. Carol Rossen (div.); 1 dau., Eve; m. Dixie Carter, May 27, 1984. Student, Suffield Acad., 1933-37, Culver Mil. Acad., 1938-42; BA with honors, Denison U., 1948. Played summer stock cos., 1947-53; organized (with wife) two-person stage prodn., touring high schs., clubs, univs., 1948-53, repertoire included a sketch based on Mark Twain's short story An Encounter with an Interviewer; appeared on TV as Abraham Lincoln, 1953; assembled solo show Mark Twain Tonight, 1953, 2005; night club performances, 1955-56; on tour U.S. TV appearances, 1954-59, in N.Y.C., 1959, 66, 76; on tour, 1960-63, TV spl., CBS, 1967; TV series, The Brighter Day, 1954-59, The Senator, 1970-71, Portrait of America (host), 1983-88, Evening Shade, 1990-94; rec. theatre presentation Mark Twain Tonight!, 1959, 1961, 1966, 1971, 2005; concert engagements, U.S., Can., Vancouver Festival, Edinburgh Festival, Saudi Arabia, European tour auspices, Dept. State with ANTA, 1959-60; performed two-character play Do You Know the Milky Way, Vancouver, also N.Y.C., 1961, Am. Shakespeare Festival, Stratford, Conn., 1962; toured two-character play Mark Twain Tonight, 1964 (Tony award, Drama Critics Circle award 1966); appeared in play The Glass Menagerie, N.Y.C., 1965; also TV movies The Whole World is Watching, 1969, A Clear and Present Danger, 1970, Travis Logan, 1971, Suddenly Single, 1971, Goodbye Raggedy Ann, 1971, That Certain Summer, 1971-72 (Emmy nomination best actor in a drama), The Pueblo, 1973 (Emmy awards for best actor in a drama, actor of year in a spl.), Sandburg's Lincoln, 1974-75 (Emmy award outstanding lead actor in a ltd. series), Our Town, 1977 (Emmy nomination outstanding lead actor in a drama or comedy spl.), The Awakening Land, 1978 (Emmy nomination outstanding lead actor in ltd. series), When Hell Was In Session, 1979, The Senator, NBC, 1970-71 (Emmy award, Best actor in dramatic series), (miniseries) North and South, 1985, North and South: Book II, 1986, Dress Gray, 1986, The Fortunate Pilgrim, 1988; plays Abe Lincoln in Illinois, N.Y.C., 1963; appeared plays Tartuffe, Lincoln Center Repertory Co., 1963-65, the Apple Tree, N.Y.C., 1967, I Never Sang for My Father, 1968, Man of La Mancha, 1968, Does a Tiger Wear a Necktie, 1969, Lake of the Woods, 1972, An American Daughter, 1997, Our Town, 2007; appeared in motion picture The Group, 1966, Wild in the Streets, 1968, The People Next Door, 1970, The Great White Hope, 1970, They Only Kill Their Masters, 1972, Jonathan Livingston Seagull (voice only), 1973, Magnum Force, 1973, The Girl from Petrovka, 1974, Midway, 1976, All the President's Men, 1976, Julia, 1977, Capricorn I, 1978, Natural Enemies, 1979, The Fog, 1980, The Kidnapping of the President, 1980, Rituals, 1980, Creepshow, 1982, Star Chamber, 1983, Girls Nite Out, 1984, Wall Street, 1987, The Unholy, 1988, Fletch Lives, 1989, The Firm, 1993, Carried Away, 1996, Cats Don't Dance (voice only), 1997, Hercules (voice only), 1997; author: Mark Twain Tonight, 1959. Mem. com. on internat. cultural exchange Nat. Council on Arts and Govt. Served with C.E. AUS, 1943-46. Recipient Vernon Rice Meml. award, 1959, Outer Circle award, 1959; spl. citation for Mark Twain Tonight N.Y. Drama Critics Circle, 1966; Torch of Liberty award Anti-Defamation League B'nai B'rith, 1972 Mem. Mark Twain Meml. Assn. Clubs: Players (N.Y.C.). Address: c/o Abrams Artists Agy 9200 W Sunset Blvd Ste 1130 Los Angeles CA 90069-3606*

HOLBROOK, HOWARD GEORGE, pharmacist; b. Worchester, Pa., July 25, 1946; s. Howard Franklin and Pauline Valentine Holbrook; m. Andrea Marie Safer, June 13, 1998; 1 child, Jeffrey M. Safer. BPharm, Mass. Coll. Pharmacy, Boston, 1976; MBA, We. New Eng., Springfield, Mass., 1994. Cert. ambulatory care U. Wis. Cmty. pharmacist Gusy's Pharmacy, Webster, Mass., 1980—2002; clin. pharmacist Milford-Whitinsville Reg. Hosp., Mass., 1990—93, DOD, 1990—93; pharmacist Boston W.Roxbury, 1993—. Mgmt. Vets. Adminstrn., Boston, 2003—06. Lt. col. US Army, 1967—70, lt. col. US Army, 1982—2003, served US Army, 2002—03, Kuwait, served US Army, 1990—90, Walter Reed. Mem.: Am. Military Surgeons, Am. Soc. Health Sys. Pharmacist, VFW, Delta Sigma Theta (pres.). Avocations: fishing, reading, exercise. Home: 3 Waite St Oxford MA 01540

HOLBROOK, JAY MACK, publishing company executive; b. Chesterfield, Idaho, Jan. 12, 1937; s. Lawrence E. and Mary Marjorie Holbrook; m. DeLene Clark, Dec. 20, 1962; children: Jalene, Lanae, Marinda, Danelle. BS, Utah State U., 1961; MA, Georgetown U., 1967, U. Wis., 1970. Contract adminstr. Dept. Navy, Washington, 1962-66; instr., asst. prof. Edgewood Coll., 1969, Brigham Young U., 1970-71, Utah State U., 1971-72, Nichols Coll., 1972-74, Cen. N.E., 1979-83, Mt. Wauchussett Community Coll., 1979-80; pub. Holbrook Rsch. Inst., Oxford, Mass., 1975—, Archive Pub., Oxford, 1990—. Sr. trainer Applicon, Burlington, Mass., 1983-84, Apollo, Chelmsford, Mass., 1984-85; bd. dirs. Holbrook Rentals, Micro Tech Supply, Archive Pub., Oxford. Author numerous publs. on Mass. vital records, census and demographic reconstrn. of colonial New Eng. Mem. Oxford Fin. Com., 1989-96, pers. bd., 1999-2003, cable adv. com., 1999-2003.

HOLBROOK, KAREN ANN, retired academic administrator, biologist; b. Des Moines, Nov. 6, 1942; married, 1973; 1 child. BS, U. Wis., 1963, MS, 1966; PhD in Biol. Structure, U. Wash., 1972. From instr. to assoc. prof. U. Wash. Sch. of Medicine, Seattle, 1971-79, vice chmn. dept. biol. structure, 1981—93, prof., 1984—93, assoc. dean sci. affairs, 1985—93; sr. v.p. & prof. U. Ga., Athens, Ga., 1993—98; pres. Ohio State U., Columbus, Ohio, 2002—07. Instr. biology Ripon Coll., 1966-69; NIH trainee, 1969-72, trainee, sr. fellow dermatology, 1976-78, mem. study sect. gen. medicine; adj. assoc. prof. med. dermatology, U. Wash., 1979-84; mem. spl. study sect. Nat. Inst. Arthritis & Metabollic Diseases, Nat. Inst. Arthritis, Diabetes & Digestive Kidney Diseases, 1985-88; adj. prof. med. dermatology, 1984-93. Named Disting. Woman Physician/Scientist, 1996; recipient Kung Sun Oh Mem prize, 34th Annual Mation Spencer Fay Nat. Bd. award, Disting. Contribn. to Rsch. Admin. award. Mem. AAAS, Am. Assn. Anatomists, Am. Soc. Cell Biology, Soc. Invest Dermatology, Soc. Pediat. Dermatology, Am. Assn. Of Univ., Nat. Assn of State Univ & Land Grant Coll., Assn of Am. Med. Coll. Commn on Higher Edn.; bd. dir. ACT, Am. Coun. On Edn., Nat. Merit Scholarship Corp, Nat. Coun. For Sci. and Environment, Huntington Bancshares, Reservoir Venture Ptnrs., Columbus Tech. Coun., Columbus Ptnrshp., Ctr. of Sci. & Industry, Columbus Downtown Dev. Corp., Ctrl. Ohio United Negro Coll. Fund, United Way of Ctrl. Ohio, Greater Columbus Area C. of C., CEOs for Cities, Columbus Sch. For Girls; Sigma Xi; trustee, Cap. So. Urban Redev. Corp. Achievements include research in fine structural & biochemical analysis of human skin including development of the human epidermis and dermis in vivo prenatal diagnosis of inherited skin diseases, structural abnormalities of the dermis in individuals with inherited disorders of connective tissue metabolism, epidermis in inherited disorders of keratinization.*

HOLBROOKE, RICHARD CHARLES ALBERT, investment banker, former ambassador; b. NYC, Apr. 24, 1941; s. Dan and Trudi (Moos) H.; children: David Dan, Anthony Andrew. BA, Brown U., 1962; postgrad., Princeton, 1969-70. Joined Fgn. Service, 1962; served in Vietnam, 1963-66; mem. White House staff, 1966-67; assigned US Dept. State; staff Paris Peace Talks on Vietnam, 1968-69; dir. Peace Corps, Morocco, 1970-72; mng. editor Fgn. Policy mag., 1972-77; cons. Commn. Orgn. Govt. for Conduct of Fgn., 1974-75; contbg. editor Newsweek Internat., 1976; asst. sec. for East Asian and Pacific affairs US Dept. State, Washington, 1977-81; v.p. Public Strategies, Washington, 1981-85; sr. advisor Lehman Bros., 1981-84, mng. dir., 1985-93; U.S. amb. to Germany US Dept. State, Berlin, 1993-94, asst. sec. state European and Can. affairs Washington, 1994-96, U.S. amb. to U.N. NYC, 1999—2001; vice chmn. Credit Suisse First Boston, NYC, 1996-99, Perseus LLC, NYC, 2001—; pres. Global Bus. Coalition on HIV/AIDS, 2001—. Chief negotiator Dayton Peace Accords, Bosnia, 1995; spl. presdl. emissary to Cyprus; mem. Trilateral Commn., chmn., Asia Society, 2002-. Author: vol. The Pentagon Papers, 1967, To End a War, 1998; co-author (with Clark Clifford): Counsel to the President, 1991; contbr. numerous articles to N.Y. Times, Washington Post, Wall St. Jour., Atlantic, other mags. and jours. Bd. dirs. Internat. Rescue Com.; chmn. Refugees Internat. Mem. Am. Acad. Berlin, Coun. Fgn. Rels., Inst. Strategic Studies; bd mem., Amer. Museum Nat. History, Nat. Endowment for Democracy, Human Genome Sciences; Fellow, Am. Acad.of Arts and Sci., 2004 Office: Perseus LLC 2099 Pennsylvania Ave NW 9th Fl Washington DC 20006

HOLBURN, ANDREA, lawyer; b. 1971; BA, Univ. Victoria, 1994; JD, Univ. No. Dakota, 1998. Bar: Wash. 1998. Assoc. atty., comml. litig. Betts, Patterson & Mines, P.S., Seattle. Contbr. articles to numerous profl. jours. Named Wash. Rising Star, SuperLawyer Mag., 2006. Mem.: ABA, Wash. State Bar Assn. Office: Betts Patterson and Mines One Covington Pl Ste 1400 701 Pike St Seattle WA 98101-3927

HOLCH, GREGORY JOHN, editor, writer; b. Tokyo, Nov. 19, 1952; (parents Am. citizens); s. Arthur Everett and Ellen Constance (O'Keefe) Holch; m. Rhonda Lyn Brauer, Sept. 7, 1989; children: Jillian Brauer, Justin Brauer. BA in English, Manhattanville Coll., 1974; MA in Am. Civilization, NYU, 1984. Editl. asst. Globe Comm., Greenwich, Conn., 1977-78, Random House Student Book Clubs, NYC, 1978-80, Bantam Books, NYC, 1981-83; assoc. editor Scholastic, NYC, 1983-85, editor, 1985-94, sr. editor, 1994—2006. Guest editor Mademoiselle mag., 1974. Author: (novels) The Things with Wings, 1998; co-author: Jungle Jokes, 1979; author: short stories; contbr. photographs to mags. Mem.: Soc. Children's Book Writers and Illustrators, Am. Radio Relay League (life). Avocations: amateur radio, photography.

HOLCOMB, DONALD FRANK, physicist, academic administrator; b. Chesterton, Ind., Nov. 8, 1925; s. Roger L. and Ethel (Frank) H.; m. Barbara Page, Aug. 26, 1950; children: Douglas Page, Jane D., Nancy M. AB, DePauw U., 1949; MS, U. Ill., 1950, PhD, 1954. Instr. U. Ill., 1954; mem. faculty Cornell U., 1954—, prof. physics, 1962—, dir. lab. atomic and solid state physics, 1964-68, chmn. dept. physics, 1969-74, 82-86, trustee, 1976-81. Cons. Corning Glass Research Lab., 1959-64, Central Inst. Indsl. Research, Oslo, Norway, 1962 Contbr. profl. jours. Served with USNR, 1944-46. Sr. vis. fellow NATO, 1962; Guggenheim fellow, 1968-69; Sci. Research Council sr. fellow, 1978 Fellow Am. Phys. Soc., AAAS; mem. Am. Assn. Physics Tchrs. (pres. 1987, Oersted medal 1996), Sigma Xi. Presbyterian. Achievements include spl. rsch. solid state physics, chem. physics, coll. physics course devel. Home: 385 Savage Farm Dr Ithaca NY 14850-6505

HOLCOMB, GENE ANN, federal loan officer; b. Munday, Tex., Jan. 11, 1937; d. L. C. Guinn, Jr. and Amerolis Magdalyn Hutcheson; m. Jerry Cobb (div.); children: Sheila Cobb, Simone Cobb. Grad. h.s., Knox City, Tex. County office clk. Farmer's Home Adminstrn. USDA, Haskell, Tex., 1970—74, county office asst. Farmer's Home Adminstrn. Knox City, 1975—92, program rev. asst. Farmer's Home Adminstrn. Tex., 1993—95, asst. loan officer Farm Security Administration Haskell, 1995—2000; ret., 2000. Asst. editor: Knox County News, 1968—70. Pres. Women's Club 1946 Study Club, Knox City, 1964—65; chmn. city-wide fund drs. Recipient Cert. Outstanding Accomplishment, USDA-Farmer's Home Adminstrn., 1976, 1987—88, Cert. Merit, 1992, Cert. Superior Performance, 1992. Mem.: Knox City Ex-Students Assn. Republican. Disciples Of Christ. Avocation: bus tours.

HOLCOMB, KEVIN MICHAEL, obstetrician, gynecologist, gynecologic oncologist; b. Bklyn., Apr. 13, 1967; married; 2 children. BA, Cornell U., Ithaca, NY, 1988; MD, NY Med. Coll., 1992. Cert. Obstetrics & Gynecology, Gynecologic Oncology. Resident, obstetrics & gynecology NY Hosp./Cornell Med. Ctr., 1992—96; fellow, gynecologic oncology SUNY-Downstate Med. Ctr., Bklyn., 1996—99; asst. clin. prof., obstetrics & gynecology Columbia Coll. Physicians and Surgeons, 2002—; dir., divsn. gynecologic oncology Beth Israel Med. Ctr., NYC. Named one of 40 Under 40, The Network Jour., 2005; recipient Nat. Faculty Tchg. award, Coun. on Residency Edn. in Obstetrics and Gynecology, 2002, 2004. Mem.: Metropolitan Gynecologic Cancer Soc. (mem. exec. coun.), Am. Cancer Soc. (bd. dir.), Sigma Pi Phi (Westchester Boule), Kappa Alpha Psi. Office: Beth Israel Med Ctr 10 Union Sq E Ste 4C New York NY 10003 Office Phone: 212-844-5729. Office Fax: 212-420-2980.*

HOLCOMB, LINDA LAINE, elementary school educator, director; d. Raymond Marcel and Eda Brunk Laine; m. Steve Alan Holcomb, Sept. 10, 1972; children: Julie Holcomb Higdon, John David. BA in Edn., Stetson U., DeLand, Fla., 1973; MA in Edn., We. Carolina U., Cullowhee, NC, 1999, EdS, 2004, student, 2002—. Lic. tchr. NC, Nat. Bd. Profl. Tchg. Standards, 2000. Tchr. Murphy Elem. Sch., NC, 1974—80; tchr. reading Andrews Elem. Sch., NC, 1983—94, Cherokee County Schs., Murphy, 1994—, dir. staff devel., 2005—06. Instr. GED Tri-County CC, Murphy, 1994—96; tchr. tnr., coord. reading Cherokee County Schs., 1998—2005, dir. Fed. Title Programs, 2007; instr. Walden U., 2002—; presenter in field. Named Tchr. of Yr., Andrews Elem. Sch., 1996, Walmart, 1997; recipient Cmty. Svc. Vol. Recognition award, Cherokee County Literacy Coun., 1994. Mem.: NEA, ASCD, Nat. Staff Devel. Coun., Reading Recovery Coun. N.Am., N.C. Assn. Educators, Internat. Reading Assn. Independent. Episcopalian. Avocations: writing, travel. Office: Cherokee County Title II Dir 911 Andrews Hwy Murphy NC 28906 Office Phone: 828-835-8483. Business E-Mail: lholcomb@waldenu.edu.

HOLCOMB, LYLE DONALD, JR., retired lawyer; b. Miami, Fla., Feb. 3, 1929; s. Lyle Donald and Hazel Irene (Watson) H.; m. Barbara Jean Roth, July 12, 1952; children: Susan Holcomb Davis, Scott H. (deceased), Douglas J., Mark E. BA, U. Mich., 1951; JD, U. Fla., 1954. Bar: U.S. Ct. Appeals (5th and 11th cirs.) 1981, U.S. Supreme Ct. 1966. Ptnr. Holcomb & Holcomb, Miami, 1955-72; assoc. Copeland, Therrel, Baisden & Peterson, Miami Beach, Fla., 1972-75; ptnr. Therrel, Baisden, Stanton, Wood & Setlin, Miami Beach, Fla., 1976-85, Therrel, Baisden & Meyer Weiss, Miami Beach, Fla., 1985-93; pvt. practice Tallahassee, Fla., 1993-95. Organizing pres. So. Fla. Migrant Legal Svcs. Program (now Fla. Rural Legal Svcs.), 1966-68. Exec. bd. So. Fla. coun. Boy Scouts Am., 1958-93; past pres., past counselor Miami chpt. Huguenot Soc. Fla. With USNR, 1947-53. Recipient Silver Beaver award, So. Fla. coun. Boy Scouts Am., 1966. Fellow Am. Coll. Trust and Estate Counsel, 1980-94, Acad. Fla. Probate and Trust Litigation Attys., 1980-95; mem. Dade County Bar Assn. (dir. 1960-71, sec. 1963-71), Miami Beach Bar Assn. (pres. 1980), Estate Planning Coun. Greater Miami, Soc. Mayflower Descs. (past pres. Miami club, past counselor state soc.), SAR (past pres. Miami chpt.), Univ. Yacht Club. Republican. Mem. United Ch. Of Christ. Home: 3538 Killarney Plaza Dr Tallahassee FL 32309-3491 Personal E-mail: lholcomb23@aol.com.

HOLCOMBE, RANDALL GREGORY, economics professor; b. Bridgeport, Conn., June 4, 1950; s. Lynn Montanye Holcombe and Gloria Gabriel (Rita) Ledbetter; m. Lora Hunt Pritchett, June 18, 1983. BS, U. Fla., 1972; MA, Va. Tech., 1974, PhD, 1976. Asst. prof. Tex. A&M U., College Station, 1975-77; prof. Auburn (Ala.) U., 1977-88, Fla. State U., Tallahassee, 1988—. Sr. fellow James Madison Inst., Tallahassee, 2004—, mem. rsch. adv. com., 1987-2004, chmn., 1991-2004; mem. editl. bd., Rev. Austrian Econs., 1987-97, Pub. Fin. Rev., 1995-2003, Quar. Jour. Austrian Econs., 1998—; adj. scholar Ludwig Von Mises Inst., 1982-; mem. Fla. Gov.'s Coun. Econ. Advisors, 2000-06; contbg. editor Independent Rev., 2004—. Author: Public Finance and the Political Process, 1983, An Economic Analysis of Democracy, 1985, Economic Models and Methodology, 1989, The Economic Foundations of Government, 1994, Public Policy and the Quality of Life, 1995, Public Finance: Government Revenues and Expenditures in the United States Economy, 1996, (with R. Sobel) Growth and Variability in State Tax Revenue, 1997, Writing Off Ideas, 2000, From Liberty to Democracy: The Transformation of American Government, 2002, Public Sector Economics, 2006, Entrepreneurship and Economic Progress, 2006; book rev. editor Pub. Choice, 2005—, mem. editl. bd., 2004—; contbr. articles to profl. jours. Mem. Fla. Gov. Coun. Econ. Adv., 2000—06. Scaife Found. fellow, 1972-73, H.B. Earhart Found. fellow, 1973-75; research grantee Earhart Found., 1979-80, 83, 89, 90, 98. Mem. Am. Econ. Assn., Pub. Choice Soc. (pres. 2006—), So. Econ. Assn., Western Econ. Assn., Soc. for Devel. of Austrian Econs. (pres. 2007). Home: 3514 Limerick Dr Tallahassee FL 32309-3139 Office: Fla State U Dept Econs Tallahassee FL 32306 Business E-Mail: holcombe@garnet.acns.fsu.edu.

HOLDAWAY, PHILLIP WAYMAN, retired environmental planner; b. San Bernardino, Calif., Jan. 8, 1947; s. Ralph Dan Holdaway, Sr. and Vera Mae Holdaway; m. Miriam June Wienholt, Aug. 19, 1967; 1 child, Aaron Matthew. BA in Geography, Calif. State U., San Bernardino, 1981. Landscape and hwy. maintenance worker Calif. Dept. of Transp., San Bernardino, 1973—80, equipment operator, 1980—87, jr. engrng. technician, 1987—89, environ. planner, 1989—92, assoc. environ. planner, 1992—2000. Author: (guidebook to historical sites) Billy Holcomb Chapter Plaque Book: 35th Anniversary, Billy Holcomb Chapter Plaque Book: 25th Anniversary, Billy Holcomb Chapter Plaque Book: 20th Anniversary; contbg. photographer: Looking Back: Amateur Adventures with Halley's Comet, 1985—86; contbr. (photographs and directions) Guidebook to Historical Plaques, 1995. Archivist Billy Holcomb Chpt. of the Ancient and Hon. Order of E Clampus Vitus, San Bernardino, 1986—. Decorated Air medal, Disting. Flying Cross, Purple Heart, Nat. Def. Svc. medal, Vietnam Campaign medal, Vietnam Svc. medal. Mem.: DAV (life), NRA (life), Am. Legion, Disting. Flying Cross Soc., San Bernardino Hist. and Pioneer Soc., Death Valley Natural History Assn. (life), Calif. Rifle and Pistol Assn. (life), Death Valley '49ers (life). Avocations: historical research, erecting historical markers, photography, camping, hiking. Home Phone: 909-475-8213.

HOLDAWAY, RONALD M., retired federal judge; b. Afton, Wyo. m. Judy Janowski, Dec. 1958; children: Denise, Georgia. BA, U. Wyo., 1957, JD, 1959. Bar: Wyo. 1959, U.S. Dist. Ct. (Wyo.), U.S. Ct. Mil. Appeals, 1960, U.S. Army Ct. Mil. Rev., U.S. Supreme Ct., 1967. Commd. 2nd lt. U.S. Army, 1960, advanced through grades to brig. gen., 1989; legal staff officer U.S. Army, Ft. Lewis, Washington, 1960-63, legal staff Hawaii, 1963-66, instr. criminal law, Judge Advocate Gen.'s Sch. Charlottesville, Va., 1966-69, staff judge advocate 1st cav. divsn. Vietnam, 1969-70, chief govt. appellate divsn. Washington, 1971-75, chief of pers., 1975-77, staff judge advocate Stuttgart, Germany, 1978-80, exec. to judge advocate gen. Washington, 1980-81, asst. judge advocate gen., 1981-83, chief judge Ct. Mil. Review, 1987-89; judge advocate U.S. Army Europe, Heidelberg, Germany, 1983-87; judge US Ct. Appeals Vets. Claims, Washington DC, 1990—2002. Decorated Bronze Star, Legion of Merit, Disting. Svc. medal with Oak Leaf Cluster, Meritorious Svc. medal with Oak Leaf Cluster, Air medal, Nat. Def. Svc. medal, Vietnam Campaign medal with 4 campaign stars, Vietnam Svc. medal, Overseas medal (3). Mem. Wyo. State Bar Assn., Assn. U.S. Army, Army Navy Club.

HOLDEN, BETSY D., former food products company executive; b. Lubbock, Tex., 1956; BA, Duke U.; MA in edn., Northwestern U., MBA, 1982. Asst. product mgr. desserts Gen. Foods Corp., 1982—84; brand mgr., venture div. Kraft Foods Inc., 1984—85, brand mgr., Miracle Whip Northfield, Ill., 1985—87, group brand mgr., confections & snacks, 1987—90, v.p. new product devel. and strategy Northfield, Ill., 1990—91, v.p., mktg., dinners, & enhancers, 1991—93, pres. Tombstone Pizza Northfield, Ill., 1993—95, exec. v.p., gen. mgr. cheese divsn., 1995—97, pres. cheese divsn., 1997—98, exec. v.p., ops., procurement, research & devel., consumer insights and E-commerce, 1998—2000; pres., CEO Kraft Foods North America, 2000—01; co-CEO Kraft Foods Inc., 2001—03, pres., global mktg. & category devel., 2004—05. Bd. dir. Kraft Foods, Tribune Co., Tupperware Corp., Western Union, 2006—. Pres. Chicago's Off the Street Club; mem., bd. Grocery Manufacturers of Amer., Evanston Northwestern Healthcare.

HOLDEN, CAROL HELEN, county official; b. Boston, Nov. 6, 1942; m. Donald B. Holden; 4 children. BA, Trinity Coll., 1964; MAT, Boston Coll., 1965. Intern U.S. Senate, 1963-64; mem. N.H. Ho. of Reps., 1984-97, vice chair children, youth and juvenile justice com.; mem. state-fed. rels. com.; asst. majority leader, 1996. Vice chair Hillsborough County Bd. Commrs., 1997—; mem. Amherst Ways and Means Commn., 1983-86; tchr., vol. coord. Del. NH Constl. Conv., 1984; pres. Amherst Women's Rep. Club, 1986-88; v.p. NH Fed. Rep. Women's Club, 1989-94, pres., 1994-95; mem. Amherst Sch. Dist. Mod., 1990—; dir. N.H. Ptnrs. in Edn., 1987—, sec., 1989—, vice chair, 1990—, chair, 1992—; mem. Gov.'s Steering Com. Volunteerism, 1991-96; mem. NH Alliance for Effective Schs., 1991-96; v.p. NH Congress Parents and Tchrs., 1984-86, 90-92; trustee NH Childrens Trust Fund, 1997-98, Child and Family Svcs., 2005-; treas. Nat. Conf. County Rep. County Ofcls., 2004-; bd. dirs. Nashua Cmty. Coun., 2002; bd. dirs. Nat. Conf. Rep. Ofcls., 1999—, treas., 2004-05, sec., 2005—, Nashua Cmty. Coun., 2002-; mem., svcs. steering com. NACO, 2005—. Mem. Nat. Assn. of Counties (v.p.), Trinity Coll. Alumni Assn. (bd. dirs. 1980-87, sec. bd. dirs. 1994-97, 2d v.p. 1997-98), NH Assn. Counties (1st v.p. 1999-01, pres. elect, 2001-03, pres. 2003), Nat. Assn. Counties (steering com. labor and employment 1999—, bd. dirs. 2002—), Boston Coll. Club of N.H. (pres. 1999-01), Vesta Roy Series (v.p. 2002-05). Avocations: travel, sailing, tennis, skiing, reading. Home: PO Box 13 Amherst NH 03031-0013 Office: Bd Commrs 329 Mast Rd Ste120 Goffstown NH 03045 Personal E-mail: ccommish@bassriver.us. Business E-Mail: ccommish@rcn.com.

HOLDEN, DONALD, artist, writer; b. LA, Apr. 22, 1931; s. Mack and Miriam (Epstein) H.; m. Wilma Shaffer, Jan. 10, 1954; children: Wendy, Blake. BA, Columbia U., 1951; MA, Ohio State U., 1952; LLD (hon.), Maine Coll. Art, 1986. Teaching asst. Ohio State U., Columbus, 1951-52; dir. pub. rels. Phila. Coll. Art, 1953-55; dir. pub. rels. and personnel Henry Dreyfuss, NYC, 1956-60; assoc. mgr. pub. rels. Met. Mus. Art, NYC, 1960-61; art cons. Fortune mag., NYC, 1962; editorial dir. Watson-Guptill Publs., 1963-79, Am. Artist mag., NYC, 1971-75. Lectr. in field; mem. faculty, mem. artist adv. bd. Scottsdale Artists Sch., Ariz. Author: Art Career Guide, 1961, rev. edits., 1967, 73, 83, Whistler Landscapes and Seascapes, 1969 (selected for inclusion in White House Libr. by Assn. Am. Pubs. 1975), Donald Holden Watercolors, 2004; under pseudonym Wendon Blake: Acrylic Watercolor Painting, 1970, Complete Guide to Acrylic Painting, 1971, Creative Color: A Practical Guide for Oil Painters, 1972, Landscape Painting in Oil, 1976, The Watercolor Painting Book, 1978, The Acrylic Painting Book, 1978, The Oil Painting Book, 1979, The Portrait and Figure Painting Book, 1979, The Drawing Book, 1980, The Color Book, 1981, Complete Guide to Landscape Painting in Oil, 1981, Painting in Alkyd, 1982, Creative Color for the Oil Painter, 1983, The Complete Painting Course, 1984, The Complete Oil Painting Book, 1989, The Complete Acrylic Painting Book, 1989, The Complete Watercolor Book, 1989, Getting Started in Drawing, 1991, The Artist's Guide to Using Color, 1992; contbr. articles to profl. publs.; editorial cons., Watson-Guptill Publs., 1979-87; sculpture, watercolors, and drawings in numerous group and one-man exhbns., including retrospective watercolor exhbn. at Butler Inst. Am. Art, Youngstown, Ohio, 1999, Contemporary Art Ctr. Va., 2000, Portland (Maine) Mus. Art, 2004, Springfield (Mo.) Art Mus., 2004, Round Top Ctr. Arts, Damariscotta, Maine, 2004; represented in collections Century Assn., N.Y., Ga. Mus. Art, U. Ga., Athens, Hickory (N.C.) Mus. Art, New Britain (Conn.) Mus. Am. Art, Springfield (Mo.) Art Mus., Wichita Art Mus., Kans., Fine Arts Museums of San Francisco, Met. Mus. Art, N.Y.C., New Orleans Mus. Art, Victoria and Albert Mus., London, Yale U. Art Gallery, New Haven, Ark. Arts Ctr., Little Rock, Ashmolean Mus., Oxford, Eng., Corcoran Gallery, Washington, Meml. Art Gallery, Rochester, N.Y., Farnsworth Mus., Rockland, Maine, Nelson-Atkins Mus. Art, Kansas City, Mo., Columbus (Ohio) Museum Art, Nat. Park Found. (Washington), Ogunquit (Maine) Mus. Am. Art, Portland (Maine) Mus. Art, Art Students League N.Y., Delaware Art Mus., Wilmington, Phila. Mus. Art, Spencer Mus. Art, U. Kans., Lawrence, Bates Coll. Mus. Art., Brit. Mus., London, Ulster Mus., Belfast, No. Ireland, Neuberger Mus. SUNY, Purchase, NAD, N.Y.C., U. N.H. Art Gallery, Durham, Albright-Knox Gallery, Buffalo, Nat. Gallery Art, Washington, Phillips Collection, Washington, Syracuse (N.Y.) U. Libr., Fitzwilliam Mus., Cambridge (Eng.) U. James A. Michener Art Museum, Doylestown, Penn, Munson Williams Proctor Inst., Utica N.Y., Butler Inst. Am. Art, Youngstown, Ohio, Palmer Mus. Art Pa. State U., University Park, U.S. Dept. State, Washington, D.C., Smithsonian Am. Art Mus., Washington, D.C., Nev. Mus. Art, Reno, Nev Recipient Adolph & Clara Obrig Prize, Nat. Acad. Design 176th Ann. Exhbn., 2001; Florsheim Art Fund grant, 1999. Mem. NAD, Artists Equity Assn., Nat. Art Edn. Assn., Maine Coast Artists, Century Assn., Salmagundi Club (JoAnn Leiser Meml. award 2005).

HOLDEN, FREDERICK DOUGLASS, JR., lawyer; b. Stockton, Calif., Nov. 21, 1949; s. Frederick Douglass and Sarah Frances (Young) H.; m. Patricia Brierton, June 25, 1988; children: Elizabeth, Andrew. BA, U. Calif., Santa Barbara, 1971; JD, U. Calif., Davis, 1974. Bar: Calif. 1974, DC 1996, US Dist. Ct. (no., ctrl., ea. and so. dists.) Calif. 1974, US Ct. Appeals (9th cir.) 1974, US Ct. Appeals (fed. cir.) 2004, US Dist. Ct. DC 1996, US Supreme Ct. 2001. Assoc. Brobeck, Phleger & Harrison LLP, San Francisco, 1974-81, ptnr., 1981—2003; chair bench-bar liaison com. U.S. Bankruptcy Ct. No. Dist. Calif., 2001—02; ptnr. Orrick, Herrington & Sutcliffe, LLP, 2003—. Mem. faculty Practising Law Inst., 1990; spkr. Nat. Conf. Bankruptcy Judges, 1987, 91, Banking Law Inst., 1986, Calif. Continuing Legal Edn. of Bar, Calif., 1983-85, Calif. State Bar, 1993; bd. dirs. Bay Area Bankruptcy Forum. Mng. editor U. Calif. Davis Law Rev., 1974. Fellow Am. Coll. Bankruptcy; mem. ABA (bus. bankruptcy com., spkr. 1991, 95), Calif. Bar Assn. (commendation 1983), San Francisco Bar Assn. (cert. appreciation 1985, 88, 90, 95, chair 2004), Internat. Bar Assn., Turnaround Mgmt. Assn. (dir., sec. 1994-96), Am. Bankruptcy Inst., Marin Audubon Soc. (chair fin. and membership, bd. dirs. 2003—), San Francisco Yacht Club, Sigma Pi (pres. 1970). Democrat. Avocations: triathlons, skiing, sailing, mountain climbing, birdwatching. Home: 140 Bella Vista Ave Belvedere CA 94920-2466 Office: Orrick Herrington & Sutcliffe LLP The Orrick Bldg 405 Howard St San Francisco CA 94105-2669 Home Phone: 415-435-2702; Office Phone: 415-773-5985. Business E-Mail: fholden@orrick.com.

HOLDEN, GEORGE FREDRIC, brewing company executive, public policy specialist, author; b. Lander, Wyo., Aug. 29, 1937; s. George Thiel Holden and Rita Zulpo; m. Dorothy, July 5, 1959; children: Lorilyn, Sherilyn, Tamilyn. BSChemE, U. Colo., 1959, MBA in Mktg., 1974. Adminstr. plastics lab. EDP, indsl chems. plant, prodn. process engring., tool control supervision, aerospace (Minuteman, Polaris, Sparrow), Parlin, NJ, Salt Lake City, Cumberland, Md., 1959-70; by-product sales, new market and new product devel., resource planning and devel. and pub. rels. Adolph Coors Co., Golden, Colo., 1971-76; dir. econ. affairs corp. pub. affairs dept., 1979-84, dir. pub. affairs rsch., 1984-86; owner Phoenix Enterprises, Arvada, 1986—; dep. treas. Jefferson County Colo. Fin. Analysis and Comm., 2003-06; mgr. facilities engring. Coors Container Co., 1976-79; instr. brewing, by-products utilization and waste mgmt. U. Wis.; cons., spkr. in field. Mem. bd. economists Rocky Mountain News, 1990-95; mem. Heritage Found. Ann. Guide to Pub. Policy Expert, 1987—, Spkrs. Bur., Commn. on the Bicentennial US Constn., 1991-93; del. Colo. Rep. Conv., 1976—; adv. Cost of Govt. Day; bd. dirs. Colo. Pub. Expenditures Coun., 1983-86, Nat. Spkrs. Assn., 1982-97, Colo. Spkrs. Assn. (bd. dirs. 1987-90), Denver Assn. Bus. Economists, 1982-97, Colo. Assn. Commerce and Industry Execs. Ednl. Found. Sr. fellow budget policy Independence Inst. Colo. "ThinkTank", 1990-95, fiscal policy, 2003—. Congregation coun. Arvada's King of Glory Luth. Ch., 1975-79, 2004-06, pres. 2004-05); Mem. US Brewers Assn. (chmn. by-products com. 1973-76, ednl. found. 1974-75, Hon. Gavel, 1975), Colo. Ind. Pubs. Assn. (bd. dirs. 2000-2003), Am. Inst. Indsl. Engrs. (dir. 1974-78), Washingtons Am. for Tax Reform Found.; Author: The Phoenix Phenomenon, 1984, Total Power of One in America, 1991 new edit., 2001; Co-author: Secrets of Job Hunting, 1972; contbr. articles to Chem. Engring. mag., 1968-76, over 400 published articles, white papers in field; over 1300 speeches, 640 appearances on radio talk shows nationwide. Home: 6463 Owens St Arvada CO 80004-2732 Office: Phoenix Enterprises PO Box 1900 Arvada CO 80001-1900

HOLDEN, HARLEY PEIRCE, retired archivist; b. Shirley, Mass., Aug. 18, 1937; s. Robert Henry Johnston and Eleanor Harriet (Harley) Holden. AB in Liberal Arts, Boston U., 1960, AM in History, 1966; SM in Libr. Sci., Simmons Coll., Boston, 1967. Cert. Harvard-Radcliffe Inst. Hist. and Archival Mgmt., 1960, Am. U.-Nat. Archives Inst. Archival Mgmt., 1966. Asst. Harvard U. Archives, Cambridge, Mass., 1960—70, asst. curator, 1970—71; univ. archivist Harvard U., 1971—2003; dir. Harvard Depository, Southborough, 1982—92; ret., 2003. Registrar, historiographer Protestant Episcopal Diocese of Mass., Boston, 1971—77, dir. libr., 1971—77; coun. mem. Colonial Soc. Mass., Boston, 1973—76; chmn. adv. com. Archives of Am. Art, Boston, 1978—99; asst. v.p. New England Depository Libr., Boston, 1982—88; lectr. in field. Contbr. articles to profl. jours. Mem. Shirley Conservation Commn., 1970—75; trustee Trinity Chapel Episcopal, Shirley, 1993—2006, chmn. bd. trustees; mem. Historic Dists. Study Com., Shirley, Mass., 1972—74; mem. coun. Shirley Hist. Soc., 1973—76. Fellow: Linnean Soc. London; mem.: Royal Geographica Soc., Mass. Hist. Soc., Harvard Meml. Soc. (hon.), Royal Horticultural Soc., Phi Alpha Theta (hon.), Phi Beta Kappa (hon.). Episc. Avocations: gardening, travel, book collecting, genealogy. Home: 6 Horse Pond Rd Shirley Center MA 01464-2714 Personal E-mail: harleyholden@comcast.net.

HOLDEN, JAMES R., state agency administrator; s. Robert J. and Donna J. Holden; m. Kristina M. Dreiband, July 25, 1998. JD, Ind. U., Indpls., 2001. Bar: Ind. 2001. Congl. aide U.S. Rep. John N. Hostettler, Bloomington, Ind., 1996—98; asst. dir. Ind. Lobby Registration Commn., Indpls., 1999—2002; dep. atty. gen. Office of Ind. Atty. Gen., Indpls., 2002—05; dep. commr., chief investigations Ind. Dept. Ins., Indpls., 2005—06; chief dep. treas. Ind. Treas. State's Office, Indpls., 2007—. Adj. prof. Ind. U., Indpls., 2003—, Purdue U., Indpls., 2003—. Precinct committeeman, ward chmn. Rep. Party, Indpls., 1998—2003; commr. Indpls. Housing Agy., 2001—03. Capt. USAR, 2004—. Recipient Chancellor's ward Disting. Tchg., IUPUI, 2006. Republican. Home: 4565 Greenthread Ct Zionsville IN 46077 Office: Office of the Treasurer of State 242 State House Indianapolis IN 46204 Home Phone: 317-769-4442; Office Phone: 317-232-6388.

HOLDEN, MARK V., lawyer; b. Worcester, Mass., Feb. 4, 1963; m. Louise Holden; children: Molly, Clay, Kate, Michael. BA cum laude, U. Mass., 1985; JD, Cath. U. of Am., 1988. Bar: DC 1988, Kans. 1997, US Dist. Ct. (Dist. DC) 1989, US Ct. Appeals (6th Cir.) 1989, US Ct. Appeals (9th Cir.) 1991, US Ct. Appeals (7th Cir.) 1993, US Ct. Appeals (DC Cir.) 1993, US Dist. Ct. (So. Dist. Tex.) 1996, US Dist. Ct. (Ea. Dist. Wis.) 1999, US Ct. Appeals (5th Cir.) 2000, US Ct. Appeals (8th Cir.) 2000. Assoc. labor law Akin Gump Strauss Hauer & Feld LLP, Washington, 1988—95; with Koch Industries, Inc., Wichita, Kans., 1995—, v.p., co-gen. counsel, sr. v.p., gen. counsel, sec., 2006—. Editor (assoc.): Catholic Univ. Law Rev., 1987—88. Mem.: ABA, DC Bar, Kans. Bar Assn. Avocation: running. Office: Koch Industries 4111 E 37th St Wichita KS 67220 Mailing: Koch Industries PO Box 2256 Wichita KS 67201 Office Phone: 316-828-5500. Office Fax: 316-828-5803.

HOLDEN, ROBERT WATSON, radiologist, educator, dean; b. Brazil, Ind., Mar. 31, 1936; s. John William and Naomi Ellen (Watson) H.; m. Miriam Ann Bognanno, June 20, 1964; children: Anne, Robert II, Jennifer. BS in Pharmacy, Purdue U., 1958; MD, Ind. U., 1963. Diplomate Am. Bd. Radiology. Intern L.A. County Gen. Hosp., 1963-64; resident radiology Vanderbilt U., Nashville, 1970-73; asst. prof. Ind. U. Sch. Medicine, Indpls., 1973-77, assoc. prof., 1977-82, prof., 1982—, prof., chmn. dept. radiology, 1991-95, dean, 1996—2000; ret., 2000. Chief vascular and interventional radiology Wishard Meml. Hosp., Indpls., 1973-79, chief radiology, 1977-91; counselor NIH, 1990-94. Contbr. over 100 articles to profl. jours. Chmn. bldg. com. 1st United Meth. Ch., Mooresville, 1988-95. Capt. U.S. Army, 1964-66. Recipient Gold medal Assn. Univ. Radiologists, 1999, Gold medal Am. Roentgen Ray Soc., 2000; named Disting. Alumnus, Purdue U. Sch. Phharmacy, 1992. Fellow Soc. Cardiovascular and Interventional Radiology, Am. Coll. Radiology (counselor, Gold medal 2005), Radiologic Soc. N.Am. (counselor), Ind. Roentgen Soc. (past pres.). Republican. Avocations: forestry, agriculture, tennis. Office: Ind U Sch Medicine fH 302 1120 South Dr Rm 302 Indianapolis IN 46202-5135 Home: 7800 Eagle Creek Overlook Dr Indianapolis IN 46254-9799 Home Phone: 317-216-1864; Office Phone: 317-274-7109. Business E-Mail: rholden@iupui.edu.

HOLDEN, STEPHEN, film critic; b. Morristown, NJ, July 18, 1941; BA, Yale U., 1963. Photo editor, staff writer, A&R executive RCA Records, 1975—76; contbr. NY Times, Village Voice, Rolling Stone, 1971—88; staff writer NY Times, 1988—. Author: Triple Platinum, 1980; contbr. various publications, poetry published in New Yorker and New Yorker Book of Poems. Recipient Grammy Award, 1986. Mem.: NY Film Critics Circle. Avocation: poetry. Office: NY Times Culture Desk 229 W 43rd St New York NY 10036 Office Phone: 212-556-1470. Office Fax: 212-556-1516.

HOLDEN, SUSAN M., lawyer; BA magna cum laude, St. Cloud State Univ., 1984; JD cum laude, William Mitchell Coll. of Law, 1988. Cert.: civil trial specialist. Law clerk Sieben, Grose, Von Holtum & Carey, Mpls., 1985—88, atty., 1988—93, ptnr., bd. dir., 1993—. Bd. dirs. Minn. Continuing Legal Edn.; mem. Commn. on Judicial Selection Minn. Supreme Ct., 1995—99. Named a Woman to Watch Minn., Bus. Jour., 2005; named one of Leading Am. Atty., Top 50 Women Super Lawyers, Top 40 Personal Injury Lawyers, Super Lawyer, 15 Attorneys of Yr., Minn. Lawyer, 2005. Fellow: Am. Bar Found.; mem.: ABA, Douglas K. Amdahl Inn of Ct., Acad. Cert. Trial Lawyers Minn., Nat. Conf. of Bar Presidents, Assn. of Trial Lawyers of Am., Minn. Trial Lawyers Assn., Minn. Women Lawyers (mem. adv. bd.), Hennepin County Bar Assn. (pres. 1999—2000, bd. dirs.), Minn. State Bar Assn. (treas. 2003, pres.-elect 2004, pres. 2005—06), Phi Alpha Delta. Office: Sieben Grose Von Holtum & Carey Ste 900 800 Marquette Ave Minneapolis MN 55402*

HOLDEN, TIM (THOMAS TIMOTHY), congressman, protective official; b. St. Clair, Pa., Mar. 5, 1957; s. Joseph F. and Catherine Siney Holden; m. Gwen Kieres. BA in Sociology, Bloomsburg U., 1980. Ins. broker; real estate agent; probation officer Schuylkill County, Pa., sheriff Pa., 1985—92; sgt.-at-arms Pa. State Ho. Reps.; mem. US Congress from 17th Pa. dist., 1993—, mem. agr. com., 1993—, vice chmn. agr. com., 2007—, chmn. minority mem. conservation, credit, energy and rsch. subcommittee, mem. transp. and infrastructure com., mem. Blue Dog Coalition. Democrat. Roman Catholic. Office: US House Reps 2417 Rayburn House Office Bldg Washington DC 20515-0001 Office Phone: 202-225-5546. Office Fax: 202-226-0996.*

HOLDEN, WILLIAM WILLARD, insurance executive; b. Akron, Ohio, Oct. 5, 1958; s. Joseph McCullem and Lettitia (Roderick) H.; m. Kim Homan, Aug. 31, 1985; 1 child, Jennifer Catharine. BA, Colgate U., Hamilton, NY, 1981. Crime ins. trainee Chubb & Son, Inc., NYC, 1981-82, exec. protection dept. mgr. San Jose, Calif., 1982-85, Woodland Hills, Calif., 1986-91; sr. v.p., mgr. Fin. Svcs. Group, Inc., Rollins, Hudig, Hall, Aon Fin. Svcs. Group, LA, 1991-2000; tng. analyst Chubb & Son, Inc., Warren, NJ, 1985-86; exec. v.p. USI of So. Calif. Ins. Svcs., Woodland Hills, 2000—05; sr. v.p. We. Region Practice Leader Acordia Risk Fin. Group, Sherman Oaks, Calif., 2005—07; mng. dir. Wells Fargo Ins. Svcs. of Calif., 2007—. Co-author manual: Chubb Claims Made Training, 1985; contbr. articles to Colgate alumni mag. Mgr., coach Campbell Little League, ?Calif., 1983-85; coach Simi Valley Girls Softball, 1995-2005; pres. Le Parc Homeowners Assn., Simi Valley, Calif., 1987-89; mem. Community Assn. Inst., LA, 1986-2004; bd. dirs. Friends of the Vols. for LA Unified Sch. Dist., 2001-03, chmn., 2001-03. Mem. Profl. Liability Underwriting Soc. (LA steering com.), Forum for Corp. Dirs. Republican. Avocations: golf, reading, hiking, swimming, softball. Office Phone: 818-464-9417. Business E-Mail: william_holden@wellsfargois.com.

HOLDENER, JUDY ANN, mathematics professor, researcher; b. Parma, OH, Sept. 14, 1965; d. Charles Dunn Newhauser and Joanne Laverne (Newhauser) Solgos; m. Eric James Holdener, June 26, 1993; children: Chase Alexander, Maxim Elias. BSc in Math., Kent State U., 1987; MSc in Math., U. Ill., 1989, PhD in Math., 1994. Tchg., rsch. asst. U. Ill., Urbana, 1987—94; asst. prof. US Air Force Acad., Colorado Springs, Colo., 1994—97, Kenyon Coll., Gambier, Ohio, 1997—2003, assoc. prof., 2003—. Cons. Wolfram Rsch. Inc., Urbana, 1989—90; vis. prof. U. Colo., Boulder, 2004—05; John B. McCoy disting. tchg. chair Kenyon Coll., 2007—. Contbr. math. papers to jours. in field. Recipient Tony M. Johnson Excellence Tchg. award, US Air Force Acad., 1995, Bd. Trustees Jr. Tchg. award, Kenyon Coll., 2003, Tomsich Sci. award, 2003. Mem.: Am. Math. Soc., Math. Assn. Am., Phi Beta Kappa. Avocations: painting, gardening, hiking, reading. Office: Kenyon Coll 307 Hayes Hall Gambier OH 43022 Office Phone: 740-427-5266. Business E-Mail: holdenerj@kenyon.edu.

HOLDER, ANGELA RODDEY, law educator; b. Rock Hill, SC, Mar. 13, 1938; d. John T. and Angela M. (Fisher) Roddey; 1 child, John Thomas Roddey Holder. Student, Radcliffe Coll., 1955-56; BA, Newcomb Coll., 1958; postgrad., Faculty of Law-King's Coll., London, 1957-58; JD, Tulane U., New Orleans, 1960; LLM, Yale U., New Haven, Conn., 1975. Bar: La. 1961, S.C. 1960, Conn. 1981. Counsel Roddey, Sumwalt & Carpenter, Rock Hill, SC, 1960-91; atty. criminal div. New Orleans Legal Aid Bur., 1961-62; counsel York County Family Ct., SC, 1962-64; asst. prof. polit. sci. Winthrop Coll., Rock Hill, 1964-74; research assoc. Yale U. Law Sch., 1975-77, exec. dir. program in law, sci. and medicine, 1976-77; lectr. dept. pediatrics Yale U. Sch. Medicine, 1975-77, asst. clin. prof. pediatrics and law, 1977-79, assoc. clin. prof., 1979-83, clin. prof., 1983-2001; prof. practice of med. ethics Duke U. Med. Ctr., Durham, NC, 2001—07, prof. emerita med. ethics and humanities, 2007—. Trustee Am. Bd. Pediatrics, 2003—; mem. com. on pediat. palliative care Inst. Medicine, 2001—02, mem. com. on clin. rsch. with children, 2002—04. Author: The Meaning of the Constitution, 1968, 3d edit., 1997, Medical Malpractice Law, 1975, 2d edit. 1978, Legal Issues in Pediatrics and Adolescent Medicine, 1977, 3d edit., 1997; contbg. editor: Prism mag., AMA; mem. editl. bd.: IRB, 1976-2000, Medicine and HealthCare, 1978-2000, Jour. Philosophy and Medicine; contbr. articles to profl. jours. Mem. Rock Hill Sch. Bd., 1967—68; chmn. bd. dirs. Family Planning Clinic, 1970—73; bd. trustees Ednl. Commn. for Fgn. Med. Grads., 1990—97, exec. com., 1997; bd. dir. Conn. Planned Parenthood, 1993—99, exec. com., 1996—99; mem. lawyers' rev. group Health Care Task Force, The White House, 1993; bd. trustees Cushing/Whitney Med. Libr. at Yale U., 1996—2001; ethics com. Leeway AIDS Hospice, New Haven, 1996—2001; alumnae bd. visitors Nat. Cathedral Sch., Washington, 2000—; cons. Artificial Reproductive Techs. Com., Ct. Ho. of Reps.; mem. adv. bd., grad. health programs Sarah Lawrence Coll., 2004—. Mem. Conn. Bar Assn., S.C. Bar Assn. (medico-legal com. 1973—), La. Bar Assn., New Haven County Bar Assn., Am. Soc. Law and Medicine (treas. 1981-83, sec. 1983-85, pres. 1986-88, bd. dirs. 1977-91). Democrat. Episcopalian. Home: 3408 Hope Valley Rd Durham NC 27707 Office: Trent Ctr Bioethics Humanities and History Medicine Box 3040 108 Seeley G Mudd Bldg Durham NC 27710 Business E-Mail: angela.holder@duke.edu.

HOLDER, CALVIN BERESFORD, history professor; b. Barbados, Sept. 28, 1946; s. Clifford Beresford and Beryl Leotta (Smith) H.; divorced; children: Aisha Margaret, Oshun Doris. AB, CCNY, 1970; AM, Harvard U., 1971, PhD, 1976. Prof. history Coll. of S.I., CUNY, N.Y., 1975—. Office: Coll SI CUNY Dept History 2800 Victory Blvd Staten Island NY 10314

HOLDER, ERIC H., lawyer, former federal agency administrator; b. NYC, Jan. 21, 1951; s. Eric H. and Miriam R. (Yearwood) H.; m. Sharon Malone; 3 children. BA, Columbia U., 1973, JD, 1976. Bar: NY 1977, DC 1980. Law clerk NAACP Legal Def. Fund, Criminal Divsn., Dept. Justice; trial atty. pub. integrity sect. US Dept. Justice, 1976-88; assoc. judge Superior Ct., Washington, 1988-93; US atty. DC US Dept. Justice, Washington, 1993-97, US dep. atty. gen., 1997—2001, acting atty. gen., 2001; ptnr. Covington & Burling, Washington, 2001—. Bd. dirs., mem. MCI; mem. ad hoc adv. group US Sentencing Commn.; chmn. external diversity adv. panel Eastman Kodak. Meyer Found.; See Forever Found. Mem. Concerned Black Men. Democrat. Office: Covington & Burling 1201 Pennsylvania Ave NW Washington DC 20004-2401 Business E-Mail: eholder@cov.com.

HOLDER, HAROLD DOUGLAS, SR., investor, hotel executive; b. Anniston, Ala., June 25, 1931; s. William Chester and Lucile (Kadle) H.; m. Anna Maria Yaccarino, 1996; children: Debra Holder Carnaroli, Harold Douglas Jr., Charlie Kadle. Student, Anniston Bus. Coll., 1949, Jacksonville State U., 1954-57, Druitt Sch. Speech, 1962. Dept. mgr. Sears, Roebuck & Co., Anniston, 1954-57, merchandising mgr. Atlanta, 1957-59, dir. coll. recruiting, 1959-61, dir. exec. devel. program, 1961, asst. personnel dir., 1962-63, store mgr. Cocoa, Fla., 1965-67, Ocala, Fla., 1963-65, opers. zone mgr. Atlanta, 1967-68, asst. gen. mgr. mdse., 1968-69, sales promotion mgr. So. area, 1968; pres., bd. dirs. Cunningham Drug Stores, Inc., Detroit, 1969-70; v.p. Interstate Stores, 1971; pres., bd. dirs. Rahall Communications Corp., 1971-73; chmn. bd., chief exec. officer, dir. Am. Agronomics Corp., 1973-86; pres. Harold Holder Leasing; mng. dir. The Holder Group, Inc., 1987—. CEO, bd. dirs. Cutler Mfg. Corp., 1989-2000, Atlas Aircraft Corp., 1987-2000; mem. exec. com., bd.

dirs. Coastland Corp., Fla., 1979-84; pres., bd. dirs. Golden Harvest, Inc., 1976-88; bd. dirs., treas. Dome Products, Inc., 1989-2000; CEO Casino Mgmt. Svcs. Internat., 1999—, Stockmen's Hotel & Casino, Red Garter Hotel & Casino, Comml. Hotel & Casino, Scoreboard Sports Lounge, The Holder Group Wigwam, LLC, 2005; chmn., CEO The Holder Hospitality Group, Inc.; CEO Silver Club Hotel & Casino, El Capitan Resort Casino, Sharkey's Nugget Casino, Sundance Casino, Model "T" Resort Casino, Charlie Holder's Casino, 2003-07, Fernley Truck-Inn and Casino, Joe's Tavern; chmn. New Dawn Resorts, Ltd., Accra, Ghana; chmn. The Holder Group Vending Co. Author: Don't Shoot, I'm Only a Trainee, 1975. Chmn., bd. dirs. Miracle, Inc., Brevard County; chmn. United Appeal, Ocala, Fla., 1964, Cocoa, Fla., 1966; bd. dirs. United Way Hillsborough County (Fla.); chmn. Heart Fund Drive, Ocala, 1964, Marion (Fla.) Com. of 100; bd. dirs. So. Coll. Placement Assn., Am. Acad. Achievement; bd. dirs. Marion chpt. ARC, Opera Arts Assn.; exec. com. Share, U. Fla.; bd. trustees U. Tampa; chmn. bd. trustees, trustee emeritus Eckerd Coll. With USMC, 1950-53. Named Harold D. Holder chair of Internat. Bus. and Fin., Eckerd Coll., Nev. Hotelier of the Yr., 2004; recipient Disting. Svc. award, Marion County 4-H Club, 1965, Golden Plate award, 1983, Champion of Higher Edn. award, 1982, Fla. NAACP Humanitarian award, 1984, Patriotic Employer award, US Dept. Def, 2005, Employer of Yr. award, Nev. Disabled Veterans Large. Mem.: Young Pres. Orgn. (past chmn. Fla. chpt.), C. of C. (chmn. beautification com., retail bus. com.), Chief Execs. Forum, Omicron Delta Kappa. Episcopalian. Office: The Holder Hospitality Group Inc 1040 Victorian Ave Sparks NV 89431-4923 Office Phone: 775-358-4771.

HOLDER, JANICE MARIE, state supreme court justice; b. Canonsburg, Pa., Aug. 29, 1949; d. Louis V. and Sylvia (Abraham) H.; m. George W. Loveland II, June 5, 1976 (div. Mar. 1987). Student, Allegheny Coll., 1967-68, Sorbonne, 1970; BS summa cum laude, U. Pitts., 1971; JD, Duquesne U., 1975. Bar: Pa. 1975, Tenn. 1979, D.C. 1988. Sr. law clk. to chief judge U.S. Dist. Ct. for Western Dist. Pa., Pitts., 1975-77; assoc. Catalano & Catalano, P.C., Pitts., 1977-79, Holt, Batchelor, Spicer & Ryan, Memphis, 1980-82; pvt. practice Memphis, 1982—87; assoc. James S. Cox & Assocs., Memphis, 1987-89; pvt. practice law Memphis, 1989-90; judge 30th Jud. Dist., Memphis, 1990-96; justice Tenn. Supreme Ct., 1996—. Solicitor Borough of McDonald (Pa.), 1978-79. Bd. dirs. Alliance for Blind and Visually Impaired, Memphis, 1985—94, Midtown Mental Health Ctr., 1995—97; trustee Memphis Bot. Garden Found., 1995—2002; mem. state coordinating coun. Tenn. Task Force Against Domestic Violence, 1994—96. Fellow: Tenn. Bar Found. (trustee 1995—99); mem.: ABA, Tenn. Trial Judges Assn. (exec. com. 1994—96), Tenn. Lawyers' Assn. for Women, Memphis Trial Lawyers Assn. (bd. dirs. 1988—90), Am. Inns Ct., Tenn. Jud. Conf. (treas. 1993—94, exec. com. 1993—96), Assn. for Women Attys. (treas. 1989, v.p. 1991, Marion Griffin-Frances Loring award 1999), Memphis Bar Assn. (bd. dirs. 1986—87, 1993—94, editor Memphis Bar Forum 1987—91, 1993—94, sec. 1993, treas. 1994, Sam A. Myar award 1990, Judge of Yr. divorce and family law sect. 1992, Chancellor Charles A. Rond award Outstanding Jurist 1992), Tenn. Bar Assn., Am. Bar Found. Office: Tenn Supreme Ct 119 S Main St Ste 310 Memphis TN 38103-3678

HOLDER, JULIE FASONE, chemicals executive; Grad. in Bus. Adminstrn., Mich. State U. Sales rep. Dow Chem. Co., San Francisco, 1975, mktg. mgr. polyurethanes bus., 1981, dist. sales mgr. Dow Latex, grp. mktg. mgr. formulation products, 1989—94, global bus. dir. performance chems. businesses, 1994, dir. sales and mktg. performance chems. bus. unit, 1997—2000, bus. v.p. indsl. chems., 2000—04, bus. v.p. specialty plastics and elastomers grp., 2004, corp. v.p. human resources, diversity & inclusion and pub. affairs, 2005—, mem. Office of the Chief Exec., 2005—. Co-founder Women Innovation Network Dow Chem. Co.; bd. dirs. Wolverine Bank, Dow Chem. Co. Found. Office: Dow Chem Co 2030 Dow Ctr Midland MI 48674

HOLDER, SALLIE LOU, training and meeting management consultant, coach; b. Cin., Jan. 25, 1939; d. David Clifford Austin and Ruth Margaret (Higby) Haver; m. Norman Horace Derwyn Holder, July 14, 1964 (div. Oct. 1975) Student, Duke U., 1957—59; BS in Home Econs. Edn., U. Md, 1962; MA in Human Resource Devel. and Edn., George Washington U., 1982; cert. Success Unltd. Network, Basic Coaching Program, 2000. Tchr. Prince Georges County Schs., Md., 1962—66; home econs. tchr. La Reine Sr. H.S., Suitland, Md., 1966—68; adult edn. Home econs. tchr. Suitland Sr. H.S, 1969—73; mgr./asst. area sales mgr. The Fabric Tree, Hyattsville, Md., 1972—75; trainer Woodward & Lothrop, Washington and Prince Georges County, 1975—79; conf. coord., non-credit short course coord. Univ. Coll. U. Md., College Park, 1979—87; analyst SYSCON, Washington, 1987—88; meeting mgmt. and tng. cons. Holder & Assocs., College Park, Md., 1988—; tng. specialist Fed. Deposit Ins. Corp., Washington, 1990; instr. Marymount U., Arlington, Va., 1990, Goucher Coll., Balt., 1991—93. Facilitator New Beginnings, Takoma Park, Md., 1983-90, chmn. planning com., facilitator co-trainer, bd. dirs., 1983-84, chmn. facilitators, 1985-86 Mem. alumni bd. Coll. Human Ecology, U. Md., College Park, 1971-93, pres., 1973-74, 77-80, sec., 1985-86, v.p., 1988-90; bd. dirs., mem., cons. lay edn. com., cmty. edn. com. Pastoral Counseling and Consultation Ctrs., 1977-86; mem. seminarian com., search com., chmn. retreat com., vestry mem. Ch. of the Nativity, Camp Springs, Md., vestryman, 1990-93, 2002-2004; mem. Fisherfolk, 1993-98, region 5 rep., 1997-99, pledge sec., 1997-98; mem. congl. care com., 1993-2005, reader, greeter, 1996—, St. Andrews Episcopal Ch., College Park; vol. monitor Smithsonian Residents Assocs. Program, 1993—; vol. usher Arena State, 1989—, Olney Theater, 2005—; membership chair, bd. dirs. Columbian Women at George Washington U., 1999-2004; mem. adv. coun. dept. bus. and mgmt. Prince Georges C.C., 1997-2004 Recipient Disting. Svc. award Alumni Bd. of Coll. Human Ecology, U. Md., 1981, Vol. award, 1991 Mem. AAUW (College Park chpt., sec. 2005-2006), ASTD (Washington chpt. employer coord. 1984-85, co-chmn. program com. 1986, chmn. meeting arrangements 1987-88, treas. 1989, Day chmn., nat. issues chair 1990, chair scholarship com. 1992, coord. spl. interest group 1993, Spl. Achievement award 1987, 88, 90, Pres.'s award 1993), Soc. Govt. Meeting Planners (program commn. 1987-88, comm. com., ann. conf. com. 1988-89, chmn. nominating com. 1990, ann. conf. presenter 1990, 93, 94, 98, bd. dirs. 1991-92, 95-97, chmn. edn. com. for 1992 ann. conf. 1995-97, newsletter editor), U. Md. College Park Alumni Assn. (bd. govs. 1989-93), Assn. Meeting Profls., Profl. Conv. Mgrs. Assn., Md. Prince Georges Alumni Assn. (v.p. 1994-99, sec. 2004—), Delmarva Depression Glass Club, Washington Met. Glass Club, Nat. Am. Glass Club, Prince Georges Hist. Soc, DAR (Toaping Castle chpt. historian 2004—), Episcopal Sr. Ministries (bd. dirs.), Art Gliner Humor Ctr. U. Md. (bd. dirs.), Nat. Interfaith Coun. On Aging (bd. dirs.), U. Pk. Women's Club, Paint Branch Garden Club. Episcopalian. Home and Office: 4102 Van Buren St University Park MD 20782-1185

HOLDING, R(OBERT) EARL, oil industry executive; b. Salt Lake City, Utah; m. Carol Holding; 3 children. BA/BS, U. Utah. Pres., CEO Sinclair Oil Corp., Salt Lake City, 1976—. Owner Sun Valley Resort, Idaho, 1977—, Grand Am. Hotel, Salt Lake City. Named one of Forbes' Richest Americans, 1999—, World's Richest People, Forbes mag., 2002—. Avocation: skiing. Office: Sinclair Oil Corp PO Box 30825 Salt Lake City UT 84130*

HOLDREN, JOHN PAUL, physicist, educator, writer; b. Sewickley, Pa., Mar. 1, 1944; s. Raymond Andrew and Virginia June (Fuqua) H.; m. Cheryl Edgar, Feb. 5, 1966; children: John Craig, Jill Virginia SB, MIT, 1965, SM, 1966; PhD, Stanford U., Calif., 1970; ScD (hon.), U. Puget Sound, 1975; DEng (hon.), Colo. Sch. Mines, 1997; DSc (hon.), Clark U., 2003. Aerodyn. engr. Lockheed Missiles & Space Co., Sunnyvale, Calif., 1966-67; theoretical physicist Lawrence Livermore Lab., Calif., 1970-71; sr. research fellow Calif. Inst. Tech., Pasadena, 1972-73; asst. prof. energy and resources U. Calif.-Berkeley, 1973-75, assoc. prof. energy and resources, 1975-78, prof. energy and resources, 1978-96, Class of 1935 prof. energy, 1991-96, chmn. grad. degree prog. in energy and resources, 1983-84; Teresa and John Heinz prof. environ. policy Harvard U., Cambridge, Mass., 1996—, dir. sci., tech. and pub. policy prog., Kennedy Sch., prof. environ. sci. and pub. policy, dept. of earth and planetary scis.; Teresa and John Heinz prof. environ. policy, dir. sci., tech, pub. policy program JFK Sch. Govt., Harvard U.; and dir. Woods Hole Rsch. Ctr., 2005—. Cons. in fusion energy Lawrence Livermore Labs., 1974—; sr. investigator Rocky Mountain Biol. Lab., Crested Butte, Colo., 1974-88; vis. fellow East-West Ctr., Honolulu, 1979-80, Max-Planck-Gesellschaft, Starnberg, Fed. Republic Germany, 1987; vis. fellow arms control program MIT, 1988; vis. prof. physics U. Rome tor Vergata, 1987; vis. scientist Woods Hole Rsch. Ctr., 1992—2005; mem. Fusion Energy adv. com. Sec. of Energy, 1991-94; mem. Pres. Clinton's Com. of Advisors on Sci. and Tech., 1994-2001. Co-editor: Man and the Ecosphere, 1971, Strategic Defences, 1987, The Cassandra Conference, 1988; co-author: Energy, 1971, Human Ecology, 1973, Ecoscience, 1977, Management and Disposition of Excess Weapon Plutonium, 1994, The Future of U.S. Nuclear Weapons Policy, 1997; co-editor: Earth and the Human Future, 1986, Conversion of Military R & D, 1999; bd. editors Bull. of Atomic Scientists, Chgo., 1984-86; contbr. to articles and rsch. papers in the field. Mem. exec. com. Pugwash Confs. on Sci. and World Affairs, London and Geneva, 1982-97, chmn., 1987-97; chmn. U.S. Pugwash Com., Cambridge, Mass., 1983-95; mem. coun. Smithsonian Instn., 1988-91; bd. dirs. McArthur Found., 1991—2005; mem. Pres.'s Com. Advisors on Sci. and Tech., 1994-2000. Recipient Gustavsen lectureship U. Chgo., 1978; MacArthur Prize fellow MacArthur Found., Chgo., 1981-86; recipient Volvo Environ. Prize, 1993, leadership award Fusion Power Assocs., 1998, award for excellence Kaul Found., 1999, Tyler Environment prize, 2000, Heinz prize in Public Policy, 2001. Fellow AAAS (pres. 2006-, co-chair nat. commn. on energy policy 2002—), Am. Acad. Arts and Scis. (vice chmn. com. on internat. security 1983—97, Kistiakowsky Meml. Lectureship 1986-87), Calif. Acad. Scis.; mem. NAE, NAS (com. internat. security and arms control 1992-2004, chmn. 1993-2004), Fedn. Am. Scientists (council, treas. 1979-80, vice chmn. 1981-84, chmn. 1984-86, bd. sponsors, 1986—, Pub. Service award 1979), Am. Phys. Soc. (Forum award 1995). Democrat. Office: Harvard U Kennedy Sch Govt BelferCtr for Sci & Internat Affairs 79 John F Kennedy St Littauer-370 Cambridge MA 02138-5801 Office Phone: 617-495-1464. Office Fax: 617-495-8963. E-mail: john_holdren@harvard.edu.

HOLDREN, SUSAN, literature and language professor, foundation administrator; b. Zanesville, Ohio, Mar. 27, 1952; d. John William and Mary Helen Straker; m. Thomas E. Holdren Jr., Sept. 6, 2003; children: Samuel, Laura. BA in English, Denison U., Granville, Ohio, 1974; MA in Interpersonal Comm., Ohio U., Athens, 1990. Prof. English Zane State Coll., Zanesville, Ohio, 1991—. Founding bd. mem. Found. Appalachian Ohio, Nelsonville, 1996—2005; pres. J.W. & M.H. Straker Charitable Trust, Zanesville, 1996—2005; dir. Unizan Bank, Zanesville, 1996—2006. Named Tchr. of Yr., Zane State Coll., 1998, 2003. Mem.: Nat. Coun. Tchrs. English. Office: Zane State Coll 1555 Newark Rd Zanesville OH 43701-2626

HOLDRIDGE, BARBARA, book editor, writer, consultant; b. NYC, July 26, 1929; d. Herbert L. and Bertha (Gold) Cohen; m. Lawrence B. Holdridge, Oct. 9, 1959; 2 children. AB, Hunter Coll., 1950. Asst. editor Liveright Pub. Corp., NYC, 1950-52; co-founder Caedmon Records, Inc., NYC, 1952, ptnr., 1952-60, pres., 1960-62, treas., 1962-70, pres., 1970-75; founder Stemmer House Pubs. Inc., Owings Mills, Md., 1975, pres., 1975—2003; founder Stemmer House, Inc., Owings Mills, 2003, pres., 2003—. Co-founder, v.p. Shakespeare Rec. So., Inc., N.Y.C., 1960-70, Theatre Rec. Soc., Inc., N.Y.C., 1964-70, BEDE Prodns., 1984, History Rec. Soc., Inc., N.Y.C., 1964, pres., 1964-70; lectr. on Ammi Phillips, 1959—; lectr. on book pub., 1992—; lectr. on Caedmon history, 1980-; adj. prof. writing media Loyola Coll., Balt., 1987-91. Author: Ammi Phillips, 1968, Aubrey Beardsley Designs from the Age of Chivalry, 1983, Chinese Cut-Out Designs of Costumes, 1989; articles on Am. paintings. Named to Hunter Coll. Hall of Fame, 1972, Nat. Women's Hall of Fame, 2001; recipient Am. Shakespeare Festival award, 1962, N.Y.C. cert. of appreciation, 1972, Lifetime Achievement award, Audio Pubs. Assn., 2001, Peabody Instl. award, 1991, Preservation Project award, Balt. County Hist. Trust, 2007. Mem. 14 West Hamilton Street Club, Phi Beta Kappa Alumni Assn. of Greater Balt. (bd. dirs.). Office Phone: 410-363-3690. Personal E-mail: stemmerhouse@verizon.net.

HOLDSCLAW, CHAMIQUE SHAUNTA, retired professional basketball player; b. Flushing, NY, Aug. 9, 1977; Grad., U. Tenn., 1999. Basketball player Washington Mystics, 1999—2005, LA Sparks, 2005—07. Named Sports Illustrated and Sporting News Nat. Women's Player of Yr., 1999, Naismith finalist, AP Women's Basketball Player of Yr., 1997—98, 1998—99, N.Y.C. Player of Yr., Rawlings/WBCA Player of Yr., Player of Yr., Columbus, Ohio Touchdown Club, 1995, Rookie of the Yr., WNBA, 1999; named one of 12 female athletes selected as inspirational role models, Women's Sports and Fitness mag., 1998; named to Kodak 25th Anniversary Team, Women's Basketball Jour., Street & Smith All-Am., three-time, USA Today All-Am., WNBA All-Star Team, 1999, 2000, 2003, All-WNBA Team, 2000, 2001; recipient Sullivan award, Gold medal, 1998 World Championships, 1997 World Qualifying Tournament, 1995 Olympic Festival, USA Basketball Player of Yr. award, 1997, ESPY's for Female Athlete of Yr. award, second consecutive Women's Basketball Player of Yr. award, 1999, Naismith award, Atlanta's Tip-Off Club, 1995, Gold medal, U.S. Olympic Team, 2000.*

HOLDSWORTH, JANET NOTT, women's health nurse; b. Evanston, Ill., Dec. 25, 1941; d. William Alfred and Elizabeth Inez (Kelly) Nott; children: James William, Kelly Elizaveth, John David. BSN with high distinction, U. Iowa, 1963; M of Nursing, U. Wash., 1966. RN, Colo. Staff nurse U. Colo. Hosp., Denver, 1963-64, Presbyn. Hosp., Denver, 1964-65, Grand Canyon Hosp., Ariz., 1965; asst. prof. U. Colo. Sch. Nursing, Denver, 1966-71; counseling nurse Boulder PolyDrug Treatment Ctr., Boulder, 1971-77; pvt. duty nurse Nurses' Offcl. Registry, Denver, 1973-82; cons. nurse, tchr. parenting and child devel. Teenage Parent Program, Boulder Valley Schs., Boulder, 1980-88; bd. dirs., treas. Nott's Travel, Aurora, Colo., 1980—; nurse Rocky Mountain Surgery Ctr., 1996—. Instr., nursing coord. ARC, Boulder, 1979-90, instr., nursing tng. specialist, 1980-82. Mem. adv. bd. Boulder County Lamaze Inc., 1980-88; mem. adv. com. Child Find and Parent-Family, Boulder, 1981-89; del. Rep. County State Congl. Convs., 1972-96, sec. 17th Dist. Senatorial Com., Boulder, 1982-92; vol. Mile High ARC, 1980; vol. chmn. Mesa Sch. PTO, Boulder, 1982-92, bd. dirs., 1982-95, v.p., 1983-95; elder Presbyn. Ch. Mem. ANA, Colo. Nurses Assn. (bd. dirs. 1975-76, human rights com. 1981-83, dist. pres. 1974-76), Coun. Intracultural Nurses, Sigma Theta Tau, Alpha Lambda Delta. Republican. Home: 1550 Findlay Way Boulder CO 80305-6922 Office: Rocky Mountain Surgery Ctr 1630 30th St # 153 Boulder CO 80301-1014

HOLE, RICHARD DOUGLAS, lawyer; b. Auburn, NY, Aug. 23, 1949; s. Robert B. and Barbara (Swift) H.; m. Deborah Elizabeth Muldoon, Jan. 8, 1972; children: Emily, Brian, Jeffrey. BA, Hamilton Coll., 1971; JD, Syracuse U., NY, 1975. Bar: N.Y. 1976, U.S. Dist. Ct. (no. dist.) N.Y. 1976, U.S. Dist. Ct. (we. dist.) N.Y. 1980. Assoc. Bond, Schoeneck & King, Syracuse, 1976—83, ptnr., 1984—. Pres. N.Y. Employee Benefits Conf., Rochester, 1987-88. Pres. Fayetteville-Manlius (N.Y.) Little League, Inc., 1988-93; pres. Eye Rsch. Inst. of Ctrl. N.Y., Syracuse, 1988-93; bd. dirs. Cystic Fibrosis Found., Syracuse, 1988-93; pres., bd. trustees United Ch. of Fayetteville, 1990-95, 98—; bd. dirs. Syracuse Symphony, 1995-2001; pres. Ctrl. N.Y. Alumni Coun. Hamilton Coll., 1999-2004; bd. dirs. United Way Ctrl. NY, 2007—. Mem.: Confrerie des Chevaliers du Tastrvin, Nat. Assn. Coll. and Univ. Attys., Onondaga County Bar Assn., NY State Bar Assn., Shameateles Country Club. Republican. Presbyterian. Office: Bond Schoeneck & King 18th Fl One Lincoln Ctr Syracuse NY 13202 Business E-Mail: holer@bsk.com.

HOLEMAN, BETTY JEAN, counseling administrator; b. Timberlake, NC, Jan. 9, 1952; d. Stanley and Mallie Alice Holeman. BS in Profl. History cum laude, NC Agrl. and Tech. State U., Greensboro, 1974, MS in Edn. Guidance, 1978. Lic. sch. counselor NC, cert. continuing edn. Journ. Learning Internat. Youth counselor Barfield Recreation Ctr., Durham, NC, 1968—69; nurse's aide ICU, VA Hosp., Durham, 1969; with PACE Program, page stacks Greensboro Pub. Libr., 1972; news editor A&T Register newspaper, 1973—74; inserter Circulation dept. Durham Herald Sun Newspaper, 1978—84; sub. tchr. Durham Pub. Schs., 1984—92. Program asst. Counseling Ctr. NC Agrl. and Tech. State U., Greensboro, intern; program adminstr. NC Agrl. and Tech. State U., Greensboro, 1974—76; hist. dept. rep. U. Senate, 1973—74. Author of poems; contbr. articles to profl. jours. Cmty. vol. Am. Diabetes Assn., Va., 2001—04. Recipient Outstanding Acad. Achievement, NC Agrl. and Tech. State U., 1973—74, Cub award, Journeyman award for continued svc., Editors award for dedicated svc.; scholar, Belk Found., 1970. Mem.: ACA, NC Assn. for Counseling and Devel., NC Sch. Counselor Assn., Phi Alpha Theta Internat. Honor Soc. in History (charter mem.), Kappa Delta Pi (sec.). Democrat. Baptist. Avocation: reading. Home: 2614 Red Valley Dr Rougemont NC 27572

HOLEMAN, RUSSELL KENT, civil engineer, director, construction executive; b. Lexington, Mo., Oct. 23, 1957; s. E.G. and Joyce Lynette (Bredehoeft) H.; m. Linda Lea Cameron, May 23, 1981; children: Jared Tyler, Chelsea Paige. BSCE, Tex. Tech. U., 1979. Registered profl. engr., Tex. Civil engr. US Army Facilities Engrs., Fort Hood, Tex., 1979-81, US Army Corps Engrs., Fort Hood, 1981-83, chief office engring., 1983-85, chief contract adminstrn. Amarillo, Tex., 1985-87, area engr., 1987-95, dir. mil. project mgmt. Tulsa, 1995—2000, asst. chief engring. and constrn., 2000—02, chief hydrology, 2002—, chief engring. and constrn. Iraq, 2006—. Facilitator U.S. Army, Ctr. for Army Leadership, Ft. Leavenworth, Kans., 1989-2001; spl. assignment for reconstruction of Iraqi oil system, 2003, 05; spl. assignment reconstruction of Iraq Pub. Infrastructure, 2006-07. Co-developer: (software) Construction Office Contract Administrator, 1983-86. Pres. Tex. Panhandle Fed. Exec. Assn., 1994; v.p. Prince of Peace Luth. Ch., Amarillo, 1988; major acct. exec. govt. sector, United Way, Amarillo, 1991, vice chmn., 1992, chmn., 1993; vice chmn. Tulsa combined fed. campaign, 1997; asst. scoutmaster Boy Scouts Am., 1996—2003, vice chmn. outer limits com., 1997-06, venturing tng. chmn., 2002-06, advisor Boy Scout Explorer Post 2001, 1998—2005, Boy Scout dist. commr. 2005-06. Recipient Engr. of Yr., Tulsa Dist., 1990, Leadership award Tulsa Dist., 1993, Comdr.'s award for civilian svc., 1998, Venturing Leadership award Boy Scouts Am., 1999, Meritorious Civilian Svc. award, 2003, Customer Care Employee of Yr., 2003, Venturing Dist. Merit award, 2006, Superior Civilian Svc. award, 2007. Mem. NSPE, Nat. Def. Indsl. Assn., Tex. Soc. Profl. Engrs., Tex. Panhandle Fed. Exec. Assn. (sec., treas. 1991-92, v.p. 1992-93, pres. 1993-94). Avocations: softball, skiing, backpacking, camping. Office Phone: 918-669-7302. Business E-Mail: russell.holeman@us.army.mil.

HOLEN, NORMAN DEAN, artist, educator; b. Cavalier, ND, Sept. 16, 1937; s. Alvin C. and Norma H. Holen; m. Ilene Gronaas, Sept. 3, 1960; children: Peter John, Alisa Ilene. BA, Concordia Coll., 1959; MFA, State U. Iowa, 1962; postgrad., U. Minn., 1972. Instr. Northwestern Coll., Orange City, Iowa, 1962-63, Concordia Coll., Moorhead, Minn., 1963-64; prof. Augsburg Coll., Mpls., 1964—2002; ret., 2002. Contbr. articles to profl. jours.; artist (commns.) Kirchbak Gardens, Richfield, Minn., King Olav, Oslo, Norway, Augsburg Coll., Mpls., King Herald V, Norway. Mem.: Allied Artists Am. (Rachel L. Armour award 1980, 1982, In Memorium award 1983), Nat. Sculpture Soc. (Bronze medal 1980, Joel Meisner award 1983), Soc. Minn. Sculptors, Artist Equity Assn. (v.p. Minn. chpt. 1973—74, chpt. pres., nat. exec. bd. 1974—75). Republican. Lutheran. Avocations: playing classical guitar, inventing tools and splints for my physically challenged students. Home: 7332 12th Ave S Minneapolis MN 55423-3343

HOLFORD, THEODORE RICHARD, biostatistician, educator; b. Columbus, Ohio, May 19, 1947; s. Charles Richard and LaVern Lucille (Lukens) H.; m. Maryellen Hutchinson Holford, Dec. 21, 1969; children: Matthew Edwin, Lesley Erin. BA in Math and Chemistry, Andrews U., 1969; PhD in Biometry, Yale U., 1973. Rsch. staff Yale U., New Haven, 1972-73, asst. prof., 1974-79, assoc. prof., 1979-89, prof., 1989—, head divsn. biostatistics, 1990-97, 2003—, dir. grad. studies, 1997—2002, acting dean pub. health, 2001. Editor: Statistical Methods in Medical Research, 1992—2005; assoc. editor Am. Jour. Epidemiology, 1989-97, Biometrics, 1984-88; contbr. articles to profl. jours. Mem. Consensus Devel. Conf. on Health Implications of Smokeless Tobacco, Washington, 1986, Epidemiology & Disease Control Study Section, Washington, 1986-89, Epidemiology Adv. Subcom. Oak Ridge (Tenn.) Assn., 1988-93. Elinor Roosevelt Cancer fellow, 1981-82; recipient Wakeman award, 1990, numerous NIH grants. Fellow Am. Coll. Epidemiology, Am. Statis. Assn.; mem. Am. Statis. Assn., 1973—, Biometric Soc., 1973—, Soc. for Epidemiologic Rsch., 1978—. Avocations: trumpet, hiking, photography. Office Phone: 203-785-2838. Business E-Mail: theodore.holford@yale.edu.

HOLIDAY, EDITH ELIZABETH, former presidential adviser, cabinet secretary; b. Middletown, Ohio, Feb. 14, 1952; d. Harry Jr. and Kathlyn (Watson) H.; m. Terrence B. Adamson, June 8, 1985; children: Kathlyn Holiday Adamson, Elizabeth Holiday Adamson; 1 stepchild, Terrence Morgan Adamson. Student, Miami U., Oxford, Ohio, 1970-71; BS with honors, U. Fla., 1974, JD, 1977. Bar: Fla. 1977, D.C. 1978, Ga. 1984. Assoc. Read Smith Shaw & McClay, Washington, 1977-83, Dow Lohnes & Albertson, Atlanta, 1983-84; exec. dir. Commn. on Exec. Legis. and Jud. Salaries, Washington, 1984-85; spl. counsel polit. action com. Fund for Am. Future, Washington, 1985-87; dir. ops. George Bush for Pres., Inc., Washington, 1987-88; chief counsel, nat. fin. and ops. dir. Bush-Quayle 88, Washington, 1988; with legal svcs. staff George Bush for Pres. Compliance Com., Washington, 1988; asst. sec. for pub. affairs and pub. liaison, counselor to sec. Departmental Offices, U.S. Dept. Treasury, Washington, 1988; gen. counsel U.S. Dept. Treasury, Washington, 1989-90; asst. to U.S. pres., sec. of cabinet Washington, 1990-93. Legis. asst. to U.S. Sen. Nicholas F. Brady, Washington, 1982—83; bd. dirs. Amerada Hess Corp., H.J. Heinz Co., White Mountain Ins. Group, Ltd., Franklin Templeton Group Funds, RTI Internat. Metals, Inc., Canadian Nat. Railway Co.; oper. trustee TWE Holdings I, II Trusts, 2002—. Recipient Alexander Hamilton award Sec. of Treasury, 1991, spl. citation John Marshall Bar Assn. Mem. Phi Delta Phi, Kappa Tau Alpha. Republican.

HOLIFIELD, MARK, retail executive; BBA, U. Tex., Austin; MBA, Baylor U. Various logistics positions H-E-B Grocery Co., 1977—86; mem. staff in logistics Frito-Lay Pepsico, 1986—88; supply chain sys. positions Dallas Sys. Corp., 1988—94; dir. transp Office Depot, Inc., Delray Beach,

Fla., 1994—96, v.p., transp., logistics, 1996—97, sr. v.p., supply chain, 1997—2003, exec. v.p. supply chain, 2003—. Office: Office Depot Inc 2200 Old Germantown Rd Delray Beach FL 33445

HOLIFIELD-KENNEDY, LINDA R., physician; b. Johnstown, Pa., July 20, 1957; d. Cleveland, Jr. and Ruth Holifield; m. Richard O. Kennedy, Sept. 1, 1990; children: Richard O. Kennedy II, Tiffani L. Kennedy. BS, UCLA, 1982; MD, SUNY, Bklyn., 1994; MPH, Johns Hopkins U., Balt., 2000. Chem. analyst Gen. Dynamics Corp., Pomona, Calif., 1982—86; med. officer The Pentagon, Washington, 2000—. Author: (rsch. articles) Hypertension Jours. Del. leader to South Africa Nat. Physician Ambassadors Program, Vienna, Va., 2005; health ministry Gethsemane Bapt. Ch., Upper Marlboro, Md., 2000—04. Recipient Randall E. Bass award, Dept. of Environ. Health Scis., Johns Hopkins U., 1999, Cert. of Appreciation, Dept. of Army, 2002. Mem.: Am. Coll. Occupl. and Environ. Medicine (assoc.; bd. dir. Washington met. chpt. 2001—03, Resident Rsch. Presentation award 2000), Am. Coll. Physician Execs. (assoc.), Am. Coll. Preventive Medicine (assoc.). Avocations: cultural arts, travel, non-fiction. Office Phone: 703-692-8849. Personal E-mail: lholifieldkennedy@yahoo.com.

HOLKUP, LINDA PATRICIA, music educator; b. Brownsville, Tex., Mar. 24, 1973; d. Santiago and Alicia Medellin; m. Eugene Matthew Holkup, June 22, 2001. BA in Music Edn., U. Tex. Pan Am., Edinburg, 1996. Choral dir. Mission Jr. High, Tex., 1996—. Mem.: Am. Choral Dirs. Assn., Tex. Choral Dirs. Assn., Tex. Music Adjudicators Assn., Tex. Music Educators Assn. (mid. sch. region chairperson 2001—04). Office: Stell Mid Sch Choir 1105 Los Ebanos Blvd Brownsville TX 78520 Home Phone: 956-618-3152; Office Phone: 956-548-8560. Personal E-mail: lpmmused@juno.com.

HOLL, DAVID B., cosmetics company executive; m. Suzanne Holl; 3 children. BS in Fin., Clemson Univ.; MBA, Univ. SC. Fin. analyst Union Tex. Petroleum; v.p. corp. capital divsn. Citibank; joined Mary Kay Inc., Dallas, 1993, v.p., fin. planning, analysis, treas., 1996, sr. v.p., CFO, treas., 1996—2001, pres., COO, 2001—06, pres., CEO, 2006—. Bd. dir. Mary Kay Inc., Cosmetic, Toiletry & Fragrance Assn.; mem. CEO Council World Fedn. Direct Selling Assn. Bd. mem. Dallas C. of C. Mem.: World Fedn. Direct Selling Assn. (CEO Coun.), Cosmetic, Toiletry, and Fragrance Assn. (bd. dir.). Office: Mary Kay Inc 16251 Dallas Pkwy Addison TX 75001-6801 also: PO Box 799045 Dallas TX 75379-9045

HOLL, JOHN WILLIAM, engineering educator; b. Danville, Ill., Feb. 20, 1928; s. William Benjamin and Anna Marie (Waldo) H.; m. Antoinette Fillhouer, Aug. 20, 1950; children— Jessica, Vanessa, Melissa, Cassandra, Alyssa, Nathan, Zachary. BSME, U. Ill., Urbana-Champaign, 1949, MSME, 1951; PhD, Pa. State U., University Park, 1958, MusB, 1996. Rsch. asst. in mech. engrng. Engrng. Experiment Sta. U. Ill., Urbana, 1949-51; rsch. assoc. Applied Rsch. Lab. Pa. State U., 1951-54, 56-58, asst. prof. engrng. rsch., 1958-59, asso. prof. aerospace engrng., 1963-67, prof., 1967-91, prof. emeritus, 1991—. Asso. prof. mech. engrng. U. Nebr., Lincoln, 1959-63; cons. in field Mem. Lincoln Symphony Orch., 1960-63; mem. Nittany Valley Symphony Orch., State College, Pa., 1969— , State Coll. Mcpl. Band, 1977—; Trustee Unitarian Ch., Lincoln, 1961-62. Served with U.S. Army, 1955-56. Fellow ASME (R.T. Knapp award 1970, 91, Melville medal 1970, Centennial medallion 1980, dedicated service award 1985); assoc. fellow AIAA; mem. Internat. Clarinet Assn., Golden Key Nat. Honor Soc., Sigma Xi, Phi Mu Alpha Sinfonia, Pi Kappa Lambda. Office: Pa State U Aerospace Engrng 227 Hammond Bldg University Park PA 16802 Home: Foxdale Village 500 E Marylyn Ave Apt D60 State College PA 16801

HOLL, ROGER ELMO, lawyer; b. Riverside, Calif., Apr. 4, 1944; s. Elmo Raymond and Thelma Almeda Holl; children from previous marriage: Bradford Eric, Charles Alden, Steward Edward. Student, U. Marburg, Germany, 1964—65; BA in History, U. LaVerne, Calif., 1966; JD, Golden Gate U., San Francisco, 1971; cert. in internat. law, Hague Acad. Internat. Law, The Netherlands; cert. in mediation, U. Wash. Bar: Alaska 1974, US Dist. Ct. Alaska 1974, US Supreme Ct. 1981. Mfg. coord. Apollo 11 telecom. sys. Lenkurt Electric, Redwood City, Calif., 1968—69; dir. cooperative edn. program U. Calif., Berkeley, 1969—71; vista lawyer program Alaska Legal Svc., Anchorage, 1972—74; assoc. atty. Debenham and Wadsworth, Anchorage, 1974, Rogers & Baldwin, Kenai, Alaska, 1977—80; pvt. practice atty. Alaska, 1980—. Hon. co-chmn. Presdl. Bus. Commn., Washington, 2002; adj. faculty U. Alaska, Anchorage, 2004—; legal adviser to three commdg. gens.; prosecutor, instr. M. P. Acad. Mem. White House Small Bus. Adv. Com.; commr. Alaska Pub. Office Commn., Anchorage, 2004—, chmn., 2007—; bd. dirs. Alaska State C. of C., 1986—87; state hearing officer adminstrv. hearings; lay pastor, deacon, youth leader Grace Brethren Ch.; trustee U. Alaska; coun. mem., pres. Kenai Peninsula CC, 1982—89, chmn.coll. coun., 1984—87; mem. governance com. U. Alaska, 1985—87. With. USMC, 1966—68, dep. JAG, dep. comdr. Alaska State Def. Force, 1987—. Named Alumnus of the Yr., U. LaVerne, 1996, Alaska Achiever, Anchorage Daily News, 1996, Alaska Businessman of the Yr., Rep. Congl. Com., 2002, Grand Marshall, City of Kenai; recipient Maritime Svc. award for Homeland Security, State of Alaska, 2002, Gov.'s Alaska Cmty. Svc. medal, Ronald Reagan Rep. Congl. Gold medal, 2004. Mem.: Kenai Peninsula Bar Assn. (pres. 1979—83, Gold Pan award), Alaska Bar Assn. (mem. ethics com. 1982—87, 1990—95, past regional chmn. fee arbitration com., mem. small firm com. 1996). Avocations: boating, fly fishing, hunting, backpacking. Office: 1500 W 33th Ave Ste 100 Anchorage AK 99503

HOLL, STEVEN MYRON, architect, educator; b. Bremerton, Wash., Dec. 9, 1947; s. Myron Leroy and Helen May Holl. BA cum laude, U. Wash., 1971; postgraduate student, Rome and London. Individual practice arch., San Francisco, 1974—76, NYC, 1977—; arch., tchr. archtl. design U. Wash., Seattle, 1979; prof. Grad. Sch. Architecture Columbia U., NYC, 1981—. Author: The Alphabetical City, 1980, Urban and Rural House Types in N.Am., 1983, Within the City, 1988, Anchoring, 1989; exhibitions include Whitney Mus. Am. Art, 1984, 1985, Facade Gallery, 1984, Architecture in Transition, Berlin, 1984, VII Triennale Milan, 1987, John Nicols Gallery, NYC, 1987, GA Gallery, Tokyo, 1987, 1992, 1997, 1999, Mus. Modern Art, NYC, 1987, 1999, 2000, Aedes Gallery, Berlin, 1989, Venice Biennial, Italy, 1991, 2002, Walker Art Ctr., 1991, Henry Art Gallery, Seattle, 1991, Can. Ctr. Architecture, Montreal, 1992, Centre de Cultura Contemporania de Barcelona, 1996, Mus. Contemporary Art, LA, 1998, Mus. Modern Art, San Francisco, 1999, Cooper-Hewitt Mus., NYC, 2000, Max Protetch Gallery, Parallax, NY, 2000, 2002, Van Allen Inst., NY, 2001, Am. Acad. Rome, 2001, Nat. Bldg. Mus., Washington, 2002, Basilica Palladiana di Vicenza, Italy, 2002, Arkitekturmuseet, Stockholm, 2003, Nat. Acad., 2006. Named Am.'s Best Arch., Time mag., 2001; recipient Progressive Architecture award, 1978, 1982, 1984, 1986—87, 1990, Nat. Endowment for Arts award, 1982, AIA award, 1985—86, 1989—90, Arnold W. Brunner prize in Architecture, Am. Acad. and Inst. Arts and Letters, 1990, Cooper Hewitt Nat. Design award in Architecture, Smithsonian Instn., 2002, NY AIA Project award for Loisium Visitors' Ctr., Langenlois, Austria, 2003, Nat. AIA award for Design Excellence for Simmons Hall, MIT, 2003, Award of Excellence for Best Design of a Parking Facility, Nelson Atkins Mus. Art, Kans. City, Mo., Internat. Parking Inst., 2004; grantee, Nat. Endowment of Arts, Grahame Found., NY State Coun. Arts, 1988; Archtl. fellow, 1979. Mem.: AIA, Alvar Aalto Found., Am. Assn. Museums, Nat. Coun. Archtl. Registration Bds. Office: Steven Holl Archts 11th Fl 450 W 31st St New York NY 10001 Office Phone: 212-629-7262. Office Fax: 212-629-7312. E-mail: mail@stevenholl.com.*

HOLLADAY, WILHELMINA COLE, interior designer, museum director; b. Elmira, NY, Oct. 10, 1922; d. Chauncy E. and Claire Elizabeth (Strong) Cole; m. Wallace Fitzhugh Holladay, Sept. 27, 1946; children: Wallace Fitzhugh, Scott Cole. BA, Elmira Coll., 1944; postgrad. art history, U. Paris, 1953—54, U. Va., 1960—61; PhD (hon.), Moore Coll. Art, 1988, Mt. Vernon Coll., 1988, Elmira Coll., 1994. Exec. sec. Howard Ludington, Rochester, N.Y., 1944-45, Chinese Embassy, Washington, 1945-48; staff Nat. Gallery of Art, Washington, 1957-59; dir. interior design div. Holladay Corp., Washington, 1970-95. Dir. Adams Nat. Bank, 1978-86, chmn., 1978-86; founder, chmn., bd. dirs., creator art collection by women (Renaissance through contemp.), Nat. Mus. Women in Arts, 1982—. Founder Archival Libr. of Periodicals, Books, Exhbn. Catalogs on Women's Art for Rsch. Purposes; bd. dirs. Am. Field Svc., 1964-80, Internat. Student House, 1973—, Leeds Castle Found.; mem. coun. Friends of Folger Shakespeare Libr., 1978-82; mem. world svc. coun. YWCA; trustee Corcoran Gallery of Art, 1980-90, The Fund for Endowment of Diplomatic Reception Rms.; mem. Mayor's Blue Ribbon Com., The Year of Visual Arts Com., Am. Acad. Rome; mem. adv. council The Girl Scouts of US; pres. Langley Sch. Decorated Order of Merit Norwegian Govt.; named laureate, Washington Bus. Hall of Fame, Washingtonian of Yr., Washingtonian Mag., 1987, Woman of Achievement, Washington Ednl. TV Assn., 1984, Woman of Distinction, Coun. Ind. Colls., 1987, Hon. Citizen, State of Tex., 1992, Hon. Athenian, Mayor of Athens, 2002; named one of 21 Leaders for 21st Century, Women's eNews, 2005; named to Women of Distinction, Birmingham So. Coll., 1991, Nat. Women's Hall of Fame, 1996; recipient Thomas Jefferson award, Am. Soc. Interior Designers, Horizon's Theatre award, 1986, Disting. Woman's award, Northwood Inst., 1987, award, Anti-Defamation League, 1987, Disting. Achievement award, Nat. League Am. Pen Women, 1991, Women Achievers award, Internat. Alliance, 1991, Key to City of Kansas City, 1991, Hon. Citizen award, State Tex., 1992, Women First award, YWCA, 1993, Women as Leaders award, The Wash. Ctr., Sears, 1994, Fellow award for disting. svc. to arts, New Orleans Mus. Art, 1997, Disting. Washingtonian award in lit. and the arts, Univ. Club Washington, 1998, Gold medal honor award, Nat. Inst. Social Scis., 2000, Honoree, Historic Georgetown Club, 2000, Leadership award, Pine Manor Coll., 2002, Nat. Women Arts award, Phoenix Art Mus. League, 2003, Visionary Woman award, Moore Coll. Art & Design, 2005, Nat. Medal Arts, Nat. Endowment Arts, 2006. Mem. Am. Assn. Mus., Am. Fedn. Art, Women's Caucus for Arts, Mus. Modern Art, Art Librs. N.Am., Coll. Art Assn., Archives Am. Art, Art Table, Smithson Soc., Internat. Women's Forum, Nat. Women's Econ. Alliance (bd. dirs. 1984—, Soaring Eagle award 1988), Internat. Women's Forum (Woman That Makes a Difference award, 1991), Women's Caucus for Art (honors, 2001), The Smithsonian Soc., Golden Cir. Kennedy Ctr., Am. News Women's Club, Capital Spkrs. Club. Episcopalian. Home: 3215 R St NW Washington DC 20007-2941 Office: Nat Mus Women Arts 1250 New York Ave NW Washington DC 20005 *You haven't failed until you quit trying.*

HOLLAND, BERNARD PEABODY, music critic; b. Norfolk, Va., Feb. 26, 1933; s. Bernard Peabody and Claudia Mildred (Emmerson) H.; m. Janet Carter, July 8, 1983 (div. July 1992); m. Elizabeth Wareham, Aug. 12, 1997. BA, U. Va., 1955. Tchr. of piano, Pitts., 1966-81; music critic, writer Pitts. Post-Gazette, 1979-80; nat. music critic NY Times, NYC, 1981—. Contbr. articles to N.Y. Times Mag., Harper's Mag., Saturday Rev. Mem. Century Assn., Phi Beta Kappa. Democrat. Episcopalian. Avocations: books, travel, all sports. Office: NY Times Culture Desk 229 W 43rd St New York NY 10036-3959 Office Phone: 212-556-1341. Office Fax: 212-556-1516.

HOLLAND, BETH, actress; b. NYC; d. Samson and Florence (Liebman) Hollander; m. Louis L. Friedman, Aug. 28, 1953 (dec. 1997); children: Ellen Lynn, Cathy Jayne; m. Richard J. Kuh, Oct. 6. Pvt. studies in acting, voice tng. Arts funding cons. N.Y. State Senate, 1974-89. Appeared in various roles on TV, film and theatre, also comedy video Your Favorite Jokes, 1988; cabaret debut, N.Y.C., 2004. Pres. Sonia Alden Found. Inc.; bd. dirs. Fla. Opera Soc., Symphony of Americas. Recipient Carbonell performance award, Theatre League of South Fla., 1996. Mem. AFTRA (pres. N.Y. chpt. 1989-91, bd. dirs., trustee Health and Retirement Funds, past treas.), SAG, English Speaking Union, N.Y. TV Acad. (past bd. dirs.), Actors Equity Assn., Twelfth Night Club, Episcopal Actors Guild (first women pres.), Players Club (libr. bd.), Lambs Club, Tower Club, Friars Club. Avocations: travel, politics, arts. E-mail: bethholland146@aol.com.

HOLLAND, BRANTI LATESSA, science educator; d. Jerry and Barbara Holland. B in Elem. Edn., Mich. U., Ypsilanti, 2001; M, Marygrove Coll., Detroit, 2006. Cert. tchr. Mich., 2001. Tchr. Detroit Pub. Schs., Detroit, Harcourt, Lansing, Mich. Adminstr. Edn. Sta., Detroit; curriculum writer mid. sch. scis. Detroit Pub. Schs. Sys., 2006, com. mem. textbook adoption, 06. Jr. girl scout leader Girl Scouts Am., Detroit, 2005—. Mem.: Mich. Sci. Tchrs. Assn., Metro Detroit Sci. Tchr. Assn. (assoc.). Christian. Avocations: reading, tutoring. Home Phone: 313-550-6663; Office Phone: 313-596-3800.

HOLLAND, CHARLES JOSEPH, lawyer; b. Ottumwa, Iowa, 1949; m. Nancy Jo Daniels; children: Tyler, Emily, Clare. BA, U. Iowa, 1971, JD (with high honors), 1977. Bar: Iowa 1977, U.S. Dist. Ct. (so. dist., no. dist.) Iowa 1977. Assoc. Hayek, Hayek & Hayek, Iowa City, 1977-81; ptnr. Hayek, Hayek, Holland & Brown, Iowa City, 1981—92; pvt. practice, 1992—2000; ptnr. Holland & Anderson LLP, 2000—. Mem. exec. coun. Nat. Conf. Bar Pres., 2003—06. Dir. Iowa City Downtown Assn., 1988-92. Mem. Iowa Coun. Sch. Bd. Attys. (chair 2004), ABA, Iowa Bar Assn. (pres. 2001-02), Johnson County Bar Assn. Office: 300 Brewery Sq 123 N Linn St PO Box 2820 Iowa City IA 52244-2820 Office Phone: 319-354-0331.

HOLLAND, DAVID K., treasurer; Grad., Brigham Young U.; MBA, San Jose State U. With Apple Computer; head capital markets sales team Paribas Capital Markets, NYC; joined Cisco Sys. Inc., San Jose, Calif., 1998, v.p., treas., 2000—, bd. dirs., 2006—. Bd. dirs. Motricity. Office: Cisco Systems, Inc 170 W Tasman Dr San Jose CA 95134*

HOLLAND, DAVID THURSTON, former editor; b. Phila., May 26, 1923; s. Rupert Sargent and Margaret Currier (Lyon) H. BA, Harvard, 1944, MA, 1946. Vice consul U.S. Fgn. Svc., Budapest, Hungary, 1945; teaching fellow Harvard U., Cambridge, Mass., 1946-49; coll. traveller Oxford U. Press, NYC, 1953-54; asst. editor Harcourt Brace, NYC, 1955-59; asst. editor Ency. Internat., Grolier Inc., NYC, 1959-62, assoc. editor Ency. Americana, 1962-65, sr. editor, 1965-85; exec. editor, 1985; editor in chief Ency. Americana Grolier Inc., Danbury, Conn., 1985-91; ret., 1991. Democrat. Episcopalian.

HOLLAND, GEORGE EDISON, JR., (ED), lawyer, utilities executive; b. Rutherfordton, NC, Dec. 2, 1952; m. Elizabeth Bird; children: Laura E., Caroline S. BA, Auburn U., Ala., 1975; JD, U. Va., 1978. Bar: Fla. 1978, US Dist. Ct. (no. dist. Fla.) 1978, US Ct. Appeals (11th cir.) 1981, US Ct. Appeals (5th cir.) 1986, US Ct. Appeals (DC cir.) 1988, US Supreme Ct. 1990. Joined Southern Co., Atlanta, 1992, sys. compliance officer; pres., CEO Savannah Electric subs., Savannah, Ga., 1997—2001; v.p. power generation/transmissions, corp. counsel Gulf Power subs., Pensacola, Fla.; exec. v.p., gen. counsel, corp. sec. Southern Co., Atlanta, 2001—. Mem.: Escambia-Santa Rosa Bar Assn. (pres. 1987—98), Fla. Bar (mem. adminstrv. law sect.), ABA (mem. pub. utility law sect.). Office: Southern Co 30 Ivan Allen Jr Blvd NW Atlanta GA 30308*

HOLLAND, JAMES R., real estate company officer; b. St. Louis, Feb. 20, 1944; s. Randolph and Thelma (Robinson) Holland; m. Helen M. Devine, Feb. 18, 1972; children: Danielle, James Randolph, Eric Marc. Student, Principia Coll., 1962—64; BFA, Ohio U., 1966; postgrad., U. Mo. Sch. Journalism, 1966. Photog. intern Nat. Geog. Soc., Washington, 1966, contract photographer for mag., 1967-68; film prodr. Christian Sci. Ctr., Boston, 1969-74; real estate developer, pres. Brownstone Properties, Inc., Boston, 1975-77; real estate broker Street & Co., Inc., Boston, 1978-82; pres. A Bit of Boston Real Estate, Inc., Boston, 1982—. Author: The Amazon, 1971, Mr. Pops-Arthur Fiedler, 1972, Tanglewood, 1973, W.O'K's Weird Wacky Wonderful World: The Art of William O'Keefe, 2006, Diamonds Are Waiting For You: Crater of Diamonds, Where Dreams Can And Do Come True, 2007; illustrator, photographer Continental and Colonial Currency of Colonical America; co-author: Photojournalism-Principles and Practice, 2d edit., 1980; contbr. articles photographs to publs., video games, textbooks; prodr.: Twinkle Toes Videos; Represented in permanent collections Truman Libr., JFK Libr., Boston Pub. Libr. Active Neighborhood Assn. Back Bay, 1972—, Boston Home and Property Owners Assn., Small Property Owners Assn., 2000—; assoc. Boston Pub. Libr.; sponsor Babe Ruth Baseball League Team, 1992—; league sponsor Back Bay, Beacon Hill and North End Little League Teams, 1999—; 10th anniversary com. Boston U. Photographic Resource Ctr. Named AAU Nat. Karate Champion, 1989; recipient World Press Competition award, 1967, Newsweek/Bolex Documentary Film award, 1969, Indls. Photography Film Competition award, 1970, Bronze medal, Internat. Film and TV Festival N.Y., 1971, 6th national ranking in weapon's form, Reeves Sport Karate Ratings, 1989. Mem.: N.Am. Sport Karate Assn. (various awards), Nat. Press Photographers (award 1966, 1967, 1968), Am. Soc. Mag. Photographers, Samuel Fletcher and Angeline Drury Soc., Friends Beverly Hills Pub. Libr. (life), Boston Athenaeum (life), Mus. Ozarks (life), Dickerson Pk. Zoo (life). Achievements include broadcast of film work on NBC, ABC, CBS, PBS, BBC, Travel Channel. Home: 208 Commonwealth Ave Boston MA 02116-2534 Office: A Bit of Boston Real Estate Inc 5 Brimmer St Boston MA 02108-1001

HOLLAND, JAMES TULLEY, retired plastics company executive; b. Pikeville, Ky., May 24, 1940; s. Thomas Joseph and Mary Alta (Tulley) Holland; m. Susan Ellen Joy; children: James Christopher, Kathleen Holland Wiesel. BA in Econs., U. Va., 1962; MBA, Am. U., 1969. With br. banking ops. United Va. Bank, Alexandria, 1965-67; with Booz Allen & Hamilton, Washington, 1967-76; treas., chief fin. officer O'Sullivan Corp., Winchester, Va., 1976-84, exec. v.p., COO, 1984-86, pres., COO, 1986—95, CEO, 1995-98, ret., 1998, also bd. dirs. Bd. dirs. Va. Nat. Bank-Winchester Region, Valley Health Sys., Valley Regional Enterprises. Trustee Glass Glen Burnie Found. Capt. US Army, 1963—65. Mem. Winchester Country Club, Farmington Country Club (Charlottesville, Va.), Belle Haven Country Club (Alexandria). Roman Catholic. Avocations: golf, reading, writing. Home: 261 Merrifield Ln Winchester VA 22602-2306

HOLLAND, JEFFREY R., religious organization administrator; b. St. George, Utah, Dec. 3, 1940; s. Frank D. and Alice (Bentley) H.; m. Patricia Terry, June 7, 1963; children: Matthew, Mary, David. BS, Brigham Young U., 1965, MA, 1966; PhD, Yale U., 1973. Dean religious instrn. Brigham Young U., 1974-76; commr. Latter Day Saints Ch. Ednl. System, 1976-80; pres. Brigham Young U., 1980-89; gen. authority, mem. 1st Quorum of the 70 LDS Ch., 1989-94; Apostle Quorum of the Twelve, 1994—. Former bd. dirs. Deseret News Pub. Co., Key Bank of Utah, Key Bancshares of Utah, Inc. Author: (books) However Long & Hard the Road, 1993, Christ & the New Covenant: The Messianic Message of the Book of Mormon, 1997, Shepherds, Why This Jubilee?, 2000, Of Souls, Symbols & Sacraments, 2001, Trusting Jesus, 2003; co-author (with Patricia T Holland): On Earth as It Is in Heaven, 1993. Mem. Am. Assn. Presidents of Ind. Colls. and Univs. (past pres.), Nat. Assn. Ind. Colls. and Univs. (former bd. dirs.), Am. Council Edn., Phi Kappa Phi. Office: LDS Church 47 E South Temple Salt Lake City UT 84150-1200

HOLLAND, JIMMIE C., psychiatrist, educator; b. Forney, Tex., Apr. 9, 1928; m. James F. Holland; 5 children. BA, Baylor U., 1948, MD, 1952. Diplomate Am. Bd. Psychiatry, Am. Bd. Neurology. Instr. to prof. SUNY, Buffalo, 1956-73; assoc. prof., assoc. attending physician to asst. dir. cons.-liaison psychiatry Albert Einstein Coll. Medicine and Montefiore Med. Ctr., Bronx, 1973-77; chair dept. psychiatry and behavioral scis., Wayne E. Chapman chair in psychiat. oncology Meml. Sloan Kettering Cancer Ctr., NYC, 1997—2003. Prof. dept. psychiatry Weill Med. Coll., N.Y.C., 1977—; cons. NIMH-USSR joint schizophrenia study Psychiat. Rsch. Inst., Moscow, 1972-73, NIMH, Rockville, Md., 1973-75; chmn. psychiatry com. Cancer and Leukemia Group B Clin. Trials, Brookline, Mass., 1976-2001. Editor: Handbook of Psycho-oncology: Psychological Care of the Patient with Cancer, 1989, Psychooncology, 1998; co-editor Jour. Psycho-oncology; author, co-author: The Human Side of Cancer, 258 jour. articles, book chpts., monographs. Bd. dirs. Cancer Care, Inc., 1979-81. Recipient Disting. Alumna award Baylor U., Waco, Tex., 1982; Am. Cancer Soc. Medal of Honor, 1994 Fellow Inst. Medicine, Am. Coll. Psychiatrists, Am. Psychiat. Assn., Acad. Psychosomatic Medicine (founding pres.), Internat. Psycho-Oncology Soc. (founding pres.), Am. Psychosocial Oncology Soc., Am. Psychosomatic Soc., Am. Soc. Clin. Oncology. Office: Meml Sloan-Kettering Cancer Ctr 1275 York Ave New York NY 10021-6094 Home Phone: 914-725-2212; Office Phone: 646-888-0026. Business E-Mail: hollandj@mskcc.org.

HOLLAND, JOEL KENT, III, entrepreneur; b. McLean, Va., 1985; Student, Babson Coll., 2005—. Teen panelist USA Today, Washington, 2000—03; founder & CEO Footage Firm LLC, Vienna, Va., 2001—; chief mktg. officer Nortel Networks Kidz Online, Inc., Washington, 2001—04; monthly columnist Entrepreneur mag., Irvine, Calif., 2002—05; news dept. intern Warner Bros., Boston, 2006; bus. devel. intern MTV Networks, NYC, 2006. Prodr. & host (TV series) Streaming Futures, 2001—. Named Bus. Student of Yr., McLean C. of C., 2002; named one of Best Entrepreneurs Under 25, Bus. Week, 2006; recipient Student Small Bus. Initiative award, Babson Coll., 2005. Mem.: Quill & Scroll Hon. Soc. Office: Footage Firm LLC 8596 Coral Gables Vienna VA 22182 also: Kidz Online Studio 120 600 W 7th St Los Angeles CA 90017 Office Phone: 703-899-5337. Office Fax: 703-852-7074. E-mail: joel@joelkentholland.com, info@footagefirm.com.*

HOLLAND, JOHN BEN, clothing manufacturing company executive; b. Scottsville, Ky., Mar. 26, 1932; s. Elbridge Winfred and Lou May (Whitney) H.; m. Margaret Irene Pecor, Jan. 31, 1954; children: John Sandra, Robert. BS in Acctg., Bowling Green U., 1959. With Union Underwear Co., Inc., Bowling Green, Ky., 1961—2001, v.p. adminstrn., 1972-74, vice chmn., 1975, chmn., CEO, 1976-96; cons., 1996—99; pres., CEO Fruit of the Loom, Inc., 2002—; chmn., CEO, Russell Corp., 2006—. Bd. dirs. Farmers Nat. Bank. Bd. dirs. Ky. Coun. Econ. Edn., Louisville, 1981-90, Ky. Advocates for Higher Edn. Inc., 1985-93, Ky. C. of C., 1987-88, Camping World Inc., 1985-97, Associated Industries of Ky., Ireland-Am. Econ. Adv. Bd., Tech. Corp. Inc.; chmn. corp. coun. Western Ky. U., devel. steering com., 1985-96; vice-chmn. West Point Pepperial, Inc., 1989-92; chmn. Intermodal Transp. Authority, 1998-2000. Mem. Bowling Green-Warren County C. of C. (bd. dirs. 1981-85), Am. Arbitration Assn. (panel 1985-93). Office: Fruit of the Loom Inc PO Box 90015 Bowling Green KY 42102-9015

HOLLAND, JOHN MADISON, retired family practice physician; b. Holden, W.Va., Oct. 7, 1927; s. Ophia I. and Lou V. (Elliott) H.; m. Mary Louise Bourne, Sept. 2, 1950; children— David, Stephen, Nancy BS,

Eastern Ky. State U., Richmond, 1949; MD, U. Louisville, 1952. Diplomate Am. Bd. Family Practice, Am. Bd. Hospice and Palliative Medicine. Intern St. Joseph Infirmary, Louisville, 1952-53; gen. practice family medicine Physicians Group, Springfield, Ill., 1955-80; med. dir. St. John's Hosp., Springfield, 1971-94, St. John's Hospice, 1995—; clin. prof. family practice So. Ill. U., Springfield, 1978—. Served to capt. USAF, 1953-55 Mem. Am. Acad. Family Physicians, Am. Acad. Hospice/Palliative Medicine. Baptist. Home: 2131 Lindsay Rd Springfield IL 62704-3242

HOLLAND, JOSEPH JOHN, retired financial executive; b. New Brunswick, NJ, Nov. 7, 1927; s. Thomas Clifford and Ruth Elizabeth (Feaster) Holland; m. Bernice T. Kearns, July 1, 1984 (dec.); 1 child, Wayne Joseph. BS magna cum laude, Mount St. Mary's Coll., 1952; MBA, Rutgers U., 1955. CPA N.J., N.Mex., Tex. Sr. acct. Peat, Marwick, Mitchell & Co., Newark, 1952—61; plant contr., ops. auditor Crane Co., NYC, 1961—65; fin. contr. Ingersoll-Rand Co., U.K., 1965—68; v.p., contr. PPD Corp., Newark, 1968—73; v.p. fin., treas. Edgcomb Steel & Aluminum Corp., Hillside, NJ, 1973—76; cons. in field North Brunswick, NJ, 1978; v.p. fin., dir. Berry Solar Products, Edison, NJ, 1978—86; dir. fin. control Berger Industries, Maspeth, NY, 1986—88; cons. Milltown, NJ, 1988—96; ret. Mem. adv. coun. Rutgers U. Acad. for Life Long Learning. With USN, 1946—48. Mem.: AICPAs, Exchange Club (New Brunswick), Sales Execs. Club of N.J. (chmn. disting. salesman award 1978), Elks.

HOLLAND, KEN, professional sports team executive; b. Vernon, BC, Can., Nov. 10, 1955; m. Cindy Holland; children: Brad, Julie, Rachel, Greg. Hockey player Medicine Hat, 1974-75, Toronto Maple Leafs, 1975-80, Hartford, 1980-83, Detroit Red Wings, 1983-84, Binghamton, Springfield, amateur scouting dir., asst. gen. mgr., gen. mgr., 1987—. Named to Binghamton Hall of Fame, 1998. Achievements include being the general manager of Stanley Cup Champion Detroit Red Wings, 1997, 1998, 2002. Office: c/o Detroit Red Wings 600 Civic Center Dr Detroit MI 48226-4408*

HOLLAND, LYMAN FAITH, JR., lawyer; b. Mobile, Ala., June 17, 1931; s. Lyman Faith and Louise (Wisdom) H.; m. Leannah Louise Platt, Mar. 6, 1954; children: Lyman Faith III, Laura. BS in Bus. Adminstrn, U. Ala., 1953, LLB, 1957. Bar: Ala. 1957, U.S. Supreme Ct. 1992. Assoc. Hand, Arendall & Bedsole, Mobile, 1957-62; ptnr. Hand, Arendall, Bedsole, Greaves & Johnston, 1963-94, mem., 1995, Hand Arendall LLC, 1996—. Mem. Mobile Jr. C. of C. (Jaycees), 1957-1968, bd. dirs., 1963-68; mem. Mobile Hist. Devel. Com., 1965-69, v.p., 1967-68; bd. dirs. Mobile Azalea Trail, Inc., 1963-68, chmn. bd., 1963-65; bd. dirs. Mobile Mental Health Ctr., 1969-76, v.p., 1972, pres., chmn. bd., 1973; bd. dirs. Mobile chpt. ARC, 1969-97, vice-chmn., 1975-77, exec. vice-chmn., 1978-80, chmn., 1980-82, life bd. dirs. emeritus, 1997—; bd. dirs. Deep South coun. Girl Scouts U.S., 1965-71, Gordan Smith Ctr. Inc., 1973, Bay Area Coun. on Alcoholism, 1973-76, Cmty. Chest Coun. Mobile County, Inc., 1976-81, Greater Mobile Mental Health-Mental Retardation Bd., Inc., 1975-81, pres., 1975-77; active Mobile Estate Planning Coun., 1981—, exec. com., 1988-97, pres., 1994-95. Lt. col. USAF, ret. Mem.: ABA, Ala. Law Found., Ala. Law Inst. (coun. 1978—), Am. Coll. Trust and Estate Counsel Found. (bd. dirs. 1990—96), Am. Coll. Trust and Estate Counsel, Mobile County Bar Assn., Ala. State Bar (chmn. sect. corp., banking and bus. law 1978—80), Camellia Club of Mobile, Bienville Club, Country Club of Mobile, Athleston Club (Mobile), Lions, Phi Delta Phi, Pi Kappa Alpha. Baptist (deacon, ch. trustee 1968-73, chmn. trustees 1971-73). Home: 3606 Provident Ct Mobile AL 36608-1534 Office: Hand Arendall LLC PO Box 123 Mobile AL 36601-0123 Office Phone: 251-694-6228. Business E-Mail: lholland@handarendall.com.

HOLLAND, MICHAEL FRANCIS, investment company executive; b. Cleve., July 8, 1944; s. Joseph Thomas and Mary Louise H.; m. Louise Grace, Aug. 20, 1966; children: Brian, Thomas, Joseph, Daniel, John, Michael Jr. AB, Harvard U., 1966; MBA, Columbia U., 1968. With Morgan Guaranty Trust Co., NYC, 1968-80, investment mgr., 1972-80, v.p., 1975-80; sr. v.p. investments Reliance Group, Inc., also Reliance Ins. Co., NYC, 1980-83; pres. Holland & Co., Inc., 1983-84; pres., chief exec. officer First Boston Asset Mgmt. Corp., 1984-89; dir., chmn. bd. dirs., chief exec. officer Global Growth and Income Fund, Inc., 1986-89; chmn., CEO Salomon Bros. Asset Mgmt., Inc., 1989-92; vice chmn. Oppenheimer & Co. Inc., 1992-94; dir. The China Fund, Inc., 1992—, Reaves Utility Fund, Inc., 2004—; gen. ptnr. The Blackstone Group, 1994-95; CEO, Blackstone Alternative Asset Mgmt. Inc., 1994—95; chmn. Holland & Co. L.L.C., 1995—; dir., chmn. State St. Master Funds Inc., 2003—. Dir. The Latin Am. Investment Fund, Inc., 1990-92; chmn. bd. dirs. Scottish Widows Investment Partners Fund, 2006—; trustee Winston Churchill Found., 2007—. Panelist: Louis Rukeyser's Wall Street, 1990-2004. Vice chmn. Harvard Coll. Fund Assoc. Program, 1998—2005; mem. com. on univ. resource, com. on faculty selection Harvard U.; trustee Vanguard Charitable Endowment Program, 1997—; mem. bd. fin. Town of New Canaan, Conn., 1997—2003; trustee Harvard Club N.Y.C. Found., 2001—05; co-chair Harvard Coll. Fund, 2005—. Mem. Harvard Club of NYC (bd. mgrs. 1998-2001, v.p., bd. mgrs. 2003-). Clubs: Racquet & Tennis; Country of New Canaan, Winter (New Canaan); Harvard of Fairfield County. Home: 1 Greenley Rd New Canaan CT 06840-3513 Office: Holland & Co LLC 375 Park Ave Ste 1903 New York NY 10152-1994

HOLLAND, MICHAEL JAMES, computer services administrator; b. NYC, Nov. 20, 1950; s. Robert Frederick and Virginia June (Wilcox) H.; Anita Garay, Jan. 5, 1981 (Aug. 1989); 1 child, Melanie. BA in Comparative Lit., Bklyn. Coll., 1972. Enlisted USN, 1975, advanced to CPO, 1989, field med. technician Okinawa, Japan, 1976-77, Camp Pendleton, Calif., 1978-79, clin. supr. naval hosp. Subic Bay, Philippines, 1979-81; dept. head Tng. Ctr. USMCR, Johnson City, Tenn., 1981-84, clin. supr. no. tng. area Okinawa, 1984-85, clin. supr. 3d marine air wing Camp Pendleton, 1985-88; cons. naval regional med. commd. USN, San Diego, 1988-90, system analyst naval med. info mgmt. ctr. detachment, 1990-92, computer svcs. adminstr. naval hosp. Guam, 1993-95, ret., 1995; svc. rep. AT&T West, 1997—2006. Mem. Fleet Res. Assn., Comm. Workers Am., Nat. City C. of C. (com. 1989-91).

HOLLAND, NORMAN NORWOOD, critic; b. NYC, Sept. 19, 1927; s. Norman Norwood and Harriette (Breder) H.; m. Jane Kelley, Dec. 17, 1954; children: Kelley, John. BS, MIT, 1947; postgrad., Harvard U., 1950, PhD, 1956; cert. in psychoanalysis, Boston Psychoanalytic Inst. From instr. to assoc. prof. MIT, Cambridge, 1955-66; McNulty prof. English SUNY, Buffalo, 1966-83; assoc. prof. U. Paris, 1971-72, 85; Marston-Milbauer eminent scholar U. Fla., Gainesville, 1983—. Cons. various pubs., 1960—, Pres's. Coun. on Obscenity, 1971, Can. Coun., 1980. Author: The First Modern Comedies, 1959, The Shakespearean Imagination, 1964, Psychoanalysis and Shakespeare, 1966, The Dynamics of Literary Response, 1968, Poems in Persons: An Introduction to the Psychoanalysis of Literature, 1973, rev. edit., 2000, 5 Readers Reading, 1975, Laughing: A Psychology of Humor, 1982, The I, 1985, The Brain of Robert Frost: A Cognitive Approach to Literature, 1988, Holland's Guide to Psychoanalytic Psychology and Literature-and-Psychology, 1990, The Critical I, 1992, Death in a Delphi Seminar, 1995, Meeting Movies, 2006. Am. Couns. Learned Socs. fellow, 1974-75, Guggenheim Found. fellow, 1979-80. Mem. Am. Acad. Psychoanalysis (sci. assoc.), Boston Psychoanalytic Soc., Modern Lang. Assn. (div. exec. com. 1975-81). Democrat. Avocation: movies. Office: U Fla Dept English Gainesville FL 32611

HOLLAND, PHILLIP KENT, aerospace engineer; b. Wichita, Kans., Oct. 10, 1959; s. Phillip Norman and Lafreda Louise (Davenport) H.; m. Linda Kay Rosenbaum, June 27, 1980 (div. Dec. 1987); m. Delaine Marie Thompson, Mar. 17, 1989. BS in Aerospace Engring., Wichita State U., Kans., 1993. Seating engr. Raytheon Aircraft, Wichita, 1979—93; R&D group engr. Interiors and Seating Group Bombardier Learjet Inc., Wichita, 1993—99; pres. Millennium Concepts Inc., Wichita, 1999—. Mem. AIAA, Soc. Aerospace Engrs., (mem. AS8049 ad hoc com. 1990-97, vice chmn. SAE seat com. 1997-2001), GAMA (seat working group 1994-2000), Aviation Rulemaking Adv. Com. (AC25.562-1 seat working group 1994-96). Republican. Greek Orthodox. Achievements include design and certification engr. on aircraft seats and interiors. Home: 4207 Spyglass Cir Wichita KS 67226-3354 Office: Millennium Concepts Inc 9050 W Monroe Cir Wichita KS 67209 Office Phone: 316-821-9300. Business E-Mail: pholland@millennium.aero.

HOLLAND, RANDY JAMES, state supreme court justice; b. Elizabeth, NJ, Jan. 27, 1947; s. James Charles and Virginia (Wilson) H.; m. Ilona E. Holland, June 24, 1972 BA in Econs., Swarthmore Coll., 1969; JD cum laude, U. Pa., 1972; LLM, U. Va., 1998; Doctorate (hon.), Widener U. Sch. Law, 2001. Bar: Del. 1972. Ptnr. Dunlap, Holland & Rich and predecessors, Georgetown, Del., 1972-80, Morris, Nichols, Arsht & Tunnell, Georgetown, Del., 1980-86; justice Del. Supreme Ct., Georgetown, Del., 1986—. Mem. Del. Bar Examiners, 1978-86; mem. Gov.'s Jud. Nominating Commn., 1978-86, sec., 1982-85, chmn., 1985-86; mem. Del. Supreme Ct. Consol. Com., 1985-86; pres. Terry-Carey Inn of Ct., 1991-94; v.p. Am. Inns of Ct., 1996-2000, pres., 2000-04; co-chair Racial and Ethnic Task Force, 1995—; adj. prof. Widener U. Sch. Law, 1991—, U. Pa. Sch. Law, 1993-94, U. Iowa Sch. Law, 1997—, Vanderbilt Law Sch., 2000—; co-chair Del. Cts. Planning Com., 1996; chair nat. jud. adv. com. fed. Office of Child Support Enforcement; Jud. Ethics Adv. Commn., 1994—; del. Code Jud. Conduct Rev. Commn., 1991-94; del. Bar Bench Media Conf., 1990—; dir. Appellate Judges' Edn. Inst., 2003—. Mem. editorial bd. Del. Lawyer Mag., 1981-85; contbr. chpt. Del. Appellate Handbook, 1985—; author Delaware Supreme Court: Golden Anniversary, 2001, The Delaware Constitution: A Reference Guide, 2002; co-editor The Delaware Constitution of 1897: The First One Hundred Years; co-author Middle Temple Lawyers and the American Revolution, 2007. Pres. adminstrv. bd. Ave. United Meth. Ch., Milford, Del. Bar Found.; hon. chmn. History of the Del. Bar in 20th Century, 1992—; active Rhodes Scholarship com., 2003—; bd. mgrs. U. Pa. Law Alumni Soc., 2004—; adv. com. on appellate rules US Jud. Conf., State judge mem., 2004-; bd. overseers Widener Law Sch., 2005-. Recipient Henry C. Loughlin prize for legal ethics U. Pa. 1972, St. Thomas More award, 1999, Alumni award of merit U. Pa. Sch. Law, 2002; named Judge of the Yr. Nat. Child Support Enforcement Assn., 1992, Hon. Master of the Bench, Lincoln's Inn, London, 2004, Judge James L. Latchum Professionalism award, 2004. Mem. ABA (standing com. lawyer competence, nat. jud. coll. adv. commn. model rules jud. disclosure enforcement 1996, appellate judge's conf. exec. com. 2001—, chmn. joint com. lawyer regulation 2002—), Am. Judicature Soc. (nat. trustee 1992—, ctr. jud. ethics, 1994, chair 1997—, Herbert Harley Award 2003), Appellate Judges Edn. Inst. (bd. dirs. 2003—), Am. Inns of Ct. Found. (trustee 1992—, nat. trustee 1996—, v.p. 1996-2000, nat. pres. 2000-04), Am. Law Inst., Del. Bar Found., Am. Inn of Ct. London, Anglo-Am. Exch. Republican. Avocations: tennis, swimming. Office: Del Supreme Ct 34 The Circle Georgetown DE 19947-1500

HOLLAND, RICHARD D., academic administrator; s. Jordan Richard and Rae Elizabeth Holland; m. Rebecca Ann Guy, Aug. 24, 1968. BS in Biology, U. W.Ala., Livingston, 1965, MS in Biology, 1967; PhD in Botany and Cell Biology, U. Tenn., Knoxville, 1970. Instr. biology U. W.Ala., 1967—70, asst. prof. biology, 1975—78, assoc. prof. biology, 1978—83, prof. biol. scis., 1983—95, chair dept. biol. scis., 1995—97, dean coll. natural scis. & math., 1997—2001, pres., 2001—; asst. prof. botany U. Tenn., 1974—75. Subject matter specialist Nat. Tchr. Exam., 1979—80; pres. Ala. Coun. U. Faculty Pres., 1979—82; mem. So. Assn. Schs. Colleges, Reaffirmation Coms., 1991—; dir. W.Ala. Regional Sci. & Engring. Fair, 1998—2000. Editor: Jour. BioPhilately, 1987—92. Mem. Black Belt Cmty. Found., Selma, Ala., 2003, Nature Conservancy Ala., Birmingham, 2004, Ala. Nat. Register Rev. Bd. Hist. Places, Montgomery, 2006; treas. Beautification Commn., Livingston, 1976; mem. Coleman Art & Culture Ctr., York, Ala., 2003. Recipient Outstanding Young Men in Am. award, Jaycees, 1970, 1976, 1980, Gilbert award for outstanding tchg. award, U. W.Ala., 1984, 1989, Disting. Svc. award, Ala. Assn. Conservation Dists., III, 1997, Silver Beaver award, Boy Scouts Am., 2005; grantee Title III fellowship, US Dept. Edn., 1970—72, Title IV fellowship, 1973—74. Mem.: Beta, Beta, Beta Nat. Biol. Honors Soc., Phi Kappa Phi. Methodist. Avocations: hiking, photography, reading, travel, history. Home: 129 Shady Heights Dr Box 297 Livingston AL 35470 Office: Univ W Ala Webb Cir Sta One Livingston AL 35470-2099 Office Phone: 205-652-3527. Office Fax: 205-652-3774. Business E-Mail: rholland@uwa.edu.

HOLLAND, ROBERT D., music educator; b. Savannah, Ga., Nov. 1, 1963; s. Jean Roger Sr. and Ruth Elizabeth Holland; m. Jill L. Potter, Apr. 14, 2007. B Music Edn., Armstrong Atlantic State U., 1995. Choir dir. Ferguson Ave. Bapt. Ch., Savannah, 1988—; band dir. Providence Christian Sch., Savannah, 1993—2004, Calvary Day Sch., Savannah, 2005—. Mem.: Ga. Music Educators Assn. Republican. Baptist. Home: 574 Mendel Ave Savannah GA 31406 Office: Calvary Day Sch 4625 Waters Ave Savannah GA 31404 Home Phone: 912-355-7140; Office Phone: 912-351-2299. Office Fax: 912-351-2280; Home Fax: 912-355-7140. Personal E-mail: mrhopus@mac.com. Business E-Mail: rholland@calvarydayschool.com.

HOLLAND, ROBERT DALE, retired judge; b. Sayre, Okla., June 10, 1928; s. Claude Henry and Alva Mae (Joyce) H.; children: Arlene, Burton Dale, Rhonda Jo. Student, Tex. A&M, 1946, Internat. Corr. Schs., 1963, 65, 67-68; PhD of Sociology (hon.), Scholars U., 1975; postgrad., Case Western Res. U., Cleve., 2003—. Miner, bonus contract engr. Phelps Dodge Corp., Bisbee, Ariz., 1946—68, spec. projects, 1968—71, safety supr., 1971—75; supr. safety, security, loss prevention officer Phelps Dodge Corp., Copper Queen Br., Bisbee, Ariz., 1975—85; probation officer Cochise County, Bisbee, 1986—87; safety dir., loss prevention dir. Spray Sys. Environ., Phoenix, 1987—93; city magistrate City of Bisbee, 1989-93; pres., owner Copper City Cons., Bisbee, 1989—. Referee & hearing officer Cochise County Juvenile Ct., 1969-78; juvenile ct. judge pro tem, 1990-93; justice ct. judge pro tem, 1991-93; bd. dirs. Southern Ariz. Safety Coun., Tucson, 1986-91. Councilman City of Bisbee, 1973-82; chmn. relief com. Salvation Army, 1980—; chmn., vice chmn. bd. dirs. Copper Queen Hosp. Corp., Bisbee, Ariz., 1977-84; With USMC, 1947-52. Mem. ACP, Ariz. Dept. Health Svcs. (state health planning and coord. coun. 1973-76, region VI health planning bd. 1973-78, treas. regional govt. orgn. 1973-78, water quality coun. 1974), Am. Mining Congress (ad-hoc com. 1980), Perfect Ashlar Lodge F&AM (master 1964, 50 yr.life mem.), Masons (Scottish Rite). Democrat. Avocations: gun collecting, reading, church work. Home and Office: PO Box 5427 206 Black Knob View Bisbee AZ 85603-5427 Office Phone: 520-432-4755. Personal E-mail: coppercityinc@cableone.net.

HOLLAND, ROSEMARY SHERIDAN, program evaluation consultant; b. Detroit, Oct. 15, 1939; d. Geoffrey Francis and Mary Ann (Beirne) Sheridan; m. Neal Holland, Sept. 1961 (div. Apr. 1968); 1 child, Daniel Holland; m. Fred Fechheimer, Nov. 29, 1974; 1 child, Steve Fechheimer. PhB, U. Detroit, 1961; MSW, U. Mich., 1969, MA, PhD, U. Mich., 1984. Tchr. Prince Georges County Bd. Edn., Seat Pleasant, Md., 1961-63; adminstrv. asst. Neighborhood Svc. Orgn., Detroit, 1969-73; dir. mental health planning Cmty. Health Planning Coun. S.E. Mich., Detroit, 1971-73; coord. adult mental health svcs. Detroit/Wayne County Cmty. Mental Health Bd., 1973-76; asst. prof. U. Detroit, 1984-89. Mem. NASW, APHA, APA. Avocations: walking, travel, reading.

HOLLAND, RUBY MAE, social welfare administrator; BA in Sociology, Shaw Coll., 1976, MA in Comparative Lit., 1978; D of Psychology, Western Mich. U., 1982; DD, Wayne Theol. Sem., 1992. Ordained min. Evangel Assn. Chs. and Ministries, 2004, ordained bishop Gospel Ministry, 2004. Adminstr. Terrell Day Care Ctr., 1980-83; instr. Reborn Acad., 1984-87; English instr. Ctrl. H.S., 1987-92; enabler Maplegrove children's program U. Mich., Dearborn, 1992—; adminstr., guidance counselor, tchr. Mothers Love, Oak Park, Mich., 1992—. Assoc. min. Unity Cathedral of Faith Ministries; mem. CEO Forums in Christ Ministries, Greater Haven of Rest; asst. pastor Lighthouse Ch. of Prayer. Mem.: Evangel Assn. Chs. and Ministries.

HOLLANDER, ANNE, writer; b. Cleve., Oct. 16, 1930; d. Arthur and Jean Hill (Bassett) Loesser; m. John Hollander, June 15, 1953 (div. 1977); children: Martha, Elizabeth; m. Thomas Nagel, June 26, 1979. BA, Barnard Coll., 1952. Author: Seeing Through Clothes, 1978, Moving Pictures, 1989, Sex and Suits, 1994, Feeding the Eye, 1999, Fabric of Vision, 2002. Guggenheim fellow, 1975. Fellow N.Y. Inst. for the Humanities (interim dir. 1995-96); mem. Costume Soc. Am., College Art Assn., PEN Am. Ctr. (pres. 1995-96), Century Assn.

HOLLANDER, DANIEL, gastroenterologist, educator; Student, UCLA, 1960; MD, Baylor U., 1964. Diplomate Am. Bd. Internal Medicine, Am. Bd. Gastroenterology. Intern Phila. Gen. Hosp., 1964-65; resident in internal medicine Med. Ctr., U. Kans., Kansas City, 1965-67; NIH rsch. fellow in gastroenterology U. Wash., Seattle, 1967-69; asst. prof. medicine Albany (N.Y.) Med. Coll., Union U., 1971-73, assoc. prof., 1973; assoc. prof. medicine, head div. gastroenterology Wayne State U., Detroit, 1973-77, prof. medicine, head div. gastroenterology, 1977—94, U. Calif., Irvine, 1978-94, prof. physiology and biophysics, 1981-94, assoc. dean for rsch. and program devel. Coll. Medicine, 1984-85, assoc. dean for acad. affairs, 1985-89, sr. assoc. dean for clin. affairs, 1989-91, chief gastroenterology Irvine Med. Ctr., 1979-94; exec. dean Sch. of Medicine U. Kans., Kansas City, 1994—96; chief med. officer Sierra Pacific Network, San Francisco, 1996-98; prof. medicine U. Calif., San Francisco, 1996-98; pres., CEO Harbor-UCLA Rsch. and Edn. Inst., 1998-2001; prof. medicine UCLA, 1998—, dir. scientific and med. initiatives and inflammatory bowel disease grants, the Broad Found., 2001—. Attending physician, attending gastroenterologist Albany Med. Ctr. Hosp., 1971-73; chief gastroenterology svc., attending physician Harper Hosp., Detroit, 1973-78; cons. in gastroenterology Children's, Detroit Gen. and VA hosps., 1973-78; chief gastroenterology VA Med. Ctr., Long Beach, Calif., 1978-80; chmn. Gastrointestinal Gerontology Rsch. Group, 1988-89; vis. scientist dept. molecular medicine U. Auckland, New Zealand, 1990-91; vis. prof., invited speaker numerous other univs., profl. meetings, confs. Author: (with G. Gitnick, N. Kaplowitz, I.M. Samloff, L.J. Schoenfield) Principles and Practice of Gastroenterology and Hepatology, 1988, (with A. Tarnawski) Gastic Cytoprotection—A Clinician's Guide, 1989, (with Porro G. Bianchi) Treatment of Digestive Disease with Sucralfate, 1989; mem. editl. bd., reviewer Can. Jour. Gastroenterology; contbr. numerous articles, revs. to profl. jours., book chpt. With USAF, 1969-71. Major USAF, 1969—71. Calif. Heart Assn. rsch. fellow, 1960; Fogarty Sr. Internat. fellow Oxford (Eng.) U., 1984-85; grantee NIH, Nat. Inst. on Aging, Nat. Insts. Arthritis, Metabolism and Digestive Diseases, Skillman Found., VA, Goldsmith Found., Internat. Pharm. Products. Mem. ACP (A. Blaine traveling scholar 1973), Am. Fedn. for Clin. Rsch. (pres. Midwestern sect. 1979-80), Am. Gastroent. Assn., Am. Physiol. Soc., Am. Soc. for Clin. Investigation, Orange County Gastroenterology Assn. (pres. 1986-87), Brit. Soc. Gastroenterology, European Assn. Gastroenterology, Western Assn. Physicians, Western Gut Club (pres. 1981-82), Alpha Omega Alpha. Office: The Eli and Edythe L Broad Found 10900 Wilshire Blvd 12th Fl Los Angeles CA 90024-6532

HOLLANDER, GERALD MARTIN, physician; b. NYC, June 28, 1947; s. Emanuel and Miriam Hollander; m. Barbara Sarah Hollander, Jan. 26, 1975; children: Aviva, Shani, Nahva. BS, CCNY; MD, SUNY, Bklyn. Resident in medicine Brookdale Hosp. Med. Ctr., Bklyn., 1973-75, fellow in cardiology, 1976-78; dir. cardiac ICU Maimonides Med. Ctr, Bklyn., 1978—, dir. cardiology, 1994-99, dir. clin. cardiology, 1999—; assoc. prof. clin. medicine SUNY Health Sci. Ctr., Bklyn., 1994—. Contbr. articles to profl. jours. Bd. dirs. Hebrew Acad. of Long Beach, N.Y., 1986—. Fellow Am. Coll. Cardiology, Am. Coll. Physicians, Am. Coll. Chest Physicians; mem. Phi Beta Kappa. Office: Maimonides Med Ctr 4802 10th Ave Brooklyn NY 11219-2844

HOLLANDER, JOHN, humanities educator, poet; b. NYC, Oct. 28, 1929; s. Franklin and Muriel (Kornfeld) H.; m. Anne Helen Loesser, June 15, 1953 (div. 1977); children: Martha, Elizabeth.; m. Natalie Charkow, Dec. 15, 1981. AB, Columbia U., 1950, AM, 1952; PhD, Ind. U., 1959; DLitt (hon.), Marietta Coll., 1982; LHD (hon.), Ind. U., 1990; DFA (hon.), Maine Coll. of Art, 1993; DHL (hon.), CUNY, 2001; DHL (hon.), New Sch. U., 2003. Jr. fellow Soc. Fellows, Harvard, 1954-57; lectr. English Conn. Coll., New London, 1957-59; instr. English Yale, 1959-61; asst. prof. English, fellow Ezra Stiles Coll., 1961-64, assoc. prof., 1964-66; prof. Hunter Coll., CUNY, 1966—77; prof. English Yale U., New Haven, 1977—, A. Bartlett Giamatti prof., 1987—, Sterling prof., 1995—2002, prof. emeritus, 2002. Vis. prof. Linguistic Inst., Inc. U., 1964; faculty Salzburg Seminar in Am. Studies, 1965; Christian Gauss seminarian Princeton U., 1962; Clark lectr. Trinity Coll., Cambridge, Eng., 2000. Author: A Crackling of Thorns, 1958, The Untuning of the Sky, 1961, Movie-Going and Other Poems, 1962, Various Owls, 1963, Visions from the Ramble, 1965, The Quest of the Gole, 1966, Types of Shape, 1968, 2d edit., 1991, Images of Voice, 1970, The Night Mirror, 1971, Town and Country Matters, 1972, The Head of the Bed, 1973, Tales Told of the Fathers, 1975, Vision and Resonance, 1975, Reflections on Espionage, 1976, 2d edit., 1999, Spectral Emanations, 1978, In Place, 1978, Blue Wine, 1979, The Figure of Echo, 1981, Rhyme's Reason, 1981, 2d edit., 1989, 3rd edit., 2000, Powers of Thirteen, 1983, (with Saul Steinberg) Dal Vero, 1983, In Time and Place, 1986, Some Fugitives Take Cover, 1988, Harp Lake, 1988, Melodious Guile, 1988, Tesserae, 1993, Selected Poetry, 1993, The Gazer's Spirit, 1995, The Work of Poetry, 1997, The Poetry of Everyday Life, 1998, Figurehead and Other Poems, 1999, Picture Window, 1993; editor: Poems of Ben Jonson, 1961, (with Harold Bloom) The Wind and the Rain, 1961, (with Anthony Hecht) Jiggery-Pokery, 1966, Poems of Our Moment, 1968, Modern Poetry: Essays in Criticism, 1968, American Short Stories Since 1945, 1968, (with Frank Kermode) The Oxford Anthology of English Literature, 1973, (with Reuben A. Brower and Helen Vendler) For I.A. Richards: Essays in His Honor, 1973, (with Irving Howe and David Bromwich) Literature as Experience, 1979, The Essential Rossetti, 1990, Animal Poems, 1994, Garden Poems, 1996, Committed to Memory, 1997, Marriage Poems, 1997, War Poems, 1999, Sonnets, 2001, (with Joanna Weber) A Gallery of Poems, 2001, American Wits, 2003, Selected Poems of Emma Lazarus, 2005, Poems Haunted and Bewitched, 2005, Selected Poetry of Vicki Hearne, 2007; assoc. editor: Raritan Quarterly, 2002—; contbg. editor: Harper's mag, 1969-71, Word and Image, 1985-91, Literary Imagination, 1999-; Art and Lit., 1985—, Lit., 1989—; assoc. for poetry Partisan Review, 1959-65; mem. poetry bd. Wesleyan U. Press, 1959-62; author numerous poems. Recipient Yale Younger Poets award, 1958, Poetry Chap Book award, 1962, award in lit. Nat. Inst. Arts and Letters, 1963, Levinson prize, 1974, Bollingen prize, 1983, Mina P. Shaughnessy award, 1963, Melville Cane award, 1990, Ambassador Book award, 1994, Gov.'s Arts award State of Conn., 1997,

Robert Penn Warren-Cleanth Brooks award, 1998, Robert Frost medal, 2007; named Poet Laureate, State of Conn., 2007-; fellow Churchill Coll., Cambridge (Eng.) U., 1967-68, NEH, 1973-74, Guggenheim Found., 1979-80, MacArthur Found., 1990-95. Mem.: Am. Acad. Arts and Scis., Am. Acad. Arts and Letters (sec. 2000—03), Am. Assn. Lit. Scholars and Critics (pres. 2000—01), Century Assn. (N.Y.C.), Phi Beta Kappa. Office: Yale U Dept English PO Box 208302 New Haven CT 06520-8302 Office Phone: 203-432-4566. E-mail: john.hollander@yale.edu.

HOLLANDER, LAWRENCE JAY, retired marketing executive; b. Chgo., Feb. 15, 1940; s. Harry and Ann Blanche Hollander; m. Sallie Sue Mines, June 21, 1964 (div. Aug. 1999); children: Marla, Amy, Rebecca. BSBA, Roosevelt U., 1963. Dir. Far East ops. Indsl. & Sci. Conf. Mgmt., Chgo., 1972-77; dir. mktg. Far East ops. Clapp & Poliak, Inc., NYC, 1978-81; pres. Expoconsul Internat. Inc., Princeton, NJ, 1981-95, EI Mktg., Inc., Princeton, 1987-94, Ctr. for Tech. Concepts, Inc., Princeton, 1988-92, Expoconsul Mktg. Group, Inc., Princeton, 1992-94; dir. corp. fin. J.S. Holdings Group, Inc., Bay Head, NJ, 1996; shareholder, investment banker J.S. Securities, Inc., Bayhead, 1995-96; pres. Entrepreneurial Mgmt. Group, Inc., Princeton, 1996—2005; ret., 2005. Bd. dir. Congregation Beth Chaim, West Windsor, N.J., 1984, Jewish Cmty. Ctr. Delaware Valley, Ewing, N.J., 1987-96, v.p. 1990-92, pres. 1993-94; bd. dir. Jewish Fedn. Mercer and Buck Counties, NJ, Pa., 1988-95, v.p., 1989-90; mem. planning bd. West Windsor Twp., N.J., 1997-2002. Mem.: Rotary Club of the Princeton Corridor (charter mem. 1986—, sec. 1990—91, sgt.-at-arms 1991—92, bd. dirs. 1992—93, 1996—2005, sgt.-at-arms 1997—98, v.p. 2001—02, pres.-elect 2002—03, pres. 2003—04). Republican. Jewish. Avocations: weight-lifting, walking, tennis. Personal E-mail: ljhceo@aol.com.

HOLLANDER, LISA ELIZABETH ELENA, geographer, educator, history professor; b. Gwelo, Zimbabwe, Sept. 10, 1961; d. Christiaan Hollander and Hazel Rosemary Beeston; life ptnr. Candace Marie Isabell, Apr. 1, 1994. BA, U. Denver, Colo., 1983; diploma, London Sch. Econs., 1985; MA, Columbia U., NY, 1987; PhD in History, U. Wyoming, 1997. Sales Hunter Douglas Duette, Denver, 1989—92; prof. history and geography Jefferson Coll., Hillsboro, Mo., 1997—. Adj. instr. geography SE Mo. State U., Cape Girardeau, Mo., 1998—2002, Maryville U., St. Louis, 2000—05; adj. instr. history U. Mo., St. Louis, 1999—2005. Recipient Linda Johnston Student Assessment award, Jefferson Coll., 1999, 2006, Student Senate Faculty award, Jefferson Coll. Student Senate, 1999, Faculty Outstanding Achievement award, Jefferson Coll. Found., 2006, Tchg. Excellence award, Gov. Mo., 2007; grantee, State of Mo., 1998, 1999. Mem.: Mo. C.C. Assn. (rep. to consortium 1997—, mem. exec. bd. 2005—), Soc. History Edn. (assoc.). Independent. Avocation: travel. Office: Jefferson College 1000 Viking Dr Hillsboro MO 63050 Home Phone: 314-544-9416; Office Phone: 636-942-3000. Business E-Mail: lholland@jeffco.edu.

HOLLANDER, NANCY, lawyer; b. NYC, Mar. 10, 1944; BA with honors, U. Mich., 1965; JD magna cum laude, U. N.Mex., 1978. Bar: N.Mex. 1978, US Dist. Ct. (dist. N.Mex.) 1979, US Ct. Appeals (10th cir.) 1980, US Supreme Ct. 1982, US Ct. Appeals (4th cir.) 1984, US Ct. Appeals (9th cir.) 1986, US Dist. Ct. (we. dist. Tenn.) 1988, US Dist. Ct. (we. dist. Tex.) 1990, US Ct. Appeals (6th cir.) 1990, US Ct. Appeals (2nd cir.) 1991, US Ct. Appeals (8th cir.) 1992, So. Ute Tribal Ct., US Ct. Appeals (5th cir.) 1993, US Dist. Ct. (no. dist. Ill.) 1996, US Dist. Ct. (no. dist. Tex.) 2004. Editor, photographer Medalist Pubs., Chgo., 1968; freelance editor and photographer Chgo., 1969—71; exec. dir. N.Mex. Civil Liberties Union, 1971—75; asst. pub. defender N.Mex. State Pub. Defender Dept., 1978—79; atty. Freedman, Boyd, Daniels, Hollander, Goldberg & Ives, P.A., Albuquerque, 1980—, ptnr., 1983—. Adj. prof. law evidence/trial practice U. N.Mex. Sch. Law, Albuquerque, 1983—; bd. regents Nat. Criminal Def. Coll., 1985—; faculty mem. Gerry Spence's Trial Lawyers' Coll., 1994—98; prog. coord. Russian Jury Trial Project, 1995—97. Contbr. articles to profl. publs. Named one of Top 50 Women Litigators, Nat. Law Jour., 2001; recipient Charlie Driscoll award, Dismas House, 1997, Henrietta Pettijohn award, N.Mex. Women's Bar Assn., 2000, Profl. Lawyer of Yr. award, N.Mex. Trial Lawyers Assn., 2006. Fellow: Am. Coll. Trial Lawyers, Am. Bd. Criminal Lawyers; mem.: Internat. Criminal Bar (mem. governing coun. 2003), Internat. Criminal Def. Attys. Assn. (bd. dirs. 2002—), NACDL (pres. 1992—93), Am. Inn Ct. (barrister 1989—92), State Bar N.Mex. (criminal law sect.), Order of the Coif. Office: Freedman Boyd Daniels Hollander Goldberg & Ives PA 20 3rd St NW Ste 700 Albuquerque NM 87102 Office Phone: 505-842-9960. E-mail: nh@fbdlaw.com.*

HOLLANDER, ROBERT B., JR., retired romance languages educator; b. NYC, July 31, 1933; s. Robert B. and Laurene (McGookey) H.; m. Jean Haberman, Apr. 23, 1964; children: Cornelia Vanness, Robert B. III. AB, Princeton U., 1955; PhD, Columbia U., 1962. Tchr. Latin and English, Collegiate Sch., NYC, 1955-57; instr. English Columbia U., NYC, 1958-62; mem. faculty dept. French & Italian Princeton U., NJ, 1962—2003, prof. European lit., 1974—2003, chmn. comparative lit., 1994—98, prof. emeritus, 2003—. Mem. Nat. Coun. on Humanities, 1974-80, 87-92, vice chmn., 1978-80; mem. N.J. Com. for Humanities, 1980-86; dir. Dartmouth Dante Project, 1982—, Princeton Dante Project, 1997—; v.p. Assn. Internat. Studi de Lingua et Lett. Italiana, 1985-94; trustee La Scuola d'Italia, N.Y.C., 1986-92, Collegiate Sch., 1990-96, vice pres. bd., 1994-96, pres. bd., 98-2001; mem. adv. bd. Ctr. for Electronic Texts in the Humanities, 1991-98, pres., 1993-98; pres. Internat. Dante Seminar, 1992-2003, bd. mem., 2003—. Author: Allegory in Dante's Commedia, 1969, Boccaccio's Two Venuses, 1977, Studies in Dante, 1980, Il Virgilio dantesco, 1983, Boccaccio's Last Fiction: Il Corbaccio, 1988, Dante's Epistle to Cangrande, 1993, Boccaccio's Dante and the Shaping Force of Satire, 1997, Dante Alighieri, 2000, Dante, 2001; editor and translator: (with T. Hampton and M. Frankel) Amorosa Visione, 1986; co-editor: L'Espositione di Bernardino Daniello da Lucca sopra la Comedia di Dante, 1989, (with Jean Hollander) Dante Alighieri, Inferno, 2000, Purgatorio, 2003, Paradiso, 2007. Trustee Nat. Humanities Ctr., 1981—, chmn. bd. trustees, 1988-91. Guggenheim fellow, 1970-71; NEH fellow, 1974-75, 82-83; recipient Gold medal of the City of Florence for work on behalf of Dante, 1988, Bronze medal of the City of Tours, 1993, John Witherspoon award in the Humanities, Com. for the Humanities, N.J., 1988, Internat. Nicola Zingarelli prize for Dantean philology and criticism, 1999, Alumni Svc. award, Princeton U., 2007; named Disting. Alumnus, Collegiate Sch., 2003; hon. citizen Certaldo, Italy, 1997. Mem. Am. Acad. Arts and Scis., Dante Soc. Am. (mem. council 1976-85, pres. 1980-85, founding editor-in-chief Electronic Bull. 1995-2004, editor 1996-2004, assoc. editor 2004—, Charles T. Davis award 2005), Am. Boccaccio Assn., Cosmos Club Washington, Princeton Club NY. Republican. Office: Princeton U Dept French and Italian E Pyne Princeton NJ 08544-0001 Business E-Mail: bobh@princeton.edu.

HOLLANDER, SAMUEL, economist, educator; b. London, Apr. 6, 1937; s. Jacob and Rachel-Leah (Bornstein) H.; m. Perlette Kéroub, July 20, 1959; children: Frances, Isaac. BSc in Econs, London Sch. Econs., 1959; MA, Princeton U., 1961, PhD, 1963; LLD, McMaster U., 1999. Asst. in instrn. Princeton U., 1962-63; from asst. prof. econs. to prof. emeritus U. Toronto, Ont., Canada, 1963—98, univ. prof. emeritus, 1998—; rsch. dir. U. Nice (CNRS), France, 1999—2000; prof. Ben Gurion U., Israel, 2000—06. Author: The Sources of Increased Efficiency, 1965, The Economics of Adam Smith, 1973, The Economics of David Ricardo, 1979, The Economics of J.S. Mill, 1985, Classical Economics, 1987, Ricardo: The 'New View'-Collected Essays I, 1995, The Economics of Thomas Robert Malthus, 1997, The Literature of Political Economy-Collected Essays II, 1998, John Stuart Mill on Economic Theory and Method-Collected Essays III, 2000, Jean-Baptiste Say and the Classical Canon in Economics, 2005. Decorated officer Order of Can.; Guggenheim fellow, 1968-69, Killam sr. fellow, 1973-75, Connaught sr. fellow, 1984-85. Fellow Royal Soc. Can. Jewish. Home: 2 Rehov Sapir 89066 Arad Israel Home Phone: 972-8-997 1664; Office Phone: 972-8-647 2305. Personal E-mail: sholland@bgumail.bgu.ac.il.

HOLLANDER, SIDNEY, computer systems engineer; b. Boston, Mar. 23, 1949; s. Morris and Edith (Feldman) H.; m. Betty Sandra Groppel, Feb. 24, 1973 (dec.). BSEE, Rensselaer Poly. Inst., 1970, MEE, 1971. Commd. 2d lt. USAF, 1971, project mgr. satellite control facility Sunnyvale, Calif., 1974-78, resigned, 1978; project engr. The Aerospace Corp., LA, 1978—2001, sys. dir. MILSATCOM, 2001—. Program systems engr. UNISYS Def. Systems, Sunnyvale, 1987-88. Lt. col. USAFR, ret. 1994. Mem. IEEE (sr. mem., chmn. Santa Clara Valley sect. 1989-90), Silicon Valley Engring. Coun. (bd. dirs. 1989-91, K-12 outreach chmn. 1990-91), San Francisco Bay Wildlife Soc. (bd. dirs. 1990-2000, pres. 1995-2000). Democrat. Unitarian-Universalist. Home: PO Box 4034 Redondo Beach CA 90277-1737 Office: Aerospace Corp MS M8/018 PO Box 92957 2350 E El Segundo Blvd Los Angeles CA 90009-2957 Office Phone: 310-336-3994.

HOLLANDER, TOBY EDWARD, education educator; b. Queens, NY, June 21, 1931; s. David and Eve (Shroot) H.; m. Harriet Goldberg, June 14, 1953; children: Marc, Deborah. BS cum laude, NYU, 1952, MBA, 1953; PhD, U. Pitts., 1960. Instr. econs. U. Pitts., 1957-58; asst. prof. Duquesne U., 1958-59; prof. Baruch Coll., CUNY, 1963-67, dean, 1967-69, vice chancellor, 1969-71; dep. commr. higher edn. N.Y. State Edn. Dept., 1971-77; chancellor N.J. Dept. Higher Edn., Trenton, 1977-90; prof. Rutgers U., 1990—2006, prof. emeritus, 2006—. Author books in field; contbr. articles to profl. jours. Served with U.S. Army, 1953-55. Mem. State Higher Edn. Exec. Officers Assn. (pres. 1977-78). Office: 889 Lawrenceville Rd Princeton NJ 08540 Personal E-mail: tedwardhollander@msn.com.

HOLLANS, IRBY NOAH, JR., retired trade association administrator; b. Christiansburg, Va., Nov. 3, 1930; s. Irby Noah and Annie May (Lester) H.; m. Frances Jo Cox, June 21, 1957; children: Susan Frances, Carol Leigh, Irby Neil. BS in Gen. Bus. Adminstrn., Va. Poly. Inst. and State U., 1953. Mgr. promotion Sta. WRVA-Radio, Richmond, Va., 1956-64, editor bus. news, 1956-64; dir. travel devel. Va. State C. of C., 1964-70, asst. exec. dir., 1970-72; exec. dir. Optical Labs. Assn., Washington, 1972-96. Instr. bus. Va. Commonwealth U., Richmond, 1965-71 Mem. Dulles (Va.) Internat. Airport Devel. Commn., 1968-76; mem. Va. Nat. Capital Airports Acquisition Study Commn., 1968-76; bd. dirs. Va. Thanksgiving Festival Inc., 1965-70, Keep Va. Beautiful, Inc., 1965-73, Central Va. Ednl. TV, 1970-72, Va. Travel Coordinating Com., 1964-72. Served to maj. USAF, 1953-72, Korea. Recipient Service award Va. Profl. Photographers Assn., 1966; Nat. award Profl. Photographers Assn. Am., 1970 Mem. Am. Soc. Assn. Execs. (cert.), Va. Pub. Rels. Conf., Nat. Assn. Wholesaler-Distbrs.-Pros Group, Am. Nat. Stds. Inst. (med. devices stds. mgmt. bd. 1973-80), Washington Soc. Assn. Execs., Va. C. of C., Vienna (Va.) Photog. Soc. (pres. 1990-92), Greater Washington Coun. Camera Clubs (exec. v.p. 1988-93), Rotary Internat. (exec. dir. 1996—). Home and Office: 5339 Cristfield Ct Fairfax VA 22032-3809 Office Phone: 703-503-9788. E-mail: ihollans@earthlink.net.

HÖLLDOBLER, BERTHOLD KARL, zoologist; b. Erling-Andechs, Germany, June 25, 1936; came to U.S., 1973; s. Karl and Maria (Russmann) H.; m. Friederike Probst, Feb. 9, 1980; children: Jakob, Stefan, Sebastian. Dr. rer. nat., U. Wurzburg, 1965; Dr. habil., U. Frankfurt a.M., 1969; D (hon.), U. Konstanz, 2000. Prof. zoology U. Frankfurt a.M., 1971-72; prof. biology Harvard U., Cambridge, Mass., 1973-90, Alexander Agassiz prof. zoology, 1982-90; prof. U. Wurzburg, Germany, 1989—. Adj. prof. U. Ariz., Tucson; rsch. assoc. Harvard U.; Andrew D. White prof. at large Cornell U., 2002—; Found. prof. Ariz. State U., Tempe, 2004—. Author: (with Edward O. Wilson) The Ants, 1990 (Pulitzer Prize for gen. non-fiction 1991), (with E.O. Wilson) Journey to the Arts, (Shortlisted for the Rhone-Poulenc Sci. Book prize, 1995, Phi Beta Kappa prize, 1995). John Simon Guggenheim fellow, 1980; recipient Sr. Scientist award Alexander von Humboldt Found., 1986-87, Gottfried Wilhelm Leibniz prize, 1989, Phi Beta Kappa prize (with E.O. Wilson) 1995, Karl Ritter von Frisch medal and Sci. prize, German Zool. Soc., 1996, Körber-prize for European Sci., 1996, Benjamin Franklin, Wilhelm v. Humboldt Prize of the German Amer. Acad. Coun. (GAAC), 1999, Werner Heisenberg medal Alexander v. Humboldt Found., Alfried Krupp Sci. prize, 2004, Treviranus medal Soc. German Biologists, 2006; named to Bavarian Maximilian Order, 2003. Fellow AAAS, Am. Animal Behavior Soc.; mem. Nat. Acad. of Sci. (fgn. mem.), Am. Acad. Sci., German Acad. der Naturforscher Leopoldina, Bayerische Acad. der Wissenschaften, Acad. Europaea, Berlin-Brandenburgische Acad., Am. Philos. Soc. (fgn. mem.), Bundesverdienstkrenz (Nat. Merit medal Germany 2000). Office: Sch Life Scis Ariz State U PO Box 874501 Tempe AZ 85287 Office Phone: 480-727-8415. Business E-Mail: bertholl@asu.edu.

HOLLE, REGINALD HENRY, retired bishop; b. Burton, Tex., Nov. 21, 1925; s. Alfred W. and Lena (Nolte) H.; m. Marla Christianson, June 16, 1949; children: Todd, Joan. BA, Capital U., 1946, DD (hon.), 1979; MDiv, Trinity Luth. Sem., 1949; D of Ministry, Ohio Consortium Religious Stdy, 1977; DD (hon.), Wittenberg U., 1989. Ordained minister Evang. Luth. Ch. Am., then bishop. Assoc. pastor Zion Luth. Ch., Sandusky, Ohio, 1949-51; sr. pastor Salem Meml. Luth. Ch., Detroit, 1951-72, Parma Luth. Ch., Cleve., 1973-78; bishop Mich. dist. Am. Luth. Ch., Detroit, 1978-87; bishop NW Lower Mich. Synod Evang. Luth. Ch., Lansing, 1988-95. Bd. dirs. Aubsburg Fortress Pub. House, Wittenberg U. Author: Planning for Funerals, 1978; contbr. to Augsburg Sermon Series. Bd. dirs. Ronald McDonald House Ctrl. Mich., 1995—, Planned Giving Luth. Social Svcs. Mich., 1995—. Recipient Pub. Svc. citation Harper Woods City Coun., 1976, Recognition for Community Svc., Detroit Pub. Schs., 1974. E-mail: rholle@juno.com.

HOLLEB, DORIS B., urban planner, economist; b. NYC, Oct. 26, 1922; m. Marshall M. Holleb, Oct. 15, 1944; children: Alan, Gordon, Paul. BA magna cum laude, Hunter Coll., 1942; MA, Harvard U., 1947; postgrad., U. Chgo., 1959-60, 65-66. Economist Fed. Res. Bd., Washington, 1943—44; freelance journalist, 1945-63; econs. cons. Chgo. Dept. City Planning, 1963—65; rsch. assoc. Ctr. Urban Studies U. Chgo., 1966-78, sr. rsch. assoc., 1978-88; dir. Met. Inst., 1973-84, professorial lectr., 1979—2004, professorial lectr. emerita, 2004—. Chmn. ednl. coun. Francis W. Parker Sch., 1963-80, cons., 1980-92, hon. trustee, 2006; adv. coun. Ctr. for Study Democratic Instns., 1975-79; nat. adv. com. White House Conf. on Balanced Nat. Growth and Econ. Devel., 1978; mem. N.E. Ill. Planning Commn., 1973-77, Chgo. Met. Area Transp. Coun., 1980-84; adv. coun. to Nat. Ctr. Rsch. on Vocat. Edn., US Dept. Edn., 1979-82, US Dept. State adv. com. internat. investment, tech. and devel., 1979-81; mem. Chgo. Plan Commn., 1986—, Nat. Coun. Humanities, 1998-03. Author: Social and Economic Information for Urban Planning, 1968, Colleges and the Urban Poor, 1972; mem. editl. bd. Ill. Issues, 1977—; contbr. articles to profl. jours Fellow: Nat. Phi Beta Kappa Soc. (bd. dirs.).

HOLLEB, MARSHALL MAYNARD, lawyer; b. Chgo., Dec. 25, 1916; s. A. Paul and Sara (Zaretsky) H.; m. Doris Bernstein, Oct. 15, 1944; children: Alan R., Gordon P., Paul D. BA, U. Wis., 1937; MBA, Harvard U., 1939; IA, 1941, JD, 1942. Bar: Ill. 1947, U.S. Supreme Ct. 1960. Assoc. Levenson, Becker & Peebles, Chgo., 1947-51; ptnr. Yates & Holleb, Chgo., 1952-59, Holleb, Gerstein & Glass, Chgo., 1960-81; sr. ptnr. Holleb & Coff, Chgo., 1982-2000; sr. counsel Wildman, Harrold, Allen & Dixon, 2000—. Chmn. bd. dirs. Urban Assocs. Chgo., Inc. Contbr. articles to profl. jours.; profiled on PBS-TV program Chicago Stories, 2001. Trustee Acorn Fund, 1971-95; life trustee Hull House Assn., pres., 1980-82; trustee emeritus nat. Bldg. Mus., Chgo. Inst. Psychoanalysis; overseer Harvard Bus. Sch. Club Chgo.; founder, life trustee, gen. legal counsel Mus. Contemporary Art Chgo.; mem. adv. bd. Landmarks Preservation Coun., Fair Housing Ctr. Home Investments Fund, Citizens Sch. Com.; mem. vis. coms. Oriental Inst. and Visual Arts U. Chgo.; bd. dirs. Intenat. Visitors Ctr., Mostly Music, Inc., Chgo. Fund. on Aging and Disability; mem. Ill. Internat. Trade and Port Promotion Adv. Com., 1982, Chgo.'s Future Project Com. of Trust, Inc., 1982, Pacific Basing Inst.; mem. nat. adv. bd. on internat. edn. programs U.S. Dept. Edn., 1981, City Chgo. Local Cultural Devel. Commn.; Mayor Daley's prin. for a day Chgo. Public Schs.; pres. Chgo. Theater Preservation Group Ltd., sec., bd. dirs. Arts Club Chgo.; bd. dirs. Chgo. Maritime Soc.; me. industry sector adv. com. on svcs. for trade policy matters U.S. Dept. Commerce, 1995-98; mem. nat. adv. com. and del. White House Conf. on Aging, 1971, 81; mem. Ill. Coun. Aging, 1961-81, chmn., 1973-81; panel mem. Ill. Statewide Comprehensive Outdoor Recreation Plan; mem. weatherization adv. com. Ill. Dept. Bus. and Econ. Devel., 1975—; mem. Ill. appeal bd. SSS, 1966-73; cons. Vt. rsch. project HUD. 1st lt. U.S. Army, Philippines and Japan, 1943-46. Recipient Humanitarian of Yr. Henry Booth House award Hull House Assn., 1979; Am. Heritage award Am. Jewish Com., 1986, Arts award Mostly Music Inc., 1986, City Brightener award Bright New City Chgo., 1987, Holleb Cmty. Svc. award, Lambda Alpha Internat., 2004. Mem. ABA, Ill. Bar Assn., Chgo. Bar Assn., Fed. Bar Assn., Am. Soc. Internat. Law, Am. Arbitration Assn. (nat. panel), Am. Inst. Planners, Nat. Assn. Housign and Redevel. Ofcls., Urban Land Inst., Harvard Law Soc. Ill. (bd. dirs.), Arts Club, Univ. Club, Bryn Mawr Country Club, Execs. Club (Chgo.), Lambda Alpha. Democrat. Office: 225 W Wacker Dr Ste 3000 Chicago IL 60606-1229 Office Phone: 312-201-2983.

HOLLEMAN, FRANK SHARP, III, lawyer; b. Seneca, SC, May 19, 1954; s. Frances (Hull) H.; m. Anne Barker, July 31, 1976; 3 children. BA magna cum laude, Furman U., 1976; JD magna cum laude, Harvard U., 1979; MS, London Sch. of Econs. and Polit. Sci., 1981. Bar: SC 1979, US Ct. Appeals (4th cir.) 1980, DC 1981, US Dist. Ct. SC 1982, US Supreme Ct. 1985. Law Clk. to hon. Harrison Winter US Ct. of Appeals (4th cir.), 1979—80; law clk. to assoc. justice hon. Harry A. Blackmun US Supreme Ct., 1981—82; assoc. Wyche Law Firm, Greenville, S.C., 1982-86, mem., 1986-93; dep. asst. atty. gen. civil divsn. U.S. Dept. Justice, Washington, 1993-94; chief of staff U.S. Dept. Edn., Washington, 1994-97; atty. Wyche Law Firm, Greenville, SC, 1997—99; dep. sec. US Dept. Edn., 1999—2000; mem. Wyche Burgess Freeman & Parham, P.A., Greenville, SC. Chmn. Greenville (SC) County Dems., 1984-88, SC Dems., 1988-90; mem. Dem. Nat. Com., 1988-90, bd. mem. Alliance Quality Edn. Knox fellow Harvard U., 1979. Mem. ABA, S.C. Bar Assn., Greenville County Bar Assn., Phi Beta Kappa, Pi Gamma Mu. Presbyterian. Editor: Harvard Law Review 1977-78; articles editor 1978-79. Office: Wyche Burgess Freeman & Parham PA 44 E Camperdown Way 29601 PO Box 728 Greenville SC 29602-0728 Office Phone: 864-242-8340. Office Fax: 864-235-8900. E-mail: fholleman@wyche.com.

HOLLEMAN, VERNON DAUGHTY, internist, educator; b. Brownwood, Tex., Oct. 1, 1931; s. Vernon Edgar and Olene Nollie (Reece) H.; m. Shirley Eyvonne Roberts, April 26, 1961; children: Richard, Joel, Douglas. BA in Chemistry and Biology, Howard Payne Coll., Brownwood, 1953; MD, Baylor U., 1958. Mem. med. staff Santa Fe Meml. Hosp. 1962-83; pres. med. staff Santa Fe Meml. Hosp., 1979-83; mem. med. staff Scott and White Hosp., 1962—; asst. chief physician Santa Fe Employees Hosp. Assn., 1962-85, med. dir., 1985—; intern Scott and White Clinic and Hosp., Temple, Tex., 1958-59, resident in internal medicine, 1959-62; dir. div. gen. internal medicine Santa Fe Ctr., Temple, Tex., 1985—; assoc. prof. internal medicine Tex. A&M Coll. Medicine, Temple, 1982—. Adj. faculty clinician Ohio Coll. of Podiatric Medicine, Cleveland, 1982-86; med. dir. Consol. Assns. Railroad Employees, 1997—. Illustrator: Aesculapian, 1957, So. Bapt. Student Union Projects, 1954-58; illustrator ltd. edit. lithographs Baylor U. Lettermans Assn., 1994; contbr. photography to books, including Colorados Biggest Bucks and Bulls, Boone and Crocket Books, Awesome Antlers, Records of North American Mule Deer; author: articles on health, preventive medicine, and numerous others. Bd. dirs Santa Fe Meml. Found.; hon. chmn. physicians adv. bd. Tex. Nat. Rep. Congl. Com. Art Instrn., Inc. scholar, 1952; recipient Centennial award Santa Fe Meml. Found., 1991. Mem. AAAS, Nat. Assn. Ret. and Vet. Railway Employees (hon. life), AMA, ACP, Am. Coll. Phys. Execs., Am. Soc. Internal Medicine, Tex. Med. Assn. (Vernon D. Holleman-Lewis M. Rampy Scott and White Centennial chair gerontology 1999), Tex. Med. Found., Am. Heart Assn. (cardiopulmonary coun.), Am. Assn. Ry. Physicians, World Med. Assn., Tex. Diabetes and Endocrine Soc., N.Y. Acad. Scis., So. Med. Assn. (life), Am. Coll. Occupl. Medicine, Am. Pain Soc., Am. Acad. Pain Mgmt. (diplomate), Am. Soc. Pain Educators (charter), Internat. Soc. Phys. Activity in Prevention of Osteoporosis (charter), Boone and Crockett Club, Tex. Taxidermy Assn., Nat. Safari Club (life), Alpha Chi, Phi Chi. Baptist. Avocations: medical history, art, hunting, photography, conservation. Office: Scott and White Clinic 600 S 25th St Temple TX 76504-5227

HOLLENBAUGH, H(ENRY) RITCHEY, lawyer; b. Shelby, Ohio, Nov. 12, 1947; m. Diane Robinson Nov. 21, 1973 (div. 1989); children: Chad Ritchey, Katie Paige; m. Rebecca U., Aug. 8, 1995. BA, Kent State U., 1969; JD, Capital U., 1973. Bar: Ohio 1973, U.S. Dist. Ct. (so. dist.) Ohio 1974, U.S. Ct. Appeals (6th cir.) 1976, U.S. Supreme Ct. 1978. Investigator Ohio Civil Rights Com., Columbus, Ohio, 1969-72; legal intern City Atty.'s Office, Columbus, Ohio, 1972-73, asst. city prosecutor, 1973-75, sr. asst. city atty., 1975-76; ptnr. Hunter, Hollenbaugh & Theodotou, Columbus, Ohio, 1976-85, Delligatti, Hollenbaugh, Briscoe & Milless, Columbus, Ohio, 1985-91, Climaco Seminatore Delligatti & Hollenbaugh, Columbus, 1991-93, Delligatti, Hollenbaugh & Briscoe, Columbus, 1993-95, Draper, Hollenbaugh, Briscoe, Yashko & Carmany, 1996-99, Carlile Patchen & Murphy LLC, Columbus, 1999—, chmn. Litig. Dept., 1999—. Mem. Ohio Pub. Defender Commn., 1988-94; chmn. Franklin County Pub. Defender Commn., 1986-92. Treas. The Gov's. Com., 1987-96, Friends With Celeste, Friends of Gov's. Residence, 1987-92, Participation 2000, 1987-91, Ohio Legal Assistance Found., 1998—. Fellow ABA Found. (chair commn. on advt. 1993-97, ho. of dels. 1993—, chair nat. conf. lawyers and reps. of media 2000-04); mem. ABA (bd. govs. 2007—), Ohio State Bar Assn. (bd. govs. 1989-94, pres. 1992-93), Columbus Bar Assn. (pres. 1987-88), Nat. Conf. Bar Pres., Nat. Assn. Criminal Def. Lawyers, Brookside Golf and Country Club. Democrat. Methodist. Avocations: golf, politics. Home: 8549 Glenalmond Ct Dublin OH 43017-9737 Office: Carlile Patchen & Murphy LLC 336 E Broad St Columbus OH 43215-3202 Home Phone: 614-799-1031; Office Phone: 614-228-6135. Business E-Mail: hrh@cpmlaw.com.

HOLLENBERG, PAUL FREDERICK, pharmacology educator; b. Phila., Sept. 18, 1942; s. Frederick Henry and Catherine (Dentzer) H.; m. Emily Elizabeth Vanootighem, May 6, 1967; children: Kathryn Mary, David Paul. BS in Chemistry, Wittenberg U., 1964; MS in Biochemistry, U. Mich., 1966, PhD in Biochemistry, 1969. Postdoctoral fellow U. Mich., Ann Arbor, 1969, U. Ill., Urbana, 1969-72; asst. prof. Northwestern U., Chgo., 1972-81, assoc. prof., 1981-84, prof. pathology and molecular biology, 1984-87; prof. pharmacology, chmn. dept. Wayne State U. Sch. Medicine, Detroit, 1987-94, U. Mich. Med. Sch., Ann Arbor, 1994—. Pharmacology test com. Nat. Bd. Med. Examiners; mem. Chem. Pathology

Study Sect. NIH, 1987-91. Co-founder, assoc. editor Chem. Rsch. in Toxicology, 1988—; assoc. editor Jour. Pharmacology and Exptl. Therapeutics; mem. editl. bd. Drug Metabolism and Disposition, British Jour. Pharmacology. Schweppe Found. research fellow, 1974-77; NIH research grantee, 1974—. Mem. Am. Chem. Soc., Am. Soc. Biochemists and Molecular Biologists, Am. Soc. Pharmacology and Exptl. Therapeutics (sec./treas. 1998-99, pres.-elect 2001-02, pres. 2002-03), Am. Assn. for Cancer Rsch., Soc. Toxicology, Internat. Soc. for Study of Xenobiotics. Avocations: reading, running, golf. Home: 1968 Woodlily Ct Ann Arbor MI 48103-9728 Office: Univ Mich 2301 MSRB III Sch Medicine 1150 W Medical Center Dr Ann Arbor MI 48109-0632 Office Phone: 734-764-8166. Business E-Mail: phollen@umich.edu.

HOLLENBERG, STEVEN MICHAEL, physician, researcher; b. Alexandria, Va., May 13, 1957; s. Jack Earl and Judith Ann H.; m. Susan Ann Colilla, Aug. 6, 1994. BA cum laude, Amherst Coll., Mass., 1978; MD magna cum laude, Emory U., Atlanta, 1984. Diplomate Am. Bd. Internal Medicine in Crit. Care Medicine and Cardiovasc. Disease. Intern, resident in internal medicine NY Hosp., 1984-87; fellow in critical care medicine NIH, Bethesda, Md., 1987-89; fellow in cardiology Johns Hopkins U., Balt., 1989-90; sr. staff fellow NIH, Bethesda, 1990-93; asst. prof. med. cardiology and critical care medicine Rush Med. Coll., Chgo., 1993—, assoc. dir. Med. ICU. Author: (with others) Harrison's Principles of Internal Medicine, 1996, Surgical Intensive Care, 1993, Cardiologic Schock, 2007, Cardiology in Family Practice, 2007; contbr. articles to profl. jours. Lt. comdr. USPHS, 1989-93. Recipient Career Devel. award Schweppe Found., 1995. Fellow Am. Coll. Cardiology, Am. Coll. Chest Physicians, Am. Heart Assn.; mem. ACP, Am. Heart Assn., Soc. Critical Care Medicine, Am. Fedn. Clin. Rsch., Alpha Omega Alpha. Office: One Cooper Plaza 366 Dorrance Camden NJ 08103 Office Phone: 856-342-2624. Business E-Mail: hollenberg-steven@cooperhealth.edu.

HOLLENDER, LARS GÖSTA, dental educator; b. Veinge, Sweden, Oct. 22, 1933; arrived in U.S., 1984; s. Gunnar Yngve and Astrid Margareta (Andersson) H.; m. Gunnel Charlotta Bergdahl, May 19, 1956 (div. 1975); children: Peter, Marie, Lena, Stefan; m. Sheridan Ellen Houston, Apr. 8, 1989; 1 child, Ashley Ellen. DDS, Sch. Dentistry, Malmö, Sweden, 1958, PhD, 1964. Diplomate Am. Bd. Oral and Maxillofacial Radiology. Assoc. prof. Sch. Dentistry, Malmö, 1964-68, prof., chair Göteborg, Sweden, 1969-87; prof., dir. U. Wash. Sch. Dentistry, Seattle, 1988—. Sec. gen. Internat. Assn. Dentomaxillofacial Radiology, 1974-85; vis. prof. UCLA Sch. Dentistry, 1980-82, U. Wash. Sch. Dentistry, 1984-87; sec./treas. Am. Bd. Oral and Maxillofacial Radiology, 1992-94, pres., 1995, councillor, 1996—. Editor-in-chief Odontologist Revy, 1964-69; contbr. over 100 chpts. to books and articles to profl. jours. Recipient Rsch. prize South Swedish Dental Soc., 1964, Rsch. prize Swedish Dental Assn., 1965, Elander Rsch. prize Gothenburg Dental Soc., 1976. Fellow Am. Acad. Oral and Maxillofacial Radiology (pres. 1997-98); mem. ADA (mem. review com. for OMFR commn. on dental accreditation 1999—), Internat. Assn. Dental and Maxillofacial Radiology (hon.), Australian Maxillofacial Radiology Soc. (hon.), Wash. State Dental Assn., King County Dental Assn. Avocations: reading, golf, cooking, travel, music. Office: Univ Wash Sch Dentistry PO Box 356370 Seattle WA 98195-6370 Office Phone: 206-543-0615. E-mail: larsholl@u.washington.edu.

HOLLERAN, KAREN ELAINE, literature and language professor; d. John Sayers and Marjorie Hughes Holleran. BA cum laude, Waynesburg Coll., Pa., 1979; MA magna cum laude, Duquesne U., Pitts., 1991. Instr. English Robert Morris U., Coraopolis, Pa., 1991—96, C.C. Allegheny County, Pitts., 1992—96; lectr. English C.C. Beager County, Monaca, 1993—94, U. Pitts., 1996; adminstrv. asst. Army Mgmt. Engring. Coll., Rock Island, Ill., 1997; asst. prof. Kaplan U., Davenport, Iowa, 2000—. Adj. instr. English Scott C.C., Bettendorf, Iowa, 1997—99. Mem. ACLU, Smithsonian Inst. Mem.: AAUW, Northeast Modern Lang. Assn. Home: 2409 Farnam St Davenport IA 52803

HOLLERBACH, SERGE, artist; b. Pushkin, Russia, Nov. 1, 1923; came to U.S., 1949, naturalized, 1955; s. Lew and Ludmila (Agapov) H. Student, Acad. Fine Arts, Munich, Germany, Art Students League. Tchr. art. Exhibited in group shows, Drawings, U.S.A., 1961, Met. Mus. Art, N.Y.C., 1966, Childe Hassam Fund Exhbn., Am. Acad. Arts and Letters, 1968; works represented in ann. exhbns., N.A.D., Am. Watercolor Soc., Audubon Artists, Nat. Arts Club; painter, designer, book illustrator. Recipient Gold medal Nat. Arts Club, 1963; prize N.A.D., 1965; Adolph and Clara Obrig prize, 1971, 76; Silver medal Am. Watercolor Soc., 1978; Gold medal Am. Watercolor Soc., 1983, Bronze medal of honor, Am. Watercolor Soc., 2002; medal and purchase Butler Inst. Am. Art, 1977; also numerous purchase awards and prizes. Mem. NAD; Mem. Am. Watercolor Soc., Audubon Artists, Nat. Soc. Painters in Casein, Allied Artists Am.

HOLLERMAN, CHARLES EDWARD, retired pediatrician; b. Turtle Creek, Pa., Apr. 22, 1929; s. Harry R. and Lena F. H.; m. Catharine, Aug. 22, 1953; children: James, Karen, Jeffrey, Pamela. BS in Chemistry, Allegheny Coll., 1951; MD, Cornell U., 1955; student, U.S. Navy Sch. Aviation Medicine, 1957. Lic. pediatrician Pa. Intern York County (Pa.) Hosp., 1955-56; pvt. practice Cochranton, Pa., 1959-60; resident in pediat. Children's Hosp., Buffalo, 1960—62; fellow in clin. nephrology SUNY, 1962-65, instr. pediatrics, 1965-66; from asst. prof. to prof. pediat. Georgetown U., 1966—75; prof. pediat. U. S.D., Vermillion, 1976—82, asst. dean clin. services; acting dean, exec. dean U. S.D. Sch. Medicine, 1977-79, dean, 1979-82, v.p. health affairs, 1979-82; chmn. dept. pediatrics Mercy Hosp., Pitts., 1982-86, v.p. med. affairs, 1985-92; chief divsn. pediat. nephrology Mercy Children's Med. Ctr., Pitts., 2000—06; v.p. med. affairs St. Joseph's Mercy Hosps., Clinton Twp., Mich., 1992-95; regional v.p. physician and clin. integration Mercy Health Ptnrs. Southwest Ohio, Cin., 1995-99. Author: Pediatric Nephrology-Medical Outline Series, 1979; contbr. in field. Served with USN, 1956-59. Fellow Am. Coll. Physician Execs. (cert. physician exec.); mem. AMA, Am. Acad. Pediats., Phi Beta Kappa (cert. pediatrician, pediat. nephrologist, med. mgr.). Home: 4550 Nature Trail Dr Allison Park PA 15101-1131

HOLLEY, CHARLES MURPHY, JR., retail company executive; b. Dallas, July 9, 1956; s. Charles Murphy Sr. and Patricia Lucille (Biel) H.; m. Shannon Spence, Apr. 27, 1996. BBA in Acctg., U. Tex., 1979; MBA in Fin., U. Houston, 1980. CPA, Tex. Sr. mgr. Ernst & Young, Ft. Worth, 1980-90; dir. internat. fin. Tandy Corp., Ft. Worth, 1991-92; mng. dir. Europe Memorex Consumer Products, London, 1992-94; v.p., CFO Wal-Mart Internat., Bentonville, Ark., 1994—2003, sr. v.p., contr., 2003—05, sr. v.p. fin., 2005—07, exec. v.p. fin., treas., 2007—. Bd. dirs. Easter Seal Soc., Tarrant County, Tex., 1987-90. Mem. AICPA, Tex. Soc. CPAs. Avocations: tennis, travel, reading. Office: Wal Mart Internat 702 SW 8th St Bentonville AR 72716-6299*

HOLLEY, CYRUS HELMER, management consulting service executive; b. Chgo., June 14, 1936; s. Cyrus Howell and Elizabeth Fay (Helmer) H.; m. Shirley Marquitta Cannon, Aug. 31, 1957; children— Barrett Cannon, Russell William BS in Chem. Engring., Tex. A&M U., 1957; LLD (hon.), Bloomfield Coll., NJ, 1998. Registered profl. engr. Vice pres. indsl. chems. BASF Wyandotte Corp., Parsippany, NJ, 1976-79; sr. v.p. minerals & chem. div. Engelhard Corp., Edison, NJ, 1979-81, v.p., exec. v.p., 1981-83, v.p., pres., chief operating officer metals div., 1983-84, sr. v.p., pres. chem. div., 1984-85, exec. v.p., chief operating officer, 1985-91; pres. Mgmt. Cons. Svcs., 1991—. CEO Oakmont Enterprises, Inc., 1993—, CSBR Properties, L.P., 1997—, Roanoke Devel. Co., L.P., 1999—, Hanna Properties, LLC, 2002—; bd. dirs. Costa Linda Beach Resort, chair, 1999-2006. Contbr. articles to profl. jours. Trustee Bloomfield Coll., 1988-97, trustee emeritus, 1997—; dir. Nat. Assn. Ptnrs. in Edn., 1990-95, 99-02, Tex. Assn. Ptnrs. in Edn., 1991-99, 2001-03, NJ Assn. Ptnrs. in Edn., 1991-99, Tex. Bus. & Edn. Coalition, 1992-96; chair Ind. Coll. Fund. NJ, 1990-92; bd. dirs. Tex. Ind. Coll. Fund, 1998-2001. Mem. AIChE. Republican. Presbyterian. Avocations: reading, golf, music. Office: Mgmt Cons Svcs 120 Oakmont Dr Trophy Club TX 76262 Business E-Mail: oakmontinc@sbcglobal.net.

HOLLEY, MICHAEL, sportswriter, sportscaster; BA in Journalism, Point Park Coll., 1992; PhD in Humane Letters (hon.), Point Park Univ., 2005. Former sports columnist Akron Beacon Jour., Cleve. Plain Dealer, Chgo. Tribune, Boston Globe; columnist, analyst Around the Horn, ESPN, 2002—04, I, Max Sports, 2004; talk show host Sports Radio WEEI, 2005—. Author: (sports books) Patriot Reign, 2004. Recipient Pulitzer Prize for Meritorious Public Svc. in Journalism, 1994. Office: WEEI Third Fl 20 Guest St Brighton MA 02135-2040

HOLLEY, RICK R., lumber company executive; BA, San Jose State Univ. Fin. mgmt. positions GE, 1974—83; asst. v.p. corp. audit Burlington No. Inc., 1983—85; v.p., CFO Plum Creek Timber Co., Seattle, 1985—94, pres., CEO, 1994—. Dir., past chmn. Am. Forest & Paper Assn.; mem. bd. gov. Nat. Assn. REITs Inc.; bd. mem. Am. Forest Found., World Forestry Ctr. Bd. mem. Children's Hosp. Found., Seattle; mem. vis. com. Univ. Wash. Sch. Med. Office: Plum Creek Timber Ste 4300 999 Third Ave Seattle WA 98104*

HOLLEY, STEVEN LYON, lawyer; b. Ft. Wayne, Ind., Apr. 5, 1958; s. Wesley Lewis and Cornelia Alice (Reeder) H. BA in History/Polit. Sci., Ind. U., 1980; JD, NYU, 1983. Bar: N.Y. 1984, U.S. Dist. Ct. (so. and ea. dist.) N.Y. 1985, U.S. Dist. Ct. (no. dist.) N.Y. 1988. Law clk. Hon. Jose' A. Cabranes, Hartford, Conn., 1983-84; assoc. Sullivan & Cromwell, NYC, 1984-90, ptnr., 1991—. Mem. Assn. Bar City of N.Y. (sec. com. on profl. and jud. ethics 1988-90). Democrat. Home: 832 Broadway New York NY 10003-4813 Office: Sullivan & Cromwell 125 Broad St Fl 34 New York NY 10004-2498 Office Phone: 212-558-4737. Business E-Mail: holleys@sullcrom.com.

HOLLEY, SUSAN L., psychologist; b. Coral Gables, Fla., 1951; d. Frank N. Holley III and Mary Lou Porlick, Robert A. Porlick (Stepfather) and Jean Holley (Stepmother); 1 child, H. Marie Warga. BA in Psychology, U. South Fla., Tampa, 1973; MEd in Counseling, U. Miami, Coral Gables, 1975; PhD in Clin. Psychology, Calif. Sch. Profl. Psychology, 1989. Cert. specialist in clin. psychology Am. Bd. Profl. Psychology, 2003, lic. clin. psychologist, cert. health svc. provider in psychology, profl. alcoholism specialist. Addiction counselor South Miami Hosp., Fla., 1979—81; therapist New Beginnings Chem. Dependency Program, Century City, Calif., 1983—84; employee assistance adminstr. Aero Med. Advisors, Westchester, Calif., 1984—86; psychology practicum Switzer Ctr. of Ednl. Therapy, Torrance, Calif., 1986—87; employee assistance counselor Entertainment Industry Referral and Assistance Ctr., Burbank, Calif., 1986—88; psychology intern Vets. Adminstrn. Psychology Dept., Brentwood, Calif., 1988—89; postdoctoral fellow, rsch. asst. Family Project, Psychology Dept. U. of Calif., LA, 1990—91; clin. psychologist, pvt. practice Gelbart & Assocs., Redondo Beach, Calif., 1992—94, Susan Holley, PhD, Lancaster, Calif., 1993—. Clin. psychologist Out patient Mental Health Unit, Edwards Air Force Base, Calif., 1994—95; staff psychologist Palmdale Hosp., Calif., 1993—96; chem. dependency therapist Torrance Meml. Hosp. Chem. Dependency Ctr., Torrance, 1992—93. Mem. Lancaster West Rotary Club, Calif., 2000—. Mem.: APA, Sierra Club (bd. mem. Miami 1980), Calif. and LA Psychol. Assn., Employee Assistance Program Assn. (assoc.; treas. 1985, newsletter editor 1991, Appreciation Plaque 1991), Lancaster West Rotary Club. Methodist. Achievements include development of and presentation on the treatment of dual diagnosis patients with bipolar disorder and chemical dependency. Avocations: dressage horseback riding, photography, swimming, dance. Office: 43535 17th St W Ste 304 Lancaster CA 93534 Office Phone: 661-942-4079. Office Fax: 661-942-3887.

HOLLI, MELVIN GEORGE, retired history professor; b. Ishpeming, Mich., Feb. 22, 1933; s. Walfred and Sylvia (Erickson) H.; m. Betsy Biggar, Aug. 12, 1961; children: Susan, Steven. Student, Suomi Coll., Hancock, Mich., 1952-54; BA, North Mich. U., 1957; MA, U. Mich., 1958, PhD, 1969. Curator manuscripts Bentley Libr., U. Mich., Ann Arbor, 1962-64; asst. prof., assoc. prof. history U. Ill., Chgo., 1965, prof., 1975—2003, prof. emeritus, 2003—, chmn. dept., 1991-94. Fulbright prof. U. Finland, 1978, 89-90. Author: Reform in Detroit, 1969, Detroit, 1975, Ethnic Chicago, 1981, 3d edit., 1995 (nonfiction prize Soc. Midland Authors 1985, Best book award Ill. Polit. Sci. Assn. 1985), Bashing Chicago Traditions, 1989, Restoration: Chicago Elects a New Daley, 1991, The Mayors: The Chicago Political Tradition, 1995, 3d edit., 2005, The American Mayor: The Best and Worst Big City Leaders, 1999; (with Paul M. Green) From Mid Century to Millennium: A View From Chicago's City Hall, 1999, (with F. Beuttler and R. Remini) The University of Illinois at Chicago: A Pictorial History, 2000, The Wizard of Washington: Emil Hurja Franklin Roosevelt and the Birth of Public Opinion Polling, 2002, (with Green) World War II Chicago, 2003; bd. editors Urban Affairs Quar., 1992-95; editor: U. Ill. Press Ethnic History in Chicago book series. Bd. dirs. Scandinavian Ctr., North Park Univ., Chgo., 1997-2006. Woodrow Wilson fellow, 1957-58; recipient Disting. Alumni award No. Mich. U., 1985. Mem. Am. Hist. Assn., Orgn. Am. Historians, Swedish Am. Hist. Soc. (mag. bd. 1990-93), Soc. Midland Authors (bd. dirs. 1989-93, 94—), Finnish-Am. Soc. of the Midwest (bd. dirs.). Business E-Mail: mholli@uic.edu.

HOLLICH, GEORGE J., psychology professor; b. Hershey, Pa., Dec. 13, 1972; s. George and Carol Hollich; m. Camille S. Rocroi; 1 child, Sebastien. BA, Lebanon Valley Coll., Annville, Pa., 1995; PhD, Temple U., Phila., 1999. Postdoctoral fellow Johns Hopkins U., Balt., 1999—2002; asst. prof. Purdue U., West Lafayette, Ind., 2002—. Contbr. articles to profl. jours. Mem.: Internat. Soc. on Infant Studies (Early Career Contribution award 2006), Soc. Rsch. Lang. Devel., Soc. Rsch. Child Devel., Internat. Soc. Infant Studies, Cognitive Devel. Soc., Assn. Psychol. Sci., APA (Early Career award 2007). Avocations: singing, tennis. Office: Purdue Univ 703 Third St West Lafayette IN 47907-2004 Office Fax: 765-494-2224. Personal E-mail: ghollich@yahoo.com. Business E-Mail: ghollich@purdue.com.

HOLLIDAY, CHAD (CHARLES O. HOLLIDAY JR.), chemicals executive; b. Nashville, Mar. 9, 1948; s. Charles O. Sr. and Ann (Hunter) H.; m. Ann Blair, June 27, 1970; children: Scot, Chad. BS in Indsl. Engring., U. Tenn., 1970; DSc (hon.), Washington Coll., Chesterton, Md., 1988, Polytechnic U., Bklyn., 2005. Registered profl. engr., Tenn. Engr. DuPont, Nashville, 1970—74, bus. analyst, fibers to product planner, 1974—78, various mfg. assignments, fibers dept. (Charleston, SC, Martinville, Va., and Seaford, Del.), 1978—84, corp. plans mgr., 1984—86, global bus. dir., Nomex, 1986, global bus. dir., Kevlar, 1987, dir. mktg., chemicals and pigments, 1988—90, v.p. then pres., Asia Pacific Tokyo, 1990—92, sr. v.p., 1992—95, exec. v.p., mem. office of chief exec., chmn. Asia-Pacific, 1995—97, pres., 1997—98, CEO, 1998—, chmn., 1999—. Chmn. World Bus. Coun. Sustainable Devel., 2000, World Bus. Coun., 2002, Catalyst, Environmental Task Force Bus. Roundtable, 2004—; mem. Singapore-U.S. Bus. Coun.; bd. dir. Hosp. Corp. Am., 2002; served on US Coun. Competiveness; founding mem. Internat. Bus. Coun.; vice-chmn. Bus. Coun., 2001. Co-author: Walking the Talk. Vice chmn. John F. Kennedy Ctr. Performing Arts; active Alliance Global Sustainability, Del. Bus./Pub. Edn. Coun., U. Tenn., Winterthur Mus. Named Tomorrow's CEO, Fortune, 1996. Mem. Japan Am. Soc. Del., Soc. Chem. Industry (vice-chmn., 2000, chmn., Am. Sect., 2002), Inst. Indsl. Engrs. (sr.), Soc. Chem. Inter-Am. Sect, NAE. Office: Dupont 1007 Market St D9000 Wilmington DE 19898*

HOLLIDAY, GUY D. "DOC", publishing executive; BS in Orgnl. Leadership, U.S. Mil. Acad., 1986; MS in Quality Sys. Mgmt. with honors, Nat. Grad. Sch., 2002. Ops. mgr. Kimberly Clark Corp., 1992—94; gen. supr. finishing ops., ops. mgr., project coord., engr. Lukens Steel, 1994—96; asst. plant mgr. NY Times printing plant NY Times, Edison, NJ, 1996—2000, dir. engring. and maintenance ops. NYC, 2000—04, v.p. advt. sales, 2004—06; sr. v.p. NY Daily News, NYC, 2006—. Capt. US Army, 1986—92, maj. US Army, 2003—04. Office: NY Times 229 W 43rd St New York NY 10036-3959

HOLLIDAY, PATRICIA RUTH MCKENZIE, evangelist; b. Jacksonville, Fla., Nov. 17, 1935; d. Robert Irving and Leona Adele (Bell) McKenzie; m. Jan. 20, 1965; children: Connie, Katheryn, Alexander. Student, Massey Bus. Coll., 1969, Luther Rice Sem., 1976; DD, Southeastern Theol. Sem., 1986, ThD, 1989, PhD, 1992. Sec. Delta Drug Corp., Jacksonville, 1965—; pres. Microfilm Ctr., Jacksonville, 1974—, Miracle Outreach Ministry, Jacksonville, 1974—; pastor Miracle World Outreach, Jacksonville; prof. Southeastern Theol. Sem., Jacksonville, 1992—; with Internat. Evang. Miracle Outreach, 2000—. Author: Holliday for the King, 1978, Be Free, 1979, Only Believe, 1980, Born Anew, 1981, The Walking Dead, 1982, Anointing Power, 1982, Signs, Wonders and Reactions, 1984, Dealing with Heresies, 1986, Marriage Answers, 1992, Solitary Satanist, 1993, Entertaining Angels of Light, 1993, The Plan: Ascended Masters, 1994, The New World Aftershock, 1994, Can. Women Preach?, 1995, New Creations, 1995, From Curses to Blessings Vols. 1, 2 & 3, 1995, Angel Fire, 1995, Can Witches Be Saved, 1996, Spirit of Idolatry, 1996, Is Halloween Pagan?, 1996, Gods of the Stars, Astrology, 1997, Gifts of the Holy Spirit, 1997, Baptism of the Holy Spirit, 1997, Deliverance Manuals, Vols. 1, 2 & 3, 1997, Spiritual Welfare Army, 1997, Spiritual Warfare - Weapons, 1997, Healing & Miracles, 1998, The Spiritual Armor of God, 1998, Children of the New Age, 1998, Prayer Warriors, 1998, Battling Territorial Spirits, 1998, New Age Inner Healing, 1999, Demons Tremble, 1999, Transference of Spirits, 1999, Experiencing Jesus, 2001, Witch Doctor and the Man-Fourth Generational Witch Doctor Finds Christ, 2001, Satan's Romper Room, 2002, Never, Never Land, 2003, The Fallen Prince, 2003, Why God Permits Heresus, 2003, Inner Healing-Body Soul and Spirit, 2004, Spirit Names, 2005, Marriage and Sex, 2005, Jesus is Deliverer, 2005, Emotional Healing, 2006, Chronicles of Narnia-World, 2006, Bewitching Spirits, 2007, Marine Demons, 2007, Healing & Miracles, 2007, Age of Aquaries, 2007, The Puppet Masters, 2007, Cosmic Consciouness, 2007, Mind Wandlers, 2007, Para Psychology, Spiritual Dimension, 2007, Religious Mysticism, 2007, Marine Spirits Under the Sea, 2007, Marriage and Sex, 2007, Orweillian Nightmare, 2007, Deliverance Schizophrenia, 2007, Emotional Healing, 2007, others; columnist Christian Courier; host (radio show): Holliday for the King, (TV program) Miracle Outreach. Sec. Four Found., Inc.; Rep. candidate Fla. Ho. of Reps., 1972; mem. Fla. Rep. Com., 1976-80; lobbyist Fla. Legislature, 1978-80; hostess Pat Holliday TV Show, Jacksonville. Recipient Rep. Gold Medal award, Nat. Rep. Congl. Com., 2004. Mem. Minutewomen of Fla. Club (founder) Univ. Women Club, Ponte Vedra Women's Club. Home: 9252 San Jose Blvd Apt 2804 Jacksonville FL 32257-9205 Office Phone: 904-733-9676. Personal E-mail: holliday_pat@hotmail.com, holliday.pat@gmail.com.

HOLLIDAY, ROBERT KELVIN, retired state legislator, publishing executive; b. Logan, W.Va., Feb. 11, 1933; s. James Kelvin and Helen Kathleen (Harris) Holliday; m. Deborah Ann Holliday; children: Kelvin, Kathleen Eddy, Stephen, Robert L., Jeffrey, Tracey, Brandon. BA, W.Va. U. Tech., 1954; MA, Marshall U., 1955. Co-owner, editor Montgomery (W.Va.) Herald, 1955—85; co-owner, editor The Fayette Tribune, 1955—85, Fayette Tribune, 1955—85, Meadow River Post, Rainelle, W.Va., 1966—85; with W.Va. Divsn. Corrections, 2001—03. Mem. W.Va. Ho. of Dels., 1963-68, W.Va. Senate, 1968-72, 80-94; adj. polit. sci. instr. W.Va. U. Inst. Tech., 1994, 99, 2000, 02-05, W.Va. State Coll., 1997-98, Bluefield State Coll., 1996, Greenbrier C.C., 1995, Glenville State Coll., 1997. Author: Tests of Faith, 1966, About Montgomery, 1956, Our Chat, 1956, A Portrait of Fayette, 1960, Politics in Fayette County, 1958. Mem. W.Va. State Dem. Exec. Com., 1978-80; pres. Fayette Needy Assn., 1960-68; chmn. Six Yr. Fayette Heart Campaign; past chmn. State Mental Health Assn.; elder Presbyn. Ch. With U.S. Army. Recipient Gov.'s Living Dream award Martin Luther King Jr., 1988, Outstanding Leadership award W.Va. NAACP, 1988, award Kanawha-Fayette Cmty. Svc., Inc., 1985-2005, Pax Reunion award Fayette Vols.; named Outstanding Legislator, W.Va. Trial Lawyers Assn., 1988, 92. Mem.: Am. Fed. of State County and Municipal Employees, W.Va.Rehab Assn. (Structural Barriers award 1988), W. Va. Edn. Assn. (Pearl S. Buck award 1982), W. Va. Mental Health Assn. (past dir.), Fayette Shrimer Club, New Rivers Nat. River (founder), Shriners, Masons (32d degree). Presbyterian.

HOLLIDAY, RONALD STURGIS, lawyer; b. Wichita, Kans., Dec. 11, 1947; s. Robert Dwight and Mary Irene (Smith) H.; m. Deborah June Winship, Aug. 29, 1975; children: Brian Joseph, Kathryn June. BA with honors, U. Kans., 1969; JD magna cum laude, U. Mich., 1972. Bar: Mich. 1972, U.S. Dist. Ct. (ea. dist.) Mich. 1972, U.S. Dist. Ct. (we. dist.) Mich. 1977, U.S. Ct. Appeals (6th cir.) 1982, Fla. 1986, U.S. Dist. Ct. (mid. dist.) Fla. 1987. Assoc. Dykema Gossett, Detroit, 1972-80, ptnr., 1980; mng. ptnr. Tampa off. DLA Piper Rudnick Gray Cary. Served to lt. JAGC, USN, 1973-76. Recipient Leadership Detroit award Greater Detroit C. of C., 1980. Fellow Mich. State Bar Found. (mem. antitrust law sect.); mem. ABA, Mich. Bar Assn., Detroit Bar Assn., Fla. Bar Assn., Sarasota County Bar Assn., Hillsborough County Bar Assn. Office: DLA Piper Rudnick Gray Cary Ste 2000 101 E Kennedy Blvd Tampa FL 33602-5149 Office Phone: 813-222-5926. Office Fax: 813-229-1447. Business E-Mail: ronald.holliday@dlapiper.com.

HOLLIDAY, THOMAS EDGAR, lawyer; b. Ft. Hood, Tex., July 3, 1948; s. William Lamont and Eileen (Fiebig) H.; children: Devon M., Trey S. BA, Stanford U., 1971; JD, U. So. Calif., 1974. Bar: Calif. 1974. Assoc. Gibson, Dunn & Crutcher LLP, LA, 1974-81; ptnr. Gibson, Dunn & Crutcher, LA, 1981—. Editor: (book, desk edition) Antitrust and Trade Regulations. Trustee S.W. Mus., L.A., 1981-98, bd. pres., 1995-97; trustee Found. for People, L.A., 1985-90, Clarkson U., 2000—; mem. L.A. Police Dept. Meml. Found. Bd. Fellow Am. Coll. Trial Lawyers; mem. Fed. Bar Assn. (exec. com. L.A. chpt. 1990, pres. 1998). Avocation: art. Office: Gibson Dunn & Crutcher LLP 333 S Grand Ave Ste 4400 Los Angeles CA 90071-3197

HOLLIEN, HARRY FRANCIS, communications engineer; b. Brockton, Mass., July 16, 1926; s. Henry Gregory and Alice Bernice (Coolidge) H.; m. Patricia Ann Milanowski, Aug. 26, 1969; children: Karen Ann, Kevin Amory, Keith Alan, Brian Christopher, Stephanie Ann, Christine Ann. BS, Boston U., 1949, MEd, 1951; MA, U. Iowa, 1953, PhD, 1955. Asst. prof. Baylor U., 1955-58, U. Wichita, 1958-62; assoc. prof. speech U. Fla., Gainesville, 1962-68, prof., 1968-98, prof. linguistics, 1976-98, prof. criminal justice, 1979-98, assoc. dir. comm. scis. lab., 1962—65, dir. comm. scis. lab., 1968—75, dir. Inst. Advanced Study Comm. Processes, 1975—84; prof. emeritus, rsch. scientist Inst. Advanced Study of Communication Processes, 1998—, assoc. dir. linguistics, 1989-91; founding dir. Inst. Advanced Study Comm. Processes U. Fla., 1984—. Vis. prof. Inst. Telecomm. and Acoustics, Wroclaw Tech. U., Poland, 1974; adj. prof. Juilliard Sch. Music, NYC, 1973—84; rsch. assoc. Gould Rsch. Lab., 1958; vis. scientist Speech Transmission Lab., Royal Inst. Tech., Stockholm, 1970; Fulbright prof. U. Trier, Germany, 1987; fencing coach U. Iowa, 1953—55; mem. comm. sci. study sect. NIH, 1963—67; mem. neurobiology merit rev. bd. VA, 1969—74; mem. Credibility Assessment Rsch. Summit, Dept. Def., 2006—; pres. Hollien Assocs., 1966—; cons. in field. Author: Current Issues in Phonetic Sciences, 1978, Acoustics of Crime, 1990, Forensic Voice Identification, 2002; assoc. editor Jour. Speech and Hearing Rsch., 1967-69, Jour. Voice, 1987—; editor The Phonetician, 1975-92; mem. edtl. bd. Jour. Comm. Disorders, 1980-91, Jour. Rsch. in Singing, 1980-83, Jour. Phonetics, 1982-85, Studia Phonetica Posnan, 1985—, Speech, Language and the Law, 1993-2002. Chmn. bd. Unitarian Fellowship, Waco, Tex., 1956-58; chmn. bd. Wild Animal Retirement Village, 1981-90. Served with USN, 1944-46; with USNR, 1946-75. Recipient Garcia/Sandoz prize Internat. Assn. Logopedics and Phoniatrics, 1971, Gould award Wm. and Harrett Gould Found., 1975, Gutzmann medal Union European Phoniatrists, 1980, Professorial Excellence award U. Fla., 1996; NIH career fellow, 1965-70, Fulbright scholar, 1987. Fellow: AAAS, Inst. Acoustics, Am. Acad. Forensic Sci. (John R. Hunt award 1988), Internat. Soc. Phonetic Scis. (sec.-gen. 1975—89, exec.v.p. 1983—89, pres. 1989—98, Kay Elemetrics prize 1987, S. Smith prize 1991, Soc. Honors 1998, hon. pres. 1999—), Am. Speech and Hearing Assn., Acoustical Soc. Am.; mem.: SAR (regional v.p. 2000—04, pres. local chpt. 2001—03, state rec. sec. 2001—03, sr. v.p. 2004—05, pres. 2005—06, Patriot medal 2003), Internat. Assn. Forensic Phonetics, Voice Found. (sci. bd., merit awards 1981, 1993), World Congress Phoneticians (permanent coun.), Japan Soc. Phonetic Scis. (hon. v.p. 1989—97), Am. Assn. Phonetic Scis. (pres. 1973—75, editor 1976—79, exec. com. 1979—82), Order Found. Patriots (chaplain, state soc. 2004—), Mayflower Descs. (gov. local chpt. 2002—05, capt. state soc. 1999—2002), Sigma Xi. Republican. Achievements include patent for apparatus using radiation sensitive switch for signalling and recording data. Home: 229 SW 43rd Ter Gainesville FL 32607-2270 Office: U Fla Inst Advanced Study Comm Processes 46 Dauer Hall Gainesville FL 32611 Office Phone: 352-392-2046 x229. Business E-Mail: Hollien@Grove.ufl.edu.

HOLLIER, LARRY HAROLD, vascular surgeon, hospital administrator, dean; b. Crowley, La., Apr. 18, 1943; s. Villere Joseph and Agnes (Guidry) H.; m. Diana Gayle Johnson, Jan. 25, 1964; children: Larry Jr., Michelle Ann. BS, La. State U., 1965, MD, 1968. Diplomate Am. Bd. Surgery, spl. qualifications in vascular surgery. Intern Charity Hosp. La., New Orleans, 1968-69, gen. surgery resident, 1969-75; vascular surgery fellow Baylor U. Med. Ctr., Dallas, 1973-74; chief vascular surgery La. State U. Med. Sch., New Orleans, 1975-80, Mayo Clinic, Rochester, Minn., 1980-87; chmn. dept. surgery Ochsner Clnic, New Orleans, 1987-93; med. dir. HCI Internat. Med. Centre, Glasgow, Scotland, 1993—96; Julius H. Jacobson II MD prof. surgery Mount Sinai Sch. Medicine, NYC, 1996—2003, chmn. dept. surgery, 1996—2003; surgeon-in-chief Mount Sinai Med. Ctr., NYC; pres. The Mount Sinai Hosp., NYC, 2002—03; dean, Sch. Medicine La. State U. Health Sci. Ctr., New Orleans, 2004—. Founder divsn. vascular surgery Mayo Clinic, Rochester, 1983; bd. mgmt. Ochsner Clinic, New Orleans, 1989-93. Editor: Vascular Surgery - Basic Science in Clinical Correlations, 1994, Haimovici's Vascular Surgery, 1995. Maj. USAF, 1970-72. Fellow ACS (young surgeons rep. 1979, pres. La. chpt. 1989); mem. Soc. Vascular Surgery (chmn. membership com. 1985-86), Soc. Clin. Vascular Surgery (pres. 1995), So. Assn. Vascular Surgery (pres. 1995), Midwestern Vascular Soc. (pres. 1988). Avocations: sailing, scuba diving. Office: LSU Med Sch 433 Bolivar New Orleans LA 70112 Office Phone: 504-568-4800. Business E-Mail: lhholl@lsuhsc.edu.

HOLLIMAN, W. G. (MICKEY), JR., furniture manufacturing executive; Founder, pres., CEO Action Industries subs. Furniture Brands Internat., 1970-96; pres., chmn., CEO, Furniture Brands Internat., St. Louis, 1996—. Office: Furniture Brands Internat Ste 1900 101 S Hanley Rd Saint Louis MO 63105-3493*

HOLLINGER, MORTON, small business owner, artist; b. Port Chester, NY; s. Max and Anna Hollinger; m. Myrna Rachel Hollinger, Mar. 30, 1958; children: Nancy Samson, Steven. BA, Syracuse U., 1949; studied with William Arrowsmith, prin. oboist, Met. Opera; studied painting with Louis Di Valentin. Pres. M.H. Pierce & Co., Stamford, Conn., 1958—. Oboist Westchester Symphony, White Plains, N.Y., 1982-85, Bronx (N.Y.) Symphony, 1986-89. Exhibitions include Studio Soto Gallery, Boston, 2004; author: Morton Hollinger Paintings, 1998. Recipient Stamford Mus. award for oil painting, 1968, Windsor-Newton award for oil painting, 1990, 1st prize for oils WEstchester County Ctr., 1958. Mem. Stamford Art Assn. Avocations: clarinet, oboe, english horn, painting. Home: 11 Ledge Terr Stamford CT 06905 Office Phone: 203-327-2970. Personal E-mail: clar@optonline.net.

HOLLINGER, PAULA COLODNY, state legislator; b. Washington, Dec. 30, 1940; d. Samuel and Ethel (Levy) Colodny; m. Paul Hollinger, Sept. 16, 1962; children: Ilene, Marcy, David. RN, Mt. Sinai Hosp. Sch. Nursing, NYC, 1961. RN NY. Pub. health sch. nurse, resident camp nurse Balt. County Dept. Health; Myasthenia Gravis specialist Acute Stroke Unit U. Md. Hosp.; clin. instr. psychiat. nursing Tuskegee Inst.; head nurse surgery intensive care unit Mt. Sinai Hosp., NY, night charge nurse emergency rm. NY; Carter del., 1976; mem. Md. Ho. of Dels., Annapolis, 1978-86, Md. Senate, Annapolis, 1987—2002, majority whip, 2000—, senate chair joint com. on health care delivery and financing, 1995—2007, chair senate econ. and environ. affairs health sub-com., 1988—2007, chair edn., health and environ. affairs com., 2003—07, majority whip, 2000—03. Chmn. adminstrv., exec., legis. rev. com., health subcom. Md. Senate, Annapolis, 1987, chmn. 1991-95, chmn. joint com. fed. rels., 1987-90, vice-chair econ. and environ. affairs com.,1995, mem. exec. nominations com., 1995—; chair health com. Nat. Conf. State Legis., , 1991-92, chair sci. and resources tech. com., 1984, com. long term care, 1985, chmn. women's network, 1993, vice chmn. 1992, 96, chmn., 1992, rep. assembly fed. issues; mem. joint oversight com. on health care cost containment, Medicaid joint com.; chmn. joint protocol com. Md. Gen. Assembly, 1998—; alt. mem. So. Legis. Conf. Coun. State Govts. Human Svcs. And Pub. Safety Com.; mem. Gov.'s Task Forces to Study: Nursing Crisis, Uses of Methlphenidate, 1997—, Class Size Reduction Programs in Md., 1998—, Alternative Methods of Coll. Financing, Joint Legis. Task Force on Organ and Tissue Donation, 1997-98, Task Forces on Violence and Extremism, Quality of Care in Nursing Facilities, 1999, AIDS; mem. Gov.'s adv. coun. on AIDS; mem. Gov.'s com. nursing issues in Md.; mem. Gov.'s commns. black and minority health, black males, chmn. health subcom.; mem. interagy. Coordinating coun. for infants and toddlers; mem. exec. com. Nat. Assn. Jewish Legislators, 1997—; mem. state adv. com. Office for Children, Youth and Families; mem. state adv. coun. organ and tissue donation awareness, 1998—; pres. Women Legislators of Md., 1986-88, v.p., 1985; lectr., spkr., guest panelist in field. Bd. dirs. Nat. Coun. Jewish Women, Safety First, 1990, Jewish Family Svcs., 1995-2007, Progress Unlimited, Inc., Juvenile Diabetes Assn. (hon.); adv. to bd. dirs. United Way Cmty. Partnership Balt.; adv. bd. Second Step, Inc., Md. Organ procurement Ctr., Inc.; bd. trustees Transplant Resource Ctr. Md., Inc., 1997-2007, Group for Independent Learning Disabled; grad. adv. coun. Notre Dame Coll.; mem. com. adolescent drug and alcohol abuse Md. Bar Assn., Environ. Matters Com.; faculty assoc. U. Md. Sch. Nursing, 1998—. Recipient Murry Guggenheim award, 1961, Bramson award Women's American ORT, 1981, Legis. award Mental Health Assn., 1983, Legislator of Yr. award Md. Nurse's Assn., 1984, Human Svc. award Constant Care Med. Ctr. 1984, Outstanding Contbns. to Edn. award Tchr.'s Assn. Balt. County, 1984, Outstanding Commitment and Dedication to Treatment of Alcoholic award Pilot House, 1984, Dedication and Commitment to Health and Environ. award Ctrl. Md. Health Sys. Agy., Edith Rosen Strauss award, 1987, Outstanding Svc. award Md. Psych. Assn., 1987, Pres.' award Md. Assn. Non-Profit Homes for Aging, 1987, Humanitarian award, Liberty Rd. Cmty. Coun., 1987, Leadership Laurel award Safety 1st Club Md., 1987, Outstanding Legis. Leadership award On Our Own Md., 1988, Outstanding Support and Devel. Rehab. Programs award Johns Hopkins Dept. Rehab., Md. Health Care Found., 1988, Legis. Honor Roll award Md. Assn. Psychosocial Svcs., 1988, Spl. award leadership Pikesville revitalization Pikesville Cmty. Growth Corp., 1988, Pres.' award Md. Assn. Home Care, 1988, Verda Welcome award for outstanding polit. achievements and pub. svc., 1989, Cmty. Svc. award Balt. Hebrew U., 1990, Physician's Asst. Appreciation award, 1991, Leadership and Commitment award Walbrook H.S. Primary Health Care Ctr., 1991, Betty Tyler Pub. Affairs award Planned Parenthood, 1992, 93, Excellence in Social Work Legislation award Md. Social Work Coalition, 1993, award Chesapeake Bay Found. Environ. Leadership, 1994, Policy Maker Leadership award Adv. for Youth, 1995, Ann. Leadership award Md. State Sch. Health Coun., 1996, Legis. award Legis. and Pub. Info. Com. Balt. County Commn. Disabilities, 1997, Legis. award Md. Retired Tchrs., 1997, award Md./D.C. Soc. Respiratory Care, 1997, Dedication and Support award Nat. Kidney Found. Md., 1998, Legis. award Md. Assn. Counseling and Devel., 1998, Sch. Health Advocacy award Sch. Nurse Inst., 2000, Outstanding Svc. award Md. Psychol. Assn., 2000, Pres.'s award Md. Nat. Capitol Home Care Assn., 2000, Presdl. award of Recognition Md. Occupl. Therapy Assn., 2001, Legis. of Yr. award, Mental Health Assn. Md., 2001, Pacesetter award Nat. Women Legis.'s Lobby, 2001, Distin. Leadership award Abilities Network and Epilepsy Found. of Chesapeake Region, 2002; named Woman of Yr., Women Realtors Anne Arundel County, 1988, Pikesville C. of C., 1989, Sen. of Yr., Md. Assn. Psychiat. Support Svcs., 1993, Oustanding Legislator, Md. Speech, Lang., Hearing Assn., 1993, Most Disting. Alumnus, Mt. Sinai Hosp. Sch. Nursing Alumnae Assn., 1998, Md.'s Top 100 Women, Daily Record, 1999, 2001, 03, Legislator of Yr. AHA, 1999, Chesapeake Bay Bound., 2004. Mem. Am. Assn. Marriage and Family Therapy (Mid Atlantic Divsn., hon., hon. licensure), B'nai Brith Women, Hadassah, Na'Amat, Orgn. for Rehab. Tng. (Bramson award 1981), Chi Eta Phi (hon.). Office: Miller Senate Bldg Annapolis MD 21401-1991

HOLLINGER, PEGGY LOUISE, elementary school counselor; b. Mobile, Ala., July 17, 1956; d. Adam Lavaughn and Louise (Baggett) H. BS, Mobile Coll., 1979; MS in Edn., Troy State U., Ala., 1982; degree in Edn., U. South Ala., 1993. Cert. counselor U. South Ala., 1990. Tchr. Baldwin County Bd. Edn., Bay Minette, Ala., 1979-90, counselor, 1990—. Baptist. Avocations: singing, reading, travel. Personal E-mail: plh71756@bellsouth.net.

HOLLINGS, FRITZ (ERNEST FREDERICK), former senator; b. Charleston, SC, Jan. 1, 1922; s. Adolph G. and Wilhelmine D. (Meyer) H.; m. Rita Louise Liddy, Aug. 21, 1971; children by previous marriage—Michael Milhous, Helen Hayne, Patricia Salley, Ernest Frederick III. BA, The Citadel, 1942, LL.D. (hon.), 1960; LL.B., U. S.C., 1947, LLD (hon.), 1980. Bar: S.C. 1947, U.S. Supreme Ct. 1952, U.S. Ct. Appeals (D.C.) 1989. Mem. S.C. Ho. of Reps., 1948-54, speaker pro tem, 1951-54; lt. gov. State of S.C., 1955-59, gov., 1959-63; pvt. practice Charleston, SC, 1963-66; U.S. senator from S.C., 1966—2005; chmn. Senate commerce, sci. and transp. com., 1987—95, 2001—03; sr. mem. Senate appropriations com., 1971—2005; chmn. commerce, justice, state, judiciary and related agencies subcoms.; sr. mem. Senate com. on the budget, 1974—2005; chmn. Senate com. on the budget, 1980—81. Mem. Hoover Commn. on Intelligence Activities, 1954—55, Pres.'s Adv. Commn. on Intergovtl. Rels., 1959—63, Pres.'s Adv. Commn. on Federalism, 1981; chmn. Legis. Coun., 1955—59, Regional Adv. Coun. on Nuclear Energy; mem. adv. com. Nat. River and Harbors Congress; del. Law of Sea Conf.; mem. Senate Dem. Policy Com., Senate Dem. Tech. and omms. om. Author: The Case Against Hunger: A Demand for a National Policy, 1970. Served to capt. U.S. Army, 1942-45, ETO, NATOUSA. Recipient Founders award S.C. Com. for Tech. Edn., 1963, Nat. Vet. award, 1968, Friend of Edn. award S.C. Edn. Assn., 1974, Neptune award Am. Oceanic Orgn., 1978, James Woodruff award Assn. U.S. Army, 1980, Nat. Future award Am. Space Found., 1984, S.C. Disting. Pub. Svc. award, 1983, Consumer Fedn. of Am. Disting. Pub. Svc. award 1985, Govt. Social Responsibility award Martin Luther King Jr. Ctr., 1986, Golden Bulldog award Watchdogs of the Treasury, 1988, Outstanding Leadership award Nat. Assn. Black-owned Broadcasters, 1988, Disting. Health Svcs. award, 1988, The Sound Dollar award, 1988-90, Hall of Leaders award Nat. Travel Industry, 1990, Disting. Svc. award Nat. Assn. Ind. Colls. and U., 1990, Nat. Security Indsl. Assn., 1990, Congl. award Nat. Coalition for Cancer Rsch., 1992, Sgt. Jasper Freedom award S.C. C. of C., 1992, No. 1 Govtl. Friend of Tourism, SE Tourism Soc., 1993, Spl. Health Recognition award N.H. Assn. Cmty. Health Ctrs., 1994; named one of Ten Outstanding Young Men U.S. Jr. C. of C., 1954, and numerous other awards. Mem. ABA, Charleston County Bar Assn., S.C. Bar Assn., Assn. Citadel Men, Hibernian Soc., Am. Legion, Univ. S.C. Law Fedn., St. Andrews Soc. Lodges: Elks, Masons. Democrat. Lutheran.

HOLLINGSWORTH, BOBBY G., career officer; m. Sue Taylor; children: Marc, Eric. Grad., Naval Flight Sch., 1965; BS in Elec. Engring., La. State Univ. Commd. comdr. USMCR, 1961, advanced through grades to maj. gen., 1999, internat. comml. airline pilot, mem., pilot; flight line officer Marine Attack Squadron 331, Beaufort, SC; embarkation officer Marine Attack Squadron 223, Chu Lai, Vietnam; landing signal officer Marine Aircraft Group 12, Chu Lai; air liaison officer 3d Marine Divsn., Phu Bai, Vietnam; asst. air liaison officer 3d Divsn. Staff; combat tactics flight instr. Marine Tng. Squadron 103, Yuma, Ariz.; capt. Boeing 767 Trans World Airlines; asst. ops. officer Marine Fighter Squadron 112, Dallas; exec. officer Marine Aircraft Group 42, Alameda, Calif.; comdr. Marine Attack Squadron 133, Alameda; asst. chief of staff 4th Marine Aircraft Wing, New Orleans; chief of staff II Marine Expeditionary Brigade, Camp Lejeune, NC; commdg. gen. USMCR Support Command, Kans. City, Mo., Fourth Force Svc. Support Group, New Orleans; dep. comdr. Jt. Task Force, Saudi Arabia; vice comdr. Marine Forces Pacific, Camp Smith, Hawaii; exec. dir. Nat. Com. Employer Support of Guard and Res., 2001—; pilot A-4 Skyhawk Fleet Marine Force Marine Corps Air Sta., Beaufort, SC; with VMA 223, MAG 12, Marine Aircraft Wing, Chu Lai. Advisor to Asst. Sec. Def. Res. Affairs US Armed Forces, rep. Nat. Chair Dept. Def. Decorated Legion of Merit, Disting. Flying Cross, Def. Meritorious Svc. medal, Air Medal with numeral 5 Combat Action Ribbon, Presdl. Unit Citation with Bronze Star, Meritorious Unit Commendation, Select Marine Corps. Res. medal with Silver Star, Nat. Def. Medal with Bronze star, Armed Forces Expiditionary medal, Vietnam Svc. medal with two Bronze Stars, Navy and Marine Corps Overseas Svc. Ribbon with two Bronze Stars, Armed Forces Res. medal with hourglass Device, Rep. of Vietnam Unit Citation, Rep. Vietnam Campaing medal with 1960 Device. Home: 12404 Grantley Ct Woodbridge VA 22192-2367 Home Phone: 314-503-4850; Office Phone: 703-862-1917. E-mail: bob.hollingsworth@osd.mil.

HOLLINGSWORTH, DEREK S., lawyer; b. Maracaibo, Venezuela, Aug. 23, 1971; m. Lara Hollingsworth; 2 children. BBA in Acctg., Baylor U., 1993, JD magna cum laude, 1997. Bar: Tex. 1997, US Supreme Ct., US Dist. Ct. (no. and so. dists. Tex.), US Ct. Appeals Fifth Cir. Briefing atty. to Justice Priscilla R. Owen Tex. Supreme Ct., 1997—98; litig. assoc. Hughes & Luce, LLP, 1998—2000; asst. dist. atty. Harris County Dist. Atty.'s Office, 2000—03; assoc. Rusty Hardin & Assocs., P.C., Houston, 2003—. Lead articles editor: Baylor Law Rev., 1996—97. Named a Rising Star, Tex. Super Lawyers mag., 2006. Mem.: Tex. Young Lawyers Assn., Houston Young Lawyers Assn., Houston Bar Assn. Office: Rusty Hardin & Assocs PC 1401 McKinney Ste 2250 Houston TX 77010 Office Phone: 713-652-9000. E-mail: dhollingsworth@rustyhardin.com.*

HOLLINGSWORTH, JACK WARING, mathematics professor; b. South Haven, Kans., Mar. 3, 1924; s. Virgil Braxton and Ethel (Waring) H.; m. Nancy Lee Harris, Sept. 14, 1950; children: Joel, Priscilla, Seth (dec.). BS in Engring. Physics, U. Kans., Lawrence, 1948, BA, 1949; MS, U. Wis., Madison, 1951, PhD, 1954. Teaching asst. U. Kans., 1947-49, U. Wis., 1949-50, computing asst., 1950-54; gen. sci. aide U.S. Naval Ordnance Lab., 1950; mathematician Gen. Electric Co., 1954-57; mem. faculty Rensselaer Poly. Inst., 1957-79, prof. math., 1961-79, supr. computer lab., 1957-70, chmn. interdisciplinary com. computer sci., 1967-73; prof. Sch. Computer Sci. and Tech./Rochester Inst. Tech., NY, 1979-86, dir., 1980-82; prof. math. Rochester Inst. Tech., 1986-96, prof. emeritus, 1996—. Mem. Bd. Coop. Ednl. Services, Saratoga-Warren Counties, 1970-79 Served to 1st lt. USAAF, 1943-45. Decorated D.F.C., Air medal with 4 oak leaf clusters, Purple Heart; Jack Hollingsworth Prize in Computer Sci. established in his honor Rennselaer Poly. Inst. Mem. Assn. Computing Machinery (treas. spl. interest group of univ. computing centers 1964-70), Am. Math. Soc., Soc. Indsl. and Applied Math., Math. Assn. Am., Sigma Xi, Tau Beta Pi, Omicron Delta Kappa, Kappa Eta Kappa. Mem. Reformed Ch. (elder). Home and Office: 55 Crestview Dr Pittsford NY 14534-2242

HOLLINGSWORTH, JOE GREGORY, lawyer; b. Indpls., Mar. 3, 1949; s. Don Roy and Marilyn Ann (Gregory) H.; m. Nancy Elaine Bartlett, Jan. 21, 1971; children: Gregory Bartlett, Grant Wagner, Brooke Ann. BA, De Pauw U., 1971; JD, Georgetown U., 1974. Bar: DC, 1975, DC Ct. of Appeals, 1975, US Ct. of Appeals Ninth Circuit, 1978, Fed. Circuit, 1982, Eleventh Circuit, 1985, Third Circuit, 1987, First Circuit, 1988, Second Circuit, 1989, Fourth Circuit, 1991, Sixth Circuit, 1993, Tenth Circuit, 1995, Seventh Circuit, 2001, Eighth Circuit, 2002. From assoc. to ptnr. McKenna, Conner & Cuneo, Washington, 1974-82; ptnr. Spriggs & Hollingsworth, Washington, 1982—. Mem. Product Liability Advisory Council, 2004—; mem. constitutional & adminstrv. law com. U.S. Chamber of Commerce Nat. Litigation Ctr. Mem.: Kenwood Country Club (Bethesda, Md.), Fed. City Club (Washington), Met. Club. Presbyterian. Avocations: tennis, running, golf, hunting, mountain climbing. Office: Spriggs & Hollingsworth 1350 I St NW Washington DC 20005 Office Phone: 202-898-5800. Office Fax: 202-682-1639. Business E-Mail: jhollingsworth@spriggs.com.

HOLLINGSWORTH, JOHN ALEXANDER, retired science and mathematics educator, writer; b. Owego, NY, Sept. 25, 1925; s. John Alexander Sr. and Florence Eve (Haley) W.; m. Winifred Louise Stoelting Hollingsworth. BS in Agr., N.C. A&T State U., 1950, MS in Adult Edn., 1985; MS in Biology, N.C. Ctrl. U., 1960; postgrad., Cornell U., 1962-63. Staff sgt. U.S. Army, 1943-46, advanced through grades to capt., 1949-57; tchr. sci. Fayetteville (N.C.) City Schs., 1959-73, coord. sci., 1968-83, coord. math., 1973-83; cons., author, artist Cherokee Village, Ark., 1985—. Dir. Emergency Sch. Assistance Act Pilot Project, Fayetteville, 1972-80; grants writer Title I and Emergency Sch. Assistance Act Pilot Project, Fayetteville, 1972-80. Co-author: (booklet) The Improvement of High School Research Through the Research Participation Program, 1968. Active Ecology Action/Common Ground, Willits, Calif.; active, charter mem. Nat. Mus. of the Am. Indian. Mem. NEA (life), Nat. Ret. Tchrs. Assn., N.C. Sci. Tchrs. Assn. (state pres. 1971-73), N.C. Assn. Educators (pres. Fayetteville unit 1970-71), N.C. Ret. Sch. Pers., N.C. Ret. Govtl. Employees Assn., Inst. Noetic Scis., Nat. Assn. Black Vets. (life). Avocations: painting, genealogy, gardening. Home: 61 Otalco Dr Cherokee Village AR 72529

HOLLINGSWORTH, JOHN ARTHUR, business educator; b. Martins Ferry, Ohio, Oct. 12, 1952; s. William Arvine and Lillian Theo (Dean) H. AAB in Retail Mktg. cum laude, Belmont Tech. Col., 1975; BSBA in Helth and Hosp. Admin., Wheeling Jesuit U., 1979, MBA, 1984; PhD in Bus. Admin., U. Miss., 1993. Cert. secondary edn. tchr., Ohio. Computer operator Stone & Thomas Co., Wheeling, W.Va., 1971-76; mgr. carpet dept. L.S. Good & Co., Wheeling, 1976-78; store mgr. Rite Aid Corp., Harrisburg, Pa., 1978-79; lectr. Belmont Tech. Col., St. Clairsville, Ohio, 1981-83; rsch. and teaching asst. U. Miss., Oxford, 1984-88; bus. admin. instr. St. John's U., NYC, 1989-94; asst. prof. bus. dept. Coll. Staten Island/CUNY, 1994-98; asst. prof. mgmt. info. sys. No State U., Aberdeen, SD, 1998—. Statis. cons. Reidenbach, Grubbs & Assoc., Jackson, Miss., 1986-87; session chair and discussant Internat. Bus. Schs. User Group, Omaha, Nebr., 1990. Poll election judge, Shadyside, Ohio, 1975-80. Selected for Group Projects Abroad to Turkey, Fulbright Program and Am. Forum Global Edn., N.Y.C., 1996. Mem. Inst. Mgmt. Sci., Acad. Mgmt., Assn. Info. Sys., Info. Resources Mgmt. Assn., Nat. Decision Scis. Inst. (session chair, discussant 1993-95, selected for New Faculty Consortium, 1993). Republican. Avocations: travel, photography, ethnography. Office: No State Univ Box 682 1200 S Jay St Aberdeen SD 57401-7155 E-mail: hollingj@northern.edu.

HOLLINGSWORTH, LARA HUDGINS, lawyer; b. Houston, Dec. 28, 1970; m. Derek S. Hollingsworth; 2 children. BA in Hist., Baylor U., 1993, JD magna cum laude, 1996. Bar: Tex. 1996, US Supreme Ct., US Dist. Ct. (all dists. Tex.), US Ct. Appeals (5th and 10th cirs.). Law clk. Staff of Sam D. Johnson, US Ct. Appeals Fifth Cir., 1996—97; briefing atty. to James A. Baker Tex. Supreme Ct., 1997—98; atty. Carrington, Coleman, Sloman & Blumenthal, P.C., Hudgins, Hudgins, and Warrick, P.C., Houston, 2000—03; of counsel Rusty Hardin & Assocs., P.C., Houston, 2003—. Tex. Civil Procedure Symposium editor: Baylor Law Rev., 1995—96. Named a Rising Star, Tex. Super Lawyers mag., 2006. Mem.: Tex. Young Lawyers Assn. Office: Rusty Hardin & Assocs PC 1401 McKinney Ste 2250 Houston TX 77010 Office Phone: 713-652-9000. E-mail: lhollingsworth@rustyhardin.com.

HOLLINGSWORTH, LAURA L., publishing executive; b. Chgo., 1967; m. John Hollingsworth; 3 children. Advt. exec., Green Bay, Wis., Olympia, Wash., Rockford, Ill., Lansing, Mich.; v.p. advt. Des Moines Register, 2002—05, gen. mgr., 2005—07, pres. & pub., 2007—. Mem. bd. Variety - The Children's Charity, Character Counts!, Iowa; mem. cmty. devel. bd. Greater Des Moines Partnership. Recipient Pres.'s Ring for Excellence in Advt., Gannett Co., Inc., 2000—04. Office: Des Moines Register PO Box 957 Des Moines IA 50306-0957 Office Phone: 515-284-8471. E-mail: lholling@dmreg.com.*

HOLLINGSWORTH, SAMUEL HAWKINS, JR., bassist; b. Birmingham, Ala., June 29, 1922; s. Samuel Hawkins and Bennie Louise Hollingsworth; m. Patricia Ann Patton, Apr. 1, 1957 (div. 1967); children: Priscilla P., Samuel Hawkins III; m. Elizabeth Mary Malezi, Dec. 31, 1974. Student, Juilliard Sch. Music, NYC, 1940-42, George Peabody Coll. Tchrs., Nashville, 1953-54. Prin. bassist Nashville Symphony, 1946-65, Chamber Symphony of Phila., 1966-68, Dallas Symphony, 1968-70, Pitts. Symphony, 1970-92, prin. emeritus, 1992-95; retired, 1995. Mem. governing bd. dirs. Nashville Symphony Orch., 1960-63; chmn. Dallas Symphony Orth Players, 1969-70. Home: 1111 Pinewood Dr Pittsburgh PA 15243-1809

HOLLINGTON, RICHARD RINGS, JR., lawyer; b. Findlay, Ohio, Nov. 12, 1932; s. Richard Rings and Annett (Kirk) H.; m. Sally Stecher, Apr. 4, 1959; children: Florence A., Julie A., Richard R. III. Peter S. BA, Williams Coll., 1954; JD, Harvard U., 1957. Bar: Ohio 1957. Ptnr. Marshman, Hornbeck & Hollington, Cleve., 1958-67, McDonald, Hopkins, Hardy &

Hollington, Cleve., 1967-69; law dir. City of Cleve., 1971-72; sr. ptnr. Baker & Hostetler, Cleve., 1969-71, 73—. Vice chair Sky Fin. Group, 1998-2004, lead dir., 1999-2003; dir. The Ohio Bank, 1958-2001; mem. adv. com. on banking policy FDIC, 2002-2006; mem. Ohio Banking Commn., 2001—, fin. dir. Hunting Valley, 2004—. Mem. Ohio Gen. Assembly, 1967-70, Cuyahoga County Rep. Ctrl. Com., 1962-66; exec. com. Ohio Rep. Fin. Com., 1971-98, Cuyahoga County Rep. Orgn., 1968-98, Geauga County Rep. Orgn., 1998—; trustee Cleve. State U., 1970-73, Greater Cleve. Hosp. Assn., 1976-82, Cleve. Mus. Natural History, 1969-81, Cleve. Zool. Soc., 1970-99, N. E. Ohio Regional Sewer Dist., 1972-73, Cuyahoga County Hosp. Found., 1968-73, Cleve. 500 Found., 1990-95, U. Findlay, 1991—, City Club Forum Found., 2005—; mem. bds. commrs. grievance and discipline Ohio Supreme Ct., 1993-95, mem. unauthorized practice of law com., 2005—. Mem. ABA, Ohio Bar Assn., Greater Cleve. Bar Assn., Sixth Cir. Jud. Conf. (life), Eighth Dist. Ohio Jud. Conf. (life), Ct. Nisi Prius, Union Club (Cleve.), The Country Club (Pepper Pike), Pepper Pike Club, Roaring Gap (N.C.) Club, Rolling Rock (Pa.) Club. Home: 13792 County Line Rd Chagrin Falls OH 44022-4008 Office: Baker & Hostetler 3200 National City Ctr 1900 E 9th St Ste 3200 Cleveland OH 44114-3475 Home Phone: 440-423-1246; Office Phone: 216-861-7623.

HOLLINRAKE, JOHN D., JR., lawyer; b. 1957; BSBA with high distinction, Univ. Ariz., 1980; JD magna cum laude, Univ. Houston, 1987. CPA 1982; bar: Wash. 1987. Ptnr., co-chair tax group Dorsey & Whitney LLP, Seattle. Named a Leading US West Coast Lawyer, Euromoney Legal Group, Super Lawyer, Wash. Law & Politics. Mem.: Seattle Internat. Tax Roundtable (chmn. 1992—93), Seattle Tax Group, Canadian Tax Found., Wash. State Bar Assn., Phi Kappa Phi, Beta Gamma Sigma, Beta Alpha Psi. Office: Dorsey & Whitney LLP Ste 3400 US Bank Ctr 1420 Fifth Ave Seattle WA 98101-4010 Office Phone: 206-903-8812. Office Fax: 206-903-8820. Business E-Mail: hollinrake.john@dorsey.com.

HOLLIS, CHARLES EUGENE, JR., finance company executive; b. Daytona Beach, Fla., Sept. 14, 1948; s. Charles Eugene and Betty Lou (Beech) H.; m. Carol Repass, Mar. 20, 1971 (div. Nov. 1993); children: Stephanie Dyane, Charles Preston, Robin Jene. AA, Dayton Beach Jr. Coll., 1968; BA, U. South Fla., 1972. CPA Fla. Asst. Deloitte Haskins & Sells, Tampa, Fla., 1972—73, sr. asst., 1973—75, sr., 1975—78, mgr., 1978—82; audit mgr. Jack Eckerd Corp., Clearwater, Fla., 1982—85; v.p. fin., contr. Freedom Savs. and Loan Assn., Tampa, 1985—87, sr. v.p., CFO, treas., 1987—88, exec. v.p., 1988—89, CenTrust Fed., Miami, Fla., 1990; supervisory fin. instn. specialist Resolution Trust Corp., Atlanta, 1990—95; exec. v.p. Beech Mgmt. Group, Inc., 1996—; portfolio mgr. GMAC Comml. Mortgage Corp., 2000—06, Capmark Finance, Inc., 2006—. Chmn. fin. and taxation com. Fla. League Cities, Tallahassee, 1979—81; mem. fin. com. Nat. League Cities, Washington, 1980—86; code enforcement bd. City of Temple Terrace, 1986—91; trustee Univ. Community Hosp., 1987—91; charter mem., treas. Northeast Sertoma, 1989—90; City councilman City of Temple Terrace, Fla., 1976—86, vice mayor Fla., 1981—82; treas. Christ Our Redeemer Luth. Ch., 1984—86, pres., 1987—88; treas. Fla. Synod-Evangelical Luth. Ch. in Am., 1988—92; pres. Oaks of Dunwordy Condominium Assn., 2005—. Recipient Disting. Service award, U. South Fla. Coll. Bus., 1972, Outstanding Alumnus award, Beta Alpha Psi, 1983. Mem.: Tampa C. of C. (Leadership Tampa 1987—88), Fin. Mgrs. Soc., Fla. Soc. CPAs, Am. Inst. CPAs, Beta Alpha Psi. Republican. Home and Office: 985 Gardendale Dr Columbia SC 29210-4906 Home Phone: 678-441-9671; Office Phone: 404-654-2366. Business E-Mail: charles_hollis@gmaccm.com.

HOLLIS, DEAN, food products executive; b. Clearwater, Fla., May 4, 1960; s. Mark C. and Lynn (Darracott) H.; m. Darla Deines, Aug. 1, 1987; children: Darrica Lyn, David William. BA in Psychology, Stetson U., DeLand, Fla., 1982. Supr. Ga.-Pacific, Houston, 1982-83, dist. mgr. Atlanta, 1983-85; sales planning mgr. The TreeSweet Cos., Houston, 1985-86, regional mgr. Atlanta, 1986-87, Conagra Frozen Foods, Atlanta, 1987-88, trade mktg. mgr. St. Louis, 1988-89, dir. sales S.E. Atlanta, 1989-90, divsn. dir.-west Scottsdale, Ariz., 1990-92, area v.p.-west, 1992, pres., 2000—05; interim pres. Grocery Foods ConAgra Foods, Inc., 2005, exec. v.p. retail products, pres., COO Consumer Foods, 2005—. Bd. advisors Stetson U., Deland, Fla., 1988. Avocations: water-skiing, reading. Office: ConAgra Foods Inc 1 ConAgra Dr Omaha NE 68102-5001 Office Phone: 402-595-4000.*

HOLLIS, DEBORAH D., systems analyst, application developer; d. Susan Tower and Allen Hollis. BS, Regis U., Denver, 1997; BA, St. John's Coll., Santa Fe, 1988; M in Computer Info. Sys., U. Denver, 1995; M in Libr. and Info. Sci., U. Wash., Seattle, 1989. Database analyst Ovid Technologies, Salt Lake City, 1998—2001; analyst Sandia Nat. Labs., Albuquerque, 2001—. Mem.: U.S. Equestrian Team, Padi Dive Soc., Arabian Horse Assn. Independent. Avocations: reading, horseback riding, scuba diving, Aikido, yoga.

HOLLIS, DONALD ROGER, management consultant; b. Warren, Ohio, Mar. 4, 1936; s. Louis and Lena (Succo) Hollis; m. Marilyn G. Morganti, Aug. 23, 1958; children: Roger, Russel Kirk, Gregory, Heather. BS, Kent State U., 1959. Regional mgr. Glidden Corp., San Francisco, 1959-65, dir. mgmt. info. svcs. Cleve., 1965-68; dir. mgmt. info. services SCM Corp., NYC, 1968-71; v.p. Chase Manhattan Bank, NYC, 1971-81; sr. v.p. First Chgo. Corp., 1981-85, exec. v.p., 1986-95, head sys., data processing, cash mgmt. and security products and quality programs, 1986-95; pres., CEO DRH Strategic Cons., Chgo., 1995—. Bd. dirs. Exss, Wausau Fin. Sys.; Life Trustee III Inst. Tech. Office: c/o Diamond 875 N Michigan Ave Ste 2300 Chicago IL 60611 Office Phone: 312-255-6975.

HOLLIS, JULIA ANN ROSHTO, critical care, medical, and surgical nurse; b. Monroe, La., June 25, 1945; d. Joseph Edward Roshto and Eleanor Coverdale Larsen; m. William Davis Hollis, Mar. 2, 1964; children: David Terrel, Julia Allison. BSN, N.E. La. U., 1976. RN, La., Ala., Miss.; cert. BCLS, ACLS. Staff nurse to head nurse E.A. Conway Hosp., Monroe, 1977-84; staff nurse, charge nurse ICU, critical care North Monroe Community Hosp., Monroe, 1984-87; staff nurse neurotrama surg. ICU U. South Ala. Med. Ctr., Mobile, 1988-89; staff nurse, charge nurse Norrell Health Care, Mobile, 1990—, Medforce Internat., New Orleans; owner Resource Mgmt., 1997. Mem. AACN, AAUW, Ala. Nurses Assn., Met. Writers Guild, Baldwin County Writers Assn. Home: 5073 Dawes Lane Ext Theodore AL 36582-9627

HOLLIS, KATHERINE MARY, information scientist, consultant; d. Albert George and Rosalyn Mary Duren; m. David Martin Hollis, Aug. 25, 1990; children: Kent David Miller, Jason Randolph Miller; children: Brittany Frances, David Christopher. MS in Nat. Security Strategy, Nat. War College, 1999; B in Polit. Sci., U. Minn., 1983. Dir. resource mgmt. installation support modules program Program Exec. Office - STD. Mgmt. Info. Sys., Ft. Belvoir, Va., 1989—93; program mgr. electronic commerce/electronic data interchange Def. Info. Sys. Agy., Falls Church, Va., 1993—96, spl. asst. to the dep., pub. key infrastructure program mgmt. office, 1999—2000; dep. dir. electronic processes initiatives coun. task force Office of the Deputy Sec. of Def., Rosslyn, Va., 1996—98; deputy dir. dept. def. Y2K office Office of the Sec. of Def., Crystal City, Va., 1998—99; exec. dir. security and privacy portfolio Electronic Data Sys., Herndon, Va., 2000—. Adv. com. Fed. Electronic Commerce Coalition, Falls Church, Va., 1999—; chair smart card integrated process team Def. Info. Sys. Agy. , 1999—2000; spkr. in field. Vol. educator Prince William County Schools, Manassas, Va., 2001. Recipient Commanders award, Dept. of the Army, Dept. of Def., 1989, Federal 100 award, Federal Computer News, 1998. Avocations: archaeology, Egyptology, travel, writing. Office: Electronic Data Sys 13600 EDS Dr (A2S-D49) Herndon VA 20171

HOLLIS, RALPH L., science educator; BS in Physics, Kans. State U., Manhattan, 1964, MS in Physics, 1965; PhD in Solid State Physics, U. Colo., Boulder, 1975. Rschr. autonetics divsn. North Am. Aviation, 1965—70; rsch. staff mem. IBM Thomas J. Watson Rsch. Ctr., 1978, mgr. advanced robotics mfg. rsch. dept., 1986—93; mem. faculty to rsch. prof. robotics Carnegie Mellon U., Pitts., 1993—. NSF/Nat. Ctr. Sci. Rsch. exch. scientist U. Pierre and Marie Curie, Paris, 1976—77; founding dir. Microdynamic Systems Lab. Carnegie Mellon U. Contbr. articles to profl. jours.; mem. editl. bd.: Jour. Micromechanics and Microengineering: Structures, Devices and Systems, IEEE Transactions on Robotics and Automation. Recipient Nakamura prize, Best Paper, Internat. Conf. Intelligent Robots and Systems, 1995, 2001. Fellow: IEEE; mem.: Am. Phys. Soc. Achievements include design of Ballbot, a robot that moves around and balances on a ball rather than legs or wheels; patents in field; research in magnetic levitation haptic interfaces, precision microassembly sys. Office: Robotics Inst Carnegie Mellon U 5000 Forbes Ave Pittsburgh PA 15213 Office Phone: 412-268-8264. Business E-Mail: rhollis@cs.cmu.edu.

HOLLIS, REGINALD, archbishop; b. Eng., July 18, 1932; emigrated to Can., 1954; s. Jesse Farndon and Edith Ellen (Lee) H.; m. Marcia Crombie, Sept. 7, 1957; children— Martin, Hilda, Aidan. BA, Cambridge U., Eng., 1954; MA, Cambridge U., 1958; BD, McGill U., Montreal, 1956; DD (hon.), U. South, 1977, Montreal Diocesan Theol. Coll., 1975. Ordained to ministry Anglican Ch. as deacon, 1956, as priest, 1956. Chaplain Montreal Diocesan Theol. Coll.; also chaplain to Anglican students McGill U., 1956-60; asst. St. Matthias Parish, Westmount, Que., 1960-63; incumbent St. Barnabas Ch., Roxboro, Que., 1963-66, rector, 1966-71, Christ Ch., Beaurepaire, Que., 1971-74; dir. parish and diocesan services Diocese Montreal, 1974-75, bishop, 1975-90; archbishop of Montreal Met. of the Ecclesiastical Province of Can., 1989-90; asst. bishop Diocese of Ctrl. Fla., Orlando, 1990-94; episc. dir. Anglican Fellowship of Prayer, 1990-94; rector St. Paul's Ch., New Smyrna Beach, Fla., 1994-97; ret., 1997. Author: Abiding in Christ, 1987. Anglican. Home: 1175 Newport Ave Ste 303 Victoria BC Canada V8S 5E6

HOLLIS, RICHARD B., pharmaceutical executive; Student, St. Mary's Coll.; BA in Psych., San Francisco State U. Product sales position Baxter Travenol (now Baxter Internat.); positions up to divsn. mgr. Imed Corp. (acquired by Warner Lambert, now part of Pfizer Inc.); western bus. unit mgr. Genentech, Inc., 1986—89; gen. mgr., v.p. mktg. and sales Instromedix, 1989—91; COO Bioject Med., 1991—94; founder, chmn., CEO Hollis-Eden Pharms., San Diego, 1994—. Office: Hollis Eden Pharms Inc 4435 Eastgate Hall Ste 400 San Diego CA 92121 Office Phone: 858-587-9333.*

HOLLIS, SHEILA SLOCUM, lawyer; b. Denver, July 15, 1948; d. Theodore Doremus and Emily M. (Caplis) Slocum (dec.); m. John Hollis; 1 child, Windsong Emily Hollis. BS in Journalism with honors, U. Colo., 1971, BS in Gen. Studies cum laude, 1971; JD, U. Denver, 1973. Bar: Colo. 1974, D.C. 1975, U.S. Supreme Ct. 1980. Trial atty. Fed. Power Commn., Washington, 1974-75; assoc. firm Wilner & Scheiner, Washington, 1975-77; dir. office enforcement Fed. Energy Regulatory Commn., Washington, 1977-80; pvt. practice, 1980—; ptnr. Vinson & Elkins, Washington, 1987-92; sr. ptnr. Metzger, Hollis, Gordon & Alprin, Washington, 1992-97; mng. ptnr. Washington office Duane Morris LLP, 1997—2004, chair Washington office, 2004—; exec. com., firm ptnrs. bd. Duane Morris LLP, 2003—. Professorial lectr. in energy law George Washington U., 1980—2000. Co-author: Energy Decision Making, 1983, Energy Law and Policy, 1989; mem. editl. bd. Oil and Gas Reporter, Pub. Utility Fortnightly; contbr. articles to profl. publs. Adv. bd. Pub. Utility Ctr. N.Mex. State U., 1986—94; adv. bd. N.Am. Energy Stds. Bd., 1998—; pres. Women's Coun. Energy and Environment, 1997—2003; bd. dirs. Am. Friends of Royal Soc., U.S. Energy Assn., chair nominating com. U. Denver scholar, 1972-73; named Woman of Yr. Women's Coun. Energy and Environment, 2003, One of 50 Key Women in Energy-Global, Commodities Now Mag., 2004; finalist Lifetime Achievement award Platt's Global Energy Awards, 2006. Fellow: ABA (chair coord. group energy law 1989—92, ho. dels. 1992—, chair coord. group energy law 1995—97, chair standing com. environ. law 1997—2000, chair bd. editors ABA Jour. 2007—, chair sect. environ., energy and resources 2001—02, standing com. fed. judiciary 2002—05, chmn. elect bd. editors 2007—, chair coun. fund for justice and edn., Finalist Lifetime Achievement Platt's Global Energy award 2006); mem.: Womens Fgn. Policy Group, Fed. Bar Assn., John Carroll Soc., Women's Bar Assn. D.C., D.C. Bar Assn., Colo. Bar Assn., Ctr. Am. and Internat. Law (trustee, v.p.), Oil and Gas Ednl. Inst. (v.p.), Energy Bar Assn. (pres. 1991—92), Am. Law Inst., Internat. Bar Assn., Comml. Bar of Eng. and Wales (hon.), Thomas More Soc. Am. (pres. 2003—05), Cosmos Club, Nat. Press Club, Dame of Malta of the Am. Assn. Roman Catholic. Office: Duane Morris LLP 1667 K St NW Ste 700 Washington DC 20006-1608 Home Phone: 202-543-3766; Office Phone: 202-776-7810. Business E-Mail: sshollis@duanemorris.com.

HOLLIS, SUSAN TOWER, history professor; b. Boston, Mar. 17, 1939; d. James Wilson and Dorothy Parsons (Moore) Tower; m. Allen Hollis, Nov. 10, 1962 (div. Feb. 1975); children: Deborah Durfee, Harrison. AB, Smith Coll., 1962; PhD, Harvard U., 1982. Cert. C.C. instr. history and humanities. Asst. prof. Scripps Coll., Claremont, Calif., 1988—91; prof. Coll. of Undergrad. Studies Union Inst., LA, 1991—93; dean coll., prof. humanities Sierra Nev. Coll.-Lake Tahoe, Incline Village, Nev., 1993—95; ind. scholar, cons. Reno, 1995—96; ctr. dir., assoc. dean Ctrl. N.Y. Ctr. SUNY Empire State Coll., Syracuse, 1996—99, assoc. prof. Rochester, 1999—2007, coord. we. region MA in Liberal Studies program, 2000—, prof., 2007—. Convener hist. studies Empire State Coll. of SUNY, 2000—03; co-chair acad. policies and learning programs com. Empire State Coll. SUNY, 2003—04, mem. academic policies and learning program com., 2001—05. Author: The Ancient Egyptian "Tale of Two Brothers", 1990; editor: Hymns, Prayers and Songs: Anthology of Ancient Egyptian Lyrics & Poetry (by John L. Foster), 1996; asst. editor: Working With No Data, 1987; co-editor: Feminist Theory and the Study of Folklore, 1993; mem. adv. bd.: KMT, A Modern Jour. of Ancient Egypt, 1991—; contbr. articles to profl. jours, encys. Music vol. Open Readings, Belmont, Mass., 1982—88; vol. Sierra Club, 1988—; problem capt. Odyssey of the Mind, Nev., 1994—95, judge NY, 1997—98; crew chief Tahoe Rim trail, 1994—96; active Masterworks Chorale, NY, 1996—99. Recipient Susan H. Turben award for excellence in scholarship, Empire State Coll., 2006. Mem.: N.Y. State Network for Women Leaders in Higher Edn. (bd. dirs. 1997—2006, assoc. coord. 1999—2000, coord. 2000—03), N.Y. Acad. Scis., Egyptological Soc. N.Y., Soc. Bibl. Lit. (co-chair Egyptology and Ancient Israel group 1995—96, chair Egyptology and Ancient Israel group 1996—2005, convenor Ancient Near East Consortium 1998—, Outstanding Svc. in Mentoring award 2003), Soc. for Study Egyptian Antiquities, Internat. Assn. Egyptologists, Am. Rsch. Ctr. Egypt, Am. Oriental Soc., Am. Folklore Soc., Am. Assn. Higher Edn., Am. Acad. Religion, Am. Recorder Soc. (Rochester NY chpt. 2004—), Incline Village/Crystal Bay C. of C. (sec., bd. dirs. 1994—95), Ka-na-wa-ke Canoe Club (bd. dirs. 1998—2000), Adirondack Mountain Club, Appalachian Mountain Club (co-leader 1987—88). Democrat. Home: 7 New Wickham Dr Penfield NY 14526-2703 Office: Empire State Coll of SUNY 1475 Winton Rd N Rochester NY 14609-5803 Office Phone: 585-224-3246. Business E-Mail: susan.hollis@esc.edu.

HOLLIS, TIMOTHY MARTIN, bank executive; b. Marietta, Ga., Nov. 13, 1962; s. Milton Joel and Mary Sylvia (Skanner) Hollis. BSBA in Mgmt., Shorter Coll., Rome, Ga., 1986. Desk supr. front desk Wyndham Hotel Co., Atlanta, 1986-87; personal banker C&S/Sovran Corp., Atlanta, 1987-90, sr. personal banker, 1990-91; asst. br. mgr., banking officer NationsBank Ga., N.A., Atlanta, 1991-92, banking ctr. mgr., 1992-95; sales mgr. Wachovia Bank, NA (formerly First Union Nat. Bank Ga.), Atlanta, 1995—97; fin. specialist, v.p. Wachovia Diversity Coun.-Ga. Gen. Bank, 1997—2005; v.p., relationship mgr. Wachovia Pvt. Adv. Banking, Atlanta, 2006—. Treas., mktg. chair, mem. fin. com., trustee Choral Guild Atlanta, 1991; bd. dirs. Artcare, Inc., Atlanta, 1991—94; docent, vol. mem. Friends of Zoo Atlanta; mem. steering com. First Night Atlanta, 1993—99, 1994 Class Atlanta Midtown Leadership Program, Atlanta Midtown Alliance, 1992—, Human Rights Campaign Fund, 1992—, GAPAC, 1993—95, AIDS Walk Atlanta, 1995—97; mem. adv. bd. Atlanta Exec. Network, 1993—96, co-chair young profls., 1996—98; mem. adv. bd. Joining Hearts Inc., 1994—99; bd. dirs. Positive Impact, 1996—97, Pets are Lovin Support, Inc., 1997—99; conf. chair First Night Internat., 1998; bd. dirs. AIDS Treatment Initiative, 1997—99, pres., 1998—99; mem. Buckhead Young Reps., Atlanta, 1989—92. Mem.: Atlanta Track Club (vol.). Methodist. Avocations: running, singing, exercise, volunteering. Home: 28 Finch Trail NE Atlanta GA 30308-2418 Office: Wachovia Banking 31 Pharr Rd 2d Fl Atlanta GA 30305 Personal E-mail: timhollis@bellsouth.net. Business E-Mail: tim.hollis@wachovia.com.

HOLLIS-SAWYER, LISA ANN, psychologist, gerontologist, researcher; d. Dale Eugene and Patricia Ann Hollis; m. Thomas Paul Sawyer, Aug. 9, 1997; 1 child, Joshua Thomas Sawyer. PhD in Indsl. Gerontol. Psychology, U. of Akron, 1996. Assoc. prof. psychology, women's studies and gerontology, gerontology program coord. Northeastern Ill. U., Chgo., 1998—. Editor (author): (book) Intersections of aging: Readings in Social Gerontology, 2000; author: (coll. textbook and instr.'s guide) Exercises in Psychological Testing Laboratory Manual, 2002, (book chpt.) Social Inequities, Health, and Healthcare Delivery, vol. XX; contbr. articles various to profl. jours. Acad. advisor Met. Family Svcs. - Seniorcare Adv. Coun., Chgo., 2000—02. Recipient Found. Faculty Rsch. and Scholarly Project grant, 4 faculty excellence awards. Mem.: Gerontol. Soc. Am. (assoc.), Sigma Phi Omega (life). Avocations: travel, photography, writing children's books, volunteering, painting. Office: Northeastern Ill U Dept Psychology 5500 N Saint Louis Ave Chicago IL 60625 Home Phone: 708-452-5245; Office Phone: 773-442-5846. Business E-Mail: l-hollissawyer@neiu.edu.

HOLLISTER, ARTHUR CLAIR, JR., epidemiologist, consultant, retired public health service officer; b. New Orleans, May 9, 1918; s. Arthur Clair Hollister and Cora Preston Odom; m. Olivia Ewing, Aug. 2, 1942; children: Arthur III, Olivia Corinna. BS, Tulane U., New Orleans, 1938, MD, 1941; MPH, Johns Hopkins U., Balt., 1948. Diplomate Am. Bd. Preventive Medicine and Pub. Health. Intern So. Bapt. Hosp., New Orleans, 1941-42; pub. health med. officer Calif. State Dept. Health, Berkeley, Sacramento, 1946-48, med. epidemiologist, 1946-83; cons. Ctr. Disease Control and NIH, Atlanta, Washington, Calif., 1950-70; lectr. UCLA Sch. Pub. Health, Berkeley, 1950-65; cons. epidemiologist Contra Costa County Social Svcs., Martinez, Calif., 1992—. State epidemiologist, chief Bur. Communicable Diseases, Calif., 1950—58; various other offices, 1958—83; mem. health svcs. study sect. NIH, Bethesda, Md., 1968—73; mem. chair health com., v.p. Adv. Coun. Aging, Martinez, 1986—, chair longterm care com., 1992—; mem. workgroup Calif. Coun. Longterm Care Integration, 2001—; apptd. sr. rep. Calif. 10th congl. dist. Nat. Silver Haired Congress, 2004—. Contbr. sci. reports and articles to profl. jours. Active City of Pleasant Hill (Calif.) Commn. Aging, 1987—92; vestry, choir mem. St. Stephen's Episc. Ch., Orinda, Calif., 1954—. 1st lt. USAAF, 1942—46, maj. USAR, 1946—51, surgeon USPHS Res., 1954—70, med. dir. USPHS ret. Fellow: ACLU, APHA (past chair epidemiology sect., governing coun.), Health Care for All, Am. Coll. Preventive Medicine; mem.: Physicians for Nat. Health Program, Calif. Physicians Alliance, Am. Epidemiol. Soc., Gray Panthers, Ret. Pub. Employees Assn., U. Calif.-Berkeley Faculty Club, Alpha Kappa Kappa, Kappa Sigma, Delta Omega. Democrat. Avocations: classical and popular piano, jazz, classic cars, real and model railroads. Home and Office: 14 Boies Ct Pleasant Hill CA 94523

HOLLISTER, WINSTON NED, pathologist; b. Milw., Mar. 23, 1942; s. Harold Arthur and Jeannette Clara (Gastrav) H.; m. Carol Jean Potter, Dec. 7, 1963 (div. May 1978); children: Timothy Carl, David Andrew; m. Margaret Ravenel Papen, Oct. 29, 1988; children: Charles Davis, Margaret Ravenel. BS in Physics, U. Wis., 1964; MD, Med. Coll. Wis., 1971. Diplomate Am. Bd. Internal Medicine, Am. Bd. Pathology. Staff pathologist St. Joseph's Hosp., Milw., 1976—; pres., CEO Franciscan Shared Lab, Wauwatosa, Wis., 1988-90; med. dir., chmn. bd. dirs. Med. Sci. Labs., Wauwatosa, 1989—2003. Cons. in field. Contbr. articles to profl. jours. Vestry mem. St. Paul's Episcopal Ch., Milw., 1978-83. Lt. USN, 1964-67. Recipient Houghton & Houghton award Med. Soc. Wis., 1971. Fellow Coll. Am. Pathologists (clin. practice com. 1984-87); mem. ACP, Am. Pathology Found. (pres. 1994-96), Oconomowoc Lake Club, Pine Lake Yacht Club. Republican. Episcopalian. Avocations: sailing, skiing, tennis, travel, music. Home: 4940 N Maple Lane Nashotah WI 53058 Office: 4940 N Maple Ln Nashotah WI 53058 Office Phone: 414-447-2021.

HOLLMAN, K. HOLLYN, lawyer; b. Jackson, Miss. m. James McCall Smith; 2 children. BA in Politics, Wake Forest U.; JD, U. Tenn. Coll. Law. Atty. McGuireWoods LLP, Washington, Waller Landsden Dortch & Davis, Nashville; gen. counsel (pub. affairs) Baptist Joint Com., 2001—. Mem.: Tenn. Bar, DC Bar. Office: Baptist Joint Com Public Affairs 200 Maryland Ave NE Washington DC 20002

HOLLOMAN, KENNETH RAYMOND, pathologist, educator; b. Akron, Ohio, Apr. 25, 1933; s. John D. and Martha N. Holloman; m. Donata L. Bridges-Holloman; children: Marc, Bruce. BS, U. Akron, Ohio, 1955; MD, Ohio State U., Columbus, 1957. Diplomate Am. Bd. Pathology, 1964. Lab. dir. Gorgas Hosp., Panama, 1965—68; pathologist St.Llukes Hosp., Denver, 1969—91; pres. Denver Area Pathology Assocs., 1987—91. Cons. Nat. Health Lab., Denver, 1992—97; chmn. dept. western medicine Sch. Oriental Medicine, Denver, 1998—2006. Col. Med. Corps US Army, 1977. Mem.: Alpha Omega Alpha, Omicron Delta Kappa. Independent. Avocations: woodworking, art, wine. Home: 5770 Oak Creek Ln Greenwood Village CO 80121

HOLLOMAN, MARILYN LEONA DAVIS, lobbyist, non profit administrator, family practice nurse practitioner, new product developer; b. Bklyn., Oct. 6, 1952; d. Leon Courbourne and Gwendolyn Omega (Crichlow) Davis; m. Theodore Albert Holloman, July 30, 1971 (div. Apr. 1975); children: Tedette Ann (dec.), Amina Omega Suedi. AAS in Nursing, Queensboro C.C., Bayside, NY, 1973; FNP, U. Miami, Coral Gables, 1980. Cert. family nurse practitioner. Founder, pres., CEO Women and Children First Inc., Miami, 1992—2004; v.p. Omega Health Network, inc., 2000—01; campaign adv./lobbyist to amb.'s dau., 2001—. Allocations panel mem. United Way, Dade County, Fla., 1989-96; mem. at large Switchboard of Miami, 1992, treas., 1993-94, sec., 1994-95; fellow Common Ground Kellogg Found./U. Miami, 1993-95; primary cand. 1996 (Fla. House Rep., Dist 101). Author: Melody's of Life, 1982; editor Health Plan Baby Book, 1985; editor, pub. Legislative Update Women and Children 1st Inc., 1994—97. Former pres. Dem. Black Caucus-Dade County chpt., 1991-92; Dem. candidate Fla. Ho. Reps., 1996; mem. Planned Giving Coun. of Dade County, 1994-95; mem. Dade County Reapportionment Task Force, 1991-92; lobbyist, adv. Am. childrent fgn.

nats. and diplomats. Amb. Dau. Campaign. Mem.: ANA (cert. specialist family nurse practitioner), Miami Parliamentary Law Unit (pres. 1993—95, v.p. 1995—97), Nat. Assn. Parliamentarians, Fla. Nurses Assn. (legis. dist. coord. 1984—99). Democrat. Achievements include patents pending for 9-11 omega buddysack, injurevac and drawstring whizz. Avocations: drama, reading, dance, travel. Home: 17 Anamosa Ct Derwood MD 20855 Office: PO Box 34653 Bethesda MD 20817 Office Phone: 301-978-9774. Personal E-mail: fnp1006@yahoo.com.

HOLLORAN, THOMAS EDWARD, business educator; b. Mpls., Sept. 27, 1929; s. Edward Francis and Florence G. (Loftus) H.; m. Patricia M. Holloran, June 26, 1954; children: Mary Patricia Harley, Anne Florence. BS, U. Minn., 1951, JD, 1955. Bar: Minn. 1955, Fed. 1955. Ptnr. Wheeler and Fredrikson, Mpls., 1955-67; exec. v.p. Medtronic, Inc., Mpls., 1967-73, pres., 1973-75; chmn., chief exec. officer Inter-Regional Fin. Group, Inc. (renamed Dain Rauscher Corp), Mpls., 1976-85; prof. mgmt. U. St. Thomas, St. Paul, 1986—2001, prof. emeritus Coll. Bus., 2001—, sr. disting. fellow Sch. Law, 2001—. Bd. dirs. Flexsteel Industries, Inc., Dubuque, Iowa; dir. emeritus Medtronic, Inc. Spl. judge Mcpl. Ct. of Shorewood, Excelsior, Tonka Bay, Greenwood and Deephaven, Minn., 1961-65; Mayor, City of Shorewood, 1971-74; chmn. Urban Coalition, Mpls., 1977-78, City of Mpls. Task Force on Tech., 1983-84; mem. Mpls.-St. Paul Met. Airports Commn., 1974-82, vice chmn., 1976-82, chmn., 1989-91; bd. trustees Coll. St. Scholastica, 1971-81, chmn., 1979-81; trustee Coll. St. Thomas, 1979-88, U. Minn. Found., 1983-85, Bush Found., 1982—2000, chmn. 1991-96; trustee Mpls. Art Inst., 1986-93, Mpls. Children's Health Ctr., 1983-84; pres. Upper M.W. Coun., Mpls., 1978-80; bd. dirs. InterStudy, Excelsior., 1975-85, Minn. Press Coun., 1982-87, mem. corp. bd. Cath. Archdiocese Mpls. and St. Paul, 1990-2007, mem. bd. St. Paul's Cath. Seminary, 2006-. With USN, 1952-54, Korea. Mem. ABA, Minn. State Bar Assn. Roman Catholic. Office Phone: 651-962-4243.

HOLLOWAY, CHARLES ARTHUR, public and private management educator; b. Whittier, Calif., May 28, 1936; s. Heber H. and Theodosia S. (Stephens) H.; m. Christina Ahlm, July 11, 1959; children: Deborah, Susan, Stuart. BSEE with honors, U. Calif., Berkeley, 1959; MS, UCLA, 1963, PhD in Bus. Adminstrn. with distinction, 1969. Sr. engr. Bechtel Corp., San Francisco, 1964-65; tchg. fellow UCLA, 1965-66; asst. prof. to prof. Stanford (Calif.) U., 1968—, Herbert Hoover prof. pub. and pvt. mgmt., 1980-91, assoc. dean acad. affairs Grad. Sch. Bus., 1980-87, 90-91, Kleiner Perkins Caufield and Byers prof. mgmt., 1991—2004, Kleiner Perkins Caufield and Byers prof. mgmt. emeritus, 2004—. Bd. dir. SRI Internat.; co-chair Stanford Ctr. Entrepreneurial Studies. Author: Decision Making Under Uncertainty: Models and Choices, 1979, Perpetual Enterprise Machine: Seven Keys to Corporate Renewal, 1994. With USN, 1959-63. Fellow Ford Found., 1966-68. Mem. Inst. Mgmt. Sci., Ops. Rsch. Soc. Am., Stanford Integrated Mfg. Assn. (co-chair 1991-95). Home: 730 Santa Maria Ave Palo Alto CA 94305-8438 Office: Stanford U Grad Sch Bus Stanford CA 94305 Business E-Mail: holloway_chuck@gsb.stanford.edu.

HOLLOWAY, CHRISTOPHER MATTHEW, brokerage house executive; b. Portsmouth, Va., Jan. 23, 1973; s. Marc Vincent and Mabel Lurlene H.; m. Susan Janrae Spears Holloway, June 26, 1999; 1 child, Erin Angela. BS in Bus. Adminstrn., Old Dominion U., Norfolk, Va., 1995, MBA, 1998. Regis. Series 4 NASD Options Prin., Series 7 Rep. N.Y. Stock Exchange, Series 24 NASD Gen. Securities Prin., Series 55 OTC Equity Trader, Series 63 NASD Uniform State Law, Series 65 NASD Regis. Investment Adv., Series 27 Fin. and Ops. Prin., Series 53 MSRB Prin. Trend analyst The Finance Co., Norfolk, Va., 1993-96; fin. analyst TFC Enterprises, Inc., Norfolk, Va., 1996-98; v.p. of ops. and compliance Investors Security Co., Inc., Suffolk, Va., 1998—, also bd. dirs. Ops. mgr. Old Dominion Investors Trust, Inc., Mutual Fund, Suffolk, Va., 1998-2004. Recipient 6 All Am. Scholar awards, U.S. Achievement Acad., 1991-95; named Outstanding Jr. Phi Kappa Phi, Norfolk, Va., 1994, Univ. Scholar Old Dominion U., Norfolk, Va., 1995, Outstanding Mgmt. Acctg. Student of Yr., Inst. of Mgmt. Acctg./Old Dominion U. Mgmt., Norfolk, Va., 1998. Mem. Inst. Mgmt. Accts., Golden Key Nat. Hon. Soc., Beta Gamma Sigma, Phi Kappa Phi. Republican. Avocations: coin collecting/numismatics, travel, auto enthusiast, antiques. Office: Investors Security Co Inc Ste 101 127 E Washington St Suffolk VA 23434 Office Phone: 757-539-2396. Office Fax: 757-925-4353. Business E-Mail: cholloway@investorssecurity.com.

HOLLOWAY, DONALD PHILLIP, lawyer; b. Akron, Ohio, Feb. 18, 1928; s. Harold Shane and Dorothy Gayle (Ryder) Holloway. BS in Commerce, Ohio U., Athens, 1950; JD, U. Akron, 1955; MA, Kent State U., 1962. Bar: Ohio 1955. Title examiner Bankers Guarantee Title & Trust Co., Akron, 1950-54; acct. Robinson Clay Product Co., Akron, 1955-60; libr. Akron-Summit Pub. Libr., 1962-69, head fine arts and music divsn., 1969-71, sr. libr., 1972-82; pvt. practice Akron, 1982—. Payroll treas. Akron Symphony Orch., 1957-61; treas. Friends Libr. Akron and Summit County, 1970-72. Mem. ABA, ALA, Ohio Bar Assn., Akron Bar Assn., Ohio Libr. Assn., Nat. Trust Hist. Preservation, Music Libr. Assn., Soc. Archtl. Historians, Coll. Art Assn., Art Librs. N.Am. Republican. Episcopalian. Avocations: art, music, travel, architecture. Home: 293 Delaware Pl Akron OH 44303-1275 Home Phone: 330-867-6147; Office Phone: 330-867-6147.

HOLLOWAY, EDWARD OLIN, human services manager; b. Rochester, NY, July 3, 1944; s. Charles Robert and Chrystal Gertrude (Darling) Holloway; m. Hama Elizabeth Farris, Dec. 23, 1967. AA, Palm Beach Jr. Coll., 1964; BA, Lenoir Rhyne Coll., 1967; MS in Pub. Health, U. N.C., 1975. From sanitarian I to sanitarian supr. I Palm Beach County Health Dept., West Palm Beach, Fla., 1969—73; from coord. emergency med. svcs. to exec. dir. dist. IX Health Planning Coun., Inc., West Palm Beach, 1975—89; sr. health and human svcs. planner bd. county commrs. Palm Beach County Dept. Cmty. Svcs., West Palm Beach, 1989—2000. Mem. faculty Pub. Health Physician Residency Program, 1990—2002, apptd. spl. advisor, 2002—; mem. accreditation five yrs. U. Miami, 1999—2004; mem. steering com. Fla. Atlantic U. Inst. Govt., 1992—2000, vice chmn., 1994—99, apptd. spl. adv., 2000—. Vol. planning staff fed. govt., 2004; chmn. dist. 9 adv. coun. Dept. Health and Rehab. Svcs., West Palm Beach, 1990—92; pres. Fla. Assn. Health Planning Agys., Inc., 1984—89; planning unit steering com. Leadership Palm Beach County, 1991; Palm Beach County data collection com. Health and Human Svcs. Planning Assn., 1992—98; mem. Interagy. Planning Group, 1994—2000; mem. sch. adv. com. Palm Beach Gardens Cmty. HS, 1994—, vice chair, 2000—03, mem. membership safety com., 2000—, mem. budget com., 2001—; appointee for customer svc. West Palm Beach VA Med. Ctr., 1997—; mem. Palm Beach County Partnership for Aging program United Way, 1998—; apptd. ex officio mem., spl. advisor Palm Beach County Citizens Adv. Com. on Health and Human Svc., 2000—, mem. planning/implementation subcom. Palm Beach County comprehensive plan, 2005—; vol. State of Fla. Dept. Health, 2000—, vol. staff, chair planning implementing and evaluation needed health and human svc. sys. improvements Guiding Principles and Ops. Comm., 2002—; vol. team to evaluate quality of care and customer svc. provided at local VA Med. Ctr. Fed. Insp. Gen.'s Office, 2002. With US Army, 1967—69, Vietnam. Decorated Bronze Star, Purple Heart, Army Commendation medal, Cross of Gallantry (Vietnam); recipient Cert. Appreciation, Wall Soc. of the Vietnam Veterans Memorial Fund, 2004, 2006, Letters of Commendation, CDC, 1980, Outstanding Svc. award, Fla. Assn. Health Planning Agys., 1989, Outstanding Achievement award, Bd. County Commrs., Palm Beach County Citizens Adv. Com. on Health and Human Svcs., 1995, Letters of Commendation, State of Fla., Lawton Chiles, 1998, Cert. of Merit, Rep. Nat. Com., 2001, Cert. Appreciation, Americans Disabled for Life Meml., 2003, Cert. Honor, Pres. 2004 Team, 2004, Cert. Commendation, Mus. US Army, 2004, Cert. of Unanimous Inclusion in Rep. Presdl. Honor Roll, Nat. Rep. Congressional Com., 2005, Congl. Order Merit, Rep. Congl. Com., 2006, Cert. Achievement, VA Med. Ctr., 2006, Cert. Appreciation, Ducks Unltd., 2007, Vietnam Vets. Meml. Fund, 2007; grantee State Fla. Dept. Transp. planning grantee, Regional Emergency Med. Svcs., 1975. Mem.: DAV (Comdrs. Club), APHA, ASPA (chpt. 102 coun. 1989—98), Fla. Environ. Health Assn., Neuropathy Assn., Nat. Alliance for Mentally Ill, Nat. Environ. Health Assn., Am. Coll. Grad. Med. Edn., Am. Legion, Vietnam Vets. Am., U. N.C. Sch. Pub. Health Alumni Assn. (bd. dirs. 1994—2001), Paralyzed Vets. Am. (life Cert. of Appreciation 2007). Republican. Lutheran. Avocations: reading, skeet shooting, machairology. Home and Office: 104 Vision Ct Palm Beach Gardens FL 33418-3859 Personal E-mail: holl1543@bellsouth.net.

HOLLOWAY, ERNEST LEON, retired university president; b. Boley, Okla., Sept. 12, 1930; m. Jan. 19, 1957; children: Ernest L., Reginald, Norman. BS, Langston U., 1952; MS, Okla. State U., 1955; EdD, U. Okla., 1970. Tchr., prin. Boley H.S., 1952-62; with Langston U., 1963—, profl. sci. higher edn., 1978—, v.p. adminstrn., 1975-77, acting pres., 1977-78, pres., 1979—2005. Mem. bd. advisors pres. Bush's Historically Black Colls. and Univs.; cons. in field. Elected to Okla. Afro-Am. Hall of Fame, 1987, Okla. Educators Hall of Fame, 1996; inducted into Okla. Higher Edn. Hall of Fame, 1999, Okla. State U. Alumni Assn.'s Hall of Fame, 2001; recipient Thurgood Marshall Scholarship Fund Edn. award, 2002, Career Achievement award, U. Okla. Mem. Okla. Higher Edn. Alumni Coun., Nat. Assn. State Univs. and Land-Grant Colls., Nat. Assn. Equal Opportunity in Higher Edn., Langston U. Alumni Assn., Alpha Phi Alpha, Phi Delta Kappa, The Lions Club, Imperial Coun. and Shriners. Home Phone: 405-466-3751; Office Phone: 405-466-3201. Personal E-mail: elholloway@sbcglobal.net.

HOLLOWAY, GORDON ARTHUR, lawyer; b. Wichita, Kans., July 27, 1938; s. George Arthur and Margurite (Bondurant) H.; m. Carol H. Criss, Sept. 1, 1960; children: Gregory Arthur, Suzanne Criss, Garrett Austin. BBA, U. Tex., 1960, JD, 1963. Bar: Tex. 1963, Colo. 1993. Assoc. McGregor, Sewell, Junell & Riggs, Houston, 1963-71; ptnr. Sewell and Riggs, Houston, 1971-93, Holloway & Rowley, 1994—. Staff sgt. Air N.G., 1964-71. Mem. Am. Bd. Trial Advocates (diplomate), Nat. Assn. Railroad Trial Counsel, Internat. Assn. Defense Counsel, Tex. Bd. Legal Specialization (cert. personal injury, civil trial law, qualified atty.-mediator), Houston Club, Intertel. Office: Holloway Rowley & Cafisch, PC 1415 Louisiana St Ste 2550 Houston TX 77002-7378 Office Phone: 713-751-0055. Personal E-mail: gordonholloway@swbell.net. Business E-Mail: gholloway@hrc-law.com.

HOLLOWAY, JACQUELINE, county commissioner; b. Knoxville, Tenn., Mar. 16, 1935; d. Clyde Herbert and Ernestine Cooper; m. George Rudolph Holloway, July 21, 1951; children: Lynda, George Jr., Michelle, Cheryl, Ingrid. AA in Bus., Cooper Inst., Knoxville, 1961; cert., U. Tenn. Ctr. Govt. Tng., 1990. Cert. pub. adminstr. U. Tenn. Biol. technician Oak Ridge Nat. Lab., Tenn., 1963—96; county commr. Anderson County, Clinton, Tenn., 1990—2002; with Tenn. Jud. Coun., 2004—. Chmn. Families First Coun., 1997—; vice chair Am.'s Promise, 1999—; bd. dirs. Anderson County Health Coun., 2000—, chmn., 2002, Quality Childcare Initiative, Tenn. Nutrition and Consumer Edn. Program; v.p. Coalition Oak Ridge Ret. Employees, 2000—03; v.p. cmty. problem solving United Way Anderson County; mem. Anderson County Headstart Policy Coun.; mem. exec. com. Anderson County Dems.; pres. Dem. Women, Tenn., 1996—98; v.p. Dem. Fedn., Tenn., 1996—2003; bd. dirs. Clinch River Home Health. Mem. Tenn. County Commn. Assn. (bd. dirs. 1991-2002), Tenn. County Svcs. Assn. Methodist. Home and Office: 102 Artesia Dr Oak Ridge TN 37830-7817 E-mail: G32284@aol.com.

HOLLOWAY, JAMES LEMUEL, III, foundation executive, retired military officer; b. Charleston, SC, Feb. 23, 1922; s. James Lemuel and Jean Gordon (Hagood) H.; m. Dabney Hix Rawlings, Dec. 14, 1942; children: Lucy Dabney Lyon, Jane Meredith. BSEE, Naval Acad., Annapolis, 1942. Cert. naval aviator, naval nuclear reactor operator. Commd. ensign USN, 1942, served in destroyers, WWII Atlantic and Pacific, 1942-45, carrier jet fighter pilot, Korean War Republic of Korea, 1951—53; comdr. jet squadron USS Valley Forge Lebanon Landings Quemoy-Matsu Def., 1958-59; comdr. 1st nuclear carrier Enterprise USN, Vietnam, 1965-67, advanced through grades to adm., 1973; comdr. carrier striking force U.S. 6th fleet Syrian invasion Jordan, 1970; comdr. U.S. 7th fleet USN, Vietnam, 1971-73, vice chief naval ops., 1973-74, mem. Joint Chiefs of Staff, Dept. Def., 1974-78, chief naval ops., 1974-78, ret., 1978; pres. Coun. Am.-Flag Ship Operators, Washington, 1981-88, Naval Hist. Found., Washington, 1982-98, chmn., 1998—. Def. and fgn. policy cons. Paine Weber, Inc., 1980-88; chmn. Dept. of Def. Spl. Rev. Group investigating Iranian hostage rescue, 1981; exec. dir. Presdl. Task Force on Combatting Terrorism, 1985; spl. envoy V.P. Bush to Middle East, 1986; commr. Predl. Blue Ribbon Commn. on Def. Mgmt., 1985, congl. Commn. on Mcht. Marine and Def., 1987-88, Presdl. Commn. on Long Term Integrated Strategy, 1987-88; U.S. rep. to South Pacific Commn., 1990-94. Tech. advisor: (film) Top Gun, 1985; author: Aircraft Carriers at War, 2007; contbr. articles to mags. Trustee St. James Sch., Md., 1962—, pres., 1989—, chmn. 1996, chmn. emeritus, 2001; bd. dirs. Olmsted Found., Washington, 1978-2000; mem. bd. advisors The Citadel, 1981-86; chmn. academic adv. bd. U.S. Naval Acad., 1983-91; chmn. Hist. Annapolis Found., Inc., 1986-96, chmn. emeritus, 1996—; pres., chmn. Naval Acad. Found., 1994-2001, chmn. emeritus, 2001—; trustee George Marshall Found., 1988-96; dir. Atlantic Coun., 1987-96; bd. visitors and govs. St. John's Coll., 1995, Bd. Mariners Mus., Newport News, Va., 1995-97, dir. emeritus. Decorated Bronze Star, Air medals (3), Legion of Merit (2), DFC, Def. DSM with 2 oak leaf cluster, Navy DSM with 4 oak leaf clusters, Order of Rising Sun (Japan), Grand Cross (Fed. republic Germany), Legion of Honor (France), Rank of Commandeur, 31 others; recipient Triennial Modern Patriot award SAR, 1994, Disting. Pub. Svc. award Navy League, 1996, Disting. Patriot award SAR, 1999, Disting. Grad. award U.S. Naval Acad., 1999, 2000; elected Nat. Wrestling Hall of Fame, 1998; named to Naval Aviation Hall of Honor, 2004. Mem. Assn. Naval Aviation (pres. 1982-91, chmn. 1991-96, chmn. emeritus 2004), Met. Club (Washington gov. 1988—, pres. 1992), Golden Eagles, Brook Club (N.Y.C.), N.Y. Yacht Club (N.Y.C.), Md. Club (Balt.), Annapolis Yacht Club, Soc. Cin., Alfalfa Club (Washington). Republican. Episcopalian. Avocation: sailing. Office Phone: 202-678-4431. Personal E-mail: xcocvan65@aol.com.

HOLLOWAY, JOHN EARLY, lawyer; b. Hampton, Va., Jan. 28, 1959; s. Gordon Duane and Patricia Grier Holloway; m. Andrea Burzyk Holloway, Apr. 15, 1989; children: Robert Forrest, Andrew McCabe. BS in Biology, Va. Mil. Inst., Lexington, 1981; JD, George Mason U., Arlington, 1987. Bar: Va., N.C., U.S. Supreme Ct., U.S. Ct. Appeals (4th cir.), U.S. Dist. Ct. (ea. dist.) Va. Law clk to Hon. Robert G. Doumar U.S. Dist. Ct. (ea. dist.) Va., Norfolk, Va., 1987—88; assoc. Hunton & Williams LLP, 1987—96, ptnr., 1996—. Hon. consul Icelandic Fgn. Ministry, 1999—. Author: To Wear the Ring, 1982. Bd. mem. Edmarc, Inc., Portsmouth, Va., 1996—. Capt. USMC, 1981—87, Grenada, Beirut. Decorated Navy Achievement medal USMC. Office: Hunton & Williams LLP 500 E Main Norfolk VA 23510 Office Phone: 757-640-5360.

HOLLOWAY, JOSH, actor; b. Calif., July 20, 1969; m. Yessica Holloway. Studied, Univ. Ga. Actor: (films) Cold Heart, 2001, Moving August, 2002, Mi Amigo, 2002, My Daughter's Tears, 2002, Sabretooth, 2002, Dr. Benny, 2003; (TV series) Lost, 2004— (Outstanding Performance by an Ensemble in a Drama Series, Screen Actors Guild award, 2006), NCIS, CSI. Named hottest hunk on TV, In Touch Weekly mag., 2006. Office: Rough Diamond Mgmt 1424 N Kings Rd West Hollywood CA 90069 Office Phone: 343-848-2900. Office Fax: 323-848-8142.

HOLLOWAY, PAUL FAYETTE, retired aerospace transportation executive; b. Hampton, Va., June 7, 1938; s. Eldridge Manning and Minnie Powell H.; m. Barbara Jane Menetch, June 23, 1956; children: Paul Manning (dec.), Eric Scott. BS, Va. Poly. Inst. and State U., 1960; postgrad., U. Va., 1961, Coll. William and Mary, 1962-63; grad. advanced mgmt. program, Harvard U., 1988; PhD (hon.), Old Dominion U., 1994. With NASA Langley Rsch. Ctr., Hampton, Va., 1960-97, aerospace technologist, 1960-69, space shuttle task group, 1969, chief space sys. divsn., 1972-75; acting dep. assoc. adminstr. Office Aeronautics and Space Tech., 1977, dir. for space, 1975-85, dep. dir., 1985-91, dir., 1991-96, acting dep. adminstr., 1992-93, ret., 1997. Cons. in field. Mem. editl. bd. Jour Spacecraft and Rockets, 1972-77, editor in chief, 1978-80; contbr. articles to profl. jours. Mem. Poquoson (Va.) Planning Commn.; v.p. local PTA; mem. coll. bd. Thomas Nelson C.C., 1997-2001. Recipient Outstanding Leadership medal NASA, 1980, Exceptional Svc. medal, 1981; Presdl. Rank award for meritorious exec., 1981, Presdl. Rank award for disting. exec., 1987, 93, Equal Opportunity medal, 1992, Disting. Svc. medal, 1992; named Peninsula Engr. of Yr., Peninsula Engrs. Club, 1996; elected to Va. Tech. Acad. Engring. Excellence, 2002. Fellow AIAA (v.p. publs. 1991-94), Am. Astronautical Soc.; mem. Internat. Acad. Astronautics, Sigma Gamma Tau. Methodist. Home: 16 N Westover Dr Poquoson VA 23662-1424 E-mail: pholloway@erols.com.

HOLLOWAY, RALPH LESLIE, anthropology educator; b. Phila., Feb. 6, 1935; s. Ralph L. and Marguerite (Grugan) H. BS in Geology, U. N.Mex., Albuquerque, 1959; PhD in Anthropology, U. Calif., Berkeley, 1964. Asst. prof. anthropology Columbia U., NYC, 1964-69, assoc. prof., 1969-73, prof., 1973—. Author: Brain Endocasts: The Paleoneurological Evidence, vol. 3 of Human Fossil Record, 2004; editor: Primate Aggression, Territoriality and Xenophobia: A Comparative Perspective, 1974; contbr. numerous articles to profl. jours. Recipient Ctr. for Rsch. into the Anthrop. Found. Tech., Ind. U. Ann. award for Outstanding Rsch., Craft award, 2002, Wilton Krogman award for disting. achievement in biol. anthropology U. Pa., 2004; Guggenheim Found. fellow, 1974; NSF grantee, 1984. Fellow AAAS, N.Y. Acad. Sci.; mem. Am. Anthrop. Assn., Am. Assn. Phys. Anthropologists, Soc. for Neurosci., Sigma Xi, Phi Beta Kappa. Avocations: trumpet, trombone, gardening, photography, genealogy. Office: Columbia U Dept Anthropology New York NY 10027 Office Phone: 212-854-4570. Office Fax: 212-854-7347. Business E-Mail: rlh2@columbia.edu.

HOLLOWAY, ROBERT CHARLES, musician, composer; b. Balt. s. George Albert and Edna Mildred (Smith); m. Leslee R. Seymour, June 4, 1960; children: Bruce, Collin, Christy, Heather, Deven, Duana. Arranger, orchestrator Alvin Ailey Dance Co., 1987; pres. Chelsea Music Svc., Inc., NYC, 1990-92. V.p. St. Croix Records. Arranger, orchestrator for ABC-TV, CBS Radio, NBC Tonight Show, Radio City Music Hall, Children's TV Workshop Sesame Street, USN Band, Boston Pops Orch., PS Classics, San Antonio Symphony, Denver Symphony, Pacific N.W. Ballet; orchestrator Le Ballet de Coeurs commd. by San Francisco Ballet, (film) Edith Piaf: Her Story.Her Songs; (Broadway musicals) Odyssey, Barnum, Peter Pan, Dancin', Sophisticated Ladies, On Your Toes, Jerome Robbins Broadway; (performers) Skitch Henderson, Enrique Madriguera, Richard Hayman, Tommy Tune, Betty Carter, Eddie Fisher, Caterina Valente, Connie Francis, Raquel Bitton, Philip Chaffin, Vt. Jazz Ensemble, Jazz Experience; composer: Prelude, Busybody, Southern Suite, Improvisations in Jazz, Celebration, Eastern Slope, Wildcat, Bone Fracture. Mem. ASCAP, Am. Soc. Music Arrangers, Am. Fedn. Musicians. Avocation: boxing. Home: 1079 Forest Rd Alstead NH 03602 E-mail: bobholloway@cheshire.net.

HOLLOWAY, ROBERT WESTER, radiochemist; b. Morrilton, Ark., Jan. 3, 1945; s. Otho and Bessie Vance (Woolverton) H.; m. Mary Ella Hamel, Dec. 31, 1970 (div.); children: David, Jason; m. Marina Borovik, March 28, 2003 BS, Harding Coll., 1967; postgrad., U. Okla., 1968; PhD, U. Ark., 1977. Asst. prof. U. Ark., Pine Bluff, 1976-79; research chemist DuPont Corp., Aiken, S.C., 1979-81; supervisory chemist EPA, Las Vegas, 1981-94; pres. Nev. Tech. Assocs., Inc., 1994—. Contbr. articles to profl. jours. Served to capt. USAF, 1967-72. Mem. Am. Chem. Soc., Health Physics Soc., Toastmasters, Optimists. Republican. Avocation: sailing. Office: Nev Tech Assocs Inc PO Box 90748 Henderson NV 89009-0748 Personal E-mail: holloway3@aol.com. Business E-Mail: roberth@ntanet.net.

HOLLOWAY, WILLIAM JUDSON, JR., federal judge; b. 1923; AB, U. Okla., 1947; LLB, Harvard U., 1950; LLD (hon.), Oklahoma City U., 1991. Ptnr. Holloway & Holloway, Oklahoma City, 1950—51; atty. Dept. Justice, Washington, 1951—52; assoc., ptnr. Crowe and Dunlevy, Oklahoma City, 1952—68; judge US Ct. Appeals (10th cir.), Oklahoma City, 1968—84, chief judge, 1984—91, sr. judge, 1992—. Mem.: FBA, ABA, Oklahoma County Bar Assn., Okla. Bar Assn. Office: US Ct Appeals 10th Cir PO Box 1767 Oklahoma City OK 73101-1767*

HOLLOWELL, JOHN W., retired urologist; b. Norfolk County, Va., July 5, 1922; s. Edward Caleb Hollowell and Marian Louise Leggett; m. Mary Louse Akert, Jan. 17, 1953; children: Heather, Mary Louise, Lesley, John. BS, Coll. William and Mary, Williamsburg, Va., 1943; MD, U. Va., Charlottesville, 1946. Diplomate Am. Bd. Urology, 1955. Resident Roosevelt Hosp., NYC, 1949—52. Cons. urology US Naval Hosp., Portsmouth, Va., 1960—85; pres. Portsmouth Acad. Medicine, 1969—70. Contbr. scientific papers to profl. jours. Chmn. Portsmouth Planning Commn., 1982—85; bd. dirs Ea. Va. Health Sys. Agy., 1976—81, Tidewater Health Care, Va., 1988—92. Lt. USNR, 1942—49, Va. Recipient Disting. Svc. award, Gen. Assembly Va., 1993. Mem.: AMA, Med. Soc. Va. (pres. 1991—92), Rotary Club (life; pres. 1978—79, Paul Harris fellow 1988). Republican. Episcopalian. Avocations: sailing, gardening.

HOLLY, KRISZTINA J., entrepreneur, academic administrator; b. Mar. 1967; BS in Mech. Engring., MIT, 1989, M in Mech. Engring., 1992. V.p. Stylus (bought by Artisoft), 1993—96; with River Run Media, 1996—99, Direct Hit Technologies (acquired by Ask Jeeves in 2000), 1999—2002; founding exec. dir., Deshpande Ctr. for Tech. Innovation MIT, 2002—06; vice provost, exec. dir. U. So. Calif. Mark and Mary Stevens Inst. Tech. Entrepreneurship and Commercialization, 2006—. Judge MIT Ann. $50K Bus. Plan Competition; bd. dir. MIT Enterprise Forum. Co-author: Visual Basic Telephony; contbr. articles to profl. publs. Named to New England Mountain Bike Trail of Fame; recipient Shimano Action Figure award, Heidi Davis award. Mem.: Internat. Bicycling Assn. (bd. dir.), New England Mountain Biking Assn. (former pres.). Achievements include with MIT Media Lab team, developed the world's first computer-generated, full-color reflection hologram; co-designed and built head-eye vision robot and developed a robotic weld-seam-tracking program for the NASA space shuttle main engine; in 1991, co-wrote a business plan for MIT that won an Entrepreneurial Competition; with Michael Cassidy and John Barrus, invented and patented, "The Stylus", a system that enabled a user to scan bar codes to order items such as groceries in 1993; with Michael Cassidy and Chris Brookins, created Visual Voice, the first Windows based computer telephony development tool. Avocations: mountain biking, backcoutry skiing, recreational trail advocate. Office: U Park Campus Office of Provost University of Southern California Los Angeles CA 90089

HOLLY, MICHAEL ANN, director; BA, Herbert & William Smith Colls., Geneva, NY, 1973; PhD, Cornell U., Ithaca, NY, 1981. Prof. Herbert & William Smith Colls., 1983—87; prof., chair U. Rochester, NY, 1987—99; dir. rsch. Clark Art Inst., Williamstown, Mass., 1999—. Author: Panofsky Foundations of Art History, 1984, Past Looking, 1997. Grantee, NEH, 1987, Guggenheim Found., 1991—92. Mem.: Coun. Libr. & Informatics Resources, Coll. Art Assn. (bd. dirs. 2000—03).

HOLLY, TIMOTHY ARNOLD, security firm executive; b. Chgo., Nov. 17, 1948; s. Timothy A. Holly and Marry Elizabeth Bozeman-Holly; m. Cynthia Andrea Scarborough, Nov. 23, 1969; children: Zakia S.E. Haile-Holly, Sordaka S.E. Haile-Holly, El-Mahdi El-Daoud E. Haile-Holly, Kafia D.E. Haile-Holly. B in Polit. Sci., Ind. U., 1977; M in Polit. Sci., U. Notre Dame, 1978; M in Law and Diplomacy, Tufts U., 1980; JD, John Marshall Law Sch., 2002. Mem. faculty U. Mass., Boston, 1978—80; rsch. staff Inst. Internat. Investment and Fgn. Trade, Washington, 1980—82; chief investment officer Royal Asset Mgmt. Co., Atlanta, 1987—92; chmn. Jefferson Acquisition Group, Inc., Atlanta, 1992—2002; chmn., CEO Red Alert Group, Inc., Atlanta, 2002—. Contbg. writer Horn of Africa Jour., NYC, 1978—80, gen. editor Fletcher Forum: Jour. Internat. Affairs, Medford, Mass., 1979—80. Founder, chmn. Bros. and Others Against Prostate Cancer, Inc., Atlanta, 2001—05; sch. rep. Assn. Profl. Schools Internat. Affairs, Washington, 1979—80. Fellow, Dorothy Compton Found., 1978—79; Dean's scholar, Fletcher Sch. Law and Diplomacy, 1979—80. Mem.: Nat. Assn. Securities Profls., Nat. Def. Transp. Assn., Fedn. Am. Scientists, Am. Soc. Indsl. Security, Internat. Assn. Counterterrorism and Security Profls., So. Ctr. Internat. Studies. Republican. Avocations: international law, intelligence, political risk analysis, counterterrorism, islamic culture. Office: Red Alert Group Inc 4279 Roswell Rd Ste 102 Atlanta GA 30342 Office Phone: 404-256-6531. Office Fax: 404-256-6532. E-mail: ceo@redalertgroup.com.

HOLLYER, A(RTHUR) RENE, lawyer; b. Wykoff, NJ, July 28, 1938; s. Richard W. and Florence (Vervaet) H.; m. Lauraine Dennis, Apr. 8, 1978; children: James Richard, Jennifer Ashley. BA, Williams Coll., 1961; MPA, Woodrow Wilson Sch., Princeton, 1963; LLB, Columbia U., 1966. Bar: N.J. 1966, U.S. Dist. Ct. N.J. 1966, N.Y. 1968, U.S. Dist. Ct. (so. and ea. dists.) N.Y. 1969, U.S. Ct. Appeals (3rd cir.) 1970, U.S. Ct. Appeals (2d cir.) 1971, D.C. 1972, U.S. Supreme Ct. 1974. Law sec. to judge chancery divsn. NJ Superior Ct., Newark, 1966-67; assoc. Olwine, Connelly, Chase, O'Donnell & Weyher, NYC, 1968-70, 72-74; asst. US atty. Dist. NJ, 1970-71; ptnr. Hollyer, Brady, Barrett & Hines, L.L.P. and predecessor firms, NYC, 1974—2007, Butzel Long, 2007—. Mem.: Assn. of Bar of City of NY (profl. discipline com. 1990—92, chmn. complaint mediation panel 1991—92, ethics com. 1992—95, profl. discipline com. 1995—98, profl. responsibility com. 1998—2001, mem. profl. discipline com. 2001—04, 2007—), NY State Bar Assn. (mem. com. procedures for judicial discipline 2001—07, mem. spl. com. to review code of jud. conduct 2003—07, NYC bar del. to NY State Bar House Del. 2003—07). Home: 50 Hamilton Rd Glen Ridge NJ 07028-1109 Office: Hollyer Brady Barrett & Hines LLP 551 5th Ave New York NY 10176-0001 Office Phone: 212-818-1110. Personal E-mail: arh-esq@worldnet.att.net. Business E-Mail: hollyer@butzel.com.

HOLLYFIELD, JOHN SCOGGINS, lawyer; b. Harlingen, Tex., Aug. 20, 1939; m. Penny Pounds, Dec. 27, 1962; children: Jon Scott, Courtney. Bar: Tex. 1968. Assoc. Fulbright & Jaworski, Houston, 1968—75, ptnr., 1975—2001, of counsel, 2001—. Lt. USNR, 1961-65. Recipient Pres.'s award Houston Bar Assn., 1986. Mem. ABA (coun. real property sect. 1986-93, sec. 1993-94, vice chair real property divsn. 1994-96, chair 1997-98, ho. of dels. 1999—2004), Am. Coll. Real Estate Lawyers (pres. 1990-91), Anglo-Am. Real Property Inst. (chair 2001). Office: Fulbright & Jaworski LLP 1301 Mckinney St Houston TX 77010-3095 Office Phone: 713-651-3717. Business E-Mail: jhollyfield@fulbright.com.

HOLM, SIR IAN, actor; b. Sept. 12, 1931; s. James Harvey and Jean (Wilson) Cuthbert; m. Lynn Mary Shaw, 1955 (div. 1965); m. Sophie Baker, 1982 (div. 1986); m. Penelope Wilton, 1991 (div. 2001); m. Sophie de Stempel, Oct. 25, 2003. Student, Royal Acad. Dramatic Art, 1950-53; LittD (hon.), U. Sussex, 1999. Actor with Shakespeare Mem. Theatre, 1954-55; in repertory, 1956; toured in Titus Andronicus, 1957; numerous roles Royal Shakespeare Co. including Henry V, Romeo and Richard III, 1958-67; plays include Moonlight, 1993, Landscape, 1994, King Lear, 1997 (Evening Std. award for Best Actor, Olivier award Best Actor and Critics Cir. award, 1998); film appearances include The Fixer, 1967, Young Winston, Alien, Chariots of Fire (named Best Supporting Actor, Cannes Film Festival, 1981, A Severed Head, Brit. Acad. Film and TV Arts, 1982, Acad. Award nomination Best Supporting Actor, 1982), Greystoke, Brazil, Dance With A Stranger, 1985, Wetherby, 1985, Dreamchild, 1985, Another Woman, 1988, Henry V, 1990, Hamlet, 1990, Kafka, 1991, The Naked Lunch, 1992, Blue Ice, 1992, Hour of The Pig, 1993, The Madness of King George, 1994, Lochness, 1994, Mary Shelley's Frankenstein, 1995, Big Night, 1995, Night Falls on Manhattan, 1995, The 5th Element, 1996, A Life Less Ordinary, 1996, The Sweet Hereafter, 1996 (Genie Best Actor award), Existenz, 1998, Simon Magus, 1998, The Match, 1998, Esther Kahn, 1999, Joe Gould's Secret, 1999, Beautiful Joe, 1999, From Hell, 2000, Lord of the Rings: The Fellowship of the Ring, 2001, The Lord of the Rings: The Return of the King, 2003, The Day After Tomorrow, 2004, Garden State, 2004, The Aviator, 2004, The Treatment, 2005, The Lord of War, 2005, Beyond Friendship, 2005, Strangers With Candy, 2005, Ratatouille (voice), 2007; TV appearances include The Lost Boys (Best Actor award Royal TV Soc., 1979), Strike, 1981, (miniseries) Game, Set and Match, 1988, The Last Romantics, 1991, (series) The Borrowers, 1992-93, others; TV appearances include Landscape, BBC, 1995, King Lear, BBC, 1997, Alice Through the Looking Glass, Channel 4, 1998, The Last of the Blonde Bombshells, 2000, The Emperor's New clothes, 2000. Awarded Knighthood by Queen of Eng.; recipient Tony award for Best Supporting Actor, 1967, Evening Std. award, 1967, 93, 97, Genie award, 1997, Olivier award, 1998. Office: First and Second Fl Offices 296 Sandycombe Rd Surrey TW9 3NG England Office Phone: 020-8332 1003. Office Fax: 020-8332 1127.

HOLM, JOY ALICE, goldsmith, psychology professor, artist, educator; b. Chgo., May 21, 1929; d. Alvin Herbert and Willette Eugenia (Miller) Holm. BFA, U. Ill., 1952; MS in Art Edn. Inst. Design, Ill. Inst. Tech., 1956; PhD in Edn., U. Minn., 1967. Tchr. art, Eng. West Chgo. H.S., 1952—54; instr., tchr. art J.S. Morton H.S. and Jr. Coll., Cicero, Ill., 1954—65; asst. prof. art & design Mankato (Minn.) State U., 1965—66; asst. prof. art Ill. State U., Normal, 1966—69; assoc. prof. art & design So. Ill. U., Edwardsville, 1969—71; assoc. prof. art, art edn. Winona (Minn.) State U., 1971—75; assoc. prof., chmn. dept. art St. Mary's Coll. of Notre Dame, Ind., 1975—76; assoc. prof. art & design, secondary, continuing edn. U. Wis., Eau Claire, 1976—78; assoc. prof. art & design Sch. Art & Design Kent (Ohio) State U., 1978—80; lectr. Jungian studies C.G. Jung Inst., Chgo., 1980—82; adj. assoc. prof. art edn. Sch. Art and Design, Sch. Edn. U. Ill., Chgo., 1981—82; lectr. U. Calif. Ext., Santa Cruz, 1983—; adj. prof. art edn., design San Jose (Calif.) State U., 1983—84; owner bus. designer-goldsmith Oak Park, Ill., 1980—82, Carmel, Calif., 1982—87, Atelier XII, Winona, 1988—. Curriculum cons. North Ctrl. Assn. Accreditation Team State of Ill., Edwardsville, 1970; regional cons. Supt. Pub. Instrn., Springfield, Ill., 1970; juror exhbns.; panelist, spkr., presenter confs., meetings. Contbr., cons. Alternative Medicine: A Definitive Guide, 1994; contbg. author: Living Science, 2003, Top 100 Scientist of 2005; contbr. articles to profl. jours; one-woman shows at J. Sterling Morton HS & Jr. Coll., 1963, Russell Art Gallery, Bloomington, 1968, Owatonna (Minn.) Art Ctr., 1980, 86; exhbns. include La Grange (Ill.) Art League (Best of Show, 1st Place award prints), 1963-64, Minn. Mus. Art, 1974-75, Craft & Folk Art Mus., L.A., 1978, The Gallery Kent State U., 1978-79, Saenger Nat. Small Sculpture and Jewelry Exhibit, 1978, Diamonds Internat., NY, 1978, Inst. Design Alumni, 1988, Internat. Biographical Ctr. Congress Exhbn., Edinburgh, Scotland, 1994, others. Fellow World Lit. Acad.; mem. AAUP, Nat. Art Edn. Assn. (rep. Wis. Women's Caucus Houston Conf. 1978, higher edn. divsn. 1961—), Am. Assn. Higher Edn., Coll. Art Assn., Soc. N.Am. Goldsmiths, Gemological Inst. Am., C.G. Jung Inst. (Chgo.), Hon. Soc. Illustrators (hon.), Internat. Soc. Study of Subtle Energies and Energy Medicine, Inst. Noetic Scis., Order of Internat. Fellowship, Alpha Lambda Delta (hon.), Phi Kappa Phi (hon.). Methodist. Office: Atelier XII PO Box 183 Winona MN 55987-0183

HOLMAN, ARTHUR STEARNS, artist; b. Bartlesville, Okla., Oct. 25, 1926; s. Newton Davis and Barbara (Hendry) H. BFA, U. N.Mex., 1951; postgrad., Hans Hofmann Sch., 1951, Calif. Sch. Fine Arts, San Francisco, 1953. One-man shows include Esther Robles Gallery, L.A., 1960, David Cole Gallery, San Francisco, 1962, 80, De Young Mus., San Francisco, 1963, San Francisco Mus., 1963, Gumps Gallery, San Francisco, 1964-66, 69, 87, Marin Civic Ctr. Gallery, 1970, 95, William Sawyer Gallery, San Francisco, 1971, 73, 74, 76, John Bolles Gallery, Santa Rosa, Calif., 1982, Braunstein, Quay Gallery, San Francisco, 1992, The Art Foundry, Sacramento, Calif., 2003; exhibited in group shows at San Francisco Mus., 1960-76, Downey Mus., L.A., 1961, 50 Calif. Artists, Whitney Mus., N.Y.C., Walker Art Ctr., Albright-Knox Gallery, Des Moines Art Ctr., 1962, U. N.C. Annual, 1965, Smithsonian Instn., Washington, 1977, Coll. of Marin, 1983, Hall of Flowers, San Francisco, 1985, 86, 20th Century Landscape Drawings, De Young Mus., San Francisco, 1989, Jan Holloway Gallery, San Francisco, 1989, Bolinas (Calif.) Mus., 1997, San Francisco Art Inst., 2001, Marin Civic Ctr. Gallery, 2005, San Geronimo Valley Art Ctr., Calif., 2006; represented in permanent collections, San Francisco Mus., Oakland Mus., Mills Coll., Stanford U., Eureka Coll., Achenbach Found., San Francisco, Rene DiRosa Art Preserve, Napa, Calif. With USAAF, 1945-46. Address: PO Box 72 Lagunitas CA 94938-0072

HOLMAN, BUD GEORGE, lawyer; b. NYC, June 30, 1929; s. Harry and Fannie Abrams (Bass) H.; m. Kathleen Barbara McLean, Sept. 1, 1961; children: Jennifer Jean, Wayne George. BBA, CCNY, 1950; LLB, Yale U., 1956. Bar: N.Y. 1956, Conn. 1979, D.C. 1982. Law sec. to judge N.Y. Ct. Appeals, 1956-58; practice in NYC, 1958—; ptnr. Kelley Drye & Warren (and predecessor firms), 1965—. Pres., chmn. bd. dirs. Sixty Sutton Corp., 1969-97; lectr. Practising Law Inst., Wage Price Inst., Young Pres. Orgn. Editor: The Bar, 1949-50, Yale Law Jour., 1955-56. Trustee U.S. Naval Acad. Found., 1978—85; bd. dirs. USO Met. N.Y., 1978—2004. Mem. Naval Res. Assn. (pres. 3d naval dist. chpts. 1973-75, mem. nat. adv. coun. 1975-94), Am. Arbitration Assn. (bd. dirs., mem. exec. com. 1991-2003), Navy League (bd. dirs. coun. N.Y. chpt. 1979-99), Yale U. Law Sch. Assn. (mem. exec. com. 1987-90, 93-96, bd. dirs.), Yale Law Sch. Assn. N.Y.C. (bd. dirs.), Met. Club, Yale Club, Beta Gamma Sigma. Democrat. Office: Kelley Drye & Warren LLP 101 Park Ave New York NY 10178-0002 Home: 60 Sutton Pl S New York NY 10022 Home Phone: 212-752-7288; Office Phone: 212-808-7729. Personal E-mail: holmanbg@aol.com. Business E-Mail: bholman@kelleydrye.com.

HOLMAN, CHARLES RAYMOND, osteopathic physician; b. Green City, Mo., July 18, 1924; s. Squire Paul and Meeda May (Daniel). Student, N.E. Mo. State U., 1943; DO, U. Health Scis., Kansas City, 1949. Intern McDowell Hosp., Phoenix, 1949-50; practice medicine specializing in family practice Kirksville, Mo., 1950-53; Cardwell Hosp., Stella, Mo., 1957-61; resident in anesthesiology Kirksville Osteo. Hosp., 1961-63; practice medicine specializing in anesthesiology Lansing Gen. Hosp., Mich., 1963-73; gen. practice medicine VA Regional Office, Cleve., 1977-81, gen. practice Phoenix, 1981-93; pvt. practice Kirksville, 1993—. Lt. USAF, 1943-45, U.S. Army, 1953-56. Mem. AMA (life), Am. Osteopathic Assn. (life), Assn. Mil. Surgeons U.S. Home: 601 W Illinois St Kirksville MO 63501-1474

HOLMAN, HALSTED REID, physician, educator; b. Cleve., Jan. 17, 1925; s. Emile Frederic and Ann Peril (Purdy) H.; m. Barbara Marie Lucas, June 26, 1949 (div. July 9, 1982); children: Michael, Andrea, Alison; m. Diana Barbara Dutton, Aug. 10, 1985; 1 child, Geoffrey. Student, Stanford U., 1942-43, UCLA, 1943-44; MD, Yale U., 1949. Med. resident Montefiore Hosp., NYC, 1952-55; staff physician Rockefeller Inst., NYC, 1955-60; prof. medicine Stanford (Calif.) U., 1960—, chmn. dept. medicine, 1960-71, co-chief, divsn. family and cmty. medicine, 1987-2001, dir. clin. scholar program, 1969-97, dir. Multipurpose Arthritis Ctr., 1977-97, co-chief, divsn. immunology and rheumatology, 1997-2000, dir. Stanford Program for Mgmt. of Chronic Disease, 1997—2001. Pres. Midpeninsula Health Svc., Palo Alto, Calif., 1975-80; mem. adv. bd. Calif Health Facilities Commn., Sacramento, 1978-81, Office Tech. Assessment, U.S. Congress, 1979-81, Inst. Advancement of Health, NYC, 1982-90; Guggenhime prof. medicine, 1960—; mem. steering com., Pacific Bus. Group on Health Breakthroughs in Chronic Care Program, 2005-; adv.commn. Santa Clara County, 2006-; mem. planning com., Assn. Am. Med. Coll. Calif. Academic Chronic Care Collaborative, 2007-. Author 2 books; assoc. editor Arthritis and Rheumatism, 1995-2000; co-editor Chronic Illness, 2004—; contbr. articles to profl. jours. Recipient Bauer Meml. award, Arthritis and Rheumatism Found., N.Y., 1964, John W. Gardner Vision award, Pathways Found., 2003. Master: Am. Coll. Rheumatology (Presdl. Gold medal 2001); fellow: AAAS (coun. 1974—79), ACP (Laureate award no. Calif. chpt. 1994, John Phillips Meml. award 2004); mem.: Improving Chronic Illness Care-R.W. Johnson Found. (Vision award 2001), Arthritis Found. (Hero Overcoming Arthritis 1998, Engalitcheff award 1999, McGuire Educator award 2000), Western Assn. Physicians (pres. 1966), Am. Soc. Clin. Investigation (pres. 1970), Assn. Am. Physicians. Democrat. Home: 747 Dolores St Stanford CA 94305-8427 Office: Stanford U Divsn Immunol and Rheumatol 1000 Welch Rd Ste 203 Palo Alto CA 94304-1808 Office Fax: 650-723-9656.

HOLMAN, JAMES, allergist; b. Jacksonville, Tex., Aug. 13, 1921; MD, U. Tex. Southwest, 1945. Diplomate Am. Bd. Allergy and Immunology. Intern Parkland Meml. Hosp., Dallas, 1945-46; resident in allergy U. Va., Charlottesville, 1947-48; fellow in medicine U. Tex. Southwest, Dallas, 1946-47, 48-50; with Presbyn. Hosp., Dallas, 1966—. Asst. clin. prof. pharmacology U. Tex. Southwest Med. Sch., 1950-83, clin. assoc. prof. internal medicine, 1981-88. Fellow Am. Acad. Allergy, Asthma and Immunology, Am. Coll. Allergy, Asthma and Immunology, Am. Coll. Clin. Pharmacology and Chemotherapy. Office: 8220 Walnut Hill Ln Ste #101 Dallas TX 75231 Home Phone: 214-363-5551; Office Phone: 214-369-1901.

HOLMAN, JAMES LEWIS, financial consultant, management consultant; b. Chgo., Oct. 27, 1926; s. James Louis and Lillian Marie (Walton) Holman; m. Elizabeth Ann Owens, June 18, 1948 (div. 1982); children: Craig Stewart, Tracy Lynn, Mark Andrew, Bonnie Gwen(dec.); m. Geraldine Ann Wilson, Dec. 26, 1982. BS in Econs. and Mgmt., U. Ill., 1950, postgrad., 1950, Northwestern U., 1954—55. Traveling auditor, then statistician, asst. contr. parent buying dept. Sears, Roebuck & Co., Chgo., 1951—54; asst. to sec.-treas. Hanover Securities Co., 1954—65; asst. to controller chem. ops. divsn. Montgomery Ward & Co., Inc., 1966—68; controller Henrotin Hosp., 1968; bus. mgr. Julian, Dye, Javid, Hunter & Najafi Associated, 1969—81, cons., 1981—84. Vol. cons., adminstrv. asst. Fiji Sch. Medicine, Suva, 1984—86, cons., 1987—89; vol. bus. cons. U.S. Peace Corps, Honduras, 1989, cons., 1989—; cons., dir., sec.-treas Comprehensive Resources Ltd., Glenview, Ill., 1982, Wheaton, 82, Walnut Creek, Calif., 82; sec.-treas. Medtran, Inc., 1980—83; sec. James C. Valenta, P.C., 1979—82; sponsored project adminstr. Northwestern U., Evanston, Ill., 1984. Sec. B.R. Ryall YMCA, Glen Ellyn, Ill., 1974—76; treas. DuPage Symphony, 1955—58; trustee Gary Meml. United Meth. Ch., Wheaton, 1961—69, 1974—77; bd. dirs. B.R. Ryall YMCA, 1968—78, DuPage Symphony, 1954—58, Goodwill Industries, Chgo., 1978—79. With USN, 1944—46. Mem.: Kiwanis (bd. dirs. Chgo. 1956—60, bd. dirs. youth found. 1957—60, pres. 1958—60). Baha'I. Home and Office: 60 N Nicoll Ave #408 Glen Ellyn IL 60137

HOLMAN, J(OHN) LEONARD, retired manufacturing corporation executive; b. Moose Jaw, Sask., Can., Aug. 30, 1929; s. Charles Claude and Lillian Kathleen (Haw) H.; m. Julia Pauline Benfield, July 18, 1953; children: Nancy Jane, Sally Joan. BS in Civil Engring., U. Alta., 1953. Pres. Consolidated Concrete Ltd., Calgary, Alta., Canada, 1969-72; dir., pres. BACM Industries Ltd., Calgary, 1972-76; exec. v.p. Genstar Corp., Calgary, 1976-79, San Francisco, 1980-87, dir. several subs. cos.; pres., CEO CBR Cement Corp., San Mateo, Calif., 1986-88, chmn. bd., 1988-89, ret., 1990. Bd. dirs., officer several nat. trade assns. Mem. Assn. Profl. Engrs. Alta. (life), Calgary Exhbn. and Stampede (hon., life, dir.), Calgary Golf and Country Club. Home: 111 Country Club Estates 111-5555 Elbow Dr SW Calgary AB Canada T2V 1H7 Personal E-mail: johnlholman@shaw.ca.

HOLMAN, L. CHARLENE, elementary school educator; b. Broken Arrow, Okla., May 22, 1964; d. Charles Edward and Nora Mae Sutton; m. Randy Holman, Apr. 12, 1986. BS, Okla. State U., Stillwater, Okla., 1986. Lic. tchr. elem. edn. Ark., 2006. Tchr. Elmdale Elem. Sch., Springdale, Ark., 1995—, coord. title i, esl, migrant, 2000—04, coord. title i and migrant, 2004—05. Mem.: Ark. State Parent Tchr. Assn. (treas.). Home: 8501 White Oak Dr Rogers AR 72756 Office: Elmdale Elementary 420 N West End St Springdale AR 72764 Home Phone: 479-790-6934; Office Phone: 479-750-8859. Personal E-mail: cholman@sdale.org.

HOLMAN, ROBERT ALAN, oceanography educator; s. Donald Morison and Frances Margaret Holman; m. Kathryn Anne Jung, Dec. 20, 1975; 1 child, Sean Fraser. BSc in Math. and Physics, Royal Mil. Coll. Can., 1972; PhD, Dalhousie U., Halifax, Nova Scotia, 1979. Prof. Oreg. State U., Corvallis, 1979—. Named Disting. Prof., Oreg. State U. Found., 2006; recipient Sec. Navy, Chief Naval Ops. Chair in Oceanography, US Navy, 2003—. Mem.: US Naval Inst., Am. Geophys. Union, Oceanography Soc. Achievements include development of Argus program. Office: Oreg State U COAS 104 Ocean Admin Bldg Corvallis OR 97331 Office Phone: 541-737-2914. Business E-Mail: holman@coas.oregonstate.edu.

HOLMBERG, ARTHUR CARL, performing arts educator, theater critic; s. Carl and Victoria Holmberg. BA in Romance Languages with highest honors, Northwestern U., Evanston, Ill., 1965; MA in Comparative Lit., Harvard U., Cambridge, Mass., 1968, PhD, 1975; cert. in Latin Am. Studies, U. Interam., Mex. City, 1963; cert. in French Lit., U. Geneva, 1966; cert. in European Theater, Inst. Avignon, France, 1974. Assoc. prof. Brandeis U., Waltham, Mass., 1994—; lit. dir. Am. Repertory Theatre, Harvard U., Cambridge, Mass., 1996—. Resident dramaturg Am. Repertory Theatre, 1987—89. Author: (critical study) Wilson; contbr. articles to profl. jours.; editor and author: theater history World Encyclopedia of Contemporary Theatre, 1996, The Lively Art, 1999, author newspaper and magazine articles, reviews. Woodrow Wilson fellow, 1965, Travelling fellow, Harvard U., 1970—71, La Carriere fellow, 1970—71, IREX grant, 1985, Mazer Faculty Rsch. grant, Brandeis U., 1966, 2004, Nat. Endowment Humanities fellowship, 2007—. Mem.: Phi Beta Kappa. Office: American Repertory Theatre 64 Brattle St Cambridge MA 02138 Office Phone: 617-495-2668. Office Fax: 617-495-1705. Business E-Mail: arthur_holmberg@harvard.edu.

HOLMBERG, TED, journalist, consultant; b. NYC, July 16, 1931; s. Teodor Holmberg and Elizabeth Codd; m. Mary Susan Bokern, Jan. 4, 1996; children from previous marriage: Ingrid Elizabeth, Erik Burns, Teodor James. BA, Bklyn. Coll., 1952; MS, Columbia U., NY, 1953. Dep. exec. editor, 1st v.p. Providence Jour., 1955—75; editor, pub Kent County Daily Times, West Warwick, RI, 1975—95; pres. Ind. News Corp., West Warwick, 1995—2000. Author: Murder Moons the Beach, 2007. Corp. US Army, 1954—55. Mem.: Columbia County Club, Providence Art Club. Home (Winter): 4715 Jamestown Rd Bethesda MD 20816 Home (Summer): 4494 Post Rd East Greenwich RI 02818 Personal E-mail: tedholmberg@earthlink.net.

HOLME, RICHARD PHILLIPS, lawyer; b. Denver, Nov. 6, 1941; s. Peter Hagner Jr. and Lena (Phillips) H.; m. Barbara June Friel, July 17, 1944; children: Daniel Friel, Robert Muir. BA, Williams Coll., Williamstown, Mass., 1963; JD, U. Colo., 1966. Bar: Colo. 1966, U.S. Dist. Ct. Colo. 1966, U.S. Ct. Claims 1990, U.S. Ct. Appeals (10th cir.) 1966, U.S. Ct. Appeals (1st cir.) 1980, U.S. Dist. Ct. D.C. 1988, U.S. Ct. Appeals (D.C. cir.) 1988, U.S. Ct. Appeals (4th cir.) 1989, U.S. Ct. Appeals (fed. cir.) 1995, U.S. Supreme Ct. 1975. Assoc. Davis, Graham & Stubbs, Denver, 1966-68, ptnr., 1972-87, 91—, mng. ptnr., D.C. office, 1987-91; dep. Denver Dist. Atty., 1969-71. Grievance com. Colo. Supreme Ct., Denver, 1979-85, civil rules com., 1994—, civil justice com., 1998—. Fellow Am. Bar Found.; mem. ABA, ABA Found., Colo. Bar Found., Colo. Bar Assn. (bd. govs. 1974-76, 85-87, 95-99, 2001-03), Denver Bar Assn. (trustee 1977-80, 1st v.p. 1997-98), Order of Coif. Presbyterian. Home: 3944 S Depew Way Denver CO 80235-3105 Office Phone: 303-892-9400.

HOLMEN, ORRIE JEFFREY, electronics company executive; b. Denver, Mar. 17, 1953; s. Orrie Joel and Eunice May (Thompson) H.; m. Mary Jane Wenzel, Apr. 21, 1984; children: Elizabeth Anne, Orrie Joel, Paul Abraham. Student, U. Colo., 1972-75, No. Ill. U., 1971. Lic. 1st class radiotelephone/gen. radiotelephone; cert. netware engr. Mgr. repair La Marche Mfg. Co., Des Plaines, Ill., 1971-72; technician Motorola Corp., Schaumburg, Ill., 1972-74; asst. mgr. Shakey's, Broomfield, Colo., 1973-75; salesman Mktg. Dept., Inc., Broomfield, Colo., 1976; pres. CBTS, Inc., Denver, 1976-78; chmn. U.S. Telephone, Denver, Dallas, Salt Lake City, Chgo. and N. Bridgton, Maine, 1978—. Cons. Marcom, Inc., Salt Lake City, 1983-84; chmn., chief exec. officer Modulex, Inc., 1989—. Author: Operations Manual, 1986, Universal Twisted Pair Wiring, 1988. Supporter Salt Lake City Rescue Mission, 1985-86; active Rep. Presdl. Task Force, 1989—; mem. Rep. Senatorial Inner Circle, 1992—; del. Rep. Conv., 1992, 94. Recipient Rep. Senatorial Medal of Freedom, 1994. Mem. Full Gospel Men's Fellowship Internat. (v.p. 1983-84), Internat. Christian Bus. Leaders, Prosperity Golf Club (Tulsa), Collin County Rep. Men's Club (v.p. 1993). Avocations: reading, scuba diving, skiing, tennis, programming. Office: US Telephone 2201 Waterview Pkwy Richardson TX 75080-2210 also: Modulex 2201 Waterview Pky MD 1 606 Richardson TX 75080-2256

HOLMÉN, REYNOLD ALGOTT EMANUEL, chemist; b. Essex, Iowa, Oct. 23, 1916; s. John Algott and Clara Amelia (Christensen) H.; m. Betty Jane Heginbottom, June 20, 1942 (dec. 1990); children: Karen C., John R., Robert C.; m. Johnnie Mae Leak, Nov. 20, 1993 (dec. 2000). AB, Augustana Coll., Ill., 1936; MS, U. Mich., 1937, PhD, 1949. Rsch. chemist DuPont Co., Phila., also Flint, Mich., 1937-46; sr. rsch. chemist ctrl. rsch. dept. 3M Co., St. Paul, 1948-55, sect. mgr. tech. info. and patent liaison, 1955-57, sect. mgr. inorganic sect., 1957-62, organic scouting mgr., 1959-62, mgr. R&D Lab., Reflective Product divsn., 1962-71, lab. mgr. R&D spl. enterprises dept., 1971-82; v.p. R&D KEMSERCH, Inc., Onamia, Minn., 1984-96; ret. Author: Kasimir Fajans: The Man and His Work, 1990. With med. corps. U.S. Army, 1941. Rackham scholar U. Mich., 1936-37; named to Wisdom Hall of Fame. Mem. Am. Chem. Soc.,

Phi Lambda Upsilon, Sigma Gamma Epsilon. Lutheran. Achievements include 20 U.S. patents; development of first catalytic dehydration of lactic acid to acrylic acid, first catalytic dehydrochlorination of alpha-chloropronic acid to acrylic acid, (with other) first sealed polycellular cube-corner retroreflective sheet, first conterfeit-resistant driver's license adopted by a state, development of first binary packaging film from two disparate solid films joined sans adhesive, improved authenticatable document construction. Home: 240 East Ave Apt 317 Mahtomedi MN 55115-2295 Personal E-mail: reholmen@aol.com.

HOLMER, ALAN FREEMAN, former trade association executive; b. NYC, July 24, 1949; s. A. Freeman and Marcia K. (Wright) H.; m. Joan Mary Ozark, June 30, 1973; children— Scott, Joy AB, Princeton U., 1971; JD, Georgetown U., 1978. Bar: D.C., Oreg. Adminstrv. asst. Senator Bob Packwood, Washington, 1972-78; assoc. Steptoe & Johnson, Washington, 1978-81; dep. asst. to pres. for intergovtl. affairs The White House, Washington, 1981-83; dep. asst. sec. for import adminstrn. Dept. Commerce, Washington, 1983-85; gen. counsel Office of U.S. Trade Rep., Washington, 1985-87; amb. Dep. U.S. Trade Rep., Washington, 1987-89; ptnr. Sidley & Austin, Washington, 1989-96; pres., CEO, Pharm. Rsch. and Manufacturers of Am., Washington, 1996—2005. Adj. prof. Georgetown U. Law Ctr., Washington, 1990; amb. and chmn. U.S. del. to Bonn Econ. Conf., 1990. Author: (with Judith H. Bello) The Antidumping and Countervailing Duty Laws: Key Legal and Policy Issues, 1987, Guide to the U.S.-Canada Free-Trade Agreement, 1990; contbr. numerous articles to profl. jours. Mem. Svcs. Policy Adv. Com., 1991-94; mem. adv. coun. Korea Econ. Inst. Am., 1992-96; trustee Met. D.C. chpt. Cystic Fibrosis Found., 1984-96, pres., 1991-94); bd. dirs. Coun. on Family Health, 1996—, Friends of the Nat. Libr. of Medicine, 1996—, Nat. Health Coun., 1999—. Recipient Disting. Cmty. Svc. award, Princeton Club Washington, 1992, Marriott Lifetime Achievement award, Arthritis Found., 2001. Mem. Internat. Fedn. of Pharm. Mfrs. (mem. coun. 1996—), Coun. Fgn. Rels. Republican.

HOLMES, ANGIE CLARK, lawyer; d. Doug Clark and Sherry Schindler; m. Frank Holmes, June 16, 2001. BS, Tex. Tech U., Lubbock, 1999; JD, Tex. Tech U. Sch. Law, 2001. Bar: Tex. 2002. Asst. dist. atty. Dallas County Dist. Atty.'s Office, 2002—; pvt. practice. Mem. Ct. Apptd. Spl. Advs., Lubbock, 1995—2000. Vol. Boys and Girls Club, Arlington, Tex., 2006, Miss Southlake Scholarship Orgn., Tex., 2005—, interview coach, 2005—. Mem.: Coll. State Bar Tex.

HOLMES, ANN HITCHCOCK, journalist; b. El Paso, Apr. 25, 1922; d. Frederick E. and Joy (Crutchfield) H. Student, Whitworth Coll., 1940, So. Coll. Fine Arts, 1944. With Houston Chronicle, 1942—, fine arts editor, 1948-89, critic-at-large, 1989-98. Author: Presence, The Transco Tower, 1985, Joy Unconfined—Robert Joy in Houston: A Portrait of Fifty Years, 1986, Alley Theater: Four Decades in Three Stages, 1986. Mem. Houston Mcpl. Art Commn., 1965-74; mem. fine arts adv. coun. U. Tex., Austin, 1967—; bd. dirs. Rice Design Alliance, Houston, 1988-91, Alliance Francaise, Houston, 1989-93, Bus. Arts Fund, Houston, 1993-96. Recipient Ogden Reid Found. award for study of arts in Europe, 1953; Guggenheim fellow, 1960-61; recipient Ford Found. award, 1965, John G. Flowers award archtl. writing Tex. Soc. Architects, 1972, 74, 77, 80 Mem.: Am. Theater Critics Assn. (founding mem. 1974, exec. com. 1975—, co-chmn. 1987—88). Home and Office: 10807 Beinhorn Rd Houston TX 77024-3008 Personal E-mail: annhholmes@aol.com.

HOLMES, ANNA-MARIE, ballerina; b. Mission City, BC, Can., Apr. 17, 1942; arrived in U.S., 1981; d. George Henry and Maxine Marie (Botterill) Ellerbeck; m. David Holmes; 1 child, Lian-Marie. Diploma, Royal Conservatory of Music. Tchr. Royal Ballet, London, 2005, Danish Ballet, Denmark, 2005, Toulous Ballet, 2005, Oslo Ballet, Norway, 2006; Royal Ballet Flanders, 2006, Atlanta Ballet, 2006, N.C. Sch. of Arts, 2006; artistic dir. Jacob's Pillow Ballet Program, 2002—06, Internat. Ballet Sch., Italy, 2006; lectr. in field. Dancer (ballets) Swan Lake, Cinderella, Romeo and Juliet, Sleeping Beauty, Bayadere, Laurencia, Paquita, Graduation Ball, Les Sylphides, Prince Igor, Giselle, Nutcracker, Firebird, Raymonda; guest appearances at numerous theatres Berlin Staarts Opera, Royal Albert Hall, London, Roy Alex, Toronto, Ont., Royal Festival Hall, London, Teatro Colon, Buenos Aires, Covent Garden, London; dancer Kirov Ballet, Leningrad, 1963, (films) Tour En L'Air, Ballet Adagio, Don Juan, Chinese Nightingale, numerous appearances on European N.Am. TV; artistic dir., prin. choreographer Tenn. Festival Ballet, Oak Ridge, 1981—, staged ballets Am. Ballet Theatre, —, Theatre of Harlem, —, Boston Ballet, 1984—, Ramonda, Am. Ballet Theatre, Met. Opera House, NYC, 2005, Corsaire, Am. Ballet Theatre, 2006, ballet mistress Ballet Theatre Francais, 1985—, tchr. Boston Ballet Co., 1985—, set Giselle Boston Ballet, 1987—; dancer Don Quixote, 1989—; mng. dir. Performing Arts/Dance Ctr., Oak Ridge, 1982—85; co-dir.: (ballets) Massimo Opera Theatre, 1993; asst. to artistic dir. Boston Ballet, 1989, dean, assoc. dir. Ctr. for Dance Edn., 1993, artistic dir., 1997—2001, guest tchr. Nervi Festival, Genoa, Italy; prodr.(film documentation): Kirov Vagonova Tchg. Sys.; artistic dir. Jackson Internat. Competition Sch., 1990, Internat. Ballet Competition Sch., 1994; choreographer Swan Lake, Tokyo, 1991, Norwegion Nat. Ballet, 1998, Sleeping Beauty Act III, Boston Ballet, 1991, Giselle, 1991, Sleeping Beauty, Boston Ballet, 1993, 1996, Tokyo, 1996, Le Corsaire, Boston Ballet, Am. Ballet Theatre, 1998, Great Performances, 1999, Met. Opera House, N.Y.C., 1999, Don Quixote, Boston Ballet, 2000; co-prodr.: Raymonda Finnish Nat. Ballet, 2003, Premier Am. Ball Theater, 2004; artistic dir. La Bayadere, Flanders-Antwerp Belgium, 2004; dir.: Jacob's Pillow Ballet Program, 2006, Ballet Adriatico, Italy, 2006. Recipient Emmy award, 2000. Office: Carnegie House 100 W 57th St Ste 11-O New York NY 10019 Office Phone: 917-365-5311. E-mail: Aellerbeck@aol.com.

HOLMES, ARTHUR S., manufacturing executive; m. Christy Holmes. BS, MS, Pa. State U.; MBA, Northwestern U. Founder, chmn., CEO Chart Industries, Inc., Cleve., 1989—; chmn. ALTEC Internat. Ltd. Partnership. Bd. dirs. 1st Bank Milw. Mem. bd. advisors Biterbo Coll.; mem. La Crosse Area Devel. Com.; mem. sch. adv. bd. U. Wis. Named Pa. State Disting. Engring. Alumnus, 1993; recipient Pope John XXIII award Viterbo Coll., 1999. Office: Chart Industries Inc 1 Infinity Corporate Centre Dr Ste 300 Cleveland OH 44125-5370 Fax: 440-753-1491.

HOLMES, BERT OTIS E., JR., retired editor; b. Milan, Tenn., Sept. 20, 1921; s. Otis E. and Mary (Lassiter) H.; m. Marian Bush, June 10, 1942 (dec. Nov. 1964); children: Bert Otis E., Richard Bush; m. Helen Hankins, July 24, 1965; children: Chris, David. AA, Magnolia A. and M. Jr. Coll., 1940; BS, So. Meth. U., 1942. Successively copy reader, makeup editor, state editor, city staff reporter, city editor Dallas Times Herald, 1946-56, news editor, 1956-60, asst. mng. editor, 1960-64, exec. editor, 1964-65, assoc. editor, 1965-90. Pres. Family Svc. Agy., 1963-68, Tex. United Community Svcs., 1970-72, Sr. Citizens of Greater Dallas, 1995-96; bd. dirs. Dallas United Fund, Dallas Community Coun.; mem. City of Dallas Sr. Affairs Commn., 2005. With AUS, 1942-46, PTO. Mem. Dallas Assembly, Sigma Delta Chi, Dallas Press Club (pres. 1957, 78-79) Methodist. Home: 4515 W Lawther Dr Dallas TX 75214-1935

HOLMES, BROOX GARRETT, lawyer; b. Mobile, Ala., Nov. 15, 1932; s. Williams Coghlan and Philomene (Boogaerts) H.; m. Laura Claire Hays, Feb. 21, 1955 (dec. 2000); children: Broox Garrett, Dupree Hays, Williams Coghlan II; m. Elsie Crain Lyons, June 5, 2004. BA, U. Ala., 1954, JD, 1960. Bar: Ala. 1960. Since practiced in, Mobile; mem. firm Armbrect Jackson LLP, 1960—. Trustee St. Paul's Episcopal Sch., chmn. bd., 1980-83. Capt. USMCR, 1954-58. Fellow Am. Coll. Trial Lawyers (state chmn. 1991-92), Am. Bar Found.; mem. ABA, Ala. State Bar (bd. commrs. 1987-93, chmn. litigation sect. 1991, pres. 1994-95), Ala. Bar Found., Mobile Bar Assn. (exec. com. 1987-93), Nat. Assn. R.R. Trial Counsel, Internat. Assn. Def. Counsel, Am. Law Inst., Ala. Law Inst., Ala. Def. Lawyers (pres. 1977-78, named one of Best Lawyers in Am. bus. and personal injury litigation), Mobile Country Club (pres. 1983-84), Mobile Touchdown Club, Athelstan Club, Delta Kappa Epsilon, Phi Delta Phi. Episcopalian. Home: 5 Holland Park Mobile AL 36608 Office: Armbrecht Jackson LLP PO Box 290 Mobile AL 36601-0290 Office Phone: 251-405-1300. Personal E-mail: bgh308@aol.com. Business E-Mail: bgh@ajlaw.com.

HOLMES, DALLAS SCOTT, judge, educator; b. LA, Dec. 2, 1940; s. Donald Cherry and Hazel (Scott) H.; m. Patricia McMichael, Aug. 21, 1965; children: Mark Scott, Tobin John. AB cum laude, Pomona Coll., 1962; MS, London Sch. Econs., 1964; JD, U. Calif., Berkeley, 1967. Bar: Calif. 1968. Assoc. Best, Best & Krieger, Riverside, Calif., 1968-74, ptnr., 1974-96; mem. Calif. Jud. Coun., 1995-96; adj. prof. Hastings Coll. Law U. Calif., San Francisco, 1990; exec. asst. to Assembly majority fl. leader, Calif. State Legislature, Sacramento, 1969-70; asst. adj. prof. Grad. Sch. Mgmt., U. Calif.-Riverside, 1977-88; lectr. UCLA Ext., 1987-2002; Superior Ct. judge, 1996—; chair Riverside Superior Ct. Jury Com., 1997-2003, 2005—; chair Calif. jud. coun. task force jury sys. improvements, 1998-2003; mem. bd. trustees, U. Calif., Riverside Found., 1983-2006; city atty. City of Corona, Calif., 1976-96; lectr. jud. local govt. and univ. ext. groups. Pres., Pomona Coll. Alumni Coun., 1973-74, Century Club, Riverside, 1974-76, Citizens Univ. Com., 1983-85, Downtown Riverside Assn., 1987-88, Torchbearers Pomona Coll., 1995-96; chmn. legal affairs com. Assn. Calif. Water Agys., 1985-91. Mem. bd. govs. State Bar Calif., 1990-93, v.p. 1992-93. Named Man of Yr., Riverside Press-Enterprise, 1962, Young Man of Yr., Riverside Jr. C. of C., 1972. Mem. Riverside County Bar Assn. (pres. 1982), Calif. State Bar Assn. (exec. com. pub. law sect. 1983-86), Am. Judicature Soc. (jury ctr. adv. com.), Riverside Rotary Club. Republican. Presbyterian. Contbr. articles on mass transit, assessment of farmland in Calif., exclusionary zoning and environ. law to profl. jours.; author proposed tort reform initiative for Calif. physicians. Office: Riverside Superior Ct 4050 Main St Riverside CA 92501-3702 Office Phone: 951-955-1482.

HOLMES, DAVID LYNN, religion educator; BA in English, Mich. State U.; MA in English, Columbia U.; MA, PhD in Religion, Princeton U.; postgrad., Columbia U., Union Theol. Sem., NYC, Duke U. Div. Sch.; DHL (hon.), Lycoming Coll., 2000. Prof. religious studies coll. of William and Mary, Williamsburg, Va., 1965—, Walter G. Mason prof. religious studies, 2005—. Instr. Carnegie-Mellon U.; vis. prof. U. Va. Author: A Brief History of the Episcopal Church, 1993, The Life of Devereux Jarratt, 1995, A Nation Mourns, 1999, The Religion of the Founding Fathers, 2003, The Faiths of the Founding Fathers, 2006, others; past ch. revs. editor: Anglican and Episcopal History; contbr. articles to profl. jours. Exec. bd. dirs. Coun. for America's First Freedom. Recipient Outstanding Faculty award, Commonwealth Va. Mem. Am. Soc. Ch. History (past exec. coun.), Hist. Soc. Episcopal Ch. (past exec. bd. dirs.), Ptnrs. for Sacred Places, Episcopal Guild of Scholars, Bishop James Madison Soc., Phi Beta Kappa. Democrat. Episcopalian. Office: Coll William and Mary Dept Religious Studies Sir Christopher Wren Bldg Williamsburg VA 23187-8795 Home Phone: 434-295-7030; Office Phone: 757-221-2177. Business E-Mail: dlholm@wm.edu.

HOLMES, DAVID RICHARD, JR., cardiologist; b. Oak Park, Ill., Nov. 21, 1945; s. David R. and Ethel B. Holmes; m. Virginia Mary Zuehlke; children: David, Joshua, Nathaniel, Jessica. BA, Princeton U., 1967; MD, Marquette U., 1971. Intern Virginia Mason Hosp., Seattle, 1971-72; fellow internal medicine and cardiology Mayo Clinic, Rochester, Minn., 1972-76, physician, 1978—, dir. cardiac catheterization lab., dir. ACC/SVS renal and iliac stenting project, 2001—, Edward W. and Betty Knight Scripps prof. cardiovasc. medicine, 2003. Mem., bd. dirs. Franciscan Skemp Hospital, 2005. Capt. USN, 1976-78. Recipient Internal Medicine Achievement award Mayo Grad. Sch., 1974; Transcatheter Therapeutics Career Achievement award Wash. Cardiology Ctr., 1995, Eugene Drake award, 2006, Dist. Scientist award Am. Coll. Cardiology, 2006, Eugene Drake award, 2006. Fellow Am. Coll. Cardiology (cardiac catheterization com. 1994-96, edn. program com., co-dir. interventional symposium 1999-2000, chmn. procedures tng. work 1999, pres.-elect Minn. chpt. 2003, trustee 2004, Disting. Scientist award 2006); mem. Soc. Cardiac Angiography and Interventions, Minn. Soc. Internal Medicine, Am. Heart Assn., Assn. Univ. Cardiologists, Interventional Andreas Gruentzig Soc. (inaugural mem.), Sigma Xi, Alpha Omega Alpha. Business E-Mail: holmes.david@mayo.com.*

HOLMES, EDWARD WARREN, dean, medical educator; b. Winona, Miss., Jan. 25, 1941; s. Edward and Mary (Hart) H.; m. Judith L. Swain, Jan. 25, 1980. BS, Washington and Lee U., 1963; MD, U. Pa., 1967. Intern Hosp. of U. Pa., 1967-68; resident in medicine Duke U. Med. Ctr., Durham, NC, 1970—71, 1973—74, fellow in metabolism, 1971—73; prof. medicine and biochemistry Duke U. Sch. Medicine, Durham, NC, 1974-91, chief divsn. metabolism, endocrinology and genetics, 1983—91; investigator Howard Hughes Med. Inst., 1974-87; prof., chmn. dept. medicine U. Pa., Phila., 1991-97; sr. assoc. dean rsch. Stanford U. Sch. Medicine, 1997-2000; dean Duke U. Sch. Medicine, Durham, 1999—2000; vice chancellor academic affairs Duke U. Med. Ctr., Durham, 1999—2000; vice chancellor health scis., dean sch. medicine U. Calif., San Diego, 2000—. Reviewer in molecular medicine. With USPHS, 1968-70. Grantee NIH. Mem. Am. Soc. Clin. Investigation, Assn. Am. Physicians. Office: Univ Calif Sch Medicine 1313 Basic Sci Bldg 9500 Gilman Dr La Jolla CA 92093-0602 Office Phone: 858-534-1501. Office Fax: 858-822-0084. E-mail: lfelix@ucsd.edu.

HOLMES, FONTAYNE, library director; BA in History magna cum laude, UCLA, 1964, MLS, 1966. Std. tchg. credential with a specialization in jr. coll. tchg. UCLA, 1979. Sr. libr., head interlibrary loan and mgr. West LA Regional br. LA Pub. Libr., 1984—87, asst. dir. brs., 1988—98, dir. ctrl. libr., 1998—99, dir. libr. facilities divsn., 1999—2002, asst. city libr., 2002—04, city libr., 2004—, South Pasadena Pub. Libr., 1987—88. Contbr. articles to profl. publs. Bd. dirs. Libr. Found. LA. Mem.: ALA (chair intellectual freedom roundtable nominating com. 1982, mem. pay equity com. 1986—87), Urban Librs. Coun. (SirsiDynix Urban Player award for Outstanding Libr. and Cmty. Leadership 2007), Calif. Libr. Assn. (chair intellectual freedom com. 1981, pres. young adult reviewers of So. Calif. 1978—80), Phi Beta Kappa. Office: LA Pub Libr Ctrl Libr 630 W 5th St Los Angeles CA 90071 Office Phone: 213-228-7515. Office Fax: 213-228-7519. E-mail: fholmes@lapl.org.*

HOLMES, HARRY DADISMAN, health care administrator; b. Houston, Aug. 8, 1944; s. Harry Newton and Ruth Eleanor (Dadisman) H.; m. Jaleea George, May 15, 2004; children: Colin George, Hillary Hunt, Ashley Elizabeth. BA, Rice U., 1966; MA, La. State U., 1968; PhD, U. Mo., 1973. Asst. prof. urban devel. U. Tenn., Knoxville, 1973—76; asst. to exec. v.p. Tex. Med. Ctr., Inc., Houston, 1976—80; dir. govt. affairs, orgnl. liaison U. Tex. System Cancer Ctr., Houston, 1980—90; asst. to pres. U. Tex. Sys. Cancer Ctr., Houston, 1981—90; v.p. govt. rels. U. Tex. M.D. Anderson Cancer Ctr., Houston, 1990—2006, pres. govtl. interface strategies, 2006; sr. v.p. Tex. Med. Ctr., 2006—. Pres., bd. dirs. City of Houston Higher Edn. Fin. Corp., 1985-; mem. Cancer Ctrs. Adminstrs. Forum, 1994—; mem. select com. on pub. issues Greater Houston Hosp. Coun., 1983-94; mem. exec. adv. bd. White, Petrov and McHone, 1987-95; mem. pub. rels. adv. coun. Tex. Med. Ctr., 1985—; founder Houston Biotech. Assn., 1986; mem. exec. com. Nat. Comprehensive Cancer Networks, 1998—2006; chair public issues com. Assn. Am. Cancer Insts., 1999-2006; mem. govt. rels. com. Am. Hosp. Assn., 1999-2000; govt. rels. com., vice chmn. Tex. Healthcare and Biosci. Inst., 2005; pres. bd. dirs. City of Houston Health Facilities Corp., City of Houston Indsl. Devel. Corp., Nat. Coalition Cancer Rsch., 2005. Mem. adminstrv. bd. St. Luke's Meth. Ch.; mem. Mayor's Task Force on Pvt. Sector Initiatives for Houston, 1981-82, Houston C.C. Found. Bd., 1992—, Greater Houston Partnership State and Fed. Com., 1989—; mem. U. Tex. Tex./Mex. Border Health Task Force, 1989-2003, exec. com., 1989-2001; pres. Houston Health Facilities Corp., 2000—, Houston Indsl. Devel. Corp., 2000—; mem. Rice U. Fund Coun., 1991-94, Nat. Cancer Ctrs. Task Force, 1991—; mem. steering com. Tex. Colorectal Cancer Plan; mem. exec. bd. Leadership Houston, 1983-86, Houston Ctr. for Humanities, 1983-86; mem. govt. rels. com. Greater Houston Hosp. Coun., 1985-95; mem. com. Instnl. Task Force on Oncology in Chile, 1986-87; exec. com. Instnl. Strategic Planning Com., 1986-95; divsn. chmn. United Way of Houston, 1983. Home: 4203 Coleridge St Houston TX 77005 Office Phone: 713-791-6182.

HOLMES, HENRY ALLEN, diplomat, educator; b. Bucharest, Romania, Jan. 31, 1933; (parents Am. citizens); s. Julius Cecil and Henrietta (Allen) H.; m. Marilyn Janet Strauss, July 25, 1959; children: Katherine Anne, Gerald Allen. AB, Princeton U., NJ, 1954; Woodrow Wilson fellow, U. Paris, 1958. Intelligence rsch. analyst Dept. State, Cameroon, 1958-59, commd. fgn. svc. officer, 1959, assigned to Am. Embassy Yaoundé, Cameroon, 1959—61, Rome, 1963-67, counselor polit. affairs Am. embassy Paris, 1970-74, sr. exec. Seminar in Fgn. Policy Washington, 1974-75; assigned as dir. Office NATO and Atlantic polit. mil. aff. Bur. European Affairs, Washington, 1975-77; dep. chief mission U.S. Embassy Dept. State, Rome, 1977-79, prin. dep. asst. sec. state for European and Can. affairs Washington, 1979-82, amb. Am. embassy Portugal, 1982-85, asst. sec. Bur. Politico Mil. Affairs Washington, 1985-89, amb. at large for burdensharing, 1989-93, asst. sec. def. for spl. ops. and low-intensity conflict, 1993-99; adj. prof. Georgetown U., 2000—. Served as capt. USMC, 1954-57. Mem. Am. Fgn. Svc. Assn., Coun. Fgn. Rels., Am. Acad. Diplomacy, Washington Inst. Fgn. Affairs, Metro Club (Washington). Episcopalian. Personal E-mail: hallenholmes@aol.com.

HOLMES, HENRY W., lawyer; b. Malden, Mass., Apr. 1, 1943; s. Henry W. Holmes BA, San Diego State U., 1966, JD, 1969. Bar: Calif. 1970, U.S. Dist. Ct. (cen. dist.) Calif. 1970, U.S. Ct. Appeals (9th cir.) 1970. Lawyer Pacht, Ross, Warne, Bernhard & Sears, LA, 1972-78; prin. Schiff, Hirsch & Schreiber, Beverly Hills, Calif., 1978-79; ptnr. Butler, Davidson & Holmes, Beverly Hills, Calif., 1979-84; counsel Cooper, Epstein & Hurewitz, Beverly Hills, Calif., 1984-94; sports and entertainment lawyer Weissman, Wolff, Bergman, Coleman, Silverman, and Holmes, Beverly Hills, Calif., 1994—2002, Greenberg Traurig LLC, Santa Monica, Calif., 2002—. Spkr. in field; adj. prof. sports UCLA; adj. prof. sports law Pepperdine U. Law Sch. Contbr. articles to profl. jours. Trustee US Women's Sports., NY, 1984—97; bd. dirs. Calif. Wildlife Ctr. Named one of Top 20 Sports Lawyers, Daily Jour., 1993, cover of So. Calif. Super Lawyers, 2005; fellow Ford Found., New Delhi, 1969—70. Mem. SAG, Beverly Hills Bar Assn., L.A. Bar Assn., Calif. Bar Assn., Am. Somoa Bar Assn., Explorer's Club. Roman Catholic. Avocations: surfing, acting, art appreciation, scuba diving. Home: 6784 Dune Dr Malibu CA 90265 also: 2450 Colorado Ave 400 East Santa Monica CA 90404-3575 Home Phone: 310-584-1973; Office Phone: 310-586-7858. Business E-Mail: holmesh@gtlaw.com.

HOLMES, JACK EDWARD, political science professor; b. Wichita, Kans., May 16, 1941; s. Herbert Paul and Marguerite Elizabeth (Duerr) H.; m. Linda Sue Pacheco, Dec. 28, 1996; stepchildren: Valerie, Cynthia, Jacqueline, Elizabeth. BA, Knox Coll., 1963; MA, U. Denver, 1967, PhD in Internat. Studies, 1972. Asst. prof. Hope Coll., Holland, Mich., 1969-72; dist. asst. Congressman Don Brotzman, Denver, 1973-75; asst. prof. Hope Coll., Holland, 1975-76, assoc. prof., 1976-87, prof., 1987—, chmn. dept. polit. sci., 1988—95, 1999—2004. Author: Mood/Interest Theory of American Foreign Policy, 1985; co-author: American Government Essentials and Perspectives, 1991, 94, 98. Campaign chmn. Ottawa County Reps., Holland, 1978, 82-96, chmn., 1997-2002, Ottawa County Bush for Pres, 2000, 2004; del. Rep. Nat. Conv., 2000; chmn. 2d Congl. Dist. Rep. Party, 2003-07. Capt. U.S. Army, 1967-69. Named to Mich. Model UN Hall of Fame. Mem. Internat. Studies Assn., Am. Polit. Sci. Assn., Holy Cross Wilderness Def. Fund. Presbyterian. Avocations: backpacking, fishing. Office: Hope Coll 208 Lubbers Hall Holland MI 49422-9000 Home Phone: 616-896-9764; Office Phone: 616-395-7543. Business E-Mail: holmes@hope.edu.

HOLMES, JAMES HILL, III, lawyer; b. Birmingham, Ala., Sept. 10, 1935; s. Houston Eccleston and Celia Lindsey (Wearn) Holmes; m. Julia (Judy) Ryman, Aug. 17, 1963; children: James H. IV, Randell Ryman, Tucker Malone. BBA, So. Meth. U., 1957, LLB, 1959. Bar: Tex. 1959, U.S. Ct. Mil. Appeals 1960, U.S. Dist. Ct. (no. dist.) Tex. 1963, U.S. Dist. Ct. (ea. dist.) Tex. 1966, U.S. Dist. Ct. (we. dist.) Tex. 1979, U.S. Ct. Appeals (5th and 11th cirs.) 1981, U.S. Supreme Ct. 1974. Ptnr. Burford & Ryburn, Dallas, 1962—. Mock trial participant Tex. Nurses Assn., 1978—86; spkr. State Bar Tex. Profl. Devel. Program, 1987—2002; co-chair adv. com. professionalism Supreme Ct. Tex., 1989—90; law sch. rep. So. Meth. U., alumni assn. bd. dirs., 2005—. Contbr. articles to profl. jours. Past mem. University Park (Tex.) Bd. Adjustment; chmn. University Park (Tex.) Planning and Zoning Commn., 1988—94; numerous other offices in civic orgns.; city councilman City of University Park, 1994—2000, 2002—04, mayor pro tem, 1998—2000, mayor, 2004—; past dir. Child Guidance Clinic; past bd. dirs. Park Cities Town North YMCA; trustee Tex. Ctr. Legal Ethics & Professionalism, 2001—03; vice chmn. adminstrv. Tex. Ctr. Legal Ethics and Professionalism, 2001—03; past dir., past pres. All Sports Assn., Dallas, 1977; pres. University Park Cmty. League, 1987—88. With USAF, 1959—62. Named one of Tex. Super Lawyers, Tex. Monthly, 2003, 2004, 2005, 2006, 2007; recipient Presdl. Citation, State Bar of Tex., 1995, Judge Sam Williams Local Bar Leadership award, 2001, Professionalism award, Coll. of the State Bar Tex., 1999, Morris Harrell Professionalism award, Dallas Bar Assn. and Tex. Ctr. for Ethics and Professionalism, 2000, Lola Wright Found. award, 2002, Jo Anna Moreland Outstanding Com. Chair award, DBA, 2002, 2003, Disting. Alumni award atty. in pvt. practice, So. Meth. U. Law Sch., 2004—05. Fellow: Tex. Bar Found., Am. Coll. Trial Lawyers; mem.: Dallas Bar Found., Patrick E. Higginbotham Am. Inn of Ct. (master 1989—95), Am. Bd. Trial Advocates (pres. Dallas chpt. 2000, named Tex. and Dallas chpts. Trial Lawyer of Yr. 2004), Tex. Bar Assn., Dallas Bar Assn. (numerous coms.), Def. Rsch. Inst. (state chmn. 1994), Internat. Assn. Def. Counsel, Assn. Def. Trial Attys., Tex. Assn. Def. Counsel (pres. 1992—93, Founder's award 1997), Dallas Assn. Def. Counsel (chmn. 1975), Blue Key, Phi Delta Theta, Phi Alpha Delta. Episcopalian. Avocations: jogging, spectator sports, outdoors. Home: 3804 Lovers Ln Dallas TX 75225 Office: Burford & Ryburn LLP 3100 Lincoln Pla 500 N Akard St Dallas TX 75201-6697 Office Phone: 214-740-3114. Business E-Mail: jholmes@brlaw.com.

HOLMES, JEAN LOUISE, real estate investor, humanities educator; b. Butler, Mo., Dec. 9, 1943; d. Victor Julius and Helen Emilia (Knapheide) Witte; m. Eugene Philmore Carter Jr., Aug. 21, 1965 (div. Aug. 1992); children: Kristin, Lance; m. Reed M. Holmes, Jan. 26, 1993. AA, Graceland Coll., Lamoni, Iowa, 1963; BA, Iowa State U., 1965; postgrad., U. Paris, 1965, Tufts U., 1973; MA in Judaic Studies magna cum laude, Hebrew Coll., Brookline, Mass., 1989; postgrad., Ratisbonne Ctr. of Judaic Studies, Jerusalem, 1993-95, Hebrew U./Yad Vashem, 1992-95, Yad Vashem/Poland, 1998. Lic. bldg. constrn. supr. Mass. Tchr. French, Iowa, Mass., 1966-69; tchg. English lang. and lit. Iowa, 1966-67; real estate broker Carter Realty, Pepperell, Mass., 1975—; pres., mgr. Viewpax Mondiale, Independence, Mo., 1982—; pres. Keshet Hashalom, Jerusalem, 1989—. Clk. Ctrl. Middlesex Multiple Listing Svc., Concord, Mass., 1980-81, v.p., 1982, pres., 1983; lectr. Remembering for the Future II, Berlin, 1994, Internat. Holocaust Scholars Conf., Mpls., 1996; dir., adj. prof. student intercultural travel to Israel, Jordan, Egypt, Park U., Mo., Graceland U., 1982—. Co-author: The Forerunners, 2003. Adv. bd. Peace Ctr., Independence, 1989-91; interfaith rels. com. Cmty. of Christ, Independence, 2000—04; dir. Maine Friendship House, 2003—; exec. com. Nat. Christian Leadership Conf. for Israel, 2001—. Recipient Friendship award Israel Ministry of Tourism, Jerusalem, 1992, Maine Preservation award, 1866 Maine Friendship House, Jaffa Am. Colony, 2004. Avocations: photography, archaeology, literature, travel. Home: PO Box 763 Pepperell MA 01463 Personal E-mail: jaffacolony@yahoo.com.

HOLMES, JEROME A, federal judge; b. Washington, Nov. 18, 1961; BA cum laude, Wake Forest U., 1983; JD, Georgetown U., 1988; MPA, John F. Kennedy Sch. Govt., Harvard U., 2000. Bar: Washington, DC 1991, Okla. 1997, Pa. 1988, US Supreme Ct. 1998, US Dist. Ct (we. dist.) Okla. 1999, US Dist. Ct (no. dist.) Okla., US Dist. Ct (ea. dist.) Okla. 2005. Law clk. to Hon. Wayne E. Alley US Dist. Ct. (we. dist.) Okla., 1988—90; law clk. to Hon. William J. Holloway US Ct. Appeals (10th Cir.), 1990—91; assoc. Steptoe & Johnson LLP, 1991—94; asst. US atty. (we. dist.) Okla. US Dept. Justice, 1994—2005; dir. Crowe & Dunlevy, PC, Oklahoma City, 2005—06; judge US Ct. Appeals (10th cir.), 2006—. Recipient John McTigue Essay award, 1988, Am. Jur award in Consumer Protection, 1988. Mem.: Okla. Bar Assn. Bd. Govs. (v.p.). Office: US Ct Appeals 333 W 4th St Ste 4-562 Tulsa OK 74103*

HOLMES, JOHN LEONARD, retired chemistry professor; b. London, Eng., Nov. 29, 1931; came to Can., 1958; s. Leonard Thomas and Jessie Ethel (Doble) H.; m. Una Jane Watts, Dec. 12, 1958 (div. 1993). children: Susan P., Jonathan B.; m. Sheila Jean Robertson, Apr. 13, 1994; stepchildren: John Fergus, Isobel Clare. BSc, London U., 1954, PhD, 1957, DSc, 1983. Postdoctoral fellow NRC, Ottawa, Can., 1958-60; I.C.I. fellow Edinburgh U., Scotland, 1960-61, lectr., 1961-62; asst. prof. U. Ottawa, 1962-65, assoc. prof., 1965-73, prof., 1973-97, emeritus prof., 1997—. Nuffield vis. prof. U. Ghana, 1971, Overbeek vis. prof. U. Utrecht, The Netherlands, 1979, Disting. vis. scholar U. Adelaide, Australia, 1984; vis. fellow Australian Nat. U., Canberra, 1993, 2000; internat. sci. exchange fellow U. Bern, 1993. Author (with C. Aubry and P. Mayer) Assigning Structures to Ions in Mass Spectrometry., 2007; editor Organic Mass Spectrometry Jour., 1976-93, European Mass Spectrometry jour., 1994-2001; contbr. over 300 articles to profl. jours. Recipient Barringer Rsch. award Can. Spectroscopy Soc., 1980, Excellence in Rsch. award, U. Ottawa, 1986, Chem. Inst. Can. medal, 1989, Herzberg award Can. Spectroscopy Soc., 1990, F.P. Lossing award Can. Mass Spectrometry Soc., 2000. Fellow Chem. Inst. Can. (medal 1989), Royal Soc. Can.; mem. Am. Soc. Mass Spectrometry, Brit. Soc. Mass Spectrometry (life), Internat. Yacht Racing Union (judge 1986-99), Can. Yachting Assn., Royal Yachting Assn. Clubs: Britannia Yacht (Ottawa). Avocations: yachting, sailing, reading, walking. Home: 121 Buell St Unit 58 Ottawa ON Canada K1Z 7E7 Office Phone: 613-562-5118. E-mail: jholmes@science.uottawa.ca.

HOLMES, KATIE (KATHERINE NOELLE HOLMES), actress; b. Toledo, Ohio, Dec. 18, 1978; d. Martin and Kathy Holmes; m. Tom Cruise, Nov. 18, 2006, 1 child, Suri. Actor: (films) The Ice Storm, 1997, Disturbing Behavior, 1998, Go!, 1999, Teaching Mrs. Tingle, 1999, Wonder Boys, 2000, The Gift, 2000, Phone Booth, 2002, Abandon, 2002, The Singing Detective, 2003, Pieces of April, 2003, First Daughter, 2004, Batman Begins, 2005, Thank You for Smoking, 2006; (TV series) Dawson's Creek, 1998—2003. Office: c/o BWR Pub Rels 9100 Wilshire Blvd West Tower 6th Fl Beverly Hills CA 90210

HOLMES, KING KENNARD, medical educator; b. St. Paul, Sept. 1, 1937; AB, Harvard Coll., 1959; MD, Cornell U., 1963; PhD in Microbiology, U. Hawaii, 1967. Diplomate Am. Bd. Internal Medicine, infectious diseases. Resident U. Wash., Seattle, 1967-68, chief resident, 1968-69, from instr. to assoc. prof. medicine, 1969-78, vice chmn. dept. medicine, 1984-89, prof. medicine, 1978—, dir. Ctr. AIDS and Sexually Transmitted Diseases, 1989—. Head divsn. pulmonary diseases USPHS Hosp., Seattle, 1969-70, asst. chief dept. medicine, 1969-83, head divsn. infectious diseases, 1970-83; dir. Sexually Transmitted Disease Clinic, Harborview Med. Ctr., 1972-79, chief med., 1984-89; mem. numerous adv. coms. Nat. Inst. Allergy & Infectious Diseases, NIH, USPHS, WHO, NAS; prin. investigator NIH, Nat. Cancer Inst., Nat. Inst. Allergy & Infectious Diseases, Nat. Inst. Child Health & Human Devel., Ctrs. Disease Control, 1983—. With USN, 1965-67. Recipient Squibb award Infectious Disease Soc. Am., 1978, Thomas Parran award Am. Venereal Disease Assn., 1983. Fellow ACP, Royal Coll. Physicians Eng.; mem. AMA, Inst. Medicine-NAS, Assn. Am. Physicians, Am. Epidemiol. Soc., Am. Fedn. Clin. Rsch. Office: U Wash Str AIDS & STDs Harborview Med Ctr 325 9th Ave MS# 359931 Seattle WA 98104-2420 Fax: 206-731-3694.

HOLMES, KRISTEN JONES, academic administrator; b. Huntsville, Ala., Oct. 3, 1971; d. Donald Wayne and June Evelyn (Johnston) Jones; m. David Paul Holmes, Dec. 27, 1993. BA in Polit. Sci., Haverford Coll., Pa., 1993; MA in Journalism, U. Ala., Tuscaloosa, 1998; postgrad., Auburn U., Ala. Legal asst. St. John and St. John, Attys., Cullman, Ala., 1993—97; office mgr., editor Harold See Campaign for Ala. Supreme Ct., Tuscaloosa, 1996; rsch. asst. U. Ala., Tuscaloosa, 1998; publs. and proposals asst. PE LaMoreaux & Assocs., Environ. Cons., Tuscaloosa, 1997—99; editor Cullman.com, Cullman, 1999; exec. officer Cullman County Home Builders Assn., Cullman, 1999—2000; media rels. coord. Wallace State C.C., Hanceville, Ala., 2000—03, dir. comms. and mktg., 2004—. Adj. instr. Wallace State C.C., Hanceville, 1999—2000; pres. Cullman City Schs. Found., 2003—05; sec. Cultural Arts Com., Cullman, 2002—04; past pres. Cullman City Schs. Found., 2005—06; group leader ednl. trip to France and Spain, 2006; group leader ednl. trip to London and Scotland, 07. Coord. Adopt-a-Mile Cullman County People Against a Littered State, 2001—03; vol. caretaker family arrivals Our Lady of the Angels Monastary, Hanceville, 2003—; mem. legis. affairs com. Cullman Area C. of C., 2000. Named Media Person of Yr., Ala. C.C. Conf., 2004; named to 2006-2007 Class of Ala. C.C. Leadership Acad.; recipient Pyramid award, Ala. Coll. Sys. Pub. Rels. Assn., 2004, 2005, 2006, Medallion award, Nat. Comms., Mktg. and Publs. Assn. Dist. II, 2005, 2006. Mem.: Nat. Comm. Mktg. and Publs. Assn. (bd. dirs. 2004—06), Nat. Comms., Pub. Rels. and Mktg. Assn., Ala. Press Assn. Avocations: rowing, reading, running, travel, horseback riding. Office: Wallace State C C 801 Main St NW Hanceville AL 35077

HOLMES, LARRY, SR., retired boxer; b. Cuthbert, Ga., Nov. 3, 1949; s. John and Flossie Holmes; children: Misty, Lisa, Belinda, Kandy, Larry Jr. Student public schs. Formerly worked in car wash, quarry, rug mill, foundry; profl. boxer, 1973—. Owner, founder Larry Holmes Enterprises, Larry Holmes Ringside Restaurant. Author: (autobiography) Against All Odds; subject: (documentaries) In the Arena. Heavyweight champion World Boxing Council, 1978-83, Internat. Boxing Fedn., 1983-85. Achievements include winning 19 of 22 amateur fights. Undefeated for a record 13 years. Office: Larry Holmes Enterprises 91 Larry Holmes Dr Ste 200 Easton PA 18042

HOLMES, LEONARD GEORGE, psychologist; b. Roanoke, Va., May 31, 1954; s. George Washington and Mary Maxine (Templeton) H.; m. Susan Rose Tankersley, June 19, 1976; children: Allison Gayle, Mary Kathleen. BA in Psychology and Religious Studies with high distinction, U. Va., 1976; MS in Clin. Psychology, Fla. State U., 1979, PhD, 1981. Lic. clin. psychologist, Va. Psychology intern William S. Hall Psychiat. Inst., Columbia, S.C., 1980-81; lectr., clin. psychologist Ctr. for Psychol. Svcs., Coll. of William and Mary, Williamsburg, Va., 1981-88, asst. dir., 1984-88; pvt. practice in clin. psychology Williamsburg, 1984—. Adj. asst. prof. psychology Coll. William and Mary, 1991—; cons. V.A. Med. Ctr., Hampton, 1985-90, coord. behavioral physiology lab., 1990—, dir. chronic pain program, 1992—; psychologist Sentara Psychol. Group, Newport News, Va., 1988-90; clin. psychologist Behavioral Medicine Inst., 1990-98; clin. psychologist Family Psychiat. Svcs., Hampton, 1998-2000; adj. asst. prof. Ea. Va. Med. Sch., 1995—; webmaster Netpsychology, 1996—, About.com Mental Health Guide, 1997-2006; founder, CEO Healing Sites Network, LLC Univ. fellow Fla. State U., 1977-78, 79-80. Mem.: Am. Psychol. Soc. Avocations: gardening, computers, fishing, hiking. Home: 102 Barlows Run Williamsburg VA 23188-9326 Office: VA Med Ctr 116B Hampton VA 23667 Office Phone: 757-722-9961 2215. Personal E-mail: leonard.holmes@gmail.com.

HOLMES, LOUIS IRA, physician assistant, educator, photojournalist; b. LA, July 16, 1943; s. Louis Issac and Mabel Jane (Walsh) H.; children: Jonathan Joseph, Kimberly Ellen, Louis Boon. AA, El Camino Coll., Torrance, Calif., 1972; cert. physician asst., U. So. Calif., 1978. Cert. Nat. Commn. Cert. Physician Assts.; cert. ACLS. Resident in surgery Norwalk Hosp.-Yale U. Sch. Medicine, 1980; nursing staff emergency dept. South Bay Dist. Hosp., Redondo Beach, Calif., 1970-75; nursing staff trauma and surg. intensive care Harbor Gen. Hosp.-UCLA Med. Ctr., Torrance, 1976-77; physician asst. Gen. Med. Corp., LA, 1979; physician asst., divsn. thoracic surgery City of Hope Med. Ctr., Duarte, Calif., 1980-81; sr. physcian asst. thoracic and cardiovascular surgery Bert Meyer MD, et al, LA, 1981-91; sr. physician asst. cardiothoracic surgery, instr. postgrad. cardiothoracic surgery residency program Cedars-Sinai Med. Ctr., LA, 1991-95; asst. prof. clin. surgery and family medicine U. So. Calif., LA, 1995—, phys. asst. in cardiothoracic surgery, 1995—. Vis. surg. instr., China; examiner Nat. Commn. on Cert. of Physician Assts., 1981—92; mem. program planning com. Masters Degree program in Health Sci. for Physician Assts., Calif. State U., Dominguez Hill, 1991—95; adj. faculty physician asst. program U. So. Calif., 1982—90, mem. adv. com., 1983—84, mem. long-range planning com., 1988—90; spkr., cons., expert witness in field; contbr. numerous color photographic images The Green Berets: Weapons and Equipment (Hans Halberstadt), 1999; bd. dirs. TV Parade Mag., 1991—2001; mem. adv. bd. Homeland Secuirty Policy Inst. Group, Inc., 2003—06; tactical weapons instr. Analytical Cons. for Security and Investigations, 2005—06; NRA cert. instr., pistol and personal def., range safety officer. Contbr. articles to profl. jours. and chpts. to books; mem. editl. bd. Clinician Reviews, 1990-96, Physician Asst. Jour., 1987-90; asst. editor Family Caregiver Mag., 2005-06; med. tech. advisor, appeared in (feature film) City of Angles, TV program on History Channel. Instr. ACLS, Am. Heart Assn., 1980-96. With Spl. Forces, US Army, 1964-70; with Calif. Army N.G., 1976-83, U.S. Army Res., 1984-91. Recipient 21 mil. decorations, including awards from US, Vietnam, Thailand, Outstanding Svc. award Physician Asst. Jour., 1989, Outstanding Svc. award, Keck Sch. Medicine U. So. Calif., 2007. Fellow Soc. Critical Care Medicine (bd. dirs. Calif. chpt. 1995), Am. Acad. Physician Assts. (ho. of dels. 1982-87, vice chair surg. coun. 1985-87, conf. planning com. 1986-88, vets. caucus chair 1986-88, advisor to bd. dirs. 1989-91), Calif. Acad. Physician Assts. (chmn. govt. affairs 1984-86, pres. 1985, Presdl. Leadership award 1986, 88), Am. Assn. Surgeons Assts. (v.p. 1988), Assn. Physician Assts. Cardiovascular Surgery (pres. 1989-91), Mil. Order World Wars (chpt. comdr. 1998-2000), Mil. Surgeons of the US, VFW, Spl. Forces Assn., Spl. Ops. Assn., Chinese Nung Commando Assn., Inc. (founding v.p. 2003-06). Republican. Buddhist. Avocations: photo journalism, running, military history. Office: Cardiothoracic Surgeons Inc 50 Bellefontaine St Ste 403 Pasadena CA 91105 Home: 24 Country Ridge Rd Pomona CA 91766-4815 Office Phone: 323-442-5849. E-mail: commanderlonny@aol.com.

HOLMES, MARK V., judge; b. NY, 1960; BA, Harvard Coll., 1979; JD, U. Chgo. Law Sch., 1983. Bar: New York, DC, US Supreme Ct., DC (2nd, 5th, 9th cir.), Ct. Fed. Claims. Assoc. Cahill, Gordon & Reindel, 1983—85; clk. Hon. Alex Kozinski, 9th Cir., 1985—87; atty. Sullivan & Cromwell, 1987—91; counsel to commrs. US Internat. Trade Commn., Washington, 1991—96; counsel Miller & Chevalier, 1996—2001; dep. asst. atty. gen. tax divsn. US Dept. Justice, Washington, 2001—03; judge US Tax Ct., Washington, 2003—. Mem.: ABA (tax divsn.). Office: US Tax Court 400 2nd St NW Washington DC 20217*

HOLMES, MICHAEL, performing arts company executive, educator; b. Palestine, Tex., June 29, 1939; s. George Washington and Marion Rebecca Holmes. Student, U. Tex. Austin, 1957—60. Tchr. Debbie Reynolds Studio, N. Hollywood, Calif., 1979—87; artistic dir. The Chandler Studio, N. Hollywood, Calif., 1988—. Prof. UCLA, 1989—93; pres., CEO Action/Reaction Theater Corp., LA, 1994—, artistic dir., 1994—, Glendale, Calif., 2003—. Actor(adapter - director): (play) Acting: The First Six Lessons (3 Drama-Logue Awards, 1990, LA Times Outstanding prodn. of the yr. in smaller theater, 1988); performer: (one man show) Michty Peculiar, 2007—; author (director - producer): (play) Ryder (L. A, Valley Theater League, Best Play; Best Dir., 1992), The Ring (4 Drama-Logue Awards; Valley Theater League Best Dir., Best Play, 1994, L.A. Times Recognition of the 10 Most Memorable Prodns. of the Yr., 1995), The Cleaning Man (Critics Choice: The LA Times, 2000); touring (one-man shows) American Peculiar, 2007—. Dir. summer theater Glendale Hist. Soc., 2001—04. Recipient Pick of the Week: Infinite Cages, Hollywood Complex, The L.A Weekly, 2000, Drama-Logue award, Drama - Logue Industry newspaper, 1990—96, Artistic Dir. awards, The Valley Theater League, 1992—95, Pick of the Week: Infinite Cages, Hollywood Complex, The LA Weekly, 2002. Mem.: AFTRA, SAG, Actors Equity Assn. Achievements include Many articles in the Los Angeles Times and other publications including a picture and story on the front page of the Los Angeles Times; featured on Broadway, films and television. Home: 13000 Burbank Blvd Sherman Oaks CA 91401 Office: The Chandler Studio 12443 Chandler Blvd North Hollywood CA 91607 Office Phone: 818-786-1045. Home Fax: 818-780-6516 ext 7. Personal E-mail: mholmes@dslextreme.com.

HOLMES, MICHAEL, health products executive; m. Gail Holmes; 2 children. With Continental Airlines; head human resources Automatic Data Processing; prin. Edward D. Jones & Co., L.P., 1996—2004; sr. v.p., chief human resources officer Express Scripts, Inc., Md. Heights, Mo., 2005—. Founder Nonprofit Improvement Assn.; mem. Social Venture Partnership; bd. mem. United Way, Mary Inst. and Country Day Sch., Webster U. Bus. Sch., Harris-Stowe State U. Bus. Sch. Office: Express Scripts Inc 13900 Riverport Dr Maryland Heights MO 63043 Office Phone: 314-770-1666.*

HOLMES, MICHAEL GENE, lawyer; b. Longview, Wash., Jan. 14, 1937; s. Robert A. and Esther S. Holmes; children: Helen, Peyton Robert. AB in Econs., Stanford U., 1958, JD, 1960. Bar: Oreg. 1961, U.S. Dist. Ct. Oreg. 1961, U.S. Ct. Appeals (9th cir.) 1961, Temp. Emergency Ct. Appeals 1976, U.S. Supreme Ct. 1976. Assoc. Spears, Lubersky, Bledsoe, Anderson, Young & Hilliard, Portland, 1961-67, ptnr., 1967-90, Lane Powell Spears Lubersky, Portland, 1990-95, of counsel, 1995. Mem. Oreg. Joint Com. of Bar, Press & Broadcasters, 1982-85, sec., 1983-84, chmn. 1985. Author Survey of Oregon Defamation and Privacy Law, ann., 1982-95. Trustee Med. Rsch. Found. Oreg., Portland, 1985-94, exec. com., 1986-94; hon. trustee Oreg. Health and Sci. Univ. Found., 1995—; trustee Portland Civic Theatre, 1962-66. Mem. Oreg. Bar Assn., Phi Beta Kappa.

HOLMES, MIRIAM H., publisher; b. Bavaria, Germany, June 2, 1951; came to U.S., 1952; d. Max J. and Mala (Rosenwasser) H.; m. Stephen H. Gelb, June 25, 1995. BA, Queens Coll., 1972; JD, Yeshiva U., 1987. Bar: N.Y. 1988. Pres. Holmes & Meier Pub., NYC, 1990—. Mem. Assn. Jewish Book Coun. (bd. dirs.), Pubs. Mktg. Assn. Office: PO Box 943 Teaneck NJ 07666 Office Phone: 201-833-2270. Business E-Mail: info@holmesandmeier.com.

HOLMES, NANCY ELIZABETH, pediatrician; b. St. Louis, Aug. 3, 1950; d. David Reed and Phyllis Anne (Hunger) Holmes; m. Arthur Erwin Kramer, May 15, 1976; children: Melanie Elizabeth Kramer, Carl Edward Kramer. BA in Psychology, U. Kans., 1972; MD, U. Mo., 1976. Diplomate Am. Acad. Pediatrics. Intern., resident in pediatrics St. Louis Children's Hosp., Washington U., St. Louis, 1976-81; pediatrician Ctrl. Pediatrics, St. Louis, 1981—. Sch. physician Sch. Dist. Clayton, Mo., 1985—92; asst. prof. clin. pediats. Washington U., St. Louis, 1993—2000, assoc. prof., 2000—, prof. clin. pediat.; cons. 1st Congregational Preschool, Clayton, 1984—86, Jewish Hosp. Daycare Ctr., St. Louis, 1993—97, Flynn Park EArly Edn. Ctr., University City, Mo., 1994—; cmty. outpatient experience Preceptor Hosp., St. Louis Children's Hosp., 1991—93, 1994—; mem. med. exec. com. St. Louis Children's Hosp., 1992—94. Vol. reading tutor Flynn Park Sch., University City, 1992—98, cub scout leader, 1993—98; mem. com. Troop 493 Boy Scouts Am., 2000—; elder Trinity Presbyn. Ch., University City, 1989—92, 1996—2001, Webster Groves Presbyn. Ch., 2006—; bd. dirs. Children's Hosp. Care Group. Fellow Am. Acad. Pediatrics; mem. AMA, Mo. State Med. Assn., St. Louis Metro. Med. Soc, St. Louis Pediatric Soc. Presbyterian. Avocations: reading, gardening, photography, travel. Office: Ctrl Pediatrics Inc 8888 Ladue Rd Ste 130 Saint Louis MO 63124-2056 Office Phone: 314-862-4002.

HOLMES, NATHANIEL J., surgeon; MD, Robert Wood Johnson Med. Sch., 1987. Diplomate Am. Bd. Surgery, 1996. Intern Robert Wood Johnson Med. Sch., Piscataway, NJ, 1987—89, resident in surgery, 1989—93; fellow in colon, rectal surgery St. Vincent Health Ctr., Erie, Pa., 1993—94; physician divsn. gen. surgery Robert Wood Johnson U. Med. Group, New Brunswick, NJ, 1994—2005; dir. colon and rectal surgery, dir. colorectal cancer program Atlantic Health System, Montclair, NJ, 2005—. Clin. asst. prof. surgery Robert Wood Johnson Med. Sch. U., New Brunswick, NJ, 1995—. Office: Ambulatory Pavilion 1 Bay Ave Ste 3 Rm 271 Montclair NJ 07042 Office Phone: 973-429-6689. Business E-Mail: nate.holmes@atlantichealth.org. E-mail: nate.holmes@ahsys.org.

HOLMES, PAUL LUTHER, political scientist, educational consultant; b. Rock Island, Ill., Mar. 7, 1919; s. Bernt Gunnar and Amanda Sophia (Swenson) H.; m. Ardis Ann Grunditz, Nov. 1, 1946; children: Mary Ann, David Stephen. BA, U. Minn., 1940; MA, Stanford U., 1949, George Washington U., 1964; EdD, Stanford U., 1968. Career officer USN, 1941-64, ret. at capt.; adminstr. Laney Coll., Oakland, Calif., 1965-70; dean Contra Costa Coll., San Pablo, Calif., 1970-71; pres. Coll. Alameda (Calif.), 1971-75, prof. polit. sci., 1975-80; dir. doctoral studies program Nova U., No. Calif., 1975-80. Cons. higher edn. Gig Harbor, Wash., 1981—; regent Calif. Luth. U., 1973-76. Decorated with medals. Mem. Stanford U. Alumni Assn., Rotary, Phi Delta Kappa. Lutheran.

HOLMES, PRIEST, professional football player; b. Fort Smith, Ark., Oct. 7, 1973; children: De'Andre, Jekovan, Corion. Postgrad in Sport Mgmt., U. Tex. Running back Balt. Ravens, 1997—2001, Kansas City Chiefs, 2001—. Spokesperson Md. Dept. Edn. Gear Up Program, McDonald House Charities; contbr. Dr. Ben Carson Scholarship Fund, Children's Miracle Net.; spkr. Ray Kroc youth achievement awards McDonald's Corp.; spkr. Youth Explosion, 2000, Urban Youth Min.; mem. Fellowship Christian Athletes. Named NFL Offensive Player of Yr., 2002, NFL All-Pro, 2002; named to Am. Football Conf. Pro Bowl Team, 2001—03. Achievements include mem. Super Bowl XXXV Champion Balt. Ravens, 2001. Office: 1 Arrowhead Dr Kansas City MO 64129

HOLMES, RICHARD BROOKS, mathematical physicist; b. Milw., Jan. 7, 1959; s. Emerson Brooks Holmes and Nancy Anne Schaffter; m. Sandra Lynn Wong, June 27, 1998. BS, Calif. Inst. Tech., 1981; MS, Stanford U., Calif., 1983. Sr. sys. analyst Comptek Rsch., Vallejo, Calif., 1982-83; staff scientist Western Rsch., Arlington, Va., 1983-85; sr. scientist AVCO Everett (Mass.) Rsch. Lab., 1985-88; prin. rsch. scientist North East Rsch. Assocs., Woburn, Mass., 1988-90; sr. mem. tech. staff Rocketdyne divsn. Rockwell Internat., Canoga Park, Calif., 1990-95; sr. staff scientist Lockheed Martin Rsch. Labs., Palo Alto, Calif., 1995-98; pres. Nutronics, Inc., Cameron Park, Calif., 1998—, Gen. Nutronics, Inc., Milpitas, Calif., 2001—. Cons. North East Rsch. Assocs., 1990. Contbr. Matched Asymptotic Expansions, 1988; contbr. articles to Phys. Rev. Letters, Phys. Rev., Jour. of the Optical Soc. Am. and IEEE Jour. of Quantum Electronics. Mem. No. Calif. Scholarship Founds., Oakland, 1977; mem. Wilderness Soc., Washington, 1989. Stanford fellow Stanford U., 1982; fellow MIT, 1990; recipient Presdl. Medal of Merit, 1992. Mem.: SPIE (conf. organizer 1995—99), AAAS, Optical Soc. Am., Am. Phys. Soc. Achievements include patents for means for photonic communication, computation, and distortion compensation; discovery of spin-two phonons. Office Phone: 408-891-0265. Personal E-mail: rholmes001@aol.com.

HOLMES, RICHARD DALE, history consultant; b. Sandown, NH, Sept. 6, 1945; s. John B. Jr. and Marjorie A. (Andrews) H.; m. Carol A. Martineau, Dec. 19, 1970; children: John B. III, Leah K. BEd, Keene State Coll., NH, 1968; MA, Rivier Coll., Nashua, NH, 1980. Cert. tchr., NH. Tchr. social studies Pelham Meml. Sch., NH, 1968-2000, chmn. dept., 1975-2000. Hist. cons., rschr. Sandown Mus., 1980-88, Chester Hist. Soc., NH, 1989—. Author: View from Meeting House Hill, 1988, Derry, 1995, Derry Revisited, 2005, Chester Revisited, 1997, Nutfield Rambles, 2007. Pres. Old Meeting House Assn., Sandown, 1987—; dir. Derry Mus., 2001—; mem. Derry Hist. Dist. Commn., 1988—, chmn. 1998—; trustee Robert Frost Farm and Mus., 2006—. With US Army, 1969-71, Vietnam. Decorated Cross of Gallantry with palm, Civic Action medal 1st class (Vietnam). Mem.: NEA, Derry Hist. Soc., Sandown Hist. Assn. (hist. cons., rschr. 1980—88, pres. 1986—87), N.H. Hist. Soc., Pelham Edn. Assn. (v.p. 1976—77), N.H. Guide Dog Users Assn., Nat. Fedn. Blind. Congregationalist. Avocations: collecting books, public speaking, research. Home: 33 Hillside Ave Derry NH 03038-2215 Office: Town Hall 48 E Broadway Derry NH 03038 Office Phone: 603-434-1247. Fax: 603-432-6131. Personal E-mail: rholmes33@comcast.net.

HOLMES, RUPERT, playwright, singer, writer; b. Northwich, Cheshire, Eng., Feb. 24, 1947; m. Liza Holmes, 1968. Grad., Manhattan Sch. Music. Piano player for bands Cuff Links and Buoys; producer (albums) for Sparks, the Sailors, Barbra Streisand; singer (albums) Widescreen, 1974, Rupert Holmes, The Singles, Pursuit of Happiness, Partners in Crime (including Escape: The Piña Colada Song and Him), Adventure, Full Circle; (plays) The Mystery of Edwin Drood, 1986 (recipient Tony awards for book, music and lyrics), Accomplice (Edgar award), Solitary Confinement, (playwright) Goosebumps, Thumbs, Swango, Say Goodnight Gracie (Carbonell award for Best Play of 2000), Curtains, 2006 (Drama Desk award outstanding book of musical, 2007); (television) Remember WENN; (author) Where the Truth Lies, 2003, Swing, 2005. Office: The Holmes Line Ste 114 717 White Plains Rd Scarsdale NY 10583 Business E-Mail: email@rupertholmes.com.*

HOLMES, STEPHEN P., hotel executive; Exec. v.p., treas., CFO HFS Inc., 1990—96, bd. dirs., 1994—97, vice chmn., 1996—97; vice chmn., bd. dirs. and chmn., CEO travel content divsn. Cendant Corp., 1997—2006, bd. dirs. hospitality svcs., 2003—06; chmn., CEO, bd. dirs. Wyndham Worldwide, 2006—. Office: Wyndham Worldwide Corp Seven Sylvan Way Parsippany NJ 07054*

HOLMES, SUZANNE MCRAE, medical/surgical nurse; b. Birmingham, Ala., June 23, 1952; d. Paul Bickman and Mabel E. (Tyler) McRae; m. Bryan Thomas Holmes, Jan. 14, 1989; 1 child, Meredith Rae. ADN, Jefferson State Coll., Birmingham, 1988. RN, Ala.; cert. BCLS instr.; cert. asthma educator, Am. Lung Assn. Staff nurse burn unit Children's Hosp., Birmingham, 1988-89; staff nurse dept. medicine Kirklin Clinic, U. Ala.-Birmingham, 1989-90, head nurse gen. medicine clinic, 1990-91, head nurse allergy clinic, 1991—2006, head nurse for pulmonary/allergy clinic, 2002—06, head nurse for pulmonary/allergy, PFT, Gastroenterology and Endoscopy Clinic, 2004; head nurse Birmingham Allergy and Asthma Specialists, P.C., 2006; staff nurse med./surg. unit Med. Ctr. East, 2007—. Facilitator and spkr. on nursing at asthma workshops Aventis Pharms., Collegeville, Pa., 1994—; mem. faculty Genecom, NYC, 1994—; operator 1-800 Allergy Info. Svc., 1991—92; vol. nurse Camp Winnataska, Birmingham, 2001—; vol. asthma nurse US Space Camp, Huntsville, Ala., 2001. Editor Allergy Update, 1991-92. Leader Girl Scouts Am., 1998—2004. Mem. Am. Coll. Allergy and Immunology, Am. Acad. Allergy, Asthma and Immunology,mem. Am. Lung Assn. (cert. asthma educator), Asthma and Allergy Found. Am. (charter bd. dirs. Ala. chpt.), Assn. Asthma Educators. Methodist. Avocations: baking, sewing, gardening.

HOLMGREN, JANET L., academic administrator; b. Chgo., Dec. 1, 1948; d. Kenneth William and Virginia Ann (Rensink) H.; m. Gordon A. McKay, Sept. 7, 1968 (div. 1990); children: Elizabeth Jane, Ellen Katherine. BA in English summa cum laude, Oakland U., Rochester, Mich., 1968; MA in Linguistics, Princeton U., 1971, PhD in Linguistics, 1974. Asst. prof. English studies Federal City Coll. (now U. DC), Washington, 1972-76; asst. prof. English U. Md., College Park, 1976-82, asst. to chancellor, 1982-88; assoc. provost Princeton U., NJ, 1988-90, vice-provost NJ, 1990-91; pres. Mills Coll., Oakland, Calif., 1991—. Mem. external adv. bd. English dept. Princeton U. Bay Area Biosci. Ctr. Author: (with Spencer Cosmos) The Story of English: Study Guide and Reader, 1986, Narration and Discourse in American Realistic Fiction, 1982; contbr. articles to profl. jours. Faculty rsch. grantee U. Md., 1978; fellow NEH, 1978, Princeton U., 1968-69, 70-72, NSF, 1969-70; recipient summer study aid Linguistic Soc. Am., Ohio State U., 1970. Mem. Assn. Ind. Calif. Colls. and Univs. (exec. com.), Nat. Assn. Ind. Colls. and Univs., Am. Coun. on Education (chair office of women in higher edn.), Calif. Acad. Sci. (coun.). Democrat. Episcopal. Avocations: travel, swimming, reading. Office: Mills Coll Office Pres 5000 Macarthur Blvd Oakland CA 94613-1301 Office Phone: 510-430-2094. Office Fax: 510-430-2256. E-mail: president@mills.edu.*

HOLMGREN, MIKE, professional football coach; b. San Francisco, June 15, 1948; m. Kathy Holmgren; children: Gretchen, Emily, Jenny and Calla (twins). BS in Bus. Fin., U. So. Calif., 1970. Coach Lincoln High Sch., San Francisco, 1971-72, Sacred Heart High Sch., 1972-74, Oakgrove High Sch., 1975-80; quarterbacks coach, offensive coord. San Francisco State U., 1981-82; quarterbacks coach Brigham Young U., 1982-85, San Francisco 49ers, 1985-89, offensive coord., 1989-92; head coach Green Bay Packers, 1992-98; gen. mgr. Seattle Seahawks, 1999—2002, head coach, exec. v.p. football ops., 1999—. Office: Seattle Seahawks Kingdome 11220 NE 53rd St Kirkland WA 98033-7595

HOLMGREN, MYRON ROGER, social sciences educator; b. Willmar, Minn., Mar. 19, 1933; s. Alfred and Cleora Victora (Scott) H.; m. Ellen Mary Shaheen, June 9, 1957; children: Brian, Mary Jo Haas. BA, Mankato State U., 1958; MA, No. Colo. State U., 1959. Instr. Grinnell (Iowa) H.S., 1959-62, Joliet (Ill.) Jr. Coll., 1962-66; instr., fin. advisor Am. Express Fin. Advisors, Joliet, 1966-72; instr. Benedictine Coll., Atchison, Kans., 1973, Moraine Valley C.C., Palos Hills, Ill., 1974-75, Minooka (Ill.) H.S., 1974-93, dept. chmn., 1984-87, dir., coach Scholastic Bowl Team, 1976-93. Local dir. Exrox Award in Humanities, 1988=93; chmn. philosophy and goals North Ctrl. Accreditation, 1987-88. Author: Profitable Pricing Techniques, 1973; contbr. articles to profl. jours. Block chmn. March of Dimes, Am. Cancer Soc., 1989, 92-93; treas. bd. dirs. The Family Counseling Agy. of Will and Grundy Counties, 1996-99; mem. vestry St. Edward's Episcopal Ch., 2002—. Grantee, Asian Found., 1962. Mem.: Internat. Platform Assn. Republican. Avocations: reading, writing, travel, gourmet cooking, market analysis. Home: 1314 Douglas St Joliet IL 60435-5814

HOLMGREN, PAUL, professional sports team executive, retired professional hockey player; b. St. Paul; m. Doreen Holmgren; children: Jason, Kirsten, Wes, Greta. Student, U. Minn. Foaward Phila. Flyers, 1975-84, Minn. North Stars, Mpls., 1984-85; asst. coach Phila. Flyers, 1985-88, head coach, 1988-91, dir. player personnel, asst. gen. mgr., 1997—2006, gen. mgr., 2006—; head coach Hartford Whalers, 1992-97. Asst. coach Team USA, World Cup Hockey, 1996, Team USA, Olympic Games, Nagano, Japan, 1998, asst. gen. mgr., Torino, Italy, 2006; gen. mgr. Team USA, World Championships, Riga, Latvia, 2006. Office: Phila Flyers Wachovia Ctr 3601 S Broad St Philadelphia PA 19148-5250*

HOLMQUEST, DONALD LEE, health organization director, nuclear medicine physician, lawyer, retired aerospace engineer; b. Dallas, Apr. 7, 1939; s. Sidney Browder and Lillie Mae (Waite) H.; m. Ann Nixon James, Oct. 24, 1972. BS in Elec. Engring., So. Meth. U., 1962; MD, Baylor U., 1967, PhD in Physiology, 1968; JD, U. Houston, 1980. Student engr. Ling-Temco-Vought, Dallas, 1958-61; electronics engr. Tex. Instruments, Inc., Dallas, 1962; intern Meth. Hosp., Houston, 1967-68; pilot tng. USAF, Williams AFB, Ariz., 1968-69; scientist-astronaut NASA, Houston, 1967-73; research assoc. MIT, 1968-70; asst. prof. radiology and physiology Baylor Coll. Medicine, 1970-73; dir. nuclear medicine Eisenhower Med. Ctr., Palm Desert, Calif., 1973-74; assoc. dean medicine, assoc. prof. Tex. A&M U., College Station, 1974-76; dir. nuclear medicine Navasota (Tex.) Med. Ctr., 1976-84, Med. Arts Hosp., Houston, 1977-85; ptnr. Wood Lucksinger & Epstein, Houston, 1980-91, Holmquest & Assocs., Houston, 1991—2004; v.p. legal affairs N.Am. Med. Mgmt., Inc., Nashville, 1995-96; practice leader profl. svcs. group McKesson Info. Solutions, San Francisco, 2002—06; CEO Calif. Regional Health Info. Orgn., San Francisco, 2006—. Asst. prof. internal medicine Baylor Coll. Medicine, Houston, 1999—. Contbr. articles to med. jours. Mem. Soc. Nuclear Medicine, Am. Coll. Nuclear Physicians, Tex. Bar Assn., Am. Fighter Pilots Assn., Sigma Xi, Alpha Omega Alpha, Sigma Tau. Home and Office: 205 Princeton Rd Menlo Park CA 94025-5217 Office Phone: 415-537-6939.

HOLMQUIST, DARREL VERNON, geotechnical engineer, arbitrator, mediator; b. Worcester, Mass., Aug. 8, 1947; s. Vernon Henry and Virginia (Simpson) H. BS in Civil Engring. with honors, U. Tex., 1974, MS in Civil Engring., 1976. Registered profl. engr., Colo. Rsch. asst. U. Tex., Austin, 1973-76; project engr. CTL/Thompson Inc., Denver, 1976-78, project mgr., 1978-84, v.p., 1984-95, pres., 1995—2001, sr. prin. cons., 2001—. Mem. steering com. Rocky Mountain Asphalt User/Prodr. Group, 1991-96; rsch. com. Colo. Transp. Inst., 1992-95; com. mem. Transp. Rsch. Bd., Washington, 1990—. Author: Engineering and Design Manual for Disposal of Excess Spoil, 1982; contbr. over 30 articles to profl. jours. Mem. tech. adv. com. Jefferson County Expansive Soils Task Force, 1994-96; pres. Suburban Met. Dist., Denver, 1987—2002. With USNR, 1966-72. Named New Prin. of the Yr., Cons. Engrs. Coun. Colo., 1989; recipient Preston Millar award Am. Coun. Ind. Labs., 1990, Appreciation award City of Denver, 1994. Fellow Am. Cons. Engrs. Coun. (pres. nat. dir. 1991-96, Orley Phillips award 2000); mem. Am. Cons. Engrs. Coun. Colo. (Pres.'s award 1996), Am. Coun. Ind. Labs. (com. chair), Am. Arbitration Assn. (mediation com. 1995—), Phi Kappa Phi, Tau Beta Pi, Chi Epsilon. Episcopalian. Avocations: scuba diving, woodworking, flying. Office: CTL/Thompson Texas 8900 Shoal Creek Bdg Austin TX 78757 Home: 511 Sarazen Loop S Georgetown TX 78628-4656

HOLMSTROM, BENGT R., economics professor; b. Helsinki, Finland, Apr. 18, 1949; s. Eric R. and Inez M. Holmstrom; m. Anneli Kuusakoski; 1 child, Sam R. BS, Helsinki U., Finland, 1969; PhD, Stanford U., Calif., 1978; PhD (hon.), U. Vaasa, 1997, Stockholm Sch. Econ., 1998, Swedish Sch. Econs. and Bus. Administrn., 2005. Corp. planner Ahlstrom Oy, Helsinki, Finland, 1972—74; asst. prof. Kellogg Sch. Mgmt. Northwestern U., Evanston, Ill., 1979—83; Edwin J. Beinecke prof. econs. and mgmt. Sch. Mgmt. Yale U., New Haven, 1983—94; Paul A. Samuelson prof. econs. MIT, Cambridge, Mass., 1994—. Dir. Nokia Oyj, Espoo, Finland, Kuusakoski Oy, Espoo. Contbr. articles to profl. jours. Lt. arty. Finnish Army Reserves. Fellow: Am. Acad. Arts and Scis., Econometric Soc.; mem.: Finnish Soc. of Sci. and Letters (fgn. mem. 1992), Royal Swedish Acad. Sci. (fgn. mem. 2001). Home: 16 John Poulter Rd Lexington MA 02421 Office: Massachusetts Institute of Technology 50 Memorial Drive Cambridge MA 02124 Home Phone: 781-888-5672; Office Phone: 617-253-0506.

HOLMSTROM, LYNDA LYTLE, sociologist, educator; b. Seattle, Apr. 23, 1939; d. Walter Wade and Dorothy Thomas Lytle; m. F. Ross Holmstrom, June 24, 1961; children: Bret, Cary. BA in Anthropology, Stanford U., Palo Alto, Calif., 1961; MA in Sociology, Boston U., 1965; PhD in Sociology, Brandeis U., Waltham, Mass., 1970. Rsch. asst. Stanford U., Palo Alto, 1961—63, Human Scis. Rsch., McLean, Va., 1963; instr. Boston Coll., Chestnut Hill, Mass., 1969—70, asst. prof., 1970—74, assoc. prof., 1974—79, prof., 1979—, chairperson dept. sociology, 1977—82. Author: The Two-Career Family, 1972; co-author: The Victim of Rape: Institutional Reactions, 1978, Mixed Blessings: Intensive Care for Newborns, 1986; contbr. articles to profl. jours. Mem.: Am. Sociol. Assn., Stanford Club New Eng. (bd. mem. 1995—), Phi Beta Kappa. Avocations: travel, photography, sports.

HOLMSTROM, TOMAS, professional hockey player; b. Pitea, Sweden, Jan. 23, 1973; married; 2 children. Left wing Detroit Red Wings, 1996—. Mem. Swedish Olympic Hockey Team, Salt Lake City, 2002, Torino, Italy, 06, Team Sweden, World Cup of Hockey, 2004. Achievements include being a member of Stanely Cup Champion Detroit Red Wings, 1997, 1998, 2002; being a member of gold medal winning Swedish Hockey Team, Torino Olympics, Italy, 2006. Avocations: fishing, woodworking, carpentry. Office: Detroit Red Wings Joe Louis Arena 600 Civic Center Dr Detroit MI 48226*

HOLNESS, GORDON VICTOR RIX, engineering executive, mechanical engineer; b. London, Sept. 6, 1939; arrived in US, 1969, naturalized, 1989; s. Ernest Arthur and Ivy A. (Rix) H.; m. Susan F. Sage (dec.); m. Audrey A. Bezz, Apr. 18, 1984. Cert., Croydon Tech. Coll., Surrey, Eng., 1962; diploma in environ. engring., Nat. Coll., London, 1964. Registered profl. engr. Mich., Minn., Tex., Conn., Calif., Kans., Colo., Fla., Ariz., NY, DC, Ala., NC, Ky., Ohio, Mo., Tenn., Ill., Ont., Can. Design engr. West Sussex County Coun., Chichester, Sussex, Eng., 1956-59, C. McKechnie Jarvis & Ptnrs., London, 1959-64, Barlow Leslie & Ptnrs., Croydon, 1964; sr. engr. R. J. Tamblyn & Ptnrs., Toronto, Ont., Canada, 1964-66; asst. chief engr. Giffels Assocs., Windsor, Ont., Canada, 1966-69; from asst. chief engr. to chmn. and CEO, bd. dirs. Albert Kahn Assocs. Inc., Detroit, 1969—2001, also bd. dirs.; ret. chmn. emeritus, 2001. Contbr. articles to profl. jours. Bd. dirs. YMCA, Mt. Clemens, Mich., 1980-82; commr. Grosse Pointe Shores Planning Commn.; trustee Grosse Pointe Shores Improvement Found. Fellow ASHRAE (chmn. energy mgmt. com. 1987, chmn. govt. affairs com. 1989, chmn. bd. policy com., bd. dirs. 2002-04, v.p. 2004-06, treas. 2007-); mem. NSPE, Am. Cons. Engrs. Coun., Chartered Inst. Bldg. Svcs. of Eng., Engring. Soc. Detroit, Mich. Soc. Profl. Engrs. (v.p. 1986, fellow 1998), Detroit Econ. Club (bd. dirs.). Republican. Presbyterian. Avocations: golf, tennis, chess, sailing. Home: 55 S Edgewood Dr Grosse Pointe Shores MI 48236-1226 Personal E-mail: gholness@comcast.net.

HOLONYAK, NICK, JR., electrical engineering educator; b. Zeigler, Ill., Nov. 3, 1928; s. Nick and Anna (Rosoha) Holonyak. BS, U. Ill., 1950, MS, 1951, PhD (Tex. Instruments fellow), 1954; DSc (hon.), Northwestern U., 1992; DEng. (hon.), Notre Dame U., 1994. Tech. staff Bell Telephone Labs., Murray Hill, NJ, 1954—55; physicist, unit mgr., mgr. advanced semiconductor lab. GE Co., Syracuse, NY, 1957—63; prof. elec. engring. and materials research lab. U. Ill., Urbana, 1963—, John Bardeen chair prof. elec. & computer engring. & physics, 1993—; mem. Center Advanced Study, 1977—. Author (with others): Semiconductor Controlled Rectifiers, 1964, Physical Properties of Semiconductors, 1989. With US Army, 1955—57. Named to, Consumer Electronics Hall of Fame, 2006; recipient Cordiner award GE, 1962, John Scott medal, City of Phila., 1975, GaAs Conf. award with Welker medal, 1976, Monie A. Ferst award, Sigma Xi, 1988, Nat. Medal Sci., NSF, 1990, Indsl. Application Sci., NAS, 1993, Centennial medal, ASEE, 1993, 50th Ann. award, Am. Elec. Assn, 1993, Japan prize, 1995, Nat. Medal of Tech. award, 2002, Internat. Global Energy prize, 2003, Lemelson-MIT prize, 2004, MRS Von Hippel award, 2004. Fellow: AAAS, IEEE (life Morris Liebmann award 1973, Jack A. Morton award 1981, Edison medal 1989, medal of honor 2003, Third Millennium medal), Internat. Engring. Consortium, Am. Phys. Soc., Am. Acad. Arts and Scis., Am. Phys. Soc., Optical Soc. Am. (Charles H. Townes award 1992, Frederic Ives medal 2001); mem.: NAS (Indsl. Application of Sci. award 1993), NAE, Lincoln Acad. Ill. (laureate 2005), We. Soc. Engrs. (Washington award 2004), Ioffe Inst. (hon.), Math. Assn. Am., Russian Acad. Scis. (fgn. mem.), Minerals, Metals and Materials Soc. (John Bardeen award 1995), Math. Assn. Am., Electrochem. Soc. (Solid State Sci. and Tech. award 1983), Tau Beta Pi (Outstanding Alumnus award 1999), Eta Kappa Nu (eminent mem. 1998, Karapetoff Eminent Mems. award 1994, eminent mem. 1998). Office: U Ill Dept Elec/Computer Engring 1406 W Green St Urbana IL 61801-2918 Home: 101 Windsor Rd 2103 Urbana IL 61802

HOLOVATY, ADRIAN, editor, web site designer; BA journalism, U. of Mo., Columbia, Mo., 2001. Online intern CopleyNet, Joliet, Ill., 2000; reporter The Columbia Missourian, 2000, columnist, 2000—01, copy editor, 2001, infographic artist, 2001; online editor The Maneater, 1999—2001; weekend producer Washington Post, Newsweek Interactive, 2001; product developer, asst. database editor The Atlanta Journal Constitution, 2002; lead developer World Online, 2002—05; editor, editorial innovations Washington Post, Newsweek Interactive, 2005—. Speaker in field. Co-recipient Web Savvy Award, U-Wire, 2000; named one of 40 Under 40, Crain's Chicago Business, 2005; recipient Online Pacemaker, Associate Collegiate Press, 2000, Batten Award for Innovations in Journalism, 2005. Achievements include design of chicagocrime.org database; holovaty.com; development of Trodo, 2002; cowroting Django opensource high-level Python Web framework. Office: c/o Washington Post PO Box 17370 Arlington VA 22216*

HOLQUIST, JAMES MICHAEL, literature educator, department chairman; b. Rockford, Ill., Dec. 20, 1935; s. Leonard and Billye Alverta (Appleby) H.; m. Lydia Landis, July 30, 1960 (div. Dec. 1972); children: Peter Isaac, Benjamin Michael, Joshua Appleby; m. Katerina Clark, Apr. 15, 1974 (div. May 1999); children: Nicholas Manning, Sebastian; m. Elise Snyder, Nov. 6, 1999. BA with highest honors, U. Ill., 1963; PhD, Yale U., New Haven, Conn., 1968; PhD honoris causa, U. Stockholm, Sweden, 2001. Asst. prof. Yale U., New Haven, 1968-72, assoc. prof., 1972-75; assoc. prof., dept. chmn. U. Tex., Austin, 1976-78, prof., 1978-80; prof. Slavic langs. and lit. dept., chmn. Ind. U., Bloomington, 1981-85; prof. comparative lit., dir. lit. major Yale U., 1986-91, chmn. coun. on Russian and East European studies, 1992-98, chmn. dept. comparative lit., 1998—2003, Northrop Frye prof. lit. theory, 2000. Co-owner Loire Wines, LLC; Christian Gauss lectr. Princeton U., 1991; NEH exchangee Soviet Acad. Scis., 1983; mem. exec. com. and editl. bd. PMLA. Author: (with Kernan and Brooks) Man and His Fictions, 1973, Dostoevsky and the Novel, 1977, reprinted, 1986; editor: (co-translator) The Dialogic Imagination: Four Essays by M.M. Bakhtin, 1981, (with Katerina Clark) Mikhail Bakhtin, 1984, Dialogism: The World of Mikhail Bakhtin, 1990, 2d edit., 2003, Philosophy of the Act, 1993; editor-in-chief: Tex. Slavic Studies, 1980; co-editor: Ind. Soviet Studies, 1982; editorial bd.: Yearbook of Comparative and Gen. Lit., 1982, Slavic Rev., 1983. Served with US Army, 1958-61. Recipient Burnes-Sewall prize for excellence in tchg. Yale Coll., 2004,Fulbright sr. specialist, 2007; Rockefeller Humanities fellow, 1983; vis. scholar Phi Beta Kappa, 1984-85; grantee NEH, 1979, Morse fellow Yale U., 1970. Mem. MLA (2d v.p. 2005, 1st v.p. 2006—), Modern Lang. Assn. (pres. 2007)Am. Assn. Advancement of Slavic Studies, Internat. Bakhtin Soc. (newsletter editor 1982—), Internat. Dostoevsky Soc., Am. Assn. Tchrs. Slavic and East European Langs., Grotesque Club, Mory's Assocs., Elizabethan Club. Democrat. Home: 455 FDR Dr Apt B-1704 New York NY 10002 Business E-Mail: michael.holquist@yale.edu.

HOLSAPPLE, CLYDE WARREN, decision and information systems educator; b. Raleigh, NC, Nov. 1, 1950; s. Van Warren and Jeanne (Rickert) H.; m. Carol Eades; children: Christiana, Claire. BS in Math., Purdue U., 1972, MS in Computer Sci., 1975, PhD in Mgmt., 1977. From asst. prof. to assoc. prof. bus. adminstrn. U. Ill., Urbana, 1978-83; vis. asst. prof. mgmt. Purdue U., West Lafayette, Ind., 1977-78, from assoc. prof. to prof. mgmt., 1983-89; prof. decision sci. and info. systems U. Ky., Lexington, 1988—, Rosenthal endowed chair in mgmt. info. systems, 1988—, chmn. dept. decision sci. and info. systems, 1993-94. Adj. prof. U. Tex., Austin, 1989—94. Co-author: Foundations of Decision Support Systems, 1981, Micro Database Management, 1984, Manager's Guide to Expert Systems, 1986, The Information Jungle, 1988, Operations Research and Artificial Intelligence, 1994, Decision Support Systems: A Knowledge-Based Approach, 1996; editor: Handbook on Knowledge Management, 2003; editor-in-chief Jour. Orgnl. Computing and Electronic Commerce, Erlbaum Corp., Mahwah, NJ, 2005-; assoc. editor Mgmt. Sci., Providence, 1991-98; area editor Decision Support Systems, Amsterdam, 1992—; contbr. over 125 articles to profl. jours. Recipient Pres.'s Acad. award Purdue U., 1970, 71, 72, Computer Educator of Yr. award Internat. Assn. for Computer Info. Systems, 1993. Recipient U. Ky. Chancellor's award outstanding tchr., 1995, R&D Excellence Program award, Ky. Sci. and Engring. Found., 2002, U. Ky. Robertson Faculty Rsch. Leadership award, 2005, AIS SIGDIS Best Jour. Paper award, 2005. Mem. IEEE, Internat. Soc. for Decision Support (co-founder, co-dir. 1989—2004), Assn. for Computing Machinery, Inst. for Operations Rsch. Mgmt. Scis., Assn. for Info. Systems, Decision Sci. Inst., Phi Beta Kappa, Phi Kappa Phi. Office: U Ky Gatton Coll Bus & Econs Lexington KY 40506-0034 Home Phone: 859-879-5055. Business E-Mail: cwhols@uky.edu.

HOLSCHER, MARK CHARLES, lawyer; b. Inglewood, Calif., 1962; BS, U. Calif., Berkeley, 1985; JD, Boalt Hall Sch. Law, U. Calif., 1988. Bar: Calif. 1988, U.S. Dist. Ct. (ctrl. dist.) Calif. 1988. Law clk. to Hon. William Keller U.S. Dist. Ct., (ctrl. dist.) Calif., LA, 1988—89; asst. U.S. atty. (ctrl. dist.) Calif. US Dept. Justice, LA, 1989—95, spl. atty. to US atty. gen. Washington, 1994—95; ptnr. O'Melveny & Myers LLP, LA, 1995—. Vice chair Nat. White Collar Crime Com., West Coast White Collar Crime Com. Named one of Top 45 Under 45, Am. Lawyer Mag., 2003; named to Chambers, Best Lawyers in Am., 2004—06. Mem.: ABA (vice chair Nat. White Collar Crime Com.), Phi Beta Kappa. Office: O'Melveny & Myers LLP 400 S Hope St Los Angeles CA 90071-2899 Office Phone: 213-430-6000. Office Fax: 213-430-6407. Business E-Mail: mholscher@omm.com.

HOLSCHUH, JOHN DAVID, federal judge; b. Ironton, Ohio, Oct. 12, 1926; s. Edward A. and Helen (Ebert) H.; m. Carol Eloise Stouder, May 25, 1952; 1 child, John David Jr. BA, Miami U., 1948; JD, U. Cin., 1951. Bar: Ohio 1951, U.S. Dist. Ct. (so. dist.) Ohio 1952, U.S. Ct. Appeals (6th cir.) 1953, U.S. Supreme Ct. 1956. Atty. McNamara & McNamara, Columbus, Ohio, 1951-52, 54; law clk. to Hon. Mell. G. Underwood U.S. Dist. Ct., Columbus, 1952-54; ptnr. Alexander, Ebinger, Holschuh, Fisher & McAlister, Columbus, Ohio, 1954-80; judge U.S. Dist. Ct. (so. dist.) Ohio, 1980—, chief judge, 1990-96. Adj. prof. law Ohio State U. Coll. Law, 1970; mem. com. on codes of conduct Jud. Conf. U.S., 1985-90. Pres. bd. dirs. Neighborhood House, Columbus, 1969-70; active United Way of Franklin County, Columbus. Fellow Am. Coll. Trial Lawyers; mem. Order of Coif, Phi Beta Kappa, Omicron Delta Kappa. Home and Office: US Dist Ct 109 US Courthouse 85 Marconi Blvd Rm 109 Columbus OH 43215-2823 Office Phone: 614-719-3310.

HOLSCHUH, JOHN DAVID, JR., lawyer; b. Columbus, Ohio, Dec. 21, 1955; s. John D. and Carol Elouise (Stouder) H.; m. Wendy G. Ellis, Sept. 22, 1984; children: Heather Elyse, John David III, Jacob Alexander. BS, Miami U., Oxford, Ohio, 1977; JD, U. Cin., 1980. Bar: Ohio 1980, US Dist. Ct. (so. dist.) Ohio 1980, US Ct. Appeals (6th cir.) 1986, US Supreme Ct. 1986, US Dist. Ct. (ea. dist.) Ky. 1987, Ky. 1991. Assoc. Santen, Shaffer & Hughes, Cin., 1980-87, ptnr., 1987-89, Santen & Hughes, Cin., 1989—. Pros. atty. City of Loveland, Ohio, 1987-92, magistrate, 1992—; magistrate Village of Fairfax, Ohio, 1999—; mem. faculty Nat. Inst. Trial Advocacy, 1990, 91, 96, 2005; participant Pretrial Civil Litigation Skills Workshop, 1991. Author: Medical Malpractice, 1986, Tort Reform Pleading, 1987, Civil Procedure, 1986, rev. edit., 1989, Damages for Plaintiff and Defense Attorneys in Ohio, 1990, 2d edit., 1991, Tort Reform Update, 1990, Masters in Trial, 2004, 2007. Recipient merit award Ohio Legal Ctr. Inst., 1986; named one of Best Lawyers in Am., 1996—. Mem.: ATLA, Internat. Soc. Barristers, Am. Coll. Trial Lawyers, Order of Barristers, Potter Stewart Inns of Ct. (emeritus mem.), Cin. Bar Found. (trustee 2001—, sec. 2006—), Cin. Bar Assn. (chmn. common pleas ct. 1991—93, trustee 1995—2004, co-chmn. bench-bar conf. 1997—98, sec. 1999—2000, v.p. 2000—01, pres.-elect 2001—02, pres. 2002—03, sec. 2006—), Hamilton County Trial Lawyers (pres. 1990—92), Ohio State Bar Assn., Ohio Acad. Trial Lawyers (trustee 1991—95, 1998—2000), Am. Bd. Trial Advs., 6th Cir. Jud. Conf. (life; del. 1983—88). Avocations: sports, travel. Office: Santen & Hughes 312 Walnut St Ste 3100 Cincinnati OH 45202-4044 Office Phone: 513-721-4450. Business E-Mail: jdh@santen-hughes.com.

HOLSEN, JAMES NOBLE, JR., retired chemical engineer; b. Palo Alto, Calif., June 20, 1924; s. James N. and Esther (Giltrud) H.; m. Nancy Schwankhaus, Feb. 24, 1950 (div.); children— James Noble III, David Edwards; m. Margot Meyer Best, Nov. 11, 1977; stepchildren— Victoria, Christopher, John. BS, Princeton U., 1948; D.Sc., Washington U., St. Louis, 1954. Registered profl. engr., Mo. Chem. engr. Olin Mathieson Chem. Corp., 1954-55; asst. prof. chem. engring. Washington U., 1955-58, assoc. prof., 1958-61, prof., 1961-73; prof. chem. engring. U. Mo.-Rolla, 1973-74, vis. prof. engring. mgmt., 1974-75; program mgr. McDonnell Douglas Corp., St. Louis, 1977-92; ret., 1992. Cons. chem. engring. and aerospace scis.; vis. prof. engring. Kabul U., Afghanistan, 1963-64, 69-73; mem. U.S. Engring. Team, Kabul, 1963-64, 69-73 Served with AUS, 1942-46 Fellow AIAA (assoc.); mem. Am. Inst. Chem. Engrs. (chmn. St.

Louis sect. 1962), Am. Chem. Soc., Am. Soc. Engring. Edn., AAAS, Ethical Soc. Sigma Xi, Tau Beta Pi Clubs: Princeton Quadrangle. Achievements include research on gas phase reaction kinetics, gaseous transport properties, materials processing in space, satellite components and structure, thermodynamics. Active in environmental affairs with St. Louis Audubon Soc. Home: 419 E Argonne Dr Kirkwood MO 63122-4523 Personal E-mail: jholsen@mindspring.com.

HOLSENBECK, GEORGE PENN, lawyer; b. Kingsport, Tenn., June 11, 1946; s. Daniel Marshall and Nancy Lyons (Penn) H.; m. Diane McClure, June 20, 1970; children: Alexander, Suzannah. BA, Yale U., 1968; JD, U. Va., 1974. Bar: Calif. 1974, U.S. Dist. Ct. (no. dist.) Calif. 1974, Pa. 1982. Assoc. Thelen, Marrin, Johnson & Bridges, San Francisco, 1974-81; atty. Bethlehem Steel Corp., Pa., 1981-83, gen. atty., asst. sec., 1983-85, asst. gen. counsel, asst. sec., 1985—92, dep. gen. counsel, sec., 1992—95; v.p., assoc. gen. counsel, corp. sec. Altria Grp., Inc. (formerly Philip Morris Co. Inc.), NYC, 1995—. Comdr. USNR, 1968. Mem. Am. Soc. Corp. Secretaries (chmn. securities law commt., 1989-92, chmn., dir., 1991-94, 1995-96), Penn. Bar Assoc., Am. Bar Assoc., St. Bar of Calif. Office: Altria Group Inc 120 Park Ave New York NY 10017 Office Phone: 917-663-4000.

HOLSINGER, JAMES WILSON, JR., cardiologist, physician; b. Kansas City, Kans., May 11, 1939; s. James Wilson and Ruth Leona (Reitz) H.; m. Barbara Jenn Craig, Dec. 28, 1963; children: Anna Elizabeth, Martha Ruth, Sarah Frances, Rachel Catherine. Student, Duke U., 1957-60, MD, 1964, PhD, 1968; MS, U. S.C., 1981; BA, U. Ky., 1997; DS (hon.), Pikeville Coll., 1996. Intern Duke U. Hosp., Durham, NC, 1964, resident in surgery, 1965, fellow in thoracic surgery, 1966, fellow in anatomy, 1966-68; resident in surgery U. Fla., Gainesville, 1968-70, fellow in cardiology, 1970-72; with VA, 1969-94; chief of staff VA Med. Ctr., Augusta, Ga., 1978-81, dir. Richmond, Va., 1981-90, Lexington, Ky., 1993-94; chief med. dir. US Dept. Vets. Affairs, Washington, 1990-93, under sec. health, 1992-93; prof. medicine and anatomy Med. Coll. Ga., Augusta, 1978-81; prof. med. and health admin. Med. Coll. of Va., Richmond, 1981-93; asst. v.p. health scis. VA Commonwealth U., Richmond, 1985-90; chancellor U. Ky. Med. Ctr., Lexington, 1994—, Wethington chair in health scis., 2001—, chancellor emeritus, 2003—; prof. medicine, surgery and anatomy U. Ky. Coll. Medicine, 1994—; profl. health care adminstrn. U. Ky. Coll. Allied Health Profls., 1994—2006; sr. v.p. U. Ky., Lexington, 2001—03; sec. Cabinet Health and Family Svcs. Commonwealth of Ky., Frankfort, 2003—05; prof. preventive medicine and health svcs. mgmt. U. Ky. Coll. Pub. Health, 2006—. Mem. com. evangelism N. Ga. conf. United Meth. Ch., 1980-81, com. 80, World Meth. Coun., 1981—, bd. discipleship Va. conf., 1982-86, lay mem., 1984-93, assoc. dist. lay leader, 1983-84, dist. lay leader, 1984-86, conf. lay leader, 1986-92, conf. chmn. health and welfare ministries, Ky., 1996-2000, Ky. conf. lay mem., 1996-00, del. gen. conf., 1988, 92, 96, 2000, del. S.E. jurisdictional conf., 1988, 92, 96, 2000; exec. com. World Meth. Coun., 1986—, treas., 1993—, gen coun. on ministries United Meth. Ch., 1988-2000, Gen. Bd. Pubs., 1992-96, bd. dirs. United Meth. Pub. House, 1996-2000, jud. council, 2000—, pres. 2004—; commr. Joint Commn. on the Accreditation of Healthcare Orgns., 1996-2002. Contbr. articles to profl. jours. Major gen. M.C., USAR, 1989-92. Master ACP; fellow Am. Coll. Cardiology, Am. Coll. Healthcare Execs. (Gold medal award 1993); mem. Am. Assn. Anatomists, Am. Heart Assn. (fellow clin. coun.), Soc. Med. Adminstrs., Internat. Brotherhood Magicians (order of Merlin with shield), Ky. Inst. Medicine, Ret. Officers Assn. (bd. dirs. 1998-2000), Assn. Theol. Schs. (bd. dirs. 2006—). Republican. Office: 121 Washington Ave Ste 107 Lexington KY 40506-0003

HOLSINGER, KENT EUGENE, biology professor, educator; b. Oregon City, Oreg., Oct. 15, 1956; s. Eugene Harold and Patricia Fay (Houston) Holsinger. BS summa cum laude in Biology, Coll. Idaho, 1978; PhD in Biol. Scis., Stanford U., Calif., 1982. Postdoctoral fellow dept. biol. scis. Stanford U., Calif., 1982, rsch. assoc. dept. biol. scis. and Dudley Herbarium Calif., 1984-86; rsch. fellow Miller Inst. Basic Rsch. in Sci., U. Calif., Berkeley, 1982-84; assoc. dept. genetics U. Calif. Agrl. Expt. Sta., Davis, 1985; adj. lectr. dept. genetics U. Calif., Davis, 1985; asst. prof. dept. ecology and evolutionary biology U. Conn., Storrs, 1986—92, assoc. prof., 1992—98, prof., 1998—, adj. prof. dept. stats., 2002—. Mem. rsch. adv. com. New Eng. Plant Conservation Prog. Contbr. numerous articles to profl. jours. Sec., trustee Conn. Mus. Natural Hist. Fellow AAAS; mem. Soc. Study of Evolution, Genetics Soc. Am., Am. Soc. Plant Taxonomists, Internat. Assn. Plant Taxonomists, Bot. Soc. Am. (treas. 2004-, Centennial award 2006), Am. Inst. Biol. Scis. (Past Pres.'s award 2007). Office: Dept Ecology and Evolutionary Biology U Conn Campus Box 4120 Storrs Mansfield CT 06269-3043 Office Phone: 860-486-4059. Office Fax: 860-486-6364. E-mail: kent@darwin.eeb.uconn.edu.*

HOLSTAD, CHRISTIAN, artist; b. Anaheim, Calif., 1972; BFA, Kans. City Art Inst., 1994. One-man shows include Sand Day: A Show of Artifacts, Absentia Art Gallery, Williamsburg, NY, 2002, one-man shows include with Chris Verene The Self-Esteem Salon: The Baptism Series, Deitch Projects, NY, 2003, one-man shows include Life is a Gift, Daniel Reich Gallery, 2002, Sonnenaufgang, Aurel Scheibler Gallery, Germany, 2003, Sonnenuntergang, Daniel Schmidt Gallery, Germany, 2003, The Birth of Princess Middlefinger, Prague Biennial, 2003, The Housekeepers, Daniel Reich Gallery, NY, 2003, Am. Express, Galeria Massimo de Carlo, Milan, Italy, 2004, Moving toward the Light, Daniel Reich Gallery, 2004, Innocent Killers, P.S. 1 Contemporary Art Ctr., Queens, NY, 2004, Gaity; Discovering the Lost Art, Kunsthalle, Zurich, Switzerland, 2004, exhibited in group shows at Midwest Bound, Chorus Gallery, Mpls., 1995, Sauna Hut Available, 1996, Cult of Claude, Here Arts Gallery, NY, 1997, exhibited in group shows, Fleshy Juggler, Brownies, NY, 1998, exhibited in group shows, Car Show, Reported Injuries Art Space, Bklyn., 1999, Slide Show, John Michael Kohler Art Ctr., Sheboygan, Wis., 2000, Zeek Sheck Collaboration, Knitting Factory, NY, 2001, Bathroom Group Show, Daniel Reich Gallery, NY, 2002, Now Playing, D'amelio Terras, NY, 2003, Calif. Earthquakes, Daniel Reich Gallery, NY, 2004, Whitney Biennial, Whitney Mus. Am. Art, 2004. Mailing: c/o Daniel Reich Gallery 537 A West 23 St New York NY 10011

HOLSTEAD, JOHN BURNHAM, retired lawyer; b. Dallas, Mar. 5, 1938; s. J.B. and Maurice (Cook) H.; m. Marilyn Morris, Nov. 23, 1963; children: Will, Rand, Scott. BA, La. Tech. U., 1959; LL.B., U. Tex.-Austin, 1962. Bar: Tex., US Dist. Ct. Tex. 1965, US Ct. Appeals (5th cir.), US Ct. Appeals (10th cir.), US Supreme Ct. 1974. Briefing clk. Tex. Sup. Ct., 1962-63; assoc. Culton, Morgan, Britton & White, Amarillo, Tex., 1963—65, Vinson and Elkins, Houston, 1965—71, comml. litig. atty., 1965—2001, ptnr., 1972; ret., 2001. Mem. bd. advisors Biology Inflamation Ctr., Baylor Coll. Medicine; spkr. on civil litigation and bus. disputes. Bd. dirs., trustee Goodwill Industries Houston, Inc. Recipient Centennial Outstanding Alumni award, La. Tech. U., 1998. Fellow Internat. Soc. Barristers, Houston Bar Found., Tex. Bar Found.; mem. ABA, Tex. Bar Assn., Houston Bar Assn., River Oaks Country Club, Houston Club. Episcopalian. Office: Vinson & Elkins 1001 Fannin St Houston TX 77002-6706 Office Phone: 713-758-2432. Business E-Mail: jholstead@velaw.com.

HOLSTEIN, WILLIAM KURT, business administration educator; b. Stamford, Conn., Nov. 19, 1936; s. Kurt Edward and Doris Christiana (Werner) H.; m. Audrey Louise Bedford, Aug. 15, 1959; children: Kurt Edward II, William Kurt Jr., Catherine Louise. BChE, Rensselaer Poly. Inst., Troy, NY, 1958; MS in Indsl. Mgmt., Purdue U., 1959, PhD in Econs., 1964. Instr., then asst. prof. indsl. mgmt. Purdue U., 1959-64; asst. prof., then assoc. prof. Harvard U. Grad. Sch. Bus. Adminstrn., 1964-72; prof. SUNY, Albany, 1972-99, disting. svc. prof., 1991-99, dean sch. of bus., 1972-81, 86-87, exec. dir. Inst. for Study of Info. Sci., 1988-96, prof. emeritus, 1999—; dir. Ctr. for Pvt. Enterprise Devel., Budapest, Hungary, 1991-93; D. Hollins Ryan prof. bus. adminstrn. Coll. William and Mary, Williamsburg, Va., 1999—2005, adj. prof., 2005—; prof. Grad. Sch. Bus. Adminstrn., Zurich, 1996—. Dir. exec. devel. programs in Singapore, Taiwan, Argentina, Switzerland, Eng. and Ctrl. Am., 1969— , cons. to industry and govt.; vis. prof. IMEDE, Lausanne, Switzerland, 1983-85. Co-author: Production Planning and Control, 1963, Casebooks in Production Management, 1968, BASIC: Concepts and Applications, 1987; author articles in field. Trustee Upsala Coll., 1969-72; mem. accreditation com., editorial adv. com., visitation teams Am. Assembly of Collegiate Schs. of Bus., 1972-81; mem. exec. com. Middle Atlantic Assn. Schs. Bus. Adminstrn., 1976-81, pres., 1980; bd. dirs. Albany Symphony Orch., 1976-99, Seagle Music Colony, 1998—; bd. dirs., treas., v.p. adminstrn. Parsons Child and Family Center, Albany, 1977-94 , pres., 1989-92; chmn. Metro 2000 Project, 1979; mem. com. on computer-aided mfg. Nat. Acad. Scis., 1980-83. Mem. Inst. Mgmt. Scis., Am. Prodn. and Inventory Control Soc. (hon.), Delta Sigma Pi, Beta Gamma Sigma. Lutheran. Home: 3104 Parkside Ln Williamsburg VA 23185-7696 Office: Coll William and Mary Mason Sch Bus Williamsburg VA 23187-8795 E-mail: William.Holstein@Mason.wm.edu.

HOLSTI, KALEVI JACQUE, political scientist, department chairman; b. Geneva, Apr. 25, 1935; s. Rudolf Woldemar and Liisa Anniki (Franssila) H.; children: Liisa, Matthew, Karina. BA, Stanford U., 1956, MA, 1958, PhD, 1961. Mem. faculty U. BC, Vancouver, Canada, 1961—, U. Killam prof. polit. sci. Canada, 1997—. Vis. prof. McGill U., Montreal, Can., 1972, Kyoto U., Japan, 1977, Hebrew U., Jerusalem, 1978, Internat. U. Japan, 1988, 92, 94; vis. fellow Australian Nat. U., 1983; cons. in field. Author: International Politics: A Framework for Analysis, 7th edit., 1994, Why Nations Realign, 1982, The Dividing Discipline: Hegemony and Pluralism in International Theory, 1985, Peace and War: International Order and Armed Conflict, 1648-1989, 1991, Change in the International System: Essays on the Theory and Practice of International Relations, 1991, The State, War, and the State of War, 1996, Taming the Sovereigns: Institutional Change in International Politics, 2004; Politica Mundial: Cambio y Conflicto: Ensayos escogidos de Kal Holsti, 2005. editor: Internat. Studies Quar., 1970-75; co-editor: Can. Jour. Polit. Sci., 1978-81. Recipient Killam Rsch. prize, 1992; Fulbright scholar, 1959-60; Can. Coun. leave fellow, 1967, 72, 78, Can. Coun. Killam Rsch. fellow, 1987-89. Fellow Royal Soc. Can.; mem. Internat. Studies Assn. (pres. 1986-87), Can. Polit. Sci. Assn. (pres. 1984-85), Finnish Acad. Scis. and Letters (fgn. mem.). Office: U BC Dept Polit Sci Vancouver BC Canada V6T 1Z1 Office Phone: 604-822-4537. Business E-Mail: holsti@interchange.ubc.ca.

HOLSTI, OLE RUDOLF, political scientist, educator; b. Geneva, Aug. 7, 1933; came to U.S., 1940, naturalized, 1954; s. Rudolf Waldemar and Liisa (Franssila) H.; m. Ann Wood, Sept. 20, 1953; children: Eric Lynn, Maija. BA with highest honors, Stanford U., 1954, PhD, 1962; MAT., Wesleyan U., Middletown, Conn., 1956. Instr., asst. prof. polit. sci., research coordinator Stanford U., 1962-67; assoc. prof. U. B.C., Vancouver, Can., 1967-71, prof., 1971-74; George V. Allen prof. polit. sci. Duke U., 1974—, chmn. dept. polit. sci., 1977-83; prof. Dept. Polit. Sci. U. Calif., Davis, 1978-79. Mem. adv. com. on hist. diplomatic documentation U.S. Dept. State, 1983-86; mem. oversight com. NSF, 1981-84; co-dir. Triangle Univs. Security Sem. Duke U., 1983-98. Author (with D.J. Finlay and R. R Fagan): Enemies in Politics, 1967; author: Analysis of Communication Content: Development in Scientific Theories and Computer Techniques, 1969, Content Analysis for Social Sciences and Humanities, 1969, Crisis Escalation War, 1972, Unity and Disintegration in International Alliances: Comparative Studies, 1973, Change in the International System, 1980, American Leadership in World Affairs: The Vietnam and Breakdown of Consensus, 1984, Pub. Opinion and Am. Fgn. Policy, 1996, 2004; co-author: International Crises, 1972, Content Analysis: Handbook with Application for the Study of Internat. Crisis, 1963, Political Science Annual, 1975, Thought and Action in Foreign Policy, 1975, The Behavior of Nations, 1976, World Politics, 1976, Diplomacy, 1979, Challenges to America, 1979, Containment, 1986, Behavior, Society and Nuclear War, 1989, Soviet-American Relations after the Cold War, 1991, Explaining the History of American Foreign Relations, 1991, 2d edit., 2004, Psychological Dimensions of War, 1991, Diplomacy, Force and Leadership, 1993, Encyclopedia of US Foreign Relations, 1997—, Pondering Postinternationalism, 2000, The New International Studies Classroom, 2000, Soldiers and Civilians: The Civil-Military Gap and American National Security, 2001, Millennial Reflections on International Studies, 2002, On The Cutting Edge of Globalization, 2005, Making American Foreign Policy, 2006; co-prodr.: American Democracy Promotion, 2000, Eagle Rules?: Foreign Policy and American Primacy in the 21st Century, 2001; assoc editor Western Polit. Quar., 1970—79, Jour. Conflict Resolution, 1967—72, bd. editors Computer Studies in the Humanities and Verbal Behavior, 1968—76, Am. Jour. Polit. Sci, 1975—80, Internat. Interaction assoc., Am. Review of Politics, editor then bd. editors Internat. Studies Quar., 1970—, Jour. Politics, 1991—, Internat. Studies Perspectives, 1999—, adv. bd. Univ. Press Am., 1976—, corr. editor Running Jour, —, corr. Racing South, —; contbr. articles to profl. jours, chapters to books. Served with AUS, 1956-58. Recipient Nevitt Sanford award, 1988, Disting. Tchrs. award Howard Johnson, 1990, Runner of Yr. award CGTC, 1985, Alumni Disting. Undergrad. Tchg. award, 1995, All-Am. award U.S. Masters Track & Field, 2000, 02; GE Found. Owen D. Young fellow, 1960-61, Haynes Found. Rsch. fellow, 1961-62, Can. Coun. Leave fellow, 1970-71, Ctr. Advanced Study in Behavioral Sci. fellow, 1972-73, Ford Found. Faculty Rsch. fellow, 1972-73, Guggenheim fellow, 1981-82, Pew Faculty fellow Harvard U., 1990; grantee Can. Coun. Rsch., 1969, NSF, 1975-77, 79-81, 83-85, 88-90, 92-95, 96-98; mem. Nat. Champion Cross Country Team (men 50-59), 1985, 88, champion, 1988; champion Tar Heel Running Tour, 1987, champion, Triple Crown Race, 1992-93; named Runner Yr., 1993, Carolina Godiva Track Club, Dave Smith award, 2007. Mem. Internat. Studies Assn. (pres. west region 1969-70, south region 1975-77, nat. pres. 1979-80, Tchr.-Scholar award Internat. Studies Assn. 2000), Internat. Soc. Polit. Psychology (coun. 1990-92, v.p. 1993-95, Nev. H. Sanford award 1988), Internat. Peace Sci. Soc. (pres. so. sect. 1975-76), Am. Polit. Sci. Assn. (coun. 1982-84, adminstrn. com. 1982-85, Disting. Lifetime Achievement award 1999, Best Fgn. Policy Paper award 2004), Can. Polit. Sci. Assn., Western Polit. Sci. Assn. (exec. coun. 1971-74), USA Track and Field (N.C. Racewalk chair 1999-2002), Phi Beta Kappa, Duke Master Runners Club, Carolina Godiva Track Club (Runner of Yr. award 1985, 93). Home: 608 Croom Ct Chapel Hill NC 27514-6706 Office: Duke U Dept Polit Sci PO Box 90204 Durham NC 27708-0204 Office Phone: 919-660-4348. Business E-Mail: holsti@duke.edu.

HOLSTON, CARLA, elementary school educator; d. Yvonne Holston. MEd, Loyola U., Chgo., 2002. Lead instr. Sylvan Learning Ctr., Chgo., 1995—97; elem. tchr. Chgo. Bd. Edn., 1997—2001, reading literacy tchr., 2001—. Recipient Delivering Results Through Innovative & Visionary Edn. award, Chgo. Pub. Schs., 2005. Home Phone: 773-288-7492; Office Phone: 773-553-1000.

HOLSTON, MICHAEL JOSEPH, lawyer, computer company executive; b. Sept. 28, 1962; BSME, U. Notre Dame, 1984; JD cum laude, Villanova U., 1987. Bar: Pa. 1987. Asst. US atty. (ea. dist.) Pa. US Dept. Justice, 1990—93; assoc. Drinker Biddle & Reath LLP, Phila., 1993—96, ptnr., 1996—2005; ptnr. litig. practice Morgan, Lewis & Bockius LLP, Phila., 2005—07; exec. v.p., gen. counsel, mem. exec. council Hewlett-Packard Co., Palo Alto, Calif., 2007—. Lectr. trial advocacy Villanova U. Sch. Law, Nat. Inst. Trial Attys. Bd. dirs. ECHOES Around the World; former bd. dirs. Bryn Mawr Fire Co. Fellow: Am. Coll. Trial Lawyers; mem.: Police Athletic League (former mem. bd. dirs.), Order of Coif. Office: Hewlett-Packard Co 3000 Hanover St Palo Alto CA 94304-1185*

HOLT, BERTHA MERRILL, state legislator; b. Eufaula, Ala., Aug. 16, 1916; d. William Hoadley and Bertha Harden (Moore) Merrill; m. Winfield Clary Holt, Mar. 14, 1942; children: Harriet Wharton Holt Whitley, William Merrill, Winfield Jefferson. AB, Agnes Scott Coll., 1938; postgrad., U. N.C. Law Sch., 1939-40; LLB, U. Ala., 1941; grad., Sch. Creative Leadership, Greensboro, NC, 1992; LLD (hon.), Agnes Scott Coll., Decatur, Ga., 2007. Bar: Ala. 1941. With Treasury Dept., Washington, 1941-42, Dept. Interior, Washington, 1942-43. Mem. N.C. Ho. of Reps. from 22d Dist., 1975-80, 25th Dist., 1980-94, chmn. select com. govtl. ethics, 1979-80, chmn. constl. amendments com., 1981, 83, mem. joint commn. govtl. ops., 1982-88, chmn. appropriation com. justice and pub. safety, 1985-88, co-chair House appropriation sub-com. transp., 1991-92, co-chair appropriation sub-com. Justice and Pub. Safety, 1993-94. Pres., Dem. Women of Alamance, 1962, chmn. hdqrs., 1964, 68; mem. NC Dem. Exec. Com., 1964-75, 95—; pres. Episcopal Ch. Women, 1968; mem. coun. NC Episcopal Diocese, 1972-74, 84-87, 95-98; chmn. budget com. 1987; chmn. fin. dept., 1973-75, parish grant com., 1973-80, mem. standing com., 1975-78; mem. Episcopal Diocese Eccles. Ct., 1998-2002; vestry mem. Ch. of Holy Comforter, 2005—, mem. bd. NC coun., 2005—; chmn. Alamance County Social Svcs. Bd., 1970; mem. N.C. Bd. Sci. and Tech., 1979-83; chair Legis. Women's Caucus, 1991-94; past bd. dirs. Hospice NC; bd. dirs. State Coun. Social Legis., pres. SCSL 1996-97, State Conf. Social Work, NC Epilepsy Assn., NC Pub. Sch. Forum, 1989, U. NC Sch. Pub. Health Adv. Bd., Salvation Army Alamance County, NC, Nursing Found., 1989, Epilepsy Found., 1989; bd. Alternatives for Status Offenders Burlington, NC, Sch. Pub. Health Adv. Bd.; bd. dirs. NC ACLU, Partnership For Children NC, 1993-98; mem. Alamance County Home Health ADv. Bd., 2005-06; bd. dirs. Ctrl. Carolina Planned Parenthood. Recipient Outstanding Alumna award Agnes Scott Coll., 1978, Legis. award for svc. to elderly Non-Profit Rest Home Assn., 1985, health, 1986, ARC, 1987, Faith Active in Pub. Affairs award NC Coun. of Chs., 1987, Ellen B. Winston award State Coun. For Social Legis., 1989, NC Disting. Women's award in gov., 1991, Disting. Svc. award Alamance County, 1992, Chi Omega award Women in Leadership, 1st ann. Hallie Ruth Allen Dem. Women award Alamance County, 1992, Disting. Svc. award Chi Omega, 1996, Svc. award Triennial Conv., Episcopal Ch. Women of US, 1997, Outstanding Alumna award U. NC, Chapel Hill, 1998, Gwyneth B. Davis award NC Assn. Women Attys., 1998, Outstanding Svc. award NC Assn. Women Attys., 1998, Disting. Alumna award U. NC,Chapel Hill, 1999, AAUW award for Edn. and Equity for Women and Girls, 2004, Lifetime Achievement 200 award Alamance County Dem. Party, 2004, Award for Outstanding Svc., NC Sr. Dems., 2005, others; named One of 5 Disting. Women of NC (Govt.), 1991; named Bertha B. Holt award in her honor NC Bar Juvenile Justice Sect., first recipient, 2004; named Bertha B. Holt Legislative Courage and Leadership award in her honor Planned Parenthood Ctrl. NC, first recipient, 2007; honored as Legis. and Scholar award Jeannette Rankin Assn. NC Women, 2005. Mem. AAUW, NOW, N.C. Women's Forums, Law Alumni Assn. U. N.C. Chapel Hill (bd. dirs. 1978-81, 1994-99), N.C. Bar Assn. (bd. dirs. sr. lawyers sect., constnl. rights sect. 1998-04, 05, juvenile justice and children's rights 1999-, chair 2002-03), English Speaking Union, N.C. Hist. Soc., Soc. Wine Educators, Les Amis du Vin, Pi Beta Phi, Phi Kappa Gamma, Delta Kappa Gamma, Phi Theta Kappa, Century Club. Address: PO Box 1111 Burlington NC 27216-1111 Personal E-mail: bholt66@triad.rr.com.

HOLT, CHIFRA, dancer, educator, choreographer, artist; b. NYC, June 8, 1933; d. Harry Halebsky and Fannie Kaminsky; m. Maroin David Willis, May 19, 1984; 1 child, Eve Jaffe. BA, CCNY, 1963; MA, UCLA, 1972. Lifetime tchg. credential in cmty. coll. Calif. Mem. dance faculty Smith Coll., Northampton, Mass., 1965—67; asst. prof., acting chair dance U. South Fla., Tampa, 1968—70; adj. prof. dance San Francisco State U., 1975—77; artistic dir., owner Chifra-Leveque Dance Ctr., San Francisco, 1976—79; assoc. prof. dance, chair Wichita State U., Kans., 1979—82; mem. dance faculty De Anza Coll., Cupertino, Calif., 1983—92, Mira Costa Coll., Oceanside, Calif., 1993—98. Choreographer (solo) Tongue of Silence, 1953, Dark Fiesta, 1965, Awakening Desert, 1972, Scenes of Men and Women, 1976, Night Mysteries, 1978, Holiday Celebration, 1979, Ripples of Joy, 1981, Beauty and the Beast, 1982, Welcome Spring, 1983, Celestial Vibrations, 1988, Seasons of My Life, 1996, Ragtime A La Carte, 1998, dancer Merry-Go-Rounders, NYC, 1955—57, Pearl Lang Dance Co., 1957—59; lead dancer, performer Paul Sanasaido Dance Co., NYC, 1958—63; artistic dir., choreographer: Mid.-Am. Dance Theatre, 1979—82; stained glass exhibits. Helpline counselor U. Calif., LA, 1971—72; bd. dirs. Corona Hist. Preservation Soc., Calif., 2005—. Grantee San Francisco State U., 1976, Met. Arts Bd., Wichita, 1979, Kans. Arts Commn., 1981. Mem.: Mensa. Avocations: theater, dance, reading, gardening, gourmet dining. Studio: 3681 Alvarado Cir Corona CA 92882 Office Phone: 909-228-4043. Personal E-mail: chifra2000@sbcglobal.net.

HOLT, DAN, library director; BA, Washburn U., 1963. Exec. dir. Dwight D. Eisenhower Libr. Presdl. Libr., Abilene, Kans., 1990—. Mem. bd. dirs. Washburn Alumni Assn. Recipient Disting. Svc. Award, Washburn U., 2002. Mem.: Ichabod Club. Office: Eisenhower Libr 200 SE 4th St Abilene KS 67410-2900 Office Phone: 785-263-6700. E-mail: dan.holt@eisenhower.nara.gov.*

HOLT, DAWN LIZABETH, paralegal; b. Sayre, Pa., Oct. 16, 1962; d. Donald E. and Julia M. Perry; m. Larry E. Holt, July 23, 2005; m. Danny W. Meyer, Feb. 2, 1983; children: Daniel K. Meyer, Danielle N. Meyer, Dane M. Meyer. Legal asst. Watson, Hollow & Reeves, Knoxville, Tenn., 1996—99, City Knoxville Law Dept., 1999—2001; paralegal Butler, Vines and Babb, PLLC, Knoxville, 2001—. Mem.: Nat. Assn. Legal Assts. (assoc.; cert. paralegal 2007, advanced cert.paralegal trial practice 2007), Tenn. Paralegal Assn. (assoc.; editor newsletter 2006—07, Mem. of Yr. award 2006). Avocations: photography, camping, travel. Office: Butler Vines and Babb PLLC 2701 Kingston Pike Knoxville TN 37919 Home Phone: 865-922-5135; Office Phone: 865-637-3531. Office Fax: 865-637-3385. Business E-Mail: lholt@bvblaw.com.

HOLT, DONALD A., agronomist, consultant, researcher, retired academic administrator; b. Minooka, Ill., Jan. 29, 1932; s. Cecil Bell and Helen (Eickoff) H.; m. Marilyn Louise Jones, Sept. 6, 1953; children: Kathryn A. Holt Stichnoth, Steven Paul, Jeffrey David, William Edwin. Grad., Joliet Jr. Coll., 1952; BS in Agrl. Sci., MS in Agronomy, U. Ill.; PhD in Agronomy, Purdue U. Farmer, Minooka, Ill., 1956-63; instr., asst. prof., assoc. prof. then prof. agronomy Purdue U., West Lafayette, Ind., 1964-82; prof., head dept. agronomy U. Ill., Urbana-Champaign, Ill., 1982-83, dir. Ill. Agr. Expt. Sta., assoc. dean Coll. Agr., 1983-96, sr. assoc. dean Coll. Agr., cons. environ. sci., 1996-2002, ret., 2002, prof. emeritus, 2003—; interim dir. Nat. Soybean Rsch. Lab., 2003—03. Cons. Deere and Co., Ottumwa, Iowa, 1978, NASA, Houston, 1979, Control Data Corp., Mpls., 1978-79, EPA, Corvallis, Oreg., 1981-90. Town Bd. commr., Otterbein, Ind., 1972-76. Fellow AAAS, Am. Soc. Agronomy (pres. 1988), Crop Sci. Soc. Am.; mem. Agrl. Rsch. Inst. (pres. 1991), Am. Forage and Grassland Coun., Ill. Forage and Grassland Coun., Gamma Sigma Delta (internat. pres. 1974-76). Republican. United Methodist. Office: U Ill 170 N5RC 1101 W Peabody Dr Urbana IL 61801-4723 Home Phone: 3879 E Forest Lodge Loop Monticello IN 47960 Home Phone: 217-356-1668. Business E-Mail: d-holt@uiuc.edu.

HOLT, FRIEDA M., nursing educator, retired academic administrator; BSN with honors, U. Colo., Boulder, 1956; MS in Cmty. Health Nursing, Boston U., 1969, EdD, 1973. RN, Ariz., Calif., Colo., Mass., Md., Pa., Wash., Liberia, W. Africa. Instr., dir. of nursing Cuttington Coll., Liberia, Africa, 1964-67; teaching fellow sch. of nursing Boston U., 1969, asst. prof. sch. of nursing, 1969-74; assoc. prof., assoc. dean for grad. studies sch. of nursing U. Md., 1975-77, dean's dep. sch. of nursing, 1975-86, prof., assoc. dean for grad. studies sch. of nursing, 1977-86, acting dean sch. of nursing, 1978, acting asst. dean sch. of nursing, 1981-82, acting chmn. sch. of nursing, 1983-84, acting dean sch. of nursing, 1986-87, prof., assoc. dean for grad. studies, dean's dep. sch. of nursing, 1987-88, prof., exec. assoc. dean. sch of nursing, 1988-89, acting dean, prof. sch. of nursing, 1989-90, prof. sch. of nursing, 1990-91, prof., dir. sch. of nursing, 1992—94, prof. emeritus, 2006—; dir. grad. programs Pa. State Sch. Nursing, 1994—2000; ret., 2000. Project dir. Primary Care Adult Nurse Practitioner Leadership grant, 1976-82, Preparation for Tchrs. in Maternal Child Nursing, judge U. Md. grad. sch. rsch. awards, 1979-84; author, project dir. Pa. State PhD Nursing Program Grant; NLN vis. for Accreditation of Baccalaureate and Masters Nursing Program, SREB/SCCEN Task Force on Grad. Edn., presenter seminars, confs., workshop; prof. emeritus U. Md. Sch. Nursing, 2006. Contbr. articles to profl. jours. Bd. dirs. Md. Nurses Found. (v.p., 1988—). Recipient VA Commendation award, 1990, Charter Trustee award Found. for Nursing of Md., 1990, Martin Luther King, Jr. Humanitarian award, 1990; named Pa. Nurse Educator of Yr., 1998. Mem. ANA, ANA (coun. nurse rschrs.), APHA, AAUP, Nat. League for Nursing, Am. Edn. Rsch. Assn., Am. Edn. Rsch. Assn., Md. Assn. for Higher Edn., Soc. for Rsch. in Nursing Edn., Sigma Theta Tau. Home: 151 Woodpecker Ln Port Matilda PA 16870 Personal E-mail: fmh16@hotmail.com.

HOLT, GEORGE, JR., information technology executive; b. New Bedford, Mass., Mar. 9, 1935; s. George and Doris Holt; m. Joan Frank (div.); 1 child, George III; m. Debra Sue Hartwell, Apr. 25, 1987; children: Laura Elizabeth, Taylor Harold. B in Mil. Sci., U. Md., 1972; M in Polit. Sci., Auburn U., Ala., 1973. Dir. Infotec Devel. Inc., Wakefield, Mass., 1984—94, Mei Tech. Corp., Lexington, 1994—98; v.p. MATCOM Corp., 1998—2000; pres., CEO AdaRose Inc., Randolph, Vt., 2000—. Co-author (book) Strategy: A Reader; contbr. articles to profl. jours. Col. USAF, 1971—84. Mem.: Rotary (pres. Randolph chpt. 2007—). Home Phone: 802-728-3664.

HOLT, GLEN EDWARD, editor; b. Abilene, Kans., Sept. 14, 1939; s. John Wesley and Helen Laverne (Schrader) H.; m. Leslie Edmonds, Jan. 29, 1994; children from previous marriage: Kris, Karen, Gordon. BA, Baker U., 1960; MA, U. Chgo., 1965, PhD, 1975. From instr. to asst. prof. Wash. U., St. Louis, 1968-82; dir. honors div. Coll. Liberal Arts, U. Minn., 1982-87; exec. dir. St. Louis Pub. Libr., 1987—2004; editor Pub. Libr. Quar., 2004—; nonprofit planning and policy cons. Cons. Chgo. Hist. Soc., 1976-79, Mo. Hist. Soc., St. Louis, 1979-87, Buffalo-Erie County Pub. Libr., 1997-98; mem. Online Computer Libr. Ctr. Pub. Libr. Adv. Com., 1991-95. Co-editor: St. Louis, 1975; co-author: Chicago, A Guide to the Neighborhoods, 1979, Measuring Your Library's Value to the Community, 2006, Library Success Stories, 2006. Recipient Cmty. Svc. award Commerce Bank, 2001; named Woodrow Wilson Found. fellow, 1963-64, Danforth fellow, 1963-68. Mem. ALA, Pub. Libr. Assn. (Charlie Robinson award 2001). Avocation: photography. Home: 4954 Lindell Blvd Apt 4W Saint Louis MO 63108-1520 E-mail: leholt@aol.com.

HOLT, HELEN, librarian, consultant, former government official; b. Gridley, Ill., Aug. 16, 1913; d. William Edward and Edna (Gingerich) Froelich; m. Rush Dew Holt, June 19, 1941 (dec. Feb. 1955); children: Helen Jane Seale, Rush Dew Holt Jr. AA, Stephens Coll., Columbia, Mo., 1932; BA, Northwestern U., Evanston, Ill., 1934, MS, 1938; postgrad., U. Mo., Columbia, U. NC, Chapel Hill, George Washington U., Washington, Marine Biol. Lab., Woods Hole, Mass. Sci. librarian, instrl. asst. Stephens Coll., 1934—37; tchg. fellow Northwestern U., 1937—38; instr. biology Nat. Park Coll., Forest Glen, Md., 1938—41; instr. sci. Greenbrier Coll., W.Va., 1955—58; mem. W.Va. Ho. of Dels., 1955—57; sec. of state W.Va., 1957—59, asst. commr. pub. instns., 1959—60; spl. asst. to commr., dir. mortgage ins. program for constrn. long term care facilities FHA, 1960—70; asst. to sec., dir. elderly programs Dept. Housing and Urban Devel., 1970—84; mem. adv. bd. Small Bus. Adminstrn., 1986—90. Cons. in field. Contbr. articles to profl. jours. Del.-at-large, vice chmn. platform com. State of W.Va. Rep. Nat. Conv., 1958; sr. citizen vol. Rep. Nat. Com., 1984; elder local Presbyn. Ch., 1975—, bd. trustees 1968-74, 80-86, bd. deacons, 1988-94; bd. dirs. Thompson Markward Hall, Nat. Alliance Sr. Citizens, Nat. Safety Coun., exec. com. Women's div. 1975-87, chmn. 1987. NSF fellow, 1956; recipient Community Svc. Human Rights award, UN Assn., 1985, Stephens Coll. Alumnae award. Fellow Am. Coll. Health Care Adminstrs. (Community Svc. award 1978); mem. Am. Health Care Assn., Nat. League Am. PEN Women (br. pres., nat. chaplain), Washington Forum (pres.), Potomac Bus. and Profl. Women (pres. 1983, Woman of the Yr. 1978), Gen. Fedn. Women's Clubs (state v.p. 1989—, other offices), The Washington Club (mem. com.), Sigma Delta Epsilon, Sigma Xi, Delta Delta Delta (dist. pres.), Zeta Mu Epsilon (nat. pres.), Zonta (bd. dirs.). Republican. Presbyterian.

HOLT, ISABEL RAE, radio program producer; b. Vineland, NJ, Oct. 5, 1946; d. Frederick Rae and Isabella A. (Foley) Steinborn; m. Robert Eugene Darby, Aug. 13, 1977 (div. 1999); children: Rachel Elisabeth Darby, Nora Odette Darby. BA in Primary Edn., Rowan U (formerly Glassboro State Coll.), 1968; postgrad., Pierce Coll., 1991-93. Dir., coord. Washington Area Free U., 1972-74; prodr. music program Sta. WGTB Georgetown U., Washington, 1972-74; prodr. music program Sta. WMGM, Atlantic City, N.J., 1974, Sta. KJAZ, Alameda, Calif., 1974-76, Sta. KPFA, Berkeley, Calif., 1974-76, Sta. KCRW, Santa Monica, Calif., 1977-88, Sta. KPCC, Pasadena, Calif., 1989-93; program dir. Boise Cmty. Radio, Idaho, 2004—06. Concert prodr.; interviewer radio programs, 1980-95; prodr. tapes for dressage/equestrian free-style riders, 1994—, riding instr., trainer, 1999-2001; riding instr. Spl. Olympics, 1999; coordinating com. Radio One. Affiliated with Idaho Cmty. Rodeo, 2007—. Mem. ACLU, Amnesty Internat., Childreach, Sierra Club. Independent. Office: 1519 N 23rd St Boise ID 83702-0409 Personal E-mail: soloirh@yahoo.com.

HOLT, JAMES FRANKLIN, retired numerical analyst, scientific programmer analyst; b. Alexander, Ark., Aug. 24, 1927; s. Edward Warbritton and Etta Turner (Ludi) H.; m. Gloria Anne Gaishin, May 5, 1963; children: Gregory James, Elizabeth Diana, Debora Anne. BA in Math., UCLA, 1953. With Pacific Mutual Ins. Corp., LA, 1953-54; assoc. engr. Lockheed Aircraft Corp., Burbank, Calif., 1954-58; mem. tech. staff Space Tech. Labs., El Segundo, Calif., 1958-61, Aerospace Corp., El Segundo, 1961-91. Author: (play) To Play's the Thing, 1963 (French Grand Prix award), Anthony Bacon a.k.a. William Shakespeare, 1994, Order Out of Chaos: Chaos, Fractals, and the Mandelbrot Set Explained, 2003, The Man Who Murdered Jack the Ripper, Death of a Programmer, 2007; internat. expert zeros of arbitrary functions, eigenvalues, non linear boundary value problems, differential algebraic equations, chaos theory, algorithms for factoring product of two primes, Riemann zeta function, numerical integration methods; papers in field. Mem. Univ. Recreation Assn. UCLA (pres. 1952-53), UCLA Student Exec. Council, Young Reps., LA, 1960-66. Cpl. USAF, 1945-48. Mem. Aerospace Profl. Staff Assn. (1st v.p. 1985-87), Shakespeare Authorship Roundtable, Alliance LA Playwrights, Mystery Writers Am. Avocations: chess, bowling, writing. Home: 3534 Mandeville Canyon Rd Los Angeles CA 90049-1022

HOLT, JOHN J., mediator, arbitrator, retired human resources specialist; b. Richmond, Va., May 7, 1931; s. Samuel L. and Susie B. Holt; m. Andrea A. Savrin; children: Brandon, Gregory, John, Keith, Derek. BS, Va. Union U., 1961; cert. in mediation, Bowie State Coll., Md., 1995. Tchr. Balt. City Schs., 1961—62; med. rschr. U. Md., Balt., 1962—69; dir. human resources U. Md. Balt. County, 1969—74, Md. Port Adminstrn., 1974—98; domestic mediator Balt., 1998—. Author: (pamphlet) Bitter Sweet Poetry, 1973, (music) A World for You and Me, 1973. Mem. Dem. Nat. Com., Md. Dem. Com.; bd. dirs. Benjamin Banneker Mus., Balt., Owen Brown Interfaith Ctr., Columbia, Md. Sgt. USAF, 1953—56. Recipient Dr. Richard Hunt Meml. Scholarship award, 1975, Cmty. Svc. award, State of Md., 1991, Gov.'s Salute to Excellence, 1994, Md. Gov.'s citation, 1996, resolution for outstanding svc., United Way, 1996. Mem.: NAACP, Md. Assn. Affirmative Action (pres.). Avocations: travel, cooking, theater, films, gardening. Home: 4115 Hanwell Rd Randallstown MD 21133 Office Phone: 410-655-0216. Fax: 410-655-0216. E-mail: anjo77@comcast.net.

HOLT, JONATHAN TURNER, public relations executive; b. New Haven, Jan. 8, 1949; s. Frederick Burton and Thelma (Turner) H. BA, Drew U., 1971. Chief adminstrv. officer Office of Policy and Analysis, FEA, Washington, 1973-76; chmn. bd. dirs. Holt, Ross Inc., Gladstone, NJ, 1977—2003; ptnr. Holt & Germann Pub. Affairs, LLC, Trenton, NJ, 1999—. Cons. U.S. Dept. Energy Regional polit. dir. Pres. Ford Com., Washington, 1976, sec./treas. Worldcom Pub. Rels. Group, Inc., 2000—, chmn., 2004—. Vice-chmn. Westfield (N.J.) Town Rep. Com., 1980-84; mem. Delaware River Basin Water Resources Assn., 1979—; chmn. bd. visitors, Drew U., 1998—, WorldCom Pub. Rels. Grp, 2005-07. NSF fellow, 1971. Mem. N.J. State C. of C., Am. Water Works Assn., N.J. Audubon Soc., Am. Assn. Polit. Cons., Pub. Rels. Soc. Am. (bd. dirs. N.J. chpt.), Nature Conservancy (trustee N.J. chpt.), Conservation Resources (dir. 2004—). Republican. Office: Holt & Germann Pub Affairs LLC 172 W State St Trenton NJ 08608 Home Phone: 908-832-0557. Business E-Mail: jholt@hgpa.com.

HOLT, KAREN ANITA YOUNG, language educator; b. Waltham, Mass., Oct. 23, 1949; d. Rexford Vernon and Linia Virginia (Duke) Young; m. Robert Jackson Holt, Dec. 30, 1974 (div. Sept. 1984). BA in English and French, Southwestern Okla. State U., 1971; MA in English, Okla. State U., 1973, postgrad., 1973-77, 86, Cen. State U., 1986. Cert. tchr., Okla. Instr. Okla. State U. Tech. Br., Oklahoma City, 1977-87; arts in edn. coord. Putnam City Schs., Oklahoma City, 1985-87; prof. Rose State Coll., Midwest City, Okla., 1987—. Dir. Righting Writing, Midwest City, 1989-91; coord. Poetry at Rose, Midwest City, 1988—, Students' Poetry, 1992—; chairperson long-range planning Cross Timbers Arts and Humanities Coun., Midwest City, 1990-91; cons. Excellence in the Arts project Kennedy Found. Sch. Bd., 1988, Okla. Writing Project, 1995. Editor: Chapbook, 1971; contbr. poetry to various publs.; poet An Evening with Oklahoma Poets, U. Okla., 1991, City Arts Conversations with the Book, 1997. Charter mem. Carpenter Sq. Theatre Vols., Oklahoma City, 1986—; mem. Rose State Coll. Speakers' Bur., Midwest City, 1990—, senator humanities divsn. faculty, 1991-94, faculty senate treas., 1993-94, acad. affairs com., 1994-96, 2004-06. Recipient honorable mention poetry award Red Dirt Press, 1988, Outstanding Prof. of Yr. award Phi Theta Kappa, 1993, keynote spkr., 1997, Excellence in Tchg. award Rose State Coll., 1996, Sister Madeleine Kisner Poetry prize Newman U., 2001; named Outstanding Honors Mentor, Rose State Coll., 2001, 02, 04; Adult Inst. for Arts scholar Okla. Arts Inst., 1990-92, Regents scholar, 1992-94; Project AIM grantee Nat. Endowment for Arts, 1986-87. Mem. Okla. Alliance for Arts Edn., Okla. Assn. Cmty. and Jr. Colls. (English chairperson 1989-90), Okla. Coun. Tchrs. of English, Rose State Coll. Faculty Assn., Rose State Coll. Founders Club, Okla. Arts Inst. Alumni Assn. Republican. Methodist. Avocations: reading, dance, film history, photography, flute. Office: Rose State Coll 6420 SE 15th St Oklahoma City OK 73110-2704 Home: 2257 NW 52nd St Oklahoma City OK 73112-8053 Home Phone: 405-858-8877; Office Phone: 405-733-7505. Business E-Mail: kholt@rose.edu.

HOLT, LEON CONRAD, JR., lawyer, chemicals executive; b. Reading, Pa., June 19, 1925; s. Leon Conrad and Elizabeth (Bright) H.; m. June M. Weidner, June 30, 1947; children: Deborah Holt Weil, Richard W. BS cum laude in Materials Sci., Engring., Lehigh U., Pa., 1948; JD, U. Pa., Phila., 1951. Bar: N.Y. 1952. With firm Mudge, Stern Williams & Tucker (attys.), NYC, 1951-53; atty. Am. Oil Co. (and predecessor co.), NYC, 1953-57; gen. atty. Air Products & Chems., Inc., Allentown, Pa., 1957-61, v.p., 1961-76, v.p. adminstrn., 1976-78, gen. counsel, 1961-78, vice chmn. bd., chief adminstrv. officer, 1978-90, also dir., mem. exec., finance, pub. policy coms. Bd. dirs. VF Corp., exec. fin. and audit coms., 1983-98. Vice chmn. Lehigh Centennial Fund, 1964-65; chmn. Allentown Bd. Ethics, 1970-74; bd. dirs. Lehigh County United Fund, 1971-83, mem. exec. com., 1971-74, campaign chmn., 1972; bd. dirs. Allentown YMCA, 1965-69, trustee, 1972-79; trustee Allentown Art Mus., pres., 1988-92; mem. Allentown Sch. Dist. Authority, 1978-86; trustee Mfrs. Alliance for Productivity and Innovation, 1981-91; mem. adv. bd. Inst. Law and Econs., U. Pa., bd. overseers Law Sch., 1985-94; mem. adv. bd. The Acad. of U. Pa.; trustee Dorothy Rider-Pool Health Care Trust, 1982-96, chmn., 1990-96; trustee Rider-Pool Found., Com. Econ. Devel., Holt Family Found.; dir. Pa. chpt. Nature Conservancy, 1991-2004, Pocono Lake Preserve; co-chmn. Partnership for Cmty. Health, 1991-94. Lt. (j.g.) USNR, 1943-46. Mem. ABA, Pa. Soc., Assn. Bar NYC, Allentown C. of C. (gov. 1965-68), Tunkhannock Creek Assn. (pres.), Alpha Tau Omega, Lehigh Country Club (bd. govs. 1970-77). Republican. Episcopalian. Office: Ste 201 1050 S CedarCrest Blvd Allentown PA 18103 Home: 2112 Kirkland Village Cir Bethlehem PA 18017

HOLT, LINDA LOUISE, elementary school educator; b. Brewton, Ala., Nov. 28, 1947; d. Fred D. and Eileen I. Holt; divorced; children: Terence J. Bostic, Jonathan D. Bostic. BS in Edn., U. Ga., Athens, 1969; MA, George Mason U., Fairfax, Va., 2004. Asst. to athletic dir. Flint Hill Sch., Oakton, Va.; lang. arts tchr. 8th grade Marsteller Mid. Sch., Bristow, Va., 2001—04; lang. arts tchr. 7-8th grade Highland Sch., Warrenton, Va., 2004—06, lang. arts tchr. 6th grade, 2006—. Usher Trinity Episcopal Ch., Manassas, Va., 2005—; bd. dirs. Boy Scouts Am., Haymarket, Va., 1989—99, merit badge counselor Nokesville, Va., 2006—07. Mem.: Nat. Coun. Tchrs. English, Phi Delta Kappa. Episcopalian. Avocations: cooking, gardening. Home: 15625 New Hope Dr Haymarket VA 20169 Office: Highland Sch 597 Broadview Ave Warrenton VA 20186

HOLT, MARJORIE SEWELL, lawyer, retired congresswoman; b. Birmingham, Ala., Sept. 17, 1920; d. Edward Rol and Juanita (Felts) Sewell; m. Duncan McKay Holt, Dec. 26, 1946; children: Rachel Holt Tschantre, Edward Sewell, Victoria. Grad., Jacksonville Jr. Coll., 1945; JD, U. Fla., 1949. Bar: Fla. 1949, Md. 1962. Pvt. practice, Annapolis, Md., 1962; clk. Anne Arundel County Circuit Ct., 1966-72; mem. 93d-99th Congresses from 4th Dist. of Md., 1973-86, mem. budget com., 1975—88, mem. joint econ. com., 1980; armed svcs. com., vice-chair Office Tech. Assessment, 1977; chair Rep. Study com., 1975-76; of counsel Smith, Somerville & Case, Balt., 1986-90. Supr. elections Anne Arundel County, 1963-65; del. Rep. Nat. Conv., 1968, 76, 80, 84, 88; mem. Pres.'s Commn. on Arms Control and Disarmament, Gov.'s Commn. on Carefirst, 2003; mem. ind. commn. USAR; bd. dirs. Annapolis Fed. Savs. Bank; adv. bd. Crestar; co-chair George W. Bush Presdl. campaign, Md., 2000. Co-author: Case Against The Reckless Congress, 1976, Can You Afford This House, 1978; mem. Fla. Law Rev., 1947. Bd. dirs. Md. Sch. for the Blind, Hist. Annapolis Found. Recipient Disting. Alumna award U. Fla., 1975, Trustees award U. Fla. Coll. Law, 1984, Alumnae Outstanding Achievement award, 1997. Mem. ABA, Md. Bar Assn., Anne Arundel Bar Assn., Phi Kappa Phi, Phi Delta Delta. Presbyterian (elder 1959). Personal E-mail: Duncan_Holt@hotmail.com.

HOLT, MAVIS MURIAL, social services administrator; b. Sturgis, SD, Apr. 30, 1932; d. Walter Raleigh and Mabel Henrietta (Krauser) Egnew; m. Howard Ray, Dec. 7, 1951; children: David Ray, Roberta Grace, Timothy Mark, Elizabeth Linda. Cert. in counseling, family issues, Multnomah Sch. of Bible, Portland, Oreg.; cert. youth at risk program, Portland State Coll.; student, North Portland Bible Coll., Long Ridge Writers Group, 1993—, Stratford Career Inst., 1999—. Mgr. The Press, Portland, 1970-71; with McDonald's Corp., Portland, 1970s; exec. dir., founder PAPYAC-Peers and Parents, Inc., Portland, 1991-97. Chairperson Neighbor Watch, Portland; block home chmn., Portland; neighborhood treas., vice chair Mill Park Neighborhood Assn., Portland, land use chair, 1993-98; vice chairperson adv. bd. David Douglas H.S., Portland; activist Neighborhood Involvement, Mill Park, City of Portland, 1985—; mem. Mid County Caring Cmty., David Douglas H.S., 1998; worker various polit. campaigns, 1995-98; mem. Gresham/East Portland C. of C., 2003—. Named Neighbor of Yr., Mid County Memo, Portland, 1994, Citizen of Month, 1997; recipient Neighborhood Plan award Mill Park Neighborhood Assn., 1995, Gateway Opportunity award City of Portland, 2000, Gift cert. Portland Environ. Bur., 2000, cert. of appreciation Mid County Caring Cmty., 2000; grantee Mill Park Nature Scape, Portland Park Bur., 1997, 2000, Howard Holt Neighborhood Park Mill Park Neighborhood Assn. grantee, 2003, use of van grantee City of Portland, 2003. Avocations: gardening, hiking, walking, local park development. Home and Office: 1235 SE 115th Ave Portland OR 97216-3567

HOLT, PETER M., professional sports team owner, agricultural products executive; b. Peoria, Ill. s. B.D. Holt; m. Julianna Hawn. Investment banker, restaurateur, Calif.; pres., CEO Holt Machinery Co., San Antonio, 1983—; owner, chmn. bd., CEO NBA San Antonio Spurs, 1996—. Commr. Tex. Dept. Parks & Wildlife; bd. dir. Free Trade Alliance-San Antonio, San Antonio Econ. Devel. Found.; corp. bd. mem. Chase Bank, San Antonio. Past chmn. United Way, San Antonio; chmn. bd. St. Mary's Hall Sch. Served to sgt. E5 US Army, Vietnam. Decorated Purple Heart, Silver Star, three Bronze Stars; named to Tex. Bus. Hall of Fame, 2004. Mem.: World Presidents' Orgn. Office: San Antonio Spurs 1 AT&T Ctr San Antonio TX 78219*

HOLT, PETER ROLF, gastroenterologist, educator; b. Berlin, Sept. 8, 1930; s. Arthur and Ruth H.; m. Joyce Weil, May 15, 1979; children: Rachel Janna, Shawn David, Tamara Naomi. BSc, U. London, 1949, MB, BS with honors, 1954. Intern London Hosp., 1954-55; asst. resident in medicine St. Luke's Hosp. Center, NYC, 1957-59; tng. fellow in medicine Mass. Gen. Hosp., Boston, 1959-61; chief gastroenterology med. Service St. Luke's Hosp. Center, NYC, 1961-96, attending physician, 1971—, Presbyn. Hosp., NYC, 1988; chief gastroenterology St. Luke's-Roosevelt Hosp. Ctr., NYC, 1996-2000; sr. scientist Inst. for Cancer Prevention, NYC, 2000—04, dir. James E. Olson Cancer Prevention Program, 2004—07, sr. scientist Strang Cancer Prevention Ctr., 2004—07; attending physician Rockefeller U. Hosp.; sr. rsch. assoc. Rockefeller U., 2007—. Mem. faculty dept. medicine Coll. Physicians and Surgeons Columbia U., NYC, 1961—; rsch. collaborator Brookhaven Nat. Lab., Upton, NY, 1973—79; prof. Columbia U., 1975—2000, prof. emeritus, 2000—, mem. Bio-engring. Inst., 1975—2000; mem. nat. sci. adv. com., nat. rev. com. Nat. Found. for Ileitis and Colitis, 1976—88, also chmn. rsch. tng. awards com.; mem. 12th work group on clin. rsch. Nat. Commn. on Digestive Disease, 1977—79; mem. Bio-engring. Inst. Inst. Human Nutrition, 1978—2000; vis. investigator Meml. Sloan-Kettering Cancer Ctr., 1988—89; Trevor Howell lectr. Brit. Geriat. Soc., 1992; Dorothy Ewerson lectr. U. Pisa, 1999; adj. sr. scientist Strang Cancer Ctr., NY, 2000—03; vis. assoc. physician Rockefeller U., 2001—, adj. prof., 2004—07; mem. Bio-engring. Inst. Comprehensive Cancer Ctr. Author, contbr. chpts. to books, articles to med. jours. Served to maj. Brit. Royal Army M.C., 1955-57. Recipient William H. Rorer award in Gastroenterology, 1965, Jannsen Lifetime Achievement award in Digestive Diseases, 2002, Internat. Solvay Nutrition award, 2002; named one of Best Doctors in Am., Castle Connoly Guide, 2002-07, Best Doctors in N.Y., N.Y. Mag., 1980-2006; NIH grantee. Fellow: ACP (gov.'s com. 1978—81); mem.: Am. Gastroenterology Assn. (pres. 1971, chmn. com. rsch. 1973—74, chmn. com. on aging 1982—86, chmn. admissions com. 1985—86, ethics com. 1997—2000, manpower and tng. com. 2001—04, internat. com. 2005—), Orgn. Mondiale de Gastro-Enterologie (chair nominating com. 1990—94, nomenclature com. and rsch. com.), N.Y. Acad. Sci., Am. Soc. Cancer Rsch., Am. Soc. Clin. Investigation, Intersoc. Com. Clin. Investigation in Digestive Disease (chmn. 1975—79). Office: Rockefeller U Box 179 1230 York Ave New York NY 10021 Office Phone: 212-327-7706. Business E-Mail: holtp@rockefeller.edu.

HOLT, ROBERT THEODORE, political science professor, educator, dean; b. Caledonia, Minn., July 26, 1928; s. Oscar Martin and Olga Linnea (Mattson) H.; m. Shirley J. Russell, Dec. 14, 1957; children: Susan Jane, Ann Carol, Sharon Linnea. AB magna cum laude, Hamline U., 1950; MPA, Princeton U., 1952, PhD, 1957. Instr. dept. polit. sci. U. Minn., Mpls., 1956-57, asst. prof., 1957-60, assoc. prof., 1960-64, prof., 1964-2001, prof. emeritus, 2001—, chmn. dept., 1978-81, dir. Ctr. for Comparative Studies in Tech. Devel. and Social Change, 1967-80, dir. rsch. devel. Coll. Liberal Arts, 1975-78, dean Grad. Sch., 1982-91, chair rsch. exec. coun., 1988-91, interim dean Coll. Liberal Arts, 1996, prof. emeritus, 2001. Bd. dirs. Coun. Grad. Schs., 1984-90, chair, 1989-90; mem. Assembly Social and Behavioral Scis., NAS, 1972-75. Author: Radio Free Europe, 1958, (with F.W. Van de Velde) Strategic Psychological Operations, 1960, The Soviet Union: Paradox and Change, 1962, (with J.E. Turner) The Political Basis of Economic Development, 1966, The Methodology of Comparative Research, 1970, Political Parties in Action, 1971, (with Turner and Chase) American Government in Comparative Perspective, 1979 With U.S. Army, 1953-55. Fellow Ctr. for Advanced Studies in Behavioral Scis., 1961-62. Mem. Am. Polit. Sci. Assn., Internat. Studies Assn., Mid West Polit Sci. Assn., Assn of Grad. Schs. (exec. com. 1985-88, chair grad. student fin. assistance com. 1986-91), 39er's Club. Episcopalian. Office: U Minn Polit Sci Dept 1414 Social Sci Tower 267 19th Ave S Minneapolis MN 55455-0499 Business E-Mail: holt@umn.edu.

HOLT, RUSH D., congressman, physics educator, researcher, consultant; b. Weston, W.Va., Oct. 15, 1948; s. Rush Dew and Helen (Froelich) Holt; m. Margaret Lancefield, 1985; 3 children. BA in Physics, Carleton Coll., Northfield, Minn., 1970; MS in Physics, NYU, 1975, PhD in Physics, 1981. Asst. prof. physics dept. Swarthmore Coll., Pa., 1980-88; Am. Phys. Soc. Congl. fellow Office of Rep. Bob Edgar of Pa., Washington, 1982-83; vis. scientist High Altitude Obs., Boulder, Colo., 1984; acting chief nuc. and sci. divsn. Office of Strategic Forces US Dept. State, 1987-89; asst. dir. Plasma Physics Lab. Princeton U., NJ, 1989—97; mem. US Congress from 12th NJ dist., 1999—, mem. edn. and labor com., mem. natural resources com., mem. permanent select com. on intelligence, chmn. select intelligence oversight panel. Bd. trustees Family and Children's Svcs. Ctrl. NJ, Planned Parenthood Mercer area, NJ; chair bd. trustees Stony Brook-Millstone Watershed Assn.; bd. dirs. Fedn. Am. Scientists Fund. Named Biotech Legislator of Yr.; recipient Cmty. Svc. award, Planned Parenthood, Sci. Coalition's Champion of Sci. award, Pub. Svc. award, Fusion Power Assocs., 1999, Congl. Support for Sci. award, Inst. Food Technologists, 2003, Outstanding Legislator award, Triangle Coalition for Sci. and Tech. Edn., 2004. Mem.: Sigma Xi (John P. McGovern Sci. and Soc. award 1999), AAAS, Am. Assn. Physics Tchrs., Am. Phys. Soc. Democrat.

Achievements include winning 5 times on "Jeopardy"; patent for a solar energy device. Office: US House Reps 1019 Longworth House Office Bldg Washington DC 20515-0001 Office Phone: 202-225-5801. Office Fax: 202-225-6025.*

HOLT, SIDNEY CLARK, journalist; b. St. Louis, Sept. 7, 1955; s. Noel Clark and Rosalee (Powell) H.; m. Jill Brodsky, Nov. 16, 1991; children: Elizabeth Summers, Victoria Edmunds. BA, Columbia U., 1979. Editor Simon & Schuster Inc., NYC, 1979-84; asst. editor Rolling Stone, NYC, 1984-85, assoc. editor, 1985-87, sr. editor, 1987-89, asst. mng. editor, 1989-90, mng. editor, 1990-97; editl. dir. US mag., NYC, 1995-97; v.p. Wenner Media, Inc., NYC, 1996-97; exec. v.p., editor-in-chief Ad Week Mags., NYC, 1998—2005; editl. dir. VNU Bus. Media, NYC, 2005—07; sr. v.p. programming 80108 Media, 2007—. Editor: The Rolling Stone Interviews: The 1980s, 1989. Bd. dirs. Fedn. Protestant Welfare Agys., N.Y.C., 1994—. Recipient Nat. Mag. award for gen. excellence, 1998. Mem. Am. Soc. Mag. Editors, Columbia Club N.Y. Democrat. Methodist. Home: 680 Titicus Rd North Salem NY 10560-2106 Office: 80108 Media PO Box 321 273 Summer St Boston MA 02210

HOLT, STEPHEN S., astrophysicist; b. NYC, May 17, 1940; s. Aaron J. and Faye E. (Schwartz) Holtz; m. Carol Ann Weissman, June 3, 1961; children: Peter David, Eric Lawrence, Laura Kimberly. BS, NYU, 1961, PhD in Physics, 1966. Instr. physics NYU, 1964—66; astrophysicist Goddard Space Flight Center, Greenbelt, Md., 1966-2000; chief high energy astrophysics NASA Hdqrs., 1980-81; dir. Lab. for High Energy Astrophysics Goddard Space Flight Ctr., Greenbelt, Md., 1983-90, dir. space scis., 1990-2000; prof. Physics Olin Coll., Needham, Mass., 2000—; prof., dir. natural scis. Babson Coll., Wellesley, Mass., 2000—. Lectr. physics U. Md., 1967-87, adj. prof. astronomy, 1988— Contbr. articles to profl. jours. Recipient medal for exceptional sci. achievement NASA, 1977, 80, medal for outstanding leadership, 1991, 2000, Presdl. meritorious exec. award, 1992, John C. lindsay Meml. award outstanding sci. achievement, 1993, NASA Disting. Svc. medal, 2000, COSPAR Internat. Coop. medal, 2004. Fellow AAAS, Am. Phys. Soc. (chair divsn. exec. com.); mem. Am. Astron. Soc. (chair div.), Internat. Acad. Astronautics, COSPAR (chair div.), Sigma Xi, Tau Beta Pi, Sigma Pi Sigma. Home: 77 Pond Ave Apt 1202 Brookline MA 02445-7115 Office: Olin Coll Olin Way Needham MA 02492-1245 E-mail: steve.holt@olin.edu. *The most important intrinsic requisites for success in experimental science are probably imagination and diligence. Very few individuals possess these in sufficient quantities to dominate the extrinsic variables which shape their careers in research, however. I consider myself fortunate to have been able to capitalize on whatever talent I possess by having my research interests aligned with funding priorities, and by being blessed with the cooperation of unselfish and stimulating colleagues.*

HOLT, THADDEUS, lawyer; b. Birmingham, Ala., Nov. 26, 1929; s. Thad and Sarah Ames (Oliver) H.; m. Waring Inge, Dec. 1, 1956 (dec. 2002); children: Sarah, Harrison. B.A., U. of South, 1951; M.A., Yale U., 1952; B.A. (Rhodes Scholar), Oxford U., 1954; LL.B., Harvard U., 1956. Bar: Ala. 1956, D.C. 1959, U.S. Supreme Ct. 1960, N.Y. 1969, Pa. 1985. Assoc. Cabaniss & Johnston, Birmingham, 1956-58; assoc. Covington & Burling, Washington, 1958-65; dep. undersec. Dept. Army, Washington, 1965-67; pres. Leacock Pennebaker Inc., NYC, 1968-69; sec. Corp. for Pub. Broadcasting, N.Y.C. and Washington, 1970-71; ptnr. Breed, Abbott & Morgan, Washington and N.Y.C., 1972-86; sole practice, Washington, Carlisle, Pa., Point Clear, Ala., 1986—. Author: The Deceivers: Allied Military Deception in the Second World War, 2004; contbr. articles to MHQ, N.Y. Times Book Rev., other mags. Recipient decoration for Disting. Civilian Service U.S. Army, 1967. Mem. Am. Law Inst., Washington Inst. for Fgn. Affairs, Met. Club (Washington). Episcopalian. Home: PO Box 440 Point Clear AL 36564 Office Phone: 251-990-7495.

HOLT, TORRY, professional football player; b. Greensboro, NC, June 5, 1976; BA in Sociology, NC State, 1999. Wide receiver St. Louis Rams, 1999—. Founder The Holt Foundation, St. Louis, 1996. Named to Pro Bowl, NFL, 2000—01, 2003—05, NFC Pro-Bowl Team, 2007. Office: St Louis Rams One Rams Way Earth City MO 63045

HOLT, WILLIAM E., lawyer, department chairman; b. Phila., Aug. 31, 1945; BBA, U. Iowa, 1967, JD with distinction, 1970. Bar: Iowa 1970, Wash. 1971. Law clk. to Hon. William T. Beeks U.S. Dist. Ct. (we. dist.) Wash., 1970-71; mem., chmn. Gordon, Thomas, Honeywell, Malanca, Peterson & Daheim, Tacoma, 1999, 2000, 2006. Adj. prof. U. Puget Sound Law Sch., 1974-75. Note editor Iowa Law Rev., 1969-70. Mem. ABA, Wash. State Bar Assn. (exec. com. real property, probate and trust sect. 1987-89), Phi Delta Phi. Office: Gordon Thomas Honeywell Malanca Peterson & Daheim PO Box 1157 Ste 2100 Tacoma WA 98401-1157 Office Phone: 253-620-6412. E-mail: holtw@gth-law.com.

HOLT, WILLIAM HENRY, retired physicist, researcher; b. San Antonio, Aug. 5, 1939; s. Joseph Marion and Mildred Louise (Ragsdale) H.; m. Margaret Ann Harrell, June 21, 1963; children: Benjamin, Andrew. BS cum laude, St. Mary's U., San Antonio, 1960; MA, U. Tex., 1962, PhD, 1967. Postdoctoral fellow, lectr. U. Man., Winnipeg, Can., 1966-69; rsch. physicist Naval Surface Warfare Ctr., Dahlgren, Va., 1969—2006; ret., 2006. Patentee; contbr. articles and papers to numerous sci. jours. and revs. Past tchr. Sunday sch. St. Matthias United Meth. Ch., Fredericksburg, Va.; past co-chmn. edn., past lay leader, past mem. pastor-parish rels. com., past chmn. coun. on ministries. Mem. Am. Phys. Soc., Can. Assn. Physicists, Materials Rsch. Soc., Sigma Xi, Sigma Pi Sigma.

HOLTAN, RAMER B., JR., lawyer; b. Wilmington, Del., Oct. 20, 1944; AB, Harvard U., 1966; JD cum laude, U. Ill., 1972; postgrad., U. Freiburg, West Germany. Bar: Wash. 1973. Mem. Perkins Coie, Seattle. Articles editor U. Ill. Law Rev., 1971-72. Mem. Order of the Coif. Office: Perkins Coie 1201 3rd Ave Fl 40 Seattle WA 98101-3029 Home Phone: 206-232-3538; Office Phone: 206-359-8400. Business E-Mail: rholtan@perkinscoie.com. E-mail: rholtan@comcast.net.

HOLTBY, KENNETH FRASER, retired manufacturing executive; b. Escanaba, Mich., May 18, 1922; s. David William and Nina Kate (Hemenway) H.; m. Bettie Roberts, June 11, 1943; children— Michael Earle, Tracy Linda Meilleur, Jeffrey Thomas, Kristen Ann Buren, Matt Fraser. BSME, Calif. Inst. Tech., 1947; SM in Indsl. Mgmt., MIT, 1961. Aerodynamicist Boeing Co., Seattle, 1947, various mgmt. positions, 1953-82, sr. v.p., 1982-87; ret. Found. mem. Pacific Sci. Ctr., Seattle, 1974—. Served to lt. USAF, 1943-46. Fellow: AIAA (hon. Aircraft Design award 1984, Laureate Bagnou prize), Brit. Royal Aero. Soc.; mem.: U.S. Nat. Acad. Engring., NRC. Avocations: tennis, skiing, sailing. Address: 6346 So Chinook Dr Clinton WA 98236

HOLTE, DEBRA LEAH, investment company executive, financial analyst; b. Madison, Wis. BA, Concordia Coll., Moorhead, Minn., 1973. Chartered Fin. Analyst, Cert. Divorce Planner. Capital markets specialist 1st Bank Mpls., 1981-83; v.p. Allison-Williams Co., Mpls., 1983-86; exec. v.p. Hamil & Holte Inc., Denver, 1986-93; pres. Holte & Assocs., Denver, Taos, N.Mex., 1993—. Active Denver Jr. League, Western Pension Com., 1986—; bd. dirs. Denver Children's Home, 1987—, treas., 1987-91, chmn. fin. com., 1987-91, v.p., 1990—, chmn. nominating com., 1991—, pres.-elect, 1994-95, bd. pres., 1995—; adv. bd. Luth. Social Svcs., 1987; co-chair U.S. Ski Team Fundraiser; bd. dirs. Minn. Vocat. Edn. Fin., Mpls., 1984-86; bd. dirs. Colo. Ballet, 1988-93, chair nominating com., 1991-93, v.p., 1992-93, chmn. bd., 1993; mem. Fin. Analyst Nat. Task Force in Bondholder Rights, 1988-90; bd. dirs. Ctrl. City Opera Guild, 1994-95, Western Chamber Ballet, 1994-96, Taos Humane Soc., 1997—; social co-chmn. The Arapahoe Fox Hunt, 1993-94; bd. dirs., mem. steering com. Denver Dumb Friends League, 2001-, mem. exec. com., 2004-, mem. audit com., 2004-; mem. exec. com., chair devel. com. Dumb Friends League, 2005—. Mem. Fin. Analysts Fedn., Denver Soc. Security Analysts (bd. dirs. 1990-97, chair ethics and bylaws com. 1987—, chair edn. com. 1988, chair membership com. 1989, rec. sec. 1990, sec. 1991, treas. 1992, program chair 1993, pres. 1994-95, dir. 1995-96).

HOLTER, ARLEN ROLF, cardiothoracic surgeon; b. Sullivan's Island, SC, Feb. 1, 1946; s. Arne and Helen (Soderberg) H.; m. Elizabeth Anne Reid, Nov. 9, 1974; children: Matthew Arlen, Peter Reid, Andrew Douglas. BS, Stanford U., 1968; MS, U. Ill., Chgo., 1971, MD, 1973. Diplomate Am. Bd. Thoracic Surgery, Am. Bd. Surgery. Intern Mass. Gen. Hosp., Boston, 1973-74, resident in surgery, 1974-78; sr. registrar in cardiac surgery South Hampton Chest Hosp., 1978; resident in cardiac surgery Yale U., New Haven, 1978-80; pvt. practice Mpls., 1980—. Instr. surgery Yale U., 1979-80. Contbr. articles to profl. jours. Recipient Franklin McLean rsch. award U. Chgo., 1973. Fellow: ACS; mem.: Mpls. Acad. Medicine, Am. Heart Assn., Soc. Thoracic Surgeons, US Triathlon Assn. (Iron Man finisher). Lutheran. Avocations: skiing, photography, triathlons. Office: 640 Jackson St Saint Paul MN 55101-2502 Office Phone: 651-254-4130. Personal E-mail: arholter@aol.com.

HOLTKAMP, JAMES ARNOLD, lawyer, educator; b. Albuquerque, Apr. 4, 1949; s. Clarence Jules and Karyl Irene (Roberts) H.; m. Marianne Coltrin, Dec. 28, 1973; children: Ariane, Brent William, Rachel, Allison, David Roberts. BA, Brigham Young U., 1972; JD, George Washington U., 1975. Bar: Utah 1976, U.S. Dist. Ct. Utah 1977, U.S. Ct. Appeals (10th cir.) 1979, Colo. 1995. Mem. staff U.S. Senate Watergate Com., Washington, 1974; atty.-advisor Dept. Transp., Washington, 1975; atty. Dept. Interior, Washington, 1975-77; assoc. Van Cott, Bagley, Cornwall & McCarthy, Salt Lake City, 1977-81, ptnr., 1981-89, Davis, Graham & Stubbs, Salt Lake City, 1989-92, Stoel Rives, Salt Lake City, 1992-97, LeBoeuf, Lamb, Greene & MacRae, Salt Lake City, 1997—2003, Holland & Hart, Salt Lake City, 2003—. Adj. prof., Law Sch. Brigham Young U., Provo, Utah, 1979—2002; adj. prof. Coll. Law U. Utah, 1995—. Co-author: Utah Environmental and Land Use Permits and Approvals Manual, 1981; contbr. articles to legal jours. Missionary LDS Ch., 1968-70; active Gt. Salt Lake coun. Boy Scouts Am., 1977—; trustee Coalition for Utah's Future, 1996-2001. Mem. ABA (vice-chmn. air quality commn. 1985-89), Utah State Bar (chmn. energy and natural resources sect. 1984-85, chmn. pub. utilities law com. 1990-93, energy and natural resources sect., Lawyer of Yr. award 1981, Disting. Svc. award 2002), Utah Mining Assn. (bd. dirs. 1999—), Rocky Mtn. Mineral Law Found. (pres. 2005-06), Utah Petroleum Assn., George Washington Law Assn. (nat. bd. dirs. 1999—). Home: 7990 Deer Creek Rd Salt Lake City UT 84121-5752 Office: Holland & Hart 60 E South Temple Ste 2000 Salt Lake City UT 84111-1031

HOLTKAMP, SUSAN CHARLOTTE, elementary school educator; b. Houston, Feb. 23, 1957; d. Clarence Jules and Karyl Irene (Roberts) H. BS in Early Childhood Edn., Brigham Young U., Provo, Utah, 1979, MEd, 1982. Cert. tchr. Utah, ESL endorsement U. Utah, 2002. 2d grade tchr. Nebo Sch. Dist., Spanish Fork, Utah, 1979-84, kindergarten tchr., 1984-85; tchr. 2d grade DODDS, Mannheim, Fed. Republic Germany, 1985-86; tchr. 3d grade Jordan Sch. Dist., Salt Lake City, 1987-92, tchr. 5th grade, 1992—2002, tchr. 6th grade, 2002—, dir. sch. choir, 1998—. Mem. NEA, JEA, ASCD, Utah Edn. Assn.

HOLTON, GERALD, physicist, educator, science historian; b. Berlin, May 23, 1922; s. Emanuel and Regina (Rossmann) H.; m. Nina Rossfort, Sept. 12, 1947; children: Thomas, Stephan. Nat. certificate elec. engring., Sch. Tech., Oxford, Eng., 1940; BA, Wesleyan U., Middletown, Conn., 1941, MA, 1942, DHL (hon.), 1981; MA, Harvard U., Cambridge, Mass., 1946, PhD, 1948; DSc (hon.), Grinnell Coll., Iowa, 1967, Kenyon Coll., Gambier, Ohio, 1977, Bates Coll., Lewiston, Maine, 1979; LLD (hon.), Duke U., Durham, NC, 1981. Instr. Wesleyan U., 1941-42, Brown U., 1942-43; staff, officers radar course and OSRD Harvard, 1943-45, various faculty positions, 1947—; rsch. prof. physics and history of sci. Harvard-Leningrad U., 1962; vis. mem. Inst. Advanced Study, Princeton, 1964; fellow Center Advanced Study in Behavioral Scis., Stanford, 1975-76. Vis. prof. MIT, 1976-94; Herbert Spencer lectr. Oxford U., 1979; Jefferson lectr. in humanities, 1981; John Simon Guggenheim fellow, 1980-81; mem. com. scholarly comm. with People's Republic of China, NAS, 1967-72, mem. com. conduct of sci., NAS, 1989-91, mem. office on pub. understanding sci., NAS, 1995-2001; mem. US Nat. Commn. on UNESCO, 1975-80, US Nat. Commn. of IUHPS, 1982-89, Coun. of Scholars, Libr. of Congress, 1980-95, US Nat. Commn. on Excellence in Edn., 1981-83; mem. adv. com. for sci. and engring. edn. NSF, 1985-93, chair, 1986-89; mem. selection bd. Albert Einstein Peace Prize, 1980—; mem. German Am. Acad. Coun. Kuratorium, 1997-2000; mem. com. interdisciplinary rsch. NAS, 2003-05. Author: Introduction to Concepts and Theories in Physical Science, 1952, 2d edit., 1985, (with D.H.D. Roller) Foundations of Modern Physical Science, 1958, Science and the Modern Mind, 1958, Science and Culture, 1965, (with others) The Project Physics Course, 1970, 75, 81, The 20th Century Sciences: Studies in Intellectual Biography, 1971, Thematic Origins of Scientific Thought: Kepler to Einstein, 1973, 2d edit., 1988, The Scientific Imagination: Case Studies, 1978, 98, (with others) Limits of Scientific Inquiry, 1979, Albert Einstein, Historical and Cultural Perspectives, 1982, 97, The Advancement of Science and Its Burdens, 1986, 98, Science and Anti-Science, 1993, Einstein, History and Other Passions, 1996, (with Gerhard Sonnert) Gender Differences in Science Careers: The Project Access Study, 1995, Who Succeeds in Science? The Gender Dimension, 1995, (with Stephen Brush) Physics, The Human Adventure, 2001, (with Gerhard Sonnert) Ivory Bridges: Connecting Science and Society, 2002, (with David Cassidy and James Rutherford) Understanding Physics, 2002, Victory and Vexation in Science: Einstein, Bohr, Heisenberg and Others, 2005, (with Gerhard Sonnert) What Happened to the Children Who Fled Nazi Persecution, 2006; founding editor-in-chief quar. Daedalus, 1957-61; mem. editl. com., editl. adv. bd. The Collected Papers of Albert Einstein, 1980-1995; contbr. articles to profl. jours. Recipient J.D. Bernal prize Soc. Social Studies Sci., 1989, Fellow AAAS (bd. dirs. 1967-71), Am. Philos. Soc., Am. Acad. Arts and Sci. (editor 1957-63, exec. bd. 1970-78, coun. 1991-95), Am. Phys. Soc. (chmn. divsn. history of physics 1992-93), Internat. Acad. History of Sci. (v.p. 1981-89), Deutsche Acad. Naturforscher-Leopoldina, Internat. Acad. Philosophy of Sci.; mem. Nat. Assoc. NAS, Am. Inst. Physics (governing bd. 1968-74, Andrew Gemant award 1989), Am. Assn. Physics Tchrs. (Robert A. Millikan medal 1967, Oersted medal 1979), History Sci. Soc. (pres. 1983-84, George Sarton medal 1989, Joseph H. Hazen Edn. prize 1998). Office: Harvard U Jefferson Phys Lab Cambridge MA 02138 Business E-Mail: holton@physics.harvard.edu.

HOLTON, GRACE HOLLAND, accountant; b. Durham, NC, Sept. 14, 1957; d. Samuel Melanchthon and B. Margaret (Umberger) Holton. BS in Math., U. N.C., Greensboro, 1978; MBA, U. N.C., Chapel Hill, 1984; M. Acctg., U. Ill., 1993. CPA NC, cert. mgmt. acct., internal auditor. Indsl. engr. Burlington Industries, Inc., Mayodan, NC, 1978—79, plant indsl. engr. Stoneville, NC, 1979—80; methods indsl. engr. Blue Cross and Blue Shield of N.C., Durham, 1980—82; fin. analyst R.J. Reynolds, Inc., Winston-Salem, NC, 1984—85; accounting cons. Ryder Truck Rental, Inc., Miami, Fla., 1985—88; contr. Ryder Jacobs (divsn. Ryder Distbn. Resources), Jessup, Md., 1988—90; grad. asst. in acctg. U. Ill., Urbana, 1990—93; contr. Salem NationaLease, Winston-Salem, 1993—94; fin. officer Chapel Hill-Carrboro City Schs., 1994—99; mgr. benefits and payroll Ryder Pub. Transp. Svcs., Cin., 1999—2000; exec. dir. budget and evaluation Charlotte-Mecklenburg Schs., 2000—02; instr. acctg. Alamance C.C., Graham, NC, 2003—. Scholar KPMG-Peat Marwick scholar, 1991—92. Mem.: AICPA, Inst. Internal Auditors, N.C. Assn. CPAs, Inst. Mgmt. Accts. Democrat. Methodist.

HOLTON, WALTER CLINTON, JR., lawyer; b. Winston-Salem, NC; s. Walter Clinton and Mabel (Hartsfield) H.; m. Lynne Rowley. BA in Polit. Sci., U. N.C., 1977; JD, Wake Forest U., 1984. Bar: N.C. 1984, U.S. Dist. Ct. (mid. dist.) N.C. 1986, U.S. Ct. Appeals (4th cir.) 1990, U.S. Supreme Ct., 1996. Asst. dist. atty. Office 21st Jud. Dist. Atty., Winston-Salem, 1985-87; assoc. White & Crumpler, Winston-Salem, 1987-88; pvt. practice Winston-Salem, 1989; ptnr. Holton & Menefee, Winston-Salem, 1989-92, Tisdale, Holton & Menefee, PA, Winston-Salem, 1992-94; U.S. atty. Office U.S. Atty. Mid. Dist. N.C., Greensboro, NC, 1994-2001; pvt. practice Grace Holton Tisdale & Clifton PA, Winston-Salem, 2001—. Democrat. Office: 301 N Main St Ste 804 Winston Salem NC 27101 Home Phone: 336-924-0557; Office Phone: 336-777-3480. Fax: 336-722-3478. Business E-Mail: wholton@ghtclaw.com.

HOLTON, WILLIAM COFFEEN, electrical engineering executive; b. Washington, July 24, 1930; s. William B. and Esther (Coffeen) H.; m. Mary Schaeffer, Aug. 5, 1953; children: Elizabeth Ashe, William Andrew, Sarah Anne. BS in Physics, U. N.C., 1952; PhD in Physics, U. Ill., 1960. Tech. staff corp. rsch. lab. Tex. Instruments, Dallas, 1960-65, mgr. quantum electronics, 1965-72, dir. advanced components lab., 1972-78, dir. R & D semicondr. group, 1978-82, mgr. strategic planning, 1982-83; dir. Semiconductor Rsch. Corp., Research Triangle Park, NC, 1984-88, sr. dir., 1989-90, v.p., 1990-95; prof. NC State U., Raleigh, 1996—, U. NC, Chapel Hill, 2004—. Lt. (j.g.) USN, 1952-54. Union Carbide fellow, 1959; recipient Dept. of Energy award, 1997. Fellow IEEE (mem. awards bd. 1999—, chair tech. field awards coun. 2005—, Phillips award 1998), Am. Phys. Soc., Electron. Device Soc. of IEEE (governing bd. 1975-98, chmn. internat. electron device meeting 1975); mem. Phi Beta Kappa, Phi Eta Sigma. Presbyterian. Home: 601 Brookview Dr Chapel Hill NC 27514-1401 Office: NC State Univ Box 8617 234B Monteith Enging Rsch Ctr Raleigh NC 27695-8617 Business E-Mail: holton@eos.ncsu.edu.

HOLTSCHNEIDER, DENNIS H., academic administrator, priest; b. Detroit, Jan. 14, 1962; BA, Niagara U., 1984; MDiv, ThM, Mary Immaculate Sem., Northampton, Pa., 1989; EdD, Harvard U., 1997. Ordained priest Roman Cath. Ch., 1989. Assoc. dean, asst. prof. St. John's U., NYC, 1996-99; exec. v.p., COO, Niagara U., Niagara Falls, NY, 2000—04; pres. DePaul U., Chicago, Ill., 2004—. Mem. N.Y. Acad. Pub. Edn. (life). Office: DePaul U 1 E Jackson Chicago IL 60604*

HOLTZ, DIANE, retail executive; Divsnl. v.p. Bloomingdale's; v.p. career merchandise & tops Ann Taylor Stores Corp., gen. mgr. merchandise, sr. v.p., 1997—2000; v.p. spl. projects design svcs. Limited Brands, Inc., 2000—02; pres. Limited Stores Limited Brands Inc., 2002—06; exec. v.p. merchandising & design Ann Taylor LOFT divsn. Ann Taylor Stores Corp., 2007. Office: Ann Taylor Stores Corp 7 Times Sq 15th Fl New York NY 10036*

HOLTZ, GILBERT JOSEPH, steel company executive; b. NYC, Jan. 23, 1924; s. Al S. and Carrie (Schindler) H.; m. Carla Kahn, July 18, 1848; children: Steven J., Robert A. Student, NYU, 1940-42. V.p. Hanger Svc. Co., Yonkers, NY, 1946-48; owner Economy Sales Co., Yonkers, 1948-50; v.p. Belvedere Space Saving Products, Inc., 1951-72; pres. Walnut Metal Industries, Inc., Yonkers, 1955-72, Belvedere Home Products Inc. (formerly 411 Walnut St. Corp.), 1962—, Holtz Realty Corp., 1962—, Walnut Assn. Inc., 1961—, Belvedere Internat. Ltd., 1970—. Patentee in field. Ward leader 2d Ward Republican County Com., Yonkers. Served with AUS, 1943-46. Decorated Bronze Star; recipient Conspicuous Svc. Cross, N.Y. State. Mem. Rotary. Home: 182 Tibbetts Rd Yonkers NY 10705-2646 Office: 937 Saw Mill River Rd Yonkers NY 10710-3230

HOLTZ, LAURENCE, artisan, photographer; b. Spangler, Pa., Jan. 9, 1949; s. Paul Omer and Helen Zita (McCombie) H.; m. Priscilla Suzanne Adsit, May 17, 1981 (div. Apr. 2005); 1 child, Samara Adsit BA, LaSalle Coll., Phila., 1974. Hand weaver, Hardwick, Vt., 1987—. Contbr. Vt. Arts Coun. Spl. Exhbn., Montpelier, Vt., fall 2000. Exhibited at Wood Gallery and Arts Ctr., Vt. Coll., Montpelier; contbr. short story and poetry to Coldspot, 1998; contbr. poetry to Exit 1, 2003; musician, vocalist First Night, St. Johnsbury, Vt., 2005, 06, 07; musician, (albums) Thatchers Pond, 2005. Mem. Ctrl. Vt. Regional Planning Commn., Montpelier, 1982, Plainfield (Vt.) Planning Commn., 1982; vol. Vt. Dept. Corrections Northeast Regional Correctional Facility, St. Johnsbury, 1998-2002; mem. Reparative Probation Bd., Barre Office, 1998-2000. Mem. New England Antiquities Rsch. Assocs., Vt. Weaver's Guild, Hardwick Area Writer's Group, Handweavers Guild Am., Alliance for Prison Justice (workshop panelist 2002). Zen Buddhist. Avocations: instrumental music, creative writing.

HOLTZ, SARA, marketing consultant; b. LA, Aug. 7, 1951; BA, Yale U., 1972; JD, Harvard U., 1975. Bar: D.C. 1975, Calif. 1982. Assoc. Brownstein, Zeidman & Schomer, Washington, 1975-77; dep. asst. dir. FTC, Washington, 1977-82; divsn. counsel Clorox Co., Oakland, Calif., 1982-90; v.p., dep. gen. counsel Nestle U.S.A., Inc., San Francisco, 1990-94; prin. Client Focus, 1996—. Mem. Am. Corp. Counsel Assn. (bd. dirs. 1986-95, chmn. 1994-95). Office: 5320 Olive Tree Ct Granite Bay CA 95746-9484

HOLTZMAN, ARNOLD HAROLD, chemical company executive; b. Phila., May 11, 1932; s. William and Rae (Shapiro) H.; m. Phyllis Raskow, June 26, 1955; children: Rosalind Ann, Linda Susan, William Lewis. BS, Drexel Inst., 1954; MS, Lehigh U., 1956, PhD, 1957. Asst. metallurgist J. Bishop & Co., Malvern, Pa., 1954; with duPont Co., various locations, 1957-89, rsch. mgr., dist. sales mgr. polymer intermediates dept. Wilmington, Del., 1973-76, mgr. new bus. programs, ctrl. R&D dept., 1976-78, mgr. health products, 1980-81, dir. devel. divsn. ctrl. R&D dept., 1982-89, cons., 1989—; freelance writer, 2007—. Pres. Action Games, Inc., 1988—; rsch. assoc. Elwyn, Inc, 1997—2001; bd. dirs. Perceptive Sys. Inc. Contbr. articles to profl. jours. Bd. dirs. Del. chpt. Alzheimer's Assn., 1992-97, pres., 1992-95; bd. dirs. Foxfire Printing Inc., 2000—; mem. sci. adv. bd. Clarity Coding, Inc., 2005—. Recipient John Price Wetherill medal Franklin Inst., 1969. Fellow Am. Soc. Metals; mem. Sigma Xi. Achievements include patentee in processing of metals and non metals. Home and Office: 208 Stonecrop Rd Wilmington DE 19810-1320 Office Phone: 302-475-5963. E-mail: holtzmana@comcast.net.

HOLTZMAN, DAVID MICHAEL, neurologist; b. St. Louis, July 31, 1961; BS in Med. Edn., Northwestern U., 1983, MD, 1985. Bd. cert. neurology. Intern/resident U. Calif., San Francisco, 1985—89, postdoctoral rsch. tng. William C. Mobley Lab., 1989—94; lab. dir. Washington U., 1994, Charlotte and Paul Hagemann assoc. prof. neurology, 2001—, prof. molecular biology and pharmacology, 2002—; Andrew and Gretchen Jones chmn. dept. neurology Washington U. Sch. Medicine, St. Louis, 2003—. Asst. prof. U. Calif., San Francisco, 1991—94. Recipient Paul Beeson Physician Faculty Scholar award in aging rsch., MetLife award for promising rsch. on Alzheimer's disease, 2002, Potamkin prize, Am. Acad. Neurology, 2003. Office: Washington Univ Sch Medicine Dept Neurology 660 S Euclid Ave Saint Louis MO 63110

HOLTZMAN, ELIZABETH, lawyer; b. Bklyn., Aug. 11, 1941; d. Sidney and Filia Holtzman. AB magna cum laude, Radcliffe Coll., 1962; JD, Harvard U., 1965; L.D.S., Regis Coll., 1975, Skidmore Coll., 1980, Simmons Coll., 1981, Smith Coll., 1982. Bar: N.Y. 1966. Assoc. Wachtell, Lipton, Rosen, Katz & Kern, NYC, 1965-67; asst. to mayor NYC, 1968-69; assoc. Paul, Weiss, Rifkind, Wharton & Garrison, 1970-72; mem. 93d-96th Congresses from 16th dist., N.Y.; vis. prof. Law Sch. and Grad. Sch. Pub. Adminstrn. NYU, 1981; dist. atty. Kings County, Bklyn., 1982-89; comptr. City of N.Y., 1990-93. Mem. Am. Jewish Commn. on the Holocaust, Nazi and Japanese War Criminal Records Interagency Working Group, 1999—; Dem. nominee U.S. Senate, 1980; N.Y. State Dem. committeewoman, 1970—72; mem. Pres.'s Nat. Commn. on U.S. Observance Internat. Women's Yr., Helsinki Watch Com., 1981—88, Select Com. on Immigration Policy, 1979—80; bd. overseers Harvard U., 1976—82; trustee Radcliffe Coll., 1999, Bklyn. Acad. Music Endowment Trust, 1999—; mem. Lawyers Com. Internat. Human Right, 1981—88. Recipient Nat. Coun. Jewish Women's Faith and Humanity award, YWCA Elizabeth Cutter Morrow award, Maccabean award N.Y. Bd. Rabbis, Alumni recognition award Radcliffe Coll. Alumnae Assn., 1973, N.J. and L.A. ACLU awards for contbns. to def. of Constn. and preservation of civil liberties, 1981, Athena award N.Y.C. Commn. on Status of Women, 1985, Woman of Yr. award N.Y. League Bus. and Profl. Women, 1985, Jan Korzak award 5th Ann. Kent State Holocaust Conf., 1986, Outstanding and Meritorious Svc. award Jewish War Vets. of U.S., 1986, Award of Remembrance Warsaw Ghetto Resistance Orgn., 1987, Gates of Freedom award State of Israel Bonds, 1987; Award of Honor United Jewish Appeal, 1988, Deed of Tzedakah award, 1991. Fellow N.Y. Inst. Humanities; mem. Assn. of Bar of City of N.Y., Nat. Women's Polit. Caucus (Outstanding Svc. award 1987), Phi Beta Kappa. Office: Herrick Feinstein LLP 2 Park Ave New York NY 10016-9302 Office Phone: 212-592-1400.

HOLTZMAN, GARY YALE, retired diversified financial services company executive; b. NYC, Aug. 7, 1936; s. Abram and Pearl (Kashetsky) H.; m. Alice A. Lang, Sept. 5, 1958; children: Bruce, Sheri, Michele. BBA, CCNY, 1958. Buyer, ops. mgr. Bloomingdale's, NYC, 1966; exec. v.p. control and ops. Jordan Marsh Co., Miami, Fla., 1967-87; sr. v.p. ops. and stores L. Luria & Sons Inc., Miami, 1987-93; exec. dir. Mar Jewish Community Ctr., Greater Miami, Fla., 1993-95; agt. Social Security Adminstrn.-TSR, 1995—2002; ret., 2002. Bd. advisers Universal Nat. Bank. Bd. dirs. Dade County Safety Coun., Miami, 1978-85, Jewish Cmty. Ctr. Greater Miami, 1983-88, Fla. Bus. Roundtable, 1975-80, Anti-Defamation League of B'nia B'rith, 1983-87; bd. advisers Opportunities Industrialization Ctr., 1982-84; pres. Michael Ann Russell Jewish Cmty. Ctr., 1984-86, bd. dirs., 1980—; life bd. dirs. Temple Beth Torah Adath Yeshurun, 1969-94, Temple B'nai Aviv, 1994-98; mem. fin. com. Temple Dor Dorim, 1998—, fin. com., 1999-2005, pres. club, 2005-, bd. dirs. 2005-; active Jewish Fedn. Broward County and Greater Miami, Miami Jewish Fedn.; com. chmn. United Way of Dade County. Lt. U.S. Army, 1958-59; capt. USAR, 1959-67. Recipient Americanism award Anti-Defamation League, 1983; recipient Adath Yeshurun Man of Yr. award, 1978 Mem. Greater Miami C. of C., Fla. Retail Fedn. Democrat. Home: 2019 Cove Ln Weston FL 33326-2336 E-mail: algari@bellsouth.net.

HOLTZMAN, JOAN KING, musician, composer; b. Aberdeen, SD, Aug. 14, 1925; d. James Wilfred and Miriam Hughes (Evans) K.; m. Wayne Harold Holtzman, Aug. 23, 1947; children: Wayne Jr., James, Scott, Karl. B in Music Edn., Northwestern U., 1947; EdMA, Stanford U., 1948. Pres. Jojo's Prodns., Austin, Tex., 1991—. Author: (with Leslie Holtzman) The Fat Rat and This and That, 1997, (with Rosario Ahumada de Diaz) Happy Times with English, 1987; composer, pianist, singer children's cassettes and CDs Jo Jo's Songs for Growing Up, 1991, Beasts, Veggies and Sospetigious Things, 1993; composer melodies song book, cassette and CD, Symphony for Simple Simon, 1984 (award of excellence Am. Symphony Orch. League, 1984); composer numerous songs. Active Save Children Fedn., 1954—, pres. 1958; vol. Austin Cerebral Palsy Ctr., 1955-59; mem. Pan Am. Round Table, 1958—, sec. 1965-66; co-founder Internat. Hospitality Com. Austin, 1960—, chmn. host families, 1960-62; pres. PTA Austin H.S., 1972; mem. Austin Arts Commn., 1977-83; mem. nat. adv. coun. Nat. Sch. Vol. Program, Washington, 1976-91; mem. adv. com. Austin Ind. Sch. Dist., 1983-91, forming future com., 1982; mem. arts plan task force City of Austin, 1985; docent, gov. mansion, 1983—; nat. class rep. Northwestern U. Sch. Music, 1977-91; mus. vol. Austin State Hosp., 1967-83; sec., bd. dirs. Austin Symphony Orch. Soc., 1966—; state bd. dirs. Very Special Arts - Tex., 1987-91; bd. dirs., chmn. coms. Child and Family Svcs., Austin, 1965-82; bd. dirs. Austin Musical Theatre, 2000-. Named Outstanding Fundraiser Austin Symphony Devel. fund drive, 1981; Festival Favorite New Tex. Choral Music Festival, Austin, 1995, Yellow Rose Tex., Tex. Gov., 1995, Vol. of Yr., 1995. Mem. Women's Symphony League Austin (pres. 1958-59, charter mem., Woman of Yr. award 1991, Outstanding Svc. First Chair award, 2007), Austin Jr. League (Vol. Extraordinaire award 1985), Mortar Bd. U. Tex. Austin (Citation award 1976), Playhouse Singers, Settlement Club, Austin Woman's Club, Univ. Ladies Club (pres. 1971-72), Sigma Alpha Iota (charter mem., pres. 1972-73, Rose of Honor award 1976). Office: Jojo's Prodns 3300 Foothill Dr Austin TX 78731-5823 E-mail: wayne.holtzman@mail.utexas.edu.

HOLTZMAN, ROBERT ARTHUR, lawyer; b. LA, July 17, 1929; s. Ruben and Bertha (Dembowsky) H.; m. Barbara Polis, June 26, 1954 (dec. 1985); children: Melinda, Mark, Bradley; m. Liliane Gurwith Endlich, July 6, 1986. BA, UCLA, 1951; LLB, U. So. Calif., 1954. Bar: Calif. 1955, U.S. Dist. Ct. (ctrl. dist.) Calif. 1955, U.S. Ct. Appeals (9th cir.) 1958. Assoc. Gang, Tyre & Brown, LA, 1954, Loeb and Loeb, LA, 1956-63, ptnr., 1964-95, of counsel, 1996—. Judge pro tem Mcpl. Ct. L.A. Jud. Dist.; lectr. Calif. Continuing Edn. of Bar. Contbr. articles to legal publs. With U.S. Army, 1954-56. Mem. ABA (dispute resolution sect., vice-chmn. arbitration com.), Calif. Bar Assn. (chmn. com. on adminstrn. of justice 1984-85), L.A. County Bar Assn., Am. Arbitration Assn. (panel arbitrators 1974—, panel mediators 1992—, arbitrator large complex case program 1993—). Office: Loeb & Loeb LLP 10100 Santa Monica Blvd Ste 2200 Los Angeles CA 90067-4164 Home Phone: 818-783-3901; Office Phone: 310-282-2280. Business E-Mail: rholtzman@loeb.com.

HOLTZMAN, ROBERT NEIL NEHEMIAH, neurosurgeon, neurologist; b. Bklyn., Aug. 11, 1941; s. Sidney and Filia (Ravitz) H.; children: Maia Merav, Jonathan Nisson, Matthew Isaac. BA, Harvard U., 1964; MD, Columbia U., 1969. Diplomate Am. Bd. Psychiatry and Neurology, Am. Bd. Neurol. Surgery. Rotating intern Harlem Hosp. Ctr., NYC, 1969-70; resident in neurology Neurol. Inst. N.Y., NYC, 1970-72, resident in neurosurgery, 1973-77; resident in gen. surgery Harbor Gen. Hosp., Torrance, Calif., 1972-73; practice medicine specializing in neurosurgery and neurology, NYC, 1977—; attending neurosurgery Met. Hosp., 2000—. Attending in neurosurgery Harlem Hosp., 1999—; attending in neurosurgery Lenox Hill Hosp., 2000; assoc. attending N.Y. Presbyn. Hosp., N.Y.C., 1996; chief of neurosurgery Cabrini Med. Ctr., 1999; assoc. clin. prof. in neurosurgery Coll. Phys. and Surgeons, Columbia U., N.Y.C., 1996; co-dir., co-founder Stonwin Med. Conf., 1983-91. Editor: Surgery of the Diencephalon, 1989, Endovascular Interventional Neuroradiology, 1995; editor, contbr.: The Tethered Spinal Cord, 1985, Surgery of the Spinal Cord: The Potential for Regeneration and Recovery, 1991, Spinal Instability, 1993; contbr. articles to med. jours. Mem.: N.Y. Soc. Neurol. Surgery, N.Y. State Neurosurg. Soc., Am. Assn. Neurol. Surgeons. Democrat. Jewish. Office Phone: 212-529-3580.

HOLTZMAN, ROBERTA LEE, French and Spanish language educator; b. Detroit, Nov. 24, 1938; d. Paul John and Sophia (Marcus) H. AB cum laude, Wayne State U., Detroit, Mich., 1959, MA, 1973, U. Mich., Ann Arbor, 1961. Fgn. lang. tchr. Birmingham (Mich.) Sch. Dist., 1959—60, Cass Tech. H.S., Detroit, 1961-64; from instr. to prof. French and Spanish, Schoolcraft Coll., Livonia, 1964—84, chmn. French and Spanish depts., 1984—2004, adj. prof. French, 2004—05, prof. emerita French and Spanish, 2005—. Trustee Cranbrook Music Guild, Ednl. Community, Bloomfield Hills, Mich., 1976-78. Fulbright-Hays fellow, Brazil, 1964. Mem. AAUW, NEA, MLA, Nat. Mus. Women in Arts (co-founder 1992), Nat. Trust, Am. Assn. Tchrs. Spanish and Portuguese, Am. Assn. Tchrs. French, Mich. Edn. Assn., U. Mich. Alumnae Club of Birmingham. Avocations: swimming, book collecting, photography, travel. Office: Schoolcraft Coll 18600 Haggerty Rd Livonia MI 45152-2696 Business E-Mail: rholtzma@schoolcraft.edu.

HOLTZMAN, WAYNE HAROLD, psychologist, educator; b. Chgo., Jan. 16, 1923; s. Harold Hoover and Lillian (Manny) H.; m. Joan King, Aug. 23, 1947; children: Wayne Harold, James K., Scott E., Karl H. BS, Northwestern U., Evanston, Ill., 1944, MS, 1947; PhD, Stanford U., Calif., 1950; LHD (hon.), Southwestern U., Georgetown, Tex., 1980. Asst. prof. psychology U. Tex., Austin, 1949-53, assoc. prof., 1953-59, prof., 1959—2003, dean Coll. Edn., 1964-70, Hogg prof. psychology and edn., 1964—2003, prof. emeritus, 2003—. Assoc. dir. Hogg Found. Mental Health, 1955-64, pres., 1970-93, spl. counsel, 1993-2003; dir. Social Sci. Rsch. Coun., 1957-63, Centro de Investigationes Sociales, Mex., 1960-70; cons. USAF, sci. adv. bd., 1969-71; basic rsch. com. NRC, 1968-71; behavioral sci. study sect. USPHS, 1957-59, mem. mental health study sect., 1960, chmn. personality and cognition rsch. rev. com., 1968-72; rsch. adv. panel Soc. Security Adminstrn., 1961-62; L.Am. adv. bd. IBM, 1985-89; dir. WHO Collaborating Ctr. in Mental Health for Tex. and Mex., 1993-2003; pres. Austin Project, 2001-03; bd. dirs. Menninger Clinic, The Learning Initiative. Author: (with B.M. Moore) Tomorrow's Parents, 1964, Computer Assisted Instruction Testing and Guidance, 1971, (with R. Diaz-Guerrero and J. Swartz) Personality Development in Two Cultures, 1975, Introduction to Psychology, 1978; (with K.A. Heller and S. Messick) Placing Children in Special Education, 1982, (with T. Bornemann) Mental Health of Immigrants and Refugees, 1990, School of the Future, 1992, Holtzman Inkblot Technique Research Guide, 1999, (with M.R. Rozenweig, Michel Sabourin and David Belanger) History of the International Union of Psychological Science, 2000; editor: Jour. Ednl. Psychology, 1966-72. Trustee Ednl. Testing Service, Princeton, 1972-74, 77-80, 83-86, J.W. and Cornelia Scarborough Found., 1977-82, Ctr. for Applied Linguistics, 1978-80, Salado Inst. Humanities, 1980-85, Population Inst., 1979-85, Menninger Atel, 1982--2003, bd. dir., 1986-, Population Resource Ctr., 1980—, chmn. bd. dirs.; dir. Sci. Rsch. Assocs., 1975-88; pres., bd. dirs. S.W. Ednl. Devel. Lab., 1974-75; mem. adv. com. computing activities NSF, 1970-73; mem. computer sci. and engring. bd. NAS, 1971-73, chmn. panel on selection and placement of mentally retarded students, 1979-82; chmn. interdisciplinary cluster on social and behavioral devel. Pres.'s Biomed. Research Panel, 1975-76; bd. dirs. Found.'s Fund for Rsch. in Psychiatry, 1973-77, chmn., 1976-77; dir. Conf. of S.W. Found., 1976-84, pres., 1978-79; mem. nat. adv. mental health coun. Alcohol, Drug Abuse, and Mental Health Adminstrn., 1978-81; mem. acad. info. sys. adv. coun. IBM, 1982-85. Commd. ensign USNR, 1944, Northwestern U. NROTC, anti-aircraft gunnery officer USNR, Pacific, lt. (jg.) USNR, 1945, flag lt. to admiral oscar badger to admiral roper USNR. Faculty Rsch. fellow, Social Sci. Rsch. Coun., 1953—54, Ctr. Advanced Study Behavioral Scis., 1962—63. Fellow APA, AAAS; mem. Tex. Psychol. Assn. (pres. 1957), S.W. Psychol. Assn. (pres. 1958), Am. Statis. Assn., InterAm. Soc. Psychology (pres. 1966-67), Am. Ednl. Rsch. Assn., Internat. Union Psychol. Scis. (sec.-gen. 1972-84, pres. 1984-88, exec. com. 1972-92), Philos. Soc. Tex. (pres. 1982-83), Sigma Xi. Methodist. Avocations: photography, gardening, travel, swimming. Home: 3300 Foothill Dr Austin TX 78731-5823 E-mail: wayne.holtzman@mail.utexas.edu.

HOLTZMANN, HOWARD MARSHALL, lawyer, judge; b. NYC, Dec. 10, 1921; s. Jacob L. And Lillian (Plotz) H.; m. Anne Fisher, Jan. 14, 1945 (dec. Aug. 1967); children: Susan Holtzmann Richardson, Betsey; m. Carol Ebenstein Van Berg, Dec. 23, 1972. AB, Yale Coll., 1942, JD, 1947; LittD (hon.), St. Bonaventure U., 1952; LLD (hon.), Jewish Theol. Sem., NYC, 1990. Bar: NY 1947. Atty. Colorado Fuel & Iron Corp., Buffalo, 1947-49; ptnr. Holtzmann, Wise & Shepard, NYC, 1949-95; judge Iran-US Claims Tribunal, The Hague, Netherlands, 1981-94; sr. claims judge, 1994—, Claims Resolution Tribunals for Dormant Accounts, Zurich, Switzerland, 1998—2002. US del. UN Commn. on Internat. Trade Law, 1975—, Hague Conf. on Pvt. Internat. Law, 1985; advisor U.S.A. Arbitration agreements with USSR, Russian Fedn., China, Hungary, Bulgaria, Czechoslovakia, Poland and German Dem. Republic. Author, editor: A New Look at Legal Aspects of Doing Business with China, 1979; co-author: (with J.E. Neuhaus) A Guide to the Unicitral Model Law on International Commercial Arbitration-Legislative History and Commentary, 1988 (cert. of merit Am. Soc. Internat. Law 1991; co-author, co-editor (with E. Kristjansdottir) International Mass Claims Processes - Legal and Practical Perspectives, 2007; contbr. chpts. to books and articles to law jours. Mem. governing coun. Downstate Med. Sch. SUNY, Bklyn., 1961-78; trustee St. Bonaventure U., Olean, NY, 1968-90, trustee emeritus, 1990—; chmn. bd. Jewish Theol. Sem., NYC, 1983-85, hon. chmn., 1985—; trustee Inst. Internat. Law, Pace U. Sch. Law, 1992—; mem. bd. advisors Lighthouse Internat. Decorated comdr. Swedish Royal Order of Polar Star; recipient Yale medal, 2006, Medal of Honor, Vienna, Austria; Assoc. fellow, Pierson Coll., Yale, 2005—, Sterling fellow, Yale U. Mem. ABA (chmn. com. code ethics comml. arbitrators 1973-77), Permanent Ct. of Arbitration (chmn. steering com. on internat. mass claims), Internat. Coun. for Comml. Arbitration (hon. vice chmn.), Am. Arbitration Assn. (hon. chmn., Gotshal Internat. Arbitration award 1980, Peacemaker award 2006), Internat. C. of C. (vice chmn. arbitration commn. 1979-2001), Stockholm Arbitration Inst. (adv. bd.), Am. Bar Found., NY County Lawyers Assn., Internat. Law Assn., Am. Fgn. Law Assn. (v.p. 1995-2003, Disting. Svc. award 1999), Internat. Bar Assn., NY State Bar Assn., Assn. Bar City of NY, Am. Soc. Internat. Law (cert. merit 1991), Soc. Profls. in Dispute Resolution, Indsl. Rels. Rsch. Assn., Am. Judicature Soc., Am. Assn. for Internat. Commn. of Jurists. Office: Ste 2000 630 Fifth Ave New York NY 10111-0100 Office Phone: 212-332-7140. Business E-Mail: holtzmannh@cs.com.

HOLTZSCHUE, KARL BRESSEM, lawyer, author, educator; b. Wichita, Kans., Mar. 3, 1938; s. Bressem C. and Josephine E. (Landsittel) H.; m. Linda J. Gross, Oct. 24, 1959; children: Alison, Adam, Sara. AB cum laude, Dartmouth Coll., 1959; LLB, Columbia U., 1966. Bar: N.Y. 1967, U.S. Dist. Ct. (so. and ea. dists.) N.Y. 1968. Assoc. Webster & Sheffield, NYC, 1966-73, ptnr., 1974-88; ptnr., head real estate dept. O'Melveny and Myers, NYC, 1988-90; pvt. practice NYC, 1990—. Adj. prof. Fordham U. Law Sch., 1990—2003; adj. prof. Bus. Sch. Columbia U., 1990—96, Law Sch., 1991. Author: Holtzschue on Real Estate Contracts, New York Practice Guide: Real Estate, Vol. 1 on Purchase and Sale, Real Estate Transactions: Purchase and Sale of Real Property, Lexis Nexis Answer Guide: New York Real Property; editor: NYSBA's Res. R.E. Forms on Hot Docs.; mem. editl. bd. Warren's Weed New York Real Property, 2003—. Trustee Soc. of St. Johnland, 1980-86, Ensemble Studio Theatre, 1986-88; bd. dirs. The Bridge, 1990—, pres., 1992-95; mem. alumni bd. Dartmouth Ptnrs. in Cmty. Svc., 1994—, founding chmn., 1994-99. Lt. j.g. USN, 1959—62. Mem.: ABA (com. on legal opinions in real estate transactions 1990—2003), Tri Bar (opinions com. 1990—99), Am. Coll. Real Estate Lawyers (vice chmn. 1992—95), Assn. Bar City NY (com. on real property law 1977—80, chmn. 1987—90, 1995—98), NY State Bar Assn. (com. on attys. opinions 1992—2003, co-chmn. com. on title and transfer 1998—2004, exec. com. real property sect. 1998—, chmn. 2007—). Episcopalian. Business E-Mail: kbholt@gmail.com.

HOLUB, MARTIN, architect; b. Prague, Czechoslovakia, Dec. 11, 1938; arrived in U.S., 1970, naturalized, 1977; s. Jan and Miloslava (Jerabkova) Holub. MS, Czech Tech. U., 1963, Acad. Art, Prague, 1966. Registered arch., N.Y., N.J., Tenn., Fla., Conn. Designer Konstruktiva, Prague, 1963-67; asst. arch. Greater London Coun., 1967-68; sr. designer R. Seifert and Ptnrs., London, 1968-69, Kahn and Jacobs, NYC, 1970-71; prin. Martin Holub Archs. and Planners, NYC, 1971—, br. office Prague, 1990—. Prin. works include Rokeby Apts., Nashville (Design award, 1976), Patricia Lane Ho. (1st prize Am. Soc. Registered Archs. Design Awards probram, 2001), Dominican Chapel, Sparkill, N.Y. (Design award Am. Soc. Registered Archs., 2002). Mem.: AIA, Archtl. League N.Y. Home: 500 E 77th St Apt 1529 New York NY 10162-0019 Office: 116 W 72nd St Fl 16 New York NY 10023-3338 Office Phone: 212-787-7644.

HOLWAY, DAVID J., labor union administrator; b. Cambridge, Mass. children: Shalie, Allei, John Conor. Attended, Boston Coll. Dep. commr. State Dept. Corrections, Mass.; chmn. Union's Health and Welfare Trust Fund; CFO Norfolk County Hospital; legis. dir., chief contract negotiator State employees Mass. Nat. Assn. Govt. Employees, pres., 2002—. Candidate St. Senate, Mass., 1986. Mem.: Mass. Dem. Com. (former chmn.), Dem. Nat. Com. (deleg. st. & nat. Dem. Conv.). Office: Nat Assn Govt Employees 159 Burgin Pkwy Quincy MA 02169 Office Phone: 617-376-0220.*

HOLWELL, PETER, management consultant; b. Mar. 28, 1936; s. Frank and Helen (Howe) H.; m. Jean Patricia Ashman, 1959; 2 chldren. BSc in Econ., London Sch. Econs. Articled clk. Arthur Andersen & Co., 1958-61, mgmt. cons., 1961-64; head univ. computing O & M unit U. London, 1967-77, sec. for acctg. & adminstrv. computing, 1977-82; clk. of the ct., 1982-85; prin. U. London, 1985-97, dir. sch. exams coun., 1988-97; mgmt. cons. Prince of Wales' Inst. Architecture, 1998-99, Chatham Hist. Dockyard Trust, 1999-2000, Leeds Castle Found., 2001. Mem. U. London Exams and Assessments Coun., 1991-96. Mem. Samuel Courtauld Avd. Bd., 1985—98; chmn. City of East London Family Health Svcs. Authority, 1994—96; trustee Leeds Castle Found., 2001—03; mem. N.E. Thames Regional Health Authority, 1990—94; chmn. St. Marks Rsch. Found. and Ednl. Trust, 1995—2000; vice chmn. coun. Wye Coll., U. London, 1995—2000, mem. coun. Sch. Pharmacy, 1996—2001; mem. Edexcel Found. Coun., 1996—97. Home: Hookers Green Bishopsbourne Canterbury Kent CT4 5JB England

HOLWELL, RICHARD J., federal judge; b. NYC, July 2, 1946; married; 2 children. BA, Villanova U., 1967; JD cum laude, Columbia Law Sch., 1970; Diploma in Criminology, Cambridge U., 1971. Bar: N.Y. 1972. Assoc. litigation atty. White & Case LLP, 1971—79, ptnr., 1971—2003; judge U.S. Dist. Ct. (So. Dist. NY), 2003—. Chairperson Panel NY State Supreme Ct. Departmental Disciplinary Com. Mem. ABA, N.Y. State Bar Assn. Office: 500 Pearl St New York NY 10007

HOLYDAY, DOUGLAS CHARLES, city councillor; b. Etobicoke, Ont., Can., July 31, 1942; s. Arthur John and Anne H.; m. Franca Palma Pellizzari, Aug. 16, 1969; children: Stephen, David. Formerly ward 6 councillor Etobicoke City Coun.; past chmn. Etobicoke Bd. Health; mayor City of Etobicoke, 1994-97; councillor City of Toronto, 1997—. Former pres., owner Holyday Ins. Brokers, Inc., Etobicoke. Founding chair Etobicoke Lakeshore Oldtimers Hockey Tournament; bd. dirs. mcpl. sect. Can. Nat. Exhbn. Assn. Avocations: golf, hockey, reading. Office: City Hall 2d Fl 100 Queen St W Toronto ON Canada M5H 2N2 Office Phone: 416-392-4002. Business E-Mail: councillor_holyday@toronto.ca.

HOLYFIELD, EVANDER, professional boxer; b. Atmore, Alab., Oct. 19, 1962; s. Annie Laura Holyfield; married; 2 children. Profl. boxer, 1985—2005; announced return to profl. boxing, 2006—. US rep. Pan-Am. Games, Venezuela, 1983; winner world title vs. Dwight Qawi, cruiserweight divsn. World Boxing Assn., 1986, winner world title def. vs. Henry Tillman by knockout, cruiserweight divsn., 87, winner world title def. vs. Ossie Ocasio by knockout, cruiserweight divsn., 87, winner world title def. vs. Dwight Qawi by knockout, cruiserweight divsn., 87, winner world title vs. James Douglas, heavyweight divsn., 90, winner world title def. vs. Larry Holmes, heavyweight divsn., 92, winner world title vs. Riddick Bowe, heavyweight divsn., 93, winner world title vs. Mike Tyson by knockout, heavyweight divsn., 96, winner world title def. vs. Mike Tyson, heavyweight divsn., 97, winner world title def. vs. Vaughn Bean, heavyweight divsn., 98, winner world title vs. John Ruiz, 2000. Performer (TV series) Dancing with the Stars, 2005. Founder Holyfield Found., 1991—. Recipient Silver medal, Pan-Am. Games, 1983, Bronze medal for light heavyweight divsn., US Olympics, LA, 1984. Achievements include being the only undefeated, undisputed cruiserweight champion; being the only 4 time heavyweight champion of the world. Office: 794 Evander Holyfield Hwy Fairburn GA 30213*

HOLYOAK, MARCEL, ecologist, educator; BS in Biology, U. London Imperial Coll., 1989; PhD in Ecology, U. London Imperial Coll., Silwood Pk., 1992. Postdoctoral rschr. Natural Environment Rsch. Ctr. Population Biology Imperial Coll. Silwood Park, 1992—94; postdoctoral rschr. Ctr. Ecology, Evolution and Behavior U. Ky., 1994—95; asst. rsch. entomologist, lectr. dept. entomology U. Calif., Davis, 1995—2000, asst. prof. dept. environ. sci. and policy, 2000—02, assoc. prof., 2002—06, prof., 2006—. Contbr. articles to profl. jours.; subeditor: Antenna, 1991—94, mem. editl. bd.: Ecology Letters, 2002—, Ecology, 2004—, Am. Naturalist, 2005—. Mem.: Union Concerned Scientists, Ecol. Soc. Am. Office: Dept Environ Sci and Policy U Calif 1 Shields Ave Davis CA 95616 E-mail: maholyoak@ucdavis.edu.

HOLZ, CARL WAYNE, retired theologian; s. Harold Otto and Gwendolyn Dee Holz; m. Rebecca Joy Osterhout, Sept. 16, 1972; 1 child, James Michael. BA, Cedarville U., Ohio, 1973; MDiv cum laude, Grace Theol. Sem., Winona Lake, Ind., 1976; ThM, Princeton Theol. Sem., NJ, 1988; PhD, Pensacola Christian Coll., Fla., 1995; DLitt (hon.), Sofia Bible U., Bulgaria, 2000; Dr.Religious Letters (hon.), Ctrl. Christian U., 2001; DD (hon.), South Fla. Bible Coll. and Sem., Deerfield Beach, 2004. Lic. preacher Conservative Bapt. Assn./Ind., 1974, ordained minister Gen. Assn. of Regular Bapt. Churches/Mich., 1975. N.Am. dir. for libr. acquisitions Sofia Bible U., Sofia, Bulgaria, 2000—02; writer/editor U.S. Army, Ft. Monmouth, NJ, 1989; humanitarian evangelist Bapt. Mid-Missions, Monrovia, Liberia, 1972. Trustee Sofia Bible U., Sofia, Bulgaria, 2000—02; cons. The Prudent Trader, Inc., NYC, 2001—03. Capt. U.S. Army, 1977—86. Decorated Silver Star Medal U.S. Army, Bronze Star Medal, Purple Heart U.S Army, Air Medal US. Army, Cross of Galantry Vietnam, 4 Army Commendation Medals Army; recipient Presdl. Cert. of Appreciation, Whitehouse, Wash. D.C., 1971. Fellow: Christian Fellowship Internat. (hon.). Personal E-mail: silverstarpurpleheart@yahoo.com.

HOLZ, GEORGE G., IV, medical educator, research scientist; b. Santa Monica, Calif., May 8, 1953; s. George G. and Mignon M. (Kiproff) Holz. BS, Cornell U., 1975; PhD, U. Ill., 1984. Rsch. fellow Tufts U. Med. Sch., Boston, 1984—89; rsch. assoc. Howard Hughes Med. Inst., Boston, 1990—93; instr. medicine Mass. Gen. Hosp.-Harvard Med. Sch., Boston, 1990—93, asst. prof. medicine, 1994—98; assoc. prof. physiology and neurosci. NYU Med. Sch., NYC, 1998—; rsch. fellow Marine Biology Lab., Woods Hole, Mass., 2000—. Corp. mem. Marine Biol. Lab., Woods Hole, Mass. Mem. All-Sectional Gymnastics Team N.Y., 1971. Recipient Rsch. award, Am. Diabetes Assn., 1996, 2000; grantee rsch. grantee, NIH;

scholar N.Y. State Regents scholar, Cornell U., 1971—75. Mem.: AAAS, Am. Diabetes Assn., Soc. Gen. Physiologists, Endocrine Soc., Soc. for Neurosci. Office Phone: 212-263-5434. E-mail: holzg01@popmail.med.nyu.edu.

HOLZ, HARRY GEORGE, lawyer; b. Milw., Sept. 13, 1934; s. Harry Carl and Emma Louise (Hinz) H.; m. Nancy L. Heiser, May 12, 1962; children: Pamela Gretchen, Bradley Eric, Erika Lynn. BS, Marquette U., 1956, LLB, 1958; LLM, Northwestern U., 1960. Bar: Wis. 1958, Ill. 1960. Tchg. fellow Northwestern U. Sch. Law, 1958-59; assoc. Sidley & Austin, Chgo., 1960; ptnr. Quarles & Brady, Milw., 1968—2002, of counsel, 2002—. Lectr. law securities regulation U. Wis. Law Sch., 1971—74; adj. prof. Marquette U. Sch. Law, 1976—91; faculty program on antitrust law Wis. State Bar Sems., 1975—82, 1989, 93; bd. dirs., sec. Creative Sharp Presentations Inc.; lectr. PLI 33rd Antitrust Inst.; lectr., spkr. in antitrust field. Bd. visitors Marquette U. Sch. Law, 1990, 93; moderator First Congl. Ch., Warnator. Capt. C.E. U.S. Army, 1960-67. Fellow: Am. Bar Found.; mem.: ABA (lectr. nat. antitrust program 1997, Robinson-Patman com., corp. counsel com., antitrust litigation com.), Marquette U. Law Alumni Assn. (bd. dirs.), Milw. Bar Assn., Wis. Bar Assn. (chmn. bus. law com. 1978—79, bd. dirs. 1978—83, chair 180 standing rev. com. 2001—, standing com. bus. law), Marquette U. Sch. Law Woolsack Soc. (bd. dirs., past pres.), Phi Delta Phi, Beta Gamma Sigma. Office: Quarles & Brady 411 E Wisconsin Ave Ste 2550 Milwaukee WI 53202-4497 Business E-Mail: hgh@quarles.com.

HOLZ, ROBERT KENNETH, retired geography educator; b. Kankakee, Ill., Nov. 3, 1930; s. Harry H. and Margaret (Conway) H.; m. Joyce F. Harpin, May 19, 1951; 1 child, Eric R. BA in Zoology, So. Ill. U., Carbondale, 1958, MA in Geography, 1959; PhD in Geography, Mich. State U., East Lansing, 1963. Asst. prof. U. Tex., Austin, 1962-67, assoc. prof., 1967-72, prof., 1972—, dir. ctr. for Middle Eastern Studies, 1991-99, Eric W. Zimmerman Regents prof., 1991-99, Eric W. Zimmerman Regents prof. emeritus, 1999—; ret., 1999. Cons. in field. Co-author: Mendes I, 1980; author, editor: The Surveillant Science, 2d edit., 1985. Staff sgt. USAF, 1951-55. Recipient Group Achievement award NASA, 1974, Urban Achievement award L.B.J. Sch. Pub. Affairs, 1984. Mem. Assn. Am. Geographers (chmn. remote sensing specialty group 1980-82, chmn. southwest div. 1971-72, medal for outstanding contbns. to remote sensing Remote Sensing Specialty Group 1998), Am. Soc. Photogrammetry, Tex. Assn. Coll. Tchrs., Am. Congress of Surveying and Mapping. Roman Catholic. Avocations: hunting, fishing, squash. Home: 2610 Fiset Dr Austin TX 78731-5614 Office: U Tex Dept Geography Austin TX 78712 Personal E-mail: holzrj@aol.com.

HOLZBACH, RAYMOND THOMAS, gastroenterologist, educator, writer; b. Salem, Ohio, Aug. 19, 1929; s. Raymond T. and Nelle A. (Conroy) H.; m. Lorraine E. Cozza, May 26, 1956; children: Ellen, Mark, James. BS, Georgetown U., 1951; MD, Case Western Res. U., 1955. Diplomate Nat. Bd. Med. Examiners, Am. Bd. Internal Medicine. Intern, asst. resident U. Ill. Research and Edn. Hosps., Chgo., 1955-56; sr. asst. resident medicine Cleve. Met. Gen. Hosp., 1959-60; asst. chief gastroenterology Case Western Res U., 1961-63; physician Gastroenterology Unit U. Hosps. of Cleve., 1961-63; instr. medicine Case Western Res. U. Sch. Medicine, Cleve., 1961-64, clin. instr. medicine, 1964-71; head gastrointestinal research unit, assoc. physician div. medicine St. Luke's Hosp., Cleve., 1967-73, dir. div. gastroenterology, 1970-73; head gastrointestinal research unit dept. medicine Cleve. Clinic Found., 1973—. Vis. prof. numerous instns. including Mayo Med. Sch., 1974, U. Calif., San Diego, 1977, U. Heidelberg, 1978, U. Pa., 1979, U. Zurich, 1980, U. Munich, 1982, U. Minn. Med. Ctr., 1985, med. ctrs., numerous Japanese univs., 1985, 92, Karolinska Inst., 1986, Royal Soc. London, 1987, Pa. State U. Sch. Med., U. Helsinki, RWTH-Aachen, Düsseldorf, Fed. Republic of Germany, U. Groningen, Utrecht, U. Amsterdam, The Netherlands, 1989, U. Perugia, Italy, Va. Commonwealth U.-Med. Coll. Va., Richmond, Christ Ch. Sch. Medicine, U. Otago, New Zealand, SUNY, Buffalo Sch. Medicine, 1990, Pontifical/Cath. U. Chile Sch. Medicine, 1991, Hiroshima U. Sch. Medicine, 1992, Kyoto U. Sch. Medicine, 1992, Sch. Medicine U. Jikei, Tokyo, 1992, Tel Aviv U., Israel Sch. Medicine, 1995, U. Leipzig, Germany, 1996, U. Heidelberg, Germany, 1996; lectr. in field. Mem. editl. bd. Gastroenterology jour., 1984-89; contbr. revs. and articles to med. jours. Served to capt. USAF, 1957-59. Recipient Alexander von Humboldt Found. Spl. Program award, 1978, 82. Fellow ACP; mem. ABA, Am. Gastroent. Assn. (rsch. com. 1976-79), Ctrl. Soc. Clin. Rsch., Am. Assn. for Study of Liver Diseases, AAAS, Am. Soc. Biol. Chemists, Am. Physiol. Assn., Biophys. Soc., Internat. Assn. Study of Liver, Am. Fedn. Clin. Rsch., Midwest Gut Club, Am. Soc. Clin. Nutrition, Ohio State Med. Assn., Sigma Xi. Unitarian Universalist. Office: Cleve Clin Found 9500 Euclid Ave Cleveland OH 44195-0001 Personal E-mail: tomholzbach@adelphia.net.

HOLZEMER, WILLIAM L., nursing educator; BS in Psychology, U. Wash.; BSN, San Francisco State U.; MS in Edn./Counseling, Miami U., Ohio; PhD in Higher Edn. Adminstrn., Syracuse U., NYC. Dir. Internat. Ctr. for HIV/AIDS Rsch. and Clin. Tng. in Nursing U. Calif., 1991—, dir. WHO Collaborating Ctr. Rsch. & Clin. Training in Nursing, 1992—, prof. cmty. health systems, Sch. Nursing, chair dept. cmty. health systems, Sch. Nursing, 1996—2001, assoc. dean internat. programs, 2002—. Vis. prof. St. Luke's Coll. Nursing, Tokyo, Thames Valley U., London; med. adv. bd. Global AIDS Interfaith Alliance. Internat. editor-in-chief Japan Acad. Nursing Scis., 2003—, editl. bd. Jour. Global AIDS Pandemic, 2003—. Recipient ONE-Calif. Award for Excellence in Nursing Scholarship, 1997, Disting. Rsch. Lectureship award, Western Inst. Nursing, 1997, Rschr. Recognition award, Assn. of Nurses in AIDS Care, 1999, Recognition award Ctr. for Ethics and Human Rights, ANA, 2000, George S. Sarlo award for Excellence in Mentoring, UCSF AIDS Rsch. Inst., 2003; fellow, Project Hope fellow, 1983; scholar, Fulbright scholar, Egypt, 1984. Fellow: Am. Acad. Nursing; mem.: Am. Nurses Found. (pres. 2002—06), Japan Acad. Nursing, Inst. Medicine (life), Coun. for Advancement of Nursing Sci. (chair 1998—2002). Office: UCSF Sch Nursing 2 Koret Way N-531C Box 0608 San Francisco CA 94143-0608 Office Phone: 415-476-2763. Office Fax: 415-476-6042. E-mail: bill.holzemer@nursing.ucsf.edu.

HOLZER, EDWIN, advertising executive; b. June 22, 1933; MusB, Yale U., 1954, MusM, 1955; postgrad., Ind. U., 1956. Acct. exec. Benton & Bowles Inc., NYC, 1959-62; account supr. William Esty Co., NYC, 1962-66, Grey Advt. Inc., NYC, 1966-68, mgmt. supr., 1968-70; exec. v.p. Grey Inc., NYC, 1970-73; pres., CEO, COO Grey-North Inc., Chgo., 1973-85; chmn., CEO, Grey Chgo. (name changed to LOIS/GGK 1988), 1988; chmn., CEO LOIS/EJL (formerly Lois/USA), Chgo., from 1988; chief marketing officer CornerDrugstore.com, 2000—.

HOLZER, HAROLD, museum and marketing executive, historian, writer; b. Bklyn., Feb. 5, 1949; s. Charles and Rose (Last) H.; m. Edith Spiegel, Feb. 27, 1971; children: Remy, Meg. BA, CUNY, Queens, 1969; diploma (hon.), Lincoln Meml. U., Harrogate, Tenn., 1988, Lincoln Coll., Ill., 1992, Ill. Coll., Jacksonville, 2006, U. Mass, Dartmouth, 2006. Editor Manhattan Tribune, NYC, 1969-73; dir. spl. projects Dept. Civic Affairs, NYC, 1973-75; press sec. to Congresswoman Bella Abzug NYC, 1975-77; communications specialist Sec. of State office, NY, 1978; dir. pub. affairs Sta. WNET (PBS), NYC, 1978-84; v.p. pub. affairs Javits Conv. Ctr., NYC, 1984-85; exec. v.p. pub. affairs Urban Devel. Corp., State of N.Y., 1985-92; chief comm. officer Met. Mus. Art, NYC, 1992-96, v.p. comm., 1996-2001, v.p. comm. and mktg., 2001—05, sr. v.p. external affairs, 2005—. Co-author: The Lincoln Image, 1984, Changing the Lincoln Image, 1985, The Confederate Image, 1987, The Lincoln Family Album, 1990, Lincoln on Democracy, 1990, Mine Eyes Have Seen the Glory: The Civil War In Art, 1993, The Union Preserved, 1999, The Lincoln Forum, 1999, The Union Image, 2000; author: The Lincoln-Douglas Debates, 1993, Washington and Lincoln Portrayed, 1993, Dear Mr. Lincoln: Letters to the President, 1993, Witness to War: The Civil War, 1996, The Civil War Era, 1996; The Lincoln Mailbag: America Writes to the President, 1998, Lincoln As I Knew Him, 1999, Abraham Lincoln, The Writer, 2000, Lincoln Seen and Heard, 2000, Prang's Civil War, 2001, State of the Union, 2002; Rediscovering Abraham Lincoln: The Lincoln Forum, 2002, The President is Shot!, 2004, Lincoln at Cooper Union: The Speech that Made Abraham Lincoln President, 2004, Lincoln in The Times, 2005, The Battle of Hampton Roads, 2006, The Emancipation Proclamation: Three Views, 2006, Lincoln Revisted, 2007, Lincoln in the Collections of Indiana Historical Society, 2007, Lincoln's White House Secretary: The Adventurous Life of William O. Stoddard, 2007, Lincoln and Freedom, 2007; contbg. editor: Americana Mag., 1991-93; writer various pamphlets on Abraham Lincoln; contbg. historian various CD-ROMS, TV spls. on C-SPAN, A&E, The History Channel, NBC, ABC, CBS, PBS; contbr. over 350 articles to popular mags., scholarly jours. and newspapers, chpts. to books Lectr. on Lincoln and Civil War; co-organizer 4 exhbns. on Lincoln and Civil War; trustee NY State Archives Partnership Trust, 1994—; mem. US Lincoln Bicentennial Commn. (appointed by Pres. Clinton), 2000, co-chmn., 2001--. Recipient Barondess/Lincoln award Civil War Round Table of NY, 1984, 91, 94, 2005, George Washington medal Freedom Found. Valley Forge, 1988, Writer of Distinction award Internat. Reading Assn., 1989, award Manuscript Soc. Am., 1996, Newman Book award Am. Hist. Print Collectors' Soc., 2000, Nevins-Freeman award, CWRT/Chgo., 2002, Lincoln prize, 2005. Mem. Abraham Lincoln Assn. (bd. dirs. 1988-95, Achievement award 1991, Lincoln prize, 2005), Lincoln Group of NY (v.p. 1979-90, pres. 1990-96, Achievement award 1988, 93, 05), State Coun. for Humanities (bd. dirs. 1991-93), Ulysses S. Grant Assn. (bd. dirs. 1996—), The Lincoln Forum (vice chmn. 1996—). Office: Met Mus of Art 1000 Fifth Ave New York NY 10028-0113 Business E-Mail: harold.holzer@metmuseum.org.

HOLZER, HARRY JOSEPH, economist, educator; b. Somers Point, NJ, Feb. 25, 1957; s. Simon and Suzanne C. (Wester) H.; m. Deborah Shulman, June 24, 1990; children Simone, Hannah, Leah. AB, Harvard U., 1978, PhD, 1983. Prof. of econs. Mich. State U., 1983—2000; chief economist US Dept. Labor, Washington, 1999; prof. public policy Georgetown U., Washington, 2000—, assoc. dean, 2004—06, interim dean, 2006. Sr. affiliate Nat. Poverty Ctr., U. Mich.; nat. fellow Programs on Inequality and Social Policy Harvard U. Author: What Employers Want, 1996, Moving Up or Moving On, 2005, Reconnecting Disadvantaged Young Men, 2006; co-editor: Shaping the American Workforce in a Changing Economy, 2007. Office Phone: 202-687-1458. Business E-Mail: hjh4@georgetown.edu.

HOLZER, JENNY, artist; b. Gallipolis, Ohio, July 29, 1950; d. Richard Vornholt and Virginia (Beasley) H.; m. Michael Andrew Glier, May 21, 1984; 1 child. Student, Duke U., 1968-70, U. Chgo., 1970-71; BFA, Ohio U., 1973, DA (hon.), 1994; MFA, RI Sch. Design, 1977; postgrad., Whitney Mus. Am. Art, 1977; DFA (hon.), RI Sch. Design, 2003, Williams Coll., 2000, New Sch. U., NYC, 2005. Resident artist Am. Acad., Rome, 2003. One-woman shows include Rüdiger Schöttle Gall, Münich, 1980, Barbara Gladstone Gallery, NYC, 1983, 86, 94, Kunsthalle, Basel, Switzerland, 1984, Des Moines Art Ctr., 1986, MIT, Cambridge, 1986, Mus. Contemporary Art, Chgo., 1987, Inst. Contemporary Art, London, 1988, Bklyn. Mus., NYC, 1988, DIA Art Found., NYC, 1989, Guggenheim Mus., NYC, 1989, Am. Pavilion, 44th Biennale, Venice, Italy, 1990, La. Mus., Humlebaek, Denmark, 1991, Albright-Knox Art Gallery, Buffalo, 1991, Walker Art Gallery, Mpls., 1991, Ydessa Hendeles Art Found., Toronto, 1992, Dallas Mus. Art, 1993, Haus der Kunst, Munich, 1993, Bergen Mus. Art, Norway, 1994, Art Tower Mito, Japan, 1994, Williams Coll. Mus. Art, Williamstown, Mass., 1995, Kunstmus. des Kantons Thurgau, Kartouse Ittingen, Warth, Switzerland, 1996, Contemporary Art Mus., Houston, 1997, Cheim & Read, NY, 1997, Yvon Lambert Gallery, Paris, 1998, 2004, Inst. Cultural Itau, São Paulo, Brazil, 1998, Centro Cultural Banco do Brasil, Rio de Janeiro, 1999, BALTIC Ctr. Contemporary Art, Gateshead, 2000, Neue Nat. Galeri, Berlin, 2001, Mus. Contemporary Art, Bordeaux, France, 2001, Monterrey, Mex., 2001, Mönchehaus Mus., Goslar, Germany, 2002, Monika Spruth Philomene Magers, 2002, 04, Kunsthaus Bregenz, Austria, 2004, NYC, 2005, others; exhibited in group shows at Documenta 7, Kassel, Germany, 1982, Contemporary Arts Ctr., Cin., 1984, Mus. Art Carnegie Inst., Pitts., 1985, Israel Mus., Jerusalem, 1986, Frankfurter Kunstverein, Frankfurt, Germany, 1986, Europa/Amerika Mus. Ludwig, Koln, 1986, Sonsbeck, Arnhem, The Netherlands, 1986, Whitney Mus. Am. Art, NYC, 1989, Mus. Contemporary Art, LA, 1989, Mus. Modern Art, NYC, 1988, 90, 96, Documenta 8, Kassel, 1987, Ctrl. Mus., Utrecht, The Netherlands, 1991, Kunsthalle, Basel, 1992, Guggenheim Mus., Soho, NYC, 1993, 96, Lenbachhaus, Munich, 1994, SITE Santa Fe, 1995, Pompidou Ctr., Paris, 1996, Biennale di Florence, Italy, 1996, Joseph Helman Gallery, NY, 1997, Kunsthalle Wien, Vienna, Austria, 1998, Nat. Gallery Australia, Canberra, 1998, Rhona Hofman Gallery, 1998, Oslo Mus. Contemporary Art, 2000; represented in permanent collections Ujazdowski Castle, Warsaw, Poland, Black Garden, Nordhorn, Germany, Erlauf (Austria) Peace Monument, Guggenheim Mus., Bilbao, Bundestag, Berlin, U. So. Calif., LA, Ludwig Mus., Aachen, Germany, Neue Nat. Galerie, Berlin, Toyota Mclpl. Mus. Art, Hamburg Kunstalle, US Fed. Courthouse, Sacramento, Allentown, Pa., Telenor Hdqr., Norway, U. Pa., Phila., Paula Matersohn-Becker Mus., Bremen, Germany, Lawrence Conv. Ctr., Pitts., Stora Target, Karlstad, Sweden, others. Recipient Golden Lion award 44th Venice Biennale, 1990, Skowhegan medal for installation Skowhegen Sch. Painting and Sculpture, N.Y., 1994, Crystal award World Econ. Forum, Cologny-Geneva, Switzerland, 1996, BMW Art car, BMW, Munich, 1999, Kaiserring award City of Goslar, Germany, 2002. Fellow Am. Acad., Berlin, 2000, Am. Acad. Rome. Avocation: reading. E-mail: studio@jennyholzer.com, gallery@cheimread.com.

HOLZER, MARC, public administrator educator; b. Feb. 28, 1945; s. Philip and Ann Lee (Blinder) H.; m. Madeleine Fuchs, Aug. 31, 1969; children: Matthew, Benjamin. BA in Polit. Sci., U. Rochester, 1966; MPA, U. Mich., 1967, PhD of Polit. Sci., 1971. Asst. prof. govt. and pub. adminstrn. John Jay Coll. CUNY, 1971-74, assoc. prof., 1975-79, prof., 1980-89; prof. I pub. adminstrn. Rutgers U., Newark, 1989—2002, prof. II pub. adminstrn., 2002—06, bd. govs., prof. pub. affairs & adminstrn., 2006—, chair grad. dept. pub. adminstrn., 2000—06, dean, sch. pub. affairs & adminstrn., 2006—. Founder, exec. dir. Nat. Ctr. for Pub. Productivity, 1975—; founder, chmn. Internat. Productivity Network, 1988—; cons. internat. and fed. depts. agys., city, state and county agys.; dir. numerous funded projects in field; mem. Croton-Harmon Bd. Edn., 1984-87, pres. 1986-87; adv. acad. bd./bd. trustees Campus Arts & Scis., Athens. Author: (with others) Managing for Improved Productivity, 1981, (with Arie Halachmi) Public Sector Productivity, 1988, (with Virginia Cherry) Public Administration Research Guide, 1991, (with Kathe Callahan) Government at Work, 1998, (with Sang-Tae Kim) Digital Governance in Municipalities Worldwide, 2005; editor: Productivity in Public Organizations, 1976, Public Productivity Handbook, 1991, (with K. Morris and W. Ludwin) Literature in Bureaucracy: Readings in Administrative Fiction, 1979, (with Ellen D. Rosen) Current Cases in Public Administration, 1981, (with Stuart Nagel) Productivity and Public Policy, 1984, (with Arie Halachmi) Strategic Issues in Public Sector Productivity, 1986, Competent Government, 1995, (with Vatche Gabrielian) Case Studies in Productive Public Management, 1995, (with Kathe Callahan and Joseph Delorio) Reinventing New Jersey, 1995, Public Service: Callings, Commitments and Contributions, 2000, (with Byong-Joon Kim) Building Good Governance, 2002, (with Mengzhong Zhang) Chinese Public Administration in Exploration, 2002, Economic Globalization and Strategies of Chinese Public Administration, 2003, Public Productivity Handbook, 2d edit., 2004, Research Resources in Public Administration, 2005, (with Se-Koo Rhee) Citizen-Driven Government Performance, 2006, Teaching Resources Guide to Public Affairs and Administration, 2007; founder, editor-in-chief Public Productivity and Mgmt. Rev., 1975—, Pub. Voices, 1994—, Chinese Pub. Adminstrn. Review, 2002—, ASPA Classics Series, 1997—, (with Jay Shafritz) Selections from the International Encyclopedia of Public Adminstration, 2001; assoc. editor Internat. Ency. Pub. Policy and Adminstrn.; assoc. editor Ency. of Pub. Adminstrn. and Pub. Policy, 2002; mem. editl. bd. Internat. Jour. Pub. Adminstrn., Pub. Adminstrn. Quar., Pub. Budgeting and Fin. Mgmt., The Pub. Mgr. (formerly The Bureaucrat), Jour. Non-Profit and Pub. Sector Mktg., Jour. Mgmt. History, Internat. Jour. Orgnl. Theory and Behavior, ASPA Classics, Internat. Rev. Pub. Adminstrn., Pub. Adminstrn. Rev., Pub. Adminstrn. and Mgmt.; contbr. numerous chpts. in books, articles to profl. jours. Founder, co-chairperson Pub. Adminstrn. Tchg. Roundtable, 1980—. Recipient Nat. Excellence in Tchg. award, Nat. Assn. Schs. Pub. Affairs & Adminstrn., 1998, Bd. Trustees award for Excellence in Rsch., Rutgers U., 2001, Southeastern Conf. Pub. Adminstrn. Sen. Peter Boorsma award, 2001, Bd. Trustees Pub. Svc. award, Rutgers U., 2002, Excellence award, Chinese Pub. Adminstrn. Soc., 2002, Human Dignity award, Rutgers U., 2004, Acad. award, Internat. City Mgmt. Assn., 2005, Presdl. Leadership award, Conf. Minority Pub. Adminstrs., 2006; fellow Rockefeller Inst. Govt., 1986—87, World Acad. Productivity Sci., 2001—. Fellow: Nat. Acad. Pub. Adminstrn.; mem.: ASPA (chmn. nat. tng. com. 1981—82, 1983—84, nat. coun. 1982—85, chairperson mgmt. sci. sect 1981—82, 1989—90, pres. N.Y. Met. chpt. 1978—79, 0799—1980, chairperson sect. humanistic, artistic and reflective expression 1993—95, chair publs. com. 1993—94, nat. v.p. 1998—99, nat. pres.-elect 1999—2000, nat. pres. 2000—01, N.Y. Met. Outstanding Acad. award 1985, N.J. Outstanding Achievement award 1992, Donald C. Stone award 1994, Charles H. Levine award 2000, Mosher award Best Article (with Patricia Julnes) 2001, Wholey Disting. Scholarship award (with Patricia Julnes) 2001). Home: 4 Giglio Ct Croton On Hudson NY 10520-2005 Office: Rutgers U Hill Hall 7th Fl 360 King Blvd Newark NJ 07102-1801 Office Phone: 973-353-5093. E-mail: mholzer@pipeline.com.

HOLZER-GARGIULO, ALEXANDRA, graphics designer, writer; b. NYC, Apr. 5, 1971; d. Hans Holzer and Catherine Buxhoeveden; m. Christopher Frank Gargiulo, Nov. 4, 1995; children: Nicole Nadine Gargiulo, Danielle Michelle Gargiulo, Samantha Alexandra Gargiulo, Matthew Michael Gargiulo. AA, Fashion Inst. Tech., NYC, 1992. Graphic designer Regency Cruise Lines, NYC, 1992—95, Inst. Internat. Rsch., NYC, 1995—98; freelancer Alexandra Holzer Gargiulo Design, Monroe, 1998—2003; freelance graphic designer, 2003—. Filmed as paranormal expert (re-release films) Poltergeist, Warner Home Video, 2007; author: (book) Lady Ambrosia-Secret Past Revealed, 2007; contbr. chapters to books; columnist: Spirit Talk UFO Digest. Mem.: Soc. Children's Book Writing & Illustration. Achievements include creating a column for KDMRadio.net Newsletter entitled 'Spirit Talk' for PAS Newsletter. Home: 11 Seely Rd Chester NY 10918 Personal E-mail: gargiulo1971@optonline.net.

HOLZMAN, D. KEITH, management consultant, record company executive; b. NYC, Mar. 22, 1936; s. Jacob Easton and Minnette Cathryn (Sternberger) H.; m. Jo Susan Handelman, Nov. 16, 1971; children: Susanne Carla, Lucas Jon, Rebecca Leigh. BA, Oberlin Coll., Ohio, 1957; MFA, Boston U., 1959. Asst. to gen. mgr. and stage mgr. N.Y.C. Light Opera, 1959, 62-64; dir. prodn. Elektra Records, NYC, 1964-70; v.p. prodn. and mfg. Elektra/Asylum/Nonesuch Records, Los Angeles, 1970-81, sr. v.p. prodn. and mfg., 1981-84; pres. ROM Records, 1987—2000; producer, arts cons. Treasure Trove, Inc., 1984—2000; mng. dir. Discovery Records, Santa Monica, Calif., 1991-98; prin. Keith Holzman Solutions Unltd., 1998—. Pres. Treasure Trove Inc.; dir. Nonesuch Records, 1980-84; music supr. Witches of Eastwick, Warner Bros., LA, 1986; bd. dirs. Plumstead Theatre Soc., LA, 1985—, Early Music Acad., LA, 1983-86, Assn. Classical Music, NYC, 1983-86, Wizard Music. Author: The Complete Guide to Starting a Record Company, 2004. Served with AUS, 1960-62. Mem. Audio Engring. Soc., Early Music Acad. (bd. dirs.) Nat. Acad. Rec. Arts and Scis., Assn. Classical Music (bd. dirs.), Plumstead Theatre Co. (bd. dirs.). Avocation: flying.

HOLZMAN, JAMES L(OUIS), lawyer; b. Bklyn., Jan. 7, 1949; s. Robert Conrad and Muriel Claire (Smith) H.; m. Jonnie Irene Frisbie; children: James Casey, Meredith Claire, Jon Carroll. BA, John B. Stetson U., 1970; JD, U. Fla., 1972. Bar: Fla. 1973, Del. 1973, U.S. Dist. Ct. Del. 1974, U.S. Dist. Ct. (so. dist.) Fla 1973, U.S. Tax Ct. 1973, U.S. Ct. Appeals (3d cir.) 1976, U.S. Ct. Appeals (fed. cir.) 1983, U.S. Ct. Appeals (2d cir.) 2001, U.S. Supreme Ct. 2002. Assoc. Prickett, Ward, Burt & Sanders, Wilmington, Del., 1973-77, ptnr., 1977-79, Prickett, Jones, Elliott, Kristol & Schnee, Wilmington, Del., 1979—, mng. ptnr., 1986-90. Author Rev. Devel. Corp. Law. Mem. ABA (sect. bus. law, chair revenue com. 2001—, chair bus. and corp. litigation com. 1996-2000, chair coun. fin. com. 2004-05, section liaison, presdl. task force on atty. client privilege, co-chair judge's task force, coun 2001-2006, mem. task force litigation reform and rules revision, mem. corp. governance com., mem. editl. bd. The Bus. Lawyer), Del. State Bar Assn. (mem. corp. law sect. coun. 1998—, vice chair 2006—), Assn. of Bar of City of N.Y., Fla. Bar, Fed. Bar Assn., Wilmington Club (trustee Tower Hill Sch. 1990-2006, pres. 2000-03). Home: 3213 Fordham Rd Wilmington DE 19807-3117 Office: Prickett Jones & Elliott 1310 N King St Wilmington DE 19801-3220 Office Phone: 302-888-6509.

HOLZMANN, GERARD JOHAN, computer science researcher; b. Amsterdam, The Netherlands, Nov. 12, 1951; s. Paulus Jacobus and Anna Christina (Hindriks) Holzmann. PhD, Delft U., Netherlands, 1979. Vis. prof. computer sci. U. So. Calif., LA, 1979-80; mem. tech. staff Bell Labs, Computer Sci. Rsch., Murray Hill, NJ, 1980-81, 83-95, disting. mem. tech. staff, 1995—2003; rschr. Delft U., 1981-83; prin. computer scientist Jet Propulsion Lab., NASA, Pasadena, Calif., 2003—. Author: Design and Validation of Computer Protocols, 1991; co-author: (with Bjorn Pherson) The Early History of Data Networks, 1995; editor: (with J.C. Gregoire and D. Peled) The Spin Verification System, 1996; author (verification sys.) Spin. Mem.: NAE. Office: Jet Propulsion Lab 4800 Oak Grove Dr Pasadena CA 91109 Office Phone: 818-393-5937. Business E-Mail: gholzmann@acm.org.

HOLZNER, BURKART, retired sociologist, educator; b. Tilsit, Germany, Apr. 28, 1931; came to U.S., 1957, naturalized, 1965; s. Hans Otto and Brigitte (Prenzel) H.; children by previous marriage: Steven, Daniel, Claire; m. Leslie Holzner; stepchildren: Sara Ruth Salmon-Cox, Weir Becket Strange. Student, U. Munich, 1949—52, student, 1953—54, U. Wis., 1952—53, postgrad., 1958—60; Diploma Psychology, U. Bonn, 1957, Dr.Phil., 1958. Grad. asst., acting instr. U. Wis., 1958—60; asst. prof. U. Pitts., 1960—63, assoc. prof., 1963—65, prof., chmn. sociology dept., 1966—80, dir. bd. visitors field staff Learning R&D Ctr., 1964—66, dir., prof. Univ. Ctr. Internat. Studies, 1998—, disting. svc. prof. internat. studies, 1999—2003, sr. rsch. assoc., prof. emeritus, 2003—. Assoc. sociologist, assoc. dir. Social Sci. Rsch. Inst., U. Hawaii, 1965-66; vis. prof. sociology, dir. Social Rsch. Centre, Chinese U. of Hong Kong, 1969-70, external examiner in sociology, 1995-98; vis. prof. U. Augsburg, 1977, Chinese Acad. Social Scis., Beijing, 1979, 80; cons. Nat. Inst. Edn., Westinghouse Electric Corp.; mem. exec. com. Pa. Coun. for Internat. Edn., 1980-89, chmn., 1980-83, 88-89. Author: Amerikanische und deutsche Psychologie, 1958, Völkerpsychologie, 1960, Reality Construction in Society, rev. edit, 1972, (with John Marx) Knowledge Application: The Knowledge System in Society, 1979; editor: (with Roland Robertson)

Identity and Authority, Explorations in the Theory of Society, 1980, (with Jiri Nehnevajsa) Organizing for Social Research, 1981, (with Zdenek Suda) Directions of Change: Modernization Theory, Research and Reality, 1981, (with Andrew Dinniman) Education for International Competence in Pennsylvania, 1988, (with Leslie Holzner) Transparency in Global Change: The Vanguard of the Open Society, 2006, (with Wenfang Tang) Social Change in Contemporary China: C.K. Yang and the Concept of Institutional Diffusion, 2007; co-editor Knowledge: Creation, Distribution, Utilization, 1985, Knowledge in Society, 1987-89. Mem. dist. export council U.S. Dept. Commerce. Recipient Philip R.A. May award for internat. svc., 1991; named hon. citizen of Johnstown, Pa., hon. mem. U. Augsburg, 1990. Mem. Am. Sociol. Assn., North Central Sociol. Assn., Pa. Sociol. Assn., Sociol. Rsch. Assn., Sozialwissenschaftlicher Studienkreis für Internationale Probleme, Internat. Soc. for Comparative Study of Civilizations (mem. U.S. coun., v.p. 1977-79), Assn. Internat. Edn. Adminstrs. (exec. com. 1986—, pres. 1990-91, Charles Klasek award for career achievement in internat. edn. 2000, sr. counselor 2001—), World Federalist Assn. Pitts. (pres. 1996-2001). Home: 1700 Grandview Ave Apt 801 Pittsburgh PA 15211-1006 Office: U Pitts Ctr Internat Studies 4116 Posvar Hall Pittsburgh PA 15260 E-mail: holzner1@pitt.edu.

HOLZWEISS, ROBERT F., archivist, educator; b. Mt. Kisco, NY, Apr. 24, 1968; s. Thomas A. and Margaret C. Holzweiss; m. Peggy C. Philpot, June 26, 1999; children: Jakob T., Nicholas G. BA, St. Bonaventure U., NY, 1990; MA, Tex. A&M U., Coll. Station, 1992, PhD, 2001. Supervisory archivist George Bush Presdl. Libr., Coll. Station, 1996—; vis. asst. prof. Tex. A&M U., 2001—. Mem.: Soc. Southwestern Archivists, Lexington Group in Transp. History, Rlwy. & Locomotive Hist. Soc. Roman Catholic. Office: George Bush Presdl Libr 1000 George Bush Dr W College Station TX 77845 Home Phone: 979-779-7661; Office Phone: 979-691-4074. Office Fax: 979-691-4030. Business E-Mail: robert.holzweiss@nara.gov.

HOM, DAVID BRIAN, surgeon; b. San Diego, 1956; s. James and Evelyn Hom; m. Lorraine Hom, 1984. BA summa cum laude, U. Calif., San Diego, 1978; MD, UCLA, 1982. Diplomate Am. Bd. Otolaryngology and Facial Plastic and Reconstructive Surgery. Gen. surg. resident U. Calif., Irvine, 1983-84; otolaryngology, head and neck surgery resident U. Mich., Ann Arbor, 1984-88; facial plastic fellow Am. Acad. Facial Plastic Surgery, Birmingham, Ala., 1988-89; asst. prof. dept. otolaryngology, head and neck surgery U. Minn., Mpls., 1989-96, assoc. prof., 1996—. Mem. otolaryngology expert adv. panel U.S. Pharmacopia Conv., Washington, 1994—; bd. dirs. Am. Bd. Facial Plastic and Reconstructive Surgery. Editor: Wound Healing for the Otolaryngologist-Head and Neck Surgeon, 1995; contbr. numerous articles to profl. jours., chpts. to books. Med. cons. NCAA, Mpls., 1996-97. NIH Rsch. grantee, 1996-2002. Fellow ACS, Am. Acad. Otolaryngology, Head and Neck Surgery (Nat. Percy Meml. Rsch. award 1991), Am. Acad. Facial Plastic and Reconstructive Surgery (chmn. rsch. 1997-2000, bd. dirs. 2005—, Nat. Ben Shuster Rsch. award 1988); mem. AAAS, Minn. Acad. Otolaryngology-Head and Neck Surgery (pres. 2005). Avocations: fishing, kayaking. Office: Univ Minn Dept Otolaryngology Box 396 420 Delaware St SE Minneapolis MN 55455

HOMAN, JEAN P., lawyer; BA, U. Hawaii, Honolulu, 1991; JD, Seattle U., 1997. Bar: Wash. 1997, Calif. 2003. Asst. city atty. Tacoma City Atty.'s Office, 1996—. Office: 747 Market St # 1120 Tacoma WA 98402

HOMAN, RALPH WILLIAM, finance company executive; b. Wilkes-Barre, Pa., June 7, 1951; s. Norman Ryan and Adelaide Bernice (Sandy) H.; m. Adelaide Almquist, Sept. 18, 2005. BS in Acctg., Wheeling Coll., 1977; MBA in Mktg., Nat. U., 1986. Paymaster Dravo Corp., Pitts., 1974-75; tax preparer H&R Block, Wheeling, W.Va., 1977; fin. services exec. NCR Credit Corp., Sacramento, 1977-84; leasing exec. CSB Leasing, Sacramento, 1984-85; pres. Convergent Fin. Svcs., Colorado Springs, Colo., 1985—, CFS Productivity Solutions, 2003—. Bd. dirs. Concord Coalition, Colorado Springs; adj. instr. bus. Colo. Mountain Coll., Leadville. Cons. Jr. Achievement, 1990—. Co-winner Name the Plane Contest Pacific Southwest Airlines, 1984; recipient Businessperson of Yr. award, Colo. Springs chpt. Future Bus. Leaders Am., 1995, 2000. Mem. The 30/40 Something Social Club (founder, pres. Sedona chpt.), Am. Assn. Boomers (pres. Pikes Peak chpt. 1992-93), Toastmasters (treas. Oak Creek chpt. 1988-89), Kiwanis (sec. 1988-89, founder, chmn. adult soccer league), Concord Coalition (bd. dirs., pres. Colorado Springs chpt.). Avocations: photography, camping, off-road motorcycling, woodworking. Home and Office: Convergent Fin Svcs 29 Mount Hope Dr Twin Lakes CO 81251-9705 Home Phone: 719-486-0695. Business E-Mail: cfssolutions@earthlink.net.

HOMANN, BRUCE KENDALL, financial analyst; s. Warren Gene Homann and Mary June Bierwirth; 1 child, Domonique Nicole. BS in Fin. Mgmt., So. Ill. U., Carbondale, 1984. Tng. mgr. USAF, Biloxi, 2003—05, fin. analyst Osan, Republic of Korea, 2005—06, divsn. chief, customer support San Antonio, 2006—. Master sgt. USAF, 2006—07, Lackland AFB, Tex. Recipient Fin. Mgmt. Educator of Yr. award, 2004. Mem.: Am. Soc. Mil. Comptrollers. Avocation: bicycling. Personal E-mail: brhomann@yahoo.com.

HOMBURGER, THOMAS CHARLES, lawyer; b. Buffalo, Sept. 16, 1941; s. Adolf and Charolotte E. (Stern) Homburger; m. Louise Paula Shemin, June 6, 1965; children: Jennifer Anne, Richard Ephraim, Kathryn Lee. BA, Columbia U., NYC, 1963, JD, 1966. Bar: Ill. 1966, US Dist. Ct. (no. dist.) Ill. 1966. Assoc., ptnr. Sonnenschein, Carlin, Nath & Rosenthal, Chgo., 1966—86, Bell, Boyd & Lloyd LLP, Chgo., 1986—2002, chmn. real estate, 2002—. Adj. prof. John Marshall Law Sch., 1989—. Contbr. articles to profl. jours. Chmn. nat. exec. com. Anti-Defamation League, 2000—03; chmn. Chgo. regional bd. Anti-Defamation League, B'nai Brith, 1986—88; mem. Glencoe Bd. Edn., Ill., 1984—89; pres. Anti-Defamation League, 2003—06 vice chmn., 2006—. Mem.: ABA (real property divsn., probate & trust law sect., fin. subcom.), Chgo. Mortgage Attys. Assn. (pres. 1975—77), Am. Coll. Real Estate Lawyers (bd. govs. 2000—03), Chgo. Bar Assn. (chmn. real property law com. 1984—85), Ill. Bar Assn. (real property sect.), Std. Club, Law Club Chgo., Lambda Alpha Internat. Home: 20 East Cedar St Apt 2F Chicago IL 60611-1149 Office: Bell Boyd & Lloyd LLP 70 W Madison St Ste 3100 Chicago IL 60602-4284 Office Phone: 312-807-4267. Personal E-mail: tc@homburger.cnchost.com. Business E-Mail: thomburger@bellboyd.com.

HOMER, WILLIAM INNES, art history educator, expert, writer; b. Merion, Pa., Nov. 8, 1929; s. Austin and Evelyn (Innes) H.; 1 child, Stacy Innes; m. Christine D. Hyer, Aug. 24, 1986. AB, Princeton U., 1951; postgrad., N.Y.U., 1952-53; MA, Harvard U., 1954; PhD, 1961. Instr. dept. art and archeology Princeton (NJ) U., 1955-59, lectr., 1959-61, asst. prof., 1961-64; assoc. prof. history of art Cornell U., 1964-66; prof. U. Del., Newark, 1966-99, chmn. dept. art history, 1966-81, 86-93; dir. index of dissertations and theses in Am. art Archives of Am. Art, Washington; vis. fellow Princeton U., 1972-73; assoc. fellow Ctr. for Advanced Studies, Nat. Gallery of Art, 1980-81. Mem. Del. Arts Coun., 1969-70, New Castle County Beautification Bd., 1967-70; adv. screening com. (overseas) Fulbright-Hays Fellowship Awards, 1970-72, chmn., 1971-72; mem. sr. fellowship panel Nat. Endowment for Humanities, 1970; mem. exhbn. com. Del. Art Mus., 1968-73, chmn. accessions com., 1974-78 Author: Seurat and the Science of Painting, 1964, Robert Henri and His Circle, 1969, Alfred Stieglitz and the American Avant-Garde, 1977, The Photographs of Gertrude Käsebier, 1979, Alfred Stieglitz and the Photo-Secession, 1983, Pictorial Photography in Philadelphia, 1984; co-author Albert Pinkham Ryder: Painter of Dreams, 1989, Thomas Eakins, His Life and Art, 1992, The Language of Contemporary Criticism Clarified, 1999, Stieglitz and the Photo-Secession, 1902, 2002; mem. editl. bd. Am. Art Jour., 1970-2005, Winterthur Portfolio, 1978-80; sr. editor Am Art Rev., 1992—. Mem. adv. com. Am. Studies Inst., Lincoln U., 1967-76; mem. corp. Mus. Am. Art, Ogunquit, Maine, 1958-92; regional adv. com. Archives Am. Art, 1979—; trustee Am. Friends Nat. Portrait Gallery, London, 1995—, Sewell C. Biggs Mus. Am. Art, 1994-97; bd. dirs. Ctr. Advanced Studies in Visual Arts Nat. Gallery Art, 1994-98. Coun. of Humanities fellow Princeton U., 1962-63; Am. Coun. Learned Socs. fellow, 1964-65; Guggenheim fellow, 1972-73; Nat. Endowment for Humanities fellow, 1980-81; Ctr. for Advanced Study U. Del. fellow, 1985-86 Fellow Royal Soc. Arts (London), New Pictorialist Soc. (dir. 1981—); mem. Coll. Art Assn. Am., Pictorial Photographers Am., Royal Photog. Soc., Welcome Soc. of Pa., Princeton Club (N.Y.C.), Nat. Arts Club, Cosmos Club, Phi Kappa Phi. Home: PO Box 4195 Greenville DE 19807 Office: U Del Dept Art History Newark DE 19716

HOMES, A. M., writer; b. Washington; BA, Sarah Lawrence Coll., 1985; MFA, U. Iowa Writer's Workshop. Tchr writing program Columbia U., NYC, 1991—. Author: (novels) Jack, 1989, In a Country of Mothers, 1993, The End of Alice, 1995, Music For Torching, 1999, This Book Will Save Your Life, 2006; (short story collection) The Safety of Objects, 1990,; playwright: The Call-In Hour, 1981, The Coffin in the Living Room, 1986; contbr. L.A. Times, Art Forum. Recipient Henfield Transatlantic Rev. award The Henfield Found., 1988; Guggenheim fellow, 1988, James Michener fellow U. Iowa, 1988-89; N.Y. Found. for Arts fellow, 1988; Helena Rubenstein fellow Whitney Mus., N.Y.C., 1988-89. Mem. PEN.*

HOMEWOOD, ELIZABETH HOLMES NASH, elementary school educator; b. Des Moines, Sept. 9, 1948; d. Henry Leighton Jr. and Catherine Anne (Cassat) Nash; m. Steven Kent Homewood, Aug. 8, 1970; children: Stephanie Leighton, Bradley Kent. BA in Child Devel., Rockford Coll., 1970, MAT, 1976. Cert. elem. tchr., Ill. Tchr. elem. Rockford Pub. Schs., Ill., 1970—2005, grant dir. Ill., 2005—. Sec. Ednl. Devel. Commn., Rockford, 1972-73; tchr. creative writing, Rockford Coll., 1975-78. Co-author: Wheels of Progress, 1989, Invent America, 1989, Focus: Rockford, 1988. Vol. Rockford Pro-Am. Golf Tournament, 1984-94, chmn. of scoreboard, 1993—; vol. Greenwich Art Fair/Beattie Festival, Rockford, 1985-90, Parents Too Soon Nutrition Class, Rockford, 1989; active Jr. League of Rockford, 1977-90; mem. exec. bd. Rockford YMCA Stingrays, sec., 1989-93; scriptwriter for Feathered Fantasy, Rockford Symphony Orch.'s Kinderkonzert, 1995; with Team Parents for U. Iowa Women's Swim Team, 1998-2000. Recipient Red Apple award, Rockford Bd. Edn., 1980, Golden Apple Tchr. of Distinction award Golden Apple Found., 1998. Mem. ASCD, Rockford Edn. Assn. (corp. cup steering com. 1991-93), PEO Sisterhood (sec. 1980-82, 84-85, treas. 2005-). Republican. Presbyterian. Avocations: running, tennis, cooking, reading, traveling with family. Home: 4241 Brendenwood Rd Rockford IL 61107-2207 Office: Roosevelt Edn Ctr 978 Haskell Ave Rockford IL 61103 Home Phone: 815-226-8563; Office Phone: 815-966-3250 ext. 4341. Personal E-mail: betsy.homewood@rps205.com.

HOMSEY, JOSEPH RICHARD, JR., lawyer; b. Oklaholma City, Jan. 3, 1947; s. Joseph Richard Sr. and Josephine Homsey; children: Jason, Lindsey. BA, SW Okla. State U., Weatherford, 1970; JD, Okla. City U., 1973. Atty., owner Jr. Homsey & Assocs., Oklahoma City, 1974—. Bd. trustees Oklahoma City U., 1986—, bd. dirs., 1999—. Author (editor): (book) The Real America Trajedy, 1977. Athletic adv. bd. chmn. Okla. City U., 1990—, dean search com. chmn., 1996, 2000. Mem.: Okla. Bar Assn., ABA. Home: 4528 N Classen Blvd Oklahoma City OK 73118

HOMSLEY, DENISE LOUISE, music educator; b. Nampa, Idaho, Sept. 9, 1949; d. Lewis Griffith and Eileen Innes Davis; m. Jon Mark Homsley, June 23, 2001; m. David Karl Stoehr, Sept. 12, 1969 (div. Jan. 4, 1982); children: Melissa Dawn (Stoehr) Joseph, Justen David Stoehr Blackburn, Regan Karl Stoehr. BA in Music, Boise State Coll., 1972; MusM in Edn., Boston U., 2007. Nat. Cert. Tchr. Music Music Tchrs. Nat. Assn., 2003. Music tchr. Ind., Boise, Idaho, 1966—75; owner, operator Stoehr Orchards, Wilder, Idaho, 1982—85; receptionist Farm Bur. Ins., Nampa, Idaho, 1997—99, Ackerley Outdoor Advt., Portland, 1999—2002; music tchr. Denise Homsley Piano Studio, Portland, 1999—2003, Jacksonville, Fla., 2003—05, Happy Valley, Oreg., 2005—06, Jacksonville, Fla., 2006—, Jacksonville Country Day Sch., 2004—05, 2006—; dir. Bravo! Music Camp, 2004—. Hotline referral adminstr. Oreg. Music Tchrs. Assn., Portland, 2001—03; adjudicator, 2005—. Children's leader Bible Study Fellowship, Caldwell, Idaho, 1992—99; pianist Happy Valley Bapt. Ch., Portland, 2001—03, 2005—06; vol. Eastside Cmty. Ch., Jacksonville, Fla., 2007. Mem.: Assn. for Supervision and Curriculum Devel., Nat. Assn. Music Edn., Fla. Music Educators Assn., Fla. State Music Tchrs. Assn. (exec. bd. rec. sec. 2006—, dist. chair student activities 2007—), Jacksonville Music Tchrs. Assn. (bd. cmty. svc. 2004, co-chair Multi-Piano Festival 2005, v.p. 2005, historian 2006, pres. 2007), Oreg. Music Tchrs. Assn. (chair focus group 2005—06), Music Tchrs. Nat. Assn. Baptist. Avocations: travel, gourmet cooking, couture sewing. Studio: 13294 Stone Pond Dr Jacksonville FL 32224 Office Phone: 904-619-5233. Business E-Mail: dh88redrose@comcast.net.

HOMSY, GEORGE, mechanical and chemical engineer, educator; Grad., U. Calif., Berkeley; PhD in chem. engring., U. Ill. Prof. engring. Stanford U.; prof. mech. engring. and chem. engring. U. Calif., Santa Barbara, 2001—. Fellow: Am. Physical Soc. (Fluid Dynamics Prize 2004); mem.: NAE, Tau Beta Pi. Office: Dept Mech and Environ Engring U Calif Santa Barbara Rm 2325 Engring II Bldg Santa Barbara CA 93106-5070 Office Phone: 805-893-2704. Office Fax: 805-893-8651. E-mail: bud@engineering.ucsb.edu.

HON, JOHN WINGSUN, physician; b. Canton, China, Aug. 21, 1947; s. Yuen-Pak and Yuk-Ying (Zhang) Hon. BA, Hunter Coll., 1972; MA, SUNY, Buffalo, 1975; DO, Kirksville Coll. Medicine, 1979. Diplomate Am. Bd. Emergency Physicians, bd. cert. emergency medicine and family practice. Enlisted U.S. Army, 1975, advanced through grades to capt., 1979; intern, resident Tripler Army Med. Ctr., Honolulu, 1979-80; gen. med. officer U.S. Army Med. Corps, Honolulu, 1979-80; intern Tripler Army Med. Ctr., Honolulu, 1979-80; gen. med. officer U.S. Army Med. Corps, Korea, Republic of Korea, 1980-81, U.S. Mil. Acad., West Point, 1981-83; attending physician Woodhull Hosp., Bklyn., 1983-86; pvt. practice Woodside, NY, 1983—2002, Elmhurst, NY, 1993—, Flushing, NY, 2002—. Attending physician Bronx Lebanon Hosp., 1987—91, Mt. Sinai Hosp., Queens, 1983—, St. John Hosp., Elmhurst, NY, 1992—, N.Y. Hosp. Dept. Medicine, 1996, Elmhurst Hosp., 1999—; clin. asst. prof. family practice N.Y. Med. Coll. Fellow: Am. Coll. Emergency Physicians; mem.: N.Y. State Osteo. Med. Soc., Chinese Am. Med. Soc. (life), Am. Osteo. Assn. Avocation: photography. Home: 10 West St Apt 33A New York NY 10004 Office: 132-07 41st Rd Flushing NY 11355 also: 86-08 Elmhurst Ave Elmhurst NY 11373 Home Phone: 212-233-4612; Office Phone: 718-424-0770. Personal E-mail: hon8song@yahoo.com.

HONAKER, BONNIE, language educator; b. Sept. 28, 1956; Tchr. Ohio County Mid. Sch., Hartford, Ky., 1991—. Mem.: Nat. Coun. Tchrs. English.

HONAKER, JIMMIE JOE, lawyer, educator; b. Oklahoma City, Jan. 21, 1939; s. Joe Jack and Ruby Lee (Bowen) H.; children: Jay Jimmie, Kerri Ruth. BA, Colo. Coll., 1963; MA, U. No. Colo., 1991; JD, U. Wyo., 1966, MS, 1995. Bar: Colo. 1966, US Dist. Ct. Colo., US Ct. Appeals (10th cir.), US Supreme Ct., Ute Indian Tribal Ct. Utah. Pvt. practice, Longmont, Colo., 1966-91. Adj. faculty Northwest Coll., Powell, Wyo., 2006—. Incorporator Longmont Boys Baseball, 1969; chmn. Longmont City Charter Commn., 1973; chmn. ch. bd. 1st Christian Ch., Longmont, 1975, 76; chmn. North Boulder County unit Am. Cancer Soc., 1978, 79. Recipient Disting. Svc. award Longmont Centennial Yr., 1971; named Outstanding Young Man, Longmont Jaycees, 1973. Mem.: US Supreme Ct. Bar Assn., Fed. Bar Assn., Internat. Assn. Landscape Ecology-US Regional Assn., Ecol. Soc. Am., Colo. Bar Assn. (interprofl. com. 1972—91, environ. law sect. 1999—), Pahaska Corral Westerners Internat., Optimist Internat., Nat. Eagle Scout Assn., Colo. Mountain Club, Alpha Tau Omega, Xi Sigma Pi, Alpha Kappa Psi, Phi Alpha Delta. Avocations: private pilot, mountain climbing.

HONAMAN, J. CRAIG, health facility administrator; b. Montclair, NJ, June 15, 1943; s. Richard Karl and Gloria (McElwain) H.; m. Dee Dee Toerpe, Dec. 31, 1971; children: Justin Craig Jr., Garman Grayson. BS, N.C. State U., 1965; MS, U. Ala., Birmingham, 1971. Sr. v.p. Bapt. Hosp., Pensacola, Fla., 1970-79; exec. v.p. Tallahassee (Fla.) Meml. Hosp., 1979-89; adminstr. Quorum Health Resources/Leesburg (Fla.) Regional Med. Ctr., 1989-91; v.p., adminstrn. home health care Meth. Med. Ctr., Jacksonville, Fla., 1991-92; pres. Kellogg Healthcare, Inc., Jacksonville, 1992-93, KNH Healthcare, Jacksonville, 1993-95; exec. dir. HomeCare Alliance of Ga., Inc., Atlanta, 1994-98; sr. v.p. Haney & Assocs., Atlanta, 1998—2001; prin. H&H Cons. Ptnrs., LLC, Atlanta, 2001—. Cons. in field, Atlanta, Ga., 1991—. Contbr. articles to profl. jours. Active Boy Scouts Am., ARC, Am. Cancer Soc., Ronald McDonald House. Capt. U.S. Army, 1966-69, Vietnam. Recipient Nat. Golden Hour award MBB Helicopter, 1988, Pub. Benefit Flying award Nat. Aeronautic Assn., 2004. Fellow Am. Coll. Healthcare Execs. (cert. health care mgr.; regent for north Ga.), Rotary. Methodist. Avocations: golf, running. Office: H&H Cons Ptnrs LLC 560 Cambridge Way NE Ste 101 Atlanta GA 30328-1007 Personal E-mail: Careerdir1@aol.com.

HONDA, MICHAEL M., congressman; b. Walnut Creek, Calif., June 27, 1941; m. Jeanne (dec. 2004); children: Mark, Michelle. BS in Biol. Sci., San Jose St. Univ., 1970, BA in Spanish, 1973, MA in Edn., 1973. Sci. tchr., Sunnyvale; prin. pub. sch.; mem. San Jose Planning Commn., 1971—81, San Jose Unified Sch. Bd., 1981—89, Santa Clara County Bd. of Supervisors, 1990—96, Calif. Assembly, 1997—2000, US Congress from 15th Calif. dist., 2001—. Conducted ednl. rsch. at Stanford; elected Reg. Whip, vice chair Congl. Asian Pac. Am. Caucus, Transp. com., Sci. com. Congress, Calif. 15th dist. Mem. edn. com. Calif. Assembly. Served Peace Corps, 1965-67. Named High Tech Legislator Yr., Am. Electronics Assn. Democrat. Office: 1713 Longworth House Office Bldg Washington DC 20515-0515*

HONDROS, CHRIS, photojournalist; b. NYC, Mar. 14, 1970; BA, NC State U., 1993. Staff photographer Getty Images News Svc., NYC. Photographer (exhibitions) Images from Kosovo, 1999, The Darkest Days of Spring: The Kosovo Refugee Crisis, 1999—2000, War in Iraq/War in Liberia, 2003, Liberia, 2004, Retrospective: 2 Years and 4 Wars, 2004, War Is, 2004, The Art of War, 2005, War in Shadows & Light, 2005, Behind War Photography, 2006, Iraq Unseen, 2006. Finalist Pulitzer Prize in spot news photography, 2003; recipient John Faber award, Overseas Press Club, 2003, Robert Capra Gold Medal award, 2006; grantee photojournalism grant, US Agy. Internat. Devel., 1999; Pew Fellowship Internat. Reporting, Johns Hopkins U., 2001. Office: 5th Fl 75 Varick St New York NY 10013 Office Phone: 917-295-5183. E-mail: hondros@aol.com.

HONEGGER, FEDERICO, artist; b. Milan, Sept. 11, 1926; s. Carlo and Maria Antonia (Casiraghi) H.; m. Lucia Serafina Carminati, Apr. 30, 1959; children: Carlo, Marco, Andrea, Anna. Baccalaureat, Coll. St. Michel, 1945; law degree, Cath. U., 1952. Textile practice Vereinigte Seidenwebereien AG, Krefeld, Germany, 1950-51; with Gaspare Honegger, Milan, Italy, 1946-59; buying mgr. Carminati Industrie Tessili SpA, Milan, 1960-82. Author: The Digital Outlook, 1984, (art project) The Ke'nosis Project, 1986 (award), Jacobs Ladder, 1989, The Eye of the Needle, 1992, Portraits, 1992, Cromatic Alphabets, 1993, Constellations, 1993, Adam's Rib, 1994, Metaphysical Alphabets, 1994, The Signs-Number of Image, 1996, The Universe of Fragments, 1996, The Profecy of Ezechiele, 1998, God All in Everybody, 1999, Soul and Body, 1999, El Shadday-The Primary Numbers, 1999, The Background, Place of Dialogue Between Thou (two) and Innumerable, 2000, Your Voice, My Voice, Our Voice: The Wise Men and the Star, 2000, From One to Two and From I to Thou, 2000, Glory, Grace and Liberty, 2001, Equal and One, 2002, Straight and Curved, 2002, Reasoned Catalogue of Works, Art Projects and Form from 1975 to 2003, 2004, The Lord Said Unto My Lord (PS. 107-108)- Birth of Heavens, 2005. Recipient Silver Palette City of Milan, 1979, Top 70 Winner Art '95 N.Y. Internat. Competition, 1995, Genius Laureate award, Am. Biog. Inst., 2005. Mem. Symbolicum Art Group (co-founder). Home and Office: Via Annunciata 23/2 20121 Milan Italy Office Phone: 0039-02-6597056. Office Fax: 0039-02-6590687. E-mail: federico.honegger@fastwebnet.it.

HONEMANN, DANIEL HENRY, lawyer; b. Balt., Oct. 20, 1929; s. Henry Letcher and Maude Elizabeth (Wilson) H.; m. Rose Ann Clark, Mar. 23, 1974; children by previous marriage: Deborah, Dori, Daniel, Donna. AB, Western Md. Coll., Westminster, 1951; JD, U. Md., 1956. Bar: Md. 1956. Practice law, Balt.; partner firm Clapp, Somerville, Honemann & Beach, 1962-85, Whiteford, Taylor & Preston, 1986—; asst. U.S. atty. Dist. Md., 1960-61. Author: (with others) Robert's Rules of Order Newly Revised, 10th edit. Served to 1st lt. inf. AUS, 1951-53. Decorated Bronze Star, Combat Inf. badge. Fellow Am. Coll. Trust and Estate Counsel, Md. Bar Found.; mem. ABA (ho. of dels. 1978-80), Md. Bar Assn. (sec. 1977-84, bd. govs. 1975-84), Balt. Bar Assn. Home: 2318 Harcroft Rd Lutherville Timonium MD 21093-2638 Office: 7 Saint Paul St Ste 1400 Baltimore MD 21202-1654 Personal E-mail: dhonemann@comcast.net. Business E-Mail: dhonemann@wtplaw.com.

HONEY, RICHARD CHURCHILL, retired electrical engineer; b. Portland, Oreg., Mar. 9, 1924; s. John Kohnen and Margaret Fargo (Larrison) H.; m. Helen Waugaman, June 8, 1952 (div. Feb. 1980); children: Leslie, Steven, Laura, Janine; m. Jo Anne Kipp, Jan. 11, 1993. BS, Calif. Inst. Tech., 1945; EE, Stanford U., 1950, PhD, 1953. Research asst. Stanford U., 1948-52; sr. research engr. microwave group Stanford Research Inst., 1952-60; tech. program coordinator Electromagnetic Techniques Lab., 1960-64, lab. dir., 1964-70, staff scientist, 1970-89, sr. prin. scientist, 1989—; 86. Dir. ILC Tech.; mem. Army Sci. Bd., 1978-84. Contbr. articles to books, encyc., profl. jours.; patentee in field. Served with USN, 1943-46. Fellow IEEE, Optical Soc. Am.; mem. Coyote Point Yacht Club, Sigma Xi. Office: SRI Internat 333 Ravenswood Ave Menlo Park CA 94025-3453

HONEYCUTT, GEORGE LEONARD, retired photographer; b. High Point, NC, Jan. 5, 1936; s. Leonard Franklin and Pearl (Reynolds) H.; m. Sandra Spencer, Mar. 29, 1955; children: George Keith, Stephen Kurt, Kevin Spencer. Student, Sch. Modern Photography, NYC, 1954. Photographer Charlotte (N.C.) News, 1959-62; Staff photographer Houston Chronicle, 1963, dir. photography, 1963-97, retired, 1997. Served with AUS, 1955-57. Recipient awards AP, awards UP, awards Headliners; 4-time winner Profl. Football Hall of Fame. Mem. Nat. Press Photographers Assn. (named Nat. Newspaper Photographer of Yr. 1962). Methodist. Office: 801 Texas St Houston TX 77002-2904

HONEYCUTT, KEVIN, construction executive, consultant; s. Larry E. and Pinky Elain Honeycutt; life ptnr. Damien Hetherington, 2001. BS in Engring. Technology, U. NC, Charlotte, 1997. Cert. in document tech. Constrn. Specifications Inst., 2002, registered constrn. mgr. V.p. land devel.

Torry Homes, Inc., Charlotte, NC, 1997—2000; project controls mgr. Constrn. Mgmt. Svcs., Charlotte, 2000—04; project mgr. Terranova Corp., Miami Beach, Fla., 2004—05; engring. cons. ZLB Plasma Svcs., Boca Raton, Fla., 2005—. Assoc. bd. mem. Metrolina Aids Found., Charlotte, 1999—2002, Metrolina YMCA, 2000—02, Ft. Lauderdale Coastal Devel. Com., Fla., 2003—03, South Beach Aids Found., Miami Beach, 2003—05. Mem.: Constrn. Specifications Inst. (assoc.). Independent. Avocations: travel, boating, weightlifting, museums, car shows. Home: 2607 Venetian Dr Boynton Beach FL 33426 Home Phone: 954-801-7866; Office Phone: 561-999-3284. Office Fax: 561-912-3005.

HONEYSTEIN, KARL, lawyer, media specialist; b. NYC, Jan. 10, 1932; s. Herman and Claire (Rosen) H.; m. Buzz Halliday, Sept. 14, 1965 (div. Dec. 1978); 1 child, Gail; m. Shauna Wood Trabert, Jan. 24, 1995. BA, Yale U., New Haven, Conn., 1953; JD, Columbia U., NYC, 1959. Bar: NY 1959. Assoc. Greenbaum, Wolff & Ernst, NYC, 1959-62; v.p. Ashley Famous Agy., NYC, 1962-69, Internat. Famous Agy., NYC, 1969-71; exec. v.p. The Sy Fischer Co., NYC and L.A., 1971-80; exec. v.p., chief operating officer The Taft Entertainment Co., L.A., 1980-88; pres. K.H. Strategy Corp., L.A., 1988—. Dir. Rhythm & Hues, Inc.; lectr. law Bklyn. Law Sch., NYC, 1973-75; mem. adv. group Wood Warren, Investment Bankers. Served to lt. j.g. USNR, 1953-56 Mem.: Internat. Acad. TV Arts and Scis., Friars Club. Office Phone: 310-273-0696. Personal E-mail: khs1@prodigy.net.

HONG, BAOMING, research scientist, engineer; b. Taizhou, China, Jan. 1, 1964; arrived in U.S., 1996; s. Mafa Hong and Linge Wang. BS, Zhejiang U., Hangzhou, China, 1986; MS, Beijing Inst. Tech., 1992; PhD, U. Mass., Dartmouth, 2002. Rsch. asst., lectr. Beijing Inst. Tech., 1986—96; rsch. asst. U. Mass., North Dartmouth, 1996—2000; sr. scientist Motion TV Inc., Campbell, Calif., 2000—01; sr. R&D engr. Media Motion Inc., Santa Clara, Calif., 2001—02; rsch. fellow Hartford (Conn.) Hosp. Inst. Living, 2003—04; rsch. scientist Yale U., New Haven, 2004—. Contbr. chpt. to book. Recipient sci. tech. award, 1992. Mem.: SPIE (mem. program com. 2001), IEEE (mem. program com. 2005). Achievements include research in semi-physical simulation technique for radio fuses. Avocations: skiing, tennis, swimming.

HONG, DONGWOO, electrical engineer; b. Seoul, Republic of Korea, Jan. 15, 1978; s. Suk-kyo Hong and So Young Han. BS cum laude, Yonsei U., Seoul, 2002; MS, U. Calif., Santa Barbara, 2005, PhD, 2007—. Intern Teradyne, Boston, 2004, Nat. Semiconductor, Santa Clara, Calif., 2005, Intel, Oreg., 2007; rsch. asst. U. Calif., Santa Barbara, 2002—, tchg. asst., 2003. Mem.: IEEE. Avocations: golf, baseball, swimming. Home: 95 Willow Springs Ln Apt 201 Goleta CA 93117 Office: U Calif Santa Barbara ECE Dept Santa Barbara CA 93106 Home Phone: 805-252-3539; Office Phone: 805-893-5678. Business E-Mail: besthdw@ece.ucsb.edu.

HONG, IN CHUL, research scientist; b. Seoul, Republic of Korea, Feb. 9, 1958; s. Sung Bae Hong and Duk Hee Yoon; m. Sun Hee Choi, May 25, 1985. B of Medicine, Yonsei U. Coll. Medicine, Seoul, 1982; PhD, Yonsei U. Grad. Sch., Seoul, 1998. Instr. Yonsei U. Coll. Medicine, Seoul, 1995—97, asst. prof., 1998—2000; rsch. fellow San Diego Microsurg. Inst., 1999—2000, 1999—2003; transplant rsch. fellow, dept. surgery U. Calif., San Diego, 2000—04; postdoctoral rsch. fellow City Hope Nat. Med. Ctr., Duarte, Calif., 2004; sr. scientist Astellas Rsch. Inst. Am., Evanston, Ill., 2004—. Hon. assoc. dir. San Diego Microsurg. Inst., 2003—04; dir. dept. surgery and ER Yonsei U. Coll. Medicine, Inchon, Republic of Korea, 1995—2000. Contbr. articles to profl.jours. Vol. dr. asst. Korean Am. Cmty. Svc., Chgo., 2005; chief mission dept. Korean United Meth. Ch. San Diego, 2002—03. Capt., dir. surgery dist. hosp. Korean Army, 1988—90, Seoul. Recipient Achievement award, Comdr. Mil. Security and Intelligence, Seoul, 1990. Mem.: Korean Surg. Soc., Korean Soc. Transplantation, Internat. Soc. Exptl. Microsurgery. Presbyterian. Avocations: travel, music, movies. Office: Astellas Rsch Inst Am 8045 Lamon Ave Skokie IL 60077

HONG, JAE-DONG, industrial engineering educator; b. Daegu, South Korea, Mar. 20, 1954; arrived in U.S., 1981; s. Hyun-Tae and Kyung-Hee (Kim) H.; m. Bong-Sun Lee, Sept. 25, 1981; children: Thomas, Christina, James. BS, Korea U., Seoul, 1979; MS, Pa. State U., 1985, PhD, 1988. Quality and process engr. Daewoo Heavy Indsl., Anyang, South Korea, 1979-81; from asst. prof. to assoc. prof. indsl. engring. tech. S.C. State U., Orangeburg, 1988-97; prof., Gov.'s disting. prof. S.C. State U. Sch. Engring. Tech. and Scis., Orangeburg, 1997—. Contbr. articles to profl. jours. Named Disting. prof., Gov. S.C., 1993. Home: 106 Fox Run Ct Orangeburg SC 29118-9791 Office: SC State U 102 Lewis Lab Orangeburg SC 29117-7722 Office Phone: 803-536-8861. E-mail: jdhong@earthlink.net.

HONG, JIANHUI, chemical engineer; BS in Chem. Engring., Tsinghua U., Beijing, 1991—96; PhD in Chem. Engring., Brigham Young U., Provo, Utah, 1996—2000. Advanced devel. engr. John Zink Co., LLC, Tulsa, 2000—06, flare process engr., 2006—. Achievements include patents for windproof flare pilot; patents pending for Steamizer XP steam assisted flares with 30-50 percent reduction of steam usage; stoichiometric meter and control method for low-NOx incinerators; development of phased array radiometers for measuring flame epicenter location and radiant fraction; global optimization of steel stack structures (flares and thermal oxidizer) with a significant cost reduction. Office: John Zink Co LLC 11920 E Apache Tulsa OK 74116 E-mail: jianhui.hong@johnzink.com.

HONG, MEI, chemistry professor; BA, Mt. Holyoke Coll., 1992; PhD, U. Calif. Berkeley, 1996. NIH postdoctoral fellow Mass. Inst. Tech., Cambridge; rsch. prof. U. Mass., Amherst; assoc. prof. chemistry Iowa State U., Ames, Iowa, 1999—. Mem. editl. bd.: Jour. Magnetic Resonance. Recipient Beckman Young Investigator award, 1999, Rsch. Corp. Innovation award, 2000, Career award, NSF, 2001, Pure Chemistry award, Am. Chem. Soc., 2003; Alfred P. Sloan Fellow, 2002. Achievements include development and application of solid-state NMR spectroscopy to investigate the structure and dynamics of membrane and insoluable fibrous proteins. Office: Dept Chemistry 1605 Gilman Hall Iowa State Univ Ames IA 50011-3111 Office Phone: 515-294-3521. E-mail: mhong@iastate.edu.

HONG, MICHAEL, communications executive; b. 1968; Sr. grp. mgr. Petry; worked for Paramount; dir., Media Rsch. Spelling Entertainment; dir., Media Analysis TBS Media Mgmt.; major sales exec. Nielson Media Rsch.; founder, CEO ImaginAsian TV, NYC, 2003—. Named one of 100 Most Influential Minorities in Cable Industry, Cable World, 2005, Top 100 Movers and Shakers, CableFax, 2005, 40 Executives Under 40, Multi-Channel News, 2006. Office: ImaginAsian TV 19 W 44th St 9th Fl New York NY 10036

HONG, SEUNGKWAN, engineering educator; b. Seoul, Republic Of Korea, Jan. 21, 1966; m. Jungmi Park. B, U. Calif., LA, 1988—91, M, 1991—93, PhD, 1993—96. Rsch. asst. U. Calif., 1992—93, 1993—96, lectr., 1997; asst. prof. U. Ctrl. Fla., Orlando, 1997—2003; assoc. prof. Korea U., Seoul, 2003—. Editor: Jour. Korea Water & Wastewater Works, 2006—. Recipient Editor's award for outstanding svc. to Jour. Environ. Engring., ASCE, 2002, Excellence in Undergraduate Tchg. award, U. Ctrl. Fla., 2002. Mem.: Membrane Soc. Korea (dir. 2005—), Korea Water & Wastewater Works Assn. (Paper award 2006), Korea Soc. Water Quality. Office: Korea Univ 1 5-ka Anam-Dong Sungbuk-ku Seoul 136-713 Republic of Korea Home Phone: 82-2-02-2232-9854. Office Fax: 82-2-02-3290-7656; Home Fax: 82-2-02-3290-7656. Business E-Mail: skhong21@korea.ac.kr.

HONG, WAUN KI, oncologist, researcher; b. Kyung gi Do, South Korea, Aug. 13, 1942; naturalized Sept. 17, 1976; s. Sung Ku and Bok Young; m. Mi Hwa Yoo, Sept. 9, 1969; children: Edward, Burton James. Student, Yon-Sei U., 1963, MD, 1967. Diplomate Am. Bd. Internal Medicine in Medical Oncology. Rotating intern Bronx-Lebanon Hosp., NYC, 1970-71; jr. med. resident Boston Vets. Affairs Med. Ctr., 1971-72, sr. med. resident, 1972-73, chief of medical oncology, 1975-84, program dir. hematology/oncology tng. program, 1982-84; teaching assoc. Sch. Medicine Boston U., 1971-73, asst. prof. medicine, 1975-79, assoc. prof. medicine, 1980-84; clin. instr. medicine Cornell U., 1973-75; attending physician in medicine Boston City Hosp., 1978-84; clin. assoc. prof. pharmacology Northeastern U., Boston, 1980-84; internist, prof. medicine M.D. Anderson Cancer Ctr., U. Tex., Houston, 1984—, chief sect. thoracic med. oncology, 1987-88, chief sect. head, neck and thoracic med. oncology, 1988-92, chmn. dept. thoracic/head and neck med. oncology, 1993—, Charles A. LeMaistre Disting. Chair in thoracic oncology. Mem. sci. adv. bd. U. Ala. Birmingham Comprehensive Cancer Ctr., 1998—, Roy Castle Lung Cancer Found., 1997—, U. Calif. San Diego Cancer Ctr., 1997—, Shanghai (China) 2d Med. U. Joint Ctr. Clin. Rsch., 1997—, Fox Chase Cancer Ctr. Population Sci. Program, 1997, Kimmel Found. on Cancer Rsch., 1996—, Yale Cancer Ctr., 1996—, Vanderbilt Cancer Ctr., Seoul Nat. U. Cancer Ctr., 1996—; Baylor Coll. Medicine SPORE program, 1995—, The Cancer Inst. of N.J., 1993-98, The San Antonio Cancer Inst., 1993—; cons. Battelle Pharms., 1997—, Taiho Pharms., 1997—, Trilex Pharms., 1996—, Sequus Pharms., 1996—, Ho-En Ctrl. Rsch. Inst., 1996—, Ilex Oncology, 1995—; Houston Vet. Affairs Med. Ctr., 1992—; adj. prof. medicine Baylor Coll. Medicine, Houston, 1991—; vis. prof. Meml. Sloan-Kettering Cancer Ctr., 1998, Boston U. Cancer Ctr., 1997, Boston VA Med. Ctr., 1997, Nat. Cancer Inst. Intramural Program, 1996, U. Minn. Cancer Ctr., 1994, Tufts U. Sch. Medicine, 1993, Dana-Farber Cancer Ctr., 1993, Johns Hopkins Oncology Ctr., 1993, Tex. Tech. U. Sch. Medicine, 1992; lectr. in medicine Tufts U., 1975-84; Am. Cancer Soc. clin. rsch. prof., 1996—; Gen. Motors Found. vis. prof. Editor: (with others) Chemoimmuno Prevention of Cancer, 1991, The Biology and Prevention of Aerodigestive Tract Cancer, 1992, Advances in the Diagnosis and Therapy of Lung Cancer, 1993, Retinoids in Oncology, 1993, Early Detection of Cancer: Molecular Markers, 1994, Head and Neck Cancer: Basic and Clinical Aspects, 1995, Head and Neck Cancer: A Multidisciplinary Approach, 1996, Lung Cancer, 2d edit., 1998, Internat. Jour. Oncology, 1996—; dep. editor Clin. Cancer Rsch., 1996—; sr. editor Clinical Cancer Research, 1994—, Jour. Molecular and Cellular Differentiation, 1992—, Cancer Rsch., 1993-97; mem. editl. bd. The Cancer Jour., 1998—, Cancer Therapeutics, 1997—, PDQ Screening and Prevention, NCI, 1993-95, Annals of Surg. Oncology, 1993—, Cancer Rsch. Therapy and Ctrl., 1993-96, Jour. Clin. Oncology, 1992-95, Cancer Prevention, 1990-93; mem. editl. adv. bd. Cancer Epidemiology, Biomarkers and Prevention, 1994-96, Jour. Nat. Cancer Inst., 1990—. Served as flight surgeon South Korean Air Force, 1967-70. Recipient AACR 17th Ann. Richard and Hinda Rosenthal Found. award, 1993, pres. citation Am. Soc. for Head and Neck Surgery, 1991; Jr. Med. Oncology fellow Meml. Sloan-Kettering Cancer Ctr., 1973-74, Sr. Med. Oncology fellow Cornell U., 1974-75, ACS Disting. Svc. award, 1993, ACS 3d Ann. Am. Cancer Soc. lectureship award, 1995, Ho-Am prize in medicine Sam-Sung Found., 1994—, M.D. Anderson faculty achievement award in cancer prevention, 1993, Milken Family Found. Cancer Rsch. award, 1990, Cancer Rsch. and Prevention Found. award for Excellence in Cancer Prevention Rsch., Am. Assn. Cancer Rsch., 2003, numerous others; also numerous federal, industry, and found. grants. Fellow AAAS; mem. AMA, ACP, Am. Radium Soc., Am. Fedn. Clin. Rsch., Assn. Am. Physicians, Am. Assn. Cancer Rsch. (bd. dirs. 1996—, publs. com. 1996—, mem. program com., subcom. on clin. investigations 1993-94, cancer prevention 1993-94, mem. task force clin. investigations 1990—, chmn. com. on clin. cancer rsch. 1995, pres.), Am. Cancer Soc. (clin. rsch. prof. 1996—, mem. med. affairs adv. group on professorships in clin. oncology, mem. nat. conf. clin. trials 1992, profl. edn. subcom. on profs. clin. oncology 1990, chmn. 1991), Am. Soc. Clin. Oncology (vice chair cancer prevention and control com. 1995-96, mem. cancer edn. com. 1995-96, mem. edn. com. 1994-96, chmn. cancer prevention and ctrl. com. 1994), Nat. Cancer Inst. (mem. adv. com. to dir. 1997—, extramural bd. sci. advisors 1996—, cancer ctrs. rev. working group 1995-96, mem. pres.'s cancer panel 1994, mem. interim combined ad hoc bd. sci. counselors 1995), Tex. Med. Assn., Radiation Therapy Oncology Group (mem. med. oncology com. 1989—, head and neck com. 1989—), Harris County Med. Soc., Soc. Head and Neck Surgeons. Office: U Tex MD Anderson Cancer Ctr 1515 Holcombe Blvd Houston TX 77030-4009

HONHART, FREDERICK LEWIS, III, academic director; b. San Diego, Oct. 29, 1943; s. Frederick Lewis Jr. and Rossiter (Hyde) H.; m. Barbara Ann Baker, Aug. 27, 1966; children: David Frederick, Stephen Charles. BA, Wayne State U., 1966; MA, Case-Western Res. U., 1968, PhD, 1972. Cert. archivist. Field rep. Ohio Hist. Soc., Columbus, 1972-73; asst. dir. univ. archives & hist. collections Mich. State U., East Lansing, 1974-79, dir., 1979—. Mem. adv. bd. Mich. Nat. Hist. Publs. & Records Commn., Lansing, 1979—; cons. in field. Creator: (microcomputer sys.), MicroMARC:amc, 1986 (Coker prize 1988), MicroMARC for Integrated Format, 1995; contbr. articles to profl. jours. Fellow Soc. Am. Archivists; mem. Internat. Coun. Archives (steering com. univ. archives sect. 2000-04, pres. univ. archives sect. 2004-06), Mich. Archival Assn. (pres. 1984-86), Midwest Archives Conf. (chair program com. 1982, 94, chair Author Awards com. 2001), Olds Forge Flying Club (pres. 2005—). Avocations: reading, sports, flying. Office: Mich State U 101 Conrad Hall East Lansing MI 48824-1327 Office Phone: 517-355-2330.

HONICKMAN, HAROLD, food manufacturing company executive; b. Phila., June 10, 1933; Grad., Widener U., 1955. CEO Honickman Affiliates, Pennsauken, N.J.; chmn. bd. Pepsi Cola, Canada Dry of N.Y. Bd. dirs. Technion Soc., B'nai B'rith, Inst. Contemporary Art, The Aperture Found. Office: Honickman Affiliates 8275 N Route 130 Pennsauken NJ 08110-1435

HONIG, AL, artist; b. Bay Shore, NY, Dec. 16, 1937; s. Harry Leon and Celia Honig; children: Steven James, Cindy Rae. Student, Md. Sch. Art and Design, Silver Spring, 1970—73, Prince Georges CC, Largo, Md., 1973—76, Coll. Marin, Ross, Calif., 1976—78. Asst. to Jim Sanborn Glen Echo, Washington, 1975; artist-in-residence Discovery Mus., Sausalito, Calif., 1997; pub. art collaboration Definestration project, San Francisco, 1997, Sampson Project, Sacramento Airport, 1998, Sidewalks of Mission St., San Francisco, 1999; lectr. in field. Sculpture, Samson, Sacramento Airport, 1998, Represented in permanent collections Miniature Mus. Modern Art, Amsterdam, Netherlands, San Jose (Calif.) Mus. Art, one-man shows include Gallerie Image Marque, Nimes, France, 1993, Brian Marki Gallery, Portland, Oreg., 1996, Tiffany & Co., San Francisco, La Luz de Jesus Gallery, LA, 1996, Hitachi Data Sys., Los Altos, Calif., 1997, Melting Point Gallery, San Francisco, 1999, Hotel Duchamp, Healdsburg, Calif., 2002, Roshambo Winery, Healdsburg, 2002, Oakland (Calif.) Mus. at City Ctr., 2004, exhibited in group shows at Melting Point, San Francisco, 1998, Pacific Rim Mems. Show, 2000, Holly Mather Modern Art, LA, 2000, La Luz de Jesus, 2002, Artemis Gallery, San Francisco, 2002, Oakland Mus. at City Ctr., 2003, Felix Culpa Gallery, Santa Cruz, Calif., 2003, 2004, San Jose (Calif.) Mus. Modern Art, 2004, Melting Pot Gallery, 2004, Varnish Fine Art, San Francisco, 2004, Atrium Gallery, 2005, others; appeared in TV, video prodns. Night Flight, NBC, 1991, CNN Nightly News, 1992, Weird TV, 1995. With USMC, 1955—59. Mem.: Pacific Rim Sculptors Group. Office: PO Box 881743 San Francisco CA 94188

HONIG, ARNOLD, physics professor, researcher; b. NYC, Feb. 28, 1928; s. Ralph and Margaret (Gershman) Honig; m. Alice Sterling, Oct. 3, 1947 (div. Nov. 1977); children: Lawrence, Madeleine, Jonathan; m. Dolly Komar, Jan. 6, 1979; stepchildren: Arne, Tanya. BA, Cornell U., 1948; MS, Columbia U., 1950, PhD, 1953. Research asst. microwave spectroscopy Columbia U., NYC, 1951-53; research physicist solid state physics U. Calif.-Berkeley, 1953-54; research fellow molecular physics École Normale Superieure, Paris, 1954-56; asst. prof. physics Syracuse U., NY, 1956-59, assoc. prof. NY, 1959-62, prof. NY, 1962—. Cons. ITT Labs., 1960—63, Gen. Atomics, 1993—96, Oxford Instruments, 1997—; ptnr., owner Sci.-Art Sys. Co., NYC, 1968—78; vis. prof. Hebrew U., Jerusalem, 1962; vis. scientist Com. a l'Energie Atomique, Saclay, France, 1965. Contbr. articles to profl. jours. Pres. Oran Meml. Pk. Assn., NY, 1981—83. Recipient Glover Meml. award, Dickinson Coll., 1966, Chancellor's citation for exceptional acad. achievement, 1999; grantee, NSF, Dept. Energy, others. Mem.: AAAS, Fedn. Am. Scientists, Am. Phys. Soc. Achievements include patents for infrared image transducer; matrix piano keyboard; production spin-polarized fuels; multi-chronal fluorescence microscope; bulk production and usage of hyperpolarized 129 Xenon; non-invasive susceptibility-based in-vivo iron measurement and imaging utilizing MRI and ESR. Avocations: music, farming. Office: Syracuse U Dept Physics Syracuse NY 13244-0001 Business E-Mail: honig@phy.syr.edu.

HONIG, BARRY HIRSH, biophysicist, educator; b. NYC, Nov. 30, 1941; s. Jacob Joshua and Bernice (Liebman) Honig; m. Marjorie Hanson, Aug. 9, 1968; children: Michael, Adam BSc in Chemistry, Poly. Inst. Bklyn., 1963; MS in Chemistry, Johns Hopkins U., Balt.; PhD in Chem. Physics, Weizmann Inst. Sci., Israel, 1968. Sr. lectr. Hebrew U., Jerusalem, 1973-78, assoc. prof., 1978-79, U. Ill., Urbana, 1979-81; prof. biochemistry and molecular biophysics Columbia U., NYC, 1981—, Howard Hughes Med. investigator, 2000—. Panel mem., cons. NIH, Washington, 1981-84, NSF, 1985; mem. sci. adv. bd. Schrödinger LLC. Contbr. articles to profl. jours.; mem. editl. bd. Biophysics Jour., Biochemistry Jour. of Molecular Biology Proteins. Dreyfus scholar Williams Coll., 1983, Merit award, NIH, 1995. Fellow Am. Acad. Arts & Scis.; mem. NAS (Alexander Hollaender award in Biophysics, 2007), Biophys. Soc. (councillor 1985-88, pres. 1990-91, Founders award, 2002), Am. Chem. Soc. Office: The Honig Lab 8th Floor Rm 815 1130 St Nicholas Ave New York NY 10032 E-mail: bh6@columbia.edu.*

HONIG, GEORGE RAYMOND, pediatrician; b. Chgo., May 5, 1936; s. Joseph C. and Raymonde S. (Moses) Honig; m. Karen R. Jacobson, Dec. 18, 1960 (dec.); children: Sharon, Debra, Robert; m. Olga M. Weiss, May 24, 1998. BS in Liberal Arts and Sci., U. Ill., 1959, MD, 1961, MS in Pharmacology, 1961; PhD in Biochemistry, George Washington U., 1966. Diplomate Am. Bd. Pediatrics, Nat. Bd. Med. Examiners. Intern Johns Hopkins Hosp., Balt., 1961-62, fellow in pediatrics, 1961-63, asst. resident in pediatrics, 1962-63; rsch. assoc. Nat. Cancer Inst. NIH, 1963-66; fellow in pediatric hematology U. Ill., Chgo., 1966-68, from asst. prof. to assoc. prof. pediat., 1968—74, prof., 1974-75, 1984—2003, prof. emeritus, 2004—, attending physician, 1968-75, dir. pediatric hematology svc., 1972-75, head dept. pediat. Coll. Medicine, 1984—2003. Attending physician, dir. divsn. hematology Children's Meml. Hosp., Chgo., 1975—83; prof. emeritus U. Ill. Coll. Medicine, 2004—. Contbr. articles to profl. jours. Mem.: AAUP, Soc. Pediatric Rsch., Am. Pediatric Soc., Am. Soc. Hematology, Am. Soc. Biochemistry and Molecular Biology, Am. Assn. Cancer Rsch., Am. Acad. Pediat., Alpha Omega Alpha. Office: U Ill Coll Medicine 840 S Wood St Chicago IL 60612-7317 Home Phone: 312-664-3769; Office Phone: 312-996-1788. Business E-Mail: ghonig@uic.edu.

HONIGBERG, CAROL CROSSMAN, lawyer; b. Salina, Kansas, Sept. 23, 1955; d. Robert Denfield and Barbara Jane (Eckberg) Crossman; m. Paul Mark Honigberg, Aug. 18, 1979; children: Michael, Margaret Ann. BA, Duke U., 1977; JD, Vanderbilt U., 1980. Bar: Va., 1980. Assoc. Hazel and Thomas, P.C., Alexandria, Va., 1980—86; propr. Hazel and Thomas, P.C., Falls Ch., Va., 1986—99; ptnr. Reed Smith LLP (formerly Reed, Smith, Hazel, and Thomas, LLP), Falls Ch., 1999—, real estate group practice leader, DC and Va. Mem. ABA (mem. real property, probate and trust sect.), Va. State Bar (mem. real property sect.), CREW Network (pres. North Va. chpt. 1998-99, nat. del. 2000-01), Urban Land Inst. (mem. urban devel. and mixed use coun.). Office: Reed Smith LLP 3110 Fairview Park Dr Ste 1400 Falls Church VA 22042 Office Phone: 703-641-4220. Office Fax: 703-641-4340. Business E-Mail: chonigberg@reedsmith.com.

HONIGMAN, STEVEN, lawyer; b. Bklyn., May 14, 1948; BA, NYU, 1969; JD, Yale U., 1972. Bar: N.Y. 1973, D.C. 1976, U.S. Supreme Ct., U.S. Ct. Appeals (2d and D.C. cirs.), U.S. Ct. Mil. Appeals, U.S. Dist. Ct. D.C., U.S. Dist. Ct. (so. and ea. dists.) N.Y. Clk. to chief judge US Dist. Ct. (ea. dist.), NY; gen. counsel Dept. Navy, Washington, 1992-98; ptnr. Thelen, Reid & Priest, 1998—2005, Miller, Singer, Raives & Brandes PC, NYC; mem. Fox Horan & Camerini LLP, NYC, 2006—. Bd.dir. DRS Technologies, Wornick Co.; dept. chief legal officer Sec. of Navy, prin. legal adv.; adv. bd. Harbor Wing Technologies Inc; bus. exec. Nat. Security. Contbr. Bd. dir. Times Sq. Grp. Recipient Disting. Pub. Svc. award Dept. Navy, 1998, Aegis Excellence award, 1995, 3rd highest civilian US Dept. Navy. Fellow Am. Bar Found.; mem. ABA (chmn. standing com. on mil. law 1986-89), NY State Bar Assn., DC Bar Assn., Assn. of Bar NYC, Yale Law Sch. Assn. (mem. exec. com.), US Naval Inst., mem. Finnish Am. C. of C., fellow CNA Corp./Ctr.Naval Analysis 1998-2000. Office: Fox Horan & Camerini 825 3rd Ave 12th Fl New York NY 10022 Office Phone: 212-480-4800. Office Fax: 212-709-0248. Business E-Mail: sshonigman@foxlex.com.

HONMA, KOICHI, pathologist, researcher; b. Shiroishi, Miyagi, Japan, Mar. 28, 1955; s. Tsuneo and Mieko (Isago) Honma; m. Kiyomi Fukuda, Nov. 27, 1986; children: Shiko, Seiji, Shino. BM, Tohoku U., 1979; MD, Dokkyo U., 1986. Instr. Dokkyo U. Sch. Medicine, Tochigi, Japan, 1981-84, asst. prof., 1984-92, assoc. prof., 1992—. Mem. sci. com. No. 9 ILO Conf., Kyoto, 1995—97; organizer internat. workshops on occupl. lung diseases, 1996—. Contbr. articles to profl. jours. Founder, diplomatic counselor London Diplomatic Acad., 2000—; mem. Asbestos Guideline Com., 2007—. Mem.: European Soc. Pathology, Pulmonary Pathology Soc., Am. Thoracic Soc., European Respiratory Soc., Deutsche Gesellschaft fur Pathologie. Avocations: music, sports. Home: Tomatsuri 3-6-45 Utsunomiya Tochigi 320-0056 Japan Office: Dokkyo U Sch Medicine Dept Pathology Kitakobayashi 880 Mibu Tochigi 321-0293 Japan Office Phone: 81-282-86-5171, 81-282-87-2129. Business E-Mail: honma@dokkyomed.ac.jp.

HONNOLD, JOHN OTIS, retired law educator; b. Kansas, Ill., Dec. 5, 1915; s. John Otis and Louretta (Wright) H.; m. Annamarie Kunz, June 26, 1939; children: Carol Honnold Davidon (dec.), Heidi Honnold Spencer, Edward. BA, U. Ill., 1936; JD, Harvard U., 1939; LLD (hon.), Capital U., 1991, Pace U., 1997. Bar: N.Y. 1940, Pa. 1953, U.S. Supreme Ct 1953. Atty. firm Wright, Gordon, Zachry & Parlin, NYC, 1939-41, SEC, 1941; chief ct. rev. br. OPA, 1942-46; mem. faculty U. Pa. Law Sch., 1946-69, 74-84, prof. law, 1952-69, 74-84, prof. emeritus, 1984; Arthur Goodhart prof. sci. of law. U. Cambridge, England, 1982-83. Mem. vis. faculty U. Beijing, 1984, U. Hawaii, 1986, U. Fla., 1988; Canterbury vis. fellow, N.Z., 1986; lectr. UN seminar, Moscow, 1990, U. Stockholm, 1990; chief internat. trade law br. UN; sec. UN Commn. on Internat. Trade Law, 1969-74; mem. faculty law sessions Salzburg (Austria) Seminar Am. Studies, 1960, chmn., 1963, 66; chief counsel Miss. Office, Lawyer's Com. for Civil Rights under Law, 1965; U.S. del., mem. drafting com. diplomatic conf. preparing uniform law for internat. sales of goods, The Hague, Holland, 1964; U.S. del UN Commn. Internat. Trade Law, 1969, 77; U.S. del. diplomatic confs. Conv. Carriage of Goods by Sea, Hamburg, 1978, Contracts for Internat. Sale of Goods, Vienna, 1980; gen. reporter 12th Internat. Congress Comparative Law, 1986 Author: (with C. Mooney, S. Harris, C. Reitz) Sales and Secured Financing, 6th edit., 1993, The Life of the Law, 1964, (with others) Commercial Law, 5th edit., 1993, Uniform Law for International Sales under the 1980 UN Convention, 1982, 3rd edit., 1999, 1991, (with others) United Nations Legal Order, 1995; contbr. articles to profl. jours. Guggenheim fellow, 1958; Fulbright sr. research scholar U. Paris, 1958; recipient Theberge award for contbn. to Pvt. Internat. Law, ABA, 1986; Lincoln Laureate, 1992.

HONORÉ, RUSSEL L., career military officer; b. Lakeland, La., 1948; s. Lloyd Honoré and Marie Udell St. Amant. BS, So. U. and A&M Coll., 1971, D (hon.) in Pub. Adminstrn.; MA, Troy State U.; LLD (hon.), Stillman Coll. Advanced through grades to lt. gen. U.S. Army, 2004; dep. commdg. gen./asst. commandant U.S. Army Infantry Ctr. and Sch., Fort Benning, Ga.; vice dir. ops. (J-3) The Joint Staff, Washington; commdg. gen., 2nd Infantry Divsn. 8th Army Eighth U.S. Army, Republic of Korea, 2000—02; comdr. Standing Joint Force Hdqs. Homeland Security U.S. No. Command, 2002—04; commdg. gen. First U.S. Army, Fort Gillem, Ga., 2004—; comdr. Joint Task Force Katrina, 2005. Decorated Def. Disting. Svc. Medal, DSM, Def. Superior Svc. Medal, Legion of Merit with four oak leaf clusters, Bronze Star Medal, Def. Meritorious Svc. Medal, Meritorious Svc. Medal with three oak leaf clusters, Army Commendation Medal with three oak leaf clusters, Army Achievement Medal, Nat. Def. Svc. Medal with two bronze svc. stars, Armed Forces Expeditionary Medal, S.W. Asia Svc. Medal with one bronze svc. star, Global War on Terror Svc. Star, Korean Def. Svc. Medal, Army Svc. Ribbon, Overseas Svc. Ribbon (4), Kuwait Liberation Medal (Saudi), Kuwait Liberation Medal (Kuwait), Joint Meritorious Unit Award; recipient Omar N. Bradley Spirit of Independence award, 2005. Office: First US Army 4705 N Wheeler Dr Forest Park GA 30297*

HONOUR, LYNDA CHARMAINE, research scientist, psychotherapist, educator; d. John Henry, Jr. and Evelyn Helen Roberta (Pietrowski) H. BA, Boston U.; MA, Calif. State U., Fullerton, UCLA; PhD, U. So. Calif. Lic. marriage, family and child psychotherapist and psychologist, Calif. Rschr. neuroendocrinology and behavioral neurosci., Calif., 1976—; pvt. practice psychotherapy Carlsbad Village, Calif., 1991—. Vis. and clin. prof. Pepperdine U., 1989—, Malibu, Calif. Sch. Profl. Psychology, Calif. State U., Long Beach, Northridge; condr. rsch. Neuropsychiat. Inst., Brain Rsch. Inst., Mental Retardation Rsch. Ctr., UCLA, Tulane U. Med. Sch., V.A. Med. Ctr., New Orleans, Salk Inst. Biol. Studies; rsch. cons. U. Calif. Med. Ctr., Irvine; cons. in rsch. or psychotherapy, 1976—; guest expert on safety issues regarding magnetic imaging Premiere Radio Network, 2001; condr. rsch. Neuropsychiat. Inst., Brain Rsch. Inst., Mental Retardation Rsch. Ctr., UCLA, Tulane U. Med. Sch., V.A. Med. Ctr., New Orleans, Salk Inst. Biol. Studies; rsch. cons. U. Calif. Med. Ctr., Irvine, Salk Inst.; cons., ad hoc reviewer (textbooks) Wadsworth/Brooks-Cole, Thomson Internat. Pub., Pacific Grove, Calif.; cons., reviewer Allyn & Bacon Pub., Boston; hon. chmn., Bus. Adv. Coun. Nat. Rep. Congl. Com.; reviewer Pearson Pub. Group. Contbr. articles to profl. jours. Named one of Top Mental Health Profls. in Am., Nat. Consumer's Rsch. Coun. Am., Washington, 2006; rsch. grantee Organon Internat. Rsch. Group, Netherlands, 1984-88. Mem. APA, Soc. for Neurosci., Internat. Behavioral Neurosci. Soc., Internat. Brain Rsch. Orgn., Calif. Assn. Marriage and Family Therapists, Sons and Daus. of Pearl Harbor Survivors, Psi Chi, Salk Inst. Alumni. Roman Catholic. Achievements include the discovery two peptides one which facilitates and one which inhibits learning and memory task performance permanently in a developmental paradigm in mice; research on the facilitation peptide reveal it can permanently reverse induced learning/memory deficit, with implications for mental retardation and other learning/memory deficit treatment; member of the research team which isolated and characterized the corticotropic hormone releasing factor, urocortin; the delineation of various effects of peptides on behavior including bipolar disorders, endogenous depression, mania and others; human research involving interface between cognition/mind and physiological processes/disease; research in the risks associated with MRI exposure; establishing new N.E. US swimming records in the 1960s; established developmental influences of peptides on cognition/learning processes; identified chemical moieties responsible for learning, memory, and cognition processing; investigating effect of cognitive process on physiological metabolisms. Avocations: quantum theory, metaphysics. Business E-Mail: DrLyndaHonour@cs.com.

HONSA, THOMAS PATRICK, secondary school educator, history professor; b. Elmhurst, Ill., Jan. 24, 1964; s. Thomas and Anna Marie Honsa; m. Laura Merle Griffin, May 21, 1988; 1 child, Aaron Patrick. AA, Manatee C.C., Bradenton, Fla., 1984; BA, U. of South Fla., Sarasota, 1986; MA, U. of South Fla., Tamp, 1997. Cert. tchr. Fla. Dept. of Edn. Tchr. Lakewood Ranch H.S., Bradenton, 1998—. Adj. prof. history Manatee C.C., Bradenton, 1998—, Eckerd Coll., Sarasota, 2004—. Designer (historic games design) Desert Storm - The Unfinished Victory, (historical games design) Balkan Storm - the Next War in Europe; contbr. articles to mags. Coord. cmty. svc. Lakewood Ranch H.S., Bradenton, 1998—2001. Named Fla. History Tchr. of the Yr., Fla. Sec. of State Office, 2005, Manatee County History Tchr. of the Yr., Manatee County Hist. Commn., 2004, Dist. Tchr. of the Yr., Manatee County Sch. Bd., 1997, Finalist, Nat. History Tchrs. of Yr. Nat. Archives, 2005. Mem.: Fla. Hist. Soc., Am. Hist. Assn. Avocations: local historical research, game design, camping. Home Phone: 941-360-8712; Office Phone: 941-727-6100.

HONSA, VLASTA, retired librarian; b. Žilina, Czechoslovakia, Sept. 1, 1924; came to US, 1951; d. František Petr and Marie (Širkova) Petrova; m. Vladimir Honsa, June 26, 1948; children: Patricia, Eva Honsa-Hogg. BA, Charles U., Prague, 1947; MLS, Ind. U., 1968. Gifts libr. Ind. U. Libr., Bloomington, 1968-70; head reference dept. Clark County Libr., Las Vegas, 1970-80, asst. adminstr., 1980-94; ret., 1994. Coord. Found. Collection, part of the Found. Ctr.'s Cooperating Collections network, Clark County Libr., 1979-94. Author: Nevada Foundation Directory, 1984, 2d edit., 1989, 3rd edit., 1994. Bd. dirs. So. Nev. Musical Arts Soc., Las Vegas, 1989-92; organized and presented fundraising workshops for cmty. fund raisers sponsored by Las Vegas-Clark County Libr. Dist., 1979-94. Recipient Ind. U. grant-in-aid to conduct rsch. of publs. in cen. Am. univs. and nat. librs., 1970, Champion award Las Vegas-Clark County Libr. Dist., 1985. Mem. ALA, AAUW, Nev. Libr. Assn., Univ. Nevada Las Vegas Faculty Club. Roman Catholic. Avocations: reading, music, arts, travel. Home: 7443 W Robin Ln Glendale AZ 85310 Personal E-mail: vhonsa@cox.net.

HOOD, ANTOINETTE FOOTE, dermatologist; b. Honolulu, 1941; MD, Vanderbilt U., 1967. Cert. dermatology. Intern Vanderbilt Affiliated Hosps, 1967-68; fellow dermatology Harvard U., 1973-75, resident dermatology, 1975-76; resident dermatology-pathology Mass. Gen. Hosp., Boston, 1976-78; faculty Johns Hopkins School of Med., 1980—93; Dir. Dermatopathology Indiana Univ. School of Med., 1993—2002; exec. dir. American Board of Dermatology, Detroit, 2001—; Dir. Dermatopathology Ea. Va. School of Med, 2002—. Office: Pariser Dermatology Specialists Ltd 601 Medical Tower Norfolk VA 23507

HOOD, DONALD CHARLES, academic administrator, psychologist, educator; b. Merrick, NY, June 2, 1942; s. David and Jessie Theresa (Vetter) H.; m. Nancy Ellen Epstein, Nov. 27, 1978. BA, Harpur Coll.-SUNY, Binghamton, 1965; MS, Brown U., 1968, PhD, 1970. Asst. prof. Columbia U., NYC, 1969-73, assoc. prof., 1973-78, prof. psychology, 1978—, James F. Bender prof. psychology, 1990—, v.p. arts & sci., 1982-87, chmn. psychology dept., 1975-78. Contbr. articles to profl. jours. Trustee Smith Coll., 1989—99, vice chair, 1991—99; trustee Harry Guggenheim Found., 1996—; trustee (fellow) Brown U., 2002—; trustee Assn. Rsch. Vision and Ophthalmology, 2004—. USPHS fellow, 1967—69, N.Y. State Coll. teaching fellow, 1965—67. Fellow: Optical Soc., Soc. Exptl. Psychology; mem.: Ea. Psychol. Assn., Assn. Rsch. Vision and Ophthalmology (trustee 2004—). Home: 450 Riverside Dr New York NY 10027-6801 Office: 415 Schernerhorn Hall 116th St And Broadway New York NY 10027 Office Phone: 212-854-4587. Business E-Mail: dch3@columbia.edu.

HOOD, EDWARD EXUM, JR., retired electronics executive; b. Boonville, NC, Sept. 15, 1930; s. Edward Exum and Nellie (Triplett) H.; m. Kay Transou, Dec. 30, 1950; children: Lisa Kay, Molly Ann. MS in Nuclear Engring., N.C. State U., 1953. Registered profl. engr., Ariz. Powerplant design engr. Gen. Electric Co., 1957-62, mgr. supersonic transport engine project, 1962-67, v.p., gen. mgr. comml. engine div., from 1968, v.p., group exec. internat. group, 1972-73, v.p., group exec., power generation group, 1973-77, sr. v.p., sector exec. tech. systems and materials sector, from 1977, vice-chmn. and exec officer, 1979-93, also bd. dirs. Served with USAF, 1952-56. Fellow AIAA; mem. Nat. Acad. Engring., Aerospace Industries Assn. (chmn. 1981)

HOOD, GLENDA E., former state official, former mayor; b. Orlando, Fla., Mar. 10, 1950; m. Charles M. Hood III; 3 children. BA in Spanish, Rollins Coll.; postgrad., Harvard U., Ga. State U. Commr. City of Orlando, Fla., 1982-92, mayor Fla., 1992—2002; sec. of state State of Fla., Tallahassee, 2003—05. Pres. Glenda E. Hood & Assocs., Inc. Vice chmn. mcpl. planning bd. City of Orlando, mem. nominating bd., chmn. task force bd. and commn. restructure; past chmn., founding mem. bd. dirs. Found. Orange County Pub. Schs.; co-chmn. Orlando Fights Back-Coalition for a Drug-Free Cmty.; bd. dirs. U. Ctrl. Fla. Found., Met. Orlando Urban League; past pres. exec. bd. Ctrl. Fla. Coun. of Boy Scouts; bd. overseers Rollins Coll. Crummer Grad. Sch. of Bus.; mem. adv. bd. Valencia C.C., Fla.- Costa Rica Inst.; past co-chmn. United Negro Coll. Fund; pres. Jr. League Orlando-Winter Park, Vol. Svc. Bur.; mem. Orange County Commn. on Children. Named Mcpl. Leader of Yr., Am. City and County Mag., 1992, one of Ten Outstanding Young Americans, U.S. Jaycees, one of Seven Outstanding Youth Floridians, Fla. Jaycees, Woman of Yr., Downtown Orlando Inc., one of Ten People to Watch, Fla. Trend, one of 100 Young Women of Promise, Good Housekeeping; recipient Willie J. Bruton award for cmty. svc. Met. Orlando Urban League, Summit award Women's Resource Ctr., Svc. to Mankind award Leukemia Soc. Am. Ctrl. Fla. chpt. Mem. Nat. League of Cities (past pres.), Fla. League of Cities (past pres.), Fla. C. of C. (past pres.), Greater Orlando C. of C. (past v.p.). Republican. Episcopalian.

HOOD, HENRY J., lawyer, energy executive; b. 1960; AB, Duke U., 1982; JD, U. Okla., 1985. Bar: 1985. With Watson & McKenzie, 1987—92; assoc. White, Coffey, Galt & Fite, 1992—95; v.p. land and legal Chesapeake Energy Corp., Oklahoma City, 1995—97, sr. v.p. land and legal, 1997—, gen. counsel, 2006—. Cons. Chesapeake Energy Corp., 1995—97. Mem.: Tex. Bar Assn., Okla. Bar Assn. Office: Chesapeake Energy Corp PO Box 18496 Oklahoma City OK 73154-0496

HOOD, JAMES BRIAN, systems engineer; b. Charlotte, NC, Dec. 22, 1940; s. Raymond V. and Stella M. (Hinson) H.; m. Patricia Ann Griffin, July 22, 1959 (div. 1979); children: Brian Russell, Pamela Elaine; m. Ramona Hamrick, June 16, 1979. BA, U. Md., 1968; MS, Troy State U., Montgomery, Ala., 1978, EdS, 1979. Cmmd. intelligence officer USAF, 1958, advanced through grades to capt., 1982, ret., 1982; sr. programs mgr. Betac Corp., San Antonio, 1982—. Recipient Commandant's trophy, Squadron Officer Sch., 1975; named Jr. Officer of Yr., Air Univ., 1977. Mem. Armed Forces Communications-Electronics Assn., Assn. Old Crows, USAF Assn., Mensa. Avocations: cooking, military history.

HOOD, JAMES CALTON, lawyer; b. Panama Canal Zone, Oct. 29, 1947; s. Robin Calton and Eleanor (Marquard) H.; m. Elise Joan Gregory, Aug. 16, 1969; children: Jamie, Molly. BA, U. N.H., 1969; JD, Georgetown U., 1972. Bar: NH 1972. Assoc. and dir. McLane, Graf, Raulerson & Middleton, PA, Manchester, NH, 1972—95; ptnr. Nixon Peabody LLP, Manchester, 1995—. Chmn. NH internat. trade adv. com. to gov. Dept. Resources and Econ. Devel. Bd. dirs. Manchester YMCA, 1982, Chmn., 1986-88; bd. dirs. NH Bus. for Social Responsibility, 2005-, Manchester Econ. Devel. Corp., 2005-; trustee St. Paul's Meth. Ch., Manchester 1985. Served to 1st lt. US Army, 1972—73. Mem. ABA, NH Bar Assn. (chmn. corp. sect. 1985), U. NH Alumni Assn. (bd. dirs. 1986-93, pres. 1992-93), Phi Beta Kappa, Phi Kappa Phi. Home: 154 Shaw St Manchester NH 03104-2760 Office: Nixon Peabody 900 Elm St Manchester NH 03101-2019 Office Phone: 603-628-4051. Office Fax: 603-628-4040. E-mail: jchood@nixonpeabody.com.

HOOD, JIM, state attorney general; m. Debbie Hood; 3 children. BA, U. Miss., JD, 1988. Asst. atty. gen. State of Miss., Jackson, Miss.; dist. atty. Third Cir. Ct. Dist., No. Miss.; atty. gen. State of Miss., 2003—. Recipient Justice Achievement award, Crime Victim's Compensation Prog., 2003. Democrat. Baptist. Achievements include prosecuted (with Dist. Atty. Mark Duncan) Edgar Ray Killen for the 1964 triple murders of civil rights workers Andrew Goodman, James Chaney and Michael Schwerner, June 2005. Office: Office of Atty Gen Dept Justice PO Box 220 Jackson MS 39205-0220 Office Phone: 601-359-3680. Business E-Mail: msag05@ago.state.ms.us.*

HOOD, LEROY EDWARD, molecular biologist, educator; b. Missoula, Mont., Oct. 10, 1938; s. Thomas Edward and Myrtle Evylan (Wadsworth) H.; m. Valerie Anne Logan, Dec. 14, 1963; children: Eran William, Marqui Leigh Jennifer. BS, Calif. Inst. Tech., 1960; MD, Johns Hopkins U., 1964; PhD in Biochemistry, Calif. Inst. Tech., 1968. Med. officer USPHS, 1967-70, staff scientist Bethesda, Md., 1967-70; sr. investigator Nat. Cancer Inst., 1967-70; asst. prof. biology Calif. Inst. Tech., Pasadena, 1970-73, assoc. prof., 1973-75, prof., 1975-92, Bowles prof. biology, 1977-92, chmn. divsn. biology, 1980-89; Gates prof. molecular biotechnology, chmn. bd. U. Wash. Sch. Medicine, Seattle, 1992—2000; co-founder, pres., dir. Inst. Systems Biology, Seattle, 2000—. Dir. NSF Sci. and Tech. Ctr. for Molecular Biotechnology, 1989-2001. Author: (with others) Biochemistry, a Problems Approach, 1974, Molecular Biology of Eukaryotic Cells, 1975, Immunology, 1978, Essential Concepts of Immunology, 1978, The Code of Codes: Scientific and Social Issues in the Human Genome Project, 1992; co-editor: Advances in Immunology, 1987, Genetics: From Genes to Genomics, 1999. Co-recipient, Albert Lasker Basic Med. Rsch. award, 1987, recipient Scientist of Yr. award, 1993, R & D Mag., Kyoto Prize, 2002, Lemelson prize MIT, 2003, Assoc. for Molecular Biology award for excellence in molecular diagnostics, 2004; named to the Nat. Inventors Hall of Fame, 2007. Mem. NAS, NAE, Am. Assn. Immunologists, Am. Assn. Sci., Am. Acad. Arts and Scis., Sigma Xi, Am. Philos. Soc., Inst. Medicine, 2004. Achievements include invention of automated DNA sequencer technique. Avocations: mountain climbing, rockclimbing, photography. Office: Inst for Systems Biology 1441 N 34th St Seattle WA 98103-8904 Office Phone: 206-732-1201. E-mail: lhood@systemsbiology.org.*

HOOD, RONALD CHALMERS, III, historian, writer; b. Florence, Ala., Apr. 2, 1947; s. Ronald Chalmers II and Elizabeth Woods (Craig) H.; m. Lucile O'Connor, Dec. 20, 1969; children: Ronald Chalmers IV, Reed Cathleen. BS, U.S. Naval Acad., 1969; MA, U. Maine, Orono, 1972; PhD, U. Md., 1979. Commd. 2d lt. USMC, 1969, advanced through grades to capt., 1973, resigned, 1982; historian, writer Johns Hopkins U., Balt., 1982—, George Mason U., Fairfax, Va., 1982—, U. Md., College Park, 1982—, Mary Washington Coll., 1999—. Lectr. Smithsonian Instn., Washington, 1988; speaker Conf. on Strategic Studies, Washington, 1985; co-chair Muscle Shoals Revisited Conf. on Future of Tenn. Valley, 1993; theatre and arts critic The Daily Jour. Author: (history monograph) Royal Republicans, 1985; co-author: (mil. history) Military Effectiveness, 1987, Body, Mind, Spirit: 75 Years of Camp Hazen YMCA, 1995; contbg. author Internat. Ency. for Military History; contbr. editorial columns to Washington Post, Richmond Times-Dispatch, Potomac News, articles to profl. jours. Asst. scoutmaster Boy Scouts Am., Woodbridge, Va., 1989—; advisor Va. State Bd. Edn., 2003-; instr. ARC, Prince William County, 1982—. Samuel Eliot Morison fellow U. Maine, Orono, 1971-72, Grad. Sch. fellow U. Md., 1975, fellow Am. Philos. Soc., 1998, sr. fellow to France Am. Coun. Learned Societies, 2000-2001. Mem. AAUP, Writers' Ctr., Smithsonian Instn., Nat. Geographic Soc. Avocations: travel, acting, bike riding, aquatic activities, cross country skiing. Home and Office: 12317 Oakwood Dr Woodbridge VA 22192-1911

HOOD, THOMAS GREGORY, minister; b. Stamford, Conn., Mar. 26, 1948; s. George E. and Shirley W. (Brundage) H.; m. Esther A. Whitcomb, July 1, 1967; children: Thomas G., Sarah D BA, Johnson State Coll., 1984; MDiv, Covington Sem., Rossville, Ga., 1986; PhD Counseling, Covington Sem., 1988. Ordained to ministry Fellowship of Christian Assemblies, 1969, Am. Bapt. Chs. in U.S.A., 1984. Asst. pastor Bethel Full Gospel Ch., Barton, Vt., 1968—71; pastor Lyndonville Full Gospel Ch., Vt., 1969—71, Sheffield Fed. Ch., Vt., 1971—74, Sutton Bapt. Ch., Vt., 1972—84, Adams Center Bapt. Ch., NY, 1984—. Del. Am. Bapt. Conv., N.Y., 1984—Author: The Lord's Prayer, 1986, A Theology of Victory, 1987, Biblical Principles, 1988; composer religious songs Mem. Am. Bapt. Mins. Coun Republican. Home: 13463 US Rt 11 Adams Center NY 13606 *It is impossible to forgive ourselves for our failures if we are unwilling to forgive others theirs. The rule we use to judge others will always reflect back on ourselves.*

HOOD, WILLIAM BOYD, JR., cardiologist, educator; b. Sylacauga, Ala., Mar. 25, 1932; s. William Boyd and Katherine Elizabeth (Anderson) H.; m. Katherine Candace Todd, May 5, 1972; 1 son, Jefferson Boyce. BS summa cum laude, Davidson Coll., 1954; MD, Harvard U., 1958. Intern Peter Bent Brigham Hosp., Boston, 1958-59, resident in internal medicine, 1959-60, 62-63; from asst. prof. to assoc. prof. medicine Harvard U., 1967-71; from assoc. prof. to prof. medicine Boston U., 1971-82; chief cardiology Boston City Hosp., 1973-82; prof. medicine U. Rochester (N.Y.), 1982-98; head cardiology unit Strong Meml. Hosp., Rochester, 1982-98; emeritus prof. medicine U. Rochester, 1998—. Cons. NIH, 1975—, NASA, 1994—; clin. prof. medicine U. Wash. Sch. Medicine, Seattle, 2000—. Mem. editorial bd. New Eng. Jour. Medicine, 1974-81, Circulation, 1980-83, Circulation Research, 1982-89, Jour. Clin. Investigation, 1984-89, Cochrane Collaboration Heart Group, 1997—; contbr. articles, revs. and editorials on cardiovascular physiology to profl. jours., chpts. to books. Served to capt. USAF, 1963-65. Research grantee NIH, 1971-98; grantee Am. Heart Assn., 1971-76. Fellow ACP; mem. Am. Soc. Clin. Investigation, Assn. Am. Physicians, Am. Heart Assn., Am. Physiol. Soc., Assn. Profs. Cardiology (past pres.), N.Y. Cardiol. Soc. (past pres.), Phi Beta Kappa, Alpha Omega Alpha. Achievements include studies on experimental and clinical myocardial ischemia and infarction, and congestive heart failure.

HOOGASIAN, SETH H., lawyer; b. Worcester, Mass., Apr. 18, 1954; BS with distinction in Mech. Engring., Cornell U., 1976; JD with distinction, Duke U., 1979. Bar: DC 1979, Md. 1989, Mass. 1993. Assoc. Shaw, Pittman, Potts & Trowbridge, Washington; ptnr. Weinberg & Green, Balt.; sr. counsel Thermo Fisher Sci. (formerly Thermo Electron Corp.), Waltham, Mass., 1990, gen. counsel, 1992—, v.p. to sr. v.p., 1996—, sec., 2001—. Mem. ABA, Mass. Bar Assn., Tau Beta Pi. Office: Thermo Fisher Sci 81 Wyman St Waltham MA 02451-1223 Office Phone: 617-622-1000. E-mail: shoogasian@thermo.com.*

HOOGENBOOM, CAROL ANNETTE, clinical neuropsychologist; b. Grand Rapids, Mich., Jan. 31; d. Cornelius Adrian and Shirley Ann (Rassi) Hoogenboom. BS, Western Mich. U., Kalamazoo, 1985, MA, 1987; PsychD, Forest Inst., Wheeling, Ill., 1993. Lic. Clin. Psychologist Ill. Dept. Fin. & Profl. Regulation, 1995. Psychometrian Crawford Consulting Svc., Chgo., 1991—92, Behavioral Health Svcs., Chgo., 1993—94; intern, resident Cermak Hosp., Chgo., 1991—92; postdoctoral Psychealth Ltd., Evanston, Ill., 1993—95; pres., adminstr. Nat. Neuropsych. Svcs., Glenview, Ill., 1995—97, clin. psychologist, 1995—97; Neuropsychologist CAH Psychological Svcs., Chgo., 1998—. Personal injury cons. Area Personal Injury Attys., Chgo., 2003—05; domestic abuse cons. Sido's Shelter, Chgo., 2004; pro bono psychol. svcs. CAH Psychol. Svcs., Chgo., 2003—; mgr. Windsor Retirement Home, LaGrange, Ill., 2006—. Author: (manual) Starting a Domestic Abuse Shelter, 2004, Anti Social Personality Disorder Is Really a Delusional Disorder, 2006. AIDS speaker Area Hosps., Chgo., 2005; Provide free depression screening through local businesses, Chgo., 2003—; motivational speaker CAH Psycholog. Svcs., Chgo., 2005—; advisor Windsor Pl. Retirement Home, LaGrange, Ill., 2006. Fellow: APA; mem.: Am. Psychol Soc., Ill. Psychol. Assn., Behavior Book Club, Psi Chi. Achievements include Numerous awards in athletics: basketball, volleyball, track, softball and cycling, including All American honors; 1st female Native Am. to obtain doctoral degree in US. Avocations: coin collecting/numismatics, computers, sports, Equality and Civil Rights Issues, building trades. Office: CAH Psychol Svcs 28 E Jackson Bldg #10-H580 Chicago IL 60604 E-mail: carolhoogenboom@yahoo.com.

HOOGLAND, ROBERT FREDERICS, lawyer; b. Paterson, NJ, Apr. 3, 1955; s. Robert J. and Lucretia H. BA, U. Fla., 1976; MBA, Rollins Coll., 1977; JD, U. Fla., 1982. Bar: Fla. 1983, U.S. Dist. Ct. (mid. dist.) Fla. 1989; cert. real estate law. Assoc. Giles, Hedrick & Robinson, Orlando, Fla., 1983-89; ptnr. Hoogland & Durket, P.A., Longwood, Fla., 1989-92, Robert F. Hoogland, P.A., Altamonte Springs, Fla., 1992—. Mem. ABA, Fla. Bar Assn., Orange County Bar Assn., Seminole Bar Assn., Voile A. Williams Inns of Court, Phi Delta Phi. Republican. Roman Catholic. Avocations: tennis, golf, fishing. Home: 139 Olive Tree Cir Altamonte Springs FL 32714-3240 Office: PO Box 160021 Altamonte Springs FL 32716-0021 Office Phone: 407-862-4909.

HOOK, HAROLD SWANSON, former management consulting executive; b. Kansas City, Mo., Oct. 10, 1931; s. Ralph C. and Ruby (Swanson) H.; m. Joanne T. Hunt, Feb. 19, 1955; children: Karen Anne, Thomas W., Randall T. BS in Bus. Adminstrn., U. Mo., 1953, MA in Acctg., 1954; grad., So. Meth. U. Inst. Ins. Mktng., 1957; postgrad., NYU, 1967-70; LLD (hon.), U. Mo., 1983, Westminster Coll., 1983. CLU, FLMI. Mem. faculty U. Mo. Sch. Bus., 1953-54; asst. to pres. Nat. Fidelity Life Ins. Co., Kansas City, Mo., 1957-60, dir., 1959-66, adminstrv. v.p., 1960-61, exec. v.p., investment com., 1961-62, pres., exec. com., 1962-66; sr. v.p. U.S. Life Ins. Co., NYC, 1966-67, dir., 1967-70, exec. v.p., mem. exec. com., 1967-68, pres., 1968-70, Calif.-Western States Life Ins. Co., Sacramento, 1970-75, chmn., 1975-79, sr. chmn., 1979-91; also bd. dirs.; mem. exec. com. Am. Gen. Corp., Houston, 1975-97, pres., 1975-81, chmn., chief exec. officer, 1978-96, also bd. dirs., chmn., 1996-97. Founder, pres. Main Event Mgmt. Corp., Houston, 1971—; bd. dirs. Duke Energy Corp.,Charlotte, N.C., Sprint Corp., Kansas City, Mo., Cooper Industries, Inc., Houston, Chase

Manhattan Corp., N.Y.C., Chase Manhattan Bank, N.Y.C., Chase Bank ofTex., Houston. Founder, mem. Naval War Coll. Found.; trustee, Baylor Coll. Medicine, Houston; coun. overseers Jesse H. Hones Grad. Sch. Adminstrn., Rice U., Houston; pres. nat. exec. bd. Boy Scouts Am., 1988-90, now mem. nat. adv. coun. Boy Scouts Am., mem. adv. bd. Sam Houston Area coun.; past pres. Houston Commerce, bd. dirs., Greater Houston Partnership (formerly Houston C. of C.), Director Emeritus. Recipient Citation of Merit U. Mo. Alumni Assn., 1965, Faculty-Alumni award U. Mo., 1978; Silver Beaver award Boy Scouts Am., 1974, Disting. Eagle Scout award, 1976, Silver Antelope award, 1989, Silver Buffalo award, 1990; Chief Exec. Officer award Fin. World mag., 1979, 82, 84, 86; named Man of Yr., Delta Sigma Pi, 1969, Outstanding Chief Exec. Officer in Multiline Ins. Industry, Wall Street Transcript, 1981-87. Fellow Life Mgmt. Inst.; mem. Mgmt. Exec. Soc., Philos. Soc. Tex., Tex. Assn. Taxpayers (bd. dirs.), Nat. Assn. Life Underwriters, Houston Assn. Life Underwriters, Forum Club (bd. govs. 1983-93), River Oaks Country Club, Petrolum Club, Econ. Club N.Y.C., Eldorado Country Club, Rotary, Beta Gamma Sigma (dirs. table 1976, nat. honoree 1984). Presbyterian. Office: Main Event Mgmt Corp 2727 Allen Pkwy Ste 1600 Houston TX 77019

HOOK, JERRY B., pharmaceutical consultant; b. Elk City, Okla., Sept. 7, 1937; m. Jacqueline H. Smith; children: Bruce, Marilyn. BS, B in Pharmacy with honors, Wash. State U., Pullman, 1960; MS, U. Iowa, 1964, PhD, 1966; DSc (hon.), John Jay Coll. Criminal Justice, CUNY, 1989. Diplomate Am. Bd. Toxicology. Assoc. prof. pharmacology Mich. State U., East Lansing, 1971-75, prof. of pharmacology, 1975-78, prof. pharmacology and toxicology, 1978-83, dir. ctr. for environ. toxicology, 1980-83; v.p. preclin. R & D Smith Kline & French Labs. Phila., King of Prussia, Pa., 1983-87, v.p. preclin. R & D worldwide, 1987-88, v.p. devel., R & D, 1988-89, SmithKline Beecham Pharms., King of Prussia, 1989-90, sr. v.p., dir. devel. R & D, 1990-93; pres., chief exec. officer Lexin Pharm. Corp., Horsham, Pa., 1993-96; pres., CEO Sparta Pharm., Inc., Horsham, Pa., 1996-98, chmn., pres., CEO, 1998-99. Burroughs-Wellcome vis. prof. U. N.D., 1981; vis. scientist Fed. Am. Soc. for Exptl. Biology Vis. Scientists for Minority Instns. Program, U. P.R. Med. Sch., 1984, Herbert H. Lehman Coll. of City U., 1985, Calif. State U., 1988, Pembroke State U., 1989; mem. adv. com. to bd. sci. counselors Nat. Toxicology Program, 1982-86; chmn. peer rev. panel of experts Nat. Toxology Program; vis. scientist John Jay Coll. Criminal Justice CUNY, 1987, mem. adv. bd. Toxicology Rsch. and Tng. Ctr., 1986-93. Author 225 publs. peer-reviewed lit., 60 book chpts., published symposia, reviews, symposia presentations. Bd. dirs. Montgomery County Community Coll. Found., 1987-89. Fellow Am. Coll. Clin. Pharmacology (hon.); mem. AAAS, Am. Soc. for Pharmacology and Exptl. Therapeutics, Internat. Union of Pharmacology (vice chmn. toxicology sect. 1987-90, chmn. toxicology sect. 1990-94), Internat. Union of Toxicology (1st v.p. 1989-92), Mid-Atlantic Chpt. Soc. of Toxicology, Soc. of Toxicology (councillor 1983-85, v.p. elect 1985-86, v.p. 1986-87, pres. 1987-88, past pres. 1988-89, IUTOX councillor). Personal E-mail: jhook0937@aol.com.

HOOK, JOHN BURNEY, investment company executive; b. Franklin, Ind., Sept. 6, 1928; s. Burney S. and Elsie C. (Hubbard) H.; m. Georgia Delis, Feb. 8, 1958; children— David, Deborah. BS, Ind. U., 1956, MBA, 1957. CPA, Ohio.; cert. fin. analyst. Store mgr. Goodman-Jester, Inc., Franklin, Ind., 1949-50; auditor Ernst & Ernst, Indpls., 1953-56; financial analyst Eli Lilly & Co., Indpls., 1957-59; gen. ptnr. Ball, Burge & Kraus, Cleve., 1966-72; pres., dir. Cuyahoga Mgmt. Corp., 1966-81; mng. ptnr. Hook Ptnrs., Cleve., 1984—96. Mem. AICPA, Am. Inst. CFAs, Union Club (Cleve.), Westwood Country Club, Ironwood Country Club (Palm Desert, Calif.). Republican. Methodist. Home: 435 Bates Dr Bay Village OH 44140 also: 73233 Ribbonwood Palm Desert CA 92260

HOOK, RALPH CLIFFORD, JR., business educator; b. Kansas City, Mo., May 2, 1923; s. Ralph Clifford and Ruby (Swanson) H.; m. Joyce Fink, Jan. 20, 1946; children: Ralph Clifford III, John Gregory. BA, U. Mo., Columbia, 1947, MA, 1948; PhD, U. Tex., Austin, 1954. Instr. U. Mo., 1947-48; asst. prof. Tex. A&M U., 1948-51; lectr. U. Tex., 1951-52; co-owner, mgr. Hook Buick Co., also Hook Truck & Tractor Co., Lee's Summit, Mo., 1952-58; assoc. prof. U. Kansas City, 1953-58; dir. Bur. Bus. Rsch. and Svcs., Ariz. State U., 1958-66, prof. mktg., 1960-68; dean Coll. Bus. Adminstrn., U. Hawaii, 1968-74; prof. mktg. U. Hawaii, 1974-96, prof. mktg. emeritus, 1996—. Vis. Disting. prof. N.E. La. U., 1979; dir. Hook Bros. Corp. Author: (with others) The Management Primer, 1972, Life Style Marketing, 1979, Marketing Service, 1983; contbr. (with others) monograph series Western Bus. Roundup; founder, moderator Western Bus. Roundup radio series, 1958-68. 1st lt. F.A., AUS, 1943-46; col. Res. Recipient alumni citation of merit U. Mo. Coll. Bus. and Pub. Adminstrn., 1969; Disting. Svc. award Nat. Def. Transp. Assn., 1977, God and Svc. award United Meth. Ch./Boy Scouts Am., 1986, Hawaii Jefferson award, 2004; named to Faculty Hall Fame Ariz. State U. Coll. Bus. Assn., 1977, Hawaii Transp. Hall of Fame, 1986, Hawaii Bus. Hall of Fame, 2000; named Educator of Yr., Western Mktg. Educators' Assn., 1998, Fellow Internat. Coun. for Small Bus. (pres. 1963); mem. Am. Mktg. Assn. (v.p. 1965-67, pres. Ctrl. Ariz. chpt. 1960-61, pres. Honolulu chpt. 1991-92, Wayne A. Lemberg award for disting. svc. 1995), Western Assn. Collegiate Schs. Bus. (pres. 1972-73), Sales and Mktg. Execs. Internat. (life), Nat. Def. Transp. Assn. (life, Hawaii v.p. 1978-82), Newcomen Soc. N.Am. (Hawaii chmn.), Pi Sigma Epsilon (v.p. for edn. programs 1990-94), Mu Kappa Tau (pres. 1996-98), Beta Gamma Sigma, Omicron Delta Kappa, Beta Theta Pi, Delta Sigma Pi (gold coun.). United Methodist. Office: U Hawaii Coll Bus Adminstrn 2404 Maile Way Bldg C Honolulu HI 96822-2223 Home: Apt 210 428 Kawaihae St Honolulu HI 96825 Home Phone: 808-395-9251.

HOOK, WILLIAM FRANKLIN, radiologist; b. Williston, ND, May 26, 1935; s. Charles Ellis and Ann (Franklin) H.; m. Margo Joanne Booth, June 21, 1958 (div. Sept. 1968); children: William, Christopher, Paul; m. Merry Jean Schimke, Nov. 26, 1968 (div. 1987); 1 child, Kari Ann; m. Linda Marie Rohrich, Aug. 18, 1988 (div. 2006). AB, Stanford U., 1957; MD, Jefferson Med. Coll., 1961. Diplomate Am. Bd. Radiology, Am. Bd. Nuc. Medicine. Staff radiologist O&R Clinic, Bismarck, ND, 1969-74, dir. nuc. radiology, 1983-98, chmn. dept. radiology, 1990-98; chief dept. radiology Bismarck Hosp., 1970-74; dir. dept. radiology Mandan (ND) Hosp., 1974-81; staff radiologist Meth. Hosps., Dallas, 1981-83, Med. Ctr. One, 1984-98; co-dir. Regional MRI Ctr., Bismarck, 1987-92. Asst. clin. prof. U. ND, 1978—. Author: Common Sense and Modern First Aid, 1967, (CD-Rom) X-Ray Film Reading Made Easy, 2001. Lt. USNR, 1961-64, col. Res. ret.; comdr. USAR hosp., Persian Gulf, 1991-92. Mem.: AMA (Physicians Recognition award 1983—86, 1986—92), 6th Dist. Med. Soc., N.D. State Radiol. Soc., Radiol. Soc. N.Am., Soc. Nuc. Medicine, Am. Coll. Radiology. Lutheran. Avocations: hunting, golf, aviation. Address: PO Box 133 12607 Pine Shadows Rd Hot Springs SD 57747 Personal E-mail: wfhook@aol.com.

HOOKER, JAMES TODD, manufacturing executive; b. Ashland, Ohio, Dec. 21, 1946; s. Melvin Todd and Harriet (Lutz) Hooker; m. Sallie Foulkrod Utz, Feb. 22, 1975; 1 child, Stephanie Rae. BSBA magna cum laude, Ashland U., 1973. From advt. mgr. to v.p. gen. mgr. Gorman-Rupp Co., Mansfield, Ohio, 1974—2003, v.p. gen. mgr. Bellville, Ohio, 2003—. Solicitor United Way, Mansfield; chmn. bd. trustees Richland County Leadership Unlimited; mem. Heritage Found.; plank owner USN Meml. Found.; chmn. bd. dirs. Mansfield Richland County Chamber Edn. Found.; pres. Richland County Bus. Adv. Coun.; moderator, bd. deacons Presbyn. Ch., 1988—89, elder, mem. Session. Decorated Vietnamese Gallantry Cross; named Ohio State Water Ski Champion, 2002. Mem.: Omicron Delta Epsilon. Republican. Home: 1090 Trout Dr Mansfield OH 44903-9144 Office: Gorman Rupp Industries 180 Hines Ave Bellville OH 44813

HOOKER, ROBERT WRIGHT, journalist; b. New Haven, July 11, 1947; s. Charles Wright and Elma (Black) Hooker; m. Ellen Ann McMackin, Apr. 13, 1974; 1 child, Matthew Wright. BA in History, Davidson Coll., NC, 1969; MA in History, Vanderbilt U., 1971. Reporter St. Petersburg (Fla.) Times, 1971-78, polit. editor, 1978, night city editor, 1979, projects editor, 1979-87, Tampa city editor, 1987, state editor, 1987-90, bus. editor, 1990-96, met. editor, 1996, asst. mng. editor, 1997-2001, dep. mng. editor, 2001—. Author: The Times and Its Times: 1884-1984, 1984. 1st lt. USAR, 1971. Recipient Nat. Edn. Reporting award, Edn. Writers Am., 1983, Best Investigative Reporting award, Am. Sports Editors Assn., 1983. Home: 2982 60th Ave S Saint Petersburg FL 33712-4524 Office: Saint Petersburg Times PO Box 1121 Saint Petersburg FL 33731-1121 Business E-Mail: hooker@sptimes.com.

HOOKER, VAN DORN, architect, educator, artist; b. Carthage, Tex., Sept. 22, 1921; s. Van Dorn and Anne (Wylie) H.; m. Marjorie Mead, June 14, 1947; children: Ann, Van Dorn III, John Hardy. Student, Coll. of Marshall, Tex., 1938-40; BArch, U. Tex., 1947; postgrad., U. Calif.-Berkeley, 1950-51. Registered architect, N.Mex., Tex. Architect, ptnr. McHugh & Hooker-Bradley P. Kidder & Assocs., Santa Fe, 1956-63; univ. architect U. N.Mex., Albuquerque, 1963-87, univ. architect emeritus, 1987—, assoc. prof. architecture, 1971-87; assoc. prof. architecture emeritus, 1987—. Architect numerous bldgs.; one-man show, Bradywine Gallery, Albuquerque, 1973, group shows include, Mus. of N.Mex., 1963, 1979; represented permanent collection, Mus. N.Mex.; author: Centuries of Hands, 1996, Only in New Mexico, 2000; contbr. articles to various publs. Trustee Albuquerque Acad., 1972-82; bd. dirs. Corrales Land Trust, 1991—. With USAAF, 1943—45. Recipient Regents medal U. N.Mex., Fergusson award U. N.Mex. Alumni Assn., 2000, Heritage Preservation award State N.Mex., 2000, John Hugh Hill award for Scholarship Achievement Coll. Marshall, 2001, award for publs. The Albuquerque Conservation, 2002, Fray Dominguez award for Rsch. N.Mex. Hist. Soc. Fellow AIA (pres. Albuquerque chpt. 1971, Silver medal We. Mountain region), Assn. Univ. Architects (pres. 1971); mem. N.Mex. Architecture Found. (pres. 1987), Santa Fe Chamber Music Festival (bd. dirs.), N.Mex. Soc. Architects (honor and merit awards, pres. 1973, Appreciation award 1987). Address: PO Box 2942 Corrales NM 87048-2942

HOOKER, WADE STUART, lawyer; b. Brockton, Mass., Sept. 23, 1941; s. Wade S. and Eleanor T. Hooker; m. Susan M. Levine, May 20, 1984; children: Thomas A., Richard P. BA, Harvard Coll., 1963; LLB, U. Va., 1966. Bar: N.Y. 1969. Assoc. Casey, Lane & Mittendorf, NYC, 1968-77; ptnr. Burlingham Underwood LLP, NYC, 1979—2001; ind. practice, 2002—. Spkr. in field. Editor-in-chief Va. Jour. Internat. Law, 1965-66; contbr. articles to profl. jours Maxwell fellow Syracuse U., Resident scholar Indian Law Inst., New Delhi, 1966-67. Mem. ABA, Assn. Bar City of N.Y. (chair aeronautics com. 2001-04), Computer Law Assn., Inc., Internat. Bar Assn., Maritime Law Assn. U.S. (chair com. maritime regulation and promotion 1990-94), Mensa. Office: 211 Central Park W New York NY 10024 Office Phone: 212-362-2696. Business E-Mail: wadehooker@post.harvard.edu.

HOOKS, AUBREY, ambassador; b. Mullins, SC, May 18, 1948; m. Jean Wilkinson; 6 children. AA, Brevard Coll., 1968; BA, U. SC, 1970; MA in econ., U. Mich., 1984. Sr. sem. 38th class US Govt.; joined Fgn. Svc., 1971—; jr. off. trainee Am. Embassy, Tel Aviv, 1971—73, econ. consular officer Warsaw, 1973—76; cultural affairs off. US Dept. of State, Washington, 1976—78; econ. off. Am. Embassy, Ankara, Turkey, 1979—83, dir. econ. sec. Port-au-Prince, Haiti, 1984—87, econ. counselor Warsaw, 1992—95; amb. to Republic of Congo US Dept. State, Brazzaville, 1996—99; charge d'Affaires Am. Embassy, Bangui, Central African Republic, 1998—99; spl. coord. for the African Crisis Response Intiative US Dept. State, 1999—2001, amb. Dem. Rep. of Congo Kinshasa, 2001—04, amb. Cote d'Ivoire Abidjan, 2004—. Mem. US Delegation to the Conf. on Security & Cooperation in Europe, Helsinki, Finland, 1992. Office: Am Embassy Abidjan 2010 Abidjan Pl Washington DC 20521-2010

HOOKS, GEORGE BARDIN, state legislator, insurance and real estate company executive; b. Americus, Ga., May 9, 1945; s. Thomas Bardin III and Rose Mary (Fay) H.; m. Gail Ann Goen, Aug. 30, 1975; children: George Bardin Jr., Mary Ann. BA, Auburn U., 1970; postgrad., Princeton U.; LLD, Mercer U. V.p. southeast region Alliance of Am. Insurers, Atlanta, 1972-77; pres. Hooks Agy. Inc., Americus, Ga., 1977—; rep. State of Ga. House Reps., 1980-90; sen. State of Ga. Senate, 1990—. Floor leader for Gov. Ga. House Reps., 1988-90, chair rules com., 1992-93, chair appropriations com., 1993—. Active bd. dirs. Ft. Valley State U., 1992—, Mercer U., 1997—. Named Legislator of Yr., Mcpl. Assn., 1992, County Com. Assn., 1993. Mem. Ga. Assn. Ins. Agts. (bd. dirs. 1978-80. legis. dir. 1974, Pres. Citation 1974, 80), Ga. C. of C. (leadership Ga. 1982), Americus C. of C. (legis. chmn.), Rotary, Kappa Alpha. Democrat. Baptist. Home: 145 Taylor St Americus GA 31709-4056 Office: PO Box 928 Americus GA 31709-0928 Home Phone: 229-924-1649; Office Phone: 229-924-2924. Business E-Mail: ghooks@legis.state.ga.us.

HOOKS, VENDIE HUDSON, III, surgeon; b. Metter, Ga., Nov. 1, 1948; s. Vendie Hudson Jr. and May (Jones) H.; m. Carolyn Anderson Braithwaite, Nov. 1, 1974; children: Hudson, Susanna, David, Katherine. BS, U. Ga., 1970; MD, Med. Coll. Ga., 1974. Diplomate Am. Bd. Surgery, Am. Bd. Colon and Rectal Surgery. Intern surgery Med. Coll. Ga. Hosps., Augusta, 1974-75, resident gen. surgery, 1975-78, chief resident gen. surgery, 1978-79; G.I. surgery fellow gen. infirmary U. Leeds (Eng.), 1979-80; colon and rectal surgery fellow U. Minn. Hosps., 1982-83; asst. prof. surgery, asst. chief sect. GI surgery Med. Coll. Ga., Augusta, 1980-85, dir. colon/rectal surgery clinic, 1980-85; attending in surgery VA Hosp., Augusta, 1980-85; from asst. clin. prof. surgery to assoc. clin. prof. Med. Coll. Ga., Augusta, 1985-2001, clin. prof., 2001—; staff surgeon Univ. Hosp., Augusta, 1985—, St. Joseph Hosp., Augusta, 1985—; attending colon/rectal surgery endoscopy Univ. Hosp., Augusta, 1986—. Dir. Southeastern Familial Polyposis Registry; bd. dirs. Richmond-Columbia County unit Am. Cancer Soc., v.p. medicine, 1985-91; mem. Ethicon Colon and Rectal Adv. Panel, 1988, Panel Specialist-Surgery, Vocat. Rehab., 1980—; mem. interview com. for med. sch. admissions Med. Coll. Ga., 1981-82, 84-85, mem. tissue com., 1983-85; chmn. familial polyposis registry com. U. Hosp. Augusta, 1986—; assoc. examiner Am. Bd. Colon and Rectal Surgery, 1995-98, mem., 1998—, v.p., 2005, pres., 2006. Contbr. articles to profl. jours.; book reviewer and abstractor in field; reviewer Gastrointestinal Endoscopy, 1985-88. Pres. med. staff U. Hosp., Augusta, Ga., 1999, Richmond County Hosp. Authority, Augusta, 1998. Recipient Continuing Med. Edn. award Am. Soc. Colon and Rectal Surgeons, 1984, 87, Spl. award for colorectal cancer control Am. Cancer Soc., 1987, Cert. of Appreciation, Am. Cancer Soc., 1991-92, Award of Excellence, Am. Cancer Soc., 1992-93; grantee Am. Soc. Hosp. Pharmacists, 1981, Smith Kline & French Labs., 1981, Merck Sharp & Dohme, 1984. Fellow ACS, Southeastern Surg. Congress, Am. Soc. Colon and Rectal Surgeons; mem. AMA (Physician Recognition award 1984-89, 1990-93, 93-96, 97-2000, 04), Med. Assn. Ga., Richmond County Med. Soc. (sec.), So. Med. Assn., Moretz Surg. Soc., Assn. for Acad. Surgeons, Ga. Gastroenterologic and Endoscopy Soc., Am. Soc. for Gastrointestinal Endoscopy, Soc. Am. Gastrointestinal Endoscopic Surgeons, Ga. Surg. Soc., Piedmont Soc. Colon and Rectal Surgeons (pres. 1992-94), Soc. Surgery Alimentary Tract, Phi Beta Kappa, Alpha Omega Alpha, Phi Kappa Phi. Methodist. Avocations: golf, hunting. Office: 1348 Walton Way Ste 6500 Augusta GA 30901-5111 Office Phone: 706-722-2118.

HOOLEY, DARLENE, congresswoman; b. Williston, ND, Apr. 4, 1939; d. Clarence Alvin and Alyce (Rogers) Olsen; m. John Hooley (div.); children: Chad, Erin. BS in Edn., Oreg. State U., Corvallis, 1961, postgraduate student, 1963-65, Portland State U., 1966-67. Tchr. Woodburn & Gervais Sch., Oreg., 1962-65, David Douglas Sch. Dist., Portland, Oreg., 1965-67, St. Mary's Acad., Portland, 1967-69; mem. City Coun., West Linn, Oreg., 1976-80, Oreg. State Ho. Reps., 1980-87; commr. Clackamas County Bd., Oreg., 1987-96; mem. US Congress from 5th Oreg. dist., 1996—, mem. energy and commerce com., mem. budget com., mem. sci. and tech. com. Vice chair Oreg. Tourism Alliance, Portland, 1991; bd. dirs. Providence Med. Ctr., Portland, 1989, Cmty. Corrections Bd., Oregon City, 1990; acting chair Oreg. Trail Found. Bd., Oregon City, 1991; mem. Urban Growth Policy Adv. Com., Portland, 1991. Named Legislator of Yr. Oreg. Libr. Assn., 1985-86, Oreg. Solar Energy Assn., 1985; recipient Spl. Svc. award Clackamas City Coun. for Child Abuse Prevention, 1989. Mem. LWV, Oreg. Women's Polit. Caucus (Woman of Yr. 1988). Democrat. Office: US House Reps 2430 Rayburn House Office Bldg Washington DC 20515-3705 Office Phone: 202-225-5711, 503-588-9100. Office Fax: 202-225-5699, 503-588-5517.*

HOOLEY, JOSEPH (JAY) L., investment company executive; BS, Boston Coll. Fin. mgmt. positions State Street Corp., Boston, 1986—; pres., CEO Nat. Fin. Data Services, 1988—90, Boston Fin. Data Services, 1990—2000; exec. v.p. investor services State Street Corp., Boston, 2002—06, vice-chmn., 2006—. Bd. mem. Boys & Girls Club of Boston; mem. corp. adv. bd. Boston Club. Office: State Street Corp 1 Lincoln St Boston MA 02111*

HOOPER, ANNE DODGE, pathologist, educator; b. Groton, Mass., July 16, 1926; d. Carroll William and Bertha Sanford (Wiener) Dodge; m. William Dale Hooper, June 17, 1952; children: Elizabeth Anne, Joan Elaine, Caroline Mae. AB, Washington U., St. Louis, 1947, MD, 1952. Diplomate Am. Bd. Pathology, Pathologic Anatomy, Clin. Pathology and Forensic Pathology. Rotating intern Virginia Mason Hosp., Seattle, 1952—53; resident in internal medicine St. Francis Hosp., Hartford, Conn., 1953—54; resident in pathologic anatomy and clin. pathology New Britain Gen. Hosp., Conn., 1954—57, Presbyn. Hosp., Phila., 1957—58; resident in forensic pathology Office Med. Examiner, Phila., 1958—60; from pathologist to acting chief lab svc. VA Hosp., Coatesville, Pa., 1960—66; dir. lab. St. Albans Hosp., Vt., 1966—69, Kerbs Hosp., St. Albans, 1966—71, Williamson Appalachian Regional Hosp., South Williamson, W.Va., 1971—73, Beckley Appalachian Regional Hosp., W.Va., 1974—76; asst. prof. pathology W.Va. Sch. Osteo. Medicine, Lewisburg, 1977, assoc. prof., 1978—97, cons. in pathology, 1997—. Lab. accreditation insp. CAP, 1992—, Am. Osteo. Assn., 1986—99; assoc. med. examiner State of W.Va., 1999—; med. missionary Kijabe Hosp., Kenya, 1998; med. missionary, pathologist Pathologists Overseas at SALFA Lab., Madagascar, 2000; med. missionary Glens Falls N.Y. Med. Missionary Found., Nueva Santa Rosa, Guatemala, 2001. Contbr. articles to profl. jours. Pres. local elem. sch. PTA, St. Albans, 1967—68; mem. profl. edn. com. W.Va. divsn. Am. Cancer Soc., Charleston, 1982—94, bd. dirs. W.Va. divsn., 1987—94, pres. Greenbrier unit Lewisburg, 1989—93; bd. dirs. ARC, Greenbrier County, W.Va., 2002—. Fellow: Am. Acad. Forensic Scis., Coll. Am. Pathologists; mem.: AMA, Am. Soc. Clin. Pathologists, Raleigh County Med. Soc., W.Va. Med. Soc. Avocations: violin, viola. Office: 63 Cedar Knoll Ronceverte WV 24970-9700 Business E-Mail: adhooper@mail.wnet.edu.

HOOPER, ANTHONY C., pharmaceutical executive; MBA in Bus. Adminstrn., U. South Africa, LLB. With South African Cyanamid Pty. Ltd., Lederle Labs., South Africa, Lederle Internat., NJ; asst. v.p. mktg. Wyeth Labs. Internat.; gen. mgr. Australia/New Zealand Bristol-Myers Squibb, 1996, mng. dir. UK and Ireland, v.p., gen. mgr. No. Europe, pres. Asia-Pacific, Mid. East and So. Africa, Internat. Medicines, 2000—01, pres. Intercontinental, Internat. Medicines, 2001—02, pres. Europe, Mid. East and Africa, Worldwide Medicines Group, 2002—04, pres. US pharms., 2004—. Office: Bristol Myers Squibb 345 Park Ave New York NY 10154-0037*

HOOPER, DANIEL LEE, music educator, composer; b. San Antonio, Tex., May 17, 1947; s. Charles Henry and Mary Eloise (Parks) Hooper. Sacred Music Master, Union Theol. Sem., NYC, 1971; MusB, Juilliard Sch. Music, NYC, 1971. Mem. faculty Millbrook (NY) Sch., 1971—72; organist, choir master Ch. of the Messiah, Rhinebeck, NY, 1972—73, All Saints' Episcopal Ch., Phoenix, 1973—87; mem. music faculty Phoenix Coll., 1990—, dir. choral studies, 2005—. Asst. dir. Mid-Hudson Cmty. Mixed Chorus, Poughkeepsie, NY, 1971—73; music dir. Mid-Hudson Opera, Poughkeepsie, NY, 1971—73; music chmn. Episc. Diocese of Ariz., Phoenix, 1975—81; founding dir. Phoenix Girls' Chorus, 1980—85; co-dir. Phoenix Oratorio Choir, 1980—84; assoc. dir. McConnell Singers Women's Cmty. Chorus, Phoenix, 1994—99, dir., 1999—; concert preview lectr. Sun City (Ariz.) Chamber Music Soc., 1999—; dir. Voices of Phoenix Coll., 2003—. Composer, lyricist: Chancel opera Abraham and Issac (Seth Bingham Composition Award, 1971); composer: (choral anthem) Festive Welcome (First Ariz. ACDA Composition Award, 2003). Asst. accompanist Phoenix Police Honor Chorus, Phoenix, 2002—07. Recipient Outstanding Young Musician award, San Antonio Optimists, 1962, Outstanding Pianist award, Sewanee Summer Music Ctr., 1965; scholar Joske Music scholar, Joske's Dept. Store and San Antonio Symphony, 1959, Juilliard Sch. Music, 1966—67. Mem.: ASCAP, Am. Choral Dirs. Assn., Nat. Assn. Tchrs. Singing, Am. Guild Organists (regional conv. co-chairman 1993—96). Independent. Episcopalian. Avocations: power walking, travel, knitting. Office: Phoenix Coll 1202 West Thomas Phoenix AZ 85013 Office Phone: 602-285-7297.

HOOPER, EDWIN BICKFORD, physicist; b. Bremerton, Wash., June 18, 1937; s. E.B. and Elizabeth (Patrick) H.; m. Virginia Hooper, Dec. 28, 1963; children: Edwin, Sarah, William. SB, MIT, 1959, PhD, 1965. Asst. prof. applied sci. Yale U., New Haven, 1966-70; physicist, dep. program leader FE Lawrence Livermore (Calif.) Nat. Lab., 1970—2003, flex term physicist, 2003—. Adv. com. Fusion Energy Bruning Plasmic Program, 2003—; mem. program adv. com. Virtual Lab. Fusion Tech., 2002—. Contbr. articles to profl. jours. Pres. Danville (Calif.) Assn., 1982-84; pres. Friends Iron Horse Trail, 1984-86; v.p. San Ramon Valley Edn. Found., 1989-90, chair sci. adv. com., 2005-; dir. Leadership, San Ramon Valley, 1990-92; mem. adv. com. East Bay Regional Pk., 2002—. Fellow Am. Phys. Soc. (bd. dirs. div. Plasma Physics 1990-91); mem. AIAA (sr.), AAAS. Office: Lawrence Livermore Nat Lab L-637 Livermore CA 94550-4436 Office Phone: 925-423-1409.

HOOPER, HENRY OLCOTT, retired academic administrator, physicist; b. Washington, Mar. 9, 1935; s. Olcott Lorin and Eleanor (Drew) H.; m. Donna Faulkingham, June 10, 1956 (div. 1992); children: Deborah, Bruce, Katherine, Michael, Andrew; m. Jeanne Riley Hughes, Mar. 2, 1996. BS in Engring. Physics, U. Maine, 1956; MS in Physics, Brown U., Providence, 1959, PhD, 1961. Asst. prof. Brown U., Providence, 1961-64; asst. prof. physics Wayne State U., Detroit, 1964-66, assoc. prof., 1966-70, prof., 1970-73; prof., chmn. dept. physics U. Maine, Orono, 1973-76, dean Grad. Sch., 1977-80, v.p. acad. affairs, 1979-80; assoc. v.p. acad. affairs, dean Grad. Coll. No. Ariz. U., Flagstaff, 1981-97, interim v.p. acad. affairs, 1993-95, assoc. provost rsch. and grad. studies, 1995-96, prof. physics, dir. Bilby Rsch. Ctr., 1997-2000; dir. sci. and math. Learning Ctr., 1998-2000;

ret., 2000; pres. John and Sophie Ottens Found., 2001—. Cons. NASA, Huntsville, Ala., 1967-68; mem. rev. panel div. ednl. programs Argonne Nat. Lab., Ill., 1982-84; mem. exec. bd. Assoc. Western Univs., 1991-97, chair 1995-96; v.p. Nat. Coun. Univ. Rsch. Adminstrs., 1991-92, pres., 1992-93. Author: College Physical Science, 3d edit., 1974, Physics and the Physical Perspective, 1977, 2d rev. edit., 1980; editor: Conf. Procs. Amorphous Magnetism, 1973. Fellow Am. Phys. Soc.; mem. AAAS, Am. Assn. Physics Tchrs. Personal E-mail: h20@ouraynet.com.

HOOPER, IAN (JOHN DEREK GLASS), retired marketing communications executive; b. London, Sept. 8, 1941; came to U.S., 1979; s. John Desmond Glass and Moira Elizabeth (White) H. Student, Coll. Distributive Trades, London, 1960-62, 65-67, Harvard U., 1979. With S. H. Benson, London, 1960-62, 65-67, Nairobi, Kenya, 1962-64; with McCann-Erickson Advt., London, 1967-79; sr. v.p., group account dir. McCann-Erickson, NYC, 1979-85; exec. v.p., mng. dir. McCann Direct, NYC, 1985-90; sr. v.p., worldwide account dir. Young & Rubicam, NYC, 1990-91; sr. v.p., account dir. Brouillard Communications, NYC, 1991-94; sr. v.p., mktg. dir. DeVries Pub. Rels., NYC, 1994-2000, COO, 2000—04; ret., 2004. Home: 180 Stony Kill Rd Canaan NY 12029 E-mail: hooperi@aol.com.

HOOPER, JOSH, advertising executive, writer, director; b. Pa., 1952; s. Henry Lloyd and Mary Katherine H.; m. Cynthia Yeiser; children: Spencer, Mason. BA, Franklin & Marshall Coll., 1974. Tchr. Lower Dauphin Sch. Dist., Hummelstown, Pa., 1974-76; prodn. mgr. Sta. WLYH-TV, Lebanon, Pa., 1976-79; producer PM Mag. Sta. WTVH-TV, Syracuse, NY, 1979-80; co-host, producer PM Mag. Sta. WGAL-TV, Lancaster, Pa., 1980-83; pres. Josh Hooper Prodns., Inc., Harrisburg, Pa., 1983-94; actor-dir., pres. A Different Look, LA, 1983-92; broadcast advt. dir. The Bon Ton, York, Pa., 1992-94; pres., creative dir. Zero Gravity Mktg. and Advt., Harrisburg, Pa., 1994—; v.p. creative direction Panoramic Visions, 2000—02. Theater dir., N.Y., Pa., Calif., 1974—; co-host Sta. WITF Auction, Hershey, Pa., 1982, 83, Easter Seals Telethon, Harrisburg, 1983, Children's Miracle Network, Lancaster, 1983; directing fellow Am. Film Inst., L.A., 1988-89; improv comedian L.A. Connection, 1989, Public Nuisance, L.A., 1989-92. Producer, dir. (TV program) Suite 10:15, 1977; exec. producer (TV kids mag.) Thresholds, 1978; actor (play) Waiting for Godot, 1985, The Winter's Tale, 1986 (film) Station to Freedom, 1987, (TV film) Lucy and Desi: Before The Laughter, 1991; dir. (short film) Collared, 1988, The Point, 1989, Bumper to Bumper, 1989. Mem. Common Cause, Washington, 1980-90; chmn. comms. Three Mile Island Pub. Interest Resource Group, Harrisburg, 1982-84; comm. chair Fox Ridge Neighbors, 1985-87; active Ctr. for Def. Info.; charter mem. Franklin and Marshall Coll. Pres.'s Farwest Adv. Coun.; bd. dirs. Parent Works Parent Edn. Ctrs.; mem. Envision Capital Region Task Force. Recipient Addy award Am. Advt. Fedn., 1987, Addy award Cen. Pa. Advt. Fedn., 1985, 87, 88, Telly award, 1987, 88, 89, 99, Gold award Creativity '96; Film Grants Panelist NEH, 1990, Vision award, Mobius award, 1997. Mem. Am. Film Inst. Alumni Assn. (past pres.), SAG, Ctrl. Pa. Ad Club (bd. dirs. 1994, 95), Capital Area Assn. for the Edn. Young Children, Success by Six. Democrat. Unitarian. Avocations: running, swimming, bicycling, boating.

HOOPER, MARCIA JACOBS, venture capitalist, former communications executive; b. Boston, July 13, 1954; d. John III and Mary Louise (Molony) Jacobs; m. James Edward Hooper III, May 31, 1986; children: Philip, Anne. BS in Chemistry, Math., Brown U., 1977; MA in Chemistry, Columbia U., 1978; MBA, Harvard U., 1985. Regional mktg. rep. IBM, NYC and Boston, 1979-83; gen. ptnr. Ampersand Ventures, Wellesley, Mass., 1985; ptnr. Viking Capital, Advent Internat.; gen. ptnr. Castile Ventures, 2002—. Bd. dirs. PolyMedica Industries, Inc., Woburn, Mass., VidCode, Inc., Waltham, Mass., OraVax, Cambridge, Mass., Micron Separations, Inc., Westborough, Mass., Bowne & Co., Inc., 2006- Faculty fellow Columbia U., 1978. Office: Castile Ventures 890 Winter St Ste 140 Waltham MA 02451*

HOOPER, MARK SCHELLER, electrical engineer, educator; b. Palo Alto, Calif., Mar. 22, 1965; s. David Chandler and Tamara Scheller Hooper. BSEE in Elec. Engring., U. Calif., Davis, 1989; MSEE in Elec. Engring., San Jose State U., Calif., 1994; PhD in Elec. and Computer Engring. and Math. minor, Ga. Inst. Tech., Atlanta, 2005. EIT Calif., 1989. Integrated circuit product engr. Nat. Semiconductor, Sunnyvale, Calif., 1992; software cons., signal processing Unitech Rsch., Madison, Wis., 1993—94; mixed signal integrated circuit design engr. Xicor, Milpitas, Calif., 1995—98; contract-directed analog integrated circuit rsch. Ga. Tech/ON Semiconductor, Atlanta, 2000—02; adj. faculty dept. elec. engring. San Jose State U., Calif., 2006; sr. application specific integrated circuit micro-electro-mech.-sys. devel. engr. Systron Donner/Schneider Electric, Concord, Calif., 2007—. Contest judge Techmaster Internat. Speech Contest, Atlanta, 2004; session chair circuits 1 tract 16th Biennial U. Govt. Industry Microelectronics Symposium, San Jose, 2006. Contbr. scientific papers. Altar boy Russian Orthodox Ch., Menlo Park/Palo Alto, Calif., 1965—78. Fellowship, ON Semiconductor, 2000—02. Mem.: IEEE (sr.), Am. Phys. Soc., Silicon Valley IEEE (treas. circuits and sys. chpt. 2006, sec. comm. chpt. 2006, sec., webmaster, solid state circuits chpt. 2006, sr. mem. advancement chair 2006—07, sec. circuits and sys. chpt. 2007, treas., webmaster, solid state circuits chpt. 2007), Toastmasters Internat. (Advanced Toastmaster Silver award 2005), IEEE-USA Career and Workplace Policy Com. (corr.). Achievements include significantly advancing the state of the art in analog integrated floating-gate circuits/arrays. Avocations: languages, classical music, travel. Home: 211 Stockbridge Ave Atherton CA 94027 Office: Systron Donner/Schneider Electric 2700 Systron Dr Concord CA 94518-1399 Office Phone: 925-682-6161. Personal E-mail: mh5@ieee.org. Business E-Mail: mhooper@systron.com.

HOOPER, MICHAEL LEE, application developer; b. July 15, 1952; Cert. in computer programming, Mid-Fla. Tech., Orlando, 1985; BA in Mgmt. Info. Sys., Coilumbia Coll., Mo., 1989. Enlisted US Army, 1973, advanced to sgt. 1st class, resigned, 1985; computer programmer Naval Tng. Sys. Ctr., Orlando, Fla., 1985—. Author: (software modeling sys.) Foreman, 1986, (software sys.) Altair, 1994. Mem.: Mensa USA. Personal E-mail: mlhooper00@aol.com.

HOOPER, ROBERT ALEXANDER, television producer, educator; b. Annapolis, Md., Apr. 13, 1947; s. P. Alexander and Louise (Hickey) H.; m. Virginia L. Gordon; 1 child, Julie Alexandra. BA in Econs., U. Calif., San Diego, 1969; JD, U. Calif., Davis, 1974; MFA in Motion Picture and TV, UCLA, 1982. Bar: Calif. 1975. Film prodr. Scripps Inst. of Oceanography, La Jolla, Calif., 1978-79, EPA, Washington, 1979-81; ind. film prodr. with ABC-TV and CBC, Del Mar, Calif., 1981-84; tv prodr. Sta. KUAC-TV, PBS, Fairbanks, Alaska, 1984-86; asst. prof. comm. Boston U., 1986-87; assoc. prof. comm. Loyola Marymount U., LA, 1987-98; exec. prodr. KPBS-TV, San Diego, 1997—2001; assoc. prof. Calif. State U., 2000—06; program head SE Asia, Inst. Global Conflict and Cooperation U. Calif., San Diego, 2005—, adj. assoc. prof. Grad. Sch. Internat. Rels. and Pacific Studies, 2006—. Vis. assoc. prof. U. Calif., San Diego, 1993, 96, UCLA, 2000; cons. CBC, Toronto, 1982-83, Radio-TV Malaysia, 1998, Fiji TV, 1996; cons. Asia-Pacific Inst. for Broadcasting Devel., 1998-99, course dir., 1998; Fulbright sr. scholar comm. program U. Sains Malaysia, Penang, 1989-90, U. South Pacific, Fiji, 1994, U. Indonesia, 2001; tng. adviser Am. Samoa Govt.-Sta. KVZK-TV, 1992; acad. specialist U. Papua New Guinea, 1995; Eisenhower fellow, Malaysia, 1996; Fulbright sr. specialist, Malaysia, 2002-04; U.S. Dept. State spkr., Indonesia, 2001, East Malaysia, 2001, Laos, 2003-06, Bangladesh, 2003-06; educator Press Inst. Bangladesh. Prodr., dir. (documentaries) Voices From Love Canal, 1978, Decisions at 1000 Fathoms, 1981, Battle at Webber Creek, 1985 (Press Club award), Alaska's Killer Whales, 1989 (Cine Golden Eagle and Silver Apple award); segment prodr. (ABC 20/20) The Deep, 1983; exec. prodr. Nature's Classic, 1998 (Press Club award, four Emmy nominations), Afoot and Afield, 1998, The Impossible Railroad, 1999 (Press Club award, Telly award, Emmy award); cons. prodr. Skin Stories (PBS), 2003; op.-editor writer, L.A. Times, San Diego Union-Tribune, 1999. Recipient Hennessy trophy, Internat. Environ. Film Festival, France, 1983. Mem. NATAS, Calif. Bar Assn., Eisenhower Fellows Assn., Fulbright Sr. Specialists Roster, Sigma Delta Chi. Democrat. Avocations: underwater photography, horseback riding. Personal E-mail: rahooper@hotmail.com.

HOOPER, ROGER FELLOWES, retired architect; b. Southampton, NY, Aug. 18, 1917; s. Roger Fellowes and Justine Van Rensselaer (Barber) H.; m. Patricia Bentley, Aug. 10, 1946; children: Judith Bayard Teresi, Rachel Bentley Zingg, Roger Fellowes III. AB, Harvard U., 1939, MArch, 1948. Ptnr. Malone & Hooper, San Francisco, 1949-60; ptnr., pres. Hooper Olmsted & Emmons, San Francisco, 1964-79; chmn. Hooper Olmsted & Hrovat, San Francisco, 1980-94, retired, 1994. Bd. mgr. Marin YMCA, San Rafael, Calif.; bd. dirs., pres. Marin Conservation League, San Rafael. Lt. comdr. USNR, 1941-45, WWII. Mem. AIA.

HOOPER, ROY B., lobbyist; b. Lawton, Okla., Mar. 19, 1947; s. Roy Basil and Frances (Castle) H.; m. Lawanna Sue James, Aug. 2, 1969; children: Blake, Mark. BS, Cameron U., 1971. Registered lobbyist 1995-. Real estate broker, Lawton, 1968-90; rep. State of Okla., Lawton, 1974-86, senator, 1986-94; ins. broker Lawton, 1966—; dir. managed care Southwestern Med. Ctr., Lawton, 1994-99, HealthBack, Oklahoma City, 1999-2000; adminstr. Okla. State and Edn. Employees Group Ins. Program, 2000—01. Pres. Cameron Former Students Assn., Lawton, 1974, Lawton Crimestoppers Orgn., 1996, S.W. chpt. Am. Heart Assn., 1995-96, Lawton Pub. Sch. Found., 1998; v.p. Lawton Bd. Realtors, 1974, KTRO, Pres.'s Ptnrs. Cameron U., Lawton Crimestoppers/Drugbusters; councilman Ward 2, Lawton, 1972-74. Sgt. E-7 USAR, 1968-74. Democrat. Baptist. Avocations: hunting, fishing, golf, horse back riding, gardening. Office: Hooper Cons 1114 Laird Lawton OK 73507

HOOPER, TOM, film and television director; Dir.: (TV series) Cold Feet, 1997, (video) EastEnders: The Mitchells-Naked Truths, 1998, (episode) EastEnders, 1999; (TV miniseries) Love in a Cold Climate, 2001; (TV films) Daniel Deronda, 2002, Prime Suspect 6, 2003 (Best Dir. Emmy nominee), Red Dust, 2004, Elizabeth I, 2005 (Emmy award for Outstanding Directing for a Miniseries, Movie or Dramatic Special, 2006); other credits include: Byker Grove, Quayside & Painted Faces, stage credits include, The Trial and A View From the Bridge.

HOOPER, WAYNE NELSON, retired clergy member; b. Toronto, Ont., Can., May 25, 1944; s. Earl Edward and Ruby Evelyn (Nelson) H.; m. Diane Elizabeth, Aug. 24, 1968; children: Tanya Joy, Craig Nelson. BA, McMaster U., 1967; MDiv, Gordon-Conwell Theol. Sem., 1970. Ordained to ministry Baptist Ch., 1970. Asst. pastor Emmanuel Bapt. Ch., Cambridge, Mass., 1967-68, First Bapt. Ch., Braintree, Mass., 1968-70; pastor Uxbridge (Ont.) Bapt. Ch., Canada, 1970-73; founding pastor Credit Valley Bapt. Ch., Mississauga, Ont., Canada, 1973-79; sr. pastor First Bapt. Ch., Orillia, Ont., Canada, 1979-83, Avenue Rd. Bapt. Ch., Cambridge, Ont., Canada, 1986-98; asst. sec. dept. Can. Missions Bapt. Conv. Ont. and Que., 1983-86; sr. pastor First Baptist Ch., Dartmouth, N.S., Canada, 1998—2003, Westview Bapt. Ch., London, Ont., Canada, 2003—05; ret., 2005. Contbr. articles to profl. jours. Mem. recruitment com. Bapt. Conv. Ont. and Que., 1973-75, mem. planning com., 1978-80, mem. coun., 1976-82, mem. exec. com., 1977-78; conv. staff rep. Ottawa and N.W. Assns., 1983-86; Bapt. Conv. Ont. and Que. rep. to Inter-Church Regional Planning Assn., 1983-86; mem. Canadian Baptist Ministries Coun., 1995-98. Mem. Can. Bapt. Fedn. (v.p. 1988-91, pres. 1991-94). Baptist. Avocations: sports, boating, stamp collecting/philately, tennis, golf. Home: 3 Cobblestone Dr Paris ON Canada N3L 4G1

HOOPER, WILLIAM EDWARD, writer, broadcast journalist; b. Tampa, Fla., Mar. 10, 1964; s. Dennis William and Doris Jean (Burkhart) H. Student, U. Tenn., 1984-87; degree cert., Profl. Acad. Broadcasting, Knoxville, Tenn., 1988. Traffic reporter K-Trans, Knoxville, 1987-93; news dir. Sta. WNOX-FM, Knoxville, 1988-90, Sta. WWZZ-FM, Knoxville, 1991-93; news reporter Sta. WKXT-TV, Knoxville, 1993-96; creator, editor Tenn. Online, 1996—; editor Tenn. Star Jour., Pigeon Forge, Tenn., 2002; news anchor WIVK, Knoxville, 2003—; freelance writer Seviercountynews.com, 2004—. Host, writer Radio Appalachia, Knoxville, 1987-92, Celebrate Knoxville, 1991, WKXT's Tenn. Bicentennial Moments, 1994-96; feature writer Foothills mag., Knoxville, 1993; host, prodr. Viewpoint Talkshow, 1994-96, freelance writing, 1998—; embedded reporter Citadel Broadcasting Corp. with 489th CABN, USA Baghdad, Iraq; civl war editor Lakeway Pubs. Inc., 2004—. Author: Images of America: Knoxville, 2003, Gunpowder and Glory: Tennessee's Wild West Legends, 2005, Images of America: Knoxville in WWII, 2006; (broadcast reports) Public Access Denied: Tennessee Statute 40-23-116, Appalachian Minorities: Behind the Spinning Wheel; syndicated columnist Banjo Newsletter, 1981; author Looking Back Column, 1997—; guest columnist So. Partisan mag., Appalachian Quar. mag.; feature writer: Tennessee Outdoors mag.; freelance broadcast news reporter S.E. Radio and TV Co.; ednl. cons. Treas. Knoxville Juvenile Diabetes Assn., 1989; trustee Nat. Medal of Honor Mus. of Mil. History, Chattanooga, 1998—; project mgr. The South Found., 1997—; bd. dirs. Tenn. Civil War Preservation Assn., 1998-00. Recipient Cert. of Appreciation, Knoxville Transit Co., 1993, Cert. of Merit, Tenn. Hist. Commn., So. Journalism award 1996, Tenn. Jefferson Davis Media award 1996, Cert. of Appreciation City of Knoxville, 1996, Robert E. Lee Media award Tenn. divsn. SCV, 1996, Merit award Tenn. Gov., 1996, Cmty. Svc. award Knox County Commn., 1996, Horace V. Wells Cmty. Svc. award East Tenn. Soc. Profl. Journalists, 1996, 1st place Investigative Reporting award, 2001, 1st place Feature Reporting award, 2001, 1st place series/package/project Reporting award, 2001, 2d place Sports Reporting award, 2001, Cert. of Merit, Tenn. Hist. Commn., 1996, 97, 98, 00, Hist. Preservation award West Tenn. Sons Confederate Nat. Pk., 1997, SCV Comdr.'s award for hist. preservation, 1999, Golden Press Card Investigative Reporting, 1999, Golden Press Card Gen. News Reporting, 1999, Comdr.'s award SCV, 1999, Cert. of Merit, Tenn. Hist. Commn., 1999, , Cert. of Merit, 2001, Pub. Svc. in Journalism award Tenn. Press Assn., 1999, 2001, Cert. of Appreciation Vietnam War Meml. Assn., 1997, Pulitzer Prize nominee Columbia Sch. of Journalism, 1999, 00, Edward Carmack Journalism award Tenn. Sons. Confed. Vets., 2000, Hist. Preservation award, 2000, Cert. of Appreciation, Native Am. Indian Movement, 2001, Pub. Svc. in Journalism award Tenn. Press Assn., 2001, medal for Disting. Pub. Svc., U.S. Dept. Def., 2001, Tenn. Conservative Union Fairness in Polit. Reporting award, 2001, East Tenn. Hist. Soc. History in Media award, 2001, US Sec. Navy medal disting. pub. svc., 2005, Mayor's award pub. svc. Knox County, Tenn., 2005; named Bard Laureate Tenn. Gen. Assembly, 2002, Letter of Commendation, U.K. House of Lords, London, 2002, Cert. of Appreciation, U.T. ROTC, 2002, Gold Press Card award East Tenn. S.P.J., 2002, E. Tenn. SPJ First Pl. Investigative Reporting Award, 2003; E. Tenn. SPJ First Pl. Series/package/Project Writing, 2003; E. Tenn. SPJ First Pl. Feature Reporting Award, 2003; First Pl. Series/package Project Reporting award, 2002, Gen. News Reporting award, 2002, Feature Reporting award, 2002; crt. of Merit, Tenn. Hist. Commn., 2002, award of Excellence, US Army Accessions Command, 2002, hon. cert. 489th Civil Affairs Battalion, USA, 2004, Patriot of Yr. award, Sons of Revolution TN Chpt., 2004, excellence award US Army Civil Affairs and Psychol. Ops. Command. Mem. Soc. Profl. Journalists (1st Pl. award radio feature reporting Atlanta chpt. 1990, Investigative Reporting award Atlanta chpt. 1994, TV-Feature Reporting award 1995, TV Deadline News award 1995, So. Journalist award 1996), East Tenn. Soc. Profl. Journalists (bd. dirs. 2003, pres. 2006, 2d term 2007, 1st place Investigative Reporting award 1999, 00, 1st place Gen. News Reporting award 1999, 00, 2d place Deadline Photography award 1999, Golden Press Card award, 1st place Feature Reporting award 2000, 2d place Series/Package Reporting award), Investigative Reporters and Editors, Masons (historian Knoxville 1990—, Meritorious cert. 1991, 92). Avocations: musician, horseback riding, whitewater caneoing, hunting, archaeology. Office: South Found Inc PO Box 7121 Knoxville TN 37921 Office Phone: 800-624-0281 ext. 325. E-mail: ed@tennesseehistory.com.

HOORT, STEVEN THOMAS, lawyer; b. Grand Rapids, Mich., Sept. 18, 1949; s. Allard Hoort and Margaret J. (Vanderkooy) Koens; m. Nancy E. Redmon, Mar. 18, 1978; 1 child, Kendra. BA with high honors, Grand Valley State Coll., Allendale, Mich., 1972; JD magna cum laude, U. Mich., 1975. Bar: Mich. 1977, US Dist. Ct. (ea. dist.) Mich. 1977, Mass. 1978, US Dist. Ct. Mass. 1978, US Ct. Appeals (1st cir.) 1978, US Dist. Ct. (we. dist.) Mich. 1993, US Dist. Ct. Colo. 2002, US Dist. Ct. (ea. dist.) Wis. 2007. Law clk. U.S. Dist. Ct. (ea. dist.) Mich., Bay City, Mich., 1975-78; assoc. Ropes & Gray LLP, Boston, 1978-84, ptnr., 1984--, co-head bankruptcy & bus. restructuring dept. Mem. ABA (bus. law sect.), Boston Bar Assn., Am. Bankruptcy Inst., Assn. Insolvency and Restructuring Adv., Order of Coif Office: Ropes & Gray LLP 1 International Pl Boston MA 02110-2624 Office Phone: 617-951-7470. Office Fax: 617-951-7050. Business E-Mail: steven.hoort@ropesgray.com.

HOOTMAN, HARRY EDWARD, educator, retired nuclear engineer, consultant; b. Oak Park, Ill., June 5, 1933; s. Merle Albert and Rachel Edith (Atkinson) H.; m. Linda P. Smith, Nov. 23, 1963; children: David, Holly, John. BS in Chemistry, Mich. Technol. U., 1959, MS in Nuc. Engring., 1962; LLB, LaSalle Ext. U., 1971, MA in English Lit., U. SC, 1999, PhD in English and Am. Lit., 2004. Registered profl. engr., SC Rsch. assoc. Argonne Nat. Lab., Ill., 1959-62; process engr. Savannah River Plant, Aiken, SC, 1962-65; rsch. assoc. reactor physics group, nuclear engring. div. Savannah River Lab., Aiken, 1965-87; with New Reactor Devel. Group, 1987-92, adv. engr. Planning, Studies and Analysis, 1992-95; ret., 1995; cons. transuranic waste disposal and incineration, radioisotope prodn., separation and shielding; instr. dept. math. and engring. U. SC, Aiken, 1979-80, 90-94, instr. dept. English, 2004—; mem. US/UK Transuranic Waste Tech. Exch., 1976-78. Author: Index to British Literary Annuals and Giftbooks 1823-1861; adv. editor The Poetess Archive, 2005—; inventor alpha waste incinerator. Bd. dirs. Central Savannah River Area Sci. and Engring. Fair, Inc., Augusta, Ga., 1972-91. Sgt. USAF, 1953-57. Mem. Am. Acad. Environ. Engrs., NSPE (local chmn. 1978-79), Am. Nuclear Soc. (local chmn. 1979-80), Am. Phys. Soc., Sigma Xi, Sigma Tau Delta, Phi Lambda Upsilon. Baptist. Home: 820 Brandy Rd SE Aiken SC 29801-7281 Personal E-mail: hhootman@bellsouth.net.

HOOTON, JAMES G., academic administrator; m. Marilyn Hooton; children: Stephanie, Joyce Ann. BA, Tex. A&M U., 1966, MBA, 1967. With Arthur Andersen, Chgo., 1976—2002, head, acctg. and audit practice, 1989, CFO, mng. partner, 2001—02; exec. vice chancellor fin. Tex. A&M Univ. Sys., 2005—. Office: Off of Exec Vice Chancellor Fin Tex A&M Univ Sys 200 Technology Way, Ste 2043 College Station TX 77845-3424 Office Phone: 979-458-6047. E-mail: jhooton@tamu.edu.

HOOVER, AMY LYNN, pilot, educator; d. Basil and Fannie Mae Hoover. BS in Geology, Tex. Christian U., Fort Worth, Tex., 1983; MS in Geology, Oreg. State U., Corvallis, Oreg., 1983, PhD in Edn., 2005. Cert. flight instr. FAA, 1992, flight instr. instrument FAA, 1995. Prin., owner McCall Mountain Canyon Flying, Idaho, 1996—2002; dir. aviation Mt. Hood C.C., Gresham, Oreg., 1998—2003; prin., owner Amy's Flight Instrn., McCall, 2001—; assoc. prof. aeronautics Ctrl. Wash. U., Ellensburg, Wash., 2003—. Wilderness river guide, chef Rocky Mountain River Tours, Idaho, 1989—92; trip leader, naturalist Baja Expeditions, La Paz, Mexico, 1986—94; event coord. Idaho Outfitters and Guides Assn., Boise, Idaho, 1989—90; charter pilot, flight instr. SP Aircraft, Boise, 1992—95; chief flight instr. bobKat Avaition, Boise, 1995—97. Contbr. chapters to books (Outstanding book award, 2005), articles to profl. jours. Dir., organizer Young Women's Aces Acad., Ellensburg, Wash., 2004—06; vol. Boise Parks and Recreation, Boise, 2001—05; mem. adv. bd. Benson H.S. Aviation, Portland, Oreg., 1999—2003. Recipient Excellence in Constrn. award, Assn. Gen. Contractors, 2006, Outstanding Tchr. award, Nat. Residence Hall Assn., 2004, Women's Achievement Award, Ctrl. Wash. U. Ctr. Student Empowerment, 2005; fellow, Ctrl. Wash. U., 2003—05; grantee, Assn. of Gen. Contractors, 2004—06, Fluor Govt. Group, 2004—06, Wolf Aviation Fund, 2004, Exptl. Aircraft Assn., 2004; scholar, Nat. Merit Corp., 1979—83, Tex. Christian U., 1980—83. Mem.: Idaho Aviation Assn., Oreg. Pilot's Assn. (v.p. 2001—02), Internat. 99's Women Pilots (Amelia Earhart scholarship 1994), Women in Aviation Internat., Nat. Assn. Flight Instrs., Exptl. Aircraft Assn. (v.p. chpt. 492 2003—05), Aircraft Owners and Pilots Assn. (life), Cen. Washington U. Alumni Assn. Avocations: cooking, kayaking, travel, music. Office: Central Washington University 400 E Univ Way MS 7515 Ellensburg WA 98926 Home Phone: 509-963-2300; Office Phone: 509-963-2300. Business E-Mail: hoovera@cwu.edu.

HOOVER, GEORGE SCHWEKE, architect; b. Chgo., July 1, 1935; s. George Milton and Antoinette (Schweke) H.; children: Sandra Jean, Ranya Sue; m. Mary Elizabeth Benoit, June 6, 1987. BArch., Cornell U., 1958. Registered architect, Colo., Calif., Tex., Minn., Ala., Tenn. Draftsman Holabird Root and Burgee, Chgo., 1957, Designer James Sudler Assocs., Denver, 1961-62; architect Ream, Quinn Assocs., Denver, 1962-65, Muchow Assocs., Denver, 1965-76; prin. Hoover Berg Desmond, Denver, 1976—. Tenured prof. arch. U. Colo. Coll. Arch. and Planning, chmn. dept. arch., 1997—; vis. lectr. U. N.Mex., Okla. State U., Harvard U., Miami U. Prin. works include Douglas County Adminstrn. Bldg., Light of the World Cath. Ch., U. Colo. Bldg., Denver, Denver Diagnostic and Reception Ctr., Labs for Atmospheric and Space Physics, U. Colo., Boulder, Colo. Acad. Master Plan, U. Ariz. Engring. Complex Master Plan, Multipurpose Arena, Nat. Western Stockshow, Nat. Wild Animal Rsch. Ctr., Colo. State U. Conf. Ctr., Storage Tech. Corp., Aerospace & Mech. Engring. Bldg. U. Ariz., Environ. and Natural Resources Bldg. U. Ariz., Master Plan Cummins Power Generation Group Hdqs., Fridley, Minn., Master Plan Fleetguard and Mfg. Plant, Cookeville, Tenn.; finalist Denver Cen. Libr. Competition, 1991; exhbn. Gund Hall Gallery, Grad. Sch. Design, Harvard U., 1986; mem. editl. bd. Avant Garde. Lt. (j.g.) USN, 1958-61. Recipient 1st Design award Progressive Arch., 1972, Citation, 1974, Design award, 1984, 87, Charles Goodwin Sands Medal for excellence in design Tau Beta Pi, Fed. Design Achievement award, 1984, Honor award Interfaith Forum on Religion, Art, and Arch., 1986, Tau Sigma Delta medal, 1991; named Outstanding Young Architect, Archtl. Record, 1974, Fellow AIA (steering com., Pitts. Corning award 1989, Nat. Honor award 1975, 83, 90, Firm of Yr. award Colo. chpt. 1991, Regional Firm of Yr. award 1992, Architect of Yr. award Colo. chpt. 1995), Nat. Acad. Design.; mem. Nat. Com. Design (steering com., chmn. awards task group 1989-92), Nat. Com. Archtl. Edn. (steering com. 1990-92). Episcopalian. Office: Art Hoover Desmond Arch 1645 Grant St Denver CO 80203-1601 also: U Colo 1250 14th St Denver CO 80202-1702 Office Phone: 303-556-5965. E-mail: hoover@ar7.com.

HOOVER, JOHN ELWOOD, former military officer, consultant, writer, educator; b. Timberville, Va., Apr. 28, 1924; s. Saylor Cornelius and Ruby Mae (Brill) H.; m. Mary Jo Cox, May 17, 1953; children: M. Kathryn, Holly H. Bullock. Student, Bridgewater Coll., Va., 1941-43, Amherst Coll., Mass., 1943-44; BS, U.S. Mil. Acad., 1947; MA, Georgetown U., 1955; postgrad., Columbia U., 1955-56, U.S. Army Command and Gen. Staff Coll., Ft. Leavenworth, Kans., 1958-59, U.S. Army War Coll., Carlisle

Barracks, Pa., 1962-63. Commd. 2d lt. U.S. Army, 1947, advanced through grades to maj. gen., 1971; with 24th Inf. Div., Japan and Korea, 1948-51, Ft. Gordon, Ga., 1951-53; faculty dept. social scis. U.S. Mil. Acad., 1955-58; bn. comdr. U.S. Army, Germany, 1959-60, Hdqrs. U.S. Army Europe, Germany, 1961-62; with Office Asst. Sec. Def. for Internat. Security Affairs, Washington, 1963-66; chief communications plans Hdqrs. Pacific Command, Hawaii, 1966-69, group comdr. Vietnam, 1969-70; exec. officer, then dir. communications systems, then dep. asst. chief staff for communication-electronics Hdqrs. Dept. Army, Washington, 1970-73; dep. comdg. gen. U.S. Army Communications Command, Ft. Huachuca, Ariz., 1973-74; dir. Joint Tactical Communications Office, Office Sec. Def., Ft. Monmouth, NJ, 1974-78; ret., 1978. Cons. command, control, comms. and mgmt.; historian emeritus U.S. Army Signal Rgt.; author and spkr. on U.S. mil. comms. history. Decorated D.S.M., Legion of Merit with oak leaf cluster, Bronze Star with oak leaf cluster, Meritorious Svc. medal, Air medal with oak leaf cluster, Joint Svc. Commendation medal, Army Commendation medal, Armed Forces Honor medal Republic of Vietnam, Staff Svc. medal (Republic of Vietnam), Vietnam Gallantry Cross with palm, Presdl. Unit citation, Meritorious Unit citation, Presdl. Unit citation Republic of Korea, Republic of Korea Order of Mil. Merit. Mem. Assn. Grads. U.S. Mil. Acad., Signal Corps Assn., Mil. Heritage Found., Silver Order Mercury, U.S. Army Signal Regiment (Disting. mem).

HOOVER, PAUL WILLIAMS, JR., lawyer; b. Little Rock, Feb. 27, 1942; s. Paul Williams and Mary Elizabeth (Lasley) H.; m. Barbara Josephine Rogers, Sept. 6, 1969; 1 child, Josephine Lasley Felton. BS, U. Ark., Little Rock, 1965; JD, U. Ark., 1969; LLM, NYU, 1970. Bar: U.S. Dist. Ct. (ea. dist.) Ark. 1969. Assoc. partner Fulk, Lovette & Mayes, Little Rock, 1970-73; mng. ptnr. Hoover Dougherty & Kooistra, Little Rock, 1973-97; ptnr. Giroir, Gegory, Holmes and Hoover, Little Rock, 1997—2001; sr. ptnr. Williams and Anderson, P.L.C., Little Rock, 2006—. Dir. Met. Nat. Bank, Little Rock, 1983—. Bd. dirs. Ark. Diabetes Assn., 1974-78, Quapaw Area Boy Scouts Coun., 1976-80, Ark. Symphony Orch., 1986-89, Florence Crittendon Home, 1994, U. Ark. for Med. Scis. Found. Fund. Mem. ABA, Ark. Bar Assn., Pulaski County Bar Assn., Rotary Club #99 (Little Rock), Fifty for Future, Country Club of Little Rock. Methodist. Avocations: duck hunting, skiing. Home: 5 Edgehill Rd Little Rock AR 72207-5443 Office: 111 Center St Ste 2200 Little Rock AR 72201-4403 Home Phone: 501-663-2992; Office Phone: 501-372-0800. E-mail: phoover@williamsanderson.com.

HOOVER, PEARL ROLLINGS, nurse; b. LeSueur, Minn., Aug. 24, 1924; d. William Earl and Louisa (Schickling) Rollings; m. Roy David Hoover, June 19, 1948 (dec. Mar. 20, 1987); children: Helen Louise, William Robert(dec.). Grad. in nursing, U. Minn., 1945, BS in Nursing, 1947; MS in Health Sci., Calif. State U., Northridge, 1972. Dir. affiliate nursing sch. Mooselake State Hosp., Minn., 1948-49; nursing instr. Anchor Hosp., County Hosp., St. Paul, 1949-51; student nurse supr. and instr. Brentwood VA Hosp., LA, 1951-52; sch. nurse LA Unified City Schs., 1963-91, substitute sch. nurse, 1991-96. Camp nurse United First Meth. Ch., winter and summer past 40 yrs.; corr. sec. Reseda Women's Club, 1st v.p.; courtesy chmn. First United Meth. Women. Mem. LA Coun. Sch. Nurses, Calif. Sch. Nurses Orgn. Democrat. Methodist. Home: 17851 Lull St Reseda CA 91335-2237

HOOVER, R. DAVID, packaging company executive; b. Straughn, Ind., June 21, 1945; BS, DePauw U., Greencastle, Ind., 1967; MBA, Indiana U., Bloomington, 1970; postgrad mgmt. program, Harvard U., 1988. Corp. fin. analyst Eli Lilly & Co., Indpls.; asst. to treas. Ball Corp., v.p., fin. & admin. agrl. sys. divsn., 1980—85, v.p., fin. & admin. aerospace sys. group, 1985—87, asst. treas., 1987—88, v.p. & treas., 1988—92, sr. v.p. & CFO, 1992—96, exec. v.p. & mem. bd. dirs., 1996—98, vice chmn. & CFO, 1998—2000, COO, 2000—01, CEO & pres., 2001—, chmn., 2002—. Bd. mem. Datum, Inc., Maxon Corp. & Energizer Holdings; mem. bd. dirs. & former chmn. Can Manufacturers Inst. Bd. mem. Nat. Food Processors Assn., Boulder Cmty. Found., DePauw U. Bd. Visitors & Bd. Trustees, Indiana U., Kelley Sch. Bus., Dean's Adv. Coun. Office: 10 Longs Peak Dr Broomfield CO 80021-2510*

HOOVER, RICHARD BRICE, astrobiologist; b. Sikeston, Mo., Jan. 3, 1943; s. Harry Laverne and Pansy Irene (Rainey) H.; m. Miriam Jackson, Aug. 15, 1970. BS, Henderson State U., 1960. Instr. in physics U. Ark., Fayetteville, 1965-66; optical scientist astrionics lab. NASA/MSFC, Huntsville, Ala., 1966-70, astrophysicist, 1970-97; astrobiology grp. leader, Space Scis. Lab., Huntsville, 1997—2001; astrobiology grp. leader NASA/Nat. Space Sci. and Tech. Ctr., Huntsville, 2001—. Dir. environ. scis. lab. UNIDEV, Inc., Huntsville, 1970-72; founder, pres. Micromega, Inc., Huntsville, 1984-86; cons. SCI, Inc., Huntsville, 1969-70, GREFCO, L.A., 1969-76, Teledyne Brown, Huntsville, 1970-71. Author: Types du Synopsis of British Diatomacaea, Original Collection of Albert Grunow for the Schizonema and Berkeleya Monograph; contbr. articles to profl. jours. Named Inventor of Yr., NASA, 1992. Fellow SPIE (bd. dirs. 1991-2002, pres. 2001), The Explorers Club; mem. Soc. Royale de Zoologie d'Anvers, Coun. Sci. Soc. Pres. (bd. dir. 2002), Am. Assn. Engring. Soc., Planetary Studies Found. (hon. life mem.). Achievements include patents in field; discovery of 13 species; genus of bacteria; species of Archaea. Avocations: diatoms, fossil collecting, antique shotguns. Home: 7706 Teal Dr SW Huntsville AL 35802-2839 Office: NASA NSSTC Marshall Space Flight Ctr VP-62 Huntsville AL 35805 Office Phone: 256-961-7770. Business E-Mail: richard.hoover@nasa.gov.

HOOVER, ROBERT ALLAN, university president; b. Des Moines, May 9, 1941; s. Claude Edward and Anna Doris H.; m. Jeanne Mary Hoover, Feb. 22, 1968 (dec. 2005); m. Leslee Hoover, Aug. 20, 2006; children: Jennifer Jill Jacobs, Suzanne Hoover Ogden. BS, Ariz. State U., 1967, MA, 1969; PhD, U. Calif., Santa Barbara, 1973. Instr. polit. sci. Utah State U., Logan, 1971-73, asst. prof. polit. sci., 1973-79, assoc. prof. polit. sci., chair polit. sci. dept., 1979-84, prof. polit. sci., 1984-91, dean Coll. Humanities, Arts and Social Scis., 1984-91; v.p. for acad. affairs U. Nev., Reno, 1991-96; pres. U. Idaho, Moscow, 1996—2003, Albertson Coll. Idaho, Caldwell, 2003—. Author: The Politics of MX: A New Direction in Weapons Procurement?, 1982, The MX Controversy: A Guide to Issues and References, 1982, Arms Control: The Interwar Naval Limitation Agreements, 1980. Bd. dirs. St. Scholastica Acad., Canon City, Colo., 1989-95, pres. 1991-95, United Way, Reno, 1994-96, Channel 5, Reno, 1991-95; bd. visitors USAF U., 1997-2003, chair, 2002-03; mem. Idaho Gov.'s Coun. for Sci. Tech., 1991-2003; chair bd. dirs. Inland Northwest Rsch. Alliance, 1998-2003; mem. pres. coun., Nat. Assn. State Univs. and Land Grant Colls., 2001-03, chair eco-terrorism task force, 2002; bd. trustees Albertson Coll. Idaho; mem. visitors group, Utah State U., 2001-03. Recipient Tchr. the Yr., Humanities, Arts and Social Scis. Coll., Utah State U., 1983—84, Dist. VII Leadership award, Coun. Advancement and Support Edn., 2002, Top Mgr. the Yr., Sales and Mktg. Execs., Boise, 2003. Mem.: Coun. Ind. Coll. Avocations: reading, skiing, jogging, piano. Office: Albertson Coll 2112 Cleveland Blvd Caldwell ID 83605-9990 Business E-Mail: rhoover@albertson.edu.

HOPCROFT, JOHN EDWARD, computer scientist, educator; b. Oct. 7, 1939; BS in EE, Seattle U., 1961; MS in EE, Stanford U., 1962, PhD in Elec. Engring., 1964. Asst. prof. Princeton (N.J.) U., 1964-67; assoc. prof. Cornell U., Ithaca, NY, 1967-71, prof., 1972—, chmn. computer sci. dept., 1987-92, assoc. dean coll. affairs Coll. Engring., 1992-93, dean Coll Engring., 1994—2001, IBM prof. engring. and applied math., 2004—. Vis. prof. Stanford U., Calif., 1970-71; mem. Info. Sci. and Tech. Office Def. Advanced Rsch. Projects Agy. (DARPA) (chair robotics working group); chmn. adv. bd. NSF, 1987-90; mem. computer sci. and telecomm. bd. NAS/NRC, 1988—, adv. com. for David and Lucille Packard Fellowships in Sci. and Tech., 1991—; mem. sci. adv. bd. USAF, Inst. for Def. Analysis, David and Lucille Packard Found., NSF. Co-author: Formal Languages and Their Relation to Automata, 1969, The Design and Analysis of Computer Algorithms, 1974, Introduction to Automata Theory, Language, and Computation, 1979, Data Structures and Algorithms, 1983, Planning, Geometry and Complexity of Robot Motion, 1987. NSF Grad. fellow, 1961-64; recipient A.M. Turing award, 1986, CRA Disting. Svc. award, 2007. Fellow IEEE (Harry H. Goode award 2005), AAAS, Am. Acad. Arts and Scis.; mem. NAE (acad. adv. bd. 1992-95), Nat. Sci. Bd., Inst. for Def. Analysis Supercomputing Rsch. Ctr., Assn. Computing Math. (Turing award 1986), Soc. for Indsl. and Applied Math., Ctr. Excellence Space Data and Info. Sci. (interim dir. 1987-88) Office: Cornell Univ Dept Computer Science 5144 Upson Hall Ithaca NY 14853-2201 Business E-Mail: jeh@cs.cornell.edu.

HOPE, HARRY JOE (JOESEPH), retired corporate communications specialist, writer; b. New London, Conn., Feb. 20, 1927; s. Harry Seth and Mary Agnes Hope; children: Lizabeth Ann, Barbara Mary. AA, Fullerton Coll., Calif., 1950. Retail sales clk. Long Beach (Calif.) Honda, 1960—65; sales mgr. BSA-19 Western States, Duarte, Calif., 1965—66; corp. dir. pub. rels. BSA/Triumph USA, Verona, NJ, 1966—70; founder, first pres. nat. trade assn. Motorcycle Industry Coun., 1968; v.p., gen. mgr. Norton Villiers Corp., Long Beach, Calif., 1970—73; mgr. bus. advertising circulation Westways Mag., Los Angeles, Calif., 1973—79; freelace writer, 1979—. Pres. Calif. Motorcycle Safety Council, 1967. Sgt. USAF, 1950—54, PTO. Recipient Kiwanian of Yr., Kiwanis Club, 1982. Mem.: Intertel, Am. MENSA. Republican. Avocations: reading, camping, chess, cribbage. Home: PO Box 205 Joshua Tree CA 92252 Personal E-mail: jhope34749@aol.com.

HOPE, KATHY MITCHELL, social studies educator; d. Walter and Vilean Mosely Mitchell; m. William Kenneth Hope, June 25, 1983; 1 child, Letitia Antoinette. BA in Edn., U. S.C., Columbia, 1977, MAT in History, 1978. Tchr. social studies Eau Claire H.S., Columbia, SC, 1979, Logan Alternative Sch., 1979—80, W.G. Sanders Mid. Sch., 1980—. Part time instr. Benedict Coll., Columbia, SC, 1991, 96; dept. head social studies W.G. Sanders Mid. Sch., mem. sch. improvement coun., 2005—06; textbook com. Richland Sch. Dist., vertical team facilitator. Mem. bd. Christian edn. Zion Bapt. Ch., sec. Arsenal Hill cir.; mem. United Christian Women's Aux. Zion Bapt. Ch. Named Outstanding Am. Tchr., Nat. Honor Roll, 2005—06, Tchr. of Yr., W.G. Sanders Mid. Sch., 2006—07. Mem.: PTA, NEA, Richland County Edn. Assn., S.C. Edn. Assn., S.C. Geog. Alliance, S.C. Coun. Social Studies, Nat. Coun. Social Studies. Avocations: meeting and talking to people, current events, game shows, westerns, mysteries. Office Phone: 803-735-3445. E-mail: khope@richlandone.org.

HOPE, MARGARET LAUTEN, retired civic worker; b. NYC; 1 son, Frederick H., III. Privately educated. Ball com. various charity fund raising events. Mem. Jr. League NYC; Everglades Club, Palm Beach, Fla.; Women's Nat. Rep. Club (NYC); St. James Club (London). Home and Office: 236 Dunbar Rd Palm Beach FL 33480

HOPE, RONALD ARTHUR, lawyer; b. Mineral Wells, Tex., Jan. 8, 1956; s. Arthur Virgil and Barbara Louise (Wester) H.; m. Mary Katharyn Howell, Oct. 3, 1987. BSBA in Acctg., U. Ark., 1978, JD, 1981. Bar: Ark. 1981, U.S.Dist. Ct. (ea. and we. dists.) Ark. 1982, U.S. Ct. Appeals (8th cir.) 1991, U.S. Supreme Ct. 1987. Atty. Howell, Price & Trice, PA, Little Rock, 1981-85; ptnr. Howell, Price, Trice, Basham & Hope, PA, Little Rock, 1985-93; shareholder Howell, Trice & Hope, PA, Little Rock, 1993-2001, Howell, Trice, Hope & Files PA, Little Rock, 2001—04; ptnr., shareholder Hope, Fuqua & Campbell PA, 2005—. City atty. City of Wrightsville, Ark., 1988—; atty. Ark. Property and Casualty Guaranty Fund. Legal com. Nat. Conf. of Ins. Guaranty Funds, 1996—. Century mem. Boy Scouts Am. Mem. ATLA, Ark. Bar Assn., Ark. Trial Lawyers Assn., Pulaski County Bar Assn., Rotary, Masons, Shriners, Phi Alpha Delta, Sigma Chi., Nat. Conf. Ins. Guaranty Funds. Methodist. Avocations: duck hunting, deer hunting, golf. Office: Hope Fuqua Campbell PA 425 West Capitol Ave Ste 400 Little Rock AR 72201-3435 E-mail: rhope@hfc-law.com.

HOPE, SAMUEL HOWARD, accreditation organization executive; b. Owensboro, Ky., Nov. 5, 1946; s. James Russell and Lorraine (Jones) H.; m. Judy Bucher, June 24, 1978. B.Mus., Eastman Sch. Music, Rochester, NY, 1967; M.Music Arts, Yale U., 1970; pupil of, Nadia Boulanger, France, 1966-67; LHD (hon.), Marywood U., 2001, Md. Inst. Coll. Art, 2007. Dean, composer-in-residence Atlanta Boy Choir Sch. Music, 1970-73, trustee, 1973—2001; vis. instr. Lee U., Cleveland, Tenn., 1973-74; exec. dir. music alumni, asso. dir. grad. profl. programs Campaign for Yale, Yale U., 1974-75; exec. dir. Nat. Assn. Schs. Music, Nat. Assn. Schs. Art and Design, Reston, Va., 1975—, Joint Commn. on Dance and Theatre Accreditation, 1978-83, Nat. Assn. Schs. Theatre, 1980—, Higher Edn. Arts Data Services, 1981—, Nat. Assn. Schs. Dance, 1981—, Working Group on Arts in Higher Edn., 1982—, Coun. of Arts Accrediting Assns., 1980—, Commn. Cmty. and Precollegiate Arts Schs., 2000—. Chmn. assembly of specialized accrediting bodies Council on Postsecondary Accreditation, 1979-82, bd. dirs., 1992-93; bd. dirs. Council Specialized Accrediting Agys., 1978-81, sec.-treas., 1979-81; mem. com. recognition Council Postsecondary Accreditation, 1984-88; chmn. adminstv. com. Found. Advancement Edn. in Music., 1986-90. Composer Piano Sonata I, 1968, II, 1971; motet Solus Ad Victimam Procedis, Domine, 1970, Blessed Be Thou Lord, 1976, Trio for Oboe, Cello and Piano, 1970, Cantata I, 1973, Cantata II, 1975, Symphonia: Psalm 145, 1982, Toccata: Psalm 117 for Organ, 1993; exec. editor Arts Edn. Policy Rev. mag., 1984—. Chmn. govt. relations com. Nat. Music Council, 1976-79, bd. dirs., 1978-84; mem. exec. com. Am. Soc. Univ. Composers, 1977-83; nat. alumni council Eastman Sch. Music, 1975-78, chmn., 1976-77; bd. dirs. Am. Music Conf., 1978-82; trustee Am. Acad. for Liberal Edn., 1997—. Recipient Composition prize Yale U., 1968, 69, 70, disting. svc. award Yale U., 2000, Ohio U., 2000, Coun. Dance Adminstrs., 2001. Mem. Coll. Music Soc., Music Educators Nat. Conf., Am. Inst. Graphic Artists, Music Tchrs. Nat. Assn., Am. Assn. for Theatre in Higher Edn., Am. Alliance for Theatre and Edn., Nat. Dance Edn. Orgn., Yale Club (N.Y.C.). Anglican. Home: 10717 Rosehaven St Fairfax VA 22030-2826 Office: 11250 Roger Bacon Dr Ste 21 Reston VA 20190-5248

HOPE, WILLIAM DUANE, retired zoologist, curator; b. Ft. Collins, Colo., June 7, 1935; s. William Earl and Lois Howe (Burnett) H.; m. Colleen Bryan, Dec. 23, 1956 (div.); children: Pam Hope Herbert, Karen Hope Van Zandt, Linda Hope Greene. BS, Colo. State U., 1957, MS, 1960; PhD, U. Calif., Davis, 1965. Systematic zoologist. dept. invertebrate zoology Nat. Mus. Natural History, Smithsonian Instn., Washington, 1964—69, curator, 1969—75, chmn. dept., 1976—81, emeritus rsch. zoologist, 2006—. Contbr. articles to profl. jours. Mem. Am. Assn. Zool. Nomenclature, Am. Micros Soc., Biol. Soc. Washington, Helminthological Soc. Washington, Soc. Nematologists, Soc. Systematic Zoology, Internat. Assn. Meiobenthologists. Democrat. Avocations: hiking, bicycling, fly fishing, birdwatching. Office: Smithsonian Instn Natural History Mus Dept Zoology Rm W212 MRC 163 Washington DC 20013-7012 Home Phone: 703-255-2881. Personal E-mail: wdhope@aol.com.

HOPEN, HERBERT JOHN, horticulture educator; b. Madison, Wis., Jan. 7, 1934; s. Alfred and Amelia (Sveum) H.; m. Joanne C. Emmel, Sept. 12, 1959; children: Timothy, Rachel. BS, U. Wis., 1956, MS, 1959; PhD, Mich. State U., 1962. Asst. prof. U. Minn., Duluth, 1962-64; prof. U. Ill., Urbana, 1965-85, prof., acting head, 1983-85; prof. horticulture U. Wis., Madison, 1985-97, prof. emeritus, 1997, chmn. dept. horticulture, 1985-91. Mem. Am. Soc. Hort. Sci., Weed Sci. Soc. Am., North Ctrl. Weed Sci. Soc., Ygdrasil, Torske Klubben, Sigma Xi. Avocations: reading, gardening. Office: U Wis Dept Hort 1575 Linden Dr Madison WI 53706-1514 Office Phone: 608-262-1490. Business E-Mail: hjhopen@wisc.edu.

HOPF, FRANK RUDOLPH, retired dentist; b. NYC, Sept. 1, 1920; s. Rudolph Aldridge and Jennie Victoria (Fusco) Hopf; m. Elsie Hedlund, Sept. 10, 1949; children: Christine, Frank, Victoria, William, Robert. BS, Purdue U., West Lafayette, Ind., 1942; postgrad., Middlesex U. Sch. Medicine, 1943—44; DDS, NYU, 1953, postgrad., 1957—61; MA, Columbia U., NYC, 1953, MPH, 1955. Asst. dir. Bur. Dental Health, NY State Dept. Health, Albany, 1956—57, regional dental dir. White Plains, 1967—90; pvt. practice dentistry specializing in periodontics Rye, NY, 1957—2003; ret., 2003. Rsch. assoc. periodontics NYU Coll. Dentistry, 1958—61; clin. asst. prof. dept. periodontics NJ Coll. Medicine and Dentistry, Jersey City, 1962—67; adj. asst. prof. dept. cmty. dentistry Columbia Sch. Dental and Oral Surgery, NYC, 1971—76; vis. prof. dept. preventive dentistry Pitts. U. Sch. Dentistry, 1967—72. Contbr. articles to profl. publs. Pres. Country Ridge Home Owners Assn., Rye Brook, NY, 1960—62. With USNR, 1944—46. Grantee, NIH, 1957. Fellow: APHA, Am. Coll. Dentists, NY Acad. Dentistry, Am. Sch. Health Assn.; mem.: AAAS, ADA, Fedn. Dentaire Internationale, Am. Soc. Dentistry for Children, Westchester Acad. Medicine, North Eastern Soc. Periodontics, Royal Soc. Health, NY State Pub. Health Assn. (pres. 1970—72), Westchester Country Club, Westchester Shore Dental Study Club (pres. 1960—61, Rye, NY), KC (4 deg.). Roman Catholic. Home: 33 Old Field Hill Rd # 7 Southbury CT 06488

HOPFENBECK, GEORGE MARTIN, JR., lawyer; b. NYC, Mar. 1, 1929; s. George Martin and Margaret Spencer (Felt) H.; m. Ruth Elizabeth Allen, June 27, 1953; children: Ann Elizabeth, James Allen. BA, Williams Coll., 1951; JD, Yale U., 1954. Bar: Colo., 1955. Assoc. Davis, Graham & Stubbs and predecessor Lewis, Grant & Davis, Denver, 1954-59, ptnr., 1959-92, of counsel, 1993—. Bd. dirs. Am. Cancer Soc. Inc., Colo. divsn., Denver, 1966-90, chmn., 1975-77; bd. dirs. Colo. Regional Cancer Ctr. Inc., Denver, 1974-81, pres., 1975-77; bd. dirs. Am. Cancer Soc. Inc., Atlanta, 1984-90, Denver Parks and Recreation Found., 1966-75; bd. dirs. Boys and Girls Clubs of Metro Denver, Inc., 1993—, chmn., 1998-2000; mem. Colo. State Pers. Bd., Denver, 1971-75, chmn., 1971-72; mem. Denver Bd. Parks & Recreation, 1961-69; trustee Kent Sch. for Girls, Denver, 1970-73; chmn. campaign com. for Gov. Love, Colo., 1966, campaign com. for McKevitt for Congress, Denver, 1970. Recipient St. George medal Am. Cancer Soc., 1982. Mem. ABA, Colo. Bar Assn., Denver Country Club (bd. dirs. 1967-70, 2002-2005), University Club (Denver) (bd. dirs. 1973-82). Republican. Episcopalian. Home: 2552 E Alameda Ave 75 Denver CO 80209 Office: 333 Logan St Ste 108 Denver CO 80203-4089

HOPFINGER, ANTON JOSEPH, education educator, consultant; m. Kathleen Hattie Hanseter, Aug. 13, 1966; children: Timothy John, Tony Joseph, Todd Michael. BS, U. Wis., Oshkosh, 1962—66; PhD, Case Western Res. U., Cleve., Ohio, 1966—69. Post doctoral fellow Harvard Med. Sch., Boston, 1969—70; prof., macromolecular sci. Case Western Res. U., 1970—81; dir., medicinal chemistry G.D, Searle & Co., Skokie, Ill., 1981—85; prof. medicinal chemistry, chemistry, bioengring. U. Ill., Chgo., 1985—2005, dir. molecular modeling and design lab., 1986—2005, prof. emeritus, 2005—; disting. rsch. prof. pharmacy U. N.Mex, Albuquerque, 2005—. Adj. prof. medicinal chemistry U. Kans., Lawrence, 1983—86; sci. adv. bd. Molecular Design Ltd., 1983—86; cons. Sterling-Winthrop Rsch. Inst., 1986—88, Bristol Myers, 1986—88, Celanese Corp., 1986—88, Sun Oil Co., 1986—90, Dow Chem. Co., 1986—90, Allied-Signal Rsch. Techs., 1989—99, Molecular Simulations, 1991—96, Eisai Co. Ltd., 1994—96, Mitotix Inc., 1998—99, Neogenesis Pharms., Inc., 1998—2002, Avon Co., 1999—, RheoGene Inc., 2002—06, various others; chmn. Gordon Rsch. Conf. Quantitative Structure-Activity Relationships, 1987; vis. prof. U. Buenos Aires, Argentina, 1991, U. Sao Paulo, Brazil, 1991, 97, U. Wutzburg, Germany, 2000; vis. rsch. prof. chemistry Oxford U., England, 1996; mem. sci. adv. bd. Locus Pharms., 2000—, US EPA, 2006—; mem. drug discovery and mechanisms of anti microbial resistance study sect. NIH, 2003—. Assoc. editor: Jour. Chem. Info. Computer Sci., 1993—, mem. editl. adv. bd.: Jour. Medicinal Chemistry, 1985—90, Anticancer Drugs, 1985—95, Computational and Theoretical Polymer Sci., 1990—, Brazilian Jour. Pharm. Rsch., 1999—. Recipient Outstanding Alumni award, U. Wis., 1972, Sigma Chi Rsch. award, Case Western Res. U., 1975, Disting. U. Scholar, U. Ill., 1998—2001; fellow, Alfred P. Sloan Found., 1971—75; grantee, NIH, NSF, Dept. Def., Dept. Energy, EPA, 1966—. Mem.: Am. Chem. Soc. (mem. editl. adv. bd. Chem. Rsch. in Toxicology 1989—93). Office: Univ New Mexico 2502 Marble NE Albuquerque NM 87131-0001 Office Fax: 505-272-0674. Personal E-mail: hopfingr@gmail.com. Business E-Mail: hopfingr@unm.edu.

HOPGOOD, HOON-YUNG, state representative; b. Inchon, South Korea, Dec. 8, 1974; BA in Polit. Sci., U. Mich., Ann Arbor, 1996; student, Northern Mich. U. Intern Office of Congresswoman Lynn Rivers, Washington, 1995; labor coordinator Mich. State AFL-CIO, 1996; with Mich. Ho. Dem. Policy Staff, 1997—99; with legislative office Office of State Repr. Raymond Basham, 1999—2001; mem. Mich. Ho. of Reps., 2002—. Mem. edu., energy and techn. com. & regulatory reform com. Mich. Ho. of Reps.; mem. Steel/Mining Caucus, Children's Caucus, Capitol Speakers Bureau. Mem. adv. bd. Council of Asian-Pacific Am. Mem.: Mich. Dem. Action Network, Dem. Club of Taylor, Mich. Young Dem., Mich. Dem. Party. Office: Mich Ho of Reps S0786 Ho Office Bldg PO Box 30014 Lansing MI 48909-7514

HOPGOOD, JAMES F., anthropologist, educator; b. Cape Girardeau, Mo., Apr. 18, 1943; s. Finley Marshall and Marjorie Louise (Schneider) Hopgood; m. Esther Berg, Jan. 29, 1966; 1 child, Myka Lynn. BA, U. Mo., 1965, MA, 1969; MPhil, U. Kans., 1971, PhD, 1976. From asst. prof. to prof. anthropology No. Ky. U., Highland Heights, 1973—2003, prof. emeritus, 2003—, chmn. dept. sociology, anthropology and philosophy, 1984-98, dir. Mus. of Anthropology, 1976—2003. Vis. instr. Washburn U., Topeka, 1969; vis. prof. Instituto Tecnologico y de Estudios Superiores de Monterrey, Mexico, 1971, U. Monterrey, 1980; profl. assoc. Asian studies devel. program East-West Ctr. and U. Hawaii, 1991, 93, 94. Author: Settlers of Bajavista: Urban Adaptation in a Mexican Squatter Settlement, 1979; editor, contbr.: The Making of Saints: Contesting Sacred Ground, 2005; mem. editl. bd. Jour. Third World Studies; contbr. articles, reports to profl. jours. Mem. edn. com. Cin. Mus. Natural History, 1992—94. Recipient Strongest Influence award, No. Ky. U. Alumni Coun., 2003, Spl. Recognition award, Ctrl. States Anthrop. Soc., 2005; Jewish Chautauqua Soc. scholar in residence, No. Ky. U., 1988—98, Sasakawa fellow, San Diego State U., 1996. Fellow: Am. Anthrop. Assn. (exec. com. 1996—98); mem.: Ctrl. State Anthropol. Soc. (exec. bd. 1989—92, pres. 1996—97, exec. bd. 1999—2001, editor CSAS Bull. 2001—07, Spl. Recognition award in photography 2005), Ky. Acad. Sci. (bd. gov. 1995—98), Sigma Xi, Lambda Alpha. Home: 4918 Corn Row Ct Independence KY 41051-8101 Business E-Mail: hopgood@nku.edu.

HOPKINS, ALISA DAWN, small business owner; b. Norton, Va., Feb. 24, 1959; d. Willard Wythe and Frances Roberta Meade; m. Jim Mat Hopkins, July 1, 2005; children: Malissa Dawn McConnell, Blaine Elzic McCoy Jr. Prin., owner Tinycare Daycare, Dryden, Va., 1989—2000, Dawn's Daycare, Coeburn, Va., 2000—. Baptist. Avocations: camping, fishing. Home and Office: Dawn's Daycare 11621 Joseph Rd Coeburn VA 24230 Home Phone: 276-395-2721; Office Phone: 276-395-2003. Personal E-mail: dawnmeade2@msn.com.

HOPKINS, SIR ANTHONY (PHILIP), actor; b. Port Talbot, South Wales, U.K., Dec. 31, 1937; s. Richard Arthur and Muriel Annie (Yeates) H.; m. Petronella Barker, Sept. 1967 (div. 1972); 1 child, Abigail; m. Jennifer Ann Lynton, Jan. 13, 1973 (div. Apr. 30, 2002); m. Stella Arroyave, Mar. 1, 2003. Student, Welsh Coll. Music and Drama, Cardiff, Wales, 1954-56, Royal Acad. Dramatic Art, London, 1961-63; DLitt (hon.), U. Wales, 1988; Fellow (hon.), St. David's Coll., Lampeter, Wales, 1992. Made London stage debut in Julius Caesar, 1964; mem. Nat. Theatre Co., 1966-73; appeared in Juno and the Paycock, 1966, A Flea in Her Ear, 1966, Three Sisters, 1967, The Dance of Death, 1967, As You Like It, 1967, The Architect and the Emperor of Assyria, 1971, A Woman Killed with Kindness, 1971, Coriolanus, 1971, The Taming of the Shrew, 1972, Macbeth, 1972, Equus (Best Actor award N.Y. Drama Desk, Best Actor award Outer Critics Circle, Best Actor award Am. Authors Celebrities Forum), N.Y.C., 1974-75, (L.A. Drama Critics award), L.A., 1977, The Tempest, L.A., 1979, Old Times, N.Y.C., 1983, The Lonely Road, London, 1985, Pravda, Nat. Theatre, London, 1985-86 (Olivier award 1985, Stage Actor award Variety Club), King Lear, Nat. Theatre, London, 1986-87, Anthony & Cleopatra, Nat. Theatre, London, 1987, M Butterfly, Shaftesbury Theatre, London, 1989, (also dir.) August, 1994; films include (debut) The Lion in Winter, 1968, Hamlet, 1969, The Looking Glass War, 1969, When Eight Bells Toll, 1971, Young Winston, 1972, A Doll's House, 1973, The Girl from Petrovka, 1974, Juggernaut, 1974, A Bridge Too Far, 1977, Audrey Rose, 1977, International Velvet, 1978, Magic, 1978, The Elephant Man, 1980, A Change of Seasons, 1980, The Bounty, 1984 (Film Actor award Variety Club), The Good Father, 1985, 84 Charing Cross Road, 1986 (Best Actor award Moscow Film Festival 1987), The Dawning, 1988, Silence of the Lambs, 1991 (Acad. award for Best Actor 1992, Best Actor award Chgo. Film Critics 1992, Best Actor award Boston Film Critics 1992, Best Actor award N.Y. Film Critics 1992, Film Actor award Variety Club 1992, Best Film Actor award BAFTA 1992), Freejack, 1992, One Man's War (TV movie), 1991, Spotswood/The Efficiency Expert, 1992, Howard's End, 1992, Bram Stoker's Dracula, 1992, Chaplin, 1992, Remains of the Day, 1993 (Acad. award nominee for Best Actor 1994, Best Actor award L.A. Film Critics Assn. 1993, Best Actor award Nat. Soc. film Critics (U.S.A.) 1993, BAFTA UK best film actor award, Guild of Regional Film Writers UK Best Actor award, Variety Club UK Film Actor award 1993, Japan Critics Best Actor in a Fgn. Film award), Shadowlands, 1993 (Best Actor award Nat. Bd. Rev. 1993, Best Actor award L.A. Film Critics Assn. 1993, Best Actor award Nat. Soc. Film Critics (U.S.A.) 1993), the Trial, 1993, The Road to Welville, 1994, Legends of the Fall, 1994, The Innocent, 1993, Nixon, 1995 (Acad. award nominee for Best Actor 1996), August, 1996, Surviving Picasso, 1996, The Edge, 1997, Amistad, 1997, The Mask of Zorro, 1998, Meet Joe Black, 1998, Instinct, 1999, Titus, 1999, Mission Impossible II, 2000, How the Grinch Stole Christmas (voice), Hannibal, 2001, Hearts in Atlantis, 2001, The Devil and Daniel Webster, 2001, Bad Company, 2002, Red Dragon, 2002, The Human Stain, 2003, Alexander, 2004, Proof, 2005, The World's Fastest Indian, 2005, All the King's Men, 2006, Bobby (also exec. prodr.), 2006, Slipstream, 2007, Fracture, 2007; BBC-TV series War and Peace (Best TV Actor award Soc. Film and TV Arts), 1972; TV shows include A Heritage and Its History, 1968, Vanya, Hearts and Flowers, Three Sisters, The Peasant's Revolt, Dickens, Danton, The Poet Game, Decision to Burn, War and Peace, Cuculus Canorus, Lloyd George, Q.B. VII, 1971, Find Me, A Childhood Friend, Possessions, All Creatures Great and Small, 1975, The Lindbergh Kidnapping Case, 1976 (Emmy award), Victory at Entebbe, 1976, Dark Victory, Mayflower: The Pilgrim's Adventure, 1979, The Bunker, 1980 (Emmy award), Peter and Paul, 1980, Othello, BBC, 1981, Little Eyolf, BBC, 1981, The Hunchback of Notre Dame, 1982, A Married Man, 1984, The Arch of Triumph, CBS, 1984, Hollywood Wives, ABC, 1984, Guilty Conscience, CBS, 1984, Blunt, BBC, 1985, the Tenth Man, CBS, 1988, Across the Lake, BBC, Heartland, BBC, Great Expectations, 1989, Disney Primetime, To Be The Best, 1990, others. Decorated Comdr. of Order of Brit. Empire, 1987, Knights Bachelor, 1993, Comdr. of Order of Arts & Letters, France, 1996; named one of Top 100 Movie Stars of All Time, Empire (U.K.) Mag., 1997; recipent Star on Hollywood Walk of Fame, 2003, Cecil B. DeMille award, Hollywood Fgn. Press. Assn., 2006. Office: Creative Artists Agy 9830 Wilshire Blvd Beverly Hills CA 90212-1804*

HOPKINS, ANTONY GERALD, history professor; b. London, Eng., Feb. 21, 1938; s. George Henry and Queenie Ethel Hopkins; m. Wendy Beech, Aug. 15, 1964; children: William Edward, John Arthur. BA with honors, U. London, 1960, PhD, 1964; Hon. D (hon.), U. Stirling, Scotland, 1996. Prof. econ. history U. Birmingham, England, 1977—88; prof. internat. history U. Geneva, 1988—94; Smuts prof. commonwealth history U. Cambridge, England, 1994—2002; Walter Prescott Webb chair history U. Tex., Austin, 2002—. Mem. Inst. Advanced Study, Princeton, NJ, 1974—75; fellow Pembroke Coll., Cambridge, 1994—2002, emeritus fellow, 2002—; spkr. in field. Author: (books) An Economic History Of West Africa, 1973; co-author (with P.J. Cain): British Imperialism 1688-1990 2 vols., 1993; editor: Jour. African History, 1972—79, Econ. History Rev., 1980—85, Cambridge Imperial and Post Colonial Studies, 1994—2003. Recipient Forkosch prize, Am. Hist. Assn., 1995; fellow, Brit. Acad., London, 1996. Avocations: running, opera. Office: Univ Tex Dept History 1 University Sta Campus Code B7000 Austin TX 78712

HOPKINS, BERNARD, professional boxer; b. Phila., Jan. 15, 1965; Profl. boxer, 1988—; ptnr. Golden Boy Promotions, 2004—; pres. Golden Boy Promotions East, 2004—. Winner vacant title vs. Wayne Powell by tech. knockout, middleweight divsn. US Boxing Assn., 1992, winner title def. vs. Gilbert Baptist by unanimous decision, middleweight divsn., 93, winner title def. vs. Roy Ritchie by tech. knockout, middleweight divsn., 93, winner title def. vs. Wendall Hall by tech. knockout, middleweight divsn., 93, winner title def. vs. Lupe Aquino by unanimous decision, middleweight divsn., 94; winner vacant world title vs. Segundo Mercado by tech. knockout, middleweight divsn. Internat. Boxing Fedn., 1995, winner world title def. vs. Steve Frank by tech. knockout, middleweight divsn., 96, winner world title def. vs. Joe Lipsey by tech. knockout, middleweight divsn., 96, winner world title def. vs. William Bo James by tech. knockout, middleweight divsn., 96, winner world title def. vs. John David Jackson by tech. knockout, middleweight divsn., 97, winner world title def. vs. Glengoffe Johnson by tech. knockout, middleweight divsn., 97, winner world title def. vs. Andrew Council unanimous decision, middleweight divsn., 97, winner world title def. vs. Simon Brown by tech. knockout, middleweight divsn., 98, winner world title def. vs. Robert Allen by unanimous decision, middleweight divsn., 99, winner world title def. vs. Antwun Echols by unanimous decision, middleweight divsn., 99, winner world title def. vs. Syd Vanderpool by unanimous decision, middleweight divsn., 2000, winner world title def. vs. Antwun Echols by tech. knockout, middleweight divsn., 00, winner world title def. vs. Keith Holmes by unanimous decision, middleweight divsn., 01; winner world title vs. Keith Holmes by unanimous decision, middleweight divsn. World Boxing Coun., 2001, winner world title def. vs. Felix Trinidad by tech. knockout, middleweight divsn., 01, Internat. Boxing Fedn., 2001; winner world title vs. Felix Trinidad by tech. knockout, middleweight divsn. World Boxing Assn., 2001; winner world title def. vs. Carl Daniels by tech. knockout, middleweight divsn. World Boxing Coun., 2002, Internat. Boxing Fedn., 2002, World Boxing Assn., 2002; winner world title def. vs. Morrade Hakkar by tech. knockout, middleweight divsn. World Boxing Coun., 2003, Internat. Boxing Fedn., 2003, World Boxing Assn., 2003; winner world title def. vs. William Joppy by unanimous decision, middleweight divsn. World Boxing Coun., 2003, Internat. Boxing Fedn., 2003, World Boxing Assn., 2003; winner world title def. vs. Robert Allen by unanimous decision, middleweight divsn. World Boxing Coun., 2004, Internat. Boxing Fedn., 2004, World Boxing Assn., 2004; winner world title def. vs. Oscar De Le Hoya by knockout, middleweight divsn. World Boxing Coun., 2005, Internat. Boxing Fedn., 2005, World Boxing Assn., 2005; winner world title vs. Oscar De Le Hoya by knockout, middleweight divsn. World Boxing Orgn., 2005; winner world title def. vs. Howard Eastman by unanimous decision, middleweight divsn. World Boxing Coun., 2005, Internat. Boxing Fedn., 2005, World Boxing Assn., 2005, World Boxing Orgn., 2005; winner title vs. Antonio Tarver, light heavyweight divsn. Nat. Boxing Assn., 2006, Internat. Boxing Orgn., 2006. Appt. Mayor's Drug and Alcohol Exec. Commn., Phila., 2006—. Named Fighter of Yr., The Ring Mag., 2001, World Boxing Hall of Fame, 2001. Office: Golden Boy Promotions Ste 350 626 Wilshire Blvd Los Angeles CA 90017*

HOPKINS, BETTY BELINDA, elementary school educator; AS, Northeast Miss. CC; BA in Music Edn., Jacksonville State U.; MA in Curriculum and Instruction, U. Miss. Cert. Nat. Bd. for Profl. Tchg. Standards. Tchr. 4th and 5th grade gifted students Saltillo Elem. Sch., Miss. Mentor Miss. State U., U. Miss. Named Wal-Mart Tchr. of Yr., 1998, Miss. Tchr. of Yr., 2006; named to Miss. Hall of Master Tchrs., 1999; recipient Presdl. Award for Excellence in Tchg. Math., 1998. Office: Saltillo Elem Sch 424 South 3rd St PO Box 1059 Saltillo MS 38866 Business E-Mail: bhopkins@lcs.k12.ms.us.*

HOPKINS, BILL EVERITT, lawyer; BA, High Point U., NC, 1990; JD, U. Tex. Sch. Law, 1995. Asst. gen. counsel State of Tex. Bd. Nurse Examiners, 1995—97, gen. counsel, 1997—98; ptnr. Thompson & Knight, LLP, Austin, Tex., 1998—. Assoc. dir. legal affairs Nat. Black Grad. Students Assn., 1996—2001, mem. bd. dirs. adv. com., 1996—2001; adminstr., regional coord. Ctrl. Tex. HS Mock Trial Competition, 1996—2005; vol. Vol. Legal Svcs. Pro Bono Clinic, 1998—; mentor Texas Appleseed Project One-to-One Mentorship Program, 1999—2001, mem. steering com., 1999—2004; mentor U. Tex. Law Sch. Career Svcs. Mentorship Program, 1999—; bd. mem. Austin Symphony Be at the Symphony Young Mem. Group, 2002—, Big Brothers/Big Sisters Ctrl. Tex., 2002—, Samaritan Ctr. Counseling, 2005—. Named one of Tex. Rising Stars, Tex. Monthly, 2006; recipient Austin Under 40 award for Law, 2006. Mem.: Austin Health Lawyers Group, Austin Black Lawyers Assn., Austin Young Lawyers Assn. (co-chair Youth Svcs. Com.), Austin Bar. Assn. (Adminstrv. Law Sect.), Am. Health Lawyers Assn. Office: Thompson & Knight LLP Ste 1900 98 San Jacinto Blvd Austin TX 78701 Office Phone: 512-469-6199. Office Fax: 512-482-5099. E-mail: william.hopkins@tklaw.com.

HOPKINS, BRENDA LUVENIA, social sciences educator, minister; b. Monroe, NC, Apr. 1, 1951; d. Willie and Marion Lomax Hopkins. BA, N.C. Ctrl. U., 1973; MA, Wingate U., 1989; ednl. specialist, Mich. State U., 2000; MDiv, No. Bapt. Theol. Sem., 2003; PhD in Ministry, Grad. Theol. Found., 2005, postgrad., 2005—; student, Hebrew U. Tchr. educator Johnson Jr. H.S., Washington, 1973—83, Coll. Moyen Gen. Enseignment, Benin, West Africa, 1983—87, Benin U., West Africa, 1983—87; tchr. educator, minister Union County Pub. Sch., Monroe, NC, 1987—96; rschr., educator Mich. State U., East Lansing, 1996—2000; minister, counselor Theol. Sem., Lombard, Ill., 2000—03, Grad. Theol. Found., South Bend, Ind., 2003—. Chaplain, counselor Good Samaritan Hosp., Downers Grove, Ill., 2001—, Alexian Brothers Med. Ctr., Elk Grove, Ill., 2003—. Vol. Peace Corps, Contonon, West Africa, 1983—84; grant writer Partnership Grant, Washington, 1982—83; pastor, chaplain Elizabeth Bapt. Ch., Monroe, 1987—96. Mem.: Ministerial Alliance (sec. 1987—), Waynes Oates Inst. (scholar 2000—03), Writers' Soc. (life scholar 2003—). Avocations: walking, swimming, piano, reading and writing French and Spanish. E-mail: luveniahop60@hotmail.com, hopkinsb@msu.edu.

HOPKINS, CHARLES L., government agency administrator; BA mechanical engring., U. of Okla.; MME, Naval Postgraduate Sch., Monterey, Calif. Sr. adv., asst. sec. for mgmt. US Dept. of the Treasury; emergency mgmt. programs dir. Mission Assurance and Security Services, IRS, US Dept. of the Treasury; dir. Office of Nat. Security Coordination, Fed. Emergency Mgmt. Agy. (FEMA) US Dept. of Homeland Security, 2005—07, asst. adminstr., Nat. Continuity Programs Directorate, FEMA, 2007; asst. sec. for ops., preparedness, security and law enforcement US Dept. of Veterans Affairs, 2007—. USN. Office: US Dept of Veteran Affairs 810 Vt Ave NW Rm A-1 Washington DC 20420 Office Phone: 202-273-5510. Office Fax: 202-273-7809. E-mail: charles.hopkins@dhs.gov.*

HOPKINS, DANIEL NELSON, materials engineer; s. Clifford Daniel and Emma Drucilla Hopkins; m. Christine Lee Hover, Sept. 23, 1972 (div. 1996); children: Amanda Christine Wickman, Adam Daniel. BS in Metall. Engring., U. Utah, Salt Lake City, 1967—72, MS in Phys. Metallurgy, 1972—73; PhD in Chem. Engring., U. N.Mex, Albuquerque, 1977—81. Registered profl. engr., Tex., 1986, nuclear plant engr., TXU Nuc. Tng. Dept., 2004. Officer USN, Pearl Harbor, Hawaii, 1973—77; rsch. scientist Los Alamos Nat. Lab., N.Mex., 1977—79; project engr. Mobil Rsch. & Devel., Dallas, 1981—86; environ. engr. US EPA, Dallas, 1986—88; prin. engr. TXU Power, Glen Rose, Tex., 1988—2006; materials engr. Shaw, Stone & Webster, Glen Rose, Tex., 2006—07, Southwest Rsch. Inst., San Antonio, 2007—. Working group flaw evaluation ASME, Tex., 1990—, subgroup evaluation standards, Tex., 1998—; advisor for master's degree candidates U. N.Tex., Denton, Tex., 1998—2002. Lt. comdr. USN, 1973—93. Decorated Meritorious Unit Commendation USN; recipient Top Industry Practice award, Nuc. Energy Inst., 1998. Mem.: ASME (codes and standards vol. 1990—2007), Nat. Assn. Corrosion Engrs. Presbyterian. Achievements include patents for four methods of enhanced oil recovery; measurement of dynamic fracture growth; four gall-resistant metallurgical surfaces; patents pending for statistical method for analyzing wall thickness data. Avocation: dance. Home Phone: 817-244-5627; Office Phone: 210-522-2934. Business E-Mail: daniel.hopkins@swri.org.

HOPKINS, DAVID R., academic administrator, educator; BA, Coll. of Wooster, MA in Tchg.; PED, Ind. U. Dept. chairperson U. Tex.-Permian Basin, Odessa; faculty mem. Ind. State U., 1988—2003, chairperson, prof. physical edn., dir. Ctr. for Fitness and Aging, 1988, adminstr. fellow to asst. v.p. to asst. v.p. to v.p. academic affairs, interim provost, interim dean Sch. Bus.; provost Wright State U., Dayton, Ohio, 2003—07, pres., 2007—. Office: Wright State U Univ Hall 3640 Colonel Glenn Highway Dayton OH 45435 Office Phone: 937-775-3035. E-mail: david.hopkins@wright.edu.*

HOPKINS, DENISE S., marketing executive; b. Dec. 18, 1965; m. Dean A. Hopkins, Dec. 30, 1989. BA, Buena Vista Coll., 1988. Account exec. Mills Fin. Mktg. & Advt., Storm Lake, Iowa, 1988-89, pers. dir., 1989-91, v.p., 1991; mem. Credit Info. Solutions Group Experian Ltd., Costa Mesa, Calif., sr. dir. mktg. Data Mgmt. Solutions, sr. dir. mktg. Bus. Mktg. Solutions, v.p. mktg. and product devel. Mktg. Info. Svcs. Mem. NAFE, Women in Communications, Inc., Bank Mktg. Assn. Office: Experian 475 Anton Blvd Costa Mesa CA 92626 Office Phone: 714-830-7000. E-mail: denise.hopkins@experian.com.*

HOPKINS, DONALD J., retired lawyer; b. Long Beach, Calif., Jan. 9, 1947; m. Ellen Colokathis, Aug. 29, 1970; children: Melanie J., Shannon R., Christopher S. AB, Stanford U., 1968; JD, Harvard U., 1971. Bar: Mass. 1971, Colo. 1974, U.S. Dist. Ct. Colo. 1974. Mem. firm Holme Roberts & Owen LLP, Denver, 1973—2004. Fellow: Am. Coll. Trust and Estate Counsel. Home: PO Box 190 9329 US Hwy 50 Howard CO 81233

HOPKINS, DONALD ROSWELL, public health physician; b. Miami, Fla., Sept. 25, 1941; s. Joseph Leonard and Iva (Major) Hopkins; m. Ernestine Mathis, June 24, 1967. BS, Morehouse Coll., 1962; MD, U. Chgo., 1966; MPH, Harvard U., 1970; DSc (hon.), Morehouse Coll., 1988, Emory U., 1994; LHD (hon.), U. Mass., Lowell, 1997; DSc (hon.), Morehouse Coll., 1999. Intern San Francisco Gen. Hosp., 1966—67; resident U. Chgo. Hosps., 1970—72; med. officer program planning and evaluation Ctrs. for Disease Control, Atlanta, 1972—74, dep. chief environ. health svc. divsn., 1974, asst. dir. ops., 1977—80, asst. dir. internat. health, 1980—84, dep. dir., 1984—87; assoc. exec. dir. The Carter Ctr., Inc., 1997—. Asst. prof. tropical pub. health Harvard U., Boston, 1974—77; chmn., advisor on internat. health rsch. Dr. Peter Bourne, White House, Washington, 1977; mem. U.S. del. World Health Assembly, Geneva, 1977—78, Geneva, 1980—86; global adv. group on immunization WHO, Geneva, 1978—79, steering com. epidemiology working group, 1980—83; cons. in field. Author: Princes and Peasants-Smallpox in History, 1983. Bd. dirs. MacArthur Found. Decorated knight Nat. Order of Mali, Order of Bifurcated Needle WHO; recipient Commd. Corps Disting. Svc. medal, USPHS, 1986, Joseph Mountin Lecture award, Ctrs. for Disease Control, 1981, John Snow award, APHA, 1997, Medal of Honor of Pub. Health, Govt. of Niger, 2004; fellow MacArthur fellow, 1995. Fellow: Am. Acad. Arts & Scis.; mem.: Inst. Medicine NAS, Am. Soc. Tropical Medicine and Hygiene, Phi Beta Kappa. Democrat. Episcopalian. Office: Carter Presdl Ctr Inc One Copenhill Bldg 453 Freedom Pkwy NE Atlanta GA 30307-1496

HOPKINS, GEORGE MATHEWS MARKS, retired lawyer, engineering executive; b. Houston, June 9, 1923; s. C. Allen and Agnes Cary (Marks) H.; m. Betty Miller McLean, Aug. 21, 1954; children: Laura Hopkins Corrigan, Edith Hopkins Collins. Student, Ga. Inst. Tech., 1943-44; BSChemE, Ala. Poly. Inst., 1944; LLB, JD, U. Ala., 1949; postgrad., George Washington U., 1949-50. Bar: Ala. 1949, Ga. 1954; registered patent lawyer, U.S.; registered profl. engr., Ga.; Can. qualified deep-sea diver. Instr. math. U. Ala., 1947-49; assoc. A. Yates Dowell, Washington, 1949-50, Edward T. Newton, Atlanta, 1950-62; ptnr. Newton, Hopkins and Ormsby (and predecessor), Atlanta, 1962-87; sr. ptnr. Hunt, Richardson, Garner, Todd & Cadenhead, Atlanta, 1987-91; ptnr. Hopkins & Thomas, 1991-95; ret., 1996; spl. asst. atty. gen. State of Ga., 2000; chmn. bd. Southeastern Carpet Mills, Inc., Chatsworth, Ga., 1962-77, Thomas-Daniel & Assocs., Inc., 1981-85, Ea. Carpet Mills, Inc., 1983-87; CEO, Airamar Chem. Engring., Inc., Doraville, Ga., 1997—. Asst. dir. rsch., legal counsel Auburn (Ala.) Rsch. Found., 1954-55; spl. asst. atty. gen. State of Ga., 1978; chmn. bd. S.E. Carpet Mills, Inc., Chatsworth, Ga., 1962-77, Thomas-Daniel & Assocs., Inc., 1981-85, Ea. Carpet Mills, Inc.; dir. Xepol Inc. Served as lt., navigator, Submarine Service USNR, 1944-46, 50-51. Mem. ABA, Ga. Bar Assn. (chmn. sect. patents 1970-71), Atlanta Bar Assn., Am. Intellectual Property Law Assn., Am. Soc. Profl. Engrs., Submarine Vets. World War II (pres. Ga. chpt. 1977-78), Phi Delta Phi, Sigma Alpha Epsilon, Atlanta Lawyers Club, Phoenix Soc., Cherokee Town and Country Club, AtlantaSoc. Episcopalian.

HOPKINS, GERALD FRANK, trade association administrator; b. La Grande, Oreg., Dec. 6, 1943; s. Albert Benjamin and Phyllis Nadine (Munn) H.; m. Mary Martha Abbott, June 9, 1967; children: Angela, Ann. BS, Ea. Mont. Coll., 1966, MS, 1967; advanced Master's degree, U. So. Calif., 1973; EdD, Calif. Coastal Coll., 2002. Grad. asst. Ea. Mont. Coll., Billings, 1966-67; tchr., adminstr. Elysian Schs., Billings, 1967-69; adminstrv. asst. Internat. Schs., Bangkok, 1969-73; prin. Nashua (Mont.) Pub. Schs., 1973-76, Roundup (Mont.) Pub. Schs., 1976-86; owner, operator Town Pump, Billings, 1986-90; exec. dir. La Grande/Union County C. of C., 1990-92; tchr., supt., adminstr. Huntington (Oreg.) Pub. Schs., 1992—. Project coord. Title I, 1996-97. Author: BJ & Boz, 1989, Humor in the Classroom, 1995; contbr. articles to profl. jours. Bd. dirs. Family Crisis Intervention, Roundup, 1983-86, Sr. Citizens Vol. Program, Roundup, 1983-86, State Reading Assn., Roundup, 1986-88, Continuing Edn. Coun., La Grande, 1990, Oreg. Trail Days., Continuing Counsel Higher Edn.; mem. Coop. Community Exch. Coun., 1983-86, hist. validation com Airport Svc. Coun., La Grande, 1991. Recipient State Disting. Title I award, Nat. Disting. Title I program, 1996-97, Oreg. Small Sch. Innovation Program, 1997, 99, Internat. Pres. Humanitarian award, 1998, Salute to Success award Oreg. Sch. Bd. Assn., 2000, 2004, Oreg. Small Sch. award of excellence, 2001, 02, Pioneer award, 2005; invitation to Oxford Edn. Round Table, 2001, 03 Mem. Small Bus. Adminstrn., Nat. C. of C., Elem. Adminstrs. Assn. (dir. ea. dist. 1988-90), Lions (internat. officer 1973-95, dist. gov. 2006-07, sec. coun. govs., Outstanding Achievement award 1986, bd. dirs. La Grande Club, Roundup of Lion Yr. 1977, 78, 79, 2d Internat. Pres.'s Humanitarian award 1978, Melvin Jones award 2002), Ambs. (assoc.) Home: 68070 Hunter Rd Summerville OR 97876-8133

HOPKINS, GROVER PREVATTE, lawyer; b. Jacksonville, Fla., Sept. 2, 1933; s. John Taylor and Capitola (Prevatte) H.; m. Ann Hutchinson, Oct. 16, 1965 (dec.); children: John, George, James, Corbin; m. Connie Jefferys, June 7, 1973. AB, Fla. State U., 1958; JD, U. N.C., 1971. Bar: N.C. 1971, Fla. 1972, D.C. 1981, U.S. Dist. Ct. (ea. dist.) N.C. 1971, U.S. Ct. Appeals (4th cir.) 1974, U.S. Supreme Ct. 1974; cert. mediator N.C. Cts., 1997. Announcer Sta. WTAL, Tallahassee, 1951-54; pub. rels. dir. Inter-Am. U., San German, PR, 1958-60; pers. mgr. Northridge Knitting Mills, San German, 1960-62; cons. bus and pers. Mayaguez, PR, Miami, Fla., 1963-69; mem. Weeks & Muse, Tarboro, NC, 1971-73, Hopkins & Assocs., Tarboro, 1973—. Served with U.S. Army, 1954-57. Mem. Inter-Am. Bar Assn. (sec. gen. 1989-91). Republican. Office: Hopkins & Geoffrion Attys Sherwood Bldg 212 N Main St Tarboro NC 27886-5008 Office Phone: 252-823-1156. Business E-Mail: jack@jackhopkins.com.

HOPKINS, HENRY HOLT, mutual fund attorney; b. Galveston, Tex., Dec. 23, 1942; s. Samuel and Winifred (Bloodgold) H.; m. Nancy Anne Vrablik, Nov. 28, 1974; children: Melissa Anne, Henry Holt Jr. BA in History, Trinity Coll., Hartford, Conn., 1965; JD, U. Md., 1968. Bar: Md. Assoc. firm Melnicove, Asch, Greenberg, Kaufman, Balt., 1968-72; v.p., chief legal counsel T. Rowe Price Group, Balt., 1987—. Bd. dir. ICI Mutual Ins. Co., Md. Bus. for Responsive Govt., 1998-, Balt. Efficiency & Economy Found., 2000-, U.S. Lacrosse Found., 2000-, Parks and People Found., Balt., 1988-2000, Garrison Forest Sch., 1991-2001, 2006-. Mem. ABA, Md. Bar Assn., Balt. City Bar Assn., Investment Counsel Assn. Am. (bd. dirs. 1987-96, 1998-2005), Investment Co. Inst. (com. mem.). Clubs: Gibson Island (Md.). Republican. Episcopalian. Avocations: tennis, golf. Office: T Rowe Price Assocs Inc 100 E Pratt St Fl 4 Baltimore MD 21202-1090

HOPKINS, HENRY TYLER, museum director, art educator; b. Idaho Falls, Idaho, Aug. 14, 1928; s. Talcott Thompson and Zoe (Erbe) Hopkins; children: Victoria Anne, John Thomas, Christopher Tyler. BA, Sch. of Art Inst., Chgo., 1952, MA, 1955; postgrad., UCLA, 1957—60; PhD (hon.), Calif. Coll. Arts and Crafts, 1984, San Francisco Art Inst., 1986. Curator exhbns., publs. LA County Mus. of Art, 1960-68; lectr. art history UCLA Ext., 1960—68; dir. Ft. Worth Art Mus., 1968-74, San Francisco Mus. of Modern Art, 1974-86; chmn. art dept. UCLA, 1991-94, dir. F.S. Wight Gallery, 1991-95, dir. Armand Hammer Mus. Art and Cultural Ctr., 1994-99, prof. art, 1999—2002, prof. emeritus, 2002—. Instr. Tex. Christian U., Ft. Worth, 1968—74; dir. U.S. representation Venice Biennial, Italy, 1970; dir. art presentation Festival of Two Worlds, Spoleto, Italy, 1970; co-commr. U.S. representation XVI Sao Paulo Biennale, Brazil, 1981; cons. NEA, mem. mus. panel, 1979—84, chmn., 1981; cons., mem. mus. panel NEH, 1976; archivist pers. archives Getty Rsch. Ctr., LA, 2005. Contbr. numerous articles to profl. jours. and mus. publs. With AUS, 1952—54. Decorated knight Order Leopold II, Belgium; recipient Spl.

Internat. award, Art LA, 1992. Mem.: We. Assn. Art Museums (pres. 1977—78), Am. Assn. Museums, Coll. Art Assn., Assn. Art Mus. Dirs. (pres. 1985—86). Home: 939 1/2 Hilgard Ave Los Angeles CA 90024-3032 Office: UCLA Art Dept 405 Hilgard Ave Los Angeles CA 90095-9000 Office Phone: 310-206-7102. Personal E-mail: hthopkins@verizon.net. Business E-Mail: hhopkins@ucla.edu.

HOPKINS, JAN, communications executive, consultant, journalist, newscaster; b. Warren, Ohio, May 22, 1947; d. Walter Charles and Lois Avelene (Botroff) Reed; m. Walter Hopkins, June 14, 1969 (div. Nov. 1981); m. Richard Trachtman, Nov. 8, 1986. Dir. news Sta. WTCL, Warren, Ohio, 1973-75; reporter, anchor Sta. WERE, Cleve., 1975-77; reporter Sta. WKBN-TV, Youngstown, Ohio, 1977-80; reporter, anchor Sta. WLWT-TV, Cin., 1980-82; assignment editor CBS News, NYC, 1983; reporter, prodr. ABC News, NYC, 1983-84; anchor bus. news CNN, NYC, 1984—2003; mng. dir., head client comms. Citigroup Pvt. Bank, 2003—05; prin., owner Jan Hopkins Group, NY, 2005—. Author: (chapter) Knight Bagehot Guide to Business Journalism, 1990, 2d edit., 2000. Bd. dirs. Girl Scouts USA, 2001—05; trustee Hiram Coll., 1988—94; adv. bd. Knight Bagehot program journalism Columbia U., NYC, 1994. Recipient Peabody award U. Ga., 1988, Front Page award Newswomen Club N.Y., 1988, Lifetime Achievement award Women's Econ. Roundtable, 2002; Knight Bagehot fellow Columbia U. Sch. Journalism, 1982-83, Front Page award NY News Women's Club, 2003 Emmy award contbn. Exporting Am. Lou Dobbs Tonight CNN, 2004; named to Hall of Excellence Ohio Found. Ind. Colls., 1993, Warren, Ohio, H.S. Disting. Alumni Hall of Fame, 1995. Mem. Econ. Club N.Y. Office Phone: 212-721-6491. Personal E-mail: jan@thejanhopkinsgroup.com.

HOPKINS, JEANNETTE ETHEL, book publisher, editor; b. Camden, NJ, Dec. 7, 1922; d. Carleton Roper and Gladys Eugenia (Hull) H. BA, Vassar Coll., 1944; MS, Columbia Sch. Journalism, 1945. Asst. to Sunday editor New Haven Register, 1945-46; reporter Providence Evening Bull., 1946-50, Oklahoma City Times, 1950-51; sr. editor Beacon Press, Boston, 1951-56, Harcourt Brace, NYC, 1956-64, Harper & Row, NYC, 1964-73; v.p. Met. Applied Res. Ctr., NYC, 1970-72, cons. editor, 1973-80, 89—; dir. Wesleyan Univ. Press, Middletown, Conn., 1980-89. Adj. prof. English Wesleyan U., 1987-89, U. N.H., 1989; propr. Portsmouth Athenaeum, 1991—. Author: Books That Will Not Burn, 1952, 14 Journeys to Unitarianism, 1951, (with K.B. Clark) Relevant War Against Poverty, 1968, Legacy: A History of the South Church Endowment, 1995. Mem. coun. Inst. Religion in an Age of Sci., 1968-72, 80-82, 88-91, mem. adv. bd. 1962-72, 82-94; mem. bd. Unitarian UN Office, 1977-80; mem. Commn. on Appraisal, Unitarian Universalist Assn., 1976-78; bd. dirs. ACLU, 1970-79, mem. nat. adv. coun., 1986—; bd. govs. Comty. Ch. N.Y., 1960-66, Unitarian-Universalist Ch., Portsmouth, 1990-93, lay min., 1991-95; trustee South Ch. Endowment Fund, 1996-99; v.p. Unitarian Fellowship for Social Justice, 1958-62. Louise Hart Van Loon fellow, Vassar Coll., 1944; recipient Disting. Alumni award Columbia Sch. Journalism, 1981. Mem.: PEN, Authors Guild. Democrat. Unitarian. Home and Office: 39 Pray St Portsmouth NH 03801-5226

HOPKINS, JEFFERY P., federal judge; b. 1960; JD, Ohio State U., 1985. Bar: Ohio 1985, U.S. Dist. Ct. (so dist.) Ohio 1986, 1986 (Fed.). Law clk. to Hon. Alan E. Norris U.S. Ct. Appeals (6th cir.), 1985-87; assoc. Squire, Sanders & Dempsey, 1987-90; asst. U.S. atty. So. Dist. Ohio, 1990-96; bankruptcy judge U.S. Dist. Ct. (so. dist.) Ohio, Cin., 1996—. Bd. dir. Fed. Judicial Ctr., mem. edn. com.; adj. prof. Coll. Law U. Cin. Mem.: Nat. Conf. Bankruptcy Judges (pres. 2006—), Am. Law Inst. of ABA (faculty bankruptcy law course), Sigma Pi Phi. Office: US Bankr Ct So Dist Ohio 221 E 4th Ste 800 Cincinnati OH 45202-4124

HOPKINS, JOHN DAVID, lawyer; b. Memphis, Feb. 8, 1938; s. John and Helen (Sweeney) H.; m. Evelyn Harry, June 8, 1963 (div. Feb. 1985); children: John David III, Katharine Jane, Matthew Foster Joseph; m. Laurie Eileen House, June 3, 1987. BA, Vanderbilt U., 1959; LLB, U. Va., 1965. Bar: Ga. 1966, D.C. 1979. From assoc. to ptnr. King & Spalding, Atlanta, 1965-93; exec. v.p., gen. counsel Jefferson-Pilot Corp., Greensboro, NC, 1993—2003; of counsel Womble Carlyle Sandridge & Rice, PLLC, Atlanta, 2003—. Bd. dirs., mem. exec. com. Rock-Tenn Co., Atlanta, 1989—; mem. bd. visitors Guilford Coll., 1994-2000; bd. dirs. U. N.C. at Greensboro Excellence Found., 1995-2003. Bd. dirs. Atlanta Ballet, 1991-93, Greensboro United Arts Coun., 1994-97, Ea. Music Festival, 1998—2005; mem. alumni coun. U. Va. Law Sch. Alumni Assn., 2000-03; trustee Children's Sch., Inc., Atlanta, 1971-79, 88-89, Nat. Assn. Children's Hosps. and Related Instns., Alexandria, Va., 1973-79. Lt. USN, 1959-62. Mem. Ga. Bar Assn. (chmn. corp. code revision com., corp. and banking sect. 1970-79), D.C. Bar Assn., Cherokee Town and Country Club (Atlanta), Highlands Country Club N.C., Amelia Island Club, Order of Coif, Omicron Delta Kappa. Episcopalian. Office: One Atlantic Ctr 1201 W Peachtree St Ste 3500 Atlanta GA 30309 Office Phone: 404-879-2429. Personal E-mail: jdhopki@yahoo.com.

HOPKINS, KAREN BROOKS, performing arts executive; b. 1951; d. Howard and Paula Brooks; divorced; 1 child, Matthew. BA in Theater Arts with honors, U. Md., 1973; MFA, George Washington U., 1980. Mem. group sales staff Am. Theater, Washington, 1973; cmty. rels. dir. Qwindo's Windo Dance Trouing Co., Washington, 1975; theater mgr., asst. dir. Chelm Players Touring Co., 1975-76, prodr., 1975-78; theater dir. Jewish Cmty. Ctr. of Greater Washington, 1976-78; devel. dir. The New Playwright's Theatre, Washington, 1978-79; devel. officer Bklyn. Acad. of Music, 1979-81, v.p. planning and devel., 1981-88, exec. v.p., 1988-98, COO and exec. v.p., 1998-99, pres., 1999—. Adj. prof. program for arts adminstrn. Bklyn. Coll., 1980-84. Author: Successful Fundraising for Arts and Cultural Organizations, 1989, 2d edit., 1997. Fundraising cons. art instns., 1979—; chair Performing Arts Ctrs. Consortium, 1994-96, Cultural Instns. Group, 2002-04; mem. adv. com. Salzburg Seminar-Alberto Vilar Project of Critical Issues for the Classical Performing Arts; ex-officio mem. N.Y.C. Cultural Affairs Adv. Commn., 2003. Recipient King Olav medal Norwegian Nat. Ballet, 1982, Dramaten medal, 1995. Office: Brooklyn Acad Music 30 Lafayette Ave Brooklyn NY 11217-1430

HOPKINS, LEE BENNETT, writer, educator; b. Scranton, Pa., Apr. 13, 1938; s. Lee Hall and Gertrude (Thomas) H. BA, Kean Coll., 1960, LLD (hon.), 1980; MS, Bank St. Coll., 1964; profl. diploma, Hunter Coll., 1966. Elem. tchr. Fair Lawn Pub. Schs., 1960—66; lang. arts supr. Bank St. Coll., NYC, 1966-68; curriculum specialist Scholastic, Inc., NYC, 1968-75; author Scarborough, NY, 1975—. Cons., vis. prof. various US and Can. colls. and univs.; bd. dirs. Soc. Sch. Librs. Internat.; lit. cons. Random House Achievement Program in Lit.; chmn. Nat. Coun. Tchrs. English poetry award com. Author: Been to Yesterdays: Poems of a Life, 1996 (The Christopher Book award and Golden Kite Honor Book award), numerous children's and junior books, poetry (awards include Nat. Coun. Tchrs. English, Tchrs. Choice award, Pa. Keystone to Reading award, Am. Inst. Graphic Arts award); contbr. articles, texts, and curriculum materials to mags., profl. jours. Recipient Lasting Contbn. to Field Children's Lit. awad U. So. Miss., 1989, Manhattan Coun. Literacy award Internat. Reading Assn., 1983, Ednl. Leadership award Phi Delta Kappa, 1980; named Keystone Author of Yr., Pa.; established Lee Bennett Hopkins Poetry award in conjunction with Children's Lit. Coun. Pa. State U., 1993—, Lee Bennett Hopkins Promising Poet award in conjunction with Internat. Reading Assn., 1995—. Mem.: Soc. Children's Book Writers and Illustrators, Internat. Reading Assn., Nat. Coun. Tchrs. of English. Avocations: reading, travel. Home and Office: 4923 Agualinda Blvd Cape Coral FL 33914 Office Phone: 239-549-9514. E-mail: lbhcove@aol.com.

HOPKINS, LEWIS DEAN, architecture educator; b. Lakewood, Ohio, Feb. 20, 1946; s. W. Dean and Harriet (Painter) H.; m. Susan Brewster Cocker, Aug. 24, 1968; children: Joshua, Nathaniel. BA, U. Pa., 1968, postgrad., 1968-69, M of Regional Planning, 1970, PhD, 1975. Asst. prof. landscape arch. Inst. Environ. Studies/U. Ill., Urbana-Champaign, 1972-79, assoc. prof. landscape arch., urban and regional planning, 1979-84, prof., head dept. urban and regional planning, 1984-97, prof. landscape arch., 1984—. Vis. lectr. dept. town and regional planning U. Sheffield, Eng., 1980; coord. grad. program in landscape arch. U. Ill., 1976-79, chair search com. for head dept. landscape arch., 1985, chair com. to evaluate dir. Inst. Environ. Studies, 1990, com. pub. adminstrn. program, 1990, campus budget strategies com., 1991-94, chancellors strategic planning com., 1993-95, campus senate, 1976-79, 82-84, chair ednl. policy com. 1978-79, senate coun. 1978-79, 82-83, budget com. 1984-86; project dir. Ill. Streams Info. sys., 1981-90; fellow Com. Instnl. Coop. Acad. Leadership Program, 1989-90; external site visit team dept. landscape arch. and environ. planning, Ariz. State U., 1990; rsch. adv. com. Ill.-Ind. Sea Grant Program, 1991—; exec. com. Office of Solid Waste Rsch., 1992-95; Fulbright sr. scholar to Nepal, 1997-98. Co-editor: (with Gill-Chin Lim) Jour. Planning Edn. and Rsch., 1987-91; mem. editl. bd. Jour. Planning Lit., Computers, Environment and Urban sys., Urban and Regional Info. Sys. Assn. Jour., Jour. Planning Edn. and Rsch., others; reviewer: European Jour. Ops. Rsch., Geographical Analysis, Internat. Regional Sci. Rev., Landscape Jour., Mgmt. Sci., Transp. Rsch., others; contbr. articles to profl. jours. Fellow Am. Inst. Cert. Planners; mem. AAUP (pres. campus chpt. 1983-84), Am. Planning Assn. (chair nominating com. Ill. chpt. 1988), Assn. Collegiate Schs. of Planning (regional rep. to exec. bd. 1989-91), Inst. Mgmt. Scis., Regional Sci. Assn., Urban and Regional Inf. Sys. Assn. for Planning Accreditation Bd. (chair site visit teams 1988, 92, 94, team mem. 1995, com. on dual degree programs 1992-93), Planning Accreditation Bd. (chair 1997—). Achievements include research in human and computer problem solving processes for incompletely defined spatial problems; land and water resources management, information, and decision support systems; comprehensive planning processes and institutions. Office: U Ill Urbana-Champaign Dept Urban/Regional Plan 611 E Taft Dr Champaign IL 61820-6921

HOPKINS, MICHAEL, communications executive; b. 1968; married; 1 child. BS in Bus. Adminstrn., Calif. State U.; MBA, Anderson Sch., U. Calif., LA. Dir., Affiliate Sales, Pacific Northwest region Fox Cable Networks, Calif., 1997, dir., Affiliate Sales and Mktg., Fox Sports West, West 2 Calif., v.p., Affiliate Sales Calif., 1999, sr. v.p., Affiliate Sales Calif. Named one of 40 Executives Under 40, Multichannel News, 2006. Office: Fox Broadcasting Company 10201 W Pico Blvd Los Angeles CA 90035

HOPKINS, MICHAEL B., lawyer; b. Houston, Sept. 25, 1969; BA with honors in Econs., U. Tex., Austin, 1992, JD, 1995. Bar: Tex. 1995, US Ct. Appeals (5th cir.) 1995, US Dist. Ct. (no., ea. and so. dists. Tex.), US Dist. Ct. (ea. dist. Mich.). Sr. atty. Loewinsohn Flegle, L.L.P., Dallas. Contbr. articles to profl. publs.; notes editor: Rev. of Litig., 1993—95. Named a Rising Star, Tex. Super Lawyers mag., 2006. Mem.: Dallas Bar Assn. Office: Loewinsohn Flegle LLP 12377 Merit Dr Ste 900 Dallas TX 75251 Office Phone: 214-572-1704. E-mail: mikeh@texasverdict.com.*

HOPKINS, NANCY HAVEN DOE, biology professor; BA, Radcliffe Coll., 1964; PhD, Harvard U., 1971. Asst. prof. MIT, Cambridge, 1973—76, assoc. prof., 1976—82, prof., 1982—, chmn. comm. on women faculty, Sch. Sci., co-chmn. council on faculty diversity, Amgen Inc. prof. molecular and devel. biology. Recipient Laya Wiesner Community Award, 2001, Women's History Month Honoree of NY Academy of Sciences, Maria Mitchell Women in Sci. award, Marie Mitchell Assn., 2004; fellow Amer. Academy of Arts and Sciences. Fellow: Am. Acad. Arts and Scis.; mem.: NAS, Inst. Med. (coun. mem. 2006—). Office: MIT E17-341 77 Massachusetts Ave Cambridge MA 02139-4301 Office Phone: 617-253-6414. Business E-Mail: nhopkins@mit.edu.*

HOPKINS, RAMONA O., psychologist, neuroscientist; BS, Westminster Coll., Salt Lake City, 1988; MS, PhD, U. Utah, Salt Lake City, 1996. Sr. rsch. assoc. LDS Hosp., Salt Lake City, Andorra, 1997—; chair, psychology dept. Brigham Young U., Provo, Utah, 1999—. Dir. neurosci. ctr. Brigham Young U., Provo, 2005—06. Contbr. articles to profl. jours. Recipient Young Scholar award, Brigham Young U., 2004. Mem.: APA (mem. sci. adv. com. 2006—), Internat. Neuropsychol. Assn., Soc. Critical Care Medicine, Am. Thoracic Soc., Soc. Neuroscience. Office: Brigham Young Univy 1082 Swkt Provo UT 84602 Office Phone: 801-422-1170.

HOPKINS, SAMUEL, retired investment banker; b. Highland, Md., Oct. 18, 1913; s. Samuel Harold and Roberta (Smith) H.; m. Winifred Holt Bloodgood, Oct. 15, 1938 (dec. Oct. 1954); children: Samuel, Henry; m. Anne E. Dankmeyer, Oct. 20, 1955; children: Robert, Frederick. BS, Johns Hopkins U., 1934; LL.B., U. Md., 1938. With Fidelity & Deposit Co. of Md., 1934-69, asst. to treas., 1934-50, asst. treas., 1950-54, sec., 1954-67, v.p., sec., dir., 1967-69; dir., mem. trust com. Equitable Trust Co., Balt., 1954-81; sec., dir. Md. Life Ins. Co., 1963-69; gen. partner Alex. Brown & Sons (investment bankers), Balt., 1970-75, ltd. partner, 1976-87. Bd. dirs. Am. Maritime Cases, Inc. Mem. adv. com. housing for elderly U.S. Housing and Fin. Agy., 1956-60; mem. Balt. Bd. Recreation and Parks, 1965-77, pres., 1965-67, 74-77, v.p., 1968-74; Rep. candidate for Congress, 1952; mem. Md. Ho. of Dels., 1950-54; Rep. candidate for mayor, Balt., 1955; del. Rep. Nat. Conv., 1976; trustee Balt. Mus. Art, Peale Mus., Sheppard and Enoch Pratt Hosp., 1972-89; trustee, v.p. State Colls. Md., 1963-70; mem. Balt. City Planning Commn., 1985-95. Lt. USNR, 1942-45. Mem.: ABA, Chartered Security Analysts, Balt. Security Analysts Soc., Md. Hist. Soc. (treas. 1956—69, pres. 1970—75, chmn. bd. trustees 1988—90). Episcopalian. Home: 45 Warrenton Rd Baltimore MD 21210-2924 Personal E-mail: annehopk@mindspring.com.

HOPKINS, STEPHEN, film director, producer; b. Jamaica, 1958; Motion picture dir., prodr. Exec. prodr. film Crossworlds, 1996; prodr., dir. Lost in Space, 1998, Under Suspicion, 2000, (TV miniseries) Traffic, 2004; dir. films Nightmare on Elm St. 5: The Dream Child, 1989, Predator 2, 1990, Dangerous Game, 1991, Judgment Night, 1993, Blown Away, 1994, The Ghost and the Darkness, 1996, The Life and Death of Peter Sellers, 2004 (Emmy award for outstanding directing for a miniseries, movie or a dramatic special, 2005), The Reaping, 2007; dir. (TV series) Tales from the Crypt, 1989, (also segment writer) Tube Tales, 1999; dir., co-exec. prodr. (TV series) 24, 2001 (nominee Outstanding Directorial Achievement in Dramatic Series Dir.'s Guild Am.). Office: care David Wirtschafter William Morris Agy 151 El Camino Dr Beverly Hills CA 90212*

HOPKINS, THOMAS DUVALL, economics professor; b. Spring Valley, Ill., Mar. 10, 1942; s. Joel Willis and Mildred (Duvall) H.; m. Jane Cole Eveleth, Apr. 20, 1968; children: Edward Eveleth, Catherine Chapin Hopkins. BA, Oberlin Coll., Ohio, 1964; MA, Yale U., 1965, M of Philosophy, 1967, PhD, 1971. Asst. prof. econs. Bowdoin Coll., Brunswick, Maine, 1968-73; cons. Irwin Mgmt. Co., Inc., Columbus, Ind., 1973-75; asst. dir. Coun. on Wage and Price Stability, Washington, 1975-81, acting dir., 1981; dep. adminstr. Office of Mgmt. and Budget, Washington, 1981-84; assoc. prof. U. Md., College Park, 1984-87; assoc. prof. econs. Am. U., Washington, 1987-88; prof. econs., Arthur J. Gosnell prof. Rochester (N.Y.) Inst. Tech., 1988-99, dean Coll. Bus., 1999—2005, prof. econs., 2005—. Cons. Adminstrv. Conf. U.S., Washington, 1986-88, Office Tech. Assessment, U.S. Congress, 1987-89, Inst. Liberty and Democracy, Lima, Peru, 1986-91, U.S. Regulatory Info. Svc. Ctr., 1990-92, Congl. Budget Office, 1991, U.S. SBA, 1993-95, 2000-02, OECD, Paris, 1994-96; seminar leader Inst. Internat. Edn., Washington, 1987-88; mem. com. on tank vessel design marine bd. NRC, Washington, 1989-91; mem. com. on taxation, fin. and pricing, 1990-93, com. on pub. policy for surface freight transp., 1993-96, com.on fed. role in marine transp. sys., 2003, Transp. Rsch. Bd., NRC; lectr. U.S. Bus. Sch. in Prague, Czech Republic, 1992-98; pub. mem. U.S. Adminstrv. Conf., Washington, 1994-95; adj. fellow Washington U. Ctr. for Study of Am. Bus., St. Louis, 1996-00; pres. U.S. Bus. Sch. in Prague, Czech Republic, 1999-06; mem. regulatory studies program adv. bd. George Mason Univ. Mercatus Ctr., 1999-05. Co-author: Tanker Spills: Prevention by Design, 1991. Mem. coun. Eastman House, Rochester, 1991—. Woodrow Wilson Found. fellow, 1964. Fellow NSF; mem. Am. Econs. Assn., Nat. Economists Club. Office: Rochester Inst Tech 107 Lomb Memorial Dr Rochester NY 14623-5608 Home Phone: 585-545-4339. Business E-Mail: thomas.hopkins@rit.edu.

HOPKINS, WILLIAM HAYES, lawyer, writer; b. Moscow, Idaho, Aug. 5, 1943; s. Bert Earl and Marie Hayes H.; m. Rachel Pomeroy, Aug. 28, 1965; children: Alaa Christina, Elizabeth Anne, Amelia Jeanne, William, Rachel G. BA, Yale U., 1965; JD, Vanderbilt U., 1968. Bar: Conn. 1968, N.H. 1969, U.S. Dist. Ct. N.H. 1969, U.S. Ct. Appeals (1st cir.) 1983. Assoc. atty. Wakefield & Ray, Plymouth, N.H., 1969-75; ptnr. Ray & Hopkins, Plymouth, 1975-88; sr. ptnr. Hopkins & Blaine, Plymouth, 1989-94; pvt. practice Plymouth, 1995—. Vice chmn. N.H. Adult Parole Bd., Concord, 1988-98; chmn. N.H. Wine Law Revision Commn., Concord, 1979-81. Mem. N.H. Bridge Assn. (pres. 1996-98), Plymouth Wine Patrol (guru 1984-93), James Hogan Bridge Club (pres. 1986-98), Yale Club N.H. (pres. 1997-99). Avocations: oenology, skiing, hiking. Home: PO Box 126 Plymouth NH 03264-0126 Home Phone: 603-783-8340; Office Phone: 603-783-9621. Personal E-mail: hpknslaw@comcast.net.

HOPKINSON, SHIRLEY LOIS, library and information scientist, educator; b. Boone, Iowa, Aug. 25, 1924; d. Arthur Perry and Zora (Smith) Hopkinson. Student, Coe Coll., 1942—43; AB cum laude, U. Colo., 1945; BLS, U. Calif., 1949; MA, Claremont Grad. Sch., 1951; EdM, U. Okla., 1952, EdD, 1957. Tchr. pub. sch., Stigler, Okla., 1946—47; tchr. Palo Verde HS., Jr. Coll., Blythe, Calif., 1947—48; asst. libr. Modesto Jr. Coll., Calif., 1949—51; tchr., libr. Fresno, Calif., 1951—52, La Mesa, Calif., 1953—55; asst. prof. librarianship, instrnl. materials dir. Chaffey Coll., Ontario, Calif., 1955—59; asst. prof. librarianship San Jose State Coll., Calif., 1959—64, assoc. prof., 1964—69, prof., 1969—. Dir. NDEA Inst. Sch. Librs., 1966; mem. Santa Clara County Civil Svc. Bd. Examiners; owner Claremont House Publishers, 1975—. Author: Descriptive Cataloging of Library Materials, Instructional Materials for Teaching the Use of the Library; editor: Calif. Sch. Libraries, 1963—64; asst. editor Sch. Libr. Assn. of Calif. Bull., 1961—63, book reviewer profl. jours.; contbr. articles to profl. jours. Honnold Honor scholar, Claremont Grad. Sch., 1945—46. Mem.: LWV (bd. dirs. 1950—51, publs. chmn.), AAUW (dir. 1957—58), NEA, ALA, AAUP, Kappa Delta Pi, Alpha Beta Alpha, Calif. Tchrs. Assn., San Diego County Sch. Librs. Assn. (sec. 1954—55), Sch. Librs. Assn. Calif. (treas. No. sect. 1951—52, com. mem.), Audio-Visual Assn. Calif., Calif. Library Assn., Bus. Profl. Women's Club, Alpha Lambda Delta, Phi Beta Kappa (scholar 1944), Delta Kappa Gamma (sec. 1994—96, legis. liaison 1996—2002, corr. sec. 2002—), Phi Kappa Phi (disting. acad. achievement award 1981). Office: 1340 Pomeroy Ave Apt 408 Santa Clara CA 95051-3658

HOPLAMAZIAN, MARK SAMUEL, hotel executive; b. Bryn Mawr, Pa., Nov. 27, 1963; s. Harry Joseph and Victoria (Sarkisian) Hoplamazian; m. Rachel DeYoung Kohler, Sept. 28, 1991; 3 children. BA, Harvard U., 1985; MBA, U. Chgo., 1989. Fin. analyst The First Boston Corp., NYC, 1985-87; mcht. banker Pritzker & Pritzker, Chgo., 1989—, sr. v.p., exec. v.p. to pres. Pritzker Org. LLC; interim pres. Global Hyatt Corp., 2006, pres., CEO, 2006—. Mem. Discovery Class of the Henry Crown Fellowship Aspen Inst., 2003—; bd. trustees Latin Sch. Chgo.; advisory bd. Facing History and Ourselves. Mem.: Beta Gamma Sigma. Avocations: japanese art, squash, golf. Office: Global Hyatt Corp 71 S Wacker St Chicago IL 60606

HOPMANN, PHILIP TERRENCE, political science educator; b. St. Louis, June 25, 1942; s. Irvin Herman and Loretta (Gerlach) H.; m. Marita Raubitschek, Aug. 24, 1968; children: Alexander Irvin, Nicholas Erich. AB, Princeton U., 1964; MA, Stanford U., 1965, PhD, 1969. Rsch. asst. Stanford (Calif.) U., 1965-67, instr., 1967-68; prof. polit. sci. U. Minn., Mpls., 1968-85, Brown U., Providence, 1985—, dir. program on global security Watson Inst. Internat. Studies, 1993—2004, dir. Internat. Rels. program, 1985-94, chair dept. polit. sci., 2005—. Cons. U.S. Inst. of Peace, 1998—; chmn. faculty exec. com. Brown U., Providence, 1994-95; Fulbright prof. Vienna Diplomatic Acad., 2005. Author: Unity and Disintergration in International Alliances, 1973, 84, The Negotiation Process and the Resolution of International Conflicts, 1996. Fulbright-Hays fellow Coun. Internat. Ednl. Exch., Belgium, 1975-76, 82-83, Jennings Randolph sr. fellow U.S. Inst. Peace, 1997-98, Fulbright fellow Orgn. Security and Cooperation in Europe, Austria, 1997-98; fellow Woodrow Wilson Internat. Ctr. for Scholars, 2004-05. Mem. Internat. Studies Assn. (editor 1980-85, v.p. 1991-92), Internat. Polit. Sci. Assn., Arms Control Assn., Am. Polit. Sci. Assn. Democrat. Home: 23 Valerian Ct Rockville MD 20852 Office: Brown U Dept Polit Sci PO Box 1844 Providence RI 02912-1844 Home Phone: 301-984-9539; Office Phone: 401-863-1571. E-mail: Philip_Hopmann@Brown.edu.

HOPP, ANTHONY JAMES, advertising agency executive; b. Detroit, Jan. 31, 1945; s. William J. and Beverly (Gildea) H.; m. Nancy Jane Dunckel, Nov. 11, 1969; children: Beth, Michael. BA in Advt./Mktg., Mich. State U., 1967, MA in Advt./Psychology, 1968. Asst. account exec. Campbell-Ewald Adv., Warren, Mich., 1968-70; account exec. Lintas Campbell-Ewald, Warren, Mich., 1970-74, account supr., 1974-75, v.p., account supr., 1975-79, sr. v.p., mgmt. supr., 1979-85, group sr. v.p., group mgmt. supr., 1985-88, exec. v.p., account dir., 1988-93, pres., 1993-95, vice chmn., 1995—97, also bd. dirs.; chmn. & CEO Lintas Campbell-Ewald (now Campbell-Ewald), Warren, Mich., 1997—. Bd. dirs. C-E Comm., Warren, Lintas Ams. Recipient Robert E. Healy award Interpublic Group of Cos., 1989. Mem. Adcraft, Hunters Creek, Bloomfield Hills Country Club, Pine Lake Country Club. Avocations: golf, hunting, boating. Office: Lintas-Campbell-Ewald 30400 Van Dyke Ave Warren MI 48093-2368

HOPP, DANIEL FREDERICK, lawyer, manufacturing company executive; b. Ann Arbor, Mich., Apr. 14, 1947; s. Clayton A. and Monica E. (Williams) H.; m. Maria G. Lopez, Dec. 20, 1968; children: Emily, Daniel, Melissa. BA in English, U. Mich., 1969; JD summa cum laude, Wayne State U., 1973. Bar: Ill. 1974, Mich. 1980. Atty. Mayer, Brown and Platt, Chgo., 1973-79, Whirlpool Corp., Benton Harbor, Mich., 1979-84, asst. sec., 1984-85, sec., asst. gen. counsel, 1985-89, v.p., gen. counsel, sec., 1989-98, sr. v.p. corp. affairs, gen. counsel, 1998—. Bd. dirs. Horizon Bank, Mich. City, Ind., Lakeland Regional Health Sys., St. Joseph, Mich., Coun. World Class Communities, Benton Harbor, Mich.; mem. City of St. Joseph Planning Commn. Served in US Army, 1969—71. Mem.: Berrien County Bar Assn., Mich. Bar Assn. Republican. Mem. Ch. Of Christ. Avocation: golf. Office: Whirlpool Corp Adminstrv Ctr 2000 N M-63 Benton Harbor MI 49022-2692*

HOPP, PHILLIP EDWARD, gifted and talented educator; s. Edward Hopp and Susan Hoffman. BS in History, Portland State U., 2000. Educator Perris Union HS Dist., Perris, Calif., 1999—2001, Val Verde HS, Perris, 2002—, chair English dept., 2004—06. Author: Healing and the Laying on of Hands, 2000, I am with You: A Dramatic and Thrilling Account of One Man's Vision of Jesus Christ, 2001; contbr. articles to profl. jours. and mags. Mem.: Mega Found. for Gifted, The Ultranet of the Global Ultra

High IQ Cmty. (iq 150+ of the ultranet 2001—03), The Internat. High IQ Soc. (hon.; platinum club 2001—03), Phi Alpha Theta. Avocations: bodybuilding, aerobics, philosophy, theology, bibliophile. Personal E-mail: res06uko@verizon.net.

HOPPE, ELIZABETH ANNE, philosopher, educator; b. Seattle, Oct. 14, 1963; d. Harley Henry and Mary Teresa Hoppe. BA in Philosophy, U. Notre Dame, South Bend, Ind., 1987; MA in Philosophy, Loyola U.-Chgo., 1990; PhD in Philosophy, DePaul U., Chgo., 2000. Assoc. prof. Lewis U., Romeoville, Ill., 1999—, peace edn. com., 2000—, chair dept. philosophy, 2004—06, chair Title III taskforce, 2006. Author (and editor): Listening: A Jour. of Religion and Culture; co-editor: From Ancient Greek to Asian Philosophy, 2007; contbr. articles to profl. jours. Collegium fellow, Collegium of Cath. Univs./Fairfield U., 2002. Mem.: Soc. for Phenomenology and Existential Philosophy, Am. Cath. Philos. Assn., Am. Philos. Assn., Delta Epsilon Sigma. Office: Lewis University One University Pkwy Romeoville IL 60446 Office Phone: 815-836-5312. Personal E-mail: ea.hoppe@hotmail.com.

HOPPE, SHERRY LEE, academic administrator; b. Chickamauga, Ga. BS magna cum laude, U. Tenn., Chattanooga, 1969, MS, 1974; EdD, U. Tenn., Knoxville, 1981. Clk. new accounts Pioneer Bank, Chattanooga, 1965-66; asst. to dir. fin. aid, sec. U. Tenn., Chattanooga, 1966-69; counselor, tchr. Chattanooga Valley High Sch., 1969-77; from coord. vets. affairs to dean Chattanooga State Tech. Community Coll., 1977-87; interim pres. Nashville State Tech. Inst., 1987-88; pres. Roane State Community Coll., Harriman, Tenn., 1988; interim pres. Austin Peay State U., Tenn., 2000—01, pres. Tenn., 2001—. Contbr. articles to jours. in field. Bd. dirs. Meth. Med. Ctr., Community Devel. Coun., Roane County, Oak Ridge Community Found., Chattanooga Area Am. Heart Assn., Multiple Sclerosis Soc., Sentenga chptr., Jr. Achievement, Chattanooga Venture, Met. Coun., Cherokee Area Coun. Boy Scouts Am., Am. Lung Assn. Southeastern Region, Sovran Bank, Henry Devel. Ctr.; account exec., sect. leader United Way, 1882-84, strategic action com., 1987; Mem. Pub. Rels. Task Force Vision 2000, 1984-85, planning adv. com. Chattanooga-Hamilton County Regional Planning Commn., 1985; chmn. Homecoming '86 Enterprise Com. Greater Chattanooga Area, Made in Chattanooga Exhbn., 1986; participator Leadership Chattanooga, Leadership Roane County. Mem. NEA, Tenn. Edn. Assn., C. of C. (pub. rels. task force 1983), Nat. Coun. Instructional Adminstrs., Am. Assn. Women in Community and Jr. Colls. (participated in Leaders of the '80s 1981), Chattanooga Indsl. Pers. Club, Chattanooga Area Pers. Assn., Rotary. Office: Austin Peay State U Office of Pres BR 125 PO Box 4576 Clarksville TN 37044 Office Phone: 931-221-7567. E-mail: hoppes@apsu.edu.

HOPPENSTEADT, FRANK CHARLES, mathematician, educator, dean; b. Oak Park, Ill., Apr. 29, 1938; s. Frank Carl and Margaret Hoppensteadt; children: Charles, Matthew, Sarah. BA, Butler U., 1960; MS, U. Wis., 1962, PhD, 1965. Instr. math. U. Wis., Madison, 1965; asst. prof. math. Mich. State U., East Lansing, 1965-68, dean Coll. Natural Sci., 1986-95; dir. sys. sci. engr. rsch., prof. math. and elec. engring. Ariz. State U., Tempe, 1995—2004; assoc. prof. NYU-Courant, 1968-76, prof., 1976-79, sr. vice provost, rsch. prof., 2004—; prof. U. Utah, Salt Lake City, 1977-86, chmn. dept. math., 1982—85. Author: Mathematical Methods in Population Biology, 1982, An Introduction to Mathematics of Neurons, 1986, 2d edit., 1997, Mathematics in Medicine and the Life Sciences, 1991, Analysis and Simulation of Chaotic Systems, 2000, Weakly Connected Neural Networks, 1997, Modeling and Simulation in Mathematics and the Life Sciences, 2001, Random Perturbation Methods, 2002. Named Christiensen fellow, Oxford U., 1994. Fellow: AAAS; mem.: IEEE, Soc. Indsl. and Applied Maths., Am. Math. Soc. (chmn. applied math. com. 1976—80), Sigma Xi. Business E-Mail: frank.hoppensteadt@nyu.edu.

HOPPER, CAROL, incentive program and trade association administrator; b. Montreal, Que., Can., Apr. 23, 1952; m. Cedric Heimrath; stepchildren: Natasha, Erik. Student, McGill U., 1972; cert., Canadian Inst. Orgnl. Mgmt., 1991. Asst. Ben Fuller Assocs., 1973-89; show dir. Nat. Ski Industries Assn., Montreal, 1989-91, exec. dir., 1991-96, dir. show svcs., 1997-98; project mgr. Chateau Travel, Carlson Mktg. Group, 1998—2002; project leader Vision 2000 Travel Group, 2002—. Mem. adv. com. sporting goods bus. program Sir Sandford Fleming Coll., 1994-98. Mem. Jr. League Montreal (bd. dirs., chmn. coms. 1987-92). Avocations: skiing, golf, reading, travel, sports. Home: 302 Perrault Rosemere PQ Canada J7A 1B9

HOPPER, DAVID HENRY, theologian, educator; b. Cranford, NJ, July 31, 1927; s. Orion Cornelius and Julia Margaret (Weitzel) H.; m. Nancy Ann Nelson, June 10, 1967 (div. June 1984); children: Sara Elizabeth, Kathryn Ann, Rachel Suzanne. BA, Yale U., 1950; BD, ThM, Princeton Theol. Sem., 1953, ThD, 1959. Ordained Presbyn. minister, 1961. Asst. prof. Macalester Coll., St. Paul, 1959-67, assoc. prof., 1967-73, James Wallace prof. of religion, 1973—2001, prof. emeritus, 2001—. Author: Tillich: A Theological Portrait, 1967 (N.J. Authors award 1968), A Dissent on Bonhoeffer, 1975, Technology, Theology, and the Idea of Progress, 1991. With USN, 1945-46. Recipient Newberry ACM Faculty fellow, 1992-93, Templeton Found. Sci./Religion Course award, 1996. Mem. Internat. Bonhoeffer Soc., Hist. of Sci. Soc., Kierkegaard Soc. Home: 1757 Lincoln Ave Saint Paul MN 55105-1954 E-mail: dhhopper@earthlink.net.

HOPPER, DENNIS, actor, writer, photographer, film director; b. Dodge City, Kans., May 17, 1936; s. Jay and Marjorie Hopper; m. Brooke Hayward, 1961 (div. 1969); 1 child, Marin; m. Michelle Phillips, Oct. 31, 1970 (div. Nov. 8, 1970); m. Doria Halprin, 1972 (div. 1976); 1 child: Ruthana; m. Katherine LaNasa, June 17, 1989 (div. April 1992); 1 child, Henry Lee.; m. Victoria Duffy, Apr. 13, 1996; 1 child. Student, San Diego pub. schs. Participated in 2002 Whitney Biennial. Appeared in films: Rebel Without a Cause, 1955, Jagged Edge, 1955, I Died A Thousand Times, 1955, Giant, 1956, The Steel Jungle, 1956, Story of Mankind, 1957, Gunfight at the O.K. Corral, 1957, From Hell to Texas, 1958, The Youngland, 1959, Key Witness, 1960, Night Tide, 1963, The Sons of Katie Elder, 1965, Queen of Blood, 1966, The Trip, 1967, Glory Stompers, 1967, Hang 'Em High, 1968, Cool Hand Luke, 1967, True Grit, 1969, Easy Rider, 1969, The Last Movie, 1971, Kid Blue, 1973, Hex, 1973, The Sky is Falling, 1975, James Dean-The First American Teenager, Mad Dog Morgan, 1976, Tracks, 1976, American Friend, 1978, Apocalypse Now, 1979, Wild Times, 1980, Out of the Blue, 1980, King of the Mountain, 1981, Renacer, 1981, Human Highway, 1981, Rumble Fish, 1983, The Osterman Weekend, 1983, Slagskämpen, 1984, My Science Project, 1985, O.C. & Stiggs, 1985, White Star, 1985, The Texas Chainsaw Massacre Part 2, 1986, Blue Velvet, 1986 (Montreal World Film Festival award 1986), Hoosiers, 1986 (Acad. award nomination 1987), River's Edge, 1987, Black Widow, 1987, Pick-up Artist, 1987, Straight to Hell, 1987, Riders of the Storm, 1988, Let it Rock, 1988, Blood Red, 1989, Flashback, 1990, Motion & Emotion, 1990, Chattahoochie, 1990, Superstar: Life and Times of Andy Warhol, 1990, Backtrack, 1991, Sunset Heat, 1991, Schneeweißrosenrot, 1991, Indian Runner, 1991, Hearts of Darkness, 1991, Paris Trout, 1991, Eye of the Storm, 1991, Super Mario Brothers, 1993, Boiling Point, 1993, True Romance, 1993, Red Rock West, 1993, Speed, 1994, Chasers, 1994, Waterworld, 1995, Search and Destroy, 1995, Carried Away, 1996, Last Days of Frankie the Fly, 1996, Cannes Man, 1996, Basquiat, 1996, Top of the World, 1997, Road Ends, 1997, Good Life, 1997, Star Truckers, 1997, Blackout, 1997, Tycus, 1998, Meet the Deedles, 1998, Sources, 1999, Lured Innocence, 1999, Justice, 1999, Jesus' Son, 1999, Bad City Blues, 1999, EdTV, 1999, Straight Shooter, 1999, Spreading Ground, 2000, Luck of the Draw, 2000, Held for Ransom, 2000, Choke, 2000, Ticker, 2001, Knockaround Guys, 2001, L.A.P.D.: To Protect and to Serve, 2001, Unspeakable, 2002, Leo, 2002, The Keeper, 2003, Out of Season, 2004, House of 9, 2004, Americano, 2005, The Crow: Wicked Prayer, 2005, Land of the Dead, 2005, (narrator) Inside Deep Throat, 2005; writer, dir. Easy Rider 1969 (Cannes Film Festival Best New Dir. award 1969), The Last Movie, 1971, Out of the Blue, 1980, Chasers, 1994, Colors, 1988, The Hot Spot, 1990, Paris Trout, 1991, Double Crossed, 1991, Sunset Heat, 1992, Nails, 1992; TV movies include The Heart of Justice, 1993, Samson and Delilah, 1996, Marlon Brando: The Wild One, 1996, The Last Days of Frankie the Fly, 1996, Jason and the Argonauts, 2000, Firestarter 2: Rekindled, 2002, The Piano Player, 2002, The Groovenians (voice), 2002, Suspense, 2003, Last Ride, 2004; TV series: Flatland, 2002, E-Ring, 2005-; exhibited photographs at Fort Worth Art Mus., Denver Art Mus., Wichita Art Mus., Cochran Art Mus., Spileto Mus., Parco Gallery, Tokyo, Osaka, Kumatomo, Japan; author: (photographic book) Out of the Sixties, 1986. Recipient Best Film award Venice Film Festival, 1971, Best Film award Cannes Film Festival, 1980. Office: Internat Creative Mgmt 8942 Wilshire Blvd Beverly Hills CA 90211

HOPPER, JACK RUDD, chemical engineering professor; b. Highlands, Tex., May 12, 1937; s. Bonnie Preston and Rosa Mae Hopper; m. Marilyn Joyce Spears, May 30, 1958; children: Connie, Bradley. Student, Lee Coll., 1957; BSChemE, Tex. A&M U., 1959; MChemE, U. Del., 1964; PhD, La. State U., 1969. Rsch. engr. Esso Rsch. and Engring., Baytown, Tex., 1959-67; asst. prof. chem. engring. Lamar U., Beaumont, Tex., 1969-72, assoc. prof. chem. engring., 1972-75, prof. chem. engring., 1975—, chair chem. engring. dept., 1974—99, dir. engring. grad. studies, 1989-99, liaison hazardous waste alternatives ctr., 1987-88, dean coll. engring., 1999—, interim assoc. provost for rsch., 2006—; interim dir Gulf Coast Rsch. Ctr., 1993-94, assoc. dir., 1995-97, dir., 1997-99, Tex. Hazardous Waste Rsch. Ctr., 1993—, Tex. Ctr. Tech. Incubation, 2004—. Cons. J. M. Montgomery, New Orleans, 1991-92, Texaco Chem., Port Arthur, Tex., 1989-90, Star Enterprise, 1990-93, Tex. Internat. Ednl. Consortium, Austin, 1991-93, Mobil Chem., 1993. Mem. editl. bd. Waste Mgmt., 1992-96, co-editor 1996-2001; contbr. articles to profl. publs. Recipient Dow Outstanding Faculty award Am. Soc. for Engring. Edn., 1971, Outstanding Alumni award Lee Coll., 1981. Fellow AIChE; mem. Tex. Soc. Profl. Engs. (Engr. of Yr. award Sabine chpt. 2004). Lutheran. Achievements include inventions in field. Office: Lamar U 4400 MLK Pkwy Beaumont TX 77705

HOPPER, STEPHEN RODGER, hospital administrator; b. Chgo., Aug. 28, 1949; s. Rodger Patterson and Dorothy Ann (Newberg) H.; m. Janet Sue Waddill, June 10, 1972; children: Nathan John, Amanda Sue. BA, Ill. Coll., 1971; MHA, U. Minn., 1974. Adminstrv. resident Rochester (Minn.) Meth. Hosp., 1973-74; dir. support svcs. Jennie Edmundson Hosp., Council Bluffs, Iowa, 1974-78; asst. adminstr. Trinity Meml. Hosp., Cudahy, Wis., 1978-83, sr. v.p. med. svcs., 1983-84; pres., chief exec. officer McDonough Dist. Hosp., Macomb, Ill., 1985—. Bd. dirs. Midamerica Nat. Bank, Canton, Ill., chmn bd., 2004-06; bd. dirs. VHA MidAm. Bd. dirs. Macomb Area Indsl. Devel., 1985—, Wesley Village, 2007—. Fellow Am. Coll. Healthcare Execs.; mem. Ill. Hosp. Assn. (past pres. region 1-B, bd. dirs. 1992-95, mem. venture corp. bd. 1999—), Macomb C. of C. (bd. dirs. 1990-94), Rotary (pres.-elect Macomb 1995-96, pres. 1996-97, asst. dist. gov. 2000-03). Avocations: golf, reading, computers, travel. Home: 112 W Totem Trl Macomb IL 61455-1272 Office: McDonough Dist Hosp 525 E Grant St Macomb IL 61455-3318 Office Phone: 309-836-1675. Business E-Mail: srhopper@mdh.org.

HOPPING, JANET MELINDA, educational association administrator; b. Washington, Dec. 27, 1943; d. Russell Leroy and Janet L. (Cloud) H. B.S., Tex. Christian U., 1965; M.Ed., Ga. State U., 1977. Edn. cert., Ga. Tchr., Littleton, Colo., 1965-68, East Point, Ga., 1969, Atlanta, 1969-78; Title IVc coordinator Fulton County Schs., Atlanta, 1978-81, middle sch. project coordinator, 1981-82; asst. prin. West Middle Sch., East Point, 1982-83; prin. Holcomb Bridge Middle Sch., Alpharetta, Ga., 1983-91, Crabapple Middle Sch., Roswell, Ga., 1991-98; exec. dir. Ga. Mid. Sch. Assn., 1998—; mem. Nat. Forum to Accelerate Mid. Grades Reform, So. Forum to Accelerate Mid. Grades Reform, Ga. Alliance of Mid. Level Excellence; co-chair Ga. Lighthouse Schs. to Watch Program; cons., trainer various sch. systems. Mem. ASCD, Am. Soc. Assn. Execs., Nat. Middle Sch. Assn. (bd. trustees 1989-91), Ga. Middle Sch. Assn. (pres. 1984-85, exec. dir. 1991—), Nat. Assn. Secondary Sch. Prins., Prins. Inst. (adv. bd.), Atlanta Com. for the Olympic Games (edn. task force mem. 1990-96, Olympic Day in Schs. steering com. 1989-96), Pi Beta Phi. Democrat. Roman Catholic. Avocations: golf, tennis. Home: 6106 Kayron Dr NE Atlanta GA 30328-4112 Home Phone: 404-252-9417; Office Phone: 404-256-4005. Personal E-mail: LHopping@aol.com.

HOPPING, RICHARD LEE, retired academic administrator; b. Dayton, Ohio, July 26, 1928; s. Lavon Lee and Dorothy Marie (Anderson) H.; m. Patricia Louise Vance, June 30, 1951; children: Ronald, Debra, Jerrold. Student, Chaffey Coll., 1947-48, U. Dayton, 1948-49, Sinclair Coll., 1948-49; BS, OD, So. Coll. Optometry, 1952, DOS (hon.), 1972; DSc (hon.), SUNY, 1995, DOS (hon.), 2004. Practice optometry, Dayton, Ohio, 1953-73; pres. So. Calif. Coll. Optometry, Fullerton, 1973-97, pres. emeritus, 1997—. Mem. Nat. Acads. of Practice, 1983—; chmn. Nat. Acad. Practice in Optometry, 1985-89; vice chmn. 13th dist. med. quality rev. com., State of Calif. Bd. Med. Quality Assurance, 1985-93; mem. adv. bd. St. Jude Hosp., 1985—2000; nat. spokesperson Better Vision Inst., 1988-2000; cons. in field. Contbr. numerous articles on vision and health care to profl. publs. V.p. Orange County coun. Boy Scouts Am., Calif., 1977-79, adv. coun., 1979-94; mem. Coun. Assocs. of Red Cross, North Orange County Svc. Ctr., 1978-80; adv. coun. YWCA, North Orange County, 1984-92. Recipient Orange County Retinitis Pigmentosa award of Excellence in field of vision care, 1988, award of Excellence Vision-America, 1991, Dirs. Choice award Optical Labs. Assn., 1995, Leo award of Excellence in Global Eye Care Nat. Eye Rsch. Found., 1995, People of Vision award Prevent Blindness Am., 1997, Lifetime Achievement award So. Coll. Optometry, 1997; named Optimist of Yr., Dayton View Optimists, 1956; named to Nat. Optometry Hall of Fame, 2003. Fellow APHA (Vision Care Disting. Achievement award 1984), Am. Acad. Optometry (chmn. primary care optometry sect. 1973-79, chmn. awards com. 1981-90); mem. Am. Optometric Assn. (pres. 1971-72, chmn. profl. enhancement adv. com. 1982-89, Calif. Optometrist of Yr. 1988, chair industry rels. com. 1989-95, chair nat. ednl. summit conf. 1990-91, chair Nat. Optometric Edn. Summit com. 1991-92, chair centennial adv. com. 1996-98, Scope of Optometric Practice Conf. 1992, vice-chmn. found. sci., edn. and charity 2006—, Nat. Optometerist of Yr. 1988, Dr. Raymond I. Meyers award 1990, Disting. Svc. award 1993), Calif. Optometric Assn. (hon. life, jud. coun., Optometrist of Yr. 1988, Paul Yarwood Meml. award 1997), Assn. Ind. Calif. Colls. and Univs. (trustee 1973-97), Optometric Ext. Programs Found. (hon. life), Assn. Schs. and Colls. of Optometry (pres. 1983-85), Ohio Optometric Assn. (pres. 1964-65, Ohio Optometrist of Yr. 1962, hon. life), Retinitis Pigmentosa Internat. (adv. exec. com. 1984-88), Dayton Jr. C. of C. (Man of Yr.), Lincoln Club of Orange County (chmn. ethics com. 1988-92). Personal E-mail: rhoppingod@aol.com.

HOPPING, WILLIAM RUSSELL, hospitality industry consultant, appraiser; b. Balt., May 3, 1947; s. Russell Leroy and Janet Louise (Cloud) H.; m. Catherine Wilson; 1 child, William Alexander. BS in Hotel Adminstrn., Cornell U., 1969; MBA, U. Denver, 1978. Mgr. Sylvania (Ohio) Country Club, 1972-77; sr. cons. Pannell Kerr Forster, Denver, 1978-82; cons. Ginther Wycoff Grp., Denver, 1982-85; pres. W.R. Hopping & Co., Inc., Denver, 1985—. Mem. adv. bd. travel and tourism dept. Arapahoe C.C., 1998. Vol., Big Bros., Inc., Denver, 1990-2000; chmn. adv. bd. U. Denver Profl. Career Devel. Prog., 1987-88, chmn. task force, Career and Placement Ctr., 1989; mem. City of Littleton Historic Preservation Bd., 2003—, chmn., 2007-. 1st lt. U.S. Army, 1970-72. Mem. Appraisal Inst., Internat. Soc. Hospitality Cons. (pres. 1990-91, chmn. 1991-93, chmn. emeritus, 1993—), Cornell Soc. Hotelmen (pres. Rocky Mountain chpt. 1984-85). Avocations: bicycling, skiing. Office: W R Hopping & Co Inc 5773 Shasta Cir Littleton CO 80123-2732

HOPPS, RAYMOND, JR., lawyer, film producer; b. Balt., July 26, 1949; s. Raymond Hopps Sr. and Ella Louise Dixon. BA cum laude, Howard U., 1971; JD, Loyola U., Chgo., 1974. Bar: Ill. 1975. CEO, art atty. Cmty. Legal Counsel, Chgo., 1972; staff and adminstr. Chgo. Vol. Legal Svcs., 1972-74; assoc. Archie B. Weston Sr. Ltd., Chgo., 1975-77; pvt. practice Chgo., 1977-78; film prodr., 1978; prodr. N.Y. Film Colony, 1979; with svc. work Internat. Econs.; owner, prodr., artist Am. Oriental Internat. Ltd., Balt., 1980—. Staff rschr. Task Force for Cmty. Broadcasting, Chgo., 1973-78; atty. cons. Assn. of AudioVisual Prodrs., Chgo., 1978; coord. N.Y. Film Colony, 1979; staff atty. Ebony Talent Assocs., Chgo. Composer: Concerto Impossible, 1987, For Your Eyes Only, 1981, Victory for the Free Planet, 1991; author: (prose) Master E, 1986; composer, author: Free Planet, 1991; writer, film prodr. for screen. Staff artist Eubie Blake Cultural Ctr., Balt., 1990—; assoc. Nat. Football League and Balt. Ravens 2001 Super Bowl Champions. With USAF, 1968-91, brig. gen. Res. Mem. NAACP, Internat. Mid. East Assn., Am. Mgmt. Assn., Equal Opportunity Found., Jim Straw Heritage Exch., WFI Corp. Democrat. Avocations: music, dance, films, walking. Office: AMI Ltd Motion Pictures PO Box 67585 Baltimore MD 21215-0016

HOPSON, CRAIG, chef; Demi chef de partie, commis chef The Grange restaurant, Hyatt Regency Sanctuary Cove, Queensland, Australia; sr. chef de partie Gekko Restaurant, Sydney; chef Berties Restaurant, Geneva, Restaurant Troigros, Paris, Restaurant Guy Savoy, Paris, Lucas Carton; exec. chef Circa Restaurant, Brisbane, Australia, 1999; sous chef Victor's, New Orleans; chef de cuisine Paris Restaurant, Phila., Picholine, NYC; chef Artisanal, NYC. Named one of NYC's Rising Stars, StarChefs.com, 2007. Office: Picholine 35 W 64th New York NY 10023 Office Phone: 212-501-7457.*

HOPSON, EDWIN SHARP, lawyer; b. Louisville, Apr. 23, 1945; s. Henry Dockins and Martha (Linton) H.; m. Jane Mayo Fitzpatrick, July 20, 1968; children: Edwin Hopson Jr., Martha. BSL, U. Louisville, 1967, JD, 1969; LLM, George Washington U., 1971. Bar: Ky. 1969, Fla. 1969, U.S. Supreme Ct. 1972, U.S. Dist. Ct. (we. dist.) Ky. 1974, U.S. Ct. Appeals (6th cir.) 1977. Atty. Solicitor's Office, U.S. Dept. Labor, Washington, 1969-72; field atty. NLRB, Balt., 1972-74; assoc. Tarrant, Combs, Blackwell & Bullitt, Louisville, 1974-77; ptnr. Tarrant, Combs & Bullitt, Louisville, 1977-80, Wyatt, Tarrant & Combs, L.L.P., Louisville, 1980—. Mem. Labor and Employment Practice Group. Co-author: The Developing Labor Law, 2002, 5th edit., 2006; editor (chpt.) How Arbitration Works, 1989, 2nd edit., 2001—; chpt. editor: Discipline and Discharge in Arbitration, 1998, supplement, 2001. Bd. dirs. Bellewood Presbyn. Children's Home, Louisville, 1988-96, pres., 1991-93; bd. dirs. Louisville Ballet, 1991-92, v.p., 1992-93, pres., 1993-94; bd. dirs. Bellewood Children's Found., 1995-02, pres., 1995-96. Fellow Coll. Labor and Employment Lawyers, Inc.; mem. ABA (co-chmn. pub. of arbitration awards subcom. 2000-03, adr. com. of labor and employment sect. 1985—), FBA (chpt. pres. 1991-92), Louisville Bar Assn. (co-chmn. labor and employment law sect. 1982-83), Ky. Bar Assn. (co-chmn. labor and employment law sect. 1987-89, mem. ho. of dels. 1996-02, chair pub. com. 1989-91, 01—, editor Bench and Bar Mag.). Republican. Presbyterian. Avocations: flying, various sports, reading. Home: 3003 Lightheart Rd Louisville KY 40222-6138 Office: Wyatt Tarrant & Combs LLP 2800 PNC Plz Louisville KY 40202-2823 Office Phone: 502-562-7360. Business E-Mail: ehopson@wyattfirm.com.

HOPSON, EVERETT GEORGE, retired lawyer; b. Stillwell, Ill., Sept. 4, 1922; s. Carman Roy and Adella (George) H.; m. Doris May Hutchins, Aug. 15, 1953 (dec.); children: Christine E., Eugene G. AA, Springfield Jr. Coll., 1942; BS, U. Ill., 1947, JD, 1949; MS in Internat. Affairs, George Washington U., 1967; disting. grad., Air War Coll., 1967. Bar: Ill. 1949, U.S. Ct. Mil. Appeals 1957, U.S. Supreme Ct. 1957. Dep. collector U.S. Treasury, IRS, Carlinville, Ill., 1949-51; commd. officer USAF, 1951, advanced to col., judge advocate, 1951-71; spl. asst. to asst. sec. def. Dept. Def., Washington, 1971; sr. atty. U.S. Postal Svc., Washington, 1972-73; dep. chief gen. law divsn. USAF, Washington, 1973-75, chief gen. law divsn., 1975-94, ret., 1994. Trustee USAF JAG Sch. Found., 1994; trustee ESL immigrant ministries United Meth. Ch., 2004. With US Army, 1943—46. Decorated Legion of Merit; recipient Presdl. Rank of Meritorious Exec., USAF, 1981, 87, 92, Freedoms Found. award, 1961, 62, 66. Mem. ABA, Ill. Bar Assn. (sr. counsellor 1999), Fed. Bar Assn., Judge Advocates Assn., Am. Inns of Ct., Phi Alpha Delta. Independent. Methodist. Avocations: coin collecting/numismatics, gardening. Home: 9719 Limoges Dr Fairfax VA 22032-1115 Personal E-mail: eghdmh@aol.com. *Helpful advice and good counsel need to make sense and be reasonable to be effective. In my professional career and in life, I have attempted, with some degree of success, to let common sense prevail and reason rule the land.*

HOPSON, JAMES WARREN, publishing executive; b. St. Louis, May 24, 1946; s. David Warren and Ruth L. (Dierkes) H.; m. Julie Ann Eastlack, Dec. 21, 1968; children: John, Benjamin, Gillian. BJ, U. Mo., 1968; MBA, Harvard U., 1973. Project mgr. Des Moines Register & Tribune, 1973-76, dir. ops., 1976-78, circulation dir., 1978-79; gen. mgr. Corpus Christi (Tex.) Caller Times, 1979-82; pub. Middlesex News, Framingham, Mass., 1982-88; pres. N.E. Group-Harte-Hanks Comms., Framingham, 1984-88; pub. The Press of Atlantic City, N.J., 1989-94; pres. Community Newspaper Co., Boston, 1994-95, Thomson Ctrl. Ohio, Newark, 1995-2000; pub. Wis. State Jour., Madison, Wis., 2000—; v.p. publishing Lee Enterprises, Madison, 2000—. Pres. Vol. Ctr. Atlantic County, 1992—; treas. DeCordova Mus., Lincoln, Mass., 1983-89, dir., 1983-89; sec. Family Health Svc. Ctrl. Ohio, 1997—, treas.; bd. dirs. Audit Bur. of Circulations, 1999—; bd, dirs. Madison Art Ctr., United Way of Dane County. 1st lt. U.S. Army, 1968-73, Vietnam. Mem. New Eng. Newspaper Assn. (chmn. circulation com. 1986-88), Mass. Newspaper Pub. Assn. (dir. 1984-88), Metrowest C. of C. (chmn. 1987-88, dir. audit bur. of circulations 1999—), Greater Madison C. of C. (bd. dirs.) Office: 1901 Fish Hatchery Rd Madison WI 53713-1248

HOPWOOD, HOWARD HOPPY PERRY, military officer; b. Mountain Top, Ark., Mar. 16, 1944; s. Ira Homer Hopwood and Hallie Mae Dunn; m. Mary M. White, Oct. 8, 1945; children: Rebecca Marie McDonell, James Howard. BS in religious Edn., So. Christian U., Montgomery, Ala., 1978. Evangelist, deacon, elder church of Christ, 1969. Sr. master sgt. Hdqs. MAC/LGME USAF, Scott AFB, Ill., 1975—79, chief master sgt. Hdqs. USAFE/LGMA Kiserslautern, Germany, 1981—85. With integrated def. sys. The Boeing Co., Oklahoma City, 1985—. Evangelist, deacon, elder ch. of Christ, Melbourne, Fla., Germany, 1975—2003. Decorated Meritorious Svc. Medal with 3 oak leaf clusters, Air Force Commendation Medal with 31oak leaf clusters, Meritorious Svc. Award. Mem.: Am. Legion (life; KS Post 0062). Conservative. Church Of Christ. Avocations: collecting military memorabilia, history, philsophy, writing, photography. Home: 2318 Ripple Creek Ln Edmond OK 73003 Personal E-mail: hophopwood@aol.com. E-mail: howard.p.hopwood@boeing.com.

HORA, HEINRICH, physicist; b. Bodenbach-Elbe, July 1, 1931; arrived in US, 1967, permanent resident, 1967; s. Otto and Elisabeth (Schneider) H.; m. Rosemarie Weiler, July 1, 1956 (dec. 2007); children: Michael, Ulrike McCluskey, Maria Carmody, Beate Steller, Dorle Minikin, Regina Law. Dipl. Phys., U. Halle-Wittenberg, Germany, 1956; Dr.rer.nat., U. Jena, 1960; DSc, U. New South Wales, 1981. Rsch. asst. to dir. R & D

Zeiss, Jena, 1956-60, Oberkochen, 1960-61; rsch. scientist IBM Lab., Boblingen, Germany, 1961-62, Max-Planck-Inst. Plasmaphysik, Garching, Germany, 1962-67, prin. rsch. scientist, 1969-75; sr. rsch. scientist Westinghouse Rsch. Ctr., Pitts., 1967-68; assoc. prof. Rensselaer poly. Inst. - Hartford Grad. Ctr., 1969-75; prof. theoretical physics, head dept. theoretical physics U. New South Wales, Sydney, 1975—92, prof. emeritus, 1992—. Adj. prof. U. Western Sydney, 1999—; vis. prof. U. Rochester, 1973-74, U. Bern, 1978-79, U. Tokyo, Weizmann Inst., 1984, U. Iowa, U. Giessen, 1985, 89, U. Osaka, 1990; sci. assoc. CERN, Geneva, Switzerland, 1990-92; Konrad-Zuse prof. elec. engring. Regensburg, 1993-95; guest prof. Osaka U., 1996; mem. convenor Dirac Funds for Theoretical Physics, U. New South Wales, 1979-92; lectr. Nuclear Club Wall St., 1978; cons. Rockford Corp., Vancouver, 1990—. Author: Laser Plasmas and Nuclear Energy, 1975, Nonlinear Plasma Dynamics at Laser Irradiation, 1979, Physics of Laser Driven Plasmas, 1981, Plasmas at High Temperature and Density, 1991, Elektrodynamik, 1994, Nonlinear Force and Ponderomotion, 1996, Innovation & Technology, 1998;: 2d edit., 2000, Laser Plasma Physics: Forces and the Nonlinearity Principle, 2000, Klimakatastrophe, 2007; author: (with others) Equation of State, 1986, Foundations of Equations of State, 2002; editor-in-chief: Laser and Particle Beams: Physics of High Energy Density, 1982—91, emeritus:, 1991—; co-editor: Laser Interaction and Related Plasma Phenomena 12 vols., 1971—93, Directions in Physics by P.A.M. Dirac, 1977, Edward Teller Lectures, 2005; mem. editl. bd.: Chinese Laser Jour., 1988—95, Czechoslovak Jour. Physics, 1992—2006; contbr. articles to profl. jours. Mem. bd. City Coun. Ottobrunn, Bavaria, 1972-75. Recipient medal Lebedev Inst. Acad. Sci., USSR, 1978, Ritter-von-Gerstner medal, 1985, German Sports Gold medal, 1982, H & E Heraeus award, 1989, Edward Teller medal, 1991, Dirac medal, 2002, Ernst-Mach-Medal, 2002; USAF grantee, 1972; vis. fellow Australian Nat. U., Canberra, 1994-98. Fellow Inst. Physics (London), Australian Inst. Physics (dir. New South Wales 1979-85); mem. Am. Phys. Soc., German Phys. Soc., Soc. Advance Fusion Energy (N.Y. dir. 1979—), Internat. Soc. for Applied Optics, Royal Soc. of NSW (councillor), Rotary. Roman Catholic. Achievements include patents in field. Home: PO Box 343 Connels Point NSW 2221 Australia Office: U New South Wales Dept Theoretical Physics Sydney NSW 2052 Australia Business E-Mail: h.hora@unsw.edu.au.

HORAHAN, EDWARD BERNARD, III, lawyer; b. Drexel Hill, Pa., Dec. 30, 1951; s. Edward Bernard and Ann Veronica (Schneeweis) H.; m. Rebecca Joy Fusco, Mar. 13, 1976; 1 child, Elizabeth Joy. BA, LaSalle Coll., Phila., 1973; JD, Yale U., 1976. Bar: D.C. 1976. Staff atty. office of gen. counsel SEC, Washington, 1976-78; staff atty. office of solicitor, plan benefits security divsn. U.S. Dept. Labor, Washington, 1978-80; assoc. Arter & Hadden, Washington, 1980-84; ptnr. Parker, Chapin, Flattau & Klimpl, Washington, 1984-88, Stroock & Stroock & Lavan, Washington, 1988-93; pvt. practice Law Offices of Edward B. Horahan III, Washington, 1993-96; counsel Groom Law Group, Washington, 1996-2001, Dechert, Washington, 2001—. Mem. ABA. Office: 1775 Eye St NW Washington DC 20006 E-mail: edward.horahan@dechert.com.

HORAK, JAN-CHRISTOPHER, filmmaker, educator, curator; b. Bad Münstereifel, Fed. Republic Germany, May 1, 1951; came to U.S., 1951; s. Jerome V. and Giselle (Offermanns) H.; m. Martha F. Schirn, May 17, 1988; 1 child, Gianna. BA, U. Del., 1973; MS, Boston U., 1975; PhD, Westfälische Wilhelms-U., Münster, Germany, 1984. Intern Internat. Mus. Photography, Rochester, NY, 1975-76, assoc. curator George Eastman House, 1984-87, curator film, 1987-90, sr. curator, 1990-94; asst. prof. film studies U. Rochester, 1985-90, assoc. prof., 1990-93, prof., 1994; dir. Münchner Filmmuseum, Munich, 1994-98; prof. Hochschule f. Fernsehen u. Film, 1995-98; dir. Archives and Collections Universal Studios, LA, 1998-00; prof. UCLA, 1999—; curator Hollywood Entertainment Mus., 2000—06; acting dir. Moving Image Archives Studies, UCLA, 2006—. Panelist, chmn. film panel NY State Coun. Arts, NYC, 1986—89; cons. USIA, 1988—90; archivists' adv. bd. The Film Found., NYC, 1990—94; v.p., pres. Assn. Moving Image Archivists, 1991—93; exec. com. Internat. Fedn. Film Archives, 1993—95, Kuratorium Junger Deutscher Film, 1995—97; peer reviewer Inst. for Mus. and Libr. Svcs., 2004—05. Author: Anti-Nazi Filme der Emigration, 1984, Fluchtpunkt Hollywood, 1986, The Dream Merchants, 1989, Lovers of Cinema: The First American Film Avant-Garde, 1995, Berge, Licht und Traum: Arnold Fanck und der deutsche Bergfilm, 1997, Making Images Move: Photography and Avant-Garde Cinema, 1997; editor: Film und Foto der 20er Jahre, 1979, Helmar Lerski, 1982; founding editor: The Moving Image, 2001—; contbr. articles to profl. jours. Recipient Louis B. Mayer award Mayer Found., Am. Film Inst., 1975; Heinrich Herz Stiftung fellow, 1979-81. Mem.: Internat. Assn. Audio-Visual Media and History, Soc. Exile Studies, Soc. Cinema Studies. Avocations: travel, skiing, swimming. Office: 545 Sierra Vista Ave Pasadena CA 91107 Personal E-mail: jchrishorak@aol.com. Business E-Mail: jchorak@ucla.edu.

HORAN, ANTHONY J., diversified financial services company executive; BS, Manhattan Coll., 1968; SM, MIT; MBA, NYU; JD, Yale Law Sch. Associated with J. Aron divsn. Goldman Sachs & Co.; associated with Law Firm of Paul Weiss, Law Firm of Jones, Day, Reavis & Pogue; atty. Bankers Trust Co.; corp. sec. J.P. Morgan Chase & Co., 1996—. Mem.: Am. Soc. Corp. Secs. (bd. dirs.). Office: JP Morgan Chase & Co 270 Park Ave New York NY 10017-2070

HORAN, DOUGLAS S., lawyer, utilities executive; b. 1949; BA, Case Western Reserve U.; MA, Johns Hopkins U.; JD, Northeastern U. Joined BEC Energy, 1977, gen. counsel, 1993—98, sr. v.p. strategy and law, gen. counsel, 1998—99; sr. v.p. strategy, law and policy NSTAR Electric & Gas Corp., Westwood, Mass., 1999—2000, sr. v.p. strategy, law and policy, sec., gen. counsel, 2000—. Bd. mem. Rsch. Bureau, Boston. Mem.: ABA. Office: NSTAR Electric & Gas Corp P1700 800 Boylston St Boston MA 02199-8003*

HORAN, GARY S., healthcare executive; BS in Economics, St. Peter's Coll., Jersey City, NJ, 1971; MS in Healthcare Adminstrn., George Washington U., Sch. Govt. and Bus., Dept. Health Care Adminstrn. V.p. hosp. ops. NYU Med. Ctr.; exec. v.p. St. Vincent's Med. Ctr., Richmond, NY; sr. v.p. St. Vincent's Hosp. and Med. Ctr., NYC; pres., CEO Our Lady of Mercy Healthcare System, Inc., Bronx, NY, 1990—2001, Trinitas Hosp., NJ, 2001—. Bd. dirs. Health Systems Agy. of N.Y.C., Daytop Village, Combined Coordinating Coun., chmn. coun.'s fin. com.; bd. govs. Am. Coll. of Healthcare Execs. Mem. Cath. Health Care Network, chmn. managed care task force; chmn. bd. dirs. Hosp. Alliance NJ; bd. dir. NJ C.ofC. Mem. Greater N.Y. Hosp. Assn. (vice chmn., bd. dirs., chmn. 2007-), Healthcare Assn. N.Y. State (bd. dirs.), Met. Health Adminstrs. Assn., Hosp. Assn. NY State (bd. dir. 1995-, former chmn.); fellow Am. Coll. Healthcare Executives (bd. gov., regent) Office: Trinitas Hosp 225 Williamson St Elizabeth NJ 07207*

HORAN, RICHARD T., JR., lawyer; b. Washington, Dec. 24, 1961; BA summa cum laude, James Madison U., 1984; JD, U. Va., 1987. Bar: Va. 1988. Law clk. to Hon. James C. Cacheris, U.S. Dist. Ct., Ea. Dist. Va., 1987—88; ptnr.-exec. com. Hogan & Hartson LLP, Mc Lean, Va., 1988—95, ptnr., 1996—, mem. exec. com., 2005—07, dir. corp., securities and fin. practice group, 2003—. Named Leading Individual Lawyer corp. mergers and acquisitions, Chambers USA: Am.'s Leading Lawyers Bus., 2005. Mem.: ABA, Va. Bar Assn. Office: Hogan & Hartson LLP 8300 Greensboro Dr Ste 1100 Mc Lean VA 22102 Office Phone: 703-610-6100. Office Fax: 703-610-6200. Business E-Mail: rthoran@hhlaw.com.

HORCHOW, S(AMUEL) ROGER, marketing consultant; b. Cin., July 3, 1928; m. Carolyn Pfeifer, Dec. 29, 1960; children: Regen Horchow Fearon, Elizabeth Horchow Routman, Sally Horchow McCauley. BA, Yale U., 1950, DLHD (hon.), 1999. Buyer Foley's, Houston, 1953-60; v.p. Neiman-Marcus, Dallas, 1960-68, 69-71; pres. Design Research, Cambridge, Mass., 1968-69, Kenton Collection, Dallas, 1971-73; chmn. Horchow Collection, Dallas, 1973-90. Author: Elephants in Your Mailbox, 1979, Living in Style, 1981; prodr. Crazy for You, 1991-95; co-prodr. Kiss Me Kate, 1999. (Broadway) Curtains, 2006; co-author: The Art of Friendship, 2005. Bd. dirs. Jefferson Award for Pub. Svc., Yale Art Galley, Com. for Preservation of the White House, Found. Art and Preservation of Embassies. Mem. Yale Club (N.Y.C.), Nantucket Yacht Club, Knickerbocker Club, Birnam Wood Club. Office: 5722 Chatham Hill Rd Dallas TX 75225-3208 Office Phone: 214-692-1954. E-mail: C4U@aol.com.

HORD, JOY M., lawyer; AB in Polit. Sci., Davidson Coll., 1992; JD, Vanderbilt Sch. Law, 1995. Ptnr. Parker, Poe, Adams & Bernstein, L.L.P., Charlotte, NC, 1995—. Office: Parker Poe Adams & Bernstein LLP 401 S Tryon St Ste 3000 Charlotte NC 28202 Office Phone: 704-372-9000. Office Fax: 704-334-4706. E-mail: joyhord@parkerpoe.com.

HORE, JOHN EDWARD, retired commodity futures educator; b. Dec. 13, 1929; s. Ernest and Doris Kathleen (Horton) H.; m. Diana King, May 3, 1958; children: Edward John Bruce, Celia Kathleen Hore Milne, Timothy Frank. BA with honors, King's Coll., Cambridge, Eng., 1952, MA, 1957. Chartered fin. analyst. Asst. sales mgr. Borthwicks, London, 1952-54; security analyst Dominion Securities, Toronto, Ont., Can., 1955-57; asst. mktg. mgr. Rio Algom, Toronto, 1957-61; dir. Bell, Gouinlock & Co., Toronto, 1961-75; v.p., dir. futures Can. Securities Inst., Toronto, 1979-94, seminar leader, 1980—2000. Founding sec. Can. Nuclear Assn.; past v.p. Brit. Can. Trade Assn. (now Brit. Can. Chamber Trade and Commerce); chmn. 1st Can. Internat. Futures Rsch. Seminar, 1985, also editor Proc., 2 vols., 1986; spkr. Can. Am. Inst. Conf. on Fin. Svcs. at Detroit-Windsor, 1989, compliance seminar Futures Industry Assn. at Alexandria, Va., 1990; chmn. Can. Futures Conf., 1986; chmn. Can. Internat. Futures Conf. and Rsch. Seminars, 1987-90, mng. editor Selected Papers 1988-91; cons. in field. Author: Trading on Canadian Futures Markets, 1984, 5th edit., 1993; co-author: CFA Inst. Standards of Practice Handbook, 1982 (Pres. Reagan Citation, 1984); co-editor: Canadian Securities Course, 1980—94. Gov. Montcrest Sch., 1970-73; mem. Commodity Futures Adv. Bd., Ont., 1989-95; apptd. mem. internat. com. Futures Industry Assn., Washington, 1988-91, rowing com. Upper Can. Coll., Toronto, 1982-86; pres. St. George's Soc. Toronto, 1978-80, chmn. edn. com., 1987. With Royal Army Ednl. Corps, 1948-49, Singapore. Mem.: CFA Inst. (bd. dirs. investment analysis stds. 1974—85, emeritus 1985), Toronto CFA Soc. (bd. dirs. 1968—71), Toronto Round Table (pres. 1999—2001), Royal Overseas League (pres. Ont. chpt. 1992—2004, vice-chmn. 2004—), Hurlingham Club (London), Arts and Letters Club Toronto (exec. com. 2000—05, treas. 2001—05), Univ. Club Toronto (bd. dirs. 1980—83, v.p. 1982—83), Leander Club (assoc.; Henley-on-Thames). Anglican. Avocations: history, music, poetry. Office: 185 Carlton St Toronto ON Canada M5A 2K7 Office Phone: 416-922-9227. Personal E-mail: johnhore@aol.com.

HORECKER, BERNARD LEONARD, retired biochemistry professor; b. Chgo., Oct. 31, 1914; s. Paul and Bessie (Bornstein) H.; m. Frances Goldstein, July 12, 1936; children: Doris Colgate, Marilyn Diamond Schnell, Linda Lally. BS, U. Chgo., 1936, PhD, 1939; Laureate honoris causa in Biol. Scis., U. Urbino, Italy, 1982. Rsch. assoc. chemistry U. Chgo., 1939-40; examiner U.S. Civil Svc. Commn., 1940-41; biochemist USPHS, NIH, Bethesda, Md., 1941-59; chief lab. of biochemistry and metabolism Nat. Inst. Arthritis and Metabolic Disease, 1956-59; professorial lectr. enzyme chemistry George Washington U., 1950-57; guest rsch.-worker Pasteur Inst., Paris, 1957-58; prof. microbiology, chmn. dept. NYU Coll. Medicine, 1959-63; prof. molecular biology, chmn. dept. Albert Einstein Coll. Medicine, 1963-72, assoc. dean for sci. affairs, 1971-72; mem. Roche Inst. Molecular Biology, Nutley, NJ, 1972-84, head Lab. Molecular Enzymology, 1977-84; adj. prof. Cornell U. Med. Coll., 1972-84, prof. biochemistry, 1984-89, prof. emeritus biochemistry, 1989, dean Grad. Sch. Med. Sci., 1984-92. Vis. prof. Albert Einstein Coll. Medicine, 1972-84; vis. prof. biochemistry U. Calif., 1954, U. Parana, Brazil, 1960, 63; vis. lectr. U. Ill., 1956; Ciba lectr. Rutgers U., 1962; Phillips lectr. Haverford Coll., 1965; vis. prof. Kyoto (Japan) U., 1967; vis. prof. biochemistry and molecular biology Cornell U., 1965; vis. prof. U. Ferrara, Italy; Reilly lectr. Notre Dame U., 1969; vis. lectr. U. Rotterdam, 1970; prof. honoris causa Fed. U. Parana, Curitiba, Brazil, 1981—; sci. adv. bd. Roche Inst. Molecular Biology, Nutley, NJ, 1967-72, chmn., 1971-72; mem. Rsch. Career Award com. Nat. Inst. Gen. Med. Scis., 1966-70; personnel com. Am. Cancer Soc., 1968-72, sci. adv. com. for biochemistry and chem. carcinogenesis, 1974-78, mem. Coun. for Rsch. and Clin. Investigation Awards, 1984-88; biology divsn. adv. com. Oak Ridge Nat. Lab., 1976-80; mem. Med. Scientist Tng. Program Sect. NIH, 1970-72. Editor Biochem. and Biophys. Rsch. Communications, 1959-89, Current Topics in Cellular Regulation, 1969-89, Archives Biochemistry and Biophysics, 1960-68; chmn. editl. bd. Archives of Biochemistry and Biophysics, 1968-84; contbr. articles to profl. jours. Recipient Paul Lewis Labs. award in enzyme chemistry, 1952, Superior Accomplishment award Fed. Security Agy., 1952, Rockefeller Pub. Svc. award, 1957, Hillebrand prize Am. Chem. Soc., 1954, Award in Biol. Scis., Washington Acad. Scis., 1954, Fulbright Travel award, 1963; Commonwealth Fund fellow, 1967. Fellow AAAS, Am. Acad. Arts and Scis.; mem. NAS, Am. Chem. Soc. (vice chmn. div. biol. chemistry 1975-76, chmn. 1976-77), Biochem. Soc. (Eng.), Swiss Biochem. Soc. (hon. mem.), Spanish Biochem. Soc., hon. mem.), Japanese Biochem. Soc. (hon. mem.), Hellenic Biochem. and Biophys. Soc. (hon. mem.), Am. Soc. Biol. Chemists (pres. 1967-68, chmn. editorial com. 1962-63, Merck award 1981), Virchow-Pirquet Med. Soc. (Neuburg medal 1981), Harvey Soc. (v.p. 1969-70, pres. 1970-71), Brazilian Acad. Sci. (hon.), PanAm. Assn. Biochem. Socs. (vice chmn. 1971, chmn. 1972, mem. exec. com. 1971-78), Indian Nat. Acad. Sci., Argentine Acad. Sci. (corr.), Phi Beta Kappa, Sigma Xi. Home: 16517 Cypress Villa Ln Fort Myers FL 33908-7609 Personal E-mail: blhorecker@comcast.net.

HOREN, JEFFREY HARRY, telecommunications executive; b. Louisville, Oct. 1, 1949; s. H. Solomon and Freda E. (Saphier) H.; m. Susan Alix Chellin, Mar. 4, 1984; children: Melissa, David. BA, U. Mich., Ann Arbor, 1971; MA, Yale U., New Haven, Conn., 1974, PhD, 1977. Econ. policy fellow Brookings Instn., Washington, 1980-81; internal cons. AT&T, Basking Ridge, N.J., 1983-87; group mgr. strategic planning Sprint Nextel, Overland Park, Kans., 1987—. Author: Scheduling of Network Television Programs, 1977. Vice chair, bd. dirs. Nat. Israel Unity Coalition. Home: 12320 Riggs Rd Overland Park KS 66209-2543

HORGAN, CORNELIUS OLIVER, applied mathematics and mechanics professor, engineering educator; m. Myra O'Callaghan; children: Olivia, David. BS, Univ. Coll., Cork, 1964, MS, 1965; PhD, Calif. Inst. Tech., 1970; DSc, Nat. U. Ireland, 1983. Lectr. U. Mich., Ann Arbor, 1970-72; sr. research assoc. U. East Anglia, Norwich, U.K., 1972-74; assoc. prof. U. Houston, 1974-78; prof. applied mechanics and math. Mich. State U., East Lansing, 1978-88; prof. applied math. and applied mechanics U. Va., Charlottesville, 1988-94, Wills Johnson prof., 1994—. Vis. prof. Northwestern U., Evanston, 1977-78, Calif. Inst. Tech., Pasadena, 1984-85, U. Pisa, Italy, 1996, 97, U. Lecce, Italy, 2001, 03, U. Ferrara, Italy, 2001, 03, U. Politecnica de Catalunya, Terrassa, Spain, 2001, 03, Dublin City U., 2007. Contbr. over 175 publs. in field of theoretical mechanics and applied math. to profl. publs. Fellow ASME (chmn. tech. com. 1981-86), Am. Acad. Mechanics; mem. Soc. Engring. Sci. (bd. dirs. 1993-99, Eringen Medal 2005), Soc. Indsl. and Applied Math., Soc. Nat. Phil., Internat. Soc. Interaction of Mechanics and Maths. (exec. com. 2000-07). Home: 2820 Meadow Vista Dr Charlottesville VA 22901-9559 Office: U Va Dept Civil Engring Thornton Hall Charlottesville VA 22904 Business E-Mail: coh8p@virginia.edu.

HORGER, EDGAR OLIN, III, retired obstetrics and gynecology educator; b. Eutawville, SC, May 30, 1937; s. Edgar Olin Jr. and Frances Durant (Jordan) H.; m. Polly Jo Collins, May 29, 1960; children: Edgar Olin IV, David Collins, Patricia Bowen. BS, Furman U., 1959; MD, Med. Coll. S.C., 1962. Cert. Am. Bd. Obstetrics and Gynecology, 1971, Am. Bd. Obstetrics and Gynecology Dvsn. Maternal-Fetal Medicine, 1974. Intern Med. U. Hosp., Charleston, SC, 1962-63, resident in ob-gyn, 1963-67; NIH fellow U. Pitts., 1967-68, asst. prof., 1968-69, Med. U. S.C., Charleston, 1969-71, assoc. prof., 1971-76, prof., 1976-90, dir. maternal-fetal medicine, 1973-90; prof. ob-gyn. U. S.C. Sch. Medicine, Columbia, 1990-2001, disting. prof., chmn., 1993-99, disting. prof. emeritus, 2001—. Mem. S.C. Bd. Med. Examiners, 1985-87. Contbr. articles to profl. jours. Adv. bd. Charleston chpt. March of Dimes, 1984-90. Capt. USAR, 1963-66. Recipient Disting. Alumnus award Med. U. S.C., 1995; USPHS fellow, 1967-68. Mem. AMA, S.C. Med. Assn., Am. Coll. Ob-Gyn. (Outstanding Faculty award dist. IV 1988, vice chmn. S.C. sect. 1993-96, chmn. 1996-98, treas. dist. IV 1997-2000, Outstanding Disting. Svc. award 2001), Coun. Res. Edn. ObGyn, South Ctrl. Ob-Gyn. Soc., South Atlantic Assn. Ob-Gyn. (exec. com. 1983-94, sec. 1987-90, v.p. 1990-91, pres.-elect 1991-92, pres. 1992-93; Lifetime Achievement award 2007), So. Perinatal Assn. (dir. Mid-Atlantic region 1974-76), Soc. Perinatal Obstetricians (dir. 1977-78), Am. Gynecol. Obstet. Soc., Am. Assn. Ob-Gyn., S.C. Ob-Gyn. Soc. (pres. 1991-92), Columbia Med. Soc., Assn. Profs. Gynecology and Obstetrics (Excellence in Tchg. award 1992), S.C. State Bd. Med. Examiners (bd. dirs. 1985-87), Wild Dunes Club, Alpha Omega Alpha. Episcopalian. Avocations: tennis, scuba diving, skiing, genealogy, bird hunting. Home: 17 Beach Club Ct Isle Of Palms SC 29451 E-mail: ehorger@aol.com.

HORI, KEIKO, English literature educator; b. Himeji, Hyogo, Japan, Jan. 18, 1954; d. Takeshi Nishiyama and Fumiko Hori; 1 child, Grace. BA summa cum laude, Osaka U., Japan, 1976, MA, 1978; postgrad., U. N.H., 1979—80, Osaka U., Japan, 1978—82. Instr. Osaka Kyoiku U., 1981-82, tenured asst. prof., 1982-87, assoc. prof., 1987-2000, prof., 2000—; instr. Osaka U., Toyonaka, Japan, 1988-90, 92-95. Vis. prof. U. Wyo., Laramie, 1986—87; vis. scholar UCLA, 2001—02. Co-author: Imeji to shite no Toshi: Gakusaiteki Toshi Bunkaron, 1996; annotator: (textbook) American Businessman: Lessons from Life, 1994; co-annotator: (textbook) American and English Ideals, 1991. Recipient Kusumoto Shogakukai award, Osaka U., 1976. Mem. Modern Lang. Assn., English Literary Soc. Japan, Japan Assn. English Romanticism, Japan Assn. Coll. English Tchrs. Office: Osaka Kyoiku U 4-698-1 Asahigaoka Kashiwara Osaka 582-8582 Japan

HORI, YUKIO, engineering educator, scientific association administrator; b. Tokyo, Aug. 22, 1927; s. Kojiro and Yoshi (Saito) H.; m. Noriko Sunabori, May 15, 1965; children: Gen, Jun, Dan. BEng, U. Tokyo, 1951, DEng, 1960. Instr. U. Tokyo, 1953-55, assoc. prof., 1955-65, prof., 1965-88, emeritus prof., 1988—; exec. dir. Japan Soc. for Promotion of Sci., 1988-94; prof., v.p. Kanazawa Inst. Tech., Tokyo, 1994—. Contbr. articles to profl. jours. Recipient Tokyo Metropolis award, 1984, Purple Ribbon medal, 1993. Japan Acad. prize, 2007. Mem. ASME, Japan Soc. Mech. Engrs. (pres. 1988-89, awards 1960, 74, 89), Japan Soc. Tribologists (pres. 1990-92, award 1982), Japan Fedn. Engring. Soc. (v.p. 1989-93), Engring. Acad. Japan (v.p. 1993-2000, adviser, 2000—). Avocation: music. Home: Kugayama 3-19-19 Suginami-ku Tokyo 168-0082 Japan Office: Kanazawa Inst Tech Akasaka 2-17-41 Minato-ku Tokyo 107-0052 Japan Office Phone: 81-3-3589-2821. Business E-Mail: hori@alum.mit.edu.

HORII, REIICHI, library director, educator; b. Kyoto, Nov. 5, 1925; s. Jiro and Mitsu Horii; m. Kazuko Ohashi, Feb. 13, 1960; 2 children. BA, Kyoto U., 1949. Lectr. Tokai U., Shimizu, Shizuoka, Japan, 1951-53, Kansai U., Suita, Osaka, Japan, 1952-57; asst. prof. Aichi (Japan) U., Toyohashi, 1957-64, prof., 1964-71, Nanzan U., Nagoya, Aichi, 1971-78, Kansai Gaidai U., Hirakata, Osaka, 1978—, dir. libr. Hirakata, Osaka, 1988—2006. Mem. com. XIII Internat. Congress of Linguists, Tokyo, 1982. Author: Dictionary of Japanese Etymology, 1983, Language and Community, 1988, Language of Kyoto, 1988, Women's Languages, 1990, Dictionary of Foreign Origin's Words, 1994, Dictionary of Osaka Dialect, 1995, Empathic Linguistics, 1996, Comparative Linguistics, 1997, Dictionary of Stereotyped Phrase, 1997, Wonder of Language, 1998, Etymological Dictionary of Kansai Dialect, 1999, General Linguistics and Japanese Linguistics, 2003, Dictionary of Semantic Change, 2003, Language in Imperial Palace, 2005, Japanese Word Histories, 2005, Outline of Kyoto Dialect, 2006, Dictionary of Kyoto Dialect, 2006. Recipient Ordre des Palmes Acad., Govt. of France, 1974, Nat. Order of Merit, 1976. Mem. Linguistic Soc. of Japan (editor 1981-82), Phonetic Soc. of Japan, Soc. French Lang. and Lit., Japan Soc. of Stylistics, Soc. of Expression-Formation Studies, Soc. of Mediterranean Studies, Shinmura Found. (chief dir. 2003-, mem. jury Shinmura prize 1982-2002). Avocation: music. Home: 43-3 Kuzuha-Nakamachi Hirakata Osaka 573-1107 Japan Office: Kansai Gaidai U 16-1 Nakamiyahigashino-cho Hirakata Osaka 573-1001 Japan

HORIKIS, THEODOROS, research scientist; b. Athens, Greece, Aug. 31, 1976; arrived in US, 2004; s. Panagiotis Horikis and Georgia Patelaki Horiki. BS in Physics, U. Crete, 1998; PhD, Imperial Coll., London, 2001. Postdoctoral fellow engring., scis., and applied math. Northwestern U., Evanston, Ill., 2004—06; rsch. assoc. dept. applied math., lectr. U. Colo., Boulder, 2006—. Office: U Colo Applied Math 526 UCB Boulder CO 80309 Office Phone: 303-492-4543. Personal E-mail: thorikis@yahoo.com. Business E-Mail: theodoros.horikis@colorado.edu.

HORINKO, MARIANNE LAMONT, former federal agency administrator; b. 1961; BS, U. Md., 1982; JD, Georgetown U., 1986. Staff scientist Nat. Cancer Inst., Bethesda, Md.; atty. Morgan, Lewis, & Bockius, LLP, Washington; atty. advisor, solid wastes & emerg. response EPA, Washington, 1990—93; pres. Clay Assocs., Inc., 1993—2001; asst. adminstr. solid waste and emer. response EPA, 2001—03, acting adminstr., 2003.

HORISZNY, LAURENE HELEN, lawyer; b. Lansing, Mich., Oct. 14, 1955; d. Walter and Jennie Ann (Pellpshen) H.; m. Richard C. Stavoe Jr., June 25, 1983; children: Andrea Kristen, Charles Ross. BA, Mich. State U., 1977; JD, Ohio State U., 1980. Bar: Mich. 1980, U.S. Dist. Ct. (ea. and we. dists.) Mich. 1980. Lawyer Consumers Power Co., Jackson, Mich., 1980-85; corp. counsel Ex-Cell-O Corp., Troy, Mich., 1985-86; sr. lawyer, asst. sec. BorgWarner Inc., Auburn Hills, Mich., 1986, v.p., gen. counsel, sec., 1993—2007, chief compliance officer, 2007—. Exec. bd. Land 'O Lakes coun. Boy Scouts Am., 1984-85. Mem. ABA, Mich. Bar Assn., Nature Conservancy. Avocations: scuba diving, cross country skiing, down-hill skiing, tennis. Office: Borg Warner 3800 Automation Ave Ste 500 Auburn Hills MI 48326-1786*

HORKEY, WILLIAM RICHARD, retired oil industry executive; b. Tulsa, Apr. 22, 1925; s. William Edward and Clara Doris (Rice) H.; m. Barbara Jeanne Williamson, Oct. 18, 1952; children: Elaine Gail, Edward Richard, Ellen Beth. BA, State U. Iowa, 1947; JD, U. Okla., 1950; grad., Advanced Mgmt. Program, Harvard U., 1962. Bar: Okla. 1950. With Gulf Oil Corp., 1950-51, Skelly Oil Co., 1951-55, Helmerich & Payne, Inc.,

Tulsa, 1955-90, sec., legal counsel, 1955-64, v.p., 1960-64, exec. v.p., 1964-87, sr. v.p., 1987-90, bd. dirs., 1957-90. Chmn. Grand River Dam Authority, Okla. Ordnance Works Authority, Woolslayer Cos. Inc., EnviroFuels Inc.; bd. dirs. Asbury Group. Bd. dirs. Tulsa United Way, 1978-88; chmn. S.E. Tulsa YMCA, 1970-72; pres. Met. Tulsa YMCA, 1972-73, Tulsa Bus. Health Group 1978-96; chmn. Tulsa chpt. ARC, 1987-88; bd. dirs. Emergency Med. Svcs. Authority, 1977-95, chmn., 1981-95; pres. Tulsa Cmty. Found. for Indigent Health Care, 1980—. Mem. ABA, Okla. Bar Assn., Tulsa County Bar Assn., Order of Coif, So. Hills Country Club, Mid-Continent Harvard AMP (Tulsa) (pres. 1969-75), Phi Delta Phi, Phi Delta Theta. Presbyterian (deacon and elder). Home: 3800 W 71st St # 3213 Tulsa OK 74132 Personal E-mail: wrh@invernessvillage.com.

HORLICK, GARY NORMAN, lawyer, educator; b. Washington, Mar. 12, 1947; s. Reuben S. and Gertrude V. (Cooper) Horlick; m. Kathryn L. Mann, June 1, 1986. AB, Dartmouth Coll., 1968; BA, MA, Diploma in Internat. Law, Cambridge U., Eng., 1970; JD, Yale U., 1973. Bar: Conn. 1974, U.S. Ct. Appeals (D.C. cir.) 1975), D.C. 1977, U.S. Supreme Ct. 1977, U.S. Ct. Internat. Trade 1979, U.S. Ct. Customs and Patent Appeals 1980. Asst. to rep. Ford Found., Santiago, Chile, 1973-74, asst. rep. Bogota, Colombia, 1974-76; assoc. Steptoe & Johnson, Washington, 1976-80; internat. trade counsel U.S. Senate Fin. Com., Washington, 1981; dep. asst. sec. U.S. Dept. Commerce, Washington, 1981-83; ptnr. O'Melveny & Myers, Washington, 1983—2002, Wilmer Cutler Pickering Hale and Dorr, LLP, Washington, 2002—. Lectr. law Yale U., New Haven, 1983-86, 2001—, World Trade Inst., U. Berne, 2000—; adj. prof. Georgetown U. Law Ctr., Washington, 1986—; lectr. various orgns.; adv. com. U.S. Ct. Internat. Trade, 1993-97; mem. permanent group of experts World Trade Orgn., 1996-2001, chmn., 1996-97. Author: WTO and NAFTA Rules and Dispute Resolution, 2003; asst. editor Jour. World Trade. Mem. ABA (chmn. standing com. on customs law 1993), Coun. Fgn. Rels., Internat. Law Assn. (mem. exec. coun. Am. br. 1983—), Internat. Bar Assn. (vice chmn. antitrust and trade law 1987-89), D.C. Bar Assn. (chmn. internat. divsn. 1984-85), Am. Soc. of Internat. Law (exec. coun. 1998-99). Office Phone: 202-663-6000. Business E-Mail: gary.horlick@wilmerhale.com.

HORLICK, RUTH, photographer; b. Frankfurt, Germany, July 17, 1921; came to U.S., 1937; d. Leo Don and Hanna Rosenstock; m. Max Horlick, 1942; children: Jeffrey, Jill, Robert. Student, Newark Sch. Fine & Indsl. Arts, U. Md., Latent Image Workshop; studied with, Lowell Anson Kenyon; student, Nikon Sch. Photography, Time Life Photography Workshop. One-woman shows include Prince George's County Arts Divsn. Gallery, 1991, Hyattsville Mcpl. Bldg., 1996, Jewish Cmty. Ctr. D.C., 1998, Colonial Theater, Annapolis, Md., 1999, U. Md. Sr. U., 1999, exhibited in group shows at Coun. Greater Md. Camera Clubs, Md. Soc. Photo Pictorialists, Prince George C.C., Internat. Artist's Support Group, New Delhi, 2000—01, Beijing, 2001, Cooper St. Gallery, Memphis, 2000, St. Petersburg, Russia, 2003, New Delhi, 2004, Open Studios-Passageways, East Pines, Md., 2005, Riderwood Celebration of the Arts, 2005, P.G. County Exec. Office, Upper Marlboro, Md., 2005, Learning and Sports Ctr. Gallery, Landover, Md., 2005, Cairo, Luxor, Aswan, 2005, Montpelier-Laurel, Md., 2006, Paint Br. Unitarian/Universalist, Adelphi, Md., 2006, Calvert House Inn, Riverdale, Md., 2006, Free State Press, Annapolis, 2006, Prince Georges County Cmty. Ctr., Hyattsville, Md., 2006—07, Harmony Hall Regional Ctr., 2006, Riderwood Village, 2006. Founding mem. Art Spin Gallery, West Hyattsville, Md. Recipient numerous awards Nikon Sch. Photography, Coun. Greater Washington Camera Clubs, Md. Soc. Photo Pictorialists, Prince George's C.C. Mem. Women in the Arts, Laurel Art Guild, Latent Image Workshop, Passageways Artists Studios, Wash. Project for the Arts Corcoran Art Gallery, Washington Ctr. for Photography, Hyattsville Cmty. Artists Alliance, Md.-Nat. Pk. and Planning Commn. Slide Bank, Rock Creek Gallery, Internat. Artist's Support Group. Avocations: foreign travel, symphonic music and opera, fine arts.

HORMATS, ROBERT DAVID, economist, investment banker; b. Balt., Apr. 13, 1943; s. Saul and Ruth H. BA, Tufts U., 1965, MA, 1966, MA in Law and Diplomacy, 1967, PhD, 1970. Research asst. Fletcher Sch. of Law and Diplomacy, 1968-69; research asso. Univ. Coll., Dar-es-Salaam, Tanzania, 1967-68; staff mem. internat. econ. affairs Nat. Security Council, 1969-73, sr. staff mem., 1974-77; sr. dep. asst. sec. for econ. and bus. affairs Dept. State, 1977-79; ambassador and dep. U.S. trade rep., 1979-81; asst. sec. state for econ. and bus. affairs, 1981-82; v.p. Goldman, Sachs and Co., 1982, mng. dir., 1998—; vice chmn. Goldman Sachs (Internat.), 1987—. Guest scholar Brookings Instn., 1973-74; vis. lectr. Princeton U., 1983, 03; mem. internat. capital markets com. N.Y. Stock Exch.; bd. dirs. Engelhard Hanovia, Inc., Irvington Inst. Immunological Rsch. Author: Making U.S. International Economic Policy, 1984, Reforming the International Monetary System, 1987, Am. Albatross: The Foreign Debt Dilemma, 1988, The Global Economy: America's Role in the Decade Ahead, 1989, International Business in the 21st Century, 1999, The Foreign Policy of the Internet, 2000, The Changing Spectrum in Asia, 2003, Abraham Lincoln and the Global Economy, 2003, The Price of Liberty: How America Pays for Its Wars, 2007; mem. editl. bd. Fgn. Policy mag., Internat. Economy mag. Mem. dean's adv. coun. John F. Kennedy Sch. of Govt., Harvard U.; mem. internat. adv. coun. Ecole dés Hautes Etudes Commercial, Montreal Decorated Legion of Honor (France); Shell Oil Co. fellow, 1967-68; Council on Fgn. Relations fellow, 1973-74; Recipient Arthur Flemming award, 1978 Mem. NY Econ. Club (pres. bd. dirs.), Internat. Longevity Inst. (bd. dirs.), Freedom House (bd. dirs.). Home: 55 E End Ave Apt 8A New York NY 10028-7935 Office: Goldman Sachs & Co 85 Broad St New York NY 10004-2456 Home Phone: 212-794-2535; Office Phone: 212-902-5347. Business E-Mail: robert.hormats@gs.com.

HORN, ALAN F., film company executive; MBA with distinction, Harvard U. With Proctor & Gamble, Tandem Prodns., T.A.T. Comm., Embassy Comm., 1973—86; pres., COO 20th Century Fox Film Corp., 1986—87; co-founder, chmn., CEO Castle Rock Entertainment, Beverly Hills, 1987—99; pres., COO Warner Bros. Entertainment, Burbank, Calif., 1999—. Bd. dirs. Univision Comm. Bd. dirs. Natural Resources Def. Coun.; vice chmn., bd. trustees Autry Mus. Western Heritage, LA; mem. bd. assocs. Harvard Bus. Sch.; founding mem., bd. dirs. Environ. Media Assn. Capt. USAF. Named one of 50 Most Powerful People in Hollywood, Premiere mag., 2004—06, Top 200 Collectors, ARTnews mag., 2006. Mem.: Hollywood Radio and TV Soc., Am. Film Inst., Acad. TV Arts and Scis., Acad. Motion Picture Arts and Scis. Office: Warner Bros 4000 Warner Blvd Burbank CA 91522-0002 Office Phone: 818-954-6000.

HORN, ANDREW WARREN, lawyer; b. Apr. 19, 1946; s. George H. and Belle (Collin) H.; children: Lee Shawn, Ruth Belle. BBA in Acctg., U. Miami, 1968, JD, 1971. Bar: Fla. 1971, Colo. 1990, U.S. Dist. Ct. (so. dist.) Fla. 1972, U.S. Tax Ct. 1974. Ptnr. Gillman & Horn P.A., Miami, Fla., 1973-74; pvt. practice Miami, 1974—. Active Miami-Dade County Health Care Task Force, Fla., 2006-07; mem. healthcare task force Miami Dade County, Fla., 2006-07. Recipient Am. Jurisprudence award Lawyers Coop. Pub. Co., 1970. Mem. ABA, ATLA, Fla. Bar, Acad. Fla. Trial Lawyers. Office Phone: 305-373-7789. Personal E-mail: lawofficehorn@msn.com.

HORN, BRENDA SUE, lawyer; b. Beech Grove, Ind., Apr. 22, 1949; d. Donald Eugene Horn and Barbara Joyce (Waggoner) Christie. AB with distinction, Ind. U., 1971; MS, Purdue U., 1975; JD summa cum laude, Ind. U., 1981. Bar: Ind. 1981, US Dist. Ct. (so. dist.) Ind. 1981. Assoc. Ice Miller, Indpls., 1981—87, ptnr., 1988—. Assoc. editor Ind. Law Rev., 1980-81. Bd. dirs. Ballet Internat., treas., 1996-2000; pres. Greenleaf Cmty. Ctr., 1992-93, 96-99, v.p., 1991, sec., 1990; v.p. Cmty. Alliance for Far East Side, 1997-98, bd. dirs. 1997-98, 2004-, hon. dir. 1998-2003; bd. dirs. Big Sisters of Ctrl. Ind., 1995-98, hon. dir., 1998-2002; bd. dirs. Indiana Edn. Savs. Authority, Cmty. Orgns. Legal Assistance Project, treas., 2001-2003, pres. 2003—. Named an Influential Women in Indpls. Ind. Lawyer and Indpls. Bus. Jour., 1998; named one of Best Lawyers in Am. 2001-02, 2002-03; named a Super Lawyer, 2004, 05, 06; Disting. fellow Indpls. Bar Found. Mem. ABA (com. on tax exempt fin.), Am. Coll. Bond Counsel (bd. dirs., v.p. 1995-98, pres. 1998-2001), Ind. Bar Assn., Indpls. Bar Assn. (bd. mgrs. 1992), Ind. Mcpl. Lawyers Assn., Nat. Assn. Bond Lawyers, Skyline Club (bd. dirs.), Phi Beta Kappa. Office: Ice Miller LLP One American Sq Ste 3100 Indianapolis IN 46282 Office Phone: 317-236-2370. Business E-Mail: brenda.horn@icemiller.com.

HORN, CARL, III, federal judge; b. 1951; BA with honors, U. Va., 1973; JD, U. S.C., 1976. Bar: N.C. 1976. Assoc. Grier, Parker, Poe, Thompson, Bernstein, Gage & Preston, Charlotte, NC, 1976-79; legal counsel, instr. Wheaton Coll., 1979-82; spl. asst. civil rights divsn. U.S. Dept. Justice, Charlotte, 1982-83, chief asst. U.S. atty. for western dist. N.C., 1987-93; ptnr. Horn & Conrad and predecessor, Charlotte, 1984-87; U.S. magistrate judge for western dist. N.C., U.S. Magistrate Ct., Charlotte, 1993—2003. Author: Fourth Circuit Criminal Handbook, 1994—, Horn's Federal Criminal Jury Instructions for the Fourth Circuit, 1997, LawyerLife: Finding a Life and a Higher Calling in the Practice of Law, 2003; editor: Michie's Fourth Circuit Criminal Reporter, 1995—, Federal Civil Practice in the Fourth Circuit, 1997, Law for Physicians, 1999; co-author and editor: The Battle for Morality in Pluralistic America, 1985; contbr. articles to law jours. Office: 401 W Trade St Ste 238 Charlotte NC 28202-1619 Office Phone: 704-350-7470.

HORN, CHARLES M., lawyer; b. Boston, Sept. 28, 1951; s. Garfield Henry and Alexandra (Matz) H.; m. Jane Charlotte Luxton, May 29, 1976; children: Andrew L., Caroline C. AB magna cum laude, Harvard Coll., 1973; JD, Cornell Law Sch., 1976. Bar: D.C. 1976, U.S. Dist. Ct. D.C. 1977, U.S. Ct. Appeals (D.C. cir.) 1977, U.S. Supreme Ct. 1980. Atty. U.S. Securities and Exchange Commn., Washington, 1976-82, br. chief divsn. enforcement, 1982-83; asst. dir. securities and corp. practices Office Comptroller of Currency, Washington, 1984—86, dir. securities and corp. practices, 1986-89; ptnr. Stroock & Stroock & Lavan, Washington, 1989-92, Mayer, Brown & Platt, Washington, 1992—2003, Mayer, Brown, Rowe & Maw LLP, Washington, 2003—07, Mayer Brown LLP, Washington, 2007—. Mem. faculty Am. Bankers Assn. Nat. Grad. Compliance Sch., 1991-92, 94, Fed. Fin. Instns. Exam. Coun. (programs off-balance-sheet risk, Trust Exams. Sch.); bd. advisors U. NC Ctr. Banking & Finance, 2004-; lectr. in field. Edit. adv. bd. Bank Acctg. and Fin., 1993—; contbr. articles to profl. jours. Mem. ABA (banking law com., com. fed. regulation securities), D.C. Bar Assn., Washington Golf and Country Club. Home: 1918 Massachusetts Ave Mc Lean VA 22101-4907 Office: Mayer Brown LLP 1909 K St NW Washington DC 20006 Home Phone: 702-341-3971; Office Phone: 202-263-3219. Business E-Mail: chorn@mayerbrownrowe.com.

HORN, DAVID C., lawyer; b. Cin., Jan. 4, 1952; BA, Yale U., 1974; JD, Vanderbilt U., 1977. Bar: Ohio 1977. Ptnr. Frost & Jacobs (now Frost Brown Todd), Cin.; asst. gen. counsel AK Steel Holdings Corp., Middletown, Ohio, 2000—01, v.p., gen. counsel, 2001—05, sec., 2003—, head human resources, 2003—04, sr. v.p., gen. counsel, 2005—. Trustee Vol. Lawyers for the Poor Found. Mem.: Butler County Bar Assn., Ohio Bar Assn., Fed. Bar Assn., ABA, Order of the Coif. Office: AK Steel Holding Corp 703 Curtis St Middletown OH 45043*

HORN, DONNA M., pharmacist, medical association administrator; BS in Pharmacy, Mass. Coll. Pharmacy and Allied Health Sci. Mgr. regulatory affairs Brooks Pharmacy, Warwick, RI, 2002—. Pres.-elect Nat. Assn. Bd. Pharmacy, 2003, pres., 2004—. Recipient Ruth Davies Flaherty Svc. award, Lambda Kappa Sigma, 1997, Alumni Achievement award, Mass. Coll. Pharmacy and Health Sci., 2003. Mem.: Boston Druggist Assn., Am. Pharmacists Assn., Mass. Pharmacists Assn. (Nathan Goldberg award 2003), Inst. Safe Medication Practices, Mass. Bd. Registration Pharmacy (bd. pres. 2003—04). Office: Regulatory Affairs Brooks Pharmacy 50 Svc Ave Warwick RI 02886 Office Phone: 401-825-3900.

HORN, HOWARD M., labor union administrator, consultant; b. Bklyn., July 31, 1938; s. Morris Norman and Yetta Horn; m. Carol Evelyn Solomon, Feb. 26, 1961 (dec.); m. Lois Bonnie Pfeffer, Nov. 10, 1997 (dec.); 1 stepchild, Ronald. Post grad. student, Harvard U., 1966. Exec. v.p. Amalgamated Meat Cutters N.Am. Local 627, NYC, 1964—81, UFCW (United Food and Commerercial Workers) Local 50, NYC, 1982—90, UFCW Local 342/50, Mineola, NY, 1991—97, cons., 1997—98. Columnist: On The Truck, 1964—90. Drug counselor N.Y. Ctrl. Labor Coun., Manhattan, 1979—89, referal com., 1975—89; county com. mem. Flushing Dem. Club, NY, 1988—. Pvt. first class US Army, 1961—63. Avocations: phongraph records, history, travel.

HORN, JOE, professional football player; b. New Haven, Conn., Jan. 16, 1972; m. Lacreshia Horn; children: Jhia, Joseph. Attended, Itawamba Jr. Coll., Miss. Wide receiver Memphis Mad Dogs, Can. Football League, 1994—95, Kans. City Chiefs, 1996—99, New Orleans Saints, 2000—06, Atlanta Falcons, 2007—. Named to Nat. Football Conf. (NFC) Pro Bowl Team, 2000—02, 2004, NFL All-Madden Team, 2000—01. Office: Atlanta Falcons 4400 Falcon Pkwy Flowery Branch GA 30542*

HORN, JOHN HAROLD, lawyer; b. Eugene, Oreg., Mar. 4, 1927; s. Harold William and Mildred A. (Truesdale) H.; m. Deloris Eileen Davis, Aug. 22, 1948; children: Lorraine, Deborah, Lisa, Darren. BS, U. Oreg., 1949, JD, 1951. Bar: Oreg. 1951, U.S. Dist. Ct. Oreg. 1957. Ptnr. Horn & Slocum, Roseburg, Oreg., 1951-65, Riddlesbarger, Pederson, Young & Horn, Eugene, 1970-74, Young, Horn, Cass & Scott, Eugene, 1974-82; pvt. practice Roseburg, 1965-70, Eugene, 1982—2005; ret., 2005. Chmn. fund raising Douglas County unit ARC, 1966, county chmn., 1968; exec. bd. Eugene Mission, 1979—; pres. bd. dirs. Jubilee Ministries, Eugene, 1980—; v.p., bd. dirs. His Word Broadcasting, 1989-91, pres. bd. dirs., 1991—. Recipient Outstanding Svc. award ARC, 1968. Mem. Oreg. Bar Assn., Douglas County Bar Assn. (pres. 1960, chmn. grievance com. 1961-62), Lane County Bar Assn., Lions (dir. Eugene chpt. 2000-2002, v.p. 2003, mem. Oreg. Lions Found. patient care com. 2004—). Republican. Avocations: aviation, golf, skiing. Home and Office: 640 Elwood Ct Eugene OR 97401-2235 E-mail: jhhorn@hotmail.com.

HORN, JOYCE ELAINE, retired music educator; d. Alfred Irving Sette and Elma Louise Robertson; 1 child, Camilla Jeanne VandenBerg. MusB, Grand Rapids Bapt. Coll.; MusM, We. Mich. U, 1972. Assoc. prof. music Cornerstone U, Grand Rapids, Mich., 1962—2007; ret., 2007—. Republican. Baptist. Avocations: reading, studying Charles Dickens, music. Home: 7355 Casade Terrace Dr SE Grand Rapids MI 49546 Office Phone: 616-949-5300 1223. Personal E-mail: jhorn218@aol.com.

HORN, KAREN NICHOLSON, investment company executive, former bank executive; b. Los Angeles, Sept. 21, 1943; d. Aloys and Novella (Hartley) Nicholson; m. John T. Horn, June 5, 1965; 1 child. BA, Pomona Coll., 1965; PhD, Johns Hopkins U., 1971. Sr. economist, bd. govs. staff FRS, Washington, 1969-71; v.p., economist First Nat. Bank, Boston, 1971-78; treas. Bell of Pa., Phila., 1978-82; pres. Fed. Res. Bank, Cleve., 1982-87; chmn., CEO Banc One Cleveland NA, Cleve.; mng. dir., head internat. pvt. banking Bankers Trust, 1996—99; mng. dir., pres. Private Client Services Marsh, Inc. (divsn. Marsh & McLennan Companies, Inc), 1999—2003; ltd. ptnr. Brock Capital Group LLC, NYC, 2004—. Bd. dirs. Eli Lilly, Simon Property Group, Fannie Mae, T. Rowe Price Mutual Funds. Office: Brock Capital Group LLC 622 Third Ave Fl 12 New York NY 10017 Office Phone: 212-209-3000.

HORN, LAWRENCE CHARLES, retired music educator; b. Abilene, Tex., July 7, 1938; s. Alonzo Horn and Isabella Wheeler Rhodes; m. Lee Ester Cross-Horn, Mar. 6, 1971; 1 child, Kenya LaDawn. BA in Music Edn., Langston U., Okla., 1961; M in Music Edn., U. Okla., Norman, 1967. Tchr. math. H.S. Abilene (Tex.) Pub. Schs., 1964—65; assoc. prof., chmn. Dept. Fine Arts Miss. Valley State U., Itta Bena, Miss., 1965—2004, ret., 1965—2004. Pvt. instr., 1967—; clarinetist Greenwood (Miss.) Cmty. Band, 2000—07; asst. dir. band Battle of the Bands Miss. Valley State U., Dallas, 1972. Dir. Miss. Valley State U. Woodwind Ensembles, 1967—2004. Served with US Army, 1962—64. Named Gospel Singer of Yr., Sch. Religious Studies, Little Rock, Ark., 1998, 2000, Christian of Yr., Tchula, Miss., Ch. of Christ, 2005. Mem.: Miss. Valley State U. Nat. Alumni Assn. (life), U. Okla. Found. (life), Langston (Okla.) U. Found. (life), Phi Delta Kappa (sec. 1967—), Omega Psi Phi (life; keeper of records and seal 1965—, sec. 1965—, Svc. award 2005). Democrat. Avocations: reading, music, singing, theater. Home: 517 Redbird Dr Greenwood MS 38930

HORN, MARIAN BLANK, federal judge; b. NYC, June 24, 1943; d. Werner P. and Mady R. Blank; m. Robert Jack Horn; 3 children. AB, Barnard Coll., 1962; student, Columbia U., 1965, NYU, 1965-66; JD, Fordham U., 1969. Bar: NY 1970, DC 1973, US Supreme Ct. 1973. Asst. dist. atty. Bronx County, NY, 1969-72; assoc. Arent, Fox, Kintner, Plotkin & Kahn, 1972-73; project mgr. Am. U. Law Sch. study on alts. to conventional criminal adjudication US Dept. Justice, 1973-75; litig. atty. FEA, 1975-76; sr. atty. office gen. counsel strategic petroleum res. br. US Dept. Energy, 1976-79, dep. asst. gen. counsel for procurement and fin. incentives, 1979-81; dep. assoc. solicitor divsn. surface mining US Dept. Interior, 1981-83, assoc. solicitor divsn. gen. law, 1983-85, prin. dep. solicitor, acting solicitor, 1985-86; judge US Ct. Fed. Claims, 1986—. Adj. prof. law Washington Coll. Law, Am. U., 1973-76, George Washington U. Sch. Law, 1992—. Office: US Ct Fed Claims 717 Madison Pl NW Washington DC 20439-0002*

HORN, PAUL M., information technology executive, crystallographer; b. NYC, Aug. 16, 1946; s. Selig S. and Agnus (Attie) H.; m. Judith Herrick; children: Lisa, Sara. BS, Clarkson Coll. Tech., 1968; PhD, U. Rochester, 1973. Prof. dept. physics and James Franck Inst. U. Chgo., 1973-79; mem. rsch. staff T.J. Watson Rsch. Ctr. IBM Corp., Yorktown Heights, NY, 1979, acting dir. phys. scis. dept. T.J. Watson Rsch. Ctr., 1987, dir. phys. scis. dept. T.J. Watson Rsch. Ctr., 1988—90, dir. silicon tech. IBM rsch divsn., 1990—94, v.p. storage, IBM rsch. divsn., dir. Almaden Rsch. Ctr. San Jose, Calif., 1994—96, sr. v.p., dir. rsch., 1996—. Contbr. articles to sci. jours.; former assoc. editor Phys. Rev. Letters, mem. editl. adv. bd. Sci. Am. Trustee NY Hall of Sci., Clarkson Industry U., Comm. Econ. Develop.; mem. indsl. adv. bd. U. Calif., Berlekey; mem. adv. bd. Gallaudet U.; mem. Coun. on Competitiveness. NSF fellow; Alfred P. Sloan Rsch. fellow, 1974-78; recipient Bertram Eugene award Am. Crystallographic Assn., 1988, Disting. Leadership award, NY Hall of Scis., 2000, Hutchinson medal, U. Rochester, 2002, Pake prize, Am. Phys. Soc., 2002. Fellow Am. Phys. Soc. (planning com.); mem. Advanced Photon Source Users Orgn. of Argonne Nat. Labs. (chmn. exec. com.), NAE. Office: IBM Corp 1 New Orchard Rd Armonk NY 10504-1722*

HORN, RONI, artist; b. NYC, 1955; BFA, RI Sch. Design, 1975; MFA, Yale U., 1978. One-woman shows include Clocktower, Inst. Art & Urban Resources, NY, 1980, Glyptothek Mus., Munich, 1983, Galerie Heinz Herzer, Munich, 1983, Burnett Miller Gallery, LA, 1985, Neuberger Mus., SUNY, 1986, Galerie Maeght Lelong, NY, 1987, Unique Forms of Deviation in Space, Mario Diacono Gallery, Boston, 1988, Paula Cooper Gallery, NY, 1989, Surface Matters, Mus. Contemporary Art, LA, 1990, Mary Boone Gallery, NY, 1991, Jablonka Galerie, Cologne, 1992, 1993, Four Watercolors, Matthew Marks Gallery, NY, 1993, Inner Geography, Balt. Mus. Art, Md., 1994, Gurgles, Sucks, Echoes, Matthew Marks Gallery, NY, 1995, Earths Grow Thick, Wexner Ctr. Arts, Columbus, 1996, You Are the Weather, Fotomuseum Winterthur, Switzerland, 1997, Patrick Painter Gallery, LA, 1998, Pi, Matthew Marks Gallery, NY, 1999, Still Water (The River Thames, for Example), Whitney Mus. Am. Art, NY, 2000, Blah, blah, hair, Blah, blah, your eyes; Blah, blah care, Blah, blah skies, Dia Ctr. Arts, NY, 2001, Clowndoubt, Matthew Marks Gallery, NY, 2002, Galerie Xavier Hufkens, Brussels, 2003, Some Thames, Art Inst. Chgo., 2004, exhibited in group shows, Corning Mus. Glass, NY, 1976, Material Object, Hayden Gallery, MIT, Cambridge, Mass., 1980, Barbara Braatten Gallery, NY, 1984, Lorence-Monk Gallery, NY, 1985, Chris Middendorf Gallery, Washington DC, 1986, Lead, Hirschl & Adler Modern, NY, 1987, Inscribed Image, Lang-O'Hara Gallery, NY, 1988, Non-representation, Anne Plumb Gallery, NY, 1989, Sculptors' Drawings, Balt. Mus. Art, 1990, Whitney Biennial, Whitney Mus. Am. Art, 1991, 2004, Drawn in teh '90s, Ind. Curators Inc., NY, 1992, Drawing the Line Against AIDS, Peggy Guggenheim Collection, Venice, 1993, Photography, Margo Leavin Gallery, LA, 1994, Works on Paper, Matthew Marks Gallery, NY, 1995, Thinking Prink: Books to Billboards, 1980-1995, Mus. Modern Art, NY, 1996, Sleight of Mind/Angle of Landscape, Ctr. Curatorial Studies Mus., Bard Coll., NY, 1997, Venice Biennial, 1997, Maverick, Matthew Marks Gallery, NY, 1998, 00, Barbara Gladstone Gallery, NY, 2000, Tenth Anniversary Exhbn., 100 Drawings & Photographs, Matthew Marks Gallery, NY, 2001, Some Chromes, Fogg Art Mus., Harvard U., 2002, Exhbns. of an Exhbn., Casey Kaplan Gallery, NY, 2003, I am the Walrus, Cheim & Read, NY, 2004, Fresh Works on Paper, 5th Anniversary Exhbn., James Kelly Contemporary, Sante Fe, NM, 2004. Recipient Awards Visual Arts, AVA 7, 1988, Moonhole Artists Assn., Bequia, 1996, Alpert Award Arts, 1998; Ford Found. Grant, 1978, Alice Kimball Traveling Fellowship, Yale U., 1978, Humanities Development Grant, Colgate U., 1983, Artist's Fellowship, Nat. Endowment Art, 1984, 1986, 1990, Guggenheim Fellowship, 1990. Mailing: c/o Mattthew Marks Gallery 523 West 24th St New York NY 10011

HORN, RUSSELL EUGENE, engineering executive, consultant; b. Yoe, Pa., May 4, 1912; s. Eugene M. and Charlotte (Snyder) H.; m. Eleanor B. Baird, Jan. 12, 1934; children: Russell Eugene, Ralph Elliot, Rosalind Emily (Mrs. Lee Kunkel), Robert Errol. BS, Pa. State U., 1933. Foreman Pa. Dept. Hwys. dist. office, York, Pa., 1933-35; draftsman, supr., designer C.S. Buchart, architect, 1935-41; exec. v.p., chief engr. Buchart Engring., 1945-59, pres., chief engr., 1959-61, Buchart-Horn, Inc., 1961-72, chmn. bd. dirs., 1972-2000. Pres. PACE Resources, inc., 1970-87, chmn. bd. dirs. 1970-2001, bd. dirs.; chmn. AAA White Rose Motor Club, 1975-78. Bd. dirs. Auto Club So. Pa.; bd. dirs. emeritus Retirement Homes of Meth. Ch., 1978—. Col. AUS, 1940-45. Mem. NSPE, Soc. Am. Mil. Engrs., Pa. Soc. Profl. Engrs. (pres. Lincoln chpt. 1961), Pa. Assn. Cons. Engrs. (pres. 1965, bd. dirs. 1966), Pa. Hwy Info. Assn. (bd. dirs.), Am. Soc. Hwy. Engrs. (nat. pres. 1962), Tech. Socs. Coun. Southeastern Pa. (chmn. 1963), Engring. Soc. York, Profl. Engrs. Pvt. Practice, Am. Concrete Inst., Assn. Pa. Constructors Assn. Hwy Ofcls. N. Atlantic States, Assn. U.S. Army Res. Officers Assn., ASCE, VFW, Cons. Engrs. Coun., Am. Legion, Pa. State U. Alumni Club (York County), Univ. Club, Lake Club, Exch. Club (Golden Deeds award 1979), Mt. Nittany Soc. Pa. State U., Masons (32 deg., Order of the Double Eagle award 1983, Legion of Freedom award 1986, outstanding engring. alumnus 1987), York County Agrl. Soc. (life), Moose Home: 1270 Brockie Dr York PA 17403-4448 Office: Pace Resources Inc 40 S Richland Ave York PA 17404-3470

HORN, RUSSELL EUGENE, JR., engineering executive; b. York, Pa., Sept. 15, 1934; s. Russell Eugene and A. Eleanor (Baird) Horn; m. Franziska Kathe Kastner (dec. 1995); children: Silvia S., Russell E. III, Monika K., Ursula F., John D.; m. Lilli Maria Funk, 2002. Sgt. lst class U.S. Army Security Agy., 1952-62; sales trainee, sales rep. Print-O-Stat, Inc., York, Pa., 1962-63, mgr., 1970-73, exec. v.p., 1976-77, pres., 1977-96, mgr. Towson, Md., 1963-70, v.p. Md., Del., 1973-76; office of pres. PACE Resources, Inc., York, 1987-96, pres., CEO, 1996—2001, chmn., pres., CEO, 2001—. Bd. dirs. Buchart-Horn, Inc., others; mem. adv. bd. Dauphin Deposit Bank-York Region, 1984-98; also officer, advisor, exec. various corps. Bd. dirs. York County chpt. ARC, 2004-07; active various ednl., charitable activities. Mem. York Area C. of C. Home: 995 Detwiler Dr York PA 17404 Office: PACE Resources Inc 40 S Richland Ave York PA 17404-3470 Office Phone: 717-852-1328. Personal E-mail: pace40@aol.com.

HORN, SHARON K., government agency administrator; B in Bus. and Econs., U. Ga.; EdM, Tex. A&M U.; PhD in Higher Edn. and Curriculum, U. Tex. Legis. fellow labor and human resources com. US Senate; secondary sch. tchr. of bus., econs. and polit. sci. Tex., Ga.; tchr. U. Tex., Tyler, S.W. Tex. State U.; assoc. dir. Program on Ednl. Policy and Orgn. Nat. Inst. Edn., 1982; dir. info. svcs. Office Ednl. Rsch. and Improvement US Dept. Edn., Washington, program officer, dir. Nat. Awards Program for Model Profl. Devel., dir. evaluation and dissemination Office Innovation and Improvement. Office: US Dept Edn FOB-6 Rm 4W332 400 Maryland Ave SW Washington DC 20202

HORN, STEPHEN, retired congressman, political scientist; b. San Juan Bautista, Calif., May 31, 1931; s. John Stephen and Isabelle (McCaffrey) H.; m. Nini Moore, Sept. 4, 1954; children: Marcia Karen, John Stephen. AB with great distinction, Stanford, 1953, postgrad., 1953-54, 55-56, PhD in Polit. Sci, 1958; M in Pub Adminstrn., Harvard, 1955. Congl. fellow, 1958-59; adminstrv. asst. to sec. labor James P. Mitchell Washington, 1959-60; legislative asst. to U.S. Senator Thomas H. Kuchel, 1960-66; sr. fellow The Brookings Instn., 1966-69; dean grad. studies and research Am. U., 1969-70; pres. Calif. State U., Long Beach, 1970-88, Trustee prof. polit. sci., 1988-93; mem. U.S. Congress from 38th Calif. dist., 1993—2003; mem. govt. reform com., transp. and infrastructure com. Sr. cons., host The Govt. Story on TV, The Election Game (radio series), 1967-69, vice chmn. U.S. Commn. on Civil Rights, 1969-80 (commr. 1980-82); chmn. Urban Studies Fellow Adv. Com., U.S. Dept. HUD, 1969-70; mem. Law Enforcement Ednl. Prog. Adv. Com., U.S. Dept Justice, 1969-70; adv. bd. Nat. Inst. Corrections, 1972-88 (chmn. 1984-87), Author: The Cabinet and Congress, 1960, Unused Power: The Work of the Senate Committee on Appropriations, 1970, (with Edmund Beard) Congressional Ethics: The View from the House, 1975. Active Pres.-elect Nixon's Task Force on Orgn. Exec. Br., 1968, Kutak Found.; vice chmn. Long Beach Area C. of C., 1984-88; co-founder Western U.S. Com. Arts and Scis. for Eisenhower, 1956; chmn. Am. Assn. State Colls. and Univs., 1985-86; mem. Calif. Ednl. Facilities Authority, 1984-93. USAR, 1954-62. Fellow John F. Kennedy Inst. Politics Harvard U., 1966-67. Fellow Nat. Acad. Pub. Adminstrn.; mem. Stanford Assocs., Stanford Alumni Assn. (pres. 1976-77), Phi Beta Kappa, Pi Sigma Alpha. Republican.

HORN, WADE FREDERICK, psychologist, former federal agency administrator; b. Coral Gables, Fla., Dec. 3, 1954; s. John David and Daisy (Anderson) H.; m. Claudia Blair, Jan. 7, 1977; children: Christiana Watson, Caroline Lindley. BA in Psychology, Am. U., 1975; MA in Clin. Child Psychology, So. Ill. U., 1978, PhD in Clin. Child Psychology, 1981. Rsch. asst. social skills devel. program Carbondale (Ill.) Elem. Schs., 1976-78; behavior analyst, psychol. cons. early childhood program Wabash and Ohio Valley Spl. Edn. Dist., Norris City, Ill., 1978-79; predoctoral intern dept. pediatric psychology Children's Hosp. Nat. Med. Ctr., Washington, 1980-81, postdoctoral clin. psychology fellow behavioral medicine rsch. lab., 1981-82; asst. prof. dept. psychology Mich. State U., East Lansing, 1982-86; vice chairperson dept. pediatric psychology, dir. outpatient psychol. svcs. dept. psychiatry Children's Hosp. Nat. Med. Ctr., Washington, 1987-88; dir. Pediatric Psychology Splty. Clinic, assoc. dir. Psychol. Clinic Mich. State U., East Lansing, 1984-86; attending staff child health care unit St. Lawrence Hosp., Lansing, Mich., 1983-84; assoc. prof. psychiatry, behavioral scis. and child health and devel. Sch. Medicine, George Washington U., 1986-89; mem. presdl. transition team Office of Pres. Elect, Washington, 1988-89; commr. Adminstrn. on Children, Youth & Families US Dept Health & Human Services, 1989—93, chief Children's Bur Washington, 1989—93, asst. sec. for children & families, 2001—07; dir. pub. sector practice Deloitte Consulting LLP, 2007—. Adj. faculty dept. pediatrics Coll. Human Medicine, Mich. State U., East Lansing, 1983-86, Pub. Policy Ibst., Georgetown U., 1993-2001; mem. Nat. Commn. Childhood Disability, 1994-95; mem. U.S. Adv. Bd. on Welfare Educators, 1996-97. Author: (with G. Greenberg) Attention Deficit Disorder: Questions and Answers for Parents, 1991; contbr. articles to profl. jours. Mem. Health Care Adv. Group for George Bush for Pres. campaign, 1987-88. Mem. Am. Psychol. Assn. (divs. clin. psychology and child clin. psychology), Assn. for Advancement Behavior Therapy, Phi Kappa Phi. Republican. Presbyterian.

HORNADAY, JON RUSSELL, professional association administrator; b. Dallas, Dec. 30, 1935; s. Walter Charles and Anna (Agnell) H.; m. Rhoda Ann Barrier, Aug. 31, 1957; children: Jon Russell Jr., David Alan (dec.). BA in Journalism, U. Tex., Austin, 1958. Sales rep. Tex. Student Publs., Inc., Austin, 1956-58; prodn. asst. Brennan-McGary-Robinson Advt., Houston, 1957; advt. and exhibit mgr. Tex. Med. Assn., Austin, 1958-59, dir. pub. rels., 1959-63, dir. pub. rels. and advt., 1964-75, dir. comm., advt. dir., 1976-87, dir. spl. svcs., 1988—. Judge ann. film festival Pub. Rels. Soc. Am., NYC, 1980. Bd. dirs., chmn. com. Tex. divsn. Am. Cancer Soc., Austin, 1968—, del. to nat. orgn., Atlanta, 1986; chmn. mem. exec. com. Friends of Performing Arts Ctr., U. Tex., Austin, 1983-87; mem. Friends of Huntington Art Gallery, 1985—. Mem. AMA (mem. adv. com. to comm. dir. 1965-68, Med. Exec. Achievement award, 2005), Tex. Pub. Rels. Assn. (pres. 1964-65), Austin Advt. Club (pres. 1964-65, Addy award 1976, 81), Internat. Assn. Bus. Communicators (pres. 1963), Am. Assn. Med. Soc. Execs., Pub. Rels. Found. Tex. (trustee 1978-84), U. Tex. Alumni Assn., Lost Creek Country Club, Tex. Spokes Sports Car Club (past pres.). Mem. Christian Ch. (Disciples Of Christ). Avocations: sports cars, photography, travel, skiing. Home: 605 Brookhaven Trl Austin TX 78746-5454 Office: Tex Med Assn 401 W 15th St Austin TX 78701-1670 Business E-Mail: jon.hornaday@texmed.org.*

HORNADAY, RICHARD H., artist, retired educator; b. Joplin, Mo., Aug. 15, 1927; s. Beecher Hoyt and Zora Hornaday; m. Margaret Ann Gardner, June 29, 1950 (div. Mar. 1972); 1 child, Emily Jane; m. Ruth Mary Miller, Nov. 26, 1972 (dec. Feb. 2002); m. Jenifer Shevis-Packard, Sept. 28, 2002. BFA, U. Iowa, 1950, MFA, 1952; student, Calif. State U., Chico. Cert. art tchr. elem. and secondary schs., Calif. Art instr. Auburn (Calif.) H.S., 1953-54; art supr. elem. sch. dist., Redding, Calif., 1954-67; instr. drawing and painting Shasta Coll., Redding, 1954-68; prof. grad. studies Calif. State U., Chico, 1968-88, chair dept. art, 1972-80, prof. emeritus, 1988—. Judge No. Calif. Art Assn., Crocker Art Mus., Sacramento, 1959. Exhibited works in solo shows at Ruthermore Gallery, San Francisco, 1959-62, Nordness Gallery, N.Y.C., 1962, Henderson Gallery, Monterey, Calif., 1963, Retrospective exhibit Redding (Calif.) Art Mus., 1983, Rosicrucian Mus., San Jose, Calif., 1985, Himovitz Pavillions Gallery, Sacramento, 1992, Watercolor Gallery, Berkeley, Calif., 1985, Vagabond Rose Gallery, Chico, Calif., 1995—; group shows include Mus. Modern Art, N.Y.C., 1962, St. Louis Art Mus., 1963, San Francisco Mus. Art, 1963, 50-Yr. Crocker-Kingsley Retrospective, Sacramento, 1985, Nat. Watercolor Okla., 1994, Nat. Watercolor Exhbn., Concord, Calif., 1996, Visual Arts Ctr. N.E. Fla., Panama City, 1996, Ariz. Aqueous XI Nat., Tubac, 1997, Ga. XVIII Nat. Watercolor Exhbn., Macon, 1997, Taos Nat. Exhbn. Am. Watercolor III, 1997, Gt. Plains Nat., Ft. Hayes, Kans., 1998, Watercolor USA, Springfield, Mo., 1998, Vagabond Rose Gallery, Chico, Calif., 2006; works in collections at Shasta Coll., Calif. State U., Chico, Iowa State U., others; subject of articles. Mem. Civic Arts Commn., Redding, 1963-78; art cons. Shasta County Supt. Schs., 1964-67, Creative Arts Ctr., Chico, 1974-75, others. Served with USN, 1945-46, PTO. Recipient awards for art. Home: PO Box 7652 Chico CA 95927-7652

HORNAK, THOMAS, retired electronics company executive; b. Bratislava, Slovakia, Oct. 14, 1924; came to U.S., 1968; s. Stefan and Elisabeth (Meer) H.; m. Vera Lautner, Mar. 15, 1958; 1 child, Thomas MSEE, Tech U., Bratislava, 1947; PhD in Elec. Engring., Tech U., Prague, Czech Republic, 1966. Sect. mgr. Tesla Radio Research Lab., Prague, 1947-61; sci. advisor Computer Research Inst., Prague, 1962-68; mem. tech. staff Hewlett Packard Labs., Palo Alto, Calif., 1968-73, mgr. research dept., 1973-91, prin. engr., 1991-99, ret., 1999. Contbr. articles to profl. jours. Patentee in field Fellow IEEE (life; assoc. editor Jour. Solid State Cirs. 1986-88, 2001—04, chmn. solid state cirs. and tech. com. 1979-81).

HORNBACH, DANIEL J., biologist, educator; BS in Biology magna cum laude, U. Dayton, 1974, MS in Biology, 1976; PhD in Zoology, Miami U., Ohio, 1980. Asst. prof. dept. biology U. Va., Va., 1980—84, Macalester Coll., St. Paul, 1984—87, assoc. prof. dept. biology, 1987—93, prof. dept. biology, 1993—97, DeWitt Wallace prof. dept. biology, 1998—, chair dept. biology, 1996—99, provost, 1993—95, 1999—2005, dean, 1999—2005. Mem. faculty Mountain Lake Biol. Sta. U. Va., 1981, 82, 84; team mem. Higginsi Eye Pearly Mussel Endangered Species Recover Team U.S. Fish and Wildlife Svc., 1995—; adj. prof. grad. faculty divsn. water quality dept. fisheries and wildlife U. Minn., 1996—. Assoc. editor: Am. Midland Naturalist, 1995—2001. Recipient Alumni Spl. Achievement award, U. Dayton, 1994; grantee, NSF, 1987, 1988, U.S. Army Corps of Engrs., 1987—90, 1996, Pew Charitable Trusts, 1990, Blandin Found., 1990—91, Minn. Dept. Natural Resources, 1990—91, 1992—93, US EPA, 1991, 1992—96, Wis. Dept. Natural Resources, 1992, 1997—98, U.S. Nat. Pk. Svc., 1993—96, 1997, 1998, 2000—02, 2001—04, 2004—, U.S. Fish and Wildlife Svc., 1994—95, Legis. Commn. on Minn. Resources, 1997—98, 1999—2001. Mem.: N.Am. Benthological Soc., Malacological Soc. London (Sir Charles Maurice Yonge award 2002), Coun. on Undergrad. Rsch., Am. Malacological Union. Office: Macalester College 1600 Grand Ave Saint Paul MN 55105*

HORNBECK, LARRY J., physicist, researcher; b. Mo. m. Laura Hornbeck; 2 children. B in Physics, Case Western Res. U., Cleveland; M in Solid State Physics, PhD in Solid State Physics, Case Western Res. U., Cleve. Mem. tech. staff ctrl. rsch. labs. Tex. Instruments, Dallas, 1973—83, sr. mem. tech. staff, 1983—93, Tex. Instruments fellow, 1993—. Contbr. articles to sci. jours. Recipient Eduard Rhein Found. Tech. award, 1995, Emmy award for Inventing Digital Light Processing Tech., Acad. TV Arts & Scis., 1998, Karl Ferdinand Braun prize, Soc. Info. Display Internat. Symposium, 1999, David Sarnoff Medal award, Soc. Motion Picture and TV Engrs., 2002, Best of Small Tech. Lifetime Achievement award, Small Times, 2004. Fellow: Internat. Soc. Optical Engring.; mem.: IEEE (Daniel E. Noble award 2004), NAE. Achievements include invention of the Digital Micromirror Device in 1987; patents in field. Mailing: 3130 Bethel Cannon Rd Van Alstyne TX 75495-3571 Fax: 214-567-5454. E-mail: l-hornbeck@ti.com.*

HORNBEIN, THOMAS FREDERIC, anesthesiologist; b. St. Louis, Nov. 6, 1930; s. Leonard and Rosalie (Bernstein) Hornbein; m. Gene Schwartz (div. 1968); children: Lia, Lynn, Cari, Andrea, Robert; m. Kathryn Mikesell, Dec. 24, 1971; 1 child, Melissa. BA, U. Colo.; MD, Wash. U. Diplomate Am. Bd. Anesthesiology. Intern King County Hosp., Seattle; resident in anesthesiology Wash. U., St. Louis, USPHS postdoctoral residency, instr. anesthesiology div., 1960—61; asst. prof. U. Wash., Seattle, 1963—67, assoc. prof., 1967—70, prof. anesthesiology, physiology and biophysics, 1970—2002, prof. emeritus, 2002—. Vice chmn. dept. anesthesiology U. Wash., Seattle, 1972—74, asst. chmn. rsch., 1974—77, chmn., 1979—93, rsch. affiliate Primate Ctr., 1980; bd. dirs. Colo. Ctr. for Alternative Medicine and Physiology, 2003—. Author: Everest the West Ridge, 1966 (rated #1 Outside Mag., 2003). Mem. bd. trustees Little Sch., Bellevue, Wash., 1982—89; bd. dirs. Colorado Ctr. Alt. Medicine and Physiology, 2003. Served to lt. comdr. USN, 1961—63. Recipient George Norlin award, U. Colo., Denver, 1970, Alumni Centennial Symposium award, 1975, Disting. Tchg. award, U. Wash., 1982. Fellow: AAAS; mem.: Inst. of Medicine, Soc. Acad. Anesthesia Chmn., Assn. Univ. Anesthetists (treas. 1969—72, pres. 1974—75), Am. Soc. Anesthesiologists (Rovenstine lectr. 1989), Am. Physiol. Soc. (editor 1967—73), Alpha Omega Alpha, Phi Beta Kappa. Avocation: mountain climbing. Office: U Wash Sch Medicine Dept Anesthesiology PO Box 356540 Seattle WA 98195-6540 Business E-Mail: hornbnt@u.washington.edu.

HORNBERGER, GEORGE MILTON, environmental science educator; b. Fountain Springs, Pa., June 22, 1942; s. George Vincent and Olive Mae (Delcamp) H.; m. Joan Marie Zackey, Aug. 28, 1965; children: Rachel Joan, George Zackey. BSCE, Drexel U., 1965, MSCE, 1967; PhD, Stanford U., 1970. Asst. prof. U. Va., Charlottesville, 1970-75, assoc. prof., 1975-84, prof., 1984—, disting. prof., 1991—, Ernest H. Ern prof., 1993—, assoc. dean for sci., 2002—. Vis. fellow Australian Nat. U., Canberra, 1977-78; vis. scientist Inst. Hydrology, Wallingford, Eng., 1980, U.S. Geol. Survey, 1990-91; hon. vis. prof. U. Lancaster (Eng.), 1984-85, Stanford U., 1990-91, U. Colo., 1997-98; mem. bd. Radioactive Waste Mgmt. of NAS, 1986-91, chmn. Commn. on Geoscis., Environment and Resources, 1996-2000; chmn. bd. Earth Scis. and Resources of NAS, 2003—, chmn., 2003—; chmn. adv. com. nuclear waste U.S. NRC, 2001-03. Author: Numerical Methods in Subsurface Hydrology, 1971, Elements of Physical Hydrology, 1998; assoc. editor Am. Geophys. Union, 1980-84; N.Am. editor John Wiley & Sons, Eng., 1986-92; editor-in-chief Water Resources Rsch., Am. Geophys. Union, 1993-96. Recipient John Wesley Powell award U.S. Geol. Survey, 1995, First Biennial medal for natural systems Australian Simulation Soc., 1995, Bownocker medal Ohio State U., 1999; elected to NAE, 1996; grantee NSF, Army Rsch. Office, EPA, Nat. Park Svc., NATO, Dept. Energy. Fellow Am. Geophys. Union (pres.-elect hydrology sect. 2004, Robert E. Horton award hydrology sect. 1993, Excellence in Geophys. Edn. award 1999), Assn. for Women in Sci.; mem. NAE, Geol. Soc. Am., Am. Geophys. Union, Sigma Xi. Home: 308 Farm Ln Charlottesville VA 22902-5324 Office: U Va Dept Environ Sci Clark Hall Charlottesville VA 22903-3188 Home Phone: 434-295-7459; Office Phone: 434-924-3437. Business E-Mail: hornberger@virginia.edu.

HORNBERGER, KEITH ROBERT, chemist; b. Balt., June 26, 1976; s. Bruce Robert and Sharon Ann Hornberger; m. Devon Nicole LaBelle LaBelle, June 29, 2002; 1 child, Noah Robert. BS with honors, U. Del., Newark, 1993—97; PhD, Columbia U., NYC, 1997—2002. Prin. scientist medicinal chemistry GlaxoSmithKline, Rsch. Triangle Park, NC, 2002—06, investigator medicinal chemistry, 2006—. Contbr. articles to profl. jours. Mem.: Am. Chem. Soc., Phi Kappa Phi. R-Consevative. Luth. Achievements include patents for medicinal chemistry patents for cancer indications. Office: GlaxoSmithKline 5 Moore Dr Research Triangle Park NC 27709 Home Phone: 919-367-8918. Business E-Mail: keith.r.hornberger@gsk.com.

HORNBY, DAVID BROCK, federal judge; b. Brandon, Manitoba, Can., Apr. 21, 1944; s. William Ralph Hornby and Retha Patricia (Fox) Sword; m. Helaine Cora Mandel, Oct. 9, 1946; children: Kirstin, Zachary. BA, U. Western Ont., 1965; JD, Harvard U., 1969. Bar: Va. 1973, Maine 1974, U.S. Supreme Ct. 1980. Law clk. U.S. Ct. Appeals, New Orleans, 1969-70; assoc. prof. U. Va. Sch. Law, Charlottesville, 1970-74; ptnr. Perkins, Thompson, Hinckley & Keddy, Portland, Maine, 1974-82; U.S. magistrate Dist. Maine, Portland, 1982-88; assoc. justice Maine Supreme Jud. Ct., Portland, 1988-90; judge U.S. Dist. Ct. Maine, 1990—; chief judge, 1996—2003. Contbr. articles to profl. jours.; editor, officer Harvard Law Rev., 1967-69. Fellow Am. Bar Found.; mem. ABA, Am. Law Inst., Maine State Bar Assn., Maine Bar Found. (bd. trustees 1990-94), Cumberland County Bar Assn. Office: US Dist Ct Edward T Gignoux Courthouse 156 Federal St Portland ME 04101-4152

HORNBY, NICK, writer; b. Maidenhead, Eng., Apr. 17, 1957; s. Sir Derek Hornby; m. Virginia Bovell (div.); 1 child, Danny; 2 children, Lowell and Jesse, with Amanda Posey. Student, Cambridge U. Author: (essay collection) Contemporary American Fiction, 1992, 31 Songs (pub. in US as Songbook), 2003, (memoir) Fever Pitch, 1992, (novels) High Fidelity, 1995, About a Boy, 1998, How to be Good, 2001 (WH Smith Fiction Award, 2002), A Long Way Down, 2005, (screenplays) Fever Pitch, 1997; editor: My Favourite Year: A Collection of New Football Writing, 1993, Speaking with the Angel, 2001; co-editor (with Nick Coleman): The Picador Book of Sportswriting, 1996; exec. prodr.: Fever Pitch, 2005. Co-founder TreeHouse Trust, London, 1997. Recipient EM Forster Award, AAAL, 1999.

HORNE, BENJAMIN DAVIES, epidemiologist; s. David Hughes and Barbara Alice Horne; m. Carolyn Joy Waisman. BSc, Brigham Young U., 1996; MPH, U. Utah, Salt Lake City, 1998, MStat, 2002, PhD, 2005. Epidemiologist, cardiovasc. dept. LDS Hosp., Salt Lake City, 1999—2005, dir. cardiovasc. and genetic epidemiology, 2005—. Mem. Ch. Jesus Christ Latter-day Saints, Salt Lake City, 1971—. Fellow, Am. Heart Assn., 2004—06; John D. Morgan fellow, Deseret Found., 2004. Mem.: SAR (pres. Utah chpt. 2006—). Office: LDS Hosp 8th Avenue & C Street Salt Lake City UT 84143 Office Phone: 801-408-5442.

HORNE, JOHN R., farm equipment company executive; b. Gary, Ind., 1938; Grad., Purdue U., 1960, Bradley U., 1964. Group v.p., gen. mgr. Navistar Internat. Transp. Corp.; pres., COO, now CEO Navistar Internat. Corp., 1995—, also bd. dirs., 1995—; pres., CEO Navistar Internat. Corp. and Internat. Truck & Engine Corp., 1995—; also chmn. bd. dirs. Navistar Internat. Corp. Mem.Soc. Automotive Engrs. (chmn. fin. com.). Office: Internatl Truck & Engine Corp PO Box 1488 Warrenville IL 60555-7488

HORNE, MARILYN BERNEICE, mezzo-soprano; b. Bradford, Pa., Jan. 16, 1934; d. Bentz and Berneice Horne; m. Henry Lewis, July 1, 1960 (div. 1974); 1 child. Student, U. So. Calif.; MusD (hon.), Rutgers U., 1970, Jersey City State Coll., 1973, Brown U., 1984, Juillard Sch. Music, 1994; DLitt (hon.), St. Peter's Coll.; LHD (hon.), Kean Coll., 1977. Vocal program dir. Music Acad. of the West, Santa Barbara, Calif., 1995—. Singer: (Operas) (debut) as Hata in The Bartered Bride, 1954, (La Scala debut) Oepidus Rex, 1969, (Met. Opera debut) as Adalgisa in Norma, 1970, (other roles) Rosina in Barber of Seville, Cleonte in The Siege of Corinth, Isabella in L'Italiana in Algieri, Carmen at Met. Opera, 1972—73, Laura in Harvest, Chgo. Lyric Opera, Marie in Wozzeck, San Francisco Opera, (appeared in) Phigenie en Tauride, Semiramide, Samson et Dalila at Met. Opera, 1987, The Ghost of Versailles, 1991, Pelléas et Mélisande, 1995, Venice Festival by invitation of Igor Stravinsky, Am. Opera Soc., N.Y.C., for several seasons, Vancouver Opera, Philharm. Hall, N.Y.C., Paris, Dallas, Houston, Covent Garden, London, roles at La Scala, Italy, Rossini Opera Festival, Pesaro, Italy, Met. Opera, 1987, (recital debuts) Madrid, Dresden, East Berlin, 1987; performer: (at inauguration) of U.S. President Clinton, 1993, ann. recital at Carnegie Hall, European tour with husband for Dept. State, 1963; rec. artist London, Columbia, Deutsche Grammaphon and RCA records, recs. include soundtrack Carmen Jones. Founder Marilyn Horne Found. Named Musician of Yr. Musical Am., 1995, Kennedy Ctr. honoree, 1995; named to Harold C. Schonberg's N.Y. Times' list of 9 All-Time, All-Star Singers in Met. Opera's 100 Years, 1984, Am. Classical Music Hall of Fame, Cin., 1999; recipient Grammy awards, 1964, 1981, 1983, 1994, Handel medallion, 1980, Premio d'Oro, Italian Govt., 1982, Commendatore al merito della Repubblica Italiana, 1983, Gold Merit medal Nat. Soc. Arts and Letters, 1987, Fidelio Gold medal, 1988, George Peabody award, 1989, Silver medal Covent Garden Royal Opera House, 1989, Disting. Dau. of Pa. Silver medal San Francisco Opera, 1990, Nat. Arts medal, 1992. Achievements include having the leading exponent florid vocal style, music of Rossini, Handel, Vivaldi. also: care Met Opera Assoc Attention: Artistic Dept Lincoln Ctr New York NY 10023 also: BMG Classics/RCA 1540 Broadway New York NY 10036-4039 Office: Music Academy of the West 1070 Fairway Rd Santa Barbara CA 93108-2899 also: Columbia Artists Management Llc 1790 Broadway # 6 New York NY 10019-1412

HORNE, MARJORIE, production stage manager, event consultant; b. Bklyn., Sept. 17, 1945; d. Clinton Davis and Pauline Sklar Horne. BA, Hunter Coll., NYC, 1990. Theater stage mgr., 1973—2004; event planner, 1999—; political and not-for-profit fundraiser, project cons. McEvoy and Assocs., NYC, 2002—. Actor: No Place to Be Somebody, over 25 other plays and musicals; stage mgr. (Broadway plays) Enchanted April, A Class Act, True West, Street Corner Symphony, Electra, St. Joan, prodn. stage mgr. over 100 prodns., including I'm Getting My Act Together and Taking It on the Road, 1978—81, Greater Tuna, 1982—85, prodns. for theater cos. including Lincoln Ctr. Theater, Nat. Actors' Theater, Manhattan Theater Club, Playwrights Horizons, 2d Stage, Cir. Repertory, NY Theater Workshop, 1973—2002, prodn. supr. Am. Theatre Wing TONY Awards, 2005—07, stage mgr., prodn. mgr. numerous corporate and pub. events including V-Day, US Open, Clinton Global Initiative, Dem. Congl. Campaign Com. Inaugural Gala Spkr. of the House Nancy Pelosi. Vol. anthropology dept. Am. Mus. Natural History, NYC; fundraiser Ferraro for US Senate, 1992; mem. Cmty. Free Dems., NYC, 1992—; pres. Nat. Women's Polit. Caucus, NYC, 1994—96, treas., 1997—99; fundraiser Catherine Abate for Senate, 1994, Catherine Abate for Atty. Gen., 1997; dir. ops, vol. coord. Ferraro for Senate, NY, 1998; dir. nomination of Hillary Rodham Clinton for US Senate NY State Dem. Conv., 2000; campaign mgr. Joyce Johnson for Assembly, NYC, 2002; campaign cons. Joyce Johnson for City Coun., NYC, 2005; charter mem. Nat. Mus. Women in the Arts, Washington, Nat. Women's History Mus., Washington. Mem.: Stage Mgrs.' Assn. (chair 1991—93, bd. dirs. 1993—2002), Actors' Equity Assn. (councillor 1994—). Democrat. Avocations: archaeology, travel.

HORNE, MICHAEL STEWART, lawyer; b. Mpls., May 10, 1938; s. Owen Edward and Adeline (DiGeorgio) H.; m. Martha Brean, Sept. 11, 1965; children: Jennifer, Katherine, Sarah, Owen. BA, U. Minn., 1959; LLB, Harvard U., 1962. Bar: D.C. 1963, U.S. Ct. Appeals (D.C. cir.) 1964, U.S. Supreme Ct. 1968, U.S. Ct. Appeals (6th cir.) 1966, U.S. Ct. Appeals (9th cir.) 1978, U.S. Ct. Appeals (4th cir.) 1979, U.S. Ct. Appeals (5th cir.) 1979, U.S. Ct. Appeals (2d cir.) 1980, U.S. Ct. Appeals (11th cir.) 1983, U.S. Ct. Appeals (8th cir.) 1984, U.S. Ct. Appeals (10th cir.) 1997. Assoc. Covington & Burling, Washington, 1964-71, ptnr., 1971—. Co-author (with T.S. Williamson and A. Herman): The Contingent Workforce, Business and Legal Strategies, 2000. Mem. ABA, D.C. Bar Assn., FCC Bar Assn., Am. Judicature Soc. Democrat. Home: 9008 Levelle Dr Bethesda MD 20815-5608 Office: Covington & Burling 1201 Pennsylvania Ave NW PO Box 7566 Washington DC 20044-7566 Personal E-mail: hornems1@verizon.net. Business E-Mail: mhorne@cov.com.

HORNE, TERRY, publishing executive; 4 children. BA, Wichita State U., 1975; MS, Okla. State U., 1982. V.p., chief ops. officer, pub. Clarksburg (W.Va.) Pub. Co., 1996—2000; v.p. & chief ops. officer Swift Newspapers, Reno, 2000—04; v.p. cmty. newspapers Ariz. Republic, 2004—07; pub. East Valley Tribune, Mesa, Ariz., 2007; pres. & pub. Orange County Register, Santa Ana, Calif., 2007—. Named Citizen of Yr., Clarksburg (W.Va.) Bd. Edn., 1998. Office: Freedom Communications 17666 Fitch Irvine CA 92614-6022 also: Orange County Register 625 N Grand Ave Santa Ana CA 92701 Office Phone: 714-796-7000. Office Fax: 714-796-3681.*

HORNE, WILLIAM MCHENRY, finance educator; b. Shreveport, La., Mar. 17, 1921; s. William McHenry and Nora (Kalmbach) H.; m. Joan Spear, Sept. 2, 1950 (div. Oct. 1974); children: Lynellyn D., William McHenry III; m. Alice Hobart, Dec. 28, 1980. BA, DePauw U., 1942; JD, Harvard U., 1949. Bar: Mass. 1949, Ind. 1949, D.C. 1955, Md. 1964. Atty., advisor U.S. Tax Ct., Washington, 1949—50; staff atty. joint com. on taxation U.S. Congress, Washington, 1953—55; assoc. Warner, Stackpole, Stetson & Bradlee, Boston, 1955—57; dir. taxes Olin Mathieson Chem. Corp. (now Olin Corp.), NYC, 1957—64; v.p. Comml. Credit Co., Balt., 1964—70; ptnr. Reed, Smith, Shaw & McClay, Pitts., Washington and Harrisburg (Pa.), 1970—73; sr. v.p., gen. tax counsel Citicorp and Citibank N.A., NYC, 1973—80; lectr. dept. mgmt. and policy Coll. Bus. Adminstrn. U. Ariz., Tucson, 1983—89; vis. prof. DePauw U., Greencastle, Ind., 1989—91. Mem. adv. com. to commr. IRS, 1969-70; past mem. tax and acctg. com. N.Y. Clearing House; past chmn. taxation com. Fin. Execs. Inst.; trustee Fin. Execs. Rsch. Found., 1975-79; fin. cons., 1980-91; bd. dirs. Ariz. Coun. Ct. Apptd. Spl. Advocates, pres., 1997-99; speaker in field. Author: Proceedings of New York University Annual Institute on Federal Income Taxation: Offers in Compromise, 1958; also chpts. to books and articles to profl. jours. Lt. USAAC, 1942-46, PTO; maj. JAGC, USAF, 1950-52. Recipient Disting. Alumni award DePauw U., Greencastle, Ind., 1976; Alfred P. Sloan fellow MIT, Cambridge, 1942. Mem. Tax Execs. Inst. (hon., pres., chmn. bd. dirs. 1968-69), Sigma Chi, Phi Beta Kappa. Avocations: hiking, water activities, travel. Home: 2465 W Tom Watson Dr Tucson AZ 85742-8531 E-mail: wmhorne@comcast.net.

HORNER, ALTHEA JANE, psychologist; b. Hartford, Conn., Jan. 13, 1926; d. Louis and Celia (Newmark) Greenwald; children: Martha Horner Hartley, Anne Horner Benck, David, Kenneth. BS in Psychology, U. Chgo., 1952; PhD in Clin. Psychology, U. So. Calif., U. Park, 1965. Lic. psychologist NY, Calif. Tchr. Pasadena (Calif.) City Coll., 1965-67; from asst. to assoc. prof. LA Coll. Optometry, 1967-70; supr. Psychology interns Pasadena Child Guidance Clinic, 1969-70; pvt. practice specializing in psychoanalysis and psychoanalytic psychotherapy NYC, 1970-83; supervising psychologist dept. psychiatry Beth Israel Med. Ctr., NYC, 1972-83, coord. group therapy tng., 1976-82, clinician in charge Brief Adaptation-Oriented Psychotherapy Rsch. Group, 1982-83; assoc. clin. prof. Mt. Sinai Sch. Medicine, NYC, 1977-91, adj. assoc. prof., 1991—; mem. faculty Nat. Psychol. Assn. for Psychoanalysis, NYC, 1982-83; sr. mem. faculty Wright Inst. LA Postgrad. Inst., 1983-85; pvt. practice LA, 1983—2004; clin. prof. dept. psychology UCLA, 1985-95; ret., 2004. Author: (with others) Treating the Neurotic Patient in Brief Psychotherapy, 1985, Object Relations and the Developing Ego in Therapy, 1979, rev. edit., 1984, Little Big Girl, 1982, Being and Loving, 1978, 3rd edit., 2005, Psychology for Living (with G. Forehand), 4th edit., 1977, The Wish for Power and the Fear of Having It, 1989, The Primacy of Structure, 1990, Psychoanalytic Object Relations Therapy, 1991, Working With the Core Relationship Problem in Psychotherapy, 1998, Chrysalis, 1999, Get Over It! Untie Your Relationship Knots and Move On, 2000, Dealing with Resistance in Psychotherapy, 2005; mem. editl. bd. Jour. Humanistic Psychology, 1986—, Am. Jour. Psychoanalysis; assoc. editor Jour. Am. Acad. of Psychoanalysis; contbr. articles to profl. jours Mem. APA, Am. Acad. Psychoanalysis (sci. assoc.), So. Calif. Psychoanalytic Soc. and Inst. (hon.). Personal E-mail: altheajane@earthlink.net.

HORNER, ANTHONY ADAM, pediatrician, educator; b. NYC, May 24, 1960; s. Harry and Joan Ruth (Frankel) H. BA in Biochemistry, U. Calif. San Diego, 1983; MD, St. Louis U., 1987. Diplomate Am. Bd. Pediatrics, Am. Bd. Allergy and Immunology. Resident in pediatrics UCLA Med. Ctr., 1990; fellow in pediatric immunology Boston Children's Hosp., 1994; asst. prof. pediatrics med. sch. U. Calif. San Diego, San Diego, 1994—. Co-principle investigator Children's Asthma Mgmt. Program, San Diego, 1994-99. Fellow Am. Acad. Pediatrics, Am. Acad. Allergy and Immunology. Achievements include rsch. in the devel. of DNA-based vaccination strategies for the treatment of disease. Office: U Calif San Diego Med Sch 9500 Gilman Dr # Mc663 La Jolla CA 92093-5004 Office Phone: 858-534-5435. E-mail: ahorner@uosd.edu.

HORNER, CARL MATTHEW, chemistry professor; b. Cicero, NY, June 4, 1930; s. Oscar Wendell and Gladys Cecilia (Horner) H. BS, LeMoyne Coll., 1952; MS, Syracuse U., 1958, PhD, 1965. Asst. prof. analytical chemistry SUNY-Oneonta, 1958-61, assoc. prof., 1961-64, prof., 1964—97, prof. emeritus, 1998—. Coord. ann. instrumental chemistry workshops, 1986-95; docent Edison Botanic Rsch. Lab., Ft. Myers, Fla., 2006—. NSF CAUSE grantee, 1979-82; NSF CSIP grantee, 1986-88; Walter B. Ford Found. grantee, 1980, 83. Mem. AAAS, Am. Chem. Soc., N.Y. Acad. Scis. Achievements include research in infrared spectroscopy and laboratory robotics. Avocations: scuba diving, photography. Home: 24 Suncrest Ter Oneonta NY 13820-4632

HORNER, CONSTANCE JOAN, federal agency administrator; b. Summit, NJ, Feb. 24, 1942; d. David Earl and Cecelia (Murphy) McNeely; m. Charles Edward Horner, May 7, 1965; children: David Bayer, Jonathan Purcell. BA in English Lit., U. Pa., 1964; MA in English Lit., U. Chgo., 1967. Dep. asst. dir. policy planning and evaluation ACTION Agy., Washington, 1981-82, acting assoc. dir. domestic & anti-poverty ops., 1982-83, dep. assoc. dir. for VISTA & service-learning, 1982-83; assoc. dir. for econs. & govt. Office of Mgmt. and Budget, Washington, 1983-85; dir. Office of Pers. Mgmt., Washington, 1985-89; deputy sec. HHS, 1989-91; asst. to pres. and dir. presdl. pers. The White House, Washington, 1991-93; mem. U.S. Commn. on Civil Rights, Washington, 1993-98. Commr. The White House Fellows Commn., Washington, 1985-89; guest scholar The Brookings Inst., Washington, 1993-05; vis. faculty Princeton (NJ) U., 1994; fellow, lectr. Johns Hopkins U., 1994-95; mem. adv. com. women in svcs. Dept. Def., 2003; bd. dirs. Pfizer, Inc., Prudential Fin., Inc., Ingersoll-Rand Co. Ltd. Bd. dirs. Annie E. Casey Found., Balt., 1994—. Fellow: Nat. Acad. Pub. Adminstrn.; mem.: Cosmos Club. Republican. Home: 3171 Porter St NW Washington DC 20008-3210

HORNER, GRACE ANN, application developer; b. Chgo., May 14, 1950; d. Harry Eugene Horner and Jeannette Lally Vollman. BS in Elem. Edn., No. Ill. U., 1972, MS in Outdoor Tchr. Edn., 1977. Cert. Control Data Inst., Ill., 1984. Optometric asst. Dr. Harry E. Horner, Optometrist, Round Lake, Ill., 1965—79; tchr. third grade Round Lake (Ill.) Area Unit Sch. Dist., 1972—73, substiute tchr., 1972—78; tchr. aide Woodlands Sch. Dist., Gages Lake, Ill., 1978—79; dir. adult edn. , field adv. No. Oakland County Girl Scout Coun., Pontiac, Mich., 1979—83; programmer Marca Med. Industries, Chicago, Ill., 1984—86, AMF Industires, Arlington Heights, Ill., 1986—87; programmer analyst Block and Co., Inc., Wheeling, Ill., 1987—. Musician: Round Lake Area Community Park District Band, 1972—79, Round Lake Area Park District Community Band, 1983—84, College of Lake County Wind Ensemble, 1977—79, 1983—84; contbr. columns in newspapers. Leader Lakeview Girl Scout Coun., Libertyville, Ill., 1972—79, mem. com., 1972—79; vestry comm. chair St. Philip's Episcopal Ch., Palatine, Ill., 1999—2001, pontice, 1986—; conv. del. Episcopal Diocese, Chgo., 1998; mem. choir, lay reader All Saints Episc. Ch., 1979—83. Mem.: Geneal. Group Wis., Nat. Geneal. Soc., Fedn. of Geneal. Societies (book reviewer 2004—), Chgo. Geneal. Soc. (workshop chmn. 1988—89, dir. 1989—92, columnist 1990—, second v.p. 1991—93, pres. 1993—95, past pres. 1995—98, Appreciation cert. 1999), Ill. State Geneal. Soc., Friends of Newberry Libr. (assoc.). Episcopalian. Avocations: genealogy, tai chi chuan, flute, singing, photography. Home Phone: 847-359-4828; Office Phone: 847-215-5951.

HORNER, HARRY CHARLES, JR., sales executive; b. Pitts., Oct. 30, 1937; s. Harry Charles and Sara Marie (Hysong) H.; m. Patricia Ann Hagarty, June 15, 1965 (div. 1981); m. Sharon Kae Wyatt, Dec. 30, 1983; children: Jeffrey Brian, Jennifer Leigh, Mark Gregory BFA, U. Cin., 1963; postgrad., Xavier U., Cin., 1963—64. Mgr. Retail Credit Co., Atlanta, 1964—68; ops. mgr. Firestone Tire and Rubber Co., LA, 1968—80; exec. v.p. Romney/Ford Enterprises Inc., Scottsdale, Ariz., 1980—85; sales mgr. Environ. Care Inc., Calabassas, Calif., 1985—93; ops. v.p. Albuquerque Grounds Maintenance, Inc., 1993—2002; gen. mgr. and ptnr. Landwork S.W., Phoenix, 2002—; gen. mgr. Mesa Constrn., Landscape and Design, Albuquerque, 2004—; project mgmt., bus. devel. Lee Landscapes, Albuquerque, 2007—. Pres., CEO The Cons. Group Cos. Ltd., Palm Desert, Calif., 1984—; pres. E. Valley Theatre Co., Chandler, Ariz., 1984-86; bd. dirs. KUNM Radio, Albuquerque Cons. Ariz. Commn. on Arts, Phoenix, 1983-84 Democrat. Mem. Lds Ch. Avocations: flying, model railroads. Office: PO Box 14912 Albuquerque NM 87191 also: Mesa Construction 514 Pope St NE Albuquerque NM 87107 Office Phone: 505-822-8722, 505-991-6881. Personal E-mail: harryh@leelandscapes.com.

HORNER, JOHN ATLEE, educational association administrator; b. Pitts., Pa., Oct. 7, 1928; s. John Atlee Horner and Dorothy Mae Brandau; m. Mary Alice Miller, Aug. 20, 1955; children: Marilyn Jean Knox, John Atlee III. AB cum laude, Kenyon Coll.; MA in ednl. adminstrn., Western Reserve U. Tchr. Blair Acad., Blairstown, NJ, 1950—52, Landon Sch., Wash., DC, 1952—53, U. Sch., Shaker Heights, Ohio, 1953—68; headmaster Harrisburg Acad., Harrisburg, Pa., 1968—78; exec. dir. Cleveland Engrng. Soc., Ohio, 1979—85; interim dir. Shaker Lakes Regional Ctr., 1988—89, 1992—93; bd. trustees and pres. Shaker Lakes Regional Nature Ctr., 1985—. Mem. editl. bd. Jour. Ednl. Thought, 1965—68. Chmn. recreation bd. City of Shaker Heights, 1968; chmn. pub. sch. United Fund, 1971. Recipient Lifetime Tchr., State of Ohio. Mem.: SAR (former v.p. gen. 1993—95), Torch Internat. (bd. mem.), Fellowship of Christian Athletes (hon. trustee), Cleve. Alumni of Kenyon Coll. (pres.), Shaker Lakes Nature Ctr. (pres.), Ret. Athletic Dir. and Coaches (pres.), Rotary Club. Avocations: golf, tennis, bridge. Home: 3008 Fontenay Rd Cleveland OH 44120 Personal E-mail: johnmagnolia@aol.com.

HORNER, JOHN ROBERT, paleontologist, researcher, curator; b. Shelby, Mont., June 15, 1946; s. John Henry and Miriam Whitted (Stith) H.; m. Virginia Lee Seacotte, Mar. 30, 1972 (div. 1982); 1 child, Jason James; m. Joann Katherine Raffelson, Oct. 3, 1986 (div. 1994); m. Celeste Claire Roach, Jan. 21, 1995 (div. 2005). Studied geology and zoology, U. Mont., 1964—66, studied geology and zoology, 1968—72, DSc (hon.), 1986, Pa. State, 2006. Rsch. asst. dept. geology, asst. curator, palenotology, dept. geological sciences, Mus. of Natural History Princeton U., NJ, 1975-82; curator paleontology Mus. of the Rockies, Mont. State U., Bozeman, 1982—; Regents prof. paleontology Mont. State U., 2001—. Rsch. scientist Am. Mus. Nat. History, N.Y.C., 1980-82; lectr. in field; Sigma XI National lecturer, 1987-1989, Phi Beta Kappa Visiting Scholar, 1997-1998. Co-author: Maia: A Dinosaur Grows up, 1985, Digging Dinosaurs, 1988 (N.Y. Acad. Sci. award 1989), Digging Up Tyrannosaurus Rex, 1993, The Complete T-Rex, 1993, Dinosaur Lives, 1997, Dinosaurs Under the Big Sky, 2001; co-editor (profl. book) Dinosaur Eggs and Babies, 1994; served as tech. advisor (films) Jurassic Park, The Lost World (Jurassic Park II), and Jurassic Park III; contbr. articles to profl. jours. With USMC, 1966-68; Vietnam. MacArthur fellow, 1986; recipient Am. Acad. Achievement award, 1993, Journalism award, Am. Assn. Petroleum Geologists, 1994, Award for Outstanding Contribution to Pub. Understanding of Geology, Am. Geolological Inst., 1995. Achievements include discovery of a new genus of duckbilled dinosaur, Maiasaura; accomplishments include: the theory of endothermic metabolism in dinosaur development, of parental nurture of new-born hatchlings, that Tyrannosaurus rex was a scavenger; excavator of the Egg Mountain cache of dinosaur nests. Home: 310 Hoffman Dr Bozeman MT 59715-5724 Office: Mus Of The Rockies Mont State U 600 W Kagy Blvd Bozeman MT 59717-2730 Business E-Mail: jhorner@montana.edu.

HORNER, MATINA SOURETIS, retired academic administrator, corporate financial executive; b. Boston, July 28, 1939; d. Demetre John and Christine (Antonopoulos) Souretis; m. Joseph L. Horner, June 25, 1961; children: Tia Andrea, John, Christopher. AB cum laude, Bryn Mawr Coll., 1961; MS, U. Mich., 1963, PhD, 1968; LLD (hon.), Dickinson Coll., 1973; LLD, Mt. Holyoke Coll., 1973; LLD (hon.), U. Pa., 1975, Smith Coll., 1979, Wheaton Coll., 1979, U. Mich., 1989; LHD (hon.), U. Mass., 1973, Tufts U., 1976, U. Hartford, 1980, U. New Eng., 1987, Bentley Coll., 1989, New Eng. Coll., 1989, Pine Manor Coll., 1989, Am. Coll. Greece, 1990; DLitt (hon.), Claremont U. Ctr. and Grad Sch., 1988, Hellenic Coll., 1990; LHD (hon.), Colby Sawyer Coll., 1991. Teaching fellow U. Mich., Ann Arbor, 1962-66, lectr. motivation personality, 1968-69; lectr. social relations Harvard U., Cambridge, Mass., 1969-70, asst. prof. clin. psychology, 1970-72, assoc. prof. psychology, 1972-89, cons. univ. health svcs., 1971-89; pres. Radcliffe Coll., Cambridge, 1972-89, pres. emerita, 1989—; exec. v.p. TIAA-CREF, NYC, 1989—2003; ret., 2003. Bd. dirs. Neiman Marcus Group, Boston Edison Co.-NSTAR, Black Rock Funds. Co-author: The Challenge of Change, 1983; contbr. psychol. articles on motivation to profl. jours. and chpts. to books. Mem. adv. coun. NSF, 1977-87, chair, 1980-86; bd. trustees Twentieth Century Fund, The Century Found., 1973—, Am. Coll. of Greece, 1983-90, Mass. Eye and Ear Infirmary, 1986-90, Com. for Econ. Devel., 1988—, vice-chmn., 1992-98; bd. trustees Mass. Gen. Hosp., Inst. Health Professions, 1988—, vice chmn., 1994, chair, 1995; bd. dirs. Coun. for Fin. Aid to Edn., 1985-89, Beth Israel Hosp., 1989-95; bd. dirs. Revson Found., 1986-92, chmn., 1992-97; bd. dirs. Women's Rsch. and Edn. Inst., 1979—, chair rsch. com., 1982—; mem. Coun. on Fgn. Rels., 1984—; exec. com. ACE Bus. Higher Edn. Forum, 1984-86; exec. com. New Eng. Colls. Fund, 1980—, 2d v.p., 1984-85, 1st v.p., 1985-88, pres., 1988-89; mem. nat. panel to study declining test scores Coll. Entrance Exam. Bd., 1976-77; exec. com., chair task force Pres.'s Commn. for Nat. Agenda for 1980s, 1979-80; adv. com. Women's Leadership Conf. on Nat. Security, 1982—; exec. com. Coun. on Competitiveness, 1986-89; chair task force on health care Challenge to Leadership Conf., 1987-89; bd. dirs. Greenwall Found., 1997, chair, 2004—; bd. dirs. Fund for City of N.Y., chair, 1997-2003. Recipient Roger Baldwin award Mass. Civil Liberties Union Found., 1982, citation of merit Northeast Region NCCJ, 1982, Career Contbn. award Mass. Psychol. Assn., 1987, Disting. Bostonian award, 1990, Ellis Island medal, 1990. Mem. NOW (nat. corp. adv. bd. of legal def. and edn. fund 1984—), Am. Laryngol. Voice Rsch. and Edn. Found. (pres.), Nat. Inst. Social Scis. (medal for outstanding svc. 1973), Phi Beta Kappa, Phi Delta Kappa, Phi Kappa Phi.

HORNER, RONALD GEORGE, musician, educator; b. Johnstown, Pa., Mar. 12, 1956; s. Clyde Melvin and Keturah Elizabeth Horner. BS, Ind. U. of Pa., 1978; MusM, Duquesne U., 1988, dip. artist, 1992; DMA, W.Va. U., 2005. Cert. profl. instrnl. Pa. Dept. of Ed., 1978. Percussionist Israel Philharm. Orch., Tel-Aviv, Israel, 1978—80; dir. of percussion studies Seton Hill Coll., Greensburg, Pa., 1983—85; sr. lectr. of music Frostburg State U, Frostburg, Md., 1983—; instr. of music U. Pitts., 1985—96; percussionist sub. Pitts. Symphony Orch., 1989—96; asst. prof. music Indiana U. of Pa., 1996—. Music dir. Arion Band of Frostburg, Md., 1995—; condr. Bedford All County Band, Pa., 2001; adjudicator Western Md. Ensemble Festival, Hagerstown, Md., 2002. Instrumentalist soloist (world premier performances) Sonus, 1991, Recitative and Scherzo, 1998, Toccata for Timpani, 2002; arranger: songs Pilgrims Chorus, 1997; author: (music method book) The Tuneful Timpanist, 2000. Mem.: SAR, Percussive Arts Soc., Soc. War of 1812, Huguenot Soc., Phi Mu Alpha Sinfonia, Delta Omicron, Pi Kappa Lambda. Republican. Methodist. Avocations: golf, skiing, classic sports cars. Home: 163 Gilmour Rd Somerset PA 15501 Office: Frostburg State U 209 Performing Arts Ctr Frostburg MD 21532 E-mail: ronhorn@aol.com.

HORNER, SHIRLEY JAYE, columnist, writing and publishing consultant; d. John and Selma (Sosna) Quentzel; m. Robert George Horner (dec. Nov. 1984); children: Charles Bruce, Neil Brian. BA, NYU, 1946; MA, Columbia U., NYC, 1948, MPhil, 1976. Instr. English L.I. U., Bklyn., 1948-49, Seton Hall U., Newark, 1949-51, Queens Coll., LI, 1953-54, Rutgers U., Newark, 1975-76; prodr. preservation experience programs Middlesex County Cultural and Heritage Commn., North Brunswick, N.J., 1980-81; editor, Fedn. Reports Nat. Fedn. State Humanities Couns., Mpls., 1981—84; columnist, writer About Books The N.Y. Times' N.J. Weekly, NYC, 1979—. Lectr. writing workshops Trenton State Coll., NJ, 1984, Seton Hall U., South Orange, NJ, 1990—91, NJ Libr. Assn., Trenton, 1990—93, NJ Inst. Tech, Newark, 1997; book rev. panelist WOR-TV, 1986; moderator, panelist Holocaust Rescuers in Italy Day Program, 1995; NEH-funded lectr. Seton Hall U., 1991; reporter (as S.J. Horner) Cultural Topics and Tri-State Regional Planning Commn., The NY Times NJ Weekly, NYC, 1979—82; founding bd. dirs. NJ Ctr. for the Book in the Libr. of Congress, 2001—; spkr. in field. Author (as Shirley Quentzel): Horace Traubel, Biographer of Walt Whitman, 1948; co-editor (as Shirley J. Horner): Ladies at the Cross-roads, 1978 (AAUW award, 1978); editor: Conserving Communities: Urban and Suburban, 1979 (award of excellence NJ Inst. Tech., 1980), (series of booklets) The Preservation Experience in Middlesex County, 1981 (Middlesex County award of distinction, 1981); prodr.: (TV program) Political Debate for '79 on Suburban Cable, 1979 (Union County award of achievement, 1980); featured author NJ Lit. Hall of Fame Authors Brunch, 1997; contbg. editor: Ency. of NJ, 2004; contbr. articles to profl. jours. Co-chmn. Bicentennial Program for Mountainside, Union County, NJ, 1974-77; del. Union County Rep. Party, Linden, NJ, 1982-88; chmn. evaluation NJ Com. for Humanities/NEH, New Brunswick, 1979-81; chmn. Union County Planning Bd., 1981-84; mem., publs. advisor NJ Hist. Commn.; trustee NJ Lit. Hall of Fame, 1987—, NJ Ctr. for the Book, Opera at Florham Fairleigh Dickinson U., Madison, NJ, 1992—; mem. historic site com. Soc. Profl. Journalists, 1989; counsellor NJ Cath. Hist. Records Commn.; publicity cons. Com. Commemorating Heroism of Aristides de Sousa Mendes, 2003, vol. Union County Med. Res. Corps, 2006. Recipient 1st pl. Journalism award NJ Press Women, 1980, 81, award for saving the life of a child Mountainside, NJ, 1968; inducted into NJ Lit. Hall of Fame, 1987, Notable Twentieth Century NJ Authors Honor Roll, 2003; NEH grantee, 1980, 90. Mem. Nat. Book Critics Cir. (bd. dirs. 1990-93, judge for NBCC awards), Images '95 Com. NJ Ctr. for Visual Arts, Nat. Arts Club (literary com. 2000—), Soc. Profl. Journalists (hist. site com. 1989), First Mogilev Podolier Friends Assn. (pres. 1996). Avocations: hiking, archaeology. Office: care NY Times NJ Weekly 1575 Brookside Rd Mountainside NJ 07092-1601 Office Phone: 908-232-2804. Personal E-mail: sjhorner@comcast.net. *How empty is the life that has not known love. Treasure the memory.*

HORNER, SYLVIA ANN, minister, real estate broker; b. Indpls., June 22, 1940; d. Bonnie Lois and Kindeth Allen Kelley (Stepfather), C. W. Burton; m. Joseph Bruce Horner, Dec. 13, 1935; children: Joseph Bradley, Lisa Monique Stephens, Reginald Lee. BA, Ind. U., Indpls., 1998. Lic. real estate broker Ind., 1967. Pastor Geist Apostolic Ch., McCordsville, Ind., 1994—. Dir. of music Geist Apostolic Ch., McCordsville, Ind., 1994—. Oil painting, Seascape (First Pl., Ind. State Fair, 1997); violinist Ind. Philharmonic Orchestra, Butler U. Orchestra. Prodr. Orchestration Praise Radio Program, 1994—98, host, 1994—98. Recipient Recognition Award, Pres. of Student Coun. Achievements include patents for carbon monoxide sensor for vehicles. Home: 509 Swan Ct Fortville IN 46040 Home Phone: 317-485-5522; Office Phone: 317-335-2454. Office Fax: 317-485-5522; Home Fax: 317-485-5522. Business E-Mail: shorner06@earthlink.net.

HORNER, WINIFRED BRYAN, humanities educator, researcher, consultant, writer; b. St. Louis, Aug. 31, 1922; d. Walter Edwin and Winifred (Kinealy) Bryan; m. David Alan Horner, June 15, 1943; children: Winifred, Richard, Elizabeth, David. AB, Washington U., St. Louis, 1943; MA, U. Mo., 1961; PhD, U. Mich., 1975. Instr. English U. Mo., Columbia, 1966-75, asst. prof. English, 1975-80, chair lower divsn. studies, dir. composition program, 1974-80, assoc. prof., 1980-83, prof., 1984-85, prof. emerita, 1985—; prof. English, Radford chair rhetoric and composition Tex. Christian U., Ft. Worth, 1985-93, Cecil and Ida Green disting. prof. emerita, 1993-97. Disting. vis. prof. Tex. Woman's U. Editor: Historical Rhetoric: An Annotated Bibliography of Selected Sources in English, 1980, The Present State of Scholarship in Historical Rhetoric, 1983, Composition and Literature: Bridging the Gap, 1983, Rhetoric and Pedagogy: Its History, Philosophy and Practice, 1995; author: Rhetoric in a Classical Mode, 1987, Nineteenth-Century Scottish Rhetoric: The American Connection, 1993, Life Writing, 1996; co-author Harbrace Coll. Hancbook, 11th edit., 1990, 12th edit., 1994, 14th edit., 1998. Named Disting. prof. Tex. Woman's U., 1999, Disting. Alumna, Washington U.; Inst. for the Humanities fellow U. Edinburgh, 1987, Rhetoric fellowship named in Winifred Homers honor U. Mo.; NEH grantee, 1976, 87; recipient Examplar award, Nat. Coun. Tchrs. English, 2003. Mem. Internat. Soc. for History Rhetoric (exec. coun. 1986), Rhetoric Soc. Am. (bd. dirs. 1981, pres. 1987), Nat. Coun. Writing Program Adminstrs. (v.p. 1977-85, pres. 1985-87), Coll. Conf. on Composition and Communication (exec. com.), Modern Lang. Assn. (mem. del. assembly 1981). Home and Office: 1904 Tremont Ct Columbia MO 65203-5467 Business E-Mail: hornerw@missouri.edu.

HORNGREN, CHARLES THOMAS, finance educator; b. Milw., Oct. 28, 1926; s. William Einar and Grace Kathryn (Manning) H.; m. Joan Estelle Knickelbine, Sept. 6, 1952; children: Scott, Mary, Susan, Catherine. BS, Marquette U., 1949, DBA (hon.), 1976; MBA, Harvard U., 1952; PhD, U. Chgo., 1955; LHD (hon.), DePaul U., 1985. CPA, Wis. Instr. U. Chgo., 1952-54, asst. prof., 1954-55, Marquette U., Milw., 1955-56; assoc. prof. U. Wis., Milw., 1956-59, U. Chgo., 1959-63, prof., 1963-65, Stanford U., Calif., 1965—. Bd. dir. ABM Industries, San Francisco. Co-author: Introduction to Management Accounting, 13th edit., 2005, Cost Accounting, 12th edit., 2006, Accounting, 7th edit., 2006, Financial Accounting, 6th edit., 2007; editor: Prentice Hall Acctg. Series. With US Army, 1944—46. Recipient Alumni Merit award Marquette U., 1973, Edmund W. Littlefield professorship Stanford U., 1973; named to Acctg. Hall of Fame, 1990. Mem. Am. Acctg. Assn. (dir. research 1964-66, pres. 1976-77, Outstanding Acctg. Educator award 1973), AICPAs (acctg. prins. bd. 1968-73, council 1978-81, Outstanding Educator award 1985), Calif. Soc. CPAs (Faculty Excellence award 1975, Disting. Prof. award 1983), Nat. Assn. Accts. (bd. regents 1981-84), Financial Acctg. Standards Bd. (adv. council 1975-79, trustee 1984-89). Home: 620 Sand Hill Rd # 407C Palo Alto CA 94304-2002

HORNICK, RICHARD BERNARD, physician; b. Johnstown, Pa., Jan. 27, 1929; s. Paul Steven and Gertrude (Cowan) H.; children: Douglas, Thomas, Marcie, Blaine; m. Susan Finnegan. AB, Johns Hopkins U., 1951, MD, 1955. Diplomate Am. Bd. Internal Medicine. Intern Johns Hopkins

Hosp., Balt., 1955-56, resident in medicine, 1956-57; faculty U. Md. Med. Sch., 1959-78, head infectious diseases, 1963-78; prof. U. Rochester, NY, 1979-87, chmn. dept. medicine NY, 1979-85, assoc. dean affiliated hosps. and external rels. NY, 1985-87; v.p. med. edn. Orlando (Fla.) Regional Healthcare System, 1988—2000. Cons. WHO, mem. Armed Forces Epidemiol. Bd., 1995-99. Contbr. articles to profl. jours. With U.S. Army, 1957-59. Master ACP (bd. govs., regent); mem., Am. Fedn. Clin. Rsch., Am. Soc. Clin. Investigation, Am. Clin. and Climatol. Assn., Assn. Am. Physicians, Infectious Disease Soc. (treas.). Home: 75 Palmer Ave Winter Park FL 32789-2529 Office: Orlando Regional Healthcare System 1414 Kuhl Ave Orlando FL 32806-2093 E-mail: rbh@orhs.org.

HORNING, BARBARA HORTENSE SCHEER, retired elementary school educator; b. San Francisco, Oct. 20, 1928; d. George Burbridge and Ruth Bonnard (Weston) Scheer; m. Dirk Jan van Mourik (dec.); 1 child, Carla van Mourik Woodworth; m. John Charles Horning (dec.). BA in tchg., San Francisco State Coll., 1950. Tchr. Berkeley Unified Sch. Dist., Berkeley, Calif., 1950—53; adminstrv. asst. U. Calif., Berkeley, 1953—57; tchr. Oak Grove Sch. Dist., San Jose, Calif., 1967—93; chair Calif. Tchrs. Assn. Profl. Relations and Responsibility, San Jose, 1980—90; demonstration tchr., summer sch. San Jose State U., San Jose, Calif., 1976—79. Bldg. rep., chair Oak Grove Sch. Dist. Calif. Tchrs. Assn., San Jose, 1970—80; overseer Coyote Grange, Calif., 2006. Sec., pres., treas. Older Womens League, Santa Clara County, 1985—; mem. Morgan Hill Sister City Com., Morgan Hill, Calif., 2005; vol. Santa Teresa Hosp., San Jose, 1985—91, El Camino Hosp., Mountain View, Calif., 1992—2005; leader Camp Fire Girls, San Jose, Calif., 1964—67; bd. mem. Unitarian Ch., San Jose, 1986—92; mem. Unitarian Fellowship, Morgan Hill, 2005—. Mem.: AAUW, Am. Assn. Univ. Women, Morgan Hill Friends Libr., Morgan Hill Hist. Soc., Calif. Retired Tchrs. Assn. (pres. 2002—07), Pine Tree Villas Homeowners Assn. (dir. 2004—06, sec. 2006—). Democrat. Unitarian. Avocations: reading, gardening, knitting, volunteering. Home: 1804 Pinecone Ct Morgan Hill CA 95037-7049 Personal E-mail: sabrejet86@charter.net.

HORNING, KATHLEEN T., library director; BA in Linguistics, U. Wis.-Madison, MLIS. Children's libr. Madison Pub. Libr., Wis.; dir. Coop. Children's Book Ctr., Sch. Edn., U. Wis.-Madison. Former pres. US Bd. on Books for Young People. Columnist (magazines) Library Sparks; author: From Cover to Cover: Evaluating and Reviewing Children's Books, 1997; co-author: Multicultural Literature for Children and Young Adults, 1980-1990, Multicultural Literature for Children and Young Adults, 1991-1996. Mem.: Assn. for Libr. Svc. to Children (pres.-elect 2005—06, pres. 2006—07, mem. exec. com. 2005—). Office: Sch of Edn U Wis-Madison 600 W park St Rm 4290 Madison WI 53706 Office Phone: 608-263-3721. Business E-Mail: horning@education.wise.edu.*

HORNISH, RONALD FREDERICK, music educator; s. Charles Everett Hornish and Louise Millard-Hornish Virginia. BS in music edn., Duquesne U., 1973—77; MusM, Northwestern U., 1983—84; D of musical arts, U. of Cin. College-Conservatory of Music, 1986—88; MA in supervision and adminstrn., North Ctrl. Coll., 2001—04. Teaching Certification in Music Pa. State Bd. of Edn., 1977, Ill. State Bd. of Edn., 1993, General Administrative Certification Ill. State Bd. of Edn., 2004, Teacher of Music NJ. Bd. of Edn., 1999. Band dir. Keystone Oaks Sch. Dist., Pitts., 1977—80; dir. of instrumental music Solanco H.S., Quarryville, Pa., 1980—83; asst. dir. of bands U. of Nev., 1984—85; dir. of bands Rocky Mountain Coll., Billings, Mont., 1985—86; asst. prof. of music/dir. of bands Bucknell U., Lewisburg, Pa., 1988—90, Grand Valley State U., Allendale, Mich., 1990—93; dir. bands Morton West HS, Berwyn, Ill., 1993—2000; music educator/fine arts tchr./band dir. Downers Grove South HS, 2000—. Guest condr., adjudicator and clinician various, 1980—2004. Musician: (professional musician-sax/clarinet) Orchestral, musicals, jazz bands, jazz combos; contbr. panelist (Music Educators Nat. Conf. NW Divsn., 1987); dir.: (director of summer arts program) Flathead Lake Music Camp (Founder and Camp Dir., 1987). Ward chmn. Dem. Nat. Party, Pittsburgh, Pa., 1988—90. Recipient Outstanding H.S. Educator, U. of Chgo., 1995, Rocky Mountain Coll. Tchr. of the Yr. Finalist, Burlington No. Found., 1986, Citation of Excellence, Nat. Band Assn., 1983, Award for Academic Excellence, Duquesne U., 1977, Pi Kappa Lambda, Northwestern U., 1984, Grammy Signature Sch. Finalist - Morton West HS, NARAS, 1999—2000, Award of Distinction for Notable Contributions to Musical Excellence, Fiesta-Val Arts, 1999, Tchr. of the Month, Morton West H.S., 1998 and 1999, Nominee for Chicagoland Outstanding Music Educator, Quinlan and Fabish, 1995, 1996, 1997, 2001; Grad. scholarship, Northwestern U., 1983—84, Jazz Performance/Cmty. Outreach, Ill. Coun. for the Arts, 2003, Grad. Doctoral scholarship, U. of Cin., 1987—88. Fellow: Pi Kappa Lambda (hon.); mem.: Coll. Band Directors Nat. Assn., Nat. Band Assn. (Pa. state exec. sec. 1980—83, Citation of Excellence 1982), Internat. Assn. of Jazz Educators, Ill. Music Educators Assn., Music Educators Nat. Conf., Mich. Sch. Band and Orch. Assn. (hon. Hon. Life Membership 1993), Phi Mu Alpha Sinfonia - Iota Chpt. Home: 100 Forest Place #P6 Oak Park IL 60301 Office: Downers Grove South HS 1436 Norfolk Downers Grove IL 60301 Personal E-mail: rfhornish@aol.com. Business E-Mail: rhornish@csd99.org.

HORNISH, SAM, JR., race car driver; b. Bryan, Ohio, July 2, 1979; Profl. race car driver Multiple World Karting Assn., 1991—95, US Formula 2000 Championships, 1996—98, Indy Racing League (IRL), Toyota Atlantics, 1999, PDM Racing, IRL Racing, 2000, IRL, 2001—. Achievements include two IRL Racing Championships, 2001-2002; youngest driver (21) ever to win Indy Car Series Race, 2001; winning Indianapolis 500, 2006, 19 career IRL victories. Office: Penske Racing 366 Penske Plz Reading PA 19602*

HORNSTEIN, JAMES E., lawyer; b. Balt., Aug. 18, 1950; BA summa cum laude, U. N.C., 1972; JD, Yale U., 1975. Bar: Calif. 1975. Law extern to Hon. Robert Zampano U.S. Dist. Ct. Conn., 1975; atty. Greenberg, Glusker, Fields, Claman & Machtinger, LA; of councel Alschuler Grossman LLP, Santa Monica. Past pres., dir., fundraising chmn. LA Legal Aid Found. Mem. ABA, State Bar Calif., Beverly Hills Bar Assn., Phi Beta Kappa, mem. Order of Grail, LA Assn. Office: Alschuler Grossman LLP Water Garden 1620 26th St 4th Fl N Tower Santa Monica CA 90404-4060 Office Phone: 310-255-9064. Office Fax: 310-907-2000. Business E-Mail: jhornstein@agsk.com.

HORNSTEIN, MARK, financial executive; b. NYC, Dec. 7, 1947; s. Joseph and Anne (Fox) Hornstein. BBA, Pace U., 1969; postgrad., NYU, 1973. Staff acct. PEat, Marwick, Mitchell & Co., NYC, 1969—70; sr. acct. Robert J. Cofini & Co., 1972—74; asst. v.p. United Va. Factors Corp., 1974—77; asst. v.p., adminstrv. head mortgage loan divsn. James Talcott, Inc., 1977—78; loan adminstrv. officer Aetna Bus. Credit, Inc., East Hartford, Conn., 1978—79; asst. v.p. A.J. Armstrong Co., Inc. (now Bankamerica Bus. Credit, Inc.), NYC, 1979—83; v.p. Leucadia Nat. Corp., 1983—. Treas. Am. Investment Co., St. Louis, 1984—; asst. v.p. Cardiff Equities Corp. (merged with Leucadia Nat. Corp.), La Jolla, Calif., 1984—86; v.p. Charter Nat. Life Ins. Co., St. Louis, 1985—93, PHLCORP, Inc. (formerly Baldwin United Corp.), Phila., 1987—; sec. Bolivian Power Co., Ltd., LaPaz, 1988—94; v.p. Transp. Capital Corp., NYC, 1992—94, chmn., pres., 1994—96. With USNR, 1970—72. Home: 25 Sutton Pl S New York NY 10022-2441 Office: 315 Park Ave S New York NY 10010-3607

HORNUNG, HANS GEORG, aeronautical engineering educator, science administrator; b. Jaffa, Israel, Dec. 26, 1934; came to U.S., 1987; m. Gretl Charlotte Frank, Jan. 29, 1960; children: Ingrid, Karl, Lisa, Jenny. BMechE with honors, U. Melbourne, Australia, 1960, M in Engring. Sci. with honors, 1962; PhD in Aeros., U. London, 1965. Rsch. scientist Aero. Rsch. Labs., Melbourne, 1962-67; lectr., sr. lectr. then reader Australian Nat. U., Canberra, 1967-80; dir. Inst. Exptl. Fluid Mechanics (DLR), Göttingen, Germany, 1980-87; dir. Grad. Aero. Labs. and Clarence Johnson prof. aero. Calif. Inst. Tech., Pasadena, 1987—2003, emeritus, 2005—. Mem. fluid dynamics panel Adv. Group. Aerospace R & D, 1983-88; mem. adv. com. Internat. Shock Tube Symposia, 1979-95; chmn. adv. com. von Kármán Inst. for Fluid Dynamics, 1984-85; mem. German del. Internat. Union Theoretical and Applied Mechanics, 1984-87; Lanchester Meml. lectr. Royal Aero. Soc., London, 1988; hon. prof. U. Göttingen; Prandtl mem. lectr. Ges. Angew. Math. and Mech., Vienna, 1988. Mem. editl. adv. bd. Experiments in Fluids jour., 1987—, Physics of Fluids, 1988-91, Ing. Archiv, 1989-96; contbr. numerous articles to profl. jours. Recipient von Karman award and medal for internat. coop. in aero. Internat. Coun. Aero. Scis.; Humboldt fellow Tech. U., Darmstadt, Germany, 1974-75. Fellow Royal Aero. Soc., Am. Inst. Aero. & Astronautics, AIAA (life), AAAS; mem. Nat. Acad. of Engring. (fgn. assoc.), Sci. mem. of bd. DLR Germany, Deutsche Gesellschaft für Luft-und Raumfahrt, Gesellschaft für angewandte Mathematik und Mechanik, Am. Phys. Soc., Royal Swedish Acad. Engring. Scis., Ludwig Prandtl Ring German Soc. Aerospace Sci. Achievements include making important contbns. in hypersonic flow theory, exptl. methods and results in real-gas flows, Mach reflection and three-dimensional separation. Office: Calif Inst Tech 1200 E California Blvd Pasadena CA 91125-0001 Business E-Mail: hans@galcit.caltech.edu.

HORNY, KAREN LOUISE, library administrator; b. Highland Park, Ill., Apr. 22, 1943; d. Hugo O. and Margaret L. (Bailey) H. AB in French Lit. magna cum laude with honors, Brown U., 1965; MLS, U. Mich., 1966. Asst. core libr. Northwestern U., Evanston, Ill., 1966-68, head core collection, 1968-71, asst. univ. libr., 1971-95; dean libr. svcs., prof. libr. sci. Mo. State U., Springfield, 1995—. Bd. editors Jour. Acad. Librarianship, 1978-81, Advances in Librarianship, 1993-98; contbr. chpts. to books and articles to profl. jours. Pres. U. Mich. Libr. Sci. Alumni Soc., 1985-86; nat. chair U. Mich. Info. and Libr. Studies Fund, 1988-90, rep. Info. and Libr. Sci. U. Mich. Alumni Bd., 1991-94; mem. alumni scholarship coun. Sch. Info. U. Mich., 1996—; mem. adv. coun. U. Ill. Grad. Sch. Libr. Sci., 1975-77; chmn. NOTIS Network Adv. com. Northwestern U., 1988-95. Recipient Disting. Alumnus award U. Mich. 1983. Mem. ALA (coun. 1983-87, divsn. pres. 1980-81, chmn. divsn. 1973-74, 76-78, chmn. various com. 1981—, rep. White Ho. conf. com. 1990-97, exec. com. White Ho. conf. on libr. and info. svcs. task force 1997-2005), Mo. Libr. Assn. (pres. 2007), Ill. Libr. Assn. (coms.), Freedom to Read Found., Brown U. Club, U. Mich. Club, Rotary Springfield Downtown, Phi Beta Kappa, Phi Kappa Phi (chpt. 170 pres., 2004-05), Beta Phi Mu. Episcopalian (subdeacon). Home: 1228 W Beekman St Springfield MO 65810-2292 Office: Mo State U 901 S National Ave Springfield MO 65897 Home Phone: 417-886-1502; Office Phone: 417-836-4525. Business E-Mail: karenhorny@missouristate.edu.

HORNYAK, JOSEPH P., lawyer; b. Silver Spring, Md., Oct. 30, 1964; BS in journalism, U. Md., College Park, 1986; JD, U. Md., 1990. Bar: Md. 1990, DC 1992. Ptnr. Holland & Knight, LLP, Washington. Office: Holland & Knight LLP Ste 100 2099 Pennsylvania Ave Washington DC 20006 Office Phone: 202-955-5564. Business E-Mail: Joseph.Hornyak@HKLAW.com.

HORNYAK, ROY ROBERT, music educator, minister; b. St. Joseph, Mo., Nov. 4, 1925; s. Roy and Mildred Gertrude Hornyak; m. Mary Margaret Lewis, Aug. 9, 1953; children: Deborah Margaret Crnkovich, Roy Robert Hornyak, Jr. BA, Ctrl. Meth. U., 1948; MusM, Ind. U., 1950; Ensign, USNR, Naval Midshipmens Sch., 1945; MusD Edn., Ind. U., 1964. Prof. music U. Cin., 1954—86; head music edn. Coll. Conservatory Music, 1967—71, head performance studies, 1976—81, assoc. dean, 1972—75; coord. of campus ministry Am. Bapt. Churches of Ohio, Granville, Ohio, 1988—97; sr. min. Hyde Pk. Bapt. Ch., Cin., 1999—2002; exec. dir. Ohio Campus Ministries, Columbus, 1989—90; music dir. Simon Winds, Cin., 1981—2003; pres. Ohio Campus Ministries, 2003—06. Moderator Miami Bapt. Associaton, Cincinnati, Ohio, 1993—96; pres. Am. Bapt. churches of Ohio, Granville, Ohio, 1997—98. Author: Attitudes Toward Contemporary American Music. Chmn. Am. Bapt. Campus Ministry at U. Cin., 1959—86. Lt. comdr. USNR, 1946—71. Recipient Disting. Alumni award, Ctrl. Meth. U., 1976, Newton C. Fedder award, 1995. Mem.: Coll. Band Directors Nat. Assoc., Phi Beta Mu (pres. 1986—88, Mu chpt., named to Hall of Fame 2006), Mil. Order of World Wars (life), Torch Club (pres. 1968—69). Office Phone: 513-922-6241. Personal E-mail: rob.hornyak@juno.com.

HOROSCHAK, MARK J., lawyer; b. Phila., Nov. 15, 1951; BA cum laude in Polit. Sci., Am. U., 1973; JD, Coll. of William and Mary, 1976. Bar: Mich. 1977, Va. 1980, NC 1996, SC 1996, US Ct. Appeals 4th Cir. 1981, US Dist. Ct. Ea. Dist. Mich. 1977, US Dist. Ct. Ea. Dist. Va. 1983, US Dist. Ct. We. Dist. NC 1996. Staff atty. GM, Detroit, 1976—80; assoc. Hunton & Williams, Richmond, Va., 1980—84; with FTC, Washington, 1984—95, atty.-advisor to chmn., 1987—88, asst. gen. counsel, 1988—89, asst. dir. Bur. Competition, 1989—95; mem. Womble Carlyle Sandridge & Rice PLLC, Charlotte, NC, 1995—, leader antitrust practice group, leader health law practice group. Mem.: ABA (vice chair healthcare com. antitrust sect. 1995—95, 1999—), Am. Health Lawyers Assn., NC Bar Assn. (chair antitrust sect. 2001—02). Office: Womble Carlyle Sandridge & Rice PLLC One Wachovia Ctr Ste 3500 301 S College St Charlotte NC 28202-6037 Office Phone: 704-331-4928. Office Fax: 704-338-7844. Business E-Mail: mhoroschak@wcsr.com.

HOROSZY, ALBERT JOHN, mathematics educator; s. Albert and Carol Horoszy. BS in Math., Coll. Misericordia, Dallas, Pa., 1996; MS in Ednl. Devel. Strategies, Wilkes U., Wilkes Barre, Pa., 2005. Cert. tchr. math. grades 7 through 12 Pa. Dept. Edn., 1996. Substitute tchr. Wilkes Barre Area Sch. Dist., 1997—98, instr. math., 1997—. Vol. Luzerne County Dem. Party, Wilkes Barre, 2000—06. Mem.: NEA (assoc.), Pa. Assn. Supervision and Curriculum Devel., Nat. Coun. Tchrs. Math., Pa. State Educators Assn. Democrat. Avocations: reading, politics, computers, baseball. Home: 580 North Franklin St Apt 3 Wilkes Barre PA 18702 Home Phone: 570-824-2240; Office Phone: 570-826-7182.

HOROVITZ, ADAM KEEFE (ADROCK, KING AD-ROCK), recording artist; b. South Orange, NJ, Oct. 31, 1966; s. Israel and Doris Horovitz; m. Ione Skye, 1991 (div. 1999); m. Kathleen Hanna, 2006. Founder, mem. Young and the Useless, 1981—83; mem. The Beastie Boys, 1983—; co-founder, mem. BS2000; co-founder Grand Royal Record Label, 1992—2001. Owner Grand Royal, Grand Royal mag., 1984—. Albums include (with Beastie Boys) Licensed to Ill, 1986, Paul's Boutique, 1989, Check Your Head, 1992, 94, Ill Communication, 1994, Some Old Bullshit, 1994, In Sound from Way Out, 1996, Def & Dumb, 1996, Hello Nasty, 1998, To the 5 Boroughs, 2004, The Mix Up, 2007, (with BS2000) BS2000, 1996, Buddy, 2000, (singles) Jimmy James, 1992, Gratitude, 1992, So What'cha Want, 1992, Sabotage, 1994, Hey Ladies, 1997, Real Men Don't Floss Up, (with BS2000) Simply Mortified, 2001, (extended play singles) Pollywog Stew, 1982, Cooky Puss, 1983, Rock Hard, 1984, Tour Shot, 1994, Sure Shot, 1994, Get It Together, 1994, Root Down, 1995, Aglio E Olio, 1995, (video) Skills to Pay the Bills, 1992, Hello Nasty, 1998, The Sounds of Science, 1999; rap artist Heart of Soul, 1988, Rap's Biggest Hits, 1990, Rap Rap Rap, 1996, Rap: Most Valuable Players, 1996; vocals Rap's Biggest Hits, 1990; prodr. Cb4, 1993, Rebirth of Cool (vol 3), 1995, Music for Our Mother Ocean, 1996, Rap Rap Rap, 1996, Rap: Most Valuable Players, 1996; (films) Krush Groove, 1985, Tougher than Leather, 1987, Lost Angels, 1989, A Kiss Before Dying, 1991, Long Road Home 1991, Roadside Prophets, 1992, Cityscrapes, 1994, Crossroads, 2002, Godspeed, 2007. Office: care Grand Royal Capitol Records 1750 Vine St Los Angeles CA 90028-5209*

HOROVITZ, ISRAEL ARTHUR, playwright; b. Wakefield, Mass., Mar. 31, 1939; s. Julius Charles and Hazel (Solberg) H.; m. Doris Keefe, Dec. 25, 1959 (div. 1974); children: Rachael Keefe, Matthew Keefe, Adam Keefe; m. Gillian Adams, July, 1981; children: Hannah Rebecca and Oliver Adams (twins) Fellow, Royal Acad. Dramatic Art, London, 1961-63; postgrad. in English, CUNY, 1972-77, MA in English, 1977; PhD (hon.), Mass. State, 1991. Am. playwright-in-residence Royal Shakespeare Co., London, 1965; lectr., 1961-75; Fanny Hurst prof. theatre arts Brandeis U., 1974-75; artistic dir. N.Y. Playwrights Lab., 1975—; founder, artistic dir. Gloucester (Mass.) Stage Co., 1980—. Prof. Columbia U. Film Sch., 2003—. Author: (plays) The Comeback, 1958, The Death of Bernard the Believer, 1960, This Play is About Me, 1961, The Hanging of Emanuel, 1962, Jump, 1962, Hop and Skip, 1963, The Killer Dove, 1963, The Indian Wants the Bronx, 1964-66, It's Called the Sugar Plum, 1965, Line, 1967, Rats, 1967, The Honest-to-God Schnozzola, 1968, Chiaroscuro (or Morning), 1968, The World's Greatest Play, 1968, First Season; (with others), collection of plays, 1968, Leader, 1969, Morning, Noon and Night, (with others), 1969, Acrobats, 1971, Play for Germs (TV), 1972, Dr. Hero, 1972, Shooting Gallery, 1972, 50 Years of Caddieing, 1999, The Wakefield Plays 3 Weeks After Paradise, 2001, Speaking Well of the Dead, 2002, A Mother's Love, 2003, Security, 2003, Cat-Lady, 2004, Sins of the Mother, 2004, Compromise, 2005, My Old Lady, 2005, The Hotel Play, 2006, Beirut Rocks, 2007, The Audition Play, 2007, The Secret of Madame Bonnard's Bath, 2007, The Bridal Dance, 2007, the Race Play, 2007; 7-play cycle including The Alfred Trilogy: Part 1-Alfred the Great, Part 2-Our Father's Failing, Part 3-Alfred Dies, 1972-77 and The Quannapowitt Quartet: Part 1-Hopscotch, Part 2-The 75th, Part 3-Stage Directions, Part 4-Spared, 1971-79; Cappella (novel), 1973; Uncle Snake, 1975, The Great Labor Day Classic, 1979, The Primary English Class, 1975, The Bottom, 1975-76, Mackerel, 1977, Sunday Runners in the Rain, 1979-80, Nobody Loves Me; (novella), 1975, The Reason We Eat, 1976; adaption Ionesco's l'homme aux Valises: Man with Bags, 1977; adaptation from Melville's Bartleby, The Scrivener, 1978; The Former One-On-One Basketball Champion; teleplays Today I Am A Fountain Pen, 1977, A Rosen by Any Other Name, 1979, The Chopin Playoffs, 1978, adaptation from Mailer's The Deer Park, 1979-80; (plays) The Good Parts, 1979—, adaptation from Dickens- Scrooge and Marley, 1980-81, Park Your Car in Harvard Yard, 1980-83, The Widow's Blind Date, 1985-88, Henry Lumper, 1984-87, Year of the Duck, 1984-87, Firebird at Dogtown, 1984-85, North Shore Fish, 1985-87, Faith, 1988, Fighting Over Beverley, 1988-93, Strong-Man's Weak Child, 1988-90, Unexpected Tenderness, 1993-94, Barking Sharks, 1995, The Chips are Down (BBC radio), 1995, Lebensraum, 1996, My Old Lady, 1996, Captains and Courage, 1996, Free Gift, 1996, One Under, 1997, Phone Tag (radio), 1997, Stations of The Cross, 1998, Fast Hands, 1999, Promises.com, 2000, 50 Years of Caddying, 2001, Man in Snow (Radio), 2001; (stage adaptations) Today I Am a Fountain Pen, A Rosen by Any Name, The Chopin Playoffs, 1986; (films) Park Your Car in Harvard Yard, 1991, Fast Eddie, 1980, The Strawberry Statement, 1971, Believe in Me, 1972, Author! Author!, 1982, Fell, 1982-83, Berta, 1982-83, Light Years, 1985-86, Wedlock, 1985-86, (with Diane Kurys) A Man in Love, 1987-88, Payofski's Discovery, 1987-88, The Deuce, 1988-90, The Pan, 1989-91, Letters to Iris, 1989-90, The Quiet Room, 1990, Strong Man, 1991-93, James Dean, 1993—, Without A Word, 1994, A Star is Born (remake), 1994, The Lounge Player, 1995—, The Widow's Blind Date, 1995, North Shore Fish, 1995, Captains and Courage, 1996, (with Istvan Szabo) Sunshine, 1998 (European Film Acad. award 2000, Best Screenplay 2000), 300 Boys, 1999 James Dean, 1999, Sunshine, 2000, The Little Shock, 2003-05, Eager to Die, 2005; contbr. to nat. mags, plays translated, pub. and performed in more than 20 langs. Recipient Vernon Rice award, 1967-68, Drama Desk award, 1967-68, Jersey Jour. best play award, 1968, Obie award, 1967-68, 68-69, French Critics prize, 1974, Christopher award, 1975, Emmy award, 1975, prix Italia-Silver Palm, 1982, L.A. Weekly Critics prize, 1984, 95, Commendation Gov. of Mass., 1984, Eliot Norton prize, 1986, Best Play award Boston mag., 1987, Lifetime Achievement award B'nai Brith, 1996, Washington Coll. Literary prize, 1996, Boston Pub. Libr. Literary Lights award, 1997, Walker Hancock prize City of Gloucester, Mass., 1999, Best Screenwriter award European Film Acad., 2000, Best Screenplay award Writers Guild Can., 2000, Star in Playwrights Sidewalk, N.Y.C., 2000, Sony RAdio award for best drama, 2002; Rockefeller fellow, 1968-69, Nat. Endowment for Arts fellow, 1974, Fulbright fellow, 1975-76, Guggenheim fellow, 1977-78. Mem. Actors Studio, New Dramatists Com., Eugene O'Neill Found., Authors' League Am. (exec. council). Achievements include being a nationally ranked masters track and road runner; most produced Am. playwright in French language. also: MCR-Agence Litteraire Paris France also: Felix Bloch Erben Hardenberg Strasse 6 D-10623 Berlin Germany E-mail: IH1996@aol.com.

HOROWITZ, BARRY ALLAN, music company executive; b. NYC, June 21, 1948; s. Henry and Tania (Aisenfeld) H.; m. Maida Barbara Schwartzberg, Oct. 9, 1977 (dec. Oct. 1994); children: Jessica, Jared; m. Patricia Szriftgiser, Mar. 9, 2006. BA, Hofstra U., Hempstead, NY, 1971. From sales staff to sr. dir. ops. Sam Ash Music Corp., Hicksville, NY, 1971-95, v.p. purchasing and merchandising, 1995—. Avocations: running, skiing, triathlons. Office: Sam Ash Music Corp 278 Duffy Ave Hicksville NY 11801-3605 E-mail: barry@samashmusic.com.

HOROWITZ, BARRY MARTIN, engineering company executive; b. Bklyn., Apr. 20, 1943; s. Isaac Harry and Clara Fireda (Weintraub) H.; m. Sheryl Robin Lang, Jan. 24, 1965; children: Hillary, Charles. BSEE, CCNY, 1965; MSEE, NYU, 1967, PhDEE, 1969. Asst. project engr. Bendix Corp., 1965-66, sr. project engr., 1967-69; project engr. Gen. Precision, 1966-67; tech. staff MITRE Corp., McLean, Va., 1969-71, group leader, 1971-74, dept. head, 1974-79, dir. spl. studies Bedford, Mass., 1979-80, tech. dir., 1980-84, v.p. strategic programs, 1984-85, v.p. programs, 1985-86, sr. v.p., gen. mgr., 1986, group v.p., gen. mgr., 1986-87, exec. v.p., chief oper. officer, also dir.; CEO Concept Five Tech, McLean, 1996-2000, chmn., 1996—. Cons. sci. adv. bd. USAF, Pentagon, Washington, 1982—, Def. Sc. Bd., Pentagon, 1988—. Contbr. articles to profl. jours. Mem. NAE, IEEE, AIAA, Armed Forces Communications and Electronics Assn. (pres. 1987-88, pres.-elect 1990, Gold medal for Engring. 1990), Ctr. Sci. and Internat. Affairs., Eta Kappa Nu, Tau Beta Pi. Avocation: musician.

HOROWITZ, CAROLE SPIEGEL, landscape contractor; b. Pitts., Mar. 24, 1940; d. Alvin Duane and Leah (Greenstein) Spiegel; m. Don Roy Horowitz, Jan. 31, 1960 (dec. July 24, 2006); children: Cindy H. Urbach, Thomas Samuel. Student, Carnegie Mellon U., 1958-61. Cert. interior hortizulturist, landscape profl. Owner Carole Horowitz Interior Design, Pitts., 1965-72; pres. Plantscape, Inc., Pitts., 1973—. Bd. dirs. Jr. Achievement Allegheny County, Pitts., 1985—95, Vocat. Rehab. Ctr., Pitts., 1989—91, United Way Allegheny County, Pitts., 1991—94, Phipps Conservatory Pitts., 2007; chmn. small bus. com. U. Pitts., 1986—92. Named Entreprenuer of the Yr., Ernst & Young and Inc. Mag., 1988; recipient Nat. Landscape award, White House and Am. Assn. Nurseryman, 1990, Entrepreneur Leadership award, YWCA, 1990, Pa.'s Best 50 Women in Bus. award, Pitts. Bus. Times, 1997. Mem.: Internat. Facility Mgmt. Assn., Associated Landscape Contractor Am. (chmn. Am. bd. govs. 1991—94, cert.), Interior Plantscape Assn. (sec., v.p. 1982—85), Longboat Key Club,

Westmoreland Country Club, Rotary (sec. downtown Pitts. chpt.). Jewish. Avocations: travel, golf, painting. Office: Plantscape Inc 3101 Liberty Ave Pittsburgh PA 15201-1400 Office Phone: 412-281-6352 230. E-mail: ch@plantscape.com.

HOROWITZ, DAVID A., history professor, writer; b. Bronx, NY, Aug. 17, 1941; s. Nathon and Dorothy Horowitz; m. Gloria Elizabeth Myers, June 23, 1996. BA, Antioch Coll., Yellow Springs, Ohio, 1964; PhD, U. Minn., Mpls., 1971. From instr. to prof. Portland State U., 1967—87, prof., 1987—. Author: Beyond Left and Right: Insurgency and the Establishment, 1997, America's Political Class Under Fire: The Twentieth Century's Great Culture War, 2003, The People's Voice: A Populist Cultural History of Modern America, 2007; author: (editor) Inside the Klavern: The Secret History of a 1920s Ku Klux Klan, 1999; co-author: On the Edge: The United States in the Twentieth Centure, 3d edit. Bd. dirs. Mus. People's Art, Bay City, Oreg., 2002—, Oreg. Cultural Heritage Commn., Portland, 1988—. Mem.: Oreg. Hist. Soc., Hist. Soc., Americans for Peace Now, Phi Kappa Phi. Home: 6034 NE 32d Pl Portland OR 97211 Office: Dept History Portland State Univ 1721 SW Broadway Portland OR 97201

HOROWITZ, DAVID CHARLES, consumer advocate, radio and television commentator, newspaper columnist, director; b. Bronx, June 30, 1937; s. Marcus Lazar and Dorothy (Lippman) H.; m. Suzanne E. Mc Cambridge, Aug. 26, 1973; children: Victoria, Amanda. BA, Bradley U., 1959; MS in Journalism, Northwestern U., 1961; DHL (hon.), Bradley U., 2002. Editor in chief Tazewell County (Ill.) Newspaper, 1956; reporter Peoria (Ill.) Jour. Star, 1957-60, Lerner Newspapers and Chgo. City News Bur., 1959-60; newscaster Sta. KCCI Radio-TV, Des Moines, 1960-62; newswriter-prodr. ABC Radio Network, NYC, 1963; Far East corr. NBC News, 1963-64; pub. affairs dir. Sta. WMCA, NYC, 1965-66; corr., edn. editor, consumer commentator KNBC News, LA, 1966-92; consumer commentator KCBS News, LA, 1993-95; syndicated columnist Creators Syndicate, LA, 1986-99; creator, host, exec. prodr. TV show Fight Back! with David Horowitz, LA, 1977-92; pres. Fight Back! Found. Consumer Edn., 1985—; syndicated newspaper, internet commentator Fight Back! Radio Reports, 1989—, Jones-Media Am., 1997—; syndicated consumer talk show Fight Back! Talk Back! Talk Radio Network, 2000—05; commentator Sta. CNBC, 1990-96; CEO Fightback.com, 1996—. Pres. Fight Back! Prodns., 1974—. Author: Fight Back and Don't Get Ripped Off, 1979, Business of Business, 1989, Fight Back! For Your Medical Health, vols. 1-4, 1993, Fight Back! at Work, 1994, five other books, 1976-; host, exec. prodr. Best Defense, 1993; exec. prodr. (CBS-TV spl.) Frog Girl: The Jennifer Graham Story (Genesis Animal Rights award 1990); spokesperson: Lowermy-bills.com, 2001-03. Patron LA County Mus. Art; bd. dirs. Nat. Broadcast Editl. Conf., Am. Cancer Soc., City of Hope; bd. advisers LA Jewish Home for Aged, Calif. divsn. Am. Cancer Soc.; mem. adv. bd. Am. Heart Assn., LA County, UCLA Publs., LA County Dist. Atty.; mem. charitable adv. com. City of LA, 1991—; hon. bd. dirs. Caring Inst., Washington, 2000—; mem. consumer adv. comm. FCC, 2003-05; hon. mayor Brentwood Cmty., L.A., 1991-98. With USNR, 1954-62. CBS fellow Columbia U., 1962-63; recipient LA City and County Pub. Svc. citation, 1979, 80, 81, 82, 83, 89, 92, Calif. State Legislature Pub. Svc. citation, 1980, 81, 82, 83, 91, 92, Spirit of Life award City of Hope, 1979, 1983, Chief US Postal Insp.'s award, 1981, 93, Emmy awards consumer reporting NTAS, 1974, 76-77, 81-86, 89, 90-05, LA Press Club award consumer reporting, 1991, News Reporting award UPI, 1983, 94, Pub. Svc. award Social Security Adminstrn., 1987, NY Internat. Film and TV Festival medal, 1984-86, Golden Mike award, 1986, Armed Forces TV Network Svcs. award, 1988, Toastmasters Internat. Leadership award, 1991, Cmty. Svc. award SBA, 1991, Excellence in Journalism award Nat. Homecare Assn., 1992, Disting. Alumni award Northwestern U., 1994, Cmty. Svc. award UCLA Ctr. Aging, 1995, AP News Reporting award, 1995, Angel award Excellence in Media, 1998, Golden Halo award Motion Picture Coun. So. Calif., 1998, Quality of Life award Proctor Health Care Found., 1998, Lifetime Achievement award Kern County Law Enforcement Found., 1999, Angel award outstanding internet website and pub. svc., 1998, 02; named to Journalism Hall of Achievement, Northwestern U., 1997, LA Press Club Best TV Feature Reporting award, 1986, 94, 97; honored David C. Horowitz Auditorium Bradley U., 2004. Mem. AFTRA (bd. dirs. L.A. chpt. 2003—, nat. bd. dirs. 2005—), ASCAP, BMI, SAG, Am. Assn. Travel Agts. (Travelers Adv. award 1991), Internat. Radio-TV Soc., Radio-TV News Dirs. Assn., The Guardians, Soc. Consumer Affairs Profls., Nat. Futures Assn. (adv. bd.), Child Passenger Safety Assn., Ill. Broadcasters Assn. (Disting. Svc. award 1986), Newspaper Creator's Assn., Writers Guild Am., Medill Journalism Sch. Alumni Assn. (pres. 1990-98), Friars Club, Overseas Press Club (NYC), Alpha Epsilon Pi, Sigma Delta Chi, Phi Delta Kappa, Omicron Delta Kappa. Avocations: writing, gardening, theater, collecting serious music, collecting contemporary art. Mailing: PO Box 49915 Los Angeles CA 90049-0915 Office Phone: 310-820-1188. E-mail: dhorowitz@fightback.com. *Life is full of compromise, but to compromise principle is to give up your self-respect. I don't want anyone to take me for a sucker, and I don't like to see anyone else taken, either. A lot of things are unfair in life. It's tough; that's the way it is. But, by heaven, if you can do something about it, do it.*

HOROWITZ, DAVID JOEL, author; b. Queens, NY, Jan. 10, 1939; s. Philip and Blanche (Brown) Horowitz; m. Elissa Krauthamer, June 14, 1959 (div.); children: Jonathan, Sarah, Benjamin, Anne; m. April Mullvain. AB, Columbia U., 1959; MA, U. Calif., Berkeley, 1961. Editor Ramparts mag., Berkeley, 1969-74; co-founder, pres. David Horowitz Freedom Ctr. (previously Ctr. for Study of Popular Culture), LA, 1988—; editor Frontpagemag.com; founder Discoverthenetworks.org. Author: Student, 1962, Shakespeare: An Existential View, 1965, The Free World Colossus, 1965, Hemispheres North and South: Economic Disparity Among Nations, 1966, Empire and Revolution: A Radical Interpretation of Contemporary History, 1969, The Enigma of Economic Growth: A Case Study of Israel, 1972, The Fate of Midas, 1973, The First Frontier, 1979; (with Peter Collier) The Rockefellers: An American Dynasty, 1976, The Kennedys: An American Drama, 1984, The Fords: An American Epic, 1987, Second Thoughts: Former Radicals Look Back at the Sixties, 1989, Second Thoughts About Race in America, 1991, Deconstructing the Left: From Vietnam to the Persian Gulf, 1991; (with Peter N. Carroll and David Lee) On the Edge: A History of America From 1890 to 1945, 1990, On the Edge: A New History of America in the Twentieth Century, 1990, Radical Son: A Generational Odyssey, 1997, Sex, Lies & Vast Conspiracies, 1998, Hating Whitey: And Other Progressive Causes, 1999, The Art of Political War And Other Radical Pursuits, 2000, Uncivil Wars: The Controversy Over Reparations for Slavery, 2002, How to Beat the Democrates and Other Subversive Ideas, 2002, Unholy Alliance: Radical Islam and the American Left, 2004; editor: Containment and Revolution, 1967, Corporations and the Cold War, 1970, Isaac Deutscher: The Man and His Work, 1971; compiler: Marx and Modern Economics, 1968, Radical Sociology: An Introduction, 1971, Counterculture and Revolution, 1972. Co-dir. 2d Thoughts project Nat. Forum Found., Washington, 1986. Office: Ctr for Study of Popular Culture 4th Fl 4401 Wilshire Drive Los Angeles CA 90010

HOROWITZ, DONALD, lawyer; b. NYC, Nov. 18, 1936; s. Louis and Ethel (Kaplan) H.; m. Rosalind Jean Odrezin Horowitz, Dec. 17, 1967; children: Louis A., Jill, Gary N. BA, Rutgers U., 1958; LLB, Columbia U., 1961. Bar: N.J. 1962, N.Y. 1983, U.S. Dist. Ct. N.J. 1962, U.S. Dist. Ct. (so. dist.) N.Y. 1986, U.S. Dist. Ct. (ea. dist.) N.Y., 1986, U.S. Ct. Appeals (3rd cir.) 1965, U.S. Tax Ct. 1972, U.S. Supreme Ct. 1966, U.S. Ct. Appeals (10th cir.) 1994; cert. civil & criminal trial atty. Supreme Ct. N.J. 1983. Asst. U.S. Atty.'s Office, Newark, 1963-66, asst.-chief criminal divsn., 1966-68, first asst., 1968-69, U.S. atty. dist. of N.J., 1969; spl. dep. atty. gen. State of N.J., 1969-70; ptnr. Cummins, Dunn, Horowitz & Pashman, Hackensack, NJ, 1969-82; sole practice Hackensack, NJ, 1982-85, 89—; ptnr. Horowitz & Jacobs, Hackensack, NJ, 1985-89. Mem. Criminal Justice Adv. Com. Bergen C.C., Paramus, N.J., 1992—. Dem. County Committeeman, Ridgewood, N.J., 1993-98. Staff Sgt. U.S. Army, 1962-68. Mem. ABA, Fed. Bar Assn. (pres. N.J. chpt. 1977-78, 79-80), Nat. Assn. Criminal Def. Lawyers, Assn. Trial Lawyers Am., N.J. State Bar Assn., Assn. Criminal Def. Lawyers of N.J. Jewish. Home: 563 Eastbrook Rd Ridgewood NJ 07450-2114 Office: 24 Bergen St Hackensack NJ 07601-5487 Personal E-mail: dhorowitzesq@earthlink.net. Business E-Mail: don@dhlawfirm.net.

HOROWITZ, DONALD LEONARD, lawyer, arbitrator, political scientist, educator; b. NYC, June 27, 1939; s. Morris and Yetta (Hibscher) H.; m. Judith Anne Present, Sept. 4, 1960; children: Marshall, Karen, Bruce. AB, Syracuse U., 1959, LLB, 1961; LLM, Harvard U., 1962, AM, 1965, PhD, 1968. Bar: N.Y. 1962, D.C. 1979, U.S. Ct. Appeals (D.C., 6th, 7th and 10th cirs.) 1970, U.S. Supreme Ct. 1969. Law clk. U.S. Dist. Ct. (ea. dist.), Pa., 1965-66; rsch. assoc. Harvard U. Ctr. Internat. Affairs, 1967-69; atty. Dept. Justice, Washington, 1969-71; fellow Coun. on Fgn. Rels./Woodrow Wilson Internat. Ctr. Scholars, Washington, 1971-72; rsch. assoc. Brookings Instn., Washington, 1972-75; sr. fellow Rsch. Inst. on Immigration and Ethnic Studies/Smithsonian, Washington, 1975-81; prof. law and polit. sci. Duke U., Durham, NC, 1980—, Charles S. Murphy Prof., 1988-93, James B. Duke prof., 1994—. Vis. prof. Charles J. Merriam scholar U. Chgo. Law Sch., 1988; vis. fellow Cambridge U., Eng., 1988; Sticerd Disting. visitor London Sch. Econs., 1998-2000, Centennial prof., 2001; vis. scholar Universiti Kebangsaan Malaysia Law Faculty, 1991; Fulbright sr. specialist, 2002; cons. Ford Found., 1977-82; mem. internat. adv. com. Office of the High Rep., Bosnia, 1998-99; McDonald-Currie Meml. lectr. McGill U., Montreal, 1980; mem. Coun. on Role of Cts., 1978-83; Opsahl lectr. Queen's U., Belfast, 2000; McDonald lectr. U. Alta., 2005; mem. Sec. of STate Adv. Com. on Democracy Promotion, 2006—. Author: The Courts and Social Policy (Nat. Acad. Public Adminstrn. Louis Brownlow prize for best book in pub. adminstrn. 1977), 1977, The Jurocracy: Government Lawyers, Agency Programs and Judicial Decisions, 1977, Coup Theories and Officers' Motives, 1980, Ethnic Groups in Conflict, 1985, A Democratic South Africa? Constitutional Engineering in a Divided Soc., 1991 (Am. Polit. Sci. Assn. Ralph J. Bunche award for best book in ethnic and cultural pluralism, 1992), The Deadly Ethnic Riot, 2001; mem. editl. bd. Ethnicity, 1974-82, Law and Contemporary Problems, 1983-84, 89-2000, Jour. Democracy, 1993—. Guggenheim fellow, 1980-81; Nat. Humanities Ctr. fellow, 1984; Carnegie scholar, 2001-2002. Fellow Am. Acad. Arts and Scis.; mem. Am. Soc. for Polit. and Legal Philosophy (v.p. 2004-07, pres. 2007—). Office: Duke University School Law Durham NC 27708-0360 Home Phone: 919-489-1017; Office Phone: 919-613-7058.

HOROWITZ, ELIOT, Internet company executive; b. 1981; BS in computer sci., Brown U. Software devel., R&D dept. DoubleClick, NYC; co-founder & chief tech. officer ShopWiki Corp., NYC, 2005—. Named one of Best Entrepreneurs Under 25, BusinessWeek, 2006. Office: ShopWiki Corp 3rd Fl 134 5th Ave New York NY 10011 E-mail: eh@shopwiki.com.

HOROWITZ, FRANCES DEGEN, academic administrator, psychology educator; b. Bronx, NY, May 5, 1932; d. Irving and Elaine Degen; m. Floyd Ross Horowitz, June 23, 1953; children: Jason Degen, Benjamin Meyer Levi. BA, Antioch Coll., 1954; EdM, Goucher Coll., 1954; PhD, U. Iowa, 1959. Tchr. elem. sch., Iowa City, 1954-56; grad. rsch. asst. Iowa Child Welfare Sta., U. Iowa, 1956-59; asst. prof. psychology So. Oreg. Coll., Ashland, 1959-61; asst. prof. home econs. U. Kans., Lawrence, 1961-62, USHPS rsch. fellow, 1962-63, assoc. prof. dept. human devel. and family life, 1964-69, prof. dept. human devel. and family life, psychology, 1969—91, chmn. dept., 1969-75, rsch. assoc., 1964-75, assoc. dean, 1975-78, vice chancellor rsch., grad. studies and pub. svc., also dean grad. sch., 1978-91, dir. Infant Rsch. Lab., 1964—91; pres. Grad. Sch. and Univ. Ctr. CUNY, 1991—2005, pres. emeritus, 2005—, Univ. prof. Grad. Sch. and Univ. Ctr., 2005—. Bd. dirs. Feminist Press; guest rsch. assoc. Bur. Child Rsch. U. Kans., 1960, Parsons State Hosp. and Tng. Ctr., Kans., 1960; vis. prof. dept. psychology Tel Aviv U., 1973—74; guest rschr. dept. pediat. Kaplan Hosp., Rehovot, Israel, 1973—74; vis. lectr. dept. psychology Hebrew U., Jerusalem, 1976, cons. rsch. programs in early edn., 1980—; pres. Ctr. for Rsch., Inc., Lawrence, 1978—91; adv. com. Carolina Inst. on Early Edn. of the Handicapped, 1978—83; reviewer NSF, 1978—91; mem. U. Kans. del. to Peoples Republic China, 1980; exch. scholar Chinese Acad. Scis., China, 1982; mem. Office Sci. Integrity Rev. Adv. Com. PHS, 1991—93; nominating com. Weizmann Women in Sci. award Am. Com. Weizmann Inst. Sci., 1994; mem. Nat. Task Force Grad. Edn., 1994—96; workforce devel. subcom. NYC Partnership, 1994—95; mem. US Nat. Com. for the Internat. Union of Psychol. Sci., 1995—97; mem. overseers' com. to visit dept. psychology Harvard U.; mem., founding adv. bd. Sackler Inst. for Human Brain Devel., 1998—; bd. dirs. Nat. Coun. for Rsch. on Women; adv. coun. Nat. Inst. Child Health and Human Devel., 1999—2004; chair nat. adv. bd. Office Child Devel., U. Pitts.; lectr. in field; cons. in field. Editor Memoir Essay, 2002—; co-editor sci. watch sect. Am. Psychologist, 1993-97; mem. editl. bd. Jour. Devel. Psychology, 1969-75, Early Childhood Edn. Quar., 1974, Devel. Rev., 1981-92, Infant Behaviour and Devel., 1984-90, Contemporary Psychology, 1986-1991; contbr. articles to profl. jours.; TV host Women to Women, 1994—. Trustee Antioch Coll., 1987-91, LI U., 1992-94; bd. dirs. Cmty. Children's Ctr., 1965-68, Douglas County Vis. Nurse Assn., 1968-69; mem. workforce devel. subcom., NYC Partnership; mem. coun. advisors, Nat. Ctr. for Children in Poverty; mem. commn. on women in higher edn. Am. Coun. on Edn. Ford Found. fellow, 1954, Ctr. Advanced Studies Behavioral Scis. fellow Stanford U., 1983-84, Alumni fellow U. Iowa Coll. Arts and Scis., 2005; recipient Trustees award medal Cherry Lawn Sch., Conn., 1971, Outstanding Educator of Am. award, 1973, Disting. Psychologist in Mgmt. award Soc. for Psychologists in Mgmt., 1993, Rebecca Rice Alumni award Antioch Coll., 1996, Sue Rosenberg Zalk award The Feminist Press, 2003; named to Women's Hall of Fame U. Kans., 1974; Spl. Commendation NYC comptroller's office, 1997, NY Women's Agenda Star award, 2002. Fellow APA (pres. divsn. devel. psychology 1977-78, mem. publs. bd. 1985-91, chief sci. adviser 1989-93, pres. 1991-94, Centennial award for Sustained Contbn. to Sci. Directorate, 1992), U. Iowa Coll. Arts and Scis. Alumni, NY Acad. Scis., Am. Acad. Arts and Scis.; mem. Soc. Rsch. in Child Devel. (editor monographs 1976-83, pres. 1997-02), Jewish Cmty. Rels. Coun. (mem. bd. 1999-2005), Hebrew Free Loan Soc. (mem. bd. 2000—), Am. Assn. on Mental Deficiency, North Ctrl. Accrediting Assn. (bd. commrs. 1977-80), Am. Psychol. Found. (pres. 1991-94), Coun. Rsch. Polic and Grad. Edn. (chair, mem. exec. com.), Assn. Grad. Schs. (mem. exec. com.), NY Women's Forum (bd. dirs. 1995-97), Nat. Assn. of State Univs. and Land-Grant Colls. (past chair commn. on human resources and social change, bd. dirs. 1999-02), Sigma Xi, Phi Beta Kappa (hon.). Home: 710 West End Ave #C/D New York NY 10025 Office: CUNY Grad Ctr 365 Fifth Ave New York NY 10016-4309 Home Phone: 212-769-9228; Office Phone: 212-817-7235. Business E-Mail: fdhorowitz@gc.cuny.edu.

HOROWITZ, GEDALE BOB, investment banker; b. NYC, June 13, 1932; s. Abraham and Florence (Bob) H.; m. Barbara Silver, Aug. 17, 1958; children: Ruth Ellen, Seth Robert. AB, Columbia U., 1953, JD, 1955. Bar: N.Y. 1956. With Salomon Bros., NYC, 1955-67, gen. ptnr., 1967-81, mng. dir., 1981-87; exec. v.p., dir. Salomon, Inc., NYC, 1981-97; sr. mng. dir. Salomon Smith Barney, 1997—, Citigroup Global Markets, Inc., 2002—. Vice chmn. bd. trustees Barnard Coll., 1976—; trustee and vice chmn. L.I. Jewish Hosp., 1982-98, chhmn., 1995-98; dir. Mspl. Assistance Corp., City of N.Y., 1989-94; bd. dirs. Jewish Cmty. Rels. Coun. on N.Y., Inc., 1989-2001, pres., 1998-2001; bd. dirs. Statue of Liberty-Ellis Island Found., Inc., 1999—; chmn. N.Y. State Local Govt. Assistance Corp., 1991-94; trustee, chmn. emeritus, exec. com. mem. North Shore/L.I. Jewish Health Sys., 1998—. Served with U.S. Army, 1956-58. Mem. Bond Market Assn. (chm. 1978-79), Securities Industry Assn. (treas. 19 87, chmn. 1991), Mcpl. Securities Rulemaking Bd. (chmn. 1977-78), Mcpl. Bond Club N.Y. (pres. 1982-83), The Bond Club of N.Y., Inc. (pres. 1994-95). Office: Citigroup Global Markets Inc 388 Greenwich St Fl 39 New York NY 10013-2339

HOROWITZ, HERBERT EUGENE, retired diplomat; b. Bklyn., July 10, 1930; s. Max and Jean (Pomerantz) Horowitz; m. Lenore Joan Glasser, Jan. 6, 1963; children: Jason, Richard. BA, Bklyn. Coll., 1952; MA, Columbia U., 1964, Fletcher Sch. Law & Diplomacy, 1965; diploma, Nat. War Coll., 1972. Econ. officer Am. Embassy, Taipei, Taiwan, 1957-62; chief China econ. unit U.S. Consulate, Hong Kong, 1965-69; chief comml. and econ. sect. U.S. Liaison Office, Beijing, 1973-75; dir. Office for Rsch. of East Asia Dept. State, Washington, 1975-78; dir. Office East-West Econ. Policy Dept. Treasury, Washington, 1979-80; consul gen. U.S. Consulate Gen., Sydney, Australia, 1981-84; dep. chief of mission U.S. Embassy, Beijing, 1984-86; amb. to Republic of Gambia, 1986-89. Lectr. history China, cons. Mem.: Am. Fgn. Svc. Assn., Diplomatic and Counselor Officers Ret., Cosmos Club. Home: 2737 Devonshire Pl NW # 111 Washington DC 20008-3454

HOROWITZ, IRVING LOUIS, publisher, educator; b. NYC, Sept. 25, 1929; s. Louis and Esther (Tepper) H.; m. Ruth Lenore Horowitz, 1950 (div. 1964); children: Carl Frederick, David Dennis; m. Mary Curtis Horowitz, 1979. BSS, CCNY, 1951; MA, Columbia U., 1952; PhD, Buenos Aires U., 1957; fellow, Brandeis U., 1958-59. Asst. prof. sociology Bard Coll., 1960; assoc. prof. social theory Buenos Aires U., 1955-58; chmn. dept. sociology Hobart and William Smith Colls., 1960-63; from assoc. prof. to prof. sociology Washington U., St. Louis, 1963-69; chmn. dept. sociology Livingston Coll., Rutgers U., 1969-73; prof. sociology grad. faculty Rutgers U., 1969—, Hannah Arendt prof. social and polit. theory, 1979—; Bacardi chair Cuban studies U. Miami, 1992—94. Vis. prof. sociology U. Caracas, Venezuela, 1957, Buenos Aires U., 1959, 61, 63, SUNY, Buffalo, 1960, Syracuse U., 1961, U. Rochester, fall 1962, U. Calif., Davis, 1966, U. Wis., Madison, 1967, Stanford U., 1968-69, Am. U., 1972, Queen's U., Can., 1973, Princeton U., 1976, U. Miami, 1992; vis. lectr. London Sch. Econs. and Polit. Sci., 1962; prin. investigator for numerous sci. and rsch. projects; sr. editl. advisor Springer Sci. Pubs.; chmn. bd. dirs., editor-in-chief Transaction/Aldine; sr. advisory editor Springer Sci. and Bus. Media, 2007—. Author: Idea of War and Peace in Contemporary Philosophy, 1957, Philosophy, Science and the Sociology of Knowledge, 1960, Radicalism and the Revolt Against Reason: The Social Theories of Georges Sorel, 2d edit., 1968, The war Game; Studies of the New Civilian Militarists, 1963, Historia y Elementos de la Sociologia del Connocimento, 1963, Professing Sociology: The Life Cycle of a Social Science, 1963, The New Sociology: Essays in Social Science and Social Values in Honor of C. Wright Mills, 1964, Revolution in Brazil: Politics and Society in a Developing Nation, 1964, The Rise and Fall of Project Camelot, 1967, rev. edit., 1976, Three Worlds of Development: The Theory and Practice of International Stratification, 1966, rev. edit., 1972, Latin American Radicalism: A Documentary Report on Nationalist and Left Movements, 1969, Sociological Self-Images, 1969, The Knowledge Factory: Masses in Latin America, 1970, Cuban Communism, 1970, 11th edit., 2003, Foundations of Political Sociology, 1972, Social Science and Public Policy in the United States, 1977, Dialogues on American Politics, 1979, Taking Lives: Genocide and State Power, 1979, 5th edit., 2001, Beyond Empire and Revolution, 1982, C. Wright Mills: An American Utopian, 1983, Winners and Losers, 1985, Communicating Ideas, 1987, Daydreams and Nightmares, 1990 (winner best biography Nat. Jewish Book Award), The Decomposition of Sociology, 1993, Subject of Festschrift: The Democratic Imagination, 1994, Behemoth: Main Currents in the History and Theory of Political Sociology, 1999, Veblen's Century: A Collective Portrait, 2002, Tributes: An Informal History of Twentieth Century Social Science, 2004, Soziale Ideologien und Politische System. Chmn. bd. Hubert H. Humphrey Inst. Ben Gurion U.; bd. mem. Alexis DeTocqueville Inst., 2003—. Recipient Harold D. Lasswell award Policy Sci. Orgn., Lifetime Achievement award Inter-Univ. Seminar on Armed Forces and Soc., Gerhart Niemeyer award Intercollegiate Studies Assn., 2003, Internat. Humanist award, 2004, Thomas S. Szasz award Ctr. for Ind. Thought, 2004, Disting. Scholarly Lifetime Achievement award Am. Sociological Assn., 2006. Fellow AAAS; founding mem, AAAS Sci and Human Rights Program; mem. AAUP, USIA (bd. advisors), Am. Polit. Sci. Assn., Nat. Assn. Scholars (bd. dirs.), Authors Guild, Ctr. for Study The Presidency, Coun. Fgn. Rels., Internat. Soc. Polit. Psychology (founder), Soc. Internat. Devel., U.S. Gen. Acctg. Office (exec. adv. bd.), U.S. Info. Agy. (exec. adv. bd. Radio and TV Marti), Nat. Assn. Scholars (bd. dirs.), Inst. for a Free Cuba, Raymond Aron Soc. (N.Am. pres. 2004-). Home: 1247 State Rd # Rt206 Princeton NJ 08540-1619 Office: Rutgers U Transaction Pubs Bldg 4051 New Brunswick NJ 08903 Office Phone: 732-445-2280. Office Fax: 732-445-3138. Business E-Mail: ihorowitz@transactionpub.com.

HOROWITZ, JACK, biochemistry educator; b. Vienna, Nov. 25, 1931; came to U.S., 1938; s. Joseph and Florence (Gutterman) H.; m. Carole Ann Sager, June 11, 1961; children— Michael Joseph, Jeffrey Frederick. BS, CCNY, 1952; PhD, Ind. U., 1957. Rsch. assoc. Columbia U., NYC, 1957-61; asst. prof. biochemistry Iowa State U., Ames, 1961-65, assoc. prof. biochemistry, 1965-71, prof. biochemistry, 1971-95, Univ. prof., 1995-2000, Univ. prof. emeritus, 2000—, chmn. dept. biochemistry, 1971-74, chmn. molecular, cellular and devel. biology program, 1977-80. Vis. scholar Rockefeller U., N.Y.C., 1968; vis. prof. Yale U., 1974-75; vis. scientist MIT, 1990-91; program dir. biophysics and biochemistry NSF, 1993-94. Contbr. articles to profl. jours. NSF fellow, 1952-54, 57-59; NIH and NSF grantee, 1961—; recipient faculty citation Iowa State U., 1989. Mem. RNA Soc., Am. Soc. Biochemistry and Molecular Biology, AAAS, Phi Beta Kappa, Sigma Xi, Phi Kappa Phi Jewish. Home: 2014 Country Club Blvd Ames IA 50014-7013 Office: Iowa State U Dept Biochemistry Biophys Ames IA 50011-0001 Business E-Mail: jhoro@iastate.edu.

HOROWITZ, MARK A., electrical engineering and computer science educator; BSEE, MSEE, MIT, 1978; PhD in Elec. Engring., Stanford U., 1984. Prof. Stanford U., Calif., 1984—, dir. Computer Systems Lab., Yahoo! Founders prof. elec. engring. and computer sci. Co-founder, dir. Rambus Inc., 1990—2005, v.p., 1990—94, chief scientist, 2005—. Contbr. articles to sci. jours. Recipient Presdl. Young Investigator award, 1985, Tech. Field award, IEEE Solid-State Circuits, 2006. Fellow: Assn. Computing Machinery, IEEE (Donald O. Pederson award in Solid-State Circuits 2006); mem.: NAE. Office: Stanford U Computer Systems Lab Gates Computer Sci Bldg 353 Serra Mall Stanford CA 94305 Office Phone: 650-725-3707. Office Fax: 650-725-6949. E-mail: horowitz@ee.stanford.edu.*

HOROWITZ, MARY **See CURTIS, MARY**

HOROWITZ, MORRIS A., retired economics professor; b. Newark, Nov. 19, 1919; s. Samuel and Anna (Litwin) H.; m. Jean Ginsburg, July 12, 1941; children— Ruth, Joel. BA in Econs., NYU, 1940; PhD in Econs., Harvard U., 1954. Mem. faculty Northeastern U., Boston, 1956—, prof. econs., chmn. dept., 1959-90, prof. emeritus, 1992—. Vice-chmn. Mass. Joint Labor-Mgmt. Com. for Mcpl. Police and Fire, 1980—; ad hoc labor arbitrator, manpower cons. Home: 1010 Waltham St Apt 341 Lexington MA 02421-8064 Office Phone: 781-861-1153.

HOROWITZ, PHILIP MARTIN, lawyer; b. Newark, Aug. 23, 1946; s. Paul and Louise (Cohen) Horowitz; m. Carol Ruth Weiner, June 28, 1970; children: Jason Benjamin, Michael. AB magna cum laude, Upsala Coll., 1970; JD, Georgetown U., 1973. Bar: Va. 1973, DC 1973. Assoc. Melrod, Redman & Gartlan, Washington, 1973-79, shareholder-dir., 1979-93, chmn. real estate dept., 1981-93; ptnr. Arter & Hadden, Washington, 1993—2002, chmn. nat. real estate practice group, 1994—2002, mem. exec. com., 1997—2001; ptnr., real estate Venable LLP, Washington, 2003—, co-chair bus. divsn., 2006—. V.p., bd. dirs. exec. com. Mentors Inc.; adj. prof. real estate planning Washington Coll. Law Am. U., 1988—; mem. exec. coun. DC Bldg. Industry Assn. With US Army, 1966—68. Mem.: Anglo-Am. Real Property Inst., Va. Bar Assn., DC Bar Assn., Am. Coll. Real Estate Lawyers (pres. 2006). Office: Venable LLP 575 7th St NW Washington DC 20004 Office Phone: 202-344-4746. Office Fax: 202-344-8300. Business E-Mail: phorowitz@venable.com.

HOROWITZ, SAMUEL BORIS, biomedical researcher, educational consultant; b. Perth Amboy, NJ, Aug. 26, 1927; s. Sol and Lillian (Levine) H.; m. Joan Hughes, June 15, 1956 (div. 1971); m. Marian Sylvia Herman, May 23, 1973 (div. 1986); 1 child, Ann Julia AB, Hunter Coll., NYC, 1951; PhD, U. Chgo., 1956. Research assoc. Eastern Pa. Psychiat. Inst., Phila., 1958-62; vis. investigator Inst. Physiol. and Med. Biophysics U. Uppsala, Sweden, 1962-63; head lab. A. Einstein Med. Ctr., Phila., 1963-72; chief cellular physiology lab. Mich. Cancer Found., Detroit, 1972-93, chmn. dept. biology, 1975-78, chmn. dept. physiology and biophysics, 1981-93. Contbr. articles to profl. jours. Served with U.S. Army, 1946-47 Fellow AAAS; mem. Am. Assn. Cancer Research, Am. Soc. Cell Biology, Sigma Xi. Home and Office: 4159 Woodland Dr Ann Arbor MI 48103-9775 Home Phone: 734-426-2403; Office Phone: 734-426-2403. E-mail: sbg3210@aol.com.

HOROWITZ, SARA, labor organizer; b. NYC, Jan. 13, 1963; BS, Cornell U., 1984; JD, SUNY, Buffalo, 1992; MPA, Harvard U., 1995. Labor atty. pvt. practice; pub. defender NYC; union organizer Nat. Health and Human Svc. Employees Union, 1199; founder, exec. dir. Working Today, 1995—. Arbitrator Am. Arbitration Assn., Task Force on Restructuring Am.'s Labor Market Institutions, MIT. Contbr. articles to profl. jours. Grantee, fellow Stern Family Fund, Rockefeller Found., Echoing Green. Office: Working Today Ste 710 45 Main St Brooklyn NY 11201 Office Phone: 718-532-1515. Office Fax: 718-222-4440. Business E-Mail: info@workingtoday.org.

HOROWITZ, SCOTT JAY, astronaut, military officer; b. Phila., Mar. 24, 1957; s. Seymour B. Horowitz and Iris D. Chester; m. Lisa Marie Kern; 1 child. BS in Engring, Calif. State U., Northridge, 1978; MS in Aerospace Engring., Ga. Inst. Tech., 1979, PhD in Aerospace Engring., 1982. Assoc. scientist Lockheed-Ga. Co., Marietta, Ga., 1982—83; commd. 2d lt. USAF, 1983; advanced through grades to col.; instr. pilot, rsch. and devel. scientist USAF, Williams AFB, Ariz., 1984—87; fighter pilot 22nd Tactical Fighter Squadron USAF, Bitburg, Germany, 1987—89; test pilot USAF 6512th Test Squadron, Edwards AFB, Calif., 1990—95; astronaut NASA, Houston, 1992—2004, ret., 2004; assoc. adminstr., exploration sys. mission directorate NASA Hdqs., Washington, 2005—; dir., space transportation and exploration A.T.K.-Thiokol, Utah, 2004—05. Adj. prof. Embry Riddle U., 1985—89; prof. Calif. State U., Fresno, 1991. Decorated Disting. Flying Cross, Exceptional Svc. medal NASA, Def. Superior Svc. medal, Def. Meritorious Svc. medal, NASA Space Flight medals (STS-75 in 1996, STS-82 in 1997, STS-101 in 2000, STS-105 in 2001); named Outstanding Young Men in Am., 1985; recipient F-15 Pilot, 22 TFS, Hughes trophy, 1988, F-15 Pilot, 22 TFS, CINCUSAFE Trophy, 1st place award Design Competition, ASME, 1978, Sys. Command Quarterly Scientific & Engring. Technical Achievement award, 1986, Combat Readiness medal, 1989, Air Force Commendation medal, 1987, 1989. Mem.: Sigma Xi Scientific Rsch. Soc., Tau Beta Pi. Achievements include 4 space flights: Pilot for STS-75 Mission (Columbia), 1996, STS-82 Mission (Discovery), 1997, STS-101 Mission (Atlantis), 2000 & crew commander STS-105 Mission (Discovery), 2001; over 5000 flying hours in fifty different aircraft. Avocations: designing and building, flying home-built aircrafts, restoring automobiles, running. Office: Astronaut Office Johonson Space Ctr Houston TX 77058*

HOROWITZ, STEVEN F., cardiologist; MD, N.Y. Med. Coll., 1972. Diplomate in internal medicine and cardiovasc. disease Am. Bd. Internal Medicine. Resident in medicine Beth Israel Med. Ctr., 1972—76; resident in cardiology, fellow in medicine Mt. Sinai Hosp., NYC, 1976—79; attending physician cardiovasc. disease Beth Israel Med. Ctr., NYC, 1988—2002; dir. cardiology Stamford (Conn.) Hosp., 2003—. Clin. prof. medicine and nuc. medicine Albert Einstein Coll. Medicine. Home: 250 Rosedale Ave White Plains NY 10605 Office: PO Box 9317 Shelburne and W Broad St Stamford CT 06904-9317 E-mail: shorowitz@stamhealth.org.

HOROWITZ, STEVEN GARY, lawyer; b. Miami Beach, Fla., Sept. 4, 1950; s. Arthur R. and Bernice (Schwamm) H.; children: Jessica Zoe, Benjamin Will, Adam Jedidiah. BA magna cum laude, Yale U., 1972; JD and M in pub. policy cum laude, Harvard U., 1978. Bar: Mass. 1979, U.S. Dist. Ct. Mass. 1979, N.Y. 1988. Asst. planner N.Y.C. Dept. Planning, 1972-74; law clk. to judge U.S. Dist. Ct., Boston, 1978-79, ct. monitor, 1979-81; assoc. Hill and Barlow, Boston, 1981-85; ptnr. Hill & Barlow, 1985-87; of counsel Cleary, Gottlieb, Steen & Hamilton, NYC, 1987-88, ptnr., 1989—. Author: Primer on Transferable Development Rights, 1979, Lender Liability for Cleaning Up Wastes, 1979, Legal Rights and Institutional Reform Litigation: Can The Judiciary Produce Results?, 1988. Bd. dirs. and gen. counsel Arts/Boston, 1983-87; cons. to Mayor of Jerusalem, 1981-83. Mem. Mass. Bar Assn. (pub. law sect. council 1985-87), Boston Bar Assn., NY State Bar Assn. (exec. com. real property law sect. 1989—), Assn. of Bar of City of NY (real property law com.), Am. Coll Real Estate Lawyers, Legal Aid Soc. (bd. dirs. 2001-06), Anglo-Am. Real Property Inst. Democrat. Jewish. Home and Office: Cleary Gottlieb Steen & Hamilton 1 Liberty Plz New York NY 10006-1404 Office Phone: 212-225-2580. Office Fax: 212-225-3999. Business E-Mail: shorowitz@cgsh.com.

HOROWITZ, WINONA LAURA See RYDER, WINONA

HOROWITZ, ZACHARY I., entertainment company executive; b. NYC, Apr. 27, 1953; s. Ben and Beverly (Lichtman) H.; m. Barbara J. Natterson; children: Jennifer Lily, Charles Samuel. BA summa cum laude, Claremont Mens Coll., 1975; JD, Stanford U., 1978. Bar: Calif. 1978. Assoc. Kaplan, Livingston, Goodwin, Berkowitz & Selvin, Beverly Hills, Calif., 1978; from sr. atty. to dir. bus. affairs West Coast CBS Records, LA, 1978-83; v.p. bus. and legal affairs MCA Records, Universal City, Calif., 1983-84, sr. v.p. bus. and legal affairs, 1984-88; from sr. v.p. bus. and legal affairs to COO Universal Music Group, Universal City, 1986-95, pres., 1995-98, pres., COO, 1999—; bd. dirs. Pressday, 2000—. Bd. dirs. Universal Victor Japan 1991-2000; mem. op. com. Motown Recording Co., L.A., 1988-93. Mem. bd. editors Stanford Law Rev., 1977-78. Nat. bd. dirs. City of Hope, 1989—, vice chmn. Music Industry chpt., 1985-86, chmn. maj. gifts com., 1986-90, nat. campaign co-chmn., 1990-91, pres., 1991-92, chmn., 1993-94, endowment chair, 1995-97, major gifts chair, 1997—, adv. bd. Nashville Celebrity Baseball Game, 1995—. Mem. NARAS (presdl. adv. com. 1996—), Record Industry Assn. Am. (bd. dirs. 1990—, fin. com. 1993—). Office: Universal Music Group 2220 Colorado Ave Fl 1 Santa Monica CA 90404-3574

HORRELL, JEFFREY LANIER, library director; b. Carbondale, Ill., Sept. 19, 1952; s. C. William and Ettelye M. (Hanser) H. BA, Miami U., Oxford, Ohio, 1975; AM in Libr. Sci., U. Mich., 1976, AM in History of Art, 1978; PhD, Syracuse U., 1995. Libr. intern Nat. Gallery of Art, Washington, 1977; asst. libr. art and architecture U. Mich., Ann Arbor, 1977-80; libr., Sherman Art Libr. Dartmouth Coll, Hanover, NH, 1981-86; Coun. Libr. Resources libr. mgmt. intern Syracuse U. Libr., 1986-87, asst. to univ. libr. for planning, 1987-88; libr., Fine Arts Libr. Harvard Coll., Cambridge, 1992-98, assoc. libr. for collections, 1998—2005; dean of libraries, coll. libr. Dartmouth Coll., Hanover, NH, 2005—. Pres. ARLIS/NA, 1987. Author: Treasures of the Hood Museum of Art, 1985; contbr. articles to profl. publs. Mem. ALA, Coll. Art Assn., Art Libr. Soc. N.Am. (pres. 1987-88), U. Mich. of Info. Studies Alumni Soc. (pres. 1997-98). Avocations: travel, photography. Office: Office of Librarian Dartmouth Coll Libr Hanover NH 03755 Office Phone: 603-646-2236. E-mail: jeffrey.l.horrell@dartmouth.edu.

HORRELL, KAREN HOLLEY, insurance company executive, lawyer; b. Augusta, Ga., July 10, 1952; d. Dudley Cornelius and Eleanor (Shouppe) Holley; m. Jack E. Horrell, Aug. 14, 1976. BS, Berry Coll., 1974; JD, Emory U., 1976. Bar: Ohio 1977. Counsel Am. Fin. Corp., 1980-81; sec., asst. sec. numerous other fin. and ins. cos.; gen. counsel numerous subsidiaries Great Am. Ins. Co., corp. counsel Cin., 1977-80, v.p., gen. counsel, sec., 1981-85, sr. v.p., gen. counsel, sec., bd. dirs., 1985—; pres. corp. svcs. Great Am. Ins. Property & Casualty Group, 1999—. Bd. dirs. Tri-Health, Inc., Bethesda, Inc, spkr. in field, 2005. Trustee Cmty. Chest, 1987—91, Seven Hills Sch., 1991—2000, v.p., 1995—99; mem. cabinet United Appeal, 1984; bd. dirs. YWCA, 1984—90, v.p. fin., 1986—89; mem. Hamilton County Blue Ribbon Task Force on Child Abuse and Neglect Svcs., 1989—91; trustee Ohio Ins. Inst., 1994—2000, chair, 1996—99, Bethesda Hosp. Inc.; chair Ohio Joint Underwriting Assn., 1992—97; trustee Berry Coll., 1999—; mem. Hamilton County Hosp. Commn., 1999—, vice chair, 2002—; bd. dirs. Children's Home, 2001—. Mem. ABA, Cin. Bar Assn. (admissions com. 1978-91, nominating com. 1987-90). Democrat. Office: Great Am Ins Co 580 Walnut St Cincinnati OH 45202-3110 Home: 11817 Quarterhorse Ct Cincinnati OH 45249-1279

HORRIGAN, BRIAN RICHARD, economist; b. Washington, Sept. 30, 1951; s. William Kienle and Eleanor Gertrude (Ahern) H. BA in Econs., Santa Clara U., 1973; MA in Econs., UCLA, 1975, PhD in Econs., 1980. Economist Fed. Reserve Bank of Phila., Research Dept., Phila., 1980-87; dir. long-term forecasting The WEFA Group, Bala Cynwyd, Pa., 1987-92; sr. economist, v.p. Loomis, Sayles & Co., Boston, 1992-2000, chief economist, 2000—. Bd. dirs. Nat. Assn. for Bus. Econs. Contbr. articles to profl. jours. Mem. Am. Econ. Assn. Office: Loomis Sayles & Co 1 Financial Ctr Fl 34 Boston MA 02111-2660 E-mail: bhorrigan@loomissayles.com.

HORRIGAN, D. GREGORY, packaging products executive; b. Des Moines, Iowa, 1943; Graduate, U. Iowa, Iowa City, 1966. Exec. v.p. Continental Can Co., 1984—87; co-founder, dir. Silgan Holdings Inc., Stamford, Conn., 1987—, co-CEO, 1994—2006, co-chmn., 2004—. Office: Silgan Holdings Inc Ste 400 4 Landmark Sq Stamford CT 06901*

HORRIGAN, JOSEPH STEWART, lawyer; b. Houston, Nov. 22, 1938; s. Joseph Raymond and Ruth (Mize) H.; children: Elizabeth, Katherine, Erin; m. Katherine K. Horrigan, Aug. 20, 1988. BA, Duke U., 1961; LLB, U. Tex., 1964. Bar: Tex. 1964, U.S. Dist. Ct. (we. and so. dists.) Tex., 1966, U.S. Ct. Appeals (5th cir.), 1981, U.S. Supreme Ct. 1995; cert. in estate planning and probate law Tex. Bd. Legal Specialization. Law clk. U.S. Dist. Ct., 1964-65, U.S. Ct. Appeals (5th cir.), 1965-66; assoc. Bryan, Suhr, Bering, & Bailey, Houston, 1966-71; ptnr. Dyche & Wright, Houston, 1973-81, Armogida & Coats, Houston, 1981-84, Coats, Yale, Holm, Horrigan & Lee, Houston, 1984-85, Horrigan & Goehrs, Houston, 1986—. Fellow: Am. Coll. Trust and Estate Counsel, Tex. Bar Found., Houston Bar Assn. (charter sustaining); mem.: ABA, State Bar Tex., Disability and Elder Law Attys., Houston Ctr. Club. Home: 2310 Mimosa Dr Houston TX 77019-6024 Office: 1600 Two Houston Ctr Houston TX 77010 Office Phone: 713-659-4200.

HORROCKS, NORMAN, librarian, educator, editor; b. Manchester, Eng., Oct. 18, 1927; arrived in Canada, 1971; s. Edward Henry and Annie (Barnes) Horrocks; m. Sandra Sheriff; children: Julie Carol, Carl Scott, Gina Louise, Anne Patricia, Sarah Helen. BA, U. Western Australia, Perth, 1960; MLS, U. Pitts., 1964, PhD, 1971. Asst. libr. Manchester Pub. Librs., 1943-45, 50-53; libr. Brit. Coun., Cyprus, 1954—55; tech. libr. State Libr. We. Australia, 1956—63; tchg. fellow U. Pitts., 1963—64, instr., 1964—69, asst. prof., 1969—71; assoc. prof. Sch. Libr. Svc., Dalhousie U., Halifax, NS, 1971—73, prof., 1973—86, dir. sch., 1972—86, dean Faculty Mgmt. Studies, 1983—86, prof. emeritus, 1995—. Vis. lectr. Perth Tech. Coll., 1961—63, U. Hawaii, 1969; ext. lectr. Pa. State Libr., 1966—70; adj. prof. Rutgers U., 1987—95; chmn. Overseas Book Ctr., Halifax, 1980—83; mem. adv. bd. sci. and tech. info. Nat. Rsch. Coun. Can., 1980—86; mem. adv. bd. com. bibliog. svcs. Nat. Libr. Can., 1980—86; v.p. editl. Scarecrow Press, Metuchen, NJ, 1986—95; editl. cons., Lanham, Md., 1995—; mem. promotion and distbn. panel Can. Coun. Editor: N. We. Newsletter, 1952—53, Jour. Edn. Librarianship, 1971—76; assoc. editor: Govt. Publ. Rev., 1973—81; contbg. editor: Libr. Jour., 1983—; contbr. articles to profl. jours. Bd. visitors Pratt Inst. Rutgers U. With Brit. Army Intelligence Corps, 1945—48. Recipient Merit award, Atlantic Provinces Libr. Assn., 1979, Disting. Alumnus award, U. Pitts., 1982. Fellow: Libr. Assn. Australia, Libr. Assn. (UK) (hon.); mem.: ALA (hon.; coun. 1972—81, exec. bd. 1977—81, coun. 1983—95, various coms., Lippincott award 1995, John Ames Humphry Online Computer Libr. Ctr. Forest Press award 2001), Order of Can. (officer 2006), Progressive Librs. Guild, NJ Libr. Assn. (Disting. Svc. award coll. and univ. sect. 1995), Australian Libr. and Info. Assn., Assn. Am. Libr. Schs. (chmn. editl. bd. 1971—76), Intelligence Corps Assn. (life), N.S. Libr. Assn. (life), Assn. Libr. and Info. Sci. Edn. (pres. 1985—86, Svc. award 1990, Profl. Contbns. award 1996), Can. Coun. Libr. Schs. (chmn. 1974—76), Halifax Libr. Assn., Can. Libr. Assn. (2d v.p. 1978—80, various coms., Outstanding Svc. to Librarianship award 1995), Am. Inst. Parliamentarians, Am. Soc. Info. Sci. & Tech. (various coms.), Bibliosmiles, Archons of Colophon (convenor 1992), Beta Phi Mu (pres. 1991—93, Kaula Gold medal 2004). Home: 2 Casavechia Ct Dartmouth NS Canada B2X 3G6 Home Phone: 902-434-7986. Business E-Mail: norman.horrocks@dal.ca.

HORSBRUGH, PATRICK, architect, educator, environologist; b. Belfast, No. Ireland, June 21, 1920; came to U.S., 1960; s. Charles Bethune and Marion Rose (McQueen) H. Diploma with honors, Archtl. Assn. Sch. Architecture, 1949; diploma city planning, U. London, 1951. With Raglan Squire and Ptnrs., London, 1956-57; vis. critic Harvard Grad. Sch. Design, 1956; with depts. architecture, planning and landscape architecture univs. Ill., N.C., 1957-58; dep. dir., then dir. Hamilton-Wentworth (Ont.) Planning Area Bd., 1958-60. Vis. prof. architecture U. Nebr., 1960-65, U. Tex., 1965-67; prof. architecture U. Notre Dame, 1967-84, prof. emeritus, dir. grad program environic studies, 1970-80; founder, chmn. bd. Environic Found. Internat., Inc., 1970-94; cons. environ. and planning issues, ednl. and design practices; adj. prof. dept. architecture Andrews U., Mich. Designer: High Paddington Project, London, 1951; co-designer: New Barbican Com. Project, London, 1954; contbr: Winston Churchill Meml. in the U.S. commemorating the Iron Curtain Speech given in Fulton, Mo.; author: High Buildings in the United Kingdom, 1952, Pittsburgh Perceived, The Form, Features and Feasibilities of the Prodigious City, 1963; editor: The Texas Conference on Our Environmental Crisis, 1966. Co-chmn. Internat. Earth Day, 1978; v.p. Channel Tunnel Assn., 1974-94; mem. Ind. curriculum adv. coun. Ind. Bd. Edn., 1986; Earth trustee Earth Soc. Found. With Royal Arty., 1938-41; with RAF Vol. Res., 1941-46. Bernard Webb fellow Academica Britannica, Rome, 1950; B.Y. Morrison Meml. lectr. U.S. Dept. Agr., 1969. Fellow Royal Soc. Arts, Royal Geog. Soc., Brit. Interplanetary Soc.; mem. Royal Inst. Brit. Architects, Royal Town Planning Inst., Am. Planning Assn., Ancient Monument Soc., Soc. Indsl. Archaeology, Soc. Protection Ancient Bldgs, Georgian Group, Nat. Trust (Gt. Britain), Irish Georgian Soc., Ry. Devel. Soc., Christopher Wren Soc. (founder, London 1995), Ecolesiological Soc. Address: 916 Saint Vincent St South Bend IN 46617-1443

HORSCH, KATHLEEN JOANNE, social services administrator, educator, consultant; b. Mpls., June 27, 1936; d. Clement Nicholas and Delta Jesse (Steckman) Simmer; m. Lawrence Leonard Horsch, Aug. 25, 1956; children: Daniel L., Timothy J., Christopher G., Catherine J., Sarah E. Student, U. Minn., 1967-73. Various positions local, state and nat. levels Am. Cancer Soc., Mpls., 1965—, pres. Hennepin County bd. dirs., 1978, hon. life mem. Hennepin Unit bd., 1992—, chmn. bd. dirs. Minn. divsn., 1984-86, hon. life mem. Minn. divsn., 1993—, sec. nat. bd. NYC, 1982-85, vice-chmn. nat. bd., 1985-87, chmn. nat. bd. Atlanta, 1987-89, past officer, dir. nat. bd., 1992-97, hon. life mem., 1997—, chair Lane W. Adams award com., 1993-98; pres. Dynamics of Vol. Effectiveness, Inc., Mpls., 1985-95. Mem. faculty Met. State U., St. Paul, 1982-94, U.S. Nat. Com./Internat. Union Against Cancer UICC, Washington, 1989-94. Mem. adv. bd. Look Good Feel Better, 1986-03, Drucker Found. Non-Profit Mgmt., 1992-03; mem. com. Joint Commn. Health, 1989; bd. govs. United Way Am., 1990-96, St. Croix area United Way, 1996-02, vice-chair, 1997; bd. govs. Youth for Understanding Internat. Exch., 1992-01, vice-chair, 1997, chair, 1998-00; bd. govs. Courage Ctr., 1993-04, vice-chair, 1996-2000, chair, 2000-02; mem. coun. Internat. Cancer Union, 1990-94, chair Campaign Orgn. Pub. Edn. and Svc. Program, 1990-94; bd. dirs. Josephson Inst. of Ethics, 1991-96; chmn. The Human Spirit Initiative, 2004—, founder, 2004-. Recipient Svc. to Mankind award, Disting. Svc. award, Am. Cancer Soc., 2006. Mem. Nat. Human Svcs. Assembly (bd. govs. 1995—), Minikahda Club. Avocations: boating, piano, swimming, hiking. Office Phone: 612-860-8468. Personal E-mail: klhorsch@earthlink.net.

HORSCH, LAWRENCE LEONARD, venture capitalist, corporate financial executive; b. Mpls., Dec. 2, 1934; s. Leonard Charles and Cecilia May (Chamberlain) H.; m. Kathleen Joanne Simmer, Aug. 25, 1956; children: Daniel Lawrence, Timothy John, Christopher Girard, Catherine Jessica, Sarah Elisabeth. BA with honors, Coll. St. Thomas, 1957; MBA, Northwestern U., 1958. Investment banker Paine Webber Jackson & Curtis, Mpls., 1961-67; v.p. N.Am. Fin. Corp., Mpls., 1967-71; pres. Eagle Investment Corp., Mpls., 1971-87; chmn., CEO Munsingwear Inc., Mpls., 1987—90; chmn. bd. Eagle Mgmt. & Fin. Corp., Mpls., 1990—. Chmn. bd. dirs. Sci. Med. Life Sys., Maple Grove, Minn., 1971-94, Leuthold Funds, Inc.; bd. dirs. Boston Scientific Corp., 1995-2003, Med. C.V. Inc., 2003-05. 1st lt. USAF, 1959-61. Mem. Fin. Analysts Fedn., Mpls Rotary, Minikahda Country Club. Home: 1404 Hilltop Rdg Saint Joseph WI 54082-2013 Office: Eagle Mgmt & Fin Corp PO Box 235 Stillwater MN 55082-0235 Office Phone: 715-549-5294.

HORSEY, DAVID, editorial cartoonist; b. Evansville, Ind., Sept. 13, 1951; m. Nole Ann Ulery; children: Darielle Jean, Daniel Rayden. BA in Comms., U. Wash., 1976; MA in Internat. Rels., U. Kent, Canterbury, Eng., 1986. Formerly govt. reporter, polit. columnist Wash. State Capitol; polit. reporter, columnist, editl. cartoonist Daily Jour.-Am., Bellevue, Wash., 1976-79; editl. cartoonist, columnist, mem. editl. bd. Seattle Post-Intelligencer, 1979—. Syndicated Tribune Media Svcs., 1986-89, 2000—, King Features/N.Am. Syndicate, N.Y.C., 1988-2000; instr. Acad. Realist Art, Seattle, 1998; propr. Horsey--Words and Picturs, Seattle, 1993—. Author: Politics and Other Perversions, 1974, Horsey's Rude Awakenings, 1981, Horsey's Greatest Hits of the '80s, 1989, The Fall of Man, 1994, One Man Show, 1999; co-editor: (anthology) Cartooing AIDS Around the World, 1992; exhibited cartoons at Art Inst. Seattle, 1992, Michael Pierce Gallery, Seattle, 1997, Shoreline C.C., 1999, others. Asst. coach North Ctrl. Little League Baseball, 1992-94; youth coach Woodland Soccer Club, 1989-98; chmn. campaign for excellence St. Benedict Elem. and Mid. Sch., 1991-93, pres. sch. commn., 1993-95. Recipient 1st place Best of the West Journalism Competition, 1995, Environ. Media award, 1995, Global Media award Population Inst., 1991, Berryman award Nat. Press Found., 1998, Pulitzer prize for editl. cartooning, 1999, 2003, numerous others. Mem. Soc. Profl Journalists (12 1st place regional awards, Susan Hutchinson Bosch award 1999), Assn. Am. Editl. Cartoonists (pres.-elect 1999-2000, pres. 2000-01). Office: Seattle Post Intelligencer PO Box 1909 101 Elliott Ave W Ste 200 Seattle WA 98119-4295 E-mail: davidhorsey@seattlepi.com.

HORSLEY, ALEX, director; b. North Ferriby, Yorkshire, England, Jan. 24, 1944; s. Alec and Susan Horsley; m. Gillian Theunissen Horsley, Aug. 1, 1992; m. Caroline Vanrenen, Dec. 30, 1963 (div. Apr. 9, 1982); children: Natasha Elisabeth Horsley-Weston, Anita Susan, Dylan Alexander. BA, Oxford U., England, 1965, MA (hon.); BA in Edn., Hull U., England, 1977; PGCE, London U., England, 1975. Headmaster Atlanta Internat. Sch., 1985—96, Internat. Sch. Beijing, 1996—98, Chinese Internat. Sch., Hong Kong, 1998—2002; exec. dir. Ctr. for the Advancement and Study Internat. Edn., Atlanta, 2004—; headmaster Friends Sch. Mullica Hill, NJ. Cons. New Concepts in Internat. Edn., Atlanta, 2002—04. V.p. Ansley Pk. Civic Assn., Atlanta, Ga., 2004—06; bd. chair Friends Sch. of Atlanta, Atlanta, Ga., 2002—06; bd. advisor Atlanta Youth Soccer Assn., Atlanta, Ga., 2003—05. Mem.: Coun. Internat. Schs. (accreditation advisor 2003—06). Office: Ctr for Advancement and Study Internat Edn 2890 N Fulton Dr Atlanta GA 30305 Home Phone: 404-888-9811; Office Phone: 404-848-9044. Office Fax: 404-848-9042.

HORSLEY, HEIDI, psychotherapist, educator, radio personality; d. Phil and Gloria Call Horsley; m. Markus Redding, June 11, 1988; children: Alexander Horsley-Redding, Samantha Horsley-Redding. MS in Mental Health Counseling, Loyola U., New Orleans, 1993; MSW, Columbia U., NYC, 1997—97; D in Psychology, U. San Francisco, 2003. Psychotherapist, rschr. FDNY CSU/Columbia U. Family Guidance Program, NYC, 2002—. Adj. prof. Columbia U., NYC, 2004—; presenter in field. Author: Healing the Grieving Heart: A Message of Hope for Grieving Teens; contbr. articles to profl. jours.; co-host (radio show) Healing the Grieving Heart, 2006—. Home Phone: 212-582-7734; Office Phone: 646-269-1664.

HORSLEY, JACK EVERETT, retired bank executive, writer, lawyer; b. Sioux City, Iowa, Dec. 12, 1915; s. Charles E. and Edith V. (Timms) H.; m. Sallie Kelley, June 12, 1939 (dec.); children: Pamela, Charles Edward; m. Bertha J. Newland, Feb. 24, 1950 (dec.); m. Mary Jane Moran, Jan. 20, 1973; 1 child, Sharon. AB, U. Ill., 1937, LLB, JD, 1939, Med./Legal Doctorate, 2001. Bar: Ill. 1939. Bd. dirs., chair Ctrl. Ill. Nat. Bank (now US Bank), 1960—, chair emeritus, 1960—87. Instr. U. Ill. ROTC, 1968—99, Sch. of the Soldier, U. Ill. ROTC, 2001, Res. Officer's Assn., 2002—05; chmn. rev. bd. Ill. Supreme Ct. Disciplinary Commn., 1973—99, 2004, adv. cons., 1976—2005; temp. prof. law NYU, NYC, 1974, 90, 98, 99, 2000—05, 2004; alumni adv. com. U. Ill. Law Forum, 1991—2000, mem. lawyers adv. coun., 1992—2005, chair, mem. heart diagnostics adv. coun., 1999—2005, mem. sr. lawyers adv. coun., 2001—03; trial laureate Ill. Trial Lawyers Acad., 1996; adv. dir. Harlan Moore Heart Rsch. Found., 2004—06; vis. prof. trial practice Fordham Law Sch., NYC, 1989—2002, 1999—2006, 2004—05, 2006—07; vis. prof. U. Berkeley Coll. Law, 1999, vis. prof, 2002, vis. prof., 2004—06; Laureata-emeritus Ill. Trial Lawyers Acad., 2000; adv. dir., cons., reviewer Am. Life League, 2001—07; lectr. in field; chair U. Ill. Law Forum, 2005; asst. treas. Harlan Moore Heart Rsch. Found., 2006; chmn. emeritus Ill. Supreme Ct. Disciplinary Commn., 2002—07; adv. dir. 1st Nat. Bank, Mattoonn, Ill., 2005—06, Ill. State Bar Assn.; atty. Ill. Cir. Judges Assn., 2006—; co-founder Lawyer

Author Soc., 2006. Narrator Poetry Interludes, Sta. WLBH-FM, 1977—2007; author: Trial Lawyer's Manual, 1967, Voir Dire Examinations and Opening Statements, Real Estate Foreclosures, 1968, Inequities to Foreclosure Appraisals, 1997, Current Development in Products Liability Law, 1969, 2d edit., 2005, Illinois Civil Practice and Procedure, 1970, 2d edit., 2006, The Medical Expert Witness, 1973, Testifying in Court, 1973, 6th edit., 2005, supplement 4th edit, 1993, The Doctor and the Law, 1975, 2nd edit., 1994, The Doctor and Family Law, 1975, The Doctor and Medical Law, 1977, 2d edit., 2004, Anatomy of a Medical Malpractice Case, 1984, 2d edit., 1993, Heartstrings of the Mind, 1998, 3d edit., 2002, Trilogy: The Frivolous Law Suit, 2000, Lincoln the Lawyer, 2002, 2d edit, 2004, Lincoln-Circuit Lawyer, 2002, suppl., 2004, Interludes of Poetry, 2004—07, Trilogy: Rembrance Lincoln, Circuit Rider Attorney; Thoughts to Ponder, 2005, Trilogy: Lincoln at Home, On Circuit, 2d edit., 2007, Rainbows: A Child's Garden of Epigrams, 2007, 2d edit., 2007; cons., reviewer All About "Biff" Story Of A Boy and His Dog; author: Persons Remembered, 2006, Corp Write-Offs On Mergers, 2006, (municipals) G.O. of Revenue, 1992, World War II, D-Day, 1994, 2d edit., 1998, (co-founder) Life's Challenges Preparation, 1999, (municipals, co-founder) World War II Air Mus, Duxford, Eng., 1999; adv. dir. World War II Air Mus, Duxford, Eng., 2005—; author: (municipals, co-founder) Trial Techniques, 1995, 4th edit., 2005, Legal Liability Exposure of Trust Co., 1996;: 2d edit., 1999, On Trust Dept. Guide-lines and Risks, 1996, On Federal Evidence and Examination, 1995—97, 1998—2005, Memories of World War II in the European Theater, 1997, U.S. Civil War, Its Military Personnel, 2d edit., 2002, 3d. edit., 2005, US Civil War: Its Major Battles, 2005, 2d supplement, 2007, Geo William Sherman: March to the Sea, 2007, (municipals, co-founder) suppl. on post World War II Reserve officer duties in mil. justice, 2000 (USAF Cross, Def. Disting. Svc. WWII Victory medal, 1945, European Theatre Svc. medal, 1943, Judge Advocate Spl. award, 1944, Spl. Svc. medal Rsch. Officer Assn., 1999, Disting. Svc. award USAF Law Dept., 1950), addendun to 2d edit., 2003, History of the Bar in East Central Illinois, 1997, History and Changes of the Bar in East-Central Illinois, 2006, Remembrances: An Autobiography, 1998, 2d edit., 2000;: supplement, 2004, Views of Christianity: Origin of Man, 1999, (pamphlet) A Doctor's Duty: Presciption Care, 1999, The Careless Doctor and Medical Malpractice, Thoughts to Ponder, 2001, Heartstrings of the Mind, 2003, "HE" Life of Christ, 2006, Foreclosure By Trustees, 2006; co-author: RN Legally Speaking, 1998, Mathew Bender Forensic Sciences, 1988, supplement, 2005, Litton Bender Forensic Sciences, 3d edit., 2003; editor: Fifty Eight Years as Attorney, 1997, Fifty Eight Years as Attorney: Twelve More Years, 2002; consulting editor Advanstar Comm., legal cons. Mast-Head, 1972—, RN Mag., Med. Econs., contbr. Forensic Scis. Texts and Treatises, 1981, 2d edit., 1999, supplement, 2004, Fed. Evidence Rules, 1988, 1996, 2001; contbr.: Fed. Evidence Rules, 2005; contbr. Fed. Evidence Rules, 2d term, 2005, Commission US Judiciary, 1998, Cross-Exam Techniques and Potential Traps, 1996, 2d edit., 2002, Eagle Forum (On Pro-Life), Alton, Ill., 1999, Christianity: The Origin of Man Creationism vs. Darwinism, 1998, Christianity: The Origin of Man and Biblical Legend, U. Ill. Law Rev., 2000, Selected Poems, Interludes of Poetry, 2001, contrb., 2004, Corp Counsel Midwest Manufacturers, 2005, cons., reviewer Civil Practice State and Fed. Cts., 1998—2001, Thoughts to Ponder, 2001; author: (pamphlet) 4th edit., 2004, My Brother and I, 1998, My Father and I, 2003, My Grandfather and I, 2003, My Great-Grandfather Dr. Arch Sampson, 2005, Prominent Persons, 2005; reviewer Current Developments in Medical Malpractice Law, supplement, 1968, 2d edit., 2004; editl. cons.: Med. Econ., 1969—2007; author: The Doctor and Business Law, 1976, 3d edit., 2004;: supplement, 2006, A Story of a Boy and His Dog, 2007, Abraham Lincoln: Selections from His Life, 2007; contbr. articles to profl. jours. Alt. del. to Rep. Platform Com., 2004; active Senatorial Reelection Com., 1993, 99; mem. exec. com. Ill. Rep. Election Campaign, 1997, 02, 04, US Supreme Ct. 1963-, 65, 69, 99, 2005; founding mem. US Supreme Ct. Hist. Soc., acting regent, 1999; pres. bd. edn. sch. dist. 100, 1946-48; bd. dirs. Harlan Moore Heart Rsch. Found., 1968-91, hon. dir., 1991-2006; vol. reader in rec. texts Am. Assn. for Blind, 1970-72, 97-98, 2000-05; chmn. exec. com. U. Ill. Law Forum, 1990-91, chair emeritus 1998-03; founding mem. Home for Law Alumni Found., Chgo., Springfield, Ill., 1998-99; pres. Res. Officers Assn. East Cen. Ill., 1988-89, 99-2000, 04-05, pres. emeritus 2001-05, chair, bd. dirs., 2000-02; founder Bertha Newland Horsley award St. John's Coll. Nursing, Springfield, Mary Jane Horsley award trophy Mattoon H.S., Ill.; mem. exec. com. Ill. Rep. Election Campaign, 1997, 06, Brig. gen. hon. res., ret., 1997; tournament judge Big Ten Debating Contest, 2001, tech. advisor, 2002, 04; 4 arguments US Supreme Ct. Bar, 1963-98; chmn. Ill. State Bar Assn. Grievance Com., 1954-55; substitute tchr. Mattoon Meth. Ch., 1988, 97, 05; co-founder scholarship Marshal Coll. Law, 2006; adv. dir. Midwest Anti-Abortion Assn., 2006; cons. Federal Rules Commn., 2006-07. Decorated Purple Heart; recipient JAG's Spl. Svc. award, Victory ribbon, ETO Svc. ribbon, Combat Zone Svc. Ribbon ETO, Extended Active Duty ribbon, Disting. Svc. award, U. Ill., 1995. Fellow Am. Coll. Trial Lawyers (co-chair membership commn. 1998, 00, acting regent 2000-01); mem. ABA, Ill. Bar Assn. (exec. coun. ins. law 1961-63, 64, 65, 66, com. chmn. banking law 1972, lectr. law course for attys. 1962, 64-65, sr. counsellor 1989-2002, chmn., 1992-99, Disting. Svc. award 1982-83), Assn. of Bar of City of NY (non-residential lic. Ct. Appeals 2005), NY Bar Assn. (non resident mem.), Coles-Cumberland Bar Assn. (v.p. 1968-00, pres. 1969-70, pres. emeritus 1971—, chmn. com. jud. inquiry 1976-80, chair meml. com. 1989-2000, mem. exec. com. 1998, sr. counsellor 1989, co-author Forensic Scis. Jour. 1991, supp., 1996, 2d edit. 1999, Life-time Achievement award 1999), Am. Arbitration Assn. (supr. nat. panel arbitrators, counsel advisor hearing officers in Ill. 1996-97, 04, 05, 06, pres. Ill. state hearing officers com. 2004), U. Ill. Law Alumni Assn. (life mem., emeritus mem. 2004, pres. 1966-67, Alumni of Month Sept. 1974, Sept. 2005, exec. com. 1990-91, Sr. Alumni of Month 2001), Ill. Appellate Lawyers Assn. (editl. cons. 2002), Soc. Legal Scribes (chair emeritus 1995-04), Ill. Def. Counsel Assn. (pres. 1967-98, chair adv. bd. 1989—, pres. emeritus 1969-03), Soc. Trial Lawyers (chmn. profl. activities 1960-61, 05-07, bd. dirs. 1966-67, 88-94, 00-04, 05), Fed. Ct. Hist. Soc. (co-chmn. 1998-03), Adelphic Debating Soc. (judge of intramural debating U. Ill. 1999, adv. judge 2005), Assn. Ins. Attys., Internat. Assn. Ins. Counsel (hon. pres. 2003), Am. Judicature Soc., Res. Officers Assn. (pres. 1997-98, chair exec. com., pres. emeritus 2002-06, hon. brig. gen. JAGD 1997), U. Ill. Alumni Assn. (exec. com. 1990-91, 04), Masons (lectr. ceremonial 32 degree Scottish Rite 2000, Sr. Master award 1992), Scabbard and Blade Soc. U. Ill. (pres. 1936, pres. emeritus 1998, bd. dirs. 1997-03), Delta Phi (exec. com. alumni assn. 1960-61, 67-68, 99-03), Sigma Delta Kappa Law Frat. (alumni advisor 2005). Lutheran. Home: 913 N 31st St Mattoon IL 61938-2271 Office Phone: 217-235-5954. *Learn from the past, work in the present, play for the future.*

HORSLEY, RICHARD DAVID, banker; b. 1942; With FDIC, Washington, 1964-66, Ernst and Ernst, NYC, 1966-72; compt. 1st Ala. Bancshares Inc., Montgomery, 1972-77, v.p., compt., 1977-82; vice chmn., exec. fin. officer Regions Fin. Corp., Birmingham, Ala., 1982—2002, also bd. dirs., 2002—. Office: Regions Fin Corp 417 20th St N Birmingham AL 35203-3203

HORSMAN, DAVID A. ELLIOTT, writer, finance company executive, educator; b. Calvert County, Md., June 28, 1932; s. Alvin W. and Bessie L. (Elliott) H. Student, U. Chgo.; BA, San Francisco State U., 1964; MA, NYU, 1967, PhD, 1970; MDiv, Episc. Div. Sch., 1984. Ordained priest, consecrated bishop Jurisdiction of Orthodox Ch. of Far Isles, 2000. Fl. dir., stage mgr. WTOP-TV, Washington, 1959-61; TV writer/producer Insight, Nat. Coun. Chs., Washington, 1961-62; English master, dir. studies Searing Sch., NYC, 1965-67; asst. prof. humanities Acad. Aeros., Flushing, N.Y., 1967-68; instr. humanities Rensselaer Poly. Inst., Troy, N.Y., 1969-70; assoc. prof., founder and coord. film sequence U. South Fla., Tampa, 1970-80; headmaster All Hallows Acad., Alexandria, Va., 1985-87; pres. Elliott Horsman & Assocs., 1988-89; fin. cons. Shearson Lehman Hutton, Inc., Balt., 1989-91; investment broker RAF Fin. Corp., Atlanta, 1991-92; exec. Josepthal, Lyon & Ross, Atlanta, 1992-93; v.p. Meyers, Pollock & Robbins, Atlanta, 1992-97; pres. Horsman Bros., Inc., 1998—. Chmn. bd. of fellows All Hallows Hall, 1998—; founder Horsman Hedge Fund, 1999 Author: The Liturgy as Communication, 1970, Introduction to Structural Description of Liturgical Dromena, 1979, (novel and screenplay) Pilgrims on Strange Strands, 1979, The Hovering Mercy and the Outstretched Hand, 2003, The Briar Patch, 2003, Christus Via, 2004. With US Army, 1957—59. Recipient Founders Day award NYU, 1971. Personal E-mail: dr.horsman@worldnet.att.net.

HORSMAN, LENORE LYNDE (ELEANORA), soprano, actress, voice educator; b. Saginaw, Mich., Apr. 21, 1931; d. George Clark and Gwendolyn (Steele) McNabb; m. Reginald Horsman, Sept. 3, 1955; children: John, Janine, Mara. BS in Music and Piano, Ind. U., 1956, MA in Theatre-Opera, 1958. profl. certs. in voice, Villa Schifanoia, Florence, Accademia Musicale Chigiana, Siena, Accademia Di Virgiliana, Mantua, Italy, Mozarteum, Salzburg. Tchrs: Tito Gobbi, Ettore Campogalliani. Dir. Mt. Clemens Studio of Music, Mich., 1950; tchr. voice, piano and acting for singers Milw. Conservatory of Music, 1964-65; dir., tchr., voice coach pvt. voice studio, 1965—; founder, dir., designer Milw. Opera Theater, 1966; vocal coach dept. opera U. Wis., Madison, 1969-70. Dir., performer Cameo Prodn., Milw., 1974, Opera for Two, Milw., 1975, Mu Phi Epsilon Sch. Music, Chgo., 1976-81; dir., tchr. pvt. voice studio, Chgo., 1976-92; voice coach Theatre X, Milw., 1977; tchr. of acting Northshore Theatre, Milw., 1978-80. More than 33 leading roles in opera, operetta, musicals and plays; performances and concerts in US and Italy. Pres. Wis. Women in the Arts, 1973-76; bd. dir. Internat. Women's Yr. Festival, Milw., 1975. Named Women of the Yr., Milw. Panhellenic Assn., 1975; recipient Career Achievement award, 1978, Singers medal of honor Amici della Lirica, Mantua, Italy, 1981, Palcoscenico Music Vocal Silver Stage award, Italy, 1981. Mem. AAUW (v.p. 1999-2000), Nat. Assn. Tchr. Singing, Nat. Opera Assn., Wis. Music Tchr. Assn., Writers' Forum, Guild for Lifelong Learning, Mu Phi Epsilon, Theta Alpha Phi. Achievements include research in belcanto teaching methods. Avocations: theater, opera, painting, poetry. Home and Studio: c/o The Astor Hotel 924 E Juneau Ave #623 Milwaukee WI 53202

HORSNELL, MARGARET EILEEN, retired historian; b. St. Paul, Jan. 3, 1928; d. Kenneth George and Mary Elizabeth (Dowd) Horsnell. BA, U. Minn., 1961, MA, 1963, PhD, 1967. Instr. history U. Minn., 1966-67; mem. faculty Am. Internat. Coll., Springfield, Mass., 1967—, assoc. prof. history, 1976-84, prof., 1984-96, chmn. dept., 1987-96, emeritus prof. history, 2006—. Vis. sr. assoc. Mem. Sch. Classical Studies, Athens, 1997—99. Author: Spencer Roane: Judicial Advocate of Jeffersonian Principles, 1986; mem. editl. bd. This Constn., 1986—88; contbr. articles to publs. Mem. adv. panel 500 Yrs. Am. Clothing, 1989—92. Recipient Tozer Found. award, 1966, McKnight Found. award, 1967; Summer grantee, Am. Internat. Coll., 1970, Alt. fellow, AAUW, 1974—75. Mem.: Am. Legal Studies Assn., So. Hist. Assn., Inst. Early Am. History and Culture, Archeol. Inst. Am., Phi Alpha Theta. Home and Office: 15 Atwood Rd South Hadley MA 01075-1601 Office Phone: 413-533-6388. Personal E-mail: horsnell@aol.com.

HORST, DEENA LOUISE, state legislator; b. Sacramento, Feb. 14, 1944; s. Orlo John and Louise Helena (Schultze) Poovey; m. Gordon Lee Horst, 1966; children: Randall, Rebecca. BSE, Emporia State U., 1966, MA, 1972; postgrad., Kans. State U., 1993—. Elem. tchr. Peabody Sch., 1966-68; mid. sch. art tchr., dept. chmn. South Mid. Sch., Unified Sch. Dist. # 305, 1968—; mem. from dist. 69 Kans. State Ho. of Reps., 1995—. Vice chmn. Kans. 2000 com., K-12 edn. com.; chmn. e-govt. com., vice chmn. higher edn. com., chmn. arts and cultural resources joint com. Kans. House of Reps.; chmn. Kans. Commemorative Coin Commn. State and nat. ofcl. U.S. Jaycee Women, 1968-84; sec. Saline County Rep. Ctrl. Com., Kans., 1992-95; mem. adv. bd. Consumer Credit Counseling, Hertzler Health Found. Named Outstanding State Pres., U.S. Jaycee Women, 1979-80; co-recipient Master Tchr. award State of Kans., 1991. Mem. C. of C., Phi Alpha, Alpha Theta Rho, Phi Delta Kappa, Epsilon Sigma Alpha (Zone Outstanding Sister award 1990), Delta Kappa Gamma. Republican. Address: 920 S 9th St Salina KS 67401-4806 Office Phone: 785-296-7653. Personal E-mail: deena@worldlinc.net.

HORST, J. ROBERT, lawyer; b. 1943; BA, Case Western Reserve U., 1965; JD, Boston U. Law, 1971. Assoc. gen. counsel Eaton Corp., Cleve., 1991—98, dep. gen. counsel, 1998—99, v.p., gen. counsel, 2000—05. Office: Eaton Corp Eaton Ctr 1111 Superior Ave NE Cleveland OH 44114-2584

HORST, TERESA DALE, music educator; b. Loudon, Tenn., May 20, 1955; d. William Jefferson and Selma Elizabeth Hamilton; m. Thomas Dale Horst, June 6, 1976; children: Thomas Dale Jr., Tiffany DeAnn. BS in Music Edn., U. Tenn., Knoxville, 1977. Program devel and dissemination Bristol City Schs., Va., 1977—79; classroom music instr., dir. devel. Highland Hills Christian Acad., Lenoir City, Tenn., 1986—96; h.s. band camp instr. various schs., Tenn., 1999—2001; dir. music Joy of Music Youth Music Schs., Knoxville, 2001—04; pvt. music instr. Tenn. Mem. Knoxville Symphony League, 2003—. Musician: East Tenn. Cmty. Band, 1990—. Vol. Hist. Mus. Lenoir City, Lenoir City, 1996—2000; office vol. Lenoir City H.S., Lenoir City, 1996—2001. Recipient Award for Tchr. Recognition as Outstanding Tchr. in State, Tenn. Gov.'s Sch. for Performing Arts, 2005, John Philip Sousa award, John Philip Sousa Found., 1973. Mem.: Tenn. Sch. Band and Orch. Assn., East Tenn. Sch. Band and Orch. Assn., Internat. Horn Soc., Music Educators Nat. Conf., Sigma Alpha Iota. Church Of God. Avocations: horseback riding, travel, scrapbooks, gardening. Home: 15906 Hotchkiss Valley Rd E Loudon TN 37774

HORSTMANN, JAMES DOUGLAS, retired academic administrator; b. Davenport, Iowa, Oct. 2, 1933; s. Leonard A. and Agnes A. (Erhke) H.; m. Carol H. Griffiths, Sept. 8, 1956; children: Kent, Karen, Diane. BA, Augustana Coll., 1955. C.P.A., Ill., Wis. Staff acct., auditor Arthur Andersen & Co., Chgo., 1955-61; v.p., controller Harry S. Manchester, Inc., Madison, Wis., 1961-65; sr. v.p. fin., treas. H. C. Prange Co., Sheboygan, Wis., 1965-83, also dir.; dir. planned giving Augustana Coll., Rock Island, Ill., 1983-85, v.p. for devel., 1985-93, v.p. planned giving, 1993-98, v.p. emeritus, 1998—; pres. Schonstedt Instrument Co., 1993-95, ret., 1995—. Chmn. Wis. Mchts. Fedn.; bd. dirs. First Wis. Nat. Bank, Fond du Lac, 1975-83; cons. Score, 2004. Chmn. Sheboygan County (Wis.) Rep. Party, 1969-70; vice-chmn. Wis. 6th Congl. Dist., 1972-73, Rock Island County Reps., 2000-02; del. Nat. Rep. Conv., 1976; campaign chmn. Sheboygan United Way, 1977, treas., 1973-75, v.p., 1975-78, pres., 1978-79; bd. dirs. Public Expenditure Survey Wis., 1981-83, Rock Island YMCA, 1986-87, Franciscan Health Care Systems, 1988-92, Christ Luth. H.S. Found., 2000-03, Alternatives for the Older Adult, 2001—, v.p. 2003, pres., 2004—, Marriage and Family Counseling, 2003—, Thrivent for Lutherans, 2003; v.p. Sheboygan Arts Found., 1973-75; v.p., bd. dirs. Sheboygan Retirement Home, 1977-83; bd. dirs. Franciscan Mental Health Ctr., 1984-94, pres., 1985-88; trustee Friendship Manor, 1993-2003, pres., 2000-02; trustee Coun. on Children at Risk, 1989-2001, Franciscan Med. Ctr., 1990-92, Cmty. Found. of the Great River Bend, 2002—, chmn., 2005; trustee Villa Montessori Sch., 1999—, pres. 2000-04; v.p. German Am. Heritage Ctr., 2000-05; treas. Trinity Vis. Nurse/Homemakers Assn., 2001, vice chair, 2004, Pathway Hospice, 2001; bd. dirs. Augustana Hist. Soc., 2001—, Quad Cities Health Initiatives, 2005—. With USN, 1955-57. Named Outstanding Fund Raising Exec. Nat. Soc. Fund Raising Execs., 1992; recipient Outstanding Svc. award Augustana Coll., 1979, Jr. Achievement Free Enterprise Found., 2003. Mem. Am. Heart Assn. (bd. dirs. Quad City chpt. 1999—, pres. 2002-), Am. Cancer Soc. (bd. dirs. Rock Island unit 1992-2001), Wis. Inst. CPAs, Ill. Soc. CPAs, Sheboygan County Assn. CPAs, Fin. Execs. Inst. (dir.), Quad-City Estate Planning Coun., Augustana Hist. Soc. (bd. dirs. 1999—), Augustana Coll. Alumni Assn. (pres. 1970-71), Econ. Club Sheboygan (pres. 1976-77), Kiwanis. Lutheran. Home: 1245 36th Ave Rock Island IL 61201-6022

HORSWELL, BRUCE BRIAN, facial surgeon; s. Ronald L. and Doris K. Horswell; m. Barbara Doreen Julius, Sept. 6, 1980; children: Bryce, Brynna, Brittany, Brocke, Brent. BA, Bemidji State U., Minn., 1974; MS, U. Minn., Mpls., 1985, DDS, 1979; MD, U. Conn., Farmington, 1991. Diplomate Am. Bd. Oral-Maxillofacial Surgery, 1988. Asst. prof. U. Conn., Farmington, 1987—90, U. Md., Balt., 1993—98; pvt. practice surgeon Maplewood Oral-Maxillofacial Surgery, St. Paul, 1998—2000; med. dir. FACES, attending surgeon Charleston Area Med. Ctr., W.Va., 2000—. Academician, rschr. U. Conn., Farmington, 1987—90, U. Md., Balt., 1993—98; clin. assoc. prof. surgery W.Va. U. Sch. Medicine, 2001—07. Contbr. articles to profl. jours., chapters to books. Hon. chair March of Dimes, W.Va., 2003. Fellow: ACS; mem.: Am. Assn. Oral-Maxillofacial Surgery, Am. Cleft Palate-Craniofacial Assn. (symposium chair annual meeting 2007). Office: FACES 830 Pennsylvania Ste 302 Charleston WV 25302 Office Phone: 304-388-2950.

HORSWILL, C. WEIR, retired obstetrician-gynecologist, photographer; b. Madison, Wis., 1924; MD, U. Wis., 1952. Diplomate Am. Bd. Ob-gyn. Intern Toledo Hosp., 1952-53; resident U. Wis. Hosp., Madison, 1956-60; hon. staff Madison Meriter Hosp.; clin. assoc. prof. ob-gyn. U. Wis. Med. Sch.; ret. Fellow ACOG, ACS; mem. Am. Coll. Sports Medicine, Cen. Assn. Obstetricians and Gynecologists.

HORT, MICHAEL, art collector; m. Susan Hort; children: Peter, Andrew, Shoshana, Rema Hort Mann(dec.). Founder Rema Hort Mann Found., NYC, 1995—. Named one of Top 200 Collectors, ARTnews mag., 2003—06. Avocation: Collector contemporary art. Office: Rema Hort Mann Found 153 Hudson St New York NY 10013

HORT, SUSAN, art collector; m. Michael Hort; children; Peter, Andrew, Shoshana, Rema Hort Mann(dec.). Founder Rema Hort Mann Found., NYC, 1995—. Named one of Top 200 Collectors, ARTnews mag., 2003—06. Avocation: Collector contemporary art. Office: Rema Hort Mann Found 135 Hudson St New York NY 10013

HORTA, JOSÉ CARLOS DE OLIVEIRA SOUSA, civil engineering consultant; b. Homoine, Mozambique, Dec. 16, 1935; s. José Maria de Sousa Horta and Maria do Carmo de Oliveira; children: Viriato, Soahanta Vololona, Maria Carmen, José Daniel. Candidate in Civil Engring., U. Liege, 1957; DSc in Earth Scis., U. Algiers, 1972, cert. in Applied Geophysics, 1973. Polit. adviser Movimento Popular de Libertação de Angola, 1959—61; geotech. and hwy. engr. Ministry Pub. Works, Algiers, 1966—73; acting dir. Civil Engring. Lab., SONATRACH, Beni Mered, Algeria, 1978—80; sr. hwy. and geotech. engr. Louis Berger Internat. Inc., Paris and East Orange, 1980—91; project mgr., regional rep. DMJM Internat., Washington, 1991—92; civil engring. cons. Lisbon, 1992—; quality lead engr ExxonMobil, Cameroon, 2000—02; design, constrn. supr. quality control expressways India, Algeria, 2003—05. Participant internat. confs. on soils, constrn. materials, road design, constrn. and maintenance, including 5th Internat. Conf. on Low-Volume Roads, Raleigh, N.C., 1991, 2d Internat. Conf. on Roads and Road Transport Problems, New Delhi, 1995. Contbr. articles to profl. jours. and confs., including Engring. Geology, Geotechnique. Mem. ASTM, Indian Roads Congress (life). Avocations: gymnastics, swimming, dance, music, reading. Home: Apt 3F Av Bombeiros Voluntários 42 1495-020 Algés Lisboa Portugal Office Phone: 351-21-4103515. Fax: 351-21-4103515. E-mail: soushort.joyc@mail.telepac.pt.

HORTA, SILVIO, scriptwriter; b. Miami, Fla., Aug. 14, 1974; Grad., NYU Film Sch., 1995. Writer: (films) Urban Legend, 1998; The Furies, 1999; writer (characters) Urban Legend: Final Cut, 2000; writer, exec. prodr.: (TV series) The Chronicle, 2001; Jake 2.0: The Tech, 2003; Jake 2.0, 2003; Ugly Betty, 2006— (NAACP Image award, Writing in a comedy series, 2007, co-recipient Writer's Guild Am. award, New Series, 2007). Mailing: Ugly Betty Raleigh Studios 5300 Melrose Ave Los Angeles CA 90038*

HORTON, CHRISTINA MARIE, literature and language educator; b. Aug. 9, 1968; BA, Calif. State U., LA. Tchr. Rio Hondo Prep. Sch., Arcadia, Calif., 1996—2006; leadership advisor Kare Youth League, Arcadia, 2005—06. Mem.: Nat. Coun. Tchrs. of English.

HORTON, DONALD J., lawyer; b. Palestine, Tex., 1946; BBA, U. Houston, 1969, JD, 1971; LLM in Labor Law, NYU, 1973. Bar: Tex. 1972. Ptnr., Labor Dept. Andrews Kurth LLP, Houston. Asst. prof. law Loyola U., Chgo., 1973—77. Assoc. editor Houston Law Rev., 1971. Mem.: Nat. Employment Law Inst., ABA (Labor Law Sect.), Tex. Bar Assn., Houston Bar Assn., Order of Barons, Phi Alpha Delta. Office: Andrews Kurth LLP 600 Travis St Ste 4200 Houston TX 77002-3090 Office Phone: 713-220-4581. Office Fax: 713-238-4285. Business E-Mail: dhorton@andrewskurth.com.

HORTON, DONALD R., construction executive; married; 2 children. B, U. Ctrl. Ark. Pres. D.R. Horton, Inc., Fort Worth, Tex., 1991—98, chmn., 1991—. Named one of World's Richest People, Forbes mag., 2007. Office: DR Horton DR Horton Tower 301 Commerce St Ste 500 Fort Worth TX 76102 Office Phone: 817-856-8200.*

HORTON, FINIS GENE, real estate manager; BA, Lyons Coll., 1974; postgrad., Ark. State U., 1974—75, U. Ctrl. Ark., 1976. Asst. v.p., cost mgr. Worthen Bank, Little Rock, 1975—81; contr. First Fed. Bank, Morrilton, Ark., 1981—82; bank auditor Superior Fed. Bank, Little Rock, Ft. Smith, Ark., 1982—91; mng. dir. Audit Svcs. Group, Little Rock, 1991—95; pres., owner Corp. Bus. Svcs., Conway, Ark., 1991—2005; owner Horton Properties, Conway, 2005—. Mem.: Nat. Fin. Assocs., Kiwanis (pres. Little Rock 1978—79, bd. dirs. 1979—81). Avocation: sports.

HORTON, FRANK ELBA, academic administrator, geographer, educator; b. Chgo., Aug. 19, 1939; s. Elba Earl and Mae Pauline (Prohaska) H.; m. Nancy Yocom, Aug. 26, 1960; children: Kimberly, Pamela, Amy, Kelly. BA, Western Ill. U., 1963; MS, Northwestern U., 1964, PhD, 1966. Faculty U. Iowa, Iowa City, 1966-75, prof. geography, 1966-75; dir. Inst. Urban and Regional Research, 1968-72, dean advanced studies, 1972-75; v.p. acad. affairs, research So. Ill. U., Carbondale, 1975-80; prof. geography and urban affairs, chancellor U. Wis., Milw., 1980-85; prof. geography, pres. U. Okla., Norman, 1985-88; prof. geography, higher edn. adminstrn., pres. U. Toledo, 1988-98, pres. emeritus, 1999—; prin. Horton & Assocs., Denver, 1999—; interim pres. So. Ill. U., 2000; interim dean coll. biol. scis. U. Mo.-Kansas City, 2001—02, exec. cons. to provost, 2003—04. Mem. commn. on leadership devel. and acad. adminstrn. Am. Coun. on Edn., 1983-85; mem. presdl. adv. com. Assn. on Governing Bds., 1986-98; dir. 1st Wis. Nat. Bank of Milw., 1980-85, Liberty Nat. Bank, Oklahoma City, 1986-89, Trustcorp. Bank, 1989-90; bd. dirs. Interstate Bakeries, 1993-2007. Author, editor: (with B.J.L. Berry) Geographic Perspectives on Urban Systems - With Integrated Readings, 1970, Urban Environmental

Management - Planning for Pollution Control, 1974; editor: (with B.J.L. Berry) Geographical Perspectives on Contemporary Urban Problems, 1973; editorial adv. bd.: (with B.J.L. Berry) Transportation, 1971-78. Co-chmn. Goals for Milw. 2000, 1981-85, Greater Milw. Com., 1980; mem. bus. devel. sub-com. Okla. Coun. Sci. and Tech., 1985-88; mem. Harry S. Truman Library Inst., 1985-88, William Rockhill Nelson Trust, 1985-88; bd. govs. Am. Heart Assn., Wis., 1980-85, Ohio Supercomputer Ctr., 1993-97; mem. exec. com. Okla. Acad. State Goals, 1986-88; trustee Toledo Symphony Orch., 1989-96, Toledo Hosp., 1989-97, Pub. Broadcasting Found. Northwest Ohio, 1989-93, Key Bank, 1990-2000, Ohio Aerospace Inst., 1990-97; chair Inter-Univ. Coun. Pres. of Ohio Public Univs., 1992-93; mem. exec. com. Com. of 100, Toledo, 1989-92. Served with AUS, 1957-60. Mem. AAAs (nat. coun. 1976-78), Assn. Governing Bds. (mem. presdl. adv. commn. 1986-95), Assn. Am. Geographers, nat. Assn. State Univs. and Land Grant Colls. (chair urban affairs div. 1983-85, chmn. Coun. of Pres. 1987-88, exec. com. 1983-88), Nat. Hwy. Rsch. Soc., Okla. Coun. on Sci. and Tech., MidAm. State Univs. Assn. (pres. 1987-88), Ohio Supercomputer Ctr. (bd. govs. 1993), Ohio Aerospace Inst. (trustee 1990—), Okla. Acad. State Goals (pres. 1987-88), Okla. State C. of C. and Industry (v.p. 1987-88), Toledo Area C. of C. (vice chmn. bd. dirs. 1991-93). Home: 288 River Ranch Cir Bayfield CO 81122-8774 Office Phone: 970-884-2102. Personal E-mail: fehorton@attglobal.net.

HORTON, JAMES WRIGHT, retired lawyer; b. Belton, SC, Dec. 24, 1919; s. John Aiken and Emmae (Tate) H.; m. Eunice Rice, Nov. 20, 1948; children— James Wright, Max Rice, Rex Rice. BA, Furman U., 1942; JD, Harvard U., 1948. Bar: S.C. 1948. Ptnr. Nettles & Horton, Greenville, SC, 1948-52; ptnr. Rainey, Fant & Horton, Greenville, SC, 1952-70, Horton, Drawdy, Marchbanks, Ashmore, Chapman & Brown, Greenville, SC, 1970-78, Horton, Drawdy, Ward & Black, Greenville, SC, 1978-91; ret., 1997. Pres. United Fund Greenville County, 1959; mem. Greenville County Sch. Trustees, 1964-70, vice chmn., 1969; pres. Greenville Family and Children's Service, 1954-55, 68-70; bd. dirs. Salvation Army, 1969—, treas., 1970-71; bd. dirs. Family and Children's Service, Greenville Mental Health Clinic, 1956-59, Greater Greenville Community Found., 1981. Col. USMCR, ret. Decorated Silver Star. Mem. Greenville County Bar Assn. (pres. 1981) Baptist (deacon 1964-69, 71-72, 86-88). Home: 2 Osceola Dr Greenville SC 29605-3013

HORTON, JARED CHURCHILL, retired diversified financial services company metal products executive; b. Greenwich, Conn., Oct. 8, 1924; s. Frederic Jared and Marcelene (Churchill) H.; m. Pauline Elizabeth Finn, June 14, 1947; children: Janette Elizabeth Hall, Cynthia Joan Carpenter, Allison Jane, Juliana Ruth. Student, Yale U., 1942; grad., Packard Jr. Coll., 1948. With PM Industries, Stamford, Conn., 1948-54; with Alleghany Corp., NYC, 1954-88, treas., 1956-88, sec., 1959-61, 63-88, v.p., 1967-88. Served to 1st lt. AUS, 1942-46. Episcopalian. Home: Coachlamp Ln Greenwich CT 06830

HORTON, JASON A., biologist; b. Geneva, NY, Dec. 28, 1976; s. David L. and Mary A. (Buckley) Horton. BS in Biology, Oswego State U., NY, 2000. Grad. rsch. asst. Upstate Med. U., 2004—. Office: Upstate Med Univ Orthopedics 3120 IHP 505 Irving Ave Syracuse NY 13210 Office Fax: 315-464-6638. Business E-Mail: hortonj@upstate.edu.

HORTON, JEANETTE, municipal government official; b. Paterson, NJ, Dec. 1, 1938; d. David and Mary (Carpenter) Potash; m. Troy Horton, Oct. 31, 1958 (dec. May 1990); m. Christos Prousalis, June 29, 1991. Student, Broward C. C., 1970—72, Barry U., 1982, Fla. Atlantic U., 1983—84, Fla. State U., 1985. Cert. master mcpl. clk. Fla. Bookkeeper Fla. Housewares, Miami, 1961—65; asst. to comptr. Gulf Stream Press, Miami, 1965—70; comptr. Chrysler Plymouth, Miami, 1970—75; mcpl. clk., fin. dir. Village of Biscayne Park, Fla., 1975—91, Bal Harbour Village, Fla., 1991—; ret., 2004. Commr. Cooper City, Fla., 1971-73. Mem. Fla. Assn. City Clks. (scholarship 1985-87, scholarship chmn. 1988-89), Am. Bus. Woman of Yr. award 1985, pres., v.p. 1985-87), Dade/Broward City Clks. and Fin. Dirs. (pres. 1992-93), Fla. City and County Mgrs. Assn., Bus. and Profl. Women (pres. 1981), Internat. Mcpl. Clks. Assn., Pers. Mgmt. Assn., Acad. for Advanced of Edn. of Mcpl. Clks. (master mcpl. clk. 2001). Democrat. Roman Catholic. Avocation: reading. Home: 5241 SW Less Davie FL 33312 Office: Village of Bal Harbour 655 96th St Bal Harbour FL 33154-2428 E-mail: retclerkfinder@aol.com.

HORTON, JOSEPH JULIAN, JR., economics and finance educator; b. Memphis, Tenn., Nov. 7, 1936; s. Joseph Julian and Nina (Williams) H.; m. Linda Anne Langley, May 30, 1964; children: Joseph Julian, Anne Adele, David Douglas. AA, Lon Morris Jr. Coll., 1955; BA, N.Mex. State U., 1958; MA, So. Meth. U., 1965, PhD, 1968; postgrad., Harvard U., 1970—71. Claims examiner Social Security Adminstrn., Kansas City, Mo., 1958-60, claims authorizer, 1960-61; with FDIC, Washington, 1967-71, fin. economist, 1967-69, coord. merger analysis, 1969-71; prof., chmn. dept. econs. and bus. Slippery Rock (Pa.) State Coll., 1971-81; vis. fin. economist Fed. Home Loan Bank Bd., Washington, 1978-79; prof., chmn. commerce divsn. Bellarmine (Ky.) Coll., 1981-82, dean W. Fielding Rubel Sch. Bus., 1982—86; dean Sch. Mgmt. U. Scranton, Pa., 1986-96; prof. Coll. Bus. Adminstrn. U. Ctrl. Ark., Conway, 1996—2001, prof. econ. and fin., 2001—. Asst. prof. George Washington U., Washington, 1968-69, U. Md., College Park, 1969-70; pres. Pa. Conf. Economists, Internat. Acad. Bus. Disciplines, Congress of Polit. Economists, U.S.A. Bd. editors Ea. Econ. Jour.; contbr. articles to profl. jours. Recipient Cokesbury award So. Meth. U., 1965; NSF Grad. fellow, 1964-66, Ford Found. Dissertation fellow, 1966-67, Harvard U. Rsch. fellow, 1970-71, Bank Adminstrn. Inst. Clarence Lichtfeldt fellow, 1981, Burk fellow. Mem. Am. Econ. Assn., Am. Fin. Assn., Internat. Acad. Bus. Disciplines (pres.), N.Am. Econs. and Fin. Assn. (bd. dirs., v.p., pres.), Ea. Econ. Assn. (v.p.). Office: U Cen Ark Dept Econ and Fin Coll Bus Adminstrn Conway AR 72035-0001 Office Phone: 501-450-5310. Business E-Mail: jhorton@uca.edu.

HORTON, LINDA RAE, lawyer; b. Louisville, Dec. 1, 1946; d. Raymond Thomas and Marcia Bryan Horton; m. Henry Ninghan Ho (dec. Jan. 1987); 1 stepchild, Michael Ho; children: Jonathan Horton, Colleen Horton; m. Carl V. Nelson Jr.; children: Cassandra Nelson, Douglas Nelson. BA, U. Ky., Lexington, 1968; JD, George Washington U., 1975; LLM, Georgetown U., Conn., 1997. Bar: Md. 1975, D.C. 1975, U.S. Supreme Ct. 1980, Brussels, Belgium (Flemish sect.) 2005. Mgmt. intern Food and Drug Adminstrn., Arlington, Va., 1968-69; legis. asst. FDA, Rockville, Md., 1970-74, chief legis. br., 1974-75, trial atty., 1975-76, assoc. chief counsel, 1976-79, dep. chief counsel, 1979-93, dir. internat. policy, 1993-99, dir. internat. agreements, 1999—2001, advisor to acting dep. commr, 2001—02; ptnr. Hogan & Hartson LLP, Washington, 2002—, chair European life sci. practice Brussels, 2004—07. Adj. prof. George Washington U. Sch. Law, Washington, 1983-85, Georgetown U. Sch. Law, Washington, 1999—. Chair editl. bd. Food and Drug Law Jour., 1985-86; FDA editl. bd. Commerce Clearing House, 2000—; mem. editl. adv. bd. Animal Pharm, 2005—, Pharm. Policy and Law, 2006—; contbr. chpts. to books and articles to profl. jours. Precinct capt. Dem. Party Ky., Jeffersontown, 1968, del. state pres. conv., Louisville, 1968; PTA fgn. lang. coord. Montgomery County Schs., Potomac, Md., 1986-89; dep. mgr., parent swim team Montgomery Swim League, Rockville, Md., 1988-90. Recipient Disting. Svc. award Dept. Health Human Svc., Washington, 1989, Meritorious Svc. award Am. Nat. Stds. Inst., 1997, Disting. Svc. award Food and Drug Law Inst., 1999, Merit award FDA, 1975, 81, 2001. Mem. ABA, Md. Bar Assn., D.C. Bar Assn., Supreme Ct. Bar, Nat. Cooperation Lab. Accreditation (bd. dirs. 1997-99), Am. Nat. Standards Inst. (bd. dirs. 1994-99), Regulatory Affairs Profl. Soc. (bd. dirs. 2001-06). Presbyterian. Avocations: travel, bridge, reading, hiking, writing. Office Phone: 322 505 0931. Business E-Mail: lrhorton@hhlaw.com.

HORTON, LOIS ELAINE, history professor; b. Buffalo, Sept. 27, 1942; d. Robert John Berry and Christine Ellen Clancy; m. James Oliver Horton, June 12, 1964; 1 child, Michael James. BA, SUNY, Buffalo, NY, 1964; MA, U. Hawaii, Honolulu, 1969; PhD, Brandeis U., Waltham, Mass., 1977. Asst. prof. social policy Howard U., 1977—79; prof. history George Mason U., Fairfax, Va., 1979—, John Adams Disting. Fulbright Chmn. Am. History, 2003. Author: Black Bostonians, 1979, In Hope of Liberty: Culture Community and Protest Among Northern Free Blacks, 1700-1860, 1997, Hard Road to Freedom: The Story of African America, 2001, Slavery and the Making of America, 2004, Von Benin nach Baltimore: Geschichte der African Americans vom Beginn des transatlanitschen Sklavenhandels bis in die neueste Zeit, 1999; editor: A History of the African American People, 1997, Slavery and Public History: The Tough Stuff of American Memory, 2006. Office: George Mason U Msn 3g1 Fairfax VA 22030

HORTON, PATRICIA MATHEWS, artist, violist and violinist; b. Bklyn., Mar. 6, 1932; d. Edward Joseph and Margaret (Briggs) Mathews; m. Ernest H. Horton Jr., Mar. 6, 1982; 1 stepchild, Carol Horton Tremblay. Student in viola, William Primrose Master Class, 1980; student, Glendale CC, Calif., 1981—90, student, 1993, student, 1999—2002, Art Ctr. Coll. Design, Pasadena, Calif., 1988-93; student in painting composition, Peter Liashkov, LA, 1993-97. Profl. musician on violin and viola, 1951-86; musician on tour U.S., Can., Cuba, 1952-57. Played with New Orleans Philharm., 1959-61, U.S. Tour of San Francisco Ballet, 1965, L.A. Civic Light Opera, 1974-80, Bolshoi Ballet Co., LA, 1975, Am. Ballet Theatre, 1974-80, N.Y.C. Opera, 1974-80, Royal Ballet of London, 1978, Alicia Alonzo's Cuban Ballet, 1979, Harlem Ballet, 1984, Deutsche Oper Berlin, 1985, also motion picture and TV soundtrack recs.; one-woman shows include Claremont (Calif.) Sch. Theology, 1997, Pasadena First United Meth. Ch., 1997, 99, La Canada Flintridge Libr., 1999. Active Dem. Nat. Com., Women's Caucus for Art. Mem. Am. Fedn. Musicians (life). Avocations: hiking local mountains, desert and beaches, studying classical guitar.

HORTON, PAUL CHESTER, psychiatrist; b. Cin., Jan. 29, 1942; s. Paul Chester, Sr. and Elizabeth Pauline (Rice) Horton; children: Paul Andrey, Alexander Robert. BA, U. Minn., 1964, MD, 1968. Diplomate Am. Bd. Psychiatry and Neurology. Rotating intern U. Cin., 1969; resident in psychiatry Yale U., New Haven, 1972; staff psychiatrist Guidance Clinic of Camden County, West Collingswood, NJ, 1972-74, Milford (Conn.) Family and Child Guidance Clinic, 1974-77; mem. faculty Sch. Medicine Yale U., New Haven, 1974-76; pvt. practice Meriden, Conn., 1974—; cons. psychiatrist Child Guidance Clinic Cen. Conn., Meriden, 1980—94, med. dir., 1994—99. Mem. faculty U. Conn. Sch. Medicine, Farmington, 1978—79; cons. Caring for Children, San Francisco, 1989—; psychiat. cons. schs. including Meriden Pub. Schs., 1999—; reviewer Am. Jour. Psychiatry, 1980—. Author: Solace, 1981, paperback edit., 1983, Japanese edit., 1985; sr. editor: The Solace Paradigm, 1988; contbr. articles to profl. jours. Active Big Bros. Orgn., Mpls., 1964—68. Lt. comdr. USN, 1972—74. Mem.: Meriden Wallingford Med. Assn., Am. Psychiat. Assn. (life), Gridiron Club. Office: 240 Pomeroy Ave Ste 205 Meriden CT 06450 Office Phone: 203-235-2505. Personal E-mail: phortonmd@aol.com.

HORTON, PHILIP W., lawyer; b. Apr. 22, 1955; BA summa cum laude, Yale Univ., 1977; JD magna cum laude, Harvard Univ., 1980. Bar: Mass. 1980, D.C. 1983. Ptnr., co-chmn. Pro Bono Com. Arnold & Porter, Washington. Mem. bd. trustees Legal Aid Soc., Washington, 1997—, sec., 2001—02, v.p., 2002—. Mem.: Washington Council of Lawyers (bd. dir. 1987—, sec. 1991—94, treas. 1995—). Office: Arnold & Porter 555 Tewlfth St NW Washington DC 20004-1206 Office Phone: 202-942-5787. Office Fax: 202-942-5999. Business E-Mail: philip.horton@aporter.com.

HORTON, ROBERT CARLTON, geologist; b. Tonopah, Nev., July 25, 1926; s. Frank Elijah and Eathel Margaret (Miller) H.; m. Beverly Jean Burhans, Dec. 5, 1952; children: Debra, Robin, Cindy. BS, U. Nev., 1949, DSc (hon.), 1985. Cert. geol. engr., 1966. Assoc. dir. Nev. Bur. Mines, Reno, 1956-66; cons. Reno, 1966-76; dir. geology divsn. Bendix Field Engring. Corp., Grand Junction, Colo., 1976-81; dir. U.S. Bur. Mines, Washington, 1981-87; dir. strategic materials rsch. U. Nev., Reno, 1987-90, assoc. dean MacKay Sch. Mines, 1989-90, assoc. dean emeritus, 1990—. Mem. Nev. Gov.'s Mining Adv. Com., 1966-72. Author: Barite Deposits of Nevada, 1962, Fluorspar Deposits of Nevada, 1963, History of Nevada Mining, 1963. Rep. candidate for Congress from Nev., 1958. Served to lt. USNR, 1944-46, 53-56, PTO. Kennecott scholar, 1948; named Engr. of Yr. Reno chpt., NSPE, 1967; recipient Outstanding Alumnus John Mackay medal, Mackay Sch. Mines, 1991. Mem. AIME (subsect. chmn. Reno 1962-63), Soc. Econ. Geologists, Mining and Metall. Soc. Am. Methodist.

HORTON, ROBERTA LAZARUS, lawyer; b. Washington, Feb. 22, 1961; BA summa cum laude, Yale U., 1983, JD, 1986. Bar: Ill. 1988, DC. Law clk. to Hon. Sam J. Ervin III Dist. Ct. Appeals (4th cir.), 1986-87; ptnr. Arnold & Porter, Wash., DC. Contbr. articles to profl. journs. Mem. Phi Beta Kappa. Office: Arnold & Porter 555 12th St NW Washington DC 20004-1206 Office Phone: 202-942-5161. Office Fax: 202-942-5999. Business E-Mail: roberta.horton@aporter.com.

HORTON, SUSAN PITTMAN, bank executive; d. Rosie Pittman; m. Stan Horton; 1 child, Alexandria Rose. BA in Bus. Adminstrn., Wash. State U., 1984. CPA. Ptnr. McFarland & Alton PS, 1989—99; pres., CEO Wheatland Bank, Spokane, Wash., 1999—, chmn., 2001—; ptnr. Deloitte and Touche, Seattle. Named one of 25 Most Powerful Women in Banking, US Banker, 2006. Mem.: Spokane Club. Avocations: barrel racing, quarter horses. Office: Wheatland Bank 222 North Wall St Spokane WA 99201*

HORTON, THOMAS EDWARD, JR., mechanical engineering educator; b. Houston, Jan. 12, 1935; s. Thomas Edward and Minnie Tolula (Sloan) H.; m. Bobbie Jean Newcomb, June 8, 1963; children— Holly Anne, Thomas Edward. BS, U. Tex., 1957, PhD, 1964; MS (Caterpillar rsch. fellow), Stanford U., 1958. Jr. mech. engr. Shell Devel. Co., Houston, 1957-58; tchg. asst., rsch. asst., rsch. scientist U. Tex., Austin, 1959-62; rsch. engr. Jet Propulsion Lab. Calif. Inst. Tech., Pasadena, 1962, sr. rsch. engr., 1963-66; asso. prof. mech. engring., rsch. engr. U. Miss., 1966-71, prof., rsch. engr., 1971-94, emeritus prof., 1994—. Dir. U.S. Army Laser Sci. Lab., Redstone Arsenal, Ala., 1975-76, Reiton Corp. of Houston; cons. Army Research Office, Jet Propulsion Lab., Marathon Oil Co., Shell Devel. Co., Exxon, Chevron, Mobil, Texaco. Contbr. articles to profl. jours.; patentee in field. Fellow AIAA (assoc.; mem. tech. coms.); mem. ASME (life; mem. tech. coms.), Am. Phys. Soc., Am. Soc. Engring. Edn. (research award Southeastern sect. 1971), Sigma Xi (pres. local chpt.), Tau Beta Pi (student adviser), Pi Tau Sigma, Phi Eta Sigma. Republican. Methodist. Home: 5100 San Felipe Rd 97E Houston TX 77056

HORTON, THOMAS W., air transportation and former telecommunications company executive; m. Janet Horton; 2 children. BBA magna cum laude, Baylor U., 1983; MBA, So. Meth. U., 1985. CPA. Mgr. fin. planning Am. Airlines, Inc., 1988—90, mng. dir. treasury, 1990—92, mng. dir. corp. acctg., 1992—94, v.p., controller, 1994—98, v.p. Europe London, 1998—2000, sr. v.p. fin. & CFO, 2000—02; sr. v.p. fin., CFO AMR Corp., 2000—02; sr. exec. v.p., CFO AT&T Corp., 2002—05, vice chmn., CFO, 2005—06; exec. v.p., fin. & planning, CFO AMR Corp., 2006—. Mem. exec. bd. Cox Sch. of Bus., So. Meth U. Bd. govs. United Way of Tri State. Office: AMR Corp 4333 Amon Carter Blvd Fort Worth TX 76155*

HORTON, WILLIAM RUSSELL, retired utilities executive; b. Toronto, Ont., Can., Aug. 25, 1931; s. Russell Burton and Freda Catherine (Middleton) H.; m. Dorothy Viva Rye, Nov. 27, 1954; children: William Russell, Robert Freeman, Douglas Lloyd, Ronald Edward. BS in Mining Engring., U. Toronto, 1955. Engr. Imperial Oil Ltd., Calgary and Camrose, Alta., Canada, 1955-56; engr., mgr. Black Sivalls & Bryson Ltd., Edmonton, Alta., 1956—65; v.p. Gamma Engring. Ltd., Edmonton, 1965-68; pres. Horton Engring. Ltd., Edmonton, 1968-2000, chmn., 2000—; mem. Alta. Pub. Utilities Bd., Edmonton, 1973-76, chmn., 1976-83; exec. v.p. Can. Utilities Ltd., Edmonton, 1984-90. Bd. dirs. Akita Drilling Ltd., Atco Utilities Bus. Group; hon. mem. Can. Assn. Members Pub. Utility Tribunals. Mem. Assn. Profl. Engrs. Geologists and Geophysicists Alta. (life). Avocations: sports, music, reading. Home: 17490 Coral Beach Rd Winfield BC Canada V4V 1C1 Office: Can Utilities Ltd 1400-909 11th Ave SW Calgary AB Canada T2R 1N6 Home Phone: 250-766-4013. Business E-Mail: wrhorton@cablelan.net.

HORUZSKO, ANATOLIJ, medical researcher; b. Pinsk, Belarus, Oct. 10, 1953; s. Pavel Horuzsko and Anna Juskevich; m. Vera Portik-Dobos, Mar. 30, 1981; children: Julia Szonja, Daniel David. MD (hon.), Pediat. Med. Sch., Leningrad, Russia, 1976; PhD in immunology and allergy, Inst. of Exptl. Medicine, Russian Acad. of Sci., Leningrad, Russia, 1980; MD, Semmelweis U. of Medicine, Budapest, Hungary, 1986; PhD in clin. immunology and allergy, Hungarian Acad. of Sci., Budapest, Hungary, 1987. Lectr., sr. lectr. Pediatric Med. Sch., Leningrad, Russia, 1979—86; sr. lectr. Nat. Inst. of Hematology and Blood Transfusion, Budapest, Hungary, 1986—92; non-clin. scientist, grade 1 Nat. Inst. for Med. Rsch., London, 1992—95; sr. rsch. scientist Med. Coll. of Ga., Augusta, 1995—98, instr., 1998—2002, asst. prof., 2002—06, assoc. prof., 2006—. Author: (over 40 studies) Dealing With Issues In Transplantation Medicine And Immunobiology. Recipient Prize of George Soros, George Soros Found., 1988, Internat. Rsch. award, Wellcome Trust, U.K., 1992—95, Internat. Human Frontier Sci. Program Orgn., Strasbourg, France, 1998, Internat. Union Against Cancer, Geneva, Switzerland, 1999, Roche Organ Transplantation Rsch. Found., Switzerland, 2001. Mem.: European Fedn. for Immunogenetics (assoc.), Hungarian Soc. for Immunology (assoc.), Brit. Soc. for Immunology (assoc.), AAAS (assoc.), Am. Assn. of Immunologists (assoc.). Office: Med Coll of Ga 1410 Laney Walker Blvd Augusta GA 30912-2615 Office Phone: 706-721-8736. Personal E-mail: horuzsko@netzero.net. Business E-Mail: ahoruzsko@mcg.edu.

HORVAT, OLGA, artist; b. Belgrade, July 23, 1963; arrived in US, 1989; d. Branko and Ranka (Peasinovic) Horvat; m. Aleksandar Filipovic, June 2, 1990; 1 child, Katharine. BA in Art, Zagreb U., Croatia, 1988; MA in Art Mgmt., Fashion Inst. Tech., 1991. Curator asst. Met. Mus. Art, NYC, 1990—91; art rsch. asst. A.J. Lederman Fine Art, Hoboken, NJ, 1991—92; art dir. Beatrice Design, Inc., NYC, 1992—94, Absolute Image, Inc., NYC, 1994—98; asst. to pres. Basically Kids, NYC, 1998—2001; art dir. Olga Horvat Art, NYC, 2001—. Exhibited in group shows at Khan Mus., Ashfelon, Israel, 2000, CASE Mus., NJ, 2001, Queens Mus. Art, NY, 2002, prin. works include Decorative Fabric Constructions, Digital Photographs, Oil Paintings, Walt Disney World Co. Named one of Outstanding Artists and Designers of the 20th Century, IBC, Cambridge, Eng., 2000; recipient Cert. of Excellence, NY Times, 1999, Twentieth Century Achievement Award, 1999. Mem.: Queens Mus. Art, Nat. Mus. Women in the Arts, Nurture Art. Avocations: tennis, aerobics, travel, gardening. Home: 13 Meadowlark Cir Peekskill NY 10566 Office: Olga Horvat Art 457 W 57th St #1704 New York NY 10019 Office Phone: 212-247-7459. Personal E-mail: ohorvat@lycos.com. Business E-Mail: olgahorvat@artlover.com.

HORVAT, VASHTI, principal; BS in Computer Info. Systems, DeVry Inst. Tech., Chgo. Cert. Yellow Belt Six Sigma; info. sys. auditor. Mgr. email mktg. Travelocity.com, 2001—03; mgr. online mktg. Piidesign, 2003—; mng. prin. Orr Consulting LLC, 2003—. Patron Internat. Inst. Mem. Nat. Heart, Lung, and Blood Inst. Heart Truth campaign, Am. Red Cross Houston Zoo Paver Program, Trees for Life, Jewish Nat. Fund-Trees Israel. Mem. ALA, Info. Systems Audit Control Assn., Nat. Women's History Mus., Am. SAP User Group, Gerson Lehman Group Coun., IT Compliance Inst., SAP Developer Network and Bus. Process Expert Cmty. Jewish. Avocations: jewelry design, yoga, golf, languages. Office: Vashti Horvat Consulting 8409 Pickwick Lane 180 Dallas TX 75225 Office Phone: 214-276-7526. Business E-Mail: info@orrconsulting.us.

HORVATH, ANNETTE, home care administrator; b. Bronx, NY, Mar. 12, 1963; d. Thomas and Roslyn DeGrazia; m. Leonard Horvath, Aug. 28, 1988; children: Jennifer, Rebecca. BSN, Lehman Coll., 1996; MS in Health Care Adminstrn., Iona Coll., 1999. RN. Case mgr. Montifiore Hosp., Bronx, 1993—98; project mgr. Jewish Home and Hosp., NYC, 1998—99, dir. patient svcs. Bronx, 1999—2000; adminstr. Americare Inc., Bklyn., 2000—01, Village Care NY, 2001—05, NY Home Health, Bklyn., 2006—07, Evercare Home Health Care Inc., 2007—. Cons. in field. Bd. mem. Black & Puerto Rican/Latino Substance Abuse Taskforce. Named Mem. of Yr., Edna A. Lauterbach, 2006. Mem.: NAFE, Assn. for Nurses in HIV/AIDS Care, Women Arts Mus., NY State Home Care Assn., Am. Coll. Health Care Execs., Women Health Mgmt., NY State Health Care Providers, Women Arts Mus. Avocations: reading, cooking. Home Phone: 718-597-5379; Office Phone: 718-319-0043. Office Fax: 347-621-5441. Business E-Mail: ahorvath28@yahoo.com.

HORVATH, DEBORA, bank executive; b. 1955; 2 adopted children. Grad., Baldwin Wallace Coll., Ohio, 1984. Joined GE, 1979; v.p., CIO Great Northern Annuity, Seattle, 1993—95, sr. v.p., 1995—97; sr. v.p., chief info. officer, chief tech. officer GE Fin. Assurance, 1997—2000, sr. v.p., chief info. officer, eBus. leader, 2000—02; mem. GE Info. Mgmt. Coun.; exec. v.p., chief info. officer Washington Mutual, Inc., 2004—. Involved with Woodland Park Zoo, Child Haven. Named one of 25 Women to Watch, US Banker, 2006; recipient CIO award, GE. Office: Washington Mutual 1201 3rd Ave Seattle WA 98101*

HORVATH, MADELON TOFT, secondary school educator; b. Cin., June 5, 1948; d. Leonard Leroy and Rosella Reeve Toft; m. Roger John Horvath, Dec. 28, 1968; children: Brent, Stacey. BA, Kent State U., Ohio, 1978; MA, Roosevelt U., Chgo., 2001. English tchr. Grand Valley Mid. Sch., Orwell, Ohio, 1979—80; English tchr., drama adv. Chardon HS, Ohio, 1980—, chair English dept., 2004—06. Mem.: Ednl. Theatre Assn. (leadership coach 1999—). Avocations: reading, travel, horseback riding, theater. Office: Chardon High Sch 151 Chardon Ave Chardon OH 44024

HORVITZ, HOWARD ROBERT, biology professor, researcher; b. Chgo., May 8, 1947; s. Oscar and Mary Horvitz; m. Martha Constantine-Paton, May 2, 1993; 1 child, Alexandra Constantine. BS in Math., BS in Econs., MIT, 1968; MA in Biology, Harvard U., 1972, PhD in Biology, 1974; MD (hon.), U. Rome, 2004. Postdoctoral fellow Med. Rsch. Coun. Lab. Molecular Biology, Cambridge, England; asst. to assoc. prof. biology MIT, Cambridge, 1978-86, prof., 1986—, career devel. assoc. prof. biology, Whitehead Inst., 1982-85, mem. sci. adv. bd. Howard Hughes program in neurosci., 1984-88, investigator Howard Hughes Med. Inst., 1988—, Whitehead prof. biology, 1999-2000, David H. Koch prof. biology, 2000—; with McGovern Inst. for Brain Rsch., 2001. Investigator Howard Hughes Med Inst., Boston, 1988—; neurobiologist, geneticist Mass. Gen. Hosp., Boston, 1989—; advisor, dept. biochemistry and molecular biology Harvard U., 1984—90; mem. neurobiology adv. bd. Cold Spring Harbor Lab., 1984—; mem. sci. adv. bd. Hereditary Disease Found., 1987—93, collaborative rsch. group adv. com., 1988—93, cure HD initiative adv. com., 1996—; mem. sci. adv. bd. Jane Coffin Childs Meml. Fund for Med. Rsch., 1989—97; sci. adv. bd. Com. on Scholarly Comm. with People's Rep. of China, U.S. NAS, 1987—93; co-organizer Gordon Conf. on Devel. Biology, 1985; organizer biennial meeting Cold Spring Harbor Internat. Conf., 1985, coms., 81, 87; mem. organizing com. biennial meeting Ea. Coast C. Elegans, Cambridge, 1988, Cambridge, 90; mem. sci. rev. com. Amyotrophic Lateral Sclerosis Assn., 1990—95, co-chair meetings, 1991, 93; lectr. Harvey Soc., 1989; macrofil steering com. spl. programme for esch and tng. in tropical diseases WHO, 1992—95; adv. bd. Umea (Sweden) Ctr. Molecular Pathogenesis, 1993—96; co-chair working group on preclin. models for cancer Nat. Cancer Inst., NIH, 1996—; mem. adv. coun. Nat. Ctr. for Human Genome Rsch., NIH, 1996—; mem. sci. adv. group Sanger Ctr., Cambridgeshire, England, 1994—; chair devel. biology rev. com. Swedish Found. for Strategic Rsch., 1996; mem. sci. adv. bd. Netherlands Cancer Inst. Site Vis. Com., 1998; mem. sci. adv. com. Warren Alpert Found. (prize), 1997—; external rev. bd. dept. molecular, cellular and devel. biology U. Colo., Boulder, 1996; mem. sci. adv. group U. Pa. Med. Ctr. Inst. Aging, 1995—; cons. sci. adv. bd. Idun Pharmaceuticals, Inc., 1993—, Axys Pharms. Inc., 1998—2002, GenPath Pharms., 2003—, Novartis Inst. for Biomedical Rsch., 2003—; mem. med. adv. bd. Gairdner Found., 2007—. Author (with others): (books) The Role of Intercellular Signals: Nav., Encounter, Outcome, 1979, Genetic Maps, 1980, Nematodes as Biol. Models, 1980, Devel. of the Nervous Sys., 1981, Repair and Regeneration of the Nervous Sys., 1982, The Nematode Caenorhabditis elegans, 1988; mem. editl. bd.: Jour. Neurogenetics, 1982—88, Jour. Neurosci., 1984—89, Devel. Biology, 1985—95, Genes and Devel., 1986—98, Cell, 1987—99, Trends in Genetics, 1987—, Neuron, 1987—90, The New Biologist, 1989—92, Genetic Analysis: Techniques and Applications, 1990—95, Current Opinion in Neurobiology, 1990—, Current Biol., 1992—95, Annual Rev. Genetics, 1993—97, Cell Death & Differentiation, 1994—, Neurobiology of Disease, 1994—2000, Jour. Exptl. Therapeutics and Oncology, 1995—, Invertebrate Neurosci., 1994—, Devel., 1986—93, Cancer Rsch., 1995—2000, Procs. of the NAS, 1997—2001, Jour. Cell Biology, 1997—2000, Genome Biology, 1999—; contbr. articles to profl. jours. Mem. adv. bd. World Health Orgn. Spl. Programme for Rsch. and Tng. in Tropical Diseases, Microfil steering com., 1992-95. Recipient Rsch. Career Devel. award, NIH, 1981—86, Spencer award in Neurobiology, Columbia U., 1986, Warren Triennial prize, Mass. Gen. Hosp., 1986, Molecular Biology award, U.S. Steel Found., 1988, Method to Extend Rsch. in Time award, NIH, 1991, V.D. Mattia award, Roche Inst. Molecular Biology, 1993, Hans Sigrist award, 1994, Charles A. Dana award for pioneering achievements in health and edn., Inst. Medicine NAS, 1995, Ciba-Drew award for biomed. sci., 1996, Rosenstiel award, Brandeis U., 1998, Passano award for the advancement med. sci., 1998, Alfred P. Sloan Jr. prize, GM Cancer Rsch. Found., 1998, Gairdner Found. Internat. award, 1999, Paul Ehrlich and Ludwig Darmstaedter prize, Frankfurt, Germany, 2000, Segerfalk award, 2000, March of Dimes prize in devel. biology, 2000, Charles-Leopold Mayer prize, French Acad. Scis., 2000, Louisa Gross Horwitz prize, 2000, Bristol-Myers Squibb award for Disting. Achievement in Neuroscience, 2001, Genetics Soc. of Am. medal, 2001, Genetics prize, Peter Gruber Found., 2002, medal of honor, Am. Cancer Soc., 2002, Wiley prize in biomed. scis., 2002, Nobel Prize in Physiology or Medicine, 2002, Alfred G. Knudson award, Nat. Cancer Inst., 2005, Centennial medal, Harvard U., 2005, Killian Faculty Achievement award, MIT, 2006; Woodrow Wilson fellow, 1968, NSF predoctoral fellow, 1968—72, Muscular Dystrophy Assn. postdoctoral fellow, 1974—77. Fellow AAAS, Am. Acad. Arts and Scis., Am. Acad. Microbiology, Am. Acad. Microbilogy; mem. Am. Assn. Cancer Rsch., NAS, Inst. Medicine, 2004, Genetics Soc. Am. (membership com. 1984-86, bd. dirs. 1990-92, 94-96, organizer ann. meeting 1989, v.p. 1994, pres. 1995), Soc. Devel. Biology (nominations com. 1989), Soc. Nematologists, Soc. Neurosci. (pub. info. com. 1993-95), Am. Soc. Cell Biology (organizing com. ann. meeting 1992, pub. policy com. 1993-96, joint steering com. pub. policy 1994-97, exec. com. 1995—), Am. Soc. Microbiology, Helminthological Soc. Washington, Am. Philos. Soc., Physiological Soc., London. Jewish. Achievements include patents in field. Office: MIT Dept Biology 68-425 77 Massachusetts Ave Cambridge MA 02139-4307 Office Phone: 617-253-4671. Office Fax: 617-253-8126. Business E-Mail: horvitz@mit.edu.*

HORVITZ, MICHAEL JOHN, lawyer; b. Cleve., Feb. 15, 1950; s. Harry Richard and Lois Joy (Unger) H.; m. Jane Rosenthal, Aug. 25, 1979; children: Katherine R., Elizabeth R. BS in Econs., U. Pa., 1972; JD, U. Va., 1975; LLM in Taxation, NYU, 1980. Bar: Ohio 1975, Fla. 1976. Assoc. Hahn, Loeser, Freedheim, Dean & Wellman, Cleve., 1975-78; counsel Hollywood, Inc., Fla., 1978-79; assoc. Jones Day, Cleve., 1980-85, ptnr., 1985-2000, of counsel, 2001—. Adv. bd. Kirtland Capital Ptnrs., L.P., 1992—; chmn. Parkland Mgmt. Co., 1992—; vice chmn. Horvitz Newspapers, Inc., 1994—; pres. H.R.H. Family Found., 1992—; chmn. H.R.H. Family Trust, 1992-2003; corp. adv. IMG Worldwide, Inc., 1999-2004, chmn. bd. dirs., 2004. Trustee Jewish Cmty. Fedn. Cleve., 1993-99, 2002-, Case Western Res. U., 1992-2005, Musical Arts Assn., 1992—, Cleve. Ctr. Econ. Edn., 1992-95, Am. Cancer Soc., Cuyahoga County unit, 1989-95, Hathaway Brown Sch., Mt. Sinai Med. Ctr., Cleve. chpt. Am. Jewish Com., 1984-95, Montefiore Home for the Elderly, 1982-90, Health Hill Hosp. for Children, 1982-95, bd. pres., 1987-89; bd. dirs. Cleve. Mus. Art, 1991—, pres. bd., 1996-2001, chmn. bd., 2001—; bd. dirs. U. Va. Law Sch. Found., 1999—, pres., 2002-05, chmn. bd., 2005; trustee Cleve. Clinic Found., 2006. Office: Jones Day 901 Lakeside Ave E Cleveland OH 44114-1190 also: Parkland Mgmt Co 1001 Lakeside Ave E Ste 900 Cleveland OH 44114-1172

HORVITZ, PAUL MICHAEL, finance educator; b. Providence, Aug. 6, 1935; s. Abraham and Rose (Gershkoff) H.; m. Carol Broomfield, Nov. 17, 1955; children: Marcia Ellen Cohen, Steven Jay. BA, U. Chgo., 1954; MBA, Boston U., 1956; PhD in Econs., MIT, 1958. Fin. economist Fed. Reserve Bank of Boston, 1957-60; asst. prof. Boston U., 1960-62; sr. economist, compt. of currency Washington, 1963-66; dir. rsch. FDIC, 1967-77; prof. banking and fin. U. Houston, 1977—2001, emeritus, 2001—. Author: Management of Bank Funds, 1981, Monetary Policy & the Financial System, 6th edit., 1987; co-editor Jour. Fin. Svcs. Rsch.; contbr. articles to profl. jours. Mem. Am. Econ. Assn., Am. Fin. Assn., Shadow Fin. Regulatory Com. Home: 150 Sugarberry Cir Houston TX 77024-7244 Home Phone: 713-780-3771; Office Phone: 713-780-3771. Personal E-mail: paulhorvitz@aol.com.

HORVITZ, STEVEN JAY, lawyer; b. Framingham, Mass., May 18, 1959; BA, Brown U., Providence, 1981; JD, Stanford U., Calif., 1984. Bar: DC 1984. Assoc. Hogan & Hartson, Washington; positions up to mng. ptnr. Cole, Raywid & Braverman, L.L.P., Washington, 1991—2006; co-ptnr.-in-charge Davis Wright Tremaine L.L.P., Washington, 2007—. Faculty mem. Practising Law Inst., NYC. Contbr. chapters to books. Mem.: Fed. Comm. Bar Assn. Office: Davis Wright Tremaine Ste 450 1500 K St NW Washington DC 20005-1272 Office Phone: 202-659-9750 ext. 9828. Office Fax: 202-452-0067. E-mail: shorvitz@crblaw.com.*

HORWICH, ALLAN, lawyer; b. Des Moines, Apr. 8, 1944; s. Joseph Maurice and Bernice (Davidson) Horwich; m. Carolyn Ruth Allen, Feb. 28, 1975; children: Benjamin, Diana, Eleanor, Flannery. AB, Princeton U., 1966; JD, U. Chgo., 1969. Bar: Ill. 1969, U.S. Dist. Ct. (no. dist.) Ill. 1969, U.S. Ct. Appeals (7th cir.) 1971, U.S. Supreme Ct. 1976, U.S. Ct. Appeals (10th cir.) 1983, U.S. Dist. Ct. (ctrl. dist.) Ill. 1990, U.S. Dist. Ct. (ea. dist.) Wis. 1995, U.S. Dist. Ct. (ea. dist.) Mich. 1995, U.S. Ct. Appeals (6th cir.) 1996. Assoc. Schiff Hardin LLP, Chgo., 1969-74, ptnr., 1975—, vice-chmn., 1989-95. Adj. prof. law Northwestern U. Sch. Law, 1999—2000, sr. lectr. law, 2000—; mem. adv. bd. Wall St. Lawyer. Contbr. articles to profl. jours. Fellow: Am. Bar Found. (life). Home: 216 W Concord Ln Chicago IL 60614-5743 Office: Schiff Hardin LLP 6600 Sears Tower Chicago IL 60606 Home Phone: 312-649-5618; Office Phone: 312-258-5618. Business E-Mail: ahorwich@schiffhardin.com.

HORWICH, ARTHUR L., medical educator; AB, Brown U., 1972, MD, 1975. Prof. genetics and pediat. Yale U., New Haven, investigator Howard Hughes Med. Inst. Recipient Basil O'Connor Rsch. award, Hans Neurath award, Protein Soc., 2001, Gairdner award, Gairdner Found., 2004; John A. Hartford Found. fellow. Mem.: NAS. Office: Dept Genetics Yale U Sch Medicine 333 Cedar St PO Box 208005 New Haven CT 06520-8005

HORWICH, GEORGE, economist, educator; b. Detroit, July 23, 1924; s. Charles and Rose (Katzman) H.; m. Geraldine Lessans, Dec. 27, 1953; children: Ellen Beth, Karen Louise, Robert Lloyd, Susan Jean. Student, Wayne State U., 1942-43, 46, Ind. U., 1943-44; AM, U. Chgo., 1951, PhD, 1954. Lectr. econs. Extension Ctrs. Ind. U., Gar and Calumet, 1949-52, instr. econs. Bloomington, 1952-55; rsch. assoc. Nat. Bur. Econ. Rsch., NYC, 1955-56; from asst. prof. to prof. econs. Purdue U., West Lafayette, Ind., 1956-99, chmn. econs. dept., 1974-78, Burton D. Morgan prof. for study pvt. enterprise, 1981-94, prof. emeritus, 1999—. Sr. rsch. assoc. Brookings Instn., Washington, 1958-62; sr. economist U.S. Dept. Energy, Washington, 1978-80; spl. asst. for contingency planning U.S. Dept. Energy, 1984; adj. scholar Am. Enterprise Inst., 1984—; collaborating scientist energy divsn. Oak Ridge Nat. Lab., 1988-94; mem. U.S. Treasury Cons. Group, Washington, 1969; cons. Fed. Res. Bank, Chgo., 1971; vis. prof. econs. U. Calif., San Diego, 1971-72, People's Univ. of China, Beijing, 1992, Kobe (Japan) U. Commerce, 1996-97; vis. scholar Victoria U., New Zealand, 1997; staff Ind. Coun. Econ. Edn., West Lafayette, 1974—, Ctr. Pub. Policy and Pub. Adminstrn., Purdue U., West Lafayette, 1977—; advisor Econ. Inst. Rsch. and Edn., Boulder, Colo., 1977—; cons. U.S. Dept. Energy, 1980-88, Fortune 500 cos., 1965—, U.S. Dept. State, Washington, 1982, 92, Hudson Inst., 1991; vis. prof. Yokohama (Japan) City U., 2000; lectr. Wabash Area Lifetime Learning Assn, 2003—. Author: Money, Capital and Prices, 1964; (with others) Costs and Benfits of a Protective Tariff on Refined Petroleum Products After Crude Oil Decontrol, 1980, Energy: An Economic Analysis, 1983; (with D.L. Weimer) Oil Price Shocks, Market Response and Contingency Planning, 1984; Responding to International Oil Crises, 1988; editor: Monetary Process and Policy, 1967, (with P.A. Samuelson) Trade, Stability, and Macroeconomics, 1974; (with J.P. Quirk) Essays in Contemporary Fields of Economics, 1981; (with E.J. Mitchell) Policies for Coping with Oil-Supply Disruptions, 1982, Energy Use in Transportation Contingency Planning, 1983; (with G.J. Lynch) Food, Policy and Politics, 1989; contbr. articles to profl. jours. With U.S. Army, 1943-46, ETO. NSF grantee; Fulbright rschr., 1996-97. Mem. Internat. Assn. Energy Econs., Am. Econ. Assn., Midwest Econs. Assn., Mont. Pelerin Soc., Nat. Assn. Scholars, Phila. Soc., Assn. Pub. Policy Analysis and Mgmt. Home: 120 Seminole Dr West Lafayette IN 47906-2116 Office: Purdue U Dept Econs 403 W State St West Lafayette IN 47907-2056

HORWITZ, BERTRAND NATHAN, finance educator; b. Chgo., Mar. 12, 1927; s. Max Solomon and Esther (Green) H.; m. Hertha Ostre Horwitz, Oct. 25, 1952; children: Eve, Neal, Mara. AB, U. Chgo., 1949, MA, 1951; PhD, U. Minn., 1962. Assoc. Russian Rsch. Ctr., Cambridge, Mass., 1960—61; Sloan tchg. fellow MIT, 1962-63; asst. prof. U. Rochester, NY, 1964-67; assoc. to full prof. Syracuse (N.Y.) U., 1967-72; prof. Binghamton (N.Y.) U., 1972—. Vis prof. U. Chgo., 1978—79, Nat. Ctr. for Indsl. Sci. and Tech., Mgmt. Devel., China, 1981—82, China, 1984; vis. prof. U. Internat. Bus. and Econs., Beijing, 1988; vis prof. Chinese U., Hong Kong, 1993—94, City U., Hong Kong, 1994—96, 1998—99, 2000; cons. UN, 1984; adj. prof. U. N.C., Asheville, 2005—. Co-author: (book) Financial Accounting and Corporate Decisions, 1982; author: (book) Accounting Controls and the Soviet Economic Reforms of 1966, 1970. With USN, 1945-46. Rsch. grantee NSF, 1979, 83; recipient Gov.'s award N.Y. State, 1992, Internat. Edn. and Bus. award U.S. Dept. Edn., 1988-91. Mem. Am. Acctg. Assn., Am. Econ. Assn., Fin. Execs. Inst. Jewish. Avocations: reading, running, foreign languages. Home: 46 Marlborough Rd Asheville NC 28804-1445 E-mail: horwitz@binghamton.edu.

HORWITZ, DAVID A., rheumatologist, educator; BA, U. Mich., 1958; MD, U. Chgo., 1962. Intern, resident Michael Reese Hosp., Chgo., 1966; rheumatology fellow Southwestern Med. Sch. U. Tex., 1969, instr. internal medicine Southwestern Med. Sch. Dallas, 1968-69; from asst. prof. to assoc. prof. medicine Sch. Medicine U. Va., Charlottesville, 1969-79, prof. medicine, 1979-80; prof. medicine and microbiology, chief divsn. rheumatology and immunology sect. Sch. Medicine U. So. Calif., LA, 1980—. Vis. prof. Clin. Rsch. Ctr., Harrow, Eng., 1976-77; vis. investigator Imperial Cancer Rsch. Fund, London, 1988-89; vis. scientist Nat. Inst. Arthritis, Musculoskeletal and Skin Diseases, NIH, Bethesda, Md., 2001-02. Contbr. more than 100 articles to profl. jours. Recipient James R. Klinnenberg award for rsch., Arthritis Found. Mem.: Am. Rheumatism Assn. (pres. 1985). Achievements include research in elucidation of lymphocytes, cytokines and immunologic circuits involved in the regulation of antibody production, characterization of pathologic abnormalities in immune regulation in subjects with Systemic Lupus Erythematosus; The generation of regulatory T cell subsets ex-vivo, and their potential for the treatment of autoimmune diseases and to prevent graft rejection. Office: Divsn Rheumatology And Immunology 2011 Zonal Ave # 711 Los Angeles CA 90089-0110 Home Phone: 310-459-6106; Office Phone: 323-442-1946. Business E-Mail: dhorwitz@usc.edu.

HORWITZ, DONALD PAUL, lawyer; b. Chgo., Feb. 5, 1936; s. Theodore J. and Lillian H. (Shlensky) H.; m. Judith Robin, Aug. 23, 1964; children: Terry Robin Kass, Linda Diane, Gail Elizabeth Miller. BS, Northwestern U., 1957; JD, Yale U., 1960. Bar: Ill. 1961, D.C. 1961, U.S. Supreme Ct. 1966; CPA, Ill. With atty. gen.'s honors program Dept. Justice, 1961-63; atty. Gottlieb & Schwartz, Chgo., 1963-66; with Arthur Young & Co. CPAs, Chgo., 1966-72, ptnr., 1971-72; exec. v.p., sec., dir. McDonald's Corp., Oak Brook, Ill., 1972-90; ptnr. Sonnenschein, Nath & Rosenthal, Chgo., 1990—. Lectr. Northwestern U. Law Sch., Grad. Sch. Commerce, DePaul U., Chgo.; bd. dirs. Bernard Tech. Inc., 1997-2004, chmn. bd., 1998-2002; sec. System Capital Corp, 1996—; trustee Evanston Northwestern Healthcare Found., 2003—. Contbr. articles to profl. jours. Trustee Goodman Theatre/Chgo. Theatre Group, 1993—96, Evans Scholars Found., Western Golf Assn., 1984—87; pres., bd. dirs. Briarwood Country Club, 1972—73; caucus nominating com. Village of Glencoe, Ill., 1975—78, vice-chmn. Ill., 1988—89; bd. dirs. Northwestern Healthcare Network, 1990—94; vice-chmn., bd. dirs., chmn. bd. Highland Park Hosp., Lakeland Health Ventures and Northwestern Network, bd. govs., 1994—2000; chmn. Midwest region Anti-Defamation League, 1994—95, mem. nat. commn., 1994—2004; exec. com. Yale Law Sch. Assn.; bd. dirs. U.S. com. United Nations Population Fund, 2003—; bd. dirs. Lakeland Health Ventures and Northwestern Network, 1986—94, McDonald's Family Charities, Inc., 2001—, Scholl Sch. Podiatry, 2001—03, Chgo. Med. Sch./Finch U. Health Scis., 1993—2003, Found. for Podiatric Edn., 2002—03. Mem.: ABA, Am. Arbitration Assn. (arbitrator panel 1991—), Chgo. Bar Found. (trustee 1990—97), Chgo. Bar Assn., Northmoor Country Club, Econs. Club, Standard Club. Office Phone: 312-876-8105. E-mail: dhorwitz@sonnenschein.com.

HORWITZ, ELEANOR CATHERINE, public information officer; b. NYC, Dec. 21, 1941; d. Fritz and Hedwig E.F. (Kramer) Jahoda; m. Paul Horwitz, Aug. 15, 1964; children: Gregory Douglas, Catherine Helen, Laura Elizabeth. BA, Swarthmore Coll., 1962; MA, NYU, 1967; MS, Cornell U., 1969; postgrad., Oreg. State U., 1969-70. Sci. tchr. New Lincoln Sch., NYC, 1962-67; coordinator outdoor edn. Lane County Int. Edn. Dist., Eugene, Oreg., 1969-70; staff writer Billerica (Mass.) Banner, 1971-72; instr., writer Mass. Audubon Soc., Lincoln, 1972-75; pub. use specialist U.S. Fish and Wildlife Service, Concord, Mass., 1975; staff writer Soc. Am. Foresters, Washington, 1975-76; mem. Mass. Gov.'s Forestry Rev. Bd., Boston, 1976-77; chief info. and edn. Mass. Div. Fisheries and Wildlife, Westborough, 1977—. Steering com. Sec.'s Adv. Group on Environ. Edn. Exec. Office of Environ. Affairs, Commonwealth of Mass., 1990-2000, 05-06, co-chair, 1992-97, chair, 1997-98; bd. dirs. Mass. Wildlife Fedn., 1986—, v.p., 1989-94, 95—, pres., 1995-97. Author: Clearcutting, A View from the Top, 1974; author, editor: Ways of Wildlife, 1977 (ACI Book award 1978); editor: (mag.) Massachusetts Wildlife, 1977—; contbr. articles to popular mags. Active Concord Natural Resources Commn., 1976-82, chmn. 1979-80; trustee Concord Land Conservation Trust, 1988—, Holbrook Island Trust, 1995-2000, Bagaduce Music Lending Libr., 2005—; MBA rep. West Concord Union Ch., 1998-2003; deacon West Concord Union Ch., United Ch. of Christ, 2003—; instr. NRA, 2003. Recipient R.E. Dimmick award Oreg. Wildlife Soc., 1970, citation Worcester County League Sportsmen's Clubs, 1987, citation Minutemen chpt. Ducks Unltd., 1987, Conservation award Mahar Fish & Game Assn., 1991, Woman of Yr. award N.E. County Quabbin Anglers Assn., 1991, Sportsman of Yr. New England Outdoor Writers, 1998, Conservation Communicator of Yr. award N.E. Conservation info. and Edn. Assn., 1999, Spl. award for Wildlife edn., Mass. Sportsmen's Coun., 2003, Disting. Svc. award Ducks Unltd., 2003, citation, 2006, Lillian Gribbons award, Mass. Sportsmen's Coun., 2005. Mem. Outdoor Writers of Am., New Eng. Outdoor Writers Assn. (membership sec. 1987-90, bd. dirs. 1987—, sec. 1990-93, 2001-03, 06—, v.p. 1993—, pres. 1994-95), Am. Forestry Assn. (life), New Eng. Conservation Info. and Edn. Assn. (chmn. 1986-87, 90-91, dir.-at-large 2000—), Mass. Wildlife Fedn., Wildlife Soc. (profl. cert., chmn. edn. com. 1974-76, 84-87, nominating com. 1990-91, Leopold award com. 1996-98, cert. of recognition 1978), Nashoba Sportsmen's Club, Concord Rod and Gun Club, Maynard Rod and Gun Club (hon.), Bucksmills Sportsmans Club. Mem. United Ch. of Christ. Office: Mass Divsn Fisheries and Wildlife Westborough MA 01581 Office Phone: 508-389-6300. Business E-Mail: ellie.horwitz@state.ma.us.

HORWITZ, ERIC M., radiation oncologist; b. Sept. 5, 1966; MD, Albany Med. Coll., 1992. Cert. Am. Bd. Radiology, Radiation Oncology. Intern and resident, radiation oncology William Beaumont Hosp., Royal Oak, Mich., chief resident; with Fox Chase Cancer Ctr., Phila., 1997—, mem. divsn. med. sci., 2003—, clin. dir., radiation oncology. Office: Fox Chase Cancer Ctr Dept Radiation Oncology 7701 Burholme Ave Philadelphia PA 19111 Address: Fox Chase Cancer Ctr 333 Cottman Ave Philadelphia PA 19111-2497 Office Phone: 215-728-2995. Office Fax: 215-214-1629.

HORWITZ, JAVAN LEE, neuropsychologist; arrived in US, 1985; s. Gary and Leonie Ruth Horwitz; m. Natalie Melina Rosales, Oct. 13, 2002. BS, U. Ariz., Phoenix, 1997; MA, Ariz. Sch. Prof. Psychology, Phoenix, 2000; D in Psychology, Argosy U., Phoenix, 2005. Trainee for pvt. practitioner, Carefree, Ariz., 1999—2000; trainee Maricopa County Hosp., Phoenix, 2000—01, Treatment Assessment Screening Ctr., Phoenix, 2001—02; mental health therapist Superstition Mountain Mental Health, Apache Junction, Ariz., 2003—04; intern VA, Ft. Meade, SD, 2004—05; postdoctoral resident neuropsychology Ind. Neuroscience Inst., Indpls., 2005—. Presenter in field. Contbr. articles to profl. jours. Com. mem., psychology adv. Ariz. Hate Crime Adv. Bd., Phoenix, 1998—99. Mem.: APA, Internat. Neuropsychol. Soc., Phi Eta Sigma. Avocations: bodybuilding, reading, martial arts. Office: St Vincent Hosp 2001 W 86th St 3rd Fl Indianapolis IN 46260

HORWITZ, PAUL, physicist; b. NYC, Dec. 4, 1938; s. Louis David and Sylvia Helen (Laibman) H.; m. Eleanor Catherine Jahoda, Aug. 15, 1964; children: Gregory Douglas Lee, Catherine Helen, Laura Elizabeth. AB, Harvard U., 1960; MS, Columbia U., 1963; PhD, NYU, 1967. Rsch. assoc. Cornell U., Ithaca, NY, 1967-69, U. Oreg., Eugene, 1969-71; prin. rsch. scientist Avco Everett Rsch. Lab., Everett, Mass., 1971-79; sr. scientist Bolt, Beranek & Newman Inc., Cambridge, Mass., 1979-91; divsn. scientist Bolt, Branek & Newman Inc., Cambridge, Mass., 1991-94; prin. scientist, 1994-97; sr. scientist The Concord Consortium, 1997—. Contbr. articles to profl. jours. Recipient Founders Day award NYU, 1969, 2 EDUCOM Nat. awards for ednl. software, 1992; Am. Phys. Soc. Congl. fellow, 1975-76; GM Corp. scholar Harvard U., 1960. Fellow AAAS; mem. Am. Ednl. Rsch. Assn. Office: 10 Concord Crossing Concord MA 01742

HORWITZ, RALPH IRVING, internist, epidemiologist, educator, dean; b. Phila., June 25, 1947; s. Sidney and Sara (Altus) H.; m. Sarah McCue, Aug. 5, 1970; 1 child, Rebecca Margaret Taylor. BS, Albright Coll., 1969; MD, Pa. State U., 1973. Diplomate Am. Bd. Internal Medicine. Intern McGill U., Royal Victoria Hosp., Montreal, Que., Canada, 1973-75; postdoctoral tng. in epidemiology, clin. scholars program Yale U. Sch. Medicine, New Haven, 1975; sr. resident Harvard U., Mass. Gen. Hosp., Boston, 1977-78; co-dir. clin. scholars program Yale U. Sch. Medicine, New Haven, 1978—2003, asst. prof. medicine, 1978-82, assoc. prof. medicine and epidemiology, 1982-88, prof., 1988—2003, chief gen. internal medicine, 1982-94, vice chmn. internal medicine, 1993-94, chmn. internal medicine, 1994—2003, Harold H. Hines Jr. Prof. Medicine and Epidemiology, 1991—2003; chief Beeson Med. Svc. Yale-New Haven Hosp., 1993—2003; v.p. med. affairs Case Western Res. U., Cleveland, Ohio, 2003—, dean sch. medicine, 2003—; dir. Case Rsch. Inst., 2003—; Arthur Bloomfield prof. and chmn. dept. medicine Stanford U. Sch. Medicine, Calif. Mem. nat. selection com. faculty scholar program Henry J. Kaiser Family Found., Menlo Park, Calif., 1987-90; mem. com. allocating resources in biomed. rsch. Inst. Medicine, Washington, 1988-89; mem. profl. standards rev. orgn., Woodbridge, Conn., 1980-82; editorial bd. The Lancet, 1991-96; past chmn. bd. dirs. Am. Bd. Internal Medicine. Contbr. over 100 articles to profl. jours. Trustee Am. Bd. Internal Medicine Found. Recipient Faculty Scholar award Kaiser Family Found., 1981-86 Fellow ACP, AAAS, Am. Coll. Epidemiology, Pa. State U. Alumni Assn.; mem. Am. Soc. Clin. Investigation, Assn. Am. Physicians, Am. Epidemiol. Soc., Inst. Medicine, New Haven Lawn Club, Union Club Cleve., Mory's. Jewish. Office: Stanford Univ Sch Medicine 300 Pasteur Dr S-102 Stanford CA 94305 Office Phone: 650-736-1484. Business E-Mail: ralph.horwitz@stanford.edu.

HORWITZ, SUSAN BAND, pharmacologist; BA, Bryn Mawr Coll., 1958; PhD in Biochemistry, Brandeis U., 1963; PhD (hon.), Universite de la Mediterranee, 2002. Postdoctoral fellow dept. pharmacology, sch. medicine Tufts U., 1963-65, Emory U., 1965-67; rsch. assoc. dept. medicine Albert Einstein Coll. Medicine, NYC, 1967-68, instr. dept. pharmacology, 1968-70, asst. prof. dept. medicine, 1970-75, asst. prof. dept. cell biology, 1973-75, assoc. prof. depts. molecular pharmacology and cell biology, 1980—, co-chair dept. molecular pharmacology, 1985—, Rose C. Falkenstein prof. cancer rsch., 1986—, assoc. dir. cancer rsch. ctr., 1991—. Mem. pharmacology-toxicology rsch. team Nat. Inst. Gen. Med. Sci., 1975-80; adv. com. Irma T. Hirschl Scientist award, 1979-85; bd. scientific counselors divsn. cancer treatment NCI, 1981-86, 87-90, mem. review com. Outstanding Investigators Grant award, 1984, ad hoc review com. in vitro and in vivo disease-oriented screening project, 1986; guest reviewer sci. adv. com. Damon Runyon/Walter Winchell Rsch. Fund, 1983,

88; vice chair Gordon Conf. Chemotherapy of Exptl. and Clin. Cancer, 1986, chair, 1987, mem. coun., 1990-93; Sterling Drug vis. prof. dept. pharmacology Boston U., 1987; mem. Charles F. Kettering selection com. Gen. Motors Cancer Rsch. Found., 1988-89, awards assembly, 1991. Contbr. articles to profl. jour., chapters to books. Recipient Rsch. Career Devel. award 1970-75, award Pharm. Mfrs. Assn., 1972, Irma T. Hirschl Career Scientists award, 1975-80, Warren Alpert Found. prize, 2005; grantee Merck, 1970, Nat. Cancer Inst., 1985-92, 92, Bristol-Myers, 1988-93; named Outstanding Woman Scientist metro N.Y.C. chpt. Assn. Women in Science, Barnard Medal of Distinction, 2003, PhRMA Found. award of Excellence, 2004. Mem. Am. Soc. Pharmacology and Exptl. Therapeutics (com. edn. and profl. affairs 1973-77), Am. Soc. Microbiology (vice chair antimicrobial chemotherapy), Am. Chem. Soc., Am. Assn. Cancer Rsch. (biochem. program com. 1983-84, Clowes award selection com. 1986-87, bd. dirs. 1987-90, spl. confs. com. 1989-92, chmn. Rhoads award selection com. 1990-91, co-chair conf. in cancer rsch. membrane transport in multidrug resistance, devel. and disease, 1991, Cain Meml. award 1992, pres., 2003-), Am. Soc. Cell Biology, Harvey Soc. (mem. coun. 1991—), Am. Acad. of Arts & Sciences, NAS. Office: A Einstein Coll Medicine Dept Molecular Pharmacology 1300 Morris Park Ave Bronx NY 10461-1926

HORWOOD, RICHARD M., lawyer; b. East Cleveland, Ohio, Apr. 7, 1940; s. Manuel L. and Esther L. (Schwartz) H.; m. Janet Hershfield, June 30, 1968; children: Sarah Ann, Daniel Lewis. BA, Colgate U., 1962; LLB, U. Pa., 1965; MBA, Am. U., 1967; LLM in Taxation, George Washington U., 1969. Bar: Ill. 1970, US Dist. Ct. (no. dist. Ill.) 1970. Ptnr. Horwood, Marcus & Berk, Chartered, Chgo., 1983—. Adv. bd. US Tax Mgmt., Washington, 1980. Contbr. articles to profl. jours. Mem. Chgo. Fund on Aging and Disabilities, 1995; bd. dirs. Chgo. Estate Planning Coun.; mem. planned giving adv. bd. Art. Inst. Chgo., Shedd Aquarium; pres. Meals on Wheels Chgo. Named one of Top 100 Attys., Worth mag., 2005—06. Office: Horwood Marcus & Berk Chartered Ste 3700 180 N LaSalle Chicago IL 60601 Office Phone: 312-606-3230. E-mail: rhorwood@hmblaw.com.*

HORYN, CATHY, newspaper editor; b. 1957; MA, Barnard Coll., 1978. Fashion editor The Wash. Post, 1992—94; fashion reporter, contr. editor Vanity Fair, 1995—99; fashion editor, chief fashion critic NY Times, 1999—. Editor: (biography) Bare Blass, 2002. Recipient Eugenia Sheppard award for fashion journalism, Coun. Fashion Designers of America, 2002. Office: NY Times Style Desk 229 W 43rd St New York NY 10036 Office Phone: 212-556-3939. Office Fax: 212-556-5999.

HOSEMAN, DANIEL, lawyer; b. Chgo., Aug. 18, 1935; s. Irving and Anne (Pruzansky) H.; m. Susan H. Myles, Aug. 7, 1960; children: Lawrence N., Joan E., Jonathan W. BS, U. Ill., 1956, JD, 1959. Bar: Ill. 1959, U.S. Dist. Ct. (no. dist.) Ill. 1960, U.S. Ct. of Appeals (7th cir.) 1969, U.S. Supreme Ct. 1976. Atty. pvt. practice, Chgo., 1959—. Mem. panel pvt. atty. trustees U.S. Bankruptcy Ct. No. Dist. Ill., 1979—; arbitrator Cir. Ct. Cook County. Trustee Ill. Legal Svcs. Fund, 1978—; v.p. Allied Jewish Sch. Bd. Met. Chgo., 1977—; v.p. United Synagogue Am., 1978—. With USAFR, 1959-65. Mem. Am. Bankruptcy Inst., Advs. Soc., Decalogue Soc. Lawyers (pres. 1981-82, award of merit 1979-80), Ill. Bar Assn. (gen. assembly, long-range planning com.), Lake County Bar Assn. (com. on bankrutpcy 1980—), Chgo. Coun. Lawyers, Comml. Law League Am., Am. Bankruptcy Inst., Nat. Assn. Bankruptcy Trustees. Home: 2151 Tanglewood Ct Highland Park IL 60035-4231 Office: Daniel Hoseman Attorney At Law PO Box 279 Highland Park IL 60035-0279 Office Phone: 847-831-4053.

HOSFORD, KITTYBELLE ADCOCK, retired education educator; d. Don and Shirley Adcock; m. Michael Hosford, May 29, 1976; children: Kali Brooke Hosford Hilke, Zachary Michael. BS, We. Carolina U., Cullowhee, NC, 1971; MA, George Wash. U., DC, 1976; PhD, U. Md., Coll. Park, Md., 1992. Speech lang. therapist Fulton County Pub. Schs., E.Point, Ga., 1972—75; learning disabilities tchr. Montgomery County Pub. Schs., Germantown, Md., 1976—83; asst. prof. Hood Coll., Frederick, Md., 1985—2006; ret., 2006. Dir. Hood Coll. Onica Prall Child Devel. Lab. Sch., Frederick, Md., 1996—2006. Mem.: Md. Assn. Tchr. Educators (pres. 2004—07).

HOSHAW, LLOYD, retired historian, educator; b. Benton, Ind., May 9, 1924; s. Walter and Gladys Ethel (Blue) H.; m. Evelyn F. Tyler, Dec. 24, 1954; children: Linda, John, James, Walter, David, Paul. BA, Goshen Coll., 1949; MA, Ind. U., 1951. Tchr. Winamac (Ind.) High Sch., 1952-55; instr. LaSalle(Ill.)-Peru-Oglesby Jr. Coll., 1955-65; history prof., dept. chair Rock Valley Coll., Rockford, Ill., 1965-88, history prof., 1988—2001; ret., 2001. Bd. dirs. Rock River Christian Coll., prof. history. Author: A History of Eastern Civilizations, Vol I., 1994, Vol. II, 1995, 2d edit., 2001. With USN, 1944—45. Mem. VFW (life), Archeol. Inst. Am. (Rockford chpt.), Ill. State Hist. Soc., Rockford Hist. Soc. Baptist. Avocations: photography, travel. Home: 1860 Charlotte Dr Rockford IL 61108-6508

HOSHIWARA, ISAO, ophthalmologist, consultant; b. Tacoma, Oct. 30, 1929; s. James Seizo; m. Yuri Hoshiwara; children: David Kazuo, Joy Yuri Boydston, Steven Tatsuo. BA in Chemistry, U. Wash., Seattle, 1952, MD, 1956. Resident eye, ear, and nose JS Pub. Health Svc., SI, surg. ophthalmologist Phoenix; rsch. ophthalmologist JS Public Health Svc., Pheonix, 1966—84; gen. ophthalmologist Group Health Puget Sound, Seattle, 1984—96. Contbr. articles to profl. jours. Vol. physician McMally Water St. Mission, NYC, 1964—64, Keiro Nursing Home, Seattle, 1985—90. Capt. US Pub. Health Svc., 1957—84. Recipient Meritorious Svc. medal, US Pub. Health Svc., 1971, Outstanding Physician award, 1972.

HOSICK, HOWARD LAWRENCE, cell biology professor, academic administrator; b. Champaign, Ill., Nov. 1, 1943; s. Arthur Howard and Eunice Irma (Miller) H.; m. Cynthia Ann Jacobson, June 15, 1968; children: Steven Cameron, Anna Elise, Rachel Victoria. BA, U. Colo., 1965; PhD, U. Calif., Berkeley, 1970. Postdoctoral fellow Karolinska Inst., Stockholm, 1970-72; asst. research biochemist U. Calif., Berkeley, 1972-73; asst. prof. Wash. State U., Pullman, 1973-78, assoc. prof., 1978-83, prof. cell biology, 1983—, chmn. dept. zoology, 1983-87, chmn. dept. genetics and cell biology, 1987-91. Vis. scientist U. Reading, Eng., 1978, B.C. Cancer Ctr., Vancouver, 2003; disting. scientist Aichi Cancer Ctr., Nagoya, Japan, 1986; vis. scholar Cambridge U., 1994; rsch. com. Am. Heart Assn., 1989; grant rev. com. Nat. Cancer Inst., 1993-2000; chair, breast cancer rsch. program, U.S. Army Med. Rsch. Command. Rev. editor In Vitro Cellular and Molecular Biology, 1986—97; contbr. articles to profl. jours. Bd. govs. Internat. Assn. Breast Cancer Rsch., 1993-2000. Recipient H.S. Boyce award, 1981, Shell Faculty Devel. award, 1984, Cancer Rsch. awards Eagles Club, 1989-2004, G. and L. Pfeiffer Rsch. Found. award, 1992; fellow NIH, NSF, Am. Cancer Soc., Damon Runyan-Walter Winchell Cancer Fund, Fogarty Internat. Ctr., 1968-2004; grantee NIH, NSF, Am. Cancer Soc., Am. Inst. Cancer Rsch., Pfeiffer Found., 1973-2004, U.S. Army, Internat. Assn. for Cancer Rsch., 2002-. Mem. Am. Soc. Cell Biology, Tissue Culture Assn., Am. Assn. Cancer Research, Internat. Assn. Breast Cancer Research. Lodges: Rotary. Democrat. Buddhist. Avocations: running, woodworking, model aviation. Office: Wash State U Sch Biol Scis Pullman WA 99164-4234 Home: 800 SE Edge Knoll Dr Pullman WA 99163-2408 Home Phone: 509-332-8687. Business E-Mail: hosick@wsu.edu.

HOSIE, SPENCER, lawyer; b. Toronto, Ont., Can., Apr. 24, 1956; BA summa cum laude, U. Calif., Berkeley, 1978; JD, U. Calif., Davis, 1981. Bar: Calif. 1981, Alaska 1982. Law clk. to Hon. Edmond W. Burke, Chief Justice Alaska Supreme Ct., 1981—82; assoc. Heller, Ehrman, White & McAuliffe, San Francisco, 1982—85; ptnr. Hosie, Frost, Large & McArthur, San Francisco, 1985—99; founder, ptnr. Hosie McArthur, LLP, San Francisco, 1999—. Editor: U. Calif. Davis Law Rev., 1980—81; mem. editl. bd.: RICO Litig. Reporter, 1984—85. Named one of Top 25 Attys. Under 45 in Calif., Calif. Lawyer, 1993, Top 10 Trial Lawyers in Am., Nat. Law Jour., 2005. Mem.: Assn. Trial Lawyers of Am., Alaska Bar Assn., Anchorage Bar Assn., Bar Assn. San Francisco, Order of Coif. Office: Hosie McArthur LLP 1 Market Spear Tower 22nd Fl San Francisco CA 94105 Office Phone: 415-247-6000. Office Fax: 415-247-6001. E-mail: shosie@hosielaw.com.*

HOSIE, THOMAS WALSH, counselor, educator; b. Buffalo; s. Frank and Mary Hosie; m. Denise Joy Hosie; 1 child, Sean Walsh. BA in History, U. Buffalo, 1966, MEd in Counseling, 1970, PhD in Counseling, 1973. Lic. profl. counselor La., 1988, cert. counselor Nat. Bd. of Cert. Counselors, 1999. Asst. prof. N.E. La. U., Monroe, 1973—77; prof., dept. head La. State U., Baton Rouge, 1977—96, Miss. State U., Starkville, 1996—. Sci. and social studies tchr. John F. Kennedy H.S., Cheektowaga, NY, 1966—68; supr. Marine Midland Trust Co. of Western N.Y., Buffalo, 1968—69; supr. of student tchr.s U. Buffalo, 1969—70; sch. counselor Hamburg Ctrl. H.S., NY, 1970—71, 1970—71, Buffalo City Schs. - Woodlawn Jr. H.S., 1970; therapist Suicide Prevention and Crisis Svc., Buffalo, 1971—72. Editor: Jour. of Counseling Svcs.; contbr. articles to profl. jours., chapters to books. Chmn. La. Profl. Counselors Bd. of Examiners, Baton Rouge, 1987—88, mem., 1995—96; v.p. for rsch. Assn. for Humanistic Edn. & Devel., Alexandria, Va., 1978—80; pres., rep. to ACA, treas. Assn. for Counselor Edn. and Supervision, Alexandria, Va., 1989—99; exec. coun. - aces rep. ACA, Alexandria, Va., 1992—95; ACA rep. Coun. for Accreditation of Counseling and Related Ednl. Programs, Alexandria, Va., 1996—99; pres. and v.p. Miss. Assoc. for Counselor Edn. and Supervision, Biloxi, Miss., 1999—2000, La. Sch. Counselors Assn., Baton Rouge, 1976—80; pres. La. Assn. for Counselor Edn. and Supervision, Baton Rouge, 1977—78; pres. and v.p. La. Assn. for Counseling and Devel., Baton Rouge, 1984—88. Recipient Counselor Educator of Yr. award, La. Sch. Counselor Assoc., 1979, Leadership and Achievement award, So. Assoc. for Counselor Edn. and Supervision, 1984, ACES Disting. Svc. award, Assoc. for Counselor Edn. and Supervision, 2002, Herbert M. Handley Outstanding Dissertation Mentor award, Mid-South Ednl. Rsch. Assoc., 2003; Vocat. Rehab. Program by Distance grant, Miss. Dept. of Vocat. Rehab., 1999 - 2003, Exptl. Evaluation of Tutorials in Problem Solving grant, Office of Naval Rsch., 2002, Measurement and Evaluation of Animated Pedagogical Agents grant, 2002, 2003. Mem.: APA, Assn. for Counselor Edn. and Supervision (pres. 1989—90, Rsch. Award & Disting. Profl. Svc. Award 1989 & 2002), Miss. Assn. of Counselor Edn. and Supervision (pres. 2000—01), La. Counseling Assn. (life; pres. 1986—87), Chi Sigma Iota. Avocation: fishing. Office: Miss State Univ PO Box 9727 Mississippi State MS 39762 Home Phone: 662-320-9312; Office Phone: 662-325-3426. Office Fax: 662-325-3263. Business E-Mail: hosie@colled.msstate.edu.

HOSKINS, ALEXANDER L. (PETE), retired zoological park administrator; b. Woodland, Calif., Sept. 1, 1947; s. Edgar and Betty (Stoner) H.; m. Sharon Paula Barr, May 19, 1990; children: Emily, David, Adam. BA in Polit. Sci., San Jose State U., 1969; MA in Pub. Adminstrn., U. Minn., 1971. Asst. to city mgr. City of Foster City, Calif., 1971-72; mgmt. analyst Mng. Dir.'s Office, City of Phila., 1972-80, exec. dir. Fairmount Park, 1980-88, commr. of streets, 1988-93; pres., CEO, Phila. Zoo, 1993—2006. Contbr. articles to various publs. Exec. v.p. Chestnut Hill Cmty. Assn., 1974-76; trustee Cmty. Leadership Seminars, 1978-80, Unitarian Soc. Germantown, 1985-87; chmn. Delaware Valley Regional Horticulture Industry Coun., 1985-86, Phila. Independence Marathon, 1985-88 Recipient ann. award for meritorious mcpl. svc. Ctrl. Phila. Devel. Corp., 1986, honor award for restoration and revitalization Pa.-Del. chpt. Am. Soc. Landscape Architects, 1986, govt. svc. award Phila. sect. ASCE, 1990, govt. award for excellence in pub. adminstrn. Phila. regional chpt. ASAP, 1991, award for engring. excellence Cons. Engrs. Coun. N.J., 1991, William V. Donaldson award for civic price PhilaPride, 1992. Mem. Am. Pub. Works Assn. (Delaware Valley exec. com. 1992—).

HOSKINS, ANTHONY GLENN, librarian; s. William Glenn and Jessie (Shields) Hoskins. BA, U. Iowa, Iowa City, 1970; MA, U. Chgo., 1990. Instr. genealogical rsch. Newberry Libr., Chgo., 1987—97; head cmty. devel. divsn. Palm Beach County Libr., West Palm Beach, Fla., 1997—2000; asst. head ref. Broward County Libr., Ft. Lauderdale, Fla., 2000—01; archivist Sonoma County Hist. Recs. Commn., Santa Rosa, Calif., 2001—; libr. Somona County History and Genealogy Libr., Santa Rosa, 2001; instr. inline genealogical rsch. Peninsula Libr. Sys., San Mateo, Calif., 2003—. Chair Sonoma County Hist. Recs. Commn., Santa Rosa, 2005—06; cons. libr. planning Stewart's Point Rancheri, Kashia Pomo Indians, Calif., 2006; dir. Sonoma County Govt. Oral History Project, Santa Rosa, 2004—; instr. Senoma State U., Rohnert Park, 2003. Author: The Ancestry of Prince Hans Georg of Ysenburg and Budingen, 1994; co-author: The Chosen Spot: Sonoma County's Rich History in Agriculture and Timber, 2002; contbr. articles to profl. jours. Pres. Sonoma County Hist. Soc., Santa Rose, 2003—, Sonoma County Geneal. Soc., Santa Rose, 2004—06. Mem.: Triple Nine Soc., Mensa. Episcopalian. Avocations: hiking, sailing. Home: 2193 Sunleaf Ln Santa Rosa CA 95403 Office: Sooma County Libr 3rd & E Sts Santa Rosa CA 95403

HOSKINS, BOB (ROBERT WILLIAM HOSKINS), actor; b. Bury St. Edmunds, Suffolk, Eng., Oct. 26, 1942; s. Robert and Elsie Lillian Hoskins; m. Jane Livesey 1967 (div. 1978); children: Alex, Sarah; m. Linda Banwell, 1982; children: Jack, Rosa. Student, Stroud Green Sch. Stage debut in Romeo and Juliet, Victoria Theatre, Stoke-on-Trent, 1968; joined Royal Shakespeare Co., 1976; stage appearances include Pygmalion, Albery, Eng., 1974, Aldwych, 1976, The World Has Turned Upside Down, 1978, Has Washington Legs?, 1978, True West, 1989, Guys and Dolls, 1981, Old Wicked Songs, 1996-97, Stage, 1996-97, As You Desire Me, 2005; TV appearances include On The Move, 1976, Pennies From Heaven, 1978, (miniseries) Flickers, 1980, Othello, 1981, The Dunera Boys, 1986, The Changeling, 1993, World War II: When The Lions Roared, 1994, David Copperfield, 1999, Don Quixote, 2000, The Lost World, 2001, Il Papa buono, 2003; film appearances include Zulu Dawn, 1980, The Long Good Friday, 1981, Cotton Club, 1984, Mona Lisa (Best Actor award Cannes Festival, Nat. Soc. Film Critics, 1987), Who Framed Roger Rabbit?, 1988, Mermaids, 1990, Heart Condition, 1990, Shattered, 1990, The Favor the Watch, 1990, The Projectionist, 1990, Hook, 1991, Passed Away, 1991, Super Mario Bros., 1992, Nixon, 1995, Michael, 1996, Cousin Bette, 1996, Twenty-Four/Seven, 1997, 1 Inch Over the Horizon, 1997, Felicias Journey, 1999, Let the Good Times Roll, 1999, Enemy at the Gates, 2001, Maid in Manhattan, 2002, The Sleeping Dictionary, 2003, Vanity Fair, 2004, Beyond the Sea, 2004, Unleashed, 2005, Son of the Mask, 2005, Truth, Divorce and the American Way, 2005, (voice) Garfield: A Tail of Two Kitties, 2006, Hollywoodland, 2006, others; actor, writer, dir. The Raggedy Rawney, 1988; actor, dir. The Rainbow, 1994; actor, exec. prodr. The Secret Agent, 1996, Mrs. Henderson Presents, 2005. Avocations: photography, gardening, playgoing. Office: Internat Creative Mgmt Ltd Oxford House 76 Oxford St London W1N 0AX England

HOSKINS, DONALD W., retired medical association administrator; BS, Queens Coll., 1953; MD, Cornell U., 1957. Diplomate Am. Bd. Internal Medicine. Chief med. officer, med. dir. , sr. v.p. med. affairs Continuum Health Ptnrs. (Beth Israel), 1997—2006; assoc. prof. clin. medicine Albert Einstein Coll. Medicine, Bronx, NY. Office: Beth Israel Med Ctr First Ave 16th St New York NY 10003

HOSKINS, H. DUNBAR, ophthalmologist, medical association administrator; b. Va. married; 3 children. MD, Med. Coll. Va. Cert. Am. Bd. Opthalmology, 1970. Chief, ophthalmology Naval Hosp., RI, 1968; exec. v.p. Am. Acad. Ophthalmology, San Francisco, 1993—; and clin. prof. ophthalmology Univ. Calif. Sch. Med., San Francisco. Chmn. St. Mary's Hosp. Med. Ctr., San Francisco, Mercy Svcs. Corp.; founder, chmn. Medem Corp.; founding dir. Am. Glaucoma Soc.; founder, dir. Glaucoma Rsch. Found. Recipient Med. Exec. Achievement award, AMA, 2005. Mem.: Internat. Coun. Ophthalmology, Am. Glaucoma Soc., Pan Am. Assn. Ophthalmology (former sec-treas.), Am. Eye Study Club. Office: Am Acad of Ophthalmology PO Box 7424 San Francisco CA 94120-7424 Office Phone: 415-561-8500. Office Fax: 415-561-8533.*

HOSKINS, JOHN HOWARD, retired urologist, educator; b. Breckenridge, Minn., Mar. 18, 1934; s. James H. and Ruth (Johanson) H.; m. Nancy Weih, Aug. 3, 1957; children: William, James, Laura, Sara. BA in History, U. Iowa, 1956; BS in Medicine, U. S.D., 1959; MD, Temple U., 1961. Diplomate Am. Bd. Urology. Practice medicine specializing in urology, Sioux Falls, SD, 1966-96; head sect. urology U. S.D. Sch. Medicine, Vermillon, 1977-93; ret., 1997. Maj. M.C. U.S. Army, 1967-69, Vietnam. Fellow: ACS; mem.: Am. Urol. Assn., Augustana Fellows, Rotary, Shriners, Masons. Republican. Methodist. Personal E-mail: jnhoskins@sio.midco.net.

HOSKINS, RICHARD JEROLD, lawyer; s. Walter Jerold and Gladys (Gaither) H.; children: Stephen Weston, Philip Richard. BA, U. Kans., 1967; JD, Northwestern U., 1970. Bar: NY 1971, Ill. 1976, US Supreme Ct. 1982. Assoc. Davis Polk & Wardwell, NYC, 1970-73; asst. US atty., So. Dist. NY, 1973-76; assoc. Schiff Hardin & Waite, Chgo., 1976-77, ptnr., 1978—. Adj. prof. U. Va. Law Sch., 1980-83, Northwestern U. Law Sch., 1992-98, sr. lectr., 1999—. Contbr. articles to profl. jours. Chancellor emeritus Episcopal Diocese of Chgo.; bd. visitors and govs. St. John's Coll. Named Hon. Canon, St. James Cathedral, Chgo.; recipient Childres Meml. award for Tchg. Excellence, Northwestern U. Sch. Law. Fellow Am. Coll. Trial Lawyers, Am. Bar Found.; mem. ABA, Ill. State Bar Assn., Chgo. Bar Assn., 7th Cir. Bar Assn., Assn. of Bar of City of NY, Chgo. Coun. Lawyers, Law Club Chgo., Met. Club (Chgo.). Episcopalian. Office: 6600 Sears Tower Chicago IL 60606 Office Phone: 312-258-5509. Business E-Mail: rhoskins@schiffhardin.com.

HOSKINS, WILLIAM JOHN, obstetrician, educator, gynecologist; b. Harlan, Ky., May 10, 1940; s. Lonnie S. and Joanne (Huff) Hoskins; m. Betty Jean Gay, Sept. 10, 1960 (div. 1985); children: Tonya J., William John Jr.; m. Iffath Abbasi Ahson, Nov. 9, 1985; children: Ahad A., Mariya A. BA, U. Tenn., Knoxville, 1962; MD, U. Tenn., Memphis, 1965. Diplomate Am. Bd. Ob-Gyn., Am. Bd. Gynecol. Oncology. Commd. lt. USN, 1966, advanced through grades to capt.; intern Jacksonville Naval Hosp., Fla., 1966-67; med. officer Destroyer Squadron 8 USN, Mayport, Fla., 1967-68; resident in ob-gyn Oakland Naval Hosp., Calif., 1968-71; staff dept. ob -gyn Pensacola Naval Hosp., 1971—74; fellow in gynecol. oncology U. Miami, Fla., 1974-76; dir. gynecol. oncology Nat. Naval Med. Ctr., Bethesda, Md., 1976—86; assoc. prof. ob-gyn Uniformed Svcs. U., Bethesda, 1976-86; ret. USN, 1986; assoc. chief gynecology svc. Meml. Sloan-Kettering Cancer Ctr., NYC, 1988-90, chief gynecology svc., 1990—, 1990—; assoc. prof. ob-gyn Cornell U. Med. Ctr., NYC, 1986—90; prof. ob-gyn. Cornell U. Med. Coll., 1990—2001, vice chmn. protocol com. gynecol. oncology group, 1993-94, vice chmn. gynecologic oncology group, 1993—2002; Avon chair gynecologic oncology rsch. Meml. Sloan-Kettering Cancer Ctr., NYC, 1995-96, dep. physician in chief disease mgmt. teams, 1996—2001; dir. Curtis & Elizabeth Anderson Cancer Ctr. at Memorial Health U. Med. Ctr., Savannah, Ga., 2001—; prof. ob-gyn. Mercer Med. Coll., Macon, Ga., 2001—, sr. assoc. dean Sch. Medicine Savannah, 2004—05. Chmn. ovarian com. Gynecol. Oncology Group, Phila., 1984-89; disting. Ga. Cancer scholar, 2001—; co-chair NCI Gyn. Cancer Steering Com., 2006—. Editor: Principles and Practice of Gynecology and Oncology, 1992, 4th edit., 2000, 4th edit., 2004, Cancer of the Ovary, 1993, Cervical Cancer and Perinvasive Peoplasia, 1996, Cancer Management: A Multidisciplinary Approach, 1996, Handbook of Gynecologic Oncology, 2000, 8th edit., 2002, Atlas of Procedures in Gynecologic Oncology, 2003; contbr. over 224 articles to profl. jours., chpts. to books. Fellow Am. Coll. Obstetricians and Gynecologists (v.p. Navy sect. 1982-83), ACS; mem. Am. Gynecol. and Obstet. Soc., Soc. Gynecol. Oncologists (sec.-treas. elect 1992, sec.-treas. 1994—, coun. mem. 1988-91, pres. 1999), Soc. Gynecol. Surgeons, Am. Radium Soc., Am. Assn Cancer Rsch., Internat. Gyn. Cancer Soc. (v.p. 2004—). Republican. Muslim. Office: Meml Sloan-Kettering Cancer Ctr 1275 York Ave Rm 2001C New York NY 10065 Office Phone: 912-350-8337. Business E-Mail: hoskiwi1@memorialhealth.com.

HOSKINS, WILLIAM KELLER, pharmaceutical executive, lawyer, mediator, arbitrator; b. Cin., Feb. 22, 1935; s. John Hobart and Gertrude Louise (Keller) H.; m. Elizabeth Ann Grimm, Aug. 5, 1961; children: Bruce, Andrew, John, Elizabeth, Allison. BA, Yale U., 1956; LLB, Harvard U., 1962. Bar: Ohio 1962, N.Y. 1982, Mo. 1983, U.S. Dist. Ct. (so. dist.) Ohio 1963, U.S. Tax Ct. 1963, U.S. Ct. Appeals (6th cir.) 1964. Assoc. Frost & Jacobs, Cin., 1962-68; gen. counsel Drackett Co., Cin., 1968-71, v.p., gen. counsel, 1971-81; assoc. gen. counsel Bristol Myers Co., NYC, 1981, spl. counsel, 1982; v.p., gen. counsel, sec. Hoechst Marion Roussell (formerly Marion Labs. Inc.), Kansas City, Mo., 1982-97; gen. ptnr. Hoskins Group, Boston, 1998—; pres. Hoskins & Assocs., Boston, 1998—; mng. ptnr. Resolution Coun., LLP, Portland, Oreg., 2002—. Chmn. household div. Soap and Detergent Assn., NYC, 1978-79, chmn. Chem. Spltys. Mfg. Assn., Washington, 1982; bd. dirs. Ferrrellgas, Inc., Kansas City, Mo., 2003-. Mem. Hamilton County Rep. Ctrl. Com., Ohio, 1970-81; sec.-treas. Marion Labs. Polit. Action Com., 1982-89; sec.-treas. polit. action com. Mid-Am. Com. Sound Govt., Lake Quivira, Kans., 1982-86; bd. dirs. Landmark Legal Found., Kansas City, 1995-2003, vice chmn., 2001-2003. Lt. (j.g.) USN, 1956-59. Mem. Mo. Bar Assn., Ohio Bar Assn., N.Y. Bar, Cin. Bar Assn., Harvard Law Sch. Alumni Assn. (bd. dirs. 1991-95). Roman Catholic. Home: 85 E India Row Apt 20B Boston MA 02110-3397 Home Phone: 617-742-4172; Office Phone: 617-742-8191. E-mail: Bhoskins98@aol.com.

HOSLER, CHARLES LUTHER, JR., meteorologist, educator; b. Honey Brook, Pa., June 3, 1924; s. Charles Luther and Miriam Deichley (Stauffer) H.; m. Gladys Cheesbrough, 1947 (div.); children:Sharon Elizabeth, David Charles, Lynn Rebecca, Peter William; m. Anna R. Stahel, 1971. Student, Bucknell U., 1943-44, MIT, 1944-45; BS, Pa. State U., 1947, MS, 1948, PhD, 1951. Faculty Pa. State U., University Park, 1948—, prof. meteorology, 1960—, head dept., 1961-65, dean Coll. Earth and Mineral Scis., 1965-85, sr. v.p. rsch., dean Grad. Sch., 1985-92. Hydrographer Pa. Dept. Forests and Waters, 1949-59; meteorol. cons., 1950—, vis. prof. colls., lectr. civic and prof. groups; condr. daily TV weather program, 1957-67; spl. rsch. microphysics of clouds; chmn. bd. atmospheric scis. and climate Nat. Acad. Scis., 1984-86; mem. Nat. Sci. Bd., 1985-94; mem. nat. adv. com. on oceans and atmosphere; chmn. bd. trustees Univ. Corp. for Atmospheric Rsch., Boulder, Colo., 1981-85. Contbr. articles to profl. jours. Served to lt. (j.g.) USNR, 1943-46; lt. comdr. Res. Fellow Am. Meteorol. Soc. (councilor, pres. 1976); mem. Nat. Acad. Engring., Am.

Geophys. Union Am. Chem. Soc. (regional lectr. 1971-72), AAAS, Sigma Xi (pres. Pa. State U. 1958, nat. lectr. 1972), Tau Beta Pi. Home: 1229 Smithfield Cir State College PA 16801-6426 Office: Pa State U 617 Walker Bldg University Park PA 16802-5014 Office Phone: 814-865-8358. E-mail: hosler@ems.psu.edu.

HOSMAN, SHARON LEE, retired music educator; b. Bisbee, Ariz., Nov. 2, 1943; d. Roy Lee and Virginia Baldwin (Bandel) H. BA, Loretto Heights Coll., 1965; MA, U. No. Colo., 1979. Tchr. Livermore (Calif.) Sch. Dist., 1965-66, Jefferson County Pub. Schs., Golden, Colo., 1966-97; ret., 1997. Faculty rep. North Area Citizens Adv. Com., Arvada, Colo., 1979-81, S.I.P.C., Arvada, 1982-83, North Area Sch. Improvement Process Com., Arvada, 1984-91, North Area Accountability com., 1991-92. Piano accompanist for sch. groups, 1965-97. Mem. NEA, DAR, Jefferson County Edn. Assn., Colo. Edn. Assn., Music Tchrs. Nat. Assn., Colo. State Music Tchrs. Assn., Denver Area Music Tchrs. Assn., Musicians' Soc. Denver, Am. Guild Organists, Hereditary Order of First Families of Mass., Smithsonian, Denver Rescue Mission, Denver Dumb Friends League, St. Luke's Hosp. Aux. (life), The Regis U. Crest Club. Republican. Episcopalian. Avocations: art, music, drama, reading, gardening.

HOSOKAWA, DAVID, advertising executive; b. 1943; Copy ed, reporter Mpls. Tribune, 1965—67; Staff writer Houston Chronicle, Tex., 1967—68; advt., mktg. consultant, 1968—76; asst mng ed. Albuquerque Journal, 1974—76; asst. pub. Sun Newspapers, Omaha, 1976—79; pres. Sunbelt Pub., 1979—84, David Hosokawa & Assoc, 1984—91; CEO TMP Worldwide, Inc., 1991—97, vice chmn. (ret.) NYC, 1997—98; chmn Voltage Factory, Atlanta, 2000—.

HOSSAIN, ANWAR, molecular biologist, educator; s. Nural Hossain and Saleha Khatoon; m. Swati Sheikh Hossain, Oct. 17, 1990; children: Labannya, Susmita. MS, U. Dhaka, Bangladesh; PhD, Tohoku U., Sendai, Japan, 1998. Rsch. assoc. M. D. Anderson Cancer Ctr., Houston, 2001—04, instr., 2005—. Mng. editor Frontiers in Bioscience, NYC, 2006—. Office: M D Anderson Cancer Ctr 7435 Fannin St Houston TX 77054 Office Phone: 713-834-6039. Office Fax: 713-834-6084. Business E-Mail: ahossain@mdanderson.org.

HOSSAIN, FAISAL, engineering educator; b. Rajshahi, Bangladesh, May 2, 1974; s. Delawer Hossain and Fazillaton Nessa; m. Sayma Rahman, May 27, 2006. BS, Banaras Hindu U., India, 1996; M in Engring., Nat. U. Singapore, 1999; PhD, U. Conn., Storrs, 2004. Asst. prof. Tenn. Tech. U., Cookeville, 2004—. Office: Tenn Tech Univ 1020 Stadium Dr Cookeville TN 38505

HOSSAIN, MARUF, research scientist; b. Chapai Nawabgonj, Rajshahi, Bangladesh, Jan. 2, 1975; s. A. H. S. and Sakina Mannan; m. Kamrun Nahar Asha; children: Faiyaz Ahnaf, Sumaiya Zahraa. BSEE, Bangladesh U. Engring. and Tech., Dhaka; MSEE, U. Ark., Fayetteville, PhD, 2004. Rsch. asst. U. Ark., Fayetteville, 2000—04; rsch. fellow U. Mo., Columbia, 2005—. Mem.: IEEE. Achievements include patents pending in field. Home: 3300 Alligator Ln Columbia MO 65202 Home Phone: 573-814-0559; Office Phone: 573-882-8135. Personal E-mail: maruf72703@yahoo.com.

HOSSAIN, MURSHED, physicist, researcher; b. Pathaliakandi, Homna, Comilla, Bangladesh, Nov. 21, 1950; came to U.S., 1979; s. Mohammad Abdul Alim and Mehar Nigar; m. Sufia Khatun, July 25, 1982; children: Chintan, Chetak. BSc with honors, Dacca U., Bangladesh, 1975, MSc, 1976; MS, Coll. William and Mary, 1981, PhD, 1983. Cert. in therapeutic radiologic physics Am. Bd. Radiology. Jr. rsch. officer Forest Rsch. Inst., Chittagong, Bangladesh, 1977-78; sci. officer AEC, Dhaka, Bangladesh, 1978-79; staff scientist Inst. for Computer Applications in Sci. & Engring. NASA Langley Rsch. Ctr., Hampton, Va., 1983-85; assoc. rsch. scientist Courant Inst. Math. Scis., NYU, 1985-88; rsch. scientist Bartol Rsch. Inst., U. Del., Newark, 1988-91, sr. rsch. scientist, 1991-97; adj. faculty Rowan U., Glassboro, NJ, 1995-97, asst. prof. dept. chemistry and physics, 1998; clin. resident Thomas Jefferson U., Phila., 1998—99, instr., 1999—2001, asst. prof., 2001—07; assoc. mem. Fox Chase Cancer Ctr., Phila., 2007—. Mng. com. B.G. Press H.S., Tejgaon, Dhaka, Bangladesh, 1974-77; v.p. Dacca U. Physics Assn., 1975-76; joint sec. Sr. Forrest Rsch. Officers Assn., Forest Rsch. Inst., 1977-78; mem. citizens adv. coun. Colonial Sch. Distr., New Castle, Del., 1992-96, mem. policy com., 1994-96, mem. gifted and talented com., 1996-97; dir. med. physics Frankford Hosp. Radiation Oncology, 2005-07. Contbr. articles to profl. jours. including Jour. Plasma Physics, Physics Fluids, Phys. Rev. Letters, Astrophys. Jour., Physics Letters, Computer Physics Comm., Phys. Rev., Med. Physics. Mem. Am. Assn. Physicists in Medicine. Achievements include research in radiation therapy physics, on plasma transport, astrophysical convection, fluid and magnetofluid turbulence theory and simulation. Home: 1015 Sweet Cherry Ct Wilmington DE 19809 Office: Fox Chase Cancer Ctr 333 Cottman Ave Philadelphia PA 19111 Office Phone: 215-728-3895. Business E-Mail: murshed.hossain@fccc.edu.

HOSSEINI, KHALED, writer; b. Kabul, Afghanistan, Mar. 4, 1965; arrived in Paris, 1976, arrived in San Jose, Calif., 1980; m. Roya Hosseini; children: Haris, Farah. BS in Biology, Santa Clara U., 1988; MD, U. Calif. San Diego Sch. Medicine, 1993. Internist residency Cedars-Sinai Hosp., LA; internist, 1996—2004, Kaiser Med. Offices, Mountain View, Calif. Author: The Kite Runner, 2003 (NY Times Bestseller, #1 Publishers Weekly paperback bestseller), A Thousand Splendid Suns, 2007. Goodwill envoy UN High Commr. for Refugees, Refugee Agy. Office: Riverhead Books 375 Hudson St New York NY 10014*

HOSSLER, DAVID JOSEPH, lawyer, educator; b. Mesa, Ariz., Oct. 18, 1940; s. Carl Joseph and Elizabeth Ruth (Bills) H.; m. Gretchen Anne, Mar. 2, 1945; 1 child, Devon Annagret. BA, U. Ariz., Tucson, 1969, JD, 1972. Bar: Ariz. 1972, US Dist. Ct. Ariz. 1972, US Supreme Ct. 1977. Legal intern to chmn. FCC, summer 1971; law clk. to chief justice Ariz. Supreme Ct., 1972-73; chief dep. county atty. Yuma County, Ariz., 1973-74; ptnr. Hunt and Hossler, Yuma, Ariz., 1974—. Instr. in law and banking, law and real estate Ariz. Western Coll.; instr. in bus. law, mktg., ethics Webster U.; instr. agrl. law U. Ariz.; co-chmn. fee arbitration com. Ariz. State Bar, 1990—; instr. employee/employer law U. Phoenix. Editor-in-chief Ariz. Adv., 1971-72. Precinct com. Yuma County Rep. Ctrl. Com., 1974-2000, vice chmn., 1982; chmn. region II Acad. Decathalon competition, 1989; bd. dirs. Yuma County Ednl. Found. (Hall of Fame 2000), Yuma County Assn. Behavior Health Svcs., pres., 1981; bd. dirs. Yuma Union H.S. Dist. Found.; coach Yuma HS mock ct. team, 1987-94; bd. dirs. friends of U. Med. Ctr., Am. Red Cross, With USN. Recipient Man and Boy award, Boys Clubs Am., 1979, Freedoms Found. award, Yuma chpt., 1988, Demolay Legion of Honor, 1991, Francis Woodward award, Ariz. Pub. Svc., 2000, named Vol. of Yr., Yuma County, 1981—82, Heart of Yuma award, 2000, voted Yuma's Best (atty.), 2001—02, 2002—03. Mem. ATLA, Am. Judicature Soc., Yuma County Bar Assn. (pres. 1975-76), Navy League, VFW, Am. Legion, U. Ariz. Alumni Assn. (nat. bd. dirs., past pres., hon. bobcat 1996, Disting. Citizen award 1997), Rotary (pres. Yuma club 1987-88, dist. gov. rep. 1989, dist. gov. 1992-93, findings com. 1996, dist. found. chair 1996-2000, co-chmn. internat. membership retention 2000-01, John Van Houton Look Beyond Yourself award 1995, Roy Slayton Share Rotary Share People award 1996, Al Face You Are the Key award 1997, Ted Day Let Svc. Light the Way award 1998, Rotary Found. citation for meritorious svc., Rotary Internat. (bd. dirs. 2004-06, bd. dirs. Katrina relief), Four Avenues of Svc. award, 2004, Internat. Svc. Above Self award, Cliff Doctorman Real Happiness is Helping Others award, Disting. Svc. award). Episcopalian (vestry 1978-82). Home: 2802 S Fern Dr Yuma AZ 85364-2919 Office: Hunt Hossler 330 W 24th St Yuma AZ 85364-6455 Mailing: PO Box 2919 Yuma AZ 85366-2919 Office Phone: 928-783-0101. Personal E-mail: dhossler@mindspring.com.

HOSTAGE, JOHN BRAYNE ARTHUR, law librarian; b. Hartford, Conn., June 10, 1952; s. John Brayne and Anne (Leonard) H. BA, Columbia U., 1974; MA in German, U. Wis., 1978, MA in LS, 1979. Cataloger U. Ill., Chgo., 1979-82, Harvard U. Law Sch. Libr., Cambridge, Mass., 1982—92; authorities libr. Harvard law Sch., Libr., 1992—. ALA/USIA libr. fellow, Berlin, 1994. Mem. ALA (editor SRRT newsletter 1984-86, coord. SRRT 1987-89); mem. Am. Assn. Law Librs., Internat. Fedn. Libr. Assns. (standing com. on cataloguing 2005—). Office: Harvard Law Sch Libr Langdell Hall Cambridge MA 02138 Office Phone: 617-495-3974. Business E-Mail: hostage@law.harvard.edu.

HOSTERT, LEONA TERESSA, retired librarian, researcher; b. Pitts., Oct. 13, 1933; d. Joseph C. and Mary T. (Chropka) Bajoras; m. Arthur H. Hostert, Aug. 9, 1958; children: Erik M., Wendy A. BS in Edn., Ind. State U., 1955; MLS, Duquesne U., 1965. Cert. secondary edn. educator Pa. Spl. libr. Am. Electronic Labs., Colmar, Pa., 1982; pres. Lee's Rsch., Lansdale, Pa., 1985—; libr. HS N. Pa. Schs., Lansdale, 1986—; ret. Access Pa. liaison N. Penn Schs., Lansdale, 1986—; bd. dirs. N. Penn Symphony, Lansdale, 1986—88; planning commr. Upper Gwynedd Twp., Lansadale, 1987—89; area rep. Lansdale Reps., Montgomery County, 1988—89. Mem.: N. Pa. Edn. Assn. (membership chair, rep. 1991—), Pa. Sch. Libr. Assn. Home: 877 Geranium Dr Warrington PA 18976

HOSTERT, SHARON ANN, elementary school educator, assistant principal; b. Joliet, Ill., Apr. 27, 1951; d. Joseph and Norma Legerski; m. Ronald Hostert, Aug. 11, 1973. BA, U. St. Francis, Joliet, Ill., 1973. Cert. tchr. Ill. Tchrs. aide Troy Schs., Shorewood, Ill., 1973—74; tchr. St. Paul The Apostle Sch., Joliet, Ill., 1974—, asst. prin., 1985—. Coord. St. Paul The Apostle Sch., Joliet, 1977—84, acting prin., 1984—85, eucharistic min., 1984—; hon. commn. congl. youth leadership coun., Washington, 2006—. Recipient Tchr. Yr., U. St. Francis, Joliet, 2005. Mem.: NCEA. Avocation: flora and jewelry design.

HOSTETTER, AMOS BARR, JR., cable television executive; b. Jan. 12, 1937; s. Amos Barr and Leola (Conroy) Hostetter; married; 3 children. BA cum laude, Amherst Coll., 1958; MBA, Harvard U., 1961. Asst. to v.p. fin. Am. & Fgn. Power Co., NYC, 1958—59; investment analyst Cambridge Capital Corp., 1961—63; co-founder, exec. v.p. Continental Cablevision, Inc., Boston, 1963—80, pres., CEO, 1980—85, chmn., CEO, 1985—96; CEO MediaOne, Inc., Boston, 1996—2000; chmn. Pilor House Assoc., LLC; chmn., CEO Continental Cablevision, Inc. (name changed to Media One), 1985—96; founder, bd. dirs. Cable Satellite Pub. Affairs Network (C-SPAN), 1979—. Bd. dirs. Commodities Corp., Princeton, NJ; trustee various mut. funds Mass. Fin. Svcs., 1985—; bd. mem. AT&T, 1999—2003. Trustee Children's TV Workshop, NYC, 1980—, New Eng. Med. Ctr. Hosp., Boston, 1982—; bd. overseers Mus. Fine Arts, Boston, 1987—; bd. dirs. Corp. Pub. Broadcasting, Washington, 1975—79, Walter Kaitz Found., 1981—. Named Man of Yr., Cablevision Mag., 1972; named one of Forbes' Richest Americans, 2006. Mem.: Internat. Radio and TV Soc., Nat. Cable TV Assn. (nat. chmn. 1973—74, dir. 1968—75, 1982—, Larry Boggs award 1975), Amherst Coll. Soc. Alumni (pres. 1982—84, exec. com. 1982—, chmn. 1987—). Office: The Pilot House Lewis Wharf Boston MA 02110

HOSTETTER, MARGARET K., pediatrician, medical educator; children: Mayme Kendrick, John Heard. BA summa cum laude, Denison U., Granville, Ohio, 1970; MD magna cum laude, Baylor Coll. Medicine, Houston, 1975. Diplomate Am. Bd. Pediatrics with subspecialty in pediat. infectious diseases. Resident Children's Hosp., Boston; fellow in pediat. infectious disease Harvard Med. Sch./Beth Israel Hosp., Boston; mem. faculty U. Minn., Mpls., 1982—98, Am. Legion Heart Rsch. prof., endowed chair, 1992—98; prof. pediats., sect. chief pediat. immunology Yale U., New Haven, 1998, founder Yale Internat. Adoption Clinic, 1998, dir. Yale Child Health Rsch. Ctr., 1998—2002; chair pediatrics, physician-in-chief Yale-New Haven Children's Hosp., 2002—; Jean McLean Wallace prof. pediat., endowed chair Yale U., New Haven, 2004—. Program dir. Pediat. Scientist Devel. Program, 1996—. Editor: Ruldoph's Textbook of Pediatrics. Co-chair Success by Six Initiative United Way of Greater New Haven, 2004—05; mem. adv. coun. Nat. Inst. Child Health and Human Devel., chair of public policy and planning sub-com.; chair, co-chair grant rev. panels Veterans Adminstrn., March of Dimes, NIH, Burroughs Welcome Fund. Named Nat. Merit Scholar; named to Best Doctors in Am.; recipient Am. Acad. Pediatrics award for Excellence in Rsch., Samuel Rosenthal award, E. Mead Johnson award, Soc. Pediat. Rsch., Maxwell Finland award, Infectious Diseases Soc. Am.; John A. and George N. Hartford fellow, 1984—87. Mem.: Pediat. Infectious Diseases Soc., Infectious Diseases Soc. Am. (elected to Inst. Medicine 2001), Soc. Pediat. Rsch., Am. Pediat. Sco., Assn. Am. Physicians, Am. Soc. Clin. Investigation, Inst. of Medicine of NAS, Alpha Omega Alpha, Phi Beta Kappa. Achievements include 5 patents in field. Office: Yale Univ Sch Medicine 333 Cedar St LMP 4085 PO Box 208064 New Haven CT 06520-8064

HOSTETTLER, JOHN NATHAN, former congressman; b. Evansville, Ind., July 19, 1961; s. Earl Eugene and Esther Aline (Hollingsworth) H.; m. Elizabeth Ann Hamman, Nov. 12, 1983; children: Matthew, Amanda, Jaclyn, Jared BSME, Rose-Hulman Inst. Tech., 1983. Reg. profl. engr. Engr. So. Ind. Gas and Electric, Evansville, 1986-94; mem. US Congress from 8th Ind. dist., Washington, 1995—2007; mem. agrl. com., homeland security com., judiciary com. Vice chair House Armed Services Comm. Special Oversight Panel on Terrorism, 2001—07. Deacon 12th Avenue Gen. Baptist, 1986-1995. Republican. Baptist.

HOSTLER, CHARLES WARREN, retired ambassador, international affairs consultant; b. Chgo., Dec. 12, 1919; s. Sidney Marvin and Catherine (Marshall) Hostler; m. Chin-Yeh Rose Hostler; 1 child, Charles Warren Jr. BA, U. Calif. at Los Angeles, LA, 1942; MA, Am. U., Beirut, Lebanon, 1955, Georgetown U., 1950, PhD, 1956. Commd. 2d lt. U.S. Air Force, 1942, advanced through grades to col., 1955; ret., 1963; dir. internat. ops. McDonnell Douglas Corp., Middle East, N.Africa, Beirut, 1965-67, mgr. internat. ops. Paris, 1963-65, mgr. internat. mktg., missiles and space, 1967-69; pres. Hostler Investment Co., Coronado, Calif., 1967—; chmn. bd. Irvine (Calif.) Nat. Bank, 1972-74; dir. Wynn's Internat., Inc., Fullerton, Calif., 1971-74; dep. asst. sec. for internat. commerce, dir. Bur. Internat. Commerce, U.S. Dept. Commerce, Washington, 1974-76; regional v.p. Mid-East and Africa, E-Systems Inc., Cairo, 1976-77; pres. Pacific SW Capital Corp., San Diego, 1977-89; ambassador U.S. Govt., Bahrain, 1989-93. Hon. consul gen. Kingdom of Bahrain, 1993—; adj. prof. polit. sci. San Diego State U., 1999—. Author: Turkism and the Soviets, 1957, The Turks of Central Asia, 1993, Soldier to Ambassador, 2004. Chmn. Calif. Contractors State Lic. Bd., 1973—79, San Diego County Local Agy. Formation Commn., 1979—89, Calif. State Park and Recreation Commn., 1983—89; pres. San Diego Consular Corps, 1996—98; chmn., bd. dirs. People-to-People Internat. Decorated Purple Heart, Legion of Merit, Legion of Honor (France); recipient decorations from 9 nations, Eisenhower Disting. Svc. award, Fgn. Affairs award for Pub. Svc., U.S. State Dept., Pub. Svc. award, U. Calif., L.A., 2005. Mem.: VFW (life), Coun. Am. Ambs., Mid. East Inst. (bd. govs. 1962—80, 1993—), Vets. of Office of Strategic Svcs., Mil. Order Purple Heart (life), Mil. Officers Assn. of Am. (life), Navy League (life). Office: 1101 First St # 302 Coronado CA 92118-1474 Personal E-mail: hostler@san.rr.com.

HOSTNIK, CHARLES R., lawyer; AB, Dartmouth Coll., 1976; JD, U. Puget Sound, 1979. Bar: Wash. 1980, U.S. Dist. Ct. (we. dist.) Wash. 1980, U.S. Dist. Ct. (ea. dist.) Wash. 1982, U.S. Ct. Appeals (9th cir.) 1983, Hoh Tribal Ct. 1984, Nisqually Tribal Ct. 1984, Puyallup Tribal Ct. 1984, Shoalwater Bay Tribal Ct. 1984, Skokomish Tribal Ct. 1984. Asst. atty. gen. Atty. Gen.'s Office State of Wash., Olympia, 1980-84; assoc. Kane, Vandeberg, Hartinger & Walker, Tacoma, 1984-87; ptnr. Anderson, Burns & Hostnik, Tacoma, 1988—. Trial and appellate judge N.W. Intertribal Ct. Sys., Edmonds, Wash., 1986—2000. Author: (chpt.) Washington Practice, 1989. Office: Anderson Burns & Hostnik 6915 Lakewood Dr W Ste A1 Tacoma WA 98467-3299 Office Phone: 253-475-4200.

HOSTON, GERMAINE ANNETTE, political science professor; b. Trenton, NJ; d. Walter Lee and Veretta Louise H. AB in Politics summa cum laude, Princeton U., 1975; MA in Govt., Harvard U., 1978, PhD in Govt., 1981. Rsch. asst. Princeton U., NJ, 1973-75; tchg. asst. Harvard U., Cambridge, Mass., 1977-78; asst. prof. polit. sci. Johns Hopkins U., Balt., 1980-86, assoc. prof. polit. sci., 1986-92; prof. polit. sci. U. Calif., San Diego, 1992—, dir. Ctr. for Democratization and Econ. Devel., 1993-99; founder, pres. Inst. Trans Pacific Studies in Values, Culture and Politics, 1999—. Vis. prof. L'Ecole des Hautes Etudes en Sci. Sociales, Paris, 1986, Osaka City U., Japan, 1990, U. Tokyo, 1991; faculty advisor Chinese lang. program Johns Hopkins U., 1981-92, undergrad. ethics bd., 1980-83, pub. interest investment adv. com., 1982-85, undergrad. admissions com., 1983-84, 86-89, pres.'s human climate task force, 1987, dir. undergrad. program, 1987, 88-89, mem. com. undergrad. studies, 1987-91, organizer comparative politics colloquium, 1987-89, dept. colloquium, 1987-89, 91-92; Japanese studies program com. U. Calif., San Diego, 1992—, Chinese studies program, 1994—, field coord. comparative politics, 1994—95, dir. grad. studies comparative politics, 1997-98; bd. dir. Inst. East-West Security Studies, NYC, 1990-97; Am. adv. com. Japan Found., 1992—; edn. abroad program com. U. Calif., 1996—; adv. com. Calif. Ctr. Asia Soc.; mem. com. tech. comms. Inst. East West Security Studies, 1997—; participant numerous workshops and seminars; lectr. in field. Author: Marxism and the Crisis of Development in Prewar Japan: The Debate on Japanese Capitalism, 1986, The State, Identity, and the National Question in China and Japan, 1994, (with others) The Biographical Dictionary of Neo-Marxism, 1985, The Biographical Dictionary of Marxism, 1986, Culture and Identity: Japanese Intellectuals During the Interwar Years, 1990, The Routledge Dictionary of Twentieth-Century Political Thinkers, 1992; mem. editl. bd. Jour. Politics, 1997—2001; contbr. articles to profl. jours. Active Md. Food Com., 1983-92, program concepts subcom. CROSS ROADS Com., Diocese of Md., 1987-88, outreach com. St. David's Episcopal Ch., Balt., standing commn. human affairs Gen. Conv. of the Episcopal Ch., 1991-97; chair peace and justice commn. Episcopal Diocese Md., 1984-87, co-chair companion diocese com., 1987-92, chair CROSS ROADS program bd., 1988-92; exec. bd. dir. Balt. Clergy and Laity Concerned, 1985-86; alternate, regular lay del. 69th Gen. Conv. of The Episcopal Ch., Detroit, 1988; trustee Va. Theol. Sem., 1988-2000; lay del. 70th Gen. Conv. of The Episcopal Ch., Phoenix, Ariz., 1991; dep. Nat. Conv. Episcopal Ch., 1988-93. Am. Legion Aux. scholar, 1972, Am. Logistical Assn. scholar, 1972-76; fellow Harvard U., 1975-77, NSF, 1975-77; Lehman fellow Harvard U., 1978-79, Fgn. Lang. and Area Studies fellow, 1978-79; fellow Am. Assn. Univ. Women Ednl. Found., 1979-80; Fgn. Rsch. scholar U. Tokyo, 1979, 82, 84, 85, 86, 91; Travel grantee Assn. Asian Studies, Japan-U.S. Friendship Commn., 1981; Internat. fellow Internat. Fedn. Univ. Women, 1982, 83; Postdoctoral grantee Social Sci. Rsch. Coun., 1983; fellow NEH, 1983; Kenan Endowment grantee Johns Hopkins U., 1984-85; fellow Rockefeller Found. Internat. Rels., 1985-88; Travel grantee Assn. Asian Studies, 1991; grantee Japan-US Friendship Commn., 1997; rsch. grantee Acad. Senate Com. on Rsch., 1996. Mem. Asia Soc. (trustee 1994—2000), Am. Polit. Sci. Assn. (mem. coun. 1991-93, mem. com. on internat. polit. sci. 1997—2003, v.p. 1998—), Assn. Asian Studies (mem. N.E. Asia coun. 1992-95, vice-chair N.E. Asia coun. 1993—94, nominated editor Jour. Asian Studies 1994, mem. coun. on fgn. rels. 1990—), Internat. Platform Assn., Pacific Coun. on Internat. Policy, Women's Fgn. Policy Group. Democrat. Episcopalian. Avocations: reading, cooking, sailing, tennis, working out. Office: 9921 Carmel Mountain Rd Ste 323 San Diego CA 92129 Home Phone: 858-549-3189; Office Phone: 888-489-0882. Business E-Mail: ghoston@myesa.com.

HOSTOVICH, JOHN LARRY, lawyer; BA in Polit. Sci., St. Vincent Coll., Latrob, Pa., 1974; AS in Specialized Tech., Triangle Tech. Inst., Greensburg, Pa., 1980; JD, Thomas Jefferson Sch. Law, San Diego, 1989. Profl. musician self-employed, Pa., 1974—85; personnel specialist US Govt. Office Personal Mgmt., Washington; mortgage atty. JP Morgan Chase, San Diego, 1993—, GMAC, Horsham, Pa., 1993—2007; atty. First Am. Title, 2007—. Composer (lyrics): (albums) Storm, 1977. Mem.: Am. Mensa (recorder 1994—96), Chinese Am. Kenpo Karate Assn. (Black Belt Rank 1980—). Avocation: Karate (black belt). Home: 1559 Russett Dr Warminster PA 18974 Office Phone: 215-323-3227. Business E-Mail: jhostovich@firstam.com.

HOTALING, ROBERT BACHMAN, urban planner, educator; b. Syracuse, NY, July 19, 1918; s. Elliot Danforth and Florence (Bachman) Hotaling; m. Janet Kelley, Nov. 20, 1943 (dec.); children: Marilyn Kelley, Brock Elliot, William Austin, Richard Chapman; m. Jeanne Bryant, July 31, 1971 (dec.); m. Phyllis Hargrave, July 27, 2001. BS in Environ. Sci. and Forestry, Syracuse U., 1942; M of Urban and Regional Planning, Mich. State U., 1952. Staff dir. McFadzean, Everly Rose and Assocs., Chgo., 1946-49; dir. state and local planning R.I. Exec. Dept., Providence, 1952-55; tech. coord. for planning Interstate hwy. systems through New Eng., R.I., Mass. and Conn., 1954-55; city planning dir., urban renewal planner Portland, Maine, 1955-57; acting dir., sec. Greater Portland Regional Planning Commn., 1956-57; prof. urban and regional planning Coll. Social Sci., Mich. State U., East Lansing, 1957-81; prof. lifelong edn. Inst. Cmty. Devel., Mich. State U., East Lansing, 1957-81; prof. emeritus Mich. State U., 1981—; assoc. McKenna and Assocs., Farmington Hills, Mich., 1992—, Freeman, Smith & Assocs., Lansing, Mich., 1992—, Pub. Sector Cons., Lansing, 1992—. Pres. Urban Cons., Inc., 1962-66; pres., owner Robert B. Hotaling and Assoc., 1949—; expert witness to law firms, state and fed. agys., philanthropic orgns.; cons., lectr., seminarian Mich. Twp. Assn., 1963-81, Mich. Mcpl. League, 1978-94; mem. Mich. State Bd. of Registration for Profl. Community Planners, 1967-81, chmn., 1970-72, 76-79; cons. to state agys., polit. orgns. and corps. Author: Michigan Local Planning Commissioners Handbook (3 edits.), Michigan Township Planning and Zoning Handbook (2 edits.); chmn. editorial com. Mich. Laws Relating to Planning (3 edits.); contbr. articles to profl. jours. Mem. Mich. State Bd. Registration for Profl. Cmty. Planners State Exam. Com., 1969, 1999, Am. Inst Planners Nat. Exam. Com. for Profl. Planners, 1977—78; mem. twp. planning commn. Meridian Twp., Ingham County, Mich., 1958—70, 1987—94, 1996—2001, chmn., 1969—70, 1998—2000, chmn. charter com., 1970—73; mem. Meridian Twp. Zoning Bd. of Appeals, 1969—70, 1987, chmn., 1969—70; mem. strategic planning com. for planning future of Meridian Twp. Gov.'s State Legis. Zoning Revision Com., 1977—79; bd. dirs. Mich. Parks Assn., 1960—68; charter mem. Am. Inst. Cert. Profl. Cmty. Planners, 1954—81; pres. Cadgewith Farms Homeowners Assn., 2002—05. Capt. C.E. US Army, 1942—46. Recipient Meritorious Svc. award Mich. Mcpl. League, 1994. Mem. Mich. Soc. Consulting Planners (bd. dirs. 1979—). Episcopalian. Home and Office: PO Box 304 Haslett MI 48840-0304 Business E-Mail: rbhjbh@aol.com.

HOTCHKISS, ANDRA RUTH, lawyer; b. Beloit, Wis., Aug. 6, 1946; d. Hilton Delos and Katherine Ruth (Huffer) H.; m. Robert K. Byron, May 31, 1977 (dec. 1978); m. Gerald Thomas Marsischky, Feb. 25, 1990. BA cum laude, Oberlin Coll., 1968; JD, Harvard U., 1971. Bar: Mass. 1971, Calif. 1982, US Dist. Ct. Mass. 1975, US Ct. Fed. Claims 1987. Dep. gen. counsel Mass. Dept. Pub. Health, Boston, 1971-78; asst. atty. gen. Mass. Dept. Atty. Gen., Boston, 1978-85; assoc. Behar & Kalman, Boston, 1985-88, Sullivan & Worcester, Boston, 1989-92, ptnr., 1992-97, of counsel, 1997—. Instr. legal writing Harvard U., Cambridge, Mass., 1984, 85. Mem. adv. com. Robert K. Byron Pub. Svc. award, 1978—; elected rep. Oberlin Coll. Nat. Alumni Coun., 1973-83, reunion gift com. co-chair, 1993. Mem. ABA, Mass. Bar Assn., Boston Bar Assn., Am. Health Lawyers Assn., Women's Bar Assn. Mass., Civil Liberties Union Mass. Avocations: flute, cross country skiing, gardening, cats, travel. Office: Sullivan & Worcester 1 Post Office Sq Boston MA 02109 Office Phone: 617-338-2811. Business E-Mail: ahotchkiss@sandw.com.

HOTCHKISS, HARLEY N., professional hockey team owner, oil industry executive; b. Tillsonburg, Ont., Can., 1927; m. Rebecca Hotchkiss; children: Paul, Brenda, John, Richard, Jeffrey. BS with high honours, Mich. State U., 1951, DSc (hon.), 2000; LLD (hon.), U. Calgary, 1996. Geologist Can. Superior Energy, 1951; with Petroleum and Natural Gas Dept. Can. Imperial Bank of Commerce, 1953; pres. Alcon Petroleum, 1959—67; pres., dir. Spartan Holdings Ltd.; co-owner Calgary Flames, 1980—, CEO, gov. Dir. Hockey Hall of Fame; chmn. bd. govs. NHL, 1995—2007; bd. dirs. Conwest Exploration Co. Ltd., Nova Corp., Alberta Energy Co., Landin Resources, Jascan Resources, TransCanada Pipelines, Telus Corp. Chmn. bd. trustees Alberta Heritage Found. for Med. Rsch.; past chmn. Foothills Hosp. Bd.; vol. United Way, Calgary Family Svc. Bur., Alberta Paraplegic Assn., Mich. State U. Found. Bd.; gov., chair Alberta Govs., Olympic Trust of Can. Served in Can. Merchant Marine, 1944—45. Decorated Officer Order of Can.; named to Can. Petroleum Hall of Fame, 2004; recipient Alberta Order of Excellence, 1998, Disting. Bus. Leader Award, 2006, Outstanding Alumni Award, Mich. State U., 1989, Disting. Hockey Alumnus Award, 1998. Mem.: Soc. of Petroleum Engrs., Am. Inst. of Metallurgical Engrs., Geological Assn. of Can., Am. Assn. of Geologists, Can. Soc. of Petroleum Geologists, Can. Inst. of Mining and Metallurgy and Petroleum, Geologists and Geophysicists of Alberta, Assn. of Profl. Engrs., Griffiths Island Club, Ranchmen's Club, Calgary Petroleum Club. Achievements include being inducted into the Hockey Hall of Fame, 2006. Office: Calgary Flames PO Box 1540 Stn M Calgary AB Canada T2P 3B9*

HOTCHKISS, HENRY WASHINGTON, real estate broker, financial consultant; b. Meshed, Iran, Oct. 31, 1937; s. Henry and Mary Bell (Clark) Hotchkiss. BA, Bowdoin Coll., 1958. French tchr. Choate Sch., Wallingford, Conn., 1959—62; v.p. Chem. Bank, NYC, 1962—80, Chem. Bank Internat., San Francisco, 1973—80; dir. corp. rels., mgr. Credit Suisse, San Francisco, 1980—87; fin. cons., 1989—; with Dan Mello Real Estate, 1994—2003, Mello & Hotchkiss Real Estate, 2003—. Bd. dirs. Calif. Coun. Internat. Trade, 1976—87; dir. Indonesia-U.S. Bus. Seminar, LA, 1979. Bd. dirs. Gordonstown Am. Found., 1986—2004, pres., 1986—99; chmn. Capt. Joshua Slocum Centennial Com., Fairhaven, Mass., 1995—98; bd. dirs. Joshua Slocum Soc. Internat., Inc., 1998—2001; assoc. bd. regents L.I. Coll. Hosp., 1969—71, pres., 1971, bd. regents, 1971—73. Capt. USAR, 1958—69. Mem.: Soc. of the Cin., SAR, Mayflower Soc., St. Francis Yacht Club (San Francisco), Explorers Club N.Y. (treas. No. Calif. chpt. 1984—86). Home: 80 Fort St Fairhaven MA 02719-2812

HOTCHNER, AARON EDWARD, author; b. St. Louis, June 28, 1920; s. Samuel and Sally (Rossman) H.; children: Timothy, Holly, Tracy. AB, LLB, Washington U., St. Louis, 1941, LHD (hon.), 1992. Bar: Mo. 1941. Practiced law in, St. Louis, 1941-42; articles editor Cosmopolitan mag., 1948-50. V.p., treas. Newman's Own, Inc.; v.p. Hole in the Wall Gang Camp. Freelance writer short stories and articles in various mags. including Sat. Eve. Post, Esquire, Readers Digest, 1950—; TV playwright Playhouse 90, 1958-60; adapted major Hemingway works for TV including For Whom The Bell Tolls, 1958, The Killers, 1959; writer screenplay Adventures of a Young Man, 1961; author: The Dangerous American, 1958, Papa Hemingway: A Personal Memoir, 1966, revised, 1999, Treasure, 1970, King of the Hill, 1972, Looking for Miracles, 1974, Doris Day, 1976, Sophia, Living and Loving, 1979, The Man Who Lived at the Ritz, 1981, Choice People, 1984, Hemingway and His World, 1989, Blown Away, 1990, Louisiana Purchase, 1996, After the Storm, 2000, Dreams of Glory, 2001, The Day I Fired Alan Ladd, 2002, (with Paul Newman) Shameless Exploitation, 2003, Everyone Comes to Elaine's, 2004, Dear Papa, Dear Hotch, 2005; playwright: The Short Happy Life, 1961, The White House, 1964, The Hemingway Hero, 1967, Do You Take This Man?, 1970, Sweet Prince, 1980, Let 'Em Rot, 1987, Welcome to the Club, 1989, Courtroom Cantata, 1995, Exactly Like You, 1996, Papa Hemingway (rev.), 1999, Exactly Like You, 1999, After the Storm, 2000, The World of Nick Adams, 2001. Founder, bd. dirs. Hole in the Wall Gang Fund. Served to maj. USAAF, 1942-46, NATOUS. Recipient Disting. Alumni award Law Sch., Washington U., 1992. Mem. Mo. Bar Assn., Writers Guild Am., Dramatists Guild, PEN, Authors Guild, Authors Guild Found. (bd. dirs.), Century Club. Address: 14 Hillandale Rd Westport CT 06880-5225 Home Phone: 203-227-9339; Office Phone: 203-222-0136. Business E-Mail: hotchner@sbcglobal.net.

HOTCHNER, HOLLY, museum director, curator, conservator; BA in Art History and Studio Art, Trinity Coll., 1973; MA in Art History, diploma conservation, N.Y. Inst. Fine Arts, 1982. Exhbns. cataloguer, collections cataloguer Mus. Modern Art, NYC, 1973-76; chief conservator N.Y. Hist. Soc., NYC, 1984-88, dir. mus., 1984-95; dir. Am. Craft Mus. (now Museum of Arts and Design), NYC, 1996—. Bd. dirs. Art Alliance for Contemporary Glass, 1999—, Friends of Fiber Art; chmn. bd. 235 E. 73rd Owners Corp., 1994-2000; mem. edn. com. Whitney Mus. Am. Art, 1994-98; mem. bd. trustees N.Y. Landmarks Conservancy, 1996—; mem. adv. bd. Friends of Contemporary Ceramics; lectr., panelist, juror in field. Fellow Am. Inst. Conservation, Internat. Inst. Conservation; mem. Am. Assn. Mus., Art Table, Phi Beta Kappa. Office: Museum of Arts and Design 40 W 53rd St New York NY 10019-6106 Office Phone: 212-956-3535.

HOTELLING, HAROLD, economics professor, lawyer; b. NYC, Dec. 26, 1945; s. Harold and Susanna Porter (Edmondson) H.; m. Barbara M. Anthony, May 4, 1974; children: Harold, George, James, Claire, Charles. AB, Columbia U., 1966; JD, U. N.C., 1972; MA, Duke U., 1975, PhD, 1982. Bar: N.C. 1973. Legal advisor U. N.C., Chapel Hill, 1972-73; instr. bus. law U. Ky., Lexington, 1977-79, asst. prof., 1980-84; asst. prof. dept. econs. Oakland U., Rochester, Mich., 1984-89; assoc. prof. econs. Lawrence Technol. U., Southfield, Mich., 1989—, chmn. dept. humanities social scis. and comm., 1994-99. Contbr. articles to profl. jours. Lt. j.g. USNR, 1968—70. Episcopalian. Home: 2112 Bretton Dr S Rochester Hills MI 48309-2952 Office: Lawrence Technol U Dept Humanities Southfield MI 48075 Office Phone: 248-204-3530. Business E-Mail: hotelling@ltu.edu.

HOTEZ, PETER JAY, research scientist, educator; b. Hartford, Conn., May 5, 1958; s. Edward Joseph and Jean (Goldberg) H.; m. Ann Elizabeth Frifield, Sept. 14, 1987; children: Matthew, Emily, Rachel, Daniel. BA magna cum laude, Yale U., 1980; PhD, Rockefeller U., 1986; MD, Cornell U., 1987. Resident Mass. Gen. Hosp., Boston, 1987-89; postdoctoral fellow Yale U., New Haven, 1989-91, instr., 1991-92, asst. prof., 1992-95, assoc. prof., 1995—; prof., chair dept. microbiology, topical med. George Wash. U. Vis. prof. Chinese Acad. Preventive Medicine, Shanghai, 1997; adv. bd. Congas Memorial Inst., Sabin Vaccine Inst. Author: Parasitic Diseases, 1995; patentee in field. Recipient Leuenhulme medal Liuenpool Sch. Tropical Medicine, 2006; named hon. prof. Chinese Acad. Preventive Medicine, 1997. Mem. Am. Soc. Tropical Medicine and Hygiene (Ashfond medal 2003), Am. Soc. Parasitologists (Wand medal 1999), Pediatric Infectious Disease Soc. (adv. bd. jour., Young Investigator award 1993), Soc. Pediatric Rsch. Home: 4547 Minuteman Dr Rockville MD 20853-1263 Office: 2300 I St NW Washington DC 20037 Home Phone: 301-570-7611; Office Phone: 202-994-3532. E-mail: photez@gwu.edu.

HOTH, STEVEN SERGEY, lawyer, educator; b. Jan. 30, 1941; s. Donald Leroy and Ina Dorothy (Barr) H.; m. JoEllen Maly, July 29, 1967; children: Andrew Steven, Peter Lindsey. AB, Grinnell Coll., 1962; JD, U. Iowa, 1966; postgrad., U. Pa., 1968, Oxford U., Eng., 1973. Bar: U.S. Ct. Appeals (8th cir.) 1966, U.S. Tax Ct. 1967, U.S. Ct. Claims 1967, U.S. Dist. Ct. Iowa 1968, U.S. Dist. Ct. ND 1968, U.S. Dist. Ct. SD 1968, U.S. Supreme Ct. 1973, U.S. Ct. Appeals (7th cir.) 1982. Law clk. to chief justice U.S. Ct. Appeals (8th cir.), Fargo, ND, 1967-68; assoc. Hirsch, Adams, Hoth & Krekel, Burlington, Iowa, 1968-72, ptnr., 1972-91; pvt. practice Burlington, 1992—. Asst. atty. Des Moines County, Burlington, 1968-72, atty., 1972-83; alt. mcpl. judge, Burlington, 1968-69; lectr. criminal law Southeastern C.C., West Burlington, 1972-82; assoc. prof. polit. sci. Iowa Wesleyan Coll., Mt. Pleasant, 1981-82; Pres. of Amerail, Inc., Iowa Truck Rail, Amerail, Inc.; pres. Burlington Truck Rail, Burlington Short Line R.R. Inc., Iowa Internat. Investments, Burlington Storage and Transfer; sec. Burlington Loading Co. Contbr. numerous articles to profl. jours. Chmn. Des Moines County Civil Svc. Commn.; trustee Charles H. Rand Lecture Trust; mem. Des Moines County Conf. Com., Des Moines County Conf. Bd.; dir. Burlington Med. Ctr. Staff Found.; moderator 1st Congl. Ch., Burlington; bd. dir. UN Assn.; clk. Burlington North Bottoms Levy and Drainage Dist.; bd. mem., pres. Burlington Cmty. Sch. Dist. Bd. Edn., chmn. commn. on ministry, mem. exec. com. Nat. Assn. Congl. Christian Chs., moderator; treas. 1st dist. Dem. Com.; bd. dirs. Legal Aid Soc. Planned Parenthood Des Moines County. Recipient Chmn.'s award ARC, 1980; Reginald Heber Smith fellow in legal aid Cheyenne River Indian Reservation, Eagle Butte, SD, 1967-68; named Lord of Foleshill. Mem. Missionary Soc.-Nat. Assn. Congl. Christian Chs., ABA (internat. sect., tax sect.), Iowa State Bar Assn. (liaison to Iowa Med. Soc.), Des Moines County Bar Assn., Am. Judicature Soc., Agrl. Law Com., Iowa Def. Coun., Iowa Archaeol. Soc., Soc. for German Am. Studies, Manorial Soc. Gt. Britain, Grinnell Coll. Alumni Assn. (bd. dirs.), Malawi Soc., Burlington-West Burlington C. of C. (bd. dirs.), Nat. Assn. Congrl. Christian Ch., Burlington Golf Club, New Crystal Lake Club (pres.), Elks, Eagles, Masons, Rotary. Office: PO Box 982 Hoth Bldg 200 Jefferson St Burlington IA 52601 Office Phone: 319-754-5000. Business E-Mail: hothlaw@mchci.com.

HOTOPP, ALICE CLAUDINE, music educator, soprano; b. Richmond, Ind., Dec. 18, 1932; d. Kenneth Lee and June Rebecca Van Ausdal; m. Thomas Leroy Hotopp, Jan. 15, 1956; children: Stephen Michael, Tonia Lee Miller, Daniel Thomas. MusB, Oberlin Conservatory, Ohio, 1954. Grad. asst. Oberlin Conservatory, 1955; pvt. voice tchr. Dayton, Ohio, 1958—; mem. voice faculty U. Dayton, Ohio, 1973—2002; singer Operation Opera, Dayton, 1975—87; singer, actress La Comedia Dinner Theater, Springboro, Ohio, 1976—77; mem. voice faculty Antioch Coll., Ohio, 1976—79; singer Opera Fun-atics, Dayton, 1979—89, Dayton Opera, 1983. Vol. Victoria Theater, Loft, Schuster Ctr., Dayton Playhouse, 1996—2006; visit supr. Erma's House, Dayton, 1999—2005. Named Ofcl. Ohio Soprano, Bi-Centennial Chorus, Interlochen, Mich., 1976; recipient cert. of achievement, Ohio Vocal Arts Network, 2000, Amici Musicae award, U. Dayton, 2002. Mem.: Nat. Assn. Tchrs. Singing (voice adjudicator 1983—2005). Achievements include a scholarship being named in her honor at the University of Dayton. Avocations: watercolor painting, travel.

HOTZ, HENRY PALMER, retired physicist; b. Fayetteville, Ark., Oct. 17, 1925; s. Henry Gustav and Stella (Palmer) H.; m. Marie Brase, Aug. 22, 1952; children: Henry Brase, Mary Palmer, Martha Marie. BS, U. Ark., 1948; PhD, Washington U., St. Louis, 1953. Asst. prof. physics Auburn U., Ala., 1953-58, Okla. State U., Stillwater, 1958-64; assoc. prof. Marietta Coll., Ohio, 1964-66; physicist, scientist-in-residence U.S. Naval Radiol. Def. Lab., San Francisco, 1966-67; assoc. prof. U. Mo., Rolla, 1967-71; physicist Qanta Metrix div. Finnigan Corp., Sunnyvale, Calif., 1971-74; sr. scientist Nuclear Equipment Corp., San Carlos, Calif., 1974-79, Envirotech Measurement Systems, Palo Alto, Calif., 1979-82, Dohrmann div. Xertex Corp., Santa Clara, Calif., 1982-86; sr. scientist Rosemount Analytical Div. Dohrmann, 1983-91; cons. Burlingame, Calif., 1991-2001; ret., 2001. Cons. USAF, 1958-62; mem. lectr. selection com. for Hartman Hotz Lectrs. in law, liberal arts U. Ark. Served with USNR, 1944-46. Named Disting. Alumnus, Fulbright Coll. Arts and Scis., U. Ark., 2006. Mem. Am. Phys. Soc., Am. Assn. Physics Tchrs., AAAS, Phi Beta Kappa, Sigma Xi, Sigma Pi Sigma, Pi Mu Epsilon, Sigma Nu Lodges: Masons. Methodist. Home: 290 Stilt Ct Foster City CA 94404-1323

HOTZ, ROBERT LEE, writer, editor; b. Hartford, Conn., Mar. 7, 1950; s. Robert B. and Joan (Willison) H.; m. Jennifer Hall Arlen, May 21, 1988; children: Michael Arlen, Robert Arlen. BA magna cum laude, Tufts U., 1973, MA, 1973. Tech. editor Intermetrics, Inc., Cambridge, Mass., 1973-76; reporter The News-Virginian, Waynesboro, 1976-79, The Pitts. Press, 1979-84; sci. writer The Atlanta Jour.-Constn., 1984-90, projects editor, 1991-93, sci. editor, 1993; sci. writer The LA Times, 1993—2007; sci. columnist Wall St. Jour., NYC, 2007—. Participant NSF Antarctica Expeditions, 1987, 95, 01. Author: Designs on Life: Exploring the New Frontiers of Human Fertility, 1991; contbr. articles to profl. publs. Recipient Sci. Journalism award AAAS, 1977, 88, 97, Ga. Best Reporting award AP, 1986, Metro Staff Pulitzer Prize spot news, 1995, Walter Sullivan award Am. Geophys. Soc., 1995, Journalism award ASCE, 1995, Media award Nat. Mental Health Assn., 1996; nominated Pulitzer prize 1986, 2004. Mem. Nat. Assn. Sci. Writers (bd. dirs.), Soc. Profl. Journalists (Ray Sprigle Meml. award 1982, 84, Nat. Mag. Writing award 2000, Non-Deadline Reporting award 2004), Sigma Xi (hon.), Nat. Press Club. Episcopalian. Home: 237 Thompson St Apt 7B New York NY 10012 Office: The LA Times NY Bur 2 Park Ave 8th Fl New York NY 10016

HOU, J. STEVE, pathologist; s. Yuanyao and Xiu Ying Hou; m. Yan Liu; children: Kevin, Kristy. MD, Weifang Med. Coll., Shandong, China, 1982. Diplomate Am. Bd. Pathology, 1998. Attending pathologist Drexel U. Coll. Medicine, Phila, 1998—. Prof., dir. surg. pathology and hematopathology Drexel U., Coll. Medicine, Phila., 2005—. Office: Drexel Univ Coll Medicine Dept Pathology 245 N 15th St Philadelphia PA 19102 Office Phone: 215-762-3753. Business E-Mail: houj1@yahoo.com.

HOU, THOMAS YIZHAO, mathematician; s. Sum-Hing Hau and Sau-Ying Yip; m. Yu-Chung Chang, Sept. 1, 2001; children: Anthony C., George C. PhD in Math., UCLA, 1987. Asst. prof. NYU, NYC, 1989—93; assoc. prof. Calif. Inst. of Tech., Pasadena, Calif., 1993—98, prof., 1998—, Charles Lee Powell prof., 2004—, dept. chair, 2000—; founding editor-in-chief, multiscale modeling and simulation Soc. for Indsl. and Applied Math., Phila., 2002—. Assoc. dir., ctr. for integrative multiscale modeling and simulation Calif. Inst. of Tech., Pasadena, 2001—; spkr. in field. Author: (research article) Physics of Fluids; contbr. articles to profl. jours. Recipient Morningside Gold medal in Applied Math., Internat. Congress of Chinese Mathematicians, 2004, Computational and Applied Scis. award, US Assn. for Computational Mechanics, 2005, James H. Wilkinson Prize in Numerical Analysis and Sci. Computing., Soc. for Indsl. and Applied Math., 2001, Francois N. Frenkiel award for Fluid Mechanics, Am. Phys. Soc., Divsn. of Fluid Mechanics, 1998, Feng Kang prize in Sci. Computing, Chinese Acad. of Scis., 1997; fellow, Alfred Sloan Found., 2000-2002. Mem.: Soc. for Indsl. and Applied Math. (editor-in-chief, multiscale modeling and simulation 2002—06), Am. Math. Soc., Phi Tau Phi Scholastic Honor Soc. (life; treas. for the nat. office 2004—06). Office: Calif Inst Inst Tech 1200 E California Blvd MC 217-50 Pasadena CA 91125 Office Phone: 626-395-4546. Business E-Mail: hou@acm.caltech.edu.

HOUCHIN, SHANNON MARIE, secondary school educator; b. Amarillo, Tex., Nov. 7, 1973; d. Edwin Lee and Jacquelynn Marie McDuffee; m. Baeron Lee Houchin, June 10, 2001. B of English, West Tex. A&M U., Canyon, 2006. Gymnastics dir., head coach Maverick Boys and Girls Club, Amarillo, Tex., 1992—96; elite sales assoc. Zales Jewelers, Amarillo, 1996—2001; owner, dir., head coach Shannon's Gymnastics, Hereford, Tex., 2001—06; elite sales assoc. Whitehall Jewelers, Amarillo, 2002—04; jr. asst. mgr. Samuels Jewelers, Amarillo, 2004—05; tchr. jr. and sr. English, coach jr. varsity cheerleading Weatherford HS, Tex., 2006—. Tchr. piano, voice Lifesongs Piano Studio, Amarillo, Weatherford, 1994—. Conservative. Avocations: horseback riding, backpacking, piano, fishing, travel. Office: Weatherford High Sch 2121 Bethel Rd Weatherford TX 76086 Home Phone: 806-282-2083; Office Phone: 817-598-2858 5158. Business E-Mail: shouchin@weatherfordisd.com.

HOUCK, ALEDA JEAN, dean; b. Ironton, Mo., Apr. 9, 1943; d. Otto Arthur and Alma Louise Bates; m. Floyd Wilson (div.); children: Jeffrey Wilson, Bradley Wilson; m. George Houck, Aug. 2, 1992. BA, Ky. Wesleyan U., Owensboro, 1969; MA, Western Ky. U., Bowling Green, 1974; EdD, Ind. U., Bloomington, 1977. Tchr. Owensboro Pub. Schs., 1969—78; prof. Morehead State U., Ky., 1978—90; assoc. dean Coll. Edn. Calif. State U., Long Beach, 1990—95, dean Coll. Edn., 1995—. Mem. editl. bd. Jour. Sch. Leadership, Jour. Humanistic Edn. and Devel.; editor Ky. Assn. Counseling and Devel. Jour., 1984—86; presenter in field. Editor (with K. Cohn and C. Cohn): Partnering to Lead Educational Renewal: High Quality Teachers, High Quality Schools, 2004; contbr. articles to profl. jours. Recipient Pres.' award for univ. svc., Morehead State U., 1985, Advancement of Women award, Pres.' Commn. Status of Women, 2004, Svc. Learning award, Blast, Long Beach, 2005. Democrat. Home: 5821 Woodboro Dr Huntington Beach CA 92649 Office Phone: 562-985-4513. Business E-Mail: houck@csulb.edu.

HOUCK, JAMES W., career military officer, lawyer; m. Susan Houck. Grad., US Naval Acad., 1980; JD, U. Mich. Law Sch., 1985; LLM in Internat. and Comparative Law, Georgetown U., 1993. Bar: Mich. Judge adv., trial counsel, sr. def. counsel Naval Legal Svc. Office, Mayport, Fla., 1985—87; staff mem. Vice Chief Naval Ops., 1987—88; exec. asst., aide Dep. JAG, 1988—89; staff atty. adminstrv. law divsn. (code 13) Office of JAG, 1989—90; legis. liaison atty. USN Office of Legis. Affairs, 1990—92; force/fleet judge adv. for comdr. US Naval Forces Ctrl. Command and US 5th Fleet, 1993—95; asst. spl. counsel Chief of Naval Ops.; dep. legal counsel Chmn. Joint Chiefs of Staff, 1996; spl. asst. legal and legis. matters Sec. Navy, 1998; fleet judge adv. for the comdr. US Fleet Forces Command and US Atlantic Fleet, 2001; exec. asst. USN JAG; head Naval Legal Svc. Office North Ctrl., 2003; spl. counsel Chief Naval Ops. Adm. Vern Clark, 2004—05; spl. asst. transformation JAG; dep. JAG, comdr. Naval Legal Svc. Command USN, 2006—. Decorated Def. Superior Svc. medal, Legion of Merit (five awards), Def. Meritorious Svc. medal, Meritorious Svc. medal (three awards), Navy Commendation medal (two awards), Navy Achievement medal. Office: USN 1200 Navy Pentagon Washington DC 20350*

HOUCK, MARK HEDRICH, engineering educator; b. Balt., May 14, 1951; s. Walter C. and Ruth Houck; m. Margaret Ann Nolan, Sept. 1, 1972; children: Timothy Daniel, Megan Hillary, Brigid Elyse B in Engring. Sci., Johns Hopkins U., Balt., 1972, PhD, 1976. Registered profl. engr., Ind., Md., diplomate, Am. Acad. Water Resources Engrs., cert. profl. hydrologist, Am. Inst. Hydrology, 2005, bd. cert., Am. Acad. Environ. Engr. Rsch. asst. prof. dept. civil engring. U. Wash., Seattle, 1975—77; from asst prof. to prof. sch. civil engring. Purdue U., West Lafayette, Ind., 1977—92; dr. of univ. Johns Hopkins U., Balt., 1989—90; prof. civil, environ. and infrastructure engring. Volgenau Sch. Info. Tech. and Engring. George Mason U. Fairfax, Va., 1992—, chair CEIE dept., 1998—2002. Pres. Omtek Engring., Inc., West Lafayette, 1983-1991; v.p. Water Resources Mgmt., Inc., Columbia, Md., 1988-89; vis. prof. Heriot-Watt U., Edinburgh, Scotland, 2003 Assoc. editor Water Resources Rsch. Jour., 1981-85; co-editor Jour. Civil Engring. & Environ. Sys., 2004-06. Fellow ASCE (chmn. water resources sys. com. 1984, chmn. emerging techs. com. 1986-88, Huber Rsch. prize 1988); mem. Am. Geophys. Union, Inst. Ops. Rsch. and Mgmt. Sci., Chi Epsilon, Sigma Xi, Omega Rho. Office: George Mason U Volgenau Sch Info Tech & Engring George Dept Civil Enviro and Infrast Eng MS 6C1 Fairfax VA 22030 Office Phone: 703-993-1737. Business E-Mail: mhouck@gmu.edu.

HOUCK, RUDOLPH S.(ROB), lawyer; b. Scranton, Pa., Nov. 15, 1947; Student, Ludwig-Maximilian Univ., Institut für ausländisches und internationales Wirtschaftsrecht, Goethe University; BA cum laude, Univ. Tex., Austin, 1969; JD, Univ. Chgo., 1972; LLM, Internat.Law Inst., Georgetown Univ., 1981. Bar: Pa. 1972, NY 1982. Ptnr., chmn., internat. group Alston & Bird LLP, NYC. Mem. Atlantik-Brücke; bd. dir. Deutscher Verein; bus. adv. bd. Am. Coun. on Germany. Office: Alston & Bird LLP 90 Park Ave New York NY 10016-1387 Office Phone: 212-210-9418. Office Fax: 212-210-9444. Business E-Mail: rhouck@alston.com.

HOUDE-WALTER, SUSAN, optics scientist, educator; b. NYC; BA, Sarah Lawrence Coll., 1976; MS, U. Rochester, 1983, PhD, 1987. Co-founder LaserMax, Inc., 1989, pres., 2000—02; prof. optics U. Rochester, 2002—. Presenter in field. Chair editl. adv. com. Optics & Photonics News, spl. editorship Jour. Non-Crystalline Solids, MRS Bulletin. Recipient 3M Faculty award for rsch. Fellow: Am. Ceramic Soc., Optical Soc. Am. (search com. 1997—98, nom. com. 1999, pres.-elect 2004, pres. 2005). Achievements include research in optical materials, especially optical glass and the molecular structure of multicomponent glasses. Office: Inst Optics Wilson Blvd Wilmont Bldg Rochester NY 14627-9000 Office Phone: 585-275-7629. Office Fax: 585-244-4936. Business E-Mail: shw@optics.rochester.edu.

HOUGGARD, SANTA CAROL HALL, family nurse practitioner, consultant; b. Ermine, Ky., Nov. 9, 1940; d. Russell L. and Ila (Amburgey) Hall; m. Byron L. Houggard, Apr. 30, 1965; children: Teresa Bramlet, Sutherland, Ronald L. Diploma, Sch. Profl. Nursing, Harlan, Ky., 1961; BSN cum laude, U. San Diego, 1981, MS in Nursing, 1983. Cert. family nurse practitioner. Staff nurse Whitesburg (Ky.) Meml. Hosp., 1961-62; nurse USN, 1962-65; pvt. duty nurse, 1965-77; nurse practitioner North County Health Svcs., San Marcos, Calif.; clin. adminstr., nurse practitioner Mountain Health Project, Campo, Calif., 1977-79; instr. U. San Diego, 1983-85; ind. contractor family nurse practitioner, Santee, Calif., 1985-88; family nurse practitioner NAVCARE, San Diego, 1988-89, Mountain Health Ctr., Campo, 1989-91, So. Indian Health Coun., 1991-95; prof. nursing Ariz. Western Coll., Yuma, Ariz., 1998—2005; freelance health info. cons. Yuma, Ariz., 2005—. Lt. (j.g.) USN, 1962-65. Mem.: Ariz. Nurses Assn., ANA, Sigma Theta Tau. Home: 12124 S Sandra Ave Yuma AZ 85367-6026 Personal E-mail: houggard@hotmail.com.

HOUGH, AUBREY JOHNSTON, JR., pathologist, physician, educator; b. Little Rock, July 20, 1944; s. Aubrey Johnston and Thelma Willeen (Miller) H.; m. Linda Ann Yaeger, June 10, 1968; children: Charles Prentiss, Robert Page. BA, Hendrix Coll., 1966; MD, Vanderbilt U., 1970. Diplomate Am. Bd. Pathology. From resident dept. pathology to assoc. prof. Vanderbilt U., Nashville, 1970—80; prof. Med. Sci. U. Ark., Little

Rock, 1980—2004, assoc. dean translational rsch., 2002—, disting. prof., 2004—. Clin. assoc. Nat. Inst. Arthritis & Metabolic Disease, Bethesda, Md., 1972-74; chief of staff U. Ark. Hosp., Little Rock, 1986-88; pres. Ark. Acad. Pathology, Little Rock, 1982-86, Coun. of Dept. Chmn. U. Ark. Coll. of Medicine, Little Rock, 1987-88; chief of staff U. Hosp. of Ark., 1986-88, 98-2000; mem. pathology test com. Nat. Bd. Med. Examiners, 1989-92, chmn., 1993-95, comp II com., 1992-95; mem. Nat. Bd. Med. Examiners, 1996-99; mem. residency rev. com. for pathology Accreditation Coun. Med. Edn., 1990-96; mem. statewide com. on bioterrorism, 2002-; mem. Ark. Med. Soc. Com. on Disaster Response, 2006-07. Author: Tumors of the Adrenal Gland, 1987; contbr. numerous articles on orthopedic diseases to profl. jours, chpts. to books; assoc. editor Human Pathology, 1988-97; editorial bds. Am. Jour. Pathology. 1986-1996, Annals of Clinical Lab. Sci., 1989-2006, Am. Jour. Clinical Pathology, 2004-. Alumni fund rep. Hendrix Coll., Conway, Ark., 1983-86; chmn. Shideler Chemistry Edn. Endowment, 1991-97, vice-chair physicians adv. com., 1996; invited keynote lectr. Odyssesy program inauguration, 2004. Served as surgeon, active duty USPHS, 1972-75, reserve, 1974-94. Basic Sci. Grantee Nat. Inst. Gen. Med. Studies, 1978, Altheimer Found., 1984, Nat. Inst. Arthritis, 1988; recipient Dirs. Commendation VA, 1980, Disting. Svc. award U. Ark., Little Rock, 1985, Disting. Alumni Hendrix Coll., 1999. Fellow Coll. Am. Pathologists (field inspector 1977-88); mem. AMA, AAUP, U.S.-Can. Acad. Pathology, Am. Soc. Clin. Pathologists, Am. Soc. Investigative Pathology, Assn. Clin. Scientists (Brown Meml. lectr 1986), Arthur Purdy Stout Soc., Assn. Pathology Chmn. (mem. publ. affairs com. 1985—, chmn. 1993-96), Orthopedic Rsch. Soc., History of Medicine Assocs. (bd. dirs. 1986-88), Assn. Am. Med. Colls. (mem. coun. academic soc. Washington 1985-89, statewide advisory com. bioterrorism, 2002—). Clubs: Bapt. Med. Dental (Memphis) (program chair 1983-84). Democrat. Avocation: fishing. Office: U Ark for Med Scis 4301 W Markham St # 517 Little Rock AR 72205-7101 Home: 209 Buckland Cir Little Rock AR 72223-4535 Home Phone: 501-868-7145; Office Phone: 501-686-5369. Business E-Mail: houghaubreyJ@uams.edu.

HOUGH, DOUGLAS RALPH, museum director; b. Brockville, Ont., Can., Oct. 13, 1928; arrived in US, 1972; s. Howard Leslie and Florence Hough; m. Marion Eileen Bell (div.); children: Deborah, Judith; m. Sarah Louies, Nov. 30, 1985. Supt. restoration Upper Canada Village, Morrisburg, Ont., Canada, 1958—73, supr. svcs., 1961—66, curator bldgs. and machinery, 1966—73; dir. crafts and presentation Edison Inst., Dearborn, Mich., 1973—82; exec. dir. Jr. Mus. Bay County, Panama City, Fla., 1983—86; dir. Mus. Man in Sea, Panama City, 1987—. Cons. Ft. Myers Nature Ctr. and Planetarium, Fla., Maritime and Sci. Tech. HS, Fla., Hale Farms, Bath, Ohio, Wheaton Village, Millville, NJ, Hist. Fayette Townsite, Mich., Ill. Rlwy. Mus., Union, Monmouth County Hist. Assn., Freehold, NJ, Conner Prairie Pioneer Settlement, Noblesville, Ind., T. T. Wentworth Mus., Pensacola, Fla., Heritage Hill State Pk., Green Bay, Wis., Iron River Hist. Mus., Mich.; lectr. in field. Host (radio show) Sta. WKGC Nat. Pub. Radio, 1991—; contbr. articles to profl. jours. Bd. advisors Algonquin Coll. Applied Arts and Tech., 1970—72. Mem.: Early Am. Industries Assn., Am. Assn. Mus. (mem. accreditation com., mem. mus. assessment program 1980—87), Fla. Assn. Mus. Home: 3100 Country Club Dr Panama City FL 32444

HOUGH, LESLIE SELDON, educational association administrator; b. Springfield, Ohio, Oct. 2, 1946; s. Donald Woodrow and Stella Alta (Finney) H.; m. Sharon Ann Cornell, May 31, 1969; children: Amity Melinda, Amanda Michelle, Leslie Elizabeth. BA, Olivet Nazarene U., 1969; MA, U. Va., 1973, PhD, 1977. Co-dir. Ohio labor history project Ohio Hist. Soc., Columbus, 1975-77; dir. archives labor urban affairs Walter P. Reuther Libr. Wayne State U., Detroit, 1992-97; dir. spl. collections Ga. State U., Atlanta, 1977-92, dir. W.J. Usery Jr. Ctr. for the Workpl., 1997—. Cons. Clayton County Water Authority, Riverdale, Ga., 1988-90, Equifax, Inc., Atlanta, 1990-92. Mem. adv. bd. Mich. Hist. Records, Lansing, 1993-97; bd. dirs. Ga. Humanities Coun., Atlanta, 1988-92. With U.S. Army, 1970-71. Democrat. Presbyterian. Avocation: running. Office: Ga State Univ WJ Usery Jr Ctr for Workpl Atlanta GA 30303 Home: 273 Orange St Apt 4 Macon GA 31201-7240

HOUGH, THOMAS HENRY MICHAEL, retired lawyer, educator; b. Midland, Pa., Aug. 4, 1933; s. Bert Patrick and Marguerite (Mullen) H.; m. Jocelyn Peltz, Aug. 20, 1956; children: Jocelyn, Thomas Henry Michael. AB, Dickinson Coll., 1955; JD, Dickinson Sch. Law, 1958. Bar: Pa. 1959, U.S. Ct. Appeals (3d cir.) 1975, U.S. Supreme Ct. 1970. Field atty. NLRB, Pitts., 1959-60; atty. United Steelworkers Am., 1960-68; ptnr. Lucchino, Gaitens & Hough, Pitts., 1968-79, Hough & Gleason, PC, Pitts., 1980-94, Barry Fasulo & Hough, PC, Pitts., 1994—2002, ret., 2002. Adj. assoc. prof. pub. sector arbitration and pub. sector collective bargaining Grad. Sch. Pub. and Internat. Affairs, U. Pitts., 1973-97.

HOUGH, WINSTON, artist; b. Hartford, Mich., July 12, 1928; s. Elbert Vere and Dorris Elizabeth H.; m. Joan Gimse, Oct. 23, 1954 (div. June 1985); m. Alice Christine Daly, Nov. 30, 1985; children: Elliott Vere, Geoffrey Winston, Elise Ingrid, Roderick Garret. BFA, Sch. Art Inst., Chgo., 1955; MA, Northeastern Ill. U., 1971. Asst. prof. art Va. Commonwealth U., Richmond, 1956-62; lectr. art U. Ill., Chgo., 1964-65; tchr. City Colls. Chgo., 1969-90. Guest lectr. art dept. State U. Ill., 1968. *Was staff artist for US Navy from 1946-48 for Jax Air News (station weekly), NAS Jacksonville; did cartoons and photo montages. Since 1952, work has been explorations of invented figures; most of these from imagination. In recent years, has been working more and more from everyday life.* One person shows include South Bend Art Ctr., 1954, Morris Gallery, N.Y.C., 1957, Palmer House Galleries, 1959, I.F.A. Gallery, Washington, 1961, Paul Theobald Book Store Art Gallery, 1978, Concordia U. Ferguson Gallery, 1987, Beverly Arts Ctr., Pillsbury Concourse Gallery, 1988, Art Reach Gallery, Columbus, Ohio, 1990; exhibited in group shows Exhbn. Momentum, 1953, Art Inst. Chgo., 1955, Valentine Mus., 1957-58, 60, Winston-Salem Gallery of Fine Arts, 1958-68, Robert Horn Gallery, N.Y.C., 1961, Roko Gallery, N.Y.C., 1964, I.F.A. Gallery, 1961-83, Evanston Art Ctr., 1973, Benjamin Galleries, 1975, Mclean County Art Ctr., Bloomington, 1987-95, 4th Presbyn. Ch., 1989; represented in pub. collections Midwest Stock Exch. Svc. Corp., Champion Fed. Savs. and Loan. Served USN, 1946—48. Recipient Birmingham Ala. Watercolor Soc. award, 1958, Best of Oils, Best of Acrylics, Rockport Pub., 1996, Best of Show, Bucktown Art Fest., 1997, Watercolor Expressions, 1999; Daniell Vandergrift scholar, 1952; Huntington Hartford Found. fellow, 1959. Mem.: Chgo. Artists Coalition. Address: 937 Echo Ln Glenview IL 60025-3327 E-mail: winalice7@mac.com.

HOUGHTALING, PAMELA ANN, communications professional, writer; b. Catskill, NY, July 8, 1949; d. Stanley Kenneth and Mildred Edythe (Fyfe) H. BA, Princeton U., 1971; M in Internat. Affairs, Russian Inst., Columbia U., 1974, cert., 1976. Internat. rels. analyst Libr. of Congress, Washington, 1974-75, US GAO, Washington, 1976-77; pub. affairs specialist IBM Corp., Washington, 1977-81; sr. external programs analyst IBM World Trade Americas/Far East Corp., North Tarrytown, NY, 1981-82; mgr. labor affairs/bus. practices US Coun. Internat. Bus., NYC, 1982-84; comms. specialist-advt. IBM Corp., Boca Raton, Fla., 1984-86, staff comms. specialist White Plains, NY, 1986-88, comms. cons., 1988-90; sr. mktg. specialist Wang Labs., Bethesda, Md., 1990-93; pub. rels. dir. STG Mktg. Comm., 1993-94; mgr. mktg. comm. Cable & Wireless, Inc., Vienna, Va., 1994-95; tech. comms. cons., journalist Falls Church, Va., 1995—98; contractor to Applied Physics Lab. Johns Hopkins U., 1998-99; mktg. mgr. Info. Tech. Lab. Nat. Inst. Stds. and Tech., Gaithersburg, Md., 2000—03, 2005, comm. mgr. Mfg. Ext. Partnership, 2005—06; fellow US Dept. Commerce Sci. and Tech., 2003—04; with Office Def. Rsch. and Engring. Dept. Def., 2003—04; contractor Office Naval Rsch., Dept. of the Navy, Arlington, Va., 2007—. Mem. AAAS, Armed Forces Comms. and Electronics Assn., Nat. Assn. Sci. Writers, Toastmasters Internat.

HOUGHTLIN, ROBERT, publishing executive; Sales positions LIFE Mag., US News & World Report; Detroit mgr. sales, launch team ESPN the Mag.; acct. mgr., DaimlerChrysler acct. Hachette Filipacchi Media US Inc., 2001—02, v.p. corp. sales, Car & Driver, 2003—04, and mgr., auto group, Detroit, 2002—03, assoc. pub., Car & Driver, v.p., corp. sales Detroit, 2004—05, v.p., pub., Car & Driver Ann Arbor, Mich., 2005—. Office: Car & Driver Hachette Filipacchi Media US Inc 2002 Hogback Rd Ann Arbor MI 48105 also: Hachette Filipacchi Media 1633 Broadway New York NY 10019 Office Phone: 734-971-3600.*

HOUGHTON, ALAN NOURSE, educational association administrator, consultant; b. Hartford, Conn., Jan. 17, 1924; m. Elizabeth T. Jones, Mar. 30, 1946; children: Alan Nourse, Elizabeth Boardman, John Barnard, Suzanne Tolles. AB cum laude, Harvard U., 1946, AM, 1951; postgrad., Columbia U., 1951, U. Conn., 1961, 62-63. Faculty Groton (Mass.) Sch., 1946-51; chmn. classics dept. Loomis Sch., Windsor, Conn., 1951-55; headmaster Pine Point Sch., Stonington, 1955-67, Renbrook Sch., West Hartford, 1967-73; exec. dir. Conn. Assn. Ind. Schs., 1974-89; ednl. cons. Madison, 1989-94. Mem. Sch. Bldg. Com., Lyme, Conn., 1959, Zoning Bd. Appeals, 1959-61, Zoning and Planning Commn., 1963-65, Bd. Fin., 1971-75, Lyme Dem. Town Com., 1957-63; trustee Blair Acad., Blairstown, N.J., Pine Point Sch., Stonington, Conn., Renbrook Sch., Country Sch., Madison, Conn.; corporator Hartford Hosp. 1st lt. USAAF, 1943-45. Decorated D.F.C., Air medal with three oak leaf clusters; Houghton Wing named for him at Pine Point Sch. Mem. Conn. Assn. Ind. Schs. (tchrs. edn. and profl. stds. rep. 1963-66, v.p., pres.), Classical Assn. New Eng., Mile Creek Beach Club (bd. govs. 1958-73), Harvard Club (N.Y.C.), Madison Winter Club, Phi Delta Kappa, Pi Eta. Home: Evergreen Woods 88 Notch Hill Rd # 124 North Branford CT 06471

HOUGHTON, AMORY, JR., former congressman; b. Corning, NY, Aug. 7, 1926; m. Priscilla Dewey Houghton; 4 children. BA, Harvard U., 1950, MA, 1952; PhD (hon.), Alfred U., 1963, Albion Coll., 1964, Cen. Coll., 1966, Clarkson Coll. Tech., 1968, Elmira Coll., 1982, Hartwick Coll., 1983, Houghton Coll., 1983. Exec. officer Corning Glass Works, 1951-86; mem. U.S. Congress from 29st N.Y. dist. (formerly 31st), Washington, 1987—2005; mem. internat. rels. com., ways and means com., chmn. oversight subcom., vice-chmn. subcom. on Africa. Mem. Grace Commn., Bus. Council N.Y. State, Bus. Adv. Commn. for Gov. N.Y., Labor-Industry Coalition for Internat. Trade. Trustee Brookings Instn. With USMC, 1945-46. Mem. Corning C. of C., Rotary. Republican.

HOUGHTON, JAMES RICHARDSON, retired manufacturing executive; b. Corning, NY, Apr. 6, 1936; s. Amory and Laura (Richardson) H.; m. May Tuckerman Kinnicutt, June 30, 1962; children: James DeKay, Nina Bayard AB, Harvard U., 1958, MBA, 1962. With Goldman, Sachs & Co., NYC, 1959—61; with Corning Glass Works, 1962—64, European area mgr. Zurich, Switzerland, 1964—68, v.p., gen. mgr. consumer products divsn., 1968—71, vice chmn. bd., dir., chmn. exec. com., 1971—83, chmn. bd., CEO, 1983—89, Corning Inc. (formerly Corning Glass Works), 1989—96; chmn., CEO Corning Inc., 2002—05, non-exec. chmn. Corning, NY, 2005—07, chmn. emeritus, 2007—. Bd. dirs. Met. Life Ins. Co., Exxon Mobil Corp.; mem. Harvard Corp. Trustee Corning Inc. Found., Corning Mus. Glass, Pierpont Morgan Libr., N.Y.C., Met. Mus. Art, Bus. Coun. With U.S. Army, 1959-60 Mem.: Laurel Valley Golf Club (Ligonier, Pa.), Rolling Rock Club, Augusta Nat. Golf Club (Ga.), Tarratine Club (Dark Harbor, Maine), Brookline Country Club (Mass.), Links Club NYC, Univ. Club, Harvard Club, River Club, Corning Country Club. Episcopalian.

HOUGHTON, KAREN THERESA, reading specialist educator, mathematics educator; d. Ralph Paul and Katherine Theresa Iacobucci; m. Harold Alan Houghton, Jan. 4, 1975; children: Brandon, Theresa. BS in Bus. Edn., Empire State Coll., 1983; MS in Edn., Coll. St. Rose, 1990. Cert. reading tchr. NY, 1997, nursery and kindergarten tchr. grades 1-6 NY, 1997. Sub. tchr. Averill Pk. Sch., NY, East Greenbush Schs., NY, Berlin and Wynantskill Schs., NY, 1988—94; remedial reading and math tchr. East Greenbush Ctrl. Schs., 1994—. Bldg. level specialist sci. D.P. Sutherland Sch., Nassau, NY, 1995—2003, bldg. level specialist math., 1997—99; tchr. cert. advanced studies reading, cert. advanced studies adminstr. SUNY, Albany, 2003—; mem., rschr. ednl. com. East Greenbush Sch. Vol. Book Ho. Stuyvesant Plz., Albany, NY, 2003—04. Mem.: ASCD, Internat. Reading Assn., Nat. Parks Conservation Assn., Nature Conservancy, Human Soc. U.S., Defenders Wildlife, Wildlife Land Trust, Nat. Wildlife Fedn. (assoc.), Nat. Pks. Conservation Assn., Arbor Day Found., Wildlife Guardians, World Wildlife Fund, Arthritis Found., Sierra Club. Avocations: reading, travel, cooking. Home Phone: 518-674-2445.

HOUGHTON, KATHARINE, actress; b. Hartford, Conn., Mar. 10, 1945; d. Ellsworth Strong and Marion Houghton (Hepburn) Grant. BA, Sarah Lawrence Coll., Bronxville, NY, 1965. Founding mem. Pilgrim Repertory Co. (Shakespeare touring co. sponsored by Ky. Arts Commn.), 1971-72, SC Arts Commn., 1972, Miss. Arts Commn., 1973, Conn. Arts Commn., St. Joseph Coll., 1974; lectr. in field. Debut on Broadway stage in A Very Rich Woman, 1965; appeared in stage plays Charley's Aunt, New Orleans Repertory, 1966, The Front Page, Broadway, 1968, Ten O'Clock Scholar, Royal Poinciana Playhouse, Fla., 1969, The Private Ear/The Public Eye, Sullivan, Ill., 1969, Sabrina Fair, Ivoryton Playhouse, 1968, The Miracle Worker, Sullivan, Ill., A Scent of Flowers (Theatre World award), Off Broadway, 1969, Misalliance, Hartford Stage Co., 1970, The Taming of the Shrew, Actors Theatre, Louisville, 1970, Poor Richard, Tartuffe, 1970, Ring Around the Moon, Hartford Stage Co., 1970, Major Barbara, The Glass Menagerie, Actors Theatre of Louisville, 1971, Play It Again Sam, Actors Theatre of Louisville, 1971, Suddenly Last Summer, Ivanhoe, Chgo., 1973, The Prodigal Daughter, Kennedy Ctr., Washington, 1973, Bell, Book and Candle, Pensacola, Fla., 1974, The Rainmaker, Ind. Repertory Co., 1975, Spiders Web, Atlanta, 1977, Hedda Gabler, Nashville, 1978, Dear Liar, Dayton, Ohio, 1978, 13 Rue de L'Amour, Ind. Repertory Co., 1978, Antigone, Nashville, 1979, Uncle Vanya, Acad. Festival Theatre, Lake Forest, 1979, Forty Carats, Radford U. Theatre, Va., 1979, A Doll's House, St. Edward's U. Theatre, Tex., 1979, The Sea Gull, Pitts. Pub. Theatre, 1979, The Glass Menagerie, Pa. Stage Co., 1980, Taming of the Shrew, Pa. State Festival, 1980, Terra Nova, Actors Theatre of Louisville, 1980, The Merchant of Venice, South Coast Repertory, Costa Mesa, Calif., 1981, A Touch of the Poet, Yale Repertory Theatre, 1983, To Heaven in a Swing, Am. Place Theatre, N.Y.C., tour various theaters, 1983-85, Sally's Gone She's Left Her Name, Am. Festival Theatre, NH, 1984-86, Vivat, Vivat Regina, Mad Woman of Chaillot, The Time of Your Life, Children of the Sun, Mirror Repertory Co., N.Y.C., 1985, A Bill of Divorcement, Westport Country Playhouse, Conn., 1985, One Slight Hitch, Charlotte Repertory Co., 1986, To Heaven in a Swing, Amherst Coll., Bowdoin Coll., 1986, and Bronson Alcott Centennial Celebration, 1988, The Hooded Eye, West Bank Downstairs Theatre Bar, 1987, Ivoryton Playhouse, 1987, Murder in the Cathedral, West Point Cadet Chapel, 1987, The Leaves of Vallombrosa, 1988, Our Town, Broadway, 1988-89, Love Letters, Ivoryton Playhouse, 1989, To Kill A Mockingbird, Paper Mill Playhouse, NJ, 1991, Best Kept Secret, A Dangerous Liaison in the Cold War, 1998, Berkshire Theatre Festival, 2000, NJ Repertory Theatre, 2001, Sch. House Theatre, Croton Falls, NY, 200l, Lettice & Lovage, Ivoryton Playhouse, 2002; motion pictures include Guess Who's Coming to Dinner, 1967, The Gardener, 1972, Eyes of the Amaryllis, 1981, Mr. North, 1987, Billy Bathgate, 1990, Ethan Frome, 1992, The Night We Never Met, 1992, Kalamazoo, 1993, Let It Be You, 1994, The Pursuit of Happiness, 2003, Kinsey, 2003; TV series The Adams Chronicles, 1975; TV mini-series I'll Take Manhattan, 1986; appeared on TV in Legacy of Fear, 1974, The Color of Friendship, 1981, (day-time serials) One Life to Live, 1989, All My Children, 1992; toured in Sabrina Fair, 1975, The Mousetrap, Arms and the Man, Dear Liar, 1976, The Streets of New York, Westport, Conn., Guildford, NH, Dennis, Mass., Denver, 1980; appeared in To True to Be Good, Acad. Festival Theatre, Lake Forest, Ill., 1977, Spingold Theatre, Waltham, Mass., 1977, Annenberg Ctr., Phila., 1977; author: (plays) To Heaven in a Swing, 1982, Merlin, 1984, Buddha, On The Shady Side, The Right Number, 1986, (book) The Marry Month of May, 1988; (stage prodns.) Phone Play, 1988, Good Grief, 1988, Mortal Friends, 1988 (stage prodn. premiere 1988), The Lick Penny Lover, 1988, Only Angels, 1997, Best Kept Secret, A Dangerous Liaison in the Cold War, 1998, Bookends, 2007, (screenplays) The Heart of the Matter, 1989, Journey to Glasnost, 1990, Good Grief, 1991, Motherman, 1993, Acting in Concert, 1994, Spot, 1996; co-author: Two Beastly Tales, 1975; editor: MHG: A Biography, 1989; written, performed in lectr. engagements: The Secret Life of Louisa May Alcott, Small Press Ctr., NYC, 1998, Women of Achievement Series, The Mount, Lenox, Mass., 2002, My Grandmother's House Near the River, Conn. River Mus., 1999, The Wadsworth Atheneum, Conn., 1999, The Hope Club, Providence, 2000, The Cosmopolitan Club, NYC, 2002, Katharine Times Three, Conn. Hist. Soc., 1999, Wadsworth Atheneum, 2000, Denver Town Hall, 2001, Met. Mus. Art., NYC, 2001, How Katharine Hepburn Became A Political Activist Without Actually Being One (Conn. Womens Hall Fame 2003), Legacy Lite, Bryn Mawr Coll., 2006; appeared Larry King Live, 2003. Mem. Dramatists Guild.

HOUGHTON, MICHAEL, geneticist; PhD, U. London, 1976. Sr. rsch. investigator human interferon genetics Searle Rsch. Labs., Buckinghamshire, England; with Chiron Corp., Emeryville, Calif., 1982—, dir. non-A non-B hepatitis rsch., v.p. hepatitis rsch. Contbr. articles to profl. jours. Recipient Karl Landsteiner Meml. award, Am. Assn. Blood Banks, 1992, Albert Lasker award Clin. Med. Rsch., 2000. Achievements include first to conduct work leading to the discovery of the virus that causes hepatitis C; development of screening methods that reduce the risk of blood transfusion-associated hepatitis in the U.S. from 30% in 1970 to virtually zero in 2000. Office: Chiron Corp 4560 Horton St Emeryville CA 94608

HOUGHTON, RAYMOND CARL, JR., education educator; b. Greenfield, Mass., May 26, 1947; s. Raymond Carl and Phyllis Irene (Richason) H.; m. Jan Marie Laws, Sept. 22, 1973; children: Raymond James, April Monica, Amy Rose BS Math., Norwich U., 1969; MS Computer Sci., George Washington U., 1975; MSEE, Johns Hopkins U., 1980; PhD Computer Sci., Duke U., 1991. Computer operator Norwich U., Northfield, Vt., 1967—69; specialist programmer power transformer dept. GE Co., Pittsfield, Mass., 1969—70, mathematician armament dept. Burlington, Vt., 1972—73; mem. tech. staff Computer Scis. Corp., Silver Spring, Md., 1974—75; data systems analyst computer security applications divsn. Nat. Security Agy., Ft. Meade, Md., 1975—78; computer scientist Inst. Computer Scis. and Tech./Nat. Bur. Stds., Gaithersburg, Md., 1978—83; instrnl. rsch. asst. dept. computer sci. Duke U., Durham, NC, 1984—91; assoc. prof. dept. math. and computer sci. Augusta State U., Ga., 1987—93; lectr. Skidmore Coll., NY, 1993—95; owner Cyber Haus, Delmar, NY, 1995—. Bd. advisers, columnist Software Engring: Tools, Techniques, Practice, 1990-94, info. sys. del., Peoples Rep. China, 2000; adj. prof. SUNY Sch. Bus., Albany, 1997-2000; mission in understanding del. People to People Amb. Programs, Vietnam, 2002; spkr. in field Contbr. articles to profl. jours.;, author history-based travel books. Town historian Bethlehem, N.Y., 2005—. 1st lt. U.S. Army, 1971-72, Vietnam Decorated Purple Heart; recipient Certs. Recognition, U.S. Dept. Commerce, 1981, 83, cert. appreciation IEEE Computer Soc., 1985 Mem.: IEEE, Assn. Computing Machinery, 101st Airborne Divsn. Assn., People to People Internat. Lutheran. Office: Cyber Haus 159 Delaware Ave #145 Delmar NY 12054-1369 Office Phone: 518-478-9798. Personal E-mail: cyhaus@msn.com.

HOUGHTON, ROBERT CHARLES, secondary school educator; b. Dover, NH, Apr. 12, 1958; s. Raymond David and Barbara Jean Houghton. Student, USCG Acad., New London, Conn., 1976-77; BA with honors, U. Calif., Riverside, 1987, postgrad., 1987-89; MA in Ednl. Adminstrn., Chapman U., 1999. Cert. tchr., adminstr., Calif. Various teaching positions, 1977-80; pharmacy technician Anaheim (Calif.) Meml./Brea (Calif.) Cmty., 1980-85; teaching asst. U. Calif., Riverside, 1988-90; instr. Mt. San Jacinto (Calif.) Coll., 1989-90; tchr. Desert Sands Unified, Indio, Calif., 1990—, interim asst. prin., 1997-98, creator P.R.I.D.E. curriculum. Counselor Chem. Awareness Network, Indio, Calif., 1990—; computer cons. Desert Sands Unified Sch. Dist., Indio, 1994—; resident tchr. Calif. State U., San Bernardino, 1994—95; asst. tour dir. Lakeland Tours, Washington, 1991—2001; magnet grant coord. Pre-Med. Acad., 2004—07. Mem. NEA, Nat. Coun. Social Studies, Nat. Geographic Soc., Calif. Tchrs. Assn., Nat. Trust Historic Preservation, Civil War Trust. Republican. Avocations: travel, photography, reading, hiking, camping. Home: 79320 Port Royal Ave Indio CA 92201-1262 Office: 81195 Miles Ave Indio CA 92201-2807

HOUK, BENJAMIN NOAH, performing company executive, choreographer; b. Seattle, Apr. 4, 1962; s. Robert Louis Houk and Marilyn Joan (Haugen) Sundin; m. Lauri-Michelle Rohde, July 11, 1991; children: Madeline, Katherine, Elizabeth, Michael, Alexandra;children from previous marriage: Marissa, Skylar. Studied dance, Amherst Ballet Acad., 1978, Jan Collum Sch. Ballet, 1979, Jo Emery Sch., 1979-80, N.Y. studios, 1980-83, Robert Joffrey Workshop, 1981, Am. Ballet Ctr., 1980-83, Pacific NW Ballet, 1983—; student, U. Wash., 1988—. Prin. dancer Pacific Northwest Ballet, Seattle, 1983—; asst. dir. Bravo Ballet Arts in Edn. Program, Seattle, 1993-96; soloist Pacific Northwest Ballet, Seattle, 1987—89, prin. dancer, 1989-96; M.C., coord. Joffrey, NYC, 1983; artistic dir., choreographer Nashville Ballet, 1996-99; artistic dir. Fort Worth Dallas Ballet, 1998—2001; dir. San Elijo Dance and Music Acad., San Marcos, Calif., 2001—. Guest artist guest artist Orange County Ballet, Ithaca, NY, 1981, Koslovs and Friends, San Francisco, 1985, Ballet Oreg., Portland, 1988, Ballet Chgo., 1989, Nev. Dance Theatre, Las Vegas, 1990, Tacoma Perf. Dance Co., 1980, Nevada Festival Ballet, 1993—94, Maui Ballet Co., 1994; grant panelist Nat. Endowment for the Arts, 1999; dance instr., lectr., 1984—. Dancer (ballets) Pacific Northwest Ballet include Romeo in The Tragedy of Romeo and Juliet, Sigfried in Swan Lake, Franz in Coppelia, The Prince in The Nutcracker, others include Albrecht in Giselle, Othello in The Moor's Pavane, choreographer Capriole Suite, 1988, By When, 1989, Shard, 1990, First Light, 1992, Schubert 2-4-5, 1994, Bete Noir, 1993, Across and Back, 1994, Nutcracker, 1995, Open Water, 1995, Aida, 1997, Passage, 1998, Swan Lake (after Petipa), 1998, Nutcracker, Calif. Ctr. for the Arts, Escondido, 1998, 2001, 2005—; TV appearance Disney Presents Bill Nye the Science Guy, 1994. Artistic dir. Benefit for the Homeless, Everett, Wash., 1990—91. Grantee Tacoma (Wash.) Arts Coun., 1986. Mem.: Am. Guild Mus. Artists. Avocations: reading, windsurfing, pottery, mountain climbing, painting. Office: 1635 Rancho Santa Fe Ste 203 San Marcos CA 92078 Office Phone: 760-410-1999.

HOUK, ERIC, economics professor; s. Wade Houk and Doris Jones. BS, Frostburg State U., Md., 1997; MS, U. Idaho, Moscow, 2000; PhD, Colo. State U., Fort Collins, 2003. Prof. econs. Calif. State U., Stanislaus, Turlock, 2003—. Contbr. articles to profl. jours. Recipient Jr. Faculty with Exceptional Promise award, Calif. State U.-Stanislaus, Coll. Arts, Letters and Scis., 2005. Office Phone: 209-667-3500.

HOUK, IRENE MILLER, dentist; b. Columbiana, Ohio, Aug. 1, 1921; d. Josiah Ellsworth and Ada Isophene (Rupert) Miller; m. George Albertus Houk, Mar. 23, 1949; children: Martha Helle, George. DDS, U. Pitts., 1944. Lic. dentist, Ohio. Gen. practice dentistry, Poland, Ohio. Sunday sch. tchr. 1st Presbyn. Ch., Columbiana, 1935-49, Emmanuel Luth. Ch., New Springfield, Ohio, 1951-2003; bd. dirs. Springfield Local Sch., New Middletown, Ohio, 1960-81, past v.p., past pres.; bd. dirs. Wittenberg U., 1962-70. Mem. ADA, Ohio Dental Assn., Corydon Palmer Dental Soc.

HOUK, KENDALL NEWCOMB, chemistry professor; b. Nashville, Feb. 27, 1943; s. Charles H. and Janet Houk; 1 child, Kendall M.; m. Robin L. Garrell. AB, Harvard U., 1964, MS, 1966, PhD, 1968. Asst. prof. chemistry La. State U., Baton Rouge, 1968-72, assoc. prof., 1972-75, prof., 1975-80, U. Pitts., 1980-86, UCLA, 1986-91, chmn. dept. chemistry and biochemistry, 1991-94. Dir. chemistry divsn. NSF, 1988—90. Contbr. articles to profl. jours. Recipient Schrodinger medal World Assn. Theoretically Oriented Chemists, 1998. Fellow AAAS, Am. Acad. Arts and Scis.; mem. Internat. Acad. Quantum Molecular Sci., Am. Chem. Soc. (Cope Scholar award 1988, James Flack Norris award 1991, award for computers in chemistry and pharm. sci. 2003). Office: UCLA Dept Chemistry Biochemistry 405 Hilgard Ave Los Angeles CA 90095-9000 E-mail: houk@chem.ucla.edu.

HOULE, JEANNE LARSON, retired music educator; d. Robert Miles and Frances Elizabeth Larson; m. Thomas Delorn Houle, Dec. 20, 1959; children: Ronald James, Lawrence Robert, Laura Houle Stephens. MusB, U. Wis., 1959; MEd, Nat. Louis U., 1992. Cert. music tchr. K-12 Wis., Ill., elem. edn. tchr. Ill. Tchr. elem. gen. and string music Madison Pub. Schools, Wis., 1959—60; tchr. music, strings Waukegan Pub. Schools, Ill., 1971—74, tchr. elem. gen. music, 1974—2001. Music dir. First Bapt. Ch. Waukegan, 1980—2005; music cons. Jeanne Houle Music, 1994—; dir. jr. orch., grade sch. choruses, madrigal instruments, h.s. musicals' pit orchestras Waukegan Pub. Schools; judge, accompanist Ill. Grade Sch. Music Assn.; tchr. Christian Youth Theater, Gurnee. Author: (field research report (277 pages) Multicultural Awareness Through Elementary General Music in Waukegan Illinois Public Schools (Med, 1992), lesson plans, District 60 Music Lessons for Classroom Teachers K-6. Facilitator bible study First Bapt. Ch., 2003—; pres. YWCA, Waukegan, 1969—71; violinist Waukegan Symphony Orch., 1965—; vocalist Bel Canto Chorus, Milw., 1997—; Waukegan ticket chmn. Ravinia Festival Assn., Highland Park, Ill., 2003—05. Recipient Cmty. Svc. award, Waukegan Pk. Dist., 2006, 2007. Mem.: Music Educators Nat. Conf., Lake County Ret. Tchrs. Assn. (membership co-chair 2004—, Cmty. Svc. award 2007), Friends Waukegan Pub. Libr. (bd. 2003—05), Friends Jack Benny Ctr. Arts, Concert Call (orch. rep. 2005—), Lake County Cmty. Concert Assn. (subscription rep.), Nat. Alliance Mentally Ill Lake County (sec. 1999—), Am. Bus. Women's Assn. (sec. 2001—, Pres.'s award 2006, Woman of Yr. 1990-91), Fellowship Am. Bapt. Musicians, Nat. Assn. Music Edn. (25 Yr. cert.), Waukegan Hist. Soc. (life), Sigma Alpha Iota (life; pres. 1957—58, Sword of Honor 1959). Baptist. Avocation: collect and demonstrate world folk instruments. Home: 819 Keith Ave Waukegan IL 60085 Home Phone: 847-623-9497; Office Phone: 847-623-9497. Personal E-mail: houleteach@aol.com.

HOULE, JEFFREY ROBERT, lawyer; b. Biddeford, Maine, July 27, 1965; s. Marcel Paul and Lois Marie (Jackson) H.; children: Grace Morgan, Hunter Jackson. AB, Boston Coll., Chestnut Hill, Mass., 1987; JD, Western New Eng. Coll., Springfield, Mass., 1991; LLM in Taxation, Cert. in Employee Benefits Law, Georgetown U., Washington, 1992, LLM in Securities Regulation, 1995. Bar: DC, NY, Conn., Mass., Maine. Pres. A.F.I. Investments, Springfield, Mass., 1988-91, Washington Capital Ventures, LP, Washington, 1995-98; law clk. Stones Solicitors, Exeter, Devon, Eng., 1989; jud. intern to the Hon. Joan Glazer Margolis US Magistrate Judge, New Haven, 1990; legal intern Office of Atty. Gen. Robert Abrams, NYC, 1990; analyst The Bur. of Nat. Affairs, Inc., Washington, 1992; assoc. Andros, Floyd & Miller PC, Hartford, Conn., 1992-94, Elias, Matz, Tiernan & Herrick LLP, Washington, 1994-98; founding ptnr. Greenberg Traurig LLP, McLean, Va., 1998—. Contbr. articles to profl. jours. With US Army, 1984-86. Mem. ABA, The Army and Navy Club, The Federalist Soc., Phi Alpha Delta. Republican. Roman Catholic. Avocations: hiking, horseback riding, swimming, scuba diving, international travel. Office Phone: 703-749-1300. E-mail: houlej@gtlaw.edu.

HOULE, JOSEPH E., mathematics professor; b. Hartford, Conn., Oct. 11, 1930; s. Joseph E. and Rena (Cyr) H.; m. Constance Deschamps, June 19, 1954; children— Marie, Joseph, Celia, Elizabeth, Amy, Bernice. AB, Cath. U. Am., 1952, MA, 1954, PhD, 1959. From instr. to assoc. prof. math. Georgetown U., 1953-62; assoc. prof. Seton Hall U., 1962-63; prof. math. Pace U., NYC, 1963-94, chmn. dept., 1963-70, dean Dyson Coll. Arts and Scis., 1971-90, vice provost, 1987-90. Dir. Ctr. for Applied Ethics, 1982-93, emeritus, 1994—; Internat. Exec. Svc. Corps. vol. exec. Ministry of Edn., Budapest, Hungary, 1991. Fellow N.Y. Acad. Scis. (chmn. sect. math. 1968-69), Phi Beta Kappa Soc.; mem. Math. Assn. Am., Sigma Xi. Roman Catholic. Home: A188 Harrogate 400 Locust St Lakewood NJ 08701-7411

HOULIHAN, GERALD JOHN, lawyer; b. Cortland, NY, Aug. 26, 1943; s. Robert Emmett and Helen (Corsi) H.; m. Claudia C. Kitchens; children: Andrea, Gerald Jr., Maureen, Katherine, Colleen. BS, U. Notre Dame, 1965; JD, Syracuse U., 1968. Bar: N.Y. 1968, U.S. Dist. Ct. (we. dist.) N.Y. 1968, U.S. Ct. Appeals (2nd cir.) 1972, U.S. Supreme Ct. 1980, U.S. Ct. Appeals (5th cir.) 1981, U.S. Ct. Appeals (11th cir.) 1981, Fla. 1985, U.S. Dist. Ct. (so. dist.) Fla. 1985, U.S. Dist. Ct. (so. dist.) N.Y. 1986, U.S. Dist. Ct. (no. dist.) Fla. 1986, U.S. Ct. Appeals (4th and D.C. cirs.) 1987, U.S. Dist. Ct. (middle dist.) Fla., 1987. Assoc. Harris, Beach, Keating et al., Rochester, NY, 1968-72; asst. U.S. atty. U.S. Atty.'s Office, Rochester, 1972-81; sr. litigation counsel U.S. Dept. Justice, Rochester, 1981-82; chief asst. U.S. atty. U.S. Atty.'s Office, Miami, Fla., 1982-85; ptnr. Steel Hector & Davis, Miami, 1985-91; mem. Greenberg, Traurig, Hoffman, Lipoff, Rosen & Quentel, P.A., Miami, 1991-95; ptnr. Houlihan & Ptnrs., P.A., 1995—2006, Ruden McClosky, 2006—. Belle L. Landry scholar Syracuse Soc. Mem. Fed. Bar Assn. (pres. 1993-94, bd. dirs. Miami chpt. 1988—), Order of Coif. Democrat. Home: 504 Aragon Ave Coral Gables FL 33134 Office: Ruden McClosky 701 Brickell Ave Ste 1900 Miami FL 33131 Personal E-mail: gjhoulihan@aol.com.

HOUNGUES, DESIRE MENSANH, dean; s. Brigitte Houngues. PhD, Boston U., 1993—97; BA, U. Benin, 1989. Cambridge Certificate Cambridge Internat. Exam., 1990. Dean Savannah Coll. of Art and Design Sch. Lib. Arts, Ga., 2002—. Office: Savannah Coll of Art and Design Charlton Savannah GA 31402 Home Phone: 912-695-5932; Office Phone: 912-695-5801. Business E-Mail: dhoungue@scad.edu.

HOUNKPEVI, FRANCK O., electrical engineer, researcher; b. Porto-Novo, Benin, Aug. 2, 1976; s. Alphonse and Virginie (Houndegla) Hounkpevi. MS in Elec. and Computer Engring., Marquette U., Milw., 2003, PhD in Elec. and Computer Engring., 2007. Tchg. asst. Marquette U., Milw., 2001—05, rsch. asst., 2003—. Reviewer Internat. Jour. Control, England, 2006—. Contbr. articles to profl. jours. Recipient Best Presentation award, Am. Control Conf., 2006; Rogers Bacon fellow, Marquette U., 2005—07, Travel grant, IEEE Control Sys. Soc. and NSF, 2006. Mem.: IEEE, IEEE Control Sys. Soc. (conf. reviewer 2005—07), Nat. Scholars Honor Soc., Eta Kappa Nu, Sigma Xi. Achievements include development of algorithms to show that chaos based encryption/secure communication methods are vulnerable to third party attacks. Home Phone: 414-736-4303; Office Phone: 414-288-6820.

HOUNSOU, DJIMON GASTON, actor; b. Benin, West Africa, Apr. 24, 1964; arrived in U.S., 1990; Actor: (films) Without You I'm Nothing, 1990, Unlawful Entry, 1992, Stargate, 1994, Amistad, 1997 (Image award for outstanding lead actor in a motion picture, 1998), Ill Gotten Gains, 1997, The Small Hours, 1997, Deep Rising, 1998, Passage du milieu, 2000, Gladiator, 2000, The Tag, 2001, Le Boulet, 2002, The Four Feathers, 2002, In America, 2002 (award for best supporting actor San Diego Film Critics Soc., 2003, Ind. Spirit award for best supporting male, 2004, Golden Satellite award for best supporting actor in a drama, 2004, Acad. award nomination for best supporting actor, 2004), Heroes, 2003, Biker Boyz, 2003, Lara Croft Tomb Raider: The Cradle of Life, 2003, Blueberry, 2004, Constantine, 2005, Beauty Shop, 2005, The Island, 2005, Blood Diamond, 2006 (Best Supporting Actor Nat. Bd. Review, 2006, Supporting Actor in a Motion Picture, NAACP Image Awards, 2007), Eragon, 2006, (guest appearance): (TV series) Beverly Hills, 90210, 1990, ER, 1999, Soul Food, 2001, Alias, 2003, 2004.*

HOUPIS, CONSTANTINE HARRY, retired electrical engineering educator; b. Lowell, Mass., June 16, 1922; s. Harry John and Metaxia (Gourokous) H.; m. Mary Stephens, Aug. 28, 1960; children: Harry C., Angella S. Student, Wayne U., 1941-43; BS, U. Ill., 1947, MS, 1948; PhD, U. Wyo., 1971. Spl. rsch. asst. U. Ill., 1947—48; devel. elec. engr. Babcock & Wilcox Co., Alliance, Ohio, 1948—49; instr. elec. engring. Wayne State U., 1949—51; prin. elec. engr. Battelle Meml. Inst., Columbus, Ohio, 1951—52; prof. elec. engring. Air Force Inst. Tech., Wright-Patterson AFB, Ohio, 1952—96, prof. emeritus, 1997—. Guest lectr. Nat. Tech. U. Athens, 1958, 99, U. Patras, 1984, Weizmann Inst. Sci., 1984, U. Strathclyde, 1995, Binghampton U., 1996; sr. rsch. assoc. Air Force Rsch. Lab., 1981-97, sr. rsch. assoc. emeritus, 1997—2006. Author: (with J.J. D'Azzo) Feedback Control System Analysis and Synthesis, 1960, 2d edit., 1966; Principles of Electrical Engineering: Electric Circuits, Electronics, Energy Conversion, Control Systems Computers, 1968; Linear Control Systems Analysis and Design: Conventional and Modern, 1975, 4th edit., 1995, (with J.J. D'Azzo and Stuart N. Sheldon) Linear Control Systems and Analysis with MATLAB, 2003, 5d edit.; (with J. Lubelfeld) Outline of Pulse Circuits; (with G.B. Lamont) Digital Control Systems: Theory Software, Hardware, 1985, 2d edit., 1992; (with S. Rasmussen) Quantitative Feedback Theory: Fundamentals and Applications, 1999, (with S. Rasmussen and Mario Garcia-Sanz) 2d edit., 2005; contbr. articles to profl. jours. Served with AUS, 1942-46. Recipient Outstanding Engr. award Dayton Area Nat. Engrs. Week, 1962, Outstanding Civilian Career Svc. award, 1997, Outstanding Engring. Alumnus award U. Wyo., 2002. Fellow IEEE; mem. Am. Soc. Engring. Edn., Am. Hellenic Edn. Progressive Assn., Tau Beta Pi, Eta Kappa Nu. Greek Orthodox. Home: 1125 Brittany Hills Dr Dayton OH 45459-1415 Office: Air Force Inst Tech 2950 Hobson Way WPAFB Dayton OH 45433-7765

HOUPT, JAMES EDWARD, lawyer; b. Calif., 1951; m. Leslie Ann Jones Houpt. BA with distinction, Calif. State U., Chico, 1976; JD cum laude, Harvard U., 1992. Bar: Va. 1992, D.C. 1992, U.S. Ct. Appeals (4th cir.) 1992, Md. 1993, Calif. 1997, U.S. Ct. Appeals (9th cir.) 1997. News dir. Sta. KNVR-FM, Paradise, Calif., 1978-80; anchor, reporter Sta. KHSL-AM-TV, Chico, 1980-85; sr. reporter Sta. KOLO-TV, Reno, 1985-89; assoc. Baker & Hostetler, Washington, 1992-97; assoc. of counsel, ptnr. Orrick, Herrington & Sutcliffe LLP, Sacramento, 1997—. Lectr. journalism Calif. State U., 1981, 85; adj. prof. law sch. U. Calif., Davis, vis. prof., 1999, 2000, reported cases Women's Resource Network v. Gourley, 2004, Thompson vs. Miller, 2003, In re Stone & Webster Inc., 2002, Berkla vs. Corel, 2002, Rosenaur vs. Scherer, 2001. Author: (booklet) Access to Electronic Records, 1990, The Libel Curtain: A Comparison of Canadian & American Libel Law, 1994, Going On-Line: Is the World Wide Web a Web for the Unwary?, 1996, Boarding a Moving Bus: Developing an Internet Risk Management Strategy, 1997, The Courts and the Internet: A Match Made in Hell?, 2000; contbr. articles to legal and gen. interest publs. With USN, 1970—74. Recipient Cert. of Merit, Calif.-Nev. AP TV-Radio Assn., 1983, 84, 86. Mem. ABA, Va. State Bar Assn., D.C. Bar, Calif. Bar Assn., VFW, Am. Legion. Avocations: photography, hiking, canoeing. Office: Orrick, Herrington & Sutcliffe LLP 400 Capitol Mall Ste 3000 Sacramento CA 95814-4497 Office Phone: 916-329-7949.

HOUPT, JEFF, energy management executive; s. Johnnie and Noreen Houpt; m. Connie Oltermann; children: Jason, Alex, Josh, Grace. BS in Nuc. Engring., Thomas Edison, Trenton, NJ, 2000. Cert. electronics technician, Electronics Technicians Assn. Internat., 1996. Elec. designer Frankfurt-Short-Bruza, Oklahoma City, 2001—04; exec. v.p., asst. sec. Energy Mgmt. & Control Synergy, Inc., Oklahoma City, 2004—. With USN, 1990—96, Norfolk, VA. Decorated Navy Achievement medal Sec. of the Navy; named one of 40 Under 40, Oklahoma City Bus., 2005. Mem.: ASHRAE, IEEE (exec. com., membership chair 2004—), U.S. Submarine Vets., Navy League, Rotary Club. Conservative. Lutheran. Avocations: hunting, fishing, reading, golf, travel. Office: EMCS Inc 36 NE 46th St Oklahoma City OK 73105 Office Phone: 405-528-3627. Business E-Mail: jhoupt@emcs.com.

HOUPT, JEFFREY LYLE, psychiatrist, educator, former dean; b. Phila., Aug. 13, 1941; s. H. Lyle and Elizabeth (McAlpine) Houpt; m. Corinne A. Anderson, Dec. 28, 1964; children: Brian Jeffrey, Eric Robert. BS in Zoology, Wheaton Coll., 1963; MD, Baylor Coll. Medicine, 1967. Diplomate Am. Bd. Psychiatry and Neurology. Intern Boston City Hosp., 1967-68; resident in psychiatry Yale U., New Haven, 1968-71; staff med. officer Oak Knoll Naval Hosp., Oakland, Calif., 1971-73; adj. asst. prof. psychiatry Presbyn. Hosp., San Francisco, 1973-75; asst. prof. to prof. psychiatry Duke Med. Ctr., Durham, NC, 1975-83; prof. psychiatry, chmn. dept. Emory U. Sch. Medicine, Atlanta, 1983-90; dean Sch. Medicine Emory U., Atlanta, 1988-96; dean Sch. Medicine, vice chancellor for med. affairs U. N.C., Chapel Hill, 1997—2004; CEO U. N.C. Health Sys., Chapel Hill, 1998—2004; exec. coach, cons. to acad. health ctrs., 2004—. Author: The Importance of Mental Health Services for General Health Care, 1979; contbr. articles to med. jours. Lt. comdr. USN, 1971-73 Fellow Am. Coll. Psychiatry (pres.), Am. Psychiat. Assn. Home: 51319 Eastchurch Chapel Hill NC 27517-8302 Office: U NC at Chapel Hill CB # 7000 Chapel Hill NC 27599-7000 Home Phone: 919-967-2871; Office Phone: 919-942-8943. E-mail: jhoupt01@bellsouth.net.

HOUPT, KAREN RAE, dermatologist; BA, U. Tex., Austin, 1978; MD, U. Tex., Houston, 1982. Diplomate Am. Bd. Internal Medicine, 1985, Am. Bd. Dermatoloty, 1992. Internal medicine intern U. Tex. Health Sci. Ctr., San Antonio, 1982—83, resident in internal medicine, 1983—85, clin. instr. in internal medicine, 1985—86; assoc. prof. internal medicine U. N.Mex. Sch. Medicine, Albuquerque, 1988—89; med. dir. dermatol. svcs. Parkland Meml. Hosp., Dallas, 1992—; dermatology resident U. Tex. Southwestern Med. Sch., Dallas, 1989—92; chief resident dermatology U. Tex. Southwestern Med. Ctr., Dallas, 1991, asst. prof. dearmatology, 1992—98, assoc. prof. dermatology, 1998—2000, assoc. prof. dermatoloty, 2002—, clin. assoc. prof. dermatology, 2000—02. Named Tex. Super Dr., Tex. Monthly Mag., 2004—06; named one of Best Drs. in Dallas, D Mag., 1999, 2002, 2003, 2005, 2006. Mem.: Am. Acad. Dermatology (Silver award 1990), Alpha Lambda Delta, Alpha Omega Alpha. Office: U Tex Southwestern Med Ctr 5323 Harry Hines Blvd Stop Dallas TX 75390-9190

HOUSE, CECIL R., utilities executive; BS, U. Va., Charlottesville; JD, Harvard Law Sch.; MBA, Columbia U., NYC. Bar: NY, Va.; cert. purchasing mgr. Assoc. Debevoise & Plimpton; ptnr. McDermott, Will & Emery, NY; v.p., asst. gen. counsel Automatic Data Processing Inc., v.p. bus. devel.; v.p. supply chain mgmt. Pub. Svc. Electric & Gas Co., v.p. customer ops.; chief procurement officer, sr. v.p. safety and ops. support Edison Internat., 2006—, chief procurement officer, sr. v.p. safety and ops. support So. Calif. Edison subs., 2006—. Office: Edison Internat 2244 Walnut Grove Ave Rosemead CA 91770-3714*

HOUSE, GEORGE R., protective services official, farmer; b. Ind., Nov. 20, 1929; s. George Rolland House Sr. and Cordelia Mae (Higgins) House; m. Edna Girt Womack, July 30, 1965; children: Geroge Rolland III, John A., Nathan D., Jessica N. B in Psychology, Fresno State U., Calif., 1966; postgrad., Calif. State U., Tuolouse, 1964—66, Calif. State U., Hayward, 1967—68. Hearing officer Stan Co. Juvenile Ct., Modesto, Calif., 1986—94; legis. Calif. State Assembly, Sacramento, 1994—2000. Republican. Ch. Of Christ.

HOUSE, JAMES STEPHEN, social psychologist, educator; b. Phila., Jan. 27, 1944; s. James Jr. and Virginia Miller (Sturgis) H.; m. Wendy Fisher, May 13, 1967; children: Jeff, Erin. BA, Haverford Coll., 1965; PhD, U. Mich., 1972. From. instr. to assoc. prof. sociology Duke U., Durham, NC, 1970-78; assoc. prof. sociology/assoc. rsch. scientist Survey Rsch. U. Mich., Ann Arbor, 1978-82, assoc. chair dept. sociology, 1981-84, prof. sociology, 1982—2005, chair dept. sociology, 1986-90, dir. Survey Rsch. Ctr., Inst. Social Rsch., 1991-2001, Angus Campbell collegiate prof. sociology and survey rsch., rsch. prof. Survey Rsch. Ctr, 2005—. Author: Work Stress and Social Support, 1981; co-editor: Sociological Perspectives on Social Psychology, 1995, A Telescope on Society, 2004; assoc. editor Social Psychology Quar., 1988-91, Jour. Health & Social Behavior, 1997-2000, Internat. Ency. of the Social and Behavioral Scis., 2001; contbr. chpts. to books and articles to profl. jours. Guggenheim fellow, 1986-87, Ctr. for Advanced Study in the Behavioral Scis. fellow, 2005-06. Fellow: AAAS, Soc. Behavioral Medicine, Am. Acad. Arts and Scis.; mem.: NAS, Soc. for Epidemiol. Rsch., Soc. for Psychol. Study of Social Issues, Acad. Behavioral Medicine Rsch., Am. Sociol. Assn., Inst. Medicine of NAS. Office: Univ Mich Inst Social Rsch PO Box 1248 Ann Arbor MI 48106-1248 Office Phone: 734-764-6526. Business E-Mail: jimhouse@umich.edu.

HOUSE, JOHN WILLIAM, otolaryngologist; b. LA, July 12, 1941; s. Howard and Helen House; m. Barbara Breithaupt, Mar. 28, 1993; children: Hans, Chris, Kurt, Steven, Kevin. BS, U. So. Calif., 1964, MD, 1967. Bd. cert. otolaryngologist 1974, bd. cert. neurologist 2004. Intern L.A. County-U. So. Calif. Med. Ctr., 1967-68; resident Glendale (Calif.) Adventist Hosp., 1971-72, L.A. County Med. Ctr., 1972-74; fellow Otologic Med. Group, LA, 1974, pvt. practice, 1975—; pres. House Ear Inst., LA, 1987—. Mem. editorial bd. Am. J. Otology, 1986—; contbr. articles to jours. in field. Admissions com. interviewer, U. So. Calif. Sch. Medicine, Los Angeles, 1976—; mem. Los Angeles County Sheriff's Res. Med. Co. Capt. U.S. Army, 1969-71. Recipient Hocks Meml. award Am. Tinnitus Assn., 1988; named Tchr. of Yr., U. So. Calif. Family Practice Dept., 1987. Fellow Am. Acad. Otolaryngology/Head and Neck Surgery; mem. AMA, Am. Neurotology Soc. (program chmn. 1976—, pres. 1998-99), Am. Otol. Soc. (past pres.), Triologic Soc., Am. Soc. Mil. Otolaryngologists, Pan-Am. Assn. Otorhinolaryngology Broncho Esophagology, Jonathan Club (Los Angeles). Avocations: skiing, computers, running, swimming. Office: House Ear Clinic Inc 2100 W 3rd St Fl 1 Los Angeles CA 90057-1922 Office Phone: 213-483-9930.

HOUSE, KAREN ELLIOTT, former publishing executive, editor, journalist; b. Matador, Tex., Dec. 7, 1947; d. Ted and Bailey Elliott; m. Arthur House, Apr. 5, 1975 (div. Sept. 1983); m. Peter Kann, June 4, 1984; children: Hillary, Petra, Jason, Jade. BJ, U. Tex., 1970; postgrad. Inst. Politics, Harvard U. Edn. reporter Dallas Morning News, 1970-71, with Washington bur., 1971-74; regulatory corr. Wall Street Jour., Washington, 1974-75, energy and agr. corr., 1975-78, diplomatic corr., 1978-84, fgn. editor NYC, 1984-89; v.p., Internat. Group Dow Jones & Co., 1989-95, pres. Internat. Group, 1995—, sr. v.p., pub. Wall St. Jour., 2002—06. Bd. dirs. Rand Corp.; mem. adv. bd. U. Tex. Austin Coll. Comm. Trustee Boston U. Recipient Edward Weintal award Georgetown U., 1980-81, Edwin Hood award Nat. Press Club, 1982, Disting. Achievement award U. So. Calif., 1984, Pulitzer prize, 1984, Overseas Press Club Bob Considine award, 1984, 88; Harvard fellow, 1982, Sr. fellow Belfer Ctr. Harvard U., 2007; named one of most powerful women, Forbes mag., 2005. Fellow: Nat. Acad. Arts and Scis.; mem.: Coun. on Fgn. Rels. (bd. dirs.). Business E-Mail: karen.house@jones.com.

HOUSE, LIANNE KAY, elementary school educator; d. Kwai Lum and Marjorie Louise Young; children: Scott Madison, Carter Marshall. BS in Art Edn. Grades K-12, U. Mo., Columbia, 1975; M in Tchg., Webster U., Kansas City, Mo., 2005. Cert. art edn. grades K-12 Mo. Dept. Edn., 1975. Elem. art specialist Raymore-Peculiar Pub. Schs., Mo., 1975—77; elem. art specialist Independence Pub. Schs., Mo., 1979—. Mem.: Nat. Art Edn. Assn., Alpha Chi Omega (life). Presbyterian. Avocations: travel, reading, cooking. Office: Sycamore Hills Elementary 15208 E 39th St Independence MO 64055 Home Phone: 913-341-1829; Office Phone: 816-478-2520.

HOUSE, STEPHEN EUGENE, information systems consultant; b. Pueblo, Colo., July 18, 1951; s. Floyd Eugene and Jewell (Brame) H.; m. Cheryl Virginia Ashby, Mar. 15, 1975; children: Deborah Lynne, Mark Stephen. BS in Bus. Info. Systems, West Coast U., 1992. Programmer Calif. Sch. Employees Assn., San Jose, 1976-79; programmer/analyst Marysville (Calif.) Joint Unified Sch. Dist., 1979-80; tech. lead Mervyns, Hayward, Calif., 1980-85, Lucky Stores, Inc., Dublin, Calif., 1985-87; project lead Northrop, Pica Rivera, Calif., 1987-92; tech. cons. Computer Profls. Inc., Charlotte, NC, 1992-97; mem. profl. staff Compuware Corp., Charlotte, 1997—.

HOUSE, W(ILLIAM) MICHAEL, lawyer; b. Birmingham, Ala., Dec. 19, 1945; s. B. William and Kathryn Regina (Cantrell) H.; m. Gina Rigby; children: Tanner, Slade, Kate. BS, Auburn U., 1968; JD, U. Ala., 1971. Bar: Ala. 1971, D.C. 1992. Legal asst. to Congressman James M. Collins, Washington, 1971-72; atty. Ala. Supreme Ct., Montgomery, 1972-76; assoc. Odom, Argo, Enslen, Montgomery, 1976-79; chief of staff Sen. Howell Heflin, Washington, 1979-86; of counsel McNair Law Firm, Washington, 1986-88; ptnr. Shaw, Pittman et al, Washington, 1988-91, Hogan & Hartson LLP, Washington, 1991—, chair legis. group. Pres. Ala. Young Lawyers, 1976; chmn. Ala. Citizens Conf., Ala. State Cts., 1974-75; co-chmn. Potomac Group Dem. Nat. Com., 1987-93; mem. bus. adv. coun. Auburn Sch. Bus., 1990-93; mem. pres.'s cabinet U. Ala., 2000—; mem. adv. coun. Blackburn Inst., 2006-. Capt. US Army, 1971—80. Named Ala. Outstanding Young Man, Ala. JC's, 1979. Mem. Ala. Bar Assn. (award of merit 1974), Am. Judicature Soc. (bd. dirs.), Soc. Internat. Bus. Fellows (bd. dirs.), Pi Kappa Alpha (bd. dirs. Meml. Found. 1980-86). Avocations: tennis, reading. Office: Hogan & Hartson LLP 555 13th St NW Ste 800E Washington DC 20004-1161 Home Phone: 202-262-2772; Office Phone: 202-637-5636. Office Fax: 202-637-5910. Business E-Mail: wmhouse@hhlaw.com.

HOUSEHOLDER, LARRY, state official, small business owner; m. Taundra Householder; children: Derek, Adam, Matthew, Nathan, Luke. Grad. in polit. sci., Ohio U., 1982. Commr. Perry County; Dist. 78 Ohio Ho. Rep., 2001—. Bd. chmn. Tri-County CAA; mem. L.F.C.P. Solid Waste Bd., Perry County Planning Commn. Coach Youth Baseball. Named Hon. State farmer, 1995. Mem.: NFIB, C.of C., Rules and Ref. Com. (chmn.), 33d Degree Scottish Rite, Aladdin Temple Shrine (amb.), Moose, Eagles, Lions, Grange, Farm Bur. Achievements include Speaker Householder running for state representative in 1996 where he has worked diligently to promote economic development, infrastructure, and improved education.

HOUSEKNECHT, KAREN L., research scientist, educator; b. Feb. 3, 1964; 1 adopted child, Aislinn 1 child, Aidan. PhD, Cornell U. Postdoctoral tng. Harvard Med. Sch.; asst. prof. endocrinology and metabolism Purdue U.; joined Pfizer, Inc., New London-Groton, Conn., 1998—, assoc. rsch. fellow, dept. cardiovascular, metabolic and endocrine disease, sr. rsch. fellow, dept. cardiovascular, metabolic and endocrine disease. Vis. prof. clin. medicine Karolinska Inst., Stockholm; past pres. Pfizer Women's Leadership Network; adj. faculty Purdue U., Salve Regina U. Author of several scientific publs. Recipient Power of Women award, 2005, Women of Innovation award for large bus. innovation and leadership, Conn. Tech. Coun., 2006.

HOUSEL, DAVID, retired athletic director; b. York, Oct. 18, 1946; m. Susan McIntosh. BA, Auburn U., 1969. News editor Huntsville (Ala.) News, 1969-70; from adminstrv. asst. athletic office Auburn (Ala.) U., 1970-72, instr. journalism, advisor newspaper, 1972-80, asst. dir. sports info., dir., asst. athletic dir., 1980-94, athletic dir., 1994—2006, athletic dir. emeritus, 2006—. Author: Saturdays to Remember, From the Desk of David Housel--A Collection of Auburn Stories. Mem. Phi Gamma Delta, Omicron Delta Kappa. Home: 1970 Canary Dr Auburn AL 36830 Office Phone: 334-844-9848.

HOUSEMAN, ALAN WILLIAM, lawyer; b. Colorado Springs, Colo., Apr. 23, 1943; s. Murl Clarence and Opal Juanita (Snyder) H.; m. Susan Hays Margolis, June 17, 1967; children: Alana Judith, Nora Suzanne. BA, Oberlin Coll., 1965; JD, NYU, 1968. Bar: Mich. 1968, U.S. Dist. Ct. (ea. dist.) Mich. 1969, U.S. Dist. Ct. (we. dist.) Mich. 1970, U.S. Ct. Appeals (6th cir.) 1973, U.S. Supreme Ct. 1976, D.C. 1979, U.S. Ct. Appeals (D.C. cir.) 1982, U.S. Ct. Appeals (3d cir.). Reginald Heber Smith fellow Wayne County Legal Services, Detroit, 1968-69; dir. Mich. Legal Services, Detroit, 1969-76; dir. research inst. Legal Services Corp., Washington, 1976-81; exec. dir. Ctr. for Law and Social Policy, Washington, 1981—. Author: (with others) Legal Services History, 1984; contbr. articles to profl. jours. Chmn. Orgn. of Legal Svcs. Back-Up Ctrs., N.Y.C., 1973-75; vice chmn. Project Adv. Group, Washington, 1974-76. Recipient Recognition award Mich. Welfare Rights Orgn., 1975, Achievement award Project Adv. Group, 1979, 88, Nat. Equal Justice award, 1994. Mem. ABA, Nat. Legal Aid and Defender Assn. (chmn. civil com. 1975-77, recipient spl. award 1973, 88, 2000), Law and Soc. Assn., Soc. Am. Law Tchrs. Democrat. Mem. United Ch. Christ. Avocations: hiking, tennis, music. Home: 1715 Crestwood Dr NW Washington DC 20011-5333 Office: Ctr for Law and Social Policy 1015 15th St NW Ste 400 Washington DC 20005 Office Phone: 202-906-8001. E-mail: ahouse@clasp.org.

HOUSEMAN, ANN ELIZABETH LORD, educational administrator; b. New Orleans, Mar. 21, 1936; d. Noah Louis and Florence Marguerite (Coyle) Lord; m. Evan Kenny Houseman, June 25, 1960; children: Adrienne Ann, Jeannette Louise, Yvonne Elizabeth. BA, Barnard Coll., 1957; MA, Columbia U., 1962; PhD, U. Del., 1969. State supr. reading Dept. Pub. Instrn., Del., 1977-79; prin. M.L. King Jr. Elem. Sch., Wilmington, Del., 1979-80; adminstr., exec. dir. Del. State Arts Coun., Wilmington, 1980-84; acting dir. Divsn. Hist. and Cultural Affairs State of Del., Wilmington, 1983-84; prin. P.S. du Pont Intermediate Sch., Wilmington, 1984-91; dir. Mid.-Atlantic States Arts Consortium, Balt., 1980-84. Adv. bd. Rockwood Mus., Wilmington, 1981-94; bd. dirs. Opera Del., Inc., Wilmington, 1984-97, pres., 1991-93, dir. devel., 1994-95, coord. adv. bd., 1996; bd. dirs. Del. Theatre Co., Wilmington, 1984-90; bd. dirs. Aux. Alfred I. duPont Hosp. for Children, 1997-2004, pres., 2000-01. Republican. Presbyterian.

HOUSEMAN, GERALD L., political science professor, writer; b. Marshalltown, Iowa, Apr. 12, 1939; s. Lawrence D. and Mary N. (Smith) H.; m. Penelope Lyon, Feb. 11, 1961 (dec. 1994); children: Christopher, Elisabeth, Victoria; m. Juliana Sujata, 1999. BA, Calif. State U., Hayward, 1965, MA, 1967; PhD, U. Ill., 1971. Asst. prof. polit. sci. Ind. U., Ft. Wayne, 1971-76, assoc. prof., 1976-82, prof., 1982-2000; ret., 2000. Vis. prof. New Coll., Durham, Eng., 1975-76, Calif. State Polytech. U., San Luis Obispo, 1983-84, U. Calif., Irvine, 1984-85, St. Mary's Coll. Calif., 1985-86, Ind. U. Coop. Program in Malaysia, 1989-90, 94, 95, Fulbright Program, Indonesia, 1993-94, Malaysia, 2000-01. Author: (with H. Mark Roelofs) The American Political System 1983, G.D.H. Cole, 1979, The Right of Mobility, 1979, City of the Right, Urban Applications of American Political Thought, 1982, State and Local Government: The New Battleground, 1986; (with Michael W. McCann) Judging the Constitution, 1989, Questioning the Law in Corporate America: Agenda for Reform, 1993, America and the Pacific Rim: Coming to Terms with New Realities, 1995, Researching Indonesia: A Guide to Political Analysis, 2004. Mem. Transit Authority Bd., Ft. Wayne, 1973-75; city planning commr., 1982-83; Dem. candidate 4th dist. Ind. U.S. Ho. of Reps., 1996. With USMC, 1954-57. Grantee NSF, 1970, Ford Found., 1973, 74, NEH, 1977-78, 87, Ind. U. fellow 1973, 74, 77; recipient Wildavsky award Best Pub. Policy Article of Yr., Policy Studies Orgn., 1994. Mem Am. Polit. Sci. Assn. (seminar grantee 1980, 81), Asian Studies Assn., Ind. Polit. Sci. Assn. (pres. 1979-80), People for Am. Way. Avocations: classical music, basketball. Address: 4706 S Thor St Spokane WA 99223-7115

HOUSEMAN, MARC ALAN, museum director; b. Washington, Mo., July 7, 1964; s. David Ellsworth and Beverly Kay Houseman; m. Christina Lynn Gravemann, Oct. 24, 1992. Funeral dir., embalmer Nieburg-Vitt Funeral Home, Washington, Mo., 1990—2001; mus. dir. Washington Hist. Soc., 2001—. Contbr. articles to newspapers, mags. Pres. Washington Hist. Preservation Commn., 1999—2003; com. mem. Washington Tourism Commn., 2000—03, Downtown Washington Inc. Design Com., 2003—06; pres. German-English Friedens Evang. Ch. Cemetery Assn., Defiance, Mo., 1997—2006; pres., bd. trustees Wildey Cemetery, Washington, 1998—2006. Mem.: Nat. Trust Hist. Preservation (assoc.), Franklin County Cemetery Soc. (assoc.; pres. 2006—06), Franklin County Hist. Soc. (assoc.), Washintgon Preservation Inc. (assoc.), Ind. Order Odd Fellows (assoc.; noble grand, dist. dep. grand master 1998—2006). Achievements include research in identifying and restoring old cemeteries. Avocations: genealogy, cemetery restoration, antiques, travel. Home: 304 High St Washington MO 63090 Office: Washington Historical Society 113 East Fourth St Washington MO 63090 Home Phone: 636-239-3988; Office Phone: 636-239-0280. Personal E-mail: museum@washmohistorical.org.

HOUSER, CONSTANCE (CONNIE) W., writer, artist; b. Goshen, NY, Aug. 16; d. Charles A. and Josephine E. Woodward; m. James (Jim) C. Houser, Sept. 21, 1972; children: J. Jackson, Katrina J. AA, Stetson U. and Palm Beach C.C., Fla., 1970; BFA, Fla. Atlantic U., Boca Raton, 1971. News, editl., features Palm Beach Post-Times, Miami Herald, Fla., 1954—62; columnist, book reviewer Palm Beach Times, Lake Worth News, Fla., 1962—69; art reviewer Art Mags., NYC, 1960—70; art features, art profiles Art Voices South, Fla., 1960—70; artist profiles Art News, 1970—89; assoc. Gordon Rule program Palm Beach CC, 1989—92. Owner 4 Points Photo Ctr., West Palm Beach, Fla., 1958—69; art tchr. for srs., computer tutor, judge art and photo competitions. Over 10 one-woman shows, Exhibited in group shows at Gallery Camino, Real, Fla., Peter Rudolph Galleries, NY, exhibitions include Soc. Four Arts Contemporary Exhibits, Ft. Lauderdale Mus. Hortt Competition; author: The Letters: Portrait of an Artist - Jim Houser, 2007; contbr. articles to profl. mags. and newspapers. Mem. Hobe Sound Art League, Fla., 1996—2004, Hobe Sound Women's Club, Fla., 1996—2006; lifetime mem. Rep. Nat. Com.; v.p. Rep. Club, West Palm Beach, Fla., 1960—80. Recipient awards, Norton Gallery of Art, West Palm Beach, 1967, Soc. of the 4-Arts, 1970—74, Art Competition awards, Hortt Mus., 1974—79. Mem.: AAUW, Nat. Soc. Arts and Letters, Gallery Players (bd. dirs., pres., v.p.), 4-Points Photo Club (pres.). Republican. Episcopalian. Home: 8338 SE Coconut St Hobe Sound FL 33455

HOUSER, DONALD RUSSELL, mechanical engineering educator, consultant; b. River Falls, Wis., Sept. 2, 1941; s. Elmont Ellsworth and Helen (Bunker) H.; m. Colleen Marie Collins, Dec. 30, 1967; children: Kelle, Kerri, Joshua. BS, U. Wis., 1964, MS, 1965, PhD, 1969. Registered profl. engr., Ohio. Instr. U. Wis., Madison, 1967-68; from asst. prof. to prof. Ohio State U., Columbus, 1968—2003, emeritus prof., 2003—, dir. Gear Dynamics and Gear Noise Rsch. Lab., 1979—2006, dir. Ctr. for Automotive Rsch., 1994-99. V.p. Gear Rsch. Inst., State Coll., Pa., 1990-99. Author: Gear Noise, 1991; contbg. editor Sound and Vibration mag., 1988-96; assoc. editor Jour. Mech. Design, 1993-94; mem. adv. bd. JSME Internat. Jour., 1996-2000; contbr. articles to profl. jours. Elder St. Andrews Presbyn. Ch., Columbus, 1972-75. Fellow ASME (legis. liaison Ohio coun. 1976-80, Century II medallion 1980); mem. Am. Gear Mfrs. Assn. (acad.), Soc. Automotive Engrs. Roman Catholic. Achievements include development of technology for measuring gear transmission error under load. Office: Ohio State U 201 W 19th Ave Columbus OH 43210 Office Phone: 614-292-5860. Business E-Mail: houser.4@osu.edu.

HOUSER, DOUGLAS GUY, lawyer; b. Oregon City, Oreg., July 11, 1935; s. Roy B. and Shirley (Knight) H.; m. Lucy Anne Latham, Sept. 1, 1961; children: Brooks Bonham, Bradley Knight, Anne Elizabeth. BA, Willamette U., 1957; JD, Stanford, 1960. Bar: Oreg. 1960. Practice in Portland, 1961—; ptnr. Bullivant, Houser Bailey PC, 1965—. Chmn. com. CLE Oreg. State Bar, 1969-70, chmn. com. jud. adminstrn., 1975, bd. bar examiners, 1970-72, mem. bd. bar govs., 1977-80, treas., 1979-80; judge protem Circuit Ct., 1973-77; gen. counsel NIKE, Inc., 1972-84, dir, 1972—; bd. overseers RAND Inst. for Civil Justice, 1998-2004; gen. counsel Soc. Registered Profl. Adjusters; former gen. counsel Pacific N.W. Life Ins. Co.; lectr. Contbr. articles to profl. publs. Legal adviser Portland Sch. Dist. 1 Race and Edn. Com., 1963-64; mem. Eagle bd. Columbia-Pacific coun. Boy Scouts Am., 1962-70; past v.p., treas., bd. dirs. Waverley Children's Home; trustee Willamette U.; bd. visitors Stanford U. Sch. Law, 1978-80, 89-91, 96-98, 98-00, Willamette U. Law Sch., 1986; past chmn. Oreg. State Jud. Fitness Commn. Named one of Best Lawyers in Am., 2007, Four Outstanding Oreg. Commn. Litigators, Chambers USA. Fellow Am. Bar Found. (life), Am. Coll. Trial Lawyers, Internat. Acad. Trial Lawyers; mem. ABA (past chmn. tort and ins. practice sect.), Multnomah County Bar Assn. (chmn. com. continuing legal edn. 1977), Oreg. Assn. Def. Counsel (dir. 1972-76, pres. 1976-77), Def. Research Inst. (bd. dirs. 1990-97, sec.-treas. 1996-97), Fedn. Def. and Corp. Counsel (chmn. bd. dirs. 1991-92), Am. Judicature Soc. (bd. dirs. 1985-88), Internat. Assn. Def. Counsel, Stanford Law Soc. Oreg., Am. Law Inst., Nat. Jud. Coll. (adv. coun. 1990—), Willamette U. Alumni Assn. (pres. 1972-74, trustee 1971—), Waverly Country Club, Arlington Club, Beta Theta Pi, Phi Delta Phi, Omicron Delta Kappa, Pi Gamma Mu. Home: 11621 SW Military Ln Portland OR 97219 Office: Bullivant Houser Bailey PC Portland OR 97204-2089 Home Phone: 503-636-1948; Office Phone: 503-228-6351. E-mail: doug.houser@bullivant.com.

HOUSER, HAROLD BYRON, epidemiologist; b. North Liberty, Ind., Nov. 22, 1921; s. Edgar Allen and Gladys Chloe (Stillson) H.; m. Clara Jane Goin, Sept. 18, 1944; children: Cristene, Edgar, John, Susan, James. AB, Ind. U., 1942, MD, 1944. Intern U.S. Marine Hosp., New Orleans, 1944-45; resident Crile VA Hosp., Cleve., 1947-49; asst. prof. medicine SUNY, Syracuse, 1952-58; asst. prof. medicine and community health Case Western Res. U., 1958-64, assoc. prof., 1965-74, prof. epidemiology, 1974-92, prof. emeritus, 1992—, chmn. dept. biometry, 1975-85, chmn. dept. epidemiology and biostats., 1985-92; cons. in field. Contbr. numerous articles to profl. jours. Served with U.S. Army, 1945-47, 49-52. Recipient Group Lasker award Am. Pub. Health Assn., 1954, Disting. Civilian award Dept. Def., 1973 Fellow Infectious Diseases Soc.; mem. Am. Epidemiol. Soc. (pres. 1991). Home: #CS 9103 5950 N Fountains Ave Tucson AZ 85704 E-mail: halhous@aol.com.

HOUSER, JIM (JAMES COWING HOUSER JR.), artist; b. Dade City, Fla., Nov. 12, 1928; s. James C. and Martha (Futch) H.; m. Constance Woodward; children: James Jackson, Katrina J. BS, Ringling Sch. Art, 1949; BFA, Fla. So. Coll., 1951; postgrad., Art Inst. Chgo., 1952; MFA, U. Fla., 1953. Represented by Rudolph Galleries, Coral Gables, Fla., 1964—90, Woodstock, NY, 1964-90; exhibited Grand Ctrl. Moderns Gallery, NYC, 1966—; represented by Gallery Camino Real, Boca Raton, Fla., 1972—, David Findlay Galleries, NYC, 1974-84, Sherry French Gallery, 1985. Sr. instr. art Ky. Wesleyan Coll., Owensboro, 1954-60, art chmn., 1964-70, dir. art gallery, 1974-91; art instr. Palm Beach C.C.; artist Notre Dame U., 1970; Cornell U., NYU, 1971: judge local and nat. art competitions; lectr. in field. One-man shows include Gallery Camino Real, Boca Raton, Fla., 1972—89, 1999, 2003, 2005—, Brevard C.C., 1973, Orlando, Fla., 1974, Cocoa, Valencia C.C., David Findlay Galleries, NYC, 1976, 1978, 1981, 1983, Northwood Inst., 1986, Palm Beach C.C., 1988, others, exhibited in group shows at Dept. State Spl. Exhbn., Washington, 1967—, Major Fla. Artist Invitational Exhbn., Sarasota, Fla., 1981—92, No. Miami Mus. Art Ctr., No. Miami, Fla., 1985, So. Fla. Invitational Exhbn., 1991, Ft. Lauderdale Mus. Art, Men's Art Northwood U., West Palm Beach, Fla., 1994, Festival Internat. Peinture, Cagnes-sur-Mer, France, 2001, Represented in permanent collections Boca Raton Mus. Art, Notre Dame U., Cornell U., NYU, Palm Beach Soc. Four Arts, U. Miami, Bethlehem Art Ctr., Pa., Dulin Gallery Art, Tenn., Syracuse U., Owensboro Mus. Art, Ky., Hunt Knight, L.A., works featured in, The Letters by Connie Houser, 2007; author: (video texts) Color for the Artist, 1975. Selection com. Palm Beach Coun. Arts, 1987; art. rev. bd. scholarship awards Palm Beach Post-Times, 1982-87. Recipient Merit award, Ft. Lauderdale Mus., 1974, Atwater Kent award, 1977, 1989, Akston Found. award, 1977, Philip Hulitar award, 1982, Four Arts award, 1992—93, Soc. Four Arts, West Palm Beach, established Connie and Jim Houser award, Contemporary Exhbn. Soc. Four Arts, 1996—2002. Mem.: Soc. of the Four Arts (Cert. of Appreciation 1996). Republican. Methodist. Avocations: music, photography, computers. Home and Office: 8338 SE Coconut St Hobe Sound FL 33455-2911

HOUSER, KEVIN, engineering educator; b. Danbury, Conn., Aug. 22, 1970; s. William and Mary Ann Houser; m. Kristen Eisenbraun, Dec. 1998. B of Archtl. Engring., Pa. State U., University Park, 1993, PhD, 1997. Registered profl. engr., Nebr.; lic. lighting profl. Asst. prof. U. Nebr.-Lincoln, Omaha, 1999—2005, assoc. prof., 2005—. Recipient Leon Gastner award, Chartered Instn. Bldg. Svcs. Engrs., 2005, Taylor Tech. Talent award, Illuminating Engring. Soc. N.Am., 2006. Office: U Nebr-Lincoln Sch Archtl Engring Omaha NE 68182-0681

HOUSER, RONALD EDWARD, lawyer, arbitrator, mediator; b. Fairbury, Nebr., Aug. 11, 1949; s. Edward Erle and Lois Charlotte (Dux) H.; m. Linda Marie Webber, June 13, 1971 (div. 1985); children: Angela Marie, Brian Edward, Darren James; m. Beatrice Virginia McMullen Bupp, July 24, 1993. DVM, U. Mo., 1974; MS, Ohio State U., 1979; JD, U. Ga., 1990. Bar: Ga. 1990, U.S. Dist. Ct. (mid., no. and so. dist.) Ga. 1990, U.S. Ct. Appeals (11th cir.) 1990, U.S. Ct. Mil. Appeals 1993, U.S. Supreme Ct. 1993. Asst. instr. Univ. Nebr., Lincoln, 1979-83; owner, mgr. Lincoln Animal Health Clinic, 1983-85; atty. Cook, Noell, Tolley, Bates & Michael, Athens, Ga., 1990—. Contbr. articles to profl. jours. Mem. Nebr. State Bd. Health, 1980-84. Mem. Nat. Lawyers Assn., Nebr. Vet. Med. Assn. (dist. pres. 1979-81), Christian Legal Soc., Res. Officers Assn., Am. Legion, Phi Alpha Delta, Sigma Xi. Avocations: sports, reading, gardening. Home: PO Box 502 Athens GA 30603-0502 Office: Cook Noell Tolley Bates & Michael LLP 304 E Washington St Athens GA 30601-2751

HOUSER, THOMAS J., lawyer; b. Belmond, Iowa, 1964; m. Susan Houser; 2 children. BA, Coll. St. Thomas, 1986; JD, U. Iowa, 1989. Bar: Iowa 1989. Sr. shareholder Davis, Brown, Koehn, Shors & Roberts, P.C., West Des Moines, Iowa. Bd. dirs. Iowa Lutheran Hosp. Found., 1993—98, Iowa Health Found., 1998—; pres., bd. dirs. Fin. Planning Assn. Iowa, 2000—01. Named one of Forty Under 40, Des Moines Bus. Record, 2003, Top 100 Attys., Worth mag., 2005—06. Fellow: Am. Coll. Trust and Estate Counsel; mem.: ABA, Iowa State Bar Assn. (mem. probate sect. coun. 2005—, mem. pres.'s task force for CLE (continuing legal edn.) reform 2005—), Polk County Bar Assn. Office: Davis Brown Koehn Shors & Roberts PC 4201 Westown Pky Ste 300 West Des Moines IA 50266 Office Phone: 515-246-7845. Office Fax: 515-243-0654.*

HOUSH, E. WILLIAM, manufacturing executive; b. West Orange, NJ, Feb. 15, 1932; m. Margot Housh; 1 child, Donna. BS in Econs., Wharton Sch., U. Pa., 1954. Various positions IBM Corp., 1954—69; dir. info. and data processing systems IBM World Trade Corp., 1965—69; pres. Cybernetics World Trade Corp., 1969—71, Wright Line Inc. subs. Barry Wright Corp., Watertown, Worcester, Mass., 1971—. V.p. United Way, chmn. campaign, 1982; chmn. bd. dirs. Ctrl. New Eng. Coll. Tech.; bd. dirs. New Eng. Coun. With USAF, 1955—57. Mem.: Bus. and Instl. Furniture Mfrs. Assn. (dir.,), Ctrl. Mass. Employers Assn. (past chmn.), Worcester. Office: Hon Industries Inc 414 E 3rd St PO Box 1109 Muscatine IA 52761-7109

HOUSHIAR, BOBBIE KAY, retired language arts educator; b. Fort Smith, Ark., Nov. 28; d. Ernest and Virgil Straham. BA, Saginaw Valley State U., 1973; MA in Elem. Edn. Adminstrn., Cen. Mich. U., 1975, Cert. Gen. Edn. Adminstrn., 1978. Elem. tchr. Saginaw (Mich.) Pub. Schs., 1973-74, jr. high tchr., 1975-76, tchr. middle sch., 1983—2005; learning ctr. coord. Saginaw Valley State U., University Center, Mich., 1974-75, instr. reading, 1974-75; tchr. ESL Refugee Ctr. of Saginaw, 1982-83. Instr. ind. study Cen. Mich. U., Saginaw, 1988-90; tutor bilingual students Delta Coll., Saginaw, 1987-96; supr./student tchrs. Saginaw Pub. Schs., 1988—; oratorical/writing instr. Saginaw Pub. Schs., 1983—. Editor: Young Writers in Michigan, 1989. Vol. Saginaw County chpt. ARC, 1996-99; mem./vol. League of Cath. Women, Saginaw, 1976—. Recipient Recognition award Saginaw Infant Mortality Coalition award, Saginaw Cooperative Hosp., 1998, Educator of Yr. award, Saginaw Coop. Hosp., 1999, Excellence in Tchg. English Writing Skills award, Saginaw Bd. Edn., 2002, Accent on Achievement award, Saginaw Pub. Sch. Bd. of Edn., 2002, others. Mem. NEA, Saginaw Edn. Assn., Mich. Edn. Assn., Nat. Coun. Tchrs. of English, ASCD, Mich. Mid. Sch. Assn., Delta Sigma Theta. Democrat. Roman Catholic. Avocations: reading, student mentor, tennis, swimming, horses. Home Phone: 989-284-5538.

HOUSTON, ALLAN WADE, professional basketball player; b. Louisville, Apr. 4, 1971; s. Wade and Alice Houston; m. Tamara Houston; 2 children. BA in African-Am. Studies, U. Tenn., 1993. Guard Detroit Pistons, 1993—96, New York Knicks, 1996—; mem. All-Star Team, 2000, 2001, US Olympic Basketball Team, Sydney, Australia, 2000. Featured sports couple (with Tamara) Swimsuit Issue, Sports Illustrated, 1999; actor: (films) Black and White, 2000; contestant (with Tamara) NBA Week, Wheel of Fortune, 2003. Named one of 99 Good Guys in Sports, The Sporting News, 2000, 2001, 2002, 2003, 2004; recipient Olympic Gold Medal, 2000. Achievements include NBA Draft first round eleventh pick, 1993. Office: New York Knicks Madison Square Garden 2 Penn Plz New York NY 10121-0101

HOUSTON, BRIAN CHRISTOPHER MICHAEL, small business owner; b. Kitchener, Ont., Canada, Dec. 27, 1938; came to the U.S., 1968; s. Brian F.C. and Patricia E. (Jones) H.; m. Carol A. Donnan, Feb. 9, 1964 (div. 1978); children: Adrienne Elizabeth, Kelly Patricia; m. Heather S. Duncan, Dec. 29, 1978. BSME, Air Force Coll., 1957; grad., Staff Command Coll., London, 1970, Staff War Coll., 1972, Police Acad., Hamilton County, Ohio, 1973; AA in Document Analysis, Lion Acad., 1991. Pres., CEO Pegasus Group Holdings Inc., Herndon, Va., 1979—, K. Investigations Inc., Herndon, 1983—. Cons. Chemform Co., Fort Lauderdale, Fla., 1976-79; chief instr., dir. Twin Oaks Ski Club, Middleton, Nova Scotia, 1963-65; cons. Washington Rsch. Bur., 1981-86. Lt. col. Royal Marines and Spl. Air Svc., 1965-79; with Royal Can. Airforce, 1957-65, ret. Recipient Bronze medallion Royal Life Saving Soc., 1963. Mem. NRA (life), Am. Soc. Tooling and Mfg. Engrs., Soc. Mfg. Engrs. (sr. mem.), Internat. Assn. Counter Terrorism and Security Profls., Am. Soc. for Indsl. Security, Masons, Harley Owners Group (life), N.Am. Hunting Club (life), Silver Wings Fraternity (life). Republican. Episcopalian. Avocations: reading, cooking, music, golf, exercise.

HOUSTON, C(LARENCE) STUART, radiologist, educator; b. Williston, ND, Sept. 26, 1927; s. Clarence Joseph and Sigridur (Christianson) H.; m. Mary Isabel Belcher, Aug. 12, 1951; children: Stanley, Margaret, David, Donald. MD, U. Man., Winnipeg, Can., 1951; DLitt, U. Sask., Saskatoon, Can., 1987. Demonstrator in anatomy U. Sask., 1960-61, teaching fellow in radiology, 1963-64, lectr., 1964-65, asst. prof., 1965-67, assoc. prof., 1967-69, prof., 1969-95, emeritus prof., 1995—, head dept. med. imaging, 1982-87. Author: To the Arctic by Canoe, 1974, Pioneer of Vision, 1980, Arctic Ordeal, 1984, R.G. Ferguson, Crusader, 1991, Arctic Artist, 1994, Steps on the Road to Medicare, 2002, Eighteenth-Century Naturalists of Hudson Bay, 2003; editor jour. Can. Assn. Radiologists, 1976-81. Recipient Roland Michener Conservation award Can. Wildlife Fedn., 1986, Douglas H. Pimlott Conservation award Can. Nature Fedn., 1988, Ralph D. Bird award Man. Naturalists' Soc., 1989, Doris Huestis Speirs award Soc. Can. Ornithologists, 1989, Eugene Eisenmann medal Linnean Soc. N.Y., 1990, Sask. Order of Merit, 1992, Officer of Order of Can., 1993. Mem. Can. Soc. for History of Medicine (pres. 1987-89), Royal Coll. Physicians and Surgeons (mem. coun. 1984-90, chmn. specialty com. 1984-88), Am. Ornithologists' Union (mem. coun. 1978-80, chmn. memls. com. 1984—, v.p. 1990-91, Marion Jenkinson Svc. award, 2004). Avocation: bird banding. Home: 863 University Dr Saskatoon SK Canada S7N 0J8

HOUSTON, DOROTHY MIDDLETON, elementary school educator; b. LaGrange, Ga., Oct. 23, 1936; d. Robert Meriwether and Marie Elizabeth (Davis) Middleton; m. Richard Gray Houston Sr., June 3, 1956; children: Jean, Ann, Richard Jr., Thomas Sandy. BS in Edn., U. Ga., 1958, MEd, 1970. Tchr. Auburn (Ga.) Elem. Sch., 1958-59; tchr. phys. edn. DuPont Manual High Sch., Louisville, 1959-62; instr. women's dept. phys. edn. U. Ga., Athens, 1970-71; tchr. phys. edn. Woodstock (Ga.) Elem. Sch., 1971-72, Brumby Elem. Sch., Marietta, Ga., 1972-77, Murdock Elem. Sch., Marietta, Ga., 1977-81; tchr. Teasley Elem. Sch., Smyrna, Ga., 1981-95; ret., 1995. Childcare program adminstr. Internat. Student Conf., Toccoa, Ga., 1986; tchr. tng. Pub. Schs. Ga., 1969-92. Mem.: Ga. Ret. Educators Assn. (area XV dir. 2004—07), Cobb-Marietta Ret. Educators (pres. 2001—02), Kappa Delta Pi, Phi Kappa Phi. Baptist. Avocations: exercise, recreational crafts, gardening. Home: 1849 Service Dr NE Marietta GA 30066-1917

HOUSTON, ELIZABETH REECE MANASCO, correctional education consultant; b. Birmingham, Ala., June 19, 1935; d. Reuben Cleveland and Beulah Elizabeth (Reece) Manasco; m. Joseph Brantley Houston; 1 child, Joseph Brantley Houston III. BS, U. Tex., 1956; MEd, Boston Coll., 1969. Cert. elem. tchr., Calif., cert. spl. edn. tchr., Calif., cert. community coll. instr., Calif.; cert. adminstr., Calif. Tchr., elem. Ridgefield (Conn.) Schs.,

1962-63; staff, spl. edn. Sudbury (Mass.) Schs., 1965-68; staff intern Wayland (Mass.) High Sch., 1972; tchr., home bound Northampton (Mass.) Schs., 1972-73; program dir. Jack Douglas Ctr., San Jose, Calif., 1974-76; tchr. specialist spl. edn., coord. classroom svcs., dir. alternative schs. Santa Clara County Office Edn., San Jose, Calif., 1976-94. Instr. San Jose State U., 1980—86, U. Calif., Santa Cruz, 1982—85, Santa Clara U., 1991—94; cons. Houston Rsch. Assocs., Saratoga, Calif., 1981—; mem. neighborhood accountability bd. County of Santa Clara Probation Dept., 2002—04. Author: (manual) Behavior Management for School Bus Drivers, 1980, Classroom Management, 1984, Synergistic Learning, 1986, Learning Disabilities in Psychology for Correctional Education, 1992. Recipient President's award Soc. Photo-Optical Instrumentation Engrs., 1979, Classroom Mgmt. Program award Sch. Bds. Assn., 1984, Svc. to Youth award, Juvenile Ct. Sch. Adminstrs. of Calif., 1989-94; grantee Santa Clara County Office Edn. Tchr. Advisor Program U.S. Sec. Edn., 1983-84. Home: 12150 Country Squire Ln Saratoga CA 95070-3444

HOUSTON, E(RNEST) JAMES, JR., banker, consultant; b. Highland Park, Mich., Sept. 25, 1939; s. Ernest James and Frieda Mary (Milligan) H.; m. Ann Draper, Dec. 16, 1961; children: James Lee, Jay Douglas, m. M. Aleen Bateman, Sept. 1, 2001, 1 child, Chanda Brae. BS in Finance, Wayne State U., 1964, MBA, 1967. Asst. v.p. Bank of the Commonwealth, Detroit, 1957-69; v.p. Birmingham Bloomfield Bank, Mich., 1969—70, pres., 1970—71; exec. v.p. Fidelity Bank Mich., 1971; pres. Houston & Assos., Inc., Birmingham, Mich., 1971—91; mgr. loan rev. Republic Bancorp Inc., Ann Arbor, 1991—93, mgr. loan control, 1993—94, loan control officer, 1994—95, v.p. loan control, 1995—2003; v.p. strategic asset mgmt. dept. Franklin Bank, N.A., Southfield, 2003—05; sr. v.p. spl. asset mgmt. dept. Franklin Bank Divsn., First Pl. Bank, Southfield, 2005. Lectr. fin. Wayne State U. Sch. Bus. Adminstrn., Detroit, 1971—. Active Bloomfield Hills Hockey Assn.; pres. pro tem Village of Bingham Farms Village Council; chmn. Southfield Twp. Citizens' Com.; v.p. Hickory Hollow Homeowners Assn.; trustee Southeastern Oakland County Water Authority; mem. Community House Assn., Birmingham; bd. dirs. CATV, Birmingham YMCA; mem. parents council Brookside Sch., Cranbrook, Mich.; pres. Brookside Sch. Dads Club; mem. Cranbrook Arena Com. Mem. Birmingham-Bloomfield C. of C., Greater Detroit C. of C. Clubs: Wayne State U. Alumni;. Lodges: Rotary. Republican. Presbyterian. Home: 7140 Round Hill Dr Apt B-1 Waterford MI 48327

HOUSTON, FRANK MATT, dermatologist; b. New Orleans, Dec. 15, 1939; s. Matt Francis and Amanda Vallie (Welch) H.; m. Helen Butler, Apr. 24, 1965; children: F. Matt, Catherine E.C., Amanda J.B. BS, La. State U., 1960, MD, 1964. Diplomate Am. Bd. Dermatology. Intern Johns Hopkins U., Balt., resident; physician, dermatologist Greensboro Dermatology Assocs., NC, 1970—. Cons. Moses H. Cone Hosp. Sys., Greensboro, NC, 1970—; adj. asst. clin. prof. dermatology U. NC Sch. Medicine, Chapel Hill, 1980—. Bd. dirs. Greensboro Hist. Mus., Greensboro Preservation Soc., Greensboro Symphony Soc., Greensboro Opera Co. Capt. U.S. Army, 1965-71. Fellow: Am. Acad. Dermatology; mem.: AMA, Am. Skin Assn. (sci. adv. com. to bd. dirs.), Royal Coll. Physicians, NC Soc. Medicine, Surf Club (Wrightsville Beach, NC), Greensboro Country Club. Republican. Episcopalian. Avocations: travel, aerobics, music. Office: Greensboro Dermatology 2704 Saint Jude St Greensboro NC 27405-3670 Home Phone: 336-288-9312; Office Phone: 336-954-7546. Personal E-mail: f_houston@bellsouth.net.

HOUSTON, GERRY ANN, oncologist; b. Baldwyn, Miss., July 16, 1953; d. Jeff Davis and Frances Holland (Agnew) Goodson; m. Terry L. Houston, Dec. 18, 1976 (dec. May 1987); 1 child, Claire Holland; m. Abe John Malouf, July 23, 1988. BA, U. Miss., 1974, MD, 1978. Diplomate Am. Bd. Internal Medicine, Am. Bd. Med. Oncology, Am. Bd. Hospice and Palliative Care. Intern U. Med. Ctr. , Jackson, Miss., 1978-79; resident U. Med. Ctr., Jackson, Miss., 1979-81, fellow oncology, 1981-83; ptnr. Jackson (Miss.) Oncology Assocs., 1987—. Staff physician Miss. Bapt. Med. Ctr., Jackson, 1983—, Ctr. Miss. Med. Ctr., Jackson, 1983—, St. Dominic Hosp., Jackson, 1983—, River Oaks Hosp., Jackson, 1983—, Univ. Med. Ctr., Jackson, 1983—; med. dir. Hospice Ministries, Jackson, 1989—; mem. exec. com. Bapt. Med. Ctr., 1994, 1998—, credentials com., 2005—, pres. staff, 2003-04; med. dir. Bapt. Comprehensive Breast Ctr., 1997— Contbr. articles to profl. jours. Chmn. exec. com. Miss. divsn. Am. Cancer Soc., 1993-95, pres., bd. dirs., 1989-93,; exec. com. Bapt. Med. Ctr., 1994, 1999-; credentials com. Bapt. Med. Ctr., 2005-. Clin. rsch. fellow, Am. Cancer Soc. Fellow ACP; mem. AMA, Nat. Hospice Orgn., Acad. Hospice Physicians, So. Assn. Oncology, Am. Soc. Clin. Oncology, Alpha Omega Alpha. Episcopalian. Avocations: jogging, reading, skiing. Office: Jackson Oncology Assocs 1227 N State St Ste 101 Jackson MS 39202-2413 Office Phone: 601-355-2485. Business E-Mail: ghouston@mbmc.org.

HOUSTON, IVAN JAMES, insurance company executive; b. LA, June 15, 1925; s. Norman Oliver and Doris Talbot (Young) H.; m. Philippa Elizabeth Jones, July 15, 1946; children: Pamela, Kathleen, Ivan Abbott. BS, U. Calif., Berkeley, 1948; postgrad., U. Man., 1948-49; LLD, U. La Verne, 1993. With Golden State Mut. Life Ins. Co., LA, 1948—62, v.p., actuary, 1962-66, sr. v.p., actuary, 1966-70, pres., CEO, 1970-77, chmn., pres., 1977-80, chmn., CEO, 1980-90, chmn., 1990—2000. Bd. dirs. First Interstate Bank Calif., Pacific Telesis Corp., Family Savs., Kaiser Aluminum and Chem. Corp., Metro-Media, Broadway Fed. Savs. and Loan. Mem. L.A. World Affairs Coun., 1970—; chmn. ctrl. region United Way, Inc., L.A., 1973-75, mem. corp. bd. dirs., 1973-80, v.p., 1973-75; bd. dirs. M & M Assn., L.A. Urban League, pres., 1977-; bd. fellows Claremont U. Ctr., 1972-80; bd. regents Loyola Marymount U., 1972-75, 79-82; bd. visitors Anderson Grad. Sch. Mgmt., UCLA, 1990-93; pres. City of L.A. Human Rels. Comm., 1993-95, 99-2000; mem. United Way of L.A, Cath. Charities of L.A. With Inf. AUS, 1944-45. Decorated Purple Heart, Bronze Star; knight comdr. Order St. Gregory the Great. Fellow Life Office Mgmt. Inst.; mem. Am. Acad. Actuaries, Am. Internat. Actuarial Assn., L.A. Actuarial Club, Conf. Cons. Actuaries (assoc.), Am. Coun. Life Ins. (dir.), Life Office Mgmt. Assn. (dir., mem. exec. com. 1972-75, chmn. 1979), Mil. Order of Purple Heart, DAV (life), Calif. C. of C. (dir.), L.A. Area C. of C. (dir.), Town Hall, Calif. Club, Cosmos Club, Kappa Alpha Psi, Sigma Pi Phi. Roman Catholic. Home: 5111 S Holt Ave Los Angeles CA 90056-1117 Personal E-mail: ihouston@aol.com.

HOUSTON, JAMES GORMAN, JR., retired state supreme court justice; b. Eufaula, Ala., Mar. 11, 1933; s. James Gorman and Mildred (Vance) H.; m. Martha Martin, Dec. 3, 1955; children: Mildred Vance, J. Gorman III. BS, Auburn U., 1955; LLB, U. Ala., 1956, JD, 1969. Bar: Ala. 1956. Law clk. to chief justice Ala. Supreme Ct., Montgomery, 1956-57; ptnr. Houston & Martin, P.C., Eufaula, 1960-85; assoc. justice Ala. Supreme Ct., Montgomery, 1985—2003, acting chief justice, 2003—04; ret., 2005; of counsel Lightfoot, Franklin & White, LLC, Birmingham, Ala., 2005—. County atty. Barbour County, Clayton, Ala., 1961-79. Contbr. numerous opinions to So. Reporter; contbr. articles to profl. jours. Mayor pro tem, alderman City of Eufaula, 1964-70; pres. Heritage Assn., Eufaula, Ala., 1979-82; mem. Ala. Commn. on Uniform State Laws. 1st lt. JAGC, USAF, 1957-60. Named Citizen of Yr., City of Eufaula, 1979; recipient Alumni Achievement in Humanities award Auburn Univ., 1993. Fellow Am. Bar Found.; mem. ABA, Ala. Bar Assn., Ala. State Bar (examiner 1979-82, disciplinary commn. 1984-85, state bar commr. 1982-85), Barbour County Bar Assn. (pres. 1975), Eufaula C. of C. (pres. 1974). Republican. Methodist. Office: Lightfoot Franklin & White LLC The Clark Bldg 400 20th St N Birmingham AL 35203-3200 Home Phone: 334-834-4414; Office Phone: 334-834-4417. Business E-Mail: ghouston@lfwlaw.com.

HOUSTON, JAMES R., government agency administrator; B in Physics, U. Calif., Berkeley, 1969; M in Physics, U. Chgo., 1970; M in Coastal and Oceanographic Engring., U. Fla., 1974, PhD in Engring. Scis., 1978. Rsch. physicist US Army Engr. R & D Ctr., Vicksburg, Miss., 1970—72, rsch. hydraulic engr., Hydraulics Lab. (HL), 1972—83, chief of rsch. divsn., Coastal Engring. Rsch. Ctr. (CERC), 1983—86, dir. Coastal Engring. Rsch. Ctr. (CERC), 1986, dir. Coastal and Hydraulics Lab. (CHL) (result of merge of CERC and HL), 1997—2000, dir. Coll. Corps. Engrs. Labs., 2000—. Published over 130 technical reports and papers. Named Eminent Spkr., Institution Engrs. (Australia); recipient Three Sr. Exec. Svc. (SES) Meritorious Presdl. Rank award, Dept. of Army R & D Achievement award, Nat. Beach Advocacy award, 1997, Morrough P. O'Brien award, Am. Shore and Beach Preservation Assn., 2003. Mem.: Phi Kappa Phi, Phi Beta Kappa. Office: US Army Engr R & D Ctr 3909 Halls Ferry Rd Vicksburg MS 39180-6199 Office Fax: 601-634-2388.

HOUSTON, JANEANNE CURRIER, vocalist, educator; d. Bryant Christiansen and Sara Jean Currier; m. Mark Lorange Ahlness, Mar. 20, 1993. BA in Performance, Ottawa U., Kan., 1975. Sr. lectr. in voice Pacific Luth. U., Tacoma, Wash., 1989—. Founder, exec. prodr. Elmgrove Prodns. Soprano (solo vocal album) The Irish Songs of Sir Hamilton Harty, 1998, soprano, exec. prodr. (solo CD album) So Great a Joy, 2001, Living Mysteries, 2002, So Much Beauty, 2004, (chamber music recording) Chamber Works, 2004, soprano, exec. prodr., commr. (composer collection) Songs of Cotton Grass, 2006, soprano, exec. prodr. (solo CD album) The Shining Place, 2006. Bd. mem., treas. Earth Day Groceries Project, Seattle, 1995—. Recipient Second Pl. winner, NW Regional Met. Opera Auditions, 1986. Mem.: Nat. Assn. Tchrs. Singing (life), Northwest Artists (founder, mng. mem.). Democrat-Npl. Avocations: gardening, birdwatching, hiking, reading, cooking. Home: 3723 SW Elmgrove St Seattle WA 98126-3418 Home Phone: 206-937-1056. Business E-Mail: houstojc@plu.edu. E-mail: janeannesoprano@comcast.net.

HOUSTON, JOSEPH BRANTLEY, JR., optical instrument company executive; b. Birmingham, Ala., June 15, 1934; s. Joseph Brantley and Inez (Graben) H.; m. Elizabeth Reece Manasco; 1 child, J. Brantley III. AB in Astronomy, U. Tex., Austin, 1956; MS, Northeastern U., Boston, 1969. Commd. 2d lt. C.E., US Army, 1956, advanced through grades to capt., 1968; optical engr. Perkin-Elmer, Wilton, Conn., 1961-64; mgr. massive optics, chief engr. underwater optical sys. Itek Corp., Lexington, Mass., 1964-71; asst. to pres. Kollmorgen E-O Divsn., Northampton, Mass., 1971-73; v.p. advanced devel. and spl. projects Itek Corp., Sunnyvale, Calif., 1973-81; founder Houston Rsch. Assocs., Saratoga, Calif., 1981—, Houston Tech. Internat., Inc., San Jose, Calif., 1991-97; founder, exec. dir. Forum for Mil. Applications of Directed Energy, Huntsville, Ala., 1989-96. Contbr. articles to profl. jours.; inventor. Recipient Outstanding Civilian Svc. medal U.S. Army, 1987. Fellow Internat. Soc. Optical Engring. (life; pres. 1977-78, advanced tech. advisor 1981-2004, Goddard award 1982); mem. Optical Soc. Am. (pres. New Eng. sect., chmn. Fabrication and Testing Tech. Group, editor Optical Workshop Notebook). Home and Office: 12150 Country Squire Ln Saratoga CA 95070-3444

HOUSTON, KEVIN TODD, speech and language pathologist; b. Chester, SC, Oct. 9, 1966; s. Ruby Olivia (Wages) H. BA in Journalism, U. S.C., 1988, MA in Speech Pathology, 1991. Grad. clinician Speech and Hearing Clinic U. S.C., Columbia, 1990; student asst. Dept. Surgery U. S.C., Columbia, 1990, Easter Seals Rehab. Ctr., Columbia, 1990; grad. clinician Brennen Elem. Sch., Columbia, 1990, Dorn Vets Hosp., Columbia, 1991; speech-lang. pathologist N.C. Sch. for the Deaf, Morganton, N.C., 1991—. Mem. Nat. Student Speech-Lang. and Hearing Assn. (U. S.C. chpt., pres. 1989-90), Midlands Assn. Hearing Impaired Children, N.C. Speech-Lang. and Hearing Assn. Avocations: sign lang., deaf culture. Home: 14 Mountain Laurel Ct Columbia SC 29223-8212

HOUSTON, PAUL DAVID, educational association administrator; b. Springfield, Ohio, Apr. 10, 1944; s. Paul Doran and Irene Almeda (Sansom) H.; m. Marilyn Kay Bowyer, Aug. 27, 1966 (div. July 1986); children: Lisa Lenore, Suzanne Elizabeth, Caroline Michelle; m. Jovel Kane, June 27, 1988 (div. Aug. 1997). BA, Ohio State U., 1966; MAT, U. NC, 1968; cert. in Advanced Study, Harvard U., 1971, EdD, 1973; D (hon.), Duquesne U., 1997. Tchr. Chapel Hill City Schs., NC, 1968—70; prin. Summit City Schs., NJ, 1972—74; asst. supt. Birmingham City Schs., Ala., 1974—77; supt. Princeton Regional Schs., NJ, 1977—86, Tucson Unified Sch. Dist., 1986—91, Riverside Unified Schs., Calif., 1991—94; exec. dir. Am. Assn. Sch. Adminstrs., Arlington, Va., 1994—. Vis. prof. Brigham Young U., Princeton U.; pres. S.W. Regional Labs. Bd., 1989-90. Author: Articles of Faith and Hope for Public Education, 1997; co-author: Exploding the Myths, 1993, The Board Savvy Superintendent, 2002, The Spiritual Dimension of Leadership: 8 Key Principles to Leading More Effectively, 2006; contbr. articles to profl. jours. Pres. NJ Interscholastic Assn.; bd. dirs. Princeton and Tucson Libr., 1977-87, YMCA, 1977-87. Finis E. Engleman scholar, 1972; recipient Richard Green Leadership award Coun. Gt. City Schs., 1991; named Exec. Educator of Month Exec. Educator, 1985; named one of 100 Outstanding Exec. Educators in N.Am., 1984, 93. Mem. Rotary (pres. 1983-84), Phi Delta Kappa. Office: Am Assn Sch Adminstrs 801 N Quincy St Ste 700 Arlington VA 22203-1730 Office Phone: 703-875-0709. E-mail: phouston@aasa.org.*

HOUSTON, RON, professional society administrator; b. Austin, Tex., 1948; BA, U. Tex., Austin, 1971, BBA, 1984, BS, 1989, M in Libr. and Info. Sci., 1995, postgrad., 1999—. Founder, dir., and trustee Soc. Folk Dance Historians, Austin, Tex., 1987—. Dir. of exhibitions, seminars, retreats and courses, 1970—; cons., rsch. libr. in field, 1989—. Author: (research reports) Folk Dance Problem Solver, 1987—, (demographic study) Folk Dance Phone Book and Group Directory, 1993—, (catalog) Folk Dance Catalogue, 1967. With USMC, 1969—71. Recipient Token of Appreciation, San Antonio Coll. Folk Dance Festival, 2003; scholar Polonia Choreographic Sch., Kosciusko Found., 1981—83; Presdl. scholar, U. Tex., 2000, Continuing Edn. fellow, 2003—04. Mem.: Nat. Folk Orgn. (corr. Preserving Our Legacy award 2007), Internat. Coun. for Traditional Music, Panna Maria Hist. Soc. (life), Soc. Folk Dance Historians (hon.; trustee 1987—), Royal Scottish Country Dance Soc. (life; cert. tchr., Miss Jean Milligan scholar 1983). Avocations: study of socio-economic and political injustice, study of the fringes of reason. Office: Soc Folk Dance Historians 2100 Rio Grande St Austin TX 78705-5578

HOUSTON, SHANNON D., school system administrator, assistant principal; d. Richard E. and Gerry M. Rice; m. Garey B. Houston, May 17, 2003; children: John B., Kathryn H. BA, Midwestern State U., Wichita Falls, Tex., 1996; MEd, Dallas Bapt. U., 2004. Asst. prin. Watauga - Birdville Ind. Sch. Dist., Tex., 2004—. Home Phone: 817-444-0302; Office Phone: 817-547-4817. E-mail: shannon_houston@birdville.k12.tx.us.

HOUSTON, STANLEY DUNSMORE, retired public relations executive; b. Toronto, July 17, 1930; s. Archibald Laing and Mary (Dunsmore) H.; m. Pauline Lennox, Oct. 20, 1955 (div. July 1975); children: Wayne Cameron, Scott Gregory, Kevin Edward; m. Suzanne Fogarty, Sept. 15, 1978 (div. Nov. 1990); 1 child, Lorraine. Grad. secondary sch., Humberside Collegiate, Toronto, 1948. Journalist editor Toronto Telegram, 1948-59; exec. v.p. Pub. Rels. Svcs. Ltd., Toronto, 1959-72; pres., chief exec. officer The Houston Group Communications Ltd., Toronto, 1972-90; chmn., chief exec. officer Edelman Houston Group, Toronto, 1990-96. Dir. L'Agence des Relationnistes de Montreal, 1974, Toronto Waterfront Coun., 1988-92, Daniel J. Edelman, Inc., Chgo.; mem. editorial adv. bd. The Sponsorship Report, Toronto. Author feature articles Macleans, Mayfair, Saturday Night; organized World Curling Championship, 1959-69, Can. Profl. Rodeo Series and Championship, 1981-; founder Can. Ladies Curling Assn. and Championship, 1960; promoted 1st Can. World Cup Ski Race, 1965; inaugurated Can. Grand Prix auto race, 1967; created duMaurier Classic (LPGA major golf event), 1974, duMaurier Coun. for Performing Arts, 1978-2000. Mem. Can. Ladies Profl. Golf (pres. 1974), Ont. M.S. Soc. (dir. 1984-87), Can. Pub. Rels. Soc., Nat. Club, World Trade Ctr., Credit Valley Golf and Country Club, Variety Club of Ont., Tent 28. Home (Winter): 4508 Nassau Rd Bradenton FL 34210

HOUSTON, STEPHEN D., anthropologist, educator; Exch. student, U. Edinburgh, Scotland, 1978—79; BA in Anthropology, U. Pa., Phila., 1980; MPhil in Anthropology, Yale U., New Haven, 1983, PhD in Anthropology, 1987. Asst. prof. Vanderbilt U., 1987—93; assoc. prof. Brigham Young U., 1994—96, prof., 1996—97, univ. prof., 1997—99, Jesse Knight U. prof., 1999—2004; prof. Brown U., Providence, 2004—. Postdoctoral affiliate dept. anthropology Yale U., 1993—94; curatorial affiliate Yale U. Peabody Mus., 1993—96; vis. scholar dept. anthropology Harvard U., 1998—99. Contbr. articles to profl. jours., chapters to books; author: Reading the Past: Maya Glyphs, 1989; co-editor: Ancient Mesoamerica, 1989—94, The Decipherment of Ancient Maya Writing, 2001, Royal Cts. of the Ancient Maya, Vols. 1 and 2, 2001. Mem.: Am. Anthrop. Assn., Soc. Am. Archaeology. Office: Dept Anthropology Brown U Box 1921 Providence RI 02912 E-mail: Stephen_Houston@brown.edu.

HOUSTON, WILLIAM ROBERT MONTGOMERY, ophthalmologist, surgeon; b. Mansfield, Ohio, Nov. 13, 1922; s. William T. and Frances (Hursh) Houston; m. Marguerite LeBau Browne, Apr. 25, 1968; children: William Erling Tenney, Marguerite Elisabeth LaBau, Selby Cabot Truitt Vanderbilt. BA, Oberlin Coll., 1944; MD, We. Res. U., 1948. Diplomate Am. Bd. Ophthalmology. Intern Meth. Hosp., Bklyn., 1948—49, Ill. Eye and Ear Infirmary, Chgo., 1949—50; resident N.Y. Eye and Ear Infirmary, 1950—52; practice medicine specializing in ophthalmic surgery Mansfield, 1952—. Fellow retinal vascular disease NYU, 1968—69; mem. staff Mansfield Gen. Hosp., NYU Bellevue Med. Ctr.; assoc. prof. clin. ophthalmology NYU Sch. Medicine. Editor: Ohio Records and Pioneer Families, 1970—. Pres. Mansfield Symphony Soc., 1965—68, Mansfield Civic Music Assn., 1965; mem. Mansfield City Sch. Bd., 1962—65, v.p., 1965. Capt. med. corps USAF, 1952—55. Recipient Honor award, Acad. Ophthalmology. Fellow: Internat. Coll. Surgeons; mem.: SR (color guard 1961—71), Ohio Geneal. Soc. (trustee 1955—), Nat. Geneal. Soc. (Merit award), N.Y. Geneal. and Biog. Soc. (life), Ohio Hist. Soc. (life). Address: 456 Park Ave W Mansfield OH 44906-3118

HOUSTOUN, FEATHER O'CONNOR, foundation administrator; b. Galveston, Tex., Aug. 24, 1946; d. Leroy A. and Bonny (Cross) Feather; m. Lawrence O. Houstoun Jr; children: Alexandra, Kate. B in Polit. Sci., U. Ariz., 1968; M in Polit. Sci., U. Tex., 1973. Rsch. dir. Rep. Party Tex., 1969-70; various positions, acting dep. asst. sec. policy devel. U.S. Dept. Housing and Urban Devel., Washington, 1971-82; exec. dir. N.J. Housing and Mortgage Fin. Agy., Trenton, 1982-86; treas. State of N.J., Trenton, 1986-90; chief fin. officer SEPTA, 1990-95; sec. Pa. Dept. Pub. Welfare, Harrisburg, 1995—99; exec. AmeriChoice; pres. William Penn Found., 2005—. Sr. visiting scholar U. Pa. Bd. dirs. N.J. State Aquarium, Phila. Devel. Corp., Center City Dist., Center City Found. Recipient L.B. Johnson Fellowship in Pub. Affairs. Fellow Nat. Acad. Pub. Adminstrs., Phi Beta Kappa, Phi Kappa Phi. Office: William Penn Found 2 Logan Sq 100 N 18th St Philadelphia PA 19103

HOUTSMA, PETER C., lawyer; b. Denver, 1951; BA in Polit. Sci. and Econs. magna cum laude, U. Colo., 1973; JD magna cum laude, Cornell U., 1976. Bar: Colo. 1976. Mem. Holland & Hart, Denver, 1976—. Mem. Am. Arbitration Assn. (panel arbitrators), Order of Coif, Phi Beta Kappa. Office: Holland & Hart PO Box 8749 Denver CO 80201-8749 Home Phone: 303-795-1715; Office Phone: 303-295-8259, 303-295-8000. Personal E-mail: phoutsma@hollandhart.com.

HOUTZ, DUANE TALBOTT, hospital administrator; b. Kansas City, Mo., Apr. 28, 1933; s. Dudley and Helen (Talbott) H.; m. Margaret McNiel; children: Erik Siegfried, Jamie Houtz Harvey. BS, U. Kans., 1955; MHA, Washington U., St. Louis, 1960. Asst. dir. Shands Teaching Hosp. and Clinics, Gainesville, Fla., 1961-65; asst. prof. Ctr. for Health and Hosp. Adminstrn., U. Fla., Gainesville, 1964-65; adminstr., exec. v.p. Baptist Med. Ctr., Montclair-Birmingham, Ala., 1965-75; hosp. dir. Alton Ochsner Med. Found., New Orleans, 1975-77; pres. Morton F. Plant Hosp., Clearwater, Fla., 1977-92, pres. emeritus, 1992—; nat. advisor to the health care industry Pershing Yoakley & Assocs., P.C., 1995-99; ptnr. Corrigo Health Care Solutions, 2000—. Chmn. Southeastern Hosp. Conf., 1986-87; chmn., pres. SunHealth Care Plans Fla., 1986-87; bd. dirs. SunHealth Enterprises Inc., SunHealth Corp.; advisor Corrigo Health Care Solutions, LLC, 1998—. Contbr. articles to profl. jours. Bd. dirs. Cmty. Svc. Coun., Birmingham, 1972-75, United Way of Pinellas County, 1987-93, campaign chmn. med. divsn., 1992-94; bd. dirs. Fla. League for Nursing, 1989-98, Bay Area Hosp. Coun./Tampa Bay Hosp. Coun., 1990-95, Morton Plant Found., 1990-96; mem. Fla. Geriatric Rsch. Bd., 1993-98; adv. bd. Jr. League Pinellas County, 1993-94; active Vets. Affairs Mgmt. Assistance Coun., 1996—; vice-chmn. Sun Coast Health Coun., 1998-2003; mem. fundraising bd. Magic Found., 2005. Capt. USAF, 1955-58. Recipient Acad. award USAF Basic Flight Sch., 1956, award of merit Fla. Hosp. Rsch. and Edn. Found., 1993, Washington U. Hosp. Adminstrn. Program Alumni of Yr. award, 1996; fellow Birmingham Bapt. Hosp. Found., 1985. Fellow Am. Coll. Healthcare Execs. (Regents award 1992); mem. Nat. League Nursing (bd. dirs.), Am. Hosp. Assn. (vice-chmn. council nursing 1983, rsch. com.), Assn. Voluntary Hosps. Fla. (bd. dirs. 1979-83, pres. 1979-80), Fla. Hosp. Assn. (trustee, bd. dirs. 1979-82), Greater Clearwater C. of C. (Outstanding Citizen selection com. 1982, bd. govs. 1984-87, bd. govs. 1987-88), Pinellas Suncoast C. of C. (adv. coun. 1984-87), Kiwanis (pres. Birmingham chpt. 1970-71), Phi Delta Theta. Personal E-mail: dhoutz1@tampabay.rr.com.

HOUTZ, RANDY L., music educator; s. Robert F. and Helen A. Houtz; children: Jay, Toni. MusB in Music Edn., Utah State U., Logan, 1976, MEd in Music Edn., 1983. Band dir. Vintah Sch. Dist., Vernal, Utah, 1976—80, Davis Sch. Dist., Bountiful, 1980—82, Weber Sch. Dist., Ogden, 1983—86, Davis Sch. Dist., Kaysville, 1986—. Assoc. condr. Salt Lake City Symphonic Winds; guest condr. honor bands. Recipient Tchr. of Yr., Kaysville Jr. High, 1993, Utah Outstanding Jr. High Music Educator, Utah Music Educators, 2000. Mem.: Music Educators Nat Cungress, Utah Music Educators Assn. (treas. 1991—99). Office: Kaysville Jr High 100 E 350 S Kaysville UT 84037 Office Phone: 801-402-7200 ext. 7279.

HOUZE, HERBERT GEORGE, writer; b. Brockville, Ont., Can., Apr. 18, 1947; s. McLean and Grace Lynham (Sayce) H.; m. Carolyn Pierce Johnson, July 8, 1972 (div. May 1990); children: Jennifer E., Alexander J. M., Andrew W.; m. Christine Mary Reinhard, Sept. 13, 1996. BA, McMaster U., Hamilton, Ont., 1969; MA, Vanderbilt U., 1971. Curator of mil. history Chgo. Hist. Soc., 1973-76; curator Winchester Mus. Buffalo Bill Hist. Ctr., Cody, Wyo., 1983-91. Advisor Royal Mil. Coll. Can. Mus., Kingston, Ont., 1979—; bd. dirs. John McLaren & Sons Distillers Ltd., London and Perth; internat. rep. Arms and Armor, Bonhams and Butterfields, San Francisco, 2004-; guest curator Wadsworth Atheneum Mus. Art, Harford, Conn., 2004— Author: Knightly Musings, 1988, The Sumptuous Flaske, 1989, To the Dreams of Youth, 1992, Winchester History, 1994, Colt Rifles & Muskets, 1996, Winchester Model 52, 1997, Winchester Bolt Action Rifles, 1998, Winchester Model 1876 Centennial Rifle, 2001,

Arming the West, 2001, Colt Presentations, 2002, Colt & Its Collectors, 2003, Samuel Colt: Arms, Art & Invention, 2006. Mem. Arms and Armour Soc. London, Armor & Arms Club N.Y., Les Amis du Musee de Liege. E-mail: herb.houze@bonhams.com.

HOVAKIMYAN, NAIRA, mathematician, educator; b. Yerevan, Armenia, Sept. 21, 1966; arrived in U.S., 1998; d. Viktor Hovakimyan and Emma Tumanyan. BS, MS in Theoretical Mechanics and Applied Math., Yerevan State U., 1988; PhD in Physics and Math., Russian Acad. Scis., Moscow, 1992. Jr. rsch. scientist Inst. Mechanics, Armenian Acad. Scis., Yerevan, 1992—94, sr. rsch. scientist, 1995—97; postdoctoral scholar INRIA (French Nat. Inst. Computer Sci. and Control), Sophia Antipolis, France, 1997—97; vis. rsch. scientist Sch. Aerospace Engring., Ga. Inst. Tech., Atlanta, 1998—2000, rsch. scientist II, 2001—03; assoc. prof. Va. Poly. Inst. and State U., Blacksburg, 2003—07, prof., 2007—. Presenter, spkr. in field. Contbr. articles to profl. jours. Recipient Internat. Best Paper award, Soc Instrument and Control Engrs., 1996, Pride@Boeing award, Boeing Co., 2004—05; fellow, Va. Tech. Coll. Engring., 2006; grantee, Soros Found., 1993—94; German Acad. Exch. Svc. scholar, Stuttgart U., Inst. for Computer Applications, 1994—95. Fellow: AIAA (assoc.); mem.: AMS, IEEE Control Sys. Soc. (sr.), Internat. Soc. Dynamic Games. Orthodox Christian. Achievements include patents for adaptive control system having direct output feedback and related apparatuses and methods; patents pending for error observer for adaptive output feedback; adaptive state estimation for unknown nonlinear processes; an improved method for adding adaptation to an existing control system applicable to non-minimum phase nonlinear systems; adaptive control with input saturation; a low-pass adaptive control design with improved transient performance. Office: Va Poly Inst and State Univ Dept AOE 215 Randolph Hall Blacksburg VA 24061-0203 Office Phone: 540-231-7989. Business E-Mail: nhovakim@vt.edu.

HOVANESSIAN, SHAHEN ALEXANDER, electrical engineer, educator, consultant; b. Tehran, Iran, Sept. 6, 1931; arrived in US, 1949; s. Alexander and Jenik (Thadeus) Hovanessian; m. Mary Mashourian Hovanessian, Sept. 17, 1960; children: Linda Larsen, Christina Tchaparian. BSEE, UCLA, 1954, MSME, 1955, PhDEE, 1958. Registered profl. engr., Calif. Research scientist Chevron Research Corp., La Habra, Calif., 1958-63; sr. scientist Hughes Aircraft Co., El Segundo, Calif., 1963-86; sr. tech. specialist Aerospace Corp., El Segundo, Calif., 1986-96; lectr. UCLA, 1962—; cons. engr. LA, 1996—. Mem. adv. group for aerospace R & D NATO, 1985-87. Author: (with Louis A. Pipes) Matrix—Computer Methods in Engineering, 1969; Digital—Computer Methods in Engineering, 1969; Radar, Detection and Tracking Systems, 1973; Computational Mathematics in Engineering, 1976; Synthetic Array and Imaging Radars, 1980; Radar System Design and Analysis, 1984; Introduction to Sensor Systems, 1988; (with Khalil Seyrafi) Introduction to Electro-Optical Imaging and Tracking Systems, 1993; editor Computers and Elec. Engring., 1973-76. Fellow IEEE (U.S. del. Moscow 1973, disting. lectr.); mem. ASME, Sigma Xi, Tau Beta Pi. Democrat. Roman Catholic. Achievements include invention of radar computer. Avocations: investments, real estate. Home: 3039 Greentree Ct Los Angeles CA 90077-2020

HOVDE, CARL FREDERICK, language professional, educator; b. Meadville, Pa., Oct. 11, 1926; s. Bryn J. and Theresse (Arneson) H.; m. Jane Hale Norris, Aug. 27, 1960; children: Katherine Hale, Sarah Theresse, Peter Bryn; m. Bertha R. Betts, 2000. BA, Columbia, 1950; MA, Princeton, 1954; PhD, 1956. Instr. English Ohio State U., 1955-58; vis. lectr. U. Muenster, W. Germany, 1958-60; mem. faculty Columbia, NYC, 1960—, asso. prof. English, 1964-69, prof. English, 1969—, emeritus, 1995, dean coll., 1968-72; chmn. Lionel Trilling Seminars. Vis. prof. U. Guanabara, Brazil, 1964, Umea, Sweden, 1989. Served with AUS, 1944-46. Fellow Villa Serbelloni, 1994. Office: Columbia Univ 602 Philosophy Hall Broadway & 116th St New York NY 10027 Home: PO Box 401 New Canaan CT 06840-0401

HOVDE, F. BOYD, lawyer; b. Mpls., Aug. 7, 1934; s. Frederick L. and Priscilla L. (Boyd) H.; m. Alice Austell, Feb. 22, 1981; children by previous marriage: Frederick R., Debra L., Kristine L., Sarah L. AB, Princeton U., 1956; JD, U. Mich., 1959. Bar: Ind. 1959, U.S. Dist. Ct. (no. and so. dists.) Ind. 1959, U.S. Ct. Appeals (7th cir.) 1960, U.S. Supreme Ct. 1977. Assoc. Ice, Miller, Donadio & Ryan, Indpls., 1959-67, ptnr., 1967-69, Townsend, Hovde & Townsend, Indpls., 1969-77; mem. Townsend, Hovde, Townsend & Montross, P.C., 1977-84, Townsend, Hovde & Montross, P.C., 1984-97, F. Boyd Hovde, P.C., 1985—, Hovde Law Firm, Indpls., 1997—2004, Hovde Dassow and Deets, LLC, Indpls., 2004—. Mem. com. on character and fitness Ind. Supreme Ct., 1976-2000, rules of practice and procedure, 1980-92. Mem. Indpls. Bar Assn. (treas. 1969, v.p. 1974, pres. 1979), ABA (del. 1980-83), Ind. Trial Lawyers Assn. (bd. dirs. 1970—, pres. 1976-77), Assn. Trial Lawyers Am., Am. Coll. Trial Laywers, Internat. Acad. Trial Lawyers, Ind. Coll. Trial Lawyers, Indpls. Jaycees (pres. 1963-64), Ind. Golf Assn. (pres. 1974-75), Western Golf Assn. (dir. 1969-81, v.p. 1972-81), Crooked Stick Golf Club (Carmel, Ind.), Pine Valley Golf Club (Celmenton, N.J.), Old Marsh Golf Club (Palm Beach Gardens, Fla.). Office: Hovde Dassow & Deets 10585 N Meridian St Ste 205 Indianapolis IN 46290 Office Phone: 317-818-3100. Business E-Mail: fbhovde@hovdelaw.com.

HOVDESTAD, WAYNE ROY, petroleum engineer; b. Kyle, Can., Feb. 8, 1958; s. Roy Osmond and Joann Shirley (Hanscam) H.; m. Michelle Diane Trew, May 17, 1980 (div. Mar. 1996); 1 child, William Roy Patrick; m. Maria Anatolievna Sinkova, Aug. 17, 1997; children: Stephanie Maria, Katherine Anna. BE, U. Saskatchewan, Can., 1979; ME, U. Calgary, Can., 1989. Engr. Texaco Can., Calgary, 1979-82, supr. engr., 1983-89; bus. engr. Texaco Inc., Houston, 1982-83; bus. devel. ESSO Can., Calgary, 1990-91; sr. engr. Petronas, Kuala Lumpar, Malaysia, 1991-94; pvt. practice Calgary, 1994-95; sr. planner Qatar Gen. Petroleum Corp., Doha, 1996-2000; sr. mgmt. Eurogas Corp., Calgary, 2000—05; v.p. Renelco Energy, Inc., 2005—06; pres. Debolt Energy Ltd., 2006—. Contbr. articles to profl. jours. Grantee Govt. Alberta, Can., 1986. Orthodox Christian. Avocation: Aikido. Home: 43 Hawkwood Rd NW Calgary AB Canada T3G1Z3 Office: Debolt Energy Ltd 230 840-6th Ave SW Calgary AB Canada T2P 3E5 Home Phone: 403-289-3273. Personal E-mail: wrhovdestad@shawlink.ca. E-mail: hovdestad@hotmail.com.

HOVEE, MARK JOHN, psychologist; b. Portland, Oreg., Feb. 20, 1954; s. Harry Juel and Janene Arden Hovee; m. Judy Lynn Pratt, Sept. 23, 2005; children: Nathanael James, Maris Alise, Claire Marie. BA in Polit. Sci., Seattle U., 1979; MA in Political Philosophy, Boston Coll., 1983; MA in Clin. Psychology, George Fox U., 1994, PsyD in Clin. Psychology, 1997; advanced cert. in peace studies, European Peace U., Stadtschlaining, Austria, 2007. Lic. psychologist Ky. Pvt. practice psychologist, Paintsville, Ky., 2002—; psychologist ARH Psych. Ctr., Hazard, Ky., 2003—04. Adj. faculty Union Inst., Cin., 1999—2003, Morehead State U., Prestonsburg, Ky., 2005—05; supr. U. Ky., Prestonsburg, 2001—04; psychologist Highlands Regional Hosp., Prestonsburg, 2001—04, 2007—, Correctin Corp. Am., Wheelwright, Ky., 2002—04; psychologist Landstuhl (Germany) Reg. Med. Ctr. U.S. Army, 2004—05; psychologist Corrections Corp. Am., Wheelwright, 2005—; presenter Transylvania U., Lexington, 2005. Contbr. articles to profl. jours.; author: Wayward Soldier: A Reserve Psychologist's Memoir and Analysis During the Second American-Iraqi War, 2007. Sgt. US Army, 1973—76, sgt. USAR, 1983—2001, capt. USAR, 2001—. Mem.: APA, Assn. Conflict Resolution, Brit. Psychol. Soc., Internat. Soc. Polit. Psychology (presenter 2004), Ky. Psychol. Assn. (presenter 2005), Rotary (presenter 2005). Democrat. Methodist. Avocations: skiing, swimming, tennis, boating, travel. Home and Office: PO Box 51 Paintsville KY 41240 Office Phone: 606-297-7315. Personal E-mail: markhovee@yahoo.com.

HOVENDICK, JAMES V., business law educator, retired aerospace engineer; b. Burt County, Nebr., Oct. 30, 1933; s. C. Vernon and Marjorie Hovendick; m. Arlene Pitre, Jan. 1, 1944; children: Karen Jeanine Hovendick-Premeaux, Michael John, Mitchell Dean, Susie Hovendick Chan, Timothy James. AA in Pre-engring., San Jacintgo Coll., 1967; BS in Econ., U. Houston, 1970, JD, 1975. Bar: State Bar Tex. 1975. Sr. aerospace engr. Ford Aerospace Corp., NASA Johnson Manned Space Ctr., Houston, 1961—79; prof. bus. San Jacinto Coll., Pasadena, Tex., 1979—2001; ret., 2001. Treas. Montgomery (Tex.) Pet Partners, Inc., 2003—06. Author: (textbook) Study Guide for Distant Learning: Introduction to Business, 1984, 9th edit., 1993. Candidate justice of the peace Galveston County, Friendswood, Tex., 1980; adult sunday sch. tchr. First Bapt. Ch. of Friendswood, Tex., 1976—99; adult sunday sch. class tchr. First Bapt. Ch. of Conroe, Tex., 2003—. With US Army, 1956—61. Mem.: ABA (assoc.), Houston Bar Assn., Montgomery County Bar Assn., State Bar Tex. (licentiate), Montgomery Country Early Ford V-8 Club (assoc.), Bentwater Country Club (licentiate), Men of Bentwater (assoc.), Men's Golf Assn., Bentwater Country Club (assoc.), Masonic Lodge 222 (assoc.), Phi Beta Lambda (advisor 1985—96, Outstanding Advisor 1986, 1987, 1989, 1992, 1993, 1994). Baptist. Avocations: golf, amateur radio, classic cars, travel. Home Phone: 936-597-6318.

HOVENKAMP, HERBERT, law educator; BA, Calvin Coll., 1969; MA, Univ. Tex., 1971, PhD, 1976, JD, 1978. Asst. instr., English, Am. Studies Univ. Tex., 1972—76, lectr., history, Am. Studies, 1976—79; assoc. prof. law Univ. Calif. Hastings Coll. Law, San Francisco, 1980—85; Ben V. & Dorothy Willie disting. prof. law, history Univ. Iowa, Iowa City, 1986—. Vis. prof., Coll. Law U. Iowa, 1984; vis. prof. Univ. Mich. Law Sch., 1986; lectr. in field. Bd. editor Journal of Legal History, 1981—, faculty advisor Hastings Journal Law, 1981—84, Journal of Corporation Law, 1987—; contbr. articles to profl. jours., chapters to books; author: Science and Religion in America: 1800-1860, 1978, Economics and Federal Antitrust Law, 1985, Enterprise and American Law: 1836-1937, 1991, Federal Antitrust Policy: The Law of Competition and Its Practices (1994, edits.: 2nd 1999, 3rd 2005), Fundamentals of Antitrust Law (Abridgement of Antitrust Law) 2002, 2nd edit. 2003, 3rd edit. 2004, 2005 & 2006 Supplements), The Antitrust Enterprise: Principle and Execution, 2006; co-author (P. Areeda & D. Turner): Antitrust Law (18 vol. + ann. supplement + end matter vol.), 1980—2006; co-author: Antitrust Law, Policy and Procedure (edits.: 1st 1984, 2nd 1989, 3rd 1994, 4th 1999, 5th 2003 teachers' manual 2004, supplement 2005); co-author: (with Mark D. Janis & Mark A. Lemley) IP and Antitrust: An Analysis of Antitrust Principles Applied to Intellectual Property Law, 2002—03; co-author: (with Sheldon F. Kurtz) American Property Law (edits.: 1st 1987, 2nd 1993, 3rd 1999, 4th 2003), The Law of Property: An Introductory Survey, 6th edit., 2005; co-author: (with Mark D. Janis & Mark A. Lemley) IP and Antitrust: An Analysis of Antitrust Principles Applied to Intellectual Property Law, 2006. Rockefeller Found. Humanities Fellow, Harvard Law Sch., 1979—80, Mark DeWolfe Howe Fellow, 1980. Fellow: Am. Coun. Learned Societies, Am. Acad. Arts & Scis. Office: 407 Boyd Law Bldg Univ Iowa Iowa City IA 52242-1113 Office Phone: 319-335-9079. Office Fax: 319-335-9098. Business E-Mail: herbert-hovenkamp@uiowa.edu.*

HOVER, CARL ARTHUR, retired minister; b. Medford, Oreg., May 12, 1936; s. Carl Arthur and Ruth Hawk Hover; m. Ellen East Dionna, June 3, 1976; children: Carla, Carl, Carson, Jonathan Wolf, Carol Wolf, Pamela Wolf, Franklin Wolf. BTh, NW Christian Coll., Eugene, Oreg., 1958; BA, U. Oreg., Eugene, 1962; MST, Tufts U., Medford, Mass., 1966, MEd, 1969. Minister Universalist Ch., Everett, Mass., 1965—67, Unitarian Ch., Sanford, Mass., 1967—76; exec. minister NE Dist. Unitarian Universalist Ch., Portland, Maine, 1972—76; sr. minister Valley Unitarian Universalist Ch., Chandler, Ariz., 1976—79, Unitarian Universalist Ch., Chelmsford, Mass., 1979—92; co-dir. Blessingwood Retreat Ctr., Corinth, Vt., 1992—2005; clinician Youth Adv., Inc., York, Pa., 2005—07. Instr. Sanford Pub. Sch., Maine, 1969—72, Rio Salado Coll., Mesa, Ariz., 1977; curriculum coun. Dover Pub. Sch., Pa., 2006—07. Ministerial com. Unitarian Universalist Congregation, York, 2006—07. Mem.: Unitarian Universalist Ret. Ministers and Ptnrs. Assn., Unitarian Universalist Ministers' Asn. Democrat. Avocations: camping, hiking, travel, gardening. Home: 1700 Palomino Rd Dover PA 17315

HOVER, JOHN CALVIN, II, banker; b. Orange, NJ, May 13, 1943; s. John Curry and Edith Margaret (Hopkins) H.; m. Jacqueline Whitley, Sept. 4, 1997; 1 child, Margaret Biddle. BA in English Lit., U. Pa., Phila., 1965, MBA in Mktg., 1967; postgrad., Aspen Inst., 1988. With Chem. Bank, 1968-76; with corp. banking and personal banking US Trust Co. of NY, NYC, 1976-80, sr. v.p., div. mgr., pvt. banking, 1980-91, exec. v.p. asset mgmt., pvt. banking group, 1991-98; retired, 1999. Chmn. U.S. Trust Pvt. Equity Fund; bd. dirs. New Hope & Ivyland R.R., Pa., Tweedy Browne Fund Inc.; former chmn. bd. overseers, U. Mus., Phila. Former trustee U. Pa., Phila. Mem. St. Nicholas Soc., 1st Troop Phila. City Cav., Soc. Colonial Wars, St. Andrews Soc., Most Venerable Order of Hosp. of St. John of Jerusalem, Knickerbocker Club, Univ. Club, Penn Club NY (bd. dirs.), Psi Upsilon. Avocation: railroadiana. Home: 72 N Main St New Hope PA 18938 Personal E-mail: jhover@erols.com.

HOVER, TRYPHENA MACHAEL, music educator; b. Clinton, Iowa, Mar. 8, 1951; d. Harold Eldred and Alvina Bell (Brink) Scott; m. Larry Odell Cooper, July 28, 1973 (dec. Oct. 1986); children: Erin Elizabeth Cooper, Jared Andrew Cooper; m. Terrance Dale Hover, June 25, 1988. B of Music Edn., NE Mo. State U., Kirksville, 1973; M of Elem. Edn., Drury U., Springfield, Mo., 1992. Cert. K-9 Art Tchr. Mo., 1976, Level 1 Am. Orff Schalwerk Assn., 1998, Level 2 Am. Orff Schalwerk Assn., 2000, Love & Logic Instr., 2002. Art & music tchr. La Plata Pub. Schs., Mo., 1973—77; curriculum writer Assembly of God Gospel Pub. House, Springfield, 1982—83; freelance decorative painter Springfield, 1984—86; music tchr. Fordland Pub. Schs., 1988—91; music & art tchr. Logan-Rogersville Pub. Schs., 1988—. Bd. mem. Children's Choirs S.W. Mo., Springfield, 2002—. Contbr. papers to profl. pubs. Ch. accompanist, choir mem. King's Chapel Assembly of God, Springfield, 1992—. Mem.: Kodaly of Ozarks ORgn. Am. Kodaly Educators, Ozark Mountain Orff Assn., Am. Orff-Schalwerk Assn., Mo. Music Educators Assn. Avocations: quilting, decorative painting, reading, interior decorating. Home: 6209 E Farm Rd 150 Springfield MO 65809 Office: Logan-Rogersville Primary Sch 7297 E Farm Rd 164 Rogersville MO 65742 Personal E-mail: tnthover@gmail.com.

HOVING, JOHN HANNES FORESTER, consulting firm executive; b. NYC, July 18, 1923; s. Hannes and Mary Alma (Gilbert) H.; m. Anne Fisher Spiers, Feb. 1, 1958; children: Christopher, Karen Anne, Katherine Jean. BA in History, U. Chgo., 1947. Radio news editor, reporter Milw. Jour., Capital Times, Madison, Wis., 1947-51; asst. to chmn. Democratic Nat. Com., 1952-54; exec. positions Kefauver, Stevenson, Johnson, Humphrey, Sanford presdl. campaigns; asst. to presdl. asst. for trade policy 1962; v.p. exec. action Air Transp. Assn. Am., Washington, 1956-64; propr. cons. firm Washington, 1964-72; sr. v.p. Federated Dept. Stores, Inc., Cin., 1972-82; pres. The Hoving Group (cons. firm), Washington, 1982—. Chmn. Washington Theol. Consortium, 1993-96; mem. adv. bd. Fashion Inst. Design Merchandising; past dep. chmn. planning Dem. Nat. Com. With AUS, 1943-46. Decorated Purple Heart, Bronze Star Mem. Am. Assn. Polit. Cons., Met. Club, Nat. Press Club, Nat. Capital Dem., Queen City Club (Cin.), Lotos Club (N.Y.C.). Home: 415 Dogleg Dr Williamsburg VA 23188 E-mail: hovings@aol.com.

HOVING, THOMAS, museum director, consultant, writer; b. NYC, Jan. 15, 1931; s. Walter and Mary (Osgood Field) H.; m. Nancy Melissa Bell, Oct. 3, 1953; 1 dau., Petrea Bell. BA, Princeton U., 1953, MFA, 1958, PhD, 1959, HHD (hon.), 1968; LHD (hon.), Hofstra U., 1966; LLD (hon.), Pratt Inst., 1967; DFA (hon.), NYU, 1968; LittD (hon.), Middlebury Coll., 1968. Staff Medieval Met. Mus. Art and The Cloisters, 1959-65, curator, 1965-66; commr. parks NYC, 1966-67; adminstr. Dept. Recreation and Cultural Affairs, 1967; dir. Met. Mus. Art, 1967-77; pres. Hoving Assocs., Inc., museum and cultural affairs cons. firm NYC, 1977—; pres. spl. mus. exhibitions The Planning Corp., 1983-91; arts and entertainment corr. ABC-TV show 20/20, 1978-84; editor Connoisseur mag., 1981-91. Author: Guide to the Cloisters, 1964, The Chase, The Capture, 1975, Kuerners and Olsons; exhbn. catalogue, 1976, Two Worlds of Andrew Wyeth: A Conversation with Andrew Wyeth, 1978, Tutankhamun, The Untold Story, 1978, King of the Confessors, 1981, Masterpiece, 1986, Discovery, 1989, Making the Mummies Dance, 1993, Andrew Wyeth: Autobiography, 1995, False Impressions, The Search for Big Time Art Fakes, 1996, Greatest Works of Art of Western Civilization, 1997, Art for Dummies, 1999, The Art of Dan Namingha, 2000, Am. Gothic, 2005, Master Pieces, The Curators' Game, 2005; contbr. articles on art, parks and recreation to profl. publs., mags. and newspapers. Past trustee Inst. Fine Arts NYU. Lt. USMC, 1953-55. Decorated knight Legion of Honor France; recipient Bronze medal Citizens Budget Com., 1966, Cue mag. award, 1966, Disting. Achievement award Advt. Club Am., 1966, Disting. Contbn. award Park Assn. N.Y.C., 1967, Elsie de Wolfe award Am. Inst. Interior Designers, 1967, Woodrow Wilson award Princeton U., 1977 Mem. AIA (hon.) Office: Hoving Assocs Inc 150 E 73rd St New York NY 10021-4362 E-mail: tomhoving@earthlink.net.

HOVLAND, ERIC JEFFREY, dean, endodontics educator; b. Oct. 9, 1946; married. Student, Lehigh U., 1964-66; BS, U. Md., 1968, DDS, 1972; MS in Adult Edn., Va. Commonwealth U., 1977; MBA in Health Care, Loyola Coll., 1980. Clin. instr. dept endodontics Med. Coll. Va., Sch. Dentistry, 1975-77; asst. prof. endodontics U. Md., Balt. Coll. Dental Surgery, 1977-82, dir. undergrad. clinics, Office Clin. Affairs, 1980—84, acting assoc. dean clin. affairs, 1981, assoc. prof. endodontics, 1982-89, chmn. dept. endodontics, 1985—93, dir. advanced splty. edn. in endodontics, 1986—87, prof. endodontics, 1989-93, acting v.p. for acad. affairs, 1991; prof. dept. endodontics La. State U. Med. Ctr. Sch. Dentistry, New Orleans, 1993—, dean, 1993—. Mem. cons. med. staff VA Hosp., New Orleans, 1994—, Med. Ctr. La., New Orleans, 1994—; cons. Northeast regional Bd. Dental Examiners, 1990-93, VA Hosp., Perry Pt., Md., the Johns Hopkins Hosp., Balt., 1980-85, U. Md. Hosp., 1978-82, others; pvt. practice endodontics, 1977-88. Contbr. articles to profl. jours., chpts. to books; mem. editorial bd. Oral Surgery, Oral Medicine, Oral Pathology, Oral Radiology, endodontics Jour., 1995—; clin. assoc. editor Balt. Coll. Dental Surgery Jour. 1975-79. With USAF, 1973—75. Fellow Internat. Coll. Dentists, Am. Coll. Dentists; mem. ADA (chmn. 1992-93, mem. adv. com. advanced edn. in endodontics 1990-96), Am. Assn. Endodontists (chmn. honors and awards com. 1997-98, nominations com. 1996, internat. rels. com. 1994-95, constitution and bylaws com. 1994-95, Pres.'s Cir. 1994-95, pres. 1993-94, others), Am. Assn. Dental Schs. (legis. adv. com. 1996—, info. tech. adv. com. 1996—, coun. of deans and house of dels. 1993—), Am. Dental Edn. Assn. (pres. 2005-2006), coun. of faculties and house of dels. 1983-86), Md. State Dental Assn. (strategic planning com. 1990, fin. com. 1985-87, others), La. State Dental Assn. (house of dels. 1994-95), New Orleans Dental Assn., Internat. Assn. for Dental Rsch., Am. Assn. for Dental Rsch., Internat. Assn. Dental Traumatology, So. Conf. of Deans and Dental Examiners (pres. 1995-96), Endodontic Soc. South Africa (hon.), Alumni Assn. of Balt. Coll. Dental Surgery U. Md. (chmn. class reunion 1982, 87), Alumni Assn. Sch. Bus. Loyola Coll. Office: La State U Sch Dentistry Office of Dean 1100 Florida Ave New Orleans LA 70119-2714 Office Phone: 504-619-8500. Business E-Mail: ehovla@lsuhsc.edu.

HOVNANIAN, ARA K., real estate developer; b. 1957; MBA, U. Pa., Phila., 1979. With Hovnanian Enterprises Inc., Red Bank, NJ, 1979—, bd. dirs., 1981—, exec. v.p. Red Bank, NJ, 1983—88, pres., 1988—, CEO, 1997—. Adv. coun. PNC Bank, Monmouth Real Estate Investment Corp., NJ. Mem. Coun. on Affordable Housing, NJ, 1985, NJ, 1990, Governor's Econ. Master Plan Commn., NJ, 1994. Office: Hovnanian Enterprises Inc 10 Highway 35 PO Box 5000 Red Bank NJ 07701-5997*

HOVNANIAN, KEVORK S., real estate developer; b. 1923; s.Stepan K. Hovnanian; married. Founder Hovnanian Enterprises Inc., Red Bank, NJ, 1959, CEO, 1967—97, chmn., 1967—. Recipient Harvard Dively Award for Leadership in Corp. Pub. Initiatives, 1992, President's Medal, NJ Inst. Tech., 1996. Office: Hovnanian Enterprises Inc 10 Hwy 35 PO Box 500 Red Bank NJ 07701-5902*

HOVSEPIAN, RONALD W., network management software company executive; b. 1961; m. Megan Hovsepian. BS, Boston Coll., 1983. Worldwide gen. mgr., industry solutions, retail sector IBM Corp., v.p., bus. develop., 1999—2000; mng. dir. Internet Capitol Group, Inc., 2000—02, Bear Stearns Asset Mgmt., 2002; exec. v.p., pres. N.Am. worldwide field ops. Novell, Inc., Waltham, Mass., 2003—05, pres., 2005—, COO, 2005—06, CEO, 2006—. Non-exec. chmn Ann Taylor Stores Corp., 2005—; bd. dirs. Novell, Inc., 2006—. Office: Novell Inc 404 Wyman St Ste 500 Waltham MA 02451

HOWALD, JOHN WILLIAM, lawyer; b. St. Louis, Dec. 21, 1935; s. Herbert John and Irene Dorothy (Weber) H.; m. Nina M. Zierendерg, June 15, 1957 (div. 1970); children: Deborah A., Catherine A., Laura A., John William; m. Betty L. Curtis, Feb. 14, 1971 (div. 1999); 1 stepchild, Tracy L.; m. Nancy J. Owens, Mar. 1, 2003. BS, U. Mo., 1957; JD, St. Louis U., 1962. Bar: Mo. 1962, U.S. Dist. Ct. (ea. dist.) Mo. 1962, U.S. Ct. Appeals (8th cir.) 1965, U.S. Supreme Ct. 1985. V.p. sales Eureka Svc. and Equip. Co., Eureka, Mo., 1959-62; ptnr. Sheehan, Furtaw & Howald, Hillsboro, Mo., 1963-64, Thurman, Nixon, Smith & Howald, Hillsboro, 1964-70, Thurman, Nixon, Smith, Howald, Weber & Bowles, Hillsboro, 1970-80, Thurman, Smith, Howald, Weber & Bowles, Hillsboro, 1989-91, Thurman, Howald, Weber, Bowles & Senkel, Hillsboro, 1991-95, Thurman, Howald, Weber, Senkel & Norrick, L.L.C., Hillsboro, 1995—. Bd. dirs. LaBarque Ent. of Jefferson County, Hillsboro, 1965-2002, Rustic Hills Resort Ltd., Hillsboro, 1968—. Mem. Mo. Ethics Commn., 1994-98, vice-chmn., 1995-96, chmn., 1996-98. Lt. (j.g.) USN, 1957-59. Recipient Spl. award, Meramec Basin Assn., 1967, 69. Fellow Am. Bar Found., Am. Coll. Trust and Estate Counsel (Mo. chmn. 1987-92); mem. ABA, Estate Planning Coun. St. Louis (pres. 1990-91), Mo. Bar Assn. (bd. govs. 1975-87, Pres. Spl. award 1979), Jefferson County Bar Assn. (pres. 1963-64). Avocations: travel, golf. Office: Thurman Howald Weber Senkel & Norrick LLC PO Box 800 One Thurman Ct 301 Main St Hillsboro MO 63050 Home: 505 Overlook Ter Eureka MO 63025 Home Phone: 636-938-9252; Office Phone: 636-789-2601. Business E-Mail: howald@thurmanlaw.com.

HOWANITZ, E. PAUL, thoracic surgeon; b. Wilkes-Barre, Pa., Jan. 15, 0950; s. Emil Paul Howanitz and Florence Schmick; m. Patricia Ann Denham, Mar. 14, 1980; children: Paul, Lauren. BS in Biology, Kings Coll., Wilkes-Barre, 1974; MD, Jefferson Med. Coll., Phila., 1978. Diplomate Am. Bd. Surgery, Am. Bd. Thoracic Surgery. Internship Thomas Jefferson U. Hosp., Phila.; gen. surgery residency Jefferson U. Hosp.;

thoracic surgery residency Ohio State U. Hosp., asst. prof. thoracic surgery Columbus, 1986—92; vascular surgery fellowship U. Kans. Med. Ctr.; cardiothoracic surgeon St. Lukes Hosp., Duluth, Minn., 1992—93; chief cardiothoracic surgery St. Joseph Med. Ctr., Reading, Pa., 1993—2005, also bd. dirs.; chief cardiothoracic surgery Reid Hosp., Richmond, Ind., 2005—. Contbr. articles to profl. jours. Fellow: ACS, Am. Coll. Cardiology; mem.: Soc. Thoracic Surgeons, Am. Coll. Chest Physicians. Avocations: skiing, travel. Office: Reid Hosp Chief Cardiothoracic Surgery 1401 Chester Blvd Richmond IN 47374

HOWARD, ALEX T., JR., federal judge; b. 1924; Student, U. Ala., 1942, student, 1946, Auburn U., 1942-44; JD, Vanderbilt U., 1950. U.S. probation officer, Mobile, Ala., 1950-51; ptnr. Johnstone, Adams, Howard, Bailey & Gordon, Mobile, 1951-86; U.S. commr. U.S. Dist. Ct. (so. dist.) Ala., Mobile, 1956—70, judge, 1986—, chief judge, 1989-94, sr. judge, 1996—. Assoc. editor Am. Maritime Cases for Port of Mobile. Served to 2d lt. U.S. Army, 1943-46. Mem. ABA, Internat. Soc. Barristers, Internat. Assn. of Ins. Counsel, Maritime Law Assn. of U.S., Southeastern Admiralty Law Inst. (dir. 1978-80), Ala. Bar Assn., Ala. Def. Lawyers Assn. (dir. late 1950's), Mobile Bar Assn. (pres. 1973). Office: 4201 Rochester Rd Mobile AL 36608-2238

HOWARD, ANDREW BAKER, lawyer; b. Watertown, NY, July 26, 1969; s. Courtland Rogers and Maryanne H.; m. Elizabeth Edge, June 8, 1996; children: Christopher Baker, Paul Andrew. BA cum laude, St. Lawrence U., 1991; JD cum laude, Union U., 1994. Bar: N.Y. 1995. Atty. Connor, Curran & Schram, Hudson, N.Y., 1994—; asst. dist. atty. Columbia County Dist. Attys., Hudson, 1995. Instr. Am. Inst. Banking, Albany, 1997—. Mem. N.Y. State Bar Assn., Columbia County Bar Assn., Justinian Soc., Columbia County C. of C. (bd. dirs.). Republican. Roman Catholic. Avocations: mountain biking, skiing, shooting. Home: 3075 Upper Main St Valatie NY 12184 Office: Connor Curran & Schram PC 441 E Allen St Hudson NY 12534-2422 Office Phone: 518-828-1521. Business E-Mail: howard@ccslawfirm.com.

HOWARD, ARTHUR ELLSWORTH DICK, law educator; b. Richmond, Va., July 5, 1933; s. Thomas Landon and Marie Antoinette (Dick) H. BA, U. Richmond, 1954; LLB, U. Va., 1961; BA with honors, Oxford U., 1960, MA, 1965; LLD (hon.), James Madison U., 1983, U. Richmond, 1984, Campbell U., 1986, Coll. William and Mary, 1991, Wake Forest U., 2000. Bar: Va., D.C. 1961. Asso. Covington & Burling, Washington, 1961-62; law clk. to Supreme Ct. Justice Hugo L. Black, Washington, 1962-64; assoc. prof. law U. Va., Charlottesville, 1964-67, prof., 1967-76, White Burkett Miller prof. law and public affairs, 1976—, assoc. dean, 1967-69, dir. Ctr. for Pub. Svc., 1988-89, Earle K. Shawe rsch. prof., 2006—. Bd. dirs. Am. Ditchley Found.; counsel sessions Gen. Assembly Va., 1969—70. Author: Commentaries on the Constitution of Virginia, 2 vols., 1974 (Phi Beta Kappa prize), The Road from Runnymede: Magna Carta and Constitutionalism in America, 1968, (with Baker and Derr) Church, State and Politics, 1982, Democracy's Dawn, 1991, Constitution-Making in Eastern Europe, 1993, Magna Carta: Text and Commentary, 1998; bd. editors The American Oxonian, 1968—, The Wilson Quar., 1977—. Chmn., exec. dir. Va. Commn. on Constl. Revision, 1968—69; chmn. Va. Commn. on Bicentennial of US Constn., 1985—92; mem. Va. Ind. Bicentennial Commn., 1966—83; vice chmn. Magna Carta Commn. Va., 1965—66; Va. sec. Rhodes Scholarship Trust, 1970—; counselor to Gov. of Va., 1982—86; bd. dirs. Am. Ditchley Found., 2003—, James Madison Meml. Found., Jamestown-Yorktown Found., 2003—; hon. mem. High Table Christ Ch., Oxford, 2002—. With US Army, 1954—56. Recipient Disting. Prof. award U. Va., 1981, Randa medal Czech Republic, 1996, George C. Marshall award internat. law and diplomacy World Affairs Coun., 2004; fellow Woodrow Wilson Internat. Ctr. for Scholars, Smithsonian Instn., Washington, 1974-75, 76-77; fellow Ctr. Advanced Studies U. Va., 1970-71, 76-77, 82-83; Rhodes scholar Oxford U., 1958-60; Disting. Vis. scholar in residence Rhodes Ho., Oxford U., 2001. Mem. Va. Bar Assn. (v.p. 1970-71), Va. Acad. Laureates (chmn. 1981-92), Lit. Soc. (Washington), Cosmos Club (Washington), Oxford and Cambridge Club (London). Episcopalian. Home: 627 Park St Charlottesville VA 22902-4654 Office: U Va Sch Law 580 Massie Rd Charlottesville VA 22903-1738 Office Phone: 434-924-3097. E-mail: adh3m@virginia.edu.

HOWARD, BLAIR DUNCAN, lawyer; b. Alexandria, Va. s. T. Brooke and Elizabeth Duncan H.; m. Catherine Cremins; children: Thomas Brooke II, Caitlin Margaret. BA, U. Va., 1960; LLB, American U., 1963. Ptnr. Howard, Leino & Howard, Alexandria, Va., 1966—. Capt. USA, 1963-65. Named a Superstar Ohio Assn. Criminal Defense Lawyers, Columbus, 1994; named one of Top Lawyers in Met. Washington, Washingtonian Mag., 1997, Va.'s Legal Elite Va. Bus. Mag., 2003, 06, Best Lawyers in Am. Fellow Am. Coll. Trial Lawyers; mem. ABA, ATLA, Alexandria Bar Assn., Va. State Bar Assn. (faculty professionalism course 1990-93). Office: Howard Morrison & Howard 1 Wall Street Warrenton VA 20186-3319 Business E-Mail: blair.howard@hmhlawfirm.com.

HOWARD, BONNIE, bank executive; BS, Univ. Mo. CPA, registered Fin. & Ops. Principal, NASD. Acct. KPMG, Ernst & Young; mng. dir. J.P. Morgan, 1988—2000; dep. auditor FleetBoston Fin. Corp., 2000—02; mng. dir. audit & risk review Citigroup Inc., NYC, 2003—04, chief auditor, mem. mgmt. com., 2004—. Mem. adv. council YWCA Acad. Women Leaders; mem. exec. steering com. Women's Health Symposium; co-chmn. Hunter Coll. High Sch. Annual Fund. Office: Citigroup 399 Park Ave New York NY 10043*

HOWARD, BRUCE ALLEN, social studies educator; b. Cleve., Tex., Mar. 24, 1962; s. Ronald James and Mary Leigh Howard; m. Stephanie Ann Traver; children: Michelle Lorrainne, Nicholas Alan, Zachary Ryan, Reagan Leigh, Herbert Glenn, Patrick Vincent. BS, Ohio State U., Columbus, 1994. Cert. secondary edn. Ga. Profl. Standards Bd., 2005. Inf. soldier US Army, Various, 1982—92; social studies tchr., football coach Mishawaka High Sch., Ind., 1995—2002; asst. football coach Earlham Coll., Richmond, Ind., 2002—03; assoc. prof. Manchester Coll., Ind., 2003—04; social studies tchr. Kell High Sch., Marietta, Ga., 2005—, asst. varsity football coach, 2006—. Mem. Youth Coun. No. Ind. Workforce Investment Bd., South Bend, 1998—2002, Ind. State Tchrs. Assn. Profl. Practices and Standards Bd., Indpls., 1999—2002. State chmn. Youth For Reagan, Columbus, 1980; intern US Ho. of Rep., Washington, 1980; state treas. Ohio Coll. Republicans, Columbus, 1980—81; mem. Franklin County Young Republicans, Columbus, 1980—82; senate page Ohio Senate, Columbus, 1980—81; campaign mem. Van Meter for Gov., Columbus, 1981—82; legislative Asst. Ohio Senate, Columbus, 1981—82; mem. Voinovich Reelection Campaign, Columbus, 1994, Daniels Gubernatorial Campaign, South Bend, Ind., 2004. Decorated Ranger Tab US Army, Master Airborne Wings, Bronze Star, Purple Heart with 3 Oak Clusters, Meritorious Svc. medal, Army Comendation medal, Armed Forces Expeditionary medal, Korean Def. Svc. Medal, Multi-National Forces and Observers medal; named Tchr. of Month, Mishawaka High Sch., 2001; recipient Courage award, 1996. Mem.: Am. Meteorological Soc., Nat. Coun. Social Studies, Am. Football Coaches Assn., VFW, Am. Legion, DAV, Am. Airborne Assn., 75th Ranger Rgt. Assn., US Army Ranger Assn., 101st Airborne Divsn. Assn. (life), Ohio State U. Alumni Assn., Ind. Chapter-101st Airborne Divsn. Assn. (life; secretary-treasurer 1996—2000), Sigma Alpha Epsilon. R-Conservative. Lutheran. Avocations: flying, fishing, hunting, piano. Home: 229 Hillcrest Ridge Canton GA 30115 Office: Kell High Sch 4770 Lee Waters Rd Marietta GA 30066 Home Phone: 770-827-2191; Office Phone: 678-494-7844. Personal E-mail: bruce.howard@cobbk12.org.

HOWARD, CARL, retired lawyer; b. Chgo., July 23, 1920; m. Kathleen Agnes Costello, May 10, 1953; 1 child, Carl. AB, DePauw U., Greencastle, Ind., 1942; JD, U. Calif., San Francisco, 1949. Bar: Calif. 1951. Supervising dep. corps. commr. State of Calif., San Francisco, 1951-69; supervisory asst., asst. house counsel Fed. Home Loan Bank of San Francisco, 1970-75; legal counsel Home Fed. Savs. and Loan Assn., San Francisco, 1976-88, chmn. bd. dirs., 1985-86; assoc. Kerner, Colangelo & Imlay, 1976-86; sole practice San Francisco, 1987—96; ret., 1997. Lt. USNR, 1942-46, PTO. Mem. State Bar Calif., Am. Legion. Republican. Roman Catholic. Avocations: walking, golf, bicycling. Home: 2450 Quintara St San Francisco CA 94116-1139

HOWARD, CAROLYN F., elementary school educator; d. Ray Harold and Julia Melba (Reagan) Wooten; 1 child, Ron R. BS, West Tex. A&M U., Canyon, Tex., 1968, MEd, 1984. Cert. mid-mgmt. West Tex. A&M U., supr. Tex. Tech, reading recovery tchr. leader Tex. Women's U. Tchr. fourth grade Amarillo ISD, Amarillo, Tex., 1968—72; tchr. first grade Vernon ISD, Vernon, Tex., 1972—73, Amarillo ISD, Amarillo, Tex., 1973—79, Cartwright #84, Phoenix, 1979—80; reading skills tchr. Amarillo ISD, Amarillo, Tex., 1980—84; title 1 coord., trainer results based monitoring, reading recovery tchr leader Region 16 ESC, Amarillo, Tex., 1984—2002; reading recovery tchr leader Portales Mcpl. Schs., Portales, N.Mex., 2002—07, literacy leader, 2002—07; ret. Quality N.Mex. examiner N.Mex. Pub. Edn. Dept., Santa Fe, 2003—05. Classroom tchr. grant, Tchr. Orgn. Dumas, 1963. Mem.: Assn. Supervision and Curriculum Devel., Reading Recovery Coun. N.Am., Panhandle Reading Assn. (pres.), Phi Delta Kappa (sec.). Baptist. Avocations: reading, walking. Office: Portales Mcpl Schs 501 S Abilene Portales NM 88130 Home: 19 Memory Pl Amarillo TX 79109

HOWARD, CECIL BYRON, retired pediatrician; b. Wallins, Ky., Apr. 16, 1927; s. William Knott and Maggie (Cawood) H.; m. Rebekah Ann Buckley, Mar. 4, 1931; children: Mark Byron, Sally Ann Howard Truxal, Maggie Elizabeth Howard Ray. BA, Vanderbilt U., 1949, MD, 1953. Intern U. Va. Hosp., Charlottesville, 1953-54; resident U. Tex. Med. Br., Galveston, 1954-56; pediatrician pvt. practice, Maryville, Tenn., 1956—2006. Dir. Christian Ch. Found. Handicapped, 1983—; elder 1st Christian Ch., Maryville, 1961-2003; scoutmaster Boy Scouts Am., 1964-79, chmn. Tuckaleechee Dist. Great Smoky Mountain Coun., 1973-75; mem. Blount County D.H.S. Child Abuse Rev. Team, 1965-2002. With U.S. Army, 1945-47. Fellow Am. Acad. Pediatrics; mem. Blount County Med. Soc. (pres. 1973), Maryville Optimist Club (pres. 1973). Republican. Avocations: hiking, piano, reading. Office: 1220 S Dogwood Dr Maryville TN 37804-5214

HOWARD, CHRISTOPHER PHILIP, management consultant, investor; b. NYC, Aug. 6, 1947; s. Murray and Hope (McGurn) H.; m. Danina Mary Hill, June 29, 1987; children: Sean, Stephen, Coby, Katherine, Sara. BA in Econs., Stanford U., 1968; MBA, Santa Clara U., 1970. Cert. mgmt. acct., bus. counselor, mgmt. cons. Cons. Ernst & Ernst, CPAs, Phoenix, 1972-74; ops. mgr. Jensen Tools & Alloys Inc., Phoenix, 1974-77; CFO Pioneer Industries, Inc., Phoenix, 1977-80; sr. v.p. Health-Tech Mgmt., Inc., Phoenix, 1980-84; mng. prin. Howard and Assocs., Inc., Phoenix, 1984-87; consulting mgr. Grant Thornton, CPAs, Reno, 1987-89; mng. dir. Howard Consulting Group, Inc., Reno, 1989—2002; faculty mem. U. Nev., Reno, 1991—2001; CEO North Star Investors, Inc., 2002—. 1st lt. USAF, 1970-72. Mem.: Inst. Cert. Mgmt. Cons., Stanford U. Alumni Assn., Inst. Cert. Bus. Counselors, Inst. Cert. Mgmt. Accts. Episcopalian. Office: NorthStar Investors 661 Sierra Rose Dr Reno NV 89511 Home: 4920 Turning Leaf Way Reno NV 89515 Office Phone: 775-954-2020. Business E-Mail: chris@northstarinvestors.com.

HOWARD, DAVID, ballet master, school administrator; b. London, June 14, 1937; came to US, 1966; s. Walter and Dorothy (Fell) Edwards. Grad., Arts Ednl. Sch., London, 1955; D (hon.), Oklahoma City U., 1998. Mem. faculty Sch. Ballet, Harkness House for Ballet Arts, NYC, 1966—; prin. tchr. Harkness Ballet Co., NYC, 1967—; dir. Sch. Ballet Harkness House for Ballet Arts, NYC, 1969—; founder David Howard Sch. Ballet, NYC, 1977; co. tchr. Am. Ballet Theatre, 1990—2002, 2002—03. Am. judicator 1st Internat. Ballet Competition, Miss., 1979; co-dir., co-founder Northeastern Ballet Summer Sch., Bard Coll., 1979; assoc. artistic dir. Catskill Ballet Theatre, 1980; founder David Howard Dance Ctr., NYC, 1986—; mem. founding bd. Swiss Profl. Sch., Zurich; guest tchr. Royal Ballet, 1986—87, 1993, 95, San Francisco Ballet, Juilliard Sch., New Sch. U., 2004—; guest tchr., coach Am. Ballet Theatre, 1990—93, 1998—99, 2000—01, tchr. training program; guest tchr., coach Bejart Ballet, 1992—94; guest tchr. Royal Ballet, 1998—2001; artistic advisor Nat. Dance Co. Mex., Mexico City, 1996—97; artistic assoc. Marin Dance Theatre, San Rafael, Calif., 1996—97; tng. David Howard Found., Seattle, Tulsa, Dallas, Erie, Pa., Boston, NYC, 1990—96; tchr. steps Broadway Dance Ballet Acad., East NYC, 1996—2001; tchr. NY On The Rd., 1996—2001, Broadway Dance Steps, 2004—05; tng. program Internat. Ballet Competition, Jackson, Miss., 1998; mem. faculty New Sch. U., NYC, 1998—2002; tng. program Internat. Ballet Competition, 2002; guest tchr., coach Royal Ballet, 2004—06. Prin. dancer London Palladium, 1955—57, soloist Royal Ballet Eng., 1958—63, Nat. Ballet Can., 1963—64, appeared in (musical) Little Me, London, 1964—66; collaborator double album ballet music:; with Royal Ballet Eng., 1957—63, Royal Ballet, 1997—2001, 1991—92; with Royal Ballet, 2003—; with Royal Ballet, 2004, Finnish Nat. Ballet, 1999, Royal Swedish Ballet, 1977—, Finnish Ballet, 2004, Hett Nat. Ballet, Holland, 2004, choreographer Rachmaninoff Suite, 1971—, Divertissement D'Adam, 1971—, Rossini Variations, 1973, Designs in Shades of Baroque, 1974, Fantasy, 1980, David Howard Shoe, Prima Soft, 2004, others; tchg. record albums include David Howard in Class, 2005, rec. (DVD) A Dancer's Class, 2004, Turns, Leaps and Bounds, 2005, Celebration, Royal Danish Ballet, 2006, Royal Ballet, 2006—, Turns and Jumps, 2005, rec. 25 video tapes, 125 CDs on ballet. Recipient Dance Master of Am. ann. award, 1983, Dance Mag. award, 2006. Mem. Regional Dance Am. (dir. pres.), royal Acad. Dancing, London Actors Equity (Adeline Genee Silver medal for male dancers 1954). Office Phone: 212-724-2149. Business E-Mail: masterteacher@rcn.com. *Have followed with great enthusiasm the growth of dance in the United States and have dedicated myself to the development of ballet training in America and bring it to a higher level. Have devoted time and effort to Regional Dance America, which reflects and contributes to the ever increasing size of ballet audiences across America. With this happening, no longer will the dancers who are developed each year have to seek employment within the long established European system of state-supported ballet houses, which is fast changing in 2005.*

HOWARD, DAVID, retired educational association administrator, writer; b. Delaware, Ohio, Sept. 24, 1929; s. Dale David and Clarine (Morehouse) H. BA, Ohio Wesleyan U., Delaware, 1953; student, Columbia U, NYC, 1961—62, student, 1986, NYU, 1985—86. Lic. tchr., attendance coordinator, N.Y. News writer Australian Broadcasting Co., Sydney, 1955; editl. asst. N.Y. Times, 1956—58; tchr. social studies N.Y.C. Bd. of Edn., 1958—82, hotel and shelter ednl. coord., 1982—89; asst. supr. N.Y.C. Truancy Patrol Teams, 1989—2005; ret., 2005. Author: Night Lights Went Out, 1966, Casa Alhambra, 1968, Picker of the Kingdom, 1999, Springtime for Kelly, 2001. Reservist FEMA, N.Y.C., 1980—. Lt. col. USAFR, 1953-75. Mem.: English Speaking Union, Mystery Writers of Am. Republican. Protestant. N.Y.C. Anchor & Saber. Home: 324 E 61st St Apt 20 New York NY 10021-8709

HOWARD, DAVID E., artist; b. NYC, Jan. 25, 1952; s. John C. and Florence (Martino) H. Student, Ohio U., 1969-71; MFA, San Francisco Art Inst., 1974. Comml. photographer, Athens, Ohio, 1969-71; tchr. photography San Francisco Ctr. for Visual Studies, 1971-74, visual artist in photography, 1975—, dir., 1975—. Vis. instr. City Coll. San Francisco; grad. instr. San Francisco Art Inst. Author: Photography for Visual Communicators, (monographs) Realities, 1976, Perspectives, 1978, The Last Filipino Head Hunters, 2001, American Artist, 1990, Objective Reality of Illusionistic Perceptions, 1970, The Hidden World of the Naga, 2003, Sacred Journey: The Ganges to the Himalayas Taschen, 2004, The World of Tattoo, 2005; photography numerous periodicals including Village Voice, N.Y.C., San Francisco Chronicle, Artweek, N.Y. Art Revs., 1990, L.A. Reader, Tribal Arts mag., 1998, 2002, Filipinas, 1998, Patagonia Mag., 2002, Vogue, 2995, Esquire Tokyo, 2005; TV Documentary series; one-man shows include G. Ray Hawkins Gallery, LA, Calif., Images Gallery N.Y.C., U. Calif. Extension, John Bolles Gallery, San Francisco, Hirshhorn Mus., Smithsonian Instn., Washington, San Francisco Art Inst., Ohio U., Athens, Thomas J. Crowe Gallery, L.A., Madison (Wis.) Art Ctr., Lehigh U., Pa., Fourth Street Gallery, N.Y.C., Intersection Gallery, San Francisco, Third Eye Gallery, N.Y.C., Ctr. for Visual Studies, San Francisco, Hutchinson Community Coll., Kans., Hank Baum Gallery, San Francisco, Martin Webber Gallery, 1986, Marc Richards Gallery, L.A., 1987, E.Z.T.V., L.A., 1987, 88, G. Ray Hawkins Gallery, L.A., 1988, Fine Arts Mus. L.I., 1989, Phila. Mus. Art, 1990, San Jose, Calif., 2000; numerous group shows including Art Commn. Gallery, San Francisco, DeYoung Mus., San Francisco, Oakland (Calif.) Mus., Palace of Fine Arts, San Francisco, Camera Work, L.A., Erie (Pa.) Art Ctr., Vorpal Gallery, 1985, Cal. State U., 1988, San Francisco Pub. Libr., 1987, Video Refuses, 1986, Hadley Martin Gallery, San Francisco, 1987, Fine Art Mus. L.I., 1989, Chandler Gallery, Seattle, 1991; represented in collections Mus. Modern Art, N.Y.C., Oakland (Calif.) Mus., San Francisco Mus. Modern Art, City of San Francisco, De Saisset Art Gallery, Santa Clara, Calif., Whitney Mus. Am. Art, Hirshhorn Mus., Smithsonian Instn., Art Ctr., Waco, Tex., Memphis Brooks Mus., Memphis, Akron (Ohio) Art Mus., Am. Mus. Natural History, N.Y.C. Spl. Collections; pvt. collections; prodr. videotape New York's East Village Art Scene, 1985, California's Art Scene, 1986, others; prodr. exptl. films: Analysis of Realities, 1974, Levels of Consciousness, 1976, Levels of Reality; prodr., dir. Art Seen, TV comml. documentary series on contemporary art televised in N.Y.C., L.A., San Francisco, Miami, Fla., Portland, Oreg., New Orleans, San Francisco, aired PBS, 1994, T.V. show Keith Haring: Artist at Work, selected segments shown Whitney Mus., Hirschhorn-Smithsonian Instn.; internat. exhbns. 10th and 13th Internat. Exhbns. Contemporay Art, Royan, France, 34thand 41st Internat. Salons of Japan, Tokyo, and 5 cities, Mex. Exhbn., Ex Convento de Carman, Guadalajara, 31st Cork Film Festival, 1986, Chgo. Film Festival, 1986, 42nd San Francisco Internatl. Film Fest., 1999, Presidio Earth Days Fest., 1999; other mus., galleries, univs. in U.S. and Europe; produced and directed films New York's East Village Art Scene, 1985, California's Art Scen, Parts 1 & 2, Levels of consciousness, Levels of Reality; presenter weekly cable TV series; Blackstar syndicated photographer, N.Y.C.; video journalist Asia-Pacific Econ. Conf., 1996, (documentary) Bill Clinton Pres. U.S. and 15 other heads of states, Manila, Philippines, 1996. Recipient San Francisco Art Festival award.

HOWARD, DAVID MILES, lawyer; b. New Rochelle, NY, May 29, 1959; s. Leon M. and Helen J. (Lepow) H.; m. Dale P. Schomer, Apr. 17, 1988; children: Rachel, Emma. AB cum laude, Princeton U., NJ, 1981; JD cum laude, U. Pa., 1984. Bar: Pa. 1984, U.S. Dist. Ct. (ea. dist.) Pa. 1984, U.S. Ct. Appeals (3rd cir.) 1996. Law clk. to Hon. Marvin Katz U.S. Dist. Ct. (ea. dist) Pa., 1984-85; assoc. Dechert Price & Rhoads, Phila., 1985-87, ptnr., 1996—; atty. White House counsel, Washington, 1987; asst. U.S. atty. U.S. Atty.'s Office, Phila., 1987-94. Lectr. U. Pa. Law Sch., Phila., 1995-97. Editor: Univ. Pa. Law Rev., 1982—84. Named 1 of Pa. "Super Lawyers" Phila. Mag. Mem.: ABA (co-chmn., subcom. corp. internal investigations), Order of the Coif. Office: Dechert LLP 2929 Arch St Philadelphia PA 19104 Home Phone: 610-649-6062; Office Phone: 215-994-2218. Business E-Mail: david.howard@dechert.com.

HOWARD, DEAN DENTON, electrical engineer, researcher, consultant; BSEE, Purdue U., 1949; MSEE, U. Md., 1951. Elec. engr. Naval Research Lab., Washington, 1949-84; cons. in elec. engring. Kaman Corp., Alexandria, Va., 1984-94; cons. to ITT Industries, Inc., 1994—. Instr. George Washington U., Washington, 1983-94. Author: (with others) Radar Handbook, 1990; co-author: Radar Handbook, 1970, Airborne Radar, 1961; contbr. articles to IEEE jour.; patentee (multiple) in monopulse radar and related fields. Served with USN, 1945-46 Recipient Radar Devel. award U.S. Navy, 1978, Meritorious Civilian Service award, 1980 Fellow IEEE; mem. Research Soc. Am. Avocation: amateur radio. Personal E-mail: dean.howard@nrl.navy.mil.

HOWARD, DONALD SEARCY, banker; b. Leadville, Colo., Aug. 13, 1928; s. Paul Parker and Amanda Jane (Searcy) H.; m. Phyllis Havey, Oct. 1, 1955; children: Steven, Julie, Rebecca, Martin BSBA, Northwestern U., 1950; MBA, Harvard U., 1955. Rsch. assoc. Bus. Sch., Harvard U., Boston, 1955-57; ofcl. asst. overseas div. Citibank, London, 1957; asst. cashier Citibank, N.A., NYC, 1959-60, asst. v.p., 1960-63, v.p., 1963-69, dep. comptroller, 1969-72; sr. v.p.-fin. Citicorp-Citibank, 1972-79, exec. v.p., chief fin. officer, 1980-88; chief fin. officer Salomon Inc., NYC, 1988-93. Mem. fin. acctg. stds. adv. com. Fin. Acctg. Bd., Stamford, Conn., 1985-88; mem. Internat. Acctg. Stds. Adv. Commn., London, 1986-93; bd. dirs. Bank Leumi U.S.A., Howard Vending, Miami, Green Garden Products LLC, Bedford, Digital Wireless Corp., L.A. Co-Author: Managing The Liability Side of the Balance Sheet, 1976, Evolving Concepts of Bank Capital Management, 1980 Chair emeritus trustees Cornerstone Sch., Jersey City, 1993-2002; trustee Vis. Nurse Assn. Ctrl. N.J., 1995-97. Lt. comdr. USNR, 1950-57, Korea. Mem. Am. Bankers Assn. (chief fin. officer's exec. com. 1984-87). Presbyterian. E-mail: Phyldonhow@aol.com.

HOWARD, DOUGLAS L., literature and language professor; b. Freeport, NY, Jan. 21, 1966; s. Philip L. and Joyce A. Howard; m. Jennifer J. Fuller, Aug. 2, 2002. BA, Adelphi U., 1988; MA, NYU, 1990, PhD, 1998. Writing ctr. coord. Suffolk County CC, Selden, NY, 2000—05, asst. academic chmn., 2005—. Co-editor: The Gothic Other, 2004; contbr. essays to profl. publs. Mem.: MLA, N.E. MLA. Office: Suffolk County CC 533 College Rd Selden NY 11784 Office Phone: 631-451-4485. Business E-Mail: howardd@sunysuffolk.edu.

HOWARD, DWIGHT DAVID, II, professional basketball player; b. Atlanta, Dec. 8, 1985; s. Dwight David and Sheryl Howard. Ctr.-forward Orlando Magic, 2004—. Mem. US Sr. Men's Nat. team FIBA World Championship, 2006. Co-founder Dwight D. Howard Found., Inc., Coll. Pk., Ga., 2004. Named McDonald's Nat. HS Player of Yr., 2004, Co-MVP, McDonald's HS All-Am. Game, 2004, Mr. Basketball, State of Ga., 2004; named to PARADE Mag. All-Am. Team, 2004, All-Rookie 1st Team, NBA, 2005, Ea. Conf. All-Star Team, 2007; recipient Naismith award, 2004, Morgan Wooten HS Player of Yr. award, 2004, Gatorade Nat. Player of Yr. award, 2004, Rich and Helen De Vos Cmty. Enrichment award, 2005. Achievements include being the first overall draft pick in the 2004 NBA draft; first player in NBA history directly out of high school to start in all 82 games during his rookie season; became youngest player in NBA history with 20 or more rebounds in a game on December 1, 2004 against the Toronto Raptors; led NBA in rebounds (1008), 2007. Mailing: Orlando Magic 8701 Maitland Summit Blvd Orlando FL 32810*

HOWARD, ELIZABETH ANN BLANTON, transportation executive; b. Spindale, NC, Mar. 14, 1934; d. John Lloyd and Monnie Clare (Geer) Blanton; m. Bill O. Howard, Aug. 13, 1950; children: Deborah Monette Howard Gustafson, Michael Ray. Real estate student, U. SC, 1965. Sales rep. Res. Life Ins. Co., Rutherfordton, NC, 1956—63; sec., salesperson Johnny Barker Real Estate, Columbia, SC, 1963—65; sec. A.M. Pullen & Co., Columbia, 1963—65; owner, mgr. Ann's Sample Shop, Columbia, 1965—81; pres. Modubilt Corp., Columbia, 1965—75, First Comml. Assocs., Inc., Columbia, 1965—75, Ann's Rag Time Van, Columbia, 1975—88; sec., treas., owner Howard's Courier Svc., Inc., Rutherfordton, 1990—2000, v.p., 2000—. Bldg. project mgr. Gen. Svc. Adminstrn., 1960's. Contbg. editor: Creative Ways to Raise Funds and Activate Alumni, 1995; contbr. History Book for Spindale United Meth. Ch. Pres. Spindale Elem. PTA, 1959, Belvedere Elem. PTA, Columbia, SC, 1963—66, Rutherford County Concert Assn., 2000—; bd. dirs. Rutherfordton, NC C. of C., 1991—92, 1996—99, 2000—01, Habitat, 2000—02. Named Sec. of Yr. WIOS Radio, Columbia SC, 1967; recipient Charles Z. Flack award, Rutherfordton, NC, 1992, award for svc. Am. Cancer Soc., 1994-96, Gov.'s award 2000. Mem. Sears Coun. of Career Women (charter), Rutherfordton Hist. Soc., Rutherfordton Ctrl. H.S. Alumni Assn. (pres. 1992—, All Class Reunion award 1992), Nat. Honor Soc.02099712 Democrat. Methodist. Achievements include holding first ever Fall Festival in Town of Spindale, NC, 2006. Avocations: travel, rehabilitation of older homes, reading. Home: 1198 Oak Springs Rd Rutherfordton NC 28139-8099 Office: PO Box 475 Spindale NC 28160-0475

HOWARD, GARY SCOTT, communications executive; b. Waukegan, Ill., Feb. 21, 1951; s. Clarence Turner Howard and Jan E. (Reimer) Searcy; m. Jacquelyn Jule Milne, Apr. 22, 1978; children: Gentry, Matthew, Chad. BS in Acctg., Colo. State U., 1973. Audit mgr. Arthur Andersen, Denver, 1973-80; v.p. Castle Pines Land Co., Denver, 1980-82; v.p. fin., treas., sec. The Sienna Co., Boulder, Colo., 1982-84; v.p., treas. United Cable TV, Denver, 1987-89; sr. v.p., treas. United Artists Entertainment Co., 1989, sr. v.p., chief adminstrv. officer, 1990—. Mem. Am. Inst. CPA's, Colo. Soc. CPA's. Roman Catholic. Avocations: hockey, sports.

HOWARD, GENE CLAUDE, lawyer, retired state senator; b. Perry, Okla., Sept. 26, 1926; s. Joe W. and Nell L. (Brown) Howard; m. Belva J. Prestidge, Dec. 28, 1979; children: Jean Ann, Joe Ted, Belinda Janice. JD, U. Okla., 1951. Bar: Okla. 1950, U.S. Ct. Mil. Appeals 1956, U.S. Supreme Ct. 1956. Ptnr. Howard & Widdows PC (and predecessors), Tulsa, 1952—; mem. Okla. Ho. of Reps., 1958-62, Okla. Senate, 1964-82, pres. pro tem, 1974-81. Mem. exec. com. Coun. State Govts., 1974—76; chmn. Okla. State and Edn. employees Group Ins. Bd., 1990—98; bd. dirs. Cubic Energy Corp., Local Okla. Bank, 1992—2004; trustee Phila. Mortgage Trust, Okla. Coll. Savs. Plan, 1998—2002. Mem. So. Growth Policy Bd., 1972—76; pres. Okla. Jr. Dems., 1954; del. Dem. Nat. Conv., 1964. With US Army, 1944—46, PTO, lt. col. USAF, 1961—62. Mem.: Phi Delta Phi, Tulsa County Bar Assn. (Outstanding Young Atty. 1953), Okla. Bar Assn. Democrat. Mem. Disciples Of Christ. Home: 2404 E 29th St Tulsa OK 74114-5619 Office: Howard Widdows PC 1500 Nations Bank Ctr 15W6 Tulsa OK 74119 Home Phone: 918-744-1119; Office Phone: 918-744-7440. Personal E-mail: howardgc@swbell.net.

HOWARD, GEORGE, JR., federal judge; b. Pine Bluff, Ark., May 13, 1924; Student, Lincoln U., 1951; BS, U. Ark., JD, 1954; LL.D., 1976. Bar: Ark. bar 1953, U.S. Supreme Ct. bar 1959. Pvt. practice law, Pine Bluff, 1953-77; spl. assoc. justice Ark. Supreme Ct., 1976, assoc. justice, 1977; justice U.S. Ct. Appeals, Ark., 1979-80; U.S. dist. judge, Eastern dist. Little Rock, 1980—. Mem. Ark. Claims Commn., 1969-77; chmn. Ark. adv. com. Civil Rights Commn. Recipient citation in recognition of faithful and disting. svc. as mem. Supreme Ct. Com. of Profl. Conduct, 1980, disting. jurist award Jud. Coun. Nat. Bar Assn., 1980, Wiley A. Branton Issues Symposium award, 1990; voted outstanding trial judge 1984-85 Ark. Trial Lawyers Assn.; inducted Ark.'s Black Hall of Fame, 1994; recipient keepers of the spirit award Univ. Ark., Pine Bluff, 1995, quality svc. award Ark. Dem. Black Caucus, 1995, Drum Major award, Ark. Martin Luther King, Jr., Commn., 2003. Mem. ABA, Ark. Bar Assn. (Disting. Svc. Pursuit Justice award 2003), Jefferson County Bar Assn. (pres.) Baptist.

HOWARD, GLEN SCOTT, lawyer, consultant; b. Birmingham, Ala., May 28, 1950; s. Jack and Bernice (Koffman) H.; m. Lauren Oldak, Sept. 2, 1978; 1 child, Gregory Alan. AB cum laude, Harvard Coll., 1971; JD, U. Chgo., 1974. Bar: DC 1976. Law clk. to chief judge US Dist. Ct., Atlanta, 1974-76; assoc. Sutherland, Asbill & Brennan, Washington, 1976-81, ptnr., 1981-96; gen. counsel, COO Fannie Mae Found., Washington, 1996-97, sr. advisor, 1997-99, sr. v.p., gen. counsel, 2000—06; pres. Strategic Philanthropy Advisors, Washington, 2006—. Performer radio show and record album: Classic Illustrated, 1984; performer Choral Arts Soc. Washington, 1980—, Washington Performing Arts Soc. Men and Women of the Gospel, 2006—; contbr. articles to profl. jours. Mem. Nat. Arts Policy Roundtable, 2006—; pres. United Arts Orgn. Greater Washington, 2000—; chair Greater Washington Bus. Philanthropy Summit, 1999—2002, Sept. 11th Fund Distbn. Com. Greater Washington, 2001—04; cmty. adv. bd. mem. John F. Kennedy Ctr. for Performing Arts, 2004—; tchr. Temple Sinai Religious Sch., 1997—; bd. dirs. Goodwill of Greater Washington, 1996—, vice-chair, 1999—2004, compliance officer, 2004—; bd. dirs. Greater DC Cares, Washington, 1997—2005, chair, 2001—03; bd. dirs. Leadership Washington, 1999—2005, Greater Washington Bd. Trade, 2002—03, Ams. for Arts, 2005—, Helen Hayes Awards, 2005—, Workforce Orgns. Regional Collaboration, 2005—. Mem.: Choral Arts Soc. Democrat. Jewish. Office: Strategic Philanthropy Advisors 2746 Jenifer St NW Washington DC 20015-1334

HOWARD, GREGORY CHARLES, lawyer; b. Jan. 20, 1947; s. Robert L. and Nonamae (Lawlor) H.; m. Kathy Arlene Steinbacher, Oct. 1, 1983. Student, Clarkson Coll., 1965-67; BS, Boston U., 1969; JD, New Eng. Sch. Law, 1975. Bar: Mass. 1975, U.S. Dist. Ct. Mass. 1975, U.S. Supreme Ct. 1979. Assoc. Carmen L. Durso, Boston, 1975-77, Norris Kozodoy & Krasnoo, Boston, 1977-79; pvt. practice Boston, 1979-80; ptnr. Hoff Ernstoff & Howard, Boston, 1980-86; pres. Gregory C. Howard, PC, Boston, 1986—. Home: 5 Eliot Ave Chestnut Hill MA 02467-1455 Office: 28 State St Ste 1100 Boston MA 02109-1775 Office Phone: 617-523-4466. Personal E-mail: gchpc@yahoo.com.

HOWARD, HARRY CLAY, lawyer; b. Rockwood, Tenn., May 1, 1929; s. Harry Clay and Julia Roe (Cannon) H.; m. Mary Helen Harrison, June 12, 1951 (dec. Dec. 1997); children: Helen Howard Porter (dec.), Anne Howard Freihofer; m. Telside Matthews Strickland, Dec. 15, 1998. BA, Vanderbilt U., 1951; LLB, Emory U., 1955. Bar: Ga. 1955. Sr. ptnr. King & Spalding, Atlanta, 1956-92, ret. ptnr., 1993—. Bd. dirs. Avondale Mills Inc. Mem. coun. Emory Law Sch., 1975-85, chmn., 1976-77; bd. dirs. Cen. Atlanta Progress Inc., 1981-85, Wesley Woods Geriatric Hosps., 1987-93, chmn., 1988-92; trustee Wesley Homes Inc., 1961-93, chmn., 1981-86; past trustee Oglethorpe U., The Lovett Sch. 1st lt. USMC, 1951-53. Mem. Am. Law Inst., State Bar Ga., Atlanta Bar Assn., Lawyers Club Atlanta, Piedmont Driving Club, Peachtree Golf Club, Highlands Country Club, Phi Beta Kappa, Omicron Delta Kappa. Office: King & Spalding 1180 Peachtree St Ste 1700 Atlanta GA 30309 Office Phone: 404-572-4835. E-mail: harrychoward@aol.com.

HOWARD, J. TIMOTHY, former finance company executive; m. Debra Howard; children: Julia, Lauren. B in Econs. magna cum laude, UCLA, M in Econs. Fin. adv. Chase Econometric Assocs., 1975; v.p., sr. fin. economist Wells Fargo Bank, San Francisco; v.p., chief economist Fannie Mae, 1982, sr. v.p. econs. and planning, exec. v.p. econs., strategic planning and fin. analysis, 1987-88, exec. v.p. asset mgmt., 1988-90, exec. v.p., CFO, 1990—2004, vice chmn., 2003—04. Bd. dirs. CarrAmerica Realty Corp. Trustee, mem. exec. com., officer The Washington Opera; trustee Holton-Arms Sch.; bd. dirs. Wharton Fin. Instns. Ctr.

HOWARD, J. WOODFORD, JR., retired political science professor; b. Ashland, Ky., July 5, 1931; s. J. Woodford and Florence Alberta (Stephens) H.; m. Valerie Hope Barclay, Apr. 10, 1960; 1 child, Elaine Howard Christ. BA summa cum laude, Duke U., 1952; M.P.A., Princeton U., 1954, MA, 1955, PhD, 1959. Instr. Lafayette Coll., Easton, Pa., 1958-59; postdoctoral fellow Harvard Law Sch., 1961-62; asst. prof. Lafayette Coll., 1959-62, Duke U., 1962-66, assoc. prof., 1966-67, Johns Hopkins U., 1967-69, prof. polit. sci. Balt., 1969-75, Thomas P. Stran prof., 1975-96, Thomas P. Stran prof. emeritus, 1996—, chmn. dept., 1973-75; ret., 1996. Author: Mr. Justice Murphy: A Political Biography, 1968, Courts of Appeals in the Federal Judicial System, 1981 (cert. merit ABA 1982); mem. editl. bd. Law and Soc. Rev., 1975-76, 78-82, Am. Polit. Sci. Rev., 1977-81, Jour. Politics, 1979-93, Johns Hopkins U. Press, 1991-93; subject of essay in The Pioneers of Judicial Behavior, edited by Nancy Maveety, 2003; contbr. articles to profl. jours. Mem. history program adv. com. Fed. Jud. Ctr., 1989-95; trustee Balt. Mus. Art; mem. music com. Balt. Symphony Orch.; bd. dirs. Shriver Hall Concert Series; vestryman Ch. of Redeemer, Balt., 1988-90. Lt. USAF, 1955-57. Named to Hall of Fame, Floyd Co., Ky., 1957; recipient Outstanding Tchr. awards and citations, Lafayette Coll., 1960, Duke U., 1966, Johns Hopkins U., 1969, 1970, 1993, Pub. award, Harcourt Coll., 2001. Mem.: Law and Soc. Assn., Am. Judicature Soc., Nat. Capitol Area Polit. Sci. Assn. (coun. 1986—89), So. Polit. Sci. Assn., Am. Polit. Sci. Assn., Filson Hist. Soc., Supreme Ct. Hist. Soc., Princeton Club (N.Y.C.), 14 Hamilton St. Club (Balt.), Phi Beta Kappa, Omicron Delta Kappa. Office: Johns Hopkins U Dept Polit Sci Baltimore MD 21218-2685

HOWARD, JACK, industrial relations specialist, consultant; b. Santa Ana, Calif., Aug. 26, 1924; s. Floyd Willie and Inez (Cooley) H.; m. Margaret Anne McKinnon, Aug. 25, 1950 (dec.); children: Marc, Anne. AB, U. Calif., Berkeley, 1948; MA, UCLA, 1952. Reporter Springfield (Ohio) Daily News, 1949-51; labor editor San Francisco Chronicle, 1952-60; chief investigator govt. information subcom. U.S. Ho. of Reps., 1960-63; spl. asst. to undersec. of Labor, 1963-64; adminstr. Neighborhood Youth Corps, 1964-66, Bur. of Work Programs, 1966-67; exec. asst. to Sec. Labor, 1968; v.p. Ednl. Scis. Programs, Inc., NYC, 1969-71; sec.-treas., cons. William Benton Found., NYC, 1971-80; asst. to pub. Ency. Brit., NYC, 1971-73; asst. dir. Twentieth Century Fund, NYC, 1974-76; asst. to pres. Am. Fedn. State, County and Mcpl. Employees AFL-CIO, 1976-97; ind. cons., 1997—. Internat. v.p. Am. Newspaper Guild-AFL-CIO, 1957-60 With AUS, 1943-46. Congl. fellow Am. Polit. Sci. Assn., 1957-58; Recipient Distinguished Svc. award Dept. Labor, 1965 Mem. ACLU. Home: 219 5th St NE Washington DC 20002-5919 Personal E-mail: howardjack@hotmail.com.

HOWARD, JAMES KENTON, academic administrator, journalist; b. June 30, 1943; s. Arthur R. and Dora G. (Utt) H.; m. Lynn M. Marsh, Sept. 23, 1982; children: Lara L., James M. BA, U. Okla., 1965, MA, 1979; Inst. Ednl. Mgmt., Harvard U., 1991. Asst. dean students U. Okla., Norman, 1965-67, asst. to pres., 1967-68, asst. to v.p. for univ. rels. and devel., 1978; editor Northland Press, Flagstaff, Ariz., 1972-77; cons. Okla. Dept. Public Safety, Oklahoma City, 1977; asst. dean student affairs Northeastern State U., Tahlequah, Okla., 1978-79, dir. univ. svcs., 1979-82, asst. prof. journalism, 1979—2004, v.p. adminstrn., 1982-91, v.p. bus. and devel., 1991—2004, trustee NSU Found., 1981—, v.p. emeritus, 2005—. Mem. Coun. Bus. Officers, Okla. State Regents for Higher Edn., 1982-04; adv. dir. BancFirst, 1995—; mem. bd. dirs. Cherokee County Ednl. Facilities Found., 2003-. Author: Ten Years With the Cowboy Artists of America, 1976. Bd. dirs. Friends of Mus. No. Ariz., 1974-77; chmn. No. Ariz. campaign March of Dimes, 1973-74; founding chmn. Cherokee County Cmty. Sentencing Coun., 1997—; No. Ariz. coord. Babbit for Atty. Gen. Campaign, 1974; trustee Flagstaff-Coconino County Pub. Libr., 1976-77, chmn. bd. trustees, 1976-77; pres. Indian Nations Soccer Coun., 1981-82; bd. dirs. Indian Nations coun. Boy Scouts Am., 1990-94, Okla. Found. for Excellence, 1996—; trustee Tahlequah Pub. Schs. Found., 1990-2000, founding chair, 1990-98; bd. dirs. Leadership Okla., 1990—, mem. exec. com., 1990-98, pres., 1994-95, mem. Class II, 1988-89; bd. dirs. Okla. Assn. of Coll. and Univ. Bus. Officers, 1993-98, pres., 1996-97; bd. dirs. Okla. Acad. for State Goals, 1993—, chair, 1999-2000; founding pres. Boys and Girls Club of Tahlequah, 1996-2000; pres., Coll. Assn. Liability Mgmt., 1996-98, 2002-2004; bd. dirs. Okla. Arts Inst., 1997-2005, Okla. Music Hall of Fame, 2000-2004, Communities Found. Okla., 2000-02, bd. govs., 2002—; founding pres. Tahlequah Comty. Found., 2003—. With USAF, 1968-72. Recipient Eason Book Collection award, 1965, Book Design award Rounce and Coffin Club of L.A., 1974-75, Citation of Profl. Merit Northeastern State U., 1991, Excellence in Okla. Leadership award, 1995, Disting. Leadership award Nat. Assn. Cmty. Leadership, 1995-96; named Outstanding Citizen, Tahlequah Area C. of C., 2005. Mem. U. Okla. Assn. (life), Nat. Cowboy Hall of Fame and Western Heritage Ctr. (life), Tahlequah Area C. of C. (bd. dirs. 1985-88), Mensa, Rotary (past pres., Paul Harris fellow), Sigma Delta Chi, Kappa Tau Alpha, Lambda Chi Alpha.

HOWARD, JAMES NEWTON, composer; b. LA, June 9, 1951; m. Rosanna Arquette, 1986 (div.); m. Sophie Howard. Prodr. for Valerie Carter, 1978; session musician with Fanny, 1974, Ringo Starr, 1974, Elton John, 1975-80, Neil Diamond, 1976, Harry Nilsson, 1976, Neil Sedaka, 1976, Yvonne Elliman, 1978, The Dudek-Finnigan-Kruger Band, 1980, Boz Scaggs, 1980, Melissa Manchester. Film scores include Wildcats, 1986, Head Office, 1986, Nobody's Fool, 1986, Never Too Young to Die, 1986, 8 Million Ways to Die, 1986, Tough Guys, 1986, Promised Land, 1987, Russkies, 1987, Campus Man, 1987, Off Limits, 1988, Everybody's All American, 1988, Tap, 1989, Major League, 1989, The Package, 1989, Coupe de Ville, 1990, Pretty Woman, 1990, Three Men and a Little Lady, 1990, Flatliners, 1990, Marked for Death, 1990, Dying Young, 1991, The Prince of Tides, 1991 (Academy award nomination best original score 1991), The Man in the Moon, 1991, King Ralph, 1991, Guilty by Suspicion, 1991, My Girl, 1991, Grand Canyon, 1991, American Heart, 1992, Glengarry Glen Ross, 1992, Diggstown, 1992, Night and the City, 1992, Falling Down, 1993, Dave, 1993, Alive, 1993, The Saint of Fort Washington, 1993, The Fugitive, 1993 (Academy award nomination best original score 1993), Intersection, 1994, Wyatt Earp, 1994, Outbreak, 1995, French Kiss, 1995 Waterworld, 1995, Restoration, 1995, Eye for an Eye, 1996, The Juror, 1996, Primal Fear, 1996, The Trigger Effect, 1996, Space Jam, 1996, Romy & Michele's High School Reunion, 1997, Father's Day, 1997, My Best Friend's Wedding, 1997, The Devil's Advocate, 1997, The Postman, 1997, A Perfect Murder, 1998, Wing Commander, 1999, Runaway Bride, 1999, Stir of Echoes, 1999, The Sixth Sense, 1999, Mumford, 1999, Snow Falling on Cedars, 1999, Dinosaur, 2000, Unbreakable, 2000, Vertical Limit, 2000, Atlantis, 2001, America's Sweethearts, 2001, Signs, 2002, Unconditional Love, 2002, The Emperor's Club, 2000, Treasure Planet, 2002, Dreamcatcher, 2003, Peter Pan, 2003, Hidalgo, 2004, The Village, 2004, Collateral, 2004, Batman Begins, 2005, King Kong, 2005, Freedomland, 2006, RV, 2006, Lady in the Water, 2006, Blood Diamond, 2006, The Lookout, 2007, Michael Clayton, 2007, The Water Horse, 2007, I Am Legend, 2007; composer for songs including (from White Nights) Prove Me Wrong, 1985, (from Cobra) Hold On to Your Vision, 1986, (from Everybody's All American) Until Forever, 1988, (from Major League) Most of All You, 1989; music condr., arranger: (film) Nothing in Common, 1986; music prodr., composer: (film) Five Corners, 1987; music condr., composer: (film) Some Girls, 1988; orchestra condr.: (TV spl.) Elton John in Australia, 1987; TV scores include (TV movies) Go Toward the Light, 1988, The Image, 1990, Somebody Has to Shoot the Picture, 1990, Descending Angel, 1990, Revealing Evidence, 1990, A Private Matter, 1992, (TV spls.) The Visit, 1987, Bedtime Story, 1987, The Hit List, 1989, Alive-The Miracle of the Andes, 1993, (TV series) Men, 1989 (Emmy award nominaton 1989), You'll Love the Ride, 1991, Middle Ages, 1992, 2000 Malibu Road, 1992, ER, 1994, The Sentinel, 1996, From the Earth to the Moon, 1998, The Fugitive, 2000, Gideon's Crossing, 2000 (Emmy award for Oustanding Main Title Theme Music, 2001); recs. include James Newton Howard and Friends, 1984. Recipient Henry Mancini award, ASCAP, 2000. Office: The Gorfaine Schwartz Agency Inc 4111 W Alameda Ave Ste 509 Burbank CA 91505-4171*

HOWARD, JAMES WEBB, brokerage house executive, engineer, lawyer; b. Evansville, Ind., Sept. 17, 1925; s. Joseph R. and Velma (Cobb) H.; m. Phyllis Jean Brandt, Dec. 27, 1948; children: Sheila Rae, Sharon Kae. BS in Mech. Engring, Purdue U., 1949; postgrad., Akron Law Sch., Ohio, 1950-51, Cleve. Marshall Law Sch., 1951-52; MBA, Case Western Res. U., 1962; JD, Western State Coll. Law, 1976. Registered profl. engr., Ind., Ohio. Jr. project engr. Firestone Tire & Rubber Co., Akron, 1949-50; gen. foreman Cadillac Motor Car div. GM, 1950-53; mgmt. cons. M.K. Sheppard & Co., Cleve., 1953-56; plant mgr. Lewis Welding & Engring. Corp., Ohio, 1956-58; underwriter The Ohio Co., Columbus, 1959; chmn. Growth Capital, Inc., Chgo., 1960-98; pvt. practice law San Diego, 1979-85. Pres. Meister Brau, Inc., Chgo., 1965-73, The Home Mart, San Diego, 1974-82; mng. agt., fin. instn. specialist FDIC/RTC, 1985-90; specialist in charge Office of FDIC-DOL, Portland, Oreg., 1986-87. Developer of "Lite" beer. Co-chmn. Chgo. com. Ill. Sesquicentennial Com., 1968. Served with AUS, 1943-46. Decorated Bronze Star, Parachutist badge, Combat Inf. badge. Mem. ASME, Nat. Assn. Small Bus. Investment Cos. (past pres.), State Bar Calif., Grad. Bus. Alumni Assn. Western Res. U. (past gov.), Masons, Tau Kappa Epsilon, Pi Tau Sigma, Beta Gamma Sigma. Presbyterian. Personal E-mail: jhoward46@cox.net.

HOWARD, JEFFREY HJALMAR, lawyer; b. N.Y.C., Aug. 23, 1944; s. Virgil Edward and Margaretta E. H.; m. Brenda H. Howard, June 19, 1966; children: Taggart Harrison, Brooke Kennedy. BA in Philosophy, Randolph-Macon Coll., 1966; postgrad. (English Speaking Union scholar) U. Edinburgh (Scotland), 1965; LLB, U. Va., 1969. Bar: D.C. 1970, U.S. Sup. Ct. 1978, Va. 1987. Law clk. Circuit Ct., Montgomery County, Md., 1969-70; assoc. gen. counsel for toxics, pesticides and solid waste U.S. EPA, Washington, 1974-76; ptnr. Crowell & Moring, 1989—; lectr. antitrust and environ. law U. Va. 1976-89; lectr. environ. law Peking U., Peoples Republic of China, 1986. Mem. ABA, D.C. Bar Assn., Va. Soc. Fellows, Order Coif, Alpha Psi Omega, Alpha Epsilon Pi, Delta Sigma Rho-Tau Kappa Alpha, Omicron Delta Kappa. Editorial bd. Va. Law Rev., 1967-69; contbr. chpts. to books and articles to profl. jours. Home: 1021 Duchess St Mc Lean VA 22102-2007 Office: 1001 Pennsylvania Ave NW Washington DC 20004-2505 Office Phone: 202-624-2909. E-mail: jhoward@crowell.com.

HOWARD, JEFFREY R., federal judge; b. Claremont, NH, Nov. 4, 1955; m. Marie Howard; 2 children. BA, Plymouth St Coll-Univ N.H., 1978; JD, Law Ctr-Georgetown U, 1981. Off. of NH atty. gen., 1981—88; dep. atty. gen. State of NH, 1988—89; U.S. atty. Dist. of NH, Concord, 1989—92; atty. gen. State of NH, 1993—97; ptnr. Choate Hall & Stewart, 1997—2001; pvt. practice Jeffrey R. Howard, Esq., 2001—02; judge US Ct. Appeals 1st Cir., 2002—. Mem. atty. gen. adv. com. Attys. Gen. Thornburg & Barr. Named Citizen of Yr., Salisbury, NH, 2000. Office: 1 Warren Rudman US Courthouse 55 Pleasant St Concord NH 03301*

HOWARD, JOHN, federal agency administrator; MD, Loyola U., 1974; M of Occupational Health, Harvard Sch. Pub. Health, 1982; JD, UCLA, 1986; LLM, George Wash. U., 1987. Bd. Certified Occupational Physician. Internist UCLA Sch. Medicine Pulmonary Fellowship Program, Cedars-Sinai Med. Ctr., LA; med. dir. and chief clinician Philip Mandelker AIDS Prevention Clinic; asst. counselor to under sec. US Dept. Health & Human Services.; asst. prof. environmental and occupational medicine U. Calif., Irvine; chief Divsn. Occupational Safety and Health, State of Calif. Dept. Indsl. Rels., 1991—; dir. Nat. Inst. for Occupational Safety and Health (NIOSH), CDC, 2002—. Spl. coord. for response to health effects of Sept. 11th US Dept. Health & Human Services, 2006—. Office: Nat Inst Ocupational Safety Hubert H Humphrey Bldg 200 Independence SW Rm 715H Washington DC 20201

HOWARD, JOHN ADDISON, former academic administrator; b. Evanston, Ill., Aug. 10, 1921; s. Hubert Elmer and Edith (Sackett) H.; m. Janette Marie Nobis, Aug. 11, 1951; children: Marie Starr, Steven Lamson, Martha Nobis, Katherine Louise. Student, Princeton U., 1939-42; BS, Northwestern U., 1947, MA, 1949, PhD, 1962; LL.D., Grove City Coll., 1972, Brigham Young U., 1976, Rockford Coll., 1980. Instr. French Palos Verdes Coll., Rolling Hills, Calif., 1947-49, dean students, 1949-51, v.p., 1950-51, pres., 1951-55; exec. vice chmn. Pres.'s Com. on Govt. Contracts, 1956-57; pres. Rockford (Ill.) Coll., 1960-77; dir. Rockford Coll. Inst., 1977-80; pres. The Rockford Inst., 1980-86, counselor, 1986-97; sr. fellow The Howard Ctr. Religion, Family & Soc., 1997—. Author: Detoxifying the Culture, 2001; contbg. author: Dilemmas Facing the Nation, 1979. Mem. U.S. Commn. on Marijuana and Drug Abuse, 1971-73, Pres.'s Task Force on Priorities in Higher Edn., 1969-70; pres. Ingersoll Found., 1983—2003. Served to 1st lt. AUS, 1942-45. Decorated Silver Star with oak leaf cluster, Purple Heart with oak leaf cluster; recipient Horatio Alger award, 1967, Educator of Yr. Religious Heritage Am., 1980. Mem. Am. Assn. Pres. Ind. Colls. and Univs. (pres. 1969-72), Phila. Soc. (pres. 1979-81), Rotary, Phi Beta Kappa. Home: 4275 Ahlstrand Dr Rockford IL 61101 Office Phone: 815-964-5819.

HOWARD, JOHN LAWRENCE, lawyer; b. Danville, Ill., May 16, 1957; s. Charles R. and Kathryn (Tormohlen) H.; m. Julia Louise Steinfirst, Oct. 13, 1984. BS, Ind. U., 1979, JD, 1982; LLM, George Washington U., 1989. Bar: Ind., 1982, US Supreme Ct., 1986, Fed. Cir. Ct., 1987, US Ct. Appeals (4th cir.), 1989. Dep. prosecutor 30th Jud. Cir., Rensselaer, Ind., 1982-84; lawyer US Office Pers. Mgmt., Washington, 1984-85; spl. asst. to gen. counsel US Consumer Product Safety Commn., Washington, 1984-85; legal counsel to chmn. US Merit Sys. Protection Bd., Washington, 1986-88; assoc. dep. atty. gen. US Dept. Justice, Washington, 1988-90; dep. counsel to v.p. Office of V.P., Washington, 1990; counsel to v.p. Dan Quayle, 1991-93; various positions Tenneco, Inc., 1993—95, gen. counsel, 1998—99; sr. v.p., gen. counsel W.W. Grainger, Inc., 2000—. Contbr. articles to profl. jours. Mem. Fed. Bar Assn., Fed. Cir. Bar Assn., Army & Navy Club Washington. Republican. Office: WW Grainger 100 Grainger Pky Lake Forest IL 60045-5201 Office Phone: 847-535-1000. Office Fax: 847-535-9243. E-mail: john_howard@grainger.com.*

HOWARD, JOHN LINDSAY, lawyer; b. Drumheller, Alta., Can., Nov. 18, 1931; s. Lindsay Lee and Nancy (Martin) H.; m. Jeannette Huguenin, Nov. 21, 1969. B.Comm., U. B.C., 1959, LL.B., 1961; LL.M., Harvard U., 1968; postgrad., McGill U., Montreal, Can., 1967. Bar: B.C. 1962, Que. 1967, Fed. Queen's Counsel 1977. Mem. Brahan, Dickerson & Howard, Vancouver, B.C., 1962-67, Tansey, de Grandpre, Montreal, 1968-71; asst. dep. minister Fed. Dept. Consumer and Corp. Affairs, Ottawa, Ont., 1971-79; sr. v.p. law and corp. affairs MacMillan Bloedel Ltd., Vancouver, 1979-96, cons., corp. dir., 1996—; dir. Investment Dealers Assn. Can., 1996—2005. Bus. law arbitrator, 1996—. Co-author: Proposals for a New Corporation Law for Canada, 1971, Proposals for a Securities Market Law for Canada, 1979. Home: PO Box 831 Sooke BC Canada V0S 1N0 Office Phone: 250-642-4489. E-mail: johnlhoward@shaw.ca.

HOWARD, JOHN VINCENT, JR., lawyer; b. San Tomé, Venezuela, Jan. 27, 1962; s. John Vincent and Diane Shirley (Page) H.; m. Val Marie Schmuhl, Aug. 24, 1991. BA in History, Washington and Lee U., 1984; LLM, U. Colo., 1987. Bar: Colo., 1987. Assoc. Brian A. Jeffrey, P.C., Evergreen, Colo., 1987; exec. v.p., gen. counsel Columbine JDS Sys. Inc., Laser Tech Color Inc.; chief intellectual property counsel Andersen Worldwide, S.C., Chgo.; chief counsel Quark Inc., Denver; sr. v.p., gen. counsel, sec. Vertis Inc., Balt., 2000—05, chief legal officer, sec., 2005—. Book reviewer Trial Talk, 1990-92. Coach Colo. High Sch. Mock Trial Team, Evergreen, 1988—; trustee Hammond-Harwood Assn., Annapolis. Mem. Kiwanis, Phi Eta Sigma, Kappa Sigma (sec. 1983). Episcopalian. Avocations: golf, skiing, creative writing, scuba diving. Office: Vertis Inc 250 W Pratt St Baltimore MD 21201

HOWARD, JOHN WAYNE, lawyer; b. Dec. 17, 1948; s. Joseph Leon and Irene Elizabeth (Silver) H.; m. Kathleen Amanda Busby, Oct. 7, 1978. BA, U. Calif., San Diego, 1971; JD, Calif. Western Sch. Law, 1976; postgrad., San Diego Inn of Ct., 1979, Hastings Coll. Advocacy, 1981; grad. Program of Instrns. for Lawyers, Harvard Law Sch., 1992. Bar: Calif. 1978, U.S. Dist. Ct. (so. dist.) Calif. 1978, U.S. Supreme Ct. 1989, Colo. 1989, U.S. Dist. Ct. (no. dist.) Calif., U.S. Dist. Ct. (ea. dist.) Calif., U.S. Ct. Appeals (9th cir.) 1995, U.S. Ct. Appeals (D.C. cir.) 1996, U.S. Ct. of Claims 1996. Assoc. Robert T. Dierdorff, San Diego, 1978—79; pvt. practice San Diego, 1979—82; ptnr. Howard & Neeb, San Diego, 1982—84; prin. John W. Howard and Assocs., San Diego, 1984—86; gen. counsel Ace Parking, Inc., 1986—89, CCCA Inc., 1989—93; pres. Individual Rights Found. Inc., 1993—95, Inst. for Constl. Rights, Inc., 1995—, JW Howard/Attys., 1995—. Jud. arbitrator Superior Ct. Calif., 1983—. Chmn. San Diego County Indigent Def. Adv. Bd., 1981-84, mem. subcom. on def. monitoring and budget for Office Defender Svcs. of San Diego County; mem. select com. on small bus. Calif. State Assembly, 1983-90; chmn. San Diego Pub. Arts Adv. Bd.; mem. San Diego County Coun. of Com. Chairs; chmn. precinct orgn. Roger Hedgecock for Supt. Campaign Com., 1976, mem. steering com., 1976; chmn. steering com. Hedgecock for Mayor, 1982, Cleator for Mayor, 1986; chmn. Muscular Dystrophy Telethon, San Diego, 1983; vice chmn. San Diego Festival of Arts, 1983-84; pres. Bowery Theatre, San Diego, 1984-89; pres., bd. dirs. La Jolla Stage Co.; founder, bd. dirs. San Diego Theatre League; 1st v.p., bd. dirs. Muscular Dystrophy Assn.; bd. dirs. Patrick Henry Meml. Found., Brookneal, Va., The Poe Mus., Richmond, Va., San Diego Med. Oncology Rsch. Found., Ilan-Lael Found., Multiple Sclerosis Soc., Am. Ballet Found., Wellness Cmty., Teatro Macara Magica; bd. dirs., chmn. legal affairs subcom. Calif. Motion Picture Coun.; mem. adv. bd. dirs. San Diego Motion Picture Bur.; mem. pub. edn. com. Am. Cancer Soc.; founder, bd. dirs. San Diego Theatre Found., 1984—; mem. 44th Congl. Dist. Adv. Com.; mem. Com. to Re-Elect Congressman Bill Lowery; mem. San Diego County 4th Dist. Adv. Com. Mem. ABA, ATLA, Calif. State Bar Assn., Am. Corp. Counsel Assn., San Diego County Bar Assn. (chmn. superior ct. com. 2002—), Consumer Attys. Assn. L.A., U. Calif.-San Diego Alumni Assn. (past v.p., bd. dirs.), Calif. Western Sch. Law Alumni Assn., Friendly Sons of St. Patrick, Delta Kappa Epsilon, Phi Alpha Delta, Enright Inn of Ct., Am. Inns of Ct. Republican.

HOWARD, JOHN W.S., mental health services professional, alcohol/drug abuse services professional, theology studies educator; b. Burlington, Nc, Mar. 11, 1956; s. John Henry and Nancy Marie (Watlington) Howard; m. Judy Carol Mayhand, Apr. 19, 1997; children: Trina Michelle Goins, Myra Helena Mayhand. Diploma in Bibl. Studies, Greensboro Bible Inst., 1988; BA, Shaw U., 1992; MDiv, Shaw U. Div. Sch., 1996; PhD in Philosophy, Atlantic Nat. U., 2005; PhD in Clin. Psychology, Windsor U., London, 2007. Adj. prof. Guilford Coll., Greensboro, NC, 2004, Barton Coll. (Lay Acad.), Wilson, NC, 2005; pres., prof. theology Guilford Theol. Acad., Greensboro, 2006—. Author: What is Faith ? (Bronze Medal for Higher Academic Achievement, 1991). Office Phone: 336-724-9016 289. E-mail: johnhoward@drugfreenc.org.

HOWARD, JOSEPH HARVEY, retired librarian; b. Olustee, Okla., Jan. 15, 1931; s. William Lester and Letitia Browder (Dickey) H.; m. Patricia Shaughnessy Schiebel, Apr. 10, 1980. B in Mus. Edn., U. Okla., 1952, MLS, 1957. Assoc. dir. pub. svcs. U. Colo. Libr., Boulder, 1960-63; vol. Peace Corps, Kuala Lumpur, Malaysia, 1963-65; head catalog dept. Washington U., St. Louis, 1956-67; asst. chief descriptive cataloging divsn. Libr. of Congress, Washington, 1967-68, chief descriptive cataloging divsn., 1968-72, chief serial record divsn., 1972-75, asst. dir. (cataloging) processing dept., 1975-76, asst. libr. for processing svcs., 1976-83; dir. Nat. Agrl. Libr., Beltsville, Md., 1983-94, ret., 1994. Author: Malay Manuscripts— A Bibliographical Guide, 1966. Served with AUS, 1952-54. Recipient Outstanding Svc. to Librarianship award U. Okla., 1979. Mem. ALA (Melvil Dewey medal 1985) Personal E-mail: jhhoward@comcast.net.

HOWARD, JOSH, professional basketball player; b. Winston-Salem, NC, Apr. 28, 1980; Student, Wake Forest U., Winston-Salem, NC. Forward-guard NBA Dallas Mavericks, 2003—. Named ACC Men's Basketball Player of Yr., 2003; named to All-Rookie 2nd Team, NBA, 2004, Western Conf. All-Star Team, 2007. Mailing: Dallas Mavericks The Pavilion 2909 Taylor St Dallas TX 75226*

HOWARD, JOYCE ANNE, elementary school educator; b. NYC, Oct. 24, 1940; d. Walter Theodore and Jessie Lillian Sattler; m. Philip Laurance Howard, Aug. 14, 1959; children: Robert, Douglas. BA Elem. Edn., Adelphi U., MA, 1976; AA, Nassau C.C. Cert. teacher k-6 N.Y.C. Tchr. North Bellmore; retirement rep. North Bellmore Dist., 1997—; exec. bd. North Bellmore Tchrs. Assn., 1997—. Cons. Nassau County Health Ctr., Nassau, NY, 1990—2000, Learn City, San Ronson, Calif., 1990—2000. Author: (Book) Windows, 2000. Recipient Lifetime award, North Bellmore Sch. PTA, N.Y., 2000. Mem.: North Bellmore Tchrs. Assn. (retirement rep. 1997—, bldg. rep. 2001—04, Recipient Lifetime award 2000, Disting. Svc. award 2005), North Bellmore Tchr. Ctr. Home: 14 Prade Ln Massapequa Park NY 11762 Office: Park Ave Sch 1599 Park Ave Merrick NY 11566 E-mail: jhow1024@aol.com.

HOWARD, KATHLEEN, computer company executive; b. Norman, Okla., Nov. 3, 1947; d. Robert Adrian and Jane Elizabeth (Morgens) H.; m. Lawrence W. Osgood, Aug. 10, 1968 (div. Sept. 1970); m. Norman Edlo Gibat, Oct. 15, 1971. Student, U. Okla., Norman, 1966—68. Typesetter Selenby Press, Norman, 1968—72; owner, pres. Noguska Industries, Fostoria, Ohio, 1973—; co-founder Home Wine Mchts., Chgo., 1976; cons. Bechtel Corp., Ann Arbor, Mich., 1980—, Gaithersburg, Md., 1980—; chairperson Am. Software Project, 1985; ptnr. Popular Topics Pubs., 1993—; cons. Xerox Corp., Rochester, NY, 1998—. Author: All You Need to Know About MSDOS, 1993; co-author, illustrator: Lore of Still Building, 1972; co-author: Making Wine, Beer and Merry, 1973, Computer Comix Mag., 1986; pres. Popular Topics Press, Inc., also jours. and bus. mgmt. software. Treas. United Way of Fostoria, 1986-88, 2d v.p. 1988-90; bd. dirs. Pvt. Industry Coun., 1988-90. Recipient Founders award Home Wine and Beer Trade Assn. Chgo., 1976. Mem. BBB, Nat. Fedn. Ind. Bus., C. of C. (bd. dirs. 1986-92), Employer's Assn. Toledo, Altrusa Internat. Club (sec. Fostoria chpt. 1984-85, pres. 1986-88, editor dist. #5 1988-90, pres. 2001-03, webmaster Dist. #5, 2004-). Avocations: painting, printing, travel, reading. Office: Noguska Industries 741 N Countyline St Fostoria OH 44830-1586 Home Phone: 419-435-1128; Office Phone: 419-435-0404. Personal E-mail: knoguska@yahoo.com. Business E-Mail: khoward@noguska.com.

HOWARD, LARRY BRUCE, forensic specialist, consultant; b. Seattle, Apr. 1, 1928; s. Walter J. and Anita S. Howard; m. Elaine Ungherini, Sept. 20, 1952; children: Randy, Rick, Laure, Lisa. BA, U. Mont., Missoula, 1945; BS, Ga. State U., Atlanta, 1988; PhD, U. Minn., Mpls., 1956. Asst. dir. Ga. crime lab. Ga. Bur. Investigations, Atlanta, 1956—71, dir. Ga. crime lab. Decatur, 1971—88; forensic scientist Mont. Crime Lab., Missoula, 1988—90; mgr. city county crime lab. Colorado Springs Police Dept., Colo., 1990—95; pvt. practice forensic sci. cons. Colorado Springs, 1995—. Editor: Am. Jour. Legal Medicine and Pathology, 1981—87, Jour. Forensic Sci., 1980—90; contbr. chpt. to book. Fellow: Am. Acad. Forensic Sci. (v.p. 1978—79, emeritus, Briggs White award 2000); mem.: So. Assn. Forensic Sci. (pres. 1973—74), Am. Soc. Crime Lab. Dirs. (chmn. 1976—77). Home: 128 Miramar Dr Colorado Springs CO 80906

HOWARD, LELAND WILLIAM, writer; b. Jackson, Tenn., Feb. 3, 1950; s. Leland William and Bernice (Ball) H. Student, U. of the South, Sewanee, Tenn., 1968—71; studied voice with, Florence Morsbach, NYC, 1971—73; cert. in French, Sorbonne, Paris, 1987; studied acting with Herbert Berghof, HB Studio, NYC, 1988; BA in English Lit. and Creative Writing, Hunter Coll., 2004. Publicist Millbrook Playhouse, Mill Hall, Pa., summer 1990; grad. tchg. asst. dept. English N.Mex. Highlands U., Las Vegas, 2005—. Coord. "The Gay Writes" Southeastern Conf. Lesbians and Gay Men, New Orleans, 1985; Michael T. Carroll lectr. N.Mex. Highlands U., Las Vegas, 2007; presenter in field. Author: (poetry) Steps Below, 1983, The Grass Hut, 1993; author: Pirouettes Get No Applause in Goldengrove, 1997, 2d edit., 2002, screenplay, 1999; contbr. articles to Impact, Gulf South Gay News, 1984, Advocate, 1985, Olivetree Rev., 1999. Mem. Doris Day Animal League, Light Opera of Manhattan, NYC, 1971, St. Cecelia Chorus, 1973, New Orleans Gay Mens' Chorus, 1983, First Nat. Gay Choral Festival, NYC, 1983. Democrat. Episcopalian. Avocations: swimming, drawing, pets, singing, theater. Home: 1012 Tilden St Las Vegas NM 87701-3867 Personal E-mail: lelandwhoward@aol.com.

HOWARD, LEWIS SPILMAN, lawyer; b. Knoxville, Tenn., Oct. 10, 1930; s. Frank Catlett and Lillian (Spilman) H.; m. Anne Robinson, Dec. 26, 1953 (div. 1976); children: Catherine C., Martha S., Lewis S. Jr., Laura A. (dec.). BSBA, JD, U. Tenn., 1953. Bar: Tenn. 1953, US Ct. Mil. Appeals 1954, US Dist. Ct. Ga. 1954, US Dist. Ct. Tenn. 1956, US Ct. Appeals (6th cir.) 1959. Ptnr. Kennerly, Montgomery, Howard & Finley, Knoxville, 1957-84, Howard & Ridge, Knoxville, 1984-99, Howard & Howard, Knoxville, 2000—. Gen. counsel The Coal Creek Co., Knoxville, 1969—, pres., 1971—. Vice chmn. Knoxville Bd. Edn., 1968-71. Capt. JAGC, USAR, 1953-56. Mem.: ABA, Tenn. Bar Assn., Knoxville Bar Assn., Cherokee Country Club. Republican. Presbyterian. Avocation: boating. Home: 1604 Kenesaw Ave Knoxville TN 37919-7863 Office: Howard & Howard 4820 Old Kingston Pike Knoxville TN 37919-6478 Business E-Mail: lsh@howardandhowardlaw.com.

HOWARD, LISA RYAN, publishing executive; b. 1971; Advt. dir. Jane and W magazines; dir. of sales Ultigo, Inc.; exec. dir. of corp. sales Condé Nast Media Grp.; pub., v.p. STYLE.COM, MEN.STYLE.COM, 2007—. Named one of 40 under 40, Advt. Age, 2007. Office: CondéNet 1166 Ave of the Americas 15th Fl New York NY 10036 Office Phone: 212-790-5100. Office Fax: 212-790-1822.*

HOWARD, LUCIA FAKONAS, retired lawyer; b. East St. Louis, Mo., July 21, 1951; BA summa cum laude, Ariz. State U., 1972; JD cuml laude, Harvard U., 1975. Bar: Ariz. 1975. Law clerk to Hon. Christopher Armstrong Mass. Ct. Appeals, 1975-76; spl. asst. on econ. devel. office of mayor City of Phoenix, Ariz., 1985, 89—. Mem. Ariz. Ctr. for Women and the Law, 1979-82, Ariz. Commn. on Salaries for Elected Ofcls., 1982-84. Commr. Phoenix Commn. on Excellence in Edn., 1989—. Mem. State Bar Ariz. (chair inst. on estate planning 1978-80, com. on pub. edn. 1979-80), Ariz. Women Lawyers Assn. (pres. 1978-81), Maricopa County Bar Found. (bd. dirs. 1984-85), Kappa Delta Pi, Alpha Lambda Delta. Home: 7540 N Silvercrest Way Paradise Valley AZ 85253-2851

HOWARD, LYN JENNIFER, medical educator; b. Buxton, Eng., Jan. 19, 1938; came to U.S., 1965; naturalized, 1971; d. Peter and Bess (Donnelly) Marsh; m. Burtis Howard, Mar. 13, 1965 (div. 1988); children: Peter Howard, Thia Howard; m. Jack Alexander, Sept. 10, 1995. BA, Oxford U., 1960, MA, BM, BCh, 1964. Diplomate Am. Bd. Internal Medicine, Am. Bd. Nutrition. Intern London Hosp., 1964-65, Kans. City Med. Ctr., 1965-66, resident, 1966-70; fellow in clin. nutrition and gastroenterology Vanderbilt Hosp., 1971-73; dir. clin. nutrition program Albany (N.Y.) Med. Coll., 1973-80, asst. prof. medicine, pediat., 1973-76, assoc. prof. medicine, pediat., 1977-84, prof. medicine, 1984—, head divsn. clin. nutrition, 1986—. Asst. dir. Clin. Studies Ctr., Albany Med. Ctr., 1973-78; attending physician Albany Med. Ctr. Hosp., 1973—; attending physician, cons. clin. nutrition Albany VA Hosp., 1973—; cons. pediat. gastroenterology St. Peter's Hosp., Albany, 1974—; med. dir. Albany Home Health Resources, 1991-92; mem. working group Nat. Commn. Digestive Diseases, 1977; mem. NIH Consensus Devel. Conf., 1978, nutrition rsch. directions, 1979, spl. study sect. clin. nutrition rsch. units, 1980, nutrition study sect., 1989-93; cons. AMA Drug Evaluations, 1982, Medicare, Blue Cross/Blue Shield S.C., 1987—; keynote spkr. Australian Soc. Parenteral and Enteral Nutrition, Perth, 1993, 1st Clin. Nutrition Symposium, Kuala Lumpor, Malaysia, 1994. Contbg. editor Nutrition Reviews, 1981-87, 89; mem. editl. bd. Jour. Drug-Nutrient Interactions, 1984, Contemporary Issues in Clin. Nutrition, 1985, Jour. Am. Soc. Parenteral and Enteral Nutrition, 1987-90; contbr. articles, abstracts to profl. jours., chpts. to books. Exec. dir. Oley Found. for Home Parenteral and Enteral Nutrition, 1983-87, pres., 1987-91, med. dir., 1991; pres. Camphill Found., Pa., 1994. Recipient Clifton C. Thorne Cmty. Svc. award, 1990, Physician of Yr. award Albany chpt. Crohn's Colitis Found. Am., 1991; elected 1st woman mem. Great Lakes Interurban Club, 1990; Major County scholar, 1956; grantee Nutrition Found., 1973-79, U.S. Dept. Agriculture, 1978-81, William F. Donner Found., 1983, Oley Found. for Home Parenteral and Enteral Nutrition Patients, 1983—, Home Health Care of Am., 1983-88, Hosp. for Incurables Found., 1987-88, 91, Schaeffer Found. for Faculty Devel., 1988. Fellow Royal Coll. Physicians, Am. Coll. Physicians, Am. Coll. Nutrition (dir. 1985-88); mem. Am. Bd. Nutrition (dir. 1980, pres. 1982-84), Brit. Med. Assn., Am. Soc. Parenteral and Enteral Nutrition (abstract selection com. 1980, nutrition support standards com. 1984, future directions com. 1991, OASIS working group 1991-92, award 1992), Am. Soc. Clin. Nutrition (rsch. com. 1978, edn. com. 1979, councilor 1982-85, chair post grad. clin. nutrition tng. com. 1983-88, clin. practice in health and disease 1991), Am. Inst. Nutrition, Am. Gastroent. Assn. (co-organizer post grad. tng. course 1987, tng. and edn. com. 1988-91, abstract selection com. 1989), N.Am. Soc. Pediat. Gastroenterology, Am. Fedn. Clin. Rsch. (abstract selection com. 1986), Alpha Omega Alpha. Office: Albany Med Coll Albany NY 12208 Office Phone: 518-262-5299.

HOWARD, MALCOLM JONES, federal judge; b. Kinston, NC, June 24, 1939; s. Clayton and Thelma (Jones) H.; m. Eloise McGinty, Nov. 24, 1964; children: Shannon Lea, Joshua Brian. BS, U.S. Mil. Acad., 1962; JD, Wake Forest U., Winston Salem, NC, 1970. Bar: NC 1970, US Ct. Appeals (4th cir.) 1973. Sec. Judge Adv. Gen. Sch., Charlottesville, Va., 1970-71; legis. counsel to sec. US Army, Washington, 1971-72; asst. US atty. Ea. Dist. NC, Raleigh, 1972-73, US dist. judge Greenville, 1988—; dep. spl. counsel to Pres. U.S. Washington, 1974; sr. ptnr. Howard Browning Sams & Poole, Greenville, S.C., 1974-88; judge Fgn. Intelligence Surveillance Ct., 2005—. With US Army, 1962-82. Office: US Dist Ct PO Box 5006 Greenville NC 27835-5006*

HOWARD, MARCIA MORALES, federal judge; b. Jacksonville, Fla., 1965; BS, Vanderbilt U., 1987; JD with honors, U. Fla., 1990. Bar: Fla. 1990, US Supreme Ct., US Ct. Appeals (11th cir.), US Dist. Ct. (middle and no. dists.) Fla. Assoc. Commander, Legler, Werber, Dawes, Sadler & Howell, 1990—91, Foley & Lardner, 1991—94, McGuireWoods LLP, 1994—98, ptnr., 1998—2003; magistrate judge US Dist. Ct. (mid. dist.) Fla., Jacksonville, 2003—07, dist. judge, 2007—. Bd. mem., sec. Jacksonville Transp. Authority, 1999—2003. Office: US Dist Ct US Courthouse 300 N Hogan St, Ste 5-111 Jacksonville FL 32202 Office Phone: 904-301-6750.

HOWARD, MARILYN, retired school system administrator; BA in Edn., U. Idaho, 1960, MSc in Edn., 1965; EdD, Brigham Young U., 1986; postgrad., Idaho State U. adj. faculty Idaho State U., U. Idaho. Tchr. jr. HS history and lang. arts, Lewiston, 1960; tchr. various elem. & secondary schs. Washington and Idaho; prin. Moscow West Park Elementary Sch., 1988—99; supervisor, devel. pre-school Moscow sch. dists., 1992—99; supt. pub. instrn. Idaho State Dept. Edn., Boise, Idaho, 1999—2006. Bd. dirs. State Bd. Edn., State Land Bd., Northwest Regional Edn. Lab. Named Outstanding Educator of Yr., Idaho State U. Chpt. Kappa Delta Pi, 2000, Idaho State U., Coll. Edn., 2000. Mem.: Internat. Reading Assn. (state coord. and state pres. (Idaho), mem. nat. rsch. and studies com.), Coun. Chief State Sch. Officers, Phi Delta Kappa. Office Phone: 208-332-6811.*

HOWARD, MARILYN KAYE, political science professor; d. Bette Grandy Howard. BA, Ohio Dominican Coll., Columbus, 1979; MA, Ohio State U., Columbus, 1991, PhD, 1999. Asst. prof. Columbus State CC, Columbus, Ohio, assoc. prof., 2006—. Ednl. cons., Columbus, Ohio, 1995—. Vol. Ohio Dominican Coll., 1993—98, Columbus Symphony Orch., Columbus, Ohio, 2001—02; book critic Ohioana Libr., 2005—07; instr. St. Christopher Cath. Ch., Columbus, 1984—86. Named Outstanding Ohio Educator, Ohio Mag., 2005; recipient Disting. Tchg. award, Columbus State CC, 1997—98, 2005—06, award, Nat. Inst. Staff & Orgnl. Devel., 1998, 2005. Mem.: Ohio Historians Assn. Liberal. Roman Catholic. Avocations: reading, needlepoint. Office: Columbus State CC 333 TL 550 East Spring St Columbus OH 43216 Office Phone: 614-287-5368. Business E-Mail: mhoward@cscc.edu.

HOWARD, MELVIN, financial executive; b. Boston, Jan. 5, 1935; s. John M. and Molly (Sagar) H.; m. Beverly Ruth Kahan, June 9, 1957; children: Brian David, Marjorie Lyn. BA, U. Mass., 1957; MS, Columbia U., 1959. Fin. exec. Ford Motor Co., Dearborn, Mich., 1959-67; v.p. adminstrn. Shoe Corps. of Am., Columbus, Ohio, 1967-70; contr., sr. v.p. fin., chief fin. officer Xerox Corp., 1970-84, exec. v.p., chmn. fin. svcs., 1984-86, vice chmn. of bd., 1986-90, bd. dirs., 1982-90; pres., CEO Ehrlich Bober Fin. Corp., 1990-92; mng. dir. Taurus Adv. Group, 1993-94. Bd. dirs. Gould Pumps, Inc., Sector Mgmt., Inc. Trustee Nursing and Home Care, Commonwealth Coll. 1st lt. AUS, 1957. Mem. Birchwood Country Club, Frenchman's Creek Country Club, Beta Gamma Sigma. Home: 5500 Collins Ave Apt 404 Miami Beach FL 33140-5530

HOWARD, MICHAEL ELIOT, historian, educator; b. London, Nov. 29, 1922; s. Geoffrey Eliot and Edith Julia Emma (Edinger) H. MA, U. Oxford, 1948, LittD, 1976, Leeds U., Eng.; DLitt, U. London, 1988. Asst. lectr. history Kings Coll. U. London, 1947-53, lectr. war studies, 1953-62; prof. war studies U. London, 1963-68; fellow higher defence studies All Souls Coll., Oxford, 1968-77; prof. history of war U. Oxford, 1977-80, regius prof. modern history, 1980-89; prof. history Yale U., New Haven, 1989-93. Pres. emeritus Internat. Inst. Strategic Studies, London. Author: The Franco Prussian War, 1961 (Duff Cooper Prize, 1962), Grand Strategy, vol. IV, 1971 (Wolfson award for history), War in European History, 1976, The Invention of Peace, 2002, The First World War, 2003, many others. Served to capt. Brit. Army, 1942-45. Decorated Mil. Cross His Majesty King George VI, comdr. Brit. Empire, companion of Honor, Order of Merit; recipient Atlantic award, NATO, 1989; created Knight Bachelor, 1986. Fellow Brit. Acad., U.S. Acad. Arts and Scis., Athenaeum Club, Garrick Club (London). Anglican.

HOWARD, MILDRED, sculptor; b. San Francisco, 1945; AA, cert. in fashion arts, Coll. Alameda, 1977; MFA in Fiberworks, John F. Kennedy U., 1985. One-woman shows include Mill Valley (Calif.) Old Post Office, 1984, Dade County Libr., Miami, Fla., 1985, Calif. State U., Hayward, 1987, Headlands Ctr. for the Arts, Sausalito, Calif., 1991, San Francisco Art Inst., 1991, Gallery Paule Anglim, San Francisco, 1991, 93, INTAR, N.Y.C., 1992, U. Art Gallery, Sonoma State U., Rohnert Park, Calif., 1992, San Jose (Calif.) Mus. Art, 1994, Hammonds House Galleries, Atlanta, 1994, Capp St. Project, San Francisco, 1994; group exhbns. include Security Pacific Gallery, San Francisco, 1992, Lew Allen Gallery, Santa Fe, 1992, Shea & Bornstein Gallery, Santa Monica, 1992, Creative Time, N.Y.C., 1992, Berkeley Art Ctr., 1992, Nina Nielsen Gallery, Boston, 1993, New Mus. Contemporary Art, N.Y.C., 1993, Calif. Crafts Mus., San Francisco, 1994, U. Calif. Berkeley Mus. Art, Sci. and Culture, 1994, Laney Coll., Oakland, Calif., 1994, The Mus. at Blackhawk, Danville, Calif., 1994, Hampton (Va.) U. Mus., 1994, Gallery Resche, Paris, 1994, Yerba Buena Ctr. for the Arts, San Francisco, 1994, Installation Gallery, San Diego, 1994, Jewett Hall Gallery, U. Maine, Augusta, 1994, CCAC, Oakland, 1994, Oakland Mus., 1994, Louis Stern Fine Arts, L.A., 1995, Gallery Concord, 1995, Gallery II, U. Bradford, 1998, City Gallery, Leicester, 1999, LewAllen Contemporary, Santa Fe, 2000, Mus. Glass: Internat. Ctr. for Contemporary Art, Tacoma, 2002, Neuberger Mus. Art Biennial, 2003, Nielsen Gallery, Boston, 2003, others; represented in permanent collections Oakland Mus., Wadsworth Athaneum, Hartford, Conn., Rene and Veronica di Rosa Found., Napa, Calif., Frederick R. Weisman Art Mus., Calif. African Am. Mus., pvt. collections. Recipient Bank of Am. award, San Francisco, 1975, Small Projects award Inter Arts Marin, San Rafael, Calif., 1984, Adaline Kent award San Francisco Art Inst., 1991, Visual Artists award Flintridge Found., 2001-02; fellow in mixed media Calif. Arts Coun., 1990, Lila A. Wallace/Reader's Digest Internat. Traveling fellow, 1992-93; grantee Calif. Arts Coun., 2003. Office: 1925 Adam Clayton Powell Jr Blvd #7L New York NY 10026-2237

HOWARD, M(OSES) WILLIAM, JR., minister; b. Americus, Ga., Mar. 3, 1946; s. M. William and Laura (Turner) H.; m. Barbara Jean Wright, July 11, 1970; children: Matthew Weldon, Adam Turner, Maisha Wright BA, Morehouse Coll., 1968, L.H.D., 1984; M.Div., Princeton Theol. Sem., 1972; D.D., Miles Coll., 1979, Central Coll., 1980; LLD, Bloomfield Coll., 2001. Ordained to ministry Am. Baptist Ch., 1974; exec. dir. Black Council, Ref. Ch. in Am., NYC, 1972-92; pres. N.Y. Theol. Sem., NYC, 1992-00; pastor Bethany Baptist Ch., Newark, 2000—. Bd. dirs. N.J. Resources; moderator Commn. of World Coun. Chs. Program to Combat Racism, 1976-78; pres. Nat. Coun. Chs., 1979-81; condr. Christmas svcs. for hostages Am. embassy, Tehran, Iran, 1979; chmn. UN Seminar on Bank Loans to South Africa, Zurich, 1981; chmn. ecumenical delegation to Syria, 1984, instrumental (with Rev. Jesse Jackson) in obtaining release of Lt. Robert O. Goodman, USN; chair religious com. to welcome Nelson Mandela to U.S.A., 1990. Researcher: Born to Rebel - Autobiography of Benjamin Elijah Mays, 1967; editor: monthly newsletter Black Caucus RCA, 1973-92; pub., producer ann. lectureship, 1975-92. Active YMCA; trustee Trenton State Coll., 1981-82, Nat. Urban League; bd. dirs. Children's Def. Fund, The Independent Sector; founding mem. People for Am. Way; pres. Am. Com. on Africa, 1987-92; bd. govs. Rutgers U., 2004—, chair, 2007-. Recipient Disting. Service award as chmn. Commn. on Justice, Liberation and Human Fulfillment, Disting. Alumnus award Princeton Theol. Sem., 1984; decorated comdr. Order Knights of Holy Sepulchre. Mem. NAACP, Assn. Theol. Schs. in U.S. and Can. (sec. 1998-2000), Coun. Fgn. Rels., Sigma Pi Phi. Baptist. Office: Bethany

Baptist Ch 275 W Market St Newark NJ 07103 Business E-Mail: mwhoward@bethany-newark.org. *Perhaps the greatest challenge to humanity today is to see that our moral and ethical development catches up, and keeps pace with, our advances in technology.*

HOWARD, NATHAN DALE, history professor; s. James Edwin and Lois Cobb Howard. BA, Harding U., Searcy, Ark., 1994; MA, Baylor U., Waco, Tex., 1996; PhD, U. Ark., Fayetteville, 2005. Asst. prof. history Wake Forest U., Winston-Salem, NC, 2005—06, U. Tenn. Martin, 2006—. Mem.: S.E. Medieval Assn., North Am. Patristics Soc. Avocations: running, baseball, sports, golf, fishing. Office: Univ Tenn Dept HIstory 322 Humanities Martin TN 38238 Office Phone: 731-881-3470.

HOWARD, RALPH O'SULLIVAN, JR., geologist, researcher; b. Mobile, Ala., Apr. 4, 1958; s. Ralph O'Sullivan Howard, Sr. and Katherine Pill Howard; m. Susanne K. M. Agenhed, Aug. 8, 1984; children: Thomas N., Daniel R. BS in Arts and Scis., U. Ala., Tuscaloosa, 1981, MS in Geology, 1990. Registered profl. geologist State Bd. Registration Prof. Geologists, Ga., 1993. Staff geologist Westinghouse Environ. Svcs., Atlanta, 1988—91; remedial project mgr. region 4 US Environ. Protection Agy., Atlanta, 1991—. Contbr. chapters to books, articles to profl. jours. Capt. US Army, 1981—85. Decorated Commendation medal US Army; named Superfund Site Assessment Mgr. of Yr., US EPA, 2006; recipient Svc. Excellence award, Westinghouse Corp., 1990, 2 Commendable Svc. Bronze medals, US EPA, 2000; scholar, US Army ROTC, 1978. Mem.: Atlanta Geol. Soc., Vasa Order Am. (chmn. 1995). Episcopalian. Avocations: rocks, camping, hiking. Home: 3568 Cold Spring Ln Chamblee GA 30341-2054 Office: US Environ Protection Agy Region 4 61 Forsyth St Atlanta GA 30303 Personal E-mail: rhjr@speedfactory.net.

HOWARD, RICHARD (JOSEPH), poet, literary translator; b. Cleve., Oct. 13, 1929; BA, Columbia U., 1951, MA, 1952; postgrad., Sorbonne, Paris, 1952-53. Lexicographer Word Pub. Co., 1953-57; Rhodes prof. of comparative lit. U. Cin. Pres. PEN-Am. Center, 1977-79 Author: (poetry) Quantities, 1962, The Damages, 1967, Untitled Subjects, 1969 (Pulitzer Prize for poetry 1970), Findings, 1971, Two-Part Inventions, 1974, Fellow Feelings, 1976, Misgivings, 1979, Lining Up, 1984, Quantities/Damages, 1984, No Traveller, 1989, Like Most Revelations: New Poems, 1994, Trappings: New Poems, 1999; (criticism) Alone With America, 1969, Passengers Must Not Ride on Fenders, 1974; editor: Preferences: Fifty-One American Poets Choose Poems from Their Own Work and from the Past, 1974, The War in Algeria, 1975, The Paris Review, Western Humanities Review; poetry editor: New Am. Review, Shenandoah, New Republic, Paris Review; translator: The Voyeur (Robbe-Grillet), 1958, The Wind (Simon), 1959, The Grass (Simon), 1960, Two Novels: Jealousy and In the Labyrinth (Robbe-Grillet), 1960, Nadja (Breton), 1961, Last Year at Marienbad (Robbe-Grillet), 1962, Mobile (Butor), 1963, Manhood: A Journey from Childhood into the Fierce Order of Virility (Leiris), 1968, Force of Circumstance (de Beauvoir), 1963, The Erasers (Robbe-Grillet), 1964, For a New Novel: Essays on Fiction (Robbe-Grillet), 1966, The Poetics of Paul Valery (Hytier), 1966, Natural Histories (Renard), 1966, History of Surrealism (Nadeau), 1967, Histoire (Simon), 1968, The Immortalist (Gide), 1970, May Day Speech (Genet), 1970, Professional Secrets: An Autobiography (Cocteau), 1970, Fall into Time (Cioran), 1970, The Battle of Pharsalus (Simon), 1971, A Happy Death (Camus), 1972, Critical Essays (Barthes), 1972, Rosa (Pons), 1972, Project for a Revolution in New York (Robbe-Grillet), 1972, The Fantastic: A Structural Approach to a Literary Genre (Todorov), 1973, Quebec versus Ottawa: The Struggle for Self-Government, 1960-1972 (Morin), 1976, The Motorcycle (Pieyre de Mandiargues), 1976, France and Algeria (Tillion), 1976, The Trouble with Being Born (Cioran), 1976, The Poetics of Prose (Todorov), 1977, Song for an Equinox (Saint-John Perse), 1977, Roland Barthes, 1977, A Lover's Discourse (Barthes), 1978 (Am. Book award nomination for translation 1979), The One Pig with Horns (De Brunhoff), 1979, New Critical Essays (Barthes), 1980, The Girl Beneath the Lion (De Mandiargues), 1980, Camera Lucida: Reflections on Photography (Barthes), 1981, The Girl on the Motorcycle (De Madiargues), 1981, The Margin (De Mandiargues), 1981, Ideologies in Quebec: The Historical Development (Moniere), 1981, Witches' Sabbath (Sachs), 1982, Le Maison de Rendez-vous (Robbe-Grillet), 1982, The Empire of Signs (Barthes), 1982, The Fashion System (Barthes), 1983, Les Fleurs du Mal (Baudelaire), 1983 (Am. Book award for translation 1984), Corydon (Gide), 1983, Drawn and Quartered (Cioran), 1983, The Conquest of America (Todorov), 1984, The Dark Brain of Piranesi and Other Essays (Yourcenar), 1984, The Complete War Memoirs of Charles De Gaulle, 1940-1946, 1984, A Strange Virus of Unknown Origin: A.I.D.S. (Leibowitch), 1985, William Marshal: The Flower of Chivalry (Duby), 1985, The Responsibility of Forms (Barthes), 1985, The Flanders Road (Simon), 1986, The Opposing Shore (Gracq), 1986, The Flowers of Manet, 1986, Michelet (Barthes), 1986, The Rustle of Language (Barthes), 1986, Le Maison de Rendez-vous and Djinn (Robbe-Grillet), 1987, Balcony in the Forest (Gracq), 1987, Return from the U.S.S.R. and Afterthoughts on My Return (Gide), 1987, Past Tense: The Cocteau Diaries, Vol. I, 1987, History and Utopia (Cioran), 1987. Recipient Harriet Monroe Meml. prize, 1969, Levinson prize Poetry Mag., 1973, Cleve. Arts prize, 1974, Am. Acad. Inst. Arts and Letters medal for poetry, 1980, PEN Am. Ctr. medal for translation, 1986, France-Am. Found. award for translation, 1987; Nat. Endowment for Arts fellow, 1987, Guggenheim fellow, 1966-67; fellow Morse Coll.; fellow Yale U.; Nat. Inst. Arts grantee, 1970 Mem.: AAAL (v.p. 2006—). Office: Am Acad Arts and Letters 633 West 155th St New York NY 10032

HOWARD, RICHARD CARL, minister; b. Toledo, Mar. 12, 1938; s. Edward Ellsworth and Hazel Marie (Brady) Howard; m. Anita Laverne Lowrie, June 8, 1962; children: Cheryl Annette Howard Langskov, Richard D. II. BA, Grove City Coll., Pa., 1960; MA, Memphis State U., 1964; postgrad., Walden U., 1986—90. Dir. Memphis Youth for Christ, 1960—62; assoc. pastor North Hollywood First Assembly, 1962—64; dean of men, dir. student life Evangelical Coll., Springfield, Mo., 1964—65; nat. coll. youth rep. Assembly of God, Springfield, 1965—68, sr. pastor Dublin, Calif., 1968—71, Peninsula Christian Ctr., Redwood City, Calif., 1971—2002, apostolic missions pastor, 2003—. Adj. faculty Asia Pacific Theol. Sem., Bangio, Philippines, 1976—, Sophia Bible Inst., Bulgaria, 1995—. Author: The Judgement Seat of Christ, 1990, Strategy for Triumph, 1991, Songs for Life, 1996, The Lost Formula of the Early Church, 1996, The Finding Times of God, 1998, This Was Your Life, 1998, Seven Biblical Steps to Personal Renewal, 2000, Restoring Restorers, 2002, The King Describes His Kingdom, 2003. Republican. Mem. Assemblies Of God. Home: 31022 S Imperial Path Ln Spring TX 77386-2965

HOWARD, RICHARD RALSTON, II, medical health advisor, researcher, financial consultant; b. Winnfield, Kans., May 26, 1948; s. Richard Ralston and Ione (Mayer) H. BBA, Loyola U., New Orleans, 1970; MPH, Tulane U., 1977, MS, 1984, DrPH, 1988. Researcher Loyola U., 1973; educator Dominican Coll., New Orleans, 1977; educator Sch. Pub. Health Tulane U., New Orleans, 1978-82, researcher Sch. Medicine, 1979-88; med. health advisor Howard Med. Clinic, Slidell, La., 1982-91; founder The Inst. Econ. Tech. Rsch., New Orleans, 1993—. NIH grantee, 1979; VA grantee, 1984. Mem. Internat. Platform Assn., Am. Assn. Individual Investors, Beta Beta Beta. Achievements include research on the impact of the health food industry on nutrition awareness, cocaine testing through quantitative tear analysis, vitamin C and ophthalmic wound healing. Home: 3531 Nashville Ave New Orleans LA 70125-4339 Personal E-mail: rhoward787@aol.com.

HOWARD, ROBERT ELLIOTT, former federal official, consultant, educator; b. Staten Island, NY, Feb. 19, 1933; s. David and Helen (Gresser) H.; m. Bulbul Batra, Mar. 24, 1957; children: Nina Howard Regan, Nicholas, Sarah. AB, Columbia U., 1952; DPhil, Oxford U., Eng., 1957. Rsch. fellow in physics Carnegie Inst. Tech., Carnegie-Mellon U., Pitts., 1958-60; rsch. physicist Nat. Bur. Standards, Washington, 1960-67; mem. profl. staff Office Mgmt. and Budget, Washington, 1968-87, dep. assoc. dir. for nat. security, 1987-90, assoc. dir. for nat. security and internat. affairs, 1990-93; vis. prof. Nat. Defense Univ., Washington, 1993-95; pres. Key Assocs., 1995—. Adj. prof. nat. security studies Georgetown U., Washington, 1993—2002; vis. rsch. physicist U.K. Atomic Energy Authority, Harwell, England, 1962. Contbr. numerous articles to profl. jours. Recipient Presdl. Meritorious Exec. award, 1987, Presdl. Disting. Exec. award, 1990; Fulbright fellow Indian Inst. Tech., New Delhi, 1966. Fellow Am. Phys. Soc. Republican. Avocations: walking, reading, arts, tennis. Office Phone: 202-337-7487. Personal E-mail: rhoward9@erols.com.

HOWARD, ROBERT FRANKLIN, observatory administrator, astronomer; b. Delaware, Ohio, Dec. 30, 1932; s. David Dale and Clarine Edna (Morehouse) H.; m. Margaret Teresa Farnon, Oct. 4, 1958; children: Thomas Colin, Alan Robert, Moira Catharine BA, Ohio Wesleyan U., 1954; PhD, Princeton U., 1957. Carnegie fellow Mt. Wilson and Palomar Obs., Pasadena, Calif., 1957-59, staff mem., 1961-81; asst. prof. U. Mass., Amherst, 1959-61; asst. dir. for Mt. Wilson Mt. Wilson & Las Campanas Obs., Pasadena, 1981-84; dir. Nat. Solar Obs., Tucson, 1984-88, astronomer, 1988-98, astronomer emeritus, 1998—. Editor: Solar Magnetic Fields, 1971; editor: (jour.) Solar Physics, 1987-98; contbr. articles to profl. jours. Mem. Am. Astron. Soc. (Hale prize 2003), Internat. Astron. Union.

HOWARD, ROBERT STAPLES, newspaper publisher; b. Wheaton, Minn., Oct. 23, 1924; s. Earl Eaton and Helen Elizabeth (Staples) H.; m. Lillian Irene Crabtree, Sept. 2, 1945; children: Thomas, Andrea, William, David. Student, U. Minn., 1942, student, 1945. Pub. various daily, weekly newspapers, 1946-55; pub. Chester, Pa. Times, 1955-61; Pres. Howard Publs. (18 daily newspapers), 1961—2002. With AUS, 1942-43; 2d lt. USAAF, 1944-45. Home: PO Box 1337 Rancho Santa Fe CA 92067-1337 Office: 2525 Pio Pico Dr Ste 202 Carlsbad CA 92008-0570

HOWARD, ROBERT T., federal agency administrator; b. Everett, Mass. m. Ciretta Howard; 2 children. Grad., Northeastern U., Texas A&M U.; M in Military Art and Sci., Army Command and Gen. Staff Coll.; grad., Nat. War Coll., 1984. Advanced through grades to maj. gen. US Army, 2004, ret., 2004; v.p., gen. mgr. analysis and learning tech. divsn. Cubic Corp.; asst. sec. info. & tech. US Dept. Veterans Affairs, Washington, 2006—. Asst. prof. math U.S. Military Acad.; profl. lectr. Am. U. Office: US Dept Veterans Affairs 810 Vermont Ave NW Washington DC 20420 Office Phone: 202-273-8842. Office Fax: 202-273-8800.*

HOWARD, RON, film director; b. Duncan, Okla., Mar. 1, 1954; s. Rance and Jean Howard; m. Cheryl Alley, June 7, 1975; 4 children: Bryce, Jocelyn, Paige, Reed. Student, U. So. Calif., Los Angeles Valley Coll. Co-chmn. Imagine Films Entertainment, LA. Actor: (theatre) The Seven Year Itch, 1956, Hole in the Head, 1963; (TV series) The Andy Griffith Show, 1960-68, The Smith Family, 1971-72, Happy Days, 1974-80, Fonz and the Happy Days Gang (voice), 1980, Mork & Mindy, 1982-83, Laverne & Shirley, 1982-83, The Fonz Hour, 1982-83, Arrested Development (voice), 2003-; (TV films) A Boy Called Nuthin, 1967, Smoke, 1970, The Migrants, 1974, Locusts, 1974, Huckleberry Finn, 1975, I'm a Fool, 1976, Act of Love, 1980, Where Have All the Children Gone, 1980, Bitter Harvest, 1981, Fire on the Mountain, 1981, Return to Mayberry, 1986; (TV appearances) Dennis the Meance, 1959, 60, Johnny Ringo, 1959, The Twilight Zone, 1959, The DuPont Show with June Allyson, 1959, General Electric Theater, 1959, Insight, 1959, The New Breed, 1962, Route 66, 1962, The Eleventh Hour, 1963, The Great Adventure, 1964, Dr. Kildare, 1964, The Fugitive, 1964, The Big Valley, 1965, Gomer Pyle, U.S.M.C., 1966, I Spy, 1966, The Monroes, 1967, Mayberry R.F.D., 1968, The F.B.I., 1968, Lancer, 1968, Land of the Giants, 1969, Daniel Boone, 1969, Gunsmoke, 1969, Lassie, 1970, Love, American Style, 1972, The Bold Ones: The New Doctors, 1972, Bonanza, 1972, M*A*S*H, 1973, The Waltons, 1974, Laverne & Shirley, 1976, 79, Happy Days, 1983, 84, The Simpsons (voice), 1998, Frasier (voice), 1999; (films) The Journey, 1959, Door-to-Door Maniac, 1961, The Music Man, 1962, The Courtship of Eddie's Father, 1963, Village of the Giants, 1965, The Wild Country, 1971, American Graffiti, 1973, Happy Mother's Day, Love George, 1973, The Spikes Gang, 1974, Eat My Dust!, 1976, The Shootist, 1976, Grand Theft Auto, 1977, More American Graffiti, 1979, Osmosis Jones (voice), 2001; dir. (films) Deed of Daring-Do, 1969, Night Shift, 1982, Splash, 1984, Cocoon, 1985, Willow, 1988, Backdraft, 1991, The Paper, 1994, Apollo 13, 1995 (DGA award dir. achievement, 1996), Ransom, 1996, Da Vinci Code, 2006; dir., prodr. (films) Edtv, 1999, How the Grinch Stole Christmas, 2000, A Beautiful Mind, 2001 (Academy award best dir., 2002, Broadcast Film Critics Assoc. award best dir., 2002, DGA award dir. achievement, 2002), The Missing, 2003, Cinderella Man, 2005; actor, dir., writer (films) Grand Theft Auto, 1977; dir., prodr., writer (films) Far and Away, 1992; dir., exec. prodr. (films) Gung Ho, 1986; dir., writer (films) Parenthood, 1989; exec. prodr. (films) Leo and Loree, 1980, No Man's Land, 1987, Vibes, 1988, Clean and Sober, 1988, The Burbs, 1989, Closet Land, 1991; prodr. (films) The Chamber, 1996, Inventing the Abbotts, 1997, Beyond the Mat, 1999, The Alamo, 2004, Inside Deep Throat, 2005, Curious George, 2006; dir. (TV films) Through the Magic Pyramid, 1981; dir., writer, (TV films) Cotton Candy, 1978; dir., prodr. (TV films) Skyward, 1980, No Greater Gift, 1985, Take Five, 1987; exec. prodr. (TV films) Skyward Christmas, 1981, When Your Lover Leaves, 1983, Into Thin Air, 1985, Student Affairs, 1999, Boarding School, 2002; prodr. Student Affairs, 1999; exec. prodr. (TV series) Maximum Security, 1984, Parenthood, 1990, Hiller and Diller, 1997, Sports Night, 1998-2000, Felicity, 1998-2002, The PJs, 1999-2001, Wonderland, 2000, The Beast, 2001, 24, 2001-, Arrested Development, 2003-, The Inside, 2005; prodr. (miniseries) From the Earth to the Moon, 1998 (Emmy award outstanding miniseries, 1998) Named one of 50 Most Powerful People in Hollywood, Premiere mag., 2004—06, 100 Most Powerful Celebrities, Forbes.com, 2007. Mem. AFTRA, SAG, Acad. Motion Picture Arts and Scis. Office: Richard Lovett Creative Artists Agy 9830 Wilshire Blvd Beverly Hills CA 90212*

HOWARD, RONALD A., systems engineer, educator; DSc in Elec. Engring., MIT, 1958. Prof. dept. mgmt. sci. and engring. Stanford U., 1965—. Founder, dir. Strategic Decisions Group; dir. Decisions and Ethics Ctr. Author: Dynamic Programming and Markov Processes, 1960, Dynamic Probabilistic Systems, 1971, Readings in Decision Analysis, 1977, READINGS on The Principles and Applications of Decision Analysis, 1984, Decision Analysis, 1996; contbr. numerous articles to profl. jours. Recipient Frank P. Ramsey medal, Operational Rsch. Soc. UK, 1986. Fellow IEEE, Informs; mem. NAE. Office: Dept Mgmt Sci and Engring Terman Engring Ctr Rm 420 Stanford U Stanford CA 94305-4026 Business E-Mail: rhoward@stanford.edu.

HOWARD, ROSCOE CONKLIN, JR., lawyer, former prosecutor; b. 1952; m. Deborah Ryan Howard; children: Ryan, Adam. AB, Brown U., 1974; JD, U. Va., 1977. Bar: Va. 1977, D.C. 1978. Summer assoc. Brown, Wood, Ivey, Mitchell & Petty, NYC, 1976; law clk. to Hon. Raymond L. Finch, Territorial Ct. V.I., Christiansted, St. Croix, 1977—78; assoc. Jones, Day, Reavis & Pogue, Washington, 1978—79, Crowell & Moring, Washington, 1979—81; staff atty. FTC, Washington, 1981—84; asst. U.S. atty. Office of U.S. Atty. D.C., 1984—87, Office of U.S. Atty. (ea. dist.) Va., Alexandria divsn., 1987—89, Office of U.S. Atty. (ea. dist.) Va., Richmond divsn., 1989—91; assoc. ind. counsel In Re Samuel R. Pierce, 1991—94; assoc. prof. law U. Kans. Sch. Law, Lawrence, 1994—97, prof. law, 1999—2001; assoc. ind. counsel In Re A. Michael Espy, 1997—98; U.S. atty. DC dist. US Dept. Justice, 2001—04; atty., ptnr. Sheppard, Mullin, Richter & Hampton LLP, 2004—05, Troutman Sanders, LLP, Washington, 2005—. Assoc. ind. counsel Office of Ind. Counsel, Alexandria, Va., 1997—98. Sec. Lawrence Pub. Libr. Found. Bd., 1997, 1998—; bd. trustees Culver Ednl. Found., Ind., 1989—97; vol. Am. Heart Assn., 1996; v.p. Culver Mil. Acad. Alumni Legion Bd., Ind., 1978—82; mem. Attorney General's Advisory Com., 2001—04; mem. editl. bd. Nat. Law Jour., 2004—; bd. dir. Canada-US Fulbright Program, 2005—. Mem.: Assn. Am. Law Schs. (adv. bd. 1996—99, exec. com. 2001—), Kans. Bar Assn. (task force on criminal justice funding 1995—96), D.C. Bar Assn., Va. Bar Assn. Home: 4405 Ivory Coast Ct Chantilly VA 20151-2426 Office: Troutman Sanders LLP 401 Ninth St NW Washington DC 20004-2134 Office Phone: 202-274-2960. Business E-Mail: roscoe.howard@troutmansanders.com.

HOWARD, RYAN JAMES, professional baseball player; b. St. Louis, Nov. 19, 1979; Student, SW Mo. State U. First baseman Phila. Phillies, 2005—. Named Major League Baseball Player Yr., Sporting News, 2006, Player Yr., Players Choice awards, 2006, Nat. League Most Valuable Player, Baseball Writers' Assn. Am., 2006; recipient Hank Aaron award, 2006, Nat. League Silver Slugger award, 2006. Achievements include winning Rookie Yr., Major League Baseball, 2005; winning HR Derby at MLB All-Star Game, 2006. Office: Phila Phillies One Citizens Bank Way Philadelphia PA 19148*

HOWARD, SHERYL ANDREA, lawyer; b. July 26, 1975; BA, Smith Coll., 1997; JD, Cornell U., 2001. Bar: NY 2002, Mass. 2002. Assoc. Foley Hoag LLP, Boston, 2002—. Named a Mass. Rising Star, Boston mag., 2005—06. Mem.: NY State Bar Assn., Mass. Bar Assn., Vol. Lawyers Arts, Women's Bar Assn. (elder law project), Boston Bar Assn. (vol. lawyers project). Office: Foley Hoag LLP Seaport World Trade Center West 155 Seaport Blvd Boston MA 02210 Office Phone: 617-832-3012. Office Fax: 617-832-7000. E-mail: showard@foleyhoag.com.

HOWARD, TERRENCE DASHON, actor; b. Chicago, Ill., Mar. 11, 1969; m. Lori McCommas, 1989 (div. 2003); m. Lori McCommas, Feb. 2005 (separated); 3 children. BS in Chem. Engring., Pratt Inst. Actor: (TV films) The Jacksons: An American Dream, 1992, The O.J. Simpson Story, 1995, Shadow-Ops, 1995, King of the World, 2000, Boycott, 2001, Lackawanna Blues, 2005 (Outstanding Actor in a TV Movie, Mini-series or Dramatic Spl., NAACP Image awards, 2006), Their Eyes Were Watching God, 2005; (TV series) Tall Hopes, 1993, Sparks, 1996, Mama Flora's Family, 1998, Street Time, 2001; (films) Who's the Man?, 1993, Mr. Holland's Opus, 1995, Lotto Land, 1995, Dead Presidents, 1995, Sunset Park, 1996, Johns, 1996, Double Tap, 1997, Butter, 1998, Spark, 1998, The Players Club, 1998, Valerie Flake, 1999, Best Laid Plans, 1999, The Best Man, 1999 (NAACP Image award for best actor, 2000, Chicago Film Critics award, 2000, Spirit award, 2000), Big Momma's House, 2000, Love Beat the Hell Outta Me, 2000, Investigating Sex, 2001, Angel Eyes, 2001, Glitter, 2001, Hart's War, 2002, Biker Boyz, 2003, Love Chronicles, 2003, Crash, 2004 (Outstanding Performance by a Cast in a Motion Picture, SAG awards, 2006, Outstanding Supporting Actor in a Motion Picture, NAACP Image award, 2006), Ray, 2004, Hustle & Flow, 2005, The Salon, 2005, Four Brothers, 2005, Animal, 2005, Get Rich or Die Tryin', 2005 (Breakthrough Performance Actor, Nat. Bd. Review, 2005), Idlewild, 2006; actor, exec. prodr.: Pride, 2007; host: (TV series) Independent Lens, 2003—07. Recipient Breakthrough Performance Actor award, Nat. Bd. Rev., 2005.*

HOWARD, TERRY THOMAS, obstetrician, gynecologist; b. Cleve., May 14, 1943; s. Henry and Paula H.; m. Phyllis C. Schaevitz, Aug. 21, 1965; children: Jennifer, Jason, Brian. AB magna cum laude, Columbia U., 1965; MD, Harvard Med. Sch., 1969. Diplomate Am. Bd. Ob-Gyn. Intern, resident gen. surgery Beth Israel Hosp., Boston, 1969-71; resident ob-gyn Boston Hosp. for Women (now named Brigham & Womens Hosp.), 1971-74; physician Chelmsford (Mass.) Med. Assocs., 1974-88, Harvard Cmty. Health Plan, Chelmsford, 1988-97, Harvard Vanguard Med. Assocs. (formerly Harvard Cmty. Health Plan), Chelmsford, 1998-2000; pvt. practice Chelmsford, 2000—. Trustee Lowell (Mass.) Gen. Hosp., 1987-2003, trustee emeritus, 2003—. Bd. dirs. Friends of the Children Concert Band, Chelmsford, 1981—, Lowell Cmty. Health Ctr., 2002-; trustee Congregation Shalom, Chelmsford, 1993-96; bd. trustees Merrimack Repertory Theatre, 2006-. Fellow Am. Coll. Obstetrics & Gynecology, Am. Coll. Surgeons; mem. Am. Soc. Reproductive Medicine.

HOWARD, THOMAS CLEMENT, surgeon; b. Austin, Tex., May 7, 1943; s. Walter Burke and Virginia Kentucky (Freeman) H.; m. Paula Cheryl Greenwald, June 7, 1969; children: Jennifer, Michael. BA, Stanford U., 1965; MD, Yale U., 1969. Diplomate Am. Bd. Surgery; cert. gen. vascular surgery. Intern in surgery Yale-New Haven Hosp., 1969-70, resident in surgery, 1970-74; instr. surgery Yale Med. Sch., New Haven, 1973-74; asst. prof. surgery U. Nebr. Med. Ctr., Omaha, 1976-80; pvt. practice Clarkson Hosp., Omaha, 1980—; pres. Surg. Ctr. the Heartland, Omaha, 1991—. Maj. M.C., U.S. Army, 1974-76. Fellow ACS; mem. Midwestern Vascular Surg. Soc., Internat. Soc. for Cardiovascular Surgery (N.Am. chpt.), Southwestern Surg. Soc. Congregationalist. Office: Surg Ctr the Heartland 823 Doctors Bldg S Tower Omaha NE 68131 Home: 11415 Iowa Cir Omaha NE 68142-1603

HOWARD, THOMAS JOSEPH, SR., editor; b. Georgetown, SC, Aug. 9, 1948; s. Lawrence Edgar Howard, Sr. and Claudia Wolf Howard; m. Ruthann O. Oberly, Nov. 4, 1967; 1 child, Thomas Joseph Howard, Jr. BA in Journalism, U. SC, Columbia, 1966—69, grad. work in journalism, 1969—70, grad. work in journalism, 1978—80. Co. clk. US Army, Ft. Benning, Ga., 1970—72; news dir. WACA Radio, Camden, SC, 1972—73; editor Wing Publs., Cayce, SC, 1973—77; pres., owner Forest Pub. Co., Columbia, 1977—80; asst. mgr. The Print Shop, Columbia, 1980—86; sr. dist. exec. Indian Waters Coun., Boy Scouts Am., Columbia, 1986—92; darkroom technician Palmetto State Printing, Columbia, 1992—93; adminstrv. asst., field inventory auditor SC Jud. Dept., Columbia, 1993—94; state editor The Times, Georgetown, 2000—. Editor: (book) Looking Through the Window, An Informal History of the Family of Henry Richardson Howard Sr. & Alice May Baker Howard, 2005. Vol. leader Boy Scouts Am., Georgetown, Columbia, Garden City Beach, Charlston, 1980—2006; precinct pres. Richland County Rep. Party, Columbia, 1975—84; eucharistic min., lector various cath. chs., Georgetown, Garden City Beach, Columbia, 1965—2006; mem. KC, Georgetown, Columbia, 1976—2006. Specialist 4th class US Army, 1970—72, Ft. Jackson, SC & Ft. Benning, Ga. Named to Chief Scout Exec. Winner's Cir., Boy Scouts Am., 1987—92; recipient Wood Badge Tng. award, 1983, Scouter's Tng. award, 1985, Dist. Merit award, 1986, Boys' Life award, 1986—92, Nat. Quality Dist. award, 1987—91, Pilot Dist., New Scout Program award, 1989—90, Writing award, SC Press Assn., 2002, 2005. Mem.: Am. Mensa (bd. mem. 1984—2006), Georgetown Breakfast Rotary Club (bd. dirs. 2000—06, pres. 2005—06). Roman Cath. Avocations: computers, reading, camping, hiking, coin collecting/numismatics. Home: 1704 Pringles Ferry Rd Georgetown SC 29440 Office: The Times 615 Front St Georgetown SC 29440 Home Phone: 843-527-6467. Personal E-mail: tjhowardsr@aol.com. Business E-Mail: thoward@gtowntimes.com.

HOWARD, TIM, professional soccer player; b. N. Brunswick, NJ, Mar. 6, 1979; Goalkeeper NY NJ MetroStars, 1998—2003, Manchester United, England, 2003—06, Everton FC, Liverpool, England, 2006—. 16 caps

U.S. Nat. Soccer team, 2002—; mem. U.S. World Cup team, 2006. Bd. dir. Tourette Syndrome Assn. NJ. Named Goalkeeper of the Yr., English Premier League, 2004. Mailing: US Soccer Fedn 1801 S Prairie Ave Chicago IL 60616

HOWARD, VIVIAN AMICK, music educator; b. Columbia, SC, Aug. 18, 1955; d. Odis Leroy and Mary Ada (Shealy) Amick; m. Thomas (Andy) Andrew Howard, July 1, 1978; children: Drew, Kathleen. B Music Edn., Lenoir-Rhyne Coll., 1977; cert. level I Orff, Westminster Choir Coll.; cert. AP music theory, Oglethorpe U. Tchr. Glen Alpine Jr. H.S., NC, 1977—78, Stanley Jr. H.S., NC, 1981—84, Harrisburg Elem. Sch., NC, 1995—2001; tchr., choral dir. Jay M. Robinson H.S., Concord, NC, 2001—. Advisor Tri-M Music Honor Soc., Concord, 2004—. Choir mem., substitute dir., organist Calvary Luth. Ch., 1982—. Mem.: Am. Choral Dirs. Assn., Music Educators Nat. Conf. Avocations: singing, piano, reading, calligraphy. Home: 2228 Quail Dr NW Concord NC 28027 Office: Jay M Robinson HS 300 Pitts School Rd SW Concord NC 28027 Office Phone: 704-788-4500. Business E-Mail: vhoward@cabarrus.k12.nc.us.

HOWARD, WILLIAM GATES, JR., electronics company executive; b. Boston, Nov. 6, 1941; s. William Gates and Mary Louise (Creager) H.; m. Kathleen Louretta Shipp, June 4, 1983. BEE with distinction, Cornell U., 1964, MS, 1965; PhD, U. Calif.-Berkeley, 1967. Asst. prof. dept. elec. engrng. and computer scis. U. Calif.-Berkeley, 1967-69; group ops. mgr. Motorola Semicondr. Group, Mesa, Ariz., 1969-76; v.p., dir. tech. and planning Motorola Semicondr. Sector, Phoenix, 1976-83; v.p., dir. R&D Motorola Inc., Schaumburg, Ill., 1983-87; sr. fellow Nat. Acad. Engrng., Washington, 1987-91; chmn. bd. dirs. Thunderbird Technologies, Inc. Bd. dirs. Ramtron Internat Corp., Xilinx, Inc., Sandia Corp.; chmn. semicondr. tech. adv. com. US Dept. Commerce, 1978-83; chmn. adv. group on electron devices Dept. Def., 1982-99, mem. def. sci. bd., 1996—; mem. study com. on tech. and implications of VLSI, NAS, 1980; chmn. vis. com. on advanced tech. Nat. Inst. Stds. and Tech., 1988-92; chmn. Def. Sci. Bd. Task Force on Microelectronics Rsch. Facilities, 1991-92; mem. Sandia Pres. Adv. Coun., 1997-2000. Author: (with D.J. Hamilton) Basic Integrated Circuit Engineering, 1976, (with B. Guile) Profiting from Innovation, 1992; patentee (with J.B. Cecil) improved reference current source, ladder termination circuit, three terminal zener diode. Fellow AAAS, IEEE (vice chmn. circuits and systems soc. 1976-78); mem. Nat. Acad. of Engrng., Sigma Xi, Phi Kappa Phi, Eta Kappa Nu, Tau Beta Pi. Office: 10642 E San Salvador Dr Scottsdale AZ 85258-6114

HOWARD, WILLIAM MATTHEW, arbitrator, lawyer, writer; b. Oak Park, Ill., Dec. 16, 1934; s. William and Martha Geraldine (Herlock) H.; children: Matthew William, Stephanie Sue. BSBA, U. Mo., 1956, JD, 1958; postgrad., U. Nice, 1976, U. London, 1977; PhD, Ariz. State U., 1995. Bar: Mo. 1958, U.S. Supreme Ct. 1986, cert.: Fla. Supreme Ct. (mediator and arbitrator). Jr. ptnr. Bryan Cave, St. Louis, 1958—66; gen. counsel, asst. to pres. U.S. Steel Co., Granite City, Ill., 1966—69; pres. Thomson Internat. Co., Thibodaux, La., 1969—70; founder, pres., chmn. bd. The Catalyst Group, Phoenix, 1970—97; dean, ctr. adminstr. The Union Inst., San Diego, 1997—99; pres. Dispute Solutions, Inc., Scottsdale, Ariz., 1999—. Mem. adj. faculty U. Mo., Columbia, 1956-58, St. Louis U., 1958-61, Ariz. State U., 1994-96, Ottawa U., 1994-96, Nova Southeastern U., 1996-97; chmn. unauthorized practice law com. Mo. Bar, St. Louis, 1964-65; chmn. bd. N.V. Vulcaansoord, Terborg, The Netherlands, 1975-78, E. Chalmers Holdings, Ltd., Glasgow, Scotland, 1977-78; exec. com. Chem. Bank, Irvine, Calif., 1985-90; vis. lectr. UCLA, 1987; arbitrator Am. Arbitration Assn., N.Y.C., 1987—, N.Y. Stock Exch., 1987—, Nt. Assn. Securities Dealers, Chgo., 1987—, Nat. Futures Assn., Chgo., 1988—, Am. Stock Exch., N.Y.C., 1988; hearing officer Mo. Dept. Natural Resources, Jefferson City, 1987-89, Internat. Ct. Arbitration, 1993—, Inter-Am. Comml. Arbitration Commn., 1993—; mem. Fla. Automobile Arbitration Bd., 1997-98; bd. dirs. Xeric Corp., Denver, Phoenix. Editor newsletter Extras, 1970—; exec. producer: (motion picture) Twice a Woman, 1979; contbr. numerous articles and revs. to various jours. Bd. dirs. U. Mo. Alumni Assn., 1986, Breckenridge (Colo.) Film Festival, 1989, Actors Theatre Phoenix, 1990; mem. club adv. bd. Phoenix Art Mus., 1990; dir. Scottsdale Cultural Coun., 1991. Mem. Am. Arbitration Assn. (regional adv. com.), Soc. Profls. in Dispute Resolution, Fla. Acad. Mediators, Nat. Inst. Dispute Resolution, Mensa, Order of Coif. Avocations: literature, travel, theater, visual arts, skiing. Office: PO Box 3438 Phoenix AZ 85030-3438 Personal E-mail: howardbill@msn.com.

HOWARD-PEEBLES, PATRICIA N., clinical cytogeneticist; b. Lawton, Okla., Nov. 24, 1941; d. J. Marion and R. Leona (prestidge) Howard; m. Thomas M. Peebles, Aug. 16, 1975. BSEd, U. Ctrl. Okla., 1963; student, Randolph-Macon Coll. Women, 1964; PhD in Zoology (Genetics), U Tex. at Austin, 1969. Diplomate Am. Bd. Med. Genetics; cert. clin. cytogeneticist, med. geneticist. Sci. and history tchr. Piedmont (Okla.) Pub. Schs., 1963-64; biochem. technician biochemistry sect. biology divsn. Oak Ridge (Tenn.) Nat. Lab., 1964-66; instr. rsch. pediatrics dept. pediatrics, instr. cytotech. U. Okla. Health Scis. Ctr., Oklahoma City, 1971-72; asst. prof., dir. Cytogenetics Lab. U. So. Miss., Hattiesburg, 1973-77, assoc. prof., dir. Cytogenetics Lab., 1977-80; assoc. prof. dept. pub. health, staff Lab. Med. Genetics U. Ala., Birmingham, 1980-81; assoc. prof., dir. Cytogenetics Lab. dept. pathology U. Tex. Health Sci. Ctr., Dallas, 1981-85, prof., dir. Cytogenetics Lab., 1985-87; prof. dept. human genetics Med. Coll. Va., Richmond, 1987—; clin. cytogeneticist, dir. postnatal lab. Genetics & IVF Inst., Fairfax, Va., 1987-98, co-dir. cytogenetics lab., 1998-2000; genetic, cytogenetic cons., 2000—. Am. Cancer Soc. postdoctoral fellow dept. human genetics U. Mich. Med. Sch., Ann Arbor, 1969-70, dept. human genetics and devel. Coll. Physicians and Surgeons, Columbia U., N.Y.C., 1970-71; genetic cons. Ellisville (Miss.) State Sch., 1973-80; attending staff dept. pathology Parkland Meml. Hosp., Dallas County Hosp. Dist., 1981-87; mem. sci. adv. com. Fragile X Found., 1985-2002; mem. Internat. Standing Com. on Human Cytogenetic Nomenclature, 1991-96. Contbr. articles to profl. jours., chpts. to books; reviewer Am. Jour. Human Genetics, Am. Jour. Med. Genetics, Clin. Genetics, Human Genetics. Fellow Am. Coll. Med. Genetics (founding mem.); mem. Am. Soc. Human Genetics, Assn. Genetic Technologists, Tex. Genetics Soc. (chmn. planning com. ann. meeting 1984), Am. Cytogenetics Conf., Delta Kappa Gamma, Sigma Xi. Bapt. Office Phone: 214-893-8635. Personal E-mail: phpeebles@yahoo.com.

HOWARDS, STUART S., urologist, educator; b. Milw., Mar. 29, 1937; s. Harvey H. and Anne (Levin) H.; m. Carter N. Howards, Aug. 20, 1966; children: Penelope P., Hugh N. BA, Yale U., 1959; MD, Columbia U., 1963. Intern in surgery Peter Bent Brigham Hosp., Boston, 1963-64, resident in urology, 1968-71; resident in surgery Childrens Hosp., Boston, 1964-65; rsch. assoc. NIH, Bethesda, Md., 1965-68; asst. prof. urology and physiology U. Va., Charlotteville, 1971-74; assoc. prof., 1974-76, prof., 1976—, chief divsn. pediat. urology, 1986—; exec. sec. Am. Bd. Urology, Charlottesville, Va. Chmn. exam com. Am. Bd. Urology, 1985-91, trustee, 1986-92, pres., 1992-93, exec. sec., 1997—; sr. urologic advisor to dir. NIDDK/NIH. Editor: Infertility in the Male, 1991, 3d edit., 1997, Adult and Pediatric Urology, 1991, 3d edit., 1995; editor Jour. Urology, 1983-2000. Maj. USPHS, 1965-68. Recipient Career Investigation award NIH, 1973-78. Fellow Am. Acad. Pediats.; mem. Am. Urol. Assn. (Golden Cystoscope award 1981, Scott award 1990, Hugh Young award 1991, Disting. Svc. award 2001), Clin. Soc. Genitourinary Surgeons, Am. Soc. Reproductive Medicine (bd. dirs. 1994-96, treas. 1996—), Soc. Andrology, Genitourinary Surgeons, Am. Assn. Genito-Urinary Surgeons (sec.-treas. 1992-97), NIDDK, NIH (sr. urology advisor to the dir., 2002—), Nat. Bd. Med. Examiners. Office Phone: 434-924-9559. Business E-Mail: ssh4e@virginia.edu.

HOWARTH, WILLIAM (LOUIS), literature and language professor, writer; b. Mpls., Nov. 26, 1940; s. Nelson Oliver and Mary Watson (Prindiville) H. BA with highest distinction, U. Ill., 1962; MA, U. Va., 1963, PhD, 1967. Instr. Princeton (N.J.) U., 1966-68, asst. prof., 1968-73, assoc. prof., 1973-81, prof. English, 1981—. Mem. exec. com. Princeton Environ. Inst.; advisor Program in Environ. Studies, Program in Am. Studies Princeton (N.J.) U.; cons. Ctr. for Edits. of Am. Authors, 1974, Rockefeller Bros. Fund, 1976, Geraldine W. Dodge Found., 1981, Nat. Geog. Soc., 1984, Corp. for Pub. Broadcasting, 1986, NEH, 1987, Nat. Rural Studies Coun., 1988, Atlantic Ctr. for Arts, 1990, Santa Fe Environ. Coun., 1991, ALA, 1993, Assn. for the Study of Lit. and Environment, 1994, Kellogg Found., 1995, Arthur Vining Davis Found., 1998, AAAS, 2000. Author: Nature in American Life, 1972, The John McPhee Reader, 1976, The Book of Concord, 1982, Thoreau in the Mountains, 1982, Traveling the Trans-Canada, 1987, Mountaineering in the Sierra Nevada, 1989, Walking with Thoreau, 2001; author book chpts.; editor-in-chief: The Writings of Henry D. Thoreau, 1972-80; mem. numerous editl. bds.; editl. adviser numerous jours. and publs.; contbr. articles to profl. jours. Woodrow Wilson Found. fellow, 1966, Henry E. Huntington Libr. fellow, 1968, NEH fellow, 1977, John E. Annan BiCentennial Preceptor, Princeton, 1973, Pew and Templeton Founds. fellow, 2000, Princeton Environ. Inst., 2004. Mem. MLA, Am. Studies Assn., Thoreau Soc. Am. (pres. 1975-76), Am. Soc. Environ. History, Am. Lit. Assn., Nat. Geographic Soc. (contract writer 1978—), Nat. Rural Studies Coun. (assoc.), Assn. for the Study of Lit. and Environ. (adv. bd.), Am. Soc. Environ. History (adv. bd.), Ctr. for Am. Places (bd. dirs.), Phi Beta Kappa. Office: Princeton U 22 McCosh Hall Princeton NJ 08544-1607

HOWAT, JOHN KEITH, retired museum executive; b. Denver, Apr. 12, 1937; s. James Bowcott and Nancy Selden (Skinker) H.; m. Anne Hadley, June 21, 1958; children: Karen Louise, Laura Anne. Grad., Phillips Exeter Acad., 1955; BA, Harvard U., Cambridge, Mass., 1959, MA, 1962. Curator Hyde Collection, Glens Falls, NY, 1962-64; Ford fellow NYU Inst. Fine Arts, 1965—66; Chester Dale fellow Met. Mus. Art, NYC, 1966—67, asst. curator dept. Am. paintings and sculpture; 1967-68, assoc. curator-in-charge, 1968-70, curator, 1970-82, chmn. depts. Am. art, 1982—2001. Mem. adv. com. archives Am. art Smithsonian Instn., 1969—; trustee Archives of Am. Art, 1988—, N.Y. Society Libr., 2002—. Author: The Hudson River and Its Painters, 1972, Frederic Church, 2005; co-author exhbn. catalogs John Frederick Kensett: An American Master, 1985, An American Paradise: The World of The Hudson River School, 1987, Art and the Empire City: New York, 1825-1861, 2000. Mem. Union Club, Grolier Club, Century Assn., The Brook. Home: 1100 Park Ave New York NY 10128-1202

HOWAT, KEVIN JOHN, publishing and healthcare services executive; b. Turtle Creek, Pa., May 22, 1953; s. Jack William and Julia (Green) H.; m. Jane Elizabeth Townsend, Sept. 30, 1984; children: Lucy, Sophia Jane. BA cum laude, Franklin & Marshall Coll., Lancaster, Pa., 1975. Exec. editor, pub. Internat. Thomson, Wadsworth, Belmont, Calif., 1979-88; new products mgr. The Learning Co., Fremont, Calif., 1988-90; sr. acquisitions editor Addison-Wesley Edn. Software, Redwood City, Calif., 1990-92; dir. strategic mktg., bus. devel. Macromedia Inc., San Francisco, 1992-94; v.p. product devel., pub. Simon & Schuster Pub., NYC, 1994-98; v.p., bus. devel., brand mgmt. Time Inc. New Media, NYC, 1998-2000; sr. v.p. bus. devel. and sales Miavita, Inc., NYC, 2000—; sr. v.p. bus. devel. Matria Healthcare, Inc. (formerly known as Miavita, Inc.), Marietta, Ga., 2005—. Founder, adv. bd. New Media Ctrs., San Francisco, 1993-94. Author CD-ROM software (awards). Program com. EDUCOM (Educational Comp. Conf.), Washington, 1990-93. Recipient Ednl. Software Product award Softward Pub. Assn., 1990. Avocations: music, mountain biking, theater, cross country skiing. Home: 51 Crow Hill Crest Mount Kisco NY 10549-3804 Office: Matria Healthcare Inc 444 Madison Ave 8th Fl New York NY 10022 Office Phone: 914-420-4718. Personal E-mail: khowat@optonline.net.

HOWDER, MURRAY LOUIS, librarian, educator; b. Washington, Aug. 10, 1932; s. William Joseph and Hilda Rose Howder. BA, George Washington U., DC, 1954; MA, Middlebury Coll., Vt., 1960; MS, Cath. U., DC, 1967. Cert. Russian Army Lang. Sch., 1950. Rsch. specialist Libr. Congress, 1960—68; assoc. mgr. Eric Facility, Bethesda, Md., 1971—79; mgr. info. svcs. Nat. Ch. Bilingual Edn., Arlington, Va., 1979—81; dir. learning and res. ctr. Washington Internat. Coll., 1981—82; adminstrv. libr. VSE Corp., Alexandria, Va., 1983—97; docent Hillwood Mus., 1998—2007. Dir. Bogart Brociner Assocs., Annapolis, Md., 1981—85; tchr. Russian, English second lang. Author: (bibliography) The Soviet Navy, 1968; co-author: (book) Library Surveys, 1971; contbr. chapters to books. Reader, bd. mem. Vol. Readers Blind, 2005—; chpt. pres. AARP, 2002—06, v.p., 2007. Sp3 US Army, 1955—57, France. Fellow, NDEA, 1959—60. Mem.: Assn. Oldest Inhabitants DC, DC Libr. Assn. (Disting. Svc. award 1988), Coun. Comm. Soc. (dir. 1980—86). Republican. Avocations: opera, theater.

HOWE, BILL, information technology executive; BS in Math., U. Waterloo; MBA, Harvard Bus. Sch. Mktg., gen. mgmt. Intel Corp., 1983—2003; pres. Intel Japan, 1998—2003; pres., CEO Azaire Networks, 2003—. Office: Azaire Networks Ste 515 4800 Great America Pkwy Santa Clara CA 95054

HOWE, CARROLL VICTOR, construction equipment company executive; b. Kearny, NJ, Dec. 12, 1923; s. Wright and Ada (Hodge) H,; m. Nancy Osborne Stivers, Nov. 24, 1951 (div.); 1 child: Gregory Carroll; m. Priscilla Howland Greene, Mar. 1, 1957 (div.); children: Gregory Carroll, Christopher David; m. Eileen Crawley Pierson, Apr. 14, 1984 (div.). BA, Princeton U., 1947; MFA, Yale U., 1950. Writer, producer Pemeho Prodns., NYC, 1950-51, free lance actor, writer, 1952-54; salesman Atlas Rigging Supply Corp., Newark, 1954-56, office mgr., 1956-57, sales mgr., 1957-58, v.p., 1958-62, pres., 1962-94, ret., 1994; pres. Arsco Industries, Inc., Newark, 1966-2000, ret., 2000. Bd. dirs. Select Ins. Group of North Am., 1987-94. Author: Best One-Act Plays, 1949-1950, 1950, (play) The Long Fall, 1950, 1957, Best Short Plays, 1917-1957, 1957. Bd. dirs., pres. 15 Tenant Shareholders, Inc., N.Y.C., 1978-81, Alumni Coun. Yale U. Grad. Sch. Drama, 1988-94; mem. bd. govs. Newark Acad., Livingston, N.J., 1990-94; mng. ptnr. Crollar Assocs. Newark, 1983-94. Served from pvt. to 2d lt. USMCR, 1942-46, 1st lt. to capt., 1951-52. Recipient Applause award N.J. Theatre Group, 1989. Mem. Wildlife Conservation Soc., USA Track & Field, Boat/US, AAII, Am. Mensa Ltd., Quadrangle Club, Princeton Club Sarasota, Yale Club of Suncoast, Westhampton Yacht Squadron (treas. 1970-72, vice commodore 1972-74, commodore 1974-76, dir. 1976-80), Bradenton Yacht Club, Ivy League Club. Humanist. Home: 2914 River Trace Cir Bradenton FL 34208

HOWE, DANIEL WALKER, historian, educator; b. Ogden, Utah, Jan. 10, 1937; s. Maurice Langdon and Lucie (Walker) H.; m. Sandra Fay Shumway, Sept. 3, 1961; children: Rebecca, Christopher, Stephen. AB magna cum laude, Harvard U., 1959; MA, Oxford U., Eng., 1965; PhD, U. Calif., Berkeley, 1966. From instr. to assoc. prof. history Yale U., 1966-73; assoc. prof. history UCLA, 1973-77, prof., 1977-92, chmn. dept., 1983-87. Harmsworth vis. prof. Am. history, Oxford (Eng.) U., 1989-90, Rhodes prof. Am. history, 1992-2002; vis. prof. Yale U., 2001. Author: The Unitarian Conscience, 1970, The Political Culture of the American Whigs, 1979, Making the American Self, 1997, What Hath God Wrought: The Transformation of America, 1815-1848, 2007. Served to lt. U.S. Army, 1959-60. Kent fellow Danforth Found., 1964-66; Charles Warren Center for Studies in Am. History fellow, 1970-71; NEH fellow, 1975-76; Guggenheim fellow, 1984-85; Huntington Libr. fellow, 1992, 94, 2002-03. Fellow: Royal Hist. Soc.; mem.: Am. Hist. Assn., Soc. Historians Early Am. Rep. (pres. 2000—01), Soc. Am Historians, Oxford and Cambridge Club (London). Episcopalian. Home: 3814 Cody Rd Sherman Oaks CA 91403-5019 E-mail: howe@history.ucla.edu.

HOWE, DRAYTON FORD, JR., lawyer; b. Seattle, Nov. 17, 1931; s. Drayton Ford and Virginia (Wester) H.; m. Joyce Arnold, June 21, 1952; 1 son, James Drayton. AB, U. Calif., Berkeley, 1953; LLB, U. Calif., San Francisco, 1957. Bar: Calif. 1958. CPA Calif. Atty. IRS, 1958-61; tax dept. supr. Ernst & Ernst, San Francisco, 1962-67; ptnr. Bishop, Barry, Howe, Haney & Ryder, San Francisco, 1968—. Lectr. on tax matters U. Calif. extension, 1966-76. Mem. Calif. Bar Assn., San Francisco Bar Assn. (chmn. client relations com. 1977), Calif. Soc. CPA's. Office: Bishop Barry Howe Haney & Ryder 2000 Powell St Ste 1425 Emeryville CA 94608-1861 Office Phone: 510-596-0888. E-mail: dhowe@bbhhr.com.

HOWE, FISHER, management consultant, retired foreign service officer; b. Winnetka, Ill., May 17, 1914; s. Lawrence and Hester (Davis) H.; m. Deborah Froelicher, June 4, 1945; children: Elizabeth, Shippen. AB, Harvard U., 1935; student, Nat. War Coll., 1948. Salesman Coats & Clarks Thread Co., NYC, 1935-40, Patons & Baldwins, Ltd., Yorkshire, England, 1936-37; mem. staff Office of Dir., OSS, Washington, London, Mediterranean, Far East, 1941-45; fgn. svc. officer Dept. State, 1945-68, spl. asst. under sec. of state, econ. affairs, 1945-46, dep. dir. Bur. Intelligence and Rsch., exec. sec., dir. exec. secretariat, 1956-58; dep. chief of mission and charge Am. Embassy, Oslo, 1958-62, The Hague, Netherlands, 1962-65; mem. policy planning coun., 1965-68; exec. dir., asst. dean Johns Hopkins U. Sch. Advanced Internat. Studies, 1968-72; dep. exec. dir. Commn. on Orgn. of Govt. for Conduct of Fgn. Policy, Washington, 1973-75; sec., gen. adv. com. Energy R & D Adminstrn., 1975-77; dir. instl. rels. Resources for the Future, Inc., 1978-82; ptnr. Lavender/Howe & Assocs., Washington, 1982—. Author: Computer and Foreign Affairs, 1968, Fund Raising and the Nonprofit Board Member, 1988, Board Member's Guide to Fund Raising, 1991, Welcome to the Board, 1995, Board Member's Guide to Strategic Planning, 1997, The Nonprofit Leadership Team: Building the Board-Executive Director Partnership, 2003. Trustee Fountain Valley Sch., Colorado Springs, Colo., Pilgrim Soc., Plymouth, Mass., STRIVE, Washington. Served to lt. USNR, 1943-44, overseas svc. Mem. Metroplitan Club (Washington), Mill Reef (Antigua). Address: Ingleside # 637 3050 Military Rd NW Washington DC 20015

HOWE, FLORENCE, literature educator, writer, publisher; b. NYC, Mar. 17, 1929; d. Samuel and Frances (Stilly) Rosenfeld. AB, Hunter Coll., 1950; AM, Smith Coll., 1951; postgrad., U. Wis., 1951—54; DHL (hon.), New Eng. Coll., 1977, Skidmore Coll., 1979, DePauw U., 1987, SUNY Coll., Old Westbury, 1992, Pace U., 2000, Chatham Coll., 2000, U. Wis., 2004. Tchg. asst. U. Wis., Madison, 1951-54; instr. Hofstra Coll., 1954-57; lectr. English Queens Coll., CUNY, 1956-57; asst. prof. English Goucher Coll., 1960-71; prof. humanities and Am. studies SUNY, Old Westbury, 1971-85; prof. English City. Coll. and Grad. Sch., CUNY, 1985-95, Grad. Sch./CUNY, 1995—2001; pres., dir. The Feminist Press at CUNY, 1970—2000, exec. dir., 2005—06, pub., 2006—. Vis. prof. U. Utah, 1973, 75, U. Wash., 1974, John F. Kennedy Inst. Am. Studies Free U. Berlin, 1978, Oberlin Coll., 1978, Denison U., 1979, MLA Summer Inst. U. Ala., 1979, Coll. of Wooster, 1980; found. edit. Women's Studies Quar., 1972-82. Author: The Conspiracy of the Young, 1970, Seven Years Later: Women's Studies Programs in 1976, 1977, Myths of Coeducation: Selected Essays, 1964-1984, 1984; editor: (with Ellen Bass) No More Masks! An Anthology of Poems by Women, 1973, Women and the Power to Change, 1975; (with Nancy Hoffman) Women Working: An Anthology of Stories and Poems, 1979; (with Suzanne Howard, Mary Jo Boehm Strauss) Everywoman's Guide to Colleges and Universities, 1982; (with Marsha Saxton) With Wings: An Anthology of Literature by and About Disabled Women, 1987; (with John Mack Faragher) Women and Higher Education in American History, 1988, Tradition and the Talents of Women, 1991, No More Masks, An Anthology of 20th Century American Women Poets, 1993, The Politics of Women's Studies: Testimony from 30 Founding Mothers, 2000, (with Jean Casella) Almost Touching the Skies: Women's Coming of Age Stories, 2000; mem. editl. bd. Women's Studies: An Interdisciplinary Jour., 1971—, SIGNS: Women in Culture and Society, 1974-80, Jour. Edn., 1976—, The Correspondence of Lydia Marie Child, 1977-81, Research in the Humanities, 1977—; contbr. articles to profl. jours. Recipient Mina Shaughnessy award, Fund for Improvement of Post-Secondary Edn., 1982—83, Rockefeller Found., Bellagio, 2001—05; grantee U.S. Dept. State, 1983, 1993; NEH fellow, 1971—73, Ford Found. fellow, 1974—75, Fulbright fellow, India, 1977, Mellon fellow, Wellesley Coll., 1979, Rockefeller Found. fellow, Bellagio, 1997. Office: The Feminist Press at CUNY 365 Fifth Ave New York NY 10016-4309 Office Phone: 212-817-7917. Business E-Mail: fhowe@gc.cuny.edu.

HOWE, HENRY FRANKLIN, ecology educator; b. Gardner, Mass., Dec. 24, 1946; s. Volney Webster and Aileen (O'Brien) H.; m. Lynn Carol Westley, Sept. 24, 1988. AB, Earlham Coll., 1968; PhD, U. Mich., 1977. Instr. biology Phillips Acad., Andover, Mass., 1971-72; asst. prof. ecology U. Iowa, Iowa City, 1978-82, assoc. prof. ecology, 1982-88; prof. ecology U. Ill., Chgo., 1988—. Co-chmn. com. Nat. Inst. Environment, Washington, 1989—, testifier, 1990. Author: Ecological Relationships of Plants and Animals, 1988, 90, 91; contbr. articles to jours. including Am. Naturalist, Ecology, Jour. Tropical Ecology. With U.S. Army, 1969-71. Fellow Smithsonian Instn., 1977-78; grantee NSF, 1979-88, 94—, Nat. Geographic Soc., 1984, USDA, 1988-93. Fellow AAAS, Am. Soc. Naturalists, Ecol. Soc. Am., Soc. for Conservation Biology (Disting. Svc. award 1992), Soc. for Study of Evolution. Achievements include research in ecology of tropical seed dispersal systems, the burn seasonality of North American prairies, experimental restoration ecology, desert ecology, argument and imagery in scientific writing. Office: Univ Ill Biol Scis (M/C 066) 845 W Taylor St Chicago IL 60607-7056

HOWE, JAMES EVERETT, investment company executive; b. NYC, Mar. 30, 1930; s. Ernest Joseph and Gladys Montgomery (Sills) H.; m. Judith DePuy Keating, May 9, 1959; children: James E. Jr., David K. BA, Williams Coll., 1952; MBA, Columbia U., 1954. Statistician J.P. Morgan & Co., NYC, 1956-59; investment assoc. Morgan Guaranty Trust Co., NYC, 1959—62, investment rsch. officer, 1963—65; sr. analyst Tri-Continental Corp., NYC, 1965-80; asst. v.p., voting shareholder J&W Seligman & Co., NYC, 1980-81; chmn. investment com. Charles Edison Fund, Newark, 1981—. Trustee Brook Found., N.Y.C., 1966-72, Charles Edison Fund, 1972—; bd. deacons Brick Presbyn. Ch., N.Y.C., 1963-66. 1st lt. USAF, 1954-56, ETO Recipient Fin. award, Wall Street Jour., 1954. Mem. N.Y. Soc. Security Analysts, CFA Inst., Machinery Analysts N.Y. (charter, pres. 1967-68), Environ. Control Analysts N.Y. (charter, pres. 1975), Jamestowne Soc., Princeton Co. (charter, gov. 1993-94), Genesee Valley Club, Nassau Club, Alpha Kappa Psi. Republican. Presbyterian. Avocation: photography. Home: 33 Keats Rd Short Hills NJ 07078-2913

HOWE, JAMES TARSICIUS, retired insurance company executive; b. Calcutta, India, Nov. 1924; came to U.S., 1975; s. Joseph Ne-Ching and Anna Su-Cheng (Huang) Hou; m. Juliana Wong, Feb. 1948; children: Christopher, Celine, Catherine, Charles, Caroline. Diploma in Bus. Adminstrn., Chinese U. Hong Kong, 1969; postgrad. in Advanced Mgmt., Lingnam Inst. Bus. Adminstrn., Hong Kong. Trainee Bank of China, Calcutta, 1942-45, various managerial positions Calcutta and, Pakistan, 1945-51; mng. ptnr. import and export firm Karachi, Pakistan, 1951-54; various exec. positions Am. Internat. Underwriters (Pakistan) Ltd., 1954-65; exec. v.p. Am. Internat. Underwriters (Far East) Inc., 1965-73; pres., mng. dir. Am. Internat. Underwriters, Hong Kong, 1973-75; asst. treas. Am.

Internat. Group, Inc., NYC, 1975—76, treas., 1976—81, v.p., 1981—92; ret., 1992. Bd. dirs., mem. audit and conduct coms. A.I.G. Life Ins. Co. Ltd., Can., A.I.G. Assurance Co., Can.; past bd. dirs., vice chmn. AICCO; ret. treas. C.V. Starr & Co., Inc., also numerous other subs.; advisor U.S. Congl. Adv. Bd.; pres., CEO China Am. Ins. Co., Ltd. Decorated knight Grand Cross Holy Sepulchre of Jerusalem, Roman Cath. Ch.; named hon. Ky. Col., 1979. Mem.: Internat. Platform Assn., Internat. Real Estate Appraisers, Internat. Real Estate Inst., Nat. Assn. U.S. Corp. Treas., Am. Mgmt. Assn., Nat. Assn. Rev. Appraisers and Mortgage Underwriters (sr.), Serra Club (N.Y.C.), Royal Hong Kong Jockey Club, Am. Club Hong Kong (life absent mem.), Royal Hong Kong Golf Club (life absent mem.), Hong Kong Country Club, Chinese Cath. Club (life), KC (grand knight Short Hills coun.), Rotary.

HOWE, JANICE W., lawyer; BA cum laude, Conn. Coll., New London, 1973; JD cum laude, Suffolk U., Boston, 1981. Bar: Mass. 1981. Asst. dist. atty. Mass.; ptnr. Bingham McCutchen LLP, Boston, co-chairperson product liability practice group. Appointed by Governor Mass. to Judicial Nominating Com. Ea. Region, 1996—2002; appointed to Spl. Judicial Nominating Com. Juvenile Ct., 1993—95. Office: Bingham McCutchen LLP 150 Federal St Boston MA 02110-1726 Office Phone: 617-951-8504. Office Fax: 617-951-8736. Business E-Mail: janice.howe@bingham.com.

HOWE, JENNIFER LYNN, secondary school educator; b. Kettering, Ohio, Dec. 8, 1975; d. Joseph Lee and Mary Spahr Taylor; m. Michael Robert Howe, Aug. 7, 2004. BA in German and English, Albion Coll., Mich., 1998; MA in Lang. Learning, Wayne State U., Detroit, 2004. Cert. in secondary edn. Mich., 1998. Fulbright tchg. asst. Helmholtz Gymnasium, Heidelberg, Germany, 1999—2000; tchr. Lake Orion H.S., Mich., 2002—. Home: 22321 Blackburn St Saint Clair Shores MI 48080 Personal E-mail: jentaylor8@hotmail.com.

HOWE, JOHN PRENTICE, III, health facility administrator, physician; b. Jackson, Tenn., Mar. 7, 1943; s. John Prentice and Phyllis (MacDonald) H.; m. Tyrrell Flawn; children: Lindsey Warren, Brooke Olmsted, John Prentice IV. BA, Amherst Coll., 1965; MD, Boston U., 1969. Diplomate Am. Bd. Internal Medicine, internal medicine and cardiovascular disease. Research assoc. cellular physiology Amherst Coll., 1963-64; research assoc. cardiovascular physiology Boston U. Sch. of Medicine, 1966-67; lectr. medicine Boston U. Sch. Medicine, 1972-73; intern Boston City Hosp., 1969-70, asst. resident, 1970-71; rsch. fellow in medicine Harvard U., 1971-73, Peter Bent Brigham Hosp., 1971-73; survey physician Framingham Cardiovascular Disease Study, Nat. Heart and Lung Inst., 1971; asst. clin. prof. medicine U. Hawaii, 1973-75; from asst. prof. medicine to assoc. prof. U. Mass., 1975-85, assoc. prof., 1977-85, vice-chmn. dept. medicine, 1975-78, asst. dean continuing edn. for physicians, 1976-78, assoc. dean profl. affairs and continuing edn., 1978-80, acad. dean, 1980-85, vice chancellor, 1980-85, acting chmn. dept. anatomy, 1982-85; pres. U. Tex. Health Scis. Ctr., San Antonio, 1985-2000; pres., CEO Project HOPE, Millwood, Va., 2001—. Prof. medicine, U. Tex. Health Sci. Ctr., San Antonio, 1985-2005; chief of staff, U. Mass. Hosp., 1978-80. Mem. editl. bd. Archives Internal Medicine, 1991—2004; contbr. articles to profl. jours., chpts. to books. Trustee S.W. Found. for Biomed. Rsch., S.W. Rsch. Inst. Maj. M.C, U.S. Army, 1973-75. Alfred P. Sloan scholar Amherst Coll., 1962-65; recipient Ruth Hunter Johnson award Boston U. Sch. of Medicine, 1969 Fellow: Am. Coll. Chest Physicians, Am. Coll. Cardiology, ACP; mem.: Bexar County Med. Soc. (exec. com. 1985—2000, 1985—2000, pres. 1996), Tex. Soc. Biomed. Rsch. (past pres.), Tex. Med. Soc. (coun. med. edn. 1986—2001, ho. of dels. 1989—2001, pres.-elect 1997—98, pres. 1998—99), Am. Heart Assn. (fellow coun. clin. cardiology), AMA (coun. on sci. affairs 1993—2001, del. ho. dels. 1995—2001), Omicron Kappa Epsilon, Alpha Omega Alpha. Avocations: tennis, skiing. Business E-Mail: jhowe@projecthope.org.

HOWE, JONATHAN THOMAS, lawyer; b. Evanston, Ill., Dec. 16, 1940; s. Frederick King and Rosalie Charlotte (Volz) H.; m. Lois Helene Braun, July 12, 1963; children: Heather C., Jonathan Thomas Jr., Sara E. BA with honors, Northwestern U., 1963; JD with highest distinction, Duke U., 1966. Bar: Ill. 1966, U.S. Dist. Ct. (no. dist.) Ill. 1966, U.S. Ct. Appeals (7th cir.) 1967, U.S. Tax Ct. 1968, U.S. Supreme Ct. 1970, U.S. Ct. Appeals (D.C. cir.) 1976, U.S. Ct. Appeals (9th cir.) 1980, U.S. Ct. Appeals (4th, 5th, 11th cirs.) 1983, U.S. Claims Ct. 1990. Ptnr. Jenner & Block, Chgo., 1966—85, sr. ptnr. in charge assn. and adminstrv. law dept., 1978—85; founding and sr. ptnr., pres. Howe & Hutton, Chgo., Washington & St. Louis, 1985—. Exec. and adv. coms. to Ill. Sec. of State to revise the Ill. Not for Profit Act, 1983-86; dir. Pacific Mut. Realty Investors, Inc., 1985-86; dir. cable TV options for pub. Chgo. Access Corp., 1995-97, Bostrom Corp., 2001—. Contbg. editor Ill. Inst. for Continuing Legal Edn., 1973—, Sporting Goods Bus., 1977-91, Meeting News, 1978-88, Meetings Mag., 1988—, Meetings and Convs., 1991—; contbr. articles to profl. jours.; legal editor Meetings and Convs., 1990—. Mem. Dist. 27 Bd. Edn., Northbrook, Ill., 1969-89, sec., 1969-72, pres., 1973-84; chmn. bd. trustees Sch. Employee Benefit Trust, 1979-85; founding bd. dirs., pres. Sch. Mgmt. Found. Ill., 1976-84; mem. exec. com. Northfield Twp. Rep. Orgn., 1967-71; bd. deacons Village Presbyn. Ch. Northbrook, 1975-78, trustee, 1981-83; mem. Arts and Music Forum, 4th Presbyn. Ch., Chgo., 1990-93; spl. advisor Pres.'s Coun. Phys. Fitness and Sports, 1983—, Duke U. Sch. of Law Bd. of Visitors (life mem.). Named Industry Leader of Yr., Meeting Industry, 1987, Sch. Bd. Mem. Yr. (twice) , Ill. State Bd. Edn.; recipient Internat. Found. PaceSetters award Hospitality Sales Mktg. Assn., 1996. Fellow Internat. Forum of Travel and Tourism Advs., Am. Soc. Assn. Execs. (vice-chmn. legal com. 1983-86), Am. Bar Found. (life); mem. ABA (antitrust sect. Nat. Inst. com., trade assn. law com. corp. banking and bus. law sect., sect. on litig., adminstrv. law sect., internat. law com., continuing edn. com., tort and ins. practice, vice-chmn. com. sports law 1986—, task force on membership benefits for disabled lawyers, standing com. meetings and travel 1988-93, spl. advisor 1993—), Acad. Hospitality Industry (dir., pres. 1994—), Ill. Bar Assn. (antitrust sect., civil practice sect., sch. law sect., adminstrv. law sect., co-editor Antitrust Newsletter 1968-70), Chgo. Bar Assn. (def. of prisoners com. 1966-83, antitrust law com. 1971—, continuing edn. com. 1977—, chmn. assn. and non-profit soc. law com. 1984-86), Am. Soc. Assn. Execs. (vice-chmn. legal com., founder legal sect.), N.Y. Soc. Assn. Execs., Acad. Hospitality Industry Attys. (founder, bd. dir., pres. 2001—), Nat. Sch. Bds. Assn. (nat. bd. dir. 1979-89, exec. com. 1981-89, sec.-treas. 1983-85, 2d v.p. 1985-86, chmn. devel. com. 1982-87, pres. 1987-88), DC Bar Assn., Am. Judicature Soc., Ill. Assn. Sch. Bds. (pres. 1977-79, bd. dir. 1971-88), Chgo. Bar Found. (life), Assn. Forum Chicagoland (assoc.), Nat. Sch. Bds. Found. (pres./trustee 1995-2002), U.S. C. of C. (legal coun. 1998—), Greater Washington Soc. Assn. Execs., Legal Club, Law Club, Mid-Am. Club, Tower Club, Univ. Club Chgo., Order of Coif, Psi Upsilon. Home: 126 W Delaware Pl Chicago IL 60610-3252 Office: 20 N Wacker Dr Ste 4200 Chicago IL 60606-9833 Office Phone: 312-263-3001. Business E-Mail: jth@howehutton.com.

HOWE, LINDA ARLENE, nursing educator, writer; b. Pitts., Dec. 12, 1948; d. Alfred Robert and Zella Jane (Lintner) Somerhalder; m. John Joseph Howe, Dec. 7, 1968; 1 child, Thomas Patrick. Diploma in nursing, Columbia Hosp., 1969; Assoc. in English, Richland Coll., 1981; BSN, U. Tex., Arlington, 1982; MS in Nursing, Tex. Woman's U., 1988; MAE in English, The Citadel, 1992; PhD in Higher Edn. Adminstrn., U. S.C., 1997. RN, Pa., S.C.; cert. BCLS, ACLS. Staff nurse Columbia Hosp., Pitts., 1969-70; staff nurse ICU Brownsville (Pa.) Hosp., 1970-72; charge nurse ICU Kennestone Hosp., Marietta, Ga., 1972-73; staff devel. dir. Autumn Breeze N.H., Austell, Ga., 1973-74; dir. nursing Hideaway Hills N.H., Austell, 1974-76; mgmt. cons. Unicare Svcs., Dallas, 1976-79; supr. ICU Meml. Hosp. of Garland, Tex., 1979-84; dir. edn. Montgomery Gen. Hosp., Olney, Md., 1984-89; dir. Roper Hosp. Sch. Nursing, Charleston, S.C., 1989-95; nurse Richland Meml. Hosp, Columbia, S.C., 1995-96; dir. Olsten Home Health Svcs., Eugene, Oreg., 1996-98; dir. critical care Valley Hosp., Santa Maria, Calif., 1998; educator St. Francis Health System, Greenville, SC, 1998—99; assoc. prof. Clemson U. Sch. Nursing, 1999—. Instr. U. Md., College Park, 1985-89; instr. English Trident Tech. Coll., Charleston, 1992-95; speaker and presenter in field; legal nurse cons., 2004— Author: Passion and Persistance: A Biography of Mary Adelaide Nutting, 1997. Leader Girl Scouts USA, Marietta, 1974-76; cub scout den mother Boy Scouts Am., Dallas, 1977-80, counselor, Dallas and Olney, 1981-88; Sunday sch. tchr. Holy Comforter Luth. Ch., 1994-96, congregational coun. sec., 1994-96; bd. dirs. Pickens County ARC, 2003-05; parish nurse Jones Ave. Bapt. Ch., 2005—. Recipient Outstanding Advisor award Student Nurses Assn. S.C., 2002, Faculty Excellence award Clemson U. Bd. Trustees, 2003, 05, Excellence in Nursing Edn. award S.C. Nurses Assn., 2002; named Instr. of Yr. Nat. Fedn. LPNs, 1990, 92 Mem. ANA (chair Hall of Fame com.), Nat. League for Nursing, S.C. League Nurses (pres.), S.C. Nurse Educators (treas. 1991-93), Am. Assn. Nurse Historians, Am. Assn. Critical Care Nurses, Sigma Theta Tau, Phi Delta Kappa. Avocations: needlecraft, gardening, music, writing. Home: 103 Hollingsworth Dr Easley SC 29640-2612 Office Phone: 864-656-5480.

HOWE, LYMAN HAROLD, III, chemist, researcher; b. Wilkes-Barre, Pa., Nov. 5, 1938; s. Lyman Harold and Esther Madeline (Smith) H.; m. Mary Louise Reinhart, June 16, 1962; 1 child, Jennifer. BS, Duke U., 1960; MS, Emory U., 1961; PhD, U. Tenn., 1966. Rsch. assoc. Emory U., 1960-61; rsch. and teaching assoc. U. Tenn., 1962-66; rsch. chemist water mgmt. TVA, Chattanooga, 1966-97. Co-author publs. in field. Fellow ASTM (water com. results advisor 1976-97, Max Hecht award 1985, Award of Merit 1993); mem. Am. Chem. Soc., Am. Contact Bridge League (reviewer environ. sci. and tech. 1989, Ace of Clubs award, 3d pl. Chattanooga Club Master of Yr. award 1989, N.Am. Bridge Championship master 2005), U.S. Chess Fedn. Clubs: Torch (1st v.p. chpt. 1981, pres. 1982-83, 2d v.p. 1984-88). Presbyterian. Home: 1241 Mountain Brook Cir Signal Mountain TN 37377-2127 Personal E-mail: lhowe007@comcast.net.

HOWE, MARTHA MORGAN, microbiologist, educator; b. NYC, Sept. 29, 1945; d. Charles Hermann and Miriam Hudson (Wagner) M.; m. Terrance Gary Cooper. AB, Bryn Mawr Coll., 1966; PhD, MIT, 1972. Postdoctoral fellow Cold Spring Harbor Lab, NY, 1972-74; asst. prof. bacteriology U. Wis., Madison, 1975-77, assoc. prof., 1977-81, prof., 1981-84, Vilas prof., 1984-86; Van Vleet prof. virology U. Tenn., Memphis, 1986—. Mem. genetic biology rev. panel NSF, 1980-82, adv. panel prokaryotic biology, 2004—; mem. gen. rsch. support rev. com. NIH, Bethesda, 1982-86, mem. microbial physiology and genetics 2 study sec., 1997-2001; mem. sci. adv. com. instnl. rsch. grants Am. Cancer Soc., 1991-94. Assoc. editor Virology, 1983-92, Genetics, 1994; mem. editorial bd. Jour. Bacteriology, 1985-90; contbr. articles to profl. jours. and books. Recipient Rsch. Career Devel. award NIH, 1978; H.I. Romnes Faculty fellow U. Wis., 1981; Amoco Teaching award U. Wis., 1981. Fellow Am. Acad. Microbiology (bd. govs. 1991-99); mem. Am. Soc. Microbiology (chmn. divsn. H 1983, councillor divsn. H 1989-91, chmn. com. on awards 1990-96, pres.-elect 1999-2000, pres. 2000-2001, past pres. 2001-2002, Eli Lilly award 1985, ASM Founders Disting. Svc. award 1999, Alice C. Evans award 2007), Am. Soc. Biochemistry and Molecular Biology, Genetics Soc. Am. (bd. dirs. 1989-91, program com. 1989-90). Office: U Tenn Dept Molecular Scis 858 Madison Ave Memphis TN 38163-0001 Office Phone: 901-448-8215. Business E-Mail: mhowe@utmem.edu.

HOWE, RICHARD RIVES, lawyer; b. Portland, Oreg., Dec. 21, 1942; s. Hubert Shattuck Jr. and Anna Gertrude (Moody) H.; m. Elizabeth Anne Crowell, Aug. 29, 1964; 1 child, Richard Rives Jr. BA, Yale U., 1964; JD, Harvard U., 1967. Bar: N.Y. 1968, U.S. Ct. Appeals (2d cir.) 1973, U.S. Dist. Ct. (so. and ea. dists.) N.Y. 1973, U.S. Supreme Ct. 1973. Assoc. Sullivan & Cromwell LLP, NYC, 1967—74, ptnr., 1974—. Exec. com. Nat. Com. Am. Fgn. Policy, Inc., 2000—. Pres., bd. dirs. Peoples' Symphony Concerts, N.Y.C., 1983—, bd. dirs. Bar Assurance and Reinsurance Ltd., Bermuda, 1994—. Mem.: ABA (com. on corp. practice, fed. regulation securities com., legal opinions com.), NY County Lawyers' Assn., NYC Bar, N.Y. State Bar Assn. (chmn. securities regulation com. 1982—86, mem. exec. com. 1982—99, chmn. 1992—93, bus. law sect.), Pi Sigma Alpha, Phi Beta Kappa. Democrat. Home: 86 Woodfield Dr Short Hills NJ 07078-1654 Office: Sullivan & Cromwell LLP 125 Broad St Fl 32 New York NY 10004-2498 Office Phone: 212-558-3612. Business E-Mail: hower@sullcrom.com.

HOWE, ROGER EVANS, mathematician, educator; b. Chgo., May 23, 1945; s. John Perry and Marilyn (Leilani) (Evans) H.; m. Carolyn (Rutter) Read Howe, Sept. 9, 1967; Nicholas Read, Katherine Joanna. BA, Harvard Coll., 1966; PhD in Math., U. Calif., Berkeley, 1969. Asst. prof. SUNY, Stony Brook, 1969-72, assoc. prof., 1972-74; prof. Yale U., New Haven, 1974—. Vis. mem. Inst. for Advanced Study, Princeton, NJ, 1971—72; guest prof. U. Bonn, Germany, 1973—74; vis. prof. Oxford (Eng.) U., 1978, Rutgers U., New Brunswick, NJ, 1989—90, U. Paris VII, 1996, Nat. U. Singapore, 1999, Hong Kong U. Sci. and Tech., 2002, Stony Brook U., 2005—06; fellow Inst. for Advanced Studies, Hebrew U. of Jerusalem, 1988; panel on math. learning NRC, 1999—2001; sci. adv. bd. Singapore Inst. Math. Scis., 2001—; math. portfolio rev. panel NSF, 2004—05; steering com., undergrad. program coord. Park City Math. Inst., 2001—06; mem. study panel RAND Math., 2000—03; mem. steering com. CBMS Math. Edn. of Tchr. Report, 1998—2001. Co-author: Non-abelian Harmonic Analysis, 1992; advisor Jour. die reine und angewandte Mathematik, 1985-97; editor Bull. Am. Math. Soc., 1988-90; mem. editl. bd. Math. Rsch. Letters, Hong Kong, 1993-96, Advances in Math., 1995-99, Transformation Groups, 1995-2001, Jour. Functional Analysis, 2000-2005; contbr. articles to profl. jours. Guggenheim Found. fellow, 1983, Japan Soc. Promotion of Sci., Tokyo, 1993. Fellow Am. Acad. Arts and Scis., Conn. Acad. Sci. and Engring., Nat. Acad. Sci.; mem. Am. Math. Soc. (editor 1989-92, chair com. on edn. 2000-04, Disting. Pub. Svc. award 2006), Math. Assn. Am. (com. Lester R. Ford award), Nat. Coun. Tchrs. Math. Office: Yale U PO Box 208283 New Haven CT 06520-8283

HOWE, ROGER T., engineering educator; BS, Harvey Mudd Coll., 1979; PhD in Engring. Sci., U. Calif., Berkeley. Asst. prof. Dept. Elec. Engring. Carnegie-Mellon U., 1984—85, MIT, 1985—87, U. Calif., Berkeley, 1987—89, assoc. dir. Berkeley Sensor & Actuator Ctr., 1987—93, assoc. prof., 1989—93, prof., 1993—2005, assoc. chair EECS Dept., 2002—05, chair Elec. Engring. Div., 2002—05, Robert S. Pepper Disting. Professorship, 2004—05; prof. Stanford U., 2005—. Mem. USAF Scientific Adv. Bd., 2004—. Recipient Presdl. Young Investigator Award, NSF, 1986. Fellow: IEEE (Cledo Brunetti Award 1998); mem.: NAE.

HOWE, WARREN BILLINGS, physician; b. Jackson Heights, NY, Oct. 25, 1940; s. John Hanna and Francelia (Rose) H.; m. Hedwig Neslanik, Aug. 7, 1971; children: Elizabeth Rose, Sarah Billings. BA, U. Rochester, 1962; MD, Washington U., St. Louis, 1965. Diplomate in family medicine and sports medicine Am. Bd. Family Practice, Nat. Bd. Med. Examiners. Intern Phila. Gen. Hosp., 1965-66; resident physician Highland Hosp./U. Rochester, 1969-71; family physician Family Medicine Clinic of Oak Harbor (Wash.), Inc., PS, 1971-92; student health physician, univ. team physician We. Wash. U., Bellingham, 1992—. Team physician Oak Harbor HS, 1972-92; head tournament physician Wash. State HS Wrestling Championships, Tacoma, 1989-2006; attending physician Seattle Goodwill Games, 1990; clin. asst. prof. U. Wash. Sch. Medicine, 1975-82; bd. dirs. Nat. Operating Com. on Stds. for Athletic Equipment. Contbr. articles to profl. jours. and chpts. to books; editl. bd. The Physician and Sports Medicine Jour., 1984—2005. Bd. dirs. Oak Harbor Sch. Dist. #201, 1975-87; chmn. Oak Harbor Citizen's Com. for Sch. Support, 1988-90. Lt. comdr. USN, 1966-69, Vietnam. Recipient Disting. Svc. award City of Oak Harbor, 1984; named to Nat. Wrestling Hall of Fame, 2003; Paul Harris fellowship Oak Harbor Rotary Club. Fellow: Am. Acad. Family Physicians, Am. Coll. Sports Medicine (chair membership com. 1986—95, Citation award 2005); mem.: Am. Coll. Health Assn., Am. Med. Soc. for Sports Medicine (Humanitarian award 2002), Wash. State Med. Assn. Episcopalian. Home: 4222 Northridge Way Bellingham WA 98226-7804 Office: WWU Student Health Ctr 2001 Bill McDonald Pkwy Bellingham WA 98225-9132 Office Phone: 360-650-3400. Business E-Mail: warrenbh@pol.net.

HOWE, WILLIAM HUGH, artist; b. Stockton, Calif., June 18, 1928; s. Edwin Walter and Eugenia (Mercante) H. AB, Ottawa U., Kans., 1951. Illustrator Western Auto Supply, Kansas City, Mo., 1952, Kansas City Mdse. Mart, 1953-56; comml. artist U.S. Army C.E., Kansas City, 1958-64, Howard Needles Tammen & Bergendoff Cons. Engrs., Kansas City, 1964-68, Urban & Regional Planning, 1968-70; freelance artist, 1970—. Exhibitions include Philbrook Art Ctr., Tulsa, Ft. Worth Children's Mus., Montserrat Gallery, N.Y.C., Witte Meml. Art Mus., San Antonio, Anthropology Mus., Chapultepec Park, Mexico City, Alice Sabatini Gallery, Topeka Pub. Libr., 2002, Powell Gardens, Kingsville, 2003; represented in permanent collections: Smithsonian Instn., Washington, Franklin Mint (Pa.), Cranbrok Inst., Bloomfield Hills, Mich., U. Mich. Exhibits Mus., Ann Arbor, Oak Knoll Mus., Clayton, Mo., Am. Mus. Natural History, N.Y.C., Denver Mus. Natural History, Am. Baptist Assembly, Green Lake, Wis., Mowbray Union, Ottawa U., Kans., Ctrl. Mo. State Coll., Warrensburg, Mich. State U., East Lansing, U. Wyo. Art Mus., Laramie, San Diego Mus. Nat. History, Balboa Park, U. Ariz., Tucson, Ill. State Mus. Art, Springfield, Mont. Hist. Soc., Helena, Wyo. State Art Mus., Cheyenne, Ariz. State U., Tempe, Milw. Pub. Mus., State Capitol Bldg., Denver, Denver Pub. Libr., Kansas City (Mo.) Mus. History Sci., Presdl. Palace, Tamazunchale, San Luis Potosi, Mexico, Ottawa (Kans.) Jr. H.S., Am. Heritage Wildlife cards Am. Butterflies, 1983, U. Kans., 1994, U. Calif. Berkeley, Allyn Mus. Entomology, Sarasota, U. Colo., Colo. State U., Calif. Acad. Scis., San Francisco, Oakland Mus., Calif., James Ford Bell Mus., U. Minn., Mpls., Coutts Art Mus., 1997; Author-artist: Our Butterflies and Moths, 1964, The Butterflies of North America, 1975, Butterfly Chart of North America, 1979, Butterfly sect. Readers Digest North American Wildlife, 1980; co-author (with Carlos R. Beutelspacher Baights), U.N.A.M., Mexico City, 1984; one man shows Caroline Kingcade Gallery, North Kansas City, Mo., 1988, Coutts Mus. of Art, El Dorado, 1997, Dallas Mus. Natural History, Fair Park, 1999, George P. Spiva Art Ctr., Joplin, Mo., 1999, Alice Sabatini Art Gallery, Topeka, 2002, Shawnee County Libr., Topeka, 2002, Heard Mus., McKinney, Tex., 2005; TV show Hoy Mismo, 1986. Mem. Ottawa Cmty. Arts Coun., Leavenworth Arts. Coun.; mem. Larry Hatteberg's "Kans. People" KAKE-TV, Wichita. Named Am. Artist Am. References, 1990. Mem. Jour. Lepidopterists Soc., Burroughs Nature Club, Audubon Soc. Mo., Ctrl. States Entomol. Soc., Los Angeles County Mus., Spiva Art Ctr., Dallas Mus. Natural History, Mus. Culture and Natural History, Harvard Bot. Mus., Olive Art Gallery, Powell Gardens, Kingsville, Mo., Salina Pub. Libr., Kans., Lawrence Pub. Libr., Kans., Coffeyville Pub. Libr., Kans., Pittsburg Pub. Libr., Kans., Hutchinson Pub. Libr., Kans., Olive Gallery, Lawrence, Kans., Chanute Art Gallery and Safari Mus., Pasco Pub. Libr., Richland Pub. Libr., Kennewick Pub. Libr. Democrat. Episcopalian. Avocation: collecting butterflies in Mexico and Guatemala.

HOWELL, ALLY WINDSOR, lawyer, editor, writer; b. Montgomery, Ala., Mar. 10, 1949; s. Elvin and Bennie Merle (Windsor) H.; m. Donna K. Graffander, Sept. 2, 1989; children: Christopher Darby, Joshua Darby, Jeremiah Graffander. BA, Huntington Coll., 1971; JD, Jones Sch. Law, 1974; LLM with hons., SUNY, Buffalo. Bar: Ala. 1974, U.S. Supreme Ct. 1977, U.S. Ct. Appeals (fed. cir.) 1983, U.S. Ct. Appeals (11th cir.) 1981, U.S. Tax Ct. 1979, U.S. Claims Ct. 1982, U.S. Dist. Ct. (mid. dist.) Ala. 1975, U. Dist. Ct. (so. dist.) Ala. 1978. Archivist Hist. Rsch. Ctr. Air U., Maxwell AFB, Ala., 1972-75; pvt. practice Montgomery, 1975-82, 83-01; atty.-editor West Group, Rochester, NY, 2001—03. Adj. prof. Faulkner U., Montgomery, 1975—, adj. prof. Jones Law Sch., 1983—85; adj. prof. Kaplan Coll., 2004; asst. atty. gen., chief legal sect. Ala. Medicaid Agy., Montgomery, 1982—83. Author: Alabama Civic Practice Forms, 1986, 3d edit., 1992, Alabama Torts Case Finder, 1988, Alabama Personal Injury and Torts, 1996, Trial Handbook for Alabama Lawyers, 2d edit., 1998, Alabama Rules of Civil Procedure Annotated, 4th edit., 2003, Tilley's Alabama Equity, 4th edit., 2004, Maryland Legislative Review Service, 2004, 05, Alabama Legislative Review Service, 2005; contr. chpts. to books. Co-founder, bd. dirs. Montgomery Inst., 2000—01; pres., treas. bd. dirs. Gay Alliance of the Genesee Valley. Hon. lt. col., aide de camp Gov. Ala., 1974. Mem. ABA (contbr. editor profl. liability newsletter, litigation sect. 1990-92, co-editor trial techniques comm. newsletter), ATLA., Montgomery County Bar Assn. (newsletter editorial com. 1984-85), Nat. Bd. Trial Adv. (cert. civil litigation 1981, 86, 91, examiner ethics, evidence and civil procedure), Nat. Lesbian and Gay Law Assn. (bd. dirs. 1999-2001, vice co-chair 2000-2001, editor newsletter 2000—01), Greater Rochester Assn. Women Attys., Women's Bar Assn. State of NY, Monroe County Bar Assn. Presbyterian. Office Phone: 585-264-1802. Personal E-mail: ahowell1@rochester.rr.com.

HOWELL, ARTHUR, lawyer; b. Atlanta, Aug. 24, 1918; s. Arthur and Katharine (Mitchell) H.; m. Caroline Sherman, June 14, 1941; children: Arthur, Caroline, Eleanor, Richard, Peter, James; m. Janet Kerr Franchot, Dec. 16, 1972. AB, Princeton U., 1939; JD, Harvard U., 1942; LLD (hon.), Oglethorpe U., 1972. Bar: Ga. 1942. Assoc. F.M. Bird, 1942-45; ptnr. Alston & Bird (and predecessor firms), 1945-89, of counsel, 1989—. Bd. dirs., gen. counsel Atlantic Steel Co., 1960-93; chmn., bd. dirs. Summit Industries, Inc., 1988-2003; bd. dirs. emeritus Enterprise Funds; chmn. emeritus bd. dirs. Crescent Banking Co.; past pres. Atlanta Legal Aid Soc.; emeritus mem. bd. dirs. Crescent Bank and Trust Co. Pres. Met. Atlanta Cmty. Svcs., 1956, dir., 1953—; pres. Cmty. Planning Coun., 1961—63; gen. chmn. United Appeal, 1955; spl. atty. gen. State Ga., 1948—55; spl. counsel, Univ. Sys. Ga. State Sch. Bldg. Authorities, 1951—70; asst. com. Ga. Corp. Code, 1967—; trustee, past chmn. Oglethorpe U.; trustee Princeton, 1964—68; emeritus trustee Atlanta Speech Sch., Westminster Schs., Atlanta, Episcopal H.S., Alexandria, Va., Morehouse Coll.; past trustee Inst. Internat. Edn., mem. exec. com., 1969—72; elder, trustee, chmn. bd. trustees Presbyn. Ch., 1985—89; past chmn. Atlanta Adv. Com. Pks. Named hon. alumnus Ga. Inst. Tech. Mem.: Am. Judicature Soc., Lawyers Club of Atlanta (past pres.), Atlanta Bar Assn., Ga. Bar Assn., ABA, Am. Law Inst. (life), Soc. Colonial Wars, Princeton Club of N.Y., Nassau Club, Homosassa Fishing Club, Capital City Club, Phi Beta Kappa. Home: 200 Larkspur Ln Highlands NC 28741-8388 Office: Alston & Bird One Atlantic Ctr 1201 W Peachtree St Atlanta GA 30309-3424

HOWELL, BENJAMIN FRANKLIN, JR., geophysicist, educator; b. Princeton, NJ, June 12, 1917; s. Benjamin Franklin and Claire M. (Mead) H.; m. Constance M. Benson, June 30, 1943 (dec.); children: Barbara Carolyn, Catherine Ann (dec.), Bonnie Andrea, James Benjamin. AB, Princeton U., 1939; MS, Calif. Inst. Tech., 1942, Ph. D., 1949. Research engr. div. war research U. Calif. at San Diego, 1942-45; geophysicist United Geophys. Co., 1946-49; faculty Pa. State U., 1949—, prof. geophysics, 1953—, head dept. geophysics and geochemistry, 1949-63; asst. dean Grad. Sch. Pa. State U. , 1968-70, assoc. dean, 1970-82, assoc. dean emeritus, 1982—. Chief cons. seismologist Vibratech Engring. Co., Hazleton, Pa., 1955-69 Author: Introduction to Geophysics, 1959, Earth and Universe, 1972, Introduction to Seismological Research: History and Development, 1990; Editor: Contributions in Geophysics in Honor of Beno Gutenberg, 1958. Fellow Am. Geophys. Union (sec. sect. tectonophysics 1956-59, sect. seismology 1959-63), Geol. Soc. Am.; mem. soc. Exploration Geophysics, Seismol. Soc. Am. (pres. 1963-64), Phi Beta Kappa, Sigma Xi. Baptist. Home: 1143 Smithfield Cir State College PA 16801-6424 Office: 402 Deike Bldg University Park PA 16802-2713 Personal E-mail: howellbf@aol.com.

HOWELL, CHARLES, III, professional golfer; b. Augusta, Ga., June 20, 1979; m. Heather Howell. Student in Bus. Mgmt., Okla. State U. Profl. golfer, 2001—. Mem. US Team Presidents Cup, 2003. Named Rookie of Yr., PGA TOUR, 2001; recipient Fred Haskins award, 2000. Achievements include winning PGA Tour events including the Michelob Championship, 2002, Nissan Open, 2007. Avocations: fishing, movies. Mailing: PGA TOUR 112 PGA TOUR Blvd Ponte Vedra Beach FL 32082*

HOWELL, CHARLES MAITLAND, dermatologist; b. Thomasville, NC, Apr. 14, 1914; s. Cyrus Maitl and Lilly Mae (Ammons) H.; m. Betty Jane Myers, Feb. 12, 1949; children: Elizabeth Myers, Pamela Jane. BS, Wake Forest U., Winston-Salem, NC, 1935; MD, U. Pa., Phila., 1937. Intern Charity Hosp., New Orleans, 1937—38; resident in medicine Burlington County Hosp., Mt. Holley, NJ, 1938—39; sch. physician Lawrenceville Sch., NJ, 1939—42; resident in pathology N.C. Baptist Hosp., Winston-Salem, 1947—48; resident in dermatology Columbia-Presbyn. Med. Ctr., NYC, 1948—50; resident in allergy Roosevelt Hosp., NYC, 1950—51; practice medicine specializing in dermatology Winston-Salem, 1951—. Mem. staff NC Bapt., Forsyth Meml. hosps.; mem. faculty Bowman Gray Sch. Medicine, Wake Forest U., 1951-86, head. sect., 1984-86, prof. dermatology, 1967-84, prof. emeritus, 1984, head sect., 1961-86, acting head sect., 1984-86. Served as officer M.C. AUS, 1942-46. Fellow Am. Acad. Dermatology, Am. Acad. Allergy; mem. N.Am. Clin. Dermatol. Soc., NY Acad. Scis., Old Town Club (Winston-Salem), Bermuda Run Country Club (Clemmons, NC). Democrat. Baptist. Home: 1100 E Kent Rd Winston Salem NC 27104-1116 Office: 340 Pershing Ave Winston Salem NC 27103-2513 Office Phone: 336-724-2255.

HOWELL, DAVID LUKE, history professor; b. Fukuoka, Japan, Nov. 2, 1959; s. Richard Wesley and Jacqueline Louise Howell; m. Koko Fujita, Feb. 26, 1984; children: Isaac Soh, Momoko Emma. BA, U. Hawaii, Hilo, 1981; PhD, Princeton U., 1989. Asst. prof. U. Tex., Austin, 1989—92; prof. Princeton (NJ) U., 1993—, chmn. dept. East Asian studies, 2005—. Author: Geographies of Identity in Nineteenth-Century Japan, 1995, Capitalism from Within: Economy, Society, and the State in a Japanese Fishery, 2005. Recipient Disting. Alumni award, U. Hawaii, 2004. Mem.: Am. Hist. Assn., Assn. Asian Studies (chmn. NE Asia coun. 2002—05, bd. dirs. 2004—05). Office: Princeton U Dept East Asian Studies Princeton NJ 08544 Home Phone: 609-497-9331; Office Phone: 609-258-4274. Office Fax: 609-258-6984.

HOWELL, DONALD LEE, lawyer; b. Waco, Tex., Jan. 31, 1935; s. Hilton Emory and Louise Howell; m. Gwendolyn Avera, June 13, 1957; children: Daniel Liege, Alison Avera, Anne Turner. BA cum laude, Baylor U., 1956; JD with honors, U. Tex., 1963. Bar: Tex. 1963. Assoc. Vinson & Elkins, Houston, 1963-70, ptnr., 1970—, mem. mgmt. com., 1980-99. Capt. USAFR, 1956—59. Fellow Am. Bar Found., Tex. Bar Found., Houston Bar Found., Am. Law Inst.; mem. ABA, Am. Coll. Bond Counsel, Houston Bar Assn., Nat. Assn. Bond Lawyers (pres. 1981-82, bd. dirs. 1979-83), Attys. Liability Assurance Soc. (Bermuda bd. dirs. 1992-2005, chmn. 2000-02, U.S. bd. dirs. 1992-2005, chmn. 2000-02), Houston Club, Houston Ctr. Club, Order of Coif, Phi Delta Phi. Democrat. Episcopalian. Office Phone: 713-758-2318.

HOWELL, EVERETTE IRL, physicist, researcher; b. Shelby, Miss., Jan. 4, 1914; s. Thomas Daniel and Helen Lundy (Eason) H.; m. Beverly Ione McLaurin, June 12, 1943; children— Everette Irl, Marcia Marie, Beverly Jeannine. BA, Miss. Coll., 1936; MS, Vanderbilt U., 1937; PhD, U. N.C., 1940. Prof. phys. sci. Belhaven Coll., 1940-48; head dept. physics Miss. State U., 1948-79, prof., 1948-79, prof. emeritus, 1979—. Summer teaching physics dept. Vanderbilt U., 1946, U. Fla., 1947; summer research participant Oak Ridge Nat. Lab., 1950, 51 Contbr. articles to sci. publs. Mem. Am. Inst. Physics, Am. Phys. Soc., Am. Assn. Physics Tchrs., Miss. Acad. Scis., Sigma Xi, Phi Kappa Phi. Presbyn. (elder).

HOWELL, GEORGE BEDELL, investment company executive; b. Schenectady, Sept. 19, 1919; s. Jesse M. and Grace (Gerhaeusser) Howell; m. Mary Barbara Crohurst, July 10, 1944; children: Raymond Gary, Terry Barbara, Janice Patricia, Nancy Jo, George Bedell Jr. BS in Adminstrv. Engring., Cornell U., 1942. With GE, 1946-59; v.p. mfg. Leece Neville Co., Cleve., 1959-61, Royal Electric Co., Pawtucket, RI, 1961-62; dir. ops. packaging equipment and product devel. Acme Steel Co. (merged with Interlake Steel Corp. 1965), 1962-64; v.p. adminstrv. svc. Interlake Steel Corp., Chgo., 1964-66, v.p. internat. divsn., v.p. Acme Products divsn., 1966-70; CEO Golconda Corp., Chgo., 1970-72; v.p. devel. Internat. Minerals & Chems. Corp., 1972-73, sr. v.p., pres. industry group, 1974-77, exec. v.p., 1977-81; pres., CEO Wurlitzer Co., 1982-86, chmn., pres., CEO, 1986-87, vice chmn., 1987-88; prin. Mid West Ptnrs., Chgo., 1988-89; gen. ptnr. Pfingsten Ptnrs., Chgo., 1989-94, ptnr., 1994—, mem. adv. com., 2002—06; chmn. Hallcrest Holding Corp., 1992-97. Chmn. bd. trustees Village of Oak Brook, Ill., 1965—73, pres., 1973—79; mem. McGraw Wildlife Found.; trustee Christ Ch., Oak Brook, vice chmn., 1992—97, trustee emeritus, 1998; mem. univ. coun. Cornell U., 2001—. Recipient Foremost Benefactor award, Cornell U., 2006; N.Y. State and Univ. scholar, 1942. Mem.: Ocean Reef Club (Fla.), Medinah Country Club. Office: 520 Lake Cook Rd Ste 375 Deerfield IL 60015-5632 Office Phone: 847-374-9140. Business E-Mail: ghowell@pfingsten.com. *Trust in God. Balance family, work, church and government service. Live every day of your life.*

HOWELL, HARLEY THOMAS, lawyer; b. Chgo., June 5, 1937; s. Harley W. and Geneva (Engelmann) H.; m. Aliceann A. McLaughlin, Apr. 23, 1983; children by previous marriage: Shelley A. Young, Rebecca L., Emily S. AB, Princeton U., 1959; JD, Yale U., 1962. Bar: Md. 1962, U.S. Supreme Ct. 1966, D.C. 1972. Law clk. to chief judge U.S. Ct. Appeals (4th cir.), 1962-63; assoc. Semmes, Bowen & Semmes, Balt., 1966-72, ptnr., 1972-92, Howell, Gately, Whitney & Carter LLP, Towson, Md., 1992-98, counsel, 1998-99; ptnr. Howell & Gately, Balt., 1999—2002, counsel, 2002—. Mem. Gov.'s Commn. to Revise Annotated Code Md., 1975-85; mem. standing com. on rules of practice and procedure Ct. Appeals of Md., 1985-2000. Bd. dirs. Balt. Symphony Orch., 1975—, sec., 1986-2003, exec. com., 1986-2005, life dir., 2005—; bd. dirs. Sinai Hosp. of Balt., 2003—, Md. Hist. Soc., 2004—; trustee Sheppard and Enoch Pratt Health Sys., Towson, 1991—. Capt. JAG Corps, U.S. Army, 1963-66. Decorated Army Commendation medal. Fellow Am. Coll. Trial Lawyers, Am. Acad. Appellate Lawyers, Md. Bar Found.; mem. ABA, Md. State Bar Assn., Bar Assn. Balt. City, Balt. County Bar Assn., D.C. Bar Assn., Fed. Bar Assn., Wine and Food Soc., Wranglers Law Club (Balt.), Am. Coll. Barristers. Home: 1012 Chestnut Ridge Dr Lutherville Timonium MD 21093-1716 Office: Howell & Gately One Charles Ctr 19th Fl 100 N Charles St Baltimore MD 21201 E-mail: hthomas37@comcast.net.

HOWELL, HOLLY LYN, athletic trainer; d. Chuck T and Sue R Howell. BS, U. of Tex. at Arlington, 2003; MEd, U. of Tex. at Tyler, 2005. Cert. athletic trainer Nat. Athletic Trainers Assn. Bd. of Certification, 2003, lic. Adv. Bd. of Athletic Trainers/Tex. Dept. of Health, 2003, cert. tchr. State Bd. for Educator Certification/Tex., 2003. Grad. asst. athletic trainer Azalea Orthop. and Sports Medicine, Tyler, Tex., 2003—05; athletic trainer/tchr. Juan Seguin H.S., Arlington, Tex., 2005—. Mem.: Tex. State Athletic Trainers Assn., Nat. Athletic Trainers Assn., S.W. Athletic Trainers Assn. Baptist. Avocations: billiards, poker, basketball, collecting sports memorabilia, collecting vinyl records. Office: Juan Seguin High School 7001 Silo Rd Arlington TX 76002 Home Phone: 817-466-1284; Office Phone: 817-375-6829, 682-867-6829. Personal E-mail: crazy_taz23@yahoo.com, crazy_taz22@yahoo.com. E-mail: hhowell@aisd.net.

HOWELL, JAMES BURT, III, retired agricultural products company sales consultant; b. Dec. 11, 1933; s. James Burt and Catharine Stanger (Sparks) H.; m. Lorraine Marie Chanatry, Feb. 18, 1995. BS with high honors, Rutgers U., 1956; MBA, U. Del., 1980. Agrl. sales rep. Allied Chem. Corp., Phila., 1957-59; sales cons. Asgrow Seed Co. subs. Upjohn Co., Vineland, NJ, 1960—99; ret., 1999. Bd. dirs. Advance Weight Systems, Inc., LaGrange, Ohio. Mem. ofcl. bd. (session) 1st Presbyn. Ch. of Cedarville, 1960—; admissions liaison officer U.S. Mil. Acad., West Point, N.Y., 1973—; chmn. Lawrence Twp. Zoning Bd. Adjustment. With U.S. Army, 1957, col. USAR. Recipient Burpee Hort. award, Rutgers U., 1955. Mem.: Res. Officers Assn. U.S., N.J. Agri-Bus. Assn. (Heritage award 2003), Vegetable Growers Assn. N.J., Nat. Def. Indsl. Assn., Alpha Zeta (Centennial Honor Roll 1997), Alpha Gamma Rho (Bros. of the Century award), Phi Beta Kappa. Home and Office: 23 Shadow Brooke Dr Bridgeton NJ 08302 Office Phone: 856-453-9765.

HOWELL, JAMES TENNYSON, allergist, immunologist, pediatrician; b. Memphis, Jan. 25, 1944; MD, U. Ark., 1970. Diplomate Am. Bd. Allergy & Immunology, Am. Bd. Pediatrics. Intern Tampa Gen. Hosp., 1970-71; resident in pediatrics Children's Med. Ctr., Dallas, 1973-76; fellow in allergy and immunology Tex., Galveston, 1976-78; with St. Edwards Mercy Med. Ctr., Ft. Smith, Ark., 1976-78. Fellow Am. Coll. Allergy, Asthma and Immunology; mem. AMA, Am. Acad. Pediatrics. Office: Cooper Clinic 6801 Rogers Ave Fort Smith AR 72903-3296

HOWELL, JEFFERSON DAVIS, JR., aerospace transportation executive, retired military officer; b. Victoria, Tex., Aug. 10, 1939; m. Janel Crutchfield; children: Jefferson Davis, III, Melissa Jane. BA in Polit. sci., U. Tex., Austin, 1961, MA in Econs., 1970. 2nd. lt. to infantry oficer USMC, 1961—64, naval aviator, 1964—73; instr. econs. U.S. Naval Acad., 1973—76; exec. officer Marine fighter attack squadron 212, 1977—80, comdr., 1978—80; staff tours include various positions Hdqtrs. Marine Corps and Pentagon; with aviation dept. Hdqtrs. Marine Corps, Washington, 1981—84, 1987—89, comdr. marine aircraft group, 1984—86, chief of staff 1st Marine Brigade Hawaii, 1986—87; asst. chief of staff for Joint Opers./sr. USN officer Hdqtrs. Allied Forces North/NATO, Kolsas, Oslo, Norway, 1989-91, asst. dep. chief of staff for aviation, 1991-92; inspector gen. USMC, 1992, comdr. 2d Marine Aircraft Wing, 1992—94; dep. comdr. Marine Forces Pacific, 1994—95; various command duties to commdr. Marine Forces Pacific/Commanding Gen., Fleet Marine Force, Camp H.M. Smith, Hawaii, 1995—98; ret., 1998; dep. program mgr., Johnson Space Ctr. Safety, Reliability and Quality Assurance Sci. Applications Internat. Corp., Houston, 1999, program mgr., safety contract, 1999—2002, sr. v.p.; dir. Johnson Space Ctr., Austin, Tex., 2002—. Decorated Def. Superior Svc. medal, Disting. Svc. medal, Legion of Merit, Bronze Star medal with Combat "V", Air medal with two individual and 25 strike/flt. awards, Navy Commendation medal with Combat "V"; recipient John Paul Jones award for Inspirational Leadership, Navy League U.S., Outstanding Leadership medal, NASA, 2003, Disting. Svc. medal, 2005. Office: NASA Johnson Space Ctr Mailcode AA 2101 NASA Pky Houston TX 77058 Home Phone: 281-488-3881; Office Phone: 281-483-5309. Business E-Mail: jefferson.d.howell@nasa.gov.

HOWELL, JOEL DUBOSE, internist, educator; b. Tex., May 11, 1953; s. Wilson and Nora (Levitas) Howell; m. Linda C. Samuelson, June 26, 1976; children: Jonathan Samuelson, Benjamin Samuelson. BS, Mich. State U., 1975; MD, U. Chgo., 1979; PhD in History and Sociology of Sci., U. Pa., 1987. Intern, resident in internal medicine U. Chgo., 1979-82; Robert Wood Johnson clin. scholar U. Pa., Phila., 1982-84; instr. U. Mich., Ann Arbor, 1984-86, asst. prof., 1986-90, assoc. prof., 1990-97, prof., 1997—, Victor Vaughan prof. history medicine, 2001—. Editor: (book) Technology and American Medicine Practice: 1880-1930, 1988, Medical Lives and Scientific Medicine at Michigan; author: Technology in the Hospital, 1995. Scholar Henry J. Kaiser Family Fedn. Faculty, 1989—92, Charles E. Culpeper Found. Med. Humanities, 1992—96. Fellow: ACP, Am. Osler Soc., Am. Assn. History Medicine. Office Phone: 734-647-4844. Business E-Mail: jhowell@umich.edu.

HOWELL, JOEL WALTER, III, lawyer; b. Jackson, Miss., Dec. 25, 1949; s. Joel W. and Elizabeth (Harris) H.; m. Wilhelmina C. Pontus, June 25, 1983. BA, Millsaps Coll., 1971; JD, Columbia U., 1974. Bar: Tex. 1974, U.S. Ct. Appeals (5th cir.) 1974, Miss. 1975, U.S. Dist. Ct. (no. and so. dists.) Miss. 1975. Ptnr. Daniel, Coker, Horton, Bell & Dukes, Jackson, 1975-80; pvt. practice, Jackson, 1981—. Adj. faculty law sch. Miss. Coll., Jackson, 1988. Contbg. editor, case notes and comments editor Columbia Jour. Transnat. Law, 1973-74. Mem. ABA, ATLA, Tex. Bar Assn., Miss. Bar (chair tech. com. 2003-04, tech. com., exec. com.), Hinds County Bar Assn. (small firm practice com. 1993-94, chair 1995, computer columnist newsletter 1996—, webmaster 1997—), Miss. Trial Lawyers Assn., Miss. Def. Lawyers Assn., Def. Rsch. Inst., Miss. Bankruptcy Conf. Home: 50 St Andrews Dr Jackson MS 39211-2466 Office: PO Box 16772 5446 Executive Pl Jackson MS 39206-4103 Office Phone: 601-362-8129. Personal E-mail: jwh3@mindspring.com.

HOWELL, JOHN FLOYD, insurance company executive; b. Mt. Juliet, Tenn., Dec. 24, 1932; s. Robert Lee and Rachel Mae (Draper) H.; m. Margaret Ann Herring, Dec. 27, 1955; children: John Floyd, Leigh Ann, Stephen Donelson. Student, Vanderbilt U., 1951-53; BA, U. Iowa, 1955, postgrad., 1955-56. Actuarial asst. Nat. Life & Accident Ins. Co., Nashville, 1963-64, asst. actuary, 1964-65, 2d v.p., 1965-71, v.p., 1971-81, sr. v.p., 1981-83, also dir.; v.p., chief actuary Ind. Life & Accident Ins. Co., 1984-88, sr. v.p., chief actuary, 1989-96, ret., 1996. Bd. dirs. Vol. Jacksonville, 1984-89, Mental Health Resource Ctr., Jacksonville, 1987-90, Fla. Meth. Bd. Pensions, 1988-96, Jacksonville Urban League, 1992-95; mem. adv. bd. Montgomery Bell Acad., 1995—. Fellow Soc. Actuaries; mem. Am. Acad. Actuaries, Richland Country Club (Nashville). Methodist. Home: 2200 Harding Pl #2 Nashville TN 37215-4145

HOWELL, JOHN REID, mechanical engineering educator, director; b. Columbus, Ohio, June 13, 1936; s. Frederick Edward and Hilma Lavilla (Kief) Howell; m. Arlene Elizabeth Pollitt, June 20, 1959 (div. 1974); m. Susan Gooch Conway, May 20, 1979; children: John Reid Jr., Keli Dianne, David Lee. BSChemE, Case Inst. Tech., Cleve., 1958, MSChemE, 1960, PhD, 1962. Registered profl. engr. Aerospace engr. NASA Lewis Rsch. Ctr., Cleve., 1961-68; assoc. prof. U. Houston, 1969-73, prof., 1973-78; dir. Energy Inst. U. Houston, 1975-78; vis. prof. mech. engring. U. Tex., Austin, 1978-79, prof., 1979-82, E.C.H. Bantel prof., 1982-90, Baker-Hughes Centennial prof. dept. mech. engring., 1990—, Ernest Cockrell, Jr. Meml. chair, 2003—, chmn. mech. engring. dept., 1986-90, dir. Ctr. for Energy Studies, 1988-91, assoc. dean for rsch. Coll. Engring., 1996-99, dir. Ctr. for Advanced Mfg., 2004—. Dir. thermal transport and thermal processing program NSF, 1994-95. Co-author: Thermal Radiation Heat Transfer, 1972, 4th edit., 2002, Design of Solar Thermal Systems, 1984, Fundamentals of Engineering Thermodynamics, 1987, 2d edit., 1992, Catalog of Radiation Configuration Factors, 2d edit., 2000, Thermodynamics, An Integrated Learning System, 2006; editor: Journal of Heat Transfer, 1995-2000; contbr. articles to profl. jours. Commr. Renewable Energy Resources Commn., Austin, 1980-81. Served to 1st lt. USAF, 1962-65. Recipient Spl. Svc. award NASA, 1965, Ralph Coats Roe award Am. Soc. Engring. Edn., 1987, Max Jakob award AIChE/ASME, 1998; named to Hon. Order Ky. Cols., 1980. Fellow ASME (life, Heat Transfer Meml. award 1991), AIAA (Thermophysics award 1990); mem. Russian Acad. Scis. (elected fgn. mem. 1999), NAE (elected mem. 2005). Office: U Tex Dept Mech Engring 1 University Sta C2200 Austin TX 78712 Office Phone: 512-471-3095. Business E-Mail: jhowell@mail.utexas.edu.

HOWELL, JULIUS AMMONS, retired plastic surgeon; b. Thomasville, NC, Apr. 14, 1914; s. Cyrus Maitland and Lillie Mae (Ammons) H.; m. Octavia Anne Southern, Oct. 20, 1951; children: Anne, Karen, Robin. LLB, Wake Forest U., 1935, BS, 1940; MD, U. Pa., Phila., 1943. Diplomate Am. Bd. Plastic & Reconstructive Surgery, Am. Bd. Otolaryngology. Chief plastic surgery sect. Bowman Gray Sch. Medicine, Winston Salem, NC, 1959-84, prof. emeritus plastic surgery, 1984-2000; lectr. Sch. Law Wake Forest U., Winston Salem, NC, 1978-94; pvt. practice Winston Salem, NC, 1984-99; ret., 1999. Mem. medico-legal com. NC Med. Soc., Raleigh, 1960-93, SE Soc. Plastic Surgery; mem. adv. com. NC Indsl. com., Raleigh, 1976-86; trustee Blue Cross/Blue Shield, Chapel Hill, 1964-68. Co-author: Plastic Surgery, 1979. Julius Ammons Howell Endowed Chair Surgery named in his honor Bowman Gray Sch. Medicine, 1995. Mem. ACS; Am. Soc. Plastic & Reconstructive Surgery (medicolegal com.), Am. Assn. Plastic Surgeons. Baptist.

HOWELL, KAREN JANE, private school educator; b. Mpls., Apr. 24, 1946; d. John and Lorraine (Quale) Borgen; m. John Morris Howell; children: Laura, John. AS in Math. and Sci., Cottey Jr. Coll., Nevada, Mo., 1966; BS in Elem. Edn. Sci. and Math., U. No. Colo., Greeley, 1968; MS Science & Gifted Education, University Of Virginia, Alexandria, Va, 1980—83. Cert. 5/6th Grade Team Tchr. 1968, 6th Grade Gifted Tchr. 1971, K-6th Gifted Program Tchr. 1983. Team tchr. John Adams and Carver Elem. Schs., Colorado Springs, Colo., 1968—73; tchr. gifted 3-6th grade Math. and Sci. Washington Mill and Stratford Landing Elem. Schs., Alexandria, Va., 1973—83; tchr. gifted program Tokeneke Elem. Sch., Darien, Conn., 1983—85; 5-8th science, 1-8 art teacher Hillel Academy, Fairfield, Ct, 1985—. Art / science docent Smithsonian Instn. and Am. Mus. Nat. History, Washington, 1974—82; guide Discovery Mus., Bridgeport, Conn., 1985—. Author: (various workshops, teaching modules) Using Art Properties With Mus. Tours, 1980-1990, 1990, (teacher's guide) Motivational Techniques, Math Manipulatives, 1988,1992, 1994. Chairperson, bd. dirs. Fairfield (Conn.) Internat. Dance Co., 1990—2002; judge Conn. State Invention Conv., Hartford, 1983—87. Recipient Presdl. award for Excellence in Sci. Tchg., State of Conn., 1989, Presdl. award for Excellence in Math. Tchg., 1989, First Sci. Tchr. award, State Sci. Fair Conn., 1996, 1st Place, Middle Schs., Conn. State Sci. Fair, 1995, 1996, 1997, 1998, 1999. Mem.: NEA, Am. Chem. Soc., Nat. Math. Tchrs. Assn., Conn. Earth Tchrs. Assn., Conn. Sci. Tchrs. Assn. (Conn. Sci. Tchr. of Yr. award 2002), Nat. Sci. Tchrs. Assn., Audubon Soc., Am. Mensa, Am. Ballet Theater (assoc.). Methodist. Avocations: ballet, jazz, dance. Office: Hillel Academy 1571 Stratfield Rd Fairfield CT 06432 Personal E-mail: j.howell@comsoc.org.

HOWELL, KATHY AILEEN, advertising executive; b. Memphis, Tenn., Mar. 14, 1952; d. Avelino L. and Kathleen Jane Saquing; m. James Mack Howell, July 9, 1971; children: Karen Klemis, James Mack Jr., Kimberly Marie, Richard Mack. Office mgr. Winston Network, Inc., Memphis, 1984—85; ops., real estate mgr. Transp. Displays Inc., Memphis, 1985—96; owner, CEO Howell Advt. Svc., West Memphis, 1996—. Mem.: Ea. Star, Quota. Republican. Baptist. Avocations: travel, camping. Office: Howell Advt Svc PO Box 5360 West Memphis AR 72301 Office Phone: 870-735-3388. E-mail: chowell3@midsouth.rr.com.

HOWELL, LAURA CLARK, biologist, educator, small business owner; d. Louie Earl Clark and Laura Elizabeth Stewart; m. Charles Samuel Howell. BS in Biology, Jacksonville State U., 1968; MS in Biology, Samford U., 1970; EdS, Jacksonville State U., 1984; postgrad., U. Ala., Birmingham. Cert. profl. tchr. Ala., profl. guidance counselor Ala., registered psychometrist Ala., cert. profl. tchr. Ga. Microbiologist Ala. Dept. Pub. Health, Anniston, 1968; tchr. biology B.B. Comer Meml. Sch., Sylacauga, Ala., 1970—71; tchr. sci., anatomy, physiology, biology, chmn. sci. dept. Wellborn H.S., Anniston, 1971—94. Adj. instr. biology Jacksonville State U., Ala., 1975, supr. student tchrs., 96; adj. instr. biology, botany, zoology Gadsden State C.C., Anniston, 1983—91. Recipient Medal and Cert. Appreciation, SAR, 2003, Educator award, United Daus. Confederacy, 1980, Martha Washington medal, SAR, 2005. Mem.: DAR (Ala. Soc. scholarship chair 2003—, field genealogist), Order Descs. of Ancient Planters (charter) (Ala. br. historian), Nat. Assn. Biology Tchrs., The Plantagenet Soc., Colonial Dames XVII Century (state historian 2005—), Ala.-Benton Geneal. Soc., Anniston Mus. League, Ala. Geneal. Soc., U.S. Daus. War of 1812, Magna Charta Dames & Barons (herald, state v.p.), The Jamestowne Soc., Athena Study Club, Persephone Garden Club, Ams. Royal Descent, Colonial Order of Crown, Knights of Most Nobel Order Garter, Kappa Delta Pi, Alpha Delta Kappa, Delta Kappa Gamma. Methodist. Office: Anniston Coin Jewelry PO Box 2534 Anniston AL 36202-2534

HOWELL, LYDIA PLEOTIS, pathologist, educator; b. Great Lakes, Ill., Oct. 19, 1957; m. Stephen Miller Howell. MD, Northwestern U. Med. Sch., Chgo., 1977—81. Lic. in anatomic & clinical pathology Am. Bd. Pathology, 1986, qualification in cytopathology Am. Bd. Pathology, 1989. Resident in pathology Temple U. Hosp., Phila., 1981—83, chief resident pathology, 1983—85; fellow cytopathology Lankenau Hosp., Wynnewood, 1985—86; vis. asst. prof. pathology Davis Sch. Medicine, U. Calif., 1986—88, asst. prof. pathology, 1988—94, dir. cytopathology, 1990—2002, assoc. prof. pathology, 1994—2000, prof. pathology, assoc. dean academic affairs, 2001—06, vice chair, dir. anatomic pathology, 2006—. Mem.: Am. Soc. Cytopathology Found., Coll. Am. Pathologists, US & Can. Acad. Pathology, Am. Soc. Cervical & Colposcopic Pathology, Am. Soc. Clin. Pathologists, Am. Soc. Cytopathology (mem. exec. bd., pres.). Office: Univ Calif Davis 4400 V St Sacramento CA 95758 Business E-Mail: lydia.howell@ucdmc.ucdavis.edu.

HOWELL, MARY L., multi-industry company executive; b. Springfield, Mass., July 10, 1952; d. Walter Edward and Mary Patricia (Landers) Lynch; m. John N. Howell, Oct. 27, 1980; 1 child, Patrick. BA, U. Mass., Amherst; grad. Advanced Mgmt. Program, Harvard U. With Textron, Inc., 1980—, exec. v.p. Washington, 1995—, chair customer leadership coun. Bd. dirs. NAM, Aerospace Industries Assn., FM Global; bd. mem. Atlantic Coun. US. Office: Textron Inc 1111 Pennsylvania Ave Ste 400 Washington DC 20004*

HOWELL, NORMAN GLEN, elementary school educator; b. Parkton, Md., May 18, 1946; m. Libby Cabeza, Sept. 20, 2005. BA in Bus. Adminstrn., U. Md.; MA in Mgmt., Webster U. Cert. tchr. grades K-8 Tex., 1990, prin. Tex., 2006. Enlisted U.S. Army, 1963, advanced through grades to command sgt. maj., ret., 1988; 5th grade tchr. El Paso Ind. Sch. Dist., 1990—2001, math leader, 2001—. Avocation: coin collecting/numismatics.

HOWELL, PEGGY HAAS, musician; b. Mechanicsburg, Pa., Dec. 22, 1949; d. Ray Leonard Haas and Mae Marie Derrick; m. Richard Stephen Howell, May 8, 1982; children: Mark, Emily. BA, Susquehanna U., 1971; student, Staatliche Hochschule fuer Musik, Hamburg, Germany, 1971; M of Sacred Music, Union Theol. Sem., 1973. Organist, choirmaster St. James's Episc. Ch., Richmond, Va., 1973—82, Ch. Good Shepherd, Ruxton, Md., 1982—95, St. John's Episc. Ch., Lynchburg, Va., 1996—. Mem. faculty Peabody Conservatory Johns Hopkins U., Balt., 1985—95; organist Goucher Coll., Towson, Md., 1988—95; dir. chorale Randolph-Macon Women's Coll., Lynchburg, 1996—2000; dir. music Glass Theater, Lynchburg, 2002—; tchr., musician Pipe Organ Encounter, Pitts., 2004; founder, dir. Jefferson Youth Chorale, Lynchburg, 2005. Recipient 2d prize, St. Albans Internat. Organ Competition, 1977. Mem.: Am. Choral Dirs. Assn., Assn. Anglican Musicians, Am. Guild Organists (sub-dean 2000—02, dean local chpt. 2002—04; Nat. Young Artists Competition 1st prize 1974). Democrat. Episcopalian. Avocations: sewing, baking. Office: St John's Episcopal Ch 200 Boston Ave Lynchburg VA 24503

HOWELL, RALPH RODNEY, pediatrician, geneticist, educator; b. Concord, NC, June 10, 1931; s. Fred Lee and Grace Mary (Blackwelder) H.; m. Sarah Vosburg Esselstyn, Nov. 19, 1960 (dec.); children: Grace Meyer, Elizabeth Eriksson, John Esselstyn. BS, Davidson Coll., 1953; MD, Duke U., 1957. Cert. Am. Bd. Pediatrics, Am. Bd. Med. Genetics/Clin. Biochem. Genetics. Intern Duke U., 1957—58, resident in pediat., 1958—59, rsch. fellow in pediat. and medicine, 1959—60; clin. assoc. and staff NIH, Bethesda, Md., 1960—64; assoc. prof. pediat. Johns Hopkins U., Balt., 1964—72; pediatrician-in-chief U. Children's Hosp. at Hermann, Houston, 1972—87, chmn. med. bd., 1972—87; David Park prof. U. Tex. Med. Sch., Houston, 1972—89, chmn. dept. pediat., 1972—87; prof., chmn. dept. pediat. U. Miami Sch. Medicine, 1989—2003, chmn. emeritus, prof., 2003—; sec. med. staff Jackson Meml. Hosp., Miami, 1992—93, v.p. med. staff, 1993—97, pres. med. staff, 1997—99; spl. asst. to dir. NICHD/NIH, Bethesda, 2003—. Cons. pediat. M.D. Anderson Hosp. and Tumor Inst., 1972-89; mem. metabolism study sect. NIH, 1973-77, chmn. maternal and child health adv. com., 1983-86; mem. exec. com. Nat. Practitioner Data Bank, 1995-98; mem. nat. clin. adv. com. Nat. Found. March of Dimes, 1973-79; chmn. sci. adv. bd. Muscular Dystrophy Assn., 1999-2007, bd. dirs., 2000—, chmn., 2007—; vis. prof. Inst. Molecular Genetics, Baylor Coll. Medicine, Houston, 1988; chief pediat. Holtz Childrens Hosp., U. Miami-Jackson Meml. Med. Ctr., 1989-2003; mem. nat. adv. coun. Nat. Inst. Child Health and Human Devel., 1999-2003; chair HHS Sec.'s Adv. Com. on Genetic Testing in Children and Newborns, 2004—. Author: (with G.H. Thomas) Selected Screening Tests for Genetic Metabolic Diseases, 1973, (with F.H. Morriss, L.K. Pickering) Role of Human Milk in Infant Nutrition, 1986; contbr. articles to profl. jours. Trustee Jackson Lab. Bar Harbor, Maine, 1985-2003; dir. Rip van Winkle Found., Claverack, N.Y., 1987-92, pres., 1992—; bd. dirs. Congl. Ch. Found., Coconut Grove, Fla., 2003-2005, Dr. John T. Macdonald Found., Coral Gables, Fla., 2003-. Served to sr. surgeon, 1960—64, USPHS. Recipient Klauber Lectureship, Greenwood Genetic Ctr., 2004. Fellow AAAS, Am. Acad. Pediat. (com. on genetics); mem. AMA (ho. of dels. 1998—), Am. Pediat. Soc., Soc. Pediat. Rsch., Houston Pediat. Soc. (pres. 1978-79), Tex. Med. Assn., Soc. Inborn Errors of Metabolism (pres. 1981), Miami Pediat. Soc., Fla. Med. Assn., Am. Coll. Med. Genetics (bd. dirs., treas. 1995-96, pres.-elect 1997-98, pres. 1999—2000), Am. Coll. Med. Genetics (found. pres. 2003—), Nat. Human Genome Rsch. Inst. (chmn. ethical, social and legal issues rev. group 1996-2003), Pi Kappa Alpha, Cosmos Club (Washington). Congregationalist. Avocations: flying, classic auto collector. Office: U Miami Sch Medicine Dept Pediatrics D-820 PO Box 16820 Miami FL 33101-6820 Office Phone: 305-243-1073. Business E-Mail: rhowell@mail.edu, rhowell@miami.edu.

HOWELL, ROBERT EDWARD, hospital administrator; b. Marietta, Ohio, Jan. 19, 1949; married; 3 children. BS, Muskingham Coll., 1971; MS in Hosp. and Health Svcs. Adminstrn., Ohio State U., 1977. Assoc. dir. U. Minn. Hosps. and Clinics, Mpls., 1980-86; exec. dir. Med. Coll. Ga. Hosps. and Clinics, Augusta, 1986-94; dir., CEO, U. Iowa Hosps. and Clinics, Iowa City, 1994—. Mem. exec. com. Accreditation Coun. for Grad. Med. Edn. Mem. Coun. Tchg. Hosps. (past chmn.), Am. Assn. Med. Colls. (exec. com.), Am. Hosp. Assn. (coord. com. med. edn.), Univ. Health System Consortium (exec. com.). Office: U VA Med Ctr 3007 McKim Hall PO Box 800809 Charlottesville VA 22908-0809

HOWELL, R(OBERT) THOMAS, JR., lawyer, former food company executive; b. Racine, Wis., July 18, 1942; s. Robert T. and Margaret Paris (Billings) H.; m. Karen Wallace Corbett, May 11, 1968; children: Clarinda, Margaret, Robert. AB, Williams Coll., 1964; JD, U. Wis., 1967; postgrad., Harvard U., 1981. Bar: Wis. 1968, Ill. 1968, U.S. Dist. Ct. (no. dist.) Ill. 1968, U.S. Tax Ct. Assoc. Hopkins & Sutter, Chgo., 1967-71; atty. The Quaker Oats Co., Chgo., 1971-77, counsel, 1977-80, v.p., assoc. gen. corp. counsel, 1980-84, v.p., gen. corp. counsel, 1984-96, corp. sec., 1994-96; of counsel Seyfarth Shaw, Chgo., 1997—. Bd. dirs. Ill. Inst. of Continuing Legal Edn., Lawyers for Creative Arts. Editor (mags.) Barrister, 1975-77, Compleat Lawyer, 1983-87. Bd. dirs. Metro. Family Svcs.; bd. dirs. Chgo. Bar Found., 1987—, pres., 1991-93; trustee 4th Presbyn. Ch., Chgo., 1989-92, pres., 1994-96; bd. dirs. Chgo. Equity Fund, 1992-96. Capt. USAR, 1966—72. Mem. ABA, Ill. Bar Assn., Wis. Bar Assn., Chgo. Bar Assn. (bd. mgrs. 1977-79, chmn. young lawyers sect. 1974-75), Lawyers Club Chgo. (pres. 2004-05), Econ. Club Chgo., Univ. Club Chgo. (bd. dirs. 1982-85, 87-88, v.p.). Presbyterian. Home: 853 W Chalmers Pl Chicago IL 60614-3233 Office: Seyfarth Shaw 131 S Dearborn St Ste 2400 Chicago IL 60603 Office Phone: 312-460-5507. Business E-Mail: thowell@seyfarth.com.

HOWELL, ROBERTA F., lawyer; b. Waukegan, Ill., June 15, 1962; d. Dale William and Judith Ann (Pringle) Sternhagen; m. Christopher W. Howell, May 28, 1983; children: Jacob, Eric, Daniel. BA with honors, U. Wis., Madison, 1984, JD, 1989. Ptnr. Foley & Lardner LLP, Madison, 1989—. Product distribution practice group leader Foley & Lardner LLP, Madison, 2005—. Co-author: CCH Product Distribution Law Guide, 1998. Mem.: State Bar of Wis., Order of Coif, Phi Beta Kappa. Office: Foley & Lardner 150 East Gilman Dr Madison WI 53703

HOWELL, SCOTT NEWELL, computer company executive, state legislator; b. Provo, Utah, Sept. 28, 1953; s. Varon L. and Kathryn (Tuttle) H.; m. Linda Skanchy, Sept. 8, 1978; children: Bryan, Bradley, Jason, Jeffrey. BA, U. Utah, 1978. With sales IBM Corp., mgr., global policy exec.; chair., Utah State Judicial Conduct Review Comm., 1990—; mem. Utah Senate, Salt Lake City, 1990—, minority leader, 1993—; mem. Nat. Conference State Legislators, 1992—. Mem. Utah info. tech. com. Utah Senate, transportation & environ. quality appropriations subcom., mem. state & local affairs standing com.; chmn. Nat. Acad. Fin., Salt Lake City, 1991-93. Bd. dirs. Utah Chpt. Nat. Children's Protection of Child Abuse, Salt Lake City, 1992-93, visually handicapped divsn. United Way, Salt Lake City, 1992-93; trustee Utah Symphony, 1994—. Mem., Nat. Academy of Finance (chair. 1990-92); Utah Info. Tech. Assoc., Intermountain Healthcare, State Legis. Leaders Found., Dem. Leadership Coun., Harvard Policy Group. Democrat. Mem. Lds Ch. Address: 319 State Capitol Salt Lake City UT 84114 Home: 5630 Lions Cross Cir Granite Bay CA 95746-9027

HOWELL, TERRY ALLEN, agricultural engineer; b. Dallas, Sept. 7, 1947; s. Levi Lowe III and Lila Lee (Allen) H.; m. Mary Sue Parkerson, Feb. 22, 1969; children: Terry A. Jr., Lisa K. Dreibrodt, Michael S. BS, Tex. A&M U., 1969, MS, 1970, PhD, 1974. Rsch. asst. Tex. A&M U., College Station, 1969-70, rsch. assoc., 1971-74; asst. prof. N.Mex. State U., Las Cruces, 1975, Tex. A&M U., College Station, 1976-79; agr. engr. USDA ARS, Fresno, Calif., 1979-83, Bushland, Tex., 1983—. Co-author: Modification of the Aerial Environment Crops, 1979, Design and Operation of Farm Irrigation Systems, 1980, Limitations to Effective Water Use in Crop Production, 1983, Irrigation of Agricultural Crops, 1991, Agricultural System Models, 2002, Encyclopedia of Water Science, 2003; co-editor, co-author: Management of Farm Irrigation Systems, 1991. Tchr. Paramount Bapt. Ch., Amarillo, 1985-94, deacon, 1987—; troop com. chmn. Boy Scouts Am., Amarillo, 1991-93. Recipient Tex. Environ. Excellence award in agr. Tex. Natural Resource Conservation Commn., 1999, Fed. Energy and Water Mgmt. award U.S. Dept. Energy, 199, Tech. Transfer award ARS, 1999, Sr. Scientist Yr. ARS, So. Plaias area, 2000. Fellow ASAE (chmn. soil and water divsn. 1987-88, Paper award 1972, 74, 80, soil and water divsn. editor 1993-97, Hancor award 2000, Tex. sect. Engr. of Yr. 2005), Am. Soc. Agronomy (A-3 divsn. chair 1999-2000); mem. ASCE (chmn. irrigation water requirements com. 1990-93, Tipton award 1997), Am. Acad. Water Resource Engrs. (diplomate 2007), Soil Sci. Soc. Am., Irrigation Assn. (life; Person of Yr. award 1995), Coun. for Agrl. Sci. and Tech., Tex. Agrl. Irrigation Assn. Office: USDA ARS PO Box 10 Bushland TX 79012-0010 Business E-Mail: tahowell@cprl.ars.usda.gov.

HOWELL, WILLIAM ASHLEY, III, lawyer; b. Raleigh, NC, Jan. 2, 1949; s. William Ashley II and Caroline Erskine Greenleaf; m. Esther Holland, Dec. 22, 1973. BS, Troy State U., 1972; postgrad., U. Ala., Birmingham, 1974-75; JD, Birmingham Sch. Law, 1977. Bar: Ala. 1977, U.S. Dist. Ct. (no. dist.) Ala. 1977, U.S. Ct. Appeals (5th cir.) 1977, U.S. Supreme Ct. 1982, U.S. Ct. Appeals (11th cir.) 1983, U.S. Dist. Ct. (mid. dist.) Ala. 1987. Atty. pub. defender divsn. Legal Aid Soc. of Birmingham, 1977—78, civil divsn. Legal Aid Soc. of Birmingham, 1978—81; dist. office atty. SBA, Birmingham, 1980—82, supervising atty. Ala. Dist., 1982—; spl. asst. U.S. Atty. (mid. dist.), Ala., 1988—, U.S. Atty. (so. dist.), Ala., 2002—. Part-time instr. legal and social environ. and human resources mgmt. Jefferson State C.C., Birmingham, 1993. Contbr. articles to profl. jours. Vol. reader Radio Reading Svc. Network for Blind, 1991—93; mem. Shelby County Econ. Devel. Coun., 1993—94, Hispanic Outreach Commn., 2000—01, Highland Crest Homeowners Assn., 2002—; del. state conv. Episc. Ch. of Ala., various yrs.; bd. dirs. Hoover Homeowners Assn., 1977—81, Southside Ministries, Inc., 1990—91, v.p. bd. dirs., 1990—91; bd. dirs. SafeHouse of Shelby County, Inc., 1990—93, vice chmn., 1991—93. Recipient Am. Jurisprudence Criminal Procedure Book award. Mem. ABA (sect. corporation, banking and bus. law), Nat. Parks and Conservation Soc. (life), Fed. Bar Assn. (sec. Birmingham chpt. 1980-81, del. nat. conv. 1993, 94, del. mid yr. meeting, 1994-95), Ala. Bar Assn. (com. on future of the profession 1978-81, 83-84, com. on quality of life 1992-93, sect. bankruptcy and corp. law, sect. bankruptcy and comml. law, sect. corp. counsel, sect. banking and bus. law), Nature Conservacy (life), Birmingham Bar Assn., Birmingham Venture Club, Sierra Club (life), Sigma Delta Kappa (v.p., Outstanding Sr. award 1977). Episcopalian. Office: US Small Bus Adminstrn 801 Tom Martin Dr Ste 201 Birmingham AL 35211-4436 Fax: 205-290-7443. E-mail: william.howell@sba.gov.

HOWELL, WILLIAM PAGE, real estate company executive; b. Carnegie, Okla., July 27, 1952; s. Herman Glen and Muriel Joyce (Raby) H.; 1 child, Blake Alexander Sewell-Howell. BS, Southwestern U., Weatherford, Okla., 1975; MS, U. Okla., 1976. Chief exec. officer, pres. Howell Assocs., Norman, Okla., 1976-84; dir. Saudi Arabian Investment Corp., Dallas, London, 1984-87; dir. acquisitions Mitsui Fudosan (N.Y.) Inc., NYC, 1987-93; prin., ptnr. Peninsula Mgmt. Corp., NYC, 1993—; pres. Howell Assocs. of N.Y., NYC, 1993—; mng. ptnr. Cushman Peninsula Asset Mgmt. Group, NYC, 1993—; chmn., pres. Boutique Hotels and Resorts, NYC, 1998—; chmn., CEO, H.A.I. Investment Advisors, NYC, 1999—; v.p. Urban Am. LLP, 2006—. Dir. adv. bd. Comml. Property News, N.Y.C., 1990—. Demographics coord. Dem. Nat. Com., Atlanta, 1976-77. Mem. Urban Land Inst., Assn. Fgn. Investors in U.S. Real Estate, Fedn. Internat. Adminstrs. de Bein Conseils Immobiliers, Japan Soc., N.Y. Real Estate Club, Internat. Devel. Rsch. Coun. Avocations: flying, skiing, skydiving, fishing, golf.

HOWELLS, JEFFREY P., computer company executive; B in Acctg., Stetson U. CPA. With Price Waterhouse, 1979—91, sr. audit mgr.; v.p. fin. Tech Data, 1991-92; CFO Tech Data Corp., 1992-93, sr. v.p. fin., CFO, 1993-97, exec. v.p., CFO, 1997—. Mailing: PO Box 6260 Clearwater FL 33758-6260 Office: Tech Data Corp 5350 Tech Data Dr Clearwater FL 33760-3122 Office Phone: 727-539-7429, 727-539-7429. E-mail: jeffery.howells@techdata.com.*

HOWER, FRANK BEARD, JR., retired banker; b. Louisville, Ky., Nov. 26, 1928; s. Frank Beard and Katharine (Coffman) H.; m. Virginia W. Barker, Dec. 30, 1954; children: Frank Beard III, William. AB, Centre Coll., Danville, Ky., 1950. With Liberty Nat. Bank, Louisville, 1950-90, exec. v.p., 1967-71, pres., 1971-90, CEO, chmn. bd. dirs., 1973-90, ret., 1990. Bd. dirs. Falls City Industries, Inc., Louisville, Bank One, Ky., Norton Health Sys., Inc., Am. Life and Accident Ins. Co., Churchill Downs Inc., Anthem Inc.; chmn. Norton Kosair Childrens Hosp., Inc., 1983-84. Trustee J. Graham Brown Found., U. Louisville; chmn. regional adv. bd. Comptr. of Currency, 1976; mem. Ky. Registry of Election Finance, 1966-70, Ky. Econ. Progress Commn., 1964-70; vice chmn. Ky.-Tenn. Export Coun.; gen. chmn. United Appeal, 1969; chmn. Greater Louisville Fund for the Arts, 1976; v.p. Louisville Philharm. Orch., 1974-75; chmn. Regional Airport Authority of Louisville and Jefferson County, Louisville Devel. Com.; bd. dirs., chmn. U. Louisville; trustee, chmn. Ky. Ind. Coll. Found.; trustee Centre Coll.; mem. Actors Theatre Bd. Maj. USMCR, 1951-52, Korea. Mem. Am., Ky. bankers assns., Robert Morris Assos., Assn. Res. City Bankers, Louisville C. of C. (pres. 1973) Republican. Episcopalian.

HOWER, PHILIP LELAND, semiconductor device engineer; b. Reading, Pa., Apr. 9, 1934; s. Frank B. and Gladys (Fox) H.; m. Suzanne Mulvey, Apr. 28, 1962; children: Benjamin L., Suzanne E. BSEE, Lehigh U., 1956; MSEE, U. So. Calif., 1958; PhDEE, Stanford U., 1967. Tech. staff Fairchild R&D, Palo Alto, Calif., 1966-71; adv. engr. Westinghouse R&D, Pitts., 1971-81; prin. scientist Unitrode Corp., Watertown, Mass., 1981-92; prin. engr. Unitrode Integrated Cirs., Merrimack, NH, 1992-99; disting. mem. tech. staff Tex. Instruments, Manchester, NH, 1999—. Contbr. 40 articles to profl. jours. Fellow IEEE (life); mem. IEEE Power Electronics Soc. (William E. Newell award 1986, disting. lectr., 1999). Achievements include patents for semiconductor device design. Home: 315 Border Rd Concord MA 01742-4625 Office: Tex Instruments 50 Phillippe Cote St Manchester NH 03101 E-mail: phil_hower@ti.com.

HOWES, BRIAN THOMAS, lawyer; b. Sioux Falls, SD, July 23, 1957; s. Thomas A. and Joyce L. (McFarland) H.; m. Robin Kay Schoonover, June 2, 1979; children: Phillip, Adam, Jason. BSBA in Acctg., BA in Polit. Sci., Kans. State U., 1979; JD, U. Kans., 1982. Bar: Mo. 1982, U.S. Dist. Ct. (we. dist.) Mo. 1982, U.S. Supreme Ct. 1989. Assoc. Shughart, Thomson & Kilroy, Kansas City, Mo., 1982-85; exec. v.p., COO, gen. counsel Tenenbaum & Assocs., Inc., Kansas City, 1985-95; ptnr., nat. dir. property tax svcs. Ernst & Young LLP, Kansas City, 1995-99; of counsel Shughart Thomson & Kilroy, P.C., Kansas City, 2000—. Pres. Nat. Coun. Property Taxation, 1999-2000. Contr. articles to profl. jours; writer, speaker in field. Bd. dirs. Kansas City Wheelchair Athletic Commn., 1987-89, Vol. Atty. Project, 1984—, Nat. Youth Sports Coaches Assn., 1994—. Mem. ABA, Kansas City Met. Bar Assn., Lawyers Assn. Kansas City, Inst. Profls. in Taxation, Internat. Assn. Assessing Officers. Episcopalian. Home: 4901 W 130th St Shawnee Mission KS 66209-1864 Office: Shughart Thomson & Kilroy PC Ste 1800 120 W 12th St Kansas City MO 64105-1929 Office Phone: 816-421-3355. Business E-Mail: bhowes@stklaw.com.

HOWES, JAMES GUERDON, communication and transportation executive; b. Balt. s. James Harold and Edna Esther (Lowman) H. BS, U. Md., 1967, MBA, 1969. Staff asst. U.S. Senate, Washington, 1965-68; regional mktg. adminstrn. Hertz Corp., Balt., 1972-75; commr. aviation Dutchess County, Poughkeepsie, NY, 1975-80; airport dir. St. Petersburg-Clearwater (Fla.) Internat. Airport, 1980-2001; CEO Atlas Comm., Tampa, 2001—. Prodr. radio programs Choral Masterpieces, 1985-95, King of Instruments, 1983-95, Sacred Classics, 1995—, other CD's and concerts. Committeeman Rep. Nat. Com. Campaign, Washington, 1974-84, Riverside Ch., N.Y.C., 1976-80; v.p. Boy Scouts Am., Largo, Fla., 1987-91, nat. coun. rep., 1992-96. Capt. USAF, 1969-72. Recipient So. divsn. Airport of Yr. Safety award, 1998; named Man of Yr., Bermuda Hotel Assn., 2004. Mem. Am. Assn. Airport Execs., Southeastern Airport Mgrs. Assn. (pres. 1993-94), Belleair Country Club. Methodist. Avocations: flying, scuba diving, classical music, photography, white water rafting. Home: 41 Pine Wood Cir Safety Harbor FL 34695-5421 Office: PO Box 5534 Baltimore MD 21285 Office Phone: 727-726-0400. E-mail: jghowes@compuserve.com.

HOWES, LORRAINE DE WET, fashion designer, educator; b. Port Elizabeth, South Africa, Dec. 24, 1933; arrived in U.S., 1957; d. Jacobus Egnatius and Johanna Elizabeth (Lowenburg) de W. Student, Sch. Fashion Design, Boston, 1957-58. Apprentice Jonathan Logan & Adam Leslie, Johannesburg, South Africa, 1953-55; apprentice, wookroom asst., model Norman Hartnell, designer to the Queen, London, 1955-57; model Peter Lumley Agy., London, 1955-57; designer, dept. mgr. Design Rsch. Inc., Cambridge, Mass., 1957-59; model Hart Agy., Boston, 1957-76; designer, mgr. Estabrook & Newell, Boston, 1959-62; designer, owner Lorraine de Wet, Boston, 1962-79; mem. adj. faculty dept. apparel design RISD, Providence, 1972-76, asst. prof., assoc. prof., 1976-82, acting head dept., 1976-79, head dept., 1979-99, prof., 1988-2000, prof. emeritus, 2000—, interim dean arch. and design, 2000-2001. Designer, cons. apparel industry and theatre, 1979—2000; dir. Hamilton Cornell Mass., 1986-2000; design and tech. edn. cons. apparel and textiles Hangzhou Econ. Commn., China, 1986-88; mem. individual grants panel Nat. Endowment for Arts, 1994. Named Faculty Mem. of Yr., RISD Alumni Assn., 1984-85; recipient John R. Frazier Excellence in Tchg. award RISD, 1993, Hon. Alumna award RISD, 1995, Helen Rowe Metcalf award 2003; named champion R.I. Pub. Links, 1983, 84. Mem.: Costume Soc. Am., Fashion Inst. Tech. Design Lab., Fashion Group. Avocation: golf. Office: RISD Dept Apparel Design 2 College St Providence RI 02903-2784

HOWES, SOPHIA DUBOSE, writer; b. Balt., Apr. 20, 1954; d. John Carleton and Marie Josephine (Meeth) Jones; m. Edward Phillip Howes, Jan. 26, 1996; 1 child, Michael Laurence. BFA with honors, NYU, 1982, MFA, 1994; JD, Fordham U., 2002. Legal asst. Skadden, Arps, Slate, Meagher & Flom, NYC, 1984-93; script reader Haft Nassiter Co., NYC, 1994; editl. assoc. Matthew Bender & Co. Inc., NYC, 1994-97. Extern Fordham U. Sch. Law, Surrogate's Ct., NYC, 1999; rsch. asst. Securities Arbitration Clinic, Fordham Law Sch., 2000, Writing Rsch., ECPAT, summer 2001. Playwright: Better Dresses, Rosetta's Eyes, 1988, 1988, Adamov, 1992, two-act play The Poisoned Kiss, 1994; mem. staff Fordham Environ. Law Jour., 1999-2000; sr. notes and comments editor, 2000-01; dir. Who's Afraid of Virginia Woolf, 2004, The Tempest, 2004. Recipient Grad. award in playwriting, NYU-Tisch Sch. Arts, 1994, Seidman award for talent, 1982. Mem. Dramatists Guild. Avocation: mountain climbing. E-mail: edwardhowes@juno.com.

HOWEY, JOHN RICHARD, architect, writer; b. New Haven, Jan. 13, 1933; s. Joseph Herman and Dorothy Pauline (Good) H.; m. Maria Andrea Hatges, Sept. 8, 1968; children: John Michael, Dorothy Anne. Student, Wooster Coll., 1951-52; BS, Ga. Inst. Tech., 1956, BArch, 1957. Registered architect Fla. With various archtl. firms, Fla., 1958—65, Ga., 1958—65; pres. John Howey, Architect, AIA, Tampa, Fla., 1965—73, John Howey Assocs., Tampa, Fla., 1973—. Pres. Baypark, Inc., Tampa, 1988—. Prin. works include coll. bldgs. U. So. Fla., 1975, Louis Pappas Restaurant, Tarpon Springs, Fla., 1975 (honor design award AIA 1976), office bldg. 101 S. Franklin St., Tampa, 1980 (Fla. Preservation award 1984), Williers Residence, Tampa, 1980 (honor design award AIA 1981), modular urban transit shelters, 1977 (U.S. patent 1980, honor design award AIA 1985), Tehran, Iran Libr. Project, 1978, Baypark Pl. apt. bldgs., Tampa, 1989 (honor design award AIA 1989, Millenium Award of Honor, 2000), others; author: The Sarasota School of Architecture, 1995; co-author: Florida Architecture, A Celebration, 2000, Florida Modern, 2004, Selected and Current Works, John Howey Associates, 2006. With C.E., U.S. Army, 1957-58. Fellow AIA (Fla./Caribbean region Design Excellence Honor award 1985, Fla. ctrl. chpt. Medal of Honor 1986); mem. Sertoma Club (bd. dirs. 1970-73), Exch. Club. Episcopalian. Avocations: photography, painting. Home: 1507 Bay Villa Pl Tampa FL 33629 Address: John Howey Assocs 121 E Whiting St Tampa FL 33602-5136 Personal E-mail: jhoweyarch@tampabay.rr.com.

HOWINGTON, JOHN, thoracic surgeon, educator; b. Nashville, Sept. 16, 1963; m. Anne Levans; children: George, Grace. MD, U. Tenn., Memphis, 1985—89. Chief thoracic surgery U. Hosp., Cin., 1999—. Assoc. prof. surgery U. Cin., 1999—. Mem. class XXVII Leadership Cin. Fellow: ACS (Ohio chpt., sec. 2004—), Am. Coll. Chest Physicians. Office: Univ Cin 231 Albert Sabin Way Cincinnati OH 45267-0558

HOWITT, ARNOLD MARTIN, academic administrator, educator; b. NYC, Jan. 6, 1947; s. Wilfred D. and Mildred (Wolch) H.; m. Maryalice Sloan; children: Matthew, Molly, Alexandra, Mark. BA, Columbia U., 1969; MA, Harvard U., 1971, PhD, 1976. Asst. prof. Brown U., Providence, 1974-76, Harvard U., Cambridge, Mass., 1976-80, assoc. prof., 1980-82, assoc. dir. Taubman Ctr. State and Local Govt., Kennedy Sch. Govt., 1983-93, exec. dir. Taubman Ctr. State and Local Govt., Kennedy Sch. Govt., 1993—, co-dir. program on emergency preparedness and crisis mgmt., 2000—. Exec. dir. Coop. Mobility Program, MIT, Cambridge, 1998-2001; cons. in field; part-time lectr. SUNY, Albany, 1984-92, U. Wash., Seattle, 1988—, dir. Exec. Session on Domestic Preparedness for Terrorism, Kennedy Sch. Govt., 1999-2003, co-dir. program on emergency preparedness and crisis mgmt., 2000—. Author: Managing Federalism, 1984; co-author, editor: Perspectives on Management Capacity Building, 1986, Countering Terrorism, 2003; contbr. articles to profl. jours. Office: Harvard U Kennedy Sch Govt 79 JF Kennedy St Cambridge MA 02138-5801

HOWITT, JOHN P., lawyer; b. LA, Jan. 22, 1953; AB magna cum laude, UCLA, 1975, JD, 1978. Bar: Calif. 1978, N.Y. 1988. Consult fgn. law, law firm of Nagashima & Ohno, Tokyo, 1981—83; ptnr. Paul, Hastings, Janofsky & Walker LLP, NYC, chmn. aviation practice group. Mem.: Order Coif. Office: Paul Hastings Janosky & Walker LLP 75 E 55th St First Floor New York NY 10022-3205 Office Phone: 212-318-6005. Office Fax: 212-230-7712. Business E-Mail: johnhowitt@paulhastings.com.

HOWLAND, BEN, men's college basketball coach; b. Lebanon, Oreg., May 28, 1957; m. Kim Zahnow; children: Meredith, Adam. BA in Phys. Edn., Weber St. U., 1979; MS in Adminstrn. and Phys. Edn., Gonazaga U., 1981. Basketball player Santa Barbara City Coll., 1976—78, Weber State U., 1978—80; profl. basketball player Uruguay, 1980; grad. asst. Gonzaga U., 1981—82; asst. coach U. Calif., Santa Barbara, 1982—94; head coach No. Ariz. U., 1994—99, U. Pitts., 1999—2003, UCLA, 2003—. Named Big Sky Conf. Coach of Yr., 1997, Nat. Coach Yr. (AP, Naismith, US Basketball Writers Assn., ESPN Mag., The Sporting News), 2002, US Basketball Writers Assn. Dist. Coach of Yr., 2002, Big East Coach of Yr., 2002, Basketball Am. Big East Coach of Yr., 2002, Basketball Times Big East Coach of Yr., 2002, Pac-10 Coach of Yr., 2006, Nat. Coach of Yr., Collegehoops.net, 2006, Dist. 15 Coach of Yr., Nat. Assn. Basketball Coaches, 2007; named to No. Ariz. U. Athletic Hall of Fame, 2004;

recipient Pitts. Tribune-Rev. City of Champions award, 2002, Dapper Dan award, honoring Pitts.'s Sportsman of Yr., 2003, Jim Phelan award, Coach of Yr., CollegeInsider.com, 2006. Achievements include coaching five conference championship teams; leading UCLA to NCAA championship game, 2006. Office: UCLA Intcol Ath BOX 951639 175 Morgan Ctr Los Angeles CA 90095-1639 Office Phone: 310-206-6276. Office Fax: 310-206-3440. E-mail: bhowland@athletics.ucla.edu.*

HOWLAND, BETTE, writer; b. Chgo., Jan. 28, 1937; d. Sam and Jessie (Berger) Sotonoff; m. Howard C. Howland (div.); children— Frank, Jacob. BA, U. Chgo., 1955. Assoc. prof. com. social thought U. Chgo., 1993-97. Author: W-3, 1974, Blue in Chicago, 1978 (1st prize Friends of Am. Writers), Things to Come and Go, 1983, Trial, 1998, Calm Sea and Prosperous Voyage, 1999. Fellow Rockefeller Found., 1969, Marsden Found., 1971, Guggenheim Found., 1978, Nat. Endowment for the Arts, 1981, MacArthur Found., 1984. Jewish.

HOWLAND, GRAFTON DULANY, financial counselor; b. NYC, Mar. 9, 1943; s. McClure Meredith and Jane Robb (Murdock) H.; m. Victoria Vincent, June 17, 1989. BA, Harvard U., 1967; MBA, U. Dallas, 1980. Cert. fin. planner/fin. counselor. Pvt. practice fin. cons., London, 1967-78; v.p. Balanced Fin. Corp., Dallas, 1981-86; chmn. Howland & Morris, Dallas, 1986-91; pres. G. Dulany Howland Adv. Corp., Dallas, 1991—. Vice chmn. Dallas Symphony Ann. Fund Dr., 1987-89. Mem. Mgmt. Inst. Cert. Fin. Planners (cert.) Dallas-Ft. Worth Soc. (bd. dirs. 1989-90, pres. 1990-91, chmn. 1991-92), Inst. Cert. Fin. Planners (nat. bd. dirs. 1992-94), Greater Dallas C. of C. (hon. life; vice chmn. ind. bus. coun. 1987-89, chmn. 1989-90) Leadership Dallas Alumni Assn., Harvard Alumni Assn. (bd. dirs. 1985-88, non-dir. com. 1988-91), Harvard Club Dallas (pres. 1983-87, chmn. 1987-89. dir. emeritus 1989—), Newport Reading Room, St. Nicholas Soc., Colonial Lords of the Manor, Tower Club, Park City Club, Idlewild Club, Terpsichorean Club. Office: G Dulany Howland Adv Corp 6116 N Central Expy Ste 518 Dallas TX 75206-5133

HOWLAND, JOAN SIDNEY, law librarian, educator; b. Eureka, Calif., Apr. 9, 1951; d. Robert Sidney and Ruth Mary Howland. BA, U. Calif., Davis, 1971; MA, U. Tex., 1973; MLS, Calif. State U., San Jose, 1975; JD, Santa Clara U., Calif., 1983; MBA, U. Minn., 1997. Assoc. librarian for pub. svcs. Stanford U. Law Library, Calif., 1975-83, Harvard U. Law Library, Cambridge, Mass., 1983-86; dep. dir. U. Calif. Law Library, Berkeley, 1986-92; dir. law libr., Roger F. Noreen prof. law U. Minn. Sch. of Law, 1992—, assoc. dean info. tech., 2001—. Questions and answers column editor Law Libr. Jour., 1986-91; memt. column editor Trends in Law Libr. Mgmt. & Tech., 1987-94. Mem. ALA, ABA (com. on accreditation 2001—), Am. Assn. Law Librs., Am. Assn. Law Schs., Am. Indian Libr. Assn. (treas. 1992—), Am. Law Inst. Office: U Minn Law Sch 120/410 Walter F Mondale Hall 229 19th Ave S Minneapolis MN 55455-0400 Office Phone: 612-625-9036. E-mail: howla001@umn.edu.*

HOWLAND, MARGARET E.C., retired librarian; b. Northampton, Mass., June 6, 1927; d. Horace Damon and Barbara Wood Clapp; m. David Frederick Howland, Mar. 28, 1948; children: David Eugene, Martha Lee. BA, Hofstra U., Hempstead, NY, 1949; MS in libr. sci., So. Conn. State Coll., New Haven, 1972; MPA, U. Mass., Amherst, 1979. Chief libr. Combustion Engring. Inc., Windsor, Conn., 1957—61; law cataloger Conn. State Libr., Hartford, 1961; chief libr. Factory Ins. Assn., Hartford, 1961—62, Travelers Rsch. Ctr. Inc., Hartford, 1962—68; adminstrv. asst. to asst. dir. U. Mass. Libr., Amherst, 1968; dir. libr. Greenfield CC, Mass., 1968—90; curator Archibald MacLeish Collection, Greenfield, 1974—; guide Hist. Deerfield Inc., Mass., 1995—2000. Coun. mem. Pocumtuck Valley Meml. Assn., Deerfield, 2002—; bd. dirs. Pioneer Valley Inst., Greenfield. Author: (book 2 vols.) Descriptive Catalog of the Archibald MacLeish Collection, 1991—92; co-author (book) Archibald MacLeish: An Annotated Bibliography, 1995; editor: (town newsletter) The Heath Herald. Mem., pres., curator Heath Hist. Soc., Mass., 1963—; mem. Heath Hist. Commn., Mass., 1991—. Fellow, Dartmouth Coll., 1981; grant to catalog the Archibald MacLeish Collection, NEH, 1990—92. Mem.: Spl. Librs. Assn. (Conn. Valley chpt. pres. 1960), Soc. Am. Archivists. Avocation: Victorian antiques collector. Home: 13 E Main St Heath MA 01346 Home Phone: 413-337-4980.

HOWLAND, RICHARD MOULTON, retired lawyer; b. Glen Cove, L.I., NY, Jan. 2, 1940; s. Richard Moulton and Natalie (Fuller) H.; m. Julie Rose Keschl, Sept. 28, 1974 (div.); children: Kimberly Merrill, Gillian Fuller. BA, Amherst Coll., 1961; JD, Columbia U., 1968. Bar: Mass. 1968. Assoc. firm Nutter, McLennen & Fish, Boston, 1968-69, DiMento & Sullivan, Boston, 1969-70; atty. for students U. Mass., Amherst, 1970-74; practice law Amherst, 1974-2000; Legal Infirmary Amherst, 1997-98; ret., 2001. Adj. prof. U. Mass., 1972-76, Western New Eng. Coll. Sch. Law, 1993-94; vis. lectr. Amherst Coll., 1983, mock trial team coach, 1989-98; mock trial team coach Tufts Coll., 1998, Deerfield Acad., 1999-2000, Southwick H.S., 1999-2000; tchr. constnl. law, history, social studies Springfield H.S. Sci. and Tech., 2001—. Co-editor: Mass. Lawyers Weekly, 1979—94; emeritus:, 1994, statistician: New Eng. Blizzard, 1996—98, Conn. Pride, 1999—2000, Springfield Sirens Pro Soccer, 1999—2000. Asst. moderator Town of Leverett, 1988—93, moderator, 1993—96; mem. Leverett Sch. Bldg. Com., 1988—89; trustee Art Inst. Boston, 1990—92, Greenfield C. C. Found., 1991—97, Amherst Regional H.S. Coun., 1993—95, Amherst Hist. Soc., 1990—95; pres. Leverett PTO, 1981—85; mem. devel. com. Pioneer Valley H.S. of the Performing Arts, 1996—97; pres. Interfaith Housing Corp., Amherst, 1984—93; bd. dirs. Leverett Craftsmen and Artists, Inc., 1986—2001, treas., 1988—89, v.p., 1988—89, pres., 1989—2001; bd. dirs. Cmty. Multisvc. Inc., Northampton, Mass., 1987—93; trustee Wildwood Cemetery Assn., 1987—; bd. dirs., sec. Responsible Hospitality Inst., 1990—95; mem. host com. Russia-Amherst Exchange City of Petrozavadsk, 1988—; del. rep. Town of Amherst to Sister City, Kanegasaki, Japan, 1992—95; chair Amherst-Kanegasaki Sister Com., 1994—95; mem. bd. career com. Hampshire-Franklin Sch., 1995—98; cert. master ofcl. U.S. Assn. Track and Field, 1996—; Western Mass. track and field ofcl., 1995—; Western Mass. football ofcl., 1995—; referee FIFA Soccer, 1997—; active Connecticut Valley Soccer Ofcls. Assn., 1995—; collegiate water polo ofcl., 1997—2000; asst. coach varsity girls soccer Amherst Regional H.S., 1995—99; v.p. Western Mass. track and field, 2002—06; mem. town mtg. Town of Amherst, mem. planning bd., 2006—. Lt. j.g. USNR, 1961—65. Named Hon. Life Citizen, Town of Leverett, Mass., 2002. Mem. ABA (chmn. profl. liability com. Gen. Practice Sect. 1987-90, chmn. certification and specialization com. Gen. Practice Sect. 1992-95, chmn. family law com. 1995-96, chmn. certification, specialization and law sch. curriculum com. 1996-98, mem. coun. 1997-2001), Mass. Bar Assn. (chmn. com. on chem. dependency, Mass. Community Svc. award 1984), Franklin Bar Assn., Hampshire Bar Assn. (del. to Mass. Bar Assn., sec., v.p. 1986), Mass. Acad. Trial Lawyers, Amherst C. of C. (pres. 1985-93, Dakin medallion 1995), Nat. High Sch. Slavic Honor Soc. (hon.), Amherst Alumni Athletic Assn. (bd. dirs. 1995—), Skating Club (past v.p., treas. 1987-96, Amherst). Democrat. Home: 326 N Pleasant St Amherst MA 01002-1706 E-mail: dick.howland@gmail.com.

HOWLAND, WILLARD J., radiologist, educator; b. Neosho, Mo., Aug. 28, 1927; s. Willard Jay and Grace Darlene (Murphy) H.; m. Kathleen V. Jones, July 28, 1945; children: Wyck, Candice, Charles, Thomas, Heather AB, U. Kans., 1948, MD, 1950; MA, U. Minn., 1958; DSc (hon.), Coll. Med. N.E. Ohio, 1990. Intern U.S. Naval Hosp., Newport, RI, 1950-51; pvt. practice medicine Kans., 1951-55; resident Mayo Clinic, Rochester, Minn., 1955-58; radiologist Ohio Valley Gen. Hosp., Wheeling, W.Va., 1959-67; prof., dir. diagnostic radiology Med. Units U. Tenn., Memphis, 1967-68; dir., chmn. dept. radiology Aultman Hosp., Canton, Ohio, 1968-87, pres. med. staff, 1978; prof., chmn. radiology coun. Coll. Medicine N.E. Ohio U., Rootstown, 1976-87, program dir. integrated radiology residency, 1976-87. Author, co-author three books and rsch. papers in field. With U.S. Army, 1945-46, USN, 1950-51. Fellow Am. Coll. Radiology; mem. AMA, Radiol. Soc. N.Am., Am. Roentgen Ray Soc., Ohio State Radiol. Soc. (pres. 1980-81), Masons. Republican. Presbyterian. Home and Office: 4521 Bishops Gate Rd NW Canton OH 44708 Office Phone: 330-479-1046. Personal E-mail: whowland1@neo.rr.com.

HOWLETT, CLIFFORD THEODORE, JR., (KIP HOWLETT), chemicals executive; b. Portland, Oreg., Oct. 19, 1945; s. Clifford T. and Lois (Ellis) H.; children: Beth, Ted, Michael; m. Marybeth Rossomando, Nov. 8, 1997. BA, Johns Hopkins U., 1967; JD, Willamette U., 1974. Bar: Oreg. 1974. Counsel, project dir. Western Environ. Trade Assn., Portland, 1973-75; v.p. environment and govt. affairs Ga.-Pacific Corp., Washington, 1988-94; vice-pres. for policy National Policy Forum, Wash., DC, 1994—. Chmn. Inter-Industry Wood Dust com., Washington, 1988—. Author: The Pitfalls and Possibilities of Planning, 1973, The Biomass Potential of Short Rotation Farms, 1977, Forest and Mill Residues as Potential Sources of Biomass, 1977. Mem. Alumni Schs. com. Johns Hopkins U., 1988—; bd. dirs. Boys and Girls Clubs of Greater Washington, 1999. With U.S. Army, 1968-70. Mem. ABA, Oreg. Bar Assn., Am. Paper Inst. (chmn. dioxin potency com. 1988—, chmn. joint occupational health study com. with Nat. Forest Products Assn. 1988—), NAM (chmn. OSHA policy com. 1988—). Home: 6635 Byrns Pl Mc Lean VA 22101-4419 Office: Chlorine Chemistry Council 1300 Wilson Blvd Arlington VA 22209-2307

HOWLETT, PHYLLIS LOU, retired athletics administrator; b. Indianola, Iowa, Oct. 23, 1932; d. James Clarence and Mabel L. (Fisher) Hickman; m. Jerry H. Howlett, Jan. 2, 1955 (dec. June 1972); children: Timothy A. (dec. Jan. 2005), Jane A. Field; m. Ronlin Royer, Dec. 30, 1977. BA, Simpson Coll., 1954. Tchr. phys. edn. Oskaloosa HS, Iowa, 1954—55; psychometrist Drake U., Des Moines, 1956-57, asst. to men's athletics dir., 1974-79; asst. dir. athletics U. Kans., Lawrence, 1979-82; asst. commr. Big Ten Conf., Inc., Park Ridge, Ill., 1982—97. Mem. football TV com. NCAA, 1980-87, women's golf com., 1983-89, chmn. com. on women's athletics, 1987-94, spl. com. women's basketball TV, 1989-90, chair com. for women's corp. mktg., 1990-94, divsn. I championship com., 1990-95, first woman chair exec. com., 1990-97, chair task force on gender equity, 1992-94, exec. dir. search com., 1993, spl. com. divsn. I football playoff, adminstrv. com., 1995-97, joint policy bd., 1995-97, sec.-treas. 1995-97, coun., 1995-97, fin. com., chair, 1995-97, treas. found. bd., 1995-97 Editor: (yearbook) Simpson Coll., 1953—54. Chair Iowa Commn. Status of Women, 1976-79; pres. Vol. Bus. of Greater Des Moines, 1969-70; chair Arts and Recreation Coun. Greater Des Moines, 1975; pres. Iowa Children's and Family Svcs., 1973; nat. pres. Assn. Vol. Bus. Am., Inc., 1972-73; mem. Jr. League Des Moines. Named to, Simpson Coll. Hall of Fame, 1985, Indianola HS Hall of Fame, 1997, NACDA Hall of Fame, 2000; recipient Alumni Achievement award, Simpson Coll., 1988, Adminstrv. Achievement award, NACDA, 1995, Honda award of Merit, 1997, Spl. award, All-Am. Football Found., 1998, Lifetime Achievement award, Ind. Sports Corp., 1997, Svc. award, Assn. Vol. Burs. Am., Inc. Mem. Nat. Assn. Coll. Women's Athletics Adminstrs. (Lifetime Achievement award 2000), Pi Beta Phi (pres. Iowa Beta chpt. 1953-54). Home: PO Box 1117 Abiquiu NM 87510-1117

HOWLETT, RAY, sculptor; b. Aug. 6, 1940; BFA, U. Nebr., Lincoln, 1963. Studio artist, LA, 1973—. Represented in permanent collections Frederick R. Weisman Art Found., LA, LA County Mus. Natural History, Sci. and Tech. Ctr., Aurora, Ill., Mus. Sci., Boston, La. Art and Sci. Mus., Baton Rouge, Lakeview Mus. Arts and Scis., Peoria, Ill., Gardiner Art Gallery Okla. State U., Stillwater, Grace Mus., Abilene, Tex., Midland Ctr. Arts, Mich., Kaleioscope Mus., Sendai-City, Japan, Springfield Art Mus., Mo., Mus. Neon Art, LA, Midwest Mus. Am. Art, Elkhart, Ind., Arts and Sci. Ctr., Pine Bluff, Ark., Masur Art Mus., Monroe, La., West Valley Art Mus., Surprise, Ariz., Butler Instn. Am. Art, Youngstown, Ohio, one-man shows include Las Vegas Art Mus., Nev., 1981, Grace Mus., Abilene, Tex., 1998, Gardiner Art Gallery Okla. State U., Stillwater, 1998, Charles MacNider Mus., Mason City, Iowa, 1998, Noel Art Mus., Odessa, Tex., 1998, Bruce Mus., Greenwich, Conn., 1998, Midland Ctr. Arts, Tex., 1999, Springfield Art Mus., Mo., 1999, Dahl Fine Art Ctr., Rapid City, SD, 1999, Canton Mus. Fine Art, Ohio, 1999, Lakeview Mus. Art and Sci., Peoria, Ill, 2000, Mus. Neon Art, LA, 2000, La. Art and Sci. Mus., Baton Rouge, 2000, Western Ill. U. Art Gallery, Macomb, 2000, West Valley Art Mus., Surprise, Ariz., 2000, Midwest Mus. Am. Art, Elkhart, Ind., 2001, Masur Art Mus., Dothan Ala., 2002, Arts and Sci. Ctr., Pine Bluff, Ark., 2002, Blanden Meml. Art Mus., Fort Dodge, Iowa, 2003, Nat. Liberty Mus., Phila., 2004, SD Art Mus., Brookings, 2005, Butler Instn. Am. Art, Youngstown, Ohio, 2006. Achievements include pioneering work in Dicroism. Home: 4230 W St Lincoln NE 68503-2827 Office Phone: 888-485-6789.

HOWLEY, JAMES MCANDREW, lawyer; b. Dunmore, Pa., Oct. 3, 1928; s. Joseph Austin and Mary Helene (Ruddy) H.; m. Mary McDade; 1 child, Maura. BS, U. Scranton, 1952; LLB, U. Pa., 1955. Bar: Pa. 1956, U.S. Dist. Ct. (mid. dist.) Pa. 1956, U.S. Ct. Appeals (3d cir.) 1960. Pvt. practice, Scranton, Northeastern Pa., 1956—. Panel mem. and speaker at various legal symposiums; chmn. and commr. Pa. State Ethics Commn.; chmn. Gov.'s Spl. Trial Ct. nomination commn., Lackawanna County, Pa., 1987; disciplinary bd. Supreme Ct. Pa. hearing com., 1987; lawyer's adv. com. U.S. Ct. Appeals (3d cir.), 1983-86, U.S. Dist. Ct. (mid. dist.) Pa., 1981-86. Chmn., trustee Marywood Coll., trustee St. Mary's Villa. Fellow Am. Coll. Trial Lawyers; mem. ABA, Pa. Bar Assn., Pa. Def. Inst., Am. Bd. Trial Advs. (cert.), Lackawanna County Bar Assn., Scranton C. of C. (bd. dirs.), Country Club of Scranton (pres. 1974-79), Friendly Sons of St. Patrick (pres. 1986). Roman Catholic. Avocation: golf. Home: 115 Maple Ave Clarks Summit PA 18411-2513 Office: 1000 Bank Towers 321 Spruce St Scranton PA 18503-1400 Office Phone: 570-346-7651. Personal E-mail: jmhowley@aol.com.

HOWLEY, PETER MAXWELL, pathology educator; b. New Brunswick, NJ, Oct. 9, 1946; s. Bartholomew Maxwell and Grace (Size) Howley; m. Ann Margaret McElwee, Aug. 23, 1969; children: Cristin, Megan, Maura. AB, Princeton U., 1968; M Med. Sci., Rutgers U., 1970; MD, Harvard U., 1972. Diplomate Am. Bd. Pathology. Intern Mass. Gen. Hosp., Boston, 1972—73; commd. lt. USPHS, 1973, advanced through grades to capt., 1985; rsch. assoc. NIH, Bethesda, Md., 1973—75; resident in pathology Nat. Cancer Inst., Bethesda, 1975—77, prin. investigator, 1977—84, lab. chief, 1984—93; chmn. dept. pathology Harvard Med. Sch., Boston, 1993—, George Fabyan prof. comparative pathology, chmn. dept., 1993—2004, Shattuck prof. pathology anatomy, 2004—. Mem. sci. adv. bd. ONYX Pharm. Co., Richmond, Calif., 1992—97, Baxter Internat., Deerfield, Ill., 1995—2006, Enanta Pharm. Co., Cambridge, Mass., 1999—2003, Millennium Pharm. Co., 2003—; chair Nat. Cancer Policy Bd., 1997—2000. Editor: The Molecular Basis of Cancer, 1996, 2nd edit., 2001, Fields Virology, 2007; contbr. over 240 articles to med. jours. Recipient Wallace P. Rowe award, Nat. Inst. Allergy and Infectious Diseases, 1986, Meritorious Svc. award, USPHS, 1989, Paul Ehrlich-Ludwig Darmstaedter prize, Govt. of Germany, 1994, Rous-Whipple award, Am. Soc. Investigative Pathology, 2004. Fellow: AAAS, Am. Acad. Microbiology; mem.: NAS, Am. Clin. and Climatol. Assn., Am. Acad. Arts and Scis., Inst. Medicine. Achievements include patent for Recombinant DNA Process Utilizing Papillomavirus DNA as a Vector. Office: Harvard Med Sch New Rsch Bldg Rm 950 77 Ave Louis Pasteur Boston MA 02115 Business E-Mail: peter_howley@hms.harvard.edu.

HOWORTH, DAVID, producer, director; b. NYC, Aug. 30, 1941; s. Marion Beckett and Dorothy Cowing) H.; m. Bea Borges, May 6, 1967. AA, Santa Ana CC, Calif., 1970; student, UCLA, 1977, Am. Film Inst., LA, 1982. V.p., co-owner Golden Coast Films, Santa Barbara, 1971-82, owner, prodr., dir., 1982—. Software developer, prodr. Internet Career Vision, Wildlife/Nature series, 1993; prodr., dir. Careers: Nursing, 1993; co-prodr., co-writer (ednl. picture) Just Beer, 1983. With USMCR, 1960-65. Recipient awards Columbus Internat. Film/Video Festival, 1993, Nat. Mental Health Assn., 1981, Excellence-Suitable for Family Viewing, No. Calif. Motion Picture and TV Coun., 1975. Mem. NATAS, AMA (acad. med. films), Internat. Interactive Comms. Soc., Greater Santa Barbara Advt. Club (pres. 1972). Avocations: historical films, records, swimming, boating. Home and Office: Golden Coast Films 102 North Hope Ave Apt 88 Santa Barbara CA 93110 Personal E-mail: gcfx@cox.net.

HOWORTH, DAVID BISHOP, retired lawyer; b. Temple, Tex., Feb. 6, 1947; s. Marion Beckett and Mary Hartwell (Bishop) H.; m. Martha Ellen Peacock, Aug. 29, 1970; children: Katherine Somerville, Emily Hartwell. BA, Yale U., 1971; JD, U. Miss., 1975. ar: N.Y. 1976, Oreg. 1990, Wash. 1996, Miss. 2000, U.S. Dist. Ct. (so. and ea. dists.) N.Y. 1977, U.S. Ct. Appeals (2d cir.) 1984, U.S. Dist. Ct. Oreg. 1990, U.S. Ct. Appeals (9th cir.) 1991. Assoc. Dewey Ballantine, NYC, 1975-77, 78-83, ptnr., 1984-90; asst. prof. law U. Miss., University, 1977—78, vis. assoc. prof. law, 2000—05; ret., 2005. Mem. ABA, N.Y. State Bar Assn., Assn. Bar City of N.Y. Home: 1420 S 10th St Oxford MS 38655 E-mail: dhoworth@olemiss.edu.

HOWREY, EUGENE PHILIP, retired economics and statistics professor; b. Geneva, Ill., Dec. 1, 1937; s. Eugene Edgar and Ellen Pauline (Boord) H.; children: Patricia Marie, Richard Philip, Margaret Ellen, Mark McCall. AB, Drake U., Des Moines, Iowa, 1959; PhD, U. NC, Chapel Hill, 1964; MA (hon.), U. Pa., Phila., 1972. Asst. prof. econs. Princeton U., NJ, 1963-69; assoc. prof. econs. U. Pa., Phila., 1969-73; prof. econs. U. Mich., Ann Arbor, 1973—2005, prof. stats., 1978—2005. Cons. Mathematica, Inc., Princeton, 1965-75; guest lectr. Inst. Advanced Studies, Vienna, 1974, 76. Contbr. articles to profl. jours. Research grantee NSF, 1975, 79, 84 Mem. Ann Arbor Bicycle Touring Soc. (pres. 1979-80), Phi Beta Kappa. Roman Catholic. Avocation: bicycling. Personal E-mail: eph@umich.edu.

HOWRY, JOE R., newspaper editor; B in History and Polit. Sci., U. Mont. Various positions with newspapers in Mont.; sports writer to city editor Nev. State Jour. and Reno (Nev.) Evening Gazette; mng. editor Salem (Oreg.) Statesman-Jour., Ventura (Calif.) County Star, 1992—2004, v.p., editor, 2004—. Office: Ventura County Star PO Box 6711 Ventura CA 93006-6711

HOWSE, JENNIFER LOUISE, foundation administrator; b. Glendale, Calif., Jan. 31, 1945; d. Benjamin McCausland and Patricia Louise (Naylor) H. BA, Fla. State U., 1966, MA, 1968, PhD in Child Lang. Devel., 1973; LHD (hon.), SUNY, Bklyn., 1990. Rsch. asst., instr. Inst. Human Devel. Coll. Edn., Fla. State U., Tallahassee, 1967-69; dir. planning and evaluation Wakulla County (Fla.) Sch. System, 1969-72; dir. NARC/HEW Liaison Project Nat. Assn. for Retarded Citizens, Govtl. Affairs Office, Washington, 1972-73; dir. Developmental Disabilities Bur., dir. Bur. Tech. Assistance and Regulation Fla. Dept. Health and Rehab. Svcs., Tallahassee, 1973-75; exec. dir. Willowbrook Rev. Panel, NYC, 1975-78; assoc. commr. N.Y. State Office Mental Retardation and Developmental Disabilities, NYC, 1978-80; state commr. for mental retardation Dept. Pub. Welfare, Harrisburg, Pa., 1980-85; exec. dir. Greater N.Y. chpt. March of Dimes Birth Defects Found., NYC, 1985-89, pres. White Plains, NY, 1990—. Advisor Ctr. for Family Life in Sunset Park, Bklyn., 1992—. Bd. dirs. Salk Inst., La Jolla, Calif.; active Pew Environ. Health Commn. Office: March Dimes Birth Defects Found 1275 Mamaroneck Ave White Plains NY 10605-5298

HOWSHAR, ERIN, lawyer; b. Creve Couer, Mo., Aug. 5, 1974; BA magna cum laude, St. Louis Univ., 1995; JD, Wash. Univ. Sch. Law, St. Louis, Mo., 1998. Bar: Wyo. 1998, Wash. 2000, U.S. Dist. Ct., Dist. Wyo., Western and Eastern Dist. Wash. 2000. Comml. litig., employment law Smyth & Mason Attys. at Law, 2000—. Contbr. articles to numerous profl. jours. Named Wash. Rising Star, SuperLawyer Mag., 2006. Mem.: Am. Bar Assn., King Co. Bar Assn., Platte Co. Bar Assn., Wyo. State Bar Assn., Wash. State Bar Assn. Office: Smyth and Mason PLLC Ste 7100 701 Fifth Ave Seattle WA 98104

HOWSON, JAMES G., photographer; b. Canton, Ohio, Sept. 2, 1916; s. Harvie George and Margaret Phietta Howson; m. Marcella Caroline Rinder. Editor, assoc. editor, sales mgr. Flow Mags. Indsl., Ohio, 1942—46; owner, mgr. Howson Advertising, Cleve., 1949—93, Indsl. Mktg. Svc., Cleve., 1956—93, Commercial Photograher, Cleve., 1980—. Mem.: Internat. Libr. of Photography, Mensa Am., Gyro Internat. Avocations: photography, sailing, flying, travel. Home: 608 Trevitt Cir W Euclid OH 44143

HOWSON, SCOTT, professional sports team executive; b. Toronto, Apr. 9, 1960; m. Antoinette Mongillo; children: Max, Rebekah, Joanna. JD, York U., Toronto, 1990. Center NY Islanders, 1985—86; gen. mgr. Cape Breton Oilers, 1994—96, Hamilton Bulldogs, 1996—2000; asst. to gen. mgr. Edmonton Oilers, 2000—01, asst. gen. mgr., 2001—07; gen. mgr. Columbus Blue Jackets, 2007—. Office: Columbus Blue Jackets 200 W Nationwide Blvd Columbus OH 43215*

HOXBY, CAROLINE MINTER, economics professor; b. Cleve., Apr. 16, 1966; d. Steven A. and Dolores K. Minter; m. Blair G. Hoxby, May 1993. AB, Harvard U., 1988; MPhil, Oxford U., Eng., 1990; PhD, MIT, 1994. Assoc. prof. econs. Harvard U., Cambridge, Mass., 1994—97, Morris Kahn assoc. prof. econs., 1997—2000, Allie S. Freed prof. econs., 2001—07; prof. Harvard Coll., Cambridge, Mass., 2005—07; prof. econs. Stanford U., 2007—. Program dir. Nat. Bur. Econ. Rsch., Cambridge, 1994; sr. advisor Brookings Instn,. Brown Ctr., Washington, 1997; disting. vis. fellow Hoover Instn., Stanford, Calif., 1998. Author: Learning from School Choice, 1998, Earning and Learning: How Schools Matter, 1999, The Economics of School Choice, 2003, College Choices: The Economics of Where to Go, When to Go and How to Pay for It, 2004; contbr. articles to profl. jours., including Am. Econ. Rev., Quar. Jour. Econs., Jour. Pub. Econs. Presenter testimony U.S. Congress, Washington, 1996-2000, mem. Nat. Bd. for Ednl. Scis. Carnegie Corp. scholar, 2000, Alfred P. Sloan Found. fellow in econs., 1999, John M. Olin Found. fellow in econs., 1998, Rhodes scholar, 1988; recipient Nat. Tas Assn. Dissertation award, 1988, Thomas B. Fordham Prize for Disting. Scholarship in Edn., 2006. Mem. Am. Econs. Assn. Office: Stanford U Dept Econs Landau Econs Bldg 579 Serra Mall Stanford CA 94305-6072 Office Phone: 650-725-3266.*

HOXIE, FREDERICK EUGENE, history professor; b. Hoolehua, Hawaii, Apr. 22, 1947; s. John Wadman and Catherine (Agee) H.; m. Elizabeth Anne Schroder, July 11, 1970 (dec. Dec. 1983); children: Silas, Charles; m. Holly Frances Hanscom, Jan. 3, 1986; stepchildren: Stephen Hoskins, Philip Hoskins. BA, Amherst Coll., 1969, PhD in Humane Letters (hon.), 1994; MA, Brandeis U., 1976, PhD, 1977; PhD in Humane Letters (hon.), L.I. U., 2000. Tchr. Phila. Pub. Schs., 1969-70; high sch. tchr. Punahou Sch., Honolulu, 1970-72; asst. prof. Antioch Coll., Yellow Springs, Ohio, 1977-82, assoc. prof., 1982-83; dir. D'Arcy McNickle Ctr. for Am. Indian History, Newberry Libr., Chgo., 1983-94, v.p. rsch. and edn., 1994-98; Swanlund prof. history U. Ill., Urbana, 1998—. Cons. Cheyenne River Sioux Tribe, Eagle Butte, S.D., 1977-78, U.S. Senate

Com. on Indian Affairs, Washington, 1989-90, Little Big Horn Coll., Crow Agency, Mt., 1990-98, Nat. Park Svc., Denver Support Ctr., 1997-98, Dept. of Justice, 2000-01, 04—. Author: A Final Promise, 1984, 2d edit., 2001, Parading Through History, 1995; co-author: The People: A History of Native America, 2007; editor: Indians in American History, 1988, 2d edit., 1997, Ency. of North American Indians, 1996, Talking Back to Civilization, 2001, Lewis and Clark and the Indian Country, 2007. Bd. dirs. Ill. Humanities Coun., Chgo., 1997-2003; trustee Nat. Mus. Am. Indian, Smithsonian, 1990-95, 2007—, Amherst Coll., 2001—07. Humanities fellow Rockefeller Found., 1984-85, fellow NEH, 1990-91, 2007—, fellow Mellon Found., 2005. Mem. Am. Hist. Assn. (program chmn. 1992), Am. Soc. for Ethnohistory (pres. 1995-96), Orgn. Am. Historians (exec. bd. 1997-2000). Avocations: running, tennis. Office: U Ill Dept History 309 Gregory Hall 810 S Wright St Urbana IL 61801-3644 E-mail: hoxie@uicu.edu.

HOXIE, JOEL P., lawyer; b. Waterloo, Iowa, Dec. 4, 1948; s. Wirt Pierce and Jeanne (Ogle) H.; m. Cynthia Ann Mast, Aug. 12, 1978; children: Robert Lewis, Laura Ann. AB, Princeton U., 1971; JD, U. Iowa, 1978. Atty. Snell & Wilmer, Phoenix, 1978—. Trustee Heard Mus., Phoenix, 1990-2004, pres. 1995-97, life trustee 2005; pres. Princeton Alumni Assn. No. Ariz., Phoenix, 1990-2003. Lt. USN, 1971-75. Mem. Nat. Bar Assn., Ariz. State Bar Assn., County Bar Assn., Securities Industry Assn. (legal and compliance divsn. 1992—), Phoenix Country Club (bd. dirs. 2001—, pres. 2006—). Methodist. Avocations: golf, tennis, swimming, hiking. Home: 5301 E Mariposa St Phoenix AZ 85018-3029 Office: Snell & Wilmer 1 Arizona Ctr Phoenix AZ 85004 Home Phone: 602-840-7752; Office Phone: 602-382-6264. Business E-Mail: jhoxie@swlaw.com.

HOXTER, CURTIS JOSEPH, international economic advisor, public relations executive, communications executive; b. July 20, 1922; s. Jacob and Hanna (Katzenstein) Hoxter; m. Grace Lewis, Feb. 4, 1945 (dec.); children: Ronald Alan, Victoria Ann, Audrey Theresa(dec.); m. Allegra Branson, Jan. 2, 1981. AB, NYU, 1948, MA, 1950. Staff contbr. AUFBAU-Reconstn., NYC, 1939-40; feature writer, reporter LI Daily Press, NY, 1940-42; editor, writer, analyst Office War Info., NYC, 1943-45; pub. info. officer Dept. State, 1945-47; dir. pub. rels. Internat. C. of C., 1948-53; info. cons. (Marshall Plan) Econ. Cooperation Adminstrn., Washington, 1950-55; exec. v.p. George Peabody and Assocs., Inc., 1953-56; pvt. practice, 1956—. Pub. rels. cons. various cos., fin. instns. and govt. agys.; columnist Scripps-Howard Newspapers; adviser U.S. Com. for UN Day; editl. advisor Internat. Economy mag.; advisor on internat. econ. and fin. problems to global agys., US Del. Disarmament Conf., London; mem. internat. adv. bd. Bus. Week Chief Exec. Roundtable; exec. dir. adv. com. to Chancellor of Austria; mem. adv. com. Grad. Sch. Internat. Rels., U. Calif., San Diego; sr. advisor to pres. European Commn. Contbr. and commentator articles to nat. jours. and newspapers. With AUS, WWII. Decorated Grand Cross of Merit Govt. of Austria, 1991, Grand Cross of Merit Govt. of Germany, 2003. Mem. Met. Club (NYC), Econ. Club NY, Leewood Country Club, Coral Beach and Tennis Club (Bermuda), Univ. Club (Washington). Office: 380 Lexington Ave New York NY 10168-0002 Home Phone: 914-636-3870; Office Phone: 212-818-0303. Business E-Mail: hoxter.inc@verizon.net.

HOY, CASEY WILLIAM, ecologist, educator; b. Berea, Ohio, Jan. 11, 1954; s. George A. and Catherine Reedy Hoy; m. Karen Ann Skubik, May 22, 1982; children: Briana Susan Hoy-Skubik, Sean Lawrence Hoy-Skubik. BS, Cornell U., Ithaca, NY, 1981, PhD, 1987. Self-employed blacksmith, Ohio, 1973—77; self-employed ipm cons. Geneva, NY, 1981—85; prof. Ohio State U., Agrl. R & D Ctr., Wooster, Ohio, 1987—2006, Kellogg endowed chair in agrl. ecosys. mgmt., 2006—. Office: Ohio State Univ Agrl Rsch and Devel Ctr 1680 Madison Ave Wooster OH 44691 Office Phone: 330-263-3611. Office Fax: 330-263-3686. Business E-Mail: hoy.1@osu.edu.

HOY, DAWN RISKE, musician, director; b. Wausau, Wis., Feb. 13, 1957; d. Robert George Riske and Mildred Minnie Hetzel; children: Martin Charles, Philip Robert, Katherine Elizabeth. BA in Music and Theology, Valparaiso U., Ind., 1980; MA in Pastoral Studies, Aquinas Inst. Theology, St. Louis, 2001. Cert. consecrated deaconess Luth. Deaconess Assn., 1980. Deaconess of music & youth St. Mark Luth. Ch., Wausau, Wis., 1988—93; min. music St. Helen Ch., Dayton, Ohio, 1993—99; dir. music ministries St. Joan Arc Ch., St. Louis, 2001—. Dir. Miami Valley Ch. Musicians, Dayton, 1994—98; pres. Luth. Deaconess Conf., Valparaiso, Ind., 2000—06. Composer: (musical anthem) You Will Not Be Left Alone. Leader Girl Scout Troop 3625, St. Louis, 2000—06. Grantee Siebert Found. grant, Luth. Deaconess Convocation, 2005. Mem.: Nat. Pastoral Musicians, Am. Guild Organists. Luth. Avocation: walking. Home: 8514 Rosemary Ave Saint Louis MO 63123 Office: St Joan Arc Ch 5800 Oleatha Saint Louis MO 63123 Home Phone: 314-397-2651; Office Phone: 314-832-2838. E-mail: riskehoy@aol.com.

HOY, GEORGE PHILIP, clergyman, county official, state legislator; b. Indpls., Feb. 5, 1937; s. Clarence Augustus Hoy and Margaret Louise (Etter) Wooley; m. Barbara J. Turpen, Aug. 11, 1957 (dec. Feb. 1987); 1 foster child, Richard H. Johnson children: Rene Hoy Riegle, Sherri Hoy Haas, Matthew Philip; m. Sandra L. Knipe, July 30, 1999; stepchildren: Wendy Knipe Bredhold, Benjamin Knipe. BA, Ky. Wesleyan Coll., 1958; MDiv, So. Bapt. Theol. Sem., 1962. Ordained to ministry United Ch. of Christ, 1962, Nat. Bapt. Conv. 1997. Pastor Union United Ch. of Christ, Evansville, Ind., 1962—72, Faith United Ch. of Christ, Ft. Wayne, Ind., 1975—80, St. Matthew's United Ch. of Christ, Evansville, 1981—87; dir. Youth Svc. Bur., Evansville, 1972—75; pastor St. Peter's United Ch. of Christ, Evansville, 1987—94; interim pastor Zion United Ch. of Christ, Henderson, Ky., 2003; mem. Ind. Ho. of Reps., 2004—, chmn. cts. and criminal code. Faculty Brescia U., Owensboro, Ky., 1970-72; chaplain Evansville State Hosp., 1966-72, Fraternal Order Police, Evansville, 1982-92, chaplain, life mem.; dir. Tri-State Food Bank, Evansville, 1987-2000; del. gen. synod Ind.-Ky. Conf., United Ch. of Christ, 1978-81; bd. dirs. Vanderburgh County Cmty. Corrections.; bd. dirs., fin. chmn. Pigeon Creek Greenway. Religion columnist Evansville Press, 1983-93. Vol. Habitat for Humanity, Americus, Ga., 1980-81; active City-County Human Rels. Commn., Evansville, 1984-93; bd. dirs. Leadership Evansville, 1987-92, Outreach Ministries, Evansville, 1987-93; regional bd. adv. Ch. World Svc., 1987-2002; mem. Bread for the World, Amnesty Internat., Police Athletic League; active Vanderburgh County Coun., 1992-2004, pres., 1994-95, v.p., 1997; property tax adjustment bd. appeals Vanderburgh County Soil and Water Conservation Dist.; chair fin. Pigeon Creek Greenway; chmn. hunger walk CROP; bd. dirs. Sustainable Cmtys. Coalition, Matthew 25 AIDS Svcs., Ark. Crisis Nursery; pres. Evansville Area Cmty. Chs.; city county data bd., preservation com., Old Liberty Bapt. Ch.; property tax replacement study commn. State of Ind.; chaplain Ctrl. Labor Coun. AFL/CIO; mem. Coalition of Inner City Neighborhoods; mem. com. Tri-State Alliance Christmas Project; mem. Hunger Task Force. Recipient Doing The Right Thing award, Evansville Psychiat. Children's Ctr., 2002, ecumenical award Evansville Area Coun. of Chs., 1987, Native Am. award Coun. of Bear, Evansville, 1988, Individual Achievement award Leadership Evansville, 1998, Martin Luther King Jr. Cmty. Svc. award Black Leadership Conf., 2000, Starfish award Tri-State Food Bank, 2000, award for outstanding svc. to foster parents, Sagamore of the Wabash award, 2000, Coalition of Inner City Neighborhoods Quality of Life award, Humanitarian award, 2006, Peace with Justice award Zion U.C.C., 2006, Mark Trail award NOAA, 2007, Mishler Lifetime Svc. award Ind.-Ky. Ch. World Svc., others; named Legislator of Yr., Ind. divsn. Isaak Walton League, 2005; named to CROP Honor Roll, 1997, Hon. Order Ky. Cols., Hall of Fame, Ctrl. H.S., 2001. Mem. NASW (Ind. Region 8 Citizen Yr. award 2007, Ind. State chpt. Citizen of Yr. award 2007), NAACP, ACLU, Internat. Brotherhood Magicians, Ind. Psychol. Assn., Tri-State Pastors Circle (pres. 1984-85), Northside Ministerial Assn., Downtown Ministerial Assn., Evansville Tri-State Assn. (pres. 1972-75), Silent Singers (hon.), Henderson Ministerial Assn., Tri-State Alliance Christmas Project Com., SW Ind. Psychol. Assn. Democrat. Avocations: music, art, drama, dance performing, model railroading. Home: 217 Cherry St Evansville IN 47713-1242 Office Phone: 812-437-9295. Personal E-mail: revgph@aol.com. Business E-Mail: h77@in.gov.

HOY, MARJORIE ANN, entomology educator; b. Kansas City, Kans., May 19, 1941; d. Dayton J. and Marjorie Jean (Acker) Wolf; m. James B. Hoy; 1 child, Benjamin Lee AB, U. Kans., 1963; MS, U. Calif., Berkeley, 1966, PhD, 1972. Asst. entomologist Conn. Agrl. Expt. Sta., New Haven, 1973-75; rsch. entomologist U.S. Forest Svc., Hamden, Conn., 1975-76; asst. prof. entomology U. Calif., Berkeley, 1976-80, assoc. prof. entomology, 1980-82, prof. entomology, 1982-92, prof. emeritus, 1992—; Fischer, Davies and Eckes prof., dept. entomology and nematology U. Fla., Gainesville, 1992—; chmn. Calif. Gypsy Moth Sci. Adv. Panel, 1982—; mem. genetics resources adv. com. USDA, 1992—, mem. adv. com. agrl. biotech., 2000—02; mem. com. on biol. threats to agrl. plants and animals NRC and NAS, 2001—02. Chmn. Calif. Gypsy Moth Sci. Adv. Panel, 1982—; mem. genetics resources adv. com. USDA, 1992—, mem. adv. com. agrl. biotech., 2000—01; F.E. Guyton disting. lectr. Auburn (Ala.) U., 1997; mem. com. on biol. threats to agrl. plants and animals NRC and NAS, 2001—02; sci. cons. transgenic insects Pew Initiative Food and Biotech. Editor, co-editor: Genetics in Relation to Insect Managment, 1979, Recent Advances in Knowledge of the Phytoseiidae, 1982, Biological Control of Pests by Mites, 1983, Biological Control in Agricultural IPM Systems, 1985, Insect Molecular Genetics, 1994, 2d edit., 2003, The Phytoseiidae as Biological Control Agents of Pest Mites and Insects: A Bibliography, 1996, Managing the Citrus Leafminer, 1996; mem. editl. bd. Internat. Jour. Pest Mgmt., Biol. Control, Biocontrol Sci. and Tech., Environ. Biosafety Rsch.; contbr. articles to profl. jours. Mem. Sec. Agr.'s adv. com. agrl. biotech.; cons. Pew Charitable Trust. Recipient citation for outstanding achievments in regulatory entomology Fla. Divsn. Plant Industry, 1995, USDA honor award Sec. of Agr., 1996, award for sci. Nat. Agri-Mktg. Assn., 1998, sr. faculty award U. Fla. chpt. Gamma Sigma Delta, 1998, Biol. Control Scientist of Yr., Internat. Orgn. Biol. Control, 2004. Fellow AAAS, Royal Entomol. Soc. London, Entomol. Soc. Am. (mem. Pacific br. governing bd. 1985, Bussart award 1986, Founder's Meml. award 1992), Coun. Agr. Sci. and Tech. (Charles Black award 2004); mem. Nat. Acad. Scis. (com. on biol. threats to agr. plants and animals), NY Acad. Scis., Am. Genetic Assn., Internat. Orgn. Biol. Control (v.p. 1984-85, Disting. Scientist award 2004), Am. Inst. Biol. Scis. (adv. coun. 1996-98, governing bd. 1999-2001), Acarological Soc. Am. (governing bd. 1980-84, pres. 1992), Soc. for Study of Evolution, Fla. Entomological Soc. (Team Rsch. award 1997, Outstanding Tchg. award 1999), Phi Beta Kappa, Sigma Xi (chpt. sec. 1979-81, Sr. Faculty Rsch. award 1996). Avocations: hiking, gardening, snorkeling. Home: 4320 SW 83rd Way Gainesville FL 32608-4131 Office: U Fla Dept Entomology and Nematology PO Box 110620 Gainesville FL 32611-0620 Home Phone: 352-335-7839; Office Phone: 352-392-1901. Business E-Mail: mahoy@ifas.ufl.edu.

HOY, RONALD RAYMOND, neurobiology educator; b. Walla Walla, Wash., Jan. 12, 1939; s. Edward and Alice (Howe) H.; m. Margaret Christina Nelson, June 1, 1980; 1 child, Timothy. BS in Zoology, Wash. State U., 1962; PhD in Biology, Stanford U., 1968. Dir. neural systems and behavior course Marine Biol. Lab., Woods Hole, Mass., 1979-84, dir. Grass fellowship program, 1988-90; prof. neurobiology and behavior to David & Dorothy Merksamer Prof. Biology Cornell U., Ithaca, NY, 1986—, chmn. dept., 1988-91. Trustee The Grass Found., 1985-88, 90—. Recipient Jacob Javits Award, Nat. Inst. Neurol. & Communication Diseases and Stroke, 1986; grantee professorship, Howard Hughes Med. Inst., 2002—. Fellow: AAAS; mem.: NIDCD (study sect. 1991—95, Exec. Coun.), Sigma Xi, Phi Beta Kappa. Office: Cornell U Sect Neurobiology and Behavior S G Mudd Hall Ithaca NY 14853 Office Phone: 607-254-4318, 607-254-4317. Office Fax: 607-254-4308. E-mail: rrh3@cornell.edu.

HOYE, J.D., foundation administrator; Youth employment counselor, Corvallis, Oreg.; assoc. supt. Oreg. Dept. Edn.; head Office of School-to-Work, Washington, 1994—98; pres., founder Keep the Change, Inc., 1998—2007; pres. Nat. Acad. Found., 2007—. Spkr. in field. Office: Nat Acad Found 39 Broadway Ste 1640 New York NY 10006 Office Phone: 212-635-2400.*

HOYE, ROBERT EARL, systems science educator; b. Warwick, RI, Jan. 12, 1931; s. S. Earl and Alice (Landry) H.; m. Patricia Buswell, Aug. 20, 1955 (dec. May 22, 2002); children: Robert Earl Jr., Joanne D., Peter M., Kathleen B. BA, Providence Coll., 1953; MS, St. John's U., NYC, 1955; PhD, U. Wis., Madison, 1973. Instr. St. John's U., 1953-55; dir. guidance Middleboro (Mass.) Pub. Schs., 1955-56, Rutland (Vt.) Pub. Schs., 1956-57; dean Champlain (Vt.) Coll., 1957-58; supt. Frontier Regional Sch. Dist., Deerfield, Mass., 1958-60; New Eng. dir. Sci. Rsch. Assocs. subs. IBM, Chgo., 1960-65; nat. dir. Learning Systems div. Xerox Corp., NYC, 1965-66; dir. Instrnl. Media Lab. U. Wis., Milw., 1966-73; asst. v.p. U. Louisville, 1974-81, prof. cmty. health Sch. Medicine, 1981-92, prof. urban policy, coord. grad. program in health systems, 1981-95, prof. edn., 1992-95, prof. emeritus, 1995—. Cons. to mgmt., Louisville, 1966—; mem. faculty health svcs. Walden U., 1988—; vis. prof. exec. leadership U. Sarasota, 1995-2001 Author: Index to Computer Based Learning, 1973; co-author: Home Health, 1996; editor Edn. Jour., 1968-73; also articles. Recipient cert. of merit San Diego State U., 1983, Grad. Teaching Excellence award U. Louisville, 1984, gold medal Project Innovation, 1984, Outstanding Faculty Mem. award Walden U., 2000. Fellow Am. Acad. Med. Adminstrs. (diplomate, chmn. editl. bd. 1986-94, dir. Ky. chpt. 2006—), Royal Soc. Health (Statesman in Healthcare Adminstrn. award 1992). Democrat. Roman Catholic.

HOYER, STENY HAMILTON, congressman; b. NYC, June 14, 1939; s. Steen T. and Jean Baldwin (Slade) H.; m. Judith Elaine Pickett, June 17, 1961 (dec. Feb. 1997); children: Susan, Stefany, Anne. BS in Polit. Sci., U. Md., 1963; LLB, Georgetown U., 1966. Bar: Md. 1966. Exec. asst. to Senator Daniel B. Brewster US Senate, 1962-66; assoc. Haislip & Yewell, Marlow Heights, Md., 1966-69, Hoyer & Fannon, District Heights, Md., 1969-81; pvt. law practice, 1981-89; mem. US Congress from 5th Md. dist., 1981—; minority whip, 2002—07; majority leader, 2007—; co-chmn. House Dem. steering com., 1989-94; ranking mem. Commn. on Security and Coop. in Europe; ranking mem. HAC. Mem. Md. Senate, 1966-79, pres., 1975-79, chmn. Prince George's County del., mem. fin., joint budget and audit coms., 1968, chmn. joint commn. on intergovtl. cooperation, 197l. Mem. Md. Bd. Higher Edn., 1979-81; mem. Balt. Council Fgn. Relations; bd. visitors U. Md. Sch. Pub. Affairs Named State Official of Yr., Md. Mcpl. League, 1971, Washingtonian of Yr., Washington mag., 1988, Champion of Pediatric Rsch., Children's Nat. Med. Ctr., 1995; named an Outstanding Young man, Md. Jaycees, 1975; recipient Excellence in Pub. Svc. award, Am. Acad. Pediatrics, 1991, Pub. Svc. award, Am. Assn. Pub. Health Dentistry, 1997, Jack Niles Medal of Honor, Pub. Employees Roundtable, 1999, Excellence in Immunization award, Nat. Partnership for Immunization, 2001, Freedom award, Nat. Assn. Secretaries of State, 2003, Leadership award, Nat. Org. on Fetal Alcohol Syndrome, 2005. Mem. U. Md. Alumni Assn. (trustee), Phi Sigma Alpha, Omicron Delta Kappa, Delta Theta Phi, Sigma Chi. Democrat. Baptist. Office: US Ho Reps 1705 Longworth Ho Office Bldg Washington DC 20515-2005*

HOYLE, SHETINA YEVETTE, librarian; b. Jackson, Tenn., Sept. 21, 1969; d. Alecia Yevette Brown; 1 child, Brandon. BFA, Lambuth U., 1991. Tchr. aide Lambuth Presch., Jackson, 1988—89; sales assoc. Goldsmith's, Jackson, 1988—89; customer svc. rep. Bancorp South, Jackson, 1991—97; libr. Jackson Madison County Libr., Jackson, 1997—. Ch. musician First Bapt. Ch., Jackson, 1989—. Mem.: Jaycees, Delta Sigma Theta. Baptist. Avocations: reading, crafts, piano, aerobics. Home: 1005 N Royal St Jackson TN 38301 Office: Jackson Madison County Libr 433 E Lafayette St Jackson TN 38301 Office Phone: 731-425-8600. Personal E-mail: syhoyle@earthlink.net.

HOYNES, LOUIS LENOIR, JR., lawyer; b. Indpls., Sept. 23, 1935; s. Louis L. and Catharine (Parker) H.; m. Judith E. Kass, Oct. 12, 1958 (div. 1979); children: Thomas M., William D., Ellen B.; m. Virginia Devin, Dec. 9, 1979. AB, Columbia U., 1957; JD cum laude, Harvard U., 1962. Bar: NY 1963, US Supreme Ct. 1967, US Dist. Ct. (so. dist.) NY, US Ct. Appeals (2d, 7th and 9th cirs.). Assoc. Willkie Farr & Gallagher, NYC, 1962-68, ptnr., 1969-90; counsel Nat. League Profl. Baseball Clubs, 1970-90; sr. v.p., gen. counsel Wyeth (formerly) Am. Home Products Corp., 1990-2000; exec. v.p. gen. counsel Am. Home Products Corp. (now Wyeth), 2000—03. Lectr. law Columbia U., N.Y.C., 1982-91; bd. dirs. Cytec Industries Inc., 1994-, US C. of C. Inst. for Legal Reform, 2002-07; trustee Food and Drug Law Inst., 1994-2002. Served to lt. USNR, 1957-59, PTO. Mem. ABA, N.Y. State Bar Assn., Assn. of City of Bar of N.Y., The Assn. Gen. Counsel. Home: 47 Cornwells Beach Rd Sands Point NY 11050-1305

HOYT, CLARK FREELAND, editor, journalist; b. Providence, Nov. 20, 1942; s. Charles Freeland and Maude Leslie (King) H.; m. Jane Ann Hauser, Sept. 30, 1967 (div. Jan. 1978); m. Linda Kauss, Aug. 22, 1988. AB, Columbia U., 1964. Research asst. to U.S. Senator, Washington, 1964-66; reporter Lakeland (Fla.) Ledger, 1966-68; politics writer Detroit Free Press, 1968-70; Washington corr. Miami Herald, 1970-73; nat. corr. Knight Newspapers, Washington, 1973-75, news editor Washington bur., 1975-77; bus. editor Detroit Free Press, 1977-79, conv. editor, 1979-80, asst. to exec. editor, 1980-81; mng. editor Wichita Eagle-Beacon, Kans., 1981-85; news editor Washington Bur., Knight-Ridder Newspapers, 1985-87, bur. chief, 1987-93, v.p. news, 1993-99, Washington editor, 1999—2006; cons. The McClatchy Co., Reston, Va., 2006—07; pub. editor NY Times, 2007—. Recipient Pulitzer prize nat. reporting, 1973. Mem. Nat. Press Club (fin. sec., bd. govs. 1975), Gridiron Club. Office: NY Times 620 8th Ave New York NY 10036 Office Phone: 703-390-1331. Business E-Mail: choyt@earthlink.net.

HOYT, COLEMAN WILLIAMS, postal consultant; b. NYC, Nov. 11, 1925; s. Colgate and Muriel (Williams) H.; m. Cecilia Lucia Guarana, Oct. 21, 1972; children: Coleman Williams, Andrew Erskine, Stephen Tecumseh. B of Naval Sci., Tufts U., 1945; BS, Yale U., 1948. With Reader's Digest Assn., Pleasantville, NY, 1948-87, mgr. book prodn., 1950-61, mgr. book subscription svc., 1961-63, mgr. subscription svc. RCA Victor Record Club, 1963-65, mgr. corp. distbn., 1965-76, v.p., dir. distbn., 1976-87; pvt. practice cons. Woodstock, Vt., 1987—. Mem. Postmaster Gen.'s Mailers Tech. Adv. Com., 1968—, chmn., 1971-73. Pub. mem. USIA inspection team, Lebanon, 1971; nat. trustee Outward Bound, Inc., 1972-88; trustee Vt. Land Trust, 1988-93, vice chmn., 1989-92. Ensign USNR, 1943-46. Recipient Disting. Svc. award U.S. Postal Svc., 1973, Donald Mumma award Graphics Comm. Assn., 1987, Miles Kimball award Mail Advt. Svc. Assn., 1987. Mem. Mag. Pubs. Assn. (chmn. postal com. 1974-80), Direct Mktg. Assn. (bd. dirs. 1973-79, chmn. govt. affairs com. 1983-86), Pub. Mems. Assn. of Fgn. Svc., Assn. Postal Commerce (bd. dirs. 1982—, Lifetime Achievement award 2006), Continuity Shippers Assn. (exec. dir. 1997—), Yale Club of N.Y., Squadron A Club, Lakota Club. Republican. Episcopalian. Home and Office: Saddlebow Farm 2351 N Bridgewater Rd Woodstock VT 05091-9670

HOYT, CREIG SIMMONS, ophthalmologist, educator; b. Pitts., Mar. 3, 1942; s. Creig Sieplein and Ruth Edice Hoyt; m. Deborah Frase, Sept. 5, 1999. BA, Amherst Coll., Mass., 1964; MD, Cornell U., NYC, 1968. Cert. ophthalmologist Am. Bd. Ophthalmology, 1977. Prof., chmn., dept. ophthalmology U. Calif., San Francisco, 1977—2006; scholar-in-residence Smith-Kettlewell Eye Rsch. Inst., San Francisco, 2006—. Bd. mem. That Man May See, San Francisco, 1999—2007. Editor: (med. jour.) British Jour. Ophthalmology (Doyne medal, 2004). Funding new musical compositions Kronos Quartet, San Francisco, 2005—07. Lt. comdr. USN, 1970—73, San Diego. Achievements include research in early surgery for congenital cataracts. Avocations: rug weaving, swimming, kayaking. Home: PO Box 1517 Gualala CA 95445-1517 Office: Univ Calif K301 16 Kirkham Beckman Vision Ctr San Francisco CA 94143 Personal E-mail: dfrase@mcn.org. Business E-Mail: choyt@itsa.ucsf.edu.

HOYT, DAVID A., bank executive; Loan officer Union Bank, Calif.; vice chair real estate, capital markets, internat. Wells Fargo & Co., 1997—98, group exec. v.p. wholesale banking, 1998—. Mem. finl svcs. roundtable, mem. adv. coun. U. So. Calif. Lust Ctr. Real Estate. Mem.: Urban Land Inst. Office: Wells Fargo & Co 420 Montgomery St San Francisco CA 94163*

HOYT, EARL EDWARD, JR., industrial designer; b. Binghamton, NY, July 16, 1936; s. Earl Edward and Lea (LaRue) H.; m. Bernice Phillips Maseritz, Aug. 20, 1960; children: Earl Edward III, Justin Phillips. B with honors in Indsl. Design, Pratt Inst., 1960. Designer Donald Deskey Assocs., NYC, 1960-65; pres. The Hoyt Group, 1965—. Instr. Sch. Visual Arts, N.Y.C., Pratt Inst., Rutgers Sch. Package Engring.; lectr. in field. Served with U.S. Army, 1954-56. Recipient awards archtl. design concept Am. Inst. Architects, 1964, Package Yr. Package Design Mag., 1970, Grand/Excellence in Design and Quality Soc. Plastic Industy, 1972, design Am. Inst. Graphic Artists Competition, 1st prize splty. design innovation-1st prize household products-1st prize communication excellence N.J. chpt. Packaging Inst. USA, 1979, package yr. Food and Drug Packaging Mag., 1978, 80, Jupiter Engring. excellence in design Western Plastics Exposition, 1980, package design excellence Clio, 1978, 81, 87, outstanding packaging achievement NJ Packaging Execs. Club, 1982-83, 86 (best of show/package yr.). Mem. Indsl. Designers Soc. Am. Republican. Achievements include patents in field. Avocations: painting, skiing, fishing, outdoor activities, guitar. Home: 5 Gathering Rd Sussex NJ 07461 Office: The Hoyt Group 5 Gathering Rd Sussex NJ 07461 Fax: 973-702-7063. Business E-Mail: hoytgrup@ptd.net.

HOYT, ERICH, conservationist, writer, researcher; s. Robert Emmet Hoyt and Betty Jane Shutrump; m. Sarah Elizabeth Wedden, Mar. 4, 1989; children: Moses Erich, Magdalen Marisa, Jasmine Elizabeth, Max Jeffrey Emmet. Freelance writer, rschr., Vancouver, Montreal, Boston, Edinburgh, 1975—; contbg. editor Equinox, Toronto, Ontario, Canada, 1982—94; sr. rsch., conservation assoc. Whale & Dolphin Conservation Soc., Chippenham, England, 2000—04, sr. rsch. fellow, 2004—. Vis. lectr. MIT, Cambridge, Mass., 1986—88, Ohio State U., Columbus, 1992, 2000; cons., designer Krent Paffett Assocs., Boston, 1986—90; cons. Internat. Plant Genetic Resources Inst., Rome, 1987, World Wildlife Fund Internat., Gland, Switzerland, 1987—92, Whale & Dolphin Conservation Soc., Bath, 1989—2000, Australian Nature Conservation Agy., Canberra, 1995, Internat. Fund Animal Welfare, East Falmouth, Mass., 1995—2000, Jason Found. Edn., Boston, 2002—03, Humane Soc. Internat., DC, 2005—06; co-dir. Far East Russia Orca Project, Petropavlovsk-Kamchatskiy, Russia, 1999—; invited expert ACCOBAMS, Monaco, 2004—; mem. IUCN Species Survival Commn. Cetacean Specialist Grp., Gland, Switzerland, 2006—; dir. marine mammals marinebio.org, Houston, 2006—. Rschr.

(academic book) Whale Watching: Worldwide Tourism Numbers, Expenditures, and Expanding Socioeconomic Benefits, 2001; author: Marine Protected Areas for Whales, Dolphins and Porpoises, (children's books) Meeting the Whales, Riding with the Dolphins, Extinction A-Z, Whale Rescue, (nonfiction books) Seasons of the Whale (Can. Outdoor Writing Best Book award, 1991), The Whale Watcher's Handbook, Orca: The Whale Called Killer, Creatures of the Deep (Outstanding Book of Yr. award, ASJA, Inc., 2002), Whales & Dolphins: The Ultimate Guide to Marine Mammals, The Earth Dwellers: Adventures in the Land of Ants (One of 25 Best Fiction & Nonfiction Books to Remember, NY Pub. Libr. Assn., 1996), (technical book) Conserving the Wild Relatives of Crops; composer: (films) The Keeper; contbg. rschr., writer, co-designer (exhibitions) How Plants Become Food, NY Botanical Garden, 1987, Rain Forest Story, Mo. Botanical Garden, 1988, scriptwriter (feature documentary film) Death Cannot Conquer, 2003; scriptwriter: (plays, feature documentary film) Cry From The Deep, 2007; author (co-editor): (anthology) Insect Lives: Stories of Mystery & Romance from a Hidden World; contbr., editor (over 450 articles to jours.). Co-organizer, mem. steering com. Internat. Fund Animal Welfare, East Falmouth, Mass., 1995—98. Finalist Wildlife award, BBC Wildlife Mag., 1988, 1992, Sci. in Soc. Book award, Can. Sci. Writers Assn., 1997, Best Book of Yr. award, Good Book Guide, 1998; recipient Environment Can. prize, Govt. Can., 1986, James Thurber Writer-in-Residence award, Thurber Ho., 1992, 2000. Mem.: Authors and Artists Conservation, Soc. Authors, European Cetacean Soc., Soc. Marine Mammalogy, Assn. Brit. Sci. Writers, Writers' Guild Gt. Britain, Am. Soc. Journalists and Authors, Inc. Achievements include research in wild killer whales in Russian waters; worldwide socioeconomics of whale watching and marine ecotourism; synthesis of whale critical habitat research with marine protected areas. Avocations: gardening, baseball, music. Personal E-mail: info@erichhoyt.com.

HOYT, HERBERT AUSTIN AIKINS, television producer; b. Buffalo, June 20, 1937; s. John Davidson Hill and Amie Dean (Aikins) Hoyt. BA, Yale Univ., 1959. Reporter Niagara Falls Gazette, NY, 1963-64; prodr., exec. prodr. WGBH Ednl. Found., Boston, 1965—2003; with Austin Hoyt Prodns., 2003—. Prodr. TV programs including The Advocates, 1969-74; Enterprise: The Wildcatter, 1981; Vietnam: A Television History, Tet 1968; L.B.J. Goes to War, 1964-65, (Emmy, Writers Guild Am. awards 1983); Reagan's New Federalism: Shift or Shaft?, 1983; The Nuclear Age, 1989; exec. prodr. Zoom, 1974-75; In Search of the Real America, 1975-78; Frontline Spl. Report: Crisis in Central America, 1985 (Peabody award), Mexico, 1988; Korea: The Unknown War, 1990; Am. Experience: Eisenhower, 1993 (Peabody award), The Windsors, 1994, 2002, The Churchills, 1996, 2003; American Experience: Carnegie, The Richest Man in the World, 1997, Reagan, 1998 (Peabody award), MacArthur, 1999 (Emmy award), PBS Millennium, 2000, American Experience: Chgo. City of the Century, 2003, Victory in the Pacific, 2005. Mem.: Somerset Club (Boston), Yale Club (N.Y.C.). Home: 11 Wright St #3 Cambridge MA 02138 Office: 90 Windom St #5 Boston MA 02134 Office Phone: 617-787-9990. Personal E-mail: austinhoyt@fastmail.fm.

HOYT, JAMES LAWRENCE, journalism educator, writer; b. Wausau, Wis., July 18, 1943; s. Lawrence Beryl and Eleanor (Kischel) H.; m. Cheryl Johannes, July 23, 1966; children: Randall James, Rebecca Cheryl, Diane Caroline. BS, U. Wis., 1965, MS, 1967, PhD, 1970; postgrad., U. Pa., 1967-68. Reporter Sta. WTMJ-TV, Milw., 1965-67; prof. journalism Ind. U., Bloomington, 1970-73; writer, editor NBC News, Washington, 1972; prof. journalism U. Wis., Madison, 1973—; dir. U. Wis. Sch. Journalism, Madison, 1981-91. Chmn. athletic bd., faculty rep. NACC Big Ten Conf. Western Collegiate Hockey Assn., U. Wis., Madison, 1991-2001. Author: Mass Media in Perspective, 1984, Writing News for Broadcast, 1994; contbr. articles to profl. jours. Named to Wis. Broadcasters Hall of Fame, 2007; recipient Carol Brewer award, Wis. AP, 1996. Mem. Assn. for Edn. in Journalism and Mass Comm. (Disting. Broadcast Educator 2002), Radio-TV News Dirs. Assn., Broadcast Edn. Assn., Internat. Radio-TV Soc. (Frank Stanton fellow 2001). Methodist. Avocation: tuba. Home: 4709 Fond Du Lac Trl Madison WI 53705-4812 Office: U Wis Sch Journalism 821 University Ave Madison WI 53706-1412 Office Phone: 608-238-1389. Business E-Mail: jlhoyt@wisc.edu.

HOYT, JOHN ARTHUR, cultural organization administrator, minister; b. Marietta, Ohio, Mar. 30, 1932; s. Claremont Earl and Margaret Adeline (Hawkins) H.; m. Gertrude Ellen Mohnkern, June 7, 1957; children: Margaret Rose, Karen Elizabeth, Anne Christine, Julie Kay. BA, Rio Grande Coll., 1954, DD, 1968; MDiv, Colgate Rochester Div. Sch., 1958; Dr honoris causa, U. Bucharest, Romania, 1995; LHD (hon.), St. Thomas U., Miami, Fla., 1998, U. St. Petersburg, Russia, 1997. Ordained to ministry Baptist Ch., 1957; pastor Allen Park (Mich.) Bapt. Ch., 1958-60, First Presbyn. Ch., Leroy, NY, 1960-64; sr. minister Drayton Ave. Presbyn. Ch., Ferndale, Mich., 1964-68, First Presbyn. Ch., Fort Wayne, Ind., 1968-70; pres. Humane Soc. U.S., Washington, 1970-91, chief exec., 1992-97; pres. emeritus, 1997—; pres. Humane Soc. Internat., Washington, 1991—97; pres., dir. Humane Soc. of Can., Toronto, 1994-98; vice chmn. bd. dirs. EarthKind Internat., Washington, London, 1991-98; pres. Earthkind, U.S., Washington, 1994-97. Author: Animals in Peril: How "Sustainable Use" is Wiping Out the World's Wildlife, 1994. Pres. Nat. Assn. Humane and Environ. Edn., East Haddam, Conn., 1970-94, chmn. bd. dirs. 1973-95; trustee Rio Grande (Ohio) Coll., 1979-86, Lake Erie Coll., Painesville, Ohio, 1986-88; bd. dirs. The Am. Fondouk, Boston, 1986-97, Earth Day 1990, 1989-90, Global Tomorrow Coalition, 1989-94; pres. World Soc. for Protection of Animals, London, 1986-90, v.p., 1990-98; dir. Ctr. Respect Life and Environment, Washington, 1986-97; dir. Internat. Ctr. Earth Concerns, Calif., 1994-; mem. Earth Charter Commn.; v.p. Internat. Devel. Conf., Washington, 1997-99, 01-03; dir. Bear Castle Property Owners Assn., Bumpbass, Va., 2001-07; hon. v.p. Inst. for Animals and Society, Balt., 2004-05. Recipient Disting. Alumnus award Rio Grande Coll., Founders award for Humane Excellence ASPCA, 1991, George T. Angell Humanitarian award Mass. SPCA, 1992, Pres.'s Disting. Ministry award Sch. of Theology at Claremont, Calif., 1995, Reverence for Life Commendation Albert Schwertzer Inst. for the Humanities, 1998. Home and Office: 320 Bear Castle Dr Bumpass VA 23024-4925 Office Phone: 540-894-4479.

HOYT, KENNETH BOYD, education educator, writer; b. Cherokee, Iowa, July 13, 1924; s. Paul Fuller and Mary Helen (Tinker) H.; m. Phyllis June Howland, May 25, 1946; children: Andrew Paul, Roger Alan, Elinore Jane. BS, U. Md., 1948; MA, George Wash. U., Washington, DC, 1950; PhD, U. Minn., 1954; EdD (hon.), Crete Coll., 1981. Tchr., counselor Northeast H.S., Md., 1948-49; dir. guidance Westminster H.S., Md., 1949-50; tchg. asst. U. Minn., 1950-51, instr. ednl. psychology, 1951-54; asst. prof. U. Iowa, Iowa City, 1954-57, assoc. prof., 1957-60, prof. edn., 1961-69; dir. Splty. Oriented Student Research Program, prof. edn. U. Md., Silver Spring, 1969-74; dir. office career edn. US Office Edn., 1974-82; disting. vis. scholar Embry Riddle Aero. U., 1982-84; disting. prof. edn. Kans. State U., 1984—2003, dir. counseling high skills vocat. tech. career options program, 1993-98, prof. emeritus, 2003—. Cons. Ordnance Civilian Personnel Agy., 1954-60, Iowa Dept. Pub. Instrn., 1954-69, U.S. Dept. Labor, 1956-68, 65—, U.S. Office Edn., 1958—, Nat. Inst. Edn., 1973—. Author: (with L.A. Van Dyke) The Drop-Out Problem in Iowa High Schools, 1958, (with C.P. Froehlich) Guidance Testing, 1960, Selecting Employees for Developmental Opportunites and Guidance Services; Suggested Policies for Iowa Schools, 1963, Career Education: Contributions to an Evolving Concept, 1976, Career Education: Where It Is and Where It Is Going, 1981, Career Education: History and Future, 2005; co-author: Career Education: What It Is and How To Do It, 1972, Career Education and the Elementary School Teacher, 1973, Career Education in the Middle Junior High School, 1973, Career Education for Gifted and Talented Students, 1974, Career Education in the High School, 1977, Counseling for High Skills, 2001, Career Education: History and Future, 2005; Editor: Counselor Education and Supervision, 1961-65; mem. editl. bd.: Personnel and Guidance Jour, 1960-63; Contbr. articles to profl. jours. With AUS, 1943—46. Fellow APA (divsn. 17); mem. Am. Counseling Assn. (pres. 1966-67, Arthur Hitchcock Outstanding Disting. Profl. Svc. award, 1994), Am. Vocat. Assn. (Outstanding Svc. award 1972), Assn. Counselor Edn. and Supervision (Disting. Svc. award 1965, Outstanding Career award 1990), Nat. Career Devel. Assn. (Eminent Career award 1981, pres. elect 1991-92, pres. 1992-93), Am. Sch. Counselors Assn., Am. Ednl. Rsch. Assn., Nat. Assn. for Industry Edn. Cooperation (vice-chmn. 1992—), Phi Delta Kappa. Address: 13816 Sheradan Ave Urbandale IA 50323 E-mail: kbhoyt@mchsi.com.

HOYT, MARY FINCH, writer, media consultant, retired federal official; b. Calif. 2 children. Free-lance mag. writer, speechwriter, formerly with Ladies' Home Jour. mag.; info. officer Peace Corps; pres. sec. to Mrs. Edmund Muskie, 1968; pres. sec. to Mrs. George McGovern, 1972; former ptnr. McClure, Schultz and Hoyt (pub. rels.).; press sec. to Mrs. Rosalynn Carter and East Wing coord. The White House, Washington, 1977-81; dir. communications Nat. Trust for Hist. Preservation, Washington, 1989-93; author, editor, media cons., 1993—. Author: American Women of the Space Age, 1966; author: (with Eleanor McGovern) Uphill: A Personal Story, 1974; author: East Wing: Politics, the Press and a First Lady, 2001. Mem. Presdl. Commn., 1977. Democrat.

HOYT, MONT POWELL, lawyer; b. Oklahoma City, Apr. 3, 1940; s. Lester Dean and Paula (Powell) H.; m. Alice Nathalie Ryan, June 15, 1974; children: Mont Powell Jr., Kathleen, Michael, Caroline. BA, Northwestern U., 1962; JD, Okla. Law Sch., 1965; M in Comparative Law, U. Chgo., 1968. Bar: Okla. 1965, Tex. 1968. Law clk. U.S. Dist. Ct., Oklahoma City, 1965; stagiaire to French advocat Paris, 1967-68; assoc. Baker & Botts, Houston, 1968-75, ptnr., 1975-92; shareholder Verner, Liipfert, Bernhard, McPherson & Hand, Houston, 1993-94; ptnr. Hughes & Luce, Houston, 1994-2001, Shook, Hardy & Bacon, Houston, 2001—04, Munsch, Hardt, Kopf & Harr P.C., Houston, 2004—06, Hoyt & Assocs., Houston, 2006—. Adj. prof. law U. Houston, 1970—76; sec. Houston Com. Fgn. Rels., 1993—; hon. consul gen. for Malaysia in Tex., 2003—. Contbr. articles to profl. jours. Bd. dirs. French Am. Found., N.Y.C., 1979-85, Mexican Cultural Inst., 1991-95, Fgn. Policy Assn., 1991-93; mem. Latin Am. adv. bd. Americas Soc., 1992—. Mem.: ABA (chmn. sect. internat. law and practice 1984—85), InterAm. C. of C. (bd. dirs. 1991—99, chmn. 1996—98), German Am. C. of C. (bd. dirs. 1978—94), Am. Arbitration Assn., Am. Soc. Internat. Law, Am. Law Inst., Internat. Bar Assn. (coun. sect. of energy and nat. resources law 1983—86), Coun. on Fgn. Rels. (chmn. Houston 1991—92), U. Chgo. Law Sch. Alumni Assn. (v.p. 1990—91), Houston Internat. Arbitration Club, Met. Club (Washington), Houston Country Club. Avocations: languages, running, international dispute resolution, amateur radio. Office: PO Box 131026 Houston TX 77219-1026

HOYT, PAMELA, nurse; b. Bronxville, NY, June 10, 1964; d. Alice Hoyt. BSN, Georgetown U., Washington, 1986. RN NY State Bd. Nursing. Sales dir. Ambulatory Pharm. Svcs., Yonkers, NY, 1996—2002; internat. nursing coord. Dreyfus Health Found., NCY, 2002—. Contbr. articles to profl. jours. Mem.: ANA, Global Health Coun., Sigma Theta Tau Internat. Nursing Honor Soc. Office: Dreyfus Health Found 205 East 64th St Ste 404 New York NY 10021 Home Phone: 914-921-4063; Office Phone: 212-750-5075. Business E-Mail: phoyt@dhfglobal.org.

HOYT, ROBERT E., dean, management educator; BS, U. Nebr.-Lincoln; MA, PhD, U. Pa. Faculty mem. Terry Coll. Bus., U. Ga., Athens, 1988—, Dudley L. Moore, Jr. chair of insurance, dept. head insurance, legal studies, and real estate, prof. corp. risk mgmt. and enterprise risk mgmt., interim dean, 2007—. Fulbright vis. prof. risk mgmt. Vienna U. of Econs., 1995; trustee Griffith Found. for Insurance Edn.; dir. Spencer Ednl. Found.; bd. mem. Athens Area Health Plan Select. Mem.: Internat. Insurance Soc., So. Risk and Insurance Assn., Risk Theory Soc., Am. Risk and Insurance Assn. (Les Strickler Innovation in Instruction Award). Office: Terry Coll Bus U Ga 206 Brooks Hall Athens GA 30602-6255 Office Phone: 706-542-4290. Office Fax: 706-542-4295. E-mail: rhoyt@terry.uga.edu.

HOYT, ROBERT F., lawyer; b. Sept. 8, 1964; BS with honors, Cornell U., 1986; MA, U. Penn., 1989, JD cum laude, 1989. Bar: Pa. 1990, DC 1991. Law clk. to to Hon. Herbert P. Wilkins Supreme Judicial Ct. Mass., 1989—90; ptnr., vice chmn. Securities, Litig. and Corp. Dept., mem. mgmt. com., mem. exec. com. Wilmer Cutler Pickering Hale & Dorr LLP, Washington, 1990—2005; spl. asst. & assoc. counsel to Pres. The White House, Washington, 2005—06; gen. counsel US Dept. Treasury, Washington, 2006—. Office: US Dept Treasury 1500 Pennsylvania Ave NW Rm 3000 Washington DC 20220 Office Phone: 202-622-0283. Business E-Mail: robert.hoyt@do.treas.gov.

HOYT, ROGER FRANKLIN, physicist, consultant; b. Evergreen Park, Ill., Aug. 16, 1949; s. William Abe and Betty Jane H.; m. Jennifer Ann, June 24, 1978; children: Elizabeth, David. BS, U. Ill., Champaign/Urbana, 1971; MS, U. Calif., San Diego, 1975, PhD, 1978. Rsch. staff IBM, San Jose, 1982-94, mgr., program dir., 1994—2002, Hitachi Global Storage Tech., 2002—04; pres. Hoyt Assocs., 2004—. Rev. panel mem Nat. Rsch. Coun., Washington, 1992—98. Mem. editl. bd. Jour. Info. Storage and Processing, 1997—2003, IEEE Transactions on Magnetics, 2003—, contbg. author Magnetic Disk Drive, 1997—; mem. editl. bd.: Micro + Nanosystems and Information Storage + Processing Systems, 2003—. Vestry mem. Episcopal Ch. Almaden, Calif., 1986-89; storage chmn., Internat. Mfg. Electronics Initiative, 1996-; bd. dirs. Santa Maria Urban Mission, San Jose, 2003—. Corp. US Army, 1971—78. Decorated Army Commendation medal. Fellow: IEEE (dir. San Francisco coun. 1996—97, editor-in-chief IEEE press 1997—98, 3d Millennium medal 2000); mem.: Magnetic Disk Heritage Ctr. (bd. mem.), IBM Acad. of Tech., N.Y. Acad. Scis., Am. Phys. Soc. Republican. Episcopalian. Achievements include patents for inventions in field. Office Phone: 408-997-1826. Personal E-mail: roger.hoyt@sbcglobal.net.

HOZUMI, MOTOO, medical educator, researcher; b. Fukushima, Japan, Mar. 12, 1933; s. Akiine and Fumi Hozumi; m. Sakiko Wakabayashi, May 4, 1963; children: Yuko, Masamichi, Ayako. BSc, Tokyo U. Edn., 1956, MSc, 1958, DSc, 1961. Rsch. mem. Nat. Cancer Ctr. Rsch. Inst., Tokyo, 1962-64, chief ctrl. lab., 1964-75; dir. dept. chemotherapy Saitama (Japan) Cancer Ctr. Rsch. Inst., 1975-93, dir., 1990-93; spl. rsch. Saitama (Japan) Cancer Ctr., 1993-96. Rsch. mem. Roswell Park Meml. Inst., Buffalo, N.Y., 1965-67; vis. prof. Showa U. Med. Sch., Tokyo, 1988-2001; cons. Japan Immunoresearch Inst., Takasaki, Japan, 1993-98. Author: Advances in Cancer Research, 1983, Ciba Foundation Symposium, 1990, Status of Differentiation Therapy, 1991, (rev. jour.) CRC Critical Rev. Oncol./Hematol., 1985, Internat. Jour. Hematology, 1998. Recipient Princess Takamatsu Cancer Rsch. Found. prize, 1974. Mem. AAAS, Japanese Cancer Assn. (councilor 1973-98, emeritus mem. 1999—), Japan Hematol. Soc. (councilor 1992-98, meritorious mem. 1999—), Am. Assn. for Cancer Rsch. Avocation: music. Home: 12-288 Fukasaku Minuma Saitama 337-0003 Japan Personal E-mail: hozumim@olive.ocn.ne.jp.

HRABAL, ANTONIN, physician, educator; b. Prilepy, Kromeriz, Czech Republic, May 21, 1957; s. Bedrich and Stepanka (Von Larisch) H. MD, Charles U., Prague, Czech Republic, 1982, PhD, 1992; DSc, U. San Jose, Costa Rica, 1998. Med. diplomate. Rschr. Charles U., Prague, 1976-88, physician, tchr., 1985-92; physician, rschr. Inst. Hippokrates, 1992-99; tchr. Palacki U., Olomouc, Czech Republic, 1989-97, 99, U. Ctr. Inst. Hippokrates, 1997—2000; prof. Hippokrates U., 2000—, Cosmopolitan U., 2000—. Chmn. Inst. Hippokrates, 1992-99; head physician U. Hosp., 1995-99; founder Found. Nadace Hippokrates, 1997-99; head rsch. Univ. Ctr., 1998-99. Mem. N.Y. Acad. Scis. Achievements include inventor of regeneration of tissues by deep stimulation through interference of electric and magnetic fields; deep brain stimulation; special immunomodulation diagnostic and therapeutic methodology therapy of autoimmune diseases, anti-aging methodology/telomeraza and hormone replacement. Home: 45053 Casa De Mariposa Indian Wells CA 92210 Home Phone: 760-200-5186. Personal E-mail: professorhrabal@yahoo.com.

HRABOWSKI, FREEMAN ALPHONSA, III, academic administrator; b. Birmingham, Ala., Aug. 13, 1950; s. Freeman A. II and Maggie (Geeter) H.; m. Jacqueline Coleman, Aug. 29, 1970; 1 child, Eric. BA, Hampton Inst., Va., 1970; MA, U. Ill., 1971, PhD, 1975. Asst. dean student svcs., vis. asst. prof. U. Ill., Champaign-Urbana, 1974-76; assoc. dean grad. studies Ala. A&M U., Normal, 1976-77; v.p. for acad. affairs, dean arts and scis. Coppin State Coll., Balt., 1977-87; exec. v.p. U. Md. Baltimore County, Balt., 1987-92, interim pres., 1992-93, dir. Meyerhoff scholarship program, 1989-93, pres., 1993—. Bd. dirs. Mercantile Safe Deposit & Trust Co., McCormick & Co. Co-author: Beating the Odds, 1998, Overcoming the Odds, 2002. Active Md. Gov.'s Commn. on State Taxes and Tax Structure, Annapolis, 1990, co-chair Md. Gov.'s Transition Policy Group on Edn., 1994-95, Gov's. Commn. on Devel. of Advanced Tech. Bus., 2003—; chair Md. Humanities Coun., Balt., 1991; bd. dirs. U. Md. Med. Sys., Balt. Mus. Art, Carnegie Instn. Washington, France/Merrick Found., Marguerite Casey Found., Md. Acad. Scis., Balt. Cmty. Found., Constellation Energy Group, Inc., Corvis Corp., Balt. Equitable Soc. Recipient 20 Yr. Outstanding Alumnus award Hampton U., 1990. Baptist. Home: 18 Aston Ct Owings Mills MD 21117-1439 Office: U Md Balt County Office of President 1000 Hilltop Cir Baltimore MD 21250-0001 Office Phone: 410-455-3880. E-mail: hrabowski@umbc.edu.*

HRABUSA, JOHN T., human resources specialist, food products executive; m. Sue Hrabusa; 4 children. BS in Bus. Adminstrn., U. Akron. Various positions in dist. mgmt. and human resource mgmt. Sherwin Williams Co.; v.p. human resources Office Depot, Inc., Publix Super Markets, Inc., Lakeland, Fla., 2004—, sr. v.p. human resources and public affairs, 2005—. Bd. dirs. James Madison Inst. Office: Publix Super Markets Inc 3300 Publix Corp Pkwy Lakeland FL 33811 Office Phone: 863-688-1188. Office Fax: 863-284-5532.

HRACHOVINA, FREDERICK VINCENT, retired osteopathic physician; b. St. Paul, Minn., Sept. 2, 1926; s. Vincent Frank and Beatrice (Funda) H.; m. Joan Halverson, July 2, 1955 BA in Chemistry, Macalester Coll., St. Paul, 1948; DO, Andrew Taylor Still U., Kirksville, Mo., 1956; student, Am. Writers and Artist Inst., Delray Beach, Fla., 2006—. Lic. osteo. surgey Minn., Fla. Chemist Mpls.-St. Paul area, 1948-51; intern Clare Gen. Osteo. Hosp., Mich., 1956-57; pvt. practice Mpls. Minn., 1957-84; asst. prof. osteo. principles and practices Nova Southeastern U. Coll. Osteo. Medicine, Ft. Lauderdale, Fla., 1985-88; founder, pres. Physician Placement Svc., Fla., 1973—, Minn., 1973—; med. dir. Associated Bioscience, Inc., Mpls., 1992, Sera-Tec Biologicals Inc., Jacksonville, Fla., 1993-94; staff physician Allegheny Biologicals, Inc., Jacksonville, 1995-96; med. dir. Serologicals, Jacksonville, 1996; med. ins. examiner Hooper Holmes, Inc., St. Petersburg, Fla., 1997—2005; ins. med. examiner Examination Mgmt. Svcs., Inc., Tampa, Fla., 1998—2005; ret., 2005. Bd. dirs. Internat. Acad. Osteopathics Medicine; lectr. Internat. Acad. Osteo. Medicine, Brussels, 1984; mem. Northlands Regional Med. Program, Inc., 1971—73, Health Svcs. Devel. Com., Regional Adv. Group; founder, faculty advisor Fla. Acad. Osteopathy Student Assn., Nova South Ea. U. Coll. Osteo. Medicine, Ft. Lauderdale, Fla., 1987; staff physician Centeon Bio-Svcs. Plasma Corp., St. Paul, 1998; v.p. med. rels., mem. adv. bd. Sinofresh Labs., Venice, Fla., 2002. Author: Microscopic Anatomy, 1952; Methods of Development of New Osteopathic Medical Colleges in the Next Millennium, 1977; contbr. articles to profl. jours. Mem. Crow Wing County Portage-Crooked Lake Preservation Soc., Minn., 1977—, Sr. Citizen Assn., Garrison, Minn., 1991—, Deerwood Civic and Commerce Assn., Deerwood, Minn., 1992—; chmn. street lights program Pinebrook South, Venice, Fla. Grantee Smith Kline & French Labs., 1973, 89, Hill Labs, Gusman Med. Equipment, 1987. Mem. Am. Coll. Osteo. Family Practice (life), Am. Osteo. Assn. (life, coun. fed. health programs, drug enforcement adminstrn. prescribers working com. 1974-75), Am. Acad. Osteopathy (life), Am. Coll. Sr. Osteo. Medicine Physicians and Surgeons, Inc. (pres., treas., bd. dirs., registered agt.), Am. Assn. Sr. Physicians, Am. Osteo. Acad. Sports Medicine (life), Am. Blood Resources Assn., Am. Assn. Blood Banks, Gulf Coast Hibiscus Soc. (presdl. liason to Venice C. of C. 1996), Minn. Osteo. Assn. (life, pres. 1965-66, exec. dir. 1966-74, pub. rels. dir. 1974-75), Assn. Osteo. State Exec. Dirs. (pres. 1970-71, dir. 1971-74, founder nat. legis. sem. 1974), Am. Coll. Osteo. Family Practice (life, lectr. Mo. chpt.), Fla. Acad. Osteopathy (trustee, chmn. audit and membership com.), Fla. Osteo Found. (v.p.), Ga. Osteo. Med. Assn. (chmn. Olympic com. 1995-96), Fla Osteo. Med. Assn. (Dade county chpt. chmn. osteo. lit. com., conv. chmn. dist. two 1994, dist. #7 Sarasota County, chmn. legis. com. dist. 11, v.p. dist. 7, long range planning com., mem. com., chmn. 175th ann. founder party, dist. v.p. mktg., chmn. mktg. com.), Fla. Osteo. Med. Assn. (fundraiser dist. 7 2006), Internat. Acad. Osteo. Medicine (trustee), Minn. Gymnastic Assn. (founder Floor Exercise 1962-72), Fla. Acad. Osteopathy Student Assn. at Southeastern Coll. Osteo. Medicine (originator, advisor), Dade-Broward Osteo. Med. County Soc., Duval County Osteo. Soc., Sarasota County Osteo. Soc., Twin-City Model A Ford Club, Pierce Arrow Soc. (sec. Fla. region 1988, news reporter Arrow Driver Midwest region, Mpls., life, founder Midwest region, 1983, dir./treas., 1983-84, gen. chmn. Midwest region swapmeet, 1990, nat. dir. 1983-84, contbr. articles to Arrow Jour.), Venice C. of C. (mem. membership com., mem. amb. com.), Cadillac LaSalle Club (founder 1978, treas. North Star region 1978-83), Classic Car Club Am. (life, membership chmn. Minn. upper midwest region 1977, sec. 1978, Gold Coast region-Fla.), Antique Auto Club. Am. (life, news reporter St. Paul chpt., Minn. region, Ft. Lauderdale region, Jacksonville region, Venice chpt., Lemon Bay region, judge at nat. meet Venice, Fla. 1997), Breakfast Club Mpls., Y.E.S. Club 1st Nat. Bank Deerwood, Minn., Scottish Rite, Valley of St. Paul, Lions (Bay Lake, Minn. del. to internat. conv., Miami, Fla., 1989), Optimist Club (dir. Mpls. 1959-62, 69-72, pres. 1970-71, gen. chmn. fl. exercise Olympic gynmastic program 1959-65), Masons (life, Capitol City #217, St. Paul), Shriners (life Zunrah Shrine Temple, fundraising com. Aadzuhma chpt.), Coll. Osteo. Medicine Mus. Andrew Still Taylor U. (life), Phi Sigma Gamma (life, nat. pres. 1987-89, pres. grand coun. and found. 1987-89, grand coun. advisor and chmn. bd.), Ascended Masters Tchg. Found., Cummer Gallery of Art and Gardens, Arlington Preservation Soc., Pierce-Arrow Mus. (life), Manasota Fossil Club, Airstream Fla. Suncoast Club, Wally Byam Caravan Club, Internat. Airstream Inc. Home: 1238 Lucaya Ave Venice FL 34285-6407

HRANITZKY, RACHEL ROBYN, lawyer; b. Irving, Tex., Mar. 16, 1968; d. Dennis Rogers and Jeanne Beverly (Crooks) H. BA, Tex. Christian U., 1987, U. Tex., 1988; JD, So. Meth. U., 1995. Bar: Tex. 1995, U.S. Dist. Ct. (no. dist.) Tex. 1997, U.S. Dist. Ct. (ea. dist.) Tex. 1999, U.S. Dist. Ct. (so. and we. dists.) Tex. 2000. Tchr. Grapevine H.S., Tex., 1989—92; clk. to Hon. Candace Tyson, 44th Dist. Ct., Dallas, 1993; assoc. coun. Mesa, Inc., 1995; sr. assoc. Hiersche, Hayward, Drakeley & Urbach, 1996—2004, Chamblee & Ryan, P.C., Dallas, 2004—05, Law Offices of Rachel R. Hranitzky, Euless, 2005—06, Office Atty. Gen., Washington, 2006—.

Rsch. asst. William V. Dorsaneo, III, 1993-95; clinic atty. So. Meth. U. Legal Clinics, Dallas, 1995. Mem. ABA, ATLA, Dallas Bar Assn., Dallas Assn. Young Lawyers, Rotary Club, Jr. League Dallas, Delta Theta Phi. Avocations: art, music, sports, cooking, dance. Home: 1200 First St 333 Alexandria VA 22314 Office: 441 Fourth St NW Ste 1060 North Washington DC 20001 Home Phone: 703-683-2828; Office Phone: 214-334-7088. Personal E-mail: rhranitzkylaw@aol.com.

HRICAK, HEDVIG, radiologist; came to U.S., 1972; MD, U. Zagreb, 1970; DMS, Karolinska Inst., 1992; Dr. (hon.), Ludwig Maximilion U., 2005. Diplomate Am. Bd. Radiology 1978. Intern in radiology Hosp. M. Stojanovic, Zagreb, 1971—72; resident in radiology St. Joseph Mercy Hosp., Pontiac, Mich., 1974—77; fellow in diagnostic radiology Henry Ford Hosp., Detroit, sr. staff diagnostic radiology, 1978—81; asst. clin. prof. diagnostic radiology U. Mich., Ann Arbor, 1979—81; from asst. prof. to assoc. prof. U. Calif., San Francisco, 1982—86, prof. radiology, urology, radiation oncology, ob-gyn., 1986—99; chief abdominal sect. dept. radiology U. Calif. Med Ctr., San Francisco, 1982—2000; chmn. dept. radiology Meml. Sloan-Kettering Cancer Ctr., NY, 1999—; prof. radiology Weill Med. Coll. Cornell U., NY, 2000—. Hon. prof. U. Zagreb, 1997; vis. prof. ovr 30 instns. Author 20 books in field; assoc. editor, Jour. of Magnetic Resonance Imaging, 2001—, Radiology, 1998—, Jour. of Women's Imaging, 1996—, others; contbr. more than 280 articles to sci. and profl. jours. Recipient Marie Curie award, Soc. Women in Radiology, 2002, Beclere medal, 2005; grantee numerous grants in field, including NIH, Nat. Cancer Inst., Am. Cancer Soc., Dept. of Def.;, numerous hon. lectureships. Fellow Am. Coll. Radiology, Internat. Soc. Magnetic Resonance in Medicine (gold medal 2003), Soc. Uroradiology (corrs. mem., pres. 2001-03); mem. Acad. Radiology Rsch. (bd. dirs. 1997—), Radiol. Soc. N.Am. (chmn. pub. info. adv. bd. 1997-2002, bd. dirs. 2003—), Soc. for the Advancement of Women's Imaging (pres. 1997-99), Calif. Acad. Medicine (pres. 1999), Croation Acad. Sci. and Art (hon.), German, Radiol. Soc. (hon.), German Roentgen Soc. (hon.) Brit. Inst. Radiologists (hon.), Inst. of Medicine. Business E-Mail: hricakh@mskcc.org.

HRICIK, LORRAINE E., bank executive; m. Nicholas DeGuercio; 2 children. B in Math. and Computer Sci., Ind. U., Pa., 1973; MBA, Columbia U., 1991. With Securities Industry Automation Corp.; exec. v.p. Chase Manhattan Bank; exec. v.p., head Treasury Services J.P. Morgan Chase, 2004—. Mem. Chase Technology Governance Bd.; chair The Clearing House Interbank Payment Co. L.L.C. Adv. Bd.; mem Federal Reserve Bank of N.Y. Payments Risk Com., N.Y. Clearing House Steering Com.; bd. dirs. Internat. Ctr. N.Y. Inductee Academy of Women Achievers, YWCA, 1990. Office: Chase Manhattan Bank 270 Park Ave Fl 12 New York NY 10017-2089

HRITONENKO, NATALI, mathematics professor, researcher; d. Vladimir Borodin and Lilia Borodina; m. Yuri Yatsenko, Oct. 15, 1955; children: Victoria, Olga Yatsenko. PhD, Belarus, Minsk, 1989, PhD in Applied Math., 1999. Assoc. prof. cybernetics dept. Kiev State U., Ukraine, 1991—96; adj. prof. dept. math scis. U. Alta., Edmonton, Canada, 1996—2000; sr. lectr. dept. math scis. U. Tex., Dallas, 2000—02; assoc. prof. dept. math Prairie View A&M U., Tex., 2002—. Mem. editl. bd. Applications and Applied Math., Internat. Jour. Ecological Econs. and Stats., Jour. Computational and Applied Math.; mem. editl. bd.: Jour. Applied Scis., Bull. Stats. and Econs.; author: 4 monographs; contbr. scientific papers. Fellow, Tex. A&M U. Sys. Regents, 2004; grantee, NSF/Assn. Women in Math., 2003, Math. Assn. Am., , Preparing Mathematicians to Educate Tchrs., NSF, 2005—06, NATO, 2006—, Gates-Marshall Found., 2006—. Mem.: Assn. Women in Math., Am. Math. Soc., Internat. Soc. Differential Equations, Internat. Fedn. Nonlinear Analysts. Avocations: travel, reading, writing. Home: 15434 Tysor Park Ln Houston TX 77095 Office: Prairie View A&M U Dept Math PO Box 519 Prairie View TX 77446-0519 Home Phone: 832-877-2827; Office Phone: 936-261-1978. Office Fax: 936-261-2088. Business E-Mail: nahritonenko@pvamu.edu.

HRITZ, GEORGE F., lawyer; b. Hyde Park, NY, Aug. 28, 1948; s. George F. and Margaret M. (Callahan) H.; m. Mary Elizabeth Noonan; 1 child, Amelia C. Hritz. AB, Princeton U., 1969; JD, Columbia U., 1973. Bar: NY 1974, DC 1978, U.S. Supreme Ct. 1979. Law clk. U.S. Dist. Ct. (ea. dist.) NY, NYC, 1973; assoc. Cravath, Swaine & Moore, NYC, 1974-77; counsel U.S. Senate Select Com. Ethics Korean Inquiry, Washington, 1977-78; ptnr. Moore & Foster, Washington, 1978-80, Davis, Weber & Edwards, NYC, 1980-2000; assoc. ind. counsel Washington, 1986-89; ptnr. Hogan & Hartson, LLP, NYC, 2000—. Mem. adv. com. U.S. Dist. Ct. (ea. dist.) NY, 1990—. Trustee Fed. Bar Found., 1998-2004; bd. dirs. exec. com. Internat. Rescue Com., 1982—; chmn. planning bd. Village of Sleepy Hollow, NY, 1993-97; bd. dirs. exec. com. Princeton in Africa, 2000—, pres., 2004—. Mem.: DC Bar Assn., Fed. Bar Coun. Office: Hogan & Hartson LLP Ste 2500 875 Third Ave New York NY 10022 Home Phone: 203-661-6944; Office Phone: 212-918-3517. Business E-Mail: gfhritz@hhlaw.com.

HRONES, STEPHEN BAYLIS, lawyer, educator; b. Boston, Jan. 20, 1942; s. John Anthony and Margaret (Baylis) H.; m. Anneliese Zion, Sept. 11, 1970; children: Christopher, Katja. BA cum laude, Harvard U., Cambridge, Mass., 1964; postgrad., U. Sorbonne, Paris, 1964-65; JD, U. Mich., 1968. Bar: Iowa 1969, Mass. 1972, US Dist. Ct. Mass. 1973, US Ct. Appeals (1st cir.) 1979, US Supreme Ct. 1991, US for the Fed. Ct., 2005, US Ct. Appeals (fed. cir.) 2006. Pvt. practice, Heidelberg, Germany, 1970-72; with Boston Legal Asst. Project, 1972—73; pvt. practice Boston, 1973-86; ptnr. Hrones and Harwood, Boston, 1986-90, Hrones and Garrity, Boston, 1990—2004, Hrones, Garrity and Hedges, LLC, Boston, 2005—. Clin. assoc. Suffolk U. Law Sch., Boston, 1979-82; faculty adv. Harvard Law Sch., 1988-2000; lectr. Northeastern Law Sch., 1998, Mass. CLE Programs, 1988—; vis. prof. law So. Federal U., Rostov, Russia, 2007; commentator CNN, Fox, MSNBC, NECN, WGBH. Author: How To Try a Criminal Case, 1982, Criminal Practice Handbook, 1995, 3rd edit., 2007, Massachusetts Jury Instructions (Criminal), 2d edit., 1999; contbr. articles to profl. jours. Trustee Orgn. for Assabet River, 1990-99; schs. and scholarship com. Harvard U., 1995-2000; fundraiser Harvard Club of Boston, 1972-, Harvard Coll. Fund, 1985-2002. Fulbright scholar, 1968-69; recipient Edward J. Duggan Pvt. Counsel award Com. for Pub. Counsel Svcs., 2000; named Super Lawyer Mass. Lawyers, 2004, 07. Mem. ACLU, Nat. Assn. Criminal Def. Lawyers, Mass. Assn. Criminal Def. Lawyers, Mass. Bar Assn., Boston Bar Assn., Nat. Lawyers Guild. Democrat. Avocations: squash, skiing, vegetable gardening, reading, travel. Home: 39 Winslow St Concord MA 01742-3817 Office: Hrones Garrity and Hedges LLC Lewis Wharf Bay 232 Boston MA 02110 Office Phone: 617-227-4019. Office Fax: 617-227-3908. Personal E-mail: sbhlaw@comcast.net.

HROVAT, DAVORIN D., engineer; Degree, U. Zagreb, Croatia; MS in Mech. Engring., U. Calif., Davis, 1976, Phd in Mech. Engring., 1979. With Ford Rsch. Lab., Dearborn, Mich., 1981—, sr. staff tech. specialist, now corp. tech. specialist. Recipient Control Engring. Practice Award, Am. Automatic Control Coun., 1999. Fellow: Am. Soc. of Mech. Engrs. (DSC Innovative Practice Award 1996); mem.: NAE, IEEE. Office: Ford Rsch Lab 2101 Village Rd Dearborn MI 48124

HRUBEC, JANE M., advertising executive; b. NYC, Sept. 20, 1942; d. A. Andrew and Beatrice (Gaines) Hrubec. BA, Briarcliff Coll., 1963. Copywriter DeGarmo-McCaffery, Inc., 1966—69, Foote-Cone-Belding, Inc., 1969—71; copy supr. Ted Bates, Inc., 1971—73; assoc. creative dir. Ogilvy & Mather, NYC, 1973—. Conf. speaker Woman Bus. Owners N.Y., Inc., NYC, 1983—84. Contbr. articles to mags. Bd. dirs. Friends of Parks, Chgo., 1976—79. Recipient Gold Medal award Art Dirs. Club, 1980, Silver award Internat. Radio's TV Festival, 1981, Gold and bronze, 1984, Adweek All-Am. Creative Team award, 1983, Clio Best Regional Campaign, 1984, Big Apple Best Humor Radio, 1984, Big Apple Best Music Radio, 1984. Democrat. Presbyn.

HRUBETZ, JOAN, retired dean, nursing educator; b. Collinsville, Ill., June 1, 1935; d. Frederick and Josephine (Nepute) H. RN, St. John's Hosp., St. Louis, 1956; BSN, St. Louis U., 1960, MA, 1970, PhD in Edn. and Counseling, 1975. Staff nurse St. John's Hosp., St. Louis, 1956-59; instr. med./surg. nursing St. Louis Mcpl. Sch. Nursing, 1960-63; asst. dir. nursing svc. Barnes Hosp., St. Louis, 1963-65, asst. dir. sch. nursing, 1965-68, ednl. cons., 1968-70, dir. sch. nursing, 1970-74; dir. undergrad. mprog. nursing St. Louis U., 1975-82, asst. to assoc. prof. nursing, 1975—, assoc. prof. pastoral health care, 1986—, dean Sch. Nursing, 1982. Lectr. in field. Contbr. articles to profl. jours. Bd. dirs. Paraquad, Inc., Ctr. Independent Living, 1985-87, hon. mem., 1987—; bd. dirs. Kenrick-Glennon Seminar, 1988, sec. bd., 1989-90; mem. adv. com. project on Clin. Edn. in Care of Elderly, 1989. Group Health Found. grantee, 1987-88, 88-89, St. Louise U. Hosps. grantee, 1980-83, others. Mem. Mo. Assn. Adminstrs. of Baccalaureate and Higher Deg. Progs. in Nursing, St. Louis Assn. Deans and Dirs. of Schs. Nursing, Am. Assn. Colls. of Nursing (adv. com. to baccalaureate data project), Am. Nurses Assn., Mo. Nurses Assn., 3rd Dist. Mo. Nurses Assn., Nat. League Nursing, Mo. League for Nursing, St. Louis Reg. League for Nursing, Midwest Alliance in Nursing (governing bd. 1985-87, chair 1986-87, resolutions com. 1987-89), Conf. Jesuit Schs. Nursing, St. Louis Met. Hosp. Assn. Office: St Louis U Sch Nursing 3525 Caroline St Rm 222 Saint Louis MO 63104-1007

HRUBY, GEORGE GEOFFREY, writer, educator; b. Cleve., Nov. 20, 1954; s. John Franklin and Mary Katherine Hruby; m. Alison Heron, Apr. 27, 2003; children: Katherine Hope, Evelyn Margaret. BA in English, Syracuse U., NYC, 1972—76; MEd in Lang. Edn., U. Ga., Athens, 1992—95, PhD in Reading Edn., 1996—2002. Ordained min. Universal Life Ch., 1982. Prodn. mgr. Jack Morton Prodns., Atlanta, 1977—79; head bartender T.G.I. Friday's, Sandy Spring, Ga., 1979—82; freelance writer, 1980—92; journalist, columnist Gwinnett Daily News/Forsyth Daily News, Gainesville, Ga., 1984—86; asst. mgr. Knickerbockers' Restaurant, Atlanta, 1987—88; owner, mgr. The Point, Atlanta, 1988—92; tchr-in-tng. Meadowcreek High Sch., 1994—95, Barrow County High Sch., 1994—95; investor, operator High-Hat Club, Athens, Ga., 1993—96; grad. asst. U. Ga., 1995—97, grad. asst. dept. reading edn., 1997—2002, post-doctoral fellow, 2002—03; asst. prof. reading and literacy edn. Utah State U., Logan, 2003—. Editl. rev. bd. mem. Reading Rsch. Quar., Newark, 2003—, Reading Rsch. and Instrn., Muncie, Ind., 2006—; bd. dirs. Am. Reading Forum, Sanibel Island, Fla., 2004—. Contbr. articles to profl. jours. Mem. Cache Chamber Music Soc., Logan, Utah, 2003—05. Fellow, Inst. of Behavioral Rsch., Cognitive Studies Group, U. Ga., 1997; scholar, Am. Reading Forum, 1999. Mem.: APA, Soc. for Neuroscience, Internat. Reading Assn., Am. Ednl. Assn. (spl. interest group chair 1999—2002), Nat. Reading Conf. Independent. Episcopalian. Achievements include research in system dynamics of literacy development. Avocations: oenology, organic gardening, travel. Office: Utah State Univ 2815 Old Main Hill Logan UT 84322 Home: 1057 E 1900N North Logan UT 84341-2075 Office Phone: 435-797-7145. E-mail: george.hruby@usu.edu.

HRUSHOVSKI, EHUD, mathematics professor; b. 1959; PhD, Univ. Calif., Berkeley, 1986. Prof. math. MIT, Hebrew Univ., Jerusalem. Co-recipient Carol Karp Prize, Assn. Symbolic Logic, 1993; recipient, 1998. Fellow: Am. Acad. Arts & Scis. Office: Inst Math 104 Einstein Hebrew Univ 91904 Jerusalem Israel Office Phone: (972)2-6586354. Office Fax: (972)2-5630702. Business E-Mail: ehud@math.huji.ac.il.

HRUSKA, ALAN J., lawyer, filmmaker; b. NYC, July 9, 1933; BA, Yale U., 1955, LL.B., 1958. Bar: N.Y. 1959, U.S. Supreme Ct. 1970. Assoc. firm Cravath, Swaine & Moore, NYC, 1958-67, ptnr., 1968—; chmn. planning and program com. 2d Circuit Jud. Conf., 1974-80; co-chmn. 2d Circuit Commn. Reduction of Burdens and Costs in Civil Litigation, 1977-80; commr. N.Y. State Exec. Adv. Commn. on Adminstrn. of Justice, 1981-83; chmn. bd. SoHo Press, Inc., 1986—; CEO The Talking Pictures Co., 2001—. Author: Borrowed Time, 1984; writer, dir.: (films) Nola, 2003; The Warrior Class, 2005; dir.: (plays) Waiting for Godot. Bd. dirs. Legal Action Ctr., 2000-06. Mem.: Actors Studio (active prodrs. and dirs. divsn.), ABA, Fund for Modern Cts. (bd. dirs. 1994—2005), Inst. Jud. Adminstrn. (trustee 1978—92, pres. 1982—85, bd. dirs. 1992—2002), Fed. Bar Coun. (trustee 1976—, pres. 1984—86), Assn. Bar City of N.Y. (sec. 1965—66), N.Y. State Bar Assn., Am. Coll. Trial Lawyers, Ctr. for Pub. Resources (exec. com. 1984—2002). Office: Cravath Swaine & Moore 825 8th Ave Fl 38 New York NY 10019-7475

HRYCAK, PETER, retired engineering educator; b. Przemysl, Poland, July 8, 1923; arrived in US, 1949, naturalized, 1956; s. Eugene and Ludmyla (Dobrzanska) Hrycak; m. Rea Meta Limberg, June 13, 1949; children: Maria(dec.) , Michael Paul, Orest W. T., Alexandra Martha. Student, U. Tubingen, Germany, 1946—48; BS with honors, U. Minn., Mpls., 1954, MS, 1955, PhD, 1960. Registered profl. engr., NJ. Adminstrv. asst. French Mil. Govt. in Germany, 1947-49; instr. mech. engring. U. Minn., Mpls., 1955-60; mem. tech. staff Bell Telephone Labs., Murray Hill, NJ, 1960-65; sr. project engr. Curtiss-Wright Corp., Woodridge, NJ, 1965; assoc. prof. mech. engring. NJ Inst. Tech., 1965-68, prof., 1968-93, dir. jet rsch. lab., 1966-93, prof. emeritus, 1993—. Participant in internat. and nat. conf. on engring. and applied sci. Contbr. articles to profl. jours.; one of original Telstar designers. Bd. dirs. Ukrainian Congress Com. Am., Mpls., 1956—60, Plast Camp, East Chatham, NY, 1963—68; v.p. Ukrainian Music Found., 1977—97; pres. Peremyschyna, 1993—. NASA grantee, 1967—68, NSF grantee, 1982—84. Mem.: ASME, AIAA (sr.), Ukrainian Acad. Arts and Scis. U.S., Shevchenko Sci. Soc., Nat. Ukrainian Acad. Engring. Scis., Am. Geophys. Union, Ukrainian Engrs. Soc. Am. (pres. 1966—67), Inst. Eviron. Scis. (sr.), Tau Beta Pi, Sigma Xi, Pi Tau Sigma. Home: 19 Roselle Ave Cranford NJ 07016-2532 Personal E-mail: mphrycak@aol.com.

HRYNKOW, SHARON HEMOND, federal agency administrator, neuroscientist, researcher; BA in Biology, RI Coll., 1983; PhD in Neuroscience, U. Conn., 1990; postdoctoral studies, U. Oslo, Norway, 1990-92. Health/sci. officer Bur. Oceans and Internat. Environ. and Sci. Affairs US Dept. State, Washington, 1992-95; sci. policy analyst Fogarty Internat. Ctr., NIH, Bethesda, Md., 1995-97, spl. asst. office of dir., 1997-99, dep. dir., 2000—04, acting dir., 2004—. Mem. adv. bd. Nat. Coun. for Internat. Health, Washington, 1997. Contbr. articles to profl., peer-reviewed journals includng Jour. Neuroscience, Developmental Brain Rsch., and others; chief drafter on strategy and policy toward internat. HIV/AIDS, US Dept. State. Recipient Lette N. Sangstad award (rsch. stipend) Oslo, Norway, 1990-92, Order of Merit, King of Norway, 2005. Mem. AAAS (Sci., Engring. and Diplomacy fellowship 1992-94), APHA, Coun. Fgn. Rels., Am. Scandinavian Assn., Norwegian Soc. of Washington, Soc. Neuroscience, Women in Neuroscience. Office: Fogarty Internat Ctr Bldg 31 Rm B2C29 31 Center Dr MSC 2220 Bethesda MD 20892-2220 Office Phone: 301-496-1415. Office Fax: 301-402-2173. E-mail: hrynkows@mail.nih.gov.

HSI, DAVID CHING HENG, plant pathologist, geneticist, educator; b. Shanghai, May 17, 1928; came to US, 1948, naturalized, 1961. s. Yulin and Sue Jean (King) H.; m. Kathy S.W. Chiang, 1952; children: Andrew C., Steven D. BSA, St. John's U., Shanghai, 1948; MS, U. Ga., 1949; PhD, U. Minn., 1951. Grad. teaching asst. U. Minn., St. Paul, 1950; postdoctoral fellow US Cotton Field Sta., Sacaton, Ariz., 1951-52; mem. faculty N.Mex. State U., Las Cruces, 1952—, prof. plant pathology and genetics, 1968-92, prof. emeritus, 1992—. Cons. AID, Pakistan, 1970; coord. external evaluation panel Peanut Collaborative Rsch. Support Program, USA, West Africa, S.E. Asia, 1993-95; acad. exch. People's Republic China, 1978, 84, 85, Republic China, 1979, 81, 82, Brazil and Argentina, 1980, Australia, 1983, South Africa, 1981; judge sr. botany N.Mex. Sci. and Engring. Fair, 1979—; adj. prof. biology U. N.Mex., 1986—. Author rsch. papers in field; co-developer new crop cultivars. Past bd. dir., treas. Carver Pub. Libr., Clovis, N.Mex.; elder 1st Presbyn. Ch., Albuquerque, workship com. chmn., 1981-82, adult edn. com. chmn., 1988-91, pers. com., 1995-98; mem. nat. adv. coun. discipleship and worship Gen. Assembly United Presbyn. Ch. USA, 1978-81, mem. nat. theol. reflections working group, 1980-81, mem. ednl. and congl. nurture unit, 1991-93, N.Mex. Child Abuse Neglect Prevention Implementation Task Force, 1993-97; mem. bd. edn. Albuquerque Pub. Schs., 1982, sec. bd. edn., 1983, v.p., 1984; bd. dir. Mid. Rio Grande Coun. Govts., 1983, 84; chair Albuquerque Sisters Cities Bd., 1986-88; 1st v.p. Albuquerque Sister Cities Found., 1995-96, pres., 1996-98; chair Albuquerque Biopark Adv. Bd., 2003-05; mem. com. higher edn. Gen. Assembly The Presbyn. Ch. (USA), 1991-93, preparation ministry com., Presbytery Santa Fe, 1993-98, chair, 1996-97; co-chair N.Mex. Advocates for Children and Families, 1993-95, vice chair, 1995-98; bd. dir. Greater Albuquerque Vol. Adminstr., 1992-95, 97-99, Project Change, 1994-98, v.p., 1996-98; v.p. Albuquerque Edn. Retirees, 1995-96, pres., 1996-98; v.p. Edn. Success Alliance, 1996-98; trustee All Faiths Receiving Home, 1997-03; trustee, Sandia Prep Sch., 2001-03; bd. dir., v.p. Explora Sci. Ctr. and Children Mus. Albuquerque, 1998—, v.p., 2002-; v.p. The Friendship Force of N.Mex., 2001, pres., 2002. Recipient Disting. Rsch. award Coll. Agr. and Home Econs. N.Mex. State U., 1971, Disting. Svc. award, 1985, Albuquerque Human Rights awad, 1997; inducted into Sr. Citizen's Hall of Fame, 1993. Fellow AAAS (hon., coun. mem. 1998-2004, Southwestern and Rocky Mountain divsn., exec. com. 1993-95, pres.-elect 1995-96, pres. 96-97); mem. Internat. Soc. Plant Pathology, Am. Phytopath. Soc. (judge Internat. Sci. and Engring. Fair 1983), Nat. Sweet Potato Collaborators Group (chmn. sprout prodn. and root piece propagation com. 1982-84), Nat. Geog. Soc., Am. Peanut Rsch. and Edn. Soc. (chmn. site selection com. 1981, award com., pres.-elect 1981, pres. 1982), N.Mex. Acad. Sci. (chmn. com. 1980, pres. 1981, 82, treas. 1984-92, dist. scientist award 1984), Nat. Assn. Acad. Sci. (pres.-elect 1992-93, pres. 1993-94), N.Mex. Chinese Assn. (pres. 1983-84, 92-93, treas. 1985-86, past bd. dir.), Chinese Am. Citizens Alliance (v.p. Albuquerque lodge 1988-92, v.p. 2002-04, pres. 2004—), Albuquerque Coun. for Internat. Visitors (v.p. 1988, pres. 1989-91), Sigma Xi (life, N.Mex. coord. centennial celebration, sr. editor commemorative pub. Frm Sundaggers to Space Exploration), Kiwanis Internat. (past pres. Clovis, past chmn. spl. program com., past bd. dir. Albuquerque). Home and Office: 2504 Griegos Pl NW Albuquerque NM 87107-2874 Personal E-mail: davidnkathyhsi@aol.com. *In grateful appreciation of my God-given talents and opportunities, my privileged academic trainings in China and U.S.A., and my professional experience and associations with world-wide scientists, I shall continue to contribute to the scientific advancement and practice, and to promote human understanding and international cooperation for the betterment of mankind and for the glorification of my Creator.*

HSI, EDWARD YANG, lawyer, venture capitalist, industrialist; b. Ann Arbor, Mich., May 30, 1957; s. Peter Hwei-Yang and Priscilla Lai-Fong (Lam) H.; m. Denise Chur-Yee Tso, Aug. 3, 1985; 2 children, Edward Yang II, Clarissa Sian Li-Hwa. BS, U. So. Calif., 1980; MBA, Duke U., 1983; JD, U. Calif., Davis, 1986. Bar: Calif. 1986, U.S. Dist. Ct. (cen. dist.) Calif. 1987, U.S. Ct. Appeals (9th cir.) 1987, U.S. Tax Ct. 1988, U.S. Supreme Court 1991. Tax intern Coca Cola Co., LA, 1983, Lear Siegler Inc., Santa Monica, Calif., 1984; assoc. Lawler, Felix & Hall, LA, 1986-87, Morrison & Foerster, LA, 1987-89, Thelen, Marrin, Johnson & Bridges, LA, 1989, Baker & McKenzie, Hong Kong, Singapore, 1989-92; of counsel Tilleke & Gibbins/Jones, Day, Reavis & Pogue, Bangkok, 1992—, Tilleke & Gibbins Cons., Ltd., Indochina, 1992—; group gen. counsel Humpuss Group Indonesia, Jakarta, Singapore, 1992-94; pres., CEO Humpuss Arun Aromatics Petrochemicals, Jakarta, Arun, Sumatra, 1994—96; exec. dir. Dharmala Group, Jakarta, 1997; vice chmn., CEO Asean Infrastructure Holdings Ltd., Jakarta, 1997—; chmn., CEO Asean Energy Group Ltd., Jakarta, 1998—. Spl. advisor to shareholders Gunung Sewu Group and Duta Anggada Group, Jakarta, 1997; founder, pres. PT Taira and Hsi Capital, 1998—2005; founder, prin. Grant Thornton Taira Hsi and Taira & Hsi, Internat. in cooperation with Kaye Scholer LLP, Jakarta, 1998—2000; advisor Govt. of Republic of Indonesia on Policy Proposal for Econ. Revitalization of Aceh as an autonomous region within a Unitary Indonesia; advisor to chmn. Indonesian Parliament DPR on a Nat. Econ. Revitalization Policy, 1998—99; mng. dir. Asia-Pacific region Mysmart Solutions, Inc., 2000—01; spl. advisor to chmn. Shingfa Group, Taipei, 2001—02; advisor Golkar Parliamentary Party of The Republic of Indonesia Del. to Taiwan, 2002; bd. dirs. DEH Asia Ltd., VBP Ltd., AO Asia Ltd., Asia Beta Capital Ltd.; co-founder, CEO New Template Media Group, LA, 2003—; COO Pacific Republic Capital, a Med. Ventures Group, 2003—. Editor: Income Taxation of Foreign Related Transaction, 5 vols., 1987; contbr. articles on tax to profl. jours. Mem. founding coun. World Peace and Diplomacy Forum, Cambridge, England, 2003—. Mem.: ABA, World Peace and Diplomacy Forum (mem. founding coun., Cambridge 2003—), L.A. County Bar Assn., State Bar Calif., U. Calif. Alumni Assn., Duke Alumni Assn., Punahou Sch. Alumni Assn., Am. C. of C.-Hong Kong, Hong Kong Assn., Indonesian Bus. Soc., Hong Kong Stanley Residents' Assn., Tuen Ng Dragon Boat Races Festival (co-chmn., ATT and Baker & McKenzie entry), Safari Club Internat., Order of Coif, Phi Kappa Tau, Alpha Mu Alpha, Phi Delta Phi. Democrat. Avocations: southeast asian art, jazz drumming, classical music, anthropology, discipleship. Home: 819 S Ridgeside Dr Monterey Park CA 91754-3724 Office: Chase Plaza 21st Fl Jalan Jenderal Sudirman Kav 21 Jakarta 12910 Indonesia E-mail: eyhsi@yahoo.com.

HSIA, IRENE YEE, electrical engineer; b. Chgo., June 10, 1963; d. Yu-ping and Ting-mei Hsia; m. George Ernest Antilla, Aug. 15, 1993; children: Katie An-yu, Sarah An-ning, Joshua An-hsia. BSEE summa cum laude, U. Calif., LA, 1984, MSEE, 1986, PhD in Elec. Engring., 1991. Asst. U. Rsch. Libr. U. Calif., LA, 1980—84, rsch. asst. Dept. Elec. Engring., 1984—91, tchg. asst. Dept. Elec. Engring., 1986—89; engr. Hughes Space and Comms., El Segundo, Calif., 1992—2000, Nanowave, Inc., El Segundo, 2000—02, Northrop Grumman Co., El Segundo, 2002—. Instr. Chinese Cultural Assn. So. Calif., Cerritos, Calif., 1982. Contbr. articles to profl. jours. Fellow, Dept. of Water and Power Sch., 1983—84, Grad. Opportunity fellowship, 1984—86; Mabel Wilson Richards scholar, 1981—83, Chancellor's scholar, 1980—81, Northrop fellowship, 1986—89. Mem.: Tau Beta Pi, Eta Kappa Nu, Phi Beta Kappa. Avocations: volleyball, basketball, dance, music, movies. Office: Northrop Grumman Co 1 Hornet Way El Segundo CA 90245

HSIA, JUDITH ANN, physician; b. Boston, Jan. 29, 1954; d. David Yi-Yung and Hsio Hsuan (Shih) H.; m. Ernest Jay Isenstadt, Jan. 28, 1983; children: Jill, Ruth. AB, Harvard Coll., 1974; MD, U. Ill., Chgo., 1978. Diplomate Am. Bd. Internal Medicine, Am. Bd. Cardiovac Disease. Intern, resident Tufts-New Eng. Med. Ctr., 1978-81; cardiology fellow George Washington U., Washington, 1981—84, asst. prof. medicine, 1988-93, assoc. prof. medicine, 1993—98, prof. medicine, 1998—. Recipient Louis N. Katz award Am. Heart Assn., 1984, Pfizer Scholar's award Pfizer Pharm., 1987. Fellow Am. Coll. Cardiology; mem. Alpha Omega Alpha. Office: George Washington Univ 2150 Pennsylvania Ave NW Washington DC 20037-3201

HSIAO, RICHARD, research and development company executive; BS, Beijing U. Sci. and Tech., 1982; PhD, U. Pa., Phila., 1986. Resident scientist AT&T Bell Labs, Murray Hill, NJ, 1985—86; devel. engr. IBM Tech. Lab, Endicott, NY, 1986—90, IBM Microelectronics, Fishkill, NY, 1990—94; rsch. scientist IBM Rsch. Ctr., San Jose, Calif., 1994—99; engring. mgr. IBM, San Jose, Calif., 1999—2002; sr. engring. mgr. Hitachi Global Storage Techs., San Jose, Calif., 2003—. Achievements include being a key contributor to IBM's world-record for the magnetic recording density demonstration; 76 patents in field. Personal E-mail: hsaioxyz@hotmail.com.

HSIAO, SHIH WEN, mechanical engineer, educator; b. Chia-Yi, China, Feb. 10, 1954; s. Yen and Ying (Chen) H.; m. Chin Yeh Wu, Jan. 22, 1980; children: Shih Wei, Man Chun, Po Han. B in Mech. Engring., Fen Chia U., 1977; M in Mech. Engring., Cheng Kung U., 1985, PhD, 1990. From engr. to project engr. China Steel Corp., Kaohsiung, 1979-91; from assoc. prof. to prof. Nat. Cheng Kung U., Tainan, Taiwan, 1991—, chmn. dept. indsl. design, 1998—2001, disting. prof., 2003—. Cons. in field.; spkr. in field. Editor: Jour. Chinese Inst. Indsl. Engrs., 2007—; editor: (editl. bd.) Design Studies, 2005—. Lt. Chinese army, 1977-79. Mem. China Indsl. Designer Soc., China Indsl. Designers Assn., China Engr. Soc., Mech. Engring. Soc. China. Buddhist. Avocations: badminton, music, jogging, mountain climbing. Office: Nat Cheng Kung U Dept Indsl Design 70101 Tainan Taiwan Office Phone: 886-6-2757575 ext. 54330. Business E-Mail: swhsiao@mail.ncku.edu.tw.

HSIEH, DIN-YU, applied mathematics professor; b. Jiangsu, Mar. 25, 1933; arrived in the U.S., 1955; s. K.S. and C. (Wei) H.; m. Lily Kwang-Fei Chow, Dec. 26, 1958; children: Paul, Daniel. BS, Nat. Taiwan U., 1954; MS, Brown U., Providence, 1957; PhD, Calif. Inst. Tech., Pasadena, 1960. Rsch. fellow Calif. Inst. Tech., 1960-63, asst. prof., 1963-68; assoc. prof. Brown U., 1968-78, prof., 1978-2000; prof., head dept. math. Hong Kong U. Sci. & Tech., 1990-96, acting dean sci., 1990-91, 92, prof. math., 1996—98; dir. Zhou Pei-Yuan Ctr. for Applied Math., Tsinghua U., Beijing, 2002—. Cons. Jet Propulsion Lab. Pasadena, 1963-67; advisor Ningbo (Peoples Republic of China) U., 1986—. Author: Asymptotic Methods, 1983, Fluid Dynamics, 1987, America, America, 1990, Amid Hills, by the Lake, 1991, Contemplating China, 1991, Wave and Stability in Fluids, 1994, Swallow Flying, 1998, Cape Dream, 2006. Mem. Am. Phys. Soc., Hong Kong Math. Soc., Edn. and Sci. Soc. (pres. 1987-90), Hong Kong Soc. Theoretical and Applied Mechanics (founding pres. 1996-97). Avocation: swimming. Office: Zhou Pei-Yuan Ctr for Applied Math Tsinghua U Beijing 100084 China

HSIEH, MARINA CING, lawyer, educator; b. Waco, Tex., Aug. 30, 1960; d. George S. C. and Rose S. C. (Pu) H. AB, Harvard U., 1982; JD, U. Calif., Berkeley, 1988. Bar: Pa., 1990; U.S. Ct. Appeals (3rd cir.) 1992; U.S. Supreme Ct. 1996. Staff Hon. Leo T. McCarthy, Lt. Gov., Calif., 1983-85; law clk. to Hon. Louis H. Pollak U.S. Dist. Ct., Phila., 1988-89; law clk. to Hon. John Paul Stevens U.S. Supreme Ct., Washington, 1989-90; asst. counsel NAACP Legal Defense and Ednl. Fund, Inc., NYC, 1990-93; acting law prof. U. Calif., Berkeley, 1993-99; asst. prof. law U. Md., Balt., 1999—2005; asst. dean academic and profl. devel. Santa Clara U. Sch. Law, Calif., 2005—. Lectr. Bar/Bri, 1996—. Author: (with others) Asian American Almanac, 1994. Mem. ACLU (bd. dirs. 1998—), Alumni of Deep Springs and Telluride Assn. Office: Santa Clara Univ Law 500 El Camino Real Santa Clara CA 95052-0448 Home Phone: 925-557-8243; Office Phone: 408-554-2764. Business E-Mail: mhsieh@scu.edu.

HSIEH, MING, information technology executive; married; 2 children. BSEE, U. So. Calif., 1983, MSEE, 1984. Rsch. devel. engr. Internat. Rectifier, 1985—87; founder, v.p. AMAX Tech., 1987—90; founder Cogent, Inc., South Pasadena, Calif., 1990, pres., chmn., CEO, 1990—. Office: Cogent Inc 209 Fair Oaks Ave South Pasadena CA 91030

HSIEH, PATRICK C., neurosurgeon; b. Taipei, Taiwan, Aug. 30, 1973; s. Jim and Mei Shui Hsieh; m. Sonya Chen, Nov. 30, 2002; children: Emily Lauren, Annabelle Elyse. BS, UCLA, 1991—95, MS, 1995—96; MD, USC Keck Sch. Medicine, LA, 1996—2001. Lic. step 1 ABNS, 2004. Rsch. scholar Howard Hughes Med. Inst., Bethesda, Md., 1998—99; neurosurgery residency Northwestern U., Chgo., 2001—. Clin. instr. UCLA, 1995—96; rsch. fellow Am. Heart Assn., NIH, Am. Pediatric Soc. Del. CSNS, Chgo., 2005—06. Mem.: CNS (assoc.), ABNS (assoc.), Golden Key (assoc.), Alpha Delta Lambda (assoc.), Phi Beta Keppa (assoc.), AOA (assoc.). Office: Northwestern Univ Neurosurgery 676 N St Clair # 2210 Chicago IL 60611 Home Phone: 312-212-1622.

HSIEH, PEI-HSUAN (PEGGY), education educator; b. Taipei, Taiwan, Feb. 15, 1978; d. Chien-Yuan Hsieh and Kuo Lin Yang. PhD, U. Tex., Austin, 2004. Adj. faculty Austin C.C., Tex., 2003—04; asst. prof. Northwestern State U., Natchitoches, La., 2004—05, U. Tex., San Antonio, 2005—. Mem.: Am. Ednl. Rsch. Assn. Office: Univ Tex 501 Durango Blvd San Antonio TX 78207 Home Phone: 832-433-0215; Office Phone: 210-458-2420. Business E-Mail: peggy.hsieh@utsa.edu.

HSIEH, TSUI-HSIA, artist, educator; b. Chia-yi, Taiwan, 1946; arrived in US, 1986; d. Wan-jin and Moo-chin Hsieh. BA, Nat. Taiwan Normal U., Taipei, 1981. Founder Jay Yuan Tong Arts Sch., Flushing, NY, 1986—; prin., owner Jay Yuan Tong Art Gallery, Flushing, 2005—. One-woman shows include Taipei Provincial Mus., 1983, Nat. Mus. History, Taipei, 1984, Princeton U., 1995, St. John's U., 1999, Hsin-Chu Cultural Ctr., Taiwan, 2002; author: Tsui-Hsia Hsieh's Paintings, 1999. Named Disting. Art Educator, Ministry Edn., Taiwan, 1982. Office Phone: 718-591-5227.

HSU, APO (CHING HSIN), conductor; b. Keelung, Taiwan, Republic of China, Oct. 7, 1956; came to U.S., 1981; d. Ying-Shyr and Yueh-Shur (Lin) H. BA, Nat. Taiwan Normal U., Taipei, 1980; MusM, Hartt Sch. of Music, 1984, artist diploma, 1985. Bassist Taipei Mcpl. Symphony Orch., 1979-80; piano instr. Kung-Jen Music Sch., Taipei, 1979-81; condr. Young People's Orch., Hartford, Conn., 1983-86; conductor Loomis Chaffee Sch., Windsor, Conn., 1985-86; asst. condr. Hartt Contemporary Players, Hartford, 1985-86; music dir. St. Cloud (Minn.) State U. Orch., 1986-91, Heartland Symphony Orch., Little Falls, Minn., 1988-91; orchestra dir. Nat. Taiwan Normal Univ., 2003—; condr. in residence Bard Coll. Condrs. Inst., 2000. Music dir. Cen. Minn. Youth Orch., St. Cloud, 1989-91; condr. in residence Peter Britt Festivals, Jacksonville, Oreg., 1990-91; bassist St. Cloud Symphony Orch., 1987-90; Affiliate Artists/NEA condr. Oreg. Symphony, 1991-94; music dir. Oreg. Mozart Players, Eugene, 1991-97; artistic dir., condr. The Women's Philharm., 1997-2001; music dir., condr. Springfield (Mo.) Symphony, 1995; faculty Interlochen, summer 2002, Okla. Arts Inst., 2002. Named one of Outstanding Young Women of Am., Com. of Outstanding Young Women of Am., 1988; Chamber Orch. Series grantee, Central Minn. Arts Coun., St. Cloud, 1989, Faculty Improvement grantee, St. Cloud State U., 1987, 88, 89. Mem. Am. Symphony Orch. League, Condr.'s Guild, Am. String Tchrs. Assn., Pi Kappa Lambda. Avocations: movies, cooking, softball, travel, hiking.

HSU, CHENG, decision sciences and engineering systems educator; b. Taipei, Taiwan, May 11, 1951; came to U.S., 1976; s. Chung-Yu and Te-Zeng (Yeh) H.; m. Susan Hsu; m. Susan; 1 child, Diana. BS in Indsl. Engring., Tunghai U., Taichung, Taiwan, 1973; MS, Ohio State U., 1978, PhD, 1983. Info. engr. China Tech. Cons., Inc., Taipei, 1975-76; grad. rsch. asst. Ohio State U., Columbus, 1977-80, grad. teaching assoc., 1980-82; asst. prof. decision scis. and engring. systems Rensselaer Poly. Inst., Troy, NY, 1982-88, assoc. prof., 1988-96, dir. undergrad. programs, 1989-91, dir. doctoral program, 1994—2001, prof., 1996—. Cons. Coopers & Lybrand, Albany, N.Y., 1988, Digital Equipment Corp., Nashua, N.H., 1991, Gen. Electric R&D, Schenectady, N.Y., 1995—; co-founder, bd. dirs. EntèrNet, Inc., 2000-04; patentee in field. Author: Enterprise Integration and Modeling: The Metadatabase Approach, 1996, Innovative Planning for Electronic Commerce and Enterprises: A Reference Model, 2000, Enterprise Collaboration: On-Demand Information Exchange for Extended Enterprises, 2006, Service Enterprise Integration: An Enterprise Engineering Perspective, 2007. Grantee GM, 1986—89, DEC, 1986—89, Johnson & Johnson, 1986—89, Aluminum Co. Am., 1992—95, Digital Equipment Corp., 1992—95, GE, 1986—95, GM, 1986—95, IBM, 1986—95, A T & T, 1987, NATO, 1988, State of N.Y., 1988, NSF, 1991—96, Samsung, 1995—98, U.S. Army, 1995—96, N.Y. State Dept. Transp., 1997—99, 2002—04. Mem. IEEE (sr.), ACM, Soc. Mfg. Engrs. (sr.), Prodn. and Ops. Mgmt. Soc., N. Am. Chinese Bus. Educators Assn. (bd. dirs. 1988-90). Republican. Home: 168 Maxwell Rd Newtonville NY 12110-4949 Office: Rensselaer Poly Inst 5219 CII Troy NY 12180-3590

HSU, CHIEH SU, applied mechanics engineering educator, researcher; b. Soochow, Kiangsu, China, May 27, 1922; came to U.S., 1947. s. Chung yu and Yong Feng (Wu) H.; m. Helen Yung-Feng Tse, Mar. 28, 1953; children: Raymond Hwa-Chi, Katherine Hwa-Ling. BS, Nat. Inst. Tech., Chungking, China, 1945; MS, Stanford U., 1948, PhD, 1950. Project engr. IBM Corp., Poughkeepsie, NY, 1951-55; assoc. prof. U. Toledo, 1955-58, Univ Calif.-Berkeley, 1958-64, prof., 1964—, chmn. div. applied mechanics, 1969-70. Sci. adv. bd. Alexander von Humboldt Found. Fed. Republic Germany, Bonn, 1985—; US nat. com. theoretical and applied mechanics US Nat. Acad. Scis., 1985-90. Author: Cell-to-Cell Mapping, 1987; contbg. author: Thin-Shell Structures, 1974, Advances in Applied Mechanics, vol. 17, 1977; tech. editor Jour. Applied Mechanics, N.Y.C., 1976-82; assoc. editor profl. jours.; author of over 106 tech. papers. Recipient Alexander von Humboldt award Fed. Republic Germany, 1986; Guggenheim Found. fellow, 1964-65; Miller Rsch. prof., U. Calif., Berkeley, 1973-74. Fellow ASME (Centennial award 1980, N.O. Myklestad award 1995) Am. Acad. Mechanics; mem. Acoustical Soc. Am., Soc. Indsl. and Applied Math., U. S. Nat. Acad. Engring., Acad. Sinica, Sigma Xi. Office: U Calif Dept Mech Engring Berkeley CA 94720-1740.

HSU, CHI-YUAN, nephrologist, researcher; b. Hong Kong, Mar. 5, 1967; arrived in U.S., 1985; s. Kwan-san and Wendy Hsu; m. Sandra Young; children: Sophia Rochelle Ming-xi, Theodore Cole Ming-ang. BS, MS, Yale U., 1989; MSc, Harvard U., 1999, MD, 1993. Instr. medicine Harvard Med. Sch., Boston, 1998—99; asst. prof. U. Calif., San Francisco, 1999—2006, assoc. prof., 2006—. Recipient Young Investigator award, Chinese Am. Soc. Nephrology, 2006. Office: U Calif San Francisco Box 0532 513 Parnassus Ave San Francisco CA 94143-0532 Home Phone: 415-731-0335; Office Phone: 415-476-2172.

HSU, C.T., architect; b. Taipei, Taiwan; arrived in US, 1974; married; 2 children. BArch, diploma in Urban Planning, Tung-hai U., Taiwan; MArch, MIT, Cambridge. Pres., mng. prin. C.T. Hsu + Assocs., P.A., Orlando, Fla., 1984—. Prin. works include Universal Studios Fla. Transp. Ctr. (Award for Excellence in Architecture, AIA Fla., 1999), Orange County Convention Ctr. West Entrance (Honor award for Design Excellence, AIA Orlando, 2004), Boone HS Adminstrn. Ctr. and Classroom Bldg. (Honor award for Design Excellence, AIA Orlando, 2004), Edgewater HS (Design award, AIA Orlando, 2004), Seminole County Softball Complex (Merit award, AIA Orlando, 2004, Award for Excellence in Architecture, AIA Fla., 1999). Recipient Outstanding Businessman of Yr. award, Rotary Club, 2006. Fellow: AIA (AIA Orlando Nils M. Schweizer Cmty. Svc. award 2005, AIA Orlando Outstanding Mem. award 2002). Office: CT Hsu + Assocs PA 820 Irma Ave Orlando FL 32803 Office Phone: 407-423-0098. Office Fax: 407-423-4793.*

HSU, DONALD I., pharmacist, educator; m. Jane S. Lee, July 27, 2002; 1 child, Nathaniel William. PharmD, Western U., Pomona, Calif., 2003. Pharmacy resident U. So. Calif., LA, 2003—05; asst. prof. Western U. Coll. Pharmacy, Pomona, 2005—07. Achievements include described the safety and efficacy of vancomycin in MRSA infections; reported the risk factors associated with fluoroquinolone-resistant Pseudomonas aeruginosa and impact on associated treatment outcomes. Office Phone: 909-469-5247.

HSU, EMILIE TIEN-JUNG, lawyer; d. Yao-Wen Hsu and Wen-Ching Lin. Baccalaureat, Lycee Gabriel Faure, Paris, 1991; AB, Columbia U., 1994; JD, Columbia Law Sch., 1997. Bar: NY 1999. Assoc. Winthrop Stimson Putnam & Roberts, NYC, 1997—98, Debevoise & Plimpton LLP, NYC, 2001—02, 2002—06, counsel, 2006—. Business E-Mail: ehsu@debevoise.com.

HSU, JIUN-JIA, engineering educator, transportation engineer; s. Teh-Nan Hsu and Shu-Li HsuLin; m. Hsiao-Ling Chang; children: Paul, Peter. BS, Feng Chia U., Taichung, Taiwan, 1995; MS, Fla. Internat. U., 1998, PhD, 2003. Registered profl. engr., Fla. Engr. Broward County Commn., Plantation, Fla., 2004—. Adj. prof. Fla. Internat. U., Miami, 2005—06. Contbr. articles to profl. publs. Recipient Outstanding Leadership award, Dept. Civil and Environ. Engring., Fla. Internat. U., 2001, Engring. Leadership award, Coll. Engring., Fla. Internat. U., 2001, Outstanding Cmty. Svc. award, 2002, Excellence in Tchg. award, Acad. for Art of Tchg., Fla. Internat. U., 2003. Mem.: Inst. Transp. Engrs. (assoc. William R. McGrath Transp. Studies scholar 2002, Best Transp. Career Brochure award 2002), Chi Epsilon, Tau Chi Alpha. Avocation: swimming. Office: Broward County Commission — Engineering 1 N University Dr Suite 300 Plantation FL 33324 Office Phone: 954-577-4585. Office Fax: 954-577-2338. Business E-Mail: jjhsu1@hotmail.com.

HSU, JONG-PING, physicist, educator; b. Po-tz, Taiwan, Feb. 17, 1939; s. Mao-Yuan Hsu and Yu-tz Huang; m. Bonnie Mei-chu Chiu, Aug. 17, 1968; children: Leonardo, Leslie. BS, Nat. Taiwan U., Taipei, 1962; MS, Nat. Tsing Hua U., Hsin-chu, Taiwan, 1965; PhD, U. Rochester, NY, 1969. Rsch. assoc. Rutgers U., New Brunswick, NJ, 1971—72; rsch. scientist U. Tex., Austin, 1972—77; sr. rsch. assoc. Marshall Space Flight Ctr., NASA, Huntsville, Ala., 1977—78; asst. prof. U. Mass., North Dartmouth, 1978—83, assoc. prof., 1983—87, prof., 1987—2001, chancellor prof., 2001—; scientist Nat. Ctr. Theoretical Sciences, Hsin-chu, Taiwan, 2004. Dir. Jing Shin Rsch. Fund, U. Mass. Dartmouth Found., 1989—; vis. scientist Ctr. Theoretical Physics, MIT, Boston, 1985—86; vis. prof. Chinese Acad. Sci., Beijing, 1999. Co-author: Lorentz and Poincare Invariance, 2001, A Broader View of Relativity, 2006. Mem. Einstein Found. Internat., Nagpur, India, 1980—87. Fellow, McGill U., Montreal, 1969—71. Achievements include research in broader perspectives on relativity, including Taiji relativity, based solely on the Principle of Relativity, and other relativity theories for which an additional postulate has been made. Avocations: classical music, walking. Office: University of Massachusetts Dartmouth 285 Old Westport Road North Dartmouth MA 02747-3233 Office Phone: 508-999-8363. Office Fax: 508-999-9115. Business E-Mail: jhsu@umassd.edu.

HSU, MING-YU, engineering educator; b. Kweiyang, Kweichow, China, Dec. 4, 1925; s. Pei-Kung and Wan-Ju (Hsiao) H.; m. Chih-Ju Yao, Jan. 1, 1952; children: Chi-Hsing, Chi-Yun, Chi-En, Chi-Che, Chi-Cheng. BE, Nat. Kweichow U., 1948; Dipl.Engr., Delft Tech. U., The Netherlands, 1959. Registered profl. engr., Ill., Ga., Fla., S.C. Prof. Cheng-Kung U., Tainan, Taiwan, 1960-68; dir. Land Devel. Commn., Taipei, 1960-68; engring. cons. Ministry of Housing & Utilities, Sehba, Libya, 1968-71; sr. engr. Philipp Holzmann Ag., Hamburg, Fed. Republic of Germany, 1971-74, Weber, Griffith & Mellican, Galesburg, Ill., 1974-80; chief engr. Chatham Engring. Co., Savannah, Ga., 1980-82; sr. cons. Hussey, Gay, Bell & DeYoung, Inc., Savannah, 1982—; prof. Savannah Coll. of Art and Design, 1986—. Designed and constructed numerous indsl. office, apt. and comml. bldgs., marine structures including docks, loading platforms, marinas, shipyards and water and waste water treatment structures. Contbr. articles on structural engring. to profl. jours. Mem. Nat. Soc. Profl. Engrs., ASCE. Home: 1115 Wilmington Island Rd Savannah GA 31410-4508 Office: Hussey Gay Bell & DeYoung 329 Commercial Dr Savannah GA 31406-3630

HSU, S. DANA, technologist; b. Tainan, Taiwan, Apr. 7, 1956; arrived in U.S., 1964; BS, George Washington U., 1978; MS, Hood Coll., Frederick, Md., 1986; JD, Am. U., Washington, DC, 1994. Bar: Md. 1995, D.C. 1996, U.S. Patent and Trademark Office 1998. Biologist NIH, Bethesda, Md., 1977—2005, technology transfer assoc., 2005—. Contbr. articles to profl. jours. Mem.: Am. Intellectual Property Law Assn. Avocations: gardening, crafts, reading. Office: NIH 6610 Rockledge Dr Rm 4076 MSC 6606 Bethesda MD 20892

HSU, STEPHEN DE, medical educator; b. Tianjin, China, June 11, 1955; arrived in U.S., 1982; s. Xukai Hsu and YunLian Qian; m. Yan Ping Wang, Dec. 5, 1995; children: Alexander, Andrew. BS, Wuhan U., China, 1982; MA, Montclair State U., 1985; PhD, U. Cinn., 1990. Fellow Sloan-Kettering Inst., NYC, 1991—95; commentor, host ESPN Internat., Bristol, Conn., 1995—98; asst. prof. Nat. U. Singapore, Singapore, 1997—98; rsch. fellow N.Y. U., NYC, 1998—99; asst. prof. Med. Coll. Ga., Augusta, 1999—2004, assoc. prof., 2004—. Contbr. articles to profl. jours. Recipient Ruth L. Kirstein Rsch. Svc. award, Nat. Cancer Inst., 1998; Rsch. grant, 2003. Mem.: Am. Assn. Dental Rsch., Am. Assn. Cancer Rsch. Achievements include invention of mega-t green tea chewing gum and mints; green tea skin care line. Avocations: travel, sports, history. Home: 4476 Woodberry Ct Evans GA 30809 Office: Med Coll Ga AD1443 Sch Dentistry Augusta GA 30912 Office Phone: 706-721-2317.

HSU, SYLVIA, dermatologist, educator; arrived in US, 1968; d. Mao Yang and Chih Jean Hsu; m. Tien Pei Wong, Dec. 27, 1986; children: Michael Gregory Wong, Kenneth Jason Wong. BA, Rice U., 1985; MD, Baylor Coll. Medicine, Houston, 1989. Cert. Am. Bd. Dermatology, 1994. Clin. asst. prof. dermatology Jefferson Med. Coll., Phila., 1994—97; asst. prof. dermatology Baylor Coll. Medicine, Houston, 1997—2000, assoc. prof. dermatology, 2000—05, prof. dermatology, 2005—. Chief dermatology Ben Taub Gen. Hosp., Houston, 2000—06. Mem.: Houston Dermatol. Soc. (pres. 2006), Phi Beta Kappa. Office: Baylor College of Medicine 6620 Main St Ste 1425 Houston TX 77030 Home Phone: 713-798-4046; Office Phone: 713-798-6131. Office Fax: 713-798-3250; Home Fax: 713-798-3250. Business E-Mail: shsu@bcm.edu.

HSU, THOMAS TSENG-CHUANG, civil engineer, educator; b. Swatow, China, July 28, 1933; came to U.S., 1958; s. Benjamin D.H. and Lucy S.K. (Ma) Zi; m. Laura H.N. Ling, July 20, 1963; children: Lynne Ling, Mia Ming. BS, Harbin Inst. Tech., China, 1957; MS, Cornell U., 1960, PhD, 1962. Engr. structural rsch. lab. Portland Cement Assn., Skokie, Ill., 1962-68; assoc. prof. structural engring. U. Miami, Coral Gables, Fla., 1968-73, prof., 1973-79, dept. chmn., 1974-78; vis. prof. dept. civil engring. Nat. Taiwan U., Taipei, 1979-80; prof. structural engring. U. Houston, 1980—, chmn., 1980-84, Moores univ. prof., 1998—. Eshbach disting. vis. prof. Tech. Inst., Northwestern U., 1991-92; prin. investigator NSF, Washington, 1970—; cons. Kaiser Transit Group, Dade County, Fla.; 1977-79. Author: Torsion of Reinforced Concrete, 1984, Unified Theory of Reinforced Concrete, 1993; contbr. articles to profl. jours. Recipient Rsch. medal Am. Soc. Engring. Edn., 1969, Award of Excellence, Halliburton Found., 1990; named Hon. Disting. Prof., Harbin Inst. Civil and Archtl. Engring., China, 1993. Fellow ASCE (Walter L. Huber Rsch. prize 1974), Am. Concrete Inst. (Leonard C. Wason medal 1965, Arthur R. Anderson award 1990). Home: 5034 Glenmeadow Dr Houston TX 77096-4212 Office: U Houston Dept Civil Environ Engring Houston TX 77204-0001 Office Phone: 713-743-4268. Business E-Mail: thsu@uh.edu.

HSUEH, CHUN-TU, political scientist, educator, foundation administrator, historian; b. Canton, Guangzhou, China, 1922; came to U.S., 1949, naturalized, 1960; m. Cordelia Teh-hua Huang, Dec. 13, 1952 (dec. 2002). Cert., China Sch. Jornalism, Hong Kong, 1939; LLB (hon.), Chaoyang U., China, 1946; grad. in English Lit., Raffles Coll., Singapore, 1946-49; MA, Columbia U., NYC, 1953, PhD, 1958; doctorate (hon.), U. San Martín de Porres, Lima, Peru, 1984, Russian Acad. Scis., 1999. Research assoc. polit. sci. Stanford U., 1959-62; lectr. history U. Hong Kong, 1962-64; vis. assoc. prof. SUNY, Plattsburgh, 1964-65; assoc. prof. U. Md., College Park, 1965-68, prof. politics, 1968-92; pres. Huang Hsing Found., Md., 1990—. Prof. Columbia U., summer 1969, 89; sr. assoc. mem. St. Antony's Coll., Oxford U., 1969; vis. prof., acting dir. Free U. Berlin, 1970; prof. Harvard U., summer 1979, 84; vis. scholar Peking U., 1983, Hebrew U., Jerusalem, 1984; disting. vis. prof. Zhongshan U., Guangzhou, China, 1983—, Wuhan U., 1984—, Peking U., 1989—, Zhejiang U., 1992—, Hunan U., 1996—, Shandong U., 1999—; adv. prof. Fudan U., Shanghai, 1985—; vis. fellow Australian Nat. U., Canberra, 1985; rsch. assoc. Ctr. for Chinese Studies U. Calif., Berkeley, 1985-86; chmn. Washington and S.E. Regional Seminar on China, 1974-81; exec. dir. Asian Polit. Scientists Group in U.S.A., 1975-2000; mem. vis. com., dept. internat. rels. Lehigh U., 1979-85; pres. Huang Hsing Found., Md., 1990—; vis. prof. U. Hong Kong, Trinity term, 1985, hon. prof., 1991-96; hon. prof. People's U., China, 1993—, Fgn. Affairs Coll., Beijing, 1996—, Jianghan U., Wuhan, China, 1987—, Ningxia U., 1992—, Nanjing Normal U., 1996—, Grad. Sch., Chinese Acad. Social Scis., 1998—, The Confucius Acad., Shandong, 1998—; trustee Jinan U., Guangzhou, China, 1989—, Nanjing Normal U., 1997—, Nanjing U., 1998—; advisor Sun Yat-sen Found., Guangzhou, 1992—; bd. dirs. Atlantic Coun. U.S., Washington, 1994-2003, Russian Rsch. Ctr. Chinese Acad. Social Scis., 1996—; hon. pres. Internat. Studies Assn., Shandong Province, 1998—; advisor Churchill Coll., U. Cambridge, 1998—, mem. exec. com. Atlantic Coun. Found., 1999—; hon. dir. Chaoyang Ctr. for Legal Studies, People's U. China, 2000—; hon. fellow Inst. Russian, East European and Ctrl. Asian Studies, Chinese Acad. Social Scis. Author: Huang Hsing and the Chinese Revolution, 1961, Chinese edit., 1980; editor, contbr. Revolutionary Leaders of Modern China, 1971, French edit., 1973, Dimensions of China's Foreign Relations, 1977, Asian Political Scientists in North America: Professional and Ethnic Problems, 1977, China's Foreign Relations: New Perspectives, 1982, Traditional Government in Imperial China: A Critical Analysis, 1982, The Chinese Revolution of 1911: New Perspectives, 1986, author/editor (books in Chinese with English title) People, Places and Politics, 1991, China and Her Neighbors: Prospects for the 21st Century, 1995, New Dimensions of China's Diplomacy, 1997, The New Russia: Politics, Economics and Diplomacy, 1997, Modernization of the Legal System and China's Economic Development, 1997, Confucianism and the Modernization of Chinese Culture, 1998, Trade and Economic Relations Between China and Russia, 1999, China and Central Asia, 1999, Sun Tzu's Art of War and Its Value in Modern Times, 1999, Social Change in the Chinese Communities in Southeast Asia after World War II, 1999, Prospects for China's Relations with Europe in the 21st Century, 2000, Japan in Turbulence, 2001, A Strategic Study of Establishing a Maritime Shandong, 2000, Europe and China in the 21st Century, 2000, Social Life and Ideas Change in Modern China, 2001, The Cradle of Modern Chinese Jurisprudence: The History of Chaoyang University, 2001, Russian Siberia and the Far East, 2002, Central and Eastern Europe in Transition, 2002, Confucianism and the Modernization of Society, 2004. Mem. Nat. Bicentennial Ethnic-Racial

Coun., 1974-76, Nat. Com. on U.S.-China Rels., 1976—; mem. adv. com. Md. Bicentennial Commn., 1975-76; mem. nat. exec. com. Caucus for New Polit. Sci., 1973-75. Named, Benefactor of Columbia U., 2004. Mem.: Am. Polit. Sci. Assn., Western Returned Scholars Assn. (hon. chmn. Found. 1994—, Beijing, overseas hon. v.p.), Assn. for Asian Studies (chmn. com. on scholars of Asian descent 1981—84). Achievements include honored benefactor Columbia U., 2004. Office: 14017 Wagon Way Silver Spring MD 20906-2065

HSUEH, EDDY C., surgeon, oncologist; b. Taichung, Taiwan, Apr. 18, 1965; s. Yuan-tu Hsueh and Chai Hsu; m. Hui-ling Lee, May 17, 1965; children: Joanne, Brandon. BA, U. Chgo., 1987, MD, 1991. Resident in gen. surgery SUNY, Bklyn., 1991—96; asst. dir. surg. oncology John Wayne Cancer Inst., Santa Monica, Calif., 1999—, dir. immunotherapy enhancement, 2000—03; assoc. prof. surgery St. Louis U., Mo., 2003—. Recipient Young Oncologist Essay award, Am. Radium Soc., 1997, Mentored Clin. Scientist Devel. award, Nat. Cancer Inst., 2000—; grantee Tech. Transfer program, Calif. Dept. Health Svcs., 2000—02. Fellow: ACS (life); mem.: AMA (licentiate), Assn. for Academic Surgery (licentiate), Soc. Surg. Oncology (licentiate Best Clin. Rsch. award 1998), Am. Assn. for Cancer Rsch. (licentiate), Am. Soc. Clin. Oncology (licentiate Merit award 1997, 1998, 2000, Young Investigator award 1999, Career Devel. award 2001—). Achievements include research in elucidating the specific immunologic response in killing tumor cells; defining the predictive factors associated with cancer patient survival; development of novel strategy for immune mediated killing of cancer cells. Avocations: reading, travel, swimming. Office: St Louis U Dept Surgery 3635 Vista at Grand Blvd Saint Louis MO 63110 Office Phone: 314-577-8566. E-mail: echsueh@msn.com.

HSUEH, WEI, pathologist, educator; b. Inner Mongolia, China, Apr. 21, 1944; d. Hsing-ruh and Yu-ing H.; m. Frank Gonzalez-Crussi, 1978. MD, Nat. Taiwan U., Taipei, 1968; PhD, Ind. U., 1972. Diplomate Am. Bd. Pathology. Assoc. pathologist Children's Meml. Hosp., Chgo., 1978—; asst. prof. pathology Northwestern U. Med. Sch., Chgo., 1978-83, assoc. prof. pathology with tenure, 1983-90, prof. pathology, 1990—2006, prof. emeritus, 2006—. Mem. GMA-2 study sect. NIH, 1992-96; mem. reversite site visit NIH/NICHD, 1992; spl. reveiwer NSF, March of Dimes, Chgo. Lung Assn., Scleroderma, NIH, 2000, 03, B.C. Health Rsch. Found., Can. Contbr. over 100 articles to profl. jours., 9 chpts. to books. Grantee Nat. Inst. Allergy and Infectious Diseases, 1979-84, NIH/Nat. Inst. Diabetes, Digestive and Kidney Diseases, 1984-2002, Nat. Inst. Child Health and Human Devel., 1994-99. Mem. Am. Assn. Investigative Pathologists, Am. Assn. Immunologists, Internat. Acad. Pathology. Office: Children's Meml Hosp 2300 N Childrens Plz Chicago IL 60614-3394 Home Phone: 773-281-4360. Business E-Mail: whsueh@childrensmemorial.org. E-mail: w-hsueh@northwestern.edu.

HU, CHENGCHENG, biostatician, medical researcher; b. Beijing; s. Zhi-ang and Hongxin Hu; m. Xiaorong Xiong, 2003. MA, Johns Hopkins U., Balt., 1995; MS, U. Wash., Seattle, 1998, PhD, 2001. Rsch. asst. Fred Hutchinson Cancer Rsch. Ctr., Seattle, 1996—2001; intern Genentech Inc., San Francisco, 1999; rsch. fellow Harvard Sch. Pub. Health, Boston, 2001—02, asst. prof. biostatis., sr. statistician, 2002—. Contbr. numerous papers in statis. methodology, AIDS, cancer, heart disease, neuroscience, and health econs. to profl. jours. Recipient Donovan J. Thompson award, U. Wash. Dept. Biostats., 1998, Best Written Paper award, Internat. Biometric Soc. Student Paper Competition, 1999. Mem.: AAAS, Internat. Biometric Soc., Am. Statis. Assn. Avocations: travel, photography. Office: Harvard Sch Publ Health 655 Huntington Ave Boston MA 02115 Office Phone: 617-432-4901. Personal E-mail: hu_cc@yahoo.com.

HU, CHENMING, engineering educator; b. Beijing, July 12, 1947; arrived in US, 1969; BS, Nat. Taiwan U., Taipei, 1968; MS, U. Calif., Berkeley, 1970, PhD, 1973. Asst. prof. elec. engring. MIT, 1973-76; prof. U. Calif., Berkeley, 1976—, Chancellor's prof., 1998-2000, Taiwan Semicondr. Mfg. Corp. Disting. prof. microelectronics, 2000—. Mgr. nonvolatile memory devel. Nat. Semicondr., Santa Clara, 1980—81; hon. prof. Beijing U., 1988, Tsing Hwa U., 1991, Chinese Acad. Sci., 1991; dir. Joint Svcs. Electronics Program, 1989—92, Indsl. Liaison Program, 1992—95; founder, chmn. Celestry Design Tech. Inc., 1995—2003; chief. tech. officer TSMC, 2001—04. Co-author: Solar Cells, 1983, Advanced MOS Device Physics, 1989, Nonvolatile Semiconductor Memory, 1991, MOSFET Modeling, 1999; contbr. articles to profl. jours. Chmn. bd. dirs. E. Bay Chinese Sch., Oakland, Calif., 1989—91. Recipient Design News Excellence in Design award, 1992, Outstanding Inventor award, 1993, R & D 100 award, 1996, Monie Ferst award, Sigma Xi, 1998, W. Y. Pang Found. award for Rsch. Excellence, 1999, Disting. Tchg. award, U. Calif., Berkeley, 1997. Fellow: NAE, IEEE (editl. bd. Trans. Electronic Devices 1986—88, Jack Morton award 1997, Solid State Cirs. award 2002, Paul Rappaport award 2004), Inst. Physics. Achievements include patents for solid state devices and technology. Office: U Calif Dept Elec Engring Computer Sci Berkeley CA 94720-0001

HU, CHI YU, retired physicist, educator; b. Szchwan, China, Feb. 12, 1933; arrived in U.S., 1957, naturalized, 1974; s. T. C. and P. S. (Yang) Hu; children: Marica, Mark, Albert, Han Chin. BS, Nat. Taiwan U., 1955; PhD, MIT, 1962. 6rsch. assoc. St. John's U., Jamaica, NY, 1962—63; asst. prof. physics Calif. State U., Long Beach, 1963—69, assoc. prof., 1968—72, prof., 1972—2005, prof. emeritus, 2006—. NSF vis. prof. UCLA, 1988—90. Contbr. articles to profl. jours. Fellow NSF summer, 1965, 1976; grantee, NSF, 1969—70, 1986—88, 1988—90, 1990—, Calif. State U. Long Beach Found., 1965, 1966, 1970, 1972, Dept. Energy, 1986—88. Mem.: Am. Phys. Soc. Office: Calif State U Dept Physics Long Beach CA 90840-0001

HU, DANIAN, history professor; MA, Case Western Res. U., Cleve., 1991; MPhil, Yale U., New Haven, 1997, PhD, 2001. Vis. asst. prof. U. Mass., Amherst, 2001—02; asst. prof. Morgan State U., Balt., 2002—03; asst. prof. dept. history CCNY, NYC, 2003—. Author: (monograph) China and Albert Einstein: The Reception of the Physicist and His Theory in China, 1917-1979, rev. ed., Ai yin si tan zai zhongguo (in Chinese). Grantee, Ctr. for History of Physics, Am. Inst. Physics, 1996; John Clarke Slater fellow, Am. Philos. Soc., 1998. Mem.: Chinese Assn. History Sci. and Tech., Assn. Asian Studies, Am. Phys. Soc., History Sci. Soc. Office: The City College of New York Hist Dept Convent Ave at 138th St New York NY 10031 Office Phone: 212-650-8927. Office Fax: 212-650-6379. Personal E-mail: danian.hu@aya.yale.edu. Business E-Mail: dhu@ccny.cuny.edu.

HU, ESTHER MING, astronomer, educator; d. David Ho Sheng Hu and Carolyn Jui Chen Hsu. BS in Physics, MIT, Cambridge, 1974; MS in Astrophysics, Princeton U., NJ, 1976, PhD in Astrophysics, 1980. Carnegie fellow Carnegie Instn. of Wash. (DC), 1980—81; rsch. assoc. U. Md./NASA Goddard Space Flight Ctr., College Park/Greenbelt, 1981—83; Space Telescope Postdoctoral Fellow Space Telescope Sci. Inst., Balt., 1983—86, rsch. assoc., 1985—86; asst. astronomer U. Hawaii, Honolulu, 1986—90, assoc. astronomer, 1990—98, astronomer, 1998—. Author: (sci. book chpt.) Our Universe. Mem.: Astron. Soc. of Pacific, Internat. Astron. Union, Am. Astron. Soc. Achievements include first to devise method for Discovering the Most Distant and Earliest Galaxies; research in Early Universe; Properties of the First Galaxies; Galaxy Evolution. Office Phone: 808-956-7190.

HU, HONGDE, mathematics professor; m. Vicky Liu; children: Lisa, Angela. BA, Pinxiang Coll., China, 1982; PhD, McGill U., Montreal, Can., 1993. Asst. prof. York U., Toronto, Ont., Canada, 1993—95; postdoctoral fellow U. Que., Montreal, 1995—96; lectr. U. Pa., Phila., 1996—99; asst. prof. Calif. State U.-Monterey Bay, Seaside, 1999—2002, assoc. prof., 2003—06, prof., 2006—, chmn. dept. math., 2006—. Vis. rschr. Stanford (Calif.) U., 1997, U. Sydney, 1998, ElectroTech. Lab., Osaka, Japan, 2000; chmn. Mathcom com. Calif. State U.-Monterey Bay, 2000—. Contbr. articles to profl. jours., confs. Grantee Agy. of Indsl. Sci and Tech., Japan, 2000. Mem.: Assn. Symbolic Logic, Am. Math. Soc., Can. Math Soc. Home Phone: 831-384-8126; Office Phone: 831-582-3851.

HU, HUA-LING WANG, writer, historian; d. Kai-ting and Shui-yan Wang; m. Chia-lun John Hu; 1 child, Carl Chun-hui. BA, Tunghai U., Taichung, Taiwan, 1959; MA, U. Colo., 1962, PhD, 1971. Instr. U. Colo., Boulder, 1963—70; assoc. prof. Nat. Chiao Tung U., Hsin Chu, 1972—74, Nat. Chung Hsin U., Taichung, 1973—74, Tunghai U., Taichung, 1973—74; asst. prof. Denver U., 1977—78; editor Jour. of Studies of Japanese Aggression against China, 1990—95. Cons. Rsch. Ctr. Nanjing Massacre, Nanjing Normal U., 2004—. Author: (short stories and novelette) Destiny of Fate, 1992, Ginling Forever: The Biography of Minnie Vautrin (Conventional Chinese characters), 1997, rev. edit. (in simplified Chinese characters), 2000, Ten Thousand days of Laughter and Tears, 1999, American Goddess at the Rape of Nanking: The Courage of Minnie Vautrin, 2000; contbr. articles to profl. jours.; appearance (documentary) Minnie Vautrin, 2003. Recipient medal of honor, Chinese Lit. and Arts, Taiwan, 1998. Mem.: Assn. for Asian Studies. Home Phone: 618-457-8734. Personal E-mail: hualinghu@aol.com.

HU, HUPING, biophysicist, lawyer; b. Wenshui, Shanxi, China, Sept. 19, 1962; arrived in US, 1987; s. Yongchang Hu and Cuifang Sun; m. Maoxin Wu, Jan. 29, 1986; children: Alice, Allen. BS, Shanxi Agrl. U., China, 1983; MS, Lanzhou U., Gansu, China, 1986; PhD, U. Ill., 1991; JD, NY Law Sch., 1998. Lic.: NY State Appellate Divsn. (2nd Dept.) 1999, bar: 1999. Rsch. asst. U. Ill., Champaign-Urbana; CEO H&W Mgmt. Corp., Champaign, 1991—93; legal asst. Bronx Dist. Atty.s Office, NYC, 1995—96; sci. cons. Stein & Associates, P.C., NYC, 1996—98; prin. Huping Hu Atty. at Law, NYC, 1999—; chief scientist Biophysics Consulting Group, NYC, 2000—. Contbr. articles to profl. jours. Recipient Best Grad. Student award, Lanzhou U., China, 1984—85. Mem.: ABA, NY State Bar Assn. D-Conservative. Achievements include founder of Scientific God Institute and Science Association for the New Millennium; proponent of the spin-mediated consciousness theory that says spins carried by nuclei in neural membranes are the linchpins between mind and brain, that is, spin is the mind-pixel; first to propose the oxygen pathway perturbation hypothesis which says that oxygen pathway perturbations by anesthetics play key roles in anesthesia; discovery of nonlocal effect of chemical substances on the brain and nonlocal chemical, thermal, and gravitational effects in water. Office: Biophysics Consulting Group 36-40 Main St Suite 306 Flushing NY 11354 Home Phone: 631-246-5654; Office Phone: 718-358-2085. Office Fax: 718-358-2086. Personal E-mail: drhu@att.net. E-mail: hupinghu@quantumbrain.org.

HU, KELLY, actress; b. Honolulu, Feb. 13, 1968; d. Herbert and Juanita. Grad., Kamehameha Sch. Co-owned Basic Bites. Actor: (films) Friday the 13th Park VIII: Jason Takes Manhattan, 1989, The Doors, 1991, Harley Davidson and the Marlboro Man, 1991, Surf Ninjas, 1993, No Way Back, 1995, Strange Days, 1995, Fakin' Da Funk, 1997, Martial Law: The Movie, 1998, Scorpion King, 2002, Cradle 2 the Grave, 2003, X-Men 2, 2003, Underclassman, 2005; (TV films) The Bold and the Beautiful, 1987, American Eyes, 1991, The Librarian: Quest for the Spear, 2004, MayDay, 2005; (TV series) Star Command, 1996, Nash Bridges, 1997—98, Sunset Beach, 1997, Hollywood Squares, 1998, Martial Law, 1998—2000; voice Star Wars: Knights of the Old Republic II-The Sixth Lords, 2004, Robot Chicken, 2005, host Asian Excellence awards, 2006, guest appearances Growing Pains, 1987, Night Court, 1988, 21 Jump Street, 1989, Tour of Duty, 1989, Melrose Place, 1994, Renegade, 1994, Malcolm & Eddie, 1998, Mad TV, 2003, Boomtown, 2003, CSI:NY, 2005, and several others. Named Miss Teen USA, 1985, Miss Hawaii, 1993. Achievements include Miss Teen USA in 1985. First Asian American female crowned Miss Teen USA; Miss Hawaii USA in 1993. Avocations: swimming, Karate (black belt). Office: c/o Innovative Artists 1505 Tenth St Santa Monica CA 90401

HU, LI, art educator; b. Shanghai, Sept. 16, 1950; s. Renzhi Hu and Keren He; m. Ping Li, Feb. 22, 1988; children: Yichen Hu, Elina Hu. BFA, Shanghai U., 1986; MFA, U. SD, Vermillion, 1993. Art designer Xiechang Sewing Machine Co., Shanghai, 1977-83; asst. prof. Shanghai U., 1986-89; assoc. prof. U. Wis., Oshkosh, 1993—2006, prof., 2006—. Solo shows include Fitton Ctr. for Creative Arts, Hamilton, Ohio, U. Wis., Oshkosh, 2006, Spartanburg County Mus. Art, SC, 2006, Chgo. Pub. Libr., 2005, Bergstrom-Mahler Mus., Neenah, Wis., Annex Gallery, U. Wis., Oshkosh, 2005, Tusculum Coll., Tenn., Rosewood Arts Ctr., 2004, North Ctrl. Coll., Naperville, Ill., 2002, Ripon Coll., Wis., 2001, Hopper House Art Ctr., Nyack, NY, 2001, So. Oreg. U., Ashland, 2001, Coll. of Siskiyous, Weed, Calif., 2000, 1078 Gallery, Chico, Calif., 2000, Lakeland Coll., Sheboygan, Wis., 2000, Morehead State U., Kent, 1999, U. Wis., Madison, 1999, Reno City Hall Gallery, 1999, Art Inst. and Gallery, Salisbury, Md., 1999, Art Ctr. in Orange, Va., 1999, Colo. State U., Ft. Collins, 1998, Coker Coll., Hartsville, SC, 1998, Linfield State Coll., McMinnville, Oreg., 1998, McHenry County Coll., Crystal Lake, Ill., 1998, Chadron State Coll., Nebr., 1997, Kansas City Artists Coalition, Kansas City, Mo., 1997, Mont. State U., Billings, 1996, Corvallis Arts Ctr., Oreg., 1996, Minnetonka Ctr. for the Art, Wayzata, Minn., 1995, Bloominton Art Ctr., Minn., 1995, U. SD, Vermillion, St. Louis CC, others; group shows include Charles Allis Art Mus., Milw., 2007, U. SD, Vermillion, U. Wis., Oshkosh, 2005, Columbia Art League, Mo. Chesterfield Arts, 2004, St. Louis CC, Calif. State U., Long Beach, 2003, Ohio State U., Mansfield, 2002, Taipai Fine Art Mus., Taiwan, 2001, Leslie Powell Gallery, Lawton, Okla., 1997, 2000, Smithtown Twp. Arts Coun., St. James, NY, 1997, Korean Cultural Ctr., LA, 1996, Medici Art Ctr., Phila., 1996, San Francisco State U. Student Ctr. Art Gallery, Calif., 1995, Berkeley Art Ctr., Calif., 1995, Royal Garden Gallery, Copenhagen, 1987, Hunte Coll., NY, 1986, Kobe Agr. Mus., Japan, 1986, Shanghai Art Mus., 1986, 87, 89, Coll. Visual Arts, St. Paul, 2001, Taipai Fine Art Mus., Taiwan, 2001 others; work collected at Sioux City Art Ctr., Iowa, U. SD, Vermillion, , Ripon Coll., Wis., Coal and Oil Corp., Ji Lu, Japan, Art Corp. of Japan-China, Kobe, Japan. Recipient Hon. Mention Okla.: Centerfold, Seventh, Leslie Powell Gallery, Lawton and the U. of Sci. and Art, Chickacha, 1997, Faculty Devel. Rsch. grant U. Wis., Oshkosh, 1995, 1996, 2007, Juror's award Berkeley Art Ctr. Assn., Calif., 1995, endowed professorship award, U. Wis. Oshkosh, 2006, others. Home: 4365 Bellhaven Ln Oshkosh WI 54904 Office Phone: 920-424-7059. Business E-Mail: hu@uwosh.edu.

HU, MEI MELVIN, interventional physiatrist; b. Ningbo, Zhejiang, China; m. Yinghong Cissy Xu; children: Angela C., Kevin C. MD, Shanghai Med. U., 1989; PhD, U. Tex. Health Sci. Ctr., Houston, 1996. Diplomate subspecialty pain medicine Am. Bd. Phys. Medicine & Rehab., 2003. Resident Zhejiang Provincial People's Hosp., Hangzhou, China, 1989—91; intern Flushing Hosp. Med. Ctr., Flushing, NY, 1998—99; resident Baylor Coll. Medicine, Houston, 1999—2002; asst. prof. dept. phys. medicine & rehab. U. Ky., Lexington, 2002—04; attending physician Pain Ctr., Mass. Gen. Hosp., Boston, 2004—05, Presbyn. Hosp. Plano, Tex., 2005—. Pvt. practice, Plano. Contbg. editor: Rehab in Rev., 2000—02. Vol. med. counselor Dallas Chinese Dr. Assn., Plano, 2005. Fellow, U. Tex., M. D. Anderson Cancer Ctr., Houston, 1996—98; grantee Am. Geriatics Soc. award, John A. Hartford Found., 2003; Clin. fellow, Mass. Gen. Hosp., Harvard Med. Sch., Boston, 2004—05. Fellow: Am. Acad. Phys. Medicine & Rehab.; mem.: Am. Assn. Neuromuscular and Electrodiagnostic Medicine, Physiatric Assn. Spine, Sports and Occupl. Rehab., Internat. Spine Intervention Soc., Am. Soc. Interventional Pain Physicians. Achievements include discovery of human fibroblast motility-stimulating factor which stimulates human sarcoma cell movement toward lung. Avocations: travel, skiing, swimming, dance, basketball. Home: 6301 Stonewood Dr #726 Plano TX 75024 Office: 2800 W 15th St Plano TX 75075 Office Phone: 214-708-6196, 972-612-9805. Personal E-mail: mmhu@hotmail.com.

HU, WEIGANG, software engineer; b. Ji-An, Jiangxi, China, Apr. 4, 1965; arrived in U.S., 1997; s. Yuanyu Hu and Jumei Fu; m. Guangping Grace Chen, Sept. 10, 2001; children: Zhengyi, Zhengjia Jennifer. BME, Nanchang Univ., 1985; PhD, Huazhong U. Sci. and Tech., Wuhan, China, 1994. Assoc. prof. Huazhong U. Sci. and Tech., Wuhan, 1994—97; post doctoral rschr. Indsl. Rsch. Inst. Swinburne - Swinburne U. of Tech., Hawthorn, Victoria, Australia, 1996—97; rsch. assoc. Wayne State U., Detroit, 1997—99; sofware engr. Ford Motor Co., Dearborn, Mich., 1999—2000, sys. analyst, 2003—; sr. project engr. Visteon Corp., Allen Park, Mich., 2000—03. Leader Chinese Soccer Club Windsor, Ont., Canada, 2000—04. Recipient Sci. and Tech. awards, Ministry Edn. China. Achievements include development of knowledge-based design and manufacturing support system; research in theories and methods of knowledge-based engineering; case-based reasoning strategy in knowledge-based engineering design. Office Phone: 313-594-2707. Personal E-mail: ae3091@yahoo.com.

HU, WINNIE, journalist; B in Polit. Sci., Princeton Univ.; M in Pub. Affairs Reporting, Univ. Md. Coll.Park. Reporter Pensacola News Jour., Dallas Morning News; metro. reporter New York Times, 1999—. Panelist New York Times Print Workshop, 2001. Author: (articles) Two Different Kinds of Math, and Two Different Spins on Employment, 2005, Home-owners are Manning Backyard Battle Stations, 2000; contbr. articles to Am. Journalism Rev. Mem.: New York Press Club (corr. sec.). Office: New York Times City Hall Room 9 New York NY 10007 Office Phone: 212-556-1947.

HU, YIPING, metallurgical engineer; b. Honghu, Hubei, China, Jan. 23, 1958; s. Zhaozhi Hu and Dingming Liu; m. Zanping Liu, Dec. 25, 1988; 1 child, Dianna. BS in Metallurgical Engring., Wuhan Inst. Tech., China, 1981; MS in Materials Sci., Mich. State U., 1996, PhD, 2000. Sr. instr. Guangdong Tech. Sch. of Light Industry, Guang Zhou, China, 1982—92; devel. engr. Quantum Laser Corp., Norcross, Ga., 1999—99; sr. engr. Honeywell-Greer Engines, Systems & Services, Greer, SC, 2000—. Mem.: Laser Inst. Am., The Minerals, Metals & Materials Soc., ASM Internat. Achievements include first to employ laser cladding technique to make rotary cutting dies, dramatically reduce production costs and greatly prolong service life; patents for multi-laser beam welding high strength superalloys; cold gas-dynamic spray repair on gas turbine engine components. Home: 18 Collier Lane Greer SC 29650 Office: Honeywell International 85 Beeco Road Greer SC 29650 Office Phone: 864-801-2174. Personal E-mail: yipinghu1@yahoo.com. Business E-Mail: yiping.hu@honeywell.com.

HU, ZHIYU, research scientist, educator; b. Kunming, Yunnan Province, China, June 30, 1965; s. Wenguo Hu and Ping Li; m. Hongzhi Li, June 2, 1965; children: Lydia, Liana. BS, Yunnan U., 1986; MA, Fisk U., 1995; PhD, U. Tenn., 2000, EMBA, 2004. Asst. engr. Kunming Inst. Tech., Kunming, Yunnan Province, 1986—90; team leader and tchr. Yangbi Detachment of Vols. in Edml. Svc., Yangbi, Yunnan Province, 1988—89; exchange vis. scholar U. Va., Charlottesville, 1990—93; gradute rsch. asst. Oak Ridge Nat. Lab., Oak Ridge, Tenn., 1995—2000; head Protiveris, Inc., Rockville, Md., 2000—02; staff scientist Oak Ridge Nat. Lab., Tenn., 2002—; rsch. asst. prof. U. Tenn., 2002—. Cons. Protiveris, Inc., Rockville, 2002—. Named Outstanding Vol. Tchr., Dept. of Edn. Yunnan Province, 1989; named to 11th Discover Mag. awards for technol. innovation, Discover Mag., 2000; recipient Southeast FLC award for excellence in tech. transfer, 2003, Excellence award in tech., Nat. Fed. Lab. Consortium, 2004. Mem.: Microscopy Soc. Am., Materials Rsch. Soc., Electrochem. Soc., Am. Physics Soc., Sigma Pi Sigma. Office: Oak Ridge Nat Lab Bethel Valley Rd PO Box 2008 Oak Ridge TN 37831-6123 Office Phone: 865-574-8461. Business E-Mail: huzn@ornl.gov.

HUA, FRED HUIZHONG, materials scientist; s. Dingfang Hua and Cai Zhang; m. Wenlian Zhou. PhD, McMaster U., 1998; B Engring, Hunan U., China, 1981. Rsch. asst. McMaster U., 1992—98; sr. rsch. engr. McDermott Tech. Inc., Alliance, Ohio, 1998—2002; sr. materials engr. Bechtel SAIC Co., LLC, Las Vegas, Nev., 2002—06, Areva NP, 2006—. Rsch. engr. Shanghai Rsch. Inst. Materials, Shanghai, 1982—91. Recipient Nat. award, Chinese Nat. Com. of Sci. & Tech., 1991/1992. Mem.: Nat. Assn. of Corrosion Engineers, Internat. (life). Achievements include research in Yucca Mountain project, which aims to secure the nuclear waste containment 1,000,000 years. Office: Yucca Mountain Project 1180 Town Center Dr Las Vegas NV 89144 Home Phone: 702-838-1185; Office Phone: 702-295-5431. Office Fax: 702-295-5965. Business E-Mail: fred_hua@ymp.gov.

HUA, NIAN GRACE, mathematician, researcher; BS in Pure and Applied Math., Tsinghua U., Beijing, 2003; DBA, Boston U., 2007. Rsch. asst. Boston U., 2004—, lectr., 2006—07. Cons. P&G Co., Boston, 2005—06. Scholar Academic Work, Social Work, and Art & Music, Tsinghua U., 1999—2003; Academic Achievement scholar, Coun. Supply Chain Mgmt. Professionals New Eng. Round Table, 2005, Grad. Sch. Mgmt. fellow, Boston U., 2004—07. Office: Boston University 595 Commonwealth Ave Boston MA 02215 Home Phone: 617-820-7637; Office Phone: 617-820-7637.

HUA, SHIPING, political science professor; b. Hebei, China, Mar. 28, 1956; came to U.S., 1987; s. Jingwen and Suxia (He) H.; m. Jia Qin; children: Xiaojia, James Hong, Eric X. BA, Tianjin Fgn. Langs. Inst., 1982; MA, Chinese Acad. Social Sci., 1986; PhD, U. Hawaii Manoa, 1993. Assoc., vis. fellow East West Ctr., Honolulu, 1990—94; assoc. prof. polit. sci. Eckerd Coll., St. Petersburg, Fla., 1996—2003, U. Louisville, 2003—; dir. Ctr. for Asian Democracy, 2006—. Editor, translator: Reporting and Writing the News, 1987; author: Scientism and Humanism: Two Cultures in Post-Mao China, 1995; editor: Chinese Political Culture, 2001, (with Yang Zhong) Political Civilization and Modernization, 2005, Reflecting on the Beijing-Taipei-Washington Triangle, 2006, (with Sujian Guo) China in the 21st Century, (with Sujian Guo) New Dimensions in China's Foreign Policy. Mem. Am. Polit. Sci. Assn., Assn. Asian Studies. Office: U Louisville Dept Polit Sci Louisville KY 40292 Home Phone: 502-290-5175. Business E-Mail: sohua002@louisville.edu.

HUA, XIANXIN, cell and cancer biology educator; b. Tongshan, Hubei, China, Aug. 27, 1962; s. Chengda Hua and Donge Jia; m. Wei Gao, June 1988; children: Connie, Michael. MD, Hubei Med. Coll., 1983; PhD, U. Tex. Southwestern Med. Ctr., Dallas, 1995. Postdoc. clin. scientist, Whitehead Inst., MIT, Cambridge, 1996-2000; asst. prof. cancer biology U. Pa., Phila., 2000—07, assoc. prof. cancer biology, 2007—. Recipient Howard Temin award Nat. Cancer Inst., 1998, Career Devel. award Burroughs Welcome Fund, 1998, Rita Allen Scholar, 2002, Am. Cancer Soc. Rsch. Scholar, 2003. Em. AAAS. Office: Univ Pa 412 BRB 2/3 421 Curie Blvd Philadelphia PA 19104-6160

HUANG, ALICE SHIH-HOU, biologist, educator, virologist; b. Nanchang, Kiangsi, China, Mar. 22, 1939; came to U.S. 1949; d. Quentin K.Y. and Grace Betty (Soong) H.; m. David Baltimore, 1968. Student, Wellesley Coll., Mass., 1957-59; BA in Human Biology, Johns Hopkins U., 1961, MA in Microbiology, 1963, PhD in Microbiology, 1966; MA (hon.), Harvard U., 1980; DSc (hon.), Wheaton Coll., Mass., 1982, Mt. Holyoke Coll., 1987, Med. Coll. Pa., Phila., 1991. Postdoctoral fellow The Salk Inst., San Diego, 1967; postdoctoral fellow dept. biology MIT, 1968-69, rsch. assoc., 1969-70; asst. prof. Harvard U. Medical Sch., 1971-73, assoc. prof., 1973-78, prof. microbiology in health scis. and tech., 1979-91; prof. microbiology and molecular genetics Harvard Med. Sch., 1979-91; dean sci., prof. biology NYU, NYC, 1991—97; sr. councilor for external rels., faculty assoc. in biology Calif. Inst. Tech., 1997—2006, sr. faculty assoc. in biology, 2007—. Program dir. NIH-Nat. Cancer Inst. Instnl. Nat Rsch. Svc. award, 1957-90; mem. com. on Biol. Scis. Yale U., Conn., 1981-85; dir. Ctr. for Pediatric Viral Diseases as part of Program on Great Neglected Diseases, Rockefeller Found., 1984-87; mem. med. rsch. and devel. command adv. com. U.S. Army, Frederick,Md., 1989-92; mem. sci. adv. bd. Inst. Molecular Cell Biology, Nat. U. Singapore, 1985-2003; N.Y. Acad. Sci., 1993; 6th Hattie Alexander Meml. lectr. Columbia U., N.Y.C., 1981; Lee Kuan Yew disting. visitor Nat. U. Singapore, 1985; chair Found. for Microbiology, N.Y., 1993; acad. adv. com. Inst. Molecular Biology, Academia Sinica, Taiwan, 1994—. Mem. editl. bd. Intervirology, 1973-90, Archive of Virology, 1975-78, Jour. Virology, 1976-93, ASM News, 1982, Microbial Pathogenesis, 1985-90, Jour. Women's Health, 1992-96; assoc. editor Revs. of Infectious Diseases, 1978-89; contbr. articles to profl. jours. Trustee Waksman Found. Microbiology, N.Y., 1986—, Keystone (Colo.) Ctr., 1993-98, U. Mass., 1987-91, Johns Hopkins U., 1992—2004, Pub. Agenda, N.Y., 2001—, Rockefeller Found., 2004—; mem. bd. overseers Shady Hill Sch., Cambridge, 1987-89. Recipient Eli Lilly award in microbiology and immunology, 1977, Alumnae Citation award Nat. Cathedral Sch., Washington, 1978, Ann. award San Francisco Chinese Hosp., 1989; Burroughs Wellcome traveling fellow to Gt. Britain, 1979. Fellow AAAS, Infectious Diseases Soc. Am., Assn. women in Sci. (Outstanding Woman Scientist award 1994); mem. Am. Soc. Microbiology (pres. 1988-89), Am. Soc. Biochemistry and Molecular Biology, Am. Soc. Virology, Am. Acad. Microbiology, Soc. Chinese Bioscientists Am. (councilor 1997-98), Acad. Sinica, Phi Tau Phi. Office: Calif Inst Tech Mail Code 147-75 Pasadena CA 91125 Home: 1225 S Grand Ave Pasadena CA 91105 Office Phone: 626-395-3446.

HUANG, BEIQING, mechanical engineer, educator; b. Anqing, Anhui, China, Oct. 6, 1967; m. Yingying Wang, Jan. 4, 1996; 1 child, Claire Felicia. B Mech. Engring., U. Electronic Sci. and Tech. China, Chengdu, 1990; M Mech. Engring., U. Alaska, Fairbanks, 2001, M Computer Sci., 2003; PhD in Mech. Engring., U. Mo., Rolla, 2007. Rsch. asst. Hangzhou Inst. Electronic Engring., China, 1990—93; lectr. U. Sci. and Tech. China, Hefei, 1993—99; grad. rschr., tchg. asst. U. Alaska, Fairbanks, 1999—2003; grad. rsch. asst. U. Mo., Rolla, 2003—. Contbr. articles to profl. jours. Recipient Sci. and Tech. award, Anhui Province, China, 1997. Mem.: ASME, AIAA. Home: 1950 Eldridge Pkwy # 9207 Houston TX 77077 Office: 3100 Wilcrest Dr Ste 240 Houston TX 77042 Home Phone: 573-202-0736; Office Phone: 573-341-6372, 713-532-2900. Business E-Mail: bh887@umr.edu.

HUANG, EUGENE YUCHING, civil engineer, educator; b. Changsha, China, Nov. 28, 1917; came to U.S., 1948, naturalized, 1962; s. Sam and Yi Yun (Chao) H.; m. Helen M. Woo, Aug. 20, 1955; children: Martha, Pearl, William, Mary, Priscilla, Stephen. *Eugene Huang's daughter, Martha, AB 1978 Harvard, PhD 1999 Columbia, is a free-lance writer. His daughter, Pearl, SB 1980 MIT, PhD 1990 Princeton, is employed as vice president, oncology proliferative diseases for Glaxo Smith Kline Co. Eugene's son, William, AB 1981 Harvard, JD 1986 Yale, PhD, 1998 University of California Berkeley, is an attorney in Washington DC. His daughter, Mary, AB 1984 Harvard, MD 1988 Duke, is an oncologist at Massachusetts General Hospital. His daughter, Priscilla, SB 1986 MIT, MBA 1990 Pennsylvania, is employed as controller for Merck Vaccines, a unit of Merck Co. His son, Stephen, BS 1990 Yale, MD 1995 Pennsylvania, is an endocrinologist at Boston Children's hospital.* MS, U. Utah, 1950; D.Sc., U. Mich., 1954. Registered profl. engr., Ill., Mich. Asst. engr. Chinese Nat. Hwy. Adminstrn., 1941-45, asso. engr., 1945-48; research asst. Engring. Research Inst., U. Mich., 1953-54; research asst. prof. civil engring. U. Ill., Urbana, 1954-58, asso. prof., 1958-63; prof. transp. engring. Mich. Tech. U., Houghton, 1963-84; acting head dept. civil engring., 1979-80; acting dean of grad. studies Mich. Tech. U., Houghton, 1981-83, prof. emeritus transp. engring., 1984—. Cons. transp. systems design, soil mechanics, 1954— Author: Overview of the American Transportation System, 1976; contbr. numerous articles on transp. design systems and research on materials for pavement to profl. jours. Recipient Faculty Research award Mich. Tech. U., 1967 Fellow ASCE; mem. AAAS, ASTM, NRC (transp. rsch. bd. 1954), Am. Soc. Engring. Edn., Assn. Asphalt Paving Technologists, Inst. Opns. Rsch. and the Mgmt. Scis., Am. Ry. Engring. and Maintenance of Way Assn., Sigma Xi, Chi Epsilon, Tau Beta Pi, Phi Tau Phi. Episcopalian. Home: 400 Garnet St Houghton MI 49931-1420

HUANG, GUIYOU, dean, English studies educator, writer; b. Xinjiang, China, Dec. 24, 1961; came to U.S., 1989; s. Huang Honglai and Dong Xiuqin; m. Yufeng Qian; 1 child, George Ian. BA in English, Qufu Tchrs. U., 1983; MA in English, Peking U., 1989; PhD in English, Tex. A&M U., 1993. Instr. Qufu Tchrs. U., 1983-86; tchg. asst. Peking U., 1986-89; editl. asst. South Ctrl. Rev. Tex. A&M U., College Station, 1989-93, lectr., 1993-95; asst. prof. Kutztown U., Pa., 1995-2000, assoc. prof., 2000—03, prof., 2003—04, dir. univ. honors program, 2000—04, chair dept. English, 2002—04; prof. English, dir. Honors Coll. Grand Valley State U., Allendale, 2004—05; dean undergrad. studies and programs St. Thomas U., Miami, Fla., 2005—07, dean, Biscayne Coll., 2007—. Author: Whitmanism, Imagism, and Modernism in China and America, 1997, The Columbia Guide to Asian American Literature Since 1945, 2006; editor: Asian American Autobiographers, 2001, Asian American Poets, 2002, Asian American Short Story Writers, 2003, Asian American Literary Studies, 2005; contbr. articles to profl. jours. Recipient Profl. Devel. awards State Sys. Higher Edn. Pa., 1997-98, 2003. Mem. MLA, Am. Lit. Assn., Am. Studies Assn., South Cen. MLA, Assn. for Asian Am. Studies, Am. Assn. Univ. Adminstrs., Am. Conf. Acad. Deans. Avocations: swimming, travel, cooking, fishing, conversation. Home: 14178 SW 54th St Miramar FL 33027 Home Phone: 305-829-6377; Office Phone: 305-474-6865. Business E-Mail: ghuang@stu.edu.

HUANG, HAN, systems engineer; b. ShenYang, LiaoNing, China, June 13, 1974; s. QiLi Huang and JingYan Zhao; m. Fang Luan, July 28, 2001. BSEE (hon.), Harbin Inst. of Tech., Heilongjiang, China, 1996; MSEE, Tsinghua U., Beijing, 2001; PhD, Poly. U., Bklyn., 2004. Cert. computer engring., NY State and Poly. U. Elec. engr. Power Simulation Co., Beijing, 1996—98; hardware engr. SunDom Electric Tech. Inc., Beijing, 1999—2000; design engr. Avionic Instruments Inc., Avenel, NJ, 2004—06; sys. planning engr. NY Power Authority, White Plains, 2006—. Author: Electric Power Quality, Advances in Soft Computing, Lecture Note in Computer Science. Recipient 1st prize Sci. and Tech., NE Power Group of China, 1997, 1st prize for excellent sci. and tech. paper, 1999; Tchg. fellow, Poly. U., 2001, Rsch. fellow, 2002—04. Master: Soc. for Indsl. and Applied Math. (assoc.); mem.: IEEE (sr.), Assn. for Computing Machinery (assoc.), Chinese Soc. Elec. Engring. (sr.), Sigma Xi, Tau Beta Pi (hon.). Achievements include design of Army 10KW Tactical Inverter System, DC/AC section main designer and project lead engineer, design of Cockpit Light Dimmer, to reduce the size, cost, weight, noise and efficiency enhancement; development of first Dynamic Voltage Restorer (DVR) in P.R. China for protection of critical loads; research in New York State power grid study to enhance its reliability and stability, development of Energy Management System and Dispatcher Training System for GuanXi Power Co; development of Flexible Dynamic Thyristor-Switched Capacitor (TSC) and Power Supply Analyzer for SunDom Electric Technology Inc; presenter of the Optimal Selected Harmonic Elimination technology; research in harmonic elimination technique and its application on General Active Power Filter (GAPF). Avocations: chess, travel, swimming, tennis, reading. Office: NY Power Authority 123 Main St White Plains NY 10601 Home: 1304 Midland Ave Apt B72 Yonkers NY 10704 Home Phone: 914-457-0242; Office Phone: 914-287-3412. Office Fax: 914-681-6932. Personal E-mail: huang.han@gmail.com. Business E-Mail: han.huang@nypa.gov.

HUANG, HAO H., music educator, department chairman; b. Jersey City, Calif., Feb. 12, 1957; s. George Chung-chi and Yi-Yin Tung Huang; m. Rachel Vetter Huang, July 30, 1984; children: Yan-Jie Micah, Yan-Han Jonah. AB in Music, Harvard U., Cambridge, Mass., 1978; MM in Piano Performance, Juilliard Sch., NYC, 1981; DMA in Musical Performance, SUNY, Stony Brook, 1985. Exec. dir., founder Belle Terre Chamber Players, 1983; asst. prof. music Sch. of Music, Converse Coll., Spartanburg, SC, 1985—91; vis. lectr. Hochschule für Musik, Weimar, Germany, 1992; exec. dir., founder Animas Music Festival, Durango, Colo., 1993—98; chair, prof. music Scripps Coll., Claremont, Calif., 1994—; prof. piano Claremont Grad. U., Calif., 1995—. Participant NEH seminar East-West Ctr., U. Hawaii, Manoa, 1998, Yale U., 1989; overseas advisor Liu Shi Kun Piano Inst., Foshan, Guangdong, China, 1999—; mem. faculty, resident artist Classical Music Festival, Eisenstadt, Austria, 2001—; vis. fellow Accademia Internazionale della Musica, Milano, Italy, 2004; vis. prof. N.Mex. State U., Las Cruces, 1998. Musician (USIA artistic amb.): (solo piano tours) Azores, Portugal, Spain, Germany, Romania, Algeria, Jordan, Bahrain, Saudi Arabia; musician: (Am. featured soloist) with Timisoara Philharmonic; musician: (piano soloist) Music in the Mountains Festival, Brevard Music Festival, Lake Tahoe Music Festival Orch/, (piano recital) An Evening with Louis Moreau Gottschalk, America's First Musical Multiculturalist, (piano soloist) Paradise Symphony Orch., (chamber music performance) 5th Internat. Assn. of Word and Image Studies Conf., (CD) Mei Duo, live, American Romantics; musician: (exec. dir., founder) (Belle Terre Chamber Players) Chamber Music Series; musician: (interviewee) (national public radio, morning edition) The "Lost" Opera of James P. Johnson and Langston Hughes; composer: (premiere of song-cycle) Change of State, based on poems by David Lloyd; author: (book chapt.) The Oekuu Shadeh of Ohkay Owingeh in Voices From Four Directons; musician: (CD) Gold Coast Trio "Live at Mondavi Center", (chamber music recital) American Composers: Music in Black and White, European Univ. Inst., Fiesole, Italy, (chamber music performance) of Ellen Taaffe Zwilich Sonata for Piano and Violin, Empiresaal, Schloss Esterhazy, Eisenstadt, (concerto soloist) Lake Tahoe Music Festival; musician: (Am. rep.) (piano recitalist) Cultural Olympiad; musician: (internat. juror) Porto Internat. Music Competition; contbr. AIDS benefit concert organizer Acad. of Friends, LA, 1997—. Named Solo Pianist, SC artist-in-residence program, 1987; named to Belle Terre Chamber Players, 1984; recipient Solo Pianist winner, David Bruce Smith Nat. Competition, 1989, Article of Yr. award, Am. Music Tchr. jour., 1995, Mary W. Johnson Faculty Achievement award for Outstanding Rsch., Creative Work and/or Performance, Scripps Coll., 1997, 1999, 2004, Mary W. Johnson Faculty Achievement award for Outstanding Tchg., 2000, Mary W. Johnson Faculty Achievement award for Outstanding Rsch., Creative Work and/or Performance, 2006; grantee City Arts grant, Nat. Endowment for Arts, Frank Huntington Beebe grant for European study, 1978, City Arts grant, Nat. Endowment for Arts, grant for European study, Frank Huntington Beebe, 1978, Odyssey grant, Mellon Found., 2003, travel grant to Xinjiang and Inner Mongolia, China, 2005, Johnson Faculty grant, Scripps Coll. Mem.: Coll. Music Soc. (Pacific So. chpt. vice-chair 1996—98). Office: Scripps Coll 1030 Columbia Ave Claremont CA 91711-3948 Home Phone: 909-624-9671; Office Phone: 909-607-3266. Office Fax: 909-607-9170. Business E-Mail: hahuang@scrippscol.edu.

HUANG, HSIEN-LU, electrical engineer; b. Hsiang-Hsiang, Hunan, China, Dec. 12, 1923; s. Shao-Ju and Ching (Yu) Huang; m. Hui-Lien Peng Huang, Jan. 1, 1947; children: Su, Na-Ching Chang, Kung, Janet Tu, Chin, Samuel Lin, Hsin, Chris Lu, Sung-Ping, Emanuel Lin, Peter Sung-an, Nina Wang. BSEE, Nat. Hunan U., 1944; MSEE, Va. Polytechnic Inst./State U., 1968, PhD in Elec. Engring., 1969. Cert. mgr. Rockwell Nat. Mgmt. Assn. Maj. Chinese Air Force, 1944-64, prodn. control chief, quality control officer, dep. squadron comdr. Nanking and Taiwan, 1944-64; assoc. prof. in elec. engring. Taipei Inst. Technology, 1960-66; instr. in elec. engring. Va. Polytechnic Inst. and State U., Blacksburg, 1968-69; asst. prof. in elec. engring. W.Va. U., Morgantown, 1970-74; devel. design engr. Barber - Colman Co., Rockford, Ill., 1975-76, Bridgeport Machines Control Co., Horsham, Pa., 1977-79; sr. elec. engr. and reliability engr. specialist Ford Aerospace and Comms. Corp., Houston, 1979-85; lead reliability engr. Rockwell Space Opers. Co., Houston, 1986-96; mem. engring. staff United Space Alliance West, Houston, 1996—. Contbr. articles to profl. publs. Elder, advisor Phila. Chinese Bible Study Fellowship, 1977—79; elder, evangelist Clear Lake Chinese Ch., Houston, 1979—; founder, coord. Space Christians Fellowship & Bible Study, Clear Lake, Houston, 1980—. Recipient Nat. Fidelity/Dilligence medal, Pres. of China, 1955, Group Achievement award, Lyndon B. Johnson Space Ctr., Houston, 1983. Fellow: AIAA (assoc.); mem.: IEEE (life), Nat. Mgmt. Assn. (cert. mgr.). Avocations: Bible study, personal evangelism, Christian fellowship, church visitation. Home: 470 Buoy Rd Webster TX 77598-2505 Office: United Space Alliance-West 600 Gemini St Houston TX 77058-2754 Office Phone: 281-282-4598. Personal E-mail: granpa.huang@gmail.com. Business E-Mail: Hsien.L.Huang@usa-spaceops.com.

HUANG, JEN-HSUN, electronics executive; b. Taiwan; m. Lori Huang; 2 children. BSEE, Oreg.State U., 1984; MSEE, Stanford U., Calif. Microprocessor designer Advanced Micro Devices; dir. coreware LSI Logic; co-founder, pres., CEO NVIDIA Corp., Santa Clara, Calif., 1993—. Trustee RAND Corp. Recipient Dr. Morris Chang Exemplary Leadership award, Fabless Semiconductor Assn., 2004, Daniel J. Epstein Engring. Mgmt. award, Univ. So. Calif. Mem.: Com. of 100. Office: NVIDIA Corp 2701 San Tomas Expy Santa Clara CA 95050*

HUANG, JIANZHONG, biomedical researcher; s. Longhe Huang and Yinzhu Xu; m. Shan Zeng, Feb. 11, 2002; children: Mary, Jason Zeng. MD, Tongji Med. U., Wuhan, China, 1980—85; Postdoctoral, Med. Coll. of Ga., Augusta, 1995—98, Columbia U., NYC, 1998—2001. Attending surgeon Health Dept. of Jiangsu, 1991. Resident in surgery Nanjing Children's Hosp., Nanjing, Jiangsu, China, 1985—91, attending surgeon, 1991—94; assoc. rsch. scientist Columbia U. Med. Ctr., NYC, 2001—. Chief divsn. of neonatal surgery Nanjing Children's Hosp., China, 1992—94; chair oral session of urology, Symposium of Pediatric Surgery 23rd Internat. Congress of Pediat., 2001. Contbr. articles to profl. jours. Recipient Aventis Young Investigator award, Eastern Coop. Oncology Group, 2003; fellow, Nat. Cancer Ctr., 2002—04; grantee, NIH, 2003—08, Nat. Cancer Inst. NIH, 2005—. Fellow: Am. Chinese Med. Assn., Southeastern Pharmacology Soc., Chinese Med. Assn.; mem.: Am. Assn. Cancer Rsch., Chinese Pediatric Surg. Assn. Achievements include invention of tumor model used to investigate effects of antitumor agents on large, metastatic tumors; discovery of regression of established tumors and metastases by a potent antiangiogenic agent. Home: 1042 Harvard Place Fort Lee NJ 07024 Business E-Mail: jh611@columbia.edu.

HUANG, JIA-SHENG JACK, optics scientist, researcher; arrived in US, 1993, naturalized, 2005; s. Chang-Sung Huang and Fang-Mei Lee; m. Ming Lee, Aug. 9, 1998; children: Ashley, Shannon. BS in Physics, Nat. Taiwan U., Taipei, 1988—92; MS in Materials Sci. & Engring., UCLA, 1993—96, PhD in Materials Sci. & Engring., 1993—97. Rsch. asst. Inst. Atomic & Molecular Scis., Academia Sinica, Taipei, 1992—93; summer internship Nat. Nano Device Lab, Hsinchu, Taiwan, 1995—96; mem. tech. staff Bell Labs, Lucent Techs., Orlando, Fla., 1997—2000; wafer fab R&D tech. mgr, scientist Ortel divsn. Emcore, Alhambra, Calif., 2000—. Tech. com. mem. Compound Semiconductor Mfg. Expo; reviewer in field. Recipient Agere Patent award, Agere Sys., 2002, 10 Yr. Anniversary award, Emcore Corp., 2007. Mem.: Huntington Tennis Club. Achievements include discovery of ultra-fast silicide line formation; polarity effect of contact failure in a paired contact structure; asymmetrical electromigration critical current density effect in multilevel interconnects; electromigration induced step-like resistance change behavior in multilevel interconnects; rippled optical spectrum of ESD stressed lasers; patents for dopant activiation of heavily-doped semiconductor by high current densities; a method of improving electromigration in semiconductor device manufacturing processes. Avocations: tennis, violin, travel, painting, basketball. Office: Emcore Ortel Divsn 2015 W Chestnut St Alhambra CA 91803 Home Phone: 323-254-4845. Office Fax: 626-293-3431; Home Fax: 323-254-4845. Personal E-mail: jshuang6@yahoo.com. Business E-Mail: jshuang@emcore.com.

HUANG, JOSEPH CHEN-HUAN, civil engineer; came to U.S., 1962, naturalized, 1972; MS in Structural Engring., Va. Poly. Inst. and State U., 1964, PhD 1988; m. Elizabeth C. Huang, Sept. 3, 1966; children: Edith, Eleanor, Evelyn, Edna. Registered profl. engr. N.Y., N.J., Pa., Del., Md., Va., W.Va., N.C., Fla., D.C. Project engr. Green Assos., Inc., Balt., 1964-68; pres. Gen. Engring. Cons., Inc., Balt., 1968-76; chmn., CEO Highlights Engring. Corp., Towson, Md., 1976—; pres. HS Mgmt. and Svcs. Corp., 1992—. Mem. ASCE, Am. Concrete Inst., NSPE, Chinese Bus. Assn. Greater Washington (pres. 1993). Author; Prestressed Steel Structures, Strategies for Business; contbr. articles to profl. jours. Home: 3506 Templar Rd Randallstown MD 21133-2428 Office: 1248 E Joppa Rd Towson MD 21286-5805 also: 1045 Taylor Ave Baltimore MD 21286-8331 also: 825 N Hammonds Ferry Rd Ste B Linthicum Heights MD 21090-1355 Office Phone: 443-416-5887. Personal E-mail: jchenhuanh@aol.com.

HUANG, JUDY, neurosurgeon; b. Taipei, Taiwan, Nov. 16, 1969; MD, Columbia U., NY, 1995. Cert. specialty bd. Am. Bd. Neurol. Surgeons, 2006. Asst. prof. neurosurgery Johns Hopkins U. Sch. Medicine, Balt., 2002—. Office: Johns Hopkins Hosp 600 N Wolfe St Meyer 8-181c Baltimore MD 21287 Office Phone: 410-502-5767. Office Fax: 410-550-0748.

HUANG, JUNMIN, chemist, researcher; b. Xiaochang, Hubei Province, China, Sept. 8, 1971; arrived in U.S., 2002; s. Qiaosheng Huang and Yuchai Ning; m. Hui Chen, Apr. 13, 1999; 1 child, Tyler Chen. PhD, Nankai U., Tianjin, China, 1999; BS in Chemistry, Cen. China Normal U., Wuhan, 1994. Asst. prof. Nankai U., Tianjin, China, 1999—2002; rsch. assoc. Vanderbilt U., Nashville, 2002—03, Miss. State U., Starkville, 2003—06; rsch. scientist U. Tex., Arlington, 2006—. Contbr. articles to profl. jours. Named Top 5 Productive Scientist, Nankai U., China, 2001; Key Tchr. Rsch. grant, Ministry of Edn., China, 2000—01. Mem.: Am. Chem. Soc., Sigma Xi. Achievements include patents pending for resolution of alpha, alpha'-Dihydroxybiaryls with a peptide chiral selector; discovery of resolution of racemic 1, 1'-bi-2-naphthol with a dipeptide chiral selector identified from a small library; highly efficient chromatographic resolution of alpha, alpha'-dihydroxybiaryls; preparation and evaluation of proline-based chiral columns; improvement of proline enantioselective stationary phases by replacing the 9-fluorenylmethoxycarbonyl group; improvement of proline chiral stationary phases by varying peptide length and linker; research in recent advances in peptide chiral selectors for electrophoresis and liquid chromatography; recent advances on the synthesis and biological activity of alpha-aminophosphonic acid derivatives. Home: 412 Summit Ave #41 Arlington TX 76013 Office: Univ Tex Dept Chemistry and Biochemistry CRB-311 Arlington TX 76019 Office Phone: 817-272-3834. Business E-Mail: jhuang@uta.edu.

HUANG, LINDA CHEN, plastic surgeon; b. Ithaca, NY, July 24, 1952; MD, Stanford U., 1979. Office: 1601 E 19th Ave Ste 3150 Denver CO 80218-1220 Office Phone: 303-831-8400.

HUANG, MARGARET, human rights advocate; BS in Fgn. Svc., Georgetown U. Sch. Fgn. Svc.; M in Human Rights, Columbia U. Sch. Internat. and Pub. Affairs. Profl. staff mem. US Senate Fgn. Rels. Com.; with Asia Found.; prog. dir. Robert F. Kennedy Meml. Ctr. Human Rights; prog. dir. US Racial Discrimination Prog. Global Rights, Washington, 2002—. Bd. dirs. Internat. Career Advancement Assn.; mem. adv. com. and screening panel Human Rights Video Project. Office: Global Rights 1200 18th St NW Ste 602 Washington DC 20036 Office Phone: 202-822-4600. Office Fax: 202-822-4606.*

HUANG, PAN MING, soil science educator; b. Pu-tse, Taiwan, Sept. 2, 1934; arrived in Can., 1965; s. Rong Yi and Koh (Chiu) H.; m. Yun Yin Lin, Dec. 26, 1964; children: Daniel Chian Yuan, Crystal Ling Hui. BSA, Nat. Chung Hsing U., Taichung, Taiwan, 1957; MSc, U. Man., Winnipeg, Can., 1962; PhD, U. Wis., Madison, 1966. Cert. prof. agrologist. Asst. prof. soil sci. U. Sask., Saskatoon, Canada, 1965-71, assoc. prof., 1971-78, prof., 1978—. Invited rsch. chair Nat. Taiwan U., 1996, 2003, 04; nat. vis. prof., head dept. soil sci. Nat. Chung Hsing U., 1975-76; mem. agr. adv. bd. Lewis Pubs., 1991—; hon. prof. Huazhong Agr. U., 1992—, Guanxi Agrl U., 1993—, Henan Agrl. U., 1996—, Langzhou U., 1999—; acad. advisor Chinese Acad. Scis., 1996—; hon. scientist Rural Adminstrn., Republic of Korea, 2004—. Author: Soil Chemistry, 1991, Environmental Soil Chemistry and Its Impact on Agriculture and the Ecosystem, 2000; mem. editl. bd.: Chemosphere, 1987—97, Pedosphere, 1990—, Trends in Agr. Sci., 1991—95, Advances in Environ. Sci., 1993, Geodema, 1994—, Soil Sci. Plant Nutrition, 1998—, Water, Air, and Soil Pollution, 1998—2001, Humic Substances in the Environment, 1998—; editor: 17 books; spl. editor, mem. editl. bd.: Water Pollution Rsch. Jour. Can., 1983—89, 1991—93, Agro's Ann. Rev. Crop Ecology, 1995—, mem. editl. adv. bd.: Trends in Soil Sci., 1995—, lead series editor: Biophysics-Chemical Processes in Environmental Systems, 2006—; contbr. over 300 articles to profl. jours., chapters to books. Bd. dirs. Saskatoon Chinese Mandarin Sch., 1977-79, Saskatoon Soc. for Study Chinese Culture, 1983—. 2d lt. Taiwan Mil. Tng. Corps, 1957-59. Recipient Soil Sci. Rsch. award, Soil Sci. Soc. Am., 2000; grantee, numerous other agys., 1965—. UN Environment Program, Nat. Scis. & Engring. Rsch. Coun., Can. Fellow: AAAS, World Innovation Found., Am. Soc. Agronomy, Soil Sci. Soc. Am. (rep. Clay Minerals Soc. 1979—83, chmn. divsn. S-9 1983—84, bd. dirs. 1983—84, editor spl. pub. 1986, Internat. Soil Sci. award com. 1986—87, assoc. editor 1987—92, Marion L. and Christie M. Jackson Soil Sci. award com. 1990—92, rep. to Internat. Union Pure and Applied Chemistry 1990—2000, fellow com. 1992—94, chmn.-elect divsn. S-2 1993—94, chmn. 1994—95, past chmn. 1995—96, spl. awards com. 1995—96, chair nominations com. divsn. S-2 1995—96, bd. dirs. 1995—96, editor spl. pub. 1998, Soil Sci. Rsch. award 2000), Can. Soc. Soil Sci.; mem.: Can. Network Toxicology (team on metal speciation 1993—96), Internat. Human Substances Soc. (leader Can. nat. chpt. 1992—2005), Internat. Union Pure & Applied Chemistry (assoc.; commn. environ. analytical chemistry 1993—95, titular mem. com. fundamental environ. chemistry

1995—97, 1999—2001, divsn. chemistry & environment 2001—05, titular mem. divsn. chemistry and environment 2006—), Internat. Assn. Study Clays (treas. 1993—2001), NY Acad. Scis., Am. Chem. Soc., Internat. Union Soil Sci. (chmn. working grp. MO 1990—2004, chmn. commn. 2.5 soil phys., chem., biol. interfacial reactions 2004—06), Sigma Xi. Avocations: music, reading. Home: 130 Mount Allison Cres Saskatoon SK Canada S7H 4A5 Office: U Sask Dept Soil Sci Campus Dr 51 Saskatoon SK Canada S7N 5A8 Home Phone: 306-373-6438; Office Phone: 306-966-6838. Business E-Mail: pmh936@usask.ca.

HUANG, ROBERT, electronics executive; BS in Elec. Engring., Kyushu U., Japan; MS, U. Rochester; MBA, MIT. Sales mgr. Advanced Micro Devices; founder Compac Microelectronics, 1980; founder, pres., CEO Synnex (formerly Compac Microelectronics), Fremont, Calif., 1992—. Office: Synnex Corporation 44201 Nobel Dr Fremont CA 94538-3178*

HUANG, ROBIN K., research scientist; b. Narragansett, RI, Mar. 5, 1973; s. Nancy and T. C. Huang. BS, MIT, 1995; MS, Stanford U., 1997, PhD, 2000. Mem. tech. staff Lincoln Lab. MIT, Lexington, Mass., 2000—. Scholar, Soc. Exploration Geophysicists, 1993—96; D.J. Lovell Scholarship, Soc. for Photoinstrumental Engrs., 1993. Mem.: IEEE (sr.; referee 2003—). Achievements include first to stimulate emission of exciton-polaritons in a microcavity; development of high power single mode semiconductor lasers. Office: MIT Lincoln Laboratory 244 Wood Street Lexington MA 02420 Home Phone: 978-663-9610; Office Phone: 781-981-4416. E-mail: huang@ll.mit.edu.

HUANG, SHAWN SHAOPING, engineer; b. Changjian, Hainan, China, Aug. 15, 1963; came to U.S., 1987; married, 1989; children: Anthony Jianfeng, Elizabeth Joanna. B in Engring., Wuhan U., China, 1983; postgrad., Peking U., Beijing, 1983-84; MS, Inst. Atomic Energy, Beijing, 1983-86; PhD, U. Idaho, 1990; MBA, U. Tex., 2004. Grad. asst. Inst. Atomic Energy, Beijing, 1984-86, rsch. assoc., project leader, 1986-87; grad. asst. U. Idaho, Moscow, 1987-90; sr. rsch. engr. Exxon Prodn. Rsch. Co., Houston, 1990-2000; prin. prof. Halliburton, Houston, 2000-01; chief engr. Conoco Phillips, Houston, 2001—. Contbr. articles to profl. jours. including Am. Chem. Abstracts and Supercritical Fluid Sci. and Tech. Vol. fund distbn. agy. United Way Gulf Coast chpt., Houston, 1996-98; vol. Idaho Spl. Olympic Games, 1988. Mem.: AIChE (mem. com.), Soc. Petroleum Engrs. (vice chmn. conf. 2004—), Tau Beta Pi. Achievements include patents pending in field. Avocations: listening to music, reading, hiking, biking. Office: Cocono Phillips 600 N Dairy Ashford Houston TX 77079-1175 Office Phone: 832-279-3834.

HUANG, SHOUHUA, electronics engineer; b. Hubei, China, Nov. 28, 1956; arrived in U.S., 1994; m. Dongmei Huang; children: Davy, Andrew, Melody. BS, Nanjing U., 1980; ME, Wuhan U., China, 1986; PhD, Beijing U. Posts and Telecom., 1992. Engr. Ministry of Aeronautics and Space China, 1980-83, Wuhan Rsch. Inst. Posts and Telecom., 1986-88; postdoctoral fellow Tsinghua U., Beijing, 1992-94; rsch. assoc. U. So. Calif., LA, 1994-95; rsch. engr. E-Tek Dynamics, Inc., San Jose, Calif., 1995-97; sr. engr. Osicom Techs., Inc., San Diego, 1997-99, Jet Propulsion Lab., Pasadena, Calif., 1999—. Translator: Guide to Programs/National Natural Science Foundation of China, 1992, 1993; contbr. articles to profl. jours. Mem.: IEEE (sr.), Internat. Soc. Optical Engring., Optical Soc. Am. Achievements include patents in field; research in 6-channel OC-48 (6x2.4 gb/s) 9,000 km WDM optical communications system; 6x2.4 Gbit/s circulating loop with 100 km DSF (Dispersion Shifted Fiber); LD characterization systems; others. Avocation: swimming. Office Phone: 818-354-0457. Business E-Mail: shouhua.huang@jpl.nasa.gov.

HUANG, THOMAS SHI-TAO, electrical engineering educator, researcher; b. Shanghai, June 26, 1936; came to U.S., 1958; s. Chien Liang and Allen (Chien) H.; m. Margaret Y. Nee, Apr. 4, 1959; children: Caroline B., Marjorie A., Thomas T., Gregory T. BS, Nat. Taiwan U., Taipei, 1956; MS, MIT, 1960, ScD, 1963. Asst. prof. MIT, Cambridge, Mass., 1963-67, assoc. prof., 1967-73; prof. Purdue U., West Lafayette, Ind., 1973-80, U. Ill., Urbana, 1980—, 1996—. Vis. prof. Swiss Inst. Tech., Zurich, U. Hannover, Federal Republic of Germany, U. Que., Can., others; cons. IBM, AT&T Bell Labs., MIT Lincoln Lab., Kodak, others. Author 6 books; editor 15 books; contbr. more than 500 articles to tech. jours. Recipient A. V. Humboldt U.S. Sr. Scientist award Alexander V. Humboldt Found., 1976-77; Honda Lifetime Achievement award, 2000, Okawa prize for info. and telecomm., 2005; Guggenheim fellow, 1971-72; fellow Japan Assn. for Promotion of Sci., 1986. Fellow IEEE (Signal Processing Soc. Tech. Achievement award 1987, Soc. award 1991, Third Millennium medal 2000, Jack S. Kilby medal 2001), Optical Soc. Am., Internat. Assn. for Pattern Recognition (King-Sun Fu Prize, 2002), Internat. Optical Engring. Soc. (Electronic Imaging Scientist of Yr. award 2006); mem. NAE, Chinese Acad. Engring. (fgn.), Chinese Acad. Scis. (fgn.). Office: Univ Ill Beckman Inst 405 N Mathews Ave Urbana IL 61801-2325 Office Phone: 217-244-1638.

HUANG, TING-CHIA, chemical engineering professor, researcher; b. Tainan, Taiwan, June 1, 1932; s. Tzuo and Nai (Yeh) H.; m. Juei-Chin Wan, Jan. 19, 1958; children: Ling-Yuang, Ling-Huei, Ping-Hsien, Chao-Cheng. BS, Nat. Cheng Kung U., Tainan, 1955; D Engring., U. Tokyo, 1979. Tchg. asst. dept. chem. engring. Nat. Cheng Kung U., 1956-60, instr., 1960-65, assoc. prof., 1965-68, prof., 1968—, chmn., dir. dept., 1981-87, v.p., 1995-97, acting pres., 1996-97; nat. chair prof. Ministry of Edn., 1997—2000. IAEA rsch. fellow Japan Atomic Energy Rsch. Inst., Tokaimura, Ibaraki-Ken, 1962; rsch. assoc. U. Houston, 1969-70; tech. cons. ChiMeng Indsl. Co., Ltd., Hsin-Hua, Taiwan, 1979-99; cons. Ministry Edn., Taipei, Taiwan, 1988-94, Kang Hsiang Lan Pharmaceutice Co., Ltd., Yung-Kan Ind. Park, Tainan Syan, Taiwan, 1989—, Vedan Enterprise Corp., Shalu Taichung, Taiwan, 1999—2004. Author: Experimental Physical Chemistry, 1963, 20th edit., 1987, Chemical Engineering Thermodynamics, 1971, Physical Chemistry, 1978, 5th edit., 1990, Experiments in Physical Chemistry, 1983, 3d edit., 1988, Physical Chemistry, 2006; regional editor Waste Mgmt. jour.; contbr. over 190 articles to profl. jours. Recipient Engring. Sci. award Hsu's Found., 1975, Engring. Acad. award Ministry Edn., 1979, Outstanding Rsch. award Ministry Edn., 1983, 84, Nat. Sci. Coun., 1986-94; named Outstanding Invited Rschr. Nat. Rsch. Coun., 1995-98. Mem. AIChE, Chinese Inst. Engrs. (best paper award 1975, 85, 96, 99, Outstanding Engring. Prof. award 1991), Chinese Inst. Chem. Engrs. (assoc. editor-in-chief jour. 1986-2000, Chin Kai-Ying award 1991, Best Paper award 1994, 95, 99, Chem. Engr. Inst. prize 1997), Chinese Chem. Soc., Soc. Chem. Engrs. Japan, Chinese Inst. Mining Engring. (Best Paper award 1989, 95), Phi Tau Phi. Avocations: reading, inventing, writing, music, ping pong/table tennis. Address: 4th fl 23 Alley 17 Ln 133 Sec 2 Chong Hua E Rd Tainan 70104 Taiwan Office: Nat Cheng Kung U No 1 Ta'-Siue Rd Tainan 70101 Taiwan Office Phone: 06-2757575 ext.62630. Business E-Mail: tchuang@mail.ncku.edu.tw.

HUANG, VERNA D., music educator; arrived in U.S., 1986; d. Jian Guo Xia and Alice Lee; m. Frank Huang (dec.); 1 child, Wayne. B in Piano Performance, Wilmington Coll., 1987; M in Piano Performance and Composition, Golden Gate Bapt. Theol. Sem., Mill Valley, Calif., 1990. Music dir. Chinese Christian Mission, Petaluma, Calif., 1987—92, Trans World Radio Sta., Cary, NC, 1992—94; piano tchr. Fremont, Calif., 1994—; pres. Spring of Spiritual Harmony, Fremont, 2000—; workshop presenter. Contbr. articles to publs. Deacon, San Francisco, 1987—99; music min., 1987—99; Sunday sch. tchr. San Francisco, Fremont, 1987—; choir condr. San Francisco, Berkeley, Fremont, 1987—. Mem.: Nat. Guild Piano Tchrs. Baptist. Avocations: reading, hiking. Personal E-mail: verna.huang@juno.com.

HUANG, WENDY WAN-JUOH, lawyer; b. Taipei, Taiwan, Aug. 3, 1966; came to the US, 1977; d. Tsung-Che and Sheree (Shen) H.; m. Kermit Marsh, July 6, 1996; children: Dermot, Connor, Morgan. BA, Cornell U., Ithaca, NY, 1988; JD, Boston U., 1992. Bar: Calif. 1993, DC 1994, NY 1994. Intern UN Com. on US-China Rels., NYC, 1986, Internat. Bus. Cons., Washington, 1987; asst. editor P.C. Mag., NYC, 1988-89; law clk. San Diego City Attys., Calif., 1990, US Atty.-So. Dist. NY, NYC, 1991, LA Dist. Attys., Calif., 1991; assoc. Law Firm of Kinkle, Rodiger & Spriggs, LA, 1992-94, Knapp, Marsh, Jones & Doran, LA, 1994-97, Burkley, Greenberg, Fields & Whitcombe, 1997—2000; chief gen. counsel Olen Cos., Newport Beach, Calif., 2000—05; exec. v.p., gen. counsel Crown Realty and Devel. Corp., Irvine, Calif., 2005—. Sec., chmn. Pacific Rim bd. govs. Calif. Chinese Bar Assn., LA, 1993—; judge pro tem, LA Superior Ct.; arbitrator LA County Bar Client Dispute Svcs.; legal cons. Sta. KPFK Radio, Voice of Am. Radio, Chinese Daily News. Writer, actress Words Across Cultures Theatre Co., LA, 1993; actress, dancer Bethune Theatre Danse, LA, 1993; editl. bd. LA Lawyer mag. Recipient Westinghouse Nat. Sci. Talent Search scholarship NSF, Washington, 1984; named a Superlawyer Rising Star, LA Mag., 2006. Mem. LA County Bar Inns of Ct., Orgn. Chinese Ams. (pres.), So. Calif. Chinese Lawyer Assn. (bd. mem.), Screen Actors Guild. Republican. Avocations: tennis, piano. Home: 8571 Edgemont Cir Westminster CA 92683-7216 Office: Crown Realty and Devel 18201 Von Karman Ave Ste 950 Irvine CA 92612 Office Phone: 949-567-5861. E-mail: whuang@crowndev.com.

HUANG, XIAO-LAN, chemist; s. Shi-Xiong Huang and Jing-Xiong Ji; m. Wei Sun, Sept. 27, 1993; 1 child, Jixiang. BSc, Nanjing Agrl. U., China, 1985, MSc, 1988; PhD, Hebrew U. Jerusalem, Rehovot, Israel, 2004. Assoc. prof. Soil and Fertilizer Inst., Anhui Acad. Agr., Hefei, 1994—2005, asst. prof., 1988—94; rschr. Hebrew U. Jerusalem, Rehovot, Israel, 1998—2004; asst. scientist, sr. rsch. assoc. U. Miami, CIMAS, RSMAS, Fla., 2005—. Recipient Anhui Sci. and Tech. Progress award, Anhui Province Govt., China, 1993, Leading Scientist for the 21 Century award, Anhui, China, 1998; fellow, Ministry Fgn. Affairs, Ministry Edn. Culture State Israel, 1998; scholar, Fund Israel-China Friendship Soc., 1999—2004. Mem.: Crop Sci. Soc. Am., Am. Soc. Agronomy, Soil Sci. Soc. Am., Am. Geophys. Union, Sigma X Sci. Soc. (hon.). Achievements include discovery of tea-arbor agroforestry in anhui, researcher and advocator; research in effect of fertilizer on the antimutagenic activity of cabbage; discovery of novel method for the nanomolar phosphate determination; research in biosolids stabilization and phosphate phytoavailability; phosphate biogeochemistry of Florida Bay. Office: Univ Miami CIMAS RSMAS 4600 Rickenbacker Causeway Miami FL 33149 Home Phone: 305-662-5031; Office Phone: 305-361-4551. Office Fax: 305-361-4447. Business E-Mail: xiaolan.huang@noaa.gov.

HUANG, XIAOZHAO, language educator; b. Beijing, 1951; s. Jiantuo Huang. PhD, Ball State U., Muncie, Ind., 1989—94. Asst. prof. U. ND, Grand Forks, 1994—2000, assoc. prof., 2000—. Contbr. articles to profl. jours. Recipient Pres. Predoctoral prize, Linguistic Assn. Can. & US, 1994, Pres. Post-Doctoral prize, 1995. Mem.: Tchrs. English Speakers Other Langs., Southeastern Conf. Linguistics, Internat. Linguistic Assn. Office: Univ ND 276 Centennial Dr Stop 7209 Grand Forks ND 58202-7209 Home Phone: 701-777-3321. Business E-Mail: xiaozhao_huang@und.nodak.edu.

HUANG, YEN TI, civil engineer; b. Taipei, Taiwan, Feb. 4, 1927; came to U.S., 1957; s. Tan Kun Huang and Mu Lin; m. Toshiko Naomi Saito Imano, July 4, 1958; 1 child, Philip Po-Wen. BSc, Nat. Taiwan U., Taipei, 1950; MASc, U. Toronto, Can., 1957; PhD, Columbia U., 1961. Registered profl. engr., Tex., N.Mex., Ont., Taiwan. Mem. rsch. staff Sperry Rand Rsch. Ctr., Sudbury, Mass., 1961-63; project geophysicist Atlantic Refining Co., Dallas, 1963-65; sr. geophysicist Geotech (subs. Teledyne Co.), Garland, Tex., 1965-68; mem. tech. staff Collins Radio Co., Richardson, Tex., 1968-70; CEO, pres. Y.T. Huang & Assocs., Dallas, 1970—, San Tai Internat. Corp., Dallas, 1973—. Adj. prof. U. Tex., Arlington. Founder of numerical transform theorem used in digital transform; patentee gyroscopic apparatus, modular inflatable dome structures, modular space framed earthquake resistant structures, modular roof structures, semi-submerged, movable, modular offshore platforms, and multipurpose offshore modular platform. Co-chmn. Tex. Asian Rep. Caucus, 1982, Spkr.'s Inner Circle, 2000; mem. Rep. Senatorial Inner Circle, 2000; conv. del. advisor from Tex., Rep. Nat. Conv., 2000. Named Rep. of Yr. representing Tex., 2001, Rep. Businessman of Yr., 2003; named to Presdl. Roundtable, 2004; recipient Outstanding Alumnus award, Nat. Taiwan U. Alumni Assn., 1999, Rep. Senatorial medal of freedom, 2002, Rep. Gold medal, 2002; scholar Econ. Coop. Am. /Joint Commn. on Rural Reconstruction Scholar, Taiwan Dept. Edn., 1951—52. Mem. ASCE (life; com. tower found. design stds. 1989-96), Internat. Soc. Offshore and Polar Engrs. (session chmn. 1991-94), N.Y. Acad. Scis., Tech. Club Dallas (v.p. 1993-95, pres.-elect 1996, pres. 1997), Rotary, Dallas Coun. on World Affairs. Unitarian Universalist. Avocations: photography, music, travel, history. Office: YT Huang & Assocs Inc/Santai Internat Corp Windy Forest Pl 9638 Greenville Ave Dallas TX 75374-4006 Office Phone: 214-348-5856. E-mail: yen853@aol.com.

HUANG, ZHONGPING, engineering educator; b. Zhejiang, China, May 7, 1964; arrived in US, 1997; s. Jinrong Huang and Laiying Pan; m. Jie Cai, May 4, 1995; children: David, Sarah. BS, Zhejiang U., Hanzhou, China, 1985, MS, 1987; PhD, U. Ky., Lexington, 2003. Mech. engr. Xizi Refrigeration, Inc., Hanzhou, 1985—87; asst. prof. Zhejiang U., Hanzhou, 1989—97, Widener U., Chester, Pa., 2004—. Vis. scientist Brookhaven Nat. Lab., Upton, NY, 1997—98, U. Ky., 1998—99. Author: Chronic Kidney Disease, Dialysis & Transplantation, 2004. Fellow, U. Ky., 2003—04. Mem.: ASME, Am. Soc. Engring. Edn., Am. Soc. Artificial Internal Organs. Achievements include patents pending for aparatus and method of enhances hemodialysis performance. Home: 1100 W Chester Pike Apt K8 West Chester PA 19382 Office: Widener U Dept Mech Engring 1 Univ Pl Chester PA 19013

HUBACH, JOSEPH F., lawyer, electronics executive; b. Cleve., Jan. 4, 1958; BA in Polit. Sci., John Carroll U., Cleve., 1980; JD, Case Western Res. U., Cleve., 1983. Bar: Ohio 1983, Tex. 1989. With Tex. Instruments, Inc., Dallas, 1984—, with law dept. Tokyo, 1990—93, v.p., asst. gen. counsel Dallas, 1998—2000; sr. v.p., gen. counsel, corp. sec. Tex. Instruments, Dallas, 2000—. Mem. adv. bd. Inst. Law and Tech. Ctr. Am. and Internat. Law. Bd. regents John Carroll U. Mem.: ABA, Ohio Bar Assn., Tex. Bar Assn. (mem. sect. intellectual property, sect. bus. law), Greater Dallas C. of C. (exec. com. bd. dirs.). Office: Tex Instruments Inc PO Box 660199 Dallas TX 75266-0199 Office Phone: 972-995-2011. Office Fax: 972-995-4360.*

HUBAND, FRANK LOUIS, educational association administrator, electrical engineer, lawyer; b. Washington, July 12, 1938; m. Carol Singer. BS, Cornell U., 1961, PhD, 1967; JD, Yale U., 1975. Bar: DC 1975, US Patent Office, 1977; registered prof. engr., Tex. Asst. prof. elec. engring. and math. scis. Rice U., Houston, 1966—72; owner, pres. Engring. Systems, Houston, 1972—73; atty., adv. FEA, Washington, 1975—76; divsn. dir. NSF, Washington, 1976—90; exec. dir. Am. Soc. Engring. Edn., Washington, 1990—; sec. gen. Internat. Assn. Continuing Engring. Edn., 2002—. Cons. Tex. Instrument, 1968-75; lectr. George Mason U., Fairfax, Va., George Washington U. Author: Protection of Computer Systems and Software, 1986. Mem. IEEE, ABA, NSPE, Am. Chem. Soc., Am. Inst. Physics. Office: Am Soc Engring Edn 1818 N St NW Ste 600 Washington DC 20036-2479 Office Phone: 202-331-3545. Office Fax: 202-265-8504. E-mail: f.huband@asee.org.

HUBBARD, ALLAN BROOKS, federal official, former chemical company executive; b. Jackson, Tenn., Sept. 8, 1947; s. George and Elizabeth (Beesley) H.; m. Kathryn Fortune, June 9, 1979; 1 child, William Fortune. BA cum laude, Vanderbilt U., 1969; MBA, JD, Harvard U. Pres. World Wide Chems., Inc., Indpls., 1977—, E & A Industries, Inc., Indpls., 1983—; dep. chief of staff to v.p. Dan Quayle The White House, Washington, 1990—92, asst. to the Pres. for econ. policy, 2005—; dir. The Nat. Econ. Coun., Washington, 2005—. Exec. dir. Pres. Coun. on Competitiveness, 1990—92; volunteer chmn. Ind. State Rep. Party, 1993—94. Bd. dirs. Indpls. Entrepreneurship Acad., The Children's Mus., Greater Indpls. Progress Com., U.S. Open Clay Court Championships, Inc.; mem. steering com. Vols. for Youth; fundraiser Vanderbilt U., numerous local art and civic groups; active various local polit. campaigns. Named Small Bus. Person of Yr., SBA, 1983. Mem. Ind. State C. of C. (bd. dirs.), Young Pres.'s Orgn., The Penrod Soc. Republican. Office: Nat Econ Coun The White House 1600 Pennsylvania Ave NW 2nd Fl W Wing Washington DC 20500*

HUBBARD, ARTHUR THORNTON, chemist, educator; b. Alameda, Calif., Sept. 17, 1941; s. John White and Ruth Frances (Gapen) H.; children: David A., Lynne F. BA, Westmont Coll., 1963; PhD, Calif. Inst. Tech., 1967. Prof. chemistry U. Hawaii, Honolulu, 1967-76, U. Calif., Santa Barbara, 1976-86; Ohio eminent scholar and prof. chemistry U. Cin., 1986-99, dir. Surface Ctr., 1986-99; dir. Santa Barbara Sci. Project, 1999—. Chmn. Ohio Sci. and Engring. Roundtable, 1990-95. Co-editor Jour. Colloid and Interface Sci., 1993—; series editor Interface Sci and Tech, 2001—; Surfactant Sci. Series; editor: Encyclopedia of Surface and Colloid Science. Mem. Am. Chem. Soc. (assoc. editor jour. Langmuir 1984-90, vice chair surface and colloid div. 1999, chair-elect 2000, chair 2001, Kendall award 1989), Electrochem. Soc. (David C. Grahame award 1993), Am. Phys. Soc. Office: Santa Barbara Sci Project PO Box 42530 Santa Barbara CA 93140-2530

HUBBARD, DEAN LEON, academic administrator; b. Nyssa, Oreg., June 17, 1939; s. Gaileon and Rhodene (Barton) H.; m. Aleta Ann Thornton, July 12, 1959; children: Melody Ann, Dean Paul John, Joy Marie BA, Andrews U., 1961, MA, 1962; diploma in Korean Lang., Yunsei U., Seoul, Korea, 1968; PhD, Stanford U., 1979. Dir. English Lang. Schs., Seoul, 1966-71; asst. to pres. Loma Linda U., Calif., 1974-76; acad. dean Union Coll., Lincoln, Nebr., 1976-80, pres., 1980-84, NW Mo. State U., Maryville, 1984—. Chair Acad. Quality Consortium, 1993-96; examiner Malcolm Baldridge Nat. Quality Award, 1993-96; judges panel Mo. Quality Award, 1994-96; adv. coun. edn. statistics U.S. Dept. Edn., 1997-99. Mem. ACE Leadership Devel. Coun., 1996-98. Avocation: classical music. Office: NW Mo State U Office of President AD143 800 University Dr Maryville MO 64468-6001

HUBBARD, ELIZABETH, actress; b. NYC; d. Benjamin Alldritt and Elizabeth (Wright) H.; divorced; 1 son, Jeremy Danby Bennett. AB cum laude, Radcliffe Coll.; postgrad., Royal Acad. Dramatic Art, London. Leading role: CBS daytime TV serial As the World Turns, 1984— (9 Emmy nominations for Best Leading Actress), NBC daytime TV serial The Doctors (Best Leading Actress Emmy), First Ladies' Diary (Best Leading Actress Emmy); appeared on Broadway in Present Laughter, Joe Egg, Time for Singing, Look Back in Anger, I Remember Mama (musical), The Physicists (Clarence Derwent award), others; appeared in off-Broadway prodn. Boys from Syracuse, Threepenny Opera (musicals); movie appearances include I Never Sang for My Father, The Bell Jar, Ordinary People, Center Stage; frequent guest TV talk shows. Former bd. dirs. Found. in Motion, U.S. Com. for Refugees, Women's Commission for Refugee Women and Children. Recipient Silver medal, Royal Acad. Dramatic Art. Mem.: NATAS (bd. govs.), AFTRA (former nat. bd. dirs.).

HUBBARD, GREGORY SCOTT, physicist; b. Lexington, Ky., Dec. 27, 1948; s. Robert Nicholas and Nancy Clay (Brown) Hubbard; m. Susan Artimissa Ruggeri, Aug. 1, 1982. BA, Vanderbilt U., 1970; postgrad., U. Calif., Berkeley, 1975-77; D in Engring. (hon.), Polytech. U., Madrid, 2006; ArtsD honoris causa, Cagswell Coll., Sunnyvale, Calif., 2007. Lab. engr. physics dept. Vanderbilt U., Nashville, 1970-73; staff scientist Lawrence Berkeley Lab. Dept. Instrument Techs., Berkeley, 1974-80; dir. rsch. & devel. Canberra Industries, Inc., Detector Products Divsn., Novato, Calif., 1980-82; v.p., gen. mgr. Canberra Semiconductor, Novato, 1982-85; cons., owner Hubbard Cons. Svcs., 1978—. Cons. SRI Internat., Menlo Park, Calif., 1979—86, sr. rsch. physicist, 1986—87; divsn. staff scientist space exploration projects office Ames Rsch. Ctr., NASA, Moffett Field, Calif., 1987—90, chief space instrumentation and studies br., 1990—92, dep. chief space projects divsn., 1992—96, assoc. dir. space directorate, 1996—97, dep. dir. space directorate, 1997—99, assoc. ctr. dir., 1999—2001, dep. ctr. dir. rsch., 2001—02, ctr. dir., 2002—06; mem. Fed. Sr. Exec. Svc., 1997—; study mgr. Mars Pathfinder Mission, 1990—91, Ames project mgr., 1992—96; mission mgr. Lunar Prospector Mission, 1994—99; founding dir. NASA Astrobiology Inst., 1998—99; Mars program dir. NASA Hdqrs., 2000—01; mem. Columbia Accident Investigation Bd.; lectr in field; Carl Sagan chair SETI Inst., 2006—; vis. scholar dept. elec. engring. Stanford U., 2006—07, cons. prof. aeronautics and astronautics dept., 2007—. Recipient Exceptional Achievement medal, NASA, 1994, 2001, Outstanding Leadership medal, 1998, 1999, 2002, DSM, 2004, Execptional Svc. medal, 2005, Laurels for Accomplishments in Space, Aviation Week, 1997, 1998, 2003, Von Karman medal in Astronautics, Am. Inst. Aeronautics and Astronautics, 2004, Carl Sagan Meml. award, Am. Astronautical Soc. and The Planetary Soc., 2006; Founders scholarship, Vanderbilt U., 1966. Fellow: AIAA (Von Karman medal 2004); mem.: IEEE, Calif. Coun. Sci. Tech., Am. Phys. Soc., Internat. Acad. Astronautics (Engring. Sci. award 2004), Nuc. Sci. Soc., Commonwealth Club Calif., Hon. Order Ky. Cols.

HUBBARD, HAROLD MEAD, energy and environmental systems consultant, retired research executive; b. Beloit, Kans., Apr. 16, 1924; s. Clarence Richard and Elizabeth (Mead) H.; m. Doreen J. Wallace, Aug. 13, 1948 (div. 1975); children: Stuart W., David D.; m. Barbara Bell Czarnecki, May 9, 1976 (div. 1987), remarried Sept. 9, 1999. BS, U. Kans., 1948, PhD, 1951; DSc (hon.), Regis U., 1984. Instr. chemistry U. Kans., Lawrence, 1949-51; rsch. chemist, rsch. mgr., lab. mgr. E. I. DuPont de Nemours & Co., Inc., Wilmington, Del., 1951-69; dir. phys. sci. Midwest Rsch. Inst., Kansas City, Mo., 1970-75, v.p. rsch., 1976-78, sr. v.p. ops., 1979-82, exec. v.p., 1983-90; dir. Solar Energy Rsch. Inst., 1982-90; Spark M. Matsunaga disting. fellow in energy and environ. U. Hawaii at Manoa, 1991-96; pres., CEO Pacific Internat. Ctr. for High Tech. Rsch., Honolulu, 1992-95. Vis. sr. fellow Resources for the Future, 1990-91; bd. dirs. Guaranty State Bank; chmn. Nat. Rsch. Coun. bd. on energy and environ. sys., 1991-96; lifetime nat. assoc. Nat. Acads. With U.S. Army, 1942-45. Mem. AAAS, Mo. Acad. Sci. (councillor at large 1977-80), Tech. Transfer Soc. (v.p. 1978-79), Am. Chem. Soc., Acad. Sci. (nat. assoc.), Am. Solar Energy Soc., Colo. Renewable Energy Soc. (pres. 1996-97), Sigma Xi, Delta Upsilon, Cosmos Club. Home: 3938 SW Linden Ct Lees Summit MO 64082-4643 Personal E-mail: hubbar@comcast.net.

HUBBARD, HARVEY HART, aeroacoustician, noise control engineer, consultant; b. Swanton, Vt., June 17, 1921; s. Horace Waite and Elbie (Hart) H.; m. Sadie Margaret Miller; children: Thomas W., Susan H., Pamela L., Walter R. BSEE, U. Vt., 1942. Engr. Westinghouse Mfg. Co., Pitts., 1942; br. chief NASA, Hampton, Va., 1945-59, asst. div. chief, 1959-80; sr. rsch. assoc. Coll. William and Mary, Williamsburg, Va., 1981-85; cons. Bionetics Inc., Hampton, 1985-87, Planning Rsch. Corp., Hampton, 1987—. Author over 130 book chpts. and tech. reports in aeroacoustics rsch. and noise control engring., 1949-99. Lt. col. USAF,

1942-45, PTO. Recipient Sonic Boom Rsch. award, 1968, Medal for Exceptional Sci. Achievement, 1969, NASA, medal for Disting. Pub. Svc., 1992. Fellow AIAA (assoc., Aeroacoustics medal 1979), Acoustical Soc. Am. (pres. 1989-90, Silver medal in noise 1978); mem. Inst. of Noise Control Engring. (pres. 1979). Presbyterian. Home: 955 Harpersville Rd Apt 2053 Newport News VA 23601

HUBBARD, HERBERT HENDRIX, lawyer; b. Balt., Sept. 20, 1922; s. Amberson Hardy and Louise Virginia (Hendrix) H.; m. Joanne Hileman Nottingham, June 5, 1948 (dec. Sept. 2002); children: Melissa Hubbard O'Donnell, Alison Hubbard Presti. JD, U. Md., Balt., 1950. Bar: Md. 1950, US Dist. Ct. Md. 1950, US Ct. Appeals (4th cir.) 1953, US Supreme Ct. 1963. Clk. to dist. judge US Dist. Ct. Md., Balt., 1950-51; assoc. France, Rouzer & Harris, Balt., 1951-52, 54-59; asst. US atty. Dist. Md., Balt., 1952-53, 1st asst. US atty., 1953-54; atty., ptnr. Weinberg & Green, Balt., 1959—98; counsel Saul Ewing, Balt., 1998—2001, of counsel, 2001—03; gen. counsel Forest Haven Nursing Home, Balt., 2001—. Founding dir. Devel. Credit Fund, Inc., Balt., 1984-96. Chmn., corp. devel. coun. Sheppard & Enoch Pratt Hosp., Balt., 1978-86. Mem. ABA, Md. Bar Assn. (founding, chmn. profl. liability ins. com. 1976-82), Bar Assn. Ins. Trust (trustee 1976-88), Legal Mut. Liability Ins. Soc. Md. (bd. dirs., 1986-2005 , sr vp., exec. com. 1986-2004, founding dir.), Order of Coif, U. Md. Law Review. Episcopalian. Avocation: bridge. Home: Blakehurst 1055 W Joppa Rd Apt 316 Towson MD 21204 Office: 701 Edmondson Ave Catonsville MD 21228 Home Phone: 410-823-0520; Office Phone: 410-747-7425 ext 50. Business E-Mail: herberth@foresthavennh.com.

HUBBARD, HOLLY ANNON, language arts educator; b. Nassawado, Va., May 27, 1976; d. George Palmer and Rhonda Allums Annon; m. Richard Lee Hubbard, July 12, 2003; 1 child, Gibson Lee. BA, Longwood U., Farmville, Va., 1998. Lic. tchr. secondary English, journalism Va. 6th grade history and lang. arts tchr. Richmond County Pub. Schs., Warsaw, 1998—2001, Accomac County Pub. Schs., Va., 2001—02; 7th grade lang. arts tchr. Northampton County Pub. Schs., Machipongo, Va., 2002—. Bd. mem. Gifted Adv. Bd., Machipongo, 2006—. Bd. mem. ESO Arts Ctr., Belle Haven, Va., 2002—06; exec. bd. mem. Ducks Unlimited, Eastern Shore. Mem.: Va. Edn. Assn. (pres. Richmond City 2000—01), Va. Mid. Sch. Assn.

HUBBARD, HOWARD JAMES, bishop; b. Troy, NY, Oct. 31, 1938; s. Howard James and Elizabeth D. (Burke) H. BA, St. Joseph's Sem., Yonkers, NY, 1960; STL, Gregorian U., Rome, 1964; DD (hon.), Siena Coll., 1977; LHD (hon.), Coll. St. Rose, 1977. Ordained priest Roman Catholic Ch., Rome, 1963; former parish priest St. Joseph's Ch., Schenectady, 1964; parish priest Cathedral Parish, Albany, 1964-65; Ordained bishop, 1977; bishop of Albany Diocese of Albany, NY, 1977—. Asst. dir. Cath. Charities, Schenectady, 1966; chaplain Convent of the Sacred Heart, Kenwood, Albany, 1966; dir. Providence House, Albany, 1966; vicar gen. Diocese of Albany, 1976; dir. Cath. Interracial Coun.; coord. Urban Apostolate, from 1972; dir. Office of Pastoral Planning, Albany, 1974-76; diocesan consultor Diocese of Albany, 1976-77. Pres. Urban League. Office: Bishop of Albany Pastoral Ctr 40 N Main Ave PO Box 6480 Albany NY 12203-1963 Address: 125 Eagle St Albany NY 12202-1718

HUBBARD, JOHN M., library and information scientist; BA in Psychology, Philosophy and Geography, Macalester Coll., St. Paul, 1995; MS in Libr. and Info. Sci., Drexel U., Phila., 2000. Instrnl. tech. specialist Haverford Coll., Pa., 1999—2001; web svcs. and electronic resources coord., sr. acad. libr. U. Wis., Milw., 2001—. Founder Library and Information Sci. Wiki, 2005. Named one of the Movers & Shakers, Libr. Jour., 2006. Mem.: ALA (life). Home: 3774 S Pine Ave Milwaukee WI 53207 Office: U Wis Milw Librs 2311 E Hartford Ave Milwaukee WI 53211 Home Phone: 414-744-0362; Office Phone: 414-229-6775. E-mail: hubbardj@uwm.edu.

HUBBARD, JOHN RANDOLPH, retired academic administrator, diplomat; b. Belton, Tex., Dec. 3, 1918; s. Louis Herman and Bertha (Altizer) H.; m. Lucille Luckett, Jan. 29, 1947 (div. Dec. 1983); children: Elisa, Melisse, Kristin. AB, U. Tex., 1938, A.M., 1939, PhD, 1950; L.H.D., Hebrew Union Coll., Los Angeles, 1971, Westminster Coll., Fulton, Mo., 1977; LL.D., Sch. of Ozarks, 1973, U. So. Calif., 1980. Pvt. sec. to ICC commr., 1939-41; teaching fellow U. Tex., 1946-48; vis. asst. prof. Brit. history La. State U., 1948; asst. prof. European history Tulane U., 1949-52, assoc. prof., 1953-58, prof., 1958-65; dean Newcomb Coll., 1953-65; vis. asst. prof. European history Yale, 1952-53; chief edn. adviser U.S. AID, India, 1965-69; v.p. for acad. affairs, provost U. So. Calif., Los Angeles, 1969-70, pres., 1970-80, pres. emeritus, 1980—, John R. Hubbard chair Brit. history, 1980—; US amb. to India, 1988-89. Vis. disting. prof. Nat. U. Taipei, Taiwan, 1981; co-chmn. Indo-U.S. Subcommn. on Edn. and Culture, 1982—. Contbr.: articles and revs. to Jour. Modern History; other ednl. jours. Mem. bd. Tulane-Lyceum Assn., 1953-65, Isidore Newman Sch., 1953-65; mem. Region 12 selection com. Woodrow Wilson Fellowship Program, also chmn., 1955-65; mem. bd. U.S. Edn. Found., India; mem. Indian adv. bd. Women's Coll. Faculty Exchange program; pres. bd. Am. Internat. Sch., New Delhi; mem. So. Calif. adv. bd. Inst. Internat. Edn.; trustee Scholarships for Children of Am. Mil. Personnel; bd. dirs. Community TV So. Calif., Los Angeles. Served as an aviator in USN, 1941-46; flight instr. and patrol plane comdr. Atlantic and Pacific fleets; lt. comdr. Res. Decorated D.F.C., Air medals (4); chevalier des Palmes Académiques; Stella della Solidarietá Italiana Italy; Order of Taj 3d degree Iran; recipient Disting. Services to Higher Edn. in U.S. award Tulane U., New Orleans, 1976; Air U. award, 1976; Disting. Alumnus award U. Tex., Austin, 1978, Alben W. Barkley medal for disitng. svc., 1989. Mem. Am., Miss. Valley hist. assns., So. Hist. Soc. (exec. council 1954-56), Anglo-Am. Hist. Soc., Assn. Ind. Calif. Colls. and Univs. (trustee), Am. Council Edn. (commn. on fed. relations 1975-77), Assn. Am. Univs. (council on fed. relations 1975-79), Orgn. Am. Historians, Conf. Brit. Studies, Am. Council Learned Socs., Phi Beta Kappa, Phi Delta Kappa, Alpha Kappa Psi, Delta Kappa Epsilon, Omicron Delta Kappa. Clubs: Royal Aero (London), Athenaeum (London); Los Angeles Country; California (Los Angeles); University (N.Y.C.); Cosmos (Washington). Office: U So Calif Dept History Los Angeles CA 90089-0001 Office Phone: 760-328-8321. *The fear of false knowledge is the beginning of wisdom.*

HUBBARD, LINCOLN BEALS, medical physicist, consultant; b. Hawkesbury, Ontario, Sept. 8, 1940; arrived in U.S., 1957; s. Carroll Chauncey and Mary Lunn (Beals) Hubbard; m. Nancy Ann Krieger, Apr. 3, 1961; children: Jill, Katrina. BS in Physics, U. NH, 1961; PhD, MIT, 1967. Diplomate Am. Bd. Radiology, cert. health physicist Am. Bd. Health Physics. Postdoctoral appointee Argonne Nat. Lab., 1966—68; asst. prof. math. and physics Knoxville (Tenn.) Coll., 1968—70; asst. prof. physics Furman U., Greenville, SC, 1970—74; chief physicist Mt. Sinai Hosp., Chgo., 1974—75, 1979—2002, Cook County Hosp., Chgo., 1975—88; prof. med. physics Rush U., 1986—; ptnr. Fields, Griffith, Hubbard & Assoc., Ltd., 1978—93; pres. Hubbard, Broadbent & Assoc., Ltd., 1993—. Author (with S.S. Stefani): Mathematics for Technologists, 1979; author: (with G.B. Greenfield) Computers in Radiology, 1984. Fellow: Am. Coll. Radiology, Am. Assn. Physicists in Medicine. Home and Office: 4113 W End Rd Downers Grove IL 60515-2307 Home Phone: 630-963-2913; Office Phone: 630-963-2913.

HUBBARD, MICHELE MASANEK, secondary school educator, soccer coach; s. Ronald Julian and Stephanie Ann Masanek; m. Rodney Wade Hubbard, July 10, 1999. BE, Bowling Green State U., Ohio, 1992; ME, Wright State U., Dayton, 2004. Tchr. Winston Woods Sch., Forest Pk., Ohio, 1994—95, Fairfield City Schs., 1995—2005. Girl's soccer coach Fairfield HS, 1994—2004, boy's asst. soccer coach, 2004—; coach Odyssey of the Mind, Ohio, 1995—98. Supporter Young Life, Fairfield, 1995—, Athletes in Action, Fairfield, 1999—, Fellowship of Christian Athletes, Fairfield, Ohio, 1999—. Nominee Ashland Tchr. of Yr., 1994, Tchr. of Yr., Walt Disney, 2000, 2004, 2006, Fairfield City Schs., 2004, Tchr. of Week, WMOH, 2004; recipient Fairfield Sch. Bell award, Fairfield City Schs., 1999, 2000, 2001, 2002, 2003, 2004, 2005, Fairfield Amb. award, 2004. Mem.: Pi Lambda Theta, Phi Kappa Phi. Democrat. Avocations: soccer, running. Office: Fairfield City Schs 255 Donald Dr Fairfield OH 45014 Personal E-mail: mro717@msn.com.

HUBBARD, RICHARD L., lawyer; b. Dallas, May 27, 1943; BA magna cum laude, Williams Coll., 1964; LLB magna cum laude, Harvard U., 1967. Bar: D.C. 1968. Law clk. to Hon. Arnold Raum U.S. Tax Ct., 1967-69; ptnr., Tax & Estates Practice Group Arnold & Porter, Washington, 1969—. Mem. Phi Beta Kappa. Office: Arnold & Porter Thurman Arnold Bldg 555 12th St NW Washington DC 20004-1206 Office Phone: 202-942-5755. Office Fax: 202-942-5999. Business E-Mail: richard.hubbard@aporter.com.

HUBBARD, R(OBERT) GLENN, dean, former federal official; b. Apopka, Fla., Sept. 4, 1958; s. Charles Whistnant and Myrtle Jean (Dabbs) H; m. Constance Pond Hubbard; children two. BA, BS, U. Cen. Fla., 1979; AM, Harvard U., 1981, PhD, 1983. Prof. economics Northwestern U., Evanston, Ill., 1983-87; Russell L. Carson prof. economics and fin. Columbia U. Bus. Sch., NYC, 1988—, prof. economics, co-dir. Entrepreneurship Program, sr. vice dean, 1994—97, dean NYC, 2004—. John M. Olin fellow, Nat. Bur. Econ. Rsch., Cambridge, Mass., 1987-88; cons., U.S. Dept. State, Dept. Energy, Internat. Trade Commn., Social Security Adminstrn., Nat. Petroleum Coun., numerous pvt. corps.; chmn., U.S. Pres. Coun. Econ. Advs., 2001-2003; dep. asst. sec. U.S. Dept. Treas., Washington, DC, 1991-92; bd. dir. MetLife Inc., 2007-, ADP, BlackRock Fin., Dex Media, KKR Fin. Corp. and Ripplewood Holdings. Editor: Asymmetric Information, Corporate Finance and Investment, 1989; contbr. numerous articles to profl. jours. Mem. Big Apple Dist. Com. Boy Scouts of Am. Grantee, NSF, 1983—. Mem. Am. Econ. Assn., Econometric Soc., Royal Econ. Assn., Am. Fin. Assn., Econ. Club NY, Univ. Club NY, Harvard Club NY, Met. Club Washington, Edgewater Beach Club of Naples. Republican. Presbyterian. Avocations: reading, theater, travel. Office: Columbia U Grad Sch Bus 3022 Broadway 609 Uris Hall New York NY 10027 Office Phone: 212-854-3493. Business E-Mail: rgh1@columbia.edu.

HUBBARD, RUTH, retired biology professor; b. Vienna, Mar. 3, 1924; arrived in US, 1938; d. Richard and Helene (Ehrlich) Hoffmann; m. Frank Twombly Hubbard, Dec. 26, 1942 (div. 1951); m. George Wald, June 11, 1958; children: Elijah, Deborah Hannah. AB, Radcliffe Coll., 1944, PhD, 1950; DSc (hon.), Macalester Coll., 1991, U. Toronto, Ont., Can., 1991, So. Meth. U., 1997, Clark U., 2003; LHD (hon.), So. Ill. U., Edwardsville, 1991. Lab. technician Tenn. Pub. Health Svc., Chattanooga, 1945-46; fellow U. Coll. Hosp. Med. Sch., London, 1948-49; Guggenheim fellow Carlsberg Lab., Copenhagen, 1952-53; rsch. fellow Harvard U., Cambridge, Mass., 1950-52, 54-58, rsch. assoc., lectr., 1958-74, prof., 1974-90, prof. emerita, 1990—. Vis. prof. MIT, Cambridge, 1972; cons. Boston Women's Healthbook Collective 1982—; Regents lectr. U. Calif, Berkeley, 2002. Author: (with Margaret Randall) The Shape of Red: Insider/Outsider Reflections, 1988; author: The Politics of Women's Biology, 1990, (with Elijah Wald) Exploding the Gene Myth, 1993, 97, 99, Profitable Promises: Essays on Women, Science and Health, 1995; editor: Women Look at Biology Looking at Women, 1979, Genes and Gender II, 1979, Biological Woman--The Convenient Myth, 1982, Woman's Nature: Rationalizations of Inequality, 1983, Reinventing Biology: Respect for Life and the Creation of Knowledge, 1995; contbr. more than 250 articles on sci. and women's issues to profl. and lay books and jours. Adv. coun. mem. Nat. Women's Health Network, Washington, 1980-85; bd. dirs. Coun. Responsible Genetics, Boston, 1982-2002, Boston Women's Health Book Collective, 1998-99; mem. adv. bd. Boston Women's Fund, 1983-85, 2000-02; mem. adv. bd. Civil Liberties Union of Mass., 1990-91, 95—, bd. dirs., 1991-95. Recipient Paul Karrer medal Swiss Chem. Soc., 1967, Peace and Freedom award Women's Internat. League for Peace and Freedom, 1985, Feminist Marathoner award Boston chpt. NOW, 1991, Disting. Svc. award Am. Inst. Biol. Sci., 1992, Luther Knight Macnair award, ACLU, 2005. Fellow AAAS; mem. Marine Biol. Lab. (trustee 1973-78, trustee emerita 1990—), Soc. Biol. Chemists, Nat. Women's Studies Assn., Phi Beta Kappa, Sigma Xi. Avocations: reading, music, yoga, swimming. Home: 21 Lakeview Ave Cambridge MA 02138-3325

HUBBARD, STANLEY STUB, broadcast executive; b. St. Paul, May 28, 1933; s. Stanley Eugene and Didrikke A. (Stub) H.; m. Karen Elizabeth Holmen, June 13, 1959; children: Kathryn Elizabeth Hubbard Rominski, Stanley Eugene II, Virginia Anne Hubbard Morris, Robert Winston, Julia Didrikke Coyte. BA, U. Minn., 1955; PhD (hon.), Hamline U., 1995, U. Minn., 2004. With Hubbard Broadcasting, St. Paul, 1951—, pres., 1967—, chmn., CEO, 1983—; past chmn. US Satellite Broadcasting Co., Inc., 1981—99. Mem. broadcast adv. com. on comm. subcom. Ho. of Reps., 1977—79; mem. adv. com. on advanced TV, FCC, 1988—95; mem. US Nat. Inf. Infastructure Adv. Coun., 1994—96. Contbr. articles to profl. jours. Chmn. St. Croix Valley Youth Ctr., 1968—; trustee Hubbard Broadcasting Found.; mem. bd. dirs. U. Minn. Found., Mpls., Assn. Maximum Svc. TV, U. St. Thomas, Minn. Bus. Partnership, Heart Rhythm Found.; past advisor Gov.'s Crime Commn., Ramsey County Ice Arena Com.; past bd. dirs. The Guthrie Theater, The Psychoanalytic Found. of Minn., Sci. Mus. of Minn., Am. Friends of Jamaica; past mem. Hazelden adv. com. Met. Airports Pub. Found. Adv. Bd.; bd. visitors U. Minn. Med. Sch., 2004; steering com. Salvation Army Twin Citites; chmn. pres. coun. Twin Cities Pub. TV, 2004. Recipient Ellis Island Medal of Honor, 2004, Mitchell Charnley award Northwest Broadcast News Assn., 1991, Internat. Humanitarian award Am. Friends of Jamaica, 1989, Arthur C. Clarke award Satellite Broadcasting and Comm. Assn., 1994, DreamMaker award Children's Cancer Rsch. Fund, 1994, Disting. Svc. award Nat. Assn. Broadcasters, 1995, Spurgeon award Boy Scouts Am., 1985, Avatar award Broadcast Cable and Fin. Mgmt., 1995, Human Rights award Am. Jewish Com., 1995, Cmty. Leadership award Mpls./St. Paul chpt. Alzheimer's Assn., 1995, Most Innovative Product award Minn. High Tech. Coun., 1995, Journalism Innovator award U. Nebr., 1996, Minn. Family Bus. award U. St. Thomas, 1996, Disting. Alumnus award Breck Sch., 1996, Minn. and Dakotas Entrepreneur of Yr. award, 1996, Heritage award US Hockey Hall of Fame, 1996, U. Minn. M Club Hall of Fame Lifetime Achievement award, 1996, Broadcasters' Found. Golden Mike award, 1997, Acad. of Achievement's Golden Plate award, 1997; named to Broadcasting and Cable Hall of Fame, 1991, Soc. Satellite Profl. Internat. Space Hall of Fame, 1992, Acad. Achievement's Golden Plate award, 1997, Broadcast Pioneer award Minn. Broadcasters Assn., 1998, John Hogan Disting. Svc. award Radio & TV News Dir. Assn., 2000, Promax TV Century award, 2003; inductee St. Croix Valley Athletics Hall of Fame, 2000, Pavek Mus. of Broadcasting Hall of Fame, 2001, ProMax TV Cent. Award, 2003, Minn. Bus. Hall Fame, 2006; named one of First Fifty Giants of Broadcasting Libr. Am. Broadcasting, 2003, Forbes' Richest Americans, 2006. Mem. Nat. Acad. TV Arts and Scis. (past chmn. bd. trustees, found. pres. 2003—, Minn. chpt. Silver Cir. award 2001, Golden Cir. award 2004), Broadcast Pioneers, Internat. Radio and TV Soc. Avocations: sailing and boating, reading, photography. Office: Hubbard Broadcasting Inc 3415 University Ave W Saint Paul MN 55114-2099 Home Phone: 651-642-4206; Office Phone: 651-642-4200. Business E-Mail: jmahoney@hbi.com.

HUBBARD, STEPHEN, cardiologist, consultant; b. May 24, 1948; BA in Zoology, U. Calif., Berkeley, 1970; MD, U. Calif., San Francisco, 1974. Cert. Am. Bd. Internal Medicine, 1977, Am. Bd. Internal Medicine, specialty bd. cert., Cardiovascular Disease, 1987, lic. Wash. State. Intern, resident internal medicine UCLA San Fernando Valley Med. Program, 1974—77; fellowship, cardiology Maricopa Med. Ctr., Phoenix, 1985—87; emergency room physician Palm Drive Hosp., Sebastopol, Calif., 1977—78; gen. internist, hospitalist/intensivist Sebastopol, Calif., 1978—82, Ukiah, Calif., 1982—85; interventional cardiologist Stevens Cardiology Group, Edmonds, Wash., 1987—2000; clin. instr. medicine U. Wash. Sch. Medicine, Divsn. Cardiology, Harborview Med. Ctr., Seattle, 2001—; attending Cardiology Consultation Svc., ECG Svc., and Coronary Care Unit, 2001—. Fellow: Am. Coll. Cardiology. Office: 4490 Eagle Harbor Dr NE Bainbridge Island WA 98110 Office Phone: 206-855-8132. Office Fax: 206-855-8139. Business E-Mail: stehub@pol.net.*

HUBBARD, TODD PHILIP, aerospace scientist; b. Johnson City, NY, Apr. 2, 1952; s. Phil and Elizabeth Joyce Hubbard; m. Deborah Lee Atkinson, Oct. 4, 1974; children: Matthew, Joshua. BA, Okla. State U., Stillwater, 1974, EdD, 2000; MS, Embry Riddle Aero. U., Dayton, Fla., 1987. Commd. 2d lt. USAF, 1974, advanced through grades to lt. col., pilot, 1974—95, comdr. svcs. squadron Beale AFB, Calif., 1993—94, ret.; reconnaisance staff officer NATO, Ramstein, Germany, 1989—92; instructional designer Boeing Aerospace Ops., Midwest City, Okla., 1995—97; instructional sys. designer III U. Okla., Oklahoma City, 1997—2005. Crew resource mgmt. instr. Eagle Sys. and Svcs., Oklahoma City, 2004—; editor jour. FAA, Oklahoma City, 2001—03, Profl. Aviation Bd. Cert., 2006—. Editor: Aviation Mental Health, 2006. Pres. PTO, Ramstein, Germany, 1991—92; Clarence E. Page endowed chmn. Clarence E. Page Found., Okla., 2005—. Decorated Humanitarian Svcs. medal, Air medal with two oak leaf clusters. Mem.: Univ. Aviation Assn. Avocations: oil painting, piano. Office: Okla State U 318 Willard Hall Stillwater OK 74078 Office Phone: 405-744-8062.

HUBBARD, WILLIAM BOGEL, planetary sciences educator; b. Liberty, Tex., Nov. 14, 1940; s. William Bogel and Marie Hubbard; m. Jean North Gilliland, June 8, 1963; children: Lynne Marie, Laurie North. BA, Rice U., Houston, 1962; PhD, U. Calif., Berkeley, 1967. Rsch. fellow Calif. Inst. Tech., Pasadena, 1967-68; asst. prof. astronomy U. Tex., Austin, 1968-72; assoc. prof. planetary scis. U. Ariz., Tucson, 1972-75, dir. Lunar and Planetary Lab., 1977-81, prof., 1975—. Cons. Lawrence Livermore (Calif.) Nat. Lab., 1972-86, NASA, 1994—; prin. investigator NASA, 1974—, NSF, 1970, 79, 83, 86-93; exch. scientist USSR Nat. Acad. Sci., 1973, mem. com. div. for planetary scis., 1985-88; mem. com. on planetary and lunar exploration NRC, 2003—. Contbr. articles to profl. jours.; assoc. editor Icarus, 1980-2003; receiving editor New Astronomy, 2004-. Fellow AAAS, Japan Soc. for Promotion of Sci., Am. Geophys. Union; mem. Am. Astron. Soc. (Gerard P. Kuiper prize 2005), Internat. Astron. Union, Am. Hereford Assn., Nat. Cattlemen's Beef Assn., Sigma Xi. Democrat. Episcopalian. Home: 2618 E Devon St Tucson AZ 85716-5506 Office: U Ariz Lunar & Planetary Lab Tucson AZ 85721-0092

HUBBARD, WILLIAM JAMES, library director; b. Grand Rapids, Mich., July 17, 1941; s. Willard Wright and Sara (Rast) H.; m. Barbara Ockun, Sept. 8, 1962; children: William, Thomas, James, Gregory. AB, Dartmouth Coll., 1963; MLS, SUNY, Geneseo, 1972. Engr., supr. Rochester (N.Y.) Telephone Corp., 1963-71; contract libr. Xerox Corp., Webster, NY, 1971-72; libr. circulation SUNY, Fredonia, 1973-75; libr. user svcs. Va. Tech., Blacksburg, 1975-80; dir. libr. svcs., dir.automation-networks, act. state libr. Va. State Libr., Richmond, 1980-88; univ. libr. Jacksonville (Ala.) State U., 1988—. Author: Stack Management, 1981; assoc. editor Ala. Librarian; contbr. articles to profl. jours. Mem. Ala. Libr. Assn., Nat. Assn. Scholars, Am. Soc. Info. Sci. and Tech., Text and Acad. Authors Assn. Office: State U Univ Libr Jacksonville AL 36265 Business E-Mail: bhubbard@jsu.edu. E-mail: williamj@hubbards.org.

HUBBE, HENRY ERNEST, financial forecaster, trading manager; b. Hamburg, Germany, Aug. 13, 1932; came to U.S., 1958; s. H.V. and Ingeborg M. (Schroeder) H.; m. Mary E. Wylie, 1961; children: John, Michael. BA, NYU, 1971, MBA, 1974. Area asistant. Bank of Am. NT&SA, San Francisco, 1958—63; asst. v.p. Citibank N.Am., NYC, 1963—74; sr. v.p. European Am. Bank, NYC, 1974—84; mng. dir. Fintech Ltd., London, 1985—96, Fintech Asset Mgmt., London, 1985—96; pres. Fintech USA Ltd., NYC, 1996—. Mem. faculty Am. Inst. Banking, N.Y.C., 1974-83; guest speaker internat. confs., profl. orgns.; panel mem. Bus. Internat., London. Creator proprietary computer software; contbr. articles to profl. jours. Mem. Beta Gamma Sigma (v.p. 1971—). Avocation: golf. E-mail: fintech@concentric.net.

HUBBELL, BILLY JAMES, lawyer; b. Pine Bluff, Ark., May 21, 1949; s. Arley E. and Mary M. (Duke) H.; m. Judy C. Webb, Feb. 21, 1981; children: Jennifer Leigh, William Griffin. BE, U. Ctrl. Ark., Conway, 1971; JD, U. Ark, Little Rock, 1978. Bar: Ark. 1978, U.S. Dist. Ct. (ea. dist.) Ark. 1978, U.S. Ct. Appeals (8th cir.) 1987. Tchr. Grady (Ark.) High Sch., 1971-78; assoc. Smith and Smith, McGehee, Ark., 1978-79; ptnr. Smith, Hubbell and Drake, McGehee, 1979-86, Griffin, Rainwater & Draper, P.A., Crossett, Ark., 1987-90; dep. prosecuting atty. Ashley County, Ark., 1989-90; dist. judge Crossett, 1991—; pvt. practice, 1991—. Candidate Ark. Ho. of Reps., Lincoln County, 1984, 10th Jud. Dist. Cir./Chancery Judge, 1998. Sgt. USAR, 1970-76. Mem. Ark. Bar Assn., S.E. Ark. Legal Inst. (chmn. 1984-85, Ashley County Bar Assn. (past pres.), Ark. Trial Lawyers Assn. Democrat. Seventh Day Adventist. Avocations: jogging, computers. Office: PO Box 574 Crossett AR 71635-0574 Office Phone: 870-364-6114. Personal E-mail: bjhubbell@alltel.net.

HUBBELL, FLOYD ALLAN, internist, educator; b. Waco, Tex., Nov. 13, 1948; s. F.E. and Margaret (Fraser) H.; m. Nancy Cooper, May 23, 1975; 1 child, Andrew Allan. BA, Baylor U., 1971, MD, 1974; MS in Pub. Health, UCLA, 1983. Diplomate Am. Bd. Internal Medicine. Intern, then resident Long Beach med. program U. Calif., Irvine, 1975-78, asst. prof. medicine, 1981-89, assoc. prof. medicine and social ecology, 1989-97, prof. medicine and social ecology, 1997—, dir. primary care internal medicine residency, 1992-97, chief divsn. gen. internal medicine and primary care, 1992—2002, dir. Ctr. for Health Policy and Rsch., 1993—2003, chair dept. medicine, 2002—. Contbr. articles to profl. jours. Fellow ACP; mem. APHA, Soc. Gen. Internal Medicine, Physicians for Social Responsibility, Assn. Profs. Medicine. Democrat. Avocations: reading, skiing, water sports. Office: Dept Medicine UCI Med Ctr 101 City Dr Bldg 200 720 Orange CA 92868-4076 E-mail: fahubbel@uci.edu.

HUBBELL, FRED SHELTON, insurance company executive; b. Des Moines, Apr. 25, 1951; s. James Windsor Jr. and Helen (Houx) H.; m. Charlotte Beyer, Aug. 28, 1976; children: Lauren, Meredith, Frederick. BA, U. N.C., 1973; JD, U. Iowa, 1976; PMD cert., Harvard Grad. Sch. Bus., 1983. Assoc. Dewey, Ballantine, Bushby, Palmer, NYC, 1976-79, Hughes, Hubbard & Reed, NYC, 1979-81, Mumford, Schrage & Zurek, Des Moines, 1981-83; v.p. Equitable of Iowa Cos., Des Moines, 1983-85; pres., chief exec. officer Younkers, Inc., Des Moines, 1985-87; pres., chief operating officer Equitable of Iowa Cos., Des Moines, from 1987, pres., chief exec. officer, bd. dirs.; chmn. Equitable Life Ins. Co. of Iowa, Des Moines; gen. mgr. ING Fin. Services Internat. N. Am., 1997—99; pres., CEO, Retail Fin. Services ING, 1997—99; chmn. exec. com. ING Fin. Services Internat., 1999—2000, ING Americas, 2000—, ING Asia/Pacific, 2000—03; exec. bd. ING Groep NV, 2000—. Contbr. articles to profl. jours. Bd. dirs. Planned Parenthood of Mid-Iowa, Des Moines, 1982—, Simpson Coll., Indianola, Iowa, 1985; bd. govs. Iowa Coll. Found., Des

Moines, 1987; trustee Mercy Hosp. Med. Ctr., Des Moines, 1984. Mem. Young Pres. Orgn., Greater Des Moines C. of C. (bd. dirs. 1985). Clubs: Wakonda, Des Moines (Des Moines). Democrat. Episcopalian. Avocations: running, golf, travel. Office: ING Americas 5780 Powers Ferry Rd NW Atlanta GA 30327

HUBBELL, ROBERT B., lawyer; BA in English and Polit. Sci. magna cum laude, Loyola Marymount U., 1978; JD magna cum laude, Loyola Law Sch., 1981. Bar: Calif., Am. Bar. Assoc. Atty. Heller, Ehrman, White, & McAuliffe, LLP, 1991—, Firmwide Managing Shareholder. Pres. Legal Aid Foundation of Los Angeles, 2000—01. Office: Heller Ehrman White & McAuliffe 333 Bush St San Francisco CA 94104 Office Phone: 213-689-7563. Office Fax: 213-614-1868. E-mail: rhubbell@hewm.com.

HUBBELL, WAYNE LESTER, ophthalmologist, educator, chemist, educator; b. Riverside, Calif., Mar. 24, 1943; s. Lester Glenn and Helyn Marie Hubbell; m. Cheryl Alice McAfee, Jan. 6, 1965; 1 child, Paul Wayne. BS in Chemistry, Oreg. State U., 1965; PhD in Chemistry, Stanford U., 1970; Doctorate (hon.), U. Pecs, Hungary, 1998. Prof. U. Calif., Berkeley, 1970—83; Jules Stein prof. ophthalmology UCLA, 1983—, assoc. dir. Jules Stein Eye Inst. Jesse W. Beams Meml. lectr. biophysics U. Va., 1994; Zuffanti lectr. chemistry Northeastern U., 1996; Alexander M. Cruickshank lectr. Gordon Rsch. Conf., 1997; Irving L. Schwartz lectr. Mt. Sinai Sch. Medicine, 1998. Contbr. articles to profl. jours. Recipient Teacher-Scholar award, Camille and Henry Dreyfus Found., Merit Rsch. award, Nat. Eye Inst., 1990—2000, Sr. Investigator award, Rsch. to Prevent Blindness, 1990, Rsch. award, Alcon Rsch. Inst., 1994, Sr. Investigator award, Rsch. to Prevent Blindness, 1999, Gold medal, Internat. Electron Paramagnetic Resonance Soc., 2000; fellow, Air Force Office Sci. Rsch.-NRC, 1969—70; fellow, Alfred P. Sloan Found., 1973—75. Fellow: Biophysical Soc. (Elisabeth Roberts Cole award 1994), Am. Acad. Arts and Scis.; mem.: Am. Chem. Soc. Achievements include development of technique of site-directed spin labeling. Office: Jules Stein Eye Inst UCLA Sch Medicine Los Angeles CA 90095 Personal E-mail: hubbellc@aol.com. E-mail: hubbellw@jsei.ucla.edu.

HUBBERMAN, RON, state official; b. Tel Aviv, 1972; naturalized, US, 1982; BA in Eng., U. Wis. Madison, 1994, BA in Psych., 1994; M, Sch. Social Svc. Adminstrn., U. Chgo., Grad. Sch. Bus.; grad., Chgo. Police Acad. Beat officer Chgo. Police Dept., tactical gang team officer, asst. dep. supt., 2002; exec. dir. Office of Emergency Mgmt. Comm., Chgo., 2005; chief of staff Office of Mayor, Chgo., 2005—. Mem. Am. Red Cross, Chgo. House. Recipient Spirit of Rogers Park award; Paul and Daisy Soros Fellowship for New Americans, 1999, Albert Schweitzer fellowship. Office: Office of Mayor 121 N La Salle Rm 507 Chicago IL 60602 Office Phone: 312-744-3300.*

HUBBS, CLARK, zoologist, researcher; b. Ann Arbor, Mich., Mar. 15, 1921; s. Carl Leavitt and Laura Cornelia (Clark) H.; m. Catherine Vickery Symons; children: Laura Ellen Hubbs Tait, John Clark, Ann Frances Hubbs Weissman. BA, U. Mich., 1942; PhD, Stanford U., 1951. Instr. zoology U. Tex., Austin, 1949-52, asst. prof., 1952-57, assoc. prof., 1957-63, prof., 1963-88, Regents prof., 1988-91, Regents prof. emeritus, 1991—, chmn. biology dept., 1974-76, chmn. zoology dept., 1978-86, with grad. faculty dept. marine sci., 1987-91; curator ichthyology Tex. Meml. Mus., 1978—. Mem. grad. faculty Tex. A&M U., 1969-83; vis. prof. U. Okla., Kingston, 1970-84; bd. dirs. Hubbs/Sea World Rsch. Inst., San Diego; faculty advisor U. de Nuevo Leon, Monterey, Mex., 1985-87; biology advisor Bd. Higher Edn., Little Rock, 1987, Jackson, Miss., 1983; leader Rio Grande Fishes Recovery Team, U.S. Interior Dept., Albuquerque, 1978—; mem. adv. com. Fish, Wildlife and Parks, U.S. Interior Dept., Washington, 1975-77; mem. sci. adv. com. Bass Anglers Sportsmans Soc., Montgomery, Ala., 1974-92; mem. environ. adv. bd. Tex. Utilities, Dallas, 1971-2001, emeritus, 2001—; chmn. inland task force, power plant sitting com., Office of Gov., Austin, Tex., 1971-72; mem. nuclear power adv. com. Tex. Energy Adv. Council, Austin, 1978-80; U.S. rep. European Ichthyological Congress, 1985-88; bd. dirs. Nature Conservancy of Tex., 1988-94; mem. rev. com. USDI, San Juan. Mng. editor: Copeia, 1971—84; contbr. articles to profl. jours. Mem. NRC Com. on Glen Canyon Releases in to the Colorado River, 1991-96; bd. dirs. Tex. Environ. Def., 1997—. Served with U.S. Army, 1942-46, PTO. Named Educator and Researcher of Yr., Tex. chpt. Am. Fisheries Soc., 1978, Student award named in his honor; recipient Excellence, Golden and Hon. awards Am. Fisheries Soc., 1988; Clark Hubbs Endowed Professorship in Zoology established in his honor, Dept. Zoology, Clark Hubbs Aquarium named in his honor. Mem. Am. Soc. Ichthyologists and Herpetologists (pres. 1987, lifetime achievement award 1992, Robert K. Johnson award 2004), Am. Inst. Fish Rsch. Biol. (pres. 1995-98), Tex. Acad. Scis. (pres. 1972-73, Disting. Scientist of Yr. 1998), S.W. Assn. Naturalists (pres. 1966-67, W.F. Blair Eminent Naturalist 1990, George M. Sutton award 1996, Clark Hubbs Student Poster award named in his honor 2000), Sociedad Iotiológica Mexicana Asociación Cientifica (hon.). Office: U Tex Sect Integrative Biology Austin TX 78712 Home Phone: 512-453-6795; Office Phone: 512-471-1176. Business E-Mail: hubbs@mail.utexas.edu.

HUBBS, DONALD HARVEY, foundation executive; b. Kingman, Ariz., Jan. 3, 1918; s. Wayne and Grace Lillian (Hoose) H.; m. Flora Vincent, June 14, 1945; children: Donald Jr., Susan Tyner, Diane Schultz, Wayne, David, Adrienne Busk. BA in Edn., Ariz. State U., 1940; JD, Southwestern U., 1956; LLD (hon.), Pepperdine U., 2005. CPA; bar: Calif. 1956. Acct. Wright and Hubbs, LA, 1945-67; pvt. practice atty. LA, 1956-81; pres., dir. Conrad N. Hilton Found., LA, 1981-98, chmn. bd., CEO, 1998—2005. Bd. dirs. TWA Airline, 1977, Vita Pakt Citrus Products Co.; regent Mt. St. Mary's Coll., 1983-98; bd. councilors U. So. Calif. Law Sch., 1992-99, Donald H. Hubbs Disting. Profs. Chair U. Houston. Hon. chief of the tribes of Kapatinga and Ohu, Ghana; spkr. So. Govs. Conf., 1986. 1st lt. (inf.) U.S. Army. Decorated Purple Heart; recipient Anne Sullivan medal Perkins Sch. for the Blind, 1992, Humanitarian award Nat. Coun. Juvenile and Family Ct. Judges, 1994, Humanitarian award Family Violence Prevention Fund, 2000, Spirit of Helen Keller award Helen Keller Internat., 1995; World Vision Hubbs scholarship, 2005. Mem. State Bar of Calif., So. Calif. Assn. for Philanthropy (pres. 1985-86), Riviera Country Club, LA Country Club. Avocations: cattle ranching, hunting, fishing, golf. Home: 1658 San Onofre Dr Pacific Palisades CA 90272-2735

HUBBS, VIOLET ELIZABETH SHAMBLIN, retired filmmaker, retired photographer; b. Charleston, W.Va., July 15, 1933; d. Charles Luke Shamblin and Lenora Edna Rust; m. Charles Taylor Hubbs, Nov. 21, 1953 (dec.); children: Elizabeth Romayne, Heather Hazlett, Holly Keith. Student, Case Western Res. U., 1951—52; AA, Mira Costa/Carlsbad Coll., 1957; Cert. in Motion Picture Arts, Brooks Inst., 1975; BA magna cum laude, UCLA, 1978, MFA, 1982. Singer, actress Camp Pendleton Marine Corps Band, Oceanside, Calif., 1952—53; tchr. drama Oceanside Parks & Recreation Commn., Oceanside, 1957; sec. The Jewish Hosp., Cin., 1960—63, US Atty. Gen., SW Ohio Dist., 1964—64; pub. rels. So. Calif. Mental Health Soc., LA, 1979—80, Inst. Rational Emotive Behaviour, 1980—81; founder, pres. VS Hubbs Productions, Inc., 1978—. Singer: (performances) Camp Pendleton Marine Corps Band (First Woman Singer in any Marine Corps Band, 1952); singer: (actress) (ktla tv/kabc national radio performances) Marines in Review and At Ease; dir.(writer, producer, editor): (documentary) Lena - A Forgotten Minority. Vice pres. Nat. Assn. Gifted Children, Cin., 1964—67; chairwoman Jr. Women's Club Western Cin., 1966—68; chmn. Child Conservation League, Cin., 1967—69; docent William O. Douglass Outdoor Classroom/Santa Monica Mountain Conservancy, Beverly Hills, 1978—80; founding mem. WCET/PBS Action Auction, Cin., 1965—66; chmn. Cin. Summer Opera Gala, 1968—69; mem. PTA, 1960—70, Beverly Hills, 1975—83; woman's com. chmn. Cin. Symphony Orch., 1967—69; chmn. United Fine Arts Fund, 1967—69; hostess Nat. Governor's Conf., 1968. With USMC, 1952—53. Mem.: AAUW (assoc.), Women Marines Assn. (assoc.), Internat. Documentary Assn. (assoc.). Home Phone: 310-276-8565.

HUBEL, DAVID HUNTER, physiologist, science educator; b. Windsor, Ont., Can., Feb. 27, 1926; s. Jesse Hervey and Elsie (Hunter) Hubel; m. Shirley Ruth Izzard, June 20, 1953; children: Carl Andrew, Eric David, Paul Matthew. BSc, McGill U., 1947, MD, 1951, DSc (hon.), 1978; AM (hon.), Harvard U., 1962; DSc (hon.), U. Man., 1983; DHL (hon.), Johns Hopkins U., 1990; DSci, U. Western Ont., 1993; DSc, Oxford U., 1994, Gustavus Adolphus Coll., 1994, Ohio State U., 1995; D (hon.), U. Madrid, 1997, Univ. Miguel, 1998; JD (hon.), Dalhousie U., 1998; D (hon.), U. Toronto, 2002; D in optometry (hon.), SUNY, 2004; D (hon.), McMaster, 2005. Intern Montreal Gen. Hosp., 1951—52; asst. resident neurology Montreal Neurol. Inst., 1952—53, fellow clin. neurophysiology, 1953—54; asst. resident neurology Johns Hopkins Hosp., 1954—55; rsch. fellow Walter Reed Army Inst. Rsch., Washington, 1955—58; sr. fellow neurol. scis. group Johns Hopkins U., 1958—59; faculty Harvard U. Med. Sch., 1959—, George Packer Berry prof. physiology, chmn. dept., 1967—68, George Packer Berry prof. neurobiology, 1968—82, John Franklin Enders U. prof., 1982—2004, res. prof. emeritus Neurobiology, 2004—. Lectr. in field; George Eastman prof., Oxford, England, 1991—92; rschr. brain mechanisms in vision; spkr. in field. With AUS, 1955—58. Recipient Trustees award, Rsch. to Prevent Blindness, 1971, Lewis S. Rosentiel award for disting. work in basic med. rsch., 1972, Karl Lashley prize, Am. Philos. Soc., 1977, Louisa Gross Horwitz prize, Columbia U., 1978, Dickson prize in medicine, U. Pitts., 1979, Ledile prize, Harvard U., 1980, Nobel prize in physiology or medicine, 1981, Outstanding Sci. Leadership award, Nat. Assn. for Biomed. Rsch., 1990, City of Medicine award, 1990, Glen A. Fry medal, Coll. Optometry, Ohio State U., 1991, First Ann. George A. Miller lectr., Cognitive Neurosci. Soc., Gerald award, Soc. Neurosci., 1993, Helen Keller award, Helen Keller Eye Rsch. Found., 1995, Wilder Penfield Lecture, Montreal Neurological Inst., 1998, Frontiers in Neuroscience Lecture, Case Western Reserve U., 2000, Disting. Canadians Spkr. Series, Corpus Christi Coll., 2001. Fellow: AAAS, Am. Acad. Arts & Scis.; mem.: NAS, Acadmica Europaea (fgn. mem.), Royal Soc. London, Am. Philos. Soc. (Karl Spencer Lashley prize 1977), Johns Hopkins U. Soc. Scholars, Spanish Soc.Ophthalmology (hon.), Assn. Rsch. in Vision and Ophthalmology (Friedenwald award 1975), Soc. for Neurosci. (Bwditch lectr. 1966), Deutsche Acad. der Naturforscher Leopoldina (Grass lectr. 1976, Gerard award 1993), Am. Physiol. Soc., Sigma Xi. Office: Harvard U Med Sch Dept Neurobiology WAB213 220 Longwood Ave Boston MA 02115-5701

HUBEN, BRIAN DAVID, lawyer; b. Inglewood, Calif., May 14, 1962; s. Michael Gerald and Dorothy (Withers) H.; m. Kathy Henson Johnson, Apr. 6, 1991; children: Kaitlin Johnson, Mariana Johnson. BA, Loyola Marymount U., 1984; JD, Loyola Law Sch., 1987. Bar: Calif. 1988, U.S. Dist. Ct. (no., ce., ea. and so. dists.) Calif. 1988, Ariz., 1994, U.S. Ct. Appeals (9th cir.) 1988, D.C. 1989, U.S. Supreme Ct. 1996. Assoc. Steinberg, Nutter & Brent, Santa Monica, Calif., 1988-89, Smith & Hilbig, Torrance, Calif., 1989-95, Robie & Matthai, LA, 1995-99; spl. master State Bar of Calif., 1995-99; ptnr. Katten Muchin Rosenman LLP, LA, 1999—. Del. L.A. County Bar Assn. State Conv., 1990-99. Mem. instl. rev. bd. Torrance Meml. Med. Ctr., 1990-95. Mem. Calif. Bar Assn., D.C. Bar Assn., L.A. County Bar Assn., Palos Verdes Peninsula Edn. Found. (trustee 2004-06), Loyola Marymount Univ. Alumni Assn. (dir., bd. dirs. 1995-01). Democrat. Roman Catholic. Avocations: travel, sports, current events. Office: Katten Muchin Rosenman LLP 2029 Century Park E 26th Flr Los Angeles CA 90067-3012 Office Phone: 310-788-4771. E-mail: brian.huben@kattenlaw.com.

HUBER, SISTER ALBERTA, academic administrator; b. Rock Island, Ill., Feb. 12, 1917; d. Albert and Lydia (Hofer) H. BA, Coll. St. Catherine, St. Paul, 1939; MA, U. Minn., 1945; PhD, U. Notre Dame, 1954. Mem. faculty Coll. St. Catherine, 1940—, prof. English, 1953-97, prof. emerita, 1997, chmn. dept., 1960-63, acad. dean, 1962-64, pres., 1964-79, pres. emeritus, 2005. Trustee Avila Coll., Kansas City, Mo., 1986-97, St. Joseph's Hosp., St. Paul, 1971-80; pres. UN Assn. Minn., 1980-81; bd. dirs. St. Paul YMCA, 1986-92. Decorated Chevalier, Ordre des Palmes Acad.; recipient Outstanding Achievement award U. Minn. Alumni Assn., 1981. Mem. Phi Beta Kappa, Pi Gamma Mu. Office: Apt 111 1322 Alton St Saint Paul MN 55116 Personal E-mail: mthom17349@aol.com.

HUBER, COLLEEN ADLENE, artist; b. Concordia, Kans., Mar. 30, 1927; d. Claude Irve and Freda (Trow) Baker; m. Wallace Charles Huber, Oct. 18, 1945 (dec.); children: Wallace Charles II (dec.), Shawn Dale (dec.), Devron Kelly (dec.), Candace Lynette, Melody Ann. Student, UCLA, 1974-78; BA cum laude, Calif. Poly. U., Pomona, 1963. Co-owner, artist The Rocket (community newspaper), Garden Grove, Calif., 1955-58; quick sketch artist Walt Disney Prodn. Co., Burbank, Calif., 1958-59; v.p., art dir. Gray Pub. Co., Fullerton, Calif., 1968-76; tchr. North Orange County Sch. Dist., La Palma, Calif., 1974-76; art dir. Shoppers Guide, Anaheim, Calif., 1976—79; pub., owner Community Woman/Huber Ad Agy., Anaheim, Calif., 1976-79; artist Bargain Bulletin Pub., Fallbrook, Calif., 1979-82; graphic artist, designer Van Zyen Pub., Fallbrook, 1982-83; cons. sales East San Diego Mag./Baker Graphics, Rancho San Diego, Calif., 1978-88; owner, artist Coco Bien Objet d'Art, Laguna Beach, Calif., 1986-92; instr. Camp Fire Inc., 1990-92, Coco Bien Objet d'Art, Temecula, Calif., 1992-93, Sun City, Calif., 1993—, Castle Rock, Wash., 1993—2004. Dir. edn. Art Acad., Orange County, 1992-94; instr. Lake Elsinore Cmty. Ctr., 1992—, San Jacinto C.C., 1997-98; 2nd v.p., membership chair, Fine Art Inst., San Bernadina Mus., San Bernardino, Calif., 1998-99, rec. sec., 2000-02. Author: Gail, 1980 (1st Pl. award 1981, 2d Pl. award 1981); artist: Yearlings (2d Pl. award 1985), Penning (1st Pl. award 1987); exhibited at Temecula Art Coun. Wild Life Art Show, 1999, San Bernardino Mus., 2001 (1st pl. award); featured artist San Bernardino Mus. Fine Arts Inst., 2001 (Best of Show 2nd Pl. 2006), Elsinore Women's Club (Best of Show, 1st and 2d pl.), 2006. Participant Art-A-Fair, Laguna Beach Festival Show. Recipient certs. North Orange County ROP, 1976-77, 2d pl. San Bernardino Art Show, 1995, Hon. Mention Nat. Orange Show, 1996, City of Lake Elsinore, 1997, 1st pl. award FAI San Bernardino Mus., 1999, 2001, Best of Show, Lake Elsinore Club Women's Art Show. Fellow Zonta (2d v.p. 1990-91), Laguna Beach C. of C. (docent gallery night 1988); mem. Exec. Women, Calif. Press Women Assn. (chmn. jr. journalism contest Orange County chpt. 1985-86, pres. 1986-87, yearly chair Taste of Valley art show 1997), The Art Inst., Temecula Art League (publicity chair), Temecula Valley Art Assn., Inst. Fine Art. Republican. Roman Catholic. Avocations: baseball fan, golf, swimming, dance, theater. Personal E-mail: cocobien@verizon.net.

HUBER, DAVID L., prosecutor; b. Louisville, Ky. BA in Polit. Sci., U. Louisville, JD, 1968. Assoc. with Mr. Fred M. Goldberg, Ky.; legis. asst. to chief legis. asst. US Senator Marlowe Cook; chief adminstrv. officer Jefferson County Govt., 1978—85; 2nd v.p. and dir. govt. rels. and compliance Capital Holding Corp.; v.p., gen. counsel Glenmore Distilleries Co.; gen. counsel to US Senator Mitch McConnell; asst. US atty. (we. dist.) Ky. US Dept. Justice, 1991—2003, US atty. (we. dist.) Ky., 2003—. Recipient Commissioner's Spl. Citation, US Food and Drug Adminstrn. Office: US Attys Office Bank Louisville Bldg 510 W Broadway Louisville KY 40202*

HUBER, DON LAWRENCE, publisher; b. Milw., Aug. 17, 1928; s. Wallace Fred and Florence (Bleck) H.; m. Joan Mac Monnies, June 23, 1951. Student, Carthage Coll., Ill., 1946-48; BS in English, Northwestern U., 1950. Sales exec. sta. WOR (radio), NYC, 1957-58; owner, gen. mgr. Sta. KALE-Radio, Pasco, Washington, 1958-60; mgr. advt. Standard Rate and Data Service, NYC, 1961-70; v.p., pub. Computer and Communication Decisions, Hayden, N.J., 1970-87, VNU Bus. Press.; pvt. practice specializing in bldg. pvt. homes, 1990—. Painter oil landscape paintings, 1990—. Served with USN, 1946-48. Mem. Sales Execs. N.Y., Navy League, Am. Artists Profl. League, Salamagundi Club, Hudson Valley Art Assn. Clubs: Northwestern University (N.Y.C.). Home and Office: 24 Rolling Dr Glen Head NY 11545-2613 Personal E-mail: donlhubr@aol.com.

HUBER, DONALD SIMON, physician; b. Clarendon, Pa., Apr. 18, 1929; s. Walter Casper and Mary Agnes (Earley) H.; m. Mary Hanks, Sept. 6, 1958; children: Donald Scott, Mark Walter, Mary Lisa. BA, Duke U., 1951, MD, 1954. Diplomate Am. Bd. Internal Medicine, Am. Bd. Allergy and Immunology. Intern Charity Hosp., New Orleans, 1954-55; resident internal medicine Tulane U. Hosp., New Orleans, 1955-56, 58-60; pvt. practice Huntsville, Ala., 1960-96 (ret. 1996); clin. assoc. prof. medicine Sch. Primary Med. Care, Huntsville, 1985—. Med. dir. Cmty. Free Clinic., 1998—. Lt. commdr. USN, 1956-58, USNR, 1958-60. Fellow Am. Coll. Allergists; mem. AMA, Am. Acad. Allergy and Immunology, Ala. Soc. Allergy and Immunology (pres. 1985), Huntsville Rotary Club (bd. dirs. 1978). Republican. Methodist. Avocation: travel. Home: 507 Holmes Ave Huntsville AL 35801 E-mail: donhuber@knology.net.

HUBER, FRANZ, retired research director; b. Nussdorf, Bavaria, Germany, Nov. 20, 1925; s. Franz and Anna (Fischer) H.; m. Lore Hedwig Schneider, Sept. 9, 1953; children: Johannes, Martin. Dr in Natural Scis., U. Munich, 1953; Dr. Habil. Natural Sci., U. Tübingen, 1960; Dr. honoris causa, U. Cologne, 1988, U. Toulouse, 1991, U. Odense, 1992, U. Zurich, 1993. Asst. prof. U. Tuebingen, 1954-60, assoc. prof., 1960-63; prof. U. Cologne, 1963-73; sci. mem. Max-Planck Soc., Seewiesen, 1973—93; dir. rsch. Inst. Behavioral Physiology, Seewiesen, 1973—93. Rsch. dir. Internat. Ctr. for Insect Physiology and Ecology, Nairobi, Kenya, 1970-74; hon. prof. U. Munich, 1978. Recipient Karl von Frisch medal German Zool. Soc., 1980, Napoleon Cybulski medal Poland Physiol. Soc., 1983. Mem. Leopoldina, Bavarian Acad. Scis., Am. Acad. Arts and Scis., Am. Philosophy Soc., Acad. Mainz Arts and Sci., Nordrhein-Westfälische Acad. Sci., Acad. Europaea London, German Zool. Soc. (hon. 2003). Home: Watzmannstr 16-Söcking D 82319 Starnberg Germany Personal E-mail: f.huber@planet-interkom.de.

HUBER, J. KENDALL, lawyer, insurance company executive; b. Norfolk, Va., Nov. 24, 1954; m. Deborah Clarke. BA, Va. Poly. Inst. and State U., 1976; JD, U. Va., 1979. Bar: Va. 1980, Md. 1981, Tenn. 1999, Mass. 2004. Sr. assoc. Piper Rudnick LLP, Balt., 1983—90; v.p., dep. gen. counsel USF&G Corp., Balt., 1990—98, Legg Mason Inc., 1998—99; v.p., dep. gen. counsel, sec. Promus Hotel Corp., Memphis, 1999—2000; exec. v.p., gen. counsel, sec. The Hanover Ins. Group, Inc., Worcester, Mass., 2000—02, sr. v.p., gen. counsel, 2002—. Lt. JACG USN, 1979—83. Office: The Hanover Ins Group Inc 440 Lincoln St Worcester MA 01653-0002 Business E-Mail: gencounsel@hanover.com.

HUBER, JANET BARLOW, librarian; d. Walter Shepherd and Evelyn Crocker Barlow; m. George Randolph Huber, Nov. 26, 1950; children: Lisa Huber Flory, Andrea Leigh. BA in History, Edn., Christopher Newport U., 1976; MS in Edn, Libr. Media, Old Dominion U., 1993. Cert. tchr. Va. Social studies tchr. Menchville H.S., Newport News, Va., 1976—79; libr. asst. Smithfield Libr., Va., 1987—90; libr. Isle of Wight Acad., Va., 1990—. Mem. Sch. Health Adv. Bd., Isle of Wight County, Va., 1990—; sponsor Scholastic Bowl, Isle of Wight Acad., Va., 1993—, Battle of the Brains Team, 2004—. Pianist/organist Bacon's Castle Bapt. Ch., Surry, Va., 1970—2006. Today's Youth Touching Past Achievers grant, 7-Eleven Inc., 2000, Ready Readers grant, Internat. Paper Co., 2005. Mem.: Va. Ednl. Media Assn. Avocations: quilting, gardening, reading. Home: 5396 Old Stage Hwy Smithfield VA 23430 Office: Isle of Wight Acad 17111 Courthouse Hwy Isle Of Wight VA 23397 Home Phone: 757-357-5446; Office Phone: 757-357-3866. Office Fax: 757-357-6886. Personal E-mail: janethuber@iwacademy.com.

HUBER, JOHN D., psychologist, consultant; b. Boise, Idaho, May 11, 1968; s. William John and Betty Annette Huber; m. Jessica R. Renz, July 8, 1995; children: John David, Phaedra Renee. D in Psychology, Carlos Albizu U., Miami, Fla., 2005. Adj. instr. SW Tex. State U., San Marcos, 1996—98; sch. psychologist Miami-Dade County Pub. Schs., 1999—2003; sr. lectr. Tex. State U., San Marcos, 2003—; lic. specialist sch. psychology Austin Ind. Sch. Dist., Tex., 2003—. Cons. in field, Austin, 1998—. Author: Program Design for Minors Adjudicated at Turner Guilord Knight. Mem.: APA, Psi Chi. Achievements include patents pending for night time sleep assistant for toddlers. Avocations: sailing, camping, fishing, music. Office: Texas State University Psychology 601 University Dr San Marcos TX 78666 Home Phone: 512-336-5044; Office Phone: 512-245-2526. Business E-Mail: jh30@txstate.edu.

HUBER, LIEZEL, professional tennis player; b. Durban, South Africa, Aug. 21, 1976; d. Jan and Sica; m. Tony Huber, Feb. 19, 2000. Profl. tennis player WTA, 1993—. Founder Liezel's Cause, 2005—. Named South African Sportswoman of Yr., 2005; named to Tour Player's Coun., 2003—04; recipient Humanitarian award, Stars for Stars, 2006. Achievements include winning 21 career doubles titles, WTA; winning 11 career doubles titles, ITF; mem. South African Fed Cup Team, 2003, South African Olympic Team, 2000. Office: WTA Hdqs One Progress Plz Ste 1500 Saint Petersburg FL 33701*

HUBER, MARIANNE JEANNE, art dealer and appraiser; b. Amboy, Ill., June 9, 1936; d. John Francis and Jeannette Marie (Wurth) Faivre; m. Robert L. Huber, Oct. 3, 1959; children: Michael Robert, Stephan Louis, Edward Francis. BA, Cardinal Stritch Coll., Milw., 1958. 6th grade tchr. St. Andrew's Sch., Rock Falls, Ill., 1958-59; jr. high tchr. Garside Sch., Mexico City, 1959-61; art dealer, cons. Huber Primitive Art, NYC and Dixon, Ill., 1963—; founder, pres. New World Art Svcs., NYC and Dixon, Ill., 1993—. Lectr., cons. Primitive Art Soc., Chgo., 1987, Freeport (Ill.) Art Mus., 1993, Indpls. Mus. Art, 1994, Nprstk Mus., Prague, Czech Republic, 1995; participant Maya Meetings, Austin, Tex., 1985—. Author: Echoes of a Distant Flute, 1984; translator: The Frida Kahlo Papers, 2007; exhibitions, The Cuna, 1980—; co-prodr., author: (documentaries) The Cuna, 1980; co-prodr., author (documentaries) Nebaj, Coztal and Chajul, 1987, author, co-prodr. The Maya Calendar, 2003—. Election judge Ogle County, Ill., 1993—; committeewoman Dem. Precinct, 2002—. Mem.: LWV, AAUW, Am. Appraisers Assn., Am. Soc. Appraisers, Nat. Mus. Women in Arts (mem. libr. bd. 2005—), Internat. Platform Assn. (gov. 1993—2001), Met. Mus. Art, Phidian Soc., Ill. Dem. Women, Delta Epsilon Sigma. Democrat. Avocations: hiking, wilderness camping, painting, piano, travel. Home and Office: 1012 Timber Trail Dr Dixon IL 61021-8934 Office Phone: 815-652-4196. E-mail: tellapple@yahoo.com.

HUBER, MARY THERESE, museum director, consultant; b. Osage, Iowa, Dec. 15, 1951; d. Robert James and Lenore Nack Huber; 1 foster child, Brandy Johnson. BFA, Mpls. Coll. Art and Design, 1977; BS in Art Edn., U. Minn., Mpls., 1983; cert. in mus. mgmt., Getty Ctr. Arts. With ednl. svcs. Mpls. Inst. Arts, supr. Arts Resource & Info. Ctr., supr. vis. svcs. dept.; dir. James & Meryl Hearst Ctr. Arts, Cedar Falls, Iowa. Bd. dirs. Cedar Falls C. of C., 1988—2000, 2001—06, Cedar Falls Cmty. Found.,

1998—. Recipient Honor, Nat. Art Edn. Assn., 1997. Mem.: Midwest Mus. Assn., Am. Assn. Mus., Cedar Valley Cultural Alliance. Office: James and Meryl Hearst Ctr Arts 304 W Seerlay Blvd Cedar Falls IA 50613

HUBER, MELBA STEWART, dance studio owner, educator, historian, writer, retailer; b. Tex., Oct. 1, 1927; d. Carl E. and Melba (Holt) Stewart; m. William C. Kinsolving Jr.; children: William Carey Kinsolving, Keith Brian Kinsolving; m. James M. Huber (dec.); 1 child, Melba Laurin. AA, Lamar Coll., 1946; student, U. Tex. Establisher, owner Melba's, Inc., McAllen, Tex., 1958—; founder McAllen (Tex.) Dance Theatre Co., 1970; tchr. Black Cmty. at Huston-Tillotson Coll., 1948—49. Columnist, tap amb. Internat. Tap Assn.; panelist St. Louis Tap Festival, NY Tradition in Tap, NY Tap Festivals. Columnist Tap Talk, NY Dance Pages, Dance and the Arts mag., 1988-97; columnist Tappin' In, Dancer mag., 1998—; prodr.: (broadway) Jelly's Last Jam. Recipient Plaudit award Nat. Dance Assn. Am. Alliance for Health, Physical Edn. and Recreation, 1970, Flo-Bert award N.Y. Com. to Celebrate Nat. Tap Dance Day, 1996, Savion Glover award St. Louis Tap Festival, 1998, Preservation of Our Heritage in American Dance award, Oklahoma City U., 1999, Women of Distinction award Detroit Tap Festival, 2000, Tradition in Tap Historian, Educator, Writer award 2005, Tex. Tap Legend award Dance Coun. Honors, 2007, 50 Yrs. in Bus. Celebration award, 2007; named for Life Achievement in the Art of Dance and Gymnastics, presented Tex. Flag Tex. State Senate, 1997; honored by Savion Glover, 2006. Mem. Tex. Assn. Tchrs. Dancing (pres. 1973-74, honoree 1997), South Tex. Dance Masters Assn. (Mem. of Yr. 1989). Home: PO Box 3664 Mcallen TX 78502-3664 Office: Melbas Inc PO Box 3664 Mcallen TX 78502-3664 Office Phone: 956-686-1411. Personal E-mail: melhuber@swbell.net, melba.huber@gmail.com.

HUBER, PAUL WILLIAM, biochemistry professor, researcher; b. Medford, Mass., July 23, 1951; s. William Francis and Catherine (Sheridan) H. BS, Boston Coll., 1973; PhD, Purdue U., 1978. NIH postdoctoral fellow U. Chgo., 1979-81, rsch. assoc., 1982-85; from asst. prof. to prof. U. Notre Dame, 1985—2003, prof., 2003—. Vis. fellow Yale U., 1997. Contbr. articles to profl. jours. Recipient John A. Kaneb award for undergrad. tchg., U. Notre Dame, 2001. Mem. AAAS, Am. Soc. Biochemistry and Molecular Biology. Home: 1215 E Irvington Ave South Bend IN 46614-1417 Office: U Notre Dame Dept Chemistry/Biochemistry Notre Dame IN 46556 Home Phone: 574-237-9156; Office Phone: 574-631-6042. Business E-Mail: phuber@nd.edu.

HUBER, RICHARD GREGORY, lawyer, educator; b. Indpls., June 29, 1919; s. Hugh Joseph and Laura Marie (Becker) H.; m. Katherine Elizabeth McDonald, June 21, 1950 (dec.); children: Katherine, Richard, Mary, Elizabeth, Stephen, Mark. BS, U.S. Naval Acad, 1942; JD, U. Iowa, 1950; LLM, Harvard U., 1951; LLD (hon.), New England Sch. Law, 1985, Northeastern U., 1987, Roger Williams U., 1996. Instr. law U. Iowa, 1950; assoc. prof. law U. S.C., 1952-54; assoc. prof. Tulane U., 1954-57, Boston Coll., 1957-59, prof., 1959-90, dean, 1970-85; disting. prof. Roger Williams U., Bristol, R.I., 1993-95; prof. New England Sch. Law, Newton, Mass., 1995-99. Adj. faculty Boston Coll., 1999-2004. Contbr. articles and book revs. to profl. jours. Past chairperson pers. and fin. coms. Mass. chpt. Multiple Sclerosis Soc.; past pres. bd. trustees Beaver Country Day Sch. With USN, 1941-47, 51-52. Mem. ABA (del., mem. coun. legal edn. 1981-85, trustee law sch. admissions coun 1983-85), Soc. Am. Law Tchrs., Assn. Am. Law Schs. (pres. 1988-89), Coun. Legal Edn. Opportunity (pres. 1975-79), Am. Judicature Soc., Mass. Bar Assn., Mass. Bar Found. Democrat. Roman Catholic. Home: 406 Woodward St Waban MA 02468-1523 Office: 885 Centre St Newton MA 02459-1148

HUBER, ROBERT, biochemist, educator; b. Munich, Feb. 20, 1937; s. Sebastian and Helene (Kebinger) H.; m. Christa Huber, 1960; children: Ulrike, Martin, Robert, Julia Diploma, Tech. Universität Munich, 1960, PhD, 1963, Habilitation, 1968; D (hon.), U. Catholic de Louvain, 1987, U. Ljubljana, 1989; D for Medicine and Surgery (hon.), U. 'Tor Vergata', 1991; D (hon.), Univ. Nova de Lisboa, 2000, U. Autónoma de Barcelona, 2000, Tsinghua U., 2003. External prof. Tech. U. Munich, 1976; prof., dir. Max-Planck-Inst. for Biochemistry, Martinsried, Germany, 1972—2005, dir. emeritus, 2005—. Hon. prof. Ocean U., Qingdao, 2002, Peking U., 2003, Sichuan U., Chengdu, 2003, Shanghai Second Med. U., 2004, Shanghai Jiao Tang U., China, 2005, U. Sevilla, 2006; Lotte Disting. prof. Seoul Nat. U., 2005; vis. prof. U. Autonoma Barcelona, 2001, Nat. U. Singapore, 2005, U. Duisburg-Essen, Germany, 2005, Cardiff U., Wales, 2007—. Editor Jour. Molecular Biology. Order for Merit for Sci. and Arts (Germany); Keilin medal Biochem. Soc. London, Richard Kuhn medal Soc. German Chemists, 1987, E.K. Frey-E. Werle meml. medal, 1989, Kone award Assn. Clin. Biochemists, 1990, Sir Hans Krebs medal, 1992, Linus Pauling medal, 1993, 94, Disting. Svc. award Miami Biotech. Winter Symposia, 1995, Max Tishler prize Harvard U., 1997, Max Bergmann medal U. Tübingen, 1997, co-recipient Nobel prize for chemistry, 1988. Fellow Royal Soc. London, Third World Acad. Scis., Am. Acad. Microbiology; mem. NAS (U.S.A.) (fgn. assoc.), European Molecular Biology Orgn. (coun. mem.), Japanese Biochem. Soc. (hon.), Am. Soc. Biol. Chemists (hon.), Swedish Soc. Biophysics (hon.), Croatian Acad. Scis. and Art (corr.), European Molecular Biology Orgn. Office: Max Planck Inst Biochem Am Klopferspitz 18 Martinsried Munich 82152 Germany Business E-Mail: huber@biochem.mpg.de.

HUBER, SCOTT, transportation services executive; b. St. Louis, 1964; BSBA, U. Mo., St. Louis, 1985, BS in Fin., 1986; JD, St. Louis U., 1989. Bar: Mo. 1989, Ill. 1990, US Ct. Appeals 8th Cir. 1990, US Dist. Ct. Ea. Dist. Mo. 1990. Sr. staff atty. Unigroup, Inc., Fenton, Mo. Mem.: Bar Assn. Met. St. Louis, ABA, Mo. Bar. Office: Unigroup Inc 1 Premier Dr Fenton MO 63026*

HUBER, WESLEY DAVID, accountant, educator; m. Mitra Elizabeth Niknam. BS, Calif. Poly. State U., San Luis Obispo, 2000; JD, Rutgers U., Camden, NJ, 2007. CPA Calif., 2002. Staff auditor Deloitte & Touche, San Jose, Calif., 2000—01; sr. acct. Petrinovich Pugh & Co., LLP, San Jose, 2001—04; tax preparer Wesley D Huber, CPA, Haddonfield, NJ, 2002—; fin. analyst Ayco Co., Parsippany, NJ, 2007—. Prof. Rutgers Sch. Bus., NJ, 2005; intern IRS, NYC, 2006; extern Hon. Gregory M. Sleet, U.S. Dist. Judge, Wilmington, Del., 2005. Asst. treas. Scaife Scholarship Alumni Assn., Oakland, Calif., 2001—04. Scaife scholar, No. Calif. Scholarship Found., 1996—99, 2005—06. Mem.: AICPA (licentiate), ABA (assoc.), Am. Assn. Atty.-CPAs (assoc.), Golden Key Nat. Honor Soc. (life), Beta Gamma Sigma (life), Phi Alpha Delta (life; treas. local chpt. 2005—06). E-mail: wesleyhuber@hotmail.com.

HUBER, WILLIAM EVAN, lawyer; b. Celina, Ohio, Mar. 10, 1943; s. W. Evan and Genevieve Rose Huber; m. E. Marie Schwaberow, June 24, 1966 (div. Aug. 1994); children: Michael D., Mark William; m. Linda Sue Nosek, Sept. 10, 2005. BS in Edn., Ohio No. U., 1965, JD, 1968. Bar: Ohio 1968, U.S. Dist. Ct. (no. dist.) Ohio 1972, U.S. Supreme Ct. 1972, U.S. Ct. Appeals (6th cir.) 1990, U.S. Tax Ct. Ohio, U.S. Dist. Ct. (no. dist.) Ohio. Asst. pros. atty. Auglaize County, Ohio, 1969-76; asst. law dir. City of St. Mary's, Ohio, 1972—79; pvt. practice St. Marys, Ohio, 1969—. Asst. law dir. City of St. Marys, Ohio, 1972-79. Mem., past pres., past state dir. St. Marys Jaycees; past state v.p. Ohio Jaycees, 1969; past state v.p. Ohio Jaycees, 1971; mem. St. Marys Sesquicentennial Com., 1972-73; past trustee, past pres. St. Marys C. of C., 1976-77; past trustee Auglaize County Mental Health Assn.; past gen. chmn. St. Mary's City United Way; mem., past chmn. St. Marys City Recreational Adv. Bd.; mem., past trustee St. Marys Cmty. Improvement Corp.; mem. Mayor's Downtown Revitalization Com.; com. mem. Ohio Bicentennial Celebration; past pres. St. Marys Nat. Little League, 1969-75, team mgr.; past chmn. St. Marys Medic-Search Com.; mem., past trustee St. Marys Cmty. Improvement Corp.; past mem., chmn. St. Marys Civil Svc. Commn., 1993-97; past trustee Auglaize County Mental Health Assn.; mem. Auglaize County Bd. Elections, 1994-97; chairperson Dem. exec. com. Auglaize County, 1992-97; bd. trustees Auglaize County Hist. Soc., 2002-05, Ohio Geneal. Soc., 2004—; mem. Wayne St. United Meth. Ch.; coach YMCA Youth Basketball, Recipient Ohio Jaycees Presdl. Honor award, 1972, Disting. Svc. award Ohio Dem. Party, 1997, Pub. Interest Pro Bono award Ohio Northern U. Coll. Law, 2001; named an Outstanding Jaycee St. Marys Jaycees, 1970. Mem. SAR, S.R., Ohio State Bar Assn., Auglaize County Bar Assn. (pres. 1975), St. Marys C. of C. (past trustee, past pres.), Allen County Geneal. Soc., Auglaize County Geneal. Soc. (pres. 2004-07), Champaign County Geneal. Soc., Shelby County Geneal. Soc., Ohio's First Families, First Families Am., First Families Allen County, First Families Auglaize County, First Families Champaign County, First Families Clark County, First Families Fairfield County, First Families Montgomery County, Ohio Soc. Civil War Families, Jr. Chamber Internat. Senate (life mem.), First Settlers Clark County, Settlers and Builders Ohio, Sons of Union Vets. Civil War, Soc. War of 1812 (adv. gen. state 2004-), Sons and Daus. Pilgrims. Office: 137 E Spring St PO Box 298 Saint Marys OH 45885-0298 Home: PO Box 298 Saint Marys OH 45885-0298 Personal E-mail: huberlaw@bright.net.

HUBERFELD, NICOLE LAUREN, healthcare educator; b. Balt. m. David Treacy, July 2, 2004. BA, U. Pa., 1995; JD, Seton Hall U., 1998. Assoc. healthcare team Wilentz, Goldman and Spitzer, Woodbridge, NJ, 1998—2000; assoc. health law group Gibbons Del Deo, Newark, 2000—02; assoc. healthcare group Wolff and Samson, West Orange, 2002—03; dir. healthcare compliance cert. program Law Sch. Seton Hall U., Newark, 2003—05, health law faculty fellow Law Sch., 2003—05; asst. prof. Coll. Law U. Ky., Lexington, 2005—. Contbr. articles to profl. jours. Team leader Komen Race for Cure, NYC, 2000—02, Lexington, 2005, Revlon Run/Walk Women's Cancers, NYC, 2000—02; vol. Habitat for Humanity, Newark, 2000—05, Lexington, 2005, fundraiser, 2000—05. Named Outstanding Woman Law Grad., Nat. Assn. Women Lawyers, 1998; recipient award, Trustees Coun. Pa. Women, 1994, Raymond DelTufo Constl. Law award, Seton Hall Law Sch., 1998. Mem.: Am. Health Lawyers Assn. (mem. fraud and abuse practice group enforcement panel 2005—), Am. Soc. Law, Medicine and Ethics. Avocations: scuba diving, yoga, travel, hiking, cooking. Office: U Ky Coll Law 258 Law Bldg Lexington KY 40506 Home Phone: 859-263-5399; Office Phone: 859-257-3281. Business E-Mail: nicole.huberfeld@uky.edu.

HUBERMAN, BENJAMIN, technology consultant; b. Havana, Cuba, Jan. 25, 1938; came to U.S., 1946; s. Henry and Marcella (Waisman) H.; m. Gisela Bialik, Oct. 13, 1963; children: Jonathan, Martin. AB, Columbia Coll., 1959; BS, Columbia U., 1960; diploma of Imperial Coll., London U., 1962. Sr. official Arms Control & Disarmament Agy., Washington, 1966-73, Nat. Security Coun., Washington, 1973-75; dir., policy evaluation Nuclear Regulatory Commn., Washington, 1975-77; sr. official Office Sci. and Tech. Policy, Washington, 1977-81; dep. sci. advisor to pres. White House, Washington, 1981; v.p. Cons. Internat. Group, Inc., Washington, 1982-88, pres., 1988-90, Huberman Cons. Group, Washington, 1990—; v.p. GBH Radio Inc., Fisher Island, Fla., 1997—. Chmn. exec. panel Chief Naval Ops. Atlantic Coun., Washington. Lt. USN, 1960-66. Fulbright scholar, London, 1960-61. Mem. Coun. Fgn. Rels., Met. Club, Cosmos Club (Washington). Home: 5012 Fisher Island Dr Miami Beach FL 33109 Office: Huberman Cons Group Ste 250 1250 Conn Ave NW Washington DC 20036

HUBERMAN, BERNARDO A., physicist; b. Buenos Aires, Nov. 7, 1943; arrived in U.S., 1966, naturalized, 1974; s. Leon and Sara Huberman; children: Lara M., Andrew D. PhD in Physics, U. Pa., 1971. Mem. rsch. staff Xerox Palo Rsch. Ctr., Calif., 1974-80, prin. scientist Calif., 1983-84, rsch. fellow Calif., 1985-2001; sr. fellow HP Lab., Palo Alto, 2001—, dir. info. dynamics lab., 2001—. Vis. scientist Inst. Laue-Langevin, Grenoble, France, 1976; cons. prof. Stanford U., Calif., 1981—; vis. prof. U. Paris, 1981, U. Copenhagen, 1993, European Sch. Bus., 1999. Author: The Laws of the Web, 2001; contbr. articles to profl. jours. Trustee Aspen Ctr. Physics, Colo., 1980—. Fellow: AAAS, Japan Soc. Promotion of Sci., Am. Phys. Soc. Office: HP Labs 1500 Page Hill Rd Palo Alto CA 94304 E-mail: huberman@hpl.hp.com.

HUBERMAN, JEFFREY ALLEN, architect; b. Boston, Jan. 2, 1942; s. Sidney H. and Miriam (Walker) H.; m. Barbara Kemp, May 16, 1964 (div.); children: Amy Beth, Marc Walker. BArch, U. Fla., Gainesville, 1964. Designer Odell Assocs., Charlotte, NC, 1964-67, Wolf-Johnson Assocs., Charlotte, 1967-69; designer, arch. Wolf Assocs., Charlotte, 1970-71; ptnr. Gantt Huberman Archs., Charlotte, 1971—. Mem. NC Bd. Architecture, 1995-2005, sec., 1996-97, treas., 1997-98, v.p., 1999-2001, pres., 2001-03. Chmn. ann. fund drive Charlotte-Mecklenburg Arts and Sci. Coun., 1975-81, v.p., 1977-78, bd. dirs., 1977; bd. dirs. Charlotte Opera Assn., 1966-82, pres., 1979-81; pres. Children's Theatre, 1984-85, bd. dirs., 1981-87; bd. dirs. Temple Beth El, 1968-83, Charlotte-Mecklenburg Cmty. Rels. Com., 1974-84, Planned Parenthood of Greater Charlotte, 1978-80, Charlotte Jr. Soccer Found., 1978-82, Tarradiddle Players, 1986-87; chmn. Charlotte Clean City Com., 1975-77; youth soccer coach, 1975-84; com. mem. Performing Arts Ctr. Adv. Ctr., 1983-85; adv. com. Charlotte/Douglas Internat. Airport, 1987-88, art adv. com., 1992—; bd. dirs. Green Hill Ctr. for NC Arts, 2000-05. Fellow AIA (chmn. honor awards com. 1972, treas. Charlotte, NC sect. 1976-77, chmn. audit com. 1987, bd. dirs. 1987-92, long range planning com. 1990, component resources com. 1992, pres. NC chpt. 1991, NC Archtl. Found. 1994, NC Gold medal 2002, NC Firm of Yr. 2006), Nat. Coun. Archtl. Registration Bd. (juror divsns. B and C archtl. registration exam. 1984-86, chmn. divsn. B graphic 1989, master jurors com. 1986, archtl. registration exam. com. 1996-97, intern devel. program com. 1998-2002, chair, 2000-02, procedures and documents com. 2000-05, chmn. 2004-05, chair reciprocity impediment task force 2002-04, So. region sec. 2003-04, bd. dirs. 2005—, 2d v.p. 2007—). Office: Gantt Huberman Architects 500 N Tryon St Charlotte NC 28202-2232 Office Fax: 704-342-9639. Business E-Mail: jhuberman@gantthuberman.com.

HUBERMAN, RICHARD LEE, lawyer; b. Lynn, Mass., Dec. 6, 1953; s. Irving Morris and Selma Edythe (Wolk) H. AB, Harvard U., 1975, JD, 1978. Bar: Mass. 1979, D.C. 1979. Atty. Office of Rail Pub. Counsel, Washington, 1978-80; counsel subcom. on commerce, consumer protection and competitiveness (formerly commerce, transp. and tourism) U.S. Ho. of Reps., Washington, 1980-95, mem. prof. staff Com. on Edn. and Workforce, 1995—97; pvt. practice Washington, 1997-98; counsel to commr. and chmn. Occupl. Safety and Health Rev. Commn., Washington, 1998—. Mem. ABA, Mass. Bar Assn., Harvard Law Sch. Assn. Clubs: Harvard (Washington). Democrat. Home: 2141 P St NW Apt 302 Washington DC 20037-1031 Office: Occupl Safety and Health Rev Commn 1120 20th St NW Washington DC 20036 Office Phone: 202-606-5723. Business E-Mail: rhuberman@oshrc.gov.

HUBER-WARRING, TONYA, education educator; b. Lackawanna, NY, Feb. 28, 1958; d. H. Joseph and Elsie Garlick H. BS, Pa. State U., University Park, 1982, MEd, 1985, PhD, 1990. Assoc. prof. Wichita State U. Coll. of Edn., Kans., 1990—2002, prof., 2002—04, St. Cloud State U., 2004—, prof., coord. social responsibility; prof. U. St. Thomas, 2004—. Cons., presenter in field; faculty internat. and overseas programs Coll. N.J., Trenton, NJ, 1997—. Author: Teaching in the Diverse Classroom: Learner-Centered Activities That Work, 1993, Quality Learning Experiences for ALL Students, 2002; editor: Internat. Jour. Curriculum Inquiry, 2006—, World Coun. for Curriculum Instrn., 2006; founding editor: Jour. Critical Inquiry Into Curriculum and Instrn., 1998—2004, assoc. editor: Multicultural Edn. Mag., —. Recipient Howard Soule Grad. fellow in Ednl. Leadership, Phi Delta Kappa, 1989. Mem.: World Coun. Curriculum and Instrn., Nat. Assn. for Multicultural Edn. (founder 1990, publs. com. 1993—2003, chair Nat. Leadership Inst. 1996, v.p. 2002—03, Svc. award 1990—98). Home: 2698 Lake Ct Dr Saint Paul MN 55112-4106 Office: St Cloud State U Human Rels and Multicultural Edn 720 4th Ave EB-B129 Saint Cloud MN 56301-4498 Office Phone: 320-308-0145. E-mail: thuber@stcloudstate.edu.

HUBSCHMAN, HENRY A., lawyer; b. Newark, Aug. 12, 1947; s. Morris and Esther (Weissman) H.; m. Joanne L. Goode; children: Lilly, Josie, Ellis, Nathan. BA summa cum laude, Rutgers U., 1969; JD magna cum laude, Harvard U., 1973, M Pub. Policy, 1973. Bar: Mass. 1973, N.J. 1974, D.C. 1974, Ohio 1994. Law clk. U.S. Dist. Ct. Mass., Boston, 1973-74; assoc. Fried, Frank, Harris, Shriver & Jacobson, Washington, 1974-77, 79-80, ptnr., 1980-92; v.p., gen. counsel, bus. devel. GE Aircraft Engines, Cin., 1992-97; pres., CEO GE Capital Aviation Svcs., Stamford, Conn., 1997—. Exec. asst. to Sec. HUD, Washington, 1977-79; bd. dir. Fed. Nat. Mortgage Assn., 1979-81. Jewish. Home: 37 Hillside Rd Greenwich CT 06830-4834 Office: GE Commll Aviation Svcs 201 High Ridge Rd Stamford CT 06905-3417

HUCAL, MICHELLE, editor; b. 1978; Degree in Journalism, Mich. State U., 2000. Assoc. editor Home Décor Buyer, Chgo.; editor Environ. Design + Constrn. mag., Troy, Mich., 2002—. Bd. dirs. US Green Bldg. Coun. Named one of 40 Under 40, Crain's Detroit Bus., 2006. Mem.: Am. Soc. Bus. Publ. Editors (Editorial Excellence award 2005). Office: Environmental Design + Contruction 2401 W Big Beaver RD Ste 700 Troy MI 48084 Office Phone: 248-244-1280. Office Fax: 248-362-5103. Business E-Mail: hucalm@bnpmedia.com.

HUCH, RONALD KIND, historian, educator; s. Emory Wallace and Anna Ophelia Huch; m. Margo Lynn Laskowski; children: Diane, Anita, Jocelyn, Elanor. BA, Thiel Coll., 1962; MA, Pa. State U., 1964; PhD, U. Mich., 1971. Asst. prof. Murray (Ky.) State U., 1967—68; from instr. to prof. U. Minn., Duluth, 1968—86; prof. Dickinson (ND) State U., 1986—92; chmn. history U. Papua New Guinea, Port Moresby, 1992—2000; prof., chmn. dept. history Ea. Ky. U., Richmond, 2000—. Cons. Ednl. Testing Svc., Princeton, NJ, 1988—. Author: The Radical Lord Radnor, 1977, Henry, Lord Brougham: Later Years, 1993, From Blacksmith Shop to Modern Hospital, 1985; co-author: Joseph Hume: The People's M.P., 1985; contbr. articles to profl. jours. Founder History Scholarships for Papua New Guineans, Port Moresby, 1996; v.p. NC chpt. AAUP, 1990—91. Recipient Solon Buck award, Minn. Hist. Soc., 1981; fellow, Am. Philos. Soc., 1971, 1975, 1977, 1981, Am. Coun. Learned Socs., 1973; summer fellow, NEH, Washington, 1988. Mem.: Anglo-Am. Historians, N.Am. Conf. Brit. Studies, Am. Hist. Assn. Avocation: horse racing. Office: Ea Ky U Dept History 521 Lancaster Ave Richmond KY 40475 Fax: 859-622-1357. Business E-Mail: ron.huch@eku.edu.

HUCHRA, JOHN PETER, astronomer, educator; b. Jersey City, Dec. 23, 1948; s. Mieczyslaw Piotr and Helen Ann Huchra; m. Rebecca M. Henderson; 1 child, Harry Matthew. BS, MIT, 1970; PhD, Calif. Inst. Tech., 1976. Ctr. fellow Ctr. Astrophysics, Cambridge, Mass., 1976-78; astronomer Smithsonian Astrophys. Obs., Cambridge, Mass., 1978-89, sr. astronomer, 1989—2005; lectr. dept. astronomy Harvard U., Cambridge, Mass., 1979-84, prof. dept. astronomy, 1984—2002, Robert O. and Holly Thomis Doyle prof. cosmology, 2002—, vice-provost rsch. policy, 2005—06, sr. adv. to provost on rsch. policy; assoc. dir. Ctr. for Astrophysics, Cambridge, Mass., 1989—98; dir. F.L. Whipple Obs., 1994-98. Mem. coun. Space Telescope Sci. Inst., Balt., 1987-95; chmn. working group on galaxy radial velocities Internat. Astron. Union, Paris, 1988—; chmn. large astron. data base working group NASA/IPAC, Washington, 1988-92; mem. astronomy and astrophysics survey Optical Panel, NAS, NRC, 1989-90; adv. bd. and vis. com. Arecibo Obs., Ithaca, NY, 1989-92; users com. Cerro Tololo Inter-Am. Obs., La Serena, Chile, 1989-91; vis. com. ESO, 1993-97; mem. NRC com. on Astronomy and Astrophysics, 1994-2001, co-chmn. 1997-2001; mem. AURA, bd. dirs., 1995-, chair, 2001-04; mem. NRC bd. on physics and astronomy, 1997-2003, chair, 2000-03; chair NOAO Future Directions Com., 1998-99; vis. prof. Cambridge U., 2003—; mem. math. and phys. sci. adv. com. NSF, 2003—; lectr. in field. Contbr. chapters to books to profl. jours. Rsch. grantee, NASA, 1979—, Smithsonian Instn., 1980, NSF, 1984-89, 99—. Fellow AAAS (Newcomb Cleve. award 1990), Am. Phys. Soc. AIP (pub. policy com. 1988-95); mem. NAS, Am. Acad. Arts and Scis., Am. Astron. Soc. (pub. bd. chmn., 1986-88, councilor 1998-2001, sci. editor Astrophys. Jour. 1998-2003), Royal Astron. Soc., Astron. Soc. of the Pacific, Am. Phys. Soc. Astrophysics Divsn. (exec. com. 1996-97), Nat. Environ. Leadership Coun., Wilderness Soc., Nat. Audubon Soc., Mass. Audubon Soc., Union of Concerned Scientists, Nature Conservancy, Trustees of Reservations, Appalachian Trail Conf., Am. Contract Bridge League, Greenpeace, Green Mtn. Club, Appalachian Mtn. Club, Sierra Club, Sigma Xi, Gamma Nu. Achievements include discovery of Comet Huchra, of nearest gravitational lens; revision of cosmic distance scale; completion of first and second Center for Astrophysics Redshift Survey; measurement of infall of our Milky Way Galaxy into the Virgo Cluster; discovery of Great Wall of galaxies, 2 Micron All Sky Survey. Office: Harvard-Smithsonian Ctr Astrophysics P 309 MS 19 60 Garden St Cambridge MA 02138-1516 Office Phone: 617-495-7375. Business E-Mail: huchra@cfa.harvard.edu.

HUCK, JOHN LLOYD, pharmaceutical executive; b. Bklyn., July 17, 1922; s. John Lloyd and Adrienne (Warner) H.; m. Dorothy Bertha Foehr, Nov. 20, 1943; children: Lloyd E., Jeanne Huck Leslie-Hughes, Virginia Huck Stalcup. BS in Chemistry, Pa. State U., 1946. Research chemist Hoffmann-LaRoche, Nutley, NJ, 1946, sales rep., 1948, dir. sales tng., 1951, asst. gen. sales mgr., 1955, dir. product devel., 1958; dir. mktg. Merck Sharp & Dohme Div., West Point, Pa., 1958; v.p. mktg. planning MSD div., 1966, v.p. sales and mktg., 1968, exec. v.p., 1969, exec. v.p., gen. mgr., 1972, pres., 1973; sr. v.p. Merck & Co., Rahway, NJ, 1975, exec. v.p., 1977, dir., 1977-86, pres., chief operating officer, 1978-85, chmn. bd., 1985-86; chmn. bd., chief exec. officer Nova Pharm. Corp., Morristown, NJ, 1986-88, chmn. bd., 1988-91. Patentee in field. Trustee Pa. State U., 1977-92, v.p., 1985-88, pres. bd., 1988-91; trustee Morristown Meml. Health Found., Inc., N.J., 1979-96, chmn. bd., 1986-88; trustee Geraldine R. Dodge Found., 1987-2003. 1st lt. USAAF, 1942-46. Alumni fellow Coll. Medicine Pa. State U., 1980, Coll. of Sci., 1983; named to Nutley Hall of Fame, 2003. Mem. Centre Hills Country Club. Republican. Home: 233 Lion's Hill Rd State College PA 16803

HUCK, L. FRANCIS, lawyer; b. Pittsfield, Mass., May 5, 1947; s. Lewis Francis Joseph and Rosemary (Ahearn) H.; m. Natalie Anne Murphy, June 10, 1978; children: Amelia Emerson, Rosemary Alice, Charles Randolph. AB, Harvard U., 1969; JD, Stanford U., 1972. Assoc. Simpson, Thacher & Bartlett, NYC, 1972-79, ptnr., 1980—, mem. exec. com. Mem. Harvard Club N.Y.C., Wee Burn Club, ABA, Bar Assn. City N.Y. Democrat. Office: Simpson Thacher & Bartlett LLP 425 Lexington Ave Fl 15 New York NY 10017-3954 Office Phone: 212-455-7025. Office Fax: 212-455-2502. Business E-Mail: lfhuck@stblaw.com.

HUCKABEE, HARLOW MAXWELL, lawyer, writer; b. Wichita Falls, Tex., Jan. 22, 1918; s. Edwin Cleveland and Gladys Idella (Bonney) H.; m. Gloria Charlotte Comstock, Jan. 10, 1942; children: Bonney M., David C., Stephen M. BA, Harvard U., 1948; JD, Georgetown U., 1951. Bar: U.S. Dist. Ct. D.C. 1952, U.S. Ct. Appeals (D.C. cir.) 1952. Lawyer Fed.

Housing Adminstrn., Washington, 1955-56, IRS, Washington, 1963-67; trial lawyer criminal sect., tax divsn. US Justice Dept., Washington, 1956-63, 1968-80, trial lawyer organized crime and racketeering sect., 1967-68. Author: Lawyers, Psychiatrists and Criminal Law, 1980, Mental Disability Issues in the Criminal Justice System: What They Are, Who Evaluates Them, How and When, 2000; contbr. articles to profl. jours. and legal publs. including Diminished Capacity Dilemma in the Federal System, 1991. Maj. U.S. Army, 1940-45, 48-55, ETO, Korea; lt. col. USAR, 1961. Methodist. Home and Office: 5100 Fillmore Ave Apt 913 Alexandria VA 22311-5048

HUCKABEE, MIKE (MICHAEL DALE), former governor; b. Hope, Ark., Aug. 24, 1955; m. Janet McCain, May 25, 1974; children: John Mark, David, Sarah. BA in Religion, Ouachita Bapt. U., Arkadelphia, Ark., 1976; postgrad., Southwestern Bapt. Theol. Sem., Ft. Worth, 1976-77; D of Humanities (hon.), John Brown Univ, 1991; D of Laws (hon.), Ouachita Baptist U., Arkadelphia, Ark., 1992. Ordained to ministry So. Bapt. Conv., 1974. Pastor Walnut Street Bapt. Ch., Arkadelphia, 1974-75, Immanuel Bapt. Ch., Pine Bluff, Ark., 1980-85, Beech Street 1st Bapt. Ch., Texarkana, Ark., 1986—96; pres. KBSC-TV, Texarkana, Ark., 1987—92, Cambridge Communications, Texarkana, Ark., 1992—96; lt. gov. State of Ark., Little Rock, 1993-96, gov., 1996—2007. Founder, past pres. Am. Christian TV Sys., Pine Bluff; pres. Ark. Bapt. Conv., 1989-91; mem. Interstate Oil and Gas Compact Commn. (past chmn.); state chmn., Delta Regional Authority; mem. Nat. Gov. Assn. (vice chmn.). Author: Living Beyond Your Lifetime: How to be Intentional About the Legacy You Leave, 2000, Quit Digging Your Grave With a Knife and Fork: A 12-Step Program to End Bad Habits and Begin a Healthy Lifestyle, 2005, From Hope to Higher Ground: 12 STOPS to Restoring America's Greatness, 2007; co-author (with John Perry): Character is the Issue: How People With Integrity Can Revolutionize America, 1997; co-author: (with George Grant) Kids Who Kill: Confronting Our Culture of Violence, 1998. So. Technology Coun., So. Internat. Trade Coun. Republican. Baptist. Avocations: hunting, fishing, reading, playing bass guitar in his band, Capitol Offense.

HUCKABY, GARY CARLTON, lawyer; b. Lanett, Ala., July 12, 1938; s. Carl Walker and Mary Evelyn (Meriwether) H.; m. Jeanne Davey Huckaby, Feb. 23, 1963; children: Gary Jr., John Stephen, Michael Stewart. BA, U. Ala., 1960, JD, 1962. Bar: US Supreme Ct. 1963, US Ct. of Mil. Appeals 1963, US Ct. Appeals (5th and 11th cirs.) 1963, US Dist. Ct. (no., middle and so. dists) Ala. 1963. Law clk. to chief justice Ala. Supreme Ct., Montgomery, 1962-63; asst. US Sen. Lister Hill, Washington, 1963; ptnr. Smith, Huckaby & Graves, Huntsville, Ala., 1966-85; dir. Ala. Ctr. for Law & Civic Edn., 1992—2001; ptnr. Bradley, Arant, Rose & White, Huntsville, 1985—2007; ret. Dir. coun. Internat. Visitors of Huntsville-Madison County, 1983-89, Tenn. Valley Boy Scouts Am., 1975-79, Mental Health Assn. Madison County, 1970-78, Ala. Law Sch. Found., 1981—; pres. Huntsville-Madison County Mental Health Bd., 1977-80, Madison County Heart Assn., 1968; active Citizens Com. on Higher Edn. of Ala. Legis., 1976, judicial sect. of Huntsville-Madison County Local Govt. Study Com., 1969. Capt. USAF, 1963-66. Fellow Am. Bar Found., Am. Coll. Trial Lawyers; mem. ABA (bd. govs. 1990-91, house of delegates, chmn. standing com. on lawyer referral and info. services 1982-85, chmn. spl. com. on delivery of legal services 1976-79, standing com. on lawyers pub. service responsibility 1987-90, consortium on legal services and the pub. 1976-79, task force on pub. edn. 1978, standing com. on lawyers in the armed forces 1971-73), Ala. State Bar (pres., bd. commrs. 1981-87, exec. com. 1982-83, 84-85, 87-88, chmn. governance com. 1986-87, action group on professionalism, disciplinary bd. 1981-87; recipient award of merit 1986), Huntsville-Madison County Bar Assn. (pres. 1977-78, chmn. grievance com. 1976, bench and bar relations 1981, convention host com. 1971, law day com. 1968), Am. Judicature Soc. (former bd. dirs.), Rotary. Democrat. Episcopalian. Home Phone: 256-534-9693; Office Phone: 256-508-1223. Personal E-mail: ghuckabysr@aol.com.

HUCKEBA, EMILY CAUSEY, retired elementary school educator; b. Carrollton, Ga., Aug. 26, 1941; d. Edward Clark and Audie Farmer Causey; m. Dale Malloy Huckeba, Aug. 27, 1961; 1 child, Catherine Nan. BS Elem. Edn., West Ga. Coll., 1962, M Edn., 1977. 2nd grade tchr. Whitesburg (Ga.) Elem. Sch., 1962—63; 1st grade tchr. Ctrl. Elem. Sch., Carrollton, Ga., 1963—68; tchr. Roopville Elem. Sch., Ga., 1968—96, substitute tchr., 1998—. Mem. alumni coun. West Ga. Coll., Carrollton, 1991—93; pilot tchr. Whole Lang. Program Roopville (Ga.) Elem. Sch., 1993—95. Charter mem. Roopville Hist. Soc., 1984—; mem. The Ga. Trust for Historic Preservation, 2001—; organist, pianist Roopville Bapt. Ch., 1960—2006; asst. organist, pianist Bethesda Bapt. Ch., 2006—, dir. children's choir, 2006—. Mem.: NEA, Ga. Ret. Educators Assn., Ga. Music Educators Assn., Carroll Heard Ret. Educators, Ga. Assn. Educators, Alpha Delta Kappa (chaplain 2006—). Baptist. Home: 1135 S Hwy 27 Roopville GA 30170-2516

HUCKIN, WILLIAM PRICE, JR., prosecutor; b. Okmulgee, Okla., Aug. 20, 1920; s. William Price and Mary Louise H.; m. Freda Croom, Nov. 15, 1947; children: William Price III, David, Elizabeth, Barbara. BA, U. Okla., 1942, LLB, 1947. Bar: Okla. 1947; U.S. Dist. Ct. (no. dist.) 1953, U.S. Dist. Ct. (we. dist.) 1950, U.S. Ct. Appeals, 1994. Asst. county atty., Tulsa, Okla., 1951-52; prosecutor, 1954-55; pvt. practice, 1956—. Apttd. city prosecutor, Tulsa. Active First Presbyn. Ch., clk. of session, permanent jud. commn. 1st lt., pilot, U.S. Army Air Corps, 1943-45. Decorated Rome Arno and Air Offensive Europe Theatre ribbon with 2 bronze stars, air medal, 1944, 2nd oak leaf cluster, 1944, unit citation, 1944. Mem. ATLA, Okla. Bar Assn., Tulsa County Bar Assn. (Disting. Svc. award 1986), Beta Theta Pi (pres. Gamma Phi chpt. 1947). Republican. Avocations: genealogy, chess. Home: 6706 S Florence Ave Tulsa OK 74136-4556 Office: 1206 Philtower Bldg 427 S Boston Ave Tulsa OK 74103-4141 Personal E-mail: huckin9@aol.com.

HUCKINS, HAROLD AARON, chemical engineer; b. Cambridge, Mass., Nov. 28, 1924; s. Harold Aaron and Julia E. (Nugent) Huckins; m. Elizabeth L. Kearns, Nov. 15, 1952; children: Richard W., Robert M., Christopher N., Patricia A., Leslie K. BSChemE, Northeastern U., Boston, 1945; ASME, Lowell Inst., 1946; postgrad., Boston U., 1947—49, U. Pitts., 1950—52. Chem. process engr., asst. project mgr. Monsanto Chem. Co., Boston-Everett, Mass., 1945—49; sr. process engr., group leader Koppers Co. Chem. Divsn., Pitts., 1949—53; mgr. pilot plants, project mgr. Sci. Design Co., Inc., NYC, 1953—66; v.p. tech. ops. Oxirane Chem. Co., Princeton, NJ, 1966—73; v.p. tech. assessment Halcon SD Group, NYC, 1973—85; pres. Princeton Advanced Tech., Inc., 1985—87. Dir. Assn. Cons. Chemists and Chem. Engrs. divsn., NYC, 1990-93, program chair, 1992-93; dir. Materials Tech. Inst., St. Louis, 1976-85; spkr. local groups/TV global energy trends; presenter in field. Co-author: The Chemical Plant, 1966; contbr. articles to profl. jours. Fellow AIChE (chair ctrl. Jersey sect. 1976-77, dir mgmt. divsn. 1981-82, dir. materials engring. and sci. divsn. 1992-93, chmn. chem. tech. materials com. 1983-84, chmn. John Fritz medal commn. 1989, chmn. entrepreneurial forum 1994-99, Chem. Engring. Practice award 1994); mem. Am. Soc. Materials, Am. Chem. Soc., Am. Ceramic Soc., Nat. Assn. Corrosion Engrs. (conf. chmn. 1984), Am. Inst. Aero. Astronautics, Comml. Devel. Assn., Mensa Internat., Country Club of Hilton Head Island, Port Royal Racquet Club, Hilton Head Ski Club (bd. dirs.). Achievements include 12 US patents for chemical process technology, four of which are for a proprietary hydrogen peroxide process. Home and Office: Princeton Advanced Tech Inc 4 Bertram Pl Hilton Head Island SC 29928-3936 Office Phone: 843-689-9211. Office Fax: 843-689-9212. Personal E-mail: hhuckins1@hargray.com.

HUCKMAN, MICHAEL SAUL, neuroradiologist, educator; b. Newark, Aug. 20, 1936; s. Louis Fillmore and Mollie (Lehman) H.; m. Beverly Joy Blachman, Aug. 2, 1964; children: Andrew Garfield, Robert Steven. AB, Princeton U., 1958; MD, St. Louis U., 1962. Rotating intern, then resident in radiology Phila. Gen. Hosp., 1962-63, 65-68; fellow in neuroradiology Edward Mallinckrodt Inst. Radiology, Washington U., St. Louis, also univ. instr. radiology, 1968-70; mem. faculty Rush Med. Coll., Chgo., 1970—, prof. radiology, 1978—; dir. sect. neuroradiology Rush U. Med. Ctr., 1970—; mem. faculty Cook County Grad. Sch. Medicine, 1972-91. Cons. Nat. Ctr. for Health Care Tech., 1980-81; sec.-gen. XVI Symposium Neuroradiologicum, 1994-98. Editor-in-chief: Am. Jour. Neuroradiology, 1989-97; mem. editorial bd. Jour. Computer Assisted Tomography, 1976-94, Radiographics, 1983-87, Applied Radiology, 1987-89; cons. editor Am. Jour. Roentgenology, 1990-91; contbr. articles to med. jours. Served with USNR, 1963-65. Spl. fellow Nat. Inst. Neurol. Diseases and Blindness, 1968-70 Fellow Am. Coll. Radiology, Coll. Physicians of Phila.; mem. AMA, Am. Soc. Neuroradiology (sec. 1980-83, pres. elect 1986-87, pres. 1987-88, editor emeritus 1998—, archivist 1998—, Gold medal 1999), Radiol. Soc. N.Am. (Gold medal 2002), Am. Soc. Head and Neck Radiology, Am. Roentgen Ray Soc., Assn. Univ. Radiologists, European Soc. Neuroradiology, Am. Soc. Pediatric Neuroradiology, World Fedn. Neuroradiol. Socs. (historian 1993-97, v.p. 1997—, pres.-elect 1998, pres. 2002—), Ill. Med. Soc., Ill. Radiol. Soc., Chgo. Med. Soc., Blockley Radiol. Soc., Soc. for Scholarly Publ., Japanese Soc. Neuroradiology (hon.), Coun. Biology Editors, Soc. Fifth Line, Indian Soc. Neuroradiology (hon. life), Sigma Xi, Phi Delta Epsilon. Clubs: Princeton Alumni of Chgo. (trustee 1982-84), Caxton. Jewish. Home: 175 E Delaware Pl Apt 7401 Chicago IL 60611-1731 Office: 1753 W Congress Pky Chicago IL 60612-3809 E-mail: m.huckman@comcast.net.

HUCKSHORN, KRISTIN, journalist; b. 1957; m. Tim Larimer; 1 child. Reporter San Jose Mercury News, 1994—98; chief polit. reporter Knight-Ridder Newspaper; dep. sports editor New York Times, 2004—. Co-founder Association for Women in Sports Writing. Grantee Am. Polit. Sci. Found. Mem.: Assoc. Press Sports Editor (APSE). Achievements include first female sports writer in US, first female corr. based in post-war Vietnam. Office: NY Times Sports Desk 229 W 43rd St New York NY 10036 Office Phone: 212-556-7371. Office Fax: 212-556-5848.

HUCLES, ANGELA KHALIA, professional soccer player; b. Va. Beach, July 5, 1978; BA in anthropology, U. Va., 2000. Soccer player, midfielder U.S. Women's Nat. Team, 2001; mem. Boston Breakers, WUSA, 2001—03, San Diego Spirit, 2003—. Columnist women's sports Boston Metro, 2002. Named First Team All-ACC, 1996, 1997, 1998, 1999, Mid Atlantic All-Star, 1996, 1997, 1998, 1999. Office: US Soccer Fedn 1801 S Prairie Ave Chicago IL 60616

HUDAK, ANDREW THOMAS, ecologist, forester, researcher; b. Grand Rapids, Minn., Oct. 29, 1966; s. Thomas Anthony and Adina Mae Hudak; m. Jeri Lynn Stewart, Aug. 19, 2006. AA, Itasca CC, Grand Rapids, 1987; BS, U. Minn., St. Paul, 1990; PhD, U. Colo., Boulder, 1999. Cert. environ. policy U. Colo., 1997, grad. tchr. U. Colo., 1999. Secondary sch. sci. tchr. US Peace Corps, Malawi, 1990—92; rsch. ecologist US Forest Svc. Pacific N.W. Rsch. Sta., Corvallis, Oreg., 1999—2001; rsch. forester US Forest Svc. Rocky Mountain Rsch. Sta., Moscow, Idaho, 2001—. Office Phone: 208-883-2327.

HUDAK, THOMAS F(RANCIS), finance company executive; b. Donora, Pa., Jan. 29, 1942; s. Thomas Joseph and Ann Marie (Petrus) Hudak; m. Dorothy Ann Palko, July 27, 1963; children: Diana Lynn, Debra Ann, Thomas David. BS, St. Vincent Coll., 1963; MBA, Ohio State U., 1968. CPA Ohio. Accountant Coopers & Lybrand, Columbus, Ohio, 1963-65; dept. mgr., data processing Western Electric Corp., Columbus, 1965-66; fin. controls mgr. Indsl. Nucleonics Co., Columbus, 1966-69; sr. v.p. fin., chief fin. officer G.C. Murphy Co., McKeesport, Pa., 1969-85, chmn. bd., 1981-85; pres. Hudak & Assocs. Treas. Mack Realty Co., McKeesport, Murphy Devel. Corp., Court House Village Co., Spotsylvania Realty Co.; bd. dirs., pres. Terry Farris STores, Inc.; mem. adv. bd. Liberty Mut. Ins. Co.; corp. comptr. PPG Industries, Inc., Pitts., 1986—89; chmn. bd. dirs., pres. Continental Plastics, Inc., 1989—95; bd. dirs. RXI Corp. Bd. dirs., pres. G. C. Murphy Co. Found. Mem.: AICPA, Peanut Butter and Nut Processors Assn., Assn. Dressings and Sauces, Assn. Spice Traders, Machinery and Allied Products Inst. (mem. fin. coun.), Nat. Assn. Corp. Dirs., Nat. Retail Mchts. Assn. (dir. fin. divsn. 1982—85), Risk and Ins. Mgmt. Soc., Fin. Execs. Inst. (bd. dirs. Pitts. chpt. 1982—85), U.S. C. of C. Personal E-mail: tfhudak@comcast.net.

HUDD, TIMOTHY R., pharmacist, educator; b. Melrose, Mass., Dec. 30, 1976; m. Timothy R. Hudd, June 2, 2007. BSc in Pharmacy, Mass. Coll. Pharmacy and Health Scis., Boston, 2000, PharmD, 2006. Lic. pharmacist Mass., Fla.; cert. infant and child CPR, standard first aid, adult CPR, ARC, 2004, disease mgr. NABP/NISPC DSM, 2003, pharmacist emergency contraceptives, Mass., 2006, pharmacy-based immunization delivery, 2006. Staff pharmacist Walgreens Pharmacy, Chelsea, Mass., 2000—03; coord. experiential edn. MCPHS, Boston, 2003—. Named Tchr. of Yr., 2005—06. Mem.: AACP, Boston Druggist Assn., Phi Lambda Sigma, Rho Chi. Home and Office: MCPHS Boston 179 Longwood Ave Boston MA 02115

HUDDLE, FRANKLIN PIERCE, JR., diplomat; b. Providence, May 9, 1943; s. Franklin Pierce and Clare (Scott) H.; m. Chanya Sawangrot, May 13, 1988; 1 child, Pavarage. BA, Brown U., 1965; postgrad., Columbia U., 1965-66; MA, Harvard U., 1970, PhD, 1978. Coord. Arabic affairs Peace Corps, Bisbee, 1968-69; instr. Harvard U., Cambridge, Mass., 1970-74; with Dept. of State, Washington and abroad, 1975—2003, charge d'affaires Rangoon, Burma, 1990-94; dir. Pacific Island Affairs, 1994-96; consul gen. Bombay, 1996-99, Toronto, 1999—2001; amb. to Tajikistan, 2001—03. Author: Libyan Arabic, 1966; author, editor: Let's Go Europe, 1972; co-author: Nationalities of the USSR, 1975; photography shows in Thailand, Nepal and Washington, 1980, 81, 84; patentee rocket coatings, 1960. Recipient Rivkin award, Presdl. Meritorious award, Sec. of State Lifetime Achievement award; Ford Found. grantee; Wayland scholar. Mem. Phi Beta Kappa. Avocations: piano, chess, ice skating. E-mail: fphuddle@hotmail.com.

HUDDLESTON, CONNIE MARIE, archaeologist, consultant; b. Owensboro, Ky., Aug. 12, 1952; d. Thomas Kenneth and Lena Carol Aldridge; m. Charles Vernon Huddleston, Feb. 4, 1973; children: Amy Cassandra, Charles Adrian. BA in Edn., U. Ky., Lexington, 1973; BS in History, Frostburg State Coll., Md., 1985; MA in Hist. Preservation, Goucher Coll., Towsen, Md., 2003. Registered profl. archaeologist Registry Profl. Archaeologists, 2003. Dir. archaeol. lab. Brockington and Assocs., Inc., Norcross, Ga., 1990—2004; prin., owner Interpreting Time's Past, LLC, Marietta, Ga., 2005—. Presenter in field. Author: (pictorial history) Marshall County. Mem. Hist. Preservation Commn., Roswell, Ga., Afghanistan, 2006—. Recipient John Williams Davis award, Frostburg Coll. Phi Alpha Theta, 1985. Mem.: Ga. Coun. Profl. Archaeologists (sec. 1999—2001, treas. 1999—2001), Soc. Ga. Archaeology, Roswell Hist. Soc. (co-pres. 2006), Soc. Hist. Archaeology. Home and Office: Interpreting Times Past LLC 3582 Clementine Ct Marietta GA 30066 Home Phone: 770-364-6512; Office Phone: 770-364-6512. Personal E-mail: itpllc@bellsouth.net.

HUDDLESTON, JOSEPH RUSSELL, retired judge, mediator, arbitrator; b. Glasgow, Ky., Feb. 5, 1937; s. Paul Russell and Laura Frances (Martin) H.; m. Heidi Wood, Sept. 12, 1959; children: Johanna, Lisa, Kristina. AB, Princeton U., NJ, 1959; JD, U. Va., Charlottesville, 1962, LLM, 1997. Bar: Ky. 1962, US Ct. Appeals (6th cir.) 1963, US Supreme Ct. 1970. Ptnr. Huddleston Bros., Bowling Green, Ky., 1962-87; judge Warren Cir. Ct. Divsn. I, Bowling Green, 1987-91, Ky. Ct. Appeals, Bowling Green, 1991—2003, sr. judge, 2003—07, mediator and arbitrator, 2007—. Mem. Adv. Com. for Criminal Law Revision, 1969-71; exec. com. Ky. Crime Commn., 1972-77. Named Ky. Outstanding Trial Judge, 1990. Fellow Am. Bar Found.; mem. ABA, Ky. Bar Assn. (ho. of dels. 1971-80), ATLA (state del. 1981-82), Ky. Acad. Trial Attys. (bd. govs. 1975-87, pres. 1978), Bowling Green Bar Assn. (pres. 1972), So. Ky. Estate Planning Coun. (pres. 1983), Rotary Internat. (Paul Harris fellow), Bowling Green-Warren County C. of C. (bd. dirs. 1987-91), Port Oliver Yacht Club (commodore), Hilton Head Plantation Yacht Club, Country Club of Hilton Head. Democrat. Episcopalian. Home (Winter): 644 Minnie Way Bowling Green KY 42101-9210 Home (Summer): 111 Governers Harbour Hilton Head Island SC 29926

HUDDLESTON, MARK WAYNE, academic administrator, political scientist, educator; b. Syracuse, NY, Dec. 31, 1950; s. Charles Proctor Huddleston and Joan Elaine Veldran; m. Melanie Kay Sharp, Nov. 19, 1983 (div. Jan. 1987); 1 child, Andrew Charles; m. Emma Elizabeth Bricker, Oct. 6, 1990; children: Katherine Anne, Giles Martin. BA in Polit. Sci., SUNY, Buffalo, 1972; MA in Polit. Sci., U. Wis., 1973, PhD in Polit. Sci., 1978. Lectr. U. Wis., Madison, 1976-77; asst. prof. SUNY, Buffalo, 1977-80, U. Del., Newark, 1980-83, assoc. prof., 1983-94, prof. polit. sci., 1994—2004, chmn. polit. sci., 1999-2000, assoc. provost, 2000—01, dean Coll. Arts and Scis., 2001—04; pres. Ohio Wesleyan U., 2004—07, U. NH, 2007—. Cons. Internat. City/County Mgmt. Assn., Bosnia-Herzegovina, 1996-2000, Kazakhstan, 1998-2000. Author: The Government's Managers, 1987, The Higher Civil Service in the U.S., 1996 (Choice award 1996), The Public Administration Workbook, 4th edit., 2000. Mem. ASPA, Am. Polit. Sci. Assn. Avocations: aviation, photography, hunting. Office: Office of Pres / U NH Thompson Hall 105 Main St Durham NH 03824 Office Phone: 740-368-3001. E-mail: mwh@owu.edu.*

HUDDLESTON, VICKI JEAN, ambassador; b. San Diego, Dec. 13, 1942; d. Howard Stevens and Duane Louise (Dickinson) Latham; m. Robert Webb Huddleston, Jan. 31, 1970; children: Robert Stevens, Alexandra Duane. BA, U. Colo., 1964; MA, Johns Hopkins U., Balt., 1975. Chief econ. sect. Am. Embassy, Freetown, Sierra Leone, 1977-80, Bamako, Mali, 1983-86; internat. economist Dept. State, Washington, 1980-82, econ. officer Office of Mexican Affairs, 1982-83, country officer for Bolivia, 1986-89, dep. dir. Office Cuban Affairs, 1989-91, dir. Office Cuban Affairs, 1991-93; charge d'affaires Am. Embassy, Port au Prince, Haiti, 1993, dep. chief of mission, 1993-95; amb. Republic of Madagascar, 1995-97; dep. asst. sec. for Africa Dept. State, Washington, 1997—99; prin. officer US Interest Sect., Havana, Cuba, 1999—2002; US amb. to Mali, 2002—05; Charge d'affaires Am. Embassy, Addis Ababa, Ethiopia, 2006. Dep. dir. Am. Inst. for Free Labor Devel., Rio de Janiero, Brazil, 1969-72, prog. officer, Lima, Peru, 1966-68. Vol. US Peace Corps, 1964-66. Am. Polit. Sci. Congl. fellow, 1988-89; fellow Kennedy Sch., Harvard U., 2005; recipient Disting. Honor award, Presdl. Meritorious Svc. award, several Superior Honor awards, Disting. Svc. award. Mem. Am. Fgn. Svc. Assn., Alumni Johns Hopkins. Presbyterian. Avocations: skiing, yoga.

HUDEL, CHESTELLA ALVIS, athletics educator; b. Temple, Okla., Jan. 13, 1931; d. James Chester and Jewel (McCain) Alvis; m. William August Hudel, June 14, 1952 (dec. June 1962); children: Mary Hudel Rinne, Nancy Hudel Parten, Joan Hudel Patrick. BS in Child Devel., Tex. Women's U., Denton, 1950. Tchr. Port Arthur (Tex.) Ind. Sch., 1950-53, Ridgewood Park Pre-Sch., Dallas, 1962-86; trainer Red Cross, Dallas, 1975—; adapted aquatics dir. YWCA, Dallas, 1975—. Trainer water safety instrs. Red Cross, Dallas, 1975-96; coach Spl. Olympics, 1993-98; educator Down's Syndrome Guild/Dallas Ind. Sch. Dist., 1994-96; counselor for breast cancer survivors Encore YWCA/Komen Found., Dallas, 1995-98' tchr. ESL, East Dallas Coop. Parish, 2006. Elder Northridge Presbyn. Ch., Dallas, 1979-2006; com. on adminstrn. YWCA, Dallas, 1980-86; active Northridge Learning Ctr. Bd., Northridge Presbyn. Ch., Dallas, 1987-2006, Bachman Recreation Ctr., Dallas, Park Cities YMCA, Dallas, 2003—, com. on integrating child devel. principles into swim program 2006-07; swim program leader Light House for the Blind, 1986-90, Tom Landry Ctr. Baylor Hosp., 2003—; resource person Parent to Parent, 1993. Named Profl. of Yr. in recognition of oustanding svcs., Red Cross, Dallas, 2004, Vol. of Yr., Helping Agys. Serving Richardson, Tex., 1990; recipient Golden Rule award, J.C. Penney, Dallas, 1983, Extra Step award, Red Cross, Dallas, 1989, Spirit of Red Cross award, 1990, Vol. Spirit award, GM, Dallas, 1992, George Washington medal of honor, Freedom Found. Valley Forge, Dallas, 1997. Mem. Assn. for Retarded Citizens (Profl. of Yr. 2005). Avocations: journal and scrapbook making, piano, bridge, bible study. Home: 8719 Coppertowne Ln Dallas TX 75243-8087 Office: 6000 Preston Rd Dallas TX 75205 Personal E-mail: aquaches@sbcglobal.net.

HUDES, NANA BRENDA, marketing professional; b. NYC, Nov. 25; d. Harry and Anita Lorraine (Seiken) Richter; m. Barton Hudes, Sept. 2, 1958 (div. Sept. 1972); children: Layne A., Michael F., Meredith A. Student, Skidmore Coll.; BA magna cum laude, Pace U., 1974; MS with honors, Coll. of New Rochelle, 1976. Dir. mail mktg. mgr. Pergamon Press, Elmsford, N.Y., 1979-80, spl. sales mgr., 1980-81; mktg. mgr. Knowledge Industry Publs., White Plains, N.Y., 1981-82, Grolier Electronic Pub., Danbury, Conn., 1982-84, dir. mktg., 1984-86; mktg. mgr. R.R. Bowker, New Providence, N.J., 1986-88, mktg. dir., 1988-91, sr. dir. mktg., 1991-99. Tchr. social studies Rye Neck (N.Y.) Mid. Sch., 1978-79; pres. NH Assocs., Mktg. Cons., 2000-01; dir. libr. mktg. Columbia U. Press, 2001—. Dist. leader, county committeeperson Dem. Party, Matawan Twp., N.J., 1964. Home: 233 E 69th St New York NY 10021-5414 Personal E-mail: nhudes@mindspring.com.

HUDGINS, DAVID DRAKE, lawyer; b. Franklin, Va., Jan. 21, 1955; s. Ira Durwood and Janet (Carter) H.; m. Ann Patrice Soch, Oct. 28, 1989; children: Drake W., Grace M., Emory P. BS, Hampden-Sydney Coll., 1977; JD, U. Richmond, 1980. Bar: Va. 1981, D.C. 1982, Md. 1992. Assoc. Cunningham & Assocs., Washington, 1981-85; ptnr. Cunningham & Hudgins, Alexandria, Va., 1985-90, Hudgins, Carter & Coleman, Alexandria, Va., 1990—99; with Hudgins Law Firm, Alexandria, 1999—. Mem. ABA, Va. Assn. Def. Attys., Assn. Def. Trial Attys., Eagle Internat. Assocs., Bar Assn. D.C., Alexandria Bar Assn., Va. Bar Assn., Fedn. of Def. and Corp. Counsel, Def. Rsch. Inst., Old Dominion Boat Club, Belle Haven Country Club, Tucker's Point Club, Commonwealth Club. Home: 909 Cameron St Alexandria VA 22314-2424 Office: Hudgins Law Firm 515 King St Ste 400 Alexandria VA 22314-3137 Office Phone: 703-739-3300. E-mail: dhudgins@hudginslawfirm.com.

HUDGINS, PAUL GRANVILLE, health facility administrator; b. Richmond, Va., July 31, 1957; s. Paul Everette and Nancy Rosamond Hudgins, Howard Porter Broaddus (Stepfather). BS in Math, James Madison U., Harrisonburg, Va., 1979. Cert. Healthstream CBT course authoring Synquest Health Edn. Sys., 2002; access mgr. Nat. Assn. Healthcare Access Mgrs., 1990, staff development educator Sentara Health Care, 1998, lic. phlebotomist Sentara Health Care, 2001; cert. choirmaster Am. Guild Organists, 1989. Quality mgmt. analyst Walter Reed Meml. Hosp., Gloucester, Va., 1980—85; mgr. outpatient svcs. Sentara Norfolk Gen. Hosp., Norfolk, Va., 1985—95, mgr. outpatient diagnostic ctr., 1992—95; mgr.

registration svcs. & scheduling Sentara Bayside Hosp., Va. Beach, 1995—97; mgr. bus. office Sentara Leigh Hosp., Norfolk, 1996—98; staff devel. educator Sentara Heatlh Care, Norfolk, 1998—2006; mgr. patient fin. svcs. & scheduling Sentara Health Care, 2006—. Moderator Sentara Edn. Coun., Hampton Roads, Va., 2001—03; cons. Norfolk State U., 2002—03; chmn. Sentara Computer Based Learning Com., Hampton Roads, 2002—04. Dir. music, organist, choirmaster Old Donation Episcopal Ch., Va. Beach, 1999—, altar guild, 2002—06; v.p. Harrington Ho. Condominium Assn., Norfolk, 1998—99. Recipient Sentara Key Contbr. award, 1997, Key Contbr. award, 2002. Mem.: Tidewater Assn. Healthcare Access Mgrs. (pres. 1989—90), Voluntary Hosp. Assn. Am. (corr.; contbr. 2002—03), Healthcare Fin. Mgmt. Assn. (assoc.; mem. 2005—06). R-Consevative. Episcopal. Avocations: travel, reading, history, genealogy. Home: 1024 Gates Ave Ste 3A Norfolk VA 23507 Office: Sentara Health Care 1441 Crossways Blvd Chesapeake VA 23320 Office Phone: 757-388-5795. Personal E-mail: pghudgins@aol.com. Business E-Mail: pghudgin@sentara.com.

HUDGINS, ROGER J., pediatric neurosurgeon; b. Albuquerque, Jan. 17, 1953; m. Patricia Hudgins; children: Tiffany, Rachel, Jack. BS in Chemisty magna cum laude, Auburn U., 1975; MD cum laude, U. Ala., 1979. Diplomate Am. Bd. Neurol. Surgery, 1985. Intern in gen. surgery U. Fla., Gainesville, 1979-80, resident in neurol. surgery, 1980-85; fellow in pediat. neurol. surgery U. Calif., San Francisco, 1985-86, clin. instr., 1985-86, asst. prof., 1986-87; attending neurosurgeon Children's Hosp., San Francisco, 1987-88, Scottish Rite Children's Med. Ctr. (now Children's Healthcare of Atlanta after merger of Egleston Children's Health Care Sys. and Scottish Rite Children's Med. Ctr.), Atlanta, 1988—, Northside Hosp., Atlanta, 1988—, Forsyth, Ga., St. Joseph's Hosp., Atlanta, 1989, Egleston Children's Hosp. (now Children's Healthcare of Atlanta), Atlanta, 1992—, Piedmont Hosp., Atlanta, 1992. Contbr. articles to profl. jours.; presenter in field. Mem. AMA, Am. Assn. Neurol. Surgery, Congress Neurol. Surgeons, Am. Soc. Pediat. Neurosurgery, Med. Assn. Ga., Calif. Med. Assn., Med. Assn. Atlanta. Lead neurosurgeon responsible for the life-saving medical treatment for spina bifida of Baby Noor, a 3-month-old Iraqi girl brought to the US in 2005. Office: Pediat Neurosurg Assoc PC 5455 Meridian Mark Rd #540 Atlanta GA 30342 also: Children's Healthcare of Atlanta at Egleston 1405 Clifton Rd Atlanta GA 30322-1062 Office Phone: 404-255-6509. Office Fax: 404-255-1686. Business E-Mail: cgreiner@pediatricneurosurgery.net.

HUDGINS, WILLIE L., JR., lawyer; b. LaCrosse, Va., Mar. 5, 1943; BB, Howard U., 1965; JD, Howard U. Law Sch., 1968. Bar: Va. 1968, DC 1971, US Supreme Ct. 1973. Dep. chief Antitrust Divsn., US Dept. Justice; atty. Collier, Shannon, Scott, PLLC, Washington. Named one of Am. Top Black Atty., Black Enterprise, 2003. Mem.: ABA, Section Antitrust Law, Va. State Bar, Washington DC Bar, US Supreme Ct. Office: Collier Shannon Scott PLLC 3050 K St NW Ste 400 Washington DC 20007 Office Phone: 202-342-8586. Business E-Mail: whudgins@colliershannon.com.

HUDIAK, DAVID MICHAEL, academic administrator, lawyer; b. Darby, Pa., June 27, 1953; s. Michael Paul and Sophie Marie (Glowaski) Hudiak; m. Veronica Ann Barbone, Aug. 28, 1982; children: David Michael, Christopher Andrew, Jonathan Joseph. BA, Haverford Coll., 1975; JD, U. Pa., 1978. Bar: Pa. 1979, U.S. Dist. Ct. (ea. dist.) Pa. 1979, NJ 1981, U.S. Dist. Ct. NJ 1981. Assoc. Jerome H. Ellis, Phila., 1978-79, Berson, Fineman & Bernstein, Phila., 1979-80; pvt. practice Aldan, Pa., 1980-81; dir. tng. paralegal program PJA Sch., Upper Darby, Pa., 1982—2005, acting dir., 1983-89, dir., 1989—2006, v.p., 1989—2006, campus pres., 2006—, also bd. dirs.; v.p., sec.-treas., bd. dirs. 7900 West Chester Pike Corp., 1994—. Mem. staff Nat. Ctr. Ednl. Testing, Phila., 1982—87; instr. Villanova U., Pa., 1985. Mem. Havertown Choristers; active U. Pa. Light Opera Co., 1977—84; mem. 10th Synod Archdiocese of Phila., 2002; active mem., parish coun., lector, cantor St. Eugene Parish. Mem.: ABA, Pa. Bar Assn., Founders Club Haverford Coll. Office: PJA Sch 7900 W Chester Pike Upper Darby PA 19082-1917 Office Phone: 610-789-6700. Personal E-mail: dhudiak@lawyer.com.

HUDIK, MARTIN FRANCIS, hospital administrator, educator, consultant, writer; b. Chgo., Mar. 27, 1949; s. Joseph and Rose H.; m. Eileen Hudik; 1 child, Theresa Margaret. AAS in Engring., Morton Coll., 1969; BS in Mech. and Aerospace Engring., Ill. Inst. Tech., 1971; BPA, Jackson State U., 1974; MBA, Loyola U., 1975; postgrad., U. Sarasota, 1975-76. Cert. health care safety mgr., hazard control mgr., hazardous materials mgr., OSHA hazardous materials response instr., hazardous materials incident comdr., disaster coord., police instr., Ill., security cert. instr., Ill. With Ill. Masonic Med. Ctr., Chgo., 1969-94, dir. risk mgmt., 1974-79, asst. adminstr., 1979-94; facilities engring. mgr. Bethany/Adv. Hosp., 1997-98; health care cons., 1995—2005; bus. mgr. St. Bernadine Parish, 2001—. Capt. tng. divsn. Cicero (Ill.) Police Dept., tng. and internal affairs divsn., aux. divsn., 1971-99, U.S. Dept. Commerce, 2000, ind. cons., 2000; instr. Nat. Safety Coun. Safety Tng. Inst., Chgo., 1977-85; cons. Coun. Tech. users Consumer Products, Underwriters Labs., Chgo., 1977-96; instr., lt. U.S. Def. Civil Preparedness Agy. Staff Coll., Battle Creek, Mich., 1977-85; liaison officer to Cook County Emergency Svcs.; asst. dir. Emergency Svcs. and disaster Agy. Town of Cicero, 1988-97; founding pres. Cook County Emergency Mgmt. Coun., 1991-92; exec. bd., pres. U.S. Postal Svc. Postal Customer Adv. Coun., Cicero, 1996-99, sec. exec. bd., 2003—; mem. exec. bd. Chicagoland Postal Adv. Coun., 1994-2006, 07—; exec. bd. advisor Cicero PCAC, 1998—. Co-chmn. Archdiocese of Chicago Deanery IV-C, 1999—2003; active Cath. Edn. Com., 2000—03; pastoral coun. Archdiocese Chgo., 2000—03; pres. sch. bd. Mary Queen of Heaven Sch., Cicero, 1977—79, 1984—86, Mary Queen of Heaven Ch. Coun., 1979—81, 1983—86, St. Leonard Parish Coun., 1998—2001, St. Bernardine Parish Coun., 2001—05, I.M.M.C. Employee Club, 1983—86. Recipient Presdl. Sports award, Amateur Athletic Union, 1978, 1980—81, Spl. Svc. award Underwriters Lab., 1992, Presdl. Sports award, Amateur Athletic Union, 2000, Meritorious Svc. award, Town of Cicero, 1990, medal of Merit, 1996, Emergency Svcs. Achievement award, 1997, Police Achievement award, 1998, Spl. Svc. award, Cook County Sheriffs Dept., 1993, Excellence in Svc. award, U.S. Postal Svc., 1997, Outstanding Effort award, 1998, Outstanding Svcs. award, Cicero Postal Coun., 1998, Svc. Recognition award, 1999, Outstanding Performance award, 2001, Volunteerism award, U.S. Postal Svc., 2002, Svc. Recognition award, Archdiocese of Chgo., 2003; scholar state scholar, Ill., 1969—71. Mem. Am. Coll. Healthcare Execs., Am. Soc. Hosp. Risk Mgmt., Nat. Fire Protection Assn., Am. Soc. SafetyEngrs. (profl.), Am. Soc. Law and Medicine, Ill. Hosp. Security and Safety Assn. (co-founder 1976, founding pres. 1976-77, hon. dir. 1977-82), Cath. Alumni Club Chgo. (bd. dirs. 1983-84, 86), Mensa, Masons (3d degree, Berwyn, Ill. chpt.), KC (mem. 4th degree cardinal coun., Svc. award 2002), Pi Tau Sigma, Tau Beta Pi, Alpha Sigma Nu. Republican. Roman Catholic. Home: 7246 W Harrison St Forest Park IL 60130-2345 Office: 6845 Riverside Dr Berwyn IL 60402-2231

HUDIS, CLIFFORD ALAN, internist, oncologist; b. Phila., 1959; m. Jane Hertzmark, Nov. 2003. BA, Lehigh U.; MD, Med. Coll. Pa., 1983. Diplomate Am. Bd. Internal Medicine, Am. Bd. Oncology. Intern, internal medicine Med. Coll. Pa., Phila., 1983-84, resident, internal medicine, 1983—87, chief med. resident; fellow, med. oncology and hematology Meml. Sloan-Kettering Cancer Ctr., NYC, 1988-91, chief, breast cancer medicine svc., assoc. attending physician; clin. asst. Meml. Hosp., NYC, 1991-94, asst. attending physician, 1994—; instr. Weill Med. Coll. Cornell U., NYC, 1991-94, asst. prof., assoc. prof. medicine. Co-leader, breast disease mgmt. team Meml. Sloan-Kettering Cancer Ctr.; co-chair Breast Com. Cancer and Leukemia Group B; mem. Breast Com. Radiation Therapy Oncology Group, Nat. Comprehensive Cancer Network. Contbr. numerous articles to profl. publs., chpts. to books; editl. bd. mem. Journal of Clinical Oncology, Clinical Cancer Research, Cancer Investigation. Mem. ACP, Am. Soc. Clin. Oncology (past chair internet svcs. com.), Am. Assn. Cancer Rsch. Office: Meml Sloan Kettering 1275 York Ave New York NY 10021-6094 Office Phone: 212-639-5449.*

HUDKINS, JOHN W., lawyer; b. Inglewood, Calif., Jan. 12, 1946; s. Ralph Emerson and Genevieve Delores H.; m. Diana Byler, Feb. 16, 1969. BA, Calif. State U., Hayward, 1968; MBA, U. Nev., Las Vegas, 1971; JD, U. of Pacific, 1976; LLM, George Washington U., 1983. Bar: Iowa 1976, Calif. 1977, U.S. Ct. Mil. Appeals 1976, Fla. 1995. Commd. 2d lt. USAF, 1968, advanced through grades to lt. col., 1983, ret., 1988; sr. counsel Aerojet-Gen. Corp., Sacramento, 1988-94; dir. bus. mgmt. Olin Ordnance, Downey, Calif., 1994-95, sr. counsel St. Petersburg, Fla., 1995-96, v.p., chief counsel, 1996-97; v.p., dep. gen. counsel Primex Tech., Inc., St. Petersburg, Fla., 1997-2001; dep. gen. counsel Gen. Dynamics Ordnance and Tactical Sys., 2001; legal counsel to bd. mgrs. Am. Ordinance, 2002—03. Bd. dirs. Vandenberg Fed. Credit Union, Lompoc, Calif., 1983-85, Prince William (Va.) County Soccer Assn., 1985-88. Mem. ABA (pub. contract law sect.), Nat. Security Indsl. Assn. (chair legal com.). Home: 7649 E Torrey Point Cir Mesa AZ 85207-1188 Home Phone: 480-985-3828.

HUDLIN, REGINALD ALAN, broadcast executive, film director, writer; b. Centerville, Ill., Dec. 15, 1961; s. Warrington W. and Helen (Cason) Hudlin; m. Chrisette Suter, Nov. 30, 2002. BA cum laude, Harvard U., 1983. Artist-in-residence Ill. State Arts Council, 1984-85; copywriter Olgivy and Mather Advt. Agy., NYC, 1986; pres. Hudlin Entertainment, NYC, 1986—; pres. entertainment, chief programming exec. Black Entertainment TV, 2005—. Vis. lectr. film U. Wis., Milw., 1985—86. Writer, dir. (short films) House Party, 1983, writer, dir., actor (films), 1990, writer House Party 2, 1991, House Party 3, 1994, exec. prodr., writer, Bébé's Kids, 1992; actor: (films) She's Gotta Have it, 1992, Posse, 1993, (voice) Joe's Apartment, 1996; dir., actor (films) Boomerang, 1992; dir.: (TV films) Cosmic Slop, 1994 (2 Cable Ace awards); (films) The Great White Hype, 1996, Serving Sara, 2002; (TV series) City of Angels, When Worlds Colitis (episode), 2000, The Bernie Mac Show, 2001, Everybody Hates Chris (pilot episode), 2005; dir., actor The Ladies Man, 2000; prodr.: (films) Ride, 1998; exec. prodr.: (TV series) The Boondocks, 2005; writer (comic books) The Black Panther, 2004, Spider-Man, 2005; co-author: Birth of a Nation, 2005. Named to Black Filmmakers Hall of Fame, 1990; recipient Best Film award, Black Cinema Soc., 1984, Lillian award, Delta Sigma Theta Sorority, 1990, Filmmakers Trophy, US Film Festival, 1990, Key to City of Newark, 1990, Nancy Susan Reynolds Award, Ctr. for Population Options, Clarence Muse Award, 1991, Starlight Award, Black Am. Cinema Soc., 1993; fellow Nat. Endowment for the Arts, 1985; grantee Prodn. Yr., Black Filmmaker Found., 1983, 1985, 1986. Mem.: Black Filmmakers Found. (co-founder 1978). Avocation: comic book collecting.

HUDNALL, JARRETT, JR., management consultant, educator, marketing professional; b. Rhome, Tex., Oct. 6, 1931; s. Jarrett and Katherine (Wilson) H.; m. Sarah Ruth Warren, Nov. 24, 1955; children: Jarrett Joseph, William Warren, Katherine Lee, Thomas Wilson. Student, Arlington State Coll., Tex., 1948-50; BBA, U. Tex., Austin, 1953, MBA, 1956; PhD, U. Ala., 1966. Lectr. U. Tex., 1955-56; asst. prof. Arlington State Coll., 1956-58; instr. U. Ala., 1958-61; asst. prof. La. Tech. U., 1961-62, assoc. prof. mktg., 1962-67, prof., head dept. bus., 1967-77; exec. Superior Supply Co., Inc., 1978-83, P&A div. Ciba-Geigy, 1983-84; v.p. Rohcar, Inc., 1984-90; prof. mgmt. and mktg. Stephen F. Austin State U., Nacogdoches, Tex., 1985-92; dean coll. bus. and commerce U. West Ala., Livingston, 1992-94; prof. mktg. Miss. U. for Women, Columbus, 1994—2002; emeritus; emeritus designee Assn. Collegiate Bus. Schs. & Programs, 2002—. Vice pres. Ctrl. Asian Cons., LLC; bd. dirs. SBI; cons. firms in chem. fertilizer, petroleum, farm equipment mfg., bus.; cons. agrl. and econ. devel. products W. Republic of Uzbekistan, 1995; vis. prof. mktg. Huron U., London, 2000, 02. Author: (with A.L. Seeyle) Compensation of Retail Department Store and Specialty Store Salesman in Major Texas Cities, 1957, Attitudes of Gulf Service Station Dealers Toward Minor Tuneup and Repair Work, 1963, An Economic Analysis of Income and Employment in a Four-State Deep South Region, 1950-60, 1966. Lt. AUS, 1953-55. Gulf Oil Corp. fellow, 1963. Mem. VFW, Am. Mktg. Assn., So. Mktg. Assn., S.W. Fedn. Allied Disciplines, Am. Collegiate Retailing Assn., So. and Southwestern Bus. Dean's Assn., Small Bus. Inst. Dirs.' Assn., Allied Acads., Kiwanis Internat., Sigma Iota Epsilon, Beta Gamma Sigma, Alpha Kappa Psi, Kappa Delta Pi, Delta Mu Delta. Democrat. Baptist. Home: 1003 Lakeview Dr Ruston LA 71270-5233 Personal E-mail: jhud@cox.net.

HUDNER, PHILIP, lawyer, rancher; b. San Jose, Calif., Feb. 24, 1931; s. Paul Joseph and Mary E. (Dooling) H.; m. Carla Raven, Aug. 6, 1966; children: Paul Theodor, Mary Carla. BA with great distinction, Stanford U., 1952, LL.B., 1955. Bar: Calif. 1955. Lawyer Pillsbury, Madison & Sutro, San Francisco, 1958—, ptnr., 1970-99, Botto Law Group, San Francisco, 1999—; rancher San Benito County, Calif., 1970—. Asst. editor: Stanford Law Rev., 1954-55; author articles on estate and trust law. Pres. Soc. Calif. Pioneers, 1976-78, Louise M. Davies Found., 2002—, Charles D. and Frances K. Field Fund, 2003—; sec.-treas. Drum Found., 2003—. Served with U.S. Army, 1956-58. Fellow Am. Bar Found.; mem. Internat. Acad. Estate and Trust Law (steering com. 1974-75, exec. coun. 1980-85), San Benito County Saddle Horse Assn., Order of Malta, Phi Beta Kappa, Pacific Union Club, Lagunitas Country Club, Frontier Boys, Bohemian Club, Rancheros Visitadores. Democrat. Roman Catholic. Office: Botto Law Group 180 Montgomery St Fl 16 San Francisco CA 94104-3104

HUDNUT, ROBERT KILBORNE, clergyman, writer; b. Cin., Jan. 7, 1934; s. William Herbert and Elizabeth (Kilborne) H.; m. Mary Lou Lundell; children by previous marriage: Heidi, Robert Kilborne, Heather, Matthew. BA with highest honors, Princeton, 1956; M.Div., Union Theol. Sem., NYC, 1959. Ordained to ministry Presbyn. Ch., 1959; asst. minister Westminster Presbyn. Ch., Albany, NY, 1959-62; minister St. Luke Presbyn. Ch., Wayzata, Minn., 1962-73, Winnetka (Ill.) Presbyn. Ch., 1975-94. Exec. dir. Minn. Pub. Interest Research Group, 1973-75; Co-chmn. Minn. Joint Religious Legis. Coalition, 1970-75. Author: Surprised by God, 1967, A Sensitive Man and the Christ, 1971, A Thinking Man and the Christ, 1971, The Sleeping Giant: Arousing Church Power in America, 1971, An Active Man and the Christ, 1972, Arousing the Sleeping Giant: How to Organize Your Church for Action, 1973, Church Growth Is Not the Point, 1975, The Bootstrap Fallacy: What The Self-Help Books Don't Tell You, 1978, This People-This Parish, 1986, Meeting God in the Darkness, 1989, Emerson's Aesthetic, 1996, Call Waiting, 1999. Pres. Greater Met. Fedn. Twin Cities, 1970—72; chmn. Citizens Adv. Com. on Interstate 394, 1971—75; mem. planning commn. City of Cottage Grove, Minn., 2001—04; chmn. Dem. Party 33d Senatorial Dist. Minn., 1970—72, Minnetonka Dem. Party, 1970—72; fusion candidate for mayor City of Albany, 1961; chmn. Philbrook for Gov. Campaign, 2004—05; nat. chmn. Presbyns. Ch. Renewal, 1971; bd. dir. Minn. Coun. Chs., 1964—70; trustee Princeton U., 1972—76, Asheville (N.C.) Sch., 1979—2003. Rockefeller fellow, 1956; named Outstanding Young Man Minnetonka, 1967; recipient Distinguished Service award Minnetonka Tchrs. Assn., 1969 Mem.: Phi Beta Kappa.

HUDNUT, WILLIAM HERBERT, III, political scientist; b. Cin., Oct. 17, 1932; s. William Herbert Jr. and Elizabeth (Kilborne) H.; m. Beverly Guidara; children: Michael Conger, Laura Anne (dec.), Timothy Norton, William Herbert IV, Theodore Beecher, George Mattheson (dec.), Christopher Shew. BA magna cum laude, Princeton U., 1954; MDiv summa cum laude, Union Theol. Sem., NYC, 1957; DD (hon.), Hanover Coll., 1967, Wabash Coll., 1969; LLD (hon.), Butler U., 1980, Anderson Coll., 1982, Franklin Coll., 1983, Martin U., 1985, Millikin U., 1987, Ind. U., 1994, Elmhurst Coll., 1996, Youngstown State U., 2002; LittD (hon.), U. Indpls., 1981; DPS (hon.), Blackburn Coll., 1987, Christian Theol. Seminary, 2004. Ordained to ministry Presbyn. Ch., 1957. Asst. min. Westminster Ch., Buffalo, 1957-60; pastor 1st Presbyn. Ch., Annapolis, Md., 1960-63; dir. Westminster Found., Annapolis, 1960-63; sr. min. 2d Presbyn. Ch., Indpls., 1963-72; mem. 93d Congress from Ind., 1973-74; dir. dept. cmty. affairs Ind. Ctrl. U., Indpls., 1975; mayor City of Indpls., 1976-91; fellow Inst. Politics Harvard U., 1992; sr. fellow Hudson Inst., Indpls., 1992-94; pres. Civic Fedn., Chgo., 1994-96; sr. resident fellow The Urban Land Inst., Washington, 1996—. Mem. Presdl. Adv. Com. on Federalism, 1981-84. Author: Minister/Mayor, 1987, The Hudnut Years in Indianapolis, 1976-1991, 1995, Cities on the Rebound, 1998, Half Way to Everywhere, 2003; editor: Union Sem. Quar. Rev., 1956-57; contbr. sermons, articles to profl. publs. Mem. Bd. Pub. Safety, Indpls., 1970-71, Rep. Nat. Com., 1987; pres. Anne Arundel County Mental Health Assn., 1961-63; pres., bd. dirs. Marion County Mental Health Assn., 1966-68, Westminster Found., Purdue U., 1969-73; bd. dirs. Cmty. Svc. Coun. Met. Indpls., 1964-68, Family Svc. Assn., 1966-72, Flanner House, 1968-72; pres. trustees Darrow Sch., New Lebanon, N.Y., 1968-75; Task Force on Fed. Deficit, 1981; mem. Adv. Commn. on Intergovtl. Rels., 1984-90; bd. dirs. Indpls. Ctr. for Adv. Rsch., 1976-91, Humane Soc., 1983-91; trustee Roosevelt Ctr. Am. Policy Studies, Washington, 1984-87; Pleasant Run Children's Home Found. bd., 1992-94, Children's Home & Aid Soc. Ill., 1994-96; co-vice chmn. Alliance for Redesigning Govt., 1992-2000; mem. Police Found. Bd., 1997—; mem. Nat. Assn. Securities Dealers Regulatory Bd., 1996-98, Nat. Adjudicatory Coun., 1998; mem. accreditation bd. Am. Planning Assn., 1998-2001; mem. Town Coun., Chevy Chase, Md., 2000-06, mayor, 2004-06; mem. Millenial Housing Com., 2000-01; bd. trustees Union Theol. Sem., 2006—. Recipient William Booth award Salvation Army, 1984, Russell G. Lloyd Disting. Svc. award Ind. Assn. Cities and Towns, 1985, Rosa Parks award Am. Assn. for Affirmative Action, 1992, Woodrow Wilson award Princeton U., 1986, Disting. Urban Mayor award Nat. Urban Coalition, 1987; named All-Pro City Mgmt. Team, City and State mag., 1986, 89, 92; fellow Nat. Acad. Pub. Adminstrn., 1994—. Mem. Columbia Club Indpls. (bd. dir. 1994-96), Cosmos Club, Chevy Chase Club, Kiwanis, Masons (33 deg.), Phi Beta Kappa. Office: The Urban Land Inst 1025 Thomas Jefferson St NW Washington DC 20007-5201 Home Phone: 301-718-0808; Office Phone: 202-624-7000. Business E-Mail: bhudnut@uli.org. *Life is relationships, and whatever we can do to enlighten and strengthen each other, in the family circle, among our friends, in business, in society at large, will help. This requires ardor and self-surrender, faith, hope and humor.*

HUDSON, ANN ELIZABETH, music educator; d. Carl Louis Maxey and Gussie Lee Mobley; m. Dewitt H. Hudson Jr. (div.); children: Dewitt(dec.), Tony Dean, Eric Donald. BS, Fla. A&M U., Tallahassee, 1955; MA in Music Edn. magna cum laude, Tex. Woman's U., Denton, 1988. Music specialist post schs., Ft. Dix, NJ, 1957—58; choral dir. pub. schs., Ocala, Fla., 1968—69, music tchr., 1974—75, 1989—, Ft. Hood, Tex., 1969—72, post schs., Frankfurt, Germany, 1972—74, Killeen, Tex., 1975—76, pub. schs., Tallahassee, 1977—78, St. Petersburg, Fla., 1980—81; chmn. Elem. Music Tchrs., Killeen, 1980—82. Pvt. music tchr. Min. of music St. Augustine Episcopal Ch., St. Petersburg, 1989—92; dir. of drama Covenant Missionary Bapt. Ch., Ocala, 2005—. Grantee Stonecrest, Summerfield, Fla., 2004, Stonecrest Ladies Club, 2005, Stonecrest Women's Aux., 2006. Mem.: Marion County Music Assn. (pres. 1995—97, presenter 1998—2000), Music Educators Nat. Conf. Avocations: acting, reading, composing. Home: 45 Pecan Pass Ocala FL 34472 E-mail: sonataina1@cs.com.

HUDSON, BARBARA, writer, actor; b. St. James, Minn., Feb. 2, 1921; d. Lloyd Edwin and Lois (Hardin) H.; m. Jesse Wilbert Powers, Oct. 27, 1946 (div. Apr. 1970); children: Jean Lois, Cathy Colleen; m. Lawrence Kneeland Dudley, Dec. 5, 1971 (div. Apr. 1979). BA, U. Iowa, 1942; MA, U. So. Calif., 1952. Tchr. drama, speech Southgate (Calif.) H.S., 1944-45; youth dir. Hollywood (Calif.) Presbyn. Ch., 1945-47; tech. writer secret publications Litton Industries, Canoga Park, Calif., 1959—61; assoc. prof. Calif. Luth. U., Thousand Oaks, 1961-75; missionary Calvary Cmty. Ch., Westlake Village, Calif., 1980—. Author: Bob Pierce, Going With God, 1956, The Henrietta Mears Story, 1958, Where Is God, 1970, The Greatest Play Ever Written, 1970, God's Power in Your Life, 1971, Bridge of Nothing Less, 1975, (videos) Women of the Bible, 1990; writer, prodr., dir. (pageant) Here I Stand, 1967, Bridge of Nothing Less, 1975, Forward in Faith, 1975, God of the Mountain, 1952-57; author numerous poems; contbr. articles to profl. jours.; internat. touring in one woman show Women of Bible, Can., Eng., Holland, Israel, USA, Hilton Head Island, Nantucket, Hawaii, 1982—. 2d lt. in 1st officer's class USMCWR, 1943—45, U.S. Recipient winner, Guideposts Story Contest, 1977, 1st pl. poetry, State of Calif., 1985, award, Ina Coolbrith Poetry Assn., 1986. Mem. DAR, Gamma Phi Beta, Zeta Phi Eta, Pi Kappa Delta Nat. Speech Farat.(Diamond award 1939, Nat. Women's Oratory award, 1940). Republican. Office: PO Box 3722 Thousand Oaks CA 91359 Home: 1851 Village Ct Thousand Oaks CA 91362 Office Phone: 805-495-4932. Personal E-mail: barbarahudsonwob@aol.com.

HUDSON, C. B., JR., insurance company executive; b. 1947; BS, Okla. Univ., 1968. With Travelers Life Ins., Hartford, Conn., 1968-74; exec. v.p. Globe Life & Accident Ins. Co., Okla. City, 1974-82; pres., CEO United Am. Ins. Co., 1982—; CEO, chmn. Torchmark Corp. Office: Torchmark Corp America 2001 Third Ave S Birmingham AL 35233

HUDSON, CAROLYN BRAUER, application developer, educator; b. Durham, NC, Dec. 17, 1945; d. Alfred Theodor and Hildegard Franziska (Wolf) Brauer; children: Paul Benjamin, Joel Stephen. BS in Math., U. NC, 1967; MA in Forestry, Duke U., 1969; MS in Geology, U. SC, 1979, PhD in Geology, 1995. Assoc. dir. office rsch. and evaluation, asst. prof. NC Ctrl. U., Durham, 1970—72; rsch. assoc. Nat. Lab. for Higher Edn., Durham, 1971—72; tchg. assoc. U. SC, Columbia, 1973—74, tchg. asst., 1990—92, tchg. assoc., 1993—, applications analyst, 1999—; vis. scientist Geol. Survey of Can., Ottawa, Ontario, 1979—82; statistician SC State Govt., Columbia, 1997—98. Mem. SC Gov's Nuc. Adv. Coun., Columbia, 2001—; tech. coord. profl. women on campus U. S.C., Columbia, 2000—05. Contbr. articles to profl. jours., photos to books and juried exhibits. Vol. area pub. sch., 1978—93; leader Boy Scouts of Am./Scouts Can., 1979—95; vol. Congaree Nat. Pk., Hopkins, SC, 1999—; mem. social action com. Tree of Life Congregation, 2007—. Named Scouting Family of Yr., Boy Scouts of Am., 1986, 1986; recipient Dist. Merit award, 1988, Silver Beaver award, 1991, Butterfield Svc. award, 1991, Shofar award, 1993, Profl. Devel. award, Profl. Women on Campus, 2000. Mem.: U. N.C. Alumni Assn. (life), Friends of Congaree Swamp (edn. com. 1996—2005, bd. dir. 2005—), Women of Reform Judaism (v.p. 1975—76), Audubon, Sierra Club (nuc. affairs subcom. 2001—07, computer chair 2003—05), Hadassah (life; bd. dir. 1983—84, mem. Jewish cmty. rels. coun. 2006—), LWV. Democrat. Jewish. Avocations: hiking, music, travel, reading, photography. Home: 115 Arcadia Springs Cir Columbia SC 29206 Office: Univ SC Univ Tech Svcs 1244 Blossom St Columbia SC 29208 Office Phone: 803-777-2358. Business E-Mail: carolyn.hudson@sc.edu.

HUDSON, CELESTE NUTTING, education educator, consultant, reading clinic administrator; b. Nashville, Sept. 18, 1927; d. John Winthrop Chandler and Hilda Bass (Alexander) Nutting; m. Frank Alden Hudson III, Dec. 30, 1948 (dec.); m. Robert Daniel Quartell, June 3, 1989; children: Frank Alden Hudson IV (dec.), Jo Ann Hudson Algermissen, Celeste Jane

Hudson Norman, Jack Winthrop N. Hudson. BS, Western Oreg. State U., Monmouth, 1952; MA, So. Ill. U., Edwardsville, 1963; PhD, So. Ill. U., Carbondale, 1973. Cert. tchr., Tenn., Oreg., Mo. Iowa. Tchr. pub. schs., Crossville, Tenn., 1949—51, Salem, Oreg., 1952—53, West Walnut Manor, Mo., 1953—54, Normandy Sch. Dist., St. Louis County, Mo., 1954—66; reading coord. Sikeston Pub. Schs., Mo., 1966—69, Charleston, Mo., 1969—72; traveling cons. Ednl. Devel. Labs., Huntington, NY, 1970—71; mem. clin. staff So. Ill. U. Reading Ctr., 1972; asst. prof. edn. St. Ambrose Coll., 1972—75, U. Tenn., Chattanooga, 1975—76; dir. children's reading clinic St. Ambrose U. (formerly St. Ambrose Coll.), 1973—94; project dir. Learning Skills Ctr. St. Ambrose U., 1976—80, from asst. prof. edn. to prof., 1976—94, prof. emeritus, 1995—. Dir. elem. edn. St. Ambrose U., 1972-94, chmn. dept. edn., 1980-84, divsn. chmn., 1984-87, faculty vice-chair, 1989-90, faculty chair, 1990-91; staff cons. Chandler Acad., 2002; cons, 2004- Author: Handbook for Remedial Reading, 1967, Cognitive Listening and the Reading of Second Grade Children, 1973, The Effect of Visual Fatigue on Reading, 1990, Longitudinal Study of Children in Clinical Reading, 1994. Active Kimberly Village Bd., Davenport, Iowa, 1976-93, Trinity Hosp. Aux., 2001-04; chmn. worship com., Asbury Meth. Ch., 1985-90, choir, 1978-98, 2005—, bell choir, 1995-97; co-chmn. Sarah Cir., 1996-9; choir St. Johns Meth. Ch., Georgetown, Tex. Mem.: AARP, DAR (Hist. Soc.), AAUW (Lit. club), AAUP, Phi Delta Kappa, Ret. Tchrs. Assn. Garfield Sch., Normandy Ret. Tchrs. Assn., Davenport Area Ret. Tchrs. Assn., Internat. Reading Assn. (Scott County coun. 1976—2003), Iowa Assn. Colls. Tchr. Edn. (exec. bd. 1989—92), Red Hat Soc., New Eng. Women (pres.-elect 1994—95, pres. 1996—2003, yearbook chmn. 2004—05), United Daus. of the Confederacy (3rd v.p. 1966—70), Tripoly Club, United Daughters of Confederacy Real Granddaughters Club, Original Music Students Club (corr. sec. 1995—96), Ret. Tchrs. Club, Quad City Women's Investment Club (treas. 2001—05), Bettendorf Lionels (treas. 1998—2002), Kappa Delta Pi (sponsor 1974—96), Phi Delta Kappa (life; internat. emeritus staus), Alpha Delta Kappa (life; past pres.). Address: St Ambrose U Box E 140 518 W Locust St Davenport IA 52803-2820 Personal E-mail: drhcnhq@aol.com.

HUDSON, CHARLES DAUGHERTY, insurance executive; b. La Grange, Ga., Mar. 17, 1927; s. J.D. and Janie (Hill) H.; m. Ida Cason Callaway, May 1, 1955; children: Jane Alice Hudson Craig, Ellen Pinson Hudson Harris, Charles Daugherty, Ida Hudson Russell. Student, Auburn U., 1945-48, LHD (hon.), 1992; LLD, La Grange Coll.; LHD (hon.), Mercer U., 1987. Ptnr. Hudson Hardware Co., La Grange, 1950-57, Hammond-Hudson Ins. Agy., La Grange, 1957-58, owner, 1958-78; pres. Hammond, Hudson & Holder INc., 1978-94, chmn. bd., 1994—. Bd. dirs., mem. exec. com. Citizens & So. Nat. Bank, La Grange, 1964-90; bd. dirs. Citizens & So. Ga. Corp., Citizens & So. Nat. Bank, Atlanta, C&S Investment Advisors, Inc., Atlanta, C&S Ga. Corp.; acting pres. La Grange Coll., 1979-80; v.p., bd. dirs. La Grange Industries, 1956—, Hudson Maddox Enterprises, 1965-95; ptnr. PCH Properties, 1981—; chmn. bd. dirs. First Annuity Corp., La Grange; bd. dirs., chmn. trust com. Nations-Bank of Ga.; chmn. Ga. Bd. Corrections, 2006-; pres. Auburn U. Found., 2006-. Recipient Pres.'s award Colonial Life Ins. Co., 1966, 69-70, 75-80, Disting. Alumni award Ga. Mil. Acad.-Woodward Acad., 1971, Disting. Svc. award Ga. Hosp. Assn., 1980, Respect Law award Optimists Assn., 1977, Van Landingham Commitment to Edn. award, 1996, Pub. Svc. award Ga. Assn. AIA, 1977, Leading Producer award Aetna Life and Casualty, 1979; Paul Harris fellow, 1984. Mem. Am. Legion, Ga. Assn. Ind. Ins. Agts., Ga. Sch. Bd. Assn. (area dir.), SAR, Amicale de Group LaFayette (hon.). Chattahoochee Valley Art Assn., La Grange C. of C. (bd. dirs.), Newcomen Soc. N.Am., Ga. Hosp. Assn. (trustee 1980—), U. Ga. Gridiron Secret Soc., Highland Country Club (chmn. bd. 1999—), Lafayette Club, Commerce Club Atlanta, Aetna Life and Casualty Presidents, Masons, Shriners, Elks, Rotary (pres. 1964-65), Sigma Alpha Epsilon, Beta Gamma Sigma. Home: 407 Country Club Rd Lagrange GA 30240-2031 Office: Hammond Hudson & Holder Inc 200 Broad St Lagrange GA 30240-2722

HUDSON, CHRISTOPHER JOHN, publisher; b. Watford, Eng., June 8, 1948; s. Joseph Edward and Gladys Jenny Patricia (Madgwick) Hudson; m. Lois Jeanne Lyons, June 16, 1979; children: Thomas, Ellen, Ronald, Timothy, Jonas. BA with honors, Cambridge U., Eng., 1969, MA with honors, 1972. Promotion mgr. Prentice-Hall Internat., England, 1969-70, area mgr. Eng., France, 1970-71, mktg. mgr. Englewood Cliffs, NJ, 1971-74, dir. mktg., 1974-76, asst. v.p., 1976; group internat. dir. I.T.T. Pub., NYC, 1976-77; pres. Focal Press, Inc., NYC, 1977-82; v.p., pub. Aperture Found. Inc., NYC, 1983-86; head publs. J. Paul Getty Trust, LA, 1986—2005; pub. Mus. Modern Art, NYC, 2005—. Author: Guide to International Book Fairs, 1976; pub. Aperture, 1983-86, J. Paul Getty Mus. Jour., 1986-2005. Mem. adv. coun. Nat. Heritage Village, Kioni, Greece; mem. trade with eastern Europe com. Assn. Am. Pubs., N.Y., 1976-79, internat. fairs com., 1986-88. Mem.: Internat. Assn. Scholarly Pubs. (sec.-gen. 1994—97, chmn. internat. contracts com.), Internat. Pubs. Assn., U.S. Mus. Publ. Group (chmn. 1989—), Internat. Assn. Mus. Publs. (Frankfurt, Fed. Republic Germany chmn. 1992—95), Hellenic Soc. (London), Travelers' Century Club (bd. dirs., v.p.), Oxford & Cambridge Club (London). Avocation: travel. Office: Mus Modern Art 11 W 53rd St New York NY 10019-5497 Office Phone: 212-708-9445. Business E-Mail: christopher_hudson@moma.org.

HUDSON, DARRIL, political scientist, educator; b. Trousdale, Okla., Dec. 18, 1931; s. Frank Wilks Hudson and Emma Lee (Jackson) Van Meter. BA, U. Calif., Berkeley, 1954; MSc in Internat. Rels., London Sch. Econs & Polit. Sci, 1960, PhD, 1965. Lectr. U. Md. Overseas Program, 1959-67; assoc. prof. Md. State Coll., Princess Anne, Md., 1967-68; prof. Calif. State U., Hayward, 1968-93, prof. emeritus, 1993—; vis. prof. Am. U., Paris, 1992-93. Resident dir. German program Calif. State U., Heidelberg, Fed. Republic Germany, 1990-91; Fulbright prof. U. Heidelberg, 1981-82. Author: A Visitor's Guide to American Home Cooking, 1989, The World Council of Churches in International Affairs, 1978, The Ecumenical Movement in World Affairs, 1968. 1st lt. Intelligence Svc., U.S. Army, 1955-58. Rsch. fellow Alexander von Humboldt Found., Bonn, Heidelberg, Fed. Republic Germany, 1966-67, 75, 89; recipient H.C. Richards prize Gray's Inn, London, 1965. Mem. Am. Friends of Paris Opera, Conservatory of Music San Francisco, San Francisco Opera Assn. Democrat. Avocations: cooking, writing, travel. Home: 443 Fair Oaks St San Francisco CA 94110-3618 E-mail: darrilh@yahoo.com.

HUDSON, DAWN EMILY, food service company executive; b. Worcester, Mass., Nov. 27, 1957; d. Kenneth Dunlap and Nancy (Selin) Hudson; m. Bruce Kershaw Beach, Aug. 31, 1980. BA, Dartmouth Coll., 1979. Asst. acct. exec., acct. exec. Compton Advt., NYC, 1979-82; product mgr. Clairol, Divsn. Bristol Myers, NYC, 1982-83; acct. supr., mgmt. supr. ptnr. Tatham-Laird Kudner Inc., Chgo., 1983-86; mgmt. supr. grp. acct. dir. sr. v.p., mng. ptnr., exec. v.p. DDB Needham, Worldwide, Chgo., 1986-94; exec. v.p., dir. client svcs. DDB Needham Worldwide NY, NYC, 1994; mng. dir. D'Arcy Masius Benton & Bowles, NY; exec. v.p. sales and mktg. Frito-Lay (subs. of Pepsi), 1996—98; sr. v.p. strategy and mktg. Pepsi-Cola N.Am., 1998—2002, pres., 2002—. Mem. editorial bd. Dartmouth Coll. Alumni Mag., 1993—. Mem. Dartmouth Coll. Alumni Coun., 1993—, career counsel grads., 1979-88. Named one of 100 Most Powerful Women, Forbes mag., 2005, 2006, 50 Most Powerful Women in Bus., Fortune mag., 2006, Next 20 Female CEOs, Pink mag. & Forté Found., 2006. Republican. Methodist. Avocations: avid tennis player, golf, skiing. Office: Pepsi Co North America 700 Anderson Hill Rd Purchase NY 10577*

HUDSON, DENNIS LEE, lawyer, retired arbitrator, federal official; b. St. Louis, Jan. 5, 1936; s. Lewis Jefferson and Helen Mabel (Buchanan) H.; children: Karen Marie, Karla Sue, Mary Ashley. BA, U. Ill., 1958; JD, John Marshall Law Sch., 1972. Bar: Ill. 1972, U.S. Dist. Ct. (so. and no. dists.) Ill. 1972. Ins. IRS, Chgo., 1962-72; spl. agt. GSA, Chgo., 1972-78, spl. agt.-in-charge, 1978-83, regional insp. gen., 1983-87; supervisory spl. agt. Dept. Justice-GSA Task Force, Washington, 1978; arbitrator Circuit Ct. Cook County, Ill., 1987-93; prof. criminal justice Coll. of DuPage, Glen Ellyn, Ill., 1996—. Adv. bd. Suburban Law Enforcement Acad., Glen Ellyn, Ill., 1999—; adv. bd. campus police Coll. DuPage, Glen Ellyn, 1999—; deacon Grace Luth. Ch., La Grange, Ill., 1977—81; lay eucharistic min. All Sts. Episcopal Ch., Western Springs, Ill., 1999—; bd. govs. Theatre Western Springs, Ill., 1978—81, Ill., 1991—92, Ill., 2005—, acting laureate Ill., 2004—, chair bd. govs. Ill., 2005—; chmn. bd. dirs. Pendulum Theatre Co., Chgo., 2001—. With US Army, 1959—61. John N. Jewett scholar, 1972, Am. Jurisprudence scholar, 1972. Mem. ABA, Ill. Bar Assn. Office: Coll Dupage Health Social and Behavioral Scis Progra 425 Fawell Blvd Glen Ellyn IL 60137

HUDSON, DONALD J., stock exchange executive; b. Vancouver, BC, Can., Sept. 26, 1930; BA in Econs. and Math., U. B.C., 1952; LLD (hon.), Simon Fraser U., 1993. With Shell Oil Co. of Can. Ltd., 1952—53; dir. sales devel. Can. Pacific Airlines, Vancouver, 1953—64; sr. v.p. Pacific div. T. Eaton Co., Ltd., Vancouver, 1964—81; pres. Vancouver Stock Exch., 1981—95. Past chmn. bd. govs. Simon Fraser U., 1988-90; past chmn. bd. trustees St. Paul's Hosp., 1983-85. Mem.: Vancouver Club, Vancouver Lawn Tennis Club.

HUDSON, EDWARD VOYLE, retired apparel executive; b. Seymour, Mo., Apr. 3, 1915; s. Marion A. and Alma (Von Gonten) H.; m. Margaret Carolyn Greely, Dec. 24, 1939; children: Edward G., Carolyn K. Student, Bellingham Normal Coll., 1933-36, U. Wash., 1938. Asst. to mgr. Natural Hard Metal Co., Bellingham, 1935—37; ptnr. Met. Laundry Co., Tacoma, 1938—39; propr., mgr. Peerless Laundry & Linen Supply Co., Tacoma, 1939—2005; ret., 2005. Propr. Ind. Laundry & Everett Linen Supply Co., 1946-74, 99 Cleaners and Launderers Co., Tacoma, 1957-59; chmn. Tacoma Pub. Utilities, 1959-60; trustee United Mut. Savs. Bank; bd. dirs. Tacoma Better Bus. Bur., 1977—; mem. regional bd., SBA, 1965. Pres. Wash. Conf. on Unemployment Compensation, 1975-76; pres. Tacoma Boys' Club, 1970; v.p. Puget Sound USO, 1972-91; elder Emmanuel Presbyn. Ch., 1974—; past campaign mgr., pres. Tacoma-Pierce County United Good Neighbors. Recipient Disting. Citizen's cert. USAF Mil. Airlift Com., 1977; U.S. Dept. Def. medal for outstanding pub. svc., 1978. Mem. Tacoma Sales and Mktg. Execs. (pres. 1957-58), Pacific NW Laundry, Dry Clearning and Linen Supply Assn. (pres. 1959, treas. 1965-75), Internat. Fabricare Inst. (dir. dist. 7, treas. 1979, pres. 1982), Am. Security Coun. Bd., Tacoma C. of C. (pres. 1965), Air Force Assn. (pres. Tacoma chpt. 1976-77, v.p. Wash. state 1983-84, pres. 1985-86), Navy League, Puget Sound Indsl. Devel. Coun. (chmn. 1967), Tacoma-Ft. Lewis Olympia Army Assn. (past pres.), Def. Orientation Civilian Assn., Elks Club (vice chmn. bd. trustees 1984, chmn. 1985-86), Shriners (potentate 1979), Masons, Scottish Rite, Jesters Club, Rotary (pres. Tacoma chpt. 1967-68), Tacoma Knife and Fork Club (pres. 1964). Republican. Home: 6250 N Park Ave Apt 106 Tacoma WA 98407-2228

HUDSON, FRANKLIN, real estate developer, lawyer; b. NYC; s. Alec N. Hudson. BBA., Sam Houston State U., 1971; JD, St. Mary's U., 1974. Bar: Tex. 1975, US Dist. Ct. Tex., US Supreme Ct., Wash., DC, US Ct. Appeals, Atlanta, New Orleans and San Francisco, Mem. Nat. Assn. Home Builders, Nat. Multi Family Council, State Bar Assn. Tex. Office: c/o PO Box 460029 Houston TX 77056-8029

HUDSON, FRANKLIN DONALD, manufacturing executive, consultant; b. Asheville, NC, July 21, 1933; s. Halbert Austin and Lillian Naomi (Cook) H.; m. Rosemary Wheatley, Dec. 1, 1956; children: Lawrence Jamison, Lauren Hudson Raabe. B.E.E., Yale U., 1955; MBA, NYU, 1962; postgrad., Pace U., 1972-75. Sales rep. RCA, NYC, 1959-62; Latin Am. gen. mgr. Fed. Pacific Electric Co., PR, 1962-68; dir. mktg. GTE Sylvania, 1968-71; dir. Home Equipment div. Singer Co., NYC, 1971-75; v.p. internat. Corometrics Med. Systems, Inc., Wallingford, Conn., 1975-78; v.p. planning and devel. Norlin Corp., White Plains, NY, 1978-81; founder, exec. v.p. Integrated Genetics, Inc., 1981-85; founder, bd. dirs. Organogenesis Inc., 1985-89; founder, pres. TSI Corp., 1987-90; founder, CEO, Protarga, Inc., 1990-93; biotech. cons., 1995—; pres., dir. VIMRX Pharms., Inc., Stamford, Conn., 1994-95. Chmn. Bio-Brite, Inc., 1990—; adj. prof. NYU, Boston U., Yale U. Bd. overseers Boston Symphony Orch., 1993—2002; asst. dir. Campaign for Yale, 1978; trustee Quinsigamond Coll., 1989—92. Capt. USAF, 1955—58. Mem.: Russell Trust Assn., Hawk's Nest Golf Club, Kittansett Club, Sippican Tennis Club, Yale Club of Treasure Coast (pres.), Tau Beta Pi. Episcopalian.

HUDSON, FREDERICK BERNARD, management consultant; b. Chgo., Oct. 29, 1947; s. Joseph Thomas and Nellie (Parham) H.; m. Yvonne Marjorie Hudson, July 9, 1994. BA, Wayne State U., 1969; postgrad., Yale U., 1969—70; MA, New Sch. Social Rsch., 1975. Registered city planner, Am. Inst. City Planners, 1979. Adminstr. cmty. rels. for N.J. Odyssey Ho., NYC, 1971-73; spl. program asst. Nat. Urban League, NYC, 1973-75; rsch. assoc. Afram Assocs., NYC, 1975; program cons. City Univ. Rsch. Found., NYC, 1975-76; project dir. Elon Michels and Assocs., Detroit, 1977—78; staff analyst Detroit City Coun., 1978-79; vis. asst. prof., coord. So. Ill. U., Edwardsville, 1979-80; dir. pub. rels. Frederick Douglass Creative Arts Ctr., NYC, 1981-82; ednl. officer Am. Bus. Inst., NYC, 1986-89; pres. Centaur Consultants, NYC, 1983—, Spectrum Imports, 1996—. Faculty Coll. New Rochelle, So. Ill. U., Ednl. Found. Dist. Coun. 37 (local of Am. Fedn. State, County and Mcpl. Employees); Am. Bus. Inst. Mgmt. and Comm.; cons. Coro Found., Asia Pacific Found., NuArtist Prodns., Art Mattan Prod., Milw. Ednl. Found., New Future Found., MicroBanking Network, AT&T, Reality Ho., Nat. Drug Prevention Week, Mothers of Harlem Bus. Incubator, Fed. Emergency Mgmt. Adminstrn., Women and Housing and Econ. Devel. Corp., Yale Coun. Cmty. Affairs, NJ Dept. Correction, candidates for state and nat. polit. offices; expert witness, presenter in field Prodr. (TV program) Take It to the Hill, 1995-99; guest and commentator numerous TV and radio programs, including HBO and ABC News; contbr. opinion columns to mags., poems to lit. jours. and anthology; co-author (jazz oratorio) Let Us Now Praise Righteous Men, 1969; author: What's In a Number? An Evaluation of a Title I Program, 1975, A Business Plan for a Multi-National Entertainment E-Commerce Business, 2000; screenwriter (TV drama) Things We Take, 1992; prodr. (TV series) The Undercover Man, 1993-95 Organizer Nat. Action Network, 1995—, Oct. 22 Movement, 2000—, Internat. Action Ctr., 2000—; hon. chmn. small bus. adv. coun. Nat. Rep. Congl. Com. Recipient Mayor's commendation, City of Newark, 1974, Emerging New Writer award, PEN, 1984, Outstanding Achievement in Poetry Silver award cup Internat. Soc. Poets, 2002, 03; name inscribed on Wall of Tolerance, Montgomery, Ala., 2002. Mem. Am. Mgmt. Assn., Film Video Arts Assn., Mensa, Women's Econ. and Cmty. Devel. Corp. Office: Centaur Consultants 1510 E 172 St Ste 4 Bronx NY 10472 Office Phone: 718-378-7109. Personal E-mail: fhdsn@aol.com.

HUDSON, HAROLD JORDON, JR., retired insurance executive; b. Kansas City, Mo., Mar. 10, 1924; s. Harold Jordan and Fannie (Jenkins) H.; m. Patricia Louise Orr, Oct. 1, 1949. BS, U. Mo., 1945, LL.B., 1948; grad., Advanced Mgmt. Program, Harvard U., 1968. Bar: Mo. 1948. Practiced in, Kansas City, until 1952; atty. Comml. Union Co., Kansas City, 1952-53, Cleve., 1953-56; with Gen. Reins. Corp., NYC, 1956-83, asst. sec., 1958-61, sec., 1961-62, v.p., 1963-68, sr. v.p., 1968-70, pres., 1970-71, 1971-72, chief exec. officer, 1971-83, chmn., 1973-83, also dir. Chmn. Reins. Assn. Am., 1975-76. Mem. Phi Delta Phi, Kappa Alpha, Brook Club, Indian Harbor Yacht Club, Greenwich Country Club, Card Sound Golf Club, Carriage Club, River Club. Office: PO Box 10350 Stamford CT 06904-2350 Personal E-mail: hhudii@aol.com.

HUDSON, JANICE WHITAKER, secondary school educator; b. Brady, Tex., Mar. 2, 1946; d. James Arthur and Virginia Olena (Thompson) Whitaker; m. David Earl Hudson; children: Tim, Chris, Amy. BA, Tex. A&I U., Kingsville, 1968, MA, 1982. Cert. edn., ESL tchr. English tchr. Presbyn. Pan Am. Sch., Kingsville, Tex., 1974—92, El Campo Mid. Sch., Tex., 1992—96, Calhoun H.S., Port Lavaca, Tex., 1996—. Part-time ESL adult edn. educator, Victoria, Tex., 1998—2004. Baptist. Avocations: outdoor activities, piano, cooking, swimming.

HUDSON, JENNIFER, singer, actress; b. Chgo., Sept. 12, 1981; Featured vocalist: (cruise ship) Disney Wonder Cruise, 2002; appeared as finalist: American Idol, 2004; actor: (films) Dreamgirls, 2006 (Best Supporting Actress, NY Film Critics Circle awards, 2006, runner-up, Best Supporting Actress award, LA Film Critics Assn., 2006, Pauline Kael Breakout award, Fla. Film Critics Cir., 2006, Breakthrough Performance award-Female, Nat. Bd. Rev., 2006, Breakthrough Performance award, Palm Springs Internat. Film Soc., Palm Springs Internat. Film Festival, 2007, Best Supporting Actress, African-American Film Critics Assn., 2006, 2006 Best Supporting Actress, Critics Choice award, Broadcast Film Critics Assn., 2007, Best Performance by an Actress in a Supporting Role in a Motion Picture, Golden Globe award, Hollywood Fgn. Press Assn., 2007, Outstanding Performance by a Female Actor in a Supporting Role, SAG, 2007, Actress in a Supporting Role, British Acad. Film and TV Arts, 2007, Acad. award best actress in a supporting role, 2007, Choice Movie Actress: Drama, Teen Choice Awards, 2007). Named Female Star of Tomorow, ShoWest, 2006, Best Actress, Black Entertainment TV (BET) Awards, 2007, Best New Artist, 2007; named one of 10 Actors to Watch, Variety, 2006, Breakthrough Actors, Movieline, 2006. Office: The DuVernay Agency c/o Ellene Miles 6605 Hollywood Blvd Ste 210 Los Angeles CA 90028*

HUDSON, JERRY E., foundation administrator; b. Chattanooga, Mar. 3, 1938; s. Clarence E. and Laura (Campbell) H.; m. Myra Ann Jared, June 11, 1957; children: Judith, Laura, Janet, Angela. BA, David Lipscomb Coll., 1959; MA, Tulane U., 1961, PhD, 1965; LL.D. (hon.), Pepperdine U., 1983; D of Comm. (hon.), Tokyo Internat. U., 1997; LHD (hon.), U. Portland, 1997, Willamette U., 1997. Systems engr. IBM, Atlanta, 1961; prof. Coll. Arts and Scis., Pepperdine U., 1962-75; provost, dean Coll. Arts and Scis., Malibu Campus, Pepperdine U., 1971-75; pres. Hamline U., St. Paul, 1975-80, Willamette U., Salem, Oreg., 1980-97; exec. v.p. Collins Found., Portland, Oreg., 1997—. Dir. Portland Gen. Co., E.I.I.A. Bd. dirs. PGE Found. Mem. Nat. Assn. Ind. Colls. (bd. dirs.), Phi Alpha Theta. Office: Collins Found 1618 SW 1st Ave Portland OR 97201-5752 Home: 2020 SW Market Street Dr Apt 402 Portland OR 97201-7719 Home Phone: 503-203-1132; Office Phone: 503-227-7171. E-mail: jhudson@collinsfoundation.org.

HUDSON, JOHN IRVIN, retired career officer; b. Louisville, Oct. 12, 1932; s. Irvin Hudson and Elizabeth (Reid) Hudson Hornbeck; m. Zetta Ann Yates, June 27, 1954; children: Reid Irvin, Lori Ann, John Yates, Clark Ray BS in Bus. Mgmt., Murray State U., 1971. Commd. 2nd lt. USMC, 1954, advanced through grades to lt. gen., 1987; comdg. officer Marine Fighter Attack Squadron 122, 1965—66; commdg. officer Marine Fighter/Attack Squadron 122, 1966—67; comdg. officer Marine Fighter Attack Squadron 115, Vietnam, 1968, Marine Corps Air Sta., Yuma, Ariz., 1977-80; asst. wing comdr. 2nd Marine Air Wing, Cherry Point, NC, 1980-81; comdg. gen. Landing Force Tng. Command/At.,4th Marine Amphibious Brigade, Norfolk, Va., 1981-83, 3rd Marine Aircraft Wing, El Toro, Calif., 1985-87, First Marine Amphibious Force, Campen, Calif., 1986-87; dep. chief staff for manpower Hdqrs. USMC, Washington, 1987-89; dir. U.S. Marine Corps Edn. Ctr., Quantico, Va., 1983-85; ret. active duty Hdqrs. USMC, Washington, 1989. Apptd. to Ariz. State Transp. Bd., 1994-2000, chmn., 1999; apptd. commr. Ariz. Power Authority, 2000—, chmn., 2006-07; apptd. bd. dirs. Greater Yuma Port Authority, chmn., 2000-02; operating bd. dirs. Yuma Regional Med. Ctr., 2001—. Decorated DFC, DSM, Bronze Star, Air medals, Silver Hawk; flew 308 combat missions in Vietnam in F-4 Phantom; inductee Early and Pioneer Naval Aviators' Assn., 1998. Mem. VFW (life), Golden Eagles, Marine Corps Aviation Assn. (life), Marine Corps Assn. (life), Marine Corps Hist. Soc. (life), Order of Daedalians (life). Avocations: sports, sailing, hunting, fishing. Home: 12439 E Del Rico Yuma AZ 85367-7366 Personal E-mail: johnihudson1@aol.com.

HUDSON, JOHN LESTER, chemical engineering professor; b. Chgo., 1937; s. John Jones and Linda Madeline (Panozzo) H.; m. Janette Glenore Caton, June 29, 1963; children: Ann, Barbara, Sarah. BS, U. Ill., 1959; MS in Engring., Princeton U., 1960; PhD, Northwestern U., 1962. Registered profl. engr., Ill. Asst. prof. chm. engring. U. Ill.-Urbana, 1963-69, assoc. prof., 1969-75; prof., chmn. dept. chem. engring. U. Va., Charlottesville, 1975-85, mem. Ctr Advanced Studies, 1985-86, prof., 1986-88, Wills Johnson prof., 1988—. Mgr. Ill. Div. Air Pollution Control, Springfield, 1974-75; cons. to various industires and govt. agys., 1966— Contbr. articles to profl. jours. Recipient sr. Humboldt prize, 1989; NSF fellow, 1962, Fulbright fellow, 1961-63, 82-83. Mem. AIChE (Wilhelm award 1991), Am. Chem. Soc. Home: 1920 Thomson Rd Charlottesville VA 22903-2419 Office: U Va Dept Chem Engring 102 Engineers Wy Box 400741 Charlottesville VA 22904-4741 Home Phone: 434-977-1085. Business E-Mail: hudson@virginia.edu.

HUDSON, KATE, actress; b. LA, Apr. 19, 1979; d. Bill Hudson and Goldie Hawn; m. Chris Robinson, Dec. 31, 2000 (separated Aug. 2006); 1 child, Ryder. Co-head (with Kurt Russell, Goldie Hawn, Oliver Hudson) Cosmic Entertainment, 2003. Actor: (films) Desert Blue, 1998, Ricochet River, 1998, 200 Cigarettes, 1999, About Adam, 2000, Gossip, 2000, Almost Famous, 2000 (Golden Globe award for Best Supporting Actress, 2001), Dr. T and the Women, 2000, The Cutting Room, 2001, The Four Feathers, 2002, How to Lose a Guy in 10 Days, 2003, Alex and Emma, 2003, Le Divorce, 2003, Raising Helen, 2004, The Skeleton Key, 2005, You, Me and Dupree, 2006; (TV series) Party of Five, 1996, EZ Streets, 1997; exec. prodr.: (TV films) 14 Hours, 2005. Named one of Most Powerful People in Hollywood, Premiere mag., 2003.

HUDSON, KATHERINE MARY, manufacturing executive; b. Rochester, NY, Jan. 19, 1947; d. Edward Klock and Helen Mary (Rubacha) Nellis; m. Robert Orneal Hudson, Sept. 13, 1980; 1 child, Robert Klock. Student, Oberlin coll., 1964-66; BS in Mgmt., Ind. U., 1968; postgrad., Cornell U., 1968-69. Various positions in fin., investor rels., communications, gen. mgr. instant photography Eastman Kodak Co., Rochester, 1970-87, chief info. officer, 1988-91, v.p., gen. mgr. printing and pub. imaging, 1991-93; pres., CEO Brady Corp., Milw., 1994—2003, chmn. bd., 2003. Bd. dirs. CNH Global N.V., Charming Shoppes, Inc. Trustee Alverno Coll., 1994—; bd. dirs. Med. Coll. Wis., 1995—. Recipient Chief of the Yr. award Info. Week Mag., 1990, Athena award Rochester C. of C., 1992, WESG Breaking Glass Ceiling award, 1993, Sacajewea award, 1995; Lehman fellow N.Y. State, 1968; named Wis. Bus. Leader of Yr., 1995. Republican. Avocations: golf, fishing, creative writing. E-mail: knh53092@yahoo.com.

HUDSON, KELLY MARIE, music educator; b. Wilmington, Del., Dec. 9, 1977; d. Victor Charles and Judith (Grezlikowski) Hudson. MusB, Shenandoah U., Winchester, Va., 2002. Music tchr., volleyball coach, colorguard instr. Caravel Acad., Bear, Del., 2000—. Recipient Tribute in Edn., Del.

Ho. of Reps., 2006. Mem.: Del. Music Educators Assn., Am. Choral Dirs.' Assn., Music Educators Nat. Conf. Avocations: volleyball, singing, scrapbooks, photography, reading. Home: 121 King William ST Newark DE 19711 Office: Caravel Acad 2801 Del Laws Rd Bear DE 19711 E-mail: suvb31@hotmail.com.

HUDSON, LEIGH CARLETON, lawyer; b. Ft. Scott, Kans., Apr. 18, 1948; s. Howard Carleton and Dorothy Delano H.; m. Marsha Ann Corn, July 30, 1971; children: Tyler William, Ryan Carleton. BS in Bus., Emporia State U., 1971; JD, Washburn U., 1975. Bar: Kans. 1975, U.S. Dist. Ct. Kans. 1975, Kansas Supreme Ct. 1975, U.S. Ct. Appeals (10th cir.) 1997. Mem. White & Hudson, Pittsburg, Kans., 1975-82, Hudson & Mullies, Fort Scott, 1982—. Contbr. articles to profl. jours. Fellow Am. Coll. Trial Lawyers (mem, state com. 1993); mem. Kans. Bar Assn. (bd. govs. 1981-87), Kans. Def. Assn. (pres. 1993), Am Bd. Trial Advs., Rotary. Home: 601 Fairway Dr Fort Scott KS 66701-3130 Office: Hudson & Mullies LLC 102 S Main St Fort Scott KS 66701-1415 Home Phone: 620-223-5645; Office Phone: 620-223-2900. Business E-Mail: leigh@hudsonmullies.com.

HUDSON, MANLEY O., JR., lawyer; b. Boston, June 25, 1932; s. Manley O. and Janet (Aldrich) H.; m. Olivia d'Ormesson, July 1, 1971 (dec. May 2000); children: Nicholas Aldrich, Antonia Maria Conchita. AB, Harvard U., 1953, LL.B., 1956. Bar: N.Y. 1964. Law clk. Justice Stanley Reed, U.S. Supreme Ct., Washington, 1956-57; assoc. Cleary, Gottlieb, Steen & Hamilton, 1958-68, ptnr. NYC, London, Paris, 1968—2001. Contbr. articles to profl. jours. Mem. Coun. Fgn. Rels., Century Assn. Office: Cleary Gottlieb Steen & Hamilton City Place House 55 Basinghall St London EC2V 5EH England Office Phone: 011 44 207 614 2200. Business E-Mail: mhudson@cgsh.com.

HUDSON, MCKINLEY, retired military officer, retired zoological park administrator; b. Cin., May 13, 1941; BS, Ctrl. State U., Wilberforce, Ohio, 1963; MS, So. Ill. U., 1974; MA, Naval War Coll., Newport, RI, 1986. Commd. 2d lt. U.S. Army, 1963, advanced through grades to col., 1985, retired, 1993, commdr. 548th composite support battalion, 1983-85, commdr. 80th area support group Chevres, Belgium, 1986-88, chief of staff mil. traffic mgmt. command Oakland, Calif., 1988-93; dep. dir. Nat. Zoological Park Smithsonian Instn., Washington, 1994—2002. Decorated Legion of Merit, Bronze Star with Oak Leaf cluster. Mem. Assn. U.S. Army, Assn. Am. Zoos and Aquariums, U.S. Army Transp. Corps. Regiment (Disting. Mem. Regiment 1993), Nat. Defense Transp. Assn. (Nat. award for disting. svc. 1992), Kappa Alpha Psi. Home: 13 Cabin Creek Ct Burtonsville MD 20866

HUDSON, MICHAEL CRAIG, political science professor; b. New Haven, June 2, 1938; s. Robert Bowman and Joan (Loram) H.; m. Vera George Wahbe, June 16, 1963; children: Leila Olga, Aida Joan. BA with honors, Swarthmore Coll., 1959; MA, Yale U., 1960, PhD, 1964; Cert. in Arabic, Princeton U., 1961. Tchr. history Am. Cmty. Sch., Beirut, 1962—63; instr. Swarthmore Coll., Pa., 1963—64; asst. prof. Bklyn. Coll., CUNY, 1964—70; assoc. prof. Johns Hopkins U., Sch. Advanced Internat. Studies, Washington, 1970—75; assoc. prof. to prof. Georgetown U., Washington, 1975—; dir. Georgetown U. Ctr. for Contemporary Arab Studies, Washington, 1976—89, 1999—2000, 2003—; Seif Ghobash prof. of Arab studies Sch. Fgn. Svc. Georgetown U., Washington, 1980—. Bd. dirs. Nat. Coun. U.S./Arab Rels., Washington; cons., lectr. U.S. State Dept.; commentator on Mid. Ea. affairs to U.S. and internat. news media; lectr. Mid. East, Europe, Japan, China, Australia univs. Mem. editl. bd. Internat. Jour. Mid. East Studies, 1980-86, Cambridge U. Press Mid. East Studies, 1989-98; author: The Precarious Republic (Lebanon), 1968, Arab Politics: The Search for Legitimacy, 1977; co-author: World Handbook of Political and Social Indicators, 1972; editor: The Palestinians: New Directions, 1990, Middle East Dilemma: The Politics and Economics of Arab Integration, 1999; contbr. numerous articles to jours. in field. Bd. dirs Ctr. for Mid. East Studies, Macquarie U., Sydney, Australia; bd. trustees Rene Moawad Found., Lebanon. Robert R. McCormick fellow Yale U., 1959-63, fellow Ford Found., 1970-71, Guggenheim fellow, 1975-76, Fulbright fellow, 1994; grantee Am. Philos. Soc., 1965, 68. Fellow Mid. East Studies Assn. N.Am. (pres. 1987); mem. Mid. East Inst., Am. Polit. Sci. Assn., Internat. Studies Assn., Coun. Fgn. Rels., Am. Inst. Yemeni Studies. Avocations: drawing, painting, book collecting, swimming, running. Office: Georgetown U Ctr for Contemporary Arab Studies Sch Fgn Svc 241 Intercultural Ctr Washington DC 20057-1020 Business E-Mail: hudsonm@georgetown.edu.

HUDSON, MICHEL COLETTE, management consultant; b. Houston; d. Arthur James and Dorothy Ann (Newton) Rutrough; m. Scott V. Hudson; 1 child, David. BA, U. St. Thomas, 1982. Cert. fund raising exec. CFRE Profl. Certification Bd., 2001. Dir. devel. info. sys. U. St. Thomas, Houston, 1983—85; coord. alumni/devel. rsch. and records U. Mo., Columbia, 1987—90, mgr. alumni/devel. rsch. and records, 1990—95; dir. devel. svcs. Seton Healthcare Network, Austin, Tex., 1995—97, v.p. devel. svcs., 1997—2001; campaign mgr. centennial campaigns The Seton Fund, Austin, 2001—01; owner Gnu Gap Consulting, Round Rock, Tex., 2001—, 501 Consulting, Round Rock, 2006—. Online instr. FUNDCLASS, 1998, 2003; instr. fund raising mgmt. cert. program U. Tex., Austin, 2000—; instr. Austin C.C. Ctr. for Cmty.-Based and Nonprofit Orgns., 2003; bd. dirs. Freelance Austin; presenter in field. Contbr. articles to profl. jours.; editor (and co-author): Prospect Research Fundamentals, 1997. Membership svcs. coord., hospitality chair Columbia Art League, 1993—95; v.p. Columbia Choral Ensemble, 1994—95; bd. dirs. Freelance Austin, 2004—. Mem.: DAR, Freelance Austin (bd. dirs. 2004—), Writers League Tex. (fundraising com. 1998—99), Am. Prospect Rsch. Assn.-Mo. Chpt. (pres., v.p., newsletter editor/pub. 1992—95), Internat. Assn. Theater and Stage Employees (trustee 1994—95), Assn. Profl. Rschrs. for Advancement (pres., conf. chair, membership svcs. dir. 1994—2001, nominations com. 2002, disting. svc. award com. mem. 2004—05, bd. dirs. S.W. chpt. 2005—, mem. 20th anniversary com. 2007, Disting. Svc. award 2003), Cir. of Friends (sec./publ. design 1997—2003). Office: 501 Consulting 1805 Gnu Gap Round Rock TX 78664 Personal E-mail: gnugap@yahoo.com.

HUDSON, ORLANDO THILL, professional baseball player; b. Darlington, SC, Dec. 12, 1977; Grad., Spartanburg Meth. Jr. Coll., SC. Draft pick Toronto Blue Jays, 1997, second baseman, 2002—05, Ariz. Diamondbacks, 2005—. Named to Nat. League All-Star Team, Maj. League Baseball, 2007; recipient Gold Glove award, 2005—06. Mailing: Ariz Diamondbacks PO Box 2095 Phoenix AZ 85001*

HUDSON, R. READ, lawyer, food products executive; b. Little Rock, Apr. 11, 1958; BSBA, U. Ark., 1980, JD, 1987; LLM, Boston U., 1988. Bar: Ark. 1988, U.S. Ct. Appeals (8th cir.) 1989, U.S. Dist. Ct. (ea. and we. dists.) Ark. 1991. With Tyson Foods, Inc., Springdale, Ark., 1992—, v.p., assoc. gen. counsel, sec., 1998—. Mem. ABA (mem. sect. on bus. law), Ark. Bar Assn., Washington County Bar Assn. Office: PO Box 2020 2210 W Oaklawn Dr Springdale AR 72762-6900*

HUDSON, RALPH P., physicist; b. Wellingborough, Eng., Oct. 14, 1924; came to U.S., 1949, naturalized, 1960. s. Harold and Ada (Jenkinson) H.; m. Nancy Brisby, July 9, 1947; children: Geoffrey R., Wendy E. BA, Merton Coll., Oxford U., 1944, MA, PhD, Oxford U., 1949; DSc (hon.), Purdue U., 2001. Sci. officer U.K. Ministry Supply, Birmingham, Eng., Montreal, Que. and Chalk River, Ont., Can., 1944-46; vis. lectr. Purdue U., 1949-50, asst. prof., 1950-51; with Nat. Bur. Standards, Washington, 1951-80, chief cryogenic physics sect., 1954-61, chief heat div., 1961-78; dep. dir. Center for Absolute Phys. Quantities, 1978-80; dir. publs. Internat. Bur. Weights and Measures, Sèvres, France, 1980-89; program dir. low temperature physics NSF, Washington, 1989-92. Cons. in field, 1993—; guest worker fundamental constants data ctr. Nat. Inst. Stds. & Tech., 1998—. Editor: Metrologia, 1980-89, editl. cons., 1995—. Mem. U.K. Home Guard, 1941-43, U.K. Atomic Energy Program, 1944-46. Recipient Silver and Gold medals Dept. Commerce, 1957; Samuel Wesley Stratton award Nat. Bur. Standards, 1964; Edward U. Condon award, 1976; Guggenheim fellow, 1960-61 Fellow Am. Phys. Soc., Franklin Inst. (John Price Wetherill medal 1962); mem. Cosmos Club (Washington). Achievements include rsch. on behavior of matter near absolute zero temperature; first to demonstrate the non-conservation of parity in the weak interactions. Home: 3152 Gracefield Rd Apt 623 Silver Spring MD 20904-5897 E-mail: ralph.hudson@nist.gov.

HUDSON, RICHARD L., retired adult education educator, minister; b. Watertown, NY, Dec. 1, 1920; s. M. A. and M. (D.) Hudson; m. Beatrice Evalin Olson, Apr. 23, 1955; 2 children. AB, Syracuse U., 1944, PhD, 1970; BD, Yale U., 1947, STM, 1950. Ordained to ministry United Meth. Ch., 1945. Asst. min. Rome (NY) Meth. Ch., 1946-48, Meth. Ch., Parish, NY, 1950-54; commentator Religion Makes News, Sta. WSYR, Syracuse, NY; dir. pub. rels. Syracuse Area United Meth. Ch., 1954-56; min. Meth. Ch., Carthage, NY, 1956-58; Cokesbury fellow, grad. asst. Syracuse U., 1958-61; mem. faculty Wyoming Sem., Kingston, Pa., 1961-64, New Eng. Coll., Henniker, NH, 1964-83, prof., 1971-83, prof. emeritus, 1983—, dean humanities, 1970-71. Adj. prof. history Post Coll., Waterbury, Conn., 1985—91, Quinnipiac Coll., Hamden, Conn., 1987—97. Author: A Burden for Souls, 1950, A Student's Guide to the New Testament, 1963, The Challenge of Dissent, 1970; editor: The Only Henniker on Earth, 1980. Chmn. Henniker HIst. Soc., 1976—83; docent Canterbury Shaker Village, 1975—83, New Haven Colony Hist. Soc., 1984—93, bd. dirs., 1988—90. Mem.: Nat. Assn. Scholars, Mayflower Soc., Tabard, Tau Theta Upsilon, Theta Chi Beta. Home and Office: 44 Cloudland Rd North Haven CT 06473-4006

HUDSON, ROBERT DONALD, dermatologist; b. Houston, Feb. 13, 1952; s. Robert Donald and Barbara Adelaide Hudson; children from previous marriage: Kacy Diane, Jessica Ann, Tifini Marie, Robert J. BS in Biology, Sowestern U., Georgetown, Tex., 1973; MD, Baylor Coll. Medicine, Houston, 1978. Diplomate Am. Bd. Dermatology. Dermatologist Laredo Dermatology Assocs., P.A., Tex., 1982—. Lectr. in field. Pres. sch. bd. Blessed Sacrament Sch., Laredo, 1986—92; sch. bd. St. Augustine Schs., Laredo, 1993—2003. Recipient Super Dr. award, Tex. Monthly Mag., 2005, 2006. Fellow: Am. Acad. Dermatology; mem.: Tex. Dermatologic Soc., Tex. Med. Assn., Alpha Omega. Avocations: hunting, fishing. Office: Laredo Dermatology Assocs PA 121 Calle Del Norte Ste 102 Laredo TX 78041 Office Phone: 956-726-1646.

HUDSON, ROBERT E., library director; Dir. Mugar Meml. Libr. Boston U., mem. faculty assembly coun. Bd. dirs. Boston Libr. Consortium. Contbr. articles to profl. jours. Office: Mugar Meml Libr Boston U 771 Commonwealth Ave Boston MA 02215 Office Phone: 617-353-3710. Office Fax: 617-353-2084. E-mail: rehuds@bu.edu.*

HUDSON, ROBERT FRANKLIN, JR., lawyer; b. Miami, Fla., Sept. 20, 1946; s. Robert Franklin and Jane Ann (Reed) Hudson; m. Edith Mueller, June 19, 1971; children: Daniel Warren, Patrick Alexander. BSBA in Econs., U. Fla., 1968, JD, 1971; cert., U. London, 1970; LLM in Taxation, NYU, 1972. Bar: Fla. 1971, N.Y. 1975. Law clk. to judge Don N. Laramore U.S. Ct. Claims, Washington, 1972-73; assoc. Wender, Murase & White, NYC, 1973-77; ptnr. Arky, Freed, Stearns et al, Miami, 1977-86, Baker & McKenzie LLP, Miami, 1986—; mem. policy com. Baker & McKenzie, Miami, 1990-93, mem. client credit com., 1992-99, mng. ptnr. Miami office, 1996-98; N. Am. Tax Practice Group Mgmt. com., 2000—03. Mem. adv. bd. Tax Mgmt., Inc., Washington, 1986—, Fgn. Investment N.Am., London, 1990—96; legal counsel to her majesty's Britanic Counsel, Miami, 1988—94. Author: Federal Taxation of Foreign Investment in U.S. Real Estate, 1986; contbr. articles to profl. jours. Bd. dirs. Camillus House, 2003—, Concert Assn. Fla., 1992—, exec. com., 1993—, vice chmn., 1994—98, 2003—05, chmn., 2005—; bd. dirs. Performing Arts Ctr. Found., 1994—, vice chmn., 2000—; bd. dirs. Fla. Philharm., 1996—97, Internat. Wine and Food Soc., 2002—, v.p., 2005—. Mem.: ABA, Internat. Trust Adv. Bd Fiduciary Trust, World Trade Ctr. (bd. dirs. 1992—94), Coll. Tax Lawyers, Internat. Tax Planning Assn., Internat. Bar Assn., Inter-Am. Bar Assn., Internat. Fiscal Assn. (v.p. S.E. region U.S. br. 1985—92, mem. exec. coun. 1987—), Fla. Bar Assn. (chmn. tax sect. 1989—90, Oustanding Spkr. 1995), Fla. Internat. Bankers Assn. (bd. dirs. 2002—), Japan Soc. S. Fla. (chmn. pub. affairs com. 1991—93, bd. dirs. 1993—2000, treas. 1995—96, pres. 1996—99), S.E./U.S. Japan Assn. Democrat. Methodist. Avocations: skiing, boating, photography, travel, hiking. Office: Baker McKenzie 1111 Brickell Ave Ste 1700 Miami FL 33131-3257 Business E-Mail: bob.hudson@bakernet.com.

HUDSON, ROBERT PAUL, medical educator; b. Kansas City, Kans., Feb. 23, 1926; s. Chester Lloyd and Jean (Emerson) H.; m. Olive Jean Grimes, Aug. 1, 1948 (div. 1963); children: Robert E., Donald K., Timothy M.; m. Martha Isabelle Holter, July 10, 1965; children: Stephen, Laurel. BA, U. Kans., 1949, MD, 1952; MA, Johns Hopkins U., 1966. Instr. U. Kans., Kansas City, 1958-59, assoc. in medicine, 1959-63, asst. prof., 1964-69, assoc. prof., 1969—, prof., chmn. history of medicine, 1969-95, ret. Author: Disease and Its Control, 1983; mem. editl. bd. Bull. History of Medicine, Balt., 1981-94; contbr. articles to profl. jours. 1st lt. U.S. Army, 1953-55. Master ACP; mem. Am. Assn. for History of Medicine (pres. 1984-86), Am. Osler Soc. (bd. govs., pres. 1987-88). Home: 12925 S Frontier Rd Olathe KS 66061-8647 Office: Kans U Med Ctr 39th And Rainbow Blvd Kansas City KS 66160-0001 E-mail: lastroma@earthlink.net.

HUDSON, ROBIN E., state supreme court justice; b. Ga., 1952; married; 2 children. BA, Yale U., 1973; JD, U. NC Sch. Law, 1976. Bar: NC 1976. Atty., Raleigh, Durham, NC, 1976—2000; judge NC Ct. Appeals, 2001—06; assoc. justice Supreme Ct. NC, 2007—. Founding steering com. mem. NC Assn. Women Attys., 1978; mem. NC Acad. Trial Lawyers, 1978—2001, bd. govs., 1993—99, chair workers' compensation sect., 1993—98; mem. Family Ct. Adv. Com., 2001—. Mem. adv. coun. NC Indsl. Commn., 1994—2000; chair NC OSHA Rev. Bd., 1994—2006. Mem.: NC Jud. Conf. (treas. 2002—), ABA Appellate Judges Conf., Nat. Assn. Women Judges, NC Assn. Black Lawyers, Wake County Bar. Assn., NC Bar Assn., Wake Women Attys., Women's Forum NC (mem. 2001—, bd. mem. & sec. 2004—05). Office: Supreme Ct NC PO Box 2170 Raleigh NC 27602-2170 also: 5417 Olde South Rd Raleigh NC 27606 Office Phone: 919-733-3723.*

HUDSON, RONALD MORGAN, aviation planner; b. Anniston, Ala., May 7, 1954; s. James Alphus and Mildred Christine (Morgan) H.; m. Marsha Carol Smith, Dec. 27, 1974 (div. Oct. 1989); children: Jereme Brandon, Sara Elizabeth; m. Connie M. Luckey, Nov. 13, 1993. BS in Aviation Mgmt., Auburn U., 1976. Aviation planner Wainwright Engring. Co., Montgomery, Ala., 1978—81, Ralph Burke Assocs., Park Ridge, Ill., 1981—85; sr. assoc. mgr. aviation Knight Architects, Engrs., Planners, Inc., Chgo., 1985—96; assoc. ptnr. Hanson Profl. Svcs. Inc., Oak Brook, Ill., 1996—. Mem. Am. Planning Assn., Am. Inst. Cert. Planners, Am. Assn. Airport Execs., Ill. Pub. Airports Assn. Avocations: biking, travel. Home: 1710 E Oakton St Arlington Heights IL 60004-5000 Office Phone: 630-990-3800. E-mail: ronaldhudson@comcast.net.

HUDSON, ROY DAVAGE, retired pharmaceutical executive; b. Chattanooga, June 30, 1930; s. Roy and Everence (Wilkerson) H.; m. Constance Joan Taylor, Aug. 31, 1956; children: Hollye Lynne, David Kendall. BS, Livingstone Coll., 1955; MS, U. Mich., 1957, PhD, 1962; MA, Brown U., 1968; LL.D., Lehigh U., 1974, Princeton, 1975. Asst. prof. pharmacology U. Mich. Sch. Medicine, 1961-66; assoc. prof. med. sci. Brown U. Sch. Medicine, 1966-70, assoc. dean grad. sch., 1966-69; pres. Hampton U., 1970-76; dir. rsch. planning and coordination Parke, Davis Pharm. Co., Ann Arbor, Mich., 1976; v.p. rsch. planning Warner Lambert/Parke-Davis Pharm. Rsch. Divsn., Ann Arbor, 1977-79; mgr. sci. liaison Upjohn Co., Kalamazoo, 1979-81, mgr. CNS diseases rsch., 1981—85, dir. CNS diseases rsch., 1985-87; v.p. pharm. rsch. divsn. Europe Upjohn Co., Brussels, 1987-90; corp. v.p. pub. rels. Upjohn Co., Kalamazoo, 1990-92, ret., 1992. Adj. prof. Black Americana studies Western Mich. U., Kalamazoo, 1993; interim exec. dir., CEO Guidance Clinic, Kalamazoo, 1993; interim pres. Livingstone Coll., Salisbury, N.C., 1995-96; dir. Parke-Davis & Co., United Va. Bank-Citizens and Marine, United Va. Bankshares, Comerica Bank-Mich., Chesapeake and Potomac Telephone Co. of Va. Contbr. articles to profl. jours., chpts. to books. Mem. screening com. Danforth Grad. Fellowships, 1962-78; mem. adv. council Danforth Grad. Fellows program Danforth Found., 1972-79; chmn. Va. Com. on Selection Rhodes Scholars, 1973; mem. Commn. on Fed. Relations, Am. Council on Edn., 1972-76, bd. dirs., 1973-76; mem. adv. council to dir. NIH, 1974—; Mem. R.I. Commn. Econ. Devel., 1967-69, R.I. Urban League scholarship com., 1966-70; mem. inst. policy commn. So. Regional Edn. Bd.; bd. dirs. Afro-Am. Soc. Conn. Coll., Kalamazoo Area Math and Sci. Ctr., Kalamazoo Area Academic Achievement Program, ARC; bd. dirs., v.p. Nat. Assn. Equal Opportunity in Higher Edn.; trustee Brown U., Livingstone Coll., Peninsula United Community Services, Spelman Coll. Served with USAF, 1948-52. Recipient Disting. Alumni award Livingstone Coll.; Outstanding Civilian Service award U.S. Army.; Danforth Grad. fellow, 1955-61 Mem. Am. Soc. Pharmacology and Exptl. Therapeutics, Peninsula C. of C., NAACP (life, 1st v.p., Golden Heritage), AAAS, N.Y. Acad. Scis., Sigma Xi, Phi Kappa Phi, Phi Sigma, Beta Kappa Chi, Kappa Delta Pi, Omega Psi Phi, Gamma Alpha, Alpha Kappa Mu. Home: 7057 Oak Highlands Dr Kalamazoo MI 49009-6580 Personal E-mail: r.d.hudson@worldnet.att.net.

HUDSON, SAUL See SLASH

HUDSON, SHERRILL W., energy executive; m. Mary Ann Hudson; 3 children. Mng. ptnr. Deloitte and Touche, LLP, Fla., 1965—2002; bd. dir. TECO Energy, Tampa, Fla., 2003—, chmn., CEO, 2004—. Bd. dir. Standard Register, Publix Super Markets, A. Duda & Sons. Treas., chmn. develop. com. Cmty. Partnership for Homeless; vice-chmn. Goodwill Industries Miami-Dade County; past chmn. Fla. Internat Univ. Found., Greater Miami C. of C., Dade Cmty. Found., Jackson Meml. Found., Am. Cancer Soc.; past pres. Orange Bowl Com., Zoological Soc. Fla. Mem.: Fla. Inst. CPAs (Outstanding CPA in Bus. & Industry 2006). Office: TECO Energy 702 N Franklin St Tampa FL 33602*

HUDSON, STANTON HAROLD, JR., public relations executive, educator, academic administrator; b. Syracuse, NY, Jan. 28, 1951; s. Stanton Harold Sr. and Lucille (Shea) Hudson. Cert. in Lang. and History, U. Caen, France, 1970; BA in History/Polit. Sci., Canisius Coll., 1972; postgrad., SUNY, Buffalo, 1974—76, Syracuse U., 1995—98, Buffalo State Coll., 2003—. Legis. asst., asst. pub. rels. dir. Erie County Rep. Com., Buffalo, 1971-73; dir. pub. rels. and fin. Greater Niagara Frontier Coun. Boy Scouts Am., Buffalo, 1977-79; dir. pub. rels. Ellis Singer & Webb Advt., Buffalo, 1979-80; asst. v.p., mgr. mktg. communications M&T Bank, Buffalo, 1980-85; exec. dir. Shea's Ctr. Performing Arts, Buffalo, 1986; pres. Hudson Mktg. Comm., Buffalo, 1987-88; sr. dir. advt. and pub. rels. Blue Cross Western N.Y., Inc., Buffalo, 1988-91; prin. Fredrickson & Hudson Assocs., Buffalo, 1991-92, Hudson & Assocs. Pub. Rels., Counselors, Buffalo, 1992—. Asst. prof. Canisius Coll., 1993—2004, dir. grad. program orgnl. comm. & devel., 1995—2004; pres., CEO Am. Lung Assn. N.Y. State, 2004—05; deputy dir. devel. and comm. Buffalo and Erie County Public Library, 2007—. Editor: (newsletter) M&T Bank Observer, 1981—82 (Project PICA Grand award United Way Buffalo and Erie County); mng. editor: newsletter Blue Cross Ink, 1991. Chmn. pub. rels. and mktg. coms. Greater Buffalo chpt. ARC, 1989—92, bd. dirs. Greater Buffalo chpt., 1991—92; bd. dirs. ARC Blood Svcs., N.Y.-Pa. Region, 1993—2003; bd. dirs., exec. com. Greater Buffalo Opera Co., 1991—93; trustee, mktg. com. Theodore Roosevelt Inaugural Nat. Hist. Site Found., 1994—, co-chair 2001 Pan Am. Expo. centennial celebration com., vice chair capital campaign, 2006—; bd. dirs. Buffalo Coun. on World Affairs, 1994—2002, co-chair mktg. com., 1994—98; Success By 6 awareness com. Buffalo and Erie County United Way, 1994—98, leadership coun., 1997—2004; bd. dirs. East Hill Found., 2000—; mem. Erie County Cultural Resources Adv. Bd., 2000—, mem. exec. com., 2003—04, 2nd vice chair, 2007—; chmn. Erie Niagara Tobacco-Free Coalition, 1999—2000, 2003—04; mem. cap. campaign cabinet Burchfield Penney Art Ctr., 2004; bd. dirs. Graycliff Conservancy, 2006—, mem. mktg. com., 2006—, mem. devel. com., 2006—, mem. exec. com., 2007; bd. dirs. Ctr. Arts U. Buffalo, 2004; bd. mgrs. Buffalo Mus. Sci., 2006—. Recipient Gold Star award, Nat. Adv. Agy. Network, 1979, Gold Quill award, Internat. Assn. of Bus. Communicators, 1984, Francis V. Hanavan Meml. award, Am. Lung Assn. We. N.Y., 1997, CEO's award, 2002, Brotherhood/Sisterhood award, Nat. Conf. for Cmty. and Justice, 1999, Pres. award, Theodore Roosevelt Inaugural Nat. Hist. Site Found., 2002. Mem.: Am. Lung Assn. (bd. dirs. We. N.Y. affiliate 1984—2004, bd. dirs. N.Y. state constituent 1986—2004, pres.-elect 1995—98, pres. 1998—2004, nat. bd. dirs. 2000—04, mem. numerous panels and coms.), Western NY Grantmakers Assn. (bd. dirs. 2002—04, 2007—, v.p. 2003—04, sec. 2007—), Coordinated Care Mgmt. Corp. (mktg. com. 1994—98), Western N.Y. Comms. Steering Com. (chair 1991—92, bd. dirs. 2007—, sec. 2007—), Am. Mktg. Assn. (v.p. comms. Buffalo/Niagara chpt. 1991—92), Pub. Rels. Soc. Am. (treas. Buffalo/Niagara chpt. 1986—89, pres.-elect 1989—90, pres. 1990—91, treas. N.E. dist. 1992, chair 1994, nat. nominating com. 1995, nat. assembly del. 1997—2000, universal accreditation bd. 1998—2000, mem. profl. devel. task force 2001—03, nat. assembly del. 2002—04, mem. Coll. Fellows 2002—, mem. ednl. affairs com. 2003—04, mem. ednl. affairs task force 2003—04, Practitioner of the Yr. Buffalo/Niagara chpt. 1993, Excalibur award 1993, 1994, 1995, 1997, Nat. Paul M. Lund Pub. Svc. award 1997, accredited 1989), Pub. Rels. Student Soc. Am. (nat. profl. advisor 1996—2000, nat. faculty advisor 2003—04), Rotary (past dir.). Avocations: theater, jazz, reading, travel, cooking. Home Phone: 716-228-2345, 716-882-2856; Office Phone: 716-228-2345. Personal E-mail: shud012851@aol.com.

HUDSON, TROY, professional basketball player; b. Mar. 13, 1976; Attended, Univ. So. Ill. Basketball player Utah Jazz, 1997—98, LA Clippers, 1998—2000, Orlando Magic, 2000—02, Minn. Timberwolves, 2002—. Achievements include leading Univ. So. Ill. in all-time 3-pointers made (225). Office: Minn Timberwolves 600 First Ave No Minneapolis MN 55403

HUDSON, WALTER TIREE, artist; b. Lynchburg, Va., Apr. 10, 1943; s. Randolph Ward Hudson and Frances Anderson Tyree. electrician diploma, pvt. investigator diploma, sex and drug counselor diploma, security and police sci. diploma, tchrs. aid diploma, computer programmer, Stratford Career Inst., 2006, ESL diploma, 2007. Owner Linchberg Folk Arts, Doggywood Lit. Prodns. Exhibitions include Hudson House, 1983, Seven Hills Art Club, 1985, The Framery, 1985—2000, Haley's Antiques, 1985—2002, Lynchburg Pub. Housing Authority, 1986—2000, Lynchburg Social Svcs., 1987—99, Lynchburg Pub. Libr., 1987—, Amelia Pride, 1988, Lynchburg Recreation Dept., 1988—2001, Daily Bread, 1989—,

Adult Daycare Ctr.-Va. Bapt. Hosp., 1989—94, Lynchburg Art Festival, 1991, Elks Nat. Home, 1992, Robert Hicks Collection, 1992, Ehrich's Opticians, 1992—2003, Va. Episcopal Sch., 1988, G.H. Vander Elst Collection, 1993, U. Tex., Houston, 1993, Lynchburg Fine Arts Ctr., Lynchburg PO, 1994, Lynchburg Voter Registration Office, 1995, Free Clinic of Va., 1995—2003, Irby L. Hudson Collection, 1995, Jacob Hunt Show, 1995—, 101 Quinlan St., 1996, Royal County Arts, 1995, Doggiewood Collection, 1996, Linchbird and Linchberg "1997", De Z Night Jump, 1997, 707 Mansfield Avenue, 1998, Ah Holloween Spring, 1998, Spring Fling, 1998—99, Blue Berg, 1998, Community Market, 1999, Linchbird, Red, White and Blue, 1999, West End Story, 1999, The Mormon Auction, 1999, WSET TV News, 1999, Cornucopia, 2000, Mental Blocks, 2000, Calif. Poly of San Luis Obispo, 2000, Linchberg Berginia, 2000, E.C. Glass HS, 2000, Lynchburg Jour., 2001, Social Svcs., 2001, Facetous Art, 2002, Art Diploma, 2003, High School Diploma, 2003, Melinda's, 2004, McCraws, 2004, Creative Writing Diploma, 2004, Automobile Mechanic Diploma, 2004, Accounting Diploma, 2005, The Best Green House, 2005, Legal Assistant Diploma, 2005, Julio Uchimura Gallery, 2007, Active Rep. Nat. Com., 2003, Ct. St. United Meth. Ch., Thomas Road Bapt. Ch., 1984. Served Airborne US Army, 1960—63. Recipient Men of Achievement award, 1996. Mem.: 82nd Airborne Div. Assn., The Statue of Liberty Ellis Island Foundation, Inc. (Millennial Certificate for Philanthropic Recognition 2000), 504th ABN Club, Blue Ridge All Airborne Club, Lynchburg Stamp Club. Republican. Mem. Lds Ch. Avocations: stamp collecting/philately, reading, walking. Home: 3475 Fort Ave Apt 326 Lynchburg VA 24501-3834

HUDSON, WILLIAM L., conductor; Studies with Anthony Gigliotti, Max Rudolph, Erich Leindorf; grad., Phila. Mus. Acad., U. Pa., Yale U.; conducting student, Tanglewood Music Festival, Curtis Inst. Music, Phila. Conservatory. Condr., music dir. Fairfax Symphony Orch., Annandale, Va. Prof. music, condr. opera prodns. and symphony orch. U. Md.; faculty mem. Conducting Inst. Am. Symphony Orch. League; music dir. Shenandoah Valley Music Festival, 1979—. Bd. dirs. No. Va. Youth Symphony, Fairfax (Va.) Chorale Soc.; mem. adv. panel Fairfax County Coun. Arts; hon. chmn. Fairfax Spotlight on Arts, 1990. Recipient Outstanding Music Dir./Condr. award Washington Area Music Assn., 1985. Office: Fairfax Symphony Orchestra 1505 Farm Credit Dr Mc Lean VA 22102-5001

HUDSON, WILLIAM L., lawyer, electronics executive; Ptnr. Brobeck, Phleger & Harrison, LLP, 1984—97, Gibson Dunn & Crutcher, LLP, 1997—99; sr. v.p., gen. counsel, corp. sec. Seagate Tech., Scotts Valley, Calif., 2000—02, exec. v.p., gen. counsel, corp. sec., 2002—. Office: Seagate Tech 920 Disc Dr Scotts Valley CA 95066*

HUDSON-ZONN, ELIZA, nurse, psychologist; b. Monrovia, Liberia, Dec. 12, 1956; arrived in U.S., 1978; d. Hartzell Gleh and Joan Eliza (Roberts) Killen; m. Henry Clay Hudson, July 28, 1979 (div. Apr. 1985); 1 child, Kimberly Clayde; m. Mawuli Sonny Zonn, July 31, 1988; 1 child, Jewel Lorraine. BA in Psychology, BSC in Nursing, U. So. Miss., 1984. RN, N.J., Tex. Pvt. duty nurse Maxim Healthcare, Inc., South Orange, NJ, 1990—; critical care nurse Midpoint Profl. Agy., East Orange, NJ, 1988; supervising nurse Interim Healthcare, Inc., Morristown, NJ, 1990—; staff nurse Montclair Gen. Hosp., NJ, 1989—91; pvt. nurse Beth-Israel Med. Ctr., Newark, 1988—92; staff nurse United Children's Hosp., Newark, 1989—92; critical care nurse Nat. Staffing Assn. Inc., East Orange, 1988—2004; DON Med. Day Care Ctr., New Cmty. Extended Care, Newark, 2003—; supr. St. Mary's Life Ctr./Pope John Paul II Pavilion, Orange, NJ, 2007. Charge nurse Cmty. Psychiat. Ctr., Houston, 1993. Rural health vol. Red Cross Liberia, Monrovia, 1973—74; women's refugees health adv. Union Sierra Leone for Liberia, 1990—95; human rights adv. Movement for Justice in Africa, 1975—; coord., health svcs. dir. Liberian Cmty. Assn. N.J., 2001; membership recruiter Student Unification Party, Monrovia, 1975—76; counselor Providence Bapt. Ch., 1975, St. Elmo Bapt. Ch., 1982. Recipient Pub. Svc. award East Miss. Bapt. Women Conv., 1972; So. Bapt. Conv. scholar, 1978-84, Nat. Bapt. Conv. scholar, 1972-84. Mem.: Nat. Staffing Assn. Skilled Home Care Nursing, Suehn Acad. Alumni Assn. (founding mem. 1995). Democrat. Avocations: reading, writing, sports, decoration, antiques. Home: 64 Hillyer St Orange NJ 07050 Office: Nat Staffing Assocs Inc 134 Evergreen Pl East Orange NJ 07018

HUDSPETH, ALMETRA KAVANAUGH, retired elementary school educator; b. San Antonio, Jan. 22, 1952; d. Wilbert L.D. Kavanaugh and Kathryn Kavanaugh Gray; m. Vernon Howard Hudspeth Jr., Aug. 17, 1974; children: Crystal LaShell, Almetra Joy. BA, St. Mary's U., San Antonio, 1974; M Edn., U. Incarnate Word, San Antonio, 1997. Cert. K-8 tchr. Tex. Tchr. Ave. D Elem. Sch. Killeen Ind. Sch. Dist., Tex., 1975—80; tchr. Graebner Elem. Sch. San Antonio Ind. Sch. Dist., 1980—2005; ret., 2005. Mem. various coms. Graebner Elem. Sch. San Antonio Ind. Sch. Dist., 1980—. Contbr. articles to profl. jours. Sunday sch. tchr. Rainbow Hills Bapt. Ch., 1988—, choir mem., 1988—. Scholar, St. Mary's U., 1970. Avocations: bowling, reading, gardening, computer games. Home: 2702 Oak Mill San Antonio TX 78251 Personal E-mail: almetra_h@yahoo.com.

HUDSPETH, CHALMERS MAC, lawyer, educator; b. Denton, Tex., Oct. 18, 1919; s. Junia Evans and Ethel (Burns) H.; m. Demaris Eleanor De Lange, Jan. 30, 1945; children: Albert James, Thomas Richard, Helen Demaris. BA, Rice U., Houston, 1940; JD, U. Tex., Austin, 1946. Bar: Tex. 1946. Pvt. practice, Houston, 1947—; of counsel De Lange Hudspeth McConnell and Tibbets LLP, 1988—; asst. prof. law U. Tex. at Austin, 1946-47; lectr. govt. Rice U., 1947—, bd. govs., 1980-89, trustee, 1982-89, trustee emeritus, 1989—. Bd. dirs. Stewart Title Guaranty Co. Contbr. articles to profl. jours. Mem. bi-racial com. Houston Ind. Sch. Dist., 1955-56; trustee, v.p. Brown Found., 1983-89. Served to lt. USNR, 1942-45. Fellow Am. Bar Found., Tex. Bar Found.; mem. ABA, Tex. Bar Assn., State Bar Tex. (dir. 1966-68, v.p. 1968-69), Houston Philos. Soc. (pres. 1964-65), Chancellors, Order of Coif, Phi Delta Phi. Office: De Lange Hudspeth McConnell & Tibbets LLP Eight Greenway Plz Ste 1300 Houston TX 77046 Office Phone: 713-871-2000. Business E-Mail: hank@dhmtlaw.com.

HUDSPETH, STEPHEN MASON, lawyer; b. Pitts., Jan. 22, 1947; s. Harold Mason and Edna Mary (Lawrenson) H.; m. Rebecca Anne Ellis, Apr. 3, 1971; children: David, Catherine. BA, MA magna cum laude, Yale U., 1968, JD, 1971. Bar: N.Y. 1973, Pa. 1973, U.S. Dist. Ct. (so. and ea. dists.) N.Y. 1973, U.S. Ct. Appeals (2d cir. 1973), Mass. 1974, U.S. Dist. Ct. (ea. dist.) Pa. 1975, U.S. Ct. Appeals (1st cir.) 1976, U.S. Ct. Appeals (3d cir.) 1977, U.S. Supreme Ct. 1980, Maine 1987. Assoc. Lord, Day & Lord, NYC, until 1979, ptnr., 1979-86, Coudert Bros., NYC, 1986—, mem. exec. com., 1990-93, also head litigation dept., 1994—. Adj. asst. prof. bus. law Wagner Coll., 1973-83. Co-author: Transfer Pricing under U.S. Law, 1995; contbr. articles to profl. jours., chpts. to books. Vestryman St. Alban's Episcopal Ch., S.I., N.Y., 1979-85, warden, 1985-87; chmn. Stewardship Commn., Diocese of N.Y., 1987-95; vestryman St. Matthew's Episcopal Ch., Wilton, Conn., 1989-92, warden, 1992-95; bd. dirs. Union Theol. Sem., 2000—. Capt. C.E., USAR, 1968-73. Mem. ABA, N.Y. State Bar Assn., Assn. Bar City N.Y., Phi Beta Kappa. Office: Coudert Bros 1114 Ave of Americas 4th Fl New York NY 10036-7710 Home Phone: 203-834-0943; Office Phone: 212-626-4442. Personal E-mail: hudspeths@comcast.com. Business E-Mail: dahuds@optonline.net.

HUDZINSKI, LEONARD GERARD, social sciences educator, researcher; b. Aug. 14, 1946; BA in Psychology and Sociology, Findlay Coll., Ohio, 1968; MSW, U. Mich., 1971; PhD, U. Pitts., 1975. Diplomate Clin. Social Work Examiners. Tchg. asst. dept. sociology Findlay Coll., 1966-68; psychology specialist Lyster Army Hosp., Ft. Rucker, Ala., 1969-70; psychiat. social worker Toledo (Ohio) Mental Health Ctr., 1972; instr. in applied social rsch. and social work Med. Coll. Ohio, 1974-77; head divsn. clin. social work Ochsner Med. Instns., New Orleans, 1977—2001; ret., 2001. Dir. Ochsner Ctr. for Elimination of Smoking; asst. clin. prof. psychiatry La. State U. Med. Ctr.; asst. clin. prof. Tulane Med. Ctr.; instr., social scis. dept., Tahoe Coll. South Lake Tahoe, Calif.; psychology and sociology faculty Lake Tahoe C.C., 2002-; program dir., adminstr. State of Ohio Epilepsy Deinstitutionalization Assistance Program, 1976-77. Contbr. articles to profl. jours.; mem. editorial bd. Headache Quar., 1989—. Bd. dirs. Biofeedback Certification Inst. Am., Wheat Ridge, Colo., 1995. With U.S. Army, 1968-70. Fellow Am. Assn. for Study of Headache; mem. Assn. for Advancement of Behavior Therapy, Assn. Applied Psychophysiology and Biofeedback, La. Assn. Applied Psychophysiology and Biofeedback (past pres.), Am. Assn. for Study of Headache, NASW, La. Assn. for Clin. Social Work Vendorship (bd. dirs., treas., pres.), ACSW, Am. Fedn. for Clin. Rsch. Home: P O Box 1182 Zephyr Cove NV 89448 Personal E-mail: lhudzinski@msn.com.

HUE, NGUYEN VAN, soil scientist, chemist, educator; arrived in US, 1974; BS in Chem. Engring., U. Saigon, Vietnam, 1972; PhD, Auburn U., Ala., 1981. Chief soil bur. Dept. Agr., Saigon, Vietnam, 1972—74; rsch. assoc. Auburn U., 1976—81, post doctoral staff, 1982—85; prof. U. Hawaii, Honolulu, 1985—. Grantee, USDA, 1986—. Mem.: Am. Chem. Soc. (corr.), Am. Agronomy Soc. (corr.), Soil Sci. Soc. Am. (corr.), Gamma Sigma Delta, Sigma Xi, Phi Kappa Phi. Home: Apt 302 1138 Hassinger Honolulu HI 96822 Office: Univ Hawaii St John 102 3190 Maile Way Honolulu HI 96822 Office Phone: 808-956-7247. Office Fax: 808-956-3894. Personal E-mail: envihue@yahoo.com. Business E-Mail: nvhue@hawaii.edu.

HUEBNER, DAVID, lawyer; b. Mahanoy City, Pa., May 7, 1960; AB summa cum laude, Princeton Univ., 1982; JD, Yale Univ., 1986. Bar: Calif. 1989, DC 1992, NY 1998, US Dist. Ct. (no., ctrl., ea. & no. Calif.), US Ct. Appeals (9th & Fed. cir.), US Ct. Internat. Trade, US Supreme Ct. Exec. asst. to Hon. Koji Kakizawa, mem. lower house of Diet, Tokyo, 1984—85; ptnr., Global Litigation practice Coudert Bros. LLP, LA, chmn., 2003—05. Adj. prof. Univ. So. Calif. Law Sch.; chmn. & commr. Calif. Law Revision Commn., 2000—04; pres. & commr. LA City Quality & Productivity Commn., 1994—97; counsel Ind. Commn. on LA Police Dept., 1991. Editor (in chief): Yale Jour. on Regulation. Henry Luce scholar. Mem.: LA Com. on Fgn. Rels. (founding mem.), Phi Beta Kappa. Office: Coudert Brothers Llp 555 S Flower St Los Angeles CA 90071-2300 Office Phone: 213-229-2900. Office Fax: 213-229-2999. Business E-Mail: huenberd@coudert.com.

HUEBNER, JEFF, art journalist, freelance writer; BA in English lit., Western Mich. U., 1982. Author: Murals: The Great Walls of Joliet, 2001, (photographs by Frank Dina) Chicago Parks Rediscovered, 2002; author, editor Chgo. Pub. Art Group mag.; co-author (with Olivia Gude): Urban Art Chicago: A Guide to Community Murals, Mosaics, and Sculptures, 2000; contbg. author Marcos Raya: Fetishizing the Imaginary, 2004; contbr. articles and art revs. to profl. jours. magazines, and newspapers. Mem.: Chgo. Art Critics Assn. Address: 1237 N Maplewood Ave Chicago IL 60622-2858 Office Phone: 773-489-2340. Personal E-mail: jeffwhuebner@mac.com.

HUEBNER, JOHN STEPHEN, geologist; b. Bryn Mawr, Pa., 1940; s. John and Elizabeth Huebner; m. Emily Mayer Zug, June 16, 1962; children: Christopher, Jeffrey. AB magna cum laude, Princeton U., 1962; PhD, Johns Hopkins U., 1967. Rsch. geologist U.S. Geol. Survey, 1967-97. Cons. NASA, 1976-78; lectr. George Washington U., 1971; sec.-treas. Am. Geol. Inst., 1974-75. Assoc. editor Jour. Geophys. Rsch., 1977-79; Contbr. articles profl. jours. Pres. Wood Acres Citizens Assn., 1977—78; sec. Cosmos Club Found., 1998—99, treas., 1999—2007. Recipient Meritorious Svc. award U.S. Dept. Interior, 1995. Fellow Mineral. Soc. Am. (bd. dirs. 1985-88, recipient MSA award 1978), Geochem. Soc. (treas. 1972-75); mem. AAAS, , Am. Geophys. Union, Geol. Soc. Washington (sec. 1972, v.p. 1991, pres. 1992, bd. dirs. 2000-01), Cosmos Club Washington (treas. 2003-07), Sigma Xi. Home: 6102 Cromwell Dr Bethesda MD 20816-3410 Personal E-mail: steve@huebners.com.

HUEBNER, MARSHALL SCOTT, lawyer; b. Feb. 13, 1967; Grad. magna cum laude, Princeton U., 1988; JD, Yale Law Sch., 1993. Bar: NY, US Dist. Ct. (ea. and so. dists.) NY, US Dist. Ct. (ea. dist.) Mich. Law clk. Hon. Pierre N. Neval, US Ct. Appeals (2nd cir.), 1993—94; assoc. Davis Polk & Wardwell, NYC, 1999—2002, ptnr., 2002—. Contbg. editor Collier Bankruptcy Practice Guide. Named a Dealmaker of Yr., Am. Lawyer mag., 2007; named an Outstanding Young Restructuring Lawyer, Turnarounds & Workouts, 2005; fellow Ford Found., 1993; scholar Fulbright scholar, 1988, Rotary scholar, 1988. Mem.: NYC Bar Assn. (chmn. Courts Subcom., Com. on Bankruptcy & Corp. Reorginization). Office: Davis Polk & Wardwell 450 Lexington Ave New York NY 10017 Office Phone: 212-450-4099. Office Fax: 212-450-3099. E-mail: marshall.huebner@dpw.com.*

HUEBNER, RUTH A., science educator, researcher; b. Milw., July 20, 1947; d. William and Barbara Sherman; m. Herbert J. Huebner, June 21, 1968; children: Beth Marie, Jeffrey William. BS, U. Wis., 1969, PhD, 1995; MS, U. Wis., Milw., 1976. Lic. psychology Ky. Bd. Psychology, 1996, occupl. therapy Ky., 1995. Staff occupl. therapist Milw. County Rehab. Hosp., 1970—71; dir. occupl. therapy Huntsville (Ala.) Rehab. Ctr., 1971—72; occupl. therapist St. Mary's Hosp. Med. Ctr., Madison, Wis., 1972—73; instr. Mt. Mary Coll., Milw., 1974—78; occupl. therapy Sch. Dist. Janesville, Wis., 1978—88; devel. specialist Riverview Learning and Devel. Ctr., Janesville, 1988—90; assoc. lectr. Occupl. Therapy Program, Madison, Wis., 1990—94; pre-doctoral internship U. of Wis. Counseling and Consultation Svc., Madison, Wis., 1994—95; assoc. prof. and prof. Ea. Ky. U., Richmond, 1995—; assoc. grad. faculty U. Ky., Lexington, 2000—; child welfare rschr. Cabinet for Health and Family Services, Frankfort, Ky., 2001—. Sr. rsch. specialist Trace R & D Ctr. of the Waisman Ctr., Madison, 1992—94; psychology cons. Bluegrass Regional Mental Health Mental Retardation Bd., Lexington, Ky., 1998—2000; rsch. cons. Hamilton Fish Inst. on Sch. Violence, Richmond, Ky., 2000—02, U. Ky., 2002—. Editor: Autism: A Sensorimotor Approach to Management, 2001; contbr. articles to profl. jours. Named Spl. Area Tchr. of Yr., Sch. Dist. Janesville, 1987. Fellow: Am. Occupl. Therapy Assn. (editl. bd. 1998—2005); mem.: APA, Nat. Coun. for Rsch. in Child Welfare (conf. planner, spl. edit. reviewer). Achievements include research in outcomes research, quality of life, and attachment and persons with disabilities. Home: 1968 Crescent Terrace Crescent Springs KY 41017 Office: Cabinet for Health and Family Services 275 East Main St 3W-A Frankfort KY 40621 Home Phone: 859-512-8051; Office Phone: 502-564-3703. Business E-Mail: rutha.huebner@ky.gov.

HUEGEL, DONNA MARIE, historian, writer, artist, archivist; b. New Hampton, Iowa, Apr. 14, 1951; d. Herbert Henry and Marceile Christoph; m. Leonard James Huegel, June 10, 1972; children: Eric, Ryan. Student, Mount Mercy Coll., 1969—72, U. Iowa, 1974, Western Wis. Tech. Coll., LaCrosse, 1999. Writer Houston County News, LaCrescent, Minn., 1994—; mus. curator LaCrescent Area Hist. Soc., 1993—. Author: Many A Grove and Orchard--The Story of John S. Harris, 1994, (anthology) America's Heartland Remembers--Stories Before, During and After 9-11, 2001, 2002, Stealing the Mississippi River.Fascinating History of the La Crescent Minnesota Area, 2006. Pres., chair PTA, Badger, Iowa, 1982—88; pres., chair art appreciation program Blanden Art Mus., Ft. Dodge, Iowa, 1982—88; sec. LaCrescent Area Hist. Soc., Minn., 1992—95. Named Edn. Vol. of Yr., Ft. Dodge Bd. Edn., 1988, La Crescent Area Hist. Soc. Outstanding Vol., 2007. Mem.: Writers' Group-LaCrosse, Wis., La Crescent Area Hist. Soc. Roman Catholic. Avocations: dance-skating, dance, singing, guitar, needlecrafts. Office Phone: 507-895-1857.

HUELSKAMP, WILLAMARIE ANN, artist; b. Covington, Ky., Sept. 16, 1959; d. Raymond Willabald and Elizabeth Louise Huelskamp; m. Ira Bennet Rubinfeld, Aug. 25, 1990; 1 child, Sonia Marie Rubinfeld. BS in Civil Engring., U. Utah, Salt Lake City, 1982, BFA, 1990. Artist Willamarie Inc., Salt Lake City, 1990—. Art tchr. Life Long Learning Program U. Utah, Salt Lake City, 1996—. 2-dimensional work on canvas, and paper, Today (Best of Show Utah Watercolor Soc., 2001), 2-dimensional mixed media, Thanksgiving (Ga. Watercolor Soc. Purchase award, 2001), 2-dimensional mixed media on canvas, Tulips/Home/ Pretty (Best of Show Utah Statewide Eccles Ctr., 2003), 2 dimensional painting on paper, Above City Creek Canyon (NW Watercolor Soc. award, 1993), 2-dimensional on paper, Circles, Spheres and Elipses (Watercolor West Juror's award, 1997), corporate and pvt. collections, Salt Lake Intenational Airport, Salt Lake C.C., The Entrada Country Club. Mem.: Utah Watercolor Soc. (assoc.). Avocations: yoga, ice skating, skiing. Office: Willamarie Inc 159 West Broadway #203 Salt Lake City UT 84101 Office Phone: 801-596-7026. Business E-Mail: willamarie@mac.com.

HUELSTER, JEFFERY JAMES, social studies educator; m. Lisa Huelster, Jan. 5, 1968; children: Cory, Samantha. BS, Ariz. State U., Tempe, 1988—91; student, Ottawa U., Phoenix, Ariz., 1993—94. Cert. Secondary Tchr. Ariz. Bd. Edn., 1995. Social studies tchr. Sandra Day O'Connor HS, Phoenix, 2002—, coach, 2002—06; football coach Cactus Shadows HS, Cave Creek, 2005—06; def. coord. Thunderbird HS, Phoenix, 2007. Vol. youth coach West Valley Soccer Club, Ariz. Sports Complex, Phoenix, 2005—06. Named State Champion Football Coach, Cactus Shadows H.S., 2006, 4A-II Coaching Staff of Yr., 2006. Mem.: Delta Sigma Phi. Office: Sandra Day O'Connor HS 25250 35th Ave Phoenix AZ 85308 Office Phone: 623-445-7270. Personal E-mail: coachjjh@yahoo.com. Business E-Mail: jeff.huelster@so.dvusd.org.

HUENEFELD, THOMAS ERNST, financial consultant, retired banker; b. Cin., July 7, 1937; s. Carl Ernst and Catherine Louise (Messer) H.; m. Catherine Ann Cogburn, Feb. 5, 1960; children: Richard Ernst, Amy Cogburn. BS in Bus. Adminstrn., U. Fla., 1961; grad. Nat. Comml. Lending Grad. Sch., U. Okla., 1975. Cert. comml. lender Am. Bankers Assn.; cert. lender-bus. banking Inst. Cert. Bankers. Mgmt. trainee Huenefeld Co., Cin., 1961—62, asst. sec., buyer, 1963—65; credit analyst First Nat. Bank Cin. (now U.S. Bank, N.A.), 1966—68, asst. cashier, 1968—69, asst. v.p., 1969—75, v.p., 1975—83, sr. v.p., 1983—96; ret., 1996. Cons. Star Banc Corp. (now U.S. Bancorp), Cin., 1997-98; dir. Wolf Machine Co., S. Eastern Materials Corp., Archiable Electric Co., Eastern Machinery Co., Ninth St. Garage, Inc., Logan & Kanawha Coal Co., Inc., Safegard Corp. Author: Pittsburgh's Historic East End: In and Around Point Breeze 1914, 2001. Bd. mgrs. Emanuel Cmty. Ctr., Cin., 1965—70, pres., 1968—70; trustee Huenefeld Meml., Inc., Cin., 1965—72, treas., 1965—69; trustee Funds for Self Enterprise, Cin., 1972—76, pres., 1973—76; trustee Cin. Musical Festival Assn., 1976—82, mem. exec. com., 1977—79; trustee Betts Ho. Rsch. Ctr., 1999—2002, mem. adv. bd., investment com., 2002—; trustee Cmty. Ltd. Care Dialysis Ctr., Cin., 1978—85, Mercantile Libr., 1979—2001, v.p., chmn. fin. com., 1983—88, life mem., 2001—; trustee Spring Grove Heritage Found., 2001—, chmn., 2004—; trustee MagnaCare Health Plan, 1988—91, v.p., chmn. fin. com., 1990—91; trustee Ohio Hist. Soc. Found., 2002—04, vice chmn., 2004; dir., treas., investment com. chmn. Pub. Libr. of Cin. and Hamilton County Found., 2004—; mem. adv. bd. Riemenschneider Bach Inst. Baldwin-Wallace Coll., 1988—; mem. history adv. bd. Cin. Mus. Ctr., 1997—; mem. adv. bd. Scarlet Oaks Retirement Com., 1998—, Emery Ctr. Corp., 1999—2002; trustee Bethesda Found., 2004—, sec.; mem. investment com. Bethesda Inc., 2004—. Mem. Am. Fin. Assn. (life), Fin. Mgmt. Assn. (life), Risk Mgmt. Assn. (life), Cin. Assn. Credit and Fin. Mgmt. (dir. 1972-76), Am. Inst. Banking, Newcomen Soc. N.Am., Ohio Hist. Soc. (life, trustee 2001-04, hon. adv. bd., 2005-), Ohioana Libr. Assn. (life), Cin. Hist. Soc. (life, trustee 1979-87, mem. exec. com. 1983-85, v.p. 1985-89), Cin. Preservation Assn. (trustee 1989-95, adv. bd. 1995—), Cincinnatus Assn. (exec. com. 1983-84), Cin. Country Club, Queen City Club, Bankers Club, The Assemblies (chmn. 1972-73), Univ. Club (bd. govs. 1982-89), Univ. Club Cin. Found. (trustee 1989-96), Fanfare (pres. 1979-80), Friends William Howard Taft Birthplace (trustee 1997-03), Sigma Chi (life). Republican. Methodist. Home and Office: 3440 Principio Ave Cincinnati OH 45208-4240

HUENEKE, MICHAEL, plastic surgeon; b. June 13, 1966; BA, U. Evansville, Ind., 1988; MD, Ind. U., 1992. Cert. Am. Bd. Plastic Surgery, 2001. Intern gen. surgery U. Tex., 1992—93, resident gen. surgery, 1992—98; resident plastic surgery Vanderbilt U., Nashville, 1998—2000; staff mem. Baptist Hosp., Nashville, Centennial Med. Ctr., Nashville; with Plastic Surgery Affiliates. Mem.: Am. Soc. Plastic Surgeons. Office: Plastic Surgery Affiliates 328 22nd Ave N Nashville TN 37203 Office Phone: 615-327-0303. Office Fax: 615-321-0242. E-mail: plasticsurgery@medscape.com.

HUENING, WALTER CARL, JR., retired consulting application engineer; b. Boston, Feb. 10, 1923; s. Walter Carl and Gladys (Whittemore) H.; m. Margaret Laurence McGeary, Aug. 5, 1944 (dec. 1986); children: Peter Carl, Susan Laurence Huening Locke; m. Elizabeth Ann Young Wright, Apr. 9, 1988. BSEE magna cum laude, Tufts U., 1944. Registered profl. engr., N.Y., Ohio. Instr. elec. engring. Tufts U., Medford, Mass., 1946-48; distbn. engr. plant engring. dept. GE, Lynn, Mass., 1948-50, application engr. indsl. power engring. Schenectady, NY, 1952-56, product planner protective devices dept. Plainville, Conn., 1956-58, design engr. vacuum cleaner dept. Cleve., 1958-59, application engr. comml. and mcpl. dept. Schenectady, 1960-62, application engr. steel mill, 1962-68, cons. application engr. indsl. power engring., 1968-89; ret., 1989. Mem. U.S. nat. com. Internat. Electrotech. Commn., tech. advisor on Tech. Com. 73 matters, 1972-89. Contbr. tech. papers to jours. and chpts. to books; patentee vacuum cleaner latch. Lt. comdr. USNR, 1944-46, 50-52, ret. Fellow IEEE (life, R. H. Kaufmann award 1988, Indsl. and Comml. Power Systems Dept. Achievement award 1989, prizes for papers 1970, 82); mem. Tau Beta Pi. Independent. Avocations: photography, collecting recorded traditional jazz music. Address: 1229 Godfrey Ln Niskayuna NY 12309-1241 Personal E-mail: whueningjr@aol.com.

HUERTA, DOLORES FERNANDEZ, labor union administrator; b. Dawson, N. Mex., Apr. 10, 1930; d. Juan and Alicia Fernandez; children: Celeste, Lori, Fidel, Emilio, Vincent, Alicia, Angela, Juanita, Maria, Elena, Ricky, Camilla. D. in Edn., U. of Pacific's Delta Community Coll.; PhD (hon.), New Coll. San Francisco, 1990, San Francisco State U., 1993, State U. of NY at New Paltz, 1999. Co-founder, first v.p. United Farm Workers of Am., Keene, Calif., 1962—. Co-founder, first v.p., bd. mem. Fund for the Feminist Majority. Recipient Martin Luther King award NAACP, Roger Baldwin award ACLU, 1993, Labor award Eugene V. Debs Found., 1993, Trumpeters award Consumers Union, Women First award YWCA, 1993, Ellis Island Medal of Freedom award; inductee Nat. Women's Hall of Fame, 1993; named one of three Women of the Year, Ms. Mag., 1998, 100 Most Important Women 20th Century, Ladies Home Journal. Office: PO Box 9189 Bakersfield CA 93389-9189

HUESTON, HARRY RAYMOND, II, criminal justice educator, researcher; b. Pitts., Aug. 8, 1949; s. Harry Raymond and Nancy Jane Hueston; m. Maryann M. Malone, Sept. 4, 1971; children: Kristina Marie

Pelican, Colleen Elizabeth Laszakovits. BS in Edn., Kent State U., Ohio, 1971; MA, Ohio State U., Columbus, 1975; PhD, U. Ariz., Tucson, 1997. Cert. police officer Ariz. Peace Officer Cert. and Tng. Bd., 1985, Ohio Peace Officer Tng. Coun., 1971, situational leadership trainer Calif. Am. U., 1983, mil. police sch. US Army, 1972. Criminal agt. iii Ohio State U. Police, Columbus, 1971—78; dir. pub. safety Loyola Marymount U., LA, 1978—85; asst. chief police U. Ariz. Police, Tucson, 1985, chief police, 1997—2000; asst. prof. criminal justice West Tex. A&M U., Canyon, 2000—06, assoc. prof. criminal justice, 2006—. Cons. HMH Tng. and Cons., Canyon, Tex., 2000—. Tchr. First Bapt. Ch., Canyon, 2003. Capt. US Army, 1971—78, Ft. Gordon, Ga. Recipient Outstanding Prof. award, West Tex. A&M U. Mortar Bd., 2005—06. Home: 3308 Mable Dr Canyon TX 79015 Office: West Texas A&M Univ PO Box 60807 Canyon TX 79016 Home Phone: 806-655-7756; Office Phone: 806-651-2421. Office Fax: 806-651-2601; Home Fax: 806-651-2601. Business E-Mail: hhueston@mail.wtamu.edu.

HUESTON, JOHN CHARLES, lawyer; b. Queens, NY, 1964; m. Mabelle Drake; children: Tara, Ryan, Kinsale, Shea. BA magna cum laude, Dartmouth Coll., 1986; JD, Yale Law Sch., 1991. Law clk. to Hon. Frank M. Johnson US Ct. Appeals (11th cir.), Montgomery, Ala., 1991—92; pvt. practice O'Melveny & Myers, LLP, 1992—2004; asst. US atty. (ctrl. dist. Calif.) US Dept. Justice, LA, 2004—06, chief Orange County divsn.; ptnr. Irell & Manella, LLP, 2006—. Atty. Enron Task Force, 2004—; adj. prof. Chapman U. Sch. Law. Notes editor: Yale Law Jour. Named a Calif. Atty. of Yr., Calif. Lawyer mag., 2007; named one of Top 20 Under 40, LA Daily Jour., Calif.'s Top 100 Leading Lawyers, Daily Jour., 25 People Who Shaped the Face of Bus. in 2006, Fortune mag., Fab 50 Young Litigators, Am. Lawyer, 2007. Office: Irell & Manella LLP 840 Newport Ctr Dr Ste 400 Newport Beach CA 92660-6324 Office Phone: 949-760-5152. E-mail: john.hueston@usdoj.com, jhueston@irell.com.*

HUESTON, TRAVIS EARL, protective services official; b. Marion, Ind., Oct. 12, 1980; s. Wilma A. Hueston-Ybarra. Telecom. operator Ind. State Police, Indpls., 2003—06; sgt. rsch. divsn. Sweetser Police Dept., Sweetser, Ind., 2003—. Mem.: Fraternal Order Police (assoc.), Phi Theta Kappa (assoc.). Office: Sweetser Police Department 113 North Main St Sweetser IN 46987 Home Phone: 765-667-3353; Office Phone: 765-384-7222. Office Fax: 765-384-5664. E-mail: sergeanthueston@sweetserpolicedepartment.com.

HUET, RAUL, psychiatrist; b. Mexico City, Jan. 25, 1953; arrived in US, 1954; s. Raul Huet Sobrado and Yolanda Juan Franco de Huet. MD, Kans. U. Sch. Medicine, 1982. Cert. diplomate Psychiatry Am. Bd. Psychiatry and Neurology. Rschr. asst. Kans. U. Sch. Medicine, Dept. Physiology, Kans. City, 1985—87; psychiatrist Labette Ctr. for Mental Health Svcs., Inc., Parsons, Kans., 1997—2004, Wyandot Ctr. for Cmty. Behavioral Healthcare, Inc., Kans. City, 2004—. Psychiatric cons. Labette County Med. Ctr., Parsons, Kans., 2002—04, Providence Med. Ctr., Kansas City, Kans., 2004—; clin. asst. prof. psychiatry Kans. U. Sch. Medicine, Dept. Psychiatry, 2005—. Author: Ischemic Colitis - Digestive Diseases, 1987. Fellow: Am Psychiat. Assn., Kans. Psychiat. Soc.; mem.: AMA, Med. Soc. Johnson and Wyandotte Counties, Kans. Med. Soc., Hispanic C. of C. Republican. Roman Catholic. Avocations: tennis, movie videos and DVDs, spy novels. Office: Wyandot Ctr for Cmty Behavioral Healthcare Inc 7840 Wash Ave Kansas City KS 66112 Home: 9536 Horton Overland Park KS 66207 Office Phone: 913-328-4600. Office Fax: 913-328-4604. Personal E-mail: rahuet@sbcglobal.net.

HUETE, LALA, costume designer; Costume designer: (films) Sal gorda, 1984; De tripas corazon, 1985; Amo tu cama rica, 1992; Belle epoque, 1992; Los Peores anos de nuestra vida, 1994; Oh, cielos, 1995; Two Much, 1995; Mi nombre es sombra, 1996; The Good Life, 1996; In Praise of Older Women, 1997; Lucky Star, 1997; Backroads, 1997; Torrente, the Stupid Arm of the Law, 1998; Talk of Angels, 1998; The Girl of Your Dreams, 1998 (Goya award Best Costume Design, 1999); Dying of Laughter, 1999; Saint Bernard, 2000; The Goalkeeper, 2000; Masterpiece, 2000; Torrente 2: Mission in Marbella, 2001; The Shanghai Spell, 2002 (Goya award Best Costume Design, 2003); Soldiers of Salamina, 2003; Di que si, 2004; Pan's Labyrinth, 2006 (BAFTA award Best Costume Design, 2007); Vete de mi, 2006.*

HUETER, ROBERT EDWARD, marine biologist, researcher; b. Balt., Apr. 13, 1952; s. Edward Milton Jr. and Patricia (Cole) H.; m. Aileen Henry, Aug. 11, 1990; stepchildren: Parker Skip, Ryan Richard. BS in Biology, U. Miami, 1974; MS in Marine Biology, U. Miami, Rosenstiel Sch. Marine & Atmospheric Sci., 1980; PhD in Zoology, U. Fla., 1988. Rsch. technician Chesapeake Biol. Lab., Solomons, Md., 1972, Va. Inst. Marine Sci., Gloucester Point, 1973-74; editorial researcher Internat. Oceanographic Found., Miami, Fla., 1977-79; grad. asst. mgr. Fla. State Mus., U. Fla., Gainesville, 1980-81, grad. teaching asst., 1982-83, 86-87, grad. rsch. asst. St. Augustine, 1984-85; postdoctoral scientist Mote Marine Lab., Sarasota, Fla., 1988-89, staff scientist, mgr. shark biology program, 1990—94, dir., Ctr. for Shark Rsch., 1992—, sr. scientist, 1994—, Perry W. Gilbert Chair in Shark Rsch., 2001—. Judge sci. fairs Fla. pub. schs., 1988—. Editor symposium vol. Vision in Elasmobranchs, Jour. Exptl. Zoology, 1990; tech. editor issue Sharks, Underwater Naturalist, 1990; contbr. articles to sci. jours. AAAS fellow, 1981; rsch. grantee NSF, 1988-89, Sport Fishing Inst., 1989, Fla. Dept. Natural Resources, 1990. Mem. Am. Elasmobranch Soc. (conservation com. 1990—), Am. Soc. Ichthyologists and Herpetologists, Soc. for Neurosci., Assn. for Rsch. in Vision and Ophthalmology. Avocations: sailing, running, tennis. Office: Mote Marine Lab 1600 Ken Thompson Pkwy Sarasota FL 34236 Office Phone: 813-388-1827. Office Fax: 941-388-4312. Business E-Mail: rhueter@mote.org.*

HUEY, CONSTANCE ANNE BERNER, mental health counselor; b. Tacoma, Wash., Jan. 20, 1938; d. Julian Boyd Berner and Beatta Kathryn (Day-Berner) Schoel; m. Donn R. Huey, July 26, 1961 (dec. June 1990); 1 child, Jennifer Anne. BA, U. Wash., 1959, MEd, 1976; cert. alcohol studies, Seattle U., 1980. Cert., lic. mental health counselor, Wash. H.S. speech and Eng. tchr., Seattle, 1959—68; tchr., supr., adminstr. U. Wash., 1968—82; instr. in addiction studies program Seattle U., 1980—86; pvt. practice, 1980—. Cons. in field; guest speaker Bastyr U.; presenter and trainer in workshops and seminars; specialist in only children. Contbg. author: We Did the Best We Could, 1993; guest on radio talk shows. Mem. Am. Counseling Assn., Seattle Counseling Assn., Women's Mental Health Assn., Nat. Assn. Alcoholism and Drug Abuse Counselors, Washington Assn. Alcoholism and Drug Abuse Counselors. Avocations: gardening, walking, reading, travel, photography. E-mail: cbhuey59@msn.com.

HUEY, JOHN WESLEY, JR., editor; b. Atlanta, Apr. 18, 1948; s. John Wesley and Helen (Cahill) Huey; m. Kathryn White (div. 1981); 1 child, John Wesley IV; m. Sue Yeargan (dec. 1986); m. Kate Ellis, 1993; 1 child, Cole. BA in English, U. Ga., 1970. Reporter DeKalb New Era, Decatur, Ga., 1972-74, Atlanta Constn., 1974-75, Wall St. Jour., Dallas, 1975-79, bur. chief Atlanta, 1979-82, mng. editor Brussels, 1982-83, editor, 1983-84, sr. spl. corr. Atlanta, 1984-86; Atlanta bur. chief, 1986—88; contbg. editor Fortune mag., 1988; editor Southpoint mag., Atlanta, 1989—90; sr. editor Fortune mag., 1990—95; mng. editor Fortune, 1995—2001; editorial dir. Time Inc., 2001—06, editor-in-chief, 2006—. Mem. adv. bd. Grady Coll., U. Ga. Served to lt. (j.g.) USN, 1970-72. Recipient Editor of the Yr., Ad Age mag., 1997. Mem.: ASME, Coun. on Fgn. Rels. Methodist. Office: Time Inc 1271 Avenue Of The Americas New York NY 10020-1300 E-mail: Laura_Whitaker@timeinc.com.*

HUEY, PEGGY J., communications educator, performing company executive; b. Lockbourne AFB, Ohio, Nov. 24, 1951; d. David Jonathon and Ann Eyman Knowlton. BA in Speech Comm./Theater, Miami U., Oxford, Ohio, 1973; AAS in Avionics Sys. Tech. and Aircrew Ops., C.C Air Force, Charleston, SC, 1978; MA in English Edn., U. South Fla., Tampa, 1987, PhD in English Lit. and Drama, 1996, post doctoral in Speech Comm., 2004—05. E-4 USAF, 1974—78; airborne comm. tech. USAF Res., Charleston AFB, SC, 1978—81, aircraft load master, 1981—92, 1st sgt., 1994—2002; tchg. asst dept. English U. South Fla., Tampa, 1989—94; instr. dept. English U. Ala., Tuscaloosa, 1994—96; instr. and facilitator Command First Sgt.'s Acad. USAF Res., Warner-Robbins AFB, Ga., 1996—2000, Non-Commissioned Officer Leadership Devel. Program USAF Res., 1996—2002; lang. trainer Cendant Mobility, Chgo., 2004—05; adj. prof. speech U. Tampa, 1998—2001, asst. prof. speech, 2002—06, vis. asst. prof. English and global issues, 2006—; instr. English and speech DeVry U., Tampa, 2007—. Program coord. Am. Heart Assn., Tampa, Fla., 1979—82, asst. exec. dir., 1982—85; mng. dir. Arts Fusion, 1985, Stageworks, 1996—; adj. instr. Hillsborough C.C., 1988—89, 2000—02; advisor English majors U. Ala., Tuscaloosa, 1994—96, trainer grad. tchg. assts. Norton Textra Connect, 1995, list mgr. and group leader Connect discussion group, 1995—96; instr. Am. Lang. Acad. U. Tampa, Fla., 2000; academic adv. com. U. Tampa, 2002—06, chair academic adv. com., 2003—06; presenter to profl. confs.; book reviewer in fields of medieval and Renaissance English lit. Contbr. chapters to books, articles to profl. jours. Mem. chmn. Grad. Student Union U. South Fla., Tampa, 1991—92. Named Joyce D. Keller Faculty/Staff Vol. of Yr., U. Tampa, 2006, commencement spkr., C.C. Air Force, Charleston AFB, 1997. Mem.: MLA, So. States Comm. Assn., Assn. Theatre in Higher Edn., South Atlantic Modern Lang. Assn. (treas. women's caucus 1998—2005), Southeastern Renaissance Conf., Internat. Spenser Soc., Marlowe Soc. Am. Achievements include member of first all female crew USAF. Avocations: gardening, reading, jigsaw puzzles. Office: U Tampa 401 W Kennedy Blvd Tampa FL 33606-1490 Home: 1404 E Sligh Ave Tampa FL 33604

HUEY, RAYMOND B., zoologist, educator; Student, Deep Springs Coll., 1961—64; AB with honors, Univ. Calif., Berkeley, 1966; MA in Zoology, Univ. Tex., 1969; PhD in Biology, Harvard Univ., 1975. Miller rsch. fellow Univ. Calif., Berkeley, 1975—77; asst. prof., zoology Univ. Wash., Seattle, 1977—80, assoc. prof., 1980—84, prof., 1984—. Recipient President's award, Am. Soc. Naturalists, 2004; grantee Guggenheim Fellowship, 1988—89. Fellow: Am. Acad. Arts & Scis. Office: Dept Biology Univ Wash Box 351800 Seattle WA 98195-1800 Office Phone: 206-543-1505. Business E-Mail: hueyrb@u.washington.edu.

HUEY, WARD L(IGON), JR., retired media executive; b. Dallas, Apr. 26, 1938; s. Ward Ligon and Irene Helen (Freeman) H.; m. Marian Kennedy Powell, Oct. 28, 1961; children: Ward L. III, David Powell. BA, So. Meth. U., 1960. Successively with dept. prodn., sales svc. mgr. local sales, regional sales mgr., gen. sales mgr. Sta. WFAA-TV, Dallas, 1960-67, sta. mgr., 1972-75; v.p., gen. mgr. Belo Broadcasting Corp., Dallas, from 1975; vice chmn. bd. dirs., pres. broadcast div. A. H. Belo Corp., Dallas, 1987—2001. Chmn. affiliate bd. govs. ABC-TV, 1981-82; chmn. bd. TV Operators Caucus, 1989. Mem. exec. com. So. Meth. U. Meadows Sch. Arts, 1986—, Goodwill Industries Dallas, 1978-79, State Fair Tex., 1992—; bd. dirs. Children's Med. Found. Tex., Dallas, 1985-94, Dallas Found., 1993—; trustee So. Meth. U., 1996—. Named Disting. Alumni, Highland Park H.S., 1998, Pioneer of Yr., Tex. Broadcasters, 2000; named to, Broadcasting and Cable Hall of Fame, 1999, Nat. TV Acad. Mgmt. Hall of Fame, 2004; recipient Disting. Alumni award, So. Meth. U., 2000. Mem. Maximum Svc. TV Assn. (vice chmn. 1988-94), TV Bur. Advt. (past bd. dirs., exec. com. 1984-88), Assn. Broadcast Execs. Tex. (bd. dirs. 1977-78), Dallas Advt. League (bd. dirs. 1975-76), Salesmanship Club Dallas (pres. 1992-93), Dallas Country Club. Methodist. Avocations: skiing, boating, swimming, golf, music.

HUFANDA, JOSEPH, dentist; DDS, U. Mich. Resident Upper Peninsula Rural Health Svcs.; co-founder Ballantyne Ctr. for Dentistry, Charlotte, NC. Mem.: Am. Acad. Cosmetic Dentistry, Charlotte Dental Soc., NC Dental Soc., Am. Dental Assn. Office: Ballantyne Ctr for Dentistry Ste K 15105 John J Delaney Dr Charlotte NC 28277 Office Phone: 704-540-2255. E-mail: drjoe@ballantynedentistry.com.

HUFBAUER, GARY CLYDE, economist, lawyer, educator; b. San Diego, Apr. 3, 1939; s. Clarence Clyde and Arabelle Maxwell (McKee) H.; children: Randall Clyde Revelle (dec.), Ellen Arabelle Scripps, Romain Clyde; m. Valerie Parra, 1996. AB, Harvard U., 1960; PhD, King's Coll., Cambridge U., Eng., 1963; JD, Georgetown U., 1980. Bar: D.C. 1980, Md. 1980. Mem. faculty dept. econs. U. N.Mex., Albuquerque, 1963-74, prof., 1970-74; dir. internat. tax staff U.S. Dept. Treasury, Washington, 1974-77; dep. asst. Sec. Treasury, Internat. Trade and Investment Policy, 1977-80; mem. firm Rose, Schmidt, Chapman, Duff & Hasley, Washington, 1980-85; dep. dir. Internat. Law Inst., Georgetown Law Ctr., Washington, 1980-82; Wallenberg prof. fin. Georgetown U., Washington, 1985-92; dir. studies Coun. on Fgn. Rels., NYC, 1997-98; sr. fellow Inst. Internat. Econs., Washington, 1982-85, 92-97, 98—. Mem. Harvard Devel. Adv. Svc., Pakistan, 1967-69; vis. prof. Stockholm Sch. Econs., 1974, Cambridge U., 1973, Georgetown U., 1975. Author: Economic Sanctions Reconsidered, 1990, World Capital Markets, 2001. Ford Found. fellow, 1966-67; Fulbright rsch. scholar, 1973 Mem. Am. Econ. Assn., Nat. Economists Club. Episcopalian. Office: Inst for Internat Econs 1750 Massachusetts Ave NW Washington DC 20036-1903 Office Phone: 202-328-9000.

HUFF, ALVIN EDWARD, retired engineer; b. Grand Rapids, Mich., Feb. 10, 1936; s. Lynn P. and Alberta (Quackenbush) Huff; m. Joyce Ann Malles Hawkins, June 24, 1995; children: Patricia Lynne Schantz, Robert Allen, Andrew Edward. A in Engring. Sci., Grand Rapids Jr. Coll., 1959; BSME, U Mich., Ann Arbor, 1962; off-site studies in plasma engring., MIT, NYC, 1964; off-site studies mass transportation phen., Oakland U., Rochester, Mich., 1969. Registered profl. engr., Md., 1967, cert. improved quality stats., Ford Seminar, Mich., 1990. Propulsion engr. Hercules Powder Co., Cumberland, Md., 1962—66; hydraulics engr. Westinghouse Air Arm, Balt., 1966—67; prin. engr. LTV Aerospace, Warren, Mich., 1967—71; engring. supr. powertrain engring. Ford Motor Co., Dearborn, Mich., 1971—97. Spl. US Army, 1955—57, Japan. Recipient Continuous Improvement Recognition Sys. Cert., Ford, 1995, Cert. Recognition for producing 1st revenue generating powertrain idea, 1996. Mem.: Detroit Engring. Soc., Nat. Soc. Profl. Engrs. Independent. Protestant. Achievements include patents for vortex injection sprayer; driver monitor system; invention of combustion additive injection sprayer; refurbishment mark 48 torpedo testing; low cost real world testing using field, commercial fleets, testing for sign-off for Ford Motor Company; parallel flow rocket nozzle used for testing boundary layer and rocket motor afterburing studies as relates to RF radar interference. Avocation: history. Home: 1076Yorick Path Wixom MI 48393

HUFF, ANN LINNEA, music educator; b. Streator, Ill., Apr. 11, 1958; d. Donald Carl Johnson and Donna Mae Lahman-Johnson; m. Daniel Maurice Huff, July 21, 1979; 1 child, Caroline Britta. B Music Edn., Ill. Wesleyan U., 1980. Choral dir. Edgewood H.S., Madison, Wis., 1988—89, Cummings H.S., Burlington, NC, 1993—94, Chapel Hill (NC) H.S., 1994—2001, Enloe H.S., Raleigh, NC, 2001—; adj. music faculty mem. U. NC, Chapel Hill, 1989—93. Clinician various camps, clinics, workshops, chs., NC. Vol. chronic illness group St. Paul's Luth. Ch., Durham, NC, 2004—. Mem.: Music Educators Nat. Conf., NC Music Educators Assn. (adjudicator, chmn. exec. bd.). Avocations: photography, hiking, nature, camping. Home: 114 Rother Ln Durham NC 27707 Office: Enloe HS 128 Clarendon Crescent Raleigh NC 27610 Office Phone: 919-856-7918.

HUFF, C(LARENCE) RONALD, sociologist, criminologist, educator; b. Covington, Ky., Nov. 10, 1945; s. Nathaniel Warren G. and Irene Opal (Mills) H.; m. Patricia Ann Plankenhorn, June 15, 1968; children: Tamara Lynn, Tiffany Dawn. BA, Capital U., 1968; MSW, U. Mich., 1970; PhD, Ohio State U., 1974. Social worker Franklin County Children's Svcs., Columbus, Ohio, 1968; social work intern Pontiac (Mich.) State Hosp. and Family Svc. Met. Detroit, 1969-70; dir. psychiat. social work Lima (Ohio) State Hosp., 1970-71; chief psychiat. social worker N.W. Cmty. Mental Health Ctr., Lima, 1971-72; grad. tchg. assoc. sociology Ohio State U., 1972-74; asst. prof. social ecology U. Calif., Irvine, 1974-76; asst. prof. sociology Purdue U., 1976-79; assoc. prof. pub. policy/mgmt. Ohio State U., Columbus, 1979-87, dir. Criminal Justice Rsch. Ctr., 1979-99, prof., 1987-99, prof. emeritus, 1999—, dir. Sch. Pub. Policy and Mgmt., 1994-99; dean Sch. Social Ecology U. Calif., Irvine, 1999—, prof. criminology, law and society, 1999—, prof. sociology, 2004—. Vis. prof. U. Hawaii, 1995; cons. Bur. Justice Stats., Nat. Inst. Justice, Nat. Inst. Corrections, Nat. Inst. Juvenile Justice and Delinquency Prevention, U.S. Senate Jud. Com., NSF, FBI, others; expert witness fed. and state cts. Author: Youth Violence: Prevention, Intervention, and Social Policy, 1999, Convicted But Innocent: Wrongful Conviction and Public Policy, 1996, (Outstanding Acad. Book award Choice Mag., 1996), The Gang Intervention Handbook, 1993, Gangs in America, 1990, 2d edit., 1996, 3rd edit., 2002, House Arrest and Correctional Policy: Doing Time at Home, 1988, The Mad, The Bad, and The Different: Essays in Honor of Simon Dinitz, 1981, Attorneys as Activists: Evaluating the American Bar Association's BASICS Program, 1979, Contemporary Corrections: Social Control and Conflict, 1977, Planning Correctional Reform, 1975, and others; mem. editl. bd. various jours.; contbr. articles to profl. jours., chpts. to books. Recipient Nat. Security award Mershon Found., 1980, prize New Eng. Sch. Law, 1981, Outstanding Tchg. award, 1985, Donald R. Cressey award Nat. Coun. on Crime and Delinquency, 1992, Paul Tappan award Western Soc. Criminology, 1993, Herbert Bloch award Am. Soc. Criminology, 1994; grantee ABA, 1974-77, Purdue U., 1978, U.S. Dept. Justice, 1978-79, 85-88, 91-95, Ohio Dept. Mental Health, 1982-83, 84-85, 85-87, Gov.'s Office Criminal Justice, 1985-88, 92-95, 98, Ohio Dept. Youth Svcs., 1989-90, Ohio State U./Ohio Bd. Regents, 1990-92. Fellow Western Soc. Criminology, Am. Soc. Criminology (exec. bd., pres.-elect 1999-2000, pres. 2000-01, Herbert Bloch award 1994); mem. Acad. Criminal Justice Scis., Nat. Coun. on Crime and Delinquency, Phi Kappa Phi, Phi Beta Delta. Office: U Calif Irvine Sch Social Ecology 300 Social Ecology I Irvine CA 92697-7050 Office Phone: 949-824-6094. Business E-Mail: rhuff@uci.edu.

HUFF, DANIEL M., music educator; b. Fairfield, Iowa, June 6, 1951; s. R. Maurice and M. Reva Huff; m. Ann L. Johnson. MusB in Edn., Ill. Wesleyan U., Bloomington, 1973; MusM, U. Wis., Madison, 1978, PhD, 1989. Tchr. music Mid-County Sch. Dist., Lacon, Ill., 1973—82; tchr. choral music Metamora HS, Ill., 1982—85; area head music edn. U. NC, Chapel Hill, 1989—. Recipient Student Undergraduate Tchg. award, U. NC Student Assn., 1999. Mem.: Am. Choral Dirs. Assn. (chmn. showchoir NC chpt. 2000—01, chmn. male choruses NC chpt. 2004—05), Music Educators Nat. Conf. Home: 114 Rother Ln Durham NC 27707 Office: Music Dept CB 3320 Hill Hall Univ North Carolina Chapel Hill NC 27599-3320 Home Phone: 919-493-4877; Office Phone: 919-962-4219. Office Fax: 919-962-3376. Business E-Mail: dhuff@email.unc.edu.

HUFF, DANN, musician, producer, singer; b. Nov. 1960; s. Ronn Huff. Co-founder, christian music band Whiteheart; co-founder, heavy metal rock band Giant. Musician (Giant) Last of the Runaways, 1989, Time to Burn, 1991; prodr.: (TV soundtrack) Jesus: The Epic Mini-Series, 2000, Desperate Housewives, 2005, (movie soundtrack) Where the Heart Is, 2000, Lilo & Stitch, 2002, Cars, 2006, Legally Blonde 2, 2003; prodr., writer, musician for artists such as Barbara Streisand, Kenney Loggins, Reba McEntire, Celine Dion, DC Talk, Shania Twain, Michael Bolton, Luther Vandross, Donna Summer, Rod Stewart, LeAnn Rimes, Kenny Chesney, Lonestar, Faith Hill, Jewel, Keith Urban, Amy Grant, Megadeth, Martina McBride, Trace Adkins, Michale McDonald, Rascal Flatts, Carrie Underwood, and many others. Recipient Musician of Yr. award for Guitar, Country Music Assn., 2004, Prodr. of Yr. award, Acad. Country Music, 2007. Office: c/o CC Entertainment PO Box 7809 Dallas TX 75209*

HUFF, DANNY W., paper products executive; b. Feb. 1, 1951; BBA, Georgia State U., 1973. CPA. Various auditing positions KMG Peat Marwick, 1793—1979; asst. to group contrs. budgets and planning to dir. corp. reporting and asst. to corp. contr. Georgia-Pacific Corp., 1979—82, dir. project analysis, 1982—84, dir. corp. finance, 1984—92, assistant treasurer, 1992—93, treasurer, 1993—96, v.p., treas., 1996—99, exec. v.p. fin., CFO, 1999—2005. Bd. dir. Lyondell Chem. Co. Former trustee Atlanta Bot. Garden; trustee Georgia State U. Named one of Best CFOs, Instl. Investor mag., 2005. Mem.: Fin. Exec. Inst., AICPA. Mailing: Lyondell Chemical Bd Directors PO Box 3646 Houston TX 77253-3646

HUFF, DENNIS LYLE, marketing professional; b. Chgo., Oct. 8, 1955; s. Barry Sanders Huff and Janada Jean (Patterson) Montgomery; 1 child, Alicia Jean; m. LouAnn Fae Gorder, Nov. 8, 1992. AS in Marine Tech., Coll. Oceaneering, 1984. Diver instr. Comml. Dive Ctr., Long Beach, Calif., 1984-87; owner Flight Shop, California City, 1987-90, Houston Export Co., 1990-92; exec. v.p. AMS, Inc., Oklahoma City, 1992-98; prin., owner Synergy Internat., Las Vegas, 1995—. With USMC, 1975-81. Avocations: skydiving, deep sea diving, camping, poetry, archaeology. Office: Synergy Internat 8687 W Sahara Ave Ste 100 Las Vegas NV 89117-5868 Home: 125 E Main St #117 American Fork UT 84003-2407

HUFF, HARRIET, artist, educator; b. Tulsa, Dec. 24, 1949; d. Roy Robert and Barbara L. Huff; m. Addison A. Gooding, Sept. 30, 1982 (div. Dec. 16, 2005); 1 child, Vanessa Ann Gooding. BFA, Calif. Coll. Arts & Crafts, Oakland, 1972; MFA, Belford U., Humble, Texas, 1998; postgrad., Pratt Art Inst., 2005, Parsons Sch. Design, 2006. Profl. fine art master printmaker/artist Harriet Huff Fine Arts, Pukalani, Hawaii, 1972—; art instr. Philbrook Art Mus., Tulsa, 1972—73; owner-art gallery De La Grabadora, Santa Fe, 1973—75; art instr. Colo. Mountain Coll., Steamboat Springs, 1978—81; owner- art gallery The Intaglio, Steamboat Springs, 1978—82; art instr. Houston Watercolor Soc., 1988—89; art instr./continuing edn. Eanes Sch. Dist., Austin, Tex., 1994—98; art instr./interdisciplinary art chair Seabury Hall Secondary Sch., Makawao, Hawaii, 2000—. Bd. dirs., gallery dir. Houston Watercolor Soc., 1988—90; pvt. art workshops A Rm. with a View Art Gallery, Pukalani, Hawaii, 1987—; printmaking studio tech. Hui No'eau Visual Art Ctr., Makawao, Hawaii, 1998—; workshop presenter Hawaii Assn. Mid. Schs., Maui Ind. Sch. Tchrs., Maui, Hawaii, 2001—. Exhibitions include Okla. Ann./Philbrook Mus., Tulsa (hon. mention, 1975), one-woman shows include ColorKing, Upper Gallery, Wichita, exhibitions include Colo. Women Artist Invitational, Crested Butte, Northwest Colo. Artists, Steamboat Springs (winter show, 1st & 2nd Pl./ summer show, 1st Pl. graphics, 1980), Delta Prints, Drawing and Crafts, Ark. Art Ctr., Little Rock, Knickerbocker, NY, one-woman shows include 20 year retrospect, Steamboat Depot, Colo., exhibitions include Internat. Art Expo, Coliseum, NYC, Le Centre Internat. d'art contemporian, Paris, Four Clover Invitational, Houston, Northwest Colo., Steamboat (2d Pl. profl., 1986), AAUW, Auburn, Calif. (purchase prize, 1971), exhibited in group shows at 15year Profl. Retrospect, Williams Ctr., Tulsa, exhibitions include Houston Watercolor Art Soc. Ann., Women Caucus for Arts Membership, Houston, one-woman shows include Steamboat Strings, Colo., exhibitions include Urantia Internat. Conf., Snow, Mass., 1990, Flagstaff, Ariz., 1997, Estes Park, Colo., 2002, one-woman shows include Holy Land Series, Westlake Meth., Austin, exhibitions include Hui No'eau Visual Art Ctr., Maui, Maui CC, U. Hawaii Cmty. Traveling Show (Windward Artist Merit Choice for ceramics), Iowa Biennial Print, U. Iowa, Nat. Print and Drawing, Oklahoma City Art Ctr., Pratt, Venice, NY, Calif. Coll. Artist South Am. Traveling Exhibit, Catherine Lorillard Wolfe, NY (2d Pl., 1974, Bronze medal 1974, Ida Becker Award, 1979), AAUW, Evanston, Ill. (Hon. Mention, 1976), Crested Butte Arts and Crafts (Hon. Mention 1977/Best of Show 1978), exhibited in group shows at Field Contemporary, Santa Fe, exhibitions include 1st Telleride Blue Grass Music Festival, Colo. Co-chair bldg. fund Westlake Meth. Ch., Austin, 1997; bd. mem., gallery dir. Houston Watercolor Soc., 1988—89. Mem.: Catherine Lorillard Wolfe Art Club (assoc.), Hui No'eau Visual Art Ctr. (assoc.), Hawaii Watercolor Soc. (assoc.). Achievements include work selected for permanent collection, Philbrook Art Museum, 2003. Office: Seabury Hall School 480 Olinda Road Makawao HI 96768 Home Phone: 808-573-0011; Office Phone: 808-572-7235. Office Fax: 808-572-7196. Personal E-mail: harriethuff@yahoo.com. E-mail: hhuff@seaburyhall.org.

HUFF, MELINDA LOUISE, art educator; m. Dennis E. Huff, June 28, 1996;; children: Miranda Lindsey Munson, Derek Thomas Munson. B in Art Edn., Northeastern State U., Tahlequah, Okla., 1970—74. Cert. Tchr. Okla. Dept. Edn., 1974. Elem. art tchr. Peters Elem., Union Pub. Schs., Broken Arrow, 1992—. Grantee, Northeastern State U., Broken Arrow, 2003; scholar, Northeastern State U., 1970. Mem.: NEA, Okla. Edn. Assn., Kappa Delta Pi, Sigma Tau Delta, Rho Theta Sigma, Alpha Chi, Delta Zeta. Office: Peters Elem 2900 West College Broken Arrow OK 74012-2100 Home Phone: 918-254-1982; Office Phone: 918-357-6759.

HUFF, ROLLA P., Internet company executive; b. Sept. 26, 1956; BS in Mgmt., Purdue U. CPA. Multiple positions NCR Corp.; fin. v.p., merger & acquisitions AT&T Corp., 1994—95; sr. v.p., CFO AT&T Wireless Services, Inc., 1995—97, pres., ctrl. US region, 1997—98; exec. v.p., CFO Frontier Corp., 1998—99, pres., COO, 1999; chmn., CEO Mpower Comm. Corp., 1999—2006; pres., CEO Earthlink, Inc., 2007—. Bd. dirs. Earthlink, Inc., 2007—. Office: Earthlink Inc 1375 Peachtree St Atlanta GA 30309 Office Phone: 404-815-0770. Office Fax: 404-815-8805.*

HUFF, WILLIAM BRAID, retired publishing company executive; b. Lynn, Mass., Apr. 18, 1950; s. Harold Butler and Mary Stewart (Braid) Huff; m. Karen Murphy, May 4, 1985; children: Thomas Murphy, Kathryn Braid. BS, Bowdoin Coll., 1972; MBA, Darthmouth Coll., 1974. CPA Mass. Staff acct. Arthur Andersen, Boston, 1974—76; contr. Affiliated Broadcasting, Boston, 1976—82, treas., 1982—86, sr. v.p., 1984—86; contr. Affiliated Publs., Boston, 1982—86, v.p., 1986—89, CFO, 1989—91, exec. v.p., CFO, 1991—97; sr. v.p., CFO Boston Globe Newspaper Co., 1992—97, pres., CFO, 1997—2001. Bd. dirs. TPR Media. Bd. dirs. Morgan Meml. Goodwill; past pres. Wayland Pub. Sch. Found. Mem.: AICPAs, Mass. Soc. CPAs, Weston Golf Club (v.p.). Republican. Episcopalian. Avocations: skiing, soccer, golf. Home: 5 Sherman Bridge Rd Wayland MA 01778-1213 E-mail: wbraidhuff@yahoo.com.

HUFFINGTON, ANITA, sculptor; b. Balt., Dec. 25, 1934; d. Norris Jackson and Agnes (Hook) H.; m. Manuel Rubin Duque, Sept. 17, 1957 (div. Nov. 1964); 1 child, Lisa Huffington Duque; m. Henry Sutter, Dec. 4, 1964. BA, CCNY, 1973, MFA, 1975. Resident La Napoule Art Found., France, 1996. One-woman exhbns. include U. Ark., Fayetteville, 1982, Valley House Gallery, Dallas, 1986, Benton Gallery, Southampton, NY, 1989, Ark. Art Ctr., Little Rock, 1990, O'Hara Gallery, NYC, 1994, 96, 99, 2001, 04, 06, U. Ctrl. Ark., Conway, 1997, Triangle Gallery, San Francisco, 1998, Lisa Kurts Gallery, Memphis, 1999, 2003, 05, 07, Morris Mus., Augusta, Ga., 2004, 06, Walton Art Ctr., Fayetteville, Ar., 2004, Jonathon O'Hara Gallery, 2006; 2-person show Lisa Kurts Gallery, 1995; 3-person shows Louis Stern Gallery, West Hollywood, Calif., 1996, Triangle Gallery, San Francisco, 1996; group exhbn. include Internat. Women's Art Festival, NYC, 1976, U. Ark., Fayetteville, 1978, 92, Ark. Arts Ctr., Little Rock, 1979-81, Territorial Restoration Gallery, Little Rock, 1981, Harris Gallery, Houston, Tex., 1981-93, Sculptural Arts Mus., Atlanta, 1982, Benton Gallery, Southampton, NY, 1988, Kornbluth Gallery, Fair Lawn, NJ, 1989, The Art Show, 7th Regiment Armory, NYC, 1989-07, Art of the 20th Century 7th Regiment Armory, NYC, 2003-04, LA Art Show, Santa Monica, Calif., Ft. Smith Art Ctr., Ark., 1990, Salon de Mars, Paris, 1992, U. Pa., Phila. US Artists Art Fair, Pa. Acad., 1992-2002, 2003, ARTexas, Dallas, 1993-94, Art Fair Seattle, 1995-97, Art Miami, 1996, 98, Triangle Gallery, San Francisco, 1996, 99, 2000, Am. Acad. Arts and Letters, NYC, 1997, Columbus Mus., Ga., and Miss. Mus. Art, Jackson, 1997, Am. Acad. Arts and Letters, 1997, Two Sculptors, Inc., NYC, 1998, Valley House Gallery, Dallas, 1998, Art Palm Beach, 1998, 99, 2000, 01, Dallas Internat. Art and Antiques Fair, 2000-02, 50th Anniversary Show, Valley Ho. Gallery, Dallas, Hist. Ark. Mus., Little Rock, 2001, Art Santa Fe, 2005, 06, 07, The Art Show, Haverstraw, 2006, 07, Telfair Mus., Savannah, Ga., 2006; permanent collections include Met. Mus. Art, NYC, 2002, others; featured in various profl. publ., mag., newspapers, and videos. Recipient Jimmy Ernst award Am. Acad. Arts and Letters, 1997, Residency award La Lapoule Art Found., 1997, Individual Artist award Gov., Little Rock, Ark., 2005, others; Visual arts fellow Ark. Arts Coun.

HUFFINGTON, ARIANNA (ARIANNA STASSINOPOULOS), writer; b. Athens, Greece, July 15, 1950; came to U.S., 1980; d. Constantine Stassinopoulos and Helen Georgiadis; m. Michael Huffington, Apr. 12, 1986 (div. 1997); children: Christina, Isabella. MA in Econ., Cambridge U., Eng., 1971. Syndicated columnist Tribune Media Svcs., 1995—; co-founder Detroit Project. Bd. mem. A Place Called Home, LA, Archer Sch. for Girls; Independent party candidate for gov State of Calif., 2003. Author: The Female Woman, 1974, After Reason, 1978, Maria Callas: The Woman Behind the Legend, 1981, Picasso: Creator and Destroyer, 1988, The Gods of Greece, 1993, The Fourth Instinct, 1994, Greetings From the Lincoln Bedroom, 1998, How to Overthrow the Government, 2000, Pigs at the Trough: How Corporate Greed and Political Corruption are Undermining America, 2003, Fanatics and Fools: The Game Plan for Winning Back America, 2004, On Becoming Fearless:.in Love, Work, and Life, 2006; guest appearances on Larry King Live, Oprah, Nightline, Inside Politics, Charlie Rose, Crossfire, Hardball, Good Morning America, Today Show, McLaughlin Group, and the O'Reilly Factor, founder, editor Huffington Post, 2005— (Webby award and People's Voice award-Blog-Political, Internat. Acad. Digital Arts and Sciences, 2006), co-host (nationally syndicated pub. radio prog.) Left, Right & Center. Named one of 100 Most Influential People, Time Mag., 2006, 50 Who Matter Now, Business 2.0, 2007; recipient Rave award for Renegade, WIRED Mag., 2007. First place, Funniest Celebrity in Washington standup comedy contest. Office: Arianna Online 1158 26th St PO Box 428 Santa Monica CA 90403 Business E-Mail: arianna@huffingtonpost.com.*

HUFFINGTON, ROY MICHAEL, business executive, former ambassador; b. Tomball, Tex., Oct. 4, 1917; s. Roy Mackey and Bertha (Michel) H.; m. Phyllis Gough, Oct. 26, 1945 (dec. Nov. 9, 2003); children: R. Michael, Terry Huffington Dittman. BS, So. Meth. U., 1938; MA, Harvard U., 1941, PhD, 1942, grad. advanced mgmt. program, 1976; LHD, So. Meth. U., 1990. Tchg. fellow Harvard U., Cambridge, Mass., 1939-42, instr. geology, 1942; sr. geologist, divn. exploration geologist Humble Oil and Refining Co., Houston, 1946-56; pres. Roy M. Huffington, Inc., Houston, 1956-83, chmn. bd., 1956-90, chmn., pres., 1993—; U.S. amb. to Austria, Vienna, 1990-93. Bd. dirs. Huffco Group, Inc., Houston; bd. dirs. Am. Petroleum Inst., Washington, 1983-90, 93—; bd. dirs. Brookings Inst., Washington, 1984-88, mem. exec. com., 1993-2002, hon. life trustee, 1988-90, 93—; chmn. Salzburg Seminar, 1994—, bd. dirs., 1992-94. Contbr. articles to profl. jours. Bd. dirs. Tex. Med. Ctr., 1989-90, 93—, Houston Mus. Natural Sci., 1981-86, Kid Care, Inc., Houston, 1993-2003; trustee Huffington Found., 1987—, Baylor Coll. Medicine, 1986-90, 93-99, trustee emeritus, 1999—, chmn. devel. bd. Huffington Ctr. on Aging, 1999—; trustee Webster U., Vienna, 1992-2002, George Bush Libr. Found., Tex. A&M U., 1993—; bd. visitors M.D. Anderson Cancer Ctr., 1980-90, 93-99, sr. mem., 1999—; bd. visitors Sheltering Arms Found. for Elderly, 1994-97, Claremont Sch. Politics and Econs., Claremont Grad. U., 1995-2002; bd. govs. Mid. East Inst., 1982-88; devel. bd. U. Tex. Health Sci. Ctr., 1981-90, 93—, life mem., 1997—; dir. The Rothko Chapel, 1996-2002, Glenwood Cemetery, 2003—; mem. leadership com. James A. Baker III Inst. for Pub. Policy, Rice U., 1993—. Lt. comdr. USNR, 1942-45, USNR, 1942-54. Decorated Bronze Star with combat V, Grosse Goldene Ehrenzeichen (Austria), 1997; recipient Alumni Achievement award Harvard U. Bus. Sch., 1982, Oil Drop award petroleum divsn. ASME, 1985, Gold Medallion Oil Pioneer award Indonesian Govt., 1985, John Rogers award Southwestern Legal Found., 1987, Disting. Alumni award So. Meth. U., 1988, Internat. Businessman of Yr. award Houston World Trade Assn., 1988, Amb. of Yr. award Diplomatic Club, Vienna, 1992, Disting. Svc. award Permian Basin sect. Soc. Econ. Paleontologists and Mineralogists, 1996, Woodrow Wilson award for corp. citizenship Woodrow Wilson Internat. Ctr. for Scholars, 2001, Henry Lawrence Gantt medal ASME, 2001, Founding Father award, Pertamina, Jakarta, Indonesia, 2002, Cmty. Advocate award Ctr. on Aging, U. Tex. Health Sci. Ctr. at Houston, 2003, Gold medal for Disting. Achievement Am. Petroleum Inst., 2003, Internat. Citizen of Yr. award Houston World Affairs Council, 2004; named to Tex. Bus. Hall of Fame, 1992. Fellow AAAS (life), Geol. Soc. Am. (trustee 1988-90, hon. found. trustee 1991—); mem. Am. Assn. Petroleum Geologists (Michel T. Halbouty Human Needs award 1991, trustee assoc. found. 1980-90, 93—), Ind. Petroleum Assn. Am. (dir. 1979-80), U.S. Oil and Gas Assn., Tex. Ind. Prodrs. and Royalty Owners Assn., Tex. Oil and Gas Assn. (dir. 1972-84, Disting. Svc. award 1988), Houston Geol. Soc., Am. Inst. Profl. Geologists, 25-Yr. Club of the Petroleum Industry, Internat. Assn. for Energy Econs. Washington (pres.'s adv. coun. 1997—), All-Am. Wildcatters (chmn. 1986-87), Asia Soc. N.Y. (chmn. 1982-89, trustee 1978-82, hon. life trustee 1989-90, 93—), Am. Austrian Found. N.Y. (trustee 1993—), The U.S. Indonesia Soc. (Washington, dir. 1994—), Coun. on Fgn. Rels., World Econ. Forum, Coun. Am. Ambs., Interferon Found. (vice chmn., co-founder, 1979-90), U.S. Navy League, Nat. Petroleum Coun., SAR, Coronado Club (Houston), The Houston Club (bd. dirs. 1967-70, v.p. 1969-70), The Houston Country Club (mem. ho. com. 1979-81), Met. Club N.Y.C. (mem. govs. adv. bd. 1974-77), Met. Club of Washington, Petroleum Club of Houston (mem. food com. 1966-67, mem. fin. com. 1969-70, bd. dirs. 1978-80, 1st v.p. 1980-81), Alpha Tau Omega (bd. govs. Found. 1993—, Disting. Alumni award 1987). Republican. Presbyterian. Office: PO Box 4337 Houston TX 77210-4337

HUFFMAN, CADY (CATHERINE ELIZABETH), actress; b. Santa Barbara, Calif., Feb. 2, 1965; d. Clifford Roy and Lorayne Dolores (Rote) H.; m. William Healy, 1994. Pvt. studies with, Nathan Lam, LA, 1983-85, Maria Gobetti, 1984-85, Bill Reed, NYC, 1987-90, Fred Kareman, 1988. Actress Broadway plays La Cage Aux Folles, 1983-84, Big Deal, 1985, The Will Rogers Follies, 1991-93, Steel Pier, 1997, The Producers, 2001-03 (Tony award best actress in a musical, 2001, Drama Desk award outstanding featured actress in a musical, 2001); (off Broadway) Gemini, 1990, Italian American Reconciliation, 1990, As You Like It, 1989, The Baker's Wife, 1982, They're Playing Our Song, 1983, Jekyll and Hyde, 1989, Dame Edna: The Royal Tour, 1999-2000, Short Talks on the Universe, 2002, The Cartells, 2006, Plain & Fancy, 2006, Surface to Air, 2007; solo show Cady Huffman: Live at Ars Nova, 2006; TV shows The Guiding Light, 1986, Another World, 1987, Pig Sty, 1995, Mad About You, 1995, Law & Order: Criminal Intent, 2001, Curb Your Enthusiasm, 2004; films Hero, 1992, Space Marines, 1996, Sunday on the Rocks, 2004 (also prodr.), Billy's Dad is a Fudge-Packer, 2004, Romance & Cigarettes, 2005, Twenty Dollar Drinks, 2006; appeared in Law & Order: Criminal Intent, 2003, Law & Order: Trial by Jury, 2005, Frasier, 2004; also appeared in more than 30 TV commls., 1985-90. Vol. recreational therapist The Lighthouse, N.Y.C., 1986-87 Recipient 3d Place award Pacific REgional Ballet Assn., 1980. Avocations: piano, swimming, dance, singing.*

HUFFMAN, D. C., JR., pharmacist, educator, health science association administrator; BS in Pharmacy, U. Ark., 1966; PhD in Pharmacy Adminstrn., U. Miss., 1971. Pharmacist Crank Drug Co., Inc., Little Rock, 1966-67; asst. prof., dir. divsn. pharmacy adminstrn. U. Tenn. Coll. Pharmacy, Memphis, 1970-73, assoc. prof., chmn. dept. pharmaceutics, 1973; exec. v.p. Am. Coll. Apothecaries, 1971—, prof., chmn. dept. pharmacy, 1974-89, vice chancellor adminstrn., 1984-89; exec. dir. NCPA Mgmt. Inst., Alexandria, Va., 1989-2000; sr. v.p. practice and mgmt. NCPA, Alexandria, Va., 1992-2000. Presenter numerous seminars. Contbr. articles to profl. jours. Archer Drug Co. scholar, 1966; recipient Lederle Faculty award, 1971; fellow NDEA, 1967-70, Am. Found. for Pharm. Edn., 1967-70. Fellow Am. Coll Apothecaries (exec. v.p.); mem. AAAS, Am. Assn. Colls. Pharmacy, Am. Pharm. Assn., Tenn. Pharm. Assn., Okla. Pharm. Assn. (hon.), Ark. Pharm. Assn. (hon. life), Am. Soc. Assn. Execs., Nat. Cmty. Pharmacists Assn., Kappa Psi, Rho Chi. Office: American College of Apothecaries 2830 Summer Oaks Dr Bartlett TN 38134-3811 Office Phone: 901-383-8119. Business E-Mail: dc@acainfo.org.

HUFFMAN, DELTON CLEON, JR., pharmacy association executive; b. St. Louis, Feb. 18, 1943; s. Delton Cleon and Kathryn (Saegesser) H.; m. Judy Hill, Aug. 11, 1962; children: Kimberly Lea, Jeffrey Keith. BS in Pharmacy, U. Ark., 1966; PhD, U. Miss., 1971. Pharmacist Crank Drug Co., Inc., Little Rock, 1966—67; asst. prof., dir. divsn. pharmacy adminstrn. U. Tenn. Coll. Pharmacy, Memphis, 1970—73, asso. prof., chmn. dept. pharmaceutics, 1973; exec. v.p. Am. Coll. Apothecaries, 1971—, also prof., chmn. dept. pharmacy, 1974—89, vice chancellor adminstrn., 1984—89; exec. dir. Nat. Cmty. Pharmacists Assn. Mgmt. Inst., Alexandria, Va., 1989—99, sr. v.p. practice and mgmt., 1992—99. Contbr. articles to profl. lit. Recipient Lederle Faculty award, 1971; NDEA fellow, 1967-70; Am. Found. for Pharm. Edn. fellow, 1967-70; Archer Drug Co. scholar, 1966. Fellow Am. Coll. Apothecaries; mem. AAAS, Am. Assn. Colls. Pharmacy, Am. Pharm. Assn., Nat. Cmty. Pharmacists Assn., Tenn. Pharm. Assn., Okla. Pharm. Assn. (hon.), Ark. Pharm. Assn. (hon., life), Am. Soc. Assn. Execs., Kappa Psi, Rho Chi. Home: 240 Lewis Fairway Cir Oakland TN 38060 Office: 2830 Summer Oaks Dr Bartlett TN 38134-3811

HUFFMAN, DURWARD ROY, academic administrator, electrical engineer; b. Little Mountain, SC, Jan. 22, 1939; s. Roy Otho and Mabel Amanda (Huffstettler) H.; m. Lillian Hope Farrell, Apr. 18, 1959; children: Donald Durward, Heatherlyn. BSEE, Heald Engring. Coll., 1963; MSEE, U. Colo., 1966; EdD in Higher Edn., U. Sarasota, 1980. Registered profl. engr., Pa. Asst. design engr. Westinghouse Elec. Corp., Sunnyvale, Calif., 1963-64; instr. elec. engring. U. Colo., Boulder, 1965-67; elec. engr. Corning Glass Works, 1967-68, sr. process control engr. Wellsboro, Pa., 1968; assoc. prof. elec.-electronic engring. tech. Luzerne County CC, Wilkes-Barre, Pa., 1968-73, chmn. dept., 1971-73; faculty Midlands Tech. Coll., Columbia, SC, 1973-75; assoc. dean Nashville State Tech. Inst., 1976-87, acting dean instrn., 1985-86; pres. No. Maine Tech. Coll., Presque Isle, 1987-2001; acad. officer Maine CC Sys., Augusta, 1994-2001, chief acad. officer, 2001—04, pres. emeritus, interim chief acad. officer, 2004—; cons. CC, 2004—. Presenter in field; chair tech. accreditation commn. Accreditation Bd. Engring. and Tech., 1989-90. Editor-in-chief, Jour. Engring. Tech., 1990-92, pub. editor, 1987-89. Mem. steering com. Ctrl. Aroostook County (Maine) Job Opportunity Zone, 1988-91; bd. dirs. Leaders Encouraging Aroostook Devel., 1988-01, sec., 1988-93; bd. dirs. Maine Rsch. and Productivity Coun., 1988-92; mem. pub. policy com. Maine Alzheimer's Assn., 2001—; mem. bd. dirs. Maine Gerontol. Soc., 2006-. Fellow Accreditation Bd. Engring. and Tech.; mem. IEEE (sr., life), Am. Soc. Engring. Edn. (divsn. engring. tech. exec. bd. 1981-82, sec. 1982-84), Am. Assn. C.C. (commn. on cmty. and workforce devel. 1995-97, com. on academic, student, cmty. devel. 1998-01), Engring. Tech. Leadership Inst. (mem. exec. com. 1978-79, 86-87), New Eng. Assn. Schs. and Colls. (chair accreditation team 1990, 95, 97, 98, team mem. 1994-96), Rotary (chair com. on vocat. svc. 1988-89, dist. 7810 scholarships subcom. 1996-00), Presque Isle Club, Eta Kappa Nu. Republican. Avocation: volunteer work. Office Phone: 207-551-1789. Personal E-mail: dhuffman@gwi.net.

HUFFMAN, EDGAR JOSEPH, oil industry executive; b. Hartford City, Ind., Aug. 24, 1939; s. Floyd Edgar and Elizabeth Jean Huffman; m. Margaret Mary Brenet, May 3, 1980; children: Donovan L. Walker, Maryanne Ramiriz. BBA, Ind. Cen. U., 1961; MA, NYU, 1968. V.p. corp. profitability Valley Nat. Bank, Phoenix, 1978—82, v.p. corp. planning, 1982—85; v.p., chief exec. officer Visa Industries Ariz., Phoenix, 1985—95. Chmn. bd. dirs. Montessori Day Schs., Inc., Phoenix, 1981. Home: 1710 E Cinnabar Ave Phoenix AZ 85020-1915 E-mail: ehuffman@mdpsc.org.

HUFFMAN, FELICITY (FLICKA HUFFMAN), actress; b. Bedford, NY, Dec. 9, 1962; m. William H. Macy, Sept. 6, 1997; children: Sofia Grace, Georgia Grace. BFA in Drama, NYU, Tisch Sch. Arts, 1988. Actress (TV films) A Home Run for Love, 1978, Lip Service, 1988, Golden Years, 1991, Quicksand:No Escape, 1992, The Water Engine, 1992, The Heart of Justice, 1993, Harrison: Cry of the City, 1996, The Underworld, 1997, A Slight Case of Murder, 1999, Snap Decision, 2001, The Heart Department, 2001, Path to War, 2002, Reversible Errors, 2004, (films) Things Change, Reversal of Fortune, 1990, Hackers, 1995, The Spanish Prisoner, 1997, Magnolia, 1999, House Hunting, 2003, Raising Helen, 2004, Christmas with the Kranks, 2004, Transamerica, 2005 (Best Actress, Nat. Bd. Review, 2005, Best Performance by an Actress in a Motion Picture-Drama, Hollywood Fgn. Press Assn. (Golden Globe award), 2006, Best Female Lead, Independent Spirit award, 2006), Georgia Rule, 2007, (TV series) Bedtime, 1996, Sports Night, 1998, Desperate Housewives, 2004— (co-recipient, Outstanding Performance by an Ensemble in a Comedy Series, Screen Actors Guild award, 2005, 2006, Outstanding Lead Actress in a Comedy Series, Emmy award, 2005, Outstanding Performance by a Female Actor in a Comedy Series, Screen Actors Guild award, 2006), (TV miniseries) Out of Order, 2003; performer: (plays) Speed-the-Plow, The Three Sisters, Boy's Life, Cryptogram (Off Broadway Theater award (OBIE), 1997); TV appearances The Human Factor, 1992, Raven, 1992, Law & Order, 1992, 1997, The X Files, 1993, Early Edition, 1996, Chicago Hope, 1997, The West Wing, 2001, Kim Possible, 2002, 2003, Frasier, 2003, The DA, 2004; co-author (with Patricia Wolff): A Practical Handbook for the Boyfriend: For Every Guy Who Wants to Be One/For Every Girl Who Wants to Build One, 2007. Recipient Best Actress award, Nat. Bd. Rev., 2005. Office: Desperate Housewives Touchstone Televison 100 Universal City Plaza Bldg 2128 Ste G Universal City CA 91608*

HUFFMAN, GERALD P., science administrator, educator; b. Steubenville, Ohio, Sept. 12, 1938; s. Sherwood John and Anne Virginia Huffman; m. Shelby-Jean Walker; children: Scott Bradley, Brad Christopher, Kirsten Ahn Rowland. PhD, W.Va. U., 1965. Rsch. scientist Fundamental Rsch. Lab., U.S. Steel Corp., Monroeville, Pa., 1965—85; pres. MacroAtom, Inc., Monroeville, 1985—86; dir. Consortium for Fossil Fuel Sci. U. Ky., Lexington, 1986—, prof. depts. chem. and materials engring. and physics, 1986—. Editor: (jour.) Fuel Processing Technology, numerous conf. procs.; contbr. 290 sci. papers to profl. jours. and books. Recipient Henry Marion Howe medal, Am. Soc. Metals, 1984, Best Fundamental Paper award South Tex. sect., AIChE, 1995, Wall of Honor award, West Liberty State Coll. Alumni Assn., 2004, 46 rsch. grants and contracts, various govt. agys. and industry, 1972—2004. Fellow: Am. Phys. Soc., Am. Chem. Soc. (chair divsn. fuel chemistry 1997—98, cert. of merit divsn. environ. chemistry 1998). Achievements include research in catalysis; coversion of coal, natural gas, and waste plastics into clean liquid fuels and hydrogen; C1 chemistry; XAFS and Mössbauer spectroscopy; electron microscopy; toxic trace metals, and fine airborne particulate matter; patents in field. Home: 908 Belmere Dr Lexington KY 40509 Office: U Ky 533 S Limestone St Lexington KY 40506-0043 Home Phone: 859-263-9927; Office Phone: 859-257-4027. Office Fax: 859-257-7215. Business E-Mail: huffman@engr.uky.edu.

HUFFMAN, GREGORY SCOTT COMBEST, lawyer; b. Austin, Tex., Dec. 19, 1946; s. Calvin Combest and Olive Agnes (Weaver) H.; m. Mary L. Murphy, Feb. 1, 1986. Student, Stanford U., France, 1966—67; BA in History with great distinction, Stanford U., 1969; postgrad., London Sch. of Econs., 1971—72; JD, Harvard U., 1973. Bar: Tex. 1973, U.S. Dist. Cts. Tex. 1974, U.S. Ct. Appeals (5th cir.) 1975, U.S. Supreme Ct. 1976. From assoc. to sr. ptnr. Thompson & Knight, Dallas, 1973—, also dir. Chief editor (monographs) Texas Free Enterprise and Antitrust Act, 1984-90, Texas Antitrust and Related Statutes, 1991—. Pres. Northern Hills Neighborhood Assn., 1980; bd. dirs. Common Cause of Tex., 1979-81, Love Field Citizens Action Commn., 1980-83, Appleseed Found., 1996-2001; adminstrv. chmn., bd. dirs. Tex. Appleseed, 1996-2001; active Tex. Supreme Ct. Adv. Com. on Professionalism. Fellow Tex. Bar Found., Dallas Bar Found.; mem. ABA (antitrust and litigation sect.), Am. Coll. Trial Lawyers, Tex. Bar Assn. (antitrust and litigation sect., chmn. unlawful practice law com. 1981-83, chmn. lawyer referral svc. com. 1982-83, bd. legal specialization 1974-77, chmn. antitrust and bus. litigation sect. 1991-92, bd. dirs. 1983—, task force on unauthorized practice of law, author of reports, presdl. citation 2000, cert. of merit 2001), Am. Bd. Trial Advocates, Dallas Bar Assn. (antitrust sect., sec.-treas. 1981, chmn. unauthorized practice law com. 1979, chmn. lawyer referral svc. com. 1980-81, chmn. profl. svcs. com. 1986-87, chmn. spkrs. com. 1999-2000, chmn. CLE com. 2001, bd. dirs. antitrust sect. 1981, 89-2002, bd. dirs. litigation sect. 1988), Harvard Law Sch. Assn. Tex. (pres. 1987-88), Tower Club Dallas, Phi Beta Kappa, Sigma Alpha Epsilon. Methodist. Office: Thompson & Knight 1700 Pacific Ave Ste 3300 Dallas TX 75201-4693 Home Phone: 214-328-3288; Office Phone: 214-969-1144. Business E-Mail: huffmang@tklaw.com.

HUFFMAN, JAMES THOMAS WILLIAM, oil industry executive; b. Norman, Okla., Mar. 27, 1947; s. Thomas William and Dorlese M. (Hicks) H.; children: Laura Anne, Christopher James. BBA, Baylor U., 1970. CPA. Mgr. Arthur Andersen & Co., Houston, 1970-76; sr. mgr. Price, Waterhouse & Co., Denver, 1976-79; v.p. Credo Petroleum Corp., 1978-80, pres., 1980-81, chmn., chief exec. officer, 1981—, also dir. Dir. Huffman Heat Exchangers Inc.; dir. XF&R, Inc.; pres., dir. SECO Energy Corp.; pres., dir. United Oil Corp. Mem. AICPA, Tex., Colo. socs. CPAs, Petroleum Landman, Ind. Petroleum Assn. Am., Ind. Petroleum Assn. Mountain State, Petroleum Accts. Soc.

HUFFMAN, JOAN BREWER, history professor; b. Springfield, Ohio, Aug. 18, 1937; d. James Clarence and Berniece (Notter) Brewer; m. James Russell Huffman, Aug. 21, 1959; children: Jill Elizabeth, Jean Elaine. AB, Ohio U., 1959; MA, Ga. State U., 1968, PhD, 1980. Adj. prof. Wesleyan Coll., Macon, Ga., 1981-82; instr. history Macon State Coll., 1968-72, asst. prof., 1972-81, assoc. prof., 1981-86, prof., 1986-2000, prof. emerita, 2000—; owner The Printed Page, Macon, Ga., 1993-97, Picture Perfect, 1995—. Chmn. History adv. com. U. Sys. Ga., 1986—87. Contbr. articles to profl. jours. Mem., bd. dirs. Oklahatchee Pk., Perry, Ga., 1966-68,

Macon State Coll. Found., 1985-90, Ga. Humanities Coun., Atlanta, 1983-87. Katharine C. Bleckley scholar English-Speaking Union, 1977; recipient Gov.'s award in the humanities, 1998. Mem. N.Am. Conf. on Brit. Studies, Am. Hist. Assn., Southern Hist. Assn. (membership com. 1988-89), Ga. Assn. Historians (pres. 1982-83), Phi Beta Kappa, Phi Alpha Theta (award 1978). Home: 135 Covington Pl Macon GA 31210-4445 Office Phone: 478-746-6365. Business E-Mail: huffmanj@bellsouth.net.

HUFFMAN, JOHN CURTIS, chemist; b. Kokomo, Ind., Dec. 9, 1941; s. Millard William and Lorene Gladys (Patmore) H.; m. Carolyn Jean Nash, Sept. 4, 1964; children: John Nash, Charles Curtis. BS in Chemistry, Ind. U., 1964, MS in Chemistry, 1968, PhD in Chemistry, 1974. Crystallographer Ind. U., Bloomington, 1968-74, dir. Molecular Structure Ctr., 1974—, sr. scientist in chemistry, 1984—, dir. Informatics Rsch. Inst., 2002—, adj. prof. informatics, 2003—. Pres. Xtelletx Software, Bloomington; cons. various drug and chem. cos. Contbr. over 1000 articles to profl. jours. Vol. Boy Scouts Am. Recipient Disting. Svc. award, Ind. U., 2006. Mem. AAAS, Am. Crystallographic Assn., Am. Chem. Soc., Am. Inst. Physics, Sigma Xi. Avocation: computer programming. Office: Ind U Chemistry Dept Bloomington IN 47405

HUFFMAN, ROBERT ALLEN, JR., lawyer; b. Tucson, Dec. 30, 1950; s. Robert Allen and Ruth Jane (Hicks) Huffman; m. Marjorie Kavanagh, Dec. 30, 1976; children: Katharine Kavanagh, Elizabeth Rooney, Robert Allen III, Simeon Ross. BBA, U. Okla., 1973, JD, 1976. Bar: Okla. 1977, U.S. Dist. Ct. (no. dist.) Okla. 1977, U.S. Ct. Appeals (10th cir.) 1978, U.S. Supreme Ct. 1982. Assoc. Huffman, Arrington, Kihle, Gaberino & Dunn, Tulsa, Okla., 1977—81, ptnr., 1981—97, Edwards & Huffmann LLP, Tulsa, 1997—2004; gen. counsel Cherokee Nation Bus., 2004—. Mem.: ABA, Fed. Energy Bar Assn., Tulsa County Bar Assn., Southern Hills Country Club (Tulsa). Republican. Roman Catholic. Home: 5937 S Columbia Ave Tulsa OK 74105-7319

HUFFMAN, VALARIE, music educator; b. Morgantown, W.Va., Jan. 5, 1973; d. Gary Huffman and Ella Marie Erickson. BA in Music Edn., Fairmont State Coll., W.Va., 1995; MusM, Ohio U., Athens, 1998; D of Musical Arts, U. Mo., Kansas City, 2003. Asst. dir. bands and orchs. Ponca City Schs., Okla., 1998—2001; asst. prof. music, dir. bands Fairmont State U., W.Va., 2003—. Mem.: Nat. Assn. Music Educators, Coll. Band Dirs. Nat. Assn., Pi Kappa Lambda, Sigma Alpha Iota (life), Kappa Kappa Psi. Office: Fairmont State University 1201 Locust Ave Fairmont WV 26554 Home Phone: 304-319-2267; Office Phone: 304-367-4206. Office Fax: 304-367-4248. E-mail: vhuffman@fairmontstate.edu.

HUFFMAN, WALTER B., retired army officer, dean, law educator; b. Keesler AFB, Miss., Oct. 8, 1944; m. Anne Robison; children: Burl, Becky, Ross. BS, Tex. Tech U., 1967, MEd, 1968, JD with highest honors, 1977. Commd. 2d lt. U.S. Army, 1968, advanced through grades to maj. gen.; judge adv. in various assignments including Desert Shield/Desert Storm, 1977-97; judge advocate gen. U.S. Army, 1997—2002; ret., 2002; dean, prof. law Sch. Law Tex. Tech. U., Lubbock, 2002—. Editor-in-chief Tex. Tech Law Rev. Decorated Legion of Merit with one oak leaf cluster, Bronze Star medal with 2 oak leaf clusters, Hungarian Disting. Svc. medal. Office: Tex Tech Univ Sch Law 18th and Hartford Lubbock TX 79409

HUFFSTETLER, PALMER EUGENE, lawyer; b. Shelby, NC, Dec. 21, 1937; s. Daniel S. and Ethel (Turner) H.; m. Mary Ann Beam, Aug. 9, 1958; children: Palmer Eugene, Ben Beam, Brian Tad. BA, Wake Forest U., 1959, JD, 1961. Bar: N.C. 1961. Practiced in Kings Mountain, NC, 1961-62, Raleigh, NC, 1962-64; with State Farm Ins. Co., Orlando, Fla., 1962; gen. legal counsel Carolina Freight Corp., Cherryville, NC, 1964-93, sec., 1969-90, sr. v.p., 1969-89, exec. v.p., 1985-93, pres., 1993-95; ret., 1995; pres., CEO Blue Chip Inc., 1997-99. Author, composer: Senior Man on Carolina Line, Fifty Years Ago. Chmn. Cherryville Zoning Bd. Adjustment, 1967-70; active N.C. Gasoline and Oil Insp. Bd., 1974-76; class chmn. Wake Forest Coll. Fund, 1971-79, decade chmn.Wake Forest Law Sch. Law Adv. Com., 1981-82; governing body, chmn. adminstrv. com. So. Piedmont Health Systems Agy., 1975-77; mem. Cherryville Econ. Devel. Commn., 1982-87, Cherryville Econ. Devel. Com., 1995-97; pres. Cherryville Devel. Corp., 1986—; bd. dirs. C. Grier Beam Truck Mus., 1982-2002, pres. 1982-96; bd. dirs. Schiele Mus., Gastonia, N.C., 1985-88, Gaston Meml. Hosp., 1990-93, vice-chmn. bd.; active N.C. Gov.'s Hwy. Safety Commn., 1985-88, Gov.'s Bus. Com., N.C., 1993-95; v.p. Ctrl. and So. Rate Bur., 1984-89; trustee Brevard Coll., 1987-93. Mem. N.C. State Bar, N.C. Bar Assn. (mem. adminstrv. bd. 1965-69, 71-72, chmn. adminstrv. bd., trustee 1970-73, fin. com. 1994-2002), First United Meth. Ch. (coun. 2002-2004). Methodist. Home: 2141 Fairways Dr Cherryville NC 28021-2115

HUFNAGEL, LINDA ANN, biology professor, researcher; b. Teaneck, NJ, Nov. 7, 1939; d. Ernest Albert and Frances Marie (Hrbek) H.; m. Dov Jaron, 1969; children: Shulamit, Tamara; m. Robert Van Zackroff, June 1984. BA, U. Vt., 1961, MS, 1963; PhD, U. Pa., 1967. Lectr. U. Pa., Phila., summer 1967; NSF postdoctoral fellow Yale U., New Haven, 1967-69; rsch. assoc. Columbia U., NYC, 1970; asst. prof. Oakland C.C., Farmington, Mich., 1970; rsch. assoc. Wayne State U., Detroit, 1971-73; lectr. biology U. R.I., Kingston, 1973-75, asst. prof., 1975-79, assoc. prof., 1979-86, prof., 1986—, dir. cen. electron microscope facility, 1973-96. NSF rsch. grantee, U. R.I., 1975, Am. Heart Assn. rsch. grantee, 1979, Steps fellow, Marine Biol. Lab., Woods Hole, Mass., 1978—79. Office: U RI Dept Cell Mol Biol Kingston RI 02881 Home Phone: 401-783-4829; Office Phone: 401-874-5914. Business E-Mail: lhufnagel@uri.edu.

HUFSTEDLER, SETH MARTIN, lawyer; b. Dewar, Okla., Sept. 20, 1922; s. Seth Martin and Myrtle (Younts) H.; m. Shirley Ann Mount, Aug. 16, 1949; 1 child, Steven. BA magna cum laude, U. So. Calif., 1944; LL.B., Stanford U., 1949. Bar: Calif. 1950. Pvt. practice, LA; assoc. Lillick, Geary & McHose, 1950-51; with Charles E. Beardsley, 1951-53; ptnr. Beardsley, Hufstedler & Kemble, 1953-81, Hufstedler, Miller, Carlson & Beardsley, 1981-88, Hufstedler, Kaus & Ettinger, LA, 1988-94; Hufstedler & Kaus, 1994-95; sr. of counsel Morrison & Foerster LLP, 1995—. Mem. Calif. Jud. Coun., 1977—78. Legis. editor Stanford U. Law Rev., 1948—49. Sec. regional planning coun. United Way, 1971-75; co-chmn. Pub. Commn. County Govt., L.A., 1975-76, 89-92; trustee AEFC Pension Fund, 1978-82; mem. Calif Citizens Commn. on Tort Reform, 1976-77; bd. visitors Stanford Law Sch., chmn., 1972-73. Lt. (j.g.) USNR, 1943-46. Mem. ABA (chmn. action commn. to reduce ct costs and delay 1979-81, mem. coun. sr. bar div. 1986-89, chmn. 1987-88), Los Angeles County Bar Assn. (trustee 1963-65, 66-70, pres. 1969-70, Shattuck Price award 1976), State Bar Calif. (bd. govs. 1971-74, pres. 1973-74, Bernard Witkin medal 2002), Am. Judicature Soc., Am. Law Inst., Am. Coll. Trial Lawyers, Am. Bar Found. (bd. govs. 1975-86, pres. 1982-84), Chancery Club (pres. 1974-75), Order of Coif, Phi Beta Kappa, Phi Kappa Phi, Delta Tau Delta. Democrat. Office: Morrison & Foerster 555 W 5th St Ste 3500 Los Angeles CA 90013-1024 E-mail: sethhufs@mofo.com.

HUFSTEDLER, SHIRLEY MOUNT, lawyer, former secretary of education; b. Denver, Aug. 24, 1925; d. Earl Stanley and Eva (Von Behren) Mount; m. Seth Martin Hufstedler, Aug. 16, 1949; 1 son, Steven Mark. BBA, U. N.Mex., 1945, LLD (hon.), 1972; LLB, Stanford U., 1949; LLD (hon.), U. Wyo., 1970, Gonzaga U., 1970, Occidental Coll., 1971, Tufts U., 1974, U. So. Calif., 1976, Georgetown U., 1976, U. Pa., 1976, Columbia U., 1977, U. Mich., 1979, Yale U., 1981, Rutgers U., 1981, Claremont U. Ctr., 1981, Smith Coll., 1982, Syracuse U., 1983, Mt. Holyoke Coll., 1985; PHH (hon.), Hood Coll., 1981, Hebrew Union Coll., 1986, Tulane U., 1988. Bar: Calif. 1950. Mem. firm Beardsley, Hufstedler & Kemble, LA, 1951-61; practiced in LA, 1961; judge LA Superior Ct., 1961-66, Calif. Ct. Appeals (2nd dist.), 1966-68, US Ct. Appeals (9th cir.), 1968-79; sec. US Dept. Edn., 1979-81; ptnr. Hufstedler & Kaus, LA, 1981-95; sr. of counsel Morrison & Foerster LLP, LA, 1995—. Emeritus dir. Hewlett Packard Co., US West, Inc.; bd. dirs. Harman Internat. Industries. Mem. staff Stanford Law Rev, 1947-49; articles and book rev. editor, 1948-49. Trustee Calif. Inst. Tech., Occidental Coll., 1972-89, Aspen Inst., Colonial Williamsburg Found., 1976-93, Constl. Rights Found., 1978-80, Nat. Resources Def. Coun., 1983-85, Carnegie Endowment for Internat. Peace, 1983-94; bd. dirs. John T. and Catherine MacArthur Found., 1983—2002; chair U.S. Commn. on Immigration Reform, 1996-97. Named Woman of Yr. Ladies Home Jour., 1976; recipient UCLA medal, 1981. Fellow Am. Acad. Arts and Scis.; mem. ABA (medal 1995), L.A. Bar Assn., Town Hall, Am. Law Inst. (coun. 1974-84), Am. Bar Found., Women Lawyers Assn. (pres. 1957-58), Am. Judicature Soc., Assn. of the Bar of City of N.Y., Coun. on Fgn. Rels. (emeritus), Order of Coif. Office: Morrison & Foerster LLP 555 W 5th St Ste 3500 Los Angeles CA 90013-1024 Office Phone: 213-892-5804. Business E-Mail: shirhufs@mofo.com.

HUFSTETLER, MARK ALLAN, historian; b. Ogden, Utah, May 27, 1958; s. Everett Howard Hufstetler and Anna Caroline Mogensen. BS, Westminster Coll., Salt Lake City, Utah, 1980; MA, Mont. State U., Bozeman, 1986. Gen. ptnr. Renewable Techs., Inc., Butte, Mont., 1990—. Cons. historian, Bozeman, 1987—. Author: (book) Forsyth: An Architectural History, Watering the Land: The Turbulant History of the Carlsbad Irrigation District, South Dakota's Railroads: An Historic Context. Mem. Soc. for Comml. Arch., 1997—2004, Mont. Preservation Alliance, Helena, 1990—93. Mem.: Western History Assn., Nat. Coun. on Pub. History, Lexington Group In Transp. History, Glacier Park Found., Soc. for Indsl. Archeology, Sigma Chi. Avocations: international travel, stamp collecting/philately, transportation history. Home: 502 N 16th Ave Bozeman MT 59715 Personal E-mail: pitamakan@mac.com.

HUG, CARL CASIMIR, JR., pharmacology and anesthesiology educator, medical ethics educator; b. Canton, Ohio, Dec. 20, 1936; s. Carl Casimir and Aimee Cecelia (McArdle) H.; m. Marilyn Ann France, May 12, 1956; children: Patricia Ann DeStephano, Michael Stephen, Joan Marie Daniel, Mary Lynn Higgins, Lori Renee Mauldin. BS in Pharmacy summa cum laude, Duquesne U., 1958; PhD in Pharmacology, U. Mich., 1963, MD with distinction, 1967. Diplomate Am. Bd. Anesthesiology 1975, recert., 1993. From instr. to assoc. prof. pharmacology U. Mich., Ann Arbor, 1963-71; from assoc. prof. anesthesiology and pharmacology to emeritus prof. Emory U. Sch. Medicine, Atlanta, 1972—, dir. cardiothoracic anesthesiology, 1982—98, dep. chmn. for rsch., 1987-95, dep. chmn. for acad. affairs, 1995—2001; faculty assoc. Emory U. Ctr. for Ethics, 1999—. Vis. rsch. prof. U. Leiden, The Netherlands, 1982, dir. Am. Bd. Anesthesiology, 1984-96, v.p. 1990-92, pres. 1992-93; bd. dirs. Found. Anesthesia Edn. Rsch. 1993-2002, v.p. 1995-98, pres. 1998-2001; councilor-at-large Assn. U. Anesthesiologists 1980-83, pres. 1984-86; vis. prof., lectr. in field, grantee in field. Author: Alfentanil: Pharmacology and Uses in Anesthesia, 1984; New Developments in Drugs Used in Anaesthesia, 1991; editor Pharmacokinetics of Anaesthesia, 1984; editor Anesthesiology, 1979-88; contbr. articles to profl. jours. Chmn. St. Francis Sch. Bd., Ann Arbor, Mich., 1967—71; coach Little League, Ann Arbor, 1967—71; active Corpus Christi Cath. Ch., Stone Mountain, Ga., 1972—96, St. John Neumann Cath. Ch., Liburn, Ga., 1997—. Recipient Lifetime Achievement award Am. Soc. Critical Care Anesthesiologists, 2002; Ralph M. Waters, MD award Ill. Soc. Anesthesiologists, 2004; named Tchr. of Yr. Emory U. Anesthesiology, 1989, Excellence in Cardiothoracic Anesthesiology award, 1998. Fellow Royal Coll. Anaesthetists (Eng., hon.), Australian and New Zealand Coll. Anaesthetists (hon.), Am. Coll. Anesthesiologists; mem. Belgian Soc. Anesthesia and Reanimation (hon.), Am. Soc. Anesthesiologists (chmn. various coms. 1976—, named Emery A. Rovenstine lectr. 1999, Disting. Svc. award 2006), Assn. Cardiac Anesthesiologists, Soc. Cardiovasc. Anesthesiologists, Am. Soc. Clin. Pharmacology and Therapeutics, Am. Soc. Pharmacology and Expl. Therapeutics. Roman Catholic. Avocations: bicycling, walking, racquetball, piano. Office: Emory Univ Hosp Dept Anesthesiology 1364 Clifton Rd NE Atlanta GA 30322-1104 Office Phone: 404-778-3917. Business E-Mail: chug@emory.edu.

HUG, PROCTER RALPH, JR., federal judge; b. Reno, Mar. 11, 1931; s. Procter Ralph and Margaret (Beverly) H.; m. Barbara Van Meter, Apr. 4, 1954; children: Cheryl Ann English, Procter J., Elyse Marie Pasha. BS, U. Nev., 1953; LLB, JD, Stanford U., 1958. Bar: Nev. 1958. Mem. Springer, McKissick & Hug, 1958—63, Woodburn, Wedge, Blakey, Folsom & Hug, Reno, 1963—77; judge US Ct. Appeals (9th cir.), Reno, 1977—2002, chief judge, 1996—2000, sr. judge, 2002—. Dep. atty. gen. State of Nev., 1971—76; v.p. dir. Nev. Tel. & Telegraph Co., 1958—77. Mem. bd. regents U. Nev., 1962—71, chmn., 1969—71; bd. visitors Stanford Law Sch.; mem. Nev. Humanities Commn., 1988—94; vol. civilian aid sect. U.S. Army, 1977. Lt. USNR, 1953—55. Named Alumnus of Yr., U. Nev., 1988; recipient Outstanding Alumnus award, 1967, Disting. Nevadan citation, 1982. Mem.: ABA (bd. govs. 1976—78), Stanford Law Soc. Nev. (past pres.), U. Nev. Alumni Assn. (past pres.), Nat. Assn. Coll. and Univ. Attys. (past mem. exec. bd.), Nat. Jud. Coll. (bd. dirs. 1977—78, 2001—, chmn. 2004—), Am. Judicare Soc. (bd. dirs. 1975—77). Office: US Ct Appeals 9th Cir US Courthouse Fed Bldg 400 S Virginia St Ste 708 Reno NV 89501-2181 Office Phone: 775-686-5949.

HUG, RICHARD ERNEST, small business owner; b. Paterson, NJ, Jan. 11, 1935; s. Gustave T. and Nelly (Rutishauser) H.; m. Lois-Ann Schack, Sept. 1, 1956; children: Donald R., Cynthia A. BS, Duke U., 1956, M in Forestry, 1957; DHL, U. Balt., 1991. Engr. forest products divsn. Koppers Co., Inc., Pitts., 1957-62, tech. rep., 1962-66, tech. sales rep., 1966-68, area sales mgr., 1968-70, mgr. product devel., 1970-72, gen. mgr. laminated products, 1972-73, v.p., gen. mgr. environ. sys. divsn., 1973-74, corp. v.p., 1973-83; pres., CEO, owner Environ. Elements Corp., Balt., 1983-88, chmn., CEO, 1988-90, chmn., 1990-95, chmn. emeritus, 1995—; owner, chmn. Deco-Sign Products, Inc., 1991—2006; owner, CEO, chmn. Hug Enterprises, Inc., 1991—; owner, chmn. The Great Am. Car Wash, etc., Inc., 1992—; dir. Hinkle-Albert Enterprise, 2001—. Mem. Md. Health Resources Planning Commn., 1984-88; bd. dirs. Nat. Aquarium, Balt., 1981-94, chmn., 1988-91; bd. dirs. Nat. Aquarium Found., 1995— Bd. dirs. Blue Cross-Blue Shield Md., 1973-94, Boy Scouts Am., Balt., 1974-85, Greater Balt. Com., 1978, 84-88, Loyola Coll. Md., 1982—, U. Md. Med. System, 1984-95, U. Md. Med. System Found., 2000—, Jr. Achievement Ctrl. Md., 1985-95, Duke U. Sch. Environ., 1986—, chair, 1988-95, Am. Auto Assn., Md., 1988—, Mid Atlantic Am. Auto Assn., 1990-2007, Md. Internat. Ctr., 1984-95, Downtown Balt. Ctr., 1991-94, Walters Art Mus., 1992-97, Environ. Forum, 1993-95, Hospice Chesapeake, 1993-98, Diehl Graphsoft, 1996-2000, Marco Group, 1985—2004, Annapolis Ctr., 2001-06; campaign chmn. United Way Ctrl. Md., 1979, 80, chmn., 1987-89; chmn. finance Ellen Sauerbrey for Gov., 1994-98, Md. Rep. Party, 1999-2000, Bob Ehrlich for Gov., 2001-06, Md. Bush for Pres. Campaign, 1999-2000, 03-04; bd. dirs. Kennedy Krieger Inst., 1981-, chair, 1984-86; bd. dirs. Ind. Coll. Fund Md., 1978-88; bd. dirs. Balt. Symphony Orch., 1989-2004, 07—, CEO coun., 1988-90, Leadership Md., 1995—, chmn., 1995-96; chmn. Baywoods of Annapolis, 1996-2006; mem. chancellor's adv. coun. U. Md., 1990-2002; bd. regents Univ. Sys. Md., 2003-06, Univ. Sys. Md. Found. Bd., 2003—; chmn. Md. U.S. Olympics Commn., 1987-88; mem. Young Pres.'s Orgn., 1974-85, chmn., 1980; bd. dirs. Inst. Human Virology, 2007—. Recipient Pres. medal Loyola Coll., 1992, Disting. Svc. award YMCA, 2005; named Md. Rep. Man Yr., 2002; named to Chimes Hall Fame, 2003. Mem. Water and Wastewater Equipment Mfrs. Assn. (bd. dirs. 1983-88), Inst. Clear Air Cos. (bd. dirs. 1980-94, pres. 1990-94), Nat. Assn. Mfrs. (bd. dirs. 1983-94), Md. Ctr. Bus. Mgmt. (bd. dirs. 1984-95, chmn. 1987-92), Md. Bus. for Responsible Govt. (bd. dirs. 1995—, chmn. 2000-04), Md. C. of C. (bd. dirs. 1981-95, v.p. 1981-84, chmn. 1985-87), Ctr. Club (bd. govs. 1993—, membership chmn. 1994-2000, v.p. 1997—, Silver Beaver award 1985, Nat. Outstanding Fund Raiser 1992). Home: 992 Stonington Dr Arnold MD 21012-1654 Office: Hug Enterprises Inc 3700 Koppers St Ste 134 Baltimore MD 21227-1020 Office Phone: 410-368-7324.

HUGANIR, RICHARD LEWIS, neuroscientist, educator, researcher; b. Phila., Mar. 25, 1953; s. George H. and Helen R. Huganir; children: Nicole R., Adam S. BS, Vassar Coll., 1975; PhD, Cornell U., 1982. Postdoctoral fellow dept. pharmacology Yale U. Sch. Medicine, New Haven, 1982—83; postdoctoral fellow lab. molecular and cellular neuroscience The Rockefeller U., NYC, 1983—84, asst. prof. lab. molecular and cellular neuroscience, 1984—87; assoc. investigator dept. neuroscience Howard Hughes Med. Inst., Balt., 1988—93, investigator, 1993—; assoc. prof. dept. neuroscience Johns Hopkins U. Sch. Medicine, 1988—93, prof., 1993—, dir. dept. neurosci., 2006—. Assoc. editor: Jour. Biol. Chemistry, 1995—2000, Jour. Neurosci., 1996—2001, mem. editl. bd.: Neuron, 1993—; contbr. chapters to books, articles to profl. jours. Recipient PDZ domains and excitatory synaptic function award, NIH, 1997—2006, Disting. Investigator award, Nat. Alliance for Rsch. on Schizophrenia and Depression, 1999—2000, Role of AMPA receptor modification in ALS award, Johns Hopkins Ctr. for ALS Rsch., 2000-2002, Regulation of the NMDA receptor signaling complex award, NIH, 2001-2006. Fellow: AAAS; mem.: NAS, Am. Soc. Biochemistry and Molecular Biology, Soc. Neurosci. (chmn. program com. 2000—02, treas. 2003—04, Young Investigator award 1991), Am. Acad. Arts and Scis. (Santiago Grisolia award 2004). Office: HHMI/Johns Hopkins Univ 904A PCTB 725 N Wolfe St Baltimore MD 21205 Office Phone: 410-955-4050. Business E-Mail: rhuganir@jhmi.edu.

HUGE, HARRY, lawyer; b. Deshler, Nebr., Sept. 16, 1937; s. Arthur and Dorothy (Vordenstrasse) Huge; m. Reba Kinne, July 2, 1960; 1 child, Theodore. AB, Nebr. Wesleyan U., 1959; JD, Georgetown U., 1963; LLD (hon.), Nebr. Wesleyan U., 2005. Bar: Ill. 1963, DC 1965, SC 1985. Assoc. Chapman & Cutler, Chgo., 1963-65; from assoc. to ptnr. Arnold & Porter, Washington, 1965-76; sr. ptnr. Donovan, Leisure, Rogovin, Huge & Schiller, Washington, 1976-92, Shea and Gould Internat., Washington, 1992-94; ptnr. Powell Goldstein Frazer & Murphy, Washington, 1995—2002, The Huge Law Firm PLLC, 2002—. Chmn., trustee United Mine Workers Health and Retirement Funds, 1973-78; chmn. bd. dirs. Hollings Cancer Ctr. Med. U. SC, Charleston; trustee Shook and Fletcher Asbestos Settlement Trust, Wilmington, Del., 2002—, Owens Corning Asbestos Settlement Trust, Wilmington, 2006—; chmn. Armstrong World Industries Settlement Trust, Wilmington. Contbr. articles to profl. jours. Pres. Voter Edn. Project, Atlanta, 1974-78; mem. Pres.'s Gen. Adv. Com. Arms Control, 1977-81; trustee Nebr. Wesleyan U., 1978—; mem. task force local govt. Greater Washington Rsch. Ctr., 1981-82; spl. master Friends for All Children, Inc., U.S. Dist. Ct. DC; mem. Nat. Tobacco Settlement Arbitration Panel, Durham, NC. With U.S. Army, 1960; officer USNG, 1960-65 Recipient Order of the Cross Terra Mariana, Republic Estonia, 2006. Mem.: ABA (co-chmn. legis. com. litig. sect. 1981), Inst. Human Virology (bd. dirs. U. Md., Balt. 1996—2001), DC Bar Assn. (bd. profl. responsibility 1976—81). Home: 25 E Battery St Charleston SC 29401-2740 Office: The Huge Law Firm PLLC Ste 502 1080 Wisc Ave Washington DC 20007 Office Phone: 843-722-1628. E-mail: harryhuge@comcast.net.

HUGENBERG, PATRICIA ELLEN PETRIE, product designer; b. NYC, Oct. 17, 1934; d. Milton John Petrie and Miriam Lois Lampke-Rubenstein-Petrie; m. George John Hugenberg, Jan. 18, 1958; 1 child, Kurt John James. Student, Briarcliff Jr. Coll., 1954, U. Calif., Berkeley, 1966. Guidette NBC, NYC, 1956; designer, resch. developer Designs for Prodn., Sausalito, Calif.; inventor games, toys, med. items, Sigi Design, San Francisco; pres. PPH Designs. Mem. pending bd. Milton & Carroll Petrie Found. for New Millenium, N.Y.C. Photographer: (book cover jacket) Baltimore; prin. works include plexiglass knitting needles, plexiglass embedded light space age stardust galaxy hammocks, space age crutch, new saddle design for mobile riding easels, kitchen veg-garnisher punch; designer (plank easels) Navel Hist. Tours, Mare Island, Air-Boat Everglade, Health care walkers and "walking sticks" canes; patents pending in field. Mem. NRA. Avocations: music, painting, horseback riding, travel, gardening. Home and Office: 10 Leeward Rd Belvedere CA 94920-2321 Office Phone: 415-435-9689, 415-435-9155. Personal E-mail: botanigirl@comcast.net.

HUGG, HAROLD J., music educator, director; b. Great Falls, Mont., Sept. 22, 1959; s. Forrest and Catherine Hugg; m. Karen K. Martin, June 15, 2002; 1 child, Jessica. MusB in Edn., Mont. State U., 1981. Cert. tchr. music Office Pub. Instrn., Mont. Dir. bands Augusta (Mont.) H.S., 1981—83; instr. elem. band Gt. Falls (Mont.) Pub. Schs., 1990—92; dir. bands East Mid. Sch., Great Falls, 1992—. Mem.: Mont. Band Masters Assn. (sec. 2002—05, treas. 2002—05), Phi Beta Mu (sec. treasure 2000—02). Home: 121 Riverview Dr E Great Falls MT 59404 Office: East Middle School 4040 Central Ave Great Falls MT 59401 Home Phone: 406-771-4740. Personal E-mail: jkbxbnd81@yahoo.com.

HUGGARD, JOHN PARKER, lawyer; b. Midland, Tex., Dec. 7, 1945; s. Peter John and Dorothy (Sampson) H. BA, U. NC, 1971, JD, 1975; MA, Duke U., Durham, NC, 1989. Bar: NC 1975, US Dist. Ct. (ea. dist.) NC 1975, US Ct. Appeals (4th cir.) 1975, US Tax Ct. 1976, US Ct. Claims 1976, US Ct. Customs 1977, US Ct. Mil. Appeals 1977, US Dist. Ct. DC 1979, US Supreme Ct. 1979, US Ct. Internat. Trade 1981, US Ct. Customs and Patent Appeals 1982; cert. fin. planner; chartered fin. cons., chartered life underwriter. Sr. ptnr. Hensley & Overby, Raleigh, NC, 1975-88, Huggard, Obiol & Blake, PLLC, Raleigh, 1988—; alumni disting. prof. Law and Econs. NC State U., Raleigh, 1975—. Author: The Adminstration of Decedents' Estates in North Carolina, 1985, North Carolina Estate Settlement Guidebook, 1995, Living Trust/Living Hell-Why You Should Avoid Living Trusts, 2004, Investing with Variable Annuities, 2005; contbr. articles to profl. publs. With USMC, 1964-68, capt. USNR. Named a Super Lawyer, Charlotte City Mag. Mem. ABA, ATLA, Am. Bus. Law Assn., NC Bar Assn., N.C. Acad. Trial Lawyers, NC Coll. Advocacy, Acad. Outstanding Tchrs., Wake County Bar Assn., Phi Beta Kappa. Democrat. Roman Catholic. Avocation: flying. Office: Huggard Obiol & Blake PLLC 124 Saint Marys St Raleigh NC 27605-1809 Home: 8304 Society Pl Raleigh NC 27615 Business E-Mail: hoblawfirm@aol.com.

HUGGETT, MONICA, performing company executive, musician; b. Eng. Studied at, Royal Acad. Music. Co-founder Amsterdam Baroque Orch., 1980, dir., 1980—87; artistic dir. Portland Baroque Orch., Oreg., 1995—. Prof. baroque violin Royal Acad. Music, London. Violinists Mozart: The 5 Violin Concertos, 1999, Vivaldi: The Four Seasons, 2000, Mozart: Violin Concertos 3 & 4, 2000, Mozart: Violin Concertos No.1, 2 & 5, 2000, Vivaldi: The Four Seasons/Four Concertos, 2000. Fellow: Royal Acad. Music. Office: Portland Baroque Orch 1020 SW Taylor St #275 Portland OR 97205-2577

HUGGINS, AMY BRANUM, music educator; b. Memphis, Dec. 20, 1954; d. Leon and Scharlene Oney Branum; m. R. David Huggins, May 8, 1976; children: Alexander, Stephanie. MusM in Edn. with Kodaly emphasis, Holy Name Coll., Oakland, Calif., 1985; MusB in Edn., Peabody Conservatory of Music, 1976. Pvt. piano instr., Balt., 1973—; early music tng. faculty prep. divsn. Peabody Conservatory of Music, Balt., 1976—83, music theory faculty prep. divsn., 1976—83, curriculum designer prep. divsn., 1976; condr., founder The Pine Grove Madrigals, Balt., 1976—; vocal music specialist Pine Grove Elem. Sch., Balt., 1976—; master tchr., supr. of student tchrs. Peabody Conservatory of Music, Shenandoah Conservatory of Music, Towson State U., U. of Md., Loyola Coll., Balt., 1978—; organizer, dir. choral festivals Balt. County Pub. Schs., Balt., 1980—90; instr. Children's Chorus of Md., Balt., 1983—86; curriculum designer Balt. County Pub. Schs., 1991; pvt. voice instr. Balt., 1997—; cons. Children's Chorus of Md., Balt., 1998—99; dir., co-founder The Am. Kodaly Inst., Balt., 2000—; instr. grad. studies program Loyola Coll. in Md., Balt., 2001—06, dir. Kodaly master's program, 2006—. Kodaly clinician, cons. Orgn. of Am. Kodaly Educators, Moorhead, Minn., 1978—, Md. United Specialists in Kodaly, Balt., 1978—; Med program dir. Loyola Coll., 2006—. Author: Elements: A Sight Singing and Rhythm Reading Book for Beginners, 1982, Kodaly, American Style, 2001, Folk Guitar for the Music Educator, 2002, 5-String Banjo for the Music Educator, 2003; columnist: The Kodaly Envoy, 2003—06; contbr. articles to profl. jours. Bd. dirs., sec. Children's Chorus of Md., 1981—83. Scholar, Mu Phi Epsilon Alumni Assn., 1975. Mem.: OAKE (chair nat. conf. planning com. 1983—85, overseer tchr. tng. com. 1983—85, chair nat. conf. planning com. 1997—98, overseer tchr. tng. com. 1997—98, overseer 1997—98), MENC, The VoiceCare Network, Soc. for Rsch. in Music Edn., Soc. for Music Tchr. Edn., Md. Music Educators Assn., Am. Choral Dirs. Assn., Orgn. of Am. Kodaly Educators (v.p. 1983—85, 1997—98), Md. United Specialists in Kodaly (sec. 1980—82, pres. 1982—84, mem. at large 1995—96, pres. 1996—98, 1998—99, 2006—), Mu Phi Epsilon. Home: 307 Southway Baltimore MD 21218 Office: Pine Grove Sch 2701 Summit Ave Baltimore MD 21234 Office Phone: 410-617-2391, 410-887-5267. Personal E-mail: amybhuggins@yahoo.com. Business E-Mail: abhuggins@loyola.edu.

HUGGINS, BOB, former college basketball coach; b. Morgantown, W.Va., Sept. 21, 1953; s. Charles Huggins; m. June Ann Fillman; children: Jenna Leigh, Jacqueline. BS magna cum laude, U. W.Va., 1977, MA in Health Adminstrn., 1978. Grad. asst. basketball coach W.Va. U., Morgantown, 1977—78, head coach, 2007—; asst. basketball coach Ohio State U., Columbus, 1978-90; head coach Walsh Coll., Canton, Ohio, 1980-83; asst. basketball coach U. Ctrl. Fla., Orlando, 1983-84; head basketball coach U. Akron, Ohio, 1984-89, U. Cin., 1989—2005, Kans. State U., 2006—07. Mem. basketball coaching staff U.S. World Univ. Games team, 1993. Founder Bob Huggins Found., 1997-98. Named Coach of the Yr. dist. 22 NAIA, 1981-82, 1982-83, area 6, 1982-83, Mid-Ohio Conf., 1981-82, 1982-83, Ohio Valley, 1984-85, Metro Conf., 1989-90, Dapper Dan Man of Yr., 1986-87, dist. 4 USBWA, 1991-92, Conf. USA, 1996-98, 98-99, 99-2000, Mideast Coach of Yr. Basketball Times, 1991-92, 95-96, Co-Nat. Coach of Yr., 1991-92 Hoop Scoop mag., finalist for AP Coach of Yr., 1991-92, Ohio Coll. Coach of Yr. Columbus Dispatch, 1991-92, 1995-96, Nat. Coll. Coach of Yr., Playboy Mag., 1992-93, Midseason Coach of Yr. USA Today, 1991-92 season, Mideast Coach of Yr. Basketball Times, 1995-96 season, Nat. Coach. of Yr. Basketball Times, 1997-98 season, The Sporting News, 1999-2000 season, ESPN.com, 2001-02 season; recipient Ray Meyer award Gt. Midwest conf., 1991-92, 92-93, Ray Meyer award Conf. USA Coach of Yr, 1997-98, 1998-99, 1999-2000. Achievements include his 517-184 record (.738) amassed during his 22 seasons as a head coach ranks him sixth in winning percentage and 18th in victories among active Division 1 mentors; his string of 12 consecutive NCAA tournament appearances is the third-longest active streak; his teams have won over 20 games in all but three of his 22 campaigns and he has averaged 23.5 victories a season, 26.3 wins per campaign over the past eight years; he has compiled a 349-112 record (.757) in his 14 years at Cincinnati, making him the most winning coach in terms of victories and percentage in the school's rich basketball history. Office: West Virginia U PO Box 6201 Morgantown WV 26506 Home Phone: 513-677-0446; Office Phone: 513-556-5847. Business E-Mail: herouxmm@email.uc.edu.*

HUGGINS, CHARLOTTE SUSAN HARRISON, retired secondary school educator, writer, travel company executive; b. Rockford, Ill., May 13, 1933; d. Lyle Lux and Alta May (Bowers) Harrison; m. Rollin Charles Huggins Jr., Apr. 26, 1952; children: Cynthia Charlotte Peters, Shirley Ann Cooper, John Charles. Student, Knox Coll., Galesburg, Ill., 1951-52; AB magna cum laude, Harvard U., Cambridge, Mass., 1958; MA, Northwestern U., Evanston, Ill., 1960, postgrad., 1971-73; cert. in conversation French, Berlitz Lang. Sch. Asst. editor Hollister Publs., Inc., Wilmette, Ill., 1959—65; tchr. advanced placement English New Trier H.S., Winnetka, Ill., 1965—97, master tchr., 1979, leader tchr., 1988. With Task Force Commn. on Grading, 1973—74; Sabbatical project 1 yr. world travel History-Lit. Prospectus; cons. Asian Studies New Trier, 1987—88; mem. New Trier Supts. Commn. on Censorship, 1991; critic tchr. Northwestern U.; cons. McDougall-Littel's Young Writer's Manual, 1985—88; asst. sponsor Echoes, 1981—, Trevia, 1982, 83; sponsor New Trier News, 1988—; pres. Harrison Farms, Inc., Lovington, Ill., 1976—; spkr. North Suburban Geneal. Soc., 1990; instr., travel expert New Trier Adult Edn. Keys to the World's Last Mysteries, 1986—; presenter in field. Author: A Sequential Course in Composition Grades 9-12, 1979, A History of New Trier High School, 1982, Passage to Anaheim: An Historical Biography of Pioneer Families, 1984, Cambodia: A Place in Time, 1987; author: (video tapes) The Glory That was Greece, 1987; author: The World of Charles Dickens, 1987; editor: Pinnacles of the Years, 2001, The Cornog Years, 2002; asst. editor newsletter: New Trier Ret. Tchrs. Active Ctrl. Sch. PTA Bd., Wilmette, Ill., 1960—64; women's bd. St. Leonard's House, Chgo., 1965—75; assocs. bd. Northwestern U. Settlement, Chgo., 1965—, pres., 1999—, fundraising com., 1997—, ctrl. bd. com., 2003—; mem. Glenbard 50th Reunion Com. Recipient Citizenship award, DAR, 1953, award, Phi Beta Kappa, 1957, Am. Legion, 1959, Cert. of Merit Graphic Arts Competition, Printing Industries of Am., 1983, 1st pl. award, Am. Scholastic Press Assn., 1990, Cert. of Merit, Am. Newspaper Pubs. Assn., 1990. Mem.: DAR (historian 1999—2000, regent 2000—02, parliamentarian 2002—), ASCD, MLA, NEA, Ill. Ret. Tchrs. Assn., Ill. Journalism Edn. Assn. (sec. 1990—97, awards chmn., bd. dirs., Life Achievement award 2001), New Trier Edn. Assn. (sec. 1992, pres.-elect 1994, pres. 1995—96, parliamentarian 2003—), Ill. Assn. Tchrs. English, Ill. Edn. Assn., Nat. Scholastic Press Assn. (conv. del. 1991, spring conf. rep. 1991—92, 1992—93, 1993—94, presenter fall and spring conv. 1993—94, spring conf. rep. 1994—95, presenter fall and spring conv. 1994—95, 1994—95, spring conf. rep. 1995—96, presenter fall and spring conv. 1995—96, 1996—, newspaper judge, All-Am. Newspaper award 1990—91, Life Achievement award 2001), Nat. Coun. Tchrs. English, Harriet Vittum Soc. (bd. dirs.), Silent Samaritan Assn. (bd. dirs. 2006), Alliance Français, Harvard U. Alumni Assn. (admissions candidate interviewer), Knox Coll. Alumni Assn. (class rep. 2005, 50 Yr. Club 2005, class donations rep.), Terra Mus. Chgo. (charter), Women Comm., Inc., Nat. Huguenot Soc., Quill and Scroll (bd. dirs. 1992—93, George Gallup award 1990), Ill. Huguenot Soc., Columbia Scholastic Press Assn. (del. 1990, newspaper judge), Jr. Aux. U. Chgo. Cancer Rsch. Bd., Northwestern U. Alumni Assn., Mary Crane League, Art Inst. Chgo. (life), Chgo. Farmers, New Trier Ret. Tchrs. Assn. (newsletter editor), Wilmette Bd. Lyric Opera (assoc.), Radcliffe Coll. Alunmae Assn., Wilmette-Kenilworth Club, Univ. Club Chgo., Women's Club Wilmette, Mich. Shores Club, Pi Beta Phi (North Shore Chgo. alumnae bd., publicity chair, 50 Yr. Club 2002). Home: 1205 Hill Rd Winnetka IL 60093 Personal E-mail: chantezch@aol.com.

HUGGINS, LOIS M., human resources specialist, consumer products company executive; BA, Franklin and Marshall Coll. Various positions Sara Lee Corp., Chgo., 1987—97; divisional v.p. human resources Sara Lee Intimate Apparel, 1997—2000; leader orgn. devel. and diversity initiative Sara Lee Corp., 2000—03, v.p. human resources, 2003—04, sr. v.p. global human resources, 2004—05, sr. v.p., chief people officer, 2005—. Co-chair global human resources steering com. Sara Lee Corp., Chgo., bd. dirs. Office: Sara Lee Corp 3 First National Plz Chicago IL 60602-4260 Office Phone: 312-726-2600. Office Fax: 312-726-3712.*

HUGGINS, MELANIE, library director; BFA in Studio Art, Winthrop U., Rock Hill, SC, 1991; MLS, U. SC, 1995. Fellow Exec. Leadership Inst. Urban Librs. Coun., Washington; with Pub. Libr. Charlotte & Mecklenburg County, 1996—2006, dir. youth and outreach svcs. NC, 2000—06; dir. St. Paul Pub. Libr., 2006—. Cons. Providence Assocs. Contbr. articles to profl. publs. Mem.: ALA. Office: St Paul Pub Libr 90 W Fourth St Saint Paul MN 55102 Office Phone: 651-266-7073. E-mail: melanie.huggins@ci.stpaul.mn.us.

HUGHES, A. N., psychotherapist; b. Ft. Meade, Md. d. G.M. and G.T. Nolen; m. E.L. Hughes, Oct. 21, 1961; 1 child, Andrew G. BS in Psychology, Rollins Coll., 1985, MA in Counseling, 1986; student in pub. speaking and human rels., Dale Carnegie Inst., 1981; student, Duke U., 1950-52. Lic. mental health counselor Nat. Bd. Cert. Counselors, nat. cert. counselor, nat. cert. gerontol. counselor. Supr. top secret control, audio/visual and small parts supply U.S. Army, Continental U.S. and Tokyo; adminstrv. sec. Sys. Devel. Corp., Rand Corp., Santa Monica, Calif.; adminstrv. asst., editor, exec. sec., adminstrv. sec. Aerospace Corp., El Segundo, Calif.; staff therapist Circles of Care, Melbourne, Fla. Developer program for leading divorce support groups for Brevard Women's Ctr. Various leadership positions PTA, Pittsford, NY, Brookfield, Wis., 1968—81; mem. Brevard Cmty. Chorus, 1991—, adv. bd., 1997; mem. Citizen's Emergency Response Team (CERT), 1999—2001; various vol. positions in several organizations in Brevard County, 1991—. Mem. DAR, Fla. Coun. on Aging, Space Coast PC Users Group, Geneal. Soc. South Brevard, Suntree Country Club, Suntree Master Homeowners Assn. (Twin Lakes rep. 1997—), Brevard County Alumnae Assn. of Kappa Kappa Gamma, Kappa Kappa Gamma. Avocations: photoimaging, fitness, genealogy, choral singing, growing orchids. Office: PO Box 410162 Melbourne FL 32941-0162

HUGHES, ALFRED CLIFTON, archbishop; b. Boston, Dec. 2, 1932; s. Alfred Clifton and Ellen Cecelia (Hennessey) H. AB, St. John's Sem. Coll., 1954; STL, Gregorian U., Rome, 1958, STD, 1961. Ordained priest Roman Cath. Ch., 1957, ordained bishop Roman Cath. Ch., 1981. Asst. pastor St. Stephen's Parish, Framingham, Mass., 1958—59, Our Lady Help of Christians, Newton, Mass., 1961—62; lectr. St. John's Sem., Brighton, 1962—65, spiritual dir., 1965—81, rector, 1981—86; aux. bishop Archdiocese of Boston, 1981—93; regional bishop of Merrimack Region, 1986—90; vicar for adminstrn. Archdiocese of Boston, 1990—93; bishop of Baton Rouge, 1993—2001; coadjutor archbishop of New Orleans Archdiocese of New Orleans, 2001—02, archbishop of New Orleans, 2002—. Chmn. com. on doctrine U.S. Cath. Conf. Bishops, 1991—94, com. on use of catechism, 1995—. Author: Preparing for Church Ministry, 1979, Spiritual Masters, 1999; chmn. editl. bd.: Nat. Dir. for Catechesis; contbr. articles to profl. jours. Recipient Mellon and Davis Founds. grant, 1976. Mem.: Catholic Theol. Soc. Am. Roman Catholic. Office: Archdiocese of New Orleans 7887 Walmsley Avenue New Orleans LA 70125-3496

HUGHES, ALLEN, music critic; b. Brownsburg, Ind., Dec. 28, 1921; s. Maurice McKinley and Bess (Collyer) H.; m. Marian Nina Berklich, Mar. 28, 1964. Student, George Washington U., 1940-42; BA, U. Mich., 1946, B.Mus., 1947; postgrad., N.Y. U., 1948-50. Lectr. music Toledo Mus. Art, 1946-47; asst. editor, critic Mus. Am., 1950-53; free-lance writer Paris, France, 1953-55; music critic N.Y. Herald Tribune, 1955-60; mem. music faculty Bklyn. Coll., 1958-60; music critic N.Y. Times, 1960-61, asst. dance critic, 1961-62, dance critic, 1962-65, music critic, 1965-86. Served to lt. (j.g.) USNR, 1943-46. Office: 1255 N Gulfstream Ave Sarasota FL 34236

HUGHES, AMY STODDART, literature and language professor; b. Holyoke, Mass., Aug. 11, 1931; d. Harold Winfield and Dorothy Robinson Stoddart; 1 child, Katherine Michele; m. Robert Marcellus Hughes (div. 1998). BA, Mt. Holyoke Coll., South Hadley, Mass., 1953; MA, Middlebury Coll., Vt., 1954; postgrad., Columbia U., NYC, 1956—57. Tchr. French Foxcroit Sch., Middleburg, Va., 1954—56, 1958—59, Ramsey H.S., NJ, 1957—58; tchr. French, dorm head Putney Sch., Vt., 1960—66; tchr. French head lang. dept., internat. advisor Mac Duffie Sch., Springfield, Mass., 1966—82; tchr. English U. Sci. and Tech. China, Hefei, China, 1982—83; tchr. French head lang. dept., internat. advisor Mac Duffie Sch., 1983—93; ret. Mem. bd. trutees Mac Duffie Sch., Springfield, 1998—2004; clerk, bd. trustees Robert M. Hughes Charter Sch., Springfield, 2002—. Author: (book) Inspiring Success, 2006. Founding mem., bd. clerk Premiss Mason Interethnic Alliance. Fellow, Columbia U., 1956—57; grantee, Fulbright Com., 1953—54. Mem.: Am. Assn. Tchrs. French. Democrat. Avocation: travel.

HUGHES, ANN HIGHTOWER, retired economist, trade association administrator; b. Birmingham, Ala., Nov. 24, 1938; d. Brady Alexander and Juanita (Pope) H. BA, George Washington U., 1963, MA, 1969. Asst. U.S. trade rep. Exec. Office of Pres., Washington, 1978-81; dep. asst. sec. trade agreements Dept. Commerce, Washington, 1981-82, dep. asst. sec. Western Hemisphere, 1982-95; dir. C & M Internat., Washington, 1995-97; ret. Recipient meritorious exec. award Pres. of U.S., 1982, 88, disting. exec. award, 1993. Avocation: breeding champion miniature Schnauzers.

HUGHES, ARTHUR HYDE, accountant, energy industry executive, accountant; b. Lansing, Mich., May 15, 1952; s. Francis Aloysius and Alice Catherine (Hyde) H.; m. Ellen Marie Krempa, Feb. 13, 1982; children: Bradley Allan, Allison Marie. BS magna cum laude, Fla. State U., Tallahassee, 1974; postgrad., U. Tex., Dallas, 1978. CPA Tex. Treas. Excella Trading Corp., Ft. Worth, 1977-79; revenue analyst gas revenue acctg. ARCO, Dallas, 1975-82, sr. acct. oil revenue acctg., 1982-85, client rep. revenue projects group, 1985-87, supr. gas data svcs., 1987-88, supr. gas sys. redevel., 1988-89, prodn. acctg. cons., 1989-90, sr. revenue compliance auditor, 1990-96; internat. acct. ARCO Algeria, 1996; pvt. practice petroleum auditing, cons., 1996-97; mgr. exploration prodn. and fin. software Allegro Devel., Inc., 1997-98; prin. cons. Oracle Energy Co., 1998-2000; oil & gas subject matter expert Akili Sys. Group, 2000-01; mgr. revenue acctg. and joint interest billing Vernon E. Faulconer, Inc., Tyler, Tex., 2001—03, contr., 2004—. Mem. Petroleum Data Exch. Steering Com., Denver, 1985-87, chmn. Gas Revenue Acctg., Data Exch. Com. (subs Petroleum Data Exch.) Dallas, 1986-87, spl. com. electronic data exch. of Coun. of Petroleum Acctg. Socs., Dallas, 1986—. Contbr. articles to profl. jours.; developer petroleum industry Gas Revenue Acctg. Data Exchange system with Gen. Elec., 1985. Alt. del. Tex. Rep. Conv., 1982; active Nat. Right to Life, Washington; active Citizen's Com. for Right To Keep and Bear Arms, Second Amendment Found. Mem. AICPA, Tex. Soc. CPAs, Petroleum Acctg. Soc., NRA (life), Tex. Rifle Assn., Ducks Unltd., Toastmasters, Gun Owner Am., Mensa, Intertel, Phi Eta Sigma, Phi Kappa Phi, Beta Gamma Sigma. Roman Catholic. Avocations: target shooting, reading, chess. Home: 1404 Woodlands Dr Tyler TX 75703-5718 Office: Vernon E Faulconer Inc Woodgate Centre Ste 160 1001 ESE Loop 323 Tyler TX 75701 Office Phone: 903-581-4382 ext 227. Personal E-mail: arthughes@suddenlink.net. Business E-Mail: ahughes@vefinc.com.

HUGHES, BLAKE, retired professional society administrator, retired publishing executive; b. NYC, June 24, 1914; s. Ferdinand Holme and Ines (de Cordova) H.; m. Betty Jean Wolf, Aug. 26, 1951; children: Diane Elizabeth, Brian Blake. Degre de civilisation, Sorbonne U., Paris, 1935; AB summa cum laude, Dartmouth Coll., 1936; postgrad., Columbia U., 1936-37. Salesman Edward B. Smith & Co., Smith, Barney & Co., investment bankers, NYC, 1936-38, N.Y. Life Ins. Co., 1939-40; promotion mgr. Engring. News Record, Constrn. Methods, McGraw-Hill Inc., NYC, 1947-50; promotion mgr., dir. mktg. Archtl. Record F.W. Dodge Corp., NYC, 1951-61; assoc. pub. Archtl. Record McGraw-Hill Inc., NYC, 1961-68, pub. Archtl. Record, 1968-80, pub. House & Home, 1976-77; pres. Internat. Inst. for Architecture, Washington, 1978-81. Author: (novels) A Lifetime's Too Short, 2002, (short stories) Good Job, 2001, Loves and Consequences, 2005, Collected Poems, 2005. Trustee Unity (Maine) Coll., 1965-75; pres. Internat. Archtl. Found., 1973-78; bd. dirs. Nat. Home Improvement Coun., 1976-77. Lt. USNR, 1940-45. Decorated Order of Fatherland War (Russia). Mem. Union Internat. Architects (archtl. critics com. 1978-80), Appalachian Housing Inst. (bd. dirs.), Charleston Artist Guild (pres. 1990-91), English Speaking Union (pres. Charleston chpt. 1995-96), Carolina Yacht Club, Phi Beta Kappa, Delta Sigma Rho. Home: 109 E Bay St Apt 2C Charleston SC 29401-2549

HUGHES, BRAD, JR., economist; b. Denver, Colo., Oct. 23, 1982; s. Brad R. Hughes, Sr. and Linda W. Hughes. BA in Econs. summa cum laude, U. Colo., 2005; MA in Econs., U. Colo., 2006. Market analyst M.B.C., Denver; bond analyst Causey, Demgen & Moore, Denver, 2007—. Witherspoon fellow Family Rsch. Coun., Washington, 2003. Contbr. articles to profl. jours. Vol. Col. Reps., Denver, 2005, Childrens Hosp., Denver, 2005. Named Witherspoon fellow, FRC, 2003. Fellow: Internat. Acad. Apologetics; mem.: Assn. Christian Economists. Office: Causey Demgen & Moore 1801 Calif #4600 Denver CO 80202 E-mail: brahughes@comcast.net.

HUGHES, BRADLEY RICHARD, finance company executive; b. Detroit, Oct. 8, 1954; s. John Arthur and Nancy Irene (Middleton) H.; m. Linda McCants, Feb. 14, 1977; children: Bradley Richard Jr., Brian Jeffrey. AA, Oakland Coll., Farmington Hills, Mich., 1974; BS in Journalism, U. Colo., Boulder, 1979, BJ, 1979, MBA in Fin. and Mktg., 1991, MS in Telecommunications, 1990. Cert. office automation profl., cert. systems profl. Buyer Joslins Co., Denver, 1979; mktg. adminstr. Mountain Bell, Denver, 1980-82; ch. cons. AT&T Info. Systems, mktg. exec. AT&T, Denver, 1983-86, acct. exec., 1986-87; mktg. mgr. U.S. West, Denver, 1987-95; dir. U. Colo. Coll. Engring., Denver, 1995—. Exec.-on-loan U. Colo. Coll. Engring. Contbr. articles to bus. publs. Bd. dirs. Brandychase Assn.; state del. Rep. Party Colo.; dir. Inst. for Govt. Innovation; bd. dirs. Olmsted Pavilion, dir. Colo. Chess Acad. Mem. IEEE, Assn. MBA Execs., U.S. Chess Fedn., Internat. Platform Assn., Mensa, Intertel, Assn. Telecom. Profls., Am. Mgmt. Assn., Am. Mktg. Assn., Info. Industry Assn., Office Automation Soc. Internat., World Future Soc., Triple Nine Soc., Internat. Soc. Philos. Inquiry, Assn. Computing Machinery. Republican. Southern Baptist. Home: 6567 S Richfield St Centennial CO 80016 Office: Qwest Comm 1801 California Ste 1920 Denver CO 80202 Personal E-mail: brad.hughes@qwest.com.

HUGHES, BRADLEY WAYNE, storage company executive; b. Gotebo, Okla., Sept. 28, 1933; 3 children. BA/BS, U. Southern Calif. Pres., Co-CEO Public Storage, Inc., Calif., 1980—91, CEO Calif., 1991—2002, chmn. Calif., 1991—; chmn., CEO Public Storage Properties XI, Inc. (renamed PS Business Park, Inc.), 1990—98, Merged Public Storage REIT's (real estate investment trust), 1994—98. Named one of Forbes' Richest Americans, 1999—, World's Richest People, Forbes Mag., 2001—; recipient Breeders' Cup Juvenile, 2003. Mem.: bd. of Breeders' Cup Ltd., bd. Thoroughbred Owners of Calif., bd. Thoroughbred Owners and Breeders Assn. Avocation: owns and breeds horses. Office: Public Storage Inc 701 Western Ave Glendale CA 91201-2349*

HUGHES, BRIGID, former editor; d. Patrick and Patricia. BA in English, Northwestern U., 1994. Intern The Paris Rev., NYC, 1995, editor, 1995—2000, mng. editor, 2000—04, exec. editor, 2004—05. Office: The Paris Review Foundation 62 White St New York NY 10013-3593

HUGHES, BYRON WILLIAM, oil industry executive; b. Clarksdale, Miss., Nov. 8, 1945; s. Byron B. and Francis C. (Turner) H.; m. Sarah Eileen Goodwin, June 23, 1973 (div.); children: Jennifer E. Hughes Crosby, Stephanie Ann. BA, U. Miss., 1968; JD, Jackson Sch. Law (now Miss. Coll. Law), 1971. Bar: Miss. 1971, U.S. Supreme Ct. 1975; cert. real estate appraiser. Atty., abstractor Miss. Hwy. Dept., 1971-76; atty., ind. landman Byron Hughes Oil Exploration Co., Jackson, Miss., 1976-92; prosecutor, child support enforcement atty. Miss. Dept. Human Svcs., 1992—. Tchr. high sch.; real estate broker. Spl. dep. Bolivar County Sheriff, Miss. Mem. ABA, Miss. Bar Assn., Hinds County Bar Assn., Bolivar County Bar Assn., Am. Judicature Soc., Nat. Assn. Real Estate Appraisers, Miss. Child Support Assn., Miss. Assn. Petroleum Landmen, Ala. Landmen Assn., Black Warrior Basin Petroleum Landmen Assn., Am. Assn. Petroleum Landmen (cert. profl. landman 1991), Ole Miss. Alumni Assn., Miss. Coll. Alumni Assn., Miss. Art Assn., Cleve. Exch. Club, Sigma Delta Kappa. Methodist. Avocations: writing, acting. Home and Office: PO Box 1485 Jackson MS 39215-1485

HUGHES, CAROLYN WRIGHT, elementary school educator, director; d. Gilbert Cornelius and Florida Bryant Wright; m. King David Hughes III, Apr. 12, 1978; children: Nicole A. Presley, King David IV. BS, Edward Waters Coll. Cert. Fla. A&M U., 1968, tchr. D.C., 1973, Fla., 1978, in ESOL Dept. Contg. Edn. Duval County, 1999. Tchr. Project Headstart, Atlanta, Washington, Lecki Elem. Sch., Washington, Greenfield Elem. Sch., Jacksonville, Fla. Asst. dir. Extended Day Greenfield Elem. Sch. Contbr. poetry to mags. Coord. United Way Greenfield Elem., 2001—05, coord. all campaign, 2002—05; mem. choir Philippian Cmty. Ch., Jacksonville, tchr. Sunday sch., asst. dist. leader. Nominee Tchr. of Yr. award, Vietnam Vets., 2005; recipient The Wall Reading Project award, V.P. Chaney, The White House, 2004. Mem.: Am. Fedn. Tchrs. Democrat. Avocations: gardening, singing, cooking, football. Home: 2510 Spring Park Rd Jacksonville FL 32207 Office: Greenfield Elementary Sch 6343 Knights Ln N Jacksonville FL 32216 Office Phone: 904-739-5249. Personal E-mail: kdh2510@comcast.net.

HUGHES, CATHERINE L. (CATHY HUGHES), radio personality, broadcast executive; b. Omaha, Apr. 22, 1947; 1 child. Student, Creighton U., HHD (hon.), 2006; student, U. Nebr. Lectr., asst. to dean comm. Howard U., Washington, 1971—73; gen. sales mgr. WHUR Radio, 1973—78; v.p., gen. mgr. WYCB Radio, 1978—80; owner, operator WOL-AM Radio, 1980—; now founder, chairperson Radio One. Trustee Lincoln U.; small bus. adv. com. Fed. Res. Bank. Bd. mem. Piney Woods Sch., Balt. Mus. Art. Named Bus. Person of the Yr., Nat. Black C. of C., 1998, Prudential Media Black Woman on Wall St., 1999; named one of 50 Most Powerful Women in Bus., Black Enterprise Mag., 2006, 100 Most Influential Black Americans, Ebony mag., 2006; recipient Mayor's Bus. award, 1995—99, Thomas A. Dorsey Leadership award, 1996, D.C. Cmty. Svc. award, 1995; scholar, Living Vision Scholarship Fund, 1995. Achievements include first to to be an African American woman to head a firm publicly traded on a stock exchange in the United States. Office: Radio One Inc 1705 Whitehead Rd Gwynn Oak MD 21207-4004

HUGHES, CHARLES E., III, plastic surgeon; b. Chgo., Mar. 19, 1943; s. Charles E. and Jane Wittig (McClintock) H.; m. Ellen Alice Schowe, Nov. 1, 1963; children: Kristian, Chad, Adnrew, Polly. BS, Northwestern U., Chgo., 1966, MD, 1969. Diploamte Am. Bd. Plastic Surgery. Fellow in surg. oncology Am. Cancer Soc., Chgo., 1973-74; resident Northwestern

U., 1974-76; asst. prof. plastic surgery Ind. U., Inspls., 1976-82; pvt. practice Geech Grove, Ind., 1983—. Contbr. articles to profl. jours. Fellow ACS (fgn. lang. editor jour. 1974-88); mem. Lipoplasty Soc. (pres. 1995—), Am. Soc. Plastic and Reconstructive Surgeons, Am. Soc. Aesthetic Plastic Surgery, Cleft Palate Soc. Avocations: exercise, sailing, reading, travel. Office: 1500 Albany St Beech Grove IN 46107-1555

HUGHES, CHRISTOPHER ADAM, conductor, educator; s. Ronald Dee and Kathleen Ann Hughes. BA magna cum laude, Western State Coll., 1994; MMus, VanderCook Coll. of Music, Chgo., 1997; PhD, U. Colo., Boulder, 2005. Lic. profl. educator Colo. Dept. of Edn. Dir. of instrumental music Grand Junction Ctrl. H.S., Grand Junction, Colo., 1994—2000; instrumental music condr. Smoky Hill H.S., Aurora, Colo., 2000—02; grad. asst./educator U. Colo., Boulder, 2002—05; asst. prof. music Lander U., Greenwood, SC, 2005—, dir. bands, 2005—. 1st v.p. Colo. Band Directors Assn., Denver, 1997—2007; honor ensemble condr., Denver, Craig, Delta, Greeley, Westminster, Arkansas Valley, Colo., 1999—2007, Greenwood, Columbia, SC, 2003, SC All-State Region Band; cmty. band condr. Performer Colo. Brass Band, 1991—, Rocky Mountain Brass Works, 2000—. Scholar Grad. Tchg./Rsch. Assistantship, U. of Colo. Mem.: Coll. Band Dirs. Nat. Assn., SC Music Educators Assn., Am. Sch. Band Dirs. Assn., Internat. Trumpet Guild, Phi Mu Alpha, Kappa Delta Pi. Avocations: restoration of 1957 Chevrolets, domestic and international travel, mountain climbing, sight seeing. Home: 106 Cornerstone Dr Greenwood SC 29649 E-mail: chughes@lander.edu.

HUGHES, CINDI BAKER, special education educator; b. Joliet, Ill., Apr. 18, 1957; d. Richard M and Evelyn M Baker; m. Forrest Rodrick Hughes; 1 child, Steven LeMond; m. Rick Tynes (dec. 1979). AA in applied sci., Waubonsee C.C., Sugar Grove, Ill., 1978; BSc, Ill. State U., Normal, 1983; M in elem. edn., Morehead State U., Ky., 1987. Tchrs. aid, deaf program Joliet Pub. Sch., 1978—80; summer counselor Lions Club of No. Ill., 1981—82, Trailways Girl Scouts, 1983; tchr. hearing impaired West Ctrl. Ill. Spl. Ed. Co-Op., Macomb, Ill., 1983—84; tchr. Jack and Jill Daycare, Joliet, Ill., 1984—85; tchr. of deaf Ky. Sch. for the Deaf, Danville, 1985—86; tchr. deaf and hearing impaired Floyd County Sch., Prestonsburg, Ky., 1986—96, tchr. hearing K-8, 1996—2004, tchr. art K-8, 2004—07, tchr. primary reading, 2007—. Sign lang. tchg. asst. Ill. State U., 1982. Exhibitions include Mountain Arts Ctr., Prestonburg, 2007. Org. Deaf Awareness Night, Ill. State U. Deaf Edn. Dept., 1981; spring pow-wow planning com. Waubonsee Cmty. Coll.; mem./trustee Mountain Christian Acad., 1999—2001, pres., 1998—2000. Grantee, Very Spl. Art of Ky., 2005; Tchr. Initiated Project grant, Ky. Arts Coun., 2004. Mem.: Ky. Edn. Assn., Ill. Tchrs. Hearing Impaired, Humane Soc. of the U.S., Creative Home Arts Club, Phi Theta Kappa. Avocations: sewing, crafts. Office: Floyd County Sch JM Stumbo Elem 6945 Ky Rte 979 Grethel KY 41631 Business E-Mail: Cindi.Hughes@floyd.kyschools.us.

HUGHES, CLYDE MATTHEW, religious denomination executive; b. Huntington, W.Va., Dec. 7, 1948; s. Donald Lee and Audrey Arlene (Stevens) H.; m. Linda May Daniels, June 10, 1972; children: Crystal, Dustin, Tina, Wesley, Timothy, Penny, Heidi, Robin. Diploma, Amb. Bible Inst., London, Ohio, 1972; BA, Cedarville Coll., Ohio, 1974; MA, Meth. Theol. Sch. in Ohio, 1980; DD, Heritage Bible Coll., Dunn, NC, 1994. Ordained to ministry Internat. Pentecostal Ch. of Christ, 1974. Pastor Internat. Pentecostal Ch. of Christ, Hillsboro, Ohio, 1981-82, nat. dir. Sunday sch. London, 1976-82, dir. ch. ministries, 1982-84, asst. gen. overseer, 1984-90, gen. overseer, chmn. gen. bd., 1990—. Mem. nat. com. Mission Am., 1997—; bd. dirs. Beulah Heights Bible Coll., Atlanta, 1982—, chmn. bd. 1990-96. Editor-in-chief The Pentecostal Leader; contbr. articles to religious publs. Chmn. bd. dirs. Locust Grove Rest Home, 1990-98. Mem. Nat. Assn. Evangs. (bd. dirs. 1990—2001), Madison County Evang. Assn. (bd. dirs. 1990-2001), London Ministerial Assn., Chs. United with Israel (bd. gov. 2002-), Mission Am. (nat. com. 1997-), Pentecostal/Charismatic Chs. N.Am. (bd. dirs. 1994—, exec. com. 2001), Internat. Pentecostal Press Assn. (N.Am. chpt. exec. com., 2001—, second v.p.). Mem. Internat. Pentecostal Ch. Of Christ. Home: 7040 Danville Rd London OH 43140-9766

HUGHES, DAN, professional basketball coach; m. Mary Hughes; children: Sara, Bryce. Grad. in Phys. Edn. and Hist., Muskingum Coll., New Concord, Ohio, 1977; MEd, Miami U., Ohio, 1978. Grad. asst. Miami U., Ohio, 1977—78; asst. coach men's basketball Mt. Union Coll., 1982—84, 1985—91, Baldwin-Wallace Coll., 1984—85, U. Toledo, 1991—96, asst. coach women's basketball, 1996—97; asst. coach Charlotte Sting, 1999, head coach, 1999, Cleve. Rockers, 2000—03; asst. commr. men's basketball ops. Mid-Am. Conf.; head coach, gen. mgr. San Antonio Silver Stars, 2005—. Named Coach of Yr., Coach of Yr., 2001. Office: San Antonio Silver Stars One AT&T Ctr San Antonio TX 78219*

HUGHES, DANIEL DAVID, performing company executive; b. Livermore, Calif., Aug. 29, 1968; s. Edwin William and Maria Eugenia Hughes. MA in Choral Conducting, San Jose State U., Calif., 2001. Artistic dir. The Choral Project, San Jose, Calif., 1996—, Silicon Valley Gay Men's Chorus, San Jose, 2002—07. Musician: Daniel Hughes Choral Series (Santa Barbara Music Publishing), So We'll Go No More A-Roving, (albums) One is the All, Winter, Water & Light, Americana, Of Christmastide, The Cycle of Life. Dir. music Frist Ch. Religious Sci., San Jose, 2006—07. Recipient Small Ensemble Category 2d Pl. award, Internat. Choral Competition, Gorizia, Italy, 1996, Large Choir Category 2d Pl. award, Llangollen Internat. Musical Eisteddfod, Wales, 2004, 3rd Pl. folk category, Calif. Internat. Choral Competition, 2007, 2nd Pl. required pieces, 2007, 1st Pl. choir's choice, 2007; Christina Cadena Meml. scholarship, San Jose State U., 1989—96. Mem.: Am. Choral Dir.'s Assn. (chmn. repertoire and standards com. We. divsn. 2000—06, Calif. state bd. mem. 2007, Student Conducting Competition 2d Pl. award 1995). Avocations: reading, pets, outdoors, films, theater. Office: The Choral Project 72 N 5th St San Jose CA 95112 Home Phone: 415-596-6594. Personal E-mail: tactus60@gmail.com.

HUGHES, DAVID HENRY, manufacturing executive; b. Orlando, Fla., Dec. 20, 1942; s. Harry C. and Pauline B. Hughes; m. Rebecca Wilkins; 1 child, Kristin E.; m. Linda Cooper, Apr. 26, 1986; children: Patrick, Shelby. BS, U. Fla., 1965, JD, 1967. Mgmt. trainee Hughes Supply Inc., Orlando, 1968-72, COO, 1972—74, pres., 1974—94, CEO, 1975—2003, chmn., 1986—. Bd. dirs. Sun Banks Inc., Orlando, SunTrust Banks Inc., Atlanta, Darden Restaurants Inc., Brown & Brown Inc. Active Orlando Regional Healthcare Sys. Mem. Fla. Bar Assn., Fla. Coun. of 100. Republican. Avocations: golf, fishing. Office: Hughes Supply 501 W Church St Orlando FL 32805

HUGHES, DAVID MICHAEL, oil industry executive, rancher; b. Knoxville, Tenn., Mar. 20, 1939; s. Cleo L. and Lucille (Farmer) H.; m. Louise Love, Mar. 17, 1960 (div. 1971); children: David Michael Jr., Sheryl Lynn; m. Elizabeth Grove, Mar. 16, 1974; children: Christopher Grove, Andrew Carter. BCE, U. Tenn., 1962. Founder, owner World Wide Divers, Inc., Morgan City, La., 1962-69; founder, past chmn. bd. Oceaneering Internat., Inc., Houston, 1969-90; founder, owner Broken Arrow Ranch, Ingram, Tex., 1975—; founder, pres. Tex. Wild Game Coop., Ingram, 1981—, Game Ranching, Inc., Ingram, 1986—. Bd. dirs. Oceaneering Internat., Inc., 1969—. Author: Broken Arrow Ranch Cookbook, 1984; patentee underwater corrosion meter, underwater camera and a device for identifying a characteristic of an object or the contents of a container. Chmn. Hist. Preservation Com., Ingram, 1986—; mem. Adv. Coun. Tex. Marine Sci. Inst., 1980-91; hon. chmn. Hunters for the Hungry, 1991—, nat. chmn. Named "Who's Who in Tex. Food and Wine", Dallas Morning News Poll, 1992; named industry pioneer Offshore Energy Hall of Fame, 1999. Mem. Assn. Diving Contractors (pres. 1967-71, Galletti award 1981), Exotic Wildlife Assn. (pres. 1987-89), Chi Epsilon (nat. conv. del. 1961). Republican. Avocations: woodworking, cooking. Home: Broken Arrow Ranch Inc PO Box 530 Ingram TX 78025-0530

HUGHES, DEANNA ELMA, psychologist; b. Jacksonville, Fla., Nov. 28, 1971; d. Victor Alexander II and Charlene Boggs Hughes. BA Psychology, Furman U., Greenville, SC, 1994; M Rehab. Counseling, Fla. State U., 1996; M Clin. Psychology, Fla. Inst. Tech., 2000, D Clin. Psychology, 2002. Lic. clin. psychologist Fla. Dept. Health. Doctoral residency Miami Vet. Med. Ctr., 2001—02; post-doctoral resident Coastal Behavioral Healthcare, Sarasota, Fla., 2002—03; clin. psychologist Tricare South, Jacksonville, 2004—; pvt. practice, nursing home cons. Jacksonville, 2004—. Com. mem. First Presbyn. Ch., Sarasota, 2003; cmty. missions, com. mem. Riverside Presbyn. Ch., Jacksonville, 2004; com. mem. Sarasota United for Responsibility, Justice and Equity. Contbr. articles to profl. jours. Mem.: APA, Fla. Psychol. Assn. Avocations: painting, music, bicycling. Office Phone: 904-504-5412.

HUGHES, DOUG, theater director; s. Barnard Hughes and Helen Stenborg; m. Lynn Fusco. Grad., Harvard U. Assoc. artistic dir. Seattle Repertory Theatre; resident dir. MCC Theater, NYC. Dir.: (Broadway plays) Frozen, 2004, Doubt, 2005— (Tony Award for best direction of a play, 2005, Outer Critics Circle award, outstanding direction of a play, 2005, Drama Desk award, outstanding director of a play, 2005, Lucille Lortel award, outstanding director, 2005), A Touch of the Poet, 2005, A Naked Girl on the Appian Way, 2005, Defiance, 2006, Inherit the Wind, 2007, (Broadway Shows) Escape: 6 Ways to Get Away (1), 2004, Escape: 6 Ways to Get Away (2), 2005, (off-Broadway) Paris Letter, 2005; (plays) Last Easter, Scattergood, Frozen, The Grey Zone (Obie award), Engaged, Flesh and Blood (Callaway award), The Beard of Avon, A Question of Mercy, John Guare's Lake Hollywood, An Experiment with an Air Pump, The House in Town, 2006, Howard Katz, 2007; co-dir.: Othello; co-prodr.: Wit (MCC award). Recipient Obie award for sustained excellence of direction, Village Voice, 2005.*

HUGHES, EDWARD F. X., healthcare educator, preventive medicine physician; b. Boston, Jan. 10, 1942; s. Joseph Daniel and Elizabeth (Dempsey) Hughes; m. Susan Lane Mooney, Feb. 11, 1967; children: Edward, John, Dempsey. BA in Philosophy, Amherst Coll., Mass., 1962; MD, Harvard U., Cambridge, Mass., 1966; MPH, Columbia U., NYC, 1969. Intern, resident surg. Columbia-Presbyn. Med. Ctr., NYC, 1966-68; instr. to assoc. prof. Mt. Sinai Sch. Medicine, NYC, 1969-77; rsch. assoc. Nat. Bur. Econ. Rsch., NYC, 1970-77; prof. prevention medicine Northwestern U. Med. Sch., Chgo., 1977—, founder, dir. ctr. health svc. policy rsch., 1977-94; prof. health industry mgmt. and mgmt. & strategy J. L. Kellogg Grad. Sch. Mgmt., Northwestern U., Evanston, Ill., 1977—, dir. health industry mgmt. program, 1980—83, co-dir. biotech. program, 2001—. Cons. Nat. Ctr. Health Svcs. Rsch., Rockville, Md., 1975-82, AMA, Chgo., 1981-83, Midwest Bus. Group on Health, Chgo., 1983-85; expert witness for providers, health Plans and pharm. firms, 1993—. Editor: Hospital Cost Containment: A Policy Analysis, 1979, A Perspective on Quality in American health Care, 1988 (Bradley award 1962, Health Career Scientist award 1973-75); mem. editl. bd. Managed Care Interface (Latiolias Honor medal 1999, Beta Gamma Sigma award), Jour. Clin. Outcomes, Group Health News, Counseline; contbr. articles to profl. jours. Health Care Financing Adminstrn. grantee, Washington, 1978-84, Ford Found., 1983-86, Robert Wood Johnson Found, 1978-82, NIH, 1983-95, Pew Charitable Trusts, 1990-92, Baxter Found., 1991-96. Fellow N.Y. Acad. Medicine, Am. Coll. Physician Execs.; mem. APHA, Americas Health Ins. Plans (acad. dir. exec. leadership program), Assn. Health Svcs. Rsch. (co-founder, v.p. 1981-83, bd. dirs. 1981-84), Assn. Tchrs. Preventive Medicine (bd. dirs. 1973-76), Med. Adminstrs. Conf., Nat. Assn. Managed Care Physicians (med. adv. bd.), Boston Latin Sch. Chgo. Club (bd. dirs. 1983-86), Chapoquoit Yacht Club (West Famouth, Mass.) Home: 810 Lincoln St Evanston IL 60201-2405 Office: Kellogg Sch Mgmt 2001 Sheridan Rd Evanston IL 60208-0814 Office Phone: 847-491-8384. Business E-Mail: efx-hughes@kellogg.northwestern.com.

HUGHES, ELIZABETH R. (BETH), lawyer; b. Easton, Md., Apr. 13, 1956; AB cum laude, Harvard Univ., 1978; JD with honors, Univ. Md., 1981. Bar: Md. 1981, DC 1999, Va. 2001. Joined Venable LLP, 1981, ptnr., chairwoman, corp. fin., mergers, acquisitions group Washington. Bd. dir. Open Door of Baltimore, Inc. Finalist Top Wash. Lawyers in corp. fin., Wash. Bus. Jour., 2004. Mem.: ABA, Va. Bar Assn., DC Bar Assn., Md. State Bar Assn. (chair, com. on corp. law 2000—01), Bar Assn. Baltimore City. Avocations: golf, fishing. Office: Venable LLP 575 7th St NW Washington DC 20004 Office Phone: 202-344-8049. Office Fax: 202-344-8300. Business E-Mail: erhughes@venable.com.

HUGHES, EUGENE MORGAN, university president; b. Scottsbluff, Nebr., Apr. 3, 1934; s. Ruby Melvin and Hazel Marie (Griffith) H.; m. Margaret Ann Romeo; children: Deborah Kaye, Greg Eugene, Lisa Ann; stepchildren: Jeff, Mark, Christi. Diploma, Neb. Western Coll., 1954; BS in Math. magna cum laude, Chadron State Coll., 1956; MS in Math., Kans. State U., 1958; PhD in Math., George Peabody Coll. for Tchrs., Vanderbilt U., 1968; LHD (hon.), No. Ariz. U., 1997; LHD, Chadron State Coll., 2003. Grad. asst. dept. math. Kans. State U., Manhattan, 1956-57; instr. math. Nebr. State Tchrs. Coll. at Chadron, 1957-58; asst. prof. math., head dept. Chadron State Coll., 1958-66, assoc. prof., 1966-69, prof. math., 1969-70, dir. rsch., 1965-66, asst. to the pres., 1966-68, dean adminstrn., 1968-70; grad. asst. dept. math. George Peabody Coll. for Tchrs., Nashville, 1962-63, 64-65, asst. to undergrad. dean, 1964, asst. to pres., 1964-65; instr. Peabody Demonstration Sch., 1963-64; prof. math. No. Ariz. U., Flagstaff, 1970-93, prof. math. emeritus, 1993—, dean Coll. Arts and Scis., 1970-71, provost univ. arts and sci. edn., 1971-72, acad. v.p., 1972-79, pres., 1979-93, pres. emeritus, 1993—; pres. Wichita State U., 1993-98, pres. emeritus, 1998—; interim pres. Ea. Ky. U., 2001; prs. Mus. No. Ariz., 2002—03. Cons. Nebr. Dept. Edn., 1966-70; mem. adv. bd. United Bank Ariz., 1980-82; mem. nat. adv. bd. Ctr. for Study of Sport in Society, 1990; mem. adv. bd. Bank IV, 1993-97; bd. dirs. NationsBank N.A. (Midwest), mem. adv. bd., 1997-98, bd. dirs. First State Bank, 1999—. Mem. staff bd. trustees Nebr. State Colls., Lincoln, 1969-70; co-dir. workshop tchr. edn. North Cen. Assn. U. Minn., 1968-70; officer fed. ednl. programs, Nebr., Ariz., 1966-93; mem. Ariz. Commn. Postsecondary Edn.; bd. fellows Am. Grad. Sch. Internat. Mgmt., 1980-93; mem. Gov.'s Com. Quality Edn., Chadron Housing Authority, 1968-70, Pres.' Commn. NCAA; mem. Ariz. State Bd. Edn., 1982-87, 90-93, pres., 1992-93; mem. Flagstaff Summer Festival, Ariz. Coun. Humanities and Pub. Policy, Mus. No. Ariz., Grand Canyon coun, Boy Scouts Am.; chair Ariz. Leadership Adv. Coun., 1990-93; mem. Ariz. Town Hall; commr. Western Interstate Commn. for Higher Edn., 1992-93; mem. Gov.'s Strategic Partnership for Econ. Devel., 1992; mem. Christopher Columbus Quincentenary Commn., 1990-91; sec., mem. Wichita/Sedgwick Partnership for Growth, 1993-97, Wichita/Sedgwick County Employment Tng. Bd., 1993-96; bd. dirs. Kids Voting Kans., 1997-98, Mus. North Ariz., 2002-03, emeritus dir., 2003—; trustee Assn. Western Univs. Inc., 1997-98. Ariz. Acad. NSF fellow, 1963, 64; recipient Chief Manuelito award Navajo Tribe, 1976, Disting. Svc. award Chadron State Coll., 1982, Flagstaff Citizen of Yr., 1988, Disting. Math. Grad. award Kans. State U., 1990, Buddy Joe Bojack Humanitarian award, 1992, Cmty. Svc. award, 1994; named Hon. Chmn. black Bd. Dirs., 1989, Outstanding Citizen, Wichita Soc. of Profl. Engrs., 1998, Kans. Soc. Profl. Engrs., 1998. Mem. Am. Assn. State Colls.and Univs. (past chmn. & mem. com. on grad. sties 1979—, bd. dirs., mem. com. on accreditation, 1980—, treas.), Math. Assn. Am. (vis. lectr. secondary schs. Western Nebr. 1962), North Cen. Assn. Colls.nd Secondary Schs. (coord. 1968-72, cons./evaluator 1977—), Nat. Coun. Tchrs. of Math., Wichita Area C. of C., Flagstaff C. of C., Blue Key, Golden Key, Masons, Elks, Rotary (past pres., Paul Harris fellow 1975), Pi Mu Epsilon, Phi Delta Kappa, Kappa Mu Epsilon, Phi Kappa Phi. Personal E-mail: ozinaz@juno.com.

HUGHES, FRANCIS P., medical association administrator; PhD. Exec. dir. Am. Bd. Anesthesiology, Raleigh, NC, 1982—. Office: Am Bd Anesthesiology 4101 Lake Boone Trl Ste 510 Raleigh NC 27607-7506

HUGHES, GRACE-FLORES, federal agency administrator; b. Taft, Tex., June 11, 1946; d. Adan Flores and Catalina San Miguel; m. Harley Arnold Hughes, May 25, 1980. BA, U. D.C., 1977; MPA, Harvard U., 1980. Sec. Dept. Air Force Kelly AFB, San Antonio, 1967-70, Pentagon-Office Sec. of Def., Washington, 1970-72; program asst., social sci. analyst HEW, Washington, 1972-78; social sci. analyst, acting dir. Office Hispanic Ams. HHS, Washington, 1978-81; vis. prof. Nebr. Wesleyan U., Lincoln, 1982-83, U. Nebr., Omaha, 1984; spl. asst. SBA, Washington, 1985-88, assoc. adminstr. for minority small bus., 1988; dir. community rels. Dept. Justice, Washington, 1988-92; pres. Grace, Inc., Alexandria, Va.; v.p. for intergovtl. affairs USTAK, LLCcs., Inc. Spl. asst. Reagan/Bush '84 Campaign, Nebr. and Washington, 1984, 50th Presdl. Inaugural, Washington, 1984-85, Office Pub. Liaison, The White House, 1985. Author: The Bureaucrat, Categorized Workforce, 1992; co-author: New Book of Knowledge, 1980; chair adv. bd. Harvard Jour. Hispanic Policy, 1989—; The Use and Abuse of Diversity Mag., 1994, Hispanic Mag., 1996. Adv. mem. U.S. Senate Rep. Task Force, Washington, 1988-91; alumni exec. bd. J.F. Kennedy Sch. Govt., Harvard U., Cambridge, Mass., 1989-93; mem. Rep. Hispanic Assembly, 1984—; apptd. by Gov. Allen of Va. to Bd. for Profl. and Occpl. Regulations, 1994—, Bd. for Agr. and Consumer Svcs., 1997—; bd. dirs. Hispanic Found. for Arts; apptd. by Pres. Bush Fed. Svc. Impasses Panel, 2000. Recipient Excellence award Nev. Econ. Devel. Corp., 1988, Leadership award Am. GI Forum, Omaha, 1989; named one of 100 Most Influential Hispanics in U.S. Hispanic Bus. Mag., 1988. Mem. Assn. Pub. Adminstrs. (Outstanding Pub. Svc. award 1990), Hispanic Bus. Roundtable, Coun. in Excellence in Govt. (prin.), Fedn. Rep. Women, Mex.-Am. Women's Nat. Assn., Univ. Club (Washington). Episcopalian. Avocations: tennis, jogging, aerobics, equestrian. Home and Office: 5208 Bedlington Ter Alexandria VA 22304-3551 Office Phone: 703-395-2863. E-mail: harley45@aol.com.

HUGHES, GREGORY, information technology executive; BS in Elec. Engring., MIT, MS in Elec. Engring. and Computer Sci.; MBA, Stanford Grad. Sch. Bus. Founder, CEO Granite Microsystems; ptnr. McKinsey & Co., 1993—2003; exec. v.p. global svcs. VERITAS Software Corp., Mountain View, Calif., 2003—. Office: VERITAS Software Corp 350 Ellis St Mountain View CA 94043

HUGHES, HARRISON G., horticulture educator; BS in Botany, Eastern Ill. U., Charleston, 1969; PhD in Plant Genetics and Breeding, Purdue U., West Lafayette, Ind., 1974. Instr., dept. horticulture Purdue U., 1973—74; tchg. faculty, dept. plant sci. SUNY, Cobleskill, 1974—76, U. RI, 1976—77; tchg./rsch. faculty, dept. horticulture Colo. State U., Fort Collins, 1977—. Vis. prof., dept. agronomy rsch. U. Ky., 1975; sabbatical leave, rsch., Fruit and Nut Clonal Repository U. Calif., Davis, 1984; summer cooperative rsch. SERI, 1991; sabbatical leave, rsch., plant molecular biology. lab USDA, Beltsville, Md., 1992, sabbatical leave, rsch., plant germoplasm preservation rsch. lab., Nat. Seed Storage Lab., Fort Collins, Colo., 98; invited spkr. in field. Contbr. articles to profl. jours.; co-author: Glossary of Plant Biotechnology and Tissue Culture, 1999. Recipient Award of Appreciation for Outstanding Svc., Colo. State U. Horticulture Club, 1991. Mem.: Am. Genetic Assn., Internat. Horticultural Soc., Internat. Plant Tissue Culture Assn., Am. Soc. for Horticultural Sci. (pres., Western regions 1991, candidate for v.p. for edn. 1994, Outstanding Grad. Educator award 1994), Beta Beta Beta, Gamma Sigma Delta, Alpha Zeta, Phi Alpha Xi, Sigma Xi. Office: Colo State U Dept Horticulture and Landscape Arch 210 Shepardson Bldg 1173 Campus Delivery Fort Collins CO 80523-1173 Office Phone: 970-491-7050. Business E-Mail: harrison.hughes@colostate.edu. E-mail: hghughes@lamar.colostate.edu.*

HUGHES, JAMES MITCHELL, epidemiologist, educator; b. Pitts., Aug. 11, 1945; s. James Paul and Adelaide (Mitchell) H.; m. Pamela Mary Parsons, June 12, 1971; children: Andrew Saban, Mitchell Parsons. BA, Stanford U., 1966, MD, 1971. Diplomate Am. Bd. Preventive Medicine, Am. Bd. Internal Medicine, Am. Bd. Infectious Diseases. Intern U. Wash., Seattle, 1971-72; epidemic intelligence svc. officer CDC, Atlanta, 1973-75; resident internal medicine U. Wash., Seattle, 1972-73, 75-76; fellow infectious diseases U. Va., Charlottesville, 1976-78; chief water-related diseases activity, asst. chief enteric diseases br. Bur. Epidemiology, CDC, Atlanta, 1978-81, chief surveillance and prevention br., asst. dir. med. sci., hosp. infections program Ctr. for Infectious Diseases, 1981-83, dir. hosp. infections program Ctr. for Infectious Diseases, 1983-88, dep. dir. Nat. Ctr. for Infectious Diseases, 1988-92, dir. Nat. Ctr. for Infectious Diseases, 1992—2005; clin. assoc. prof. Emory U., Atlanta, 1993-2001, clin. prof. dept. medicine Sch. Medicine, 2001—05, dir. program in global infectious diseases Sch. Medicine, dir. Ctr. for Global Safe Water, Rollins Sch. Pub. Health, 2005—. Clin. assoc. prof. divsn. geographic medicine, dept. medicine, U. Va., Charlottesville, 1979-82; clin. asst. prof. divsn. infectious dieases, dept. medicine Emory U., Atlanta, 1981-93; staff physician Atlanta VA Hosp., 1989—; adj. prof. dept. epidemiology Rollins Sch. Pub. Health, Emory U., 1994—2005. Contbr. articles to profl. jours., chpts. in books. Baseball coach North Decatur (Ga.) Youth Assn., 1981-90; pres. Westchester Sch. PTA, Decatur, 1986-87. Asst. surgeon gen. USPHS, 1973-75, 76—2005. Recipient Meritorious Svc. medal USPHS, Atlanta, 1986, Outstanding Svc. medal, 1989, Disting. Svc. medal, 1997. Fellow ACP, AAAS, Infectious Diseases Soc. Am.; mem. APHA, Inst. of Medicine, Am. Soc. Microbiology, Am. Soc. Tropical Medicine and Hygiene, Am. Epidemiol. Soc., Royal Soc. Tropical Medicine and Hygiene, Soc. Epidemiol. Rsch., U. So. Calif. Alumni Assn. (bd. govs. 1995-97), Stanford U. Alumni Club Ga. (pres. 1980-82). Avocations: sports, travel. Office: Ste 446 1462 Clifton Rd NE Mailstop 1370/004/1AD Atlanta GA 30322 Home Phone: 404-378-0222; Office Phone: 404-727-3113. Business E-Mail: jmhughe@emory.edu.

HUGHES, JEFFREY A., art history educator; m. Terri F. Reilly, June 19, 1993; 1 child, Jackson Reilly. PhD, U. Iowa, Iowa City, 1988. Prof. art histroy and criticism Webster U., St Louis, 1988—. Dir. grad. program in art Webster U. Office: Webster U 470 E Lockwood Saint Louis MO 63119

HUGHES, (ROBERT) JOHN, journalist, educator; b. Neath, Wales, Apr. 28, 1930; came to U.S., 1954; s. Evan John and Dellis May (Williams) H.; m. Vera Elizabeth Pockman (div. 1987); children: Wendy Elizabeth, Mark Evan; m. Peggy Janeane Jordan, 1988; 1 child, Evan Jordan. LLD (hon.), Colby Coll., 1978; HHD (hon.), So. Utah U., 1994; LHD (hon.), Salt Lake CC, 2007. Africa corr. Christian Sci. Monitor, 1955-61, Far East corr., 1964-70, editor Boston, 1970-79, columnist, 1985—, dir. radio broadcasting, 1987-89; pres. Hughes Newspapers, Orleans, Mass., 1977-85; assoc. dir. USIA, Washington, 1981-82; dir. Voice of Am., Washington, 1982; asst. sec. of state Dept. State, Washington, 1982-85; prof. comm. Brigham Young U., Provo, Utah, 1991—96, 2007—; editor Deseret News, Salt Lake City, 1997—2006. Pres., pub., editor Concord Comm., Rockland, Maine, 1989-91; chmn. Pres. Bush Commn. on U.S. Govt. Internat. Broadcasting, 1991, Presdl./Congressional Commn. Broadcasting to People's Republic China, 1992; asst. sec.-gen. UN, NYC, 1995. Author: The New Face of Africa, 1961, Indonesian Upheaval, 1967. Nieman fellow, Harvard U.,

1961-62; recipient Pulitzer prize, 1967, Sigma Delta Chi, 1977. Mem. Am. Soc. Newspaper Editors (past pres.), Coun. Fgn. Rels., Overseas Press Club (Best Reporting from Overseas 1970). Office: Brigham Young Univ Dept Comm Provo UT 84602

HUGHES, JOHN RUSSELL, neurologist, educator; b. DuBois, Pa., Dec. 19, 1928; s. John Henry and Alice (Cooper) H.; m. Mary Ann Dick, June 14, 1958; children: John Russell Jr. (dec.), Christopher Alan, Thomas Gregory, Cheryl Ann. AB summa cum laude, Franklin and Marshall Coll., 1950; BA with honors, Oxford U., Eng., 1952, MA with honors, 1955, DM (hon.), 1976; PhD, Harvard U., 1954; MD, Northwestern U., 1975. Neurophysiologist NIH, 1954-56; dir. electroencephalography dept. Meyer Hosp., SUNY, 1956-63; dir. div. lab. scis., including electroencephalography Northwestern U. Med. Center, 1963-77, prof. neurology, 1968—; dir. EEG and Epilepsy Clinic, U. Ill. Med. Center, 1977—; staff U. Ill. Hosp., Community Hosp., Geneva, Delnor Hosp., St. Charles; dir.neurophysiology Humana-Michael-Reese Med. Ctr., 1992—. Cons. Chgo. VA Westside Hosp., Mercyville and Copley Meml. Hosp., Aurora, Ill., others; participant debate on brain death BBC-TV; bd. dirs. Am. Bd. EEG and Neurophysiology; participant Am. Med. EEG Assn.; rep. Internat. Fedn. EEG and Clin. Neurophysiology lectr. tour of Africa, 1989; keynote speaker Internat. Course of Neurophysiology, Oxford U., 1993, invited speaker, 1996, 99, 02, 05; invited spkr. Damascus Med. Sch., Syria, 1998, Royal Soc. of Medicine, London, 2003; lectr. in field. Author: Functional Organization of the Diencephalon, 1957, Atlas on Cerebral Death and Coma, 1976, Chinese Translation, 1997, Japanese Translation, 1998, EEG in Clinical Practice, 1982, 2d edit., 1994, EEG Evoked Potentials in Psychiatry and Behavioral Neurology, 1983, JFK and Sam, 2005; contbr. articles to profl. jours. Command Surgeon, USAR, 1986-90, with Army Med. R & D Command, 1990—, mobilization replacement for maj. gen., comdr. Recipient Alumni award Franklin and Marshall Coll., 1978, Lifetime Achievement award Am. EEG and Clin. Neurophysiol. Soc., 2000. Mem. Am. Electroencephalography Soc. (treas. 1965-68), Eastern Electroencephalography Soc. (sec.-treas. 1961-64), Ctrl. Electroencephalography Soc., Am. Med. EEG Assn. (bd. dirs.), Am. Bd. EEG and Neurophysiology (bd. dirs.), Internat. EEG and Clin. Neurophysiology (bd. dirs.), Am. Acad. EEG (bd. dirs.), Brit. Soc. of neurophysiology (hon.), Chgo. Acad. Medicine, Am. Epilepsy Soc., Am. Physiol. Soc., Soc. Neuroscis., Am. Acad. Neurology, Phi Beta Kappa, Sigma Xi (lectr. 1960—) Achievements include research on coding in central nervous system, new theory on neural mechanisms in olfaction, electro-clin. correlations in different types of epilepsy, organic aspects in juvenile delinquency. Home: 720 Roslyn Ter Evanston IL 60201-1722 Office: U Ill Consultation Clinic Epilepsy 912 S Wood St Chicago IL 60612-7325 E-mail: JHughes@uic.edu. *Always be ahead of your colleagues in every endeavor by having done it before they do. Do what you must do now to leave time for innovation later.*

HUGHES, JOHN W., film producer, director, screenwriter; b. Lansing, Mich., Feb. 18, 1950; m. Nancy Ludwig; children: John III, James. With Needham Harper & Steers, Chgo.; copywriter, creative dir. Leo Burnett Co.; editor National Lampoon; founder, pres. Hughes Entertainment, 1985—. Screenwriter: National Lampoon's Class Reunion, 1982, National Lampoon's Vacation, 1983, Mr. Mom, 1983, Nate and Hayes, 1983, National Lampoon's European Vacation, 1985, (as Edmond Dantes), 101 Dalmations, 1996, Maid in Manhattan, 2002, Just Visiting, 2001; screenwriter, prodr.: Pretty in Pink, 1986, Some Kind of Wonderful, 1987, The Great Outdoors, 1988, National Lampoon's Christmas Vacation, 1989, Home Alone, 1990, Career Opportunities, 1990, Dutch, 1991, Home Alone 2: Lost in New York, 1992, Dennis the Menace, 1993, Baby's Day Out, 1994, Miracle on 34th Street, 1994, 101 Dalmations, 1996, Flubber, 1997, Home Alone 3, 1997, Reach the Rock, 1998; screenwriter, dir.: Sixteen Candles, 1984, Weird Science, 1985; screenwriter, dir., prodr.: The Breakfast Club, 1985, Ferris Bueller's Day Off, 1986, Planes, Trains and Automobiles, 1987, She's Having a Baby, 1988, Uncle Buck, 1989, Curly Sue, 1991; prodr.: Only the Lonely, 1991, NewPort South, 2001; TV writer: Home Alone 2, 2002, National Lampoon's American Adventure, 2000. Recipient Commitment to Chgo. award, 1990; named NATO/ShoWest Prodr. of Yr., 1990. also: c/o Michael Wimer Creative Artists Agy 9830 Wilshire Blvd Beverly Hills CA 90212-1804

HUGHES, J(OHNSON) DONALD, history professor, editor; b. Santa Monica, Calif., June 5, 1932; s. Johnson and Vannelia Anna (Blanchfield) H.; m. Pamela Louise Peters, June 8, 1964; children: Peter, Melissa, Joy. AB, UCLA, 1954; STB, Boston U., 1957, PhD, 1960; postgrad., Am. Sch. Classical Studies, Greece, 1966-67. Asst. prof. history U. Denver, 1967-72, assoc. prof. history, 1972-77, prof. history, 1977—, Evans prof., 1994—, chair dept. history, 2000—01. Author: Ecology in Ancient Civilizations, 1975; In The House of Stone And Light, 1978 (Nat. Pk. Service award 1977-78); North American Indian Ecology, 1983, Pan's Travail: Environmental Problems of the Ancient Greeks and Romans, 1994, An Environmental History of the World: Humankind's Changing Role in the Community of Life, 2001, The Mediterranean: An Environmental History, 2005, What is Environmental History?, 2006; editor: Ecological Consciousness, 1981, The Face of the Earth: Environment and World History, 2000; editor Environ. Rev., 1983-85, mem. editl. bd., 1986-95, Environ. Ethics, 1981-89, Environ. History, 1995—, Nature and Culture, 2006—. Boston U. fellow, 1957; Danforth Found. assoc., 1965—; Lindbergh grantee, 1987. Mem. Am. Inst. Archaeology, Am. Soc. Environ. History (exec. bd. 1983-85, Disting. Svc. award 2000), European Soc. Environ. History, Forest History Soc., Denver Mus. Nature and Sci. (rsch. assoc.), Am. Hist. Assn., Phi Beta Kappa. Home: 2580 S University Blvd Apt 1001 Denver CO 80210-6159 Office: U Denver Dept History Denver CO 80208-0001 Business E-Mail: dhughes@du.edu.

HUGHES, KAREN PARFITT, federal agency administrator; b. Paris, Dec. 27, 1956; m. Jerry L. Hughes; 1 child, Robert. BA in English, So. Meth. U., 1977, BFA in journalism, 1977. Television reporter KXAS-TV, Dallas/Ft. Worth, Tex., 1977—84; Tex. media coord. Reagan/Bush Campaign, 1984; media cons. Rep. Party of Tex., 1985—91, exec. dir., 1991—94; dir. comm. to Gov. George W. Bush State of Tex., 1994—2001; dir. comm. Bush-Cheney campaign, 2000; counselor to Pres. The White House, Washington, 2001—02; advisor Bush-Cheney campaign, 2004; under sec. for pub. diplomacy & pub. affairs US Dept. State, Washington, 2005—. Author: Ten Minutes From Normal, 2004. Office: US Dept State 2201 C St NW Rm 7261 Washington DC 20520

HUGHES, KENT HIGGON, economist; b. Portland, Oreg., Feb. 23, 1941; s. John Kenneth and Gwladys (Higgon) H.; m. Virginia Carrington Sammon; children: John Kenneth, Jeff, Krista. BA, Yale U., 1962; LLB, Harvard U., 1965; PhD, Washington U., 1976. Bar: D.C. 1971. Fellow Internat. Legal Ctr., Sao Paulo, Brazil, 1967-69; atty. Urban Law Inst., Washington, 1970-71; legis. counsel Office of Sen. Vance Hartke, Washington, 1971-72; analyst Congl. Rsch. Svc., Washington, 1973-76; sr. economist Joint Econ. Com., Washington, 1977-82; legis. dir. Office Sen. Gary Hart, Washington, 1983-84; staff dir. trade subcom. Ho. Reps. Fgn. Affairs Com., Washington, 1985-87; chief economist Dem. policy com. U.S. Senate, Washington, 1987-90; pres. Coun. on Competitiveness, 1990-93; assoc. dep. sec. of commerce U.S. Dept. of Commerce, Washington, 1993-99; pub. policy scholar Woodrow Wilson Internat. Ctr., Washington, 1999-2001; dir. Sci., Tech. Am. and Global Economy Program Woodrow Wilson Ctr., 2001—04, dir. Program on Sci., Tech. Am. & Global Economy, 2005—. Author: Trade, Taxes, Transnationals, 1979, Building the Next American Century, 2005; contbr. articles to profl. jours. Mem. ABA, Am. Econ. Assn., D.C. Bar Assn. Avocations: languages, rugby, collecting political memorabilia. Home: 4961 Allan Rd Bethesda MD 20816-2721 Office: Woodrow Wilson Internat Ctr One Woodrow Wilson Plaza 1300 Pennsylvania Ave NW Washington DC 20004-3027 Business E-Mail: kent.hughes@wilsoncenter.org.

HUGHES, KEVIN JOHN, lawyer; b. St. Cloud, Minn., July 27, 1936; s. Fred James and Valeria Mary (Spaniol) H.; m. Joanne Margaret Robertson, July 27, 1936; children: Anne, Thomas, Jennifer, James, Emily. BA in Philosophy and Polit. Sci., St. John's U., Collegeville, Minn., 1958; JD, U. Minn., 1962. Bar: Minn. 1962, U.S. Dist. Ct. Minn. 1963, U.S. Ct. Appeals (8th cir.) 1973, U.S. Supreme Ct. 1973. Law clerk Minn. Supreme Ct., 1962-63; assoc. Fred J. Hughes Atty., St. Cloud, 1963; ptnr. Hughes Thoreen & Sullivan, Hughes Thoreen Mathews & Knapp, St. Cloud, 1964-94, Hughes Mathews PA, St. Cloud, 1994—. Bd. dirs. Ctrl. Minn. Cmty. Found., United Way, YMCA. 1st lt. US Army, 1959. Mem.: Am. Health Lawyers Assn., Minn. State Bar, St. Cloud C. of C. Home: 295 Waite Ave S Saint Cloud MN 56301-7335 Office: Hughes Mathews PO Box 548 Saint Cloud MN 56302-0548 Business E-Mail: khughes@hughesmathews.com.

HUGHES, LIBBY, writer; b. Pitts., Aug. 11, 1932; d. Lloyd Alfred and Vera Abby (Walker) Pockman; m. R. John Hughes, Aug. 20, 1955 (div. 1988); children: Wendy E., Mark E BA, U. Ala., 1954; MFA, Boston U., 1955. Profl. actress, Kenya, South Africa, 1955—59; drama critic and feature writer Cape Cod Newspapers, 1977—86, assoc. pub., 1977—81, pub., 1981—85. Pres. Desert Starfield Prodn., 1994 Author: Bali, 1969, Margaret Thatcher, 1989, Benazir Bhutto, 1990, Nelson Mandela, 1992, Good Manners for Children, 1992, H. Norman Schwarzkopf, 1992, West Point, 1992, Valley Forge, 1992, Colin Powell, 1996, School Manners Workbook, 1998, Christopher Reeve, 1997, Tiger Woods, 2000, Yitzhak Rabin, 2001, George W. Bush, 2003, John Grisham, 2004, Ronald Reagan, 2005, (with Marian R. Carlson) American Genius: Henry Wadsworth Longfellow, 2006; editor: Ginger Rogers Autobiography, 1989, 91; playwright: Sin in the Attic (Chatham Drama Guild award 1999-2000), Pasta and Curry (New Opera and Musical Theatre Initiative award 2000), Here Come the Bullies, 2004, 2nd edit, 2006, Weapon in Her Pocket, 2006, Tiger, Tiger Hits the Ball and That's not All!, 2006, 37 others; theater critic, reviewer www.capecodtoday.com Bd. dir. Wisdom Inst., 1984-86, Cape Cod Mus., 1984-86 Recipient Songwriting award, Eventide Arts Festival Cape Cod, 2001, 2003, 2005, 2006, Life Achievement award, Emma Willard Sch., 2005. Mem. ASCAP, Dramatists Guild, Authors Guild, Ala. Wildlife Rescue Svc. (pres. 1988-89), Nat. Soc. Arts and Letters (chpt. pres. 1984-86, protocol officer 1984-86), Nat. League Am. Pen Women Avocations: theater, news, wildlife, rhodesian ridgebacks. Home (Winter): 993 Memorial Dr #301 Cambridge MA 02138 Personal E-mail: libhughes@aol.com.

HUGHES, LINDA J., newspaper publisher; b. Princeton, BC, Can., Sept. 27, 1950; d. Edward Rees and Madge Preston (Bryan) H.; m. George Fredrick Ward, Dec. 16, 1978; children: Sean Ward, Kate Ward. BA, Victoria U., Can., 1972; LittD (hon.), Athabasca U., 1997; diploma in journalism (hon.), Grant MacEwan C.C., Edmonton, Alta., Can., 1999; LLD (hon.), U. Alberta, 2003. With Edmonton Jour., Alta., Canada, 1976—, from reporter to asst. mng. editor Alta., 1984-87, editor Alta., 1987-92, pub. Alta., 1992—. Southam fellow U. Toronto, Ont., Can., 1977-78; recipient Disting. Citizen award Grant MacEwan C.C., 1999, Dist. Alumni award U. Victoria, 2000. Office: Edmonton Journal 10006 101st St PO Box 2421 Edmonton AB Canada T5J 2S6 E-mail: lhughes@thejournalcanwest.com.

HUGHES, LYNN NETTLETON, federal judge; m. Olive (Allen). BA, U. Ala., 1963; JD, U. Tex., 1968; LLM, U. Va., 1992. Bar: Tex., 1966. Pvt. practice, Houston, 1966-79; judge Dist. Ct. Tex., Houston, 1979-85; U.S. dist. judge So. Dist. Tex., Houston, 1985—. Adj. prof. South Tex. Coll. Law, 1973-03, U. Tex., 1990-91, 00-01, mem. bd. visitors, 2006-; Tex. del. Nat. Conf. State Trial Judges, 1983-85; cons. Tex. Jud. Budget Bd., 1984; lectr. Tex. Coll. Judiciary, 1983; mem. task force on revision rules of civil procedure Supreme Ct. Tex., 1993-94; cons. on constrn. Moldova, 1993, European Cmty., 1989, Ukraine, 1995, Romania, 1996, Albania, 1997; mem. jud. adv. bd. Law and Econs. Ctr., George Mason U., 1999—. Mem. adv. bd. Houston Jour. Internat. Law, 1981—, chmn., 1989-99. Trustee Rift Valley Rsch. Mission, 1978—; mem. St. Martin's Episcopal Ch.; dir. Houston World Affairs Coun., 1997—, co-chair 1999-2000. Mem.: FBA (bd. dirs. Houston chpt. 1986—89), ABA, Am. Inns of Ct. XV (pres. 1986—92), Houston Philos. Soc. (exec. com. 2000—03), Am. Anthrop. Assn., Am. Soc. Legal History, Am. Judicature Soc., Tex. State Bar (selection, compensation and tenure state judges com. 1981—85, ct. cost, delay and efficiency com. 1981—90, vice chmn. 1982—83, nominations com. jud. sect. 1983, vice chmn. 1984—86, liaison with law schs. com. 1987—92, plain lang. com. 1989—96), Houston Bar Assn., Maritime Law Assn., Am. Law Inst., Coun. on Fgn. Rels., Houston Com. Fgn. Rels. (chmn. 2003—04). Office: US Ct Hse 11122 515 Rusk St Houston TX 77002-2605 Home: PO Box 61565 Houston TX 77208 Office Phone: 713-250-5900. Business E-Mail: lnh@txs.uscourts.gov.

HUGHES, MALCOLM KENNETH, dendrochronologist, educator, administrator; b. Matlock, Derbyshire, Eng., July 24, 1943; came to U.S., 1986; s. Joseph Kenneth and Gladys Bertha (Linahen) H.; children: Rachel Janet, Daniel John. BSc in Botany and Zoology with honors, U. Durham, Eng., 1965, PhD, 1970. Rsch. fellow Soil Biology Inst. U. Aarhus, Denmark, 1968-69; rsch. fellow Botany Dept. U. Durham, 1969-71; lectr. II in ecology Biology Dept. Liverpool Poly., England, 1971-73, sr. lectr. in ecology, 1973-80, prin. lectr. in ecology, 1980-82, reader in ecology, 1982-86; prof., Lab. of Tree-Ring Rsch. U. Ariz., Tucson, 1986—; dir. div. global change Ariz. Rsch. Labs., 1989-92; vis. fellow Coop. Inst. Rsch. in Environ. Sci. U. Colo., Boulder, 1992-93. Internal/external examiner degree candidates Coun. for Nat. Acad. Awards and Univs. Oxford, Durham, East Anglia, Ulster, Aix-Marseille, and Auckland, 1974—; external examiner degree studies in ecology New Coll., Durham, 1978-85; external examiner ecology Inst. Biology, Eng., 1980-86; mem. combined sci. studies bd. Coun. Nat. Acad. Awards, Eng., 1983-86; mem. rev. panel arid lands scis. acad. program U. Ariz., 1990, chmn. rev. panel remote sensing acad. program, 1991, mem. rev. panel stats. dept., 1991, chmn. com. on global change faculty of sci., 1986—, chmn. coord. com. on global change, 1988-92; organizer Global Dendroclimatology Workshop, 1978-82; mem. terrestrial life scis. grants com. Natural Environment Rsch. Coun., Eng., 1982-85, mem. advanced courses rev. panel, 1984-85; mem. U.S. Nat. Com. for Internat. Union Quaternary Rsch., 1988—; mem. organizing com. 1989 Global Change Inst. Univs.' Corp. for Atmospheric Rsch., 1988-89; mem. paleoclimatology adv. panel NOAA, 1989-91; mem. adv. panel. earth system history NSF, 1990; mem. tech. adv. panel Western Region Nat. Inst. Global Environ. Change U.S. Dept. Energy, 1990-92; mem. com. on geophys. and environ. data NAS, 1994—; mem. exec. com. and com. on global chage, Inst. for the Study of Planet Earth, involved with Climate Assessment Project for the Southwest; lectr., presenter in field. Author: (with P.M. Kelly, J.R. Pilcher, V.C. LaMarche Jr.) Climate from Tree Rings, 1982; contbr. numerous articles to profl. jours. Bd. trustees Nat. Inst. Global Environ. Change, 1992—. Grantee Royal Soc. London, 1973-79, Natural Environment Rsch. Coun., 1974, 81, Sci. and Engring. Rsch. Coun., 1981, Commn. of European Communities, 1984, NSF, 1989, 90, NOAA, 1990, U.S. Nat. Park Svc., 1991, NATO, 1980, 84, 86. Fellow Royal Meteorol. Soc.; mem. Am. Geophys. Union, Brit. Ecol. Soc. (sec. energy and prodn. biology group 1972-78, mem. meetings com. 1972-78, coun. 1984-86). Achievements include establishment of climate record in Brit. Isles tree rings; reconstruction of temperatures in pre-instrumental times, e.g. in Scotland and Kashmir, of drought frequency in Calif. from giant sequoia tree rings; research conducted with colleagues concluded that the Northern Hemisphere was the warmest it has been in 2,000 years. The research was known as the "hockey-stick" graph because it compared the sharp curve of the hockey blade to the recent sharp rise in temperatures and the stick's long shaft to centuries of previous climate stability. Office: U Ariz Lab Tree-Ring Rsch PO Box 210058 West Stadium 293 Tucson AZ 85721 Office Phone: 520-621-6470. Business E-Mail: mhughes@ltrr.arizona.edu.

HUGHES, MARIJA MATICH, law librarian; b. Belgrade, Yugoslavia; came to U.S., 1960, naturalized, 1971; d. Zarija and Antonija (Hudowsky) Matich. BA in Music, Mokranjac, Belgrade; BA in English, U. Belgrade and Calif. State U.; MLS, U. Md.; student, McGeorge Sch. Law; MHA in Health Care Adminstrn., George Washington U., 1985, M. in Adminstrv. Scis., 1989. Counselor, gen. mgr. Career Counseling Service, Sacramento, Calif., 1962-64; sec. to mgr. Sacramento State Coll., 1965-66; student librarian High John program U. Md., Fairmont Heights, 1967; reference librarian Calif. State Law Library, Sacramento, 1968; head reference library-faculty liaison librarian Hastings Coll. Law U. Calif., San Francisco, 1969-72; head law librarian AT&T, Washington, 1972-73; chief law librarian Nat. Clearinghouse Library, U.S. Commn. on Civil Rights, Washington, 1973-86; tech. info. specialist U.S. Dept. Labor, OSHA, Tech. Date Ctr., 1988—; owner, pub. Hughes Press. Author (compiler): The Sexual Barrier, Legal and Econ. Aspects of Employment, vols. 1 and 2, 1970—73, The Sexual Barriers: Legal, Medical, Economic and Social Aspects of Sex Discrimination, 1977, Computer Health Hazards, 1990, 1993, Computer Health Hazards, Eng. translation, 1996, Sick From Computers, 1994, Computers, Antennas, Cellular Telephones and Power Lines Health Hazards, 1996, Shadow at the Ball, 2001; contbr. articles to profl. jours. Mem. Am. Assn. Law Librs., Bioelectromagnetics Soc., Consumer Utilities Bd. Home: 2400 Virginia Ave NW Apt C501 Washington DC 20037-2644 Office Phone: 202-293-2686.

HUGHES, MARY ALICE, adult education educator, consultant; b. Natchitoches, La. d. J. Wesley and Mary Odeal (Ferguson) Stephens; children: Cary Wendell, Andrea Michelle. BA, Northwestern State U., 1960, MEd, 1982, postgrad., 1984; EdD in Developmental Edn./Instrnl. Systems and Tech., Grambling State U., 2003. Cert. tchr., La. Tchr. Caddo Parish-Linwood Jr. High Sch., Shreveport, La., 1960-64, St. Tammany Parish-Salmen High Sch., Slidell, La., 1967-69, Rapides Parish-Adult Edn. Ctr., Alexandria, La., 1971—99; coord., tchr. JTPA Acad. Remediation High Sch. Program, Alexandria, La., 1991-93; tchr. La. Bus. Coll., Alexandria, La., 1987-89; coord., tchr. St. Frances Cabrini Hosp.: Workplace Literacy Project, Alexandria, La., 1991—97; edn. cons. and site coord. workplace tng. Willamette Industries/Weyerhauser Co., 1999—. Staff assoc. tchr. tng., assessment team mem. diagnostic/prescriptive evaluations, Youth Challange Program, 1993; coord. Mobile Automated Learning Lab, 1994; mentor adult edn. and insvc. grant Northwestern State U., 1991, cons. tng. tchrs. adult learners grant, 1993, evaluator Adult Learning Project grant program, 1993—; tutor in field; evaluator grant proposals Bur. Adult and Cmty. Edn., Baton Rouge, 1992-94; cons. Natchitoches Parish Workplace Literacy Grant, 2000-01; supr. grad. assts. La. Tech., Grambling State U.; presenter in field. Participant support projects Battered Women's Program, Alexandria, Shepard Ctr., Alexandria, Food Bank; rep. Gov.'s Forum on Literacy in the Workforce in Yr. 2000, Baton Rouge, 1991. Named Tchr. of Yr., La. Assn. Pub. Community and Adult Educators, 1987-88, named to Nat. Dean's List, 1991; recipient All Am. Scholar award U.S Achievement Acad., 1990. Mem. La. Assn. Pub. Community and Adult Educators (state bd. dirs. 1981-88, state conv. coord. 1986), Assoc. Profl. Educators La., La. Ret. Tchrs. Assn., Phi Delta Kappa. Methodist. Avocations: redesigning jewelry, collecting carousels, nurturing houseplants. Personal E-mail: ash.121@suddenlink.net.

HUGHES, MARY KATHERINE, lawyer; b. July 16, 1949; d. John Chamberlain and Marjorie (Anstey) Hughes; m. Andrew H. Eker, July 7, 1982. BBA cum laude, U. Alaska, 1971; JD, Willamette U., 1974; postgrad., Heriot-Watt U., Edinburgh, Scotland, 1971. Bar: Alaska 1975. Ptnr. Hughes, Thorsness, Gantz, Powell & Brundin, Anchorage, 1974—95; mcpl. atty. Municipality of Anchorage, 1995—2000; of counsel Hughes, Thorsness, Powell, Huddleston & Bauman, 2001—05; Alaska state dir. Office US Senator Lisa Murkowski, 2005—. Talk show host AM 700 KBYR, 2002—. Trustee Willamette U., 1997—; bd. visitors WUCL, 1978—2001; bd. dirs. Alaska Repertory Theatre, 1986—88, pres., 1987—88; commr. Alaska Code Revision Commn., 1987—94; bd. visitors U. Alaska, Fairbanks, 1994—2002, bd. regents, 2002—, chair bd. regents, 2005—; bd. dirs. Anchorage Econ. Devel. Corp., 1989—, chmn., 1994; mem. Providence Anchorage Adv. Coun., 1993—2005, Providence Alaska Found., 1998—2005, chair, 2002—04; lawyer rep. 9th Cir. Jud. Conf., 1995—2000; pres. Alaska Bar Found., 1984—98, trustee, 2001—, Athena Soc., 2003—; bd. dirs. Alaska Humanities Forum, 2006—. Fellow: U. Alaska Found. (trustee 1990—), Am. Bar Found.; mem.: Internat. Mcpl. Lawyers Assn. (state chair 1995—96, regional v.p. 1997—2000), Anchorage Assn. Women Lawyers (pres. 1976—77), Alaska Bar Assn. (bd. govs. 1981—84, pres. 1983—84), Soroptimists (pres. 1986—87), Delta Theta Phi. Republican. Roman Catholic. Home: 1592 Coffey Ln Anchorage AK 99501-4977 Office Phone: 907-274-6290. E-mail: mkhughes@acsalaska.net.

HUGHES, MARY SORROWS, artist; b. Washington, Oct. 28, 1945; d. Howard Earl and Martha Jane (Summerville) Sorrows; m. Frank Broox Hughes, May 22, 1967; 1 child, Broox Bradley. BA in Art, Centenary Coll., 1967, BA in Edn., 1978. Draftsman for civil engring. dept. Texaco, New Orleans, 1967-70; art studio owner, freelance artist Shreveport, La., 1979—. Illustrator Total Tales, 1984; included in The Best of Watercolor, 1995, Best of Watercolor: Painting Color, 1997, Floral Inspirations, 1998, Splash 7: The Qualities of Light, 2002, The New Creative Artist by Nita Leland, 2006; represented in permanent collections Southwestern Electric Power Co., Shreveport, Burgess Corp. Collection, Calif.; featured artist Watercolor Mag., 2003; featured artist donor Phila. House Auction and Fund Raiser for AIDS, 2003. Bd. dirs. Child Care Svcs., Inc. of N.W. La., Shreveport, 1987-91, pres., 1991; Artport Airport Exhibit and Fundraiser for AIDS, Shreveport, 1991-2007; worker Habitat for Humanity, Shreveport, 1992, 94; trustee St. Luke's Meth. Ch., Shreveport, 1993-95, chair bldg. com., 1986; bd. dirs. Shreveport Art Guild, Friends of the Meadows Mus., 2000-03. Named one of 10 Artists for Highway Haiku, 2002; recipient Gary, Field, Landry & Bradford award, La. Women Artists, 1994. Mem.: La. Watercolor Soc. (signature mem., Pres. award Internat. Show 2005), Hoover Watercolor Soc. (pres. 1986, treas., publicity chair, others, Jurors Choice award 2001, Transparent Watercolor award 2003, Jurors Choice award 2006, Transparent Watercolor award 2006), La. Artists (pres. 1994, 1998), Watercolor West (Yarka St. Petersberg Mdse. award 1995, Signature Mem. award 1996, W. Burgess Purchase prize 1998), Southwestern Watercolor Soc. (Signature Mem. award 1991, Edgar A. Whitney award 1992, Ansel Merchandise award 1999, Canson-Talons Inc. award 2000), Med. Aux. Wives Club. Democrat. Avocations: exercise, gardening, travel, reading, flute. Home: 530 Atkins Ave Shreveport LA 71104-4448 Studio: 1700 Creswell Ave Shreveport LA 71101-4726 Office Phone: 318-222-2912. Business E-Mail: maryhughes@marysorrowshughes.com.

HUGHES, MICHAEL RANDOLPH, evangelist; b. Newport News, Va. s. Luke Jr. and Patsy Ruth (Jewell) H.; m. Carolyn Delight Williamson, Mar. 20, 1981; children: Amanda, Patsy. Diploma, Memphis Sch. Preaching, 1976; cert. in theology, Ala. Christian Sch. Religion, 1982, BA, 1984; MS, Troy State U., 1987; MA, So. Christian U., 2001; PhD, Wiltshire U., 2005. Min. Newport News Ch. of Christ, 1977-80, 81-83, Ch. of Christ of Clyattville, Ga., 1980-81, 83-85, City Boulevard Ch. of Christ, Waycross, Ga., 1985-87, Hampton (Va.) Ch. of Christ, 1988-92; instr. Bible Ga.

Christian Sch., Dasher, 1985-87; min. Green's Lake Road Ch. of Christ, East Ridge, Tenn., 1992-97; min., elder Marion (Ark.) Ch. of Christ, 1997—; prof. So. Christian U., Montgomery, Ala., 1999—. Dir., instr. Bible, Idlewild Christian Camp, Surry, Va., 1977-80; youth worker Ga. Christian Children's Home, Dasher, 1985-87; missionary Mil. Outreach, Germany, 1988-90, Chs. of Christ, India, Malaysia, Taiwan, 1992—; program analyst HB Software, 1996—; co-founder, co-owner HB Software, 1997—. Author: Tax Record System, 1980; contbr. articles to relgious publs. Cmty. organizer North End Huntington Heights Preservation Assn., Newport News, 1977—80; tax preparer VITA, Valdosta, Ga., 1986—87; mem. Ark. Gov.'s Steering Com. on Abstinence Edn., 2000—01; elected ofcl., chmn. Crittenden County Ark. Rep. Ctrl. Com., 2000—02; chmn. 1st Cong. Dist. Ark./Ea. Region, 2002—03; chmn. ea. region 1st Congl. Dist. Rep. Party of Ark., 2002—. Recipient award of merit Memphis Sch. Preaching, 1977. Mem. Givens Orgn., Memphis Sch. Preaching Alumni Assn. (bd. dirs. 1991-95, 98—). Avocations: coin collecting/numismatics, tennis, bowling. Home: 72 Military Rd PO Box 209 Marion AR 72364-0209 Office: Marion Ch Christ PO Box 209 Marion AR 72364-0209 Office Phone: 870-759-1849. E-mail: borninva@aol.com.

HUGHES, MIKE, advertising executive; b. Washington, May 27, 1948; s. James Richard and Ann Marie (Lucas) H.; m. Ginny Lee Ferguson, Apr. 12, 1975; children: Preston Ferguson, (dec.)Jason Christopher. BA, Washington & Lee U., 1970. Reporter Richmond News Leader, Va., 1965-70, copy editor, reporter Va., 1970; reporter Richmond Times Dispatch, 1967-70; copywriter Clinton E. Frank Advt., 1971-72, Martin & Woltz Advt., Richmond, 1973; creative dir. Lawler & Ballard, Richmond, 1974; founder, ptnr. Hughes Wynne, Richmond, 1975-78; exec.v.p., creative dir. Martin Agy., Richmond, 1978-99, dir., 1983-99, vice chmn., 1986-99, ptnr., 1999—; dir. Alan Newman Rsch., Richmond, 1982—. Contbr. articles to Richmond mag. Mem. adv. bd. N.Y. Art Dirs. awards, 1978—, CA mag. awards, 1978—. Mem. One Club for Copy and Art (One Show awards 1978—), Advt. Club of Richmond (bd. dirs., v.p. scholarship chmn., Addy awards chmn., program chmn., pub. svc. chmn., Addy awards). Home: 7501 Riverside Dr Richmond VA 23225-1244 Office: Martin Agy One Shockoe Plz Richmond VA 23219-4132

HUGHES, NICHOLAS MELVIN, mining company executive; b. Lordsburg, N.Mex., Dec. 15, 1913; s. Nicholas and Sara Ellen Hughes; m. Melba Ruth Morrow Boland; children: Nicholas Melvin Jr., Craig Morrow; m. Jean Abbott, May 14, 1943; children: Kathryn Melba, RoseMary. CEO, pres., dir. Minenex Corp., Las Vegas, Nev., Hughes Exploration and Mining Corp., Las Vegas. With Merchant Marines, WW II. Avocations: mining, geology, early western history. Office Phone: 702-858-0300.

HUGHES, PHIL (PHILIP J. HUGHES), professional baseball player; b. Mission Viejo, Calif., June 24, 1986; s. Philip Hughes Sr. and Dorianne Hughes (Stepmother). Pitcher NY Yankees, 2007—. Named Minor League Player of Yr., NY Yankees, 2005; named one of Top 100 Prospects, Baseball Am., 2007. Mailing: Yankee Stadium 161st St and River Ave Bronx NY 10451 Office Phone: 718-293-4300.*

HUGHES, PHILIP S. H., dermatologist; b. Flandreau, SD, Feb. 5, 1944; s. Philip F. H. Pugh and Elizabeth L. Ramsdell; m. Jane Barbara Lindell, June 14, 1969; children: Elizabeth, Alexander, Audrey. BS, Iowa State U., Ames, 1965; MD, U. Iowa, Iowa City, 1969. Diplomate Am. Bd. Dermatology. Intern Iowa Meth. Hosp., Des Moines, 1969—73; resident dermatology U. Tex. Med. Br., Galveston, 1973—76; pvt. practice dermatology San Antonio, 1976—. Capt. Med. Corp. US Army, 1970—73. Fellow: Am. Acad. Dermatology; mem.: Alpha Omega Alpha. Avocations: sailing, bicycling, skiing. Office: Hughes Dermatology 7940 Floyd Curl Dr San Antonio TX 78229

HUGHES, RAY HARRISON, minister, religious organization administrator; b. Calhoun, Ga., Mar. 7, 1924; s. J.H. and Emma Hughes; m. Marian Euverla Tidwell; children: Janice, Ray H., Donald, Anita. AA, Lee Coll.; BA, Tenn. Wesleyan Coll.; MS, EdD, U. Tenn.; LittD, Lee Coll., Cleveland. Ordained to ministry Ch. of God, 1950. Pastor Fairfield Ch. of God (Ill.), 1945-46; pastor North Chattanooga Ch. of God, 1948-52; organized churches in Spain, Md., Ill., Tenn., Ga., North Chattanooga Ch. of God, 1948-52; Nat. Sunday Sch. and youth dir., 1952-56; pres. Lee Coll., Cleveland, Tenn., 1960-66, 82-84; pres. theol. seminary Ch. God Sch. Theology, 1984-86; Md.-Del.-D.C. overseer Ch. of God, 1956-60, 3rd asst. gen. overseer, 1966-68, 92-94, mem. exec. coun., 1956-60, 62-82, 86-90, 92-96, 99-2000, exec. dir. gen. bd. edn., 1970-72, 2d asst. gen. overseer, 1968-70, 1st asst. gen. overseer, 1970-72, 76-78, 86-90, 94-96. Gen. overseer, 1972-74, 78-82, 96, Ga. overseer, 1974-76; spkr. for convs., preaching missions, ministers retreats. Author: Planning for Sunday School Programs, 1960, Order of Future Events, 1962, What is Pentecost?, 1963, The Effect of Lee College on World Missions, 1963, The Transition of Church Related Junior Colleges To Senior Colleges, 1966, Church of God Distinctives, 1968, The Outpouring of the Spirit, Dynamics of Sunday School Growth, 1980, Pentecostal Preaching, 1981, Who is the Holy Ghost, 1992, Lord, Show Us Thy Glory, 1997, The Cross: Love's Necessity, 1999, The Rapture and Revelation, 2000; editor the Pilot; contbr. articles to profl. jours. Chmn. Pentecostal Fellowship of N.Am., Pentecostal World Conf., 1989-98, Hall of Prophets Ch. of God Theol. Sem. Mem. Nat. Assn. Evangelicals (pres.), Pi Delta Omicron, Phi Delta Kappa. Address: PO Box 4815 Cleveland TN 37320-4815

HUGHES, ROBERT G., foundation administrator; BA, DePauw U.; MA, Ohio State U.; PhD in behavioral sciences, Johns Hopkins U. Post-doctoral fellow U. Calif., San Francisco; mem. faculty Ariz. State U.; joined The Robert Wood Johnson Found., Princeton, NJ, 1989, now chief learning officer. Office: The Robert Wood Johnson Found PO Box 2316 College Rd E and Rt 1 Princeton NJ 08543 Office Phone: 888-631-9989.

HUGHES, ROBERT HARRISON, former agricultural products executive; b. Puunene, Hawaii, Mar. 23, 1917; s. Robert Edwin and Alice Thayer (Walker) H.; m. Nadine Jeannette Hegler, Aug. 24, 1940 (div. 1983); children: Robert Lawrence, Linton Alice, Carole Nadine.; m. Judith R. Gething, Jan. 28, 1983. B.Sc. in Sugar Tech, U. Hawaii, 1938. With Hawaiian Comml. & Sugar Co., 1939—62, sugar mill supt., 1962—65; prodn. mgr., v.p. tech. services C. Brewer & Co., Ltd., Honolulu, 1965-69, sr. v.p. Hawaiian ops., 1969-77, exec. v.p., 1977-80, dir. subs., 1966-80; pres. Hawaiian Sugar Planters Assn., Aiea, 1981—86; dir. Mauna Loa Resources Inc., 1986-95. Mem. bd. regents U. Hawaii, 1961-66; trustee Hawaii Conf. Found., 1966-85, Hawaii Loa Coll., 1980-89, Moloka'i Mus. and Cultural Ctr., 1984-91, Hawaiian Hist. Soc., 1990-94, U. Hawaii Found., 1963-65, 73-78, pres., 1967-68; bd. dirs. Hawaii Multi-Cultural Ctr., 1979-81, Samaritan Counseling Ctr. Hawaii, 1985-91; chmn. adv. bd. Cancer Rsch. Ctr., Hawaii, 1979-81; pres. Hawaii conf. United Ch. of Christ, 1962-63. Mem. Hawaiian Sugar Planters Assn. (dir. 1972-80), Hawaiian Hist. Soc, Home: 1080 S Beretania #902 Honolulu HI 96814-1445

HUGHES, STANLEY JOHN, retired mycologist; b. Llanelli, S. Wales, Sept. 17, 1918; emigrated to Can., 1952, naturalized, 1967; s. John Thomas and Gertrude (Roberts) H.; m. Lyndell Anne Rutherford, Oct. 11, 1958; children— Robert Conway, Glenys Anne, David Stanley. B.Sc. with honors, U. Wales, Aberystwyth, 1941, M.Sc., 1943, D.Sc., 1954. Asst. to adv. mycologist Nat. Agrl. Advisory Ser. U. Wales, 1941-45; asst. mycologist Commonwealth Mycological Inst., Kew, England, 1945-52; mycologist Research br. Agr. Can. Central Exptl. Farm, Ottawa, Ont., 1952-58, sr. mycologist, 1958-62; prin. mycologist Rsch. br. Agr. Can. Central Exptl. Farm (Ctr. for Land and Biol. Resources Rsch., 1962-83; hon. rsch. assoc., 1983—. Sr. Rsch. fellow New Zealand Dept. Sci. and Indsl. Rsch., 1963; Exchange scientist Nat. Rsch. Councils of Can. and Brazil, 1974. Contbr. articles in field to profl. jours. Recipient Jakob Eriksson Gold medal, 1969; George Lawson medal, 1981 Fellow Royal Soc. Can., Linnean Soc. London (fgn. mem.); mem. Mycological Soc. Am. (pres. 1975; Disting. mycologist award 1985); British Mycological Soc. (fgn. v.p. and honorary mem. 1987), Internat. Mycological Assn. (v.p. 1977-83, hon. v.p. XVI internat. botanical congress 1999). Home: 360 Hamilton Ave Ottawa ON Canada K1Y 1C5 Office: Ea Cereal/Oilseed Rsch Ctr Agrl and Agri-Food Can Ctrl Exptl Farm Ottawa ON Canada K1A 0C6 Personal E-mail: sjhughes@sympatico.ca.

HUGHES, STEPHEN H., virologist, researcher; PhD, Harvard U. Post-doctoral rsch. with Dr. J. Michael Bishop and Harold Varmus U. Calif., San Francisco; sr. staff investigator Cold Spring Harbor Lab.; established the Gene Expression in Eukaryotes Sect.(subsequently called the Retroviral Replication and Vector Design Sect.) ABL Rsch. Program, 1984—88, dep. dir., 1988—95; dir. Molecular Basis of Carcinogenesis Lab., 1995—99; chief, retroviral replication lab. HIV Drug Resistance Program, Nat. Cancer Inst., 1999—, chief, vector design and replication sect. Researcher Rutgers U., Ctr. of Advanced Biotechnology and Medicine, Piscataway, NJ, 1987—; co-organizer, retroviruses and viral vectors mtgs. Cold Spring Harbor Lab.; co-organizer, annual mtg. on Oncogenes. Named one of Most Frequently Cited AIDS Researchers, Science Watch, 1996. Partnered with Edward Arnold in 1987 at Rutgers University Laboratory, Center of Advanced Biotechnology and Medicine, to work with a 30 member research team to develop a trio of drugs that are believed to destroy HIV, the virus that causes AIDS, tenifovir, or the DAPY (diarylpyrimidine). Office: Nat Cancer Inst HIV Drug Resistance Program NCI-Frederick PO Box B Bldg 539 Frederick MD 21702-1201 Office Phone: 301-846-1619. Office Fax: 301-846-6966. Business E-Mail: hughes@ncifcrf.gov.

HUGHES, SUE MARGARET, retired librarian; b. Cleburne, Tex. d. Chastain Wesley and Sue Willis (Payne) H. BBA, U. Tex., Austin, 1949; MLS, Tex. Woman's U., Denton, 1960, PhD, 1987. Sec.-treas. pvt. corps., Waco, Tex., 1949-59; asst. in public svcs. Baylor U. Libr., Waco, 1960-64, acquisitions libr., 1964-79, acting univ. libr., summer 1979, dir. Moody Libr., 1980-89; interim univ. libr. Baylor U., Waco, 1989-91, spl. materials cons., 1991-92; ret., 1992. Bd. advs. Baylor U. Libr., 2006—. Mem. AAUP, ALA, Tex. Libr. Assn., AAUW, Brazos Forum, Hist. Waco Found., Altrusa Club, Delta Kappa Gamma, Beta Phi Mu, Beta Gamma Sigma. Methodist.

HUGHES, THOMAS A., lawyer, utilities executive; BS, Mo. Valley Coll.; JD, Univ. Mo. Gen. counsel Mo. Pub. Svc. Commn.; staff atty. Detroit Edison, Mich. Consol. Gas Co., 1978—83, regulatory atty. supr., 1983—88, gen. atty., regulatory affairs, 1988—93, assoc. gen. counsel, mgr., 1993—98, asst. v.p., mgr., assoc. gen. counsel, 1998—2001, v.p. gen. counsel, 2001—; and chief compliance officer DTE Energy, 2005—. With US Army, 1963—65, artillery. Mem.: Met. Detroit Bar Assn. Found., Am. Corp. Counsel Assn. (Mich. chpt.), Mich. Bar Assn. Office: DTE Energy Co 2000 2nd Ave Detroit MI 48226-1279*

HUGHES, THOMAS C., JR., lawyer; b. Chgo., Nov. 2, 1949; s. Thomas and Mattie Hughes; children: Tiffanie, Talease, Thomas, Timothy, Tatiana. BA, U. Ill., Champaign-Urbana, 1971, MA, 1973, JD, 1976. Bar: Ill. 1977, Calif. 1987, Colo. 1989, Tex. 1990, US Dist. Ct. (ctrl. ea. dist.) Ill. 1978, US Ct. Appeals (7th cir.) 1983, US Supreme Ct. 1982. Pvt. practice, atty., counselor at law Law Offices of Thomas C. Hughes. Jr, 1977—88; sr. dep. county counsel, trial atty. Office County of San Diego, Calif., 1989—. Instr., lectr. bus. law Calif. State U., 1987—89; asst. prof. bus. law Ill. Wesleyan U., Bloomington, 1978—79; asst. prof. bus. law, social instns. Parkland Coll., Champaign, Ill., 1974—76; instr. sociology U. Ill., 1971—73; reader, presenter McGill Sch. of Success for Children, San Diego, 2003—; child abuse prevention com. San Diego County Dist. Atty., 1994; diversity action com. San Diego County Health and Human Svcs., 1995. Chmn. legal divsn. NAACP, Champaign, 1978—79; commr. City Planning Commn. Champaign, Ill., 1982; commr. jud. nominees evaluation com. State Calif., 2002—06; People to People del. to South Africa, 2005; spkr., presenter, black history month spkr. San Diego CountyFamily Resource Ctr., 2005. Mem.: San Diego County Bar Assn., Phi Alpha Delta, Alpha Phi Alpha (life).

HUGHES, THOMAS JOSEPH ROBERT, mechanical engineering educator, consultant; b. Bklyn., Aug. 3, 1943; s. Joseph Anthony and Mae (Bland) H.; m. Susan Elizabeth Weh, July 1, 1972; children: Emily Susan, Ian Thomas, Elizabeth Claire. B.M.E., Pratt Inst., Bklyn., 1965; M.M.E., Pratt Inst., 1967; MA in Math., U. Calif.-Berkeley, 1974, PhD in Engring. Sci., 1974; Doctorate (hon.), U. Catholique de Louvain, Belgium, 2003. Mech. design engr. Grumman Aerospace, Bethpage, NY, 1965-66; R & D Gen. Dynamics, Groton, Conn., 1967—69; lectr., asst. rsch. engr. U. Calif., Berkeley, 1975-76; assoc. prof. structural mechanics Calif. Inst. Tech., Pasadena, 1976-80; assoc. prof. mech. engring. Stanford U., Calif., 1980-82, prof. Calif., 1983—, chmn. divsn. applied mechanics, 1984-88, 94—, chmn. dept. mech. engring., 1988-89; founder, chmn. CENTRIC Engring. Sys., Inc., 1990-99. Galileo vis. prof. Scuola Normale Superiore, Pisa, Italy, 1999; Eshbach vis. prof. Northwestern U., 2000; cons. in field. Author: A Short Course in Fluid Mechanics, 1976, Mathematical Foundations of Elasticity, 1983, The Finite Element Method: Linear Static and Dynamic Finite Element Analysis, 1987, Computational Inelasticity, 1998; editor: Nonlinear Finite Element Analysis of Plate and Shells, 1981, Computational Methods in Transient Analysis, 1983; editor Jour. of Computer Methods in Applied Mechanics and Engring., 1980—; contbr. numerous articles to profl. jours. Recipient Computational Mechanics prize Japan Soc. Mech. Engrs., 1993. Fellow AAAS, ASME (Melville medal 1979, Worcester Reed Warner medal 1998), AIAA, ASCE (Huber prize 1978), Internat. Assn. Computational Mechanics (pres. 1998-2002, Gauss-Newton medal), Am. Acad. Mechanics, U.S. Assn. Computational Mechanics (pres. 1990-92, von Neumann medal 1997), Nat. Acad. Engring, Am. Acad. Arts & Scis.; mem. Sigma Xi, Phi Beta Kappa. Office: U Tex at Austin 1 University Sta C0200 201 E 24th St ACES 6 412 Austin TX 78712-0027 Business E-Mail: hughes@ices.utexas.edu.

HUGHES, THOMAS LOWE, foundation executive; b. Mankato, Minn., Dec. 11, 1925; s. Evan Raymond and Alice (Lowe) H.; m. Jean Hurlburt Reiman, May 7, 1955 (dec. Dec. 1993); children: Thomas Evan, Allan Cameron; m. Jane Dudley Casey Kuczynski, Nov. 25, 1995. BA summa cum laude, Carleton Coll., 1947, LHD (hon.), 1974; BPhil and MA in Politics (Rhodes scholar), Balliol Coll., Oxford U., Eng., 1949; LLB, JD, Yale U., 1952; LLD (hon.), Washington Coll., 1973, Denison U., 1980, Fla. Internat. U., 1986; HHD (hon.), Washington and Jefferson Coll., 1979. Bar: Minn. 1952, US Supreme Ct. 1960, US Dist. Ct. DC 1968. Profl. staff mem. U.S. Senate Subcom. on Labor and Labor-Mgmt. Relations, Com. on Labor and Pub. Welfare, 1951-52; assoc. prof. polit. sci. and internat. rels. U. So. Calif., 1953; asso. prof. polit. sci. and internat. relations Trinity Coll., Tex., 1954, George Washington U., 1957-58; exec. sec. to gov. of Conn., 1954-55; legis. counsel Sen. Hubert Humphrey, 1955-58; adminstrv. asst. U.S. Rep. Chester Bowles, 1959-60; spl. asst. to under sec. state Dept. State, 1961, dep. dir. intelligence and research, 1961-63, dir. intelligence and research with rank of asst. sec. state, 1963-69; minister, dep. chief mission Am. embassy, London, 1969-70; planning and coordination staff Dept. State, 1970-71; pres., trustee Carnegie Endowment for Internat. Peace, 1971-91, pres. emeritus, hon. trustee, 1991—. Former chmn. nuclear proliferation and safeguards adv. panel Office Tech. Assessment, Congress US; co-chmn. Coun. PR-US Affairs; internat. adv. bd. Battelle, Pacific Northwest Nat. Lab.; vis. sr. rsch. fellow German Hist. Inst., Washington. Author: The Hohenzollerns; editor: Indian Chiefs of Southern Minnesota; mem. editorial bd. Fgn. Policy Mag., 1971—, chmn., 1971-91; contbr. articles to profl. jours. Vol. Kibbutz Ein Hashofet, Israel, 1950; trustee, sec. German Marshall Fund US, 1972-82; mem. Trilateral Commn., 1973-83; trustee Am. Inst. Contemporary German Studies, Am. Acad., Berlin, Social Sci. Found., U. Denver; past bd. govs. Ditchley Found., Eng.; vis. com. Ctr. for Internat. Studies, Harvard U., 1971-76; bd. visitors Ctr. for German and European Studies, Georgetown U.; bd. dirs. Arms Control Assn.; adv. coun. Woodrow Wilson Sch., Princeton U.; mem. adv. bd. Fundacion Luis Munoz Marin, San Juan, PR; chmn. US-UK Bicentennial Fellowships Com. on Arts, 1975-78; adv. com. Hubert H. Humphrey Inst. Pub. Affairs U. Minn.; staff dir. platform com. Dem. Nat. Conv., 1960. Maj. JAGC, USAF, 1952-54. Recipient Arthur S. Fleming Outstanding Pub. Svc. award, 1964. Mem. Inst. Internat. de Geopolitique Paris, NY Coun. Fgn. Rels., Inst. Current World Affairs (trustee), Internat. Inst. Strategic Studies London (trustee Am. com.), Am. Acad. Diplomacy, Am. Assn. Rhodes Scholars, Washington Inst. Fgn. Affairs (pres., exec. com.), Atlantic Coun. US (bd. dirs.), Oxford-Cambridge Assn. Washington (former chmn.), Women's Fgn. Policy Group, New England Hist. Geneal. Soc., Scottish Genealogy Soc., Soc. Mayflower Descs., Mid-Atlantic Club (chmn.), Cosmos Club, Century Assn. (NYC), Oxford (Eng.) Union, Knight of St. John (Johanniterorden, Balley Brandenburg), Phi Beta Kappa, Phi Delta Phi. Episcopalian. Office: German Hist Inst 1607 New Hampshire Ave NW Washington DC 20009-2562 Office Phone: 301-656-1420. Personal E-mail: thoshughes@aol.com.

HUGHES, THOMAS MORGAN, III, lawyer; b. Racine, Wis., June 14, 1949; s. Thomas Morgan and Rosemary (Navratil) H.; m. Teresa Lee Cloud, Aug. 10, 1974; 1 child, Gwyneth Leigh. B.B.A., U. Wis.-Madison, 1971; J.D., St. Louis U., 1974. Bar: Ark. 1974, U.S. Dist. Ct. (ea. dist.) Ark. 1974. Sole practice, Beebe, Ark., 1974-78; ptnr., Hughes & Hughes, Searcy, Ark., 1978—; instr. Ark. State U., Beebe, 1975. City atty. City of Beebe, 1975-76; treas. Beebe Indsl. Devel. Corp., Beebe, 1983—; judge City Ct., Beebe, 1985-87, Beebe Mcpl. Ct., 1987-2002, White County Beebe Dept., 2002-04. Mem. White County Bar Assn. Prs. 1996), Beebe C. of C. (pres. 1984—), Kiwanis (pres. 1981-82, bd. dirs. 1979—). Independent. Home: 807 W Louisiana St Beebe AR 72012-2623 Office: Hughes & Hughes PO Box 91 Searcy AR 72145-0091 Office Phone: 501-268-0504.

HUGHES, THOMAS PARKE, history professor; b. Richmond, Va., Sept. 13, 1923; s. Hunter Russell and Mary Bronaugh (Quisenberry) H.; m. Agatha Chipley, Aug. 7, 1948; children: Thomas P. (dec.), Agatha H., Lucian P. BME, U. Va., Charlottesville, 1947, PhD, 1953; D (hon.), Royal Inst. Tech., Stockholm, 2000, Northwestern U., Evanston, Ill., 2001. Instr. U. Va., Charlottesville, 1951-54; asst. prof. history Sweet Briar (Va.) Coll., 1954-56; assoc. prof. history Washington and Lee U., Lexington, Va., 1956-63, MIT, Cambridge, 1963-66; prof. history Inst. Tech., So. Meth. U., Dallas, 1969-73; mem. faculty U. Pa., Phila., 1973-94, prof. history and sociology of sci., 1973-94, Andrew W. Mellon prof., 1987-94, prof. emeritus, 1994—. Vis. assoc. prof. history Johns Hopkins U., Balt., 1966-69; Torsten Althin prof. Royal Inst. Tech., Stockholm, 1985-90; founding rsch. prof. Tech. Univ., Darmstadt, Germany, 1986-87; vis. rsch. prof. Wissenschaftszentrum Berlin, 1988-94; vis. prof. MIT, 1991, 93, 94—, E.T.H. Zürich, 1997, Stanford U., 1999—2001. Author: Elmer Sperry: Inventor and Engineer, 1971 (Dexter prize), Networks of Power: Electrification in Western Society 1880-1930, 1983 (Dexter prize), American Genesis: A Century of Invention and Technological Enthusiasm 1870-1970, 1989 (Pulitzer Prize finalist); editor: (with Agatha C. Hughes) Lewis Mumford: Public Intellectual, 1990, Rescuing Prometheus, 1998, Systems, Experts, and Computers, 2000, Human-Built World, 2004. Chmn. NRC com., 1996—99; mem. adv. coun. Smithsonian Inst., 1984—90. Served to lt. (j.g.) USN, 1943—46. Fulbright postdoctoral fellow, Germany, 1958—59, NSF fellow, 1975, Inst. Advanced Study fellow, Berlin, 1983, Guggenheim fellow, 1986. Mem. NAE, Soc. History of Tech. (pres. 1978-80, Leonardo da Vinci medal 1984), Soc. Social Studies Sci. (Bernal prize 1990), History of Sci. Soc. (coun. 1976-79), Am. Acad. Arts and Scis., Johns Hopkins U. Soc. Scholars, Swedish Royal Acad. Engring. Scis., Am. Philos. Soc., Phi Beta Kappa. Business E-Mail: thughes@sas.upenn.edu.

HUGHES, VESTER THOMAS, JR., lawyer; b. San Angelo, Tex., May 24, 1928; s. Vester Thomas and Mary Ellen (Tisdale) H. Student, Baylor U., 1945—46; BA with distinction, Rice U., 1949; LLB cum laude, Harvard U., 1952. Bar: Tex. 1952, US Supreme Ct., US Tax Ct., US Ct. Appeals (5th and 11th cirs.), US Ct. Fed. Claims. Law clk. US Supreme Ct., 1952; assoc. Robertson, Jackson, Payne, Lancaster & Walker, Dallas, 1955-58; ptnr. Jackson, Walker, Winstead, Cantwell & Miller, Dallas, 1958-76, Hughes, Luce, Hennessy, Smith & Castle, Dallas, 1976—, Hughes & Hill, Dallas, 1979-85, Hughes & Luce, Dallas, 1985—. Bd. dirs. Exell Cattle Co., Amarillo, Tex., LX Cattle Co., Amarillo, Sammons Enterprises, Inc.; adv. dir. First Nat. Bank Mertzon; sr. tax counsel Cmtys. Found. of Tex., Inc.; adv. com. Tex. Supreme Ct., 1985-93. Contbr. articles on fed. taxation to profl. jours. Bd. dirs. Juvenile Diabetes Found. Inc., Dallas, 1982—; trustee Dallas Bapt. U., 1967-77; v.p., trustee, exec. com. Tex. Scottish Rite Hosp. for Children, 1967—; bd. overseers vis. com. Harvard Law Sch., 1969-75. 1st lt. JAGC US Army, 1952-55. Named one of Best Lawyers in Dallas, D Mag., 2003, 2005. Mem.: Tex. Bar Found. (Outstanding Fifty-Yr. Lawyer award 2003), State Bar Tex. (Outstanding Tex. Tax Lawyer award 2003), Am. Coll. Trust and Estate Counsel, Ctr. Am. & Internat. Law, Am. Coll. Tax Counsel, Am. Law Inst. (coun. 1958—), Dallas Bar Assn., Tex. Bar Assn., ABA (mem. coun. sect. taxation 1969—73), Harvard Club (NYC), Met. Club (Washington), Order Ea. Star, Masons, Sigma Xi, Phi Beta Kappa. Democrat. Baptist. Avocations: travel, community and church activities, reading. Office: Hughes & Luce 1717 Main St Ste 2800 Dallas TX 75201-7342 Office Phone: 214-939-5433. Office Fax: 214-939-5849. Business E-Mail: hughesv@hughesluce.com.

HUGHES, WALTER THOMPSON, pediatrician, educator; b. Cleve., May 16, 1930; s. Walter Thompson and Millie Hasentine (Collette) H.; m. Frances J. Skinner, Nov. 24, 1957; children: Carla, Gregory, Christopher. MD, U. Tenn., 1954. Diplomate Am. Bd. Pediatrics. Resident in pediatrics U. Tenn. Coll. Medicine, Memphis, 1955-57, prof. pediatrics and microbiology, 1969-77, prof. pediatrics, 1981—; mem. St. Jude Children's Rsch. Hosp., Memphis, 1969-77, mem., chair dept. infectious diseases, 1981-95; mem. staff Walter Reed Army Med. Ctr., Ft. Detrick, Md., 1957-59; pvt. practice pediatrics Cleve., 1959-61; instr. to prof. U. Louisville Sch. Medicine, 1961-69; Eudowood prof. pediatrics, dir. div. infectious diseases Johns Hopkins U. Sch. Medicine, Balt., 1977-81; Arthur Ashe chair in pediat. AIDS rsch. St. Jude Children's Rsch. Hosp., Memphis, 1993-98, emeritus mem., 1998—. Capt. U.S. Army, 1957-59. Fellow Am. Acad. Pediatrics; mem. Am. Pediatric Soc., Infectious Diseases Soc. Am., Soc. Pediatric Rsch., Pediatric Infectious Diseases Soc. (pres. 1983-85). Republican. Methodist. Home: 854 River Park Dr Memphis TN 38103-0804 Office: St Jude Children's Rsch Hosp 332 N Lauderdale St Memphis TN 38105-2729 Home Phone: 901-528-9460; Office Phone: 901-495-3485. Personal E-mail: FU5774832@aol.com. Business E-Mail: walter.hughes@stjude.org.

HUGHES, WILLIAM JOHN, former congressman, diplomat; b. Salem, NJ, Oct. 17, 1932; s. William W. and Pauline H.; m. Nancy L. Gibson; children: Nancy Lynne, Barbara Ann, Tama Beth, William John. AB, Rutgers U., 1955, JD, 1958, LLD (hon.), 1995; LHD (hon.), Mt. Vernon Coll., 1984; LLD (hon.), Richard Stockton State Coll., 1994, Glassboro State Coll., 1992; AA (hon.), Cumberland County Coll., 1994; AS (hon.), Atlantic Cape Cmty. Coll., 2004. Bar: N.J. 1959. Ptnr. Loveland, Hughes & Garrett, Ocean City, NJ, 1968-78; 1st asst. pros. atty. Cape May County,

NJ, 1960-70; mem. 94th-103rd Congresses from 2d N.J. dist., Washington, 1974-95; amb. to Panama U.S. Dept. State, 1995-98; Clifford P. Case prof. pub. affairs Rutgers U., 1997, prof., 1999—2003; disting. scholar ethics and pub. policy Richard Stockton Coll. N.J., Pomona, 1999—; of counsel Riker, Danzig, Scherer, Hyland & Perretti, LLP, 2000—. Founder William J. Hughes Ctr. for Pub. Policy, Richard Stockton Coll.; bd. govs. Shore Meml. Hosp., Sommers Point, NJ, 1972—76; bd. trustees Shore Meml. Hosp. Found., 2001—, Ocean City Tabernacle Assn., 2002—; bd. dirs. South Jersey Industries, South Jersey Gas, 2002—. Recipient Ann. Planning award Am. Planning Assn., 1979, Disting. Citizen award Atlantic Area coun. Boy Scouts Am., 1982, Legislator of Yr. award VFW, 1982, Pres.'s award Nat. Dist. Attys. Assn., 1982, Legis. Leadership award Nat. Assn. Chain Drug Stores, 1984, Humanitarian citiation Food Mktg. Chain Drug Stores and N.J. Food Council, 1984, Legis. award Nat. Assn. Police Orgns., 1984, Legis. Achievement award Fed. Law Enforcement Officers Assn., 1984, Man of Yr. award Girl Scouts Am., 1986, Legis. award N.J. Foster Parents Assn., 1986, Leo Fraser Super Achiever award Juvenile Diabetes Found., 1987, Arthur E. Armitage Sr. Disting. Alumni award Rutgers U., 1987, Disting. Info. Processing Pub. Service award Data Processing Mgmt. Assn., 1987, Rutgers U. medal, 1992, Distinction in Pub. Svc. award Am. Rivers, 1993, Congressional Advocacy award, 1994, Spirit of South Jersey award South Jersey Devel. Coun., 1994, Career Achievement award in pub. svc. N.J. Edn. Assn., 1995; named Congressman of Yr., Nat. Assn. Police Orgns., 1986, Hall of Disting. Alumni award Rutgers U., 1997, Jefferson medal award N.J. Intellectual Property Law Assn., 1995, Judge John F. Gerry award for adminstrv. justice, 2000, South Jerseyan of Yr. award Rand Inst.,2003 Pub. Affairs, Rutgers U. Fellow Am. Bar Found.; mem. ABA, N.J. Bar Assn., Ocean City Hist. Soc. (bd. dir. 1972-76), Ocean City C. of C. (bd. dir. 1960—), Exch. of Ocean City Club (pres. 1965-66, Nat. Big E. award 1965), Masons (master lodge, Worshipful Master 1969). Democrat. Episcopalian. Home: 1019 Wesley Rd Ocean City NJ 08226-4754 Home Phone: 609-399-2551. Personal E-mail: ambjack1@aol.com.

HUGHES-TEBO, JACQUELINE EMMA, regional coordinator; b. Baltimore, Md., Feb. 10, 1968; d. Hugh Price Hughes Jr. and Reta Theresa Hughes; m. Donald W. Tebo, Jr. BA in Psychology, Coll. Notre Dame Md., Balt., 1990; MBA, U. Phoenix, Columbia, Md., 2001; doctoral canidate, Capella U., 2005—. CPR, First Aid, and AED Instructor ARC, 2002. Armorer USMC Reserves, Savannah, Ga., 1988—99; counselor Mgmt. Tng. Corp., Washington, 1992—99; counseling mgr. Adams and Assocs., Laurel, Md., 1995—96; regional coord., info. systems specialist TCU Manpower Tng. Dept., Rockville, Md., 1999—. Innovation com. mem. Mgmt. Tng. Corp., Randallstown, Md., 1993; cultural diversity coord. Adams and Assocs., Laure, Md., 1995—96. Author: (poetry) Look, 1999. Chair, Relay for Life Am. Cancer Soc., 2002—03. Mem.: AAUW, NAFE. Avocations: travel, volunteer work. Personal E-mail: jetebo@comcast.net.

HUGHEY, JAMES FLETCHER, JR., lawyer; b. Jacksonville, Fla., Aug. 15, 1945; s. James Fletcher and Geraldine (Hammack) Hughey; m. Janice Johnson, Aug. 15, 1968; children: James Fletcher III, Elizabeth Bond. AB, U. Ala., 1967, JD, 1970; LLM in Taxation, NYU, 1972. Bar: Ala. 1970. Assoc. Balch & Bingham, Birmingham, Ala., 1972—77, ptnr., 1978—, chair exec. com., mng. ptnr., 1990—. Mem. exec. bd. Greater Ala. coun. Boy Scouts Am.; trustee Daniel Found. Ala., 1996—; bd. dirs. United Way Ctrl. Ala., 1993—, Leadership Birmingham, 1991—, Leadership Ala., 1995—, Lakeshore Found., Lakeshore Hosp., 1978—91, chmn., 1986—87. Fellow: Am. Law Found., Am. Bar Found.; mem.: ABA, Ala. Law Inst., Birmingham Bar Assn., Ala. State Bar (bd. bar examiners 1982—86), Brimingham C. of C., U. Ala. Law Sch. Alumni Assn. (pres. 1992), Birmingham Country Club (pres. 1996), Rotary Club Birmingham (pres. 2005). Episcopalian. Office: Balch & Bingham LLP PO Box 306 1710 6th Ave N Birmingham AL 35201-2015 Home Phone: 205-870-8345; Office Phone: 205-226-3469. Business E-Mail: jhughey@balch.com.

HUGHEY, RICHARD KOHLMAN, writer, lawyer; b. Chgo., July 6, 1934; BA cum laude, Santa Clara U., Calif., 1958, JD cum laude, 1963. Bar: Calif. 1964, U.S. Ct. Appeals (9th cir.) 1964, U.S. Supreme Ct. 1972. Atty. Pacific Gas & Elec. Co., San Francisco, 1963-69, Berry, Davis & McInerny, Oakland, Calif., 1969-71; ptnr. Caputo, Liccardo, Rossi & Kohlman, San Jose, Calif., 1971-75; lectr. law, dir. CLE Santa Clara U., 1975-80; mng. editor Bancroft-Whitney Co., San Francisco, 1980-91, Lawyers Coop. Pub. Co., Rochester, NY, 1992-94; history and lit. biography writer, 1995—; columnist Mountain Democrat, Placerville, Calif., 1997—. Author: Jeffers Country Revisited: Beauty Without Price, 1996, Computer Technology in Civil Litigation, 1990, Trial Lawyers Manual, 1978, Jeffers in Antrim, 2003, El Dorado: California's Empire County, 2003, Golden Girl, 2003, Bullion Bead, 2004; co-author: Petroglyphs: Poetry and Fiction, 1994, Hey Lew: Homage to Lew Welch, 1997; editor: Am. Jury Trials, 1980—90, Proof of Facts, 1982—90; bd. editors Calif. State Bar Jour., 1972—75, editor-in-chief Santa Clara Law Rev., 1961—63. Avocation: photography.

HUGHSON, MICHAEL DONALD, pathologist, researcher, medical educator; b. Long Beach, Calif., May 3, 1941; s. Robert Marshall and Ellen Ruby Hughson; m. Virginia Ophelia Segrest, Mar. 11, 2006; children: John Michael, Charles Robert, Elizibeth Ann. BA, Fla. State U., 1966; MD, Med. U. SC., Charleston, 1971. Lic. anatomical & clin. pathology Americal Bd. Pathology, 1979. Asst. prof. pathology Med. U. SC., Charleston, 1975—81; clin. assoc. prof. pathology U. Tex., El Paso, 1982—89; assoc. prof. pathology U. Okla. Health Scis. Ctr., Oklahoma City, 1989—94; chief pathology & lab. medicine Vets. Adminstrn. Med. Ctr., Northport, NY, 1994—97; prof. pathology U. Miss. Med. Ctr., Jackson, Miss., 1997—. Chmn., dept. pathology U. Miss. Med. Ctr., Jackson, 1998—2005. Contbr. chapters to books. Kidney And Hypertension Rsch. grant, NIH, Am. Heart Assn., 1998—. Achievements include research in chronic renal disease and hypertension. Home: 116 Azalea Trails Dr Brandon MS 39047 Office: U Miss Med Ctr 2500 North State St Jackson MS 39216-4505 Home Phone: 601-992-6001; Office Phone: 601-984-1540. Office Fax: 601-984-1531. E-mail: mhughson@pathology.umsmed.edu.

HUGO, JANET, director; m. Doug Hugo; 2 children. BA, Pa. State U., 1971; MA in Gifted Studies, Miss. U. for Women; PhD in Tech. and Edn., Miss. State U., 2000. Dean academic affairs Miss. Sch. for Maths. and Scis., Ark. Sch. for Math., Scis. and Arts, Hot Springs, 2001—06, dir., 2006—. Pres. Nat. Consortium of Specialized Secondary Schs. for Maths., Sci. and Tech. Office: Ark Sch for Math, Sci and Arts 200 Whittington Ave Hot Springs AR 71901 Office Phone: 501-622-5100. Office Fax: 501-622-5108.*

HUGO, NORMAN ELIOT, retired plastic surgeon, educator; b. Beverly, Mass., Sept. 23, 1933; s. Victor Joseph and Helen Bernadette (Box) Hugo; m. Geraldine P Tonry, Oct. 10, 1959; children: Helen, William, Geraldine, Norman, Catherine. BA, Williams Coll., Williamstown, Mass., 1955, DSc (hon.), 1989; MD, Cornell U. Med. Coll., Ithaca, NY, 1959. Diplomate (dir 1982-88, vice chmn 1987-88, residency rev comt, accreditation coun, grad med educ, 1994-98) Am Bd Plastic Surg. Intern, resident Cornell U. Surg. Svc., Bellevue Hosp., NYC, 1959-63; resident NY Hosp.-Cornell Med. Ctr., 1963-65, univ. instr. surgery, 1966-65; asst. prof. Ind. U.; asst. chief plastic surgeon Walter Reed Army Med. Ctr., 1967-69; assoc. prof. U. Chgo., 1969-71; chief plastic and reconstructive surgery Michael Reese Hosp., Chgo., 1969-71, Passavant Hosp., Chgo., 1971-79; assoc. prof. Northwestern U., Chgo., 1971-82; dir. plastic surgery Lakeside VA Hosp., 1971-77; chief plastic and reconstructive surgery Columbia U.-Presbyn. Med. Ctr., NYC, 1982-95; prof. Columbia U. Coll. Physicians & Surgeons, 1982-98, prof. emeritus, 1998—; ret., 1998. Maj MC AUS, 1967—69. Mem.: AMA (del 1983—88), ACS, Am. Burn Soc., NY Acad. Sci., Soc. Head and Neck Surgeons, Assn. Acad. Surgery, Am. Cleft Palate Soc., Plastic Surg Rsch. Coun., Chgo. Soc Plastic Surg (secy 1979—81, vpres 1981—82), Am. Soc. Aesthetic Plastic Surgery (secy 1979—82), Am. Assn. Plastic and Reconstructive Surgery (trustee 1982—84), Am. Soc. Plastic and Reconstructive Surgeons (trustee 1981—84, historian 1982—84, vpres 1985—86, pres-elect 1986—87, pres 1987—88, bd dirs educ found), Touchdown Club Am. (dir. 2002—06), Union Club (gov. 2002—, NYC), Williams Club. Home: 37 Carriage Ln New Canaan CT 06840-4401 Office: Columbia U Coll Physicians and Surgeons 161 Fort Washington Ave New York NY 10032-3713 Office Phone: 203-966-2434. Personal E-mail: normanehugo@msn.com.

HUGUENEL, JEAN M., pharmaceutical executive, director, legal assistant; d. Edward G. and Katherine P. Huguenel. BS, Montclair State U., NJ, 1988. Legal asst. Honeywell Internat. Inc., Morristown, NJ, 1986—93, AT&T Capital Corp., Morristown, 1993—98, Bryan Cave LLP, NY, 1998—99; paralegal Pharmacia Corp., Peapack, NJ, 1999—2003; sr. legal coord. Schering-Plough Corp., Kenilworth, NJ, 2003—04; assoc. dir. legal affairs NovaDel Pharma Inc., Flemington, NJ, 2004—. Mem.: Soc. Corp. Secs.and Governance Profls. Home: 77 Crickhollow Crt Hillsborough NJ 08844 Office: NovaDel Pharma Inc 25 Minneakoning Rd Flemington NJ 08822 Home Phone: 908-874-5335; Office Phone: 908-782-3431 2120. Office Fax: 908-782-1295. Business E-Mail: jhuguenel@novadel.com.

HUH, JOAN, lawyer; d. Jung and Woon Huh. AB (hon.), Dartmouth Coll., Hanover, NH, 1993—97; JD, U. So. Calif., Los Angeles, 1998—2002, MBT, 2001—02. Supreme Ct.: Calif. 2003, US Dist. Ct. (ea. dist.): Calif. 2005, US Dist. Ct. (no. dist.): Calif. 2005. Law clk. Third Jud. Dist. Ct., Yerington, Nev., 2002—03, Supreme Ct. Nev., Carson City, 2003—03; staff atty. US Bankruptcy Ct., Dist. Utah, Salt Lake City, 2003—04; assoc. Felderstein Fitzgerald et al., Sacramento, 2006—. Mem. Sacramento Valley Bankruptcy Forum, 2006—, Asian/Pacific Bar Assn. of Sacramento, 2006—, Sacramento County Bar Assn., 2006—. Office: Felderstein Fitzgerald et al 400 Capitol Mall Ste 1450 Sacramento CA 95814 Office Phone: 916-329-7400. E-mail: jhuh@ffwplaw.com.

HUHEEY, MARILYN JANE, ophthalmologist, educator; b. Cin., Aug. 31, 1935; d. George Mercer and Mary Jane (Weaver) Huheey. BS in Math., Ohio U., Athens, 1958; MS in Physiology, U. Okla., 1966; MD, U. Ky., 1970. Diplomate Am. Bd. Ophthalmology. Tchr. math. James Ford Rhodes H.S., Cleve., 1956-58; biostatistician Nat. Jewish Hosp., Denver, 1958-60; life sci. engr. Stanley Aviation Corp., Denver, 1960-63, N.Am. Aviation Co., LA, 1963-67; intern U. Ky. Hosp., 1970-71; emergency room physician Jewish Hosp., Mercy Hosp., Bethesda Hosp., Cin., 1971-72; ship's doctor, 1972; resident in ophthalmology Ohio State U. Hosp., Columbus, 1972-75; practice medicine specializing in ophthalmology Columbus, 1975—. Mem. staff Univ. Hosp., Grant Hosp., St. Anthony Hosp., 1975—79; clin. asst. prof. Ohio State U. Med. Sch., 1976—, dir. course ophthalmologic receptionist/aides, 1976; mem. Peer Rev. Sys. Bd., 1986—92, mem. exec. com., 1988—92; mem. Ohio Optical Dispensers Bd., 1986—91; bd. dirs. Ctrl. Ohio Radio Reading Svc., 1997—2003; mem. Ohio Bd. Cosmetology, 1999—. Mem. United Way, mem. planning com., 1992—93; Dem. candidate Ohio Senate, 1982. Fellow: Am. Acad. Ophthalmology; mem.: LWV, AAUP, Herb Soc., Grandview Area Bus. Assn., Columbus Coun. World Affairs, Life Care Alliance (pres. sustaining bd. 1987—88), Am. Coun. the Blind (bd. dirs. 1995—96), Columbus EENT Soc., Ohio State Med. Assn. (dr.-nurse liaison com. 1983—87), Ohio Soc. Prevent Blindness (chmn. med. adv. bd. 1978—80), Franklin County Acad. Medicine (mem. profl. rels. com. 1979—82, mem. legis. com. 1981—89, mem. edn. and program com. 1981—88, chmn. 1982—85, chmn. cmty. rels. com. 1987—90, chmn. resolution com. 1987—92, mem. fin. com. 1988—92), Ohio Ophthalmol. Soc. (bd. govs. 1984—89, del. to Ohio State Med. Assn. 1984—88), Am. Assn. Ophtalmologists, Columbus Area Women's Polit. Caucus, Federated Dem. Women Ohio, Columbus C. of C., Mercedes Benz Club (bd. dirs. 1981—83), Wicked Investment Club (pres. 1999—2004, treas. 2005—), Columbus Met. Club (mem. forum com. 1982—85, mem. fundraising com. 1983—84, chmn. 10th anniversary com. 1986), Colubmus Bus. and Profl. Women's Club, Zonta (mem. program com. 1984—86, chmn. internat. com. 1983), Phi Mu. Home: 2396 Northwest Blvd Columbus OH 43221-3829 Office: 1335 Dublin Rd Ste 25A Columbus OH 43215-1000 Office Phone: 614-488-8836. E-mail: mhuheey.1@yahoo.com.

HUHMANN, MAUREEN BRIGITTE, dietitian, researcher; b. Perth Amboy, NJ, Dec. 12, 1977; d. Alexander L. and Christina A. Huhmann. BSc, Coll. St. Elizabeth, Morristown, NJ, 1999; MSc, U. Medicine & Dentistry NJ, Newark, 2003, D in Clin. Nutrition. Registered dietitian Commn. on Dietetic Registration, 2000. Clin. nutritionist Raritan Bay Med. Ctr., Perth Amboy, 1999—2003; tchg. asst. dept. nutrition sci. Rutgers U., New Brunswick, NJ, 2000—01; nutritionist in pvt. practice Woodbridge, NJ, 2001—02; asst. prof. U. Medicine & Dentistry of NJ, 2003—; adj. faculty Coll. St. Elizabeth, 2004—05. Evidence analyst Am. Dietetic Assn., Chgo., 2005—06, lead evidence analyst, 2006—, nutrition fact sheet reviewer, 2006—. Contbr. textbook, ,; author: articles in jours. and newsletters. Mem. NB Tomorrow's Get Fit Coalition, New Brunswick, NJ, 2003, N.J. Cancer Control Plan, Nutrition and Phys. Activity Workgroup, Trenton, 2003. Recipient Claire W. Boothe scholarship, Coll. St. Elizabeth, 1995—99, Presdl. scholarship, 1995—99, Academic Excellence award, Coll. St. Elizabeth Dietetic Internship, 2000, Nabisco scholarship for Dietetic Internship Students, Coll. St. Elizabeth, 2000, Recognized Young Dietitian of Yr., NJ Dietetic Assn., 2006, Julie O'Sullivan Maillet Rsch. award, Am. Dietetic Assn., 2006; grantee, Dietitians in Nutrition Support, Am. Dietetic Assn., 2006; scholar, State of NJ, 1995—99; Margaret Yardley Fellowship, NJ State Fedn. of Women's Clubs of GFWC, 2006. Mem.: Dietitians in Nutrition Support (mem. web devel. com. 2004), Oncology Nutrition Practice Group (assoc. editor 2004), NJ Soc. for Parenteral and Enteral Nutrition, Am. Soc. Nutrition, Am. Soc. Enteral and Parenteral Nutrition, NJ Dietetic Assn., Am. Dietetic Assn. Achievements include research in the impact of medical nutrition therapy by a registered dietitian on outcome in cancer patients; the impact of dysphagia screening on identification of dysphagia risk and appropriateness of diet order in acute stroke patients; prevalence and usage patterns of complementary and alternative medicine among cancer patients; the impact of medical nutrition therapy provided by a registered dietitian on clinical outcomes; the role of diet in the management of inflammatory bowel disease. Avocations: travel, swimming. Office: Univ Medicine & Dentistry NJ 195 Little Albany St New Brunswick NJ 08903 Home Phone: 732-709-3135; Office Phone: 732-235-8508. Office Fax: 732-235-8808. Business E-Mail: huhmanma@umdnj.edu.

HUHN, THERESA J., social studies educator; b. Springfield, Ill., Feb. 4, 1953; d. Paul Alford and Stella Marie Price; m. Richard Paul Huhn, May 26, 1973; children: Rachel Langford, Trevor Jon. BE, St. Mary Coll., Leavenworth, Kans., 1975; MEd, U. Kans., Lawrence, 1992. Lic. K-9 tchr. Kans. Elem. tchr. Sacred Heart Sch., Leavenworth, 1975—77; kindergarten tchr. KinderCare Daycare, Lansing, Kans., 1983—84; para profl. Lansing Unified Sch. Dist., 1984—86; tchr. St. Patrick Sch., Leavenworth, 1986—. Actor: River City Players, 1980. Auxilary mem. Leavenworth County Fire Dept., Lansing, 2004—; cantor St. Francis de Saies, Lansing, Kans., 1979—. Independent. Roman Catholic. Home: 601 N 2d Ter Ct Lansing KS 66043

HUHS, JOHN I., lawyer; b. Galveston, Tex., Sept. 18, 1944; s. Roy E. and Martha Mae (Hansen) H.; m. Vivian C. Swindley, 1970 (div. 1978); m. Renee J. Stillings, 2005. BA, U. Wash., 1966; MBA with honors, JD with honors, Stanford U., 1970. Bar: NY 1971, DC 1981. Internat. cons. Satra Cons. Corp., NYC, 1970—74; sr. staff White House Office Mgmt. & Budget Nat. Security, Internat. Affairs, Washington, 1973—76; ptnr. Pisar & Huhs, NYC, 1976—85; sr. v.p., gen. counsel Tendler, Beretz Assocs., Ltd., NYC, 1985-87; pvt. practice NYC, 1987-88; sr. ptnr., chmn. internat. practice LeBoeuf, Lamb, Greene & MacRae LLP, NYC, 1989—, founder Moscow office, founder Almaty office; prof. Stanford Law Sch., 2007—. Prin. Ctr. for Excellence in Govt., 1984—99. Contbr. articles on internat. law, bus. and fin. to profl. jours.; comment editor Stanford Law Rev., 1967-69. Mem. bd. visitors Stanford Law Sch., 1996-98, 2004-07. Mem.: ABA (chmn. com. on Soviet and Ea. European law 1982—85, chmn. com. internat. comml. trans. 1985—90, coun. sect. internat. law and practice 1988—92, ABA rep. to Union Internat. Advs. 1991—94), DC Bar Assn., NY State Bar Assn. (chmn. internat. investment devel. com. 1987—91), Assn. of Bar of City of NY (internat. trade com. 1987—89, com. Newly Ind. States of former Soviet Union 1989—2000), 175 E. 74th Corp. (pres.), U. Club NYC, Order of Coif. Office: LeBoeuf Lamb Greene MacRae LLP One Embarcadero Ctr San Francisco CA 94111-3619 Office Fax: 415-951-1180. Business E-Mail: jhuhs@llgm.com.

HUHTALA, MARIE THERESE, federal agency administrator, former ambassador; b. LA, Mar. 26, 1949; d. Joseph E. Sr. and Rosemary E. (Williamson) Mackey; m. Eino A. Huhtala Jr., July 10, 1971; children: Karen Rose, Jorma David. BA in French, Santa Clara U., 1971; diploma, Nat. War Coll., 1988; MA, Laval U., 1995. Joined Fgn. Svc., Dept. State, Washington, 1972; consular officer Am. Embassy, Paris, 1973-75; vice consul U.S. Consulate, Chiang Mai, Thailand, 1976-79; secretariat staff officer Fgn. Svc., Dept. State, Washington, 1979-80, congl. rels. officer, 1980-81, country officer for Chad, 1981-83, polit. officer U.S. Consulate Gen. Hong Kong, 1985-87, chief East Asian assignments, bur. pers. divsn. Washington, 1988-90, dep. dir. Vietnam, Laos and Cambodia affairs, 1990-92, consul gen. U.S. Consulate Gen. Que., Canada, 1992—95; dep. chief mission U.S. Embassy, Bangkok, 1998—2001; U.S. amb. to Malaysia US Dept. State, 2001—04, dep. asst. sec. E. Asian & Pacific affairs Washington, 2004—. Bd. dirs. Orchestre Symphonique de Que., 1992—. Recipient Superior Honor award, Dept. of State, Meritorious Honor award. Mem. Am. Fgn. Svc. Assn., Acad. Polit. Sci., Nat. War Coll. Alumni Assn., Rotary Club of Que. (hon.). Roman Catholic. Achievements include speaks fluent French and Thai. Avocation: choral singing.

HUIE, CAROL P., information science educator; b. Kingston, Jamaica; AAS, Hostos CC, NYC, 1986; BSc, Lehman Coll., NYC, 1988; MS, CCNY, 1994; postgrad., CUNY, 1994—99, Nova Southeastern U., 2001—. Patient acct.coord. New Rochelle Med. Ctr., New Rochelle, NY, 1988-91; coll. lab tech. Hostos Community Coll., Bronx, NY, 1991-98, instr., 1994—2000, asst. professor, 2000—. Mem.: IEEE, Assn. Computing Machinery, Schomburg Ctr. Rsch. Black Culture, Consortium for Computing in Small Colls., CUNY Acad. for Humanities and Scis., Delta Pi Epsilon. Office Phone: 718-518-6550. Business E-Mail: chuie@hostos.cuny.edu.

HUITT, JIMMIE L., rancher, oil and gas industry executive, real estate developer; b. Gurdon, Ark., Aug. 21, 1923; s. John Wesley and Almedia (Hatten) H.; m. Janis C. Mann, Oct. 30, 1945; children— Jimmie L., Jr., Allan Jerome BS in Chem. Engring., La. Tech. U., 1944; MS in Chem. Engring., U. Okla., 1948, PhD, 1951. Research engr. Mobil Oil Corp., Dallas, 1951-56, Gulf Research Co., Pitts., 1956-67; ops. coordinator Kuwait Oil Co., London, 1967-71; gen. mgr. Gulf Oil-Zaire, Kinshasa, 1971-74; mng. dir. Gulf Oil-Nigeria, Lagos, 1974-76; sr. v.p., exec. v.p. Gulf Oil Exploration and Prodn. Co., Houston, 1976-81, pres., 1981-85; rancher Four Jays Ranch, Industry, Tex., 1986—. Contbr. articles to profl. jours.; patentee in field Served to 1st lt. U.S. Army, 1944-47 Mem. Soc. Petroleum Engrs. (chmn. various coms. 1956—), Masons, Shriners. Republican. Office: Four Jays Ranch PO Box 236 Industry TX 78944-0236

HUIZENGA, H. WAYNE, entrepreneur, professional sports team executive; b. Evergreen Park, Ill., Dec. 29, 1939; s. G. Harry and Jean (Riddering) Huizenga; m. Martha Jean Pike, Apr. 17, 1972; children: H. Wayne Jr., H. Scott, Ray, Pamela Ann. Student, Calvin Coll., 1957-58. Vice chmn., pres., COO Waste Mgmt. Inc., Oak Brook, Ill., 1968-84; chmn. Huizenga Holdings, Inc., Ft. Lauderdale, Fla., 1984—; chmn., CEO Blockbuster Entertainment Corp., Ft. Lauderdale, 1987-94; owner Fla. Marlins, Miami, 1992-99, Fla. Panthers, Sunrise, Fla., 1993—2001; chmn. Boca Resorts, Inc., Boca Raton, Fla., 1996—2004, AutoNation Inc., Ft. Lauderdale, 1994—2002. Owner Miami Dolphins and Dolphins Stadium. Mem. Fla. Victory Com., 1988-89, Team Repub. Nat. Com., Washington, 1988-90; organizer Broward Victory 90 PAC, Ft. Lauderdale, 1989-90. Recipient Entrepreneur of Yr. award Wharton Sch. U. Pa., 1989, Excalibur Award Bus. Leader of Yr. News/Sun Sentinel, 1990, Silver Medallion Brotherhood award Broward Region Nat. Conf. Christians and Jews, 1990, Laureates award Jr. Achievement Broward and Palm Beach Counties, 1990, Jim Murphy Humanitarian Award The Emerald Soc., 1990, Entrepreneur of Yr. award Disting. Panel Judges Fla., 1990, Man of Yr. Billboard/Time Mag., 1990, Man of Yr. Juvenile Diabetes Found., 1990, Fla. Free Enterpriser of Yr. award Fla. Coun. on Econ. Edn., 1990, commendation for youth restricted video State of Fla. Office of Gov., 1989, Hon. Mem. Appreciation award Bond Club Ft. Lauderdale, 1989; named one of 400 Richest Ams. Forbes mag., 2006; honored with endowed teaching chair Broward Community Coll., 1990. Mem. Lauderdale Yacht Club, Tournament Players Club, Fisher Island Club, Ocean Reef Club, Cat Cay Yacht Club, Coral Ridge Country Club, Linville Ridge Country Club. Avocations: golf, collecting antique cars. Office: Huizenga Holdings 450 E Las Olas Blvd Ste 1500 Fort Lauderdale FL 33301-4212

HUIZENGA, JOHN ROBERT, nuclear chemist, educator; b. Fulton, Ill., Apr. 21, 1921; s. Harry M. and Josie B. (Brands) H.; m. Dorothy J. Koeze, Feb. 1, 1946; children: Linda J., Jann H., Robert J., Joel T. AB, Calvin Coll., 1944; PhD, U. Ill., 1949. Lab. supr. Manhattan Wartime Project, Oak Ridge, 1944-46; instr. Calvin Coll., Grand Rapids, Mich., 1946-47; assoc. scientist Argonne Nat. Lab., Chgo., 1949-57, sr. scientist, 1958-67; professorial lectr. chemistry U. Chgo., 1963-67; prof. chemistry and physics U. Rochester, 1967-78, Tracy H. Harris prof. chemistry and physics, 1978-91, Tracy H. Harris prof. emeritus chemistry and physics, 1991—, chmn. dept. chemistry, 1983-88. Vis. prof. Joliot-Curie Lab., U. Paris, 1964-65, Japan Soc. for Promotion of Sci., 1968; chmn. Nat. Acad. Sci.-NRC Com. on Nuclear Sci., 1974-77; mem. energy rsch. adv. bd. Dept. Energy, 1984-90; numerous adv., vis. coms. to univs., govt. and nat. labs. Author: (with R. Vandenbosch) Nuclear Fission, 1973; (with W.U. Schröder) Damped Nuclear Reactions, 1984; Cold Fusion: The Scientific Fiasco of the Century, 1992; contbr. articles to profl. jours. Fulbright fellow Netherlands, 1954-55; Guggenheim fellow Paris, 1964-65; Guggenheim fellow Berkeley, Calif., 1973; Guggenheim fellow Munich, W.Ger., 1974; Guggenheim fellow Copenhagen, 1974; recipient E.O. Lawrence award AEC, 1966, Leroy Rundle Grumman medal, 1991; named Disting. Alumnus Calvin Coll., 1975 Fellow AAAS, Am. Phys. Soc., Am. Acad. Arts and Scis.; mem. NAS (chmn. NAS-NRC com. on nuclear and radiochemistry 1988-91), Am. Chem. Soc. (award for nuclear applications in chemistry 1975), Phi Beta Kappa, Sigma Xi, Phi Kappa Phi. Home: 43 McMichael Dr Pinehurst NC 28374-6702 Personal E-mail: johnrhuizenga@earthlink.net.

HUKINS-RODRIGUE, DANA ANN, nurse; b. Raceland, La., Nov. 1, 1964; d. Herman Cecil and Diana Ann (Chiasson) H. BSN, Nicholls State U., Thibodaux, La., 1986; postgrad., Nicholls State U., 2004—. RN La. Nurse II, staff pediatrics nurse South La. Med. Ctr., Houma, 1986-88; pub. health nurse III Lafourche Parish Health Unit, Thibodaux, 1988—2003; pub. health nurse IV, hosp. coord., bioterrorism nurse Region 3 Office Pub. Health, Thibodaux, 2003—04; nurse, student health svcs. Nicholls State

U., Thibodaux, La., 2004—07; nurse Audubon Pediat. LLC, Houma, 2007. Mem. Nicholls State U. Nursing Honor Soc., Sigma Theta Tau (Xi Zeta chpt.). Office: Audubon Pediat LLC 216 Mystic Blvd Houma LA 70360 also: La Tech Coll 900 Youngs Rd Morgan City LA 70380 Personal E-mail: dhrodrigue@bellsouth.net.

HULBERT, JARL O., music educator; b. Corona, Calif., Aug. 7, 1974; s. Thomas Foster and Wenche Lise Hulbert; m. Irene Tsuey-Lin Chang, June 12, 1999; 1 child, Avagail Beatrice. MusB, U. of Redlands, Calif., 1996; MusM, U. Ariz., Tucson, 1999; PhD in Hist. Musicology, U. Md., College Park, 2006. Coord., instr., dir. Artist Music Edn. Ctr., Balt., 1999—; adj. prof. music St. Mary's Coll. of Md., St. Mary's City, 2000—02, CC Balt. County, Essex, 2000—; asst. to coord. William Kapell Internat. Piano Competition U. Md., College Park, 2002—03, coord., 2006—07, adj. lectr. music, 2004—06, adj. prof. music, 2006—. Bible instr. Balt. Chinese Bapt. Ch., 2000—03. Recipient 1st prize Green Valley Piano Competition, Green Valley Concert Assn., Ariz., 1998; Ambassadorial scholar, Rotary Internat., 1996—97. Mem.: Music Tchrs. Nat. Assn. (nationally cert. music tchr. 2005), Am. Musicological Soc. (Irving Lowens Musicology Rsch. award 2001). Avocation: birding. Office: Artist Music Edn Ctr 9333 A Belair Rd Baltimore MD 21236 Home Phone: 410-256-4407; Office Phone: 410-256-7320. E-mail: info@artistmusiceducation.com.

HULBERT, MARK J., financial analyst, columnist; B, Haverford Coll., Pa., 1977. Founder, pres. Hulbert Fin. Digest, Annandale, Va., 1983—2002; columnist MarketWatch.com (acquired Hulbert Fin. Digest), 2002—, Barron's Online, 2004—; fin. columnist NY Times. Co-author: Interlock: The Untold Story of American Banks, Oil Interests, the Shah's Money, Debts & the Astounding Connections Between Them, 1982, Hulbert Guide to Financial Newsletters, 1993. Bd. trustees Sidwell Friends Sch. Office: Hulbert Fin Digest MarketWatch 5051B Backlick Rd Annandale VA 22003 Address: MarketWatch 825 Battery St San Francisco CA 94111 also: Fin Columnist NY Times 229 W 43rd St New York NY 10036 Office Phone: 703-750-9060. Business E-Mail: mhulbert@marketwatch.com.

HULBERT, RICHARD WOODWARD, lawyer; b. Cambridge, Mass., Sept. 24, 1929; s. Woodward Dennis and Clifford (Halliday) H.; m. Dorothy Marie Hanni, Apr. 21,1954; children: Jonathan, Ann, Laura, Mary. AB, Harvard U., 1951, LLB, 1955. Bar: N.Y. 1956. Assoc. Cleary, Gottlieb, Steen & Hamilton LLP, NYC, 1955-65, ptnr., 1966-83, 89-96, Paris, 1983-89, mng. ptnr., 1979-84, sr. counsel, 1997—. Lectr. in law U. Calif., Berkeley, 1988; adj. prof. NYU Law Sch., 1990—; vis. prof. law Am. U. Armenia, 2004; vice chmn. internat. ct. arbitration Internat. C. of C., 1994-99, mem. commn. internat. arbitration, 2001-. Trustee Bklyn. Bot. Garden, 1982-98, 99-, Bklyn. Mus., 1992-04. Sheldon fellow in history Harvard U., 1951-52 Mem. ABA, N.Y. Bar Assn., Assn. of Bar of City of N.Y., Bklyn. Bar Assn., N.Y. County Lawyers Assn., Am. Law Inst. Democrat. Home: 141 Henry St Brooklyn NY 11201-2501 Office: Cleary Gottlieb Steen & Hamilton LLP 1 Liberty Plz New York NY 10006-1470 Office Phone: 212-225-2050. Business E-Mail: rhulbert@cgsh.com.

HULBERT, STEPHEN THOMPSON, academic administrator; BS in Edn., Worcester State Coll., Mass., 1966; MEd, U. Mass., Amherst, 1968; DEd, SUNY, Albany, 1972. Dir. student activities and residence life Western New England Coll., Springfield, Mass., 1968-70; cons. Univ. Assocs. Inc., Washington, 1971-72; exec. asst. to the pres. Mansfield (Pa.) U., 1972-77; v.p. for fin. and adminstrn. Slippery Rock (Pa.) U., 1977-88; v.p. adminstrv. svcs., treas. bd. trustees U. Northern Colo., Greeley, 1988-91, interim pres., 1991, sr. v.p., 1992-94, provost, v.p. for acad. affairs, 1994-96; commr. higher edn., CEO R.I. Bd. of Govs. for Higher Edn., Providence, 1996-99; chancellor U. Mont.-Western, Dillon, 1999—2003; pres. Nicholls (La.) State U., 2003—. Chair bd. dirs. La. Campus Compact. Mcpl. coun. Grove City, Pa., 1986-88; adv. bd. Franklin Regional Hosp., Franklin, Pa., 1985-88; mem. exec. bd. Longs Peak coun. Boy Scouts Am., 1991-96, disting. citizen com. chair, 1992, others; mayor's adv. task force City of Greeley, 1992-96, U. No. Colo. Found., Inc., 1991-96, R.I. Children's Crusade Higher Edn., 1996-99, U. No. Colo. Rsch. Corp., Inc., 1988-96, chair 1994-96, vice chair 1992-94, corp. treas. 1988-92; steering com. Edn. Comms., 1988—99; bd. govs. Colo. Alliance for Sci., 1995-96. Mem. Nat. Assn. Intercollegiate Athletics (coun. pres.), Frontier Athletic Conf. (chair coun. pres. 2000-03), Southland Conf. (bd. dirs. 2003—). Office: Nicholls State U PO Box 2001 Thibodaux LA 70310 Home: 111 Acadia Dr Thibodaux LA 70301 Office Phone: 985-448-4003. Business E-Mail: stephen.hulbert@nicholls.edu.

HULBURT, LUCILLE HALL, artist, educator; b. Portland, Oreg., Oct. 31, 1924; d. Allen Bergen and Agnes Edna (Davis) Hall; m. Frank Theodore Hulburt, Nov. 28, 1943; children: Robert, Carol Davalos, Clarke. Grad. h.s., Whitefish, Mont. Asst. milliner, illustrator Hat Co., NYC, 1944; cafe owner, operator San Diego, 1950—52; profl. artist Vancouver, Wash., 1978—; resident artist Artist's Gallery 21, Vancouver, 1988—. Tchr. children and adult art clases, schs. and home studio, Vancouver, 1978—; artist in residence Wash. State Arts Commn., 1987-88; co-founder, coop. Artists Gallery 21, Vancouver, 1988—; cons. nat. Western Art Show and Auction, Trails West, Vancouver; organizer, com. mem. ann. Summer Art at the Ctr., Vancouver, 1986; judge/jurist art exhibits. Founder, pres. Boundary Assn. Retarded Children, Bonners Ferry, Idaho, 1964-65; com. mem. 1st Bldg. Com., Columbia Arts Ctr., Vancouver, 1980-81; bd. mem. Local Arts Promotion, Vancouver, 1992, 93. Recipient Best of Show award Western Art Show and Auction, Chinook, Mont., 1983, 84, Cmty. Svc. award Arts Coun., Clark County, Wash., 1988, Windsor-Newton award Watercolor 91, 1991. Mem. S.W. Wash. Watercolor Soc. (co-founder, pres. 1979, 80, 84), Soc. Washington Artists (Grumbacher Silver medal 1990), Am. Artists Profl. League, Order Ea. Star (life), N.W. Watercolor Soc. Avocations: gardening, sewing, swimming. Office Phone: 360-693-5291.

HULER, ROBERT JAY, surgeon; b. Detroit, Jan. 29, 1957; s. Morris Henry and Barbara Ann Huler; m. Kylene Keiko Hodge, May 13, 1984. BS in Pharmacy, U. Mich., Ann Arbor, 1980; MD, U. Mich., 1984. Diplomate Ind., 1984. Orthopaedic surgeon in spine surgery Ind. U. Med. Ctr., Indpls., 1990—99, OrthoIndy, Indpls., 1999—. Fellow: Scoliosis Rsch. Soc. (life); mem.: N.Am. Spine Soc. (life). Office: OrthoIndy 8450 Northwest Blvd Indianapolis IN 46278 Business E-Mail: rhmd@att.net.

HULET, ERVIN KENNETH, retired nuclear chemist; b. Baker, Oreg., May 7, 1926; s. Frank E. and Marjorie (Suiter) H.; m. Betty Jo Gardner, Sept. 10, 1949 (dec. Jan. 1992); children: Carri, Randall Gardner. BS, Stanford U., 1949; PhD, U. Calif., Berkeley, 1953. AEC grad. student U. Calif. Radiation Lab., Berkeley, 1949-53; research chemist nuclear chemistry div. Lawrence Livermore Nat. Lab., Livermore, Calif., 1953-66, group leader, 1966-91, ret., active emeritus, 1991—. Achievements include discovery of divalent oxidation state in actinide elements; co-discovery of symmetric fission in actinides. Served with USNR, 1944-46. Fulbright scholar Norway; Welch Found. lectr., 1990; recipient Am. Chem. Soc. award for Nuc. Chemistry, 1994. Fellow AAAS, Am. Inst. Chemists (chmn. Golden Gate chpt. 1992); mem. Am. Chem. Soc. (chmn. divsn. nuclear chemistry and tech. 1987, award in nuclear chemistry 1994), Am. Phys. Soc. Achievements include co-discovery of Element 106; discovery of bimodel fission. Personal E-mail: ekhulet@comcast.net.

HULET, RANDALL GARDNER, physics professor; b. Walnut Creek, Calif., Apr. 27, 1956; s. Ervin Kenneth and Betty Jo (Gardner) H.; m. Lourdes Teresa Hernandez, Aug. 16, 1980; children: Benjamin Hernandez, Gabriella Alison. BS in Physics, Stanford U., 1978; PhD in Physics, MIT, 1984; PhD (hon.), Utrecht Univ., 2002. Rsch. asst. MIT, Cambridge, Mass., 1978-84, rsch. assoc., 1984-85; Nat. Rsch. Coun. postdoctoral fellow Nat. Inst. Standards and Tech., Boulder, Colo., 1985-87; asst. prof. physics Rice U., Houston, 1987-92, assoc. prof. physics, 1992-96, prof., 1996-99, Fayez Sarofim prof. physics, 1999—. Contbr. articles to profl. jours. Alfred P. Sloan fellow, 1988; Nat. Inst. Standards and Tech. grantee, 1988-91; recipient Presdl. Young Investigator's award NSF, 1989, Exceptional Sci. Achievement medal NASA, 2004 Fellow: AAAS, Am. Phys. Soc. (I.I. Rabi prize 1995); mem.: Am. Acad. Arts and Scis. Office: Rice U Dept Physics and Astronomy MS61 Houston TX 77251 Business E-Mail: randy@rice.edu.

HULKA, JAROSLAV FABIAN, obstetrician, gynecologist; b. NYC, Sept. 29, 1930; s. Jaroslav Hugo and Milada (Touskova) H.; m. Barbara E. Sorenson, Nov. 13, 1954; children— Carol Ann, Gregory Fabian, Bryan Herbert. BA, Harvard U., 1952; MD, Columbia U., 1956. Diplomate: Am. Bd. Ob-Gyn. Intern Roosevelt Hosp., NYC, 1956-57; resident Sloane Hosp. for Women, Columbia-Presbyn. Med. Center, NYC, 1957-60; Josiah Macy, Jr. fellow Columbia-Presbyn. Med. Center, 1960-61; practice medicine specializing in Ob-Gyn, 1961—; asst. prof. Ob-Gyn U. Pitts. Sch. Medicine, 1961-66, asso. mem. grad. faculty, 1962-66, acting chmn. dept. ob-Gyn, 1963-64; assoc. prof. dept. ob-Gyn Sch. Medicine, U. N.C., Chapel Hill, 1967-76, prof. dept. ob-Gyn and dept. maternal and child health, 1976-96, prof. emeritus dept. ob-gyn.; prof. emeritus dept. maternal and child health U. N.C. Sch. Pub. Health, Chapel Hill. Author: Textbook of Laparoscopy, 1985, 3d edit., 1997; patentee in field. Assoc. dir. Carolina Population Center, 1967-74. Recipient Excel award Soc. of Laparoendoscopic Surgeons, 1994. Fellow ACOG; mem. Soc. for Gynecol. Investigation, Am. Assn. Gynecol. Laparoscopists (pres. 1980), Am. Fertility Soc., Soc. Reproductive Surgeons (founding), N.C. State Bar (bd. legal specialization 1990-96), Planned Parenthood Fed. Am. (chair nat. med. com. 1991-94), Soc. Physicians for Reproductive Choice and Health (founding). Achievements include development of and teaching of worldwide use of clips for female sterilization by laparoscopy; demonstration of local anesthesia for safer procedures. Home: 2317 Honeysuckle Rd Chapel Hill NC 27514-1716 Personal E-mail: jhulka@unc.edu.

HULKOWER, MARK J., lawyer; BS with honors, Cornell U., 1980; JD magna cum laude, Georgetown U., 1984. Bar: Pa. 1985, DC 1986. Law clerk US Ct. of Appeals, DC Circuit, Washington, 1984—85; asst. US atty. Ea. Dist., Va., 1989—95; ptnr., white collar criminal defense practice Steptoe & Johnson LLP, Washington, 1995—. Lecturer US Dept. Justice, FBI; adjunct prof. George Washington U. Office: Steptoe & Johnson LLP 1330 Connecticut AveNW Washington DC 20036 Office Phone: 202-429-6221. Office Fax: 202-429-3902. Business E-Mail: mhulkower@steptoe.com.

HULL, ANTHONY E., real estate company executive; Investment banking position Morgan Stanley & Co., Inc., 1984—90; various sr. fin. exec. positions Paramount Comm., 1990—94; CFO DreamWorks LLC, 1996—2003; exec. v.p. fin. Cendant, 2003—06; exec. v.p., CFO, treas. Realogy Corp., Parsippany, NJ, 2006—. Office: Realogy Corp 1 Campus Dr Parsippany NJ 07054 Office Phone: 973-407-2000. Office Fax: 973-407-7004.*

HULL, BRETT A., retired professional hockey player, former commentator; b. Belleville, Ont., Can., Aug. 9, 1964; s. Bobby Hull; m. Alison Curran, May 27, 1997 (div.); children: Jude, Jayde, Crosby; m. Darcie Schollmeyer, July 21, 2006. Student, U. Minn., Duluth, 1984-86. Forward Calgary Flames, 1986—88, St. Louis Blues, 1988—96, Dallas Stars, 1999—2001, Detroit Red Wings, 2001—04, Phoenix Coyotes, 2004—05; spl. asst. to pres. Dallas Stars, 2006—07, spl. advisor hockey ops., 2007—; studio analyst NHL on NBC, 2006—07. Player NHL All-Star 1st Team, 1990—92, US Olympic Hockey Team, Nagano, 1998, Salt Lake City, 2002, Team USA, World Cup of Hockey, 1996, 2004. Named NHL Player of Yr., The Sporting News, 1989—90, 1991—92, All-Star Game MVP, 1992; named to NHL All-Star Game, 1989, 1990, 1992—94, 1996, 1997, 2001; recipient Lady Byng Meml. Trophy, 1989, 1990, Hart Meml. Trophy, 1990—91, Dodge Ram Tough award, 1989—90, 1990—91, Lester B. Pearson award, 1990—91. Achievements include leading the NHL in goals, 1989-92; being a member of the World Cup Champion Team USA, 1996; being a member of the Stanley Cup Champions Dallas Stars, 1999, Detroit Red Wings, 2002; being a member of silver medal winning USA Hockey Team, Salt Lake City Olympics, 2002; having his number, 16, retired by St. Louis Blues, 2006. Office: c/o Dallas Stars 2601 Avenue of the Stars Frisco TX 75034*

HULL, CATHY, artist, illustrator; b. NYC, Nov. 4, 1946; d. Max H. and Magda M. (Stern) H.; m. Neil S. Janovic; 1 child, Julie. BA, Conn. Coll., 1968; cert., Sch. Visual Arts, NYC, 1970. Instr. illustration and portfolio Sch. Visual Arts, NYC, 1983-94, Parsons Sch. Design, NYC, 1994—. Juror The 6th World Cartoon Gallery, Skopje, 1974, Soc. Pub. Designers, N.Y.C., 1982, Soc. Illustrators, N.Y.C., 1983, The Biennale of Humor, Fredrikstad, Norway, 1987, The 6th Internat. Simavi Cartoon Competition, Istanbul, Turkey, 1988 Contbr. to anthologies, books, mags. and newspapers including Time, Penthouse, Newsweek, Esquire, Playboy, MSNBC, Fortune, Wall Street Jour., Washington Post, Forbes, Chgo. Tribune, Ency. Brit., Disney, Sports Illustrated, N.Y. Times, Bus. Week, Travel and Leisure, Money, others; group shows include The 17th Nat. Print Exhbn., Bklyn., 1970, AIGA Show, N.Y.C., 1970-71, 74, Printing Industries Am., 1971, Soc. Illustrators, 1973, 80, 85, 94, 01, World Cartoon Gallery, Skopje, former Yugoslavia, 1972-75, Art Dir.'s Club, 1974, 82, Internat. Cartoon Exhbn., Istanbul, Turkey, 1974, Switzerland, 1974, 78, 80, 82, 90, Athens, Greece, 1975, Soc. Publ. Designers, 1974, 82, Musée de Beaubourg, Paris, 1977, Pacific Design Ctr., L.A., 1980, The Md. Inst., 1981, Scottsdale (Ariz.) Ctr. for Arts, 1981, Soc. Newspaper Design, 1984-85, Butler Inst. Am. Art, Youngstown, Ohio, 1983, Am. Peace Poster Exhibit, 1985, Quebec City Exhbn., Society of Illustrators, 2002; represented in permanent collections including Mus. Caricatures and Cartoons, Basel, Switzerland, Soc. Illustrators Advt. Ann. show, Smithtown Twp. Arts Coun.; designer and pub. playing cards sold at Cooper Hewitt Mus., N.Y., N.Y. Pub. Libr., L.A. County Mus. Art, St. Louis Art Mus., Chgo. Mus. Art, Nat. Mus. Scotland, Seibu, Japan, Contemporary Mus. of Honolulu, Contemporary Mus. San Diego, High Mus. Atlanta, Meml. Exhbn., Mus. Am. Illustration, 2002, Herbert F. Johnson Mus. of Art, 2002, Cornell U., Karikatur and Cartoon Mus., Basel, Switzerland, 2003, Mus. Am. Illustration, 2005, RSVP Portraits Show, N.Y. Times Show and The Ripple Effect, Mus. of Am. Illustration, 2006. Exec. bd. Friends of the H.S. Art and Design, 2002—. Office: 180 E 79th St New York NY 10021-0437 Business E-Mail: chull@nyc.rr.com.

HULL, CHARLES WILLIAM, retired special education educator; b. East St. Louis, Ill., Feb. 23, 1936; s. William Semple Hull and Jessie Marie (Brennan) Poole; m. Beverly Kay Julian, Aug. 19, 1967; 1 child, William Kenneth. BA in Econs., Cen. Meth. Coll., 1964; MEd, Olivet Nazarene Coll., 1974; AA (hon.), Joliet Jr. Coll., 1987. Tchr. elem. grades Taft Sch., Lockport, Ill., 1965-67; tchr. spl. edn. S.W. Cook County Coop. Assn. Spl. Edn., Oak Forest, Ill., 1967-99; ret., 1999. Represented in permanent collections Tchr.'s Ret. Office Bldg., Springfield, Ill. Mem. Nat. Trust Hist. Preservation; past bd. dirs., v.p., chmn. fund raising Easter Seals Will and Grundy Counties; dist. leader Am. Cancer Soc., 1984, residential campaign chmn., 1985; vol., mem. adv. bd. Big Bros.-Big Sisters Will County; mem. Cub Scouts com. Boy Scouts Am., 1980—81, commr. Rainbow coun., bd. dirs. troop 61; Will County walkathon chmn. March of Dimes, 1979; chmn. Canal Days events Will County Hist. Soc., 1987, pres., 1989; mem. Lockport Area Geneal. Hist. Soc.; bd. dirs. Joliet Project Pride, Will G. Project Pride, 2000—06; life mem. Friends Ill. and Mich. Canal; mem. Pleasant Hill Hist. Soc., Cumberland County Farm Bur., Tenn., 2005—06; choir, past trustee Faith United Meth. Ch. With USMC, 1955—58. Named to Joliet/Will County Hall of Pride, 2002; recipient Congl. medal of Merit, 1985, Frederick Bartleson Meml. award, Will County Hist. Soc., 1985, Citizen of the Week award, Sta. WBBM, Chgo., 1985, Leadership award, Am. Cancer Soc., 1985, Outstanding Svc. award, Big Bros.-Big Sisters Will County, letter of commendation, Pres. of U.S., 1986, 1989, Disting. Svc. award, Joliet Jr. Coll., 1987, Citizen of the Month award, Southtown Economist. Mem.: KC (plaque), Tenn. Hist. Soc., Ill. Ret. Tchrs. Assn., Will County Old-Timers Baseball Assn., Coalition Citizens with Disabilities Ill. (life), White County Hist. Soc. (life), 1st Marine Divsn. Assn., Joliet Area Ret. Tchrs. Assn., Royal Order Scotland, Lions (pres. Manhattan club 1984, chmn. youth and fgn. exch. dist. 1986—87, bd. dirs. Lockport chpt.), Scottish Rite Club, Medina Temple, Shriners (pres. Joliet club 1983, Shriner of the Yr. 1989), Am. Legion, Masons (life 32 degree). Republican. Methodist. Home: PO Box 429 Pleasant Hill TN 38578 E-mail: beehul@earthlink.net.

HULL, CLIFFORD, SR., military officer; b. Carbondale, Pa., Jan. 4, 1935; s. Charles Henry and Phyliss Marie Hull; m. Erna T. Schwaiger, July 4, 1955; children: Steven R., Clifford J. Jr., Peter J., Paul A. Enlisted US Army, 1952, engr. Vietnam, 1967—68, advanced through grades E-7, 1972, mil. assistance advisor Vietnam, 1970—71. Decorated 3 Bronze Star medals US Army, Bronze Star medal for valor, Army Commendation medal, Army Commendation medal for valor, Honor medal 2d class Republic of South Vietnam, Cross of Gallantry with palm. Avocation: gardening.

HULL, CORDELL WILLIAM, engineering, construction, and project management executive, investor; b. Dayton, Ohio, Sept. 12, 1933; s. Murel George and Julia (Barto) H.; m. Susan G. Ruder, May 10, 1958; children: Bradford W., Pamela H., Andrew R. B of Engring., U. Dayton, 1956; MS, MIT, 1957; JD, Harvard U., 1962; doctorate (hon.), Dominican U. Registered profl. engr., Mass.; bar: Ohio 1962; lic. contractor Calif. Atty. Taft, Stettinius & Hollister, Cin., 1962-64, C & I Girdler, Cin., 1964-66; gen. counsel, treas., pres. C&I Girdler, Internat., Brussels, 1966-70; v.p. Bechtel Overseas Corp., San Francisco, 1970-73; pres., dir. Am. Express Mcht. Bank, London, 1973-75; v.p., treas. Bechtel Corp. and Bechtel Power, San Francisco, 1975-80; pres. Bechtel Fin. Svcs., San Francisco, 1975-82; v.p., CFO Bechtel Group Inc., 1980-85; pres. Bechtel Power Corp., 1987-89, dir.; chmn. Bechtel Enterprises, 1990-95. Bd. dirs. Fremont Group, Inc., 1980—2006; former chmn. audit commn. Gilead Scis., 2001—04; mem. Accenture Energy Adv. Bd.; mgr. HWC LLC; former chmn. adv. com. U.S. Eximbank; former mem. svcs. policy com. Office of U.S. Trade Rep. Former trustee Dominican Coll.; former bd. trustees U. Dayton. Mem. Pacific Union Club, Menlo Country Club, Pasadera Country Club. also: HWC LLC 400 Oyster Point Blvd Ste 540 South San Francisco CA 94080 Home Phone: 650-328-5356.

HULL, DAVID GEORGE, aerospace engineering educator, researcher; b. Oak Park, Ill., Mar. 27, 1937; s. John Lawrence Hull and Elizabeth Christine (Carstensen) Meyer; m. Meredith Lynn Kiesel, June 2, 1962 (div. July 1980); children: David, Andrew, Matthew; m. Vicki Jan Poole, June 30, 1983; children: Katherine, Emily. BS, Purdue U., 1959; MS, U. Wash., 1962; PhD, Rice U., 1967. Staff assoc. Boeing Sci. Research Labs., Seattle, 1959-64; research assoc. Rice U., Houston, 1964-66; asst. prof. U. Tex., Austin, 1966-71, assoc. prof., 1971-77, prof., 1977-85, M.J. Thompson Regents prof., 1985—. Cons. several aerospace cos. Assoc. editor 2 jours.; author: Optimal Control Theory for Applications, 2003; author: Fundamentals of Airplane Flight Mechanics, 2007; reviewer several engring. jours.; contbr. over 55 articles to profl. jours. Recipient/co-recipient more than 50 grants and contracts; recipient award Best paper, AAS/AIAA Space Flt. Mechanics Conf., Albuquerque, 1995. Fellow AAS, AIAA (assoc., atmospheric flight mechanics tech. com. 1974-77, guidance and control tech. com. 1984-87); mem. Delta Tau Delta (treas. Purdue U. 1958-59) Office: U Tex ASE/EM C0600 Austin TX 78712-0235 Office Phone: 512-471-4908. Business E-Mail: dghull@mail.utexas.edu.

HULL, EDMUND J., former ambassador; b. Keokuk, Iowa, Dec. 1949; married; 2 children. Diploma with honors, Princeton U.; postgrad. in strategic issues with Sir Michael Howard, Oxford U., 1986—87. Numerous positions including dir. No. Gulf Affairs during the Gulf War; dep. chief of mission and charge d'Affaires U.S. Embassy, Cairo, 1993—96; former dir. Office of Peacekeeing; former acting coord. for counterterroism U.S. Dept. of State, U.S. amb. to Yemen Sana'a, 2001—04. Vol. Peace Corps, Tunisia, 1971—73. Recipient Meritorious Honor award, Superior Honor awards, U.S. Dept. of State, Baker-Wilkins award, 1995.

HULL, FRANK MAYS, federal judge; b. Augusta, Ga., Dec. 9, 1948; d. James M. Hull Jr. and Frank (Mays) Pride; m. Antonin Aeck, Apr. 16, 1977; children: Richard Hull Aeck, Molly Hull Aeck. AB, Randolph-Macon Women's Coll., 1970; JD cum laude, Emory U., 1973. Bar: Ga. 1973, US Ct. Appeals (5th cir.) 1973, US Dist. Ct. (no. dist.) Ga. 1974, US Ct. Appeals (11th cir.) 1982. Law clk. to Hon. Elbert P. Tuttle US Ct. Appeals (5th cir.), Atlanta, 1973—74; assoc. Powell, Goldstein, Frazer & Murphy, Atlanta, 1974—80, ptnr., 1980—84; judge State Ct. Fulton County, Atlanta, 1984—90, Superior Ct. Fulton County, Atlanta, 1990—94, US Dist. Ct. (no. dist.) Ga., 1994—97, US Ct. Appeals (11th cir.), 1997—. Mem. commn. on family violence State of Ga., 1992—94, commn. on gender bias in jud. sys., 1988—90. Mem. Leadership Atlanta, 1986—, program co-chair criminal justice com., 1988—89; Sunday sch. tchr. Cathedral St. Philip, Atlanta, 1983—88, children's com., 1981—82, outreach com., 1989—91; bd. dirs. Met. Atlanta Mediation Ctr., Inc., 1976—79, Atlanta Vol. Lawyers Assn., 1988—91. Fellow, AAUW, 1973—. Mem.: ABA (fin. sec. long range planning com. tort and ins. practice sect. 1979—82, chmn. contract documents divsn., forum com. on constrn. industry 1983—85, editl. staff jour. 1981—85, vice chmn. fidelity and surety law com. 1978—85), Nat. Assn. Women Judges, Ga. Assn. Women Lawyers, Atlanta Bar Assn., Am. Judicature Soc. (bd. dirs. 1990—96), Ga. Bar Assn., Order of Coif. Office: US Ct of Appeals 56 Forsyth St NW Rm 300 Atlanta GA 30303-2289*

HULL, FREDERICK ALBERT, artist, writer; b. Norfolk, Va., July 27, 1931; s. William Barr and Velma Beatrice Hull; m. Joan Arnold, Aug. 4, 1956; children: Frederick William, Christopher John. BA in Art, Calif. State U., Sacramento, 1971, MPA, 1977. Chief of design dept. Reed & Reese Corp., Pasadena, Calif., 1961—63; asst. br. chief graphic br. 323 Flying Tng. Wing, Mather AFB, Calif., 1963—72; art and prodn. editor The Navigator mag. Dept Air Force, Mather AFB, Calif., 1972—87; syndicated cartoonist Adventure Features Syndicate newspapers, Glendale, Calif., 1976—90; instr. journalism Calif. State U., Sacramento, 1981; dir., writer, artist Hull Features Syndicate, Am. Internat. Features, Calif. and Mo., 1991—95; sr. signature artist, master painter No. Calif. Artists Inc., Carmichael, 1995—; also bd. dirs. No. Calif. Artists Inc. NCA, Carmichael. Designer, publ. asst. dir. Calif. State Mil. Mus., Sacramento, 1982-92; mem. art show and promotion bds. Sacramento Fine Art Ctr., Carmichael, 1997—. Maj. U.S. Army, 1954-56, with Calif. State Mil. Reserve, 1982-96. Recipient numerous nat. and internat. juried show awards for oil painting. Mem.: Sigma Delta Chi, Phi Kappa Tau. Avocations: sailing, bike riding, jogging, weightlifting, woodworking. Home: 2512 G St Sacramento CA 95816-3610 E-mail: fredhull@cwnet.com.

HULL, GERALD W., JR., lawyer; b. Newark, 1940; BBA, U. Miami, 1962; LLB, Rutgers U., 1965. Bar: NJ 1965. Legal sec. to Hon. Arthur Lewis Superior Ct., NJ appellate divsn.; sr. real estate ptnr., co-head, real estate practice group Drinker Biddle & Reath LLP, Florham Park, NJ; mng. ptnr., 2002—; and mem., mgmt. com. Drinker Biddle & Reath LLP. Recipient Lifetime Achievement award in Real Estate, Nat. Assn. Industrial and Office Properties, 1996. Office: Drinker Biddle & Reath LLP 500 Campus Dr Florham Park NJ 07932-1047 Office Phone: 973-549-7000. Office Fax: 973-360-9831. Business E-Mail: gerald.hull@dbr.com.

HULL, HERBERT MITCHELL, botanist, researcher; b. La Jolla, Calif., Aug. 19, 1919; s. Daniel Ray and Emma (Kammeyer) H.; m. Mary Randall Mattison, Mar. 4, 1950; children: Laurinda Lee, Daniel James. AA, Pasadena City Coll., 1939; BS, U. Calif., Berkeley, 1946; PhD, Calif. Inst. Tech., 1951. Research fellow Calif. Inst. Tech., 1949-52; plant physiologist U.S. Dept. Agr., Tucson, 1952-78; prof. renewable natural resources U. Ariz., 1966-85, prof. emeritus, 1985—. Served as meteorologist and pilot USAAF, 1941-46. Fellow AAAS, Ariz.-Nev. Acad. Sci.; mem. Am. Soc. Plant Biologists, Bot. Soc. Am., Sigma Xi, Alpha Zeta. Presbyterian. Home: 4040 W Sweetwater Dr Tucson AZ 85745-9757

HULL, ISABEL VIRGINIA, history professor; BA, Univ. Mich., 1970; MPhil, Yale Univ., 1973, PhD, 1978. John Stambaugh prof. history Cornell Univ. Author: Absolute Destruction (Ralph Waldo Emerson Book award, 2005). Recipient Leo Gershoy award, Am. Hist. Assn., 1997, Berkshire Prize, Berkshire Conf. Women Historians, 1997. Fellow: Am. Acad. Arts & Scis. Office: Dept History 431 McGraw Hall Cornell Univ Ithaca NY 14853-4601 Office Phone: 607-255-6747. Business E-Mail: ivh1@cornell.edu.*

HULL, J(AMES) RICHARD, retired lawyer; b. Keokuk, Iowa, Dec. 5, 1933; s. James Robert and Alberta Margaret (Bouseman) H.; m. Patricia M. Kiesner, June 14, 1958; children— Elizabeth Ann Hull Whims, James Robert, David Glen. BA, Ill. Wesleyan U., 1955; JD, Northwestern U., 1958. Bar: Ill. 1958, Fla. 1978. V.p., sec., gen. counsel Honeggers & Co., Inc., Fairbury, Ill., 1959-65, also bd. dirs.; staff atty. Am. Hosp. Supply Corp., Evanston, Ill., 1965-68, chief atty., asst. sec., 1968-70, corp. sec., 1970-71, corp. sec., corp. gen. counsel, 1971-79, gen. counsel, 1979-84; sr. v.p., sec., gen. counsel Household Internat. Inc., Northbrook, Ill., 1984-93, sr. v.p., of counsel, 1993-94; ret. Mem. planning com. Northwestern U. Corp. Counsel Inst., 1992-93, chmn. Northwestern Corp. Counsel Ctr., 1993. Bd. trustees, bd. visitors Ill. Wesleyan U.; pres. Prestancia Cmty. Assn. Fellow Am. Bar Found., Am. Law Inst.; mem. ABA, Ill. Bar Assn., Fla. Bar Assn., Chgo. Bar Assn. (chmn. corp. law dept.), North Shore Gen. Counsels, Northwestern U. Sch. Law Alumni Assn. (pres.), Sigma Chi, Legal Club (Chgo.), Law Club (Chgo.), Skokie Country Club (Glencoe, Ill.), Gator Creek Golf Club (Sarasota, Fla.), T.P.C. Club (Prestancia, Fla.), Prestancia Cmty. Assn. (pres. 1995-96), Champion Hills Golf Club (Hendersonville, N.C.), Hendersonville Country Club. Home (Winter): 4634 Mirada Way #24 Sarasota FL 34238 Home: 301 Piney Knoll Ln Hendersonville NC 28739-7510 E-mail: dph4634@aol.com. *Success will come to those who plan and rehearse. Set your goals, define your strategies and implement your tactics. Your goals must always determine and never justify the means toward achievement.*

HULL, JANE DEE, former governor, state legislator; b. Kansas City, Mo., Aug. 8, 1935; d. Justin D. and Mildred (Swenson) Bowersock; m. Terrance Ward Hull, Feb. 12, 1954; children: Jeannette Shipley, Robin Hillebrand, Jeff, Mike. BS in elem. edn., U. Kans., 1957; postgrad. in polit. sci., Ariz. State U., postgrad. in econs., 1972-78; grad., Josephson Sch. of Ethics, 1993. Former state legislator Ariz. Ho. of Reps., Phoenix, 1979—93, spkr. pro tem, 1993, chmn. ethics com., chmn. econ. devel., 1993, mem. legis. coun., 1993, mem. gov.'s internat. trade and tourism adv. bd., 1993, mem. gov.'s strategic partnership for econ. devel., 1993, mem. gov.'s office of employement implementation task force, 1993, spkr. of house, 1989—93, house majority whip, 1987-88; former sec. of state State of Ariz., Phoenix, 1995—97, former gov., 1997—2003; pub. del. to the UN, 2004—05. Author (edited by Michael S. Josephson and Wes Hanson): The Power of Character; author: Character in Soc.: The Challenge of Pub. Svc.; contbr. opinion pieces to periodicals and newspapers. Mem. dean's coun. Ariz. State U., 1989—92; assoc. mem. Heard Mus. Guild; mem. Maricopa Med. Aux., Ariz. State Med. Aux., Valley Citizens League, Charter 100, Ariz. Women's Forum; hon. chmn. Race for the Cure; hon. bd. mem. Teach for Am.; assoc. mem. Cactus Wren Rep. Women; mem. Freedom Found., North Phoenix Rep. Women, 1970; Trunk 'N Tusk Legis. Liaison Ariz. Rep. Party, 1993; mem. Gov.'s Emergency Coun., Ariz. -Mex. Commn., Phoenix Commn. on Internat. Rels.; Ariz. chmn. George W. Bush for Pres., 2000; mem. Adv. Coun. Hist. Preservation; chmn. Western Gov.'s Assn., 2002, Border Gov.'s Assn., 2002; bd. dir. Morrison Inst. for Pub. Policy, Beatitudes D.O.A.R., 1992, Ariz. Town Hall, Ariz. Econs. Coun. Recipient Econ. Devel. award, Ariz. Innovation Network, 1993, Spl. Achievement award, Nat. Notary Assn., 1997, Appreciation award, No. Ariz. U. Sch. of Forestry students, 2000. Mem. Nat. Orgn. of Women Legislators, Am. Legis. Exch. Coun., Nat. Rep. Legislators Assn. (Nat. Legislator of Yr. award 1989), Soroptimists (hon.). Republican. Roman Catholic.

HULL, JOHN DANIEL, IV, lawyer, writer; b. Washington, Feb. 27, 1953; s. John Daniel III and Arlene (Reemer) Hull. BA cum laude, Duke U., Durham, NC, 1975; JD, U. Cin., 1978. Bar: DC 1980, US Dist. Ct. DC 1983, US Ct. Appeals (DC cir.) 1984, US Ct. Appeals (10th cir.) 1986, Md. 1989, Pa. 1989, US Dist. Ct. (we. dist.) Pa. 1989, US Ct. Appeals (3d cir.) 1989, US Supreme Ct. 1989, Calif. 2002, US Dist. Ct. (so. dist.) Calif. 2002, US Dist. Ct. Md. 1992. Legis. asst. 93d & 96th U.S. Congresses, Washington, 1974, 78-81; assoc. Rose, Schmidt & Dixon, Washington, 1981-87, ptnr., 1988-92, Hull McGuire PC, Pitts., Washington, and San Diego, 1992—. Agt. US Film and TV Industry, 2002—. Author: (blog) What About Clients?, 2005; co-editor: International Directory of Business Terms and Symbols, 2001; mem.: U. Cin. Law Rev., 1976—77, editor student articles:, 1977—78. Mem. planning bd. Rancho Bernardo Calif., 1998—2004. Fellow Congress of Ctr. for Internat. Legal Studies, Salzburg, Austria. Mem.: ABA, Calif. Bar Assn., Internat. Bar Assn., Md. Bar Assn., Bar Assn. DC, Internat. Bus. Law Consortium (Austria and London, mem. bus. devel. group), Tara Club, Duke Club. Office: Hull McGuire PC 32d Fl US Steel Tower 600 Grant St Pittsburgh PA 15219-2702 also: Hull McGuire PC 888 17th St NW Ste 1200 Washington DC 20006 also: Hull McGuire PC Merrill Lynch Bldg 701 B St Fl 10 San Diego CA 92101 Business E-Mail: jdhull@hullmcguire.com.

HULL, LEANNE VON NEUMEYER, public relations and communications executive, research consultant, writer; d. F. Louis and Greta Catherine (Clifford) von Neumeyer; children: Marc Lane, Kristin LeAnne, Michael Lane, Jamie Laird, Jeremy Leif, Breton Louis. Rschr., writer, owner Heritage Tree, Arcadia, Calif., 1970—; CEO von Neumeyer & Assocs., 1996—; project mgr., prodn. asst. One Light, KCM Prodns., 1999—; dir. comms. Vision Film Festival Vision in Arts Coun., 2001—. Internat. bd. advisors, dir. protocol, mem. scholarship grant rev. com. Neeley Scholarship Found., 1988-89; dir. pub. comm. Ch. of Jesus Christ of Latter-day Saints, Foothill and Glendale regions, Calif., 1975-92, dir. cmty. rels., 1984-92, asst. dir. area coun., 1984; adminstrv. asst. Calif. Pub. Affairs Dept., L.A., 1990—; seminar coord. R.E.D.I., Inc., L.A., 1982-91, corp. rels. dir., 1984-91; design cons. H.M.J. Fine Jewelers Time & Eternity Collection, L.A., 1985-95; mem. nat. adv. coun. motion picture studio Brigham Young U., Provo, Utah, 1986-89; adminstrv. dir. Pasadena Geneal. Libr., Calif., 1977-82; writer, co-prodr. KBIG, Sideband Div. Radio, L.A., 1979-80; exec. assoc. adminstr. Calif. Bicentennial Found. for the U.S. Constn., 1987; regional cons. Latter-Day, Sentinel Newspaper, L.A., 1985-89, exec. dir., 1988-89; mem. Brigham Young U. Marriott Sch. Bus. Mgmt. Soc., L.A., 1990—; mem. com. on child pornography legis. chmn. pub. info. portfolio com., 1988-91, L.A. County Commn. on Obscenity & Pornography, 1988-91; internet moderator 21stRenaissance-.com, 1999. Author: Honored Heritage, 1975, Woman's Place of Honor, 1976, Prologue and Tapestry, 1976, Moments with the Prophets, 1977, Southern California: The Earthquake Threat, 1981, Quake!: Preparing Home, Family and Community, 1982, DreamQuest: Along the Trail, 1982, The Peregrine Papers, 1986, Bridget 'Biddy' Smith Mason: Her Legacy Among the Mormons, 1996, Etherea, 1999, Preparing Home and Family, 1999, (novel and screenplay) The Dreamin' Jar, 2000, (screenplay) Snow Search, 2000; columnist Heritage Tree Foothill Intercity News, Knight-Ridder Pub., 1977-79; contbg. writer Women's Exponent Southern California edit., Sentinal: Journalism series, 1978-80; contbr. articles to profl. jours.; art exhibits include Wilshire Alma Exhibit, 1985, The Grand Artists Hall, 1986-88. Pres. Daus. Utah Pioneers-Los Angeles County, 1983-85; prodr. Calif. Gov.'s Gala, Philadelphia 1776; dir. protocol L.A. County Law Enforcement Conf., 1990; dir. recept. protocol State of Calif. Law Enforcement Conf. on Child Pornography, 1990; chmn. So. Calif. Task Force on Pornography, 1989-92; instr. earthquake preparedness and survival Arcadia chpt. ARC, L.A., 1983-85; mem. Cmty. Coordinating Coun., Arcadia, 1983-86; mem. exec. bd. Calif. Utah Women, L.A., 1977-79, 85-86, chmn. L.A. County Commn. Pub. Rels. Portfolio, 1988; exec. dir. Neeley Scholarship Found., 1989-91; coord. planning com. California '96: One Hundred Fifty Years LDS Sequicentennial, 1994—; display coord. L.A. Temple Hill Visitors Ctr., 1994-96; lineage rsch. dir. von Neumeyer-Burches & Assocs., 1992-96; specialist Y2K Task Force on Family Preparedness, 1998—. Recipient Best of Exhibit award Sculptor's West Workshop, 1982, cert. of recognition L.A. County, 1989, cert. appreciation L.A. County, 1990. Mem. Nat. Assn. Female Execs., Found. for Ancient Rsch. and Mormon Studies, Mormon Hist. Assn., Assn. Latter-Day Media Artists (assoc. editor Voice of ALMA 1978-83, exec. bd. 1977-81, chmn. spl. events 1985-90, internat. bd. govs. fellow 1981-83), Am. Film Inst., Deseret Bus. and Profl. Assn., Marriott Bus. Mgmt. Soc. (L.A. chpt.), Assn. L.D.S. Pub. Rels. Profls., Pub. Rels. Soc. Am. (L.A. chpt.), Nat. Mus. Women in the Arts (charter), Arcadia Tournament of Roses Assn., Arcadia C. of C. (chmn. industry commn. of women's divsn. 1983-85, mem. exec. bd. 1985-86). Avocations: sculpting, painting. Office: 1591 E Temple Way Los Angeles CA 90024-5801 E-mail: mirialara@aol.com, PublicAffairsLA@aol.com.

HULL, LEWIS WOODRUFF, manufacturing executive; b. Scranton, Pa., Oct. 16, 1916; s. Robert Alonzo and Clara Lucelia (Woodruff) H.; m. Margaret (Burns) Carson, June 7, 1947; children: Arthur, Martha, Stephen, Rebecca. BS in Chem. Engring., MIT, 1938. Divsn. mgr. F. J. Stokes Co., Phila., 1938—52; pres. Hull Corp., 1952—2002, Hull Vac Pump Corp., Ivyland, Pa., 2003—, Hull Freeze-dry Corp., Ivyland, 2003—. Bd. dir. Hull Internat. Ltd., Girvan, Scotland, Hull-Japan Ltd., Tokyo, Advanced System Design, Evergreen, Colo., Willow Grove Bancorp, Maple Glen, Pa., Pa. Free Enterprise Found., Erie, Pa. (v.p.); dir. Mid-Atlantic Employers Assn., Trooper, Pa. Contbr. articles to profl. jours.; patentee in field. Bd. dir. Heritage Conservancy, Doylestown, Pa. Mem. Plastics Pioneers Assn. (past pres.), Am. Vacuum Soc. (past pres.), Soaring Soc. Am. (former sec.), Rotary. Republican. Avocations: sailplaning, tennis. Home: 277 W Bristol Rd Southampton PA 18966-1070 Office: Hullvac Pump Corp 73 Steamwhistle Dr Warminster PA 18974-4875 also: Hull Freeze-Dry Corp 73 Steamwhistle Dr Warminster PA 18974 Business E-Mail: lhull@hullvacpumps.com.

HULL, MCALLISTER HOBART, JR., retired university administrator; b. Birmingham, Ala., Sept. 1, 1923; s. McAllister Hobart and Grace (Johnson) H.; m. Mary Muska, Mar. 23, 1946; children: John McAllister, Wendy Ann. BS with highest honors, Yale U., 1948, PhD in Physics, 1951. Tech. asst. Los Alamos (N.Mex.) Lab., 1944-46; from instr. to assoc. prof. physics Yale U., 1951-66; prof. physics, chmn. dept. Oreg. State U., 1966-69, SUNY, Buffalo, 1969-72, dean Grad. Sch., 1972-74, dean. grad. and profl. edn., 1974-77; provost U. N.Mex., 1977-85, counselor to pres., 1985-88, prof. emeritus physics, 1988—. Adviser to supt. schs., Hamden, Conn., 1958-65. Author: Rider of the Pale Horse: A Memoir of Los Alamos and Beyond, 2005, others; author papers, chpts. to books, articles in encys. Bd. dirs. Western N.Y. Reactor Facility, 1970-72; trustee N.E. Radio Obs. Corp., 1971-77; pres. Western Regional Sci. Labs., 1977; chmn. tech. adv. com. N.Mex. Energy Rsch. Inst., 1981-83, mem., 1983-88; co-chmn. Nat. Task Force on Ednl. Tech., 1984-86. Served with AUS, 1943-46. Faculty fellow Yale U., 1964-65. Fellow Am. Phys. Soc.; mem. Am. Assn. Physics Tchrs. (chmn. Oreg. sect. 1967-68). Personal E-mail: machull@unm.edu. *Experience says that everyone is sometimes wise, no one is always wise. One mustdevelop the willingness to listen for wisdom from whatever source, the judgment to identify it, the skill to use it: only in this way can one's talents, however modest or extensive, be optimally enhanced and the number of wasted efforts minimized.*

HULL, PHILIP GLASGOW, lawyer; b. St. Albans, Vt., Feb. 17, 1925; s. Charles Herman and Gladys Gertrude (Glasgow) H.; m. Gretchen Elizabeth Gaebelein, Oct. 24, 1952; children: Jeffrey R., Sanford D., Meredyth Hull Smith. AB, Middlebury Coll., 1949; LLB, Columbia U., 1952. Bar: N.Y. 1952, Fla. 1977. Staff mem. subcom. on adminstrn. internal revenue laws, com. on ways and means U.S. Ho. of Reps., Washington, 1951; assoc. Winthrop, Stimson, Putnam & Roberts, NYC, 1952-63, ptnr., 1964-97, sr. counsel, 1998-2000, Pillsbury Winthrop, NYC, 2001—05, Pillsbury Winthrop Shaw Pittman, 2005—06. Mem. Sch. Revenue Com., Cold Spring Harbor, N.Y., 1963-65; bd. dirs. Eagle Dock Found., Cold Spring Harbor, 1971-74, People's Symphony Concerts, N.Y.C., 1977—2005, L.I. Philharm., 1979-81; trustee L.Am. Mission, Miami, Fla., 1969-79; elder Ctrl. Presbyn. Ch., Huntington, N.Y., 1956-78; mem. nat. mssions bd. United Presbyn. Ch., U.S.A., 1967-73; trustee Madison Avenue Presbyn. Ch., N.Y.C., 1989-94, pres., 1993-94; mem. Lloyd Harbor Conservation Adv. Coun., 1973-77. With U.S. Army, 1943-46. Ellis fellow, Kent scholar, Stone scholar Columbia U. Mem. Am. Coll. Trust and Estate Counsel, NY State Bar Assn., Christian Legal Soc. (bd. dirs. 1984-97), Fellowship Christians in Univs. and Schs. (trustee 1983-90), Univ. Club NYC (bd. dirs. 1986-90), Cold Spring Harbor Beach Club, Blue Key, Phi Beta Kappa. Office: Pillsbury Winthrop 1540 Broadway New York NY 10036-4039 Home Phone: 609-426-6785.

HULL, RAYMOND WHITFORD, public relations executive; b. Cohoes, NY, Oct. 13, 1946; s. Raymond W. and J. Ruth (Barber) H. BS, Syracuse U., 1971. Spl. asst. to Gov. Nelson A. Rockefeller, Albany, N.Y., 1971; conf. asst. to commr. N.Y. State Dept. Environ. Conservation, Albany, 1971-74; exec. dir. Spl. Joint Legis. Commn. on Petroleum Distbn., Albany, 1974-75; asst. headmaster Hoosac Sch., Hoosick, N.Y., 1975-77; area coordinator N.Y. State Assembly, Albany, 1977-79; staff dir. N.Y. State Senate Com. on Energy, Albany, 1979-85; dir. pub. affairs Niagara Mohawk Power Corp., Albany, 1985-89; pub. affairs cons. Albany, 1990-96; assoc. commr. N.Y. State Dept. Motor Vehicles, Albany, 1996—. V.p. Rensselaer City Sch. Bd., N.Y., 1981-86; treas. bd. trustees Hoosac Sch., 1974-81, Rennsselaer City Hist. Soc., 1980—, pres., 1994; trustee Rennselaer county hist. Soc., 1986-94. Mem.: Ft. Orange (Albany); SAR (N.Y.C.). Republican. Episcopalian. Avocations: historical architecture, art. Home: The Patroon Agts House 15 Forbes Ave Rensselaer NY 12144-1622 E-mail: RayHull@aol.com.

HULL, ROBERT F., JR., (BOB), consumer products company executive; B in Acctg., U. N.C., Charlotte, BBA. CPA. Controller Side Show, Inc., 1997—99; v.p. fin. planning and analysis Lowe's Cos., Inc., 1999—2003, sr. v.p., CFO, 2003—04, exec. v.p., CFO, 2004—. Office: Lowes Cos Inc 1605 Curtis Bridge Rd Wilkesboro NC 28697*

HULL, ROBERT JOE, lawyer; b. Ft. Monmouth, NJ, Dec. 16, 1944; s. Thurman Beuford and Helen Louise (Bracey) H.; m. Susan Diane Hull, Mar. 12, 1966; 1 child, Robert Steven. BA, U. Tex., 1966, JD, 1969. Bar: Tex. 1969, Calif. 1970, U.S. Dist. Ct. (ctrl. dist.) Calif. 1970, U.S. Ct. Appeals (9th cir.) 1970, U.S. Tax. Ct. 1971, U.S. Supreme Ct. 1992. Assoc. Sheppard, Mullin, Richter & Hampton, LA, 1969-76, ptnr., 1976-98, Bracewell & Patterson LLP, Houston, 1998—. Co-author: Representing Start-Up Companies, 1992, (annual) ABA Sales & Use Tax Handbook; mem. editorial bd., contbr. Jour. Multistate Taxation, 1991—. Mem. Tex. Bar Found., Club at Escondido, Houstonian Golf Club, Houston Club. Republican. Episcopalian. Avocation: golf. Home: 2607 Sutton Ct Houston TX 77027-5246 Office: Bracewell & Giuliani LLP S Twr Penzoil Pl 711 Louisiana St Ste 2300 Houston TX 77002-2770 Home Phone: 713-355-6087; Office Phone: 713-221-1589. Business E-Mail: joe.hull@bgllp.com.

HULL, ROGER HAROLD, foundation and former academic administrator; b. NYC, June 18, 1942; s. Max Harold and Magda Mary (Stern) H.; children: Roberto Franklin, Lincoln Macgregor. AB cum laude, Dartmouth Coll., 1964; LL.B., Yale U., 1967; LL.M., U. Va., 1972, SJD, 1974; LHD (hon.), Rockford Coll., 1988; LLD (hon.), Beloit Coll., 1992; DCl (hon.), Union Coll., 2005; DHL (hon.), Albany Coll. Pharmacy, 2006. Bar: N.Y. 1968. Assoc. firm White & Case, NYC, 1967—71; spl. counsel to gov., Va., 1971—74; spl. asst. to chmn., dep. staff dir. Interag. Task Force Law of Sea, NSC, 1974—76; v.p. devel. Syracuse U., 1976—79, v.p. devel. and planning, 1979—81; pres. Beloit (Wis.) Coll., 1981—90, Union Coll., Schenectady, NY, 1990—2005, pres. emeritus, 2005—; chancellor Union U., Schenectady, 1990—2005; pres. Help Yourself Found., Schenectady, 2005—. Mem. U.S. del. Law of Sea Conf., 1974-76; adj. prof. Syracuse Univ. Law Sch., 1976-81; bd. visitors Coll. William and Mary, Williamsburg, Va., 1970-74; mem. pub. instns. task force Assn. Gov. Bds., 1975. Author: The Irish Triangle, 1976; co-author: Law and Vietnam, 1968. Co-founder, vice chair Schenectady 2000. Named Schenectady County Person of Yr., 1998, Patroon, 1999, Schnectady C. of C. Exec. of Yr., 2002; recipient Cmty. Leadership award, 1999 Golden Apple award Schenectady Sch. Sys., 2004; Roger Hull Place named by City of Schenectady 2005, Hull Plaza at Union Coll., 2005. Mem. Am. Soc. Internat. Law, Univ. Club Home and Office: Help Yourself Found 1090 Avon Rd Schenectady NY 12308 Office Phone: 518-280-5735. Business E-Mail: rhull@hyfdn.org.

HULL, THOMAS GRAY, federal judge; b. 1926; m. Joan Brandon; children: Leslie, Brandon, Amy. Student, Tusculum Coll.; JD, U. Tenn., 1951. Atty. Easterly and Hull, Greeneville, Tenn., 1951-63; mem. Tenn. Ho. of Reps., 1955-65; atty., prin. Thomas G. Hull, 1951-72; chief clk. Tenn. Ho. of Reps., 1969-70; judge 20th Jud. Cir., Greeneville, Morristown and Rogersville, Tenn., 1972-79; legal counsel to Tenn. Gov. Lamar Alexander, 1979-81; judge U.S. Dist. Ct. (ea. dist.) Tenn., 1983—. Served as cpl. U.S. Army, 1944-46. Mem. Tenn. Bar Assn. (chmn. East dist. com. 1969), Greenville Bar Assn. (pres. 1969-71), Tenn. Jud. Conf. (del. 1972-79, vice chmn. 1974-75, com. to draft uniform charges for trial judges). Republican. Office: Office of US Dist Judge 220 W Depot St Greeneville TN 37743

HULL, WILLIAM EDWARD, theology studies educator; b. Birmingham, Ala., May 28, 1930; s. William Edward and Margaret (King) H.; m. Julia Wylodine Hester, July 26, 1952; children: David William, Susan Virginia. BA, Samford U., 1951; MDiv, So. Bapt. Theol. Sem., Louisville, 1954, PhD, 1960; postgrad., U. Gottingen, Germany, 1962—63, Harvard U., 1971. Ordained to ministry Bapt. Ch., 1950. Pastor Beulah Bapt. Ch., Wetumpka, Ala., 1950-51, Cedar Hill Bapt. Ch., Owenton, Ky., 1952-53, 1st Bapt. Ch., New Castle, Ky., 1953-58; from instr. to assoc. prof. So. Bapt. Theol. Sem., Louisville, 1954-67, prof., 1967-75, dean theology and provost, 1969-75; pastor 1st Bapt. Ch., Shreveport, La., 1975-87; provost Samford U., Birmingham, 1987-96, Univ. prof., 1987-2000; theologian in residence Mountain Brook Baptist Ch., Birmingham, 1991; rsch. prof. Samford U., Birmingham, 2000—. Author: Gospel of John, 1964, Broadman Bible Commentary, 1970, Beyond the Barriers, 1981, Love in Four Dimensions, 1982, The Christian Experience of Salvation, 1987, Southern Baptist Higher Education: Retrospect and Prospect, 2001, The Quest for Spiritual Maturity, 2004, The Four-Way Test: Core Values of the Rotary Movement, 2004; (with others) Professor in the Pulpit, 1963, The Truth That Makes Men Free, 1966, Salvation in Our Time, 1978, Set Apart for Service, 1980, Celebrating Christ's Presence Through the Spirit, 1981, The Twentieth Century Pulpit, Vol. II, 1981, Minister's Manual, 1983-87, 2000, 5th edit., 2005, Biblical Preaching: An Expositor's Treasury, 1983, Preaching in Today's World, 1984, Heralds to a New Age, 1985, Getting Ready for Sunday: A Practical Guide for Worship Planning, 1989, Best Sermons 2, 1989, The University Through the Eyes of Faith, 1998, Putting Women in Their Place: Moving Beyond Gender Stereotypes in Church and Home, 2003, Distinctively Baptist: Essays on Baptist History, 2005, Gladly Learn, Gladly Teach: Living Out One's Calling in the 21st Century Academy, 2005; contbr. articles to profl. jours. Mem. Futureshape Shreveport (La.) Commn., 1985-87. Recipient Denominational Svc. award Samford U., 1974, Liberty Bell award Shreveport Bar Assn., 1984, Brotherhood and Humanitarian award NCCJ, 1987, Charles D. Johnson Outstanding Educator award Assn. So. Bapt. Colls. and Schs., 1999, Samford U. Alumnus Yr., 2005. Mem. Nat. Assn. Bapt. Profs. Religion (pres. 1967-68), Am. Acad. Religion, Soc. Bibl. Lit., The Club (Birmingham), Vestavia Country Club (Birmingham), Rotary, Phi Kappa Phi, Phi Eta Sigma, Omicron Delta Kappa. Baptist. Home: 435 Vesclub Way Birmingham AL 35216-1357 Office Phone: 205-726-4030. Business E-Mail: wehull@samford.edu.

HULLIHEN, KAREN A., chemist; married, June 21, 1980; children: Elaine J., Theresa L. BS, Youngstown State U., Ohio, 1995. Lab. technician Kent State U., Ohio, 2001—03, acad. lab. coord. Middlefield, Ohio, 2003—. Office: Kent State U 15825 Old State Rd Middlefield OH 44062 Office Fax: 440-632-1622. Business E-Mail: khullihe@kent.edu.

HULLIN, TOD ROBERT, aerospace transportation executive; b. Seattle, May 28, 1943; s. Jack Elmer Hullin and Floretta Elizabeth Light; m. Susan Lee Kanz, 1967. BA in Bus. Adminstrn., U. Wash., 1966. Staff asst. domestic coun. The White House, Washington, 1973—74, assoc. dir. domestic coun. for housing and community devel., 1974—76, prin. dep. asst. sec. def. for pub. affairs, 1976—77; v.p. Interstate Gen. Corp., St. Charles, Md., 1977—83; pres. Interstate Condominiums, Inc., 1981-83, 1981—83; v.p. comm./pub. affairs G.D. Searle Pharms., Skokie, Ill., 1983—86; v.p. corp. affairs SmithKline Beecham Labs., Phila., 1986—91; v.p. comm. Time Warner, NY, 1991—97; sr. v.p. comm. The Seagram Company, 1998—2000; exec. v.p. global public policy and N.A. comm. Vivendi Universal, 2000—02; sr. v.p. comm. The Boeing Co., Chgo., 2003—06, sr. v.p. pub. policy & comm., 2006—. 1st lt. US Army, 1967—69. Recipient Army Commendation medal, Outstanding Pub. Sfc. award, Dept. of Def., 1977. Mem. Nat. Assn. Home Builders, Urban Land Inst., Greater Washington Bd. Trade, U. Wash. Alumni Assn. (pres. San Francisco Bay Area chpt. 1982-83), Eureka (Ill.) Coll. Arts Coun., Army Navy Country Club, Sigma Nu; dd. dirs. Phila. Drama Guild, Balch Inst. for Ethnic Studies. Office: The Boeing Co 1200 Wilson Blvd Arlington VA 22209

HULLS, JAMES ROBERT, emergency physician; b. Columbus, Ohio, Sept. 5, 1947; s. Charles Robert and Margaret Rose (Chichka) Hulls; m. Suzanne Lynn Evans, Dec. 18, 1971; children: Michelle, Kristin. BA, Ohio State U., 1969, MD, 1973. Diplomate Am. Bd. Emergency Medicine, Am. Bd. Forensic Examiners, 2004. Resident U. South Fla., Tampa, 1973—74; emergency physician U. Cmty. Hosp., Tampa, 1974—2006, asst. dir. emergency dept., 1993—96, 1998—99; asst. dir. Franklin, Favata Hulls,

Md., 1989—2004; dir. emergency dept. Suncoast Hosp., Largo, Fla., 2005—06; peer review officer quality control Tampa Bay Emergency Physicians, 2006—. Med. advisor City of Tampa Fire Rescue, 1978—96; clin. preceptor emergency medicine Nova U. Coll. Medicine, 1994—99, clin. asst. prof., 1999—2002; preceptor physician assts. program U. Nebr., 1998—99; mem. control bd. Pinellas County Emergency Med. Svcs., 2005—. V.p. North Hillsborough chpt. Am. Heart Assn., 1996—97, pres., 1997—98. Fellow: Am. Coll. Emergency Physicians; mem.: AMA (life), Hillsborough County Med. Assn. (mem. editl. bd. 1993—, restaurant reviewer Bulletin mag. 1997—99, 2001—, v.p. 2006—07). Methodist. Avocations: photography, travel, diving, swimming. Office: Univ Cmty Hosp 3100 E Fletcher Ave Tampa FL 33613-4613

HULME, JANET A., physical therapist, writer, small business owner; b. Seattle, July 2, 1946; d. John C. and Anna C. (Wick) Bower; children from previous marriage: Erika, Abigail. BS, U. Mont., Missoula, 1968; MA, Stanford U., Palo Alto, Calif., 1970. Owner Janet Hulme Rentals, Missoula, Mont., 1971—; dir., prof. phys. therapy U. Mont., 1979—88; pvt. practice Phoenix Phys. Therapy, 1987—97; owner Bagels on Broadway, 1993—96; owner, publ. Phoenix, Inc., 1994—; prin. Phoenix Seminars, 1994—. Author: Beyond Kegels, 2d edit., 1994, Fibromyalgia A Handbook for Self-Care and Treatment, 3d edit., 1994, Beyond Kegels Book II, 1996, Geriatric Incontinence, 1998, Bladder and Bowel Issues in Kids, 2002, Pelvic Rotator Cuff in Human Function, 2004. Mem.: Am. Assn. Biofeedback, Am. Phys. Therapy Assn., Kiwanis. Office: Phoenix Inc PO Box 8231 Missoula MT 59807-8231

HULME, PAUL G., chemicals executive; b. Eng. Grad. in Bus. Studies, U. Manchester, Eng. Chartered acct. Various positions in fin., acctg. and info. systems ICI; global ops. dir. polyurethanes Huntsman Corp., Salt Lake City, 1999—2000, v.p. performance chems., 2000—03, divsn. pres. advanced materials, 2003—06, divsn. pres. materials and effects, 2006—. Office: Huntsman Corp 500 Huntsman Way Salt Lake City UT 84108 Office Phone: 801-584-5700.*

HULON, WILLIE T., federal agency administrator; b. Memphis, 1957; BA, Rhodes Coll., 1979. Police officer, Memphis, 1980—83; spl. agent FBI, 1983—91, supervisory spl. agent violent crimes and major offenders squad San Antonio, 1991—95, spl. agent violent crimes fugitive unit Washington, 1995—96, asst. inspector inspection divsn., 1996—97, chief interstate theft govt. reservation crimes unit, 1997—2000, asst. spl. agent in charge St. Louis, 2000—01, chief inspector, 2001, spl. agent in charge Detroit, dep. asst. dir. counterterrorism divsn. Washington, exec. asst. dir. nat. security br., 2006—. Office: FBI 950 Pennsylvania Ave Washington DC 20535*

HULSE, CARL, newspaper executive; m. Kim Hulse; children: Nicholas, Benjamin. BS, Ill. State U., 1976. With Gainesville Sun, Fla., 1989—91; reporter NY Times, 1991—93, Washington bur. chief, 1994—, chief Congl. corr., Washington bur., 2004—. Office: NY Times Washington Bur 7th Fl 1627 I St NW Washington DC 20006-4007 Office Phone: 202-862-0381. Office Fax: 202-862-0340. E-mail: cahuls@nytimes.com.

HULSE, ROBERT DOUGLAS, biotechnologist; b. Niagara Falls, NY, Aug. 16, 1943; s. Robert Edwin and Helen Louise (Kenny) H.; m. Nancy Louise Musser, Aug. 20, 1966 (div. 1986); children: Anne Warren, Robert Alexander; m. Karen Alice Karlberg, Dec. 31, 1987. AB, Princeton U., 1965; SMChemE, MIT, 1966, SM in Mgmt., 1968. Mgr. bus. analysis Halcon Internat. Inc., NYC, 1968-73, dir. bus. planning, 1973-76; v.p., gen. mgr. Halcon Catalyst Industries, Little Ferry, NJ, 1976-82; v.p. planning & devel. Engelhard Industries, Iselin, NJ, 1982-84; pres., chief exec. officer i-STAT Corp., Princeton, NJ, 1984-86, Sunstone Inc., Dayton, NJ, 1986-87; vice chmn. Princeton Entrepreneurial Resources, 1988-90; pres., chief exec. officer SDTX Technologies, Inc., Princeton, 1989—; v.p. bus. devel. Enzon, Inc., Piscataway, NJ, 1991-94; exec. dir. The Sage Group, Bridgewater, NJ, 1995—, also bd. dirs.; gen. ptnr. SAE Ventures, New Canaan, Conn., 1997-2001; pres., COO Hemispherx Biopharma, Inc., Phila., 1996—97, 2005—06. Cons. in field; pres., dir. Captiva Technologies, Princeton, 1989—; bd. dirs. SDTX Technologies, Inc., Princeton, Carnegie Venture Resources, Inc., Princeton, Sage Group, Branchburg; adv. bd. Commercialization Ctr. for Innovative Tech., New Brunswick Dir. Gotham Light Opera Soc., N.Y.C., 1969-73; treas. Bloomingdale House of Music, N.Y.C., 1979-84. Named Univ. scholar Princeton U., 1961. Mem. The Licensing Execs. Soc., Soc. Competitive Intelligence Profls., Controlled Release Soc., Princeton Club NY, The Union League Club, Doubles, Sigma Xi, Phi Beta Kappa. Republican. Episcopalian. Avocations: chess, tennis. Office: Sage Group 3322 Rte 22 W Bldg 2 Ste 201 Somerville NJ 08876 Office Phone: 908-231-9644 21. Personal E-mail: Doughulse@aol.com.

HULSE, RUSSELL ALAN, physicist; b. NYC, Nov. 28, 1950; s. Alan Earle and Betty Joan (Wedemeyer) Hulse. BS, Cooper Union, 1970; MS, U. Mass., 1972, PhD, 1975. Rsch. assoc. Nat. Radio Astronomy Observatory, Charlottesville, Va., 1975—77; mem. tech. staff Princeton U. Plasma Physics Lab., 1977—80, staff rsch. physicist, 1980—84, rsch. physicist, 1984—92, prin. rsch. physicist, 1992—2007. Vis. prof. physics, math., sci. edn. U. Tex., Dallas, 2004—07, assoc. v.p. for rsch. and econ. devel., 2005—07, regental prof., assoc. v.p. for strategic initiatives, 2007—; bd. dirs. Battelle Meml. Inst. Contbr. articles to profl. jours. Recipient Nobel prize in physics, 1993. Fellow: AAAS, Inst. Physics, Am. Phys. Soc.; mem.: Am. Astron. Soc. Achievements include discovery of first binary pulsar - a twin star system that provides a rare natural laboratory in which to test Albert Einstein's prediction that moving objects emit gravitational waves. Avocations: target shooting, birdwatching, canoeing, hiking, hunting.

HULSEBOSCH, DANIEL JOSEPH, historian, educator; b. Scarsdale, NY, Nov. 6, 1965; s. Edward J. and Jane Mangan Hulsebosch. AB, Colgate U., 1987; JD, Columbia U., 1991; AM, Harvard U., 1993, PhD, 1999. Assoc. prof. Sch. of Law St. Louis (Mo.) U., 1999—2005; prof. NYU Sch. Law, NYC, 2005—. Cons. in field. Author: Constituting Empire: New York and the Transformation of Constitutionalism in the Atlantic World, 1664-1830, 2005; contbr. articles to profl. jours. Fellow Samuel I. Golieb fellowship, N.Y. U. Sch. of Law, 1998—99; grantee Whiting fellowship in the Humanities, Harvard U., 1996—97. Mem.: Am. Hist. Assn. (Littleton-Griswold Book prize 2006), Am. Soc. Legal History (John Phillip Reid Book prize 2006), Omohundro Inst. for Early Am. History and Culture (assoc.), Phi Beta Kappa. Office: NYU Sch Law 40 Washington Sq S New York NY 10012 E-mail: daniel.hulsebosch@nyu.edu.

HULSHOF, KENNY CHARLES, congressman; b. Sikeston, Mo., May 22, 1958; m. Renee Lynn Howell; 1 child. BS in Agr. Econs., U. Mo., Columbia, 1980; JD, U. Miss. Sch. Law, 1983. Bar: Mo. 1983, Miss. 1983. Asst. pub. defender 32nd Mo. Jud. Circuit, 1983—86; asst. pros. atty. Cape Girardeau County, Mo., 1986—89; spl. prosecutor Mo. Atty. Gen. Office, 1989—96; mem. US Congress from 9th Mo. dist., 1997—, mem. ways and means com., mem. budget com., mem. health subcommittee, mem. social security subcommittee. Rep. candidate for Boone County Prosecutor, 1992, US Congress, 1994, 96; mem. MU Farm Ho. Found. Named Statesman of Month, Jefferson City, Mo. News Tribune, 1993; recipient Lon O. Hocker award, Trial Advocacy, Mo. Bar Assn., 1992, Nat. Energy Leadership award, Nat. Biodiesel Bd., 2004. Mem.: Boone County, Mo. Farm Bur., NRA, Nat. Dist. Atty. Assoc., Mo. Bar Assn., Miss. Bar Assn., Ducks Unlimited. Republican. Roman Catholic. Office: US House Reps 409 Cannon House Office Bldg Washington DC 20515 Office Phone: 202-225-2956. Office Fax: 202-225-5712.*

HULTGREN, DENNIS EUGENE, farmer, management consultant; b. Union County, SD, Mar. 19, 1929; s. John Alfred and Esther Marie (Johnson) H.; m. Nelda Ethelyn Olson, Aug. 3, 1957; children: Nancy Hultgren Forsythe, Jean Hultgren Doty, Jahn Dennis, Ruth Dorothy Hultgren Henneman. Farmer, Union County, 1953—. Commr., chmn. Union County Planning and Zoning Bd., 1972-83; mem. bd. bylaw revision Union County Electric Co., 1983-85. Author: To Korea and Back Home Again a Reminisce, 2006, The Queen of the Neighborhood, A Reminisce, 2007. Pres. bd. Union Creek Cemetry, 1958—; pres. bd. mgrs. Union-Sayles Watershed Dist., 1965-70; exec. bd. SD Farm Bur., Union County, 1996—, pres., 1998—; treas. Sioux Valley Twp., Union County, 1980—; treas., bd. dirs. W. Union Sch., 1957-67; chmn. Union County Sch. Bd., 1961-68; pres. Alcester Sch. Bd., SD, 1970-77; chmn. Alcester PTA, 1967-68; mem. tech. bd. rev. Southeastern Coun. Govts., Sioux Falls, 1976-77; bd. dirs. Siouxland Interstate Met. Planning Coun., Sioux City, 1977-83, sec. coun. ofcls., 1978-83; bd. dirs. Old Opera House Cmty. Theater, Akron, Iowa, Akron Area Action Assn., 1983-85, Akron Devel. Corp., 1985-90; Rep. precinct committeeman, 1970, Union County Rep. Ctrl. Com., 1970—; chmn. SD State Bd. Equalization, 1987-95, SD State Resolutions Com.; mem. synod stewardship bd. Western Iowa Synod Luth. Ch., 1987-90, elected synod assembly bus. and coun. com., 1991-93, synod bus. and coun. com., 1997-99, synod coun. Western Iowa Synod, 1997-2000; SD del. Rep. nat. Conv., New Orleans, 1988. Served with AUS, 1951-53, Korea. Decorated Combat Infantry Badge, 3 Bronze Battle Stars; recipient Outstanding Dedication and Svc. award Old Opera House Cmty. Theatre, 1984, Sioux City Siouxland Disting. Citizen award Siouxland Interstate Met. Planning Coun., 1983, Jefferson award Sta. KELO-TV, 1985, Outstanding Cmty. Svc. award Lions Internat., 1985. Mem.: VFW (Alcester, SD, vice-comdr. 1995—97, comdr. 2000—02), NRA, Nat. Cattlemen's Assn., SD Livestock Feeders Assn., Farmers Union (exec. bd. Union County 1987—90), Farm Bur., 224 Infantry Regiment Assn., Associated Sch. Bds. SD (Merit award 1976), Am. Legion (exec. bd. Akron 1978—92, comdr. Akron 1980—81, historian 1981—96, trustee 1983—90, comdr. Akron 1985—86, vice comdr. 9th dist. 1989, chmn. athletics and contest com. Dept. of Iowa Am. Legion 1991—92, judge adv. 9th dist. Iowa 1993—, trustee 1996—, chmn. athletics and contest com. Dept. of Iowa Am. Legion 1997—99, 2002—03, comdr. 9th dist. Dept. of Iowa 1992—93). Lutheran (mem. bd. 1967-70, 82-84, 90-93, 2001-2007, lay chmn. 1970, 82-93, chmn. centennial com. 1974, chmn. 125th anniversary com. 1999, chmn. ch. bd. 2001-03). Address: Hulteboda Farm 47953 309th St Akron IA 51001-7575

HULTIN, JERRY MACARTHUR, academic administrator, former dean; b. Lansing, Mich., May 17, 1942; s. Arthur Frederick and Donna (Prevey) H.; m. Jill Foreman, June 27, 1965; children: Jeremy Foreman, Jedd Foreman. BA, Ohio State U., Columbus, Ohio, 1960—64; JD, Yale Law Sch., New Haven, CT, 1969—72. Bar: Ohio 1972, U.S. Dist. Ct. (so. dist.) Ohio 1973, U.S. Ct. Appeals (6th cir.) 1975, U.S. Supreme Ct. 1979. Ptnr. Taylor and Hultin, Columbus, Ohio, 1972—74, Moots, Hultin, Weinberger & Cope, Columbus, Ohio, 1975—80; coo Hydron and HydroHorse, Columbus, Ohio, 1980—82; ceo Novatech, Columbus, Ohio, 1982—83; chmn. Hultin & Associates, Inc., Columbus, Ohio, 1984—94; ptnr. Jefferson Partners, Washington, 1994—97; under sec., Dept. Navy US Dept. Def., Washington, 1997—2000; dean Stevens Inst. of Tech., Hoboken, NJ, 2000—05; pres. Polytechnic U., Bklyn., 2005—. Chief coun. Joint Select Com. on Workers Compensation, Columbus, 1975-76; exec. com. CETA Strike Force, Columbus, 1983-84; trustee, chmn. Savs. & Loan Assurance Corp., Columbus, 1985-88; bd. dirs. Fed. Home Loan Mortgage Corp., McLean, Va.; mem. Chief of Naval Ops. Exec. Panel, 1994—. Sponsor (book and study) The Global Century: Globalization and National Security. Chmn. Columbus Cable Commn., 1977-78; pres. ACTV-Access Cable, Columbus, 1984-86; treas., chmn. Participation 2000, Inc., 1988—. Lt. USN, 1964—69, Vietnam, Western Pacific and California. Decorated Navy Unit Commendation and various Vietnam-era medals US Dept. Def., Disting. Pub. Svc. Medal, Dept. Navy. Mem.: Nat. Economist Club. Achievements include development of Revolution in Business Affairs in Department of the Navy; Navy Marine Corps Intranet; Thirty Something for young naval officers. Avocations: running, squash, tennis, golf, music. Office: President Polytechnic U 6 Metro Tech Ctr Brooklyn NY 11201 Business E-Mail: hultin@poly.edu.

HULTQUIST, THOMAS ROBERT, meteorologist; s. Henry Gustav and Alice Marie Hultquist; m. Carol Ann Gould, Sept. 27, 1997. Diploma in Meteorology, Lyndon State Coll., Lyndonville, Vt., 1988—92. Forecaster NOAA/Nat. Weather Svc., Grand Rapids, 1994—2001, sci. and ops. officer Marquette, Mich., 2001—. Mem.: Am. Meteorol. Soc. Achievements include research in re-examination of the 9-10 November 1975 Edmund Fitzgerald Storm using today's technology. Office: NOAA/National Weather Svc 112 Airpark Dr Negaunee MI 49866 Home Phone: 906-249-1193; Office Phone: 906-475-5782 766.

HULTSTRAND, CHARLES JOHN, architect; b. Mt. Vernon, Ohio, Dec. 26, 1951; s. Donald M. and Marjorie R. (Richter) H.; m. Kathi, Brooke, Andrew, Caroline, Clay, Kristi, Scott. BSE, Princeton U., 1974; MArch, Rice U., 1977. Registered architect, S.C. Assoc., project designer Golemon & Rolfe Architects, Houston, 1977-83; prin., exec. v.p., dir. of design The Boudreaux Group, Inc., Columbia, SC, 1983—2003; ptnr., dir. design Neal-Prince & Ptnrs., Greenville, SC, 2003—. Guest lectr. Clemson (S.C.) U. Coll. Architecture, 1993-2005, Cornerstone Nat. Conf. 2005; mem. steering com. Onions & Orchids Award Program, Columbia, 1988, jury mem., 1989; mem. steering com. Columbia R/UDAT Commn., 1987; v.p. Terrace Lake, Inc.; bd. dirs. Columbia Devel. Corp., Faith and Form, 2005-. Pres. parent tchr. fellowship Ben Lippen Sch., Columbia, 1991-94, mem. bd. mgrs., 1991—, v.p. bd., 1995-2000; mem. fundraising com., 1993-2002; deacon Cornerstone Presbyn. Ch., Columbia, 1988-91, First Presbyn. Ch., Columbia, 1997-99, 2000-03, vice chmn., 2001-02, chmn., 2003; mem. bd. Faith & Form, 2005-; pres. Yokemen Svc. Orgn., 1982-83; vol. ARC Hurricane Hugo Relief, 1990, SCETV Fundraising, Columbia, 1991; mem. sch. com. Princeton Alumni Assn., 2000-05. Named Columbia Small Bus. Person of Yr., Greater Columbia C. of C., 2003; recipient AIA SC Honor Award, Columbia Internat. U. Prayer Towers, 1988, St. Francis of Assisi Episcopal Ch., 1988, Brick Assn. of Carolinas Pres. Award, St. Christopher's Episcopal Ch., 1996, Merit Award Columbia Chpt. AIA, 1996, SC Conservatory, 1996, Clemson U. Student Housing, 1996, Honor Award Brick Assn. of Carolinas, 1998, Honor Award, USC Athletic Practice Faculty, 1999, Historic Columbia Found. Preservation Award, Flinn Hall Classroom Bldg., 2000, Bldg. of Yr. Award for Archtl. Steel, The Berkeley Bldg., Con/Steel Alliance, 2003. Mem. AIA (pres. S.C. chpt. 1996, v.p./pres.-elect S.C. chpt. 1995, sec.-treas. S.C. chpt. 1993-94, chmn. spkrs. bur. 1988-90, dir. Columbia sect. 1988-90, chmn. govt. affairs commn. S.C. chpt. 1990-93, bd. dirs., advisor intern devel. program 1990-94, state engr.'s com. 2002-03, 2005), S.C. Archtl. Soc. (bd. dirs./sec. 1997-99), Columbia Design League (bd. dirs. 1997-98), Columbia Coun. Archs. (pres. 1986-87, bd. dirs. 1984-87), Princeton Alumni Assn. S.C. (treas. 1990-94), Greater Columbia C. of C. Avocations: reading, walking, tennis, golf. Office: Neal-Prince & Ptnrs Ste 300 110 W North St Greenville SC 29601 Office Phone: 864-235-0405. E-mail: chuck@neal-prince.com.

HULTSTRAND, DONALD MAYNARD, bishop; b. Apr. 16, 1927; s. Aaron Emmanuel (H.) and Selma Avendla (Liljegren) Hultstrand; m. Marjorie Richter, June 11, 1948; children: Katherine Ann, Charles John; m. Ann Haselwood, Feb. 18, 2006. BA summa cum laude, Macalester Coll., 1950; BD summa cum laude, Colgate-Rochester Theol. Sem., 1974; DD (hon.), Nashotah Divinity Sch., 1986, Bexley Hall Sem., 2003. Ordained priest Episcopal Ch., 1953, consecrated bishop Episcopal Ch., 82. Vicar St. John's Episcopal Ch., Worthington, Minn., 1953—57; rector Grace Meml. Ch., Wabasha, Minn., 1957—62, St. Mark's Episcopal Ch., Canton, Ohio, 1962—68, St. Paul's Episcopal Ch., Duluth, Minn., 1969—75; assoc. rector St. Andrew's Episcopal Ch., Kansas City, Mo., 1968—69; exec. dir. Anglican Fellowship of Prayer, 1975—79; rector Trinity Episcopal Ch., Greeley, Colo., 1979—82; bishop Episcopal Diocese of Springfield, Ill., 1982—91; exec. bd. Episcopal Radio (TV Found.), Atlanta, 1982—87, Anglican Fellowship of Prayer, 1968—93; adv. bd. Episcopal Boys' Homes, Salinas, Kans., 1983—91; com. of execs. Ill. Conf. Chs., 1982—91; mem. House of Bishops, 1982—, mem. Minn. Standing Com., 1970—73. Chmn. Minn. Examining Chaplains, 1954—61; chaplain Pews-action Fellowships U.S.A., 1983—92; pres. Living Ch. Found., 1992—2002; advisor Diocesan Youth of Minn., 1956—60. Author: The Praying Church, 1978, And God Shall Wipe Away All Tears, 1968, Intercessory Prayer, 1972, Upper Room Dialogues, 1980, Revelations of Effective Prayer, 1995; co-author: The Parish as a Center of Prayer, 1996. Bd. dirs. Sr. Citizens Housing, Duluth, Minn., 1972—75, St. Luke's Hosp., Duluth, 1969—75; pres. Low-Rent Housing Project, Greeley, 1979—82. With USNR, 1945—46. Named hon. canon, Diocese of Ohio, Cleve., 1967; recipient Disting. Svc. award, Young Life Minn., 1974. Mem.: Pi Phi Epsilon. Episcopalian.

HUM, VANCE YORK, technology consulting executive; b. San Francisco, Apr. 19, 1948; s. Bing Wai and Jean Bik-Tsun (Pong) H.; children: Matthew Ta, Christina Lee, Jonathan Derek-Lee. BSEE, U. Md., 1971, postgrad., 1983—, George Washington U., 1977—83. Engr. Singer-Link Divsn., Silver Spring, Md., 1970; engr., field engr. Bendix Field Engring., Columbia, Md., 1971-72; primary examiner U.S. Patent & Trademark Bd., Arlington, Va., 1972-83; v.p. ops. Cheung Labs. Inc., Lanham-Seabrook, Md., 1983-86; v.p. fin. Cheung Labs. Inc., Lanham-Seabrook, Md., 1985-86; v.p. ops. Century Techs., Inc., Silver Spring, 1988-89; CEO, bd. dirs. Marc's Distbg., Inc., Jessup, Md., 1987-88; CEO, pres. I.M. Systems Group, Inc., Kensington, Md., 1986-87, 89—. Chmn. bd. dirs. I.M. Systems Group, Inc., Md., 1989—; chmn. audit/supervisory com. Lee Fed. Credit Union, Washington, 1977-83; adv. bd. Pacific Savs. and Loan Assn., McLean, Va., 1979-80; chmn. strategic planning com. Nat. Assn. Corp. Dirs., Balt.-Washington, 1989; mem. No. Va. Technology Coun., 2001. Troop treas. Boy Scouts Am., Bethesda/Chevy Chase, Md., 1993—; hon. co-chmn. Bus. Adv. Coun.; active Nat. Rep. Congrl. Com. Mem. Herndon (Va.) C. of C. , Monte Jade Sci. and Tech. Assn. Greater Washington DC Area (bd. dirs. 1999-). Avocations: tennis, golf, Karate, skiing, gardening, jiu-jitsu. Office: IM Sys Group Inc 3401 Bexhill Pl Kensington MD 20895-3105 Office Phone: 240-833-1889. Business E-Mail: humv@imsg.com.

HUMANN, L. PHILLIP, bank executive; BA, Auburn U., Ala., 1967, MS, 1969. Chmn., CEO Trust Co. Bank, Atlanta, 1985—89; exec. v.p. SunTrust Banks, Inc., Atlanta, 1989—90, sr. v.p., 1990—91, pres., 1991, CEO, 1998—2006, chmn., 1998—2006, exec. chmn., 2007—. Mem. bd. dirs. Coca-Cola Enterprises Inc., Equifax Inc., Haverty Furniture Cos., Inc. Office: SunTrust Banks Inc PO Box 4418 Atlanta GA 30308-4418 Office Phone: 404-588-7711. Office Fax: 404-827-6173.*

HUMAYUN, MARK S., ophthalmologist, educator; BS, Georgetown U., 1984; MD, Duke U. Med. Sch., 1989; PhD in Biomedical Engring., U. NC, Chapel Hill, 1994. Cert. Am. Bd. Ophthalmology, 1995, lic. Calif., 1993, Md., 1994, Fla., 1994. Intern Roanoke Meml. Hosp., 1990; resident Duke Eye Ctr., NC, 1990—93, clin. preceptor NC, 1993—95; fellowship Wilmer Opthalmological Inst., John Hopkins U., 1994—95, asst. prof. Md., 1995—99, assoc. prof., dir. Intraocular Retinal Prothesis Lab. Md., 2000—01; prof., ophthalmology and biomedical engring. U. So. Calif., 2001—; assoc. dir. rsch. Doheny Retina Inst. (affiliated orgn. Doheny Eye Inst. at the U. So. Calif. Sch. Medicine), LA, 2001—. Retinal cons. Columbia Med. Plan, 1996—97; vis. prof. Kresge Eye Inst., Detroit, 1998, Oakland Eye Inst., Rochester, Mich., 1998; bd. mem. Springer Serres BMP-BME, Calif., 2001—; dir., NSF Biomimetic Microelectronics Systems Engring. Rsch. Ctr. U. So. Calif.; clin. affiliation U. So. Calif., Keck Sch. Medicine; invited lectr. numerous univs. and assns. Author: numerous peer- and non-peer-reviewed articles and book chapters. Named Innovator of Yr., R&D Mag., 2005; recipient William and Mary Greve Scholars award: Rsch. to Prevent Blindness, 1997, Jules Stein Living Tribute award, 2002; grantee numerous rsch. grants. Mem. Am. Ophthal. Soc., Am. Acad. Ophthalmology, AMA, Assn. Rsch. in Vision and Ophthalmology, Biomed. Engring. in Medicine and Biology Soc., IEEE Engring. in Medicine and Biology Soc., Biomedical Engring. Soc., The Macula Soc., Retina Soc., Vitreous Soc., Soc. Neuroscience, Am. Soc. Retinal Specialists, Wilmer Resident Assn., Bd. Sci. Counselors for Nat. Space Biomed. Rsch. Inst., Pacific Coast Oto-Ophthalmological Soc. (hon.) sole or co-inventor of patents for retinal prostheses, retinal microstimulation, intraocular drug delivery, opthalmic surgical devices (cannulas), implantable retinal electrode arrays, and methods for training visual prosthesis. Office Phone: 323-442-6335. Office Fax: 323-442-6519. Business E-Mail: humayun@usc.edu.

HUMBERT, KIMBERLY RAMSAY, secondary school educator; b. Brookville, Pa., Jan. 20, 1972; d. Carl Frederick Ramsay and Linda Carol Ramsay-Marietta, Jon Robert Marietta (Stepfather); m. Scott A. Humbert, Feb. 1, 1997; 1 child, Matthew Scott. BS in Edn., Slippery Rock U., Pa., 1996. Cert. tchr. Commonwealth Pa., 1996. Student tchr. New Brighton (Pa.) Area Sch. Dist., 1996; sub. tchr. Mt. Gallitzin Acad., Baden, Pa., 1997, Connellsville Area Sch. Dist., Pa., 1997—98; tchr. English lang. arts Connellsville Area Sr. HS, 1998—. Med. coord., coach Fayette County Spl. Olympics, Connellsville, Pa., 1998—99, pub. rels. coord., 1999—2003, sec., coach, 2003—05, mentor, 2006—07, cooperating tchr., 2007; conselor children's recreation United Cerebral Palsy, Butler, Pa., 1993—96, counselor adult recreation, edn., 1993—96; tchr. music, dir. program vacation bible sch. First Bapt. Ch. Fairchance, Pa., 1998—2001; dir. vacation bible sch., bell choir dir., mem. praise and worship team, deaconess Ctrl. Fellowship Ch., Connellsville, Pa., 2003—. Named Educator of Yr., Fayette C. of C., 1999—2004; named to Nat. Honor Roll Outstanding Am. Tchrs., 2005—06; recipient DisneyHand Tchr. awards, Walt Disney Co., 2005. Mem.: NEA (assoc.), Pa. State Edn. Assn. (assoc.), Phi Sigma Sigma (assoc.). Conservative-R. Baptist. Avocations: rock climbing, singing, cross stitch. Office: Connellsville Area School District 201 Falcon Drive Connellsville PA 15425-5599 Home Phone: 724-628-5386; Office Phone: 724-628-1350. Office Fax: 724-628-0280. E-mail: khumbert@casdfalcons.org.

HUMBLE, MONTY GARFIELD, lawyer; b. Cameron, Tex., Dec. 20, 1951; s. Don Garfield Humble and Betty Sue (Maedgen) French; m. Donell Lou Moss, Mar. 12, 1976 (div. June 1981); m. Macy A. Melton, Oct. 23, 1993; children: Megan Elizabeth, John Marshall, Nicole Marie, Crawford Melton. BA, U. Tex., 1974, JD, 1976. Assoc. Clark, Thomas, Winters and Shapiro, Austin, Tex., 1972-82, Vinson & Elkins, Houston, 1982-86, ptnr. Dallas, 1986—. Bd. dirs. Ft. Worth Ballet, 1990-94, Dallas Opera, 1987-92, Tex. Gen. Counsel Forum, 2001-2003, Tex. Nanotech. Initiative, 2002—; gen. counsel Superconducting Super Collider Devel. Authority, 1987-94; active Leadership Dallas, 1988, Greater Dallas Planning Coun.; legal adv. Dallas City Charter Revision Com., 1990; adv. coun. U. Tex. Dallas External Rsch., 2002—. Fellow Dallas Bar Found., Tex. Bar Found.; mem. ABA, State Bar Tex., Nat. Assn. Bond Lawyers (steering com. 1985-87, 94-96, bd. dirs. 2001-06, treas. 2002-03, pres.-elect 2003-04, pres. 2004-05, past pres. 2005-06), Am. Coll. Bond Coun., Dean's Roundtable, U. Tex. Sch. Law, Health Care Fin. Mgrs. Assn. (bd. dirs.

1990-92), Crescent Club, Bent Tree Country Club, Phi Beta Kappa. Republican. Office: Vinson & Elkins LLP 2001 Ross Ave Ste 3700 Dallas TX 75201-2975 Office Phone: 214-220-7746. E-mail: mhumble@velaw.com.

HUME, BRIT (ALEXANDER BRITTON), journalist; b. Washington, June 22, 1943; s. George and Virginia Powell (Minnigerode) H.; m. Clare Stoner, Feb. 10, 1965 (div. 1992); children: Louis, Virginia, Alexander Jr. (dec.); m. Kim Schiller, June 1, 1993. BA, U. Va., 1965. Reporter Hartford Times, Conn., 1965-67, UPI, Hartford, Conn., 1967, Balt. Evening Sun, 1968; fellow Washington Journalism Ctr., 1969; reporter Jack Anderson Column, Washington, 1970-72; freelance journalist Washington, 1973; cons. ABC News, Washington, 1973-76, corr., 1976-97, Capitol Hill corr., White House corr., 1989—96; columnist Washington Post Writers Group, 1987-99; joined FOX News Channel, Washington, 1996, chief Washington corr., mng. editor, 1997—, anchor Special Report with Brit Hume. Contbr. World News Tonight with Peter Jennings, Nightline and This Week ABC News; regular panelist FOX News Sunday; contbr. news analysis FOX News Channel, oversee news content. Author: Death and the Mines, 1971, Inside Story, 1974. Recipient Emmy award, 1991; Sol Taishoff Award for Excellence in Broadcast Journalism, Nat. Press Found., 2003; named Best in Bus. by Am. Journalism Rev., 1992, 94 Mem. Met. Club, Chevy Chase Club, St. Andrews Soc. Episcopal. Office: FOX News Channel 400 N Capitol St NW Ste 550 Washington DC 20001-1502

HUME, CAMERON R., ambassador; b. Jan. 18, 1947; married; 4 children. Grad., Princeton U.; LLB, Am. U. With US Dept. State, 1970—, vice consul Palermo, advisor on human rights U.S. Mission to UN, mem. Sec. of State's planning staff, desk officer South Africa, polit. counselor Damascus, Beirut, dir. field sch. Tunis, advisor on Middle East, U.S. Mission to UN, 1986-90, sr. advisor, 1990, dep. chief of mission U.S. Embassy to Holy See Rome, 1991-94, minister-counselor for polit. affairs U.S. Mission to UN, 1994-97, US amb. to Democratic Republic of Algeria Alger-Gare, 1997—2000, spl. adv. to permanent rep. to UN NYC, 2000—01, US amb. to Republic to South Africa Pretoria, 2001—04, charge d'affaires US Embassy Khartoum, Sudan, 2005, US amb. to Indonesia Jakarta, 2007—. Author: The United Nations, Iran and Iraq: How Peacemaking Changed, 1994, Ending Mozambique's War: The Role of Mediation and Good Offices, 1994, Mission to Algiers: Diplomacy by Engagement, 2006; contbr. articles to profl. jours. Coun. on Fgn. Rels. fellow, 1975-76, Harvard U. Ctr. for Internat. Affairs fellow, 1989-90; U.S. Inst. of Peace guest scholar, 1994. Office: DOS Amb 8200 Jakarta Pl Washington DC 20521-8200*

HUME, ELLEN HUNSBERGER, media analyst, educator, journalist; b. Chevy Chase, Md., Apr. 24, 1947; d. Warren Seabury and Ruth (Pedersen) H.; m. John Shattuck, Feb. 14, 1991; 1 child, Susannah; stepchildren: Jessica, Rebecca, Peter. BA, Harvard U., 1968; PhD (hon.), Daniel Webster Coll., 1990, Kenyon Coll., 2001. Reporter Somerville (Mass.) Jour., 1968-69; feature writer Santa Barbara (Calif.) News Press, 1969-70; pub. service dir., copy writer KTMS Radio, Santa Barbara, 1970-72; edn. reporter Ypsilanti (Mich.) Press, 1972-73; bus. reporter Detroit Free Press, 1973-75; met. reporter L.A. Times, 1975-77, congl. reporter Washington, 1977-83; White House corr., polit. writer Wall St. Jour., Washington, 1983-88; exec. dir. Shorenstein Ctr. on Press and Politics Harvard U., Cambridge, Mass., 1988-93; moderator The Editors TV program, Montreal, Que., 1990-93; adj. lectr. Kennedy Sch. Govt., 1991-93, Medill Sch. Journalism, 1993-94; founding dir. Ctr. on Media and Soc., U. Mass., Boston, New Eng. Ethnic Newswire. Commentator Washington Week in Rev. PBS-TV, 1973—88, CNN, 1993—97; exec. dir. The Democracy Project PBS, 1996—98; bd. dirs. Shorenstein Ctr. Fellow Kennedy Inst. Politics, Harvard U., 1981, Annenberg Washington Program, 1993—95. Mem.: Coun. on Fgn. Rels. Episcopalian. Address: 121 Hunnewell Ave Newton MA 02458 Business E-Mail: ellen.hume@umb.edu.

HUME, FREDERICK RAYMOND, electronics executive; b. LA, Feb. 23, 1943; s. Laurence Frederick and Willetta Fredericka (Balderson) H.; m. Betty Ruth Dudley, Mar. 30, 1963; children: Joy Anne Sprague, Frederick William III. Student, Calif. State U., Long Beach, 1960-61, Biola Coll., 1961-62. Test engr. Autoretics div. Rockwell, Anaheim, Calif., 1964-67, research engr., 1967-72; mgr. new products John Fluke Mfg. Co. Inc., Everett, Wash., 1972-76, div. gen. mgr., 1976-80, v.p., 1980-88; v.p., gen. mgr. Keithley Investments, Cleve., 1988—. Bd. dirs. Artech Corp., Seattle, 1985—. Author: Transactions of IEEE, 1973. Inventor radio frequency power testing equipment, broadband spectral intensity measurement system. Chmn. Wash. High Tech. Coordinating Bd., Seattle, 1983-87; co. chmn. Jr. Achievement, Seattle, 1984. Mem. Higher Edn. Fin. Assn. (bd. dirs. 1987—), Am. Electronics Assn. (bd. dirs. 1982-86), Nat. Acad. Sci. (panel mem. 1986—), Electronics Edn. Found. (bd. dirs. 1985—), Soc. Mfg. Engrs. (sr. mem. 1983—), Precision Measurements Assn. (pres. 1978-79). Avocation: literature. Office Phone: 425-367-6213. Business E-Mail: humef@dataio.com.

HUME, JAMES BORDEN, foundation administrator, director; b. Halifax, NS, Can., Nov. 6, 1950; s. Thomas White and Elizabeth Mae (Spears) Hume; m. Penelope Ann Morris, June 3, 1972; children: Kathryn Ann, David Stuart. BA, U. Calgary, Alta., Can., 1972. Chartered Acct. V.p. TIW Industries Ltd., Ottawa, Ont., Canada, 1978-80; pres. Hume Mgmt. Cons. Ltd., Calgary, 1980-85, Kanesco Holdings Ltd., Calgary, 1985—. Pres. The Kahanoff Found., 1984—; bd. dirs. Can. West Found., Ecotrust Can., Southwestern Resources Group, The Kahanoff Found., Calgary, Paget Resources. Fellow, Inst. Chartered Accts., 2002. Mem.: Can. Inst. Chartered Accts. Office: Kahanoff Found 101 6th Ave SW Ste 105 Calgary AB Canada T2P 5K7 Office Phone: 403-237-7896. Business E-Mail: info@kahanoff.com.

HUME, SUSAN RACHEL, finance educator; b. Englewood, NJ, Aug. 25, 1952; d. Philip and Anna Ann (Petrowski) Nachtigal; m. John Elliott Hume, Dec. 27, 1975; children: Philip John, Scot Elliott. BA, Douglass Coll., 1974; MBA, Rutgers U., 1976; PhD, CUNY, 2003. Bank analyst N.Y. Fed. Res. Bank, 1976-77, sr. credit analyst, 1977-79; sr. comml. loan officer 1st Pa. Bank, Phila., 1979-81; asst. v.p. Mfrs. Hanover Trust Co., NYC, 1982-83, v.p., 1983-84, dept. head, hedge funding and asset liability mgmt., 1984-88; adj. assoc. prof. fin. and econs. Rider Coll., 1988-90; asst. adj. prof. Fairleigh Dickinson, Madison, NJ, 1991-93; adj. prof. dept. fin. and econs. Baruch Coll., NYC, 1993—. Mem. Douglass Alumnae Endowment Fund Fin. Com., 1985—; pres. Douglass Coll. Class of 1974, 1990-; mem. internat. seminar interest rate risk mgmt. N.Y. Inst. Fin., N.Y.C., 1990-92. Mem. choir, Sunday Sch. tchr. Presbyn. Ch., Glendale; mem. investment com. Glendale Presbyn. Ch.; active Boy Scouts Am., PTO Cedar Hill and Ridge H.S.; former chairperson McGinn Elem. Sch. PTA Reading Program. Recipient Heller alumni award Rutgers U., 1976. Mem.: Beta Gamma Sigma.

HUMES, EDWARD, journalist, writer; married; 1 child. Grad., Hampshire Coll., Amherst, Mass. Author: Buried Secrets, 1992, Bad Cop, 1992, Mississippi Mud, 1994 (Edgar award finalist), No Matter How Loud I Shout, 1996 (PEN Center USA award for rsch. non-fiction, 1997, Best Book of Yr. Investigative Reporters and Editors of Am.), Mean Justice, 1999, School of Dreams, 2003, Over Here: How the GI Bill Transformed the American Dream, 2006. Recipient Pulitzer Prize for beat reporting, 1989. Mailing: Author Mail care Harcourt Books Ste 1900--525 B St San Diego CA 92101

HUMES, GRAHAM, investment banker; b. Williamsport, Pa., Oct. 8, 1932; s. Samuel and Elenor (Graham) H.; m. Elizabeth Schwartz Hershey, June 17, 1978; children: Margaret, Kathryn, Malcolm, Elizabeth, John Hershey, Lisa Hershey. BA, Williams Coll., 1954; MBA, Harvard U., 1958. Mng. ptnr. Butcher & Singer, Inc., Phila., 1958-74; sr. v.p. Girard Bank-Mellon Bank, Phila., 1974-87; mng. dir. Legg Mason Wood Walker, Inc., Phila., 1987-93; founder, gen. dir. CARESBAC, St. Petersburg, Russia, 1993-95. Bd. dirs. Brunschwig & Fils, North White Plains, NY, Baltic Cranberry Corp., St. Petersburg, Russia, George M. Leader Family Corp., Hershey, Pa.; trustee Fgn. Policy Rsch. Inst., Phila., Presbyn. Children's Village, Rosemont, Pa. Mem. Merion Cricket Club, Phila. Club, Harvard Bus. Sch. Club. Republican. Home: 7 Montgomery St Cherry Valley NY 13320

HUMES, HARVEY DAVID, nephrologist, educator, director; b. Honolulu, Nov. 20, 1947; s. William and Nancy Humes; m. Dolores Humes; 1 child, Michael David. BA, U. Calif., Berkeley, 1969; MD, U. Calif., San Francisco, 1973. Diplomate Am. Bd. Internal Medicine. Intern Moffit Hosp. and U. Calif. Hosps., San Francisco, 1973—74; resident U. Calif. Hosps., San Francisco, 1974—75; clin. fellow nephrology U. Pa. Hosp., Phila., 1975—76; rsch. fellow lab. kidney & electrolyte physiology Peter Bent Brigham Hosp., Boston, 1976—77; from instr. to asst. prof. medicine Peter Bent Brigham Hosp./Harvard Med. Sch., Boston, 1977—79; from asst. prof. to assoc. prof. internal medicine U. Mich., Ann Arbor, 1979—86, prof. internal medicine, 1986—, John G. Searle prof., chmn. internal medicine, 1996—2000; founder, gen. ptnr., mgr. EpiGenesis, LLC; founder Nephros Therapeutics, Inc.; founder, chair sci. adv. bd. RenaMed Biologics, Inc.; founder, pres., dir. Chelux Medica, Inc.; chmn. med. adv. bd. Natural Therapeutics, Inc.; founder, pres., chief sci. officer Innovative BioTherapies; founder, chief sci. officer, dir. Nephrion, Inc. Mem. sci. adv. bd. NephRx, Renal Solutions, Inc.; cons. Dow Chem.; dir., chief Nephrology Rsch. Labs., U. Mich., Ann Arbor, 1980-81; chief med. svc. VA Med. Ctr., Ann Arbor, 1983-96. Editor: Current Opinion in Internal Medicine, 2001—; editor-in-chief: Kelley's Textbook of Internal Medicine, 1997—2001; mem. editl. bd. Am. Jour. Medicine, 1997—2006; mem. editl. bd.: Seminars in Nephrology, 1993—, Internat. Yearbook of Nephrology, 1989—; contbr. articles to profl. jours. Grantee Nat. Kidney Found., 1981-85, 87-88, PHS, 1987—, Am. Heart Assn., 1982-87, 94-95. Fellow: AAAS, ACP; mem.: Am. Soc. Artificial Internal Organs (trustee), Ctrl. Soc. Clin. Rsch. (past pres.), Nat. Kidney Found. Mich., Nat. Kidney Found. (Pres. award), Internat. Soc. Nephrology, Am. Fedn. Clin. Rsch., Am. Soc. Nephrology, Am. Heart Assn., Am. Soc. Clin. Investigation, Assn. Prof. Medicine, Am. Physiol. Soc., Phi Beta Kappa, Alpha Omega Alpha. Achievements include development of bioartificial kidney; research in cellular basis of acute renal failure, biochemical basis of aminoglycoside-induced acute renal failure, cyclosporine nephrotoxicity, lipid alterations in ischemic acute renal failure, free-radical-induced mitochondrial injury, molecular basis of renal repair in acute renal failure, molecular basis of kidney tubulogenesis. Office: U Mich Med Sch SPC 5651 4520 MSRB I, 1150 W Medical Ctr Ann Arbor MI 48109 Office Phone: 734-647-8018. Business E-Mail: dhumes@umich.edu.

HUMES, WILLIAM D., information technology executive; BA economics, UCLA. Sr. audit mgr. PriceWaterhouseCoopers; sr. dir. Ingram Micro, 1998—2002, corp. v.p., controller, 2002—04, sr. v.p., CFO, 2005—. Office: c/o Ingram Micro 1600 E St Andrew Place Santa Ana CA 92799*

HUMICK, THOMAS CHARLES CAMPBELL, lawyer; b. NYC, Aug. 7, 1947; s. Anthony and Elizabeth Campbell (Meredith) H.; m. Nancy June Young, June 7, 1969; 1 child, Nicole Elizabeth Campbell. BA, Rutgers U., 1969; JD, Suffolk U., 1972; postgrad., London Sch. Econs.-Polit. Sci., 1977-78. Bar: N.J. 1972, U.S. Ct. Appeals (3d cir.) 1976, U.S. Supreme Ct. 1977, N.Y. 1981. Law clk. Superior Ct. N.J., 1972-73; assoc. Riker, Danzig, Scherer & Debevoise, Newark and Morristown, NJ, 1973-77; ptnr. Francis & Berry, Morristown, 1978-84, Dillon, Bitar & Luther, Morristown, 1985-92, Schenck, Price, Smith & King, Morristown, 1992—. Arbitrator U.S. Dist. Ct. N.J., 1985; del. Jud. Conf. 3d Jud. Cir. U.S., 1975—79; dist. X ethics com. NJ Supreme Ct., 1983—87; jud. selection com. Morris County, NJ, 1995—96. Contbg. author: Valuation for Eminent Domain, 1973; co-author: From Roslyn to Remedies, NJ Law Jour., 2005; mem. editl. bd. Suffolk U. Law Rev., 1970-71, N.J. Lawyer, 1993-94; contbr. articles to profl. jours. and mags. Trustee Peck Sch., 1993-98; trustee Richmond Fellowship N.J., 1982-89, pres., 1984. Mem.: ABA, FBA, Am. Bd. of Trial Advocates, Morris County Bar Assn. (trustee 1995—2000), NJ Bar Assn., Bay Head Yacht Club. Presbyterian. Home: PO Box 152 Morristown NJ 07963-0152 Office: Schenck Price Smith & King 10 Washington St Morristown NJ 07963-0905 Business E-Mail: tcch@spsk.com.

HUML, DONALD SCOTT, manufacturing executive; b. Lake Geneva, Wis., May 8, 1946; s. Robert Francis and Shirley (Roberts) H.; m. Joyce Cora Featherstone, Oct. 2, 1965; children: Tiffany Lynn, Alison Michelle, Andrew Scott. BBA, Marquette U., 1969; MBA, Temple U., 1980. Mgr. treasury ops. Allis-Chalmers Corp., West Allis, Wis., 1970-73; dir. fin. services CertainTeed Corp., Valley Forge, Pa., 1973-75, asst. treas., 1975-78, v.p., treas., 1978-81, v.p., comptroller, 1981-83, v.p., div. pres., 1983-86, v.p., group pres., 1986-89, v.p., chief fin. officer, 1989-90; v.p., CFO Saint-Gobain Corp., Valley Forge, Pa., 1990-94; sr. v.p., CFO Snap-on Inc., Kenosha, Wis., 1994—2002; exec. v.p., CFO Greif, Inc., Delaware, Ohio, 2002—. Mem. adv. bd. Marquette U. Sch. Bus. Adminstrn. Mem. Am. Mgmt. Assn., Fin. Execs. Inst., Conf. Bd. CFO Coun., Leading CFOs, Beta Gamma Sigma. Republican. Roman Catholic. Avocations: tennis, running, reading. Office: Greif Inc 425 Winter Rd Delaware OH 43015 Home: PO Box 346 Boca Grande FL 33921 Office Phone: 740-549-6137. Business E-Mail: don.huml@greif.com. E-mail: dhuml@columbus.rr.com.

HUMMEL, DANA D. MALLETT, librarian; BA in art history, Smith Coll., Northampton, Mass., 1957; postgrad., Def. Lang. Inst., 1961, Inst. Mex.-N.Am., 1962; MA in Libr. and Info. Sci., Denver U., 1968; postgrad., Cath. U. Am., Washington, 1974, postgrad., 1981, Nat. War Coll., 1976, No. Va. Bus. Sch., Falls Ch., 1978; diploma, U. Italiana Stranieri, Perugia, Italy, 1997. Head libr., adminstrn. Howard AFB, Libr., Panama, 1969—70; asst. libr. Holmes Intermediate Sch., 1970-71; tchr. Spanish, substitute tchr. J.E.B. Stuart HS, 1972-77; sec., Office of Exec. Dir. Africa The World Bank, 1978-79; personal sec. rector Falls Church, Va., 1979—81; mgr. Info. Svcs. Ctr. BDM Internat., subs. Ford Aerospace Co. (now Northrop Grumman), McLean, Va., 1981-88; pres. Monterey, Calif. Mem. vestry Falls Church Epis. Ch., 1982; del. Rep. State Conv., 1981, 86; pres. Ravenwood Civic Assn., 1979-82; rep. Mason Dist., Fedn. Civic Assns.; mem. ann. plan rev. task force Mason Dist., 1981-82; gov. trustee Fairfax County Pub. Libr. Bd., 1982-88, chmn. bd. trustees; lead fund raiser Smith Coll., 1998-2002; active St. Boniface Epis. Ch.; v.p. bd. dirs. Carriagehouse II, 2006, pres., 2007—. Named Outstanding Woman of Yr., Fairfax County Bd. Suprs. and Com. of Women, 1982. Mem. AAUP, ALA, Am. Soc. Info. Sci., Spl. Libr. Assn., Va. Libr. Assn., DC Libr. Assn., Women in Def., Villa D'Este Assn. (bd. dirs. 1995-98, pres. 1997-98), Jr. League Sarasota, Fla., Tournament Players Club Prestancia, Fla., The Field Club, Marie Selby Bot. Gardens, The Smith Club of Sarasota (v.p. 2005-07), Sarasota PC Users Group. Home: 4933 Kestral Park Way N Sarasota FL 34231-2346

HUMMEL, DONALD KEITH, priest; b. Newark, Nov. 24, 1949; s. Donald Willard Hummel and Viola Susan Liebiedz. AB in Humanities, Providence Coll., 1971; MA in Ednl. Psychology, Montclair Coll., Upper Montclair, NJ, 1973; MDiv in Pastoral Ministry, Immaculate Conception Sem., Mahwah, NJ, 1982; Cert. Advanced Study in Pastoral Counseling and Psychotherapy, Blanton-Peale Grad. Inst., NYC, 1983; DMin in Pastoral Ministry, St. Mary's Sem. and U., Balt., 1991. Ordained priest Roman Cath. Ch., 1978, cert. master chaplain Internat. Conf. Police Chaplains; addictions counselor Matt Talbot Inst. Tchr. religious studies, humanities East Orange Cath. HS, NJ, 1971—74; deacon Our Lady of Mercy, Jersey City, 1977; priest St. Cecilia's Ch., Kearny, NJ, 1978, parochial ficar, 1978—82, Our Lady of Fatima Ch., North Bergen, NJ, 1982—89; parochial vicar St. Helen's Ch., Westfield, NJ, 1997—2000; chaplain, dir. campus ministry Immaculate Heart Acad., Washington Twp., NJ, 1989—95; pastor St. Bartholomew the Apostle Ch., Scotch Plains, NY, 2000—05; dir. Continuing Edn. and Ongoing Formation of Priests, 2005—; assoc. dir. Formation for Permanent Diaconate, 2006—. Life mem. nat. Cath. com. on scouting Boy Scouts Am., nat. chaplain, 2001—04, past nat. chaplain, 2004—; cert. priest, counselor Project Rachel post-abortion counseling; champalin Scotch Plains Fire Dept.; head task force confl. assistance program, mem. adv. bd. Prevention Links; active Boy Scouts Am., mem. NE region exec. bd. Named Ecclesitical Knight of Grace, Sacred Mil. Constantinian Order St. George, 1999; recipient Outstanding Svc. and Commitment award, Mothers Against Drunk Driving, Alan M. Augustine Prevention award, Prevention Links, numerous awards, including Scouter's Tng. award, Boy Scouts Am., Dist. award of Merit, Silver Beaver award, Silver Antelope award, Disting. Scoutmaster award, Disting. Commr. award, Bronze Pelican award, Silver St. George award, Bronze Benemerenti medal for Disting. Svc. to Cath. Youth, 2004, Monsengior John J. Kiley award for disting. svc. in youth ministry. Mem.: KC (4th degree), SAR, ACA, UNICO Internat., NJ State Assn. Chiefs of Police (chief 2005, chaplain), Fellowship Christian Firefighters, NJ State Police Tng. Commn., NJ Paid Fire Chiefs Assn., NJ Traffic Officers Assn., Internat. Conf. Police Chaplains, Assn. Death Edn. and Counseling (cert. thanatologist), Assn. Adult Devel. and Aging., Am. Soc. Ethics, Religion and Values in Counseling, Am. Assn. Christian Counselors, Am. Sch. Counselors Assn., Nat. Cath. Con. on Alcoholism and Related Drug Problems, Nat. Fedn. Priests' Coun., Nat. Orgn. Continuing Edn. Roman Cath. Clergy, Am. Mensa Ltd., Orders and Medals Soc. Am., Sons Union Vets. of Civil War, Gen. Soc. War of 1812, Union County Emerald Soc., Mil. Order VFW US, Two Hundred Club Union County, Psi Chi, Alpha Phi Omega. Home: 332 Madison Hill Rd Clark NJ 07066-2227 Office: Roman Catholic Archdiocese Newark 171 Clifton Ave PO Box 9500 Newark NJ 07104-0500

HUMMEL, GREGORY WILLIAM, lawyer; b. Sterling, Ill., Feb. 25, 1949; s. Osborne William and Vivian LaVera (Guess) H.; m. Teresa Lynn Beveroth, June 20, 1970; children: Andrea Lynn, Brandon Gregory. BA, MacMurray Coll., 1971; JD, Northwestern U., 1974. Bar: Ill. 1974, U.S. Dist. Ct. (no. dist.) Ill. 1974. Assoc. Rusnak, Deutsch & Gilbert, Chgo., 1974-78; ptnr. Rudnick & Wolfe, Chgo., 1978-97; mem. Bell, Boyd & Lloyd LLP, Chgo., 1997—. Mem. vis. com. dept. music U. Chgo. Editor Jour. Criminal Law & Criminology Northwestern U., 1973-74; co-author: Illinois Real Estate Forms, 1989; contbr. articles to law jours. Mem. gov. coun. Luth. Gen. Hosp. Advocate Health Care Sys.; trustee Mac Murray Coll., Jacksonville, Ill., 1986-2001; trustee, sec.-treas. Homes for Children Found; bd. advisors Chgo. area coun. Boy Scouts Am., ChildServ; trustee Nat. Inst. Constrn. Law and Practice; mem. steering com. Increment Fin. Coalition Coun. Devel. Fin. Authorities. Mem. Internat. Bar Assn. (past co-chmn. com. internat. constrn. projects), Am. Coll. Constrn. Lawyers (past pres.), Urban Land Inst. (trustee), Urban Land Inst. Found. (gov.), Chgo. Dist. Coun. (past chmn.), Lambda Alpha Internat. (Ely chpt. past pres.), Econ. Club (Chgo.). Office: Bell Boyd & Lloyd LLP 3 1st Nat Plaza 70 W Madison St Ste 3300 Chicago IL 60602-4207 Office Phone: 312-807-4253. E-mail: ghummel@bellboyd.com.

HUMMEL, JOHN, information technology executive; Head, info. sys. Specialty Labs. Inc., Santa Monica, Calif., Brim, Inc., Portland, Oreg., Health Svc. Pharmacy/Option Care, Vancouver, Wash.; dir., sys. integration Sutter Health, Sacramento, 1997—99, chief info. officer, 1999—2002, sr. v.p., info. tech., 2002—. Commnr. Certification Commn. for Healthcare Info. Tech. Office: SVP Info Tech Sutter Health 2200 River Plz Dr Sacramento CA 95833

HUMMEL, KEITH R., lawyer; b. Bklyn., June 3, 1965; BA, Univ. Notre Dame, 1987; JD magna cum laude, Georgetown Univ., 1990. Bar: NY 1991. Assoc. Cravath Swaine & Moore LLP, NYC, 1990—98, ptnr., litig., 1998—. Notes and comments sr. editor Georgetown Law Jour. Mem.: Order of Coif. Office: Cravath Swaine & Moore LLP Worldwide Plz 825 Eighth Ave New York NY 10019-7475 Office Phone: 212-474-1772. Office Fax: 212-474-3700. Business E-Mail: khummel@cravath.com.

HUMMEL, MARGARET P., state representative; b. Binghamton, NY, Mar. 24, 1940; m. Manfred K. Hummel; four children. BA, Coll. New Rochelle, 1962; MA, Boston Coll., 1968, St. Michaels Coll., 1981. Mem. Vt. Ho. of Reps., 1996—2004. Mem. Underhill Selectboard, 1992—2001; chair Underhill Planning Commn.; mem. Burlington Sch. Gifted and Talented Task Force; trustee U. Vt., 1999—2005. Roman Catholic. Home: 262 Lake Ave # 1 Newton Highlands MA 02461-1210

HUMMEL, PATRICIA, pediatric nurse practitioner, researcher; b. Clarion, Iowa, June 9, 1955; d. James and Gladys Arndorfer; m. David Hummel, May 1, 1982; children: Dawn, Jamie, Tyler. ADN, Iowa Ctrl. C.C., Ft. Dodge, 1975; BA in Nursing, U. Kans., Lawrence, 1982; MA in Nursing, U. Iowa, Iowa City, 1988. Cert. neonatal nurse practitioner, Nat. Cert. Corp., 1984, pediat. nurse practitioner, ANCC, 1988. RN pediats. Mary Greeley Hosp., Ames, Iowa, 1975—76, U. Minn. Hosp., Mpls., 1976—77; RN neonatal ICU U. Iowa Hosp., Iowa City, 1977—78; RN pediat. ICU and neonatal ICU Children's Mercy Hosp., Kansas City, Mo., 1978—82; nurse clinician, RN Mercy Hosp. Med. Ctr., Des Moines, 1982—85; RN pediat. ICU St. Lukes Hosp., Cedar Rapids, Iowa, 1985—88; RN neonatal ICu and pediat. Ctrl. DuPage Hosp., Winfield, Ill., 1988—89; pediat. nurse practitioner DuPage County Health Dept., Wheaton, Ill., 1989; clin. nurse specialist Sherman Hosp., Elgin, Ill., 1989—94; nurse practitioner neonatal ICU Loyola U. Med. Ctr., Maywood, Ill., 1994—, coord. neonatal devel. follow-up program, 1996—. High-tech pediat. home nursing staff Concerned Care, St. Charles, Ill., 1988—89; clin. instr. Aurora U., Ill., 1988—89, Coll. DuPage, Glen Ellyn, Ill., 1989; adj. instr. No. Ill. U., Dekalb, 1992; cons. and educator in field, Batavia, Ill., 2000—; mem. neonatal pain control working group mem. Nat. Inst. Child Health and Human Devel. and FDA-Divsn. Pediatric Drug Devel., NIH, Bethesda, Md., 2003—05. Primary author: N-PASS (Neonatal Pain, Agitation and Sedation Scale); contbr. articles to profl. jours. Recipient Outstanding Nurse Recognition, March of Dimes, 2003; grantee, Loyola U. Med. Ctr. Quality Improvement Dept. and Nursing Dept., 2001, Am. Nurses Found., 2006. Mem.: ANA, Acad. Neonatal Nursing, Nat. Assn. Neonatal Nurses (rsch. grantee 1988, Advanced Practice Leadership award 2004), Sigma Theta Tau. Office: Loyola University Medical Center 2160 S First Ave Maywood IL 60153 Office Phone: 708-327-9055. Business E-Mail: phummel@lumc.edu.

HUMPHREY, CHARLES EDWARD, JR., lawyer; b. Detroit, Jan. 20, 1943; s. Charles Edward and Betty Jane (Bixby) H.; children: Jennifer Jane Castle, Jordan Susan Trigler. BBA, U. Mich., 1964, JD cum laude, 1968, MBA, 1968. Bar: Mich. 1968, Tex. 1971, Colo. 1982. Assoc. Evans & Luptak, 1968; atty., fin. adviser SEC, Washington, 1969-71; ptnr. Foreman & Dyess, Houston, 1971-81; pres. Ptnrs. Oil Co., Houston, 1981-82; ptnr. Kirkland & Ellis, Denver, 1982-87; pres. Addoms & Humphrey (a bus. devel. co.), 1986-88; of counsel Cohen, Brame & Smith, 1987—88; pres. Vector Video, Inc., 1987-89, Venture Capital Investments, 1989—. Chmn.

Advanced Cable Systems, Inc., 1989-99; mng. ptnr. Signature Stes., 1989-98; founder Tournament of Champions of Poker, 1999, chmn., 1999-2001; founder, mng. ptnr. Team Pegasus, 1998-2001; author, web-master www.gambling-law-us.com, 2003—. Bd. dirs. Houston Civil Liberties Union, 1973-77, treas., 1975-77; pres. Tex. Civil Liberties Union, 1978-79, Ctrl. City Opera House Assn., 1982-84. Mailing: 1755 Swadley St Lakewood CO 80215 E-mail: cehjr@umich.edu.

HUMPHREY, CHRISTINE M., lawyer; b. Louisville, Fla., Sept. 1972; d. James Melvin and Carol Ann Probus. BA, Bellarmine Coll., Ky., 1994; JD magna cum laude, U. Miami, Fla., 2003. Bar: Fla. 2004. Investigator US FDA, 1994—97, med. device specialist Tampa, Fla., 1997—2000, compliance officer Miami, 2000—02, advisor Rockville, Md., 2002—03, investigator, Divsn. Import Ops. & Policy, 2002—03; pres. Humphrey & Assocs. PA, Miami, 2004—06; shareholder Fuerst Humphrey Ittleman, Miami, 2006—. Cons. Rodriguez O'Donnell Ross Fuerst, Miami, Fla., 2003—04. Named Investigator of Yr., US FDA, 1999, Compliance Officer of Yr., 2002. Mem.: Fla. Bar Assn. (assoc.; mem. adv. com. 2007). Home: 521 Santurce Ave Coral Gables FL 33143 Office: Fuerst Humphrey Ittleman 1001 Brickell Bay Dr Ste 2002 Miami FL 33131 Home Phone: 305-740-9413; Office Phone: 305-350-9690. Business E-Mail: chumphrey@fuerstlaw.com.

HUMPHREY, CRAIG REED, social studies educator; b. Grand Rapids, Mich., Oct. 14, 1942; s. Roger and Ruth Reed Humphrey; m. Catherine Elaine Clark, Aug. 6, 1966; children: Michelle Ruth, Gwen Allison. BA, Bowling Green State U., 1964; MA, Brown U., 1967, PhD, 1971. Asst. prof. Coll. William and Mary, Williamsburg, Va., 1969—71, Pa. State U., University Park, 1971—77, assoc. prof., 1977—2001, assoc. prof. emeritus of sociology and demography, 2001—. Vis. assoc. prof. rural sociology U. Wis., Madison, 1987; vis. assoc. prof. Yale U., New Haven, 1996—97. Co-author: Environment, Energy and Society, 1982, Environment, Energy and Society: A New Synthesis, 2002, Environment. Energy and Society: Exemplary Works, 2003. Pres. Cmty. Land Trust, State College, Pa., 2002—03, sec., 2004—06; elected coun. mem. State Coll. Borough Coun., 2004—07. Recipient Rose Cologne Vol. Yr., Land Trust, 2007. Mem.: Rural Sociol. Soc. (assoc. editor 2002—04), Am. Sociol. Assn. (chair sect. on environment and tech. 1986—88, Disting. Contbn. award 2003). Democrat. Episcopalian. Avocations: sailing, gardening, writing, physical fitness. Home: 227 W Prospect Ave State College PA 16801 Office: Pa State Univ Dept Sociology 215 Oswald Tower University Park PA 16802 Office Phone: 814-865-2527. Business E-Mail: ch8@psu.edu.

HUMPHREY, DEBORAH A, medical educator, internist; d. Stephen T. and Etta M. Bereheiko; m. Barry Humphrey, Apr. 16, 1983; children: Sean W., Daniel J., Sarah A. BA in Chemistry, U. South Fla., Tampa, 1980, BA in Psychology, 1987, BS in Biology, 1987; D in Osteo. Medicine, Nova Southeastern U., Ft. Lauderdale, Fla., 1991. Diplomate Am. Bd. Internal Medicine, 1996. Asst. prof. U. South Fla., Tampa, 1995—. Contbr. chapters to books, articles to profl. jours. Sunday sch. instr. St. Andrews United Meth. Ch., Brandon, Fla., 2004—07. Named Disting. Physician, Fla. Med. Assn., 2006; named one of Florida's Best Doctors, Fla. Monthly, 2006; recipient Marcus award for Excellence in Internal Medicine, Marcus Family, 1995. Fellow: Am. Soc. Internal Medicine, ACP; mem.: So. Med. Assn. Office: Univ SFla 4 Columbia Dr #630 Tampa FL 33606 Office Phone: 813-259-0670. Office Fax: 813-259-0679. Business E-Mail: dhumphre@health.usf.edu.

HUMPHREY, DIANA YOUNG, fundraiser; b. Balt., Feb. 7, 1938; d. Edwin Parson and Elizabeth Miller (Hoskins) Young; m. David Henry Carls, July 27, 1963 (div. Dec. 17, 1997); children: Peter Van Patten Carls, Elizabeth Roy Carls, Susan Montanye Carls; m. George Lee Humphrey, May 22, 1999. AB, Smith Coll., Northampton, Mass., 1960. Lic. real estate broker, Mass., 1978. Fgn. rights sales Little, Brown & Co., Inc., Boston, 1960-63; speech writer DNA Rsch., NYC, 1963-64; vol. fund raiser John V. Lindsay, NYC, 1964-65, Smith Coll., Northampton, Mass., 1970-75, 90-95, Smith Coll. Club, Concord, Mass., 1976-89, Jr. League of Boston, 1967—; bd. mem. devel. Ctr. House, Inc., Boston, 1981-94; fund raiser events Boston Symphony Orch., 1975—; dir. edn. Hawthorne Ptnrs. Inc. Fund raising, events Mass. Soc. for Prevention of Cruelty to Children, Boston, 1997—. Editor: Huntington Hartford Gallery Modern Art, N.Y.C., 1963. Speechwriter, Nelson A. Rockefeller Presdl. campaign, NYC, 1963-64; active John V. Lindsay for Mayor, NYC, 1964-65; chmn. Wayland Planning Bd., Mass., 1976-81, Wayland Housing Partnership, 1987-2004; adv. com. REACH, Waltham, Mass., Bay Cove, Boston; active Patriots' Trail coun. Girl Scouts U.S. Mem. Jr. League of Boston, Weston Golf Club. Episcopalian. Avocations: golf, travel, gardening, singing, politics. Home: 42 Cutting Cross Way Wayland MA 01778-3845

HUMPHREY, DUDLEY, lawyer; b. Dec. 1933; AB, Duke U., 1955; JD with honors, U. N.C., 1961. Bar: N.C. 1961. With Kilpatrick Stockton LLP, Winston-Salem, NC. Mem.: ABA (ho. dels.), N.C. State Bar (pres. 2003). Office: Kilpatrick Stockton LLP 1001 W Fourth St Winston Salem NC 27101-2400 Home Phone: 336-765-4115. Business E-Mail: dhumphrey@kilpatrickstockton.com.

HUMPHREY, LOIS ELLEN, librarian; b. Coos Bay, Oreg., Aug. 21, 1932; d. James Follett Houston and Lillette Anna (Carlson) Lanway; m. Thomas Harold Humphrey, Aug. 29, 1952; children: Denise, Ellen, Megan, Jane. BS, U. Oreg., 1959, MLS, 1969. Librarian Marshfield H.S., Coos Bay, 1959—60, Coquille (Oreg.) H.S., 1976—95. Mem. adv. bd. Coos County Edn. Svc., Coos Bay, 1977—90; life mem. Friends Coos Bay Libr. Mem.: DAR, Coquille Edn. Assn. (bldg. rep. 1982, 1984, v.p. 1989—90, pres. 1990—91), Coos Bay Libr. Assn. (life), Wilsonville Tuesday Quilters, Northwest Quilters, Coos Sand and Sea Quilters (charter), Lake County Mus. (life), Friends of Wilsonville Libr. (life), South Coast Wave Walkers (v.p. 1991), Cmty. Concert Assn. Coos Bay (bd. dirs. 1965—95), Coos Hist. Soc. (life), Coos Bay Jr. Women's Club (pres. 1962—63), South Coast Running Club (treas. 1988—90), Sons and Daus. Oreg. Pioneers (life), Delta Kappa Gamma (scholarship com.), P.E.O. Sisterhood (state area edn. chmn., chpt. pres. 2000—02). Episcopalian. Home: 6576 SW Stratford Ct Wilsonville OR 97070-6787 Personal E-mail: loishumphrey@hotmail.com.

HUMPHREY, LOUISE IRELAND, civic worker, equestrienne; b. Morehead City, NC, Nov. 1, 1918; d. R. Livingston and Margaret (Allen) Ireland; m. Gilbert W. Humphrey, Dec. 27, 1939; children: Margaret (Mrs. K. Bindhart), George M. II, Gilbert Watts. Educated pvt. schs. Nurse's aide ARC, 1944-64. Past. dir. Nat. City Bank, Cleve., Nat. City Corp., Cleve. 1981-86. Trustee Mus. Arts Assn.; hon. trustee, past pres. Vis. Nurse Assn.; hon. trustee Lake Erie Coll.; life trustee United Way Cleve.; trustee Archbold Med. Ctr. and Hosp., Thomasville, Ga.; hon. trustee Case Western Res. U., Bus. Coun. Internat. Understanding Inc.; bd. dirs. Monticello (Fla.) Opera Ho.; mem., former trustee, 2d v.p. Jr. League Cleve.; past pres., hon. chmn. bd. dirs. Met. Opera Assn.; bd. dirs. Lincoln Ctr., Thomas County Entertainment Found.; past pres. No. Ohio Opera Assn.; mem. adv. bd. Coll. Vet. Medicine U. Fla., Gainesville; mem. Ohio Arts Coun., 1975—85; treas., trustee Wildlife Conservation Fund Am.; former master Foxhounds Chagrin Valley Hunt, Gates Mills, Ohio; past dir., zone v.p. U.S. Equestrian Team Inc., now hon. life dir.; mem. Garden Club Cleve.; bd. dirs., past pres. Nat. Homecaring Coun.; treas., bd. dirs. Wildlife Legis. Fund Am. Conservation Fund; past pres. bd. dirs. Thomasville Cultural Ctr.; bd. dirs. Cmty. Found. North Fla.; commr. Fla. Game & Fresh Water Fish, 1984—99. Home: Box 91102 Woodfield Springs Plantation Tallahassee FL 32309

HUMPHREY, OWEN EVERETT, retired education administrator; b. Wautoma, Wis., Oct. 25, 1920; s. Marion A. and Flora A. (Helms) H.; m. Billye A. Cox, Apr. 6, 1946 (dec. Dec. 1974); children: Reba, Ivye. BS, U. Wis., Whitewater, 1947; MS, U. Ark., 1949; advanced cert., U. Ill., 1954. Life gen. supervisory cert. grades K-14. Elem. classroom tchr. Four Corners Sch., Plainfield, Wis., 1941-42; jr. high art and sci. tchr. Jefferson Sch., Sheboygan, Wis., 1947-48; elem. classroom tchr. and prin. Holcomb, Mo., 1949-50, Lincoln Sch., Mattoon, Ill., 1950-55; supervising prin. various elem. schs., Peotone, Ill., 1955-57; elem. tchr. Nameoki Sch., Granite City, Ill., 1957-59; elem. prin. Maryville Sch., Granite City, 1959-67; curriculum coord. Sch. Dist. #9, Granite City, 1967-79; adminstrv. asst. Regional Supt. of Schs., Madison County, Ill., 1979-81, 85-87; ret., 1987. Leader parent study groups Ea. Ill. U., Mattoon, 1950-54; PTA field unit organizer Ill. Congress of Parents and Tchrs., Mattoon, 1952-54; coord. local dist. planning Sch. Dist. #9, Granite City, 1973-79; rep. Ill. State Curriculum Coun., Springfield, 1980-81. Co-author: The Greening of Gateway East, 1984; contbr. poetry to Nat. Libr. of Poetry anthologies; contbr. articles to profl. jours. Dir. chorus Area Coun. PTA, Mattoon, 1950-54, Granite City Area Coun. PTA, 1957-59; dir. Granite City Elks Mixed Chorus, 1958-60; actor Creative Arts Theatrical Soc., 1992--. Sgt. U.S. Army Infantry, 1942-45, ETO. Recipient Area Coun. PTA award Granite City, Ill., 1979. Mem. NEA (life), ASCD (life), Ill. ASCD (life, bd. dirs.), Internat. Poets Soc. (life), Creative Arts Theatrical Soc. (bd. govs.), Miners Inst. Found. (bd. dirs. 2002-03), Phi Delta Kappa (Gateway East chpt. sec., historian, v.p., pres., Svc. Key award 1984, George H. Reavis Assoc. award 1991). Avocation: composing music and lyrics. Home: 1609 Wellington Dr Granite City IL 62040-2572 Personal E-mail: oweneh@aol.com.

HUMPHREY, PATRICK PAUL, pharmacologist; b. Pietersburg, South Africa, Jan. 28, 1946; s. Gordon William and Judith Suzanne (LeRoux) H.; m. Mary Frances Letford, Sept. 14, 1968; children: Patrick Tobias, Damian Paul, Joel Anthony. B Pharmacy with honors, U. London, 1968, PhD in Pharmacology, 1972. Qualified pharmacist. Lectr. physiology dept. St. Mary's Hosp. Med. Sch., London, 1971-72; rsch. leader dept. pharmacology Allen and Hanbury, Ware, Eng., 1972-80; head dept. pharmacology Glaxo Group Rsch. Ltd., Ware, 1980-83, dir. divsn. pharmacology, 1983-92; dir. Glaxo Inst. Applied Pharmacology, U. Cambridge, England, 1992—2001; hon. prof., 1994—2001; dir. Glaxo Wellcom Headache Rsch. Group, 1999—2001; exec. v.p. rsch. Theravance (formerly Advanced Medicine), South San Francisco, Calif., 2001—. Mem. com. for receptor nomenclature and drug classification Internat. Union Pharmacology, 1990-2002, mem. exec. com., 1998-2002; chmn. receptor nomenclature com. Serotonin Club, 1987-93. Co-editor: Serotonin: Actions, Receptors, Pathophysiology, 1989, Receptor Classification, 1997, The Triptans, 2001; editor Brit. Jour. Pharmacology, 1984-90; team leader drug discovery and devel. Anti-Migraine Drug Sumatriptan (trademarks Imitrex and Imigran), 1972-92. Recipient Mullard award Royal Soc., 1997, OBE award, 1999. Fellow Royal Pharm. Soc.; mem. Am. Gastroenterological Assn., Brit. Pharm. Soc., Soc. Neurosci., Internat. Headache Soc. Roman Catholic. Avocations: fishing, tennis, gardening, ornithology. Office: Theravance Inc 901 Gateway Blvd South San Francisco CA 94080 Office Phone: 650-808-3704. E-mail: phumphrey@theravance.com.

HUMPHREY, SAMUEL STOCKWELL, town official, physicist; b. Canton Center, Conn., Apr. 25, 1923; s. Harold William and A. Genevieve (Stockwell) H.; m. Mary Elizabeth Mills, Feb. 4, 1945; children: Warren Mills, Kenneth Stockwell, Marianne Ruth. BS, U. Conn., 1948; MA, Wesleyan U., Middletown, Conn., 1950; postgrad., U. Utah, 1961-63. Enlisted USAF, 1942, advanced through grades to lt. col., 1966, ret., 1971; physicist Wesleyan U., 1948-51; cons. physicist Canton, Conn., 1971-74; tchr. physics Canton (Conn.) High Schs., 1973-74, real estate broker, 1975-93; first selectman Town of Canton, 1983-87, selectman, 1989-91, mem. bd. fin., 1997—; mgr. Cherry Brook Farm LLC. Dir. Conn. Conf. Municipalities, Conn. Interlocal Risk Mgmt. Agys. (CIRMA), 1987; bd. dirs. Sundown Ski Patrol, Inc.; mem. policy bd. and exec. com. Capitol Region Coun. of Govts., 1983-87; cons. physicist RCA, Burlington, Mass., 1971-74, Martin Marietta, Orlando, Fla., 1971-72; co-founder Simsbury (Conn.) Bank & Trust Co.; researcher in field. Author, editor numerous studies and reports. Trustee, treas. 1st Congl. Ch., Canton Ctr., 1972-85; chmn. Hist. Dist. Commn., Canton, 1972-80, Mcpl. Bd. Fin., Canton, 1975-83, 97—; justice of peace State of Conn., 1974—. Recipient numerous awards and decorations USAF and Philippines; Wesleyan U. fellow, 1948-50. Mem. Optical Soc. Am. (emeritus), Air Force Assn., Conn. Christmas Tree Growers Assn. (bd. dirs. 1984-90, v.p. 1990, pres. 1992-95), New Eng. Christmas Tree Assn. (dir. 1990—), Selman Field Hist. Assn. La. (dir. 2005—), Hanscom Flying Club (Bedford, Mass., pres. 1955-59), Skiesta Club (pres. 1964-68), Sigma Xi (assoc.), Sigma Pi Sigma. Republican. Mem. United Ch. of Christ. Avocation: ski patrol. Home: Box 150 96 Barbourtown Rd Canton Center CT 06020-0150 Office Phone: 860-693-4066. E-mail: sshumphrey@aol.com.

HUMPHREY, STEPHEN M., paperboard company executive; b. Oct. 10, 1944; BS, Siena Coll., 1967. With GE Co., 1967—81; pres. on-hwy. products bus. Rockwell Internat. Corp., 1981—94; chmn., pres., CEO Nat. Gypsum Co., Charlotte, NC, 1994—96; pres, CEO Riverwood Internat. Corp, Atlanta, 1997—2003; also bd. dirs. Riverwood Internat. Corp., Atlanta; pres., CEO Graphic Packaging Corp. (formerly Riverwood Internat. Corp.), Atlanta, 2003—06, vice-chmn., 2007. Office: Graphic Packaging Corp 814 Livingston Ct Marietta GA 30067*

HUMPHREY, WATTS SHERMAN, information technology executive, writer; b. Battle Creek, Mich., July 4, 1927; s. Watts Sherman Humphrey and Katharine (Strong) Osborne; m. Barbara Fallon, May 22, 1954; children: Katharine Pickman, Lisa Fish, Sarah DeCamello, Watts Jr., Peter, Erica Jarrett, Christopher. BS in Physics, U. Chgo., 1949, MBA, 1951; MS in Physics, Ill. Inst. Tech., 1950; PhD in Software Engring. (hon.), Embry Riddle Aero. U., 1998. Electronics engr. Fermi Inst. U. Chgo., 1949-51, dir. sci. pers. Chgo. Midway Lab., 1951-53; mgr. computing devel. Sylvania Electric Products, Natick, Mass., 1953-59; instr. computer design Northeastern U., Boston, 1956-59; with IBM, White Plains, NY, 1959-86, mgr. teleprocessing systems devel., 1959-64, dir. systems application engring., Armonk, N.Y., 1964-65, dir. time sharing systems, White Plains, 1965-66, dir. programming, 1966-68, v.p. tech. devel., Armonk, 1968-70, dir. Endicott (N.Y.) Labs., 1970-72, dir. policy devel., Armonk, 1972-79, dir. tech. assessment, White Plains, 1979-83, dir. programming quality and process, Poughkeepsie, N.Y., 1983-86; dir. software process program Software Engring. Inst. Carnegie Mellon U., Pitts., 1986-91, fellow, 1991—. Chmn. adv. bd. IBM Systems Rsch. Inst., N.Y.C., 1973-82. Author: Switching Circuits with Computer Applications, 1958, Managing for Innovation, Leading Technical People, 1987, Managing the Software Process, 1989, A Discipline for Software Engineering, 1995, Managing Technical People, Innovation, Teamwork and the Software Process, 1997, Introduction to the Personal Software Process, 1997, Introduction to the Team Software Process, 1999, Winning with Software: an Executive Strategy, 2002, PSP: A Self-Improvement Process for Software Engineers, 2005, TSP: Landing a Development Team, 2006, TSP: Coaching Development Teams, 2006; contbr. numerous articles to profl. jours.; (mem. editl. bd.) Jour. Sys. and Software, 1988-96, Software Process, Improvement and Practice, 1996-, Empirical Software Engring., 1996-. Bd. examiners Malcolm Baldridge Nat. Quality Award, 1991; sci. adv. com. Std. System Ctr. USAF, 1989-92. With USN, 1944-46. Recipient Aerospace Software Engineering award Am. Inst. of Aeronautics and Astronautics, 1993, Boeing award for leadership and innovation in software process improvement, 2000, Nat. medal of Tech., Pres. U.S., 2003; Watts Humphrey Software Quality Inst. in Chennai, India, named in his honor, 2000. Fellow IEEE (editorial bds. Spectrum 1982-83, The Institute 1982-83, reviewer Software 1984, Computer 1984, IBM System Jour. 1989); mem. Assn. for Computing Machinery, Inst. for Radio Engrs. (chmn. computer sect. 1959). Democrat. Achievements include patents in field. Avocations: running, piano, bridge. Office: Carnegie Mellon U Software Engring Inst 4500 5th Ave Pittsburgh PA 15213-2612 Business E-Mail: watts@sei.cmu.edu.

HUMPHREYS, DONALD D., oil industry executive; BS in Indsl. Engring. and Mgmt., Okla. State U., 1971; MBA, U. Pa. Wharton Sch. Bus., 1976. Sys. analyst Exxon Corp., 1976, sr. fin. advisor contr.'s dept. NYC, 1986—88, v.p., contr., 1997—99, asst. treas., 1997, v.p., contr., 1997—99; fin. reporting mgr. Exxon Co. Internat., 1988, asst. gen. auditor; upstream contr. Exxon Co., USA, 1990; fin. dir. Exxon Cos., Kuala Lumpur, Malaysia, 1993—97; v.p., contr. ExxonMobil Corp., Irving, Tex., 1999—2004, v.p., treas., 2004—06, sr. v.p., treas., mem. mgmt. com., 2006—. Bd. gov. Okla. State U. Found. Served in US Army, 1972—74. Mem.: Conf. Bd. Coun. Fin. Execs., Am. Petroleum Inst., Fin. Execs. Internat. Office: Exxon Mobil Corp 5959 Las Colinas Blvd Irving TX 75039-2298 Office Phone: 972-444-1000.*

HUMPHREYS, KENNETH KING, engineer, educator, professional society administrator; b. Pitts., Jan. 19, 1938; s. Meredith Harold and Olga (Adamitis) H.; m. Harriet Elizabeth Moss, May 6, 1961; children: Kenneth King, Keith Alan, Kevin James, Karen Elizabeth. BS, Carnegie Inst. Tech., 1959, postgrad., 1961-62, U. Pitts., 1965; MS, W.Va. U., 1967; PhD, Kennedy Western U., 1990. Registered profl. engr., Pa., N.C., W.Va.; cert. cost engr. U.S., Mex., Internat. Tech. asst. Applied Research Lab.-U.S. Steel Corp., 1959-60, tech. assoc. Monroeville, Pa., 1960-62, asst. technologist Universal, Pa., 1962-63, assoc. research engr., 1963-65; cost engr. W. Va. U. Coal Research Bur., Morgantown, 1965-67, sr. staff and cost engr., 1967-71, asst. dir., 1971-81; asst. prof. Coll. Mineral and Energy Resources-W. Va., Morgantown, 1970-73; assoc. prof. Coll. Mineral and Energy Resources-W. Va. U., Morgantown, 1973-76, prof., 1976-82, adj. prof., 1982-92, asst. to dean, 1971-77, chmn. minerals program, 1978-81, asst. dean acad. affairs, 1979-82; exec. dir. Am. Assn. Cost Engrs., 1971-92. Engring. cons. metallurgy and fuel tech., 1963—82; engring. cons. cost engring. and project mgmt., 1993—. Author: Basic Cost Engineering, 1981, 2d edit., 1986, 3d edit., 1996, What Every Engineer Should Know About Ethics, 1999; editor: Control and Management of Capital Projects, 2d edit., 1992, reprint edit., 1998; co-author, co-editor: Basic Mathematics and Computer Applications for Coal Preparation and Mining, 1983; co-author, assoc. editor: Coal Preparation, 4th edit., 1979; co-author, editor: Project and Cost Engineers' Handbook, 4th edit., 2005; co-author, co-editor: Mechanical Estimating Guidebook, 5th edit., 1987, 6th edit., 1995; co-author, editor: Jelen's Cost and Optimization Engineering, 3d edit., 1991; editor: Effective Project Management Through Applied Cost and Schedule Control, 1996; contbr. articles to prof. jours.; patentee in field. Leader Allegheny Trails, Piedmont and Mountaineer area couns. Boy Scouts Am., 1961—, dist. commr. Mountaineer area coun., 1969-72, dist. tng. chmn., 1972-74, 90, chmn. coun. tng., 1975-77, exec. bd., 1987-89, leadership devel. com., area 6 East Cen. region, 1977-79, dist. commr. Piedmont coun., 1996-97, rechartering com., 1997-99, asst. dist. commr., 1999-2002, asst. coun. commr., 2003—, internat. rep., 2001-; deacon 1st Presbyn. Ch., Morgantown, W.Va., 1968-70, ruling elder, 1972-75, 90-92, pres. congregation, 1975-77; deacon Waldensian Presbyn. Ch., Valdese, N.C., 1995-97, treas., 1995-96; ruling elder Fairview Presbyn. Ch., Lenoir, N.C., 2007—. Recipient Silver Beaver award Mountaineer Area Coun. Boy Scouts Am., 1973, Disting. Silver Beaver award Boy Scouts Am., 1990; recipient dist. award of merit Mountaineer Area Coun. Boy Scouts Am., 1969, Woodbadge award Mountaineer Area Coun. Boy Scouts Am., 1971, 50-Year Vets. award Boy Scouts Am., 1998, Het Schaap mit vijf Poten award Royal Netherlands Industries Fair, 1977; named Hon. West Virginian Gov. West Virginia, 1974. Fellow NSPE (life mem.), Assn. Cost Engrs. U.K. (Tony Jarvis Outstanding Paper award 2006), Assn. Advancement Cost Engring. Internat. (nat. chmn. 1969-71, 1998-2004, Mem. of Moment, nat. bd. dirs. 1971, exec. dir. 1971-92, award of merit 1993, award recognition 1979, Brian Dunfield Edn. award 2007, B. Danfield Edn. award, 2007, pub. Cost Engring. mag. 1981-92, co-editor trans. 1982-92, pres. No. W.Va. sect. 1989-91, pres. Catawba Valley, Charlotte, N.C. sect. 1994-96, regional rep. 1996—), Profl. Engrs. N.C. (ethics steering com. 1995—, coun. of fellows 2005—, chmn. ethics com. 1999-2001, Engr. of Yr. award 1999), Assn. Italiana di Ingegneria Economica; mem. Soc. Mexicana de Ingenieria Economica Financiera y de Costos (Mex.), So. African Project Control Inst. (hon. life, regional rep. 1996—), Internat. Cost Engring. Coun. (sec.-treas. 1976-2006, asst. sec. 2006-, disting. internat. fellow, Outstanding Paper awards 1996, 98), W.Va. Soc. Profl. Engrs. (bd. dirs. 1971-76, 83-92, v.p. 1980-81, pres. 1982-83, W.Va. Engr. of Yr. 1986), Morgantown Soc. Profl. Engrs. (pres. 1969-70, bd. dirs. 1970-76), Am. Assn. Engring. Socs. (bd. govs. 1979-83), Coun. Engring. Splty. Bds. (pres.-elect 1990-92, pres. 1992-93), Sigma Xi, Beta Theta Pi (asst. gen. sec. 1987-91), Alpha Phi Omega. Democrat. Home and Office: 1168 Hidden Lake Dr Granite Falls NC 28630-8592

HUMPHREYS, PAUL WILLIAM, philosophy educator, consultant; b. London, Jan. 17, 1950; came to U.S., 1971; s. William Edward and Florence C. (Didcock) H.; m. Diane Gail Snustad, July 14, 1984; children: Emily Victoria, Alexandra Elizabeth. BSc, U. Sussex, UK, 1971; MA, MS, Stanford U., 1974, PhD, 1976. From asst. to assoc. prof. philosophy U. Va., Charlottesville, 1978-91, prof., 1991—, chmn., 1996—97, 1999—2004; v.p. Assn. for Founds. Sci., 1995-99. Seminar dir. NEH, Va., 1991, 95; cons. EPA, CDC, BCG; vis. prof. CNRS, Paris, France, 2005. Author: Chances of Explanation, 1989, Extending Ourselves, 2004; editor: Synthese, 1991—98, Foundations of Science, 1993—98, Oxford Studies in the Philosophy of Science, 1999—. Recipient Fulbright travel award, 1971, Scholars award NSF, 1984, 2006. Mem.: Philosophy Sci. Assn. (gov. bd. 1997—2000), Am. Philos. Assn. (chmn. CIC 2007—, bd. officers 2007—), Keswick Soc. (chmn. 2000—). Home: 323 Kent Rd Charlottesville VA 22903-2409 Office: U Va Dept Philosophy PO Box 400780 Charlottesville VA 22903-4780

HUMPHREYS, RICHARD STEPHEN, history professor, researcher; b. Hutchinson, Kans., Aug. 11, 1942; s. Richard Sexton and Virginia Edna Humphreys; m. Gail Claire Simons, Dec. 27, 1964; children: Cymbre Gay Van Fossen, Michael Stephen, Brian Edward. BA, Amherst Coll., Mass., 1964; PhD, U. Mich., Ann Arbor, 1969. Asst. prof. history SUNY, Amherst, 1969—75; vis. asst. prof. U. Chgo., 1975—80; prof. history U. Wis., Madison, 1981—90; prof. history and islamic studies U. Calif., Santa Barbara, 1990—. Bd. dirs. U. Calif. Press, Berkeley. Author: From Saladin to the Mongols, 1977, Islamic History: A Framework for Inquiry (named one of Disting. Academic Books, 1991), Between Memory and Desire: the Middle East in a Troubled Age, 1999, Mu'awiya: From Arabia to Empire, 2006; editor: Internat. Jour. Mid. East Studies, 1994—99. Fellow, NEH, 1972, 1987, 1989, Inst. Advanced Study, Princeton, NJ, 1980—81, All Souls Coll., Oxford U., 2006. Mem.: Am. Coun. Learned Societies (del. 2005—), Am. Hist. Assn., Medieval Acad. (councilor 1998—2000), Mid. East Studies Assn. (pres. 2000—01). Office: Univ California Dept History Santa Barbara CA 93106-9410 Office Phone: 805-893-2316.

HUMPHREYS, ROBERT RUSSELL, lawyer, arbitrator, consultant; b. Eugene, Oreg., May 7, 1938; s. Russell Wallace and Roberta Lois (Bennett) H.; m. Natalia Dimitrievna Lucenko; children: Tatyana Roberta, Grigori Robert. BA, U. Wash., 1959; LLB, George Washington U., 1965. Bar: Va. 1965, DC 1966, US Dist. Ct. (DC) 1966, US Ct. Appeals (DC cir.) 1985, US Ct. Appeals (4th cir.) 2000, Ct. Fed. Claims 2001, US Ct. Appeals (1st cir.) 2003, US Supreme Ct. 2007. Law clk. Barco, Cook & Patton, Washington, 1963-64, Keller & Heckman, Washington, 1964; mgr. pub.

affairs services Air Transport Assn. Am., Washington, 1965-66; asst. to v.p. fed. affairs, 1966-71; spl. counsel com. on labor and human resources U.S. Senate, Washington, 1971-77; commr. Rehab. Svcs. Adminstrn., HEW, Washington, 1977-80; ptnr. Hoffheimer & Johnson, Washington, 1980-83, Humphreys & Mitchell, Washington, 1983-88; cons. MARC Assocs., Inc., Washington, 1988-94; pvt. practice Washington, 1988—, 1991-95; arbitrator State of NC, 1988—, hearing officer, 2002; pres., CEO Jennings Randolph Inst., Washington, 1998—. Spkr. nat., internat. confs. Author: Compliance Manual on Americans with Disabilities Act; contbr. articles to profl. jours. Incorporator, bd. dirs., treas., counsel Nat. Ctr. for Barrier-Free Environ., 1975-77, 81-84; bd. dirs. Va. Spl. Olympics, 1982-84. Recipient Jennings Randolph award, Rudolph-Sheppard Vendors Am., 1992, 2006. Mem. DC Bar Assn., George Washington U. Law Alumni Assn., Am. Coun. of Blind (assoc.), Randolph-Sheppard Vendors of Am. (assoc.), Phi Delta Phi. Achievements include being the prin. Senate draftsman for Black Lung Benefits Act, 1972, Rehab. Act, 1973, Randolph-Sheppard Act Amendments, 1974, Black Lung Benefits Reform Act, 1977. Office Phone: 202-363-2200. Personal E-mail: humphreyslaw@att.net.

HUMPHREYS TROY, PATRICIA, foundation administrator; b. Birmingham, June 3, 1946; m. Stephen Richard Troy; 1 child, David. BS in Edn., Auburn U., 1968, MEd, 1969; cert. advanced study in edn., Loyola Coll., 1989; cert., Inst. Orgn. Mgmt., U.S. Chamber at U. Del., 1999; MBA, U. Kans., 2005. Cert. assn. exec. Grad. tchg. asst. Auburn U., 1968—69; asst. libr. McKendree Coll., 1969—71; adj. instr. Chapman Coll., 1972—75; libr. Wroxeter-on-Severn, 1978—80; adminstrv. dir., media dir. Chesapeake Acad.1, 1980—89; pres., CEO Bay Media Inc., 1989—, Next Wave Group LLC, 2001—; CEO, Facetswoman, Inc., 2004—. Past vice-chair bd. trustees, chair strategic planning com. Anne Arundel Health Sys. and Anne Arundel Med. Ctr.; exec. dir., adminstr. Assn. for Women in Comms., 1996—2005; exec. dir. Mid-Atlantic Carwash Assn., 2002—, Md./D.C. Soc. Clin. Oncology, 2006—; bd. dirs. membersnow.com. Unit pres. Am. Cancer Soc., 1986—92; pres. Panhellenic of Annapolis, 1976, Cultural Arts Found. Anne Arundel County, 1995—99, Greater Severna Park Coun., 1990—93; chair Small Area Plan for Severna Park, Anne Arundel County, 1997—2002, Anne Arundel County Cancer Control Task Force, 1994—96; bd. trustees, founding vice chair Chesapeake Acad., 1980—; grad. Leadership Anne Arundel; founding chair Assn. for Severna Park Improvement, Renewal and Enhancement, Inc., 1994—; chair bd. dirs. Stop the Silence, 2006. Named Independence Day Parade Grand Marshal, Greater Severna Park Chamber, 1993, Bus. Leader of Yr., Anne Arundel Trade Coun., 1996, Women in Bus. Advocate, Md. Small Bus. Assn., One of Md.'s Top 100 Women, Daily Record, 1997, 1999, 2001, Cmty. Activist of Yr., Taste of the Bay Mag., 2006, Entrepreneur of Yr., Annapolis and Anne Arundl County C. of C., 2006; recipient Exec. citation for cmty. svc., Anne Arundel County, 1999, Disting. Alumni award, Leadership Anne Arundel, 1997, TWIN award, Anne Arundel County YWCA, 1996, Anne Arundel County Cmty. Svc. award, YWCA, 2005, AA County Svc. award. Mem.: Am. Soc. Assn. Exec. (cert.), Anne Arundel Trade Coun./Annapolis and Anne Arundel County Chamber (edn. chmn. 1990—), Am. Bus. Women's Assn. (pres. Severn River/Md. Capital chpt. 1980—81, Woman of Yr. Severn River 1991, Bus. Assoc. of Yr., Severn River 1992, named among Top 10 Women in Bus. 2003), Women in Comms. (pres. Md. profl. chpt. 1991—92, Georgina Mac Dougall Davis award 2004). Office: 550M Ritchie Hwy 271 Severna Park MD 21146 Home Phone: 410-544-1538; Office Phone: 410-647-8402, 410-647-5002. E-mail: pat@facetswoman.com.

HUMPHRIES, ASA ALAN, JR., biologist, educator, dean; b. Anniston, Ala., Sept. 6, 1924; s. Asa Allen and Myree (Adamson) Humphries; m. LaNelle Wright, Sept. 10, 1949 (dec. 1969); children: Susan Myree, David Alan, Ann Wesley; m. Laurie Cecilia Lee, July 22, 1972; 1 child, Laura Catherine. AB, Emory U., 1948, MS, 1949; AM, Princeton U., 1952, PhD, 1953. Instr. biology Emory U., Atlanta, 1949-50, from asst. prof. to assoc prof. dept. biology, 1954-67, prof. biology, 1967-81, chmn. dept. biology, 1974-81; anatomy instr. U. Va. Sch. Medicine, Charlottesville, 1953-54; prof. Transylvania U., Lexington, Ky., 1981-94, prof. emeritus, 1994—, v.p., dean, 1981-83, exec. v.p., dean, 1983-91, dean spl. programs, 1991-94, dean emeritus, 1994—. Mem. editl. bd.: U. Press Ky., 1981—94; contbr. articles to profl. jours. Trustee Lexington Clin. Found., 1986—2005; bd. dirs. Ky. Inst. Internat. Studies, 1990—94, Operation Read, Lexington, 1993—99, 2001—02. With US Army, 1943—46. Recipient Ann. Rsch. award, Assn. S.E. Biologists, 1956, Transylvania medal, 2001; fellow, NATO, NSF, Procter, Princeton U., 1952—53; grantee Rsch., NSF, NIH, Rockefeller Found. Mem.: AAAS, Soc. Devel. Biology, Optimist Club Internat., Alpha Tau Omega, Omicron Delta Kappa (leadership hon.), Sigma Xi. Democrat. Home and Office: 2009 Des Cognets Ln Lexington KY 40502-3040 Personal E-mail: asa.humphries@verizon.net.

HUMPHRIES, EDWARD FRANCIS, lawyer; b. S.I., NY, May 25, 1957; s. Robert Edward and Joan D. (Mauter) H.; m. Colleen Kennedy, July 21, 1990; 1 child, Stephen Edward. BBA magna cum laude, Bernard M. Baruch Coll., 1981; JD, Fordham U., 1984. Bar: N.J. 1984, U.S. Dist. Ct. N.J. 1984, N.Y. 1985, U.S. Dist. Ct. (ea. and so. dists.) N.Y. 1985, U.S. Dist. Ct. (we. dist.) N.Y. 1987, Pa. 1990, Hawaii 1990, U.S. Supreme Ct. 1990, U.S. Dist. Ct. Hawaii 1991; lic. capt. USCG. Assoc. Amabile & Erman, Bklyn., 1984-86, 87-92, ptnr., 1993—; assoc. Pegalis & Wachsman, Great Neck, NY, 1986-87. Trustee Soc. Hill East Condominium Assn., East Brunswick, N.J., 1987-90, pres., 1988-90; co-chmn. Homeowners Assn. Coun. East Brunswick, 1988-90; vice-chmn. East Brunswick Planning Bd., 1989-90; pres. East Brunswick Rep. Club, 1989-91; mem. strategic planning com. Staten Island Acad., 2003-05 Recipient Morton Wollman medal in mgmt. Bernard M. Baruch Coll., 1981. Mem. NY State Bar Assn., Hawaii State Bar Assn., Princess Bay Boatman's Assn. (vice commodore 2002-06, bd. dirs. 2002—), Richmond County Yacht Club (mem. house com. 2007—), Beta Gamma Sigma, Sigma Iota Epsilon. Republican. Roman Catholic. Home: 451 Manor Rd Staten Island NY 10314-2963 Office: Amabile & Erman 1000 South Ave Staten Island NY 10314-3430

HUMPHRIES, JIMMY, set designer, educator; b. DC, June 6, 1954; s. James Hugh and Mary Humphries; m. Linda Lee Hall, Dec. 28, 2004; m. Mary Hannum, June 2, 1979 (div. July 1, 2004); 1 child, James III. BA in Studio Art, So. Ark. U., Magnolia, 1978; MA in Theatre Prodn., U. Idaho, Moscow, 1980, MFA in Theatre Design, 1986. Instr. Kearney State Coll., Nebr., 1980—85; asst. prof. Tex. A&M U., College Station, 1986—92; assoc. prof. Wittenberg U., Springfield, Ohio, 1992—. Artstic staff Tex. Shakespeare Festival, Kilgore, Tex., 1991—. Named to Hall of Fame, Ohio Ednl. Theatre Assn.; recipient Internat. Siglo de Oro award in scenic design for The Gambler, 1991, award in set design for The Devils, Tex. Non-Profit Theatres, 1992, Globe award for MacBeth, San Antonio Theatre, 1999, ACTF citation citation in scenic design for,The Skin of Our Teeth, Kennedy Ctr., 1999, award for set dressing for Proof, Ostrander Memphis Theatre, 2004. Mem.: United Scenic Artists. Home: 5409 Stoneridge Dr Springfield OH 45503 Office: Wittenberg Univ PO Box 720 Springfield OH 45501

HUMPHRIES, JOAN ROPES, psychologist, educator; b. Bklyn., Oct. 17, 1928; d. Lawrence Gardner and Adele Lydia (Zimmermann) Ropes; m. Charles C. Humphries, Apr. 4, 1957; children: Peggy Ann, Charlene Adele. BA, U. Miami, 1950; MS, Fla. State U., 1955; PhD, La. State U., 1963. Registered lobbyist State of Fla. Part-time instr. psychology dept. U. Miami, Coral Gables, Fla., 1964—66; prof. behavioral studies dept. Miami-Dade Coll., 1966—. Presenter, lectr. in field cruise ship Costa Romantica. Editl. staff, maj. author The Application of Scientific Behaviorism to Humanistic Phenomena, 1975, Rev. Edit., 1979; prodr. & host, Sigma Series video, cert. for TV Strategies in Global Modern Academia: Issues and Answers in Higher Education, 1993—94, Strategies in Global Modern Academia: Issues and Answers in Higher Education II, 1995; prodr.: (video series) Strategies in Global Modern Academia: Issues and Answers in Higher Education, III, 1996—97, Strategies in Global Modern Academia: Issues and Answers in Higher Education, IV, 2001—02, W2RN (cert.). Mem. Biofeedback Del., China, Hong Kong, 1995; mem. Citizen Amb. Program Psychic Arts Del. to Russia, 1997; mem. Citizen Amb. Program Am. Mus. Natural History; life mem. Pastorius Home Assn., Inc., 2001; mem. Citizen Amb. Program Vizcayans Mus., Alden Kindred of Am., Inc.; mem. Citizen Amb. Program Nat. Trust Hist. Preservation, The Charles F. Menninger Soc., People to People; mem. ladies aux. Fla. Soc. SAR; mem. Nat. Mus. Women in Arts; mem. women's history month com. Jr. Honor Women Recognition, women's leadership seminar. Recipient award in hon. of women recognition, Women's Hist. Month com. and Women's Leadership Seminar, 2003. Mem.: AAUP (past v.p. Fla. conf. 1986—88, pres. of chpt., Miami-Dade Coll. 1986—, mem. exec. bd. Fla. conf. 1989—90, former v.p., sec. Miami-Dade Coll.), AAAS, AAUW (life; former v.p. Tamiami br. 1983—88, Appreciation award 1977), APA (life), Dade-Monroe Psychol. Assn., Fla. Psychol. Assn., Biofeedback Soc. Am. (pres. 1990—), Noetic Scis., NY Acad. Scis. (life), Assn. Applied Psychophysiology and Biofeedback, Inst. Evaluation, Diagnosis and Treatment (past v.p. 1975—87, pres. 1987—, former bd. dirs.), Internat. Soc. for Study Subtle Energies and Energy Medicine (charter), Physicians for Social Responsibility, Am. Psychol. Soc. (charter), Am. Inst. Parliamentarians, (Biltmore Hotel) Coral Gables, Pilgrim John Howland Soc., Hist. Homeowners Coral Gables, Heredity Order Descs. of Colonial Govs., Regines in Miami, North Campus Spkrs. Bur. (Cmty. Lecture Series award), Internat. Platform Assn. (bd. govs. 1979—, Silver Bowl award 1993), Mexico Beach C. of C. (bus. 1991—95), Colonial Dames 17th Century, Soc. Mayflower Descs. (elder William Brewster colony), Cellar Club, Coral Gables Country Club (life), Jockey Club (life), Phi Lambda Pi, Phi Lambda (Founder's Plaque 1976, Appreciation award 1987). Democrat. Achievements include research in biofeedback and human consciousness. Home: 1311 Alhambra Cir Coral Gables FL 33134-3521 Office Phone: 305-443-8433.

HUMPHRIES, JOHN O'NEAL, cardiologist, educator, dean; b. Columbia, SC, Oct. 22, 1931; s. Arthur Lee and Helen Elliott (O'Neal) H.; m. Mary Ellen Cregan, Mar. 13, 1954; children: Arthur Thomas, Ellen Cregan, John Elliott. BS, Duke U., 1952; MD, Johns Hopkins U., 1956. Diplomate Am. Bd. Internal Medicine (mem. bd. subsplty. cardiovascular disease 1974-79). Intern Johns Hopkins Hosp., 1957; asst. resident Osler Med. Service, Osler Med. Svc., 1958-60, resident physician pvt. med. svc., 1962-64, staff physician, 1962-79; rsch. fellow in cardiology U. London, St. George's Hosp., 1960-61, Johns Hopkins U. Med. Sch., 1956-57, 61-62, mem. faculty, 1964-79, Robert L. Levy prof. cardiology, 1975-79, prof. medicine, 1976-79; O.B. Mayer Sr. and Jr. prof. medicine U. S.C., Columbia, 1979-86, prof. medicine, 1979-96; disting. prof. medicine, dean emeritus, 1997—; chmn. dept. medicine U. S.C., Columbia, 1979-87, dean Sch. Medicine, 1983-94. Contbr. articles to med. publs.; mem. editl. bd. various jours. Bd. dirs. Md. Ballet, Balt., 1975-78. Master ACP (bd. govs. for S.C. chpt. 1986-90), Am. Coll. Cardiology (bd. govs. for Md. chpt. 1973-76); mem. Am. Fedn. Clin. Rsch., Am. Heart Assn. (fellow coun. clin. cardiology, chmn. postgrad. edn. com., exec. com. 1972-75), Cen. Md. Heart Assn. (pres. 1972-73), Md. Heart Assn. (pres. 1976-77), Assn. Univ. Cardiologists, Am. Clin. and Climatol. Assn., Alpha Omega Alpha. Office: U SC Sch Medicine Columbia SC 29208-0001

HUMPHRIES, M. CLAYTON, JR., lawyer; b. Opelika, Ala., Mar. 8, 1953; BA cum laude, Birmingham-So. Coll., 1975; JD, U. Ala., 1978. Bar: Ala. 1978. Law clk. Ala. Supreme Ct., 1978—79, U.S. Dist. Ct. Ala. (mid. dist.), 1980; v.p., gen. counsel Westpoint Stevens, Inc., West Point, Ga. Mem.: ABA, Ala. State Bar Assn.

HUND, THOMAS N., rail transportation executive; BA in Bus. Adminstrn., Loyola U.; MBA, U. Chgo., 1988. Acct. Burlington No. Santa Fe Corp., 1983-89, asst. v.p., contr., 1989-90, v.p., contr., 1990-95, sr. v.p., CFO, 1999-2000, exec. v.p., CFO, 2001—. Mem.: AICPA. Office: Burlington No Santa Fe Corp PO Box 961056 Fort Worth TX 76161-0056 Office Phone: 817-867-6100.*

HUNDER, GENE GERALD, rheumatologist, educator; b. Lake City, Minn., Feb. 7, 1932; s. Tilman James and Melita Henrietta (Bremer) H.; m. Ingeborg Anne Hanson, May 6, 1990; children: Heidi, Jennifer, Gregory,Grant, Naomi, Stephanie. Student, St. Olaf Coll., 1950—52; BA, U. Minn., Mpls., 1954, MD, 1958, MS, 1963. Diplomate Am. Bd. Internal Medicine. Intern. Strong Meml. Hosp., Rochester, N.Y., 1958-59, resident, 1959-61, Mayo Clinic, Rochester, Minn., 1961-64; instr. internal medicine Mayo Grad. Sch., Rochester, Minn., 1966-67, asst. prof. internal medicine, 1968-73, assoc. prof., 1973-78, prof., 1978—, full mem. internal medicine, 1981—, cons. internal medicine and rheumatology; head sect. rheumatology Mayo Clinic, 1976-81; prof. internal medicine Mayo Clinic May Clinic Coll. Med. Scis., Rochester, Minn., 1978—. Chmn. rheumatology rsch. com., 1976-81, 87, clin. investigator tng. program Mayo Grad. Sch., 1981-84, chmn. div. rheumatology 1987-96; Philip Showalter Hench lect. Ariz. Med. Soc., Phoenix, 1965; Charles W. Thomas lectr. Med. Coll. Va., Charlottesville, 1979; Carl Pearson lectr. Los Angeles County Med. Assn., 1983; Henry J. Lehrhoff lectr. Clarkson Hosp., Omaha, 1989, Nana Swartz lectr. Swedish Med. Soc., 1994, Gilbert Galens Meml. lectr. William Beaumont Hosp., Detroit, 1995; Clemmeson lectr. Danish Soc. Rheumatology, 2006. Co-author: Physical Examination of the Joints, 1978; editor: Rheumatology, 1978, Atlas of Rheumatology, 1998, 2002, 2005, Mayo Clinic on Arthritis, 1999, 2002, 2006; assoc. editor: Jour. Lab and Clin. Medicine, 1979-81; editor Jour. Current Opinion in Rheumatology, 1992-2000, Jour. Arthritis Care and Rsch., 2000-05; mem. editl. bd. Jour. Rheumatology, 1982—, Jours. Musculoskeletal Medicine, 1983-2001, Annals Internal Medicine, 1998-2001, ISI List of Frequently Cited Clin. Investigators. Mem. ho. dels. Arthritis Found., Atlanta, 1980-83, trustee, 1985; mem. exec. com. Minn. Arthritis Found., Mpls., 1984-90. Nu Sigma Nu scholar, 1955, Minn. Med. Found. acad. scholar, 1955. Fellow ACP; mem. AMA, Am. Bd. Internal Medicine, AAAS. Ctrl. Soc. Clin. Research (mem. program com.), Am. Soc. Clin. Rheumatology (pres.), Am. Coll. Rheumatology (mem. exec. com. 1976-77, v.p. cen. region 1987, pres. cen. region, 1989, bd. dir. 1988-92, Master award 1997, Disting. Rheumatologist 2004), Phi Beta Kappa, Alpha Omega Alpha. Republican. Lutheran. Office: Mayo Clinic 200 1st St SW Rochester MN 55905-0002 Home: 59488 367th Ave Zumbro Falls MN 55991-9725 Office Phone: 507-284-2511. Business E-Mail: ghunder@mayo.edu.

HUNDERT, EDWARD M., former academic administrator, educator; b. Woodbridge, NJ; m. Mary Hundert; 3 children. BS in Math. and History of Sci. and Medicine, summa cum laude, Yale U., 1978; MA in Philosophy, Politics and Econs., first class honors, Oxford U., 1980; MD, Harvard U., 1984. Diplomate Am. Bd. Neurology and Psychiatry. Med. intern Mount Auburn Hosp., Cambridge, Mass., 1984—85; resident in adult psychiatry, rsch. fellow, Labs. for Psychiatric Rsch. McLean Hosp., Belmont, Mass., 1985—88, chief resident, 1987—88; clin. fellow in psychiatry Harvard Med. Sch., Boston, 1984—88, instr. psychiatry, 1988—90, asst. prof. psychiatry, 1990—93, asst. prof. med. ethics, 1990—97, assoc. dean for student affairs, 1990—97, assoc. master, William B. Castle Soc., 1992—97, assoc. prof. psychiatry, 1994—97, faculty fellow, Harvard U. Mind/Brain/Behavior Initiative, 1996—99; prof. psychiatry U. Rochester Sch. Medicine and Dentistry, 1997—2002, prof. med. humanities NY, 1997—2002, sr. assoc. dean for med. edn., 1997—2000, dean, 2000—02; pres. Case Western Res. U., Cleve., 2002—06, prof. biomed. ethics, 2002—. Asst. psychiatrist McLean Hosp., Belmont, 1988—94, hosp. ethicist, 1988—97, assoc. psychiatrist, 1995—97; psychiatrist Strong Meml. Hosp., Rochester, NY, 1997—2002. Author: Philosophy, Psychiatry and Neuroscience: Three Approaches to the Mind, 1989, Lessons from an Optical Illusion: On Nature and Nurture, Knowledge and Values, 1995. Mem.: Phi Beta Kappa. Office: Case Western Res U Adelbert Hall 216 10900 Euclid Ave Cleveland OH 44106-7001

HUNDLEY, JAMES W., III, think-tank executive, consultant, researcher; b. Balt., June 19, 1950; s. James W. Jr. and Virginia (Baird) H. BA, Princeton U., 1972; MBA, Loyola Coll., Balt., 1985. Exec. dir. Balt. Zoo, 1978-86; dir. corp. rels. World Wilflife Fund, Washington, 1986-88; devel. dir. Nat. Geog. Soc., Washington, 1988-94; sr. cons. The Conservation Co., Washington, 1992-94; prin. Hundley Assocs., Washington, 1994-96; dir. N.Y. office Rand Corp., NYC, 1996—. Home: 280 Park Ave S Apt 26E New York NY 10010-6135 Office: Rand Corp 215 Lexington Ave New York NY 10016

HUNDLEY, NORRIS CECIL, JR., historian, educator; b. Houston, Oct. 26, 1935; s. Norris Cecil and Helen Marie (Mundine) H.; m. Carol Marie Beckquist, June 8, 1957; children: Wendy Michelle Hundley Harris, Jacqueline Marie Hundley Reid. AA, Mt. San Antonio Coll., 1956; AB, Whittier Coll., 1958; PhD (Univ. fellow), UCLA, 1963. Instr. U. Houston, 1963-64; asst. prof. Am. history UCLA, 1964-69, assoc. prof., 1969-73, prof., 1973-94, prof. emeritus, 1994—, chmn. exec. com. Inst. Am. Cultures, 1976-93, chmn. univ. program on Mex., 1981-94, acting dir. Latin Am. Ctr., 1989-90, dir. Latin Am. Ctr., 1990-94. Exec. com. U. Calif. Consortium on Mex. and the U.S., 1981-86; adv. com. Calif. water atlas project Calif. Office Planning and Research, 1977-79 Author: Dividing the Waters: A Century of Controversy Between the United States and Mexico, 1966, Water and the West: The Colorado River Compact and the Politics of Water in the American West, 1975, The Great Thirst: Californians and Water 1770s-1990s, 1992, Las aguas divididas: Un siglo de controversia entre México y Estados Unidos, 2000, The Great Thirst: Californians and Water-A History, 2001; co-author: The Calif. Water Atlas, 1979; co-author: California: History of a Remarkable State, 1982; editor: The American Indian, 1974, The Chicano, 1975, The Asian American, 1976; co-editor: The American West: Frontier and Region, 1969, Golden State Series, 1978-2002; mng. editor Pacific Hist. Rev., 1968-97; mem. editl. bd. Jour. San Diego History, 1970-79, Calif. Hist. Soc., 1980-89; contbr. articles to profl. jours. Bd. dirs. John and LaRee Caughey Found., 1983-2000, Henry J. Bruman Ednl. Found., 1983-2003, Forest History Soc., 1987-93. Recipient award of merit Calif. Hist. Soc., 1979; Am. Philos. Soc. grantee, 1964, 71, Ford Found. grantee, 1968-69, U. Calif. Water Resources Ctr. grantee, 1969-72, 91, 2000, Sourisseau Acad. grantee, 1972, NEH grantee, 1983-89, Hewlett Found. grantee, 1986-89, U. Calif. Regents faculty fellow in humanities, 1975, Guggenheim fellow, 1978-79, Hist. Soc. So. Calif. fellow, 1996—; Whitsett lectr., 2000. Mem. Am. Hist. Assn. (exec. coun. Pacific Coast br. 1968-97, v.p. 1993-94, pres. 1994-95), Western History Assn. (coun. 1985-88, 93-97, pres. 1994-95, Winther award 1973, 79), Orgn. Am. Historians. Office: UCLA Dept History Los Angeles CA 90095-1473 E-mail: hundley@history.ucla.edu.

HUNDLEY, SHELLI, mathematics educator; b. Mesa, Ariz., July 27, 1982; d. Jared Max and Beryl Hundley. BA in Secondary Edn. Math., Ariz. State U., Tempe, 2003; MAT, Grand Canyon U., Phoenix, 2005. Math. educator Mesa Pub. Schs., 2004—. Mem.: Nat. Coun. Math. Tchrs. Mem. Lds Ch. Office: Mesa Pub Schs Skyline HS 845 S Crismon Mesa AZ 85208 Business E-Mail: shundley@mpsaz.org.

HUNDSDORFER, BETH, reporter; Reporter Belleville (Ill.) News-Democrat. Co-recipient Best Cmty. Svc. award, So. Ill. Editl. Assn. Better Newspaper Contest, 2003, Grand award in Print, Nat. Headliner Awards, 2007, Robert F. Kennedy Journalism award for Domestic Print, 2007. Office: Belleville News-Democrat 120 S Illinois St Belleville IL 62220-2130 Office Phone: 618-239-2570. E-mail: bhundsdorfer@bnd.com.

HUNDT, REED ERIC, management consultant, former federal agency administrator; b. Ann Arbor, Mich., Mar. 3, 1948; s. Neal H. and Viola (Pullan) H.; m. Elizabeth Ann Katz, Oct. 26, 1980; children: Adam Elias, Nathaniel Pullan, Sara. BA, Yale U., 1969, JD, 1974. Bar: U.S. Dist. Ct. Md. 1974, U.S. Ct. Appeals (4th cir.) 1975, U.S. Dist. Ct. (cen. and no. dists.) Calif. 1976, U.S. Ct. Appeals (9th cir.) 1976, U.S. Supreme Ct. 1977, U.S. Tax. Ct. 1978, U.S. Ct. Appeals (3d cir.) 1979, U.S. Dist. Ct. D.C. 1980, U.S. Ct. Appeals (D.C. cir.) 1980. Law clk. to presiding justice U.S. Ct. Appeals (4th cir.), Balt., 1974-75; assoc. Latham & Watkins, Washington, 1975-81, ptnr., 1982-94; chmn. FCC, Washington, 1994-97; prin. Charles Ross Ptnrs., LLC, Washington, Md., 1997—; sr. advisor McKinsey & Co. Inc., 1997—. Mem. adv. com. and tchr. Yale Law Sch. and Yale Sch. of Mgmt.; bd. dirs. Allegiance Telecom, Inc., Northpoint Commn. Inc., Phone.com, Inc., Global Connect Partners, Core Express, Inc., Sigma Networks, Novell Inc., 1998—, Intel Corp., 2001—; spl. adv. Madison Dearborn Partners; venture ptnr. Benchmark Capital. Book rev. editor Yale U. Law Rev., 1974-75; Author: You Say You Want A Revolution: A Story of Information Age Politics, 2000, In China's Shadow: The Crisis of American Entrepreneurship, 2006 Mem. Environ. Task Force of Dem. Policy Com., Washington, 1986. Named one of 50 Who Matter Now, Business 2.0, 2007; recipient Voice for Children Leadership award, Disting. Svc. award, Nat. Assn. of Elem. Sch. Principals, Nat. Assn. of Sec. Sch. Principals, Helen Keller Outstanding Pub. Svc. award, Am. Found. for the Blind. Mem. ABA.*

HUNEYCUTT, ALICE RUTH, lawyer; b. New Haven, Jan. 10, 1951; d. C. Jerome and Alberta (Piner) H.; m. Howard Mark Bernstein, Nov. 28, 1981; children: Ashley Laughton, Laura Whitney. BA in History, Duke U., 1972; JD, Miami U., Fla., 1979. Bar: Fla. 1980, U.S. Dist. Ct. (so. dist.) Fla. 1980, U.S. Ct. Appeals (5th cir.) 1980, U.S. Dist. Ct. (mid. dist.) Fla. 1982, U.S. Ct. Appeals (11th cir.) 1982. Corp. counsel Burger King Corp., Miami, 1980-82; assoc. Stearns Weaver Miller Weissler Alhadeff & Sitterson, P.A., Tampa, Fla., 1982-84, ptnr., 1984—. Bd. dirs. Am. Heart Assn., Tampa, 1986-91, chmn. elect, 1988-89, chmn. 1990-91. Mem. ABA (corp., banking and bus law sect.), Fla. Bar Assn. (pres.'s Pro Bono Svc. award 1987), Fla. Assn. Women Lawyers. Democrat. Methodist. Home: 1400 72nd Ave NE Saint Petersburg FL 33702-4610 Office: 401 E Jackson St Ste 2200 Tampa FL 33602-5251 Office Phone: 813-222-5031. E-mail: ahuneycutt@swmwas.com.

HUNG, CHIN-CHENG, artist, educator; s. Chao-Ho and Fen Chen Hung; m. Hsiu-Yuan Cheng, Oct. 1, 1992; 1 child, Jared. MFA in Painting, Savannah Coll. of Art and Design, 1999. Cert. technician of screen printing Taiwan Govt., 1997. Commd. 2d lt. Taiwan Army, 1987, advanced through grades to maj., 1996; platoon leader 10th Corps, Taiwan Army, Taichung, 1987—88, co. asst. comdr., 1988—91; retinue (aide) of maj. gen. Penghu Frontier Def. Corps, Taiwan Army, Makung, Penghu County, 1991—93; bn. asst. comdr. 8th Corps, Taiwan Army, Gaoxiong, 1993—95, officer of propaganda dept., 1995—97; prof. of found. studies Savannah Coll. of Art and Design, Savannah, Ga., 1997—. Guest lectr. Chinese calligrapgy, watercolor, and painiting Youth Activity Ctr., China Youth Corps, Makung, Penghu County, Taiwan, 1991—94; art dir. dept. fine arts 8th Corps, Taiwan Army, Gaoxiong, 1995—97; ind. artist, Savannah, Ga. One-man shows include Person, Place, and Thing, 1999, Candid Sight, 2000, Anatomy of Life Drawing, 2002, group exhibition, Thousand People Fine Arts Show (First Pl., 1983), Far from Home 1999 International Student Exhibition (Hon. Mention Award, 1999), Dimensions 1999 (So. Cmty. Bank & Trust Award, 1999), Faculty Show '99, Looking at Color, The Art of Drawing, Pastels U.S.A., Men at Art, Group Show of Fine Arts

Department, 7th Annual National Juried Pastel Competition 2001, Prints, Drawings and Pastels, Out of the Classroom, Pastels on High International Exhibition 2001 (Mdse. Award, 2001), Renaissance in Pastel (Strathmore Artists Products Pastel Paper, 2001), 10th Annual National Pastel Painting Exhibition (First Pl., 2001), School of Fine Arts Faculty Exhibition, Atlanta Chinese Artist Association Annual Member's Exhibition, Oh, Baby, Chromaception, 2002, Graduation Show, Atlanta Chinese Artist Association Annual Member's Exhibition, Vision 2002, Chromaception, 2003, Contemporary Focus: Mirroring the Creative Self, 32nd Annual Exhibition for "Pastel Only, The Armed Forces Juried Fine Arts Exhibition, Provincial Juried Fine Arts Exhibition, The Army 8th Corps Fine Arts Exhibition, National Juried Fine Arts Exhibition, Alexander Hall Open Studios, The Commemorative Exhibition of Mr. Jing-Guo (First Pl., Chinese calligraphy and watercolor, 1987), interview (scad tv), Candid Sight; musician: (interview) musical performance (Hansheng Broadcasting Station), musical performance (Central Broadcasting Station), musical performance (Broadcasting Corporation of China); interview (scad tv), Chromaception, 2002, magazine (the pastel journal), Finalists of Pastel 100, Figure category, magazine (pastel artist international), Master Pastel Artists of the World - United States Showcase; musician: (musical performance) Confession (The Best Vocalist and The Best Music, 1987), (performance) musical performance (Chinese Television Service), musical performance (China Television Co. Ltd, musical performance (Taiwan Television Enterprise); contbr. articles to profl. jours. Decorated Medal of Pao Star, Taiwan Army, Medal of Brilliant Star, Medal of Loyalty and Diligence,; recipient 1st pl. in Chinese calligraphy, Keelung City Fine Arts Exhbn., City of Keelung, Taiwan, 1985, Best Vocalist for 2d Ann. Golden Panpipe Prize mus. competition, Dept. of Def., Taiwan, 1995, Cert. of Hon. Citizenship, Taiwan Govt., 1997, Outstanding Achievement Award in Screen Printing, Taipei City Profl. Tng. Ctr., 1997, Purchase award, Internat. Birthday Illustration Competition, Savannah Coll. of Art and Design, 1998, Popular Vote award, 32d Ann. Exhbn. for Pastel Only, Pastel Soc. of Am., 2004. Mem.: Atlanta Chinese Art Assn., Chinese-Am. Acad. and Profl. Assn. in Southea. US, Pastel Soc. Am., Coll. Art Assn. Achievements include selected for Sotheby's International Young Art 2001 Program, The Lovers series of paintings featured in New York, Tel Aviv, Israel, and Artlink online auction in 2000; pastel painting featured in The Pastel Journal as a finalist for 2d Annual Pastel 100 competition in 2001; paintings featured in New American Paintings magazine for its Open Studios 2001 Southern Competition. Avocations: painting and drawing, travel, singing, musical instruments. Home: 14 Steeple Run Way Savannah GA 31405 Office: Savannah Coll of Art and Design 420 E Anderson St Savannah GA 31401 Home Phone: 912-232-0748; Office Phone: 912-525-6621. Office Fax: 912-525-6606; Home Fax: 912-232-0748. Personal E-mail: chung3@comcast.net. Business E-Mail: chung@scad.edu.

HUNG, DONALD LU-CHENG, electrical engineer, computer engineer, educator; s. Timothy Teh-Ying Hung and Sophia Ren-Fan Wu; m. Judith Yee Hung; 1 child, Leonard. BSEE, Tongji U., 1982; MS, Case Western Res. U., 1986, PhD, 1990. Asst., assoc. full prof. Gannon U., Pa., 1990—95, Wash. State U., 1995—99, San Jose State U., Calif., 1999—. Vis. prof. The Chinese U. Hong Kong, 1998—99; guest prof. Tongji U. Shanghai, 2005—; steering com. mem. 8th Joint Conf. Info. Scis., Salt Lake City, 2005; chair 8th Internat. Conf. Computer Sci. and Informatics, Salt Lake City, 2005. Mem.: IEEE (sr.), Eta Kappa Nu (hon.). Office: San Jose State U One Washington Sq San Jose CA 95192-0180 Home Phone: 510-651-5622. Business E-Mail: dhung2@email.sjsu.edu.

HUNG, JAMES CHEN, engineering educator, consultant; b. Foochow, Republic of China, Dec. 18, 1929; s. David Shen and Pearl C. (Chao) H.; m. Sufenne Huang, Apr. 3, 1958; children: John Y., Samuel M., Stephen T. BEE, Nat. Taiwan U., 1953; MEE, NYU, 1956, DEng, 1961. Registered profl. engr., Tenn. Instr. NYU, 1956-61; asst. prof. U. Tenn., Knoxville, 1961-62, assoc. prof., 1962-65, prof., 1965-84, disting. service prof., 1984-99, prof. emeritus, 1999—. V.p. Poly-Analytics, Inc., Knoxville; hon. prof. Nanjing U. Aerospace and Astrophysics, 1989, South China U. Tech., 1994, Hunan U., Peoples Republic of China, 1996; cons. prof. Northwestern Poly. U., Chongging U., S.W. China Tchrs. U., 1984—. Contbr. articles to profl. jours. Recipient Technology award NASA, 1969, Cert. NASA, 1970, Brooks Disting. Engring. Prof. award, U. Tenn., 1973. Fellow: IEEE (editor IEEE Trans. on Indsl. Electronics 1991—95, gen. chmn. internat. symposium on indsl. electronics, Xian, China 1992, gen. chmn. internat. conf. indsl. tech. 1994, 1996, tech. activity bd. 1998—99, gen. chmn. internat. symposium on indsl. electronics, L'Aquila, Italy 2002, tech. track chair internat. conf. indsl. elecs. 2003, 2004, gen. chair internat. conf. indsl. tech. 2005, hon. gen. chair internat. conf. factory automation and emerging tech. 2005, gen. co-chair internat. conf. factory automation and emerging. tech. 2007—, Anthony J. Hornfeck Svc. award 1995, Eugene Mittelmann Achievement award 2000, Millennium medal 2000), Indsl. Electronics Soc. (v.p. 1996, pres.-elect 1997, pres. 1998—99, chair nomination com. 2003—); mem.: Phi Kappa Phi, Eta Kappa Nu, Tau Beta Pi, Sigma Xi. Methodist.

HUNG, MEI-JONG CHOW, social worker; b. Taipei, Taiwan, Republic China, Oct. 7, 1937; s. Wen-tung Yeh Chow; m. Chao-huang Hung, Mar. 24, 1964; children: Jennifer Ching-yi, John Ching-tsung. BS, Nat. Taiwan U., 1960; MSW, Simmons Coll. Sch. Social Work, 1963. Cert. hypnotherapist; social worker. Mental health counselor Taipei Pub. Health Teaching Demonstration, 1963-66; asst. prof. Taiwan U., 1964-66; social work supr. Johns Hopkins Hosp., Balt., 1969-71; pvt. practice social work Columbia, Md., 1972—. Vol. cmty. recreational social work, 1988—; co-prodr. Opera Internat., Washington, 1999—, prodr., 2002—. Fellow, WHO. Mem.: NASW, Acad. Cert. Social Workers. Home and Office: 7255 Meadow Wood Way Clarksville MD 21029-1714 Address: PO Box 140 Fulton MD 20759-0140

HUNG, WU, art historian, educator; Student, Ctrl. Acad. Fine Arts, Beijing; PhD in Early Chinese Art, Harvard Univ. Rsch. staff, Palace Mus. Forbidden City, Beijing, 1973—78; Harrie A. Vanderstappen disting. svc. prof., Chinese art history Univ. Chgo., and dir., Ctr. Art of E. Asia; also consulting curator Smart Mus. Art. Author: Monumentality in Early Chinese Art, 1995, Three Thousand Years of Chinese Painting, 1997, Transience, 1999. Fellow: Am. Acad. Arts & Scis. Office: Art History Univ Chgo 166 Cochrane Woods Art Ctr 5540 S Greenwood Ave Chicago IL 60637 Office Phone: 773-702-0274. Business E-Mail: hungwu@uchicago.edu.*

HUNGAR, THOMAS G., federal agency administrator, lawyer; BS, Williamette U., 1984; JD, Yale U., 1987. Law clk. to Hon. Alex Kozinski US Ct. Appeals (9th cir.), 1987—88; law clk. to Justice Anthony M. Kennedy US Supreme Ct., Washington, 1988—89; asst. solicitor gen. US Dept. Justice, Washington, 1992—94, dep. solicitor gen., 2003—; ptnr., assoc. Gibson, Dunn & Crutcher LLP, 1994—2003. Office: US Dept Justice Rm 5137 950 Pennsylvania Ave NW Washington DC 20530

HUNGER, J(OHN) DAVID, business educator; b. May 17, 1941; s. Jackson Steele and Elizabeth (Carey) H.; m. Betty Johnson, Aug. 2, 1969; children: Karen, Susan, Laura, Merry. BA, Bowling Green State U., Ohio, 1963; MBA, Ohio State U., 1966, PhD, 1973. Selling supr. Lazarus Dept. Store, Columbus, Ohio, 1965-66; brand asst. Procter and Gamble Co., Cin., 1968-69; asst. dir. grad. bus. programs Ohio State U., Columbus, 1970-72; instr. Baldwin-Wallace Coll., Berea, Ohio, 1972-73; prof. U. Va., Charlottesville, 1973-82; strategic mgmt. prof. Iowa State U. Coll. Bus., Ames, 1982—2006; strategic mgmt. scholar in residence St. John's U., 2006—. Prof. bus. George Mason U., Fairfax, Va., 1986-87; past pres. bd. dirs. Iowa State U. Press; cons. to bus., fed. and state agys. Author (with T.L. Wheelen): Strategic Management and Business Policy, 1983, 10th rev. edit., 2006, An Assessment of Undergraduate Business Education in the U.S., 1980, Cases in Strategic Management and Business Policy, 10th rev. edit., 2006, Essentials of Strategic Management, 1997, 4th edit., 2007, Concepts in Strategic Management and Business Policy, 10th rev. edit., 2006; contbr. articles to profl. jours. Capt. Mil. Intelligence, U.S. Army, 1966-68. Decorated Bronze Star. Mem. Acad. Mgmt., N.Am. Case Rsch. Assn. (past pres.), Soc. for Case Rsch. (past pres.), Strategic Mgmt. Soc., US Assn. for Small Bus. and Enterpreneurship (past v.p.). E-mail: jdhunger@iastate.edu.

HUNGERFORD, CONSTANCE CAIN, art educator; b. Chgo., Apr. 26, 1948; d. Craig John and Jocelyn Enid (Mason) Cain. B.A., Wellesley Coll., 1970; M.A., U. Calif.-Berkeley, 1972, Ph.D., 1977. Instr. to prof. history of art Swarthmore (Pa.) Coll., 1975—, chmn. dept. art, 1981-86. Exbitions include Ernest Meissonier Musee der Veaux Arts, Lyons, 1993; contbr. articles to profl. jours. Samuel H. Kress nat. fellow, 1973-75; Am. Council Learned Socs. grantee-in-aid, 1978; Am. Philos. Soc. grantee 1980. Mem. Coll. Art Assn. Am., AAUW (award 1983), Phi Beta Kappa. Office: Swarthmore Coll Dept Art 500 College Ave Swarthmore PA 19081-1306

HUNGERFORD, DAVID SAMUEL, orthopedic surgeon, educator; b. Rochester, NY, May 4, 1938; s. Francis Samuel and Marjorie Ellen (Wilson) H.; m. Uta-Heide Jung, July 20, 1962; children: Marc Wilson, Kyle Sasha, Lars Daniel. BA, Colgate U., 1960; MD, U. Rochester, 1964. Diplomate Am. Bd. Orthopaedic Surgery. Asst. prof. orthopaedic surgery Johns Hopkins U., Balt., 1972-78; chief orthopaedic surgery VA Hosp., Balt., 1975-80, Good Samaritan Hosp., Balt., 1972—, chief div. arthritis surgery, 1979—2001; assoc. prof. orthopaedic surgery Johns Hopkins U. Sch. Medicine, Balt., 1978-86, prof. orthopaedic surgery, 1987—. Cons. Balt. City Hosp., 1972-85, Children's Hosp., 1972-80, East Balt. Med. Ctr., 1972-78; co-dir. Johns Hopkins U. Ctr. for Osteonecrosis Rsch. and Edn., 1995—; bd. dirs. Nat. Osteonecrosis Found. Author: Progress in Orthopaedics, 1977, Ischemia and Necroses of Bone, 1980, Total Knee Arthroplasty: A Comprehensive Approach, 1984, Total Hip Arthroplasty: A New Approach, 1984, Bone Circulation, 1984, Disorders of the Patello Femoral Joint, 1990, Videobook of Total Knee Arthroplasty, 1994; founding editor Jour. Arthroplasty, 1985-93. Elder Cen. Presbyn. Ch., Balt., 1974-83; dir. Crippled Children's United Rehab. Effort, 1997—, Christian Orthopaedic Ptrs., 1997—; chmn. bd. Med. Assistance Program Internat., 1998—. Maj. U.S. Army, 1969. Recipient George Hoyt Whipple award, 1965; named Disting. So. Orthopedist, So. Orthopedic Assn., 2002; Colgate U. scholar, 1956-59, GM scholar, 1956-59, U. Rochester scholar, 1959-61, Girdlestone Meml. scholar Oxford U., Eng., 1969-70; fellow USPHS, Paris, 1961-62, Carl Berg traveling fellow, 1973. Mem. Johns Hopkins Med. and Surg. Soc., Md. Orthopaedic Soc., Arthritis Found., Hip Soc., Am. Assn. Orthopaedic Surgeons, Am. Assn. Hip Knee Surgeons, Soc. Internat. de Chirurgie Orthopedique et de Traumatologie, Knee Soc. (pres. 1994), Girdlestone Orthopaedic Soc. (chmn. 2005-). Republican. Home: 10715 Pot Spring Rd Cockeysville Hunt Valley MD 21030-3019 Office: Good Samaritan Hosp Profl Office Bldg G-1 5601 Loch Raven Blvd Baltimore MD 21239-2991 also: Johns Hopkins U Sch Medicine Dept Orthopaedic Surgery Baltimore MD 21205 Home Phone: 410-561-4383; Office Phone: 410-532-4732. Business E-Mail: dhunger@jhmi.edu.

HUNGERFORD, GARY A., insurance executive, columnist, writer, editor; b. Bklyn., Apr. 20, 1948; s. Gene and Ann Hungerford; m. Eleanor Haragsim, 1969. BBA cum laude, Coll. Ins., NYC, 1974; MBA, Coll. Ins., 1978; grad., U.S. Army Svc. Rifle Small Arms Firing Sch., 1992. CPCU, AIS, ASLI. With Guardian Life Ins. Co., 1965-67, Providence Washington Ins. Co., 1967-68, The Atlantic Cos., 1968-74, Midland Ins. Co., 1974-76, Drake Ins. Co. of N.Y., 1976-78, Mead Reinsurance Corp., 1978-80, Yorktown Indemnity Co., 1980-82, Tri-County Facilities, Ltd./Tri-County Facilities N.J., Inc., 1982-85; pres., CEO Spl. Risk Facilities, Ltd., Lindenhurst, N.Y., 1985—; chmn., CEO CompuPub. Svcs., Ltd., Lindenhurst, 1987—; chmn. Hungerford Arms Co., Ltd., Lindenhurst, 1988—; v.p., dir. Protective Ins. Agy., Ridgewood, N.Y., 1983—. Past editor, pub. Lindenhurst's Chamber News, 1990—95, former columnist, South Bays' News, Suffolk Alliance of Sportmen's Newsletter, The Bullet. Author: NYSRPA's Education and Training Directory, 1992, History of New York State Rifle and Pistol Association, 1997, Atlantic Mutual's No-Fault Automobile Insurance Manual, 1972; contbr. articles to profl. jours. Sponsor U.S. Olympic Shooting Team; life mem. N.Y. State Conservation Coun.; mem. Glock Sport Shooting Found.; mem. small bus. adv. com. N.Y. Senate; mem. Rocky Mountain Elk Found. With US Army, 1968—70. Mem.: NRA (life; mem. field support team, polit. preference com. 1992, mem. Inst. Legis. Action, mem. Polit. Victory Fund, cert. firearms instr., Golden Eagles), Rocky Mtn. Elk Found., Nat. Assn. Federally Lic. Firearms Dealers, L.I. Computer Assn., Nat. Assn. Desktop Pubs., Ind. Ins. Agts. NY, Profl. Ins. Wholesalers Assn., Profl. Ins. Agts. NY, Casualty and Surety Soc. NY, Ind. Ins. Agts. Assn., Soc. Ins. Rsch., Soc. CPCU, Law Enforcement Alliance Am. (life), Coastal Conservation Alliance, Wildlife Forever, Coll. Ins. MBA Soc., Conservation Alliance NY (life), Citizen's Com. for Right to Keep and Bear Arms (life), Shooter's Com. Polit. Edn. (life), Theodore Roosevelt Conservation Assn. (life), Coll. Ins. Alumni Assn., Lindenhust C. of C. (past chmn.), Izaak Walton League, L.I. Dahlia Soc., L.I. Beach Buggy Assn., NY State Rifle and Pistol Assn. (life; past bd. dirs., past chmn. fin. com., past chmn. range com., past printing com., past hist. com., past omnibus com.), United Gamefish Anglers, Inc. (life), N.Y. Sportfishing Fedn. (life), Varmint Hunters Assn. (life), Gun Owners Am. (life), Free Hunters (life), M-1 Carbine Collectors Assn., Garand Collectors' Assn., Northeastern Arms Collectors Assn., Internat. Game Fish Assn., Suffolk Alliance Sportsmen (del., firearms chmn., past v.p., dir.), Bass Anglers' Sportsman's Soc., Whitetails Unlimited, Nassau County Fish and Game Assn., Old Bethpage Rifle and Pistol Club (trustee), N.Am. Hunting Club (life), Lindenhurst Lions. Republican. Avocations: chess, fishing, hunting, shooting sports, computers, photography. Office: Spl Risk Facilities Ltd 101 N Wellwood Ave Lindenhurst NY 11757-4001

HUNGWE, KEDMON NYASHA, education educator, researcher; b. Harare, Zimbabwe, May 2, 1956; s. Elliott Bera and Chipo Hungwe; m. Chipo Mazimbe, Sept. 4, 1982; children: Ruvimbo Gamuchirai, Tendeukai Ratidzo, Tsitsi Fadzai, Manjere Mwarianesu. BS, U. Rhodesia, Harare, Zimbabwe, 1978; MS, U. Wis., Madison, 1987; PhD, Mich. State U., East Lansing, 1999. Lic. secondary tchr. Ministry of Edn., Zimbabwe. Tchr. Harare H.S., Harare, Zimbabwe, 1981—83; lectr. Ministry of Edn. in Zimbabwe, Harare, 1984—85, U. of Zimbabwe, Harare, 1987—2002; asst. prof. Mich. Technol. U., Houghton, Mich., 2002—. Cons. Dept. for Internat. Devel., UK, So. Ctr. for Energy and Environment. Contbr. book; editor: (web site) African cinema: a new series of reviews, criticism and theory; contbr. articles to profl. jours. Mem. Children's Performing Arts Workshop, Zimbabwe; jury mem. Zimbabwe Film Festival, Harare. Fellow, Candice Thoman Found. fellow, 1994—95, Robert Mugabe fellow, Mich. State U., 1992—97; scholar, World U. Svc. scholar, 1976—78, US AID scholar, 1985—87. Mem.: Nat. Coun. of Tchrs. of Math., Am. Ednl. Rsch. Assn. (mem.), Phi Kappa Phi. Methodist. Achievements include research in filmmaking in Southern Africa. Avocations: reading, travel, film critic. Office: Michigan Technological University 1400 Townsend Dr Houghton MI 49931 Office Phone: 906-483-8302. Business E-Mail: khungwe@mtu.edu.

HUNKE, DAVID L., publishing executive; b. Houston; m. Janet Hunke; children: Evan, Jenna. BS, U. Kans., Lawrence, 1974. With Kansas City Star; dir. advt. Miami Herald; with Gannett Co. Inc., 1992—, exec. v.p. for mktg. Cin. Enquirer and Cin. Post Ohio, 1997-99, pub., pres. digital edits. Rochester Dem. and Chronicle NY, 1999—2005; pres., pub. Detroit Free Press, Gannett Co. Inc., Mich., 2005—; CEO Detroit Newspaper Partnership, Mich., 2006—. Recipient Lifetime Humanitarian award, Lifetime Assistance Found., 2004. Office: Detroit Free Press 600 West Fort St Detroit MI 48226 E-mail: dhunke@dnps.com.*

HUNKELE, LESTER MARTIN, III, retired federal agency administrator; b. Bklyn., Aug. 16, 1947; s. Lester Martin, Jr. and Agnes Veronica (Tarpey) Hunkele; m. Diane Kathryn Sotiridy, Mar. 30, 1974. BS, U.S. Mil. Acad., 1969; MS in Constrn. Engring., Purdue U., 1975; diploma, Indsl. Coll. Armed Forces, 1988. Registered profl. engr., Va., cert. plant engr.; constrn. mgr., LEED accredited profl. Commd. 2d lt. U.S. Army, 1969, advanced through grades to capt., 1979; lt. col. USAR, 1990; ret., 1995; logistics officer 809 Engring. Bn., 1970-71, engr. officer Thailand, 1970-71; engr. officer army enging. sch. U.S. Army, Ft. Belvoir, Va., 1971-74, asst. area engr. Balt. dist. C.E., 1975-79, resigned Washington, 1979; civil engr. office chief engrs. Dept. Army, Washington, 1979-81, asst. chief constrn. mgmt. office chief army res., 1981-83; asst. head facilities HQs USMC, Washington, 1983-85; dir. facilities office asst. sec. def. res. affairs Dept. Def., Washington, 1985-88, prin. dir. materiel and facilities, 1988-89; dep. asst. sec. for facilities Dept. Vets. Affairs, Washington, 1989-92, dep. asst. sec. facilities oversight, 1992-93; exec. dir. Pa. Ave. Devel. Corp., Washington, 1993-96; exec. project mgr. Gen. Svcs. Adminstrn., Washington, 1996; project exec. Clark Constrn. Group, 1996-99; assoc. v.p. DMJMH&N, Arlington, Va., 1999-2001, v.p., 2001—02, sr. v.p., 2002—04; pres. Hunkele Cons., Mililani, Hawaii, 2004—. Mem.: CMAA, NSPE (mem. govt. adv. group), ASCE, Soc. Am. Mil. Engrs. (dir. Washington chpt. 1984—88), Assn. Facilities Engrs., Urban Land Inst., West Point Soc. (co-founder Annapolis chpt. 1986—), Fed. Exec. Inst. Alumni Assn. (membership chmn. 1987), Lambda Alpha. Avocations: sailing, skiing, scuba diving. Home: 95-1016 Inana St Mililani HI 96789 Home Phone: 808-638-2002; Office Phone: 443-995-6897. Personal E-mail: leshunkele@yahoo.com.

HUNKER, JEFFREY, dean; B in Engring. and Applied Physics, Harvard Coll.; PhD in Bus. Adminstrn. in Managerial Econs., Harvard Bus. Sch. Cons. Boston Consulting Group; dir. Crit. Infrastructure Assurance Office (CIAO) U.S. Dept. Commerce, dep. asst. to sec., sr. policy advisor sec.; v.p., mergers, and acquisitions Kidder Peabody and Co., NY; sr. dir. crit. infrastructure, nat. security coun. Clinton Adminstrn. , 1996—2000; dean Heinz Sch. Carnegie Mellon U. , 2001—. With Dept. Commerce Nat. Security Coun. Mem. Photography Coun. Mus. Modern Art (MOMA). Achievements include development of 1st-ever national strategy for cyber-security and protecting critical information, Internet, and computer systems; President's 2000 Cyber-Security Summit with internet leaders; Partnership for Critical Infrastructure Security, a national organization with over 130 Frotune 500 companies as members. Office: H John Heinz III Sch Pub Policy & Mgmt Carnegie Mellon U Pittsburgh PA 15213-3890 Home Phone: 412-802-8380; Office Phone: 412-268-4897. Business E-Mail: jhunker@andrew.cmu.edu.

HUNKINS, RAYMOND BREEDLOVE, lawyer, rancher; b. Culver City, Calif., Mar. 19, 1939; s. Charles F. and Louise (Breedlove) H.; m. Mary Deborah McBride, Dec. 22, 1967; children: Amanda, Blake, Ashley. BA, U. Wyo., 1966, JD, 1968. Ptnr. Jones, Jones, Vines & Hunkins, Wheatland, Wyo., 1968—. Local rules com. U.S. Dist. Ct., 1990—; spl. counsel U. Wyo., Laramie, State of Wyo., Cheyenne; mem. faculty Western Trial Adv. Inst., 1993—95, Wyo. Supreme Ct. Commn. Jud. Salary and Benefits, 1996—98; owner Thunderhead Ranches, Albany and Platte Counties, Wyo.; gen. ptnr. Split Rock Land & Cattle Co.; spl. asst. atty. gen., Wyo.; founder, pres. Wyo. chpt. Federalist Soc. for Law and Pub. Policy Studies, 2003—04; vice chmn. bd. dirs. BH Inc. Chmn. Platte County Reps., Wheatland, 1972-74, chmn. adv. coun. Coll. Commerce and Industry, U. Wyo., 1978-79; bd. dirs. U. Wyo. Found., 1996-2002, Found. Laramie, 2002—, Laramie Peak Mus., 1989-2004; bd. advisors Am. Heritage Ctr., 1995-99; mem. Gov.'s Crime Commn., 1970-78; pres. Wyo. U. Alumni Assn., 1973-74, commr. Wyo. Aeronautics Commn., 1987-98; Rep. candidate for Gov. Wyo., 2002, Rep. nominee for Gov. Wyo., 2006; Wyo. del. Rep. Nat. Conv., 2004. With USMCR, 1956-60. Recipient Outstanding Advisor award Phi Delta Theta, 1968, Big Horn Mountain Roundup Pax Irvine award, 1989, Disting. Alumnus award U. Wyo., 2005. Fellow Am. Coll. Trial Lawyers (Wyo. state chmn. 1998-2000, nat. ethics com. 2000—), Internat. Soc. Barristers, Am. Bd. Trial Advs.; mem. ABA (aviation com. 1980-86, forum com. on constrn. industry litigation sect.), Wyo. Bar Assn. (chmn. grievance com. 1980-86, mem. com. on civil pattern jury instrns. 1999-2002, state bar-law sch. com., bench-bar rels. com.), Wyo. Trial Lawyers Assn. (past pres.) Office: Jones Jones Vines & Hunkins PO Drawer 189 9th and Maple Wheatland WY 82201

HUNLEY, JOHN DILLARD, retired historian, ombudsman; b. Bluefield, W.Va., Aug. 24, 1941; s. Henry Cleveland and Nell Hunley; m. Cheryl Jean Ewers, Mar. 15, 1967; children: Kelly Denise Humphrey, Michael Glen. PhD, U. of Va., 1973. Asst. prof. Allegheny Coll., Meadville, Pa., 1972—77; historian USAF, various locations, 1980—91, NASA Hdqs., Washington, 1991—95; chief historian NASA Dryden Flight Rsch. Ctr., Edwards, Calif., 1995—2001, human capital project mgr., 2003—06, ombudsman, 2005—06. Adj. prof. Solano C.C., Fairfield, Calif., 1988—89; Ramsey fellow Smithsonian Nat. Air and Space Mus., Washington, 2001—02; adj. prof. Calif. State U., San Bernardino, 2003—04. Author: (manuscript) The Development of Propulsion Technology for U.S. Space-Launch Vehicles, 1926-1991 (AIAA History Manuscript award, 2006), (chpt.) To Reach the High Frontier, (history/biography) The Life and Thought of Friedrich Engels: A Reinterpretation, (history) Boom and Bust: Society and Electoral Politics in the Duesseldorf Area, 1867-1878, The Development of Propulsion Technology for U.S. Space Launch Vehicles, 2007; contbr. articles to profl. jours. Capt. USMC, 1963—66. Recipient Woodrow Wilson fellowship, Woodrow Wilson Nat. Fellowship Found., 1963, Air Force History Program Monograph award, USAF History Program, 1990. Mem.: Soc. for the History of Tech., German Studies Assn., Am. Hist. Assn. Democrat. Avocation: travel. Home: 6211 Linden Ave Rialto CA 92377-4454 Home Phone: 909-820-7374. Personal E-mail: dillh@roadrunner.com. Business E-Mail: dill@hunleys.us.

HUNNEWELL, RICHARD, art historian, educator; s. Reginald and Frances Whittier Hunnewell; m. Anne White, July 22, 1967; children: Joshua Richard Whittier, Isaac Nicholas White. BA, Colby Coll., Waterville, Maine, 1967; MA, Boston U., 1972, PhD, 1983. Prof. art history Plymouth State U., NH, 1980—, coord. art history program, 1980—, chmn. gen. edn. com., 1981—87, chmn. silver arts ctr. arch. search com., 1993—96, co-dir. Frost Faculty Ctr. Learning and Tchg. Excellence, 2003—06. Mem. NH. Humanities Coun., Concord, 1990—94. Coord. Speare Hosp. Art Project, Plymouth, 1985—89; liturgy com. chmn. Ch. of Holy Spirit Episcopal, Plymouth, 1986—2006. Recipient Disting. Tchg. award, Plymouth State U., 1994, Whiting award for Rsch. and Travel, Whiting Found., 1995. Mem.: Phi Kappa Phi, Historians of Netherlandish Art, Coll. Art Assn., Delta Phi Alpha, Phi Beta Kappa. Avocations: travel, reading, gardening, cooking. Office: Plymouth State U D&M Bldg MSC 21 Plymouth NH 03264 Home Phone: 603-536-4015; Office Phone: 603-535-2546. Office Fax: 603-535-2938. Business E-Mail: rhunnewell@plymouth.edu.

HUNNICUTT, CHARLES ALVIN, lawyer; b. LaGrange, Ga., Dec. 7, 1950; s. William Oliver and Mary Olivia (Leggett) Hunnicutt. BS, Am. U., 1972; JD, U. Ga., 1975; LLM, U. Brussels, Belgium, 1976. Bar: Ga. 1975, D.C. 1978, U.S. Dist. Ct. D.C. 1978, U.S. Ct. Appeals (D.C. cir.) 1978, U.S. Ct. Internat. Trade 1980, U.S. Ct. Appeals (fed. cir.) 1981, U.S. Supreme Ct. 1981. Dep. dir. State of Ga. Office, Brussels, 1975-76; ops.

mgr. Presdl. Pers. The White House, Washington, 1976-77; exec. asst. to under sec. internat. trade U.S. Dept. Commerce, Washington, 1977-80; legal advisor to chmn. Internat. Trade Commn., Washington, 1980-87; ptnr. Robins, Kaplan, Miller & Ciresi, Washington, 1987—96, mng. ptnr., 1989—91, ptnr., 1999—2005, mem. exec. bd., 2003—04; advisor to Govt. of Ukraine on accession to Gen. Agreement on Tariffs and Trade World Trade Orgn., Kiev, 1994-95; asst. sec. for aviation and internat. affairs U.S. Dept. Transp., Washington, 1996-99; ptnr. Troutman Sanders LLP, Washington, 2005—. Adj. prof. Am. U. Coll. Law, Washington, 1988—91. Bd. visitors U. Ga. Sch. Law., 2000—04. Mem.: ABA (internat. trade steering com., air and space law forum), Internat. Bar Assn., Am. Soc. Internat. Law (exec. coun. 1999—2002, chair budget com. 2000—04, co-chair ann. meeting program com. 2006—07), Washington Fgn. Law Soc. (pres. 1987—88), Ga. State Bar, Bar Assn. D.C., Internat. Aviation Club (bd. dirs. 2001—06, pres. 2004—05). Democrat. Presbyterian. Office: Troutman Sanders LLP 401 9th St NW Ste 1000 Washington DC 20004-2134 Office Phone: 202-274-2957. Personal E-mail: hunnca@aol.com. Business E-Mail: charles.hunnicutt@troutmansanders.com.

HUNNICUTT, VICTORIA ANNE WILSON, educational consultant; b. Tyler, Tex., July 23, 1944; d. Leroy G. and N. Joseline (Bobo) Wilson; m. John Walter Hubble, July 29, 1967 (div. Oct. 1972); m. Buford D. Hunnicutt, Aug. 1, 1982. BA, Emory and Henry Coll., 1966; MEd, Mercer U., 1970; Ed Specialist, U. Ga., 1993; EdD, Ga. So. U., 1998. Tchr. Spanish/English Marion (Va.) Sr. H.S., 1966-67; tchr. Spanish Ballard Hudson Middle Sch., Macon, 1967-68; reading specialist Robins AFB Sch. System, Warner Robins, Ga., 1973-74, Spanish tchr., 1968-70, classroom tchr., 1970-86, computer/sci. specialist, 1986-90, prin. Robins Elem. Sch., 1991, curriculum coord., 1990-99; asst. prof. Early Childhood Ga. Coll. and State U., 1999—2004. Adj. prof. Tift Coll., Forsyth, Ga., 1985-88, Ft. Valley State Coll., 1993-99. Treas. Bibb County Dem. Women, Macon, Ga., 1986-88, membership chair 1989-93. Mem.: NSTA, ASCD, Nat. Coun. Tchrs. English, Aerospace Edn. Found. (nat. bd. trustees 1998—, nat. sec. 2000—03, Tchr. of Yr. 1995, Jane Shirley McGee award 1990, Medal of Merit 1990, Exceptional Svc. award 1997, George C. Hardy award for excellence in aerospace edn. 1999, Pres.'s citation 2001), Air Force Assn. (treas. chpt. 296 1989—91, v.p. 1991—92, v.p. for aerospace edn. chpt. 296 1991—2004, v.p. for aerospace edn. Ga. State AFA 1992—, regional v.p. for aerospace edn. 1997—), Ocmulgee Audubon Soc. (edn. chair 1986—93), Nat. Audubon Soc., HOPE Coun. (pres. 1994—95), Internat. Reading Assn., Ga. Coun. of Internat. Reading Assn., Bus. and Profl. Womens Club (Woman of Achievement local, regional, and state levels 1999), Phi Delta Kappa (chpt. sec. 2002—04). Democrat. Methodist. Avocations: reading, gardening. Office Phone: 478-745-0495, 478-745-0495. E-mail: vhunnictt@direcway.com.

HUNSAKER, BARRY, JR., lawyer; b. Mesa, Ariz., May 4, 1950; BS, Tex. A&M U., 1972, MS, 1973, PhD, 1976; JD, U. Tex., 1979. Bar: Tex. 1979. Ptnr. Vinson & Elkins, LLP; sr. v.p., gen. counsel EOG Resources, Inc., Houston, 1996—. Bd. dirs. Houston Pub. Libr. Mem.: State Bar Tex., Order of Coif, Tau Beta Pi, Sigma Gamma Tau, Phi Kappa Phi. Office: EOG Resources Inc 333 Clay St PO Box 4362 Houston TX 77002*

HUNSPERGER, ELIZABETH JANE, art and design consultant, educator; b. Phila., Aug. 30, 1938; d. Francis Charles and Elizabeth Julia Thorpe; m. Robert George Hunsperger, Sept. 13, 1958; 1 child, Lisa Marie. AA in Design, Santa Monica Coll., Calif., 1974; student, UCLA, 1975-76; BA in Art History, U. Del., Newark, 1978; postgrad., Rutgers U., 1978-81; MA in Edn., Del. State Coll., 1993; EdD in Ednl. Tech., U. Del., Newark, 2006. Designer Huntingdon Mills, Phila., 1960-63, Rothschild's, Ithaca, NY, 1963-65, Cornell U., Ithaca, 1965-67; freelance designer Malibu, Calif., 1967-76; art and design cons., lectr. Art & Sci. Assocs., Newark, Del., 1980—2001, Galena, Md., 2001—. Art tchr. Cath. Diocese of Wilmington, 1988-95, Kent County HS, Md., 2002-; art and spl. edn. tchr. Red Clay Consolidated Sch. Dist. A.I. duPont HS, Greenville, Del., 1995-97, Shorehaven Sch., Chesapeake City, Md., 1997-99, A.I. duPont Inst., Wilmington, Del., 1999—; with Leech Sch., 1994; cons. Arts and Sci. Assocs., Ednl. and Design Svcs., Newark, Del., 1995—; coord. Delmarva Edn. Action Learning Project; educator Kent County Pub. Schs., Md., 2002. Exhbns. include Malibu Art Assn. Show, 1973-74, Newark Art Show, 1987-88. Founding mem. bd. dirs., v.p. Newark Housing Ministry, Inc., 1983-94, pres., 1989-91; social concerns com. and drug and alcohol task force Del.; active Coun. Exceptional Children. Recipient Outstanding Svc. award YWCA, Santa Monica, Calif., 1972, award of recognition Mission-hurst, 1982, Gov.'s Vol. of the Yr. award State of Del., 1990. Mem. Nat. Art Edn. Assn., Am. Craft Coun., Art Educators of Del. (bd. dirs., pres.), Soroptimist Internat., Debutante Assembly Club (N.Y.C.). Episcopal. Home: 14040 S Mill Rd Galena MD 21635 Personal E-mail: elizabeth_hunsperger@usa.net.

HUNSTEIN, CAROL, state supreme court justice; b. Miami, Fla., Aug. 16, 1944; AA, Miami-Dade Jr. Coll., 1970; BS, Fla. Atlantic U., 1972; JD, Stetson U., 1976, LLD (hon.), 1993. Bar: Ga. 1976; U.S. Dist. Ct. 1978; U.S. Ct. Appeals 1978; U.S. Supreme Ct. 1989. Atty. Hunstein & Hunstein, Atlanta, 1976-84; judge Superior Ct. of Ga. (Stone Mt. cir.), 1984-92; justice Supreme Ct. of Ga., Atlanta, 1992—, presiding justice, 2005—. Chair Ga. Commn. on Gender Bias in the Judicial System 1988-1991; pres. Coun. of Superior Ct. Judges of Ga., 1990-91; adj. prof. Sch. Law Emory U., 1991—; former chair State Commn. on Child Support, 1992, 1993, 2000; former mem. Chief Justice's Commn. on Professionalism. Bd. dirs. Ga. Campaign Adolescent Pregnancy Prevention, 1992—. Recipient Clint Green Trial Advocacy award 1976, Women Who Made A Difference award Dekalb Women's Network 1986, Outstanding Svc. commendation Ga. Legislature, 1993, Cmty. Svc. award Emory U. Legal Assn. for Women Students., 1993, Gender Justice award Ga. Commn. Family Violence, 1999, Margaret Brent award ABA, 1999; inducted to Fla. Atlantic U. Hall of Fame, 1993. Mem. Ga. Assn. of Women Lawyers, Nat. Assn. of Women Judges (dir. 1988-90), Bleckley Inn of Ct., State Bar Ga. (mem. com. women and minorities in profession 2006, Commitment to Equality award). Office: Supreme Ct Ga 244 Washington Street Atlanta GA 30334-9007 Office Phone: 404-656-3475. Business E-Mail: hunsteic@gasupreme.us. E-mail: hunsteic@supreme.courts.state.ga.us.

HUNSUCKER, ROBERT DUDLEY, physicist, electrical engineer, educator, researcher; b. Portland, Oreg., Mar. 15, 1930; s. Robert Deets and Johnnie Morris (Kuykendal) H.; m. Judith Mary Cotter, Apr. 28, 1956 (dec. Nov. 1980); children: Edith Louise, Jeanne Marie, Cynthia Lee; m. Phyllis Marie Hoover, July 25, 1981. BS in Physics, Oreg. State U., 1954, MS in Physics, 1958; PhD in Elec. Engring., U. Colo., 1969. Asst. prof. Geophysics Inst. U. Alaska, Fairbanks, 1958-64, assoc. prof. Geophysics Inst., 1971-78, prof. Geophysics Inst., 1978-87, prof. emeritus physics and elec. engring., sr. cons., 1988—; physicist Nat. Bur. Stds., Boulder, Colo., 1964-67; sr. project leader ITS Office of Telecom. Sci., Boulder, 1967-71. Radio propagation cons.; adj. prof. Pa. State U., 1993, 1995—96, Oreg. Inst. Tech., 1995—2002. Author 2 Tech. Books; editor in chief: Radio Sci., 1995—2002, assoc. editor: URSI Radioscience Bull., 1998—2005; contbr. more than 100 articles to profl. jours. Served to lt., chief engr., boat group comdr. USNR, 1948—67. Fellow AAAS, IEEE (Alaska Engr. of Yr. Alaska sect. 1988, recipient outstanding achievement award IEEE region 6 1988); mem. Am. Geophys. Union, U.S. Commn. Internat. Union of Radio Sci., Sigma Xi, Sigma Pi Sigma, Eta Kappa Nu. Republican. Lutheran. Avocations: fishing, radio, writing, flying. Office Phone: 541-885-8786. Business E-Mail: rdhrpc1@charter.net.

HUNSUCKER, (CARL) WAYNE, architectural firm executive, educator; b. Morganton, NC, Feb. 16, 1945; s. Earnest Howard and Reba (Laughridge) H.; m. Edith Mabel Whittaker Guisto, May 23, 1990; children: Wendy Edith Guisto, Bret Thomas Guisto. Student, Old Dominion Coll.; BFA, Coll. William and Mary, 1968; BArch with Distinction, U. Ariz., 1975. Lic. architect, Calif., Nev., Idaho, Oreg., Wash., Ariz.; cert. Nat. Coun. Archtl. Registration Bds. Archtl. draftsman Woodmoor Corp., Colorado Springs, Colo., 1971-72; architect-in-training James Gresham & Assocs., Tuscon, 1975-76; prin., pres. Hummel Hunsucker Archs., Boise, Idaho, 1976—, prin.-in-charge office ops. Spokane, Wash., 1998—. Part-time draftsperson Forrest Coile & Assocs., Newport News, Va., 1959-63; asst. instr. U. Ariz. Prin. works include U.S. Courthouse and Fed. Office Bldg., Boise, Idaho, Earl F. Chandler Bldg., Boise, Benton County Jud. Facility, San Francisco, Orchard Pl. Office Complex, Boise, 1st Security Bank addition and remodel, Nampa Main Br., Blue Cross Idaho, Idaho N.G. Armory Annex, Boise, various bldgs. Mt. Home AFB (Citation and Design awards Dept. Air Force), Mountain Home Town Jr. High Sch. addition; co-author: (text books) Architectural Drafting, 1976, Neighborhood Planning - Case Study of the Sam Hughes Neighborhood. Bd. dirs. Ada County Hist. Soc., 1989-90, Boise; mem. Lincoln Day Banquet Com., Boise, 1984-86; mem. licensing bd. Idaho Outfitters and Guides, 1996—; bd. mem. Bldg. Owners and Mgrs. Assn., Boise chpt., 1998. 1st lt. U.S. Army, 1969-71, Vietnam. Recipient Citation award USAF, Best Stand Alone Bldg. award TAC Air Force, 1984, Henry Adams Fund for Excellence award. Mem. AIA (state pres. 1990, pres. ctrl. sect. Idaho chpt. 1988, Silver medal 1976), Nat. Coun. Archtl. Registration Bds. Avocations: bird hunting, fishing, boating. Office: Hummel Architects PA 2785 N Bogus Basin Rd Boise ID 83702-0911

HUNT, ALBERT R., editor; b. Charlottesville, Va., Dec. 4, 1942; s. Albert R. and Ann G. (Lillard) H.; m. Judy C. Woodruff, Apr. 5, 1980; children: Jeffrey Woodruff, Benjamin Woodruff, Lauren Ann Lee. BA in Polit. Sci., Wake Forest U., 1965. Reporter Wall St. Jour., NYC, 1965-67, Boston, 1967-69, Washington, 1969-71, polit. reporter, 1972-83, bur. chief, 1983-93, exec. Washington editor, 1993—2005; mng. editor, govt. reporting Bloomberg News, Washington, 2005—. Author: (with others) American Elections of 1980, American Elections of 1982, American Elections of 1984, Elections American Style, 1987; participant in TV program CNN Capital Gang. Bd. visitors Wake Forest U., Winston-Salem, N.C., 1979-85, trustee, 1987; sr. adv. bd. Shorenstein Barone Ctr. for Press, Politics and Pub. Policy, Harvard U., Cambridge, Mass.; pres. Dow Jones Newspaper Fund, 1993-2002. Mem. Am. Polit. Sci. Assn. (congl. fellowship adv. com. 1981—). Office: Bloomberg News 1399 New York Ave NW Washington DC 20005

HUNT, BARNABAS JOHN, priest, religious organization administrator; b. Sayre, Pa., Jan. 6, 1937; s. Clarence Elmer and Margarite Frances (Bennett) H. BS in Edn., Pa. State U., 1958; postgrad., Elmira Coll., 1960—61, Portland State U., 1969—70, Clackamas CC, 1970—71, Mt. Hood CC, 1973—74. Joined Soc. St. Paul, 1961, ordained priest Episcopal Ch. 1984, installed and seated as hon. canon of St. Paul's Cathedral, San Diego, 2000. HS tchr. Pub. Schs., Candor, NY, 1958-61; headmaster St. Luke's Sch., Soc. St. Paul, Gresham, Oreg., 1961-66; lic. adminstr. St. Jude's Nursing Home, Inc., Portland and Sandy, Oreg., 1964-73; assoc. rector Soc. St. Paul, Palm Desert, Calif., 1975-89, rector, 1989—; brother in charge St. Paul's Press, Sandy, Oreg., 1969-76. Treas. Desert Samaritans for Elderly, Palm Desert, Calif., 1997-98. Mem. Tri-County Bd., Oreg. Agy. on Aging, 1971-76; pres. Sandy C. of C., 1972; mem. Sandy City Coun., 1975-76, candidate for City Coun., City of Palm Desert, 1986; pres. St. Jude's Home, Inc., Oreg., 1989—; pres. adv. bd. The Carlotta, 1985-92, vice chmn. resource devel. fund bd., 1993-97; bd. dirs. St. Paul's Episcopal Home, Inc., San Diego, 2000—, Campus Redevel. Com., 2005; chpt. mem. St. Paul's Episcopal Cathedral, San Diego, 2000—; bd. dirs. Uptown Faith Cmty. Svc. Ctr., San Diego, 2004—, Dorcas Ho., Tijuana, Mex., 2005—. Fellow Am. Coll. Health Care Adminstrs. (pres. Coll. Found. 1984-87); mem. Nat. Guild Churchmen (pres. 1982—), Conf. on Religious Life in Anglican Communion (v.p. 1992-97, archivist 1982—). Episcopalian. Home and Office: Soc of St Paul Inc PO Box 34548 San Diego CA 92163-4548 Fax: 619-542-8585. E-mail: anbssp@earthlink.net.

HUNT, BONNIE, actress; b. Chgo., Sept. 22, 1961; m. John Murphy, July 8, 1988 (separated). Actor: (films) Rain Man, 1988, Beethoven, 1992, Dave, 1993, Beethoven's 2nd, 1993, Only You, 1994, Now and Then, 1995, Jumanji, 1995 (Saturn award for best actress), Getting Away with Murder, 1996, Jerry Maguire, 1996, Kissing a Fool, 1998, A Bug's Life (voice), 1998, Random Hearts, 1999, The Green Mile, 1999, Monsters, Inc. (voice), 2001, Stolen Summer, 2002, Cheaper By the Dozen, 2003, Loggerheads, 2005, Cheaper by the Dozen 2, 2005, (voice) Cars, 2006; (TV series) Davis Rules, 1992, The Building, 1993; actor, prodr. The Bonnie Hunt Show, 1995 (Founder's award Viewers for Quality TV awards 1996); actor, dir., writer (films) Return to Me, 1998 (TV series) Life With Bonnie, 2002-04. Office: Creative Artists Agy 9830 Wilshire Blvd Beverly Hills CA 90212-1825

HUNT, BONNIE JO, art association administrator, writer, soprano; d. Guy Lester II and Arlene McLaughlin Robbins; m. Lawrence John Hunt, Aug. 23, 1968. BA, U. Mont., Missoula, 1966; MA, Am. U., Cairo, 1978; studied with William Pearce Herman, studied with Julia Monroe, studied with Anatole Orfeonov, studied with Anatole Orfeonov. Hwy. dept. hostess State of Mont., Helena, 1966—67; arts specialist Ford Found., NYC, 1978—80; founder, pres., CEO Artists of Indian Am., Inc., Albuquerque, 1980—. Panelist, reader NEA, Washington, 1987—93; panelist future funding for the arts MIT, Boston, 1994; founder, exec. editor Mad Bear Press Publ., Albuquerque, 1997—. Singer (soprano): San Francisco Opera Co., 1967—68; co-author: The Lone Wolf Clan, 11 vols., 1997—2007. Vol. in country tng. Peace Corps, Zaria, Nigeria, 1968—69; vol. pub. rels. tng. Indian Pueblo Cultural Ctr., Albuquerque, 1999—2007. Named Miss. Mont. Centennial Queen, State of Mont., 1964, Guest of Honor, Rio Grande Valley Celtic Festival, Albuquerque, 2002; named one of Outstanding Am. Women, AARP, 1989. Avocations: reading, sewing, hiking, dance. Office: Artists Indian Am Inc 6636 Mossman Pl NE Albuquerque NM 87110

HUNT, CARLTON CUYLER, JR., physiologist, educator; b. Waterbury, Conn., Aug. 11, 1918; s. Carlton Cuyler and Adele F. (Weidemann) H.; m. Marion Hall, July 3, 1965. BA, Columbia U., 1939; MD, Cornell U., 1942. Intern N.Y. Hosp., 1942-43, asst. resident, 1946; research fellow Cornell U., 1946-48, instr. physiology, 1948; sr. fellow NRC, 1948-52; asst. prof. Johns Hopkins, 1951-52; assoc. Rockefeller Inst., 1952-55; prof. physiology Albert Einstein Coll. Medicine, 1955-57; prof. physiology, chmn. dept. U. Utah, 1957-64, Yale Sch. Medicine, 1964, 68; prof. and head dept. physiology and biophysics Washington U. Sch. Medicine, St. Louis, 1967-83, prof., 1983—95; vis. prof. (now emeritus) Univ. NC, Chapel Hill, 1995—. Hon. research assoc. U. Coll., London, Eng., 1962-63; vis. prof. Collège de France, Paris, 1984-86; mem. adv. panel NSF, 1958-59, NIH, 1959-62. Served as med. officer AUS, 1943-46. Fellow Am. Acad. Arts & Scis. Spl. research sensory receptors.*

HUNT, CRAIG A., lawyer, paper company executive; BA in Econ., U. Kansas, JD. Atty., gen. corp. law Shook, Hardy & Bacon, Kansas City, Mo.; sr. counsel, asst. sec. Jefferson Smurfit, 1993—98; sr. v.p., sec., gen. counsel Smurfit-Stone Container Corp., Chgo., 1998—. Office: Smurfit-Stone Container 150 N Michigan Ave Chicago IL 60691*

HUNT, DAVID EVANS, lawyer; b. Wilkes-Barre, Pa., May 10, 1953; s. James Dixon and Twyla (Burkert) H.; m. Denise M. Barbera, Aug. 21, 1976 (div. 1984); 1 child Christopher Evans; m. Elizabeth S. Pearce, Sept. 5, 1987; children: Alexandra Stacy, Thomas Dixon. AB, Dartmouth Coll., 1975; JD, U. Chgo., 1978. Bar: N.Y. 1979, U.S. Dist. Ct. (so. and ea. dists.) N.Y. 1979, Maine 1982, U.S. Dist. Ct. Maine 1982, U.S. Tax Ct. 1982, Fla. 1999. Assoc. Debevoise & Plimpton, NYC, 1978-81; ptnr. Pierce, Atwood, Scribner, Allen, Smith & Lancaster, Portland, Maine, 1981-92, McCandless & Hunt, Portland, Maine, 1992-97; sole practitioner Portland, 1997—. Adj. prof. U. Maine Law Sch., Portland, 1991—92, Portland, 2000—02. Co-author: Maine Will and Trust Forms Annotated, 1994, Maine Estate Administration, 1996. Officer, dir. Maine Estate Planning Coun., Portland, 1986-94. Fellow: Am. Coll. Trust and Estate Counsel (state chair 1997—2001, regent 2001—03); mem.: ABA, Cumberland County Bar Assn., N.Y. State Bar Assn., Maine State Bar Assn., Fla. Bar, Woodlands Club. Roman Catholic. Avocations: classical Latin, skiing. Home: 6 Highland St Portland ME 04103-3005 Office: 511 Congress St Portland ME 04101-3411 Office Phone: 207-773-5100. Business E-Mail: dhunt@mainewills.com.

HUNT, DAVID FORD, lawyer; b. Ft. Worth, Apr. 7, 1931; s. John Greffrey and Bernice (Ford) H. BS, North Tex. State U., 1954; JD, Vanderbilt U., 1960. Bar: Tex. 1961, U.S. Dist. Ct. (no. dist.) Tex., U.S. Dist. Ct. (we. dist.) Tex., U.S. Dist. Ct. (ea. dist.) Tex.U.S. Ct. Appeals (5th and 11th cir.), U.S. Supreme Ct. Law clk. to U.S. dist. judge No. Dist. Tex., 1960-62; pvt. practice, Dallas, 1962-94; ptnr. Jenkens & Gilchrist, P.C., Dallas, 1980-92, of counsel, 1993-94; atty. pvt. practice, Denton County, Tex., 1995—. Chmn. com. on admissions Dist. 6 Tex. State Bd. Law Examiners, 1978-87 Contbr. articles to legal jours. Co-chmn. pollwatchers com. Dallas County Republican Com., 1964; Sec. Bootstrap Ranch, 1972-74; pres. So. Methodist U. Lambda Chi Edn. Found., 1972-76, dir. Internat. Lambda Chi Edn. Found., 1966-68. Served with AUS, 1954-56. Mem. Tex. Bar Assn., Tex. Bar Found., Vanderbilt U. Law Sch. Alumni Assn. (pres. Dallas chpt. 1972-75), Lambda Chi (chancellor 1966-68). Home and Office: 1849 Bridle Bit Rd Flower Mound TX 75022-6571

HUNT, DONALD FREDERICK, chemistry professor; b. Hyannis, Mass., Apr. 25, 1941; s. Sheldon Leslie and Vena Elizabeth (Knowles) H.; m. Linda Lee Carson, June 12, 1965; children: Amanda Montgomery, Caroline Moore. BS in Chemistry, U. Mass., 1962, PhD in Chemistry, 1967. Asst. prof. chemistry U. Va., Charlottesville, 1967-73, assoc. prof., 1973-78, prof., 1978-93, Univ. prof. chemistry and pathology, 1993—. Recipient Charles H. Stone award ACS-Piedmont Sect., 1990, Va.'s Outstanding Scientist award Va. Sci. Mus., 1992, Pehr Edman award Methods in Protein Sequence Analysis Conf., 1992, Disting. Contbn. award Am. Soc. for Mass Spectrometry, 1994, The Christian B. Anfinsen award Protein Soc., 1996, Thomson medal award Internat. Soc. Mass Spectrometry, 2000. Mem. Am. Chem. Soc. (Chem. Instrumentation award 1997, Frank H. Field and Joe L. Franklin award 2000). Office: U Va Chemistry Dept McCormick Rd Charlottesville VA 22901 E-mail: dfh@virginia.edu.

HUNT, EARL STEPHEN, federal agency administrator; b. Chattanooga, Nov. 28, 1948; s. Earl Gladstone, Jr. and Mary Anne (Kyker) Hunt; m. Edeltraut Gilgan, Sept. 6, 1986. BA with honors, Emory and Henry Coll., 1971; MA, Am. U., 1973; PhD, U. Va., 1979; MLS, CAS, Syracuse U., 2000. Instr. Fla. So. Coll., Lakeland, 1980-81; edn. cons. Nashville, NYC, 1980-82; editor, cons. Washington, 1982-86; sr. rsch. analyst US Dept. Edn., Washington, 1986—94, sr. internat. rels. specialist internat. affairs staff Office Sec., 2002—; planning dir. Nat. Libr. Edn., 1995—2002; mgr. US Network Edn. Info., 1997—. Mem. drug prevention task force US Dept. Edn., Washington, 1986—89; cons. US Dept. Labor, Washington, 1990—, NSF, Washington, 1990—, US Trade Rep., Washington, 1999—, US Dept. Homeland Security, Washington, 2001—; mgr. US network for edn. info. UNESCO, Coun. Europe, 1997—; US expert, adviser G8 Negotiations, 2005—06. Co-editor: (book) The Apocalyptic Premise: Nuclear Arms Debated, 1982; author: Drug Prevention Curricula, 1993, Mapping the World of Education: The Comparative Database System, 1994, Professional Workers as Learners, 1992, A Guide to the International Interpretation of U.S. Education Program Data, 1993; co-author: Classification of Instructional Programs (CIP), 1990, 2000; contbr. articles to profl. jours. Mem. Sangamore-Brooks Ln. Citizens' Assn., Bethesda, Md., 1990—. Grantee, USIA, 1982. Mem.: Nat. Assn. Fgn. Student Advisers-Assn. Internat. Edn., European Assn. Internat. Edn., Nat. Contract Mgmt. Assn., Phi Delta Kappa, Blue Key, Phi Gamma Mu, Alpha Phi Omega (life). Methodist. Avocations: reading, travel, gardening, cooking. Home: 5209 Sangamore Rd Bethesda MD 20816-2324 Office: US Dept Edn Internat Affairs Office 105 RM 6W108 400 Maryland Ave SW Washington DC 20202 Office Phone: 202-401-3710. Business E-Mail: stephen.hunt@ed.gov.

HUNT, EFFIE NEVA, retired dean, literature educator; b. Waverly, Ill., June 19, 1922; d. Abraham Luther and Fannie Ethel (Ritter) H. AB, MacMurray Coll. for Women, 1944; MA, U. Ill., 1945, PhD, 1950; postgrad., Columbia U., 1953, Univ. Coll., U. London, 1949-50. Keypunch operator U.S. Treasury, 1945; spl. librarian Harvard U., 1947, U. Pa., 1948; Instr. English U. Ill., 1950-51; librarian Library of Congress, Washington, 1951-52; asst. prof. English Mankato State Coll., 1952-59; prof. Radford Coll., 1959-63, chmn. dept. English, 1961-63; prof. Ind. State U., 1963-86; dean Ind. State U. (Coll. Arts and Scis.), 1974-86, dean and prof. emerita, 1987—. Author articles in field. Fulbright grantee, 1949-50 Mem. AAUP, MLA, Nat. Council Tchrs. English, Am. Assn. Higher Edn., Audubon Soc. Home: 3365 Wabash Ave Apt 4 Terre Haute IN 47803-1655 Office: Ind State U Root Hall Eng Dept Terre Haute IN 47809-0001

HUNT, ELIZABETH HOPE, psychologist; b. Hattiesburg, Miss., Oct. 14, 1943; d. Emory Spear and I. Elizabeth (Burkett) Hunt; m. John Volney Allcott, III, Sept. 9, 1978; children: Hunt Volney Allcott, Elizabeth Hunt Allcott. AB, Sweet Briar Coll., 1965; MSW, U. Pa., 1971; PhD, U. Oreg., 1980. Lic. psychologist Oreg. Peace Corps vol., Santiago, Chile, 1967—69; civil rights specialist Region III HEW, Phila., 1971—74; doctoral fellow Rehab. Rsch. and Tng. Ctr., U. Oreg., Eugene, 1974—77; intern Phila. Child Guidance Ctr., U. Pa., 1977—78; psychologist in pvt. practice Eugene, 1980—. Rschr., civic activist. Contbr. articles to profl. jours. Bd. dirs. Lane County Relief Nursery for Abused and Neglected Children, 1981—84; activist, bd. dirs. Eugene Edn. Found., 1993—2002; vol. psychologist Friends of Torture Survivors, 1993—2004; founder Allcott/Hunt Scholarship for Recent Immigrants; philanthroper Wellsprings Quaker Friends Sch., Eugene; steering com. clerk Quaker North Pacific Yearly Meeting Religious Soc. of Friends, 2003—05. Grantee, Nat. Inst. Handicapped Rsch., 1977—79. Mem.: Lane County Psychologists Assn., Oreg. Psychol. Assn., APA. Home: 2650 Cresta De Ruta St Eugene OR 97403-1849 E-mail: bhunt5425@comcast.net.

HUNT, ELLEN, minister, evangelist; b. Ocala, Fla., Nov. 7, 1951; d. Roosevelt Sr. and Vera Hunt; m. Earmon Rucker, Jr. (div.); children: Angela Brown Jesaly, Ruby Earmon Rucker III. At, CFCC C.C., Ocala, Fla., PFGC Biblical Coll. Lic. pastor, evangelist. Pastor Salvation and Praise Ministry, Winston-Salem, NC, PFGC Ministry, Ocala, Fla., Ch. of Living God, United Holiness. Evangelist PFGC Ministry, 1980—; convalescent visitor Salvation and Praise Ministry, Winston-Salem, NC, 2001—; homeless ministry. Democrat. Pentacostal. Avocations: visiting sick and elderly, praying for sick and afflicted. Home: 1829 Pleasant St Winston Salem NC 27107

HUNT, EVERETT CLAIR, engineering educator, researcher, consultant; b. Stamford, Conn., Dec. 28, 1928; s. Benjamin G. and Dorothy (Griffith) H.; m. Jay Kilby, July 12, 1952; children: Gerilyn, Scott, Erik. BS in

Engring., US Mcht. Marine Acad., Kings Port, NY, 1951; MS in Engring., Rensselaer Polytech. Inst., Troy, NY, 1958; MS, Northeastern U., Boston, 1972; DSc, Eurotech., Palo Alto, Calif., 1988. Registered profl. engr., Mass.; chartered engr., U.K. Engr. GE, Schenectady, NY, 1954-65, project mgr. Lynn, Mass., 1965-66, cons. Schenectady, 1966-67, engring. mgr. Portland, Maine, 1967-69, mgr. quality control Lynn, 1969-75; dir. Sun Shipbuilding, Chester, Pa., 1975-79; prof. U.S. Mcht. Marine Acad., Kings Point, NY, 1979-84; dir. rsch., prof. Webb Inst., Glen Cove, NY, 1984-92; pvt. practice cons., 1992—. Adj. prof. Widner Coll., Chester, Pa., 1978-79; cons. engr. 1993-2005. Author: Marine Engineering Economics and Cost Analysis, 1994; editor, author: Modern Marine Engineering, Vol. I, 1999, Vol. II, 2002; patentee forced circulation steam generator. Lt. USN, 1951-52, Korea. Recipient Bronze medal U.S. Dept. Transp., 1984. Fellow Inst. Marine Engrs.; mem. Pan-Am. Inst. Naval Engrs. Republican. Anglican. Avocations: hiking, mountain climbing, sailing, canoeing. Home and Office: PO Box 308 Warner NH 03278-0308

HUNT, FRANCIS HOWARD, retired navy laboratory official; b. Emporia, Kans., Apr. 12, 1919; s. Frederick Raymond and Mabel (Holmes) Hunt; m. Kathleen McLean, June 4, 1945 (dec. Sept. 1992); children: Deborah Mary, Laurie Jane, Peter Raymond; m. Mary Alice Fish, July 16, 1993. BA, Wesleyan U., 1941. Supr. records Columbia U. divsn. War Research, New London, Conn., 1941—43, tech. editor, writer, 1943—44; with U.S. Navy Underwater Sound Lab., Fort Trumbull, New London, Conn., 1945—70, successively asst. to asst. tech. dir., 1945—47, staff asst. to tech. dir., head tech. info. divsn., 1947—60, assoc. tech. dir. for administrn., 1960—70; assoc. dir. center operations Naval Underwater Systems Ctr., Newport, RI, 1970—76. Mem. East Lyme Zoning Bd. of Appeals, 1956—, sec., 1960—78, chmn., 1978—97; past charter mem. East Lyme Flood and Erosion Control Bd.; mem. Conn. Fedn. Planning and Zoning Agencies. Bd. dir. East Lyme Pub. Libr., 1962—83, Child Guidance Clin. So.Eastern Conn., 1959—62; planning com. East Lyme Jr. HS; past mem. Niantic (Conn.) Boy Scout Com.; justice of peace, 1985—; past mem. East Lyme Rep. Town Com.; bd. dir. East Lyme Nursing Assn., 1964—66. With AUS, 1944—45. Decorated Purple Heart, Bronze Star Medal WWII, Battle of the Bulge, Conn. Veterans Wartime Svc. Medal; named Melvin Jones Fellow for Dedicated Humanitarian Services, Lions Clubs Internat. Found., 1997; recipient Outstanding mem. Town Commn., East Lyme C. of C., 1972, 1981. Mem.: VFW (life), IEEE (life), Disabled Am. Vets., Nat. Assn. Ret. Fed. Employees, Gov. William Bradford Compact, Conn. Soc. SAR (mem. bd. mgrs. 1980—87, registrar 1984—87, Patriot medal 1987, Silver good citizenship medal 1992), Conn. Huguenot Soc. (pres. 1990—96), Conn., Lebanon, Columbia hist. socs., Soc. Colonial Wars in Conn., Soc. of Cin. in Conn., Soc. Mayflower Descendents in Conn., Nat. Huguenot Soc. (chaplain gen. 1993—95), New Eng. Historic Geneal. Soc., R.I. Geneal. Soc., Conn. Soc. Genealogists, Lions (pres. Niantic club 1959—60). Baptist. Home: 2 Strawberry Ln Niantic CT 06357-1936

HUNT, FRANKLIN GRIGGS, lawyer; b. Jenks, Okla., Dec. 21, 1930; s. John Wesley and Alta (Johnson) H.; m. Marilyn Glenn Maxfield, July 12, 1958; children— Laura Suzanne, Molly Frances. AB, Harvard U., 1952, LL.B., 1959. Bar: N.Y., 1960. Assoc. Lord, Day and Lord, NYC, 1959-64, ptnr., 1965-93, of counsel, 1993-94; sr. advisor Morgan, Lewis & Bockius, NYC, 1994—. Assoc. editor Am. Maritime Cases, 1982-92; contbr. articles to profl. jours. Mem. adv. bd. Inst. Intercultural Studies, NYC, 1985—; bd. dirs. Friends of Archaeology, Office Archaeol. Studies, Mus. N.Mex. Lt. (j.g.) USN, 1952—55. Mem. ABA, N.Y.C. Bar Assn., Maritime Law Assn. U.S., AAAS, Am. Phys. Soc., Soc. for Am. Archaeology. Avocations: ballet, archaeology. Home: 43 W 61st St Apt 22M New York NY 10023-7618 Home Phone: 212-956-3420. Personal E-mail: hunt@cybermesa.com.

HUNT, FREDERICK TALLEY DRUM, JR., association executive; b. Martinique, French West Indies, Sept. 19, 1947; s. Frederick Talley Drum and Eleanor Conly H.; m. Acacia Lynn Graham, Dec. 4, 1976. Ba, Vanderbilt U., 1970. Medal hon. specialist and ceremonies U.S. Army, Washington, 1971—73; dir. program devel. manufactured Housing Inst., Washington, 1973-74; pres. Hunt Assocs., Washington, 1974-75; asst. dir. field svcs. Nat. Assn. Life Underwriters, 1975-77; dir. comm., govt. liaison Am. Acad. Actuaries, Washington, 1977-80; pres. Soc. Profl. Benefit Adminstrs., 1980—. Pres., owner Hunt Mgmt. Sys., 1982—; advisor White House, Congress, fgn. govts., others; spkr. in field. Contbr. articles to profl. jours. Mem.: Soc. Cin., Miles River Yacht Club, Met. Club. Home: Westmoreland Hills 5308 Blackistone Rd Bethesda MD 20816-1803 also: 228 Riverside Rd Edgewater MD 21037-1505 Office: 2 Wisconsin Cir Ste 670 Chevy Chase MD 20815

HUNT, GEORGE WAYNE, real estate appraiser; b. Beaumont, Tex., Jan. 21, 1932; s. James Crittenden Hunt and Mary Ahava Godkin; m. Eva Patrice Tolman, Aug. 5, 1961; children: Scott Norman, Sharon Leslie. BS, Calif. Poly Tech., Pomona, 1964; MA in Mgmt., Nat. U., San Diego, 1986; JD, Newport U., Newport Beach, Calif., 1998. Mfg. liaison Aerojet Gen. Corp., Sacramento, 1956—61; appraiser County of San Diego, 1964—82; real estate appraiser ind. contractor, San Diego, 1982—92. With USN, 1949—53. Mem.: VFW, Am. Legion, Mensa. Avocations: reading, puzzles, exercise, singing, motorcycling. Home: 14712 Roberto Rio Rd Poway CA 92064 Personal E-mail: wphunt@sbcglobal.net.

HUNT, GEORGE WILLIAM, priest, magazine editor; b. NYC, Jan. 22, 1937; s. George Aloysius and Grace Winifred (Jordan) H. AB, Fordham U., 1961, MA, 1963; PhL, Woodstock Coll., 1961, STL, 1967; STM, Yale U., 1968; PhD, Syracuse U., 1974; DHL (hon.), Spring Hill Coll., 1991, Loyola Coll., Balt., 1993, Fairfield U., 1996. Joined S.J., 1954; ordained priest Roman Cath. Ch., 1967. Asst. prof. St. Peter's Coll., Jersey City, 1968-70; assoc. prof. Le Moyne Coll., Syracuse, N.Y., 1973-81; vis. prof. Georgetown U., Washington, 1983-84; pres., editor in chief Am. mag., NYC, 1984-98; dir. Arch. Hughes Inst. of Religion and Culture Fordham U., Bronx, N.Y., 1999—. Author: (literary criticsm) John Updike and the Three Great Secret Things, 1980 (Christianity lit. award 1981), John Cheever: The Hobgoblin Company of Love, 1983.Y Trustee Boston Coll., 1985—, Carnegie Coun. on Ethics and Internat. Affairs, 1986—, Holy Cross Coll., Worcester, Mass., 1990—, Loyola Coll., Balt., 1994—, Le Moyne Coll., Syracuse, 1995—; trustee emeritus U. Detroit, 1984—. Roman Catholic. Home and Office: Fordham U Arch Hughes Inst Religion and Culture 441 E Fordham Rd Bronx NY 10458-5149

HUNT, GORDON, lawyer; b. LA, Oct. 26, 1934; s. Howard Wilson and Esther Nita (Dempsey) H. BA in Polit. Sci, UCLA, 1956; JD, U. So. Calif., 1959. Bar: Calif. 1960. Law clk. Appellate Dept., Superior Ct. LA County, 1959-60; mem. firm Behymer & Hoffman, LA, 1960-65; partner firm Behymer, Hoffman & Hunt, LA, 1965-68; ptnr. firm Munns, Kofford, Hoffman, Hunt & Throckmorton, Pasadena, 1969—90; mem. Hunt, Ortman, Blasco Palff and Rossell Inc., Pasadena, 1990—2007, Hunt, Ortman, Palff, Nieves, Lubka, Darling and Mah, Inc., Pasadena, 2007—. Lectr. UCLA, various yrs.; chmn. legal adv. com. Assoc. Gen. Contractors Calif., 1985; arbitrator LA Superior Ct., State of Calif. Author: Construction Surety and Bonding Handbook; co-author: California Construction Law, 16th edit.; contbr. numerous articles to legal jours. Named a Super Lawyer in Constrn. Law, 2004, 2005, 2006, 2007. Mem. ABA, Calif. Bar Assn. (del. Conv. 1964-69), LA County Bar Assn. (real property com. 1965-66, exec. com. 1970-72, sec. 1972-73, vice chmn. 1972-75, chmn. real property sect. 1975-76, co-chmn. continuing edn. bar com. 1969-71, Outstanding Real Estate Lawyer award 2000, Outstanding Achievement in Constrn. Law 2004, named one of Best Lawyers in Am., 2006), Am. Arbitration Assn. (arbitrator, mediator). Office: 301 N Lake Ave Fl 7 Pasadena CA 91101-4108 Office Phone: 626-440-5200. Business E-Mail: hunt@huntortmann.com.

HUNT, GREGORY C., music educator; b. Tawas City, Mich., May 18, 1963; s. Charles A. and A. Eleanor Hunt; m. Diana L. Shampo, June 14, 1986; children: Amber M., Michelle L., Bethany A. MusB in edn., Northern Mich. U., Marquette, 1985. Cert. music tchr. Mich., 1985. Dir. bands Atlanta Cmty. Schs., Mich., 1985—89, Gwinn Area Pub. Schs., Mich., 1989—95, Iron Mountain Pub. Schs., Mich., 1995—97; dean music camp Michigamme United Meth. Inst., Mich., 1995—2007; dir. bands Norway-Vulcan Area Schs., Mich., 1997—. Choral dir. Trinity United Meth. Ch., Iron Mountain, 1998—2007, computer tech. specialist, 2002—. Musician: (drummer) Phil Lynch Jazz Trio, (bass trombonist) Jimmy Dorsey Orch.; dir.: (jazz bands) opening for Glenn Miller, Jimmy Dorsey, Ed Shaughnessy and Maynard Ferguson, 2001—06. Mem. mission team Appalachia Svc. Project, 1993—98; choir dir. Trinity United Meth. Ch., Iron Mountain, 1998—2007. Named Most Influential Educator, Kellogg Found. Mem.: Wis. Sch. Music Assn. (adjudicator 2001—, Menominee River Conf. Honors Jazz Band Dir. 2006), Mich. Sch. Band and Orch. Assn. (assoc.; adjudicator 1993—2007, Dist. 14 Tchr. of Yr. 2000), Mich. Edn. Assn., Lions Clubs Internat. (pres. 2006—07). Methodist. Avocations: jazz drumming, restoring classic cars, camping, boating. Home: 713 Maple St Norway MI 49870 Home Phone: 906-563-5278; Office Phone: 906-563-9542 31. Personal E-mail: ghunt@norwaymi.com. Business E-Mail: ghunt@norway.k12.mi.us.

HUNT, H(AROLD) KEITH, retired business management educator, marketing consultant; b. Apr. 16, 1938; married; 8 children. BS in Mktg. and Mgmt., U. Utah, 1961, MBA, 1962; PhD in Mktg., Northwestern U., 1972. Instr. Imperial Valley Coll., El Centro, Calif., 1962-64; teaching asst. Northwestern U., 1964-66, instr., 1966-67; asst. prof. bus. adminstrn. and journalism U. Iowa, 1967-73; cons., staff mem. Office Policy Planning and Evaluation, FTC, Washington, 1973-74; assoc. prof. bus. adminstrn. U. Wyo., Laramie, 1974-75; assoc. prof. bus. mgmt. Brigham Young U., Provo, Utah, 1975-78, prof., 1978—2005. Participant, chmn. various workshops, seminars, meetings; research expert, cons., expert witness on consumer research FTC, 1974-81; cons., expert witness div. drug advt. FDA, 1975-82; cons., adv. on consumer research Consumer and Corp. Affairs Can., 1978-82. Editor: Advances in Consumer Research, vol. 5, 1977; co-editor conf. proc. (with Frances Magrabi) Interdisciplinary Consumer Research, 1980, (with Ralph Day) Consumer Satisfaction/Dissatisfaction and Complaining Behavior, 8 vols., 1975-85, Jour. 1988-2005 Elected to Orem City Coun., Utah, 1986-93. Recipient Maeser Research award Brigham Young U., 1981; scholar-in-residence adv. dept. U. Ill., 1979; vis. research scholar Coll. Home Econs., U. Ala., 1980; vis. research scholar dept. mktg. and transp. U. Tenn., 1981; NSF grantee, 1975-77 Mem. Assn. Consumer Research (pres. 1979, exec. sec. 1983-2000, 1st Disting. Svc. award 1989), Am. Acad. Advt. (pres. 1982-83, exec. sec. 1983-86, elected fellow 1987), Am. Mktg. Assn., Soc. Consumer Psychology, Am. Council on Consumer Interests, Beta Gamma Sigma, Kappa Tau Alpha, Omicron Delta Epsilon, Phi Kappa Phi Home: 835 E High Country Dr Orem UT 84097-2370

HUNT, HAZEL ANALUE STANFIELD, retired accountant; b. Butler, Mo., Apr. 4, 1921; d. Vernon Arthur and Myrrl Millicent (Henderson) Stanfield; m. Marvie Avanell Hunt, July 25, 1942; 1 child, Roger LeRoy Grad., Sawyer Sch. Bus., LA, 1939. Supr., bookkeeper, sec. Nethercutt Labs., Santa Monica, Calif., 1940—45; v.p., treas. Dwyer-Curlett, Inc., LA, 1946—86; ret., 1986. Pres. Nat. Assn. Accts., West L.A., 1970-96, other offices Mem. DAR, Clan Henderson Soc. U.S., Beta Sigma Phi (pres. 1942, other offices) Presbyterian. Home: 1575 E Washington Blvd Apt 312 Pasadena CA 91104-2663 Personal E-mail: hash@mailstation.com.

HUNT, HELEN (HELEN ELIZABETH HUNT), actress; b. LA, June 15, 1963; m. Hank Azaria July 17, 1999 (div. Dec. 18, 2000); 1 child Makena' Lei Gordon Carnahan with Matthew Carnahan. Attended, UCLA. TV guest appearances include Amy Prentiss, 1974, The Swiss Family Robinson, 1975-76, The Fitzpatricks, 1977, The Bionic Women, 1978, Weekend, Mary Tyler Moore Show, 1977, Family, 1976, 1980, Facts of Life, 1980, Knots Landing, 1980, 1981, Darkroom, 1981, Gimmie a Break!, 1982, It Takes Two, 1982, Highway to Heaven, 1985, St. Elsewhere (several episodes between 1984-86), The Hitchiker, 1987, China Beach, 1990, The Trials of Rosie O'Neill, 1990, My Life and Times, 1991, Friends, 1995; TV movies include Pioneer Woman, 1973, All Together Now, 1975, Death Scream, 1975, Having Babies, 1976, The Spell, 1977, Transplant, 1979, Angel Dusted, 1981, I Think I'm Having a Baby, 1981, The Best Little Girl in the World, 1981, The Miracle of Cathy Miller, 1981, Child Bride of Short Creek, 1981, Desperate Lives, 1982, Quarterback Princess, 1983, Bill: On His Own, 1983, Choices of the Heart, 1983, Sweet Revenge, 1984, Shooter, 1988, American Playhouse: Land of Little Rain, 1989, Incident at Dark River, 1989, Into the Badlands, 1991, Murder In New Hampshire: The Pamela Wojas Smart Story, 1991, In the Company of Darkness, 1993, Twelfth Night, or What You Will, 1998, Empire Falls, 2005; TV series Mad About You, 1992-99 (also prodr. 3 episodes, dir. 5 episodes)(Emmy nomination, Lead Actress - Comedy, 1993, 94, Golden Globe award for Best Actress, musical or comedy, 1994, 95, Emmy award for Best Leading Actress in a Comedy series, 1996); films include Rollercoaster, 1977, Girls Just Want To Have Fun, 1985, Waiting to Act, 1985, Trancers, 1985, Empire, 1985, Peggy Sue Got Married, 1986, Project X, 1987, Stealing Home, 1988, Miles From Home, 1988, The Frog Prince, 1988, Next Of Kin, 1989, Trancers II, 1991, The Waterdance, 1992, Only You, 1992, Bob Roberts, 1992, Mr. Saturday Night, 1992, Trancers III, 1992, Sexual Healing, 1993, Kiss of Death, 1995, Twister, 1996, As Good As It Gets, 1997 (Acad. award Best Actress in a Leading Role 1997), Twister: Ride It Out, 1998, Dr. T and the Women, 2000, Pay It Forward, 2000, Cast Away, 2000, What Women Want, 2000, Curse of the Jade Scorpion, 2001, A Good Women, 2004, Bobby, 2006; plays include: Life (X)3, 2003; (voice) Galtar and the Golden Lance, 1985, The Nativity, 1986, The Easter Story, 1989, Captain Planet and the Planeteers, 1990, The Simpsons, 1998. Named one of 50 Most Beautiful People, People Mag., 1998. Address: Connie Tavel Mgmt 9171 Wilshire Blvd Beverly Hills CA 90210-5530

HUNT, JAMES BAXTER, JR., lawyer, former governor; b. Guilford County, NC, May 16, 1937; s. James Baxter and Elsie (Brame) Hunt; m. Carolyn Joyce Leonard, Aug. 20, 1958; children: Rebecca Hunt Hawley, James Baxter Hunt III, Rachel Nilender, Elizabeth Amigh. BS in Agrl. Edn., N.C. State U., 1959, MS in Agrl. Cons., 1962; JD, U. N.C., 1964. Bar: N.C. 1964. Econ. advisor H.M. Govt. of Nepal for Ford Found., 1964—66; ptnr. Kirby, Webb and Hunt, 1966—72; lt. gov. State of N.C., 1973—77, gov., 1977—85, 1993—2001; ptnr. Poyner and Spruill, Raleigh, NC, 1985—93; atty. Womble Carlyle Sandridge & Rice, Raleigh, 2001—. Originator, bd. dirs. Triangle East; chmn. N.C. State U. Emerging Issues Forum; bd. visitors Wake Forst U.; founding chmn. Nat. Bd. for Profl. Tchg. Stds., 1987, Nat. Ctr. for Pub. Policy and Higher Edn., 1998; chmn. James B. Hunt, Jr. Inst. for Ednl. Leadership and Policy. Author: Rally Around the Precinct, 1968. Trustee Atlantic Christian Coll.; mem. Carnegie Forum on Edn. and Econ. Task Force on Tchg. as a Profl., 1986; chmn. Nat. Commn. on Tchg. and Am.'s Future, 1994; trustee Carnegie Corp.; state pres. Young Dems., 1968; del. Dem. Nat. Conv., 1968; mem. Sec. of Edn.'s Commn. on Future of Edn., 2005. Named Outstanding Young Man of Yr., Wilson Jr. C. of C., 1969, Outstanding Govt. Ofcl. in Cmty. Edn., Nat. Assn. Cmty. Edn., 1977; recipient 1st Harry S. Truman award, Nat. Young Dems., 1975, James Bryant Conant award, Edn. Commn. States, 1984, Nat. 4-H Outstanding Alumnus award, 1984, Soil Conservation Honors award, 1986, Child Health Adv. award, Am. Acad. Pediat., 1994, Friend of Edn. award, Horace Mann League, 1999. Mem.: Nat. Govs. Assn. (chmn. task force on technol. innovation mem. exec. com., chmn. edn. com. states and nat. task force on edn. for econ. growth 1982—83, leadership team on controlling crime and violence 1994, chmn. nat. edn. goals panel 1997—). Presbyterian. Office: Womble Carlyle Sandridge & Rice 150 Fayetteville St Mall Ste 2100 PO Box 831 Raleigh NC 27602

HUNT, JAMES CALVIN, physician, academic administrator; b. Lexington, NC, Sept. 11, 1925; s. James Lee and Sarah Della (Frank) Hunt; m. Irene Kivett, Sept. 17, 1949; children: James Calvin, Michael S., Cynthia Irene. AB, Catawba Coll., 1949; MD, Bowman Gray Sch. Medicine, 1953; MS, U. Minn., 1958; ScD, Wake Forest U., 1992. Diplomate Am. Bd. Internal Medicine. Intern N.C. Bapt. Hosp., Winston-Salem, 1953-54; resident, fellow Mayo Grad Sch. Medicine, Rochester, Minn., 1954-58; practice medicine, specializing in internal medicine (cardiovasc.-renal diseases) Rochester, 1958-78; cons., instr. to asst. prof. dept. medicine Mayo Clinic and Mayo Med. Sch., 1958-63, assoc. prof., chmn. divsn. nephrology, 1963-72, prof., chmn. dept. medicine, 1973-78; prof., assoc. dean clin. ednl. programs Mayo Med. Sch., 1972-74; prof. medicine U. Tenn., Memphis, 1978—, dean Coll. Medicine, 1978-81, v.p. health affairs, chancellor Univ. Health Scis. Ctr., 1981-93, univ. disting. prof., dir. clin. scholars program, 1993—2001, v.p. health affairs, chancellor emeritus, 2001—. Adv. coun. Nat. Heart, Lung and Blood Inst. NIH, 1976—81. Contbr. articles to profl. jours. Pres. Nat. Kidney Found., 1973—76; mem. Congl. Tech. Adv. Coun., 1987—96; bd. dirs. Memphis Downtown Neighbors Assn., 1995—99, pres., 1997—98; mem. adv. bd. Goals for Memphis, 1987—95; bd. dirs. YMCA, Memphis, Memphis Riverfront Devel. Corp., 1999—, sec., 2000—02; trustee Le Bonheur Children's Med. Ctr., 1981—93, Christian Bros. Coll., 1983—96; mem. cmty. adv. bd. Bapt. Meml. Hosp., 1986—; bd. dirs. Bapt. Meml. Coll. Health Scis., 1995—2005, chair acad. affairs com., 1998—2005; mem. adv. bd. Rhodes Coll. With USAAF, 1943—46, ETO. Recipient Disting. Svc. award, Bowman Gray Sch. Medicine, Wake Forest U., 1975, Disting. Alumnus award, Catawba Coll., 1974, Educator of the Yr. award, Memphis State U., 1986, Outstanding Alumnus award, Mayo Found., 1991, Gift of Life award, Nat. Kidney Found., 1991. Fellow: ACP, Am. Heart Assn. (mem. coun. circulation), Am. Coll. Cardiology; mem.: AMA, Am. Soc. Clin. Pharmacology and Therapeutics, Am. Soc. Internal Medicine, Coun. High Blood Pressure Rsch., Soc. Nuc. Medicine, Internat. Soc. Hypertension, Internat. Am. Socs. Nephrology, Sigma Xi, Phi Rho Sigma, Alpha Omega Alpha. Home and Office: 3381 Moss Rose Dr Memphis TN 38115-4263 Office Phone: 901-547-9437.

HUNT, JAMES L., lawyer; b. Chgo., Oct. 20, 1942; BA magna cum laude, DePauw U., 1964; JD, Northwestern U., 1967. Bar: Calif. 1967. Atty. McCutchen, Doyle, Brown & Enersen, San Francisco, 1967, ptnr., chmn. firm, 1988—91, 1999—2001, chmn. litig. dept., 1991—95; ptnr. Bingham McCutchen LLP, San Francisco, 2001—, chmn. litig. practice group. Atty. rep. 9th Cir. Jud. Conf., 1991-94; bd. dirs. The Lurie Co.; trustee The Lurie Found. Assoc. editor: Northwestern U. Law Rev., 1966-67. Bd. dirs. San Francisco Giants; bd. visitors Northwestern U. Law Sch., 1989—. Named a No. Calif. Super Lawyer, Law & Politics & SF Mag., 2004. Mem. Am. Coll. Trial Lawyers, Phi Beta Kappa, Order Coif. Office: Bingham McCutchen LLP 3 Embarcadero Ctr Ste 18000 San Francisco CA 94111-4003 Office Phone: 415-393-2212. Business E-Mail: james.hunt@bingham.com.

HUNT, JOHN EDWIN, insurance company executive, consultant; b. Ozark, Ala., Jan. 13, 1918; s. Tim Atticus and Ada (Arnold) H.; m. Winnifred Prichard; children: Jacqueline, John Edwin Jr., Geoffery, Scott, Richard; md. 2d Leona Snowden. Student, Columbus U., Washington, 1938-40, Pace U., 1940-41; diploma in banking, Am. Inst. Banking, 1942; diploma in ins., Travelers Ins. Co., 1944. Aide to regional adminstr., chief auditor Fed. Housing Adminstrn., Washington, 1938-40; with trust dept. Riggs Nat. Bank, Washington, 1940-42; asst. trust officer Fla. Nat. Bank, Jacksonville, 1942-44; asst. mgr. Travelers Ins. Co., Jacksonville, 1944-45, gen. agt. regional br., 1945-58; pres. John E. Hunt & Assocs., Tallahassee, 1972-84; chmn. bd. dirs. Hunt Ins. Group-Spl. Law Enforcement Agy. and Self-Ins. Fund Adminstrn., Tallahassee, 1984-97; pres. John Hunt & Assocs., Miami, Fla., 1958-72; chmn. emeritus Hunt Ins. Group, Tallahassee, 1997—. Pres. Ins. Cons. and Analysts, Tallahassee, 1972-95. Past chmn. pvt. industry coun. Pres. Reagan's Job Tng. Partnership Act; past mem. Gov's Adv. Coun. for Ins.; founder Fla. Police Chiefs Edn. & Rsch. Found., Inc.; trustee, mem. pres.'s coun. Fla. So. Coll., Lakeland, 1986-97. trustee emeritus, 1997—. Mem. Fla. Assn. Surplus Lines, Fla. Assn. Ins. Agts., Com. of 99 (past pres., bd. dirs., law enforcement com. 1984-85), Greater Miami Mortgage Brokers Assn. (pres. 1964-65), Fla. Jr. C. of C. (nat. dir., state v.p. 1950-52), Fla. Police Chiefs Assn. (hon., life), Fla. Sheriffs Assn. (hon., life), Killearn Golf and Country Club, Fla. Econ. Club, Tiger Bay Club, Govs. Club, Masons, Shriners, Elks (life). Republican. Avocation: yachting. Home: PO Box 14015 Tallahassee FL 32317-4015 Office: Hunt Ins Group Inc 3606 Maclay Blvd S Tallahassee FL 32312

HUNT, JOHN MORTIMER, JR., classical studies educator; b. Bryn Mawr, Pa., Sept. 21, 1943; s. John Mortimer and Ruth Pierson (Ott) H. AB, Lafayette Coll., 1965; MA, Bryn Mawr Coll., 1968, PhD, 1970. From asst. prof. to assoc. prof. classical studies Villanova (Pa.) U., 1970-91, prof., 1991—, chmn. dept. classical studies, 1993-99, dir. classical studies, 1999—. Instr. Latin Lafayette Coll., Easton, Pa., 1970; vis. assoc. prof. U. Calif., Santa Barbara, 1978—80. Mem. editl. bd. Classical Philology, 1976—2001; contbr. articles to profl. publs. Grad. fellow, Cornell U., 1965—66. Mem.; Delano Kindred, Roger Williams Family Assn., Colonial Soc. Pa., Soc. Colonial Wars in Pa., Soc. Mayflower Descs. Pa. (state historian 1999—2000, editor The Pa. Mayflower, Most Disting. Pilgrim award 2003), Pa. Soc. S.R., Franklin Inn Club, Ancient and Honorable Artillery Co. Mass. Episcopalian. Avocations: genealogy, early American history, opera. Office: Villanova U Dept Humanities and Augustinian Trads Villanova PA 19085-1699 Home Phone: 610-688-2630; Office Phone: 610-519-4678. Personal E-mail: jhunt001@comcast.net. Business E-Mail: john.hunt@villanova.edu.

HUNT, J(ULIAN) COURTENAY, artist; b. Jacksonville, Fla., Sept. 17, 1917; s. Julian Schley and Ruth Rosalind (Loftin) Hunt. Student, Ringling Sch. Art, Farnsworth Sch. Art. Tchr. pvt. classes painting. One-man shows include Cummer Gallery, Jacksonville, exhibited in group shows at Palm Beach Art Gallery, Soc. Four Arts, Palm Beach, Audubon Artists Am., N.Y.C., Allied Artists Am., Atlanta High Mus., St. Augustine (Fla.) Art Assn., Sarasota (Fla.) Art Assn., Nortno Art Gallery Palm Beaches, Represented in permanent collections U. Fla., Gainesville, Jacksonville U., City Hall of Jacksonville, Duval County Cir. Ct., Jacksonville Ind. Life Ins Co., P.A.S.T.A. Gallery, St. Augustine, Fla. With USAF, ETO. Home and Office: 2248 Carnes St Orange Park FL 32073 Office Phone: 904-264-9998.

HUNT, KAY NORD, lawyer; b. Carver, Minn., June 26, 1955; d. Edward John and Carol Valentine (Lunde) Nord; m. Gary C. Hunt, June 25, 1977 (div. Dec. 1987). BA summa cum laude, Gustavus Adolphus Coll., 1977; JD, Marquette U., 1981. Bar: Wis. 1981, Minn. 1982, US Dist. Ct. (ea., we. dist. Wis. 1981, Minn. 1982), US Ct. Appeals (7th, 8th cir. 1982), US Supreme Ct. 2000. Law clk. Wis. Ct. Appeals, Milw., 1981-82; atty., appellate litig. Lommen Nelson Cole & Stageberg, Mpls., 1982—. Adj. prof. Univ. St. Thomas Sch. Law, 2003—. Bd. mem. Ramsy County Humane Soc., St. Paul, 1997—. Mem. ABA, Am. Acad. Appellate

Lawyers, State Bar Wis., Minn. State Bar Assn., Minn. Def. Lawyers (amicus curia com.), Hennepin County Bar Assn., Amdahl Inn of Ct. Office: Lommen Nelson Cole & Stageberg 2000 IDS Ctr 80 S 8th St Minneapolis MN 55402-2100 Office Phone: 612-336-9341. Office Fax: 612-339-8064. Business E-Mail: kay@lommen.com.

HUNT, KEVIN J., food products executive; BA, Dartmouth Coll.; MBA, Columbia Univ., 1976. With Ralcorp Holdings, Inc., St. Louis, 1985—, corp. v.p., 1995—2003, pres., co-CEO, 2003—, bd. dirs., 2004—05; CEO Bremner, Inc., 1995—, Nutcracker Brands, Inc., 2003—. Office: Ralcorp Holdings Inc ste 2900 800 MarketSt Saint Louis MO 63101 Office Phone: 314-877-7000. Office Fax: 314-877-7666.*

HUNT, LAWRENCE HALLEY, JR., lawyer; b. July 15, 1943; s. Lawrence Halley Sr. and Mary Hamilton (Johnson) H.; m. Katherine Collins; children: Caroline Smith, Laura Hamilton, Darwin Halley. AB, Dartmouth Coll., 1965; cert., Inst. d'Etudes Politiques, Paris, 1966; JD, U. Chgo., 1969. Bar: N.Y. 1970, Ill. 1971, U.S. Ct. Appeals (9th cir.) 1980, U.S. Ct. Appeals (2d cir.) 1981, U.S. Supreme Ct. 1981. Assoc. Davis Polk & Wardwell, NYC, 1969-70, Sidley & Austin, Chgo., 1970-75; ptnr. Sidley Austin LLP and predecessor firms, Chgo., 1975—; mem. exec. com. Sidley Austin, Chgo., 1985—2002. Mem. securities adv. com. Ill. Sec. of State, Springfield, Ill., 1977—87; prof. grad. program fin. svcs. law Ill. Inst. Tech.-Chgo.-Kent Coll. Law, 1987—99; dir. Melanoma Rsch. Found., 2006—. Mng. editor U. Chgo. Law Review, 1968-69; contbr. aticles to profl. jours. James B. Reynolds scholar Dartmouth Coll., 1965-66. Fellow: Am. Bar Found., Ill. Bar Assn.; mem.: ABA (com. on commodity regulation, past chmn. subcom. on futures commn. merchants, past mem. exec. coun.), Internat. Bar Assn. (past chmn. bus. law com. sub-com. futures and options), Indian Hill Club, Mid-Day Club. Avocations: hockey, golf. Office: Sidley Austin LLP One South Dearborn St Chicago IL 60603 Office Phone: 312-853-7000. Business E-Mail: lhunt@sidley.com.

HUNT, LINDA, hospital administrator; Pres., CEO St. Joseph's Hosp. and Med. Ctr., Phoenix. Named Bus. Leader, Tribute to Women Awards, Maricopa County YWCA, 2001. Mem.: Am. Assn. of Med. Colleges (rep.). Office: St Joseph's Hosp and Med Ctr 350 W Thomas Rd Phoenix AZ 85013

HUNT, LORRAINE T., former lieutenant governor; b. Niagara Falls, NY, Mar. 11, 1939; Student, Westlake Coll. Music. Former pres., CEO Perri Inc.; founder, also bd. dirs. Continental Nat. Bank; lt. gov. State of Nev., 1998—2007; pres. Nev. State Senate, 1999—2007. Bd. dirs. First Security Bank Nev.; chmn. bd. trustees Las Vegas Convention and Visitors Authority; former commr. and vice chair Nev. Commn. on Tourism; dir. Nev. Hotel/Motel Assn.; vice chmn. Nev. Motion Picture Found., Nev. Motion Picture Commn. Commr. Clark county Commn., 1995-99; mem. cmty. bd. Wells Fargo Bank Named U.S. Small Bus. Adv. of the Yr., 1989, Nev. Restaurateur of Yr., 1992, Rep. Woman of Yr., 1996, Woman of Yr., Nev. Ballet Theater, 1998; recipient Govs. award for excellence in bus., 1987, Free Enterprise award, 1993, First Lifetime Achievement award, Govs. Conf. on Tourism, 1993. Republican.*

HUNT, MARK ALAN, museum director; b. Topeka, May 21, 1949; s. Ira B. and Marjorie May (McConnell) H.; m. Cynthia E. Rush, Feb. 21, 1976; children: Alexander Rush, Alice Claire. BA magna cum laude, Washburn U., 1971; MA, Cooperstown Grad. Programs, N.Y. State U. Coll., Oneonta, 1982; grad., Mus. Mgmt. Inst. U. Calif., Berkeley, 1983. Dir. Plymouth (Mich.) Hist. Mus., 1976; curator exhibits Kans. Hist. Soc., Topeka, 1976, asst. dir. mus., 1976-79, dir. mus., 1979-88, dir. mus. and hist. sites, 1988-90; dir. Nat. Scouting Mus., Murray (Ky.) State U., 1990-96, Ronald Reagan Presdl. Libr. and Mus., Simi Valley, Calif., 1996-2000; dep. dir./curator Franklin D. Roosevelt Libr., Hyde Park, NY, 2000—. Cons. Menninger Found., 1980, Nat. Endowment Humanities, 1974, 75, 77, 1978, Mus. Assessment Program; instr. mus. adminstrn., U. Kans., 1987-89; mem. adv. coun. Ea. Ill. U. Hist. Adminstrn. Program, 1992-96. Contbr. articles to profl. jours. Bd. dirs. Mulvane Art Ctr., Washburn U., 1988-89, Land Between the Lakes Assn., 1994-96; mem. master planning com. Ward-Meade Hist. Park, 1986-89; mem. Bus. Coun. for Arts, 1990-96; grad. Leadership Murray, 1994, Murray Tourism Commn., 1995-96; mem. Ventura County (Calif.) Cultural Tourism Collaborative, 1998-2000, Moorpark (Calif.) Coll. Found. Bd., 1999; bd. dirs. World Affairs Coun. Mid-Hudson Valley, 2003-05. Recipient award for excellence, Kans. Mus. Assn., 1991; Wiseman scholar, 1967—68, Washburn scholar, 1968—71, Clark fellow, 1973—74, Alumni fellow, Washburn U., 1998. Mem. Am. Assn. State and Local History (chmn. state membership com. 1976-85, cons., mem. program com. ann. meeting 1988, 92, mem. edn. com. 1981-84, mem. local arrangements com. ann. meeting 1985, mem. membership task force 1993-97, mem. nat. governing coun. 1991-95, mem. profl. std. and ethics com. 2001-04, mem. CEO transition task force 2004—, presdl. sites and librs. com. 2003—), Mountain Plains Mus. Assn. (mem. bd. 1977, Kans. rep.), Calif. Assn. Mus. (dist. rep. on CAM bd. 1998-99), Kans. Mus. Assn. (pres. 1978-80, Excellence award 1991), Ky. Assn. Mus. (bd. dirs. 1994-96), Am. Assn. Mus. (mem. accreditation vis. com., mem. mus. studies task force 1988-89), Southeastern Mus. Assn. (bd. dirs. 1995-96), Murray-Calloway County C. of C., Rotary Internat., Kappa Sigma, Phi Kappa Phi. Methodist. Home: 16 Yates Blvd Poughkeepsie NY 12601-5006 Office: Franklin D Roosevelt Libr 4079 Albany Post Rd Hyde Park NY 12538-1917 Office Phone: 845-486-7746. Business E-Mail: mark.hunt@nara.gov.

HUNT, MARY ALICE, retired humanities educator; b. Lima, Ohio, Apr. 14, 1928; d. Blair T. and Grace (Henry) H. BA, Fla. State U., Tallahassee, 1950, MA, 1953; PhD, Ind. U., Bloomington, 1973. Instr., librarian Fla. State U., Tallahassee, 1955-61, asst. prof., 1961-74, assoc. prof., 1974-82, prof., 1982-95, assoc. dean, 1986-95, prof. emerita, 1995—. Author: Transitions: An Informal History of a School Celebrating its 50th Anniversary, 1997; co-author: Multimedia Indexes, Lists, etc., 1975; editor: Multimedia Approach To Children's Literature, 1983, (periodical) Fla. State U./SLIS Alumni Newsletter, 1966-95, Florida Libraries, 1961-67; assoc. editor: Folders of Ideas for Library Excellence, 1991. Mem. Sr. Ctr. Art Coun., 2004—06. Recipient Art Vol. of Yr. award, Sr. Ctr. Art Coun., 2004. Mem. ALA (councilor at large 1986-94, 96-2000), Southeastern Libr. Assn., Fla. Assn. Media in Edn., Delta Kappa Gamma, Pi Lambda Theta, Pi Kappa Phi, Beta Phi Mu. Avocations: gardening, reading, photography, pastel drawing and watercolor painting. Home: 1603 Kolopakin Nene Tallahassee FL 32301-4733 Business E-Mail: mhunt@mailer.fsu.edu.

HUNT, MARY REILLY, organization executive; b. NYC, Apr. 17, 1921; d. Philip R. and Mary C. (Harten) Reilly; m. Robert R. Hunt, Apr. 10, 1943,; children: Marianne Schram, Philip R., Robert R., Elise Hannah. Student, CCNY, 1939; DHL (hon.), Thomas More Coll., 2005. Tax investigator Ind. Dept. Revenue, 1970-80; pres. Ind. Right to Life, 1973-77; treas. Nat. Right to Life Com., Washington, 1974, 77, 78, mem. exec. com., 1974, 76-81, vice chmn., 1976, exec. dir., 1978, dir. devel., 1979-94, v.p. devel., 1994-97, hon. bd. mem., 1983—; v.p. devel. Nat. Life Ctr., Woodbury, 1997—; pres. Mary Reilly Hunt & Assoc., Inc., South Bend, Ind., 1985—. Bd. dirs., v.p. YWCA, 1968-73, bd. dirs. Mental Health Assn. St. Joseph Co., 1972-78; candidate for state legis., 1988; mem. St. Joseph County Rep. Women precinct com., South Bend, 1964-79, alt. del. to Nat. Rep. Conv., 1976, 84, 88, 92; mem. Souht Bend Symphony Women's Assn.; mem. Coun. for Nat. Policy, 1988—, mem. exec. com., 2000-06. Recipient St. Patrick's medal St. Patrick's Coll. and Sem. (Ireland), 1996. Mem. NAFE, Women Bus. Owners, Am. Soc. Sovereign Mil. Order of Malta. Republican. Roman Catholic. Avocations: gardening, antiques. Office: Nat Life Ctr 1102 N Lafayette Blvd South Bend IN 46617-1136

HUNT, MAURICE ARTHUR, language educator, researcher; b. Lansing, Mich., Oct. 30, 1942; s. Elmore Clare and Irene Elizabeth H.; m. Pamela Helene Coyle, June 24, 1978; children: Alison, Jeffrey, Andrew, Thomas. BA, U. Mich., 1964; MA, U. Calif., Berkeley, 1966, PhD, 1970. Instr. English Coll. Marin, Kentfield, Calif., 1970-73; lectr. English Dominican Coll., San Rafael, Calif., 1974-75; vis. asst. prof. English Ariz. State U., Tempe, 1980-81; from asst. to assoc. prof. English Baylor U., Waco, Tex., 1981-93, prof. English, 1993—2003, rsch. prof., 2003—, chair dept. English, 1996—2007. Adv. bd. writing ctr. Tex. A&M U., College Station, 1985—; dir. Baylor Advanced Placement Inst., Waco, 1994-95, Baylor Freshman Composition Program, Waco, 1982-98; exec. com. South Ctrl. Renaissance Conf., College Station, 1988-90, v.p., 2005-06, pres., 2006-07; pres. Coll. Conf. Tchrs. English, 2005—06; mem. so. regional, nat screening com. Fulbright Grants. Author: Shakespeare's Romance of the Word, 1990, Shakespeare's Labored Art, 1995, Shakespeare's Religious Allusiveness: Its Play and Tolerance, 2004, Shakespeare's As You Like It: Late Elizabethan Culture and Literary Representation, 2007; editor: Approaches to Teaching The Tempest and Other Late Romances, 1992, The Winter's Tale: Critical Essays, 1995, Approaches to Teaching Shakespeare's Romeo and Juliet, 2000, Approaches to Teaching Shakespeare's Othello, 2005; US editor English Studies, 2007-; assoc. editor Papers on Lang. and Lit., 1996-, The Upstart Crow: A Shakespeare Jour., 1990-; mem. editl. bd. Shakespeare and the Classroom, 1993-; contbr. articles to profl. jours. Fundraiser United Way Bay Area, San Francisco, 1976-80; bd. dirs. Alameda County Tng. and Employment Bd., Oakland, Calif., 1977-78. Rsch. grantee Baylor U., 1986—; named to Greater Lansing Area Sports Hall of Fame, Portland HS Sports Hall of Fame, Mich. Mem. MLA (mem. New Variorum Shakespeare com., 2004—), Shakespeare Assn. Am., South Ctrl. Renaissance Conf. (mem. exec. com. 1984-85, program chair 2005-06), Internat. Assn. Univ. Profs. English, Phi Beta Kappa. Democrat. Episcopalian. Avocations: jogging, sports. Home: 321 Oakwood Ln Hewitt TX 76643-3027 Office: One Bear Pl # 97404 Waco TX 76798-7404 Office Phone: 254-710-1768. E-mail: maurice_hunt@baylor.edu.

HUNT, MICHAEL O'LEARY, wood science and engineering educator; b. Louisville, Dec. 9, 1935; s. George Henry and Tressie (Truax) H.; children: Elizabeth H. Schwartz, Lynne T. Lattimer, Michael O. Jr. BS, U. Ky., 1957; M.Forestry, Duke U., 1958; PhD, N.C. State U., 1970. Product engr. Wood Products div. Singer Co., Pickens, SC, 1959-60; asst. prof. wood sci. Purdue U., West Lafayette, Ind., 1960-70, assoc. prof., 1970-79, prof., 1979—, dir. Wood Rsch. Lab., 1979—2002. Contbr. articles over 80 articles to profl. jours. Chmn. campus preservation com. Wabash Valley Trust for Historic Preservation, Lafayette. Recipient Servaas Meml. award Hist. Landmarks Found. of Ind., 1994, H. Fannon award Lafayette Neighborhood Housing Svcs., 1998, Downie Meml. award Wabash Valley Trust, 2002. Mem. Forest Products Soc. (pres. 1990-91, Fred Gottschalk Meml. award 1984), Soc. of Wood Sci. and Tech., Assn. Preservation Tech., Rotary. Achievements include patent for lightweight, high-performance structural particleboard. Office: Purdue Univ Wood Rsch Lab West Lafayette IN 47907-2033 Business E-Mail: huntm@purdue.edu.

HUNT, RAY LEE, petroleum company executive; b. 1943; s. H. L. and Ruth (Ray) Hunt; m. Nancy Ann Hunt; 5 children. BBA, So. Meth. U., 1965. With Hunt Oil Co., Dallas, 1958—2004; former chmn. Hunt Oil. Co., Dallas; chmn., pres., CEO Hunt Consolidated Inc., Dallas, 1994—. Exec. com., bd. trustees So. Mich. U.; bd. trustees Ctr. for Strategic & Internat. Studies, Washington; bd. trustees. So. Methodist Univ., Dallas; bd. mem. Presdl. Fgn. Intelligence Adv. Bd., 2001; bd. dir. Halliburton Co., 1998, King Ranch, Inc., Pepsico, Inc., The Cooper Inst., Electronic Data Sys., Dallas; chmn. bd. Fed. Res. Bank, Dallas; exec. com. Southwestern Medical Found., Dallas. Named one of Forbes' Richest Americans, 1999—, World's Richest People, Forbes mag., 2001—; named to Tex. Bus. Hall of Fame, 1992. Mem.: Am. Petroleum Inst. (exec., pub. policy com., chmn. 1991—94). Office: Hunt Consolidated Inc 1445 Ross At Field Dallas TX 75202*

HUNT, RICHARD, sculptor; b. Chgo., Sept. 12, 1935; BA, Sch. of Art Inst. Chgo., 1957. Instr. Sch. Art Inst. Chgo., 1960-61, U. Ill., Chgo., 1960-62. Vis. prof. Chouinard Art Sch., L.A., 1964, Northern Ill. U., De Kalb, summer 1968, Northwestern U., Evanston, Ill., 1968-69; vis. artist Yale U., New Haven, 1964, Purdue U., Ind., 1965, Wis. State U., Oshkosh, 1969, So. Ill. U., Carbondale, 1969, Washington U., 1977-78; artist cons. Hobart Welding Sch., Troy, Ohio, 1969; artist-in-residence, Eastern Mich. U., Ypsilanti, 1988. Prin. works include individual exhibitions: U. Notre Dame, Ind., 1966, Cleve. Mus. Art, 1967, Milw. Art Ctr., 1967, Fisk U., Nashville, 1968, Mus. Modern Art N.Y., 1971, Art Inst. Chgo., 1971, U. Iowa, 1975, Balt. Mus. Art, 1980, Columbia U., N.Y., 1981, Bklyn. Artist Cultural Assn., 1982, Terry Distenfass Gallery, N.Y., 1983, 84, 86, Gwenda Jay Gallery, Chgo., 1991, Louis Newmann Gallery, 1991, Shiduni Gallery, Santa Fe, 1992; group exhibitions: World's Fair, Seattle, 1962, World Festival of Negro Art, Dakar, Senegal, 1966, 100 Artist, 100 Years: Alumni of Sch. Art Inst. Chgo, 1979, also collections at Met. Mus. Art N.Y., Mus. Modern Art, N.Y., Whitney Mus., N.Y., Albright-Knox Art Gallery, Buffalo, Hirshorn Mus. and Sculpture Garden, Washington, Cleve. Mus. Art, Art Inst. Chgo., Milw. Art Ctr., William Nelson Rockhill Gallery Art, Kansas City, Mo., Nat. Mus. Israel, Jerusalem, Dorsky Gallery. Bd. dirs. Coll. Art Assn., 1972-76, Am. Coun. for Arts, 1974—; trustee Mus. Contemporary Art, Chgo., 1975-79; mem. Nat. Coun. Arts, 1968-74, Ill. Arts Coun., 1970-75. Served with U.S. Army, 1958-60. James Nelson Raymond Travel fellowship Art Inst. Chgo., 1957, Guggenheim fellowship, 1962, Tamarind fellowship Artist Ford Found., 1965, Cassandra Found. fellowship, 1970; recipient Logan Prize, 1956, 61, 62, Palmer Prize, 1957; named Outstanding Chicagoan in the Arts Chgo. Jr. C. of C., 1971. Address: Printworks Gallery 311 W Superior St Ste 105 Chicago IL 60610-3548

HUNT, ROBERT G., construction company executive; b. Feb. 15, 1948; BS in bus., Ball State U.; MS in Engring., Purdue U. Joined Huber, Hunt & Nichols Inc., Indpls., 1974, from field engr. to divsn. mgr., pres. Phoenix and Tampa, CEO Indpls., 1999—; pres. The Hunt Corp., Indpls.; CEO, chmn. Hunt Constrn. Corp. Office: Hunt Construction Group 2450 S Tibbs Ave Indianapolis IN 46241

HUNT, RONALD J., dean, dental educator; DDS, U. Iowa, 1973, MS in dental pub. health, 1982. Diplomate Am. Bd. Dental Pub. Health, 1986. Assoc. prof., dental ecology U. NC Sch. Dentistry, 1986—88, prof., dental ecology, 1990—92, asst. dean, 1992—98, assoc. dean academic affairs, 1992—98; dean, Harry Lyons Prof. Va. Commonwealth U. Sch. Dentistry, Richmond, Va., 1999—. Disting. vis. scholar U. Adelaide, Australia, 1990. Fellow: Pierre Fauchard Acad. Found., Am. Assn. Dental Schools. Office: PO Box 980566 Richmond VA 23298 Office Phone: 804-827-2077. Business E-Mail: rjhunt@vcu.edu.

HUNT, SARAH MINCEY, elementary school educator; b. Claxton, Ga., Aug. 1, 1946; d. Herbert Mincey and Wincey Beatrice Benjamin, Berether Mills Mincey (Stepmother); m. Richard Murray Hunt, Sr., Oct. 3, 1967; children: Richard Hunt, Jr., Sherod Montrell. BBA, Ft. Valley State U., Ga., 1982; MEd, U. Phoenix, Ariz., 2004. Cert. gifted tchr. Ga., 2000, tchr. leader Bibb County Bd. Edn., Ga., 2002. Mortgage broker Sm Hunt Mortgage Co., Macon, Ga., 1980—94; social studies & math tchr. Mcevoy Mid. Sch., Macon, 1992—2000; social studies & lang. arts tchr. Bibb County Bd. Edn., 2000—. State dir. Women Excellence, Macon, Ga., 1996—2007. Mem.: NSTA, Nat. Social Studies Coun., Ga. Educators Assn., Nat. Educators Assn. Personal E-mail: s.f.mince@cox.net.

HUNT, SHARON ANN, cardiologist; b. Cleve., Oct. 2, 1946; MD, Stanford Univ. Sch. Med., 1972. Cert. Cardiovascular Medicine, Heart, Lung Transplantation Am. Bd. Internal Medicine, Internal Medicine Am. Bd. Internal Medicine. Intern Stanford Univ., med. dir., heart transplant program, and prof., medicine. Recipient Wyeth Senior Achievement award in Clin. Transplantation, Am. Soc. Transplantation, 2007. Office: Cardiovascular Medicine CVRB H2146 MC 5246 300 Pasteur Dr Stanford CA 94305 Office Phone: 650-498-6605. Office Fax: 650-725-1599.*

HUNT, SWANEE G., public policy educator, former ambassador; b. Dallas, May 1, 1950; m. Charles Alexander Ansbacher; 3 children. BA, Tex. Christian U., 1972; MA, Ball State U., 1976; MA in Religion, Iliff Sch. of Theology, 1977, PhD (hon.), 1986, Webster U., 1994. Pres. Hunt Alternatives Fund, 1981—; co-founder Karis Community, 1980-83; min. pastoral care Capital Heights Presbyn. Ch., 1983; vice chair Denver Community Mental Health Commn., 1983-87; with Gov. Policy Acad. on Families and Children at Risk, 1989-90; chair Colo. Coord. Coun. Housing and the Homeless, 1989-92; U.S. amb. to Austria, 1993-97; dir. Women and Pub. Policy Program, Kennedy Sch. Govt. Harvard. Composer The Witness Cantata, 1985; author: This Was Not Our War: Bosnian Women Reclaiming the Peace, 2004; syndicated columnist Scripps Howard. Bd. dirs., co-founder Women's Found. Colo.; chair Mayor's Human Capital Agenda Coun., 1992-93; co-chair Denver Initiative Children and Families; mem. UN High Commn. on Refugees; mem. Internat. Crisis Group, Internat. Alert. Recipient Martin Luther King Humanitarian award U. Colo., 1992, NCCJ, 1992, Denver Urban Ministries, 1991, United Meth. Ch., 1989, Internat. Women's Forum, 1989, Sta. KUSA-TV, 1989, Caring Connection, 1989, Nat. Mental Health Assn., 1985, Mental Health Assn. Colo., 1984, 94, Mile High award United Way, 1993, Am. Heritage award Anti-Defamation League, 1995, Cordon Bleu du Saint Esprit Peace award, 1996, Humanitarian Lifetime Svc. award Denver Holocaust Awareness, 1997, Together for Peace award 1997, 3 decorations Austrian Govt., 1997, Amb. award The Conflict Ctr., 1997, Inst. for Internat. Edn. award, 1998, PEN New Eng. award, 2005. Office: 168 Brattle St Cambridge MA 02138-3309 also: Harvard Univ Kennedy Sch Government 79 JFK St Cambridge MA 02138-5801 Office Phone: 617-547-8921. Business E-Mail: swanee_hunt@huntalternatives.org.

HUNT, T(HOMAS) W(EBB), retired religion educator; b. Mammoth Spring, Ark., Sept. 28, 1929; s. Thomas Hubert and Ethel Clara (Webb) H.; m. M. Laverne Hill, July 22, 1951; children: Melana Claire Hunt Monroe. MusB, Ouachita Bapt. U., 1950; MusM, N. Tex. State U., 1957, PhD, 1967. Faculty Southwestern Bapt. Theol. Sem., Ft. Worth, 1963-87; life cons. for prayer Lifeway Christian Resources, Nashville, 1987-94; ret. Bapt. Sunday Sch. Bd., Nashville, 1994. Lectr. in field; confs. on the five continents; mem. adv. coun. Life Action Ministries, John Franklin Ministries; mem. bd. ref. Union U., Prayer Power Ministries. Author: The Doctrine of Prayer, 1985, Music in Missions, 1986, The Disciple's Prayer Life, 1988, Church Ministry Prayer Manual, 1994, The Mind of Christ, 1995, In God's Presence, 1995, From Heaven's View, 2002, The Life-Changing Power of Prayer, 2002, Prayer and Kingdom Advance, 2004; author: (with Claude King) Pray in Faith, 2007; composer: Gentle Guide, 1960, Voluntary on Old Hundreth, 1963; founder, author: course in music in missions; composer: (CD) Improvisations on Classic Hymns, 2006. Home: 3915 Cypress Hill Dr Spring TX 77388-5798 Office Phone: 281-288-7209. E-mail: lhhunt@sbcglobal.net. *In a rapidly changing world, we rely on a God who does not change.*

HUNT, VALERIE VIRGINIA, electrophysiologist, educator; b. Larwill, Ind., July 22, 1916; d. Homer Henry Hunt and Iva Velzora Ames. BS in Biology, Fla. State Coll., 1936; MA in Physiol. Psychology, Columbia U., 1941, EdD in Sci. Edn., 1946; DD, Phoenix Inst., San Diego, 1984. Sci. tchr. Anniston (Ala.) H.S., 1936-38; asst. anatomy nursing dept. Columbia U., NYC, 1939-40; chmn. health edn. Boston YWCA, 1942-43; instr. Columbia U. Tchrs. Coll. and Coll. Physicians and Surgeons, NYC, 1943-46; asst. prof. U. Iowa, Iowa City, 1946-47; assoc. prof., dir. divsn. phys. therapy UCLA, 1947-64, prof. physiology, dir. electromyographic lab., 1964-80, prof. emeritus, 1980—; dir. BioEnergy Fields Lab. BioEnergy Fields Found., Malibu, Calif., 1980—; CEO Malibu Pub. Co., 1995—. Cons. Nat. Bd. YWCA, 1943-46, Nat. Early Childhood Edn., 1948-50, UCLA Sch. Engring. Prosthetics Inst., 1949-51, Calif. Dept. Edn., 1950-60, Chrysler Motor Co. Space Divsn. Rsch., 1952, NASA Space Biology, 1958, Grand Kamalani Wellness Ctr., Maui, Hawaii; field reader U.S. Dept. HEW, 1958-65; reviewer sci. textbooks McMillan Pub., Prentice-Hall, McGraw-Hill, W.B. Saunders & Co., 1959-67; cons. Fetzer Found. Energy Field Rsch., 1989, Heart Math Found., 1992. Author: Recreation for the Handicapped, 1955, Corrective Physical Education, 1967, Movement Education for Preschool, 1972, Guidelines for Movement Behavior: Curricula for Early Childhood Education, 1974, Infinite Mind: Science of the Human Vibrations of Consciousness, 1996, Mind Mastery Meditations, 1997, Naibhu, 1998; contbr. articles to profl. jours. Pres. United Cerebral Palsy, L.A., 1947-51; mem. adv. com. Harlan Shoemaker Clinic for Neurol. Disabilities, 1948-53; bd. dirs. Found. for Jr. Blind, 1949-52, Crippled Children Soc., 1953-58, YWCA, L.A., 1955-65; adv. com., Internat. Congress for Exceptional Children, 1964-72, Rory Found., L.A., 1998—; vestry bd. mem. St. Matthew Episcopal Ch., L.A., 1965-69. Rsch. grantee USPHS, 1957-61, Adelphi Found., 1960-63, Rolf Found., 1965-71; recipient Heritage award Calif. Dance Educator Assn., 1987, N.B. Rudman award Found. Exceptional Leadership, 1995; Dame Order of St. John of the Ams., 1996. Mem. NSF, N.Y. Acad. Scis., Pi Lambda Theta, Kappa Delta Pi. Avocations: travel, gardening, music, art, lecturing. Office: BioEnergy Fields Found PO Box 6653 Malibu CA 90264-6653 Home Phone: 310-589-2748; Office Phone: 310-457-4694. Business E-Mail: vhunt@bioenergyfields.org.

HUNT, WAYNE ROBERT, SR., non-profit organization executive; b. Mt. Holly, NJ, Feb. 23, 1948; s. Edward Middleton Sr. and Sarah Isabel (Pope) H.; m. Elizabeth Evans Caputi, Oct. 23, 1982; children: Brandi Leigh, Wayne Robert Karr, Joshua David, Jacob Cody. BSBA, William Jewell Coll., 1970; MPA, Rutgers U., 1993; student, Command and Gen. Staff Coll., 1995. Cert. pub. mgr., facilitator. Mgr. Edward M. Hunt & Son Inc., Mt. Holly, 1970—79; spl. staff officer mech. sect., engring. divsn. NJ Dept. Def., Trenton, 1979—82, asst. bur. chief facilities mgmt. bur., 1982—88; contracting officer/bur. chief installations divsn. ops. bur. NJ Dept. Mil. and Vets. Affairs, Lawrenceville, 1986—94, dir. installations divsn., 1994—99, chief info. officer, 1999—2003, chief fin. & info. officer, fiscal and adminstrv. svs. divsn., 2003—04; chief of staff N.G. Assn. U.S., 2005—. Field assoc. orgnl. leadership devel. sec. Nat. Guard Bur., 1986-92. Deacon New Life Christian Ch.; past pres. Union Fire Co. #2. Lt. col. NJ Army Nat. Guard, 1970—; Bn. Comdr.; anti-terrorism- force protection sect. chief; sch. bd. dirs., Morrisville Sch. Bd., 2001-2004, sec., 2004—. Decorated Meritorious Svc. medal, (5) Army Commendation medals; recipient Proclamation for Svc. to State, Gov. James J. Florio, 1993, Cert. of Recognition, Drumthwacket Found., 1992, Letter of Appreciation, NJ Statue of Liberty Svc., NJ Dept. Mil. and Vets. Affairs Group award, 1995, Rancocas Valley Regional H.S. VIP Hall of Fame, 1997, NJ State Teamwork Award, 2002, Gov. McGreevey's Achievement Coin, 2003; letter of appreciation from Gov. McGreevey, 2003; named Man of Yr., 2004. Mem. ASPA (Cert. Achievement 2002), Am. Mgmt. Assn., Pub. Sector Mgr. Assn., NJ Soc. Cert. Pub. Mgr., Am. Acad. Cert. Pub. Mgr. (past pres.), N.G. Exec. Dir. Assn. (1st v.p., 2d v.p., chmn. nominations com., by-laws com.), N.G. Assn. US (Dist. Svc. medal 2003, Man of Yr.

2003), ABI (Medal of Honor 2003), N.G. Assn. NJ (sec. 1987-2004, Pres.'s award 1997), 114th Regtl. Assn., Trenton Arty. Officers Assn., Enlisted Assn. NJ, Masons (32 degree), Nat. Assn. Chief Info. Officers, Nat. Assn. State Mil. Resource Mgrs.; Elks, Pi Alpha Alpha. Avocations: golf, camping, jogging, weight training. Office: Nat Guard Assn of US One Massachusetts Ave Washington DC 20001 Home: 287 Belle Isle Dr Union Hall VA 24176-4081 Home Phone: 540-576-1094; Office Phone: 202-408-5895. E-mail: hu114@aol.com.

HUNT, WILLIAM B., pulmonologist; b. Lexington, NC, Sept. 27, 1927; s. William B. and Maxine (Cox) H.; married; children: William B., III, Anne, Alex, Sarah. BS, Wake Forest U., 1948; MD, Bowman Gray Sch. Medicine, Winston Salem, NC, 1953. Diplomate Am. Bd. Internal Medicine, Am. Bd. Allergy and Immunology. Intern, resident U. Va., Charlottesville, 1953-55, resident, fellow, 1957-59, assoc. prof., 1960-75, asst. dean Sch. Medicine, 1972-75; fellow gastroenterology Bowman Gray Sch. Medicine, Winston Salem, 1959-60; instr. internal medicine N.Y. Med. Coll., NYC, 1959-60; from clin. assoc. prof. medicine to clin. prof. medicine East Carolina Sch. Medicine, Greenville, NC, 1975—; staff physician Craven Regional Med. Ctr., New Bern, NC, 1975—, med. dir. cardiopulmonary svcs., 1975-95. Cons. N.C. Health Dept., TB Control Br., 1997-2000; TB control physician Craven County Health Dept., 1999—; mem. N.C. TB Peer Rev. Com., 1996—. Pres. Ea. Area Health Edn. Ctr., 1990-95. Recipient Douglas Southhall Freeman award Va. Lung Assn., 1975, Disting. Alumnus award Bowman Gray Sch. Medicine, 1973, Robert Bageant award Va. Soc. Respiratory Care, 1987. Fellow Am. Coll. Chest Physicians, Am. Thoracic Soc., Am. Coll. Physicians; mem. N.C. Med. Soc. (councillor 1978, exec. com. 1981), Va. Thoracic Soc. (pres. 1974), N.C. Thoracic Soc. (pres. 1984), N.C. Lung Assn. (pres. 1986), Craven Pamlico Jones Med. Soc. (pres. 1984). Democrat. Episcopalian. Avocations: skiing, golf, flying, sailing, tennis. Home: 1617 King Mountain Rd Charlottesville VA 22901

HUNT, WILLIAM EDWARD, SR., lawyer, retired state supreme court justice; b. Feb. 28, 1923; BA, U. Mont., LLB, 1955. Bar: Mont. 1955, US Dist. Ct., Mont. 1956, US Supreme Ct. Atty. Liberty County, Chester, Mont., 1957—70; dir. Mont. Aeronautics Commn., 1970—75; judge Mont. First Worker Compensation Ct., 1975-81; justice Mont. Supreme Ct., Helena, 1985—2000; of counsel Hunt Law Firm, Helena, 2000—. Contbr. articles to law jours. Trustee Mont. Legal Svc., 1968—71. Capt. US Army, 1947—65. Mem.: Mont. Legal Found. (dir. 2003—). Office: Hunt Law Firm 310 E Broadway St Helena MT 59601-4237 Office Phone: 406-442-8552. Office Fax: 406-495-1660.*

HUNT, WILLIAM W., investment company executive; B, Bates Coll.; M internat. bus., Univ. SC. Equity rsch. & trading positions Swiss Bank Corp. Internat., Tokyo; sr. investment officer Japan & Korea AIG Japan; joined State Street Corp., 1994; mng. dir. State Street Global Advisors, Tokyo; CEO State Street Japan; exec. v.p. internat. bus. State Street Global Advisors, 2001—05, pres., CEO, 2005—; vice-chmn. State Street Corp., Boston, 2006—. Mem. bd. overseers Boston Symphony Orch., Mus. Fine Arts Boston. Mem.: Japan Soc. Boston (bd. dir.). Office: State Street Corp 1 Lincoln St Boston MA 02111*

HUNT-COFFEY, NANCY, library director; b. Glendale, Calif. BA in English Lit., Occidental Coll., LA; MLS, PhD student, UCLA. Tech. cons. Glendale CC, Calif.; with LNX team Glendale Pub. Libr., 1992, mgr. LNX cmty. info. utility, exec. analyst/automation svcs. coord., asst. dir., dir., 2004—. Ex officio bd. mem. Assocs. of Brand Libr. and Arts Ctr.; bd. dirs. Friends of Glendale Pub. Libr. Contbr. articles to profl. publs. Office: Glendale Pub Libr 222 E Harvard St Glendale CA 91205 Office Phone: 818-548-2030. Office Fax: 818-548-7225. E-mail: nhunt-coffey@ci.glendale.ca.us.

HUNTEN, DONALD MOUNT, planetary scientist, educator; b. Montreal, Can., Mar. 1, 1925; came to U.S., 1963, naturalized, 1979; s. Kenneth William and Winnifred Binnmore (Mount) H.; m. Isobel Ann Rubenstein, Dec. 28, 1949 (div. Apr. 1995); children: Keith Atherton, Mark Ross; m. Ann Louise Sprague, May 21, 1995. B.Sc., U. Western Ont., 1946; PhD, McGill U., 1950. From research asso. to prof. physics U. Sask. (Can.), Saskatoon, 1950-63; physicist Kitt Peak Nat. Obs., Tucson, 1963-77; sci. adv. to asso. adminstr. for space sci. NASA, Washington, 1976-77; prof. planetary scis. U. Ariz., Tucson, 1977-88, Regents prof., 1988—. Cons. NASA, 1964—. Author: Introduction to Electronics, 1964; (with J.W. Chamberlain) Theory of Planetary Atmospheres, 1987; contbr. articles to profl. jours. Recipient Pub. Svc. medal NASA, 1977, 85,96, medal for exceptional sci. achievement, 1980, Space Sci. award Com. on Space Rsch., 2000. Mem.: AAAS, Can. Assn. Physicists (editor 1961—63), Royal Soc. Can., Nat. Acad. Scis., Internat. Assn. Geomagnetism and Aeronomy, Internat. Union Geodesy and Geophysics, Internat. Astron. Union, Am. Astron. Soc. (chmn. divsn. planetary scis. 1977), Am. Geophys. Union (John Adam Fleming medal 1998), Am. Phys. Soc., Cosmos Club (Washington), Explorers Club. Home: 3445 W Foxes Den Dr Tucson AZ 85745-5102 Office: U Ariz Dept Planetary Scis Tucson AZ 85721-0001 Business E-Mail: dhunten@lpl.arizona.edu.

HUNTER, BEVERLY CLAIRE, research scientist, educator; b. Pitts., Apr. 19, 1941; d. Eldon Claire and Ethel Mae (Kamer) Roberts m. Harold G. Hunter, Jan. 7, 1966; children: Cynthia Claire, Gregory Shawn. BA cum laude (Nat. Merit scholar), U. Pitts., 1963. Cert. Geographic Info. Sys. George Mason Univ., 2003. Computer programmer U.S. Navy, 1964-65; systems engr. IBM Corp., 1965-66; dir. instructional programming Human Resources Rsch. Orgn., Alexandria, Va., 1966-68, sr. staff scientist, 1970-87; staff scientist Matrix Rsch., Alexandria, 1969; lead scientist BBN Corp., 1993-98, NSFf, program mgr. rsch. on tchg. and learning, 1989—93; scientist Boston Coll., 1998-99; pres. Piedmont Rsch. Inst., Amissville, Va., 1999—. Cons. U.S. Congress, U.S. Office Edn., Bell Labs., Telenet Comms.: pres. Targeted Learning Corp., 1983-89; adj. prof. U. San Francisco, 1985-86; v.p. Piedmont Rsch. Ctr., 1979-80; peer reviewer. Co-author: Learning Alternatives in U.S. Education: Where Student and Computer Meet, 1975, Computer Literacy, 1982; Author: My Students Use Computers, 1984 Guide to Learning Resources for Users of IBM Personal Computers, Scholastic U.S. History Data Bases, 1985, Scholastic U.S. Government Data Bases, 1985, Scholastic Life Science Data Bases, 1985, Scholastic Physical Sciences Data Bases, 1985, Scholastic World Geography Data Bases, 1986, Scholastic Poetry and Mythology Data Bases, 1986, Scholastic Literature Data Bases, 1986, Scholastic Constitution Then and Now Data Files, 1987, Scholastic Weather and Climate Data Files, 1987, Working with the U.S. Congress, 1988, Online Searching in the Curriculum, 1989; Scientists at Work hypermedia data base; editor Edn. and Computing Internat. Jour.; contbr. articles to publs. Grantee, N.S.F., 1979—2003. Mem.: Va. Assn. Mapping and Land Info. Sys., Rappahannock Friends and Lovers of Our Watershed (bd. dir.), Rappahannock League Environ. Protection, Nature Conservancy. Office: Piedmont Rsch Inst 130 Mossie Ln Amissville VA 20106-4152

HUNTER, BILLY (G. WILLIAM), sports association administrator, lawyer; b. Cherry Hill, NJ, Nov. 5, 1942; Grad., Syracuse U.; JD, Howard U., 1969, U. Calif., Berkeley, 1970. US atty. (no. dist.) Calif. US Dept. Justice, 1976—83; pvt. practice defense and entertainment industry litigator; exec. dir. NBA Players Assn., 1996—. Football player Wash. Redskins and Miami Dolphins, 1965—66. Named to Little League Mus. Hall of Excellence, 2000. Office: NBA Players Assn 2 Penn Plz Ste 2430 New York NY 10121

HUNTER, BYNUM MERRITT, retired lawyer; b. Greensboro, NC, June 13, 1925; s. Hill McIver and Annie (Merritt) H.; m. Ann Fulenwider, June 22, 1957 (div. 1968); children: Ann Shirley, Mary Parker; m. Mary Lane Yancey, Aug. 7, 1969 (div. 1978); m. Mary Bonneau McElveen, June 13, 1980; 1 son, Bynum Jr. AB, U. N.C., 1945, JD, 1949. Bar: N.C. 1949. Ptnr. Smith Moore LLP, 2005; ret., 2005. Served with USNR, 1943-46, 51-53. Fellow Am. Coll. Trial Lawyers, Am. Bar Found. (life mem.); mem. ABA, Internat. Assn. Def. Counsel, Am. Judicature Soc., Greensboro Bar Assn. (pres. 1965-66) 4th Cir. Jud. Conf., N.C. Bar Assn., Zeta Psi, Phi Delta Phi. Clubs: Rotary. Home: 710 Country Club Dr Greensboro NC 27408-5714 Office: Smith Moore LLP Ste 1400 PO Box 21927 300 N Green St Greensboro NC 27420-1927 Office Phone: 336-378-5200. Business E-Mail: bynum.hunter@smithmoorelaw.com.

HUNTER, CHERYE RENEE, counselor; b. Newnan, Ga., Sept. 26, 1962; d. Johnnie Lee and Minnie Lee Hunter; m. Mosapa Echane (div.); 1 child, Jertez A. BA, Sam Houston State U., Huntsville, Tex., 1984; MSW, Howard U., Washington, 2003. Commd. lt. US Army, 1984, advanced through grades, resigned, 1994; correctional officer D.C. Dept. Corrections, DC, 1986—88; dep. sheriff Alexandria Sheriff's Office, Va., 1988—91; case mgr. Alexandria Cmty. Diversion Program, 1991—95; classification counselor Alexandria Sheriff's Office, 1995—. Avocations: photography, travel, writing, cooking, poetry. Home: 9669 Franklin Woods Pl Lorton VA 22079

HUNTER, COREY RYAN, secondary school educator; b. Williamsport, Pa., Sept. 4, 1977; s. Craig Ralph and Kathie Lee Hunter; m. Kimberly Rochelle Myers, June 23, 2001. BA, Susquehanna U., Selinsgrove, Pa., 1999; MA, Bucknell U., Lewisburg, Pa., 2004. Chemistry educator, head girls tennis coach Johnsonburg Area HS, Pa., 1999—2002, head baseball coach, 2000—02; chemistry educator St. Mary's Area HS, Pa., 2000; chemistry educator, asst. baseball coach Montoursville Area HS, Pa., 2002—. Mem.: NEA, Montoursville Area Edn. Assn. (bldg. representatitve, adv. bd. 2004—), Alpha Lambda Delta. Achievements include invention of synthesis and characterization of 20 new mononuclear gold(I) complexes. Avocations: baseball, hockey, tennis, travel. Office: Montoursville Area HS 100 North Arch St Montoursville PA 17754 Home Phone: 570-321-9198; Office Phone: 570-368-2611.

HUNTER, DONALD FORREST, lawyer; b. Mpls., Jan. 30, 1934; s. Earl Harvey and Ruby Cecilia (Lagerson) H.; m. Marlys Ann Zilge; Jeffrey, Cheri, Kathryn. BA, U. Minn., 1961, JD, 1963. Bar: Minn. 1963, US Dist. Ct. Minn. 1965, US Ct. Appeals (8th cir.) 1965, Ill. 1977, US Dist. Ct. (no. dist.) Ill. 1991, US Supreme Ct. 1986. Assoc., then ptnr. Gislason, Dosland, Hunter & Malecki, New Ulm, Minn., 1963-76; exec. v.p., sec., gen. counsel Wirtz Prodn. Ltd. Ice Follies/Holiday on Ice, Chgo., 1976-79; ptnr. Gislason, Dosland, Hunter & Malecki, Mpls., 1979-99; of counsel Gislason & Hunter, 1999—. Chmn. bd. dirs. Chgo. Milw. Corp., 1977-81; pres. Chgo. Milw. R.R., 1977-81; bd. dirs. First Security Bank, Chgo.; bd. dirs., officer First Security Bancorp, Inc., Chgo., 1993—; bd. dirs., sec. Wirtz Corp., Chgo. Blackhawk Hockey Team and related cos.; bd. dirs. First Miami Bancorp, Inc Fellow Am. Coll. Trial Lawyers; mem. ABA, Minn. Bar Assn. (bd. of govs. 1973-76), 5th Dist. Bar Assn. (pres. 1971-72), Hennepin County Bar Assn., US Supreme Ct. Hist. Assn. Office: Gislason & Hunter 701 Xenia Ave S Ste 500 Minneapolis MN 55416 Office Phone: 763-225-6000. Personal E-mail: hdonaldf@aol.com. Business E-Mail: dhunter@gislason.com.

HUNTER, DUNCAN LEE, congressman; b. Riverside, Calif., May 31, 1948; m. Lynne Layh, 1973; children: Robert Samuel, Duncan Duane. Attended, U. Calif., Santa Barbara, U. Mt., 1966—67; BSL, Western State U., 1976, JD, 1976. Bar: Calif. 1976. Pvt. practice, San Diego; mem. U.S. Congress from 52nd Calif. dist., 1981—, mem., chmn. armed svcs. com. Mem. Congressional Jobs and Fair Trade Caucus; co-chair Congressional Task Force on Bowhunting, Nat. Security Caucus. With U.S. Army, 1969-71, Vietnam. Decorated Air medal, bronze star. Mem. Navy League. Republican. Baptist. Office: US Ho Reps 2265 Rayburn Ho Office Bldg Washington DC 20515-0552*

HUNTER, DURANT ADAMS, executive search company executive; b. North Adams, Mass., Nov. 25, 1948; s. Richard Andrew and Lucy (Adams) H.; m. Sara Hoagland, June 10, 1978; children: John, Abigail. AB, U. NC, 1971; MPA, George Washington U., 1973. Staff asst. to Congressman Silvio O. Conte U.S. Ho. of Reps., Washington, 1971-72; program dir. Internat. Mgmt. and Devel. Inst., Washington, 1973-74; asst. v.p. J.P. Morgan Co., NYC, 1974-81; v.p., COO James Hunter Machine Co., North Adams, 1981-83; exec. v.p. HM Internat., Wellesley, Mass., 1983-85; mng. dir. Boyden Internat., Boston, 1985-89; ptnr. Gardiner Stone Hunter Internat., Boston, 1989-92; pres., CEO Pendleton James Assocs. Inc., Boston, 1992-2000; CEO Whitehead Mann Inc., 2000—03, Ridgeway Ptnrs., LLC, 2003—. Mem. Wellesley Planning Bd., 1983-86; bd. dirs. Boys and Girls Clubs, Boston, 1988—, Wide Horizons Children's Svcs., Waltham, Mass., 1989—, Mass. Cultural Coun.; trustee The Wang Ctr. Performing Arts, Boston, 1995—; bd. dirs. Mass. Cultural Coun. Mem.: Wianno Club, Hole-in-the-Wall Golf Club, Ekwanok Country Club, Royal Automobile Club, The Country Club, Univ. Club, Bus. Assoc. Club (pres. 1989). Home: 153 Ridgeway Rd Weston MA 02493-2724 Office: Ten Post Office Sq Ste 960 Boston MA 02109 Business E-Mail: andy.hunter@ridgewaypartners.com.

HUNTER, EARLE LESLIE, III, retired professional association executive; b. Juneau, Alaska, Nov. 23, 1929; s. Earle and Mary Uinta (Kirk) H.; m. Helen Doreen Dawson, Jan. 19, 1954; children: Barbara, James, Robert. BS, Ill. Coll. Optometry, Chgo., 1956, OD, 1957, DOS, 1988, New Eng. Coll. Optometry, 1995. Practice optometry, Juneau, 1957-59, McMinnville, Oreg., 1959-71; dir. clinics Pacific U., Forest Grove, Oreg., 1971-74; dir. primary care Am. Optometric Assn., St. Louis, 1974-78, asst. exec. dir., 1978-84, interim exec. dir., 1984-85, dep. exec. dir., 1985-87, exec. dir., 1987-95; ret., 1995—99; spl. asst. to the dean U. Mo. Sch. Optometry, 1999-2001. Sec. Z.80 com. Am. Nat. Stds. Inst., 1974-95. Contbr. articles to profl. jours. County chmn. various gubernatorial campaigns; vice chmn. Oreg. Health Commn., 1971-74. Named Optometrist of Yr., Oreg. Optometric Assn., 1971, Jr. Citizen of Yr., Jaycees, McMinnville, 1961. Fellow APHA, Am. Acad. Optometry; mem. Optical Soc. Am., Am. Soc. Assn. Execs. (com. 1981-93), St. Louis Soc. Assn. Execs. (pres. 1983-84), U.S. C. of C. (assn. com.), Tomb and Key, Univ. Club (St. Louis), Masons, Elks, Beta Sigma Kappa. Republican. Episcopalian. Avocations: sailing, golf. Home: 213 Orchard Ave Saint Louis MO 63119-2523

HUNTER, FORREST WALKER, lawyer; b. Arlington, Va., Jan. 25, 1950; s. Dallas Walker and Ann Arsell (Wheat) H.; m. Susan Gladys Zsamer, June 8, 1974; children: Andrew Chastain, Alison Christian. BA, U. Va., 1972; JD, Emory U., 1975. Bar: Ga. 1975, U.S. Dist. Ct. (no. dist.) Ga. 1978, U.S. Ct. Appeals (5th cir.) 1978, U.S. Ct. Appeals (11th cir.) 1981, U.S. Dist. Ct. (mid. dist.) Ga. 1982, U.S. Dist. Ct. (so. dist.) Ga. 1983, U.S. Ct. Appeals (6th cir.) 1988, U.S. Dist. Ct. (we. dist.) Mich. 1994, U.S. Ct. Appeals (7th cir.) 1996, U.S. Dist. Ct. (ea. dist.) Tex. 1999, U.S. Dist. Ct. (no. dist.) Ind. 2002. Atty. Office Chief Counsel IRS, Dept. Treasurey, Washington, 1975-77, sr. atty. Office. Regional Counsel Atlanta, 1977-81; assoc. Jones, Bird & Howell and Alston & Bird, Atlanta, 1981-85; ptnr., labor, employment litig. Alston & Bird LLP, Atlanta, 1985—. Bd. dirs. Boys and Girls Clubs of Metro Atlanta, 1984. Named one of Legal Elite, Ga. Trend, 2004, Super Lawyers, Atlanta Mag., 2005. Mem. Am. Health Lawyers Assn., Ga. Acad. Hosp. Attys., Lawyers Club Atlanta, Atlanta Bar Assn., U. Va. Alumni Assn., Emory U. Alumni Assn. Office: Alston & Bird LLP 1 Atlantic Ctr 1201 W Peachtree St NW Atlanta GA 30309-3424 Office Phone: 404-881-7190. Business E-Mail: forrest.hunter@alston.com.

HUNTER, FRANCES ELLEN CROFT, music educator; b. Greensboro, NC, Jan. 25, 1941; d. John Wilkins Croft Sr. and Zara Louise Fisher Croft; m. C. Linwood Hunter, Jan. 25, 1964 (dec. Sept 2, 1996); 1 child, Leticia Collette. BFA, Ohio U., Athens, 1962. Cert. tchr. music N.C., Ohio. Tchr. music Hoke County Schs., Raeford, NC, 1962—64, Harnett County Schs., Johnsonville, NC, 1964—65, Fayetteville City Schs., NC, 1965—70, Ft. Bragg Schs., NC, 1971—2001. Singer Cumberland Oratorio Singers, Fayetteville, 2003, bd. dirs., 2004—; singer and accompanist Stars and Stripes Singers, Fayetteville, 2003. Composer: Here's Looking At You Yr. 2000, 1987. Vol. Fayetteville Festival of Flight, 2003, Teen Involvement Projects, Inc.; vol. reader svc. for blind Southeastern NC Radio Reading Svc. Inc., 2004. Recipient Svc. award, Music Educators Nat. Conf./N.C. Music Educators Assn., 1999, Cert. of Retirement, Dept. Def. Edn. Activity, 2001. Mem.: Nat. Assn. Ret. Fed. Employees, NC Ret. Govt. Employees' Assn., Music Educators Nat. Conf. Lutheran. Avocations: reading, dance.

HUNTER, HARLEN CHARLES, orthopedic surgeon; b. Estherville, Iowa, Sept. 23, 1940; s. Roy Harold and Helen Iola (King) H.; m. JoAnn Wilson, June 30, 1962; children: Harlen Todd, Juliann Kristin. BA, Drake U., 1962; DO, Coll. Osteo. Med. and Surgery, Des Moines, 1967. Diplomate Am. Osteo. Bd. Orthop. Surgery, Am. Osteo. Acad. Sports Medicine. Intern Normandy Osteo. Hosp., St. Louis, 1967-68, resident in orthops., 1968-72, chmn. dept. orthops., 1976-77; founder Orthopedics and Sports Medicine, PC, Bedford, Ind.; chmn. dept. surgery Bedford Regional Med. Ctr., 2002—04. Founder, orthop. surgeon Mid-States Orthop. Sports Medicine Clinics of Am., Ltd. Sports Med. Ctrs., Chesterfield, Mo., Fairview Heights, Ill., Jerseyville, Ill., Herman, Mo., 1977-99, Hunter Trauma Team, 1988-92; founder, pres. Life Style Health Systems, 1992; assoc. prof. orthop. Kansas City Coll. Osteopathy, 1993, Pikeville Coll. Osteopathic Medicine, 2005—; adj. prof. Lake Erie Coll. Osteo. Medicine, 1995—; staff Normandy Osteopathic, 1972-90, Outpatient Surgery Ctr., St. Louis, 1990-99, Luth. Med. Ctr., 1989-99, St. Joe's of Kirkwood, 1990-99, Bedford Med. Ctr., Dunn Meml.; clin. instr. Kirksville Coll. Osteo. Medicine; orthop. cons., team physician to high schs.; pres. Health Specialists, Inc.; program dir. sports medicine Family Physicians, 1993-94; host weekly TV program Raceology Weekly Spl. on Motorsports; med. adv. bd. Mo. Athletic Activities Assn.; cons. sports medicine Sports St. Louis newspaper; founder Ann. Sports Medicine Clinic for Trainers and Coaches, 1 yr. fellowship in sports medicine; adj. clin. assoc. prof. Coll. Osteo. Surgery, Des Moines; orthop. surgeon Iowa State Boys Basketball Tournament, 1966-85; founder Mobile Sports Medicine Semi Truck, 1988, Hunter Sports Medicine Clinic, Belleville, Ill.; sponsor U.S. Biathalon Assn., 1989; staff photographer Ind. Motor Speedway, 1973—, Daytona Internat. Speedway, 1979-96, ARCA, 2000—, USAC, 2005—; adv. bd. Motorsport Rsch. Group Human Performance Internat., Daytona Beach, Fla., 1990—; mem. Sports Medicine Commn. Ind. State Med. Assn.; lectr. in field Co-author: Motorsports Medicine, 1992; host daily radio program Making a Difference, For Your Health; radio host Racing USA with Dr. Hunter, 2006; contbr. articles to profl. jours. Pres. adv. bd. Bedford Salvation Army; candidate Lawrence County Commr., 2004. Recipient Clinic Spkr. award Iowa H.S. Baseball Coaches Assn., 1982, 83, Hall of Fame award Mo. Athletic Trainers Assn., 1987, Sibley Medallion award for outstanding svc. Lindenwood U., Ann. Outstanding Soccer Player of Yr. award Mo. Athletic Club, Hunter 100 Stock Car Race, Peveley, Mo., Bob Scott Photography award Indpls. Motor Speedway, 2002; named Businessman of Yr., Nat. Rep. Congl. Com., 2003; Harlen C. Hunter Sports Complex named in his honor Lindenwood U., St. Charles, Mo., 1988. Fellow Am. Coll. Osteo. Surgeons, Am. Osteo Acad. Orthops. (past chmn. com. on athletic injuries), Am. Osteo. Acad. Sports Medicine; mem. Am. Osteo. Assn., Mo. Assn. Osteo. Physicians and Surgeons (Medallion award 1990), Am. Coll. Sports Medicine, Am. Orthop. Soc. Sports Medicine (del. sports medicine exch. program to China 1985), AMA, Am. Coll. Occupl. Medicine, Ind. Med. Assn. (sports medicine com. 1999—), Ind. Osteo. Assn. (bd. trustees 2003-), St. Louis Met. Med. Assn., Sports Car Club Am. (med. dir. pro racing 1989-91), World Congress Motorsport Scis., St. Louis Auto Racing Club (Amb. award 1989, 91), 500 Old Timers Club, The Butler Soc., Elks, Lions, Masons, Shriners. Republican. Methodist. Home: 604 Heltonville Rd E Bedford IN 47421-9250 Home Phone: 812-278-8130; Office Phone: 812-275-1234. Business E-Mail: drsptmed@insightbb.com.

HUNTER, HERBERT ERWIN, aerospace engineer; b. Washington, June 11, 1934; s. Herbert C. and A. Paula (Dieterich) H.; m. Helen Louise Shelhorse, June 11, 1956 (div. 1978); children: Erwin, David, Shirley Black, Patricia Copeland, Linda Markiewicz; m. Jeanne Theresa Parent, Nov. 25, 1978; stepchildren: Richard Kinsella, William Kinsella, Katey McMahon, Philip Kinsella. BS in Aerospace Engring., U. Md., 1956; MS in Aerospace Engring., Calif. Inst. Tech., Pasadena, 1957, PhD in Aerospace Engring., 1960. Dept. mgr. AVCO Corp., Wilmington, Mass., 1963-73; pres., founder, chmn. bd. dirs. Adapt Svc. Corp., Reading, Mass., 1973-83; assoc. fellow Nichols Rsch. Corp., Huntsville, Ala., 1983-94; co-founder Applied Data Trends, Inc., Huntsville, 1994, pres., 1994-2000, pres. emeritus, 2000—, dir., 1994—2004. Dir. QPC, Inc., 2000-2004. Contbr. articles to Jour. Aerospace Scis., Jour. Math Physics, Jour. Climate Applied Meteorology, Jour. Atmospheric Ocean Tech. With USAF, 1960-63. Mem. AAAS, AIAA, Am. Meteorol. Soc., Soc. of Photo-Optical Instrumentation Engrs. Baptist. Home: 8912 Hogan Dr SE Huntsville AL 35802-3436 Office: Applied Data Trends Inc 215 Wynn Dr Ste 321 Huntsville AL 35805 Personal E-mail: herbhunter@aol.com.

HUNTER, HOLLY, actress; b. Conyers, Ga., Mar. 20, 1958; d. Charles Edwin and Opal Marguerite (Catledge) Hunter; m. Janusz Kaminski, May 20, 1995 (div. Dec. 21, 2001); 2 children. BFA, Carnegie-Mellon U., 1980. Actress: (films) The Burning, 1981, Swing Shift, 1984, Broadcast News, 1987 (Acad. Award nomination for best actress, 1988), Raising Arizona, 1987, End of the Line, 1988, Always, 1989, Miss Firecracker, 1989, Animal Behavior, 1989, Once Around, 1991, The Piano, 1993 (Cannes Film Festival Award for best actress, 1993, Golden Globe for best actress, 1994, Acad. Award for best actress, 1994), The Firm, 1993 (Acad. Award nomination for best supporting actress, 1994), Home for the Holidays, 1995, Copycat, 1995, Crash, 1996, Hurly-burly, 1997, A Life Less Ordinary, 1997, Living Out Loud, 1998, Jesus' Son, 1999, Things You Can Tell Just By Looking at Her, 2000 (Emmy nomination for best supporting actress in a miniseries or movie, 2001), Woman Wanted, 2000, Timecode, 2000, O Brother, Where Art Thou, 2000, Moonlight Mile, 2002, Levity, 2003, Little Black Book, 2004, The Incredibles (voice), 2004, Nine Lives, 2005, The Big White, 2005; (TV) Svengali, 1983, An Uncommon Love, 1983, With Intent to Kill, 1984, A Gathering of Old Men, 1987, Roe vs. Wade, 1989 (Emmy for best actress in a miniseries or special, 1989), Crazy in Love, 1992, The Positively True Adventures of the Alleged Texas Cheerleader-Murdering Mom, 1993 (Emmy for best actress in a miniseries or special, 1993, CableACE award for best actress in a movie or miniseries, 1994), Harlan County War, 2000 (Emmy nomination for best actress in a miniseries or movie, 2000), When Billie Beat Bobby, 2001 (Emmy nomination for best actress in a miniseries or movie, 2001); (Broadway stage prodns.) Crimes of the Heart, 1982, The Wake of Jamey Foster, 1982, Impossible Marriage, 1998; (regional stage prodns.) Buried Child, A Doll's House, Artichoke; (other stage prodns.) include A Lie of the Mind, L.A., Battery, N.Y.C., Miss Firecracker Contest, 1984, The Person I Once Was, N.Y.C.; Actress, exec. prodr.: (films) Thirteen, 2003 (Acad. Award nomination for best supporing actress, 2004, Golden Globe nomination for best supporting actress, 2004, Screen Actors Guild Award nomination for best supporting actress, 2004); (TV series) Saving Grace, 2007-. Bd. dirs. Calif. Abortion Rights Action League.*

HUNTER, HOWARD OWEN, academic administrator, law educator; b. Brunswick, Ga., Oct. 14, 1946; m. Susan Frankel, Nov. 27, 1971; 1 child, Emily Atwood Plotkin. BA in Russian Studies, Yale U., 1968, JD, 1971. Bar: Ga. 1971, Supreme Ct. Ga., 1998. Assoc. atty. Hogan & Hartson, Washington, 1971-72, Hansell, Post, Brandon & Dorsey, Atlanta, 1972-76; asst. prof. Emory U. Sch. Law, Atlanta, 1976-79, assoc. prof., 1979-82, assoc. dean, 1979-80, prof., 1982—, prof. law, dean, 1989-2001, provost, exec. v.p. for acad. affairs, 2001—03; prof. of law, pres. Singapore Mgmt. U, Singapore, 2004—; prof. of law and dean emeritus Emory U, Atlanta, 2004—. Dir. Ga. Vol. Lawyers for the Arts, Inc., 1975-89, sec., 1975-77, treas., 1978-80, v.p., 1980-82, pres., 1984-87; vis. prof. law U. Va. Sch. Law, Charlottesville, 1982-83, Ctrl. European U, Budapest, 1999; hon. prof. law U. Hong Kong, 1986; vis. Mills E. Godwin prof. law Coll. William & Mary, Williamsburg, Va., 1989, vis. McWilliam prof. of Comml. Law Sydney U, 2004; mem. Chief Justice Commn. on Professionalism, 1990—, Supreme Ct. Commn. on Indigent Def., 2000—; bd. trustees Fed. Def. Program, 1991-97; lectr. in field. Author: Freedom of Information Handbook: Georgia, 1979, Modern Law of Contracts: Breach and Remedies, 1986, supplements, 1987, 88, 89, 90, 91, 92, 93, Modern Law of Contracts: Formation, Performance, Relationships, 1987, supplements, 1988, 89, 90, 91, 92, 93, Modern Law of Contracts, revised edit., 1993, supplements, 1994, 95, 96, 97, 98, 2d rev. edit., 1999, supplements, 2000, 01, (with Mogens Pedersen) Recent Reforms in Swedish Higher Education, 1980; contbr. articles to profl. jours.; mem. editl. bd. Jour. of Contract Law, 1988—. Member (appeals bd.) Competition Comm. of Singapore, 2006—; bd. dir. Singapore Internat. C. of C., 2005—, Workforce Devel. Authority of Singapore, 2005—, The Enterprise Challenge of Singapore, 2005—, Nat. Research Found. of Singapore, 2006—; bd. of governors American C. of C., Singapore, 2006—. Fulbright Sr. scholar U. Sydney, 1988, recipient Amicus Curiae award. Mem. ABA 1972, Assn. Am. Law Schs.1976, Am. Law Inst. (mem. consultative com. on revisions to article 2 of UCC), State Bar Ga. (mem. editl. bd. Ga. State Bar Jour. 1977-82), Decatur-DeKalb Bar Assn., Atlanta Bar Assn. (vol. lawyer project on illegal Cuban immigrants 1985-87, vol. lawyer in representation of Cuban inmates at fed. prison in Talladega, Ala. 1988, bd. dirs. internat. transaction sect. 1995—), Inst. Continuing Legal Edn. (vice-chmn. bd. trustees 1993-97), Inst. Continuing Judicial Edn. (bd. trustees 1989-2001), Ga. Vol. Lawyers for Arts Inc.(bd. dir. 1975-1989, pres. 1985-1987, bd. adv. 1997-2004) Avocations: bicycling, jogging, fishing, travel. Office: Singapore Mgmt U 81 Victoria St Administration Bldg 81-14-03100 Singapore 188065 Office Phone: 65 6828 0181. Business E-Mail: howardhunter@smu.edu.sg. E-mail: hunter@emory.edu.*

HUNTER, IAN W., engineering educator, researcher; BSc, U. Auckland, 1974, MSc, 1975, DCP, 1976, PhD, 1980. Hatsopoulos prof. mech. engring., prof. biol. engring. MIT, Cambridge, dir. BioInstrumentation lab. Achievements include research in nanostructured actuator polymers, optimization of conducting polymer actuators, model-based control of mechanically active materials. Office: MIT BioInstrumentation Lab 77 Massachusetts Ave Rm 3-154 Cambridge MA 02139 Office Phone: 617-253-4763. Office Fax: 617-252-1849. E-mail: ihunter@mit.edu.

HUNTER, JACK DUVAL, retired lawyer; b. Elkhart, Ind., Jan. 14, 1937; s. William Stanley and Marjorie Irene (Upson) H.; m. Marsha Ann Goodsell, Nov. 14, 1958 (dec.); children: Jack (dec.), Jon, Justin. BBA, U. Mich., 1959, LLB, 1961. Bar: Mich. 1961, Ind. 1962. Atty. Lincoln Nat. Life Ins. Co., Ft. Wayne, Ind., 1961-64, asst. counsel, 1964-68, v.p., gen. counsel, 1975-79, sr. v.p., gen. counsel, 1979-86, exec. v.p., gen. counsel, 1986-99. Asst. gen. counsel, asst. sec. Lincoln Nat. Corp., Ft. Wayne and Phila., 1968-71, gen. counsel, 1971-2002, v.p., 1972-79, sr. v.p., 1979-86, exec. v.p., 1986-2002. Life trustee Ind. Nature Conservancy, chmn. bd. trustees, 1993-95. Recipient Oak Leaf award Nature Conservancy, 1997. Mem. ABA, Ind. State Bar Assn., Allen County Bar Assn., Assn. Life Ins. Counsel (pres. 1995-96, Anderson Disting. Svc. award 2002), Am. Coun. Life Ins. (chmn. legal sect. 1991). Personal E-mail: jack.hunter2@verizon.net.

HUNTER, JACK E., retired judge; b. Alexandria, La., May 24, 1945; s. William A. and Lucy A. Hunter; m. Marcela Sanchez, Aug. 12, 1989 (div. Dec. 2001). BBA, U. Houston, 1969; JD, South Tex. Coll. Law, Houston, 1974. Bar: Tex., bd. cert. criminal law: Tex. 1st asst. dist. atty., acting dist. atty. Nueces County Dist. Atty.'s Office, Corpus Christi, Tex., 1977—83; chief judge Corpus Christi Mcpl. Ct., Corpus Christi, Tex., 1983—86; state dist. judge 94th Dist. Ct., Corpus Christi, Tex., 1987—2006; ret., 2006. Adv. com. legal asst. program Del Mar Coll., Corpus Christi, 1990—; past adj. prof. arts and humanities Tex. A&M C.C., Corpus Christi. Author: From The Bench, 2005, Osaka Spa Murders, 2005, Drug Running, 2007; contbr. articles to legal jours. Past chmn. Nueces County Gang Task Force; past adv. chair Leadership Corpus Christi XXII; adminstrv. judge Nueces County Bd. Judges; past chmn. Nueces County Juvenile Bd.; founder Texans Against Gangs; past dist. chmn. Boy Scouts Am. Sp4 US Army, 1970—72. Recipient Spirit of Benevolence award, Coastal Bend Coun. Alcohol and Drug Abuse, 1998, Citizen of Yr. award, Arthritis Found. Corpus Christi, 2000; fellow, Tex. Bar Found. Mem.: Corpus Christi Bar Assn. (chmn. continued legal edn. 1989—, Cecil Burney Humanitarian award 1990), Teen Ct. Inc. (co-founder, pres. 1990—). Democrat. Roman Catholic. Avocations: reading, exercise, travel. Office: 94th Dist Ct Nueces County Courthouse 901 Leopard St Corpus Christi TX 78401 Business E-Mail: drehler@nueces.esc2.net.

HUNTER, JAMES AUSTEN, JR., lawyer; b. Phoenix, June 19, 1941; s. James Austen and Elizabeth Aileen Hunter; m. Donna Gabriele, Aug. 24, 1973; 1 child, James A. AB, Cath. U. Am., 1963, LL.B., 1966. Bar: N.Y. 1967, Pa. 1975, U.S. Supreme Ct. 1974. Assoc. firm Sullivan & Cromwell, NYC, 1967-74; assoc. firm Morgan, Lewis & Bockius, LLP, Phila., 1974-77, ptnr., 1977—. Home: 1001 Red Rose Ln Villanova PA 19085-2118 Office: Morgan Lewis & Bockius LLP 1701 Market St Philadelphia PA 19103-2903 Home Phone: 610-527-7618; Office Phone: 215-963-5381. E-mail: jhunter@morganlewis.com.

HUNTER, JAMES EDWARD, chemist, consultant; b. Phila., May 4, 1945; s. James Bruce and Ruth Moyer (Lenker) H.; m. Marilyn Kay Jones, Aug. 24, 1968; children: Melanie Kay, Timothy Edward. BS in Chemistry, Lehigh U., 1967; MS in Biochemistry, U. Wis., 1969, PhD in Biochemistry, 1974. Staff nutritionist Procter & Gamble Co., Cin., 1974-92, staff toxicologist, 1992-95, staff toxicologist regulatory affairs, 1995-96; adj. prof. chemistry Cin. State Tech. and Cmty. Coll., 1997-98, U. Cin., 1998—. Mem. biol. subcom. of tech. com. Inst. of Shortening and Edible Oils, Inc., Washington, 1981-93, chmn. biol. subcom., 1985-93; mem. human nutrition bd. of sci. counselors USDA, Washington, 1990-92; mem. oral health com. and subcom. on fatty acids and health Internat. Life Scis. Inst., Washington, 1985-92. Editor: (booklet) Food Fats and Oils, 5th edit., 1982, 6th edit., 1988, 7th edit., 1994; contbr. numerous articles to profl. jours. including Jour. Am. Oil Chemists Soc., Am. Jour. Clin. Nutrition. V.p., chmn. fundraisers St. Xavier H.S. Music Promoters Bd., Cin., 1992-94; sec., mem. com. mgmt. Powel Crosley Jr. YMCA, Cin., 1980-86, sec., 1982-86; cubmaster Boy Scouts Am., Cin., 1985-87. With U.S. Army, 1969-71. Mem.: Am. Soc. for Nutrition, Am. Chem. Soc. (chair various local coms.), Am. Oil Chemists Soc. (bd. dirs., treas. local chpt. 1990—93), Runners Club Greater Cin. (v.p. 1994—95, sec. 1995—), Tau Beta Pi, Sigma Xi, Phi Beta Kappa. Avocations: ragtime piano, running, swimming, photography, woodworking. Business E-Mail: hunterje@email.uc.edu.

HUNTER, JAMES GALBRAITH, JR., lawyer; b. Phila., Jan. 6, 1942; s. James Galbraith and Emma Margaret (Jehl) H.; m. Pamela Ann Trott, July 18, 1969 (div.); children: James Nicholas, Catherine Selene; m. Nancy Grace Scheurwater, June 21, 1992. B.S. in Engring. Sci., Case Inst. Tech., 1965; J.D., U. Chgo., 1967. Bar: Ill. 1967, U.S. Dist. Ct. (no. dist.) Ill. 1967, U.S. Ct. Appeals (7th cir.) 1967, U.S. Ct. Claims, 1976, U.S. Ct. Appeals (4th and 9th cirs.) 1978, U.S. Supreme Ct. 1979, U.S. Dist. Ct. (cen. dist.) Ill. 1980, Calif. 1980, U.S. Dist. Ct. (cen. and so. dists.) Calif. 1980, U.S. Ct. Appeals (5th cir.) 1982, U.S. Ct. Appeals (fed. cir.) 1982. Assoc. Kirkland & Ellis, Chgo., 1967-68, 70-73, ptnr., 1973-76; ptnr. Hedlund, Hunter & Lynch, Chgo., 1976-82, Los Angeles, 1979-82; ptnr. Latham & Watkins, Hedlund, Hunter & Lynch, Chgo. and Los Angeles, 1982—. Served to lt. JAGC, USN, 1968-70. Mem. ABA, State Bar Calif., Los Angeles County Bar Assn., Chgo. Bar Assn. Clubs: Metropolitan (Chgo.), Chgo. Athletic Assn., Los Angeles Athletic. Exec. editor U. Chgo. Law Rev., 1966-67. Office: Latham & Watkins Sears Tower Ste 5800 Chicago IL 60606-6306 also: 633 W 5th St Los Angeles CA 90071-2005

HUNTER, J(AMES) PAUL, literature and language professor, literary critic; b. Jamestown, NY, June 29, 1934; s. Paul W. and Florence I. (Walmer) H.; children: Debra, Lisa, Paul III, Anne, Ellen Harris. AB, Ind. Central Coll., 1955; MA, Miami U., Oxford, Ohio, 1957; PhD, Rice U., 1963. Instr., U. Fla., Gainesville, 1957-59, Williams Coll., Williamstown, Mass., 1962-64; asst. prof. U. Calif., Riverside, 1964-66; assoc. prof. English Emory U., Atlanta, 1966-68, prof., 1968-80, chmn. dept., 1973-79; prof. English, dean Coll. Arts and Sci., U. Rochester, NY, 1981-86; prof. English U. Chgo., 1987—, Chester D. Tripp prof. humanities, 1990-96, Barbara E. and Richard J. Franke prof. humanities, 1996—2001; dir. Franke Inst. for the Humanities, 1996—2001, Franke prof. emeritus, 2001—; prof. of English U. of Va., 2001—. Gen. editor Bedford Cultural Edits., 1994—. Author: The Reluctant Pilgrim, 1966, Occasional Form, 1975, Norton Introduction to Poetry, 9th edit., 2007, Norton Introduction to Literature, 9th edit., 2005, New Worlds of Literature, 2d edit., 1994, Before Novels, 1990; co-editor: Rhetorics of Order/Ordering Rhetorics, 1989; editor: Norton Critical Edition of Mary Shelley's Frankenstein, 1996. Sr. advisor Andrew W. Mellon Found., 1999—. Guggenheim fellow, 1976-77, NEH fellow, 1985-86, Nat. Humanities Ctr. fellow, 1986, 95-96. Mem. MLA, Am. Soc. 18th Century Studies (2d v.p. 1994-95, 1st v.p. 1995-96, pres. 1996-97, Louis Gottschalk prize 1991), Southeastern Am. Soc. 18th Century Studies (pres. 1977-78), Soc. Atlantic MLA (pres. 1992-93), N.E. Am. Soc. 18th Century Studies (pres. 1982-83), Ill. Humanities Coun. (chair 2000-04), Fedn. State Humanities Couns (chmn. bd. 2005—). Home Phone: 773-536-4691; Office Phone: 312-458-9978. Business E-Mail: jph7f@virginia.edu.

HUNTER, JODY JEAN, association executive, conservationist; b. Glen Cove, NY; d. William T. and Lois Hunter; m. Joseph A. Herbert, Jr., Nov. 30, 1998; stepchildren: Mary Herbert, Nancy Herbert. BS in Park Mgmt. and Conservation magna cum laude, U. N.H., 1980. Cert. in food svc. sanitation, Fairfax County, 1985. Park mgr. Fairfax County Park Authority, Fairfax, Va., 1980-86; adminstrv. asst. The Wilderness Soc., Washington, 1988-89, Internat. Chiropractors Assn., Washington, 1986-88, membership coord. Arlington, Va., 1989-93, dir. membership svcs., 1993—. Spl. events coord. Arlington Uncommon Market Food Coop., 1990—, bd. dirs., 1987—91, sec., 1989; vol. No. Va. Regional Park Authority, Fairfax Station, 1999, Arlingtonians for a Clean Environment , 2000—; vol. membership coord. No. Va. Land Trust, 2000—, Signature, Gunston and Shakespeare Landsberg theaters, 1996—. Mem.: U.S. Pub. Info. Rsch. Group, Save the Manatee Soc., The Nature Conservancy, Nat. Honor Soc., Am. Soc. Assn. Execs., Sr. Key U. Honor Soc., Phi Kappa Phi. Avocations: wildflower appreciation, nature walking, edible foods identification, world-wide adventure travel.

HUNTER, JOEL CARL, clergyman, educator; b. Shelby, Ohio, Apr. 18, 1948; s. Wilbur Westerman and Jean Ellen (Bashore) H.; m. Becky Gaylene Beeson, July 2, 1972; children: Joshua, Isaac, Joel. BS in Edn., Ohio U., 1970; MDiv, Christian Theol. Sem., Indpls., 1973, D Ministry, 1974; D Humanities (hon.), Belhaven Coll., 2005. Ordained to ministry United Meth. Ch., 1975. Assoc. min. Bradley United Meth. Ch., Greenfield, Ind., 1970-71, Southport (Ind.) United Meth. Ch., 1971-74; sr. min. Faith United Meth. Ch., Princeton, Ind., 1974-78, Mt. Auburn United Meth. Ch., Greenwood, Ind., 1978-85, Northland Cmty. Ch., Longwood, Fla., 1985—. Chmn. Min.'s Forum, Orlando, Fla., 1993—; adj. prof. practical theology Ref. Theol. Sem., Orlando; bd. dirs. Gospel to the Unreached Millions; pres.-elect Christian Coalition of Am., 2006. Author: Prayer, Politics, and Power, 1988, The Challenging Road, 1995, Finding Your Purpose, 1995, Overcoming Adversity, 1996, Learning to Love, 1997, Transforming Faith, 1998, The Journey to Spiritual Maturity, 2001, Right Wing, Wrong Bird, 2006; also articles; radio broadcast Fit for the Journey, 1996—. Bd. dirs. Liberty Coun., Orlando, 1994-97; cons. Cmty. Issues Forum, Orlando, 1993—, Interfaith Alliance, Orlando, 1995, World Evang. Alliance, Global Pastors' Network, The Jobs Partnership of Fla, Christian Peacemaking Resources, Inc.; tchr. Worldview Seminar, Orlando, 1995; chmn. Northland Found. for Arts and Edn., Longwood, 1995—; paradigm Pioneer Leadership Network, Tyler, Tex., 1995—; adv. bd. mem. Belhaven Coll., Man in the Mirror Ministries, Vision Orlando, Christian HELP, New Man Mag. Mem.: Nat. Assn. Evangelicals. Avocations: mentoring, art student, weight-lifting, running. Office: Northland Cmty Ch 530 Dog Track Rd Longwood FL 32750-6546*

HUNTER, JOHN C., III, chemicals executive; b. LaGrange, Ga., Mar. 1, 1947; BS in Chem. Engring., Ga. Inst. Tech., 1969; MBA, U. Houston, 1977. Joined Monsanto Co., 1969, pres. fibers, 1997; pres., COO, CEO, chmn. Solutia, Inc. Lt. U.S. Army, 1970-72. Address: 575 Maryville Center Dr Saint Louis MO 63141

HUNTER, JOHN ORR, retired college president; b. Newfane, NY, Mar. 17, 1933; s. Alexander and Jane (Robertson) H.; m. Lyla Beth Brown, Aug. 31, 1957; children: Elaine, John, Susan, Elizabeth. BA, U. Buffalo, 1959, MA, 1964; EdD, SUNY, Buffalo, 1968; postgrad., St. Bonaventure U., NY, Harvard U., Cambridge, Mass., 1976. Prof. Niagara C.C., Sanborn, NY, 1963-69, dean, 1969-78; pres. Coll. Lake County, Grayslake, Ill., 1978-86, Alfred State Coll., NY, 1986-93; founding pres. Cambria County CC, Pa., 1994—; pres. W.Va. No. CC, 2000—; ret. Spl. cons. FEPADE, El Salvador, 1988-94; mem. Afred Tech. Resources, Inc., 1990—; bd. dirs. Bank of Highland Park, Ill. Author: Values and the Future: Models of Community College Development, 1979; contbr. articles to jours. in field. Trustee Nioga Libr. System, 1973-78; mem. Abbott Scholarship Found., 1979-86, Lake County SBA Corp., 1980-86, Ill. Community Coll. Bd. Planning Adv. Com., 1980-81, Lake County Econ. Devel. Commn., 1981-86, exec. coun. Steuben Area Boy Scouts Am., 1987-88; chmn. Wellsville adv. bd. Salvation Army, 1988—; bd. dirs. Hornell YMCA, 1989—. lst lt. arty. US Army, 1954-57. Recipient award Lake County Freedom Found.; N.Y. Jaycees pub. speaking champion, 1964. Mem. US Navy League (hon.), Ill. Coun. Pub. Community Coll. Presidents (curriculum com. chmn. 1981-82, econ. devel. com. chmn. 1983-84, sec., treas., 1984-85, chmn. elect 1985-86), Ill. Bd. Higher Edn. (spl. com. on undergrad. edn. reform 1985-86), Pres. Assn. of Colls. of Tech. Home: 82 Scott St Hornell NY 14843-2258 Home Phone: 607-324-1277. Personal E-mail: drjohnohunter@aol.com.

HUNTER, J(OHN) ROBERT, insurance consumer advocate; b. New Orleans, Nov. 20, 1936; s. J. Robert and Alberta M. (Cox) H.; m. Carole A. Means, Mar. 6, 1976; children: Laura Jeanne, James Douglas, John Robert, III. BS, Clarkson U., Potsdam, NY, 1958; grad. Program for Sr. Mgrs., Harvard U., Cambridge, Mass., 1976. Dir. of ins. Atlantic Mut. Ins. Co., 1960-61; supervisory actuary Ins. Svcs. Office, NYC, 1961-67; asst. actuary Mut. Ins. Rating Bur., NYC, 1967-71; chief actuary Fed. Ins. Adminstrn., HUD, Washington, 1971-74, acting adminstr., 1974-76, adminstr., 1976-77, dep. fed. ins. adminstr., 1977-80; founder, pres. Nat. Ins. Consumer Orgn., 1980-93; ins. commr. State of Tex., 1993-94; dir. ins. Consumer Fedn. Am., Arlington, Va., 1994—. Author: Taking the Bite Out of Insurance, 1980, Profitability and Investment Income in Property Casualty Insurance, 1983, Insurance in California, 1986, Pay at the Pump Private No Fault Auto Insurance, 1992, Proposition 103 Revisited: A Consumer Triumph, 1993, Auto Insurance, Progress but More to Be Done, 1995, America's Distrous Disaster Insurance System, 1998, Premium Deceit, 1999, Texas Tort Reform's Incredible Shrinking Savings, 1999, Changes in State Insurance Department Resources, 2000, California Auto REgulation The Best in Nation, 2001, Medical Malpractice Insurance: Stable Losses/Unstable Rates, 2005, Home Insurance Rates Rise Sharply, 2003, Insurers Undermine Terrorism Insurance Law, 2003, White Paper on Insurance Profits, 2007. Pres. Freeport Cmty. Chorale, NY, 1970-71; pres., founder Rockville Musical Theatre, Md., 1974-75; vestryman Christ Ch., Alexandria, 1982-84, 91-93. Recipient award for excellence Sec. HUD, 1977, Ester Peterson award for consumer lifetime achievement Consumer Fedn. Am., 2002. Fellow Casualty Actuarial Soc.; mem. Am. Acad. Actuaries, Internat. Actuarial Assn. Home: 2202 24th St N Arlington VA 22207-4904 Office Phone: 703-528-0062. Personal E-mail: loonlakeme@aol.com.

HUNTER, JOHN STUART, statistician, consultant; b. Holyoke, Mass., June 3, 1923; s. John and Irene (Robinson) H.; m. Edna Taylor Martz, Sept. 19, 1952; 3 children: m. T.J. Hirasuna, Aug. 13, 1977; 2 children: m. Vonna Halford, Aug. 28, 1982; 4 children: m. S. Thomas, May 1, 1987; 2 children. PhD in Exptl. Stats., N.C. State U., 1954, MS in Engring. Math, 1949, BS in Elec. Engring, 1947; DSc (hon.), NC State U., 2004. Staff statistician Am. Cyanamid Co., 1954-59; with Statis. Techniques Research Group, 1957-59, Math. Research Center, U. Wis., 1959-61; assoc. prof. Princeton, 1962-67; prof. engring. Princeton U., 1968-82, prof. emeritus, 1982—; statistician in residence U. Wis., 1967-68. Lectr. Korean Standards Research Inst., 1979, Nat. Center: Indsl. Sci. and Tech. Mgmt. Devel., Dalian, People's Republic of China, 1981, 82; mem. staff com. nat. statistics Nat. Acad. Scis., 1975-76, mem. com., 1976-82, chmn. com. pres.'s of statis. socs., 1976-79; chmn. panel Nat. Bur. Standards, 1977-80. Author, cons., lectr. in field; founding editor: Technometrics, 1959-63. Served with AUS, 1942-46. Recipient S.S. Wilks medal U.S. Army, 1987. Fellow Am. Statis. Assn. (v.p. 1990, pres. 1993, Founder's award 1995), Am. Soc. Quality (hon., Shewhart medal, 1971, Youden award 1977, Ott award 1979, Deming medal 1987, Statistician of Yr. award 1987), AAAS (coun. mem. 1974-77, chmn. com. on fellows 1977); mem. NAE, Biometrics Soc., Inst. Math. Stats., Royal Statis. Soc., Internat. Stats. Inst. Clubs: Cosmos. Episcopalian. Home: 15 Meadow Lks Apt U7 Hightstown NJ 08520-3315

HUNTER, LARRY DEAN, lawyer, broadcast executive; b. Leon, Iowa, Apr. 10, 1950; s. Doyle J. and Dorothy B. (Grey) H.; m. Rita K. Barker, Jan. 24, 1971; children: Nathan (dec.), Allison. BS with high distinction, U. Iowa, Iowa City, 1971; AM, U. Mich., Ann Arbor, 1974, JD magna cum laude, 1974, CPhil in Econs., 1975. Bar: Va. 1975, Mich. 1978, Calif. 1992. Assoc. McGuire, Woods & Battle, Richmond, Va., 1975-77; asst. counsel, internat. counsel Clark Equipment Co., Buchanan, Mich., 1977-80; ptnr. Honigman, Miller, Schwartz & Cohn, Detroit, 1980-93; asst. gen. counsel Hughes Electronics Corp., LA, 1993-98, corp. v.p., 1998—2001, sr. v.p., gen. counsel El Segundo, Calif., 2002—03, DIRECTV, Inc., El Segundo, Calif., 1996-98; chmn., pres. DIRECTV Japan Mgmt., Inc., Tokyo, 1998-2000; exec. v.p. legal and human resources, gen. counsel, sec. DIRECTV Group, El Segundo, Calif., 2004—. Mem. faculty Wayne State U. Law Sch., Detroit, 1987-89. Mem. Order of Coif. Home: 1101 S Catalina Ave Redondo Beach CA 90277 Office: The DIRECTV Group Inc 2230 E Imperial Hwy El Segundo CA 90245 Office Phone: 310-964-0723. E-mail: larry.hunter@directv.com.*

HUNTER, LARRY LEE, retired electrical engineer; b. Versailles, Mo., Mar. 5, 1938; s. Donnan Kleber and Molly Opal (Roe) H.; m. Marcella Ann Avey, Feb. 1, 1959; children: Cynthia Lynn Hunter Morency, Stuart Roe. BSEE, U. Mo., 1963; MBA, Fla. Inst. Tech., 1984. Radar sys. test engr. McDonnell Aircraft Corp., St. Louis, 1963—65; design engr. Magnavox Co., Urbana, Ill., 1965—66, R&D engr., 1966—67; project engr. LTV Electrosystems, Garland, Tex., 1967—68, sys. engr., 1968—70; program mgr. Dorsett Electronics, Tulsa, 1970—73, Harris Corp., Melbourne, Fla., 1973—75, bus. area mgr., 1975—85; v.p. mktg., engring., program mgmt. Teledyne Lewisburg, Tenn., 1985—88; pres. L.H. Assocs., Columbia, Tenn., 1988—90; founder, gen. mgr. Precision Cable divsn. AMP Inc., Harrisburg, Pa. and Greensboro, NC, 1990—96, dir. global cable sys. bus. group, 1996—97; pres. L. Hunter Assocs., Inc., Tampa, Fla., 1997—2001. Contbr. articles to profl. jours. Mem.: IEEE (sr.), EE Scholastic (hon.), Eta Kappa Nu. Republican. Methodist. Achievements include invention of medical thermometer. Avocations: hunting, fishing, golf. Home: 16309 E Course Dr Tampa FL 33624-1127 Personal E-mail: lhunter8@verizon.net.

HUNTER, LESLIE GENE, history educator; b. Meadville, Pa., Sept. 26, 1941; s. George Harper and Gladys Laverne (Bowland) H.; m. Cecilia Aros, Aug. 15, 1969; children: Louis, Raquel, Daniel, Joseph. BA in History, U. Ariz., 1964, MA in History, 1966, PhD in History, 1971. Asst. prof. Tex. A&M U., Kingsville, 1969-74, assoc. prof., 1974-81, prof., 1981—, Regents prof., 1998—, chmn. dept. history, 1986-90, 91-96. Mem. faculty exch. Kiev (Ukraine) Policy Inst., 1991. Author: The 75th Anniversarh History of Texas A&M University, 2000; editor: Historic Kingsville, Texas, 1994; author (computer software) Missions in Spanish Tex., 1987; editor Jour. South Tex., 1997—;mem. editl. bd. Jour. South Tex., 1989—, Social Studies Texan, 1989—; contbr. articles to profl. jours. Chair hist. rev. bd. City of Kingsville, Tex., 1987—; amb. Inst. Texan Culture, 1994—. Mem. AAUP, Tex. Coun. Social Studies, Tex. Computer Edn. Assn., South Tex. Hist. Assn., S.W. Mission Rsch. Ctr., Phi Alpha Theta. Democrat. Episcopalian. Avocation: computer technology. Office: Tex A&M U Dept History Kingsville TX 78363 Home: PO Box 3104 Kingsville TX 78363-8332 Business E-Mail: kflgh00@tamuk.edu.

HUNTER, LOUIS G., retired aerospace engineer; b. Coleman, Tex., June 10, 1933; s. Louis G. and Bobbie Clary Hunter; m. Catherine Moody Hunter, Apr. 20, 1959; children: Steve, Becky, Julianna, Jeff, Kate, Blake. BS in Mech. Engring., Brigham Young U., Provo, Utah, 1958, MS in Mech. Engring., 1963; PhD in Aerospace Engring., U. Tenn., Knoxville, 1969. Commd. 2d lt. USAF, 1958; advanced through grades to lt. col. USAF Res., 1984; engr. N.Am. Aviation, Downey, Calif., 1963—65, Aro, Inc., Tullahoma, Tenn., 1972—77; specialist sr. Lockheed Martin, Ft. Worth, 1978—2002; ret.; part-time tchr. remedial math. Tarrant County Coll., Ft. Worth. Assoc. prof. physics Motlow State Coll., Tullahoma, 1970—76. Contbr. articles to profl. jours. Decorated Commendation medal USAF; recipient Advancement Aerospace Scis. award, AIAA, 1986; PhD fellow, N.Am. Aviation, 1965—68. Achievements include patents for development and design of pulse detonation engines and their application for propulsion and soot blowers for coal power plants. Avocations: genealogy, music, sports. Home: 1005 Jessica Dr Burleson TX 76028

HUNTER, MARK JOHN, lawyer, photographer; b. Alpena, Mich., Dec. 22, 1956; s. Francis Raymond and Evelyn Joan (Hoodlet) Hunter. BA in US History, Mich. State U., East Landing, 1979, BA in Graphic Design, 1981; A in Concrete Tech., Alpena C.C., Mich., 1987; JD, Ohio No. U., Ada, 1995. Bar: Mich. 1996. Freelance photographer, Alpena, 1974—; mfg. mgr. Concrete Product Industry, Mass., 1987—89; attendant Hunter Funeral Home, Alpena, 1995—; pvt. practice Alpena, 1996—. Columnist: The Alpena News, 2005—. Ex-officio mem. Alpena County Planning Commn., 1999—2002; vice chmn. Alpena County Rep. Com., 2001—02; mem. Alpena County Rep. Exec. Bd., 2003—, mem. exec. com., 2003—04; del. Mich. Rep. Conv., 2004; bd. dirs. Sunrise Mission Shelter, Alpena, 2000. Mem.: World Wildlife Fund, Mich. Land Use Inst., Eagles Club of Ossineke, Moose Lodge. Avocations: political theory, prisoners of conscience, world development, reading biographies. Office: 310 W Chisholm St Alpena MI 49707 Office Phone: 989-356-3171.

HUNTER, MICHAEL, publishing executive; b. Atlanta, Dec. 11, 1941; s. Joel H. and Eleanor Johnson; m. Katherine Garlick, Aug. 2, 1975. BA cum laude, Harvard U., 1964; postgrad., Columbia U., 1965-67. Dir. Spectrum Books, Prentice-Hall Inc., Englewood Cliffs., NJ, 1974-80; pres. Gen. Pub. div. Prentice-Hall Inc., Englewood Cliffs., NJ, 1980-85; pres. Hunter Pub. Co., NYC, 1985—. Mem. Am. Assn. Pubs. (exec. council Gen. Pub. div.) Clubs: University (N.Y.C.). Office: Hunter Pub Co 130 Campus Plz Edison NJ 08837-3936 Home: 222 Clematis St West Palm Beach FL 33401 Office Phone: 561-835-2022. Business E-Mail: michael@hunterpublishing.com.

HUNTER, MILTON, construction company executive, retired career military officer; b. Houston, May 1, 1943; married; 2 children. BS in Archtl. Engring., Wash. State U., 1967; M in Engring., U. Wash., 1978; grad. Exec. Devel. Program, U. Va., 1988; postgrad., Tex. A&M U., 1990, Harvard U., 1994; DSc (hon.), N.J. Inst. Tech., 1997. Registered profl. engr., D.C. Commd. 2d lt. U.S. Army, 1967, advanced through grades to maj. gen.; instr. Tactical Bridging br., dept. applied engring. U.S. Army Engr. Sch., Ft. Belvoir, Va.; comdr. and dist. engr. Seattle Dist. U.S. Army CE, comdg. gen., divsn. engr. South Pacific, San Francisco, chief of staff Washington, comdg. gen., divsn. engr. North Atlantic divsn. N.Y., condg. gen., divsn. engr. North Atlantic divsn. Washington, 1997-2000, dep. chief of engineers., dep. comdr., 2000—01; sr. v.p. infrastructure and tech. group Parsons Corp., Pasadena, Calif., 2002—. Decorated Legion of Merit (2), Bronze Star medal, DSM, others; recipient Disting. Alumni award Wash. State U., 1991; named to Outstanding Young of Am., 1979. Fellow Soc. Am. Mil. Engrs.; mem. Army Engr. Regtl. Assn., Assn. U.S. Army, Tau Beta Pi. Office: Parsons Corp 100 W Walnut St Pasadena CA 91124

HUNTER, PATRICIA RAE (TRICIA HUNTER), state official; b. Appleton, Minn., June 15, 1952; d. Harlan Ottowa and Clara Elizabeth (Tryhus) Hunter; m. Clark Waldon Crabbe, May 28, 1978 (dissolved July 1994); 1 child, Marcantonio Samantha. AS in Nursing, Good Samaritan Hosp., Phoenix, 1974; BSN, U. San Diego, 1981; MSN, UCLA, 1985. RN, cert. oper. rm. nurse. Surg. svcs. educator Stanford (Calif.) Hosp., 1983-85; oper. rm. supr. Alexian Bros., San Jose, Calif., 1985-86; dir. surg. svcs. Cmty. Hosp. Chula Vista, Calif., 1986-89; mem. Calif. State Assembly, San Diego, 1989-92; spl. asst. Gov. Wilson Office Statewide Health Planning and Devel., Sacramento, 1993-94; commr. Calif. Med. Assistance Commn., Sacramento, 1994—98, sr. v.p., mng. dir., 1998—2002, The Flannery Group, San Diego, 1997—2002; prin., owner Govt. Rels. Group, Inc., 2004—. Cons. hosp., Monterey, Calif., 1984—, Summit Schs., Ontario, Calif., 1992—93. Mem. adv. bd. Alzheimers Assn., San Diego, 1990—92, Arthritis Found., 1990—92; pres. Calif. Rep. League, 1995—97; bd. dir. Am. Nurses Found., 2007—. Named Rookie Legislator of the Yr., Calif. Psychol. Assn., 1990, Legislator of the Yr., Calif. Nurse Practitioners Assn., 1992; recipient Alice Pauly award, Nat. Women Polit. Caucus San Diego, 1991. Mem.: NWPC, ANA (v.p. 1982—85), Bus. and Profl. Orgn., Assn. Oper. Rm. Nurses, Rotary (bd. dir. 1993—94), Sigma Theta Tau (Leadership award 1991). Republican. Lutheran. Home: 3260 E Fox Run Way San Diego CA 92111-7723 Office: Govt Rels Group Inc 1121 L St Ste 409 Sacramento CA 95814 Office Phone: 916-447-7821. Business E-Mail: grg@govrelationsgroup.com.

HUNTER, RICHARD EDWARD, retired physician; b. Worcester, Mass., May 30, 1919; s. William and Catherine (Powers) H.; m. M. Minta Shaw, Jan. 30, 1993 (dec.); children: Todd Wayne, Elayne Cheryl, Jill Elizabeth, Amy Louise. AB, Clark U., 1941; MD, Boston U., 1944. Diplomate Am. Bd. Ob-Gyn. Intern Worcester City Hosp., 1944-45; resident gen. surgery Framingham (Mass.) Union Hosp., 1947; resident ob-gyn Mercy Hosp., Balt., 1947-49; practice medicine specializing ob-gyn Worcester, 1949—; prof. dept. ob-gyn U. Mass., Worcester, 1976—, chmn. dept. ob-gyn, 1976-89, emeritus prof., 1989—; ret., 1999. Contbr. articles to med. jours. Served with US Army, 1945-47. Mem. ACS, ACOG, New Eng. Assn. Gynecologic Oncologists, Soc. Gynecologic Oncology, Boston Obstetric Soc., New Eng. Cancer Soc., Am. Soc. Clin. Oncology, Soc. Gynecologic Surgeons, Royal Soc. Medicine. Republican. Home: 406 Browning Ln Worcester MA 01609 Office: 55 Lake Ave N Worcester MA 01655-0002

HUNTER, RICHARD SAMFORD, JR., lawyer; b. Montgomery, Ala., May 8, 1954; s. Richard Samford and Anne (Arendell) H.; m. Jane Messer, June 28, 1981; children: Richard Samford III, Benjamin Arendell. Student, Berklee Coll. of Music, 1974—75; BA, U. N.C., 1977; JD, Cumberland Sch Law of Samford U., 1980. Bar: N.C. 1980, U.S. Dist. Ct. (ea. and ctrl. dists.) N.C. 1981. Assoc. Green & Mann, Raleigh, N.C., 1980-82, Smith, Debnam, Hibbert & Pahl, Raleigh, 1982-85; ptnr. Futrell, Hunter & Bingham, Raleigh, 1985-97. Program chmn. media law U. NC, Chapel Hill, 1983-84; faculty NCATL Nat. Inst. Trial Advocacy, 1987; lectr., spkr. in field. Author: How to Try a Civil Case, 1986, Traumatic Medicine, 1988, Insurance Law for the General Practitioner, 1992, North Carolina Bar Assn. Desk Book, 1992, Traumatic Medicine, 1988, Inadequate Offer? Try that P.I. Case, 1995; composer, performer (TV musical) The Tomorrow Show, 1975; contbr. articles to profl. jours. and mags. including Trial Briefs Mag., Fourth Quarter. Corp. fund raiser United Way, Wake County, NC, 1984-85; clergy's sermon evaluation com. Christ Episc. Ch., Raleigh; bd. dirs. Raleigh Chamber Music Guild, 1986-88, Food Bank of NC, 1990—. Fellow So. Trial Lawyers Assn., Roscoe Pound Found.; mem. ABA (litig. sect.), ATLA, Am. Bd. Trial Advocs. (cert., v.p. 2004, ea. dist. NC chpt. diplomate, pres. 2005), NC Bar Assn. (litig. sect.), Wake County Bar Assn. (bd. dirs. 1987-88, chmn. 1988), Assn. Trial Lawyers Am. (Stalwart fellow Roscoe Pound Found.), NC State Bar, NC Acad. Trial Lawyers (chmn. spkrs. bur. 1984-85, bd. govs. 1986—, v.p. pub. svc. and info. com. 1988-90, v.p. membership 1990-91, v.p. legis. 1991—, pres. 1993-94, exec. com. 1987-94, chmn. auto torts sect. 1998-99, edn. com. 1985-88, pres.-elect 1992-93, bd. dirs. 1984-87, co-chair auto torts sect. 1998-99, U. NC journalism press law seminar, 1983-84, seminar chmn. 1986, 88, 95), Kiwanis, Sphinx, Phi Alpha Delta. Democrat. Avocations: sports, music, hunting, fishing. Home: 813 Graham St Raleigh NC 27605-1124 Office: 127 W Hargett St Ste 104 Raleigh NC 27601 Office Phone: 919-831-8722. Office Fax: 919-831-8734. Personal E-mail: hunteratty@aol.com.

HUNTER, ROBERT CHARLES, entertainment executive; b. Furstenfeldbruk, Germany, Apr. 2, 1948; s. John Columbus and Ellen Gertrude (Genge) H.; m. Rebecca Ann Hendrick, Oct. 31, 1972 (div. 1998); children: Amy Catherine, Emily Jane, Brandon Charles; m. Diane Ladd, Feb. 14, 1999. BA, Coll. Artesia, 1969. V.p. C-B Truck Lines, Inc., El Paso, Tex., 1969-74; with distbn. mgmt. Frito Lay, Inc., Dallas, 1974-78; sr. dir. Franchise Svcs., Inc., Wichita, Kans., 1978-81, v.p., 1981-84; v.p. restaraunt franchising Pizza Hut, Inc., Wichita, 1984-86; pres. and CEO PepsiCo Food Systems, Dallas, 1986-98; chmn., CEO Exxcell Entertainment, Inc., 1999—. Active Dallas Easter Seals Soc. for Children, 1992-96, mem. adv. coun., 1992—; pres. Young Audiences Greater Dallas, 1989-91; founder, chmn. David J. Ewing Scholarship Fund, 1991—, Tex. Christian U. Parents Coun., 1991-96; mem. Tex. Christian U. New Frontier Bd., 1994-97; North Tex. U. Hotel and Restaurant Adv. Bd., 1994-97; bd. dirs. S.W. Family Inst., Dallas, 1989-92, Ctr. for Non-Profit Mgmt., 1992-98, The Child Care Group, 1995—; chmn. fin. com. Northwood U. Arts Program Bd., 1993-94; mem. Dallas Assembly, 1994—; chmn., CEO StarWay Soc., 1999—. Mem. Young Pres. Orgn., U. S. C. of C. (bd. dirs. 1995—), Dallas Mus. Art Assocs., Dallas Theater Ctr., Northwood Club. Methodist. Avocations: golf, scuba diving, skiing, boating. Office: Exxcell Entertainment Inc 5956 Sherry Ln Ste 1000 Dallas TX 75225-8021 Home: 1204 Stratford Dr Richardson TX 75080-2917

HUNTER, ROBERT GRAMS, retired language educator; b. Milbank, SD, Nov. 12, 1927; s. Donald Raymond and Esther (Grams) H.; m. Anne Ziesmer, Aug. 25, 1956; children: Timothy, Catherine. BA, Harvard, 1949; MA, Columbia, 1957, PhD, 1962. Instr. Robert Coll., Istanbul, Turkey, 1949-52; successively instr., asst. prof., asso. prof. Dartmouth, 1959-70; Kenan prof. English Vanderbilt U., Nashville, 1970-82; Frensley prof. English So. Meth. U., Dallas, 1982-97; ret., 1997. Author: Shakespeare and the Comedy of Forgiveness, 1965, Shakespeare and the Mystery of God's Judgments, 1976. Served with AUS, 1952-54. Home: 5923 Hillcrest Ave Dallas TX 75205-2262

HUNTER, STEVEN L., medical center administrator; b. Alton, Ill., Oct. 3, 1953; s. Samuel and Harriet (Wetstein) H.; children: Ryan, Jeff, Victoria. BS in Med. Tech. summa cum laude, Ea. Ill. U., Charleston, 1975; cert. in med. tech., Carle Found. Hosp., Urbana, Ill., 1975; MHA, St. Louis U., 1978. Cert. med. technologist Am. Soc. Clin. Pathologists. Various staff and mgmt. positions Cardinal Glennon Hosp. and Christian Hosp. N.E., St. Louis, 1975-78; asst. adminstr. St. Elizabeth Med. Ctr., Granite City, Ill., 1978-81, v.p. corp. planning & mktg., 1981-87; COO Incarnate Word Hosp., St. Louis, 1987-90; pres., CEO St. Mary's Health Ctr., Jefferson City, Mo., 1990—93; pres. St. Anthony's Hosp., Oklahoma City, 1993—98; regional pres. SSM Healthcare, Oklahoma City, 1998—2005; CEO Covenant Health Sys., Lubbock, Tex., 2005—07, Provena Health, Mokena, Ill., 2007—. Mem. faculty dept. human resource mgmt. Webster U., St. ZLouis; bd. dirs. Missouri River Home Health Agy., 1991—. Bd. dirs. ARC, 1992—, Lincoln U. Found., 1991—, Tri-City YMCA; mem. governing body Jefferson City Area United Way, 1991—. Recipient Malclom Baldridge Nat. Quality award, 2002. Fellow Am. Coll. Health Care Execs.; mem. Mo. Hosp. Assn. (by-laws com. 1991—, medicaid com. 1991—). Office: Provena Health 19065 Hickory Creek Dr Ste 300 Mokena IL 60448

HUNTER, TERRY K., artist, educator, director; s. Samuel A. and Audrey Bernice Hunter; m. Gilda Cobb Hunter, Aug. 30, 1975. BS, Fla. A&M U., 1973; MFA, Ohio State U., 1977; PhD, Fla. State U., 1988. Tchr. Dan McCarty Mid. Sch., Ft. Pierce, Fla., 1973—75; prof. art SC State U., Orangeburg, 1977—2000, Claflin U., Orangeburg, 2000—06; exec. dir. FACETS, Orangeburg, 2006—. Cons., master tchr. SC Gov.'s Sch. for the Arts, Greenville, 1981, 82, 1986—96; cons. item devel. test SC State Dept. Edn., Columbia, 1996—2000; cons., mem. design com. SC Arts Commn., Columbia, 1995; mus. dir. Arthur Rose Mus., Claflin U., Orangeburg, curator 8 exhbns., 2004—06; dir. Upper Room Graphic Edits. Studio, Arts Run the Spectrum. Exhibited in group shows at Apex Mus., African American Mus. Nassau County, Hempstead, NY, 2004, Arthur Rose Mus., Claflin U., Orangeburg, S.C., 2005, Sumter (S.C.) Gallery Art, 2006, Nat. Ctr. for Study Civil Rights and African Am. Culture, Montgomery, Ala., 2007, one-man shows include Gridded Connections, Nat. Ctr. Study Civil Rights and African Am. Culture, Ala. State U., 2007. Com. chair SC Nat. Heritage Corridor, Orangeburg, 2004—; design chair African Am. monument SC Ho. of Reps., Columbia, 1998—2001; leader Heritage Corridor Hub Designation, Orangeburg, 2006. Named Exemplary Art Educator, Youth Art Celebration, Columbia, 2004, 2005. Mem.: Coll. Art Assn., SC Art Edn. Assn. (Arts Advocate of Yr. 2005), Nat. Art Edn. Assn. Avocations: graphic design, photography. Home: 112 Estate Ct Orangeburg SC 29115-8168 Office: FACETS Orangeburg SC 29115 Office Phone: 803-534-8911. Home Fax: 803-516-8033. Personal E-mail: tkhurges@bellsouth.net.

HUNTER, THOMAS ROGERS, political science professor; b. Kinston, NC, Dec. 19, 1963; s. Carl Doering and Doris Jean (Martin) Hunter; m. Nicole Ann Hager, June 17, 2006. BA, U. Va., Charlottesville, 1986, MA in History, 1990, JD, 1990; PhD, Johns Hopkins U., Balt., 2001. Bar: NC 1990. Law clk. to Hon. Donald S. Russell US Ct. Appeals (4th cir.), Spartanburg, SC, 1990—91; instr. Sch. Law U. Ark., Fayetteville, 1992—95; asst. prof. Hendrix Coll., Conway, Ark., 2000—01; vis. asst. prof. Auburn U., Ala., 2002—05; asst. prof. U. W. Ga., Carrollton, 2005—. Co-author: History of Legal Education in the United States, 1998. Named Prof. of the Yr., U. Ark., 1995, Sigma Kappa, 2005; Bryanston fellow, 1986—87, Hopkins fellow, Dean's Tchg. fellow, Johns Hopkins U., 1995—2000. Mem.: So. Hist. Assn., NC Bar, Am. Polit. Sci. Assn., Phi Detla Phi, Phi Alpha Theta. Presbyterian. Home: 221 Overlook Ct Dallas GA 30157 Office: U W Ga Carrollton GA 30117 Office Phone: 678-839-4994.

HUNTER, TONY (ANTHONY REX), molecular biologist, educator; b. Ashford, Kent, Eng., Aug. 23, 1943; arrived in U.S., 1971; s. Ranulph Rex and Nellie Ruby Elsie (Hitchcock) H.; m. Philippa Charlotte Marrack, July 19, 1969 (div. 1974); m. Jennifer Ann Maureen Price, June 8, 1992; children: Sean Alexander Brocas, James Samuel Alan. BA, U. Cambridge, Eng., 1965, MA, 1966. Rsch. fellow Christ's Coll., U. Cambridge, 1968-71, 73-75; rsch. assoc. Salk Inst., San Diego, 1971-73, asst. prof., 1975-78, assoc. prof., 1978-82, prof., 1982—, Am. Cancer Soc. rsch. prof., 1992—. Adj. prof. biology U. Calif. San Diego, La Jolla, 1982—. Contbr. articles to sci. jours. Recipient award, Am. Bus. Found. Cancer Rsch., 1988, Katharine Berkan Judd award, Meml. Sloan-Kettering Cancer Ctr., 1992, Internat. award, Gairdner Found., 1994, Hopkins Meml. award, 1994, Mott prize, GM Cancer Rsch. Found., 1994, Feodor Lynen medal, 1999, J. Allyn Taylor Internat. prize in medicine, John P. Robarts Rsch. Inst. and C.H. Stiller Meml. Found., 2000, Keio Med. Sci. prize, Keio U. Med. Sci. Fund, Tokyo, 2001, Sergio Lombroso award in cancer rsch., Weizmann Inst. Sci., 2003, City of Medicine award, Durham Health Ptnrs., 2003, Medal of Honor, Am. Cancer Soc., 2004, Kirk A. Landon prize, Am. Assn. Cancer Rsch., 2004, Prince of Asturias award for sci. and tech. rsch., 2004, Louisa Gross Horwitz prize, Columbia U., 2004, Wolf Found. prize, Israel, 2005, Daniel Nathans Meml. award, Van Andel Inst., 2005, Herbert Taylor award, Am. Soc. Biochemistry and Molecular Biology, 2007, Pasarow award Cancer, Robert J. and Claire Pasarow Found., 2006. Fellow Am. Acad. Arts and Scis., Royal Soc. London, Royal Soc. Arts, Mfrs. and Commerce; mem. NAS, European Molecular Biology Orgn. (assoc.), Inst. Medicine, Am. Philos. Soc. Avocations: white water rafting, desert camping. Home: 4578 Vista de la Patria Del Mar CA 92014-4150 Office: Salk Inst Biol Studies Molecular-Cell Biology Lab 10010 N Torrey Pines Rd La Jolla CA 92037-1099 Office Phone: 858-453-4100 1385.

HUNTER, TORII KEDAR, professional baseball player; b. Pine Bluff, Ark., July 18, 1975; m. Katrina Hall; children: Torii Jr., Monshadrik. Draft pick Minn. Twins, 1993, outfielder, 1997—. Mem. South squad Jr. Olympics, 1992. Named Gatorade Ark. Player of Yr., 1993; named to Am. League All-Star Team, 2002, 2007; recipient Gold Glove award, 2001—06, Carl R. Pohlad award, 2004. Office: Minn Twins Metrodome 34 Kirby Puckett Pl Minneapolis MN 55415*

HUNTER, VICTOR LEE, marketing executive, consultant; b. Garrett, Ind., Mar. 1, 1947; s. John Joseph and Martha May (Brown) H.; m. Linda Ann Loudermilk, Dec. 19, 1969; children: Jed, Andrew, Matthew, Holly. BS, Purdue U., 1969; MBA, Harvard U., 1971. Dir. mktg. Kreuger, Inc., Green Bay, Wis., 1971-75; pres. B&I Furniture, Milw., 1975-81, Hunter Bus. Group, LLC, Milw., 1981—. Bd. dirs. Wm. K. Walthers Co., Milw. Author: Business-to-Business Marketing: Creating a Community of Customers, 1997. Lay leader United Meth. Ch., Whitefish Bay, Wis., 1985; mem. exec. com. Greater Milw. Conv. and Visitors Bur. Mem. Direct Mktg. Assn., Wis. Pres.' Orgn., Strategic Accounts Mgmt. Assn. (bd. dirs.), Dean's Leadership Coun. Prudue U. Coll. Sci. Office: Hunter Business Group PO Box 12970 Milwaukee WI 53212-0970 Office Phone: 414-203-8066. Business E-Mail: vhunter@hunterbusiness.com.

HUNTER, WILLIAM CURT, dean, finance educator; BS, Hampton Inst., 1970; MBA in Fin., Northwestern U., 1972, PhD in Fin. and Environment, 1978. Asst. prof. fin. Chgo. State U., 1975—77; asst. prof. banking and fin. U. Ga., Athens, Ga., 1977—80; asst. prof. bus. adminstrn. Emory U., Atlanta, 1980—84, assoc. prof. fin., 1986—94; prof. fin., dir. rsch. Grad. Sch. Bus., Atlanta U., 1984—85, prof. fin., chmn. Fin. Dept., 1985—86; vis. scholar Dept. Rsch. Fed. Res. Bank of Atlanta, 1986—88, rsch. officer, sr. fin. economist, 1988—90; sr. v.p., dir. rsch. Fed. Res. Bank of Chgo., 1995—2003; dean, disting prof. fin. U. Conn. Sch. Bus., 2003—06; dean Henry B. Tippie Coll. Bus., U. Iowa, 2006—. Vis. prof. Bd. Govs. of Fed. Res. Sys., Washington, 1982; disting. vis. chaired prof. Hong Kong Poly. U., 2001—03. Contbr. articles to profl. jours. Office: Henry B Tippie Coll Bus C120 Pappajohn Bus Bldg U Iowa Iowa City IA 52242-1994 Office Phone: 319-335-0866. Office Fax: 319-335-0860. E-mail: curt-hunter@uiowa.edu.

HUNTER, WILLIAM DENNIS, lawyer; b. Boise, Idaho, June 26, 1943; s. William Gregory and Lorene (Persilla) H.; m. Jane Emily Porter, Apr. 30, 1966; children: Keith Alan, Elise Aubrey. BA, Stanford U., 1965; JD, U. Calif., San Francisco, 1973. Bar: Calif. 1973, U.S. Dist. Ct. (no. dist.) Calif. 1974, U.S. Ct. Appeals (9th cir.) 1974, U.S. Supreme Ct. 1996. Assoc. Pettit & Martin, San Francisco, 1973-79, ptnr., 1980-92, counsel, 1993-95, Collette & Erickson LLP, San Francisco, 1995-2000; regional counsel The Nature Conservancy, San Francisco, 2000—. Bd. dirs. City Celebration, Inc., San Francisco, 1984-91, pres., 1989-91. Recipient Service award Calif. Nature Conservancy, 1987. Mem. ABA, Calif. State Bar Assn., San Francisco Bar Assn., Nat. Assn. Installation Devel. (regional dir. 1993-2000), Order of coif. Democrat. Office: The Nature Conservancy 201 Mission St 4th Fl San Francisco CA 94105

HUNTER, WILLIAM MICHAEL, electrical engineer, civil engineer technician; b. Detroit, Oct. 5, 1956; s. William Ray and Delores Patricia Hunter; m. Carolyn Ann Cox, July 29, 2000. Student, Nashville State Tech., 1980—81, Vanderbilt U., Nashville, 1980—81; degree in civil engring., Tenn. Tech. U., Cookville, 1982; degree in elec. engring., Tenn. State U., Nashville, 1983. With USAF, Vietnam, 1974—75, weapons specialist Dvis Monthan AFB Tucson, 1975—77; with US Army, Fayetteville, NC, 1977—86, with Spl. Ops. Command 5th Group Fort Bragg; civil engr. Hwy. Dept. Tenn., Nashville, 1986—90; elec. engr. State of Tenn., Nashville, 1990—93. Asst. chmn. Engrs. of Am., Atlanta, 1985—89. Staff sgt. US Army and USAF, 1973—90. Decorated Silver Star, 2 Bronze Stars, Purple Heart, 4 Army Commendation medals; named Airman of Yr., 1975. Avocations: hunting, fishing, shooting.

HUNTER BLAIR, PAULINE CLARKE, author; b. Kirkby-in-Ashfield, Eng., May 19, 1921; d. Charles Leopold and Dorothy Kathleen (Milum) Clarke; m. Peter Hunter Blair, Feb., 1969. BA with honors, Somerville Coll., Oxford U., Eng., 1943. Free-lance writer, 1948—. Lectr. Author (writing as Pauline Clarke): (novels) The Pekinese Princess, 1948, The Great Can, 1952, The White Elephant, 1952, Smith's Hoard, 1955, The Boy with the Erpingham Hood, 1956, Sandy the Sailor, 1956, James, The Policeman, 1957, James and the Robbers, 1959, Torolv The Fatherless, 1959, 2d edit., 1973, The Lord of the Castle, 1960, The Robin Hooders, 1960, James and the Smugglers, 1961, Keep the Pot Boiling, 1961, The Twelve and the Genii, 1962 (Libr. Assn. Carnegie medal, 1962, Lewis Carrol Shelf award, 1963, Deutsche Jugend Buchpreis, 1968), Silver Bells and Cockle Shells, 1962, James and the Black Van, 1963, Crowds of Creatures, 1964, The Bonfire Party, 1966, The Two Faces of Silenus, 1972; author: (under pseudonym Helen Clare) Five Dolls in a House, 1953, Merlin's Magic, 1953, Bel The Giant and Other Stories, 1956, Five Dolls and the Monkey, 1956, Five Dolls in the Snow, 1957, Five Dolls and Their Friends, 1959, Seven White Pebbles, 1960, Five Dolls and the Duke, 1963, The Cat and the Fiddle and Other Stories from Bel, the Giant, 1968; author: (writing as Pauline Hunter Blair) The Nelson Boy, 1999, A Thorough Seaman, 2000, Warscape, 2001, Jacob's Ladder, 2003; book reviewer, contbr.: Times Lit. Supplement. Mem.: Brit. Soc. Authors. Home: Church Farm House Bottisham Cambridge CB25 9BA England Office: care Curtis Brown Ltd Haymarket House 28/29 Haymarket London SW1Y 4SP England also: care John Cushman Assocs Inc 24 E 38th St New York NY 10016-2502 Office Phone: 01223/811223.

HUNTERTON, C. STANLEY, lawyer; BA, Syracuse U., NY, 1970, JD, 1974. Bar: Nev. Spl. atty. Organized Crine and Racketeering Sect. U.S. Dept. Justice, Detroit, 1975—78, Las Vegas, 1978—84; dep. chief counsel Pres.'s Commn. Organized Crime, 1984—85; atty. Hunterton and Assocs. Law Firm, 1986—2002; sr. v.p., gen. counsel, corp. sec. Sierra Pacific Resources, Reno, 2002—. Spl. counsel Ethics Rev. Bd. City Las Vegas; mem. election practice com. State Bar Nev. Named to Best Lawyers in Am., Bus. Litig., 2005—06. Master: Nev. Am. Inns Ct.; fellow: ACTL; mem.: State Bar Assn. Nev. (mem. standing com. judicial ethics and election practice), Clark County Bar Assn. Avocations: tennis, golf. Office: Sierra Pacific Resources 6100 Neil Rd Reno NV 89511*

HUNTINGTON, HILLARD GRISWOLD, economist; b. Boston, Apr. 10, 1944; s. Hillard Bell and Ruth Smedley (Wheeler) H.; m. Honor Mary Griffin, Sept. 30, 1972; children: Honora Redmond, Emma Anne Hillard. BS, Cornell U., 1967; MA, SUNY, Binghamton, 1972, PhD, 1974. Staff economist Fed. Energy Adminstrn., Washington, 1974-77; dir., sr. economist Data Resources, Inc., Washington, 1977-80; exec. dir. Energy Modeling Forum Stanford (Calif.) U., 1980—. Vol. U.S. Peace Corps., Pub. Utilities Authority, Monrovia, Liberia, 1967-69; vis. rsch. assoc. Inst. Devel. Studies, U. Nairobi, Kenya, 1972-73; mem. joint U.S.-U.S.S.R. Nat. Acad. Sci. Panel on Energy Conservation, 1986-90; peer rev. panel Nat. Acid Precipitation Assessment Program Task Force, Ctrs. for Excellence Govt. Can., Nat. Petroleum Coun., Commn. for Environ. Coop. N.Am.; cons. Argonne Nat. Lab., Electric Power Rsch. Inst., others. Editor Macroeconomic Impacts of Energy Shocks, 1987, N. Am. Natural Gas Markets: selected tech. studies, 1989, Designing Competitive Electricity Markets, 1998. Life fellow Clare Hall, Cambridge (Eng.) U. Sr.fellow U.S. Assn. for Energy Econs. (sr., pres. 1997), Internat. Assn. Energy Econs. (v.p. publs. 1990-92, program chmn. N.Am. conf., program chmn. internat. conf.), Am. Statis. Assn. (com. on energy stats. 1992-94), Am. Econ. Assn. Home: 305 Hermosa Way Menlo Park CA 94025-5821 Office: Stanford U 450 Terman Ctr Stanford CA 94305-4026 E-mail: hillh@stanford.edu.

HUNTINGTON, JAMES CANTINE, JR., retired equipment manufacturing company executive; b. Detroit, Mar. 21, 1928; s. James Cantine and Joanna (Donlon) H.; m. Bettyanne Hopkins, Sept. 21, 1973; children: James, Ann, Patricia, Carol, Judith, Amy. B.E.E., Cornell U., 1950. Mktg. exec. Harnischfeger Corp., Milw., 1953-62; cons. Milw., 1962-64; mgr. Colt Industries, Beloit, Wis., 1964-67; v.p., dir. Clark Equipment Co., Buchanan, Mich., 1967-76; sr. v.p. Am. Standard, Inc., 1976-88; ret., 1988.

Served with AUS, 1945-47, 50-53. Mem. Constrn. Industry Mfrs. Assn., Delta Kappa Epsilon, Tau Beta Pi, Eta Kappa Nu. Home: 613 Twin Pine Rd Pittsburgh PA 15215-1568

HUNTINGTON, LAWRENCE SMITH, investment banker; b. NYC, June 13, 1935; s. Prescott B. and Sarah H. (Powell) H.; m. Olivia Hallowell (div.); children: Christopher Bowditch, Charles Stewart Butler, Matthew Hallowell; m. Caroline Ballard BA, Harvard U., 1957; LL.B., New York Law Sch., 1964, LLD (hon.), 1998. With Fiduciary Trust Co. Internat., NYC, 1961-2000, pres., CEO, 1973-99, chmn. bd., CEO, 1983-2000. Dir. Bus. Execs. for Nat. Security, 1993-2000, Woods Hole Rsch. Ctr., 1994—, chmn., 1997—; bd. dirs. Continuum Health Ptnrs., 1996—, chmn., 2007—. Bd. dirs. St. Luke's-Roosevelt Hosp., NYC, 1974, chmn., 1975-81, 96-2001; bd. dirs. World Wildlife Fund, Washington, 1977-96, chmn., 1984-86, mem. nat. coun., 1996-2002; bd. dirs. Trinity Ch., NYC, 1987-2006; bd. dirs. Citizens Budget Com., N.Y.C., 1970—, trustee, 1970-2004, chmn. 1978-84, The Commonwealth Fund, 1989-2004, N.Y. Law Sch., 1984-2004, chmn., 1992-97, Opsail, 1992—; mem. adv. bd. N.Y. State Common Retirement Fund Investment Com., 1981-87; dir. Josiah Macy, Jr. Found., 1981—, chmn. 2004—; trustee Santa Fe Inst., 1988-98; trustee South Street Seaport, 1988—, chmn., 1999-2006; mem. adv. bd. NASD Internat. Mkts., 1994-99. Lt. USCG, 1959-61 Mem.: Explorers Club, NY Yacht Club (trustee, commodore 2002—04), Am. Alpine Club, Century Assn. Office Phone: 212-717-8633.

HUNTINGTON, LISA LYNEE, music educator; b. Jackson, Miss., Dec. 14, 1979; d. David Everett and Deborah Glynn Sandifer Rockett; m. Courtney Aaron Huntington, Feb. 8, 2003. BA in Music, U. of La., Monroe, 2001; postgrad., U. La., Monroe, 2001—. Cert. tchr. piano La. Music Teachers Assn. Office mgr., appt. setter St. James Agy., Monroe, La., 1996—98; student accompanist U. of La., 1997—2001; piano tchr. Lisa Rockett Piano Studio, Monroe, 1997—2003; schedule organizer, trainer Chili's Bar and Grill, West Monroe, La., 1998—2000; tchr. piano and voice Huntington Music Co., Monroe, 2003—04; piano tchr., dir. Huntington Ctr. for the Arts, Monroe, 2004—; accompanist Grace Episcopal Sch., Monroe, 2003—, music tchr., 2005—. Dir. Summer Music Camp, Monroe, 2000—. Mem. Katrina Relief Com., Monroe, 2005—06; vol. Refuge of Hope, Monroe, 2005—06; mem. linen guild Alter Guild, Monroe, 2004—06; music tchr. Vacation Bible Sch., Monroe, 2004—05; Sunday sch. tchr. Christian Edn., Monroe, 2006. Master: Monroe Dist. Music Tchrs. Assn. (assoc.; v.p. 2004—06, sec. 1998—2003, rally chmn. 2004—06), La. Music Tchrs. Assn. (assoc.; advt. chair 2005—06), Jr. Piano Festival (assoc.; co-chair 1998—2003); mem.: Music Teachers Nat. Assn. (assoc.), Music Educators Nat. Club (assoc.), Am. Choral Dirs. Assn. (assoc.), Monroe Music Coterie (assoc.). Conservative. Anglican. Avocations: tennis, reading, travel, musicals, writing. Office: Huntington Ctr for the Arts 509 Bres Ave Monroe LA 71201 Office Phone: 318-812-2787. Office Fax: 318-998-0204; Home Fax: 318-998-0204. Business E-Mail: lhuntington@huntingtonarts.net.

HUNTINGTON, RAYMOND J., education center executive; m. Eileen Huntington. Grad., Dartmouth Coll., Hanover, NH. Sr. bus. analyst Fortune 50 corp.; instr., math and stats.; pres., co-founder, chmn. Huntington Learning Ctr., Oradell, NJ, 1977—; chmn. Parents' Souce. Achievements include founding the oldest supplemental education provider in the US. Office: Huntington Learning Ctr 496 Kinderkamack Rd Oradell NJ 07649-1512 Office Phone: 201-261-8400.*

HUNTINGTON, ROBERT HOWARD, business management executive; b. Mpls., Mar. 25, 1955; s. Robert Howard and Cecelia (Benchak) H.; m. Susan Mary McCafferty; children: Ashley, Aidan. BA, Middlebury Coll., 1978, MA, 1983; MBA, Dartmouth Coll., 1985; EdD, Harvard U., 1997. Asst. mgr. Gen. Foods Corp., White Plains, NY, 1987—89, mgr., 1989—91, dir., 1991—96; v.p. Allied Domecq Quick Svc. Restaurants, White Plains, NY, 1996—. Tchg. fellow grad. sch. edn. Harvard U., Cambridge, Mass., 1991-92, instr. summer sch., 1991; tchg. asst. Harvard Ext. Sch., 1988-90; bd. trustees Lasell Coll., Newton, Mass., 1998—. Bd. dirs. First Parish Unitarian-Universalist, Medfield. Fellow: Phi Beta Kappa; mem.: Sierra Club. Home: 70 Adams St Medfield MA 02052-1614 Office: Allied Domecq Quick Svc Restaurants 14 Pacella Park Dr Randolph MA 02368-1773

HUNTINGTON, SAMUEL PHILLIPS, political science educator; b. NYC, Apr. 18, 1927; s. Richard T. and Dorothy S. (Phillips) H.; m. Nancy Alice Arkelyan, Sept. 8, 1957; children: Timothy Mayo, Nicholas Phillips. BA, Yale U., 1946; MA, U. Chgo., 1948; PhD, Harvard U., 1951. Instr. govt. Harvard U., Cambridge, Mass., 1950-53, asst. prof. govt., 1953-58, prof., 1962—, Thomson prof. govt., 1967-81, Clarence Dillon prof. internat. affairs, 1981-82, Eaton prof. sci. of govt., 1982—, chmn. dept., 1982-95; Albert J. Weatherhead univ. prof., 1995—. Research assoc. def. policy Brookings Instn., Washington, 1952-53; faculty research fellow Social Sci. Research Council, N.Y.C., 1954-57; asst. dir. Inst. War and Peace Studies, Columbia U., 1958-59, research assoc., 1958-63, assoc. dir., 1959-62, assoc. prof. govt., 1959-62, Ford research prof., 1960-61; research assoc. Ctr. for Internat. Affairs, Harvard U., 1963-64, mem. faculty, 1964—, exec. com., 1966—, assoc. dir., 1973-78, acting dir., 1975-76, dir., 1978-89; dir. John M. Olin Inst. for Strategic Studies, 1989-2000; vis. fellow All Souls Coll., Oxford (Eng.) U., 1973; coordinator security planning Nat. Security Council, 1977-78; trustee Inst. Def. Analysis, 1985-98; cons. numerous govt. agys.; chmn. Harvard Acad. Internat. & Area Studies, 1996—. Author: The Soldier and the State, 1957, The Common Defense, 1961, Political Order in Changing Societies, 1968, American Politics: The Promise of Disharmony, 1981, The Third Wave: Democratization in the Late Twentieth Century, 1991, The Clash of Civilizations and the Remaking of the World Order, 1996; co-author: Political Power: USA-USSR, 1964, The Crisis of Democracy, 1975, No Easy Choice: Political Participation in Developing Countries, 1976; editor: Changing Patterns of Military Politics, 1962, The Strategic Imperative, 1982; co-editor: Foreign Policy (quar.), 1970-77, Authoritarian Politics in Modern Society, The Dynamics of Established One-Party Systems, 1970, Global Dilemmas, 1985, Reorganizing America's Defense, 1985, Understanding Political Development, 1986, Culture Matters: How Values Shape Human Progress, 2000; also articles. Chmn. coun. on Vietnamese studies S.E. Asia Devel. Adv. Group, 1966-69; mem. Presdl. Task Force on Internat. Devel., 1969-70, Commn. on U.S.-Latin Am. Rels., 1974-76, Commn. on Integrated Long-Term Strategy, 1986-88, Commn. on Protecting and Reducing Govt. Secrecy, 1995-97; trustee Internat. Devel. Found., 1969-76. Served with AUS, 1946-47. Recipient Silver Pen award Jour. Fund, 1960, Grawemayer World Order award, 1992; fellow Ctr. for Advanced Study in Behavioral Scis., Stanford, 1969-70. Fellow Am. Acad. Arts and Scis.; mem. Internat. Polit. Sci. Assn. (coun. 1973-75), Coun. on Fgn. Rels., Interrnat. Inst. Strategic Studies, Am. Polit. Sci. Assn. (coun. 1969-71, v.p. 1984-85, pres.-elect 1985-86, pres. 1986-87). Office: Harvard Acad for Internat and Area Studies 1737 Cambridge St Cambridge MA 02138-3016

HUNTLEY, HORACE, history professor; b. Birmingham, Ala., Dec. 5, 1942; s. Theodore Huntley and Mattie Lee Mason; m. Barbara Jean Young, Mar. 14, 1943; children: Falona Renae Glenn, Marcus Malik. BA, U. of Minn., Mpls., 1970; MA, Syracuse U., 1972; PhD, U. Pitts., 1977. Prof. of history U. of Ala., Birmingham, 1976—; dir. oral history project Birmingham Civil Rights Inst., 1994—. Cons. in field. Author: Black Workers' Struggle for Equality in Birmingham, From Pipe Shop To Wall Street - The Life and Times of Terry Harris; contbr., , articles to profl. jours. and mags. Presenter Ala. Humanities Found., Birmingham; mem. Leadership Birmingham, Birmingham Festival of Arts; founding mem. Birmingham Civil Rights Inst., 1992—94; co-chair Birmingham Civil Rights Mus. Task Force, 1981—84; reader NEH, Washington; pres. So. Conf. on Afro-American Studies, Birmingham. With USAF, 1961—65. Mem.: Nat. Black Cultural Soc. (founding mem.), Birmingham Hist. Soc., So. Hist. Assn. (assoc.), Assn. for Study of Afro Am. Life and History (assoc.; v.p.), Omega Psi Phi (assoc.). Independent. Baptist. Avocations: travel, option trading. Home: 839 2nd St SW Birmingham AL 35211 Office: U Ala Dept History Birmingham AL 35211 Home Phone: 205-252-8706; Office Phone: 205-934-5634. Personal E-mail: hhuntley@bellsouth.net. Business E-Mail: hhuntley@uab.edu.

HUNTLEY, JAMES ROBERT, government official, international affairs scholar; b. Tacoma, July 27, 1923; s. Wells and Laura H.; m. Colleen Grounds Smith, May 27, 1967; children by previous marriage: Mark, David, Virginia, Jean. BA in Econs., Sociology magna cum laude, U. Wash., 1948, postgrad., 1951; MA in Internat. Rels., Harvard U., 1956. Cons. Wash. Parks Recreation Commn., Olympia, 1949-51; exch. of persons officer U.S. Fgn. Svc., Frankfurt, Nuremberg, Germany, 1952-54; dir. cultural ctr. USIA, Hof/Saale, Germany, 1954-55; USIA postgrad. scholar Harvard U., 1955-56; asst. to Pres.'s coord. for Hungarian relief Washington, 1956; European regional affairs officer USIA, Washington, 1956-58; dep. pub. affairs officer U.S. Mission to European Cmtys., Brussels, 1958-60; mem. U.S. Del. to Atlantic Congress, London, 1959; sec. organizing com. Atlantic Inst., Brussels and Milan, 1960, exec. officer and co-founder Paris, 1960-63; dir. Atlantic Inst. (N.Am. Office), Washington, 1963-65; founder, sec. Com. Atlantic Studies, 1963-65; sec. edn. com. NATO Parliamentarians Conf., Brussels, 1960-64; program assoc., internat. affairs divsn. Ford Found., NYC, 1965-67; sec. gen. Coun. Atlantic Colls., London, 1967-68; ind. writer, cons., lectr., internat. affairs Guildford, England, 1968-74; founder, sec. Assn. Mid-Atlantic Clubs, 1970-74; founder, sec. gen. Standing Conf. Atlantic Orgns., 1972-74; rsch. fellow, sr. advisor to pres. on internat. affairs Battelle Meml. Inst., Seattle, 1974-83; pres., CEO Atlantic Coun. of U.S., Washington, 1983-85; ind. cons., author internat. affairs. European corr., environ. affairs Saturday Rev./World, 1972-74; Corrs. World Wide, London, 1970-74; European corr. Non-Profit Report, 1970-74. Author: The NATO Story, 1965; (with W.R. Burgess) Europe and America - The Next Ten Years, 1970, Man's Environment and the Atlantic Alliance, 1972, Uniting the Democracies, 1980, Pax Democratica—A Strategy for the 21st Century, 1998, 2d edit., 2001, An Architect of Democracy: Building a Mosaic of Peace, 2006; contbr. articles to profl. jours. Bd. dirs. Internat. Standing Conf. Philanthropy, 1969-74, Assn. to Unite Democracies, 1976-94, Seattle Com. Fgn. Rels., 1975-78, World Affairs Coun. Seattle, 1975-83, adv. bd. 1986—, Bainbridge Island Land Trust, 1994-97; founding chmn. Coms. for a Cmty. of Democracies, 1979-92; co-founder 21st Century Found., 1987-91; mem. adv. bd. 21st Century Trust, London, 1988—; co-founder Next Century Initiative, 1992-95, New Century Initiative, 1996-99, pres. 1996-98; co-founder, v.p. Coun. for Cmty. of Democracies, 1999—. Carnegie fellow U. Wash., 1949-51; recipient Disting. Eagle Scout award 1995; named Kappa Sigma Man of Yr., 1999 Mem. Rainier Club (Seattle), DACOR (Washington). Home and Office: 1213 Towne Rd Sequim WA 98382-8849 E-mail: huntleypax@olypen.com. *For a full life, embrace a worthy cause. Mine is the unity of the democracies. America's most precious asset is its free political system. It can be successfully defended only if we merge our force, our hearts and our fortune with like-minded peoples. Like-mindedness is not simply a gift of history; it must be cultivated. My life's aim has been to forge consensus among the democracies as a prelude to the creation of a free, just, and durable world order.*

HUNTLEY, ROBERT STEPHEN, newspaper editor; b. Winston-Salem, NC, Mar. 6, 1943; m. Linda Fabry; children: Kristine Elizabeth, Katherine Vallie. BA in Journalism, U. N.C., 1965. Reporter UPI, various locations, 1965-69, writer, editor broadcast and gen. news depts. Chgo., 1969-77, exec. editor nat. broadcast dept., 1977-78; bur. chief Commodity News Svc., Chgo., 1978-79, U.S. News & World Report, Chgo., 1979-82, assoc. editor Washington, 1982-85, sr. editor, 1985-86; reporter, rewrite specialist Chgo. Sun Times, 1986-90, met. editor, 1990-91, asst. mng. editor/metro, 1991-97; editl. page editor, 1997—. Bd. dirs. City News Bur., Chgo, 1993-97, pres., 1996; media fellow Hoover Instit. Stanford U., 2001. Author (with Truman K. Gibson): Knocking Down Barriers: My Fight for Black America, 2005. V.p. Ill. Freedom of Info. Coun., 1994. Recipient Stick-O-Type award for feature writing Chgo. Newspaper Guild, 1987, Appreciation cert. for outstanding contbns. to freedom of info. Nat. Ctr. Freedom of Info. Studies at Loyola U.-Chgo., 1993. Office: Chgo Sun-Times 350 N Orleans Chicago IL 60654 Office Phone: 312-321-2535. Business E-Mail: shuntley@suntimes.com.

HUNTLEY, WILLIAM BARNEY, religious studies professor; b. Feb. 19, 1933; AB, Duke U; BD, Yale U; PhD, Duke U. Chaplain Westminster (Mo.) Coll., Mo., 1964—74, chmn. divsn. humanities, 1969-72, dean of students, 1972-74; assoc. dean Waseda U., Tokyo, 1986-87; chair dept. religious studies U. Redlands (Calif.), 1977-82, 84-86, 1997—2007, dir. Asian studies program, 1991—2002, Crawford prof. of religious studies, 2000—. Contbr. articles to profl. jours. Scholar-in-residence Reitaku U., Kashiwa, Japan, 1988-89. Address: 1474 Pacific St Redlands CA 92373-6936 Office: U Redlands 1200 E Colton Ave PO Box 3080 Redlands CA 92373-0999 Office Phone: 909-793-2121. Office Fax: 909-793-2029.

HUNTOON, MAJ. GEN. DAVID H., JR., military officer; Grad., US Mil. Acad., West Pt., 1973; M. in Mil. Arts & Sciences, CGSC Sch. Advanced Mil. Studies, 1988; MA, Georgetown U. Commd. 2d. lt. US Army, 1973, advanced through grades to Maj. Gen.; inf. officer, 1973—86; sr. war plans officer XVIII Airborne Corps. Directorate of Plans, Ft. Bragg, NC, dep. dir. plans, dir. plans; inf. comdr. Camp Casey, Korea; chief of plans CJ3. Combined Forces Command & UN Command, Yongsan; comdr. 3d. US Inf. Regiment, Ft. Myer, Va., 1995—97; exec. officer to chief of staff US Army, 1997—99; asst. divsn. comdr. 1st Cav. Divsn., Ft. Hood, Tex., 1999—2000; dep. comdt. US Army Command & Gen. Staff Coll., Ft. Leavenworth, Kans., 2000—02; dir. strategy, plans & policy Army G3, The Pentagon, 2002—03; comdt. US Army War Coll., Carlisle Barracks, Pa., 2003—. Decorated Legion of Merit-6th award, Bronze star, Expert Infantryman's badge; nat. security fellow, Hoover Inst., 1994—95. Office: US Army Garrison 45 Ashburn Dr Carlisle PA 17013-5006*

HUNTOON, NANCY, security manager; b. LA, Dec. 12, 1957; d. James Keith and Mary Elizabeth Huntoon. BS, U. Md., College Park, 1990. Card ops. technician NW Fed. Credit Union, Herndon, Va., 1995—2000, call ctr. asst. mgr., 2000—05, security mgr., 2005—. Instr. ARC, Fairfax County, Prince William Co., Va. Office: Northwest Federal Credit Union 200 Spring St Herndon VA 20170 Home Phone: 703-476-4134; Office Phone: 703-709-8900. Business E-Mail: nhuntoon@northwestfcu.org.

HUNTRESS, WESLEY THEODORE, JR., research scientist; b. Washington, Apr. 11, 1942; s. Wesley Theodore and Elizabeth Agnes (Moran) H.; m. Roseann Albano, June 22, 1973; 1 child, Garret. BS, Brown U., 1964; PhD, Stanford U., 1968. Scientist Jet Propulsion Lab., Pasadena, Calif., 1968-88; dep. dir earth sci. NASA, Washington, 1988-90, dir. solar system exploration, 1990-93, assoc. adminstr. space sci., 1993-98; dir. geophys. lab. Carnegie Instn. Washington, 1998—2007. Former mem. adv. coun. sci. com. NASA.

HUNTSBERRY, FREDERICK D., film company executive; Bachelor's degree, Boston U. Mgr., mergers and acquistions Europe Gen. Electric, 1985—97; v.p. TV bus. devel. Universal Pictures Corp., 1997—98; sr. v.p., CFO Universal Studios TV and Networks Group, 1998—2001, Universal Studios, 2001—02; exec. v.p., CFO Vivendi Universal Entertainment, 2002—04; exec v.p. NBC Universal TV Distbn., 2004—06; interim pres., CEO Paramount Pictures Corp., 2005, COO, 2006—. Office: Paramount Pictures Corp 5555 Melrose Ave West Hollywood CA 90038

HUNTSMAN, JON MEADE, chemicals executive; b. Blackfoot, Idaho, 1937; m. Karen Huntsman; 1 child, Jon Jr. BS, U. Pa., Phila., 1959; MBA, U. So. Calif., LA, 1970. With Olson Bros, Inc., North Hollywood, Calif., 1961; assoc. adminstr. HEW, spl. asst. to the pres., 1971-72; with Huntsman Container Corp., Salt Lake City, 1972-83, Huntsman Chem. Corp, Salt Lake City, 1982—; CEO Huntsman Corp., Salt Lake City, 1996-2000, chmn., 2000—. Bd. mem. Chem. Mfrs. Assn., Am. Plastics Coun. Author: Winners Never Cheat, 2005. Bd. mem. ARC, Wharton Sch. U. Pa., Primary Children's Med. Ctr. Found.; Pres. mission LDS Ch., Washington, 1980-83; founder, chmn. Huntsman Cancer Inst. Named Top chem. ind. CEO, 1994, hon. citizen, Republic of Armenia, Humanitarian of Yr., Larry King, 2002; named one of 50 Most Generous Philanthropists, BusinessWeek, 2005, Forbes' Richest Americans, 2006. Office: Huntsman Corp 500 Huntsman Way Salt Lake City UT 84108-1235 Office Phone: 801-532-5200.*

HUNTSMAN, JON MEADE, JR., governor, former federal agency administrator; b. Palo Alto, Calif., Mar. 26, 1960; s. Jon Meade and Karen (Haight) H.; m. Mary Katherine Cooper, Nov. 18, 1983; children: Mary Anne, Abigail, Elizabeth, Jon III. AB, U. Pa., 1987. Spl. asst. to chmn. Rep. Nat. Com., Washington, 1982; staff asst. The White House, Washington, 1983; state dir. UT Reagan-Bush campaign, Salt Lake City, 1984; v.p., dir. Huntsman Pacific Chem. Corp., Taipei, Taiwan, 1987-88; dep. asst. sec. Internat. Trade Administrn., Washington, 1989-90; dep. asst. sec. commerce for E. Asia and Pacific Affairs US Dept. Commerce, Washington, 1990-91; US amb. to Singapore US Dept. State, 1992—93; dep. US trade rep. & US trade amb. Office U.S. Trade Rep., Washington, 2001—03; chmn., CEO Huntsman Family Holdings Co. LLC, 2003—04; gov. State of UT, Salt Lake City, 2005—. Chmn. U.S.-China Comml. Commn. Groups, Washington, 1990-91, U.S.-Mongolia Trade Facilitation Group, 1990-91; exec. sec. U.S.-Thailand Joint Comml. Commn., 1990-91, U.S. Pacific Islands Joint Comml. Commn., 1990-91; pres., CEO Huntsman Cancer Found., 1995-2001. State dir. Utah Reagan-Bush campaign, Salt Lake City, 1984; chmn. Utah Reagan-Bush Inaugural Com., Salt Lake City, 1985; nat. del. Rep. Conv., 1984, 86. Mem. Internat. Club Washington, Asia Soc. Republican. Mem. Lds Ch. Office: Office of Gov UT E Office Bldg Ste E220 PO Box 142220 Salt Lake City UT 84114 Office Phone: 801-538-1000. Office Fax: 801-538-1528.*

HUNTSMAN, LAWRENCE DARROW, lawyer, director; b. Jan. 21, 1934; s. Orson Lawrence and Vera Maude (Day) H.; m. Lynn Maroe; children by previous marriage: Laura, Kathleen, Marguerite, Holbrook. Bar: Va. 1959, D.C. 1961. Clk. D.C. Superior Ct., 1959-60; asst. corp. counsel D.C., 1960-64, Miller, Brown & Gildenhorn, 1964-69; ptnr. Brown, Gildenhorn & Statland, Washington, 1969-75; pres. Pan Mediterranean Shipping Corp., 1975-82, Assorted Techs. Inc., 1994-97; dir. Ashley Corp.; gen. counsel KeyByte Techs., Inc., 1993-97. Mem. D.C. Bar Assn., Va. Bar Assn. Home: 223 Harpers Ferry Dr Locust Grove VA 22508 Office: 223 Harpers Ferry Dr Locust Grove VA 22508-5149 Office Phone: 540-972-3545. E-mail: ldhuntsman@earthlink.net.

HUNTSMAN, LEE L., former academic administrator, director; BSc in Elec. Engring., Stanford U., 1963; PhD in Biomedical Engring., U. Pa., 1968. Dir, ctr. for bioengineering U. Wash., 1980—96, assoc. dean for sci. affairs, sch. of medicine, 1993—96, provost, v.p. acad. affairs Seattle, 1997—2002, interim pres., 2002—03, pres., 2003—04, pres. emeritus, 2004—. Mem. Whitaker Found. Governing Com., 1994—98; chmn. Working Gorup on Rev. of Bioengineering and Tech. Instrumentation Develop. Rsch. for the Ctro for Sci. Rev of the NIH, 1998. Fellow: Am. Ins. of Med. and Biol. Engring., Am. Assn. for the Advancement of Sci.

HUNTSMAN, PETER R., chemicals executive; Grad., U. Utah, Salt Lake City. Pres. Olympus Oil Corp., 1986; v.p. to sr. v.p., gen. mgr. Huntsman Polypropylene Corp., 1987—94; sr. v.p. Huntsman Chem. Corp., Huntsman Packaging Corp.; pres., COO Huntsman Corp., 1994—2000, pres., CEO, dir., 2000—. Office: Huntsman Corp 500 Huntsman Way Salt Lake City UT 84108 Office Phone: 801-584-5700.*

HUNTTING, CYNTHIA COX, artist; b. San Francisco, Sept. 2, 1936; d. E. Morris and Margaret (Storke) Cox; m. Edward Tyler Huntting Jr., Mar. 8, 1969 (div. 1974). BA, Smith Coll., 1958; San Francisco Art Inst., 1959. Artist Emporium White House, San Francisco, 1958-61; artist, staff Pace Program Stanford U., 1962-64; artist World Affairs Council No. Calif., San Francisco, 1964-67; artist pvt. practice San Francisco, 1968—. Mem. Modern Art Council Bd. San Francisco Mus. Modern Art, 1970-78. Active Jr. League San Francisco, Inc. Mem. Town and Country, Calif. Tennis, Met. Club. Republican. Episcopalian. Avocations: tennis, fly fishing. Home and Office: 2720 Lyon St San Francisco CA 94123-3815

HUNTWORK, JAMES RODEN, lawyer; b. Milw., May 6, 1948; s. Daniel Lawrence and Gladys (Roden) H.; m. Patience Tipton Huntwork, July 7, 1972; children: Andrew Stuart, Sarah Noel. BA with distinction, Shimer Coll., 1968; JD, Yale Law Sch., 1972; MA Econs., Yale U., 1973. Bar: Mass. 1972, Ariz. 1977. Atty. Sullivan & Worcester, Boston, 1972-77, Jennings, Strouss & Salmon, Phoenix, 1977-91, Fennemore Craig, Phoenix, 1992-98, Salmon, Lewis & Weldon, Phoenix, Ariz., 1998—. Dir. exec. com. Phoenix Econ. Growth Corp., 1987-91; state ballot security chmn. Ariz. Rep. Party, Phoenix, 1992-2006; originator The Comml. Law Project for Ukraine, 1991—; mem. Ariz. Ind. Redistricting Commn., 2000-. Co-recipient Judge Learned Hand Human Rels. award Am. Jewish Com., 1992. Mem. ABA, Ariz. Bar Assn., Maricopa County Bar Assn., Phoenix C. of C. (N.Am. Free Trade Task Force 1991-95). Republican. Office: Ste 200 2850 E Camelback Rd Phoenix AZ 85016-4316 Office Phone: 602-801-9077. Business E-Mail: jrh@slwplc.com. E-mail: jrh@huntwork.net.

HUNTZICKER, WILLIAM EDWARD, journalism educator, writer; b. St. Paul, Aug. 18, 1946; s. Kenneth Verndale and Edith Hale (Bennion) H.; m. Linda DeLaurenti, 1974; children: James William, Rachel Lyn. BA in History, Mont. State U., 1968; MA in Am. Studies, U. Minn., 1973, PhD, 1978, cert. social studies, 1989. Ranch hand various family ranches, Miles City, Mont., 1964; electronic tech. Teledyne, Inc., Miles City, 1965; reporter, photographer Miles City Daily Star, 1966-67; reporter, editor Associated Press, Mpls., 1968-69; writer U. Minn. News Svc., Mpls., 1970-79; asst. prof. journalism U. Wis., River Falls, 1979-86; media writer Minn. Ho. of Reps., St. Paul, 1987; lectr. sch. of journalism and mass communication U. Minn., Mpls., 1988-97; asst. prof. mass comm. Bemidji (Minn.) State U., 1997-99; writer/editor Minn. Hist. Soc., St. Paul, 1999—2002; asst. prof. mass comm. St. Cloud State U., 2003—. Freelance Wis. corr. St. Paul Pioneer Press, 1984-86; editl. advisor The Minn. Daily, U. Minn., 1989-90, 92-97. Author: The Popular Press: 1833-65, 1999; contbr. articles to profl. jours. Chair parks com. Marcy Holmes Neighborhood Assn., Mpls., 1977-86, pres., 1981-82, sec., 1982-83, bd. dirs., 2003-05; co-pres. SE Mpls. Planning and Coord. Com., 1982-83, sec., 1978-79; tour guide Mpls. River City Trolley, 2002-06. Congregationalist. Home: 415 8th St SE Minneapolis MN 55414-1223 Office Phone: 320-308-4203. Personal E-mail: huntzicker@earthlink.net. Business E-Mail: wehuntzicker@stcloudstate.edu.

HUO, BONNIE KWAN, artist; b. China, Nov. 23, 1949; d. Hok Pui and Tai Wah; m. Rex W.C. Huo, Feb. 10, 1972; 1 child, Alina BA, U. Calif., Berkeley, 1971; postgrad. diploma in edn., U. Hong Kong, 1972. Sole proprietor Chinatelier, Hong Kong, 1987—. One-woman exhibits include Kowloon Shangrila Hotel, Hong Kong, 1989, Shenzhen Art Mus., China, 1993, Letty's Gallery, Vancouver, 1994, Pristine Harmony Art Ctr., Taipei, 1995, Modest Art Gallery, Toronto, Traditional Chinese Cultural Soc., Montreal, 1996, Melbourne Chinese Mus. & Sydney Chinese Culture Ctr., 1998, World Jour. Gallery, San Francisco, 2000, World Jour. Gallery, L.A., U. Indpls., Shenzhen Art Mus., 2003; represented in permanent collections Singapore Nat. Mus., Shenzhen Art Mus., Australia Chinese Mus., U. Indpls., Sotheby's Fine Modern Chinese Painting Auction. Recipient Cert. of Honor Suprs. of City and County of San Francisco and numerous art awards. Mem. Hong Kong Arts Devel. Coun. (examiner), Watercolor Rsch. Soc. (dir.), Hong Kong Zonta Club (com.). Avocations: travel, attending cultural events, reading, poetry. Home Fax: (852) 2838-9362. Personal E-mail: ufomail77@gmail.com.

HUO, JINSHAN, materials scientist; arrived in U.S., 1997; BS, Chongqu-ing U., China, 1983, MS, 1989; PhD, Oreg. Health and Sci. U., 2004. Asst. engr. Shanxi Heavy Vehicle Plant, China, 1983—85; instr. Xihua U., Chengdu, China, 1988—95, assoc. prof., 1995—97; rsch. asst. Grad. Inst. Sci. and Tech. Oreg. Health and Sci. U., Beaverton, 1997—2004; postdoctoral fellow Air Liquide, Countryside, Ill., 2004—05; materials scientist Fujimi Corp., Tualatin, Oreg., 2005—. Project contractor Intel Corp. and Oreg. Health and Sci. U., Hillsboro, Oreg., 2001—02. Co-author: Electrochemistry New Research, 2005, Microelectronics Applications Using Chemical Mechanical Planarization, 2007; contbr. articles to profl. jours. Named Outstanding Young Tchr., Sichuan Province Edn. Com., China, 1995; recipient Sci. Achievement cert., Sichuan Province Sci. Com., 2004. Mem.: Electrochem. Soc., Sigma Xi. Achievements include design of system and method for controlling temperature and detecting time of uniform temperature; non-destructive thermal uniformity detector; electrochemical mechanical polishing system; patents pending for methods of electopolishing patterned substrates, electrochemical planarization system and method of electrochemical planarization. Office Phone: 503-972-9454. Personal E-mail: jinshan_huo@yahoo.com.

HUO, XIAOMING, mathematician, educator; PhD, Stanford U., 1993—99. Prof. Ga. Inst. of Tech., 1999—. Contbr. articles to profl. jours. Recipient First Prize In Internat. Math. Olympiad, IMO orgn. com., 1989. Mem.: Inst. of Math. Stats. Achievements include development of var. toolboxes for signal processing. Office: School of ISyE 765 Ferst Dr Atlanta GA 30332 E-mail: xiaoming@isye.gatech.edu.

HUPE, DONNA MARIE, education educator; b. Jeannette, Pa., Oct. 15, 1951; d. Donald Spencer and Mary Agnes Ludwig; m. David William Hupe, Aug. 11, 1973; 1 child, Jennifer Anne Martin. BS in Elem. Edn., Slippery Rock U., Pa., 1973, MEd, 1980. Cert. elem. tchr. Pa., 1973. Visual perception therapist D. T. Watson Home for Crippled Children, Sewickley, Pa., 1975—78; elem. tchr. Seneca Valley Sch. Dist., Harmony, Pa., 1978—2006; adj. lectr., prof. St. Vincent Coll., Latrobe, Pa., 2006—. Recipient Profile Tchr. award, Campbell's Soup and Family Cir. Mag., 1989, Profl. Best award, Learning Mag., 1989; Just Do It! grantee, Nike Corp., 1991, Fulbright Meml. Fund scholar, 2003. Mem.: Seneca Valley Edn. Assoc. (pres.). Home: PO Box 4361 Hidden Valley PA 15502 Office: Saint Vincent Coll 300 Fraser Purchase Rd Latrobe PA 15650 Home Phone: 814-444-1116. Personal E-mail: hoopd2@zoominternet.net.

HUPP, JAMES R., dean, dental educator; b. Iron Mountain, Mich. m. Carmen Hupp, June 19, 1976; children: Jamie, Justin, Joelle, Jordan. BS in biol. sciences, U. Calif., Irvine, 1973; DMD cum laude, Harvard Sch. Dental Medicine, 1977; MD, U. Conn. Sch. Medicine, 1982; JD, Rutgers U., Newark, 1995; MBA, Loyola U., 2000. Diplomate American Board of Oral and Maxillofacial Surgery, 1982. Resident in oral-maxillofacial surgery U. Conn. Sch. Dental Medicine, 1980; intern in internal medicine UCLA Med. Ctr., 1983; asst. prof. dept. oral-maxillofacial surgery Vanderbilt U. Sch. Medicine, Nashville, 1983—85; chief oral-maxillofacial surg. svc. V.A. Med. Ctr., Nashville, 1983—85; dir. oral-maxillofacial surg. svc. Met. Nashville Gen. Hosp., 1983—85; asst. prof. dept. surgery U. Conn. Sch. Medicine, 1985—89; asst. prof. dept. oral-maxillofacial surgery U. Conn. Sch. Dental Medicine, 1985—89; assoc. chief of staff, J. Dempsey Univ. Hosp. U. Conn. Health Ctr., 1987—89, dir. oral-maxillofacial surgery residency, 1988—89; chair, assoc. prof. oral-maxillofacial surgery U. Medicine and Dentistry N.J., 1989—94, dir. oral-maxillofacial surgery residency program, 1992—93, chair dept. dental medicine, 1994, dir. divsn. oral-maxillofacial surgery, Univ. Hosp., 1994; chair, prof. oral-maxillofacial surgery U. Md. Dental Sch., Baltimore, 1994—2002; chair dept. dentistry U. Md. Med. System, Baltimore, 1994—2002; CEO U. Md. Oral-Maxillofacial Surgical Associates, 1994—2002; dir. oral-maxillofacial surgery residency program U. Md. Med. Ctr., Baltimore, 1996—99, 2001; dean U. Miss. Sch. Dentistry, 2002—, prof. oral-maxillofacial surgery, 2002—. Mem. editl. bd. Oral Surgery, Oral Medicine and Oral Pathology, 1993—; team dentist Baltimore Ravens, NFL, 1996—97; adj. prof. oral surgery/pharmacology U. Pa. Sch. Dental Medicine, 1997—. Editor-in-chief (textbook) "Five-minute Clinical Consult"; co-editor: (textbook) "Contemporary Oral and Maxillofacial Surgery", "Oral-Maxillofacial Infections". Fellow: Pierre Fauchard Acad., Am. Assn. Oral and Maxillofacial Surgeons (mem. rsch. sect. 1985—), Am. Coll. Surgeons, Am. Coll. Dentists; mem.: S.E. Soc. of Oral and Maxillofacial Surgeons, Am. Assn. Dental Rsch., Internat. Assn. Dental Rsch., AMA, ADA, Am. Dental Edn. Assn., Am. Bd. Oral and Maxillofacial Surgeons (dir. 1996—, mem. fin. com. 1999—, mem. exec. com. 2000—, sec.-treas. 2000—01, v.p. 2001—02, pres. 2002—03). Office: 2500 N State St Jackson MS 39216 Office Phone: 601-984-6000. Office Fax: 601-984-6014. Business E-Mail: jhupp@sod.umsmed.edu.

HUPP, MICHAEL M., lawyer; b. Norfolk, Nebr., Oct. 29, 1957; s. Andrew L. and Lorraine M. Hupp; m. Lauren Hupp, Sept. 21, 1990; children: Anna, Elizabeth, William. BS in Constrn. Mgmt., U. Nebr., Lincoln, 1980; JD, U. Nebr., 1984. Atty. McGill Koley, Omaha, 1984—87; shareholder Koley Jesson P.C., Omaha, 1988—. Bd. dirs. Cath. Charities, Omaha, 2003—, Child Saving Inst., Omaha, 2002—, Skutt Cath. HS, Omaha, 1997—2003, chmn., 2002—03. Mem.: ABA, Omaha Bar Assn., Nebr. Bar Assn. Office: Koley Jessen PC 1125 S 103d St Ste 800 Omaha NE 68124-1079 Office Phone: 402-390-9500. Business E-Mail: mike.hupp@koleyjessen.com.

HUPPE, ALEX, public relations executive; b. Princeton, NJ, June 18, 1947; s. Bernard F. and Mary Lois (McMaster) Huppe. BA with honors, Harpur Coll., 1969; MA, U. Va., Charlottesville, 1971. Prof. English Western Piedmont C.C., Morganton, NC, 1971-79, asst. to pres., 1979-80; asst. dean Boston U., 1980-85; dir. news Dartmouth Coll., Hanover, NH, 1985-95; dir. pub. affairs Harvard U., Cambridge, Mass., 1995—99, v.p., cons., 1999—. Rschr. Smith/Huppe Rsch., Boston, 1980—85; adj. prof. English Maine Maritime Acad., 2002—; adv. bd. Harpur Coll., 1998—. Co-author: (book) Alaska National Communication Program, 1982; mem. editl. bd.: Binghamton U. Pres. River City Arts, 1993—95; U.S. election observer Gabon, 2005; chmn. bd. dirs. Celo Health and Edn. Corp., Burnsville, NC, 1973—78; bd. dir. Assocs. Boston Pub. Libr., 1997—2002, Castine Hist. Soc., 2001—, SUNY Binghamton Alumni, 2003—. Mem.: NATAS (New Eng. chpt. gov. 1983—87, dir., Disting. Svc. award 1987), Ivy League News Dirs. (sec. 1988—91), Pub. Rels. Soc. Am. (exec. bd. counselors higher edn. 1998). Avocations: sailing, skiing, auto restoration. Personal E-mail: alexhuppe@aol.com.

HUPPER, JOHN ROSCOE, retired lawyer; b. NYC, June 16, 1925; s. Roscoe Henderson and Dorothy Wallace (Healy) Hupper; m. Joyce Shirley McCoy, June 14, 1952; children: John R. Jr., Gail J., Craig W. AB, Bowdoin Coll., 1949; LLB, Harvard U., 1952. Bar: NY 1954, US Supreme Ct. 1960. Assoc. Cravath, Swaine & Moore LLP, NYC, 1952—60, ptnr., 1961—95; ret., 1996—. Trustee Allen-Stevenson Sch., 1968—96; bd. dirs. Travelers Aid Soc., NY, 1962—79, Legal Aid Soc., NYC, 1971—76; overseer Bowdoin Coll., 1970—82, trustee, 1982—95. With US Army, 1943—46. Fellow: Am. Coll. Trial Lawyers; mem.: ABA, NY Supreme Ct. (mem. com. character and fitness appellate divsn. 1st dept. 1992—, spl. master 1982—), Assn. Bar City of NY, NY State Bar Assn., Down Town Assn., Union Club, Univ. Club, Apawamis Club. Republican. Office: Cravath Swaine and Moore LLP 825 8th Ave New York NY 10019-7475 Office Phone: 212-474-1313. Business E-Mail: jhupper@cravath.com.

HUR, SU-RYONG, physician, anesthesiologist; b. Korea, Feb. 8, 1942; arrived in US, 1966; s. Hyung Keun and JaeKyung (Kim) H.; m. Myung Ja; children: Jennifer, Steven, Michelle. MD, Seoul Nat. U., 1966. Diplomate Am. Bd. Anesthesiology. Intern Union Hosp., Fall River, Mass., 1966-67; resident St. Vincent's Hosp, Worcester, Mass., 1967-68, Mass. Gen. Hosp., Boston, 1968-71; staff anesthesiologist St. Michael's Hosp., 1975—; asst. prof. anesthesiology Med. Coll. Wis., 1971-75, mem. clin. faculty anesthesiology, 1976—, asst. prof. anesthesiology Milw., 2005—; staff anesthesiologist Firoedtert Meml. Luth. Hosp., 2004—. Contbr. articles to profl. jours. Fellow Am. Coll. Anesthesiologists; mem. AMA, Internat. Anesthesia Rsch. Soc., Am. Soc. Anesthesiologists, Korean Am. Med. Assn., Wis. Soc. Anesthesiologists, State Med. Soc. of Wis., Med. Soc. of Milw. County, Milw. Soc. of Anesthesiologists. Office: Froedtert Lutheran Memorial Hosp Anesthesia Dept 9200 W Wisconsin Ave Milwaukee WI 53226-3596 Office Fax: 414-805-6147, 414-805-6147; Home Fax: 262-241-3415.

HURAS, WILLIAM DAVID, retired bishop; b. Kitchener, Ont., Can., Sept. 22, 1932; s. William Adam and Frieda Dorothea (Rose) H.; m. Barbara Elizabeth Lotz, Oct. 5, 1957; children— David, Matthew, Andrea. BA, Waterloo Coll., Ont., 1954; BD, Waterloo Sem., Ont., 1963; MTh, Knox Coll., Toronto, Ont., 1968; MDiv, Waterloo Luth. U., 1973; DD (hon.), Wilfred Laurier U., Waterloo, 1980, Huron Coll., London, Ont., 1989. Ordained to ministry Luth. Ch. in Am., 1957. Pastor St. James Luth. Ch., Refrew, Ont., 1957-62, Advent Luth. Ch., North York, 1962-78; bishop Eastern Can. Synod Luth. Ch. in Am., Kitchener, 1978-85, Eastern Synod Evangel. Luth. Ch. in Can., 1986-98; ret., 1998. Exec. com. Can. sect. of Luth. Ch. in Am., 1969-79, Luth. Merger Commn., Can., 1978-85; pres. Luth. Coun. Can., 1985-88; chmn. Group Svcs. Inc., Evangelical Luth. Ch. in Can., 1993—2001; mem. Anglican-Luth. Jt. Working Group, 1995-2001. Bd. govs. Waterloo Luth. U., 1966-75, Waterloo Luth. Sem., 1973-75, 78-2004. Mem. Order of St. Lazarus of Jerusalem (Ecclesiastical Grand cross 1985). Lutheran. *We are called by God and God covets an affirmative response. To say "yes" to God is to say "yes" to all of life and to all of God's people.*

HURD, BYRON THOMAS, retired publishing executive; b. Roseville, Mich., 1933; s. Clark Frank and Evelyn (Sybelden) H.; m. Barbara Jean Ekeroth; children: Thomas E., Roger A., J. Douglas, James B. BSBA in Advt. and Mktg., Wayne State U., 1954. Sales mgr. Detroit Free Press, 1954—55, Milne & Jones, Royal Oak, Mich., 1955—56, Detroit Times, 1956—59; account mgr. Milne Circulation Sales, Inc., Bloomfield Hills, Mich., 1959—65; agt. Bankers Life Co., Des Moines, 1965—66; promotion mgr. Chgo. Today, Chgo. Tribune, 1966—74; owner, cons. Circulation Specialists, Homewood, Ill., 1974—77; exec. dir. circulation The Star Newspapers, Chicago Heights, Ill., 1977—95; ret., 1995. Panelist, discussion leader, session master, com. mem. No. Ill. Newspapers Assn., DeKalb. Contbr. Publishers handbook, 1988. Elder, pres. governing bd. Flossmoor (Ill.) Cmty. Ch., 1988. Mem. Ctrl. States Circulation Mgrs. Assn., Suburban Newspapers Am. (conf., sem. com.), Audit Bur. Circulation (voting rep.), Circulation Mgmt. Ill., Rotary (dir. cmty. svc. 1978-79, dir. internat. svc. 1979-80, sec. 1981-82, v.p. 1982-83, pres. 1983-84, dist. dir. pub. rels. 1984-86, dist. govs. aide 1986-87, dist. dir. vocat. svc. 1987-88, host Soviet Emerging Leaders 1988, Finnish 1989, dist. dir. group study exch. with India 1990, dist. conf. com. master ceremonies 1987-88, dist. conf. com. chmn. 1989-90), Flossmoor Country Club (sports and pastimes com. 1988), Marietta Country Club, Internat. Golfing Fellowship of Rotary (life), U.S. Golfing Fellowship of Rotary (life). Avocations: golf, drawing, painting. Personal E-mail: bbhurd@gmail.com.

HURD, GALE ANNE, film producer; b. LA, Oct. 25, 1955; d. Frank E. and Lolita (Espiau) Hurd; m. James Cameron, 1985 (div. 1989); m. Brian DePalma, July 20, 1991 (div.); 1 child; m. Jonathan Hensleigh, June 19, 1995. Degree in econs. and communications, Stanford U., 1977. Dir. mktg. and publicity, co-prodr. New World Pictures, LA, 1977-82; pres., prodr. Pacific Western Prodns., LA, 1982—. Owner Vertical Wine Bistro, Pasadena, Calif. Prodr.: (films) The Terminator, 1984 (Grand Prix Avoiriaz Film Festival award), Aliens 1986 (nominated for 7 Acad. awards, recipient Best Sound Effects Editing award, Best Visual Effects award Acad. Picture Arts & Scis.), Alien Nation (Saturn award for best sci. fiction film), The Abyss, 1989 (nominated for 4 Acad. awards, Best Visual Effects award), The Waterdance, 1991 (2 TFP Spirit awards, 2 Sundance Film Festival awards), Cast a Deadly Spell, 1991 (Emmy award), Raising Cain, 1992, No Escape, 1994, Safe Passage (Beatrice Wood award for Creative Achievement), 1994, The Ghost and the Darkness,(Acad. award) 1996, The Relic, 1996, Going West in America, 1996, Dante's Peak, 1997, Virus, 1997, Dead Man on Campus, 1997, Armageddon, 1998, Dick, 1999, Clockstoppers 2002, The Hulk, 2003 (TV series) Adventure, Inc., 2002, Punisher, 2004, Aeon Flux, 2005, (TV pilot) Coven, 2004; exec. prodr.: (films) Switchback, 1997, Tremors, 1990, Downtown, 1990, Terminator 2, 1991 (winner 3 Acad. awards), Witch Hunt, 1994, Sugartime, 1995, Terminator 3, 2004, Punisher, 2004, Hulk 2, 2007, Punisher 2, 2007; creative cons. (TV program) Alien Nation, 1989-90. Juror Focus Student Film Awards, 1989, 90; chmn. Nicholl Fellowship Acad. Motion Picture Arts & Scis., 1989—; mem. Show Coalition, 1988—; mem. Hollywood (Calif.) Women's Polit. Com., 1987—; mem. U.S. Film Festival Juror; bd. dirs. IFP/West, Artists Rights Found.; trustee Am. Film Inst.; bd. dirs. L.A. Internat. Film Festival, Coral Reef Rsch. Found., Ams. for a Safe Future; mentor Peter Stark Motion Picture Producing Program, Sch. of Cinema-TV, U. of So. Calif., Women in Film Mentor Program. Recipient Spl. Merit award Nat. Assn. Theater Owners, 1986, Stanford-La Entrepreneur of Yr. award Bus. Sch. Alumni L.A., 1990, Fla. Film Festival award, 1994, Women in Film Crystal award, 1998, Ind. Vision award Temucala Film Festival, 2001, Nat. Bd. Rev. Prodr.'s award, 2004, Global Green Millennium award, 2004, Israel Film Festival Visionary award, 2004, Saturn awards, Donald Reed award, 2004; named Prodr. of Yr., Stunt Awards, 2003. Mem. AMPAS (prodr.'s br. exec. com. 1990—, chair festival grants com.), Am. Film Inst. (trustee 1989—), Americans for a Safe Future (bd. dirs. 1993—), Prodr.'s Guild Am. (bd. dirs.), Women in Film (bd. dirs. 1989-90, 2000—03), Inst. for Rsch. on Women and Gender (nat. adv. panel 1997-2000), Feminist Majority, The Ocean Consrvancy (bd. dirs. 2001—, Heal the Bay (adv. bd.), Reef Check Internat. (adv. bd.), Seakeepers Soc., Mulholland Tomorrow, The Trusteeship (bd. dirs. 2006-), Explorers Club (N.Y.C.), Jamestowne Soc., Nat. Soc. DAR, Phi Beta Kappa. Avocations: scuba diving, paso fino horses. Office: Valhalla Motion Pictures 8530 Wilshire Blvd Ste 400 Beverly Hills CA 90211 Office Phone: 310-360-8540.

HURD, HEIDI M., dean, humanities and law educator; b. Laramie, Wyo., Oct. 19, 1960; d. Carroll Parsons and Jeanne Marie H.; children: Gillian K.J. and Aidan A. (twins). BA with honors, Queen's U., Kingston, Ont., Can., 1982; MA, Dalhousie U., Halifax, NS, Can., 1984; JD, U. So. Calif., LA, 1988, PhD, 1992. Asst. prof. U. Pa. Law Sch., Phila., 1989-94, prof. law and philosophy, 1994—2002, assoc. dean, 1994-96, co-dir. Inst. Law and Philosophy, 1998—2000; Herzog rsch. prof. law U. San Diego, 2000—02; dean, prof. philosophy, David Baum prof. law U. of Ill. Coll. Law, 2002—. Vis. asst. prof. dept. philosophy U. Iowa, Iowa City, 1991-92; vis. prof. law U. Va. Law Sch., Charlottesville, 1997-98. Author: Moral Combat, 1999; contbr. articles to profl. jours. Office: U Illinois College Law Dean Office 504 E Pennsylvania Ave Champaign IL 61820-6909 Office Phone: 217-333-9857. E-mail: hhurd@law.uiuc.edu.

HURD, JOSEPH KINDALL, JR., obstetrician, gynecologist; b. Hoisington, Kans., Feb. 12, 1938; MD, Harvard U., 1964. Cert. ob.-gyn. Intern Boston City Hosp., 1964-65, resident in surgery, 1965-66; resident in ob.-gyn. Bronx (N.Y.) Mcpl. Hosp. Ctr., 1966-70; with Walson Army Hosp., Ft. Dix, NJ, 1970—72, Lahey Clinic Med. Ctr., Burlington, Mass., 1972—, chair dept. gynecology, 1988—2000. Clin. instr. surgery Harvard U., 1972—; clin. asst. prof. Tufts U. Sch. Medicine, Boston, 1996—. Named one of Top 100 Black Physicians in Am., Black Enterprise Mag., 2001. Fellow Am. Coll. Ob.-Gyn., ACS; mem. AMA, Nat. Med. Assn. Office: Lahey Med Ctr 41 Mall Rd Burlington MA 01805-0001 Home Phone: 781-235-5912; Office Phone: 781-744-8495. Business E-Mail: jkhurd@massmed.org.

HURD, MARK V., computer company executive; b. NYC, Jan. 1, 1957; m. Paula Hurd; 2 children. BBA, Baylor U., Waco, Tex., 1979. With NCR Corp., 1980—2005; sr. v.p. Teradata Solutions Group (divsn. NCR Corp.), 1998—2000; COO Teradata (divsn. NCR Corp.), 2000—02; exec. v.p. NCR Corp., 2000—01, co-pres. Dayton, Ohio, 2001—02, COO, 2002—03, CEO, 2003—05; pres., CEO Hewlett-Packard Co., Palo Alto, Calif., 2005—06, chmn., pres., CEO, 2006—. Bd. dirs. Hewlett-Packard Co., 2005—. Co-author (with Lars Nyberg): The Value Factor: How Global Leaders Use Information. Bd. visitors Fuqua Sch. Bus. Duke U.; bd. trustees, Dayton Area Chap. Am. Red Cross. Named one of 50 Who Matter Now, CNNMoney.com Bus. 2.0, 2006, 2007. Avocation: tennis. Office: Hewlett Packard Co 3000 Hanover St Palo Alto CA 94304-1185 Office Phone: 650-857-1501. Office Fax: 650-857-5518.*

HURD, MARY K., civil engineer, writer; BSCE, Iowa State U., Ames; postgrad, U. Chgo., U. Mich., U. Ill. Assoc. editor spl. tech. publs. Am. Concrete Inst., 1966-67, staff engr. Detroit, 1967-76; engr.-writer, cons., 1976-80, 90—; engring. editor Concrete Constrn. Mag., Addison, Ill., 1983-90, editor, 1981-83; pres. Engr. Publs., Farmington Hills, Mich. Past chmn. bd. dirs. Concrete Improvement Bd. Author: Formwork for Concrete, 1963, 7th edit., 2005; contbr. articles in field to profl. jours. including Constrn. Specifier, Concrete Internat., Jour. Am. Concrete Inst., Internat. Jour. of Ferrocement, Revista IMCYC Mexico, Pub. Works, Concrete Constrn., Concrete Prodr., PCI Jour., presenter and organizer in field. Recipient Profl. Achievement in Engring. Citation award Iowa State U., 1982, Outstanding Achievement award Concrete Improvement Bd. Detroit, 1990, Anson Marston medal Iowa State U. Coll. Engring., 2004; named one of 125 Top People of Past 125 Years in Constrn. Industry. Mem. ASCE (life), Am. Concrete Inst. (hon. mem., past mem. bd. dirs., organizing chmn. com. 124 concrete aesthetics, com. 347 formwork for concrete, past pres. Mich. chpt., Constrn. Practice award 1982, 88, Delmar L. Bloem Disting. Svc. award 1990, 2006, Arthur Y. Moy award Mich. chpt. 1994, Henry C. Turner medal 1995), Am. Soc. Concrete Contractors, Precast/Prestressed Concrete Inst. (profl.), The Concrete Soc. (U.K.), Tau Beta Pi, Phi Kappa Phi. Address: 33742 Lyncroft Rd Farmington Hills MI 48331-3647 Office Phone: 248-474-1369.

HURD, NICOLE FARMER, director; d. Lawrence William and Susan Farmer; m. William Lewis Hurd, May 31, 1997; children: Monica Katharine, Matthew Lawrence. BA, U. Notre Dame, Ind., 1992; MA, Georgetown U., Washington, 1996; PhD, U. Va., Charlottesville, 2002. Adminstrv. officer Georgetown U., Washington, 1995—96; asst. dean for rsch. U. Va., Charlottesville, 2002—05, founding dir. Ctr. for Undergrad. Excellence, 2002—; dir. Coll. Guide Program, Charlottesville, Va., 2005—. Coll. Access grantee for Va., Jack Kent Cooke Found., 2004—, Dupont fellow, U. Va., 2001—02, Marchant fellow, 2001—02. Mem.: Am. Hist. Assn., Am. Acad. Religion, Nat. Assn. Fellowship Advisors, Nat. Coll. Access Network, Omicron Delta Kappa. Home: 1011 Wildmere Pl Charlottesville VA 22901 Office: U Va PO Box 400874 Charlottesville VA 22904 Home Phone: 434-244-2907; Office Phone: 434-924-6058. Office Fax: 434-924-3832. E-mail: nhurd@virginia.edu.

HURD, RICHARD NELSON, pharmaceutical executive; b. Evanston, Ill., Feb. 25, 1926; s. Charles DeWitt and Mary Ormsby (Nelson) H.; m. Jocelyn Fillmore Martin, Dec. 22, 1950; children: Melanie Gray, Suzanne Dewitt. BS, U. Mich., 1946; PhD U. Minn., 1956. Chemist Gen. Electric Co., Schenectady, NY, 1948-49; R&D group leader Koppers Co., Pitts., 1956-57; rsch. chemist Mallinckrodt Chem. Works, St. Louis, 1957-63, group leader, 1963-66, Comml. Solvents Corp., Terre Haute, Ind., 1966-68, sect. head, 1968-71; mgr. sci. affairs G. D. Searle Internat. Co., Skokie, Ill., 1972-73, dir. mfg. and tech. affairs, 1973-77; rep. to internat. tech com. Pharm. Mfrs. Assn., Skokie, Ill., 1973-77; v.p. tech. affairs Elder Pharms., Bryan, Ohio, 1977-81; v.p. rsch. & devel. U.S. Proprietary Drugs & Toiletries div. Schering-Plough Corp., Memphis, 1981-83; v.p. sci affairs Moleculon, Inc., Cambridge, Mass., 1984-88; v.p. regulatory affairs Pharmaco-LSR, Inc., Austin, Tex., 1989-94; prin. Hurd & Assocs., Inc., Evanston, Ill., 1994—. Contbr. articles to profl. jours.; patentee in field. Mem. Ferguson-Florissant (Mo.) Sch. Bd., 1964-66; bd. dirs. United Fund of Wabash Valley (Ind.), 1969-71. With USN, 1943-46, 53-55. E.I. DuPont de Nemours & Co., Inc. fellow, 1956. Fellow AAAS; mem. Am. Acad. Dermatology (life), Am. Soc. Photobiology, Am. Chem. Soc., N.Y. Acad. Sci., Am. Pharm. Assn., Am. Assn. Pharm. Scientists, Food and Drug Law Inst., Drug Info. Assn., Sigma XI, Mich. Shores Club (Wilmette, Ill.). Presbyterian. Achievements include codevelopment of Ralgro and Oxsoralen; research in thioamides as a class of organic compounds; development of macrocyclic synthetic routes for natural products; development of psoralens for photochemotherapy of dermatologic disorders. Home Phone: 847-864-9773. Personal E-mail: hurdreg@earthlink.net.

HURDLE, CLINT, professional athletics manager; b. Big Rapids, Mich., July 30, 1957; m. Karla Hurdle; 1 child, Ashley. Player KC Royals, 1977—81, Cin. Reds, 1982, NY Mets, 1983—85, 1987, St. Louis Cardinals, 1986; hitting instr. Colo. Rockies, 1994—96, mgr., 2002—. Office: Co Rockies 2001 Blake St Denver CO 80205

HURET, BARRY S., marketing professional, consultant; b. NYC, 1938; s. Benjamin and Anna (Berko) H.; m. Marilynn Moskowitz, Feb. 1961; children: Abbey, Eric. BA with honors, Cornell U., 1961; MBA with distinction, NYU, 1970. Asst. sales engr. Westinghouse Corp., Pitts., 1962-64; sales engr. MultiAmp Corp., Cranford, N.J., 1964-65; sales engr., regional mgr., nat. sales mgr. Gould, Inc., St. Paul, 1965-77; successively mktg mgr., v.p. mktg., v.p. new bus. ventures Exide Corp., Horsham, Pa., 1977-82; nat. sales mgr. battery sales div. Panasonic Indsl. Co., Secaucus, N.J., 1982-86, asst. gen. mgr. battery sales group, divsn. head, 1986-97; pres., CEO Huret Assocs., Inc., A Battery Cons. Co., 1997—. Leader Gerson Lehrman Group; former sr. counselor Mastushita Storage Battery Co. Am.; past chmn. battery sect. accessory divsn. Electronic Industries Assn.; exec. rev. bd. Power 94, Power 95, Power 96; cons. Battery Rsch. Lab. Rutgers U., GIGA ExperNet; chmn. Battery Sessions, Battery Track Portable by Design, 1998—; cons. ibattery.com, 1998—2006; expert witness battery litigation, 1999—. Author: A User Friendly Guide to Selecting Rechargeable Batteries. 1st lt. US Army, 1961—62. Recipient

Hector Lazo Meml. Mktg. award NYU, 1970, Alumni Key, 1970. Mem. Cornell U. Alumni (former v.p. class of 1959), Phi Beta Kappa. Home: 484 Kings Rd Yardley PA 19067-4652 Personal E-mail: bhuret@comcast.net.

HURLBERT, ROGER WILLIAM, information technology executive; b. San Francisco, Feb. 18, 1941; s. William G. and Mary (Greene) H.; m. Karen C. Haslag, Nov. 6, 1982; children: Sage, Mica, Chula, Monk, Morris, Cassie, Bella. BS in Community Devel., So. Ill. U., 1965. Newspaper editor and reporter various, San Francisco Bay Area, 1958-62; pvt. practice investigation Ill., 1963-65; advisor San Francisco Planning Urban Rsch. Assn., 1969-87; pres. Sage Info. Svcs., Glen Ellen, Calif., 1988—. Compiler U.S. Land Data Base, 1972—. Pres. Haight-Ashbury Neighborhood Coun., San Francisco, 1959-61. With U.S. Army, 1966-68, Vietnam. Recipient Cert. of Merit, San Francisco Coun. Dist. Mchts. Assn., 1972. Mem. Real Estate Info. Profls. Assn. (sec. 1998-03), Direct Mktg. Assn., Mail Advt. Svc. Assn. Internat., League of Men Voters (v.p. 1959—), Internat. Assn. of Assessing Officials. Democrat. Office: Sage Info Svcs 13606 Arnold Dr PO Box 1832 Glen Ellen CA 95442-1832

HURLBURT, HARLEY ERNEST, ocean modeling and prediction scientist; b. Bennington, Vt., Apr. 12, 1943; s. Paul Rhodes and Evelyn Arlene (Lockhart) H.; m. Cheryl Elaine Finch, Jan. 10, 1998. BS in Physics, Union Coll., Schenectady, NY, 1965; MS, Fla. State U., 1971, PhD in Meteorology, 1974. NASA trainee Fla. State U., 1970-72; postdoctoral fellow advanced studies program Nat. Ctr. Atmospheric Rsch., Boulder, Colo., 1974-75; staff scientist JAYCOR, Alexandria, Va., 1975-77; oceanographer Naval Rsch. Lab. and related orgns., Stennis Space Ctr., Miss., 1977—, br. head, 1983-85, sr. scientist ocean modeling and prediction, 2000—. Adj. faculty marine sci. U. So. Miss., Stennis Space Ctr., 1993—; adj. faculty meteorology Fla. State U., Tallahassee, 1995—; nat. adv. panel satellite surface stress working group NASA, 1981-84, minerals mgmt. svc. interagy. adv. group, 1982-89, world ocean circulation experiment working group on numerical modeling, 1984-96, USN space oceanography working group, 1986-89; co-chmn. working group on global prediction sys., ocean prediction workshop, 1986; internat. working group on acoustic monitoring of world ocean Sci. Com. Oceanic Rsch., 1991-98; internat. working group on modelling subarctic North Pacific circulation North Pacific Marine Sci. Orgn., 1994-95; sci. steering team Internat. Global Ocean Data Assimilation Experiment, 1998—; mem. NASA High Resolution Ocean Topography Sci. Working Group, 2001, NASA Wide Swath Ocean Altimeter Sci. Working Group, 2002-03; project leader eddy-resolving global ocean prediction model devel. USN, 1987—; mem. steering team Philippines Straits Experiment Office Naval Rsch., 2007—. Contbr. numerous articles to profl. jours. V.p. Burgundy Citizens Assn., 1976-77. Weather officer USAF, 1965-69. Scholar Union Coll., 1965; recipient Disting. Scientist medal 13th Internat. Colloquium, Liege, Belgium, 1981, Publ. award for best basic rsch. paper Naval Ocean R & D Activity, 1980, 90; grantee Office Naval Rsch., 1975-77, 84—, Dept. Energy, 1975-78, Tex. A&M U., 1976, Office of Naval Tech., 1987-93, Space Warfare Sys., 1989-94, Advanced Rsch. Projects Agy., 1993-95, Strategic Environ. Rsch. and Devel. Program, 1994-95, Def. Dept. High Performance Computing Challenge, 1997—, Nat. Ocean Partnership Program, 1997—; case study on Eddy-resolving Global Ocean Modeling and Prediction included in 2000 Computerworld Smithsonian Collection archived in Smithsonian's Nat. Mus. Am. History's permanent rsch. collection. Mem. Am. Meteorol. Soc., Am. Geophys. Union, Oceanography Soc., Phi Sigma Kappa, Sigma Xi (Kaminski Publ. award 1991), Sigma Tau, Chi Epsilon Pi. Methodist. Achievements include research on the oceanic onset of El Nino and the dynamics of loop current eddy shedding in the Gulf of Mexico; discovery of the impact of upper ocean-topographic coupling via flow instabilities on upper ocean current pathways, including the Gulf Stream in the Atlantic and the Kuroshio in the Pacific; transition of the world's first eddy-resolving global ocean prediction system to the Naval Oceanographic Office for operational use. Home: 507 Hermitage Ct Pearl River LA 70452-3903 Office: Naval Rsch Lab Code 7304 Bay Saint Louis MS 39529 Office Phone: 228-688-4626. E-mail: hurlburt@nrlssc.navy.mil.

HURLBUT, ROBERT HAROLD, health care services executive; b. Rochester, NY, Mar. 9, 1935; s. Harold Leroy and Martha Irene (Fincher) H.; m. Barbara Cox, June 14, 1958; children: Robert W., Christine A. Hurlbut. Student, Coll. Hotel Adminstrn., Cornell U., 1953-56; PhD (hon.), St. John Fisher Coll, 2006. Adminstr. and dir. Pillars Nursing Home, Rochester, 1956—80, Elmcrest Nursing Home, Churchville, NY, 1960—75, Elm Manor Nursing Home, Canandaigua, NY, 1960—75, Penfield Nursing Home, Rochester, 1963—75, Avon Nursing Home, NY, 1964—75, Newark Nursing Home, NY, 1965—75, Lakeshore Nursing Home, Rochester, 1972—75. Bd. dir. HSBC; organizer, adminstrv. dir. hdqrs. Rohm Svcs. Corp., Rochester, 1964—; organizer, pres. hdqrs. Vari-Care Inc., Rochester, 1969—93; adv. bd. mem. Cornell Hotel Sch., NY, 2003—; commr. N.Y. State Ins. Fund, 1982—, chmn. bd., 2006—. Trustee St. John Fisher Coll., 1983—98, trustee emeritus; trustee U. Rochester, 2001—, mem. adv. bd.; trustee Eastman Dental Ctr. Found.; pres. Hurlbut Trust, 1994; mem. bd. dir. Strong Meml. Hosp., 1984—, chmn. bd. dir., 2004—06; life coun. mem. Cornell U. Recipient Compeer award, 2001, George Eastman Medal award, U. Rochester, 2006. Fellow Am. Coll. Health Care Adminstrs.; mem. Greater Met. C. of C. (past chmn. bd. dirs.), Genesee Valley Club, Oak Hill Country Club, Cornell Soc. Hotelmen, Meml. Art Gallery, NY State Sheriff's Assn., Smithsonian, Rochester MUs. and Sci. Ctr., Lambda Chi Alpha. Home: 200 Sheldon Rd Honeoye Falls NY 14472-9316 Office: Hurlbut Trust 740 East Ave Rochester NY 14607-2107 Office Phone: 585-271-1650.

HURLEY, ALFRED FRANCIS, historian, academic administrator emeritus, retired air force officer; b. Bklyn., Oct. 16, 1928; s. Patrick Francis and Margaret Teresa (Coakley) H.; m. Joanna Helen Leahy, Jan. 24, 1953; children: Alfred F., Thomas J., Mark P., Claire T., John K. BA summa cum laude, St. John's U., 1950; MA, Princeton U., 1958, PhD, 1961. Enlisted USAF, 1950, commd. lt., 1952, tng. officer, instr. navigator, 1952—56; from instr. to asst. prof. history USAF Acad., 1958—63, prof., head dept. history, 1966—80, prof. emeritus, 1990—; navigator, exec. officer USAF Hdqrs., Germany, War Plans Staff, Joint Chiefs of Staff, 1963—66; bd. mem. Acad. Bd., 1977-80; advanced through grades to brig. gen. USAF, ret., 1980; v.p. adminstrv. affairs U. North Tex. (formerly North Tex. State U.), Denton, 1980-82, pres., chancellor, 1982-2000, prof. history, 1981—; chancellor U. North Tex. Sys., 2000—, pres. emeritus, 2002—. Mem. adv. com. USAF hist. program sect. USAF, Washington, 1982-86, chmn., 1984-86; mem. bd. visitors Air U., 1993-97. Author: Billy Mitchell, Crusader for Air Power, 1964, (rev. edit.), 1975; contbg. author: Winged Shield, Winged Sword, History of the USAF, 1997; co-editor: Air Power and Warfare, 1979; pub. Air Power History, 2006—. Decorated Legion of Merit (2); Guggenheim fellow, 1971-72, Eisenhower Inst., Smithsonian fellow, 1976-77; recipient Pres.'s medal St. John's U., 1990. Mem.: Tex. Philos. Soc. (pres. 2003—04, bd. dirs. 2004—), Dallas Citizens Coun. (bd. dirs. 2000—02), North Tex. Commn. (bd. dirs. 1986—2000, chmn. 1995—97, bd. dirs. 2004—), Alliance for Higher Edn. of North Tex. (trustee 1983—89, chmn. coun. of pres. 1989—90), Tex. Coun. Pub. Univ. Pres. and Chancellors (chmn. 1987—89), Coalition Urban and Met. Univs. (co-chair 1993—2002, mem. exec. com. 2002—04), Am. Hist. Assn. (chmn. NASA fellowship com. 1993—94), Am. Coun. Edn. (commn. leadership 1993—96), Am. Assn. State Colls. and Univs. (coun. state reps. 1989—92), Air Force Hist. Found. (trustee 1980—), Am. Mil. Inst. (trustee 1973—78, 1981—85). Roman Catholic. Home: 828 Skylark Dr Denton TX 76205-8012 Office: U North Tex Dept History Denton TX 76203-0650 Business E-Mail: hurley@unt.edu.

HURLEY, ALLYSON KINGSLEY, dentist; b. Buffalo, June 15, 1949; d. Norman and Marion (Legler) Kingsley; m. Lawrence Joseph Hurley, May 28, 1977; children: Michael William, Kathryn Elizabeth. Student, Barat Coll., 1967-68; degree in dental hygiene, Marquette U., 1970, BS, 1971; DDS, Howard U., 1977. Pvt. practice dental hygiene, Washington, 1971-77; resident VA Hosp., Lyons, N.J., 1977-78; gen. practice dentistry Chatham, N.J., 1978—. Attending dentist Overlook Hosp., Summit, NJ, 1979—, dir. resident adminstrn., 1980-85, edn. com., 1981-86; clin. instr. dental hygiene Union County Tech. Inst., Scotch Plains, NJ, 1979-81, selection com. for dental dept., 1987; coord. kindergarten-4th grades dental health program Chatham Boro Sch. Sys., 1978-92; active oral cancer screening program Chatham Boro Jr. Women's Club, 1980-82. Editor, contbg. author newsletter Word of Mouth, 1981—; author Your Child's Teeth, 1984; contbg. author: Love Is the Best Medicine, 2001; one-woman shows include Morris Twp. Mcpl. Bldg., Gallery 54, Libr. of the Chathams, Borus Gallery, Fiddleheads, Johns Island, S.C., New Providence Libr.; exhibited in group shows at Overlook Hosp., Summit, Summit Coll., Unitarian Ch., Libr. of Chathams, Summit Libr., Chatham Mcpl. Bldg., Kiawah Island Cmty. Assn.; field contbr. Nature Photographer. Alumni recruiter Marquette U., Morris County, N.J., 1977-83; bd. dirs. Am. Cancer Soc., Morris County, 1981-83; chair Scholarship Found. of the Chathams, Inc., 1985-95. Recipient Art awards, Chatham Women's Club, 2001, 2002, 2004, 3d pl. award, S.C. Wildlife Mag., 2005, 2006, 2d pl. award, 2007. Master Acad. Gen. Dentistry (Lifelong Learning award 2006); fellow Internat. Acad. Dental-Facial Esthetics; mem. ADA, AAUW, Am. Acad. Cosmetic Dentistry (accredited, Gold medals 2001, 03, 06), N.Am. Nature Photography Assn., NJ Acad. Cosmetic Dentistry (pres. 2000-02), Tri-County Dental Soc. (bd. dirs. 1982-83), Internat. Dental Lectr., Internat. Platform Assn., NY Acad. Scis., NJ Assn. Women Bus. Owners, Assn. Media Photographers, Nat. Assn. Photoshop Profls., Drew Art Assn., Chatham Twp. Art League, Columbia U. Dental Study Club, No. NJ Women's Study Club (pres. 1980-82, 86-, sec. 1983-86), Newcomer's Club Chatham Township, Milburn-Short Hills Art League, Acad. Esthetic and Restorative Dentistry Study Club Republican. Roman Catholic. Office: Allyson Kingsley Hurley DDS 585 Main St Chatham NJ 07928-2104 Home Phone: 973-638-2924; Office Phone: 973-635-0698. E-mail: akhurley@aol.com.

HURLEY, ANDREW JOHN, musician; b. Milwaukee, May 31, 1980; Drummer Fall Out Boy, 2003—, Project Rocket. Musician (with Project Rocket): (albums) New Years Revolution, 2003; musician: (with Fall Out Boy) Take This to Your Grave, 2003, From Under the Cork Tree, 2005, Infinity on High, 2007, (songs) Sugar, We're Going Down, 2003 (MTV2 award, MTV Video Music Awards, 2005), Dance, Dance, 2005 (Choice music single & Choice rock track, Teen Choice Awards, 2006, Viewer's Choice award, MTV Video Music Awards, 2006); actor: (films) Rock 'n' Roll Frankenstein, 1999. Recipient Choice Music Rock Group award, Teen Choice Awards, 2006. Office: Fall Out Boy Inc Box 219 1187 Wilmette Ave Wilmette IL 60091

HURLEY, CHAD MEREDITH, Internet company executive; b. Jan. 24, 1977; s. Donald and JoAnn; m. Kathy Clark. BA in Fine Art, Ind. U. of Pa., 1999. First user-interface designer PayPal Inc., 1999—2002; design cons. several tech. companies, 2002—05; co-founder, CEO YouTube Inc. (sold to Google in 2006), 2005—. Design cons.: (films) Thank You for Smoking, 2005. Named (with Steve Chen) Webby Person of the Yr., 2007; named one of 50 Who Matter Now, CNNMoney.com Bus. 2.0, 2006, The World's Most Influential People, TIME mag., 2007, 25 Most Influential People in Web Music, Powergeek 25, 2007. Achievements include logo design for PayPal.*

HURLEY, CHERYL JOYCE, book publishing executive; b. Pitts., Oct. 30, 1947; d. John and Violet der Norsek; m. Kevin Hurley, July 27, 1974. Lang. and lit. cert., Université de Lyon, France, 1968; AB, Ohio U., 1969; MA, U. Mich., 1971. Research assoc. MLA, NYC, 1972-74, dir. spl. programs, 1974-79; pub. The Library of America, NYC, 1979—88, pres., 1988—. Cons. in field. Contbr. articles to profl. jours. Trustee French Inst./Alliance Francaise, 1992—, v.p., exec. com., 1994—, chmn. libr. com., 1996—, Samuel H. Kress Found., 1999—; adv. com. N.Y. 100 Centennial, 1997-98; mem. humanities adv. coun. N.Y. Pub. Libr., 1996—; mem. dean's adv. bd. Rackham Grad. Sch. U. Mich., 2000-; mem. vis. com. printed books Pierpont Morgan Libr., 2005-. Rackham fellow, 1969—70. Mem.: Assn. Internationale de Bibliophilie, Am. Antiquarian Soc. (councillor 1999—), Bridgehampton Club, Colony Club, Grolier Club, Century Assn., Phi Beta Kappa. Home: 1172 Park Ave New York NY 10128-1213 Office: Libr of Am 14 E 60th St New York NY 10022-1006

HURLEY, CORNELIUS KEEFE, JR., law educator; b. Boston, Oct. 16, 1945; s. Cornelius Keefe and Mildred G. (Anholt) Hurley; children: Emma, Eleanor, Cornelius. AB, Coll. of Holy Cross, 1968; JD, Georgetown U, 1974; PMD, Harvard U., 1986. Bar: Mass. 1974, US Supreme Ct. 1980, DC 1981. Law clk. McCarty & Noone, 1971—72; legis aide to Congressman Thomas O'Neill, 1973—74; bd. govs. Fed. Res. Sys., Washington, 1974—81, asst. gen. counsel, 1981; v.p., gen. counsel Shawmut Nat. Corp., Boston, 1981—88, dir. human resources, 1988—89; ptnr. The Secura Group, Washington, 1990—97. Prof. Boston U., 2003—, dir. Morin Ctr. for Banking and Fin. Law, 2005—; lectr. in field. Editor: International Banking: US Laws and Regulations, 1984. Mem.: DC Bar Assn., Mass. Bar Assn. Office: Boston U Morin Ctr for Banking and Fin L 765 Commonwealth Ave, Rm 1524 Boston MA 02215 Office Phone: 617-353-3023. E-mail: ckhurley@bu.edu.*

HURLEY, DEAN C., bank executive, lawyer; b. South Weymouth, Mass., Oct. 16, 1954; s. Dean C. and Neva (Richards) H.; m. Laura Ann Beck, Apr. 5, 1997; children: Mackenzie Katherine, Caroline Jeanette, Margaret Neva, Dean C. III. BS, Fairleigh Dickinson U., 1976, MBA, 1978; JD, N.Y. Law Sch., 1985. Bar: N.J. 1985, D.C. 1986. Asst. ops. mgr. Fieldcrest Mills, Inc., NYC, 1976-77; spl. projects mgr. Citicorp Credit Svcs. Inc., NYC, 1978-86; v.p., dir. fin. planning First Jersey Nat. Corp., Jersey City, 1986-88; v.p. asset strategies A/L. Mgmt. Dae Ichi Kangyo Bank div. The CIT Group, 1988-95; v.p. portfolio sales group Meenan, McDevitt & Co., Inc., 1996-98; v.p. debt, currencies, commodities and derivatives comml. mortgage acquisitions group Société Générale, NYC, 1998—2003, dir. debt, currencies, commodities and derivatives comml. mortgage backed securitization group, 2003—. Active Christian Ctr.; trustee, recording sec. Livingston Symphony Orch., 1993-97. Mem.: Nat. Assn. Securities Dealers, Omicron Delta Epsilon, Phi Delta Phi. Republican. Avocations: flying, boating. Home: 23 Cider Mill Ln Port Murray NJ 07865-3202 Office: Société Générale 1221 Avenue Of The Americas New York NY 10020-1001

HURLEY, DENIS R., federal judge; b. 1937; BS, U. Pa., 1959; MBA, Columbia U., 1962; LLB, Fordham U., 1966. Assoc. Bond, Schoenck and King, Syracuse, N.Y., 1966-68; prin. asst. dist. atty. Dist. Attys. Office, Suffolk County, N.Y., 1968-70; assoc., then ptnr. Pike, Behringer & Hurley (and successor firms), Riverhead, N.Y., 1970-82; judge N.Y. State Family Ct., 1983-87; acting justice N.Y. Supreme Ct., Suffolk County, 1987-88; judge N.Y. State County Ct., Suffolk County, 1988-91; fed. judge U.S. Dist. Ct. (ea. dist.) N.Y., Bklyn., 1991—, now sr. judge. Adj. prof. Touro Law Sch., Huntington, NY, 1995—97. Office: US Dist Ct PO Box 9014 Central Islip NY 11722-9014

HURLEY, ELIZABETH (LIZ HURLEY), actress, model; b. Hampshire, Eng., June 10, 1965; m. Arun Nayar, Mar. 2, 2007; 1 child, Damian Charles. Student, London Studio Ctr. Head devel. Simian Films, London and L.A., 1994—; model, cosmetic rep. Estee Lauder. Actress (films) Die Tote Stadt, 1987, Rowing with the Wind, 1988, Bloody Atlantic, 1991, The Orchid House, 1991, Passenger 57, 1992, El Largo Invierno, 1992, Beyond Bedlam, 1993, Goldeneye, 1995, Mad Dogs and Englishmen, 1995, Dangerous Ground, 1997, Austin Powers: International Man of Mystery, 1997, Permanent Midnight, 1998, Edtv, 1999, My Favorite Martian, 1999, Austin Powers: The Spy Who Shagged Me, 1999, The Weight of Water, 2000, Bedazzled, 2000, Double Whammy, 2001, Serving Sarah, 2002; (TV movies) Act of Will, 1989, Death Has A Bad Reputation, 1990, The Orchid House, 1991, Sharpe's Eneny, 1994, The Shamrock Conspiracy, 1995, Samson and Delilah, 1996, Harrison Cry of the City, 1996; (TV series) Aria, 1987, Inspector Morse, 1988, Cristabel, 1989, Rumpole and the Barrow Boy, 1989, The Young Indiana Jones Chronicles, 1992, Sharpe II, 1995; host (TV spl.) The World of James Bond, 1995; actor, exec. prodr. (films) Method, 2004; prodr. (films) Extreme Measures, 1996, Mickey Blue Eyes, 1999. Office: Creative Artists Agy 9830 Wilshire Blvd Beverly Hills CA 90212-1804*

HURLEY, FRANCIS T., retired archbishop; b. San Francisco, Jan. 12, 1927; Grad., St. Patrick Sem., Menlo Park, Calif., Cath. U. Am. Ordained priest Roman Cath. Ch., 1951, consecrated bishop 1970. With Nat. Cath. Welfare Conf., Washington, asst. sec., 1958—68; assoc. sec. Nat. Cath. Welfare Conf. (now U.S. Cath. Conf.), 1968—70; titular bishop Daimlaig, aux. bishop Diocese of Juneau, Alaska, 1970—71, bishop, 1971—76; archbishop Archdiocese of Anchorage, 1976—2001, archbishop emeritus, 2001—. Roman Catholic.

HURLEY, FRANK THOMAS, JR., realtor; b. Washington, Oct. 18, 1924; s. Frank Thomas and Lucille (Trent) H.; m. Betty Guisinger, Aug. 9, 1997. AA, St. Petersburg Jr. Coll., 1948; BA, U. Fla., 1950. Reporter St. Petersburg Evening Independent, Fla., 1948-53; editor Arcadia Tribune, Calif., 1956-57; reporter Los Angeles Herald Express, 1957; v.p. Frank T. Hurley Assocs., Inc. realtors, 1958-64, pres., 1964—. Author: Surf, Sand and Post Card Sunsets, 1977, Pass-a-Grille Vignettes, 1999. Elected St. Petersburg Beach Bd. Commrs., 1965—69; chmn. Pinellas County Traffic Safety Coun., 1968—69; apptd. mem. Pinellas County Hist. Commn., 1993—, chmn., 2003; pres. Pass-A-Grille Cmty. Assn., 1963; mem. St. Petersburg Mus. Fine Arts, St. Pete Beach Aesthetic and Hist. Rev. Bd., chmn., 1994—96; apptd. mem. Pinellas County Sesquicentennial Coord. Com., 1995; pres. Gulf Beach Bd. Realtors, 1969; bd. govs. Palms of Pasadena Hosp., 1979—86. With USAAF, 1943—46. Recipient Vol. of Yr. award, 2006, Disting. Svc. award, Fla. Trust for Hist. Preservation's, 2007. Mem. Fla. Assn. Realtors (dir., dist. v.p. 1971), St. Petersburg Suncoast Assn. Realtors (life, Ambassadors award 1994), St. Petersburg Beach C. of C. (dir., pres. 1975-76, Citizen of Yr. award 1983), Fla. Hist. Soc., Ky. Col., Am. Legion, Pass-A-Grille Yacht Club (bd. govs.), Sigma Delta Chi, Sigma Tau Delta. Home: 2808 Sunset Way Saint Petersburg Beach FL 33706-4133 Office: 2506 Pass A Grille Way Saint Petersburg Beach FL 33706-4160 Office Phone: 727-367-1949.

HURLEY, GRADY SCHELL, lawyer; b. New Orleans, Nov. 29, 1954; s. Daniel Patrick and Joycelyn Mary (Schell) H.; children: Joshua, Benjamin, Mary Elizabeth, William, John. BA, Tulane U., 1976, JD, 1979, LLM, 1981. Bar: La. 1979, U.S. Dist. Ct. (ea., mid. and we. dists.) La. 1979, U.S. Ct. Appeals (5th and 11th cirs.) 1980, U.S. Supreme Ct. 1986. Assoc. Jones, Walker, Waechter, Poitevent, Carrere and Denegre, New Orleans, 1979-84, ptnr., 1984—. Bd. dirs. Tulane Admiralty Law Inst., 2006—. Editor: Damages Recoverable in Maritime Matters, 1984, Briefly Speaking, 1993. Mem. ABA (House of Delegates, 2003-06, chmn. subcom. on wrongful death and workers compensation 1990-94), Fed. Bar Assn., La. Bar Assn. (dist. rep. young lawyers sect. 1986, La. Bar examiner 1989—, elected Bar Found. appt. jud. liasion comm., 2005), New Orleans Bar Assn. (chmn. maritime law com. 1990-92, exec. bd. 1994-2003, pres.-elect 2001, pres. 2002), New Orleans Bar Found. (v.p. 2006, pres. 2007), Am. Inns of Court (chpt. pres. 2004-06), Maritime Law Assn. (maritime pers. com., proctor, chmn. offshore industires com., bd. dirs.), S.E. Admiralty Law Inst. (bd. dirs. 2004-06), Tulane U. Alumni Assn. (bd. dirs. 1986-96, pres. 1995, chmn. 35th ann. ednl. conf.), Mariner Club, New Orleans Bar Found. (v.p., 2005). Republican. Roman Catholic. Avocations: sports, reading, painting, movies. Office: Jones Walker Waechter Poitevent Carrère & Denègre 201 St Charles Ave Ste 5000 New Orleans LA 70170-5100 Office Phone: 504-582-8225.

HURLEY, JOHN KENNETH, real estate company and merchant banking executive; b. Washington, Nov. 28, 1931; s. Frank T. and Lucille (Trent) H.; m. June Carol Morgan, June 19, 1954 (div. 1976); children: Sean Kenneth, Kathleen Patricia; m. Joyce Carol Winemiller, Mar. 30, 1980 (div. 1990). AA, St. Petersburg Jr. Coll., 1952; BS, Fla. State U., 1954; MBA, Suffield U., 1995, PhD, 2005, Canterbury U., 2000. Chmn. of bd. Frank T. Hurley Assocs., Inc., St. Petersburg Beach, Fla., 1954—; pres. Hurley Marine Corp., St. Petersburg Beach, 1980—, Pass-a-Grille Trading Co., St. Petersburg Beach, 1982—, J. Kenneth Hurley Co., St. Petersburg Beach, 1984—. Ptnr. Joyce Hurley Natural Food Products, St. Petersburg Beach, 1982-94; mng. dir. Baytree Investors, St. Petersburg Beach, 1993-97; guest lectr. more than 40 colls. and univs. Pub. Palma Ceia - MacDill News, Tampa, Fla., 1972-76; pub. poet in numerous periodicals and anthologies. Bd. dirs. Orthomolecular Research Ctr., St. Petersburg Beach, 1955-85; chmn. Zoning and Planning Bd., St. Petersburg Beach, 1968-71; pres. Friends St. Petersburg Beach Library, 1976-78. Mem. Am. Philos. Assn., Gulf Beach Seminole Bd. Realtors, Slocum Soc., Ky. Coll., Cauliflower Alley Club. Republican. Mem. United Ch. of Christ. Club: Pass-a-Grille (Fla.) Yacht (sec. 1978-80). Avocations: yachting, passenger vessel certified master. Home: 2122 W Vina Del Mar Blvd Saint Petersburg FL 33706-2842 Office: 2506 Pass A Grille Way Saint Petersburg FL 33706-4160

HURLEY, KATHY LEE, mental health services professional, director; d. Essie B. and Dent R. Hurley, J.C. Crowson (Stepfather); m. Edmond J. Moloney, Dec. 13, 2002; 1 child, Breckin M. Moloney. BA, U. Ctrl. Fla., 1985; AA, MS, Nova U., 1988; PhD, Maimonides U., Ft. Lauderdale, Fla., 2003. Diplomate Am. Bd. of Sexologists; cert. social work counselor Fla. Sr. counselor Ctr. for Drug-Free Living, Kissimmee, Fla., 1991—94; program mgr. Grove Counseling Ctr., Sanford, 1994—95; sr. counselor Stewart-Marchman Ctr., Daytona, Fla., 1995—99; clinician Children's Home Soc., Daytona, 1999—2000, Three Springs, Daytona, 2000—03; clin. dir. Devereux of Fla. Found., Orlando, 2003—. Cons. Sch. Bd., Daytona, 2000—03. Exec. com./vol. Dem. Party, Daytona, 2000—02; choirister, musician Grace Episcopal Ch., Port Orange, Fla., 2000—02; tchr., counselor First Bapt. Ch., Daytona, 1997—2001; musician, vocalist Rima Ridge Bapt. Ch., Ormond Beach, Fla., 1995—97, Ch. of Christ, Longwood, Fla., 1992—95. Recipient High Scholastic Achievement award, Nova U., 1986—88; grantee, Daytona Beach C.C., 1982. Mem.: Nat. Assn. of Forensic Counselors (assoc.; cert.), Assn. for the Treatment of Sexual Abusers (assoc.), Am. Assn. of Christian Counselors (assoc.), Am. Counselor's Assn. (assoc.), Am. Mental Health Counselor's Assn. (assoc.; voting mem. 2000—05). Democrat. Avocations: piano, singing, acting, travel, swimming. Home Phone: 407-568-3418; Office Phone: 407-296-5300.

HURLEY, LAWRENCE JOSEPH, lawyer; b. Plainfield, NJ, Nov. 17, 1946; s. Luke Michael and Gertrude Marie (Bremer) Hurley; m. Allyson J. Kingsley, May 28, 1977; children: Michael William, Kathryn Elizabeth. BS, U. Dayton, 1969; JD, Cath. U. Am., 1974. Bar: NJ 1974, US Dist. Ct. NJ, 1974, D.C. 1976, NY 1980, US Ct. Appeals (3rd cir.) 1980, US Dist. Ct. (ea. and so. dists.) NY 1981, US Ct. Appeals (2nd cir.) 1981, US Ct. Appeals (DC cir.) 1982. Law clk. Superior Ct. NJ, New Brunswick, 1974-75; assoc. Lynch, Mannion, Lutz & Lewandowski, New Brunswick,

1975-76, Stryker, Tams & Dill, Newark, 1976-79; atty. AT&T, Basking Ridge, NJ, 1979-85; chief asst. prosecutor econ. crimes and ofcl. corruption Morris County Prosecutor's Office, Morristown, NJ, 1985—89; ptnr. Voorhees & Acciavatti, Morristown, 1989-91; sr. atty. AT&T, 1991—96; labor and employment counsel Lucent Techs., Murray Hill, NJ, 1996—99; mng. labor and employment corp. counsel Lucent Techs., Inc., 1999—2001, mng. litigation, labor and employment counsel, 2001—05; law v.p. Lucent Techs., inc., 2005—07; counsel Bryan Cave, LLP, NYC, 2007—. With. US Army, 1969—71. Decorated Bronze Star, Army Commendation medal. Fellow Coll. Labor and Employment Lawyers; mem. ABA (litig. sect. 1976-86, 2001—, labor law sect. 1981-86, 1991—, criminal law sect. 1985-91, labor law sect. 1991—), NJ State Bar Assn. Office: Bryan Cave LLP 1290 Ave of the Americas New York NY 10104-3300 Office Phone: 212-541-2322. Business E-Mail: lawrence.hurley@bryancave.com.

HURLEY, R. BRUCE, lawyer; b. Harlingen, Tex. BSS, Southwestern Univ., 1986; JD cum laude, Univ. Houston, 1989. Bar: Tex. 1989. Ptnr., Litigation Practice Group King & Spalding, LLP, Houston. Mem. Greater Houston Partnership; bd. mem. Univ. Houston Law Ctr. Fellow: Houston Bar Found.; mem.: Houston Volunteer Lawyers Assn., Def. Rsch. Inst., ABA, State Bar Tex., Houston Bar Assn., Tex. Accountants & Lawyers for the Arts. Office: King & Spalding LLP 1100 Louisiana Houston TX 77002 Office Phone: 713-276-7383. Office Fax: 713-751-3290. Business E-Mail: bhurley@kslaw.com.

HURLEY, REBECCA, lawyer; Grad. summa cum laude, U. Tex., Austin, 1976; JD summa cum laude, So. Meth. U., 1982. Law clk. to Hon. Irving L. Goldberg, US Ct. Appeals (5th cir.), 1982—83, Hon. Warren E. Burger, US Supreme Ct., 1983—84; pvt. practice Dallas; shareholder, chair Bus. Transactions Practice Group Patton Boggs LLP, 2000—02; v.p. compliance Triad Hospitals, Inc., Plano, Tex., 2002—04, sr. v.p., assoc. gen. counsel, chief compliance officer, asst. sec., 2004—05, sr. v.p., gen. counsel, sec., 2005—. Office: Triad Hospitals Inc 5800 Tennyson Parkway Plano TX 75024 Office Phone: 214-473-7000.*

HURLEY, WILLIAM JOSEPH, retired information technology executive; b. NYC, June 14, 1939; s. William and Anna Rita (Hubschman) Hurley; m. Dorothy Ann Mellett, Sept. 23, 1961 (dec.); children: William, Terrianne, Barbara, Daniel; m. Marianne F. Jordan, Mar. 17, 1990. BBA, Pace U., 1968, MBA, 1973. Dir. info. sys. Gen. Foods Corp., White Plains, NY, 1973—79; dir. sys. devel. Securities Industry Automation Corp., NYC, 1979; dir. mgmt. info. sys. Schering Plough Corp., Kenilworth, NJ, 1979—81, sr. dir. mgmt. info. sys., 1981—83, v.p. mgmt. info. svc., 1983—88; v.p. world wide info. sys. Technicon Corp., Tarrytown, NY, 1988—90; dir. info. sys. Miles Inc., Tarrytown, 1990—95; ret., 1995. Pres. New City (N.Y.) Vol. Fire Engine Co. 1, 1979—81; commr. New City Fire Dist., 1983—94. With USMC, 1956—59. Mem.: Assn. Sys. Mgmt. (v.p. 1981), Soc. Info. Mgmt., Am. Legion. Republican. Roman Catholic. Avocation: financial planning. Home: Unit 504 3150 N A1A Fort Pierce FL 34949-8868 Office Phone: 772-466-5908. Personal E-mail: bhurley317@aol.com.

HURLIN, DAN, theater director; Artistic dir. Andy's Summer Playhouse, Wilton, NH, 1987—93; instr. Bowdoin Coll., Bennington Coll., Barnard Coll., Princeton U., Sarah Lawrence Coll.; dir. Pupet Lab at Arts St. Ann's, Bklyn. Dir.: No(thing so powerful as) Truth, 1995, Constance and Ferdinand, 1991, The Jazz Section, 1989, A Cool Million, 1990, Quintland, 1992, The Day the Ketchup Turned Blue, 1997, The Shoulder, 1998, Everyday Uses for Sight, 2000, Hiroshima Maiden, 2004. Recipient Village Voice OBIE award, 1990, N.Y. Dance and Performance aAward, A.K.A. Bessie, 2000, Alpert award in the Arts, 2004; Guggenheim fellow, 2002. Office: 72-74 E 3rd St #5B New York NY 10003

HURLOCK, JAMES BICKFORD, retired lawyer; b. Chgo., Aug. 7, 1933; s. James Bickford and Elizabeth (Charls) Hurlock; m. Margaret Lyn Holding, July 1, 1961; children: James Bickford III, Burton Charls, Matthew Hunter. AB, Princeton U., 1955; BA, Oxford U., 1957, MA, 1960; JD, Harvard U., 1959. Bar: N.Y. 1960, U.S. Supreme Ct. 1967. Assoc. White & Case, NYC, 1959—66, ptnr., 1967—2000; ret., 2000. Bd. dirs. Orient Express Hotels, Ltd., Stolt-Nielsen S.A., Acergy S.A. Trustee NY Presbyn. Hosp., Woods Hole Oceanographic Inst.; chmn. Parker Sch. Fgn. and Comparative Law. Recipient Rhodes scholarship, 1955. Mem.: ABA, Am. Law Inst., N.Y. State Bar Assn., N.Y. Yacht Club, River Club. Republican. Episcopalian. Home: 46 Byram Dr Greenwich CT 06830-7008 Office: White & Case 1155 Avenue Of The Americas New York NY 10036-2787 Office Phone: 212-819-8282. Personal E-mail: jhurlock46byram@aol.com.

HURNYAK, CHRISTINA KAISER, lawyer; b. Noblesville, Ind., Dec. 22, 1949; d. Albert Michael and Lois Angie (Gatton) Kaiser; m. Cyril Hurnyak, June 24, 1972. BA cum laude, Wittenberg U., 1972; JD, SUNY-Buffalo, 1979. Bar: N.Y. 1980, Pa. 1996, US Dist. Ct. (we. dist.) Pa. 1998, bd. cert. civil trial adv.: Nat. Bd. Trial Advocacy. Mem. support staff McKinsey & Co., Inc., mgmt. cons., Chgo., 1972-75; law clk. Justice Norman J. Wolf, N.Y. Supreme Ct., Buffalo, 1980-81; assoc. Dempsey & Dempsey, Buffalo, 1979-80, 81-90, Grossman, Levine & Civiletto, Niagara Falls, N.Y., 1990-95, Tarasi & Tarasi, PC, Pitts., 1998—. Mem.: ABA, AAJ, PAAJ, Pa. State Bar Assn., Allegheny County Bar Assn. Democrat. Lutheran. Office: Tarasi & Tarasi PC 510 3rd Ave Pittsburgh PA 15219-2107 Office Phone: 412-391-7135.

HURON, RODERICK EUGENE, minister, writer; b. Chesapeake, Ohio, Dec. 5, 1934; s. Raymond Clarence and Minnie Opal (Williams) Huron; m. Autumn June Hostetter, July 24, 1956; children: Lila Kay Huron Albinger, Eric Scott, Sara Lynn Huron Myers. BA, Ky. Christian Coll., 1956; MEd, U. Pitts., 1967; postgrad., U. Akron, 1968—70. Ordained to ministry Christian Chs. and Chs. of Christ, 1958; cert. meeting profl., lic. amateur radio operator. Min. Highlawn Ch. of Christ, Huntington, W.Va., 1956—57; youth min. 1st Christian Ch., Canton, Ohio, 1957—62; min. LaBelle View Ch. of Christ, Steubenville, Ohio, 1962—67, West Akron Ch. of Christ, Ohio, 1968—71; missionary Toronto Christian Mission, 1971—75; sr. min. North Industry Christian Ch., Canton, 1976—84; dir.-elect N.Am. Christian Conv., Cin., 1984—86, conv. dir., 1986—97; pres. Meeting Excellence, 1997—2001; min. of membership devel. Lakeside Christian Ch., Ft. Mitchell, Ky., 1997—2001, min. involvement Lakeside Park, 1997—2001; dir. svc. learning Cin. Christian U., 2001—05, adj. prof., 2005—. Guest on various TV and radio programs. Author: Do You Know Who You Are, 1976, Checkpoint, 1979 (Sherwood E. Wirt award Billy Graham Evangelist Assn.), Christian Minister's Manual, 1984 (Gold Medallion Merit award Evang. Christian Pub. Assn.), Say Hello to Life, 1984, Bible Stories for Children, 1995, Love, Laughter, and Leadership: The Ministry of Wayne B Smith, 2004; contbr. articles to religious jours. Republican. Mem. Christian Ch. E-mail: rod.huron@ccuniversity.edu.

HURST, CHARLES WILSON, lawyer; b. Salt Lake City, July 4, 1957; s. John Vann and Myra (Kasik) Piscane; m. Karen Buck, Jan. 5, 1985; children: Jeanette Q., Daniel C., Brian K., Matthew C., Robert W. Student, U. Chgo., 1975-77; BA cum laude, Wesleyan U., Conn., 1979; JD, Duke U., 1983. Bar: Pa. 1983, U.S. Dist. Ct. (ea. dist.) Pa. 1985, Calif. 1986, U.S. Dist. Ct. (cen. dist.) Calif. 1990. Assoc. Saul, Ewing, Remick & Saul, Phila., 1983-85, Wyman Bautzer Kuchel & Silbert, Orange County, Calif., 1985-89, ptnr., 1990, Snell & Wilmer LLP, Orange County, 1990—. Trustee Pegasus Sch., 1996—2005, vice chair, 2003—05; treas. Pacific Club Impact Found., 2004—05, sec., 2005—; bd. dirs. Pacific Art Found., 1994—2000, treas., 1994—96. Mem. ABA (comml. leasing com. of real property, probate and trust law sect.), Orange County Bar Assn. Office: Snell & Wilmer 600 Anton Blvd Ste 1400 Costa Mesa CA 92626-7689 Office Phone: 714-427-7012. Business E-Mail: churst@swlaw.com.

HURST, DEBORAH, pediatric hematologist; b. Washington, May 9, 1946; d. Willard and Frances (Wilson) H.; m. Stephen Mershon Senter, June 14, 1970; children: Carlin, Daniel. BA, Harvard U., 1968; MD, Med. Coll. Pa., 1974. Diplomate Nat. Bd. Med. Examiners, Am. Bd. Pediatrics, Am. Bd. Pediatric Hematology-Oncology. Intern Bellevue Hosp., NYU Hosp., NYC, 1974-75, resident in pediatrics, 1975-76; ambulatory pediatric fellow Bellevue Hosp., NYC, 1976-77; hematology, oncology fellow Bellevue Hosp., Columbia U., NYC, 1977-80; assoc. hematologist Childrens Hosp. Oakland, Calif., 1980-92; asst. clin. prof. U. Calif. San Francisco Med. Ctr., 1992—2004; med. dir. Bayer Corp., Berkeley, Calif., 1992-98; sr. dir. clin. devel. Chiron Corp., Emeryville, Calif., 1998—2006; sr. clin. scientist bio-oncology Genentech, Inc., South San Francisco, Calif., 2006—. Hematology cons. Assn. Asian/Pacific Community Health Orgns., Oakland; dir. Satellite Hematology Clinic/Valley Childrens Hosp., Fresno, Calif., 1984-92; cons. state dept. epidemiology Calif. State Dept. Health, Berkeley, 1992; chelation cons. lead poisoning program Childrens Hosp., Oakland, 1986-92. Contbr. articles to profl. jours. Vol. cons. lead poisoning State Dept. Epidemiology and Toxicology, Berkeley, 1986-92. Fellow Am. Acad. Pediatrics; mem. Am. Soc. Hematology, Am. Soc. Gene Therapy, Am. Soc. Clin. Oncology, Am. Soc. Pediat. Hematology/Oncology. Office: Genentech Inc 1 DNA Way South San Francisco CA 94080-4990 Personal E-mail: hurst.deborah@gene.com.

HURST, FRANCES See MAYHAR, ARDATH

HURST, GREGORY SQUIRE, investment company executive, theater director and producer; b. Oak Park, Ill., Dec. 1, 1947; s. Claude Squire Hurst and Marcia (Tooker) Allen; m. Joyce Barbara Baum, Apr. 4, 1981; children: Alexander Squire, Adam Spencer. BS, Miami U., Oxford, Ohio, 1969; MA, U. Wis., 1973; MFA, U. NC, 1975; postgrad., U. Pa., 2003. Dir. theater Wayland Acad., Beaver Dam, Wis., 1969-73; instr. acting U. NC, Chapel Hill, 1973-75; chmn. theater dept. Tarkio Coll., Mo., 1975-77; producing artistic dir. Pa. Stage Co., Allentown, 1979-88, George St. Playhouse, New Brunswick, NJ, 1988-97; sr. v.p. investments, fin. advisor UBS, NYC, 1999—, ins. coord. br. office, 2001—, wealth mgmt. spkrs. bur., 2004—, mentoring program, 2004—, pres. coun., 2004—06, chmns. club, 2007—. Artistic dir. Mule Barn Theatre, Tarkio, 1975-77; mem. theater panel Mo. Arts Coun., St. Louis, 1975-77, Pa. Coun. Arts, Harrisburg, 1982-85; cons. Found. Devel. Am. Profl. theatre, NYC, 1983; on-site evaluator Nat. Endowment Arts, Washington, 1984-97; mem. mus. theater task force Rockefeller Found., Phila., 1985; founding mem. Playmakers Reperatory Theatre, 1975; vis. prof. Rutgers U., 1989; sr. lectr. Duke U., 1995-96. Librettist (mus. play) Song of Myself, 1981; stage dir. (world premieres) Feathertop, (with Beth Leavel) Great Expectations, (with Hinton Battle) Shim Sham, (with John Spencer) Walk out of Water, (with Estelle Parsons) Forgiving Typhoid Mary (named One of Best 5 Plays in Am., Time mag. 1991), Greetings, (with Paul Guilfoyle) Copperhead, (with Cady Huffman and John Cullum) Jekyll and Hyde, (with Joel Higgins, Christine Andreas) Fields of Ambrosia, West End London Aldwych Theatre, 1996, (with Michael Rupert) Relativity, Sing a Christmas Song, (with Laura Innes and Gabrielle Carteris) Les Liaisons Dangereuse; nat. tour The Acting Co. The Glass Menagerie; prodr. (with Calista Flockhardt) Zara Spook and Other Lures, (with Bebe Neuwirth) Just So, (with Victoria Clark) Opal, (with Alison Janey) Idioglossia, (With Eli Wallach and Anne Jackson) Spanky & the Fitz; dir. TV shows General Hospital, One Life to Live, Another World, The Guiding Light. Area leader Allentown and Cen. Jersey United Way, 1981-92; exec. v.p., bd. dirs. Stage Dirs. and Choreographers Found., 1989-92, pres., 1992-98, East Coast Dirs. Coun. Recipient Downtown Improvement award City of Allentown, 1987, Outstanding Contbn. award Theatre Assn. Pa., 1988, Vision, dedication, leadership award SDC Found., 1998; Tony nomination for best musical Swinging On A Star; named Best Dir. in NJ Belmont Avenue Social Club, 1994, Les Liaisons Dangereuse, 1989. Mem. Soc. Stage Dirs., Dramatist Guild, Dirs. Guild Am. (coun. mem. 1997-99), Actors Equity Assn., U. NC NJ Alumni Club (pres. 1999—), Knights of the Vine, NY Food and Wine Soc., Phi Kappa Tau. Democrat. Avocations: golf, antiques, travel, swimming, gourmet cooking, wine collecting. Home: 3 Fernwood Ct East Brunswick NJ 08816-3333 Office Phone: 212-370-7698. E-mail: gsquireh@aol.com, gregory.hurst@ubs.com.

HURST, HEATHER, illustrator; b. Aug. 14, 1975; BA, Skidmore Coll., 1997. Archeological artist and illustrator focusing on creating representations of Mesoamerican structures. Exhibitions include Nat. Gallery Art, Washington, Peabody Mus. Nat. History, illustrations published in National Geographic and Arqueologia Mexicana. Named MacArthur Fellow, John D. and Catherine T. MacArthur Found., 2004. Achievements include the reproduction of the Maya murals of Bonampak.

HURST, LAWRENCE, orthopedic surgeon; MD, U. Vt., 1973. Cert. Orthopedic Surgery, 1980, added qualifications hand surgery, 1989. Surgeon Stony Brook Orthopedic Associates, PC, 1979; chmn. and program dir. SUNY, Stony Brook, prof. orthopedic surgery, chief divsn. hand surgery. Named one of Medical Marvels, NY Mag., 2006. Mem.: Am. Soc. Surgery of Hand. Office: Stony Brook Univ Dept Orthopedics T-18 Health Sciences Ctr Stony Brook NY 11794-8181 also: Orthopedics 14 Technology Dr Ste 11 East Setauket NY 11733-3464 Office Phone: 631-444-3145. Office Fax: 631-444-8894. E-mail: lhurst@surg.som.sunysb.edu.*

HURST, LELAND LYLE, natural gas company executive; b. Mooreland, Okla., Oct. 16, 1930; s. Lewis Walter and Ellen Sarah (Riggs) H.; m. Karen Lee Lamkin, Jan. 24, 1969; children: Courtney Anne, Caroline Leigh. BS in Indsl. Engring., Okla. State U., 1952; MS in Petroleum Engring., U. Tulsa, 1958. Registered profl. engr., Okla. With Amoco Prodn. Co., 1958-80; engr. Amoco Prodn. Co. (various locations), 1958-68; staff engr. Amoco Prodn. Co., Calgary, Alta., Canada, 1968-70, div. engr. supr. Denver, 1970-73, area supt. Liberal, Kans., 1973-74, asst. div. engr. Denver, 1974-75, gas sales mgr., 1975-80; v.p. Amoco Gas Co., Houston, 1980-81, pres., dir., 1981-86; v.p. mktg. KN Energy Inc., Gasco Inc., 1986-87; v.p. interstate ops., exec. v.p. Gasco Inc., 1987-88, sr. v.p. ops., 1988-95, also bd. dirs., 1992-95; exec. v.p., dir. Indsl. Mechanics Inc., 1987-95, Sunflower Pipeline Co., 1988-95, Rocky Mountain Gas Co., 1992-95, 1992-95, No. Gas Co. Wyo., 1992-95, 1992-95. Bd. dirs., v.p. KN Front Range Oper. Co., KN Wattenberg Co., KN Wattenberg Ltd. Liability Co.; bd. dirs. RMNG Gathering Co., TCP Gathering Co.; v.p. Panola/Rusk Gatherers, Am. Energy Holdings, Inc., Am. Gas Storage, L.P., Am. Gathering, L.P., Am. Processing, L.P., Am. Oil and Gas Corp., Am. Pipeline Co., Am. Webb, Inc., AOG Holdings, Inc., AOG Mgmt., Inc., Caprock Pipeline Co., Red River Gas Pipeline Corp., Red River Pipeline, L.P., RRP Fin. Corp., Webb/Duval Gatherers, Westar Transmission Co., 1995. With Chem. Corps U.S. Army, 1953-55. Served with Chem. Corps, U.S. Army, 1953-55. Mem. Rocky Mountain Gas Men's Assn. (bd. dirs. 1977), Soc. Petroleum Engrs. (editl. com. 1953-55), Rocky Mountain Oil and Gas Assn. Colo. (pres. 1995-97, indsl. mechanic chmn. 1995-2004), Natural Gas Men of Houston-New Orleans (v.p.), Houston Club, Denver Petroleum Club. Republican.

HURST, ROBERT JAY, security firm executive; b. NYC, Nov. 5, 1945; s. Kurt and Jeanette (Sachs) Hurst; m. Soledad Deleon Hurst; children from previous marriage: Alexander, Amanda. BA, Clark U., 1966; M in Govt. Adminstrn., U. Pa., 1968, Pub. Fin. fellow, 1969. With investment banking divsn. Merrill Lynch, Pierce, Fenner & Smith, Inc., NYC, 1969-74, v.p., 1974, Goldman, Sachs & Co., NYC, 1974-80, gen. ptnr., 1980—2000, mem. mgmt. com., 1990—2000, co-head investment banking div., 1990—96, head investment banking div., 1996—99, mem. exec. com., 1995—2000, vice chmn., 1999—2000, bd. dir.; CEO 9/11 United Svcs. Group, 2001—. Trustee Whitney Mus. Am. Art, 1998—, pres., 2002—; trustee coun. Nat. Found. for Tchg. Entrepreneurship, bd. dir.; mem. bd. overseers Wharton Sch., U. Pa., coun. on fgn. relations, com. for econ. devel.; trustee Com. Econ. Develop., Ctrl. Pk. Conservancy; bd. trustees Manhattan Inst.; trustee coun. Nat. Gallery Art; bd. dir. Air Clic Inc., NYC 2012, IDB Holding Ltd., Constellation Energy Group, VF Corp; chmn. Jewish Mus., 1997—2002. Recipient Louis Marshall Award, Jewish Theological Soc., 2000. Mem.: Maroon Creek Club (Aspen), Atlantic Golf Club (Bridgehampton), U. Club. Mailing: c/o Whitney Mus Am Art 945 Madison Ave New York NY 10021

HURT, JOHN VINCENT, actor; b. Chesterfield, Eng., Jan. 22, 1940; s. Arhould Herbert and Phyllis (Massey) H.; m. Annette Robertson, 1962 (div. 1964); m. Donna Peacock, Sept. 6, 1984 (div. 1990); Joan Dalton, Jan. 24, 1990 (div. 1996); children: Alexander, Nicholas; m. Anwen Rees Meyers, Feb. 2005. Student, Royal Acad. Dramatic Art, 1960-62; LittD (hon.), U. Derby, 2002, U. Hull, 2006. Actor: (plays) including Chips with Everything, 1962, Hamp, 1964, Little Malcolm and His Struggle Against the Eunuchs, 1966, Man and Superman, 1969, The Caretaker, 1972, Travesties, 1974, The Shadow of a Gunman, 1978, (films) including (debut) The Wild and the Willing, 1962, A Man for All Seasons, 1966, Before Winter Comes, 1969, Mr. Forbush and the Penguins, 1971, Little Malcolm, 1974, Spectre, 1977, The Disappearance, 1978, The Shout, 1978, Alien, 1978, Midnight Express, 1978, The Elephant Man, 1980, Heaven's Gate, 1981, History of the World Part I, 1981, Night Crossing, 1982, Watership Down, 1982, The Osterman Weekend, 1982, The Hit, 1983, Champions, 1983, '1984', 1985, Rocinonte, 1985, From the Hip, 1986, Jake Speed, 1986, Vincent, 1987, White Mischief, 1987, Aria, 1987, Scandal, 1989, Frankenstein Unbound, 1989, The Field, 1990, Windprints, 1990, King Ralph, 1991, I Dreamt I Woke Up, 1991, Lapse of Memory, 1991, L'Oeil Qui Ment, 1992, Crime and Punishment, 1993, Monolith, 1993, Forraderi, 1994, Second Best, 1994, Even Cowboys Get the Blues, 1994, Rob Roy, 1995, Wild Bill, 1995, Two Nudes Bathing, 1995, Saigon Baby, 1995, Love and Death on Long Island, 1997, Contact, 1997, Bandyta, 1997, The Commissioner, 1998, The Climb, 1998, Night Train, 1998, All the Little Animals, 1998, Le Chateau des singes (voice), 1999, You're Dead, 1999, If.Dog.Rabbit, 1999, New Blood, 1999, The Tigger Movie (voice), 1999, Lost Souls, 2000, Captain Corelli's Mandolin, 2001, Tabloid, 2001, Harry Potter and the Sorcerer's Stone, 2001, Miranda, 2002, Crime and Punishment, 2002, Owning Mahowney, 2003, Dogville (voice), 2003, Hellboy, 2004, Short Order, 2005, Valiant (voice), 2005, Manderlay (voice), 2005, The Skeleton Key, 2005, Shooting Dogs, 2005, V for Vendetta, 2005, The Proposition, 2005, Outlander, 2006, The Oxford Murders, 2007, Lecture 21, 2007; (TV films) include The Naked Civil Servant, 1974, Caligula in I Claudius, 1974, Crime and Punishment, 1979 (Emmy award 1979), The Storyteller, 1986, Poison Candy, 1987, Scandal, 1988, The Investigation: Inside a Terrorist Bombing, 1990, Who Bombed Birmingham (Granada TV), 1990, Journey to Knock, 1991, Red Fox (BBC), 1991, Dark at Noon, 1991, London Vertigo (play) 1991, Six Characters in Search of an Author, (BBC) 1992, Great Moments In Aviation, 1992, Prisoners in Time, 1995, Krapp's Last Tape, 2000, Bait, 2002, The Alan Clark Diaries, 2004, Pride, 2004; (TV miniseries) Picture Windows, 1995, Watership Down (voice), 1999. Recipient Brit. Academy award, Brit. Oscar, Golden Globe award, Brit. Emmy. Mem. Brit. Equity, Screen Actors Guild, Am. Acad. of Arts and Scis., AFTRA. Mailing: ICM 76 Oxford St London W1D 1BS England

HURT, NATHAN HAMPTON, JR., mechanical engineer; b. Clifton, Mo., June 7, 1921; s. Nathan Hampton Sr. and Mary Lillian (Mayo) H.; m. LuCretia Ann Cutler, Feb. 16, 1946 (dec. 1980); children: Steven Eugene, Mark Lindsay; m. Karin Elisabeth Tuttle, Aug. 30, 1980; 1 stepchild, Christine Yvonne Reed; adopted children: Audrey Barbara, Nikki Alexandra. Student in mech. engring., Mont. Sch. Mines, 1944, U. So. Calif., 1944-46; BS in Mech. Engring., U. Colo., 1947. With Goodyear Tire and Rubber Co., Akron, Ohio, 1947—87, program mgr. Rio de Janeiro, 1959-62; plant mgr. Akron Rubber Chems. Plant, 1962-63, Logan, Ohio, 1963-68; supt. plant engring. Goodyear Atomic Corp., Piketon, 1952—56, mgr., 1968—72, gen. mgr., 1977—85, pres., 1985—87, ret., 1987; mgr. bus. devel. Los Alamos Tech. Assocs., Piketon, 1987—94; v.p. IDM Environ. Corp., Oak Ridge, Tenn., 1994-98; dir. Sharp and Assocs., Oak Ridge, 1998—2000; cons., 2000—. Mem. Chief Logan Coun. Boy Scouts Am., 1970-80; bd. dirs. Ross County Med. Ctr., Chillicothe, Ohio, 1974. Mem.: ASME (pres. 1991—92), Kiwanis (lt. gov. 2005—06). Home and Office: 3775 Hiawatha Dr Lake Havasu City AZ 86404-3559 Home Phone: 928-854-2440; Office Phone: 928-854-2440. Office Fax: 928-854-2439. E-mail: hurtnhjr@npgcable.com.

HURT, WILLIAM, actor; b. Washington, Mar. 20, 1950; s. Henry Luce III (Stepfather) and Claire; m. Mary Beth Supinger, 1971 (div. 1981); m. Heidi Henderson, Mar. 5, 1989 (div. 1992); children: Sam, William Jr.; children: Alexander Devon, Jeanne. BA in Drama, Tufts U., 1972; student, Juilliard Sch.; ArtsD (hon.), U. Arts, 2006. Joined Oreg. Shakespeare Festival, 1975; performed regularly with Ashland Shakespeare Festival, Oreg.; joined Circle Repertory Theatre, NYC, 1977. Actor: (theatre) including Henry V, 1977, My Life, 1977, Ulysses in Traction, Lulu, 1978, Fifth of July, 1978, Hamlet, 1979, Mary Stuart, 1979, Childe Byron, 1981, The Diviners, 1981, The Great Grandson of Jedediah kohler, 1982, Richard II, 1982, A Midsummer Night's Dream, 1982, Hurlyburly, 1984, Joan of Arc at the Stake, 1985, Love Letters, 1989, Beside Herself, 1989, Ivanov, 1991, (films) Altered States, 1980, Eyewitness, 1981, Body Heat, 1981, The Big Chill, 1983, Gorky Park, 1983, Kiss of the Spider Woman, 1985 (Best Actor Award, Cannes Film Festival, 1985, Acad. Award for best actor, 1986), Children of a Lesser God, 1986 (Acad. Award nomination for best actor, 1987), Broadcast News, 1987 (Acad. Award nomination for best actor, 1988), A Time of Destiny, 1988, The Accidental Tourist, 1988, I Love You To Death, 1990, Marilyn Hotchkiss' Ballroom Dancing and Charm School (voice), 1990, Alice, 1990, The Doctor, 1991, Until the End of the World, 1991, The Plague, 1992, Mr. Wonderful, 1993, Trial by Jury, 1994, Second Best, 1994, Secrets Shared with a Stranger, 1994, Smoke, 1995, Michael, 1996, Jane Eyre, 1996, A Couch in New York, 1996, Loved, 1997, Dark City, 1998, Lost in Space, 1998, One True Thing, 1998, The Big Brass Ring, 1999, Sunshine, 1999, Do Not Disturb, 1999, The 4th Floor, 1999, The Simian Line, 2000, Artificial Intelligence: AI, 2001, The Contaminated Man, 2001, Rare Birds, 2001, Changing Lanes, 2002, Nearest to Heaven, 2002, Tuck Everlasting, 2002, The Tulse Luper Suitcases: The Moab Story, 2003, The Blue Butterfly, 2004, The Village, 2004, A History of Violence, 2005 (Best Supporting Actor, NY Film Critics Circle, 2005), Neverwas, 2005, Syriana, 2005, The Legend of the Sasquatch (voice), 2006, Beautiful Ohio, 2006, The Good Shepherd, 2006, Mr. Brooks, 2007, (TV films) Verna: USO Girl, 1978, All the Way Home, 1981, The Miracle Maker (voice), 2000, The Flamingo Rising, 2001, Master Spy: The Robert Hanssen Story, 2002, Frankenstein, 2004, Hunt for Justice, 2005, (TV miniseries) The Best of Families, 1977, Dune 2000, (TV series) Riviere-des-Jeremie, 2001. Recipient 1st Spencer Tracy Award for outstanding screen performances and profl. achievement, UCLA, 1988. Office: c/o Hilda Quille/William Morris 151 S El Camino Dr Beverly Hills CA 90212-2704*

HURT, WILLIAM HOLMAN, investment management company executive; b. LA, Mar. 29, 1927; s. Holman G. and Mary E. (Ortloff) H.; m. Sheridan Ann Stephens, Aug. 10, 1950 (div. May. 1970); children: Kelley

Anne Hurt Purnell, Kathleen Constance, Courtney Diana Hurt MacMillan; m. Sarah Sherman, May 28, 1970. BS magna cum laude, U. So. Calif., 1949; MBA, Harvard U., 1951. With Dean Witter & Co., Los Angeles, 1951-71, ptnr., 1959, sr. v.p., 1968-70, exec. v.p., dir., mem. exec. com., dir. mktg. and rsch., 1969-71; chmn. exec. com. Capital Rsch. Co., 1972-77; chief exec. office Capital Group, Inc., LA, 1978-82; chmn. Capital Strategy Rsch., Inc., 1982—. Adv. com. Coldwell Banker Funds, 1978-99. Mem. bd. councilors Grad. Sch. Bus., U. So. Calif., L.A., 1978-88, vis. com., 1990-96; bd. dirs. L.A. Children's Hosp., 1985—. Served with USNR, 1945-46. Mem. Calif. Club, L.A. Athletic Club, N.Y. Athletic Club, Phi Kappa Phi, Beta Gamma Sigma, Kappa Alpha. Republican.

HURTADO, RODRIGO CLAUDIO, allergist; b. Chile, 1939; MD, U. Chile, Santiago, 1964. Diplomate Am. Bd. Allergy and Immunology, Am. Bd. Pediatrics. Intern U. Chile, 1964, resident, 1968-71; fellow allergy and infectious diseases Georgetown U., Washington, 1972-74; pvt. practice Washington, 1974—; clin. asst. prof. Georgetown U. Med. Sch., Washington, 1974—. Mem. Am. Acad. Pediatrics and Immunology, Am. Acad. Allergy Asthma and Immunology, Am. Acad. Pediatrics, Am. Coll. Allergy. Office: 3450 N Beauregard St Alexandria VA 22302-1200

HURTADO LEE, CLARA ISABELLE, voice educator, singer; b. Salt Lake City, Apr. 30, 1978; d. Victor Arturo Hurtado and Clara Lovisa Lyman; m. Joshua Lane Lee, May 5, 2001. MusB in Vocal Performance, U. Utah, Salt Lake City, 2001, MusM in Vocal Performance, 2003. With La Musica Lirica, 2002—03; pvt. practice voice instr. Provo, Utah, 2003—; with Utah Light Opera Co., Salt Lake City, 2005, Utah Opera Co., 2005. Mem.: Nat. Assn. Tchrs. Singing (social com. 2005—).

HURTEAU, GILLES DAVID, retired obstetrician, gynecologist, educator, dean; b. Cornwall, Ont., Can., Nov. 28, 1928; s. Joseph A. and Antoinette (St-Laurent) H.; m. Janine Anita Carriere, June 16, 1956; children: Michele, Jean, Louise, Pierre, Gilles Andre. BA, U. Ottawa, 1951; MD, CM, McGill U., 1955. Licentiate, Med. Council Can., 1956; cert. in ob-gyn. Instr. and clin. asst. Yale U. Med. Sch., New Haven, 1961-62; asst. prof. U. Ottawa Med. Sch., Ont., 1963-66, assoc. prof. Ont., 1966, prof. and chmn. dept. ob-gyn Ont., 1967-76, dean Sch. Medicine Ont., 1976-89, dean faculty health scis. Ont., 1978-89; exec. dir./registrar Royal Coll. Physicians and Surgeons Can., Ottawa, 1990-95. Bd. govs. U. Ottawa, 1995-2007, vice chmn. bd., chmn. exec. bd. govs. 2003-07; bd. dirs. Assoc. Med. Svcs. Inc., 2000-05, chmn., 2004-05. Mem. editl. bd. European Jour. Ob-Gyn and Reproductive Biology, 1970-78; contbr. articles to profl. jours., chpts to books. Mem. coun. Ottawa-Carleton Dist. Health Coun., 1978-84; jt. rsch. rev. task force Ont. Coun. Health, 1977-81; bd. dirs. Ont. Cancer Treatment and Rsch. Found., 1983-92, Physicians Svcs. Inc. Found. Ont., 1984-86, 95-2001. Fellow Royal Coll. Physicians and Surgeons Can. (coun. 1970-78, v.p. 1976-78), Royal Coll. Physicians Ireland (1994—); mem. Coun. Ont. Faculty of Medicine (1976-89), Assn. Can. Med. Colls. (pres. 1981-82). Home: 31 Durham (Priv)-Unit 203 Ottawa ON Canada K1M 2J1 Personal E-mail: gilles.hurteau@sympatico.ca. *Ce que nous connaissons est peu de chose; ce que nous ignorons est immense.*

HURTER, ARTHUR PATRICK, economist, educator; b. Chgo., Jan. 29; s. Arthur P. and Lillian T. (Thums) Hurter; m. Florence Evalyn Kays; children: Patricia Lyn, Arthur Earl. BSChemE, MSChemE, Northwestern U., MA in Econs., PhD in Econs., Northwestern U. Chem. engr. Zonlite Rsch. Lab., Evanston, Ill., 1957-58; assoc. dir. Rsch. Transp. Ctr., Northwestern U., Evanston, 1963-65; asst. prof. dept. Indsl. Engring. and Mgmt. Scis. Tech. Inst., Northwestern U., 1962-66, prof., 1970—; prof. of transp., 1992—; chmn. dept. Northwestern U., 1969-89, assoc. prof. fin. Grad. Sch. Mgmt., 1969-70, prof., 1970—. Faculty mem. Newspaper Mgmt. Ctr., Transp. Ctr., 1989—; cons. U. Chgo., ESCOR, Sears Roebuck & Co., Standard Oil of Ind., Ill.; bd. dirs. Ill. Environ. Health Rsch. Ctr., 1972-77; mem. com. Sci. Tech. Adv., Ill. Inst. Natural Resources, 1980-84. Author: The Economics of Private Truck Transportation, 1965, Facility Location and the Theory of Production, 1989; contbr. articles to profl. jours. Pres. Coun. St. Scholastical H.S., 1972-80; elder Granville Ave. Presbyn. Ch., 1976-89; deacon 1st Presbyn. Ch., Evanston, trustee, 2003-06. Grantee Resources for the Future, 1964, Office of Naval Research, 1965, NSF, Social Sci. Research Council dissertation fellow Mem. Am. Econ. Assn., Regional Sci. Assn., Ops. Research Soc. Am., Inst. Mgmt. Scis., Inst. Indsl. Engrs., Sigma Xi, Phi Lambda Upsilon, Tau Beta Pi, Alpha Pi Mu (Disting. Engr. award). Home: 1505 W Norwood St Chicago IL 60660-2414 Office: Dept Indsl Engring Mgmt Sci Technological Inst Northwestern U Evanston IL 60208-0001 Office Phone: 847-491-3414. Business E-Mail: hurter@iems.northwestern.edu.

HURTTGAM, MARK HOWARD, information technology manager; s. Howard John Hurttgam and Frances Imogene Middleton. BA, Wayne State U., Detroit, 1982. Info. tech. mgr. Royal Oak Name Plate Co. Inc., Roseville, Mich., 1984—. Columnist (periodical) Bowler's Digest. Recipient Bowler of Yr. award, Nat. Amateur Bowlers Inc., 1995, 1998. Mem.: Profl. Bowlers Assn., US Bowling Congress (life), Mensa. Republican. Lutheran. Avocation: classical music. Personal E-mail: mhurttgam@comcast.net.

HURWICZ, LEONID, economist, educator; b. Moscow, 1917; arrived in U.S., 1940; LLM, U. Warsaw, Poland, 1938; DSc, Northwestern U., Evanston, Ill., 1980; D honoris causa (hon.), U. Autónoma de Barcelona, Spain, 1989; D of Econs. honoris causa (hon.), Keio U., Tokyo, 1993; LLD (hon.), U. Chgo., 1993; D honoris causa (hon.), Warsaw Sch. Econs., Poland, 1994; Dr.rer.pol honoris causa (hon.), U. Bielefeld, 2004. Rsch. assoc. Cowles Commn. U. Chgo., 1944—46; from assoc. prof. to prof. Iowa State U., Ames, 1946—49; prof. econ., math. and stats. U. Ill., 1949—51, U. Minn., Mpls., 1951—99, Regents' prof., 1969—88, Regent's prof. emeritus, 1988—, Carlson prof. econs., 1989—92, prof. econs., 1992—. Vis. prof. econs. Stanford U., Calif., 1955—56, 1958—59, Harvard U., Cambridge, Mass., 1969—71, U. Calif., Berkeley, 1976—77, Northwestern U., Evanston, Ill., 1988—89, U. Calif., Santa Barbara, 1998, Calif. Inst. Tech., 1999, U. Mich., Ann Arbor, 2002; Fisher lectr. U. Copenhagen, 1963; hon. prof. Ctrl. China U. Sci. and Tech., Wuhan, 1984; vis. lectr. People's U., Beijing, 1986, Tokyo U., 1982, Hebrew U., Jerusalem, 1993, Australian Econometric Mtgs., Melbourne, 1997; vis. Fulbright lectr. Bangalore U., India, 1965—66; vis. disting. prof. econs. U. Ill., 2001; invited lectr. Chuo U., Keio U., UN U., Inst. Adv. Studies (symposium participation), Tokyo, 1999, Symposium Devel. Western China, Chongqing, 2000, Pub. Econ. Theory Conf. Warwick U., England, 2000; cons. Econ. Design, Istanbul, 2000, Ctr. China U. Sci. and Tech., Wuhan, 2000, Peking U., 2000. Co-author (co-editor (with K.J. Arrow): Studies in Resource Allocation Processes, 1977; co-author: (co-editor (with K.J. Arrow and J. Uzawa) Studies in Linear and Non-Linear Programming, 1958; co-author: (co-editor (with J.S. Chipman) Prefences, Utility and Demand, 1971; co-author: (co-editor (D. Schmeidler and H. Sonnenschein) Social Goals and Social Organization, 1985; editor: Econ. Design, 1993, Review of Econ. Design, 1997, Jour. of pub. Econ. Theory, 1999, Advances in Mathematical Economics, 1999, Econs. Bull., 2001; mem. adv. bd.: Jour. of Math. Econs.; contbr. articles to profl. jours. Recipient Nat. medal Sci., 1990; fellow, Ctr. Advances Studies in Behavioral Scis., 1955—56; scholar Sherman Fairchild Disting. scholar, Calif. Inst. Tech., 1984—85. Fellow: Am. Econ. Assn. (disting., lectr. 1972), Econometric Soc. (pres. 1969); mem.: NAS, Am. Acad. Arts and Scis. Office: Univ Minn Dept Econs 271 19th Ave S Minneapolis MN 55455-0430 Home Phone: 612-728-0388. E-mail: hurwicz@umn.edu.

HURWITZ, ANDREW D., state supreme court justice; AB in Pub. and Internat. Affairs, Princeton U., 1968; JD, Yale U., 1972. Bar: Conn. 1973, Ariz. 1974, U.S. Dist. Ct. Ariz. 1975, U.S. Ct. Appeals (9th cir.) 1975, U.S. Supreme Ct. 1976, U.S. Dist. Ct. Conn. 1977, U.S. Ct. Appeals (2d cir.) 1977, U.S. Tax Ct. 1987, U.S. Ct. Appeals (7th cir.) 1987. Law clk. to Hon. Jon O. Newman U.S. Dist. Ct. Conn., 1972; law clk. to Hon. J. Joseph Smith U.S. Ct. Appeals, 1972—73; law clk. to Hon. Potter Stewart U.S. Supreme Ct., 1973—74; with Meyer Hendricks et. al., 1974—80, 1984—95, 1983—95, Osborn Maledon, 1995—2003; assoc. justice Ariz. State Supreme Ct., Phoenix, 2003—. Chief of staff Ariz. Gov. Bruce Babbitt, 1980—83, Ariz. Gov. Rose Mofford, 1988; mem. Ariz. Bd. of Regents, 1988—96, pres., 1992—93; co-chair of transition team Ariz. Gov. Janet Napolitano, 2002; vis. prof. law, civil procedure Ariz. State U., 1994—95, disting. vis. from practice, 2001, adjunct prof. law, ethics, supreme ct. litigation, legislative process, civil procedure, 1977—80, 1988, 2002. Mem. bd. dirs. Ariz. Ctr. for Law in Public Interest, 1986—88, Children's Action Alliance, 1999—2003, sec., 2002—03; chair City of Phoenix Neighborhood Improvement Com., 1986—88, City of Phoenix Street Environment Com., 1989—90. Mem.: State Bar of Ariz. (Com. on Rules of Professional Conduct 1985—90, Examination & Bar Review Com. 1986—87), Phi Beta Kappa. Office: Ariz State Supreme Ct Adminstrv Office Cts 1501 W Washington Phoenix AZ 85007 Office Phone: 602-542-4532.*

HURWITZ, ANN, lawyer; b. Portsmouth, Va., Aug. 19, 1953; d. Frederick Dean and Mildred (Wood) Hardy; m. Mitchell Seth Hurwitz, May 30, 1981. BA, U. S.C., 1977; JD, U. N.C., 1980. Bar: Tex. 1983, D.C. 1981, N.C. 1980. Assoc. Thompson, Pikrallidas & Schott, Alexandria, Va., 1980-82, Smith, Underwood, Carmichael & Floyd, Dallas, 1982-84, Evans, Fernandez, Forgerson & Hurwitz, Dallas, 1984-86, Smith, Underwood & Hunter, Dallas, 1987-88; ptnr. Smith & Underwood, Dallas, 1988; mng. ptnr. Dallas off. DLA Piper Rudnick Gray Cary, Dallas. Contbr. articles to profl. jours. Named a Texas Super Lawyer, 2003—04. Mem. ABA (franchising subcom of the small bus. com. of bus. law sect. of corp., banking and bus. law), Tex. State Bar Assn. (franchising com. of intellectual property law sect.), Dallas Bar Assn., N.C. Bar Assn., D.C. Bar Assn. Democrat. Baptist. Office: DLA Piper Rudnick Gray Cary 1717 Main St Dallas TX 75201-4605 Office Phone: 214-743-4521. Office Fax: 214-743-4545. Business E-Mail: ann.hurwitz@dlapiper.com.

HURWITZ, JOHANNA (JOHANNA FRANK), writer; b. NYC, Oct. 9, 1937; d. Nelson and Tillie (Miller) Frank; m. Uri Hurwitz, Feb. 19, 1962; children: Nomi, Beni. BA, Queens Coll., 1958; MLS, Columbia U., 1959. Libr. children's sect. N.Y. Pub. Libr., 1959-64; lectr. in children's lit. Queen's Coll., NYC, 1965-69; libr. Calhoun Sch., NYC, 1968-75, New Hyde Park (N.Y.) Sch. Dist., 1975-77; libr. children's sect. Great Neck (N.Y.) Pub. Libr., 1978-92. Author: Busybody Nora, 1976, Nora and Mrs. Mind-Your-Own-Business, 1977, The Law of Gravity, 1978, Much Ado About Aldo, 1978, Aldo Applesauce, 1979, New Neighbours for Nora, 1979, Once I Was a Plum Tree, 1980, Superduper Teddy, 1980, Aldo Ice Cream, 1981, Baseball Fever, 1981, The Rabbi's Girls, 1982, Tough-Luck Karen, 1982, Rip-Roaring Russell, 1983, DeDe Takes Charge!, 1984, The Hot and Cold Summer, 1984, The Adventures of Ali Baba Bernstein, 1985, Russell Rides Again, 1985, Hurricane Elaine, 1986, Yellow Blue Jay, 1986, Class Clown, 1987, Russell Sprouts, 1987, The Cold and Hot Winter, 1988, Teacher's Pet, 1988, Anne Frank: Life in Hiding, 1988, Hurray for Ali Baba Bernstein, 1989, Russell and Elisa, 1989, Astrid Lindgren: Storyteller to the World, 1989, Class President, 1990, Aldo Peanut Butter, 1990, School's Out, 1991, E Is for Elisa, 1991, Roz and Ozzie, 1992, Ali Baba Bernstein, Lost and Found, 1992, The Up and Down Spring, 1993, Make Room for Elisa, 1993, Leonard Bernstein: A Passion for Music, 1993, New Shoes for Silvia, 1993, A Word to the Wise, 1994, School Spirit, 1994, A Llama in the Family, 1994, Ozzie on His Own, 1995, Birthday Surprises, 1995, Elisa in the Middle, 1995, Even Stephen, 1996, Down and Up Fall, 1996, Spring Break, 1997, Ever-Clever Elisa, 1997, Helen Keller: Courage in the Dark, 1997, Faraway Summer, 1998, Starting School, 1998, A Dream Come True, 1998, Llama in the Library, 1999, Just Desserts Club, 1999, Summer with Elisa, 2000, Peewee's Tale, 2000, One Small Dog, 2000, Lexi's Tale, 2001, Russell's Secret, 2001, Oh No, Noah!, 2002, PeeWee & Plush, 2002, Dear Emma, 2002, Ethan, Out & About, 2002, Ethan at Home, 2003, Elisa Michaels, Bigger and Better, 2003, Fourth Grade Fuss, 2004, The Unsigned Valentine, 2006, Mostly Monty, 2007, Squirrel World, 2007. Recipient Bluebonnet award Tex. Libr. Assn., 1987, Wyoming Indian Paintbrush award 1987, W.Va. Children's Book award 1989, Sunshine State award Fla. Libr. Assn., 1990, Miss. Children's Book award Miss. Libr. Assn., 1990, S.C. Children's Book award, 1990, Garden State award N.J. Sch. Libr. Assn., 1991, 94, Weekly Reader Book Club award, 1993, Land of Enchantment award N.Mex., 2004. Mem. PEN, Author's Guild, Soc. Children's Book Writers, Amnesty Internat. Address: 10 Spruce Pl Great Neck NY 11021-1904

HURWITZ, SOL, writer, consultant; b. Washington, Aug. 31, 1932; s. Morris Aaron and Rose (Honig) H.; m. Nina Deutch, May 3, 1959; children: Linda, Mark Aaron, Laura. BA, Harvard U., 1953, postgrad., 1955—56, advanced mgmt. program, 1977. Various communication and broadcasting positions, Washington, 1956-60, NYC, 1960-66; assoc. dir. info. Com. for Econ. Devel., NYC, 1966-67, dir. info., 1967-72, v.p., 1972-80, sr. v.p., 1980-90, pres., 1990-97, trustee, 1990—. Bd. dirs. Albert Shanker Inst., Washington. Contbr. articles to N.Y. Times, Washington Post, Christian Sci. Monitor, Barron's, Harvard Mag., others. Trustee Rye (N.Y.) Bd. Edn., 1970-76; overseer Colby Coll., Waterville, Maine, 1980-2001. With USN, 1953-55. Mem. Coun. on Fgn. Rels., Harvard Club N.Y.C., Manursing Island Club (Rye). Avocations: single sculling, hiking, tennis, music, theater. Home and Office: 800 Forest Ave Rye NY 10580-3202

HUSA, KAREL, composer, conductor, educator; b. Prague, Czech Republic, Aug. 7, 1921; came to U.S., 1954, naturalized, 1959; s. Karel and Bozena (Dongresova) H.; m. Simone Perault, Feb. 2, 1952; children: Catherine, Anne-Marie, Elizabeth, Caroline. M summa cum laude, Conservatory and Acad. Music, Prague, 1945, M summa cum laude, 1947; lic. for conducting, Ecole Normale de Paris, 1947; grad., Conservatoire de Paris, 1948; MusD (hon.), Coe Coll., 1976, Cleve. Inst., 1985, Ithaca Coll., 1986, Baldwin-Wallace Conservatory, 1991, Hartwick Coll., 1997, New Eng. Conservatory, 1998, Acad. Musical Arts, Capital U., 2006; DHL (hon.), Coll. St. Vincent, 1996; ArtsD (hon.), Masaryk U., Czech Republic, 2000, Acad. Musical Arts, 2000; DFA (hon.), U. Ctrl. Ark., 2006. Guest condr. Czechoslovak Radio, Prague, 1945-46; guest condr. orchs. in Hamburg, Germany, Brussels, Paris, Zurich, Switzerland, Suisse Romande, London, Manchester, England, Prague, Stockholm, Hong Kong, Singapore, Japan, Cin., Buffalo, NYC, Boston, Rochester, NY, Balt., San Diego, Syracuse, NY; faculty Cornell U., Ithaca, NY, 1954—, prof. music, 1954—, dir. univ. symphony and chamber orchs., 1972-92, Kappa Alpha prof. music emeritus. Composer: Symphony, 1953, Fantasies for Orchestra, 1957, Divertimento for Brass, 1959, Poem for Viola and Orchestra, 1959, Elegy and Rondeau for Saxophone and Orchestra, 1961, Divertimento for String Orchestra, 1948, String Quartet No. 2, 1952, Portrait for String Orch., 1953, Mosaiques for Orch., 1961, Fresque for Orchestra, rev, 1964, Sonatina for Piano, 1943, Sonatina Violin and Piano, 1945, Sonata for Piano, 1949, Evocations of Slovakia for Clarinet, Viola and Cello, 1951, Eight Duets for Piano, 1955, Twelve Moravian Songs, 1956, Poem for Viola and Orchestra, 1962, Serenade for Woodwind Quintet and Orch., 1963, Concerto for Brass Quintet and Orch., 1965, Two Preludes; flute, clarinet, bassoon, 1966, Music for Percussion, 1966, Concerto for alto saxophone, concert band, 1967, String Quartet No. 3, 1968 (Pulitzer prize 1969), Music for Prague; for Band, 1968, for Orch., 1969, Apotheosis of this Earth for Winds, 1970, Concerto for Percussion and Winds, 1971, Two Sonnets from Michelangelo for Orch., 1971, Concerto for Trumpet and Wind Orch., 1973, Apotheosis of this Earth for Chorus and Orch., 1973, Sonata for Violin and Piano, 1972-73, The Steadfast Tin Soldier; for narrator and orch., 1974, Sonata for Piano, No. 2, 1975, Monodrama, ballet for orch., 1975, An American Te Deum; for mixed chorus, baritone solo, band and organ, 1976, for orch., 1978, Landscapes for Brass Quintet, 1977, Fanfare for Brass Ensemble, 1980, Pastoral for Strings, 1980, Three Moravian Songs, 1981, The Trojan Women, ballet for orch., 1981, Sonata a Tre, 1982, Concerto for Wind Ensemble, 1982 (Sudler award 1983), Cantata, 1983, Smetana Fanfare for Wind Ensemble, 1984, Variations for Violin, Viola, Cello and Piano, 1984 (Friedheim award 1986), Symphonic Suite for Orch., 1984, Intrada for Brass Quintet, 1984, Concerto for Orch., 1986, Concerto for Organ and Orch., 1987, Frammenti for Organ solo, 1987, Concerto for Trumpet and Orch., 1987, Concerto for Violoncello and Orch., 1988 (Grawemeyer award 1993), String Quartet No. 4, 1990, Youth Overture, 1991, Cayuga Lake (Memories), 1992, Concerto for Violin and Orch., 1993, Five Poems for Wood-Wind Quintet, 1994, Les Couleurs Fauves, 1995, Midwest Celebration Fanfare, 1996, Celebration for Orch., 1997, Postcard from Home, 1997, Song, for Mixed Chorus, 2000, Sonatina for Flute and Piano, 2003, Cheetah for Wind Ensemble, 2006, others; commns. from, UNESCO, Koussevitsky Found., Nat. Endowment for Arts, Friends of Music at Cornell, Fine Arts Found. Chgo., Ithaca Coll., U. Ga., Chgo. Symphony Orch., Butler U., Washington Music Soc., Coe Coll., NY Philharm., U. So. Calif., Kerze Found., also others.; editor: French Baroque Music: Reconstructions of Old French Baroque works by Lully and Delalande, 1961-68. Recipient prize Prague Acad. Arts, 1948, French Govt. award, 1946-47, L. Boulanger award, 1952, Pulitzer prize in music, 1969, Acad. Inst. Arts and Letters award, 1989, Grawemeyer award U. Louisville, 1993, Serge Koussevitzky Music Found. award, 1993, Czech Republic's medal of merit of 1st degree Pres. V. Havel, 1995, medal of Honor, City of Prague, 1998; Guggenheim fellow, 1964-65. Mem. Internat. Inst. Arts and Letters (life), AAAL, Belgian Royal Acad. Arts and Scis., Am. Music Ctr., Internat. Soc. Contemporary Music, French Soc. Composers, Am. Fedn. Musicians, Kappa Gamma Psi (hon.), Kappa Kappa Psi (hon.), Delta Omicron (hon.), Phi Mu Alpha (hon.). Avocations: painting, sports. Home: 1 Belwood Ln Ithaca NY 14850 Office: Karel Husa Archive & Gallery Sch Music Ithaca Coll Ithaca NY 14850 Office Phone: 607-257-7018. *As long as there will be museums, concerts, orchestras, libraries, our works will be measured against the masterpieces of the past. For this reason, the search for technical perfection must continue even today, in addition to new ideas and contents. One cannot exist without the other.*

HUSAR, LINDA S., lawyer; b. Chgo., Sept. 12, 1955; BS summa cum laude, Boston U., 1977; JD magna cum laude, Loyola Law Sch., 1980. Bar: Calif. 1980, US Dist. Ct. (no., ea., so., and ctrl. dists.) Calif. 1981, US Ct. Appeals (9th cir.) 1981. Ptnr., labor & employment dept. Thelen Reid & Priest LLP, LA. Mem.: LA County Bar Assn. (Labor Law Sect.), ABA (Labor Law Sect.), Calif. State Bar. Office: Thelen Reid & Priest LLP 333 S Hope St Ste 2900 Los Angeles CA 90071-3048 Office Phone: 213-576-8017. Office Fax: 213-687-1817. Business E-Mail: lshusar@thelenreid.com.

HUSAR, RUDOLF BERTALAN, mechanical engineering educator; b. Martonos, Yugoslavia, Oct. 29, 1941; came to U.S., 1966; s. Ga'bor and Ilona Huszar; m. Janja Djukic, Oct. 8, 1967; children: Maja, Attila. Degree in mech. engring., U. Zagreb, Croatia, 1962; diploma in mech. engring., Tech. U., Germany, 1966; PhDME, U. Minn., 1971. Design technician W. Hofer, Krefeld, Germany, 1962-63; rsch. asst. Tech. U., Berlin, 1963-66; from rsch. asst. to assoc. U. Minn., Mpls., 1966-71; rsch. fellow Calif. Inst. Tech., Pasadena, 1971-73; prof. Washington U., St. Louis, 1973—. Vis. prof. U. Stockholm, 1976; co-chmn. Interagy. Com. Health and Environ. Effects of Advanced Energy Tech., 1978; coop. program mem. Devel. and Appin. Space Tech. Air Pollution, EPA/NASA, 1978; dir. Ctr. for Air Pollution Impact and Trend Analysis (CAPITA), St. Louis, 1979—; mem. com. on atmospheric-biospheric interactions NAS, 1979-81. Editor: Atmospheric Environment, 1980, Indojaras, 1980; mem. adv. bd. Environ. Sci. Tech., 1980; contbr. chpt. to: Air Quality Criteria for Particulate Matter, EPA, 1995. Rsch. fellow U. Glasgow, Scotland, 1965, U. Minn., 1966-71; grantee, EPA, 1973—, NOAA, 1991—, U.S. Dept. Def., 1989-92. Mem. Air & Waste Mgmt. Assoc., Ges. Aerosolforschung. Office: Wash U CAPITA PO Box 1124 Saint Louis MO 63188-1124

HUSAR, WALTER GENE, neurologist, neuroscientist, educator; b. Jersey City, Sept. 24, 1956; s. Walter and Ksenia H. (Dawybida) H. BS in Biology summa cum laude, St. Peter's Coll., Jersey City, 1978; MS in Microbiology, Rutgers U., 1982; MD, UMDNJ-N.J. Med. Sch., 1988. Diplomate Nat. Bd. Med. Examiners; lic. physician, N.J., N.Y. Adj. instr., then adj. lectr. microbiology St. Peter's Coll., 1979-84; intern in neurology and internal medicine U. Medicine and Dentistry N.J., Newark, 1988-89, resident, then adminstrv. chief resident in neurology, 1989-92, instr. dept. neuroscis. to asst. prof. neuroscis., 1992-99, 99—, attending physician dept. neuroscis. U. Hosp. Newark, 1992—; staff attending physician VA Med. Ctr., East Orange, NJ, 1992—; cons. physician dept. medicine divsn. neurology Holy Name Hosp., Teaneck, NJ, 1992—2003; attending physician St. Clare's Hosp. (formerly N.W. Covenant Med. Ctr.), Denville, NJ, 1997—; pvt. practice Denville, 1997—; regional staff Newton (N.J.) Meml. Hosp., 2001—05; staff Kindred Hosp. Morris County, Dover, NJ, 2004—. Mem. bd. health Twp. of East Hanover, N.J., 1993—, v.p., 1996-97, pres., 1998-2003; mem. stroke coun. Am. Heart Assn., 1992-96. Fellow Acad. Medicine N.J.; mem. AMA, Med. Soc. N.J., Morris County Med. Soc., Am. Acad. Neurology (assoc.), Am. Assn. Electrodiagnostic Medicine (assoc.). Home: 10 Christine Dr East Hanover NJ 07936-3039 Office: Ctrl Morris Neurology 170 E Main St Rockaway NJ 07866-3530 Office Phone: 973-625-8888. Business E-Mail: dochusar@centralmorrisneurology.com.

HUSARIK, ERNEST ALFRED, educational administrator; b. Gary, Ind., July 2, 1941; m. Elizabeth Ann Bonnette; children: Jennifer, Amy. BA in History, Olivet Nazarene U., 1963; MS in Ednl. Adminstrn., No. Ill. U., 1966; PhD in Ednl. Adminstrn. and Curriculum Devel., Ohio State U., 1973. Supt. Ontario (Ohio) Pub. Schs., 1973—75, Euclid (Ohio) Pub. Schs., 1975—86, Westerville (Ohio) Pub. Schs., 1986—2000, Carmel Clay Sch. Corp., 2000—01; ednl. specialist MS Cons., Inc. Past pres. Sch. Study Coun. Ohio; gd. govs. Westerville Fund; mem. adv. and distbn. com. Martha Holden Jennings Found.; pres. Westerville chpt. Am. Heart Assn.; past chmn. Franklin County Ednl. Coun.; past mem. alumni adv. coun. Ohio State U.; past pres. Euclid C. of C., Ohio. Named Ohio Supr. of Yr., 1994; named one of top 100 Edn. Adminstrs. N.Am., Exec. Educator, 1993. Mem.: ASCD, Hamilton-Boone County Ednl. Svc. Ctr. (chmn.), Franklin County Area Supt.'s Assn. (exec. com.), Ind. Assn. Pub. Sch. Supts., Ohio Assn. Supervision and Curriculum Devel., Ohio State U. Edliners (pres.), Sci. amd Math. Achievement Required for Tomorrow, Ohio Math. and Sci. Coalition (exec. bd.), Buckeye Assn. Sch. Adminstrs. (bd. dirs., pres., Disting. Svc. award 2001), Am. Assn. Sch. Adminstrs., Olivet Nazarene U. Alumni Assn. (past mem. alumni bd. dirs.), Carmel C. of C., Westerville Area C. of C. (bd. dirs.), Rotary (pres. Westerville, Rotarian of Yr.), Sigma Tau Delta, Phi Delta Kappa (past chpt. pres.). Office: 1029 Wood Glen Rd Westerville OH 43081-3240 E-mail: edwardH568@aol.com.

HUSARIK, STEPHEN, music educator; b. Chgo., May 23, 1944; s. Stephen Husarik Sr. and Inez Medley. MusB with honors, U. Ill., 1970, MusM, 1972, postgrad., 1972-77; PhD, U. Iowa, 1983. Tchg. asst. U. Ill., Urbana, 1972-74; lectr. Sampson C.C., Clinton, NC, 1976; tchg. asst. U. Iowa, Iowa City, 1977, 79; instr. Lewis U., Lockport, Ill., 1978, Trinity Coll., Palos Hills, Ill., 1980; instr. music and humanities Moraine Valley

Coll., Palos Hills, Ill., 1984-89; head carillonneur Westark Coll., Ft. Smith, Ark., 1995—, instr. humanities and music, 1992—2001; prof. humanities and music history U. Ark., Ft. Smith, 2002—. Sr. editor Am. Keyboard Artists, 1987-92; co-author: A History of Westark College, 1999, (online question database) Reality Through the Arts, 2000; editor Who's Who in the Humanities, 1990-92; rec. artist: (piano solos) Pictures at an Exhbn. by Mussorgsky, Scott Joplin and the Ragtime Classics; contbr. numerous articles to profl. jours. and mags Field reader Coun. for Post-Secondary Edn., Washington, 1987; chair tech. com. U. Ark. Ft. Smith, 2004-05 Recipient Nat. Edpress Assn. award, 1987, Master Tchr. award Whirlpool, 2000, Tchr. of Yr. award Ark. Distance Learning Assn., 2002, Excellence in Online Tchg. award Ark. Distance Learning Assn., 2003, European Travel sabbatical, fall 2005, Walter L. Brown award Ark. Hist. Assn., 2006; grantee NEH, 1984, 89, 94, Ark. Humanities Coun., 1997. Mem. Am. Musicol. Soc., Am. Liszt Soc., Guild of Carillonneurs of N.Am., Coll. Music Soc., Nat. Assn. Humanities Edn. (newsletter editor 1993-94, bd. dirs., 2007), Westark Coll. Assn. (chair 1999), Ark. Music Educators Conf. (bd. dirs. 2004). Office Phone: 479-788-7555. Business E-Mail: shusarik@uafortsmith.edu.

HUSBAND, BERTRAM PAUL, lawyer; b. LA, Aug. 15, 1950; s. Bertram Perry and Ruth (Eatough) H.; m. Beverly Ruth Hyams, May 1, 1987 (div. March 6, 2003); children: Joseph Bertram, Daniel James, David Paul; m. Evelyn Concepcion Ferrer, Apr. 20, 2006. BA, Occidental Coll., 1972; JD, UCLA, 1977. Bar: Calif. 1977, U.S. Dist. Ct. (cen. dist.) Calif. 1978, U.S. Ct. Appeals (9th cir.) 1979, U.S. Dist. Ct. (so. dist.) Calif. 1980, U.S. Dist. Ct. (no. dist.) Calif. 1988, U.S. Tax Ct. 1987. Assoc. Coskey, Coskey & Boxer, LA, 1978-79, Cooper, Epstein & Hurewitz, Beverly Hills, Calif., 1979-81; pvt. practice LA, 1981-84; ptnr. Husband & Morris, LA, 1984-89, Husband & Roberts, L.A. and Encino, Calif., 1989-91; pvt. practice Encino, 1991-94, Valencia, Calif., 1994-97, Burbank, Calif., 1997—2002, Universal City, Calif., 2002—. Adj. prof. law Pepperdine U., Malibu, Calif., 1978—79; lectr. in field. Author equine law column Jour. Agrl. Taxation and Law, 1987-93; writer, producer (ednl. video) Fighting Back: Successfully Representing Your Horse Business to the IRS, 1991; editl. adv. bd. Am. Horse Coun. Tax Bulletin, 1994—. Registered judge Am. Horse Shows Assn., 1975-94; recommended judge Equestrian Trials Inc., 1988-94; dir., gen. counsel Burbank Internat. Children's Film Festival, 2000-03. Fellow, Am. coll. Equine Attys., 2005. Mem. ABA, L.A. County Bar Assn. (chmn. pro bono oversight com. tax sect. 1987-88, officer entertainment tax com. of tax sect. 1993-96, chair 1995-96), Beverly Hills Bar Assn. (exec. com. entertainment sect. 1992-96), San Fernando Valley Bar Assn. (chair tax sect. 1993-94), Calif. State Bar (tax sect. com. 2003, lectr. seminar 1988, 2003), Internat. Arabian Horse Assn. (vice chair fed. tax study com. 1979-92), Association Internationale du Film d'Animation (Hollywood chpt., dir. 1997-2003, gen. counsel 1997—), World Arabian Horse Orgn. Mem. Ch. of Christ. Avocation: speculative fiction. Office: 10 Universal City Plz Ste 2000 Universal City CA 91608 Office Phone: 886-780-8899. Business E-Mail: Paul.Husband@Husbandlaw.com.

HUSBANDS, ANDY, chef; b. Seattle, 1970; Sous chef East Coast Grill, Cambridge, Mass., 1992—93, exec. chef, 1993—95; worked at Elizabeth Berry's Organic farm, Abique, N.Mex., 1995; co-owner, exec. chef Tremont 647, Boston, 1996—, Sister Sorel, Boston, Rouge, Boston, 2002—. Participant Pork, The Other White Meat campaign, Nat. Pork Bd. Author: The Fearless Chef, 2004. Adv. bd. Boston Operation Frontline; co-chair Boston Taste of Nation. Named Chef/Restaurateur of Yr., Share Our Strength, 2004; named one of 5 Celebrated Chefs in Country, Nat. Pork Bd., 2005, Boston's Rising Stars, StarChefs.com, 2006. Mem.: UFO Social Club, Que BBQ team (Vt. State Champions 2002, Team of Yr. Yahoo Cup 2002—03, NH State Champions 2003—05, New England Regional BBQ Champions 2004). Office: Tremont 647 647 Tremont St Boston MA 02118 Office Phone: 617-266-4600.*

HUSBY, DONALD EVANS, engineering company executive; b. Mpls., Nov. 30, 1927; s. Olaf and Elsie Louise (Hagen) H.; m. Beverly June Tilbury, Sept. 24, 1949. BS, S.D. State U., 1952. Student engr., jr. asst., sr. engr., mgr. new products Westinghouse Electric Corp., Cleve., 1952-72; engring. mgr., v.p. engring. lighting div. Harvey Hubbell, Inc., Christiansburg, Va., 1972-76; pres. Elliptipar Inc., West Haven, Conn., 1976-78; fellow engr., mgr. engring. sect. Westinghouse Electric Corp., Vicksburg, Miss., 1978-82; engring. mgr. new products devel. Cooper Industries Crouse-Hinds LTG Products div., 1982-84; utility sales mgr. central region Cooper Lighting, Mpls., 1985-89; chief exec. officer Husby & Husby Inc., Madison, Minn., 1990—. Mem. indsl. adv. counsel Underwriters Labs.; provider ednl. seminars in lighting, tech. expert for NVLAP, NIST, U.S. Dept. Commerce. Contbr. articles to profl. jours.; patentee in field. With USN, 1945—47. Fellow Illuminating Engrs. Soc. (chmn., sec., dir., Disting. Service award 1989); mem. Internat. Municipal Signal Assn., Soc. Plastics Engrs., Nat. Elec. Mfrs. Assn., Am. Nat. Standards Inst., Am. Soc. Quality Control, Am. Soc. Engring. Physicists, Miss. Engring. Soc., D.C. Soc. Profl. Engrs., Designers Lighting Forum., Mensa Internat., Toastmasters Internat. Mem. Christian Ch. Home and Office: 705 5th Ave PO Box 66 Madison MN 56256-0066 Home Phone: 320-598-7786; Office Phone: 320-598-7786.

HUSE, FRANK PETER, lawyer; b. Indpls., Apr. 13, 1948; s. Frank Pershing and Betty (Goldsmith) Huse; m. Suzanne Grace Sims, Apr. 20, 1948; children: Christopher James, Patrick Daniel. BS, JD, Ind. U., 1975; MBA, Butler U., 1980. Bar: Ind. 1980, US Dist. Ct. (so. dist.) Ind. 1975. Asst. trial counsel, sr. atty. Blue Cross-Blue Shield Ind., Indpls., 1976—81; gen. counsel United Presdl. Life Ins. Co., Kokomo, Ind., 1981—87, gen. counsel, sec., 1987—93, sr. v.p. law and human resources, 1993—98; sr. v.p., assoc. gen. counsel Mutual of Omaha Cos., Nebr., 1998—. Mem.: ABA. Republican. Roman Catholic. Home: 2122 S 183rd Cir Omaha NE 68130-2744 Office: Mutual of Omaha Mutual of Omaha Plaza Omaha NE 68175

HUSEBOE, ARTHUR ROBERT, American literature educator; b. Sioux Falls, SD, Oct. 6, 1931; s. Carl and Lillian Ruth (Auby) H.; m. Doris Louise Eggers, May 27, 1953. BA, Augustana Coll., 1953; MA, U. S.D., 1956; PhD, Ind. U., 1963; LHD (hon.), Dana Coll., 1984. Teaching assoc. Ind. U., Bloomington, 1959-60; instr. U. S.D., Vermillion, 1960-61; prof. Augustana Coll., Sioux Falls, SD, 1961—. Pres. S.D. Humanities Found., Sioux Falls, 1994-96, Fedn. of State Humanities Couns., Washington, 1988-91; exec. dir. Nordland Heritage Found., Sioux Falls, 1980-, Ctr. Western Studies, Augustana, 1989—; NEH regional heritage chair, 1989-06. Author: An Illustrated History of the Arts in South Dakota, 1989, Sir George Etherege, 1987, Herbert Krause, 1985, Sir John Vanbrugh, 1976. Bd. dirs. S.D. Symphony, Sioux Falls, 1966-2005; mem. Nordland Fest Assn., Sioux Falls, 1975-. With U.S. Army, 1953-55. Recipient Gov.'s award in the Arts State of S.D., 1989; NEH grantee, 1975-77, 79-83, 92-94; named to S.D. Hall of Fame, 2001. Mem. MLA, We. Lit. Assn. (pres. 1976-77), Norwegian-Am. Hist. Assn., S.D. State Hist. Soc. Lutheran. Avocations: travel, theater, classical music. Home: 813 E 38th St Sioux Falls SD 57105-5939 Office: Ctr for Western Studies Box 727 Augustana Coll Sioux Falls SD 57197-0001 Business E-Mail: arthur.huseboe@augie.edu.

HUSHEN, JOHN WALLACE, manufacturing executive; b. Detroit, July 28, 1935; s. J. Wallace and Hilda Carol (Jean) H.; m. Margaret Corinne Aho, Apr. 25, 1959 (div. May 1978); children: Susan Lisa, Jane Louise, Peter Matthew; m. Lane Gay Johnston, Feb. 8, 1985 (div. May 2002); 1 child, John Case. BA, Wayne State U., 1958. Reporter The Detroit News, 1959-66; campaign press sec. Griffin for Senate, Mich., 1966; press sec. U.S. Senator Robert P. Griffin, Washington, 1967-70; dir. pub. info. U.S. Dept. Justice, Washington, 1970-74; dep. press sec. Pres. Gerald R. Ford, Washington, 1974-76; dir. govt. relations Eaton Corp., Washington, 1976-79, dir. pub. affairs Cleve., 1979-81, v.p. govt. rels. Washington, 1981-91, v.p. corp. affairs Cleve., 1991-99. Trustee Citizens League Rsch. Inst., Cleve., pres., 1998-2000; trustee YMCA, Cleve. Mem.: Senate Press Secs. Assn. (pres. 1969—70), Former Senate Aides, St. Andrews South Golf Club, Elkdale Country Club, Capitol Hill Club.

HUSKEY, DOW THOBERN, lawyer; b. Sept. 23, 1946; s. Dow Thobern Huskey and Helen (Weathersbee) Morris; m. Julie Beth Courson, May 17, 1975; children: Dow, III, Whitney. BS, Samford U., 1970; JD, Cumberland Sch. Law, 1976. Bar: Ala. 1977, U.S. Dist. Ct. (mid. dist.) Ala. 1977, U.S. Ct. Appeals (5th cir.) 1977, U.S. Ct. Appeals (11th cir.) 1981, U.S. Supreme Ct. 1981. Ptnr. Huskey & Etheredge, Dothan, 1977—82, Johnson Huskey Hornsby & Etheredge, Dothan, 1982—87; pvt. practice Dothan, 1987—. Author: (non-fiction) Landlord and Tenant, The Law in Alabama, 1980, Damages, The Law in Alabama, 1985. Pres. Houston County chpt. Am. Cancer Soc., Dothan, Ala., 1979—81, Houston County chpt. Ala. Soc. Crippled Children and Adults, Dothan, 1982—83. Mem.: Soc. Ala. Def. Lawyers Assn., Am. Judicature Soc., Assn. Trial Lawyers Am., Nat. Assn. Coll. and Univ. Attys., Ala. Trial Lawyers Assn. (bd. govs. 1980—85), Rotary (pres. 1990—91). Republican. Episcopalian. Home: 27 Hampton Way Dothan AL 36305-6319 Office: 112 W Adams St Dothan AL 36303-4528 Office Phone: 334-794-3366.

HUSKEY, HARRY DOUGLAS, information and computer science educator; b. Whittier, NC, Jan. 19, 1916; s. Cornelius and Myrtle (Cunningham) H.; m. Velma Elizabeth Roeth, Jan. 2, 1939 (dec. Jan. 1991); children: Carolyn, Roxanne, Harry Douglas, Linda; m. Nancy Grindstaff, Sept. 10, 1994. BS, U. Idaho, 1937; student, Ohio U., 1937—38; MA, Ohio State U., 1940, PhD, 1943. Temp. prin. sci. officer Nat. Phys. Labs., England, 1947; head machine devel. lab. Nat. Bur. Stds., 1948; asst. dir. Inst. Numerical Analysis, 1948-54; assoc. dir. computation lab. Wayne U., Detroit, 1952-53; assoc. prof. U. Calif., Berkeley, 1954-58, prof., 1958-68, vice chmn. elec. engring., 1965-66, prof. info. and computer sci. Santa Cruz, 1968-85, prof. emeritus, 1985—, dir. Computer Ctr., 1968-77, chmn. bd. info. sci., 1976-79, 82-83. Vis. prof. Indian Inst. Tech., Kanpur; (Indo-Am. program), 1963-64, 71, Delhi U., 1971; cons. computer divsn. Bendix, 1954-63; vis. prof. MIT, 1966; mem. computer sci. panel NSF, Naval Rsch. Adv. Com.; cons. on computers for developing countries UN, 1969-71; chmn. com. to advise Brazil on computer sci. edn. NAS, 1970-72; project coord. UNESCO/Burma contract, 1973-79; mem. adv. com. on use microcomputers in developing countries NRC, 1983-85. Co-editor: Computer Handbook, 1962. Recipient Disting. Alumni award Idaho State U., 1978, Pioneer award Nat. Computer Conf., 1978, IEEE Computer Soc., 1982; named U.S. sr.scientist award Fulbright-Alexander von Humboldt Found., Mathematisches Institut der Tech. U. Munich, 1974-75, 25th Ann. medal ENIAC; named to U. Idaho Alumni Hall of Fame, 1989. Fellow AAAS, IEEE (edit. bd., editor-in-chief computer group 1965-71, Centennial award 1984), Brit. Computer Soc.Computer Soc. India; mem. Am. Math. Soc., Math. Assn. Am., Assn. Computing Machinery (pres. 1960-62), Am. Fedn. Info. Processing Socs. (governing bd. 1961-63), Sigma Xi. Achievements include designing SWAC computer, Bendix G-15 and G-20 computers. Office: U Calif Computer & Info Sci Santa Cruz CA 95064 Home: 518 Summit Glen Ct Spartanburg SC 29307 Personal E-mail: harryhuskey@yahoo.com.

HUSMAN, CATHERINE BIGOT, retired insurance company executive, consultant; b. Des Moines, Feb. 10, 1943; d. Edward George and Ruth Margaret (Cumming) Bigot; m. Charles Erwin Husman, Aug. 5, 1967; 1 child, Matthew Edward. BA with highest distinction, U. Iowa, 1965; MA, Ball State U., 1970. Actuarial asst. Am. United Life Ins. Co., Indpls., 1965—68, assoc. actuary, 1971—74, group actuary, 1974—84, v.p., corp. actuary, 1984—97, v.p., chief actuary, 1997—2002; cons., 2002—04. Mem. group tech. com. Mut. Life Ins. Co., 1986-98; mem. profitability studies com. Life Office Mgmt. Assn. Inc., 1991-99. Mem. women's adv. com. United Way Ctrl. Ind., 1991—93; mem. Exec. Svc. Corps, 2002—, asst. treas., 2005—06; docent Pres. Benjamin Harrison Home, 2002—; vol. Indpls. Mus. Art, 2002—05, Clowes Meml. Hall, 2002—, Indpls. Civic Theater, 2002—, Ronald McDonald House, 2004—; bd. dirs., mem. fin. com. St. Elizabeth's Home, 1991—99, sec., 1994, mem. exec. com., treas., 1995; bd. dirs., mem. adminstrv. svcs., mem. exec. com. Heritage Place, 1993—99, treas., 1995—99. Fellow Soc. Actuaries; mem. Am. Acad. Actuaries, Actuaries Club Ind., Ky. and Ohio, Actuarial Club Indpls. (pres. 1979-80), Phi Beta Kappa. Republican. Roman Catholic. Avocations: reading, tennis. Home: 13530 Belford Ct Carmel IN 46032-8209 Personal E-mail: cbhusman@earthlink.net.

HUSSAIN, MEHBOOB, medical educator; s. Dilawar and Zohra Hussain; m. Shazi Naiyer, June 16, 2006. MD, U. Zurich, 1989. Instr. Harvard Med. Sch., Boston, 1999—2000; asst. prof. NYU, NYC, 2003—04, U. Chgo., 2004—05, Johns Hopkins U., Balt., 2005—. Sci. advisor Regenetech LLC, Houston, 2003—. Editor: (textbook) Molecular Basis of Pancreas Endocrine Development and Function. Grantee, Juvenile Diabetes Rsch. Found., 1998—2002, 2003—07, NIH, 2003—; scholar, Swiss NSF, 1995—96, Juvenile Diabetes Rsch. Found., 1997—98. Mem.: Endocrine Soc. Am. (assoc.), Am. Diabetes Assn. (assoc.), Mass. Med. Soc. (assoc.), Swiss Med. Assn. (assoc.). Achievements include discovery of bone marrow stem cells for the treatment of Diabetes Mellitus. Office: Johns Hopkins U 600 N Wolfe St Baltimore MD 21287 Office Phone: 410-502-5761. Office Fax: 410-502-5779. E-mail: mhussai4@jhmi.edu.

HUSSAIN, MOINUDDIN SYED, geologist, engineer, consultant; b. Hyderabad, India, Dec. 28, 1931; s. Karimuddin Syed and Hafeeza Begum (Khan) H.; m. Aziza Moin Quadri, Aug. 20, 1942; children: Qutub, Ayesha, Arju. BS, Osmania U., Hyderabad, 1954; DIC, Imperial Coll., London, 1963; MS, London U., 1964. Registered profl. geologist, Calif. Asst. groundwater geologist Groundwater Devel. Orgn., Lahore, Pakistan, 1955-56; test geologist Std. Vacuum Oil Co. (ESSO), Karachi, Pakistan, 1956-62; superintending geologist Oil and Gas Devel. Corp., Karachi, Pakistan, 1962-69; mgr. exploration/projects Dawood Petroleum Ltd., Karachi, Pakistan, 1969-73; project geologist Hallenbeck McCoy and Assoc., Berkeley, Calif., 1973-75; sr. geologist Dow Chem. Co., USA, Houston, 1975-81; sr. internat. geologist Union Tex. Petroleum Corp., Houston, 1981-85; cons. Hycarbex, Inc., Houston, 1985-93; cons. in petroleum, energy, groundwater Katy, Tex., 1993—. Mem. adv. bd. Petroland Exploration Inc., Houston, 1985—; advisor Dawood Group of Industries, Karachi, 1969-73; del. to Pakistan, U.S. Dept. of Energy; mem. (with Dept. of Energy) Presdl. Mission to Pakistan, 1994-95. Founding mem. Internat. Explorationist Group, Houston, 1984. Mem. Am. Assn. Petroleum Geologists (cert. geologist, alt. del. 1984, Cert. of Recognition award 1987), Bangladesh Geol. Soc. (life), Pak-Am. Petroleum Soc. (founder 1983), Houston Geol. Soc. (Svc. award 1985). Republican. Muslim. Achievements include research on petroleum potential of Pakistan and Bangladesh resulting in several oil and gas discoveries; introduction of API stds. in these countries to replace Soviet technology; establishment of oil producing trend in San Marcos Arch area, Tex. thru Austic Chalk Formation; preparation of feasability studies for establishment of refineries, power plants, fertilizer plants, pig iron plants, LPG projects; design of oil and gas pipelines groundwater resource evaluation and development, basin evaluation, project development and implementation; petroleum exploration and development in the Middle East and Far East; petroleum crude and products market development. Office: Petroland Exploration Inc PO Box 218341 Houston TX 77218-8341 Personal E-mail: energyexpln@yahoo.com. Business E-Mail: energyexpln@att.net.

HUSSAIN, SYED TASEER, biomedical researcher, educator; b. Lahore, Pakistan, Sept. 18, 1943; came to U.S., 1970; s. S. Fayyaz and Riaz (Fatima) H. BS, Punjab U., Pakistan, 1963, BS with honors, 1964, MS, 1965; PhD, U. Utrecht, Netherlands, 1969. Postdoct. fellow Am. Mus. Natural History, NYC, 1970—72; instr. Howard U. Coll. Medicine, Washington, 1972-73, asst. prof., 1973-76, assoc. prof., 1977-85, prof. anatomy, 1985—. Dir. gen. Pakistan Mus. of Natural History, Pakistan Sci. Found., Islamabad, 1985-87; grants reveiwer NSF, 1980—, NATO, 1987—, Nat. Geog. Soc., 1985—; frequent invited spkr. on evolutionary processes, biological changes, climate change and human health. Author, co-author over 60 publs. and several book chpts., contbr. articles to profl. jours. Grantee Smithsonian Instn., 1974-94, NSF, 1977—, Nat. Inst. Environ. Health Scis., 1994. Fellow Pakistan Acad. Geol. Scis.; mem. AAAS, Am. Assn. Anatomy, Soc. Vertebrate Paleontology. Achievements include research in evolution in locomotion and hearing mechanism in mammals; human health and forced climate change; influence of increased temperatures on diseases. Office: Howard Univ Coll Medicine 520 W St NW Washington DC 20001-2337

HUSSAM, ABUL, chemistry professor; BSc with honors in Chemistry, U. Dhaka, Bangladesh, 1975, MSc in Chemistry, 1976; PhD in Analytical Chemistry, U. Pitts., 1982. Assoc. prof. dept. chemistry and biochemistry George Mason U., Fairfax, Va. Contbr. articles to sci. jours. Recipient Grainger Challenge Gold award, NAE, 2007. Achievements include invention of the SONO filter, a household water treatment system for eliminating arsenic. Office: Dept Chemistry and Biochemistry George Mason U 4400 University Dr Fairfax VA 22030 Office Phone: 703-993-1085. E-mail: ahussam@gmu.edu.*

HUSSEY, JOHN FRANCIS, physician, geriatrician; b. Richmond Hill, NY, Jan. 6, 1951; s. John F. Sr. and Jean (Peczyinski) H.; m. Ann Pelley, Sept. 10, 1979; children: Leo, Nicholas. BS in Biology, St. Johns U., 1972; MD, Creighton U., 1976. Family practice intern, resident St. Joseph's Hosp., Omaha; pvt. practice, Augusta, Maine, 1982-90; med. cons. Augusta Mental Health Inst., 1990-95; geriatrician, psychiatry cons. Togus (Maine) VA Hosp., 1995—. Capt. USPHS, 1979-82. Fellow Am. Acad. Family Physicians; mem. Am. Geriat. Soc., Kennebec County Med. Assn. (treas. 1995-96, pres. 1996-97), Am. Heart Assn. Office: VA Hosp 1 VA Ctr Sta 171 Augusta ME 04330-6795 E-mail: jfhmd@msn.com.

HUSSEY, KENT J., consumer products company executive; With United Techs. Corp., Astechnologies, Inc., Conair Group; v.p., CFO Regina Co., 1991—94, ECC Internat., 1994—96; bd. dirs. Spectrum Brands, Inc., 1996—, exec. v.p. fin. and adminstrn., CFO, 1996—98, pres., COO, 1998—2001, 2002—06, pres., CFO, 2001—02, CEO, 2007—. Bd. dirs. Am. Woodmark Corp. Office: Spectrum Brands Inc 6 Concourse Pky Ste 3300 Atlanta GA 30328 Office Phone: 770-829-6200.*

HUSSEY, WILLIAM BERTRAND, retired diplomat; b. Bellingham, Wash., Oct. 23, 1915; s. Bertrand Brokaw and Ruth (Axtell) Hussey; m. Fredricka Boone, Dec. 31, 1940 (div. 1957); children: Crhistina, Pamela, Eva, William Bertrand, Peter; m. Piyachart Bunnag, May 20, 1959. BS, Boston U., 1938; postgrad., UCLA, 1939-40, Naval War Coll., 1953-54. Asst. housing mgmt. supr. U.S. Housing Authority, 1941-42; chmn. London (Eng.) Liaison Group, also State Dept. rep., 1948-52; spl. State Dept. rep., Rome, 1949, Paris, 1950. Chmn. regional conf., Dhahran, Saudi Arabia, 1949; chief civil-mil. rels. sect., Munich, 1952—53; adminstr. officer, Frankfurt, Germany, 1953—55; attache, Rangoon, Burma, 1955—56; consul, Chiengmai, Thailand, 1957—59; acting dep. chief plans and devel. staff Bur. Ednl. and Cultural Affairs, Dept. State, 1959—60, dep. chief cultural presentations divsn., 1960—61; mem. del. regional confs., Beirut, Kampala, Uganda, 1960; group leader Nat. Strategy Seminar, Asilomar, Calif., 1960; counselor embassy, Lome, Togo, 1961—65, Biantyre, Malawi, 1965—66; chargé d'affaires Am. embassy, Maseru, Lesotho, Tananarive, Madagascar, 1966—67, Port Louis, Mauritius, 1967—68, UN Devel. Programme Western Pacific, Apia, Western Samoa, 1969—74; del. UN Law of Sea Conf., 1975—80; assoc. v.p. LA Olympic Organizing Com., 1982—84; dir. govt. rels. Statue of Liberty Centennial, Liberty Weekend, 1986; cons. in field. With U.S. Mcht. Marine, 1930—33, served to lt. comdr. USN, 1942—48, ETO, PTO, capt. USNR. Recipient Superior Svc. award, Sec. of State, 1986. Address: 5563B Via Portora Laguna Woods CA 92637-6960

HUSSMAN, WALTER E., JR., publishing executive; b. Texarkana, Tex., 1947; s. Walter E. and Betty (Palmer) Hussman; m. Robena Kendrick; 3 children. B in Journalism, U. NC, 1968; MBA, Columbia U. Gen. mgr. Camden News, Ark.; v.p. & gen. mgr. Palmer Newspapers (name changed to WEHCO Media), Hot Springs, Ark., 1973; pres./CEO WEHCO Media, Inc., Little Rock; pub., owner Ark. Democrat, Little Rock, 1974—91; pres., CEO Ark. Democrat-Gazette, Little Rock, 1991—. Prin., owner Camden (Ark.) News, El Dorado (Ark.) News-Times, Hot Springs (Ariz.) Sentinel-Record, Magnolia (Ark.) Banner-News, Texarkana (Tex.) Gazette, KWEH FM radio, Camden, KCMC AM radio, Texarkana, KTAL FM and TV, Texarkana, Shreveport, La. Bd. visitors U. N.C., Chapell Hill, NC. Office: Ark Dem Gazette 121 E Capitol Ave Little Rock AR 72201 also: WEHCO Media Inc PO Box 2221 Little Rock AR 72203 Office Phone: 501-378-3400.*

HUST, BRUCE KEVIN, lawyer; b. Cin., Aug. 16, 1957; s. George Julius and Shirley Mae (Glaser) H. BA, U. Cin., 1979; JD, No. Ky. U., 1985. Bar: Ohio 1986, US Dist. Ct. (so. dist.) Ohio 1987, US Ct. Appeals (6th cir.) 2000. Pvt. practice, Cin., 1986—; trial counsel Hamilton County Pub. Defender's Office, Cin., 1988—2000. Vol. Lawyers Project, Cin., 1986—87, 1990—; precinct exec. mem. Hamilton County Rep. Ctrl. Com., 1988—. With Ohio Naval Militia, 1988—94, mass comm. specialist USN, 1994—. Mem. Ohio State Bar Assn., Cin. Bar Assn., Ohio Assn. Criminal Def. Lawyers, Masons, Odd Fellows. Mem. United Ch. of Christ. Avocations: reading, current events, politics, writing and performing comedy. Home: 4247 Delridge Dr Cincinnati OH 45205-2025 Office: 917 Main St 2d Fl Cincinnati OH 45202 Office Phone: 513-421-7700.

HUSTAD, THOMAS PEGG, marketing educator, association executive; b. Mpls., June 15, 1945; s. Thomas Earl Pegg and John Charles and Dorothy Helen (Anderson) H.; m. Sherry Ann Thomas, Jan. 30, 1971; children: Kathleen, John. BS in Elec. Engring., Purdue U., 1967, MS in Indsl. Mgmt., 1969, PhD in Mktg., 1973. Cert. new product devel. profl. Vis. asst. prof. Purdue U., West Lafayette, Ind., 1971-72; asst. prof. Faculty of Adminstrv. Studies York U., Toronto, Ont., Can., 1972-74, assoc. prof., 1974-76, assoc. prof., mktg. area coord., 1976-77; assoc. prof. mktg. Kelley Sch. Bus. Ind. U., Bloomington, 1977—82, prof., 1982—2006, chmn. MBA program, 1983—85, Nestlé Hustad prof., 2007—. Chmn. program Ind. U. Ann. Bus. Conf., 1983, 84, co-founder Exec. Forum; adj. prof. philanthropic studies, 1992—96; vis. prof. City U. Hong Kong, 1997, Ljubljana U., Slovenia, 1998, 2000, Steinbeis U., Berlin, 1998—2000, CEU Bus. Sch., Budapest, Hungary, 2003—; exec. dir. Ind. U. Internat. Bus. Forum, 1981—85; cons. N.Am. corps. Govt. of Can.; condr. seminars for U.S., Singapore, Can., European, Asian and Venezuelan industry; mem. selection com. Outstanding Corp. Innovator award, 1978—; interim dir. Johnson Ctr. for Entrepreneurship and Innovation, 2004—05. Author: Approaches to the Teaching of Product Development and Management, 1977, (with others) PDMA Handbook of New Product Development, 1996, 2d edit., 2005; editor: International Competition: The American Challenge, 1986, Managing the Product Development Process, 1989, Product Development: Prospering in a Rapidly Changing World, 1990, Born to Play: A Discography and Performance Guide for the Career of Ruby Braff, 2007; founder, editor Jour. Product Innovation Mgmt., 1986-2000; contbr. articles to books and profl. jours. Fulbright fellow, 1987, fellow Ind. U. Ctr. Entrepreneurship and Innovation, John Kosin Faculty fellow, 1993-03; Crawford fellow of Product Innovation, 1993—; recipient Eli Lilly MBA Tchg. Excellence award, 1990, Editorship award Elsevier Sci. Pub. Co., 1993, Kelley award innovative tchg., 1999, Kelley Svc. award 2000, Anbar Emerald Golden prize practical applications and originality, 2000; named Best Best Tchr., Bus. Week Mag.; Thomas P. Hustad Best Paper award named in his honor, 1998—, Nestlé-Hustad endowed professorship created in his honor Nestlé, Ind. U., 2007. Mem.: PDMA Found. (bd. dirs. 2004—), European Inst. Advanced Studies in Mgmt. (chair ann. conf. 2003, mem. governing bd. 1992—), Product Devel. and Mgmt. Assn. (v.p. confs. 1979, pres.-elect 1980, pres. 1981, dir. 1982—83, chmn. publ. com. 1982—84, sec./treas. 1984—96, mgr. assn. office 1984—96, bd. dirs. 1984—2000, 2004—, program. chmn. 3rd ann. conf., Presdl. award 1987), Am. Mktg. Assn. (award 1973), Brown U. Alumni Assn. (Assoc. Alumni award 1963), Internat. Assn. Jazz Record Collectors, Ancient and Hon. Arty. Co., Beta Gamma Sigma, Tau Beta Pi, Phi Eta Sigma. Home: 3101 Daniel St Bloomington IN 47401-2421 Office: Ind U Kelley Sch Bus 1309 E 10th St Bloomington IN 47405-1701 Office Phone: 812-855-1160. Business E-Mail: hustad@indiana.edu.

HUSTED, RUSSELL FOREST, research scientist; b. Lafayette, Ind., Apr. 4, 1950; s. Robert Forest and Miriam Ruth (Jackson) H.; m. Nancy Lee Driscoll, Oct. 25, 1969 (div. Feb. 1986); children: Jacqueline Marie, Randall Forest; m. Ruth Elaine Hurlburt, Nov. 12, 1988. BS in Chemistry with highest distinction, Colo. State U., 1972; PhD in Pharmacology, U. Utah, 1976. Post-doctoral fellow dept. medicine U. Iowa, Iowa City, 1976-79, rsch. scientist dept. medicine, 1979-81, 1982—; asst. prof. U. Conn. Sch. Medicine, Farmington, 1981-82. Contbr. articles to profl. jours. Mem. Parks and Recreation Com., North Liberty, 1997—. Mallinckrodt scholar Colo. State U., 1968. Mem. AAAS, Am. Soc. Nephrology, Am. Physiol. Soc., Soc. Gen. Physiology, N.Y. Acad. Sci., Sigma Xi. Democrat. Methodist. Office: Univ Iowa 3180 Medical Labs Iowa City IA 52242 Home Phone: 319-626-6354; Office Phone: 319-335-7618. Business E-Mail: russell-husted@uiowa.edu.

HUSTED, WILLIAM ARMSTRONG, sales executive; b. London, Feb. 25, 1937; s. John Grinnell Wetmore and Helen Armstrong Husted. *Descendant of the original settlers of Greenwich, CT. On mother's side of family, I am a descendant of John Alden, who came over to the U.S. on the Mayflower.* BS, Hobart Coll., 1959. Jr. analyst group actuarial divsn. Met. Life Ins. Co., NYC, 1959-60, sr. analyst group actuarial divsn. dividend sect., 1961-63, sr. retention analyst group customer rels. and adminstrn. staff, 1964-70; distbr. Amway, Bedford, NY, 1976-98; ind. bus. owner Quixtar, Bedford, NY, 1999—. Mem. Rep. Presdl. Legion of Merit, Washington, 1980—; mem. nat. adv. bd. Black America's Polit. Action Com., Hagerstown, Md., 1996—; rep. Congrl. Order of Liberty, 1993, Congl. Order of Freedom, 1995; founding prodr. GOP-TV, 1994—; nat. mem. Libr. of Congress, Washington, 1990— (mem. chmn. adv. bd., 1995); hon. educator St. Joseph's Indian Sch., 1997—; life mem. Rep. Nat. Com., 2002—; mem. scholarship com. Am. Indian Edn. Found., 2004—; mem. guardian of the wild, Nat. Wildlife Fedn., 2004—; hon. trustee Am. Indian Relief Coun., 2007. Royal Patronage bestowed Principality of Hutt River Province, 1994-95. Mem.: Consumer Reports (life), Kappa Alpha Soc. (mem. exec. coun. 1962—65). Episcopalian. Avocations: collecting stamps, signed first edition books and fine antiques. Home and Office: 46 Greenwich Rd Bedford NY 10506-1509 Office Phone: 914-234-3981.

HUSTING, PETER MARDEN, advertising consultant; b. Bronxville, NY, Mar. 28, 1935; s. Charles Ottomar and Jane Alice (Marden) H.; m. Carolyn Riddle, Mar. 26, 1960; children: Jennifer, Gretchen, Charles Ottomar; m. Myrna Diaz, May 11, 1996. BS, U. Wis., 1957; grad., Advanced Mgmt. Program, Harvard U., 1974. Sales rep. Crown Zellerbach Corp., San Francisco, 1958-59; media analyst Leo Burnett Co., Chgo., 1959-61, time buyer, 1961-62, asst. account exec., 1962-63, account exec., 1963-68, v.p., account supr., 1968-72, sr. v.p., account dir., 1972-79, group exec., 1979-86, exec. v.p., 1979-92, dir. human relations internat., 1986-92, also bd. dirs., ret., 1992; pres. Husting Enterprises, Chgo., 1993—. Dir. Columbian Mutual Life Ins. Co., Harley-Davidson Customer Funding Corp. Trustee Shedd Aquarium Soc., Chgo., 1980-94, hon. life trustee, 1995—; bd. dirs. Chgo. Better Govt. Assn., 1976-92, Leadership Coun. Met. Open Cmtys., Chgo., 1980-86, Lyric Opera Guild, 1971-78, Chgo. Forum, 1969-76. Served with AUS, 1958. Mem.: Indian Hill (Winnetka) (bd. govs. 1975-79), The Valley Club (Montecito, Calif.), Coral Casino Club (Santa Barbara). Avocations: flying, swimming, hunting, trekking, golf. Office: Husting Enterprises 150 S Wacker Dr Ste 3100 Chicago IL 60606-4103

HUSTON, ANGELA C., lawyer; b. Tulsa, Jan. 23, 1973; BS cum laude, Tex. Woman's U., 1995; JD, Baylor U. Sch. Law, 2001. Bar: Tex. 2001, US Dist. Ct. (no. dist. Tex.) 2001. Assoc. Holmes Firm, P.C., Dallas. Mem. Assoc. Leadership Coun., 2005—06. Named a Rising Star, Tex. Super Lawyers mag., 2006. Mem.: Internat. Coun. Shopping Ctrs., Real Estate Coun., Tex. Young Lawyers Assn., Dallas Bar Assn. Office: Holmes Firm PC 14911 Quorum Dr Ste 340 Dallas TX 75254 Office Phone: 469-916-7700. E-mail: angela@theholmesfirm.com.*

HUSTON, ANJELICA, actress; b. Santa Monica, Calif., July 8, 1951; d. John and Enrica Huston; m. Robert Graham, May 23, 1992. Student, Loft Studio. Actress appearing in Hamlet, Roundhouse Theatre, London, Tamara, Il Vittorale Theatre, L.A.; appeared in films including A Walk with Love and Death, 1969, Hamlet, 1969, Sinful Davey, 1969, Swashbuckler, 1976, The Last Tycoon, 1976, The Postman Always Rings Twice, 1981, Rose for Emily, 1982, This is Spinal Tap, 1984, The Ice Pirates, 1984, Prizzi's Honor, 1985 (Academy award for best supporting actress 1985, N.Y.Film Critics award 1985, L.A. Film Critics award 1985), Captain Eo, 1986, Gardens of Stone, 1987, The Dead, 1987 (Best Actress award Ind. Filmakers 1987), Mr. North, 1988, A Handfull of Dust, 1988, Witches, 1989, Crimes and Misdemeanors, 1989, Enemies, A Love Story, 1989 (Acad. award nomination 1990), The Grifters, 1990 (Acad. award nomination 1991), The Addams Family, 1991, The Player, 1992, Addams Family Values, 1993, Manhattan Murder Mystery, 1993, The Crossing Guard, 1995, The Perez Family, 1995, Buffalo '66, 1997, Phoenix, 1998, Ever After, 1998, The Golden Bowl, 2000, The Man From Elysian Fields, 2000, The Royal Tenenbaums, 2001, Blood Work, 2002, Barbie as Rapunzel, (voice only), 2002, Daddy Day Care, 2003, Kaena: The Prophecy (voice only), The Life Aquatic with Steve Zissou, 2004, These Foolish Things, 2006, Art School Confidential, 2006, Material Girls, 2006; TV films include The Cowboy and the Ballerina, 1984, Family Pictures, 1993, And The Band Played On, 1993, Buffalo Girls, 1995, The Kentucky Derby, 2002, Iron Jawed Angels, 2004 (Golden Globe award for best supporting actress series, miniseries or TV movie, 2005), Covert One: The Hades Factor, 2006; dir. (films) Bastard Out of Carolina, 1996, (TV films) Riding the Bus with My Sister, 2005; dir, prodr., actor (films) Agnes Browne, 1999; TV mini-series include Lonesome Dove, 1989, The Mists of Aalon, 2001; TV guest appearances Laverne & Shirley, 1976, Inside the Actors Studio, 1994. Office: Internat Creative Mgmt c/o Toni Howard 8942 Wilshire Blvd Beverly Hills CA 90211-1934

HUSTON, DANIEL CLIFF, geophysicist; b. Anchorage, June 29, 1955; s. Arthur Cliff and Allie Mae (Ogdon) H.; m. Holly Hunter, Oct. 10, 1992; children: Lana Marie, Hayley Allison. BS in Geology and Geophysics, U. Hawaii, 1980, marine option program cert., 1980; MA in Geological Scis., U. Tex., 1987. Surveyor Trans Alaska Pipeline, 1975-78; geologist R&M Cons., Anchorage, 1980; geophysicist U.S. Minerals Mgmt. Svc., Anchorage, 1981-83; rsch. asst. Miss. Canyon Project, Austin, 1983-84; project SEER U. Tex. Inst. Geophysics, Austin, 1983-87; geophys. intern Sohio Petroleum Co., San Francisco, summer 1984; geophysicist leader advanced seismic methods group Unocal Sci. and Tech. Divsn., Brea, Calif., 1987-90; sr. geophysicist Unocal Oil and Gas Divsn., Houston, 1991-96; founder, v.p. Hunter 3-D Inc. (geophys. consulting firm), 1996—, Creekside Exploration, Inc. (oil and gas exploration firm), 1999—. Pres. Creekside Exploration, Inc., 1999—; presenter in field. Contbr. articles to profl. jours. Fellow U. Tex. Indsl. Assocs., 1983. Mem. Am. assn. Petroleum Geologists, Soc. Exploration Geophysicists (presenter workshop 1984, ann. conv. 1986, regional conv. 1989). Methodist. Avocations: travel, scuba diving, skiing, weightlifting, reading. Home: 1635 Creekside Dr Sugar Land TX 77478-4203

HUSTON, JOHN CHARLES, law educator; b. Chgo., Mar. 21, 1927; s. Albert Allison and Lillian Helen (Sullivan) H.; m. Joan Frances Mooney, Aug. 1, 1954; children: Mark Allison, Philip John, Paul Francis James; m. Inger Margareta Westerman, May 4, 1979 (dec. 2003); m. Heather Van Nuys, June 24, 2007. AB, U. Wash., 1950, JD, 1952; LLM, N.Y. U., 1955. Bar: Wash. 1952, N.Y. 1964, U.S. Dist. Ct. (we. dist.) Wash. 1953, U.S. Ct. Appeals (9th cir.) 1953, U.S. Tax Ct. 1977, U.S. Supreme Ct. 1993. Assoc. Kahin, Carmody & Horswill, Seattle, 1952—53; tchg. fellow NYU Law Sch., 1953—54; asst. prof. NYU, 1954—57; asst. co-dir. U. Ankara Legal Rsch. Inst., Turkey, 1954—55; asst. prof. Syracuse (NY) U., 1957—60, assoc. prof., 1960—65; prof. Syracuse U., NY, 1965—67; prof., assoc. dean U. Wash., Seattle, 1967—73, prof. law, 1973—96, prof. emeritus, 1996—. Of counsel Carney, Badley, Smith & Spellman, Seattle, 1987—2002, Smith McKenzie Rothwell & Barlow, P.S., Seattle, 2002—07, Smith Law Partnership, Seattle, 2007—; vis. prof. U. Stockholm, 1986, U. Bergen, 1989, Bond U., Australia, 1991. Author: (with Redden) The Mining Law of Turkey, 1956, The Petroleum Law of Turkey, 1956, (with Mucklestone and Cross) Community Property: General Considerations, 1971, (with Price and Treacy) 4th edit., 1994, (with Sullivan and others) Administration of Criminal Justice, 166, 2d edit., 1969, (with Miyatake and Way) Japanese International Taxation, 1983, supplements through 1997, (with Cross and Shields) Community Property Desk Book, 1977, 2d edit., 1989, supplement, 1997, (with Williams) Permanent Establishment, 1993. With USNR, 1945-46; capt. USAFR. Mem.: ABA, Internat. Fiscal Assn. (past regional v.p., past mem. coun.), Japanese Am. Soc. Legal Studies, King County Bar Assn., Wash. State Bar Assn. (chmn. tax sect. 1984—85), Am. Coll. Trust and Estate Coun. Office: Second & Seneca Bldg Ste 1800 Seattle WA 98101 Personal E-mail: huston@seanet.com.

HUSTON, JOHN WILSON, military officer, historian; b. Pitts., Mar. 6, 1925; s. James Leslie and Kathryn Rachel (Ray) H.; m. Dorothy Winters Bampton, Aug. 27, 1960; children: Ann, John. BA, Monmouth Coll., 1948; MA, U. Pitts., 1950, PhD, 1957. Served as 1st lt. USAAF, 1943-45; advanced through grades to maj. gen. USAF Res., 1976; recalled to active duty as chief Office of Air Force History, Dept. Air Force, Washington, 1976—; lectr. history U. Pitts., 1949-56; prof. U.S. Naval Acad., Annapolis, 1956-76, prof. emeritus, 1994—, chmn. dept. history, 1971-76. Vis. prof. U. Rochester, 1964, Ball State U., 1965, 67, U. Md., 1969; Disting. vis. prof. USAF Acad., 1994-95. Author: American Air Power Comes of Age: General Henry H. "Hap" Arnold's World War II Diaries, 2001. Decorated D.S.M., D.F.C. with oak leaf cluster, Air medal with 3 oak leaf clusters, Joint Service Commendation medal, Air Force Commendation medal. Home: 115 E Lake Dr Annapolis MD 21403-4444 Office: Hdqrs USAF AF/CVAH Bolling Afb Washington DC 20332-0001

HUSTON, JOYCE A., entertainment and publishing company executive; d. Herman and Loyce (Pickens) Huston; m. Z. Lipsky, July 21, 2001. BSBA, U. Redlands, 1988; postgrad., Rockhurst Coll. Continuing Edn. Ctr., 2000—. Trumpeter, vocalist, arranger Albert King Blues Band, St. Louis, 1980—82; word processing specialist TRW, Los Angeles, Calif., 1986—88; pres. UniSun Prodns., Las Vegas, Nev., 1993—; project controls engr., sys. analyst U.S. DOE (Bechtel SAIC, TRW, SAIC Contractors), Las Vegas, Nev., 1989—. Webmaster, spokesperson Las Vegas Fibromyalgia/Chronic Fatigue Syndrome Support Group; presenter in field. Prodr.(composer, singer, trumpeter, synthesizers): (CD) Soul Stir Fry; composer: Songs Forever; musician (front trumpeter): The Music Man with Tony Randall, 1978; musician: (trumpeter) (albums) Howard University Jazz Ensemble; performer: Bill Pinkney and the Original Drifters, 1992, Shower of Stars, 2000; performer: (one woman show) Fitzgerald's Hotel & Casino, 1997; author: The Black O'Kelleys in America, 1998. Recruiter asst. Rainbow Coalition, Washington, 1982; Census 2000 program asst. African Am. Cmty. Coalition of So. Nev., Las Vegas, 2000; mem. P.U.S.H Coalition, St. Louis, 1978—79. Recipient Dr. Barbara O'Rourke award, Las Vegas Fibromyalgia/Chronic Fatigue Syndrome Support Group, 2006. Mem.: Las Vegas Blues Soc., Clark County Geneal. Soc., Las Vegas Songwriters Assn. (assoc.), Nat. Spiritualist Assn. of Chs. (assoc.). Democrat. Avocations: genealogy, computers, music, reading, swimming. Office: UniSun Prodns 2375 E Tropicana Ave Ste 353 Las Vegas NV 89119 Office Phone: 702-391-3040. Personal E-mail: thelady@msjoyce.com.

HUSTON, JULIA, lawyer; d. Dennis and Evelyn Bilbe Huston; m. Donald Larson. BA, BS, magna cum laude with distinction, Boston U., 1987; EdM, Harvard U., 1989; JD magna cum laude, Boston U., 1992. Ptnr. Bromberg & Sunstein LLP, Boston, 1995—. Office: Bromberg & Sunstein LLP 125 Summer St Boston MA 02110 Office Phone: 617-443-9292.

HUSTON, KENT ALLEN, rheumatologist; b. Wichita, Kans., May 14, 1944; s. George W. and Elizabeth H.; m. Janet Kay Heims, June 12, 1968 (div. 1985); children: Kent K., Heather J., Elizabeth K.; m. Susan Jolene Held, Dec. 2, 1990; 1 child, Boris H. BA, U. Kans, lawrence, 1966; MD, U. Kans, Kansas City, 1970. Diplomate Am. Bd. Internal Medicine and Rheumatology. Intern Wesley Med. Ctr., Wichita, 1970-71; resident in internal medicine Mayo Clinic, Rochester, Minn., 1971-75, fellow in rheumatology, 1975-77; pres. Mid-Am. Med. Cons., Kansas City, Mo., 1977-91, Ctr. Rheumatic Disease, Kansas City, 1991—. Preceptor U. Kans. Sch. Medicine, 1978—; clin. assoc. prof. U. Mo.-Kansas City Med. Sch., 1982—; mem. organizing com. Mid-Am. Rehab. Hosp.; dir. Mo. State Regional Arthritis Ctr., 1988—. Contbr. to profl. publs. Bd. dirs. Western Mo. chpt. Arthritis Found., 1980-90, chmn. med. and sci. com., 1984-87; mem. Mo. Arthritis Adv. Bd., Jefferson City, 1984—. Capt. USAF, 1971-73. Fellow ACP; mem. AMA, Am. Soc. Internal Medicine, Am. Coll. Rheumatology, Southwest Clin. Soc., Kansas City Met. Med. Soc., Kansas City Rheumatism Soc. (pres. 1991—). Avocations: backpacking, tennis, golf, photography, woodworking. Office: Ctr Rheumatic Disease 4330 Wornall Rd Kansas City MO 64111-3217 Office Phone: 816-531-0930.

HUSTON, LANA M., lawyer; b. Jamestown, NY, Jan. 1, 1981; d. Dale E. and Joan B. Huston. BA, St. Bonaventure U., NY, 2001; JD, SUNY, Buffalo, 2004. Bar: NY. Assoc. Bly, Sheffield, Bargar Pillittieri & McCallum, Jamestown, 2004—. Treas., bd. dirs. Chautauqua Regional Youth Symphony, Jamestown, 2006—. Home: 426 Park St Jamestown NY 14701 Office: Bly Sheffield Bargar Pillittieri & MacCallum 3 Lakeview Ave Jamestown NY 14701

HUSTON, MARGO, journalist; b. Waukesha, Wis., Feb. 12, 1943; d. James and Cecile (Timlin) Bremner; m. James Huston, Dec. 9, 1967 (div.); 1 son, Sean Patrick. AB in Journalism, Marquette U., 1965. Editl. asst. Marquette U., Milw., 1965—66; feature editor, reporter Waukesha Freeman, Wis., 1966—67; feature reporter Milw. Jour., 1967—70, reporter Spectrum, women's and food sects., 1972—79, editl. writer, 1979—84, polit. reporter, 1984—, asst. picture editor, 1985—91, copy editor, 1992—95; reporter Milw. Jour Sentinel (merger Milw. Jour. and The Sentinel), 1995—99; mem. working bd. Cath. Herald, 2000—01; freelance journalist Milw., 2001—. Instr. mass comm. U. Wis., Milw. Mem. Milw. Restorative Justice Task Force, 2004. Recipient Penney-Mo. award for consumer abortion series, 1977, Pulitzer Prize for investigation into plight of elderly, 1977, Clarion award, 1977, Knight of Golden Quill award, Milw. Press club, 1977, Wis. AP writing award, 1977, Spl. award Milw. Soc. Profl. Journalists, 1977, Penney-Mo. Paul Myhre award for excellence, 1978, By-Line award Marquette U. Coll. Journalism, 1980, Wis. UPI Best Editl. award, 1982, Wis. Women's Network award for journalist achievement for women's issues, 1983, Dick Goldensohn Fund award, 1991, 1st place award for investigative reporting Inland Press Assn., 1997, 98, 2d award Enterprise interpretive reporting Wis. Newspaper Assn., 1998; Wis. Arts Bd. Lit. Arts grantee, 1992. Mem. European Project for Interreligious Learning (founder, cert. in Muslim-Christian Dialogue 2004), Milw. Press Club (Hall of Fame 2000). E-mail: margo.huston@gmail.com.

HUSTON, SAMUEL RICHARD, health facility executive; b. Newton, Iowa, Apr. 21, 1940; s. Marshall Dwight and Miriam Evelyn (Peake) H.; m. Ann M. Huston; children: Carmen Colleen, Christopher Dwight. BA, U. No. Iowa, 1962; MA, State U. Iowa, 1964. Asst. adminstr. med. ctr. Hosp. of Vt., Burlington, 1964-66; assoc. dir. No. New Eng. Regional Med. Program, Burlington, 1966-68; asst. adminstr. Univ. Hosp. Cleve., 1968-70, from assoc. adminstr. to exec. v.p., COO, 1972—86; assoc. dir. Duke Hosp., Durham, NC, 1970-72; pres., CEO Lehigh Valley Hosp. Ctr., Allentown, Pa., 1986—87, Allentown Hosp.-Lehigh Valley Hosp. Ctr., Pa., 1987—90; CEO Lehigh Valley Health Network, Lehigh Valley Hosp., Allentown, Pa., 1990—93; pres., CEO St. Luke's Med. Ctr., Cleve., 1994-97, St. Luke's Found. of Cleve., 1997-99; prin. Jay Alix and Assocs., 1999-2000; pres., CEO ViaHealth Sys., Rochester, NY, 2000—06; ret. Avocations: reading, music, hunting, golf. Home: 5 Roxbury Ln Pittsford NY 14534 E-mail: sam.huston@viahealth.org.

HUSTON, VELVALI DEAYXA, elementary school and voice educator; d. Armanda de Jesús and Maria Ayxa Mercado; m. Ralph Eugene Huston, III, Apr. 23, 1986; children: Jesse Aragon, Maxillian Frost. MusB, U. Pacific, Stockton, Calif., 1972; tchg. credential, Calif. State U. Monterey Bay, Marina, 1999. Vocal performer Hidden Valley Opera, Carmel Valley, Calif., 1973—83; pvt. English lang. tchr. to preschool thru music Hamburg, Germany, 1987—88; pvt. voice tchr. Gilroy H.S., Calif., 1990—93, Santa Catalina Sch., Monterey, Calif., 1990—98, Robert Louis Stevenson Sch., Pebble Beach, Calif., 1990—98; 1st grade bilingual tchr. Salinas City Elem. Sch. Dist., Calif., 1999—. Mem. fine arts com. Salinas City Elem. Sch. Dist., 2006. Named Outstanding Student Tchr., Delta Kappa Gamma Monterey Chpt., 1999. Mem.: Nat. Assn. Tchrs. Singing. Avocations: acting, singing, knitting, cultural anthropology. Home: 432 West St Salinas CA 93901

HUSTRULID, WILLIAM A., mining engineer, consultant; BS in Mineral Engrng., U. Minn., 1962, MS in Rock Mechanics, 1965, PhD in Rock Mechanics, 1968. Asst. prof. Colo. Sch. Mines, 1968—71, assoc. prof., 1971—72, prof. emeritus, 1994—; assoc. prof. U. Utah, 1974—76, prof., 1977—94, 2000—05, prof. emeritus mining engrng., 2005—; ind. cons. Hustrulid Mining Svcs., Bonita Springs, Fla., 2005—. Contbr. articles to sci. jours.; co-author: Open Pit Mine Planning & Design, 1994, Slope Stability in Surface Mining, 2001, Underground Mining Methods: Engineering Fundamentals and International Case Studies, 2001; author: Blasting Principles for Open Pit Mining, 1999. Mem.: Soc. Mining, Metallurgy and Exploration (Daniel C. Jackling award 2002), Royal Swedish Acad. Engrng. Scis. (fgn.), NAE. Office: Hustrulid Mining Svcs 333 Renaissance Blvd Bonita Springs FL 34134-7006 Office Phone: 239-947-0222. E-mail: whustrulid@aol.com.*

HUSZAGH, FREDRICK WICKETT, lawyer, information technology executive, educator; b. Evanston, Ill., July 20, 1937; s. Rudolph LeRoy and Dorothea (Wickett) H.; m. Sandra McRae, Apr. 4, 1959; children: Floyd McRae, Fredrick Wickett II, Theodore Wickett II. BA, Northwestern U., 1958; JD, U. Chgo., 1962, LLM, 1963, JSD, 1964. Bar: Ill. 1962, U.S. Dist. Ct. D.C. 1965, U.S. Supreme Ct. 1966. Market rschr. Leo Burnett Co., Chgo., 1958-59; internat. atty. COMSAT, Washington, 1964-67; assoc. Debevoise & Liberman, Washington, 1967-68; asst. prof. law Am. U., Washington, 1968-71; program dir. NSF, Washington, 1971-73; assoc. prof. U. Mont., Missoula, 1973-76, U. Wis., Madison, 1976-77; exec. dir. Dean Rusk Ctr., U. Ga., Athens, 1977-82; prof. U. Ga., 1982—2003, prof. emeritus, 2004—. Chmn. TWH Corp., Athens, 1982—; chmn. Profession Mgmt. Techs., Inc., Athens, 1993-96; cons. TWH Scv. Corp.; cons. Pres. Johnson's Telecommunications Task Force, Washington, 1967-68; co-chmn. Nat. Gov.'s Internat. Trade Staff Commn., Washington, 1979- 81. Author: International Decision-Making Process, 1964, Comparative Facts on Canada, Mexico and U.S., 1979; editor Rusk Ctr. Briefings, 1981-82; contbr. articles to publs. Mem. Econ. Policy Coun., N.Y.C., 1981-89. NSF grantee, 1974-78. Republican. Presbyterian. Office: U Ga Law Sch Athens GA 30602 Business E-Mail: huszagh@uga.edu.

HUSZAR, ANDREW LOUIS, school psychologist; b. Schenectady, NY, Apr. 23, 1974; s. Arthur Donald and Ruth Ann Huszar; 1 child, Kara A. AAS, Hudson Valley CC, 1999; BS in Social Work and Psychology summa cum laude, U. Albany, 2001; MS, Coll. St. Rose, 2004. Cert. sch. psychologist SUNY, 2004. Intern N.E. Parent and Child Soc., Schenectady, NY, 1998; intern Grant Pk. Sch., N.E. Parent and Child, Schenectady, NY, 1999; inter probation officer Rensselaer County Probation, Troy, NY, 2000—01; sch. psychologist Galway Ctrl. Sch., NY, 2003—. Club leader Banana Split (Galway Sch.), NY. Mem.: NASP, NY Assn. Sch. Psychologists, Phi Alpha. Home: 2966 Curry Rd Ext Schenectady NY 12303

HUSZAR, CARL GEORGE, social studies educator; b. Greensburg, Pa., Sept. 15, 1948; s. Edward George and Mary Jane Huszar; m. Kathleen Kovac, May 2, 1970; children: Stephanie Anne, Zachary Carl. BA, U. Pitts., 1970, EdM, 1976. Cert. secondary prin. U. Pitts., 1982, Letter of Eligibility U. Pitts., 1984. Tchr., social studies dept. chmn. Norwin Sch. Dist., North Huntingdon, Pa., 1974—, secondary asst. prin., 1985—87. Summ sch. prin. Westmoreland County C.C., Youngwood, Pa. Mem. cmty. affairs com. Norwin C. of C., Irwin, 1998—2006, mem. cmty. adv. bd., 1998—2005; mem. Lincoln Hwy. Heritage Corridor Com. for Westmoreland County, Ligonier, Pa., 2001—06; mem. cmty. adv. bd. Mercy-Jeannette Hosp., Pa., 2002—04; William Penn amb. 56th Ho. of Rep. Dist., North Huntingdon, Pa., 2000; pres. Norwin Hist. Soc., Irwin, 1995—2007. With US Army, 1971—73. Decorated Good Conduct medal US Army, Nat. Def. Svc. medal, Army Commendation medal; named Educator of Yr., Norwin Mid. Sch. East, 2002, Tchr. of Excellence Honoree, Tchr. Excellence Ctr., 2005—06; recipient Outstanding Tchr. Recognition award, St. Vincent Coll., 2005—06. Mem.: NEA, Nat. Coun. for the Social Studies, Norwin Edn. Assn., Early Am. Coppers, Am. Legion. Democrat. Roman Catholic. Avocations: basketball, baseball, coin collecting/numismatics, bicycling. Home: 10050 John Dr North Huntingdon PA 15642 Office: Norwin High School 251 Mc Mahon Dr North Huntingdon PA 15642 Home Phone: 724-863-0834; Office Phone: 724-861-3005.

HUT, A. STEPHEN, lawyer; b. Dec. 6, 1946; BA, Univ. Pa., 1968; JD magna cum laude, Harvard Univ., 1972. Bar: DC 1974. Ptnr., vice chmn. Litigation dept., co-chmn. pro bono & cmty. svc. com. Wilmer Cutler Pickering Hale & Dorr, Washington. Acting spl. asst. to gen. Counsel U.S. Dept. Def., Washington, 1977; trustee Council for Ct. Excellence, 1991—, mem. exec. com., 1994—98, 2001—. Editor (note): Harvard Law Rev.; contbr. articles to profl. jours. Mem.: Phi Beta Kappa. Office Phone: 202-663-6235. Office Fax: 202-663-6363. Business E-Mail: stephen.hut@wilmerhale.com.

HUTCHENS, JEROME ENOS, psychiatrist; b. Indpls., Aug. 12, 1929; s. Fay Enos Hutchens and Mary Elizabeth Duning; m. Eva Ruiz; children: Richard, James, Craig, Jay, Linda, Babetts, Marla. BA, Earlham Coll., Richmond, Ind., 1952; MD, U. Tex. Med. Sch., Galveston, 1956; post grad. in Radio Therapy, Vanderbilt U., Nashville, 1969, post grad. in Psychiatry, 1969—72. Lic. physician Tex., Mont., Ind., Ga., Wis., Idaho. Intern Madison Gen. Hosp. (now Meriter Hosp.), Wis., 1956—57; resident radiotherapy Vanderbilt U. Hosp., Nashville, 1968—69, resident psychiatry, 1969—72; pvt. practice gen. medicine Milw., 1956—68; pvt. practice psychiatry Nashville, 1972—73; forensic psychiatrist Fed. Correctional Inst., Ft. Worth, 1973—74; locum tenens emergency room physician Tex., 1974—77, Nev., 1974—77, Tenn., 1974—77; pvt. practice gen. medicine Houston, 1977—81; psychiatrist., med. dir. Brazos Valley Mental Health Mental Retardation, Bryan, 1986; adolescent psychiatrist Big Spring State Hosp., 1987—92; psychiatrist III Mental Health Mental Retardation Assn. Harris County, Houston, 1993—94; locum tenens physician gen. medicine Houston area, 1994—. Mem.: Am. Psychiatric Soc. Republican. Soc. Of Friends. Avocations: classical music, investments, exercise. Mailing: 7827 Prestwood Dr Houston TX 77036-2820

HUTCHENS, TYRA THORNTON, pathologist, educator; b. Newberg, Oreg., Nov. 29, 1921; s. Fred George and Bessie (Adams) H.; m. Betty Lou Gardner, June 7, 1942; children: Tyra Richard, Robert Jay, Rebecca (Mrs. Mark Pearsall). BS, U. Oreg., 1943, MD, 1945. Diplomate: Am. Bd. Pathology, Am. Bd. Nuclear Medicine. Intern Minn. Gen. Hosp., Mpls., 1945—46; AEC postdoctoral research fellow Reed Coll., Med. Sch. U. Oreg., 1948—50; NIH postdoctoral research fellow Med. Sch. U. Oreg., 1951—53; mem. faculty Oreg. Health Scis. U., 1953—, prof., chmn. dept. clin. pathology, 1962—87, prof. emeritus, 1987—, prof. radiotherapy, 1963—71, allied health edn. coord., 1969—77. Vis. lectr. radiobiology Reed Coll., 1955, 56 Contbr. articles to profl. jours. Mem. adv. bd. Oreg. Regional Med. Program, 1968-75; mem. statuatory radiation adv. com. Oreg. Bd. Health, 1957-69, chmn., 1967-69; founding trustee Am. Bd. Nuc. Medicine, 1971-77, 82-84, sec., 1973-75, 84-85; voting rep. Am. Bd. Med. Specialties, 1973-78, chmn. com. long range planning, 1976-78; mem. sci. adv. bd. Armed Forces Inst. Pathology, 1978-83; chmn. Portland Com. on Fgn. Affairs, 1990-91. Lt. (j.g.) M.C., USNR, 1946-48. Charter mem. Acad. Clin. Lab. Physicians and Scientists, Soc. Nuc. Medicine (de Hevesey Nuc. Medicine Pioneer award 1995), Am. Coll. Nuc. Physicians; mem. AMA, Oreg. Pathologists Assn. (pres. 1968), Pacific N.W. Soc. Nuc. Medicine (pres. 1958), Coll. Am. Pathologists (bd. govs. 1967-74, pres. 1977-79, chmn. commn. on internat. affairs 1979-83, chmn. planning com. 1987 World Congress Pathology), Am. Soc. Clin. Pathologists (bd. registry med. technologists 1967-71), World Assn. of Socs. of Pathology (bur. of pathology 1981-87, 89-93, v.p. 1985-87, pres. 1989-91, chmn. commn. on world stds. 1981-86, Gold Headed Cane award 1995), World Pathology Found. (pres. 1987-89, trustee 1989-91), Assn. Clin. Pathologists (hon.), Italian Soc. Lab. Medicine (hon.), Phi Beta Kappa, Sigma Xi, Alpha Omega Alpha. Achievements include research radioactive carbon tracer studies of lipid metabolism, clinical radioisotope techniques. Home: 17480 Holy Names Dr 413 Lake Oswego OR 97034 Personal E-mail: tyhutch@comcast.net.

HUTCHEON, DUNCAN ELLIOT, physician educator; b. Kindersley, Sask., Can., June 21, 1922; s. Robert Scott and Anne (McGibbon) H.; m. Jean-Marie Kirkby, June 7, 1946. MD, U. Toronto, Can., 1945, BSc in Medicine, 1947; DPhil, St. Catherine's, Oxford U., Eng., 1950. Diplomate Am. Bd. Internal Medicine, Am. Bd. Clin. Pharmacology. Intern Toronto Gen. Hosp., 1945-46; asst. prof. to prof. pharmacology and medicine Univ. Medicine and Dentistry N.J. Med. Sch., Newark, 1957-91, prof. emeritus, 1991—; pres. CINE, Inc., Comms. in Edn., Oak Park, Ill., 1991—. Editor: Jour. Clin. Pharmacology, 1978-85; contbr. to basic and clin. pharmacology. Mem. Drug Utilization Review Coun. NJ, 1977-86; pres. Inst. Sci. Edn. and Tech., 1999-2003; prodr., dir. Percy Julian Symposia Sci. Edn., 2000-03. Capt. Royal Can. Army Med. Corps, 1943—46. Fellow Nat. Rsch. Coun. Can., 1948-50. Fellow ACP, AAAS; Am. Coll. Clin. Pharmacology (founder, first pres. 1971-76), Sigma Xi. Office Phone: 708-383-2883. Personal E-mail: duncan.hutcheon@sbcglobal.net. Business E-Mail: cinechic@aol.com.

HUTCHEON, LINDA ANN, English language educator; b. Toronto, Aug. 24, 1947; d. Vincent Roy and Elisa (Rossi) Bulfon Bortolotti; m. Michael Alexander Hutcheon, May 30, 1970. BA, U. Toronto, 1969, PhD, 1975; MA, Cornell U., 1971. Prof. McMaster U., Hamilton, Ont., Canada, 1976-88, U. Toronto, 1988—95, 1995—. Vis. prof. U. Toronto, 1980-81, 81-82, 84-85, U. Wis., Madison, 1995, U. Ga., 1998, U. Queensland, Australia, 2001, U. Mich. Inst. for the Humanities, 2003. Author: Narcissitic Narrative, 1980 (choice award, 1980), Formalism and the Freudian Aesthetic, 1984, A Theory of Parody, 1985, 2000, A Poetics of Postmodernism, 1988, The Canadian Postmodern, 1988, The Politics of Postmodernism, 1989, 2002, Splitting Images, 1991, Irony's Edge, 1995, A Theory of Adaptation, 2006; author: (with M. Hutcheon) Opera: Desire, Disease, Death, 1996, Bodily Charm: Living Opera, 2000, Opera: The Art of Dying, 2004; assoc. editor: RS/SI, 1982—84, U. Toronto Quar., 1993—; mem. (editl. bd.) Texte, Toronto, 1983—, English Studies in Can., 1984—94, Italian Canadiana, 1984—, Textual Practice, 1987—2003, Can. Rev. Comparative Lit., 1987—, Can. Poetry, 1987—93, PMLA, 1990—92, Essays on Can. Writing, 1992—, Contemporary Lit., 1992—, Modern Fiction Studies, 1993—, CLIO, 1994—, Parallax (U.K.), 1994—. Recipient Killam prize Hunanities, 2005; Woodrow Wilson Found. fellow, 1969, Social Scis. and Humanities Rsch. Coun. Can. fellow, 1983, 93-95, 96-99, 2000-03, 04—, co-fellow maj. collaborative rsch. initiatives, 1996-2000; Can. Coun. fellow, 1972-75, Killam Found. fellow, 1978-80, 86-88, Connaught fellow, 1991-92, Guggenheim fellow, 1992-93. Fellow Am. Acad. Arts and Scis. (Killiam prize in humanities 2005); mem. MLA (del. assembly 1985-88, exec. coun. 1992-96, 2d v.p. 1998, 1st v.p. 1999, pres. 2000), AAAS (elected), Assn. Can. Coll. and Univ. Tchrs. English (exec. mem. 1978-81), Can. Comparative Lit. Assn. (sec.-treas. 1981-83), Internat. Comparative Lit. Assn. (coord. com. lit. history 1992-97) Home Phone: 416-604-9471; Office Phone: 416-978-6616.

HUTCHEON, PETER DAVID, lawyer; b. SI, NY, Sept. 11, 1943; s. Peter and Helen Christine (Buckley) H.; m. Elizabeth Ann Demy, June 8, 1969 (div. Jan. 1986); children: Rececca Leigh, Douglas Ian; m. Barbara Mary Silver, Feb. 14, 1986; 1 child, Peter Silver. BA, Williams Coll., 1965; postgrad., Ludwig-Maximilian Universitát, Munich, 1965-66; JD, Harvard U., 1969. Bar: N.Y. 1970, N.J. 1975. Assoc. White & Case LLP, NYC, 1968—75, Norris, McLaughlin & Marcus, P.A., Somerville, NJ, 1975—76, mem., 1976—. Chmn. N.J. Corp. and Bus. Law Study Commn., 1989—2001; mem., sec. adv. com. N.J. Bur. Securities, 1993—2001, chmn., 1994—2001. Contbr. articles to profl. jours. Chmn. bd. mgrs. St. Andrews Soc. of N.Y., 1986—87; deacon United Reformed Ch., Somerville, 1977—80; elder Bound Brook Presbyn. Ch., 1996—99. Dankstipendium scholar, Fed. Republic of Gemany Govt., 1965. Mem. ABA (chmn. sect. of sci. and tech. 1986-87, Martin I. Lubaroff award bus. law sect. 2005), N.J. State Bar Assn. (chmn. banking law sect. 1982-83, chmn. corp. and bus. sect. 1990-92), N.Y. State Bar Assn., German-Am. Lawyers Assn., Nat. Conf. of Lawyers and Scientists (del. 1988-91), Princeton Area Alumni Assn. of Williams Coll. (pres. 1981-89), Clan Donald (N.Y.). Avocations: wine tasting, singing. Office: Norris McLaughlin & Marcus PA PO Box 1018 721 Rt 202/206 Somerville NJ 08876 Office Phone: 908-722-0700 ext. 216. Business E-Mail: pdhutcheon@nmmlaw.com.

HUTCHEON, WALLACE SCHOONMAKER, historian, educator; b. NYC, June 27, 1933; s. Wallace Schoonmaker and Dorothy Mae (Tate) Hutcheon; m. Margaret Marie Crossen, Sept. 29, 1963; children: Dorothy Lee, Hillary Ann. BS in Agrl. Econs., Pa. State U., 1954; MA in History, George Washington U., 1969, MPhil in History, 1971, PhD in History, 1975. Commd. ensign USNR, 1955, advanced through grades to comdr., 1970; comm. officer Fawtulant Naval Air Sta., Key West, Fla., 1955-59; edn. officer USS Kitty Hawk, 1962-64; air intelligence officer CVW-2, 1964-66, intelligence analyst DIA, 1966-70; released to inactive duty, 1970; lectr. George Mason U., Fairfax, Va., 1970; instr. St. Marys Coll., Md., 1971; from asst. prof. to assoc. prof. history No. Va. CC, Annandale, 1971—80, prof., 1980—, head dept., 1974—, asst. chmn. divsn. social scis. and pub. svcs., 1979—2003, asst. dean Liberal Arts, 2003—. Mgmt. tng. cons. Health Resources Adminstn., HEW, Hyattsville, Md., 1978; cons. mil. evaluations program Am. Coun. Edn., Washington, 1980; cons. coll. history textbooks Houghton-Mifflin Co., Boston, 1992—; pub. spkr. Mariners Mus., DC Historian Luncheon, others. Mem. adv. bd. ann. edits. Dushkin Pub. Co.; author: Robert Fulton: Pioneer of Undersea Warfare, 1981; contbr. manuscripts collection to U.S. Navy History Divsn. Mem. History of City of Fairfax Roundtable, 1995—98; history day judge George Mason U., 1990—2002. Recipient Outstanding Contbns. to Edn. award, Alumni Fedn. No. Va. CC, 1993, 1995, 2003, Golden Apple award, Student Govt., 1999—2000. Mem.: U.S. Capitol Hist. Soc., No. Va. Assn. History (bd. dirs. 1994, v.p. 1994), Orgn. Am. Historians, U.S. Naval Inst., 1885 Club, Delta Chi. Democrat. Episcopalian. Avocations: swimming, reading, music, theater. Home: 4425 Village Dr Fairfax VA 22030-5642 Office: No Va CC 8333 Little River Tpke Annandale VA 22003-3743 Business E-Mail: whutcheon@nvcc.edu.

HUTCHER, NEIL EDWARD, surgeon; b. NYC, Dec. 31, 1941; MD, Med. Coll. Va., Richmond, 1965. Cert. Am. Bd. Surgery, 1974. Intern surgery Med. Coll. Va. Hosp., 1965—66, resident, 1968—72, fellow, 1970—72; clin. asst. prof. Va. Commonwealth U./Med. Coll. Va., Richmond, 1976—2002, clin. assoc. prof., 2003; staff mem. St. Mary's Hosp., Richmond, 1976, Henrico Drs. Hosp. - Forest, Richmond, 1976, Henrico Drs. Hosp. - Parham, Richmond, 1976, Retreat Hosp., Richmond, 1976, Chippenham/Johnston, Richmond, 1976; faculty mem. surgery Va. Commonwealth U./Med. Coll. Va. Hosps., Richmond, 1986, Hunter Holmes McGuire/Vets. Affairs Med. Ctr., Richmond, 1986; chmn. dept. surgery St. Mary's Hosp.; physician Commonwealth Surgeons, Ltd., Richmond. Featured: newspapers USA Today. Fellow: Am. Coll. Surgeons; mem.: AMA, Am. Bd. Surgery, Am. Soc. Bariatric Surgery (sr. past pres.). Office: Commonwealth Surgeons Ltd St Marys Med Bldg N 5855 Bremo Rd Ste 506 Richmond VA 23226-1925 Office Phone: 804-285-3225. Office Fax: 804-285-0360.

HUTCHESON, JACK ROBERT, hematologist, medical oncologist; b. Rock Hill, SC, Dec. 26, 1946; s. Jack Robert and Lillian Massey (Dunlap) H.; m. Charlene Marie Dixon, Sept. 14, 1974; children: Gregory Allen, Julia Lynn. BS in Biology, Wake Forest U., 1969; MD, Med. U. S.C., 1973. Diplomate in internal medicine, hematology, oncology Am. Bd. Internal Medicine. Straight med. intern U. Md. Hosp., Balt., 1973-74, resident in medicine, 1974-76; fellow in hematology Med. U. S.C., Charleston, 1976-78; fellow in oncology Emory U., Atlanta, 1978-79; oncologist, hematologist Oncology and Hematology Assocs. of S.W. Va. Inc., Roanoke, 1979—; med. dir. Carilion Health Sys. Oncology Svc. Line, Roanoke, 1996—. Instr., assoc. investigator in hematology Med. U. S.C./VA Hosp., Charleston, 1977-78; assoc. prof. medicine U. Va., Roanoke. Contbr. articles to med. jours. Pres. Scottish Soc. Va. Highlands, Roanoke, 1996, 2000, 01; chair com. on smoking cessation Va. br. Am. Cancer Soc., Roanoke, 1980; mem. Vets. Corps. of Artillary, N.Y. Decorated officer brother Most Venerable Order of Hosp. of St. John of Jerusalem, Caballero Grand Cruz Order Don Carlos I (Portugal); recipient Berson Yalow award, Soc. Nuclear Medicine, 1977; grantee for hematology, VA Career Devel., 1977—78. Fellow ACP; mem. Am. Soc. Clin. Oncology, Am. Soc. Hematology, St. Andrews Soc. Presbyterian. Avocations: Jaguar auto restoration, genealogy, Scottish/Celtic activities, bagpipes. Home: 2860 S Jefferson St Roanoke VA 24014-3320 Home Phone: 540-982-2430. Personal E-mail: jhut@aol.com. Business E-Mail: jack.hutchesonjr@usoncology.com.

HUTCHESON, JAMES STERLING, retired physician, allergist; b. Richmond, Va., Apr. 17, 1936; s. James P. and Daisy-Clarke (Lorentz) H.; m. Nancy Montgomery Sanders, May 20, 1961; children: Anne Farrar McCausland, Betsy Dulaney. Student, Roanoke Coll., Va., 1953-55; BA, U. Va., 1955-57; MD, The Johns Hopkins U., 1957-61. Diplomate Am. Bd. Allergy and Clin. Immunology. Intern in medicine U. Va., Charlottesville, Va., 1961-62; resident in medicine Med. Coll. Va., Richmond, Va., 1962-64; fellow in allergy and immunology U. Va., Charlottesville, Va., 1964-65; asst. prof. medicine Med. Coll. Va., 1967-68; staff Nalle Clinic, Charlotte, 1968-89; pvt. practice Carolina Asthma and Allergy Ctr., 1990—2005, ret., 2005. Founder Allergy Clinic USAF Acad. Hosp., Colo., 1965-67; cons. Blue Cross/Blue Shield of NC, 1985-2002; adj. assoc. prof. pediats. U. NC Sch. Medicine, Carolinas Med. Ctr., Charlotte, 1997-2000. Bd. trustees Charlotte County Day Sch., 1974-85; bd. dirs. Friends of Music Queens Coll., 1994-96. Capt. USAF M.C. Fellow Am. Acad. Allergy, Asthma and Immunology, Am. Coll. Allergy, Asthma and Immunology; mem. Southeastern Allergy Assn., NC Soc. Allergy and Clin. Immunology (former pres.). Episcopalian. Avocations: gardening, hiking, classical music, reading. Home: 334 Green Cove Rd Sugar Mountain Banner Elk NC 28604 Personal E-mail: sthutch@skybest.com.

HUTCHESON, JERRY DEE, manufacturing company executive; b. Oct. 31, 1932; s. Radford Andrew and Ethel Mae (Boulware) H.; m. Lynda Lou Weber, Mar. 6, 1953; children: Gerald Dan, Lisa Marie, Vicki Lynn. BS in Physics, Ea. N.Mex. U., 1965; postgrad., Temple U., 1962, U. N.Mex., 1965. Registered profl. engr., Calif. Rsch. engr. RCA, 1959—62; sect. head Motorola, 1962—63; rsch. physicist Dikewood Corp., 1963—66; sr. mem. tech. staff Signetics Corp., 1966—69; engrng. mgr. Litton Sys., Sunnyvale, Calif., 1969—70, Fairchild Semiconductor, Mountain View, Calif., 1971; equipment engr., group mgr. Teledyne Semiconductor, Mountain View, 1971—74; dir. engring. DCA Reliability Labs., Sunnyvale, 1974—75; founder, prin. Tech. Ventures, San Jose, Calif., 1975—; CEO VLSI Rsch., Inc., San Jose, 1981—, chmn., 2004—. Contbr. articles to profl. jours. Dem. precinct committeeman, Albuquerque, 1964—66. With USAF, 1951—55. Mem.: NSPE, Am. Soc. Test Engrs., Soc. Photo-Optical Instrumentation Engrs., Semiconductor Equipment and Materials Inst., Calif. Soc. Profl. Engrs., Profl. Engrs. Pvt. Practice, Masons. Presbyterian. Office: VLSI Rsch 2880 Lakeside Dr 350 Santa Clara CA 95054-2822 Office Phone: 408-453-8844.

HUTCHESON, MARK ANDREW, lawyer; b. Phila., Mar. 29, 1942; s. John R. and Mary Helen (Willis) H.; m. Julie A. Olander, June 13, 1964; children: Kirsten Elizabeth, Mark Andrew II, Megan Ann. BA, U. Puget Sound, 1964; LLB, U. Wash., 1967. Bar: Wash. 1967, U.S. Dist. Ct. (we. and ea. dists.) Wash., U.S. Ct. Appeals (9th cir.), U.S. Supreme Ct. Staff counsel Com. on Commerce U.S. Senate, Washington, 1967-68; assoc. Davis Wright Tremaine, Seattle, 1968-72; ptnr. Davis, Wright Tremaine, Seattle, 1973—; mng. ptnr., chief exec. officer Davis Wright Tremaine, Seattle, 1989-94; chmn. Davis, Wright Tremaine, Seattle, 1994—. Mem., co-founder labor law com. Nat. Banking Industry, 1984—. Co-author: Employer's Guide to Strike Planning and Prevention, 1986; contbr. articles to profl. jours. Chmn., trustee Virginia Mason Hosp., Seattle, 1980-2003, Overlake Sch., Redmond, Wash., 1984-89, Epiphany Sch., Seattle, 1982-84, Legal Aid for Wash. Fund, 1991-2003; bd. dirs. Vis. Nurse Svcs., Seattle-King County, 1985-88; trustee Pacific N.W. Ballet, 1991-99, Pacific N.W. Assn. Ind. Schs., 1996-98. Nelson T. Hartson scholar U. Wash., 1966; Deerfield fellow Heritage Found., Deerfield, Mass., 1963. Mem. ABA (health care forum, employment law sect.), Seattle-King County Bar Assn. (employment law sect.), Am. Acad. Hosp. Attys., Am. Hosp. Assn. (labor rels. adv. com. 1978—), Coll. Labor and Employment Lawyers, Greater Seattle C. of C. (bd. dirs. 1991-94), Rainier Club, Seattle Tennis Club, Univ. Club, Order of Coif. Episcopalian. Avocations: sailing, tennis, skiing, reading, travel. Office: Davis Wright Tremaine 1201 3rd Ave Ste 2200 Seattle WA 98101-3045 Office Phone: 206-628-7678, 206-757-8065. Business E-Mail: markhutcheson@dwt.com.

HUTCHESON, THOMAS WORTHINGTON, trade association administrator; b. Lake Forest, Ill., July 1, 1958; s. Harold Randolph and Minna Margaret (Adams) Hutcheson. BA, U. Mass., 1980, MEd, 1987, EdD, 1993. Instr. edn. U. Mass., Amherst, 1987-89, v.p. Grad. Student Senate, 1988-89, rsch. asst. dept. econs., 1989-91; rsch. cons. Nat. Priorities Project, Northampton, Mass., 1991-92; estate cons. Sandwich, Mass., 1996-99; music critic The Recorder, Greenfield, Mass., 1996-99; project coord. Bonnyvale Environ. Edn. Ctr., Brattleboro, Vt., 1996-99, cons., 1992; policy asst. Organic Trade Assn., Greenfield, Mass., 1999-2000, policy coord., 2000—02, assoc. policy dir., 2002—06, regulatory and policy mgr., 2006—. Musician; arranger choral work: Welcome, Yule!, 1994—; dir.: Shapeshifters Vocal Quartet, 1997—2001, 2004—; contbr. articles to profl. jours. Chmn. Pub. Transp. Com., Amherst, 1989—90; mem. Franklin Regional Planning Bd., Greenfield, 1993—, chmn., 2002—06, mem. local emergency planning com., 2002—04; mem. Overall Econ. Devel. Program Policy Com., Greenfield, 1996—99, Greater Franklin Regional Comprehensive Econ. Devel. Strategy Com., 1999—, mem. governing bd., 2004—; chmn. Com. Elec. Industry Deregulation, Greenfield, 1996—99. Mem.: Am. Soc. Assn. Execs., Am. Planning Assn. Democrat. Mem. Soc. Of Friends. Avocations: Morris dance, traditional music. Home: 21 Madison Cir Greenfield MA 01301-2723 Office: Organic Trade Assn 60 Wells St Greenfield MA 01301-9654 Personal E-mail: thutcheson@ota.com.

HUTCHINGS, GEORGE HENRY, food company executive; b. Fort Worth, June 23, 1922; s. George H. and Emma (Harder) H.; m. Edith Van Gils, Mar. 23, 1946 (dec.); children: Mark Dennis Lisa Ellen; m. Elizabeth T. Storey, Apr. 10, 1968 (dec.). Student, Tex. A&M, 1940-42. Analyst mktg. research Frito Food Mfg., Dallas, 1946, mgr. mktg. research Los Angeles, 1946-57, div. sales mgr. San Mateo, Calif., 1958-60, div. gen. mgr., 1961, v.p., 1961-62; v.p. for ops. Western zone, 1962—; pres. Nalley's, Inc., Tacoma, 1964, Nalley's div. W.R. Grace & Co., 1966—, ret. Tacoma, 1972-81; pres. Wash. Beverages, Inc., Tacoma, 1972-81. Dir., mem. exec. com. Puget Sound Nat. Bank, Tacoma; cons. 1964-83; dir. mem. examining com. Key Bank of Wash., Tacoma, 1993-94, ret., 1994. Served to capt. USAAF, 1942-46. Decorated D.F.C., Air medal with 7 clusters. Mem. Masons. Baptist. Home: 7419 North St SW Tacoma WA 98498-5213 *A man must know what he stands for before he can logically take a stand against anything.*

HUTCHINGS, JOHN BARRIE, astronomer, researcher; b. Johannesburg, July 18, 1941; arrived in Can., 1967; BSc, Witwatersrand U., Johannesburg, 1962, MSc, 1964; PhD, U. Cambridge, Eng., 1967. Rsch. scientist Dominion Astrophysics Obs., NRC Can., Victoria, B.C., Canada, 1967—. Author numerous rsch. papers and revs., 1964—. Recipient Gold medal Sci. Coun. B.C., 1983, Royal Jubilee medal, 2002. Fellow Royal Soc. Can.; mem. Internat. Astron. Union, Am. Astron. Soc., Can. Astron. Soc. (Beals award 1982). Office: Dominion Astrophysics Obs 5071 W Saanich Rd Victoria BC Canada V9E 2E7 Home Phone: 250-656-5457; Office Phone: 250-363-0018. E-mail: john.hutchings@nrc.ca.

HUTCHINGS, PETER LOUNSBERY, retired insurance company executive, director; b. NYC, Nov. 1, 1943; s. Robert Spaulding and Kathryn Eleanor (Lounsbery) H.; m. Marsha Kayser, May 27, 1966 (div. 1980); children: Michael, Daniel; m. Martha Deborah Wolfgang, Jan. 16, 1983 BA, Yale U., 1964. CLU, ChFC, FSA. Mem. actuarial program MONY, NYC, 1964-68, dir. group systems, 1969, asst. v.p., 1970-73; v.p., actuary Blue Cross and Blue Shield of Greater N.Y., NYC, 1973-77, sr. v.p., 1977-83; ptnr. Kwasha Lipton, Fort Lee, N.J., 1983-87; exec. v.p., CFO Guardian Life Ins. Co. Am., NYC, 1987—2001. Pres. bd dirs. 300 CPW Corp., 1995-98; pres., bd. dirs. Park Ave. Life (Guardian sub.), 1998-2001, Vis. Nurse Svc. of N.Y., 1999—; bd. dirs. Well Choice. Active 14th St. Bus. Improvement Dist., N.Y.C., 1992-99, pres., 1995-99; bd. dirs. 14th St.-Union Sq. Local Devel. Corp., 1993-99, Children's Orch. Soc., 1999—, Downtown Alliance, 2000-02, Rubin Mus. Art, 2002—; mem. N.Y. Organ Donor Network, 2002—, Friends of Wertheim Nat. Wildlife Refuge, 1999-2002. Fellow Soc. Actuaries; mem. Am. Acad. Actuaries, Actuarial Soc. Greater N.Y. (pres. 1992-93), Med. Health and Rsch. Assn. Avocations: photography, music, travel. Home: 300 Central Park W Apt 14B New York NY 10024-1513 E-mail: mdwplh@mac.com.

HUTCHINS, DIANE ELIZABETH RIDER, librarian; b. Kearny, NJ, June 25, 1951; d. Thomas Lindsay and Dorothy Jane (Sommer) Rider; m. Clifford James Hutchins, Feb. 14, 2002. MusB magna cum laude, Westminster Choir Coll., 1973; MLS, Fla. State U., 1993. Intern preservation dept. U. Fla., Gainesville, 1993; intern free-net libr. Tallahassee Free-Net, 1993; reference libr. Broward County Main Libr., Ft. Lauderdale, Fla., 1994-95; libr., instr. Art Inst. Ft. Lauderdale, 1995-96, dir. Learning Resource Ctr., 1996-98; dean Nevin C. Meinhardt Meml. Libr., 1998-99; collection devel. coord. Washington State Libr., Olympia, 1999—2002, program mgr. collection mgmt., 2002—06, program mgr. for preservation and access svcs., 2006—. Vice chair, assoc. mem. com. S.E. Fla. Libr. Info. Network, 1996-97, chair assoc. mem. com., 1997-98, ex officio mem. bd. dirs. S.E. Fla. Libr. Info. Network, 1996-99; spl. librs. rep. Fla. Libr. Network Coun., 1998-99. Soloist St. Paul's Chapel, Columbia U., N.Y.C., 1973, Ch. of St. Mary the Virgin, N.Y.C., 1974. Recipient Outstanding Leadership award Wash. State Libr., 2000; Fla. State U. fellow, 1993-94, Coll. Tchg. fellow, 1992-93; Louis Shores scholar, 1992-93. Mem. Spl. Librs. Assn. (dir. Fla. and Caribbean chpt. 1997-99, Fla. rep., steering com. South Atlantic Regional conf. 1997-99), New Eng. Hist. Geneal. Soc., Geneal. Soc. Southwestern Pa., Geneal. Soc. of N.J., Phi Kappa Phi, Beta Phi Mu. Avocations: cooking, genealogy, gardening, reading. Office: The Wash State Libr Office of Sec of State PO Box 42460 Olympia WA 98504-2460 Office Phone: 360-704-7137. Business E-Mail: dhutchins@secstate.wa.gov.

HUTCHINS, JOAN MORTHLAND, manufacturing executive, farmer; b. Pasadena, Calif., Aug. 8, 1940; d. Andrew and Constance Amelia (Gordon-Grant) Morthland; children: Andrew E. Bush, Georgia R. Bush, Alan S., Paul M. AB, Radcliffe Coll., 1961; degree (hon.), Royal Coll. Music, London, 1979; AAS, SUNY, Farmingdale, 1985. Jr. mathematician Shell Devel. Co. (Shell Oil), Emeryville, Calif., 1961-63; mathematician Corp. for Econ. and Indsl. Rsch., London, 1964-65; mgmt. cons. McKinsey & Co., NYC, 1965-67; v.p. devel. Compotite Corp., LA, 1985-87, pres., 1987-89, pres., CEO, 1989—. MBH Farms, Inc., Elizaville, NY, 1986-2001, chmn., 2001—. Editor McKinsey & Co. Mgmt. Scis. News Bull., 1965-67; contbr. articles to profl. jours. Mem. bd. overseers Harvard U., Cambridge, Mass., 1994—2000, pres., 1999—2000, mem. overseers vis. com. Harvard athletic dept., 1986—91, mem. overseers vis. com. Arnold Arboretum, 1995—2004, chmn., 1997—2004, mem. overseers vis. com. Harvard Grad. Sch. Edn., 1995—, vice chmn., 2003—, mem. overseers vis.

com. Harvard music dept., mem. nominating com. for overseers and HAA dirs., 2000—04; mem. adv. bd. Harvard U. Com. on Environment, 2001—04; bd. dirs., v.p. Royal Music Found., NYC, 1978—90; trustee Bowdoin Coll. Summer Music Festival, Brunswick, Maine, 1978—88, L.I. Biol. Assn., Cold Spring Harbor, NY, 1986—88. Recipient Harvard medal, 2004. Mem. Am. Nat. Stds. Inst. (nat. waterproofing stds. com. 1988—), Harvard Alumni Assn. (bd. dirs. 1990-93, nominating com. overseers and dirs., 2000-03), Harvard-Radcliffe Club LI (pres. 1988-90). Avocations: skiing, music, sports, ice hockey, travel. Office: Compotite Corp 355 Glendale Blvd Los Angeles CA 90026-5032

HUTCHINS, LAURA FULPER, physician, medical educator; b. Trenton, NJ, 1952; MD, U. Ark., 1977. Diplomate Am. Bd. Internal Medicine, Am. Bd. Med. Oncology, Am. Bd. Hematology. Intern, then resident in internal medicine U. Ark., Little Rock, 1977-80, fellow in hematologic oncology, 1980-83; mem. staff Univ. Hosp., Little Rock; prof. medicine U. Ark. Med. Scis., Little Rock, dir., divsn hematology/oncology, Virginia Clinton Kelly Endowed Chair for Clin. Breast Cancer Rsch. Contbr. articles to profl. jours. Mem. Am. Soc. Hematology, Am. Soc. Clin. Oncology. Office: Univ Ark Med Scis 4301 W Markham St Little Rock AR 72205-7101 Office Phone: 501-686-8511. Business E-Mail: hutchinslauraf@uams.edu.*

HUTCHINS, MICHAEL, non-profit scientific society administrator, conservation biologist; b. Algona, Iowa, May 20, 1951; s. Russell Duane and Elaine June (Norlin) H.; m. Song Hui Choe, May 20, 2000; children: Alexandra Lin, Fascione-Hutchins, Shani Else, Chantal Else. BS in Psychology and Anthropology, U. Wash., 1975, postgrad., 1979, PhD in Animal Behavior Psychology, 1984. Grad. instr. U. Wash., Seattle, 1979-84, acting asst. prof., 1984—85; curatorial intern mammalogy N.Y. Zool. Soc., Bronx, 1986-87, conservation biologist, 1987-88; coord. rsch. Bronx Zoo/N.Y. Zool. Park, Bronx, 1988-90; dir. conservation and sci., William Conway chair Am. Zoo and Aquarium Assn., Silver Spring, Md., 1990—2005; exec. dir. ZooThink, Inc., 2006—. Assoc. adj. prof. grad. program in conservation biology and sustainable devel., U. Md., College Park, 1994—; sr. fellow Ctr. for Conservation and Behavior, Dept. of Pschology, Ga. Inst. Tech., 2005—; exec. dir., CEO The Wildlife Soc., Bethesda, Md., 2005—; cons. Disney Wildlife Conservation Fund and Animal Kingdom Project; active World Conservation Union's Species Survival Commn. Invasive Species and Conservation Breeding Specialist Groups; adv. bd. Ency. The World's Zoos; co-chmn. Bushmeat Crisis Task Force, 1999-2004, Butterfly Conservation Initiative, 2002-05, Human-Wildlife Conflict Collaboration, 2006—. Author, editor: Ethics on the Ark: Zoos, Animal Welfare and Wildlife Conservation, 1996, Second Nature: Environmental Enrichment for Captive Animals, 1997, Great Apes and Humans: Ethics of Co-Existence, 2001; primary editor: Smithsonian Press Book Series-Zoo and Aquarium Biology and Conservation, 1995-2004, Johns Hopkins U. Press, 2005—; series editor Grzimek's Animal Life Ency., 17 vols., 2003; assoc. editor Zoo Biology, 1990—; editor Internat. Zoo Yearbook, 2005—; contbr. articles to profl. jours. Bd. dirs. Renewable Nat. Resource Found., Bethesda, Md. Named Alumnus of Yr., Highline CC, Midway, Wash., 1992; grantee NSF, Washington, 1996, Nat. Fish and Wildlife Found., Washington, 1996; field assoc., conservation fellow NY Zool. Soc., Bronx, 1990. Mem. AAAS, Wildlife Soc., Am. Zoo and Aquarium Assn. (profl. assoc.), Soc. for Conservation Biology, Coun. Engring. and Sci. Soc. Execs. Democrat. Avocations: photography, paleontology, hiking, travel, scuba diving. Office: The Wildlife Soc 5410 Grosvenor Ln Ste 200 Bethesda MD 20814-2144 Home Phone: 301-625-9545; Office Phone: 301-897-9770. Personal E-mail: michael@wildlife.org.

HUTCHINS, ROBERT AYER, architectural consultant; b. NYC, Oct. 19, 1940; s. Robert Senger and Evelyn Reed (Brooks) Hutchins; m. Saran Niel Morgan, Jan. 4, 1964; children: Amey, Elisabeth, Margaret. BA, Harvard U., 1962, MArch, 1965; MDiv, McCormick Theol. Sem., 1992. Cert. Nat. Coun. Archtl. Registration Bds., 1976; lic. architect, Ill. Architect Skidmore, Owings & Merrill, Chgo., 1966—89, ptnr., 1980—89. Pres. Chgo. Architecture Found., 1983—86, v.p., 1986—89. Housing adv. Protestants for the Common Good, 2000—02; bd. dirs. Lincoln Park Zool. Soc., Chgo., 1976—91; bd. govs. Met. Planning Coun., Chgo., 1977—2004; bd. trustees McCormick Theol. Sem., 1990—91. Mem.: AIA (corp.), Chgo. Presbytery Property Ministries, Chgo. Cultural Affairs Adv. Bd. (vice chmn. 1984—90).

HUTCHINS, TRAVER, publishing executive; B in History and Econs., U. Minn. Advt. salesman Working Mother; with Sassy, Success, Working Woman; mgr. corp. sales Lang Comm.; pres., CEO, founder MediZine, Inc., NYC, 1997—. Office: Medizine Inc 500 5th Ave # 19 New York NY 10110-0002 Office Phone: 212-695-5581. Office Fax: 212-695-2936. E-mail: traver@medizine.com.*

HUTCHINSON, (W.) ASA, lawyer, former federal agency administrator; b. Bentonville, Ark., Dec. 3, 1950; s. John M. and Coral (Mount) Hutchinson; m. Susan Burrell; children: Asa III, Sarah, John, Seth. BS in Acctg., Bob Jones U., 1972; JD, U. Ark., 1975. Bar: Ark., US Supreme Ct., US Ct. Appeals (5th and 8th cirs.). City atty. City of Bentonville, Ark., 1977—78; US atty. (we. dist. Ark.) US Dept. Justice, 1982-85, adminstr. Drug Enforcement Adminstrn. Washington, 2001—03; ptnr. Karr & Hutchinson, Ft. Smith, Ark., 1986-96; mem. US Congress from 3rd Ark. dist., 1996—2001; under sec. for border and transp. security US Dept. Homeland Security, Washington, 2003—05; co-founder Hutchinson Group, LLC, Little Rock, 2005—; ptnr., chair litig. divsn. Venable LLP, Washington, 2005—. Judiciary com. US Congress, subcommittee crime, subcommittee constn., transp. and infrastructure com., subcommittee Water Resources and Environment, subcommittee aviation, intelligence com., ethics com., intellectual property subcommittee; co-chair Freshmen Bipartisan Campaign Fin. Reform Task Force; apptd. to Spkrs. Task Force for Drug-Free Am.; chmn., Ark. State Rep. Com., 1990-95; past mem. Ark. Jud. Ethics Commn., Ark. Election Commn., Ark. Election Law Revision Commn.; condr. democracy workshops in Russia, 1994; del. White House Conf. Aging, 1995; past bd. mem. Western Ark. chpt. Alzheimer's Assn.; mem. bd. dirs. SAFLINK Corp., 2005-, CEO Hutchinson Grp, Little Rock, Ark. Named one of Ten Outstanding Young Leaders in Ark., Ark. Jaycees, 1986. Republican. Office: Venable LLP 575 Seventh St NW Washington DC 20004 Office Phone: 202-344-4000. E-mail: ahutchinson@venable.com.

HUTCHINSON, DOUGLAS K., chemist; BS in Chemistry, Rose-Hulman Inst. Tech., Terre Haute, Ind., 1977; MS in Organic Chemistry, Ohio State Univ., 1980; PhD in Organic Chemistry, Purdue Univ., 1987. Rsch. investigator Abbott Lab., Abbott Park, Ill. Co-recipient Fred Kagan Lead Finding award, 1995. Mem.: Am. Chem. Soc. (Award for Team Innovation 2007, 31st Northeast Regional Indsl. Innovation award 2003). Achievements include recipient 12 US patents inc. being co-inventor of linezolid, which became the basis of Zyvox. Office: Abbott Laboratories 100 Abbott Park Rd North Chicago IL 60064-3500 Office Phone: 847-937-6100.*

HUTCHINSON, DOUGLAS TRUMAN, surgeon; b. Ann Arbor, Mich., Mar. 28, 1958; s. Harry D. and Betty L. Hutchinson; children: Eric, Steven. BS in Engring., U. Mich., Ann Arbor, 1980; MD, Jefferson Med. Coll., Phila., 1984. Assoc. prof. U. Utah Orthopaedic Ctr., Salt Lake City, 1990—. Dir. hand and micorsurgery fellowship U. Utah, Dept. Orthopaedics, 1997—; dir. sect. hand surgery Veteran's Adminstrn. Med. Ctr., Salt Lake City, 1991—, Shriners Hosp. Crippled Children, Salt Lake City, 1994—; adj. assoc. prof. U. Utah, Coll. Engring., 1998—, U. Utah Health Scis. Ctr. Phys. Therapy, 1998—, U. Utah Health Scis. Ctr. Divsn. Pediat., 2002—. Physician Interplast, Inc., Mountain View, Calif., 1998—2002. Mem.: Utah Med. Soc., Utah Orthopaedic Soc. (founding mem. 2001), Assn. Fellowship Directors, Jefferson Orthopaedic Soc., Internat. Wrist Investigators Workshop, Orthopaedics Overseas, Am. Soc. Surgery of the Hand, Salt Lake County Med. Soc., Am. Acad. Orthopaedic Surgeons, Shriners Hand Surgeons. Office: University of Utah Orthopaedic Center 590 Wakara Way Salt Lake City UT 84108 Home Phone: 801-278-3150; Office Phone: 801-587-5453. Office Fax: 801-587-5411.

HUTCHINSON, EDNA M., home care nurse; b. Phoenix, Mar. 13, 1940; d. William Henry and Mary L. Hutchinson; children: Wendell, Antoinette, Lynette, Mary Maxine. Cert., San Diego C.C., 1981, Grossmont C.C., El Cajon, Calif., 1988. Cert. electrocardiographic technologist, Calif.; sec. sci. lab. Calif. Nurse asst., Phoenix, 1965—66, San Diego, 1966—69; med. asst. Med. Clinic, San Diego, 1980—85; electrocardiogram tech. Maricopa County Hosp., Phoenix, 1989—91; home care nurse Home Health Care, San Diego, 1991—. Songwriter Hill Top Records, Hollywood, Calif., 2000—. Author: (book) Inspiration Songs and Poems, 2000; songwriter In the Beginning, 2000, Jesus in the Inside, 2000; author: Etches in Time, 1997, (songs) God Creation, 2000; co-author: Best Poems and Poets, 2000, Poetry's Elite's Best Poets of 2001, 2001; contbr. over 400 poems to pubs. Daycare provider County of Riverside, Calif., 2001. Finalist Top Model, San Diego, Calif., 1976; named Ten Best Dressed, 1983; recipient Editor's Choice award for Outstanding Achievement in Poetry, State of Md., 1997, Poet of Merit award, Internat. Soc. Poets, 1997, Achievement award, Creative Writing Skills, 1999, Cert., Wall of Tolerance Nat. Campaign, 2001. Avocations: reading, music, songwriting.

HUTCHINSON, JAMES S. (JAMIE), lawyer; b. Detroit, June 26, 1952; BA, St. Lawrence Univ., 1974; JD, Vanderbilt Univ., 1979. Bar: Ga. 1979, DC 2000. Joined Alston & Bird LLP, 1979, ptnr., leader, employee benefits, exec. compensation group Washington. Staff mem. Vanderbilt Law Rev., 1977—78, exec. articles editor, 1978—79. Exec. bd. Literacy Action, Inc. Fellow: Am. Coll. Employee Benefits Counsel; mem.: ABA, Phi Beta Kappa. Office: Alston & Bird LLP 10th Fl North Bldg 601 Pennsylvania Ave Washington DC 20042-2601 Office Phone: 202-756-3359. Office Fax: 202-756-3333. Business E-Mail: jhutchinson@alston.com.

HUTCHINSON, LESLIE JULIAN, preventive medicine physician; b. Cin., June 22, 1957; s. Joseph Edward and Evelyn (Moss) H.; m. Stephanie Ellyn Leffingwell, Dec. 22, 1989. BS, Xavier U., 1978; MD, U. Cin. Coll. of Medicine, 1984; MPH, The Johns Hopkins U., 1990. Diplomate in occupl. medicine Am. Bd. Preventive Medicine; MD, Calif., Ga.; registered hazardous substances profl. Chemist EPA, Cin., 1982; Ctrs. for Disease Control vis. program staff fellowship Nat. Inst. for Occupl. Safety and Health, Cin., 1984; resident in internal medicine Wright State U., Dayton, Ohio, 1984-85; med. officer Agy. for Toxic Substances and Disease Registry, Atlanta, 1986-92; occupl. medicine resident Emory U., Atlanta, 1992-93; adj. assoc. prof. environ. and occupl. health Emory U. Sch. Pub. Health, Atlanta, 1990—; pres. HLM Consultants, Atlanta, 1993—. On-site peer reviewer Tex. Air Control Bd., Galveston, 1987-88; mem. Emory U. Acad. Adv. Coun. on Occupl. and Environ. Health, Atlanta, 1989—; v.p., chief med. officer Internat. Inst. Environ. Risk Mgmt., U. S.W. Tex., San Marcos, 1997—. Contbr. articles to profl. jours. Instr. med. coll. admission text preparation program for minority students Atlanta U., 1987-90. Recipient Performance Mgmt. and Recognition System award Dept. Health and Human Svcs., 1989, Spl. Act or Svc. award Dept. of Health and Human Svcs., 1992, Xavier U. Achievement and Nat. Merit scholarships, Xavier Biology prize. Mem. Nat. Environ. Health Assn., Delta Omega, Alpha Omega Alpha, Sigma Pi Sigma. Avocations: photography, oriental philosophy. Office: HLM Consultants 214 Wynfield Way Auburn GA 30011-2849 Personal E-mail: hlm@mindspring.com. Business E-Mail: hlm@hlmconsultants.com.

HUTCHINSON, LYNDA RONETTE (BILLIE HOLIDAY JR., PRINCESS OF JAZZ, MUNCHIE), vocalist, musician, comedian, actress; b. Queens, NY, Dec. 28, 1965; d. Roy Radcliff and Rachel Isabella (Outten) Hutchinson; children: Myisha Daunique Odom, Zaire chase Arzelle. Student, L.I. U., Bklyn., 1991—96. Founder, CEO Diva Soul Records, 2003—. Singer: (performer) Empire Tech. Sch., 1989, L.I. U., 1991, Two Steps Down Jazz Club, 1992—94, Titus Walker's Ujjaama Black Theatre, 1991, St. Nick's Pub, 2000—, Apollo Theatre, 2000, 2001, Lenox Lounge Jazz Club, 2002—, Cotton Club, 2002—, (contestant) Showtime at the Apollo, 1994, Sylvia's 30 Anniversary, 1993; performer: TV show The Cut, 2005, radio; author: (book of poetry) Lend Me Your Ear, 1992; singer: (performance) Ciprianis, 2005, Bet at the Cotton Club, 2006; prodr., performer: CD Princess Billie Live at the Lenox Lounge, 2006. Participant Nat. Action Network Freedom March, 1993. Finalist NYC Housing Authority Talent Search, 1998; recipient Cert. achievement, Internat. Mannequins, Inc., 1995, Certification award, Project Enterprise, 2002, Mel Edwards award, 2003. Mem.: Harlem Arts Alliance, New Amsterdam Musical Assn. Home: Apt 16-G 2370 First Ave New York NY 10035 Personal E-mail: divasoulrecords@hotmail.com.

HUTCHINSON, MICHAEL PHILIP, education educator; b. Canadian, Tex., Mar. 31, 1970; s. Albert and Genevieve Raparata Hutchinson; m. Kittie Leigh Hutchinson, Dec. 17, 2004; 1 stepchild, Claude Clayton Emory Sewell IV;children from previous marriage: Alisa Marie, Genevieve Shea-Leigh 1 stepchild from previous marriage, Robert Emmett Spoon. Student, Macon State Coll., 1990—92, U. Ga., 2000, Acad. Health Scis., 2005—. Cert. CPR instr., registered EMT. With Houston Med. Ctr., Warner Robins, Ga., 1990, Med. Ctr. Ctrl. Ga., Macon, 1991—92; nursing asst. Caremasters Med. Svcs., Griffin, Ga., 1994—95, AA Quality Care, Inc., Macon, 1995—96, Tender Loving Care, Inc., Macon, 1996; rehab. nurse tech. Healthsouth-Ctrl. Ga. Rehab. Hosp., Macon, 1996; surg. tech., attendant maintenance and housekeeping Piedmont Sports Medicine and Orthop. Complex: Surgery Ctr., Macon, 1996—2002; health occupations faculty, adv. Sandersville (Ga.) Tech. Coll., 2002—03; surg. tech. Field Foot and Ankle Clinic, Griffin, 2003—04; health occupations faculty Mary Persons HS, 2004—, Ctrl. Ga. Tech. Coll., 2004—. With USNG, sgt. US Army, 2005—06. Decorated Achievement medal U.S. Army, Army Commendation medal; recipient Cert. of Recognition, Sec. Def., 1991, Cert. of Excellence, Ga. Army N.G., 1999, Cert. of Appreciation, Med. Ednl. Devel., Inc., 2000, NATO medal, Sec. Gen., 2001. Office Phone: 478-992-2631. Business E-Mail: mhutchinson@centralgatech.edu.

HUTCHINSON, PETER ARTHUR, artist; b. London, Mar. 4, 1930; arrived in U.S., 1953; s. Arthur William Woodhams and Linda Mary Woodhams (West) Hutchinson. BFA, U. Ill., 1960. Author: Dissolving Clouds, 1996, Thrown Rope, 2006; contbr. articles, short stories to profl. jours.; one-man shows include John Gibson Gallery, NYC, 1969-80, Holly Solomon Gallery, 1980-90, James Mayor Gallery, London, 1996, Galerie Damasquine, Brussels, 1997, Galerie Bugdahn und Kaimer, Düsseldorf, Germany, 1998, 2005, 07, Galerie Helga De Alvear, Madrid, 1998, Kunstverein, Ulm, Germany, 1998, Biennale De France, Lyon, 1998, Galerie Lucien-Durand, Paris, 1999, Galerie Blancpain/Stepczynski, Geneva, 2001, 04, Lance Fung Gallery, NYC, 2002, Frederieke Taylor Gallery, NYC, 2005, FRAC Limousin, Limoges, France, 2006-07; exhibited in group shows at Mus. Modern Art, NYC, 1969, Acad. Art, Berlin, 1988, Herter Gallery, U. Mass. Traveling Exhbn., 1989, Torch Gallery, Amsterdam, 1998, 2005, DNA Gallery, Provincetown, 1994-2006, Fondacion Joan Miro, Barcelona, 2004, Echigo-Tsumari Art Triennial, Japan, 2003, Musée Pompidou, Paris, 2007. Active Fine Arts Work Ctr., Provincetown, Mass., 1979-85, 88-89; artists bd. Studio Art Ctr Internat. Art Found., 2006—. Fellow Aspen Ctr. for Arts, 1970-71, NEA, 1974, D.A.A.D., Berlin, 1988; grantee Adolph and Esther Gottlieb Found., 1987, Krasner-Pollack Found., 1989. Mem. Am. Rock Garden Soc. Avocations: botany, history, biology, horticulture. Home: 10 Holway Ave Provincetown MA 02657-1327 Personal E-mail: peterhutchinson@comcast.net.

HUTCHINSON, THOMAS CUTHBERT, ecology and environmental educator; b. Sunderland, Eng., Feb. 18, 1939; emigrated to Can., 1967; s. Walter and Margaret Amelia (Bell) H.; s. Vivien Coyne, Sept. 8, 1961 (div. 1981); 1 dau., Sally Louise; m. Magda Havas, 1982. BS with honors in Botany, Manchester U., Eng., 1960; PhD in Ecology, Sheffield U., Eng., 1966. Sir James Knott fellow Newcastle (Eng.) U., 1964-67; asst. prof. dept. botany Toronto U., 1967-71, assoc. prof., 1971-74, prof., 1974-90, chmn. dept., 1976-82; assoc. dir. Inst. Environ. Scis., U. Toronto, 1974-76; prof. faculty of forestry U. Toronto, 1978-90; prof., chair environ. and resource study Trent U., Peterborough, Ont., 1991-94, prof. environ. resource studies program, 1994—. Com. environ. quality criteria NRC Can.; dir. Oliver Ecol. Ctr., Trent U., 1999—; chmn. Can. Polar Commn., 2005-. Co-author: Environmental Consequences of Nuclear War, 1986; editor: Heavy Metals in Environment, 1977, Acid Rain Effects on Forests, Crops and Wetlands, 1987; co-editor: Acid Rain Effects on Vegetation, 1980; editor: Environ. Revs., 1990—2004; assoc. editor: Jour. Applied Ecology, —, Ecotoxicology, —, Environ. Pollution, —, Environ. Health, —; contbr. articles to profl. jours. Mem. Royal Agrl. Winter Fair Ont. Com., 1992—. Recipient Faculty Alumni award U. Toronto, 1984, Civic medal City of Toronto, 1991. Fellow Royal Soc. Can. (Miroslaw Romanowski medal 1998), Explorers Club; mem. Am. Agronomy Soc., Coun. of Nat. Scis. and Engring. Rsch. (pres. 1994—2002), Can. Bot. Assn. (George Lawson medal 1982, Trent faculty rsch. award 1998), Am. Ecol. Soc., Brit. Ecol. Soc., Arctic Inst. N.Am., Rare Breeds Can. (bd. dirs. 1992-2003), Can. Cotswold Longwool Assn. (sec.-treas. 1993—). Home: RR # 2 Indian River ON Canada K0L 7B8 Office: Trent U Environ Resource 1600 W Bank Dr Peterborough ON Canada K9J 7B8 Business E-Mail: thutchinson@trentu.ca.

HUTCHINSON, TIM, former senator; b. Bentonville, Ark., 1949; children: Jeremy, Tim, Joshua. MA in Polit. Sci., U. Ark. Co-owner, mgr. Sta. KBCV-FM, 1982-89; mem. 94th-98th Congresses from Ark., 1984-88, 106th Congress from 3rd Ark. dist., 1993; senator from Ark. U.S. Senate, 1997—2003; sr. advisor, pub. policy & law practice Dickstein Shapiro LLP, Washington, 2003—. Instr. history John Brown U., Siloam Springs, Ark.; mem. U.S. Senate armed svcs. com., health, edn., labor and pensions, com., vets.' affairs com., spl. subcom. on aging. Active Northwest Ark. C.C. Found. Named rep. of Yr. Ark. Fraternal Order Police, 1988, 90, Ark. Assn. of Chiefs of Police, 1990, 91. Mem. Bentonville Bella Vista C. of C., Bentonville Kiwanis Club. Republican. Baptist. Office: Dickstein Shapiro LLP 1825 Eye St NW Washington DC 20006-5403 Office Phone: 202-420-3600. Business E-Mail: hutchinsont@dicksteinshapiro.com.*

HUTCHISON, ANDREW SANDFORD, archbishop; b. 1938; m. Lois Hutchison; 1 child, David. LTh, Trinity Coll., 1969, DD (hon.), 1994, Montreal Diocesan Theol. Coll., 1993; DCL (hon.), Bishop's U., 2003. Ordained deacon, 1969; asst. curate Christ Ch., Toronto, 1969; ordained priest, 1970; rector Parish of Minden, Haliburton Highlands, Ontario, 1970-74, St. Francis Ch., Toronto, 1974-81, St. Luke Ch. East York, Toronto, 1981-84; dean Christ Ch. Cathedral, Montreal, 1984-90; consecrated bishop, 1990; Bishop of Montreal, 1990—2004; bishop ordinary Can. Forces, Ottawa, 1997—2004; Archbishop of Ecclesiastical Province of Can., 2002—04; Primate of Can., 2004—. Past pres. Montreal Diocesan Theol. Coll.; vis. Bishop's U., Lennoxville. Bd. governors Lakefield Coll. Sch., Ontario, 1994—97. Recipient Jerusalem Prize, Can. Zionist Fedn., 1999, Alan Rose Award, Can. Jewish Congress. Office: 80 Hayden St Toronto ON M4Y 3G2 Canada Office Fax: +1 416 924 0211. Business E-Mail: primate@national.anglican.ca.

HUTCHISON, BARBARA BAILEY, singer, songwriter; Recipient Grammy award for Best Musical Album for Children "Sleepy Time Lullabyes", 1996. E-mail: barbara@bbhsings.com.

HUTCHISON, CLAUDE B., JR., federal agency administrator; Grad., U. Calif., Berkeley; MBA, Harvard U. Chmn. Smith and Crowley Inc.; mng. dir. strategic mktg. group LEGC, Inc.; dir. Office Asset Enterprise Mgmt. Dept. Vets. Affairs, Washington, 2001—. Capt. USNR, ret. Office: US Dept Vets Affairs Mgmt 810 Vermont Ave NW Washington DC 20420 Office Phone: 202-273-7130. E-mail: claude.hutchison@va.gov.

HUTCHISON, KAY BAILEY, senator; b. Galveston, Tex., July 22, 1943; d. Allan and Kathryn Bailey; m. Ray Hutchison; four children. BA, U. Tex., 1992, LLB, 1967. Bar: Tex. 1967, US Supreme Ct., 1977. TV news reporter, Houston, 1969-71; pvt. practice law, 1969-74; press sec. to Anne Armstrong Rep. Nat. Com., 1971; vice-chair Nat. Transp. Safety Bd., 1976-78; asst. prof. U. Tex., Dallas, 1978-79; sr. v.p., gen. counsel Republic Bank Corp., Dallas, 1979-81; prin. Boyd-Levinson, Ltd., Houston and Dallas, 1981-91; mem. Tex. Ho. of Reps., 1972-76; elected treas. State of Tex., 1990; US Senator from Tex. Washington, 1993—. Chmn., bd. visitors, US Military Acad. at West Point, US Delegate to Commn. on Security and Cooperation in Europe (The Helsinki Commn.); owner McCraw Candies; co-founder Fidelity Nat. Bank; mem. com. appropriations, US Senate, com. commerce, sci., and transp., com.rules and adminstrn., com. veterans affairs. Author: (books) American Heroines: The Spirited Women Who Shaped Our Country, 2004. Recipient Eagle award valued commitment to our nation's Hispanic Cmty., 1993, Silver Ingot Ward Coastal Conservation Assn, 1997, CLEAT award, 2000, Nat. Family Mil. Assn. award, 2001, Nat. Leadership award Hispanic Assn. Coll. and U., 2002, Congl. Leadership award Women's Fgn. Policy Grp., 2004, Disting. Pub. Svc. award Alliance for Aging Rsch., 2004, Adam Smith Fed. Elected Official medal Bus. Industry Polit. Action Com., 2004, Wetland Sponser of Yr. award Ducks Unlimited, 2005, Disting. Pub. Svc. award Am. Legion Nat. Comdr., 2006, Outstanding Legislator award Assn. US Army, 2006, Charles Dick Medal of Merit Nat. Guard Assn. Tex., 2006; named Rep. Woman of Yr. Nat. Fedn. Rep. Women, 1995, Outstanding U. Tex. Alumnus, 1995, Texan of Yr. Tex. Legis. Conf., 1997, Mr. South Tex. Washington's Birthday Celebration Assn., 2005, Legislator of Yr. Deep East Tex. Coun. of Govt., 2005; named to Tex. Women's Hall of Fame, 1997, named one of 100 Most Influential Texas Women of the Century Tex. Women's Chamber of Commerce, 1999, 100 Most Powerful Women in World, Forbes mag., 2005. Fellow, U. Tex. Law Alumni Assn. (pres. 1985-86). Republican. Episcopalian. Office: US Senate 284 Russell Senate Bldg Washington DC 20510-4304 also: District Office Ste 1160 Lock Box 606 10440 North Central Expressway Dallas TX 75231-2223 Office Phone: 202-224-5922, 214-361-3500. Office Fax: 202-224-0776, 214-361-3502.

HUTCHISON, LARRY M., lawyer; b. Des Moines, Iowa, Jan. 29, 1954; BBA, U. Iowa, 1976; JD, Drake U., 1979. Bar: Iowa 1979. Gen. counsel Torchmark Corp., 1994—97, v.p., gen. counsel, 1997—99, exec. v.p., gen. counsel Birmingham, Ala., 1999—. Mem.: Iowa Bar Assn. Office: Torchmark Corp 2001 Third Ave S Birmingham AL 35233

HUTCHISON, MARK STEVENSON, lawyer; b. Syracuse, NY, Apr. 28, 1965; s. Edward Ross and Jean Marie (King) H.; m. Robin Jones (dec. 2003); children: James Mark, Anne Catherine, Colton Lee; m. Amanda Wise. BS, Millsaps Coll., 1987; JD, Miss. Coll., 1990. Bar: Miss. 1990, U.S. Dist. Ct. (so. dist.) Miss. 1990. Assoc. Richard Schartz & Assocs., Jackson, Miss., 1990; lawyer Miss. Asbestos Assn., Jackson, 1990-91; pvt. practice Jackson, 1991—. Hall scholar Millsaps Coll., Jackson, 1983,

Regents scholar SUNY, Albany, 1983. Mem. ABA, Am. Trial Lawyers Assn., Delta Theta Phi (officer 1988-90). Office: 5269 Keele St Ste A Jackson MS 39206-4322 Office Phone: 601-366-8911.

HUTCHISON, RAY RAY (E. RAY), lawyer; b. Rockwall, Tex., Sept. 16, 1932; children: Brenda, Julie. BBA with honors, So. Meth. U., 1957, JD cum laude, 1959. Bar: Tex. 1959. Mem. Tex. Ho. Reps., Dallas County, 1972-76, mem. intergovtl. affairs com., chmn. standing subcom. on urban affairs, state affairs, rules com., chmn. full legis. com., Constitutional Revision, intergovtl. affairs com.; mng. ptnr. Hutchison Boyle Brooks & Fisher, Dallas and Austin, Tex., 1969—95; of counsel Vinson & Elkins LLP, Dallas, 1996—. Assoc. editor Southwestern Law Jour. Del. Tex. Constitutional Conv., 1974, mem. local govt. and submission and transition coms.; chmn. Tex. Reps., 1975-78; mem. Rep. Nat. Com., 1975-78, exec. com., 1976-78. Served with USN, 1950-54. Mem. Order of Woolsack, Barristers Fraternity, Delta Theta Phi, Phi Eta Sigma. Office: Trammell Crow Ctr 2001 Ross Avenue Suite 3700 Dallas TX 75201 E-mail: rhutchison@velaw.com.

HUTCHISON, STANLEY PHILIP, retired lawyer; b. Joliet, Ill., Nov. 22, 1923; s. Stuart Philip and Verna (Kinzer) H.; m. Helen Jane Rush, July 25, 1945; children: Norman, Elizabeth. BS, Northwestern U., 1947; LLB, Ill. Inst. Tech., 1951. Bar: Ill. 1951. Legal asst. Washington Nat. Ins. Co., Evanston, 1947-51, asst. counsel, 1951-55, asst. gen. counsel, 1955-58, assoc. gen. counsel, 1958-60, gen. counsel, 1960-63, v.p., gen. counsel, dir., 1963-66, exec. v.p., gen. counsel, dir., 1966-67, exec. v.p., gen. counsel, sec., dir., 1967-70, chmn. exec. com., 1970-73, vice-chmn. bd., 1974-75, chmn. bd., CEO, 1976-88; pres. Wash. Nat. Corp., 1970-83, CEO, 1978-88, chmn. bd., 1983-88; ret., 1988-98. Bd. dirs. Washington Nat. Corp. Pres.'s coun. Nat. Coll. Edn., 1977-88, adv. coun. Kellogg Grad. Sch. Mgmt. Northwestern U., 1981-88; bd. dirs. Evanston Hosp. Corp., 1983-88. Lt. (j.g.) USNR, 1942-46. Mem. Assn. Life Ins. Counsel, Am. Coun. Life Ins. (bd. dir. 1977-81, 84-88), Ill. Life Ins. Coun. (bd. dir. 1978-86, pres. 1983-85), Inc. Econs. Soc. Am. (bd. dir. 1977-85, chmn. 1981-82), Health Ins. Assn. Am. (bd. dirs. 1982-88, chmn. 1987-88). Home: 7501 E Thompson Peak Pky #501 Scottsdale AZ 85255 E-mail: carefreesh@aol.com.

HUTCHISON, VICTOR HOBBS, biologist, educator; b. Blakely, Ga., June 15, 1931; s. Joseph Victor and Veva (Hobbs) H.; m. Theresa Dokos, Dec. 14, 1952; children: Victoria Ann, John Christopher, David Michael, Kenneth Hobbs. BS, N. Ga. Coll., 1952; MA, Duke U., 1956, PhD, 1959; grad., U.S. Army Command and Gen. Staff Coll. Instr. Duke U., 1957-58, faculty fellow, So. Fellowship Fund fellow, 1958-59; mem. faculty U. R.I., 1959-70, prof. biology, 1968-70; dir. Inst. Environ. Biology, 1966—70; prof., chmn. dept. zoology U. Okla., Norman, 1970-80, George Lynn Cross rsch. prof. zoology, 1979-2001, rsch. prof. emeritus, 2001—. Rsch. prof. Universidad de Los Andes, Bogotá, Colombia, 1965-66; prin. investigator Nat. Geog. Soc.-U. R.I. herpetological expdn. to Colombia, 1964-65, Nat. Geog. Soc.-U. Okla. expdns. to Lake Titicaca, 1975, Cameroon, 1981. Editor Animal Natural History series, 1991—; rsch. and articles on heat tolerances of lower vertebrates, effects of day-length on metabolism and temperature tolerance of lower vertebrates, physiology of lower vertebrates, physiol. ecology of amphibians and reptiles, respiration in amphibians, behavioral thermoregulation. With US Army, 1952—54, col. med. svc. corp. USAR. Decorated Army Commendation medal, Meritorious Svc. medal; Guggenheim fellow, 1965-66. Fellow AAAS; mem. Am. Inst. Biol. Sci., Am. Soc. Ichthyologists and Herpetologists (pres. 1988), Am. Physiol. Soc., Ecol. Soc. Am., Herpetologists League (exe. com. 1968-71), Soc. Study Amphibians and Reptiles (bd. govs. 1986-88, pres. 1998-99), Explorers Club, Sigma Xi, Phi Sigma, Phi Kappa Phi, Oklahomans for Excellence in Sci. Edn.(founder, 2002). Achievements include demonstration of facultative endothermy in brooding pythons; research on role of skin in amphibian respiration; development of standardized method for determination of critical thermal maximum in animals. Home: 2010 Crestmont Ave Norman OK 73069-6414 Office: U Okla Dept Zoology Norman OK 73019-0001 Office Phone: 405-325-6721. Business E-Mail: vhutchison@ou.edu.

HUTH, EDWARD JANAVEL, internist, educator, editor; b. Phila., May 15, 1923; s. Edward Gaston and Suzanne Madeleine (Janavel) H.; m. Carol Elizabeth Monnik, Apr. 6, 1957; children: John Edward, James Janavel. BA, Wesleyan U., Middletown, Conn., 1945; MD, U. Pa., 1947. Diplomate Am. Bd. Internal Medicine, Nat. Bd. Med. Examiners. Intern Hosp. of U. Pa., 1947-48, resident medicine, 1949-51, ward physician, 1951-61; mem. Diagnostic Clinic, 1959-61; postdoctoral fellow Life Ins. Med. Research Fund, 1952-53; spl. research fellow USPHS, Univ. Coll. Hosp., London, Eng., 1957-58. Asst. instr. pharmacology U. Pa. Sch. Medicine, Phila., 1948-49, assoc. in medicine, 1951-58, asst. prof. medicine, 1958-61; assoc. prof. comparative medicine Sch. Vet. Medicine, 1963-68; adj. asst. prof. medicine U. Pa. Sch. Medicine, 1966-71, assoc. prof. clin. medicine, 1971-74, adj. clin. prof. medicine, 1974-78, adj. prof. medicine dept. medicine Assoc. Faculty, 1978-91; asst. prof. medicine Woman's Med. Coll., Phila., 1961-62, assoc. prof., 1962-65; chmn. com. on 4th edit. CBE Style Manual Coun. Biology Editors, 1971-78, chmn. com. on 6th edit., 1990-95; biomed. comms. study sect. NIH, 1972-76; chmn. subcom. 10 of Com. Z39 Am. Nat. Stds. Inst., 1974-77; mem. UNISIST Working Group on Primary Sources of Info., UNESCO, Paris, 1973-74; bd. regents Nat. Libr. Medicine, 1979-83; office med. applications of rsch. NIH, 2001—; expert com. on info. devel. and dissemination US Pharmacopeia, 2002-05. Author: Medical Style and Format, 1987, How to Write and Publish Papers in the Medical Sciences, 1990, Writing and Publishing in Medicine, 1998, SI Units for Clinical Medicine, 1998, Medicine in Quotations, 2000, 2d edit., 2006; asst. editor Annals of Internal Medicine, 1960-63, assoc. editor, 1963-71, editor, 1971-90, editor emeritus, 1990-93, 95—, book rev. editor, 1990-93, 95-96, interim editor, 1994-95; editor Online Jour. Current Clin. Trials, 1991-94, also articles; mem. editl. bd. Nat. Med. Jour. India, 1991—, Transactions and Studies of the Coll. Physicians Phila., 2002—04; mem. adv. bd. Croatian Med. Jour., 1998—; rev. editor Pa. Geneal. Mag., 2003. Sec. Harriton Assoc., Bryn Mawr PA, 1991-2005. With AUS, 1943—46. Fellow ACP, AAAS (coun. 1968, editor Online Jour. Current Clin. Trials 1991-94), Royal Coll. Physicians (London), Am. Med. Writers Assn. (pres. 1967-68); mem. Coun. Biology Editors (dir. 1970-75, chmn. 1973-74), European Assn. Sci. Editors, Coll. Physicians Phila. (chmn. Wood Inst., Libr. and Mus. com. 2004-06, chmn. sect. on med. history 2005—06), Soc. for Scholarly Pub. (dir. 1988-92), Phi Beta Kappa, Sigma Xi, Alpha Omega Alpha, Zeta Phi. Democrat. Home and Office: 1124 Morris Ave Bryn Mawr PA 19010-1712

HUTH, GEOFFREY ANTHONY, archivist, artist; b. Burlingame, Calif., May 25, 1960; s. Donald Edward Huth and Maureen Elizabeth Tanner; m. Nancy Anne Frye, Feb. 11, 1984; children: Erin Mallory, Timothy Liam. BA in English, Vanderbilt U., Nashville, 1982; MA in English, Syracuse U., NY, 1986; MLS, SUNY, Albany, 1989. Field archivist, capital dist. labor history project U. Albany, SUNY, 1989—90; records mgmt. coord. Albany-Schoharie-Schenectady BOCES, Latham, NY, 1990—91; sr. pub. records mgmt. specialist NY State Archives, Albany, 1991—93, regional adv. officer, 1993—99, mgr., electronic records svc., 1999—2000, mgr., records svc. devel., 2000—04, mgr., records adv. svc., 2004—05, dir., govt. records svc., 2005—. Cons., spkr. in field. Author: (poems) Wreadings, 1987, Peristyle, 1989, Ghostlight, 1990, Water Vapour, 2005, Out of Character, 2007, (technical booklet) Retention and Disposition of Records, 2000, Managing E-Mail Effectively, 2002 (Notable Document Award, NY Libr. Assn., 2002), Conducting Needs Assessments for New Recordkeeping Systems, 2002, Managing Imaging and Micrographics Projects, 2003, Indexing Minutes, 2003; co-author (technical booklet) Preparing for the Worst: Managing Records Disasters, 2004; author: (dictionary) Familiar Words: How We Speak Alone Together, 1996; exhibitions include Miami Beach Convention Ctr., 1992, U. Pa. Libr., Phila., 1997, Neuberger Mus. Art, Purchase Coll., NY, 1998—99, Ayers-Knisely Gallery, Arts Ctr. of the Capital District, Troy, NY, 2000—01, Ohio State U., Columbus, 2002, Aldrich Mus. Contemporary Art, Ridgefield, Conn., 2002, Hordaland Kunstenter, Bergen, Norway, 2005, The Nave Gallery, Somerville, Mass., 2005, Bury Art Gallery, UK, 2005, Durban Segmini Gallery, Miami, 2005, UBU Studio, Portland, Maine, 2006, Gallery 324, Cleve., 2006. Mem.: Capital Area Archivists NY (pres. 1991—93), ARMA (pres. Albany chpt. 1993—96, Chpt. Mem. of Yr. 1996), Lake Ont. Archives Conf. (chair 1997—98), Mid-Atlantic Archives Conf. (chair 2005—07, Svc. award 1998, 2005), Soc. Am. Archivists (chair electronic records sect. 2002—03, chair govt. records sect. 2005—06). Home: 875 Central Pkwy Schenectady NY 12309 Home Phone: 518-372-7742; Office Phone: 518-474-6926. Office Fax: 518-486-4923. Personal E-mail: geofhuth@gmail.com. E-mail: ghuth@mail.nysed.gov.

HUTH, JOHN E., physicist, educator; b. Mar. 1958; AB in Physics, Princeton U., 1979; PhD, U. Calif., Berkley, 1985. Postdoctoral scientist Fermi Nat. Accelerator Lab., 1985—87, Wilson fellow, 1987—90, staff scientist, 1990—93; prof. Harvard U., 1993—, chmn. dept. physics. Office: Harvard U Dept Physics 236 Lyman Lab Cambridge MA 02138

HUTH, WILLIAM EDWARD, lawyer; b. South Bend, Ind., July 26, 1931; s. Edward Andrew and Margaret Mary (Emonds) H.; m. Mary Pamela Hall, Aug. 11, 1962; children: Katharine Louise, Stephen Edward (dec.), Alan Edward. BS, U. Dayton, 1952; JD, Yale U., 1957. Bar: N.Y. 1958, U.S. Dist. Ct. (so. dist.) N.Y. 1959, Mich. 1962, U.S. Dist. Ct. (ea. dist.) Mich. 1962, U.S. Supreme Ct. 1969, Pa. 1975, Conn. 1978. Assoc. Kelley, Drye, Newhall & Maginnes, NYC, 1958—61; group counsel Chrysler Corp., Detroit, 1962—72; ptnr. Ziegler, Dykhouse, Wise & Huth, Detroit, 1973—74; assoc. gen. counsel Westinghouse Electric Corp., Pitts., 1974—76; asst. sec., asst. gen. counsel Combustion Engring., Inc., Stamford, Conn., 1976—90; ptnr. Huth, Grinnell & Flaherty, Stamford, 1991—2000. Adj. prof. law Wayne State U., Detroit, 1969-74, Pace U. Sch. of Law, 1999-2001 Contbr. articles to profl. publs. 1st lt. AUS, 1952-54. Mem. ABA (antitrust sect., internat. law sect., dispute resolution sect.), Am. Arbitration Assn. (Blue Ribbon Panel Arbitrators, internat. panel, internat. arbitration com.), ICC Arbitration Com., US Coun. Internat. Bus. (ICC arbitration com.), Internat. Bar Assn., Conn. Bar Assn., Assn. Bar City NY (arbitration com.), Westchester-Fairfield Corp. Counsel Assn. (pres. 1987, bd. dirs. 1984-88), Woodfield Village Assn., (pres. 2006), Yale Club NYC, The Army and Navy Club (Washington), Indian Harbor Yacht Club (Greenwich), Order of Coif. Roman Catholic. Home: 39 Balmaha Ct Fairfield CT 06825-1173 Office: PO Box 320298 Fairfield CT 06825 Home Phone: 203-371-6110; Office Phone: 203-372-1202. Personal E-mail: huthwe@ix.netcom.com.

HUTSON, JEFFREY WOODWARD, lawyer; b. New London, Conn., July 19, 1941; s. John Jenkins and Kathryn Barbara (Himberg) Hutson; m. Susan Office, Nov. 25, 1967; children: Elizabeth Kathryn, Anne Louise. AB, U. Mich., 1963, LLB, 1966. Bar: Ohio 1966, Hawaii 1971. Assoc. Lane, Alton & Horst, Columbus, Ohio, 1966-74, ptnr., 1974—. Arbitrator commercial construction panel Am Arbitration Asn, 1976—. Trustee, vice-chair 6 Pence Sch., 1983—88; mem. com. creeds and professionalism Ohio Supreme Ct, 1989—90; chair bd. dirs. N.W. Counseling Svcs., 1990—92; regional v.p. Def. Rsch. Inst., 1991—93. Lt comdr USNR, 1967—71. Fellow: Columbus Bar Found., Ohio State Bar Found., Am. Arbitration Assn., Am. Coll. Trial Lawyers, Am. Bar Found.; mem.: Internat. Assn. Def. Counsel, Columbus Bar Assn. (chair constrn. law com. 2004—06), Ohio Assn. Civil Trial Attys., Ohio Bar Assn., Athletic Club, Scioto Country Club. Avocations: bicycling, reading, music. Office: Lane Alton & Horst Two Miranova Pl Ste 500 Columbus OH 43215 Office Phone: 614-233-4747. Business E-Mail: jhutson@lanealton.com.

HUTSON, JOHN D., dean, retired military officer; b. 1946; m. Paula Smith; children: Christy, Melissa. Grad., Mich. State U., 1969; JD, U. Minn., 1972; LLM, Naval Justice Sch., Newport, RI, 1980. Bar: Mich. Commd. 2d lt. USN, 1969, advanced through grades to rear adm., 1997, ret., 2000; chief def. counsel, chief trial counsel Naval Law Ctr., Corpus Christi, Tex., 1973—75; legal officer Naval Air Station, Point Mgu, Calif., 1975—77; instr. Naval Justice Sch., Newport, RI, 1977—80; legis. counsel, Office Legis. Affairs USN, 1980—84; staff judge advocate & adminstrv. officer Portsmouth Naval Shipyard, Kittery, Maine, 1984—87; exec. officer Naval Legal Svc. Office, Newport, RI, 1987—89; staff judge advocate & exec. asst. to comdr. Naval Investigative Command, Washington, 1989, dir. legis., 1989—92; exec. asst. to judge advocate gen. USN, 1992—93; commdg. officer Naval Legal Svc. Office, Naples, Italy, 1994-96; commanding officer Naval Justice Sch., 1996-97; judge advocate gen. USN, Washington, 1997—2000; pres., dean Franklin Pierce Law Ctr, Concord, NH, 2000—. Decorated Legion of Merit (with two gold stars), Disting. Svc. medal, Meritorious Svc. medal (with two gold stars), Navy Commendation medal, Navy Achievement medal. Office: Franklin Pierce Law Ctr Two White St Concord NH 03301*

HUTSON, MARTHA GILLON, social studies educator, consultant; b. Greenwood, Miss., Sept. 19, 1948; d. Earl L. and Peggy McKee Gillon; m. Jerrell B. Hutson, Dec. 21, 1974; 1 child, Ellen Hutson Brewer. BA, William Carey Coll., Hattiesburg, Miss., 1970; MA, U. So. Miss., Hattiesburg, Miss., 1972. Secondary tchr. social studies Hattiesburg Pub. Schs., Miss., 1971—78, Clinton Pub. Schs., 1981—2000; adj. instr. Miss. Coll., 1993—2000, instr., 2000—. Mem. adv. bd. Miss. Geog. Endowment Fund, Jackson, 1990—; mem. tchr. of yr. advisory bd. South Ea. Regional Vision Edn. Author: (on line lesson plans) Mississippi History NOW, 2000—. Pres. Old Towne Clinton (Miss.) Homeowners Assn., 1995—2000; mem. Arts Coun. Clinton, 1997—2000. Recipient Miss. Tchr. of Yr., Nat. TOY Program and Miss. Dept. Edn., 1997—98, Alumni Achievement award, William Carey Coll., 1998; grantee, Miss. Geog. Endowment Fund, 2003—06. Mem.: NEA, Miss. Assn. Educators, Nat. Coun. Geographic Edn., Nat. Coun. Social Studies, Miss. Coun. Social Studies, Miss. Geog. Alliance (co-dir., outstanding tchr. cons. 1998), Miss. Hist. Soc. (bd. dir. 2005—). Avocation: antiques. Home: 403 W Madison Clinton MS 39056 Office: Miss Coll Box 4006 Clinton MS 39058

HUTSON, MELVIN ROBERT, lawyer; b. Decatur, Ala., Dec. 7, 1947; s. John Robert and Katie Louise (Waddell) H.; children: Melvin, Rachael, Katie, Jamie. BS, U. Ala., 1968, JD, 1971. Bar: Ala. 1971, Ga. 1972, S.C. 1975, D.C. 1978. Atty. NLRB, Atlanta, 1971-73; ptnr. Thompson Mann & Hutson, Greenville, SC, 1974-98, Melvin Hutson, PA, Greenville, 1998—. Bd. dirs. Primesco, Inc., Mut. Savs. Life Ins. Co., Inc. Chmn. bd. dirs. World Cancer Rsch. Fund, London, 1994-96; chmn. AGC Labor Lawyers Coun., 1989-90, Am. Inst. Cancer Rsch., 1982—. Mem. ABA (mem. com. on devel. of law under nat. labor rels. act 1977—, chmn. litigation sect., subcom. on labor mgmt. litigation). Home: 1307 N Main St Greenville SC 29609-4716 Office: PO Box 88 Greenville SC 29602-0088 Office Phone: 864-241-4000. Business E-Mail: mel.hutson@scbar.org.

HUTT, PETER BARTON, lawyer; b. Buffalo, Nov. 16, 1934; s. Lester Ralph and Louise Rich (Fraser) H.; children: Katherine Zurn, Peter Barton, Sarah Henderson, Everett Fraser. BA magma cum laude, Yale U., 1956; LLB, Harvard U., 1959; LLM, NYU, 1960. Bar: N.Y. 1959, D.C. 1961, U.S. Supreme Ct. 1967. Assoc. Covington & Burling, Washington, 1960-68, ptnr., 1968—71, 1975—2004, sr. counsel, 2004—; chief counsel FDA, Washington, 1971-75. Bd. dir. Andora, Inc., Cambridge, Mass., CV Therapeutics Inc., Palo Alto, Calif., Favrille, Inc., San Diego, Momenta, Inc., Cambridge, Mass., Ista Pharms., Inc., Irvine, Calif., Pervasis Therapeutics, Inc., Boston, Introgen Therapeutics, Inc., Houston, Xoma, Inc., Berkeley, Calif., Calif. HealthCare Inst., San Diego, Life Line Screening, Cleve., Concert Pharms., Inc., Lexingto, Mass., 2006—, Keck Grad. Inst. Applied Life Sci., Claremont, Calif., 2007, Aeras Global TB Vaccine Found., Rockville, Md.; adv. com. to dir. NIH, 1976—81; com. on rsch. tng. NAS, 1976—80; counsel to Alcoholic Beverage Med. Rsch. Found., 1984—85, chmn. bd. dir., 1986—92; mem. Nat. Com. to Rev. Current Proc. for Approval of New Drugs for Cancer and AIDS, Nat. Cancer Inst., 1988—90; mem. nat. bd. Scripps Clinic and Rsch. Found., La Jolla, 1977—85, 1990—95; mem. internat. bd. Scripps Instns. of Medicine and Sci., 1995—2002, Ctr. for Study Drug Devel., Tufts U. Ctr., 1976—99, Ctr. for Advanced Studies, U.Va., 1982—2002, Inst. for Health Policy Analysis, 1982—, Am. Pharm. Inst., Washington, 1988—92; com. on food laws and regulations Inst. Food Tech.; adv. com. Progress and Freedom Found., 1994—97; adv. bd. Frazier Healthcare Investments, Seattle, 1993—99, Sprout Group, NY and Menlo Park, 1993—, Polaris Venture Ptnrs., Waltham, 1995—, Vanguard Medica Ltd., Guildford, England, 1993—99, Columbia U. Sch. Pub. Health, 1997—2004, Sherbrook Capital Health & Wellness Fund, Lexington, Mass., 1999—, Burrill Neutraceuticals, San Francisco, 2000—, New Leaf Venture Ptnrs., NY, 2005—, Menlo Park, Calif., 2005—, Sirtris Phrams., Inc., Cambridge, Mass., 2006—, Magen BioScis., Inc., Cambridge, 2006—; panel mem. US Congl. Office Tech. Assessment; adv. bd. Kearny Venture Ptnrs., San Francisco, 2006—; lectr. on food and drug law Harvard U., 1994—, Stanford U., 1998; panel on adminstrv. restructuring NIH, Nat. Acad. Pub. Adminstrn., 2004—06; mem. working group AIDS divsn. Nat. Inst. Allergy and Infectious Diseases, 2005—06; mem. sci. bd. subcom. on state of FDA sci. FDA, 2006—. Author: (with Patricia Wald) Dealing with Drug Abuse, 1972, (with Richard Merrill, Lewis Grossman) Food and Drug Law, 2007, (with Bruce Kuhlik) Understanding Export Law, 1998; editor-in-chief U.S. Food Labeling Law, 1991—; contbg. editor: Legal Times of Washington, 1978-86; mem. editl. bd. various jours.; editor: Food and Drug Law: An Electronic Book of Harvard Law School Student Papers. Bd. dirs. Sidwell Friends Sch., Washington, 1976-84; bd. dirs. Legal Action Ctr., N.Y.C., 1976-2003, vice-chmn., 1984-98; bd. dirs. Found. for Biomed. Rsch., 1976-, vice chmn., 1989—; trustee Washington Lawyers Com. for Civil Rights and Urban Affairs, 1976—, Food and Drug Law Inst., 2001-05; bd. dirs. Soc. Risk Analysis, 1985-88, 89-92, counsel, 1992—; mem. vis. com. Harvard Sch. Pub. Health, 1980-86. Recipient award of merit FDA, 1972, 75, Disting. Svc. award HEW, 1974, Underwood-Prescott award MIT, 1977, Disting. Alumni award FDA, 2005, Lifetime Achievement award Found. Biomed. Rsch., 2005; named Leading Food and Drug Lawyer Legal Times, 2005. Fellow: Soc. Risk Analysis; mem.: Inst. Medicine of NAS (Devel. of Drugs and Vaccines Against AIDS roundtable 1988—94, bd. on health care svcs. 1998—2002). Episcopalian. Home: 124 S Fairfax St Alexandria VA 22314 Office: Covington & Burling 1201 Pennsylvania Ave NW Washington DC 20004-2401 Office Phone: 202-662-5522. Business E-Mail: phutt@cov.com.

HUTTENBACK, ROBERT ARTHUR, academic administrator, educator; b. Frankfurt, Germany, Mar. 8, 1928; s. Otto Henry and Dorothy (Marcuse) H.; m. Freda Braginsky, July 12, 1954; 1 dau., Madeleine Alexandra. BA, U. Calif. at Los Angeles, 1951, PhD, 1959; postgrad., Sch. Oriental and African Studies, U. London, Eng., 1956-57. Mem. faculty Calif. Inst. Tech., Pasadena, 1958-78, asst. prof., 1960-63, assoc. prof., 1963-66, prof. history, 1966-78, master student houses, 1958-69, dean students, 1969-72, chmn. div. humanities and social scis., 1971-77; chancellor U. Calif., Santa Barbara, 1977-86. Cons. Jet Propulsion Lab., Pasadena, 1966-68 Author: British Relations with Sind, 1799-1843, An Anatomy of Imperialism, 1962, (with Leo Rose and Margaret Fisher) Himalayan Battleground-Sino-Indian Rivalry in Ladakh, 1963, The British Imperial Experience, 1966, Gandhi in South Africa, 1971, Racism and Empire, 1976, (with Lance Davis) Mammon and the Pursuit of Empire, 1986, Kashmir and the British Raj, 2004. Served to 1st lt. U.S. Army, 1951-53. Home Phone: 805-388-4617; Office Phone: 805-388-4617. E-mail: huttenback@earthlink.net.

HUTTENLOCHER, JANELLEN, psychology educator, psychologist; b. Buffalo, Feb. 17, 1932; d. Allen and Sylvia (Holtz) Burns; m. Peter Huttenlocher, June 13, 1954; children: Daniel, Anna, Carl. BA, U. Buffalo, 1953; MA, Radcliffe Coll., 1958, PhD, 1960. Instr., research fellow Harvard U., Cambridge, Mass., 1960-62, research fellow in cognitive studies, 1962-66, lectr. social relations, 1964-66; assoc. prof. psychology and edn. Columbia U., NYC, 1966-72, prof. psychology and edn., 1972-74; William S. Gray prof. edn. and behavioral scis., chair U. Chgo., 1974—. Mem. behavioral devel. study sect. Nat. Inst. Child Health and Devel., 1971-74 Mem. editorial bd.: Jour. Experimental Child Psychology, 1970-74, Cognitive Psychology, 1972-76, Psychol. Rev., 1982—; contbr. numerous articles to profl. jours. Recipient Nat. Inst. Child Health and Devel. award, 1969-74; NIMH fellow, 1954; fellow Harvard U., 1960-62 Fellow Am. Acad. Arts & Scis.; mem. Am. Psychol. Assn., Psychonomic Soc., Soc. Research in Child Devel., Phi Beta Kappa Office: Behavioral Scis Beecher 413 Univ Chgo 5848 S University Ave Chicago IL 60637 Business E-Mail: hutt@ccp.uchicago.edu.*

HUTTER, ADOLPH MATTHEW, JR., cardiologist, educator; b. Fond du Lac, Wis., Feb. 22, 1937; s. Adolph Matthew and Janet (Kay) H.; m. Sylvia H. Murray, June 18, 1960; children: Janice Marie, Adolph Joseph, Elizabeth Kay, Matthew Murray, Jonathan James. BS summa cum laude, Georgetown U., 1959; MD, U. Wis., 1963. Diplomate Am. Bd. Internal Medicine, Am. Bd. Cardiovascular Diseases; lic. physician, Mass. Med. intern Strong Meml. Hosp., Rochester, N.Y., 1963-64; clin. assoc. Nat. Cancer Inst., Bethesda, Md., 1964-66; asst. resident Strong Meml. Hosp., 1966-67, assoc. resident, 1967-68; fellow in medicine (oncology) Georgetown U. Sch. Medicine, Washington, 1965-66; clin. and rsch. fellow in cardiology Mass. Gen. Hosp., Boston, 1968-70; instr. medicine Harvard U. Med. Sch., Boston, 1970-72, asst. prof., 1972-76, assoc. prof., 1976-99, prof., 1999—. Vis. prof. 100 univs. and med. ctrs., 1979-96; asst. in medicine Mass. Gen. Hosp., 1970-72, asst. physician, 1972-76, assoc. physician, 1976-84, physician, 1984—, assoc. dir. CCU, 1970-81, dir., 1981-86, chmn. med. intensive care coord. com., 1986-94; cardiologist Boston Bruins hockey team, 1972—, New Eng. Patriots football team, 1982—. Contbr. over 100 articles to med. jours. Trustee The Roxbury Latin Sch., 1988-90, mem. soc. of fellows, 1995—. Recipient Howard H. Blakeslee award, Am. Heart Assn., 1974; fellow, Roxbury Latin Sch. Fellow: AAAS, ACP, European Soc. Cardiology, Am. Coll. Cardiology (mem. program com. on sci. sessions 1975—76, mem. credentials com. 1976—83, asst. sec. 1981—82, chmn. 1981—83, mem. long-range planning com. 1981—83, trustee 1981—85, mem. ACCEL com. 1982—90, sec. 1984—85, chmn. 1987—90, mem. ACCEL edn. bd. 1987—90, trustee 1987—95, mem. strategic planning com. 1988—92, v.p. 1990—91, mem. exec. com. 1990—94, pres. 1992—93, past pres. 1993—94, mem. chmn. award com. 1993—95, mem. ACCEL edn. bd. 1993—, chmn. govt. rels. com. 1993—, chmn. chpt. rels. com. 1993—, mem. tech. and practice exec. com. 1994—, moderator, convs. expert 2004—, editl. bd. 2004—), CLin Coun. Am. Heart Assn. (mem. com. on postgrad. edn. 1972—75, mem. com. on sci. sessions program 1973—75, mem. sci. sessions com. 1979—81, vice chmn. com. on cardiovasc. disease of elderly 1987—90); mem.: Mass. Med. Soc., Am. Clin. and Climatol. Assn., U. Wis. Med. Alumni Assn., Alpha Omega Alpha. Roman Catholic. Avocations: golf, gardening. Business E-Mail: ahutter@partners.org.

HUTTER, PAUL J., lawyer; b. 1954; m. Mary Hutter; 3 children. JD, U. Santa Clara; MBA, Pepperdine U.; LLM, Judge Advocate General's Sch., 1987. Bar: Ct. Appeals Vet. Claims, US Supreme Ct., Calif., Hawaii, Va.

Pvt. practice atty., Honolulu; staff atty., appellate atty. Balt. Regional Counsel, Washington, asst. regional counsel, dep. asst. regional counsel; acting asst. sec. policy & planning US Dept. Vets Affairs, Washington, asst. gen. counsel mgmt. & ops., acting gen. counsel. Prosecutor, internat. lawyer, staff judge advocate, comdr. Army Judge Advocate Gen. Corps. Colonel (ret.) USAR, judge adv. USAR. Office: Office of General Counsel US Dept Veterans Affairs 1722 Eye St NW Washington DC 20421 E-mail: paul.hutter@va.gov.*

HUTTER, TERESA ANN, art educator; b. Great Bend, Kans., Jan. 25, 1952; d. Harry and Wilma Witterstaetter; children: Trina, Troy. BA in Art Edn., U. Ctrl. Okla., 1987. Nat. bd. cert. tchr. Tchr. art Mustang Pub. Schs., Okla., 1988—; tchr. art camp So. Nazarene U., Bethany, Okla., 1996—2000; host Internat. Children's Art Exhbn., 1995, 2001; tchr. art Jr. Tng. Pks. Assn. Edn. program Okla. C.C., 1994—95. Okla. state judge state reflections program PTA, Oklahoma City, 1996—97. Mem.: NEA, Mustang Area Reading Coun., Nat. Art Edn. Assn., Okla. Edn. Assn., Okla. Art Edn. Assn. (sec. 1992—94, treas. 1994—98, chmn. young talent in Okla. 1998—2000, chmn. we. region div. 1998—2000, chmn. Okla. elem. div. 2000—04, newsletter editor 2004—06, pres. 2006—, Okla. Elem. Art Educator of Yr. 1995, Okla. Art Educator of Yr. 2000, Youth Arts Month Svc. award 1996, 2000), Delta Kappa Gamma (music chmn. 2000—01). Republican. Methodist. Avocations: reading, pottery, flute, hand bells. Office: Mustang Pub Schs 906 S Heights Dr Mustang OK 73064 Business E-Mail: huttert@mustangps.org.

HUTTING, LORI A., language educator; b. Livonia, Mich., May 6, 1969; d. Bill Roberts and Grace Pergande; m. Matt Hutting, July 8, 2000; children: Deegan, Dainan. BA, Mich. State U., East Lansing, 1992; MA, Saginaw Valley State U., Mich., 1997. Englsh tchr. Lyceo Jean Bart, Dunkerque, France, 1992—93; French, English tchr. Ostego H.S., Mich., 1993—94; elem. French tchr. Bay City Pub. Schs., Mich., 1994—99; French, English tchr. DeWitt Pub. Schs., Mich., 1999—. Mem.: Nat. Network Early Lang. Learning, Am. Coun. Tchg. Lang., Am. Assn. Tchrs. French. Avocation: saxophone. Office: DeWitt Pub Schs PO Box 800 Dewitt MI 48820

HUTTLER, STEPHEN B., lawyer; b. Newport, RI, Sept. 19, 1949; BA cum laude, Syracuse U., 1971; JD, Georgetown U., 1974; attended, U. Munich, Germany. Bar: DC 1975, US Supreme Ct. 1980. Assoc. to ptnr. Shaw Pittman LLP, Washington, 1974—2003, mng. ptnr., 2003—05; ptnr. Real Estate Practice Pillsbury Winthrop Shaw Pittman LLP, 2003—, vice chmn. Washington, 2005—. Editor: Law & Policy in Internat. Bus. Trustee Wash. Nat. Opera. Mem.: ABA, Urban Land Inst. Office: Pillsbury Winthrop Shaw Pittman 2300 N St NW Washington DC 20037-1128 Office Phone: 202-663-8121. Office Fax: 202-663-8007. Business E-Mail: stephen.huttler@pillsburylaw.com.

HUTTNER, CONSTANCE S., lawyer; b. Youngstown, Ohio, 1958; BS in Cellular Immunology, Ohio State U., 1977; JD magna cum laude, Boston Coll., 1980. Bar: NY 1981. Ptnr., patent litigation Skadden, Arps, Slate, Meagher & Flom, LLP, NYC; ptnr. Buchanan Ingersoll & Rooney PC, NYC, 2007—. Co-chmn., Patent Litigation Seminar Practising Law Institute, 2001. Author: Unfit for Jury Determination: Complex Civil Litigation and the Seventh Amendment Right of Trial By Jury, Boston Coll. Law Review, Vol. XX, No. 3, 1979, Markman Practice, Procedures and Tactics, Patent Litigation, Practising Law Inst., 1999, 2000, Markman Practice, Procedures and Tactics, Patent Litigation Strategies Handbook, ABA Sect. of Intellectual Property Law, 2000. Order of the Coif. Mem.: Am. Intellectual Property Law Assn., NY Intellectual Property Law Assn., Phi Beta Kappa. Office: Buchanan Ingersoll & Rooney PC One Chase Manhattan Plz 35th Fl New York NY 10005*

HUTTNER, SIDNEY FREDERICK, librarian; b. Portal, ND, Feb. 18, 1941; s. Frederick W. and Fern May (Nolting) H.; m. Elizabeth Ann Stege, Oct. 24, 1981; 1 child, Erica Marie. BA in Tutorial Studies, U. Chgo., 1963, MA in Philosophy, 1969. Asst. head spl. collections U. Chgo. Libr., 1970-80; head George Arents Rsch. Libr. Syracuse (N.Y.) Libr., 1980-84; curator spl. collections U. Tulsa Libr., 1984-98; head spl. collections U. Iowa Librs., 1999—. Author: A Register of Artists, Engravers, Booksellers, Bookbinders, Printers and Publishers in New York City, 1821-1842, 1993, The Lucile Project website. Fellow Woodrow Wilson Found., 1963-64. Avocation: bookbinding. Home: 5 Glendale Cir Iowa City IA 52245-3208 Office: Spl Collections U Iowa Librs Iowa City IA 52240-1420 Office Phone: 319-335-5922. Business E-Mail: sid-huttner@uiowa.edu.

HUTTON, CAROLE LEIGH, executive editor; b. Framingham, Mass., Aug. 23, 1956; d. James and Norma Inez (Vitali) Hamilton; m. Tom Huff. B Journalism, Mich. State U., 1978. Editor Natick (Mass.) Sun, 1978—79; reporter, city editor, mng. editor Hammond (Ind.) Times, 1979—87; dir. publs. CNA Ins. Cos., Chgo., 1987—88; day city editor, accent editor Detroit News, 1988—90; city editor Detroit Free Press, 1992—95, dep. mng. editor for news, 1995—96, mng. editor, 1996—2002, exec. editor, 2002—03, pub. and editor, 2004—05; v.p. news Knight Ridder Newspapers, 2005—07; v.p. & exec. editor San Jose (Calif.) Mercury News, 2007—. Tutor Detroit Pub. HS, 1994—94. Named one of 100 Most Influential Women in S.W. Mich., Crain's Detroit Bus.; recipient Local News Coverage award, Hoosier State Press Assn., 1982. Mem.: AP Mng. Editors, Mich. AP Editors Assn. (pres., bd. dirs. 2000—), Am. Soc. Newspaper Editors, IAP Mng. Editors. Office: San Jose Mercury News 750 Ridder Park Dr San Jose CA 95190 Office Phone: 408-920-5000. Office Fax: 408-288-8060.*

HUTTON, DELVIN DWAYNE, retired theology studies educator, minister; b. Auburn, Nebr., Aug. 24, 1934; s. Chester P. and Helen M. Hutton; m. Gertrude E. Obermeyer, Aug. 19, 1956; children: Charisse E., Tamyra L. Tomlinson, Celeste R., Stephen J. BA, Pacific Luth. U., Parkland, Wash., 1956; BD, Wartburg Theol. Sem., Dubuque, Iowa, 1960; ThM, Harvard Div. Sch., Cambridge, Mass., 1962, ThD, 1970. Ordained Evang. Luth. Ch. Am., 1964. Asst. prof. religion Dana Coll., Blair, Nebr., 1964—68, assoc. prof. religion, 1968—78, prof. religion, 1978—99; ret. Vis. prof. U. Nebr., Omaha, Wartburg Theol. Sem., Pacific Luth. Theol. Sem.; interim pastor various chs. Evangelical Luth. Ch. Am., Nebr., 1999—. Author: From One King to Another, 1973. Vol. Habitat for Humanity, Nebr., 1990—. Scholar, Luth. Brotherhood Ins. Co., 1956, 1960, Rockefeller Found., 1963—64. Avocations: gardening, music, reading, sports, travel. Home: 2233 Colfax St Blair NE 68008 Business E-Mail: dthutton@huntel.net.

HUTTON, EDWARD LUKE, medical products executive; b. Bedford, Ind., May 5, 1919; s. Fred and Margaret (Drehobl) H.; m. Kathryn Jane Alexander; children— Edward Alexander, Thomas Charles, Jane Clarke BS with distinction, Ind. U., 1940, MS with distinction, 1941; LLD (hon.), Ind. U., Cumberland Coll., 1992. Dep. dir. Joint Export Import Agy. (USUK), Berlin, 1946-48; v.p. World Commerce Corp., 1948-51; asst. v.p. W.R. Grace & Co., 1951-53, cons., 1960-65, exec. v.p., gen. mgr. Dubois Chems. div., 1965-66, group exec. Specialty Products Group and v.p., 1966-68, exec. v.p., 1968-71; cons. internat. trade and fin., 1953-58; fin. v.p., exec. v.p. Ward Industries, 1958-59; pres., CEO Chemed Corp., Cin., 1970—93, chmn., 1993—2004, non-exec. chmn., 2004—; chmn. Omnicare, Inc., Cin., 1981—2003, non-exec. chmn., 2003—. Chmn. bd. dirs. Nat. San. Supply Co., 1983-97; E. Hutton Internat. scholarship program establisher, Ind. U., 2003; bldg. funder, Hutton Sch. Bus., Cumberland Coll., Williamsburg, Ky., 2004. Co-chmn. Pres.'s Pvt. Sector Survey on Cost Control, exec. com., subcom.; former trustee Millikin U., 1973-84. 1st lt., U.S. Army, 1945-47. Recipient Disting. Alumni Svc. award Ind. U., 1987. Mem. AAUP (governing bd. dirs. 1958—), Econ. Club, Princeton Club, Univ. Club, Queen City Club, Bankers Club. Home: 6680 Miralake Ln Cincinnati OH 45243-2722 Office: Chemed Corp 255 E 5th St Ste 2600 Cincinnati OH 45202-4700 Business E-Mail: edward.hutton@chemed.com.

HUTTON, ESSEX CLARK, SR., adult education educator; b. Mesa, Ariz., Oct. 31, 1940; s. Joseph Hutton and Pauline Trenella Ratliff; children: Essex Jr., Tanya Natasha. AA in bus. mgmt., San Diego Evening Coll., 1974; BA in pub. adminstrn., San Diego State U., 1980. Cert. tchr. Calif., 2000. Welfare appeals officer San Diego Welfare Dept., 1971—80; adj. lectr. City Colls. of Chgo., 1982—83; sub. tchr., 1992—; employment devel. supr. Vietman Vets. of Calif., Sacramento, 1998—2003; adult edn. tchr. Scramento City Unified Sch. Dist., 2000—03. Workforce investment act rep. Vietnam Vets. of Calif., Sacramento, 1994. Author poems. Chief warrant officer US Army, 1960—92. Mem.: MENSA. Democrat. Avocations: writing, poetry, reading. Home: 4042 New York Ave #1404 Fair Oaks CA 95628 Personal E-mail: essexhutton@aol.com.

HUTTON, G. THOMPSON, lawyer; b. Greensboro, NC, Oct. 1, 1946; s. Charles Coble and Annie (Lee) H.; m. Mara; children: Jason, Jennifer, Logan, Nate. BA with honors, U. N.C., 1968; JD, Columbia U., 1971. Bar: N.Y. 1972, U.S. Dist. Ct. (so. dist.) N.Y. 1976, U.S. Ct. Appeals (2nd cir.) 1976. Assoc. Shea & Gould, NYC, 1971-79, ptnr., 1979-89; founding ptnr. Hutton Ingram, Yuzek Gainen Carroll & Bertolotti, NYC, 1989-99; pvt. practice, 1999—. Pres. Geoffrey Beene, Inc., 2004—, CEO, 2004—, chmn. bd., 2004—. Mem. adv. bd. Meml. Sloan-Kettering Inst.; trustee Geoffrey Beene Found., 2007—; bd. dirs. Geoffrey Beene Cancer Rsch. Ctr., NYC. Harlan Fiske Stone scholar. Mem. ABA, NY State Bar, Assn. Bar of City NY, Order Old Well Honor Soc., Phi Beta Kappa, Phi Eta Sigma, Gamma Beta Phi. Avocations: golf, music, swimming, skiing, nature conservancy. Office: 13 E 69th St Ste 2R New York NY 10021-4968 E-mail: gthompsonhutton@aol.com.

HUTTON, JOHN EVANS, JR., surgeon, educator, retired military officer; b. NYC, Sept. 9, 1931; s. John Evans and Antoinette (Abbott) H.; m. Barbara Seward Joyce, Apr. 15, 1961; children: John III, Wendy, James, Elizabeth. BA, Wesleyan U., 1953; MD, George Washington U., 1963. Diplomate: Am. Bd. Surgery, Am. Bd. Med. Examiners. Commd. 2d lt. USMC, 1953, advanced through grades to capt., 1962; discharged USMCR; commd. capt. U.S. Army, 1963, advanced through grades to brig. gen., 1989, intern, resident in gen. surgery Walter Reed Army Med. Ctr. Washington, 1963-68, fellow vascular surgery, 1969-70, asst. chief vascular surgery, 1970-71, mem. staff gen. surgery svcs., 1969-71, chief dept. surgery, 1981-84, White House physician, 1984-86, physician to the Pres. Ronald Reagan, 1987—88, chief surgeon 91st Evacuation Hosp., Republic of Vietnam, 1968—69, chief vascular surgery, asst. chief gen. surgery Letterman Army Med. Ctr., 1971-74, chief gen. and vascular surgery, program dir., gen. surgery residency Letterman Army Med. Ctr. San Francisco, 1975-81; comdr. 47th Field Hosp., Honduras, 1984; commanding gen. Madigan Army Med. Ctr. U.S. Army, Tacoma, 1989-92; ret., 1992; prof. surgery, chief div. gen. surgery, dept. surg. Uniformed Svcs. U. Sch. Medicine, Bethesda, Md., 1992—, mem. faculty senate, 1996—99, mem. students promotion com., 1993-96, 2002—05, mem. instl. rev. bd., 1993-96, mem. com. appointments, promotion and tenure, 1998-99, pres. elect faculty senate, 1997; pres. faculty senate Uniformed Svcs. U. Health Scis., Bethesda, 1998. Assoc. clin. prof. surgery U. Calif., San Francisco, 1978-81, mem. dean's adv. group Uniformed Svc. U. Health Sci., 1998-99; assoc. prof. surgery, vice chmn. dept. surgery Uniformed Svcs. U. Health Scis., Bethesda, 1981-84, prof. surgery, 1985—; clin. prof. surgery Tulane U. Sch. Medicine, 1988—, George Washington Sch. Medicine, Washington, 1985—. Contbr. articles, photographs to profl. publs., chpts. to books. Mem. men and boys choir Grace Cathedral, San Francisco, 1971-75. Decorated D.S.M., Bronze Star, Meritorious Svcs. medal with oak leaf cluster, Army Commendation Medal, Navy Commendation Medal, Joint Svc. Commendation Medal, Vietnam Svc. medal with four bronze svc. stars, Nat. DSM with two bronze svc. stars, Naval Occupation medal, WWII, Vietnam Honor medal 1st class, Vietnam Cross of Gallantry; recipient Barron Dominique Larrey award for excellence in surgery, Disting. Svc. medal, Uniformed Svcs. U. Sch. Medicine, 2000. Fellow: ACS; mem.: Internat. Soc. Vascular Surgery, Soc. Vascular Surgery, Soc. Med. Cons. Armed Forces (councilor 1988—89, v.p. 2000, pres. 2001), Acad. Medicine Washington D.C., Chesapeake Vascular Soc., Soc. Mil. Vascular Surgery, Am. Assn. Surgery of Trauma, Soc. Clin. Vascular Surgery, Bay Surg. Soc. (hon.), U.S. Naval Acad. Sailing Squadron, Severn Sailing Assn., St. Francis Yacht Club (membership com. 1978—81). Republican. Episcopalian. Avocations: music, photography, sailing, sports. Home: 1707 Priscilla Dr Silver Spring MD 20904-1610 Office: Uniformed Svcs U Health Scis Dept Surgery 4301 Jones Bridge Rd Bethesda MD 20814-4712 Office Phone: 301-295-9822. Business E-Mail: jhutton@usuhs.mil.

HUTTON, PAUL ANDREW, historian, educator, writer; b. Frankfurt, Germany, Oct. 23, 1949; s. Paul Andrew and Louise Katherine (Johnson) Hutton; m. Vicki Lynne Bauer, 1972 (div. 1985); 1 child, Laura; m. Lynn Terri Brittner, Dec. 31, 1988 (div. 1996); children: Lorena, Paul; m. Tracy Lee Cogdill, Aug. 7, 2001. BA, Ind. U., 1972, MA, 1974, PhD, 1981. Editorial asst. Jour. Am. History, Bloomington, Ind., 1973-77; instr. history Utah State U., Logan, 1977-80, asst. prof., 1980-84, U. N.Mex., Albuquerque, 1984-86, assoc. prof., 1986-96; prof. U. N. Mex., Albuquerque, 1996—2006, disting. prof., 2006—. Author: Phil Sheridan and His Army, 1985; editor: Custer and Hist Times, 1981, Ten Days on the Plains, 1985, Soldiers West, 1987, The Custer Reader, 1992, Frontier and Region, 1997, (series) Eyewitness to the Civil War, 1991—93; writer, co-prodr. (TV series) Frontier: The Decisive Battle, 2000, Boone & Crockett: The Hunter Heroes, 2003, Investigating History, 2004—05; writer, co-prodr.: (films) Daniel Boone and the Westward Movement, 2002; The Wilderness Road: Spirit of a Nation, 2004; assoc. editor: Western Hist. Quar., 1977—84; editor: N.Mex Hist. Rev., 1985—91. Active Little Bighorn Battlefield Indian Meml. Adv. Com., Nat. Park Svc., 1994—2002. Recipient Evans Biography award, Brigham Young U., 1986, Paladin award, Mont. Hist. Soc., 1991, Western Heritage award, Nat. Cowboy Hall of Fame, 1996, 1999, 2003, 2005; Mead Disting. Rsch. fellow, Huntington Libr., 1988. Mem.: Writers Guild Am. West, Western Writers Am. (exec. bd. 1997—99, pres. 2002—04, exec. dir. 2007—, Spur award 1985, 2002, 2004, 2006, Pres. award 1998, Stirrup award 2000, 2004), Soc. Mil. History, Western Hist. Assn. (exec. dir. 1990—2006), Orgn. Am. Historians (Ray A. Billington award 1986). Office: U NMex MSC06 3760 Dept History Albuquerque NM 87131-0001 Business E-Mail: hutton@unm.edu.

HUTTON, ROBERT LEE, pathologist; b. Corpus Christi, Tex., Nov. 5, 1969; s. Rollin Lee Hutton and Billie Karen Rex; m. Sherry Lynn Murphy, Sept. 11, 1992; children: Misty Dawn Murphy, Amber Rose, Robert Lee, Crystal Lynn. BS in Physics, Math., U. Tex., Austin, 1992. Lic. physician La. State Bd. Med. Examiners, 2004. Transitional intern Brooke Army Med. Ctr., Fort Sam Houston, Tex., 2002—03, pathology resident, 2003—. Cubmaster, com. mem. Boy Scouts Am., Alamo Area Coun., San Antonio, 2005—07. Capt. US Army, 1993—2007, Brooke Army Med. Ctr. Decorated ARCOM with Oak Leaf Cluster, AAM with Oak Leaf Cluster USArmy. Mem.: Coll. Am. Pathologists. Achievements include research in primary peritoneal serous borderline tumors, adult-type granulosa cell tumors of the testis. Home: 5418 Stormy Autumn San Antonio TX 78247 Office: Brooke Army Med Ctr 3856 Roger Brooke Dr Fort Sam Houston TX 78247 Home Phone: 210-654-4921; Office Phone: 210-219-3572. Personal E-mail: rhutton1@satx.rr.com.

HUTTON, TIMOTHY, actor; b. Malibu, Calif., Aug. 16, 1960; s. Jim and Maryline H.; m. Debra Winger, March 16, 1986 (div. 1990); 1 child, Emmanuel Noah; m. Aurore Giscard d'Estaing, Jan. 21, 2000; 1 child, Milo. Appeared in TV movies Zuma Beach, 1978, Best Place to Be, 1979, Baby Makes Six, 1979, Friendly Fire, 1979, Young Love, First Love, 1979, Father Figure, 1980, The Oldest Living Graduate, 1980, Sultan and the Rock Star, 1980, A Long Way Home, 1981, We're Family Again, 1981, Zelda, 1993, The Golden Spiders: A Nero Wolfe Mystery, 2000, Deliberate Intent, 2000, WW3, 2001, 5ive Days to Midnight, 2004, Avenger, 2006; films include Ordinary People, 1980 (Best Supporting Actor Acad. award 1981, Golden Globe award for Best Motion Actor in a Supporting Role, New Star of Year in a Motion Picture 1981), Taps, 1981, Daniel, 1983, Iceman, 1984, Turk 182, 1985, The Falcon and the Snowman, 1985, Made in Heaven, 1987, A Time of Destiny, 1988, Everybody's All-American, 1988, Betrayed, 1988, Torrents of Spring, 1990, Q & A, 1990, The Temp, 1993, The Dark Half, 1993, French Kiss, 1995, Scenes from Everyday Life, 1995, The Substance of Fire, 1996, Mr. and Mrs. Loving, 1996, Beautiful Girls, 1996, City of Industry, 1997, Playing God, 1997, Deterrence, 1998, The General's Daughter, 1999, Deterrence, 1999, Just One Night, 2000, The Lucky Strike, 2000, Sunshine State, 2002, Secret Window, 2004, Kinsey, 2004, Turning Green, 2005, Last Holiday, 2006, Stephanie Daley, 2006, The Kovak Box, 2006, Heavens Fall, 2006, Falling Objects, 2006, Off the Black, 2006, The Good Shepherd, 2006, The Last Mimzy, 2007; TV series A Nero Wolfe Mystery (also exec. prodr., dir.), 2001-02, Kidnapped, 2006-07; Broadway includes Prelude to a Kiss, 1990, Babylon Gardens, 1991; dir. video Drive, 1984 (The Cars song); dir. episode Amazing Stories, 1985 (Grandpa's Ghost). Office: Creative Artists Agy 9830 Wilshire Blvd Beverly Hills CA 90212-1804*

HUTTON, WILLIAM MICHAEL, manufacturing executive; b. Herrin, Ill., June 15, 1948; s. William T. and Violet (Childress) Hutton; m. Lois A. Piontkowski, Sept. 7, 1968; children: Cynthia L., Pamela. BS in Mgmt. Scis., So. Ill. U., 1972; grad. in decision scis., MIT, 1986; MA in Ops. Mgmt., Norwich U., 1991; grad. in exec. leadership, U. NC, 1998; PhD in Bus. Adminstrn., Kennedy-Western U., 2003. Cert. foodservice profl., SME mfg. engr. Mgr. machining ops. Ingersoll-Rand, Phillipsburg, NJ, 1973-83; mgr. of mfr. Bendix Aerospace Corp., Eatontown, NJ, 1983-84; v.p. ops. Follett Corp., Easton, Pa., 1984-87, pres., COO, 1988-95; CEO Wilkra Co., Inc., Portland, Pa., 1995, also bd. dirs.; ptnr. Filtration Mfg. Co.; founder, CEO Omega Tools, Inc. Cons. to small mfg. co.; tech. transference orgnl. adaptation consulting Natural Gas Industry; dj. prof. DeSales U.; exec. in residence So. Ill. U., 1991—, guest lectr. Coll. Bus.; guest lectr. Moravian Coll.; bd. dirs. Bustin Industries; presenter in field. Author: (book) Competitive Strategy, A Heuristic Model for Linking Manufacturing and Marketing, 1992, Organizational Adaptation Through Strategic Reorientation, A Study of the Gas Distribution Industry; contbr. articles to profl. publs. Chmn. adv. bd. Coll. Bus. and Adminstrn., So. Ill. U., 1989—, Ben Franklin Inst., 1991—; bd. dirs. Forum Lehigh Valley. Named to Hall of Fame Coll. Bus., So. Ill. U., 1994; recipient Alumni Achievement award, 1992, Ben Franklin Innovation award, 2002. Mem.: Acad. Mgmt., Soc. Mfg. Engrs., Ducks Unlimited, Grouse Soc., Young Pres.'s Orgn., So. Ill. U. Alumni Assn. Republican. Roman Catholic. Avocations: fly fishing, hunting. Home: 4640 Hillview Dr Nazareth PA 18064-8525 Office: Omega Tools Co Inc 969 Postal Rd Allentown PA 18104 Business E-Mail: hutton@otipa.com.

HUTTON, WINFIELD TRAVIS, management consultant, educator; b. LA, Aug. 17, 1935; s. Travis Calhoun and Frances (Gardemann) H. BS in Mgmt. summa cum laude, Ohio State U., 1956, MBA, 1957, PhD, 1959. Consumer economist Fed. Res. Bank Atlanta, 1959—62; prof. econs. Hunter Coll., CUNY, 1962—68; prof. European divsn. U. Md., 1968—79, 1993—99; prof. Troy State U.-Europe, Germany, 1979—93. Cons. on mgmt., mktg. and econs. in Europe, 1968—. Author: (mgmt. computer simulations) City Finance, 1994, Simanage, 1998; author computer programs for rsch. stats.; contbr. articles to profl. jours. Lay reader St. Alban's Episcopal Ch., Kaiserslauten, Germany, 1981-88. Mem. AAUP, Am. Mktg. Assn. (manuscript reviewer 1983-94), Am. Econ. Assn., Beta Gamma Sigma. Office: Palmer House 6059 S Redwing St Seattle WA 98118-6020

HUURMAN, WALTER WILLIAM, pediatric orthopaedic surgeon, educator; b. Rochester, NY, Mar. 16, 1936; s. Walter U. and Anna Mae (Lennon) H.; m. Lindsay Ann McGuiness, Dec. 16, 1967; children: Sean Patrick, Anne Lindsay. BS, U. Notre Dame, 1958; MD, Northwestern U., 1962. Diplomate Am. Bd. Orthop. Surgery. Intern Cook County Hosp., Chgo., 1962—63; flight surgeon USS Hornet, San Diego and Vietnam, 1964—66, NAS Miramar, San Diego, 1966—68; resident in orthop. surgery Naval Regional Med. Ctr., Oakland, Calif., 1968—71; dir. pediat. orthop. USN, Oakland, 1973—77; prof. pediat. and orthop. U. Nebr., Omaha, 1977—, prof. emeritus, 2006—; dir. pediat. orthop. U. Nebr./Children's Meml. Hosp., Omaha, 1977. Bd. dirs. Nat. Alumni, Northwestern U. Mem. editl. bd. Jour. Pediat. Orthop., 1981-83, Jour. Bone and Joint Surgery, 1983-87, Pediat. in Rev., 1995-2000; reviewer Clin. Orthop. and Related Rsch., 1985—, Jour. Am. Acad. Orthop. Surgeons, 1998—; contbr. articles to sci. and profl. jours Pres., chmn. bd. dirs. Nebr. Arthritis Found., 1984. Capt. USN, 1963-77; res., 1980-95, ret. Fellow ACS, Am. Acad. Orthop. Surgery, Am. Acad. Pediat. (chmn. orthop. sect. 1986-89, mem. exec. com. sect. on sports medicine, 1992-2000); mem. AMA, Am. Orthop. Assn., Omaha Midwest Clin. Soc. (pres. 1994), Nebr. Orthop. Soc. (pres. 2000-07), Pediat. Orthop. Soc. N.Am.(bd. dirs. 1994-2000), Acad. Orthop. Soc., Northwestern U. Feinberg Sch. Medicine Alumni Assn. (pres. 2005-07) Roman Catholic. Office: U Nebr Med Ctr 600 S 42nd St Omaha NE 68198-1002 Office Phone: 402-492-9767. Personal E-mail: whuurman@ix.netcom.com.

HUVAERE, JASON, production company executive; b. 1974; Attended, Northwood U., 1993. Pres., dir. ops. Paxahau Promotions Grp., L.L.C., Ferndale, Mich., 1998—. Prodr.: Movement 2006, Detroit's Electronic Music Festival. Named one of 40 Under 40, Crain's Detroit Bus., 2006. Office: Paxahau Promotions Group LLC 326 Hilton Ferndale MI 48220

HUVOS, ANDREW, internist, cardiologist, educator; b. Budapest, Hungary, Apr. 23, 1930; came to U.S., 1950; s. Julian Gyula and Magdolna (Matyas) H.; m. Monique Chatriot, June 8, 1959; children: Christine, Anne, Philip. Student, Free U. Brussels, 1948-50, Harvard U., 1951; MD, Boston U., 1955. Diplomate Am. Bd. Internal Medicine, Am. Bd. Cardiovasc. Disease. Resident in medicine Yale-New Haven Med. Ctr., 1955-59; fellow in cardiology Mass. Gen. Hosp., Boston, 1961-63; physician-in-charge cardiac catheterization lab. Univ. Hosp., Boston, 1963-70; chief cardiology Faulkner Hosp., Boston, 1970-74, chief medicine, 1974-95; lectr. medicine Harvard Med. Sch., Boston, 1974-86; lectr. medicine and physiology Boston U. Sch. Medicine, 1976—95; prof. medicine Tufts U. Sch. Medicine, Boston, 1985-97, prof. emeritus, 1997—. Dir. Tufts Assoc. Health Plan, 1979-81. Contbr. articles to med. jours., chpts. to books. Chmn. bd. trustees Ecole Bilingue, Inc., Arlington, Mass., 1970-74; trustee Boston Med. Libr., 1981-85. Capt. M.C., U.S. Army, 1959-61. Recipient Excellence in Teaching award Boston U. Sch. Medicine, 1974; USPHS grantee, 1977-83. Fellow: ACP, Mass. Med. Soc. (del., mem. com. on med. edn. 1981—95), Am. Heart Assn., Am. Coll. Chest Physicians (pres. New Eng. States chpt. 1981—83), Am. Coll. Cardiology; mem.: Roxbury Clin. Record Club, Dorchester Med. Club, Alpha Omega Alpha. Presbyterian. Avocations: opera, classical music.

HUWILER, JOAN P., public relations executive, consultant; b. New Haven, Conn., June 15, 1963; d. Paul F. and Joan E. (Tickey) H. BA in Comm., Southern Conn. State Univ., 1985; MS in Journalism, Boston Univ., 1990; MBA, U. New Haven, 2006. Account coord. Coates Pub.

Rels. subs. Mason & Madison Advertising, Bethany, Conn., 1985-86; devel. fund raiser Atty. Gen. Joe Lieberman, Hartford, Conn., 1986; dep. press sec. Office Atty. Gen., State of Conn., Hartford, Conn., 1986-89; media dir. NOW Legal Def. and Edn. Fund, NYC, 1990-92; cons., 1992-96; exec. dir. Schooner Inc., New Haven, Conn., 1992-93; comms. officer Cmty. Found. for Greater New Haven, New Haven, Conn., 1996-99; mktg. and comm. mgr. S. Ctrl. Regional Water Auth., New Haven, 1999—. Teaching asst. Boston Univ., 1989-90; pub. info. officer Hamden Bd. of Edn., 1984-85; writer, cons. Bank Mart, Bridgeport, Conn., 1985-86. Recipient Vanguard spl. merit award Women in Comm., 1991, Forty Under Forty award Bus. Times New Haven, 1999; named one of 20 Noteworthy Women, Bus. Times New Haven, 2000. Democrat. Avocations: reading, cooking, gardening. Office: S Ctrl Conn Regional Water Auth 90 Sargent Dr New Haven CT 06511-5918

HUXLEY, SIR ANDREW (FIELDING), physiologist, educator; b. London, Eng., Nov. 22, 1917; s. Leonard and Rosalind (Bruce) H.; m. Jocelyn Richenda Gammell Pease, July 5, 1947 (dec. Mar. 2003); children: Janet Rachel, Stewart Leonard, Camilla Rosalind, Eleanor Bruce, Henrietta Catherine, Clare Marjory Pease. BA, Cambridge U., Eng., 1938, MA, 1941, ScD (hon.), 1978; MD (hon.), U. Saar, 1964, Marseille U., 1979, Humboldt U., Berlin, 1985, Ulm U., 1993, Charles U., Prague, 1998; DSc (hon.), U. Sheffield, Eng., 1964, U. Leicester, 1967, London U., 1973, U. St. Andrews, Scotland, 1974, U. Aston, Birmingham, Eng., 1977, U. Western Australia, 1982, Oxford U., 1983, U. Pa., 1984, Harvard U., 1984, U. Keele, 1985, East Anglia U., 1985, U. Md., 1987, Brunel U., 1988, U. Hyderabad, 1991, Glasgow U., 1993, Witwatersrand U., 1998; LLD (hon.), U. Birmingham, 1979, Dundee U., 1984; Dr (hon.), York U., 1981, Toyama Med. and Pharm. U., 1995; DHL (hon.), NYU, 1982. Mem. rsch. staff Anti-Aircraft Command, 1940-42, Admiralty, 1942-45; fellow Trinity Coll., Cambridge, 1941-60, 90—, hon. fellow, 1967-90, master, 1984-90, dir. studies, 1952-60, Tarner lectr., 1988. Demonstrator dept. physiology Cambridge U., 1946—50, asst. dir. rsch. dept. physiology, 1951—59, reader exptl. biophysics, 1959—60; Jodrell prof. U. Coll. London, 1960—69, Royal Soc. rsch. prof., 1969—83; emeritus prof. London U., 1983—, hon. fellow, 1980—; fellow Royal Soc. London, 1955—, Croonian lectr., 1967, mem. coun., 1960—62, 1977—79, pres., 1980—85; Herter lectr. Johns Hopkins U., 1959; Jesup lectr. Columbia U., 1964; Forbes lectr., 66; Florey lectr., 82; Blackett Meml. lectr., 84; Fullerian prof. Royal Inst., London, 1967—73; Hans Hecht lectr., Chgo., 1975; Sherrington lectr Liverpool U., 1976—77; Centenary Colloquium lectr. Berlin Inst. Physiology, 1977; Cecil H. and Ida Green vis. prof. U. B.C., 1980; 6th ann. Darwin lectr., 82; Romanes lectr. Oxford U., 1983; Tarner lectrs. Trinity Coll., Cambridge, 1988; Maulana Abul Kalam Azad Meml. lectr., New Delhi, 91; C.G. Bernhard lectr. Stockholm, 1993; Davson lectr. Am. Physiol. Soc., 1998; Wartenweiler lectr. Internat. Soc. Biomechanics, Calgary, 1999. Author: Reflections on Muscle, 1980; editor Jour. Physiology, 1950-57, chmn. bd. Publs. on analysis of nerve conduction (with Hodgkin), physiology of striated muscle, devel. of interference microscope and ultramicrotome. Trustee Brit. Mus. (Natural History), 1981-90, Sci. Mus., 1984-88; mem. Agrl. Rsch. Coun., 1977-80, Nature Conservancy Coun., 1985-88, Animal Procedures Com., 1987-95. Decorated knight bachelor, Order of Merit, Grand Cordon of Sacred Treasure Japan; recipient (with A.L. Hodgkin and J.C. Eccles), Nobel Prize for physiology or medicine, 1963, Swammerdam medal, Soc. for Advancement of Natural Scis., Medicine and Surgery, Amsterdam, 1997, Copley medal, Royal Soc., 1973; fellow, Imperial Coll. Sci., Tech. and Medicine, 1980, Queen Mary and Westfield Coll., 1987, Royal Holloway and Bedford New Coll., 1994. Fellow Royal Acad. Engring. (hon.), Inst. Biology (hon.), Royal Soc. Can. (hon.), Royal Soc. Edinburgh (hon.), Royal Coll. Physicians (hon.), Acad. Med. Sci. (hon.), Indian Nat. Sci. Acad. (fgn.); mem. Physiol. Soc. (hon., rev. lectr. on muscular contraction 1973), Internat. Union Physiol. Scis. (pres. 1986-93), Brit. Biophys. Soc., Found. for Sci. and Tech., Royal Acad. Scis., Letters and Fine Arts Belgium (assoc.), Muscular Dystrophy Campaign (chmn. med. research com. 1974-81, v.p., 1981—), Royal Instn. Gt. Britain (hon.), Anat. Soc. Gt. Britain and Ireland (hon.), Am. Acad. Arts and Scis. (hon.), Am. Philos. Soc. (Penrose lectr. 1986), Brit. Assn. Advancement Sci. (pres. 1976-77), Leopoldina Acad. (hon.), NAS (U.S.) (fgn. assoc.), Royal Acad. Medicine Belgium (assoc.), Dutch Soc. Scis. (fgn.), Royal Danish Acad. Sci. (hon.), Am. Soc. Zoologists (hon.), Royal Irish Acad. (hon.), Japan Acad. (hon.). Home and Office: Manor Field 1 Vicarage Dr Grantchester Cambridge CB3 9NG England

HUXLEY, MARY ATSUKO, artist; b. Stockton, Calif., Mar. 5, 1930; d. Henry K. and Kiku H. (Kisanuki) Taniguchi; m. Harold Daniels Huxley, 1957. Student, Armstrong Coll., Berkeley, Calif., 1950, San Francisco Art Inst., 1968; pvt. studies with, Thomas C. Leighton, 1970—75. Art show judge regional art clubs, corps., pvt. orgns., and county fairs, 1972-2005. One-woman shows include Artists' Coop., San Francisco, 1973, 75-76, Univ. Club Invitational, San Francisco, 1976, I. Magnin, San Mateo, 1976, Palo Alto Med. Found., 1992, Galerie Genese, San Mateo, 1993; exhibited in group shows at Catharine Lorillard Wolf Art Club, NYC, 1979, Knickerbocker Artists of Am., NYC, 1979, Salmagundi Club Ann., NYC, 1981, Butler Inst. Am. Art, Youngstown, Ohio, 1982, Am. Artists Profl. League, NYC, 1982-83, 86-88, Oil Painters of Am., Gallery at Long Grove, Ill., 1993-94, Taos, N.Mex., 1997, Oil Painters of Am., Jones & Terwilliger Gallery, Carmel, Calif., 1997, San Francisco Ann. Art Festival, 1970-74, Renaissance Gallery, Santa Rosa, Calif., 1973, Paramount Theater, Oakland, Calif., 1974, Met. Club, San Francisco, Marin Soc. Artists, Ross, Calif., 1976, 79, Soc. Western Artists, San Francisco, 1976, 78, 80, Peninsula Art Assn., Belmont, Calif., 1980, Fresno Fashion Fair, Calif., 1981, 84, De Saisset Gallery, U. Santa Clara, Calif., 1979, Lodi Ann. Grape and Art Festival, Calif., 1970-79, 81, San Mateo County Floral Fiesta, 1975-79, 81, Charles & Emma Frye Mus. Gallery, Seattle, 1975, Redwood City Women's Club, 1978, Fremont Art Assn., 1987-89, John Muir Med. Ctr., 1999-2000, 3 Com-Synopsis, 2000-01, others; represented in numerous pvt. and corp. collections. Recipient Marjorie Walter Spl. award San Mateo County Exhbn., 1975, Gold medallion and 1st award San Mateo County Fair Fine Arts Exhbn., 1976, Best of Show award Cultural Arts of Palo Alto and Palo Alto Art Club, 1979, Best of Show and 1st award U. Art Ctr. and Palo Alto Art Club Ann., 1981, Spl. Merit award Oakland Art Assn., John Muir Med. Ctr. Ann., 1989, 1st award Burlingame Art Soc. Anns., 1976, 77, 1st award Redwood City Women's Club Ann. Flower Show, 1978, 1st award Soc. Western Artists Palo Alto Med. Ctr. Ann., 1983, 1st award Soc. Western Artists John Muir Med. Ctr. Ann., 1986, 1st award Fremont Art Assn. Ann., 1989, numerous others. Fellow Am. Artists Profl. League; mem. Soc. Western Artists (signature, trustee 1986-97, bd. dirs. 1972-75, 98, chmn. juried exhbns. 1972-81), Oil Painters Am. (signature), Allied Artists Am., Marin Soc. Artists (signature). Studio: PO Box 5467 San Mateo CA 94402-0467

HUXLIN, KRYSTEL RALUKA, neuroscientist, educator; b. Bucharest, Romania, Apr. 8, 1969; d. Raymond Will and Mary Ellen Huxlin; m. Keith Webster Nehrke, Sept. 13, 1997; 1 child, Jaenelle Marie Nehrke. BSc, U. Sydney, Australia, 1987—91, PhD, 1991—94. Rsch. asst. prof. U. Rochester, NY, 1999—2002, asst. prof., 2002—. Contbr. chapters to books. Bd. mem. Rochester Squash Racquets Assn., NY, 1997—2004. Recipient Beverly Steward Meml. prize, U. Sydney, 1987; fellow, Australian NH&MRC, 1995—97, Australian Med. Found., 1994—95; grantee, McDonnell-Pew Found., 2000—04, Bausch & Lomb Inc., 2001—, CEIS/NYSTAR, 2002—, Schmitt Program on Integrative Brain Rsch., 2003—05, NIH/NEI, 2004—; scholar, Juvenile Diabetes Found. Internat., 1988, Australian NH&MRC, 1991—94, Brit. Coun., 1992, Australian NH&MRC, 1990; Robert E. McCormick scholar, Rsch. Prevent Blindness Found., 2005. Mem.: Faculty for Undergraduate Neurosci., Assn. for Rsch. in Vision and Ophthalmology, Soc. for Neurosci., Vision Sciences Soc., Rsch. to Prevent Blindness (assoc.; ophthal. assoc. 2004—). Achievements include patents pending for computerized training and evaluation of visual discrimination abilities; research in the neural and molecular substrates of visual recovery after permanent visual cortical damage in adulthood; the optical consequences of corneal wound healing following laser refractive surgery. Avocations: squash, Irish dancing, horseback riding, hiking, violin. Office: U Rochester Med Ctr Box 314 601 Elmwood Ave Rochester NY 14642 Home Phone: 585-533-2294; Office Phone: 585-275-5495. Office Fax: 585-473-3411. Business E-Mail: huxlin@cvs.rochester.edu.

HUXTABLE, ADA LOUISE, architecture critic; b. NYC; d. Michael Louis and Leah (Rosenthal) Landman; m. L. Garth Huxtable. AB magna cum laude, Hunter Coll.; postgrad., Inst. Fine Arts, NYU; degree (hon.), Harvard U., Yale U., NYU, Washington U., U. Mass., Oberlin Coll., Miami U., RI Sch. Design, U. Pa., Radcliffe Coll., Oberlin Coll., Smith Coll., Skidmore Coll., Md. Inst., Mt. Holyoke Coll., Trinity Coll., LaSalle U., Pace Coll., Pratt Inst., Colgate U., Hamilton U., Williams Coll., Rutgers U., Finch Coll., Emerson Coll., LI U., Cleve. State U., Bard Coll., Fordham U., Parsons Sch. Design, Mass. Coll. Art, Nottingham U., U. Mich. Asst. curator architecture and design The Museum of Modern Art, NYC, 1946-50; Fulbright fellow for advanced study in architecture and design Italy, 1950, 52; free-lance writer, contbg. editor to Progressive Architecture and Art in America, 1950-63; architecture critic N.Y. Times, NYC, 1963-82, mem. editorial bd., 1973-82; Cook lectr. in Am. instns. U. Mich., 1977; Hitchcock lect. U. Calif.-Berkeley, 1982. Corp. vis. com. Harvard U. Grad. Sch. Design, Sch. Visual and Environ. Arts; mem. adv. bd. Am. Trust Brit. Libr.; archtl. cons. Nat. Gallery, London, J. Paul Getty Trust, L.A., San Francisco Pub. Libr., Mus. Contemporary Art, Chgo., Kansas City Art Mus.; archtl. critic The Wall Street Jour., 1996—. Author: Pier Luigi Nervi, 1960, Classic New York, 1964, Will They Ever Finish Bruckner Boulevard?, 1970, Kicked a Building Lately?, 1976, The Tall Building Artistically Reconsidered: The Search for a Skyscraper Style, 1985, Goodbye History, Hello Hamburger 1986, Architecture Anyone? 1986, The Unreal America: Architecture and Illusion, 1997, Frank Lloyd Wright, 2004. Recipient 1st Pulitzer prize for disting. criticism, 1970, Spl. award Nat. Trust for Historic Preservation, 1971, Archtl. Criticism medal AIA, 1969, medal for lit. Nat. Arts Club, 1971, Diamond Jubilee medallion City N.Y., 1973, Mayor's Cultural award, 1984, Woman of Yr. award AAUW, 1974, Sec.'s award for conservation U.S. Dept. Interior, 1976, Thomas Jefferson medal U. Va., 1977, Archtl. Criticism medal Acad. d' Architecture Française, 1988; Guggenheim fellow for studies in Am. architecture, 1958, MacArthur fellow, 1981-86, fellow Ctr. for Scholars and Writers, N.Y. Pub. Libr., 1999-00; Henry Allen Moe prize Humanities Am. Philosophical Soc., 1992. Fellow Am. Acad. Arts and Scis., Royal Inst. Brit. Architects (hon.), AAAL; mem. AIA (hon.), Am. Acad. Arts and Letters, Soc. Archtl. Historians. Home: 969 Park Ave New York NY 10028-0322

HUYBRECHTS, STEVEN MARC, space system technologist; b. Dover, NH, Dec. 29, 1969; s. Marc Huybrechts and Brigitte Duces, John Strawhorn (Stepfather) and Ellida Yngente (Stepmother); m. Wendy Marie Cubbison, Oct. 11, 2002; children: Rachel Johnson, Caden, Taryn, Mia. BSc in Physics and Computer sci., McGill U., Montreal, Can., 1991; MS in Aero. and Astron. Engring., Stanford U., 1992, PhD in Aero. and Astron. Engring., 1995. Rschr. Ctr. for Spacecraft Component Tech., Kirtland AFB, N.Mex., 1992—99, chief, 1999—2002; prin. dir., C3, space spectrum Office Sec. of Def., Pentagon, DC. Recipient Sci. and Tech. Achievement award, Air Force Materiel Command, 1997, Arthur S. Fleming award, Flemming Found., Georgetown U., 2000, Stellar award, 2000, Rotary Nat. Space Achievement award, 2000, Pres.'s award, Nat. Def. U., 2004. Fellow: AIAA (sub-com. chair, conf. chair 1999—2002). Achievements include development of many enabling technologies for future space systems.

HUYGENS, REMMERT WILLIAM, architect; b. Haarlem, Netherlands, Apr. 19, 1932; came to U.S., 1956, naturalized, 1963; s. Willem and Antoinette (Bruynzeel) H. Diploma dept. architecture, Amsterdam HTS, 1955. With Marcel Breuer, NYC, 1956; pvt. practice Wayland, Mass., 1960—2005, Woodbine, Ga., 2005—. Prin. works include: Campus Rivers Country Day Sch., Weston, Mass., 1960, Longy Concert Hall, Cambridge, Mass., 1966, Interfaith Religious Ctr. Columbia, Md., 1967, campus N.H. Coll., Manchester, 1969-81, The Village of Loon Mountain, Lincoln, N.H., 1973-, Cath. Med. Ctr. Manchester, 1974, Milford (Conn.) Pub. Libr., 1976, Village Green at Stowe, Vt., 1980—, rsch. bldgs. for Biogen Inc., Cambridge and Geneva, 1980, Indian Head Nat. Bank, Nashua, N.H., 1981, Pub. Libr., Framingham, Mass., 1982, Teradyne Circuits Inc., Nashua, 1983, Riverview office tower, Cambridge, 1985, Cochituate Place office bldg., Framingham, 1986 One Memorial Drive office tower, Cambridge, 1986, Constitution Office Complex, Boston, 1987, Water's Edge Resort, Westbrook, Conn., 1987, Franklin Park Zoo, Boston, 1989, Ipswich (Mass.) Country Club, 1989; office parks, residential cmtys. and pvt. residences in U.S., Holland, France, Switzerland, Malaysia, corp. hdqs. and rsch. facilities for Genzyme Corp., Enzytech Inc., BioSurface Technology Inc., ImmunoGen Inc., Digital Equipment Corp., urban planning Guangzhou, China, 100 story office tower, Guangzhou, China, 1990, work exhibited at N.Y. Archtl. League, N.Y. Mus. Modern Art, N.Y., Brockton Art Ctr., Boston Arch. Ctr.; works pub. in numerous books and jours., U.S., Eng., Holland, Italy, Japan, France, Belgium, Germany, China, others, including: Arch. Record, Archtl. Forum, AIA Jour., Am. Home, House and Garden, Progressive Arch., House Beautiful, N.Y. Times, Boston Globe. Recipient Abu-Dhabi Conf. Ctr. award, 1st award Internat. Masonry Inst., Modern Architecture award, Coun. Architecture, Modernism and Environment, France, 2001, others. Fellow AIA (Progressive Architecture Design awards, Honor awards New Eng. regional coun., award of merit R.I. chpt., Conn. Soc. Archs./AIA Design award). Office: R W Huygens FAIA Arch 140 Lakes Blvd 212 Kingsland GA 31548 Office Phone: 912-729-6548. Business E-Mail: huygensarchitect@tds.net.

HUYNH, MY HANG VO, chemist, researcher; b. Saigon, Vietnam, May 30, 1962; arrived in US, 1985; d. Louis Huynh and Ngoc Thom Thi Huynh-Dang; MA in Math. (hon.), SUNY, Geneseo, 1991, MS with honors in Chemistry, 1991; PhD, SUNY, Buffalo, 1998. Postdoctoral rsch. assoc. U. NC, Chapel Hill, 1998—2000; postdoctoral fellow Los Alamos Nat. Lab., N.Mex., 2000—02, rschrs. synthetic organic and inorganic chemist divsn., dynamic and energetic materials divsn., DE-1, High Explosive and Sci. Tech. Group, 2002—. Featured 26 nat. and 13 internat. media appearances; contbr. articles to profl. jours. Named one of Outstanding Scientists of 21st Century, 2004, 2006, 2000 Outstanding Scientists of the 21st Century, 2005; recipient Found. Presdl. Scholarship award, SUNY, Geneseo, 1989—90, Outstanding Adult Student award, 1991—92, Postdoctoral Disting. Performance award, 2002, Dept. Chemistry Supplemental award, SUNY, Buffalo, 1992—93, Mattern-Tyler award, SUNY, Buffalo, 1995—96, Excellence in Tchg. award, 1996—97, R&D 100 award, Los Alamos Nat. Lab., 2005, 2006, Individual Disting. Licensing award, 2005, Individual Disting. Performance award, 2005, Health and Safety award, Nat. Registry Environ. Profls., 2006, Ernest Orlando Lawrence award in Chemistry, Dept. Energy, 2006, Internat. Medal of Honor, 2007, Best-in-Class Pollution Prevention award, Dept. Energy and Nat. Nuc. Security Assn., 2007; fellow, Los Alamos Nat. Lab., 2001—; Found. Presdl. scholar Co-curricular activities, SUNY, Geneseo, 1989—90, Paul R. Neureiter scholar, 1990—91, Gordon M. Harris Chemistry fellow, SUNY, Buffalo, 1992—95. Mem.: ACS, Pi Mu Epsilon. Achievements include patents in field; discovery of green primary explosives. Office: Los Alamos Nat Lab Dynamic Experimentations Divsn DE-1 High Explosive Sci and Tech MS P918 Los Alamos NM 87545 Office Phone: 505-667-9668, 505-667-3762. Personal E-mail: osmium2003@yahoo.com. Business E-Mail: huynh@lanl.gov.

HUZAR, ELEANOR GOLTZ, historian, educator; b. St. Paul, June 15, 1922; d. Edward Victor and Clare (O'Neill) Goltz; m. Elias Huzar, June 21, 1950 (dec. Dec. 1950); m. Bruce I. Granger, Oct. 11, 1991. BA, U. Minn., 1943; MA, Cornell U., 1945, PhD, 1948. Instr. history Stanford U., Palo Alto, Calif., 1948-50; asst. prof. classics U. Ill., Urbana, 1951-55; assoc. prof. history S.E. Mo. Coll., Cape Girardeau, 1955-59; assoc. prof. classics Carleton Coll., Northfield, Minn., 1959-60; prof. history Mich. State U., East Lansing, 1960-90, chmn. program in classical studies, 1965-90. Mem. selection com. Nat. Endowment for Humanities, Washington, 1979-84, Coun. for Internat. Exchg. Scholars, Washington, 1979-81, Mich. Rhodes Scholars, Ann Arbor, 1981-84, Prix de Rome, Am. Acad., NYC, 1978-80. Author: Mark Antony: A Biography, 1978; contbr. articles and revs. to profl. jours. George Boldt fellow, Cornell U., 1947—48. Mem. Classical Assn. of Mid. West and South (pres. 1984-85), Am. Hist. Assn., Am. Philol. Assn., Archael. Inst. Am. (local pres. 1979-80), Mich. Classical Conf. (pres. 1984-85), Am. Acad. in Rome (adv. coun. 1963-92, exec. com. 1970-73, 88-92), Am. Sch. in Athens (mng. com. 1964-92), Phi Beta Kappa, Phi Kappa Phi. Democrat. Roman Catholic. Avocations: hiking, skiing, travel. Home: 2945 Lincoln Dr Apt 132 Saint Paul MN 55113-1341

HWANG, BEONGBOK, engineering educator; s. Suckeun Hwnag and Jungsoon Park; m. Soonmin Hong, July 15, 1985; 1 child, Jungkyu. PhD in Engring., U.C. Berkeley, Calif., 1991. Prof. Inha U., Inchon, Republic of Korea, 1993—2005. Office: Inha Univ 253 Yonghyun Dong Incheon 402-751 Republic of Korea Home Phone: 416-512-2799; Office Phone: +8232-860-7387. Personal E-mail: bbhwang@inha.ac.kr.

HWANG, CHAN S., physiatrist, consultant; s. Chonsok Jonathan Hwang and Duksoon Amy Pak; m. Esther Miran Park, June 21, 1992; children: Nathaniel Chanoong, Nicole Mina, Natalie Anna, Noelle Emily. MD, Loma Linda U. Sch. Medicine, Calif., 1994. Diplomate Am. Bd. Phys. Medicine and Rehab., 1999, Am. Bd. Electrodiagnostic Medicine, 2004, lic. physician Wash., 2003. Physician Meml. Clinic, Olympia, Wash., 1998—2001, Park's Med. Clinic, Lakewood, Wash., 1998—2001; pvt. practice Puyallup, Wash., 2001—. Ind. cons. UBC, Inc., Puyallup, 2001—; physician Electrodiagnosis and Rehab. Assoc. Tacoma, 2002—05. Contbr. articles to profl. jours. Writer online answers Bibleinfo.com, Spokane, 2005—07. Recipient Scholl Recognition award. Fellow: Am. Assn. Neuromuscular and Electrodiagnostic Medicine, Am. Acad. Phys. Medicine and Rehabilitation. Achievements include development of lifestyle modification recommendations in clinical pain management practice. Avocation: violin. Office: 126 15th St SE Puyallup WA 98372 Home Phone: 253-568-0021; Office Phone: 253-445-8663. Office Fax: 253-445-8342.

HWANG, CORDELIA JONG, retired chemist; b. NYC, July 14, 1942; d. Goddard and Lilly (Fung) Jong; m. Warren C. Hwang, Mar. 29, 1969; 1 child, Kevin. BA, Barnard Coll., 1964; MS, SUNY, Stony Brook, 1969. Rsch. asst. Columbia U., NYC, 1964-66; analytical chemist Veritron West, Inc., Chatsworth, Calif., 1969-70; asst. lab. dir., chief chemist Pomeroy, Johnston & Bailey Environ. Engrs., Pasadena, Calif., 1970-76; chemist Met. Water Dist. So. Calif., LA, 1976-79, rsch. chemist, 1980-91, sr. chemist, 1992—2000, sr. rsch. chemist, 2001—05. Mem. Joint Task Group on Instrumental Identification of Taste and Odor Compounds, 1983-85, Joint Task Group on Nitrosamines, 2004; instr. Citrus Coll., 1974-76; chmn. Joint Task Group on Disinfection by-products: chlorine, 1990. Mem. AAUW (chmn. edn. found. Palos Verdes Peninsula br. 2005—), Am. Chem. Soc., Am. Water Works Assn. (life).

HWANG, DAVID HENRY, playwright, screenwriter; b. LA, Aug. 11, 1957; s. Henry Yuan and Dorothy Yu (Huang) H.; m. Kathryn A. Layng, Dec. 17, 1993; 1 child, Noah. BA in English, Stanford U., 1979; postgrad., Yale Drama Sch., 1980-81. Playwright: FOB, 1980 (Obie award 1981), The Dance and the Railroad, 1981 (CINE Golden Eagle award 1982), Family Devotions, 1981, Sound and Beauty, 1983, The Sound of a Voice, 1984, As the Crow Flies, 1986, Rich Relations, 1986, M. Butterfly, 1988 (Tony award for best play 1988, Outer Critics Circle award for best Broadway play 1988, Pulitzer prize for drama nomination 1988), Yellow Face, 2007, (musicals) 1000 Airplanes on the Roof, 1988, Bondage, 1992, Face Value, 1993, Trying to Find Chinatown, 1996, Golden Child, 1996-98 (Obie award 1997, Tony nomination Best Play 1998), The Silver River, 1997, (adaptation) Peer Gynt, 1998; librettist: The Voyage, 1992; screenwriter: (films) M. Butterfly, 1993, Golden Gate, 1994, (television) Forbidden Nights, 1990. Mem. Pres.'s Com. Arts and Humanities, 1994—. Fellow Rockefeller Found., 1983, Guggenheim Found., 1984, Nat. Endowment Arts, 1987; recipient Drama-Logue award 1980, 86, 98, John Gassner award, 1988. Mem. Dramatists Guild (bd. dirs. 1988—). Democrat. Office: Writers & Artists Agy care William Craver 19 W 44th St Ste 1000 New York NY 10036-6095 also: Creative Artists Agy 9830 Wilshire Blvd Beverly Hills CA 90212-1804*

HWANG, DENNIS (DENNIS HWANG-JUNG-MOAK), graphic computer artist; b. Knoxville, Tenn., Mar. 31, 1978; arrived in Korea, 1983, arrived in Am., 1992; Logo designer Google Inc., 2000—, asst. webmaster. Appalachian Arts Fellow award, World's Fair Park, Knoxville, Tenn., 2003. Designed his first logo for Google on the Fourth of July in 2000, at the request of Larry Page and Sergey Brin, and has been designing the specialty logos since that time. Mailing: Google Inc 1600 Amphitheatre Parkway Mountain View CA 94043

HWANG, JAE-KWANG, physicist, researcher; b. Seoul, Republic of Korea, Apr. 23, 1961; arrived in U.S., 1996; s. Jung-Sup Hwang and Jung-Sun Yun; m. Kyung-Saeng Annette Koh, Sept. 15, 1966; children: Joseph Cheol-Jean, Sherrina Yeh-Eun. BS, Yonsei U., Seoul, 1984, MS, 1986, PhD, 1992. Sr. rsch. assoc. Vanderbilt U., Nashville, 1996—. Contbr. articles to profl. jours. Mem.: Am. Physics Soc. Achievements include development of new nuclear half-life measurement technique; Identification of first gamma transitions in several nuclei such as 109Mo, 109Tc and 147Pr. Office: Vanderbilt Univ Physics Dept Box 1807 Station B Nashville TN 37235 Business E-Mail: jae-kwang.hwang@vanderbilt.edu.

HWANG, JASON KAO, composer, violinist, music educator; b. Lake Forest, Ill., May 12, 1957; s. Kao and Sheila Hwang; m. Gennevieve Lam, Jan. 1986. BFA, NYU, 1979. Lectr. Ctrl. Conservatory, Beijing, 1997; adj. instr. NYU, 2000—; lectr. Bklyn Coll., 2002, 2006. Mem. adv. com. New World Records, NYC; panelist Nat. Endowment for the Arts, Washington, 2002, Fund for U.S. Artists at Internat. Festivals, NYC, 1997. Composer: (chamber opera) The Floating Box, A Story in Chinatown, 2005 (chosen by Opera News one of top 10 opera recs. in 2005), (film) Tea and Justice, 2007; violinist, composer (CD) Unfolding Stone, 1990, Urban Archaeology, 1996, Caverns, 1994, Edge, 2006, Local Lingo, 2007, (dance score) Unbroken Thread, 2003, dir., composer (documentary film) Afterbirth, 1983, violinist, co-arranger M Butterfly, Broadway and nat. tour., 1988—91, composer, violinist du Maurier Ltd. International Jazz Festival, Vancouver, Can., 1993, Jazz Spektakel, Wuppertal, Germany, 1995, Nickelsdorf Konfrontationen Festival, Nickelsdorf, Austria, 1995, Whitney Mus. Contemporary Art at Phillip Morris, NYC, 1996, Inst. Contemporary Art, Boston, 1996, Internat. Festival Musique Actuelle, Victoriaville, Que., Can., 1996, Beijing Internat. Jazz Festival, 1997, Vision Festival, NYC, 1998, 2006—07, The Freer Gallery, Washington, 1999, violinist with Sin Cha Hong, Pusan, Seoul and Tae Koo, South Korea, 1992, with Reggie Workman Ensemble, Austria, Switzerland, 1993, with Anthony Braxton Quintet, Internat. Akbank Festival, Istanbul, Turkey, 1995, with Henry Threadgill Soc. Situation Dance Band, Verona Jazz Festival, Verona, Italy, 1996, with Vladimir Tarasov Ensemble for New and Improvised Music, Lithuania, Moscow and Arkhengelsk, Russia, 1997. Fellow, NJ State Coun. on the Arts, 1996, 2002; grantee, Greenwall Found., 1995, Nat. Endowment for Arts, Opera/Musical Theater, 1995, Mary Flagler Cary Charitable Trust, 1995, 1999, Meet the Composer/New Residencies, 1998—2000, Fund for U.S. Artists at Internat. Festivals and Exhbns., 1997, NY Cmty. Trust, 1999, Rockefeller Found. Multi-Arts Prodn. Fund, 2000, Puffin Found., 2001, Nat. Endowment for the Arts, 1999, Margaret Fairbanks Jory Copying Assistance Program of the Am. Music Ctr., 2001. Mem.: Am. Fedn. Musicians (Local 802). Home Phone: 201-653-3646.

HWANG, JIMMY JOHN, internist, oncologist; b. Lakeland, Fla., Sept. 18, 1969; MD, U. Pitts., 1995. Cert. Internal Medicine, Med. Oncology, Hematology. Intern, medicine U. Pitts., Pa., 1996, resident Pa., 1998; fellow U. Pitts. & Pitts. Cancer Inst., Pa., 1998—2001; staff mem., Lombardi Cancer Ctr. Georgetown U. Hosp., Washington, 2002—, asst. prof. medicine, 2002—. Office: Lombardi Cancer Ctr Georgetown U Hosp 3800 Reservoir Rd NW Washington DC 20007 Office Phone: 202-444-1287, 202-444-8154. Office Fax: 202-444-2886. Business E-Mail: jh96@georgetown.edu.*

HWANG, KAREN, research scientist; BA in Comm., U. Pa., Phila., 1990; EdM in Counseling Psychology, Rutgers U., New Brunswick, NJ, 1995, EdD in Counseling Psychology, 2005. Psychology student extern Children's Specialized Hosp., Mountainside, NJ, 1998—99; rsch. asst. Kessler Med. Rehab. Rsch. and Edn. Corp., West Orange, NJ, 1996—2000, rsch. fellow, 2005—; pre-doctoral rsch. fellow U. Medicine and Denistry N.J., Newark, 2000—01; psychology intern Hunterdon Developmental Ctr., Clinton, NJ, 2003—04. Disability adv. Alliance for Disabled in Action, Edison, NJ, 2002—03; bd. dirs. AUTONOMY, Danvers, Mass., 2006; peer counselor Kessler Med. Rehab Rsch. & Edn. Corp., West Orange, NJ, 1992—2003. Scholar, Ethel Louise Armstrong Found., 2000—01. Mem.: APA, Am. Assn. Spinal Cord Injury Psychologists and Social Workers (assoc.). Avocation: community radio. Office: Kessler Med Rehab Rsch & Edn Corp 1199 Pleasant Valley Way West Orange NJ 07052 Home Phone: 908-753-3903; Office Phone: 973-324-3566. E-mail: khwang@kmrrec.org.

HWANG, TZU-YANG, minister; b. Kaohsiung, Taiwan, Republic of China, Sept. 21, 1953; came to U.S., 1985; d. Chi-Chou and Iu-Chih (Tsai) Huang; m. Wei-Chih Shih Hwang, Sept. 6, 1980; 1 child, Mu-Hsuan. MDiv, Tainan Theol. Sem., 1980; ThM, Princeton Sem., NJ, 1986; PhD, Chinese for Christ Theol. Sem., Rosemead, Calif., 1990. Ordained to ministry Presbyn. Ch. Chairperson, min. Presbytery's Zrhlin Dists. Ch., Chanphwa, Taiwan, 1981-83; min., lectr., sr. editor Tainan Theol. Sem., 1983-85; founder, min. The Youth Fellowship of Kingston Presbyn. Ch., Princeton, 1985-86; head of religion edn., lectr. Good Shepherd Formosan Presbyn. Ch., Monterey Park, Calif., 1987—89, Chinese for Christ Theol. Sem., 1987—90, chmn. theology and philosophy, dean students, sr. editor, 1990-94; founder., hon. chair, pres., prof., CEO Am. Chi Chou Theo-Philosophical Inst., 1995—. Vis. scholar Harvard U. Div. Sch., Duke U. Div. Sch., 1991—92; sr. pastor, founder, pres. Light Christ Ch.; chmn., pres., incorporator, bd. dirs., founder, CEO Light Christ Found., 1994—; sec.-gen. Ministry of Culture; amb.-gen. United Cultural Conv.; others. Contbr. numerous articles to profl. jours. chpts. to books. With Chinese Def., 1972—. Named Noble Laureate, Greatest Intellectuals of the 21st Century; named one of Greatest Lives, Greatest Minds, Greatest Living Legends; recipient Nobel Peace prize, Legion of Honor, Distinction cert., UN, Lifetime Achievement award, World Congress Arts, Scis. and Comms., Outstanding Profl. Achievement award. Mem. Am. Acad. Religion, Soc. Biblical Literature, ABIRA (internat. and continental gov., internat. Order of Ambassadors), Internat. Biog. Ctr. (dir. gen. honors list), Assn. IBC (advisor dir. gen., hon. dir. gen., dep. dir. gen.), Internat. Order of Merit (bd. mem.), Leading Intellectuals of World (founding charter mem., noble mem. and world laureate), Harvard Coperative Soc., Comdrs. Club, Disabled Am. Vets., World Order Edn., Sci. and Culture, World Acad. Letters, Order Am. Amb. (founder, sovereign amb. goodwill), Internat. Amb. Goodwill (founder, mem. cabinet), World Peace and Diplomacy Forum (pres., presdl. edition and dedication). Home and Office: 11768 E Roseglen St El Monte CA 91732-1446 Office: Am Chi Chou Theo Phil Inst 11804 Hemlock St El Monte CA 91732-1413 Office Phone: 626-579-4727.

HWANG, WEI-CHIN, psychology professor; s. Yuan-Tzu and Shu-Chin Hwang. BA in Psychology, U. Utah, Salt Lake City, 1997, BA in Asian Studies, 1997; PhD in Clin. Psychology, U. Calif., LA, 2003. Lic. clin. psychologist CA, 2004, Utah, 2004. Asst. prof. U. Utah, Dept. Psychology, Salt Lake City, 2003—06, Claremont McKenna Coll., Dept. Psychology, Calif., 2006—. Psychology pvt. practice, Pasadena & Claremont, Calif., 2006—. Contbr. scientific papers. Faculty com. mem. Claremont McKenna Coll., 2006, U. Utah, Salt Lake City, 2003—06. Recipient Clayton award, U. Utah, 2006; Grad.fellowship, Phi Kappa Phi Honor Soc., 1997, Minority Fellowship Program Grad. fellow, APA, 1997—2000, Eugene Cota Robles Grad. fellowship, UCLA, 1997—2001, fellowship, Okura Mental Health Leadership Found., 2002, Minority Fellowship Program Psychology Summer Inst. fellowship, APA, 2005, Proposal Initiative grant, U. Utah, 2005, OBSSR Summer Inst. on Clin. Trials fellowship, NIH, 2006. Fellow: Taiwan Psychology Network, Faculty Mentor; mem.: Divsn. 45, Soc. for Psychol. Student of Ethnic Minorities Issues, Asian APA, APA. Office: Claremont McKenna Coll Dept of Psych 850 Columbia Ave Claremont CA 91801 Office Phone: 909-607-2762. Office Fax: 909-621-8419. Business E-Mail: whwang@cmc.edu.

HWANG, YUJONG, information scientist, educator; b. Seoul, Kyungki, Jan. 20, 1971; s. Sang-kuk Hwang and Young-hee Kim; m. Sung E. Kong, July 2, 1999; children: Esther J., David J. BS in Bus. Adminstrn., Hankuk U. Fgn. Studies, Seoul, 1996, MBA in MIS and Acctg., 1998; PhD in Bus. Adminstrn., U. S.C., Columbia, 2003. Instr. U. S.C., Columbia, 2001—03; asst. prof. DePaul U., Chgo., 2003—. Contbr. articles to profl. jours. Computer instr. West Alliance Ch., Warrenville, Ill., 2005—06. Mem.: Global Info. Tech. Mgmt. Assn. (assoc.), Assn. Info. Systems (assoc.), Beta Gamma Sigma (hon.). Avocation: swimming. Office: DePaul Univ 1 E Jackson Blvd Chicago IL 60604 Home Phone: 630-904-8921; Office Phone: 312-362-5487. Office Fax: 312-362-6208. E-mail: yhwang1@depaul.edu.

HYBELS, BILL, Pastor; b. Kalamazoo, 1952; m. Lynn Hybels; 2 children. BA Biblical Studies, Trinity Coll., hon. Phd of Divinity. Founder, sr. pastor Willow Creek Assn., South Barrington, Ill., 1992—. Author: (novels) Who You Are When No One's Looking, 1987; co-author Becoming a Contagious Christian, 1995, Too Busy Not to Pray, 1997, Philippians: Run the Race, 1999; author Courageous Leadership, 2002, The Volunteer Revolution, 2004, Just Walk Across the Room: Simple Steps Pointing People to Faith, 2006. Named one of 25 Most Influential Evangelists in America, Time Magazine, 2005. Achievements include leading a network of 10,500 churches and training more than 100,000 pastors each year. Office: Willow Creek Community Church 67 East Algonquin Rd Barrington IL 60010 Office Phone: 847-765-5000. E-mail: info@willowcreek.org.*

HYBL, WILLIAM JOSEPH, lawyer, foundation administrator; b. Des Moines, July 16, 1942; s. Joseph A. and Geraldine (Evans) H.; m. Kathleen (Horrigan), June 6, 1967; children: William J. Jr., Kyle Horrigan. BA, Colo. Coll., 1964; JD, U. Colo., 1967. Bar: Colo. 1967. Asst. dist. atty. 4th Jud. Dist. El Paso and Teller Counties, 1970—72; pres., dir. Garden City Co.; chmn., CEO, trustee El Pomar Found., Colorado Springs, Colo., 1973—; vice chmn. Broadmoor Hotel, Inc., 1987—; pres. U.S. Olympic Com., 1991—92, 1996—2000; chmn. and CEO U.S. Olympic Found., 2002—; chmn. IFES, 2003—; nat. commr. US Nat. Commn. UNESCO, 2005—; western interstate commr. Higher Edn. (WICHE), 2005—. Dir. USAA, San Antonio, Kinder Morgan Inc., Houston, First Bank Holding Co., Lakewood, Colo.; mem. Colo. Ho. of Reps., 1972-73; spl. counsel The White House, Washington, 1981; U.S. Rep. to 56th Gen. Assembly of UN, 2001-02; bd. dirs. Vail Valley Found. Pres. Air Force Acad. Found.; sec., vice chmn. bd. U.S. Adv. Commn. on Pub. Diplomacy, 1990-97; civilian aide to sec. of army, 1986—; bd. trustees Colo. Coll. Capt. U.S. Army. 1967-69. Republican. Office Phone: 719-577-5712. Business E-Mail: wjhybl@elpomar.org.

HYDE, ALAN LITCHFIELD, retired lawyer; b. Akron, Ohio, Nov. 4, 1928; s. Howard Linton Hyde and Katharine (Pennington) Litchfield; m. Charlotte Griffin Ross, July 10, 1954; children: Elizabeth Hyde Moore, Pamela. AB magna cum laude, Amherst Coll., 1950; JD, Harvard U., 1953. Bar: Ohio 1953, U.S. Dist. Ct. (no. dist.) Ohio 1955. Assoc. Thompson, Hine and Flory, Cleve., 1953-64, ptnr., 1964-93; ret., 1993. Hon. consul, Mexico, 1969—74. Contbr. articles to profl. jours. Trustee Planned Parenthood Greater Cleve., Inc., 1960-79, 80-81, pres. bd. trustees, 1977-79; sec., gen. counsel Greater Cleve. Growth Assn., 1972-74, 86-88, bd. dirs., 1974-80, 82-86, 88-93; trustee Cleve. World Trade Assn., 1978-81; trustee Cleve. Coun. World Affairs, 1980-93, mem. exec. com., 1980-83. Mem. ABA, Inter-Am. Bar Assn. (coun., com. on Latin Am. Devel.), Greater Cleve. Internat. Lawyers Group, Tavern Club (Cleve.), Chagrin Valley Hunt Club (Gates Mills, Ohio). Republican. Episcopalian.

HYDE, CLARENCE BRODIE, II, oil industry executive; b. Ft. Worth, Oct. 22, 1937; s. Clarence Edgar and Frances McCain (Williams) H.; m. Sylvia Flower, June 5, 1960; children: C. Brodie III, Brooke Allison, Brett Kinlock, Blair Elizabeth. BS, Tex. Wesleyan Coll., 1961, LLD (hon.), 1996; MBA, U. Tex., 1963; grad., So. Meth. U., 1973. V.p., asst. mgt. lending group, chmn. loan com. Ft. Worth Nat. Bank, 1964-76; ind. oil prodr. Ft. Worth, 1976-78; pres., chmn. bd. Hyde Oil & Gas Corp., Ft. Worth, 1978—; pres. Hyde Resources Corp., 1997—, Hyde Energy Corp., 1993—. Exec. com., dir. River Plz. Nat. Bank, Ft. Worth, 1983-86; trustee, v.p., treas. The Hyde Found., Ft. Worth, 1981—. Bd. dirs. Tarrant County chpt. Salvation Army, 1969-79, chmn. bd., 1972-74; trustee Trinity Valley Sch., Ft. Worth, 1970; mgmt. com. Camp Amon Cartr, Ft. Worth, 1970-76, adv. mem., 1976—; trustee Tex. Wesleyan Coll., 1971-96, chmn. bd., chmn. exec. com., 1990-94; bd. dirs. Big Bros. Tarrant County, 1971; trustee W.A. Moncrief Radiation Ctr., Ft. Worth, 1971-99, v.p., 1986-99; bd. dirs., mem. exec. Harris Hosp., Ft. Worth, 1971-88, Harris Meth. Health Systems, 1983-87; bd. dirs., treas. Tarrant County chpt. ARC, 1971-73, bd. dirs., 1989-91; bd. dirs., exec. com. Ft. Worth Opera Assn., 1971-99, v.p., treas., 1972-74; bd. dirs., exec. com. Hurst-Euless (Tex.)-Bedford Hosp., 1973-80; bd. dirs. Ft. Worth Arts Coun., 1972-95, pres., 1973-75; chmn. Cmty. Pride Campaign, 1972; bd. dirs. Ann Waggoner Scholarship Fund, 1984—; fin. com. Ft. Worth Country Day Sch., 1985-89; pres. MRC-Trans Co. (subs. Moncrief Radiation Ctr.), 1987-94; bd. dirs. Cancer Care Svcs., 1994-95, adv. bd. dirs., 1995—; dir. Ft. Worth Pub. Libr. Found., 1996-2002. Named Alumnus of Yr., Tex. Wesleyan Coll., 1985. Mem. Ind. Petroleum Assn. Am., Tex. Ind. Prodrs. & Royalty Owners Assn., Tex. & Southwestern Cattle Raisers Assn., Tex. Hosp. Assn., Rivercrest Country Club, Shady Oaks Country Club (Ft. Worth), Steelechase Club (Ridotto), Ft. Worth Petroleum Club, Crescent Club (Dallas). Republican. Methodist. Avocations: hunting, fishing, travel. Home: 8 Westover Rd Fort Worth TX 76107-3103 Office: Hyde Oil & Gas Corp 6300 Ridglea Pl Ste 1018 Fort Worth TX 76116-5778

HYDE, DAVID ROWLEY, lawyer; b. Norwalk, Conn., Aug. 21, 1929; s. Thomas Arthur and Mary Julia (Sass) H.; m. Valerie Rosemary Worrall, Dec. 30, 1961; children: Meredith Ellen, Timothy Worrall. AB, Yale U., 1951, LL.B., 1954. Bar: Conn. 1954, N.Y. 1956, U.S. Supreme Ct. 1969. Assoc. Cahill Gordon & Reindel, NYC, 1954-59, 64-65, ptnr., 1966-90, sr. counsel, 1991—2006; with U.S. Atty.'s Office, 1959—63, chief civil divsn., 1961—63. Home: 35 W 12th St New York NY 10011-8501

HYDE, GERALDINE VEOLA, retired secondary school educator; b. Berkeley, Calif., Nov. 26, 1926; d. William Benjamin and Veola (Walker) H.; m. Paul Hyde Graves, Jr., Nov. 12, 1949 (div. Dec. 1960); children: Christine M. Graves Klykken, Catherine A. Graves Okerlund, Geraldine J. Graves Hansen. BA in English, U. Wash., 1948; BA in Edn., Ea. Wash. U., 1960, MA in Edn., 1962. Cert. tchr. K-16, Wash.; life cert. specialist in secondary edn., Calif. English educator Sprague (Wash.) Consol. Schs., 1960-62, Bremerton (Wash.) Sch. Dist., 1962-63, Federal Way (Wash.) Sch. Dist., 1963-66; English, journalism and Polynesian humanities educator Hayward (Calif.) Unified Sch. Dist., 1966-86; ret., 1986. Charter mem. Hist. Hawaii Found., Honolulu, 1977-; founding mem. The Cousteau Soc., Inc., Norfolk, Va., 1973-; life mem. Hawaiian Hist. Soc., Honolulu, 1978-; mem. Molokai Mus. and Cultural Ctr., Kaunakakai, 1986-, Bishop Mus. Assn., Honolulu, 1973-, Mission House Mus., Honolulu, 1994, Bklyn. Hist. Assn., N.Y., 1994, Berkshire Family History Assn., Pittsfield, Mass., 1994-, Richville (N.Y.) Hist. Assn., 1994-, Swanton (Vt.) Hist. Soc., 1998-, N.Y. Geneal. and Biog. Soc., 1999-, New Eng. Hist. Genealogic Soc., 1998-, Gouverneur Hist. Assn., NY, 1998-, New Wing Luke Asian Mus., Seattle, 1994, Upham Family Soc., Inc., Melrose, Mass., 2001-, Calif. Ret. Tchrs Assoc. 2003, RHS Golden Grads, 2006—. Mem. Libr. Congress Assocs. (charter), Nature Conservancy of Hawai'i, Smithsonian Inst. (contbg.), Nat. Geog. Soc., Nat. Trust Historic Preservation, U. Wash. Alumni Assn. (life), Ea. Wash. U. Alumni Assn. (life). Episcopalian. Avocations: historic and ecologic preservation, genealogy, shell collecting, needlecrafts, crafts. Home: 2050 Springfield Drive 470 Chico CA 95928

HYDE, HENRY JOHN, retired congressman; b. Chgo., Apr. 18, 1924; s. Henry Clay and Monica (Kelly) Hyde; m. Jeanne Simpson, Nov. 8, 1947 (dec. 1992); children: Henry J., Robert, Laura, Anthony. Student, Duke U., 1943-44; BS, Georgetown U., 1946; JD, Loyola U., Chgo., 1949. Bar: Ill. 1950. Mem. Ill. Gen. Assembly, 1967-74, majority leader, 1971—72; mem. US Congress from 6th Ill. dist., 1975—2007; mem. jud. com.; chmn. jud. com., 1995—2001; chmn. internat. rels. com., 2001—07. Author: For Every Idle Silence, 1985, Protecting Our Property Rights: Is Your Property Safe From Seizure?, 1995; cinematographer:. Served in USN, 1944—46. Mem.: Chgo. Bar Assn. Republican. Roman Catholic. Achievements include being appointed by House of Representatives to conduct impeachment proceedings against Judge Harry E. Claiborne of the US District Court of Nevada, 1986; being appointed by House of Representatives to conduct impeachment proceedings against President Bill Clinton, 1998.

HYDE, LAWRENCE HENRY, JR., manufacturing executive; b. Cambridge, Mass., July 10, 1924; s. Lawrence Henry and Catherine I. (McMahon) H.; m. Lois A. Crehan, May 31, 1947; children— Abigail Ellen, Stephen Lawrence, Lawrence Henry III. AB, Harvard U., 1946, MBA, 1947. With Ford Motor Co., 1947-65, dir. internat. purchasing office, 1960-62; v.p. Philco, 1962-64; with Harris Corp., Cleve., 1965-73; from dir. internat. ops. to group v.p. internat. Am. Motors Corp., Detroit, 1974-83, v.p. internat., 1974-77; group v.p., pres. AM Gen. Corp., 1977-81, exec. v.p., 1982-83; with LTV Corp., 1983-85; divsn. pres. AM Gen., 1983-85; with Harris Graphics Corp., 1985-86, also chmn. bd. dirs.; with Sonex Rsch., Inc., 1986—2003, also chmn. bd. dirs., 1986-93. Chmn. Karnak Investments, Ltd., Bermuda; chmn. U. Investment Fund, Cairo; trustee Am. U., Cairo.

HYDE, MANLY RICHARD, thoracic surgeon; s. William Herbert and May Georgina Hyde; m. Mary Jane Hyde; children: Elizabeth Jane, Mary Catherine. BA, Pacific Union Coll., 1972; MD, Loma Linda U. Sch. Medicine, 1976. Diplomate Thoracic Surgery Am. Bd. Thoracic Surgery, General Surgery Am. Bd. Surgery, Surgical Critical Care Am. Bd. Surgery, Testamur Naspe Exam Heart Rhythm Soc. Cardiothoracic surgeon So. Calif. Med. Group, Los Angeles, 1989—; attending cardiac surgeon Loma Linda (Calif.) U. Med. Ctr., 1986—88. Vol. physician ADRA, Washington. CEO Click411, Inc. Recipient Alumnus of Yr. award, Can. U. Coll. Alumni Assn., 1999. Fellow: ACS; mem.: AMA, Western Thoracic Assn., Am. Coll. Chest Physicians, Soc. Thoracic Surgeons. Avocations: internet devel., vol. med. work. Office: Cardiac Surgery Kaiser Hosp 1526 N Edgemont St 3rd Fl Los Angeles CA 90027 Home Phone: 661-284-2646. Business E-Mail: manly.r.hyde@kp.org.

HYDE, THOMAS D., lawyer; b. Kansas City; BA in English, U. Kans., 1970, MBA, 1982; JD, U. Mo., 1975. Atty. Stubbs & Mann, Kansas City, Mo.; with Emerson Electric, St. Louis, Manville Corp., Denver, Continental; sr. v.p., pres., gen. counsel and CFO MNC Special Assets Bank, Balt.; with Raytheon Co., Lexington, Mass., 1992—2001, v.p., gen. counsel, 1994—98, sr. v.p., gen. counsel, corp. sec., 1998—2001; exec. v.p., corp. sec. Wal-Mart Stores, Inc., 2001—. Office: Wal-Mart Stores, Inc 702 SW Eighth St Bentonville AR 72716 Office Phone: 479-277-0627. Business E-Mail: tdhyde@wal-mart.com.

HYERS, THOMAS MORGAN, physician, biomedical researcher; b. Jacksonville, Fla., June 16, 1943; s. John and Joan (Clemens) H.; m. Elizabeth Mclean, June 12, 1965; children: Justin, Adam. BS, Duke U., 1964, MD, 1968. Diplomate Am. Bd. Internal Medicine, Am. Bd. Pulmonary Diseases. Intern in medicine Cleve. Met. Gen. Hosp., 1968-69; asst. chief Nat. Blood Resource Br., Nat. Heart, Lung and Blood Inst., NIH, 1971-72, pulmonary disease adv. com., 1983-86; resident in medicine U. Wash., Seattle, 1972-74; chief resident, instr. medicine, 1974-75; fellow in pulmonary diseases U. Colo. Health Scis. Ctr., Denver, 1975-76, research fellow Cardiovascular Pulmonary Research Lab., 1976-77, asst. prof. medicine, staff physician respiratory care, assoc. investigator, 1977-82; research assoc. Denver VA Med. Ctr., 1979-82; assoc. prof. medicine, dir. div. pulmonary diseases St. Louis U. Med. Ctr., 1982-85, prof. medicine, divsn. dir., 1985-98; dir. NIH Specialized Ctr. Research in Adult Respiratory Failure, 1983-93. Contbr. articles to profl. jours. Served to comdr. USPHS, 1969-71. Named hon. Ky. col. grantee NIH, Nat. Heart, Lung and Blood Inst. Fellow ACP, Am. Coll. Chest Physicians; mem. Am. Heart Assn. (mem. councils on thrombosis and cardiopulmonary disease), Internat. Soc. Thrombosis and Haemostasis, Am. Lung Assn. (Eastern Mo. chpt.), Am. Fedn. Clin. Research, Am. Physiol. Soc., Western Soc. Clin. Investigation, Am. Thoracic Soc., Phi Beta Kappa. Office: CARE Clin Rsch 533 Couch Ave Ste 140 Saint Louis MO 63122-5561 Office Phone: 314-909-9779. E-mail: studies@careinternet.com.

HYLAND, GEOFFREY FYFE, retired energy executive; b. Montreal; B in Engring., McGill U., Montreal, 1966; MBA, York U., Toronto, Ont., Can., 1972. Pres., COO Shaw Industries Ltd, Toronto, Ont., Canada, 1987, pres., CEO, 1994—2005, ret., 2005. Bd. dir. ShawCor Ltd., Enerflex Sys., Ltd., Exco Techs. Ltd., Fortis Inc. Home Phone: 519-941-5880; Office Phone: 416-567-7429. Business E-Mail: hylands@can.rogers.com.

HYLAND, GREGORY E., home building products executive; BA, MBA, Univ. of Pitts. Various positions Rockwell Internat.; v.p. mktg. sales Anderson, Greenwood & Co., 1991—93, exec. v.p., 1993—94; pres., Anderson, Greenwood & Co. Keystone Internat., 1994; various positions to group pres., corp. officer Keystone Internat. (acquired by Tyco, 1997); pres. engineered products group, flow control div. Tyco Internat.; pres. indsl. products segment Textron, Inc., 2002, chmn., CEO Textron golf, turf & specialty products, 2000—02; exec. v.p. US fleet mgmt. solutions Ryder Sys. Inc., 2004—05; pres., CEO, chmn. Walter Industries, Inc., Tampa, Fla., 2005—06; chmn., pres., CEO Mueller Water Products, Atlanta, 2006—. Office: Mueller Water Products 1200 Abernathy Rd Atlanta GA 30328*

HYLAND, WILLIAM FRANCIS, retired lawyer; b. Burlington, NJ, July 30, 1923; s. Theodore J. and Margaret M. (Gallagher) H.; m. Joan E. Sharp, Apr. 20, 1946; children: William Francis, Nancy E. Hyland Wiley, Stephen J., Emma L. Hyland McCormack, Margaret M. Hyland Frank, Thomas M. BS in Econs, U. Pa., 1944, LL.B., 1949; D.H.L., Hahnemann Med. Sch. and Hosp., 1976. Bar: NJ 1949, U.S. Supreme Ct. 1960. Of counsel Riker, Danzig, Scherer, Hyland & Perretti, Morristown, NJ; atty. gen. NJ, 1974-78; ret., 2006. Mem. N.J. Gen. Assembly from Camden County, 1954-61, speaker of house, 1958, acting gov., N.J., 1958; chmn. N.J. Sports and Expn. Authority, 1978-82, commr., 1974-84; pres. N.J. Bd. Pub. Utility Commrs., also mem. cabinet govs. Meyner, Hughes, Byrne, N.J., 1961-68, 74-78; chmn. N.J. Atomic Energy Council, 1968-69, N.J. Commn. Investigation, 1969-71; co-chmn. Reapportionment Commn.; chmn. Brazilian Mission Com., 1962-65; permanent del. Fed. Jud. Conf. 3d Circuit.; del.-at-large Dem. Nat. Conv., 1964, del., 1968; assoc. trustee U. Pa., 1960-74. Served as officer USNR, 1943-46, ETO, PTO. Decorated knight Order of St. Gregory (Pope Paul VI), 1964; recipient Distinguished Service award Camden County Jaycees, 1954, Outstanding Young Man in Govt. N.J. award N.J. Jaycees, 1958, Myrtle Wreath award Camden County So. N.J. region Hadassah, 1977, Pub. Service award Anti-Defamation League of B'nai B'rith, 1982; named Outstanding Citizen of N.J. Advt. Club. N.J., 1979 Mem. ABA (fellow N.J. chpt.), Camden County Bar Assn. (pres. 1959), Nat. Assn. R.R. and Utilities Commrs. (exec. com. 1965-68), Nat. Assn. Attys. Gen. (exec. com. 1975-78, v.p. 1976, pres. elect 1977-78), Phi Kappa Psi. Home: 309 Bridgeboro Rd Apt 2345 Moorestown NJ 08057-1427

HYLANDER, JESSICA S., lawyer; BA, Miami U., 1999; JD, U. Mich., 2003. Bar: Ohio 2003, Ct. of Appeals Sixth Cir., US Dist. Ct. Southern Dist. Ohio. Assoc. Dinsmore & Shohl LLP, Cin. Named one of Ohio's Rising Stars, Super Lawyers, 2006. Mem.: Ohio State Bar Assn., Cin. Bar Assn. Office: Dinsmore & Shohl LLP 255 E Fifth St Ste 1900 Cincinnati OH 45202-4700 Office Phone: 513-977-8200. Office Fax: 513-977-8141.

HYLBERT, PAUL W., construction executive; Various field and corp. pos., including mngr. dir. Wickes Europe, and sr. v.p. and gen. mgr. Wickes Lumber, 1966—90; pres. PrimeSource, 1990—2001; pres., CEO Lanoga Corp., Redmond, Wash., 2001—06; CEO Pro-Build Holdings Inc., So. Plainfield, NJ, 2007—. Mem.: Nat. Bldg. Materials Distbrs. Assn. (pres. 1993). Office: Pro-Build Holdings Inc 1 Cragwood Rd South Plainfield NJ 07080*

HYLLA, LINDA KAY, sister, social worker; b. Granite City, Ill., Mar. 1, 1961; d. Leonard Albert and Loretta Ann Hylla. BA, Fontbonne U., 1987; MSW, Washington U., St. Louis, 1992. Entrance into Sisters of Divine Providence, 1980; LCSW 1995. Coord. youth and human svc., Granite City, Ill., 1992—95; child care worker St. Elizabeth Med. Ctr., Granite City, 1986—95, outpatient therapist, 1995—2000; vocations dir. Sisters of Divine Providence, Bridgeton, Mo., 2000—. Clin. supr. pvt. practice, Madison, Ill., 1998—; founder Quest Ho., Madison, Ill. Contbr. poetry poetry.com. Bd. dirs. New Opportunities, Madison, 1989—91; chmn. bd. Rm. at the Inn Homeless Shelter, St. Louis County, 2002—03. Named an Internat. Poet of Merit, Internat. Soc. Poets, 2002; named to TREND Hall of Fame, 2000; Vocation grantee, KC, 2003. Office: Sisters of Divine Providence 3415 Bridgeland Bridgeton MO 63044 Office Phone: 618-660-9736. Personal E-mail: srlindahylla@hotmail.com.

HYLTON, KEVIN NATHANIEL, musician, composer; b. Detroit, Mar. 16, 1960; s. Kenneth Niles and Ethel Williams Hylton. BA, Yale U., New Haven, 1982. Arts cons., tchg. artist Mus. for African Art, NYC, 1991—. Composer: (recordings) Mbira Sanctuary; musician; contbr. soundtrack; musician: (CD) African Voices, Ancestral Callings, When I Start to Play, African Dreams (Parent's Choice award, 2005); composer: Heritage OP, 1997; musician, composer: Spirit Ensemble, 1985. Active WBAI Pacifica,

NYC, 2000—07. Named Accompanist of the Yr., Attitude Mag., 1996—97. Mem.: NAACP (life). Avocations: african dance, tai chi, yoga, drums, flute. Office: Kevin Nathaniel Hylton/Gwenyambira Prod PO Box 1948 New York NY 10013-0873 Home Phone: 718-230-8439; Office Phone: 212-969-0847. Personal E-mail: kevinmbira@hotmail.com.

HYLTON, THOMAS JAMES, author; b. Reading, Pa., Dec. 20, 1948; s. William Harold and Mary Harriet (Kitzmiller) H.; m. Frances Wismer, Aug. 31, 1970. BA, Kutztown U. of Pa., 1970. Reporter The Mercury, Pottstown, Pa., 1970-86, editl. writer, 1986-94. Author: Save Our Land, Save our Towns: A Plan for Pennsylvania, 1995; prodr., host (PBS) Save Our Land, Save Our Towns, 2000. Co-founder Trees Inc., Pottstown, 1983; co-founder Preservation Pottstown, 1984, 10,000 Friends of Pa., 1998. Recipient Am. Planning Assn. award, 1988, 90, 94, Honor award Nat. Trust for Hist. Preservation, 1997, Pulitzer prize for editl. writing, 1990; Pulliam fellow, 1993. Republican. Presbyterian. Home: 222 Chestnut St Pottstown PA 19464-5508 Office Phone: 610-323-6837. Personal E-mail: thomashylton@comcast.net.

HYMAN, ABRAHAM, electrical engineer; b. Bklyn., Mar. 8, 1934; s. Rubin and Regina (Holzman) H.; m. Marianne Daniel, June 19, 1955; children: Debra Hyman Rathauser, Lori Hyman Rones, Karen Hyman Cantor. BEE, Poly. Inst. Bklyn., 1952; MS, Newark Coll. Engring., 1954. Registered profl. engr., N.Y. Chief elec. engr. Med. Equipment R&D Lab., Fort Totten, NY, 1955-64; head lab. Office Naval Rsch., Port Washington, NY, 1964-66; tech. adminstr. AEC, Upton, NY, 1966-71; supr. indsl. hygienist Dept. Labor, Westbury, NY, 1971-80, regional indsl. hygienist NYC, 1980-84; mgr. health and safety Unisys Corp., Great Neck, NY, 1984-95; safety and health cons. New Hyde Park, NY, 1995—. Adj. prof. York Coll., Queens, NY, 1974—78; cons. Poison Control Ctr., Mineola, NY, 1981—; adj. assoc. prof. Staten Island Coll., NY, 1983—95; lectr. Queensboro C.C., Queens, NY, 1994—96. Patentee in field. Bd. dirs. Am. Lung Assn., East Meadow, 1974-99. Mem. IEEE, Am. Acad. Environ. Engrs. (diplomate), NSPE, Am. Conf. Indsl. Hygienists, Sci. Rsch. Soc. Am., Sigma Xi. Avocations: photography, swimming, bicycling. Home and Office: 142 Claudy Ln New Hyde Park NY 11040-1635

HYMAN, ALAN BARRY, lawyer; b. Balt., Apr. 22, 1947; s. Henry and Estelle (Datkyn) H.; m. Sharon Susan Albert, June 22, 1968; children: Cori Ann, Marcie Allison. BA, NYU, 1968, JD, 1971. Bar: N.Y. 1971. Ptnr. Summit Rovins & Feldesman, NYC, 1971-86; ptnr., head bankruptcy & reorganization practice group Proskauer Rose LLP, NYC, 1986—. Lecturer Turnaround Industry Conference, US Trustee Symposium, Am. Bankruptcy Inst., Inst. for Internat. Rsch. Mem. Bar Assn. City N.Y., Bankruptcy Lawyers Bar Assn.; fellow Am. Coll. of Bankruptcy Lawyers. Office: Proskauer Rose LLP 1585 Broadway Fl 27 New York NY 10036-8299

HYMAN, ALBERT LEWIS, cardiologist, educator; b. New Orleans, Nov. 10, 1923; s. David and Mary (Newstadt) Hyman; m. Neil Steiner, Mar. 27, 1964; 1 child, Albert Arthur. BS, La. State U., 1943; MD, 1945; postgrad., U. Cin., U. Paris, U. London, Eng. Diplomate Am. Bd. Internal Medicine. Intern Charity Hosp., 1945-46, resident, 1947-49, sr. vis. physician, 1959-63; resident Cin. Gen. Hosp., 1946-47; instr. medicine La. State U., 1950-56, asst. prof. medicine, 1956-57; asst. prof. Tulane U., 1957-59, assoc. prof., 1959-63, assoc. prof. surgery, 1963-70, prof. rsch. surgery in cardiology, 1970—, prof. clin. medicine Med. Sch., 1983—, adj. prof. pharmacology Med. Sch., 1974—, dir. Cardiac Catheterization Lab., 1957—, Mayerson meml. lectr. in physiology, 2000; prof. medicine in cardiology La. State U. Sch. Medicine; physician in cardiology, dept. medicine Brigham and Women's Hosp. Harvard Med. Sch., Boston, 2007—. Vis. physician Touro Hosp., Touro Infirmary, electrocardiographer; vis. physician Hotel Dieu Hosp.; chief cardiology Sara Mayo Hosp., electrocardiographer, Metairie Hosp., St. Tammany Hosp.; internat. sci. com. IV Internat. Symposium Pulmonary Circulation Charles U., Prague; vis. prof. SUNY, Stony Brook, 2001, U. South Ala. Med. Sch., 2001; vis. prof. medicine Harvard Med. Sch., Boston, 2006; lectr. in field; cons. in field. Mem. editl. bd. Jour. Applied Physiology; contbr. articles to profl. jours. Recipient award for rsch., Hadassah, 1980, Vis. Scientist award, Wellcome Found., U. Coll., London, 1991, Albert Hyman award for excellence in cardiology, Tulane U. Med. Sch., 1997, Disting. Achievement award in sci. and rsch., Orlean Parish Med. Soc., 2001; Tulane Med. Sch. Sect. on Cardiology fellow, 1997. Fellow: ACP, Am. Fedn. Clin. Rsch., Am. Coll. Cardiology, Am. Coll. Chest Physicians; mem.: AAUP, N.Y. Acad. Scis., N.Am. Soc. Pacing and Electrophysiology, Am. Physiol. Soc., New Orleans Surg. Soc. (hon.), So. Med. Soc. (Seale-Harris award 1988), So. Soc. Clin. Investigation (chmn. membership com.), Am. Soc. Pharmacology and Exptl. Therapeutics, La. Heart Assn. (v.p. 1974, Albert L. Hyman Ann. Rsch. award, Wellcome Rsch. Found. Vis. Scientist award U. Coll. London 1992, Disting. Achievement award for outstanding sci. contbns. to cardiopulmonary medicine), Am. Heart Assn. (chmn. sci. com. cardiopulmonary coun. 1981, fellow coun. circulation, fellow coun. clin. cardiology, chmn. cardiopulmonary coun., mem. editl. bd. Circulation Rsch., Jour. Applied Physiology, Am. Jour. Physiology, Heart Disease and Stroke, mem. rsch. com. bd. dirs., mem. coun. cardiopulmonary medicine, regional rep. coun. clin. cardiology, vice-chmn. rsch. com., Dickinson Richards Meml. lectr. 1986, Disting. Sci. Achievement award 1990, Dickinson Richards Meml. lectr. 1992, Disting. Achievement award 1992, Disting. Sci. Achievement award 1993, Disting. Achievement award 1993), Alpha Omega Alpha. Achievements include research in cardiopulmonary circulation. Home: 1501 Beacon St Apt 903 Brookline MA 02446 Office Phone: 617-935-6774. Business E-Mail: aahyman@tulane.edu.

HYMAN, BRADLEY CLARK, biology professor, geneticist; b. San Diego, May 14, 1952; s. Richard M. and June M. Hyman; m. Leone P. Hyman, June 22, 1975; children: Derek L., Kyle R. BA, U. Calif., San Diego, 1974; PhD, UCLA, 1980. Prof. U. Calif., Riverside, 1983—, dir. interdisciplinary grad. program in genetics, 1998, faculty dir. CaTEACH sci./math. initiative, 2005—. Editor-in-chief Jour. Nematology, 2000—03. Vice chmn. citizens oversight com. Riverside Sch. Bond, 2003—07. Recipient Disting. Tchg. award, U. Calif., Riverside, 2001. Fellow: AAAS; mem.: Soc. Nematologists (mem. exec. bd. 1993—2000, Svc. Award 2003, Svc. award 2004), Golden Key Internat. Honor Soc. Achievements include research in mitochondrial DNA recombination; rolling circle amplification of mitochondrial DNA. Avocation: college athletics. Office: U Calif Riverside Dept Biology 900 University Ave Riverside CA 92521-047 Office Phone: 951-827-5911. Office Fax: 951-827-4286. Business E-Mail: bhyman@ucr.edu.

HYMAN, BRUCE MALCOLM, ophthalmologist; b. N.Y.C., May 22, 1943; s. Malcolm A. and Sylvia S. H.; AB, Columbia U., 1964; MD, NYU, 1968. Intern in surgery Albert Einstein Coll. Medicine/Bronx Mcpl. Hosp., 1968-69; resident in ophthalmology Manhattan Eye, Ear and Throat Hosp., N.Y.C., 1971-74; pvt. practice medicine specializing in ophthalmology, N.Y.C., 1974—; tchr. attending surgeon Manhattan Eye, Ear and Throat Hosp., 1974—; med. cons. U.S. Seaplane Pilots Assn., 1975—, Health Ins. Plan Greater N.Y., 1977—; ophthalmologist to Hotel Trades Coun., Hotel Assn. N.Y.C., 1974—; attending ophthalmologist Roosevelt Hosp., N.Y.C., 1979—, dir. adult outpatient ophthalmology, 1980—; police surgeon N.Y.C., 1977—, dep. chief police surgeon, 1978—; attending ophthalmologist Doctors Hosp., 1979—, Le Roy Hosp., 1979—, St. Luke's Hosp., 1980—; outpatient ophthalmologist N.Y. Hosp., 1975-77; clin. ophthalmologist Columbia Coll. Physicians and Surgeons, 1981—. Served with USPHS, 1969-71. Diplomate Am. Bd. Ophthalmology. Fellow ACS; mem. N.Y. State, N.Y. County med. socs., Am. Acad. Ophthalmology and Otolaryngology. Contbr. articles to profl. jours. Office: 133 E 64th St New York NY 10021-7045

HYMAN, EDWARD, financial analyst, economist; B, Univ. Tex., 1967; MBA, MIT, 1969. Positions through vice-chmn. C.J. Lawrence, 1972—91; co-founder, chmn. Internat. Strategy & Investment Group, NYC, 1991—. Bd. dir. Capital Trust Inc. Named #1 Wall St. Economist, Institutional Investor Mag. Office: ISI Group 40 W 57 th St New York NY 10019 Office Phone: 212-446-5000.

HYMAN, JEROME ELLIOT, lawyer; b. Rosedale, Miss., Dec. 26, 1923; s. Mose and Mary Ann (Sprecher) H.; m. Isabelle Miller, July 1, 1960. AB, Coll. William and Mary, 1944; LL.B. magna cum laude (Fay diploma), Harvard U., 1947. Bar: N.Y. 1949, D.C. 1960. Mem. fgn. funds control staff Dept. Treasury, U.S. Mil. Govt., Frankfurt and Berlin, Germany, 1945-46; law clk. to judge U.S. Ct. Appeals, Boston, 1947-48; assoc. firm Cleary Gottlieb, Steen & Hamilton LLP, NYC, 1948-58, ptnr., 1959-93, sr. counsel, 1994—; trustee, mem. exec. com. Practising Law Inst., NYC, 1972-97, v.p., 1979-86, pres., 1986-96, chmn. bd. trustees, 1996-97, chmn. emeritus, 1997—; sr. v.p., gen. counsel Pan Am World Airways, Inc., 1982-84. Mem. bd. editors Harvard Law Rev., 1945-47. Pres. Lexington Dem. Club, NYC, 1956-58; counsel NY Com. for Stevenson, 1956; del. various Dem. state and jud. convs.; alumni mem. Harvard Law Sch. Placement Com., 1976-79; nat. chmn. maj. gifts com. Harvard Law Sch. Fund, 1978-80; mem. overseers com. to visit Harvard Law Sch., 1986-92; trustee Lawyers' Com. for Civil Rights Under Law, 1981—; trustee Citizens Budget Commn., NYC, 1991-94, trustee emeritus, 1994—; trustee Coll. of William and Mary Found., 1997-03, trustee emeritus, 2003—; mem. dean's adv. bd. Harvard Law Sch., 2000—, exec. com., 2003—. Fellow Am. Bar Found., Phi Beta Kappa Soc.; mem. ABA, Assn. Bar City N.Y. (chmn. com. corp. law 1984-87), Am. Law Inst., Am. Judicature Soc., N.Y. County Lawyers Assn., Tribar Opinion Commn., Harvard Law Sch. Assn. N.Y.C. (trustee 1980-83, v.p. 1984-85, pres. 1985-86), Nat. Harvard Law Sch. Assn. (mem. coun. 1990-93, mem. exec. com. 1991-93). Home: 1125 Park Ave Apt 10B New York NY 10128-1243 Office: Cleary Gottlieb Steen & Hamilton LLP One Liberty Plaza New York NY 10006-1470 Home Phone: 212-831-8537; Office Phone: 212-225-2010. Business E-Mail: jhyman@cgsh.com.

HYMAN, LAWRENCE ROBERT, psychiatrist; b. Amsterdam, NY, Dec. 7, 1940; s. Morris Arthur and Bertha (Berkman) H.; m. Lois Armstrong Wilson, June 27, 1978; children: Elyse Michelle, Michael Louis, Joshua William. BA, Ohio Wesleyan U., 1963; MD, Chgo. Med. Sch., 1968. Intern then resident U. Wis., Madison, 1968-72; guest worker NIH, Bethesda, Md., 1973-76; asst. prof. Johns Hopkins Sch. Medicine, Balt., 1976-78; resident George Washington U., Washington, 1978-80; asst. clin. prof. U. Md., Balt., 1981-84; pvt. practice Columbia, Md., 1981—; active staff dept. psychiatry Howard County Gen. Hosp., Columbia, Md., 1981—; CEO Orchard Hill Treatment Ctr. for Chem. Dependency, Columbia, 1987-93; pvt. practice gen. psychiatry Columbia; CEO, med. dir. Howard Behavioral Health, Inc., 2003—; med. dir. Lawrence R. Hyman MD and Assocs., 1993—, Vis. Speakers Bureau, Lilly, Forest, Wyeth & Janssen Pharm. Cos., 2003—. Cons. Family Therapy Inst., Rockville, Md., Pfizer Pharma, 2004, others; bd. dirs. Closecall Am., Inc. Contbg. editor Gould Med. Dictionary, 1979; contbr. articles to profl. jours. Adv. bd. Nat. Kidney Found., Balt., 1971. Maj. M.C., AUS, 1972-76. Recipient USPHS Rsch. Career Devel. award, 1977; NIH fellow, 1972; NIH grantee. Mem. Am. Psychiat. Assn., Md. Psychiat. Soc., Med. and Chirurgical Faculty State of Md., Howard County Med. Soc., Am. Orthopsychiat. Assn. Avocations: sailing, marathons. Home: 3681 Folly Quarter Rd Ellicott City MD 21042-1452 Office: # 201 11055 Little Patuxent Pky Columbia MD 21044 Home Phone: 410-531-2638; Office Phone: 301-997-8847. E-mail: lrhymanmd@aol.com.

HYMAN, LEONARD STEPHEN, financial consultant, economist, writer; b. NYC, June 5, 1940; s. Milton and Elsie (Reiter) Hyman; m. Judith N. Siegel, July 4, 1965; children: Andrew S., Robert C. BA, N.Y. U., 1961; MA, Cornell U., 1965. Fin. analyst Chase Manhattan Bank, NYC, 1965-72; ptnr. H.C. Wainwright & Co., NYC, 1972-77; v.p. Wainwright Securities, NYC, 1977-78; v.p., head utility rsch. group Merrill Lynch Capital Markets, NYC, 1978-94, 1st v.p., 1987-94; pres. Pvt. Sector Advisors, Inc., Sleepy Hollow, NY, 1994—. Mem. lunar energy enterprise case study task force NASA, 1988—89; mem. bd. advisors Electric Power Rsch. Inst., 1993—99, Enertech Capital, 1999—, Excelergy, 2000—05, Internat. Found. Rsch. Exptl. Econ., 2000—; mng. dir. Fulcrum Internat., Ltd., 1995—96; sr. industry advisor Salomon Smith Barney, Inc., 1997—2002; sr. advisor R.J. Rudden Assocs., 2002—. Author: America's Electric Utilities, 1983; co-author: The New Telecommunications Industry, 1987, The Water Business, 1998, A Blueprint for Transmission, 1999, Energy Risk Management: A Primer for the Utility Industry, 2006; editor: The Privatization of Public Utilities, 1995; mem. editl. bd. Forum for Applied Rsch. and Pub. Policy, 1993—2002, Cogeneration and Competitive Power Jour., 1999—2002; contbr. articles to profl. pubs. Mem. adv. com. U.S. Congress-Office Tech. Assessment, Washington, 1983, 1986—87, 1987—88, 1992—93; mem. elec. reliability panel N.Am. Elec. Reliability Coun., 1997; mem. Pa. Task Force Electric Utility Efficiency, Harrisburg, 1982—83. Mem.: AAAS, Inst. Chartered Fin. Analysts, Fin. Analysts Fedn., N.Y. Soc. Security Analysts, Soc. Utility Regulatory Fin. Analysts (bd. dirs.), Phi Beta Kappa. Democrat. Jewish. Avocations: travel, bicycling, music, canoeing. Home and Office: Private Sector Advisors Inc 34 Fremont Rd Tarrytown NY 10591-1118 Office Phone: 631-348-4090 x238. Business E-Mail: lhyman@rjrudden.com.

HYMAN, LESTER SAMUEL, lawyer; b. Providence, July 14, 1931; s. Carl and Alice (Adelman) H.; m. Helen Reeder Sidman, Sept. 19, 1959 (div. 1982); children: David, Andrew, Elizabeth. AB, Brown U., 1952; LLB, Columbia U., 1955. Bar: D.C. 1955, Mass. 1955, U.S. Supreme Ct. 1957. Atty. SEC, Washington, 1955-57; chief asst. to Gov. State of Mass., Boston, 1962-64, sec. commerce, 1964-65; sr. cons. HUD, Washington, 1966-67; ptnr. Leva, Hawes & Symington, Washington, 1969-82; founding ptnr. Swidler & Berlin, Washington, 1982—2007, sr. of counsel, 2007—. Lectr. John F. Kennedy Sch. Govt. Harvard U., 1968-69; bd. dirs. CDS Internat., 1988-94. mem. Internat. Oberver Team for nat. election in Haiti, 1990; v.p. Health Record Network, 2005—; chmn. legal adv. bd. Ctr. Advanced Def. Studies, 2007—. Author: U.S. Policy Towards Liberia, 1822-2003: Unintended Consequences?, 2003. Bd. dirs. Ctr. Nat. Policy, Washington, 1980—; bd. advisors Close-Up Found.; bd. govs. Am. Jewish Commn., 1980-84; Dem. chmn., Mass., 1967-69, del. Dem. Nat. Conv., 1968, mem. Dem. Charter Reform Commn., 1970, D.C. Cmty. Humanities, 1988-90; bd. dirs. C.C. of Brit. V.I., 1989—, Young Artists, 1989-94; mem. adv. bd. Internat. legal Studies Program, Washington Coll. Law, Am. U., 1990—; apptd. by Pres. Clinton to Franklin Delano Roosevelt Meml. Commn., 1994; trustee Norton Simon Mus. of Art, Pasadena, Calif., 1995-97, U. D.C. Found, 2002, U. D.C., 2003—; mem. U.S. Presdl. Del. to Guatamalan Peace Accord Signing, 1996; bd. dirs. Brit. V.I. Nat. Park Trust, 1999; bd. dirs. Liberia Support Group, 2005-, Partnership for Democracy and Human Rights, 2005—; trustee U. D.C., 2004. Named Outstanding Young Man of Yr., Greater Boston Jr. C. of C., 1964. Mem. Performing Artists Soc. Am. (mng. dir. 1997), Internat. Intellectual Property Inst. (dir. 1998—). Home: 3826 Van Ness St NW Washington DC 20016-2228 Office: Swidler Berlin 3000 K St NW Ste 300 Washington DC 20007-5116 Home Phone: 202-363-3079; Office Phone: 202-373-6509. Personal E-mail: lshyman@aol.com. Business E-Mail: lshyman@swidlaw.com.

HYMAN, MICHAEL BRUCE, judge; b. Elgin, Ill., July 26, 1952; s. Robert I. and Ruth Hyman; m. Leslie Bland, Aug. 14, 1977; children: Rachel Joy, David Adam. BSJ with honors, Northwestern U., 1974, JD, 1977. Bar: Ill. 1977, U.S. Supreme Ct. 1989. Asst. atty. gen. Antitrust divsn. State of Ill., Chgo., 1977—79; trial atty. Much Shelist Freed Denenberg Ament & Rubenstein, Chgo., 1979—85, ptnr., 1985—2006; judge Cir. Ct. of Cook County, Ill., 2006—. Chmn. panelist various continuing legal edn. seminars. Columnist Editor's Briefcase, CBA Record, 1988-90, 93—2004, The Red Pencil, 1986-89; contbr. chpt. to book, articles to profl. jours.; host (cable TV program) You and the Law, 1995-2004. Trustee North Shore Congregation Israel, Glencoe, 1980-89, 95-2001, v.p., 1987-89. Mem.: ABA (assoc. editor 1985—89, sect. litig., chmn. antitrust litig. com. 1987—90, mng. editor 1989—90, editor-in-chief Litig. News 1990—92, task force on civil justice reform 1991—93, chmn. monographs and unpub. papers com. 1992—95, editor-in-chief Litig. Docket 1995—2001, Tips From the Trenches 2001—02, co-jud. divsn. mem. chair 2002—04, chmn. consumer and personal rights litig. com. 2002—05, exec. com. lawyer's conf. 2002—, jud. divsn. ann. meeting. co-chair 2004—05, atty.-client taskforce 2005—, sec. 2005—06), Chgo. Bar Found. (bd. dirs.), Decalogue Soc. Lawyers (co-chair CLE programs 2001—04, trustee 2001—, fin. sec. 2002—03, rec. sec. 2003—04, pres. 2004—05), Am. Soc. Writers on Legal Subjects (chair book award com. 1997—, bd. dirs., treas. 2005—), Ill. Bar Assn. (antitrust coun. 1981—87, vice chair, sec., co-editor newsletter 1982—85, chmn. coun. 1985—86, rep. on assembly 1986—92, chmn. bench and bar sect. coun. 1990—91, professionalism com. 1992—95, chair 1993—94, rep. on assembly 1994—99, vice chair ARDC com. 1995—96, cable TV com. 1995—2005, chair ARDC com. 1996—97, chair 1997—99, bench and bar sect. coun. 1998—2003, rep. on assembly 2001—04), Chgo. Bar Assn. (editor-in-chief CBA record 1988—90, 1992—94, CBA News 1994—98, vice-chair class action com. 1999—2000, chair 2000—01, bd. mgrs. 2003—04, 2d v.p. 2003—04, editor-in-chief CBA record 2003—, 1st v.p. 2004—05, pres. 2005—06). Jewish. Avocations: writing, Abraham Lincoln.

HYMAN, MILTON BERNARD, lawyer; b. LA, Nov. 19, 1941; s. Herbert and Lillian (Rakowitz) Hyman; m. Sheila Goldman, July 4, 1965; children: Lauren Davida, Micah Howard. BA in Econs. with highest honors, UCLA, 1963; JD magna cum laude, Harvard U., 1966. Bar: Calif. 1967. Assoc. Irell & Manella LLP, LA, 1970-73, ptnr., 1973—. Co-author: Partnerships and Associations: A Policy Critique of the Morrisey Regulations, 1976, Consolidated Returns: Summary of Tax Considerations in Acquisition of Common Parent of Subsidiary Member of Affiliated Group, 1980, Tax Aspects of Corporate Debt Exchanges, Recapitalization and Discharges, 1982, Tax Strategies for Leveraged Buyouts and Other Corporate Acquisitions, 1986, Preservation and Use of Net Operating Losses and Other Tax Attributes in a Consolidated Return Context, rev. edit., 1992, Collier on Bankruptcy Taxation, 1992, Real Estate Workouts and Bankruptcies, 1993, Current Corporate Bankruptcy Tax Issues, 1993, Tax Strategies for Corporate Acquisitions, Dispositions, Financing, Joint Ventures, Reorganizations, and Restructurings, 1995; author: A Transactional Encounter with the Partnership Rules of Subchapter K: The Effects of the Tax Reform Act of 1984, 1984, Net Operating Losses and Other Tax Attributed of Corporate Clients, 1987. Past pres., bd. dirs. Sinai Temple, West Los Angeles, Calif. Capt. JAGC, U.S. Army, 1967-70. Sheldon traveling fellow Harvard U., 1966-67. Mem. ABA (chmn. com. affiliated and related corps. 1981-83, chmn. corp. tax com. 1999-2000), Calif. State Bar Assn., Am. Law Inst. (fed. income tax project tax adv. group 1976—), Masons, Phi Beta Kappa. Jewish. Office: Irell & Manella LLP Ste 900 1800 Avenue Of The Stars Los Angeles CA 90067-4276

HYMAN, MONTAGUE ALLAN, lawyer, educator; b. NYC, Apr. 19, 1941; s. Allan Richard and Lilyan P. (Pollock) H.; m. susann Podell, Jan. 25, 1965; children: Jeffrie-Anne, Erik. BA, Syracuse U., 1962; JD, St. Johns U., 1965. Bar: N.Y. 1965, U.S. Dist. Ct. (so. and ea. dists.) N.Y. 1967, U.S. Ct. Appeals (2d cir.) 1982, U.S. Supreme Ct. 1973. Assoc. Warburton, Hyman, Deeley & Connolly, Mineola, NY, 1965-67; ptnr. Hyman & Deeley, 1967-69, Koeppel, Hyman, Sommer, Lesnick & Ross, 1969-72, Hyman & Hyman, P.C., Garden City, 1972-80, Costigan, Hyman, Hyman & Herman, P.C., Mineola, 1980-87, Certilman, Haft, Balin, Buckley, Adler & Hyman, 1988—, Certilman Balin Adler & Hyman, 1988—. Lectr. Hofstra U., Adelphi U., Columbia Appraisal Soc., Practicing Law Inst.; counsel Edn. and Assistance Corp. Contbr. articles to profl. jours. Bd. trustees North Shore L.I. Jewish Health System. Mem. Nassau County Bar Assn., N.Y. State Bar Assn., Inst. Property Taxation. Office: Certilman Balin Adler & Hyman LLP 90 Merrick Ave East Meadow NY 11554-1571 Home Phone: 516-883-4814; Office Phone: 516-296-7075. E-mail: ahyman@certilmanbalin.com.

HYMAN, MORTON PETER, private equity investment company executive; b. NYC, Jan. 9, 1936; s. Irving S. and Dora (Pfeffer) H.; m. Chris Oliphant Stern, Mar. 18, 1979; children: Sarah Anne, David Jacob. BA, Cornell U., 1956, LLD with distinction, 1959; DHL (hon.), N.Y. Med. Coll. Bar: N.Y. 1960. Assoc. Proskauer Rose Goetz & Mendelsohn, NYC, 1959-63; officer, dir. Overseas Discount Corp., NYC, 1963—2002, Overseas Shipholding Group, Inc., NYC, 1969—2003, CEO, 1999—2003, also chmn., bd. dirs.; CEO MPH Enterprises, LLC, NYC, 2003—. Vice chmn. bd. Discount Bank and Trust Co., 1999-2002. Bd. editors Cornell Law Rev. Vice-chmn. N.Y. State Health Planning Commn., 1977-78; mem. Pub. Health Coun. N.Y., 1971-95, vice chmn., 1975-85, chmn., 1985-95; co-chmn. N.Y. State Health Issues Forum; chmn. N.Y. State Health Care Capital Policy Adv. Com., 1982-94; chmn. bd. trustees Beth Israel Med. Ctr., Continuum Health Ptnrs, Inc.; chmn. bd. trustees St. Luke's-Roosevelt Hosp. Ctr.; vice chmn. N.Y. Eye and Ear Infirmary; vice-chmn. bd. regents L.I. Coll Hosp.; chmn. N.Y. State Joint Exec. and Legis. Task Force on Delivery of Health Care, 1977-80; chmn. N.Y. State Joint Exec. and Legis. Com. on Residential Health Care Facilities, 1977-80; trustee The Brearley Sch., 1993-97; mem. pres. coun. United Hosp. Fund; bd. dirs. United Jewish Appeal Fedn., 1986-91; mem. bd. overseers Albert Einstein Coll. Medicine of Yeshiva U. 2d lt. AUS, 1956-57. Fellow N.Y. Acad. Medicine; mem. N.Y. Bar Assn., Harmonie Club, Order of Coif, Phi Kappa Phi. Republican. Home: 998 5th Ave New York NY 10028-0102 Office: MPH Enterprises LLC 667 Madison Ave New York NY 10021

HYMAN, PAULA E(LLEN), history professor; b. Boston; d. Sydney Max and Ida Frances (Tatelman) H.; m. Stanley Harvey Rosenbaum, June 7, 1969; children: Judith Hyman Rosenbaum, Adina Hyman Rosenbaum. BJED, Hebrew Coll., Brookline, Mass., 1966; BA, Radcliffe Coll., 1968; MA, Columbia U., 1970, PhD, 1975; degree (hon.), Jewish Theol. Sem., 2002. Asst. prof. Columbia U., NYC, 1974-81; assoc. prof. history Jewish Theol. Sem., NYC, 1981-86; dean. Sem., Coll. Jewish Studies, 1981-86; Lady Davis vis. assoc. prof. Hebrew U., Jerusalem, 1986; Lucy Moses prof. history Yale U., New Haven, 1986—. Author: From Dreyfus to Vichy, 1979, The Emancipation of the Jews of Alsace, 1991, Gender and Assimilation in Modern Jewish History, 1995, The Jews of Modern France, 1998; co-author: The Jewish Woman in America, 1976; co-editor: The Jewish Family: Myths and Reality, 1986, Jewish Women in America: An Historical Encyclopedia, 2 vols., 1997; editor: My Life as a Radical Jewish Woman, 2002; series editor Ind. U. Press, Bloomington, 1982—; contbg. editor Sh'ma Mag., N.Y.C., 1977—; contbr. articles to publs. Vice chmn. Zionist Acad. Coun., N.Y.C., 1982-83. NEH summer grantee, 1977; Am. Coun. Learned Socs. fellow, 1978; grantee N.Y. Coun. for Humanities, 1980; NEH fellow, 1986-87. Fellow Am. Acad. Jewish Rsch. (treas. 1995—, v.p. 1999-); mem. Am. Hist. Assn. (com. 1983), Assn. for Jewish Studies (bd. dirs. 1978-81, 83-85, 86—, v.p. for membership 1995-97), Nat. Found. Jewish Culture (chair acad. adv. com. 1996—), Leo Baeck Inst. (bd. dirs. 1979—), Yivo Inst. for Jewish Rsch., Phi Beta Kappa. Jewish. Office: Yale U Dept History New Haven CT 06520

HYMAN, ROGER DAVID, lawyer; b. Oak Ridge, Tenn., Apr. 23, 1957; s. Marshall Leonard and Vera Lorraine (McKinney) H.; m. Elsa Laurencio; children: Cristina Alicia, James Marshall. BA, Vanderbilt U., 1979; JD, U. Tenn., 1984. Clk. Oak Ridge Nat. Lab., 1977-78, 81; air personality, news reporter Stas. WKDA, WKDF, Nashville, 1979; program dir. Sta. WBIR-FM, Knoxville, Tenn., 1979-80; assoc. atty. Hindman & Holt, Attys., Knoxville, Tenn., 1984-85; asst. atty. gen. State of Tenn., Knoxville, 1986-95; with Law Offices of Roger D. Hyman Powell, Tenn., 1995-97; ptnr. Hyman & Carter, PLLC, Powell, Tenn., 1997—. Bd. dirs. Knoxville Christian Sch., 1991-93. Democrat. Mem. Ch. of Christ. Home: 2713 Windemere Ln Powell TN 37849-3782 Office: Hyman & Carter PLLC PO Box 1304 Powell TN 37849-1304 Home Phone: 865-947-5577; Office Phone: 865-947-0533. Personal E-mail: RDHymanLAW@aol.com.

HYMAN, STEVEN EDWARD, academic administrator, physiatrist, educator; BA summa cum laude, Yale U., 1974; BA with honors, MA in History and Philosophy of Sci., U. Cambridge, Eng., 1976; MD cum laude, Harvard U., 1980. Diplomate Am. Bd. Psychiatry and Neurology. Intern in medicine Mass. Gen. Hosp., Boston, 1980-81, clin. and rsch. fellow in endocrinology and neurology, 1983-84, rsch. fellow in molecular biology, 1984-88, dir. rsch. dept. psychiatry, 1990-96, dir. divsn. addictions, 1992-95, supr. psychiatric residents, 1984—, dir. neurosci. and biolo. psychiatry curriculum for residents, lectr., 1986—; clin. fellow in medicine Harvard U., Boston, 1980-81, clin. fellow in psychiatry, 1981-84, rsch. fellow in genetics, 1984-87; from instr. in psychiatry to asst. prof. psychiatry Harvard Med. Sch., Boston, 1987-92, assoc. prof. psychiatry, 1993-98, prof. psychiatry, 1998—; dir. NIMH, Rockville, Md., 1996—2001; provost Harvard U., Cambridge, Mass., 2001—. Mem. sci. coun. NARSAD, 1996—; mem. adv. com. Howard Hughes Med. Inst., 1998—, Riken Brain Scis. Inst., Tokyo. Author: (with G.W. Arana) Handbook of Psychiatric Drug Therapy, 1987, 2d edit., 1991, 3d edit. (with G.W. Arana, J.R. Rosenbaum), 1995, (with E. Nestler) The Molecular Foundations of Psychiatry, 1993, Molecular Neuropharmacology: Foundation for Clinical Neuroscience, 2001; editor numerous textbooks; mem. editl. bd. Jour. Geriat. Psychiatry and Neurology, 1987-96, Psychosomatics, 1988-96, Harvard Rev. Psychiatry, 1992—, Am. Jour. Med. Genetics, 1992—, Jour. Neurochemistry, 1994—, Archives Gen. Psychiatry, 1996—, Molecular Psychiatry, 1996—, Neurobiology of Disease, 1996—. Mellon fellow, 1974-76, Dupont-Warren fellow, 1983-84, Laughlin fellow Am. Coll. Psychiatry, 1983; recipient Laughlin award Nat. Psychiatric Endowment Fund, 1984, Physician Scientist award NIDDK, 1985-90, Philip Isenberg award for best tchr. selected by graduating residents McLean Hosp., 1985, Rsch. Scientist Devel. award level 2, 1995-96. Mem. APA, Inst. Medicine, Am. Coll. Neuropsychopharmacology, Soc. Neurosci., Soc. Biolo. Psychiatry; Fellow, Am. Academy Arts & Sciences, 2004. Office: Harvard U University Hall Harvard Yard Cambridge MA 02138 Office Phone: 617-496-5100.*

HYMAN, URSULA H., lawyer; BA, Immaculate Heart Coll., 1973; MEd, Loyola Marymount Coll., 1977; JD, U. So. Calif., 1983. Bar: Calif. 1983. With Latham & Watkins, LA, 1983—, ptnr., 1990—. Founding mem. ad hoc com. Chpt. 9 Reform. Bd. dirs. Calif. Philharmonic. Named LA Super Lawyers, LA Mag., 2004, 2005, 2006. Mem.: ABA, L.A. Women's Lawyers Assns., Nat. Assn. Bond Lawyers, L.A. County Bar Assn., State Bar Calif., Order of the Coif. Office: Latham & Watkins LLP 633 W Fifth St Ste 4000 Los Angeles CA 90071 Office Phone: 213-485-1234. Business E-Mail: ursula.hyman@lw.com.

HYMEL, L(EZIN) J(OSEPH), lawyer, former prosecutor; b. Baton Rouge, July 2, 1944; s. Lezin Joseph Sr. and Alma K. Hymel; m. Linda N. Hymel, Oct. 6, 1973; children: Traci Lyn, Shea Roach Bonaventure, Kimberly Kaye. BS in Geology, La. State U., 1966, JD, 1969. Bar: La., U.S. Dist. Ct. (ea. dist.) La., U.S. Dist. Ct. (mid. dist.) La., U.S. Dist. Ct. (we. dist.) La., U.S. Ct. Appeals (5th cir.). Pvt. practice, Baton Rouge, 1969—70; staff atty. Office State Atty. Gen., Baton Rouge, 1970—71, asst. atty. gen., 1972—78, dir. criminal divsn., 1992—93; asst. dist. atty. Office 19 Jud. Dist. Atty., Baton Rouge, 1978—79; city judge Baton Rouge City Ct., 1980—83; state dist. ct. judge criminal divsn. 19th Jud. Dist. Ct, Baton Rouge, 1983—90, state dist. ct. judge civil divsn., 1991—92; US atty. Office US Atty., Dept. Justice, Baton Rouge, 1994—2001; ptnr. Sharp Hymel Cerniglia Colven Weaver & Davis, Baton Rouge, 2001—04, Hymel, Davis & Peterson, Baton Rouge, 2005—. Office: Hymel Davis & Petersen 10602 Coursey Blvd Baton Rouge LA 70816

HYMEL, MELISSA K., librarian; Adminstrv. libr. Pointe Coupee Parish Libr., New Roads, La. Bd. dirs. Greater Pointe Coupee C. of C., New Roads, La. Recipient NY Times Libr. award, 2006. Mem.: Southeastern Libr. Network (SOLINET), Southeastern Libr. Assn. Office: Pointe Coupee Libr 201 Claiborne St New Roads LA 70760 Office Phone: 225-638-9841. Office Fax: 225-638-9847. E-mail: mkhymel@yahoo.com.

HYMES, DELL HATHAWAY, anthropologist, educator; b. Portland, Oreg., June 7, 1927; s. Howard Hathaway and Dorothy (Bowman) H.; m. Virginia Margaret Dosch, Apr. 10, 1954; 1 adopted child, Robert Paul; children: Alison Bowman, Kenneth Dell; 1 stepchild, Vicki (Mrs. David Unruh). BA, Reed Coll., 1950; MA, Ind. U., 1953, PhD, 1955; postgrad., UCLA, 1954-55; degree (hon.), U. Turino, Italy, 2002, U. Mass., Amherst, 2005. From instr. to asst. prof. Harvard U., 1955-60; from assoc. prof. to prof. U. Calif., Berkeley, 1960—65; prof. anthropology U. Pa., 1965-72, prof. folklore and linguistics, 1972-88, prof. sociology, 1974-88, prof. edn., 1975-88, dean Grad. Sch. Edn., 1975-87; prof. anthropology and English U. Va., 1987-90, Commonwealth prof. anthropology, 1990-98, Commonwealth prof. English, 1990-98, emeritus, 1998—. Bd. dirs. Social Sci. Rsch. Coun., 1965-67, 69-70, 71-72. Author: Language in Culture and Society, 1964, The Use of Computers in Anthropology, 1965, Studies in Southwestern Ethnolinguistics, 1967, Pidginization and Creolization of Languages, 1971, Reinventing Anthropology, 1972, Foundations in Sociolinguistics, 1974, Soziolinguistik, 1980, Language in Education, 1980, In Vain I Tried to Tell You, 1981, (with John Fought) American Structuralism, 1981, Essays in the History of Linguistic Anthropology, 1983, Vers la Competence de Communication, 1984, Ethnography, Linguistics, Narrative Inequality, 1996, Now I Know Only So Far, 2003; assoc. editor: Jour. History Behavioral Scis., 1966-93, Am. Jour. Sociology, 1977-80, Jour. Pragmatics, 1977—; contbg. editor: Alcheringa, 1973-80, Theory and Society, 1976-96; editor: Language in Society, 1972-92; poetry editor Anthropology and Humanism, 2003-05; editl. bd.: New World Studies U. Va. Trustee Ctr. for Applied Linguistics, 1973-78. With AUS, 1945-47. Fellow Ctr. Advanced Study Behavioral Scis., 1957-58, Fellow Clare Hall, Cambridge, Eng., Guggenheim fellow, 1969-70, Nat. Endowment for Humanities sr. fellow, 1972-73. Fellow Am. Acad. Arts and Scis., Am. Folklore Soc. (pres. 1973-74), Brit. Acad.; mem. Am. Anthrop. Assn. (exec. bd. 1968-70, pres. 1983), Am. Assn. Applied Linguistics (pres. 1986), Linguistic Soc. Am. (exec. bd. 1967-69, pres. 1982), Coun. on Anthropology and Edn. (pres. 1978), Consortium Social Sci. Assns. (pres. 1984-85), Folklore Fellows Finland. Home: 205 Montvue Dr Charlottesville VA 22901-2022 Personal E-mail: dhymes@adelphia.net.

HYNES, AEDHMAR, public relations executive; b. Galway, Ireland; married; 4 children. Degree in econs., Univ. Coll., Galway; postgrad. diploma in mktg. Account mgr. Text 100, 1990—96, regional dir. N.Am. San Francisco, 1996—2000, CEO, 2000—. Bd. dir., in charge of client svc. Text 100, 1996. Office: Text 100 26 W 17th 2nd Fl New York NY 10011 Home Phone: 415-593-8400, 415-593-8408; Office Phone: 212-529-4600. Office Fax: 212-989-7149; Home Fax: 415-593-8401.

HYNES, BRIAN, lawyer, lobbyist; b. 1971; s. Stephen and Kathleen. BA in Speech Comm., Univ. Ill., 1992; JD, Loyola Univ., 1996. Bar: Ill. Ptnr. Shefsky & Froelich, Ltd., Chgo.; prin. Ill. Gov. Cons. Group, LLC, Chgo.; outside gen coun. Ill. Finance Authority. Past mem. bd. dir. Ill. Devel. Fin. Authority; past commr. S.W. Home Equity Assurance Commn.; spkr. in field. Contbr. articles to numerous profl. jours. Mem. bd. dir. Internat. Visitors Ctr. Chgo., Chgo. Gateway Green; co-chmn. Chgo. Green Tie Ball, 2003—06. Named one of 40 Under 40, Crain's Chgo. Bus., 2005. Office: Shefsky & Froelich, Ltd Ste 2800 111 E Wacker St Chicago IL 60601 Office Phone: 312-836-4030. Office Fax: 312-527-4011.

HYNES, DANIEL W., comptroller; b. Chgo., July 20, 1968; m. Christina Kerger Hynes, June 1999; 1 child, Charlie. BS in Econ., Computer Applications, U. Notre Dame, 1990; JD with honors, Loyola U. of Law, 1993. Health care atty. Chgo. law firm; comptroller State of Ill., Chgo., 1998—. Mem. Abraham Lincoln Assn., James Jordan Boys and Girls Club, Pediatric AIDS Chgo., Chgo. Coun. on Global Affairs, City Club, Planned Parenthood. Mem.: Ill. State Bar Assn., Am. Bar Assn., Chgo. Conv. and Tourism Bur., Ill. Govt. Fin. Officers Assn., Econ. Club. Office: Office of Comptroller 201 Capitol Springfield IL 62706-0001 Office Phone: 217-782-6000.*

HYNES, GARRY, theater director; b. Ballaghadereen, Ireland; Grad., U. Coll. Galway; LLD (hon.), Nat. Coun. for Ednl. Awards, Nat. U. Ireland, 1997. Founder Druid Theatre Co., Galway, Ireland, 1975—, artistic dir., 1975—90, 1994—, The Abbey Theatre, 1990—94. Prodns. include: The Playboy of the Western World, Bailegangaire, Conversations on a Homecoming, Wood of the Whispering, 'Tis a Pity She's a Whore, Lovers' Meeting, The Loves of Cass McGuire, The Beauty Queen of Leenane (Tony award for dir. of a play 1998), The Leenane Trilogy, A Whistle in the Dark, King of the Castle, The Plough and the Stars, The Power of Darkness, Famine, Portia Coughlan, The Man of Mode, The Love of the Nightingale, The Colleen Bawn, The Lonesome West, A Skull in Connemara, Mr. Peter's Connections, Sive, 2002, On Raftery's Hill, 2000; dir. Big Maggie, 2001, Crimes of the Heart, 2001, Sharon's Grave, 2003, Goodfather, 2003, My Brilliant Divorce, 2003, Sive, 2003, The Well of the Saints and The Tinker's Wedding (double bill), 2004, The Playboy of the Western World, 2004, DruidSynge Edinburgh Internat. Festival, Mpls., NYC, Galway Arts Festival and Dublin Theatre Festival, 2005, The Shadow of the Glen, 2005 The Well of the Saints, 2005, The Year of the Hiker, 2006, The Empress of India, 2006, Leaves, 2007, Translations, Biltmore Theatre, NY, 2007. Recipient award for best dir. The Irish Times/Electricity Supply Bd. Irish Theatre Awards, 2002. Office: Druid Theatre Co Chapel Ln Galway Ireland Business E-Mail: info@druid.ie.

HYNES, MARY ANN, lawyer, food products executive; b. Chgo., Oct. 26, 1947; d. Ernest Mario and Emma Louise (Noto) Iantorno; m. James Thomas Hynes, Jan. 25, 1969; children: Christina, Nicholas. BS, Loyola U.; JD, John Marshall Law Sch., 1971, LLM in Taxation, 1975; MBA, Lake Forest Grad. Sch. Bus., 1993. Bar: Ill. 1971, U.S. Dist. Ct. (no. dist.) Ill. 1971. Exec. editor, law editor Commerce Clearing House, Inc., Riverwoods, Ill., 1971-79, asst. sec, counsel, 1979, v.p., gen. counsel, 1979—95; chief legal officer Wolters Kluwer US Corp., Riverwoods, Ill., 1996—98; sr. v.p., gen. counsel, sec. Sundstrand Corp., Rockford, Ill., 1998—99; sr. v.p., gen. counsel, chief legal officer IMC Global Inc., Lake Forest, Ill., 1999—2004; sr. v.p., gen. counsel, corp. sec. Corn Products Internat., Inc., Westchester, Ill., 2006—. V.p., bd. dirs., exec. com. Chgo. Crime Commn.; mem. nat. strategy forum Midwest Coun. Nat. Security; adv. coun. Chgo. Symphony Orch. Chorus; deanery del. Chgo. Archdiocesan Pastoral Coun.; pres. local sch. bd., 1984-87; corp. coun. inst. planning com. Northwestern U. Sch. Law; mem. pres.' coun. Mus. Sci. and Industry, Chgo. Mem. ABA (coun., corp. law depts. com., litigation sect.), Ill. Bar Assn. (corp. law dept. sect. chair), Chgo. Bar Assn., Internat. Bar Assn., Women's Bar Assn., Ill. (former bd. dirs., found. adv. bd.), Internat. Fedn. Women Lawyers, Am. Corp. Counsel Assn., Am. Soc. Corp. Secs., Computer Law Assn., Justinian Soc. Lawyers, Law Club Chgo., Legal Club Chgo. (exec. com. 1987), Chgo. Club. Roman Catholic. Avocations: scuba diving, skiing. Office: Corn Products Internat 5 Westbrook Corporate Ctr Westchester IL 60154 Office Phone: 708-551-2600.*

HYNES, PATRICIA M., lawyer; b. NYC, Jan. 26, 1942; BA, CUNY, 1963; LLB, Fordham U., 1966. Bar: NY 1966, US Dist. Ct. (so. and ea. dists.) NY 1969, US Ct. Appeals (2d cir.) 1982. Law clk. to Hon. Joseph C. Zavatt US Dist. Ct. (ea. dist.) NY, 1966-67; asst. US atty. (so. dist.) NY US Dept Justice, 1967—82, mem. civil divsn., 1967-71; chief consumer fraud unit US Dept. Justice, 1971-78, chief ofcl. corruption and spl. pros. unit, 1978-80, exec. asst. U.S. atty., 1980-82; ptnr. Milberg Weiss Bershad Hynes & Lerach LLP, NYC, 1983-99; of counsel Milberg Weiss Bershad & Schulman LLP, NYC, 2000—06, Allen & Overy LLP, NYC, 2006—. Adj. prof. law Fordham U., 1978—83; lectr. trial advocacy Harvard U. Law Sch., 1983; lectr. Practising Law Inst.; chmn. merit selection panel for NY magistrate judges US Dist. Ct. (so. dist.) NY, 2002—; mem. dept disciplinary com. of appellate divsn. Supreme Ct. First Jud. Dept., 2005—. Mem. editl. bd. NY Law Jour., 1994—. Chairperson NY Regional Consumer Protection Coun., 1971—72; mem. Gov.'s Exec. Adv. Com. on Adminstrn. Criminal Justice, 1981—82, NY Gov.'s Commn. on Govt. Integrity, 1987—90, Mayor's Adv. Com. on Jud., 1994—2001, NYC Charter Revision Commn., 2002. Named one of 50 Top Women Lawyers, Nat. Law Jour., 1998, 2001, The 50 Most Influential Women Lawyers in Am., 2007. Fellow: Am. Coll. Trial Lawyers; mem.: ABA (chair govt. litig. com. litig. sect. 1984—87, chair securities litig. com. 1987—89, coun. litig. sect. 1989—92, chair pre-trial practice and discovery com. 1992—94, standing com. on fed. jud. 1995—2000, chair 2000—01, criminal justice sect.), Legal Aid Soc. (bd. dir. 1998—, chair bd. dir. 2004—06), Am. Law Inst. (spl. advisor 1995—2001), NY State Bar Assn., Fed. Bar Coun. (trustee 1983—91, treas. 1987—90, v.p. 1990, 1996—2002), Assn. Bar City NY (consumer affairs com. 1974—78, criminal law com. 1980—84, police law and policy com. 1981—83, sec. 1982—84, ho. dels. 1983—84, exec. com. 1984—88, second century com. 1988—92, del. to ABA, ho. dels. 1990—94, chair fed. cts. com. 1992—95, del.,), Am. Law Inst. (spl. advisor 1995—2001), Fordham Law Alumni Assn. Office: Allen & Overy LLP 1221 Ave Americas New York NY 10020 Business E-Mail: patricia.hynes@allenovery.com.*

HYNES, RICHARD OLDING, biology researcher, educator; b. Nairobi, Kenya, Nov. 29, 1944; s. Hugh Bernard Noel and Mary Elizabeth (Hinks) Hynes; m. Fleur Marshall, July 29, 1966; children: Hugh Jonathan, Colin Anthony. BA with honors, U. Cambridge, Eng., 1966, MA, 1970; PhD, MIT, 1971. Asst. prof. biology MIT, Cambridge, 1975-78, assoc. prof., 1978-83, prof. dept. biology, 1983—, assoc. head dept. biology, 1985-89, head, 1989-91, dir. Ctr. for Cancer Rsch., 1991-2001, Daniel K. Ludwig prof. cancer rsch., 1999—; investigator Howard Hughes Med. Inst., Chevy Chase, Md., 1988—. Gov. Wellcome Trust, 2007—. Author: Fibronectins, 1990; editor: Tumor Cell Surfaces and Malignancy, 1979; contbr. articles to profl. jours. Recipient Internat. award, Gairdner Found., 1997; Guggenheim Found. fellow, 1982. Fellow: AAAS, Royal Soc. London, Am. Acad. Arts and Scis.; mem.: Inst. Medicine NAS (co-chair adv. com. Human Embryonic Stem Cell Rsch. 2006—). Office: MIT Ctr Cancer Rsch E17-227 77 Massachusetts Ave Cambridge MA 02139-4307 Office Phone: 617-253-6422. Business E-Mail: rohynes@mit.edu.

HYNES, SAMUEL, language educator, writer; b. Chgo., Aug. 29, 1924; s. Samuel Lynn and Margaret (Turner) H.; m. Elizabeth Igleheart, July 28, 1944; children: Miranda, Joanna. BA, U. Minn., 1947; MA, Columbia U., 1948, PhD, 1956. Mem. faculty Swarthmore Coll., 1949-68, prof. English lit., 1965-68; prof. English Northwestern U., Evanston, Ill., 1968-76, Princeton U., 1976-90, Woodrow Wilson prof. lit., 1978-90, Woodrow Wilson prof. lit. emeritus, 1990—. Author: The Pattern of Hardy's Poetry, 1961 (Explicator award, 1962), William Golding, 1964, The Edwardian Turn of Mind, 1968, Edwardian Occasions, 1972, The Auden Generation, 1976, Flights of Passage, 1988, A War Imagined, 1990, The Soldiers' Tale, 1997 (Robert F. Kennedy Book award, 1998), The Growing Seasons, 2003; editor: Further Speculations by T.E. Hulme, 1955, The Author's Craft and Other Critical Writings of Arnold Bennett, 1968, Romance and Realism, 1970, Complete Poetical Works Thomas Hardy, Vol. I, 1982, Vol. II, 1984, Vol. III, 1985, Vols. IV and V, 1995, Thomas Hardy, 1984, Complete Short Fiction of Joseph Conrad, vols. I-III, 1992, vol. IV, 1993. Served to maj. USMCR, 1943-46, 52-53. Decorated Air medal, DFC; recipient award in lit. Am. Acad. Arts and Letters, 2004; Fulbright fellow, 1953-54, Guggenheim fellow, 1959-60, 81-82, Bollingen fellow, 1964-65, Am. Coun. Learned Socs. fellow, 1969, 85-86; NEH sr. fellow, 1973-74, 77-78, 89-91. Fellow Royal Soc. Lit.; mem. Phi Beta Kappa. Home: 130 Moore St Princeton NJ 08540-3359

HYNES, THOMAS JOHN, academic administrator; b. Brighton, Mass., Nov. 19, 1949; 1 child, Thomas Patrick. BS in Math., U. Mass., 1971; MA, U. N.C., 1972; PhD, U. Mass., 1976. Asst. prof. Baylor U., Waco, Tex., 1975—78; from asst. prof. to assoc. prof. to dean U. Louisville, 1978—90, dean Coll. Arts and Scis., 1990—96; v.p. acad affairs U. West Ga., Carrollton, 1996—, acting pres., 1999—2000, 2006—. Chmn. bd. trustees Nat. Debate Tournament, Del., 1987—2002. Author: Counterplan: Theory and Practice, 1987, The Last Frontier, 1990, Aging in America, 1988; editor: Comm. Edn., 2002—04, on-line Jour. Distance Learning Adminstrn., 1998—. Mem. Ga. Commn. Holocaust, 2000—04; bd. dirs. Carroll Tomorrow, Carrollton, 1999—2000, Ga. Humanities Coun., 2004—. Mem.: Nat. Comm. Assn. (mem. internat. discussion and debate 1985—88, chmn. bd. finance 2002—04, mem. exec. com. 2002—), Woodcock Soc., Rotary (mem. internat. svcs. coun. 0199—). Avocations: running, cooking, travel. Office: Office Academic Affairs Maple St Carrollton GA 30118 Office Phone: 678-839-6445. Business E-Mail: thynes@westga.edu.

HYNES, THOMAS N. (TOBY), automotive company executive; BBA, Hillsdale Coll.; MBA, Stanford U. Various key positions in sales and ops. Ford Motor Co., 1969, regional mgr. Ford and Lincoln-Mercury divsns., pres., COO Primus Fin. divsn., 1995-99; pres., gen. mgr. Gulf States Toyota Inc., Houston, 1999—. Office: Gulf States Toyota 7701 Wilshire Pl Dr Houston TX 77040*

HYNES, VIRTNER GILMORE, rehabilitation services professional; b. Phila., Nov. 24, 1943; s. George Marcus and Virginia Pauline Hynes. BA, Rowan U., Glassboro, NJ, 1979. Tchr. Sch. Dist. Phila., 1985—90; vocat. rehab. counselor Office Vocat. Rehab., Phila., 1990—. Organist St. Peters Hope Luth. Ch., Phila., 1995—. Singer: Delaware Valley Opera Co., 1993. With US Army, 1965—67. Recipient Svc. award, African Am. Luth. Assn., Phila., 1996, Customer Svc. award, Office Vocat. Rehab., 2004, Svc. award, St. Michael's Luth. Ch., Phila., 2004. Mem.: Am. Guild Organists. Avocations: languages, theater. Home: 6312 Ross St Philadelphia PA 19144 Office: OFfice Vocat Rehab 444 N 3d St 5th Fl Philadelphia PA 19123

HYODO, HARUO, radiologist, educator; b. Honai-cho, Japan, Mar. 3, 1928; B of Medicine, Tokushuma U., 1959, MD, 1966. Chief clinic of radiology Nat. Kochi Hosp., 1963-65; chief divsn. of radiology Ehime Prefectural Ctrl. Hosp., 1970-77; prof. dept. radiology Dokkyo U. Sch. Medicine, Mibu, Japan, 1977—90; dir. emeritus Ikeda Meml. Hosp., Sukagawa, Japan, 1990—; asst. dir. Fukuda Meml. Hosp., Mooka, 1993—2006. Guest prof. Dokkyo U. Sch. Medicine, 1994-2006, Tenjin (China) 2d Med. Coll., 1986-2006. With Japanese Navy, 1944—45. Mem. Japanese Radiol. Soc. (cert. radiologist), Japanese Soc. Med. Imaging Tech. (pres. ann. gen. mtg. 1989-90), Japan Biliary Assn. (hon.; pres. ann. congress 1987-88), Japanese Med. Imaging Tech. Assn. (councilor 1980-95), Japanese Soc. Interventional Radiology (hon.). Achievements include patents in field. Avocations: photography, motoring, bowling, fishing. Home: 1-9-3 Saiwai-chou Mib-machi Shimotsuga-gun Tochigi 321-0203 Japan Office: Fukuda Meml Hosp 3-10 Namiki-chou Mooka Tochigi 321-43 Japan Business E-Mail: hyodo283@green.ocn.ne.jp.

HYSLOP, DAVID JOHNSON, retired arts administrator; b. Schenectady, June 27, 1942; s. Moses McDickens Hyslop; m. Sally Fefercorn, Aug. 12, 1995; 1 child, Alexander. BS in Music Edn., Ithaca Coll., 1965. Elem. sch. vocal music supr., Elmira Heights, N.Y., 1965-66; mgr. Elmira Symphony Choral Soc., 1966; asst. mng. dir. Minn. Orch., Mpls., 1969-72; gen. mgr. Oreg. Symphony Orch., Portland, 1972-78; exec. dir. St. Louis Symphony Soc., 1978-89, pres., 1989-91, Minn. Orch., 1991—; ret. Bd. dirs. Am. Symphony Orch. League, 1988-96, chmn., 1994, mem. exec. and nominating coms., 1990-93; bd. dirs. Minn. Citizens for Arts, Mpls. Downtown Coun., 1992-97, Mpls. Visitors and Conf. Bur., 1996-98; mem., co-chmn. arts edn. task for Mo. Arts Coun., 1989-90; mem. rec. panel Nat Endowment for Arts, 1986-88, mem. challenge grant panel, 1987-88, mem. music overview panel, 1987-88, mem. music creation and presentation panel, 1999; chmn. music and performing arts com. Regional Commerce and Growth Assn., St. Louis, 1987-89; bd. dirs. Minn. State Fair Found., 2002-. Martha Baird Rockefeller grantee, 1966. Mem. Am. Symphony Orch. League (chmn. major mgrs. and policy com. 1985-87, orch. mgmt. fellowship program 1979-88, orch. assessment program 1988), Regional Orch. Mgrs. Assn. (founder), Minn. Orchestral Assn., Mpls. Club, Arena Club. Avocations: basketball, travel, reading, study of German. Home: 2019 Irving Ave S Minneapolis MN 55405-2521 Office: Minn Orch 1111 Nicollet Mall Minneapolis MN 55403-2477 E-mail: dhyslop@mnorch.org.

HYSLOP, NEWTON EVERETT, JR., infectious disease specialist; b. Newton, Mass., 1935; AB, Harvard U., 1957, MD, 1961. Diplomate Am. Bd. Allergy and Immunology, Am. Bd. Internal Medicine, Am. Bd. Infectious Disease. Intern Mass. Gen. Hosp., Boston, 1961-62, resident in medicine, 1962—63, fellow in infectious disease, 1966—68; rsch. assoc. lab. immunology Nat. Inst. Allergy and Immunology, Bethesda, Md., 1963—65; resident in medicine Peter Bent Brigham Hosp., Boston, 1965—66; with Tulane U. Med. Ctr., New Orleans, 1984—; prof. medicine Tulane U., 1984—2006, prof. emeritus, 2006—. Instr. to asst. prof. Harvard Med. Sch., 1965—85; asst. to assoc. physician Mass. Gen. Hosp., 1965—85; Moseley traveling fellow and vis. scientist dept. biochemistry U. Oxford, 1968—69; chief infectious disease sect. Tulane Sch. Medicine, 1984—2006; founder and prin. investigator Tulane-La. State U. AIDS Clin. Trials unit, 1987—96, co-prin. investigator, 1996—2006; med. dir. HIV/AIDS/TB In-Patient unit, Charity Hosp., 1991—2006; clin. head HIV disease mgmt. initiative, health care svcs. divsn. La. State U. Health Scis. Ctr., 1999—. Fellow ACP, Infectious Dis. Soc.; mem. Am. Assn. Immunologists, Am. Soc. Microbiology, Assn. Subspecialty Professors. Office: Tulane U Sch Medicine Infectious Diseases Sect SL87 1430 Tulane Ave New Orleans LA 70112-2699 Home Phone: 504-891-1541; Office Phone: 504-988-7316. Business E-Mail: nhyslop@tulane.edu.

HYTIER, ADRIENNE DORIS, French language educator; d. Jean and Katharine (Hytier) Matson. BA summa cum laude, Barnard Coll., 1952; MA, Columbia U., 1953, PhD, 1958. Instr. French Vassar Coll., Poukeepsie, NY, 1959—61, asst. prof., 1961—66, assoc. prof., 1966—70, prof. French, 1970—96, Lichtenstein Dale prof. French, 1974—96. Vis. assoc. prof. Columbia U., 1966, U. Calif., 1968—69. Editor for French lit.: The 18th Century: A Current Bibliography Since 1970, 25 vols., Two Years of French Foreign Policy: Vichy 1940-42, 1958, 2d edit., 1974, Les Dépêches diplomatiques du Comte de Gobineau en Perse, 1959, La Guerre, 1975, 4th edit., 1991; contbr. articles to profl. jours. Decorated chevalier des Palmes

Académiques; fellow, Guggenheim Found., 1967—68. Mem. MLA, Am. Soc. 18th Century Studies, Internat. Soc. 18th Century Studies, Phi Beta Kappa. Home: 71 Raymond Ave Poughkeepsie NY 12603-0372 Office: Vassar Coll Box 372 Poughkeepsie NY 12604-0001

IACOBUCCI, EDWARD E., air transportation and former software company executive; BS in Systems Engring., Ga. Inst. Tech. Co-founder, v.p., chief tech. officer Citrix Systems Inc., 1989—91, chmn., 1991—2000; founder, chmn. WingedFoot Svcs. LLC, West Palm Beach, Fla., 2000; co-founder, CEO DayJet, 2002. Bd. dir. SCO Group, Inc., Lindon, Utah, 2000—. Named one of 50 Who Matter Now, Business 2.0, 2007. Home: 3300 Airport Rd Ste 401 Boca Raton FL 33431-6479*

IACOBUCCI, FRANK, lawyer, judge, former academic administrator; b. Vancouver, BC, Can., June 29, 1937; s. Gabriel and Rosina (Pirillo) I.; m. Nancy Elizabeth Eastham, Oct. 31, 1964; children: Andrew Eastham, Edward Michael, Catherine Elizabeth. B of Commerce, U. BC, 1959, LLB, 1962; LLM, Cambridge U., Eng., 1964, Diploma in Internat. Law, 1966; LLD (hon.), U. Toronto, 1989, U. BC, 1989, U. Ottawa, 1995, U. Victoria, 1996, Law Soc. Upper Can., 2000, McGill U., 2003, U. Waterloo, 2003, U. Calabria, Italy, 2003, Queen's U., 2005, York U., 2005; D of Sacred Letters (hon.), U. Trinity Coll. in U. Toronto, Toronto, 2005. Bar: Ont. 1970, Queen's Counsel, 1986. Assoc. Dewey Ballantine et al, NYC, 1964-67; assoc. prof. law U. Toronto, 1967-71, prof. law, 1971-85, assoc. dean faculty of law, 1973-75, v.p. internal affairs, 1975-78, dean faculty of law, 1979-83, v.p., provost, 1983-85; vis. fellow Wolfson Coll., Cambridge, England, 1978; dep. min. of justice and dep. atty. gen. Govt. of Can., Ottawa, Ont., 1985-88; chief justice Fed. Ct. of Can., Ottawa, 1988-90; justice Supreme Ct. Can., Ottawa, 1991—2004; interim pres. U. Toronto, 2004—05; atty. Torys LLP, 2005—. Mem. Permanent Ct. of Arbitration, 1997-2004; former cons. Ont., Alta., Can. govts.; mem. Ont. Securities Commn., Toronto, 1982-85; dir. Cambridge Can. Trust, 1984-91; mem. Can. Jud. Coun., 1988-91, exec. com., edn. com.; gov. Can. Jud. Ctr., 1989-91; gov. Nat. Jud. Inst., 1992-2004; mem. adv. coun. Internat. Ctr. Criminal Law Reform and Criminal Justice Policy, 1991-93, dir. 1993-2004; Walter S. Owen vis. prof. U. BC, 2005-06; Oscar M. Ruebhausen Fellow Yale U., 2005-06; mentor Trudeau Found., 2005-07; advisor Can. Pension Plan Investment Bd., 2005—; mem. Can. adv. bd. Gen. Motors of Can., 2006—; bd. dirs. Torstar Corp., 2004-, chmn., 2005—; bd. dirs. Tim Hortons Inc., 2006-; chair Higher Edn. Quality Coun. Ontario, 2006—, Dean's Adv. Coun. Nat. Bus. Law Ctr. U. BC, 2005—; chair Rhodes Scholarship Selection Com., Ontario, 2006—; commr. internal inquiry Govt. of Can., 2007—. Co-author: Canadian Business Corporations, 1977, Cases and Materials on Partnerships and Canadian Business Corporations, 1983; co-editor: Materials on Canadian Income Tax, 6th edit., 1985; contbr. chpts. to books, articles to profl. jours. Mem. Islington Residents and Ratepayers Assn., 1971-85; dir. Multicultural History Soc., Ont., 1976-88; v.p. Nat. Congress Italian Cans., 1980-83, dir. Toronto dist., 1979-83; v.p. Can. Inst. Advanced Legal Studies, 1981-85, bd. govs., 1981-85, 91-98; mem. adv. com. Faculty of Law, McGill U., 1996-2004; mem. adv. bd. Inst. Can. Studies, U. Ottawa, 1998-2004. Decorated Commendatore dell'Ordine Al Merito della Repubblica Italiana; named hon. citizen, Mangone, Italy, 1996, Cepagatti, Italy, 2001, Grimaldi, Italy, 2003; recipient Law Soc. medal, Law Soc. Upper Can., 1987, Ordine al merito, Nat. Congress Italian Canadians, Toronto Dist., 1989, 125th Anniversary of Confedn. Can. medal, 1992, Lion d'Or award, Ordre des Fils d'Italie au Can., Montreal, 1995, Cosentino dell'Anno award, Fedn. of Clubs Cosentini of Ont., 1995, Man of the Yr. award, Can. Italian Bus. and Profl. Assn. Toronto, 1985, Italo-Can. of the Yr. award, Confratellanza Italo-Canadese, Vancouver, 1985, Man of Yr. award, Brotherhood Interfaith Soc., Vancouver, Can., 1999, Medaglia d'Argento del Pres. della Repubblica Italiana, 2000, Can.-Italian Nat. award, 2000, Premio Italia nel mondo, Italy in the World award, 2001, Valigia d'Oro award, 2002, Dist. Svc. award, Ont. Bar Assn., 2003, Anthony P. Pantages medal, Justice Inst. BC, 2004, Italiani nel Mondo award, Rome, Italy, 2004, Arbor award, U. Toronto, 2005, Lifetime Achievement award, U. BC Law Alumni Assn., 2005, Lifetime Achievement award, Law Sch., 2006, F.R. Scott award, McGill U. Faculty Law, 2006; Newton Rowell fellow, Can. Inst. Internat. Affairs, 1962, McKenzie-King Traveling fellow, U. BC, 1963, hon. fellow, St. John's Coll., Cambridge U. Fellow Am. Coll. Trial Lawyers (hon.); mem. Can. Bar Assn., Ontario Law Comm., 2006-, Supreme Ct. Advocacy Inst. (chair 2007—), Univ. Club of Toronto, The Queens Club, Sigma Tau Chi, Phi Gamma Delta (Disting. Fiji award 1987). Avocations: tennis, golf. Home: 17 Wilgar Rd Etobicoke ON Canada M8X 1J3 Office: Torys LLP Ste 3000 Box 270 TD Centre 79 Wellington St West Toronto ON Canada M5K 1N2 Office Phone: 416-865-8217.

IACOCCA, LEE (LIDO ANTHONY), venture capitalist, retired automotive executive; b. Allentown, Pa., Oct. 15, 1924; s. Nicola and Antoinette (Perrotto) I.; m. Mary McCleary, Sept. 29, 1956 (dec. May 16, 1983), children: Kathryn Lisa Hentz, Lia Antoinette Nagy; m. Peggy Johnson, Apr. 17, 1986 (annulled 1987); m. Darrien Earle, March 30, 1991 (div. 1994) BS, Lehigh U., 1945; ME, Princeton U., 1946. With Ford Motor Co., Dearborn, Mich., 1946-78, successively mem. field sales staff, various merchandising and tng. activities, asst. dirs. sales mgr. Phila., dist. sales mgr. Washington, 1946-56, truck mktg. mgr. div. office, 1956-57, car mktg. mgr., 1957-60, vehicle market mgr., 1960, v.p., gen. mgr., 1960-65, v.p. car & truck group, 1965-69, exec. v.p., 1967-69, pres., 1970-78; pres., COO Chrysler Corp., Highland Park, Mich., 1978-79, chmn., CEO, 1979-93; prin. Iacocca Partners, 1994—; pres. Lee Iacocca & Associates, Inc.; founder EV Global Motors, 1999—, Olivio Premium Products, 2000—. Co-author: (with William Novak) Iacocca: An Autobiography, 1984, (with Sonny Kleinfeld) Talking Straight, 1988, (with Catherine Whitney) Where Have All the Leaders Gone?, 2007; actor (TV appearances) Miami Vice, 1986 Chmn. The Statue of Liberty-Ellis Island Found., 1982; founder, The Iacocca Found., 1984- Wallace Meml. fellow Princeton U. Mem. NAE, Tau Beta Pi. Clubs: Detroit Athletic. Office: Lee A Iacocca 16760 Schoenborn St North Hills CA 91343-6108 also: Iacocca Foundation 17 Arlington St 4th Fl Boston MA 02116*

IACONO, JAMES MICHAEL, research and development company executive, nutrition educator; b. Chgo., Dec. 11, 1925; s. Joseph and Angelina (Cutaia) I.; children: Lynn, Joseph, Michael, Rosemary. BS, Loyola U., Chgo., 1950; MS, U. Ill., 1952, PhD, 1954. With U.S. Army Nutrition Ctr., Letterman Army Hosp., Denver, 1954—58; assoc. prof. biochemistry and exptl. medicine U. Cin. Sch. Medicine, 1958—70; chief Lipid Nutrition Lab. Nutrition Inst. Agrl. Rsch. Svc. USDA, Beltsville, Md., 1970-75, dep. asst. adminstrv. nat. program staff Washington, 1975-77, assoc. adminstr. office human nutrition, 1978-82, dir. Western Human Nutrition Rsch. Ctr. San Francisco, 1982-94. Prof. nutrition Sch. Pub. Health UCLA, 1987—. Author over 100 rsch./tech. publs. and chpts. in books relating to nutrition and biochemistry and lipids. With US Army, 1944—46. Recipient Rsch. Career Devel. award NIH, 1964-70. Fellow Am Heart Assn. (coun. on arteriosclerosis and thrombosis), Am. Inst. Chemists; mem. Am. Inst. Nutrition, Am. Soc. Clin. Nutrition, Am. Oil Chemists Soc. Personal E-mail: jiacono25@aol.com.

IAMELE, RICHARD THOMAS, retired law librarian; b. Newark, Jan. 29, 1942; BA, Loyola U., LA, 1963; MSLS, U. So. Calif., 1967; JD, Southwestern U., LA, 1976. Bar: Calif. 1977. Cataloger U. So. Calif., LA, 1967-71; asst. cataloger L.A. County Law Libr., 1971-77, asst. ref. libr., 1977-78, asst. libr., 1978-80, libr. dir., 1980—2005; ret., 2005. Mem. ABA, Am. Assn. Law Librs., Calif. Libr. Assn., So. Calif. Assn. Law Librs., Coun. Calif. County Law Librs. (pres. 1981-82, 88-90). Office Phone: 213-629-3531.

IAMMARTINO, NICHOLAS R., corporate communications executive; m. Eileen Iammartino. B in Chem. Engring., Cooper Union; M in Chem. Engring., NYU; MBA in Fin., Adelphi U. Process engr. Esso Rsch. and Engring. Co., 1969-71; bus. and tech. news writer Chem. Engring. mag. McGraw-Hill, 1971-76; chem. industry securities analyst Merrill Lynch, 1976-78; from sr. writer to bus. pubs. mgr. dept. corp. comm. Celanese Corp., 1979-85; corp. mgr. fin. comm. and adminstrn. Philip Morris, Inc., 1985; dir. fin. comm. Borden, Inc., N.Y., 1986-89, dir. external comm. N.Y., 1989, dir. pub. affairs N.Y., 1994-95, v.p. pub. affairs Columbus, Ohio, 1995—. Bd. dirs. Borden Found., Inc.; mem. assn. bd. Columbus Zool. Pk. Assn. Office: Borden Inc 180 E Broad St Columbus OH 43215-3799

IAMRATANAKUL, SUPACHART, educational consultant; b. Bangkok, Sept. 2, 1977; s. Somphob and Nantawee Iamratanakul. B of Engring., Kasetsart U., Bangkok, 1998; MS in Elec. and Computer Engring., Portland State U., 2002, MS in Engring. and Tech., 2003. Tchg. Portland State U., 2000—02, 2003—; cons. Intel Corp., Hillsboro, Oreg., 2004—. Office: Portland State U Portland OR 97201

IANNICELLI, JOSEPH, chemical company executive, consultant; b. NYC, Aug. 5, 1929; s. Peter and Catherine (Gugliotti) I.; m. Betty Peterson, June 28, 1978; children: Mark, Rex, Gina. SB, MIT, 1951, PhD, 1955. Rsch. chemist Textile Fibers, E.I. DuPont, Wilmington, Del., 1955-60; tech. dir. Clay Div. J.M. Huber, Macon, Ga., 1960-70; founder, chief exec. officer Aquafine Corp., Brunswick, Ga., 1970—, Aero-Instant Corp., Brunswick, Ga., 1988—; co-founder IMPEX Corp., Brunswick, Ga., 1988—. Cons. Consol. Goldfields Australia, Sydney, 1976-78, Rio Tinto, Madrid, 1980-82, Hoganes, Malmo, Sweden, 1984. Author: Evaluation and Comparison of Crossfield and Solenoid Field Magnetic Filters, 1981; co-author: A Survey-Benneficiation of Industrial Minerals, 1980; contbr. over 30 articles to profl. jours. Pres. Ga. Tidewater Conservation Assn., Brunswick, 1991—92; govt. appointment as mem. Jekyll Island (Ga.) Citizens Resource Coun., 1995—97; foreman Glynn County Grand Jury, Brunswick, 1989; chmn. Glynn County Bd. Edn., 2002; bd. dirs. Jekyll Island (Ga.) Citizens Assn., 1992—96, pres., 1993—95. Recipient Rsch. grant NSF, 1980, 84, Elec. Power Rsch. Inst., 1980, Resolution of Commendation, Ga. Ho. of Reps., 1995. Fellow Am. Inst. Chemists; mem. Tech. Assn. of Pulp and Paper Industry (chmn. pigments com. 1971-72). Achievements include more than 100 patents in field. Home: 28 Saint Andrews Dr Jekyll Island GA 31527-0901 Office: Aquafine Corp 3963 Darien Hwy Brunswick GA 31525-2423 Office Phone: 912-265-2000.

IANNIELLO, JOSEPH R., broadcast executive; BBA, Pace U., NY; MBA, Columbia U., NYC. With KPMG; dir. fin. planning CBS Corp., NYC, 1997—2000, sr. v.p. fin., treas., 2005—; v.p. corp. devel. Viacom, 2000—05, sr. v.p., treas., 2005. Bd. dirs. New Alternatives for Children. Mem.: AICPA, NY Soc. Pub. Accts. Office: CBS Corp 51 W 52nd St New York NY 10019-6188

IANNOTTI, JOSEPH PATRICK, orthopedic surgeon; b. NYC, Dec. 16, 1954; s. Frank Thomas and Victoria (Artuso) I.; 1 child, Matthew; m. Karen Bloomberg, July 26, 2003. BS, Fordham U., 1975; MD, Northwestern U., 1979; PhD in Cell Biology, U. Pa., 1987. Diplomate Am. Bd. Orthopaedic Surgery. Resident in orthopedic surgery U. Pa., Phila., 1979-83, chief resident, 1983-84, asst. prof. orthopedic surgery, 1984-93, assoc. prof., 1993-97, prof., 1997-2000; chief of shoulder svc. Hosp. of U. Pa., Phila., 1988-2000; chmn. dept. orthopedic surgery Cleve. Clinic Found., 2000—; prof. Cleve. Clinic Lerner Sch. Medicine. Author, editor: Rotator Cuff Disorders, 1992; editor: Basic Science Orthopaedics, 1994, The Shoulder Evaluation and Management, 1999, 2006, Complex and Revision Problems in Shoulder Surgery, 1998, 2005; contbr. over 200 articles to profl. jours. NIH postdoctoral fellow U. Pa., 1980-81; recipient career devel. award NIH, 1984-89, DeForest Willard award U. Pa., 1984; N.Am. travel fellow Am. Orthopaedic Assn., 1985, Am. Brit. Can. fellow, 1993. Fellow Am. Acad. Orthopaedic Surgeons; mem. Orthopaedic Rsch. Soc., Am. Shoulder and Elbow Surgeons (pres. 2005-06), Acad. Orthopaedic Soc., Pa. Orthopaedic Soc. Office: Cleve Clinic Found 9500 Euclid Ave # A-41 Cleveland OH 44195-0001 Office Phone: 216-445-5151. Business E-Mail: iannotj@ccf.org.

IANNUZZI, JOHN NICHOLAS, lawyer, author, educator; b. NYC, May 31, 1935; s. Nicholas Peter and Grace Margaret (Russo) I.; m. Carmen Marina Barrios, Aug. 1979; children: Dana Alejandra, Christina Maria, Nicholas Peter II, Alessandro Luca; children from previous marriage: Andrea Marguerite, Maria Teresa. BS, Fordham U., Bronx, NY, 1956; JD, N.Y. Law Sch., 1962. Bar: Conn. 1967, Conn. 1967, NY, 1977, Wyo. 1994, US Dist. Ct. (so. and ea. dists.) NY 1964, US Dist. Ct. (no. and we. dists.) NY 1965, US Ct. Appeals (2d cir.) 1965, US Supreme Ct. 1971, US Dist. Ct. Conn. 1978, US Tax Ct. 1978, US Ct. Appeals (5th and 11th cirs.) 1982, US Ct. Appeals (4th cir.) 1988, US Ct. Appeals (1st cir.) Wyo. 2003, US Ct. Appeals (3d cir.) Wyo. 2006. Assoc. Law Offices of H.H. Lipsig, NYC, 1962, Law Offices of Aaron J. Broder, NYC, 1963; ptnr. Iannuzzi & Iannuzzi, NYC, 1963—. Adj. prof. trial advocacy Fordham U. Law Sch., 1987-2003. Author: (fiction) What's Happening, 1963, Part 35, 1970, Sicilian Defense, 1974, Courthouse, 1977, J.T., 1984, Condemned, 2006, (non-fiction) Cross-Examination: The Mosaic Art, 1984, Trial Strategy and Psychology, 1992, Handbook of Cross-Examination, 1999, Handbook of Trial Strategy, 2000. Mem. ABA, N.Y. County Bar Assn., N.Y. Criminal Bar Assn., Columbian Lawyers Assn., Lipizzan Internat. Fedn. (v.p.), Roman Catholic. Home: 118 Via Settembre 9 Rome Italy Office: Iannuzzi & Iannuzzi 74 Trinity Place New York NY 10006 also: 775 Park Ave Huntington NY 11743-3976 also: 345 Franklin St San Francisco CA 94102-4427 also: 11377 West Olympic Los Angeles CA 90064 also: 266 Post Rd E Westport CT 06880 also: 1592 Pine Ave W Montreal PQ Canada also: Trinity Pl Nassau The Bahamas Office Phone: 212-227-9595. Business E-Mail: jni@iannuzzi.net.

IANNUZZI, SALVATORE, information technology executive; married; 3 children. BS in Acctg., St. Francis Coll. With KPMG, Bear Sterns; various sr. leadership positions, including chief adminstrv. officer, COO Europe, COO Global Investment Bank Bankers Trust/ Deutsche Bank; chief adminstrv. officer CIBC World Markets, 2000—04; former non-exec chmn. Symbol Technologies, Holtsville, NY, sr. v.p., chief adminstrv. and fin. officer, 2005—, interim pres., CEO, 2005, pres., CEO, 2006—07; bd. dir. Monster Worldwide Inc., NYC, 2006—, chmn., CEO, 2007—. Office: Monster Worldwide Inc 39th Fl 622 Third Ave New York NY 10017*

IANNUZZI SUCICH, MICHELE F., physician; BS, Siena Coll., Loudonville, NY, 1994; MD, SUNY, Syracuse, NY, 1998. Diplomate Am. Bd. Family Practice, 2001. Internship West Jersey Meml. Family Practice, 1998—2001; resident Virtua, Voorhees, NJ; physician Modena Family Practice, NY, 2003—. Contbr. articles to profl. jours. Fellow, U. Conn. Health Ctr., 2001—03. Mem.: Am. Acad. Family Practice. Office Phone: 845-883-5176. Office Fax: 845-883-5177.

IAPALUCCI, SAMUEL H., financial executive; b. Cresson, Pa., July 19, 1952; s. Anthony F. and Dorthy (Quartz) I.; m. Berniece Reichert, June 5, 1976; children: Amanda Berniece, Cara Elizabeth. BS, St. Francis Coll., Loretto, Pa., 1974; MBA, Duquesne U., 1980. CPA, Pa. Audit sr. Coopers & Lybrand, Pitts., 1974-76; asst. v.p. Equibank, N.A., Pitts., 1976-78; with Allegheny Internat., Inc., Pitts., 1978-91, v.p., treas., 1987-90, v.p., CFO, 1990, cons., 1990-91; v.p., CFO OHM Corp., Findlay, Ohio, 1991—; CFO CH2M Hill Companies, Greenwood Village, CO, sr. v.p., CFO, sec. Mem. AICPA, Pa. Inst. CPAs, Fin. Execs. Inst., Findlay Country Club. Avocations: golf, tennis, reading.

IAQUINTA, LEONARD PHILLIP, academic administrator, writer, consultant, not-for-profit fundraiser; b. Kenosha, Wis., Aug. 1, 1944; s. Anthony Sam and Mary Natalie (Gallo) I. BJ, Northwestern U., 1966; M in Journalism, Columbia U., 1967. Dir., cons. World Studies Data Bank Acad. for Ednl. Devel., NYC, 1969-76; dir. field svcs. for alumni rels. Northwestern U., Evanston, Ill., 1977-81; dir. nat. alumni program Columbia U., NYC, 1981-82; devel. officer, alumni dir. Bklyn. Coll. (CUNY), 1982-86; dir. devel. and alumni affairs Ind.-Purdue Univs., Ft. Wayne, 1986-95, Northeastern Ill. U., Chgo., 1995-2001; asst. dean, dir. devel. and alumni rels. Coll. Engring. and Applied Scis. U. Wis., Milw., 2001—03, devel. officer, 2003—04; comm. and fund raising cons., 2005—; prin. Excellence in Comm., Inc., 2004—; dir. spl. gifts U. Wis.-Parkside, Kenosha, 2005—07. Spkr. various profl. confs. Assoc. editor: Notes on Negotiating, 1974; contbr. articles to profl. jours.; chpts to books; author various devel. manuals. Exec. dir. Kenosha United Way, 1976-77, mem. campaign cabinet, 2003, bd. dirs., 2007—; mem. fund adv. com. Greater Milw. Found., 2003—; mem. devel. com. and resource devel. svc. adv. com. Alliance for Children and Families. Recipient 4 nat. alumni programming and fundraising awards Council for Advancement and Support of Edn., 1981, 84, 88, 98; 15 Who Care awards, Vol. Connection of Switchboard of Ft. Wayne, 1990. Mem. Assn. Fundraising Profls., Alliance for Nonprofit Mgmt., Assn. Consultants for Nonprofits, East Wis. Planned Giving Coun., Soc. Profl. Journalists, Racine-Kenosha Estate Planning Coun. (bd. dirs.), Rotary (pres.-elect, dir. Kenosha). Mem. Congregational Ch. Avocations: gardening, reading, enjoying the arts, travel. Home and Office: 9507 74th St Kenosha WI 53142-8194 Office Phone: 262-716-6605. Personal E-mail: LPIaquinta@cs.com.

IATROPOULOS, MICHAEL JOHN, health research executive, pathology educator; b. Athens, Greece, Nov. 8, 1938; came to U.S. 1966; s. John Michael and Marina (Yancoglu) I.; m. Barbara Jeanne McNeil, Aug. 27, 1966; children: John Michael, Mary Ellen. AB, Athens Coll., Greece, 1958; MD, U. Tuebingen, Ger., 1964; Dr.Med.Sc., U. Tuebingen, 1965. Research assoc./resident Div. Biomed. Sci., Brown U., Providence, 1966-67; resident dept. internal medicine U. Cologne, Germany, 1967-68; instr. pathology div. biomed. sci. Brown U., 1968-70; resident dept. pathology U. Mo., Columbia, 1970-71; spl. fellow toxicology CEPT Albany (N.Y.) Med. Coll., 1972-74; asst. prof. ICES Albany Med. Coll., Alamogordo, N.Mex., 1974-77, assoc. prof., dep. dir., 1977-78; dept. head MRD Am. Cyanamid Co., Pearl River, NY, 1978-89; head regulatory pathology and histopathology Am. Health Found., Valhalla, NY, 1989-99; pres. Labpath Mgmt., Inc., Suffern, NY, 1989-99. Prof. pathology N.Y. Med. Coll., N.Y., 1989—. Author: New Anticancer Drugs, 1983, Gastrointestinal Toxicology, 1986, Carcinogenicity, 1988, Toxicokinetics and New Drug Development, 1989, Toxicokinetics, 1993, Principles and Methods in Toxicology, 2001, 07; assoc. editor Jour. Toxicologic Pathology, 1999—. Fellow Acad. Toxicol. Scis., Internat. Acad. Toxicologic Pathology (hon., bd. dirs. 2000-06); mem. Soc. Toxicology, Soc. Toxicologic Pathologists (councillor 1981-86), Internat. Fedn. Soc. Toxicologic Pathologists (sec.-gen. 1989-95), Japanese Soc. Toxicologic Pathology (hon. mem.), Home: 6 Bruce Ct Suffern NY 10901-3310 Office: NY Med Coll Dept Pathology Grasslands Rd Valhalla NY 10595

IAVARONI, MARC (MARCUS JOHN), professional basketball coach, retired professional basketball player; b. Jamaica, NY, Sept. 15, 1956; m. Caroline Iavaroni; children: Kenton, McCray, Jackson. Grad., U. Va., 1978. Draft pick NY Knicks, 1978; forward Italy and Spain, 1978—81, Phila. 76ers, 1982—84, San Antonio Spurs, 1984—86, Utah Jazz, 1986—89, Milan, 1989—91; grad. asst. U. Va.; asst. coach Bowling Green State U., 1992—94, Cleve. Cavaliers, 1997—99, Phoenix Suns, 2002—07; asst. coach, dir. player devel. Miami Heat, Fla., 1999—2002; head coach Memphis Grizzlies, 2007—. Achievements include winning an NBA Championship as a member of the Phila. 76ers, 1983. Office: Memphis Grizzlies 191 Beale St Memphis TN 38103*

IAVICOLI, MARIO ANTHONY, lawyer; b. Camden, NJ, Aug. 11, 1939; s. Vito Anthony and Angelina Jessie (Marchionese) I.; m. Arlene V. LeDonne, July 6, 1963; children— Michelle, Denise, Laura. BME, Drexel U., 1962; JD, U. Pa., 1965. Bar: NJ 1965. Assoc. Samuel P. Orlando, Camden, 1965-66, Ballen & Batoff, Camden, 1966-68; ptnr. Maressa, Console & Iavicoli, Berlin, NJ, 1968-72; first asst. prosecutor Camden County, 1972-74; pvt. practice Pennsauken, NJ, 1974-79, Haddenfield, 1980—; counsel to spkr. N.J. Gen. Assembly, 1970-72, N.J. Automobile Ins. Study Commn., 1970-74, Camden County Charter Study Commn., 1974, Camden County Republican party, 1974-76, N.J. Rep. party, 1976—; solicitor Haddenfield Borough, 1980—. Author: No Fault and Comparative Negligence in New Jersey, 1973; Drafter: N.J.'s No Fault Law and other companion legislation, 1970-73. Chmn. Camden County Rep. Com., 1978—; Rep. state committeeman, 1976—; mem. Electoral Coll. from, N.J., 1976; solicitor Pennsauken Twp., 1975—; Vice pres. Haddonfield Home Sch. Assn., 1972-73; Bd. dirs. Drexel U. Class Endowment Fund; trustee Haddonfield Civic Assn. Named One of N.J.'s 5 Outstanding Young Men, 1974; recipient Ocean County Bar Assn. award, 1975 Mem. Camden County Jr. C. of C. (counsel 1967-68), ABA (ho. of dels., 2004—, pres. 2003-04), N.J. Bar Assn., Camden County Bar Assn (trustee 1996-98, sec. 1998-99, treas. 1999-2000, 2d v.p. 2000-01, 1st v.p. 2001-02, pres.-elect 2002-03, pres. 2005—, del. to ABA Ho. Dels. 2004—), Sons of Italy, Drexel U. Alumni Assn. (v.p. 1991—), Rotary. Roman Catholic. Avocations: golf, reading, travel. Home: 340 Marquis Rd Haddonfield NJ 08033-4011 Office: 43 Kings Hwy W Haddonfield NJ 08033-2128 Home Phone: 856-429-8009; Office Phone: 856-429-0201. Personal E-mail: miavicoli@comcast.net, mario.iavicoli@verizon.net.

IBACH, ROBERT DANIEL, JR., library director; b. Lynch, Nebr., Dec. 31, 1940; s. Robert Daniel Sr. and Mabel Bertine (Selstad) I.; m. Paula Joanne Hubbling, June 11, 1977. B.R.E., Detroit Bible Coll., 1963; BD, Grace Theol. Sem., Winona Lake, Ind., 1966, ThM, 1969; MLS, Ind. U., 1975. Ordained minister, 1989. Libr. Grace Coll. and Sem., Winona Lake, 1969-86; library dir. Dallas Theol. Sem., 1986—. Archaeologist Heshbon (Jordan) Expedition, 1971-76; library cons. Inst. of Holy Land Studies, Jerusalem, 1989, Seteca, Guatemala City, 2001, 04; peer evaluator So. Assn. Colls. and Schs., 1990-2006. Author: Archaeological Survey of the Hesban Region, 1987; contbg. author: Hesban After 25 Years, 1994, Dictionary of Biblical Imagery, 1998; periodical revs. editor: Bibliotheca Sacra, 1988—; contbr. articles to profl. jours., 1972—. Mem. Soc. Bibl. Lit., Am. Theol. Libr. Assn., Am. Libr. Assn., Tex. Libr. Assn. Home: 3229 Colby Cir Mesquite TX 75149-1875 Office: Dallas Theol Sem 3909 Swiss Ave Dallas TX 75204-6496

IBAÑEZ, ALVARO, museum director, patent design company executive, artist; b. Bucaramanga, Santander, Colombia, Jan. 18, 1951; came to U.S., 1981; s. Epimenio and Maria Delia (Muñoz) I.; m. Marta Cecilia Arias, Dec. 30, 1971 (div. Dec. 1991); children: Carlos Humberto, Alvaro Antonio, Diana Saray, Sandra; m. Denise DeVries, Sept. 6, 1997; children: Elena, Austin, Paul, Delia Denise. Fine arts, David Manzur Acad., Bogotá, Colombia, 1972; structural draftman, ACADITEC, Bogotá, Colombia, 1974. Elem. tchr. German Pena Sch., Bogotá, Colombia, 1971; with sales dept. Grolier Internat., Bogotá, Colombia, 1973-74; civil engring. draftsman Adminstrv. Dept. Cmty. Action, Bogotá, Colombia, 1974-76; gen. ins. mgr. Gilabert & CIA, Santa Marta, Colombia, 1976-77; farmer El Roble Ranch, Santa Marta, Colombia, 1976-77; sales mgr. Onix Ltda., Bucaramanga, Colombia, 1977-78; owner, mgr. Distrisiba Ltda., Bucaramanga, Colombia, 1977-80; sales mgr. Coramex Andina Ltda., Bogotá, Colombia, 1980-81; with Radian, Inc., Alexandria, Va., 1984—, Birch, Stewart, Kolasch & Birch, Falls Church, Va., 1985—, Diversified Technologies, Alexandria, Va., 1986—; founder Sunrise Studio Gallery, Kilmarnock, 1996—, Pennie & Edmonds, L.L.P., Washington, 1998—, A-Ibañez Mus., Kilmarnock, 2006, Aim Abanez Mus., 2006—. Freelance Pub. Health Ctr., Bogotá, Colombia, 1971-74, Guillermo Victorino SA, Bogotá, 1973-74, Felix A. Clavijo Co., Bogotá, 1973-75, Metron Publicity, Bucaramanga, Colombia, 1977-80, Tulio Ramirez, 1980-81, Fabio Hernandez Salazar, Bogotá, 1980-81; with Lascaris Design Group Internat., Washington, 1984; founder A-Ibañez Mus. One-man shows include Georgetown Streets, Washington, 1981, Sovran Bank CC, Springfield, Va., 1985; exhibited in group shows at David Manzur Acad., Bogotá, Colombia, 1974, Dicas Fine Arts Ctr., Bogotá, Colombia, 1979, Santander Indsl. U., Bucaramanga, Colombia, 1979, Arlington Ctr., Va., 1982, Falls Church Recreation Park, Va., 1982, Latin Am. Art League, Alexandria, Va., 1991, Desfile de las Americas, Washington, 1993, Martin Luther King Meml. Libr., Washington, 1994, 96, Art Mus. Ams.-Orgn. Am. States, Washington, 1994, Strathmore Hall Arts Ctr., North Bethesda, Md., 1994, AT&T, Oakton, Va., 1994, Washington, 1994, Cultural Mexican Inst., Washington, 1994, Montgomery County Exec. Office Bldg., Rockville, Md., 1994, Bell Atlantic, Arlington, Va., 1994, Silver Spring, Md., 1994, Torpedo Factory Art League, Alexandria, Va., 1994, Moscoso Gallery, Washington, 1995, Fla. Mus. Hispanic and Latin Am. Art, Miami, 1995, Montgomery County Exec. Office Bldg., Rockville, Md., 1995, NASA Hdqs., Washington, 1995, Pan Am. Health Orgn., Washington, 1995, SED Ctr., Washington, 1996, (retrospective) Falls Church (Va.) Recreation Ctr., 1997, Bell Atlantic Hdqrs., Arlington, Va., 1997, D.C. Arts in the Alley/Georgetown U., Washington, 1998, Moca Gallery, Washington, 1998, Del Ray Artisans, Alexandria, 1998, Barnes & Noble Seven Corners, Falls Church, 1998, Rappahannock Westminster Canterbury, Kilmarnock, Va., 2002, Museo Regional Queretaro Mexico, 2005, Sunrise Studio Gllery, 2006. Sponsor World Vision, Tacoma, Wash., 1987—, Child Devel. Ctr., Falls Church, Va., 1989—, Crystal Cathedral, Glandale, Calif., 1992—, Beverley Hills United Meth. Ch., Alexandria, Va., 1997, Arts in the Alley Georgetown, D.C., 1998. Recipient 1st prize drawing Prismacolor Contest, 1958. Mem. Worldwide Fine Art Promotions, Hispanic Museo Art, Art League, Torpedo Factory. Republican. Avocations: paint, gardening, music, travel. Home: A Ibañez Art Design Inc PO Box 1060 197 Whittaker Line Kilmarnock VA 22482-3123 Office Phone: 804-435-2880. E-mail: aibanez@rivnet.net.

IBANEZ, MANUEL LUIS, academic administrator, biologist, educator; b. Worcester, Mass., Sept. 23, 1935; s. Ovidio Pedro and Esperanza Fe (Perez) I.; m. Jane Marie Bourquard, Oct. 16, 1970; children: Juana Lia Cristina, Vincent Ovidio, William Dayan, Marc Albert BS cum laude, Wilmington Coll., 1957; MS, Pa. State U., 1959, PhD, 1961. Asst. prof. Bucknell U., Lewisburg, Pa., 1961-62; postdoctoral fellow UCLA, 1962; sr. biochemist IICA de la OEA, Turrialba, Costa Rica, 1962-65; assoc. prof., chmn. dept. U. New Orleans, 1965-70, prof., 1977-90, assoc. dean grad. sch., 1978-82, assoc. vice chancellor acad. affairs, 1982-83, acting vice chancellor, 1983-85, vice chancellor acad. affairs, provost, 1985-89, prof. emeritus, 1990—; pres. Tex. A&M U., Kingsville, 1989-98, named disting. prof. biology, 1998, pres., prof. emeritus; ret., 2000. Bd. regents Smithsonian Instn.; adj. prof. biology Delmar CC, 2000—. Author: Basic Biology of Microorganisms, 1972; contbr. articles to profl. jours. Regent Smithsonian Inst., 1994-2006, regent emeritus, 2006—; mem. Alliance for Good Govt., New Orleans, 1980. NSF coop. fellow, 1958-61 Mem. Am. Assn. State Colls. and Univs., Kingsville C. of C. (pres. 1991), Rotary, KC, Sigma Xi Democrat. Roman Catholic. Avocations: chess, tennis, bicycling, collections.

IBARGUEN, ALBERTO, foundation administrator, former newspaper executive; b. Rio Piedras, PR, Feb. 29, 1944; s. Albert E. and Angelica (Bigas) I.; m. Susana E. Lopez, Jan. 8, 1969; 1 child, Diego. BA in History, Wesleyan U., Middletown, Ct., 1966; JD, U. Pa., 1974. Bar: Conn. 1974. Atty. Legal Aid Soc., Hartford, Conn., 1974-76; dir., counsel Conn. Election Commn., Hartford, 1976-77; ptnr. Cloud & Ibarguen, Hartford, 1977-78; atty. Updike, Kelly & Spellacy, Hartford, 1978-79; dep. gen. coun., v.p. public affairs, v.p. pvt banking Conn. Nat. Bank, Hartford, 1979-84; sr. v.p. Hartford Courant, 1984-86; exec. v.p. ops. Newsday/N.Y. Newsday, NYC, 1986-95; pub. El Nuevo Herald, Miami, Fla., 1995-98; v.p. The Miami Herald, 1995-98, pub., 1998—2004; chmn. Miami Publishing Co., 1998—2005; pres., CEO John S. & James L. Knight Found., Miami, 2005—. Bd. dirs. Lincoln Ctr. for Performing Arts, N.Y.C., 1990-96, Dade County Found., Com. to Protect Journalists, Fla. Philharm., Pub. Broadcasting Sys., 1997—; trustee Wesleyan U., 1992-95, Smith Coll., 1995-97; mem. bus. commn. Met. Mus. Art, 1990-95. Mem. N.Y. Athletic Club. Office: Knight Found Wachovia Fin Ctr Ste 3300 200 S Biscayne Blvd Miami FL 33131

IBARRA, IRENE M., foundation administrator; b. 1952; m. Armando Quiroz. JD, U. Wash.; MPA, U. Denver, MS in Social Work in Community Svcs. & Social Planning; sr. exec. program, Harvard U. Dep. mgr. Dept. of Social Services City of Denver, 1984—87; former exec. dir. Dept. Health & Human Services State of Colo., 1987—91; atty., corp. & bus. law Hillis, Clark, Martin and Peterson, Seattle; COO Alameda Alliance for Health, 1996—98; CEO Alameda Alliance for Health, 1998—2003; dir. LA Health Action, 2003—05; exec. v.p. Calif. Endowment, 2005—06; pres., CEO The Colorado Trust, Denver, 2006—. Mem. Calif. Performance Review Commn. Trustee Blue Shield of Calif. Found., Casey Family Programs, 2003—. Office: The Colorado Trust 1600 Sherman St Denver CO 80203 E-mail: irene@coloradotrust.org.

IBBOTSON, ROGER G., financial educator; b. Chgo., May 27, 1943; s. Arthur E. and Margaret B. I.; m. Jody L. Sindelar, 1983. BS, Purdue U., 1965; MBA, Ind. U., 1967; PhD, U. Chgo., 1974. Economist Bank of Japan, 1969; bond portfolio mgr., treas.'s office U. Chgo., 1971-75, asst. prof. fin. Grad. Sch. Bus., 1975-79, sr. lectr. fin. and exec. dir. Ctr. for Research in Security Prices, 1979-84; prof. Yale U. Sch. Mgmt, 1984—; chmn. Ibbotson Assocs., Inc., Chgo., 1979—2006; chmn., CIO Zebra Capital Mgmt., 2001—. Recipient Graham and Dodd award, 1980, 82, 84, 2001, 2003, 2006, James Vertin award AIMR, 2002. Mem. Am. Fin. Assn., Am. Econ. Assn., Fin. Mgmt. Assn. Author: (with Rex Sinquefield) Stocks, Bonds, Bills, and Inflation, 3d edit., 1982, (with Gary Brinson) Global Investments, 1993, (with J.C. Francis) Lifetime Financial Advice 2007 (with Chen, Milevsky, Zhu), Investments, 2002. Home: 75 Old Hartford Tpke Hamden CT 06517-3524

IBE, BASIL OBIJIAKU, biochemist, educator; b. Rafin Kada, Nigeria, Apr. 20, 1949; arrived in US, 1981, naturalized, 1996; s. Dennis Ibe and Katrina Amole Okafor; m. Mary Lynn Anderson, Aug. 18, 1979; children: Solomon Ajika, Bronze Obinna, Ndukaku Dayton, Nnejiuwa Ugochukwu. BS, Pepperdine U., LA, 1977; MS, Idaho State U., 1979; PhD, U. Tex., 1984. Cert. in Aromatherapy Australasian Coll. of Herbal Studies, 2002. Asst. instr. Dept. of Pharmacology, Univ. of Tex. Southwestern Med. Ctr., Dallas, 1984—87; rsch. assoc. Coll. of Pharmacy, U. Colo., Boulder, 1987—88; asst. prof. pediat. David Geffen Sch. of Medicine at UCLA, LA, 1988—95, assoc. prof. pediat., prof. pediat., 2001—. Dir. cell culture facilities LA Biomedical Rsch. Inst., Torrance, Calif., 1998—, dir. summer rsch. fellowship program, 2003—. Research scientist (rsch. publs.) General Area of Perinatal Pulmonary Adaptation. Deacon First Christian Ch., Torrance, 1996—, elder, 1996—; 2d vice moderator Disciples of Christ, Pacific SW Region, Altadena, Calif., 2000. Grant, Sickle Cell Disease Rsch. Found. Greater LA, 1992—95, Harbor-UCLA Rsch. and Edn. Inst., 1998—99, Nat. Heart Lung and Blood Inst., NIH, Bethesda, Md., 2004—. Mem.: Assn. African Biomedical Scientists, Inc. (v.p.), Am. Chem. Soc. (assoc.), Am. Soc. of Pharmacology and Exptl. Therapeutics (assoc.), Toastmasters Internat. (assoc.; pres. 1991, Able Toastmaster 1994), Rho Chi, Pharmacy Soc. (assoc.), Phi Kappa Phi (assoc.). Democrat. Mem. Christian Church (Disciples Of Christ). Avocations: story telling, sports, photography, religion. Office: LA Biomedical Rsch Inst 1124 W Carson St Torrance CA 90502 Home Phone: 310-530-6154; Office Phone: 310-222-1966. Office Fax: 310-222-3887; Home Fax: 310-222-3887. Business E-Mail: ibe@labiomed.org.

IBEKWE, ABASIOFIOK MARK, soil scientist, educator; b. Ukanafun, Nigeria, Nov. 5, 1956; arrived in U.S., 1979, naturalized, 1994; s. Mark Rueben and Nko (Essien) Ibekwe; m. Mary Brown, May 11, 1985 (div.); m. Anieno Amos Ideh, Jan. 6, 1996; children: Uwakmfon, Emem, Idara. BS, N.C. Agr. and Tech. State U., 1983, MS, 1984, MS, 1990; PhD, U. Md., 1995. Rsch. asst. N.C. Agr. and Tech. State U., Greensboro, 1984-90; rsch. technologist Roche Biomed. Lab., Burlington, Vt., 1989-90; supr. Mid State Farms, Siler City, NC, 1985-88; rsch. asst. U. Md., College Park, 1990-93, tchg. asst., 1993—. Rsch. microbiologist USDA-ARS, Riverside, Calif.; assoc. rsch. scientist Wash. State U., Pullman. Contbr. articles to profl. jours. including Jour. Environ. Quality, Jour. Applied Microbiology, Applied Microbiol. and Biotech., others. Gen. sec. Nigerian Profls., Washington, 1992—. Mem.: Soil Soc. Am., Soil S.C. Soc., Environ. S.C. Tech., Am. Soc. Microbiology, Soil Sci. Soc. Am., Am. Soc. Agronomy, Phi Sigma Eta. Avocations: photography, soccer, volleyball, dance. Home: 6983 Harvest Ln Riverside CA 92506-3744 Office: USDA 215 Johnson Rd Pullman WA 99163-8831 Office Phone: 951-369-4828. Business E-Mail: aibekwe@ussl.ars.usda.gov.

IBEN, ICKO, JR., astrophysicist, educator; b. Champaign, Ill., June 27, 1931; s. Icko and Kathryn (Tomlin) I.; m. Miriam Genevieve Fett, Jan. 28, 1956; children: Christine, Timothy, Benjamin, Thomas. BA, Harvard U., 1953; MS, U. Ill., 1954, PhD, 1958. Asst. prof. physics Williams Coll., 1958-61; sr. rsch. fellow in physics Calif. Inst. Tech., Pasadena, 1961—64; assoc. prof. physics MIT, Cambridge, 1964-68, prof., 1968-72; prof. astronomy and physics, head dept. astronomy U. Ill., Champaign-Urbana, 1972-84, prof. astronomy and physics, 1972-89, disting. prof. astronomy and physics Urbana, 1989—99, disting. prof. emeritus, 2000; holder of Eberly family chair in astronomy Pa. State U., 1989-90. Vis. prof. astronomy Harvard U., 1966, 68, 70; vis. fellow Joint Inst. for Lab. Astrophysics U. Colo., 1971—72; vis. prof. astronomy and astrophysics U. Calif., Santa Cruz, 1972; vis. prof. physics and astronomy Inst. for Astronomy U. Hawaii, 1977; adv. panel astronomy sect. NSF, 1972—75; vis. com. Aura Observatories, 1979—82; vis. scientist astronomical coun. Union Soviet Socialist Rep. Acad. Sci., 1985; sr. vis. fellow Australian Nat. U., 1986; vis. prof. U. Bologna, Italy, 1986, Hokkaido U. Grad. Sch. Sci., 2001; sr. rsch. fellow U. Sussex, England, 1986; George Darwin lectr. Royal Astronomical Soc., London, 1984; McMillin lectr. Ohio State U., 1987; vis. eminent scholar U. Ctr. Ga., 1988; guest prof. Christian Albrechts U. Kiel, 1990; sr. fellow Nicolaus Copernicus Astron. Ctr., Warsaw, 2002. Contbr. articles to profl. jours. John Simon Guggenheim Meml. fellow, 1985—86, Japan Soc. for Promotion of Sci. fellow, U. Tokyo, 1985, Niigata U., 1990, vis. Japan Soc. for Promotion of Sci. Eminent Scientist, Hokkaido U., 2003—04. Fellow Royal Astron. Soc. (Eddington medal 1990); mem. Am. Astron. Soc. (councilor 1974-77, Henry Norris Russell lectr. 1989), U.S. Nat. Acad. of Scis., Internat. Astronom. Union. Home: 3910 Clubhouse Dr Champaign IL 61822-9280 Office: U Ill Dept of Astronomy 1002 W Green St Urbana IL 61801-3074

IBENDAHL, JEAN AYRES, retired elementary and secondary educator; b. Bement, Ill., June 10, 1918; d. Charles Edward and Minnie Nora (Burns) Ayres; m. Calvin Frederick Ibendahl, Dec. 31, 1958. BS, U. Ill., Urbana-Champaign, 1952, MEd, 1957. Cert. elem. and secondary edn. educator, Ill. Tchr. Union Grove Sch. Hillsboro Pub. Schs., Ill., 1938—39, 1940—41, tchr. Burbank Sch., 1939—40; secondary educator Wilmington Unit Dist., Ill., 1952—53, elem. educator, 1942—52; tchr. social studies Lakeview Jr.-Sr. H.S., Decatur, Ill., 1953—57; tchr. biology DuQuoin H.S., Ill., 1966—67; substitute tchr., 1967—80; ret., 1980. A founder Ag in the Classroom Program, 1984. Author: Pork Primer, 1977. Dir. Nat. Livestock and Meat Bd. Chgo., 1966-72, Perry County Health Dept., Pinckneyville, 1992; pres. Ill. Porkettes, 1974-76, Ill. Agri-women, 1978-80, 1988-89; sec. Perry County Pub. Bldg. Com., Pinckneyville, Ill., 1984—; bd. mem. Rend Lake Coll. Found., 1988-94; candidate state rep., 115th Dist., Ill., 1992; coord. Perry County Bush/Quayle Campaign, 1992; founder Perry County Jail Mus., 1994, chmn., 1993-97; v.p. Perry County Hist. Soc., 1995-; 4H leader, 1984-88; founder, dir. Ill. Ag Leadership Found., 1986. Named to Ill. Hall of Fame, 1996, Agrl. Leadership Wall, Ill. Dept. Agrl. Springfield, 2007; named Silver Haired Congresswoman, 12th dist., 1996; recipient Land of Lincoln award Ill. Pork Prodrs., 1983. Mem. Am. Agri-Women (awards com. 1992, Leaven award 1982), Ill. Agri-Women (regional dir. 1990—), So. Ill. Agrl. Bus. Assn., Perry County Home Ext. (first vice chmn. 1989-91, 1994-95, cultural arts chmn. 1992—), Perry County Hist. Soc. (v.p. 1992—), LWV, P.E.O., Order of Ea. Star. Republican. Methodist. Avocations: reading, travel, sewing, antiques. Home: Apt 6 912 N Washington St Du Quoin IL 62832-1232

IBERS, JAMES ARTHUR, chemist, educator; b. LA, Calif., June 9, 1930; s. Max Charles and Esther (Imerman) I.; m. Joyce Audrey Henderson, June 10, 1951; children: Jill Tina, Arthur Alan. BS, Calif. Inst. Tech., 1951, PhD, 1954. NSF post-doctoral fellow , Melbourne, Australia, 1954-55; chemist Shell Devel. Co., 1955-61, Brookhaven Nat. Lab., 1961-64; mem. faculty Northwestern U., 1964—, prof. chemistry, 1964-85, Charles E. and Emma H. Morrison prof. chemistry, 1986—. Recipient Disting. alumni award Calif. Inst. Tech., 1997. Mem. NAS, Am. Acad. Arts and Sci., Am. Chem. Soc. (inorganic chemistry award 1979, Disting. Svc. in the Advancement of Inorganic Chemistry award 1992, Linus Pauling award 1994), Am. Crystallographic Assn. (Buerger award 2002). Office: Northwestern U Dept Chemistry Evanston IL 60208-3113 Home: 990 N Lake Shore Dr 17C Chicago IL 60611-1366 Business E-Mail: ibers@chem.northwestern.edu.

IBOLD, CATHERINE BUHALY, lawyer, director; BS in Bus. Adminstrn., U. Fla., Gainesville, 1983; JD, U. Miami, Fla., 1993. Bar: Fla. 1993. Gen. counsel Cypress Cos., Orlando, Fla., 1999—2003; sr. dir., legal dept. Winn-Dixie Stores, Inc., Jacksonville, Fla., 2005—. Recipient Pro-bono award, Dade County Bar Assn. Mem.: Am. Corporate Counsel Assn. (chpt. founder, v.p.), Am. Mediation Assn. (assoc.), Duval County Bar Assn. (assoc.), Fla. Bar Assn. (assoc.). Office: Winn-Dixie Stores Inc 5050 Edgewood Ct Jacksonville FL 32254 Business E-Mail: catherineibold@winn-dixie.com.

ICAHN, CARL CELIAN, investor; b. Queens, NY, Feb. 16, 1936; m. Liba Icahn, 1979 (div. 1999); children: Brett, Michelle; m. Gail Golden, 1999. BA in Philos., Princeton U., NJ, 1957; postgraduate student, NYU Sch. Medicine. Apprentice broker Dreyfus Corp., NYC, 1960-63; options mgr. Tessel, Patrick & Co., NYC, 1963-64, Gruntal & Co., 1964-68; chmn., pres. Icahn & Co., NYC, 1968—; chmn. bd. Starfire Holding Corp. (formerly Icahn Holding), 1984—; chmn. ACF Industries Inc., St. Charles, Mo., 1984—; chmn. bd., pres., CEO Trans World Airlines Inc., NYC, 1985—93; chmn. bd. Am. Real Estate Ptnrs., 1990—, Am. Property Investors Inc., 1990—, Am. Railcar Industries, 1994—, Maupintour Holdings, LLC, 1998—2002; pres. Stratosphere Corp., 1998—2004; chmn. bd. GB Holdings (now Am. Real Estate Ptnrs.), 2000—, XO Comm., 2003—, ImClone Systems Inc., 2006—. Bd. dirs. Cadus Pharm. Corp., 1993—. Founder Icahn House, NYC, Carl C. Icahn Charter Sch., NYC. Served in US Army, 1960—61. Named one of Top 200 Collectors, ARTnews mag., 2004, Forbes Richest Ams., 2006, World's Richest People, Forbes mag., 2007. Avocation: Collector Old Masters and Impressionist art. Office: XO Communications 11111 Sunset Hills Rd Reston VA 20190 also: Icahn & Co Inc 82 Beaver St New York NY 10005 Office Phone: 703-547-2000.*

ICAHN, GAIL GOLDEN **See GOLDEN, GAIL**

ICE, CARL R., rail transportation executive; married; 2 children. BS in Indsl. Engring., Kans. State U., 1979. With indsl. engring. dept. Santa Fe Rlwy., 1979, positions in ops., fin. and info. systems, v.p. adminstrn., 1992—94, v.p. carload bus. unit, 1994, v.p. exec., 1994—96; (Santa Fe Rlwy. merged with Burlington No. Rlwy. in 1995); v.p., chief mech. officer Burlington No. Santa Fe Corp., 1996—99, v.p. ops. north, 1999, sr. v.p. ops., 1999—2000, exec. v.p., COO, 2000—. Bd. dirs. Transp. Tech. Ctr. Inc. Mem. engring. adv. bd. Kans. State U. Coll. Engring. Mem.: Inst. Indsl. Engrs. Office: Burlington No Santa Fe Corp PO Box 961056 Fort Worth TX 76161-0056 Office Phone: 817-867-6100.*

ICE CUBE, (O'SHEA JACKSON), rap artist, actor; b. LA, June 15, 1969; s. Hosea and "Moms" Doris Jackson.; m. Kim Jackson, 1992; 4 children. Attended, Phoenix Inst. Tech. Founder Lynch Mob Records, LA. Founder Cubevision Prodn. Co. Albums: (with NWA) Straight Outta Compton, 1989, (solo) Amerikkka's Most Wanted, 1990, Kill At Will, Death Certificate, 1991, The Predator, 1992, Lethal Injection, 1993, War & Peace, Vol. 1, 1998, War & Peace, Vol. 2, 2000, Laugh Now, Cry Later, 2006; Actor (films) Boyz n the Hood, 1991, Trespass, 1992, Higher Learning, 1995, Anaconda, 1997, I Got the Hook Up, 1998, Three Kings, 1999, Ghosts of Mars, 2001, Barbershop, 2002, Torque, 2004, xXx: State of the Union, 2005; actor, screenwriter (films) The Glass Shield, 1995; actor, prodr. (films)All About the Benjamins, 2002, Friday After Next, 2002, Barbershop 2: Back in Business, 2004, Are We There Yet?, 2005, Are We Done Yet, 2007; actor, exec. prodr. (films) Friday, 1995, Dangerous Ground, 1997, The Players Club, 1998, Next Friday, 2000, Barbershop 2: Back in Business, 2005; exec. prodr. (films) Beauty Shop, 2005. Office: Priority Records 6430 W Sunset Blvd Los Angeles CA 90028-7901*

ICE-T, (TRACY MARROW), rap artist, actor; b. Newark, Feb. 16, 1958; m. Nicole Austin, 2004; children: Tracy Marrow Jr., Letesha Marrow. Albums: Rhyme Pays, 1987, O.G. Original Gangster, 1991, (with King Tee) Havin' a T Party, 1991, Body Count, 1992, Home Invasion, 1993, The Classic Collection, 1993, (with Body Count) Born Dead, 1994, 7th Deadly Sin, 1999, Greatest Hits: The Evidence, 2001, Gang Culture, 2004, Gangsta Rap, 2006; actor: (films) Breakin', 1984, Breakin' 2, 1984, New Jack City, 1991, Ricochet, 1991, Trespass, 1992, Why Colors?, 1992, Surviving the Game, 1994, Tank Girl, 1995, Johnny Mnemonic, 1995, Mean Guns, 1997, The Deli, 1997, Beyond Utopia, 1997, Crazy Six, 1998, Final Voyage, 1999, Corrupt, 1999, The Wrecking Crew, 1999, Sonic Impact, 1999, The Heist, 1999, Frezno Smooth, 1999, Urban Menace, 1999, Stealth Fighter, 1999, Corrupt, 1999, Guardian, 2000, Gangland, 2000, Luck of the Draw, 2000, The Alternates, 2000, Stranded, 2001, Kept, 2001, Crime Partners, 2001, 3000 miles to Graceland, 2001, Point Doom, 2001, Deadly Rhapsody, 2001, 'R Xmas, 2001, Ticker, 2001, Out Kold, 2001, Ablaze, 2001, On the Edge, 2002, Tracks, 2002, (TV films) Exiled, 1998, The Disciples, 2000, (TV Series) Players, 1997-98, Law and Order: Special Victims Unit, 2000-; author: The Iceberg/Freedom of Speech, Just Watch What You Say, 1989, The Ice Opinion, 1994. Office: Priority Records 6430 W Sunset Blvd Los Angeles CA 90028-7901

ICHEL, DAVID W., lawyer; b. Newark, May 14, 1953; BA, Duke U., 1975, JD, 1978. Bar: N.Y. 1979, N.J. 1978, D.C. 2004, U.S. Supreme Ct. 1983, U.S. Ct. Appeals (2nd cir.) 1984, U.S. Ct. Appeals (9th cir.) 1985, U.S. Dist. Ct. (so. dist.) N.Y. 1979, U.S. Dist. Ct. (ea. dist.) N.Y. 1980, U.S. Dist. Ct. N.J. 1978. Ptnr. Simpson Thacher & Bartlett, NYC, 1978—. Mem. bd. MFY Legal Svcs., Inc., bd. visitors Duke Law Sch., NYC Bar (chair products liability com.), Am. Law Inst. Mem. Phi Beta Kappa. Office: Simpson Thacher & Bartlett 425 Lexington Ave Fl 15 New York NY 10017-3954 Office Phone: 212-455-2563. E-mail: dichel@stblaw.com.

ICHILOV, NEHEMIA, principal, consultant; m. Lisa Ichilov; 2 children. BA, Rutgers U.; M, Jewish Theol. Sem. of Am., NYC. Professoriate cert. U. Ctrl. Fla., 2003, lic. prin. Nat. Bd. of Lic. Spiritual leader Congregation Shalom of Williamsburg, Orlando, Fla., 2002—05; head of sch. Jerome Lippman Jewish Cmty. Day Sch., Akron, Ohio, 2003—. Mem. curriculum adv. com. JSkyway, Boston; adj. asst. prof. Siegal Coll., Cleve. Fellow Steinberg Leadership Inst., Anti-Defamation League; merit fellow, Whizin Inst. for Jewish Family Edn. Mem.: ASCD, Network for Rsch. in Jewish Edn., Am. Edn. Rsch. Assn., Assn. Dirs. of Ctrl. Agys., Kappa Delta Pi. Office: Lippman Day Sch 750 White Pond Dr Akron OH 44320 Home Phone: 330-351-3500; Office Phone: 330-836-0419. Office Fax: 330-869-2514. E-mail: nammie_ichilov@jewishakron.org.

ICHINO, YOKO, ballerina; b. Los Angeles, Cali. m. David Nixon. Studied with Mia Slavenska, LA. Mem. Joffrey II, NYC, Joffrey Ballet, NYC, Stuttgart Ballet, Fed. Republic Germany; tchr. ballet, 1976; soloist Am. Ballet Theatre, 1977-81; guest appearances, 1981-82; prin. Nat. Ballet Can., Toronto, Ont., 1982-90. Various guest appearances including World Ballet Festival, Tokyo, 1979, 85, Tokyo Ballet, 1980, with Alexander Godunov and Stars, summer, 1982, Sydney Ballet, Australia, N.Z. Ballet, summer 1984, Ballet de Marseille, 1985-87, Deutsche Opera Ballet Berlin, 1985-90, Munich Opera Ballet, 1987-90, Australian Ballet, 1987, 89, Staatsoper Berlin, 1989, 90, Komische Opera, Berlin, 1991-93, David Nixon's Dance Theater, Berlin, 1990, 91, Birmingham Royal Ballet, 1990-93, Deutsche Opera Ballet, Berlin, 1994-95; tchr. Australian Ballet, 1989, Birmingham Royal Ballet, 1991, 93, Nat. Ballet of Can., 1993, Cullberg Ballet, Sweden, 1994, Nat. Ballet Sch., 1994, 95, Ballet de Monte-Carlo, 1994, Geneva Ballet, 1995-98, Nederlands Dance Theater, 1995, Rambert Dance, 1995, Royal Winnipeg Ballet, 1999; tchr. numerous ballet workshops; dir. profl. program Ballet Met, 1995-2003; guest master tchr., coach No. Ballet Theatre, 2002—. First Am. trained woman recipient medal Third Internat. Ballet Competition, Moscow, 1977. Office: No Ballet Theatre West Park Centre Spen Ln Leeds LS16 5BE England

ICHIYAMA, DENNIS YOSHIHIDE, art educator, educational association administrator; b. Aiea, Hawaii, May 28, 1944; s. Edwin Kiyotada and Florence Fusae (Inoshita) I. BFA, U. Hawaii, 1966; MFA, Yale U., 1968; postgrad., Allgemeine Gewerbeschule, Basel, Switzerland, 1975-77. Instr. U. Bridgeport, Conn., 1968-70; sr. graphic designer Graphic Communications Ltd., Hong Kong, 1970-71; instr. Carnegie-Mellon U., Pitts., 1971-74; asst. prof. Cornell U., Ithaca, NY, 1974-75; assoc. prof. Ind. U., Bloomington, 1977-78; asst. prof. U. Ill., Chgo., 1978-79; assoc. prof. Wichita (Kans.) State U., 1979-81; prof., chmn. divsn. art and design Purdue U., West Lafayette, Ind., 1985-92, head dept. visual and performing arts, 1993—. Design cons. US Postal Svc., Washington, 1986, Purdue U. Press, West Lafayette, 1989—, Interior Design Educators Coun., Ithaca, 1985-87; vis. scholar U. Iowa Ctr. for Book, 1990; fellow Ctr. for Artistic Endeavor Purdue U., Sch. Liberal Arts, 1992, 2003-; artist-in-residence Hamilton Wood Type & Printing Mus., Wis., 1999-2000, Ctr. for Book and Paper Arts, Columbia Coll., Chgo., 2005, Minn. Ctr. Book Arts, Mpls., 2006; bd. dir. Coll. Art Assn., 2002-, v.p. coms., 2006-, chair nominating com., 2006-, chair profl. devel. fellowships in art history and visual arts, 2006-, mem. exec. com, 2006-, mem. conf. com., 2006-, mem. budget and fin. com., 2006-, chair task force, 2006-. Design work exhbns. in Can., US, Germany, Finland, France, Czechoslovakia; exhibited in shows at Centre Georges Pompidou, 1985, Poster Biennale, Warsaw, 1982, Biennale of

Graphic Design, Brno, Czechoslovakia, 1982, 92, Columbia U. Rare Book and Manuscript Libr., Ctr. Book and Paper Arts, Columbia Coll., Chgo., 2006; represented in collection of the Plakatsammlung of Kunstgewerbemuseum, Zurich, Rochester Inst. Tech. Libr., NY, Lahti Art Mus., Finland, Stern Book Arts and Spl. Collections Ctr., San Francisco Pub. Libr., Purdue U. Librs., Ruth and Marvin Sackner Archive of Concrete and Visual Poetry; author essays in Contemporary Designers, 1985, T Y P O G R A M S, Pure Type Forms, 2000, The Hamilton Type Specimen Sheets Portfolio, 2001, book revs.; book reviewer Choice (ALA, Assn. Coll./Rsch. Librs.). Recipient Typographic Excellence award Type Dirs. Club, 2006; grantee Nat. Endowment for Humanities, 1984; IAC master fellow Ind. Arts Commn., 1985, 2001; grantee Nat. Endowment for Arts, 1989, Individual Artist program Indian Art Commn., 2001-03, 05-06; fellow Prix du Rome, Am. Acad. Rome, 2006-07. Mem. Am. Ctr. for Design, Am. Inst. Graphic Arts, Graphic Design Educators Assn., Alliance Typographique Internat., Internat. Soc. Typographic Designers, Soc. Typographic Arts, Nat. Coun. Art Adminstrs. (nat. bd. dirs. 1998—), Internat. Coun. Fine Arts Deans, Coll. Art Assn. Am. (nat. bd. dirs. 2002—), Arts Ind. (state coun. 1993-99), Hui na opio o Hawaii (advisor 1986-93), Greater Lafayette Mus. Art. Buddhist. Avocations: swiss posters, artists books, Chinese and Japanese seals, printing history, hand bookbinding and letterpress printing. Office: Purdue U Dept Visual and Performing Arts Bldg 552 W Wood St West Lafayette IN 47907-2002 Home Phone: 765-743-0440; Office Phone: 765-494-3071. E-mail: diad@purdue.edu.

IDASZAK, JEROME JOSEPH, economic journalist; b. Chgo., Dec. 28, 1945; s. Joseph Edward and Estelle Charlotte (Grelecki) I.; m. Geraldine Rae Fehst, Sept. 4, 1976; children: Alexander Jerome, Joshua Adam. B.Journalism, Northwestern U., Evanston, Ill., 1967, M.Journalism, 1968. Reporter Rockford Morning Star, Ill., 1968-70; reporter Chgo. Tribune, Deerfield, Ill., 1974-76; fin. reporter Chgo. Sun Times, 1976-82, fin. columnist, 1982-90, Washington corr., 1985-90; freelance writer and editor, 1991; assoc. editor Kiplinger Washington Editors, 1992—. Fin. commentator Sta. WBBM-AM, Chgo., 1984-85; contbr. Sta. WBEZ-FM, Chgo., 1987-93; grad. journalism instr. Northwestern U., 1984; instr. Washington Intern Inst., 2002-04, 06. Author: (newspaper series) Farm problems, 1983 (Peter Lisagor award 1984); Asian economy & growth, 1979 (Peter Lisagor award 1980). Vol., U.S. Peace Corps, 1970-72. Brookings Instn. fellow, 1979. Mem. Soc. Profl. Journalists, Nat. Returned Peace Corps. Vols., Chgo. Headline Club (bd. dirs. 1980-85, pres. 1984-85).

IDE, ROY WILLIAM, III, lawyer; b. Geneva, Ill., Apr. 23, 1940; s. Roy William and Jenny (Coleman) Ide; m. Gayle Marie Oliver, Jan. 21, 1967; children: Logan, Jennifer, Lucienne. BA cum laude, Washington and Lee U., 1962; LLD, U. Va., 1965; MBA, Ga. State U., 1972. Bar: Ga. 1967, D.C. 1994, U.S. Ct. Appeals (5th and 11th cirs.) 1967, U.S. Supreme Ct. 1969. Law clk. Judge Griffin Bell U.S. Ct. Appeals (5th cir.), 1965—66; assoc. King & Spalding, Atlanta, 1966—71; ptnr. Huie, Sterne & Ide, Atlanta, 1971—77, Kutak Rock (and predecessor firm), Atlanta, 1978—92, mng. ptnr., Atlanta office; ptnr. Long, Aldridge & Norman; sr. v.p., spl. counsel E.F. Hutton and Co., Inc., 1985—87; spl. counsel, mng. dir. Prescott, Ball & Turben, 1988—89; gen. counsel, sec., sr. v.p. Monsanto Co., 1996—2001; with McKenna Long & Aldridge LLP, 2002—. Former bd. dirs., mem. exec. com. Atlanta Com. for Olympic Games; counselor U.S. Olympic Com., 1996—2002; bd. dirs. AFC Enterprises. Named one of Atlanta's Five Outstanding Men of Yr., 1976; recipient Arthur Van Briesen award, Nat. Legal Aid and Defender Assn., 1977. Mem.: ABA (ho. of dels., chair young lawyer's divsn. 1976, chair gen. practice sect. 1983—84, chair spl. com. on drug crisis 1991—92, 1992—93, pres. 1993—94), Ga. Bar Assn. (bd. govs.). Office: McKenna Long & Aldridge LLP 303 Peachtree St NE Ste 5300 Atlanta GA 30308 E-mail: bide@mckennalong.com.

IDEKER, TREY, computational and molecular biologist; b. Memphis, June 24, 1972; s. Raymond Edwin Ideker, Mary Lou Ideker; m. Kristyn Gray. BS in Elec. Engring. and Computer Sci., MIT, 1994, MS in Elec. Engring. and Computer Sci., 1995; PhD in Molecular Biotechnology, U. Wash., 2001. Rsch. scientist Loral Infrared and Imaging Sys., Lexington, Mass., 1991—95; database cons. Klinikum Rechts der Isar, Munich, 1995—96; rsch. fellow Whitehead Inst., Cambridge, 2001—03; asst. prof. to assoc. prof. dept. bioengineering U. Calif., San Diego, 2003—. Cons. Genstruct, Cambridge, 2001—, Pfizer, Cambridge, 2001—. Fellow, Achievement Rewards for Coll. Scientists, 1996—98. Mem.: Internat. Soc. for Computational Biology. Achievements include pioneering research in the nascent field of systems biology; invention of methods for modeling cellular systems and circuitry. Avocations: running, piano, guitar, scuba diving, travel. Office: U Calif San Diego Bioengring 9500 Gilman Dr La Jolla CA 92093-0412 E-mail: trey@bioeng.ucsd.edu.

IDING, ALLAN EARL, lawyer; b. Milw., Apr. 29, 1939; s. Earl Herman and Erna Adeline (Albrecht) I.; m. Anne Louise Chaconas, July 9, 1961; children: Kent Earl, Krista Anne Templeman, Bradford A., Andrea Beth Brozynski. BS, Marquette U., 1961, LLB, 1963; DHL (hon.), Nashotah House, 1990. Bar: Wis. 1963, U.S. Dist. Ct. (ea. dist.) Wis. 1963, U.S. Ct. Appeals (7th cir.) 1963. Law clk. U.S. Ct. Appeals (7th cir.), Chgo., 1963—64; assoc. Whyte Hirschboeck Dudek, S.C., Milw., 1964—71, mem., 1971—2006, sr. counsel, 2006—. Trustee Nashotah House, 1976—, Wis. Scottish Rite Bodies; mem. Wauwatosa Police and Fire Commn., Wis., 1978-83.; pres., bd. dirs. Wis. DeMolay Found., Milw., 1985—, Wis. Health and Ednl. Facilities Authority, 1978-85, Todd Wehr Found., Inc., Nashotah House Found., Inc. Mem. Blue Mound Golf and Country Club, Masons (grand master Wis. 1981-82). Republican. Episcopalian. Avocation: golf. Home: 9212 Wilson Blvd Wauwatosa WI 53226-1729 Office: Whyte Hirschboeck Dudek Ste 1900 555 E Wells St Milwaukee WI 53202 Office Phone: 414-978-5427. Business E-Mail: aiding@whdlaw.com.

IDLE, ERIC, actor, scriptwriter, film producer, lyricist; b. South Shields, Eng., Mar. 29, 1943; Pres. The Cambridge Footlights, 1964-65. TV shows include The Frost Report, Monty Python's Flying Circus, 1969-74, Rutland Weekend TV, 1975, Suddenly Susan, 1999-2000; films include And Now For Something Completely Different, 1971, Monty Python and the Holy Grail, 1975, The Rutles, 1978, Monty Python's Life of Brian, 1979, Monty Python Live at the Hollywood Bowl, 1982, Monty Python's The Meaning of Life, 1983, Yellowbeard, 1983, National Lampoon's European Vacation, 1985, Transformers: The Movie, 1986, The Adventures of Baron Munchausen, 1988, Nuns on the Run, 1990, Too Much Sun, 1991, Mom and Dad Save the World, 1993, Splitting Heirs, 1993, Casper, 1995, The Wind in the Willows, 1996, Burn Hollywood Burn, 1998, Dudley Do-Right, 1999, South Park: Bigger, Longer and Uncut (voice), 1999; writer (broadway plays): Spamalot, 2005 (Drama Desk award, outstanding lyrics, 2005, Grammy award, Best Musical Show Album, 2006); author The Greedy Bastard Diary: A Comic Tour of America, 2005. Office: Grant & Tani Inc 9100 Wilshire Blvd Ste 1000 Beverly Hills CA 90212-3415 also: William Morris 151 S El Camino Dr Beverly Hills CA 90212-2704

IDOL, ANNA CATHERINE, magazine editor; b. Chgo., July 8, 1941; d. Melvin Oliver and Louise Hildegard (Bullington) Lokensgard; m. William Ross Idol, Oct. 25, 1959 (div. Mar. 1962); 1 child, Laura Jeanne; m. Michael Wataru Sugano, Jan. 28, 1990. BS, Lake Forest Coll., Ill., 1980; MBA, Northwestern U., Evanston, Ill., 1982. treas. Chgo. Women in Pub., Chgo., 1970-71. Editor Rand McNally Co., Chgo., 1968-78, product mgr. adult reference, 1983-84; founder, pres. Bullington Laird, Inc., Chgo., 1986—; mng. editor Elks Mag., Chgo., 1997—. Pub.: Center Within, 1988 (award Heartsong Rev. 1989); writer, concept advt. alert, 1990 (Harvey Comm. award). Pres. Am. Buddhist Assn., 1985-93; mem. bd. Buddhist Temple Chgo., 1985-93; v.p. Buddhist Coun. Midwest, 1985-89. Democrat. Buddhist. Avocations: wilderness adventure, travel, reading. Office: Elks Mag 425 W Diversey Pkwy Chicago IL 60614-6196 Office Phone: 773-755-4894. Business E-Mail: annai@elks.org.

IDOL, JAMES DANIEL, JR., chemist, educator, inventor, consultant; b. Harrisonville, Mo., Aug. 7, 1928; s. James Daniel and Gladys Rosita (Lile) I.; m. Marilyn Thorn Randall, 1977. AB, William Jewell Coll., 1949; MS, Purdue U., 1952, PhD, 1955, D.Sc. (hon.), 1980. With Std. Oil Co., Ohio, 1955—77, rsch. supr., 1965—68, rsch. mgr., 1968—77; mgr. venture rsch. Ashland Chem. Co., Columbus, Ohio, 1977—79, v.p., dir. corp. R & D, 1979—88; disting. prof. materials sci. and ceramics sch. engring. Rutgers U., New Brunswick, NJ, 1988—2006, dir. polymer sci. ctr. for advanced materials via immiscible polymer processing, 2002—. Adv. bd. NSF Presdl. Young Investigators Awards, Nat. Inst. Sci. and Tech., 1997—; cons. in field; lectr. chem. engring. dept. Northwestern U., 1978, Stanford U., 1982-83, U. Calif., Berkeley, 1986, Yale U., 1988 U. Chgo., 1998; lectr. Lawrence Berkeley Lab., 1985-86; v.p., program coord. 1st N.Am. Chem. Congress, 1975; program coord. 1st Pacific Rim Chem. Cong., 1979; indsl. rep. U.S. Coun. for Chem. Rsch., 1983—, governing bd., 1985—; panel on frontiers in fossil fuel energy rsch. NRC, 1986, com. on tracking toxic wastes, 1989-93, panel on polymers in the environ. Internat. Union of Pure and Applied Chemistry, 1996, com. on energy conservation in processing of indsl. materials; adv. bd. U. Tex., Tex. A&M, Ohio State U., Purdue U., Okla. State U., Ariz. State U., U. Mass., Case Western Reserve U., 1965-75; com. polymers recycling Internat. Union Pure and Applied Chem., 1993—; mem. U.S. Coun. Chem. Rsch., 1981-89, gov. bd. 1985-88. Chmn. editl. adv. bd.: Indsl. & Engring. Chemistry Jour., 1976—84, mem. editl. adv. bd.: Chem. and Engring. News, 1977—81, Am. Chem. Soc. Symposium Series, 1978—84, Advances in Chemistry Seris, 1979—84, Chem. Week Mag., 1980—82, Sci., 1986—91, Jour. Applied Polymer Sci., 1988—; contbr. chapters to books, articles to profl. jours., handbooks and encys. Active Cleve. Welfare Fedn. Recipient Modern Pioneer award NAM, 1965, Disting. Alumnus citation William Jewell Coll., 1971 Fellow AAAS, Am. Inst. Chemists (life; bd. dirs. 1981—, vice-chmn. 1986, chmn. 1987, Chem. Pioneer award 1968, Mems. and Fellows lectr. 1980); mem. Nat. Acad. Engring., Soc. Plastics Industry, Soc. Mfg. Engrs.-Composite Group, Am. Chem. Soc. (indsl. and engring. chemistry divsn., chmn. 1971, chem. innovator designation Chem. and Engring. News mag. 1971, adv. bd. Petroleum Rsch. Fund, 1974-76, Joseph P. Stewart Disting. Svc. award 1975, Creative Invention award 1975), Am. Mgmt. Assn. (R&D coun. 1985-88, Coun. award for Disting. Svc. pkg. coun. 1989-97, mfg. and tech. coun. 1997—), Dirs. of Indsl. Rsch., Am. Inst. Chem. Engrs., Licensing Execs. Soc., Soc. Plastics engrs., Indsl. Rsch. Inst. (rep., chmn. bd. editors 1983-86), Plastics Pioneers Assn., Soc. Chem. Industry (Perkin medal 1979), Ind. Acad. Sci., Catalysis Soc. (Ciapetti award/lectureship 1988), Cleve. Athletic Club, Cosmos Club (Washington), Worthington Hills Country Club, Masons, Shriners, Sigma Xi, Alpha Chi Sigma, Theta Chi Delta, Kappa Mu Epsilon, Alpha Phi Omega, Phi Gamma Delta. Mem. Christian Ch. (Disciples Of Christ). Achievements include invention of process for manufacture acrylonitrile (over 80 plants in 30 countries). Also oxidation process for manufacture of acrylic acid practiced worldwide; patents in field. Office: Dept Ceramic & Materials Eng 607 Taylor Rd Rutgers Univ Piscataway NJ 08854-8065 Home Phone: 614-888-5091. E-mail: jdidol@rci.rutgers.edu.

IDOS, MARGARITA DE LEON, elementary school educator; b. Cabanatuan, Philippines, Oct. 16, 1975; arrived in U.S., 2002; d. Martin Nunez de Leon and Julia Macam Pagdanganan; m. Rey Vejerano Idos, June 10. AB in Psychology, Ateneo de Manila U., 1996, MEd, 1999; student in Reading, U. Philippines, 1999—; cert., U. San Diego, 2003, U. Calif., San Diego, Calif., 2004. Tchr. Ateneo Grade Sch., Philippines, 1996—2002; lead tchr. Children's World, San Diego, 2002; tchr. Paradise Hills Elem. Sch., San Diego, 2002—. Substitute tchr. San Diego Unifed Sch. Dist., 2002, San Ysidro Sch. Dist., San Diego, 2002, Chula Vista Sch. Dist., 2002—03. Actor: Moneo Children's Theater. Recipient Eaglet award, Ateneo Grade Sch., 2002; scholar, Alemo de Manila U., 1992—96. Mem.: Nat. Tchrs. Assn., San Diego Edn. Assn., Calif. Reading Assn., Internat. Reading Assn., Filipino Am. Educators Assn. San Diego County, PTA (tchr. rep. 2005—). Office: Paradise Hills Elem 5816 Alleghany St San Diego CA 92139 Office Phone: 619-479-3145.

IDZIK, DANIEL RONALD, retired lawyer; b. Depew, NY, Jan. 20, 1935; s. Daniel Henry and Ann Mary (Kolakowski) I.; m. Kathleen Osborne, Oct. 6 1989; children by previous marriage: Christopher, Rebecca, Laura, Susan. BS, SUNY, Buffalo, 1956; LLB, Harvard U., Cambridge, Mass., 1963. Bar: NY 1964. Exec. v.p. US Nat. Student Assn., Phila., 1956-57; assoc. sec. World Univ. Svc., Geneva, 1957-60; chief counsel NY State Senate Com. on Labor and Industry, Albany, 1965; from assoc. counsel to gen. counsel Booz, Allen & Hamilton, Inc., NYC, 1967-98; ret., 1998. Chmn. Philharmonia Virtuosi, Westchester County, NY, 1988-90, pres. 1987-88, bd. dirs. 1985-91; pres. Coun. for Arts in Westchester, 1983-85, bd. dirs., 1980-85; chmn., Friends of Neuberger Mus., Purchase, NY, 1991-93, pres., 1990, bd. dirs., 1987-97; bd. dirs. Buffalo State Coll. Found., 1985—, Jacob's Pillow, 1996—, LongBoat Key Ctr. Arts, 2000-, pres., 2002-04, Pierian Spring Acader. Recipient Disting. Alumni award SUNY Buffalo, 1986, Arts award Coun,. for the Arts in Westchester, 1990. Mem. Harvard Club of NY (mem. bd. mgrs. 1997-2000). Business E-Mail: daniel_idzik@post.harvard.edu.

IDZIK, MARTIN FRANCIS, lawyer; b. Depew, NY, Apr. 2, 1942; s. Daniel Henry and Ann Mary (Kolakowski) I.; m. Patricia Ann O'Brien, Aug. 7, 1965; children: Andrew, Amy. BS, Canisius Coll., 1963; JD, U. Notre Dame, 1966. Bar: N.Y. 1966. Assoc. Phillips, Lytle et al., Buffalo, 1971-76, ptnr., 1977-78, Jamestown, NY, 1979—. Bd. trustees Randolph Children's Home, 1993—99. Acting village justice, East Aurora, N.Y.,1972-79; bd. dirs. Chautauqua County Humane Soc., 1989-93, Downtown Jamestown Devel. Task Force, 1988-92, Jamestown YMCA, 1985-87, N.Y. State affiliate of Am. Heart Assn., 1983-85, Southwestern chpt. Am. Heart Assn., 1981-85, Jamestown Cmty. Learning Coun., 1995-2001, Roger Tory Peterson Inst., 2000—; chmn. fund for the Arts in Chautauqua County, 1984-88; pres. Arts Coun. Chautauqua County, 1982-84, United Way South Chautauqua County, 2000-01; mem. Jamestown Civic Ctr. Task Force, 1982-86, N.Y. State Mgmt. Atty.'s Conf., 1978—. Capt. JACG, U.S. Army, 1967-71. Mem. ABA, N.Y. State Bar Assn., Erie County Bar Assn., Jamestown Bar Assn. (pres. 1991-92), No. Chautauqua County Bar Assn., Sportsmen's Club (Stow, N.Y.). Office: Phillips Lytle LLP 8 E 3rd St PO Box 1279 Jamestown NY 14702-1279 Office Phone: 716-483-3903. Business E-Mail: midzik@phillipslytle.com.

IENNER, DONALD S., former recording industry executive; b. Oct. 8, 1951; Co-founder,exec. v.p. Millennium Records, 1977—83; v.p. promotion, later exec. v.p., gen. mgr. Arista Records, 1983—89; pres. Columbia Records, NYC, 1989; chmn. Columbia Records Group, NYC, 1994—2004; pres., CEO Sony Music Label Group, US, NYC, 2004—06, chmn., 2006.

IERARDI, ERIC JOSEPH, school system administrator; b. Bklyn., May 11, 1950; s. Joseph and Angelina (Vitale) Ierardi. BA, St. Francis Coll., 1973; MEd, Fordham U., 1987. Asst. dir. James A. Kelly Local Hist. Studies Inst., 1973; St. Francis Coll. tchr. St. Bartholomew's Sch., 1974-78; tchr. Our Lady of Grace Sch., Bklyn., 1978-86, St. Mary Star of Sea Sch., 1986-87, asst. on edn. to Bklyn. borough pres., 1979; dist. rep., mgr. Congressman Stephen J. Solarz, 1981-82; prin. St. Francis Xavier Sch., Vicksburg, Miss., 1987-89, St. Francis Paola Sch., Bklyn., 1989-91, St. Pius V, Jamaica, Queens, NY, 1991-96; adminstr. David A. Boody Intermediate Sch. 228, Bklyn. Instr. Hinds CC, Bklyn.; U.S. del. Gruppo Savoia, 2000. Author: Gravesend: The Home of Coney Island, 1975, Gravesend: Brooklyn, Coney Island & Sheepshead Bay, 1996, Brooklyn in the 1920s, 1998; contbg. editor: Bklyn. Mag., 1978—79. Past mem. Cmty. Planning Bd. 11, Bklyn.; commr. deeds City of N.Y.; past pres. Gravesend Dem. Club. Decorated knight His Royal Higness Prince Victor Emmanuel IV of Savoy; named Hon. Mayor, Gravesend, Eng., 1977, Knight Officier, Order of Merit Savoy, 2002, Honor Guard, Royal Tombs at Pantheon Rome, 2003; recipient Calabrian of the Yr. award, Brutium Cultural Club, 1979. Mem.: Gravesend Hist. Soc. (pres.), Columbia Tchrs. Assn., Assn. Tchrs. Social Studies, U. S. Fla. Club, Circolog Culturale Club, Order Sons of Italy. Democrat. Roman Catholic. Home: PO Box 5 Upper Black Eddy PA 18972-0005 Office: IS 228 228 Avenue S Brooklyn NY 11223-2746 Office Phone: 718-375-7635 228. Personal E-mail: ericierardi@aol.com.

IEYOUB, RICHARD PHILLIP, lawyer, former state attorney general; b. Lake Charles, La., Aug. 11, 1944; s. Phillip Assad and Virginia Khoury Ieyoub; m. Caprice Brown, Feb. 3, 1995; children: Amy Claire, Nicole Anne, Brennan Jude, Richard Phillip Jr., Khoury Myhand, Christian Brown, Anna Michael. BA in history, McNeese State U., 1968; JD, La. State U., 1972. Bar: La. 1972, U.S. Supreme Ct. Spl. prosecutor to atty. gen. State of La., Baton Rouge, 1972—74; assoc. Camp, Carmouche, Lake Charles, 1974—76; mem. Stockwell, Sievert, Lake Charles, 1976—78, Baggett, McCall, Singleton, Ranier, Ieyoub, Lake Charles, 1978—; pvt. practice Lake Charles; dist. atty. Calcasieu Parish, 1985—92; atty. gen. State of La., 1992—2004; ptnr. Couhig Partners, Baton Rouge, 2004—. Instr. criminal law McNeese State U.; chmn. La. Drug Policy Bd. Active La. Commn. on Law Enforcement; apptd. by gov. to adv. bd. D.A.R.E., La.; chmn. New Orleans Met. Crime Task Force, Gov's. Military Adv. Commn.; active President's Commn. on Model State Drug Laws, 1992—; parish coun. Immaculate Conception Cathedral Parish, Lake Charles; bd. dirs. S.W. La. Health Counseling Svcs., Crime Stoppers of Lake Charles, St. Jude Children's Rsch. Hosp., 1998—99; vice-chmn. La. coord. Coun. on the Prevention of Drug Abuse and Treatment of Drug Use; bd. dirs. La. State U. Alumni Assn. Named Outstanding Pub. Ofcl. for Diocese Lake Charles, 1990; recipient Disting. Alumnus award, McNeese State U., 1994, Legis. Leadership award, Nat. Coun. Against Drinking and Driving, 1996, Ochsner Humanitarian award, 1998. Mem.: ABA (vice-chmn. prosecution function com.), So. Attys. Gen. Assn. (elected chmn.), S.W. La. Bar Assn. (exec. com. 1979), Nat. Coll. Dist. Attys. (bd. regents 1991), La. Dist. Attys. Assn. (pres., bd. dirs. 1989—90), Nat. Assn. Attys. Gen. (exec. working group on prosecutorial rels.), Nat. Dist. Attys. Assn. (pres., bd. dirs. 1990—91), La. Bar Assn. (lectr. criminal law), Nat. Assn. Criminal Def. Lawyers, Assn. Trial Lawyers Am., Sierra Club. Democrat. Roman Catholic. Office Phone: 225-612-4670. Business E-Mail: rieyoub@couhigpartners.com.

IFFT, LEWIS GEORGE, III, company administrator; b. Uniontown, Pa., July 21, 1951; s. Lewis George Jr. and Miriam Katherine Wilson; m. Kathleen Marie Andersen, Mar. 26, 1983; children: Christopher Andrew, Jonathan Lewis. BS in Bus. Adminstrn., Bowling Green State U., Ohio, 1973; MBA, Rensselaer Polytechnic Inst., Troy, NY, 1979. Ops. mgr. Battery Products Divsn. Union Carbide Corp., 1973-80; asst. reg. mgr. Eastern Region TransAmerica Corp., Elizabeth, NJ, 1980-82, reg. mgr. Eastern Region, 1982, regional mgr. Central Region Chgo., 1983—89; v.p. The Fred Barbara Co., Chgo., 1989-90; v.p., gen. mgr. Global Intermodal Sys., 1990—; regional v.p., mem. exec. com. Con Global Industries, San Ramon, Calif., 1992—2004. Mem. bd. dirs. Global Intermodal Systems, Inc., San Ramon, Calif. Presbyterian. Office: Con Global Industries 11700 Wallisville Rd Houston TX 77013-3421 Personal E-mail: lgifft@cgini.com.

IFFY, LESLIE, medical educator; b. Budapest, Hungary, May 17, 1925; arrived in U.S., 1969; s. Zoltan and Rozsa (Lantos) Iffy; m. Margaret Lesniak. MD, U. Budapest, Hungary, 1949; MD (hon.), U. Budapest, 1993. Diplomate Am. Bd. Ob-Gyn. Resident, fellow Országos Testnevelési és Sportegészségügyi Intézet Hosp. Ministry of Health, Budapest, 1951-56; fellow U. Wash., Seattle, 1964; asst. prof. Temple U., Phila., 1969-70; assoc. prof. U. Ill., Chgo., 1971-72, Jefferson Med. Coll., Phila., 1972-73; prof. U. Medicine and Dentistry of N.J., Newark, 1974—; dir. obstetrics U. Hosp., Newark, 1974—. Editor: Perinatology Case Studies, 1978, 1985, Obstetrics and Perinatology, 1981, Operative Perinatology, 1984, Operative Obstetrics, 1992, 3d edit., 2006; contbr. articles to profl. jours. Recipient Dr. Robert Jardine Rsch. prize, U. Glasgow, 1963, award for Disting. Svc., U. Medicine and Dentistry N.J., 2005, Semmelweis Meml. award, U. Budapest, 1993, 2005; rsch. fellow, Ford Found., Seattle, 1964, hon. fellow, Hungarian Obstet. Soc., 1986. Fellow: Royal Coll. Surgeons (Can.); mem.: Am. Coll. Legal Medicine (bd. dirs. 1989—95), Royal Faculty Physicians and Surgeons (Glasgow, Scotland) (licentiate), Romanian Soc. Obstetricians and Gynecologists (hon.), Ctrl. Assn. Ob-Gyn. (life), Royal Coll. Physicians (Edinburgh, Scotland) (licentiate), Chgo. Gynecol. Soc. Avocations: music, chess, literature, art. Home: PO Box 550 5 Robin Hood Rd Summit NJ 07901 Office: NJ Med Sch UMDNJ 150 Bergen St Newark NJ 07103 Office Phone: 973-972-5838. Personal E-mail: liffy@comcast.net.

IFILL, GWEN, moderator, political reporter; b. Queens, NY, Sept. 29, 1955; d. O. Urcille Ifill, Sr. and Eleanor Ifill. BA in Comm., Simmons Coll., Boston, 1977; recipient of 15 hon. degrees. Food columnist Boston Herald American, 1977—80; covered nat. and local affairs for Baltimore Evening Sun, 1981—84, Washington Post, 1984—91; White House corr., journalist NY Times, 1991—94; chief congl., polit. corr. NBC News, 1994—99; panelist Washington Week; moderator, mng. editor Washington Week with Gwen Ifill, Pub. Broadcasting Svc. (PBS) and WETA-TV, 1999—; sr. corr., back-up anchor The NewsHour with Jim Lehrer, Pub. Broadcasting Svc. (PBS), 1999—. Bd. dir. Harvard U. Inst. Politics, Com. to Protect Journalists, Mus. TV and Radio, U. Md. Philip Merrill Coll. Journalism; spkr. in field. Covered Bill Clinton's rise from So. gov. to Pres. US, 1992—93, moderator first v.p. debate, 2004. Fellow: Am. Acad. Arts & Sciences. Methodist. Office: Washington Week Pub Broadcasting Svc 2775 S Quincy St Arlington VA 22206 Address: The NewsHour with Jim Lehrer Pub Broadcasting Svc 3620 27th St S Arlington VA 22206 Office Phone: 703-998-2600, 703-998-2137.

IGALI, BARALADEI DANIEL, Olympic athlete, coach, motivational speaker; b. Eniwari, Bayelsa, Nigeria, Feb. 3, 1974; arrived in Can., 1994, naturalized, 1998; s. Leimokumo and Grace Igali, adopted s. Maureen Matheny. Student in Mass Comm., Nigeria; student, Simon Fraser U.; BA in Criminology, Simon Fraser U., Burnaby, B.C., Can., 2001, postgrad., 2002—. Pres. Daniel Igali Found. Mem. Can. Olympic com. Named Nat. Wrestling Champion, Nigeria, 1990, African Wrestling Champion, Cairo, 1993, World Champion Wrestler, Ankara, Turkey, 1998, Athlete of Yr., Can., 1999, 2000, 6 Time Can. Nat. Wrestling Champion, 1998—, 4 Time Nigerian Nat. Champion, 1991—94, 2 Time African Champion, 1992—94, Hon. Can. Soldier; recipient Wrestling Gold medal, Olympics, 2000. Avocations: Kabaddi, watching wrestling movies, soccer, surfing the Internet. Office: 8876-140 St PO Box 16531 Surrey BC Canada V3W 2P5 Home: 128-8655 King George Hwy Surrey BC Canada V3W 5C4 Personal E-mail: danieligali@aol.com, dynamiteigali@hotmail.com, daniel.igali@gmail.com.

IGER, BOB (ROBERT ALLEN IGER), entertainment company executive; b. NYC, Feb. 10, 1951; s. Arthur and Mimi Iger; m. Willow Bay, Oct. 7, 1995; children: Max, William;children from previous marriage: Kate, Amanda. BA magna cum laude, Ithaca Coll., 1973. Studio supr. ABC-TV, 1974—76; various positions ABC-TV Sports, 1976—85; v.p. prog. planning, devel. ABC Sports, 1985—87, v.p. prog. planning & acquisition,

1987—88; exec. v.p. ABC TV Network Grp., 1988—89, pres., 1992—94, ABC Entertainment, 1989—92; exec. v.p. Capital Cities/ABC Inc., NYC, 1993—94, pres., COO, 1994—96; pres. ABC, Inc., NYC, 1996—99; chmn. ABC Grp., 1999—2000; pres. Walt Disney Internat., 1999—2000; pres., COO The Walt Disney Co., Burbank, Calif., 2000—05, pres., CEO, 2005—. Bd. dirs. The Walt Disney Co., 2000—, Lincoln Ctr. Performing Arts, NYC; bd. trustees Am. Film Inst. Bd., Mus. TV and Radio, Ithaca Coll. Trustee Ithaca Coll. Named one of 50 Who Matter Now, CNNMoney.com Bus. 2.0, 2006; recipient Trustee award, Nat. Acad. TV Arts & Scis., 2005. Office: The Walt Disney Co 500 S Buena Vista St Burbank CA 91521-0001*

IGGERS, GEORG GERSON, history professor; b. Hamburg, Germany, Dec. 7, 1926; came to U.S., 1938, naturalized, 1949; s. Alfred G. and Lizzie (Minden) I.; m. Wilma Abeles, Dec. 23, 1948; children: Jeremy, Daniel, Karl Jonathan. BA, U. Richmond, 1944, DHL, 2001; AM, U. Chgo., 1945, PhD, 1951; postgrad., New Sch. Social Rsch., 1945-46; PhD (hon.), Philander Smith Coll., 2002, Technische U., Darmstadt, Germany, 2006. Instr. U. Akron, Ohio, 1948-50; assoc. prof. Philander Smith Coll., Little Rock, 1950-57; from assoc. prof. to prof. Dillard U., New Orleans, 1957-63; assoc. prof. Roosevelt U., Chgo., 1963-65; prof. history SUNY, Buffalo, 1965—, disting. prof., 1978-97, chmn., 1981-84, disting. prof. emeritus, 1997—. Mem. Conf. Group Ctrl. European History, vice chmn., 1989-90, chmn., 1990-91; vis. prof. U. Ark., Fayetteville, 1956-57, 64, U. Rochester, 1970-71, U. Leipzig, Germany, 1992; vis. assoc. prof. Tulane U., New Orleans, 1958-60, 63; vis. scholar Technische Hochschule Darmstadt, Germany, 1991, Forschungsschwerpunkt zeithistorische Studien, Potsdam, Germany, 1993; fellow Woodrow Wilson Ctr. Internat. Scholars, Washington, 1993-94; vis. prof. Aarhus (Denmark) U., 1998, Zentrum für Zeithistorische Forschung, Potsdam, Germany, 1998, U. New Eng. (Australia), 1999, Internat. Forschungszentrum Kulturwissenschaften, Vienna, 2000, U. Vienna, 2002. Author: The Cult of Authority, 1958, The German Conception of History, 1968, New Directions in European Historiography, 1975, Geschichtswissenschaft im 20 Jahrhundert, 1993, Historiography in the Twentieth Century, 1997; co-author (with Wilma Iggers): Zwei Seiten der Geschichte, 2002; co-author: English: Two Lives in Uncertain Times, 2006; editor (with Harold T. Parker): International Handbook of Historical Studies, 1979, The Social History of Politics, 1986; editor: (with James Powell) Leopold von Ranke and the Shaping of the Historical Discipline, 1990, Ein anderer historischer Blick Beispiele ostdeutscher Sozialgeschichte, 1991, Marxist Historiography in Transformation, 1991; co-editor: Storia della Storiografia jour., Geschichtswissenschaft der DDR als Forschungsproblem, Historische Zeitschrift, Sonderband 27, 1998; mem. editl. bd. Zeitschrift für Geschichtswissenschaft, History and Theory. Bd. dirs., counselor Draft and Mil. Counseling Ctr., Buffalo, 1967-89; bd. dirs.Citizens Coun. Human Rels., Buffalo, 1965-95; chmn. edn., exec. coms. NAACP, Little Rock, 1951-56, chmn. edn. com., New Orleans, 1957-63, bd. dirs, Buffalo, 1965— , chmn. edn. com., 1965-75, co-chmn. health com., 1979-85. Fellow Guggenheim Found., 1960-61, Rockefeller Found., 1961-62, NEH, 1971-72, 78-79, 85-86, Ctr. Interdisciplinary Rsch., Bielefeld, Fed. Republic Germany, 1986-87; hon. fellow Fulbright Commn. 1978-79, 85-86, 87; recipient Kittler award Technische Hochschule Darmstadt, 1988, Alexander von Humboldt Rsch. prize 1993. Mem. Internat. Commn. Historiography (v.p. 1980-95, pres. 1995-2000, exec. com. 1980-2005), Am. Hist. Assn., Acad. Scis. of German Dem. Republic (fgn. mem. 1990-92). Office: Dept History Park Hall SUNY Buffalo NY 14260-4130 Home: Schillerstrasse 50 D 37083 Göttingen Germany Home Phone: 011-49-551-740 38. Personal E-mail: iggers@buffalo.edu.

IGIETSEME, JOSEPH UGBODAGA, biomedical researcher, educator; b. Agenebode, Edo State, Nigeria, Feb. 17, 1955; s. Igietseme Omogbako Ugbodaga and Adishetu Omosi Igietseme; m. Veronica Emeke Onwude; children: Gabriel Ugbodaga, Nene Veronica, Jojackson Ugbodaga. PhD, Georgetown U., Washington, 1988. Chief molecular pathogenesis lab. Ctrs. Disease Control and Prevention, Atlanta, 2002—. Prof. Morehouse Sch. Medicine, Atlanta, 2002—. Scholar, NIH, 1996—. Mem.: Am. Assn. Immunologists (life), Nigerians in the Diaspora Orgn. (gen. sec. 2005). Achievements include research in immunology, infectious disease and vaccines. Home: 982 Carlisle Rd Stone Mountain GA 30083 Office: Ctrs Disease Control C 17 1600 Clifton Rd Atlanta GA 30333 Home Phone: 404-299-5624; Office Phone: 404-639-3352. Office Fax: 404-639-3199; Home Fax: 404-343-6571. E-mail: jigietseme@cdc.gov.

IGLAUER, EDITH, writer, reporter; b. Cleve., Mar. 10, 1917; arrived in Can., 1976; d. Jay and Bertha G. (Good) I.; m. Philip Hamburger, Dec. 24, 1942 (div. 1966); children: Jay Philip Hamburger, Richard Shaw Hamburger; m. John Heywood Daly, Mar. 1, 1976 (dec. Feb. 1978); m. Franklin White, Feb. 25, 2006. BA, Wellesley Coll., 1938; MS, Columbia U., 1939; LLD (hon.), U. Victoria, Can., 2006. Freelance writer, 1939—. Author: The New People, The Eskimo's Journey Into Our Time, 1966 (Outdoor Sci. Club award), Denison's Ice Road, 1975, 4th edit., 2005, Inuit Journey, 1979, revised edit., 2000, Seven Stones: A Portrait of Arthur Erickson, Architect, 1981, Fishing with John, 1988, 3d edit., 2000 (Shortlisted Gov. Gens. award), The Strangers Next Door, 1991; contbr. articles to newspapers and popular mags. Geneva scholar Sch. Internat. Studies, 1937; recipient Woodrow Wilson Prize in modern politics Wellesley Coll., 1938, Cleve. Creative Achievement in Lit. award Womens City Club, 1983, Short-Listed, Gov. Gen's award for Non-Fiction, Can., 1988. Mem. Authors Guild, Writers Union Can., Francis Point Marine Pk. Soc., Cosmopolitan Club NY, The Cleve. Play House Club. Democrat. Avocations: swimming, travel, cooking. Home: PO Box 116 VON 1S0 Garden Bay BC Canada Office: The New Yorker Mag 4 Times Sq New York NY 10036-6561 Personal E-mail: edaly@dccnet.com.

IGLESIAS, DAVID CLAUDIO, former prosecutor; b. Jan. 1958; m. Cynthia J. Iglesias; 4 children. BA, Wheaton Coll., 1980; JD, U. N.Mex. Asst. atty. gen. N.Mex Atty. Gen. Office; asst. city atty. City of Albuquerque, 1991—94; spl. asst. to sec. transp. White Ho. Fellowship, 1995; chief counsel N.Mex Risk Mgmt. Legal Office, 1995—98; gen. counsel N.Mex Taxation and Revenue Dept., 1998—2001; assoc. Walz and Assoc., Albuquerque; US atty. N.Mex US Dept. Justice, 2001—06. Comdr. JAGC USNR.*

IGLESIAS, EMMA MARIA, economics professor; b. La Coruña, Spain, Oct. 11, 1974; arrived in U.S., 2004; BSc in Econs., U. La Coruña, 1997; MSc in Econs. and Econometrics, U. Exeter, England, 1999; PhD in Econs., Cardiff U., Wales, 2002. Tchg. asst. Cardiff U., 2000—02; postdoctoral rsch. fellow U. Exeter, 2002—03; asst. prof. U. Alicante, Spain, 2003—04, Mich. State U., East Lansing, 2004—. Jour. referee. Contbr. articles to profl. jours. Grantee, Econ. and Social Rsch. Coun., England, 2000—02, Mich. State U., 2005—07; Postdoctoral Rsch. fellow, Econ. and Social Rsch. Coun., England, 2002—03. Mem.: Econometric Soc. (assoc.). Office: Michigan State Univ 101 Marshall Adams Hall East Lansing MI 48824 Home Phone: 517-256-6119; Office Phone: 517-353-9916. Business E-Mail: iglesia5@msu.edu.

IGLESIAS, MARIA ESTRELLA, language educator, writer; b. Granada, Spain, Jan. 11, 1952; arrived in U.S.A., 1977; d. Severiano Iglesias-Galindo and Dolores Tortosa-Orihuela; m. Christopher H. Maurer, Mar. 2, 1977; children: Daniel, Pablo. BA in Journalism, Temple U., 1978; MA in Spanish Lit., U. Pa., 1980. Tchr., Spanish U. Sch. Nashville, 1990—2000; assoc. dir., edn. tchr., U. Ill., 2000—04. Co-author: Temas: Invitacion a la Literature Hispanica, 1994, Dreaming in Clay on the Coast of Miss.: Love and Art at Shearwater, 2000. Democrat. Avocation: jewelry making.

IGLEWICZ, BORIS, statistician, educator; b. Omsk, USSR, Oct. 11, 1939; arrived in US, 1952, naturalized, 1959; s. Solomon and Faiga (Brucker) Iglewicz; m. Raja Brody, May 24, 1973; children: David, Alana. BS, Wayne State U., 1962, MA, 1963; PhD, Va. Poly. Inst., 1967. Instr. math. Mich. Tech. U., 1963—64; asst. prof. stats. Case We. Res. U., Cleve., 1967—69; assoc. prof. stats. Temple U., Phila., 1969—74, prof., 1974—, dir. Ph.D. program in stats., 1970—76, chmn. dept., 1978—82, dir. biostats. group, 1992—93, dir. biostats. rsch. ctr., 1993—. V.p., dir. Meco Metals Corp., 1974; vis. prof. Harvard U., 1984—85. Author: (with J. Stoyle) An Introduction to Mathematical Reasoning, 1973, (with D.C. Hoaglin) How to Detect and Handle Outliers, 1993; contbr. articles to profl. jours., chpts. to books. NIH fellow, 1964-67; advanced rsch. fellow Harvard U., 1978; recipient Musser Leadership award, 2001, Don Owen award 2003. Fellow: Am. Statis Assn. (pres. Phila. chpt. 1981—83, W.J. Youden award 2001), Royal Statis. Soc.; mem.: Internat. Stats. Inst., Am. Soc. Quality (sr.), Inst. Math. Stats., Biometric Soc., Beta Gamma Sigma, Pi Mu Epsilon, Sigma Xi. Home: 1912 Rolling Ln Cherry Hill NJ 08003-3328 Office: Temple U 1810 N 13th St Dept Stats Philadelphia PA 19122 Office Phone: 215-204-8637. Business E-Mail: borisi@temple.edu.

IGNACZAK, EDWARD B., health products executive; m. Mary Ann Ignaczak. V.p. account mgmt. and sales ValueRx, 1996—97, v.p., gen. mgr. Core Bus. Unit, 1997—98; v.p., gen. mgr. Nat. Employer Divsn. Express Scripts, Inc., Md. Heights, Mo., 1998—2002, sr. v.p. sales and account mgmt., 2002—. Office: Express Scripts Inc 13900 Riverport Dr Maryland Heights MO 63043 Office Phone: 314-770-1666.*

IGNARRO, LOUIS J., pharmacology educator; b. Bklyn., May 31, 1941; m. Sharon Elizabeth Williams, July 1997; 1 child from previous marriage. BA in Pharmacy, Columbia U., 1962; PhD in Pharmacology, U. Minn., 1966; degrees (hon.), U. Madrid, Lund U., U. Gent, U. NC. Postdoctoral rsch., Lab. Chem. Pharmacology Nat. Heart, Lung and Blood Inst., NIH; head, biochem, anti-inflammatory program Geigy Pharmaceuticals, 1968—73; asst. prof., pharmacology Tulane Univ. Sch. Medicine, New Orleans, 1973—79, prof., pharmacology, 1979—85; prof. dept. molecular and med. pharmacology UCLA Sch. Medicine, 1985—. Contbr. articles to profl. jours. Recipient Edward G. Schlieder Found. award, 1973, Merck Rsch. award, 1974, Rsch. Career Devel. award, USPHS, 1975—80, Nobel prize in physiology or medicine, 1998; fellow postdoctoral, NIH, 1966—68. Mem.: NAS, Alpha Omega Alpha (hon.). Achievements include research in biochemical, physiological, and pathophysioilogical roles of nitric oxide and cyclic GMP in mammalian cell function; the transcriptional, translational and catalytic regulation of constitutive and inducible nitric oxide synthases; the role of other biochemical pathways in the regulation of biosynthesis and metabolism of nitric oxide; the biochemical and chemical mechanisms by which nitric oxide elicits cytotoxic effects on invading target cells and microorganisms; the role of nitric oxide as a neurotransmitter in non-adrenergic non-cholinergic neurons innervating various issues. Office: UCLA Sch Medicine Dept Molecular & Med Pharmacology 23-315 Chs 10833 Leconte Ave Los Angeles CA 90095-1735

IGNATIEV, ALEX, physics researcher; b. Wehingen, Germany, Feb. 14, 1945; U.S. citizen; married; two children. BS, U. Wis., 1966; PhD in Material Sci., Cornell U., 1972. Postdoctoral fellow material sci. SUNY, Stony Brook, 1971—73; from asst. prof. to assoc. prof. physics and chemistry U. Houston, 1974—83, prof. physics and chemistry, 1983—2003, disting. prof., physics, chemistry & elec. and computer engring., 2003—; assoc. dir. Magnetic Info Rsch. Lab., 1984-89. Mem. energy lab. U. Houston, 1975—; lectr. physics Aarhus U., Denmark, 1977-78; Fulbright sr. scholar, 1983; assoc. dir. Space Vacuum Epitaxy Ctr., 1986-88, dir. 1988—; task leader Tex. Ctr. for Superconductivity, 1987—; dir. Tex. Ctr. superconductivity and advanced materials, 2002-. Assoc. editor Vacuum, Space Forum, Research Trends; contbr. numerous articles to profl. jours. Mem. AIAA, AAAS, ASME, IEEE, SPIE, Internat. Acad. Astronautics, Am. Phys. Soc., Am. Vacuum Soc., Am. Chem. Soc., Internat. Solar Energy Soc, The Materials Rsch. Soc., Sigma Xi. Business E-Mail: ignatiev@uh.edu.

IGNATOWSKI, TRACEY A., research scientist, educator; b. Buffalo, Mar. 6, 1968; d. Geoffrey J. and Janice A. Ignatowski; m. Kenneth J. Wojciechowski, Sept. 13, 1997; children: Alaina M. Wojciechowski, Andrew M. Wojciechowski. BS, U. Buffalo, 1990, PhD, 1995. FACScan flow cytometry cert. Becton-Dickinson Immunocytometry Sys., 1995. Predoctoral fellow dept. pathology U. Buffalo, SUNY, Buffalo, 1990—95, rsch. asst. prof. dept. anesthesiology, 1997—99, rsch. asst. prof. dept. pathology & anat. scis., 1999—; postdoctoral fellow dept. pharmacology and physiology U. Rochester Med. Ctr., NY, 1995—97. Co-author: Methods in Molecular Biology, NeuroImmune Biology: Cytokines and the Brain; editl. adv. bd. Immunological Investigations, 1998—; contbr. articles to profl. jours. Recipient Postdoctoral Fellow Poster Competition award, AIDS, Drugs Abuse, and Neuroimmune Axis Neuroscience Satellite Meeting, 1995, Outstanding Poster Presentation award, European Soc. Intensive Care Medicine, 1999; grantee, Sigma Xi, 1995; Young Investigator Travel grantee, AIDS, Drugs Abuse, and Neuroimmune Axis Neuroscience Satellite Meeting, 1995, 1996, Mark Diamond Rsch. grantee, SUNY, Buffalo, 1994, Travel grantee, Am. Soc. Investigative Pathology, Exptl. Biology, 1995, Young Investigator grantee, Nat. Alliance Rsch. Schizophrenia and Depression, 1999, Rsch. grantee, United Spinal Assn., 2004—06. Mem.: Internat. Assn. Study Pain, Ea. Pain Assn., Soc. Neuroscience (Rochester chpt. Notter Award, Postdoctoral Fellow Poster Competition award 1997), Golden Key, Alpha Epsilon Delta. Avocations: reading, gardening, exercising, travel. Office: U Buffalo 3435 Main St Buffalo NY 14214 Office Phone: 716-829-3102. Business E-Mail: tai1@buffalo.edu.

IGNERI, DAVID SEBASTIAN, elementary school educator; b. Bklyn., July 4, 1944; s. Marco and Margaret (Marzullo) I.; m. Nancy Reilly Goldberg, Feb. 9, 1969 (div. Nov. 1974); 1 child, Lisa Anne; m. Elisabeth Kenyatta Strachan, Aug. 4, 1990; 1 child, Giovanni. BS in Edn., Brockport State U., 1966; MS in Edn., Long Island U., 1969, MA in History, 1972; profl. cert. in African studies, St. John's U., 1976; PhD in Am. Colonial History, Union Inst., 1992; MALS in Am. Studies, Stony Brook U., 1997. Cert. elem. tchr. K-6, social studies tchr. 7-12, N.Y. Elem. tchr. Centereach (N.Y.) Pub. Schs., 1967-68, Brentwood (N.Y.) Pub. Schs., 1968-70, Patchogue Medford (N.Y.) Pub. Schs., 1970-98. Lectr. on historic topics, N.Y., 1988—; adj. prof. history Dowling Coll., Oakdale, N.Y., 1999-2001, L.I. Univ., 2002-2004. Recipient Commendation letters Town of Brookhaven, 1988, 93, longevity awards Brookhaven Recreation Dept., 1985, 90. Roman Catholic. Home: 23 E 6th St Patchogue NY 11772-2315 Personal E-mail: docandmrs.ig.1@verizon.net.

IGUSA, JUN-ICHI, mathematician, educator; b. Japan, Jan. 30, 1924; arrived in U.S., 1953; s. Shiro and Rui (Fukushima) I.; m. Yoshie Yamamoto, Oct. 7, 1948; children: Kiyoshi, Takeru, Mitsuru. MA, Tokyo Imperial U., 1945; PhD, Kyoto U., Japan, 1953. Assoc. prof. Kyoto U., 1949—55; rsch. assoc. Harvard U., 1953-55; mem. faculty Johns Hopkins U., 1955—, prof. math., 1961-93, prof. emeritus, 1993—, J.J. Sylvester chair, 1986-93. Chmn. bd. dirs. Japan-U.S. Math. Inst. Johns Hopkins U., 1987-93. Author: Theta Functions, 1972, Forms of Higher Degree, 1978, Local Zeta Functions, 2000; editor-in-chief: Am. Jour. Math., 1978-93. Decorated Order of Sacred Treasure medal Japan. Mem. Math. Soc. Japan, Am. Math. Soc., Phi Beta Kappa. Home: 14209 Greencroft Ln Hunt Valley MD 21030-1111

IHARA, MICHIO, sculptor; b. Paris, Nov. 17, 1928; naturalized, U.S., 2001; s. Usaburo and Shigeko (Shinkai) I.; m. Doreen Joyce Kaplan, July 7, 1966; 1 child, Akeo. BFA, Tokyo U. Fine Arts, 1953. Fulbright fellow MIT, 1961-62, rsch. assoc., 1962-64; instr. Musashino U. Fine Arts, Tokyo, 1966-69. One-man shows Kanegis Gallery, Boston, 1964, Tokyo Gallery, 1970, Staempfli Gallery, N.Y.C., 1977, 80, 84; numerous group shows in Japan and U.S., 1957-74; important works include marble mural Chuokoron Pub. Co, Tokyo, 1957; copper relief 275 Wyman St. Office Bldg, Waltham, Mass., 1963; altar canopy Josenji Temple, Tokyo, 1965; metal screen Imperial Theatre, Tokyo, 1966; relief Internat. Christian U, Tokyo, 1967, Fuji Film Co. Bldg, Tokyo, 1969; sculpture Internat. Sculptors Symposium, Osaka, 1970, Wellesley (Mass.) Office Park, 1973, Fitchburg (Mass.) Pub. Library; civic sculpture, Auckland, N.Z., 1977, Constellation Place, Balt., 1978; metal screen Rockefeller Center, N.Y.C., 1978, Neiman-Marcus, Beverly Hills, Calif., New World Hotel, Hong Kong, Pavilion Hotel, Singapore; wall sculpture S.E. Bank, Miami, 1983; suspended sculptures Marriott Marquis Hotel, N.Y.C., 1985, wall sculpture Harvard U., 1985, 89, wind sculpture, Tallahassee City Hall, 1989, tower sculpture Tokyo City Hall, 1991, suspended sculptures AT&T Plaza, Chgo., 1991, Colorado Springs Airport, 1994, Wall Sculpture Ikenoue Ch., Tokyo, 1995, suspended sculpture Lorillard Headquarters, N.C., 1997, interactive sculpture Cyclelight, Boston 1st Night, 1993, suspended sculpture New Eng. Med. Ctr. Hosp., Boston, 2000, sculptures Yokohama Crematorium, Japan, 2002, suspended sculpture Crowne Plz. Hotel, N.Y., 2002, Suspended Sculpture 101 Constitution Ave. Bldg., Washington, D.C., 2003, suspended sculpture Riverside Meth. Hosp., Columbus, Ohio, 2004, Shinsegae Dept. Store, Seoul, Republic of Korea, 2006. Trustee The Artists Found. Mass. JDR 3d Fund grantee, 1970-71; recipient award Mass. Council Arts and Humanities, 1974, Nat. Inst. Arts and Letters/Am. Acad. Arts and Letters award in art, 1973, award Fgn. Min. of Japanese Govt., 1999; Graham Found. fellow, 1963-64; MIT Center for Advanced Visual Studies fellow, 1970-73 Mem. Japan Artists Assn. Address: 63 Wood St Concord MA 01742-2225 Home Phone: 978-369-3731; Office Phone: 978-369-3731. Personal E-mail: michio.ihara@sprintmail.com.

IHDE, DON, philosopher, educator; b. Hope, Kans., Jan. 14, 1934; s. Melvin Millard and Nell Pearl (Reikeman) I.; m. Carolyn W. Ihde (div.); children: Leslie Ann, Lisa Ihde-Costa, Eric Martin; m. Linda Einhorn, Apr. 4, 1985; 1 child, Mark Hillel. BA, U. Kans., 1956; MDiv, Andover Newton Theol. Sem., 1959; PhD, Boston U., 1964; prof. (hon.), El Rosario U., Bogota, Columbia, 1982. Asst. prof. So. Ill. U., Carbondale, 1964-67, assoc. prof., 1968-69, SUNY, Stony Brook, 1969-70, prof., 1971-86, dean humanities and fine arts, 1985-90, leading prof., 1986—, disting. prof., 1997—. Author: Hermeneutic Phenomenology, 1971, Sense and Significance, 1973, Listening and Voice, 1976, Experimental Phenomenology, 1977, Technics and Praxis: A Philosophy of Technology, 1979, Existential Technics, 1983, Conequences of Phenomenology, 1986, Technology and the Life World, 1990, Instrumental Realism, 1991, Philosophy of Technology, 1993, Postphenomenology, 1993, Expanding Hermeneutics, 1998, Bodies in Technology, 2001; editor: The Conflict of Interpretations (Paul Ricouer); (with Richard M. Zaner) Phenomenology and Existentialism, 1973, Selected Studies in Phenomenology and Existential Philosophy, vol. IV, 1974, Interdisciplinary Phenomenology, vol. VI, 1977; (with Hugh J. Silverman) Selected Studies in Phenomenology and Existential Philosophy, vols. IX, XI, 1985, (with Evan Selinger) Chasing Technoscience, 2003; mem. editorial bd. Ind. U. Press, Northwestern U. Press. Recipient Jr. award So. Soc. for Philosophy and Psychology, 1966; summer rsch. fellow So. Ill. U., 1966, 67, 68, 69; Fulbright rsch. fellow U. Paris, 1967-68, sr. fellow NEH, 1972, vis. rsch. fellow Australian Nat. U., 1985, vis. scholar U. Sydney, 1991; grantee SUNY, Stony Brook, 1970, NSF, 1981. Mem. AAAS, Am. Philos. Assn. (mem. program com. 1976, 88, nominating com. 1981-83), Am. Psychol. Assn. (mem. sect. D), Heidegger Conf., Husserl Circle, Merleau-Ponty Circle, Nat. Assn. Sci., Tech. and Soc., Soc. Phenomenology and Existential Philosophy (exec. co-dir. 1972-75, 81-84), Soc. Philosophy and Tech. (bd. dirs. 1983-86, editor Ind. series), Phi Beta Kappa. Office: SUNY Dept Philosophy Stony Brook NY 11794-0001 Office Phone: 631-632-7575. Business E-Mail: dihde@notes.cc.sunysb.edu.

IHENACHO, DAVID ASONYE, campus chaplain; s. Simeon Ihenacho Onuoha and Grace Manumgbede Osumpere. BA in Philosophy, Bigard Meml. Sem., 1982, BA in Theology, 1987; MA in Religious Studies, Fordham U., 1995; PhD in Religious Studies, Marquette U., 1999. Asst. editor The Leader Newspaper, Owerri, Imo State, Nigeria, 1982—83; assoc. editor The Guide Newspaper, Ahiara, 1988—94; pastor St. Paul's Parish, Amuzu, 1990—92; rector Mother Ch. Cathedral, Ahiara, 1992—94; chaplain, tchr. Edgewood H.S., Madison, Wis., 1997—98; chaplain Beloit Cath. H.S., 1998—99; resident parochial vicar St. Patrick and St. Joseph Parish, Doylestown And Rio, 1999—2000; chaplain, adj. instr. Sacred Heart U., Fairfield, Conn., 2000—01; chaplain L.I. U., Bklyn., 2001—. Author: The Community Of Eternal Life, African Christianity Rises, 2 Volumes. Instr. Bible Study Group, Bklyn., 2001—05. Scholar, Marquette U., 1997—99. Mem.: Cath. Bibl. Assn., Soc. Bibl. Lit. Independent. Christianity. Avocations: writing, sports, music, travel. Home Phone: 718-253-4004; Office Phone: 718-488-3359. E-mail: davidihenacho@hotmail.com.

IHRIE, ROBERT, oil, gas and real estate company executive; b. Phila., Jan. 4, 1925; s. Theodore Richard and Ella Martha (Anderson) I.; m. Dorothy Myrtle Waltz, July 8, 1944 (div. 1983); children: Robert Jr., Richard William, David Wayne, Nancy Ellen; m. Nancy Jean Joseph, June 8, 1984. BS, valedictorian, Ursinus Coll., 1943; MBA with high distinction, Harvard U., 1947. Process engr., econ. analyst, foreman, head tng. dept. head bus. analysis dept. Esso Std. Oil Co., Baton Rouge, 1947—59; head demand/supply coord. planning dept. Exxon Corp., NYC, 1959—62; asst. dep. adminstr. AID, asst. sec. state Dept. State, Washington, 1962—64; v.p. Lippincott and Margulies, Inc., NYC, 1965—68; sr. v.p. Am. Trading and Prodn. Corp., Balt., 1968—, bd. dirs. Bd. dirs. Am. Trading Real Estate Properties, Balt. With U.S. Army, 1943-46. Baker scholar Harvard Grad. Sch. Bus., 1947; recipient Presdl. Citation. Mem. Am. Contract Bridge League (life master 1977). Presbyterian. Avocations: roller dance skating, coaching softball, theater, travel. Home: 212 E Ridgely Rd Lutherville Timonium MD 21093-5239 Office: Am Trading & Prodn Corp PO Box 238 Baltimore MD 21203-0238

IHRIG, JUDSON LA MOURE, chemist; b. Santa Maria, Calif., Nov. 5, 1925; s. Harry Karl and Luella (LaMoure) I.; m. Gwendolyn Adele Montz, July 22, 1950; children: Kristin, Neil Marshall. BS, Haverford Coll., 1949; MA, Princeton U., 1951, PhD, 1952. Asst. prof. chemistry U. Hawaii, 1952-58, assoc. prof., 1958-72, prof., 1972-94, dir. honors program, 1958-64, 87-95, dir. liberal studies program, 1973-79, chmn. chemistry dept., 1981-86, prof. emeritus, 1994—. Cons. chemistry local firms. Author publs. in field. Served with AUS, 1945-46. Mem. Am. Chem. Soc., Phi Beta Kappa, Sigma Xi. Home: 386 Wailupe Cir Honolulu HI 96821-1525 Office: U Hawaii 2545 The Mall Honolulu HI 96822-2233 Office Phone: 808-956-4590.

IIDA, SHUICHI, physicist, educator; b. Kobe, Hyogo-Ken, Japan, Jan. 30, 1926; s. Shunzoh and Sono (Ueda) Iida; m. Kyoko Matsuoka, Apr. 29, 1955; children: Mariko Takahara, Junko Kose. BS in Physics, U. Tokyo, 1947, PhD in Physics, 1958. Asst. prof. U. Tokyo, 1952-58, assoc. prof., 1958-68, prof., 1968-86, prof. emeritus, 1986; prof. Teikyo U., Sagamiko, Kanagawa, Japan, 1988-89, Utsunomiya, Japan, 1989-96. Vis. prof. AT&T Bell Labs., Murray Hill, NJ, 1961—63. Contbr. articles to profl. jours. Mem.: Japan Inst. Metals, Magnetics Soc. Japan, NY Acad. Scis., Japan Soc. Powder and Powder Metallurgy, Physics Soc. Japan, Magnetics Soc.

of IEEE, Am. Physics Soc. Achievements include research in ferrites; grand unifying frame for physics; electromagnetism; joint-use of MKSP and SI unit systems; correct representation for electromagnetic momenta; solution of Poincaré paradox; transient energy principle; proof for perfect diamagnetism of perfect conductors; essential q-number theory in biophysics; frontier notion principle; wave particle dualism; EPR problem; cold fusion; livelex f3 structure or filamentary current loops for c-number structure of lepton and hadron particles; electromagnetic origin of particle masses; trefoiled knot structure for proton; electromagnetic origin of weak and strong interactions; contra-particles for neutrinos and pions; Iida diagram for parity violation problems; chipped photon mechanism for redshifts and denial of big-bang cosmology; finding of Iida metric with denial of black hole having surpassed Schwarzschild metric with Einstein equation; Iida structure for electronic order of magnetite; symmetric location of proton for hydrogen bond of ice; proposal for ECTJ mechanism for flagellar motor and strict proof for unified unrestricted Larmor diamagnetism and cyclotron motion; research in solely protons and Iida pions in nuclei; discovery of third fire or explosive proton-electron annihilation in type II supernovae: via-Iida pion spin aligned protons for neutron stars and magnetic flux quantization for all elementary particles; idea of fourth fire or colossal Iida pion-proton annihilation explosion for transmigrating universe with galaxies; idea for GRBs due to ignition of third fire for approaching or colliding celestial bodies by colossal magnetic field around neutron star; proposal of Iida equation for dark matter in Halos of galaxies, moon, molecular mass of muon neutrinos having been deduced. Home and Office: 4-23-11 Funabashi Setagaya-ku Tokyo 156-0055 Japan Office Phone: 81 03 3483 5218. Business E-Mail: s.iida.prof.em.tokyo@proof.ocn.ne.jp.

IJAZ, MANSOOR, news correspondent; b. 1961; s. Mujaddid Ahmed Ijaz. BS in Physics (magna cum laude), Univ. Va., 1983; MS in Mech. Engring., MIT, 1985. Founder, chmn. The Crescent Partnerships, 1991—; foreign affairs and terrorism analyst FOX News Channel, 2001—. Mem. Coun. on Fgn. Rels. Contbr. to editl. pages of Financial Times, Wall Street Journal, NY Times, LA Times, Washington Post, Newsweek and International Herald Tribune. Office: FOX News Channel 400 N Capitol St NW Ste 550 Washington DC 20001

IJIRI, YUJI, finance educator; b. Kobe, Japan, Feb. 24, 1935; came to U.S., 1959; s. Takejiro and Hiroko (Hanno) I.; m. Tomoko Nishimura, June 17, 1962; children: Lisa, Yumi. LLB, Ritsumeikan U., Kyoto, Japan, 1956; MS, U. Minn., 1960; PhD, Carnegie Mellon U., 1963; LLD (hon.), DePaul U., 1990; DSc in Bus. Adminstrn. (hon.), Bryant Coll., 1991. CPA, Japan. Staff mem. Price Waterhouse & Co., Tokyo, 1957-59; asst. prof. grad. sch. bus. Stanford (Calif.) U., 1963-65, assoc. prof. grad. sch. bus., 1965-67; prof. grad. sch. indsl. adminstrn. Carnegie Mellon U., Pitts., 1967-75, Robert M. Trueblood prof. acctg. and econs. Tepper Sch. Bus., 1975-87, 1987—. Cons. Gulf Oil Corp., Pitts., 1968-85. Co-author: Skew Distributions and the Sizes of Business Firms, 1977, Kohlers Dictionary for Accountants, 6th edit., 1983, New Directions in Creative and Innovative Management, 1988; author: Momentum Accounting and Triple-Entry Bookkeeping, 1989; editor: Creative and Innovative Approaches to the Science of Management, 1993. Named inductee Acctg. Hall of Fame, Ohio State U., 1989. Fellow Acctg. Researchers Internat. Assn. (pres. 1979-81); mem. Am. Acctg. Assn. (pres. 1982-83, Outstanding Educator 1987), Fin. Execs. Inst. (chpt. bd. dirs. 1977-81), Beta Alpha Psi. Home: 5 Bayard Rd Apt 118 Pittsburgh PA 15213-1904 Office: Tepper Sch Bus Carnegie Mellon U Pittsburgh PA 15213 Business E-Mail: ijiri@cmu.edu.

IKARD, FRANK NEVILLE, JR., lawyer; b. Wichita Falls, Tex., June 26, 1942; s. Frank Neville and Jean (Hunter) I.; children: Frank III, Jean, Charles; m. Kathleen P. Ikard, Feb. 14, 1998. BA, U. Tex., 1965, JD, 1968. Bar: Tex. 1968; cert. Tex. Estate Planning and Probate Law Bd. of Legal Specialization. Assoc. then ptnr. Clark, Thomas, Winters, & Shapiro, Austin, Tex., 1968-84; mng. ptnr. Jenkens & Gilchrist, Austin, 1985-88; ptnr. Johnson & Gibbs, Austin, 1988-92, Ikard & Golden, Austin, 1992—. Bd. dirs. Paramount Theatre, Austin, 1988-89, pres. bd. dirs., 1991-92; mem. Greater Austin Crime Commn. Fellow Am. Coll. Probate Counsel, Tex. Bar Found.; mem. Am. Coll. Trust and Estate Coun. (fiduciary litigation com. 1991-2001), Tex. Acad. Real Estate (pres. probate and trust law coun. 1988-89), State Bar Tex. (chmn., sec.-treas. legis. com. real estate, probate trust law sect. 1983-84, coun. chmn.), Travis County Bar Assn., Tarry House, Headliners, U. Tex. Club. Avocations: fly fishing, photography. Home: 1102 Claire Ave Austin TX 78703 Office: Ikard and Golden 400 W 15th St 975 Austin TX 78701-1600 Office Phone: 512-472-2884. Business E-Mail: fni@ikardgolden.com.

IKAWA-SMITH, FUMIKO, anthropologist, educator; arrived in Canada, 1960; d. Jokei and Sachi Ikawa; m. Takao Sofue, Jan. 1955 (div. 1958); m. Philip Edward Lake Smith, Nov. 1959; 1 child, Douglas Philip Edward. BA, Tsuda Coll., Tokyo, 1953; student Tokyo Met. U., 1954-55; AM in Anthropology, Radcliffe Coll., 1958; PhD in Anthropology, Harvard U., 1974. Asst. prof. McGill U., Montreal, 1968—74, assoc. prof., 1974—79, chmn. dept. anthropology, 1975—80, prof., 1979—2003, dir. Ctr. East Asian Studies, 1983—88, chmn. dept. East Asian langs. and lits., 1983—88, assoc. acad. vice prin., 1991—96. Vis. prof. Canadian studies Kwansei Gakuin U., Japan, 1996-97. Editor: Early Palaeolithic in South and East Asia, 1978, Proc. of First Meeting of The Social Scis. Assn. Can., 1989; mem. editl. bd. Anthrop. Sci., 1998-2002. Decorated Order Sacred Treasure, Gold Rays with Rosette Japan. Fellow Am. Anthrop. Assn. (exec. at-large archeology divsn. 1988-90), Current Anthropology (assoc.); mem. Pacific Sci. Assn. (life), Soc. Am. Archeology, Soc. for East Asian Archaeology (pres. 2004—), Japan Studies Assn. Can. (acting pres. 1988-90, pres. elect 1998-99, pres. 1999-2000, 04—), Indo-Pacific Prehistory Assn. (exec. com. 1990-98), Can. Asian Studies Assn. (chair Japan com. 1991-94), Quebec-Japan Bus. Forum (bd. 1998-2000). Avocations: horticulture, piano. Home: 3955 Ramezay Ave Montreal PQ Canada H3Y 3K3 Office: McGill U Dept Anthropology 855 Sherbrooke St W Montreal PQ Canada H3A 2T7 Office Phone: 514-398-4300. E-mail: fumiko.ikawa-smith@mcgill.ca.

IKE, JUSTUS, biology professor; arrived in US, 1972; s. John and Selina Ike; m. Ojiugo Ike, Nov. 20, 1979; 1 child, Uloma. BA in Biology, Dana Coll., Blair, Nebr., 1975; MS in Biology, Atlanta U., 1979, PhD in Biology, 1984. Asst. prof. Fisk U., Nashville, 1984—89, assoc. prof., 1989—, asst. prof. United Negro Coll. Fund Premedical, 1985—93, acting chmn. dept. biology, 2003—07. Vis. prof. Vanderbilt U., Nashville, 1992, Nashville, 1993—94. Grantee, Nat. Inst. Child Health and Human Devel., 2000, Army Rsch. Office, 2004. Office: Fisk Univ 1000 17th AVe North Nashville TN 37208

IKEDA, CLYDE JUNICHI, plastic and reconstructive surgeon; b. Kobe, Japan, 1951; s. Paul Tamotsu and Kazu Ikeda. BA, SUNY, Binghamton, 1973; MD, N.Y. Med. Coll., Valhalla, 1979. Resident St. Vincent Hosp., NYC, 1979-83, Francis Meml. Hosp., San Francisco, 1983-86; med. dir. Burn Ctr. St. Francis Meml. Hosp., San Francisco, 1992—2001, med. examiner, 1993—, med. dir. Wound Healing Ctr., 1994—2001; dir. Hosp. de la Familie, 2000—06, v.p., med. dir., 2006—. Asst. clin. prof. plastic surgery U. Calif., San Francisco, 1998-2003, assoc. clin. prof. plastic surgery, 2003—; adj. clin. prof. surgery Stanford Sch. Medicine, 2004—. Recipient Edward Weisband Disting. Alumni award, Binghamton U., 2003, medal of honor, Alumni Assn. N.Y. Med. Coll., 2004. Fellow ACS. Office: 1199 Bush St Ste 640 San Francisco CA 94109-5977

IKEDA, KAZUYOSI, physicist, poet; b. Fukuoka, Japan, July 15, 1928; s. Yosikatu and Misao (Misumi) I.; m. Mieko Akiyama, Nov. 20, 1956; children: Hiroko Ikeda Yamaguti, Yosihumi. 1st degree Rigakusi, Kyushu U., Fukuoka, Japan, 1951, DSc, 1957; D Environ. Sci. (hon.), Internat. Earth Environment U., 1993; DLitt (hon.), London Inst. Applied Rsch., 1995; diploma of honor, Inst. Affaires Internat., 1995, European Acad. Arts, 1999, Internat. Assn. Educators World Peace, 1999, Internat. Rels., 1999, Inst. Intercultural Studies Ala., 1999; DSc (hon.), World Acad., 1995; DHum honoris causa, Intl Acad. Culture/Polit. Sci., 1999. Asst. dept. physics Kyushu U. Faculty Sci., Fukuoka, 1956-60, assoc. prof. dept. physics, 1960-65; assoc. prof. dept. applied physics Osaka (Japan) U. Faculty Engring., 1965-68, prof. theoretical physics dept. applied physics, 1968-89, prof. theoretical and math. physics dept. math. scis., 1989-92, prof. emeritus, 1992—. Pres. Internat. Earth Environment U., Japan, 1995—, prof. theoretical physics, 1992—; bd. adv. coun. Ansted U., 1999—; prof. Internat. Assn. Educators for World Peace, 1999—. Author: ter Haar's Thermostatistics, 1960, Modern Developments in Thermodynamics, 1974, Statistical Thermodynamics, 1975, Mechanics Without Use of Mathematical Formulae--From a Moving Stone to Halley's Comet, 1980, Invitation to Mechanics--From the Fundamentals of Calculus to the Motion of a Comet, with Appendix on a comet in ancient times, 1985, (collection of poems) Bansyoo Hyakusi, 1986, Basic Mechanics, 1987, Basic Thermodynamics--From Entropy to Osmotic Pressure, 1991, The World of God, Creation and Poetry, 1991, Poems on the Hearts of Creation, 1993, Mountains, 1995, North South East and West, 1996, Graphical Theory of Relativity, 1998, Hearts of Myriad Things in the Universe, 1998, Kazuyosi's Poetry on the Animate and the Inanimate, 1998, Poems on Love and Peace, 1998, Songs of the Soul, 1999, Hearts of Innumerous Things in Heaven and Earth, 2000, Kazuyosi's Poems on Myriad Things-For Global Brotherhood and World Peace, 2001, The World of Hearts, 2002, Peace Offerings, 2003, Men and Nature, 2003, Spring Rain, 2003, Universal Songs, 2004, Paeans to Spirit, 2004, Journeys of Heart, 2005, Rainbows to Flowers, 2005; editor Modern Poetry, 1996—; contbr. more than 100 articles to sci. profl. jours.; author serialized poems of seven and five syllable metre, more than 30 lit. books, more than 60 lit. articles, reviews, and essays on poetry; haiku, tanka, Chinese classical fixed-form poetry; translations of Shakespeare's Sonnets into Japanese poems in seven and five syllale metre. Hon. founder, Japan rep. Olympoetry Movement, 1992—. Recipient Yukawa Commemorative Scholarship award Yukawa Found., 1954, World Biographical Hall of Fame award Hist. Preservations Am., 1990, prize Catania e il suo Vulcano, Accademia Ferdinandea Sci. Lettere Arti, 1994, Order of Good Neighbors, Olympoetry Movement Fund, 1996, Albert Einstein Acad. Cert. award for outstanding achievement Albert Einstein Internat. Acad. Found., 1998, Internat. Artistic-Literary prize of Primavera Catanase, Accademia Ferdinandea, Sci. Lettere Arte, 1997, Pandit prize Indian Coun. Natural Medicine Rsch., 1999, Diplome de Reconnaisance Edn. Ecologique, Assn. Internat. des Educateus pour la Paix Mondiole, 1999, Diplome ad Honores, Acad. Europeene des Arts, 1999, Diploma of Honor, Internat. Assn. Educators for World Peace, 1999, Diploma in Internat. Rels. Inst. for Internat. Rels. and Intercultural Studies of Ala. U., 1999, Prize Oscar 2000, Accademia Ferdinandea Sci. Lettere Arte, 2000, Gran Premio d'Autore, Edizioni U., 2000, New Millennium Michael Madhusuden award for best poetry Michael Madhusuden Acad., 2000, Oscar prize, 2000, Accademia Ferdinandea Sci. Lettere Arte, 2000, New Millenium Michael Madhusudan award Best Poetry Michael Madhusudan Acad., 2000, Netaj Subbash Chandra Bose Nat. award for Excellence in field of poetry and environ. sci. Jagruthi Kiran Found., 2001, Internat. Lit. prize Libro d'Oro Edizioni U., 2001; named Knight of Yr., Internat. Writers and Artists Assn., 1995, Knight Templar Order, Lofsensic Ursinius Order, Holy Grail Order, Universal Knights Order, San Ciriaco Order, 1995, Order of Pegasus Highest Degree, Olympoetry Movement Fund, 1996, Pandit prize, Indian Coun. of Natural Medicine and Rsch., 1999, Cultural Doctorate in Poetical Lit., World U. Roundtable, 1999, Best World Poet of Yr. award Poets Internat., 1999, Poet of Millennium award Internat. Poets Acad., 2000, Grand prize author Edizioni Universum, 2000, Netaji Subbash Chandra Bose Nat. award excellence in poetry and environ. sci. Jigruthi Kiran Found., 2001, Premio Letterario Internat., Global Peace and Friendship award India-European Union Friendship Soc., 2001, Knight Commander of Sovereign Order of Ambrosini's, 2001, Ivory Eagle award Home of Letters, 2001, Sphatika (India) Internat. Poet award Supreme Governing Body of Sphatika Prakashana, 2001, Internat. Peace prize United Cultural Conv. USA, 2002, Mandakini Lit. award Internat. Poetry Soc. Bareilly, 2002, Excellence in World Poetry award Internat. Poets Acad., 2002, Voice of Kolkata award Kolkata Lit. Soc., 2003; decorated Knight comdr. Sovereign Order of Ambrosini's, 2001. Libro d'Oro Edizioni Universum, 2001, Golden Book Internat. prize for Sto Mikrokosmo, Edizioni U., 2003, Star of Asia award Poets Internat., 2003, Master Diploma Special Honours in Science and Poetry, World Acad. Letters, 2004, Einstein Chair of Science award, World Acad. Letters, 2004, Silver Book Prize for Universal Songs, Edizioni Universum, 2004, Author of the Year award, Edizioni Universum, 2004, Golden Pen prize, Edizioni Universum, 2004, Omaggio a Dennis Kann Internat. Poetry Prize, Edizioni Universum, 2004, Award of Homage to Dante Alighieri for the Poetical Work Rainbows, 2004, Award of Alessandra Manzoni for Poetical Work Buddhist Images, Edizioni Universum, 2005, Region of Honor award, United Cultural Convention, 2005. Fellow United Writers' Assn. (life), World Lit. Acad. (life), Internat. Poets Acad. (life, Internat. Eminent Poet award 1993); mem. NY Acad. Scis., Am. Biog. Inst. Rsch. Assn. (dep. gov. 1989—, continental gov. 1998—), World Inst. Achievement (life), Lifetime Achievement Acad. (life, Golden Acad. award 1991), Phys. Soc. Japan (com. mem. 1970—, exec. com. centenary 1976-77, chmn. Osaka br. 1976-77, 83-84, editor jour. 1976-78), Internat. Biog. Assn. (life patron 1990-, bd. govs. 2004-), Internat. Biog. Ctr. (dep. dir. gen. 1989—, vice consul 2002—), World Acad. Arts and Culture (life), World Congress of Poets (life), Confedn. Chivalry (mem. grand coun. 1991—, Chevalier Grand Cross 1991), Accademia Ferdinandea Scienze Lettere Arti (academician of honor 1994—), Order Internat. Fellowship (charter 1994—), World Parnassians Guild Internat. (hon. dir. 1995—), Acad. M.I.D.I. (senator 1995—), Coun. of States for Protection of Life (senator 1995—, minister plenipotentiary for Asian States 1999—), Academia Argentina (academician 1995—), Internat. Parliament for Safety and Peace (Medalla al Merito 1995, senator 1999—, Minister plenipotentiary for Japan 1999—), Modern Poets Soc. (bd. dir. 1996—), Modern Poetry (editor 1996-), Rock Pebbles (editor, 2004—), Titas (editl. advisor 2005—), Accademia Internazionale Trinacria Lettere-Arte-Scienze (academician of merit 1997—), Leading Intellectuals of the World (founding charter mem. 1998—), Sci. Fac. Cambridge (founder mem. 2000-), Metverse Muse (lit. life chief patron, 2000-), Internat. Govs. Club, London Diplomatic Acad. (founder 2000—), Planet Soc., Profs.-Students Coalition Unification North East West South (chmn. Osaka U. br. 1987—), Profs. World Peace Acad. (dir. Osaka br. 1988—), Nat. Coalition Unification North East West South (chmn. Osaka br. 1988—), World Peace Acad. (academician 1999—), Academie Scientifique Internat. Vie Univers (sci. academician environ. scis. 1999—), Academia Ecologia (hon. 1999—), Internat. Poetry for Peace Assn. (regional coord. Japan and Asia Pacific 2000—), Jagruthi Kiran Found. (hon. life 2000—), Am. Order of Excellence (founding mem. 2000—), Michael Madhusudan Acad. (chief exec. 2001—), Karuna India Soc. (patron-in-chief 2001—), Chetana Lit. Group (patron-in-chief 2001—), Katha Kshetre (patron 2001—), Inst. der Affaires Internationales (corr. mem., rep. Japan 2002—), Internat. Honour Soc. (founding mem. 2002—), Home of Letters (chief patron 2002-), Voice of Kolkata (patron-in-chief 2003-), Acad. Indo-Asian Lit. (hon. fellow mem 2003-), Brain Wave English Lit-Q (patron 2002-), Creative Writing Criticism Acad.(adv. bd. 2003-), Titiksha (editl. bd. 2003-), Rsch. Soc. Communication in English (hon. adv. bd 2003-), Internat. Writers and Artists Assn. (dir. 2004-), Comissione di Lettera Internat. (exec. mem. 2004-), OMEGA Welfare Organization (patron-in-chief 2004-), Cyberwit Net. Home: Nisi-7-7-11 Aomadani Minoo-si Osaka 562-0023 Japan Office: Osaka U Fac Engring Dept Math Scis 2-1 Yamadaoka Suita-si Osaka 565-0871 Japan

IKEDA, TSUGUO (IKE IKEDA), retired social services administrator; b. Portland, Oreg., Aug. 15, 1924; s. Tom Minoru and Tomoe Ikeda; m. Sumiko Hara, Sept. 2, 1951; children: Wanda Amy, Helen Mari, Julie Ann, Patricia Kiyo. BA, Lewis & Clark Coll., Portland, 1949; MSW, U. Wash., Seattle, 1951. Social group worker Neighborhood House, Seattle, 1951-53; exec. dir. Atlantic St. Ctr., Seattle, 1953-86; pres. Urban Partnerships, Seattle, 1986-88, Tsuguo "Ike" Ikeda and Assoc., Seattle, 1988—2004; ret., 2004. Cons. Commn. on Religion and Race, Washington, 1973, North Northeast Mental Health Ctr., Portland, 1985, others; affirmative action cons. NASW, Washington, 1977; conf. coord. Beyond the Mask of Denial Wash. State Conf. on Drug/Alcohol/Substance Abuse in the Asian/Pacific Islander Cmtys., 1993; coord. Minority Mental Health Colloquium in Wash., 1994-95; coord. Asian Pacific Islander Coming Home Together Summit-95, Tacoma, Asian Pacific Bi-Ann. Leadership Conf., 1995-96, craftsmanship trainer, 1996-98; Tsuguo "Ike" Ikeda, Pub. Svc. ann. award established in 1987; trainer region II Dept. Children and Family Svcs., Yakima, Wash., 1997, API Cons. and Tng. Project, 1998. Author: Ike's Principles, 2007. Mem. Nat. Task Force to develop standards and goals for juv. delinquency, 1976; mem. Gov.'s Select Panel for social and health svcs., Olympia, Wash., 1977; chmn. Asian Am. Task Force, Community Coll., Seattle dist., 1982, King County Coordinated Health Care Initiative Client Edn., Mktg. Subcom., 1993; div. chmn. social agys. Seattle United Way campaign, 1985; vice-chmn. Wash. State Com. on Vocat. Edn., Olympia, 1985-86, chmn. 1986-87; chmn. regional adv. com. Dept. Social and Health Svcs., 1990-91; mem. Gov. Mike Lawry's Commn. on Ethics Govt., Campaign Practices, 1993—; mem. exec. task force King County Dept. Youth Svcs., 1996-97. With Mil. Intelligence Lang. Sch., 1945-46. Decorated Presdl. Unit Citation Spl. Svcs. U.S. Army Mil. Intelligence Svc.; named Cmty. Treasure, United Way of King County, 1996; recipient cert. appreciation, U.S. Dept. Justice, Washington, 1975—76, Am. Dream award, Cmty. Coll. Dist., Seattle, 1984, Asian Counseling & Referral Svc., 1991, 1995, Wing Lake Mus., 1991—92, Atlantic St. Ctr., 1992, Seattle Chinese Post, 1992, Bishop's award, U. Meth. Ch., Tacoma, Wash., 1984, Cmty. Svc. award, Seattle Rotary Club, 1985, Outstanding Citizen award, Mcpl. League, Seattle and King County, 1986, Outstanding Leadership award, Dept. Social and Health Svcs., 1993, Cmty. award, South Pacific Islander Program Seattle Pub. Schs., 1993, Pasasalmat award, Filipino Youth Activities, 1993, Brass Ring award, Asian Am. Polit. Alliance, 1993, Comm. Svc. award, Asian Counseling and Referral Svc., 1994, award, Gen. Bd. Global Ministries, United Meth. Ch., 1995, Disting. Alumnus award, Multicultural Alumni Partnership U. Wash. Alumni Assn., 1996, Alvirita Little Svc. award, Therapeutic Health Svc., 1999, Nordstrom Cmty. award, 1999, U.S. Presdl. Unit citation for meritorious svcs., Mil. Intelligence Svc., 2001, Local Hero award, Bill and Melinda Gates Found., United Way Campaign, 2001, Disting. Alumnus award, U. Wash. Sch. Social Work, 2005, Nonprofit Assistance Ctr. award, 2006. Mem. NASW (chpt. pres., Social Worker of Yr. 1971, Social Work Pioneer 1995), Vol. Agy. Exec. Coalition (pres., Outstanding Cmty. Svc. award 1979), Ethnic Minority Mental Health Consortium (chmn., Outstanding Leader 1992, David E. "Ned" Skinner Cmty. Svc. award 1990), Minority Exec. Dirs. Coalition (organizer, mem. chmn. 1980-86), U. Wash. Nikkei Alumni Assn.(Disting. Alumnus award, 2005). Democrat. Methodist. Avocations: stamp collecting/philately, World War II memorabilia.

IKENBERRY, HENRY CEPHAS, JR., lawyer; b. Cloverdale, Va., Mar. 23, 1920; s. Henry Cephas and Bessie (Peters) I.; m. Margaret Sangster Henry, July 3, 1943; children: Anna Catherine Ikenberry Fawell, Mary Margaret Ikenberry Rauck. BA, Bridgewater Coll., 1947; JD, U. Va., 1947. Bar: Va. 1947, W.Va. 1948, D.C. 1948, U.S. Supreme Ct. 1954, U.S. Ct. Claims 1972, U.S. Ct. Appeals (fed. cir.) 1982. Asso. firm Steptoe & Johnson, Washington, 1947-49, 50-53, partner, former chmn. exec. com., 1953-85, of counsel, 1986-92; asst. counsel Gen. Aniline & Film Co., NYC, 1949-50. Mem. com. on unauthorized practice D.C. Ct. Appeals, 1972-76. Ruling elder Chevy Chase Presbyn. Ch., Washington, 1970-72; trustee Mary Baldwin Coll., Staunton, Va., 1979-92, mem. exec. com., 1987-92; life mem., dean's counsel U. Va. Sch. Law; hon. trustee Bridgewater Coll., 2000—. Lt. comdr. USNR, 1941-46, ETO, PTO, Okinawa, The Philippines. Recipient Alumni citation Bridgewater Coll., 1960; named Ky. col., 1973 Mem. Bar Assn. D.C. (chmn. com. on corp. law 1960-61, com. comml. bus. law 1969-72), Raven Soc., Am. Legion, Metropolitan Club, Chesapeake Bay Yacht Club, Chevy Chase Club, Talbot Country Club (Easton, Md.), Order of Coif, Phi Delta Phi, Tau Kappa Alpha. Home: Pine Lodge 26783 Miles River Rd Easton MD 21601-5013 also: PO Box 1518 Easton MD 21601-8929

IKENBERRY, STANLEY OLIVER, education educator, director, former university president; b. Lamar, Colo., Mar. 3, 1935; s. Oliver Samuel and Margaret (Moulton) Ikenberry; m. Judith Ellen Life, Aug. 24, 1958; children: David Lawrence, Steven Oliver, John Paul. BA, Shepherd Coll., 1956; MA, Mich. State U., 1957, PhD, 1960, LHD (hon.); LLD (hon.), Millikin U.; LHD (hon.), Millkin U., Ill. Coll., Rush U., W.Va. U., Towson State U., U. Nebr., Bridgewater Coll., Va., Bradley U., Shepherd Coll., Roosevelt U., Juniatta Coll., Pa., 2003, Northeastern U. Instr. office evaluation svc. Mich. State U., 1958—60, instr. instl. rsch. office, 1960—62; asst. to provost for instl. rsch., asst. prof. edn. W.Va. U., 1962—65, dean coll. human resources and edn., assoc. prof. edn., 1965—69; prof., assoc. dir. ctr. study higher edn. Pa. State U., 1969—71, sr. v.p., 1971—79; pres. U. Ill., Urbana, 1979—95, pres. emeritus, Regent prof., 1995—; pres. Am. Coun. on Edn., Washington, 1996—2001. Bd. dirs. Aquila Inc., Kans. City; pres. bd. overseers Tchrs. Ins. and Annutiy Assn./Coll. Retirement Equities Fund. Named hon. alumnus, Pa. State U. Fellow: Am. Acad. Arts and Scis.; mem.: Cosmos Club (Washington), Comml. Club Chgo. Office: U Ill 347 Education 1310 S 6th St Champaign IL 61820

IKLÉ, FRED CHARLES, former federal agency administrator, policy advisor, defense expert; b. Fex, Switzerland, Aug. 21, 1924; s. Fritz A. and Hedwig M. (Huber) I.; m. Doris Eisemann, Dec. 23, 1959; children: Judith, Miriam. MA in Social Sci, U. Chgo., 1948, PhD in Sociology, 1950. Rsch. assoc. Columbia Bur. Applied Social Rsch., 1950—53; mem. social sci. dept. Rand Corp., Santa Monica, Calif., 1954—61, head social sci. dept., 1968—72; research assoc. Ctr. for Internat. Affairs Harvard U., 1962-63; prof. polit. sci. Mass. Inst. Tech., 1964-67; dir. U.S. ACDA, Washington, 1973-77; chmn. Conservation Mgmt. Corp., 1978-81, 88—; under-sec. for policy Dept. Def., Washington, 1981-88; Disting. scholar Ctr. for Internat. and Strategic Studies, 1988—. Mem. Dept. Def. Policy Bd.; mem. Nat. Com. on Terrorism, 1999-00, Gov. Smith Richardson Found., 1996—; dir. U.S. Com. for Human Rights in North Korea. Author: The Social Impact of Bomb Destruction, 1958, How Nations Negotiate, 1964, Every War Must End, 1971, 3d edit., 2005, Annihilation From Within, 2006. Mem. Internat. Inst. Strategic Studies, Coun. Fgn. Rels., Met. Club. Republican. Home: 7010 Glenbrook Rd Bethesda MD 20814-1223 Office: Ctr Strategic & Internat Studies 1800 K St NW Washington DC 20006-2202 Personal E-mail: guichet2@comcast.net.

IKLÉ, RICHARD ADOLPH, lawyer; b. Mineola, NY, Mar. 25, 1930; s. Adolph M. and Ruth Clark; children: Roger Scott, Lisa Kristina, Richard Keith. BA, Amherst Coll., 1953; JD, Columbia U., 1960. Bar: N.Y. 1961, Fla. 1975. Ptnr. Thacher, Proffitt & Wood, NYC., 1960—90; supervisory counsel FDIC, NYC, NJ, Washington, 1990—. Deacon Cmty. Ref. Ch., Manhasset, NY, 1975—80, elder, 1980—82. Lt. USNR, 1953—56. Mem.: ABA, Fla. Bar Assn., N.Y. State Bar Assn., Manhasset Bay Yacht Club (Port Washington, N.Y.), Phi Delta Phi. Avocations: sailing, hiking.

IKOSSI, KIKI, electrical and computer engineer; b. Nicosia, Cyprus, Dec. 23, 1954; came to U.S., 1978; d. George J. and Margarita K. (Vavlitis) Ikossi; children: Georgia-Charithea, Michael-George. BSEE, Nat. Tech. U., Athens, Greece, 1977; MS, U. Cin., 1982, PhD, 1986. Rsch./tchg. asst. U. Cin., 1980-86; sr. rsch. scientist Universal Energy Sys., Dayton, Ohio, 1986-90; asst. prof. elec. and computer engring. La. State U., Baton Rouge, 1990-96, tenured assoc. prof., 1996-99; rsch. elec. engr. Naval Rsch. Lab., Washington, 1999—2003; pres. I-Cube, 2003—; prof. George Mason U., Fairfax, Va., 2004—. Rsch. fellow Navy-Am. Soc. Engring. Edn. Naval Rsch. Lab., Washington, 1991—99; rsch. fellow US Dept. Commerce, 2000—, tech. adv., 2006—; reviewer NSF, NASA, ASEE, LEQSF, Washington, 1993—; sr. summer faculty rsch. fellow Naval Rsch. Lab., Washington, 1992—98; evaluator ABET. Contbr. articles to profl. publs. Recipient 7 awards for contbns., Am. Soc. Engring. Edn./Navy, 1991—98, DON Contbn. award, 1999, 2000, Tech. Transfer award, 2000, 2001, Alan Berman Outstanding Rsch. Publs. award, US Navy, 1998, Individual Invention award, 2003; fellow U. Cin. coun. rsch., 1982, 1983, 1979—85; grantee USN, La. Quality Support Edn., 1991—; Rsch. grant, NSF. Mem.: AAUW, AAIP, AAAS, IEEE (sr.; reviewer 1991—99, mem. tech. program com. IMS MTTS 1996—, co-chmn. 1999—2002, sec. dir. program MTTS Wash., N.Va. chpt. 1999—2002, IMS PA competition organizer 2003—04, sec. 2004, treas. 2005, vice chair 2006, chair Washington sect. 2007, chmn. subcom. high power devices MTT, chair IMS TPC high power), Women in Engring. (vice chair 2001—02, Washington area affinity group vice chair 2002—03, chair 2003), Electrochem. Soc. Metall., N.Y. Acad. Sci., Washington Acad. Sci. (founding mem.), Am. Soc. Engring. Edn., Assn. Women in Sci., Soc. Women Engrs. Achievements include refinement of method of moments for deep level transient spectroscopy studies in Semiconductors Devices on explorildory materials; one of the first scientists to incorporate antimonides in III-V compound microelectronic devices; two patents in process; patentee indium phosphide microelectronic device processing. Office: 6275 Gentle Ln Alexandria VA 22310-2260 Office Phone: 703-960-0261. E-mail: ikossi@ieee.org.

IKOUEBE, BASILE, ambassador; b. July 1, 1946; married; 6 children. Student, Internat. Inst. Pub. Adminstrn., Paris, Inst. Polit. Studies, Bordeaux, France. Chief internat. orgns. divsn. Ministry Fgn. Affairs Govt. Republic of the Congo, 1974, prin. pvt. sec. to min. fgn. affairs, 1975—77, sec. to Ministry Fgn. Affairs, 1977—79, trainee France, 1980—82, diplomatic advisor to head of state, 1982—92, min., prin. pvt. sec. to head of state, 1987, amb.-at-large, 1994—95, sec. Ministry Fgn. Affairs and Cooperation, 1996—98, amb., permanent rep. to UN NYC, 1998—. Office: Permanent Mission of Republic of the Congo to UN 14 E 65th St New York NY 10021 Office Phone: 212-744-7840. Office Fax: 212-744-7975. E-mail: congo@un.int.

IKUTA, SANDRA SEGAL, federal judge; b. LA, June 24, 1954; m. Ed Ikuta; 1 child. Student, Stanford U., 1972—74; AB, U. Calif. Berkeley, 1976; MS, Columbia U., 1978; JD, UCLA, 1988. Law clk. to Hon. Alex Kozinski US Ct. Appeals (9th Cir.), 1988—89; law clk. to Justice Sandra Day O'Connor US Supreme Ct., Washington, 1989—90; assoc. O'Melveny & Myers LLP, 1990—97, ptnr., 1997—2004; dep. sec., gen. counsel Calif. Resources Agy., 2004—06; judge US Ct. Appeals (9th cir.), 2006—. Office: US Ct Appeals 95 Seventh St San Francisco CA 94103*

ILACQUA, ROSARIO SALVATORE, securities analyst; b. Albany, NY, Aug. 12, 1927; s. Anthony and Carmela (Gerasia) I. BS, Siena Coll., 1950; MS, Columbia U., 1955. Chartered fin. analyst. With L.F. Rothschild, NYC, 1957-87, ptnr., 1972-87; with Nikko Securities, 1987-90, Rothschild Inc., 1990-99, Monness, Crespi, Hardt & Co., 2000—. With USNR, 1945-46. Mem. Nat. Assn. Petroleum Investment Analysts (pres. 1977), N.Y. Soc. Security Analysts, Oil Analysts Group N.Y. (pres. 1972), Assn. for Investment Mgmt. and Rsch. (chmn. corp. info. com.), N.Y. Athletic Club. Home: 2 Horatio St Apt 15J New York NY 10014-1645 Office: 767 Third Ave New York NY 10017 Home Phone: 212-924-8925; Office Phone: 212-838-7575.

ILAGAN, ARTEMIO B., territorial agency administrator; Dir. Guam Dept. Revenue & Taxation; acting banking and ins. commr., securities adminstr., real estate commr., and tax commr. Office: Guam Dept Revenue & Taxation PO Box 23607 Barrigada GU 96921 Office Phone: 671-635-1817. Office Fax: 671-633-2643. E-mail: ilagan@revtax.gov.gu.

ILCHMAN, WARREN FREDERICK, academic and foundation administrator, educator; b. Denver, Sept. 6, 1933; s. Frederick Warren and Imogene (Trovinger) I.; m. Alice Crawford Stone, June 11, 1960; children: Frederick Andrew Crawford, Alice Sarah Crawford. BA, Brown U., 1955; PhD, Cambridge U., Eng., 1959. Asst. prof. Ctr. Devel. Econs. Williams Coll., Williamstown, Mass., 1960-64; from asst. prof. to prof. polit. sci. U. Calif., Berkeley, 1965-73, dir. Ctr. South and Southeast Asian Studies, 1970-73; vis. prof., rsch. assoc. Ctr. Population Studies, Harvard U., Cambridge, Mass., 1973-74; prof. polit. sci. and econs., dean arts and scis. Grad. Sch., Boston U., 1974-76; program adviser internat. divsn. Ford Found., NYC, 1976-80; v.p. for rsch. and grad. studies SUNY, Albany, 1980-83, provost Nelson A. Rockefeller Coll. Pub. Affairs and Policy, 1983-87, dir. Rockefeller Inst. Govt., 1983-87, exec. v.p., 1987-90; pres. Pratt Inst., Bklyn., 1990-93; exec. dir. ctr. Philanthropy Ind. Univ., Indpls., 1993-97; dir. Paul and Daisy Soros Found., NYC, 1998—. Author: Professional Diplomacy in the U.S, 1961, New Men of Knowledge and the Developing Nations, 1966, Professionals as Agents of Change, 1968, The Political Economy of Change, 1969, rev. edit., 1998 (translated into French, Spanish, Japanese, Hindi and Arabic), Political Economy of Development, 1972, Comparative Public Administration and The Conventional Wisdom, 1973, Policy Sciences and Population, 1975, Education and Employment: The Policy Nexus, 1976, New York in the Year 2000, 1986, Caring and Coping, 1986, Capacity to Change, 1997, Philanthropy and the World's Tradition, 1998, The Lucky Few and the Worthy Many: Selecting the World's Future Leaders, 2004. Bd. dirs. The Masters Sch., The Gen. Theol. Sem., Westchester Cmty. Found.; mem. Am. Friends of the Anglican Ctr. in Rome. Marshall scholar U.K.; recipient Harbison prize Danforth Found., 1969 Mem. Am. Soc. Pub. Adminstrn. (Burchfield award 1965), Asia Soc., Am. Polit. Sci. Assn., N.Y. Acad. Pub. Adminstrn. (Al Smith award), Assn. Asian Studies, Nat. Acad. Pub. Adminstrn., Univ. Club, Bronxville Field Club, Phi Beta Kappa. Episcopalian. Home: 18 Highland Cir Bronxville NY 10708-5908 Office: Paul and Daisy Soros Fellowship Program 400 W 59th St New York NY 10019-1105 Office Phone: 212-547-6926. Business E-Mail: wilchman@sorosny.org.

ILES, EILEEN MARIE, bank executive, risk management consultant, accountant; b. Highland Park, Ill., Sept. 29, 1965; d. Dennis Jay and Ida Sigrid (Calderelli) Connolly; m. Kenneth Robert Iles, Dec. 14, 1985; children: Kevin Andrew, Eric Robert. Student, U. Ill., Chgo., 1983—85; BBA in Acctg. and Mktg. Mgmt., U. N.Mex., 1988, M in Acctg., 1992. CPA. Acct. Charter Bank for Savs., Albuquerque, 1989-90, bank acctg. supr., 1990-91, asst. contr., 1991-2000, asst. v.p., 1992-2000; engagement mgr. Crowe Chizek & Co., LLC, Oak Brook, Ill., 2000, sr. engagement mgr., 2000—03, exec., 2003—. Instr. acctg. U. N.Mex., Albuquerque, 1994-99, Albuquerque Tech. Vocat. Inst., 2000; cons. in field. Mem.: Assn. Cert. Fraud Examiners, Inst. Internal Auditors, Inst. Mgmt. Accts. Office: One MidAm Plz PO Box 3697 Oak Brook IL 60522-3697 E-mail: eiles@crowechizek.com.

ILES, GREG, writer; b. Germany, 1960; Grad., U. Miss., 1983. Band founder Frankly Scarlet; guitarist Rock Bottom Remainders. Author: Spandau Phoenix, 1992, Black Cross, 1995, Mortal Fear, 1997, The Quiet Game, 1999, 24 Hours, 2000, Dead Sleep, 2001, Sleep No More, 2003, The Footprints of God, 2003, Blood Memory, 2005, Turning Angel, 2005. Mailing: Author Mail - Scribner Books Simon & Schuster 1230 Ave of Americas New York NY 10020

ILES, ROGER DEAN, business educator; b. Detroit, June 11, 1950; s. Virgil Llewellyn and Mary Elizabeth (Lynn) I.; m. Gail Ann Swatzell, Jan. 10, 1971; 1 child, Gwendolyn Christine. AA, Regents Coll., 1990; BS magna cum laude, Crichton Coll., 1992; MBA, U. Memphis, 1997. Enlisted USN, 1969, advanced through grades to chief electronics technician, 1969-89; ret., 1989; switchman Mich. Bell Telephone Co., Dearborn, 1968-69; controller, alumni advisor Crichton Coll., Memphis, 1989-99; faculty U. Memphis, 2005—. Adj. faculty Crichton Coll., Memphis, 1998—2005, U. Memphis, 1998—2005; chmn., mgr. Shade Tree Engring., Inc., Munford, Tenn., 1992—; online faculty U. Phoenix, 2003—05, faculty Memphis campus, 2003—05. Bd. dirs. U. Memphis Alumni Assn., 2004—. Mem.: Gideons Internat. (area dir., pres. Tipton County South Camp). Republican. Baptist. Avocations: auto racing, target shooting. Home: 59 Jennifer Cv Munford TN 38058-4056 Office: Fogelman Coll Business and Econs The Univ Memphis Memphis TN 38152 Office Phone: 901-678-3414. Business E-Mail: riles@memphis.edu.

ILETT, FRANK, JR., trucking executive, educator; b. Ontario, Oreg., June 21, 1940; s. Frank Kent and Lela Alice (Siver) I.; m. Donna L. Andlovec, Apr. 3, 1971; children: James Frank, Jordan Lee. BA, U. Wash., 1962; MBA, U. Chgo., 1969. CPA Idaho, Ill., Wash. Acct. Ernst & Young, Boise, Cleve., Spokane, 1962-69, mgr. Boise, 1970-72, regional mgr. San Francisco, 1972-73; treas. Interstate Mack, Inc., Boise, 1973-81, pres., CEO, 1981-82; pres. Interstate NationLease, Inc., Boise, 1975-81, Contract Carriers, Inc., Boise, 1983-89, Ilett Transp. Co., Boise, 1985-90; chmn. Carriers/West, Inc., Salem, Oreg., 1986-89; CFO, White GMC Trucks, 1988-92; v.p., CFO, May Trucking Co., Payette, Idaho, 1992-94; acct., mng. ptnr. F. Ilett, PLLC, Boise, 1994—. Spl. lectr. Boise State U., 1964-67, 94—, St. Mary's Grad. Sch., Moraga, Calif., 1989-92; cons. Calif. Hosp. Commn., 1973, Idaho Hosp. Assn., 1974; chmn. Mack Truck Western Region Distbr. Coun., 1979-82; nat. distbr. adv. com. Mack Trucks, Inc., 1980-82; dir. stds. enforcement Idaho State Bd. Accountancy, 1983-84; contr. Idaho Stampede, 2002—. Contbr. articles to profl. jours. Recipient Outstanding Prof. award KPMG, 2003, 05; named Arthur Andersen Outstanding Acctg. Prof., 1996, 2001 Mem.: Inst. Mgmt. Accts., SAR, Gen. Soc. Mayflower Descs., Crane Creek Country Club, Shriners, Masons, Alpha Kappa Psi (Outstanding Bus. Prof. award 1997, named Disting. Faculty Mem., Coll. Bus. 2002). Episcopalian. Home: 1701 Harrison Blvd Boise ID 83702-1015 Office: 1910 University Dr Boise ID 83725 Home Phone: 208-389-4624; Office Phone: 208-426-2568. Business E-Mail: filett@boisestate.edu.

ILGEN, DOROTHY L., arts foundation executive; Asst. dir. Mo. Arts Coun.; exec. dir. Kans. Arts Commn., Ind. Arts Commn., Indpls., 1995—. Active numerous coms. and commns. various local, state, regional, and nat. orgns.; bd. dirs. Mid-Am. Arts Alliance, Arts Midwest, mem. program planning com.; bd. dirs., mem. planning and budget com., nominating com. Nat. Assembly of State Arts Agys.; panelist arts design panel NEA, Nat. Access Task Force. Office: Indiana Arts Commission 150 W Market St Ste 618 Indianapolis IN 46204

ILICH, JASMINKA Z., dietician, educator; Registered dietitian Am. Dietetic Assn., 1991. Assoc. prof., dir. bone and mineral metabolism lab. U. Conn., Storrs, 1998—2005; prof. Fla. State U., Tallahassee, 2005—. Recipient Excellence in Rsch. award, U. of Conn., 2002, 2005; grantee, USDA, 2001—05, 2005—. Fellow: Am. Coll. Nutrition (life Best Rev. Paper award 2001); mem.: Am. Dietetic Assn., Am. Soc. Clin. Nutrition, Am. Soc. Bone and Mineral Rsch. Office: Florida State Univ 418 Sandels Bldg Tallahassee FL 32306-1493 Office Phone: 850-645-7177. Office Fax: 850-645-5000. Business E-Mail: jilichernst@fsu.edu.

ILIESCU, RADU, medical educator; MD, U. Medicine and Pharmacy, Iasi, 2001, PhD, 2005. Rsch. assoc. Max Delbruck Ctr. Molecular Medicine, Berlin, 2001—03; postdoctoral fellow U. Miss. Med. Ctr., Jackson, 2004—05, instr., 2005—. Fellow rsch. fellow, Ernst Schering Rsch. Found., 2000; Marie Curie fellow, EU, 2001—02. Mem.: Soc. Free Radical in Biology and Medicine, Am. Heart Assn., Am. Physiol. Soc. (postdoctoral fellow 2005—, Rsch. Recognition award water and electrolyte homeostasis sect. 2006, Caroline tum Suden Profl. Opportunity award 2005, 2007). Office: U Miss Med Ctr 2500 North State St Jackson MS 39216 Business E-Mail: riliescu@physiology.umsmed.edu.

ILINICH, OLEG, chemist, researcher; b. Zhabinka, Belarus, Sept. 7, 1947; s. Mikhail Georgievich and Valentina Mikhailovna Ilinich; m. Irina Nicole Kireyeva, Mar. 20, 2000; m. Galina Nikolaevna Linkova, Sept. 3, 1969 (div. Apr. 1, 1992); 1 child, Inna Olegovna. MS, Inst. Tech., Leningrad, USSR, 1969; PhD, Boreskov Inst. of Catalysis, Novosibirsk, Russia, 1978, DSc in Chemistry, 1997. Jr. rsch. scientist Boreskov Inst. of Catalysis, Novosibirsk, Russia, 1969—77, rsch. scientist, 1978—82, sr. rsch. scientist, 1987—96, lead rsch. scientist, 1997—2000; head rsch. lab. Rsch. Inst. of Chem. Industry, Novosibirsk, Russia, 1982—86; dir. rsch. Inst. of Rsch. in Catalysis, Villeurbanne, France, 2000—00; sr. chemist Engelhard Corp., Iselin, NJ, 2001—06, BASF Catalysts, LLC, Iselin, 2006—. Author: (chpt.) Annual Review of Materials Research, Polyphenylene Oxide and Modified Polyethylene Oxide Membranes; contbr. articles to profl. jours. Grantee, Internat. Sci. Found., 1992, Russian Found. for Basic Rsch., 1993-1994, Internat. Sci. Found., 1993-1994, Internat. Assn. Advancement Sci., 1994-1996, The Netherlands Orgn. for Sci. Rsch., 1997-1999, Russian Found. for Basic Rsch. and Internat. Assn. Advancement Sci., 1999-2000. Mem.: AIChE, Am. Chem. Soc. Achievements include patents for catalysis and separation membranes. Avocations: scuba diving, tennis, jogging. Home: 12 Kimberly Ct Monmouth Junction NJ 08852 Office: BASF Catalysts LLC 101 Wood Ave Iselin NJ 08830 Home Phone: 732-355-1180; Office Phone: 732-205-7043. Business E-Mail: oleg.ilinich@basf.com.

ILITCH, MARIAN, professional hockey team and food service executive; m. Michael Ilitch; children: Denise Ilitch Lites, Ron, Mike Jr., Lisa Ilitch Murray, Atanas, Christopher, Carole. Co-owner, sec.-treas. Little Caesar Internat., 1959—, Detroit Red Wings, 1982—; sec.-treas. Olympia Arenas, Inc. (Olympia Entertainment Inc.), 1982—; co-owner, sec.-treas. Fox Theatre, 1987—, Detroit Tigers, 1992—, Little Foxes Fine Gifts, 1992—, The Second City, 1993—, Olympia Devel. LLC, 1996—, Hockeytown Cafe, 1999—, Blue Line Distributing, Uptown Entertainment, Champion Foods; co-founder, vice-chmn. Ilitch Holdings, Inc., 1999—. Recipient Pacesetter Award, Roundtable for Women in Foodservice, 1988, Nat. Preservation Honor Award, 1990. Office: Ilitch Holdings Inc Fox Office Ctr 2211 Woodward Ave Detroit MI 48201-3400

ILITCH, MICHAEL, professional hockey team and food products executive; m. Marian Ilitch; children: Denise Ilitch Lites, Ron, Mike Jr., Lisa, Atanas, Christopher, Carole. Founder, owner Little Caesars Restaurant, 1959—; owner, pres. Detroit Red Wings Hockey Team, 1982—; founder Blue Line Distbg., Am.'s Pizza Cafe; owner Olympia Arenas, Inc. (formerly Olympia Stadium Corp.), 1983—, Adirondack Red Wings Hockey Team, Detroit Dir. of Arena Football League; owner, chmn., former pres. Detroit Tigers Baseball Team; chmn. Ilitch Holdings, Inc. Little Caesars Love Kitchen program, 1985—. With USMC, 4 yrs. Named one of 400 Richest Americans, Forbes mag.; named to Hockey Hall of Fame, 2003; recipient Lester Patrick trophy, 1991, Bus. Statesman award, Harvard Bus. Sch. Club Detroit, 1990, Joe Louis award, Sports Illustrated Mag. and Detroit Inst. Arts, Humanitarian of Yr. award, March of Dimes. Office: Detroit Red Wings 600 Civic Center Dr Detroit MI 48226-4419 also: Detroit Tigers Tiger Stadium 2100 Woodward Ave Detroit MI 48201-3470 also: Little Caesars Enterprizes 2211 Woodward Ave Detroit MI 48201-3467

ILKIN, BAKI, diplomat, Turkish government official; Turkish amb. to Copenhagen; spl. advisor to fgn. min. Govt. of Turkey; Turkish amb. to The Hague; Turkish amb. to USA Washington, 1998—; now acting undersecretary Ministry of Foreign Affairs, Ministry of Foreign Affairs Acting Undersecretary, Ankara, Turkey. Office: 821 United Nations Plaza 10t Fl New York NY 10017 Fax: 202-659-0744.

ILL, CHARLES, III, information technology executive; BS in Mech. Engring., Lehigh U., MBA in Fin. Sales and mktg. IBM, 1978—2003, former v.p. worldwide software geo. sales, mktg. and tech. team; exec. v.p. worldwide sales BEA Systems, Inc., San Jose, Calif., 2003—. Office: BEA Systems Inc 2315 N First St San Jose CA 95131

ILLANES, DIEGO SEBASTIAN, obstetrician, gynecologist; b. Cordoba, Argentina, Apr. 23, 1977; s. Luis Eduardo Illanes and Marta Lucia Vidal; m. Katarina Muckova, Feb. 25, 2005; 1 child, Julia. MD, Cath. U., Cordoba, 1999. Rsch. assoc. in medicine Brigham and Womens Hosp., Harvard Med. Sch., Boston, 2001—04; gross anatomy instr. Harvard Med. Sch., Boston, 2003—04; ob-gyn. intern physician Albany Med. Coll., NY, 2004—05; ob-gyn. resident physician U. Mass., Worcester, 2005—. Contbr. articles to profl. jours. Named Best Gross Anatomy Lab Instr. of Yr., Harvard Med. Sch., 2004, Berlex Tchg. award, U. Mass., 2006; recipient Gross Anatomy award, Cordoba Nat. U., 1995. Mem.: AMA, Am. Assn. Gyn. Laparoscopists (resident mem. 2005), Am. Coll. Ob-Gyn. (jr. fellow 2004). Office: Univ Mass Meml Med Ctr 119 Belmont St Jaquith 4 Worcester MA 01605 Home Phone: 508-254-5252; Office Phone: 508-334-1000. Business E-Mail: illanesd@ummhc.org.

ILLE, BERNARD GLENN, insurance company executive, director; b. Ponca City, Okla., Feb. 8, 1927; s. Frank Louis and Marie (Cornwell) Ille; m. Mary Lou Allen, Aug. 23, 1952; children: Meredith, Les, Frank. BBA in Fin., U. Okla., 1950. CLU. Agt. Phoenix Mutual Life, Hartford, Conn., 1950-54; gen. agt. Farmers and Bankers Life, Wichita, Kans., 1954-56; asst. v.p. agy. United Founders Life, Oklahoma City, 1956-58, agt. v.p., 1958-60, exec. v.p., dir. agy., 1960-66, pres., 1966-88, pres., CEO, 1988-94, First Life Assurance Co., Oklahoma City, 1994—; pres. BML Cons., Oklahoma City, 1994—; apptd. receiver Mid-Continent Life Ins. Co., Oklahoma City, 1999-2000. Chmn. audit com. LSB Industries, bd. dirs., Quail Creek Bank, chmn audit commn.; bd. dirs. Landmark Nat., Am. Stock Exch. Organizer Big Bros., Oklahoma City, 1960; past pres., organizer Nat. Football Found., Oklahoma City, 1969. Recipient Young Pres. Orgn. award, 1966, Kappa Alpha Man of Half Century award, U. Okla. Mem.: Exec. Svc. Corps. Okla. (chmn.), Okla. Assn. Life Ins. Cos. (past pres.), Okla. Life Ins. Guaranty Assn. (chmn. 1984—94), Kiawah Country Club (Kiawah Island, S.C.), Palm Beach Golf and Polo Club (West Palm Beach), Carmel (Calif.) Valley Golf and Country Club, La Quinta Golf and Country Club (Palm Springs), Petroleum Club, Oak Tree Golf and Country Club, Quail Creek Golf and Country Club (Okla. City, Okla.) (organizer), Order Knights of Holy Sepulchre. Democrat. Roman Catholic. Home: 11004 Magnolia Park Oklahoma City OK 73120-5210 Office: BML Cons PO Box 21080 Oklahoma City OK 73156-1080 Office Phone: 405-755-8404. Office Fax: 405-755-8289.

ILLES, GEORGE MAXIMILIAN, retired food products executive; b. St. Louis, Sept. 11, 1912; s. Arpad Enoch Illes and Mary Sylvina Martin; widowed; children: Eleanor Illes Carosella, George M. Jr. BA, Rice Inst., 1933. Co-owner, chmn. bd. Illes Seasoning and Flavors, Dallas, 1945—89, chmn. emeritus. Mem. Dallas Art Mus., 1960—90, Santa Fe Art Mus., 1991—2007, Houston Art Mus., 2002—07. Lt. USNR, 1941—45. Mem.: Am. Inst. Conservation, Dallas Country Club, Phi Beta Kappa. Roman Catholic. Avocations: art, painting, English tea caddies and artifacts. Office: 2200 Luna Rd Ste 120 Carrollton TX 75006

ILLNER-CANIZARO, HANA, physician, researcher, oral surgeon; b. Prague, Czechoslovakia, Nov. 2, 1939; came to U.S., 1968; d. Evzen Pospisil and Emilie (Chrastna) Pospisilova; m. Pavel Illner, June 14, 1963 (div. 1981); children: Martin Illner, Anna Illner; m. Peter Corte Canizaro, Nov. 1, 1982. MD, Charles U., Prague, 1961. Diplomate Am. Bd. Oral Surgery. Resident in oral surgery Inst. of Health, Pribram, Czechoslovakia, 1961-63; attending physician Oral Surgery Clinic, Prague, 1963-68; rsch. assoc. dept. surgery U. Tex. Southwestern Med. Sch., Dallas, 1969-72, instr. surgery, 1972-74, U. Wash. Sch. Medicine, Seattle, 1974-77; asst. prof. surgery Cornell U. Med. Coll., NYC, 1977-81, assoc. prof. surgery, 1981-83, Tex. Tech U. Health Scis. Ctr., Lubbock, 1984-88, prof. surgery, 1988—. Site visitor NIGMS Postdoctoral Tng. Grant, Bethesda, Md., 1987. Mem. editorial bd. Circulatory Shock, N.Y.C., 1981—; manuscript reviewer Surgery, Gynecology and Obstetrics, Chgo., 1985—; contbr. chpts. to books, articles to profl. jours. Grantee NIH, 1979-83, 87-92, Tex. Tech U. Health Scis. Ctr., 1985-86, U.S. dept. Army, 1988-90; Fogarty Sr. Internat. fellow, 1991-92. Mem. Shock Soc. Avocations: remodeling of historical homes, gardening, skiing, pottery. Home: 4622 8th St Lubbock TX 79416-4722 Office: Tex Tech U Health Scis Ctr 3601 4th St Lubbock TX 79430-0001

ILLSTON, SUSAN Y., federal judge; b. 1948; BA, Duke U., 1970; JD, Stanford U., 1973. Ptnr. Cotchett, Illston & Pitre, San Francisco, 1973-95; judge U.S. Dist. Ct. (no. dist.) Calif., San Francisco, 1995—. Author: Insurance Coverage in a Toxic Tort Case, A Guide to Toxic Torts, 1987, California Complex Litigation Manual, 1990. Active Legal Aid Soc. San Mateo County, Svc. League San Mateo County. Recipient Appreciation for Vol. Svcs. cert. No. Dist. Calif. Fed. Practice Program, 1989, Svc. and Appreciation cert. 1992. Mem. ABA, ATLA, Assn. Bus. Trial Lawyers, San Mateo County Bar Assn. (Eleanor Falvey award 1994), State Bar Calif. (mem. jud. coun., mem. ethics com. 1975-79, mem. com. on women in law 1985-87, mem. jud. nominees evaluation commn. 1988, mem. exec. com. on litigation 1990-93), Calif. Women Lawyers, Calif. Trial Lawyers Assn., Trial Lawyers for Pub. Justice. Office: US Dist Ct No Dist Calif PO Box 36060 450 Golden Gate Ave San Francisco CA 94102-3661

ILOGIENBOH, CAROLINE O., protective services official, publishing executive; b. Ubiaja, Edo, Nigeria, July 31, 1957; arrived in U.S., 1987; d. Augustine Asa and Esther Oniha Omoifo; m. Ephraim Eghehi Ilogienboh, Feb. 26, 1988; children: Ebinehita, Ofure, Nemedia. BA, U. Alta., Edmonton, Alta., Can., 1982. Cert. criminal justice counselor Addiction Profls. Cert. Bd NJ. Adminstrv. officer Nigerian Telecom., Lagos, 1983—87; social worker Cmty. Svc. N.J., East Orange, 1988—89; probation officer Superior Ct. N.J., East Orange, 1989—; pub. Sun Rose Pubs., East Orange, 2001—. Author: Jayda's Story-Lost at Crossroads, 2001, The Return of Tyreek, 2002, Nowhere to Hide, 2004, Hatcher's Room: Men Only, 2006, poetry. Mem. adv. bd. Minority Concerns Com., Newark, Essex County Coalition Teen Pregnancy, Sch. Based Com., Orange, NJ. Recipient Appreciation award, Probation Assn. N.J., Atlantic City, 2001. Mem.: Watchung Heights Neighborhood Assn. (program chair 1999—). Avocations: reading, travel, swimming, writing, sewing. Address: PO Box 2314 East Orange NJ 07019 Office: Essex Vicinage Probation Svcs 7th Fl 60 Evergreen Pl East Orange NJ 07018 Personal E-mail: carolineilo@yahoo.com.

ILSE-NEUMAN, URSULA, curator; d. Hermann Ilse and Charlotte Troeltsch; m. Lawrence Donald Neuman; 1 child, Andreas Neuman. BA, Hunter Coll., NY, 1977; MA, The New Sch., NYC, 1992; postgrad., Bard Graduate Ctr. Studies Decorative Arts, NYC, 1998—2002. Curator Mus. Arts and Design, NYC, 1992—. Exhbn. juror various nat. and internat. orgns.; curator Corporal Identity - Body Lang., 2003, essayist, 03. Curator, essayist, editor (book) Made in Oakland: The Furniture of Garry Knox Bennett, 2001, (exhbn. catalog) None That Glitters: Perspectives on Jewelry in the Donna Schneier Collection, 2002, Radiant Geometries: Fifteen International Jewelers, 2001; author: (exhbn. catalog) Cabinets of Curiosities: Cabinets of Wonder and Delight; curator, essayist, editor (exhbn. catalog) Corporal Identity-Body Language, 9th Triennial for Form and Content, USA and Germany, 2003; author: (exhbn. catalog) Treasures from the Vault: Contemporary Jewelry, Schmuck, 2006, Glass Wear, 2007, (Essay) Worthy of the Muses: The Furniture of John Eric Byers, 2001; contbr. essays and articles to publs., selections to exhbn. catalogs; curator, essayist, editor Six Continents of Quilts: The Museum of Arts & Design Collection, 2003; mem. editl. adv. bd.: Metalsmith Mag. Fellow, Bard Grad. Ctr., 1999—2002, 20th Century Visual Arts fellow, Grad. Ctr., CUNY, 1992. Mem.: Glass Art Soc., Coll. Art Assn., Am. Mus.Assn., Internat. Curators Assn., Art Table, Furniture Soc. (mem. adv. bd. 1999—2002), Phi Beta Kappa. Office: Mus Arts and Design 40 W 53d St New York NY 10019 Office Phone: 212-956-3535 x 119. Personal E-mail: ursula.neuman@madmuseum.org. Business E-Mail: uneuman@nyc.rr.com.

ILSON, BERNARD, public relations executive; b. NYC; s. Abraham and Goldie Itzkowitz; m. Carol Ruth Geller; children: David, James. BA, Bklyn. Coll.; MA, Columbia U.; PhD, NYU, 1998. Writer NBC TV, NYC, 1955-57, David Alber Assocs., NYC, 1957-58; v.p. Rogers, Cowan and Brenner, NYC, 1958-63; pres. Bernie Ilson, Inc., NYC, 1963—. Founder Hall Fame Am. Humor; past/present clients include Ed Sullivan Show, Beatles Shea Stadium, All in the Family, Monkees, Patridge Family, Grammy Awards, Entertainer Yr. Awards, Motown Records, Tony Bennett, Liberty Mut. Ins. Co., Control Data Corp., Am. Soc. Hypertension, Missoula Children's Theater, Silver Dollar City, Branson, Mo., Mack Ave. Records, Stax Records, Bell Records, Grand Ole Opry, Hee Haw, Negotiation Inst., Liberty Mut. Legends Golf, NBC TV Network, Simon and Schuster, City Mobile Tricentennial, Sister to Sister Found., Games Workshop, Marketplace series on pub. radio, Soupy Sales, Ken Burns Statue Liberty TV spl, Boston Pops 4th July TV spl., Ticketron, Candid Camera, Proctor & Gamble Corp., World Almanac, Sister to Sister Everyone Has a Heart Found., M.T.H. Electric Trains, Senior Bowl, Art of Negotiation (book). Watercolor artist: Bklyn. Mus. Biennial Watercolor Show, 1954; one-man shows: Keulik Gallery, NYC, Nemisis Galley, NYC; pub., founder Ilson's Inside Information, 1991—; guest appearances (Beatles expert) CBS-TV, ABC Radio Network, Westwood One Radio Network, CNN TV Network. Mem. Writers Guild Am., Acad. TV Arts and Scis., Country Music Assn., Mobile C. of C., Kappa Delta Pi. Clubs: Explorers. Avocations: painting, fishing. Office: 65 W 55th St New York NY 10019-4913 Home Phone: 212-319-7255; Office Phone: 212-245-7950. Personal E-mail: ilson@aol.com.

ILTIS, HUGH HELLMUT, botanist, educator, environmental advocate; b. Brno, Czechoslovakia, Apr. 7, 1925; arrived in US, 1939, naturalized, 1944; s. Hugo and Anne (Liebscher) I.; m. Grace Schaffel, Dec. 20, 1951 (div. Mar. 1958); children: Frank S., Michael George; m. Carolyn Merchant, Aug. 4, 1961 (div. June 1970); children: David Hugh, John Paul; m. Sharyn Wisniewski Nov. 3, 2006. BA, U. Tenn., 1948; MA, Washington U., St. Louis and Mo. Bot. Garden, 1950, PhD, 1952; PhD (hon.), U. Guadalajara, Mex., 2007. Rsch. asst. Mo. Bot. Garden, 1948-52; asst. prof. botany U. Ark., 1952-55; asst. prof. U. Wis.-Madison, 1955-60, assoc. prof., 1960-67, prof., 1967-93, prof. emeritus, 1993—, curator herbarium, 1955-67, dir. univ. herbarium, 1967-93, dir. emeritus, 1993—. Vis. prof. U. Va., Biol. Sta., 1959; expdns. to Costa Rica, 1949, 89, Peru, 1962-63, Mex., 1960, 71-72, 77-79, 81-82, 84, 87-88, 90, 93-96, Guatemala, 1976, Ecuador, 1977, St. Eustatius, P.R., 1989, USSR, 1975, 79, Nicaragua-Honduras, 1991, Venezuela, 1991, Hawaii, 1967; adv. bd. Flora N.Am., 1970-73, Gov. Wis. Commn. State Forests, 1972-73; rsch. assoc. Mo. Bot. Garden, Bot. Rsch. Inst. Tex.; co-instigator Reserva Biosfera Sierra de Manantlán, Jalisco, Mex.; lectr. in field. Co-author: Flora de Manantlan, Jalisco, Mexico, 1995, Siola, vol. 13, 1995, Atlas of the Wisconsin Prairie and Savana Flora, 2000; co-author: (with T.S.Cochrane) Checklist of the Vascular Plants of Wis., 2001; editor: Extinction or Preservation: What Biological Future for the South American Tropics?, 1978; contbr. articles to profl. jours. With US Army, 1944—46, ETO. Recipient Biologia award, U. Tenn., 1948, Presdl. Merit cert., Mex., 1987, Feinstone Environ. award, SUNY, Syracuse, 1990, Conservation award, Conservation Coun. Hawaii, 1990, Nat. Wildlife Fedn. Spl. Achievement award, 1992, Puga medal, U. de Guadalajara, Mex., 1994, Disting. Alumnus award, Mo. Bot. Garden, 1999. Fellow AAAS, Linnean Soc. (London); mem. Am. Inst. Biol. Scis., Bot. Soc. Am. (Merit award 1996, Centennial award 2006), Soc. Econ. Botany (Econ. Botanist of Yr. award 1998), Am. Soc. Plant Taxonomists (Asa Gray award 1994), Internat. Assn. Plant Taxonomy, Soc. Bot. Mex., Soc. Study Evolution, Ecol. Soc. Am., Wis. Acad. Arts, Sci. and Letters, Forum for Corr.-Internat. Ctr. Integrative Studies, Nature Conservancy (co-founder and trustee emeritus Wis. chpt., Nat. Oakleaf award 1963), Wilderness Soc., Sierra Club, Nat. Parks Assn., Citizens Natural Resources Assn. Wis., Natural Resource Def. Coun., Environ. Def. Fund, Friends of Earth, Population Connection, Negative Population Growth, Soc. Conservation Biology (Disting. Achievement award 1994), Natural Areas Assn., Sigma Xi, Phi Kappa Phi. Achievements include co-discovery of Zea diploperennis, Z. nicaraguensis (wild species of the maize genus) and Lycopersicon chmielewskii (high sugar-content wild tomatoes). Home: 2784 Marshall Pky Madison WI 53713-1023 Office: U Wis Dept Botany 430 Lincoln Dr Madison WI 53706-1313 Home Phone: 608-256-7247; Office Phone: 608-262-2792. Office Fax: 608-262-7509. Personal E-mail: swis@charter.net. *If we are to remain healthy and sane, we must concern ourselves with the concept of an Optimum Human Environment, one which must include large portions of the wild and natural environment that shaped our bodies and minds through natural selection over the past millions of years. Hence, only in the preservation of nature, of the world's wild ecosystems and their species, and in a clear comprehension of evolution and the consequent urgent need to reduce both the world's human population and its unsustainable trashing of the environment, can we find the foundations for a meaningful new ethic that will insure a livable world for our children. For their sake, we have to become good ancestors and learn to live within sustainable limits.*

ILTZ, JASON L., pharmacist, educator; b. Odessa, Wash., Aug. 23, 1971; s. Dorothy A. and Ronald E. Frederick; m. Kaylene J. Plinski, June 12, 1993; children: Aleyna N., Jason T., Jaron D. B of Pharmacy, Wash. State U., Pullman, 1996; PharmD, Wash. State U., Spokane, 1997. Clin. pharmacy specialist Group Health Coop., Spokane, 1997—2006; asst. prof. Wash. State U. Coll. Pharmacy, Spokane, 1997—2001, clin. asst. prof., 2001—07, clin. assoc. prof., 2007—; clin. pharmacy specialist Integrated Health Profls., Spokane Valley, Wash., 2006—. Mem.: Nat. Inst. for Stds. in Pharmacist Credentialing (cert. disease mgr.), Am. Assn. Colls. Pharmacy, Am. Soc. Cons. Pharmacists, Nat. Home Infusion Assn., Spokane Pharmacy Assn. (pres. 2001—02, Presdl. Leadership award 2001). Office: Wash State Univ Coll Pharmacy PO Box 1495 Spokane WA 99220-1495 Home Phone: 509-979-1926; Office Phone: 509-924-1826. Office Fax: 509-358-7744. Business E-Mail: iltzj@wsu.edu.

IM, HYEPIN CHRISTINE, not-for-profit developer; BS, U. Calif., Berkeley; MBA, U. So. Calif.; MDiv, Wesley Theological Seminary. Sponsorship mgr. Calif. Sci. Ctr., community gifts mgr.; venture capitalist Renaissance Capital Partners; founder & pres. Korean Churches for Community Develop., 2001—. Lecturer & speaker Christian Community Develop. Assn., Nat. Council of Korean So. Baptist Churches, US Dept. of Housing and Urban Develop., Asian Am. for Equality, So. Calif. Conference of AME Churches; Am. Memorial Marshall fellow German Marshall Fund, 2001. Pres. Korean Am. Coalition, 1995—96; mem. Pacific Council, 2001—; state commr. Calif. Svc. Corps. Office: Korean Churches for Community Develop PO Box 76146 Los Angeles CA 90076-0146 Office Phone: 213-985-1500. Personal E-mail: hyepin@gmail.com.

IM, JAEMO, research scientist; permanent resident, US. s. Jong Tae Lim and Gae Ja Chun; m. Su Young Cho, Jan. 19, 1973; children: Julia Jeongwon children: Joanna Juwon. MS, Stanford U., 1991; PhD, Northwestern U., 1998. Process engr. Applied Materials, Santa Clara, Calif., 1991—93; rsch. assoc. Argonne Nat. Lab., Ill., 1998—2000; device scientist Agere Systems, Alhambra, Calif., 2000—04, Emcore, Alhambra, 2004—. Author: (book) Ferroelectric Thin Films, 1997, In Situ Real-Time Characterization of Thin Films, 2000; contbr. articles to profl. jours. Mem. Light of Love Mission Ch., Pasadena, Calif., 2001—. Fellow, Seiwha Found., 1988; scholar, Northwestern U., 1994. Mem.: Materials Rsch. Soc. (Grad. Student award 1998), Sigma Xi (assoc.). Achievements include patents pending for elimination of destructive processes in capacitors for non-volatile ferroelectric random access memories; design of 10 Gb/s Avalnche Photo Detector; 40 Gb/s PIN Photo Detector; research in designed and constructed a novel in-situ real time surface characterization system (ToF-ISARS); microwave frequency electric-field tunable devices. Home: 3571 Emanuel Dr Glendale CA 91208 Office: Emcore 2015 West Chestnut St Alhambra CA 91803 Office Phone: 626-293-3632. Personal E-mail: jaemue@hotmail.com, imjaemue@yahoo.com. Business E-Mail: jaemo@emcore.com.

IM, SUBIN, marketing educator; PhD, U. of N.C., Chapel Hill, 1999. Asst. prof. U. of Wash., Tacoma, 1999—2002, San Francisco State U., 2003—. Contbr. articles to profl. jours. Mem.: Am. Mktg. Assn. Office: San Francisco State U 1600 Holloway Ave San Francisco CA 94132

IMADE, LUCKY OSAGIE, political scientist, educator; b. Kano, Nigeria, Dec. 18, 1957; arrived in U.S., 1983; s. Gabriel Agho and Jant Agho Imade; m. Ayowie H. Imade, Dec. 31, 1991; children: Olivia, Lucky Imade, Jr. BA, Shaw U., 1987; MA, Clark U., Atlanta, 1993, PhD, 1995. Instr. polit. sci. Ga. Perimeter Coll., Atlanta, 1995—97; coord. internat. programs Shaw U., Raleigh, NC, 1997—. Fulbright scholar, 1999—2000. Mem.: Edo Soc. Rsch. (pres. 1999—). Avocations: soccer, reading, tennis, travel, basketball. Office: Shaw U 118 E South St Raleigh NC 27601 E-mail: limade@shawu.edu.

IMAMURA, MICHIAKI, cardiac surgeon, pediatric and congenital cardiothoracic surgery; PhD, Hokkoido U. Grad, Sch, Medicine, Japan, 1992; MD, Hokkaido U. Sch. Med., Japan, 1988. Cert. Bd. Gen. Surgery, Japanese Soc. Surgery, 1992, Ednl. Commn. Fgn. Med. Graduates, 1995, Bd. Japanese Assn. for Thoracic Surgery, 1999, US Med. Licensing Examination, 2002. Resident Hokkaido U. Sch. Medicine, Japan, 1993, fellow, 1995—96, Cornell U. Med. Coll., NYC, 1993—95, Cleve. Clin. Found., Ohio, 1996—99; cardiac surgeon, pediatric and congenital cardiothoracic surgery Ark. Children's Hosp.; asst. prof. U. Ark. Med. Sciences. Contbr. articles to profl. jours. Office: Ark Childrens Hosp 800 Marshall St Slot 653 Little Rock AR 72202 Address: 4301 W Markham Little Rock AR 72205*

IMAN, RONALD L., statistician, consultant; b. Phillipsburg, Kans., Oct. 1, 1940; s. I. J. Iman and E. Lucille Hofaker; m. V. Rae Forssberg, Apr. 10, 1960; children: Deborah Iman Schaefer, Susan Rae White. BS, Kans. State U., Manhattan, 1962; MS, PhD, Kans. State U., 1973; MA, Emporia State U., Kans., 1965. Instr. Kans. State U., Manhattan, 1970—73; asst. prof. We. Mich. U., Kalamazoo, 1973—75; disting. mem. tech. staff Sandia Nat. Labs., Albuquerque, 1975—96; pres. SW Tech. Cons., Albuquerque, 1995—. Author: (textbooks) A Data-Based Approach to Statistics, A Data-Based Approach to Statistics, Concise Edit., Modern Business Statistics 2e, Modern Business Statistics, A Modern Approach to Statistics, Introduction to Modern Business Statistics. Pres. ch. coun. Faith Luth. Ch., Albuquerque, 2006—07; mem. Kans. State U. Found., Manhattan, 2000—07, Kans. State Univ. Alumni Assn., 2003—07. Recipient Disting. Svc. award, Kans. State U., 1996, Disting. Alumni award, Emporia State U., 1996, Highly Cited Rschr. award, Inst. Sci. Info., 2004—. Fellow: Am. Statis. Assn. (pres. 1994, exec. com. mem. 1984—96). Lutheran. Avocation: golf. Home and Office: SW Tech Cons 1065 Tramway Ln NE Albuquerque NM 87122

IMAN, (IMAN ABUDULMAJID), model; b. Somalia, July 25, 1955; m. Spencer Haywood (div. 1987); 1 child, Zulekha; m. David Bowie, Apr. 24, 1992; 1 child, Alexandria Zahra. Student, U. Nairobi, Kenya. Joined Wilhelmina Model Inc., 1975; introduced to U.S. Iman's Kikois; host Project Runway Can.; founder, CEO Iman Cosmetics, 1994—. Global amb. Keep a Child Alive, 2006—. Appearences include (films) The Human Factor, 1979, Out of Africa, 1985, Star Trek VI, 1986, No Way Out, 1987, Surrender, 1987, House Party II, 1991, Exit to Eden, 1994, The Deli, 1997, Omikron: The Nomad Soul, 1999, (TV) Heart of Darkness, 1994; (TV series) Miami Vice, The Cosby Show, In the Heat of the Night; author: I Am Iman, 2001, (with Tia Williams) The Beauty of Color: The Ultimate Beauty Guide for Skin of Color, 2005.*

IMANA, JORGE GARRON, artist; b. Sept. 20, 1930; came to U.S., 1964, naturalized, 1974. s. Juan S. and Lola (Garron) I.; m. Cristina Imana; children: George, Ivan. Grad. fine arts acad., U. San Francisco Xavier, 1950. cert. Nat. Sch. for Tchrs., Bolivia, 1952. Prof. art. Nat. Sch. Tchrs., Sucre, 1954-56; prof. biology Padilla Coll., Sucre, 1956-60; head dept. art Inst. Normal Simon Bolivar, La Paz, Bolivia, 1961-62; propr., mgr. The Artists Showroom, San Diego, 1973—. Over 100 one-man shows of paintings in U.S., S. Am., and Europe, 1952—, including: Gallery Banet, La Paz, 1965, Artists Showroom, San Diego, 1964, 66, 68, 74, 76, 77, San Diego Art Inst., 1966, 68, 72, 73, Constrast Gallery, Chula Vista, Calif., 1966, Univ. de Zulia, Maracaibo, Venezuela, 1969, Spanish Village Art Ctr., San Diego, 1974, 75, 76, La Jolla Art Assn. Gallery, 1969, 72-93, Internat. Gallery, Washington, 1976, Galeria de Arte L'Atelier, La Paz, 1977, Mus. Nat., La Paz, 1987, 88, Casa del Arte, La Jolla, Calif., 1987, Simon Patino Found., Bolivia, 1994; numerous group shows including: Fine Arts Gallery, San Diego, 1964, Mus. Modern Art, Paris, 1973; exhibits in galleries of Budapest, Hungary, 1975, Moscow, 1975, Warsaw, Poland, 1976; represented in permanent collections: Mus. Nat., La Paz, Mus. de la Univ. de Potosi, Bolivia, Mus. Nat. de Bogota, Colombia, S. Am. Ministerio de Edn., Managua, Nicaragua, Bolivian Embassy, Moscow and Washington, also pbt. collections in U.S., Europe and Latin Am.; executed many murals including; Colegio Padilla, Sucre, Bolivia, 1958, Colegio Junin, Sucre, Bolivia, 1959, Sindicato de Construccion Civil, Lima, Peru, 1960. Hon. consul of Bolivia, So. Calif., 1969-73. Served to lt. Bolivian Army, 1953. Recipient Mcpl. award Sucre, Bolivia, 1985, Gold medal, Bolivian Govt., 2003, Disting. Svc. Gold medal, Marisoal de Ayacucho, Bolivia, 2006. Mem. San Diego Art Inst., San Diego Watercolor Soc., Internat. Fine Arts Guild, La Jolla Art Assn. Home: Apt 212 2510 Torrey Pines Rd La Jolla CA 92037-3424 Office Phone: 858-452-7096.

IMANAKA, MITCHELL AKIO, lawyer; b. Honolulu, Nov. 26, 1954; s. Herbert Toshiyuki and Nell Haruko (Chan) I.; m. Marie Mie Miyamoto, June 1, 1986. BA, U. Hawaii, 1976; JD, Georgetown U., 1979. Bar: Hawaii 1979. Ptnr. Dwyer Imanaka & Schraff (now Imanaka Kudo & Fujimoto), Honolulu, 1979—. Adj. prof. law U. Hawaii, 1990—; instr. real estate continuing edn., 1989—; cons. condominium and time sharing, Honolulu, 1982—. Mem. ABA, Hawaii Bar Assn. (real property and fin. svcs. sect.), Honolulu Club, Plaza Club, Elks, Lions, Phi Beta Kappa, Phi Kappa Phi. Avocation: golf. Office: Imanaka Kudo & Fujimoto TOPA Fin Ctr Fort St Tower 17th Fl 745 Fort St Honolulu HI 96813 Office Phone: 808-521-9500. Office Fax: 808-541-9050.

IMBARUS, AURA, language educator, consultant; b. Sibiu, Romania, July 2, 1971; arrived in US, 1997; d. Stefan Ioan and Aurelia Imbarus; m. Mihai Chiorean, Sept. 2, 1996. BA, Lucian Blaga U., Sibiu, 1995, MA, 1996, PhD, 2002. Cert. tchr. Calif. Asst. prof. English State U. Lucian Blaga, Sibiu, 1995—97; English tchr. Le Conte Humanities Magnet, LA, 1998—2000; English instr. LA City Coll., 1999—2000; English tchr. West H.S., Torrance, Calif., 2000—. English instr. Sylvan Learning Ctr., LA, 1998—99, LA Harbor Coll., Wilmington, Calif., 2000—, Long Beach (Calif.) City Coll., 2002—; ESL instr. El Camino Coll., Torrance, 2001—; interview operator Gallup Pool, Sibiu, 1993—97; head news dept. Radio Contact, Sibiu, 1993—97; mem. editl. bd. Jour. Hosp. Librarianship. Author: Research of Language & Literature, 2000; contbr. articles to profl. jours. Named Outstanding H.S. Tchr., U. Calif., 2001—02. Mem.: AAUW, MLA, Nat. Coun. Tchrs. English, Calif. Tchrs. Assn. Avocations: reading, swimming, ice skating, painting. Home: # 463 384 S Miraleste Dr San Pedro CA 90732-6068 Office: West HS 20401 Victor St Torrance CA 90503 Personal E-mail: auraimbarus@hotmail.com.

IMBEAU, STEPHEN ALAN, allergist; b. Portland, Oreg., Nov. 25, 1947; s. David A. and Marjory Anne (Jacobsen) I.; m. Shirley Ruth Burke, Aug. 18, 1979; children: Stephanie Frances, Andrew Paul, Charles Burke. BA, U. Calif., Berkeley, 1969; MD, U. Calif., San Francisco, 1973. Diplomate Am. Bd. Internal Medicine, Am. Bd. Allergy. Intern U. Wis., Madison, S.C., 1973-74, resident in internal medicine, 1974-75, resident in allergy, 1976-78, resident in infectious diseases, 1978-79; pvt. practice Florence, S.C., 1980—. Budget and control bd. S.C. Data Oversight Coun., 1993—98; founder Coastal Growth Ptnrs. (a Venture Capital Co.), 1997; bd. dirs. Joint Coun. Allergy and Immunology; gen. ptnr. Venture Fund, 2001—, Coastal Growth Ptnrs., 1997—, Trelys Investments, Venture Capital Co., 1997—; co-owner profl. hockey team Columbia Infernos; mem. practicing physicans adv. coun. U.S. HHS Health Care Financing Adminstrn., 2000—03; commr. S.C. Dept. Mental Health, 2003—05. Contbr. articles to profl. jours. Chmn. Florence Symphony Orch., 1985-91; bd. dirs. Big Bros., 1989-92, Am. Lung Assn., 1982-86, Florence County Progress, chmn. 1993-95; mem. SC Mental Health Commn., 2003-05; trustee SC Venture Capital Fund, 2005—. Fellow ACP; mem. AMA (SC alt. del. 1992-98), Am. Acad. Allergists, SC Med. Soc. (trustee 1988-90, sec. bd. 1990-94, treas. 1995-97, S.C. Ambassador of the Yr. 1995, pres.-elect 1997, pres. 1998-99, del. to AMA 2004-), Am. Acad. Allergy, Asthma and Immunology (alt. del. to AMA 1999—2004), Joint Coun. Allergy Immunology (bd. mem., sec. 2002-04, treas. 2004-06, pres.-elect 2006—), Florence County Med. Soc. (pres. 1984-85), Lions (pres. 1987-88). Avocations: reading, hunting, stamp collecting/philately. Home: 950 Park Ave Florence SC 29501-5734 Office: 8W E Cheves St Ste 420 Florence SC 29506-2769 Office Phone: 843-679-9335. Personal E-mail: stephenimbeau@yahoo.com.

IMBER, ANNABELLE CLINTON, state supreme court justice; b. Heber Springs, Ark., July 15, 1950; m. Ariel Barak Imber (dec. 2001); 1 child, William Pierce Clinton. BA magna cum laude, Smith Coll., Northampton, Mass., 1971; postgrad., Inst. for Paralegal Tng., 1971, U. Houston, Tex., 1973-75; JD, U. Ark., 1977. Atty. Wright, Lindsey & Jennings Law Firm, Little Rock, Ark., 1977-88; apptd. cir. judge (5th divsn.) Pulaski and Perry Counties, Ark., 1984, elected chancery and probate judge (6th divsn.) Ark., 1989-96; elected assoc. justice Ark. Supreme Ct., 1997—. Bd. dirs. Ark. Advs. for Children and Families, 1985-90, pres. 1986-88; bd. dirs Pulsaki County Hist. Soc., 1992-95, Congregation B'Nai Israel, 1988-92, 2001-05, Kiwanis Club 1995-98, YMCA of Greater Little Rock and Pulaski County, 1986-1988, 1991-1999, 2007—, Our House-A Shelter for Homeless, 1992-2006, St. Vincent Devel. Found., 1989-93, UAMS Med. Ctr. Dept. Pastoral Care and Edn., 1996-2005. Mem. ABA, AAUW, Nat. Assn. Women Judges, Ark. Bar Assn. (sec.-treas., 1982-1986), Ark. Women Exec., Assn. of Ark. Women Lawyers (pres. 1980-81, Judge of the Year award 1994), Pulaski County Bar Assn. (bd. dirs. 1982-84). Office: Ark Supreme Ct Justice Bldg 625 Marshall St Little Rock AR 72201-1054 Office Phone: 501-682-6867. Business E-Mail: annabelle.clinton-imber@arkansas.gov.

IMBER, GERALD, plastic surgeon; b. NYC, Jan. 9, 1941; s. George Howard and Rose (Weiss) I.; children: Peter, Jason, Gregory. MD, SUNY, 1966. Diplomate Am. Bd. Plastic Surgery. Intern LI Jewish Med. Ctr., 1966-67; resident Kaiser Hosp., LA, 1970-72, USAF Griffiss AFB Hosp., Rome, NY, 1970-72, NY Presbyn. Hosp.-Cornell Med. Ctr., NYC, 1972-74, attending surgeon, 1974—, clin. asst., prof. of surgery; dir. Imber Clinic, NYC, 1982—. Author: Youth Corridor, 1997, For Men Only, 1998, Absolute Beauty, 2005. Trustee Inwood House, NYC, 1998—. Capt. USAF, 1968—70. Mem. Am. Soc. Plastic Surgeons, NE Soc. Plastic Surgeons, NY State Med. Soc., NY County Med. Soc. Avocations: polo, sailing. Office: Imber Clinic 1009 5th Ave New York NY 10028-0155 Office Phone: 212-472-1800. Business E-Mail: drimber@drimber.com.

IMBERT, RICHARD CONRAD, insurance company executive, real estate developer; b. NYC, Jan. 30, 1941; s. Henry A. and Patricia (Boyer) I.; married; children: Peter, Cynthia, Elise; m. Susan Fusaro. Underwriter Ins. Co. N.Am., Hempstead, NY, 1961—64; sales exec. Ashby Lee Biedler, Inc., NYC, 1964—67, pres., 1967—74, Fisher-Biedler, Inc., Amityville, 1974—85, Am. Profl. Agy., Inc., Amityville, 1974—, R.C.I. Industries Inc., Amityville, 1980—, IMP Properties, Inc., Amityville, 1975—; pres., CEO Windmill Manor Farms, Inc., 2000—. V.p. L.I. Polymers, Hauppauge, NY, 1988; bd. dirs., chmn. bd. Polymerix, Inc., NJ, 1985-91; ptnr. Sheraton Hotel, Hauppauge. Chmn. bishop's appeal com. St. Martin of Tours Roman Cath. Ch., Amityville, 1985, trustee, 1987-90, bishop's coun of stewarts, 1990; mem. Rep. Senatorial Inner Circle, Pres. Adv. Com.; trustee L.I. Aquarium, Bay Shore, NY, 1997; dep. commr. of police Amityville Police Dept., 2000—. Named Man of the Yr., L.I. Aquarium, 2000. Mem. NY State Thorobred Owners Assn., Southward Ho Country Club (West Islip, NY), Unqua Corinthian Yacht Club (commodore 1981-82), Chub Cay Club. Republican. Avocations: yachting, scuba. Office: RCI Industries Inc 95 Broadway Amityville NY 11701-2728

IMBRESCIA, MARCIA, landscape company executive; BA in Mktg. and Journalism, grad. cert. in landscape design. Media dir. Drumbeater; owner Peartree Designs, Wellesley Hills, Mass., 2003—. Mem. com. on Guidelines for Human Embryonic Stem Cell Rsch. NAS, 2005—; mem. adv. com., Human Embryonic Stem Cell Rsch. NRC and Inst. Medicine., 2006—. Mem. Am. Juvenile Arthritis Orgn., 1996—98, 2001, chairperson, 2002—03; bd. trustee, nat. and chpt. vol. Arthritis Found. Recipient Vol. of Yr., Mass. Chpt. Arthritis Found., 1992. Office: Peartree Designs 51 River St Wellesley Hills MA 02481

IMBRIE, ANDREW WELSH, composer, educator; b. NYC, Apr. 6, 1921; s. Andrew C. and Dorothy (Welsh) I.; m. Barbara Cushing, Jan. 31, 1953; children: Andrew, John (dec.). AB, Princeton U., 1942; MA, U. Calif.-Berkeley, 1947; DMusic (hon.), San Francisco Conservatory of

Music, 2004. Instr. music U. Calif., Berkeley, 1947, 49-51, asst. prof., 1951, assoc. prof., 1957-60, prof., 1960-91, Jerry and Evelyn Hemmings Chambers chair dept. music, 1989-92. Composer-in-residence Tanglewood Music Ctr., Lenox, Mass., summer 1991; guest prof. Brandeis U., 1982, U. Ala., 1992, U. Chgo., 1994, 96-97, Northwestern U., 1994, NYU, 1995, Fromm prof., Harvard U., fall, 1997. Compositions include 3 symphonies, 5 string quartets, trios, sonatas, songs, orchestral and choral works, works for various chamber ensembles, Angle of Repose (opera), Three Against Christmas, 3 piano concerti, concerti for violin, cello and flute, Dance-cantata Prometheus Bound, Requiem in memoriam John Imbrie (Grammy award nomination 2000), Adam (cantata), From Time to Time (for woodwinds, percussion and string quartet). Bd. dirs. Koussevitzky Found.; bd. govs. San Francisco Symphony, 1982-91. Recipient Circle award N.Y. Music Critics, 1943-44; Alice M. Ditson fellow Columbia U., 1946-47; fellow Am. Acad. in Rome, 1947-49; grantee Nat. Inst. Arts and Letters, 1950; Guggenheim fellow, 1953-54, 60-61; merit award Boston Symphony Orch., 1955; creative arts award Brandeis U., 1958; Naumburg award, 1960; grantee Nat. Found. on Arts and Humanities; composer in residence Am. Acad. Rome, 1967-68; recipient Walter Hinrichsen award Columbia U., 1971 Mem. Am. Acad. Arts and Letters, Am. Acad. Arts and Scis., Phi Beta Kappa. Clubs: Bohemian (San Francisco). Home: 2625 Rose St Berkeley CA 94708-1920

IMBROGNO, CYNTHIA, judge; b. 1948; BA, Ind. U., Pa., 1970; JD cum laude, Gonzaga U., 1979. Law clk. to Hon. Justin L. Quackenbush U.S. Dist. Ct. (Wash. ea. dist.), 9th circuit, 1980-83; law clk. Wash. State Ct. of Appeals, 1984; civil rights staff atty. Ea. Dist. of Wash., 1984-85, complex litigation staff atty., 1986-88; with Preston, Thorgrimson, Shidler, Gates & Ellis, 1988-90, Perkins Coie, 1990-91; magistrate judge U.S. Dist. Ct. (Wash. ea. dist.), 9th circuit, Spokane, 1991—. Office: 740 US Courthouse 920 W Riverside Ave Spokane WA 99201-1010

IMEL, ELIZABETH CARMEN, retired physical education educator; b. Galesburg, Ill., Oct. 21, 1936; d. Leo Henry and Anna Imel. BS in Edn., Ill. State U., Normal, 1957; MA, U. Iowa, Iowa City, 1964, PhD, 1966. Instr. rsch. methods, dance, physical edn., kinesiology U. Iowa, Iowa City, 1962—64; prof. Ill. State U., Normal, 1964—95; ret., 1995. Pres. Ill. Dance Assn., 1978—80. Editor: AAHPERED Periodical, 1968—70, Focus on Dance VIII Dance Heritage, 1977. Active Ill. Arts Commn., 1981—82, Citizen's Rev. Commn., San Marcos, 2000—02; chmn. San Marcos Arts Commn., 2003—05; fundraising adv. bd. Tex. State U., 2005—06; sec., bd. mem. Lyndon B. Johnson Mus., San Marcos; pres.-elect Friends of the Cemetery, San Marcos; regent DAR. Mem.: Heritage Assn. San Marcos (bd. dirs. 2000—06). Lutheran. Home: PO Box 1248 San Marcos TX 78667

IMEL, JOHN MICHAEL, lawyer; b. Cushing, Okla., Aug. 4, 1932; s. Arthur Blaine and Hazel Monnet (Kelly) I.; m. Patricia Ann Carney, July 31, 1954; children: Blythe Michele, Kathryn Ann, Dixie Lynn, Sally Louise. BS, U. Okla., 1954, JD, 1959. Bar: Okla. 1959, U.S. Dist. Ct. (no. dist.) Okla. 1961, U.S. Ct. Appeals (10th cir.) 1961, U.S. Supreme Ct. 1962, U.S. Dist. Ct. (we. dist.) Okla. 1967, U.S. Dist. Ct. (ea. dist.) Okla. 1971. Asst. atty. County of Tulsa, 1959—60; mcpl. judge City of Tulsa, 1960—61; U.S. atty. U.S. Dept. Justice, Tulsa, 1961—67; ptnr. Moyers, Martin, Santee Imel & Tetrick, Tulsa, 1967—. Regent U. Okla., Norman, 1981-88, chmn., 1987-88; trustee Children's Med. Ctr., Tulsa, 1979-84. Capt. USNR, 1954-77. Fellow Am. Bar Found., Am. Coll. Trial Lawyers (state chmn. 1987-88); mem. Am. Inns of Ct. (program chmn. 1989-90, Exemplary Leadership award 1996), So. Hills Country Club (bd. govs. 1993-99), Tulsa Club (pres. 1990), Rotary (pres. 1968-69). Democrat. Methodist. Avocations: golf, swimming, tennis, reading. Home: 3920 E 58th Pl Tulsa OK 74135-7823 Office: Moyers Martin Santee Imel & Tetrick 401 S Boston Ste 1100 Tulsa OK 74103 Home Phone: 918-742-4923; Office Phone: 918-582-5281. Business E-Mail: imel@moyersmartin.com.

IMENDE-COONEY, ELIZABETH F., literature educator, consultant; d. Thomas Blinco and Rebecca Imende. BA in English, Wake Forest U., Winston-Salem, NC, 1998; MEd, Harvard U., Cambridge, Mass., 1999. Cert. cons. Rsch. for Better Tchg. Tchr. Lexington HS, Mass., 1999—2002; HS tchr. Internat. Sch., Hanover, Germany, 2002—03; English tchr. New Eng. Sch. English, Cambridge, 2003—04; adj. prof. High Point U., NC, 2004—05; co-dir. Amani Children's Found., Winston-Salem, 2004—05; ednl. cons. Rsch. for Better Tchg., Acton, Mass., 2005—. Keynote spkr. Kenya Girls HS, Nairobi, 1997; staff developer, cons. Colegio Flamenco, San Salvador, El Salvador, 2004; cons., rschr. Madison Park and Thalana HS, South Africa, 2006; staff developer Kwa Zulu Natal, South Africa. Author, editor (ESL series) The Grammar Plus, 2006. Bd. dirs. Amani Children's Found., Winston-Salem, 2005—. Recipient MINT award, Mass. Dept. Edn., 1999, Scholar for the Dream award, Nat. Coun. Tchrs. of English, 2006. Mem.: ASCD. Home and Office: 52R Beacon St Somerville MA 02143 Office Phone: 617-833-1995. Personal E-mail: eimende29@aol.com. Business E-Mail: cooney@rbteach.com.

IMEOKPARIA, REMI, healthcare educator, department chairman; b. Abeokuta, Nigeria; m. Michael Imeokparia, Sr.; children: Ayo Nemedia, Osi Lola, Michael Jr., Osereme Lara, Sade Nene. MD, Kharkov State Med. Inst., Russia, 1974; MPH, U. Sydney, Australia, 1982; PhD, U. S.Fla., Tampa, 1992. Asst. prof. U. Ill., Springfield, 1993—98, assoc. prof., 1998—, dept. chair, 1999—; adj. asst. prof. SIU Sch. Medicine, Springfield, 1997—. Prof., scholar Rotary Internat., Springfield, 2001—02. Bd. mem. Internat. Health & Devel. Network, 1999—2007, v.p. non-profit orgn., 2003—07; mem. Am. Cancer Soc., Springfield, 1994—99. Recipient Outstanding Faculty award, U. Ill., 1995; grantee Rsch. grant, Ill. Dept. Pub. Health, 2005; Ill. Pub. Health Leadership Inst. fellow, U. Ill., 1997. Mem.: APHA, Ill. Pub. Health Assn. Business E-Mail: imeokparia.remi@uis.edu.

IMESCH, JOSEPH LEOPOLD, bishop; b. Grosse Pointe Farms, Mich., June 21, 1931; s. Dionys and Margaret (Margelisch) I. BS, Sacred Heart Sem., 1953; student, N.Am. Coll., Rome, 1953-57; STL, Gregorian U., Rome, 1957. Ordained priest Roman Cath. Ch., 1956. Sec. to Cardinal Dearden, 1959—71; pastor Our Lady of Sorrows Ch., Farmington, Mich., 1971—77; titular bishop of Pomaria, aux. bishop of Detroit, 1973—79; asst. bishop N.W. region, 1977—79; bishop of Joliet Ill., 1979—2006.

IMHOFF, KATHLEEN RUTH TOSTRUD, library administrator; b. Superior, Wis., Sept. 9, 1945; d. Gerhard Lars Oliver Tostrud and Dorothea Henrietta (Panzenhagen) Tostrud Stream; m. Clement T. Imhoff, Aug. 10, 1968; children: Ethan Charles, Eliot Clifford. BA in English, Valparaiso U., Ind., 1967; MA, U. Wis., 1968. Dir. Horseshoe Bend Regional Libr., Dadeville, Ala., 1968—73; head mobile info. svcs. Atlanta Pub. Libr., 1973—74; cons. libr. svcs. State Libr. Wis., Madison, 1974—75; dir. Bur. Pub. and Coop., Madison, 1975—77, Chattahoochee Regional Libr., Columbus, Ga., 1977—80; asst. dir. Broward County Libr., Ft. Lauderdale, Fla., 1980—90; dir. Harrison Regional Libr., Columbiana, Ala., 1990; exec. dir., CEO Lexington Pub. Libr., Ky., 2003—. Dir. Solinet, Atlanta, 1988-91; instr. Auburn U., Ala., 1971-73. Contbr. chpts. to books: Bibliographic Access in Europe, 1990, Interlending and Document Supply, 1991; contbr. numerous articles to profl. jours. Pres. Montevallo HS PTA, Ala., 1993-94. Recipient John Cotton Dana award, 1972, Internat. Study award ALA/Pub. Libr. Assn., 1989, Bumblebee Cannot Fly award Omnisystems Internat., 1992, Disting. Svc. award SE Fla. Libr. Info. Network, 2003. Mem. AAUW, ALA (councilor chpt. 1989—), Shelby County Art Assn. (historian 1992-93), Optimist Club (2nd v.p. 1994-95). Office: Lexington Pub Libr 140 E Main St Lexington KY 40507 Office Phone: 859-231-5599. E-mail: kimhoff@lexpublib.org.

IMHOFF, WALTER FRANCIS, investment banker; b. Denver, Aug. 7, 1931; s. Walter Peter and Frances Marie (Barkhausen) I.; m. Georgia Ruth Stewart, June 16, 1973; children: Stacy, Randy, Theresa, Michael, Robert. BSBA, Regis U., Denver, 1955; D Pub. Svc. (hon.), Regis U., 1991. Asst. v.p. Coughlin & Co., Denver, 1955-60; pres., chief exec. officer Hanifen, Imhoff Inc., Denver, 1960-2000; mng. dir. Stifel, Nicolaus & Co., 2000—. Guest lectr. U. Colo., 1976 Trustee Regis Coll., 1975—95, treas., 1976—79, vice chmn., 1981, chmn., 1982—89, life trustee, 1998—; bd. dirs. NCCJ, 1980—89, chmn., 1986—89, life trustee, 1998—; bd. dirs. Arapahoe Libr. Found., 1990—94, Channel 6 Ednl. TV, treas., 1996—97, vice chmn., 1997—98, chmn., 1998—99; bd. dirs. Highland Hills Found., 1993—, Denver Area coun. Boy Scouts Am., 1986—, v.p., 1989—2003; bd. dirs. St. Joseph's Hosp., mem. exec. com., 1991, vice chmn., 1994, chmn., 1995—98; bd. dirs. Kempe Children's Found., 1992, chmn., 1994—97; bd. dirs. 9 Who Care, 1998—2006, Caring for Colo., 2001—; chmn. Colo. Concern, 1988—2007, St. Joseph Hosp. Found., 2004—; chmn. exec. com. 2% Club, 2000—; trustee Irish Cmty. Ctr., 2001. Named Outstanding Alumnus Regis Coll., 1970 Mem. Bond Club Denver (pres. 1965), Colo. Mcpl. Bond Dealers Assn. (pres. 1973), Mid-Continent Securities Industry Assn. (dir. 1972-75), Securities Industry Assn. (chmn. S.W. region 1991-95, dir. 1993-96), Nat. Assn. Security Dealers, Pub. Securities Assn. (dir. 1972-75), Denver C. of C. (bd. dirs. 1986-91, treas. 1989-91), Rose Hosp. Found., Centennial C. of C. (vice chmn.), NCCJ, Alpha Kappa Psi, Alpha Sigma Nu. Clubs: Denver (pres. 1981-82). Republican. Roman Catholic. Home: 10432 E Ida Pl Greenwood Village CO 80111-3753 Office: 1125 17th St Ste 1600 Denver CO 80202-2024 Business E-Mail: wimhoff@hanifen.com.

IMIG, DAVID GREGG, education educator, retired educational association administrator; b. Normal, Ill., July 25, 1939; s. Donald John and Margaret Winifred (Gregg) I.; m. Carol Janet Rowley, June 18, 1961; children: Douglas R., Mark D., Scott R., Jennifer C. BA, U. Ill., 1961, MA, 1964, PhD, 1969. Tchr. Nyakato Secondary Sch., Bukoba, Tanzania, 1961—63; edn. officer AID mission to, Sierra Leone, 1966—68, devel. officer Liberia, 1968—70; dir. govtl. rels. Am. Assn. Colls. for Tchr. Edn., Washington, 1970—80, exec. dir., 1980—90, CEO, 1991—2005, pres. emeritus, 2005—; prof. of practice U. Md. Coll. Edn., 2006—. Chair adv. commrs. Edn. Commn. of the States, 1987-88; chair Nat. Policy Bd. for Edn. Adminstrn., 1989-91; sec. Nat. Coun. Econ. Edn., 1992-95; mem. tchr. edn. exec. bd. Nat. Coun. for Accreditation, 1980—. Contbr. Tchrs. for East Africa fellow Tchrs. Coll., Columbia U., 1961, Inst. Edn. fellow, London, 1961, Makerere U. fellow, Kampala, 1961, Hanna fellow Hoover Inst., 1995. Mem. Am. Ednl. Rsch. Assn., Inst. Ednl. Inquiry (sr. assoc.), Phi Delta Kappa, Kappa Delta Pi. Office: U Md 2311 Benjamin Bldg College Park MD 20742-1175 Office Phone: 301-405-8657. E-mail: dimig@umd.edu.*

IMIG, WILLIAM GRAFF, lawyer, lobbyist; b. Omaha, Aug. 13, 1941; s. Jacob H. and Gretchen I.; m. Joyce, Dec. 18, 1976; children: Scott, Kari, Steven BA, Cornell U., 1963, LLB, 1965. Bar: Colo. 1965, U.S. Ct. Appeals (10th cir.) 1965, U.S. Supreme Ct. 1969. V.p., shareholder Ireland, Stapleton, Pryor & Pascoe, Denver, 1970-92; pvt. practice, Denver, 1992—. Colo. counsel Property Casualty Ins. Assn. Am., Des Plaines, Ill., 1971—; Colo. legis. counsel Allstate Ins. Cos., 1982—; mem. bd. arbitrators NASD Dispute Resolution. Bd. editors Cornell Law rev., 1964-65. Chmn. Colo. Gov.'s Auto Insurance Task Force, 2002; trustee Colo. chpt. Nat. Multiple Sclerosis Soc., 1995-2000. Capt. JAGC, U.S. Army, 1966-70. Mem. Colo. Bar Assn. (bd. govs. 1974-77), Colo. Assn. Commerce and Industry (chmn. tort reform coun., chmn. auto ins. roundtable), City Club of Denver, Denver Law Club, Phi Kappa Phi. Republican. Episcopalian. Home and Office: 1011 S Valentia St #40 Denver CO 80247

IMMEL, BARBARA KAY KEPHART, management consultant; b. Bakersfield, Calif., July 31, 1956; m. Joseph Herbert Immel, Jr., Aug. 31, 1979; children: Joseph Herbert Immel, III, Elizabeth Logan. BA in English, U. Calif., Santa Barbara, 1978, single subject tchg. credential, 1979; grad., Stanford Profl. Pub. Course, 1981, Stanford U. Exec. Pub. Course, 1982, grad., 2002, Buckley Sch. Pub. Speaking, 2000, grad., 2001. Asst. to pres. Vet. Practice Pub. Co., Santa Barbara, 1980—81; tech. editor I-III Syva Co., Palo Alto, Calif., 1982—86; adminstr. Syntex Corp., Palo Alto, 1986—92; compliance mgr. Chiron Corp., Emeryville, Calif., 1993—95; cons. pres. Immel Resources, LLC, Petaluma, Calif., 1995—. Vol. libr. Career Action Ctr., Palo Alto, Calif., 1982—86; instr. U. Calif. Berkeley Ext., 1995—2000, co-dir. drug devel. course, 1998—2000; guest lectr. undergrad. pharmacology course U. Calif., Berkeley, 1999—; cons. in field. Columnist: Biopharm mag., 1996—2007; contbr. articles to profl. jours., Dekker's Ency. of Pharm. Tech.; editor-in-chief Immel Report, 2004—. Scholar Pres. scholar, U. Calif. Santa Barbara, 1974—78. Mem.: Pharm. Rschrs. and Mfrs. Am. (tng. com. 1988—92), Parenteral Drug Assn. (tng. com. 1993—96). Avocations: reading, travel. Office Phone: 707-778-7222. Personal E-mail: immel@immel.com.

IMMELMAN, TREVOR, professional golfer; b. Cape Town, South Africa, Dec. 16, 1979; m. Carminita Immelman, 2003; 1 child, Jacob. Profl. golfer, 1999—. Named PGA TOUR Rookie of Yr., 2006. Achievements include winner, Cialis Western Open on the PGA Tour, 2006; winning European Tour events including the Tusker Kenya Open, 2000, South African Airways Open, 2003, 04, Deutsche Bank-SAP Open TPC of Europe, 2004; winner, other events including the Vodacom Players Championship, South Africa, 2000, Dimension Data Pro-Am, South Africa, 2003. Mailing: PGA European Tour Wentworth Dr Virginia Water Surrey GU25 4LX England*

IMMELT, JEFFREY R., diversified technology and services company executive; b. Cincinnati, Ohio, Feb. 19, 1956; s. Joseph and Donna Immelt; m. Andrea Allen, 1986; 1 child. BA in Applied Math., Dartmouth Coll., 1978; MBA, Harvard U., 1982. With GE Corp. Mktg., 1982; various positions GE Plastics, 1982-89; v.p. consumer svc. GE Appliances, 1989-91, v.p. worldwide mktg. and product mgmt.; v.p., gen. mgr. GE Plastics Am., 1992-96; pres., CEO GE Med. Sys., 1997—2000; pres., chmn. elect GE Co., 2000—01, chmn., CEO, 2001—; chmn. NBC Universal, 2007—. Bd. dirs. Catalyst, Robin Hood, NYC. Named Man of the Year, Fin. Times, 2003, CEO Coach of Yr., Am. Football Coaches Found., 2006. Office: GE 3135 Easton Tpke Fairfield CT 06431-0002*

IMMELT, STEPHEN J., lawyer; b. Columbus, Ohio, Dec. 27, 1951; s. Joseph Francis and Donna (Wallace) I.; m. Susann Randolph Carroll, June 7, 1976; children: Catherine Carroll, Molly Maccubbin. BA, Yale U., 1974; JD, U. Md., 1977. Bar: Md. 1977, D.C. 1995, U.S. Dist. Ct. Md. 1978, U.S. Dist. Ct. D.C. 1988, U.S. Ct. Appeals (4th cir.) 1978, U.S. Ct. Appeals (D.C. Cir.) 1988, U.S. Ct. Appeals (6th and 9th cirs.) 1992. Law clk. to Hon. Harrison L. Winter U.S. Ct. Appeals (4th cir.), Balt., 1977-78; asst. U.S. atty. U.S. Dept. Justice, Balt., 1979-83; assoc. Piper & Marbury, Balt., 1978-79, 85-86, ptnr., 1986-89; mng. ptnr.-Balt. office Hogan & Hartson, Balt., 1989—, dir. litig. practice group. Mem. adv. bd. Johns Hopkins U. Sch. Nursing, Balt., 1990-98. Bd. dirs. Md. chpt. The Nature Conservancy, Chevy Chase, 1985-96, Valleys Planning Coun., Towson, Md., 1991-97, Balt. Zoo, 1994-2000, Balt. Choral Arts Soc., 1994-2000. Democrat. Avocations: golf, skiing, bicycling, gardening, outdoors. Office: Hogan & Hartson LLP 111 S Calvert St Ste 1600 Baltimore MD 21202-6191 Office Fax: 410-659-2757, 410-639-6981. Business E-Mail: sjimmelt@hhlaw.com.

IMMERGUT, KARIN J., prosecutor; b. Bklyn. BA, Amherst Coll., 1982; JD, U. Calif., Berkeley, 1987. Bar: Calif. 1987, Vt. 1995, Oreg. 1996. Asst. US atty. Central. Dist., Calif., 1988—94; atty. Gravel & Shea, Burlington, Vt., 1994—96, Covington & Burling, Washington, 1987—89; assoc. independent counsel Office Independent Counsel, Washington, 1998; dep. dist. atty. Portland, Oreg., 1996—98; asst. US atty. dist. Oreg. US Dept. Justice, 1998—2001, US atty. dist. Oreg. Oreg., 2003—. Office: US Attys Office Mark O Hatfield US Courthouse 1000 SW Third Ave Ste 600 Portland OR 97204-2902 Office Phone: 503-727-1000.*

IMMERGUT, MEL M., lawyer; b. Bklyn., 1947; BA, U. Pa., 1968; JD, Columbia U., 1971, MBA, 1972. Bar: N.Y. 1972. Ptnr., Global Corp. Dept. Milbank, Tweed, Hadley & McCloy, NYC, 1980—, chmn., 1995—. Bd. dir. Legal Aid Soc.; trustee & past pres. Am. Col. Investment Counsel; trustee Eye Bank for Sight Restoration; past pres. Billfish Found.; bd. vis. Columbia Univ. Law Sch. Mem. Council on Fgn. Rels., ABA, N.Y. State Bar Assn., Assn. Bar City N.Y. Office: Milbank Tweed Hadley & McCloy 1 Chase Manhattan Plz Fl 47 New York NY 10005-1413 Office Phone: 212-530-5730. Office Fax: 212-530-5219. Business E-Mail: mimmergut@milbank.com.

IMMERMAN, MICHAEL, director; b. Rochester, NY, Oct. 5, 1945; m. Katrina Immerman, Aug. 11, 1968. PhD, U. N.Mex, Albuquerque, 1986. Dir. rsch. SW Indian Poly. Inst., Albuquerque, 1980—86, supervisory edn. specialist, 1986—92. Assoc. prof. N.Mex Highlands U., Las Vegas. Author: (textbooks) The Other Side Of The Desk. Mem.: Phi Kappa Phi. Home and Office: N Mex Highlands U 1026 8th St Las Vegas NM 87701 Office Phone: 505-454-3548. Personal E-mail: immerman@nmhu.edu.

IMMERMAN, NEIL, academic administrator, computer science educator; BS, MS, Yale U., 1974; PhD, Cornell U., 1980. Grad. program dir., prof. computer sci. U. Mass., Amherst. Author: (book) Descriptive Complexity, 1999. Co-recipient Gödel prize in theoretical computer sci., 1995; recipient Guggenheim fellowship, 2003—04. Fellow: Assn. for Computing Machinery. Office: U Mass Dept Computer Sci Rm 374 140 Governor's Dr Amherst MA 01003-9264*

IMMKE, KEITH HENRY, lawyer; b. Peoria, Ill., Jan. 18, 1953; s. Francis William and Pearl Lenora (Kime) I. BA, U. Ill., 1975; JD, So. Ill. U., 1978. Bar: Ill. 1978, U.S. Dist. Ct. (so. and ea. dist.) Ill. 1979. Assoc. Lawrence E. Johnson & Assocs., P.C., Champaign, Ill., 1979-87; staff atty. Dept. Ins. State Ill., Springfield, 1987-88; asst. legal counsel Office Fire Marshal State Ill., 1988—. Mem. ABA, Ill. State Bar Assn., U. Ill. Alumni Assn., Phi Kappa Phi, Pi Sigma Alpha, Phi Alpha Delta. Office: State Ill Office Fire Marshal Div Petroleum and Chem Safety 1035 Stevenson Dr Springfield IL 62703-4259 Office Phone: 217-785-0969.

IMMROTH, BARBARA, library and information scientist; AB, Brown U., 1964; MA in Librarianship, U. Denver, 1965; PhD Libr. & Info. Sci., U. Pitts., 1980. Sch. cert. Duquesne U., 1975. Free-lance indexer; instr. State Libr. Pa., U. Pitts.; asst. libr. Brown U. Libr.; libr. U. Denver Libr.; children's libr. Carnegie Libr.; prof. U. Tex. Grad. Sch. Libr. & Info. Sci., Austin. Author: Texas in Children's Books, 1986; co-author: Teaching Texas History: An All-Level Resource Guide, 1985, 1989; co-editor: Achieving School Readiness: Public Libraries & the First of the National Education Goals, 1995, Library Service to Youth of Hispanic Heritage, 2000; contbr. chapters to books, articles. Recipient Certificate of Excellence, Am. Assn. U. Women, 1999; grantee, U. Tex. Centennial Programs, 1982—84, US Dept. Edn., 1994, Tex. State Libr. & Archives Commn. & Tex. Libr. Assn., 1998—99, Fast Tex, U. Tex. Austin, 1998; scholar Advanced Rsch. Inst., U. Ill. GSLIS, 1990; Summer Rsch. award, U. Tex. U. Rsch. Inst., 1984, U. Tex. Temple Teaching fellowship, 1988—89, 1997—98, 2001—02. Mem.: ALA (libr. rsch. round table, intellectual freedom roundtable, Chgo. conf. program intellectual freedom com. 1978—82, appts. com. 1989—90, trustee 1991—95, v.p. Freedom to Read Found. 1994—95, chair rsch. & stats. com. 1991—95, chair nominating com. 1997—98, internat. rels. com. 1998—2000, councilor at large 1983—87, 1992—96, 2000—04, ALSC councilor at large 1987—88, 2000—04, Beta Phi Mu award 2007), Tex. Libr. Assn. (exec. com. Tex. Assn. Sch. Librs. 1991—92, pres. 1997—98, chair scholarship & rsch. com. 1999—2000), Assn. Libr. & Info. Sci. Edn. (faculty devel. com. 1994—95), Assn. Specialized & Cooperative Libr. Agys., Assn. Libr. Svc. to Children (Newbery-Caldecott com. 1979, pres. 1989—90, past pres. 1990—91, internat. rels. com. 1991—93, Caldecott com. 1999), Am. Assn. Sch. Librs., Delta Kappa Gamma, Phi Delta Kappa, Beta Phi Mu (nat. pres. 1999—2001, chair nominating com. 2001—02, chair scholarship com. 2001—03). Office: U Tex at Austin Sch of Info SZB 564 1 University Sta D7000 Austin TX 78712-0390 Office Phone: 512-471-3875. E-mail: immroth@ischool.utexas.edu.*

IMPARATO, ANTHONY MICHAEL, vascular surgeon, educator, researcher; b. NYC, July 29, 1922; s. Silverio and Olga (Santilli) I.; m. Agatha Maria Petriccione, Dec. 19, 1943; children: Maria April Imparato , Karen Elsa Imparato Cotton. AB, Columbia U., 1943; MD, NYU, 1946. Diplomate Am. Bd. Surgery; cert. spl. qualifications in gen. vascular surgery. Intern U.S. Naval Hosp., Bklyn., 1946-47; fellow in anatomy NYU Med. Sch., 1949-50; successively intern, asst. resident in surgery, resident, chief resident in surgery NYU Med. Center Bellevue Hosp., 1950-56; mem. faculty NYU Med. Center, 1956—, dir. div. vascular surgery, 1975-92, prof. surgery, 1975—2000, prof. emeritus surgery, 2000—. Leader People-to-People delegation in vascular surgery: western Europe 1982, Soviet Union, 1985; ops. com. "Cooperative VA Study on Asymptomatic Carotid Stenosis", 1983-87 and Nascet, 1987-92; hon. pres. Societa Italiana Prevenzione Ictus Cerebrale, 1997, 98; lectr. in field. Contbr. over 175 articles in field, over 35 chpts. to textbooks. Served as officer M.C. USNR, 46-49, 50. Grantee NIH, 1976-81. Fellow ACS, Am. Coll. Cardiology; mem. Am. Heart Assn. (fellow Stroke Coun.), Am. Surg. Assn., Soc. for Vascular Surgery (pres. 1984-85), Internat. Cardiovascular Soc., Soc. Clin. Vascular Surgery, Soc. Angiologia Uruguay, Royal Australasian Coll. Surgeons (hon.), Soc. Internat. Chirurgie, N.Y. Regional Vascular Soc. (co-founder, pres. 1982-84), N.Am. Soc. Pacing and Electrophysiology (founding mem.), James IV Assn. Surgeons (dir., treas.), Lithuanian Vascular Soc. (hon.), Alpha Omega Alpha. Office: NYU Faculty Practice Area 530 1st Ave Ste 6-f New York NY 10016-6402 Home Phone: 727-867-8504; Office Phone: 212-263-7311. Business E-Mail: amimparatomdprnj@aol.com.

IMPELLIZERI, JOHN C. (JACK), mathematics educator; s. Jack W. and Catherine Impellizeri; m. Mary T. Blaney, Aug. 28, 1982; children: Traci A., Jack P., Jeremy J. BA, SUNY, New Paltz, 1973, MS in edn., 1978. Cert. tchr. NY State Edn. Dept. Math. tchr. Uniondale Pub. Schools, NY, 1985—. Founder/pres. JMI Computer Svcs., Freeport, NY, 1985—; adj. assoc. prof. math/computer/stats. dept. Nassau Cmty. Coll., Garden City, NY, 1999—. Author: Basic Mathematics Workbook, (newspaper column) Hyde Pk. Townsman, Anderson Sch.; author, editor, publisher Archbishop Molloy Coun. Yearbook, editor, author, publisher (monthly newsletter) The Molloy Monitor (3rd Pl. Nassau County Bull. Contest, Nassau/Suffolk Chpt. KC, 1998), dir., prodr. (video presentation) RST Presents Lawrence Road JHS; contbr. articles to newspapers. Former first aid instr. ARC, Mineola, NY; founder Yesterday, Today & Tomorrow Entertainment

Group, Freeport, NY, 1978—2005, dir., 1978—2005, performer, 1978—2005; former emt/crew chief Port Jefferson Ambulance Corps, NY; former firefighter Freeport Fire Dept. Emergency Co. #9, Freeport; former choral mem. masterwork chorus Masterwork Chorus & Orch., Morristown, NJ; former emt instr. Franklin Gen. Hosp., Lynbrook, NY; former choral mem. St. Cecilia Chorus, NYC; former chief timer, scorer NY Region Sports Car Club Am.; former v.p. sch. bd. Our Holy Redeemer, Freeport, former leader folk group, former co-leader Antioch Weekends, former choir mem. adult choir. Mem.: Internat. Coun. Webmasters, Nassau Reading Coun., Nat. PTA, Adj. Faculty Assn. (assoc.), Uniondale Teachers Assn. (assoc.), Padre Pio 4th Degree Assembly (assoc.), Friends for LI Heritage (life), KC (webmaster, publr. www.knightsite.com, former mem. supreme coun. internet steering com., former coord. internet workshop, #1 KC Website in World 1997, Website of Yr. 2003, listed #15 in Top 40 Cath. Websites in World 1997), Archbishop Molloy KC Coun. (assoc.; grand knight 1998—2000). Roman Catholic. Home Phone: 516-379-1938. Personal E-mail: knightsite@optonline.net.

IMPELLIZZERI, ANNE ELMENDORF, insurance company executive, non-profit executive; b. Chgo., Jan. 26, 1933; d. Armin and Laura (Gundlach) Elmendorf; m. Julius Simon Impellizzeri, Oct. 12, 1961 (dec.); children: Laura, Theodore (dec.). BA, Smith Coll., 1955; MA, Yale U., 1957. CLU; ChFC. With Met. Life Ins. Co., NYC, 1959—79, from asst. v.p., corp. social responsibility to v.p. group ins., 1979—88; v.p. N.Y.C. Partnership, NYC, 1988-90; pres., CEO Blanton-Peale Inst., NYC, 1990-98; exec. dir. Russel Wright's Manitoga, Garrison, NY, 1998—2001. Bus. urban issues coun. The Conf. Bd., 1981—85; bd. dirs. Bard Music Festival, 1990—; trustee Smith Coll., 1991—96; bd. dirs. Scenic Hudson, 1997—, treas., 1999—2002, sec., 2004—; trustee Nuveen Mut. Funds, 1994—2004. Trustee Lakeland Bd. Edn., Westchester County, NY, 1967-71, pres., 1970-71; bd. dirs. Nat. Safety Coun., 1974-80; trustee Cold Spring Spl. Bd. for Comprehensive Plan, 2006—; pres. Am. Assn. Gifted Children, 1975-85, chair, 1985-90. Named to Acad. of Women Achievers, YWCA NY, 1978; Fulbright grantee, 1955-56. Mem. Yale Club NYC, Smith Coll. Club N.Y., Women's City Club N.Y. (bd. mem. 2002-06, v.p. 2004-06), Yale Alumni Assn. (bd. govs. 1985-88), Phi Beta Kappa.

IMPERATO, JOSEPH JOHN, lawyer, composer; b. Jersey City, Mar. 14, 1956; s. Joseph Francis Imperato and Edith Roslyn (Dubin) Schwimmer. Student, Oberlin Coll., 1974-76; BA, Fla. State U., 1978, JD, 1981. Bar: Fla. 1983; court-cert. forensic audio expert, 2003. Trial atty., tng. instr. Office of Pub. Defender, Miami, Fla., 1982—. Lectr., mock trial coach Dade County sec. schs. and univs., Miami, 1993—; owner ImperaTunes Music, 1997—. Composer musical scores Fox TV Network, 1992-94; composer comml. jingles, 1975— (Addy award 1976), original songs, 1974— (Billboard Mag. Songwriting award 1995); composer, producer original childrens' musicals, 1997—2000. Mem. ASCAP, Audio Engring. Soc. Office: Office of Pub Defender 1320 NW 14th St Miami FL 33125-1609

IMPERIAL, HENRY L., internist; b. Irosin, Philippines, Apr. 24, 1963; s. Joaquin Sr. and Avelina (Li) I. BS in Med. Tech., Far Ea. U., 1984, MD, 1988. Diplomate Am. Bd. Internal Medicine. Med. resident in primary care internal medicine U. Medicine and Dentistry N.J. Robert Wood Johnson Med. Sch., New Brunswick, 1991-94; primary care/internal medicine physician Brownsville (Tex.) Cmty. Health Ctr., 1994—, asst. med. dir., 1996, med. dir., 1996—. Cmty. faculty East Tex. Area Health Edn. Ctr., 1995—; performance improvement program chmn. Brownsville Cmty Health Ctr., 1996—; clin. asst. prof. cmty. faculty U. Tex. Med. Br., Galveston, 1997—; clin. asst. prof. U. Tex. Health Sci. Ctr., San Antonio, 2000—05; clin. assoc. prof., 2005—. Pres. student coun. Far Ea. U. Sch. of Med. Tech., 1983-84. Fellow ACP; mem. AMA (Physicians Recognition award 1997—), Tex. Med. Assn./Cameron Willacy Med. Soc., Migrant Clinicians Network. Roman Catholic. Avocations: wine, chess. Office: Brownsville Cmty Health Ctr 2137 E 22nd St Brownsville TX 78521-2908 Office Phone: 956-548-7400. Office Fax: 956-546-2056. E-mail: hlimperial@hotmail.com.

IMPERIOLI, MICHAEL, actor; b. Mt. Vernon, NY, Jan. 1, 1966; m. Victoria Imperioli; children: Isabella, Vadim. Co-founder, co-artistic dir. Studio Dante, NYC, 2003—. Actor: (films) Alexa, 1988, Lean on Me, 1989, Goodfellas, 1990, Jungle Fever, 1991, Malcolm X, 1992, Fathers & Sons, 1992, Night We Never Met, 1993, Household Saints, 1993, Joey Breaker, 1993, Men Lie, 1994, Amateur, 1994, Postcards from America, 1994, Scenes From a New World, 1994, Hand Gun, 1994, Bad Boys, 1995, The Basketball Diaries, 1995, Clockers, 1995, Flirt, 1995, Dead Presidents, 1995, The Addiction, 1995, Trouble, 1995, I Shot Andy Warhol, 1996, Girls Town, 1996, Girl 6, 1996, Sweet Nothing, 1996, Tree's Lounge, 1996, Last Man Standing, 1996, Blixa Bargeld Stole My Cowboy Boots, 1996, Under the Bridge, 1997, Office Killer, 1997, The Deli, 1997, A River Made to Drown In, 1997, On the Run, 1999, Summer of Sam, 1999, Auto Motives, 2000, Love in the Time of Money, 2002, Stuey, 2003, My Baby's Daddy, 2004, (voice) Shark Tale, 2004,: (TV films) Firehouse, 1997, Witness to the Mob, 1998, Disappearing Act, 2000, Hamlet, 2000, The Five People You Meet in Heaven, 2004; (TV series) The Sopranos, 1999—2007 (Emmy award Outstanding Supporting Actor in a Drama Series, 2004); (plays) Aven' U Boys, Displaced Persons, Half Deserted Street, The Writing on the Wall, Little Blood Brother, Late Fragment, 2005, Chicken, 2007; writer: films Summer of Sam, 1999. Office: c/o The Endeavor Agy 10th Fl 9601 Wilshire Blvd Beverly Hills CA 90212*

IMPOCO, JIM, editor; married. Tokyo bur. chief to nat. bus. corr. US News & World Report, 1988—2000; asst. mng. editor Fortune mag., NYC, 2000—03; Sunday Bus. editor NY Times, NYC, 2003—05; dep. editor Conde Nast Portfolio, 2005—.

IMRAN, AYESHA, internist; b. Karachi, Pakistan, Feb. 13, 1967; came to U.S., 1993; d. Muhammed Iqbal Ali Khan and Rasheed Fatima Iqbal; m. Muhammed Imran, Mar. 18, 1993; children: Sarah, Saba, Ahmed Ismail, Ishaq. BA, U. Karachi, 1986, MBBS, 1992. Cert. Am. Bd. Internal Medicine. House officer in surgery and medicine Dow Med. Coll. Civil Hosp., Karachi, 1992-93; rsch. asst. Rush Presbyn. St. Lukes Med. Ctr., Chgo., 1994—95; resident in internal medicine Chgo. Med. Sch., 1996—99; practice primary care internal medicine Chgo., 1999—2002; fellow in geriat. Loyola U., Maywood, Ill., 2002—. Social worker Patients Welfare Assn., Pakistan, 1985, Pediats. Dept., Pakistan, 1990. Mem. ACP. Avocations: current news, travel, cooking. Home: 204 Bridle Path Cir Oak Brook IL 60523-2615 E-mail: geriatrics2@yahoo.com.

IMRAY, THOMAS JOHN, radiologist, educator; b. Milw., Nov. 11, 1939; s. George William and Genevieve (Bresnehan) I.; m. Carla Marie Rake, Aug. 17, 1963; children: John Scott, Jean Ann, Jeff William. BA, Marquette U., 1961, MD, 1965. Diplomate Nat. Bd. Med. Examiners, Am. Bd. Radiology (guest examiner 1975-76, 79, 85-2002). Intern St. Mary's Hosp., San Francisco, 1965-66; resident in radiology U. Minn., Mpls., 1966-70, instr., 1969-70; asst. prof. Med. Coll. of Wis., Milw., 1973-77, assoc. prof., 1977-80, U. Calif., Irvine, 1980-82; prof. and chmn. dept. radiology U. Nebr. Med. Ctr., Omaha, 1982-96, prof. dept. radiology, 1996—2005, prof. emeritus radiology, 2005—. Vis. prof. Vanderbilt U., Nashville, 1976, 82, U. Wis., Madison, 1978, SUNY Downstate Med. Ctr., Bklyn., 1978, Harvard Med. Sch., Boston, 1980, Loyola U. Sch. Medicine, Maywood, Ill., 1980, UCLA-Wadsworth VA Hosp., 1981, UCLA, 1982 Northwestern U. Sch. Medicine, Chgo., 1984, Meth. Hosp., Indpls., 1984, U. Mo., Kans. City, 1985, U. Iowa, Iowa City, 1986, U. Ark., Little Rock, 1987, Keio U. Sch. Medicine, Tokyo, 1989, Mich. State U., 1993. Contbr. articles to profl. jours. Mem. Tech. Task Force on Diagnostic Radiology Nebr. Dept. Health, 1983-84; Major U.S. Army M.C., 1970-73. Co-recipient Magna Cum Laude in Sci. Exhibits award Am. Soc. Neuroradiology, 1987; GE grantee, 1985-87. Fellow Am. Coll. Radiology; mem. AMA (rep. to radiology residency rev. com., 1987), Radiol. Soc. N. Am. (award 1981, 82), Am. Coll. Radiology (com. on satellite communications 1981-83), Am. Roentgen Ray Soc. (award 1986), Assn. Univ. Radiologists, Soc. Chmn. Acad. Radiology Depts., Am. Soc. Uroradiology, Nebr. State Radiol. Soc., Nebr. State Med. Assn., Omaha Metro Med. Soc., Omaha Mid-West Clin. Soc. (hosp. and svc. exhibits com. 1984, award 1986), Omaha C. of C. (task force on edn. 1983-85, edn. coun. steering com. 1984, edn. coun. 1985), Rotary Internat. (program com. 1986), Marquette U. Club (bd. dirs. Omaha chpt., 1987), Alpha Omega Alpha (alumni and faculty mems. com., 1986). Roman Catholic. Avocation: swimming. Office: Nebr Health Sys Dept Radiology 981045 Nebr Med Ctr Omaha NE 68198-1045

IMRE, CHRISTINA JOANNE, lawyer; b. Gary, Ind., Oct. 25, 1950; d. Joseph and Ruth Leone I.; m. Richard Long, Dec. 31, 1991. BA, Mt. St. Mary's Coll., LA, 1972; MA, U. Notre Dame, 1974; JD, Loyola Law Sch., LA, 1980. Bar: Calif. 1980, US Ct. Appeals (9th cir.) 1982, US Dist. Ct. (ctrl. dist.) Calif. 1983, US Dist. Ct. (no. dist.) Calif. 1988, US Dist. Ct. (so. dist.) Calif. 1995, US Supreme Ct. 2000. Assoc. Lascher & Lascher, Ventura, Calif., 1980-83, Law Office of Errol Berk, Ventura, Calif., 1983-84, Pachter, Gold & Schaffer, LA, 1984-87; sr. atty. Kornblum & McBride, LA, 1987-89; ptnr. Horvitz & Levy LLP, Encino, Calif., 1989—2000, Crosby, Heafey, Roach & May, Los Angeles, 2000—02, Sedgwick, Detert, Moran & Arnold, LLP, Los Angeles, 2002—. Bd. govs. Calif. Continuing Edn. of Bar, Berkeley, Calif., 1996-2000; chair Calif. Continuing Edn. of Bar Joint Adv. Com., Berkeley, 1995; editorial bd. L.A. Lawyer Mag., L.A., 1996-99; cons. Handling Civil Appeals, Berkeley, 1996, Calif. Trial Practice, Berkeley, 1995; lectr. in field. Editor-in-chief: Loyola of Los Angeles International & Comparative Law Journal, 1979-80; monthly columnist CEB Civil Litigation Reporter; contbr. articles to profl. jours. and chpts. to books. Named one of 50 Most Powerful Women in LA Law, LA Business Journal, 1998; Loyola Law Sch. fellow, 1979-80, U. Notre Dame fellow, 1972-74; named Southern Calif. Super Lawyer, LA Mag., 2003-. Mem. L.A. County Bar Assn., Defense Rsch. Inst., So. Calif. Defense Counsel Assn. Avocations: music, shakespeare, history, philosophy. Office: Sedgwick Detert Moran & Arnold LLP 801 S Figueroa St 19th Fl Los Angeles CA 90017 Business E-Mail: christina.imre@sdma.com.

IMUS, DEIRDRE (COLEMAN), health facility administrator, writer; m. Don Imus; 1 child, (Frederick) Wyatt. BA in internat. rels., Villanova U. Co-founder, co-dir. with Don Imus The Imus Cattle Ranch for Kids with Cancer, Ribera, N.Mex., 1998—; founder, pres. The Deirdre Imus Environ. Ctr. Pediat. Oncology, Hackensack U. Med. Ctr. Launched Greening the Cleaning products with husband (Don Imus) Imus Ranch Foods. Author: The Imus Ranch: Cooking for Kids and Cowboys, 2004, (book series) Green This! Volume 1: Greening Your Cleaning, 2007; guest appearances The Today Show, The View, & Martha, 2007, featured in magazines Prevention, InStyle, Town & Country, New Jersey Life & Blueprint, 2007. Named Women of Substance and Style, Organic Style mag. Achievements include completed several triathlons and ran the NYC marathon twice, in the time of 3 hours 31 minutes; instituting an environmentally sound award winning program called 'Greening the Cleaning' in The Deirdre Imus Environ. Ctr. Pediat. Oncology, Hackensack U. Med. Ctr. Office: Deirdre Imus Environ Ctr for Pediat Oncology David Jurist Rsch Bldg Rm 240 30 Prospect Ave Hackensack NJ 07601*

IMUS, DON (JOHN DONALD IMUS JR.), radio personality; b. Riverside, Calif., July 23, 1940; m. Deirdre Coleman; 1 child, (Frederick) Wyatt;children from previous marriage: Nadine, Toni, Elizabeth, Ashleigh. Radio host WNBC, 1971-88, WFAN, 1988—2007; TV host MSNBC, 1996—2007. Co-founder, dir. Imus Cattle Ranch for Kids with Cancer, Ribera, N. Mex., 1998-; launched food line, Imus Ranch Foods to help fund work of Ranch, also Greening the Cleaning products with wife, Deirdre; co-owner (with Fred Imus) Imus Ranch Coffee, Mohegan Sun Casino, Uncasville, Conn. Author: God's Other Son; co-author: (with Fred Imus) Two Guy's Four Corners, 1997; actor Odd Jobs, 1986; appeared on Prime Time Live, 20/20, Larry King, David Letterman, CBSs 48 Hours, 60 Minutes, The Today Show. Host radiothon CJ Found. for Sudden Infant Death Syndrome (also dir. emeritus), the Tomorrow's Children's Fund, and the Imus Ranch, 1990-; raised money for the construction of a Don Imus/WFAN Pediatric Ctr. for Tomorrow's Children, Hackensack Med. Ctr., NJ. With USMC, 1957—59. Recipient Marconi award, 1990, 1992, 1994, 1997, Humanitarian award (with Deirdre Imus), Cancer Rsch. and Treatment Fund, 2004; named Major Market Personality of the Year, Syndicated Personality of the Year; Named to Emerson Radio Hall Fame, Nat. Assn. Broadcasters Broadcasting Hall of Fame; named Time Mags. Most Influential Ams., 1997. Office: Westwood One Entertainment 1675 Broadway New York NY 10019-5820 also: care WFAN-AM 34-12 36th St Astoria NY 11106*

IMWINKELRIED, EDWARD JOHN, law educator; b. San Francisco, Sept. 19, 1946; s. John Joseph and Enes Rose (Gianelli) I.; m. Cynthia Marie Clark, Dec. 30, 1978; children— Marie Elise, Kenneth West BA, U. San Francisco, 1967, JD, 1969. Bar: Calif. 1970, Mo. 1984, U.S. Supreme Ct. 1974. Prof. law U. San Diego, 1974-79; prof. law Washington U., St. Louis, 1979-85, Edward L. Barrett jr. prof. law, 2004—; prof. law U. Calif.-Davis, 1985—. Disting. faculty mem. Nat. Coll. Dist. Attys., Houston, 1978— Author: Evidentiary Foundations, 1980, 6th rev. edit., 2005, Uncharged Misconduct Evidence, 1984, rev. edit., 1999, The New Wigmore: Evidentiary Privileges, 2002; co-author: McCormick, Evidence, 6th edit., 2006, Materials for Study of Evidence, 1983, 6th edit., 2007, Scientific Evidence, 1986, 4th edit., 2007, Pretrial Discovery: Strategy and Tactics, 1986, rev. edit., 2004, Courtroom Criminal Evidence, 1987, 4th edit., 2005, California Evidentiary Foundations, 1988, 3d edit., 2000, Dynamics of Trial Practice, 1989, 3d edit., 2002, Exculpatory Evidence, 1990, 3d edit., 2004, Florida Evidentiary Foundations, 1991, 2d edit., 1997, Illinois Evidentiary Foundations, 1991, 2d edit., 1997, Texas Evidentiary Foundations, 1992, 3d edit., 2005, New York Evidentiary Foundations, 1993, 2d edit., 1997, Evidentiary Distinctions, 1993, Colorado Evidentiary Foundations, 1997; contbg. editor Champion pub. Assn. Criminal Def. Lawyers, 1983, Criminal Law Bull. Mem. Am. Acad. Forensic Sci., ABA (continuing edn. com. 1983-84), Am. Assn. Law Schs. (chmn. evidence sect. 1983) Democrat. Roman Catholic. Avocation: jogging. Home: 2204 Shenandoah Pl Davis CA 95616-6603 Office: U Calif Law Sch Davis CA 95616 Office Phone: 530-752-0727. Business E-Mail: ejimwinkelried@ucdavis.edu.

INABINET, GEORGE WALKER, JR., retired state agency administrator; b. Cameron, SC, Sept. 24, 1927; s. George Walker and Elizabeth (Wolfe) I.; m. Helen Ruth Davis, Sept. 27, 1947; children: Pamela Ruth, Jeffrey Walker. Cert. EE, S.C. Area Trade Sch., Columbia, 1949; Bus. Mgmt. degree, U. S.C., 1951; electronics engr. cert., Nat. Radio Inst., Washington, 1967. Asst. dir. S.C. Dept. Hwys., Columbia, 1951-53; adminstr. transp. S.C. Dept. Edn., Columbia, 1953-90. Chmn. Boy Scouts Am., Sandy Run, S.C., 1965-70; pres. Sandy Run Cmty. Club, 1966-70, S.C. Football Ofcls. Assn., Columbia, 1971-72; mem. White House Coun. on Youth, Washington, 1972-76; chmn. Calhoun County Tri-Centennial Commn., 1970; chmn. adminstrn. bd. Mt. Zion United Meth. Ch., Sandy Run, 1952-75; mem. Gov.'s Com. on Comm.; vice chmn. Calhoun County Planning Commn., 1996—, Calhoun County Planning Com.; pres. ch. coun. Sandy Run Luth. Ch. Named to S.C. Football Ofcls. Hall of Fame, 2000. Mem. Assn. Pub. Safety Communications Officers (pres. 1979-81), Assn. Pub. Communications Officers (v.p. 1979-80, pres. 1980-81), S.C. Assn. Pupil Transp. (v.p. 1981-82, pres. 1982-83), Columbia Civitan Club (pres. elect), Am. Legion (chmn. state oratorical com. 1989-97, mem. nat. commn. on Americanism), Masons, Shriners. Avocations: golf, fishing, swimming, sports. Home: Windy Hill 2496 Old State Rd Swansea SC 29160-9350 Office Phone: 803-920-1171.

INAGAMI, TADASHI, biochemistry professor; b. Kobe, Japan, Feb. 20, 1931; m. Masako Araki, Nov. 12, 1961 BS, Kyoto U., 1953, DSc, 1963; MS, Yale U., 1955, PhD, 1958. Rsch. staff Yale U., New Haven, 1958—59, rsch. assoc., 1962—66; rsch. staff Kyoto U., Japan, 1959—62; instr. biochemistry Nagoya City U., Japan, 1962; asst. prof. biochemistry Vanderbilt U., Nashville, 1966—69, assoc. prof., 1969—74, prof. biochemistry, 1975—91, dir. hypertension rsch. ctr., 1979—95, Stanford Moore prof. biochemistry, 1991—, prof. medicine, 1992—. Contbr. numerous articles to profl. jours. Fulbright fellow, 1954-55; recipient Roche Vis. Prof. award, 1980, Humboldt Found. award, 1981, Spa award Belgium Nat. Funds Sci. Rsch., 1985, Ciba award High Blood Pressure Res Coun., 1986, Sutherland prize Vanderbilt U., 1990, Charles Park award for Excellence in Rsch., 2002, Okamoto Internat. award Japan Vascular Disease Rsch. Found., 1994. Res Achievement award, 1995, award for excellence in cardiovascular rsch. Bristol Meyers Squibb, 1996, award Japan Acad., 1996, Jokichi Takamine award Japan Cardiovasc. Endocrine-Metabolism Soc., 1998, Merit award NHLBI, 2000 Mem.: Japan Soc. Cardiovascular Endocrinol. Metabolism, Japan Soc. Biochemistry, Japan Soc. Hypertension, Internat. Soc. Hypertension, Am. Soc. Hypertension, Soc. Neurosci., Am. Soc. Cell Biology, Am. Heart Assn. (Rsch. Achievement award 1994), Am. Soc. Pharmacology and Therapeutics, Am. Chem. Soc., Endocrine Soc., Am. Physiol. Soc., Am. Soc. Biol. Chemists and Molecular Biologists, Japan Soc. Agrl. Chemistry (hon.), Japan Endocrine Soc. (hon.). Office: Vanderbilt U Sch Medicine Dept Biochemistry 23D Ave S And Pierce Ave Nashville TN 37232-0146 Home Phone: 615-373-0036; Office Phone: 615-322-4347. Business E-Mail: tadashi.inagami@vanderbilt.edu.

INAN, ZABRIN, psychiatrist; d. Sabit and Czatdana Inan; children: Eden Inan-Lynch, Gabriel Inan-Lynch(dec.). BS magna cum laude, Loyola U., 1989; MD, U. Ill., 1994. Am. Bd. Psychiatry and Neurology. Child, adolescent and adult psychiatrist Linden Oaks Hosp., Naperville, Ill., 2001—02; child and adolescent psychiatrist Helen Ross McNabb Ctr., Knoxville, Tenn., 2002; pvt. practice Chicago, 2002—, Northbrook, Ill., 2002—. Contbr. articles to profl. jours. including Psychiatry & Psychopharmacology. Inst. Juvenile Rsch., Child and Adolescent Psychiatry fellow, U. Ill., Chgo., 2001. Mem.: Ill. State Psychiat. Inst., Ill. Med. Soc. (licentiate), Am. Psychiatry Assn. (licentiate), Am. Acad. Child & Adolescent Psychiatry (licentiate). Avocations: tennis, ballet. Office: 680 N Lake Shore Dr Ste 917B Chicago IL 60611 Office Phone: 312-286-1785.

IÑÁRRITU, ALEJANDRO GONZÁLEZ, film director, producer; b. Mexico City, Aug. 15, 1963; married. Dir. Televisa, Mexico; founder Zeta Films, 1991. Dir.: (films) Timbre, El, 1996, Powder Keg, 2001; dir., prodr. (films) Amores perros, 2000, 11'09''01 - September 11 (Mexico segment), 2002, 21 Grams, 2003, Babel, 2006 (Best Dir. Prize, Cannes Film Festival, 2006, Best Motion Picture-Drama, Golden Globe award, Hollywood Fgn. Press. Assn., 2007), exec. prodr. Nine Lives, 2005, Toro negro, 2005.*

INCANDELA, GERALD JEAN-MARIE, artist; b. Tunis, Tunisia, Feb. 19, 1952; came to U.S., 1977; s. Laurent and Gilda (Solina) I. BA, Janson De Sailly, Paris, 1970; postgrad., U. of Nanterre, Paris, 1971-73. One man shows include Felicity Samuel Gallery, London, 1978, Gallery Jean Chauvelin, Paris, 1978, Charles Cowles Gallery, NY, 1981, Robert Fraser Gallery, London, 1984, Mus. Modern Art, Oxford, Eng., 1986, Paul Kasmin, NY, 1988, SEBU, Japan, 1990; exhbns. in group shows at Hal Bromm Gallery, 1975, Grey Art Gallery, 1977, Corcoran Gallery, 1978, Jacksonville Mus., Fla., 1981, The Drawing Ctr., NYC, 1982, Met. Mus. of NYC, 1982, Mus. of Modern Art, 1983, Walker Art Ctr., 1986, J. Paul Getty Mus., Santa Monica, 1998, Galerie Beyeler, Basel, 2002. Home and Office: 88 Lexington Ave New York NY 10016-8943 Office Phone: 212-679-7568.

INCAPRERA, FRANK PHILIP, internist; b. New Orleans, Aug. 24, 1928; s. Charles and Mamie (Bellipanni) I.; m. Ruth Mary Duhon, Sept. 13, 1952; children: Charles, Cynthia, James, Christopher, Catherine. BS, Loyola U. of South, 1946; MD, La. State U. Med. Sch., 1950. Diplomate Am. Bd. Internal Medicine. Intern Charity Hosp., New Orleans, 1950-51, resident, 1951-52, VA Hosp., New Orleans, 1952-54; practice medicine specializing in internal medicine New Orleans, 1957-97; med. dir. Internal Medicine Group, 1973-97, chief med. officer, 1997-99. Med. dir. Owens-Ill. Glass Co., New Orleans, 1961-85, Kaiser Aluminum Co., Chalmette, La., 1975-84, Tenneco Oil Co., Chalmette, 1978-84, Luth. Nursing Home, 1990-99; assoc. med. dir. Cigna Health Plan of La., 1991-99; co-founder Med. Ctr. E. New Orleans, 1975; clin. assoc. prof. medicine Tulane U. Sch. Medicine, 1971-87, clin. prof. medicine, 1987-99, clin. prof. medicine La. State U., 1994-; adv. bd. Healthcare New Orleans, 1991-96; mem. New Orleans Bd. Health, 1966-70. Bd. dirs. Meth. Hosp., 1971-97, sec. 1992-96, Chateau de Notre Dame, 1977-92, New Orleans Opera Assn., 1975—; mem. New Orleans Human Rels. Com., 1968-70; bd. dirs. Emergency Med. Svcs. Coun., 1977-86, pres. La. southeastern region, 1979-81; bd. dirs. New Orleans East Bus. Assn., 1980-99, v.p. 1981-83; bd. dirs. Luth. Towers, 1988-89, Peace Lake Towers, 1988-89, La. State U. Med. Ctr. Found. Bd., 1989-91, Cristo Sana, 1997—; mem. pastoral care adv. com. So. Bapt. Hosp., 1982-83; mem. pres.'s adv. bd. coun. Loyola U. of South, 1989-96; mem. Mayor's Mil. Adv. Com., New Orleans, 2001—. Capt. USAF, 1955-57. Named Man of Yr., St. Gabriel Holy Name Soc., 1964; recipient Lifetime award Outstanding Svc., Cefalutana Soc., La., 1998, Pres.'s award, New Orleans East Bus. Assn., 2000, Andrew Jackson Higgins award, Mayor's Mil. Adv. Com., 2002, Founders award, Italian-Am. Fedn. of the S.E., 2003, Spirit Charity award, Med. Ctr. La. Found., 2005. Master: ACP (gov. 1995—99, Laureate award 1993); mem.: AMA, La. Soc. Internal Medicine (exec. com. 1975—98, pres. 1983—85), La. State Med. Soc. (v.p. 1975—76, Continuing Med. Edn. award for Outstanding Contributions to advancement of continuing med. edn. in La. 2001), La. Occupl. Medicine Assn. (pres. 1971—72), New Orleans Acad. Internal Medicine (pres. 1969), Orleans Parish Med. Soc. (sec. 1972—74, Outstanding Physician award 2000), La. Med. Soc. (v.p. 1975—76), Am. Coll. Physicians Execs., Am. Geriatrics Soc., La. State U. Med. Sch. Alumni Assn. (pres. 1989—90, Alumnus of Yr. 1996), New Orleans East C. of C. (dir. 1979—85), Optimists Club (bd. dirs. New Orleans 1964—69), Blue Key, Order of St. Louis, Alpha Omega Alpha (Beta chpt., Vol. Clin. Faculty award 2003), Delta Epsilon Sigma. Home: 2218 Lake Oaks Pky New Orleans LA 70122-4345 Personal E-mail: fincaprera@aol.com.

INCE, LAUREL T., music educator; b. Gonzales, Tex. m. Joe C. Ince; children: Joe C. Ince, Jr.(dec.) , Mark A., Susan I. Burns, William C. BMus, Trinity U., 1950. Piano tchr. Ince Piano Studio, Gonzales, 1950—. Performer various internat. workshops, Austria, Can., Switzerland, Scotland, France; south ctrl. coord. music Link Found., 1990—; chmn. founders coun. Internat. Festival Inst. at Round Top, 2007—. Contbr. articles to profl. jours. Advisor City Coun., Gonzales; accompanist First Bapt. Ch., Gonzales; pres. Sesame Club, Gonzales. Recipient Tchr. of Yr. award, Austin Music Tchrs. Assn., 1995, Pillar of the Point award, Inspiration Point Fine Arts Colony; Tex. fellow, Music Tchrs. Nat. Assn. Mem.: Music Tchrs. Nat. Assn. Found. Fund (Tex. chair), Nat. Guild Piano Tchrs., Tex. Music Tchrs. Assn. (state pres., Tchr. of Yr. award 1995), Nat. Fedn. Music Clubs (life; chmn. FAMA 1991, co-chmn. nat. conv. 2005, recording sec., lectr., performer, Tex. rep. to bd. dirs.), Tex. Fedn. Music

Clubs (founder jr. state festival 1975, state pres.), Sigma Alpha Iota (life). Avocations: entertaining, travel. Home: 723 St Francis Str Gonzales TX 78629 Home Phone: 830-672-3757. Home Fax: 830-672-5808. Personal E-mail: ljince@stx.rr.com.

INCHIOSA, MARIO ANTHONY, JR., pharmacologist; b. Weehawken, NJ, Jan. 9, 1929; s. Mario and Christina Inchiosa; m. Elisabeth Harris Stamm, Aug. 14, 1977; m. Valerie Norma Stoppani, July 4, 1955 (dec. Jan. 10, 1972); children: Maria Valerie Warburton, Mario Emil, Andrew Stamm. BS, Rutgers U., 1950, MS, 1953; PhD, U. Ill., 1956. Postdoctoral fellow Argonne Nat. Lab., Ill., 1956—58; sr. rsch. scientist N.Y. State Dept. Mental Hygiene, SI, NY, 1958—60; rsch. assoc. Med. Sch. Harvard U., Boston, 1960—66; prof. pharmacology N.Y. Med. Coll., Valhalla, NY, 1966—. Cons. U.S. FDA, Washington, 1996—. Contbr. articles to profl. jours. Grantee, USPHS, Nat. Heart Inst., NIH, 1967—69, USPHS, Nat. Heart and Lung Inst., NIH, 1970—74, Am. Heart Assn., 1987—90, Berlex Labs., Inc., 1998—2001. Mem.: Soc. Cardiovasc. Anesthesiologists, Internat. Anesthesia Rsch. Soc., Am. Soc. Pharmacology and Exptl. Therapeutics. Achievements include patent for intravenous phenoxybenzamine for treatment of reflex sympathetic dystrophy. Office: New York Med Coll Basic Science Bldg Valhalla NY 10595 Office Phone: 914-594-4129. Business E-Mail: mario_inchiosa@nymc.edu.

INCROPERA, FRANK PAUL, mechanical engineering educator; b. Lawrence, Mass., May 12, 1939; s. James Frank and Ann Laura (Leone) I.; m. Andrea Jeanne Eastman, Sept. 2, 1960; children: Terri Ann, Donna Renee, Shaunna Jeanne. BSME, MIT, 1961; MS, Stanford U., 1962, PhD, 1966. Jr. engr. Barry Controls Corp., Watertown, Mass., 1959; thermodynamics engr. Aerojet Gen. Corp., Azusa, Calif., 1961; heat transfer specialist Lockheed Missiles and Space Co., Sunnyvale, Calif., 1962-64; mem. faculty Purdue U., 1966-98, prof. mech. engring., 1973-98, head dept., 1989-98; dean of engring. U. Notre Dame, Ind., 1998—2006, Clifford and Evelyn Brosey prof. mech. engring., 1998—. Cons. in field. Author: Introduction to Molecular Structure and Thermodynamics, 1974, Fundamentals of Heat Transfer, 1985, 90, 96, 2001, 06; Fundamentals of Heat and Mass Transfer, 1981, 85, 90, 96, 2001, 06, Liquid Cooling of Electronic Devices by Single-Phase Convection, 1999; also articles. Recipient Solberg Teaching award Purdue U., 1973, 77, 86, Potter Teaching award, 1973, Von Humboldt sr. scientist award Fed. Republic Germany, 1988; named One of the 100 most frequently cited engrs. in the world Inst. for Sci. Info., 2000. Fellow AAAS, ASME (Melville medal 1988, Heat Transfer Meml. award 1988, Worcester Reed Warner award 1995); mem. Am. Soc. Engring. Edn. (Ralph C. Roe award 1982, George Westinghouse award 1983), Nat. Acad. Engring. Achievements include invention of bloodless surg. scalpel. Office: U Notre Dame Coll Engring 257 Fitzpatrick Hall Notre Dame IN 46556 Business E-Mail: fpi@nd.edu.

INCULET, ION I., electrical engineer, educator, science association director, consultant; b. Iasi, Moldova, Romania, Feb. 11, 1921; arrived in Can., 1948; s. Ion C. and Ruxanda (Basota) I.; m. Marion Elsie Smith, Aug. 25, 1951; children: Richard, Catherine, Diana. Diploma in engring., Politechnica, Bucuresti, Romania, 1944; M in Engring. Sci., Laval U., Que., 1962; DTechSc (hon.), Bucuresti U., Romania, 1993; DSc (hon.), We. Ont. Can. U., 1996. Advance devel. engr. Can. GE, Peterborough, Ont., 1948-56, mgr. engring., Que., 1956-64; prof. elec. engring. U. Western Ont., London, 1964—, dir. environ. engring., 1966-68, dir. Applied Electrostatics Rsch. Ctr., 1986—. Pres. Elstat, Ltd., London, 1972—; cons. in field. Author: 1 book; contbr. over 110 articles to profl. jours., book chpts.; holder 27 patents. Recipient T.C. Keefer medal Can. Soc. Civil Engring., 1994-95. Fellow IEEE (Centennial medal 1984), Can. Acad. Engring., Inst. Electrostatics of Japan; mem. NSPE (engring. medal 1984), Industry Applications Soc. IEEE (Outstanding Achievement award 1983), Romanian Acad. (hon.). Avocation: skiing. Home: 81 Lloyd Manor Crescent London ON Canada N6H 3Z4 Office: U Western Ont Engring Bldg Electrostatics Rsch Ctr London ON Canada N6A 5B9 Office Phone: 519-661-2002. Business E-Mail: iinculet@uwo.ca.

INDIANA, ROBERT (CLARK), artist; b. New Castle, Ind., Sept. 13, 1928; Student, John Herron Sch. Art, 1945-46, Munson-Williams-Proctor Inst., 1947-48, Skowhegan Sch. of Painting and Sculpture, summer 1953; student (scholarship); B.F.A., Chgo. Art Inst., 1953; student, U. Edinburgh, Scotland, 1953-54; D.F.A. (hon.), Franklin and Marshall Coll., 1970, U. Ind., 1977; DFA (hon.), Colby Coll., Waterville, Maine, 1981. Artist-in-residence Ctr. Contemporary Art, Aspen, Colo., 1968. Exhbns. include, Mus. Modern Art, 1961, 63, Dallas Mus. Contemporary Arts, 1962, San Francisco Mus. Art, 1962, Art Inst. Chgo., 1963, Beaverbrook Art Gallery, Fredericton, N.B., 1963, Tate Gallery, London, Eng., 1963-64, Washington Gallery Modern Art, 1963, Whitney Mus., 1963, Guggenheim Mus., 1963, Albright-Knox Art Gallery, Buffalo, 1963, Am. Cultural Center, Paris, France, 1963, Gemeente Mus., The Hague, Netherlands, 1964, U. Ill. at Champaign, 1965, Worcester (Mass.) Art Mus., 1965, White House Festival Arts, 1965, Stedelijk Mus., Amsterdam, Wurttembergischer Kunstverein, Stuttgart, U. St. Thomas, Houston, Smithsonian Instn., 6th Biennale San Marino, Carnegie Inst., Royal Dublin Soc., Documenta IV, Germany, Whitney Mus. Am. Art, 1975, Corcoran Gallery, 1975, San Francisco Mus. Art, 1975, Fine Arts Gallery San Diego, 1976, Dallas Mus. Fine Arts, 1976, Josly Art Mus., Omaha, 1976, Greenville (S.C.) County Mus., 1977, Va. Mus. Fine Arts, 1977, Lafayette (La.) Natural History Mus. and Planetarium, 1977, Colby Coll. Mus. Art, 1982, Nat. Mus. Art, 1984, Salama-Caro Gallery, London, 1991, Royal Acad. London, 1991, Portland Mus. Art, Maine, 1991, Museo Nacional Reina Sofia, Madrid, 1992. Numerous one-man shows at, Stable Gallery, N.Y.C., 1962, 64, 66, Rolf Nelson Gallery, LA, 1965, Stedelijk van Abbemuseum, Eindhoven, Holland, Mus. Haus Lange, Krefeld, Germany, Galerie Schmela, Dusseldorf, Germany, 1966, Wurttembergisher Kunstverein, Stuttgart, Germany, 1966, Inst. Contemporary Art U. Pa., 1968, Gallery Denise Rene, 1972, McNay Inst., San Antonio, Herron Art Mus., Indpls., 1977, Santa Fe Mus., 1976, Indpls. Mus. Art, 1977, Osuna Gallery, Washington, 1981, Art Ctr., Waco, Tex., 1982, Marisa del Re Gallery, 1990, Susan Sheehan Gallery, NYC, 1991, Frederick R. Wiesman Art Mus. Mpls., 1995, Terra Mus. Art., Chgo., 1995, Fla. Internat. U., Miami, 1995, Indpl. Mus. Art, 1996, Musee d'Art Moderne et d'Art Conemporain, Nice, France, 1998, Portland Mus. Art, Maine, 1999, Gana Ctr., Seoul, Republic of Korea, 1999, Indpls. Mus. Art, 2000, Galleria Ateneo de Caracas, Venezula, 2001, Galerie Denise Rene, 2001, Scottsdale Mus. Contemporary Art, 2002, Peace Paintings, 2003, Paul Kasmin Gallery, NY, 2003, Michael Kohn Gallery, Calif., 2003, C&M Arts, NYC, 2003, Gallery Hyundai, 2004, Waddington Galleries, London, 2004, Price Tower Arts Ctr., Okla., 2004, Olin Art Ctr., Bates Coll., 2005, Paul Kasmin Gallery, 2005, Price Arts Ctr., 2005, MECA, 2006, others; designer: sets and costumes The Mother of Us All; executed mural for N.Y. State Bldg., N.Y. World's Fair, 1964-65; illusr. "Numbers", 1968; represented in permanent collections, Mus. Modern Art, Whitney Mus., Finch Coll., N.Y.C., Albright-Knox Gallery Art, Larry Aldrich Mus., Ridgefield, Conn., Balt. Mus. Art, Detroit Inst. Arts, Walker Art Center, Mpls., Rose Art Mus. of Brandeis U., Sheldon Meml. Art Gallery of U. Nebr., Washington Gallery Modern Art, Stedelijk Mus., Amsterdam, Holland, Stedelijk van Abbemuseum, Eindhoven, Holland, Von der Heydt Mus., Wuppertal, Germany, Mus. Hans Lange, Krefeld, Germany, Art Gallery of Toronto, Carnegie Inst., Krannert Art Mus., U. Ill., Los Angeles County Mus., Mich. U. Mus. Art, LOVE sculpture, Monaca, 1991, Fla. 1998, NYC 2000, many other sculptures and permanent exhibits throughout the world. With USAF, 1946—49. Decorated Medal of Merit; Albert A. List Found. grantee for inaugural poster of N.Y. State Theatre, Lincoln Ctr., 1964; Brown Travelling fellow Art Inst. Chgo., 1953; honored by Gov. Ind., 1973. Mem. Delta Phi Delta (pres. Zeta chpt. 1951-52); Royal Soc. Arts. Mailing: Star of Hope PO Box 808 Vinalhaven ME 04863-0432

INDIC, PREMANANDA, education educator, researcher; m. Mridhu Ramanath, May 5, 1993; children: Anagha M., Arnav A. Bin Tech, U. Calicut, India, 1992, M in Tech, 1995; PhD, Cochin U. of Sci. & Tech., India, 2001. Lectr. in elec. engring. Cochin (India) U. of Sci. & Tech., 1996—2001; rsch. fellow Harvard Med. Sch., Boston, 2001—04; instr. U. Mass Med. Sch., Worcester, 2005—. Author: (rsch. article) Jour. of Theoretical Biology, Jour. of Biological Rhythms. Fellow GATE, Govt. of India, 1993—95; Postdoctoral Fellowship in Medicine, Harvard Med. Sch., 2001—04. Mem.: Soc. for Rsch. on Biol. Rhythms, Sleep Rsch. Soc., Soc. for Math. Biology. Achievements include estimation of amplitude recovery dynamics of biological clock in the human brain using an integrated dynamic and stochastic model. Office: U Mass Med Sch 55 Lake Ave N Worcester MA 01655 Home Phone: 508-845-2399; Office Phone: 508-856-6283. Business E-Mail: premananda.indic@umassmed.edu.

INDIVIGLIA, SALVATORE JOSEPH, artist, retired military officer; b. NYC, Nov. 16, 1919; s. Joseph and Alfonsina Barbara (Gaeta) I.; widower Jan. 1986; children: Barbara Ann (dec.), Joseph (dec.), Lawrence, Dianne. BA, Pratt Inst., 1948; AS, U.S. Naval Acad., 1976. Mural painter asst. Crimi Studio, NYC, 1939-42; art dir. Advt. Printin Co., NYC, 1946-63; art tchr. Mechanics Inst., NYC, 1962-66; v.p. Vogue Wright Studios, NYC, 1963-80; dir. art Electrographic Corp., NYC, Chgo., 1968-70; artist, account exec. Chelsea Photo/Graphics, Inc., NYC, 1981-84. Ofcl. USN combat artist, Washington, 1960-89. Exhibited in group shows at Smithsonian Inst. Operations Palette, 1965, Joe and Emily Lowe Found., 1955, 1963 (Liquitex award, 1997); painter Am. Artist Mag., 1971; McLean Libr. Collection Hofstra U. WWII Posters, 2004; painter watercolors USN Combat Art Collection, N.Y. State Naval Militia, 1962, 1991, 1994, 1996—2007, US Navy Combat Art 1964-1967, Vietnam, —, " Homeless Veterans" Nassau County Vets. Svc. Agy., 2005—, featured USN combat artist, Channel 12 TV, N.Y., 2001; paintings of Vietnam ops. in 1967, 2005—, Franklin Sq. Hist. Soc., 2005—, Represented in permanent collections Hofstra U. McLean Collection (now Salvatore J. Indiviglia Collection). Hon. chair Brigade Activities Ctr. US Naval Acad., Annapolis, Md., 1994. Comdr. USNR, 1962—67. Decorated U.S. Navy Commendation medal, Croce Al Merito Di Guerra (Italy), Vietnamese Cross of Gallantry with palm; recipient U.S. Naval Acad. Supt.'s award, 1983. Roman Catholic. Avocations: playing guitar, singing country & western music. Home: 974 Lorraine Dr Franklin Square NY 11010-1813 Office Phone: 516-775-3447.

INDURSKY, ARTHUR, lawyer; b. Bklyn., Jan. 1, 1943; s. David and Anne (Levine) I.; m. Deanne Fiedler, Mar. 26, 1967; 1 child, Blake. BBA, CCNY, 1964; JD, Bklyn. Law Sch., 1967. Bar: N.Y., 1968. Entertainment counsel Columbia Pictures, NYC, 1969-72; mng. ptnr. Grubman Indursky & Schindler P.C., NYC, 1973—. Bd. dirs. Alliance Artists and Rec. Cos.; guest spkr. Can. Rec. Industry Seminar, 1986, Entertainment Law Soc., Bklyn. Law Sch., 1987, 92, Copyright Soc., 1988, Disting. Alumni Lecture Series Bklyn. Law Sch., 1989, Hofstra Law Sch., 1995. Bd. dirs. T.J. Martell Found. for Leukemia, Cancer and AIDS Rsch., 1993—. Recipient 1st Ann. Alumni Achievement award Bklyn. Law Sch., 1992, Outstanding Leadership award Meml. Sloan Kettering Cancer Ctr., 1994, City of Hope award, 1995, Jule Styne Humanitarian award Childrens Hearing Inst., 1998. Office: Grubman Indursky & Schindler PC 152 W 57th St New York NY 10019-3310

INDYK, MARTIN S., think-tank executive, former ambassador; b. London, July 1, 1951; m. Jill Collier; children: Jacob, Sarah. BE, Sydney U., 1972; PhD in Internat. Rel., Australian Natl. U., 1977. Spec. asst. to the pres. & sr. dir. for Near East & So. Asian affairs NSC, 1993—95, deputy dir. current intelligence for the Mid-East Australia, 1978; exec. dir Washington Inst. for Near East Policy, 1985—93; US amb. to Israel US Dept. State, Tel Aviv, 1995—97, 2000—01, asst. sec. Near Ea. affairs Washington, 1997-2000; sr. fellow The Brookings Inst., Washington, 2001—, dir., Saban Ctr. for Middle East Policy, 2002—. Office: Saban Ctr for Middle East Policy The Brookings Inst 1775 Mass Ave NW Washington DC 20036

INFANTE, ISA MARIA, political scientist, educator, lawyer, writer; b. Santo Domingo, Dominican Republic, Sept. 8, 1942; d. Rafael Infante and Dolores Nieves; 1 child, Nina Maria. BA, U. Calif., Santa Cruz, 1973; MA in Comparative Polit. Sys., Yale U., 1975; PhD in Polit. sci., U. Calif., Riverside, 1977; JD, Northeastern U., 2005. Mgmt. trainee Calif. Savs. and Loan Assn., LA, 1960—61; asst. fgn. corr. L.A. Times, Mexico City, 1961—62; bus. enterprise officer LA, 1962—64; regional mgr. Strout Realty, Pasadena, Calif., 1964—66; entrepreneur retail stores L.A., Lake Elsinore, Anaheim, Calif., 1966—70; exec. dir. coll. adult rehab. program U. Calif., Riverside, 1970—71; dir. nat. immigration bd. Nat. Lawyers Guild, LA, 1977; acad. adv. to provost Antioch Coll. West, Antioch U., San Francisco, 1977—78; sr. devel. officer U.S. Human Resources Corp., San Francisco, 1978; spl. asst. to Sarah Weddington, Esq. Interdepartmental Task Force on Women, White House, Washington, 1978—79; policy fellow and program officer Inst. for Ednl. Leadership/Fund for Improvement of Postsecondary Edn., HEW, Washington, 1978—79; assoc. dean Labor Coll. Empire State Coll., SUNY, NYC, 1979—81; pres. Iml Assocs, internat. cons., 1980—. Prof. polit. sci., dir. L.Am. studies dept. Jersey City State Coll., Jersey City, 1983—86; pres. Nat. Hispanic Coalition, Washington, 1978—80; notary pub., 1980—82; mem. Am. Coun. on Edn., 1980—82, Cmty. Bd. 12, Borough of Manhattan, NY, 1980—82; pres. Free, Inc., 2005—. Author (with others): Field Preparation Manual, 1973; contbg. author: Voices From the Ghetto, 1968, The Politics of Teaching Political Science, 1978, Labor Studies Jour., 1981, Political Affairs, 1984. Bd. dirs. Nagle House Co-op, NYC, 1980—82, Solidaridad Humana, Inc., NYC, 1980—82; trustee Ctr. for Integrative Devel., NYC, 1979—82; world chair Dem. Party of Knox County, Tenn.; Mayoral candidate City of Knoxville. Pease Barker scholar, 1972—73, Marius de Brabant scholar, 1970—71, Rsch. scholar, NEH, Washington, 1984. Fellow: Am. Polit. Sci. Assn.; mem.: ATLA, NAFE, ABA, Knoxville Bar Assn., Women's Bar Found. of Mass., Nat. Women's Health Networn, Nat. Women's Polit. Caucus, Univ. and Coll. Labor Assn., L.Am. Studies Assn., Am. Ednl. Rsch. Assn., Internat. Polit. Sci. Assn., Soc.Internat. Devel., Progressive Women's Coalition, Yale Club of Boston, Yale Club of N.Y.C. Home: 601 Gill Ave Knoxville TN 37917-7233 Office Phone: 865-637-4074. Personal E-mail: isainfante@bellsouth.net. Business E-Mail: isa@aya.yale.edu.

INGALLS, MARIE CECELIE, former state legislator, retail executive; b. Faith, SD, Mar. 31, 1936; d. Jens P. and Ida B. (Hegre) Jensen; m. Dale D. Ingalls, June 20, 1955; children: Duane (dec.), Delane. BS, Black Hills State Coll., 1973, MS, 1978. Elem. tchr. Meade County Schs., Sturgis, SD, 1957-72, Faith Sch. Dist. 46-2, 1973-76; elem. prin. Meade Sch. Dist. 46-1, Sturgis, 1976-81; owner, operator Ingalls, Sturgis, 1978-99; mem., asst. majority whip S.D. House Reps., Pierre, 1986-92; lobbyist S.D. Legislature. Bd. dirs. S.D. Retailers Assn., 1990—98, treas., 1992—93. Former sec. S.D. Rep. Orgn; Rep. nominee S.D. Commr. Sch. and Pub. Lands, 1998. Recipient Woman of Achievement award City of Sturgis, 1986, Retail Bus. of Yr. 1998. Mem. S.D. Cattlewomen, S.D. Stockgrowers (edn. chair), S.D. Farm Bur. (bd. dirs. dist. V 1993-2001, 03—, dist. dir. women's com. 2003-05 women's chair 2005—), Meade County Farm Bur., Faith C. of C. (pres. 1989), Sturgis C. of C. (past bd. dirs.), Key City Investment Club. Republican. Lutheran. Avocations: knitting, crocheting, piano, reading, golf. Home: 17054 Opal Rd Mud Butte SD 57758 Personal E-mail: mcingalls@gwtc.net.

INGATO, ROBERT JOSEPH, lawyer; b. July 3, 1960; m. Anna B. Ingato. BSBA with honors, Bucknell U.; JD with honors, Cornell U. With AT&T Capital Corp., 1988—98, exec. v.p., gen. counsel, 1996—98; exec. v.p. Newcourt Credit Grp. Inc., 1998—99; exec. v.p., dep. gen. counsel CIT Group Inc., Livingston, NJ, 1999—2001, exec. v.p., gen. counsel, 2001—, sec., 2002—. Bd. trustees Liberty Sci. Ctr., NJ Hist. Soc.; mem. exec. com. Morris County Am. Heart Assn. Office: CIT Group Inc 1 CIT Dr Livingston NJ 07039 Office Phone: 973-740-5000. Office Fax: 973-886-5527.*

INGBAR, DAVID H., physician, researcher; b. Boston, Aug. 1, 1953; s. Sidney H. and Mary Lee Ingbar; m. Mary E. Meighan, Oct. 14, 1991. BA, Reed Coll., 1974; MD, Harvard Med. Coll., 1978. Diplomate Am. Bd. Internal Medicine. Intern then resident U. Wash., Seattle, chief resident; pulmonary fellow Yale U., New Haven, 1982-85, asst. prof. medicine, 1985-91; assoc. prof. medicine U. Minn., Mpls., 1991-98, prof. medicine, physiology and pediat., 1998—, dir. pulmonary, allergy and critical care divsn., 2001—. Dir. med. ICU and respiratory care Yale New Haven Hosp., 1986-91, U. Minn., 1991—; pres. Assn. Pulmonary and Crit. Care Medicine Program Dir., 2003-04. Mem.: Am. Thoracic Soc. (pres. 2007—). Office: U MN Pulmonary & Critical Care Dept Medicine MMC 276 UMMC 420 Delaware St SE Minneapolis MN 55455-0374 Office Phone: 612-624-0999. Business E-Mail: ingba001@umn.edu.

INGBER, LARRY H., lawyer; b. NYC, Apr. 2, 1959; BS, SUNY, Albany, 1979; JD, Rutgers U., 1983. Bar: NY 1984, NJ 1984, Fla. 1984, US Tax Ct., US Dist. Ct. Ea. Dist. NY, US Dist. Ct. So. Dist. NY. Ptnr. Wilson, Elser, Moskowtiz, Edelman & Dicker LLP, Garden City, NY. Mem.: Nassau County Bar Assn., NY State Bar Assn. Office: Wilson Elser Moskowitz Edelman & Dicker LLP Ste 510 666 Old Country Rd Garden City NY 11530 Office Phone: 516-228-8900. Office Fax: 516-228-0200. Business E-Mail: ingberl@wemed.com.

INGBERMAN, SIMA BLUMENFELD, real estate company officer; b. Berlin, Nov. 10, 1947; arrived in U.S., 1956; children: Nina Ingberman Genauer, Abraham, Efram. BA, Bklyn. Coll., 1970, MA in Art History, 1978; PhD in Art History, CUNY, 1987. Ptnr. Blumenfeld Partnership, 1998—2003; gen. ptnr. Ingberman Assocs., 2003—. Author: ABC - International Constructivist Architecture, English, German and Japanese edits., 1994. Avocation: collecting architecture and design posters.

INGE, DEANDRES GATES, mathematics educator; b. Jackson, Miss., May 6, 1967; d. Andrew Jr. and Dorothy Jean (Cannon) Gates; m. Victor de Porres Inge, June 27, 1992; children: Alexander Vincent, Arin Victoria. BEd, Jackson State U., 1990; MEd, Auburn U., Montgomery, Ala., 1998. Cert. tchr. La. Kindergarten tchr. East End Elem. Sch., Selma, Ala., 1990—91; 3d grade tchr. Meadowview Elem. Sch., Selma, 1991—2006; math. specialist Ala. State Dept. Edn., Wallace Coll., Selma, 2006—. Test administrator Am. Coll. Testing, Selma, 1992—, Scholastic Aptitude Test, Selma, 2000—; test evaluator Johns Hopkins U., Balt., 2006. Sen. Hank Sanders Edn. grantee, 2003, John Hinman fellow, Internat. Paper Co., 2001. Mem.: NEA, Nat. Coun. Tchrs. Math., Ala. Edn. Assn. Home: 2601 Springdale St Selma AL 36701 Office: Wallace CC Selma 3000 Earl Goodwin Pkwy Selma AL 36702

INGE, MILTON THOMAS, American literature and culture educator, author; b. Newport News, Va., Mar. 18, 1936; s. Clyde Elmore and Bernice Lucille (Jackson) I.; m. Betty Jean Meredith, 1958 (div. 1977); 1 child, Scott Thomas; m. Tonette Long Bond, 1982 (div. 1991); 1 stepchild, Michael Gordon Bond; m. Donaria Romeiro Carvalho, 1998. BA, Randolph-Macon Coll., 1959; MA, Vanderbilt U., 1960, PhD, 1964. Instr. English Vanderbilt U., 1962-64; asst. prof. Am. thought and lang. Mich. State U., 1964-68, assoc. prof., 1968-69; assoc. prof. English Va. Commonwealth U., Richmond, 1969-73, prof., 1973-80, chmn. dept. English, 1974-80; prof., chmn. dept. English, Clemson U., SC, 1980-84; resident scholar in Am. studies USIA, Washington, 1982-84; prof. humanities Randolph-Macon Coll., Ashland, Va., 1984—. Reader English Composition Test Coll. Entrance Exam Bd., 1967, 69, 77, 80; Va. Cultural Laureate, 92; dir. USIA Summer Inst. in Am. Studies, 1993—95; liberal studies disting. scholar-in-residence U. Louisville, 2003. Author: Donald Davidson: Essay and Bibliography, 1965, (with T.D. Young) Donald Davidson, 1971, The American Comic Book, 1985, Comics in the Classroom, 1989, Great American Comics: 100 Years of Cartoon Art, 1990, Comics as Culture, 1990, Faulkner, Sut, and Other Southerners, 1992, Perspectives on American Culture: Essays on Humor, Literature, and the Popular Arts, 1994, Anything Can Happen in a Comic Strip: Centennial Reflections on an American Art Form, 1995, William Faulkner: Overlook Illustrated Lives, 2006; editor: (books) Sut Lovingood's Yarns, 1966, 2d edit. 1987, High Times and Hard Times, 1967, Agrarianism in American Literature, 1969, A.B. Longstreet, 1969, Faulkner: A Rose for Emily, 1970, Wm. Byrd of Westover, 1970, Studies in Light in August, 1971, Frontier Humorists: Critical Views, 1975, Ellen Glasgow: Centennial Essays, 1976,(with J. Bryer and M. Duke) Black American Writers: Bibliographic Essays, 2 vols., 1978, Handbook of American Popular Culture, Vol. I, 1978, Vol. II, 1980, Vol. III, 1981, 3 vols. rev. and expanded edits., 1989, Concise Histories of American Popular Culture, 1982, (with E.E. MacDonald) James Branch Cabell: Centennial Essays, 1983, (with J. Bryer and M. Duke) American Women Writers: Bibliographical Essays, 1983, Huck Finn Among the Critics: A Centennial Selection, 1984, rev. edit., 1985, Truman Capote: Conversations, 1987, Naming the Rose: Essays on Umberto Eco's "The Name of the Rose", 1988, Handbook of American Popular Literature, 1988, A Nineteenth Century American Reader, 1988, The Comics, 1991, (with Sergei Chakovsky) Russian Eyes on American Literature, 1992, Dark Laughter: The Satiric Art of Oliver W. Harrington, 1993, Why I Left America and Other Essays of Oliver W. Harrington, 1993, William Faulkner: The Contemporary Reviews, 1994, (with James E. Caron) Sut Lovingood's Nat'ral Born Yarnspinner: Essays on George Washington Harris, 1996, Mark Twain's A Connecticut Yankee in King Arthur's Court, 1997, The Achievement of William Faulkner: A Centennial Tribute, 1998; Conversations with William Faulkner, 1999, "Co. Aytch," or a Side Show of the Big Show and Other Sketches by Samuel R. Watkins, 1999, Charles M. Schulz: Conversations, 2000, (with Ed Piacentino) The Humor of the Old South, 2001, (with Dennis Hall) Greenwood Guide to American Popular Culture, 4 vols., 2002, The New Encyclopedia of Southern Culture: Literature, vol. 9, 2007; editor Resources for American Literary Study, 1971-79, American Humor: An Interdisciplinary Newsletter, 1974-79, Studies in American Humor, 2004—; gen. editor Greenwood Press Bio-Bibliographies and Reference Guides in Popular Culture, Cambridge U. Press Am. Critical Archives, U. Press Miss., Great Comic Artists and Conversations with Comic Artists Series; book reviewer: Nashville Tennesseean, Richmond Times-Dispatch. Bd. dirs. Friends of Richmond Pub. Libary; bd. dirs. San Francisco Acad. Comic Art, James Br. Cabell Libr. Assocs., Va. Commonwealth U., Edgar Allen Poe Mus. Recipient Bd. Govs. award Am. Cultural Assn., 1999, Disting. Prof. award, Randolph Macon Coll, 2004; fellow So. Fellowship Fund, 1959-62, Newberry Libr., 1987, Va. Found. Humanities, 1987, 93; grantee Fulbright-Hays, 1967-68, 71, 79, 88, 94, Mich. State U., 1965, 66, 68, Am. Philos. Soc., 1970, Clemson U., 1981, NEH, 1986, 91, 92; recipient Disting. Alumnus award Randolph-Macon Coll., 1995. Mem. MLA (hon. life, del. assembly 1976-78, 2001-03, chmn. elections com. 1980), South Atlantic MLA (program com. 1982-85, chmn. 1986, v.p. 1987, pres. 1988-89), Am. Studies Assn., Popular Culture Assn., Am. Humor Studies Assn. (pres. 1978, 88, Charlie award 1996), Soc. Study So. Lit. (exec. coun. 1971-73, 78-80, 86-88), Melville Soc., Ellen Glasgow Soc. (exec. coun. 1974-84, pres. 1987-88), Mus. Cartoon Art (nominating com. Hall of Fame 1975-95), European Assn. Am. Studies, So. Studies Forum (founder, exec. coun. 1988—), Popular Culture Assn. in South (v.p. 1987-88, pres. 1988-89), Mark Twain Cir. (chmn. nominating com. 1987-88), Mark Twain Cir. Am.

(hon.), Cosmos Club, Phi Beta Kappa (key reporter), Omicron Delta Kappa, Pi Delta Epsilon, Lambda Chi Alpha. Home: PO Box 129 Ashland VA 23005-0129 Home Phone: 804-262-7439; Office Phone: 804-752-7282. Business E-Mail: tinge@rmc.edu.

INGELS, JACK EDWARD, horticulture educator; b. Indpls., Mar. 28, 1942; s. Carl Eugene and Mary Louise (Fultz) I. BS, Purdue U., 1964; MS, Rutgers U., 1966; postgrad., Ball State U., 1968-70. Rsch. asst. Rutgers U., New Brunswick, N.J., 1964-66; prof. SUNY, Cobleskill, 1966-89, disting. teaching prof., 1990—. Hort. cons. J.C. Penney Corp., N.Y.C., 1966-69; landscape designer, 1966—; hort. and/or landscape cons. numerous small cos., 1970—; pres. J. Ingels Assoc., 1991—. Author: Landscaping: Principles and Practices, 6th edit., 2003, Ornamental Horticulture: Science, Operations, and Management, 3d edit., 2000. Chmn. Cobleskill Restoration and Devel., Inc., 1991—, bd. dirs., 1988—; pres. Timothy Murphy Gourmet Soc., 1989—; mem. Schoharie County Coun. on Arts, Cobleskill, Albany Inst. of History and Art; bd. dirs. Cobleskill Partnership, 1996—. Named Nat. Landscape Educator of Yr., Profl. Land Care Network, 2007; named one of Top Ten Landscape Educators in Am., Landscape Mgmt. mag., 1995. Mem. Associated Landscape Contractors Am., Northeastern N.Y. Nursery Assn., Genesee-Finger Lakes Nursery Assn., Univ. Club (Albany, N.Y.), Moose, Elks. Avocations: gourmet cooking, landscape garden history, travel. Home: 139 Jay St Cobleskill NY 12043 Office: SUNY Horticulture Dept Cobleskill NY 12043 Business E-Mail: ingelsje@cobleskill.edu. *To teach is a privilege that permits me to touch lives. To teach well is my obligation.*

INGELS, MARTY, agent, broadcast executive; b. Bklyn., Mar. 9, 1936; s. Jacob and Minnie (Crown) Ingerman; m. Jean Maire Frassinelli, Aug. 3, 1960 (div. 1969); m. Shirley Jones, 1977. Founder Ingels Inc., 1975—; formed Stoneypoint Prodns., 1981; TV and motion picture producer U.S. and Abroad; mgr. of Shirley Jones. Star: Dickens and Fenster series, ABC-TV, 1964; co-star: Pruitts of Southampton, 1968-69; films include Armored Command, 1962, Horizontal Lieutenant, 1965, Busy Body, 1967, Ladies Man, 1966, If It's Tuesday This Must Be Belgium, 1970, Wild and Wonderful, 1965, Guide for a Married Man, 1968; numerous TV appearances. Active various charity drives. Achievements include Owning the world's largest celebrity brokerage service, 1974; widely noted as the Henry Kissinger of Madison Avenue. Office: Network Prodns 4531 Noeline Way Encino CA 91436

INGERMAN, PETER ZILAHY, systems analyst, consultant; b. NYC, Dec. 9, 1934; s. Charles Stryker and Ernestine (Leigh) Ingerman; m. Carol Mary Pasquale, Dec. 19, 1970 (div. May 1980); m. Colleen Frances McGaffey, Sept. 13, 1996. AB, U. Pa., 1958, MSEE, 1963; PhD, Greenwich U., 1991. Cert. data processor, computer programmer, sys. profl., chartered engr. Brit. Engring. Coun., 1990, chartered IT profl. Brit. Computer Soc., 2004, chartered scientist Brit. Sci. Coun., 2005; CLU; cert. EMT. Rsch. investigator U. Pa., Phila., 1958-63; tech. dir. programming rsch. Westinghouse, Balt., 1963-65; mgr. RCA, Cherry Hill, NJ, 1965-72; sr. staff cons. Equitable Life Assurance Soc. of U.S., NYC, 1972-77; ind. computer cons. Willingboro, NJ, 1977—. Adj. prof. computer sci. Pratt Inst. Tech., 1968—73; mem. working groups Internat. Fedn. Info. Processing, 1962—82; rep. Conf. Data Sys. Langs., 1967—71, Am. Nat. Stds. Inst., 1960—71; bd. dirs. Compliance, Inc. Peer reviewer: Open-Source Ency., 2000—; author: (book) A Syntax-Oriented Translator, 1966; contbr. articles to profl. jours. Bd. dirs. Providence Ho., 1991—94, vice chair, 1991—94; mem. Willingboro Emergency Squad, 1982—90, 2002—, bd. officers, 1986—89, 2003—; bd. dirs. Crossroads Runaway Program, Inc., 1981—82, Compliance, Inc., 1989—92. Fellow: Brit. Computer Soc. (life); mem.: AAAS, IEEE (life; tech. bd. givs. social implications sect. 2007—), Assn. Humanistic Psychologists, Brit. Computer Soc. USA (treas. 2004—), Internat. Transactional Analysis Assn., NJ Acad. Scis., Ind. Computer Cons. Assn. (treas. 1999—2001), Brit. Engring. Coun., Am. Cryptogram Assn., Data Processing Mgmt. Assn. (cert.), Assn. Computing Machinery, Assn. Former Intelligence Officers, Am. Guild Organists (co-dean S.W. Jersey chpt. 1997—98, dean 1998—99, treas. 1999—2005), Mensa, Triple Nine Soc., Upsilon Pi Epsilon, Sigma Xi (life). Achievements include patents for electronic circuits. Office: 40 Needlepoint Ln Willingboro NJ 08046-1997 Office Phone: 609-871-7474. Business E-Mail: pzi@ingerman.org.

INGERSOLL, CAROLINE YEE, director; d. Paul Yee and Violet Kau; m. Richard King Ingersoll, Aug. 31, 1968; children: Kristin Paula Juk Yee, Karin Eleanor Juk Ling. BA, Occidental Coll., 1966; tchg. credential, U. Calif., Berkeley, 1967; MA, U. Ill., 1970; MBA, U. Hawaii, 1982. Tchr. Willard Intermediate Sch., Berkeley, 1967—69, Maine Twp. HS, Park Ridge, Ill., 1970—73; mktg. and bus. planner GTE Hawaiian Tel. Co., Honolulu, 1984—97; dir. internat. advancement and prin. gifts U. Hawaii Found., Honolulu, 1997—. Bd. dirs., sec. LWV, Honolulu, 1995—98; bd. dirs. Hawaii Symphony Orch., Honolulu, 1998, YWCA, 1997—2003. Home: 944 Waiholo St Honolulu HI 96821 Office: Univ Hawaii Found 2444 Dole St Bachman Hall 101 Honolulu HI 96822

INGERSOLL, PAUL MILLS, banker; b. Phila., Apr. 13, 1928; s. John H.W. and Frances Paul (Mills) I.; m. Eleanor S. Koehler, Oct. 6, 1951; children: Eleanor Ingersoll Sylvestro, Rita W., Frances M. BA, Princeton U., 1950. With Provident Nat. Bank, Phila., 1963-78, v.p. adminstrn. and exec. mgmt., 1969, sr. v.p. retail banking divsn., 1969-73, pres., chief adminstrv. officer, 1973-78. Pres., bd. dirs. Beaver Mgmt. Corp.; bd. dirs. Haverford Trust Co.; cons. Christie, Manson & Woods Internat., Inc. Trustee Emeritus Drexel U., Bryn Mawr Hosp., Pa. 1st lt. AUS, 1950-52. Recipient Human Rights award Am. Jewish Com., 1973. Mem. Merion Cricket Club, State in Schuylkill, The Cts., The Rabbit. Democrat. Episcopalian.

INGERSOLL, RICHARD KING, lawyer; b. Algoma, Wis., Aug. 13, 1944; s. Robert Clive and Bernice Eleanore (Koehn) I.; m. Caroline Soi-Keu Yee, Aug. 31, 1968; children: Kristin Paula Juk-Yee, Karin Eleanor Juk-Ling. BBA, U. Mich., 1966; JD, U. Calif.-Berkeley, Berkeley, 1969. Bar: Ill. 1969, Hawaii 1973. Asst. prof. U. Ill.-Champaign, Champaign, 1969-70; assoc. Sidley & Austin, Chgo., 1970-73; ptnr. Rush, Moore, Craven, Kim & Stricklin, Honolulu, 1973-88, Gelber, Gelber, & Ingersoll, Honolulu, 1989—. Spkr. tax law seminars. Author various law materials. Mem. ABA (taxation, bus. and internat. law coms.), Waialae Country Club (sec.). Home: 944 Waiholo St Honolulu HI 96821-1226 Office Phone: 808-524-0155. Business E-Mail: ringersoll@ggik.com.

INGERSOLL, WILLIAM BOLEY, lawyer, real estate developer; b. Washington, Sept. 21, 1938; s. William Brown and Loraine (Boley) I.; m. Carolyn Grace Potter, Sept. 8, 1963; children: William Brett, Courtney Lynn, Wayne Brandon, Dana Lee. BS, Brigham Young U., 1964; JD, Cath. U. Am., 1968. Bar: Va. 1968, D.C. 1969. Atty. Office of Corp. Counsel D.C., 1967-69, Office Gen. Counsel HUD, 1969-70; ptnr. Fried, Klewans, Ingersoll & Bloch, Washington, 1970-72; pres. Ingersoll and Bloch Corp., Washington, 1972—; of counsel Holland & Knight, Washington, 1998—. Mng. ptnr. JC Assocs. Real Estate Devel., Washington, 1973—; gen. counsel Am. Resort Devel. Assn.; chmn. Trust Communities Inc., Washington, 1999—, Power Corp., Washington, 2000—; lectr. in field. Co-editor-in-chief Land Devel. Law Reporter, Land Trends, 1973—, The Digest of State Land Sales, 1976—, Time Sharing Law Reporter, 1980—, D.C. Real Estate Reporter, 1982—, Real Estate Opportunity Report, 1986; contbr. in field. Bd. dirs. Nat. Timesharing Coun., 1981—; mem. Garrison Presdl. Commn., 1984; mem. bd. adv. J. Ruben Clark Law Sch., 1987-93, chmn., 1991-93; bishop McLean (Va.) Ward, LDS Ch.; mem. nat. adv. com. Inside Real Estate, 1985—. Mem. ABA, FBA, D.C. Bar Assn., Va. Bar Assn., Va. Assn. Trial Lawyers, Land Devel. Inst. (vice chmn.), Brigham Young U. Alumni Assn. (bd. dirs. 1984-92), Order of Coif, Univ. Club Washington, Boca Raton (Fla.) Resort and Club. Home: 713 Potomac Knolls Dr Mc Lean VA 22102-1421 also: Holland & Knight Ste 100 2099 Pennsylvania Ave NW Washington DC 20006-1816 Office Phone: 202-955-3000, 301-299-4174. Business E-Mail: william.ingersoll@hklaw.com.

INGHAM, NORMAN WILLIAM, literature educator, genealogist; b. Holyoke, Mass., Dec. 31, 1934; s. Earl Morris and Gladys May (Rust) I. AB in German and Russian cum laude, Middlebury Coll., 1957; postgrad. Slavic philology, Free U. Berlin, 1957—58; MA in Russian lang. and lit., U. Mich., 1959; postgrad. in Russian lang. and lit., Leningrad State U., 1961—62; PhD in Slavic langs. and lit., Harvard U., 1963. Cert. genealogist. Postdoctoral rschr. Czechoslovak Acad. Scis., Prague, 1963—64; asst. prof. dept Slavic langs. and lits. Ind. U., Bloomington, 1964—65; asst. prof. Harvard U., Cambridge, Mass., 1965—70, lectr., 1970—71; assoc. prof. U. Chgo., 1971—82, prof., 1982—2006, chmn. dept., 1977—83, dir. Ea. Europe and USSR lang. and area ctr., 1978—91, prof. emeritus, 2006—. Mem. Am. Com. Slavists, 1977-83; mem. com. Slavic and Ea. European studies U. Chgo., 1979-91, chmn., 1982-91, also other coms.; dir. Ctr. for East European and Russian/Eurasian Studies, 1991-96; cert. genealogist, 1994—. Author: E.T.A. Hoffman's Reception in Russia, 1974; editor: Church and Culture in Old Russia, 1991; co-editor: (with Joachim T. Baer) Mnemozina: Studia litteraria russica in honorem Vsevolod Setchkarev; mem. editorial bd. Slavic and East European Jour., 1978-87, adv. bd., 1987-89; assoc. editor Byzantine Studies, 1973-81; contbg. editor The Am. Genealogist, 1995—; contbr. and translator articles and book revs. Fulbright fellow, 1957-58, vis. fellow Dumbarton Oaks Ctr. for Byzantine Studies, 1972-73. Mem. Am. Assn. Advancement Slavic Studies (rep. coun. on mem. instns. 1985-96, area rep. nat. adv. com. for Ea. European lang. programs 1985-96), Am. Assn. Tchrs. Slavic and East European Langs., Early Slavic Studies Assn. (v.p. 1993-95, pres. 1995-97), Chgo. Consortium for Slavic and East European Studies (v.p. 1982-84, 98, pres. 1984-86, 98-2000, exec. coun. 1992-94), Phi Beta Kappa. Home: 128 Pleasant St Granby MA 01033-9551

INGLE, ROBERT P., retail executive; b. 1933; married. Grad., U. Miami, 1958. Sales rep. Kraft Foods, Miami, Fla., 1958-61; produce mgr. Colonial Stores, Asheville, N.C., 1961-63; chmn., dir. Ingles Markets Inc., Black Mountain, NC, 1963—2004, CEO, 1963—. Office: Ingles Markets Inc 2913 US Hwy 70 E Black Mountain NC 28711*

INGLES, ERNIE BOYCE, academic administrator, library director; b. Calgary, Alta., Can., Dec. 30, 1948; s. Robert Howard and Muriel E. (Boyce) I.; m. Claire E. Chapman, Aug. 28, 1971; 1 child, Erin. BA, U. Calgary, 1970, MA, 1973; MLS, U. B.C., Can., 1974. Head dept. rare books U. Calgary, 1974-78; exec. dir. Can. Inst. of Hist. Microre Prodns., Ottawa, Ont., Can., 1978-84; univ. librarian U. Regina, Sask., Can., 1984-90; dir. libraries U. Alberta, 1990-95, assoc. v.p. learning sys., 1995—. Compiler: Canada: The Printed Record, 1981, Canada: World Bibliographical Series, 1990, Bibliography of Canadian Bibliography, 1994. Exec. dir., founder Northern Exposure to Leadership Inst., 1993—; trustee Ottawa Pub. Libr. Bd., 1982-84. Recipient Ruth Cameron medal, U. B.C., 1974, Marie Tremaine medal for bibliography, 1996; named Outstanding Acad. Librarian, Can. Assn. of Coll. and Univ. Librs., 1994, Innovator of Year, Can. Info. Tech., 1996. Mem. Can. Libr. Assn. (pres. 1990-91), Bibliog. Soc. of Can. (pres. 1989-91), Hist. Soc. Alta. (exec. dir. 1977-78). Avocation: riding. Address: 1-3J University Hall Edmonton AB Canada T6G 2J9

INGLIS, BOB (ROBERT DURDEN), congressman; b. Savannah, Ga., Oct. 11, 1959; m. Mary Anne Williams, Aug. 7, 1982; children: Robert D. Jr., Mary Ashton, Anne McCullough, Mabel Andrews, Sara Meade. AB summa cum laude in Polit. Sci., Duke U., 1981; JD, U. Va. Sch. Law, 1984. Atty. Leatherwood, Walker, Todd & Mann P.C., Greenville, SC, 1986—92, 1999—2004; mem. US Congress from 4th SC dist., 1993—98, 2005—, mem. sci. and tech. com., ranking mem. energy & environment subcommittee, mem. fgn. affairs com., co-chair hydrogen and fuel cell caucus. Chmn. 4th Congl. Dist. South Carolinians to Limit Congl. Terms; mem. Leadership Greenville Class XVI; loaned exec. Greenville County United Way, 1987; mem. exec. com. Greenville County Rep. Party; mem. exec. com. First Monday in Greenville. Mem. SC Bar Assn., Greenville County Bar Assn., Phi Beta Kappa. Republican. Presbyterian. Office: US House Reps 330 Cannon House Office Bldg Washington DC 20515 Office Phone: 202-225-6030. Office Fax: 202-226-1177.*

INGOLD, CATHERINE WHITE, academic administrator; b. Columbia, SC, Mar. 15, 1949; d. Hiram Hutchison and Annelle (Stover) White; m. Wesley Thomas Ingold, June 13, 1970; 1 child, Thomas Bradford Hutchison. Student, U. Paris-Sorbonne, 1969; BS in French with honors, Hollins Coll., 1970; MA in Romance Langs., U. Va., 1972, PhD in French, 1979; DHum honoris causa, Francis Marion U., Florence, SC, 1992. Assoc. prof. romance langs. Gallaudet U., Washington, 1973-88, dir. hons. program, 1980-85, dean arts and scis., 1985-86, provost, v.p. acad. affairs, 1986-88; pres. Am. U. of Paris, 1988-92, Curry Coll., Milton, Mass., 1992-96. Dir. Nat. Fgn. Lang. Ctr.; bd. dir. U. Md. Recipient Prix Morot-Sir de Langue et Littérature françaises (Hollins). Phi Beta Kappa. Episcopalian. Home: 2015 N Brandywine St Arlington VA 22207-2200 Office: Nat Fgn Lang Ctr Patapsco Bldg Ste 2132 5201 Paint Branch Pkwy College Park MD 20742 Business E-Mail: cwingold@nflc.org.

INGOLD, KEITH USHERWOOD, chemist, educator; b. Leeds, Eng., May 31, 1929; s. Christopher Kelk and Edith (Usherwood) I.; m. Carmen Cairine Hodgkin, Apr. 7, 1956; children: Christopher Frank (dec.), John Hilary, Diana Hilda. BSc with honors in Chemistry, U. Coll., London, 1949; DPhil, Oxford U., Eng., 1951; DSc (hon.), U. Guelph, 1985; LLD (hon.), Mt. Allison U., 1987; DSc (hon.), St. Andrews U., Scotland, 1989, Carleton U., 1992, McMaster U., 1995; LLD (hon.), Dalhousie U., 1996; Laurea Honoris Causa in Biology, U. Ancona, Italy, 1999. Postdoctoral fellow NRC Can., Ottawa, 1951-53, rsch. officer, 1955-77, assoc. dir. chemistry, 1977-90, disting. rsch. scientist, 1990—. Adj. prof. U. Guelph, Ont., Can., 1985-87, Brunel U., U.K., 1983-94, Carleton U. Ottawa, Can., 1991—, St. Andrews U., U.K., 1997—; postdoctoral fellow U. B.C., 1953-55; vis. scientist Chevron Rsch. Co., Richmond, Calif., 1966, Univ. Coll., London, 1969, 72, Ford Motor Co., 1971, Esso Rsch. and Engring. Co., Linden, N.J., 1973, U. Western Ont., 1975, 1993, Iowa State U., 1975, U. Bologna, Italy, 1975, 93, U. Adelaide, Australia, 1979, U. Grenoble, France, 1983, Australian Nat. U., 1987, 99, 2005, U. Freiburg, Germany, 1990-91, U. Essen, Germany, 1990, U. Dusseldorf, Germany, 1991, U. Leiden, The Netherlands, 1992-93, U. St. Andrews, Scotland, 1977, 98. Decorated Order of Can., 1995; recipient Can. Silver Jubilee medal, 1977, Queen Elizbeth II Golden Jubilee medal, 2002, Humboldt Sr. Rsch. Fellowship award, Germany, 1989, Veris award, 1989, Lansdown Visitor award U. Victoria, B.C., 1990, Mangini prize U. Bologna, 1990, Izaak Walton Killam Meml. prize Can. Coun., 1992, Gold medal Natural Scis. and Engring. Coun. Can., 1998; Carnegie fellow U. St. Andrews, Scotland, 1977; vis. fellow Japan Soc. for Promotion of Sci., 1982, Italian Nat. Rsch. Coun., 1983; Nat. Sci. Coun. Republic China lectr., 1992. Fellow Royal Soc. Can. (treas. 1979-81, Centennial medal 1982, Henry Marshall Tory medal 1985), Royal Soc. (London, Davy medal 1990, Royal medal 2000), Chem. Inst. Can. (medal 1981, Syntex award for phys. organic chemistry 1983), Univ. Coll. (London), Royal Soc. Edinburgh (hon.); mem. Am. Chem. Soc. (award petroleum chemistry 1968, Pauling award 1988, Arthur C. Cope scholar 1992, James Flack Norris award phys. organic chemistry 1993), Chem. Soc. (award kinetics and mechanism 1978), Can. Soc. Chem. (v.p. 1985-87, pres. 1987-88, Alfred Bader award in organic chemistry 1989), Royal Soc. Chemistry (Ingold lectr. 1990), World Innovation Fund (hon.). Achievements include research papers on free radical chemistry. Home: 72 Ryeburn Dr Ottawa ON Canada K1V 1H5 Office: Nat Rsch Coun of Can Ottawa ON Canada K1A 0R6 Office Phone: 613-990-0938. Business E-Mail: keith.ingold@nrc.ca.

INGOLE, SUDEEP PRABHAKAR, engineering educator, researcher; s. Prabhakar Gangaram and Vascthala Prabhakar Ingole; m. Vidya Premanand Nagrale, Jan. 5, 2004; 1 child, Prasenjeet Sudeep. BS in Engring., Visveswaraya Nat. Inst. Tech., Nagpur, India, 1999; MS in Engring., Indian Inst. Sci., Bangalore, India, 2001; PhD in Mech. Engring., U. Alaska, Fairbanks, 2005. Rsch. asst. Indian Inst. Sci., 2000—02; doctoral sci. asst. GKSS Rsch. Ctr., Geesthact, Germany, 2002—03; vis. scholar Tex. A&M U., College Station, 2004—05, postdoctoral rsch. assoc., 2005, lectr. Galveston, 2005—. Mem., bd. dirs., v.p. rsch. & tech. devel. Prasen Tech Pvt., Ltd., Mumbai, India, 2007—. Contbr. articles to profl. jours. Grantee Chmns. grant, Gordon Rsch. Conf., 2004, 2006. Mem.: Am. Soc. Metals, Minerals, Metals and Materials Soc., Soc. Tribologists and Lubrication Engrs. Achievements include research in tripartite fundamental research areas with the utilization of an atomic force microscope to study nanomechanical tribological properties; multi-length scales wear modes and surface mechanical properties using an atomic force microscope; boron coatings on refractory metals for biological applications; surface analysis using an AFM; surface texture and frictional behavior using the friction force microscope. Home: 7820 Seawall Blvd #218 Galveston TX 77551 Office: Texas A&M Univ 200 Seawolf Pky Galveston TX 77553-1675 Office Fax: 409-741-7153. Personal E-mail: isudeep@yahoo.com. Business E-Mail: ingoles@tamug.edu.

INGOLFSSON-FASSBIND, URSULA G., music educator; b. Zurich, Switzerland, Dec. 22, 1943; arrived in U.S., 1980; d. Franz Bernardin Fassbind and Gertrud M. Schmucki; m. Ketill Ingolfsson; children: Katla Soffia, Judith, Mirjam, Bera Bjorg. Nat. tchrs. diploma, Conservatory Zurich, 1965, soloist diploma, 1968; postgrad., U. Ariz., 1969—70. Tchg. asst. Conservatory Zurich, 1966—68; with Reykjavik (Iceland) Music Coll., 1970—79, Settlement Music Sch., Phila., 1987—2000; founder, dir., tchr., performer Leopold Mozart Acad. and Franz Fassbind Found., Phila., 2001—. Founder, dir. Leopold Mozart Chamber Music Concerts, 2002—. Grantee Excellency in Tchg. grant, Wilmington (Del.) Piano Co., 2003. Mem.: Am. Composers Guild, Music Tchr. Nat. Assn. Democrat. Avocations: painting, gardening. Home and Office: Leopold Mozart Acad 4833 Pulaski Ave Philadelphia PA 19144 Office Phone: 215-848-1370. Personal E-mail: lmozartacademy@aol.com.

INGRAHAM, ALEC, mathematics professor; b. North Billerica, Mass., Oct. 17, 1946; s. Chester Doane Ingraham and Margaret Helen Blakely. BA in History, U. Mass., Boston, 1970, MA in Math., 1975. Lectr. math. Newbury Coll., Boston, 1975—78; prof. math. So. NH U., Manchester, NH, 1976—, chair math. dept., 1984—. Chair Billerica Hist. Commn., Mass., 2000—; treas., vice chair Middlesex Canal Commn., Billerica, 1997—; state del. Am. Math. Assn. of Two Year Coll., Memphis, 1993—2001. Mem.: Early Am. Industries Assn., NH Tchrs. Math., Billerica Hist. Soc. (pres. 1997—2000), Math. Assn. Am. (dept. liaison 2002—), New England Math. Assn. Two Yr. Colls. (bd. mem. 1998—2002). Office: So NH Univ 2500 N River Rd Manchester NH 03106

INGRAHAM, LAURA, lawyer, political commentator; b. Glastonbury, Conn., June 19, 1964; BA in Russian and English lit., Dartmouth Coll.; JD, U. Va. Sch. of Law, 1991. Speechwriter White House and Dept. Edn. and Transp., 1986—88; law clerk to Supreme Ct. Justice Clarence Thomas and Ralph K. Winter , US Ct. Appeals Second Cir., 1992—93; criminal def. lawyer Skadden, Arps, Slate, Meagher & Flom, Wash., DC, 1993—96; host Watch It! with Laura Ingraham, MSNBC, 1996—2000, nat. syndicated radio program, The Laura Ingraham Show, 2001—. Co-founder The Dark Ages Weekend. Author: The Hillary Trap: Looking for Power in All the Wrong Places, 2000, Shut Up & Sing: How the Elites in Hollywood, Politics.and the UN are Subverting America, 2003; contbr. NY Times, Wash. Post, LA Times, San Francisco Chronicle. Office: Talk Radio Network PO Box 3755 Central Point OR 97502

INGRAM, CHARLES CLARK, JR., energy executive; b. Dec. 10, 1916; s. Charles Clark and Winnie (Edwards) I.; m. Maxine Waterbury, Jan. 29, 1939; children: James C., Jack R. BS, U. Okla., 1940; LLD, Oral Roberts U., 1983. Registered profl. engr., Okla. With Oneok Inc., Tulsa, 1940—, pres., 1966-71, CEO, 1966-81, chmn., 1966-87, chmn. emeritus, 1987—. Former chmn. bd. trustees Frontiers of Sci. Found. of Okla., Inc., 1973-74; former adv. bd. Downtown Tulsa Unlimited; former bd. govs. Am. Citizenship Ctr., Oklahoma City; mem. pres.'s bd. visitors, chmn. Tulsa Engring. Coun., U. Okla. Maj. AUS, WWII, 1941-46. Named to Okla. Hall of fame, 1982. Mem. AIME, Am. Assn. Petroleum Geologists, Am. Gas Assn. (chmn. 1979-80), So. Gas Assn. (past pres.), Engrs. Soc. Tulsa, Okla. State C. of C. (pres. 1981), Oklahoma City C. of C., Tulsa C. of C., Nat. Alliance Businessmen (chmn. Ea. Okla. and Tulsa 1973-74), Propeller Club U.S., Summit Club, So. Hills Country Club (gov., past pres.), Cedar Ridge Country Club (Tulsa), Masons, Sigma Tau, Sigma Gamma Epsilon. Baptist. Office: Oneok Inc 100 W 5th St PO Box 871 Tulsa OK 74102-0871

INGRAM, CHARLES OWEN, priest, educator; b. Lee County, Miss., Oct. 23, 1929; s. Leonard Thaddeus and Elizabeth Owen Ingram; m. Frances Chick Hyde, Jan. 8, 1977 (dec.); m. Dorothy Ann Lott, Aug. 29, 1952 (dec.); 1 child, Charles Mark. BS, U. Memphis, 1950, MA, 1958; BD, Southwestern Theol. Sem., Ft. Worth, 1953; PhD, U. Ariz., Tucson, 1967. Ordained priest Bishop Kenneth Woollcombe of Christ Ch. Cathedral, Oxford, 1975. Missionary Sudan Interior Mission, Addis Ababa, Ethiopia, 1954—57; headmaster, chaplain Decamere Boys' Home, 1955—57; dir. U. Ariz. Learning Ctr., Tucson, 1962—87, asst. prof. psychology, 1967—72; deacon St. Stephan's House, Oxford, England, 1974—75; vicar St. Andrews Episcopal Ch., Tucson, 1975—81, rector, 1981—93. Pres. standing com. Diocese of Ariz., Phoenix, 1984, 85, 87; chmn. bd. Found. Campus Ministry, Tucson, 1982—88, A Place Apart, Ecumenical Retreat Ctr., Tucson, 1985—91. Founder New Start Program Acad. Assistance for Minority Students, U. Ariz., 1967, Frensdorff House for Persons with AIDS, Tucson, 1988—, St. Andrew's Bach Soc., Tucson, 1989—; dep. Bicentennial Gen. Conv. of Episcopal Ch., LA, 1985. Mem.: Gibbs Soc., Soc. St. Mary (assoc.), Phi Alpha Theta. Democrat. Episcopalian. Avocations: art, travel. Home: 6380 E Printer Udell Tucson AZ 85710

INGRAM, DAVID B., entertainment company executive; b. Dec. 13, 1962; m. Sarah LeBrun; 1 child, Henry LeBrun. BA in History cum laude, Duke U., 1985; MBA in Mktg., Vanderbilt U., 1989. Dir. rsch. Duke U. Capital Campaign Office, Durham, NC, 1985-87, dir., found. Young Alumni for The Capital Campaign, 1986-87; asst. to treas. Ingram Industries, Inc., Nashville, 1989-91; dir. sales Ingram Entertainment Inc., La Vergne, Tenn., 1991-92, asst. v.p. sales, 1992-93, v.p. major accounts, 1993-94, pres., COO, 1994—96, pres., chmn., 1997—. Chmn. bd. visitors The Duke Primate Ctr., 1987; bd. dir. Montgomery Bell Acad.; owner Ingram Entertainment Holdings Inc., La Vergne, Tenn., DBI Distributing Inc., Memphis, Golden Brands Beverage Distributors, San Francisco. Mem.: Video Software Dealers Assn. (nat. bd. dir.), Green Spring Valley Hunt Club, Caves Valley Golf Club, Belle Meade Country Club, Golf Club Tenn., Delta Tau Delta. Avocations: golf, bicycling, running, tennis, hunting, reading, investments. Office: Ingram Entertainment Inc Two Ingram Blvd La Vergne TN 37089

INGRAM, DENNY OUZTS, JR., lawyer, educator; b. Kirbyville, Tex., Mar. 23, 1929; s. Denny Ouzts and Grace Bertha (Smith) I.; m. Ann Elizabeth Rees, July 11, 1952; children: Scott Rees, Stuart Tillman. BA, U. Tex., 1955, JD with honors, 1957. Bar: Tex. 1956, N.Mex. 1967, Utah 1968. Editor Kirbyville Banner, 1949-50; mem. Tex. Ho. of Reps., 1951-52; assoc. Graves, Dougherty, Gee and Hearon (and predecessors), Austin, Tex., 1957, 59-60, partner, 1961-66; asst. prof. law U. Tex., 1957-59, U. N.Mex., 1966-67; prof. U. Utah, 1968-77; ptnr. McGinnis, Lochridge, and Kilgore, Austin, 1977-90, of counsel, 1991—; prof. law Tex. Wesleyan U. Sch. Law, 1991—. Vis. prof. U. Calif., Davis, 1973-74, U. Tex., summers 1968, 75, U. San Diego, 1993; research fellow Southwestern Legal Found., lectr. in field Contbr. numerous articles to law revs., chpts. to books; assoc. note editor: Tex. Law Rev., 1956-57. Research dir. Utah Constn. Revision Com., 1969-71, 73-74. Served with U.S. Army, 1951-54. Fellow Am. Coll. Trust and Estate Counsel, Am. Coll. Tax Counsel, Tex. Bar Found.; mem. ABA, Am. Law Inst. (life), Tex. Bar Assn., Utah Bar Assn., N.Mex. Bar Assn., Chancellors, Order of Coif, Phi Delta Phi. Democrat. Episcopalian. Home: 4055 Hildring Dr E Fort Worth TX 76109-4712 Office: Tex Wesleyan U Sch Law 1515 Commerce St Fort Worth TX 76102-6572

INGRAM, DOUGLAS STEPHEN, lawyer; b. Aug. 31, 1962; BS magna cum laude, Ariz. State U., 1985; JD summa cum laude, U. Ariz., 1988. Bar: Calif. 1988. Atty. Gibson, Dunn & Crutcher, 1988—96; assoc. gen. counsel, asst. sec. Allergen, Inc., Irvine, Calif., 1998—2000, exec. v.p., gen. counsel, sec., 2000—. Mem.: ABA, Am. Soc. Corp. Secretaries, Am. Corp. Counsel Assn., State Bar Calif., Orange County Bar Assn., Order of Coif. Office: Allergan Inc 2525 Dupont Dr PO Box 19534 Irvine CA 92623-9534 Office Phone: 714-246-4535. Office Fax: 714-246-4971. E-mail: ingram_doug@allergan.com.*

INGRAM, GEORGE, manufacturing executive; b. Montclair, NJ, Dec. 10, 1920; s. George and Frances Elizabeth (Watts) I.; m. Olive May Holtz, Feb. 15, 1947 (dec. Dec. 1999); children: Patricia (Mrs. S. K. Bone), George III (dec.), Sara, John. BS, Yale U., 1942; MS, Stevens Inst. Tech., 1948. Registered profl. indsl. engr., Pa. Indsl. engr. RCA, 1942-45; cons. mgmt. engr. Stevenson, Jordan & Harrison, Inc., NYC, 1945-51; controller Riegel Paper Corp., 1951-57, Raytheon Co., Lexington, Mass., 1957-60, v.p., 1960-61, v.p. fin., 1961-63, sr. v.p., dir., supr. corp. staff, CFO and acquisitions, 1963—68; sr. v.p. Champion Internat., Inc., NYC, 1968-69, exec. v.p., 1969-72, dir., 1968-72; pres., CEO. dir. Reed-Ingram Corp., NYC, 1972-77, cons., 1977-83. Pres. Dionis Corp., Nantucket, Mass., 1977-87; chmn. bd., dir. Deerfield Splty. Papers, Inc., 1973-77, Oneida Packaging Products, Inc., 1973-77, Canadian Glassine Co., Ltd., 1973-77; chmn., sec., dir. Arctos Corp., Quaker Hill, Conn., 1980-86; pres., treas., dir. Fitchburg Engring. Corp., Mass., 1980-86; dir. M/A Com, Inc., Burlington, Mass., 1968-91. Trustee Coll. of Wooster, Ohio, 1970-88. Mem.: ASME, Fin. Execs. Inst. (past pres. Boston chpt., past chmn. nat. com. securites and exchanges regulation), Mory's Assn., Phi Gamma Delta. Republican. Episcopalian. Home and Office: 88 Notch Hill Rd Apt 324 North Branford CT 06471 Office Phone: 203-481-5956. Personal E-mail: geoingram@comcast.net.

INGRAM, GEORGE CONLEY, judge; b. Dublin, Ga., Sept. 27, 1930; s. George Conley and Nancy Averett (Whitehurst) I.; m. Sylvia Williams, July 26, 1952; children: Sylvia Lark, Nancy Randolph, George Conley. AB, Emory U., 1949, LLB, 1951. Bar: Ga. 1952. City atty. City of Smyrna, Ga., 1958-64, City of Kennesaw, Ga., 1964; judge Cobb County Juvenile Ct., 1960-64, Superior Ct., Cobb Jud. Cir., 1964-68; justice Supreme Ct. Ga., 1973-77; spl. asst. atty. gen. State of Ga., 1979-86; ptnr. Alston & Bird, Atlanta, 1977-98; sr. judge State of Ga., 1998—. Staff, faculty Judge Adv. Gen. Sch. US Army, U. Va., 1952—54. Former trustee Agnes Scott Coll., Kennesaw Coll. Found., Emory U.; trustee Cobb Cmty. Found., Eleventh Cirs. Hist. Soc. Inc.; emeritus mem. Emory Law Sch. Coun.; past pres. Cobb County YMCA, Cobb Landmarks Soc.; former chmn. ofcl. bd. 1st Meth. Ch. of Marietta, trustee. 1st lt. JAGC, USAR, 1952-54. Recipient Emory U. medal, Disting. Svc. award Kennesaw Mountain Jaycees, 1961, award Ga. Jaycees, 1961, Disting. Citizen award City of Marietta, Ga., 1973, award Emory Law Sch. Alumni Assn., 1985, Len Gilbert Leadership award Cobb County C. of C., 1985, Cobb County Citizen of Yr. award, 1990; named an hon. life mem. Ga. PTA. Fellow Am. Bar Assn. Found., Am. Coll. Trial Lawyers, Internat. Soc. Barristers, Am. Acad. Appellate Lawyers, Marietta-Cobb Mus. Art; mem. ABA, Am. Law Inst., State Bar Ga. (Tradition of Excellence award 1987), Cobb and Atlanta Bar Assn., Ga. Arbitrators Forum, Old War Horse Lawyers Club, Cobb County C. of C. (Pub. Svc. award 1970, Turner award in family law 2002) Georgian Club (bd. mem., founding chmn.), Rotary (award for vocat. excellence 1999), Order of Coif (hon.), Phi Delta Phi, Omicron Delta Kappa. Methodist.

INGRAM, JACK, musician; b. Nov. 15, 1970; Student, So. Methodist U., Dallas. Signed to Big Machine Records, Nashville, 2005—. Singer: (albums) Jack Ingram, 1995, Live at Adair's, 1995, Lonesome Question, 1995, Livin' or Dyin', 1997, Flutter, 1997, Hey You, 1999, Electric, 2002, Live at Billy Bob's Texas, 2003, Live at Gruene Hall: Happy Happy, 2004, Acoustic Motel, 2005, Live Wherever You Are, 2006, This is It, 2007, (songs) Wherever You Are, 2006, Love You, 2006 (Wide Open Country Video of Yr., Country Music TV awards, 2007). Office: c/o George Couri CSE 98 San Jacinto Blvd Ste 430 Austin TX 78701 also: Big Machine Records 1219 16th Ave S Nashville TN 37212 Office Phone: 615-324-7777. E-mail: artistinfo@bigmachinemail.com.*

INGRAM, JEFFREY CHARLES, lawyer, educator; b. Santa Barbara, Calif., Apr. 8, 1953; s. John Samis and Jeanne Lorraine (McLaughlin) I.; m. Mary Jane Fenner, Mar. 9, 2002; children: Jeffrey C. II, Michael K., Kara Jeanne. Student, Miami U., Oxford, Ohio, 1971-72; BS, Suffolk U., 1974; JD cum laude, So. Calif. Inst. Law, 1979. Bar: Calif. 1979, U.S. Ct. Appeals 1979, U.S. Dist. Ct. (cen. dist.) Calif. 1982, U.S. Dist. Ct. (ea. dist.) Calif. 1990. Assoc. McGahan & Engle, Ventura, Calif., 1979-82, Henderson & Smith, Ventura, 1982-87; mng. atty. Borton, Petrini and Conron, Santa Barbara, Calif., 1987-88; ptnr. Ingram & Assocs., Penn Valley, Calif., 1988—. Prof. Oxnard (Calif.) Coll., 1981-88, U. Calif., Santa Barbara, 1983-88; commr. Nevada County Airport, 1999—; dir. Penn Valley Fire Protection Dist., 2000—. Author: (photography book) Come and Get It, 1972; dir., producer of movie Come and Get It, 1972. Mem. Rep. Party Central Com., 1998—2000. Mem. ABA, Assn. Trial Lawyers Am., Barrister's Club (bd. dirs. 1981-83). Avocations: flying, golf. Office: Ingram & Assocs 10520 Spenceville Rd Penn Valley CA 95946-9413 Office Phone: 530-432-1996. Business E-Mail: ingramlaw@starband.net.

INGRAM, KENNETH FRANK, retired state supreme court justice; b. Ashland, Ala., July 7, 1929; s. Earnest Frank and Alta Mary (Allen) I.; m. Judith Louise Brown, Sept. 3, 1954; children: Jennifer Lynn Ingram, Kenneth Frank Jr. BS, Auburn U., 1951; LLB, Jones Law Sch., 1963. Bar: Ala. 1963, U.S. Dist. Ct. (no. dist.) Ala. 1965, U.S. Dist. Ct. (mid. dist.) Ala. 1966. City councilman City of Ashland, Ala., 1956-58; mem. Ho. of Reps., Ala., 1958-66; presiding judge 18th Jud. Cir. Ct., Ala., 1968-87; judge Ala. Ct. Civil Appeals, Montgomery, 1987-89, presiding judge, 1989-91; assoc. justice Ala. Supreme Ct., Montgomery, 1991-97. Mem., chmn. Ala. Jud. Inquiry Commn., 1979-87. Contbr. articles on jud. ethics to profl. pubs. With USMC, 1952-54. Mem. Ala. Bar Assn., Masons. Democrat. Meth. Avocations: woodworking, metalcrafting, tennis, swimming. Home: 264 1st St N PO Box 729 Ashland AL 36251-0729

INGRAM, MARTHA RIVERS, publishing executive; b. Charleston, SC, Aug. 20, 1935; m. E. Bronson Ingram (dec. 1995), Oct. 4, 1958; children: Orrin Henry III, John Rivers, David Bronson, Robin. BA in History, Vassar Coll., 1957. V.p., pub. affairs Ingram Industries Inc., Nashville, 1979—95, mem., bd. directors, 1981—, chmn. bd. dirs., 1995—. Bd. dirs. Baxter Internat., Weyerhaeuser Co., Ashley Hall, Vassar Coll., Harpeth Hall Sch., Ingram Micro Inc.; mem. adv. bd. Kennedy Ctr. for Performing Arts, Washington. Chmn. Tenn. Bicentennial Commn., 1996; bd. dirs. Tenn. Performing Arts Ctr., Nashville Ballet, Nashville Opera, Nashville Inst. for Arts, Nashville Symphony, Nashville Cmty. Found.; past chmn. United Way's Alexis de Tocqueville Soc.; founder, bd. dirs. Tenn. Repertory Theater; chmn. bd. trustees Vanderbilt U., 1999-; co-founder Ingram Charitable Fund, 1995. Named one of Richest Americans, Forbes, 2001—, World's Richest People, 2001—; named to Jr. Achievement Nat. Bus. Hall of Fame, 1999, SC Bus. Hall of Fame, 1999; recipient Mary Harriman Cmty. Leadership award, Jr. League Internat., Inc., 1999, Golden Plate award, Acad. Achievement, 2004, Joe Kraft Humanitarian award, Cmty. Found., 2006. Mem. Nashville Area C. of C. Office: Ingram Industries Inc One Belle Mead Pl 4400 Harding Rd Nashville TN 37205-2244*

INGRAM, ORRIN HENRY, II, transportation executive; s. Martha Rivers and E. Bronson Ingram. Grad., Vanderbilt U., 1982. With Ingram Industries Inc., Nashville, 1982—, co-pres., 1995—99, bd. dirs., 1999—2005, pres., CEO, 1999—; chmn. Ingram Barge Co., Nashville. Mem. adv. bd. SunCom; Bd. dirs. eSkye.com, Boys and Girls Club Mid. Tenn., Friends of Warner Pks., Vanderbilt Cancer Ctr. (chmn. 1998-), Bapt. Hosp. Corp.; bd. govs., chmn. U.S. Polo Assn Office: Ingram Industries Inc 1 Belle Mead Pl 4400 Harding Rd Nashville TN 37205-2244

INGRAM, RICHARD THOMAS, retired president, consultant, writer; b. McKeesport, Pa., Sept. 29, 1941; s. Henry Stephen and Jean Catherine Ingram; m. Mollie Mangan Brown, Apr. 6, 1968; children: Kirsten Collins, David Thomas. BS, Indiana U. Pa., 1963; MEd, U. Pitts., 1964; EdD, U. Md., 1969. Tchr. h.s. Monroeville Sch. Dist., Monroeville, 1963—64; dir. psychometric svcs. U. Md., College Park, 1965—69; adj. instr. U. So. Calif., 1976, U. Va., 1971—79; program assoc. Assn. Governing Bds. of Univs. and Colls., Washington, 1971—74, exec. dir., 1974—79, exec. v.p., 1978—92, pres., 1992—2005; ret., 2005. Dir. United Educators Ins. Risk Retention Group, Inc., Washington, 1988-99, Am. Coun. on Edn., 1995-96; adv. commr. Edn. Commn. of States, Denver, 1985-95; trustee Dickinson Coll., Pa., 1995-2002, Coun. for Advancement and Support of Migley Edn., 2006—; trustee Allegheny Coll., 2007—. Editor, author: Governing Public Colleges and Universities, 1993, Governing Independent Colleges and Universities, 1993. Trustee U. Charleston, W.Va., 1980—89, Connelly Sch. Holy Child, Potomac, Md., 1987—93, Dickinson Coll., Pa., 1996—2002. Capt. US Army, 1969—71, Vietnam. Recipient Disting. Alumni award Ind. U. Pa., 1992, Outstanding Alumnus Citation, Pa. Coll. Alumni Assn., 1994, Coll. Edn. Alumni Assn. award U. Md., 1996. Mem.: Cosmos Club. Avocations: skiing, fly fishing. Home: 12017 Gregerscroft Rd Potomac MD 20854-2148

INGRAM, ROBERT D., lawyer; b. Cobb County, Ga. m. Kelly Ingram; 2 children. B, Kennesaw Coll., Ga.; JD, Emory Univ. Sch. of Law, Atlanta. Ptnr. Moore, Ingram, Johnson & Steele LLP, Marietta, Ga. Named a Spl. Master for disciplinary proceedings, Ga. Supreme Ct. Mem.: Ga. Inst. Continuing Legal Edn. (chair), Fed. Jud. Screening Panel, State Bd. Worker's Compensation (chmns. adv. coun.), State Disciplinary Bd. (mem. review panel), Cobb County Bar Assn. (past pres.), State Bar of Ga. (bd. gov. 1993—, chair bench and bar com. 1996—2005, exec. com. 1999, pres. 2005—06, chair Found. freedom commn.). Office: Moore Ingram Johnson & Steele 192 Anderson St PO Box 3305 Marietta GA 30061-3305 Office Phone: 770-429-1499.

INGRAM, SAMUEL WILLIAM, JR., retired lawyer; b. Utica, NY, Mar. 20, 1933; s. Samuel William and Mary Elizabeth (Rosen) I.; m. Jane Austin Stokes, Sept. 30, 1961; children: Victoria, William BS, Vanderbilt U., 1954; LLB, Columbia U., 1960. Bar: NY 1960. Assoc. Sullivan & Cromwell, NYC, 1960-67; assoc. Shea Gallop Climenko & Gould, NYC, 1967-68; ptnr. Shea & Gould and predecessors, NYC, 1968-89, Ingram, Yuzek, Gainen, Carroll & Bertolotti LLP, NYC, 1989—2006; ret., 2006. Bd. dirs. Legal Aid Soc., N.Y.C., 1974-86, sec., 1978-86; trustee Green Mountain Valley Sch., Waitsfield, Vt., 1984-87. Served to 1st lt. USMC, 1954-57 Mem. ABA, N.Y. State Bar Assn., Assn. of Bar of City of N.Y. Avocation: athletic and outdoor activities. Home: 332 Long Ridge Rd Pound Ridge NY 10576-2005 Personal E-mail: singram@ingramllp.com.

INGRAM, THEODORE FRANCIS, transportation executive; b. St. Louis, Mo., Sept. 9, 1950; s. Melvin Theodore and Laverna Ruth Ingram; m. Christine Clare Loechl; children: Theodore, Jr Francis, Jason Allen. MS in mgmt., Lindenwood U., 1979—83. Mgr. train ops. Union Pacific RR, Shreveport, La., 1984—88, mgr. terminal ops. Little Rock, 1988—90, dir. of safety, health, environment, 1992—95, dir. quality and transp., 1995—96, merger cons., 1996—2000, dir. transp. ops. Los Angeles, 2000—. Human resource cons. Union Pacific RR, Omaha, 1990—92. Recipient Alpha Sigma Tau Honor Soc., Lindenwood U., 1983. Mem.: Sigma Chi Frat. Achievements include development of behavior based safety system for UPRR. Avocation: baseball historian. Office: Union Pacific Railroad 4145 Washington Blvd Los Angeles CA Home Phone: 714-761-0626. E-mail: tingram2@up.com.

INGRAM, WILLIAM THOMAS, III, mathematics professor; b. McKenzie, Tenn., Nov. 26, 1937; s. William Thomas and Virginia (Howell) I.; m. Barbara Lee Gordon, June 6, 1958; children: William Robert, Kathie Ann, Mark Thomas. BA, Bethel Coll., 1959; MS, La. State U., 1961; PhD, Auburn U., 1964. Instr. Auburn U., Ala., 1961-63; instr. math. U. Houston, 1964-65, asst. prof., 1965-68, assoc. prof., 1968-75, prof., 1975-89, U. Mo., Rolla, 1989—2003, prof. emeritus, 2003—, chmn., 1989-98. Contbr. articles to profl. jours. Mem. Am. Math. Soc., Math. Assn. Am. (Disting. Tchg. award 2003). Presbyterian. Avocation: photography. Home: 284 Windmill Mountain Rd Spring Branch TX 78070 Office: Univ Mo Rolla Dept Math and Statistics Rolla MO 65409-0020

INGRASSIA, ANTHONY FRANK, human resource specialist; b. Middletown, NY, Sept. 22, 1926; s. Joseph and Mary (Dina) I.; m. Eleanor Mae Birkholz, Aug. 9, 1952 (dec.); children: Michael, Mary, Steve, Laura, Anne, Jane, Lisa, Timothy. BA, U.Wis., 1948. Sports writer Milw. Sentinel, 1948-62; exec. v.p. Milw. Newspaper Guild, 1952-62; asst. dir. Dist. Coun. 48 Am. Fedn. State, County, Mcpl. Employees, AFL-CIO, Milw., 1962-64; labor rels. specialist, labor rels. dir. US P.O. Dept., Washington, 1964-69; dir. office labor-mgmt. rels. US CSC, Washington, 1970-78; asst. dir. labor-mgmt. rels. US Office Pers. Mgmt., Washington, 1979-82, asst. dir. agy. compliance and evaluation, 1982-86, dep. assoc. dir. pers. sys. and oversight, 1986-90, chmn. fed. prevailing rate adv. com., 1990-96; vice chmn., acting chmn. Fed. Salary Coun., Washington, 1992-95, vice chmn., 1995-2000. US del. ILO Pub. Employee Conf., Geneva, 1975-77, 86; spkr. seminar on collective bargaining U. Tel Aviv, 1979; cons. civil svc. reform Govt. Hungary and Poland, Budapest and Warsaw, 1991; cons. civil svc. Govt. of Saudi Arabia, Riyahd, 1986. Vol. Arlington (Va.) Food Assistance Ctr., 1992-97, Hospice, 1996-2002; ombudsman No. Va. Long Term Care Program, 1999-2003. Recipient presdl. rank awards Disting. Govt. Exec., 1980, Meritorious Govt. Exec., 1988. Mem. Soc. Fed. Labor Rels. Profl. (outstanding contbn. to fed. labor rels. award 1983-87), KC. Roman Catholic. Avocations: gardening, golf. Home: 12206 Cathedral Dr Lake Ridge VA 22192

INGRASSIA, LAWRENCE, editor; BA in Journalism, U. Ill., 1974. Reporter Chgo. Sun-Times, 1974—78; reporter Chgo. Bur. The Wall St. Jour., 1978—79, reporter Mpls. Bur., 1979—83, dep. bur. chief London Bur., 1983—86, bur. chief London Bur., 1993—98, bur. chief Boston Bur., 1986—93, spl. project editor, editor, money and investing group, 1999—2003, asst. mng. editor money and investing group, 2003—04; bus. and fin. editor The N.Y. Times, NYC, 2004—. Office: The New York Times 229 W 43rd St New York NY 10036*

INGRASSIA, PAUL JOSEPH, publishing executive; b. Laurel, Miss., Aug. 18, 1950; s. Angelo Paul and Regina M. (Iacono) I.; m. Susan Marie Rougeau, Sept 29, 1973; children— Adam, Charles, Daniel BS, U. Ill., 1972; MA, U. Wis., 1973. Editorial writer Lindsay-Schaub Newspapers, Decatur, Ill., 1973-76; staff reporter Wall St. Jour., Chgo., 1977-80, news editor, 1980-81, bur. chief Cleve., 1981-85, Detroit, 1985-93, sr. editor, 1993-94; asst. v.p. Dow Jones Telerate, 1994-95; v.p. news svcs., exec. editor Dow Jones & Co., 1995-98; exec. editor, COO Dow Jones Newswires, 1996-98, pres., 1998—. Author: (with Joseph B. White) Comeback: The Fall and Rise of the American Automobile Industry, 1994 Recipient Pulitzer prize for beat reporting, 1993, Gerald Loeb award, 1993, Disting. Svc. to Journalism award U. Wis., 1995. Mem. U. Ill. Alumni Assn. (bd. dirs. 1980-87). Roman Catholic. Home: 111 Division Ave Summit NJ 07901-3050 Office: Harborside Fin Ctr 600 Plaza Two Jersey City NJ 07311-1103

INGRASSIA, TIMOTHY J., investment banker; b. 1965; m. Stephanie Ingrassia. Co-head, consumer products, retail, healthcare cos. Goldman Sachs & Co., NYC. Bd. dir. Alliance TRACE Media. Named a Top Dealmaker, Dealmaker mag., 2006; named Br. Volunteer Yr., Dodge Br. YMCA, 2006. Office: Goldman Sachs & Co 85 Broad St New York NY 10004 Office Phone: 212-902-1000. Office Fax: 212-902-3000.*

INGWALL, JOANNE S., medical educator; b. Syracuse, NY, Oct. 23, 1941; m. Richard Ingwall. PhD, Cornell U., Ithaca, NY, 1968; LHD honoris causa (hon.), LeMoyne Coll., Syracuse, NY, 2004. Prof. medicine, physiology Harvard Med. Sch., Boston, 1991—; sr. biochemist Brigham and Women's Hosp., Boston, 1991—, vice-chair for faculty devel. in medicine, dir. Boston, 1988—. Author: more than 140 articles in peer-reviewed sci. jours.; 63 articles, revs., book chpts., editls. Mem. med. adv. bd. Bioenergy, Inc, Mpls., 2006. Recipient Disting. Alumni award, LeMoyne Coll., 1993, John MacArthur Rsch. Svc. award, Brigham and Women's Hosp., 1999, A. Clifford Barger Excellence in Mentoring award, Harvard Med. Sch., 2000, Disting. Svc. award, Internat. Soc. Magnetic Resonance in Medicine, 2001; grantee numerous grants, NIH, 1973—. Fellow: Am. Physiol. Soc.; mem.: Am. Heart Assn. Office: Brigham and Women's Hosp NMR Lab 221 Longwood Ave Boston MA 02115 Office Phone: 617-732-6994. Business E-Mail: jingwall@rics.bwh.harvard.edu.

INGWERSEN, MARTIN LEWIS, water transportation executive; b. Sandusky, Ohio, Nov. 5, 1919; s. John Christian and Irene Catherine (Hinkey) Ingwersen; m. Blanche Robinson, Apr. 26, 1947; children: Brenda, Richard Charles, Martin Lewis. BS, U. Notre Dame, 1941; postgrad., Western Res. U., 1941, Princeton U., 1943. Asst. to hull supt. Gt. Lakes Engring. Works, Ashtabula, Ohio, 1941-43, asst. supt., 1946-49; supt. plant Am. Ship Bldg. Co., Buffalo, 1948-50; mgr. plant Toledo, 1950-52, Lorain, Ohio, 1952-53; v.p. ops., 1954-58; v.p., works mgr. Ingalls Shipbldg. Corp., Pascagoula, Miss., 1958-65, v.p. ops., 1965-67; pres. Md. Shipbldg. and Drydock Co., Balt., 1967-68; exec. v.p. Lockheed Shipbldg. Co., Seattle, 1968-73; pres. Lockheed Shipbldg. and Constrn. Co., Seattle, 1973-76, exec. v.p. office of pres., 1976-86, trustee, 1973-86; cons. shipbldg. and ship repair, 1986—. Bd. dirs. Puget Sound Bridge and Dry Dock Co., Colby Crane & Mfg. Inc. Served to lt. USNR, 1943—46. Mem.: Am. Soc. Naval Engrs., Soc. Naval Archs. and Marine Engrs., Am. Bur. Shipping, Navy League, Notre Dame Club Vero Beach, Propeller Club U.S. Roman Catholic. Home and Office: 940 Turtle Cove Ln #304 Vero Beach FL 32963 Home Phone: 772-492-5075; Office Phone: 772-492-5075. Personal E-mail: mingwersen@aol.com.

INHOFE, JAMES M., senator; b. Des Moines, Nov. 17, 1934; m. Kay Kirkpatrik; children: Jim, Perry, Molly, Katy. BA, U. Tulsa, 1973. Pres. Quaker Life Ins. Co.; mem. Okla. Ho. Reps., 1967—69, Okla. State Senate, 1969—77; mayor City of Tulsa, 1978-84; mem. 1st Dist. Okla. Ho. of Reps., 1987-94; US Senator from Okla., 1994—. Com. environment and public works US Senate, com. armed services. Mem. Tulsa Airport Authority, Tulsa Area Safety Coun. Served with US Army, 1955—56. Recipient Democracy award, Internat. Found. Election Systems, 1996, William S. Lee award leadership, Nuclear Energy Inst., 2001, Nat. Guardian award, Lincoln House Heritage Inst., 2002. Mem.: Friends of Am. Diabetes Assn. Republican. Presbyterian. Office: US Senate 453 Russell Senate Bldg Washington DC 20510-0001 also: District Office Ste 530 1924 South Utica Ave Tulsa OK 74104-6511 Office Phone: 202-224-5754, 918-748-5111. Office Fax: 202-224-6008, 918-748-5119. E-mail: jim_inhofe@inhofe.senate.gov.*

INIGO, RAFAEL MADRIGAL, retired electrical engineering educator; b. Madrid, June 18, 1932; arrived in U.S., 1963; s. Rafael G. and Francisca V. (Madrigal) I.; m. Eliana Soto, Apr. 29, 1961; children: C. Paulina, Alvaro A. Ing. El., U.T.F. Santa Maria, Val Chile, 1957; MSEE, U. Va., 1965, DSc in EE, 1966. Registered profl. engr., Va. Elec. engr. Branden Coppe Co., Coya, Chile, 1957-61; asst. prof. elec. engring. U.T.F. Santa Maria, Valparaiso, Chile, 1961-66; prof. elec. engring. UT Santa Maria, Valparaiso, 1966-68; assoc. prof. elec. engring. Va. Mil. Inst., Lexington, 1968-74, prof. elec. engring., 1974-78; assoc. prof. elec. engring U. Va., Charlottesville, 1978-85, prof. elec. engring., 1986-97, prof. emeritus, 1997—. Invited prof. U. Deusto, Spain, 1981, 83, 93, U. Seville, Spain, 1988, Rovira Virgili U., Tarragona, Spain, 2000. Author: Teoria de Circuitos, 1977, Vision por Computador, 1986, Robots Industriales Manipuladores, 2002; contbr. articles to profl. jours. Helen Wessel fellow U. Va., 1959, AID fellow U.S. Govt., 1963; Fulbright scholar U. Tech. Nat. Faculty Cordoba, Argentina, 1997. Avocations: photography, canoeing. Office: U Va Thornton Hall Dept Elec Engring Charlottesville VA 22903-6073 E-mail: rafainigo@earthlink.net.

INK, DWIGHT A., government agency administrator; b. Des Moines, Sept. 9, 1922; s. Dwight P. and Edna (Craun) I.; m. Margaret Child, Aug. 31, 1948; children: Stephen, Bruce, Lawrence, Barbara, Lauri; m. Donna A. Wolf, Feb. 14, 1981. BS, Iowa State U., 1947; MA, U. Minn., 1951. Budget and personnel officer City of Fargo (N.D.), 1948-50; chief mcpl. water sect. Bur. Reclamation Dept. Interior, Bismark, ND, 1950-51; chief reports and statistics br. Savannah River Ops. Office AEC, Oak Ridge, 1952-55, exec. asst. to chmn. Washington, 1958-59, asst. gen. mgr., 1959-66; 1st asst. sec. for adminstrn. HUD, Washington, 1966-69; asst. dir. for exec. mgmt. Office of Mgmt. and Budget, Washington, 1969-73; dep. adminstr., acting adminstr. GSA, Washington, 1973-76, acting adminstr., Mar.-July 1985; exec. dir., pres. personnel project mgmt. CSC, Washington, May-Nov. 1977; v.p. Nat. Consumer Coop. Bank, Washington, 1980-81, U.S. Synthetic Fuels Corp., Washington, 1982-84; ind. cons. McManis and Assocs., Washington, 1984-85; asst. adminstr. USAID, Washington, 1985-88; pres. Inst. of Pub. Adminstrn., NYC, 1988-93, pres. emeritus, 1994—. Exec. dir. Alaska Reconstrn. Commn.; pres. Am. Consortium Internat. Pub. Adminstrn., 1980-83; adminstr. Cmty. Svcs. Adminstrn., Washington, 1981; chmn. White House Task Force on Edn., 1965; bd. dirs. N.Am. Mgmt. Coun., 1989-93; vice chair nat. adv. bd. Ctr. Study of Presidency. Chmn. Charter Commn. S.C., 1955; mem. exec. com. Ga.- Carolina Council Boy Scouts Am., 1954-55. Served to capt. USAR, 1942-58. Recipient Arthur Fleming award as one of the 10 Outstanding Young Men in Govt. U.S. C. of C., 1961, Disting. Svc. award AEC, 1966, Outstanding Achievement awards U. Minn., 1969, Iowa State U., 1986, Disting. Svc. award GSA, 1975, Outstanding Leadership award Assn. Govt. Accts., 1976, Commrs.

award for Disting. Svc., CSC, Pub. Adminstr. of Yr. award Brigham Young U., 1978. Mem. Am. Pub. Works Assn. (bd. dirs.), Am. Soc. Pub. Adminstrn. (pres. 1978-79, Lifetime Achievement award for Distinguished Pub. Svc., 2001—), Nat. Civil Service League (bd. dirs., career service award 1966), Pub. Adminstrn. Service (bd. dirs.), Nat. Acad. Pub. Adminstrn. (trustee), Internat. Inst. Adminstrv. Sci. (v.p. 1980-86), Coun. on Fgn. Rels., Delta Sigma Rho, Phi Kappa Phi. Home: 43725 Collett Mill Ct Leesburg VA 20176-1626

INKELES, ALEX, sociology educator; b. Bklyn., Mar. 4, 1920; s. Meyer and Ray (Gewer) K.; m. Bernadette Mary Kane, Jan. 31, 1942; 1 child, Ann Elizabeth BA, Cornell U., 1941; postgrad., Washington Sch. Psychiatry, 1943-46; MA, Cornell U., 1946; PhD, Columbia U., 1949; AM (hon.), Harvard U., 1957; student, Boston Psychoanalytic Inst., 1957-59; prof. (hon.), Faculdade Candido Mendez, Rio de Janerio, 1969, Faculdade Candido Mendez, 2002. Social sci. research analyst Dept. State and OSS, 1942-46; cons. program evaluation br., internat. broadcasting div. Dept. State, 1949-51; instr. social relations Harvard U., Cambridge, Mass., 1948, lectr., 1948-57, prof. sociology, 1957-71, dir. studies social rels. Russian Rsch. Ctr., dir. studies social aspects econ. devel. Ctr. Internat. Affairs, 1963-71, rsch. assoc., 1971-79; Margaret Jacks prof. edn., prof. sociology Stanford U., Calif., 1971-78, prof. sociology, 1978-90; sr. fellow Hoover Inst., 1978—; prof. emeritus, 1990—. Mem. exec. com. behavioral sci. div. NRC, 1968-75; lectr. Nihon U., Japan, 1985. Author: Public Opinion in Soviet Russia, 1950 (Kappa Tau Alpha award 1950, Grant Squires prize Columbia 1955); with R. Bauer, C. Kluckhohn) How the Soviet System Works, 1956, (with R. Bauer) The Soviet Citizen, 1959, Soviet Society (edited with H.K. Geiger), 1961, What is Sociology?, 1964, Readings on Modern Sociology, 1965, Social Change in Soviet Russia, 1968, (with D.H. Smith) Becoming Modern, 1974 (Hadley Cantril award 1974), Exploring Individual Modernity, 1983; editor: (with Masamichi Sasaki) Comparing Nations and Cultures, 1996, National Character: A Psychosocial Perspective, 1997, One World Emerging? Convergence and Divergence in Industrial Societies, 1998; editor-in-chief Ann. Rev. Sociology, 1971-79; editl. cons. Internat. Rev. Cross Cultural Studies; editl. bd. Ethos, Jour. Soc. Psychol. Anthropology, 1978; editor Founds. Modern Sociology Series; adv. editor in sociology to Little, Brown & Co.; contbr. articles to profl. jours. Recipient Cooley Mead award for Disting. Contbn. in Social Psychology, 1982; fellow Ctr. Advanced Study Behavioral Sci., 1955, Founds. Fund Research Psychiatry, 1957-60, Social Scis. Research Council, 1959, Russell Sage Found., 1966, 85, Fulbright Found., 1977, Guggenheim Found., 1978, Bernard van Leer Jerusalem Found., 1979, Rockefeller Found., 1982, Eisenhower Assn., Taiwan, 1984; NAS Disting. Scholar Exchange, China, 1983; grantee Internat. Rsch. and Exchs. Bd., 1989, NSF, 1989. Fellow AAAS (co-chmn. western ctr. 1984-87, chmn. Talcott Parsons award com. 1988-93), Am. Philos. Soc., APA; mem. NIMH, Nat. Inst. Aging (monitoring com. health retirement survey 1990—), Nat. Acad. Scis. (corr. human rights com. 1986-88, mem. com. on scholarly comms. with People's Republic of China, chmn. panel on social sci. and humanities, NRC panel on issues in democratization 1991-92), Am. Sociol. Soc. (coun. 1961-664, v.p. 1975-76), Ea. Sociol. Soc. (pres. 1961-62), World Assn. Pub. Opinion Rsch., Am. Assn. Pub. Opinion Rsch., Inter-Am. Soc. Psychology, Sociol. Rsch. Assn. (exec. com. 1975-79, pres. 1979), Soc. for Study Social Problems. Home: 1001 Hamilton Ave Palo Alto CA 94301-2215 Office: Stanford U Hoover Instn Stanford CA 94305 Home Phone: 650-327-4197; Office Phone: 650-723-4856. Business E-Mail: inkeles@hoover.stanford.edu.

INKLEY, JOHN JAMES, JR., lawyer; b. St. Louis, Nov. 7, 1945; s. John James Sr. and Morjorie Jane (Kenna) I.; m. Catherine Ann Mattingly, Apr. 13, 1971; children: Caroline Marie, John James III. BSIE, St. Louis U., 1967, JD, 1970; LLM in Taxation, Washington U., St. Louis, 1976. Bar: Mo. 1970, U.S. Dist. Ct. (we. dist.) Mo. 1970, U.S. Dist. Ct. (ea. dist.) Mo. 1975, U.S. Tax Ct. 1975, U.S. Supreme Ct. 1975. Assoc. Padberg, Raack, McSweeney & Slater, St. Louis, 1970-73; ptnr. Summer, Hanlon, Summer, MacDonald & Nouss, St. Louis, 1973-81; city atty. City of Town and Country, Mo., 1979-84, spl. counsel Mo., 1984-88; ptnr. Hanlon, Nouss, Inkley & Coughlin, St. Louis, 1981-83; ptnr., chmn. banking and real estate dept. Suelthaus & Kaplan, St. Louis, 1983-91; ptnr. Armstrong Teasdale LLP (and predecessor firm), St. Louis, 1991—; co-chmn. bus. svcs. group, 1993-2000; exec. com. St. Louis, 1994—. Mem. ABA, Mo. Bar Assn., Bar Assn. Met. St. Louis. Roman Catholic. Home: 35 Muirfield Ln Saint Louis MO 63141-7382 Office: Armstrong Teasdale LLP 1 Metropolitan Sq Ste 2600 Saint Louis MO 63102-2740

INKSTER, CHRISTINE DAVIS, librarian, educator; b. Scranton, Pa., Aug. 3, 1943; d. Gordon W. and Mary Elizabeth (Murphy) Davis; m. Robert Paul Inkster, June 7, 1965; children: Matthew, John, Benjamin. BA in English, U. Wyo., 1965, MA in English, 1975; MLS, U. Pitts., 1979; EdD, U. Minn., 1995. English tchr. Wash. Jr. High Sch., Chgo. Heights, Ill., 1965-66, Laramie (Wyo.) Jr. High Sch., 1966-68, 79-89, Laramie (Wyo.) High Sch., 1969-75, Ea. Wyo. Coll., Torrington, 1975-78; ref. libr., prof. St. Cloud (Minn.) State U., 1989—. Teacher, trainer Wyo. Writing Project, Laramie, 1979-89. Contbr. articles to profl. jours. Vol. Sch. Dist. 742, St. Cloud, 1989—. Mem. NEA, AAUW (newsletter editor 1990-94, Outstanding Newsletter award 1991, 92, ednl. equity chair 1994-96), Minn. Ednl. Media Orgn. (region chair 1992-94, Emerging Leader award 1991), Phi Kappa Phi (chpt. sec. 1992-96), Phi Delta Kappa. Democrat. Lutheran. Avocations: reading, singing, playing piano. Home: 716 10th Ave S Saint Cloud MN 56301-4241 Office: St Cloud State U Learning Res Svcs MC140H Saint Cloud MN 56301 Office Phone: 320-308-4930. Business E-Mail: cinkster@stcloudstate.edu.

INKSTER, JULI, professional golfer; b. Santa Cruz, Calif., June 24, 1960; m. Brian Inkster, July, 1980; 2 daughters. Student, San Jose State U., Calif. Mem. LPGA, 1983—. Mem. US Solheim Cup teams, 1992, 98, 2000, 02, 03, 05; mem. US World Cup Team, 1980, 82. Named a Collegiate All-Am., 1979, 1981—82; named Rookie of Yr., LPGA, 1984; named to LPGA Tour Hall of Fame, 1999, World Golf Hall of Fame, 2000; recipient Rookie of Yr., Golf Digest, 1983, Espy, Outstanding Woman Golfer, ESPN, 2000, William and Mousie Powell award, LPGA, 2004. Achievements include winning 31 career LPGA events including the Du Maurier Classic in 1984, the Kraft Nabisco Championships in 1984 and 1989 and Safeway International in 2006; winner, 7 majors inclusing the McDonald's LPGA Championship, 1999, 2000, and the US Women's Open, 1999, 2002; winner, US Women's Amateur Title, 1980-82. Office: c/o LPGA 100 International Golf Dr Daytona Beach FL 32124-1082*

INLOW, JENNIFER KAY, chemistry professor, researcher; d. James G. and Karen J. McCulloch; m. Mark H. Inlow, Aug. 16, 1997. BA, Jamestown Coll., 1995; PhD, Tex. A&M U., 2001. With Ariz. Rsch. Labs. Divsn. Neurobiology, Tucson, 2001—03; instr. chemistry Ind. State U., Terre Haute, 2003—04, asst. prof. chemistry, 2004—. Mem. Grad. Christian Fellowship U. Ariz., Tucson, 2001—03, Intervarsity Christian Fellowship Tex. A&M U., College Station, 1996—2001; sanctuary computer operator World Gospel Ch., Terre Haute, 2005—06. Grantee, Ind. State U. Ctr. Tchg. and Learning, 2005; scholar, NIH, 2003; Franklin Rsch. grantee, Am. Philos. Soc., 2005. Mem.: Am. Chem. Soc. Avocations: weightlifting, walking. Office: Ind State U Det Chemistry Terre Haute IN 47809 Office Phone: 812-237-2242.

INLOW, RUSH OSBORNE, chemist; b. Seattle, July 10, 1944; s. Edgar Burke and Marigale (Osborne) I.; m. Gloria Elisa Duran, June 7, 1980. BS, U. Wash., 1966; PhD, Vanderbilt U., 1975. Chemist, sect. chief U.S. Dept. Energy, Argonne, Ill., 1975-78, chief nuclear safeguards br. Cruise missile sys. Ops. Office Albuquerque, 1983-84; program mgr. Navy strategic sys., 1984-85; dir. weapon programs divsn., 1985-88; dir. prodn. ops. divsn., 1988-90; asst. mgr. safeguards and security, 1990-94; asst. mgr. nat. def. programs, 1994-96; dep. mgr., 1996-2000; prin. mem. tech. staff Sandia Nat. Labs., 2000—. Apptd. Fed. Sr. Exec. Svc., 1985. Served with USN, 1966-71. Tenn. Eastman fellow, 1974-75; recipient Pres. Meritorious Exec. awrd The White House, Pres. Clinton, 1994. Mem. Am. Chem. Soc., Sigma Xi. Republican. Episcopalian. Home Phone: 505-797-8375. Business E-Mail: roinlow@sandia.gov.

INMAN, BOBBY RAY, retired electronics executive; b. Rhonesboro, Tex., Apr. 4, 1931; s. Herman H. and Mertie F. (Hinson) I.; m. Nancy Carolyn Russo, June 14, 1958; children: Thomas, William. BA, U. Tex., 1950; grad., Nat. War Coll., 1972. Commd. ensign U.S. Navy, 1952, advanced through grades to adm., 1981; asst. naval attache Stockholm, 1965-67; exec. asst., sr. aide to vice chief naval ops. Washington, 1972-73; asst. chief staff intelligence on staff comdr. in chief U.S. Pacific Fleet, 1973-74; dir. Naval intelligence Dept. Navy, Washington, 1974-76; vice dir. Def. Intelligence Agy., 1976-77; dir. Nat. Security Agy., Ft. Meade, Md., 1977-81; dep. dir. CIA, 1981-82; chmn., pres., chief exec. officer Microelectronics and Computer Tech. Corp., Austin, Tex., 1983-86; chmn. bd., chief exec. officer Westmark Systems, Inc., Austin, 1986-89; pvt. investor Austin, 1990—; prof., Lyndon B. Johnson Centennial chair in nat. policy U. Tex. Decorated Def. D.S.M., Navy D.S.M., Legion of Merit, Def. Superior Service medal, Meritorious Service medal, Nat. Security medal, Joint Services Commendation medal. Office: 301 Congress Ave Ste 1350 Austin TX 78701

INMAN, JAMES RUSSELL, claims consultant; b. Tucson, May 24, 1936; s. Claude Colbert and Myra Eugenia (Langdon) Inman; m. Charleen M. Bowman Inman, Feb. 22, 1964 (div. 1977); m. Margaret Williams Kendrick, Apr. 26, 1996 (dec. Feb. 2002). Student, Pomona Coll., Claremont, Calif., 1954-60. Supr. res. dept. Honnold Libr. Claremont Coll., 1959-60; supr. casualty claims CNA Ins., LA, 1961-70; asst. mgr., asbestos specialist, head entertainment claims Firemen's Fund, L.A., Beverly Hills, 1970—83; pres. Wilnor Corp., LA, 1982—. Claims auditor dirs. and officers claims Harbor/Continental Ins., L.A., 1984-86; claims mgr. Advent Mgmt., L.A., 1987, Completion Bond Co., Century City, Calif., 1988; asst. to pres., claims specialist Am. Multiline Corp., L.A., 1988-92; sr. claims specialist Reliance Ins. Co., Glendale, Calif., 1992-94; expert witness in entertainment claims field. Mem. First Century Families: Calif.; mem. com. Baldwin Hills Dam Disaster, 1968-72; pres. Alcohol Info. Ctr., LA, 1983-85; trustee Woodbury U., 2005-07. Mem. LA Athletic Club, Wilshire Country Club, Sloane Club (London), Rotary Internat. Avocations: classic cars, American and English silver. Home: 623 S Arden Blvd Los Angeles CA 90005-3814

INMAN, JONATHAN RUSSELL, mechanical engineer; b. Fort Belvoir, Va., Jan. 10, 1980; s. Charles Scott Inman and Cheri Inman Luster. BS in Mech. Engring., Va. Poly. Inst. and State U., Blacksburg, 2004. Registered engr., Va., 2004. Engr. II electronic cooling water, chilled water Northrop Grumman Newport News, Va., 2004—. Organizer, vol. Toys for Tots, Roanoke, Va., 1998—2003. Sgt. USMC, 1998—2003. Mem.: ASHRAE (assoc.), ASME (assoc.), Am. Legion (assoc.). Avocations: running, history, reading, drawing, cooking. Office: Northrop Grumman Newport News 4101 Washington Ave Newport News VA 23607 Home Phone: 571-334-8654; Office Phone: 757-688-4445.

INMAN, LARRY JOE, basketball coach; b. Summer County, Tenn., Jan. 3, 1948; m. Bobby Gene Follis; children: Jody, Latrice, Tiffany. BS, Austin Peay State U., Clarksville, Tenn., 1970; M, Tenn. State U., 1977. Head coach basketball Gallatin (Tenn.) H.S., 1970-73, Mt. Juliet (Tenn.) H.S., 1973-78; head coach women's basketball Mid. Tenn. State U., Murfreesboro, 1978-86, Ea. Ky. U., Richmond, 1987—. Named Coach of Yr., Ohio Valley Conf., 1979—80, 1982—83, 1984—85, 1990—91, 1994—95, 1996—97, 2001, Man of Yr., 2001; recipient Coach of Yr., Ohio Valley Conf., 2005. Mem.: Womans Basketball Coaches Assn. Office: Eastern Ky U Womens Athletic Dept Lancaster Ave Richmond KY 40475 Office Phone: 859-622-2127. Business E-Mail: larry.inman@eku.edu.

INMAN, MARIANNE ELIZABETH, academic administrator; b. Berwyn, Ill., Jan. 9, 1943; d. Miles V. and Bessee M. (Hejtmanek), Plzak; m. David P. Inman; Aug 1, 1964. BA, Purdue U., 1964; AM, Ind. U., 1967; PhD, U. Tex., 1978. Dir. Comml. Div. World Instruction and Translation, Inc., Arlington, Va., 1969-71; program staff mem. Ctr. for Applied Linguistics, Arlington, 1972-73; lectr. in French No. Va. Community Coll., Bailey's Crossroads, 1973; faculty mem., linguistic researcher Tehran (Iran) U., 1973-75; intern mgmt. edn. rsch. & devel. S.W Ednl. Devel. Lab., Austin, Tex., 1977-78; asst. prof., program dir. Southwestern U., Georgetown, Tex., 1978; dir. English lang. inst. Alaska Pacific U., Anchorage, 1980-87, chairperson all-U. requirements, 1984-88, assoc. dean acad. affairs, 1988-90; v.p. dean of coll. Northland Coll., Ashland, Wis., 1990-95; pres. Ctrl. Meth. Univ., Fayette, Mo., 1995—. Contbr. Pres. Commn. Foreign Lang. and Internat. Studies, Washington, 1978-79; manuscript evaluator The Modern Lang. Jour., Columbus, Ohio, 1979-84; cons. Anchorage Sch. Dist., 1984-90; cons., evaluator The Higher Learning Commn. of N. Cen. Assn. Colls. and Schs., Chgo., 1990—; mem. dean's task force Coun. on Ind. Colls., 1993-95; pres. Ind. Colls. and Univs. Mo., 1996-00. Co-author: English for Medical Students, 1976; co-author and editor: English for Science and Engineering Students, 1977; contbr. articles to profl. jours. Treas. Alaska Humanities Forum, Anchorage, 1982-87; mem. Anchorage Matanuska-Susitna Borough Pvt. Industry Coun., 1983-86, Sister Cities Commn., Anchorage, 1984-90; mem. Multicultural Edn. Adv. Bd., Anchorage, 1987-90; with speakers bur. Wis. Humanities Com., 1992-95, Mcpl. Libr. Bd., 1993-95; active Mo. Humanities Coun., 1997-03, 04—, vice chmn., 2005—07, chmn., 2007-; bd. dirs. Mo. Colls. Fund, Ind. Colls. and Univs. of Mo.; mem. bd. Great Rivers Coun. Boy Scouts Am., 1996—; mem. presdl. adv. com. Mo. Coordinating Bd. for Higher Edn. Named Fellow of Grad. Sch., U. Tex. Austin, 1977-78, Nat. Teaching Fellow, Alaska Pacific U., Anchorage, 1980-81; recipient Pub. Svc. award Sister Cities Commn., Anchorage, 1987, Kellogg Found. Nat. fellowship, Battle Creek, Mich., 1988-91. Mem. LWV, Nat. Assn. Women Edn., Nat. Assn. Ind. Colls. and Univs. (bd. dirs. 2005-, chair policy and pub. rels. com. 2007-), Am. Assn. Higher Edn., Am. Coun Tchg. Fgn. Langs., Nat. Assn. Schs. and Colls. of United Meth. Ch. (bd. dirs.), Tchrs. English to Speakers Other Langs., Nat. Coun. Tchrs. English, Gold Peppers, Mortar Board, Alpha Chi, Alpha Lambda Delta, Delta Rho Kappa, Kappa Delta Pi, Omicron Delta Kappa, Phi Kappa Phi, Pi Delta Phi, Pi Lambda Theta, Sigma Delta Pi, Sigma Epsilon Pi, Sigma Kappa. Avocations: community theater, hiking, camping, fishing. Office: Central Methodist U 411 Central Methodist Sq Fayette MO 65248-1198 Business E-Mail: minman@centralmethodist.edu.

INMAN, SAMANTHA MAE, music educator; b. Peoria, Ill., Aug. 29, 1985; d. David McMillen II and Patricia Mae Inman. MusB in Music Theory and Flute Performance, Baldwin-Wallace Coll., Berea, Ohio, 2007. Music libr. asst. Jones Music Libr., Baldwin-Wallace Coll., 2003—06, tchg. asst. music theory, 2006—07, rsch. asst. music history, 2006—07; tutor in solfege and piano Baldwin-Wallace Coll. Learning Ctr., 2004—07. Presdl. scholar, Baldwin-Wallace Coll., 2003—07, Gund Student-Faculty Rsch. grantee, 2006—07, Va. Hejduk Ocasek Women's Club scholar, Women's Club at Baldwin-Wallace Coll., 2005—06. Mem.: Nat. Flute Assn., Soc. Music Theory, Dayton C. Miller Honor Soc., Mu Phi Epsilon (corr. sec. 2005—07). Home: 2008 N North St Peoria IL 61604 Home Phone: 309-682-4222.

INMAN, WILLIAM PETER, lawyer; b. Cleve., June 29, 1936; s. James B. and Lillian (Frances) I.; m. Judith A. Clay, Feb. 5, 1994; children: William Peter, Elizabeth, David. Student, Miami U., 1954-55; BA, Ohio State U., 1958; JD, Case Western Res. U., 1960, MBA, 1966. Bar: Ohio 1960, Tex. 1985. Tax accountant U.S. Steel Corp., Cleve., 1960-63; asso. trust counsel Central Nat. Bank of Cleve., 1963-66; atty. Sherwin-Williams Co., Cleve., 1966-67, tax counsel, 1967, mgr. tax dept., 1967-68, corporate dir. taxes, 1968-69, asst. sec., dir. taxes, 1969-71, sec., dir. taxes, 1971-75, v.p., sec., asst. treas., 1975-78, v.p., treas., chief fin. officer, 1978-80; v.p. fin., chief fin. officer RTE Corp., Waukesha, Wis., 1980-83; fin. cons. Houston, 1983-85; corp. sec., gen. counsel Mera Bank, Phoenix, 1985-88; gen. counsel CADTEL Sys. Inc., Phoenix, 1988-95, Ariz. Bus. Assocs., L.L.C., Phoenix, 1995—. Mem. Greater Cleve. Growth Assn., 1969-80; Trustee Ohio Pub. Expenditure Council, 1969-80, v.p., 1970-73, pres., 1973-75, chmn. bd., 1975-77. Mem. Am. Soc. Corp. Secs., Fin. Execs. Inst., Cleve. Treasurers Club, N.A.M., Ohio Mfrs. Assn., Am., Ohio, Greater Cleve., Tex., Maricopa County, Ariz. bar assns., Estate Planning Council of Cleve., Tax Execs. Inst., Phi Delta Phi, Beta Gamma Sigma, Beta Alpha Psi. Home and Office: 5702 E Sylvia St Scottsdale AZ 85254-4364

INNES, DEBORAH, bank executive; 3 children. V.p., treasury mgmt. Amegy Bank of Texas (subsidiary of Southwest Bancorporation of Texas, Inc.), Houston, 1992—94, exec. v.p., treasury mgmt., 1994—, exec. v.p., retail banking, 2005—. Bd. secy. and chair of volunteer services I Have a Dream, Houston; bd. mem. ESCAPE Family Resource Ctr., Juvenile Diabetes Rsch. Found., Houston. Named one of 25 Women to Watch, US Banker mag., 2005, 25 Most Powerful Women in Banking, US Banker, 2006. Office: Amegy Bank of Texas 4400 Post Oak Pkwy Houston TX 77027-7459*

INNES, KENNETH FREDERICK, III, lawyer; b. San Francisco, May 15, 1950; s. Kenneth F. Jr. and Jean I.; m. Patricia Ann Graboyes, May 12, 1973; children: Kenneth F. IV, Julia Christine. BA, San Francisco State U., 1972, JD, 1984. Bar: Calif. 1984, U.S. Dist. Ct. (no. dist.) Calif. 1987, U.S. Dist. Ct. (ea. dist.) Calif. 1988. Tchr. secondary schs., Red Bluff, Calif., 1973-74; postal clk. U.S. Postal Svc., Vallejo, Calif., 1977-84, postal insp. Denver, 1984-87; regional atty. U.S. Postal Inspection Svc., Memphis, 1987-90, fin. auditor, 1990-92, regional atty. San Francisco, 1992—. Capt. USMCR, 1974-77. Mem. ABA, Calif. Bar Assn., Mensa, Elks. Democrat. Roman Catholic. Home: 157 Heartwood Ct Vallejo CA 94591-5638 Office: US Postal Insp Svc PO Box 882528 San Francisco CA 94188-2528

INNIS, DANIEL EUGENE, dean, consultant; b. Columbus, Ohio, Apr. 7, 1963; s. Eugene A. and Jeanie A. Innis; m. Margaret C. Moody, Aug. 17, 1985 (div. Jan. 2007); children: Benjamin D., Nicholas R., Emily A. BA, Ohio U., 1985; MBA, Miami U., Ohio, 1986; PhD, Ohio State U., Columbus, 1991. Asst. ops. analyst Warner-Lambert Co., Morris Plains, NJ, 1986—88; prof. Ohio U., Athens, 1991—98, assoc. dean, 1999—2002; dean U. Maine, Orono, 2002—07, U. NH, 2007—. Mem. Healthcare Charities, Bangor, Maine, 2006. Recipient Doctoral Dissertation award, Coun. Logistics Mgmt., 1992. Mem.: Coun. Supply Chain Mgmt. Profls., Am. Mktg. Assn., Rotary. Conservative. Methodist. Avocations: weight training, bicycling, outdoor activities. Home Phone: 207-866-0868; Office Phone: 207-581-1968. Personal E-mail: daninnis@adelphia.net, daninnis@mac.com. Business E-Mail: dan.innis@unh.edu. E-mail: innis@maine.edu.

INNIS, PAULINE, writer, publishing company executive; b. Devon, England, Dec. 8, 1917; came to U.S., 1954; m. Walter Deane Innis, Aug. 1, 1959 (dec. 1991). Student, U. Manchester, U. London. Author: Hurricane Fighters, 1962, Ernestine or the Pig in the Potting Shed, 1963, The Wild Swans Fly, 1964, The Ice Bird, 1965, Wind of the Pampas, 1967, Fire from the Fountains, 1968, Astronumerology, 1971, Gold in the Blue Ridge, 1973, My Trails (transl. from French), 1975, Prayer and Power in the Capital, 1982, The Secret Gardens of Watergate, 1987, Attention: A Quick Guide to Armed Services, 1988, Desert Storm Dairy, 1991, The Nursing Home Companion, 1993, Bridge Across the Seas, 1995, The Gospel of Joseph, 1998, I've Smashed the Devil's Window, 1999; co-author: Protocol: The Complete Handbook of Diplomatic, Official and Social Usage, 1977. Bd. dirs. Washington Goodwill Industries Guild, 1962-66; membership chmn. Welcome to Washington Club, 1961-64; co-chmn. Internat. Workshop Capital Spkr.'s Club, 1961-64; pres. Children's Book Guild, 1967-68; dir. Ednl. Commn., bd. dirs. Internat. Conf. Women Writers and Journalists, Nat. Arboretum, 1992-96; criminal justice com. D.C. Commn. on Status of Women; founder vol. program D.C. Women's Detention Ctr.; chmn. women's com. Washington Opera, 1977-79; mem. Liaison Com. Med. Edn., 1979-85; nat. trustee Med. Coll. Pa., 1980—; mem. Edn. Commn. for Fgn. Med. Grads., 1986-97. Named Hoosier Woman of Yr., 1966. Mem. Soc. Women Geographers, Authors League, Smithsonian Assocs. (women's bd.), English-Speaking Union, Spanish-Portuguese Group D.C. (pres. 1965-66), Br. Inst. U.S., Am. Newspaper Women's Club (pres. 1971-73), Internat. Soc. Poets (disting.), Internat. Clubs (co-chair 1997), Venerable Order St. John Jerusalem (comdr.), Internat. Neighbors Club. Home: Washington, DC. Died Aug. 18, 2007.

INNIS, ROY EMILE ALFREDO, foundation executive; b. St. Croix, V.I., June 6, 1934; s. Alexander and Georgianna (Thomas) I.; m. Doris Valdena Funnye, Feb. 13, 1965; children: Roy Jr. (dec.), Alexander (dec.), Cedric, Patricia, Corinne, Kwame, Niger, Kimathi Mugabe. Student, CCNY, 1953-58. Chem. technician Vick Chem. Co., 1961-63; research asst. cardiovascular research labs. Montefiore Hosp., 1963-67; mem. CORE, 1963—, edn. chmn. Harlem group, 1964-68, chmn., 1965-68, 2d nat. vice chmn., 1967-68, asso. nat. dir., 1968, nat. dir., 1968-70, nat. chmn., nat. dir., 1970-82, nat. chmn., 1982—; founder and chmn. CORE Cmty. Sch., Bronx, NY, 1977. Exec. dir. Harlem Commonwealth Council, 1967-68; 1st ofcl. N.Am. del. Orgn. African Unity, Ethiopia, 1973, Uganda, 1975 Contbr.: chpt. to The Endless Crisis, 1973, Black Economic Development, 1970; pub.: chpt. to Profiles in Black, 1976. Served with AUS, 1950-52. Research fellow Met. Applied Research Center, 1967 Office: 817 Broadway New York NY 10003-4709 Home Phone: 914-961-1697; Office Phone: 212-598-4000. Personal E-mail: corenyc@aol.com.

INOS, RITA HOCOG, retired school system administrator; MA in Sch. Adminstrn. and Supervision, San Jose State U., 1983; EdD in Ednl. Planning, Policy and Adminstrn, USC, 1993. Commr. No. Mariana Islands Pub. Sch. System, Saipan, 2002—06; ret.

INOUE, MICHAEL SHIGERU, industrial and electrical engineer; b. Tokyo, June 27, 1936; came to U.S., 1956; s. Takajiro and Kazu (Morimoto) I.; m. Mary Louise Shuhart, Sept. 23, 1965; children: Stephen M., Rosanne E., Marcus S., Joanne K., Suzanne T. BSEE magna cum laude, U. Dayton, 1959; MSE, Johns Hopkins U., 1963; MSIE, Oreg. State U., 1964, PhD, 1967. Registered profl. engr., Oreg., Calif.; cert. data processor. Sr. rsch. engr. Black and Decker Mfg. Co., Towson, Md., 1960-62; prof. Oreg. State U., Corvallis, 1966-82; mgr. Kyocera Internat., Inc., San Diego, 1982—84, v.p., 1986—2002, sr. advisor, 2002—04; hon. consul gen. of Japan by the Govt. Japan US Dept. State, San Diego, 2006—. Mem. adv. bd. Coll. Arts and Scis. San Diego State U., 2001-, Asia Media Inc., 2007-. Co-author: Introduction to Operation Research & Management Science, 1975, Circulo de Qualidad, 1982, Pacific Saury, 1971. Adv. bd. mem. Sch. Arts and Letters, San Diego State U. Recipient Grad. Rsch. award IBM, 1965, Asian Heritage award, 2007; named to Engring. Hall of Fame Oreg. State U., 2007. Fellow Global Bus. Devel. Inst.; mem. Inst. Indsl. Engrs. (Oreg. Indsl. Engr. of Yr. award 1976), Japan Soc. of San Diago and Tijuana (pres. 2001-03, pres. emeritus 2003-),

Ikerana Internat. of San Diego (hon.). Republican. Roman Catholic. Address: 1250 Sixth Ave Ste 226 San Diego CA 92101 Office Phone: 619-233-6873. Office Fax: 619-702-5035. Personal E-mail: hcgjapan@gmail.com.

INOUE, SHUN, sociologist; b. Sendai, Miyagi, Japan, Sept. 8, 1938; s. Noboru and Tadako (Ishihara) I.; m. Mayako Shigematsu, Mar. 14, 1967. BA, Kyoto U., 1963, MA, 1965. Asst. lectr. Kyoto U., 1967-70; lectr. Kobe U. Commerce, 1970-72; assoc. prof. Osaka Nat. U., Japan, 1972-80, prof., 1980-96, Kyoto U., 1996—2002, Konan Women's U., Kobe, Japan, 2002—. Author: The Loss of Meaning in Death, 1973, A Sociology of Play and Games, 1977, Play and Culture, 1981, A Social Psychology of Lies and Lying, 1982, A Choice of Nightmares, 1992, The Sociology of Sport and Art, 2000, The Martial Arts in Modern Japan, 2004; co-author: Introduction to Sociology, 1993; editor: A Sociology of Contemporary Culture, 1998, Contemporary Sociology Series, 26 vols., 1995-97, Studies in the Sociology of Sport, 1999, Sociology of the Self and Others, 2005. Mem. Japan Sociol. Assn. (pres.), Japan Soc. Sport Sociology, Kansai Sociol. Assn. Home: 3-23-13 Nagaoka Nagaokakyo-shi Kyoto 617-0823 Japan Office: Konan Women's U 6-2-23 Morikitamachi Higahsinada-ku Kobe 658-0001 Japan

INOUE, YUKIKO, educational research educator; b. Nigata, Japan, Apr. 28, 1953; d. Tomohei and Ine Soma. PhD in Edn., U. of Memphis, 1997. Assoc. prof. of ednl. rsch. U. of Guam, Mangilao, Guam, 2001—06, prof. of ednl. rsch., 2006—. Tanka poet (collection of tank poems) Roses, You Must Be published by Mellen Poetry Press (Humanities Scholar of the Yr., Guam Humanities Coun., 2003). Recipient Faculty award for excellence in rsch., U. Guam, 2000, 2006, Gov.'s award for excellence in higher Edn., Govt. Guam, 2001. Mem.: Am. Ednl. Rsch. Assn. Avocations: reading, writing. Home: POBox 5375 UOG Sta Mangilao GU Office: University of Guam School of Education UOG Sta Mangilao GU 96923 Home Phone: 1-671-734-4914; Office Phone: 1-671-735-2447. Office Fax: 1-671-734-3651; Home Fax: 1-671-734-3651. Business E-Mail: yinoue@uog9.uog.edu.

INOUYE, DANIEL KEN, senator; b. Honolulu, Sept. 7, 1924; s. Hyotaro and Kame Imananga; m. Margaret Shinobu Awamura, June 12, 1949 (dec.); 1 child, Daniel Ken. AB in Govt. and Economics, U. Hawaii, 1950; JD, George Washington U., 1952. Bar: Hawaii 1953. Dep. pub. prosecutor, Honolulu, 1953-54; pvt. practice, 1954—; mem. Hawaii Territorial Ho. of Reps., 1954-58, Hawaii Territorial Senate, 1958-59, US House of Reps., 1959—63; senator from Hawaii US Senate, 1963—; mem. Senate Armed Svcs. Com., 1963—71; sec. Senate Dem. Conf., 1978-88; chmn. Dem. Steering Com., Senate Appropriations Com., 1971—; chmn. subcom. def., mem. Commerce Com., 1969—77; chmn. Senate Select Com. on Intelligence, 1976—79; ranking mem. subcom. budget authorizations Select Com. on Intelligence, 1979-84; chmn. Select Com. Indian Affairs, 1989—94, vice-chmn., 1990—; mem. Select Com. on Presdl. Campaign Activities, 1973-74; chmn. Sen. select com. Secret Mil. Assistance to Iran and Nicaraguan Opposition, 1987; co-chmn. Com. on Comm., Sci., Tech., 2005—. Mem. Senate Watergate Com., 1973-74; sr. counselor Kissinger Commn., 1984; chmn. Senate Dem. Ctrl. Am. Study Group, 1984. Co-author (with Lawrence Elliott): Journey to Washington, 1967. Active YMCA, Boy Scouts Am. Keynoter; temporary chmn. Dem. Nat. Conv., 1968, rules com. chmn., 1980, co-chmn. conv., 1984. Pvt. to capt. AUS, 1943-47. Decorated Medal of Honor, D.S.C., Bronze Star, Purple Heart with cluster; decorated Grand Cordon of the Order of the Rising Sun, Govt. Japan, 2000; named 1 of 10 Outstanding Young Men of Yr. U.S. Jr. C. of C., 1960; recipient Splendid Am. award Thomas A. Dooley Found., 1967 Golden Plate award Am. Acad. Achievement, 1968, Spirit of Hope award USO, 1999, Advocacy Conf. Congl. award Nat. Breast Cancer Coalition, 2002, Friend of Coast award Am. Coastal Coalition, 2002, Doughboy award U.S. Army, 2002, Sonny Montgomery award Nat. Guard Bur., 2003, Congressional Am. Spirit Medallion Nat. D-Day Mus., 2004, Leadership award Nat. Marine Sanctuary Found., 2005, Lifetime Achivement award Air Force Assn., 2005, Bryce Harlow award Bryce Harlow Found., 2006; Daniel K. Inouye Bldg. of Walter Reed Army Inst. Rsch., Naval Med. Rsch. Ctr., Bethesda, Md. dedicated in his honor, 2001; Hart-Dole-Inouye Fed. Ctr., Battle Creek, Mich. named in his honor, 2003. Mem. Disabled Am. Veterans (past comdr. Hawaii), Honolulu C. of C., Am. Legion (Nat. Comdr.'s award 1973); Clubs: Lion. (Hawaii), 442d Veterans (Hawaii). Democrat. Methodist. Home: 469 Ena Rd Honolulu HI 96815-1749 Office: US Senate 722 Hart Senate Bldg Washington DC 20510-0001 also: Prince Kuhio Fed Bldg Rm 7-212 300 Ala Moana Blvd Honolulu HI 96850-4975 Office Phone: 202-224-3934, 808-541-2542. Office Fax: 202-224-6747, 808-541-2549.*

INOUYE, WAYNE RYO, computer company executive; b. Yuba City, Calif., Aug. 25, 1952; m. Shannon Inouye; children: Lauren, Josh. Student in Biology, U. Calif. Berkeley, 1971—72. Founder No. Calif. Mktg., 1978; with Good Guys, 1986—95, head audio merchandising, 1986; mgr. Computer-Retailing Divsn. Best Buy, 1995—2001; pres., CEO eMachines, Inc. (acquired by Gateway, Inc.), Irvine, Calif., 2001—04, Gateway Inc., Irvine, Calif., 2004—06, advisor, 2006. Avocations: guitar, golf.

INSANA, RONALD GERARD, newscaster; b. Buffalo, Mar. 31, 1961; s. Arthur Joseph and Adelia (Pilato) I. BA, Calif. State U., Northridge, 1984. Prodn. asst. Fin. News Network, LA, 1984, prodr., 1985, news anchor, 1985—91, mng. editor, 1990—91; news anchor Cable News Bus. Channel-TV, Ft. Lee, NJ, 1991—, news anchor, Street Signs, sr. analyst, 2006—. Regular contbr. NBC's Today, Nightly News with Tom Brokaw, Imus in the Morning, others. Author: Traders' Tales, 1999, The Message of the Markets, 2000, Trend Watching: How to Avoid Wall Street's Next Fads, Manias and Bubbles, 2002; prodr., writer: instrnl. videotape Winning Entrepreneurial Style, 1986, columnist: Money Mag., USA Today, 2003—. Bd. dirs. N.Y.C. chpt. Jr. Achievement, 1994. Named one of top 100 business news journalists of the century, TJFR Group, 1999; recipient Emmy nom. for 9/11 coverage, 2001. Roman Catholic. Office: Cnbc 1 Cnbc Plz Englewood Cliffs NJ 07632-3313 Home: 4 Boulder Rd Tenafly NJ 07670-2206

INSCHO, EDWARD WILLIAM, physiology educator; b. Owego, NY, July 25, 1954; BA in Biology, Mercyhurst Coll., 1976; MS in Biology and Exptl. Medicine, St. Thomas Rsch. Inst., 1978; PhD in Physiology, U. Cin., 1987. Rsch. asst. Biology and Cancer Rsch. Lab. Mercyhurst Coll., Erie, Pa., 1972—76; grad. rsch. asst. dept. biology St. Thomas Rsch. Inst., Cin., 1976—78; lab. asst. dept. neurophysiology Inst. Devel. Rsch., Cin., 1978—80; grad. rsch. asst. dept. physiology and biophysics U. Cin. Coll. Medicine, 1980—87, lab. instr. dept. physiology, 1983—86, med. tutor dept. physiology, 1984—85; physiology lectr. U. Ala., Birmingham, 1988; rsch. instr. dept. physiology Tulane U. Sch. Medicine, New Orleans, 1989—91, rsch. asst. prof. dept. physiology, 1991—92, asst. prof. dept. physiology, 1992—97, assoc. prof. dept. physiology, 1997—2000; prof. dept. physiology Med. Coll. Ga., 2000—. Reviewer Am. Jour. Physiology: Renal, Heart, Regulatory, Hyptersion, Jour. Clin, Investigation, Mineral and Electrolyte Metabolism, Jour. Hypertension, Jour. Am. Soc. Nephrology, Clin. Sci., Kidney Internat., Jour. Cardiovasc. Pharmacology, Circulation Rsch., Brit. Jour. Pharmacology, Pflugers Archives, Jour. Vascular Rsch.: Nature-medicine, Current Hypertension, Reviews, Endocrinology, Hypertension, Microcirculation, Nephron; mem. editl. bd. Am. Jour. Physiology, Hypertension, Clin. Soc., Current Hypertension Revs.; contbr. articles to profl. jours. Recipient Rsch. fellowship NIH, 1984-87, 87, 88, Univ. Rsch. Coun. Travel award U. Cin., 1984, 85, Eckstein Meml. Fund Travel award, U. Cin., 1984, Amgen Young Investigator award Nat. Kidney Found., 1992, 93, Harry Goldblatt award 1998, Young Scholars award Am. Soc. Hypertension, 2000. Mem. Am. Physiol. Soc. (travel award 1993), Am. Heart Assn. (coun. kidney and cardiovasc. disease, travel award 1989, Established Investigator award 1995—, fellow of coun. high blood pressure rsch. 1996). Office: Med Coll Ga Dept Physiology CA #3137 1120 15th St Augusta GA 30912 Home Phone: 706-855-0790; Office Phone: 706-721-5615. Business E-Mail: einscho@mail.mcg.edu.

INSCHO, JEAN ANDERSON, retired social worker, landscape artist; b. Camden, NJ, Oct. 31, 1936; d. George Myrick and Alfrida Elizabeth (Anderson) Hewitt; m. James Ronald Inscho, June 4, 1955 (div. Mar. 1982); children: James Ronald Jr., Cynthia Ann, Michael Merrick. BA, Fla. Atlantic U., 1971; MA in Coll. Teaching, Auburn U., 1974, postgrad., 1998-99. Instr. So. Union State Jr. Coll., Wadley, Ala., 1973-75; social worker Jefferson County Dept. Human Resources, Birmingham, Ala., 1976-77, Shelby County Dept. Human Resources, Columbiana, Ala., 1977-78, Houston County Dept. Human Resources, Dothan, Ala., 1978-98. Adj. instr. Troy State U., Dothan, 1984-97. Bd. dir., v.p. Adolescent Resource Ctr., 1992-93, sec., 1993-95; mem. Alzheimer's Assn. EPDA fellow Auburn U., 1973, 74. Mem.: Am. Horticultural Therapy Assn. (Ga.-Ala. chpt.), Wiregrass Master Gardeners (pres. 1994—95), Ala. Master Gardeners Assn. (bd. dir., sec. 2003—, sec. 2003, recipient award 2004, Outstanding Svc. and Dedication award 2004), Dist. 7 State Employees Assn. (polit. action com. rep. 1994—98), Ala. State Employees Assn. (bd. dir.), Am. Daffodil Soc. Episcopalian. Avocations: gardening, needlecrafts, church activities.

INSEL, MICHAEL S., lawyer; b. NYC, Apr. 19, 1947; s. Ralph David and Lillian Ruth (Solomon) I.; married; 1 child, Louis Leo. BA, Duke U., 1969; JD, NYU, 1973. Bar: N.Y. 1974, Fla. 1984. Assoc. Kelley Drye & Warren, NYC, 1973-82, ptnr., 1982—; pres. French Am. Vintners LLC. Bd. dirs. Kobrand Corp., N.Y.C., Maison Louis Jadot, S.A., Beaune, France, L & L, S.A., Boe, France, Western Wine Svcs., Inc., North Bergen, N.J., Kobrand Found., N.Y.C., The Kopf Family Found., Inc., St. Francis Vineyards, Sonoma, Calif., Domaine Carneros, Napa, Calif.; chmn. Goodwill Industries, Astoria, N.Y.; trustee Elsie del Fierro Charitable Trust, N.Y.C., 1985—, Barbara Bell Cumming Found., N.Y.C., 1991—. Mem.: ABA, Fla. Bar Assn., NY State Bar Assn. Avocations: sailing, golf, opera. Office: Kelley Drye & Warren 101 Park Ave Fl 30 New York NY 10178-0062 Office Phone: 212-808-7933. Business E-Mail: minsel@kelleydrye.com.

INSEL, THOMAS R., federal agency administrator, psychiatrist; m. Deborah Insel; 2 children. BA, Boston U., 1971, MD, 1974. Intern Berkshire Med. Ctr., Pittsfield, Mass.; resident Langley Porter Neuropsychiatric Inst., U. Calif., San Francisco; clin. assoc. Clin. Neuropharmacology Br. NIMH, NIH, 1979, various adminstrv. and leadership positions including head Sect. Comparative Studies of the Brain and Behavior, Lab. Clin. Sci., 1979—94; prof. psychiatry Emory U., Atlanta, 1994—2002, dir. Yerkes Regional Primate Rsch. Ctr., 1994—99, also dir. Ctr. Autism Rsch.; dir. Ctr. Behavioral Neuroscience, Atlanta, 1999—2002, NIMH, NIH, 2002—. Recipient A.E. Bennett Award, Soc. Biol. Psychiatry, 1986, Curt Richter Prize, Internat. Soc. Psychoneuroendocrinology, 1991, Outstanding Svc. Medal, USPHS, 1993, Disting. Alumnus Award, Boston U. Sch. Medicine, 1997, Disting. Investigator Award, Nat. Alliance for Rsch. of Schizophrenia and Depression. Fellow: Am. Coll. Neuropsychopharmacology; mem.: Inst. Medicine. Achievements include initiating and developing the first program for the study of adults with obsessive-compulsive disorder in the US, NIMH, 1979-84. Office: Nat Inst Mental Health Rm 8184 MSC 9663 6001 Executive Blvd Bethesda MD 20892-9663 Office Phone: 301-443-3673. E-mail: ti4g@nih.gov.

INSKEEP, STEVE, radio personality; m. Carolee Inskeep; 1 child, Ava. BA, Moorehead State Univ., Kentucky, 1990. Radio host Public Radio NYC; with Nat. Publ. Radio (NPR), 1996—, Morning Edition host, 2004—. Contbr. articles to numerous profl. jours. and newspapers. Recipient Nat. Headliner award, Press Club of Atlantic City, 2003, Alfred I duPont-Columbia U. Silver Baton award for Coverage of Iraq, 2004, 2007, Robert F. Kennedy Journalism award, 2006. Office: NPR 635 Mass Ave NW Washington DC 20001*

INSLEE, JAY ROBERT, congressman; b. Seattle, Feb. 9, 1951; s. Frank and Adele Inslee; m. Trudi Anne Inslee, Aug. 27, 1972; children: Jack, Connor, Joe. BA in Econs., U. Wash., Seattle, 1973; JD magna cum laude, Willamette U. Sch. Law, Salem, Oreg., 1976. Atty. Peters, Fowler & Inslee, Selah, Wash., 1976-92; mem. Wash. State Ho. Reps. from 14th dist., 1988-92, US Congress from 4th Wash. dist., 1993-95; atty. Gordon, Thomas, Honeywell, Malanca, Peterson and Daheim, Seattle, 1995-96; regional dir. region 10 US Dept. Health and Human Svcs., Seattle, 1997-98; mem. US Congress from 1st Wash. dist., 1999—, mem. energy and commerce com., mem. resources com. Charter mem. Hoopaholics, 1988—. Democrat. Office: US Ho Reps 403 Cannon Ho Office Bldg Washington DC 20515-4701 Office Phone: 202-225-6311.*

INSLER, STANLEY, philologist, educator; b. NYC, June 23, 1937; AB, Columbia Coll., 1957; postgrad., U. Tubingen, 1960-62; PhD, Yale U., 1963. Mem. faculty Grad. Sch., Yale U., 1963—, now prof. Sanskrit and comparative philology. Cons. NEH Contbr. numerous articles on ancient langs. and lits. of India and Iran to profl. publs; translator Songs of Zarathustra. Recipient fellowships Ford Found., fellowships Woodrow Wilson Found., fellowships Yale U. Mem.: Societe Asiatique, Assn. Française des Sanskritists, Royal Asiatic Soc. Gt. Brit. and Ireland, Philological Soc., Cambridge, Eng., Deutsche Morgenlandische Gesellschaft, Am. Oriental Soc. (pres., fin. dir.), Am. Acad. Arts and Scis. Office: Yale U Dept Linguistics Box 208236 New Haven CT 06520-8236 Office Phone: 203-432-2455. Business E-Mail: insler-stanley@yale.edu.

INSOGNA, ANTHONY M., lawyer; b. Bklyn., Sept. 5, 1967; BS in Organic Chemistry, NYU, 1989, MS in Bio-organic Chemistry, 1990; JD, Fordham Univ., 1994. Admitted to practice: US Patent and Trademark Office 1991, bar: NY 1995, DC 1996, Calif., US Ct. Appeals (fed. cir.), US Supreme Ct., US Dist. Ct. (so. dist.), Calif. Researcher, chemistry departments Columbia Univ. and NYU; law clk., biotechnology group Pennie & Edmonds LLP; now ptnr.-in-charge San Diego office Jones Day. Mem. selection com. 2006 UCSD Chancellor's Assoc. Annual Faculty Excellence Awards, 2006. Named one of Top 20 Under 40 attorneys in Calif., Daily Jour., 2005; named to the list of 2006 So. Calif. Super Lawyers, Law & Politics, 2006. Mem.: ABA, NY Intellectual Property Law Assn., NY State Bar Assn., Am. Chem. Soc., Sigma Xi. Office: Jones Day Ste 300 12750 High Bluff Dr San Diego CA 92130-2083 Office Phone: 858-314-1130. Office Fax: 858-314-1150. Business E-Mail: aminsogna@jonesday.com.*

INSULZA, JOSÉ MIGUEL, international organization official, former Chilean government official; b. June 2, 1943; m. Georgina Núñez Reyes; children Francisca, Javier and Daniel. Student, St. George' Coll., U. Chile, Facultad Latinoamericana de Ciencias Sociales, U. Mich. Prof. polit. theory U. Chile, 1973; prof. polit. scis. Pontificia U. Católica de Chile, 1973; pol. adviser Ministry Fgn. Rels., Santiago, Chile, 1973, head multilateral econ. affairs dept., 1990-94, under-sec. fgn. affairs, 1994; dir. Diplomatic Acad., 1973; rschr., then dir. Instituto de Estudios de Estados Unidos, Centro de Investigación y Docencia Económicas, Mex., 1981-88; prof. U. Autónoma de Mex., 1990-94; dep. chair Internat. Cooperation Agy., 1990-94; min. sec. of the pres. Govt. of Chile, Santiago, 1994-99, min. interior, 1999-2000, 2000—05; sec. gen. OAS, Washington, 2005—. Mem. Consejo Chileno de Relaciones Internacionales, Consejo de Redacción, Nexos Mag. Office: OAS 17th St & Constitution Ave NW Washington DC 20006*

INTRILIGATOR, DEVRIE SHAPIRO, physicist; b. NYC; d. Carl and Lillian Shapiro; m. Michael Intriligator; children: Kenneth, James, William, Robert. BS in Physics, MIT, 1962, MS, 1964; PhD in Planetary and Space Physics, UCLA, 1967. NRC-NASA rsch. assoc. NASA, Ames, Calif., 1967—69; rsch. fellow in physics Calif. Inst. Tech., Pasadena, 1969—72, vis. assoc., 1972—73; asst. prof. U. So. Calif., 1972—80; mem. Space Scis. Ctr., 1978—83; sr. rsch. physicist Carmel Rsch. Ctr., Santa Monica, Calif., 1979—; dir. Space Plasma Lab., 1980—. Cons. NASA, NOAA, Jet Propulsion Lab.; chmn. NAS-NRC com. on solar-terrestrial rsch., 1983-86, exec. com. bd. atmospheric sci. and climate, 1983-86, geophysics study com., 1983-86; U.S. nat. rep. Sci. Com. on Solar-Terrestrial Physics, 1983-86; mem. adv. com. NSF Divsn. Atmospheric Sci. Co-editor: Exploration of the Outer Solar System, 1976; contbr. articles to profl. jours. Recipient 3 Achievement awards NASA, Calif. Resolution of Commendation, 1982. Mem.: AAAS, Am. Geophys. Union, Am. Phys. Soc., Cosmos Club. Achievements include being a participant Pioneer 10/11 missions to outer planets; Pioneer Venus Orbiter, Pioneers 6, 7, 8 and 9 heliocentric missions. Home: 140 Foxtail Dr Santa Monica CA 90402-2048 Office: Carmel Rsch Ctr PO Box 1732 Santa Monica CA 90406-1732

INTRILIGATOR, MARC STEVEN, lawyer; b. Oceanside, NY, July 14, 1952; s. Alan and Sally (Jacobs) I.; m. Roxann Kathleen Hoff, Aug. 28, 1977; children: Seth Adam, Joshua Ross, Daniel Benjamin. BA, SUNY, Binghamton, 1974; JD, Boston U., 1977. Bar: N.Y. 1978. Assoc. Dreyer and Traub, NYC, 1977-83, assoc. ptnr., 1984-85, sr. ptnr., 1985-96; of counsel Fischbein Badillo Wagner Harding, NYC, 1996—2005; mem. Cozen O'Connor, NYC, 2005—. Projects editor: Boston U. law rev., 1976-77. Past pres. Croton Jewish Ctr., Highlands Country Club. Mem. ABA, Assn. Bar City N.Y., Hollow Brook Golf Club (founding mem.), Barefoot Landing Resort Golf Club, Tau Epsilon Phi. Office: Cozen O'Connor 909 3rd Ave New York NY 10022-4731 Office Phone: 212-453-3801. Business E-Mail: mintriligator@cozen.com.

INTRILIGATOR, MICHAEL DAVID, economist, educator; b. NYC, Feb. 5, 1938; s. Allan and Sally Intriligator; m. Devrie Shapiro; children: Kenneth, James, William, Robert. SB in Econs., MIT, 1959; MA, Yale U., 1960; PhD, MIT, 1963. Asst. prof. econs. UCLA, 1963—66, assoc. prof., 1968—72, prof., 1972—, prof. dept. polit. sci., 1981—, prof. dept. policy studies, 1994—, dir. Ctr. Internat. and Strategic Affairs, 1982—92, 2000—02; dir. Jacob Marschak Interdisciplinary Coll., 1977—; dir. Burkle Ctr. Internat. Rels., 2000—02. Cons. Inst. Def. Analysis, 1974—77, ACDA, 1968, Rand Corp., 1962—65; sr. fellow Milken Inst., 1998—. Author: Mathematical Optimization and Economic Theory, 1971; author: (with Ronald Bodkin and Cheng Hsiao) Econometric Models, Techniques, and Applications, 1996; author: (with others) A Forecasting and Policy Simulation Model of the Health Care Sector, 1979; mem. adv. editl. bd.: Math. Social Scis., 1983—; editor (assoc. editor): Jour. Optimization Theory and Applications, 1979—91, Conflict Mgmt. and Peace Sci., 1980—; co-editor: (series) Handbook sin Economics, 1980—, Advanced Textbooks in Economics, 1972—; editor (with Kenneth J. Arrow): (book) Handbook of Mathematical Economics, 3 vols., 1981—85; editor: (with Zvi Griliches) Handbook of Econometrics, 3 vols., 1983—86; editor: (with B. Brodie and R. Kolkowicz) National Security and International Stability, 1983; editor: (with H. A. Jacobsen) East-West Conflict: Elite Perceptions and Political Opinions, 1988; editor: numerous others; contbr. articles to profl. jours. Recipient Disting. Tchg. award, UCLA, 1966, Warren C. Scoville Disting. Tchg. award, 1976, 1979, 1982, 1984; fellow Woodrow Wilson, 1959—60, MIT, 1960—61, Ford, 1967—68. Fellow: AAAS, Econometric Soc.; mem.: Russian Acad. Sci., Coun. Fgn. Rels., Internat. Inst. Strategic Studies. Office: UCLA Dept Econs Los Angeles CA 90095-0001 Office Phone: 310-825-4144. Business E-Mail: intriligator@econ.ucla.edu.

INUI, THOMAS SPENCER, physician, educator; b. Balt., July 10, 1943; s. Frank Kazuo and Beulah Mae (Sheetz) Inui; m. Nancy Stowe, June 14, 1969; 1 child, Tazo Stowe. BA, Haverford Coll., 1965; MD, Johns Hopkins U., 1969, ScM, 1973. Diplomate Am. Bd. Internal Medicine. Intern Johns Hopkins Hosp., Balt., 1969—70, resident in internal medicine, 1970—73; clin. scholar Johns Hopkins U., Balt., 1971—73, chief resident, instr., 1973—74; chief of medicine USPHS Indian Hosp., Albuquerque, 1974—76; chief gen. medicine, dir. health svc. rsch. Seattle VA Med. Ctr., 1976—86; dir. Robert Wood Johnson clin. scholars program U. Wash., Seattle, 1977—92, prof. dept. medicine and health svcs., 1985—92, head div. gen. internal medicine, 1986—92; prof., chmn. of dept. ambulatory care and prevention Harvard Med. Sch. and Harvard Pilgrim Health Care, Boston, 1992—2000; pres., CEO Fetzer Inst., 2000—01, Regenstrief Inst., Indianapolis, 2002—. Scholar-in-residence Assn. Am. Med. Coll., 2002. Contbr. articles to profl. publs. Surgeon USPHS, 1974—76. Fellow: ACP; mem.: APHA (mem. coun. 1988—90), Inst. Medicine, Soc. Tchrs. Family Medicine, Assn. Health Svcs. Rsch., Am. Fedn. Med. Rsch., Soc. Gen. Internal Medicine (pres. 1988—89, mem. coun. 1983—89), Alpha Omega Alpha, Phi Beta Kappa. Office: Regenstrief Institute 1050 Wishard Blvd RG-6 Indianapolis IN 46202 E-mail: tinui@iupui.edu.

INWANG, ROSIE L., education educator; b. Corinth, Miss., Sept. 1, 1941; MEd, DePaul U., Chgo., 1982. CNNI CISCO, 1999, cert. CNNI networking instr. CISCO, 2000. Prof. Olive-Harvey Coll., Chgo., 1982—2000, dean, career & tech. edn. programs, 2000—05; prof. East-West U., Chgo., 1983—85. Pres. faculty coun. Olive-Harvey Coll., 1987—96, dir., 1993—96, tech prep. coord., 1994—2000, pres., 1998—2000; exec. sec. faculty coun. City Colls. Chgo., 1992—95, coord., office info. sys. dist. wide faculty com., 1993—95, dist. computer info. sys. programs chmn., 2001—04, adminstrv. facilitator, dist. wide computer info. sys. faculty com., 2001—04. Panelist WYCC TV 20, Chgo., 1994, Chgo. Area Radio Talk Show, 2004; graduation spkr. Adv. Trinity Sch. Respiratory, Chgo., 2003. Recipient Appreciation award, 1990, 1990, Chancellor Recognition award, 1994, Student Govt. Appreciation award, 1998, Appreciation award, Student Govt. Assn., 1998, Disting. Professorship award, Bd. Trustees, Olive-Harvey Coll., 1998—99, Appreciation Outstanding Svc. award, 2001, Outstanding Svc. Appreciation award, 2001, Outstanding Ptnr. award, Chgo. Pub. Schs., 2004, Student Adv. award, Olive-Harvey Coll. Nursing Dept., 2004, Appreciation & Dedication award, Adv. Trinity Sch. Respiratory Care, 2004. Mem.: Black Faculty and Staff Higher Edn., Am. Assn. Women Cmty. Colls. (Phenomenal Woman award 1999), Phi Theta Kappa (hon. Recognition & Support award 2004). Home: 7434 S Merrill Ave Chicago IL 60649-3211 Office: City Colls Chgo Olive-Harvey 10001 S Woodlawn Ave Chicago IL 60628 Personal E-mail: rinwang@talkamerica.net. Business E-Mail: rinwang@ccc.edu.

INZETTA, MARK STEPHEN, lawyer; b. NYC, Apr. 14, 1956; s. James William and Rose Delores (Cirnigliaro) I.; m. Sharon Inzetta; children: Michelle, Margot, Mallory. BBA summa cum laude, U. Cin., 1977; JD, U. Akron, 1980. Bar: Ohio 1980, U.S. Dist. Ct. (no. dist.) Ohio 1980. Legal intern City of Canton, Ohio, 1979-80; assoc. W.J. Ross Co., LPA, Canton, 1980-84; v.p., asst. gen. counsel, chief compliance officer Wendy's Internat. Inc., Columbus, Ohio, 1984—. Instr. real estate law Stark Tech. Coll., Canton, 1983; adj. prof. bus. ethics Ohio Dominican U., 2004—. Case and comment editor: Akron Law Rev., 1979-80. Bd. dirs. Brookside Village Civic Assn., 1985—87, treas., 1986—87; bd. dirs. Ct. Apptd. Spl. Advocates of Franklin County, Ohio, Dublin Cmty. Counselling Ctr.; legis.

dir. Children's and Parents' Rights Assn., 1996—97, chmn., 1997—, State of Ohio Child Support Guidelines Commn., 1995—97, 1999—2001; treas. State of Ohio Task Force on Family Law and Children, 1998—2001; asst. coach Worthington Kilbourne H.S. Varsity Girls Lacrosse Team, 2002; chmn. campaign Earle Wise Appellate Judge, North Canton, Ohio, 1982; instr. religious edn. St. Peter's Cath. Ch. Recipient Am. Jurisprudence award Lawyers Coop. Pub. Co., 1978, Dir. of Yr. award North Canton Jaycees, 1982, Presdl. award of honor, 1984, Dist. Dir. award of honor Ohio Jaycees, 1984, Vol. of Yr. award Children's Rights Coun., 2001. Mem. ABA, Ohio Bar Assn., North Canton Jaycees (bd. dirs. 1981-82, v.p. 1982-83, pres. 1983-84), North Canton C. of C. (bd. dirs. 1983-84). Roman Catholic. Office: Wendy's Internat Inc 4288 W Dublin Granville Rd Dublin OH 43017-1442 Home: 10535 Wellington Blvd Powell OH 43065 Home Phone: 614-848-6238; Office Phone: 614-764-6746. Personal E-mail: mark_inzetta@wendys.com.

IOANNOU, CONSTANTINOS ELIA, accountant; b. Neon Chorion Kythreas, Nicosia, Cyprus, June 21, 1956; s. Elias and Eleni I.; m. Florentia Savva, June 29, 1986; children: Christina, Marina, Elias, Elina. Trainee Norton Keen Chartered Accts., London, 1976-80; sr. auditor Fraser Keen Chartered Accts., London, 1980-82; mgr. Ioannou & Co. Chartered Accts., London, 1982-86, ptnr., 1986—. Mng. dir. Wonderful Ltd., 1996—; dir. Manor Hostels Ltd., London, 1996—, Hartan Investments Ltd., London, 1996—, Manor Properties (London) Ltd., 1996—. Gov. All Saints Ch. of England Primary Sch., London, 1998—, St. John the Bapt. Greek Sch., London, 1996—; treas. St. John the Bapt. Ch., London, 1998—. Fellow Inst. of Chartered Accts. in Eng. and Wales; mem. North London Soc. of Chartered Accts. (chmn. 1998-2000), London Soc. of Chartered Accts. (governing com., treas. 2002-2004, v.p. 2004—, dep. pres. 2005-06, pres. 2006—). Avocations: reading, walking, cinema, golf, nature watch. Office: Ioannou & Co 407 Green Ln London N4 1EY England Home Phone: 020 8445 6623; Office Phone: 020 8341 4543. Fax: 020-83408655. E-mail: mail@ioannou-and-co.com.

IOCONO, JOSEPH ANTHONY, pediatric and trauma surgeon; b. Phila., Pa., Mar. 14, 1967; s. Antonio Francis and Marie Iocono; m. Susan Granieri; children: Amanda Danielle, Lauren Victoria. BS, Boston Coll., Chestnut Hill, Mass., 1989; MD, Jefferson Med. Coll., Phila., 1993. Bd. cert. gen. surgery Am. Bd. Surgery, 2004, spl. cert. pediat. surgery Am. Bd. Surgery, 2006. Asst. prof. surgery and pediat. Ky. Children's Hosp., Lexington, 2003—, dir. pediatric trauma svcs., 2004—; asst. dir. minimally invasive surgery U. Ky., Lexington, 2004—. Spkr. in field. Active Makenna Found., Lexington, 2004. Fellow: ACS. Conservative. Avocation: travel. Office: Kentuckey Childrens Hospital Division of Pediatric Surgery Lexington KY 40536 Home Phone: 859-271-8179; Office Phone: 859-323-5625. Office Fax: 859-323-5289; Home Fax: 859-323-5289. Business E-Mail: jiocono@uky.edu.

IOLANA, PATRICIA ELVIRA, foundation administrator, consultant; b. Kenosha, Wis., June 15, 1965; d. Richard Schenkel and Maria Johanna Van Dijk; m. Howard Clark (div. Jan. 2005); children: Konane Sage, Kaipo'i Chace. Student, Grand Valley State U., 1988—90; AA with honors, U. Hawaii, 1993; BA magna cum laude, U. No. Colo., 1995; student, Calif. State U., 2005—. Owner Performance Initiatives, Kailua-Kona, 1995—. Program creator Aloha Performing Arts Ctr., Kealakekua, Hawaii, 1997—98; advisor, funds adminstr. West Hawaii Tobacco Free Coalition, Kailua-Kona, 2001—07; advisor County Hawaii Mayor's Office, Hilo, 2002; playwright-in-residence The Artists' Gym, 1998—2000; presenter in field. Author: (plays) A Matter of Opinion, 1995, The Gatehouse, 1998; dir.: (plays) A Matter of Opinion, 1995, 1997, 1998, 2000, 2004, MacBeth, 2004, Bang Bang You're Dead, 2006; prodr.(creator): Banned, 1995, Love Letters, 1998, Gypsy, 1998; dramaturge: The Rose Tattoo, 1995; Hamlet, 1997; Othello, 2005; Romeo and Juliet, 2006; author: The Graffiti Subculture: A Social and Linguistic Community, 1995, The Women of Greek Drama: Social Casting of Gender Roles in Ancient Greek Society, 1995, False Witnesses: The Morality of Arthur Miller's The Crucible, 1996, Huaka'i oka Pu'uwai, 2006; contbr. articles to profl. jours. Bd. pres. Aloha Performing Arts Ctr., Kealakekua, 1996—98; founder, bd. chair The Poliokekoa Advocacy Group, Kailua-Kona, 2004—; sr. advisor The Aloha Teen Theatre, Kealakekua, 2004—. Scholar, U. No. Colo. English Dept., 1994—95. Mem.: Internat. Soc. for Religion, Lit. and Culture, Am. Acad. Religion, Sacred History Soc., Sigma Tau Delta (Zeta Psi pres. 1994—95). Avocations: theater, reading, gardening, interior decorating. Office: Performance Initiatives 73-4327 Malu Pl Kailua Kona HI 96740 Office Phone: 808-987-2470.

IOMMI, TONY (FRANK ANTHONY IOMMI), musician; b. Birmingham, England, Feb. 19, 1948; m. Maria Sjöhölm, 1999. Founding mem., guitarist Black Sabbath, 1969—. Musician: (albums) Iommi, 2000, Fused, 2005; musician: (with Black Sabbath) Black Sabbath, 1970, Paranoid, 1971, Master of Reality, Black Sabbath vol. 4, 1972, Sabbath Bloody Sabbath, 1973, Sabotage, 1975, Technical Ecstasy, 1976, Never Say Die!, 1978, Heaven & Hell, 1980, Live at Last, 1980, The Mob Rules, 1981, Live Evil, 1982, Born Again, 1983, The Seventh Star, 1986, The Eternal Idol, 1987, Headless Cross, 1989, TYR, 1990, Dehumanizer, 1992, Cross Purposes, 1994, Forbidden, 1995, Sabotage, 1996, Past Lives, 2002. Named to Rock and Roll Hall of Fame, 2006. Office: Sanctuary Records Group Ltd Sanctuary House 45-53 Sinclair Rd London W14 0NS England

IONESCU TULCEA, CASSIUS, research mathematician, educator; b. Bucharest, Rumania, Oct. 14, 1923; naturalized, 1967; s. Ioan and Ana (Caselli) Ionescu Tulcea; m. Alexandra Bellow, 1956 (div. 1969). MS, U. Bucarest, 1946; PhD, Yale, 1959. Mem. faculty U. Bucarest, 1946-57, assoc. prof., 1952-57; research assoc. Yale U., 1957-59, vis. lectr., 1959-61; assoc. prof. U. Pa., 1961-64; prof. U. Ill., Urbana, 1964-66, Northwestern U., Evanston, Ill., 1966-90, prof. emeritus, 1990—. Author: Hilbert Spaces (in Rumanian), 1956, A Book on Casino Craps, 1980, A Book on Casino Blackjack, 1982; co-author: Probability Calculus (in Rumanian), 1956, Calculus, 1968, An Introduction to Calculus, 1969, Honors Calculus, 1970, Topics in the Theory of Liftings, 1969, Sets, 1971, Topology, 1971, A Book on Casino Gambling, 1976; contbr. articles to profl. jours. Recipient Asachi prize Rumanian Acad., 1957. Office: Northwestern U 2033 Sheridan Rd Evanston IL 60208-0830

IOSSIFOVA, ALBENA ROUMENOVA, business educator, researcher; b. Bourgas, Bulgaria, Apr. 11, 1971; d. Rumen Dimov Yosifov and Zlatka Kostova Gradinarova; m. Hristov Emil Ivanov, June 17, 2000. B in Info. Sys., Econ. U., Vazna, Bulgaria, 1995; M in Info. Sys., Econ. U., Varna, Bulgaria, 1995; PhD in Bus. Adminstrn., U. Minn., Mpls., 2004. Asst. prof. Slippery Rock U., Pa., 2004—. Mem.: Decision Sci. Inst., Prodn. and Ops. Mgmt. Soc. Avocations: yoga, folk dancing. Office: Slippery Rock Univ 1 Morrow Way ECB 313A Slippery Rock PA 16057

IOVINE, JIMMY, recording industry executive; b. Bklyn., Mar. 11, 1953; s. Jimmy Iovine Sr.; m. Vicki Iovine. Former engr. The Record Plant, NYC, 1973; ind. prodr., co-head Interscope Records, 1991—. Prodr.: (albums) Patti Smith's Easter, Tom Petty's Damn the Torpedoes, 1979, Tom Petty's Hard Promises, 1981, Tom Petty's Long After Dark, 1982, Stevie Nicks' Bella Donna, 1981, Stevie Nicks' The Wild Heart, 1983, Stevie Nicks' Rock A Little, 1985, Pretenders' Get Close, 1986, U2's Rattle & Hum, 1989. Office: c/o Interscope Comm 10900 Wilshire Blvd Ste 1230 Los Angeles CA 90024-6532

IP, T. Y. STEVEN, plastic surgeon; Grad., UCLA; MD, U. Tex. Cert. Am. Bd. Plastic Surgery, Am. Bd. Surgery. Trainee in gen. surgery Columbia U., NYC; trainee in gen. surgery, chief resident St. Lukes/Roosevelt Hosp. Ctr., NYC; trainee in aesthetic, plastic & reconstructive surgery, chief resident Duke U. Med Ctr.; pvt. practice Newport Beach, Calif. Affiliated Hoag Meml. Hosp., Newport Beach Surgery Ctr., Irvine Regional Med. Ctr., Fountain Valley Regional Hosp. Work profiled in Glamour mag. Mem.: Am. Soc. Laser Medicine & Surgery, Orange County Med. Assn., Am. Coll. Surgeons, Am. Soc. Plastic Surgeons. Office: 351 Hospital Rd Ste 319 Newport Beach CA 92663 Office Phone: 949-548-0300. Office Fax: 949-548-2896. E-mail: TYStevenIpMD@mindspring.com.*

IPPEN, ERICH PETER, electrical engineer, educator, physicist; b. Fountain Hill, Pa., Mar. 29, 1940; s. Arthur Thomas and Elisabeth Anne (Wagenplatz) I.; m. Dorothea Ellen Swansen, Sept. 24, 1966; children: Erich Peter, Jason Timothy. SB, MIT, 1962; MS, U. Calif., Berkeley, 1965, PhD, 1968. Mem. tech. staff Bell Labs., Holmdel, NJ, 1968-80; vis. prof. MIT, Cambridge, 1977-78, prof. elec. engring., 1980—, Elihu Thomson prof. elec. engring., 1987—, prof. physics, 1996—. Cons. Bell Labs., 1981-2000, Allied Corp., Mt. Bethel, NJ, 1982-90, MIT Lincoln Lab., 1999—. Contbr. articles to profl. jours.; patentee in field. Recipient Edward Longstreth medal Franklin Inst., 1982, Harold E. Edgerton award Soc. Photo-Optical Instrumentation Engrs., 1989, John Scott award City of Phila., 1991, Disting. Engring. Alumnus award U. Calif., Berkeley, 2000, MIT Killian award, 2001. Fellow Am. Acad. Arts & Scis., Optical Soc. Am. (former pres., R.W. Wood prize 1981, C.H. Townes award 2004, Frederic Ives medal 2006), IEEE (Morris E. Leeds award 1983, Quantum Electronics award 1997), Am. Phys. Soc. (Arthur L. Schawlow prize 1997); mem. NAS, NAE, Sigma Xi. Office: MIT Dept Physics Rm 36 319 77 Massachusetts Ave Cambridge MA 02139-4307 Office Phone: 617-253-8504. E-mail: ippen@mit.edu.*

IPSEN, CAROL ANNE, psychiatrist, educator; b. Schenectady, NY, Jan. 9, 1951; d. Peter Grover and Joan Stevens (Wilson) I.; m. James Donald Alpert, Aug. 14, 1976; 1 child, Kathryn Ipsen Alpert. BS, U. Mich., 1972; MD, U. Rochester, NYC, 1978. Diplomate Am. Bd. Psychiatry and Neurology. Intern U. Colo. Med. Ctr., Denver, 1978-79, resident in psychiatry, 1979-82; staff psychiatrist Ft. Logan Mental Health Ctr., Denver, 1982-84; pvt. practice, Denver, 1982-85, Albany, N.Y., 1985—; clin. asst. prof. Albany Med. Coll., 1986—. Mem. Am. Psychiat. Assn. (ethics com. Albany chpt. 1988—). Office: 1240 New Scotland Rd # 204 Slingerlands NY 12159 Office Phone: 518-439-5624.

IPSEN, GRANT RUEL, state legislator, insurance and investments professional; b. Malad, Idaho, Nov. 6, 1932; s. Nephi Ruel and Ada (Hughes) I.; m. Edna Wayne Hughes, July 27, 1956; children: Edna Gaye, LeAnn, Garin Grant, Shawna Lee, Wayne Ruel. BA, Brigham Young U., 1961. CPA, CLU, ChFC. Acct. Ernst & Ernst, Boise, Idaho, 1961-64; sales dept. Mut. of N.Y., Boise, 1964—93; mem. Idaho Senate, Dist. 17, Boise, 1992—2002; ret. Mut. of N.Y. Active Boy Scouts Am., 1945—; co-convener Boise Religious Freedom Com., 1991-94. With U.S. Army, 1956-58. Named Agt. of Yr., Boise Assn. Life Underwriters, 1978, Man of Yr., Mut. of N.Y., 1982. Mem. Million Dollar Round Table (life), Brigham Young Univ. Alumni (bd. dirs. 1987-93). Republican. Mem. Lds Ch. Avocations: reading, outdoor recreation, hiking, travel.

IQBAL, SYMA U., information technology executive; b. Karachi, Sind, Pakistan, Dec. 24, 1967; d. Hafeezuddin and Feroze Munshi; m. Umair Iqbal, Nov. 29, 1995; 1 child, Hamza. BComm, U. Karachi, Pakistan, 1989. Assoc. Chartered Acct., Inst. Chartered Accountants of Pakistan, 1995; cert. profl. Oracle U., 2001. Audit supr. Ernst & Young Pakistan, Karachi, Sind, Pakistan, 1989—93; Oracle applications functional cons. Softech Microsystems, Karachi, Sind, Pakistan, 1999—2000; mgr. accounts Security Leasing Corp. Ltd. - A Merrill Lynch, USA and CDC, UK Co., Karachi, Sind, Pakistan, 1994—99; Oracle financials cons. Amtex Systems Inc, NYC, 2001—. Bus. cons., ERP fin. applications Bi-State Devel. Agy. of St Louis, Mo., 2003; Oracle financials specialist Ingersoll Rand - Air Solutions Group, Davidson, NC, 2003, Ingersoll Rand - Constrn. and Mining Group, Annandale, NJ, 2002—03; Oracle financials cons. GE Power Systems, Milpitas, Calif., 2002; Oracle fin. applications - functional specialist Human Resource Adminstrn., NYC, 2001—02. Achievements include design of Business Process re-engineering architecture for financial applications at Ingersoll Rand - ASG; Business Process re-engineering architecture - NY City Human Resource Administration; Business process re-engineering documentation at GE Power Systems. Office: Amtex Systems Inc 50 Broadway Suite 801 New York NY 10004 Home: 382 Marywood Ct Ballwin MO 63021-6323 Office Phone: 314-982-1400. Personal E-mail: syma_iqbal@hotmail.com.

IQBAL, ZAFAR, neuroscientist, biochemist, educator; b. Lucknow, India, July 12, 1946; came to U.S., 1972, naturalized, 1979; s. Shujaat Ali and Saleha (Begum) Siddiqui. Cert. proficiency in French, Lucknow U., 1965; PhD, All India Inst. Med. Scis., New Delhi, 1971. Jr. research fellow Council Sci. and Indsl. Research, India, 1963-66, research fellow, 1967-68; research scholar Directorate Gen. Health Services, India, 1966-67; asst. research officer Indian Council Med. Research, 1968-71; research assoc. in physiology, investigator Ind. U. Sch. Medicine, Indpls., 1972-82, asst. prof. med. biophysics, 1977-82, asst. prof. biochemistry, 1979-82; asst. prof. neurology and neurosci. Northwestern U. Sch. Medicine, Chgo., 1982-85; assoc. prof. pharmacology Chgo. Med. Sch., 1985-88; assoc. prof. neurology Northwestern U. Inst. for Neuroscience, Chgo., 1989-95; adj. prof. neurology and neurosci. Northwestern U. Med. Sch., 1995—; mem. Northwestern U. Ctr. Devel. Biology, Chgo., 1989—; health sci. specialist VA Cen. Office Med. Rsch. Svc., Washington, 1995—. Contbg. author: Macromolecules in Storage and Transfer of Biological Information, 1969, Macromolecules and Behavior, 1972, Growth and Development of the Brain, 1975, Mechanism, Regulation and Special Function of Protein Synthesis in the Brain, 1977, Peripheral Neuropathies, 1978, Neurochemistry and Clinical Neurology, 1980, Calcium-Binding Proteins, 1980, Axoplasmic Transport, 1981, Calcium and Cell Function, 1982; editor: Axoplasmic Transport, 1986, Recent Progress in Polyamine Research, 1986, The Physiology of Polyamines, 1987; mem. editorial bd. Neurochem. Rsch.; contbr. articles to profl. jours. Bd. dirs. India Cultural Coord. Cmty. Rsch. grantee NIH, 1973-77, Muscular Dystrophy Assn. Am., 1975-77, 94-97, Am. Cancer Soc., 1979-80, NSF, 1981, 84, Juvenile Diabetes Found., 1981, Am. Diabetes Assn., 1980; recipient internat. travel award NSF, 1984, Fidia Rsch. Found. award, 1987, UN Devel. Program Internat. Expert award, 1987, 93, award Am. Soc. for Biochemistry and Molecular Biology, 1994. Mem. AAAS, Am. Physiol. Soc., Indian Acad. Neuroscis., Soc. Biol. Chemists (India), Internat. Brain Rsch. Orgn., Internat. Soc. Neurochemistry (award 1994), Soc. Neurosci., Am. Soc. Neurochemistry, Ind. Acad. Sci. (chmn. cell biology 1982-83), N.Y. Acad. Scis., Biophys. Soc., Soc. Exptl. Biology and Medicine, Assn. Scientists of Indian Origin Am. (counselor 1986—), Ameer Khusro Soc. Am. (v.p.), Lucknow Rschrs. Assn. in Am., All-Indian Inst. Med. Scis. Assn., Assn. of Communal Harmony in Asia, Orgn. of Univ. Communal Harmony, Aligarh Alumni Assn. Washington (sec.), Lucknow U. Alumni Assn., Global Orgn. People of Indian Origin (sec.-gen. 2003-), Nat. Coun. Indian Orgns. (bd. dirs.). Home: 19105 Warrior Brook Dr Germantown MD 20874 Personal E-mail: z_iqbal_19105@yahoo.com. Business E-Mail: iqbzaf@mail.va.gov. E-mail: raabta_india@yahoo.com.

IQBAL, ZAFAR MOHD, biochemist, molecular biologist, pharmacologist, cancer researcher, toxicologist, consultant; b. Hyderabad, India, Dec. 12, 1938; came to U.S., 1965, naturalized, 1973; s. M.A. and Haleemunissa (Begum) Rahim. BSc, Osmania U., 1958, MSc, 1962; PhD, U. Md., 1970. Diplomate Am. Bd. Forensic Medicine, Am. Bd. Forensic Examiners. Fellow in molecular pharmacology Nat. Cancer Inst./NIH, Bethesda, Md., 1971-74; asst. prof. pharmacology Case Western Res. U., Cleve., 1974-76; assoc. dir. ERC programs in occupational toxicology U. Ill. Med. Ctr., Chgo., 1980-81, assoc. prof. microbiology, 1977-80, assoc. prof. occupational medicine and environ. health, 1976-93, assoc. prof. preventive medicine, 1982-93; faculty grad. coll. U. Ill., Chgo., 1977-93, dir. Carcinogenesis Labs., 1983-93, chair recombinant DNA instnl. com., 1982-93; chair HIV hazards in rsch. com. U. Ill. Grad. Coll. Faculty, Chgo., 1976-93; dir. Toxicology-Cancer, Chgo., 1987—; affiliate Lurie Cancer Ctr. Northwestern U., Chgo., 1996—. Cons. in field to OSHA, 1980-81, Clements Assocs., 1976-79, Expert Resources, 1982—, Ill. Cancer Coun., 1981-82, Toxicology Cancer, 1987—; lectr. continuing edn.; grant reviewer study sects. NIH; program project reviewer Nat. Cancer Inst., 2000; merit grant reviewer VA, 1981-82; mem. tech. bd. panel Gt. Lakes Protection Fund, 1989—; participant profl. confs.; NSF-Coun. Sci. and Indsl. Rsch. exch. scientist, 1981; sponsor, trainer India-U.S. exch. scientists NSF, 1985-86; peer reviewer: (jours.) Sci., Cancer Rsch., Jour. Biochem., Toxicology, Carcinogenesis, others, also books and films; spl. advisor RRL (India) Dirs., 1980-86; mem. U.S. AID's-Asia Environ. Partnership and Environ Tech. Network Asia, 1994—, Environ. and Tech. Network Asia-Latin Am. Program, 1996—; chair recombinant DNA com. U. Ill., Chgo., 1983-93; contbr. WHO Internat. Agy. for Rsch. Cancer, Tallinn, 1975, Budapest, 1979, Tokyo, 1981, Banff, 1983; mem. exec. bd. sci. and tech. advs. Am. Bd. Forensic Exams., 1997—. Author, editor: Molecular Mechanisms of Toxic Response; Pancreatic Carcinogenesis Mechanisms; editor Jour. Molecular Toxicology and Carcinogenesis; mem. editl. adv. bd. Forensic Examiner, 1995—, editl. bd. 2002—; exec. bd. sci. and tech. advisors Am. Bd. Forensic Examiners, 1996—; contbr. more than 100 articles to profl. jours. NSF-CSIR exch. scientist, 1981; sponsor, trainer India-U.S. Exch. Scientists, NSF, 1985-86; spl. advisor RRL (India) Dirs., 1980—; pres. Rahim Meml. Found., 1995—. Fellow Coun. Sci. and Indsl. Rsch., India, 1963-65; Fogarty Internat. fellow Nat. Cancer Inst., NIH, 1970-71, staff fellow, 1971-74; grantee Nat. Cancer Inst./NIH, Nat. Inst. Occupational Safety and Health, EPA, State of Ill., 1974-93. Fellow Am. Coll. Forensic Examiners (life, diplomate, bd. cert. forensic medicine, editl. bd. advisors 1995—); mem. AAAS, Am. Assn. Cancer Rsch., Am. Pancreatic Assn., N.Y. Acad. Scis., Am. Chem. Soc., Soc. Toxicology, Am. Coll. Toxicology, Nat. Registry of Forensic Examiners, B.E.S.T. N.Am., Registry Global World Leaders, Soc. Toxicology (molecular biology, carcinogenesis and mechanism splty. sects.), NIHAA, Sigma Xi. Office: Toxicology-Cancer PO Box 60267 Chicago IL 60660-0267 Personal E-mail: toxicancer@yahoo.com.

IRAFAJKO, ROBERT RICHARD, science administrator; b. Chgo., Sept. 3, 1931; s. Edward Michael and Mildred Eleanor (Simo) R.; m. Mary Ann Filipi, June 24, 1954 (div. 1979); children: Rorie Rae, Ronald Raymond, Robin Rene, Rod Richard, Rebecca Rae.; m. Anne Thorne Sloan, Jan. 26, 1982; 1 son, Andrew Sloan. BA, Coe Coll., Cedar Rapids, Iowa, 1953; MS, U. Iowa, Iowa City, 1958, PhD, 1960. Rsch. assoc. Merck Sharp and Dohme, West Point, Pa., 1960-61; rsch. scientist Microbiol. Assos., Bethesda, Md., 1961-66; v.p., gen. mgr. Med. Rsch. Cons., Rockville, Md., 1966-69; v.p. R & D, N.Am. Biols., Rockville, 1969-74; pres. Biofluids, Inc., Rockville, 1974-99, Bonheur Inc., Keswick, Va., 1999—. Pres. Tysan Serum, Inc., Rockville, 1974-2000, Kytaron Inc, Rockville, 1987-99; breeder thoroughbred horses, 1980—. Contbr. 23 articles to profl. jours. Chmn. PVAAU Swimming Program, Washington, Md. and Va., 1973-76; bd. dirs. Montgomery County Swim League, Montgomery County, Md., 1968-76. Served with USAF, 1954-55. Mem. AAAS, NY Acad. Scis., Am. Soc. Microbiology, Tissue Culture Assn., Am. Horse Council, Horsemans Benevolent and Protective Assn. Republican. Presbyterian. Avocations: scuba diving, photography, collecting stamps, travel. Home and Office: 1349 Queenscroft Keswick VA 22947-2731 Personal E-mail: bonheur421@aol.com.

IRANI, KLINE R., oil, gas and chemical company executive; b. Beirut, Jan. 15, 1935; came to U.S., 1953, naturalized, 1956; s. Rida and Naz I.; children: Glenn R., Lillian M., Martin R. BS in Chemistry, Am. U. Beirut, 1953; PhD in Phys. Chemistry, U. So. Calif., 1957. Rsch. scientist, then sr. rsch. scientist Monsanto Co., 1957-67; assoc. dir. new products, then dir. research Diamond Shamrock Corp., 1967-73; with Olin Corp., 1973-83, pres. chems. group, 1978-80, corp. pres., dir. Stamford, Conn., 1980-83, COO, 1981-83; chmn. Occidental Petroleum Corp. subs. Occidental Chem. Corp., Dallas, 1983-94; CEO Occidental Petroleum Corp., subs. Occidental Chem. Corp., Dallas, 1983-91; chmn. Can. Occidental Petroleum Corp. Ltd., Calgary, 1987-99; exec. v.p. Occidental Petroleum Corp., LA, 1983-84, pres., COO, 1984-91, pres., 1991—96, chmn., CEO, 1991—2005, chmn., pres., CEO, 2005—. Bd. dirs. Am. Petroleum Inst., KB Home Corp., TCW Group. Author: Particle Size; also author papers in field; numerous patents in field. Co-chmn. Am. U. Beirut; trustee U. So. Calif., St. John's Hosp.; bd. govs. Los Angeles Town Hall, Los Angeles World Affairs Coun.; adv. bd. Rand Ctr. Mid. East Pub. Policy. Mem. Nat. Petroleum Coun., Am. Inst. Chemists, Am. Chem. Soc., Sci. Rsch. Soc. Am., Indsl. Rsch. Inst., The Conf. Bd., The CEO Roundtable, Am. Petroleum Inst. (bd. dirs.), Am. Chem. Soc., Nat. Assn. Mfrs., Nat. Com. US-China Rels., Sigma Xi, US-Saudi Arabian Bus. Coun. Office: Occidental Petroleum Corp 10889 Wilshire Blvd Los Angeles CA 90024-4201

IRBY, ELDON ELMORE, military officer, banker; b. Wichita, Kans., Dec. 19, 1934; s. Floyd Anderson and Bernice (Elmore) Irby; m. Sharon Elaine Lapp, Aug. 13, 1957; children: Frank Owen, Debra Lynn, Carol Anne. A in Bus. Adminstrn. magna cum laude, Muskingum Area Tech. Coll., Zanesville, Ohio, 1979. E7 warrant officer USN, 1952—74; banking officer Bancohio Nat. Bank, Zanesville, 1979—90; ret. Ordinance officer USN, 1956—74. Mem.: SAR, VFW, Navy Nuc. Weapons Assn., Am. Legion, Phi Theta Kappa. Republican. Avocations: genealogy, travel.

IRBY, HOLT, lawyer; b. Dodge City, Kans., July 4, 1937; s. Jerry M. and Virgie (Lorean) I.; m. LaVerne Smith, May 27, 1956; children: Joseph, Kathy, Kay, Karon, James. BA, Tex. Tech. U., 1959; JD, U. Tex., 1962. Bar: Tex. 1962, U.S. Dist. Ct. (no. dist.) Tex. 1963. Asst. city atty. City of Lubbock, Tex., 1962-63; assoc. Hugh Anderson, Lubbock, 1963-66; gen. counsel, sec. Merc. Fin. Corp., Dallas, 1966-69; gen. counsel, v.p. Ward Food Restaurants, inc., Dallas, 1969-71; pvt. practice, Garland, Tex., 1971—. Mem. lawyer referal com. State Bar Tex., 1977, 78. Mem. bd. deacons First Bapt. Ch., Garland, 1979-90, chmn., 1976-77; bd. dirs. Garland Assistance Program, 1980, Habitat for Humanity of Greater Garland, Inc., 1997-2001, Dallas Life Found., 1980-90, Toler Children's Cmty., 1983-85; bd. dirs. Garland Civic Theatre, 1986—, pres., 1990-91, 92-93, v.p., 1991-92; mem. Garland Drug Task Force, 1990; deacon South Garland Bapt. Ch., 1992—, chmn., 1993-94, 98-99, 2002-03. Mem. Tex. Trial Lawyers Assn., Tex. Assn. Bank Counsel, Tex. Bar Assn., Garland Bar Assn. (bd. dirs. 1986-96, sec. 1992-93, v.p. 1993-94, pres. 1995-96), Dallas Bar Assn., Praetor Legal Frat. (named outstanding mem. 1962), Lubbock Jaycees (dir. 1963-65), Kiwanis (dir. 1973-74). Office: Bank of Am Tower 705 W Avenue B Ste 110 Garland TX 75040-6241 Business E-Mail: holt@irby-spencer.com.

IRBY, KATHERINE SCOTT ROCHE, educational association administrator; b. Roanoke, Va., Sept. 22, 1970; d. Francis DeLorme and Katherine (Aliff) Roche; m. Jeffrey Irby, Dec. 1, 1992; children: Quinton Chancellor Scott, Cullen Austin Day. BBA in Mgmt. summa cum laude, Am. Intercontinental U., Ga., 2006, AA in Adminstrn. with honors, 2005, MEd in Instrnl. Tech., 2007. Exec. ops. mgr. BIS-Mktg., Kitty Hawk, NC, 1991—99; program dir. NC Coop. Ext. Svc., Manteo, NC, 1999—. Participant, coach, mentor Optimist Internat., Roanoke, 1978—88; vol.

Roanoke City Spl. Events, 1984—88, Greater Raleigh Ct. Civic League, Roanoke, 1984—88, Currituck Soccer Assn., NC, 1998—2000; mem. implementation and program devel. com. CareerSmarts Initiative/NC State U., Raleigh, 1999—2000; vol. Currituck Pks. and Recreation Soccer, 2000—05; vice-chair Dare County Youth Ctr. Adv. Bd., Kill Devil Hills, NC, 2002—06; mem., monitoring/needs chair. Dare County Juvenile Crime Prevention Coun., Manteo, 2002—; mem. bldgs. and grounds task force Dare County Pks and Recreation, Manteo, 2005; mem. child care com. State of the Child, Nags Head, NC, 2005—06, mem. use of free time com., 2005—06; vol. Relay for Life, Kill Devil Hills, 2005—, OBX Marathon EXPO, Kill Devil Hills, 2006; co-chair Dare County Youth Coun. Adv. Bd., Kill Devil Hills, 2006—. Recipient Spotlight award, RCI, 1998, Deborah Benbow Legacy award, NC Dept. Juvenile Justice and Delinquency Prevention, 2004. Presbyterian. Home: 141 Pinewood Acres Dr Powells Point NC 27966 Office: NCCES 517 Budleigh St Manteo NC 27954 Home Phone: 252-491-2343; Office Phone: 252-473-4290. Office Fax: 252-473-3106. Personal E-mail: kats1970@yahoo.com. Business E-Mail: katherine_irby@ncsu.edu.

IREDALE, NANCY LOUISE, lawyer; BS summa cum laude, Georgetown U., 1969; JD, Yale U., 1972. Bar: D.C. 1973, Calif. 1977. Tax counsel to Senator William Brock Senate Fin. Com., 1976; ptnr. Paul Hastings, Janofsky & Walker, LA. Named one of Top 100 LA County Super Lawyers, Law & Politics Media, 2004, Top 50 Female Super Lawyers, Super Lawyers Tax, 2006. Fellow: Am. Coll. Tax Counsel; mem. Yale Law Sch. Assn. (exec. com. 1982-85), Phi Beta Kappa, Phi Beta Kappa Alumni (councilor alpha assoc.). Office: Paul Hastings Janofsky & Walker LLP 515 S Flower St Fl 25 Los Angeles CA 90071-2228 Office Phone: 213-683-6232. Office Fax: 213-627-0705. Business E-Mail: nancyiredale@paulhastings.com.

IRELAN, ROBERT WITHERS, retired metal products executive; b. Takoma Park, Md., Mar. 10, 1937; s. Charles Morris and Julia Mae (McKenzie) I.; m. Barbara Lucille Mitchell, Mar. 21, 1959; children: Robert Withers Jr., Jonathan M. BS, U. Md., 1960. Copy reader, copy editor Wall St. Jour., Washington, 1960—66; assoc. editor Nation's Bus. Mag., Washington, 1966—68; rep. pub. rels. Kaiser Industries Corp., Oakland, Calif., 1968—70; exec. asst. to chmn. Kaiser Affiliated Cos., Oakland, 1970—79; mgr. corp. rels. Kaiser Aluminum & Chem. Corp., Oakland, 1979—82, regional v.p. pub. affairs midwest Ravenswood, W.Va., 1982—85, corp. v.p. pub. rels. Oakland, 1985—97, Maxxam Inc., Houston, 1990—99; ret., 1999. Vis. lectr. dept. comm. U. of the Pacific, Stockton, Calif., 2001-02; instr. U. Calif., Davis Ext., 2003—. Co-author, co-editor: Lessons of Leadership, 1967. Mem. U. Md. Alumni Assn., Rancho Murieta Country Club. Democrat. Lutheran. Avocations: golf, travel, theater, sports, reading. Home: 6798 Terreno Dr Rancho Murieta CA 95683 Personal E-mail: golfbob@calweb.com.

IRELAND, BETTY, state official; b. Charleston, W. Va., 1945; m. Sam Haddad; children: Chuck, Andy, Alex, Janie. Teacher W. Va. Pub. Sch. Sys.; owner Retirement Sys. & Svc., Charleston, W.Va., 1977—83; v.p. & head pension div. Trust Dept. Nat. Bank of Commerce, Charleston, 1983—89; pension cons. & mgr. employee benefits Jackson Kelly PLLC, 1989—98; exec. dir. W.Va. Consolidated Pub. Retirement Bd., 1998—2002; pres., CEO Jackson & Kelly Solutions LLC, 2002—05; sec. state State of W. Va., Charleston, 2005—. Mem. City of Charleston Bd. of Zoning Appeals, W.Va., 1985—86; rep.-at-large Charleston City Coun., W.Va., 1987—91; citizen expert Pub. Safety Retirement Task Force of Joint Legis. Com. on Pensions & Retirement, W.Va., 1991—92. Republican. Office: Office Sec State Bldg 1 Suite 157 K 1900 Kanawha Blvd East Charleston WV 25303-0770 Office Phone: 304-558-6000. Office Fax: 304-558-0900. Business E-Mail: wvsos@wvsos.com.*

IRELAND, DAVID, artist; b. Bellingham, Wash., 1930; Student, Western Wash. State U., Bellingham, 1948—50; BAA, Calif. Coll. Arts and Crafts, Oakland, 1953; postgrad., Laney Coll., Oakland, 1972—74; MFA, San Francisco Art Inst., 1974. One-man shows include Arts Club Chgo., 1996, Ctr. Arts Yerba Buena Gardens, San Francisco, 1996, Gallery Am. Acad., Rome, 1997, Gallery Paule Anglim, San Francisco, 1998, one-man shows include, 2001, 2006, Freedman Gallery, Reading, Pa., 2000, Jack Shainman Gallery, NYC, 2000, Christopher Grimes Gallery, Santa Monica, Calif., 2001, Oakland Mus. Calif., 2003—04, Addison Gallery Am. Art, Phillips Acad., Andover, Mass., 2003—04, Sheldon Meml. Art Gallery and Sculpture Garden, U. Nebr., Lincoln, 2003—04, Santa Barbara Mus. Art, Calif., 2003—04, numerous others. Office: Gallery Paule Anglim 14 Geary St San Francisco CA 94108-5702

IRELAND, HERBERT ORIN, retired engineering educator; b. Buckley, Ill., June 12, 1919; s. Harvey Glenn and Anna Estella (Perkinson) I.; m. Mary Leota Austin, Mar. 1, 1941; children: Orin Lee, Marin Fae, Jeanne Lu. BS, U. Ill., 1941, MS, 1947, PhD, 1955. From research asst. to prof. civil engring. U. Ill., Urbana, 1946-79, emeritus, 1979—. Cons. soil mechanics and found. engring., 1946—. Contbr.: sect. to Structural Engineering Handbook, 1968; also articles profl. jours. Served from 2d lt. to maj., C.E. AUS, 1941-46. Fellow Am. Soc. C.E., Geol. Soc. Am.; mem. Am. Ry. Engring. Assn., Sigma Xi, Tau Beta Pi, Chi Epsilon. Methodist. Home: 1132 E Township Road 209 Gilman IL 60938-6114 E-mail: oireland@netzero.net.

IRELAND, JAY, broadcast executive; m. Valerie Ireland; 2 children. BA, St. Lawrence Univ., 1977. Fin. mgmt. prog. GE, Lynchburg, Va., 1980—82, corp. audit staff, 1982—88; various fin. and prod. mgmt. positions GE Plastics, Pittsfield, Mass., 1988—90; mng. dir. Polymerland-Europe, Holland, 1990—93; mgr., corp. investor com. GE, Fairfield, 1993—95, v.p., corp. staff, 1995—97; CFO GE Plastics, 1997—99; pres. NBC TV stations, 1999—2004, NBC Universal TV stations, NYC, 2004—06, NBC Universal TV stations & Network Ops., NYC, 2006—. Exec. com. The Quills; bd. dir. ValueVision Media, TV Bur. of Advert., Maximum Svc. TV. Trustee St. Lawrence Univ; trustee, treas. Norman Rockwell Mus., Stockbridge, Mass. With US Army. Office: NBC Universal TV 30 Rockefeller Plz New York NY 10112*

IRELAND, KATHY, actress, apparel designer; b. Glendale, Calif., 1962; d. John and Barbara Ireland; m. Greg Olsen, 1988; children: Erik, Lily, Chloe. CEO, chief designer Kathy Ireland Worldwide. Designer Kathy Ireland Brand began 2000, appearances in Sports Illustrated's Ann. Swimsuit Issues, 25th Anniversary Show Swimsuit Edit., Kathy Ireland LPGA Championship, ESPN, 2001; films include: Alien from L.A., 1988, Necessary Roughness, 1991, Mom and Dad Save the World, 1992, National Lampoon's Loaded Weapon I, 1993, The Player, Mr. Destiny, Amore, Backfire; TV films include Beauty and the Bandit, 1994, Danger Island, 1994, Miami Hustle, 1995, Gridlock, 1996, Once Upon A Christmas, 2000, Twice Upon A Christmas, 2001; TV appearances include: Down the Shore, The Edge, Tales from the Crypt, Without a Clue, Grand, Charles in Charge, Perry Mason, Boy Meets World, Melrose Place, The Watcher, Deadly Games, Sabrina the Teenage Witch, Suddenly Susan, Gun, Cosby, Touched by an Angel, Pensacola, For Your Love, Strong Medicine. Recipient Entrepreneur of Yr., 2001, Mother of Yr., 2004, Received Good Housekeeping Seal, 2004, Bus. Owner of Yr., 2004, Entrepreneural Champian award, 2005. Office: Kathy Ireland Worldwide 15th Fl 10900 Wilshire Blvd Los Angeles CA 90024-4341 Office Phone: 310-557-2700.

IRELAND, OLIVER, lawyer; BA, Yale Univ., 1970; JD, Univ. Tex., 1974. Assoc. gen. counsel bd. mems. office FRS, Washington, 1985-2000; vice-pres., assoc. gen. coun. Fed. Res. Bank Chgo.; ptnr. Morrison Foerster, Washington, 2000—; atty. Fed. Res. Bank Boston. Office: Morrison Foerster Ste 5500 2000 Pennsylvania Ave NW Washington DC 20006-1888 Office Phone: 202-887-1500. Office Fax: 202-887-0763.

IRELAND, PATRICIA, lawyer; b. Oak Park, Ill., Oct. 19, 1945; d. James Ireland and Joan Filipek; m. James Humble, 1968. BA, U. Tennessee, 1966; JD, U. Miami Law Sch., 1975; degree (hon.), U. R.I., U. Mass. Coll. Law, U. Ind., Sweetbriar Coll. Flight attendant Pan Am. World Airlines, 1967-75; ptnr. Stearns, Weaver, Miller, Weissler, Alhadeff & Sitterson, Miami; nat. pres. NOW, 1991—2001; of counsel Katz, Kutter, Alderman, Bryant & Yon, 2001—03; campaign mgr. Carol Moseley Braun for pres., 2004; of counsel Phillips, Richard & Rind, 2005—. Author: What Women Want, 1996. Mailing: PO Box 1569 Homestead FL 33090-1569 Office Phone: 305-412-8322. Personal E-mail: patriciaireland2@aol.com. Business E-Mail: pireland@phillipsrichard.com.

IRELAND, PATRICK, artist; b. Ireland, 1928; came to U.S., 1957; One-man shows include Betty Parsons Gallery, 1970, 1974, Corcoran Gallery Art, Washington, 1974, Los Angeles County Mus. Art, 1974, Seattle Art Mus., 1977, Fogg Art Mus., 1981, Smithsonian American Art Mus., 1985, Everson Mus., 1987, Orpheus Gallery, Belfast, 1989, Butler Inst. Am. Art, 1994, Brigham Young U., 1995, Eaton Fine Art, West Palm Beach, 1999, Fenton Gallery, Cork, 2006, retrospective, Beyond the White Cube, Dublin City Gallery, 2006, Grey Art Gallery, NYC, 2007, exhibited in group shows at Inst. Contemporary Art, London, 1967, Hirshhorn Mus., 1976, Documenta 6, 1977, Bienale, Venice, 1980, Yale U. Art Gallery, 1982, Bklyn. Mus., 1983, Detroit Inst. Arts, 1987, Museo Tamayo, Mexico City, 1991, Langage et Pouvoir, Paris, 1996, Artists of the Millenium, UN, N.Y.C, 1999, Joyce in Art, Royal Hibernian Acad., Dublin, 2004, others, Represented in permanent collections Centre George Pompidou, Paris, Met. Mus. Art, N.Y.C., Nat. Gallery Art, Washington, Nat. Gallery, Australia, Irish Mus. Modern Art, Dublin, Nat. Gallery of Ireland, Hugh Lane Gallery Modern Art, Detroit Inst. Art, Smithsonian Am. Art Mus., Washington, Hirshhorn Mus., others. Mem.: Nat. Coll. Art & Design (assoc.). Studio: 15 W 67th St New York NY 10023-6226

IRELAND, RODERICK L., state supreme court justice; b. Springfield, Mass. m. Alice Alexander. BA, Lincoln U., 1966; JD, Columbia U., 1969; LLM, Harvard U., 1975; PhD, Northeastern U., 1998. Atty. Neighborhood Legal Service, NYC, 1969; staff atty. Harvard Ctr. for Law & Education, Mass., 1970; chief atty. then dep. exec. dir. Roxbury Defenders Com., 1971—73; hearing officer Mass. Civil Service Commn., 1973—75; legal counsel Roxbury Dist. Ct. Clinic, 1974—77; assoc. Burnham, Stern and Shapiro, 1975; asst. sec., chief legal counsel Mass. Exec. Office of Adminstrn. & Fin., 1975—77; chmn. State Bd. of Appeal on Motor Vehicle Liability Policies & Bonds, 1977; assoc. justice Boston Juvenile Ct., 1977—90, Mass. Appeals Ct., 1990—97, Mass. Supreme Jud. Ct., 1997—. Judge Boston Juvenile Ct., 1977, 90, Mass. Appeals Ct., 1990-97. Author: Massachusetts Juvenile Law, 1993. Mem. Eliot Congregational Ch. Recipient Boston Covenant Peace prize, 1982, Jud. Excellence award, Mass. Judges Conference, 1996, Lawyers Weekly, 2001. Mem.: Boston Bar Assn. (Haskell Cohn Disting. Jud. Service award 1990), Mass. Bar Assn. (Jud. Excellence award 2001). Office: Supreme Jud Ct John Adams Courthouse One Pemberton Sq Boston MA 02108-1735*

IRENAS, JOSEPH ERON, judge; b. Newark, July 13, 1940; s. Zachary and Bessie (Shain) Irenas; m. Nancy Harriet Jacknow, Jan. 1, 1962; children: Amy Ruth, Edward Eron. AB, Princeton U., 1962; JD cum laude, Harvard U., 1965; postgrad., NYU Sch. Law, 1967-70. Bar: N.J. 1965, N.Y. 1982. Law sec. to justice N.J. Supreme Ct., 1965-66; assoc. McCarter & English, Newark, 1966-71, ptnr., 1972-92; judge U.S. Dist. Ct., Newark, 1992—2002, sr. judge, 2002—. Trustee Hamilton Investment Trust, Elizabeth, NJ, 1980—83; mem. N.J. Supreme Ct. Dist. Ethics Com., 1984—86, vice chmn., 1986; adj. prof. law Rutgers Sch. Law, Camden, 1985—86, Camden, 1988—97, Camden, 1999—2002, N.J. Bd. Bar Examiners, 1986—88. Contbr. Chmn. bd. trustees United Hosps. of Newark, 1982—83; trustee United Hosps. Found., 1985—92, United Way Essex County, 1988—92, treas., 1990—92. Fellow: Am. Bar Found., Royal Chartered Inst. Arbitrators (London); mem.: ABA, Camden County Bar Assn., N.J. Bar Assn., Am. Law Inst., Union League Club, Nassau Club. Jewish. Office: Mitchell H Cohen US Courthouse One John F Gerry Plaza PO Box 2097 Camden NJ 08101-2097 Home Phone: 609-921-3828; Office Phone: 856-757-5223.

IREY, ROBIN ELIZABETH, performing company executive, performing arts educator; b. Arlington Heights, Ill., Dec. 29, 1971; d. James Delloyd and Jacquelyn Myers Irey. BA in Orgnl. Comm., No. Ill. U., DeKalb, 1995, BFA in Dance Performance, 1995; cert. of completion, Ballet Intensive of Moscow, Chgo., 2003, cert. of completion, 2004. Cert. dance educator Chgo. Nat. Assn. Dance Masters. Dance capt. Busch Gardens, Tampa Bay, Fla., 1995—96; claim rep. Allstate Ins. Co., Northbrook, 1996—99; soloist Northwest Ballet Ensemble, Schaumburg, 1996—98; owner and artistic dir. Cary-Grove Performing Arts Ctr., Cary, 1999—. Benefactor Joe Irey Meml. Scholarship, Cary, Ill., 1990—, Cary Grove Performing Arts Ctr. Dance Scholarships, 1999—; participant Chgo. Marathon, 2005, Chgo. Distance Classic, Indpls. Mini-Marathon, 2006; founder and com. mem. Disaster Aid Needs Cmty. Effort, Cary, Ill., 2005; com. mem. and benefit performer Dana Floor Legacy Fund, 2005, Invisable Children Crisis in Uganda, 2006. Mem.: Chgo. Area Runners Assn., Dance Masters of Wis., Chgo. Nat. Assn. Dance Masters. Democrat. Unitarian Universalist. Avocation: running. Home: 574 Cary Woods Cir Cary IL 60013

IRGANG, CAROLE A., marketing executive; b. Apr. 4, 1964; BS, Ithaca Coll., 1986. Exec. v.p. Grey Worldwide, 1988—2006; dir. total comms. planning MediaCom, 2003—05; pres. Red Shoes Mktg., 2006—07; sr. v.p. integrated mktg. comms. Kraft Foods, 2007—. Named a Woman to Watch, Advt. Age, 2007. Mem.: Advt. Ednl. Found. Office: Kraft Foods Three Lakes Dr Northfield IL 60093 Office Phone: 847-646-2000.*

IRICK, DAVID KIM, engineering educator, consultant; b. Knoxville, Tenn., Sept. 22, 1955; s. Tyson Lloyd and Callie Sexton Irick; m. Carol Elizabeth Gibbs, Aug. 5, 1978; 1 child, Lauren Elizabeth. BS in Mech. Engring., U. Tenn., Knoxville, 1980, MS, 1995, PhD, 1997. Cert. profl. engr., Tenn. Bd. Engring. Examiners, 1986. Engring. specialist Lockheed Martin, Oak Ridge, Tenn., 1984—97; rsch. asst. prof. U. Tenn., 1997—. Cons. David Irick Engring. Cons., Heiskell, Tenn., 1997—. Grantee Grad. Automotive Tech. Edn. Ctr. Excellence, US Dept. Energy, 2005—. Mem.: Soc. Automotive Engrs., Soc. Mfg. Engrs. Avocation: auto racing. Home: 916 Gamble Dr Heiskell TN 37754 Office: U Tenn 414 Dougherty Hall Knoxville TN 37996 Home Phone: 865-924-7441. Office Fax: 865-974-5274. Personal E-mail: davidirick@gmail.com. Business E-Mail: dki@utk.edu.

IRICK, LARRY D., lawyer, energy executive; b. 1956; BS, Emporia State U.; JD, Duke U. Bar: 1982. With Westar Energy, Inc., Topeka, 1999—, v.p., gen. counsel, corp. sec. Office: Westar Energy Inc 818 S Kansas Ave PO Box 889 Topeka KS 66601-0889 Office Phone: 785-575-1625.

IRICK, MICHAEL L., systems analyst, educator; s. Lloyd and Janet M Irick; m. Lynnette M. Youngman, Dec. 28, 1996; children: Sean M., Connor J. BS in Computer Tech., Purdue U., W.Lafayette, Ind., 1995; MS in Info. Sci., Ind. U., Bloomington, 2003. Cert. ReportNet product profl. Cognos Corp., 2006, PowerPlay product profl. Cognos Corp., 2006; project mgmt. Ind. U., 2004. Sys. engr. Joseph Graves Assoc., Inc., Indpls., 1995—98; programmer, analyst USA Grp., Inc., Fishers, Ind., 1998—99; sr. sys. analyst HealthCare Grp., LLC, Indpls., 1999—. Adj. prof. computer & info. tech. Purdue U., Indpls., 2005—. Mem.: Data Warehousing Inst., Assn. Computing Machinery. Baptist. Avocations: computers, music.

IRISH, GEORGE BUTLER, media company executive; b. Decatur, Ill., Feb. 27, 1944; s. Thomas Bone and Carolyn Elizabeth (Gilman) I.; m. Mary Rettig (dec. 2005), Jan. 29, 1966; children: Sandra Lynn, Christine Marie. BA, Millikin U., 1968, PhD (hon.). With dept. advt. sales Decatur Herald & Rev., 1966-67; asst. mgr. personnel Lindsay-Schaub Newspapers, Decatur, 1967-72, mgr. personnel, 1972-76; bus. mgr. Midland (Mich.) Daily Newspapers, 1976-79, gen. mgr., 1979-80, pub., 1980-82, Midland (Tex.) Reporter-Telegram, 1982-84, Beaumont (Tex.) Enterprise, 1984-88, San Antonio Light, 1988-93; group pub. The Hearst Corp., Beaumont, 1985-88, v.p., 1993—98, sr. v.p., 1998—; pres. Hearst Newspapers, 1998—. Pres. Midland Newspapers, Inc., 1982-84; com. chmn. Inland Daily Press Assn., Chgo., 1983—. Mem. bd. counselors St. Elizabeth Hosp., Beaumont, 1987, task force Job Creation and Econ. Devel., Austin, Tex., 1986-87; bd. dirs. San Antonio Econ. Devel. Found., 1988—, San Antonio Med. Found., 1990—, San Antonio Symphony (bd. dirs. 1988-93), Jr. Achievement S. Tex. 1988-93 (exec. com. 1990-93; trustee Southwest Rsch. Inst.; mem. governing coun. San Antonio Edn. Partnership; trustee Millikin U., Decatur, Ill., Incarnate Word Coll.; mem. devel. bd. U. Tex., San Antonio; mem. bd. visitors Trinity U.; mem. devel. bd. U. Tex. Health Sci. Ctr. at San Antonio; mem. exec. com. United Way of San Antonio, 1989—, vice chmn. ann. campaign, 1992, chmn. comm. com., 1989—; mem. exec. bd. Alamo Area Coun. Boy Scouts Am. Named Paul Harris fellow Rotary Internat., 1984 Citizen of the Yr. Sales and Mktg. Exec., 1987; recipient Disting. Service award Jaycees, 1976, Jr. Achievement Silver Leadership award, 1992, Community Svcs. award Brooks Heritage Found., 1992, Golden Rule award J.C. Penney, Merit Loyalty award Millikin U., 1993; honoree People of Vision Soc. To Prevent Blindness, 1992; named Newspaper Leader of Yr. Tex. Daily Newspaper Assn., 1992. Mem. Tex. Daily Newspaper Assn. (pres. 1987-88), Am. Press Assn. (adv. bd.), So. Newspaper Pub. Assn., Am. Newspaper Pub. Assn., San Antonio C. of C. (bd. dirs. 1989-91), Tex. C. of C. (bd. dirs. 1991—, Rotary (various coms.). Clubs: Dominion Country (San Antonio, chmn. bd. 1992—). Roman Catholic. Office: Hearst 250 W 55th St New York NY 10019-5201

IRISH, JAMES DAVID, oceanographer, educator; b. Bay City, Mich., Dec. 7, 1943; s. Don Delance Irish and Louise Sarah Clark; m. Peggy Ann Thompson, Mar. 27, 1965. BS, Antioch Coll., Yellow Springs, Ohio, 1967; PhD in Oceanography, Scripps Instn. Oceanography, La Jolla, Calif., 1971. Rsch. asst. prof. applied physics lab. U. Wash., Seattle, 1972—79; rsch. assoc. prof. U. NH, Durham, 1979—91, rsch. prof., 2006—; sr. rsch. specialist Woods Hole Oceanog. Instn., Mass., 1991—2006. Contbr. over 40 articles to profl. jours. Chmn. planning bd. City Madbury, NH, 1984—91. Recipient Al Vine Sr. Tech. Staff award, Woods Hole Oceanog. Instn., 2002. Mem.: IEEE, Am. Geophys. Union, The Oceanog. Soc., Marine Tech. Soc. Achievements include development of use of compliant elastic tether moorings; and testing of Acoustic Doppler Current Profilers, moored conductivity sensors, and the use of bottom pressure measurements of ocean currents; acoustic sediment concentration and bedload transport sensors. Office: Univf NH 24 Colovos Rd Durham NH 03824 Home Phone: 603-742-8765; Office Phone: 603-862-1916.

IRISH, JOEL DAVID, anthropologist; b. Mpls., Sept. 6, 1957; s. Lloyd Donald and Violet Esther (Heller) I.; m. Carol Diann McCracken, July 23, 1994. BS, Mankato State U., 1980; MS, Ariz. State U., 1984, PhD, 1993. Faculty assoc. Mankato (Minn.) State U., 1983-84; teaching assoc. Ariz. State U., Tempe, 1985-88, faculty assoc., 1989-92; archeologist USDA Forest Svcs., Sitka, Alaska, 1990-91; project archaeologist Lobdell and Assocs., Anchorage, 1992; physical anthropologist Office Cultural Resource Mgmt., Tempe, 1989-94; asst. prin. investigator Louis Berger & Assocs., Inc., Phoenix, 1993-94, prin. investigator, 1994-95; asst. prof. U. N.Mex., Albuquerque, 1995-98; assoc. prof., curator phys. anthropology U. Alaska Fairbanks, 1998—. Adj. prof. Ariz. State U., Tempe, 1993-96. Contbr. articles to profl. jours. Grantee, NSF, Washington, 1991, 2001, Nat. Geographic Soc., 2006, WGNNGR-GRGN Found., 2006. Mem. Am. Assn. Physical Anthropology, Am. Anthrop. Assn., Soc. Am. Archaeology, Dental Anthropology Assn. (sec.-treas. 1992-95, co-editor newsletter 1990-95, pres. 2002-04), Sigma Xi, Phi Kappa Phi. Achievements include determination of biological affinity estimates of 50 late-pleistocene through modern African samples based on dental discrete traits; study on late Paleolithic through post-dynastic peoples of Egypt and Nubia. Office: U Alaska Fairbanks Dept Anthropology PO Box 757720 Fairbanks AK 99775-7720 Office Phone: 907-474-6755. E-mail: ffjdi@uaf.edu.

IRISH, LEON EUGENE, lawyer, non-profit organization executive, educator; b. Superior, Wis., June 19, 1938; s. Edward Eugene and Phyllis Ione (Johnson) I.; m. Karla W. Simon; children: Stephen T., Jessica L., Thomas A., Emily A. BA in History, Stanford U., 1960; JD, U. Mich., 1964; D.Phil in Law, Oxford U., Eng., 1973. Law clk. to Assoc. Justice U.S. Supreme Ct. Byron R. White, 1967—68; cons. Office Fgn. Direct Investments, Dept. Commerce, 1968; spl. rep. sec. def. 7th session 3d UN Conf. Law of Sea; mem. Caplin & Drysdale, chartered, Washington, 1968—85; prof. law U. Mich. Law Sch., Ann Arbor, 1985—88; ptnr. Jones, Day, Reavis & Pogue, Washington, 1988—93; v.p., sr. counsel Aetna Life and Casualty Co., Hartford, Conn., 1993-95; pres., chmn. Internat. Ctr. Not-for-Profit Law, Washington, 1992—2002; pres., CEO United Way Internat., Alexandria, Va., 1996; sr. legal cons. World Bank, 1997—2001. Adj. prof. Georgetown U. Law Ctr., 1975-85, Cath. U. Am. Sch. Law, 2003—; regent Am. Coll. Tax Counsel, 1986-89; mem. IRS Commr.'s Adv. Group, 1987; bd. dirs., sec. Vols. Tech. Assistance, 1978-2005, Found. for Devel. of Polish Agr. 1988-2003; vis. fellow World Bank, 1995-96; vis. prof. law Ctrl. European U., Budapest, 1998—, Temple U., 2002-03, pres. Internat. Ctr. Civil Soc., 2002-; bd. dirs. Enterprise Works/VTA, 2004-; mem. nat. coun. UN Assn. USA, 2004-. Contbr. articles to legal jours. Mem. ABA, D.C. Bar Assn., Am. Law Inst., Am. Coll. Tax Counsel, Coun. on Fgn. Rels., Am. Coll. Employee Benefits Coun., Internat. Soc. Third Sector Rsch. Democrat. Home: 304 Kyle Rd Crownsville MD 21032-1843 Personal E-mail: leon.irish@gmail.com.

IRIYE, AKIRA, historian, educator; b. Tokyo, Oct. 20, 1934; s. Keishiro and Naoko (Tsukamoto) I.; m. Mitsuko Maeda, May 14, 1960; children: Keiko, Masumi. BA, Haverford Coll., 1957; PhD, Harvard U., 1961. Instr. in history Harvard U., Cambridge, Mass., 1961-64, lectr. in history, 1964-66; asst. prof. history U. Calif., Santa Cruz, 1966-68; assoc. prof. U. Rochester, 1968-69, U. Chgo., 1969-71, prof., 1971-89, disting. service prof., 1983-89, chmn. dept. history, 1979-85; prof. history Harvard U., 1989—91, Charles Warren prof. history, 1991—2005, Charles Warren rsch. prof. history, 2005—, chmn. dept. history, 2002—04. Vis. prof. Ecole des Hautes Etudes en Sciences Sociales, Paris, 1986-87, London Sch. Econs., 1992. Author: books, including After Imperialism, 1965, Across the Pacific, 1967, Pacific Estrangement, 1972, The Cold War in Asia, 1974, Power and Culture, 1981, The Origins of the Second World War in Asia and the Pacific, 1987, China and Japan, 1992, The Globalizing of America, 1993, Cultural Internationalism and World Order, 1997, Japan and the Wider World, 1997, Global Community, 2002; editor: The Chinese and the Japanese, 1980, other books. John Simon Guggenheim fellow, 1974-75 Mem. Am. Hist. Assn. (pres. 1988), Am. Acad. Arts and Scis., Orgn. Am. Historians, Soc. Historians Am. Fgn. Relations (pres. 1978) Office: Harvard U Dept History Cambridge MA 02138

IRIZARRY, DORA L., federal judge; b. San Sebastian, Puerto Rico, Jan. 26, 1955; 1 child. BA, Yale U., 1976; JD, Columbia U., 1979. Bar: NY 1981. Asst. dist. atty Bronx County, NY, 1979—87, Appeals Bur., 1979—81, NYC Spl. Narcotics Prosecutor, 1981—95, NY County, 1987—95; judge Criminal Ct. NYC, 1995—97, NY State Ct. Claims, 1997—2002; of counsel Hoguet Newman & Regal LLP, 2002—04; judge US Dist. Ct. (ea. dist.) NY, 2004—. Mem. 2d Cir. Fed.-State Jud. Coun. Mem.: Fed. Bar Coun., Fed. Judges Assn., Bar Puerto Rican Bar Assn., Com. on the Bench, Assn. Judges Hispanic Heritage (pres. 1997—2002), Fed. Bar Eastern Dist. NY, Fed. Bar Southern Dist. NY, NY State Bar. Office: 225 Cadman Plaza E Brooklyn NY 11201 Office Phone: 718-613-2150. Office Fax: 718-613-2156.

IRMAS, AUDREY MENEIN, not-for-profit developer; m. Sydney Milton Irmas Jr., June 26, 1949 (dec.); children: Deborah, Robert, Matthew. Co-founding trustee Audrey & Sydney Irmas Charitable Found., 1983—, projects include Audrey & Sydney Irmas Campus of the Wilshire Blvd. Temple, Audrey & Sydney Irmas LA Youth Ctr., many others; bd. trustees Mus. Contemporary Art, LA, 1992—, past pres., chmn.; trustee Hirshhorn Mus. and Sculpture Garden, Washington; bd. govs. ctr curator studies Bard Coll., NY. Named one of Top 200 Collectors, ARTnews mag., 2004. Avocation: Collector contemporary art, photography. Office: Audrey & Sydney Irmas Charitable Found Ste 364 16830 Ventura Blvd Encino CA 91436-2797 Office Phone: 818-382-3313. Office Fax: 818-382-3315.

IROH, JUDE ONWUEGBU, chemistry professor; b. Umulogho Obowo, Nigeria, Sept. 2, 1958; came to the U.S., 1986; s. Konkwo and Rita (Akuichi) I.; children: Bright Jude Obinna, Jude Onwuegbu Jr. BS in Applied Chemistry, U. Jos Jos, Nigeria, 1980; MS in Polymer Sci. and Tech., U. Manchester, 1984; PhD in Materials Sci., U. Conn., 1990. Grad. asst. Fed. U. Tech., Owerri, Nigeria, 1981-84, asst. lectr., 1985-86, lectr. II, 1986-90; grad. asst. U. Conn., Storrs, 1986-90; postdoctoral fellow Temple U., Phila., 1990-91; asst. prof. chemistry U. Cin., 1991-97, assoc. prof., 1997—. Student cons. engr. UTRC, Hartford, Conn., 1989; cons. G-Cat Co., Hartford, 1990-95. Advocate, mentor U. Cin., 1992-95, faculty advisor, 1993-95. Mem. Am. Chem. Soc., SAMPE, AIChE (assoc.), Adhesion Soc. (award com. 1993—). Achievements include patent for electrochemical method and product; co-inventor electrochemical technique for insi.tu impregnation of graphite fiber-polyimide composites. Office: U Cin 408B Rhodes Hall Ml12 Cincinnati OH 45221-0001 Home: 3877 Breeders Cup Ct Mason OH 45040-3814

IRONS, JEREMY JOHN, actor; b. Cowes, Eng., Sept. 19, 1948; s. Paul Dugan and Barbara Anne (Sharpe) Irons; m. Sinead Moira Cusack, Mar. 28, 1978; children: Samuel James, Maximilian Paul. Performer: (plays) John the Baptist in Godspell, 1973, Mick in The Caretaker, 1974, Petruchio in The Taming of the Shrew, 1975, Harry Thunder in Wild Oats, 1976—77, James Jameson in Rear Column, 1978, The Real Thing, 1984 (Tony award, 1984), Harry Thunder in Wild Oats, 1986, Richard II, Leontes in Winter's Tale, The Rover, Henrik in Embers, 2006, (films) Nijinsky, 1979, The French Lieutenant's Woman, 1981, Betrayal, 1982, Moonlighting, 1982, The Wild Duck, 1983, Swann in Love, 1983, The Mission, 1985, Chorus of Disapproval, 1988, Australia, 1988, Dead Ringers, 1988 (Best Actor N.Y. Film Critics' Circle, 1988), Danny, the Champion of the World, 1989, Reversal of Fortune, 1990 (Acad. award for Best Actor, 1991, Golden Globe for Best Actor, 1991), Kafka, 1991, Waterland, 1992, Damage, 1992, M. Butterfly, 1993, The House of the Spirits, 1994; performer: (voice) The Lion King, 1994; performer: Die Hard with a Vengeance, 1995, Stealing Beauty, 1996, Lolita, 1997, The Chinese Box, 1997, Man in the Iron Mask, 1998, Dungeons and Dragons, 2000, Fourth Angel, 2000, And Now Ladies and Gentlemen, 2001, Callas Forever, 2001, Mathilde, 2003, Being Julia, 2003, Merchant of Venice, 2004, Kingdom of Heaven, 2004, Casanova, 2004, Inland Empire, 2006, Eragon, 2006, (TV films) Charles Ryder in Brideshead Revisited, 1980—81, Alex Hepburn in The Captain's Doll, 1982, Tales from Hollywood, 1992, Longitude, 1999, Last Call, 2001, Elizabeth I, 2005 (Emmy award for Outstanding Supporting Actor in a miniseries or movie, 2006, Best Performance by an Actor in a Supporting Role in a Series, Mini-Series or Motion Picture Made for TV, Golden Globe, Hollywood Fgn. Press Assn., 2007, Outstanding Performance by a Male Actor in a TV Movie or Miniseries, SAG, 2007); performer: (voice). Decorated officier des Artes et Lettres (France). Address: Hutton Mgmt 4 Old Manor Close Askett Bucks HP27 9NA England

IRONS, PAULETTE RILEY, state legislator, lawyer; b. New Orleans, May 19, 1953; d. Florida Wilson; m. Alvin L. Irons; children: Marseah Irons Delatte, Paul-Alvin. BBA, Loyola U., New Orleans, 1975; JD, Tulane U., 1991. Bar: La. 1991. Sr. cons. Small Bus. Devel. and Mgmt. Inst., New Orleans, 1992-93; mem. La. Ho. of Reps., Baton Rouge, 1992-94, La. Senate, Baton Rouge, 1994—. Vice-chmn. transp., hwys. and pub. works com., mem. health and welfare com., formr mem. fin. com., pres. women's caucus,1998, sgt.-at-arms legis. black caucus, 1993-95; sr. cons. Small Bus. Devel. and Mgmt. Inst., New Orleans, 1992-93; adj. prof. Tulane U. Law Clinic, New Orleans, fall 1995; atty. 1st City Ct., New Orleans, 1996-98; atty. Recorder of Mortgages Office, New Orleans, 1997—; adv. bd. women's network Nat. Conf. State Legislators, Denver, 1996—. Pres. bd. dirs. La. Initiative on Teen Pregnancy Prevention, 1995-2001; bd. dirs. New Orleans Area Literacy Coalition. Recipient Woman of Excellence award 2d Bapt. Ch., 1994, Outstanding African Am. Woman, Tulane Black Law Students, 1996, Good Housekeeping award, 2001; named Legislator of Yr., New Orleans Alliance for Good Govt., 1995. Fellow Japan Soc.; mem. LWV, AAUW, Nat. Order Women Legislators, Nat. Order Black Elected Legislators, Women for a Better La., Ind. Women's Orgn., La. League Good Govt. Democrat. Avocations: reading, travel. Address: La Senate Ofc PO Box 94183 Baton Rouge LA 70804-9183 Office: Jud Civil Dist Ct 421 Loyola Ave Room 200B New Orleans LA 70112 Office Phone: 504-592-9250.

IRONS, WILLIAM GEORGE, anthropology educator; b. Garrett, Ind., Dec. 25, 1933; s. George Randall and Eva Aileen (Veazey) I.; m. Marjorie Sue Rogasner, Nov. 4, 1972; children: Julia Rogasner, Marybeth Rogasner. BA, U. Mich., 1960, MA, 1963, PhD, 1969; postgrad., London Sch. Econs., 1964—65. With Army C.E., 1956-58; asst. prof. social rels. Johns Hopkins U., 1969-74; asst. prof. anthropology Pa. State U., 1974-78; assoc. prof. anthropology Northwestern U., Evanston, Ill., 1978-83, prof., 1983—. Cons. Nat. Geog. Soc., NSF, AAAS, Social Sci. Rsch. Coun., Time-Life Books, U. Wash. Press, Random House, Worth Pubs., Rutgers U. Press, U. Tex. Press, Pelenum Press, Oxford U. Press, Cornell U. Press. Author: Perspectives on Nomadism, 1972, The Yomut Turkmen, 1975, Evolutionary Biology and Human Social Behavior, 1979, Adaptation and Human Behavior, 2000; mem. bd. editors Evolution and Human Behavior. With AUS, 1954-56. Recipient Lifetime Achievement award Commn. on Nomadic Peoples, Internat. Union Anthrop. and Ethnol. Scis.; grantee NSF, 1973, 76, 83, 85, 86, Ford Found., 1974, Harry Frank Guggenheim Found., 1976. Fellow AAAS, Am. Anthrop. Assn.; mem. Assocs. in Current Anthropology, Human Behavior and Evolution Soc. (pres. 2001-03), Internat. Soc. Human Ethology, Internat. Soc. for Behavioral Ecology, Ctr. for Advanced Studies in Religion and Sci., Inst. for Religion in an Age of Sci., Evolutionary Anthropology Soc. (pres. 2004—), Phi Kappa Phi. Achievements include research on Turkmen of Iran, human behavioral ecology, evolutionary ethics. Home: 2604 Payne St Evanston IL 60201-2133 Office: Northwestern U Dept Anthropology 1810 Hinman Ave Evanston IL 60208-0809 Business E-Mail: w-irons@northwestern.edu.

IRSAY, JAMES STEVEN, professional football team owner; b. Lincolnwood, Ill., June 13, 1959; s. Robert Irsay and Harriet Pogerzelski; m. Margaret Mary Coyle, Aug. 2, 1980; children: Carlie Margaret, Casey Coyle, Kalen. B in Broadcast Journalism, So. Meth. U., 1982. With Balt. Colts., from early 1970's; owner, CEO Indpls. Colts, 1997—. Bd. dirs. Noble Ind. Composer, performer single Hoosier Heartland, 1985, single and video Go Colts, 1985, Colors, 1990. Bd. dirs. United Way Ctrl. Ind.; dir. Greater Indpls. Progress Com. Achievements include purchased in auction Jack Kerouac's orignial scroll of On the Road, 2001. Avocations: weightlifting, guitar, song writing. Office: Indpls Colts 7001 W 56th St Indianapolis IN 46254-9725 also: Indianapolis Colts PO Box 535000 Indianapolis IN 46253

IRVIN, LORETTA REGAN, elementary school educator; d. Robert William and Doris Lee Regan; m. Warren D. Irvin (dec.); children: Christopher Ronald, Patricia Anne Alford, Kelli Elaine. Master's degree, Ga. State U., 2002. Lic. T-5 Ga. Profl. Stds. Commn. Tchr. Cobb County Sch. Sys., Marietta, Ga., 1974—. Sunday sch. tchr. United Meth. Ch., Dallas and Marietta. Grantee, Women's Jr. League of Cobb County, 1990. Mem.: CEC, Ga. Assn. of Educators. Democrat. Methodist. Avocation: gardening. Home Phone: 770-975-0474; Office Phone: 678-594-8252. Personal E-mail: lorirvin@hotmail.com.

IRVIN, MICHAEL JEROME, sportscaster, retired professional football player; b. Ft. Lauderdale, Fla., Mar. 5, 1966; s. Walter and Pearl Irvin; m. Sandy Harrell, 1990; 4 children. BA in Bus. Mgmt., U. Miami, 1988. Wide receiver Dallas Cowboys, 1988—99; analyst, Sunday NFL Countdown ESPN, 2003—06. Actor: (films) The Longest Yard, 2005. Named NFL All-Pro, 1991, NFL Pro Bowl MVP, 1991; named to Nat. Football Conf. Pro Bowl Team, 1991—95, The NFL 1990's All Decade Team, The Pro Football Hall of Fame, 2007. Achievements include being a member of 3 Super Bowl Championship teams with the Dallas Cowboys, 1993, 1994, 1996.*

IRVIN, MICHAEL P., lawyer; b. Ft. Worth, Apr. 29, 1950; BA, U. Tex., 1972; JD, U. Houston, 1975. Bar: Tex. 1975. Atty. Fulbright & Jaworski L.L.P., Houston, 1975—83, ptnr., 1983—, and head, energy and real property dept. Mem. ABA, Houston Bar Assn., State Bar Tex., Phi Delta Phi, Order of the Barons. Office: Fulbright & Jaworski LLP 1301 McKinney St Ste 5100 Houston TX 77010-3031 Office Phone: 713-651-3705. Office Fax: 713-651-5246. Business E-Mail: mirvin@fulbright.com.

IRVIN, PATRICIA LOUISE, lawyer; b. Great Lakes, Ill., Mar. 11, 1955; d. Jesse Lewis and Eleonore Hortense (Wetterrainer) I. AB summa cum laude, Princeton U., 1976; JD, Harvard U., 1979. Bar: NY, Wash., DC. Assoc. Milbank, Tweed, Hadley & McCloy, NYC, 1979-87, ptnr., 1988—; dep. asst. sec. def. Clinton Adminstrn., 1993—96; ptnr. Shaw Pittman, Wash.; exec. v.p. and gen. counsel New Urban Entertainment TV; v.p. Andrew W. Mellon Found., NYC, 2005—. Trustee Cooper Union Advancement Sci. & Art, 1988-92, Princeton U., 1990—; bd. dirs. Legal Aid Soc., 1988—, exec. com., 1990—, Legal Def. Ednl. Fund NAACP, 1989—, exec. com. 1990—; mem. Coun. Fgn. Rels., 1991—. Mem. ABA, Assn. of Bar of City of N.Y. (jud. com. 1985-88, com. minorities legal profession 1988-90, nominating com. 1990-91), Met. Black Bar Assn., Nat. Bar Assn., Am. Law Inst., Assn. Black Princeton Alumni. Office: Andrew W Mellon Found 140 E 62nd St New York NY 10021 Office Phone: 212-500-2525. Office Fax: 212-500-2302. Business E-Mail: pi@mellon.org.

IRVINE, JOHN ALEXANDER, lawyer; b. Sault Ste. Marie, Ont., Can., Mar. 10, 1947; s. Alexander and Ruth Catherine (Woolrich) I.; children from previous marriage: John Alexander, Allison Brooks; m. Lynda Kaye Myska Jenkins, May 24, 1981; children: James Woolrich, William Myska. BS, Auburn U., 1969; JD, Memphis State U., 1972. Bar: Tenn. 1972, Ohio 1982, Tex. 1985. Law clk. U.S. Dist. Ct. (we. dist.) Tenn., 1972-73; asst. dist. atty. gen. 15th Jud. Cir. Tenn., 1973-78; assoc. Glankler, Brown, Gilliland, Chase, Robinson and Raines, Memphis, 1978-81; asst. gen. counsel Mead Corp., Dayton, Ohio, 1981-84; ptnr. Porter & Clements, Houston, 1984-87; prin. Boyer, Norton & Blair, 1987-89; ptnr. Thelen, Marrin, Johnson & Bridges, 1989-94, mng. ptnr. Houston office, mem. mgmt. com., 1991-94; ptnr. Porter & Hodges, L.L.P., 1995—, chmn. litig. practice group, 2002—04, mem. mgmt. com., 2000—02, 2005—. Bd. dirs. Make-A-Wish Found. Tex. Gulf Coast, 1985-86; governing dir., trustee Houston Symphony Orch., 2006—. Fellow Tex. Bar Found. (sustaining life; chair Region 4 nominating com. 2000), Houston Bar Found. (sustaining life; named Tex. Super Lawyer 2003, 04, 06); mem. ABA (vice chmn. com. corp. counsel, litig. sect. 1989-91, co-chmn. intellectual properties litig. com. 1996-99, co-chmn. trial practice com. 2000-2003, mem. task force judiciary 2003-, co-chmn. cle programs & evaluations), Internat. Assn. Def. Counsel, Am. Arbitration Assn. (bd. arbitrators), Nat. Assn. Securities Dealers (bd. arbitrators), Tex. Bar Assn., Tenn. Bar Assn., Fed. Bar Assn. (treas. 1997-98, v.p. 1998-99, pres.-elect 1999-2000, pres. 2000—), Memphis Bar Assn. (YLS, bd. dirs. 1976, treas. 1977), Ohio Bar Assn., Houston Bar Assn., Coll. State Bar Tex., Memphis State U. Law Sch. Alumnae Assn. (pres. 1975-76, 77-78), 5th Cir. Ct. Appeals Bar Assn., U.S. C. of C. (coun. on antitrust policy 1983—), Phoenix Club of Memphis (bd. dirs. 1977-79), Def. Rsch. Inst., Champions Golf Club, Promontary Ranch Club, Coronado Club, Briar Club. Republican. Presbyterian. Avocations: sports, travel, reading. Home Phone: 713-626-3428; Office Phone: 713-226-6605. Personal E-mail: jirvine@porterhedges.com.

IRVINE, JUDITH TEMKIN, anthropologist, educator; b. Balt., Mar. 10, 1945; BA, Harvard U., Cambridge, Mass., 1966; PhD in Anthropology, U. Pa., 1973. Asst. prof. to assoc. prof. to prof. dept. anthropology Brandeis U., Mass., 1972—99; prof. anthropology U. Mich., Ann Arbor, 2000—. Chair dept. anthropology Brandeis U., 1987—90, U. Mich. Contbr. articles to profl. jours., chapters to books. Grantee Guggenheim fellowship, 2005. Fellow: Am. Acad. Arts & Scis. Office: U Mich Dept Anthropology 101 West Hall 1085 S Univ Ave Ann Arbor MI 48109-1107 Business E-Mail: jti@umich.edu.

IRVINE, ROBERT, chef; Cert. Exec. Chef Am. Culinary Fedn. Culinary cons. Bali, Jakarta, Ho Chi Minh City; exec. chef cruise ships; dir. culinary ops., exec. chef Trump Taj Mahal, Caesars Atlantic City; dir., food services, exec. chef Resorts Atlantic City; founder Irvine Grp., 2003—. Culinary dir. Taste of LPGA; team coord. Children Uniting Nations Oscar Dinner, 2005. Host (TV series) Dinner: Impossible, Food Network. Recipient Chef's Five Diamond award, Am. Acad. Hospitality Sciences, 1998—2006. Office: Resorts Atlantic City 1133 Boardwalk Atlantic City NJ 08401*

IRVINE, WILLIAM BURRISS, management consultant; b. Wheeling, W.Va., July 20, 1925; s. Russell Drake and Elizabeth (Carney) I.; m. Allen Claywell; children: William, Mary, Edward. BA in Econs., Cornell U., 1949. V.p. Basil L. Smith Sys., Phila., 1949-66; pres. Pa. Graphic Arts, Inc., Phila., 1966-78, Classified Devel. Corp., Bryn Mawr, Pa., 1978—, Nat. Media Svcs., Wilmington, NC, 2003—. Pres. Victor O'Neil Studios divsn. Herff Jones, Inc., N.Y.C., 1972-75; trustee Cornell Delta Phi Ednl. Found., N.Y., 1985; bd. dirs. Main Line Sch. Night, 1998. Author: Treasury of College Humor, 1947. Bd. dirs. Family and Neighborhood Inst., Wilmington, NC. Mem. St. Elmo Club of Phila., St. Elmo Club of N.Y., Lake White Club, Delta Phi (sec. 1960-62). Republican. Roman Catholic. Office Phone: 910-342-9177. Personal E-mail: classdev@zoomnet.net.

IRVING, GEORGE STEVEN, actor; b. Springfield, Mass., Nov. 1, 1922; s. Abraham and Rebecca (Sack) Shelasky; m. Maria Karnilova, Oct. 17, 1948; children: Alexander, Katherine. Student, Leland Powers Sch. of Theatre, Boston, 1941. Actor (on Broadway) play, Oklahoma, 1943, Lady in the Dark, 1943, Call Me Mister, 1946, Along Fifth Avenue, 1949, Gentlemen Prefer Blondes, 1949, Two's Company, 1952, Me and Juliet, 1953, Can-Can, 1954, Bells Are Ringing, 1957, The Beggar's Opera, 1957, The Good Soup, 1957, Irma La Douce, 1960, Romulus, 1962, Bravo Giovanni, 1962, Seidman and Son, 1962, Tovarich, 1963, A Murderer Among Us, 1964, Alfie, 1964, Anya, 1965, Galileo, 1967, The Happy Time, 1968, Promenade, 1969, An Evening With Richard Nixon, 1972 (Drama Desk award), Irene, 1973 (Tony award for best supporting actor 1973), On Your Toes, 1983, Me and My Girl, 1986, Cinderella, The Merry Widow, NY City Opera, 1994, The Chocolate Soldier, 2005, A Mother, A Daughter, And A Gun, 2005; stock and touring prodns. E-mail: gsirving@earthlink.net.

IRVING, GEORGE WASHINGTON, III, veterinarian, researcher, small business executive; b. NYC, Apr. 25, 1940; s. George Washington Jr. and Frances (Connell) I.; m. Alice Marie Graves, Dec. 21, 1968; 1 child, George Washington IV. BS, U. Md., 1962; DVM, Purdue U., 1965; MS, Tex. A&M U., 1970. Diplomate Am. Coll. Lab. Animal Medicine, Am. Coll. Vet. Preventive Medicine. Commd. 1st lt. USAF, 1966, advanced through ranks to col., 1984; base veterinarian Niagara Falls Internat. Airport, NY, 1966, 388th Tactical Fighter Wing, Korat, Thailand, 1966-67; base veterinarian Wilford Hall USAF Med. Ctr., Lackland AFB, Tex., 1968; asst. chief vet. edn. br. USAF Sch. Aerospace Medicine, San Antonio, 1970-75; chief divsn. lab. animal medicine Armed Forces Inst. Pathology, Washington, 1976-79; grad. Armed Forces Staff Coll., 1975-76, Air War Coll., 1977; program mgr. Air Force Office Sci. Rsch., Bolling AFB, DC, 1979-82, dir. life sci., 1982-83; USAF liaison U.S. Army Med. R & D Command, Ft. Detrick, Md., 1983-84, dir. med. chem. def. rsch. program, 1984-87; cons. to surgeon gen. USAF, Washington, 1983-95; dir. Armed Forces Radiobiology Rsch. Inst., Bethesda, Md., 1987-91; staff dir. Human Systems Ctr., Brooks AFB, Tex., 1991-94, vice comdr., 1994-95, dir. re-engring., 1995-96; ret. USAF, 1996; v.p. Conceptual MindWorks, Inc., 1996—, v.p. sci. and tech. support svcs. Instr. grad. rsch. program NIH, Bethesda, 1976-85; merit rev. VA, Washington, 1978-84; cons. Stunkard, Miller Assocs., Bowie, Md., 1976-79; mem. site proposal team dept Homeland Security Nat. Bio and Agrl. Def. Facility. Editor: Selected Topics in Laboratory Animal Medicine, 15 vols., 1971-75; contbr. articles to jours. and chpts. to books; editor: Contemporary Topics in Laboratory Animal Sciences, 1995-97. Vice-min. Secular Franciscan Order, Holy Name Province, 1989-91; min. Tex. Dist., Sacred Heart Province, 1992-94, Los Tres Compañeros/The 3 Companions Region, 1994-98; co-chair capital campaign com., St. Joseph Honey Creek Cath. Ch., 2001- , mem. pastoral coun., 2002-05 , chmn. pastoral coun., 2005; mem. San Antonio site proposal team Dept. Home and Security, Nat. Bio and Agro Def. Facility. Decorated Legion of Merit with oak leaf cluster, Def. Superior Svc. medal, Air Force Commendation medal, Army Commendation medal, Meritorious Svc. medal, Joint Svc. Commendation medal, Vietnam Svc. medal. Fellow Aerospace Med. Assn.; mem. AVMA, D.C. Vet. Med. Assn. (pres. 1982), Am. Assn. for Lab. Animal Sci. (pres. nat. capital area br. 1981-82, v.p. 1998, pres. 1999), San Antonio-Austin Life Scis. Assn., Brooks Aerospace Found. (treas., CFO), Brooks Heritage Found., Brooks AFB Rod and Gun Club (pres. 1973-74), San Antonio Greater C. of C. (mem. Mil. Transformation Task Force 2006—). Republican. Roman Catholic. Office: Conceptual MindWorks Inc Ste 377 9830 Colonnade Blvd San Antonio TX 78230 Office Phone: 210-737-0777. Business E-Mail: girving@teamcmi.com.

IRVING, GITTE NIELSEN, secondary school educator; b. Copenhagen, Nov. 5, 1954; came to U.S., 1976; d. Sven Aage and Aase (Espersen) Nielsen; m. Richard Frederick Irving, June 5, 1976; children: Erik Christian, Emilie Jessica. BA, U. Iceland, Reykjavik, 1976; MEd, Lesley Coll., 1977. Cert. elem. tchr., spl. edn. tchr., Mass.; cert. by Mass. Gen. Hosp. in use of Orton-Gillingham strategies for remediation of dyslexia, 1989. Spl. edn. aide Brookline (Mass.) Pub. Schs., 1977-78; spl. edn. tchr. Ashland (Mass.) Pub. Schs., 1978-81, Greater Lawrence Ednl. Collaborative, Andover, Mass., 1981-82; owner, dir. Comprehensive Academics, Inc., Winchester, Mass., 1983—. Tutor The Rivers Sch., Weston, Mass., 1998—; mem. com. early edn. planning Winchester Pub. Schs., 1986; com. missions and social concerns United Meth. Ch., Winchester, 1987, co-chair, 1988-91; adv. coun. Spl. Edn. Parents, Winchester, 1985-2001; mem. com. on sch. configurations, subcom. to Sch. Com., Winchester, 1991-92; spkr. European League of Mid. Level Edn. Ann. Conf., Amsterdam, The Netherlands, 1996. Editor spl. edn. presch. newsletter, 1985-86; guest columnist Winchester Star, 1986. V.p. Neighborhood Coop. Nursery Sch., Winchester, 1988-90; mem. sch. improvement coun. Muraco Elem. Sch., Winchester, 1993-95; parents' coun. exec. com. mem., Simmons Coll., Boston, 2006-. Avocations: reading, furniture refinishing, knitting and needlework, gardening. Home: 12 Stone Ave Winchester MA 01890-1332 Office: Comprehensive Acads 573 Main St Winchester MA 01890-2900 Office Phone: 781-729-3686. Personal E-mail: Gitte@dkirvings.com.

IRVING, JANELL NAKIA, management consultant; b. Gary, Ind., Mar. 23, 1980; d. Janice Morris Morris and Dennis Edward Irving. BS, Stephens Coll., Columbia, 2002; MA, Purdue, Hammond, 2004. Ceo, founder Visionaries Oper. to Improve Christian Entrepreneurship Consulting Inc., Gary, Ind., 2002—07; grants writer Purdue North Ctrl., Westville, Ind., 2006—. Composer: (play) Built on Solid Ground: This History of African American Praise. Mem.: Phi Delta Kappa (sec. 2006—07). Achievements include national wall of tolerance. Personal E-mail: janellirving@voiceincorporated.com.

IRVING, JEFFREY ALAN, management consultant, educator, lawyer; b. NYC, May 20, 1947; s. Herbert and Florence (Rapoport) I.; m. Maureen Pickett, July 20, 1988; children: Tara, Michael. BSBA cum laude, U. Denver, 1969; JD, U. Okla., 1973; MBA with honors, Harvard U., 1980. Bar: NY 1974, admitted to practice: US Dist. Ct. (Ea. Dist.) NY 1975, US Dist. Ct. (So. Dist.) NY 1975, US Ct. Appeals (2nd Cir.) 1975, US Supreme Ct. 1978. Legal intern Legal Aid Soc., Norman, Okla., 1972-73; assoc. Pincus, Hutner, Seeman & Hasen, NYC, 1973-74; exec. v.p., gen. counsel Global Sysco divsn. Sysco Corp., Garden City, NY, 1974-91; pres. food svcs. divsn. Seabrook Bros. and Sons. Inc., 1991-92. Founder, mng. dir. cons. firm, Great Neck NY; mem. faculty Hofstra U. Coll. Bus. Adminstrn. Editor: Human Rights Rsch. Coun. Jour., 1972—73; contbr. articles to Inc. mag. and Food Svc. Distbr. mag. Bd. dir. LI chpt. March of Dimes, 1975—91. Mem.: Freight Users Assn. NY (pres. 1978, bd. dir. 1975—92), Nassau County Bar Assn. (ethics com. 1974—80), Bar NY. Republican. Avocations: tennis, sailing. E-mail: icgnewyork@att.net.

IRVING, JOHN WINSLOW (JOHN WALLACE BLUNT JR.), writer; b. Exeter, NH, Mar. 2, 1942; s. Colin F.N. and Frances (Winslow) I.; m. Shyla Leary, Aug. 20, 1964 (div. 1981); children: Colin, Brendan; m. Janet Turnbull, June 6, 1987; 1 child, Everett. Student, U. Pitts., 1961-62, U. Vienna, 1963-64; BA, U. N.H., 1965; M.F.A., U. Iowa, 1967. Asst. wrestling coach Phillips Exeter Acad., 1964-65; asst. prof. English Windham Coll., 1967-69, 70-72, Mt. Holyoke Coll., 1975-78; writer-in-residence U. Iowa, 1972-75; with Bread Loaf Writer's Conf., 1976, Brandeis U., 1978-79; asst. wrestling coach Northfield Mt. Hermon Sch., 1981-83, Fessenden Sch., 1984-86; head wrestling coach Vermont Acad., 1987-89. Author: (novels) Setting Free the Bears, 1969, The Water-Method Man, 1972, The 158-Pound Marriage, 1974, The World According to Garp, 1978, The Hotel New Hampshire, 1981, The Cider House Rules, 1985 (Academy award for best adapted screenplay 2000), A Prayer for Owen Meany, 1989, A Son of the Circus, 1994, A Widow for One Year, 1998, The Fourth Hand, 2001, Until I Find You, 2005 (Publisher's Weekly hardcover bestseller list); (collections) Trying to Save Piggy Sneed, 1996; (nonfiction) An Introduction to Great Expectations, 1986, An Introduction to A Christmas Carol, 1996, My Movie Business: A Memoir, 1999; contbr. short stories and revs. to other publs. Rockefeller Found. grantee, 1971-72; Nat.

Endowment for Arts fellow, 1974-75, Guggenheim fellow, 1976-77; Recipient Nat. Book award, 1980, O. Henry award, 1981, Golden Plate award, Acad. Achievement, 2005; inducted into Nat. Wrestling Hall of Fame, 1992, Am. Acad. of Arts and Letters, 2001.*

IRVING, PAUL HOWARD, lawyer; BFA with highest honors, NYU, 1975; JD, Loyola Marymount U., LA, 1980. Bar: Calif. 1980, US Dist. Ct. (ctrl. dist.). Chief exec., mng. ptnr. Manatt, Phelps & Phillips, LLP, LA, 1999—2006, chmn., 2007—. Adj. prof. Loyola Law Sch., 1980—85; exec. com. mem. Anti-Defamation League Pacific S.W. Region; bd. dirs. Chanin Capital Ptnrs., Prospect Fin. Advs., LLC; spkr. in field. Mem. nat. coun. Human Rights First; bd. dirs. Operation Hope; nat. co-chair Hope Coalition Am.; mem. bd. trustees and exec. com. New Rds. Sch. Named Mgr. of Yr., LA Daily Jour. and San Francisco Daily Jour., 2002; named one of Top 25 Up-and-Coming Legal Stars in Calif., 1993. Mem.: Calif. Bar Assn. Office: Manatt Phelps & Phillips LLP 11355 W Olympic Blvd Los Angeles CA 90064-1614 Office Phone: 310-312-4196. Office Fax: 310-312-4224. E-mail: pirving@manatt.com.*

IRVING, THOMAS L., lawyer; b. Salt Lake City, Apr. 29, 1951; BA in Chem. magna cum laude, U. Utah, 1974; JD, Duke U., 1977. Bar: DC 1977; US Ct. Appeals (fed. cir.); US Patent Office. Mem. Finnegan, Henderson, Farabow, Garrett & Dunner, Washington. Co-author: Chemical Patent Law, Patent Resources Group, 1996-2005. Recipient Am. Jurisprudence Book award Duke U. Sch. Law 1976; named one of best lawyers in intellectual property law, Best Lawyers in Am., 2006. Mem. ABA, Am. Intellectual Property Law Assn. (chmn. CAFC dist. ct. subcommittee 1985-87, chmn. CLE subcommittee 1988-89, chmn. 1989-1991, bd. dirs. 1991—), Am. Chem. Soc., Phi Beta Kappa, Phi Kappa Phi. Achievements include specializing in due diligence, patent prosecution, reissue, reexamination, patent interferences and counseling, including prelitigation and infringement and validity analysis. Office: Finnegan Henderson Farabow Garrett & Dunner LLP 901 New York Ave NW Washington DC 20001-3315 Office Phone: 202-408-4082. Office Fax: 202-408-4400. Business E-Mail: irvingt@finnegan.com.

IRWIN, BILL, actor, clown; b. Santa Monica, Calif., Apr. 11, 1950; s. Horace and Elizabeth Irwin; m. Martha Roth. BA in Theatre Arts, Oberlin Coll.; grad., Ringling Brothers and Barnum & Bailey's Clown Coll. Actor & writer (plays) The Regard of Flight, 1987, Largely New York, 1989; actor: (plays) The Accidental Death of an Anarchist, Fool Moon (Spl. Tony Award for Live Theatrical Presentation), The Goat, or Who is Sylvia?, 2002, Who's Afraid of Virginia Woolf?, 2005 (Tony Award for best performance by a leading actor in a play, 2005), Trumbo, 2005 (Barrymore award, outstanding leading actor in a play, 2005); (films) Manhattan by Numbers, 1993, Stanley's Gig, 2000, How the Grinch Stole Christmas, 2000, The Laramie Project, 2002, Igby Goes Down, 2002, The Truth About Miranda, 2004, The Manchurian Candidate, 2004, Lady in the Water, 2006. Named to Internat. Clown Hall of Fame, 1999.

IRWIN, DONALD PAULDING, lawyer; b. NYC, Oct. 15, 1944; s. Donald McDonald and Sarah Paulding (Ray) Irwin; m. Stoner Winslett; children: Louise Porcher Gray, Elizabeth Sinclair, Alex W. Pankoff, Caroline Winslett. AB, Princeton U., 1965; JD, Yale U., 1971, MA in Polit. sci., 1971. Bar: Va. 71, DC 77. Assoc. Hunton & Williams, Richmond, Va., 1971—78, ptnr., 1978—. Mem.: Commonwealth Club (Richmond), Country Club of Va., Met. Club (Washington). Republican. Episcopalian. Avocation: golf. Home: 403 Harlan Cir Richmond VA 23226-1634 Office: Hunton & Williams Riverfront Plz E 951 E Byrd St Richmond VA 23219-1535 Office Phone: 804-788-8357. E-mail: dirwin@hunton.com.

IRWIN, GERALD PORT, physician; b. Muncie, Ind., July 11, 1945; s. Francis Inlow and Helen Marcella (Morgan) I.; m. Martha Sue Vincent, Mar. 10, 1946; 1 child, Tamara Suzette. AB in Biol. Sci., Ind. U., 1968; MD, Ind. U., Indpls., 1972. Diplomate Am. Bd. Family Physicians. Intern and resident Ball Meml. Hosp., Muncie, Ind., 1972-73; pvt. practice Alexandria, Ind., 1973—. Med. dir. Richland Twp. Fire Dept., Anderson. Mem. AMA (Physician Recognition award 1992-95, 98-2001, 2007—), Am. Acad. Family Physicians,Ind. State Med. Assn., Ind. Assn. Family Physicians, Lions, Elks. Methodist. Avocations: computers, backpacking. Office: PO Box 124 Alexandria IN 46001-0124 Home Phone: 765-724-6252; Office Phone: 765-724-7711.

IRWIN, GLENN WARD, JR., medical educator, physician, academic administrator; b. Roachdale, Ind., July 18, 1920; s. Glenn Ward and Elsie (Browning) I.; m. Marianna Ashby; children: Ann Graybill Irwin Warden, William Browning, Elizabeth Ashby Irwin Schiffli. BS, Ind. U., Bloomington, 1942; MD, Ind. U., Indpls., 1944; LLD (hon.), Ind. U., 1986, Marian Coll., 1987. Diplomate: Am. Bd. Internal Medicine. Intern Meth. Hosp., Indpls., 1944-45; resident in internal medicine Ind. U. Med. Ctr., Indpls., 1945-46, 48-50; mem. faculty Ind. U., Indpls., 1950—, instr. , asst. prof. then assoc. prof., 1950-61, prof. medicine, 1961-86, prof. emeritus, 1986, dean Sch. Medicine, 1965-73, dean emeritus, 1986, v.p., 1974-86; chancellor Ind. U.-Purdue U., Indpls., 1973-74, chancellor emeritus, 1989. Sr. assoc. Ind. U. Found. Bd. dirs. Goodwill Industries of Ctrl. Ind., Indpls., Greater Indpls. Progress Com., Greater Indpls. YMCA, Walther Med. Rsch. Inst., Walther Oncology Ctr., Indpls. Health Inst., Eiteljorg Mus. Western Art and the Am. Indian; elder 2d Presbyn. Ch. Served to capt. M.C. U.S. Army, 1946-48. Recipient Disting. Alumnus award Ind. U. Sch. Medicine, 1972, Otis R. Bowen Physician County Service award, Benjamin Harrison award, Ind. Acad. award; named Sagamore of the Wabash, Gov. of Ind., 1961, 79, 86. Fellow ACP (gov. for Ind. 1964-70); mem. AMA, Ind. State Med. Assn., Marion County Med. Soc., Ind. Soc. of Chgo., 500 Festival Assn., James Whitcomb Riley Meml. Assn. (bd. govs. 1986—), Newcomen Soc., Sigma Xi, Alpha Omega Alpha, Beta Gamma Sigma, Sigma Theta Tau. Clubs: Columbia (Indpls.), Contemporary (Indpls.), Meridian Hills Country, Skyline (bd. dirs.). Lodges: Masons (33 degree), Rotary. Home: 8025 N Illinois St Indianapolis IN 46260-2938 Office: Ind U-Purdue U at Indpls 1120 South Dr Indianapolis IN 46202-5135 Home Phone: 317-255-7445; Office Phone: 317-274-5160. E-mail: drglenni@aol.com.

IRWIN, IVAN, JR., lawyer; b. Dallas, Dec. 10, 1933; s. Ivan and Charlotte Irwin; m. Carol Eklund; children: Catherine Ann, Ivan III (dec.), Margaret Lynn, Kevin. BA, So. Meth. U., 1954, LLB, 1957. Bar: Tex. 1957. Assoc. Fulbright & Jaworski, Houston, 1957-60; ptnr. Shank, Irwin, Conant, Lipshy & Casterline, Dallas, 1960-90, Vinson & Elkins, Dallas, 1990-94; vice chmn. Hunt Petroleum Corp., Dallas, 1994—. Contbr. articles to profl. publs. Bd. dirs., trustee trust fund Dallas Lighthouse for Blind; bd. dirs. Anita N. Martinez Ballet Folklorico, Dallas, 1991-92; trustee Dallas Mus. Art, 1988-99. Mem. Dallas Bar Assn. (corp. coun. and internat. bar sects.). Avocations: photography, golf, tennis. Office: Hunt Petroleum Corp 1601 Elm St Ste 4700 Dallas TX 75201 Business E-Mail: ii@huntpetroleum.com.

IRWIN, JOHN DAVID, electrical engineering educator; b. Mpls., Aug. 9, 1939; s. Arthur Fowle and Virginia I.; m. Patricia Edith Watson, Aug. 26, 1961; children: Geri Marie, John David, Laura Lynne. BEE, Auburn U., Ala., 1961; MS, U. Tenn., 1962, PhD, 1967. Mem. tech. staff Bell Labs., Holmdel, NJ, 1967—68; supr. Bell Labs, Holmdel, 1968—69; asst. prof. elec. engring. Auburn U., 1969—72, assoc. prof., 1972—73, assoc. prof., head dept., 1973—76, prof., head dept., 1976—. Earle C. Williams Eminent Scholar and dept. head, 1993—; pres. Southeastern Ctr. for Elec. Engring. Edn., Orlando, Fla., 1983—84. Hon. prof. Chinese Acad. Sci., Inst. for Semiconductors, Beijing, 2004. Author: (with Nelson and Carroll) Introduction to Computer Logic, 1975, (with E.R. Graf) Industrial Noise and Vibration Control, 1979, Basic Engineering Circuit Analysis, 1984, 8th edit. (with R.M. Nelms), 2005, (with V.P. Nelson, H.T. Nagle, B.D. Carroll, J.D. Irwin) Digital Logic Circuit Analysis and Design, 1995, (with D.V. Kerns) Introduction to Electrical Engineering, 1995, On Becoming An Engineer, 1997; editor-in-chief The Industrial Electronics Handbook, 1997, Emerging Multimedia Computer Communication Technologies. Fellow IEEE (editor jour. Indsl. Electronics 1982-83, Centennial medal 1984, A.H. Hornfeck Svc. award Indsl. Electronics Soc. 1986, Region III Outstanding Educator award 1989, Meritorious award Edn. Soc. 2005, Ednl. Activities Bd. V.P.'s Recognition award, 2006), Am. Soc. Engring. Edn. (Elec. and Computer Engring. Disting. Educator award 2001); mem. IEEE Edn. Soc. (pres. 1989-90, IEEE-Indsl. Electronics Soc. Achievement award 1991, IEEE Edn. Soc. award 1991, IEEE Edn. Soc./Soc. McGraw Hill Jacob Millman award 1993, Undergrad. Tchg. award 1998, Third Millennium medal 2000, Richard M. Emberson award 2000). Roman Catholic. Home: PO Box 2740 Auburn AL 36831-2740 Office: Auburn U Dept Engring Auburn AL 36849 Business E-Mail: jdirwin@eng.auburn.edu.

IRWIN, JOHN ROBERT, oil and gas industry executive; b. Melbourne, Australia, July 24, 1945; came to U.S., 1969; s. Robert L. and Daisy O. I.; m. Margo E. Mayon, 1979; children: Joshua R., Elizabeth J. BE with honors, Melbourne U., M Engring. Sci., 1969; MS in Indsl. Adminstrn., Purdue U., 1970; AMP, Harvard Bus. Sch., 1990. Registered profl. engr., Australia. Mgmt. program Kerr-McGee Corp., 1970-72; ops. and mgmt. positions Transworld Drilling Co. (sub. Kerr-McGee Corp.), 1972-75; mgr. ops. Transworld Drilling Co., Sharjah, Nigeria and La., 1975-79, Atwood Oceanics, Inc., Houston, 1979-80, gen. mgr., 1980, v.p., 1980-88, exec. v.p., 1988-92; pres., CEO, 1992—. Bd. dirs. Atwood Oceanics, Inc., Offshore Tech. Conf., 1999-2007; chmn. Internat. Assn. Drilling Contractors, 2000. Recipient Young Entrepreneur of Yr. Energy award, Gulf Coast, Ernst & Young, 2006. Fellow: Inst. Engrs. Australia; mem.: Melbourne U. Football Club. Avocations: reading, history, Australian Rules football. Office: Atwood Oceanics Inc PO Box 218350 Houston TX 77218-8350

IRWIN, JOHN THOMAS, humanities educator; b. Houston, Apr. 24, 1940; s. William Henry and Marguerite Harriet (Hunsaker) I.; m. Laura Elizabeth Scott, Sept. 23, 1978 (div. 1991); m. Meme Amosso, May 29, 1993. BA, U. St. Thomas, 1962; MA, Rice U., PhD, 1970. Supr. public affairs library NASA Manned Spacecraft Center, Houston, 1966-7; asst. prof. English, Johns Hopkins U., 1970-74, prof. writing seminars, 1977—, Decker prof. in humanities, 1984—, chmn., 1977-96; editor Ga. Rev., U. Ga., 1974-77. Author: Doubling and Incest/Repetition and Revenge, 1975, expanded edit., 1995, The Heisenberg Variations, 1976, American Hieroglyphics, 1980, The Mystery to a Solution, 1994, Just Let Me Say This About That, 1998, As Long As It's Big, 2005, Unless the Threat of Death Is Behind Them: Hard-Boiled Fiction and Film Noir, 2006; editor: Johns Hopkins Press Fiction and Poetry series, 1978—, Words Brushed by Music, 2004, So the Story Goes, 2005; mem. editl. bd. Hopkins Review, Poe Studies, Ariz. Quar.; contbr. articles to profl. jours. Served with USNR, 1963-66. Recipient John Gardner medal Rice U., 1970, Christian Gauss prize, 1994, Scaglione prize for comparative lit., 1994, Helen C. Smith Meml. award Tex. Inst. Letters, 2006; Danforth fellow, 1962, Guggenheim fellow, 1991. Mem.: Am. Acad. Arts and Scis., Tudor and Stuart Club, F. Scott Fitzgerald Soc., Faulkner Soc., Poe Studies Assn. (v.p. 1995—97), Assn. Lit. Scholars and Critics. Home: 5313 Springlake Way Baltimore MD 21212-3413 Office: Johns Hopkins U Writing Seminars Gilman 135 Baltimore MD 21218 Office Phone: 410-516-6287. Business E-Mail: jirwin@jhu.edu.

IRWIN, JOHN WESLEY, publisher; b. Toronto, Ont., Can., July 11, 1937; s. John Coverdale Watson and Annie Elizabeth (Hiltz) I.; m. Marjorie Eleanor Gray, Dec. 16, 1961; children— John Joseph, Marjorie Elizabeth, Peter David Gordon, Andrew James Gray. BA with honours, U. Toronto, 1959; LLD honoris causa, McMaster U., 1999. Tchr., 1959-60; pres. Book Soc. Can. Ltd. (ednl. books), Agincourt, Ont., 1960-83, Irwin Pub. Inc., 1983-89, Ednl. Project Resources Can. Ltd., Willowdale, Ont., Canada, 1994—96, Scripture Union-Can., 1997—2005. Chmn. bd. trustees McMaster Div. Coll., Hamilton, Ont., 1988-99. Recipient Canadian Confedn. medal, 1967 Mem. Assn. Canadian Pubs. (treas. 1977), Canadian Edn. Assn., Can. Copyright Inst. (gov. 1970-77, 81-99), Inter-Varsity Christian Fellowship Can. (hon. life; dir. 1973-2003, chmn. 1979-91), Canadian Feed the Children (chmn. 1992-95), Peiromai Club (Toronto), Empire Club. Anglican. Home: 81 Bayview Ridge Willowdale ON Canada M2L 1E3 E-mail: jirwinc617@rogers.com.

IRWIN, MARILYN M., librarian, educator; BS, Ind. U., 1972, MLS, 1983, PhD in Libr. and Info. Sci., 1991. Asst. govt. publications dept. Ind. U. Libraries, Bloomington, Ind., 1972—77, assoc. libr., 1993—98, libr., 1998—; cataloger edn. libr. Ind. U., 1977—79, manuscripts cataloger Lilly Libr., 1979—84; dir. ctr. for disability info. & referral Ind. Inst. on Disability and Cmty., Ind. U., 1984—; asst. prof. Sch. Libr. and Info. Sci., Ind. U., 1993—98, assoc. prof., 1998—. Mem.: Ind. U. Librarians Assn., Ind. Fedn. Coun. for Exceptional Children, Assn. Ind. Media Educators, Ind. Libr. Fedn., Ind. Assistive Tech. Standards Implementation Grp., Young Adult Libr. Services Assn., Am. Assn. Sch. Librarians, Assn. for Specialized and Coop. Libr. Agencies (councilor 2001—04, mem. bd. dirs., exec. com. 2001—, pres. 2006—07), ALA. Office: Sch Libr and Info Sci Ind U 755 W Michigan U13100 Indianapolis IN 46202-5195 Office Phone: 317-278-2376. Office Fax: 317-278-1807.*

IRWIN, MARY JANE, engineering educator; b. Cairo, Ill., July 14, 1949; BS in Math., Memphis State U., 1971; MS in Computer sci., U. Ill., 1975, PhD in Computer sci., 1977; Doctorate (hon.), Chalmers U., Sweden, 1997. Grad. rsch. and grad. tchg. asst. computer sci. U. Ill., Champaign-Urbana, 1972—77; asst. prof. computer sci. Pa. State U., University Park, 1977—83; rsch. staff Supercomputing Rsch. Ctr. Inst. for Def. Analysis, Bowie, Md., 1986; assoc. prof. computer sci. Pa. State U., University Park, Pa., 1983—89, dept. head computer sci., 1991—93, prof. computer sci. & engring., 1989—99, disting. prof. computer sci. & engring., 1999—2003, A. Robert Noll chair in engring., computer sci. & engring., 2003—, Evan Pugh prof. computer sci. & engring., 2006—. Recipient Premier Rsch. award, Pa. State U./Product Safety Engring. Soc., 2001, You Make a Difference award, Pa. State U./WEP, 2003, Marie R. Pistilli award, Design Automation Conf., 2004, Disting. Svc. award, Computing Rsch. Assn., 2006, Howard B. Palmer Faculty Mentoring award, Pa. State U., 2006. Fellow: IEEE (Cert. of Appreciation 1993—95, fellow 1994, Best Paper award 2003), Assn. Computing Machinery (Leadership award 1993, fellow 1996, Best Paper award 2003, Disting. Svc. award 2005); mem.: Spl. Interest Group on Embedded Systems, Spl. Interest Group on Computer Arch., Spl. Interest Group on Design Automation (Disting. Svc. award 2005), Nat. Acad. Engring. Office: Dept Computer Sci & Engring 348C Info Sciences & Tech Bldg Pa State U University Park PA 16802

IRWIN, MIRIAM DIANNE OWEN, publishing executive, writer; b. Columbus, Ohio, June 14, 1930; d. John Milton and Miriam Faith (Studebaker) Owen; m. Kenneth John Irwin, June 5, 1960; 1 child, Christopher Owen. BS Home Econs., Ohio State U., 1952, postgrad., 1961—62. Editl. asst. Am. Home Mag., NYC, 1953—56; salesman Owen Realty, Dayton, Ohio, 1957—58, Clevenger Realty, Phoenix, 1958—59; home economist Columbus and So. Ohio Electric Co., 1959—60; pub. Mosaic Press, Cin., 1977—. Owner Bibelot Bindery, 1987—; ptnr. Owen & Irwin, 1978—2005. Author: Lute and Lyre, 1977, Forty is Fine, 1977, Miriam Mouse's Survival Manual, 1977, Miriam Mouse's Costume Collection, 1977, Miriam Mouse's Marriage Contract, 1977, Miriam Mouse, Rock Hound, 1977, Silver Bindings, 1983; editor: Tribute to the Arts, 1984, Chunging, 1996; contbg. author: Publisher's Favorite, 1988; Corals of Pennekamp, 1979. Daytime crew chief Wyoming Life Squad, Ohio, 1966—71. Recipient Norman Forgue award, 2000. Mem.: Miniature Book Soc. (chair 1987—89, past bd. dirs., Glasgow cup 2003), Studebaker Family Nat. Assn. (archivist 2000—, bd. dirs.). Presbyterian. Avocation: book collecting. Home and Office: 358 Oliver Rd Cincinnati OH 45215-2615 Personal E-mail: mirwin@cinci.rr.com.

IRWIN, PETER C., not-for-profit fundraiser; b. Hartford, Conn., Apr. 26, 1964; s. David Henry Irwin and Diane Elaine Campbell. MusB, Syracuse U., 1987. Dir. pub. rels. and devel. Met. Sch. for Arts, Syracuse, NY, 1994—96; exec. dir. Leukemia and Lymphoma Soc. Am., Syracuse, 1996—98; nat. dir. field campaigns Am. Diabetes Assn., Alexandria, Va., 1998—2003; exec. dir. Cystic Fibrosis Found., Liverpool, NY, 2003—04; ind. cons. Syracuse, 2004—05; individual giving officer Ithaca Coll., 2005—06; dir. devel. Friends of Jowonio, Syracuse, 2006—. Pvt. voice instr., 1987—; cons. CNY Jazz Arts Found., Syracuse, 2004—05, Wit's End Players, Syracuse, 2004—06. Mem. Civic Morning Musicals, Syracuse, 1993—, Cmty. Health Charities, Syracuse, 1997—2004, Children's Miracle Network, Syracuse, 1989—94, Nat. Soc. Fundraising Execs., 1998—2000, CNY Assn. Music Tchrs., 2006—; mem. bd. dir. Wit's End Players, 2006—. Mem.: Performing Arts Medicine Assn. (mem. exec. com. 1995—99), Nat. Assn. Tchrs. of Singing (2d pl. voice competition 1987, 1989, 3d pl. voice competition 1990, 1991), Syracuse Opera. Home: 915 Bellevue Terr Syracuse NY 13204 Personal E-mail: pirwin0426@usadatanet.net.

IRWIN, PETER JOHN, orthopaedic surgeon; b. East St. Louis, Ill., July 7, 1934; s. Peter and Anne (Sokalski) Iwasyszyn; m. Kathryn Swanson, June 15, 1960; children: Kathryn Linda, Mary Elizabeth, Amy Marie, Kenneth John, James Patrick. BS in Biology, St. Louis U., 1955, MD, 1959. Diplomate Am. Bd. Orthopedic Surgery, Am. Bd. Forensic Medicine. Intern Creighton Meml. St. Joseph Hosp., Omaha, 1959-60; resident in orthop. surgery U. Ark. Med. Ctr., Little Rock, 1961-65, tchg. staff, 1965-97; pvt. practice Fort Smith, Ark., 1965-97; mem. staff St. Edward Mercy Med. Ctr., 1965-97; ret., 1997. Mem. staff Sparks Regional Med. Ctr., 1965—97, chief staff, 1979, bd. dirs., 1980—87. Lt. comdr. M.C. USN, 1966—68. Fellow: ACS, Am. Acad. Orthop. Surgeons (councillor 1983—89); mem.: AMA, Am. Soc. Sports Medicine, Am. Orthop. Soc. Sports Medicine, So. Orthop. Assn., Mid-Ctrl. States Orthop. Soc. (pres. 1979—80), Clin. Orthop. Soc., Mid-Am. Orthop. Assn. (founding mem., pres. 1993—94), Ark. Orthop. Assn. (pres. 1976—77), Sebastian County Med. Soc. (pres. 1997), So. Med. Assn., Ark. Hand Club.

IRWIN, PHILIP DONNAN, lawyer; b. Madison, Wis., Sept. 6, 1933; s. Constant Louis and Isabel Dorothy (Elfving) I.; m. Sandra L. McMahan, Sept. 14, 1985; children: Jane Donnan, James Haycraft, Victoria Wisnom, Philip Donnan Jr. BA, U. Wyo., 1954; LLB, Stanford U., 1957. Bar: Wyo. 1957, Calif. 1958. Assoc. O'Melveny & Myers, LA, 1957-65, ptnr., 1965-2000, of counsel, 2000—. Mem. planning com. Inst. Fed. Taxation of U. So. Calif. Law Ctr., 1976—, chairperson, 1995-98; spkr. legal seminars. Contbr. articles legal jours. Trustee Mackenzie Found., Los Angeles, 1969—. Recipient Dana Latham Meml. Lifetime Achievement award, LA County Bar Assn. (Taxation Sect.), 2002. Mem.: Calif. Club (L.A.). Republican. Episcopalian. Office: O'Melveny & Myers 400 S Hope St Rm 1835 Los Angeles CA 90071-2899 Office Phone: 213-430-6467. Business E-Mail: pirwin@omm.com.

IRWIN, R. ROBERT, lawyer; b. Denver, July 27, 1933; s. Royal Robert and Mildred Mary (Wilson) Irwin; m. Sue Ann Scott, Dec. 16, 1956; children: Lori, Stacy, Kristi, Amy. Student, U. Colo., 1951-54; BS in Law, U. Denver, 1955, LLB, 1957. Bar: Colo. 1957, Wyo. 1967. Asst. atty. gen. State of Colo., 1958-66; asst. divsn. atty. Mobil Oil Corp., Casper, Wyo., 1966-70; prin. atty. No. Natural Gas Co., Omaha, 1970-72; sr. atty., asst. sec. Coastal Oil & Gas Corp., Denver, 1972-83; ptnr. Baker & Hostetler, 1983-87; pvt. practice Denver, 1987—. Mem.: Rocky Mountain Oil and Gas Assn., Colo. Bar Assn., Denver Law Club. Republican. Office: 650 S Alton Way Apt 4D Denver CO 80247-1669 Business E-Mail: rrisas@msn.com.

IRWIN, RICHARD DENNIS, electrical engineering educator; b. Albany, Ga., Mar. 27, 1958; s. Vernon Hugh and Martha Lucille (Carson) I.; children: Katherine Virginia, Thomas Ralph, Elizabeth Martha. BSEE, Miss. State U., Starkville, 1980; MS, Miss. State U., 1983; PhD, Miss. State U., Starkville, 1986. Registered profl. engr., Ohio. Instr. Miss. State U., 1983-86; assoc. sr. staff engr. Control Dynamics Co., Huntsville, Ala., 1986-87; asst. prof. Ohio U., Athens, 1987-90, assoc. prof., 1990-96, prof., 1996—, chair Sch. EECS, 1997—2002, Grad. chair, 1993—97, Thomas prof. engring., 2001—02; dean and moss prof. of engring. tech. Russ Coll. of Engring. and Tech., Athens, 2002—. Cons. Control Dynamics Co., Huntsville, 1988, Systran, Dayton, Ohio, 1991, Wright State U., Dayton, 1990-92, Nichols Rsch., Huntsville, 1992; mem. steering com. Southeastern Symposium on Sys. Theory, 1988—, gen. chmn., 1994; chair Ohio Engring. Deans Coun. Contbr. articles to Jour. Guidance, Control, Dynamics, Jour., Astron. Sci., Jour. Materials Engring. and Performance, Jour. Optimal Control and Applications, others. Recipient Outstanding Achievement award Ohio Soc. Profl. Engrs., 1989, Russ Rsch. award, 1993, Outstanding Mgmt. award NASA, 2001, Outstanding Project Mgmt. award NASA, 2002; NASA faculty fellow, 1988, 89, 90; grantee NASA, 1988-95, Dept. Edn., 1999-2002 Fellow AIAA (assoc.); mem. IEEE (sr.), Am. Astron. Soc., Am. Soc. Engring. Edn., Internat. Fedn. for Automatic Control (aerospace tech. com. 2000—, vice chair 2002-05), Sigma Xi, Phi Kappa Phi, Tau Beta Pi, Eta Kappa Nu. Achievements include development of frequency domain system identificaiton techniques for flexible systems; demonstration of control system design using experimental data models, first Internet accessible flexible structures control lab. Office: Ohio U Stocker 151 Athens OH 45701 Home Phone: 740-590-2691; Office Phone: 740-593-1479. Business E-Mail: irwind@ohio.edu.

IRWIN, ROBERT JAMES ARMSTRONG, investment company executive; b. Buffalo, June 27, 1927; s. Robert J.A. and Dorothy (McLean) I.; m. Donna Henwood, Sept. 10, 1966; children: William Baird, Elaine Mitchell, Elizabeth Flora, Robert J.A. IV, Ronald Henwood, Derrick Millet. BA, Colgate U., 1949; postgrad., U. Buffalo, 1949-50, Babson Inst. Finance, Wellesley, Mass., 1952-53. With Marine Trust Co. Western N.Y., Buffalo, 1958-66; v.p. Marine Midland Banks, Inc., NYC, 1966-69, sr. v.p., 1969-71; exec. v.p. Dreyfus-Marine Midland Mgmt. Corp., 1970-72; sr. exec. v.p. Niagara Share Corp., Buffalo, 1972-74, pres., 1974-92, CEO, 1988-92, also bd. dirs.; chmn. bd., CEO, treas. ASA Ltd., 1993—2004; chmn., pres., treas. ASA (Bermuda) Ltd., 2004—07; CEO, chmn., pres., treas. ASA Ltd., 2007—. Bd. dirs. Boys Club of Western N.Y., 1953; adv. bd. Hauptman Woodward Med. Rsch. Inst., 1975—; trustee Baird Found., 1965—, Old Ft. Niagara Assn., 1986—, Ridley Coll. Scholarship Fund, Inc., James H. Cummings Found., 1978—, N.Y. State Hist. Assn., Shaw Festival Found. Mem. Saturn Club, Buffalo Canoe, Royal Canadian Yacht (Toronto), Univ. (N.Y.C.). Office: 11 Summer St Buffalo NY 14209-1210

IRWIN, ROBERT W., medical educator; b. Rochester, NY, July 25, 1958; s. Thomas and Penny Irwin; life ptnr. Floyd Gonzales; 1 child, Jane Elizabeth Hasbrouck-Lay. BS, U. N.Mex, Albuquerque, 1976—88, MD, 1988—92. Diplomate La., 1992, NC, 2001, Fla., 2005. Instr. phys. medicine & rehab. Rehab. Inst. Chgo., 1997—98; asst. prof. phys. medicine & rehab. La. State U., New Orleans, 1998—2001, Wake Forest U., Winston-Salem, NC, 2001—05; asst. prof. phys. medicine & rehab. Miller Sch. Medicine U. Miami, Fla., 2006—. Fellow: Am. Bd. Electrodiagnostic Medicine, Am. Bd. Phys. Medicine & Rehab., Am. Acad. Phys.

Medicine & Rehab. Avocations: swimming, running. Office: Univ Miami Miller Sch Medicine PO Box 016960 D-461 Miami FL 33101 Home Phone: 305-460-1833. Office Fax: 305-585-1340. Business E-Mail: rirwin@med.miami.edu.

IRWIN, ROBERT WALTER, artist; b. Long Beach, Calif., Sept. 12, 1928; s. Overton Ernest and Goldie Florence (Anderberg) I.; m. Adele; 1 child, Anna-Grace. Doctorate (hon.), San Francisco Art Inst., 1979, Otis Parson Sch. Art Design, 1992. Pvt. practice art, 1952—; tchr. Chouinard Art Inst., LA, 1957-58, UCLA, 1962, U. Calif., Irvine, 1968-69. John J. Hill prof., lectr. U. Minn., 1981; J. Paul Getty lectr. U. So. Calif., L.A., 1986; Cullinan prof., lectr. Rice U., Houston, 1987-88. Author: Notes Towards a Model.On the Nature of Abstraction, 1977, Being and Circumstances, 1985. Founding mem. Mus. Contemporary Art., L.A., 1981-84. Guggenheim fellow, 1966-67, Mac Arthur fellow, 1984-89. Mem.: AAAL. Office: 32 E 57th St 2nd Fl New York NY 10022*

ISAAC, CHARLES EDWARD, environmental scientist, director; b. Vermilion, Alta., Can., Apr. 29, 1963; s. Vincent Wilfred and Anne Eleanor Isaac; m. Loretta Suzanne Szeligowski, May 23, 2003. BSc, U. Alta., Edmonton, 1985, MSc, 1987; MBA, U. San Diego, 1992. Environ. scientist, Edmonton, 1988—90; prodn. and ops. mgr. Karl Strauss Breweries, San Diego, 1991—98; rsch. mgr. Universal Preservation Techs., San Diego, 1998—2001; dir. bioprocess devel. Diversa Corp., San Diego, 2001—. Mem.: Soc. Indsl. Microbiology. Achievements include patents for vitrification of biological products. Avocations: physical fitness, travel, golf. Office: Diversa Corp 4955 Directors Pl San Diego CA 92121 Home Phone: 619-987-2232; Office Phone: 858-526-5351. Business E-Mail: cisaac@diversa.com.

ISAAC, KAKKATTUKUZHY M., engineering educator, researcher; b. Piravom, India, May 10, 1948; s. Kakkattukuzhy U. and Sosamma Mathai; m. Angela G. George; children: Maya Ann Lunnemann, Andrew John. B of Tech., Indian Inst. Tech., Madras, 1971; PhD, Va. Polytech Inst. and State U., Blacksburg, 1982. Assoc. prof. U. Mo., Rolla, 1991—2000, prof. aerospace engring., 2000—. Fellow: AIAA (assoc.). Office: U Mo 1870 Miner Cir Rolla MO 65409

ISAAC, STEVEN RICHARD, business executive, academic administrator, educator, owner; b. Utica, NY, Dec. 19, 1947; s. Anthony Richard and Camille Cecilia (Potaro) I.; m. Martha Cash, Oct. 9, 1982; children: Charles Wesley, Spencer Anthony. BA in English, U. Buffalo, 1969; MS in Edn./Comm., Syracuse U., 1973; postgrad. in bus. adminstrn. program, Fordham U., 1978. Prin. Media Design Assocs., NYC, 1973—75; dir. multimedia products Am. Mgmt. Assn., NYC, 1975—78; ptnr. Tng. by Design, Inc., NYC, 1978—79; founder, chmn. and CEO Martin Direct, Inc. (formerly The Stenrich Group Inc.), NYC, 1979—96; founder, CEO Martin Interactive, 1995—96; bd. dirs., exec. v.p., COO, Martin Agy., 1996; exec. v.p., sector oper. officer Cadmus Comm. Corp., Richmond, Va., 1996—99; CEO DMW Worldwide, 2000—02; exec. v.p. DIMAC Holdings, 2000—02; mng. dir. Interactive Mktg. Inst., adj. prof. exec. MBA program Va. Commonwealth U., Grad. Sch. Bus., Sch. Mass Comm., Richmond, 2002—; prin., owner Isaac Enterprises, LLC, 2003—; CEO Halyard Ednl. Ptnrs., 2006—. Bd. dir. Charlottesville Venture Group, Va.; mem. adv. bd. DMW Direct; chmn. bd. Halyard Edn. Ptnrs., 2006—. Author: Words for Phone: Writing Winning Telephone Scripts; contbr. articles to profl. jours. Mem. cmty. adv. bd. 1st Capital Bank; bd. dirs., past mem., Shady Grove YMCA, Nat. Tax Edn. Coun. Mem.: Direct Mktg. Assn. (past chair Agy. Leaders Group), Commonwealth Club. Methodist. Office Phone: 201-377-3001. Personal E-mail: steve@stevenrisaac.com. Business E-Mail: sisaac@elearners.com.

ISAAC, SUSAN VICTORIA, literature and language professor, department chairman; b. Sevierville, Tenn., Aug. 27, 1970; d. Robert Carl Wells and Elaine Joann Tallman, Dolores Wells (Stepmother); m. Walter Lon Isaac, Aug. 18, 1993. MA, East Tenn. State U., Johnson City, 1997. Asst. prof. English Ga. Mil. Coll., Milledgeville, Ga., chair of humanities, 2000—. Author fiction. Mem. St. Stephen's Episcopal Ch., Milledgeville, Ga., 2000—06. Recipient Moore Family Fund award, Ga. Mil. Coll., 2004. Mem.: Sigma Tau Delta (life), Phi Kappa Phi (life). Avocations: writing, reading, stained glass, gardening. Office Phone: 478-445-1469.

ISAAC, TERESA ANN, former mayor, lawyer; b. Lynch, Ky., July 3, 1955; d. Samuel Thomas Sr. and Barbara Ann (Thomas) I.; children: Jacob, Alicyn. BA, Transylvania U., 1976; JD, U. Ky., 1979. Bar: Ky. 1979, U.S. Dist. Ct. (ea. dist.) Ky. 1979, U.S. Ct. Appeals (6th cir.) 1980, U.S. Supreme Ct. 1981, U.S. Ct. Appeals (D.C. cir.) 1984. Pvt. practice, Lexington, Ky., 1979—; vice mayor City of Lexington, 1993-99, mayor, 2003—07. Asst. atty. Fayette County Prosecutors Office, Lexington, 1986-88; judge U. Ky. Trial Adv. Competition, Lexington, 1981; assoc. prof. dept. govt. and law Eastern Ky. U., 1983-88; acting dir. Eastern Ky. U. Paralegal Program, Richmond, 1985; legal counsel Ky. Women's Heritage Mus., Inc., 1986, v.p., 1987; selected as one of six Arab-Am. elected ofcls. to monitor the first Palestinian elections, 1996; econs. and govt. prof. Lexington C.C., 1996-97; mem. bldg. com. Fayette County Justice Ctr., 1997. Editor newsletter At Issue, Lexington Forum, 1983-85; pub. The Full Ct. Press, 1986—; author: Sex Equity in Sports Leadership: Implementing the Game Plan in Your Community, 1987. Mem. Lexington Human Resources Adv. Bd., 1982-85, Ky. Displaced Homemaker Adv. Bd., Lexington, 1982-84, NCAA Final Four Host Com., Lexington, 1985; chmn. Ky. Women's Suffrage Day Celebration, 1986—; project dir. Sports Equity Program-Model for South, Ky., 1986—; mem. Philmarm. Guild, 1986—; chmn. Ky. Nat. Women in Sports Day Celebration, 1988; mem.-at-large Lexington-Fayette Urban County Coun., 1990—; bd. dirs. Ky. World Trade Ctr., 1993-97, Housing Found., 1993-97; bd. control Ky. H.S. Athletic Assn., 1993-97; mem. adv. bd. LPGA Jr. Girls Golf Club, 1993-97; mem. Criminal Justice Commn., 1993-97; mem. nat. adv. bd. Dems. 2000, 1993-97; mem. Mil. Support Com., 1997; exec. dir. Lexington Fair Housing Coun., 1999—. Named Best Elected Ofcl. in the Bluegrass, 1994; named one of Top 16 Women in Bus., 1995, 50 Most Powerful People in Sports, 1997; recipient Outstanding Svc. award Lexington Forum, 1985, Woman of Achievement award Miss Ky. Pageant, 1996, Pub. Advocacy award Nat. Assn. Women Bus. Owners, 1998, Sports Equity Leadership award, 1999, Georgia Powers Polit. Courage award Women's Polit. Caucus, 2006, Najeeb Halaby Pub. Svc. award Arab Am. Inst., 2007. Mem. ABA (exec. com. delivery of legal svcs. to women, chair 1987-88, spl. com. on housing and urban devel. law, recipient Silver Key award 1979), AAUW (sec. 1986, state bd. dirs. 1987-88) Fed. Bar Assn., Ky. Bar Assn. (bd. of editors 1983-85, mem. Task Force on Gender Bias in Cts. 1987—), Ky. Acad. Trial Lawyers Assn., Am. Soc. for Pub. Adminstrn., Am. Assn. for Paralegal Edn., Nat. Assn. Women Lawyers (brief bank coord. 1985—), ACLU (chairperson legal panel 1983—), League of Women Voters (voter svc. com. 1985—), Ky. Women Advs. (treas. 1987—, v.p. 1988), Leadership Am., Ky. Women's Polit. Caucus (pres. 1992-93), Lexington C. of C., Phi Mi (legal advisor 1985—). Democrat. Roman Catholic. Avocation: running marathons. Office Phone: 859-245-5933. Business E-Mail: teresa.isaac@kysu.edu.

ISAAC, WILLIAM MICHAEL, brokerage house executive, retired government agency administrator; b. Bryan, Ohio, Dec. 21, 1943; s. Charles R. and Ruth L. (Hallberg) I.; m. Carma Sue Dunbar, Aug. 15, 1965 (div. 1993); m. Christine Verney, Nov. 16, 1997; children: David M., Stephanie A., Lennon G., Quinn V. BS, Miami U. Oxford, Ohio, 1966, LLD (hon.), 1984; JD summa cum laude, Ohio State U., 1969. Bar: Wis. 1969, Ky. 1974, D.C. 1986. Mem. firm. Foley & Lardner, Milw., 1969-74; v.p., gen. counsel, sec. First Ky. Nat. Corp., Louisville, 1974-78; chmn. FDIC, Washington, 1978-85; ptnr. Arnold & Porter, Washington, 1985-93; chmn. The Secura Group, Washington, 1985—, Secura Burnett Co. LLC, San Francisco, 1992—; mem. Depository Instns. Deregulation Com., 1981-85, Bush Task Group, 1982-85; chmn. Fed. Fin. Instns. Exam. Coun., 1983-85, Isaac Property Cos., 1992—. Bd. dirs. MPS Group, Inc., Jacksonville, Fla., TransUnion Corp., Chgo. Co-author: Bank Holding Companies: A Practical Guide to Bank Acquisitions and Mergers, 1972; contbr. articles on banking to profl. jours. Mem. nat. coun. Coll. Law, Ohio State U., Columbus, 1980—; mem. bus. adv. coun. Miami U., Oxford, Ohio, 1982—; trustee Miami U. Found., 1988-96; bd. dirs. Ohio State U. Found., The Cmty. Found. of Sarasota County; chmn.-elect Goodwill Ind.; chmn. Isaac Properties Group. Mem. ABA, Wis. Bar Assn., Ky. Bar Assn., Fed. Nat. Mortgage Assn. (adv. bd. 1989-90). Republican. Office: The Secura Group 1921 Gallows Rd Ste 950 Vienna VA 22182 Office Phone: 703-749-1560. Personal E-mail: billisaac@comcast.net.

ISAACMAN, ALAN L., lawyer; b. Harrisburg, Pa., July 12, 1942; BS, Pa. State U., 1964; JD, Harvard U., 1967. Bar: Calif. 1968, U.S. Ct. Appeals (1st, 2nd, 4th, 9th and 10th cirs.) 1968, U.S. Supreme Ct. 1968. Law clk. to Hon. Harry Pregerson US Dist. Ct. (ctrl. dist.) Calif., 1969—70; sr. ptnr. Isaacman, Kaufman & Painter, Beverly Hills, Calif. Lectr. in field; mem. bd. dirs. New Frontier Media, Inc., 1999—. Fellow: Am. Coll. Trial Lawyers. Office: Isaacman Kaufman & Painter Ste 850 8484 Wilshire Blvd Beverly Hills CA 90211

ISAACMAN, JARED, entrepreneur; b. 1983; Dir. info. systems Merchant Svcs., Inc., NJ; founder, CEO & dir. ops. United Bank Card, Inc., NJ, 1998—. Named a Mover & Shaker, Transaction World, 2005; named one of Best Entrepreneurs Under 25, BusinessWeek, 2006. Office: United Bank Card Inc PO Box 4006 Clinton NJ 08809 Office Phone: 800-201-0461, 908-638-5326. Office Fax: 908-638-4219. E-mail: jared@unitedbankcard.com.

ISAACS, AMY FAY, political organization executive; b. Phoenix, Nov. 11, 1946; d. Richard and Bessie (Wagner) Hamburger; m. John David Isaacs, Oct. 6, 1974; children: Rachel Elizabeth, Stanley Richard. Student, U. Cologne, Germany, 1967-68; BA, Am. U., 1969; MA, Sch. for Internat. Tng., Brattleboro, Vt., 1970. With AID, Washington, 1965-66; tchr. English, Turkish Am. Univs. Assn., Istanbul, 1969; direct mail and fundraising cons., Washington, 1986-87; sr. coord. communications Planned Parenthood Fedn. Am., Washington, 1987-89; various positions Ams. for Dem. Action, Washington, 1969-86, nat. dir., 1989—. Observer del. Liberal Internat., Stockholm, 1984; del. Am. Coun. on Germany, Berlin, Dallas, 1985-87; mem. fin. com. Dukasis for Pres., Washington, 1987-88; mem. quality of care com. Group Health Assn., Washington, 1987-93. Democrat. Jewish. Home: 2018 Pierce Mill Rd NW Washington DC 20010-1023 Office: Ams for Dem Action 1625 K St NW Ste 210 Washington DC 20006-1611

ISAACS, GARVIN ALFRED, lawyer; b. Carnegie, Okla., Apr. 3, 1945; s. Garvin and Ellen Isaacs; m. Beth Kimrey, July 4, 1994; children: eleanor, Jennifer. BA, Tex. Christian U., 1967; JD, Oklahoma City U., 1974. Bar: Okla. 1974, N.Mex. 1987, U.S. Dist. Ct. (no., ea. and we. dists.) Okla. 1975, U.S. Ct. Appeals (10th cir.), 1977. Asst. dist. atty. Dist. Atty.'s Office, Oklahoma City, 1974-75; 1st asst. pub. defender Pub. Defender's Office, Oklahoma City, 1976-78; instr. Nat. Coll. Criminal Def., Oklahoma City, 1979—; pvt. practice Oklahoma City, 1979—. Instr., bd. mem. Trial Lawyers Coll.; instr. Western Trial Advocacy Inst. Mem. ATLA, Oklahoma City Def. Lawyers Assn., NACDL (life). Avocations: painting, photography. Office: 123 NW 8th St Oklahoma City OK 73102-5804 Office Phone: 405-232-2060. Office Fax: 405-232-9035.

ISAACS, GERALD WILLIAM, retired agricultural engineering educator, consultant; b. Crawfordsville, Ind., Sept. 3, 1927; s. William Paul and Verna Ethel (Johnson) I.; m. Phyllis Joyce Seaton, Aug. 22, 1948; children: Joyce Irene (dec.), David Gerald, Donald Phillip, Joseph Lee (dec.), Susan Verna, Linda Kay. BSEE, Purdue U., 1947, MSEE, 1949; PhD in Agrl. Engring., Mich. State U., 1954. Registered profl. engr., Fla. Grad. asst. agrl. engring. dept. agrl. engring. Mich. State U., E. Lansing, 1952-54; instr. agrl. engring. Dept. Argl. Engring, Purdue U., W. Lafayette, Ind., 1948-52, from asst. prof. agrl. engring to prof. agrl. engring., 1954-1964, prof., head dept. argl. engring., 1964-81; prof., chmn. dept. agrl. engring. U. Fla., Gainesville, 1981-91, prof. emeritus, 1991—. Cons. engr. various mfg. and legal firms, 1958—. Contbr. articles to profl. jours. Recipient Massey Ferguson Gold medal Am. Soc. Agrl. Engrs., 1991, Silver medal Max Eyth Gesselschaft, Germany, 1979. Mem. Polish Acad. Sci., Rotary Internat. (dir. 1976-78, Paul Harris fellow 1993), Am. Soc. Agrl. Engrs. (nat. pres. 1982-83), Soc. German Engrs. (hon. corr. mem.); Verien Deuthes Ingeneurs (corr.). Lutheran. Avocations: photography, travel, music. Office: U Fla Dept Agrl and Biol Engring Frazier Rogers Hall Gainesville FL 32611 Personal E-mail: isaacsg@bellsouth.net. Business E-Mail: isaacs@ufl.edu.

ISAACS, HAROLD, history professor; b. Newark, Dec. 19, 1936; s. Albert Lewis and Bertha (Wohl) I.; m. Doris Carol Mack, Apr. 25, 1974. BS in History, U. Ala., University, 1958, MA in History, 1960, PhD in History, 1968. Grad. tchg. fellow hist. U. Ala., Univ., 1959-62; instr. hist. Memphis State U., 1962-65; asst. prof. hist. Ga. Southwestern State U., Americus, 1965-70, assoc. prof. hist., 1970-79, prof. hist., 1979—2005, prof. emeritus hist., 2006. Bd. dirs. World Communities Theater, Ctr. Third World Studies, 2005—; bd. advs. Ency. Developing World; scholar cons. Jimmy Carter Residency Program, Author: Jimmy Carter's Peanut Brigade, 1977; founder, editor Jour. of Third World Studies, 1984—. Advisor Young Dems., Ga. Southwestern State U., 1965-80, chmn. faculty capital campaign, 2003; founder, coord. Third World in Perspective Program Seminar Series, 1981—; coord. Black Leaders Lecture Series, 1981. Recipient Tchr. of Yr. award Alpha Phi Alpha, 1982, Outstanding Svc. award Americus Early Bird Civitan Club, 1983, Outstanding Historian and Humanitarian award SABU, 1994, Presdl. Citation for Disting. Svc., 1995, Outstanding Svc. to African Am. and Third World Studies SABU 1996-97, 1997, All-Africa award African Studies and Rsch. Forum, 2001, Africa Excellence in Scholarship and Svc. award, 2006, Internat. Lincoln Ctr. Disting. Leadership and Scholarship award, 2003, faculty award Univ. Sys. Ga. Regents' Hall of Fame, 2004, Grand Marshal Spl. Svc. award, Ga. Southwestern State U., 1994-2005, Presdl. Medallion award, 2006. Mem. Assn. Third World Studies, Inc. (founder, pres., exec. dir., 1983-91, treas. 1983-97, proceedings editor 2002—, Presdl. award 1992, Harold Isaacs award). Democrat. Jewish. Home: 180 Lakeshore Dr Americus GA 31719-8233 Office: Ga Southwestern State U Dept History & Polit Sci 800 Wheatley St Americus GA 31709 Office Phone: 229-931-2078. Business E-Mail: hisaacs@americus.net.

ISAACS, JONATHAN WILLIAM, oil industry executive; b. Chgo., Apr. 9, 1957; s. Kenneth Sidney and Ruth Elizabeth (Johnson) I. BA, Lake Forest Coll., 1980. Prin. Kenisa Oil Co., Northbrook, Ill., 1980—, Kenisa Drilling Co., Denver, 1986—, broker and appraiser of oil, gas, and water rights, cons. for water rights Baca Ranch. First to utilize Diamonium Phosphate Drilling Mud in Denver Julesburg Basin biodegradable into fertilizer, (HN4) 2 HPO 4; inventor downhole non-metalic oil well tubing system. Mem. NRA, Nat. Skeet Shooting Assn., Ind. Petroleum Assn., Denver Assn. Petroleum Landmen, Rowland Ward, Rep. Mens Club, Exmoor Country Club, Alpha Nu Chi Psi. Nat. Groundwater Assn. Republican. Avocations: dressage, shooting.

ISAACS, JOSEPH C., medical association administrator; BS in Psychology, City Coll. of NY; MS in Hlth. Svcs. Mgmt., U. Mo. Mayor pro tem City of Greenbelt, Md., 1986—91; various positions Nat. Hlth. Policy Forum; former pres., CEO Nat. Hlth. Council; various positions Am. Hospital Assn.; former exec. dir. Am. Occupational Therapy Assn., Bethesda; CEO Nat. Infertility Assn., 2004—07; exec. dir. Assn. of Women's Hlth., Obstetric and Neonatal Nurses, Washington, 2007—. Adv. panel mem. Alzheimer's Assn., Am. Liver Found., Am. Med. Assn., Am. Soc. of Assn. Exec., March of Dimes, Nat. League of Cities, Pharma. Manuf. and Rsch. Assn.; chair Nat. Coalition for Oversight of Assisted Reproductive Tech.; consultant CDC. Fellow, Am. Soc. of Assn. Exec. Office: Assn of Women's Hlth, Obstetric and Neonatal Nurses Ste 740 2000 L St NW Washington DC 20037*

ISAACS, NICHOLAS STEPHEN, music educator, director; b. Beaconsfield, Buckinghamshire, Eng., June 16, 1945; arrived in U.S., 1977; s. Leonard Isaacs and Marianne Bardas; MA in Medieval History (hon.), St. Andrews U., Scotland, 1968; licentiate in piano, Guildhall Sch. Music and Drama, London, 1974; DMA in piano, Stanford, 1986. Music instr. United World Coll. of Atlantic, St. Donats, Wales, 1973—77; music sch. dir. Cmty. Sch. Music and Arts, Mountain View, Calif., 1985—. Curriculum develop. Music Tchrs. Assn. Calif., Santa Clara U., Cmty. Sch. Music and Arts, United World Coll., 1973—; music instr. Foothill Coll., Los Altos Hills, Calif., 1985—86; judge U.S. Open, San Francisco Bay Area, 1984—; lectr. in piano Santa Clara U., Calif., 1993—; choral dir., pianist Congl. Cmty. Ch., Sunnyvale, Calif., 1998—2003; pianist, organist Bethany Luth. Ch., Menlo Park, Calif., 2003—. Recipient Achievement award, Coun. of Arts for Palo Alto, Calif., 1985; scholar, English Speaking Union, Stanford U., 1977—81. Avocations: Scrabble, cats, cooking, old recordings, singing. Office: Cmty Sch Music and Arts 230 San Antonio Cir Mountain View CA 94040 Office Phone: 650-917-6800 ext. 313. Personal E-mail: nsisaacs@hotmail.com.

ISAACS, ROGER DAVID, public relations executive; b. Boston, Oct. 23, 1925; s. Raphael and Agnes (Wolfstein) I.; m. Joyce R. Wexler, Oct. 23, 1949; children: Gillian, Jan. Student U. Wis., 1943; AB, Bard Coll., 1949. With Pub. Rels. Bd., Inc., Chgo., 1948—, account supr., 1948-51, ptnr., 1951-60, exec. v.p., 1960-66, pres., 1966-75, chmn., pres., 1975-86; chmn. PRB, a Needham Porter Novelli Co., Chgo.; exec. v.p., gen. mgr. Doremus Porter Novelli, Chgo., 1986-89; sr. counselor Porter/Novelli, Chgo., 1989-91, The Fin. Rels. Bd., Inc., Chgo., 1991—. Bd. dirs. North Bank, Chgo. Past bd. dirs. Anti-Defamation League Chgo., Jewish Family and Cmty. Svc., Sr. ctrs. Met. Chgo., Highland Park Hosp., Met. Crusade of Mercy, Suburban Fine Arts Ctr., Asthma and Allergy Found., Spertus Coll.; cmty. adv. bd. Sta. WBEZ; bd. dirs. Chgo. Crime Commn.; libr. vis. com. Spertus Inst.; life bd. dirs. Evanston Northwestern Healthcare Found. With AUS, 1943-45. Decorated Purple Heart. Mem. Pub. Rels. Soc. Am. (accredited), Met. Club, Publicity Club Chgo., Birchwood Club Home: 1045 Hillcrest Rd Glencoe IL 60022-1215 Personal E-mail: joroisaacs@aol.com.

ISAACS, SUSAN, writer, scriptwriter; b. Bklyn., Dec. 7, 1943; d. Morton and Helen (Asher) I.; m. Elkan Abramowitz, Aug. 11, 1968; children: Andrew, Elizabeth. Student, Queens Coll., 1965, DHL (hon.), 1996; LittD (hon.), Dowling Coll., 1988. From editorial asst. to sr. editor Seventeen mag., NYC, 1965-70; freelance writer, 1970-76. Author: Compromising Positions, 1978, Close Relations, 1980, Almost Paradise, 1984, Shining Through, 1988, Magic Hour, 1991, After All These Years, 1993, Lily White, 1996, Red, White and Blue, 1998, Brave Dames and Wimpettes: What Women Are Really Doing on Page and Screen, 1999, Long Time No See, 2001, Any Place I Hang My Hat, 2004, Past Perfect, 2007; screenwriter Compromising Positions, 1985; screenwriter, co-producer Hello Again, 1987. Trustee Queens Coll. Found.; bd. dirs. North Shore Child and Family Guidance Assn; adv. bd. Nassau County Coalition Against Domestic Violence; trustee Walt Whitman Birthplace Assn. Recipient Writers for Writers award Poets and Writers, 1996, The John Steinbeck award, 1999. Mem. PEN, Internat. Thriller Writers, Mystery Writers Am. (pres. 2001-02), Nat. Book Critic Circle, Poets and Writers (bd. dirs. 1994—, chmn. 1998—), Authors Guild, Internat. Assn. Crime Writers, Feminists for Free Expression, Creative Coalition, Am. Soc. Journalists and Authors. Jewish.

ISAACSON, ALLEN IRA, lawyer; s. Bernard and Sylvia Isaacson; m. Dena Mishkoff, Mar. 8, 1970; 1 child, David Andrew. AB, Princeton U., 1960; LLB, Yale U., 1963; postgrad., U. Melbourne, Australia, 1963—64; LLM in Taxation, NYU, 1973. Bar: NY 1966. Assoc. Fried, Frank, Harris, Shriver & Jacobson, LLP, NYC, 1966-70, ptnr., 1970—2004, of counsel, 2004—. Fulbright fellow, 1963—64. Mem. ABA, N.Y. State Bar Assn., NYC Bar Assn Home: 15 W 81st St New York NY 10024-6022 Office: Fried Frank Harris Shriver & Jacobson LLP 1 New York Plz Fl 22 New York NY 10004-1980 Office Phone: 212-859-8180. E-mail: allen.isaacson@ffhsj.com.

ISAACSON, MILTON STANLEY (JIM), research and development company executive, engineer; b. Dayton, Ohio, Apr. 23, 1932; s. Max and Sylvia Mariam (Kirsin) I.; m. Joan Sue Koor, Sept. 4, 1955; children: Julie Fay, Jill Ellen, Jan Lynn. BSEE, Ohio State U., 1955. Registered profl. engr., Ohio. Design engr., mgr. quality control, divsn. mgr., dir. R & D Globe Industries, Dayton, 1957—70; pres. Nu-Tech Industries, Inc., Trotwood, Ohio, 1970—. Officer, bd. dirs. Food Svcs., Dayton, 1970-95. Bd. dirs. Grace House Sexual Abuse Resource Ctr., Dayton, 1985—, pres., 1985-89; bd. dirs. Temple Israel Found., 1987-90, pres., 1990; v.p. Jewish Fedn. Greater Dayton, 1984—; bd. dirs. Big Bros./Big Sisters of Greater Dayton, 1965-95, pres., 1978-79; bd. dirs. Old Time Newsies, 1969—, pres., 1991-92. 1st lt. USAF, 1955-57. Recipient Dr. Alan F. Wasserman Leadership award Jewish Fedn. Dayton, 1972, Boss of the Yr. award Nat. Trail chpt. Am. Bus. Womens Assn., 1975, Outstanding Pub. Svc. award Sta. WKEF, Dayton, 1979, Outstanding Svc. award Big Bros./Big Sisters of Greater Dayton, 1977, 88, 304 Cmty. svc. award, 2002, Hon. Judge Carl D. Kessler Meml. award The Grace House, 1991. Mem. IEEE, Rotary (pres. Trotwood club 1989, sec. 1993—), Eta Kappa Nu. Achievements include patents for brushless DC motors and medical devices. Avocations: fishing, travel. Office: Nu-Tech Industries Inc 5905 Wolf Creek Pike Dayton OH 45426-2439 Office Phone: 937-298-6636.

ISAACSON, ROBERT LEE, neurobehavioral scientist, educator; b. Detroit, Sept. 26, 1928; s. Emil Alfred and Evelyn (Johnson) I.; m. Susan Doherty, Dec. 16, 1956 (div. 1972); children: Gunnar, Lars, Mary Ingrid, Mary Christina; m. Ann W. Braden, Dec. 31, 1974; stepchildren: Richard, Milly Braden AB Psychology, U. Mich., 1950, MS Psychology, 1954, PhD Psychology, 1958. Co-dir. U. Fla. Ctr. for Neurobiol. Sci., Gainesville, 1970—78; grad. rsch. prof. U. Fla., Gainesville, 1977—78; disting. prof. psychology SUNY, Binghamton, 1978—, dir. Ctr. Neurobehavioral Sci., 1978—88, Bartle prof., 1998—; prof. U. Cordoba, 2002; hon. prof. Nat. U. Cordoba, Argentina, 2000. Author: Limbic System, 2d edit., 1982; co-author: Fluoride in the Drinking Water, 2006; deditor: (with others) Expression of Knowledge, 1982, The Hippocampus, vols. 3-4, 1986, The Vulnerable Brain and Environmental Risks, vols. 1-2, 1992, vol. 3, 1994. Pres. Alachua County Assn. for Retarded Children, Gainesville, 1973-75; chmn. dist. III Human Rights Advocacy Com., Gainesville, 1975-77. Served with USN, 1950-53, Korea Holloway fellow U.S. Navy, 1946-50; grantee NSF, NIH, U.S. Army Surgeon Gen., NIMH. Fellow APA, AAAS; mem. Internat. Behavioral Neurosci. Soc. (councilor 1991-95, pres. 1999, Myers Lifetime Achievement award 2002), Soc. for Neurosci. (pres. ctrl. N.Y. chpt. 1982-84), Assn. Neurosci. Depts. Programs, Am. Physiol. Soc., Sec. Health Rehab. Svcs. State of Fla. (Blue Ribbon com. 1976), Nat. Rsch.

Coun. (subcom. on fluoride in drinking water, 2003-06) Office: SUNY Dept Psychology Binghamton NY 13902-6000 Office Phone: 607-777-6764. Business E-Mail: isaacson@binghamton.edu.

ISAACSON, SAMUEL B., lawyer; b. Johnstown, Pa., June 28, 1957; BA magna cum laude, Dickinson Coll., 1979; JD, Pa. State Univ., 1982. Bar: Pa. 1982, Ill. 1983, DC 1985. Ptnr., head of Chgo. Litigation group DLA Piper Rudnick Gray Cary, Chgo. Mem.: ABA, Ill. State Bar Assn., Chgo. Bar Assn., Def. Rsch. Inst., Lawyers Club Chgo., Fedn. of Insurance & Corp. Counsel, Phi Beta Kappa. Office: DLA Piper Rudnick Gray Cary Suite 1900 203 N LaSalle St Chicago IL 60601-1293 Office Phone: 312-368-2163. Office Fax: 312-251-5827. Business E-Mail: samuel.isaacson@dlapiper.com.

ISAACSON, STEVEN ROBERT, surgeon; b. Bronx, NY, 1947; BS, Pa. State U., 1969; MD, Thomas Jefferson U., Phila., 1973. Bd. cert. radiation oncology Am. Bd. Radiology, bd. cert. otolaryngology Am. Bd. Otolaryngology. Attending physician Columbia Presbyn. Med. Ctr., 1988—; intern surgery Abington Meml. Hosp., 1973—74, resident surgery, 1974—75; resident otolaryngology U. Pa., 1975—78; resident radiation oncology SUNY Health Sci. Ctr., Bklyn., 1985—88; co-dir. Ctr. for Radiosurgery Columbia Presbyn. Med. Ctr., 1998—. Asst. prof. radiation oncology and otolaryngology Columbia Coll. Physicians and Surgeons Columbia U., NYC, 1990—94, assoc. clin. prof. radiation oncology and clin. otolaryngology, 1994—98, assoc. clin. prof. head and neck surgery in dentistry, 1998—2005, clin. prof. radiation oncology (in neurol. surgery), 2005—. Office: Columbia Presbyn Med Ctr BHN-BII Dept Rad Oncol 622 W 168th St New York NY 10032-3720

ISAACSON, WALTER SEFF, think-tank executive, writer; b. New Orleans, May 20, 1952; s. Irwin and Betsy (Seff) I.; m. Cathy Wright, Sept. 15, 1984; 1 child, Elizabeth Carter. BA, Harvard U., 1974; MA, Oxford U., Eng., 1976. Reporter Sunday Times London, 1976-77; reporter, columnist States-Item, New Orleans, 1977-78; staff writer Time mag., NYC, 1978-79, polit. corr. Washington, 1979-81, assoc. editor NYC, 1981-84, sr. editor, 1985-91, asst. mng. editor, 1991-93; editor New Media Time Inc., NYC, 1993—95; mng. editor Time mag., NYC, 1995—2000; editl. dir. Time Inc., NYC, 2000—01; chmn., CEO CNN News Group, 2001—03; pres., CEO The Aspen Inst., Washington, 2003—. Bd. dirs. Reader's Digest Assn., Tulane U., Nat. Constn. Ctr., Shakespeare Theatre of Washington, United Airlines Corp.; vice-chairperson La. Recovery Authority; chmn. bd. Teach for Am. Author: Pro and Con, 1983, Kissinger: A Biography, 1992, Benjamin Franklin: An American Life, 2003, Einstein: His Life and Universe, 2007; co-author: The Wise Men, 1986 (Harry Truman Book prize 1987). Chmn. bd. Teach for Am. Rhodes scholar, 1974; recipient Overseas Press Club award, N.Y.C., 1981, 84, 87. Mem. Coun. Fgn. Rels., Century Assn., Met. Club of Washington. Office: Aspen Institute One Dupont Cir Ste 700 Washington DC 20036 Office Phone: 202-736-5840.

ISAF, FRED THOMAS, lawyer; b. Jacksonville, NC, Nov. 18, 1950; s. Thomas Fred and Rowanda (Maloof) Isaf; m. June J. Jeffcoat, Aug. 18, 1973; children: Julie, Thomas, Christa. BA, Duke U., 1972; JD, Emory U., 1975, LLM in Taxation, 1978. Bar: Ga. 1975, US Tax Ct. 1978. Shareholder Roberts and Isaf, PC, Atlanta, 1986-94, Roberts, Isaf & Summers, PC, Atlanta, 1994-99; ptnr. McGuire Woods LLP, Atlanta, 1999—2003, Atlanta mng. ptnr., 2003—. Dir. Pinecrest Acad., Atlanta, 1995—2002. Named a Ga. Super Lawyer, Law and Politics and Atlanta Mag., 2004, 2005; named Ga. Super Lawyers, Law and Politics, Atlanta Mags., 2004, 2005. Mem.: State Bar Ga., Cherokee Town and Country Club (sec. 1993, bd. dirs. 1994—2000, v.p. 1997, pres. 1998—99), Order of Barristers, Order of the Coif. Office: McGuire Woods Ste 2100 1170 Peachtree St Atlanta GA 30309 Office Phone: 404-443-5712. Business E-Mail: fisaf@mcguirewoods.com.

ISAKI, LUCY POWER SLYNGSTAD, lawyer; b. Jersey City, Oct. 21, 1945; d. Charles Edward and Ann Mary (Power) Slyngstad; m. Paul S. Isaki, Aug. 26, 1967. BA summa cum laude, Seattle U., 1973; JD cum laude, U. Puget Sound, 1977. Bar: Wash. 1977. Case worker San Joaquin County Welfare, Stockton, Calif., 1968-70, Alameda County Welfare, Oakland, Calif., 1971-73; legal intern King County Prosecutor's Office, 1976-77; law clk. to hon. Justice Hamilton Wash. Supreme Ct., 1977-78; ptnr. Bogle & Gates, Seattle, 1978—99; sr. asst. atty. gen. State of Wash., 1999—2006; mem. exec. team for Atty. Gen. Gregoire, Seattle, 2001—04; Wash. state risk mgr., sr. asst. dir., legal counsel, risk mgmt. contracts divsn. Office Fin. Mgmt., State of Wash., 2006—. Cons. Region X, HHS, 1975; chair task force on alternative dispute resolution Atty. Gen. Gregoire, 1993-94; mem. sentencing guidelines commn. State of Wash., 2006—. Bd. dirs. King County Family Svcs., Seattle, 1982-84, Wash. State Coun. Crime and Delinquency, 1981, Northwest Kidney Ctr., 2001—, vice chair, 2003-05, chair, 2005—; treas. Mother's Against Violence in Am., 1994; trustee emeritus U. Puget Sound, 1985—, Seattle Youth Symphony, 1995, Ea. Wash. U., 1998-99; chmn. law sch. bd. visitors Seattle U., 1984-96; trustee Legal Found., Wash., 1992-95, sec. bd. dirs. 1993, v.p. bd. dirs. 1994, pres. 1995; pres. Kinnear Vistas Homeowners' Assn., 2003-05. Dean's scholar U. Puget Sound, 1976-77; recipient Disting. Law Grad. award U. Puget Sound, 1984, Majis award Seattle U., 1997. Mem. Wash. Women Lawyers (pres. Seattle-King County chpt. 1982, v.p. 1984), ABA (ho. of dels. 1995-97), Wash. State Bar Assn. (bd. govs. 2000-03), King County Bar Assn. (sec. 1986-87, trustee 1987-90, treas. 1995-97, 1st v.p. 1998, pres. 1999-2000, chair govt. lawyers sect. 2004—), U. Puget Sound Law Alumni Soc. (pres. 1979). Democrat. Office: Office of Fin Mgmt PO Box 41027 Olympia WA 98504-1027 Office Phone: 360-902-3058. E-mail: lucy.isaki@ofm.wa.gov.

ISAKOFF, SHELDON ERWIN, chemical engineer; b. Bklyn., May 25, 1925; s. Harry and Rebecca I.; m. Anita Ginsburg, Aug. 18, 1946; 1 son, Peter D. BS, Columbia U., 1945, MS, 1947, PhD, 1952. Guest fellow Brookhaven Nat. Lab., Upton, NY, 1949-50; with E.I. duPont de Nemours & Co., Inc., Wilmington, Del., 1951-90, dir. engring. research and devel., 1975-90, ret., 1990. Mem. Nat. Materials Adv. Bd., 1980-82; adj. prof. Columbia U., 1990—; trustee, United Engring. Trust, 1992-98, pres., 1995-97. Vice chair bd. Chem. Heritage Found., 1992-94, chair, 1995-98. With USNR, 1943-46. Recipient Egleston medal Columbia U., 1994, Alumni medal, 1996. Fellow AIChE (past dir., Founders award 1980, Inst. lectr. 1984, materials divsn. award 1986, v.p., pres.-elect 1989, pres. 1990, Thomas H. Chilton award, Wilmington sect. 1994, Mgmt. Divsn. award 1997, Van Antwerpen award 1997), AAAS; mem. NAE, Am. Chem. Soc., Sigma Xi, Tau Beta Phi, Phi Lambda Upsilon. Home: 102 Center Mill Rd Chadds Ford PA 19317-9212 E-mail: isakoffshe@aol.com.

ISAKOWITZ, STEVEN JEFFREY, federal agency administrator, aeronautical engineer; b. 1961; BS, MS in Aeronautics and Astronautics, MIT. Comml. space cons. Booz Allen Hamilton; project mgr. and sys. engr. Lockheed Martin; policy analyst & mgr. Office Mgmt. & Budget, Exec. Office of the Pres., branch chief sci. and space programs; comptr. NASA, dep. assoc. adminstr. exploration sys. mission directorate, 2005—07; CFO US Dept. Energy, 2007—. Recipient Presidential Disting. Rank award, Outstanding Leadership medal, NASA. Office: US Dept Energy Forrestal Bldg 4A-253 1000 Independence Ave SW Washington DC 20585*

ISAKSEN, ROBERT L., retired bishop; b. Bklyn. m. Beverly Sievertsen; children: Elisabeth, Lois. BA, Concordia Coll., Moorhead, Minn., 1957; MDiv, Luther Sem., St. Paul, 1961; STM, N.Y. Theol. Sem., 1971; DD (hon.), Upsala Coll., 1990. Ordained to ministry Am. Luth. Ch., 1961. Vicar St. Timothy Luth. Ch., Chgo., 1960; pastor Bethlehem, Bronx, NY, 1961-62, St. Peters, Bronx, 1962-68, Bethlehem, Baldwin, NY, 1972-81; Bronx Luth. coord. Planning Assn. of Bronx Luth. Chs., 1968-72; mission dir. Am. Luth. Ch., 1981-87; bishop New Eng. Synod Evang. Luth. Ch. in Am., Worcester, Mass., 1987-2000; ret.; interim pastor Stavanger Internat. Ch., Stavanger, Norway, 2003; transition pastor Trinity Luth. Ch., Great Barrington, Mass., 2003—04. Vis. prof. Yale Divinity Sch., 2001; adv. bishop to Bd. for Outreach, Evang. Luth. Ch. in Am., 1988-91, adv. bishop to Ch. Coun., 1992-97; chair Boston Ch. Leaders Covenant, 1995-96; pres. New Eng. Conf. Ch. Leaders, 1993. Bd. dirs. Luth. Immigration and Refugee Svcs., N.Y.C., 1983-87. Mem., Hendrick Hudson Male Chorus, 2002-. Lutheran. Home: 175 Ashley Hill Rd Brainard NY 12024 E-mail: bpisak1@yahoo.com.

ISAKSON, JOHNNY (JOHN HARDY ISAKSON), senator, former congressman; b. Atlanta, Ga., Dec. 28, 1944; m. Dianne (Davison) Isakson; children John, Kevin, Julie BBA, U. Ga., 1966. Pres. Northside Realty, Atlanta, 1979—98; CEO Fairgreen Capital LP, Atlanta, 1996—99; mem. Ga. Ho. of Reps., 1976—90, Republican leader, 1983—90; mem. Ga. St. Senate, 1994—96, U.S. Congress from 6th Ga. dist., 1999—2005; US senator from Ga., 2005—. Chmn. Ga. State Bd. Edn., 1996—99; mem. com. environment and public works US Senate, com. health, edn., labor and pensions, com. small bus. and entrepreneurship, com. veterans affairs. Winner spl. election to succeed Rep. Newt Gingrich, who resigned, 1999; represented Cobb County in the Ga. legislature 17 yrs.; Rep. candidate for gov. of Ga., 1990, Rep. primary candidate for US Senate, 1996; Sunday sch. tchr. Mt. Zion Meth. Ch., 1978—; adv. bd. Fed. Nat. Mortgage Assn.; bd. trustees Kennesaw State U., Ga.; bd. dirs. Ga. Club, Metro Atlanta C. of C., Ga. C. of C., Riverside Bank. Served with USAF, 1966—67, served as SSG with Ga. Nat. Guard, 1967—72. Recipient Best Legis. in Am. award, Rep. Nat. Com., 1989, Disting. Svc. award, Ga. Mcpl. Assn., Guardian Small Bus. award, Nat. Fedn. Independent Bus., Hero of Taxpayers award, Americans for Tax Reform, Tax fighter award, Nat. Tax Limitation Com., Blue Key award, U. Ga., 1998. Mem.: Realty Alliance (pres.), Nat. Assn. Realtors (exec. com.). Republican. Methodist. Office: US Senate 416 Russel Senate Office Bldg Washington DC 20510 also: One Overton Park Ste 970 3625 Cumberland Blvd SE Atlanta GA 30339-6406 Office Phone: 202-224-3643, 770-661-0999. Office Fax: 202-228-0724, 770-661-0768.*

ISAYEV, AVRAAM ISAYEVICH, polymer engineer, educator; b. Privolnoe, Azerbaijan, Russia, Oct. 17, 1942; s. Isai S. and Basia Isayev; m. Lubov M. Dadasheva, July 26, 1969; 1 child, Daniela. MSChemE, Azerbaijan Inst. Oil & Chem., Baku, 1964; PhD in Polymer Engring., USSR Acad. Scis., Moscow, 1970; MS in Applied Math., Inst. Electronic Machine Bldg., Moscow, 1975. Rsch. assoc. State Rsch. Inst. Nitrogen Industries, Severodonetsk, Russia, 1965—66; predoctoral Inst. of Petrochem. Synthesis Russia Acad. Sci., Moscow, 1967—69, rsch. assoc., 1970—76; sr. rsch. fellow Israel Inst. Tech., Haifa, 1977—78; sr. rsch. assoc. Cornell U., Ithaca, NY, 1979—83; assoc. prof. Inst. Polymer Engring., U. Akron, Ohio, 1983—87, prof., 1987—2001, dir. mold tech., 1987—, disting. prof., 2001—, dir., 2006—07. Guest prof. U. Aachen, Germany, 1986, U. Linz, Austria, 1993, Kyoto Inst. Tech., Japan, 1996, Inst. Polymer Rsch., Dresden, Germany, 1997, U. Sao Carlos, Brazil, 1997; expert on plastics processing technologies, Malaysia, 1995. Author: (monograph) Rheology, 2006; editor: Injection Compression Molding Fund, 1987, Modelling of Polymer Processing, 1991, Liquid Crystalline Polymer Systems Technological Advances, 1996, Rubber Recycling, 2005; mem. editl. bd. Advances in Polymer Tech., 1989—90, Jour Elastomers and Plastics, 1992—, Progress in Polymer Processing Series, 1993—, Jour Applied Polymer Sci., 1995—, Jour. Polymer Engring., 1997—; contbr. articles Internat. Ency. of Composites, Ency. of Polymer Sci. and Engring., Ency. of Matter, Sci. and Tech. and others. Expert witness US Ho. of Reps., Washington, 1988; expert US Army Rsch. Office, 1991; rev. panel NSF, Washington, 1991, 94, 2000-04. NASA fellow, 1985; recipient Laureate of Young Scientists USSR Acad. Scis., 1970, Cert. of Appreciation, U. Akron Bd. Trustees, 1988, 93, Outstanding Rschr. award U. Akron Alumni Assn., 1996, Silver medal The Inst. Materials, London, 1997, Vinogradov prize G. V. Vinogradov Soc. Rheology, Moscow, 2000, Omnova Solutions Signature Univ. award, Akron, 2000, 02, Cert. Recognition for Exemplary Svc., Mortar Bd. and Omicron Delta Kappa, 2003; named Disting. Corp. Inventor, Am. Soc. Patent Holders, 1995. Mem. Am. Chem. Soc. (Melvin Mooney Disting. Tech. award rubber divsn. 1999), NY Acad. Scis., Soc. Plastics Engrs. (Cert. of Recognition 1994), Polymer Processing Soc. (treas. 1989-91), Soc. Rheology. Jewish. Achievements include patents in field of self-reinforced composites, devulcanization of rubbers and decrosslinking of crosslinked plastics; in-situ copolymerization in polymer blends, carbon molding, multi-layer conductive and nonconductive polymers; research in polymer, composite and nanocomposite processing. Office: U Akron Inst Polymer Engring 230 S Forge St Akron OH 44325-0301 Office Phone: 330-972-6673. Business E-Mail: aisayev@uakron.edu.

ISBELL, DAVID BRADFORD, lawyer, educator; b. New Haven, Feb. 18, 1929; s. Percy Ernest and Dorothy Mae (Crabb) I.; m. Florence Bachrach, July 21, 1971; children: Christopher Pascal, Virginia Anne, Nicholas Bradford. BA, Yale U., 1949, LLB, 1956. Bar: Conn., 1956, DC 1957. Assoc. Covington & Burling, Washington, 1957-59, 61-65, ptnr., 1965-98, sr. counsel, 1998—; asst. staff dir. U.S. Commn. on Civil Rights, Washington, 1959-61. Lectr. Sch. Law U. Va., 1962—, Georgetown U. Law Ctr., 1996—. Bd. dirs. ACLU, 1965-92; chmn. exec. bd. Vets. Consortium Pro Bono Program, 1992-05. 2nd lt. US Army, 1951-53. Mem.: ABA (mem. ho. dels. 1986—96, chmn. com. on ethics & profl. responsibility 1991—94), D.C. Bar (gov. 1978—82, pres. 1983—84), Cosmos Club. Home: 3709 Bradley Ln Bethesda MD 20815-4256 Office: Covington & Burling 1201 Pennsylvania Ave NW Washington DC 20004 Office Phone: 202-662-5518. Personal E-mail: disbell@cov.com.

ISBISTER, JENEFIR DIANE WILKINSON, microbiologist, researcher, educator, consultant; b. Rahway, NJ, June 4, 1936; d. Edwin Guy and Alvira Marie (Andrews) Wilkinson; m. James David Isbister, July 23, 1960; children: Wendy Jill Isbister Kalavritinos, Kirstin Ann Isbister Hammond. BS, Newberry Coll., SC, 1957; MS in Med. Tech., Jefferson Med. Sch., Phila., 1958; PhD in Microbiology, U. Md., 1977. Med. technologist Princeton (N.J.) Hosp., 1958-60; instr. med. tech. sch. George Washington U., Washington, 1960-62, rsch. asst., 1976-77; rsch. microbiologist Environ. Biospherics, Inc., Rockville, 1978-80; group leader environ. microbiology dept. Atlantic Rsch. Corp., Alexandria, Va., 1980-89; pvt. practice cons. microbiologist Potomac, Md., 1989—; sr. tech. advisor ARCTECH, Inc., Chantilly, Va., 1989-92. Adj. prof. George Mason U., 1988-92, rsch. prof., 1992—; cons. Orkand Corp., Silver Spring, Md., 1979-80, U.S. DOE, Pitts., 1988-89; cons. Advancis Pharm., Gaithersburg, Md., 2001—, mem. sci. adv. bd., 2003-. Contbr. to book, articles to profl. jours. Sci. fair judge Montgomery and Fairfax County Schs., Md. and Va., 1975—; bd. dirs. Bedford (Pa.) Springs Music Festival, 1984-89. Va.-Carolina Chem. Corp. scholar, 1953; recipient Congl. High Tech. award Congl. Caucus for Sci. and Tech., 1985. Mem. ASTM (vice chair 1983-92, 99-2002), Am. Soc. for Microbiology, Am. Soc. for Clin. Pathologists, Cosmos Club, Phi Kappa Phi, Phi Sigma, Chi Beta Phi. Episcopalian. Avocations: reading, music, tennis, restoring old houses and furniture. Home: 9521 Accord Dr Rockville MD 20854-4302 Office: George Mason U Rm 303E Prince William II 10900 University Blvd Manassas VA 20110 Business E-Mail: jisbiste@gmu.edu.

ISCHINGER, WOLFGANG, ambassador, diplomat; b. Stuttgart, Germany, Apr. 6, 1946; married; 3 children. Student, U. Bonn, Germany, U. Geneva, Switzerland; law degree, 1972; MA in Internat. Law, Internat. Rels. and Econ., Fletcher Sch. of Law and Diplomacy, 1972—73; postgrad., Harvard U. Asst. to cabinet UN sec. gen., NYC, 1973; with German Fgn. Svc., 1975—, mem. policy planning staff, 1977—79, diplomat German Embassy Washington, 1979—82; mem. cabinet Fgn. Min., Bonn, Germany, 1982—90, pvt. sec., 1985—87; dir. Cabinet and Parliamentary Affairs; min. counselor, head polit. sect. German Embassy, Paris, 1990—93; dir. policy planning staff German Fgn. Office, Bonn, 1993—95, dir. gen. polit. affairs, 1995—98, state sec. (dep. fgn. min.), 1998—2001, mem. high level German-Russian Strategy Group, 2000—01; amb. to US Embassy of Germany, Washington, 2001—06; amb. to Eng., 2006—. Bd. dirs. East-West Inst., NY, Am. Field Svc., Fletcher Sch. Law and Diplomacy, Alfred-Herrhausen-Gesellschaft (Deutsche Bank). Avocations: skiing, mountain climbing. Office: Embassy of Fed Republic of Germany 23 Belgrave Sq London SW1X 8PZ England Office Phone: 0044 207 824 1301. Business E-Mail: amboffice@german-embassy.org.uk.

ISDELL, (EDWARD) NEVILLE, beverage company executive; b. Downpatrick, County Down, Ireland, June 8, 1943; came to U.S., 1989; s. Edward Neville and Margaret (Smith) I.; m. Pamela Anne Gill, Jan. 10, 1970; 1 child, Cara Anne. BA in Social Sci., Cape Town U., Republic of South Africa, 1965; PMD, Harvard Bus. Sch. Mgmt. trainee Edgars Stores Ltd., Johannesburg, 1966, Copperbelt Bottling Co., Kitwe, Zambia, 1966-68; various positions The Coca-Cola Co., Atlanta, Zambia, South Africa, 1968—80, regional mgr. Sydney, Australia, 1980—81; pres. Coca-Cola Bottlers Philippines, Inc., Manila, 1981—85; pres., Central European div. The Coca-Cola Co., Essen, West Germany, 1985—89, sr. v.p., pres. Northeast Europe and Africa group Atlanta, 1989-92, sr. v.p., pres. Northeast Europe and Middle East group, 1993—95, pres., Greater Europe Group, 1995—98; chmn., CEO Coca-Cola Beverages plc, England, 1998—2000; CEO Coca-Cola Hellenic Bottling Co. S.A., 2000—01, vice chmn, 2001; sr. internat. cons. to CEO Doug Daft The Coca-Cola Co., 2001—04, chmn., CEO, 2004—. Bd. dirs. Coca-Cola Co., Sun Trust Bank; chmn. US-Russian Bus. Coun. Mem. Ch. of Ireland. Office: The Coca-Cola Co PO Box 1734 Atlanta GA 30301

ISEKEIJE, SOLOMON ROWLAND, artist, educator; s. Rowland Afehide and Caroline Mama Isekeije. MFA, Norfolk State & Old Dominion U., Va., 2002. Asst. prof. arts Hampton U., Va., 2003—, Norfolk State U., Va., 2003—. Juror Harmitage Found., Norfolk, Va., 2006; mem. Artificium Humanitas, Chesterfield, Va., 2006—, Richmond, Va., 2006—, So. Graphics Coun., 2007—. Recipient Merit award, Nat. Youth Svc. Corp, Taraba State, Nigeria, 1992, Stockly Garden Arts Festival, 1999, Disting. Artist award, Yongsan Internat. Artist Assn., Seoul, 2006. Mem.: S.E. Artists Assn., So. Graphics Coun., Coll. Arts Assn. Office: Norfolk State and Hampton University 700 Park Ave Norfolk VA 23504 Home Phone: 757-487-0060; Office Phone: 757-823-8417. Office Fax: 757-823-8844. Personal E-mail: solomonisekeije@hotmail.com. Business E-Mail: sisekeije@nsu.edu.

ISELIN, JOHN JAY, academic administrator; b. Greenville, SC, Dec. 8, 1933; s. William Jay and Fannie Harrington (Humphreys) I.; m. Josephine Lea Barnes, Sept. 8, 1956; children: William Jay II, Benjamin Barnes, Josephine Lea, Fannie I. Minot, Alison Jay Russell. AB, Harvard U., 1956, PhD, 1965; BA, U. Cambridge, Eng., 1958, MA, 1963; degree (hon.), Adelphi U., LI U., Lander Coll. Rsch. fellow Brookings Inst., Washington, 1960-61; sr. writer Congl. Quar., Washington, 1961; corr.-editor Newsweek mag., 1962-65, sr. editor nat. affairs, 1965-69; v.p., pub. Harper & Row Publs. Inc., NYC, 1969-71; pres., trustee Ednl. Broadcasting Corp., Channel 13, sta. WNET, NYC, 1971-87; pres. The Cooper Union for the Advancement of Sci. and Art, NYC, 1988-2000; dir. Marconi Internat. Fellowship Found., 2000—. Adj. prof. Columbia U., 2000—. Mem. bd. overseers Harvard U., 1970-76; mem. Acad. Polit. Sci., mem. Nat. Geog. Soc., Josiah Macy Jr. Found., Ventures in Edn.; Waterford Inst.; mem. Cathedral of St. John the Divine, N.Y. State Archives Inst. Recipient Disting. Citizen award trustees SUNY. Mem. Coun. on Fgn. Rels., Century Club, Harvard Club of N.Y.C. Office: Marconi Foundation 500 Mudd Hall Columbia Univ New York NY 10027 Home: 149 E 96th St New York NY 10128 Office Phone: 212-854-7676. Business E-Mail: jji9@columbia.edu.

ISELY, HENRY PHILIP, association and business executive, integrative engineer, writer, educator; b. Montezuma, Kans., Oct. 16, 1915; s. James Walter and Jessie M. (Owen) I; m. Margaret Ann Sheesley, June 12, 1948 (dec. 1997); children: Zephyr, LaRock, Lark, Robin, Kemper, Heather Capri; m. Jelica Kungulovska, 2001. Student, South Oreg. Jr. Coll., Ashland, 1934-35, Antioch Coll., Yellow Springs, Ohio, 1935-37. Organizer Action for World Fedn., 1946-50, N.Am. Coun. for People's World Conv., 1954-58, World Com. for World Constl. Conv., 1958, sec. gen., 1959-66, World Constn. and Parliment Assn., Lakewood, Colo., 1966—; organizer worldwide prep. confs. World Constnl. Convention, 1963, 66, 67, 1st session People's World Parliament and World Constl. Conv., Switzerland, 1968; editor assn, jour. Across Frontiers, 1959—; co-organizer Emergency Coun. World Trustees, 1971, World Constituent Assembly, Innsbruck, Austria, 1977, Colombo, Sri Lanka, 1978-79, Troia, Portugal, 1991; organizer Provisional World Parliament 1st session, Brighton, Eng., 1982, 2nd Session, New Delhi, India, 1985, 3d Session, Miami Beach, Fla., 1987; mem. parliament, 1982—. Sec. Working Commn. to Draft World Constn., 1971-77, pres. World Svc. Trust, 1972-78; co-founder Builder Found., Vitamin Cottages, 1955—, (chmn. bd. dir s., 1985—), pres. Earth Rescue Corps., 1984-90, sec.-treas. Grad. Sch. World Problems, 1984-99, pres., 1999—, cabinet mem. Provisional World Govt. , 1987—, pres. World Govt. Funding Corp., 1986—, Emergency Earth Rescue Adminstrn., 1995—, co-organizer Global Ratification and Elections Network, 1991—(sec. 1992—), prin. organizer 4th session Provisional World Parliament, Barcelona, Spain, 1996, 5th session, Malta, 2000, organizer first More Oxygen for the World conf., San Antonio, 1998; prof. world problems Grad. Sch. World Problems, 1990—; organizer Com. Five Global Expositions, 2001—. Author: The People Must Write the Peace, 1950, A Call to All Peoples and All National Governments of the Earth, 1961, Outline for the Debate and Drafting of a World Constitution, 1967, Strategy for Reclaiming Earth for Humanity, 1969, Call to a World Constituent Assembly, 1974, Proposal for Immediate Action by an Emergency Council of World Trustees, 1971, Call to A Provisional World Parliament, 1981, People Who Want Peace Must Take Charge of World Affairs, 1982, Plan for Emergency Earth Rescue Administration, 1985, Plan for Earth Finance Credit Corporation, 1987, Climate Crisis, 1989, Technological Breakthroughs for A Global Energy Network, 1991, Bill of Particulars: Why the U.N. Must Be Replaced, 1994, Manifesto for the Inauguration of World Government, 1994, Call to the Fourth Session of the Provisional World Parliament, 1995, Fifth Session, 1997, Critique of the Report of the Commission on Global Governance, 1995, Using Credit Cards and Electronic Accounting to Initiate New Global Accounting, Credit and Finance System, 1996, Double Jeopardy and the Phytoplankton Project, 1997, The Fallacy of Treating Labor as a Commodity, 2000, The Immediate Economic Benefits of World Government, 2000, The First Fifteen Global Ministries of World Government, 2002; co-author, editor: A Constitution for the Federation of Earth, 1974, rev. edit., 1991, also author several other world legis. measures adopted at Provisional World Parliament, 1968-96; co-author: Plan for Collaboration in World Constituent Assembly, 1991, Creator treatment for screen drama History Hangs by a Thread, 1993; designer: prefab modular panel sys. constrn., master plan Guacamaya project, Costa Rica; planner five world fairs, five sessions World Parliament, 2000. Candidate for U.S. Congress, 1958. Recipient hon. rsch. doctorate in edn., 1989, Honor award Internat Assn. Educators for World Peace, 1975, Ghandi medal, 1977, Honor award Internat Soc. Universalism, 1993. Mem. ACLU, Am. Acad. Polit. Sci., Fellowship of Reconciliation, World Union, World Federalist Assn., World Future Soc., Earth

Island Inst., Populatin Reference Bur., Earth Action, People's Congress, Life Ext. Found., Interfaith Alliance, Internat. Assn. for Hydrogen Energy, Friends of Earth, Wilderness Soc., Solar Energy Soc., Sierra Club, Amnesty Internat., World Resources Inst., Human Rights Watch, Nat. Nutritional Foods Assn., Environ. Def. Fund, Greenpeace, Ctr. for Study of Democratic Instns., War Resistors League, Audubon Soc., Worldwatch Inst., Internat. Assn. Constl. Law, Earth Regeneration Soc., Zero Population Growth, Cancr Control Soc., Mt. Vernon Country Club, Lakewood Country Club. Socialist. Home: Lookout Mountain 241 Zephyr Ave Golden CO 80401-9589 Office: 8800 W 14th Ave Lakewood CO 80215-4817 Office Phone: 303-233-3548. Fax: 303-237-7685, 303-526-7933. E-mail: wcparliament@uswest.net.

ISEMAN, MICHAEL DEE, medical educator; b. St. Paul, Mar. 3, 1939; s. Manuel Wessel and Eileen Catherine (Croghan) I.; m. Joan Marie Christensen, Aug. 31, 1963; children: Thomas Michael, Matthew Charles. BA in History, Princeton U., 1961; MD, Columbia U., 1965. Intern, jr. resident in medicine Columbia Svc., Bellevue Hosp., NYC, 1965-67; sr. resident in medicine Columbia Svc., Harlem Hosp., NYC, 1969-70; fellow pulmonary medicine Harlem Hosp., NYC, 1970-72; assoc. dir. pulmonary svc. Denver Gen. Hosp., 1972-82; chief clin. mycobacteriology svc. Nat. Jewish Med. and Rsch. Ctr., Denver, 1982—2004. Asst. prof. medicine U. Colo. Sch. Medicine, Denver, 1973-79, assoc. prof. medicine, 1979-89, prof., 1989—. Author: A Clinician's Guide to Tuberculosis, 1999; assoc. editor Am. Rev. Respiratory Diseases, N.Y., 1984-89; editor-in-chief Internat. Jour. Tuberculosis and Lung Disease, 1997-2003. Pres. Am. Lung Assn. Colo., Denver, 1982-83; alumni trustee Princeton U., 1981-85. Lt. comdr. USN, 1967-69. Prin. investigator devel. and evaluation of drugs for treatment of mycobacterium avium in AIDS, NIH, 1984-1992. Fellow ACP, Am. Coll. Chest Physicians; mem. Am. Thoracic Soc. (v.p. 1983-84). Presbyterian. Avocations: rowing, skiing, tennis, photography, history. Office: Nat Jewish Med and Rsch Ctr 1400 Jackson St Denver CO 80206-2762 Business E-Mail: isemanm@njc.org.

ISEMINGER, GARY HUDSON, philosophy educator; b. Middleboro, Mass., Mar. 3, 1937; s. Boyd Austin and Harriet Herring (Hudson); m. Andrea Louise Grove, Dec. 18, 1965; children: Andrew, Ellen. BA, Wesleyan U., 1958; MA, Yale U., 1960, PhD, 1961. Instr. philosophy Yale U., 1961-62, Carleton Coll., Northfield, Minn., 1962-63, asst. prof., 1963-68, assoc. prof., 1968-73, prof., 1973-94, William H. Laird prof. philosophy and liberal arts, 1994—2002, Stephen R. Lewis, Jr. prof. philosophy and liberal learning, 2002—04, emeritus, 2004—. Vis. fellow Kings Coll., London, 1966, U. Lancaster, 1991; chair student-faculty adminstrn. com. Carleton Coll., 1970-71, dept. philosophy, 1972-75, 86-89, 98—, ednl. policy com., 1973-74, English dept. rev. com., 1973-74, com. Lucas Lectrs. in Arts, 1977-81, presdl. inauguration, 1987, edn. dept. rev. task force, 1988, Am. studies program rev. com., 1992, mem. tenure and devel. rev. com., 1985-87, Coll. Coun., 1987, Coll. Marshall, 2001-04; acad. vis. London Sch. Econs., 1971; vis. prof. philosophy U. Minn., 1979, Mayo Med. Sch., 1986, 87, U. Lancaster, 1994, Trinity Coll. Dublin, 2000, Lingnan U., Hong Kong, 2003; Belgum meml. lectr. St. Olaf Coll., 1997; vis. lectr. Uppsala (Sweden) U., 2005; panelist divsn. fellowships NEH, 1980, 91; commentator Minn. Pub. Radio, 1981; dir. London arts program Associated Colls. Midwest, 1982; cons. Harvard U. Press, Univ. Calif. Press, Prentice-Hall, Cornell U. Press, Holt, Rinehart and Winston, Vanderbilt U. Press, Jour. Aesthetics and Art Criticism, Dialogue, Notre Dame Jour. Formal Logic, Jour. of Philosophy and Phenomenological Rsch., Inquiry; external reviewer, evaluator various philosophy depts.; presenter in field. Author: An Introduction to Deductive Logic, 1968, Logic and Philosophy: Selected Readings, 1968, 2d edit., 1980, Knowledge and Argument, 1984, Intention and Interpretation, 1992, The Aesthetic Function of Art, 2004; mem. editl. bd. Am. Philos. Quar., 1989-92, Jour. of Aesthetics and Art Criticism, 1993—; contbr. articles, revs. to profl. jours. Mem. Minn. Humanities Commn., 1984-90, chair 1988-89 Grantee NSF Coun. Philos. Studies, 1968, Bush Found., 1983, Sloan Found. 1984, Faculty Devel. Endowment, 1989, 94, 2000, NEH, 1990, 91; recipient summer stipend NEH, 1971, 78, Disting. Alumnus award Wesleyan U., 1993; Woodrow Wilson fellow, 1958, fellow Univ. Coll., London, 1975, 78, Inst. Adv. Studies in the Humanities, U. Edinburgh, 1985; vis. scholar Cambridge U., 1996, York U., 2002. Mem. AAUP (pres. Carleton chpt. 1967-68), Am. Philos. Assn. (program com. western divsn. 1982, task force on the philosophy major 1989-90, program com. ctrl. divsn. 1991, chmn. com. on tchg. philosophy 1993-96, com. to award Matchette prize in philosophy 1993-95, bd. officers 1993-96), Am. Soc. Aesthetics (trustee 1996-99), Minn. Philos. Soc. (pres. 1978-79), Phi Beta Kappa (pres. Carleton chpt. 1968-69). Avocations: timpani, jazz vibraphone, choral singing. Office: Carleton College One North College St Northfield MN 55057-4002 E-mail: giseming@carleton.edu.

ISENBERG, ABRAHAM CHARLES, shoe manufacturing company executive; b. Lynn, Mass., Feb. 24, 1914; s. Louis and Alice (Lown) I.; m. Thelma F. Sisenwine, Oct. 30, 1938; children: Gerald, Lee Carol, Edward. BS, Wharton Sch., U. Pa., 1935. Cert. paralegal vol., county ct. mediator, lic. mediator, Fla. With Consol. Nat. Shoe Corp., Norwood, Mass., 1935—, exec. v.p., 1967-68, pres., CEO, 1968-72, chmn. bd., treas., 1972-74. Vice chmn. shoe divsn. Greater Boston area Combined Jewish Philanthropies, 1968—. Bd. dirs. New Eng. Anti-Defamation League of B'nai B'rith. Mem. Two Ten Assocs. (bd. dirs. 1956—, v.p. 1969—), Am. Footwear Assn. (bd. dirs. 1968, regional v.p. 1970—), Am. Footwear Inst. (trustee 1970-74), Boston Boot and Shoe Club (exec. com. 1967—, v.p. 1969, pres. 1973), Brandeis U. Men's Assocs. (bd. dirs. 1966—), Beta Sigma Rho. Clubs: Hebrew Rehab. Ctr. Men's (bd. dirs. 1970-72), B'nai B'rith (bd. dirs. 1979—). Home: 2480 N Park Rd Apt 314 Hollywood FL 33021 Personal E-mail: abethelma@webtv.net. *I have found that being honest and ethical with those I associated with in business or community affairs was the most rewarding behavior I could follow. I realize that some who act entirely contrary to these principles appear to be very successful, but I would not want success on those terms.*

ISENBERG, ANN MARIE, psychologist; b. Bellefonte, Pa., Sept. 30, 1949; d. Melvin William and Edna Saby Isenberg. BA in Psychology, Pa. State U., 1982; PhD in Clin. Psychology, Mich. State U., 1991. Lic. psychologist Del., 1998, Pa., 2005. Rehab. counseling specialist VA-Vet Ctr., St. Paul, 1989—90; tech. asst., rschr. Louise Guerney, PhD, University Park, Pa., 1991—93; psychologist-in-tng. L.T. Clayton & Counseling Assocs., State College, Pa., 1993—98; outpatient therapist Altoona Regional Health Sys., Pa., 1999—2005; psychologist Susquehanna Valley Profl. Assn., 2005—. In-plant rep., Corning-Asahi EAP Design, State College, 1993—96; agy. rep. to Centre County Coun. Human Svcs. L.T. Clayton & Counseling Assocs., State College, 1995—98; bd. mem. Ctrl. Pa. Drug & Alcohol Tng. Consortium, State College, Pa., 1995—98; behavioral health svc. rep. to hosp. safety com. Altoona Regional Health Sys., 2002—05. Contbr. Vol. AAUW, State College, 1994—, Centre County Dem. Party, 1992—. Mem.: APA, Pa. Psychol. Assn., Ctrl. Pa. Civil War Round Table, Psi Chi, Phi Kappa Phi, Phi Beta Kappa, Alpha Delta Pi. Democrat. Episcopalian. Avocations: reading, antiques, walking, music, films. Home: 721 S Sparks St State College PA 16801 Home Phone: 814-238-6103; Office Phone: 814-867-0670. Personal E-mail: amifriend2@msn.com.

ISENBERG, HENRY DAVID, microbiology educator; b. Giessen, Germany, Mar. 9, 1922; came to U.S., 1937, naturalized, 1943; s. Gerson and Flora (Gruenebaum) I.; m. Lila S. Grossman, Feb. 15, 1948; children: Ina Pepi Isenberg Stein, Gerald Alan. BS, CCNY, 1947; MA, Bklyn. Coll., 1951; PhD, St. Johns U., 1959. Diplomate Am. Bd. Med. Microbiology (chmn. 1976-79, Disting. Svc. award 1994). Asst. dir. Angrist Labs., 1947-54; chief microbiology L.I. Jewish Med. Ctr., New Hyde Park, NY, 1954-97, chief emeritus, cons., 1997—2002, chief emeritus microbiology (pathology), dir. infection control (medicine), 2002—05, chief emeritus, 2005—; cons. clin. microbiology Mt. Sinai Med. Ctr., 1997—2001; cons. Univs. Space Rsch. Assn., 1998—; asst. clin. prof. orthopedic surgery SUNY Downstate Med. Ctr., Bklyn., 1963-68, assoc. clin. prof. orthopedic surgery, 1968-71, professorial lectr. orthopedic surgery, 1971-89. Prof. clin. pathology SUNY Health Sci. Ctr., Stony Brook, 1970-89; clin. prof. microbiology and immunology U. South Fla. Sch. Medicine, 1982-87; prof. lab. medicine Albert Einstein Coll. Medicine, 1989-96, prof. pathology, 1996-05, prof. emeritus, 2005—; cons. in microbiology NASA, 1990—; lectr. pathology Mt. Sinai Sch. Medicine, 1998-2001 Editor Jour. Clin. Microbiology, 1974-79, editor-in-chief, 1979-89; editor CRC Critical Revs. in Microbiology, 1978-81; editor in chief: CRC Forum in Bacteriology; sect. editor Manual of Clin. Microbiology, 4th edit.; editor: Manual of Clinical Microbiology, 5th edit.; editor-in-chief Clinical Microbiology Procedures Handbook, 1991-2002, 2d edit. 2002-04, Essential Procedures in Clinical Microbiology, 1997-2002; mem. editl. bd. Applied Microbiology, 1969-74; contbr. numerous articles to profl. jours. and books; patentee in field. Served with U.S. Army, 1943-45. Named Microbiologist of Yr. Lab World Mag., 1978; recipient Kimble awrd, 1980; Profl. Recognition award Am. Bd. Microbiology/Am. Acad. Microbiology, 1994. Fellow Am. Acad. Microbiology (bd. govs.), N.Y. Acad. Scis., Am. Inst. Chemists, Infectious Disease Soc. Am., N.Y. Acad. Medicine; mem AAAS, Am. Soc. Microbiology (Becton-Dickinson award 1979, Alexander C. Sonnenwirth Meml. Lectr. award 1989, Disting. Svc. award N.Y. br. 1991, nat. 1996, hon. mem. 1999), Harvey Soc., Sigma Xi. Jewish. Home: 26910 Grand Ctrl Pky Apt 22D Floral Park NY 11005-1022 E-mail: hisenberg@nyc.rr.com.

ISENBERG, JANE FRANCES, writer, retired language educator; b. Paterson, NJ, Aug. 27, 1940; d. Hymen and Marian Alma (Spitz) Siegendorf; m. Donald Windham Isenberg, Aug. 19, 1962 (dec. June 1985); children: Rachel, Daniel; m. Philip J. Tompkins, Dec. 20, 1997. BA in English, Vassar Coll., Poughkeepsie, NY, 1962; MA in English, Southern Conn. State Coll., 1971; PhD in Applied Linguistics, N.Y.U., 1993. English tchr. Richard C. Lee, James Hillhouse H.S., New Haven, Conn., 1962-69; tchr. South Central C.C., New Haven, Conn., 1969-77; dir. Outreach Program Human Resources Adminstrn., New Haven, Conn., 1976-77; tchr. Goddard Coll., Plainfield, Vt., 1975-77; prof. English Hudson County C.C., Jersey City, N.J., 1979—. Tchr. Yale U., New Haven, summers 1977-78, Stevens Inst. Tech., Hoboken, NJ, summer 1982; bd. trustees Jewish Family and Counseling Svcs., Bayonne, NJ, 1994—, The Hudson Sch., Hoboken, NJ, 1979-89, Stevens Coop. Sch., Hoboken, 1978-84; presenter in field. Author: Going by the Book: The Role of Popular Classroom Chronicles in the Professional Development of Teachers, 1994 (James N. Britton award Nat. Coun. Tchrs. English 1994); (novels) The 'M' Word, 1999, Death in a Hot Flash, 2000, Mood Swings to Murder, 2000, Midlife Can Be Murder, 2001, Out of Hormone's Way, 2002, The Proof is in The Patch, 2003, Hot and Bothered, 2003, Hot on the Trail, 2004, Hot Wired, 2005; co-editor Award Winning Papers, 1993—. Grantee Am. Studies, Yale U., New Haven, Conn., 1965, NDEA, Wesleyan U., Middleton, Conn., 1966; recipient Mid-Career fellowship Princeton (NJ) U., 1991-92. Mem. MLA, Hudson County Country Club Profl. Assn., Hudson Reading Coun., Lang. Educators Appying Reflection Now, Nat. Coun. Tchrs. English, NJ Edn. Assn., NJ Reading Assn., NY Metro. Assn. for Developmental Edn., NY State TESOL. Home Phone: 425-391-6941. Personal E-mail: janeisenberg@aol.com.

ISENBERG, STEVEN LAWRENCE, retired publishing executive; b. Detroit, Oct. 19, 1940; s. A.G. Jerry and Lucille (Potaschnik) Isenberg; m. Barbara Lee Levy, Nov. 26, 1967; 1 child, Christopher Michael. BA in English, U. Calif., Berkeley, 1962; BA in English Lang. and Lit., Oxford U., Eng., 1964, MA, 1966; JD, Yale U., 1976; DHL (hon.), Adelphi U., 2000. Bar: N.Y. 1976. Asst. to dir. Bur. Budget, NYC, 1967—68; chief staff, asst. to mayor Office of Mayor, NYC, 1969—73; litigator Breed, Abbott and Morgan, NYC, 1976—82; asst. to pub. Newsday, LI, NY, 1982—83; pub., CEO So. Conn. Newspapers, Stamford, 1983—86; assoc. pub. Newsday, N.Y. Newsday, NYC, 1986—90; pub. Sports, Inc., NYC, 1987—88; exec. v.p. mktg. L.A. Times, 1991—92; deputy pub. Newsday/N.Y. Newsday, Melville, 1992—95; pub. N.Y. Newsday, 1994—95. Reuters fellow Green Coll., Oxford, 1997; vis. prof. U. Calif., Berkeley, 1996; chmn. bd. trustees Adelphi U., Garden City, NY, 1997—2001, pres. ad interim, 1999—2000, chmn. emeritus, 2001—; lectr. Yale Coll., 1999; vis. scholar, lectr. The New Sch., 1999; vis. prof. humanities Polytechnic U., Bklyn., 2000; Batten prof. pub. policy Davidson (N.C.) Coll., 2001; vis. prof. humanities U. Tex., Austin, 2002—. Pres. adv. bd. U. Calif. Coll. Letters and Scis., Berkeley; emeritus chmn. bd. trustees Adelphi U., LI; bd. dirs. Franklin & Eleanor Roosevelt Inst.; mem. presdl. campaign staff Robert F. Kennedy, 1968, John V. Lindsay, 1972; bd. dirs. Mcpl. Arts Soc., Com. to Protect Journalists. Hon. fellow, Worcester Coll., Oxford, 2006. Mem.: Coun. Fgn. Affairs, Century Assn., Yale Club. Democrat. Jewish. Home: Apt 3N 151 Central Park W New York NY 10023-1514

ISENSEE, PAUL RALPH, music educator, minister; b. Eugene, Oreg., Nov. 18, 1947; s. Ralph Henry and Joy Louise Isensee; m. Rebecca Russau Isensee, Jan. 5, 1974; children: Jonathan, Derrie, Courtney. BA, Seattle Pacific U., 1969; MDiv, Western Bapt. Seminary, 1973, M Ch. Music, 1977; DMA, Southwestern Bapt. Theol. Seminary, 1991. Music dir. Hinson Meml. Bapt. Ch., Portland, Oreg., 1972—73; min. of edn. and music First Bapt. Ch., Albany, Oreg., 1973—77; min. music Cmty. Bapt. Ch., Manhattan Beach, Calif., 1977—84, Northwest Bible Ch., Ft. Worth, 1984—92; prof. Southeastern Bible Coll., Birmingham, Ala., 1992—93; min. music Calvary Bapt. Ch., Canton, Mich., 1993—2002; dean, sch. music and performing arts Phila. Biblical U., Langhorne, Pa., 2002—. Mem.: Nat. Assn. Sch. Music, Am. Choral Dir. Assn. Office: Phila Biblical U 200 Manor Ave Langhorne PA 19047

ISERBYT, CHARLOTTE THOMSON, researcher, writer, educational consultant; b. Bklyn., Oct. 26, 1930; d. Clifton Samuel and Charlotte Deyer Thomson; m. Johan Louis Iserbyt, Sept. 26, 1964; children: Robert Louis, Samuel Thomson. Diploma in Secretarial, Exec., Academic Studies with honors, Katharine Gibbs Sch., 1949. Social worker ARC, Anderson AFB, 1953—55; sec. to amb. US Dept. State, Pretoria, South Africa, 1959—60, Brussels, 1961—63; co-founder Guardians Edn. Maine, Camden, 1978—2000; sr. policy advisor US Dept. Edn., Washington, 1980—82; pres. 3D Rsch. Co., Bath, Maine, 1999—. Freelance writer, 1973—2005; host, guest radio talk shows, 1999—2005. Author: (books) Back to Basics Reform or.OBE.Skinnerian International Curriculum, 1985, 2d edit., 1993, the deliberate dumbing down of america.A Chronological Paper Trail, 1999, 3d edit., 2003; contbr. articles various profl. jours. and newspapers. Elected sch. bd. mem. Camden-Rockport Sch. Dist., 1976—79. Mem.: DAR. Independent. Roman Catholic. Avocations: languages, collecting old books, history. Home: 519 River Rd Dresden ME 04342 Home Phone: 207-442-7899; Office Phone: 207-737-4730. Personal E-mail: dumbdown00@yahoo.com.

ISERSON, KENNETH VICTOR, bioethicist, writer, medical educator; b. Washington, Apr. 8, 1949; s. Isadore I. and Edith (Swedlow) I.; m. Mary Lou Sherk, June 16, 1973. BS, U. Md., 1971, MD, 1975; MBA, U. Phoenix, 1987. Diplomate Am. Bd. Emergency Medicine, Nat. Bd. Med. Examiners; cert. in Thanatology: Death, Dying and Bereavement, Assn. Death, Dying and Counseling, 2003. Intern surgery Mayo Clinic, Rochester, Minn., 1975; resident emergency medicine Cin. Gen. Hosp., 1976-78; capt. USAF, 1978-80; chmn. emergency dept. Tex. A&M Coll. Medicine, Temple, 1980-81; asst. prof. surgery U. Ariz. Coll. Medicine, Tucson, 1981-84, residency dir. emergency medicine, 1981-91, assoc. prof. surgery, 1984-92; dir. Ariz. Bioethics Program U. Ariz., Tucson, 1991—, prof. surgery, 1992—2001; prof. emergency medicine U. Ariz. Coll. Medicine, Tucson, 2001—; supervisory med. officer Disaster Med. Assistance Team AZ-1 Dept. Homeland Security, 2002—. Pres. Iserson Assocs. Ltd., Tucson, 1984—; vis. scholar Ctr. Clin. Med. Ethics U. Chgo., Pritzker Sch. Medicine, 1990-91. Author: Iserson's Getting Into a Residency: A Guide for Medical Students, 1988, 7th edit., 2006, Death to Dust: What Happens to Dead Bodies?, 1994, 2nd edit., 2001, Non-Standard Medical Electives in the U.S. and Canada, 1997, 2nd edit., 1998, Get Into Medical School! A Guide for the Perplexed, 1997, 2nd. edit., 2004, Grave Words: Notifying Survivors About Sudden Unexpected Death, 1999, (video and slide sets) The Gravest Words, 2000, Demon Doctors: Physicians as Serial Killers, 2002; sr. editor: Ethics in Emergency Medicine, 1986, 2nd edit., 1995; mem. editl. bd. Cambridge Quar., 1991—, Jour. Emergency Medicine, 1985—; contbr. sci. articles to profl. jours. Med. dir. So. Ariz. Rescue Assn., Pima County, 1983—. Fellow Am. Coll. Emergency Physicians (life): mem. AMA, Med. Soc. US and Mex. (treas. 2002-03, v.p. 2003-04, pres. 2004-06), Soc. Acad. Emergency Medicine (pres. 1984-85), Wilderness Med. Soc. (bd. dir. 1987-91). Office Phone: 520-626-2398. E-mail: kvi@u.arizona.edu.

ISH, DANIEL RUSSELL, law educator, academic administrator; b. Loon Lake, Sask., Can., Aug. 28, 1946; s. Leme Jay and Obeline Delia (Sicotte) I.; m. Diane Maureen Cote, Sept. 2, 1967 (div. 1970); m. Bonnie Jeanne Bolger, Dec. 22, 1970; children: Jason Bolger, Rachel Bolger. LLB, BA, U. Sask., 1970; LLM, Osgoode Hall Law Sch., Toronto, Ont., Can., 1974. Bar: Alta. 1971, Sask. 1979; called to Queen's Counsel, 1991. Lawyer H. Lloyd MacKay, Banff, Alta., Canada, 1970-71; asst. prof. law McGill U., Montreal, Que., Canada, 1972-75; assoc. prof. U. Sask., Saskatoon, 1975-80, prof. law, 1980—, asst. dean law, 1977-78, dean, 1982—88, 1996—97, 2002—04; dir. Ctr. for Study of Coops., 1989-95. Author: The Taxation of Canadian Co-operatives, 1975, The Law of Canadian Co-operatives, 1981, Co-operatives in Principle and Practice, 1992, Legal Responsibilities of Directors and Officers in Canadian Cooperation, 1996. Pres. Univ. Credit Union, Saskatoon, 1979-80. Fulbright fellow, Stanford U., 1995—96. Mem. Law Found. Sask. (trustee 1982-88, 2002—), Law Soc. Sask. (bencher 1982-88, 2002—). Avocations: skiing, running. Office: U Sask Coll Law Saskatoon SK Canada S7N 5A6 Office Phone: 306-966-5870.

ISHAK, WAGUIH WILLIAM, psychiatrist; b. Port Said, Egypt, Oct. 16, 1964; s. William Makram IsHak and Nawara Yacoub Dawoud; m. Asbasia A Mikhail-IsHak, M.D.; children: William Waguih, Michael Waguih. MD, Cairo U., 1987. Dir., psychiatry residency tng. program Cedars-Sinai Med. Ctr., LA, 2001—, med. dir., adult outpatient psychiatry, 2003—. Assoc. dir., psychiatry residency program NYU Sch. of Medicine, NYC, 1998—2001. Editor: Outcome Measurement in Psychiatry: A Critical Review (Reviews in the Am. Jour. of Psychiatry and Psychiat. Services, 2003). Fellow: Am. Psychiat. Assn. Achievements include development of Online screening tests for psychiatric disorders. Office: Cedars-Sinai Medical Center 8730 Alden Dr Thalians W-157 Los Angeles CA 90048 Office Phone: 310-423-3481. Office Fax: 310-423-3497.

ISHAK-BOUSHAKI, MUSTAPHA, research scientist, physicist; s. Moh Ishak-Boushaki and Malika Beggar; m. Samia Boucetta; children: Adam, Zak. PhD, Queen's U., Kingston, Ont., Can., 2002. Assoc. rschr. Princeton U., NJ, 2003—05; asst. prof. U. Tex.-Dallas, Richardson, 2005—. Author: (sci. computer program sys.) An Online Interactive Geometric Database: Including Exact Solutions of Einstein's Field Equations, 2002 (highlight of 2002, Classical and Quantum Gravity Jour.). Fellow, Natural Scis. and Engrng. Rsch. Coun. Can., 2002—04. Mem.: Am. Astronomy Soc., Am. Phys. Soc. Achievements include discovery of large scale intrinsic ellipticity-density correlation from the Sloan Digital Sky Survey and implications for weak lensing surveys; research in decisive answers to dark energy questions from cosmic complementarity and lensing tomography; aninverse approach to Einstein's equations for non-conducting fluids; exact solutions with w-modes; perfect fluid models in non-comoving observational spherical coordinates. Home: 2401 W Spring Creek Pkwy # 2909 Plano TX 75023 Office: U Tex Dallas Dept Physics 2601 N Floyd Rd PO Box 830688 FO23 Richardson TX 75023 Home Phone: 972-883-2815; Office Phone: 972-883-2815. Business E-Mail: mishak@utdallas.edu.

ISHAQ, ASHFAQ, foundation administrator, economist, educator; BA, Govt. Coll., Lahore, Pakistan; MPA, U. Punjab; PhD in Econs., George Washington U. Economist World Bank; faculty mem. George Washington U.; founder, exec. dir. Internat. Child Art Found., Washington, DC, 1997—. Guest lectr. US Foreign Svcs. Inst. Author: Success in Small & Medium Scale Enterprises, 1987; founder, editor ChildArt mag., 1998—. Grantee Hesselbein Cmty. Fellowship, Peter Drucker Found., 2001. Mem.: Internat. Acad. Digital Arts and Scis. (adv. bd. mem.), World Psychiatry Assn. Office: Internat Child Art Found Ste 1225 1350 Connecticut Ave NW Washington DC 20036 Office Phone: 202-530-1000.

ISHERWOOD, CHARLES, theater critic; Contbg. writer The Advocate; theater reviewer Variety mag., LA, 1993, chief theater critic, 1998—2004; theater critic NY Times, NYC, 2004—. Office: NY Times Culture Desk 229 W 43rd St New York NY 10036 Office Phone: 212-556-7411. Office Fax: 212-556-1516.

ISHIBASHI, AKIRA, mechanical engineer, educator; b. Fukuoka, Japan, Aug. 24, 1931; s. Hajime and Miyako Ishibashi; m. Minako Kato, July 20, 1964; children: Meiko Hirai, Motoko Shiga, Haruko Alderson. B in Engrng., Kyushu U., Fukuoka, 1955, M in Engrng., 1958, D in Engrng., 1962. Lectr. Kyushu U., Fukuoka, 1961—63, assoc. prof., 1963—71; prof. Saga (Japan) U., 1971—97, Kumamoto (Japan) Inst. Tech., 1997—2000, Sojo U., Kumamoto, 2000—05, 2005—. Author: (book) Gear Technology, 1977. Recipient Gear Grinding Machine award, Japan Soc. Mech. Engrs.; grantee, Mazda Found., Ministry of Edn., 1998. Achievements include development of intermittent gear grinding machine; mirror-like finishing of gear tooth surfaces using cubic-boron nitride wheel; of tribological characteristics of used engine oils; reduction in running noise of planetary gear drives. Avocations: carpentry, fishing. Home: 3-20-5, Shimoyamato, Nishi-ku Fukuoka 819-0052 Japan Personal E-mail: a-ishibashi@mx71.tiki.ne.jp.

ISHIGURO, KAZUO, writer, scriptwriter; b. Nagasaki, Kyushu, Japan, Nov. 8, 1954; arrived in Eng., 1960; s. Shizuo and Shizuko (Michida) I.; m. Lorna Anne MacDougall, May 9, 1986; 1 child. BA in Lit. and Philosophy, U. Kent, Canterbury, 1978; MA in Creative Writing, U. East Anglia, Norwich, 1980. Grouse beater for Queen Mother Balmoral Castle, Aberdeen, Scotland, 1973; cmty. worker Renfrew Social Works Dept., Renfrew, Scotland, 1976; residential social worker W. London Cyrenians Ltd., England, 1979-80, resettlement worker, 1981-83. Author: A Pale View of Hills, 1982 (Winifred Holtby award Royal Soc. Lit. 1983), An Artist of the Floating World, 1986 (Whitbread Book of Yr. 1986), The Remains of the Day, 1988 (Booker prize 1989), The Unconsoled, 1995, When We Were Orphans, 2000, Never Let Me Go, 2005; screenwriter: (films) The Saddest Music in the World, 2003, The White Countess, 2005, (TV films) A Profile of Arthur J. Mason, 1984 (Best Short Film award Chgo. Film Festival 1985), The Gourmet, 1984. Recipient Officer of Brit. Empire award for literature, 1995. Avocations: music, guitar, piano, cinema. Address: c/o Amanda Urban ICM 40 W 57th St New York NY 10019

ISHII, AKIRA, parasitologist, allergist, malariologist; b. Kochi, Japan, July 11, 1937; s. Katsuhiko and Fusae Ishii; m. Fuyuko Ishii, Mar. 20, 1968; children: Ken, Shin. MD, U. Tokyo, 1964, D Med. Sci., 1969; MSc, U. London, 1970. Cert. malaria advanced epidemiology. Rsch. assoc. Inst. Infectious Disease, U. Tokyo, 1969-74; asst. prof. Toyko Med. and Dental U., 1974-78, Inst. Med. Sci., U. Tokyo, 1978-79; prof. Miyazaki (Japan) Med. Coll., 1979-84, Okayama (Japan) U. Med. Sch., 1984-90; dir. dept. parasitology NIH, Tokyo, 1990-95; prof. Jichi Med. Sch., 1995—2003, prof. emeritus, 2003—; prof. Jissen Women's U., Tokyo, 2005—; prof. hon. China Med. U., Shenyoung, 2001—. Com. mem. Japanese Internat. Coop. Agy., Tokyo, 1978—89; panel mem. U.S.-Japan Coop. Med. Program Parasitic Diseases, 1991—95, China-Japan Parasitology Seminar. Fellow: Royal Soc. Tropical Medicine and Hygiene, Am. Soc. Tropical Medicine and Hygiene; mem.: German-Japan Assn. for Protozoan Diseases, Japanese Soc. Pub. Health, Japan Assn. Internat. Health (pres., councilor, mem. exec. bd.), Japanese Soc. Infectious Disease (councilor), Japanese Soc. Allergologists (merit mem.), Japanese Soc. Med. Ent. Zoology (Soc. prize), Japanese Soc. Tropical Medicine (councilor), Japanese Soc. Parasitology (councilor, Koizumi prize, Katsurada prize). Avocations: mountain climbing, golf. Home: 1-14-11 Matsubara Setagayaku Tokyo 156-0043 Japan Home Phone: +81-03-3325-9366. Business E-Mail: ishiiaki@jichi.ac.jp.

ISHII, ANTHONY W., judge; b. Santa Ana, Calif., 1946; AS, Reedley Jr. Coll., 1966; PharmD, U. Pacific, 1970; JD, U. Calif., Berkeley, 1973. Dep. city atty. City Atty.'s Office, Sacramento, 1975; dep. pub. defender County of Fresno, 1979; pvt. practice Fresno, 1979—83; justice ct. judge Parlier-Selma Judicial Dist., Fresno, Calif., 1983—93; mcpl. ct. judge Central Valley Mcpl. Ct., Fresno, Calif., 1994—97; judge U.S. Dist. Ct. (ea. dist.) Calif., 1997—. Office: Fed Bldg, Rm 3654 US Courthouse 1130 O St Fresno CA 93721-2201

ISHII, YOSHINORI, environmental science educator, science writer; b. Tokyo, Mar. 14, 1933; s. Kichijiro and Kei Ishii; m. Hiroko Hisamune, Nov. 24, 1963; children: Yutaka, Makoto, Akira. BS, U. Tokyo, 1955, ED, 1977. Exploration geophysicist Teikoku Oil Co., Tokyo, 1955; rsch. geophysicist Japan Petroleum Exploration Co., Tokyo, 1955-67, sr. geophysicist, 1970-71, Japan Nat. Oil Corp., Tokyo, 1967-70; assoc. prof. geophysics U. Tokyo, 1971-78, prof. geophysics, 1978-93, prof. emeritus, 1993—; dep. dir. gen. Nat. Inst. Environ. Studies, Ibaraki, Japan, 1994-96, dir. gen., 1996-98; prof. Toyama U. Internat. Studies, 2000—06. Mem. Sci. Coun. of Japan, Tokyo, 1988-91. Author: Introduction to Remote Sensing, 1981, Geophysical Engineering, 1988, Energy and Global Environmental Problems, 1995, Environmental Studies for Citizens, 2001, The Last Battle for Oil, 2006, co-author several books; contbr. numerous articles to profl. jours. Mem. Engring. Acad. Japan, Soc. Exploration Geophysicists of Japan (pres. 1984-85, 1988-89, Best Paper award, Tokyo, 1976), Remote Sensing Soc. Japan, (v.p. 1981-88, pres. 1990-92), Japanese Assn. for Petroleum Tech. (v.p. 1982-86), The Mottainai Soc. (pres. 2006-). Avocations: golf, computers.

ISHIKAWA-FULLMER, JANET SATOMI, psychologist, educator; b. Hilo, Hawaii, Oct. 17, 1925; d. Shinichi and Onao (Kurisu) Saito; m. Calvin Y. Ishikawa, Aug. 15, 1950; 1 child, James A. Ishikawa; m. David W. Fullmer, June 11, 1980. B of Edn., U. Hawaii, 1950, MEd, 1967, MEd, 1969, PhD, 1976; postgrad., Queen's Med. Ctr., 1980—82. Diplomate Am. Acad. Pain Mgmt. Postdoctoral trainee Queen's Med. Ctr., intern pain diagnosis tng., biofeedback/self-hypnosis tng.; prof. Honolulu Bus. Coll., 1953-59; prof., counselor Kapiolani C.C., Honolulu, 1959-73; prof., dir. counseling Honolulu C.C., 1973-74, dean of students, 1974-77; psychologist, pres., treas. Human Resources Devel. Ctr., Inc., Honolulu, 1977—. Cons. United Specialties Co., Tokyo, 1979, Filipino Immigrants in Kalihi, Honolulu, 1979—84, Grambling State U., La., 1980, La., 81, Legis. Ref. Bur., Honolulu, 1984—85, Honolulu Police Dept., 1985; co-founder Waianae Child and Family Ctr., Hawaii, 1979—92. Co-author: Family Therapy Dictionary, 1991, Manabu: The Diagnosis and Treatment of a Japanese Boy with a Visual Anomaly, 1991; contbr. articles to profl. jours. Commr. Bd. Psychology, Honolulu, 1979—85; co-founder Kilohana United Meth. Ch. and Family Ctr., 1993—. Recipient Outstanding Educator award, Grambling State U., 1977, Pres.'s award, 1984, Disting. Benefactor award, U. Hawaii Coll. Edn., 2004, Disting. Alumna award, 2005. Mem.: ACA, APA, Hawaii Psychol. Assn., Delta Kappa Gamma (sec., v.p. scholarship 1975, Outstanding Educator award 1975, Thomas Jefferson award 1993, Francis Clark award 1993, Donor Recognition award 2004), Pi Lambda Theta (sec. 1967—68, v.p. 1968—69, pres. 1969—70, 1996—98, Disting. Pi Lambda Theta award 2007). Avocations: jogging, tennis, dance. Office: Human Resources Devel Ctr 1750 Kalakaua Ave Apt 809 Honolulu HI 96826-3725 Office Phone: 808-942-2072.

ISHIMARU, AKIRA, electrical engineering educator; b. Fukuoka, Japan, Mar. 16, 1928; came to U.S., 1952; s. Shigezo and Yumi I.; m. Yuko Kaneda, Nov. 21, 1956; children: John, Jane, James, Joyce. BSEE, U. Tokyo, 1951; PhD, U. Wash., 1958. Registered profl. engr., Wash. Engr. Electro-Tech. Lab, Tokyo, 1951-52; tech. staff Bell Telephone Lab, Holmdel, NJ, 1956; asst. prof. U. Wash., Seattle, 1958-61, assoc. prof., 1961-65, prof. elec. engring., 1965-98, prof. emeritus, 1998—. Vis. assoc. prof. U. Calif., Berkeley, 1963-64; cons. Jet Propulsion Lab., Pasadena, Calif., 1964—, The Boeing Co., Seattle, 1984—. Author: Wave Propagation & Scattering in Random Media, 1978, Electromagnetic Wave Propagation, Radiation and Scattering, 1991; editor: Radio Science, 1982; founding editor Waves in Random and Complex Media, U.K., 1990. Recipient Faculty Achievement award Burlington Resources, 1990; Boeing Martin professorship, 1993. Fellow IEEE (editl. bd., Region VI Achievement award 1968, Centennial medal 1984, Antennas and Propagation Disting. Achievement award 1995, Heinrich Hertz medal 1999), IEEE Geosci. and Remote Sensing (Disting. Achievement award 1998, Third Millennium medal 2000), Acoustical Soc. Am., Optical Soc. Am. (assoc. editor jour. 1983), Inst. Physics U.K. (chartered physicist); mem. NAE, Internat. Union Radio Sci. (chmn. commn. B, John Howard Dellinger Gold medal 1999). Home: 2913 165th Pl NE Bellevue WA 98008-2137 Office: U Wash Dept Elec Engring PO Box 352500 Seattle WA 98195-2500 Home Phone: 425-885-0018; Office Phone: 206-543-2169. Business E-Mail: ishimaru@ee.washington.edu.

ISHIMARU, STUART JON, commissioner, lawyer; b. San Jose, Calif., Dec. 15, 1957; s. Kenzo and Toshiko M. (Suzuki) I.; m. Agnieszka Fryszman; 2 children AB, U. Calif., Berkeley, 1980; JD, George Washington U., 1983. Bar: Calif. 1983. Advance person Mondale for Pres. Campaign, Washington, 1984, Dukakis/Bentsen Com., Boston, 1988; asst. counsel. com. on judiciary U.S. Ho. Reps., Washington, 1984-91, mem. profl. staff, com. on armed svcs., 1991—93; acting staff dir. US Commn. Civil Rights, Washington, 1993—94; counsel to asst. atty. gen. civil rights divsn. US Dept. Justice, Washington, 1994—99, dep. asst. atty. gen. civil rights divsn., 1999—2001; commr. US Equal Employment Opportunity Commn., Washington, 2003—. Lectr. Kogod Coll. Bus. Adminstrn., Am. U., Washington, 1988. Mem. ABA. Democrat. Methodist. Office: US Equal Employment Opportunity Commn 1801 L St NW Washington DC 20507 Home Phone: 202-462-8012; Office Phone: 202-663-4052. E-mail: stuart.ishimaru@eeoc.gov.

ISHITANI, TERRENCE TAKATSUGU, education educator, researcher; b. Kyoto; s. Toshiaki and Kyo Ishitani. MS, Fla. State U., Tallahassee, 1999; PhD, U. Iowa, Iowa City, 2000. Rschr. Ind. State U., Terre Haute, 2001—; asst. prof. U. Memphis, 2007—. Editor: New Directions for Institutional Research. Grantee, Am. Ednl. Rsch. Assn., 1999, Rsch. grantee, 2002. Mem.: Assn. Instl. Rsch. Home Phone: 812-298-8021; Office Phone: 812-237-2306.

ISHLER, HAROLD LEROY, JR., retired physician; b. Lock Haven, Pa., Mar. 16, 1941; s. Harold and Marqueta (Guiser) I.; m. Suzanne McNeilly, July 17, 1965; children: Stephanie, Stephen. BS, Pa. State U., 1963; MD, Jefferson Med. Coll., 1967. Diplomate Am. Bd. Family Practice. Resident East Baton Rouge Parish Med. Soc., 2000; pres. La. Acad. Family Physicians, 2000—01; physician Ochsner Clinic Found., Baton Rouge; ret., 2007. Home: 4838 Elm Shadow Dr Baton Rouge LA 70817-1819

ISHMAEL, ANTIONETTE ROSE, elementary school educator, writer; d. Carmen Frank and Virginia Marie Vigliaturo; m. Phil L. Ishmael, May 31, 1980; children: Patrick Jude, Dominic Gerard, Anthony Phillip. BA in Edn., Rockhurst U., Kansas City, Mo., 1981; MA, Webster U., Kansas City, 2006. Cert. tchr. Mo., 1981, Kans., 1981. Pub. rels. St. Mary's H.S., Independence, Mo., 1983—85; tchr. Holy Cross Sch., Kansas City, 1992—94, St. Bernadette Sch., Kansas City, 1994—99, Visitation Cath. Sch., Kansas City, 1999—2007, St. James Acad. H.S., 2007—. Choreographer, dir. Italian Festival, Kansas City, 1990—94; docent Kans. City Mus., 1984—87; pub. rels. specialist St. Bernadette's Ch., Kansas City, 1995—99. Dir.: (plays) Seven Brides for Seven Brothers, 2004—, Bye Bye Birdie, 2006—; contbr. short stories to lit. publs. Com. chmn. Boy Scouts Am., Kansas City, 1989—93; founder, pres. NE Moms and Tots, Kansas City, 1987—94. Recipient Hon. Mention, Ct. TV, 1995, Bronze Pelican award, Boy Scouts Am., 1995; grantee Excellence in Tchg. award, Kans. City Star, 1995; Fellowship grantee, Diocese Kans. City -St. Joseph, 1996, 2003. Mem.: Nat. Cath. Edn. Assn. (assoc.). Conservative. Roman Catholic. Avocations: travel, knitting, writing, volleyball, coaching.

ISIK, FRANK, plastic surgeon; b. Izmir, Turkey, Nov. 20, 1960; married. MD, Mt. Sinai U., 1985. Diplomate Am. Bd. Plastic and Gen. Surgeon, cert. Am. Bd. Surgery. Assoc. prof. U. Wash., Seattle, 1995—2003, prof. plastic surgery, 2003—07; with Polyclinic, Seattle, 2007—. Examiner Am. Bd. Plastic Surgery. Assoc. editor Jour. Plastic & Reconstructive Surgery. Named one of Seattle's Top Doctors, Seattle mag. Mem.: Am. Soc. Plastic Surgery. Office: Polyclinic 1145 Broadway Seattle WA 98122 Office Phone: 206-543-5516, 206-860-4566. Office Fax: 206-543-8136. Business E-Mail: isik@u.washington.edu.*

ISKANDAR, HARRIS, attache; b. Bandung, Indonesia, Apr. 29, 1962; s. Iro Suratman Dendadibrata and Siti Romlah (late); m. Rooslyndiani Iskandar, Sept. 15, 1961; children: Ariza Indarika, Tanya Nabila, Raihan Aufareza. PhD, Syracuse U., NYC, 1994. Faculty mem. Indonesian Open U., Jakarta, Indonesia, 1986—97; project mgr., ctrl. program coordinating unit Ministry of Nat. Edn., Jakarta, 1997—2004, dep. dir., directorate for vocat. edn., 2003—04; edn. and culture attache Embassy of the Republic of Indonesia, Washington, 2004—. Nat. cons. World Bank Office Jakarta, Jakarta, 1995—97. Vice chmn. Edn. Bd., Dist. Sukabumi, Sukabumi, Indonesia, 2002—04, Sch. Com., Jr. Secondary Sch. No 13 Jakarta, 2002—04. Recipient President's Award of Excellence, World Bank, 2000. Mem.: Am. Indonesian Culture and Edn. Found. (bd. dirs. 2004). Home: 4814 Fort Sumner Drive Bethesda MD 20816 Office: Embassy of the Republic of Indonesia 2020 Massachusetts Ave NW Washington DC 20036 Home Phone: 301-229-8679; Office Phone: 202-775-5232. Office Fax: 202-775-5235; Home Fax: 301-229-6273. Personal E-mail: harris_iskandar@verizon.net. E-mail: h_iskandar@embassyofindonesia.org.

ISKENDERIAN, MARY ELLEN, bank executive; b. 1958; d. Ara Iskenderian; m. Gregory Owen Lipscomb, Oct. 26, 1991. BS in internat. econ., Georgetown U. Sch. Fgn. Svc.; MBA, Yale Sch. Orgn. With World Bank Group, Washington, 1989—2006; mgr. fin. markets, Europe II dept. Internat. Fin. Corp. (IFC), regional head fin. markets, Latin Am. & Caribbean dept., dir. South Asia regional dept., dir. global fin. markets portfolio, dir. partnership devel.; pres. & CEO Women's World Banking, NYC, 2006—. Bd. dirs. Nat. Bank Commerce, Tanzania, ShoreCap Internat. Office: Womens World Banking Lbby 8 W 40th St New York NY 10018*

ISLAM, MOHAMMAD, chef; m. Malika Ameen. Chef The Dining Room, The Ritz Carlton, Chgo., Jean Georges; exec. sous chef Mercer Kitchen, NYC; exec. chef Chateau Marmont, LA, 2003—, The Standard Hollywood, 2003—. Named one of LA's Rising Stars, StarChefs.com, 2006. Avocations: hiking, mountain climbing, skiing. Office: Chateau Marmont 8221 W Sunset Blvd Los Angeles CA 90046 Office Phone: 323-656-1010.*

ISLAM, MUHAMMAD AZADUL, physicist, educator, researcher; b. Bogra, Bangladesh, Dec. 23, 1951; came to U.S., 1975; s. Muhammad Mohsin Ali and Amena Khatun; m. Aziza Gole Afroz, July 24, 1987; children: Crescent Mamnun, Cosmo Hasibul. BSc with honors, Dhaka U., Bangladesh, 1974; MS, U. Ala., 1977; MPhil, Columbia U., 1979, PhD, 1981. Tchg. asst. U. Ala., Tuscaloosa, 1975-77; faculty fellow, then head tchg. asst. Columbia U., NYC, 1977-79; grad. rsch. asst. Columbia Radiation Labs., NYC, 1979-81; postdoctoral fellow Joint Inst. Lab. Astrophysics, U. Colo., Boulder, 1981-83; asst. prof. San Diego State U., 1983-85; asst. prof. physics SUNY, Potsdam, 1985-89, assoc. prof., 1989-97, prof., 1997—, chmn. dept., 1999—2002. NEH vis. scholar Columbia U., N.Y.C., 1993; vis. scholar MIT Cambridge, 1993, Ctr. for Astrophysics Harvard U., 1995. Author: Test Yourself Physics, 1999, Beyond Ordinary Light, 2003; contbr. articles to profl. publs. Talent and merit scholar Comilla Bd. Edn. Mem. AAAS, United Univ. Profs., N.Y. State United Tchrs., Am. Fedn. Tchrs., Islamic Soc. N.Am. (trustee Potsdam chpt. 1990—), N.Y. Acad. Scis., Am. Phys. Soc., Sigma Xi, Sigma Pi Sigma. Avocations: reading, travel, history. Home: 6 Poplar St Potsdam NY 13676-2113 Office: SUNY Dept Physics Potsdam NY 13676 Office Phone: 315-267-2284.

ISLAM, SALEEM, pediatric surgeon, researcher; b. NYC, Nov. 25, 1967; s. Naseem and Swaleha Islam; m. Shehla P. Peshimam, Feb. 14, 1993; children: Rubab, Nazli, Feryal. MD, Aga Khan U., Karachi, Pakistan, 1992; MPH, U. Mass., Amherst, 2006. Diplomate Am. Bd. of Surgery, spl. cert. in pediat. surgery Am. Bd. of Surgery. Intern U. Mass., worchester, 1995—96, resident, 1995—2001; fellow U. Mich., Ann Arbor, 2001—03; asst. prof. of surgery U. Fla., Gainsville, 2003—, dir. pediat. minimal invasive surgery. Dir. extracorporeal membraine oxygenation U. of Miss. Med. Ctr., Jackson, 2004—. Contbr. scientific papers to profl. jours. Mem.: Assn. of Acad. Surgeons, Assn. of Surg. Edn., Children's Oncology Group, Internat. Pediat. Endosurgery Group, Am. Acad. of Pediats., Am. Pediat. Surg. Assn, Mass. Med. Soc.

ISLAM, SAMANTHA, civil engineer, researcher; b. Khulna, Bangladesh, Nov. 5, 1975; US19999; d. Nazrul and Mira Islam; m. Akhter B. Hossain, July 1996. BS, Bangladesh U. Engring. and Tech., Dhaka City, 1999; MS, Purdue U., West Lafayette, Ind., 2002, PhD, 2005. EIT Ala., 2006. Project engr. Volkert & Assocs., Mobile, Ala., 2006—. Rschr. U. South Ala., Mobile, 2005; presenter in field. Contbr. articles to profl. jours. Active supporter PETA, Mobile; worker Adopt-A-Road, West Lafayette, Ind., 1999—2003; supporter, subscriber Habitat For Humanity, Mobile, 2003—06, Frat. of Police, Mobile, 2003—05; subscriber United Way, Mobile. Nominee C.V. Wootan Meml. award in Policy and Planning Cate, Coun. U. Transp. Ctrs., 2002; scholar Merit scholar, Bangladesh U. Engrng. and Tech., 1994—99;, Bangladesh Govt., 1992. Mem.: ASCE (assoc.), Soc. Women Engrs., Inst. Transp. Engrs. (assoc.), Purdue U. Alumni Assn., Bangladesh Student Assn. Purdue U. Achievements include design of highways and interstates; research in concrete materials; highway safety, traffic accidents, costs of accidents, transportation planning and design of highways and interstates. Office: Volkert and Associates 3809 Moffett Rd Mobile AL 36618 Home Phone: 251-607-7371. Personal E-mail: samanthaislam@gmail.com. Business E-Mail: sislam@volkert.com.

ISLER, RAYMOND EARL, engineer; s. Walter Coy and Christine Isler; m. Leonia Annette Denning, Sept. 11, 1999. AAS, Durham Tech. C.C., 2004; BS, NC Ctrl. U., 1981—87. Professional Server Expert IBM Corp./NC, 1997, PSG Entry Level Education IBM Personal Systems Group/NC, 1993, Netfinity Server Support Specialist IBM PC Inst./NC, 1997, IBM Professional Server Specialist IBM PC Inst./NC, 1998, Project Management Fundamentals I IBM Global Campus/NC, 1999, Web Page Design Durham Tech. Cmty. Coll./NC, 2003, Certificate of Achievement: IBM Advanced FASt/Fibre Storage Workshop IBM PC Inst., 2004, A+, Network+, MCP(Microsoft Certified Professional), Security+, and CC NC State U., 2005. Dietary svc. aide sr. Duke U. Med. Ctr., Durham, NC, 1978—84; vol. math and computer asst./tutor NCCU Dept of Math & Computer Sci., 1984—88; math tutor and computer lab asst. NCCU-Summer Ventures In Sci. & Math., Durham, NC, 1988—88; mfg. support test IBM Corp., Rtp, NC, 1988—93; math tutor, computer lab asst. NC Ctrl. U., 1989; customer support tech. specialist IBM Corp., Rsch. Triangle Pk., NC, 1993—97, us lead server tech. specialist, 1997—99, ww svc. & support devel. engr./staff scientist, 1999—2001, ww xseries svc. planner, 2001—03, profl. field engr., 2004—05, tech. project mgr., 2005—. Mem. NCCU Alumni Assn., 1988. Recipient IBM Personal Sys. Group Tech. Acheivement, IBM Corp., 1999, IBM Tech. Achievement, 1996, IBM Tech. Server Achievement, 1997. Mem.: NC Acad. of Sci. (assoc.), Math. Programming Soc. (assoc.), Am. Math. Soc. (assoc.), Math. Assn. of Am. (assoc.), NCCU Math & Computer Sci. Club (assoc.; treas. 1985—86, pres. 1986—87). Home: Po Box 1680 Durham NC 27702-1680 Office: IBM Corp 3039 Cornwallis Rd Research Triangle Park NC 27709 Home Phone: 919-781-8673; Office Phone: 919-254-5419. Personal E-mail: ncman7@netzero.com. E-mail: reisler@us.ibm.com.

ISLEY, SARA, chemist, educator; BA, Cornell Coll., 2001; PhD, U. Minn., Mpls., 2007. Undergraduate rsch. asst. dept. chemistry U. Iowa, Iowa City, 2000; math. tutor dept. chemistry Cornell Coll., Mount Vernon, Iowa, 2000—01; tchg. asst. dept. chemistry U. Minn., Mpls., 2001—02, rsch. asst. dept. chemistry, 2002—, head gen. chemistry tchg. asst. dept. chemistry, 2002—. Mem. grad. student workshop com. U. Minn., peer adv. chemistry grad. students, mem. oral presentation peer rev. group; presenter in field. Contbr. articles to profl. jours. Recipient Am. Inst. Chemists award, Dept. Chemistry, Cornell Coll., 2000—01; grantee, Sigma Delta Epsilon Grad. Women in Sci., 2007, Grad. and Profl. Student Assembly, 2007; scholar, Cornell Coll., 1997—2001; Sarah Frances Bush scholarship, Math. Cornell Coll., 2000—01. Mem.: Am. Chem. Soc. (exec. bd. younger chemists com. Minn. chpt. 2006, Organic Chemistry award 1999, Analytical Chemistry award 2000). Office Phone: 612-624-3803.

ISMACH, ARNOLD HARVEY, retired journalism educator; b. NYC, Dec. 28, 1930; s. Louis and Augusta (Lacher) I.; m. Judy Daniels, June 20, 1959 (div. 1975); children: Richard, Theresa. BA, U. Okla., 1951; MA, UCLA, 1970; PhD, U. Wash., 1975. News editor Union-Bulletin, Walla Walla, Wash., 1954-56; reporter, editor Sun-Telegram, San Bernardino, Calif., 1956-69; prof. journalism U. Minn., Mpls., 1973-85; dean journalism U. Oreg., Eugene, 1985-94, prof. journalism, 1994-97. Cons. Pub. Rels. Ctr., L.A., 1970-75; pres. Comm. Rsch. Ctr., Mpls., 1973-85. Co-author: New Strategies, 1976, Enduring Issues, 1978, Reporting Processes, 1981. Pres. Planned Parenthood S.W. Oreg., 1998-99; dir. ACLU Oreg., 1994-2001. Sgt. U.S. Army, 1951-54. Mem. Soc. Profl. Journalists, Assn. for Edn. in Journalism. Democrat. Avocation: photography. Business E-Mail: aismach@uoregon.edu.

ISMAIL, ABU ZAFAR MOHAMED, physics professor, researcher; b. Keymore, India, Oct. 9, 1930; arrived in U.S., 1982; s. Abulkhair Mohamed and Zakiya Yusuf; children: Atif Zafar, Khurram Zafar, Faiza N. Zafar, Mona S. Zafar. MSc, Panjab U., Lahore, Pakistan, 1952, MA, 1954; BA with Honours, Cambridge U., Eng., 1958; DPhil in Elem. Particle Physics, Oxford U., Eng., 1964. Tchr. St. Mary's High Sch., Sukkur, Pakistan, 1952-53; instr. Mumtaz Coll., Khairpur Mirs, Pakistan, 1954-56; lectr., sr. lectr. Sind U., Hyderabad, Pakistan, 1958-65, assoc. prof., 1965-71, prof., 1971-72, Tripoli (Libya) U., 1972-82; prof. physics Daemen Coll., Amherst, N.Y., 1983—. Cons. Sci. First Inc., Buffalo, 1991-2004. Contbr. articles on high energy nuclear physics to profl. jours. Scholar Pakistan Ministry Edn., 1953; fellow Colombo PLan, 1960. Mem. Am. Assn. Physics Tchrs., Inst. Physics U.K. Republican. Avocations: photography, writing fiction, stamp and book collecting. Home: 130 Breezewood Common East Amherst NY 14051-1425 Office: Daemen Coll 4380 Main St Amherst NY 14226-3592 Office Phone: 716-839-8374. Business E-Mail: zismail@daemen.edu.

ISMAIL, NAHED, microbiologist, immunologist; d. Abd El Sadek Ismail and Awatef Nawar; m. Ayman Al-Hendy; children: Mohamed Al Hendy, Omar Alhendy. MD, Med. Sch., Tanta, Egypt, 1988; MSc, U. Toronto, Can., 1996; PhD, U. Sask., Can., 2000. Lic. physician Ministry of Health, Egypt, 1988. Assoc. dir. U. Tex. Med. Br., Galveston, 2000, asst. prof., 2003. Grantee NIH. Mem.: Am. Soc. for Microbiology (assoc.). Achievements include research in host-microbial interaction. Office: Univ Tex Med Br 301 University Blvd Galveston TX 77555 Home Phone: 281-727-8799; Office Phone: 409-772-3111.

ISMAIL, TAREK, lawyer; b. Alexandria, Egypt, Sept. 22, 1969; BA in Economics, Carleton Coll., Northfield, Minn., 1991; JD, U. Ill. Coll. Law, 1994. Bar: Northern Dist. Ill. 1994, US Dist. Ct., Fed. Cir. 1995. Clerk US Dist. Ct., Northern Dist. Ill., 1994—95; assoc. Mayer, Brown & Platt, 1995—2000; ptnr. Bartlit Beck Herman Palenchar & Scott LLP, Chgo., 2000—. Named one of Litigation's Rising Stars, The Am. Lawyer, 2007. Office: Bartlit Beck Herman Palenchar & Scott LLP Courthouse Pl 54 W Hubbard St Chicago IL 60610 Office Phone: 312-494-4400. Office Fax: 312-494-4440.*

ISMAIL, YAHIA H., dentist, prosthodontist; arrived in USA, 1962, naturalized; s. Hassan and Horia (Soloman); m. Launa Lutz, Sept. 5, 1968; children: Alan Kareem, Zane Zaid. DDS, Cairo U., 1959; MS in Prosthondics, U. Pitts., 1965, DMD, 1973, PhD in Psychology and Higher Edn., 1973. Cert. Nev., Penn. Instr. Dental Sch. Cairo U., 1959—62; asst. prof. prosthodontics U. Pitts., 1962—68, assoc. prof., 1968—73, prof., 1973—2005, dir. prosthodontic grad. program, 1970—, chmn. dept. prosthodontics, 1973—2005; dir. acad. affaris, internat. affairs and grad. edn. Dental Medicine, U. Pitts., 1995—2001; dir. Reconstructive Dentistry Inst., Las Vegas; prof. emeritus, prosthodontics U. Pitts. Pa. Vis. prof., Paris and Marseille, France, Cairo and Alexandria, Egypt, European U., Brussels; mem. staff VA Hosp., Montefiore Hosp., Univ. Med. Ctr. Hosp., St. Margaret's Hosp. Contbr. over 60 articles to profl. jours., three textbooks, gave 120 lectures and presentations, and taught numerous continuing edn. courses. Bd. dirs. Ridgewood Civic Assn., 1969-73; cubmaster Allegheny Trails council Boy Scouts Am.; coach Youth Soccer League Allegheny County. Recipient Chancellor's Pub. Svc. award, 1995. Fellow Internat. Coll. Dentists, Am. Coll. Dentists, Royal Soc. Medicine, Am. Coll. Oral Implantologists, Internat. Congress Oral Implantologists, Am. Acad. Implant Prosthodontics (pres. elect 1989-90, pres. 1990-92); mem. ADA,

Internat. Assn. Dentofacial Abnormalities (bd. dirs., sec., treas. 1973-77), Internat. Congress Oral Implantologists (v.p. 1985-86, pres. 1988-89), Am. Prosthodontic Soc. (internat. circuite courses humanities citation), Pa. Prosthodontic Assn. (past pres.), Prosthodontic Soc. Western Pa. (past pres.), Dental Soc. Western Pa. (bd. dirs.), Am. Coll. Oral Implantologists (pres. 1984-86), Am. Coll. Prosthodontists, Am. Assn. Dental Schs., Internat. Assn. Dental Rsch., Univ. Club, Omicron Kappa Upsilon, Am. Dental Assn., Penn. Dental Assn., Nev. Dental Assn. Democrat. Achievements include: Established the first graduate program in Implant Dentistry in the United States; trained more than 100 specialists in Prosthodontics. Avocations: Skiing, boating, walking, reading, art, travel. Home Phone: 702-254-3137. *Talk about ideas and philosophies rather than other people.*

ISOGAI, MASAHARU, international corporate strategist, retired apparel executive; b. 1939; AMP, Harvard U., 1985. With Ogiya, 1958-76, Jusco Co. Ltd., 1976-88, bd. mem., 1992—94; exec. v.p., gen. mgr. Jusco USA, Inc., 1988-96, sr. advisor, 1996-99; dir. Talbots, 1993-99; chmn. Revman, 1994-99; ret., 1999. Mem. Japanese Youth Goodwill Mission to U.S., 1964. Mem. Japanese Am. Assn. N.Y. (bd. dirs.), Assn. for Better N.Y. (hon. mem. exec. com., spl. amb. from Japan). Office: 401 E 34th St Apt S5J New York NY 10016-6611 Business E-Mail: misogainy@earthlink.net.

ISOM, O(TTIS) WAYNE, thoracic surgeon, educator; b. Lubbock, Tex., Feb. 9, 1940; m. Pat Isom; 5 children. Undergraduate studies, Tex. Tech; MD, U. Tex. Southwestern Med. Sch., 1965. Cert. Surgery, Thoracic Surgery. Med. intern Parkland Hosp., Dallas, 1965—66, gen. surgery resident, 1966—70; cardiothoracic resident NYU Med. Ctr., 1970—72; with faculty NYU Sch. Medicine, prof. surgery, dir. cardiothoracic tng. prog., 1978—85; chmn. dept. cardiothoracic surgery NY-Cornell Med. Ctr. (before the NY Hosp. and Presbyn. Hosp. merged to become NY Presbyn. Hosp.), 1985; Terry Allen Kramer prof of cardiothoracic surgery NY Presbyn.-Weill Cornell Med. Ctr., chmn., dept. cardiothoracic surgery, cardiothoracic surgeon-in-chief. Spkr. in field. Contbr. articles to profl. jours., chapters to books. Recipient Bugher Found. award for Achievement in Cardiovascular Sci. and Medicine, Hero With a Heart award, Nat. Marfan Found., 2000, Humanitarian award, Larry King Cardiac Found. & NYSAE Edn. Rsch. Found. Mem.: Am. Heart Assn. (bd. mem., NYC), Am. Coll. Surgeons, Am. Assn. for Thoracic Surgery. Office: 525 E 68th St M-404 New York NY 10021 Office Phone: 212-746-5151. Office Fax: 212-746-8828. Business E-Mail: owisom@med.cornell.edu.*

ISONG, ENÓ, public health service officer; d. Clement Nyong and Nne C. Isong; m. O. Felix Obi; 1 child, Felix Nyong Obi. BA, U. of Calabar, Calabar, Cross River State, Nigeria, 1987; MA, Howard U., Washington, 1993. News editor/reporter AKBC-TV, Uyo, Akwa Ibom State, Nigeria, 1988—90; assoc. editor/columnist TRA Pubs., Albany, Ga., 1990—91; cons. Internat. Ctr. The Smithsonian Instn., Washington, 1993—94; program officer Creative Assoc. Internat. Inc., Washington, 1995—98; sr. program officer The Henry J. Kaiser Family Found., Washington, 1998—. Recipient USAA award, The US Achievement Acad., 1993. Mem.: APHA.

ISQUITH, AARON DAVID, real estate broker, consultant; b. Bklyn., Jan. 12, 1949; s. Santley and Rita Isquith; m. Janet Louise Rosenzweig; 1 child, Daniel Benjamin. BA in English, CUNY, Bklyn., 1970, MA in Musicology, 1976; MS in Acctg., CW Post Sch. Profl. Acctg., Greenvale, NY, 1976. Lic. real estate broker NY State. Vp fin. and adminstrn. Transtech Svc. Network, Rosedale, NY; broker real estate Warren Lewis Realty Assoc., Bklyn., 1998—. Interim exec. dir. Bklyn. Conservatory of Music; cons. in field. Pres. 34 Plz. Owners' Corp., Bklyn. Home: 6284 North Camino de Michael Tucson AZ 85718 Office: Warren Lewis Realty Assoc 123A Seventh Ave Brooklyn NY 11215 Home Phone: 917-816-0363; Office Phone: 718-638-6500 204. Personal E-mail: aaronisquith@gmail.com. Business E-Mail: isquith@warrenlewis.com.

ISQUITH, FRED TAYLOR, lawyer; b. NYC, June 6, 1947; s. Stanley and Rita (Hoskwith) Isquith; m. Susan Nora Goldberg, May 23, 1976; children: Fred, Rebecca. BA, CUNY, 1968; JD, Columbia U., 1971. Bar: N.Y. 1972, U.S. Dist. Ct. (so. and ea. dists.) N.Y. 1975, U.S. Ct. Appeals (2d cir.) 1975, DC 1976, U.S. Supreme Ct. 1983, U.S. Ct. Appeals (8th cir.) 1985, U.S. Ct. Appeals (3d cir.) 1986, U.S. Dist. Ct. (no. dist.) N.Y. 1988, U.S. Ct. Appeals (4th cir.) 1990, U.S. Dist. Ct. (we. dist.) Mich. 1992, U.S. Dist. Ct. Ariz. 1994, U.S. Dist. Ct. (ctrl. dist.) Ill. 1996, U.S. Dist. Ct. Colo. 1999, U.S. Dist. Ct. Nebr. 2000, U.S. Ct. Appeals (1st cir.) 2000. Assoc. Fulbright & Jaworski, NYC, 1971-75, Kaye Scholer et al, NYC, 1975-80; ptnr. Wolf Haldenstein Adler Freeman & Herz, NYC, 1980—. Lectr. Am. Conf. inst., N.Y. State Bar Assn., N.Y. County Bar Assn., others; mediator Supreme Ct. State of N.Y.; arbitrator Am. Arbitrator Assn.; lectr. in field; bd. dirs. 103 E. 84th St. Corp., Sheinkopf, Ltd. Author: An Introduction to Securities Arbitration, 1994, Real Estate Exit Strategies, 1994, Fundamental Strategies in Securities Litigation, 2000, Federal Civil Practice, 2000, A Scalpel in Your Hand Litigation as a Tool for Forcing Responsible Corporate Guidance, 2002, Anatomy of a Deposition: Preparation for a Deposition in a Complex Financial Case, 2002, The Seven Year Itch: A Survey of Experience Under the 1995 Amendments to the Security Laws, 2003, Wolf in Sheeps Clothing: Tort Reforms, 2004; author: (with Thomas Burt) Ethics: Going Astray By Small Steps, 2004; author: A Flexible Approach to Loss Causation, 2005, A SEC Monopoly Will Not Work, 2007; editor, columnist: Class Act. Mem. devel. com. Friends Sem., NYC, 1998—2004; clk., mem. vestry St. Thomas Ch. Fifth Ave., NYC, 2002—. Mem.: NASCAT (pres.), ABA (mem. internet com. anti-trust law sect.), Bklyn. Bar Assn. (mem. civil practice law and rules com., mem. fed. cts. com., mem. legis. com.), Assn. Bar City of N.Y. (mem. fed. cts. com.), DC Bar Assn., N.Y. County Lawyers Assn. (chmn. bus. torts), N.Y. State Bar Assn. (mem. com. securities, mem. com. legis., securities industry sect.), Columbia Club. Office: Wolf Haldenstein Adler Freeman & Herz 270 Madison Ave New York NY 10016-0601 Home Phone: 212-628-4545; Office Phone: 212-545-4600. Business E-Mail: isquith@whafh.com.

ISRAEL, ALLEN D., lawyer; b. Seattle, Nov. 28, 1946; m. Nettie Israel. BSME, U. Wash., 1968, MBA, 1971, JD, 1978. Bar: Wash. 1978. Ptnr. Foster Pepper PLLC, Seattle, 1978—. Office: Foster Pepper PLLC 1111 3rd Ave Ste 3400 Seattle WA 98101-3299 Office Phone: 206-447-8911. Business E-Mail: IsraA@Foster.com.

ISRAEL, BARBARA A., healthcare educator; MPH, DPH, U. NC, Chapel Hill, 1982. Asst. prof. U. Mich., Ann Arbor, 1982—88, assoc. prof. Sch. Pub. Health, 1988—94, prof. Sch. Pub. Health, 1994—, chair dept. HBHE Sch. Pub. Health, 1995—99. Editor: (book) Methods in Community-Based Participatory Research for Health; contbr. articles to profl. jours. Mem.: APHA (Early Career award 1991), SOPHE (Disting. Fellow award 2005). Office: University of Michigan SPH 109 S Observatory Ann Arbor MI 48109-2029 Office Phone: 734-647-3184.

ISRAEL, BARRY JOHN, lawyer; b. Rockford, Ill., Mar. 14, 1946; s. Robert John and Bettie Jane (Erickson) I.; childn: Alison, Ashley, Brenna. BA, U. So. Calif., LA, 1968; JD, George Washington U., 1974. Bar: Calif. 1975, D.C. 1976, U.S. Supreme Ct. 1978, U.S. Dist. Ct. Mariana Islands 1985. Assoc. Clifford & Warnke, Washington, 1975-83; ptnr. Stovall, Spradlin, Armstrong & Israel, Washington, 1983-86, Dorsey & Whitney, Washington, 1988-92, Stroock, Stroock & Lavan, Washington, 1992-95. Spl. counsel, pres. Federated States of Micronesia, 1982-84; spl. asst. atty. gen. Territory Guam, 1990-95; chmn. bd., CEO Danao Internt. Holdings Co., Ltd.; bd. dirs. Jadora Ltd. Author: Investment Guides to the Federated States of Micronesia and the Republic of the Marshall Islands, 1989. 1st lt. U.S. Army, 1969-72. Democrat. Avocations: travel, tennis. Address: 24/7 Dinh Tien Hoang Dist 1 Ho Chi Minh City Vietnam Personal E-mail: barryjon@aol.com.

ISRAEL, DAVID, journalist, scriptwriter, film producer; b. NYC, Mar. 17, 1951; s. Hyman and Edith Oringer I.; m. Lindy De Koven, Aug. 8, 1987. BS in Journalism, Northwestern U., 1973. Reporter Chgo. Daily News, 1973-75; columnist Washington Star, 1975-78, Chgo. Tribune, 1978-81, L.A. Herald Examiner, 1981-84; chmn., pres. Big Prodn., Inc., LA; prod., writer OCC Prodn., LA, 1985-88; exec. prodr., writer Lorimar TV, LA, 1988-92, Paramount Pictures, Hollywood, Calif., 1992-93; writer, exec. prodr. Stephen J. Cannell Prod., Inc., Hollywood, 1993-95. Dir. office of Pres., Los Angeles Olympic Organizing Com., 1984; exec. prodr. House of Frankenstein, NBC, Universal, 1997, exec. prodr. Mutiny, NBC, 1999, Y2K, NBC, 1999, Tremors, SciFi, 2002-03. Supervising prodr., writer: A Comedy Salute to Baseball, NBC, 1985; supervising prodr., writer: Fast Copy, NBC, 1985-86; co-creator, supervising prodr.: Crimes of the Century, 1987-88; co-exec. prodr., writer: Midnight Caller, NBC, Lorimar TV, 1988-91, The Untouchables, Paramount TV, 1992-93; exec. prodr., writer: Jake Lassiter: Justice on the Bayou, NBC, Stephen J. Cannell Prodn., 1995; exec. prodr., writer: Pandora's Clock, NBC, Citadel Entertainment, 1996; consulting prodr., writer, Turks, CBS Studios, USA, 1998-99; coord. prodr. Monday Night Football, ABC Sports, 2000-01. Commr. LA Meml. Coliseum Commn., 2005—, v.p., 2007—; bd. dirs. Calif. Govs. and First Lady's Conf. on Women and Families, Calif. Sci. Ctr., 2004—, Calif. State Alliance, 2004—06, exec. com., 2004—06. Mem. AFTRA, Writers Guild Am., Chgo. Athletic Assn., Beverly Hills Tennis Club. Office: c/o Bob Broder & Chris Von Goetz ICM 10250 Constellation Blvd Los Angeles CA 90067

ISRAEL, JEROLD HARVEY, law educator; b. Cleve., June 14, 1934; s. Harry and Florence S. (Schoenfeld) I.; m. Tanya M. Boyarsky, Sept. 28, 1959; children: Lewis, Laurie, Daniel BBA, Western Res. U., 1956; LLB, Yale U., 1959. Bar: Ohio 1959, Mich. 1967. Law clk. to Justice Potter Stewart U.S. Supreme Ct., Washington, 1959-61; asst. prof. Law Sch. U. Mich., Ann Arbor, 1961-64, assoc. prof., 1964-67, prof., 1967-96, Alene and Allan F. Smith prof., 1983-96, prof. emeritus, 1996—; Ed Rood Eminent Scholar in trial advocacy and procedure U. Fla. Coll. Law, Gainesville, 1993—. Exec. sec. Mich. Law Revision Commn., 1972-92; co-reporter Uniform Rules of Criminal Procedure, Nat. Conf. Commrs. Uniform State Laws; Alene and Allen F. Smith prof. emeritus U. Mich., Ann Arbor, 1996—. Co-author: Criminal Procedure Treatise, 1999, White Collar Crime, 2003, Criminal Procedure Hornbook, 2004, Principles of Criminal Procedures: Investigation, 2004, Principles of Criminal Procedure: Post-Investigation, 2004, Criminal Procedure and the Constitution, 2005, Modern Criminal Procedure, 2005. Office: U Fla Law Sch Gainesville FL 32611-2038 Home Phone: 352-335-2700; Office Phone: 352-273-0966. Business E-Mail: israel@law.ufl.edu.

ISRAEL, KIMBERLY HELD, lawyer; b. Jacksonville, Fla., Aug. 7, 1969; d. Edwin W. and Leslie (Edwards) Held; m. Jonathan Bruce Israel, Apr. 2, 1995; children: Eliza, Allie, Ayden. BA, Vanderbilt U., 1991; JD, U. Fla., 1994. Assoc. Moseley, Warren, Prichard & Parrish, Jacksonville, 1995—99, ptnr., 2000—04, Held & Israel, 2004—. Mem. editl. bd. SEALI, Ga., 2002—04. Bd. dirs. Jewish Cmty. Alliance, 2002—04; chmn. editl. bd. Jacksonville Jewish News, 2004—06; bd. dirs. Jacksonville Jewish Fedn., 2004—06. Recipient Young Leadership Award, Jax Jewish Fedn., 2000. Mem.: FBA, ABA, Women Bus. Owners of North Fla., Comml. Law League Am., Am. Bankruptcy Inst., Fed. Bar Assn. (treas. Jacksonville chpt. 2003—04, sec. 2004—05, v.p. programs 2005—06, v.p. membership 2006—), Maritime Law Assn., Jacksonville Women Lawyer's Assn., Jacksonville Bar Assn., Fla. Bar. Jewish. Office: Held & Israel 1301 Riverplace Blvd 1916 Jacksonville FL 32207 Office Phone: 904-398-7038. Office Fax: 904-398-4283. Business E-Mail: khisrael@hilawfirm.com.

ISRAEL, MARTIN HENRY, astrophysicist, educator, academic administrator; b. Chgo., Jan. 12, 1941; s. Herman and Anna Catherine Israel; m. Margaret Ellen Mitouer, June 20, 1965; children: Elisa, Samuel. SB, U. Chgo., 1962; PhD, Calif. Inst. Tech., Pasadena, 1969. Asst. prof. physics Washington U., St. Louis, 1968-72, assoc. prof., 1972-75, prof., 1975—, assoc. dir. McDonnell Ctr. for Space Scis., 1982-87, acting dean faculty arts and scis., 1987-88, dean faculty, 1988-94, vice chancellor, 1994-95, vice chancellor acad. planning, 1995-97. Com. on space astronomy and astrophysics NRC, 1976-79; high energy astrophysics mgmt. ops. working group NASA, 1976-84, co-chair Cosmic Ray Program Working Group, 1980-87, space and earth scis. adv. com., 1985-88, chair Particle Astrophysics Magnet Facility Definition Team, 1985-87, astrophysics coun., 1986-87, prin. investigator Heavy Nuclei Expt. High Energy Astronomy Obs., 1971-89, structure and evolution of the universe subcom., 1996-99, chair ACCESS steering com., 1998-2000, mem. Space Sta. Utilization adv. subcom., 1998-2002, mem. GSFC Space Sci. vis. com., 1997-2001, chair, 2000-01, chair sci. ballooning roadmap team, 2004-07; mem. GSFC Ctr. Dir.'s Vis. Com., 2000-01; chair Space Sci. Working Group, Assn. Am. Univs., 1983-85; chair nat. organizing com. 19th Internat. Cosmic Ray Conf., 1985, 1982-85. Contbr. articles on cosmic ray astrophysics and observation of elemental and isotopic composition of cosmic rays to profl. jours. Sloan Found. fellow, 1970; recipient Exceptional Sci. Achievement award NASA, 1980. Fellow Am. Phys. Soc. (chair astrophysics divsn. 1980-81); mem. Am. Astron. Soc. (mem. exec. com. high energy astrophysics divsn. 1982-84), AAUP, AAAS. Home: 2 Valley View Pl Saint Louis MO 63124-1810 Office: Washington U Campus Box 1105 1 Brookings Dr Saint Louis MO 63130-4899 Office Phone: 314-935-6263. Business E-Mail: mhi@wuphys.wustl.edu.

ISRAEL, RICHARD STANLEY, investment banker; b. Oakland, Calif., Sept. 27, 1931; s. Sybil Noble, July 29, 1962; children: Richard Lee, Lynne, Lawrence. BA, MA, U. Calif., Berkeley, 1953. Copy editor San Francisco Chronicle, 1953-59; publicist CBS TV Network, LA, 1959-62; sr. v.p. Rogers & Cowan, Beverly Hills, Calif., 1962-69, Cantor, Fitzgerald, Beverly Hills, Calif., 1969-73; pres. Sponsored Cons. Svcs., LA, 1973—; managing ptnr. Mason, Israel & Ptnrs., Beverly Hills, Calif. Bd. dirs. Hurst Labeling Systems. Pres. North Beverly Dr. Homeowners Assn., Beverly Hills, 1986-88; v.p. Temple Emanuel, Beverly Hills, 1988-93, L.A. chpt. Juvenile Diabetes Found. Internat, 1987—. With U.S. Army, 1956-58. Recipient Alumni citation U. Calif. Alumni Assn., Berkeley, 1984. Mem. L.A. Venture Assn. (pres. 1987), Assn. for Corp. Growth (pres. bd. dirs. L.A. chpt.). Democrat. Avocations: volleyball, travel. Office: Mason Israel & Ptnrs 8929 Wilshire Blvd Ste 214 Beverly Hills CA 90211-1951 Office Phone: 310-208-1234. Business E-Mail: dick@masonisrael.com.

ISRAEL, ROBERT ALLAN, statistician; b. NYC, Mar. 30, 1933; s. John J. and Ray (Sladkus) I.; m. Barbara Diane Johnston, Jan. 26, 1953; children: John, Richard, Deborah, Pamela, James, Michael. BA, Hofstra Coll., 1954; MS, Columbia U., 1957. Med. analyst Md. State Health Dept., Balt., 1959-63, chief div. statis. rsch., 1963-66; chief mortality stats. br. Nat. Ctr. for Health Stats., Washington, 1966-68, dir. div. vital stats., 1968-72, assoc. dir. for ops., 1972-75, dep. dir., 1975-92, assoc. dir. for internat. stats., 1992-95, ret., 1995. Head WHO collaborating ctr. for disease classification for North Am., 1975-95, ret., 1995; dep. exec. dir. Internat. Inst. for Vital Registration and Statistics, 1997—2005. Co-author: The Methods and Materials of Demography, 1973; co-editor: Encyclopedia of Biostatistics, 1997. Recipient Superior Svc. award U.S. Pub. Health Svc., 1972, 79, scholarship N.Y. State Bd. Regents, 1950-54, fellowship U.S. Public Health Svc., 1956-58, Special Recognition award Asst. Sec. for Health. Fellow APHA (stats. sect. award 1986), Am. Statis. Assn.; mem. Internat. Statis. Inst., Internat. Assn. Ofcl. Stats. Home: 16910 E Laney Ct Fountain Hills AZ 85268 E-mail: risrael@ix.netcom.com.

ISRAEL, STEVEN JAY, congressman; b. Bklyn., May 30, 1958; s. Howard and Madeline Israel; m. Marlene Budd; children: Carly, Elana. AA, Nassau Cmty. Coll., Garden City, NY, 1978; student, Syracuse U., NY, 1978—79; BA in Polit. Sci., George Washington U., 1982. Congl. aide Staff of US Rep. Richard Ottinger of NY, Washington, 1979-83; cons. Steve Israel Assn., Huntington, NY, 1985—; asst. county exec. County of Suffolk, Hauppauge, NY, 1988-92; mem. Huntington Town Bd., NY, 1993—2001; exec. dir. Inst. on the Holocaust and Law, Huntington, 1998-2000; mem. US Congress from 2nd NY dist., 2001—, mem. appropriations com., asst. Dem. whip. Author/editor: Great Jewish Speeches, 1994. Founder Ctr. for Prejudice Reduction, Great Neck, NY, 1990; dir. Pederson-Krag Ctr., Huntington, 1996; founder, dir. LI Fgn. Affairs Forum, Mingola, NY, 1998. Named Legislator of Yr., United Jewish Appeal Fedn. NY, 2005; recipient Govt. Leadership award, United Cerebral Palsy Assn. Greater Suffolk, Inc., 2005, Interethnic Racial Harmony award, Found. Ethnic Understanding, 2006. Mem.: Nature Conservancy, Audubon Soc., Sons of Italy (assoc. Purple Aster award 1999), NAACP (life). Democrat. Jewish. Avocations: writing, historical research. Office: US House Reps 432 Cannon House Office Bldg Washington DC 20515 Office Phone: 202-225-3335. Office Fax: 202-225-4669.*

ISRAEL, WERNER, physicist, educator; b. Berlin, Oct. 4, 1931; s. Arthur and Marie (Kappauf) I.; m. Inge Margulies, Jan. 26, 1958; children: Mark Abraham, Pia Lee. BSc, U. Cape Town, 1951, MSc, 1954; PhD, Trinity Coll., Dublin, 1960; DSc (hon.), Queen's U., Kingston, Ont., 1987; Docteur honoris causa, U. Francois Rabelais, France, 1994; DSc (hon.), U. Victoria, B.C., Can., 1999. Asst. prof. physics U. Alta., Canada, 1958-68, prof., 1968-85, Univ. prof., 1985-96; adj. prof. dept. physics and astronomy U. Victoria, Canada, 1996—; hon. prof. dept. physics and astronomy U. B.C., Canada. Sherman Fairchild disting. scholar Calif. Inst. Tech., 1974-75; vis. prof. Dublin Inst. Advanced Studies, 1966-68, U. Cambridge, 1975-76, Institut Henri Poincare, 1976-77, U. Berne, 1980, Kyoto U., 1986, 98; vis. fellow Gonville and Caius Coll., Cambridge, 1985; fellow Can. Inst. for Advanced Rsch., 1986—. Editor: Relativity, Astrophysics and Cosmology, 1973; co-editor: General Relativity, An Einstein Centenary Survey, 1979, 300 Years of Gravitation, 1987. Decorated officer Order of Can.; recipient Izaak Walton Killiam Meml. prize, 1984, Medal in Math. Physics, Ctr. de Recherche Math./Can. Assn. Physicists, 1995, Tomalla Found. for Gravitational Rsch. prize, 1996. Fellow Royal Soc. Can., Royal Soc. (London); mem. Can. Assn. Physicists (medal of Achievement in Physics 1981), Internat. Soc. Gen. Relativity and Gravitation (pres. 1997-2001). Jewish. Office: U Victoria Dept Physics Astronomy Victoria BC Canada V8W 3P6 Business E-Mail: israel@uvic.ca.

ISRAELACHVILI, JACOB NISSIM, chemical engineer; b. Tel Aviv, Aug. 19, 1944; came to U.S., 1986; s. Haim Israelachvili and Hela (Noma) Galili; m. Karina Haglund, Sept. 14, 1971; children: Josefin, Daniela. BA, U. Cambridge, 1968, MA & PhD, 1972. Prof. U. Calif., Santa Barbara, 1986—. V.p. Internat. Assn. Colloid & Interface Scientists, 1986-89. Author: Intermolecular and Surface Forces, 1985, 2d edit., 1991; contbr. articles to profl. jours. Fellow Australian Nat. U., Canberra, 1974-86, Rsch. fellow U. Stockholm, Sweden, 1972-74; recipient Matthew Flinders medal, 1986. Fellow Royal Soc. London, Australian Acad. Sci.; mem. AIChE (Alpha Chi Sigma award 1991), NAS, Nat. Acad. Engrng. (fgn. assoc.). Home Phone: 805-252-5568; Office Phone: 805-893-8407. Business E-Mail: jacob@engineering.ucsb.edu.

ISRAELITE, DAVID M., music publishing executive, prosecutor; b. 1968; BA, William Jewell Coll.; JD, U. Mo. Dir. polit. and govt. affairs Rep. Nat. Com., 1999—2001; dep. chief staff, chief counsel to US Atty. US Dept. of Justice, Washington, 2001—05; pres. & CEO Nat. Music Publishers' Assn., Washington, 2005—. Campaign mgr., adminstrv. asst. Senator Christopher Bond, Mo., 1998. Office: Nat Music Pubs Assn Ste 705E 101 Constitution Ave Washington DC 20001 Office Phone: 202-742-4375. Office Fax: 202-742-4377.*

ISRAILI, ZAFAR HASAN, pharmacologist, educator; b. Moradabad, India, July 2, 1934; came to U.S., 1961, naturalized, 1977; s. Siddiq Hasan and Zahida Khatun I.; m. Sally Jean Smith, Oct. 24, 1970; children: Shahnaz Joy, Taj Hasan, Rana Shereen. BSc, Aligarh M. U., 1951, MSc, 1953; PhD, U. Kans., 1968. Lectr. chemistry Aligarh M. U., 1953-54, sr. rsch. scholar, 1954-57; rsch. asst., jr. sci. officer AEC India, 1957-61; rsch. assoc. U. Kans., 1968-69; sr. rsch. chemist Alza Corp., Lawrence, Kans., 1969-70; asst. prof. medicine and chemistry Emory U., Atlanta, 1970-75, assoc. prof. chemistry, 1975-78, assoc. prof. medicine, 1975—, prof. chemistry, 1978—. Rsch. pharmacologist Atlanta VA Med. Ctr., Decatur, 1979-87; sci. staff Grady Hosp., Atlanta, 1974—; adj. prof. chemistry Ga. Perimeter Coll., 2004—. Editor Ethnicity and Disease, 1997—; assoc. editor Drug Metabolism Revs., 1974—, Venezuelan Jour. Hypertension, 2005-, Revista Latino Americana Hipertension, 2006—; mem. editl. bd. Drug Devel. Rsch., 1979—, Archives Venezuelan Pharm. Ter., 1983—, Am. Jour. Ther., 2003-; contbr. articles to profl. jours., chpts. to books. Recipient Asia Found. award, 1962; Merit scholar Aligarh M. U., 1953; Merck Sharpe & Dohm grantee, 1977, 85, 87, NIH grantee, 1978-83, VA grantee, 1979-87, Am. Heart Assn. grantee, 1989-91. Mem. Am. Soc. Clin. Pharmacology and Therapeutics, Am. Soc. Pharmacology and Exptl. Therapeutics, Soc. Exptl. Biology and Medicine, Am. Assn. Cancer Rsch., Am. Aging Assn., Am. Chem. Soc., Am. Soc. Hypertension, Chem. Soc. London, Internat. Soc. for Study Xenobiotics, Interam. Soc. Clin. Pharm. Therapeutics (pres.-elect 1997-2000, pres. 2000—), Internat. Soc. on Hypertension in Blacks, Am. Heart Assn., Sigma Xi, Rho Chi, Phi Lambda Upsilon. Muslim. Home: 3567 Cloudland Dr Stone Mountain GA 30083-4005 Office: Emory Univ Sch Medicine Dept Medicine 69 Jesse Hill Jr Dr Atlanta GA 30303-2607 Office Phone: 404-616-5176. Business E-Mail: zisrail@emory.edu.

ISSA, DARRELL E., congressman; b. Cleve., Nov. 1, 1953; m. Kathy; 1 child, William. AA, Kent St. U.; BA, Siena Heights U., 1976. Founder, CEO Directed Electronics, Vista, Calif., 1982—99; mem. US Congress from 49th (formerly 48th) Calif. dist., 2001—. Mem. House com. on Internat. Rels., House Judiciary com., House com. on Small Bus., Permanent Select Com. on Intelligence Co-chair Calif. Civic Rights Initiative, 1996 Served in US Army, 1970—80. Recipient Entreprenuer Yr. award, Inc. mag., 1994, Angel of the Yr. award, N County Solutions for Change, 2004, Ellis Island Medal of Honor. Past chmn. Consumer Electronics Assn., former govr. Electronic Indus. Alliance; bd. dirs. Bus.-Industry Political Action com., San Diego Econ. Devel. Assn., Greater San Diego County Chamber of Commerce; past pres. Am. Task Force for Lebanon; served bd. trustees Siena Heights U. Republican. Protestant. Office: 211 Cannon House Office Bldg Washington DC 20515-0549*

ISSACHAROFF, SAMUEL, law educator; b. 1954; BA, Binghamton U., 1975; JD, Yale U., 1983. Law clk. to Judge Arlin M. Adams US Ct. Appeals 3rd Cir.; practiced law Washington; joined law faculty U. Tex., 1989, Joseph D. Jamail Centennial Chair in Law; joined law faculty Columbia U., NYC, 1999, Harold R. Medina prof. procedural jurisprudence; Bonnie and Richard Reiss prof. constl. law NYU Sch. Law, NYC, 2005—. Fellow: Am. Acad. Arts and Sciences. Office: NYU Sch Law 40 Washington Sq S, 411J New York NY 10012 Office Phone: 212-998-6580. Office Fax: 212-995-4881. E-mail: samuel.issacharoff@nyu.edu.

ISSELBACHER, KURT JULIUS, internist, educator; b. Wirges, Germany, Sept. 12, 1925; arrived in U.S., 1936, naturalized, 1945; s. Albert and Flori (Strauss) Isselbacher; m. Rhoda Solin, June 22, 1955; children: Lisa, Karen, Jody, Eric. AB, Harvard U., 1946, MD cum laude, 1950; ScD (hon.), Northwestern U., 2001. Intern, then resident Mass. Gen. Hosp., Boston, 1950—53, chief gastrointestinal unit, 1957—89, chmn. com. rsch., 1967, Cancer Ctr., 1987—2003, dir. emeritus, 2003—; investigator NIH, 1953—56; prof. medicine Harvard Med. Sch., 1966—, chmn. exec. com. depts. medicine, 1968—97, Mallinckrodt prof. medicine, 1972—97, disting. Mallinckrodt prof. medicine, 1998—, chmn. univ. cancer com., 1972—87. Mem. governing bd. NRC, 1987—90; mem. sci. bd. FDA, 1993; acad. liaison Novartis Biomed. Rsch. Inst., 2002—; trustee Marine Biol. Labs., 2004—; editor Harrison's-on-line, 1999—. Editor-in-chief (Harrison): Principles of Internal Medicine, 1976, 1991—99. Recipient award for disting. achievement in nutrition, Bristol-Myers Squibb, 1991, Sci. Bd. FDA, 1993—97, Tree of Life award, Jewish Nat. Fund, 2001. Fellow: ACP (John Phillips award for disting. achievement in clin. medicine 1989); mem.: NAS (chmn. food and nutrition bd. 1983—88, mem. exec. com., mem. coun. 1987—90, chmn. com. on risk assessment of hazardous air pollutants 1991—94), Inst. Medicine of NAS, Assn. Am. Physicians (pres. 1977—78, Kober medal 2001), Am. Gastroenterology Assn. (pres. 1974—75, Julius Friedenwald medal for outstanding achievement in gastroenterology 1985), Am. Acad. Arts and Scis. Achievements include research in molecular and genetic changes in malignant cells, metastasis in breast and colon cancer. Home: 20 Nobscot Rd Newton MA 02459-1523 Office: Cancer Ctr Mass Gen Hosp 139 13th St Charlestown MA 02129-2023 Office Phone: 617-726-5610. E-mail: KIsselbacher@partners.org.

ISSELL, BRIAN F., oncologist, internist; b. Auckland, New Zealand, Sept. 29, 1943; MD, U. Otago, New Zealand, 1971. Diplomate Am. Bd. Internal Medicine, Am. Bd. Oncology. Intern U. Otago-Otago Hosp., 1971, resident, 1972-75; fellow in med. oncology M.D. Anderson Hosp., Houston, 1976-78; mem. staff Queens Med. Ctr., Honolulu, 1988; dir. cancer rsch. ctr. U. Hawaii, Honolulu, 1988—; prof. medicine U. Hawaii John A. Burns Sch. Medicine, Honolulu, 1988—. Prof., researcher Cancer Rsch. Ctr. Hawaii. Fellow Royal Australasian Coll. Physicians, ACP; mem. AMA, Am. Soc. Clin. Oncology, Hawaii Med. Assn., Am. Assn. Cancer Rsch. Office: Cancer Rsch Ctr Hawaii 1236 Lauhala St Honolulu HI 96813-2424 Business E-Mail: brian@crch.hawaii.edu.*

ISSHIKI, MASAYUKI, sociologist, educator, dean; b. Suzuka, Japan, Oct. 21, 1950; s. Mikio Isshiki and Michiko Isshiki-Fujii; m. Miwa Terada, Dec. 28, 1988. BA in Sociology, Sussex Coll., 1980, D in Sociology, 1986. V.p. Sanas Corp., Yokkaichi, Japan, 1980-83; rsch. scientist Triad PCL, Hong Kong, 1986-91; ptnr. Triad Cons., Suzuka, Japan, 1991-93; prof. Suzuka Internat. U., 1994—, dean grad. sch., 2002—. Author: Economic Development in Southeast Asia, 1991, Development of Bamboo, 1992, U.S. Watch, 1995—. Avocations: skiing, farming. Home and Office: Rm C-101 15-11 Minami-Ejima Suzuka Mie 510-0235 Japan E-mail: misshiki@mecha.ne.jp.

ISSLER, HARRY, lawyer; b. Cologne, Germany, Nov. 14, 1935; came to U.S., 1937; s. Max and Fanny (Grunbaum) I.; m. Doris Helen Lukow, June 1, 1958; children: Adriane P. Schorr, M. Valerie Priestley, Stephanie L. Beck. BS, U. Wis., 1955; JD, Cornell U., 1958. Bar: N.Y. 1958, U.S. Supreme Ct. 1962, U.S. Ct. Mil. Appeals 1967, U.S. Dist. Ct. (so. and ea. dists.) N.Y. 1960, U.S. Customs Ct. 1964, U.S. Tax Ct. 1964; cert. specialist in civil trial advocacy Nat. Bo. Trial Advocacy. Assoc. Wing & Wing, NYC, 1958-60; assoc. Fuchsberg & Fuchsberg, NYC, 1960-62; ptnr. Issler & Fein, NYC, 1963-68, Shaw, Issler & Rosenberg, NYC, 1968-70; pvt. practice NYC, 1970-79; ptnr. Issler & Scrage, P.C., NYC, 1980-99; sr. ptnr. The Law Firm of Harry Issler PLLC, NYC, 1999—. Arbitrator Civil Ct., NY County, 1979-91; hearing officer NY State Tax Appeals, 1975-77, Supreme Ct. NY, NY County Med. Malpractice Panel, 1980-91; judge advocate NY State; neutral evaluator mediation panel Supreme Ct., NY County, 1997—; charter mem. Trial Lawyers Care, Inc. Book reviewer: NY Law Jour., 2001—. Trustee NY State Mil. Ednl. Found., 1997-2000; exec. v.p. Sutton Area Cmty., Inc., 2000-07; v.p. 50 Sutton Pl. South Owners, Inc., 2002-03; pres. 50 Sutton Pl. South Owners Corp., 2003-05. With U.S. Army, 1958-59, NY Army N.G., 1963-88, ret. brig. gen., 1988. Ford Found. scholar, 1951-55. Mem. ABA, N.Y. State Bar Assn., Assn. of Bar of City of N.Y., Am. Trial Lawyers Assn., N.Y. State Trial Lawyers Assn., 42d Infantry Divsn. Officers Club (N.Y.C.pres. 1979-80), Officers Club (U.S. Mcht. Marine Acad.), 42d Infantry Rainbow Divsn. Assn. (pres. 1989), Phi Alpha Delta, Pi Lambda Phi (Omega chpt. pres. 1953-54). Home: 50 Sutton Pl S New York NY 10022-4167 Office: 110 E 59th St 25th Fl New York NY 10022 Office Phone: 212-371-0200. Business E-Mail: harryissler@lawyer.com.

ISTEL, JACQUES ANDRE, mayor; b. Paris, Jan. 28, 1929; came to US, 1940, naturalized, 1951; s. Andre and Yvonne Mathilde Cremieux I.; m. Felicia Juliana Lee, June 14, 1973; 1 dau. by previous marriage, Claudia Yvonne. AB, Princeton U., NJ, 1949. Stock analyst Andre Istel & Co., NYC, 1950, 55; pres. Parachutes Inc., Orange, Mass., 1957-87, Intramgmt. Inc., NYC, 1962-80; chmn. Pilot Knob Corp., 1982—; mayor Town of Felicity, Calif., 1986—; curator Ctrl. Point for Memories, Calif., 1992—. Pres. VI World Parachuting Championships, 1962; capt. U.S. Parachuting team, 1956, master of sports, USSR, 1956, capt., team leader, 1958; chmn. Mass. Parachuting Commn., 1961-62; life hon. pres. Internat. Parachuting Commn., Fedn. Aero. Internat., 1965-; chmn. Hall of Fame of Parachuting, 1973—, Imp. Co. water commn. 1997—; founder Nat. Collegiate Parachuting League, 1957, World Commemorative Ctr., 1993; co-leader Nat. Geog. Soc. Vilcabamba Expdn., 1964. Author: Coe the Good Dragon at the Center of the World, 1985, Coe le Bon Dragon au Centre du Monde, 1985; editor in granite Museum Walls, 2001—; contbr. articles to encys., profl. jours.; patentee in field. Trustee Inst. for Man and Sci., 1975-82; bd. dirs. Marine Corps Scholarship Found., 1975-85; founder Mus. History Granite, 2005—. Served with USMC, 1952-54; lt. col. Res. Recipient Leo Stevens award, 1958, Diplome Paul Tissandier, 1969, Air and Space medal, 2003, Official Citation, Mass. State Senate, 2007; decorated chevalier de la Legion D'Honneur; named Hon. Citizen Yuma, Ariz., 2007; world record holder for parachuting, 1961. Mem. Nat. Aero. Assn. (bd. dirs. 1965-68), Fedn. Internat. des Centres (pres. 1990—), Cercle de l'Union Interalliée (Paris), Marine Corps Res. Officers Assn., DAV (life), Racquet and Tennis Club (NYC), Princeton Club (NYC). Home: Northview Felicity CA 92283 also: 10 rue Galilée 75116 Paris France Office: 1 Center Of The World Plz Felicity CA 92283-7777 Office Phone: 760-572-0100. Personal E-mail: ctrworld@aol.com.

ISTOCK, VERNE GEORGE, retired bank executive; b. Sept. 20, 1940; BA in Econs., U. Mich., 1962, MBA in Fin., 1963. Credit analyst trainee NBD Bancorp, Inc., Detroit, 1963—66, group head, 1971-77, head U.S. divsn., 1977-82, sr. v.p., 1979-82, exec. v.p., 1982-85, vice chmn., dir., 1985-93, chmn., CEO, 1994-95, also bd. dirs.; chmn. NBD Bank; pres., CEO First Chgo. NBD Corp., Chgo., 1995-98, chmn., 1996-98; chmn. bd. Bank One Corp., Chgo., 1999—2000, pres., 2000; ret., 2000. Bd. dirs. Kelly Svcs. Inc., Masco Corp., Rockwell Automation, Inc. Bd. dirs. Chgo. Coun. Fgn. Rels., Chgo. Crime Commn. Mem. U. Mich. Alumni Assn. (past pres., lifetime dir.), Bankers Roundtable (past dir.), Econ. Club Chgo. (past dir.), Mich. Bus. Roundtable (past bd. dirs.), Comml. Club of Chgo., Econ. Club Detroit (past dir.), Ill. Bus. Roundtable (past dir.).

ISTOK, CHRISTINE MARKWARD, retired executive director social service agency, consultant; b. Washington, July 5, 1947; d. George Albert and Mary Ruth (Stalcup) Markward; m. Donald Phillip O'Sullivan, June 27, 1985. Sec. Gas Distributors Info. Svc., Washington, 1966-70; adminstr. asst. Nat. Airlines, Washington, 1970-71; office mgr. Tire Industry Safety Coun., Washington, 1971-75; pres. Type-Right Exec. Sec. Svc., Washington, Pitts., 1976-91; exec. dir. Eastside Cmty. Ministry, Zanesville, Ohio, 1991—2001. Chair FEMA Emergency Bd., Muskingum, Morgan and Perry Counties, Ohio, 1994-97, 99-2000; chair United Way Exec. Dirs. Coun., 1994-97, United Way agy. relations com. 2000-03, allocations com. 2002-04; v.p. Muskingum County Hunger Network, Zanesville, 1993-99. Author: Write a Good Resume, 1976. Mem. task force Literacy Coun., 1993—2000; mem. steering com. Muskingum County Operation Feed, 1992—99; trustee Disability Network of Ohio-Solidarity, 2001—; mem Zanesville City Sch. Bldg. Adv. Coun., Ohio, 2001—03; v.p. Muskingum County Women's Rep. Club, 1994, sec., 1995; mem. Downtown Clergy Assn., 1992—, pres., 1995—96; bd. dirs. Human Care Ministry, Ohio dist. Luth. Ch., Mo. Synod, PRO-Muskingum, 1995—2000; commr. Mo. Synod Luths. to Commn. on Religion in Appalachia, 1996—98; chair human care bd. Trinity Evang. Luth. Ch., 2003—; bd. dirs. Muskingum County Women's Coalition, 1994—97, Families and Children First Coun., 1995—2000, Interfaith Response to Ohio Disaster, 1988—91, Luth. Social Svcs. Emergency Assistance Com., 1998—99, Muskingum County Family Adv. Team, 2000—01. Recipient Cert. of Achievement for Mil. Family Support, U.S. Army, 1991, Excellence in Cmty. Svc. award Aid Assn. Luths., 1993, Excellence in Cmty. Svc. award Muskingum County DAR, 1994, Positive Action award, NOW, 1997, YWCA Woman of Achievement award, 1997, Americanism award VFW, 1992, Cmty. Involvement award Richvale Grange, 1997, Cmty. Citizen award State of Ohio Grange, 2000; named Outstanding Cmty. Vol. Zanesville Daybreak Rotary Club, 1997. Mem.: Nat. Multiple Sclerosis Soc. (program com. Buckeye chpt. 2001—04), Muskingum County Respiratory Assn. (bd. dirs. 2001—, sec., bd. dirs. 2003—), Disability Network Ohio Solidarity (trustee 2001—), Richvale Grange, Kiwanis (Zanesville chpt. bd. dirs. 1997—99, spiritual aims com. chair Dist. 18 of Ohio 1998—99). Avocations: creative writing, music. Office: Eastside Cmty Ministry 221 Stillwell St PO Box 965 Zanesville OH 43702-0965 Personal E-mail: chrissyduck@hotmail.com.

ISTOMIN, MARTA CASALS, retired school president, performing company executive; b. PR, Nov. 2, 1936; d. Aquiles and Angelica M. (Martinez) Montanez; m. Pablo Casals, Aug. 3, 1957 (dec. 1973); m. Eugene Istomin, Feb. 15, 1975. Student, Mannes Coll. Music, NYC, 1950-54; Mus.D. (hon.), World U., PR, 1972; L.H.D. (hon.), Marymount Coll., 1975; Doctorate (hon.), U. P.R., 1984, Dickinson Coll., Carlisle, Pa., 1986; D (hon.), Shenandoah Coll., 1986, Interam. U., PR, 1989. Prof. cello Conservatory Music, San Juan, P.R., 1961-64; vis. prof. cello Curtis Inst., Phila., 1974-75; co-chmn. bd., music dir. Casals Festival, 1974-77; artistic dir. John F. Kennedy Center for Performing Arts, Washington, 1980-90; dir. gen. Evian Music Festival, France, 1990—; pres. Manhattan Sch. Music, NYC, 1992—2005, ret., 2005. Mem. Nat. Coun. on Arts, 1990; cons. Latin Am. ednl. projects. Trustee Marlboro Sch. Music and Festival; trustee Marymount Sch., NYC, World U. Recipient Puerto Rican Fedn. Women's Clubs award, 1967; award for cultural achievements City of San Juan, 1975; Nat. Conf. Puerto Rican Women award, 1975; Casita Maria medal for outstanding contbns. to culture N.Y.C., 1978; Outstanding Contbns. Performing Arts in Nation's Capitol award, 1983; Family Place Outstanding Community Service award, 1986; Mayor's Excellence in Service Arts award, Washington, 1986; Nat. Fedn. Music Clubs citation, 1987; named Outstanding Woman of Yr. P.R., 1975; Woman of Achievement Sta. WETA-TV, Washington, 1981; Order of Isabella the Cath. govt. Spain, 1986; Officer, Order Arts and Letters govt. France, 1986; Officer's Cross Order Merit govt. Fed. Republic Germany, 1987. Mem. Nat. Coun. on the Arts. Roman Catholic. Office: Manhattan School Music 120 Claremont Ave New York NY 10027-4698

ISTOOK, ERNEST JAMES, JR., (JIM), former congressman, lawyer; b. Ft. Worth, Feb. 11, 1950; s. Ernest James and Dessie Cordelia Lyne Istook; m. Judy Lee Bills, 1973; children: Amy, Butch, Chad, Diana, Emily. BA in Journalism, Baylor U., Waco, Tex., 1971; JD, Okla. City U. Sch. Law, 1976. Reporter State Capitol Stas. KOMA-TV, Oklahoma City, 1972—73, WKY-Radio, Oklahoma City, 1973—76; dir. Okla. Alcoholic Beverage Control Bd., 1977-78; asst. legal counsel to Gov. David Boren Staff of Okla., 1978; dir. Warr Acres C. of C., 1982-86; mem. city coun. City of Warr Acres, Okla., 1982-86; atty. Istook & Assocs., 1983-93; mem. Okla. State Ho. Reps., 1987—93, US Congress from 5th Okla. dist., 1993—2007, mem. appropriations com., 1993—2007, vice chmn. homeland security appropriations subcommittee. Bd. mem. Okla. County Met. Libr. Sys., 1982—86, chair, 1985—86. Named Taxpayer Friend of Yr., 1991, One of Ten Best Legislators, 1992. Mem.: Kappa Nu. Republican. Mem. Lds Ch.

ITABASHI, HIDEO HENRY, coroner, pathologist, educator, consultant; b. LA, July 7, 1926; s. Masakichi and Mitsuko (Kobayashi) I.; m. Yoko Osawa, Feb. 3, 1952; children: Mark Masa, Helen Yoko. AB, Boston U., 1949, MD, 1954; postgrad., Yale U., 1949—50. Diplomate in neuropathology Am. Bd. Pathology. Intern U. Mich. Hosp., Ann Arbor, 1954-55, resident in neurology, 1955-58; assoc. rsch. neurologist U. Calif., San Francisco, 1958-60, asst. clin. prof., 1964-65; asst. neuropathologist Langley Porter Neuropsychiat. Inst., San Francisco, 1960-65; cons. Neuropathologist San Francisco Gen. Hosp., 1964-65; assoc. prof. neurology, pathology U. Mich. Med. Sch., Ann Arbor, 1968-71; prof.-in-residence pathology and neurology UCLA, 1975-93, prof. emeritus, 1993—, acting vice chair dept. pathology Sch. Medicine; acting chair pathology Harbor-UCLA Med. Ctr., 1990-91; cons. neuropathology dept., chief med. examiner-coroner Los Angeles County, 1977—. Cons. VA Hosp., Sepulveda, Calif., 1977-92; spl. fellow in neuropathology Nat. Inst. Neurol. Diseases and Blindness, 1958-60. Contbr. numerous articles on neurol. disorders to med jours. Fellow Am Acad. Forensic Scis.; mem. Am. Assn. Neuropathologists (sr.), Am. Acad. Neurology (sr.). Office: County LA Dept Coroner 1104 N Mission Rd Los Angeles CA 90033 Home Phone: 310-377-0664.

ITANO, HARVEY AKIO, biochemistry educator; b. Sacramento, Nov. 3, 1920; s. Masao and Sumako (Nakahara) I.; m. Rose Nakako Sakemi, Nov. 5, 1949; children: Wayne Masao, Glenn Harvey, David George. BS, U. Calif., Berkeley, 1942; MD, St. Louis U., 1945; PhD, Calif. Inst. Tech., 1950; DSc (hon.), St. Louis U., 1987. Intern City of Detroit Receiving Hosp., 1945-46; commd. officer USPHS, Bethesda, Md., 1950-70, advanced through grades to chief, sect. on chem. genetics, Nat. Inst. Arthritis and Metabolic Diseases, NIH, 1962-70, mem. hematology study sect., NIH, 1959-63, research fellow then sr. research fellow, Calif. Inst. Tech. Pasadena, 1950-54; prof. Dept. Pathology U. Calif. San Diego, La Jolla, 1970-88, prof. emeritus, 1988—. Vis. prof. Osaka (Japan) U., 1961-62, U. Chgo., 1965, U. Calif., San Francsico, 1967; cons. sickle cell anemia, mem. hematology study sect. 1953-63, various sickle cell anemia rev. coms., 1970-81, NIH, Bethesda. Editor: (with Linus Pauling) Molecular Structure and Biological Specificity, 1957; contbr. articles to profl. jours. George Minot lectr., AMA, 1955; Japan Soc. for Promotion of Sci. fellow, Okayama U., 1983-84. Mem. NAS, Am. Acad. Arts and Scis., Am. Chem. Soc. (Eli Lilly award in Biol. Chemistry 1954), Am. Soc. Biochemistry and Molecular Biology, Am. Soc. Hematology, Internat. Soc. Hematology, Phi Beta Kappa, Sigma Xi, Alpha Omega Alpha. Office: U Calif Dept Pathology 9500 Gilman Dr La Jolla CA 92093-0612

ITKIN, IVAN, nuclear scientist, mathematician; b. NYC, Mar. 29, 1936; s. Abraham Aaron and Eda (Kreger) I.; m. Judith Ann Weiss, Aug. 19, 1962 (div. 1975); children: Marc Eric, Laurie Rachel; m. Joyce Lee Hudak, July 12, 1975; 1 child, Max Eugene. BSChemE, Poly. Inst., Bklyn., 1956; M in Nuclear Engring., NYU, 1957; PhD in Math., U. Pitts., 1964; D of Pub. Svc. (hon.), Chatham Coll., 1994. Assoc. scientist Bettis Atomic Power Lab. Westinghouse Electric Corp., Pitts., 1957-59, scientist, 1959-64, sr. scientist, 1964-71, fellow scientist, 1971-73; mem. Pa. Ho. of Reps., Harrisburg, 1973-98; dir. Office Civilian Radioactive Waste Mgmt. U.S. Dept. Energy, Washington, 1999-2001. Majority caucus chmn. Pa. Ho. of Reps., 1982-90, majority whip, 1990-92, majority leader, 1993-94, Democratic whip, 1995-98; Dem. nominee for Pa. gov., 1998; chmn. sci., tech., and resource planning com. Nat. Conf. State Legislators, Denver, 1988; del. Dem. Nat. Conv., 1984, 96; U.S. presdl. elector, 1992, 96. Election judge 19th Dist., 14th Ward, Pa., 1966-68; chmn. 14th Ward Dem. Com., Pitts., 1970-72. Recipient Keystone award Alcoholism and Addiction Assn., 1983, Award of Appreciation, Nat. Fedn. Blind, 1983, Disting. Svc. award Pa. Coll. Optometry, 1986; named House Mem. of Yr., Pa. Jewish Coalition, 1983. Mem. ACLU, Am. Nuclear Soc., Am. Jewish Congress, B'nai B'rith. Home: 3200 N Ocean Blvd Unit 606 Fort Lauderdale FL 33308-7155 Personal E-mail: iitkin@bellsouth.net.

ITO, NOBORU, electric power industry executive; b. Qindao, Santon, China, Dec. 17, 1921; s. Eisho and Raiko (Watanabe) I.; m. Sachiko Tsuchiya (dec. Nov. 1978); children: Junko, Kyoko. B, Tohoku U., 1946, D, 1973. Engr. Toyo Comm. Co., Kawasaki, 1946—50, Oi Electric Co., Tokyo, 1950—57, chief rschr. Yokohama, 1964—69, dir., 1970—83, cons., 1984—91; pres. Leo-B Corp., Yokohama, 1992—. Scientist Tokyo U., 1960-63, 89-91; lectr. Yamagata U., 1982-83; scientist U. So. Calif., LA, 1985-86. Recipient invention prize Japan Inst. Invention, 1982, dir. prize Sci. and Tech. Agy. of Japan, 1982, yellow ribbon prize Japan Govt., 1984. Mem. IEEE (sr.), NY Acad. Scis., Japan Phys. Soc., Japan Merits Club. Avocations: languages, travel. Office: Leo-B Corp R1012 6-13-53 Kikuna Kohokuku Yokohama 222 Japan

ITO, YOICHIRO, pathologist, researcher; b. Osaka, Japan, Dec. 22, 1928; came to U.S., 1968, naturalized, 1978; s. Taichi and Ai (Kubota) I.; m. Ryoko Tanioka, Dec. 23, 1963; children: Koichi, Shin. MD, Osaka City U., Japan, 1958. Intern U.S. Yokosuka (Japan) Naval Hosp., Yokosuka, Japan, 1958—59; resident in pathology Cleve. (Ohio) Met. Gen. Hosp., 1959—61, Michael Reese Hosp., Chgo., 1961—63; instr. physiology Osaka (Japan) City U. Med. Sch., 1963—68; vis. scientist Nat. Heart, Lung and Blood Inst. NIH, Bethesda, Md., 1968—78, med. officer Nat. Heart, Lung and Blood Inst., 1978—. Recipient 1st pl. award ann. sci. rsch. presentation at Cleve. Met. Gen. Hosp., 1960, Tech. Excellence award for devel. blood cell separator, 1979; Fulbright exch. scholar, 1959-63; WHO rsch. travel fund grantee Nat. Inst. Med. Rsch., London, 1968. Mem. N.Y. Acad. Scis., Kenshinkai. Achievements include research on innovation in separation science, including continuous development of countercurrent chromatography, cell separation methods; initiated and developed countercurrent chromatography; patentee coil planet centrifuge, rotating-seal-free flow-through centrifuge, pH-zone-refining countercurrent chromatography, centrifugal precipitation chromatography; continuous-flow cell separation method based on cell density, spiral disk assembly for high-speed countercurrent chromatography. Home: 6003 Melvern Drive Bethesda MD 20817 Office: NIH Bldg 50 Rm 3334 9000 Rockville Pike Bethesda MD 20892-8014 Home Phone: 301-530-8746; Office Phone: 301-496-1210. E-mail: itoy2@mail.nih.gov.

ITOH, TATSUO, engineering educator; b. Tokyo, May 5, 1940; BS, Yokohama Nat. U., Japan, 1964, MS, 1966; PhD, U. Ill., 1969. Registered profl. engr., Tex. Rsch. assoc. U. Ill., Urbana, 1969-71, rsch. asst. prof., 1971-76; sr. rsch. engr. Stanford Rsch. Inst., Menlo Park, Calif., 1976-77; assoc. prof. U. Ky., Lexington, 1977-78, U. Tex., Austin, 1978-81, prof., 1981-90, Hayden Head prof., 1983-90; prof.and TRW endowed chair UCLA, 1991—. Guest rschr. AEG-Telefunken, Ulm, Fed. Republic of Germany, 1979; vis. prof. Def. Acad. Japan, 1991, U. Leeds, Eng., 1994—; hon. vis. prof. Nanjing Inst. Tech., China; hon. prof. Beijing Aeronautical and Astron. U., China, 1995—; adj. rsch. officer Comms. Rsch. Lab., Ministry of Post and Telecom., Japan, 1994; cons. Tex. Instruments, Dallas, 1979, Hughes Aircraft. Editor (guest): Transactions, 1991. Recipient Engring. Found. faculty awards, 1980-81, Billy and Claude Hocott Disting. Rsch. award, 1988, Disting. Alumnus award U. Ill., 1990, Shida award Min. of Post and Telecom., Japan, 1998, Japan Microwave prize Asia-Pacific Microwave Conf., 1998. Fellow IEEE (Millennium medal 2000, MTT Disting. Microwave Educator award 2000), Nat. Acad. Engring.; mem. Microwave Theory and Techniques Soc. (hon. life; editor 1983-85, pres. 1990, jour. editor Microwave and Guided Wave Letters 1991-94), Internat. Sci. Radio Union (chmn. USNC commn. D 1988-90, chmn. commn. D 1993-96, long range planning com. 1996—), Inst. Electronics and Comm. Engrs., Nat. Acad. Engring. Achievements include invention of the millimeter-wave line; quasi-optical mixer; non-contact ID; high power photo detector. Office: UCLA Dept Elec Engring Los Angeles CA 90095-0001 Home: 12 Eastfield Dr Rolling Hills CA 90274-5226 Office Phone: 310-206-4820. Business E-Mail: itoh@ee.ucla.edu.

ITTS, ELIZABETH ANN DUNHAM, retired psychotherapist, consultant; b. Columbus, Ohio, May 11, 1928; d. Dalton Dee and Elizabeth Farrell (Beck) Dunham; m. Frank Joseph Itts, June 23, 1951; children: Cynthia Ann Robbins, Mark Dunham, Deirdre Elizabeth Jones, Andrea Lee Schoenfeld. Student, St. Mary of the Springs, Columbus, Ohio, 1946-47; BFA in Archtl. Design, Ohio State U., 1950; MS in Edn. Guidance, Youngstown State U., Ohio, 1979. Lic., cert. counselor Nat. Bd. Cert. Counselors. Dir. activity ctr. pilot program Mahoning County Health Dept., Youngstown, 1974-76; dir. Career Devel. Ctr. for Women, Youngstown, 1978-79; asst. to dir. Youngstown State U. Alumni Assn., 1979-81; pvt. practice psychotherapist, cons., 1981-85, 87-92; dir. career planning, placement and spl. programs Kent State U., Salem, Ohio, 1985-87. Writer grants funding for workshops, 1978-79; established career planning and placement office Kent State U., Salem, 1985, initiated and developed human svcs. tech. degree, 1986-87; writer acad. challenge grants; chmn. curriculum devel. Inst. Learning Retirement Youngstown State U., 1994-2000. Mem. Planning and Zoning Commn., Canfield, Ohio, 1980-90, Ohio Speakers Forum, 1990, Friends of Art (Butler Art Gallery), Youngstown, 1965—, Ohio Hist. Soc., Columbus, 1984—; chmn. nominating com. United Way Scholarship Commn., Youngstown, 1978-82; mem. Youngstown 2010 Revitalization, Northea. Ohio Regional Consortium. Mem. Ea. Ohio Counselor's Assn., Jr. Women's League, Youngstown State U. Alumni (life), Ohio State U. Alumni (life). Roman Catholic. Avocations: painting, sculpture, poetry. Home: 1323 Red Tail Hawk Ct Unit 1 Youngstown OH 44512-8026

ITURBIDE, GRACIELA, photographer; b. Mexico City, May 16; married, 1962; children: Manuel, Claudia, Mauricio. Student, U. Nat. Autanoma Mexico, 1969—72. Asst. Manuel Breva. Exhibitions include Galeria José Clemence Orosco, Mexico City, 1975, Midtown Y Gallery, N.Y.C., 1976, Centre Georges Pompldeu, Paris, 1982. Recipient prize, UN Internat. Labor Orgn., 1986, W. Eugene Smith award, 1987; Consejo Mexicano de Fotografia grantee, 1983, Guggenheim Found. grantee, 1987. Mem.: Mexican Coun. Photography (founding mem.). Office: c/o Robert Miller Gallery 524 W 26th St New York NY 10001

IULIANO, ROBERT W., lawyer; b. Waltham, Mass. m. Susan Iuliano; children: Jeff, Ben. Degree, Harvard U., 1983; JD, U. Va., 1986. Bar: Mass. 1987. Law clk. to Chief Judge Levin Campbell US Ct. Appeals (1st cir.); atty. Choate, Hall & Stewart; prosecutor US Atty.'s Office, Boston, 1991—94; atty. Harvard U., Cambridge, Mass., 1994—2000, dep. gen. counsel, 2000—03, v.p., 2003—, gen. counsel, 2003—. Trustee Goodnow Libr., Sudbury, Mass., 2002. Office: Harvard Univ Massachusetts Hall Cambridge MA 02138 Office Phone: 617-496-4179.*

IUZZINI, JOHNNY, chef; Pastry chef Payard Patisserie, Paris, Laduree, Paris, Restaurant Daniel, NYC, Jean Georges, NYC. Named one of Ten Best Pastry Chefs, Pastry Art & Design; recipient Outstanding Pastry Chef award, James Beard Found., 2006. Office: Jean Georges Trump International Hotel and Tower 1 Central Park W New York NY 10012 Office Phone: 212-299-3900.*

IVANCHENKO, LAUREN MARGARET DOWD, pharmaceutical executive; b. West Orange, NJ, Mar. 20, 1958; d. Bernard Peter and Virginia (Morsell) Dowd; m. John Ivanchenko, Aug. 12, 1990; 1 child, Liana Katherine. BS in Psycho.-Biology, Albright Coll., 1980; postgrad., Rutger's U., 1991—92; MBA, St. Joseph's U., 2002. Sales Bourroughs Wellcome Co., Rsch. Triangle Pk., NC, 1981—84, acct. mgr. med. ctr., 1984—96; therapeutic area specialist Glaxo Wellcome, Inc., 1996—2000; sr. exec. clin. specialist Glaxo Smith Kline, Inc., 2000—. Mem.: Am. Epilepsy Soc., N.J. Epilepsy Soc. (mem. profl. adv. bd. 2001—), Nat. Exch. Club, Beta Gamma Sigma, Phi Delta Sigma. Avocations: piano, reading.

IVANHOE, ROBERT J., lawyer; b. NYC, 1953; BA, Johns Hopkins U., 1975; JD, Am. U., 1978. Bar: N.Y. 1979. Ptnr. Dreyer and Traub, NYC; now shareholder, mem. exec. com., chair nat. real estate practice Greenberg Traurig, LLP, NYC. Sr. editor Am. U. Law Review, 1977-78. Mem. Omicron Delta Kappa, Pi Sigma Alpha. Office: Greenberg Traurig LLP MetLife Bldg 200 Park Ave New York NY 10166 Office Phone: 212-801-9333. Office Fax: 212-801-6400. Business E-Mail: ivanhoer@gtlaw.com.

IVANICK, CAROL W. TRENCHER, lawyer; b. Springfield, Mass., Mar. 6, 1939; d. Joseph George and Daisy Wolf; m. Michael Ira Trencher, July 30, 1960 (div. Feb. 1984); children: Christopher, Daniel, Deborah; m. Peter Alan Ivanick (div. 1998). BA, Wellesley Coll., 1959; JD, Yale U., 1962. Bar: N.Y. 1963. Assoc. Cleary, Gottlieb et al, NYC, 1962-67; ptnr. Dewey, Ballantine LLP, NYC, 1976—2004, of counsel, 2004—. Chmn. adv. com. Pension Benefit Guaranty Corp., Washington, 1978-80; visiting lectr. Yale Law Sch., New Haven, Conn., 1978-79, 82-83. Avocations: ceramics, bowling, tennis. Home: 110 Riverside Dr New York NY 10024-3715 Office: Dewey Ballantine 1301 Avenue Of The Americas New York NY 10019-6022 Office Phone: 212-259-7800. E-mail: civanick@dbllp.com.

IVANKOVICH, ANTHONY D., anesthesiologist, educator; b. Debeljaca, Yugoslavia, Mar. 25, 1939; came to U.S., 1965; m. Olga Ivankovich. MD, U. Zagreb, Croatia, 1963. Lic. physician, Ill.; diplomate Am. Bd. Anesthesiology. Resident in internal medicine County Hosp. Nunberg, Fed. Republic Germany, 1963-65; rotating intern Edgewater Hosp., Chgo., 1966; resident in anesthesiology U. of Chgo. Hosps., 1967-68; asst. prof. anesthesiology Stritch Sch. Medicine Loyola U., Maywood, Ill., 1970-71; instr. anesthesiology Pritzker Sch. Medicine U. Chgo., 1969, assoc. prof. anesthesiology, 1972-74; faculy Sch. Medicine Cook County Postgrad., Chgo., 1975—85; prof. anesthesiology Rush Med. Coll. Rush Univ. Med. Ctr., 1980; dir. Rush Pain Ctr., chmn. anesthesiology Rush U. Med. Ctr., Chgo., 1980—2006. Dir. anesthesia rsch. Michael Reese Med. Ctr., Chgo., 1971—74, attending anesthesiologist, 1971—74, Stritch Sch. Medicine, Loyola U., Chgo., 1970—71, lectr. in anesthesiology, 1971—81; cons. anesthesiology Suburban TB Sanatorium, Hinsdale, Ill., 1970—71, Shriners Hosp. for Crippled Children, Chgo., 1977—82; chief oper. rm. svcs. 801st Gen. Hosp., USAR, Lincolnwood, Ill., 1971—73, chief surgery, 1973—74, assoc. chief profl. svcs., 1974—76; chmn. anesthesiology Ill. Masonic Med. Ctr., Chgo., 1974—80, Rush U. Med. Ctr., Chgo., 1980—2006, chmn. coun. surg. chmn. divsn. surg. scis. and svcs., 1992—94, dir. Surg. Svcs., assoc. v.p., 1993—2007, dir. Women & Children's Hosp., assoc. v.p., 1994—2007, pres. med. staff, trustee, 2005—; assoc. examiner Am. Bd. Anesthesiology, 1978; presenter in field. Author: (books) Nitroprusside and Other Short-Acting Hypotensive Agents, 1978, (book chpts. with others) Perspective in High Frequency Ventilation, 1983, Current Controversies in Thoracic Surgery, 1986, Anesthesia and ENT Surgery, 1987, Liposomes as Drug Carriers, 1987, Effective Hemostasis in Cardiac Surgery, 1988, Adjuncts to Cancer Therapy, 1989, Advances in Anesthesia, 1990, Cardiothoracic and Vascular Anesthesia Update, 1991, Cardiothoracic and Vascular Anesthesia Update, 1991, Clinical Anesthesia, 1992, Clinical Anesthesia Updates, 1992, Liposomes in Drug Delivery, 1992; contbr. articles and abstracts to profl. jours. Fellow Am. Coll. Anesthesiologists; mem. AMA, Internat. Assn. for Study of Pain, Internat. Anesthesia Rsch. Soc., Am. Soc. Anesthesiologists, Am. Heart Assn., Am. Coll. Chest Physicians, Am. Pain Soc., Pan Am. Med. Assn., Soc. for Intravenous Anesthesia, Ill. Med. Soc., Ill. Soc. Anesthesiologists, Soc. Neurosurg. Anesthesia and Neurologic Supporting Care, Midwest Pain Soc., Chgo. Med. Soc., Chgo. Soc. Anesthesiologists, Inst. of Medicine of Chgo., Chgo. Heart Assn., Sigma Xi. Office: Rush Univ Med Ctr Dept Anesthesiology 1653 W Congress Pkwy Chicago IL 60612-3833 Office Phone: 312-942-3137. E-mail: aivankov@rush.edu.

IVANOV, ILIYAN, psychiatrist, researcher, artist; b. Burgas, Bulgaria, July 18, 1963; MD, Varna Med. Inst., Bulgaria, 1990. Diplomate in psychiatry Am. Bd. Psychiatry and Neurology, 2004. Clin. instr. Varna Med. Inst., 1990—94; intern Maimonides Med. Ctr., Bklyn., 1996—97, resident, 1997—2000, Mt. Sinai Med. Ctr., NYC, 2000—03; asst. prof. psychiatry Mt. Sinai Sch. Medicine, NYC, 2005—. Co-founder Curb Group Arts. Exhibitions include Albright Knox Art Mus., 9th Annual D.U.M.B.O. Art Festival, Toronto Spring Salon. Bd. dirs. NY Coun. on Child and Adolescent Psychiatry, NYC, 2000—. Grantee, NIDA, AACAP, 2005—. Home: 235 E 95th St New York NY 10128 Office: Mount Sinai Sch Medicine One Gustave L Levy Pl New York NY 10029 Office Phone: 646-387-6080. Personal E-mail: iliyani@yahoo.com. Business E-Mail: iliyan.ivanov@mssm.edu.

IVANOV, KAMEN PETKOV, engineering educator; b. Veliko Tarnovo, Bulgaria, July 20, 1927; s. Petko Ivanov Angelov and Paraskeva Stoyanova Christova; m. Varbina Ivanova Miteva, Oct. 20, 1957; 1 child, Chavdar. Diploma in Commn. Engring., Czech Tech. U., 1952; PhD in Elec. Engring., Moscow Engring. Inst., 1961. Design and support engr. Electronics Works, Sofia, Bulgaria, 1953—55; tchg. asst., dept elec. engring. Sofia Tech. U., Bulgaria, 1956—57; sr. engr. Inst. Physics Bulgarian Acad. Sci., 1962—63; rsch. scientist Inst. Electronics Bulgarian Acad. Sci., 1963—65, sr. rsch. scientist, head dept. microwaves, 1965—90; guest prof. Fernuniversitaet Hagen, Germany, 1990—2000; instr. of electrodynamics Ill. Inst. Tech., Chgo., 2000—. Spkr. in field; ofcl. rep. Danube countries mgmt. com. European Microwave Confs., 1978—83, mem. tech. program com.; v.p. Internat. Conf. Microwave Ferrites of E. European Countries, 1978—80, pres., 1980—82. Author: Phase Shifters and Control Devices, 1990; guest editor: Microwaves, Antennas, and Propagation, IEE Procs., 1993, mem. editl. bd.: Electronic Letters, 1972—76; contbr. articles to profl. jours. Recipient Medal of Merit, Polish Acad. Scis., 1987; grantee, European Union Commn. Sci. Rsch., 1993, rsch. on anisotropic waveguides, Fern U. Mem.: Czechoslovakia-Bulgarian Friendship Soc. (disting. mem.). Avocation: violin. Office: Ill Inst Tech 3301 S Dearborn Chicago IL 60616

IVANOV, LYUBEN DIMITROV, naval architecture researcher, educator; b. Varna, Bulgaria, Apr. 14, 1941; came to U.S., 1991; s. Dimitar Dimov and Petra Christova (Grozdeva) I.; m. Svetlana Zekova, Aug. 14, 1965 (div. July 1977); children: Ognyan, Iskra; m. Irina Radeva, Aug. 18, 1977; stepchildren: Ivelin, Michaela. Diploma for Naval Architecture, Higher Naval Sch., Varna, Bulgaria, 0164; PhD, Leningrad Shipbuilding Inst., Russia, 1970. Chartered engr., U.K. Designer Inst. for Shipbuilding, Varna, 1964-66; asst. Tech. Univ., Varna, 1966, reader, head of dept., 1970-74, vice-dean for rsch., 1975-76, vice-dean for continuing edn., 1985-86, dean of faculty of shipbuilding, 1987-89, reader on ship structures, 1989-91; sr. engr. Am. Bur. Shipping, NYC, 1991—. Vis. researcher Univ. Newcastle upon Tyne, U.K., 1974-75; dep. dirs. Inst. for Shipbuilding, Varna, 1986-87, mng. dir. 1987-89; v.p. Bulgarian Shipbuilding Corp., Varna, 1987-88. Mem. editorial bd. Marine Structures Jour., 1988-93. Founder, sec. Union of Bulgarian Scientists in Shipbuilding, Varna, 1982. Recipient badge of Honor, Presidium of the Union of Bulgarian Scientists, Sofia, 1984. Mem. Royal Instn. Naval Architects/U.K. (mem. internat. standing com. practical design of ships and mobile units symposium 1987-93), Soc. Naval Architects and Marine Engrs. Achievements include research in application of probabilistic methods in ship structures design and analysis. Home: 12 Brentwood Oaks Ct The Woodlands TX 77381-2525 Office: Am Bur Shipping ABS Plaza 16855 Northchase Dr Houston TX 77060-6006 Office Fax: 281-877-5820. Business E-Mail: livanov@eagle.org.

IVE, JONATHAN, information technology executive, product designer; b. London, 1967; Studies design and art, Northumbria U., Eng., 1985; BA, Doctorate, Newcastle Polytechnic. Ptnr. Tangerine, London, 1989—92; with Apple Computer, Inc., Cupertino, Calif., 1992—, head, design team, 1996—, sr. v.p. indsl. design apple computers, 1998—. Work widely exhibited in Europe, N.Am. and Asia, forming permanent collections at many museums. Named as having the greatest impact on popular culture, BBC poll, 2002, New Media Hero, British Interactive Media Assn., 2003, Most Admired in the Creative Industries, Creative Review Peer Poll, 2003, No. 1 on the list. British Culture's Top 50 Movers and Shakers, BBC 3, 2004, Comdr. of the Most Excellent Order of the British Empire (CBE), 2005; named one of Best and Brightest, Esquire, 2002, Details, 2002, 25 Masters of Innovation, BusinessWeek, 2006; recipient Designer of Yr. prize, Design Mus. London, 2003, Product Designer of Yr. award, BluePrint Magazine, 2004, President's award for Outstanding Contribution to the Industry, Design and Art Direction Awards, 2005. Fellow: Royal Soc. Arts (Inaugural medal for Design Achievement 1999, awarded title of Royal Designer for Industry 2003). Lead designer of the following launches: iMac, 1998; Apple iBook, the 22″ Cinema Display, PowerMac G4 Tower and iSub, 1999; Apple G4 Cube, 2000; Titanium PowerBook G4 and iPod portable MP3 Player, 2001; sunflower-inspired iMac with 15″ and 17″ floating screens, 2002; eMac, 2002; Apple 12″ PowerBook and 17″ Powerbook, 1″ thick and 6.8 lbs, world's slimmest and lightest 17″ notebook computer, 2003, iMac G5, 2004, iPod Shuffle, 2005, Mac Mini, 2005, iPhone, 2007. Office: Apple Computer Inc 1 Infinite Loop Cupertino CA 95014 Office Fax: 408-974-2113.*

IVENS, MARY SUE, microbiologist, medical mycologist; b. Maryville, Tenn., Aug. 23, 1929; d. McPherson Joseph and Sarah Lillie (Hensley) Ivens. BS, East Tenn. State U., Johnson City, 1949; MS NIH rsch. trainee, Tulane U. Sch. Medicine, New Orleans, 1963; PhD, La. State U. Sch. Medicine, New Orleans, 1966; postgrad., Emory U. Sch. Medicine, Atlanta, 1960. Diplomate Am. Bd. Microbiology. Dir. microbiol. and mycol. labs. Lewis-Gate Hosp., Roanoke, Va., 1953—56; rsch. mycologist Ctrs. Disease Control, Atlanta, 1957—60; rsch. assoc. La. State U. Sch. Medicine, New Orleans, 1963—66; instr. medicine La. State U., 1966—72, instr. microbiology, 1966—72, clin. prof., 1972—. Dir. micology lab. La. State U. Sch. Medicine, 1963—72, lectr. sch. dentistry, 1968—70; assoc. prof. natural scis. Dillard U., New Orleans, 1972—; assoc. Marine Biol. Lab., Woods Hole, Mass., 1978—; cons. in field; mem. exec. bd. Trinity Dental Assn., 2006. Contbr. articles to profl. jours. Commr. conf. on ctr. Mycotic sera WHO, 1969; mem. La. assn. def. counsel expert witness bank, 1985—; bd. dirs. La. coun. Girl Scouts US, Cmty Relationships Greater New Orleans, Zoning Bd. River Ridge, La.; mem. exec. bd. River Ridge Civic Assn., 1982—98, sec., 1982—84; chmn. pers. bd. Riverside Bapt. Ch., River Ridge; dir. outreach First Bapt. Ch., New Orleans, 1989—97; chmn. gold medal award com. Sigma Xi, 1978. Recipient Rosicrucian Humanitarian award, 1981; fellow Macy, MBL, 1978—79; grantee NSF, NIH. Mem.: Nat. Inst. Sci., AAAS, Am. Soc. Microbiology (Nat. com. on membership 1983—87), Med. Mycological Soc. Am., Internat. Soc. Human and Animal Mycology, Sigma Xi. Office: Dillard U Div Natural Sci New Orleans LA 70122 Home: 809 Prestwick Dr Maryville TN 37803-6757

IVER, ROBERT DREW, dentist; b. Miami, Fla., Feb. 6, 1947; s. William Henry and Jeanette (Minden) I.; m. Lisa Marie Stettner-Iver, May 5, 1974. Student, Ohio State U., Columbus, 1965-66, U. Miami, 1966-68; DDS, Georgetown U., Washington, DC, 1972. Lic. yachtsmaster USCG Approved Capts. Pvt. practice dentistry, Miami Beach, Fla., 1974—. Bd. dirs. Cmty. Svc. Sunset Islands. Lt. USNR, 1968-81. Fellow ADA, Gold Coast Dist. Dental Soc.; mem. Fla. Dental Assn., East Coast Dist. Dental Soc., Acad. Gen. Dentistry, Miami Beach Dental Soc., Gold Coast Acad. Gen. Dentistry, South Fla. Dist. Dental Soc., Esthetic Dental Assn., Nature Conservancy, Am. Radio Relay League, N.Am. Fishing Club, Dade Radio Club Miami, Everglades Amateur Radio Club, Miami Rod and Reel Club. Avocations: sports fishing, ham radio operating. Office: 1205 Lincoln Rd Ste 203 Miami FL 33139-2365

IVERS, DONALD LOUIS, retired federal judge; b. San Diego, May 6, 1941; s. Grant Perrin and Margaret (Ware) I.; married; 3 children. AA, N.Mex. Mil. Inst., Roswell, 1961; BA, U. N.Mex., Albuquerque, 1963; JD, Am. U., Washington, 1971. Bar: U.S. Dist. Ct. (D.C. 1972), U.S. Ct. Appeals (D.C. cir.) 1972, U.S. Ct. Mil. Appeals 1972, U.S. Supreme Ct. 1975. Assoc. Brault, Graham, Scott, Brault, Washington, 1972-78; chief counsel Republican Nat. Com., Washington, 1978-81; gen. counsel 1980 Rep. Nat. Conv. Site Selection Com., 1979-80; chief counsel Fed. Hwy. Adminstrn., 1981-85; counselor to sec., chmn. sec.'s safety rev. task force US Dept. Transp., 1984-85; gen. counsel VA, 1985-89; acting gen. counsel US Dept. Vets. Affairs, 1989-90, asst. to the sec., 1990; judge US Ct. Appeals Vets. Claims, 1990—2004, chief judge, 2004—05; ret., 2005. Capt. U.S. Army, 1963-68, Vietnam, lt. col. Res., ret. Republican. Personal E-mail: iversd41@cox.net.

IVERS, JOHN JOSEPH, language educator, dean; s. Albert Thomas Ivers and Florence Gertrude Meinhardt; m. Connie Lynn Laird, June 5, 1979; children: John Joseph, Nathaniel Nicholas, Heidi Lynn. BA, Brigham Young U., 1982, MA, 1984; EdD, U. N.C., Greensboro, 1990. Prof. fgn. langs. Ricks Coll. / Brigham Young U. - Idaho, Rexburg, Idaho, 1989—; assoc. dean Coll. Lang. and Letters Brigham Young U. - Idaho, Rexburg, 2005—06, dept. chair fgn. lang. dept., 2006—. Dir. tchg. tune-up course for faculty Brigham Young U. - Idaho, Rexburg, 1990—95, dir. Summer Honors Inst., 1998—2001, coord. secondary edn. fgn. langs., 2001—05. Contbr. articles to profl. jours. Co-founder, co-dir. fgn. lang. program Madison Mid. Sch., Rexburg, 1993—2002; charter rep. Boy Scouts Am., Rexburg, 1995—97, charter orgn. head, 2002—07; bishop LDS Ch., Rexburg, 2002—07. Named Disting. Faculty Mem., Brigham Young U. - Idaho, 2003; recipient Hon. Faculty award, Ricks Coll., 1996. Democrat. Lds Ch. Home: 145 Birch Ave Rexburg ID 83440 Office: Brigham Young U - Idaho Rexburg ID 83460-0825 Home Phone: 208-356-5893. Business E-Mail: iversj@byui.edu.

IVERS, LOUISE H., art history professor; life ptnr. Allen R. Guerrero. BFA, Boston U., 1964; MA, U. N.Mex., Albuquerque, 1967, PhD, 1975. Prof. art history Calif. State U. Dominguez Hills, Carson, 1971—. Newsletter editor Long Beach Heritage, Calif., 1990—. Author exhbn. catalogs. Fellow, U. N.Mex., 1966—70; grantee, Women's Archtl. League, 1994, Calif. State U. Dominguez Hills, 1999—2000, Evalyn M. Bauer Found., 2004; Travel fellow, Del Amo Found., 1977, U. Found. grantee, Calif. State U. Dominguez Hills, 1984. Mem.: Soc. Archtl. Historians. Office: Calif State U Dominguez Hills 1000 E Victoria St Carson CA Office Phone: 310-243-2549. Business E-Mail: livers@csudh.edu.

IVERSON, ALLEN EZAIL, professional basketball player; b. Hampton, Va., June 7, 1975; s. Ann Iverson; m. Tawana Turner, Aug. 31, 2001; children: Allen II, Tiaura, Isaiah Rahsaan. Student, Georgetown U., 1994—96. Basketball player Phila. 76ers, 1996—2006, Denver Nuggets, 2006—. Mem. US Olympic Basketball Team, Athens, 2004. Founder Cross Over Found. Named AP First Team All-Am., 1994, NBA Rookie of Month, Apr., Nov., 1997, MVP Schick Rookie game, 1997, Schick Rookie of Yr., 1997, All-Star game MVP, 2001, NBA MVP, 2001; named to first All-NBA Team, 1999, 2001, second All-NBA Team, 2000, 2002, 2003, Ea. Conf. All-Star Team, NBA, 2000—06, Western Conf. All-Star Team, 2007. Achievements include being the 1st player selected in 1996 NBA draft. Avocations: drawing, reading. Office: Denver Nuggets 100 Chopper Cir Denver CO 80204*

IVERSON, KRISTINE ANN, federal agency administrator; b. Elgin, Ill, Aug. 15, 1953; d. Theodore and Vivian (Schumaker) I. BA, DePauw U., Greencastle, Ind., 1975; MA, George Mason U., 1985; postgrad., Va. Poly. Inst. and State U., 1978. Legis. aide Rep. John B. Conlan, Washington, 1975-76; legis. asst. Sen. Orrin G. Hatch, Washington, 1977-81, sr. policy advisor, 1993-94, legis. dir., 1995—2001; employment policy dir. Senate Labor and Human Resources Com., Washington, 1981-88, minority staff dir., 1988-92; asst. sec. congl. intergovernmental affairs US Dept. Labor, Washington, 2001—. Cons. Reagan-Bush Transition, 1980 Pres. The Ron Freeman Chorale, Arlington, Va., 1987-2000; steering com. George Mason U. Tech. Forum, 1983; del. 11th Dist. Rep. Conv., Fairfax, Va., 1992; mem. DePauw U. Alumni Bd., Greencastle, Ind., 1993-99; mem. Bd. of Visitors 2000-03. Recipient Young Alumni award DePauw U., Greencastle, 1993, John C. Stennis Congrl. fellow, 1999-2000. Mem. Alpha Omicron Pi;mem. The Falls Ch. (Episcopal). Avocations: music, sports. Office: US Dept Labor Congressional Intergovt Affairs 200 Constitution Ave NW Washington DC 20210

IVERSON, PETER JAMES, historian, educator; b. Whittier, Calif., Apr. 4, 1944; s. William James and Adelaide Veronica (Schmitt) I.; m. Kaaren Teresa Gonsoulin, Mar. 7, 1983; children: Erika, Jens, Tim, Scott. BA in History, Carleton Coll., 1967; MA in History, U. Wis., 1969, PhD in History, 1975. Vis. asst. prof. Ariz. State U., Tempe, Ariz., 1975-76; from asst. prof to prof. U. Wyo., Laramie, Wyo., 1976-86; coord. divsn. social and behavioral scis. Ariz. State U., Phoenix, 1986-88, prof. history Tempe, Ariz., 1988—, regents prof. history, 2000—. Panelist, reviewer Nat. Endowment Humanities, Washington, 1986—; vis. prof. Carleton Coll., 1991. Author: The Navajos: A Critical Bibliography, 1976, The Navajo Nation, 1981, Carlos Montezuma, 1982, The Navajos, 1990, When Indians Became Cowboys: Native Peoples and Cattle Ranching in the American West, 1994, Barry Goldwater: Native Arizonan, 1997, We Are Still Here: American Indians in the 20th Century, 1998, Riders of the West: Portraits From Indian Rodeo, 1999, Diné: A History of the Navajos, 2002; co-editor: Indians in American History, 1998; editor: The Plains Indians of the 20th Century, 1985, For Our Navajo People: Din+248 Letters, Speeches, and Petitions, 1900-1960, 2002; co-editor: Major Problems in American Indian History, 1994, 2d edit., 2001; assoc. editor The Historian, 1990-95; editl. bd. Pacific Hist. Rev., 1986-88, Jour. Ariz. History, 1987-89, Social Sci. Jour., 1988-96, Montana: The Magazine of Western History, 1993—, Western Historical Quarterly, 2000-02. Acting dir. McNickle Ctr. for History of Am. Indian, Newberry Libr., 1994-95, mem. adv. bd., 1993-2003; bd. dir. Ariz. Humanities Coun., 1993-99; chmn. Wyo. Coun. Humanities, 1981-82; mem. Heard Mus., Phoenix, 1986—, Desert Bot. Garden, Phoenix, 1986—. Recipient Chief Manuelito Appreciation award Navajo Nation, 1984, Disting. Achievement award Carleton Coll. Alumni Assn., 1992, Lifetime Achievement award Am. Indian Hist. Assn., 1999, Him-Dak Eco-Mus. Svc. award Ak-Chin Indian Cmty., 2001, We. Writers Am. Spur award, 2002, Outstanding Doctoral Mentor award ASU Grad. Coll., 2002, Outstanding rsch. award ASU Alumni Assn., 2005; fellow Newberry Libr., Chgo., 1973-74, NEH, 1982-83, 99-2000, Kellogg Found., Battle Creek, Mich., 1982-85, Guggenheim Found., 1999-2000; Disting. Pub. scholar, Ariz. Humanities Coun., 1999. Mem.: Am. Soc. Ethnohistory (coun. 1991—93, chmn. program com. 1994, chmn. prize com. 1987), We. Social Sci. Assn. (pres. 1988—89), Orgn. Am. Historians, We. History Assn. (chmn. prize com. 1991, co-chmn. program com. 1995, coun. 1995—98, pres. elect 2003—04, pres. 2004—05). Office: Ariz State U Dept History Tempe AZ 85287-4302 Business E-Mail: peter.iverson@asu.edu.

IVERSON, ROBERT LOUIS, JR., retired internist, physician; b. Borden, Ind., Sept. 3, 1944; s. Robert L. and Agnes Maxine (Knight) Iverson; m. Elsa Maschmeyer, Sept. 9, 1967 (div. 1982); children: Nathan, Kirsten; m. Deborah A. Budd, June 16, 1984 (dec. May 1996); children: Richard, Colin; m. Amy M. Neidert, May 9, 1998. Student, Wabash Coll., 1962-64; BA, Ind. U., 1970, MD, 1974, Intern, 1974-75. Diplomate Am. Bd. Internal Med., diplomate in critical care medicine, Am. Bd. Internal Med. Intern Ind. U., Indpls., 1974-75; resident (internal med.) Methodist Hosp., Indpls, 1975-77, co-dir. critical care, mem. tchg. staff dept. medicine, 1977-84; fellow in critical care med. U. So. Calif. Shock Rsch. Unit, Ctr. for Critically Ill, LA, 1977; vis. lectr. U. So. Calif., LA, 1977; co-dir. critical care, teaching staff, Dept. of Med. Methodist Hosp., 1977-84; asst. prof. medicine Wayne State U., Detroit, 1984-96, assoc. prof. clin. medicine, 1996-2000; dir. med. affairs Hutzel Hosp., Detroit, 1996-97, vice chief med. staff, 1995-97, dir. ICU, 1986-2000, chief critical care medicine, 1988-2000; chief critical care svcs. Vassar Bros. Hosp., Poughkeepsie, NY, 2000—02; ret., 2002. Mem. bd. Rudgate Neighborhood Assocs., Bloomfield Hills, Mich. 1996-98; mem. physician leadership coun. Detroit Med. Ctr., 1996-2000; participant Ind. Malpractice Rev. Panels, 1981-85; chief med. officer Oakland County (Mich.) Sheriff's Dept., 1997-2000, tactical med. officer Spl. Response Team (SWAT), 1997-2000. Author: (with others) Respiratory Care of the Neurosurgical Patient, 1983, Septic Shock in Critical Care Clinics, 1988; established adminstrv. core curriculum for intensivists Critical Care Clinics, 1993; contbr. abstracts and articles to profl. jours. Med. advisor to Ind. Coun. Emergency Response Teams, 1980—85; mem. Ind. Symphonic Choir, 1970—84, trustee, 1983—84; hon. dep. sheriff Marion County Sheriff's Dept., 1982—84; bd. dirs. City of Bloomfield Hills, Mich., Rudgate Neighborhood Assn., 1996—98; pres. Ashley Homeowners Assn., Inc., 2004—. With US Army, 1964—67, Vietnam. Fellow: ACP, Am. Coll. Chest Physicians; mem.: AMA (Physicians Recognition award 2002—05, 2005—), Sarasota County Med. Soc., Fla. State Med. Soc., Wayne County Med. Soc. (elected del. 1990—91), Soc. Critical Care Medicine, Fla. Sheriffs Assn., Phi Beta Kappa. Avocations: music, shortwave radio communications, sailing, astronomy, astrophotography. Home: 5421 Ashley Pkwy Sarasota FL 34241 Personal E-mail: robertive@msn.com.

IVERSON, THOMAS EDWIN, retired academic administrator, mathematician, educator; b. Hamilton, Mont., June 4, 1938; s. Andrew Ivar and Helen Ruth (Wagar) I.; m. Doris Diane Douglass, June 12, 1960; children: Paul, Philip, Mark. BA, Westmont Coll., 1960; MA, Wash. U., 1964; PhD, Claremont Graduate Sch., 1975. Math. instr. Pitzer Coll., Claremont, Calif., 1970-74; asst. prof. math. Seattle Pacific U., 1974-76; interim dean Ctrl. Coll., Pella, Iowa, 1993-94, prof. math. and computer sci., 1976—2002, interim pres., 1997-98, provost, sr. v.p., 1998—2002; ret., 2002. Vis. prof. math. and computer sci. Moi U., Kenya, East Africa, 1988-89. Exec dir. Friendship Internat. Ctr. for Christian Studies in Romania, 2003—; Iowa area Rep. STEER Inc., Bismarck, ND, 2004—; with On with Life, Ankeny, Iowa, 2000—. Republican. Mem. Reformed Ch. Am. Avocation: ranch in montana. Personal E-mail: iversont@central.edu.

IVERSON, WARREN PHILIP, retired microbiologist, research scientist, consultant; b. Plymouth, Wis., Sept. 2, 1923; s. Barthold Alfred Iverson and Edna Catherine Hall; m. Margaret Ellen Golibart, Feb. 4, 1956; 1 child, Martin Philip; 1 child, Mary Katherine. BA, U. Wis., Madison, 1944; PhD, Rutgers U., New Brunswick, NJ, 1949. Cert. corrosion engr. Cancer rschr. McArdle Meml. Lab., Madison, Wis., 1944; microbiologist Parke-Davis, Detroit, 1949—52, U.S. Army Biol. Labs., Frederick, Md., 1952—67, Nat. Bur. Stds. (now Nat. Insts. Sci. and Tech.), Washington, 1967—85. Lectr. bacteriology U. Md., Frederick, 1957—61; U.S. del. biol. corrosion group Orgn. Economic Co-operation and Devel., 1965—66; cons. Three Mile Island, Harrisburg, Pa., 1979; cons. Kufic monument deterioration Govt. of Egypt, Cairo, 1982. Contbr. scientific papers. Vice comdr. U.S. Coast Guard Aux., 1963—73; adult edn. instr. history of writing Thomas Johnson HS, Frederick, Mo., 1990. Medic inf. US Army, 1944—46, ETO. Recipient Charles Thom award, Soc. Indsl. Microbiology, 1974, Silver medal, Dept. Commerce, 1974; Commonwealth fellow, Rutgers U., 1949. Mem.: AAAS, Am. Soc. Microbiology (emeritus), Nat. Assn. Corrosion Engrs. (emeritus). Avocations: reading, classical music, Japanese technical papers. Home: 1208 Beechwood Dr Frederick MD 21701-4242

IVES, COLTA FELLER, museum curator, educator; b. San Diego, Apr. 5, 1943; m. E. Garrison Ives, June 14, 1966; 1 child, Lucy Barrett. BA, Mills Coll., 1964; MA, Columbia U., 1966. Staff Met. Mus. Art, NYC, 1966—, curator in charge prints and photographs, 1975-93, curator dept. drawings and prints, 1993—; guest scholar J. Paul Getty Mus., 2002. Adj. prof. Columbia U., 1970-87, NYU Inst. Fine Arts, 2001—. Author: The Great Wave, 1974, Art Libraries Assn. award, 1975, The Flight Into Egypt, 1972, R. Rauschenberg Photos In and Out City Limits: New York, 1981, French Prints in the Era of Impressionism and Symbolism, 1988, Toulouse-Lautrec in the Metropolitan Museum of Art, 1996; co-author: The Painterly Print, 1980, Pierre Bonnard: The Graphic Art, 1989, Daumier Drawings, 1992, Goya in the Metropolitan Museum of Art, 1995, The Private Collection of Edgar Degas, 1997 (Best Show of 1997-98 N.Y.C. Mus. Internat. Assn. Art Critics), Romanticism and the School of Nature, 2000, The Lure of the Exotic: Gauguin in New York Collections, 2002, A Private Passion: Winthrop Collection, Harvard University, 2003 (Best Mus. Catalog of 2003 Assn. Art Mus. Curators), Wrightsman Pictures, 2005, Vincent van Gogh: The Drawings, 2005 (Best Mus. Exhbn. in Eastern U.S. 2005, Best Hist. Show of 2005-06). Chmn. grants com. Met. Mus. Art, 1986-87; bd. dirs. Bidwell House Mus., Mass. Mem. Print Coun. Am. (exec. bd. 1975-77, 84-87, v.p. 1989-93), Assn. Art Mus. Curators (exec. bd. 2002-04, bd. dirs. 2003-04), Assn. Profl. Landscape Designers, Grolier Club.

IVES, EDWARD DAWSON, folklore educator; b. White Plains, NY, Sept. 4, 1925; s. Warren Livingston and Millicent Clarissa (Dawson) I.; m. Barbara Ann Herrel, Sept. 8, 1951; children— Stephen John, Nathaniel Edward, Sarah Ruth AB, Hamilton Coll., 1948; MA, Columbia U., 1950; PhD, Ind. U., 1962; LLD, U. P.E.I., 1986; DLitt, Meml. U., Newfoundland, 1996. Instr. English Ill. Coll., Jacksonville, 1950-53; lectr. CCNY, 1953-54; instr. English U. Maine, Orono, 1955-62, asst. prof., 1962-64, assoc. prof., 1964-69, prof. folklore, 1969-99, chmn. anthropology dept., 1983-89; dir. Northeast Archives Folklore and Oral History, 1971-99, Maine Folklife Ctr., 1992-99, emeritus, 1999—. Author: Larry Gorman: The Man Who Made the Songs, 1964, reprinted 1993, Lawrence Doyle: The Farmer-Poet of Prince Edward Island, 1971, Joe Scott: The Woodsman-Songmaker, 1978, The Tape Recorded Interview, 1980, reprinted 1995, George Magoon and the Down East Game War, 1988, reprinted 1993, Folksongs of New Brunswick, 1989; (with Bruce Jackson) The World Observed, 1996, The Bonny Earl of Murray, 1997, Drive Dull Care Away, 1999. Served with USMC, 1943-46 Guggenheim fellow, 1965—66. Fellow Am. Folklore Soc.; mem. Oral History Assn. Home: 1392 River Rd Bucksport ME 04416-9708 Office Phone: 207-825-3079. E-mail: sandy_ives@umit.maine.edu.

IVES, H. BRYAN, III, lawyer; b. Charlotte, NC, Sept. 13, 1955; BS in Acctg. with honors, Univ. NC, Chapel Hill, 1977, JD with high honors, 1980. Bar: NC 1980. Ptnr., group leader, capital mkts. practice Alston & Bird LLP, Charlotte, NC. Articles editor NC Law Rev. Mem.: Am. Coll. Tax Counsel, Order of Coif. Office: Alston & Bird LLP Ste 4000 Bank of Am Plz 101 S Tryon St Charlotte NC 28280-4000 Office Phone: 704-444-1002. Office Fax: 704-444-1111. Business E-Mail: bives@alston.com.

IVES, J. ATWOOD, financial executive; b. Atlanta, May 1, 1936; s. Stephen Bradshaw and Ellen (Atwood) I.; m. Elizabeth Saalfield; children: Ian, Anna, Benjamin. BA in Econs., Yale U., 1959; MBA, Stanford U., 1961; AMP, Harvard U., 1975. CPA, Calif. Acct. Price, Waterhouse & Co., San Francisco, 1961-64; fin. analyst Textron, Inc., Providence, 1964-66; ptnr., v.p. Paine Webber Jackson & Curtis, 1966-74; dir. Gen. Cinema Corp., Chestnut Hill, Mass., 1970—91, sr. v.p. fin., CFO, 1974-83, exec. v.p., CFO, 1983-84, vice-chmn., CFO, 1985-91, mem. office of chmn., 1983-91; vice-chmn., CFO The Neiman Marcus Group, Inc., 1987-91, also bd. dirs.; trustee Eastern Enterprises, 1989—2000, chmn., CEO, 1991-2000. Ind. chmn. trustees 93 mut. funds advised by Mass. Fin. Svcs. Co., 2004- , trustee, 1992-; corp. adv. bd. Carroll Sch. Mgmt., Boston Coll.; bd. dirs. Keyspan Corp., 2000-2004. Hon. trustee Mus. Fine Arts, Boston; bd. overseers WGBH Edn. Found.; founding trustee Beacon Hill Village. With U.S. Army, 1961-62. Recipient award Haskins and Sells Found., 1961 Home: 17 W Cedar St Boston MA 02108-1211 Personal E-mail: 41mantell@hotmail.com.

IVES, SAMUEL CLIFTON, minister; b. Farmington, Maine, Nov. 13, 1937; s. Alfred H. and Alice (Smith) I.; m. Jane Petherbridge, June 6, 1959; children: Bonnie, Stephen, Jonathan. BA, U. Maine, 1960; MDiv, Boston U., 1963, D in Ministry, 1983; D (hon.), West Va. Wesleyan, 2004. Pastor Cape Elizabeth (Maine) United Meth. Ch., 1962-68, First United Meth. Ch., Bangor, Maine, 1968-73; dir. Maine Conf. Coun. on Ministries, Winthrop, Maine, 1973-77; sr. pastor Waterville (Maine) United Meth. Ch., 1977-86; dist. supt. So. Dist. United Meth. Ch., Portland, Maine, 1986-92; elected bishop United Meth. Ch., assigned to W.Va., Charleston, 1992—2004; ret., 2004. Del. Gen. Conf. United Meth. Ch., 1972, 76, 80, 84, 88, 92; exec. com. Maine Coun. Chs., 1981-92, 2006—; pres. Appalachian Devel. com., 1996-2000; v.p. W.Va. Coun. of Chs., 1996-2000. Mem. Gen. Bd. Discipleship United Meth. Ch., 1984-92, pres. Gen. Commn. on Religion and Race, 1996-2000, mem. coun. bishops; pres. Gen. Bd. Ch. and Soc., 2000-04; nat. co-pres. Meth. Fedn. for Social Action, 2006—. Mem. Assn. Couples for Marriage Enrichment (cert. leader and trainer 1979—). Home: 10 Quaker Lane Portland ME 04103

IVESTER, M(ELVIN) DOUGLAS, investment company executive, retired beverage company executive; b. New Holland, Ga., Mar. 26, 1947; s. Howard Edward and Ada Mae (Pass) Ivester; m. Victoria Kay Grindle, Mar. 20, 1969. BBA cum laude, U. Ga., 1969. Acct. Ernst & Ernst, Altanta, 1969—75; mgr. Ernst & Whinney, Atlanta, 1975—79; asst. contr., dir. corp. auditing The Coca-Cola Co., Atlanta, 1979—91, v.p., contr., 1981—83, sr. v.p. fin., 1983—84, sr. v.p., CFO, 1985—89; pres. European Cmty. Group, 1980—90, Coca-Cola USA, 1990—91, Coca-Cola N.Am. Group, 1991—93, prin. oper. officer, 1993—94, pres., COO, 1994—97, also bd. dirs., chmn., CEO, 1997—2000, ret., 2000; pres. Deer Run Investments LLC, 2001—. Bd. dirs. Georgia Pacific Corp., Sun Trust, Inc., S One Corp.; trustee, dir. U. Ga. Found.; bd. trustees Emory U., 1998—.

IVEY, DENISE HASSELL, publishing executive; b. 1950; m. Michael Ivey; 1 child, Forest. BS, La. State U., 1978. CPA. With Gannett Co., Inc., 1983—; v.p. East regional group Gannett Co, Inc., v.p. South newspaper group, 1991—94, pres. Gulf Coast newspaper group, 1994—2006; pres. Mid-South group Gannet Co., Inc., 2006—; asst. contr. Gainesville (Ga.) Times, 1983-84, contr., 1984, pres., pub., 1986, Herald-Dispatch, Huntington, W.Va., 1989; v.p. & pub. Pensacola (Fla.) News Jour., 1991—94, pres. & pub., 1994—2006, Louisville Courier-Jour., 2006—. Bd. dirs. Leadership Louisville Ctr., 2007—. Mem.: Southern Newspaper Pubs.' Assn., Ky. Press Assn. Office: Courier-Jour 525 W Broadway PO Box 740031 Louisville KY 40201-7431 Office Phone: 502-582-4101. E-mail: publisher@courier-journal.com.*

IVEY, DONALD JAMES, historian, archivist; b. San Francisco, Calif., Nov. 5, 1961; s. James Burnett and Evelyn (Rogers) Ivey; m. Mylene Espineda Chiong, Feb. 24, 1992; 1 child, John. Student, U. Fla., Gainesville, 1979—80; BA cum laude, U. Ctrl. Fla., Orlando, 1983, MPA, 1987. Curator Lake Wales Mus. and Cultural Ctr., Fla., 1987—89, Cartoon Mus., Orlando, Fla., 1989—94; curator collections Heritage Village-Pinellas County Hist. Mus., Largo, Fla., 1994—2003; mgr. archives and records City El Paso, Tex., 2003—05; mgr. Ctr. History Family Medicine Am. Acad. Family Physicians Found., Leawood, Kans., 2005—. Instr. Pinellas County Geneal. Soc., Largo, Fla., 1996; chmn. exhibits subcom. Fla. African Am. Heritage Celebration Pinewood Cultural Ctr., Largo, 2001—03; adv. bd.mus. profl. studies program U. South Fla., St. Petersburg, Fla., 2001—02; adv. bd. pub. programs and exhibits St. Petersburg Mus. History, Fla., 2002—03; mem. border regional archives group City of El Paso, 2003—05. Author: A Pocket History of Pinellas County, 1997, Guide to the Library and Archives of Heritage Village - Pinellas County Historical Museum, 1997, 7th edit., 2003; author: (prodr.) (films) Heritage Village, the Pride of Pinellas, 1997, Punta Pinal: A History of Pinellas County, 1997; co-author: Pennants Over Pinellas: A History of Major League Baseball in Pinellas County 1914-1998, 1998, Proceedings of the Florida Cattle Frontier Symposium, 2003; contbr. articles to hist. jours.; author: websites. Mem. libr. planning com. Fla. Botanical Gardens Pinellas County Extension Svc., 1998—2003; bd. trustees Greater Largo Libr. Found., Fla., 2001—02. Recipient Employee Suggestion award, Pinellas County, 1997, Bd. County Commrs. award, 2000, Employee Recognition award, 2002, Spl. Rsch. and Exhibiting award, Pinellas County African Am. History Mus., 2002. Mem.: Med. Mus. Assn., Med. Libr. Assn. (history health scis. sect.), Kans. City Area Archivists, Archivists and Librarians History Health Scis., Am. Assn. State and Local History, Pinellas Mus. Assn. (dir. 2002—03, v.p. 2002—03, co-founder), U. Ctrl. Fla. Alumni Assn., Phi Kappa Phi, Delta Upsilon. Avocations: history, writing. Office: Am Acad Family Physicians Found 11400 Tomahawk Creek Pkwy Leawood KS 66211

IVEY, ELIZABETH SPENCER, retired physicist, educator; b. Schenectady, NY, Apr. 21, 1935; married, 1957 (div.), remarried, 1982; 5 children. BS in Physics, Simmons Coll., 1957; MA in Tchg., Harvard U., 1959; PhD in Mech. Engring. Acoustics, U. Mass., 1976. Prof. physics Simmons Coll., 1958-59, Bucknell U., 1960-63, Colo. State U., Ft. Collins, 1964-68, assoc. dean faculty, 1982-85, Louise Wolff Kahn prof., from 1985; prof. physics Smith Coll., 1969-90, chmn. dept. physics, 1983-90; prof. physics, provost Macalester Coll., St. Paul, 1990-95; prof. mech. engring., provost U. Hartford, West Hartford, Conn., 1995-2000, provost emerita, 2000—, prof. emerita mech. engring., 2000—. Vis. prof. Yale U., 1982. Bd. dirs. Minn. Inst. Talented Youth, 1990-95, World Press Inst., 1990-93, St. Paul Area United Way, 1990-95, Women's Edn. and Leadership Fund, Hartford, 2005—; trustee Hartford Coll. Women, 1995-2005, Mitchell Coll. 2003-; corporator Simmons Coll., 2000-05. Recipient Woman Engr. award Soc. Women Engrs., 1988, Simmons Coll. Alumnae Achievement award, 2007. Fellow AAAS, Assn. Women in Sci.; mem. Acoustical Soc. Am., Am. Assn. Physics Tchrs., Assn. Women in Sci. (bd. dirs. 2001—, pres.-elect 2003-04, pres. 2004-06). Home Phone: 860-286-8682. Personal E-mail: ivey@hartford.edu.

IVEY, JACK TODD, lawyer; b. Galveston, Tex., Apr. 26, 1967; s. Jack Lyndon Ivey and Catherine Ann (Kemmerer) Harward; m. Jane Marie Gurley, May 7, 1994. BA in Econs., U. Tex., Austin, 1989; JD, So. Tex. Coll. Law, 1992. Bar: Tex. 1993, U.S. Dist. Ct. (so. dist.) Tex. 1994, U.S. Dist. Ct. (ea. dist.) 1998, U.S. Ct. Appeals (5th cir.) 1998, U.S. Supreme Ct. Tex. 1993; bd. cert. personal injury trial law Tex. Bd. Legal Specialization, 2004. Assoc. Holland & Stephens, Houston, 1993-95, Holland & Assocs., Houston, 1995-97; ptnr. Ivey & Kadlec, Houston, 1997—; founder, ptnr. North Kirkwood Properties, LP, 2002—. Vol. HTLF Adopt-a-Sch., Houston, 1993-99; dir. Harris County MUD 355, 2004-06. Named Tex. Rising Star Super Lawyer, Tex. Monthly Mag., 2004, 2005, Top Lawyers in Houston, Tex. Mag., 2006, 2007, Super Lawyer in Personal Injury Law, Tex. Monthly Mag., 2007. Fellow Houston Bar Found., Houston Bar Assn. (com. mem. 1995-97); mem. Tex. Trial Lawyers Assn. (sustaining mem.), Houston Trial Lawyers Assn. (bd. dirs. 1999—), Houston Trial Lawyers Found. (bd. dirs. 1996-99), Coll. of the State Bar (1997, 2005-07). Home: 1136 N Kirkwood Rd Houston TX 77043-4543 also: 727 Diamond Leaf Ln Houston TX 77079 Personal E-mail: jti@iveyandkadlec.com.

IVEY, JAMES FREDERICK, JR., physician; b. Orlando, Florida, Apr. 30, 1939; s. James Frederick and Naomi Nell (Milner) I.; m. Nancy Joan Martin, Aug. 5, 1961 (dec. July 2004); children: Mary Nell, James Thomas, John Mark, Samuel Svc., Daniel Dominic; m. Pamela Jean Monroe, Aug. 6, 2005. BS in Biology, Duke U., Durham, NC, 1960, U. Fla., Gainesville, 1960; MD, Emory U., Atlanta, 1964. Diplomate Am. Bd. Family Practice with cert. of added qualifications in geriatrics; FAA sr. aero. med. examiner. Intern Duval Med. Ctr., Jacksonville, Fla., 1964-65; resident Emory U./VA Hosp., Atlanta, 1965-66; physician Clermont, Fla., 1968-69; pvt. practice Palmer, Alaska, 1969-74; owner, physician Valley Med. Ctr., Inc., Palmer, Alaska, 1974-91; staff physician Lakeside Med. Ctr. and Family Care, Lakeland, Fla., 1991-92; pvt. practice Lakeland, Fla., 1992-95; staff physician Polk Gen. Hosp., Bartow, Fla., 1995-96, Family First Med. Ctr., Gainesville, Fla., 1996; med. dir. Trenton Med. Ctr., Fla., 1996—2001; physician for jails Levy and Dixie counties, Fla., 2001—07; physician Marion Regional Juvenile Detention Ctr., Fla., 2001—05; med. authority First Step Adolescent Care, Gainesville, Fla., 2003—07; med. staff Trenton Med. Ctr., Fla., 2001—, Urgent Care Ctr. Gainesville, Fla., 2007—. Med. dir. Palmer Pioneer Home, Alaska, 1979—91, Nugens Ranch, Wasilla, 1983—91, Starting Point, Inc., Wasilla, 1989—91, Arbors at Lakeland Nursing Home, Lakeland, Fla., 1992—96; courtesy clin. asst. prof. dept. cmty. health and family medicine U. Fla. Sch. Medicine. Former med. dir., co-founder Mat-Su Coun. Prevention of Alcoholism and Drug Abuse, Wasilla, Alaska, past chmn. bd. dirs.; elder and lay pastor United Presbyn. Ch., USA. Capt. USAF, 1966—68. Mem. Am. Acad. Family Physicians (pres. Alaska chpt. 1976); Christian Med. and Dental Soc.; Alpha Tau Omega, Phi Kappa Phi, Phi Chi; mem. Trinty United Meth. Ch. Republican. Avocations: golf, music, cosmology, history, philosophy. Home: 6711 NW 38th Ter Gainesville FL 32653 Office: Trenton Med Ctr Inc PO Box 640 911 S Main St Trenton FL 32693-3239 Office Phone: 352-463-1100. Personal E-mail: jivey1@cox.net.

IVEY, JUDITH, actress; b. El Paso, Tex., Sept. 4, 1951; d. Nathan Aldean and Dorothy Lee (Lewis) I.; m. Tim Braine, 1989; children: Maggie, Thomas Carter. BS, Ill. State U., 1973. Actress in stage plays: The Sea, 1974, The Philanthropist, Hay Fever, Romeo and Juliet, Two Gentlemen of Verona, Mourning Becomes Electra, 1975, Don Juan, Cactus Flower, As You Like It, Design for Living, 1976, The Goodbye People, The Moundbuilders, Oh, Coward, Much Ado About Nothing, 1977-78, Bedroom Farce, 1979, Dusa, Fish, Stas and VI, 1980, Piaf, 1980-81, The Dumping Ground, 1981, The Rimers of Eldritch, 1981, Pastorale, 1982, Two Small Bodies, 1982, Steaming, 1982-83 (Tony award 1983, Drama Desk award 1983), Second Lady, 1983, Hurlyburly, 1984 (Tony award 1985, Drama Desk award 1985), Precious Sons, 1986, Blithe Spirit, 1987, Mrs. Dally Has a Lover, 1988, Park Your Car in Harvard Yard, 1991, The Moonshot Tape, 1994 (Obie award 1994), A Fair Country, 1996, A Madhouse in Goa, 1997, The Subject Was Roses, 2006; (films) Harry and Son, 1984, The Lonely Guy, 1984, The Woman in Red, 1984, Compromising Positions, 1985, Brighton Beach Memoirs, 1986, Hello Again, 1987, Sister Sister, 1987, Miles from Home, 1988, In Country, 1989, Everybody Wins, 1990, Love Hurts, 1991, There Goes the Neighborhood, 1992, Washington Square, 1996, A Life Less Ordinary, 1997, Devil's Advocate, 1997, Without Limits, 1998, The Stand-In, 1999, Mystery, Alaska, 1999, What Alice Found, 2003; (TV films) The Shady Hill Kidnapping, 1980, Dixie Changing Habits, 1982, Piaf, 1984, We Are The Children, 1986, The Long, Hot Summer, 1985, Jesse and the Bandit Queen, 1986, Decoration Day, 1990, Frogs!, 1991, Her Final Fury: Betty Broderick, the Last Chapter, 1992, Other Mothers, 1993, On Promised Land, 1994, Almost Golden: The Jessica Savitch Story, 1995, The Summer of Ben Tyler, 1996, What the Deaf Man Heard, 1997, Texarkana, 1998, Half a Dozen Babies, 1999; (TV series) Down Home, 1990-91, Designing Women, 1992-93, The Five Mrs. Buchanans, 1994; (TV miniseries) Rose Red, 2002; guest appearances Cagney & Lacey, 1982, Buddies, 1995, Will & Grace, 2002, Law & Order:Special Victims Unit, 2005, Related, 2005; dir. (stage) Fugue, 2007.*

IVEY, KAY ELLEN, state official; b. Repton, Ala., Oct. 15, 1944; d. Boardman Nettles and Barbara Elizabeth Ivey. BS, Auburn U., 1967; cert. in mktg., U. Colo., 1975; cert. in banking, U. South Ala.; cert. in Strategic Leadership for State Execs., Duke U., 1989. Tchr., coach forensics Rio Linda (Calif.) High Sch., 1968-69; asst. v.p. Mchts. Nat. Bank, Mobile, Ala., 1970-79; cabinet officer Office of the Gov., State of Ala., Montgomery, 1979-81; reading clk. Ala. Ho. Reps., 1981-82; exec. v.p. St. Margaret's Hosp. Found., 1982-85; dir. govt. affairs Ala. Commn. Higher Edn., 1985—98; treas. State of Ala., 2003—. Owner, cons. Ivey Enterprises, Montgomery, 1982—; speaker in field. Editor (audio-visual presentation) What Price Freedom (award of Excellence), 1976, St. Margaret's Hosp. Heart tabloid, 1983. Mem. adv. bd. Sch. Bus. Auburn U., 1980-83; candidate Ala. State Auditor, 1982; sec. Ala. div. Am. Cancer Soc., 1985—; bd. dirs. Ala. Girl's State Sch., 1983-85, Stetson Hoedown Rodeo Queen's Pageant, Montgomery, Montgomery YMCA; bd. trustees Sheriff's Boys and Girls Ranches.; charter trustee, Ala. Banking Sch. Mem. Indsl. Developers Ala., Young Men's Bus. Orgn., Pub. Relations Council Ala. (bd. dirs. 1976-82), DAR (state chmn. 1985-86), Ala. Young Bankers (past pres.), Ala. Bankers Assn. (chmn. edn. com., cons.), Ala. Forestry Assn., Alpha Gamma Delta (disting. citizen award 1986), Montgomery Rotary Club (dir., Paul Harris award), Homemakers Am. (hon.), Future Farmers Am. Republican. Presbyterian. Avocations: horseback riding, public speaking. Office: State Treasurers Office Rm S-106 600 Dexter Ave Montgomery AL 36104 Office Phone: 334-242-7500. Office Fax: 334-242-7592. Business E-Mail: alatreas@treasury.alabama.gov.*

IVEY, STEPHEN DAVID, lawyer; b. Glen Ridge, NJ, Jan. 15, 1953; s. Henry Franklin and Sylvia (Berg) I. BA in History, Polit. Sci., Pa. State U., 1975; JD, Georgetown U., 1978. Bar: Pa. 1978, U.S. Dist. Ct. (ea. dist.) Pa. 1979, U.S. Ct. Appeals (3d cir.) 1979, U.S. Supreme Ct. 1982, U.S. Ct. Appeals (fed. cir.) 1984. Law clk. to judge Supreme Ct. Pa., Phila., 1978-81; pvt. practice Phila., 1981—. Office: 325 S 16th St Philadelphia PA 19102-4936 Office Phone: 215-985-1558.

IVEY, SUSAN M., tobacco company executive; b. Schenectady, NY, Oct. 31, 1958; m. Trevor Ivey, 1997. BS, U. Fla., Gainesville, 1980; MBA, Bellarmine U., 1987. Trade mktg. repr. Brown & Williamson Tobacco Corp., 1981—83, dist. sales mgr., 1983, dir. mktg. Far East, head internat. brands U.K. London, 1990—94, dir. mktg. British Am. Tobacco Hong Kong, 1994—96, mgr. internat. brands London, 1996—99, sr. v.p. mktg. Louisville, 1999—2000, pres., CEO, 2001—04; chmn. RJ Reynolds Tobacco, 2004—; pres., CEO Reynolds American Inc., Winston-Salem, NC, 2004—, chmn., 2006—. Bd. dirs. Reynolds American Inc., 2004—. Bd. mem. Bellarmine Univ.; mem. Committee of 200. Named one of 100 Most Powerful Women in Bus., Fortune mag., 2005—06, 50 Most Powerful Women in Bus., 2006. Office: Reynolds American Inc 401 N Main St Winston Salem NC 27101*

IVEY, THOMAS J., lawyer; b. Leeds, Yorkshire, UK, 1967; BA cum laude, UCLA, 1989; JD, U. Calif. Boalt Hall Sch. Law, 1992. Bar: Calif. 1993. Ptnr. Skadden. Co-chair PLI's seminar on Vulture Capital and Corporate Restructuring, 2002, PLI's seminar on Current Trends in Convertible Debt, 2003; guest lectr. UC Berkeley's Sch. Law. Contbr. article to firm website. Bd. mem. Bus. United in Investing, Lending and Devel. Office: Skadden 525 U Ave Ste 1100 Palo Alto CA 94301 Office Phone: 650-470-4522. Office Fax: 888-329-3302. Business E-Mail: tivey@skadden.com.*

IVIE, EVAN LEON, computer science educator; b. American Fork, Utah, May 15, 1931; s. Horace Leon and Ruth (Ashby) Ivie; m. Betty Jo Beck, Mar. 29, 1957; children: Dynette, Mark, Joseph, Robert, Ann, Rebecca, John, James, Mette, Emily, Peter. BS, BES, Brigham Young U., 1956; MS, Stanford U., 1957; PhD, MIT, 1966. Instr. MIT, Cambridge, 1960—66; mem. tech. staff Bell Labs., Murray Hill, NJ, 1966—79; prof. computer sci. Brigham Young U., Provo, Utah, 1979—; pres. Ivie Computer Corp., Provo, 1979—. Expert witness on computers for 12 lawsuits, 1983—; instr., dir. Joseph Smith Acad., Ill., 2002—06. Leader Boy Scouts Am., 1954—83; mem. Warren Sch. Bd., NJ, 1975—78; pres. GeneSys Found., 2006—; developer Pioneer Ancestral Past, Utah Sesquicentennial, 1997. 1st lt. USAF, 1957—60. Recipient Fulbright scholarship, Kiev Poly. Inst., Ukraine, 1992—93; fellow, Stanford U., 1956—57. Mem.: IEEE (sr.), Assn. Computing Machinery. Republican. Mem. Lds Ch. Achievements include invention of Data Base Computers, 1972; Programmer's Workbench, 1975; Electronic Yellow pages, 1978; Reader's Workbench, 1984. Business E-Mail: evan@ivies.org, evan@cs.byu.edu.

IVINS, MICHAEL LEE, musician; b. Omaha, Mar. 17, 1963; m. Catherine Ivins. Co-founder, bassist The Flaming Lips, 1983—; engr. Tarbox Road Studios, Fredonia, NY, 2001—. Musician: (albums) The Flaming Lips, 1985, Hear it Is, 1986, Oh My Gawd!!!.The Flaming Lips, 1987, Telepathic Surgery, 1989, In a Priest Driven Ambulance, 1990, Hit to Death in the Future Head, 1992, Transmissions from the Satellite Heart, 1993, Clouds Taste Metallic, 1995, Zaireeka, 1997, The Soft Bulletin, 1999, Yoshimi Battles the Pink Robots, 2002 (Grammy award, Best Rock Instrumental Performance, 2003), At War with the Mystics, 2006 (2 Grammy awards: Best Rock Instrumental Performance, Best Non-Classical Engineered Album, 2007), Spider-Man 3 soundtrack, 2007. Office: c/o Scott Booker Hellfire Enterprises Ltd 1208 Chowning Ave Edmond OK 73034*

IVORY, BENNIE L., executive editor; b. Hot Springs, Ark., June 19, 1951; With Sentinel-Record, Hot Springs, Ark., 1969—79; mng. editor Clarion-Ledger, Miss., 1989—93; exec. editor Florida Today, 1993—95, The News Journal, Del., 1995—97; exec. editor, v.p. news group The Courier-Journal, Louisville, 1997—. Named Editor of Yr., 1994; recipient Pres.'s Ring award (10-time winner), Gannet Co., 1994—2004, Signet award, 2005, Robert G. McGruder award for Diversity Leadership, Freedom Forum, 2004. Mem.: Am. Soc. Newspaper Editors, Nat. Assn. Black Journalists. Office: The Courier Journal 525 W Broadway Louisville KY 40202-2137 Mailing: Courier Journal PO Box 740031 Louisville KY 40201-7431 Office Phone: 502-582-4295. E-mail: bivory@courier-journal.com.*

IVORY, JAMES FRANCIS, film director; b. Berkeley, Calif., June 7, 1928; s. Edward Patrick and Hallie Millicent (DeLoney) Ivory. BFA, U. Oreg., 1951; MA in Cinema, U. So. Calif., 1957. Ptnr. Merchant Ivory Prodns., NYC, 1963—. Dir.: (films) Venice: Theme and Variations, 1957, The Sword and the Flute, 1959, The Householder, 1963, The Delhi Way, 1964, Shakespeare Wallah, 1965, The Guru, 1969, Bombay Talkie, 1970, Adventures of a Brown Man in Search of Civilization, 1971, Savages, 1972, Autobiography of a Princess, 1975, The Wild Party, 1975, Roseland, 1977, Hullabaloo over Georgie and Bonnie's Pictures, 1978, The Five Forty Eight, 1979, The Europeans, 1979, Jane Austen in Manhattan, 1980, Quartet, 1981, Heat and Dust, 1983, The Bostonians, 1984, A Room with a View, 1986 (Acad. Award nominee for best dir.), Maurice, 1987 (Silver Lion shared award with Ermanno Olmi for best dir. Venice Film Festival, 1987), Slaves of New York, 1989, Mr. and Mrs. Bridge, 1990, Howards End, 1992 (Acad. Award nominee for best dir., Cannes Internat. Film Festival 45th Anniversary Prize), The Remains of the Day, 1993 (Academy award nominee, Best dir., 1993), Jefferson in Paris, 1995, Surviving Picasso, 1996, A Soldier's Daughter Never Cries, 1998, The Golden Bowl, 2000, Le Divorce, 2003, The White Countess, 2005; films (sets and costumes) Handel's Apollo e Dafne Maggio Musicale, Florence, 1997; contbr. articles to profl. jours. Cpl. US Army, 1953—55. Recipient Comdr. des Arts et Lettres (France), 1996, 1996; Guggenheim fellow, 1973. Mem.: Dirs. Guild Am. (D.W. Griffith award 1995). Democrat. Roman Catholic. Office: Merchant Ivory Prodns 250 W 57th St Ste 1824/5 New York NY 10107-1913 E-mail: contact@merchantivory.com.

IVRA, AUGUSTINE LAFRANCHINIAX, pre-school educator; b. Memphis, Tenn., July 24, 1948; s. A J Stuckey and Rosie Elizabeth Weston; children: Terris, Thomas, Arvell. BA, Calif. State Dominguez Hills, 1978. Tchr. Los Angeles Unified Sch. Dist., 1970—. Head tchr. Parent Adv. Com., Los Angeles, 1993—. Mem. Block Club, 1982—. Mem.: United Teachers Los Angeles. Avocations: travel, gardening, antiques.

IVRY, ALFRED LYON, philosophy educator, historian; b. Bklyn., Jan. 14, 1935; s. Morris and Belle (Malamud) I.; m. Joann Saltzman, June 15, 1958; children: Rebecca, Jonathan, Sara Beth, Jessica. BA, Bklyn. Coll., 1957; MA, Brandeis U., 1958, PhD, 1963; D.Phil., Oxford U., Eng., 1971. From asst. prof. to assoc. prof. Cornell U., Ithaca, NY, 1967-74; Leon Yassenoff prof. Ohio State U., Columbus, 1974-76; Walter S. Hilborn prof. Mid. Eastern Studies Brandeis U., Waltham, Mass., 1976—89; Skirball prof. of Jewish Thought NYU, 1989—2006, prof. Middle East studies, 1989—2006, prof. emeritus, 2006—, dir. grad. studies, 1993—95. Co-chmn. Colloquium in Medieval Philosophy, Boston, 1977-81, 84-89; chmn. Colloquium in Medieval Philosophy NYU, 1990-2000; dir. NYU Medieval and Renaissance Ctr., 2002-04. Mem. editl. bd. Univ. Press of New Eng., 1982, 84, 86; editor: (translator) Al-Kindi's Metaphysics, 1974, Moses of Narbonne: Perfection of the Soul, 1977, Alexander Altmann: The Meaning of Jewish Existence, 1991, Averroes' Middle Commentary on Aristotles De anima, 1994, English-Arabic edit., 2002, medieval Hebrew edit., 2003. Trustee Boston Hebrew Coll., 1981-87, adj. prof., 1983-90. Fulbright fellow, 1963-65, 72, 1982-83; grantee NEH, 1978-79, 80-81 Fellow Am. Oriental Soc., Am. Philos. Assn., Assn. for Jewish Studies (bd. dirs. 1971-74), Medieval Acad. Am., Soc. Medieval and Renaissance Philosophy (bd. dirs. 1985-90, v.p. 1993-94, pres. 1995-96), Am. Acad. for Jewish Rsch. (bd. dirs. 1989-2000). Jewish. Business E-Mail: ai1@nyu.edu.

IVY, CONWAY GAYLE, paint company executive; b. Houston, July 8, 1941; s. John Smith and Caro (Gayle) I.; m. Diane Ellen Cole, May 25, 1973; children: Brice McPherson, Elizabeth Cole. Student, U. Chgo., 1959-62, MBA, 1968; MA in Econs., 1972, postgrad., 1973-74; BS in Natural Scis., Shimer Coll., 1964; postgrad., U. Tex., 1964-65. Geol. asst. John S. Ivy, Houston, 1965-72; securities analyst Halsey Stuart & Co. and successor Bache & Co., Chgo., 1974-75; dir. corp. planning Gould Inc., Rolling Meadows, Ill., 1975-79; v.p. corp. planning and devel. Sherwin-Williams Co., Cleve., 1979-88; v.p., treas., 1989-92; v.p. corp. planning and devel., 1992—. Pres. Ivy Minerals Inc., Boise, Idaho, 1978—. Author numerous analytincal reports on brokerage industry. Trustee Michelson-Morley Centennial Celebration, 1987, Cleve. Inst. Music, 1983-94, treas., 1987-90, vice chmn., 1990-94. Mem. Am. Econs. Assn., Soc. Mining and Metallurgy and Exploration, am. Inst. Mining Engrs., Houston Club, Phi Gamma Delta. Republican. Office: 101 Prospect Ave NW Cleveland OH 44115-1093

IVY, JOHN L., medical educator, researcher; b. Portsmouth, Va., Dec. 26, 1946; BS in Phys. Edn., Old Dominion U., 1970; MA in Exercise Physiology, U. Md., 1974, PhD in Exercise Physiology, 1976. Tchr. phys. edn. and sci. Thomas Eaton Jr. H.S., Hampton, Va., 1970; biology and physiology tchr., asst. football coach, head golf coach Kecoughtan H.S., Hampton, Va., 1971—73; asst. prof. biokinetics rsch. lab. dept. phys. edn. Temple U., Phila., 1976—77; rsch. assoc. Human Performance Lab., Ball State U., Muncie, Ind., 1976—77; postdoctoral fellow dept. preventive medicine Washington U. Sch. Medicine, St. Louis, 1978—80; asst. prof. dept. phys. edn. Coll. Health and Sch. Medicine dept. pharmacology U. S.C., Columbia, 1980—82; asst. prof. dept. kinesiology and health edn. Coll. Edn. U. Tex., Austin, 1982—84, assoc. prof. dept. kinesiology and health edn. Coll. Edn., 1984—89, prof., dir. exercise scis. labs. dept. kinesiology and health edn. Coll. Edn. and divsn. pharmacology Coll. Pharmacy, 1989—, Margie Gurley Seay Centennial prof., 1998—, chmn. dept. kinesiology and health edn., 1999—, Teresa Lozano Long endowed chair. Cons. clin. diabetes and nutrition sect. NIH, Phoenix, 1985—87; cons. com. mil. nutrition rsch. U.S. Army, 1987—88; mem. adv. bd. performance team Women's Athletic Dept. U. Tex., 1988—94; cons. Sports and Cardiovasc. Nutritionists, 1989—92, outside mem. long range planning com., 1989—90; cons. Shaklee U.S., Inc., 1988—93; mem. adv. bd. Q Health Club, 1994—96; cons. U.S. Olympic Com. Sports Medicine com. nutrition, 1992—94; mem. com. mil. nutrition and rsch. rev. panel NAS, 1995—99. Contbr. articles to profl. jours., chapters to books; jour. reviewer Am. Jour. Physiology, Endocrinology and Metabolism, 1993—2001, Jour. Optimal Nutrition, 1993—96, Diabetes, 1987—88, Internat. Jour. Sports Nutrition, 1995—, sect. editor physiology Rsch. Quar. for Exercise and Sport, 1988—91, mem. editl. bd. Medicine and Sci. in Sports and Exercise, 1987—2001, Am. Jour. Physiology, 1995—2001, Internat. Jour. Sport Nutrition, 1997—, reviewer Jour. Applied Physiology, Am. Jour. Physiology, Medicine and Sci. in Sports and Exercise, Internat. Jour. of Sports Medicine, Rsch. Quar., Am. Jour. Clin. Nutrition, Diabetes, Jour. Clin. Investiagation, Internat. Jour. Sports Nutrition, presenter in field. Recipient Nat. Rsch. Svc. award, NIH, 1978—80; grantee, Tex. Heart Assn., Ross Products, Pfizer, Inc., Shaklee U.S., Inc., U.S. Olympic Rsch. Com. Fellow: Am. Acad. Kinesiology Phys. Edn., Am. Coll. Sports Medicine (midwest chpt. 1977—79, southeast chpt. 1980—82, Tex. chpt. bd. trustees 1985—86, bd. trustees rep. for basic and applied sci. 1986—89, ambassador 1986—90, Tex. chpt. exec. dir. 1986—91, organizer, chair symosium diabetes and exercise I regulation of muscle 1988, organizer, chair symposium diabetes and exercise I regulation of muscl 1988, mem. rsch. rev. com. 1991—95, Tex. chpt. bd. trustees 1992—95); mem.: Am. Soc. Clin. Nutrition, Inc., Am. Inst. Nutrition, Am. Diabetes Assn. (mem. nutrition scis. and metabolism coun. 1991—93, mem. exercise coun. 1991—93, sec. exercise coun. 1991—93, program chair exercise coun. 1993, organizer, chair symposium role of exercise and phys. activity in the 1992, organizer, chair symposium exercise through the ages 1994, grantee 1996, rsch. award 1996), Am. Physiol. Soc., Sigma Xi, Phi Epsilon Kappa. Office: U Tex Bellmont Hall Rm 710 Dept Kinesiology and Health Edn Austin TX 78712 Office Phone: 512-471-1273. E-mail: johnivy@mail.utexas.edu.

IVY, ROBERT ADAMS, JR., architect, editor-in-chief; b. Columbus, Miss. m. Holly Ivy; children: Virginia Edmunds, Robert Adams, Benjamin Ledyard. BA cum laude, U. South, 1969; MArch, Tulane U., 1976. Consulting arch., Columbus, 1981-96; editor-in-chief Archtl. Record Mag., NYC, 1996—; editl. dir., v.p. McGraw-Hill Constrn. Publs. Author: Fay Jones: Architect, 1991; editor Architecture South mag., 1993-96; prodr., screenwriter (documentary film) 1,000 Homes. Pres. Greater Columbus, 1987-89; co-founder Greater Columbus Learning Ctr., Inc.; trustee Columbus-Lowndes Libr., 1984—, chmn., 1987, 91; vestry mem. St. Paul's Episcopal Ch., Columbus, 1985-87; adv. bd. The Dwelling Pl., Ctr. for So. Culture, 1993—; commr. U.S. Pavilion Biennale di Venezia, 2002, 04. Lt. USNR, 1970-73. Fellow AIA (bd. dirs. 1993-96), Philippine Inst. Archs.; mem. Am. Architecture Found. (bd. regents 1993-96), Miss. Inst. of Arts and Letters (bd. dirs. 1993—), Inst. Urban Design, Rembrandt Club, Century Assn. Office: Archtl Record 2 Penn Plz New York NY 10121-0101

IWAI, WILFRED KIYOSHI, lawyer; b. Honolulu, Aug. 21, 1941; s. Charles Kazuo and Michiko (Sakimoto) I.; m. Judy Tomiko Yoshimoto, Mar. 1, 1963; children: Kyle K., Tiffany Seiko. BS in Bus., U. Colo., 1963, JD, 1966. Bar: Hawaii 1966, Colo. 1966, U.S. Dist. Ct. Hawaii 1966, U.S. Ct. Appeals (9th cir.) 1966. Dep. corp. counsel State of Hawaii, Honolulu, 1966-71; assoc. Kashiwa & Kanazawa, Honolulu, 1971-75; ptnr. Kashiwa, Iwai, Motooka & Goto, Honolulu, 1975-82, Iwao, Motooka & Goto, Honolulu, 1982—93, Iwai, Motooka, Goto & Morris, Honolulu, 1993—94, Iwai, Motooka & Morris, Honolulu, 1994—2001, Iwai & Morris, Honolulu, 2001—02; atty. pvt. practice, Honolulu, 2002—. Mem. ABA, Hawaii Bar Assn Office: PO Box 61392 Honolulu HI 96839 Office Phone: 808-988-2889.

IWANIEC, HENRYK, mathematics professor; b. Elblag, Poland, 1947; Grad., U. Warsaw, 1971, PhD, 1972. Faculty to prof. dept. math. Rutgers, State U. NJ, New Brunswick, 1989—. Contbr. articles to profl. jours.; author: Elem. and Analytic Theory of Numbers, 1985, Topics in Classical Automorphic Forms, 1997, Spectral Methods of Automorphic Forms, 2002; co-author: Analytic Number Theory, 2004. Recipient Frank Nelson Cole prize, Number Theory, Am. Math. Soc., 2002, Ostrowski prize, 2002. Fellow: NAS. Office: Dept Math Hill Ctr-Busch Campus Rutgers U 110 Frelinghuysen Rd Piscataway NJ 08854-8019 E-mail: iwaniec@math.rutgers.edu.

IWATA, JON C., computer company executive; BA in Pub. Rels., San Jose State U. Joined IBM Corp., San Jose, Calif., 1984, various media rels. and nternal comm. positions Armonk, NY, 1989—94, dir. corp. pub. rels., 1994, v.p., 1995—2002, sr. v.p. comm., 2002—. Office: IBM Corp 1 New Orchard Rd Armonk NY 10504*

IWRY, J. MARK, lawyer; b. Balt., May 15, 1950; s. Samuel and Nina Iwry; m. Daryl A. Lander, June 5, 1988; 1 child, Jonathan Lander. BA, Harvard Coll., 1972; M in Pub. Policy, Kennedy Sch. Govt, 1976; JD, Harvard U., 1976. Bar: D.C. 1977, U.S. Dist. Ct. D.C., U.S. Ct. Appeals (4th and D.C. cirs.), U.S. Supreme Ct. Assoc. Covington & Burling, Washington, 1977-85, ptnr., 1985-92; dep. benefits tax counsel U.S. Dept. Treasury, Washington, 1992-95; benefits tax counsel US Dept. Treasury, Wash., DC, 1995—2001; of counsel Sullivan & Cromwell LLP, Wash., DC, 2004—. Adj. assoc. prof. George Wash. U., Wash., 1981-83, sr. adv. Retirement Security Project, rsch. prof. Pub. Policy Georgetown U., sr. staff mem. Urban-Brookings Tax Policy Ctr., staff dir. & mem. Bipartisan Presidential Transition Study Grp. John F. Kennedy Sch. Govt. Harvard U., nonresident sr. fellow Brookings Instn. Contbr. articles to various profl. journs. Rsch. grantee Harvard U. Ctr. European Studies, 1971, Treasury's Exceptional Svc. award, 2001. Mem. ABA (chmn. employee benefits com., task force on separation from svc., sect. on taxation 1987-91), D.C. Bar Assn. (chmn. employee benefits com., sect. on taxation 1989-92, nominating com., 1990, tax policy com., 1989-92), Office: Sullivan & Cromwell LLP 1701 Pennsylvania Ave NW Washington DC 20006 Office Phone: 202-956-6960. Office Fax: 202-293-6330. Business E-Mail: communications@brookings.edu.

IX, ROBERT EDWARD, food products executive; b. Woodcliffe, NJ, Oct. 15, 1929; s. William Edward and Helen Elizabeth (Gorman) I.; m. Mildred Gilmore, June 27, 1959; children: Helen Adele, Alesia Gilmore, Robert Owens Gilmore, Julia Ryan, Christopher Prouty. AB, Princeton U., 1951; MBA, Wharton Grad. Sch., U. Pa., 1956; LL.D. (hon.), Marymount Coll., 1978, Sacred Heart U., Conn., 1984. Mgmt. cons. Arthur D. Little Inc., Cambridge, Mass., 1956-64; mktg. dir. Browne-Vintners Co., Distillers Corp.-Seagrams Ltd., NYC, 1964-66; v.p. mktg. Schweppes (USA) Ltd., NYC, 1966-68, pres., 1968; pres., chief exec. officer Cadbury Schweppes Inc., Stamford, Conn., 1970-78; chmn., chief exec. officer Am. region Cadbury Schweppes P.L.C., 1976-86. Bd. dirs. Cadbury Schweppes P.L.C., London, N.E. Bancorp Inc., Union Trust Co., New Eng. Frozen Foods, Inc., Am. Thread Co., Binney & Smith Inc., Royal Doulton Co. Inc., Loctite Corp., Health Waters Inc., Chase Packaging Corp., O'Shaughnessy Funds, Inc. Trustee Marymount Coll., also chmn.; trustee Greenwich (Conn.) Acad., Trinity Pawling Sch. (N.Y.); mem. adv. council N.Y. Med. Coll., Valhalla, N.Y. Served to lt. comdr. USNR, 1951-55. Decorated Knight Sovereign Mil. Order Malta. Mem. Young President's Orgn., World Bus. Coun., Chief Execs. Forum, SW Area Commerce and Industry Assn. Conn. (dir. 1970-80 , chmn. bd. 1976-77), Def. Orientation Conf. Assn. (dir.), Grocery Mfrs. Am. (dir. 1981-85), U.S. Navy League (dir. Conn.), Univ. Club (N.Y.C.), Belle Haven Club (Greenwich), Greenwich Country Club, Landmark Club (Stamford, chmn. bd. govs.). Roman Catholic. Personal E-mail: cbix@optonline.net.

IYENGAR, ARUN K., computer scientist; s. Raja M. and Chung Wha L. Iyengar; m. Louise O. Knapp, Jan. 18, 1992; 1 child, Roger A. BA in Chemistry summa cum laude, U. Pa., 1985; MS in Computer Sci., MIT, 1988, PhD in Computer Sci., 1992. Software design engr. Hewlett-Packard Co., Chelmsford, Mass., 1992—95; rsch. staff mem. IBM Rsch., Yorktown Heights, NY, 1995—; master inventor IBM, Yorktown Heights, NY, 2001—. Contbr. scientific papers to profl. jours. Recipient Scholastic Achievement award, Am. Chem. Soc., 1985, Best Paper award, Internat. World Wide Web Confs., 2001, 2003—04, Pat Goldberg Meml. Best Paper award, IBM, 2005; Grad. fellow, NSF, 1985—90. Mem.: IEEE (sr.; treas. 1998—2000, vice chair 2000—03, chair tech. com. on internet 2003—), Assn. Computing Machinery (co-editor-in-chief Trans. on Web 2005—), Internat. Fedn. Info. Processing (U.S. nat. del. 1999—, chair working group 6.4 on Internet applications engring. 2000—), Sigma Xi. Achievements include invention of and implementation of widely used methods for improving computer performance; patents for determining how changes to underlying data affect cached objects; systems and methods for persistent and robust memory management; preserving state information in a continuing conversation between a client and server networked via a stateless protocol; new method for debugging optimized computer programs; other national and international patents in field. Office: IBM TJ Watson Rsch Ctr PO Box 704 Yorktown Heights NY 10598 Home Phone: 914-302-6117. Business E-Mail: aruni@us.ibm.com.

IYER, KISHORE, transplant surgeon; b. Trichur, India, Nov. 19, 1960; s. Devaraja Ramakrishna and Kamala Iyer; m. Lakshmi Kishore, Mar. 23, 1986; children: Anup Kishore, Divya Kishore. MBBS, Stanley Med. Coll., Chennai, India, 1984. Attending transplant surgeon U. of Nebr. Med. Ctr., Intestinal Rehabilitation Program, Omaha, 1999—2003, Children's Meml. Hosp., Chgo., 2003—; assoc. prof. surgery Northwestern U. Sch. of Medicine, Chgo., 2005—. Dir., intestinal transplant program Children's Meml. Hosp., Chgo., 2003—. Trustee Oley Found., Albany, NY, 2005—06. Recipient Brit. Assn. of Pediatric Surgeons prize, Brit. Assn. of Pediatric Surgeons, UK, 1998, Excellence in Academic Medicine award, Ill. Dept. of Pub. Aid, 2004—06. Fellow: Am. Coll. Surgeons, Royal Coll. Surgeons. Achievements include research in studies identifying plant sterols as contaminants in parenteral nutrition that may contribute to development of parenteral nutrition associated liver disease. Office: Children's Meml Hosp 2300 Children's Plaza Box # 57 Chicago IL 60614 Office Phone: 773-883-6187. Office Fax: 773-975-8534. Business E-Mail: kiyer@childrensmemorial.org.

IZAGUIRRE, GEORGE, microbiologist; b. LA, Dec. 4, 1944; s. Hector Manuel and Graciela Izaguirre. BA in Biology, Calif. State U., Northridge, 1973. Lab asst. Bio-Sci. Lab., Van Nuys, Calif., 1968—72; jr. chemist Met. Water Dist. So. Calif., 1973—77, microbiologist, 1977—2007. Project adv. com. mem. Am. Water Works Assoc. Rsch. Found., Denver, 1990—93. Contbr. articles various profl. jours. With US Army, 1966—68, Tex. Decorated Letter of Commendation US Army. Mem.: N. Am. Lake Mgmt. Soc., Am. Soc. Microbiology, Am. Water Works Assn., Internat. Water Assn. Episc. Avocations: gardening, singing, reading, travel. Office: Met Water Dist 700 Moreno Ave La Verne CA 91750 Personal E-mail: georgeize@yahoo.com.

IZARD, JOHN, lawyer; b. Hartford, Conn., Mar. 4, 1923; s. John and Elizabeth (Andrews) I.; m. Mary Bailey, apr. 16, 1955; children: Sarah Izard Pariseau, John Jr., David Bailey. BS, Yale U., 1945; LLB, U. Va., 1949. Bar: Ga. 1950. Assoc. King & Spalding, Atlanta, 1949-52, ptnr., 1952—91. Mem. Adminstrv. Conf. U.S., Washington, 1978—82. Author, pub.: A Traveler's Table, 2002; editor-in-chief Va. Law Rev., 1948; contbr. articles to legal periodicals. Mem. Nat. Com. To Study Antitrust Laws and Procedures, Washington, 1978; trustee Episcopal Media Ctr., Atlanta, 1988—2004, chmn., 1992-96; trustee U. Va. Law Sch. Found., Charlottesville, 1974-97, Alliance for Christian Media, Atlanta, 2004—; founding chmn. Sr. Citizens Svcs. of Met. Atlanta, 1967. Lt. (j.g.) USNR, 1944-46, PTO. Mem. ABA (chmn. antitrust sect. 1974-75), Ga. Bar Assn. (chmn. antitrust sect. 1969-71), Atlanta Legal Aid Soc. (pres. 1960), Lawyers Club Atlanta, Capital City Club (bd. dirs. 1976-79), Peachtree Golf Club, Piedmont Driving Club. Democrat. Episcopalian. Home: 4061 Glen Devon Dr NW Atlanta GA 30327-3613 Office: King & Spalding 1180 Peachtree St NE 29th Fl Atlanta GA 30309 Office Phone: 404-572-4752.

IZAURRALDE, ROBERTO CÉSAR, science educator, researcher; b. Paraná, Argentina, Nov. 5, 1948; s. Hermenegildo Roberto Izaurralde and Elida Nahir Pelayo; m. María Cristina Quiroga Jakas, Oct. 11, 1972; children: Octavio Rafael, María Renée, Bernarda María, Arthur Benjamin. Agronomist Engr., Nat. U. of Córdoba, 1967—72; MS, Kans. State U., 1980—81, PhD, 1982—84. Asst. prof. Nat. U. of Córdoba, Argentina, 1976—86; grad. rsch. asst. Kans. State U., Manhattan, 1982—84; rsch. assoc. U. Alta., Edmonton, Canada, 1986—90, from asst. to assoc. prof., 1990—97; staff scientist Pacific NW Nat. Lab., Washington, 1997—2001; staff scientist, lab. fellow Joint Global Change Rsch. Inst., College Park, Md., 2004; adj. prof. U. Md., College Park, 2002—. Exec. sec. Córdoba U. Exptl. Farm, 1978—80; faculty coun. mem. Nat. U. of Córdoba, 1986—86; cons. Greenhouse Gas Emissions Consortium, Edmonton, Canada, 1995; exec. com. mem. Consortium for Agrl. Soils Mitigation of Greenhouse Gases, Coll. Pk., Md., 2001—; rsch. leader Carbon Sequestration in Terrestrial Ecosystems Rsch. Ctr., Coll. Pk., Md., 2002—. Fellowship, Fulbright Program, 1980—81. Fellow: Soil Sci. Soc. Am., Am. Soc. Agronomy; mem.: AAAS, Am. Geophysical Union. Achievements include research in sustainable agricultural production; simulation modeling of anhydrous ammonia retention in soil; simulation modeling of biogeochemical cycles; simulation modeling of climate change impacts on agriculture, water resources and ecosystems; leadership in developing soil carbon sequestration as a tool to mitigate global warming. Avocations: classical music, bicycling. Office: Joint Global Change Rsch Inst 8400 Baltimore Ave Ste 201 College Park MD 20740-2496 E-mail: cesar.izaurralde@pnl.gov.

IZENBERG, JERRY, sportswriter, columnist, author; b. 1930; Sportswriter & columnist Newark Star-Ledger, 1963—; columnist Newhouse Syndicate. Author: At Large, with Jerry Izenberg, 1968, The Rivals, 1968, How Many Miles to Camelot?: the All-American Sports Myth, 1972, Championship: the NFL Title Games plus Super Bowl, 1973, Great Latin Sports Figures: Proud People, 1976, The Greatest Game Ever Played, 1988, The Jerry Izenberg Collection (The Sportswriters Eye), 1989, No Medals for Trying: A Week in the Life of a Pro Football Team, 1990, New York Giants: Seventy Five Years, 1999; prodr.(or director, writer, narrator): of over 30 TV specials (Emmy award for writing & directing "A Man Named Lombardi"). Founder & pres. Project Pride, NJ. Nominee Pulitzer Prize (15 nominations); named NJ Sportswriter of the Year (5 awards); named to Nat. Sportscasters & Sportswriters Hall of Fame, 2000, NJ Literary Hall of Fame, Athletic Hall of Fame, Rutgers Univ.-Newark; recipient Red Smith award, Assoc. Press Sports Editors, 2000. Office: The Star-Ledger 1 Star-Ledger Plz Newark NJ 07102

IZENSTARK, JOSEPH LOUIS, retired radiologist, physician, educator; b. Chgo., Mar. 29, 1919; s. Paul and Flora (Berger) I.; m. Elizabeth Kaplan, June 25, 1944; 1 child, Susan Rebecca. BA, U. Calif., Berkeley, 1948; MD, U. Calif., San Francisco, 1951. Diplomate Am. Bd. Radiology, Am. Bd. Nuc. Medicine. Intern USPHS, Chgo., 1951—52; resident Kern Gen. Hosp., Bakersfield, Calif., 1952—53; resident in radiology Cedars of Lebanon Hosp., LA, 1955—56; chief radiology resident Los Angeles County Harbor Gen. Hosp., Torrance, 1957—58; practice medicine Inglewood, Calif., 1953—55; practice radiology Bakersfield, 1971—99; dir. radiology Imperial Hosp., Inglewood, 1959—60; asst. prof. radiology Tulane U., 1960—62, assoc. prof., 1963; assoc. prof. radiology Emory U., 1963—67, dir. nuc. medicine, 1963—67; prof. radiology U. So. Calif., 1969—72; prof. health scis. Bakersfield State Coll., 1973—83; ret., 2005. Chief nuc. medicine Cedars of Lebanon Hosp., 1968-71; med. dir. edn. Bakersfield Meml. Hosp., 1983-87; spl. cons. radiol. health USPHS, Calif. Bur. Radiol. Health, U.S. Army; mem. La. Atomic Energy Adv. Coun.; dir. nuc. medicine Crawford W. Long Meml. Hosp.; mem. USPHS Commn. on Radiation Exposure Evaluation, Med. Bd. Calif., 1982-91. Author: Anatomy and Physiology for X-ray Technicians, 1961; contbr. articles to profl. jours. With AUS, 1941-45. Recipient Cert. of Merit, City of New Orleans, 1962, Physician of Yr. award Bakersfield Meml. Hosp., 1988, Outstanding Physician Contbns. to Medicine award Calif. State Assembly, 1992. Fellow Am. Cancer Soc., Am. Coll. Radiology; mem. Soc. Nuclear Medicine (pres. So. Calif. chpt. 1976), So. Valley Radiol. Soc. (pres. 1975), Kern County Med. Soc. (pres. 1978). *Set your goal in a definite clear outline taking each step one at a time, as if climbing a ladder. Think about your goals; don't talk about them. Concentrate your abilities, your studies, your friends while denying yourself luxuries. Make your own decisions; stick by them. Don't have regrets. Be honest, sincere, and dedicated without regard to time. Finally, don't give up the fight— stick to your goal.*

IZEVBIGIE, ERNEST B., biomedical researcher; b. Benin, Nigeria; arrived in US, 1982; s. Benjamin I. and Esther E. (Obasohan) Izevbigie; m. Karen M. Izevbigie; 1 child, Ernest O. Jr. BSc, Tenn. State U., 1986; MSc, U. Tenn., 1988; PhD, Mich. State U., East Lansing, 1996. Dir. quality control Four Stars Products, Inc., Bridgeton, NJ, 1988—89; pvt. practice Sewell, NJ, 1989—91; rsch. asst. Mich. State U., 1992—96; fellow NIH, Bethesda, Md., 1996—98; asst. prof. biology Jackson State U., Miss., 1999—2004, assoc. prof. biology, 2004—. Mem. editl. bd.: Med. Sci. Monitor Internat., Cellular and Molecular Biology; contbr. chapters to books, articles to profl. jours. Named Inaugural Mem. award, Internat. Biog. Ctr. Leading Scientists World, 2005; named to Leading Scientists of World, IBC, 2005; scholar, Nat. Ctr. for Minority Health and

Disparity/NIH, 2004. Mem.: Am. Soc. Nutritional Sci., Soc. Exptl. Biology and Medicine, Am. Soc. Biochemistry and Molecular Biology, Sigma Xi, Gamma Sigma Delta. Achievements include patents for phytochemotherapy for cancer. Avocations: reading, jogging, swimming. Office: Ctr for Environ Health Jackson State Univ 1400 Jr Lynch St Jackson MS 39217 Office Phone: 601-979-3464. Business E-Mail: ernest.b.izevbigie@jsums.edu.

IZUCHUKWU, JOHN IFEANYICHUKWU, industrial engineer, mechanical engineer; b. Uke, Nigeria, May 6, 1955; arrived in US, 1976; s. Michael Chike and Cecilia Obiageli (Ikeakor) I.; m. Michele Anthea Palmer, July 22, 1989; children: Michael, John, Joseph. BS in Indsl. Engring., U. Portland, 1980, MS in Mech. Engring., 1984; PhD in Indsl. Engring., Northeastern U., Boston, 1994; MBA, Northwestern U., Evanston, Ill., 2002. Registered profl. engr., Mo. Base mgr. OEM Mfg., Digital Equipment Corp., Portland, Oreg., 1980-85; computer-aided software engring. mgr. Digital Equipment Corp., Marlboro, Mass., 1985-87, mgr. mech. design automation, 1987, mgr. concurrent engring. and application ctr. for tech. Rochester, NY, 1989-91, group mgr. aerospace product strategy Marlboro, 1991-93, worldwide strategy mgr., integrated product devel., 1993-95; team leader, R & D Ethicon Endo-Surgery, Inc., Cin., 1995-98; sr. dir. global rsch., devel. and engring. Mallinckrodt, Inc., St. Charles, Mo., 1998-2001; pres., CEO VITALTECH, Inc., 2001—; CEO Core Devices, Inc., 2001—. Adj. prof. decision scis. Babson Coll., Wellesley, Mass., 1994—95, St. Louis U., 2001—, U. Mo., Rolla. Contbr. articles to engring. jours., including Jour. Mfg. Sci. and Engring.; patentee in field. Mem. ASME, Inst. Indsl. Engring. (sr. mem.). Home: 18002 Pine Canyon Ct Wildwood MO 63005-4938 Office: Mallinckrodt Inc PO Box 5840 Saint Louis MO 63134-0840 Personal E-mail: jizuchukwu@aol.com, john.izuchukwu@sbcglobal.net.

IZZI, JOHN, mathematics educator, writer, actor; b. Providence, Dec. 31, 1931; s. Joseph and Elizabeth (Kinney) I.; m. Barbara Ann Freethy, Dec. 18, 1954; children: Kathleen, Donna, James; m. Patricia Margaret Crowley, Aug. 27, 1979; children: John, Matthew, Jessica. BA, Providence Coll., 1953; MEd, RI Coll., 1965; postgrad., U. Vt., 1959, postgrad., 1960, postgrad., 1963, Seton Hall U., 1961, Yale U., 1966, Boston U., 1968—70. Tchr. LaSalle Acad., Providence, 1955-58, Warren (RI) HS, 1958-60, Warwick (RI) Vets. HS, 1960-62, 2003—04, Pilgrim HS, Warwick, 1962—66, 1999—2001, head math. dept., 1968-72, Seekonk (Mass.) HS, 1966-67; state supr. math. Mass. Dept. Edn., 1967-68; head math. dept. Toll Gate HS, Warwick, 1972—88, 2001—02; coord. secondary sch. RI Hosp., 1988-89; tchr. math., sci. Westport (Mass.) HS, 1989-91, math. adviser, biology, sci. tchr.; adj. faculty Bristol (Mass.) C.C., 1992-94. Dir. Prep. Inst., Warwick, Math. Edn. Svc., Providence, 1965-66, Toll Gate Metrication Project, Warwick, 1972-73; textbook reviewer AAAS, 1968-74; book reviewer Phi Delta Kappan, 1974-76; pres. Smallstate Co., Warwick, 1975—; prin. Warwick Adult Edn., 1987-88; ext. lectr. U. RI, 1976—; math. coach Toll Gate Acad. Decathlon State Champions, 1985, New Eng. Math. League Divsn. Champions, 1989-90; creator 1st federally funded sch. metrication project in US, 1972, Izzi Metric Slide Chart, 1974, Izzi Decimal Notation, 1974; dir. Smallstate Math. Inst., Warwick, 1989-90, Smallstate Scholarship Svc., Warwick, 1991-93; pres. Smallstate Pub., 1994-96; advisor Am. Security Coun., 1973-79; pres. P & J Izzi Assocs., Warwick, 1997-99; metrication cons. Nat. Coun. Tchrs. Math., 1973—, computer software reviewer, textbook reviewer, 1981-88; adj. faculty C.C. RI, 1981-85, Bristol (Mass.) C.C., 1992-94; editl. adviser New England Mathematic Jour., 1982-85; metrication cons. State Depts. Edn., New Eng., Pa. and NY, 1977-80. Author: Metrication, American Style, 1974, Looking at the Metric System, 1977, Adult Metric Guide, 1977, Basic Metric Competency Test, 1977, My Irish, Voices of America, 1991; actor: (TV) Brotherhood, 2004—06, Waterfront, 2004—06; contbr. articles to publs. Mem. Mass. Gov.'s Hwy. Safety Act Com., 1967-68. With US Army, 1953-55. NSF grantee 1959-61, 63, 66, 68-70; recipient Disting. Achievement award Ednl. Press Assn. Am., 1974; named Best Math. Tchr. Am., Ky. Ednl. TV, 1990. Mem. ASCD, NEA, Am. Fedn. Tchrs., Nat. Coun. Tchrs. Math., Am. Assn. Sch. Adminstrs. Metric Assn., Assn. Tchrs. Math. New Eng., New Eng. Regional Metric Assn. (edn. commr. 1976-80), Mass. Dept. Edn. Assn. (v.p. 1967-68). Home and Office: 243 Greenwood Ave Warwick RI 02886-2015 Office Phone: 401-737-8119. Personal E-mail: johnizzi@aol.com.

IZZO, HERBERT JOHN, language and linguistics educator, researcher; b. Saginaw, Mich., July 17, 1928; s. Joseph Anthony and Eleanor Bertha (Karau) I.; m. Barbara Suzanne McLaughlin, Sept. 22, 1958 (div); children: Victoria Sue Gutierrez, Alexander John, Sylvia Rachel Hunter, Daniel Stanley; m. Olga Frances Koutna, Dec. 30, 1989. BA in Spanish, U. Mich., 1950, MA in Spanish and Italian, 1951, BS in Chemistry, 1953, PhD in Linguistics, 1965. Chargé de cours Huê (Vietnam) U., 1958-59; instr. Spanish U. Ariz., Tucson, 1960-61; instr. Spanish and linguistics Stanford (Calif.) U., 1961-64; asst. prof. Spanish San Jose (Calif.) State U., 1964-68; from assoc. to prof. linguistics U. Calgary, Alberta, Canada, 1968-88, prof. emeritus, 1988—. Vis. asst. prof. fgn. langs. Mansfield (Pa.) State Coll., 1957; vis. prof. Romance linguistics U. Mich., Ann Arbor, 1977-78, 93-94; vis. prof. linguistics U. Bucharest, Romania, 1975-76; vis. prof. Italian, Stanford U., 1990-91; vis. scholar Romance lang. U. Mich., 1996-99, classics 2004-, adv. bd. Quaderni d'Italianistica, Can., 1979-91. Author: Tuscan and Etruscan, 1972; editor: The Sixth LACUS Forum, 1980, Italic and Romance, 1985; editor for linguistics Can./Am. Jour. Italian Studies, 1988-2002; translator Lost Papers of Ludwig von Mises, 1998-2001, 05—, Italian Dialect Studies of Carl L. Fernow, 2003. Bd. dirs. Fathers Alberta, Calgary, 1986-87. Grad. fellow U. N.Mex., 1953, Award for Advanced Study, Am. Coun. Learned Socs., 1963, Fulbright-Hays award U.S. Dept. State, 1966, 75. Mem. Am. Assn. Italian Studies, Linguistic Assn. Can. and U.S. (conf. organizer 1978), N.Am. Assn. for History of Lang. Scis. (v.p. 1977-80), Am. Assn. Tchrs. Italian (life), Linguistic Soc. Am. (life), Am. Classical League, Am. Assn. Tchrs. of Spanish and Portuguese (life), Can. Soc. Italian Studies (nominating com. 1977-78, adv. bd. 1974-80), Internat. Soc. Phonetic Scis., Nat. Assn. Scholars, Phi Beta Kappa, Phi Kappa Phi, Sigma Delta Pi. Avocations: music, history. Home: 2515 Deake Ave Ann Arbor MI 48108-1330 E-mail: hizzo@umich.edu.

IZZO, RALPH, utilities executive; b. NYC, Oct. 20, 1957; s. Luigi and Angelina (Barone) I.; m. Karen Ann Danowski, July 14, 1984. BS, Columbia U., 1978, MS, 1979, PhD, 1981. Coal pyrolysis researcher Exxon Rsch. and Engring., 1978; staff physicist plasma physics lab. Princeton (N.J.) U., 1981-86; adj. prof. physics Trenton (N.J.) State Coll., 1982, 91; legis. asst. U.S. Sen. Bill Bradley, Washington, 1985; policy advisor N.J. Gov. Thomas H. Kean, Trenton, 1986-90; dir. new site devel. Concord Resources Group, Lawrenceville, N.J., 1990-92; mgmt. positions PSE&G, Newark, 1992—98, v.p. corp. planning, appliance services, utility ops., 1998—2003, pres., COO, 2003—06, PSEG Inc., Newark, 2006—07, chmn., pres., CEO, 2007—. Mem. Princeton Plasma Physics Lab. Adv. Com., Pinelands Rsch. and Mgmt. Coun. (ex-officio) Gov.'s Sci. Adv. Com., Princeton Plasma Physics Lab. Speakers Bur., N.J. Dept. Environ. Protection Radon Adv. Com.; designee N.J. Commn. on Sci. and Tech., Gov.'s Task Force on Mkt. Based Pricing Electricity; mem. Gov.'s Roundtable on Superconductivity, 1989; bd. dir. Am. Elec. Power Rsch. Inst., Am. Gas Assn., NJ Utilities Assn. Contbr. articles to profl. jours. Alternate commr. NE Low-level Radioactive Waste Compact; chmn. Plainsboro Zoning Bd., Bread for the World, Local Offering Letters on Childhood Immunization; bd. dir. NJ C. of C., NJPAC; trustee Rutgers Univ. Bus. Sch., Partnership for a Drug-Free NJ, NJ Network Found.; co-chmn. Drumthwacket Found.; mem. adv. com. NJ Atty. Gen. Office of Counter-terrorism. Am. Phys. Soc. Congl. Sci. fellow, 1985, IEEE fellow, 1982, NSF fellow, 1979-82, Columbia U. fellow, 1978. Mem. Am. Phys. Soc., Scientists' Inst. for Pub. Info. Office: PSEG Inc PO Box 570 Newark NJ 07101 Office Phone: 973-430-7000.*

IZZO, THOMAS, college basketball coach; b. Iron Mountain, Mich., Jan. 30, 1955; m. Lupe Izzo; 1 child, Raquel. Grad., No. Mich. U., 1977. Head coach Ishpeming (Mich.) H.S., 1977-79; asst. coach No. Mich. U., 1979-83; with Mich. State U., East Lansing, 1983—, head coach, 1995—. Asst. coach Goodwill Games, 2001; head coach USA Pan Am. Games, 2003. Named to No. Mich. U. Hall of Fame, 1990, Upper Peninsula Hall of Fame, 1998; Divn. I Nat. Coach of Year by Nat. Assn of Basketball Coaches, 2001. Office: Mich State U Athletic Dept 222 Breslin Ctr Jensen Fieldhouse East Lansing MI 48824

JAAKKOLA, MARITTA SYLVIA, respiratory medicine consultant, researcher; b. Helsinki, Mar. 9, 1959; d. Juha V. and A. Kyllikki (Sihvonen) Keso; m. Jouni J.K. Jaakkola, Dec. 13, 1980. MD, U. Helsinki, 1984, DSc, 1994, specialist in pulmonary medicine, 1995; diploma in epidemiology and biostats., McGill U., Montreal, Que., Can., 1990. Lic. in clin. medicine. Resident in internal medicine Kiljava (Finland) Hosp., 1986-87; rsch. fellow dept. epidemiology and biostats. McGill U., 1987-89; resident in pulmonary medicine Helsinki U. Ctrl. Hosp., Helsinki, 1989-92, Riks Hosp., Oslo, 1995, U. Helsinki, 1989-92, sr. registrar, 1992-94; cons. in pulmonary medicine Finnish Inst. Occupl. Health, Helsinki, 1996—. Visiting assoc. prof. Dept. Epidemiology Sch. Hygiene and Pub. Health Johns Hopkins U., Balt., 1997-98, asst. prof. 1999—. Author textbook in respiratory medicine, 1997. Rsch. fellow Acad. Finland, 1992. Mem. European Respiratory Soc., Am. Thoracic Soc. Avocations: films, aerobics.

JAAR, BERNARD GEORGES, nephrologist, researcher; b. Port-au-Prince, Haiti, Oct. 2, 1961; came to France, 1988; s. Georges Saïd and Denise Marie (Dabdoub) J.; m. Addolorata Nocera, Oct. 31, 1987; 2 children: Stephanie, Gabriel Georges. MD, State U. Haiti, 1987; Specialist in Nephrology, Necker Sch. Medicine, Paris, 1992; Diploma in AIDS, St.-Antoine Sch. of Medicine, Paris, 1993; MPH, Johns Hopkins U., 2005. Intern Gen. Hosp. State U. Haiti, Port-au-Prince, 1986-87; comty. medicine resident Ministry of Pub. Health, Arcahaie, Haiti, 1987-88; vol. dr. Ctrs. for Devel. and Health, Port-au-Prince; intern Dialysis Svc. Tenon Hosp., Paris, 1988-89; researcher Hematopoiesis Lab. St.-Antoine Hosp., Paris, 1989-90; resident ICU St. Louis Hosp., Paris, 1990-91, nephrology svc. Tenon Hosp., Paris, 1991-92, clin. asst., 1992-94; rsch. fellow Johns Hopkins Med. Instn., Balt., 1995—97; resident in internal medicine Grad. Hosp., Phila., 1997—2000; fellow in nephrology Johns Hopkins Hosp., Balt., 2000—02; asst. prof. medicine Johns Hopkins Sch. Medicine, Balt., 2002—; staff nephrologist Nephrology Ctr. of Md., 2004—. Contbr. articles to profl. jours. Valedictorian State U. of Haiti, 1987, Necker Sch. of Medicine, 1992; recipient Boehringer Mannheim prize, France, 1992, Richard Ross Clinican Scientist award Johns Hopkins Sch. Medicine, 2003. Fellow Am. Soc. Nephrology; mem. ACP, French Soc. Nephrology, Am. Heart Assn., Internat. Soc. Nephrology. Roman Catholic. Avocations: jogging, travel, history books, soccer. Office: 2024 E Monument St Ste 2-500 Baltimore MD 21287-0007

JABARA, MICHAEL DEAN, real estate developer, former technology entrepreneur; b. Sioux Falls, SD, Oct. 26, 1952; s. James M. and Jean Marie (Swiden) J.; m. Gundula Beate Dietz, Aug. 26, 1984; children: James Michael, Jenna Mariel. Student, Mich. Tech. U., 1970-72; BSBA, U. Calif., Berkeley, 1974; MBA, Pepperdine U., 1979. Mgr. original Sprint project team So. Pacific Communications Corp., 1976-78; network product mgr. ROLM Corp., 1978-81; cons. McGraw Hill Co., Hamburg and London, 1982—83; founder and CEO Friend Techs. Inc. (merger VoiceCom Sys., Inc., now Premiere Techs., Inc.), San Francisco, 1984—88; pres. Voice-Com Ventures, San Francisco, 1988-93; mng. dir. Telecom, EMS Group Ltd., London, 1993-95; owner Red Rock Ptnrs., Ltd., Las Vegas, Nev., 1993—; chmn. bd. and COO Bingo Card Minder Corp., Stateline, Nev., 1996; owner TOIR LLC, Glenbrook, 1998-99, NewHoldings, Ltd., Las Vegas, 2000—; dir. Bus. Devel. Kummer Kaempfer Bonner & Renshaw, Las Vegas, 2002—05; co-owner Highrise Ptnrs. Ltd., Las Vegas, 2004—05; prin. and owner Summit Realty, Utah, 2005—, Brian Hess, Utah, 2005—; pres., CEO Altitude Devel. Co., Las Vegas, 2006—. Registered rep., sr. advisor Silver Pacific Advisors, LLC, 2004—; trustee Nev. Devel. Authority, 2002—05. Patentee in field. Bd. dirs. Tahoe-Douglas C. of C.; chmn. Tahoe Citizens Com., 1995-2000. Mem.: Mich. Tech Alumni Assn., U. Calif. Berkeley Bus. Alumni, Pepperdine Bus. Alumni, Las Vegas Jaguar Club. Avocations: classic cars, flying, sailing. Office: Summit at Brian Head LLC 4750 W Flamingo Rd Ste A Las Vegas NV 89103 Office Phone: 702-696-9001. Business E-Mail: mjabara@brianhesscondos.com.

JABBAR, ABDUL, physician, educator, gastroenterologist; b. Multan, Punjab, Pakistan, Oct. 14, 1968; s. Muhammad Sharif and Hajira Bibi; m. Nosheen Jabbar, Nov. 12, 2000; 1 child, Ayyan. MD, Nishtar Med. Coll., Pakistan, 1992. Clin. instr. U. Louisville, 2002—03, asst. prof., 2003—. Consulting gastroenterologist Gastroenterologist Group U. Louisville, 2002—; staff attendant VA Hosp. Contbr. rsch. and med. lit. revs. Gastroenterology/Hepatology fellow, Am. Bd. Internal Medicine, 2002. Mem.: Am. Coll. Gastroenterology. Achievements include research in guidelines for intagastric versus intrajejunal feeding. Home: 9911 Fringe Tree Ct Louisville KY 40241 Office: 530 S Jackson St Louisville KS 40202 Home Phone: 502-412-7995; Office Phone: 502-852-6991. Office Fax: 502-852-0846. Personal E-mail: ajh5@hotmail.com.

JABER, RAJAA, physician, educator; b. Beirut, Apr. 22, 1956; arrived in US, 1986; d. Ali Jaber and Maymana Majzoub; m. Jeffrey Trilling, May 19, 1991; children: Stefan Trilling, Adam Trilling. BS, Am. U. Beirut, 1977, MD, 1982. Diplomate Am. Bd. Family Practice., 1988, Am. Holistic Med. Assn., 2005. Chmn. Collaboration Health and Healing, Setauket, NY, 1996—2003; dir. Wellness and Chronic Illness Program, Setauket, 2000—; clin. assoc. prof. dept. family medicine SUNY, Stony Brook, NY, 1998—2006, clin. assoc. prof. dept. prevention medicine, 2007—. Co-dir. nutrition course SUNY Med. Sch., Stony Brook, 2004—; tchr. self care and integrative medicine. Avocations: dance, hiking. Office: SUNY Stony Brook Dept Family Medicine Stony Brook NY 11790-8461 Office Phone: 631-444-0624. Business E-Mail: rjaber@notes.cc.sunysb.edu.

JABLONSKI, ROBERT LEO, architect; b. Chgo., Mar. 28, 1926; s. Leo Frank and Rose (Domian) J. BS, U. Ill., 1950. Lic. architect Ill., 1950; cert. Nat. Coun. Archtl. Registration Bd., 1965. Chief planner Nat. Council YMCA, Chgo., 1957-64; assoc. Univ. architect U. Ill., Chgo., 1964-69; coordinating architect U. Chgo., 1969-70; dir. bldg. programs City of Chgo., 1970—2003; prin. Robert Jablonski Mgmt. Svcs., Chgo., 2003—. Combat infantry US Army, ETO. Decorated Purple Heart medal, 2 battle stars. Mem.: Assn. Lic. Arch. Roman Catholic. Avocations: tennis, swimming. Office Phone: 773-775-2289.

JABLONSKI, ZYGMUNT, lawyer; b. Gdynia, Poland, May 14, 1953; MA with distinction, A. Mickliewicz U., 1977; JD magna cum laude, U. Miami, 1985. Bar: Fla. 1985, DC 1986, US Ct. Appeals (Fed. Cir.) 1986, US Ct. Internat. Trade 1986. Atty. Steptoe & Johnson, Washington, 1985—86, Wilkie Farr & Gallagher, Washington, 1986—92, Skadden Arps Slate Meagher & Flom, Washington, 1992—94; sr. v.p., gen. counsel, sec. Unisource Worldwide Inc., Norcross, Ga. Mem.: ABA. Office: Unisource Worldwide Gen Counsel Law Dept 6600 Governors Lake Pkwy Norcross GA 30071 Office Phone: 770-209-6557.

JABS, AURA LEE, minister, educator; b. Lewistown, Mont., Apr. 21, 1932; d. Stephen Ellias and Mabel Harriet Sande; m. Edward Henry Jabs, June 20, 1954; children: Mark Allan, Mary Kay, David Stephen. BS, Mont. State U., 1954; MDiv, Iliff Sch. Theology, 1982, MA in Religion, 1983. Ordained to ministry United Presbyn. Ch., 1984. Tchr. Spanish Gallatin County H.S., Bozeman, Mont., 1953—54; tchr. English Box Elder H.S., 1954—55; tchr. English, French Williams Bay H.S., Wis., 1957—58; tchr. English Am. Dependent Sch., Molesworth AFB, England, 1959—60; pastor Vale (Oreg.) United Meth. Ch., Oreg., 1984—90, Southside Blvd. United Meth. Ch., Nampa, 1990—93, Sutherlin/Wilbur United Meth. Churches, Sutherlin, Oreg., 1993—2002. Bd. trustees Oregon-Idaho Conf., Portland, 1988—90; chair Ctrl. Dist. Com. Superintendency, Bend, 1989—90; mem. So. Dist. Leadership Team, Eugene, 2002—04, Conf. Bd. of Elders Task Force, Portland, 2004—. Vol. driver Silver Key, Colorado Springs, 1976—78; sr. deaconess United Ch. Christ, Colorado Springs, 1976—79; bd. mem. Sutherlin/Oakland Emergency Food Pantry, Oreg., 1993—2002; vol. Suicide Crisis Hotline, 1983—84. Recipient Iliff Preaching prize, Iliff Sch. Theology, 1982. Methodist. Avocations: reading, travel, photography, computers. Home Phone: 541-440-5227.

JACCACI, AUGUST THAYER, JR., social architect, educator; b. NYC, Mar. 9, 1937; s. August Thayer and Helen Jenkins Jaccaci; m. Robin Charboneau Middleton, June 28, 1963 (div. June 1982); children: Anthony, Alexander; m. Joanne Karen Hobbs, Aug. 28, 1999. BA, Harvard Coll., 1960, MA in Tchg., 1964; MFA, R.I. Sch. Design, 1965. Tchr., coach Rutland (Vt.) H.S., 1960—61; admissions officer, coach Harvard Coll., Cambridge, Mass., 1961—63; admissions officer, tchr. R.I. Sch. Design, Providence, 1963—65; tchr., coach Phillips Acad. Andover, Mass., 1965—68; arts adminstr., lectr. Boston Coll., Newton, 1968—75; adminstr., coach Lawrence Acad., Groton, Mass., 1976—78; tchr. Burke Mountain Acad., East Burke, Vt., 1983—85; social arch. Unity Scholars, New Gloucester, Maine, 1998—2003. Pres. Metamatrix Assoc., Thetford, Vt., 1978; founder Nature Planning Network, New Gloucester, 2005; ski coach, team capt. FIS World Ski Championships, Vail, Colo., 1989; guest lectr. Stanford Bus. Sch.; cons. Motorola, Fannie Mae, Pillsbury, AT&T, P.W. Minor, Micromentor, Chase Manhattan Bank, J.C. Penney, Polaroid, Vt. Agy. Human Svcs., Arthur Anderson, Xerox, Vol. Hosp. Assn. Am., Toronto Dominion Bank, No. Telecom, Canada, IMD, Europe, Credit Suisse, Europe, Brit. Petroleum, Europe; spkr. in field nat. and internat. Represented in permanent collections, Addison Gallery Am. Art; author: CEO: Chief Evolutionary Officer, 1999, General Periodicity, 2000. Candidate for gov., Vt., 1992, Vt., 1994. Recipient Svc. to Humanity Award, PW Minor Co., 2000, Earl award, Religious Futurist, 2002. Mem.: World Future Soc. (pres. Boston chpt. 1975), Creative Edn. Found. (tchr. 1972—2005, Leadership, Svc. and Commitment award 1990, Disting. Leadership award 2005). Avocations: skiing, rowing, hiking. Home: 626 Penney Rd New Gloucester ME 04260 E-mail: unityscholars@earthlink.net.

JACHE, ALBERT WILLIAM, retired chemistry professor, academic administrator, research scientist; b. Manchester, NH, Nov. 5, 1924; s. William Frederick and Esther (Ruemely) J.; m. Lucy Ellen Hauslein, June 14, 1948; children: Ann Gail, Ellen Ruth, Philip William, Heidi Verena. BS, U. N.H., 1948, MS, 1950; PhD, U. Wash., 1952. Sr. chemist Air Reduction Co., Murray Hill, NJ, 1952-53; rsch. assoc. dept. physics Duke U., 1953-55; asst. prof. dept. chemistry Tex. A&M U., College Station, 1955-58, assoc. prof., 1958-61; cons. Ozark Mahoning Co., Tulsa, 1960-61, assoc. rsch. dir., 1961-64; sr. rsch. assoc. Olin Mathieson Chem. Corp. (now Olin Corp.), New Haven, 1964-67, sect. mgr., 1965-67, cons., 1967-75; prof. chemistry Marquette U., Milw., 1967-90, prof. emeritus, 1990—, chmn. chem. dept., 1967-72, dean Grad. Sch., 1972-77, assoc. acad. v.p. for health scis., 1974-77, assoc. v.p.-acad. affairs, 1977-85; scientist-in-residence Argonne (Ill.) Nat. Lab., 1985-86, scientist, 1991-96, temporary appointment, 1991-96; with ChemLab, 2000—. Program coordination com. Med. Center S.E. Wis.; lectr. U. Tulsa, 1963-64, New Haven Coll., 1967; cons. Allied Chem. Corp., 1977-78, 2000-; salt panel com. remediation buried and tank wastes NAS/NRC, 1996-97. Trustee Milw. Sci. Ednl. Found.; pres. Milw. Sci. Ednl. Trust, 1973—; trustee Argonne Univs. Assn., 1977-80; chmn. Assn. Grad. Schs. in Cath. Univs., 1973-75; mem. AUA nuclear engring. edn. com. U. Chgo, 1977-89, chmn., 1984, sec., 1989; double bass player River Cities Symphony Orch., 1997-2001, Evergreen Comty. Orch., 1994—, Evergreen String Ensemble, 1994-2000, Marietta Chamber Orch., 1994-97. With AUS, 1942-46. Fellow AAAS (Sr. Scientists and Engrs. Am.), Am. Inst. Chemists; mem. Am. Chem. Soc. (chmn.-elect, program chmn. div. fluorine chemistry 1981, chmn. div. fluorine chemistry 1982), Sigma Xi, Omicron Kappa Upsilon, Alpha Sigma Nu. Achievements include research and numerous patents in the area of inorganic fluorine chemistry with emphasis on anhydrous hydrogen fluoride as a solvent or reaction medium and Hypofluorite chemistry. Home and Office: 301 Ohio St Marietta OH 45750-3139 Personal E-mail: albert@jache.com.

JACHINO, DANEEN L., legal administrator; b. Chgo., Feb. 16, 1947; d. James and Lee Jachino. BA, DePaul U., 1985; MBA, Ill. Inst. Tech., 1995. Asst. buyer Chas A. Stevens, Chgo., 1967—70; sec. Lord, Bissell and Brook, Chgo., 1970—78; adminstrv. asst. to Judge David Linn Ill. Appellate Ct., Chgo., 1978—85; legal asst., sr. legal asst. Kirkland and Ellis, Chgo., 1986—95; mgr. mergers/acquisitions clearance Kirkland and Ellis LLP, Chgo., 1995—2005, dir. mergers/acquisitions clearance, 2006—. Presenter Fed. Trade Commn., Washington, 2002. Contbr. chapters to books. Vol. underprivileged children Shama Ministries; mem. Art Inst. Chgo., 1995—, Friends of Park, Chgo., 2002—, Lincoln Park Zoo, Chgo., 2004—. Mem.: Alzheimer's Assn. (support group facilitator 2001—, steering com. memory walk 2003, 2005, co-chair 2006—07, pub. policy com. 2007—, bd. dirs. Greater Ill. chpt. 2007—). Roman Catholic. Avocations: running, sailing, skiing, bicycling. Office: Kirkland & Ellis LLP 200 E Randolph Dr Chicago IL 60601 Office Phone: 312-861-2137. Business E-Mail: djachino@kirkland.com.

JACHNA, JOSEPH DAVID, photographer, educator; b. Chgo., Sept. 12, 1935; m. Virginia Kemper, 1962; children: Timothy, Heidi, Jody. BS in Art Edn., Inst. Design, Ill. Inst. Tech., 1958, MS in Photography, 1961. Part-time photographic asst. Derwin Studio Darkroom, Chgo., 1953-54; photo-technician Eastman Kodak Labs., Chgo., 1954; photographer's asst. DeSort Studio, Chgo., 1956-58; free-lance photographer Chgo., 1961—; instr. photography Inst. Design, Ill. Inst. Tech., Chgo., 1961—69; assoc. prof. U. Ill., Chgo., 1969—75, prof., 1976—2001, prof. emeritus, 2001—. One-man shows include Art Inst. Chgo., 1961, St. Mary's Coll., Notre Dame, Ind., 1963, U. Ill., Chgo., 1965, 77, Lightfall Gallery Art Ctr., Evanston, Ill., 1970, U. Wis., Milw., 1970, Ctr. for Photog. Studies, Louisville, 1974, Nikon Photog. Salon, Tokyo, 1974, Afterimage Gallery, Dallas, 1975, Visual Studies Workshop Gallery, Rochester, N.Y., 1979, Chgo. Ctr. for Contemporary Photography, 1980, Focus Gallery, San Francisco, 1981, Photogenesis, Albuquerque, 1983, Andover (Mass.) Gallery, 1984, Chgo. State U., 1985, Tweed Mus. Art, Duluth, Minn., 1986, Gallery 954, Chgo., 1993, State of Ill. Galleries, Chgo., Lockport and Springfield, 1994, Fermilab, Batavia, Ill., 1995, Stephen Daiter Gallery, Chgo., 2000, Bruce Silverstein Gallery, N.Y.C., 2003, City Gallery Photography, Chgo., 2007; exhibited in group shows at Art Inst. Chgo, 1963, 83, MIT, Cambridge, 1968, Walker Art Ctr., Mpls., 1973, 89, Renaissance Soc. Gallery U. Chgo., 1975, Mus. Contemporary Art, Chgo., 1977, 96—, Mus. Art RISD, Providence, 1978, Carpenter Ctr. Visual Arts, Harvard U., Cambridge, 1981, Nexus, Atlanta, 1983, Nat. Mus. Art., Washington, 1984, San Francisco Mus. Modern Art, 1985, Internat. Ctr. Photography, Tucson, 1992, Gallery 312, Chgo., 1996, Stockholm Subway, Sweden, 1999, Hyde Park Art Ctr., Chgo., 2001, Stephen Daiter Gallery,

Chgo., 2002, 2003, Taken by Design: Photography at the Inst. of Design, 1937-1971, Art Inst. Chgo., 2002; represented in permanent collections, Mus. Modern Art, N.Y.C., Internat. Mus. Photography, George Eastman House, Rochester, N.Y., MIT, San Francisco Mus. Modern Art, Mpls. Inst. Arts, Art Inst. Chgo., Ctr. Photog. Studies, Louisville, Ctr. for Creative Photography, U. Ariz., Tucson. Ferguson Found. grantee, 1973, Nat. Endowment for Arts grantee, 1976, Ill. Arts Council, 1979; Guggenheim fellow, 1980. Home and Studio: 5707 W 89 Pl Oak Lawn IL 60453-1225 Personal E-mail: jjachna@sbcglobal.net.

JACK, JANIS GRAHAM, judge; b. 1946; RN, St. Thomas Sch. Nursing, 1969; BA, U. Balt., 1974; JD summa cum laude, South Tex. Coll., 1981. Pvt. practice, Corpus Christi, Tex., 1981-94; judge U.S. Dist. Ct. (so. dist.) Tex., Corpus Christi, 1994—. Jud. mem. The Maritime Law Assn. U.S. Mem. ABA, Fed. Judges Assn., Fifth Cir. Dist. Judges Assn., Nat. Assn. Women Judges, Jud. Conf. Com. Info. Tech., Tex. Bar Found., State Bar Tex., The Philos. Soc. Tex., Order of Lytae, Phi Alpha Delta. Office: US Dist Ct 1133 N Shoreline Blvd Corpus Christi TX 78401

JACK, MORGANN TAYLLOR, writer, artist; d. William H. and Emma Lee (Williams) Blanks; m. Charles D. Jack, July 21, 1957 (dec. Sept. 20, 1979). AA in Fine Arts, Allan Hancock Coll., 1975. Editl. asst. The Cycler Champlin Oil Co. house organ, Ft. Worth, 1957; columnist, reporter, corr. Santa Barbara News-Press, Lompoc, Calif., 1961—64; freelance journalist AP, Springfield (Mass.) Rep., 1966—68; staff reporter features, 1st editor weekend entertainment supplement, Lompoc Record, 1968—71; feature writer Lompoc Valley News, 1980—84; feature writer, cover artist Cen. Coast Mag., Santa Maria, Calif., 1989—90. Guest artist Binnenheide Art Exhbn., Kevelaer, Germany, 1994. Creator, editor, artist (monthly mag.) Space 'n Lace, VAFB, Calif., 1961—63, (weekly newsletter) Reeflector, Recife, Brazil, 1964—65; commd. garden sculpture, for Lompoc Mayor (reception benefitting Lompoc Mus.), 1978; illustrator (book) A Word About Birds in Rhyme Time, 1984; commd. art, Office Idaho State Treas., 1988—93. Mem. Santa Barbara County Commn. for Women, 1999—2000. Recipient regional awards, juried art shows and competitions, 1951—86, Plaque in Appreciation of Outstanding Comty. Svcs., City of Lompoc, 1968—71. Mem.: Santa Barbara Mus. Art, Nat. Mus. Women in the Arts (charter mem.). Avocations: travel, reading. Home: PO Box 598 Lompoc CA 93438

JACKEL, LAWRENCE, publishing executive; b. NYC, July 25; s. Solomon and Sylvia (Fisher) J.; m. Ellen Jane Koons, Sept. 29, 1985; children: Kenneth Isaac, Molly Laurie, Sarah Kate. BBA, CCNY, 1961, MBA, 1966. Acct. Aviquipo, Inc., NYC, 1961-62; fin. exec. Litton Industries, NYC, 1962-68; group controller Alloys Unltd., Inc., NYC, 1968-69; v.p. fin. Litton Ednl. Pub., Inc., NYC, 1969-72, 1969-72, pres. Delmar Pubs. div. Albany, NY, 1973-80, 1973-80, exec. v.p., pres. NYC, 1976-80; owner, pres. Tab Books Inc., 1980-90, 1980-90; group v.p. McGraw Hill, Blue Ridge Summit, Pa., 1990-92; pres. Jackel Group Inc.-Cons. and Pubs., Venice, Fla., 1992-93; vice chmn., CEO, owner Lectorum Publs., Inc., NYC, 1993-96; chmn. Promotional Sales Books LLC, NYC, 1996—; lit. agt. Waterside Prodn. Co., 2006—. Mem.: Univ. Club. Democrat. Jewish. Home: 1771 Ringling Blvd Apt 1203 Sarasota FL 34236 Office Phone: 941-364-3601. Personal E-mail: jackelpub1@verizon.net.

JACKENDOFF, RAY SAUL, linguistics educator; b. Chgo., Jan. 23, 1945; s. Nathaniel and Elaine Muriel (Flanders) J.; m. Hildy Dvorak; children: Amy Sarah, Beth Liana, Daniel Nathan. BA, Swarthmore Coll., 1965; PhD, MIT, 1969. Instr. UCLA, 1969-70; asst. prof. linguistics Brandeis U., Waltham, Mass., 1971-73, assoc. prof., 1973-79, prof., 1979—2005, prof. emeritus, 2006—, chmn. linguistics and cognitive sci., 1979-92, 2002—05; prof. philosophy Tufts U., Medford, Mass., 2005, Seth Merrin prof. philosophy, 2005—, co-dir. Ctr. for Cognitive Studies, 2005—; external faculty Santa Fe Inst., 2006—. Author: Semantic Interpretation in Generative Grammar, 1972 (Arts Humanities award Coun. Grad. Schs. in U.S. 1974), X-Bar Syntax: A Study of Phrase Structure, 1977, Semantics and Cognition, 1983, (with F. Lerdahl) A Generative Theory of Tonal Music, 1983, Consciousness and the Computational Mind, 1987, Semantic Structures, 1990, Languages of the Mind, 1992, Patterns in the Mind, 1993, The Architecture of the Language Faculty, 1997, Foundations of Language, 2002, (with P. Culicover) Simpler Syntax, 2005, Language, Consciousness, Culture, 2007; mem. editl. bd. Music Perception, Cognitive Sci., Studia Linguistica, Natural Lang. and Linguistic Theory, Trends in Cognitive Scis. Soloist Boston Pops Orch., 1980. Recipient Jean Nicod prize in cognitive philosophy, 2003; Guggenheim fellow, 1993-94, fellow Wissenschaftskolleg zu Berlin, 1999-2000. Mem. Linguistic Soc. Am. (exec. com. 1996-99, 2002-05 pres 2003), Soc. for Philosophy and Psychology (pres. 1990-91), Am. Acad. Arts and Scis. Jewish. Home: 79 Goden St Belmont MA 02478-2934 Office: Tufts U Ctr Cognitive Studies Medford MA 02155

JACKER, CORINNE LITVIN, playwright, writer; b. Chgo., June 29, 1933; d. Thomas Henry and Theresa (Bellak) Litvin. Student, Stanford U., 1950-52; BS, Northwestern U., 1954, MA, 1955, postgrad., 1955-56. Editor Liberal Arts Press, 1959-60, Macmillan Co., 1960-63, Scribner's, 1963-65; story editor Sta. WNET-TV, NYC, 1969-71, CBS-TV, NYC, 1972-74; instr. playwrighting NYU, 1976-78; vis. prof. playwriting Yale U., 1979-81. Adj. prof. Princeton U., 1986, 88, Columbia U., 1988-99, Breadloaf Sch. of English, 1988, NYU, 1990-91, U. Ga., 1995—2003; sci. cons. Benton Project for Broadcasting, U. Chgo., 1988-90. Exec. story editor, head writer (TV series) Best of Families, PBS, N.Y.C., 1975-77; head writer (TV series) Another World, 1981-82; author: Man, Memory, and Machines, 1964 (N.Y. Pub. Library 50 Best Books of Yr. 1964), Window on the Unknown, 1966 (AAAS 50 Best Books of Yr. 1966), A Little History of Cocoa, 1966, The Black Flag of Anarchy, 1968 (Pubs. Weekly 25 Best Books of Yr. 1968), The Biological Revolution, 1971, The Chocolate Bar Bust, 1994; playwright: The Scientific Method, 1970, Seditious Acts, 1970, Travellers, 1973, Breakfast, Lunch, & Dinner, 1975, Bits and Pieces, 1975 (Obie award 1975), Harry Outside, 1975 (Obie award 1975), Night Thoughts & Terminal, 1976, Other People's Tables, 1976, My Life, 1977, After the Season, 1978, Later, 1979, Domestic Issues, 1981, In Place, 1982, Songs from Distant Lands, 1985, (adaptation) Hedda Gabbler, 1989, The Island, 1991, (adaptation) Three Sisters, 1992, In the Dark, 1993, Light, 1993, Getting Home, 1994, A New Life, 1995, The Promised Land, 1995, The Machine Age, 1996, Parties, 2000; TV writer, including: 3 episodes Actors' Choice, NET, 1970 (Emmy citation 1970), Virginia Woolf: The Moment Whole, NET, 1972 (CINE Golden Eagle award 1972); story editor: 4 episode series Benjamin Franklin, CBS, 1974 (Emmy citation 1974); The Adams Chronicles, 1975 (Peabody award 1975); Bicentennial Minutes, 1975, Loose Change, 1978, 3 episode series, NBC, 1978, 3 episodes of Best of Families, NET, 1978, The Jilting of Granny Weatherall, NET, 1980, Night Thoughts and Terminal BBC, 1978, Overdrawn at the Memory Bank, NET, 1983 (Rotterdam Film Festival, Am. Film Inst. Video Feature Film Festival). Rockefeller Found. grantee, 1979-80; residency Villa Serbelloni, Bellagio, Italy, 1987. Mem. Dramatists Guild, Writers Guild Am. East, PEN Home and Office: 110 W 86th St New York NY 10024-4049 Office Phone: 212-496-9698. E-mail: jacaranda@verizon.net.

JACKIW, ROMAN, physicist, researcher; b. Lublinec, Poland, Nov. 8, 1939; came to U.S., 1949; s. Nicholas and Zenobia (Kostyk) J.; m. So-Young Pi, Sept. 4, 1981; children: Simone Ahlborn, Nicholas, Stefan Pi. BA, Swarthmore Coll., 1961; PhD, Cornell U., 1966; Doctorate (hon.), U. Uppsala, Sweden, 2000, U. Torino, Italy, 2000, Bogolyubov Inst., Kyiv, Ukraine, 2003. Jr. fellow Harvard Soc. of Fellows, Cambridge, Mass., 1966-69; from asst. prof. to Jerrold Zacharias prof. physics MIT, Cambridge, 1969—. Vis. prof. Rockefeller U., N.Y.C., 1977-78, U. Calif., L.A., Santa Barbara, 1980, Columbia U., N.Y.C., 1989-90. Contbr. over 200 articles to profl. jours. Alfred P. Sloan fellow Sloan Found., 1969-71, J.S. Guggenheim fellow Guggenheim Found., 1977-78; recipient Dannie Heineman prize in math. physics Am. Phys. Soc., 1995, Dirac medal and prize Internat. Ctr. for Theoretical Physics, Trieste, Italy, 1998. Fellow Am. Acad. of Arts and Scis., Am. Phys. Soc.; mem. NAS, Nat. Acad. Scis. Ukraine (fgn. mem.). Achievements include research on fundamental processes in nature. Office: MIT MIT CTP 6-403 77 Massachusetts Ave Cambridge MA 02139-4307 Office Phone: 617-253-4830.

JACKLEY, MARTIN J. (MARTY JACKLEY), prosecutor; b. 1970; BS in Electrical Engring., SD Sch. Mines & Tech., 1992; JD, U. SD, 1995. Bar: SD 1995, Minn. 1997, US Dist. Ct. SD 1997, US Ct. Appeals (8th cir.) 1998, US Supreme Ct. 1999. Law clk. to Hon. Richard Battey US Dist. Ct. SD, Rapid City, 1995—97; spl. asst. atty. gen. State of SD, 2001—05; ptnr. Gunderson, Palmer, Goodsell & Nelson LLP, Rapid City, 2002—06; US atty. dist. SD US Dept. Justice, Sioux Falls, SD, 2006—. Recipient Abe award, Pennington County Republican Party. Office: US Attys Office PO Box 3303 Sioux Falls SD 57101 Home Phone: 605-271-4414; Office Phone: 605-330-4400. Business E-Mail: marty.j.jackley@usdoj.gov.

JACKMAN, HUGH, actor; b. Sydney, NSW, Australia, Oct. 12, 1968; s. Chris Jackman; m. Deborra-Lee Furness, Apr. 11, 1996; adopted children: Oscar Maximilian, Ava Eliot. BA in Journalism, U. of Technology, Sydney; student, Actor's Ctr., Sydney; grad., Western Australian Acad. Performing Arts, Perth, 1994. Actor: (TV series) Correlli, 1995, Snowy River: The McGregor Saga, 1993, Halifax f.p: Afraid of the Dark, 1998, Oklahoma!, 1999; (films) Hey Mr. Producer, 1998, Paperback Hero, 1999, Erskineville Kings, 1999, X-Men, 2000, Someone Like You, 2001, Swordfish, 2001, Kate & Leopold, 2001, Standing Room Only, 2002, X2, 2003, Van Helsing, 2004, The Fountain, 2006, X-Men: The Last Stand, 2006, Scoop, 2006, The Prestige, 2006, (voice) Flushed Away, 2006, Happy Feet, 2006,; (Broadway debut) The Boy from Oz, 2003— (Tony award best actor in a musical, 2004, Drama Desk award best actor in a musical, 2004), (other stage appearances) Beauty and the Beast, Oklahoma!, Carousel, 2002; host Tony Awards, 2003, 2004, 2005 (Emmy award, outstanding individual performance in a variety or musical program, 2005).*

JACKMAN, LLOYD MILES, chemistry professor; b. Goolwa, Australia, Apr. 1, 1926; came to U.S., 1967; s. Charles Stuart and Florence Olive (Green) J.; m. Marie Alma Sandow, 1950; children— Richard Miles, Donald Charles, Andrew Thorpe. BSc, U. Adelaide, Australia, 1945, BSc with honors, 1946, MSc, 1948, PhD, 1951. Asst. lectr. organic chemistry Imperial Coll., London, 1952, lectr., 1953; reader U. London, 1961—62; prof., head dept. organic chemistry U. Melbourne, Australia, 1962—67; prof. chemistry Pa. State U., University Park, 1967—91, prof. emeritus, 1992—. Author: Applications of NMR in Organic Chemistry. Beit fellow U. London, 1951-52; NSF sr. fgn. fellow, 1965; Guggenheim fellow, 1973-74; Wilsmore fellow chemistry, Melbourne, Australia; recipient Humboldt award, Fed. Republic Germany, 1977, 89. Fellow AAAS, Chem. Soc. London, Am. Chem. Soc., Royal Australian Chem. Inst. Home: 710 Glenn Rd State College PA 16803-3414 Office: 152 Davey Lab University Park PA 16802-6300 E-mail: lmj@psu.edu.

JACKMAN, ROBERT ALAN, retail executive; b. NYC, Mar. 22, 1939; s. Joseph and Kate Queenie (Silverman) J.; m. Lois Wiederschall, June 10, 1962; children: Jennifer Sharon, Deborah Lynn. BS, U. Bridgeport, 1961. Dir. sales Mattel Inc., Hawthorne, Calif., 1963-75; sr. v.p. mktg. and sales Tyco Industries Inc., Moorestown, NJ, 1975-78; gen. mgr. Aurora Products Inc., Stamford, Conn., 1978-80; ptnr. Scott Lancaster Jackman Mills Atha, Westport, Conn., 1980-83; pres., CEO Leisure Dynamics Inc. divsn. Coleco Industries, Westport, 1983-86; with Oak Tree Publs., San Diego, 1983-87; exec. v.p. Coleco Industries Inc., West Hartford, Conn., 1986-88; gen. mgr. Tomy Am., Inc., Southport, Conn., 1988-90, also bd. dirs.; owner Yes I Can, 1990—. Cons. Harvard U. Bus. Sch. Club, N.Y.C., 1984. Patentee in field. With USAR, 1961—62. Recipient Disting. Alumni award U. Bridgeport (Conn.), 1986. Mem. U. Bridgeport Mktg. Coun., Mission Hills Country Club (Rancho Mirage, Calif.). Avocations: tennis, music, reading. Home: 8 Via Elegante Rancho Mirage CA 92270-1969 Office: 35 325 Date Palm Dr Ste 131 Cathedral City CA 92234-7031 Office Phone: 760-321-1717. E-mail: bob@yesican.com.

JACKMAN, RODERICK VICTOR, distance learning educator; b. Salt Lake City, Dec. 30, 1949; m. Linda Jackman; children: Candace Linda, Roderick Dustin, Sean Larsen. AS in Gen. Edn., Brigham Young U., Provo, 1974; BS in Med. Sociology, U. Utah, 1976, MS in Health Sci., 1979, postgrad. in pub. adminstrn., 1979—81; BS in Biochemistry, Westminister Coll., Salt Lake City, 1997. Chemistry Utah State Office of Edn., 1981, Sociology Utah State Office of Edn., 1981, Medical Anatomy and Physiology Utah State Office of Edn., 1981, Health Occupations Utah State Office of Edn., 1981, Health Science/Health Technology Utah State Office of Edn., 1981, Health Education Utah State Office of Edn., 1981, Advanced Health Science Utah State Office of Edn., 1981. Distance edn. instr. Alpine Sch. Dist., American Fork, Utah, 1981—, Utah Valley State Coll., Orem, 1985—2003, Salt Lake C.C., 2003—. Surg. asst.; advisor Health Occupation Students Am., 1986—; bd. dirs. Utah Health Students Am., 1986—88; pres. health divsn. Utah Vocat. Assn., 1986—87, pres., 1988—89; so. rep. health dept. bd. Edn. Health Divsn. Utah Assn. for Career and Tech., 2005—; head soccer coach Pleasant Grove (Utah) HS, 1982. Recipient Vocat. Excellence award, Utah Health Occupation Students Am., Outstanding Svc. award, Health Occupation Students Am., 1986—2005, Extra Mile Tchg. award, Alpine Sch. Dist., 1989, 2005, Outstanding Tchr. award, Utah Vocat. Assn., 1990, Outstanding Svc. to Edn. award, Utah State Bd. Edn., 1997, Golden Apple Tchr. award, Alpine Sch. Dist., 1997, Outstanding Instr. award, Utah Vocat. Assn., 1998, Students Choice award, Utah Valley State Coll., 1999, Outstanding Interactive Course award, 2002, Award of Merit, Assn. for Career and Tech. Edn., 2006, Extra Mile award, Pleasant Grove H.S., 2005. Home: 748 S Sunny Ln Orem UT 84058 Office: Alpine Sch Dist /Mountain View 665 W Center Orem UT 84057 Home Phone: 801-226-2383; Office Phone: 801-227-2400 150. Personal E-mail: rjackman@alpine.k12.ut.us.

JACKMAN, STEVEN H., lawyer, electronics executive; Bar: Fla. V.p., corp. counsel Sanmina-SCI, San Jose, Calif. Office: Sanmina-SCI Corp 2700 N First St San Jose CA 95134 Office Phone: 408-964-3630. Office Fax: 408-964-3636. E-mail: steven.jackman@sanmina-sci.com.*

JACKSON, ALAN, musician, lyricist; b. Newnan, Ga. s. Eugene and Ruth Jackson; m. Denise Jackson; children: Mattie, Ali. Student, W. Ga. Coll. Albums include Here in the Real World, 1990, Don't Rock the Jukebox, 1991 (Acad. Country Music album of yr.), A Lot About Livin' (and a Little 'Bout Love), 1992 (2 Grammy nominations, Best Country Male Vocal & Song for Chattahoochee, Acad. Country Music album of yr., 1993), Honky Tonk Christmas, 1993, Who I Am, 1994, The Greatest Hits Collection, 1995, Everything I Love, 1996, High Mileage, 1998, Under the Influence, 1999, When Somebody Loves You, 2000, Drive, 2002, What I Do, 2004, Like Red on a Rose, 2006, Live at Texas Stadium, 2007; songs & singles include Don't Rock the Jukebox, 1991 (Acad. Country Music single record of yr., 1991, ASCAP country song of yr., 1992) Chattahoochee, 1993 (Acad. Country Music single record of yr., Country Music Assoc. single & music video of yr., 1993, song of yr., 1994) Where Were You (When the World Stopped Turning), 2002 (Grammy, best country song). Named country songwriter of yr., ASCAP, 1992, male vocalist of yr., Acad. Country Music, 1994, 1995, entertainer of yr., Country Music Assoc., 1995; recipient Triple Play award, 1990, 1991, 1992. Office: Alan Jackson Fan Club PO Box 121945 Nashville TN 37212-1945 also: Arista Records 7 Music Cir Nashville TN 37203

JACKSON, ALAN JAY, prosecutor; b. 1965; Grad., U. Tex., Austin; law degree, Pepperdine U., Malibu, Calif. Bar: Calif. 1994, US Dist. Ct. (ctrl. dist. Calif.) 1994. Dep. dist. atty. hardcore gang unit LA County Dist. Atty.'s Office, dep. dist. atty. major crimes divsn. Faculty mem. prosecuting gang violence Ernest F. Hollings Nat. Advocacy Ctr., Columbia, SC. Office: LA County Dist Attys Office 210 W Temple St Ste 18000 Los Angeles CA 90012 Office Phone: 213-974-3535. Office Fax: 213-893-0150.

JACKSON, ALLEN KEITH, retired museum administrator; b. Rocky Ford, Colo., July 22, 1932; s. Monford L. and Leliah Jean (Hipp) Jackson; m. Barbara May Hollard, June 13, 1954; children: Cary Vincent, Deborah Kay, Edward Keith, Fredrick James. BA, U. Denver, 1954; postgrad., Cambridge U., Eng., 1955; Th.M. (Elizabeth Iliff Warren fellow), Iliff Sch. Theology, 1958; PhD, Emory U., 1960. Instr. sociology Emory U., 1958-60; chaplain, asst. prof. religion and sociology Morningside Coll., Sioux City, Iowa, 1960-62, dean coll., 1962-67; pres. Huntingdon Coll., Montgomery, Ala., 1968-93; dir. Idaho Mus. Natural History, Idaho State U., Pocatello, 1993—98; exec. dir. Nat. Heritage Ctr., 1998—2002; ret., 2002—. Past pres. Montgomery Area United Appeal. Fulbright scholar, Cambridge U., 1955, honor fellow, Emory U., 1960. Mem.: Ala. Coun. Advancement Pvt. Colls. (pres. 1975—81), Ala. Assn. Ind. Colls. and Univs. (pres. 1969—71), Rotary, Phi Kappa Phi, Beta Theta Pi, Omicron Delta Kappa, Phi Beta Kappa. Home: 633 W Mcnabb Rd Inkom ID 83245-1502 *A worthy aim it seems to me, is to seek the Truth and to share the truths you find.*

JACKSON, ALPHONSO ROY, secretary of housing and urban development; b. Marshall, Tex., Sept. 9, 1946; s. Arthur Todd and Henriette (Green) Jackson; m. Marcia A. Jackson, June 18, 1988; children: Annette Watkins, Lesley Jackson. BS, Truman State U.(formerly N.E. Mo. State), 1968, MA, 1969; JD, Washington U., St. Louis, 1973. Asst. prof. criminal justice and polit. sci. U. Mo., St. Louis, 1973—77; dir. pub. safety City of St. Louis, 1977—81, dep. exec. dir., Housing Authority, 1981—82; dir., cons. svcs. Laventhol & Horwath, St. Louis, 1982-87; CEO Dept. of Pub. and Assisted Housing, Washington, 1987-89; pres. and CEO Housing Authority/City of Dallas, 1989-96; dep. sec. US Dept H.U.D., Washington, 2001—04; acting sec. US Dept. H.U.D., Washington, 2003—04, sec., 2004—. Cons. other city govts.; adj. prof. U. Mo., St. Louis; mem. bd. commrs. Planned Indsl. Expansion City of St. Louis, 1978—; bd. dirs. St. Louis Local devel. Co., 1978—. Contbr. Bd. dirs. Zale-Lipshy Hosp., Dallas, 1992, Truman State U., 1995, Tex. So. U., 1998, Children's Med. Ctr., Dallas, 1994; chmn. Gen. Svcs. Commn. State of Tex., Austin, 1998; mem. task foce edn. Mo. Gov., 1975-76, Sister Cities Internat., 1976-81. Recipient Chmn.'s award Nat. Boys and Girls Clubs of Am., 1997; fellow Kellogg fellow Ctr. Biology nat. Sys., Washington U., 1970-71, U. Oxford, 1977, Danforth Found., 1981, The Aspen Inst. Fellow: Kappa Alpha Psi; mem.: Nat. Bar. Assn., Anniversary Club. Democrat. Roman Catholic. Avocations: jogging, golf, reading. Office: US Dept HUD Robert C Weaver Federal Bldg 451 7th St SW Rm 10000 Washington DC 20410-1047*

JACKSON, ANDREW PRESTON, library director; b. Bklyn., Jan. 28, 1947; s. Walter Luther Sr. and Bessie (Lindsey) J. BS, CUNY, 1990, MLS, 1996; pub. librs. profl. cert., SUNY. Asst. supr. pers. processing unit Human Resources Adminstrn. Agy. Child Devel. Pers. Dept., NYC, 1968-70, coord. pers. svcs., 1970-76; customer rels. mgr., contracts mgr. Robinson Chevrolet, Novato, Calif., 1976-79; office mgr. Sesame Press, Inc., NYC, 1979-80; exec. dir. Langston Hughes Cmty. Libr. and Cultural Ctr., Corona, NY, 1980—. Lectr. Black history, NYC, 1986—; cons. evaluating Black heritage collections; adj. lectr. York Coll., CUNY, 2001—; tng., devel. and orgn. cons. Roosevelt Pub. Libr., 2006—. Author: Queens Notes: A Work In Progress, Facts About the Forgotten Borough of Queens New York, (foreword) African American Almanac, 9th edit., 2003; contbg. author: Handbook of Black Librarianship, Turn the Page and Don't Stop Sharing Successful Chapters in Our Lives with Youth, 2006; contbr. articles to profl. jours. Chmn. social svcs. adv. coun. Cmty. Planning Bd. Areas 3 and 5, 1984—87; treas. No. Blvd. Mchts. Assn., Corona, 1985—99; cmty. adv. coun. York Coll., 1997—; active NY State Freedom Trails Commn., Queens Underground RR Com., 1997—; bd. trustees The Renaissance Charter Sch., 1999—; convenor Churchman's fellowship Corona Congl. Ch., 1987—89; nat. adv. bd. CDF Langston Hughes Libr., 2001—03; cmty. adv. bd. Elmhurst (NY) Hosp. Ctr., 1983—97; bd. dirs. York Coll. Alumni Inc., Jamaica, NY, 1990—93, 1996—99, Queens Pub. TV, 1986—; vice chair cmty. adv. bd. Otis Bantum Correctional Ctr., N.Y.C. Dept. Corrections, Rikers Island, NY, 1990—95. Staff sgt. (E-5) USAF, 1964—68, Vietnam. Decorated Bronze Star; named Man of Yr., Nat. Assn. Negro Bus. and Profl. Women's Club, Inc., 1991, Disting. Grad., Queens Coll. Grad. Sch. Libr. and Info. Scis., CUNY, 2006; named to East Elmhurst Alumni Inc. Hall of Fame, 1998; recipient Ombudsman award, 1982, Cmty. Svc. award, East Elmhurst Track Club, 1986, Tabernacle Cmty. CME Ch., Nat. Assn. Univ. Women (north shore br.), Outstanding Leadership in Queens award, Queens Fedn. Chs., 1988, Cmty. award, East Elmhurst-Corona Civic Assn., 1989, cert. of appreciation, Kiwanis, 1991, Cmty. Svc. award, Minority Mgmt. Assn., NYC, 1992, cert. of recognition, August Martin HS, 1992, Gov.'s award African-Ams. of Distinction, NY State Gov., 1994, Disting. Grad. award, Nat. Assn. Equal Opportunity in Higher Edn., 1994, cert. of honor, Queens Borough Pres., 1994, Youth Devel. award, 115th Police Precinct Coun., 1994, Giving It Back award, W.C. Bryant HS, 1995, Disting. Alumni award, York Coll. Alumni Assn., Inc., 1996, Fulfilling the Dream award, CBS-TV, 1996, Scroll of Honor, 4W Cir. of Arts and Enterprise, 1996, Cmty. Svc. award, Nat. Coun. Negro Women, 1997, Elmcor Alumni Assn., 1998, Concerned African-Am. of Flushing, 1998, Lamplighter award, Queens Borough Pub. Libr., 1999, Cmty. Svc. award, NY Firre Dept. African Heritage Soc., 2000, Outstanding Contbns. award, Combined Treasury Dept., 2001, Appreciation award, Grace Episcopal Ch., 2001, Cmty. Person of Yr. award, Delta Beta Zeta, 2001, Recognition award, NY State Atty. Gen., 2002, Cmty. Activist award, United for Progress Dem. Club, Cmty. Svc. award, Corona Congl. Ch., 2002, Cultural award, Key Women of Am., 2002, Cmty. Leader of Yr. award, Alpha Kappa Alpha, 2003, Pinnacle award, Jack and Jill of Am., Inc., 2005, Legend award, Barnes Hist. Soc., 2005, Cmty. Leadership award, First Child Soc., 2007. Mem.: ALA Black Libr. Caucus (v.p. 2002—04, pres. 2004—, Libr. Advocacy award 1999, Libr. Outreach award 1999, Profl. Devel. award 2007), ALA, NAACP (life), LI Libr. Assn., Reforma, NY Black Librs. Caucus, Libr. Adminstrn. and Mgmt. Assn., Pub. Librs. Assn. Avocations: speaking with youth, reading, writing. Home: 94-24 30th Ave East Elmhurst NY 11369 Office: Roosevelt Pub Libr 27 W Fulton Ave Roosevelt NY 11575 Home Phone: 718-397-9261; Office Phone: 516-378-0222. Business E-Mail: apjackson@roosevetlibrary.org.

JACKSON, ANNE (ANNE JACKSON WALLACH), actress; b. Allegheny, Pa., Sept. 3, 1926; d. John Ivan and Stella Germaine (Murray) J.; m. Eli Wallach, Mar. 5, 1948; children: Peter, Roberta, Katherine. Studied with Sanford Meisner and Herbert Berghof at Neighborhood Playhouse; attended Lee Strassberg, Actor's Studio; DFA, South Hampton Coll. Tchr. Herbert Berghoff Sch. Profl. debut: Cherry Orchard; mem. Am. Repertory Co.; Broadway plays include: Summer and Smoke, Oh, Men! Oh, Women!, Middle of the Night, Major Barbara, Rhinoceros, Luv, Waltz of the Toreadors, Diary of Anne Frank, 1978, Twice Around the Park, 1982-83, Nest of the Woodgrouse, 1984, Café Crown, 1989, Love Letters, 1991-92, Lost in Yonkers, 1992, In Person, 1993, The Flowering Peach, 1994, off-Broadway plays: Tennessee Williams Remembered, 1999, Mr. Peter's Connection, 1998, Down the Garden Path; London stage performances of The Typists, The Tiger, 1966; film appearances include: So Young, So Bad, 1950, Secret Life of an American Wife, 1968, Dirty Dingus McGee, 1970, Lovers and Other Strangers, 1970, The Shining, 1980, Sam's Son, 1985, Funny About Love, 1992, Folks, 1992, Johnnie Twenties, 1998, Something Sweet, 2000; TV appearances include: 84 Charing Cross Road, Private Battle, Everything's Relative, 1987, Law & Order, 1997, Education of Max Bickford, 2002; TV films: Family Man, Golda I and II, Out on a Limb, Baby M, 1988, The Rescuers: The Lady on the Bicycle, 1997; author: (autobiography) Early Stages, 1979. Recipient Obie award. Mem.: Actor's Studio (life). Office: care Paradigm 200 W 57th St Ste 900 New York NY 10019-3211

JACKSON, BEVERLEY JOY JACOBSON, columnist, educator; b. LA, Nov. 20, 1928; d. Phillip and Dorothy Jacobson; m. Robert David Jackson (div. Aug. 1964); 1 child, Tracey Dee. Student, U. So. Calif., UCLA. Daily columnist Santa Barbara News Press, 1968-92, Santa Barbara Ind., 1992—94; internat. lectr., 2003. Nat. lectr. Santa Barbara History, History of China Recreated, Chinese Footbinding, Shoes for Bound Feet, China Today; freelance writer, fgn. corr. Author: Dolls and Doll Houses of Spain, 1970; (with others) I'm Just Wild About Harry, 1979, Spendid Slippers: A Thousand Years of an Erotic Tradition, 1997, Ladder to the Clouds-Intrigues and Traditions of Chinese Rank, 1999, King Fisher Blue, 2002, Shanghai Girl Gets All Dressed Up, 2005, The Grand Tour of Asia 1910, 2006. Bd. dirs. Santa Barbara br. Am. Cancer Soc., 1963-92; art mus. coun. LA Mus. Art, 1959-96, docent, 1962-64, costume coun., 1983-92; exec. bd. Channel City Club, 1969-2004; adv. bd. Storyteller Sch. Homeless Children, Santa Barbara Hist. Soc. Mus., Coun. Christmas Cheer, Women's Shelter Bldg., Direct Relief Internat., Nat. Coun. Drug and Alcohol Abuse, Santa Barbara Choral Soc., Am. Oceans Campaign, Hospice Santa Barbara, 1981-92, Stop AIDS Coun., Arthritis Found.; bd. dirs. So. Calif. Com. for Shakespear's Globe Theatre, Friends U. Calif. Libr., Santa Barbara; chmn. Santa Barbara Com. for Visit Queen Elizabeth II, 1982—; founder costume guild Santa Barbara Hist. Soc.; curator Chinese collections Santa Barbara Hist. Mus.; hon. bd. Santa Barbara Salvation Army, Ensemble Theatre Santa Barbara. Mem.: PEN, Commanderie Bordeaux San Francisco. Home: PO Box 5118 Santa Barbara CA 93150-5118 Personal E-mail: bevjack@silcom.com.

JACKSON, BOBBY RAND, minister; b. Wilson, NC, Dec. 14, 1931; s. Joel John and Bessie Francis (Mayo) J.; m. Martha Jane Ketteman, May 30, 1953; children: Stephen Rand, Philip Wayne. BA, Free Will Bapt. Bible Coll., Nashville, 1954; MA, Bob Jones U., Greenville, SC, 1955. Ordained to ministry Free Will Baptists Ch., 1951. Evangelist Free Will Baptists Ch., Nashville, 1955—; asst. moderator Nat. Assn. Free Will Baptists, Nashville, 1972-77, moderator, 1978-87, mem. exec. com., 1972-87, chmn. exec. com., 1978-87, presiding officer of gen. bd., 1978-87. Author: Messages That Matter, 1960, Six Steps to Successful Living, 1962, Awakening in the Wilderness, 1965, Beyond the Stars, 1966; soloist: record albums Softly and Tenderly, 1968, Then Sings My Soul, 1969, Fill My Cup, Lord, 1970, My God and I, 1978, Songs from Two Generations, 1985. Mem. Free Will Bapt. Bible Coll. Alumni Assn., Bob Jones U. Alumni Assn. Home: 1412 E 14th St Greenville NC 27858-4734 E-mail: bjea@suddenlink.net.

JACKSON, BRIAN KELLY, economics professor; b. Tacoma, Wash., Jan. 2, 1960; s. Gary Bill and Betty Ann Jackson; m. Kathy Louise Isaacs; children: Katie Anne, Jonathan Brian. BS, Northea. Okla. State U., Tahlequah, 1982; MS, U. Okla., Norman, 1984; PhD, Okla. State U., Stillwater, 2005. Imagery scientist U.S. Govt./CIA, Washington, 1985—87; instr. math. Collin County C.C., McKinney, Tex., 1988—90, Connors State Coll., Warner, Okla., 1990—2001; prof. math. and econs. Okla. Wesleyan U., Bartlesville, 2003—. Author: (article) Jour. Econs., 2006. Office: Okla Wesleyan Univ 2201 Silver Lake Rd Bartlesville OK 74006 Business E-Mail: bjackson@okwu.edu.

JACKSON, BRIAN MATTHEW, musician, educator; b. Detroit, May 31, 1972; s. Susan D and Elliot J Jackson. BS in Sociology & Philosophy, Western Mich. U., 1994; MA, Calif. Inst. Integral Studies, San Francisco, 1999. Musician Infinite Volume, Memory Systems, I Am Spoonbender, 1996—; sr. quality assurance engr. Rocket Network, San Francisco, 1999—2001; instr. Touro Coll., New York City, 2002—. Music event promoter Form8 /Synth, San Francisco, 2001—03. Vol. Drug Policy Alliance, NYC, 2004. Recipient Academic Achievement award, Sociology Dept., Western Mich. U., 1993, Best Club to Hear the Future, San Francisco Bay Guardian, 2001, Best Pickup Spot for HAL 9000, San Francisco Weekly, 2002; scholar, Western Mich. U., 1990—94. Mem.: Alpha Kappa Delta, Golden Key. Liberal. Achievements include first to develop independent, digital record producing techniques. Avocations: consciousness studies, computers, audio technology, chess, electronic music. Home Phone: 212-228-5750. E-mail: info@form8.com.

JACKSON, CANDINE LEE, performing arts, English and speech educator; b. Lynwood, Calif., Sept. 4, 1947; d. Larry Barney and Juanita Florine Cagan; m. Kirk Allan Jackson, Nov. 24, 1991; 1 child, Yvonne Franz. AA, Long Beach City Coll., Calif., 1969; BA, Calif. State U., Long Beach, 1973; edn. credential, Calif. Luth. U., Thousand Oaks, 1978; MPH, Calif. State U., Northridge, 1987. Engish and speech instr. Northwest HS, Cedar Hill, Mo., 1999—2002; performing arts instr. Herculaneum (Mo.) HS, 2002—06; team instr. hons. English and speech team Hillsboro HS, Mo., 2006—. Intern The Muny Opera and U. Mo.-St Louis, 1996—2000; region 6 coord. Tonkinese Breed Assn. Mem.: MNEA (assoc.), Cat Fanciers' Assn (steering com. 1999—). Home: 1102 Crystal Heights Crystal City MO 63019 Office: Hillsboro HS 120 Leon Hall Pkwy Hillsboro MO 63050 Home Phone: 636-931-5432; Office Phone: 636-789-0010. Personal E-mail: kjcjsing@sbcglobal.net.

JACKSON, CARLAYNE E., neurologist, educator; d. Carlton Joseph and Romayne Lucille Mertens; m. E. Penn Jackson, July 21, 1984; children: Carenn E., Caitlyn Claire. BS, Tex. A&M U., College Station, 1983; MD, 1987. Prof. medicine, neurology U. Tex. Health Sci. Ctr., San Antonio, 2006—. Office: University of Texas Health Science Cente 7703 Floyd Curl Dr MC 7883 San Antonio TX 78229-3900 Office Phone: 210-567-1945. Office Fax: 210-567-1948.

JACKSON, CARLTON LUTHER, history professor, writer; b. Blount, Ala. s. Luther Harrison and Winnie Forrestor Jackson; m. Patricia Ann Dow, Jan. 30, 1954; children: Beverly, Daniel, Matthew, Hilary. BA, Birmingham U., Ala., 1958, MA, 1959; PhD, U. Ga., Athens, 1963; degree (hon.), U. Argentina, Buenos Aires, 1976. From mem. staff to disting. prof. We. Ky. U., Bowling Green, Ky., 1961—96, disting. prof. history, 1996—. Mem. selection com. Fulbright Found., Washington, 1991—96. Author: Hattie: The Life of Hattie McDaniel, 1996. Sgt. USAF, 1951—55. Fellow, Fulbright Found., 1989—90. Mem.: Fulbright Assn. (life). Episcopalian. Office: Western Ky Univ Dept History Bowling Green KY 42101 Office Phone: 270-745-5730. Business E-Mail: carlton.jackson@wku.edu.

JACKSON, CAROL E., federal judge; BA, Wellesley Coll., 1973; JD, U. Mich., 1976. With Thompson & Mitchell, St. Louis, 1976-83; counsel Mallinckrodt, Inc., St. Louis, 1983-85; magistrate US Dist. Ct., Ea. Dist. Mo., 1986-92, dist. judge, 1992—, now chief judge. Adj. prof. law Washington U., St. Louis, 1989-92. Trustee St. Louis Art Mus., 1987-91; dir. bi-state chpt. ARC, 1989-91, Mo. Bot. Garden. Mem. Nat. Assn. Women Judges, Fed. Magistrate Judges Assn., Mo. Bar, St. Louis County Bar Assn., Bar Assn. Metro. St. Louis, Mound City Bar Assn., Lawyers Assn. St. Louis. Office: US Dist Ct Eagleton US Courthous Ste 14-148 111 S 10th St Saint Louis MO 63102

JACKSON, CHARLES ANTHONY, music educator, radio personality; b. Metuchen, NJ, July 17, 1960; s. Edwin Francis and Sally Ann Jackson; m. Blair Kirby Nesbit, May 19, 1989. MusB in Performance/Tuba, U. No. Colo., 1984; MEd in Curriculum and Instrn., U. Phoenix, Las Vegas, Nev., 2005. Cert. K-12 music tchr. Nev. Prin. tuba Va. Symphony Orch., Norfolk, 1986—89; dir. orchestras, chmn. dept. Durango H.S., Las Vegas, 1998—2003; dir. orchestras Silverado H.S., Las Vegas, 2003—; host Nev. Pub. Radio, Las Vegas, 2004—05. Music dir. Las Vegas Brass Band, 2000—; condr. Las Vegas Youth Philharm. Orch., 2006—; freelance tuba , bass, and cimbasso player. With US Army, 1985—96. Decorated achievement medals, commendation medals U.S. Army. Independent. Presbyterian. Avocations: reading, crossword puzzles, Civil War history, collecting historic recordings. Home: 3136 Waterview Dr Las Vegas NV 89117 Office: Silverado HS Silver Hawk Ave Las Vegas NV 89123 Home Phone: 702-233-5990; Office Phone: 799-5790. Personal E-mail: chuckjackson1@cox.net. Business E-Mail: caj940@interact.ccsd.net.

JACKSON, CHARLES IAN, writer, consultant; b. Keighley, Yorkshire, Eng., Feb. 11, 1935; s. Harry Sydney and Nellie (Crabtree) J.; m. Margaret Cochrane Storrie, July 10, 1963 (div. 1987); 1 child, Janet Clare Louise; m. Merlyn Hayward Farina (Martin), Aug. 16, 2001. BA, London U., 1956; MS, McGill U., 1959, PhD, 1961. Lectr. in geography London Sch. Econ., 1959-69; head econ. geography sect. Can. Dept. Energy, Mines and Resources, Ottawa, Ont., 1969-71; dir. planning and priorities Ministry of State for Urban Affairs, Ottawa, Ont., Canada, 1972-78; sr. econ. affairs officer UN Econ. Commn. Europe, Geneva, 1978-81; exec. dir. Sigma Xi, New Haven, 1981-87. Cons. water resources UN Econ. Commn. Europe, 1966-67; cons. German Marshall Fund U.S., 1975-77, Ford Found., 1977, Environment Can., 1994-95; rsch. dir. Can. Ho. of Commons Standing Com. on Environment, 1991-92; dir. Chreod Ltd., 1993-97; assoc. fellow Timothy Dwight Coll., Yale U. Translator tech. lit. from French; editor Letters from the 49th Parallel 1857-73, 2000, The Arctic Journals of William Scoresby the Younger 1811-1813, 2003, and other books in field; author: Does Anyone Read Lake Hazen?, 2002, articles on history, resource mgmt. and geography; co-author Great Lakes: Great Legacy?, 1990; columnist (monthly mag.) Notes from Ptolemy, 1969-99. Recipient Darton prize Royal Meteorol. Soc., 1962; recipient Evan Durbin prize Inst. Econ. Affairs, 1964. Mem. Hakluyt Soc. (coun. 1967-69), Champlain Soc., Soc. History of Discoveries, Can. Nautical Rsch. Soc. Business E-Mail: ian.j@cshore.com.

JACKSON, CHARLES WAYNE, food products and former telecommunications industry executive; b. Louisville, June 3, 1930; s. Wayne O. and Geneva Drake J.; m. Sallie I. Lambert, June 21, 1952 (div. Feb. 1980); m. Elizabeth J. Soptic, June 1, 1979; children: Thomas, Carol E., Charles N. BEE, Ga. Inst. Tech., 1952. Student engr. AT&T, Cin., 1954-55, dist. plant engr. Jacksonville, Fla., 1955-56, comml. rep to acctg. asst. Atlanta, 1956-59, transmission systems engr. to plant design engr. Kansas City, 1963-66; project mgr. to dir. major project Western Elec. Co., NYC, 1966-69; engr. dir. TWX coord. to bus. relations dir. AT&T, NYC, 1969-75; dir. pvt. lines rates Long Lines Co., Somerset, NJ, 1975, dir. pvt. lines rates to dir. planning Bedminster, NJ, 1975-81; dir. data prog. svcs. to dir. svc. devel. mktg. dept. AT&T, Bedminster, 1981-87; cons. pvt. practice Brandenburg, Ky., 1987-90; v.p. H&R Block Franchise, 1990-92; owner Squire Taber Apple Orchard, 1992—2000. V.p. Echo Enterprises, Inc., 1991—. 1st. lt. U.S. Army, 1952-54. Mem. Elks. Methodist. Avocations: photography, horticulture. Home and Office: 7829 Caenen St Lenexa KS 66216

JACKSON, CHEYENNE, actor; b. July 12, 1975; Actor: (Broadway plays) All Shook Up, 2005 (Theatre World award), Xanadu, 2007, (Off-Broadway) Altar Boyz, 2004, The Agony and the Agony, 2006, (regional theatre) Anything Goes, Tales of Hoffman, Kismet, Cinderella, Kiss Me Kate, Cendrillon, Gifts of the Magi, The Secret Garden, Children of Eden, South Pacific, Damn Yankees, Joseph and the Amazing Technicolor Dreamcoat, Carousel, Grease, Beowulf, West Side Story, Most Happy Fella, Hair, Rocky Horror Show; (films) Curiosity, 2005, United 93, 2006; guest appearances All My Children, 2005, Larry King Live, 2006, former back-up singer for Vanessa Williams, Heather Headley and Liza Minnelli. Mailing: c/o Rogers & Cowan Floor 5 640 Fifth Ave New York NY 10019*

JACKSON, CURTIS JAMES **See FIFTY CENT**

JACKSON, CYNTHIA ANN, medical association administrator, health consultant; b. Hornell, NY, Feb. 13, 1960; d. William Thompson and Carol Ann (Dailey) Moss; m. Robert Dale Jackson, Dec. 2, 2000; m. Clinton Newell Colvin, Mar. 3, 1984 (div. Oct. 10, 1994); stepchildren: Brandi Louise Moss, Robert Dale II children: Christopher David Colvin, Cassandra Lynn Colvin. Assocs. in Environ. Health Tech., Merritt Coll., Oakland, Calif., 1985; B of Occupl. Health and Safety magna cum laude, Nat. U., San Diego, 1987, M of Forensic Sci., 1989. Lic. practical nurse, U. of N.Y.; registered environ. health secialist, ServSafe instr. Nat. Restaurant Assn., cert. pest control applicator Va. Dept. of Agr. and Consumer Svcs., food safety mgr. Nat. Registry of Food Safety Profls., spl. conservator of the peace Commonwealth of Va. Dept. of Criminal Justice Svcs. Cook Coachlight Steakhouse, Hornell, 1978—79; head preventive medicine dept. Naval Med. Clinic, Phila., 1992—94, Naval Hosp. Camp Pendleton, Calif., 1995—98, 1st Med. Bn., Camp Pendleton, 1998—2001, Mil. Sealift Command, Norfolk, Va., 2001—04; environ. health specialist Chesapeake Health Dept., Va., 2004—; hosp. corpsman Naval Regional Med. Ctr., Bremerton, Wash., 1980—81; preventive medicine technician U.S. Naval Hosp., Yokosuka, Japan, 1982—84, Naval Hosp. San Diego, 1984—89; surface force ind. duty corpsmen instr. Naval Sch. of Health Scis., San Diego, 1989—92; officer recruit Officer Indoctrination Sch., Newport News, RI, 1992. Mgr. bio-hazardous waste Naval Hosp. Camp Pendleton Marine Corps Base, 1995—98; legal officer 1st Med. Bn., Camp Pendleton, 1998—2001, equal opportunity officer, 1998—2001, mem. awards bd., 1998—2001; environ. health cons. Miliatry Sealift Command, Norfolk, 2001—04; health promotion mgr. Mil. Sealift Command, Norfolk, 2001—04, inspector shipboard material assessments and readiness team, 2001—04, mem. awards bd., 2001—04; environ. health cons. Chesapeake Health Dept., Va., 2004—, epidemiology rep., 2004—; chmn. rabies control bd. Naval Hosp. Camp Pendleton Marine Corps Base, Camp Pendleton, 1995—98, mem. infection control com., 1995—98, mem. base water steering com., 1995—98, mem. quality rev. bd. for child care, 1995—98, mem. hazardous material control mgmt., 1995—98, mem. wellness adv. com., 1995—98; environ. health officer cons. 1st Med. Bn., Camp Pendleton, 1998—2001, health promotion mgr., Semper Fi fit coord., 1998—2001. Co-author: Field Biomedical Waste Program; author, exhibitor: poster bd. Med Cap Results in Kenya, Africa. Decorated Navy Marine Corps Commendation Medals (3) USN, Navy Achievement Medals (2), Good Conduct Medals (3), Rifle and Pistol Expert Medals (2), Seven Letters of Commendation, Thirty-five Letters of Appreciation, Twenty Certs. of Recognition; named Employee of the Quar., Chesapeake Health Dept., 2005; recipient Four Certs. of Appreciation, 2004—05. Mem.: Tidewater Environ. Health Assn., Nat. Environ. Health Assn., U.S. Naval Inst., Women's Meml. (chartered mem.). Methodist. Avocations: bass fishing, camping, arts and crafts, sewing. Home: 1129 Cherrytree Ln Chesapeake VA 23320 Office: Chesapeake Health Dept 748 N Battlefield Blvd Chesapeake VA 23320 Home Phone: 757-436-5597; Office Phone: 757-382-8679. Personal E-mail: ehscynthia@yahoo.com. Business E-Mail: cynthia.jackson@vdh.virginia.gov.

JACKSON, CYNTHIA L., lawyer; b. Houston, May 6, 1954; BA, Stanford U., 1976; JD, U. Tex., 1979. Bar: Tex. 1979, Calif. 1980. Mem. Heller, Ehrman, White & McAuliffe, Palo Alto, Calif., 1983—99, Baker & McKenzie, Palo Alto, 1999—. Mem. ABA. Office: Baker & McKenzie 660 Hansen Way Palo Alto CA 94304-1044 Office Phone: 650-856-5572.

JACKSON, DARREN RICHARD, retail executive; b. Detroit, Nov. 13, 1964; s. Richard Dennis and Connie May (Ellis) J.; m. Terry Ann Hall, May 28, 1988; children: Ryan David, Bridget Caffrey. BS in Acctg., Marquette U., 1986. CPA, Wis. Supr. KPMG Peat Marwick, Milw., 1985-89; dir. fin. reporting Carson, Pirie, Scott & Co., Milw., 1989-90, dir. treasury svcs., 1990-91, v.p., treas., CFO, 1992-1998; CFO, Full-line Store Div. Nordstrom, Inc.; sen. v.p. fin. & treas. Best Buy Co., Inc., Mpls., 2000-2001, sr. v.p., CFO, 2001—02, exec. v.p., CFO, 2002—. Office: Best Buy Co 7075 Flying Cloud Dr Eden Prairie MN 55344*

JACKSON, DARRYL W., federal agency administrator; BA, Lincoln U., 1974; JD, Howard U., 1977. Narcotics chief U.S. Dept. Justice, Washington, dep. chief, acting chief spl. prosecutions sect., U.S. atty. for DC, lead atty. organized crime drug enforcement task force, exec. asst. U.S. atty. for ops.; asst. sec. of commerce for export enforcement U.S. Dept. Commerce, 2005—; ptnr. Arnold & Porter, LLP. Vis. Howrey prof. George Washington U.; disting. lectr. Cath. U. Office: US Dept Commerce Herbert Clark Hoover Bldg 14th St and Constitution Ave NW Rm 3731 Washington DC 20230 Office Phone: 202-482-1561. Office Fax: 202-482-4173.

JACKSON, DEBORAH CHERYL, mathematician; b. Melbourne, Australia, Feb. 2, 1955; d. Frederick Arthur and Beryl Victoria (Potter) Trueman; m. Clive Warwick Jackson, Jan. 6, 1990. BA double honors, Monash U., Clayton, Victoria, 1978, PhD, 1981; Assoc. in Music, Australian Music Exam. Bd., 1986. Tutor Monash U., 1981—83, sr. tutor, 1984—85; lectr. Swinburne U. Tech., Hawthorn, Australia, 1986—98; reviewer Math. Revs., Ann Arbor, Mich., 1983—. Contbr. articles to profl. lit. Chair Victorian Algebra Group, 1996—2003. Recipient Commonwealth postgrad. rsch. award, 1979—81; scholar Australian Commonwealth U. scholar, Monash U., 1973. Mem.: Math. Assn. Am., Victorian Algebra Group, Australasian Assn. Engring. Edn., Australian Stat. Soc., Inst. Math. Stats., Am. Math. Soc., Australian Math. Soc. Anglican.

JACKSON, DONALD WILSON, political science professor, lawyer; b. Houston, May 15, 1938; s. Enoch Wilson and Ozella Rae J.; m. Joanne Shea, Apr. 20, 1985; children: Daniel Wilson, Michael Oden. BA, So. Meth. U., Dallas, 1959; JD, So. Meth. U., 1962; PhD in Polit. Sci., U. Wis., Madison, 1972. Bar: Tex. 1962, Supreme Ct. 75. Assoc. Storey, Armstrong & Steger, Dallas, 1962—67; instr. polit. sci. So. Meth. U., 1967—68; asst. prof. polit. sci. Idaho State U., Pocatello, Idaho, 1970—74; jud. fellow Supreme Ct. U.S., Washington, 1974—75; Herman Brown prof. polit. sci. Tex. Christian U., Ft. Worth, 1975—, dir. Ctr. for Civic Literacy, 2006—. Author: An Introduction to Political Analysis: The Theory and Practice of Allocation, 1978, Even the Children of Strangers: Equality Under the U.S. Constitution, 1992 (Oustanding Book on Human Rights, Gustavus Myers Center for Human Rights, 1993), The United Kingdom Confronts the European Convention on Human Rights, 1997; editor: Presidential Leadership and Civil Rights Policy, 1995; co-editor: Comparative Judicial Review and Public Policy, 1992; editor (assoc.): Governments of the World: A Global Guide to Citizens' Rights and Responsibilities, 2006. Bd. dirs. ACLU, NYC, 2000—01, Quaker United Nat. Com., NYC, 1997—2000; mem. adv. bd. Am. United for Separation of Ch. and State, Washington, 1995—2001, bd. trustees, 2005—, exec. com. mem., 2006—; bd. dirs. Tex. affil. ACLU, Austin, 1992—2001. Named Outstanding Prof. in North Tex., N. Tex. Assn. Phi Beta Kappa, 1984, Tex. Piper Prof., Minnie Stevens Piper Found., 2003; recipient Citizenship Participation: Bill of Rights award, Tarrant County LWV, 1995, Silver Spur award, Planned Parenthood of North Tex., 1997. Mem.: We. Polit. Sci. Assn., Internat. Polit. Sci. Assn. (sec.-treas. 1997—2000, mem. rsch. com. comparative jud. studies), Am. Polit. Sci. Assn. (sec. treas. law and cts. sect. 1996—99), Phi Beta Kappa. Avocations: backpacking, golf. Office: Tex Christian U TCU Box 297021 Fort Worth TX 76129-0001 Home Phone: 817-763-5364; Office Phone: 817-257-7468. Office Fax: 817-257-7397; Home Fax: 817-377-4368. Personal E-mail: djj1955@sbcglobal.net.

JACKSON, DYLAN E., lawyer; b. Eugene, Oreg., June 7, 1970; BA, Univ. Wash., 1996; JD, Univ. Montana, 1996. Bar: Mont. 1996, US Dist. Ct., Dist. Montana 1997, Wash. 1999, US Dist. Ct., Western Dist. Wash. 2000. Assoc. atty., civil litig. Wilson Smith Cochran Dickerson, Seattle. Contbr. articles to numerous profl. jours. Named Wash. Rising Star, SuperLawyer Mag., 2006. Mem.: State Bar Assn. Montana, Cascade Co. Young Lawyers Div. (v.p. 1997—99), Cascade Co. Bar Assn. Office: Wilson Smith Cochran Dickerson 1700 1215 Fourth Ave Seattle WA 98161

JACKSON, EDWIN ATLEE, retired physicist, educator; b. Lyons, NY, Apr. 18, 1931; s. Frederick Wolcott and Helen Jean (Carroll) J.; m. Cynthia Ann Gregg; children: Eric Hugh, Mark Wolcott. BS in Physics, Syracuse U., NY, 1953, MS in Physics, 1955, PhD in Physics, 1958. Asst. lectr. Brandeis U., Waltham, Mass., 1957—58; postdoctoral Airforce Cambridge Rsch. Ctr., Bedford, Mass., 1958—59; rsch. staff Princeton U., NJ, 1959—61; asst. prof. U. Ill., Urbana, 1961—64, assoc. prof., 1964—77, physics prof., 1977—98, prof. emeritus, 1998—. Dir. ctr. for complex systems rsch. Beckman Inst. U. Ill., Urbana, 1989-98; vis. faculty FOM-Inst. Voor Plasma Fysica, Jutphaas, The Netherlands, 1967-68; vis. staff Los Alamos Sci. Lab., N.Mex., 1971; vis. prof. Chalmers U., Göteberg, Sweden, 1984; JIFT prof. Nagoya U., Japan, 1984; core rschr. Santa Fe Inst., 1992-98. Author: Equilibrium Statistical Mechanics, 1968, Perspectives of Nonlinear Dynamics, vol. 1, 1989, vol. 2, 1990, Japanese transl., 1994, Exploring Nature's Dynamics, 2001; contbr. more than 80 articles to profl. jours. Fellow Am. Phys. Soc. Business E-Mail: eaj@uiuc.edu.

JACKSON, ERIC ALLEN, philatelist; b. Long Beach, Calif., Jan. 3, 1955; s. Allen Joseph and Janice Meredith (Lyen) J.; m. Theresa Kathleen Strauss Jackson, Mar. 21, 1975 (div. Jan. 1997); children: Amy Marie, Jared Brady, Luke Allen; m. Tamara Jane Kaufman, July 18, 2002. Student, Chapman Coll., Orange, Calif., 1973-75. Owner pvt. practice, Anaheim, Calif., 1973-81; cons. William C. Tatham Stamp Co., Whittier, Calif., 1979-81; owner Whittier (Calif.) Philatelic Svcs., 1981-87; pvt. practice Herndon, Va., 1987-88, Leesport, Pa., 1988—. Expert com. The Philatelic Found., N.Y.C., 1979—, Am. Philatelic Soc., State College, Pa., 1979—, Profl. Stamp Expertising, Newport Beach, Calif., 1987—; bd. dirs., v.p. Am. Revenue Assn., Rockford, Iowa, 1980—, pres., 2001—; cons. Scott Pub. Co., Sidney, Ohio, 1980—. Contbr. articles to profl. jours. Mem. Am. Stamp Dealers Assn. (bd. dirs. 1998—, pres. 2005—), Am. Philatelic Soc., Am. Revenue Assn., Collectors Club of N.Y., Revenue Soc. Great Britain, Berks County C. of C., Berks County Hist. Soc., Nat. Trust for Historic Preservation. Republican. Avocations: antiques, baseball, fishing, music. Home: 230 Eagleview Dr Mohrsville PA 19541 Office: Eric Jackson Co PO Box 728 Schoolside Pla Ste A-1 Leesport PA 19533-0728 Home Phone: 610-926-0120; Office Phone: 610-926-6200. E-mail: eric@revenuer.com.

JACKSON, ERIC MICHAEL, marketing executive, writer, media specialist; s. Ronald and Teresa Jackson. BA in Econs. with honors, Stanford U., 1998. Bus. cons. Arthur Andersen LLP, San Francisco, 1998—99; dir. of mktg. PayPal Inc., Mountain View, Calif., 1999—2002; v.p. of mktg. (interim) PayPal, an eBay Co., Mountain View, Calif., 2003—03; founder, pres. World Ahead Media, Torrance, 2003—. Adv. bd. The Stanford Rev. Nonprofit Corp., Palo Alto, Calif., 1996—2004; bd. of dirs. World Ahead Media, Torrence, Calif., 2003—; adv. bd. thevanguard.org, Little Rock,

2004—; spkr. in field; media commentator in field. Author: (book) The PayPal Wars: Battles with eBay, the Media, the Mafia, and the Rest of Planet Earth (USA Book News Best Books 2004, 2004, Writers Notes Book award- Best Bus. Book, 2005, Non-Fiction Book of Yr. award Book Festival, 2005); editor: (newspaper) The Stanford Review, 1996. Mem. Coun. for Nat. Policy, 2004, Nat. Fedn. of Rep. Assemblies, 2004. Recipient Jeff Skoll Cmty. award, eBay Inc., 2002; grantee, Stanford U., 1998. Mem.: Publishers Mktg. Assn. Christian.

JACKSON, FELICITY ANNE, performing arts organization administrator; b. Hitchin, Hertfordshire, Eng., Apr. 16, 1949; d. Brian John and Jacqueline Anne (Barnes) J. BA with honors, Cambridge U., Eng., 1970; B Philosophy, Exeter U., Eng., 1972. Planning coord. Glyndebourne Festival, Sussex, Eng., 1979-82; head artistic planning Nat. Opera, Brussels, 1982-84; casting mgr. Glyndebourne Festival, Sussex, Eng., 1988-90; casting cons. Leipzig Opera, Germany, 1990-92, Netherlands Opera, Amsterdam, Holland, 1990-92; artistic adminstr. Can. Opera Co., Toronto, Can., 1992-94; dir. artistic adminstrn. Glimmerglass Opera, N.Y., 1994-97; gen. mgr. European Union Opera, London, 1997-98; casting cons. Fla. Grand Opera, 2000—01, ensemble dir., casting mgr., 2001—06; assoc. dir. Chgo. Opera Theater, Chgo., 2006—. Avocations: canoeing, travel. E-mail: fjackson@fgo.org.

JACKSON, FRANCIS JOSEPH, research and development company executive; b. Providence, May 23, 1932; s. Francis Joseph and Mary Elizabeth (Ryan) J.; m. Mary Veronica Brennan, Sept. 1, 1956 (div. Mar. 1983); children: Mary Cecilia, Paul Francis, Thomas Edward.; m. Nancy M. McMahon, May 21, 1983. BS magna cum laude, Providence Coll., 1954; MSc, Brown U., Providence, 1957, PhD, 1960. Rsch. assoc. Brown U., 1959-60; sr. scientist Bolt Beranek & Newman Inc., Cambridge, Mass., 1960-68, divsn. v.p., 1968-77, v.p., 1977-79, sr. v.p., 1979-98, cons., 1998-99. Adj. prof. Cath. U., 1973-77. Contbr. articles to profl. jours. Recipient Personal Achievement award Providence Coll., 1989, 75th Diamond Jubilee award Providence Coll., 1992. Fellow Acoustical Soc. Am.; mem. IEEE (sr.), Am. Inst. Physics, Cosmos, Winchester Country Club (bd. dirs. 1992-94), Delta Epsilon Sigma. Home and Office: 14A Plato Ter Winchester MA 01890-2229

JACKSON, FRANK G., mayor; b. Cleve., Ohio, Oct. 4, 1946; s. George Jackson, Rose Jackson; m. Edwina Jackson, 1975. BA in urban studies and history, Cleve. State U., M in urban affairs; JD, Cleve. Marshall Coll. of Law. Former night clerk Cleve. Municipal Ct., Cleve.; past asst. city prosecutor Cleve.; councilman Cleve. City Coun., Cleve., 1989—2001, coun. pres., 2001—05; mayor Cleve., 2006—. US Army, Vietnam. Office: City Hall Rm 202 601 Lakeside Ave Cleveland OH 44114*

JACKSON, GARY LEE, security consultant; b. Houston, Sept. 15, 1947; s. Charles Andrew and Ruth Willma (Tew) Jackson; m. Meridel May Pettyjohn, Apr. 3, 1973; children: Gary Lee II, Thomas Jonathan. BA cum laude in polit. sci., Trinity U., 1965—69; PhD in govt., Georgetown U., 1969—85. Cert. Information Systems Security Professional (CISSP) Internat. Info. Systems Security Certification Consortium, 2002. Sr. info. security systems engr. Sci. Applications Internat. Corp., Herndon, Va., 1997—2002; homeland security cons. Northrop Grumman Corp., Alexandria, Va., 2002—. Fellow in polit.-mil. studies Ctr. for Strategic and Internat. Studies, Washington, 1995—96. Asst. troop scoutmaster Boy Scouts of Am., Derwood, Md., 1989—91. Maj. US Army, 1974—94, Ariz., Germany, Tex., Md., Va. Decorated Legion of Merit US Army, Army Commendation medal, Meritorious Svc. medal. Mem.: NRA, Armed Forces Comm. & Electronics Assn., Am. Legion, Mil. Officers Assn. Am., Assn. US Army, World Future Soc., Am. Polit. Sci. Assn., Inst. Ops. Rsch. & Mgmt. Scis., VFW. Conservative. Christian. Avocations: football, camping, watch collecting, book collecting. Home: 17336 Founders Mill Dr Derwood MD 20855 Office: 8211 Terminal Rd Lorton VA 22079 Office Phone: 571-642-6696. Personal E-mail: jacksondoc@yahoo.com. E-mail: gary.jackson@ngc.com.

JACKSON, GEORGE ARTHUR, dean, educator; b. Milton, Fla., Dec. 24, 1942; s. Nemiah and Sarah Jackson; m. Clemmye Oliver, Aug. 24, 1968; children: Terri R. Carson, Toni R. Lampley. BA, Bethune-Cookman Coll., Daytona Beach, Fla., 1963; MA, N.C. A&T U., Greensboro, NC, 1968; PhD, Mich. State U., East Lansing, Mich., 1976. Asst. dean students, dir. spl. programs Oakland U., Rochester, Mich., 1971—78; dir., minority student affairs Iowa State U., Ames, Iowa, 1978—93, asst. v.p. student affairs, 1987—94, adj. assoc. prof. Coll. Edn., 1987—, spl. asst. to provost, 1994—2005, dir. George Washington Carver Doctoral Fellowship Program, 1994—, asst. dean Grad. Coll., 1994—. Cons. Noel-Levitz Conf. Retention and Graduation, New Orleans, 2001—03; co-prin. investigator alliance grad. edn. and the professorate Iowa State U., 2001—06. Author: Helpful Hints for Advising & Counseling Minority Students in Predominantly White Institutions, 1987, Saving the Other 2/3: Practices & Strategies for Improving the Retention & Graduation of African American Students in Predominantly White Institutions, 2003; contbr. articles to profl. jours. Pres., chmn. bd. Black Cultural Ctr., Ames, 2001—06, Iowa African Am. Hall Fame, Ames, 2002—06. Recipient Martin Luther King Humanitarian award, Martin Luther King, Jr. Ctr. Social Change, Atlanta, Ga., 1979, Outstanding Service award, Black Graduate Student Assn., Iowa State U., 1988, Outstanding Rsch. award, Mid-Am. Assn. Ednl. Opportunity Program Pers., 1995, Iowa Man of the Yr. Leadership award, KUCB Radio, Des Moines, Iowa, 1995, Presdl. Svc. award, Iowa State U. Office of Pres., 2005, Mary McCloud Bethune Educator of Year award, Iowa Juneteenth Observance Arts & Edn. Com. Mem.: NAACP (life; pres. Ames br. 1996—2006), Nat. Alliance Black Sch. Educators, Coun. Grad. Schs., Golden Key (founder Iowa State U. chpt. 1987—2004, adv. Iowa State U. chpt. 1987—2004). Democrat. Home: 2801 Greensboro Dr Ames IA 50014 Office: Iowa State University Graduate College 1137 Pearson Hall Ames IA 50011-2206 Home Phone: 515-292-1120; Office Phone: 515-294-1386. Office Fax: 515-294-3003. Business E-Mail: gajacks@iastate.edu.

JACKSON, GEORGE LYMAN, retired nuclear medicine physician; b. Arlington, Mass., Dec. 17, 1923; s. William and Alice (Tenney) J.; m. Alyce Verne Yeager, Sept. 7, 1946; children: Scott Douglas, Carole Elizabeth, Diane Priscilla, Richard Lee. BS cum laude, Franklin and Marshall Coll., 1944; MD, U. Pa., 1948. Diplomate: Am. Bd. Internal Medicine, Am. Bd. Nuclear Medicine. Intern Hosp. U. Pa., 1948-49, resident, 1949-52; practice medicine specializing in internal medicine Harrisburg, Pa., 1952-63; dir. med. edn., acting med. dir. Harrisburg Hosp., 1963-68, dir. undergrad. fellowships, 1968-69, head sect. nuclear medicine, 1965-75, med. dir. dept. nuclear medicine, 1975-89. Asst. prof. medicine Hahnemann Med. Coll., 1963-68, assoc. prof., 1968-70; clin. assoc. prof. M.S. Hershey Med. Centre, Pa. State U., 1970-76, clin. prof., 1976-90; dir. Harrisburg Hosp. Sch. Nuclear Medicine Tech.; adj. faculty Harrisburg Area Community Coll., Millersville State Coll.; cons., chmn. med. adv. com. Lebanon (Pa.) VA Hosp., 1968-75; nuclear medicine adv. Pa. Dept. Edn., Pa. Med. Soc., Pa. Blue Shield. Author: Of Thee I Sing, 1993, The Eclectic Club of Harrisburg, 1997, 150th Anniversary of St. Paul's Lutheran Church, 2005, Ebenezer Tolman and Benedict Arnold's Canadian Expedition 1775-1776, 2006, Ebenezer Tolman and Benedict Arnold's Quebec Campaign 1775-1776, 2007; contbr. articles to profl. jours. Mem. Cen. Dauphin Sch. Bd., 1971-73; bd. dirs. Bethesda Mission, Harrisburg Hosp. Med. Edn. and Rsch. Found.; bd. dirs. New Hope Ministries, 1987-93, pres. 1988-93; chmn. archives and collections com. No. York County Hist. and Preservation Soc., 1998-2000. With USNR, 1942-45. Fellow ACP (govs. com. for coll. affairs 1969-76, gov. 1976-80, laureate 1985), Soc. Nuclear Medicine, Am. Coll. Nuclear Physicians (bd. regents), Am. Coll. Nuclear Medicine; mem. Am. Thyroid Assn., Pa. Soc. Internal Medicine (past pres.; chmn. liaison com.), Pa. Coll. Nuclear Medicine (pres.), Joint Rev. Com. Nuclear Medicine Tech., Phi Beta Kappa, Alpha Omega Alpha. Lutheran. Home: 22 N Baltimore St Dillsburg PA 17019-1210 *The efforts of my adult life have been directed primarily at three priorities— family, profession, church. Success in achieving any of these is a consequence of a combination of providence, help from others and personal attributes. Help from others involves, principally, my family (in its largest sense) and of these my wife is most important. She is a source of understanding, wise counsel, inspiration, support and balance. My associates help significantly by their dedication, industry and responsibility. Personal attributes are hard work, absolute honesty, religious belief, and a conviction that the only justification for my professional life is to help the sick patients whom I am privileged to serve.*

JACKSON, GERALDINE, entrepreneur; b. Barnesville, Ga., Oct. 30, 1934; d. Charles Brown and Christine (Maddox) Jackson; 1 child, Prentiss Andrew. Nurses aide Grady Hosp., Atlanta, 1953—54; mail handler U.S. Post Office, Cicero, Ill., 1966—70; sec., tour guide Walgreens Lab., Chgo., 1970—74; credit clk. Sterling Jewelers, Atlanta, 1974—2000; receptionist Willie A. Watkins Funeral Home, Atlanta, 2000—. Mem. Nat. Law Enforcement Officer Meml. Fund; assoc. mem. presdl. task force Rep. Nat. Com.; active Sacred Heart League. Mem. AARP, DAV, NAACP, Nat. Assn. Police Orgn., Internat. Assn. Chief Police, Ga. Sheriff's Assn., Nat. Right to Life. Democrat. Home: 1890 Myrtle Dr SW Apt 422 Atlanta GA 30311-4954 Office Phone: 404-758-1731.

JACKSON, GUIDA MYRL, writer, editor, literature educator; b. Clarendon, Tex., Aug. 30; d. James Hurley and Ina (Benson) Miller; m. Prentice Lamar Jackson (div. Jan. 1986); children: Jeffrey Allen, William Andrew, James Tucker, Annabeth Broomall Dugger; m. William Hervey Laufer, Feb. 14, 1986 (dec. Nov. 2006). BA, Tex. Tech U.; MA, Calif. State U., 1986; PhD, Greenwich U., 1990. Tchr. secondary sch. English, Houston Ind. Sch. Dist., 1951—53, Ft. Worth Ind. Sch. Dist., 1953—54; pvt. tchr. music, freelance writer, Houston, 1956—71; editor newsletter Tex. Soc. Anesthesiologists, Austin, 1972—80; editor-in-chief Tex. Country Mag., Houston, 1976—78; mng. editor lit. mag. Touchstone, Houston, 1976—. Contbg. editor Houston Town and Country mag., 1975—76; book editor Arte Publico, 1987—88; editor, pub. Panther Creek Press, 1999—; lectr. English U. Houston, 1986—95; instr. Montgomery Coll., 1996—2006; freelance writer, Houston, The Woodlands, Tex., 1978—. Author: (novels) Passing Through, 1979, A Common Valor, 1980; (play) The Lamentable Affair of the Vicar's Wife, 1989, Showdown at Nosegay Cottage, 1997, The Man From Tegucigalpa, 1998, Julia is Peculiar; (biog. reference) Women Who Ruled, 1990 (best reference lists award Libr. Jour. and Sch. Libr. Jour. 1990), (nonfiction) Virginia Diaspora, 1992, Virginia Diaspora CD-ROM, 2001, (lit. reference) Encyclopedia of Traditional Epic, 1994 (best reference list award ALA), (lit. reference) Traditional Epics: A Literary Companion, 1995, Encyclopedia of Literary Epics, 1996; (reference) Women Rulers Throughout the Ages, 1999; (fiction) The Other Texas, 2005; editor: Heart to Hearth, 1989, African Women Write, 1990, Fall From Innocence, Memoirs of the Great Depression, 1998; (nonfiction) Legacy of the Texas Plains, 1994, Through the Cumberland Gap, 1995, The Patchwork Mind, 2006, Darning the Patches, 2007. Mem.: Houston Writers Consortium, Writers' Forum, Montgomery Lit. Arts Coun., Dramatists Guild, Woodland Writers Guild, Houston Writers Guild, PEN Ctr. West, Women in Comm. Avocations: music, gardening, poetry. Personal E-mail: panthercreek3@hotmail.com.

JACKSON, HAROLD, journalist; b. Birmingham, Ala., Aug. 14, 1953; s. Lewis and Janye (Wilson) J.; m. Denice Estell Pledger, Apr. 30, 1977; children: Annette Michelle, Dennis Jerome. BS in Journalism and Polit. Sci., Baker U., 1975. Reporter Birmingham Post-Herald, Ala., 1975-80, UPI, Birmingham, Ala., 1980-83, state news editor, 1983-85; asst. nat. editor Phila. Inquirer, 1985-86; asst. city editor Birmingham News, Ala., 1986-87, editorial writer, 1987-94; editl. page writer The Balt. Sun, 1994-99; commentary editor Phila. Inquirer, 1999—2004, dep. editl. page editor, 2004—. Journalist-in-residence Loyola Coll., Balt., 1997-98; Freedom Forum vis. prof. U. Ala., 1993-94. Trustee Baker U., 1997—2005. Recipient Pulitzer Prize for editl. writing, 1991; Petter Jennings fellow Nat. Constl. Ctr., 2007. Mem. Nat. Assn. Black Journalists (Journalist of Yr. award 1991), Birmingham Assn. Black Journalists (pres. 1987-90), Soc. Profl. Journalists (Green Eyeshade award 1989), Phila. Assn. Black Journalists. Presbyterian. Avocations: reading, exercise. Home: 57 Fox Hollow Ln Sewell NJ 08080-3139 Office: 400 N Broad St Philadelphia PA 19130-4015 Office Phone: 215-854-2555.

JACKSON, HARRY ANDREW, artist; b. Chgo., Apr. 18, 1924; s. Harry Shapiro and Ellen Grace Jackson; m. Theodora Rehard DuBois, 1946 (div.); m. Grace Hartigan, 1948 (div.); m. Claire Rodgers, 1950 (dec.); m. Joan Hunt, 1951 (div.); m. Sarah Mason, Sept. 10, 1962 (div.); children: Matthew, Molly; m. Tina Lear, Aug. 11, 1973 (div.); children: Jesse, Luke, Chloe. Diploma, H.S., 1945; LLD (hon.), U. Wyo., 1986. Founder fine art foundry, Camaiore, Italy, 1964—, Harry Jackson Studios, Italy, 1965—; CEO Harry Jackson Studios (formerly Wyo. Foundry Studios, Inc.), Cody, Wyo., 1971—; founder Western Arts Found., 1974—; foundry ptnr. Jackson-Mariani Fine Art Foundry, Camaiore, Italy, 1985-98; founder Harry Jackson Art Mus., Cody, Wyo., 1994. Author: Lost Wax Bronze Casting, 1972, New York School Abstract Expressionists, 2000; one man exhbns. include Ninth St. Show, N.Y.C., 1951, Tibor de Nagy Gallery, N.Y.C., 1952, 53, Martha Jackson Gallery, N.Y.C., 1956, M. Knoedler & Co., N.Y.C., 1960, Amon Carter Mus., Fort Worth, 1961, 68, Kennedy Galleries, N.Y.C., 1964, 68, Smithsonian Instn., Washington, 1964, Whitney Gallery Western Art, Cody, 1964, 81, Mont. Hist. Soc., 1964, NAD, 1965, 68, Nat. Cowboy Hall of Fame, Oklahoma City, 1966, XVII Mostra Internazionale d'Arte, Premio del Fiorino, Florence, Italy, 1966, Pennational Artists Ann., Pa., 1967, Mostra de Arte Moderna, Convento di S. Lazzaro, Camaiore, 1968, Am. Artists Profl. League, N.Y., 1968, Cowboy Artists Am., 1971-76, S.W. Mus., L.A., 1979, Smith Gallery, N.Y.C., 1981, 85, Buffalo Bill Hist. Ctr., 1981, Palm Springs Desert Mus., 1981, Mpls. Inst. Art, 1982, Camaiore, Italy, 1985, Met. Mus. Art, N.Y.C., 1987; represented in permanent collections Met. Mus. Art, NAD, Nat. Mus. Am. Art, Nat. Portrait Gallery, Washington, Her Majesty Queen Elizabeth II, Sandringam Castle, Eng., Am. Mus. of Gt. Britain, Bath, Eng., U.S. State Dept., Washington, Lyndon Baines Johnson Meml. Libr., Austin, Tex., Ronald Reagan Meml. Libr., Santa Barbara, Calif., Whitney Gallery Western Art, Plains Indian Mus., Buffalo Bill Hist. Ctr., Cody, Wyo., Wadsworth Atheneum, Hartford, Conn., Alberta Glenbow Mus., Calgary, Can., Univ. So. Calif., Stanford (Calif.) Univ., Love Libr. Univ. Nebr., Lincoln, Portsmouth (R.I.) Abbey, S.W. Mus., Gene Autrey Mus., L.A., Nat. Cowboy Hall of Fame, Oklahoma City, Gilcrease Mus., Tulsa, Fort Pitts Mus., Pitts., Amon Carter Mus., Pro Rodeo Cowboy Hall of Fame, Colorado Springs, Colo., Eiteljorg Mus., Indpls., Shelburne (Vt.) Mus., Columbus (Ga.) Mus. Arts & Scis., Oreg. Hist. Soc., Portland, Salt Lake City Art Ctr., Norfolk (Nebr.) Arts Ctr., Aspen (Colo.) Art Mus., Woolaroc Mus., Bartlesville, Okla., U. Wyo. Art Mus., Laramie, Mont. Hist. Soc., Helena, Norton Mus., Shreveport, La., Columbia U., N.Y.C., Trout Gallery Dickinson Coll., Carlisle, Pa., Ctrl. Wyo. Coll., Riverton, N.W. C.C., Powell, Wyo., Baylor Sch., Chattanooga, Orme Sch., Mayer, Ariz., others; commd. works include (sculpture) William R. Coe Commn., 1959, 60, Fort Pitt Mus., 1964, 73, Plains Indian Mus., Cody, Wyo., Ctrl. Wyo. Coll., Riverton, 1978, 81, Piazza della Chiesa, Capezzano, Pianore, Italy, 1985, Great Western Savs. & Loan, Santa Barbara, Calif., 1985, John Wayne monumental sculpture Beverly Hills, Calif, 1981, 84, (portrait busts) Met. Mus. Trustees, C. Douglas Dillon, 1985, 87, (portrait) "John Wayne" TIME cover, Aug. 8, 1969 (Nat. Best Cover Art award Am. Inst. Graphic Arts 1969), (paintings) Whitney Gallery Western Art, Cody, 1960, 66, (mural) R.K. Mellon. Served with USMC, 1942-45. Decorated Purple Heart with gold star; recipient Gold medal NAD, 1968; grantee Fulbright, 1954, Italian Govt., 1956, 57. Fellow NAD (academician), RISD, Nat. Acad. Western Art, Nat. Sculpture Soc., Am. Artists League; mem. Bohemian Club (San Francisco). Office: PO Box 2836 Cody WY 82414-2836 also: Via Monteggiori 55040 Camaiore Lucca Italy Office Phone: 307-587-5508. Office Fax: 307-587-6362. Business E-Mail: lora@harryjackson.net.

JACKSON, HENRY NATHANIEL, clothing designer; b. Boston, July 8, 1958; s. Henry Nathaniel Jackson and Rita Louise (Drummond) McCollin. BA, Parsons Sch. of Design, 1979. Designer for Oscar De La Renta, NYC, 1978-79; designer of couture Valentino Ltd., NYC, 1979-80; designer, ptnr. H.N.J. Design House, NYC, 1980-82; costume designer CBS Search for Tomorrow, NYC, 1982-84; designer, owner H.N.J., Boston, 1984-86; costume designer NBC Young and the Restless, LA, 1986-90; owner, designer H.N.J., Boston, NYC, Milan, 1990-94; costumer designer H.N.J./ABC All My Children, NYC; designer Gallery of Wearable Art, 2004—. Cons. Gillian Swonnel Ltd., Boston, 1993, Kazu Inc., Boston, Tokyo, 1993-94. Specialty work for films such as Ford Fairlane and Leonard, Part 6; costume designer in field. Fund raiser Am. Breast Cancer Assn., Boston, 1993. Recipient Am. Next Great Designer award Internat. Ladies, 1978, Garment Workers Union, 1979, Rising Star award Ashanti Oil Corp., 1981. Mem. Oxford Club, English Speaking Union. Democrat. Roman Catholic. Avocations: hobbies, law, caberet singing, charity event planning, real estate, travel. Office: Gallery of Wearable Art 34 67th St New York NY 10021

JACKSON, HERB, artist, educator; b. Raleigh, NC, Aug. 16, 1945; s. Walter H. and Virginia (Rogers) Jackson; m. Laura Dudley Grosch, June 9, 1967; children: Leif, Ulysses. BA, Davidson Coll., NC, 1967; postgrad., Philips Universität; MFA, U. NC, 1970. William H. Williamson prof. art Davidson Coll., NC, 1969—, chmn. dept. art NC, 1977-94; dir. Art Gallery, 1974-95; mem. artist adv. bd. Mint Mus. Art, Charlotte, NC, 1979-85. Bd. adv. Light Factory, Charlotte, 1990—, NC Dance Theater, NC, 1998. One-man shows include: Mint Mus. Art, Charlotte, 1973, U. Nev., Reno, 1973, Rahr Mus., Manitowoc, Wis., 1973, Jane Haslem Gallery, Washington, 1974, Nielsen Gallery, Boston, 1974, Impressions Gallery, Boston, 1975, 81, Hahn Gallery, Phila., 1976, Dryden Gallery, Charlotte, 1976, Van Straaten Gallery, Chgo., 1977, Frances Aronson Gallery, Atlanta, 1978, NC Mus. Art, Raleigh, 1979, Rowe Gallery, U. NC, Charlotte, 1979, Southeastern Ctr. for Contemporary Art, Winston-Salem, NC, 1981, Phyllis Weil Gallery, NYC, 1981, 83, 85, 87, 88, 90, Princeton Gallery Fine Art, 1982, 83, Oxford Gallery, Eng., 1982, DBR Gallery, Cleve., 1983, 84, Mint Mus. Art, Charlotte, 1983, Springfield Mus. Art, Mo., 1983, Asheville Mus. Art, NC, 1983, NAS, Washington, 1983, Cheekwood Art Ctr., Nashville, 1983, Reading Art Mus., Pa., 1984, Gulbenkian Found., Lisbon, Portugal, 1984, Huntsville Mus. Art, Ala., 1984, Jerald Melberg Gallery, Charlotte, 1984, 85, 87, 88, 90, 92, 93, 94, 96, 97, 98, 99, Fay Gold Gallery, Atlanta, 1986, 88, 92, Cumberland Gallery, Nashville, 1987, 96, Judy Youens Gallery, Houston, 1988, Peden Gallery, Raleigh, 1988, 92, 93, Asheville Mus. Art, 1988, Allene Lapides Gallery, Santa Fe, 1989-90, Maurine Littleton Gallery, Washington, 1990, Hickory Mus. Art, NC, 1993, St. Johns Mus. Art, Wilmington, NC, 1993, Bi-Nat. Cultural Ctr., Arequipa, Peru, 1994, parchman Stremmel Gallery, San Antonio, 1995-2001, Somerhill Gallery, Chapel Hill, NC, 1995, 98, 2006 Christa Faut Gallery, Cornelius, NC, 1996, 97, 99, 2000, 02, 03, 05, 07, La. Tech U., Ruston, 1999, Lmar Dodd Art Ctr., La Grange, Ga., 1999, Greenville (NC) Mus. Art, 2000, Les Yeux du Monde, Charlottesville, Va., 2001, 04, 07, GSI Fine Art, Cleve., 2001, Fayetteville Mus. Art, NC, 2002, The Art Preserve, Charlotte, 2004, McColl Ctr. Visual Art, 2007; numerous group shows, 1962—, latest being Internat. Print Biennale, Bradford, Eng., 1979, Mint Mus., Charlotte, 1979, 81, Southeastern Ctr. Contemporary Art, Winston-Salem, 1979, Internat. São Paulo Bienal, 1979, Spring Mills Ann. Competition, Lancaster, SC, 1980, Weatherspoon Gallery, Greensboro, NC, 1980, Impressions Gallery, Boston, 1980, Associated Am. Artists, Phila., 1980, Am. Acad. and Inst. Arts and Letters, NYC, 1981, 1987, Bklyn. Mus. Art, 1981, World's Fair, Knoxville, Tenn., 1982, Davos, Switzerland, 1983, Palazzo Venezia, Rome, 1984, Miss. Mus. Art, 1984, U. Denver, 1984, Albuequerque Mus. Art, 1985, Fla. State U., 1985, St. John's Mus. Art, Wilmington, 1986, U. Tex., San Antonio, 1987, Contemporary Arts Ctr. New Orleans, 1988, Kunstsammlungen der Veste Coburg, Fed. Republic Germany, 1988, Lorenzelli Fine Art, Milan, 1989, Exhbn. Hall of Union of Moscow Artists, Moscow, 1989, Samuel P. Harn Mus., Gainesville, Fla., 1990, New Orleans Mus. Art, 1995, Shanxia Govt. Art Gallery, Xian, China, 1996, Morris Mus. Art, Augusta, Ga., 1997, Mus. Del Vidrio, Monterey, Mex., 1999, Vanessa Suchar Fine Arts, London, 2000, Thomas McCormick Gallery, Chgo., 2002; represented in permanent collections: Balt. Mus. Art, Phila. Mus. Art, Victoria and Albert Mus., London, Whitney Mus. Art, NYC, Mpls. Inst. Arts, Nat. Acad. Sci., Washington, Indpls. Mus. Art, Bklyn. Mus., USIA, Japan, U. Wis., Sheboygan, Yale U., New Haven, Mus. Fine Arts, Boston, NY Pub. Libr., Libr. of Congress, Washington, Mint Mus., Charlotte, So. Ill. U., Edwardsville, Kalamazoo Inst. Arts, Mus. Fine Arts, Springfield, Mass., Utah Mus., Salt Lake City, U. Nebr., Lincoln, U. Calif., Riverside, Minn. Mus. Art, St. Paul, Brit. Mus., London, others. Fellow Southeastern Ctr. for Contemporary Art Southeastern Seven, 1981, N.C. Visual Arts, 1984, Nat. Endowment for Arts and So. Arts Fedn., 1986, Boswell Family Faculty, 2006; recipient N.C. award, 1999, Hunter-Hamilton Love of Tchg. award, 2003. Mem. Coll. Art Assn., So. Graphics Coun., Charlotte Artists Coalition (dir. 1980-81), Mecklenberg-Charlotte Arts and Sci. Coun. (dir. 1977-79), Southeastern Coll. Art Conf. Home: PO Box 10 Davidson NC 28036-0010 Office: PO Box 7117 Davidson NC 28035-7117 Home Phone: 704-892-1723; Office Phone: 704-894-2358. Office Fax: 704-894-2691. Business E-Mail: hejackson@davidson.edu. *The artist's integrity is all he truly has, after all the trends, fads and movements have faded into history. I try to make art which will stand as a personal statement.*

JACKSON, HOWELL E., law educator; b. NYC, Jan. 4, 1954; BA magna cum laude, Brown U., 1976; JD, Harvard U., 1982, MBA magna cum laude, 1982. Bar: DC 1984. Law clk. to Justice Thurgood Marshall US Supreme Ct.; assoc. Arnold & Porter, Washington; asst. prof. law Harvard Law Sch., Cambridge, Mass., 1989—94, prof., 1994—, Finn M.W. Caspersen and Household Internat. Prof. Law, 1999—2004, assoc. dean rsch. and spl. programs, 2001—03, vice dean adminstrn. and budget, 2003—, James S. Reid, Jr. Prof. Law, 2004—. Office: Harvard Law Sch 1563 Massachusetts Ave Cambridge MA 02138 Office Phone: 617-495-5466. Office Fax: 617-496-5156. Business E-Mail: hjackson@law.harvard.edu.

JACKSON, HUNTER, health products executive; PhD in Psychobiology, Yale U., New Haven; postgrad. dept. neurosurgery, U. Va. Assoc. prof. dept. anatomy U. Utah, Salt Lake City; CEO, chmn. bd., founder NPS Pharms., Inc., Salt Lake City, 1986—, pres., 1994—.

JACKSON, J. DAVID, lawyer; b. York, Pa., 1949; BA magna cum laude, St. Olaf Coll., 1971; JD summa cum laude, Washington U., 1974. Bar: Minn. 1974. Law clerk 8th cir. U.S. Ct. Appeals, 1974-75; ptnr., trial practice group Dorsey & Whitney, Mpls. Mem. Order of Coif. Office: Dorsey & Whitney Ste 1500 50 S 6th St Minneapolis MN 55402-1498 Office Phone: 612-340-2760. Office Fax: 612-340-2807. Business E-Mail: jackson.j@dorsey.com.

JACKSON, JACK P., lawyer; b. NYC, Aug. 4, 1958; BA cum laude, Fordham U., 1979; MBA, Columbia U., 1983; JD, Columbia U. Sch. Law, 1983. Bar: NY 1984. Ptnr., corp. dept. Proskauer Rose LLP, NYC. Named Harlan Fiske Stone Scholar; named one of Top 100 Minority Bus. Leaders

NYC, Crain's NY, 2003, Am. Top Black Atty., Black Enterprise, 2003; recipient Whitney M. Young award, Greater NY Coun. Boy Scouts Am., 1999. Mem.: Assn. Bar City NY (mem. task force on minorities, mem. banking law com. 1997—). Office: Proskauer Rose LLP 1585 Broadway New York NY 10036-8299 Office Phone: 212-969-3140. Office Fax: 212-969-2900. Business E-Mail: jjackson@proskauer.com.

JACKSON, JACQUELINE DOUGAN, literature educator, writer; b. Beloit, Wis., May 3, 1928; d. Ronald Arthur and Vera Arlouine (Wardner) Dougan; m. Robert Sumner Jackson, June 17, 1950 (div. 1973); children—Damaris Lee, Megan Trever, Gillian Patricia, Jacqueline Elspeth. BA, Beloit Coll., 1950, H.H.D., 1977; MA, U. Mich., 1951; D.Litt., MacMurray Coll., 1976. Instr. English Kent (Ohio) State U., 1964-68; prof. lit. U. Ill. (formerly Sangamon State U.), Springfield, 1970—. Writer, presenter: radio shows The Author is You, U. Wis. WHA Sch. of Air, 1969-78, Reading and Writing and Radio, WSSU, Springfield, Ill., 1975-94; author: Julie's Secret Sloth, 1953, The Taste of Spruce Gum (Notable Book award 1966), 1966 (Dorothy Canfield Fisher award 1967), Missing Melinda, 1967, Chicken Ten Thousand, 1968, Spring Song, 1969, The Orchestra Mice, 1970, The Endless Pavement, (with William Perlmutter), 1973, Turn Not Pale, Beloved Snail, 1974, Stories from the Round Barn, 1997, More Stories from the Round Barn, 2002; author-illustrator: The Paleface Redskins, 1958, The Ghost Boat, 1969; illustrator: (Chad Walsh) Knock and Enter, 1953. Mem. Phi Beta Kappa. Home: 816 N 5th St Springfield IL 62702-5215 Home Phone: 217-544-2916. Business E-Mail: jjack1@uis.edu.

JACKSON, JAMES F., nuclear engineer, educator; b. Ogden, Utah, Aug. 15, 1939; s. Allyn Boyd and Virginia (Dixon) J.; m. Joan Borger, Aug. 25, 1960; children: James D., Bret A., Tracy L., Wendy L. BS, U. Utah, Salt Lake City, 1961; MS, MIT, Cambridge, 1962; PhD, UCLA, 1969. Rsch. engr. Atomics Internat., LA, 1962066; nuclear engr. Argonne Nat. Lab., Idaho Falls, Idaho, 1969-72, group leader Argonne, Ill., 1972-74; assoc. prof. Brigham Young U., Provo, Utah, 1974-76, adj. prof., 1998—; cons. Los Alamos Nat. Lab., N.Mex., 1974-76, group/div. leader N.Mex., 1976-82, dep. assoc. dir. N.Mex., 1979-81, div. leader N.Mex., 1983-84, assoc. dir. N.Mex., 1984-86, dep. dir. N.Mex., 1986-98, staff mem. N.Mex., 1998-99, cons. N.Mex., 1999—2006, Atomic Safety and Licensing Bd. Panel, US Nuc. Regulatory Commn., 2006—. Contbr. articles to jours. in field. Mem. atomic safety and licensing bd. panel US Nuc. Regulatory Commn., 2006-. Recipient E.O. Lawrence award Dept. Energy, Washington, 1983. Mem. NAE, Am. Nuclear Soc. (safety div. 1967—, exec. com. 1977-80), Tau Beta Pi. Republican. Mem. Lds Ch. Avocations: history, motorsports, photography. Home: 536 Sheffield Dr Provo UT 84604-5666

JACKSON, JAMES SIDNEY, psychologist, educator; b. Detroit, July 30, 1944; s. Pete James and Johnnie Mae (Wilson) J. BS, Mich. State U., 1966; MA, U. Toledo, 1970; PhD, Wayne State U., 1972. Probation counselor Lucas County Juvenile Ct., Toledo, 1967-68; tchg. and rsch. asst. Wayne State U., Detroit, 1968-71; from asst. prof. to prof. psychology U. Mich., Ann Arbor, 1971—, faculty assoc. Rsch. Ctr. Group Dynamics, 1971—86, dir. Rsch. Ctr. Group Dynamics, 1996—2005, faculty assoc. Inst. Gerontology, 1976—, dir. program rsch. on Black Ams., 1976—2005, faculty assoc. Ctr. Afro-Am. and African Studies, 1982—, rsch. prof., 1986—, assoc. dean Rackham Sch. Grad. Studies, 1987-92, prof. pub. health, 1990—, Daniel Katz Collegiate prof., 1994-95, Daniel Katz Disting. Univ. prof. psychology, 1995—; Hill Disting. vis. prof. U. Minn., Ann Arbor, 1995; dir. Ctr. Afro-Am. and African Studies U. Mich., Ann Arbor, 1998—2005, dir. Inst. Social Rsch., 2005—. Chair sociol. psychology tng. program U. Mich., 1980-86, 93-96; cons. Emergency Sch. Aid Project, 1973-74, Commn. on Equal Opportunity in Psychology, 1970, Project to Provide Psychol. Svcs. to Head Start Programs, 1973-74, European Econ. Commn. Project on Racism, Xenophobia and Immigration, 1989—; mem. com. on aging and com. on status of Black Ams., panel on race, ethnicity and health in later life, Nat. Acad. of Scis.; mem. com. on African Am. Population Year 2000 and 2010 U.S. Census Bur.; mem. nat. adv. com. Boston Mus. Sci., 1998-2002; mem. Nat. Adv. Coun. on Aging, NIH, 1996-99; mem. bd. sci. counselors, Nat. Inst. Aging; invited rschr. Ecole des Hautes Etudes en Scis. Sociales, Paris, 1992-2004; disting. lectr. gerontology UCLA, 1992; mem. steering com. Nat. Acad. Aging Soc., 1995—. Author: The Black American Elderly: Research on Physical and Psychosocial Health, 1988, African American Elderly, 2d edit., 1997, (with Gurin P., Hatchett S.) Hope and Independence: Blacks Response to Electoral and Party Politics, 1989, Life in Black America, 1991, (with Chatters L., Taylor R.) Aging in Black America, 1993, (with H. Neighbors) Mental Health in Black America, 1996, (with R. Taylor and L. Clatters) Family Life in Black America, 1997; editor: New Directions: African Americans in a Diversifying Nation, 2000; editl. cons. Jour. Behavioral and Social Scientists; editl. bd. Jour. Gerontology, Applied Social Psychology Ann., Psychol. Bull., Jour. Social Issues; cons. editor Psychology and Aging; contbr. articles to profl. jours. Bd. dirs. Pub. Commn. on Mental Health, Ronald McDonald House, Ann Arbor, 1993—; bd. trustees Greenhills Sch., Ann Arbor, 1997-2003, v.p., 2002-03. Recipient Disting. Faculty Svc. award U. Mich., 1976, Harold R. Johnson Diversity Svc. award U. Mich., 2000, Orgn. Black Alumni Achievement award Wayne State U., 2005, James McKeen Cattell Fellow award Assn. for Psychol. Sci., 2005; Urban Studies fellow Wayne State U., 1969-70; NSF fellow, 1969; Sr. Postdoctoral fellow Groupe d'Études et de Recherches sur la Science, École des Hautes Études en Sciences Sociales, 1986-87; Sr. Ford Found. Minority Postdoctoral fellow, 1986-87; Fogarty Sr. Internat. fellow, 1993-94; Robert W. Kleemeier award for rsch., Gerontol. Soc. Am. Fellow APA (divs. 9-20, policy and planning bd., fin. com. 1984-86, award for early contbns. 1983, Tenth Anniversary Peace and Social Justice award Soc. for the Study of Peace, Conflict and Violence, Peace Psychology divsn. 2000, com. on internat. rels., 1999-02, chair 2001-02, Disting. Career Contbns. ro Rsch. award Divsn. 45, 2001), AAAS (past chmn. sect. social, econ. and polit. scis.), Am. Psychol. Soc., Gerontol. Soc. Am. (task force on minority issues in gerontology, chmn. 1988-92, ann. sci. conv. program com., Minority Task Force Mentoring award 2003, Disting. Mentorship in Gerontology award behavioral and social sci. sect. 2004); mem. Assn. Advancement of Psychology (trustee 1973-89, chmn. 1978-80), Inst. of Medicine, Nat. Acad. Scis., Black Students Psychol. Assn. (nat. chmn. 1970-71), Assn. Black Psychologists (nat. chmn. 1972-73), Soc. Psychol. Study of Social Issues, World Future Soc., Assn. Behavioral and Social Scientists, Gerontol. Soc. Am. (chair behavioral and social scis. sect. 1997-98), Internat. Platform Assn., NIMH (nat. mental health coun. 1989-93, panel on equal access com. on instl. cooperation 1989-92), Psi Chi, Alpha Phi Alpha. Home: 340 Orchard Hills Dr Ann Arbor MI 48104-1832 Office: U Mich 5110 Inst Social Rsch 426 Thompson St Ann Arbor MI 48104-2321 Home Phone: 734-623-7783; Office Phone: 734-763-2491. Business E-Mail: jamessj@umich.edu.

JACKSON, JANET (DAMITA JO), vocalist, dancer; b. Gary, Ind., May 16, 1966; d. Joseph and Katherine J.; m. James DeBarge, Sept. 7, 1984 (annulled Nov. 18, 1985), m. René Elizondo, March 31, 1991 (div. March 13, 2000). Albums include Janet Jackson, 1982, Dream Street, 1984, Control, 1986, Rhythm Nation 1814, 1991, janet, 1993, Design of a Decade: 1986-1996, 1995, The Velvet Rope, 1997, All For You, 2001 (Grammy award, Best Dance Recording, 2002), Damita Jo, 2004, 20 Y.O., 2006; actress (TV series) Good Times, 1977-1979, A New Kind of Family, 1979, Diff'rent Strokes, 1981-1982, 1984, Fame, 1984-1985; (films) Poetic Justice, 1993 (Academy award nomination Best Original Song 1993), Nutty Professor II: The Klumps, 2000. Recipient 6 Am. Music awards, 1987, 1988, 1991, 5 Grammy nominations, MTV Video Vanguard award, 1990, Grammy award, Best R&B song 1994 for "That's the Way Love Goes" with Terry Lewis and James Harris III; MTV Best Female Video for "If", named one of 50 Most Influential African-Americans, Ebony Mag. 2004. Office: Creative Artists Agency 9830 Wilshire Blvd Beverly Hills CA 90212-1825

JACKSON, JASON M., military officer, educator; b. Troy, Ohio, June 29, 1972; s. Charles B. and Linda S. Jackson; m. Sheryl Ann Tegeler, Sept. 2, 1995; children: Noah B., Grace H. BS in Math., Purdue U., W.Lafayette, Ind., 1991—95; MS in Computer Info. Sys., U. Phoenix, 2001—03. Cert. software engring. mgmt., Air Force Inst. Tech., Ohio, 2005; acquisition level I - prodn., quality & mfg. Def. Acquisition U., sr. navigator US Air Force, Tex., 2004, navigator US Air Force, Tex., 1997, simulator course Air Mobility Command, 2004. Chief navigator Detachment 3, Air Mobility Command, Air Ops. Squadron, Little Rock Air Force Base, Ark., 2004—; adj. prof. info. sys. Kaplan U., Ft. Lauderdale, Fla., 2006—. Nat. adminstrv. cons. Arnold Air Soc., Dover, Del., 1995—. Editor: (tng. & procedures manual) Arnold Air Society Manual 1, 1995—2005 (Air Force Assn., Exceptional Svc. award, 2005). 3rd ann. outstanding rep. Carnegie Mellon Software Engring. Inst., Pitts., 2006. Maj. USAF, 1995—, Little Rock AFB. Decorated Joint Svc. Achievement medal Dept. Def., medal NATO, Yugoslavia, NATO,Kosovo, Air medal USAF, Europe, Aerial Achievement medal, Air Force Commendation medal, Air Force Achievement medal, Joint Meritorious Unit award, Combat Readiness medal, Armed Forces Svc. medal, various other medals. Mem.: IEEE, Carnegie Mellon Software Engring. Inst., Purdue Griffin Soc., Purdue Alumni Assn. (life), VFW (life), Res. Officer's Assn. (life), Air Force Assn. (life Medal of Merit award 2001), Internat. Soc. Mensa. Roman Cath. Office: 88 ABW/CVI Bldg 110 Rm 101 5440 Skeel Ave Dayton OH 45432 Home Phone: 501-626-8456; Office Phone: 937-522-2568. Home Fax: 501-255-6425. Personal E-mail: jacenj@ieee.org. Business E-Mail: jason.jackson@wpafb.af.mil.

JACKSON, JEANINE E., ambassador; BS, Hastings Coll.; MS, Fla. Tech. Consular officer Jeddah Consulate Gen., Saudi Arabia; pers. officer Hong Kong and Consulate Gen.; gen. services. officer Kenya; mgmt. counselor Afghanistan; coord. for Iraq transition US Dept. State, amb. to Burkina Faso, 2006—. Office: US Dept State 2440 Ouagadougou Pl Washington DC 20521-2440

JACKSON, JEANNE PELLEGREN, apparel executive; b. Denver, Aug. 10, 1951; d. John James and Barbara (Grove) Pellegren; m. Douglas Emmett Jackson, Nov. 23, 1984; children: Lindsay, Craig. BS in Fin., U. Colo., 1974; MBA, Harvard Bus. Sch., 1978. Buyer, mgr. Bullocks Dept. Stores, LA, 1978-85; v.p. merchandise mgr. to sr. v.p. direct mail pvt. brands Saks Fifth Ave., NYC, 1985-89; sr. v.p. merchandising Walt Disney Attractions, Orlando, 1989-92; exec. v.p. merchandising Victoria's Secret, Columbus, Ohio, 1992-95; CEO Banana Republic, 1996-2000, Wal-Mart.com, 2000—. Instr. mktg. U. So. Calif., L.A., 1979-81; adv. bd. Navy Exch., Norfolk, Va., 1991—. Bd. dirs. Orlando Mus. Art, 1990-92. Republican. Avocations: skiing, tennis. Office: Walmartcom 135 Constitution Dr Menlo Park CA 94025

JACKSON, JESS S., vintner; JD, U. Calif. Practice, San Francisco; now pres. Kendall-Jackson Winery Ltd., Santa Rosa, Calif., chmn. bd. dirs. Founding mem. Family Winemakers of Calif. Named one of Forbes' Richest Americans, 2006. Mem. Calif. Bar Assn. Office: Kendall-Jackson Winery Ltd 421 Aviation Blvd Santa Rosa CA 95403-1069

JACKSON, JESSE LOUIS, political organization worker, clergyman; b. Greenville, SC, Oct. 8, 1941; s. Noah Robinson, Charles Henry (Stepfather) and Helen Burns Jackson; m. Jacqueline Lavinia Brown, 1963; children: Santita, Jesse Louis Jr., Jonathan Luther, Yusef DuBois, Jacqueline Lavinia. Student, U. Ill., 1959-60; BA in Sociology and Economics, NC AT State U., 1964; student, Chgo. Theol. Sem., 1964—66, MDiv, 2000; degree (hon.), NC AT State U., Pepperdine U., Oberlin U., Oral Roberts U., U. RI, Howard U., Georgetown U. Ordained to ministry Baptist Ch., 1968; Chgo. dir. Operation Breadbasket project, So. Christian Leadership Conf., Chgo., 1966—67, nat. dir., 1967-71; founder, exec. dir. Operation PUSH (People United to Serve Humanity), Chgo., 1971—96; founder PUSH-Excel and PUSH for Econ. Justice, 1977—96; founder, nat. pres. Nat. Rainbow Coalition Inc., Chgo., 1984—96; shadow senator from DC US Senate, Washington, 1991—96; founder, nat. pres. Rainbow/Push Coalition, Inc., Chgo., 1996—; spl. envoy of the President & Sec. State for the Promotion of Democracy in Africa US Dept. State, Washington, 1997; founder The Wall St. Project, 1997—. Candidate for Dem. nomination US Presdl. Election, 1983—84, 1987—88; lectr. for high schs., colls., prof. audiences in Am., Europe. Host, Both Sides with Jesse Jackson, CNN, 1992-2000; Author: Straight From the Heart, 1987, Keep Hope Alive, 1989; co-author: (with Jesse L. Jackson, Jr.) Legal Lynching: Racism, Injustice, and the Death Penalty, 1996, It's About the Money: How You Can Get Out of Debt, Build Wealth, and Achieve Your Financial Dreams!, 1999. Active Black Coalition for United Cmty. Action, 1969. Recipient Presdl. Award Nat. Med. Assn., 1969, Humanitarian Father of Year Award Nat. Father's Day Com., 1971, Presdl. Medal of Freedom, 2000; named Third Most Admired Man in Am. Gallup Poll, 1985, one of six new leaders on the rise US News World Report, 100 Most Influential Black Americans, Ebony mag., 2006. Address: Rainbow PUSH Coalition 930 E 50th St Chicago IL 60615-2702

JACKSON, JESSE LOUIS, JR., congressman; b. Greenville, SC, Mar. 11, 1965; m. Sandra Jackson; children: Jessica Donatella, Jesse L. III. BS in Bus. Mgmt., NC A&T U., 1987; MA in Theology, Chgo. Theol. Sem., 1990; JD, U. Ill., 1993. Natl. field dir. The Rainbow Coalition, 1993—95; mem. US Congress from 2d Ill. dist., Washington, 1995—, mem. house appropriations com., 1997—. Co-chair, comm. group Dem. Policy Com.; mem. Congressional Black Caucus, Congressional Steel Caucus. Author: Legal Lynching: Racism, Injustice and the Death Penalty, 1996, It's About the Money, 1999, A More Perfect Union: Advancing New American Rights, 2001. Named one of 100 Most Influential Black Americans, Ebony mag., 2006. Democrat. Baptist. Office: US Ho Reps 2419 Rayburn Ho Office Bldg Washington DC 20515-1302 Office Phone: 202-225-0773. Office Fax: 202-225-0899. E-mail: webmaster@jessejacksonjr.org.*

JACKSON, JEWEL, retired state agency administrator; b. June 3, 1942; d. Willie Burghardt and Bernice Jewel (Mayberry) Norton; children: Steven, June Kelly, Michael, Anthony. With Calif. Youth Authority, 1965-91, group supr. San Andreas & Santa Rosa, 1965-67, youth counselor Ventura, 1967-78, sr. youth counselor Stockton, 1978-81, parole agt., 1986, treatment team supr., program mgr. Whittier & Ione, 1981-91; ret., 1991. Owner Access Legal Document Assistance; v.p., mem. bd. nonprofit orgn. New Toyz Assn. Past bd. dirs. Samuel Hancock Christian Sch.; past pres. San Joaquin Valley Girls Horsewomen's Assn.; bd. dirs., regional dir. New Toyz Assn. Mem. Internat. Egg Art Guild. Avocations: reading, decorative egg art, decoupage. Home and Office: 1410 Delta Dr Cedar Hill TX 75104 Home Phone: 972-291-9385; Office Phone: 209-466-3570. Personal E-mail: accesslda@sbcglobal.net.

JACKSON, JIMMIE L., retired music educator, organist; b. Lakeland, Fla., Mar. 22, 1935; s. Amos Jackson and Essie M. Jackson (Hollie); m. Mary L. Wolfe, June 24, 1961. MusB, Boston U., 1973, MusM, postgrad., Boston U., 1976—. Cert. tchr. Mass. Dept. Edn., 1973. Choir dir., organist First Bapt. Instl. Ch., Lakeland, Fla., 1948—53, St. Michael's & All Angels Episcopal Ch., Tallahassee, 1954—56, Phila. Bapt. Ch., 1955—56, Grace Ch. (Van Vorst), Jersey City, 1956—57, Temple Menorah, Bloomfield, 1956—57, Peoples Bapt. Ch., Boston, 1957—59; office mgr. Samuel Hurwitz Co., 1961—70; choir dir., organist St. James African Orthodox Ch., Oston, 1962—63, Grant A M E Ch., Boston, 1963—69, St. Cyprian's Episcopal Ch., 1969—83; dir. adminstrn. & fin. The Ecumenical Ctr. Roxbury Inc, 1970—72, interim exec. dir., 1972; choral dir. Weston H.S., 1973—74; instr. k-12 music Wellesley Pub. Schs., 1974—88; clinician Mass. Music Educators All-State Conf., Lowell, 1979; choir dir., organist 195th Conv., Episcopal Diocese, Boston, 1980—80, St. Bartholomew's Episcopal Ch., Cambridge, 1984—85; min. music Peoples Bapt. Ch., Boston, 1986—93; program dir., dept. head, music and art Boston Latin Sch., 1988—99; music dir., organist Union United Meth. Ch., 1994—99. Adj. clin. instr. Boston U., 1979—80; adjudicator Boston Pops Auditions, Ayer, 1975, New Eng. Music Festival Assn., Rutland, Vt., 1976—79. Mem. Garrison-Trotter Neighborhood Assn. Inc., Boston, 1978—; pres. The Couples Club Peoples Bapt. Ch., 1976—93. With US Army, 1959—60. Recipient award, Union United Meth. Ch., 1996. Mem.: Mass. Music Educators Assn. (assoc.), Music Educators Nat. Conf. (assoc.), Am. Guild Organists (assoc.), Am. Choral Dirs. Assn. (life). Home: 76 Cheney St Dorchester MA 02121-2511 Home Phone: 617-445-5023.

JACKSON, J(OHN) DAVID, physicist, researcher; b. London, Ont., Can., Jan. 19, 1925; arrived in US, 1957, naturalized, 1988; s. Walter David and Lillian Margaret Jackson; m. Barbara Cook, June 26, 1949; children: Ian, Nan, Maureen, Mark. BS in Physics and Math., U. Western Ont., 1946, DSc (hon.), 1989; PhD in Physics, MIT, 1949. Rsch. assoc. dept. physics MIT, Cambridge, 1949; from asst. prof. to assoc. prof. math. McGill U., Montreal, Que., Canada, 1950-57; from assoc. prof. to prof. physics U. Ill., Urbana, 1957-67; prof. U. Calif., Berkeley, 1967-92, dept. chair, 1978-81, prof. emeritus, 1993—. Vis. fellow Cambridge (Eng.) U., 1970; acting head theory group Fermilab, Batavia, Ill., 1972-73; head physics divsn. Lawrence Berkeley Lab., 1982-84; dep. dir. SSC Cen. Design Group, Berkeley, 1985-87; vis. sr. rsch. fellow Oxford (Eng.) U., 1988-89; mem. vis. com. Argonne Nat. Lab., CERN, SSC Lab., Stanford Linear Accelerator Ctr., others. Author: Physics of Elementary Particles, 1958, Classical Electrodynamics, 1962, rev. edit., 1975, 3d edit., 1998, Mathematics for Quantum Mechanics, 1962, reprinted 2006; also contbr. numerous articles to profl. publications; editor Ann. Rev. Nuclear and Particle Sci., 1977-93 J. S. Guggenheim Found. fellow, 1956-57, Ford Found. fellow, 1963-64. Fellow Am. Phys. Soc.; mem. NAS (elected 1990), Am. Acad. Arts and Scis. (elected 1989), ACLU (life). Avocations: hiking, swimming, scientific bibliophily. Address: Lawrence Berkeley Nat Lab 50A5104 Berkeley CA 94720 Office Phone: 510-486-4490.

JACKSON, JOHN E., gas industry executive; Grad. cum laude in Bus. Adminstrn., Baylor U., Waco. CPA. Staff acct. Arthur Young & Co., Ft. Worth, 1979; various treasury, contr. and acctg. positions including CFO Gathering, Processing & Mktg. divsn. Union Pacific Resources, 1981—99; v.p., contr. Duke Energy Field Svcs. (joint venture of Duke Energy and Philips Petroleum), 1999—2001, v.p., CFO, 2001—02; sr. v.p., CFO Hanover, Houston, 2002—04, pres., CEO, bd. dirs., 2004—. Office: Hanover 12001 N Houston Rosslyn Houston TX 77086 Office Phone: 281-447-8787.*

JACKSON, JOHN EDWARD, adult education educator, retired military officer; b. Rapid City, SD, Feb. 11, 1949; s. William Edward Joseph and Bettye Davis (Williams) J.; m. Valerie Lee McGilton, June 5, 1971; children: Gina Marie, Brian Howard. BA in Univ. Studies, U. N.Mex., 1971; MEd, Providence Coll., 1976; MS in Mgmt., Salve Regina U., 1983, cert. of advanced grad. studies, 1998; grad. mgmt. devel. program, Harvard U., 1997. Commd. USN, 1971, advanced through grades to capt., ret., 1998; disbursing officer USS Hunley AS-31, Charleston, SC, 1972-74; food svc. officer Naval Edn. and Tng. Ctr., Newport, RI, 1974-76; supply officer USS Joseph Strauss DDG-16, Pearl Harbor, Hawaii, 1976-78; data processing dept. dir. Nava. Supply Ctr., Pearl Harbor, 1978-80; prof. Ctr. Continuing Edn. U.S. Naval War Coll., Newport, 1980-83, prof. dept. nat. security decision-making, 1994-96, dean Coll. Continuing Edn., 1996—, assoc. dean for Distance Education, 2000—, dir. devel. and long range planning, 2002—; divsn. dir. Navy Fleet Material Support Office, Mechanicsburg, Pa., 1983-86; curricular officer U.S. Naval Postgrad. Sch., Monterey, Calif., 1986-90; supply officer USS Sierra AD-18, Charleston, 1990-92; exec. officer Naval Supply Ctr., Charleston, 1992-94; mil. chair logistics Naval War Coll., Newport, RI, 1994—. Speechwriter USN, 1978—. Former editor-in-chief newsletter The Oakleaf; editor: Logistics Leadership Series; contbr. articles to profl. jours. Mem. Soc. Logistics Engrs., Navy Supply Corps Assn. (bd. dirs. 1983-96, pres. 1994-96), Naval War Coll. Found., U.S. Naval Inst. (liaison officer). Home: 7 Mast Ct Middletown RI 02842-7212

JACKSON, JOHN HOLLIS, JR., lawyer; b. Mongomery, Ala., Aug. 21, 1941; s. John Hollis and Erma (Edgeworth) J.; m. Rebecca Mullins, May 27, 1967; 1 child, John Hollis III. AB, U. Ala., 1963, JD, 1966. Bar: Ala. 1966, U.S. Dist. Ct. (no. dist.) Ala. 1969, U.S. Ct. Appeals (11th cir.) 1993. Pvt. practice, Clanton, Ala., 1967—. County atty. Chilton County Commn., Clanton, 1969-; mcpl. judge Clanton, 1971-99, city atty., 1999—; dir. First Nat. Bank, Clanton, 1974-83; mem. adv. bd. Colonial Bank, Clanton, 1983-2003; mcpl. judge, Jemison, Ala., 1984—. Bd. dirs. Chilton-Shelby Mental Health Bd., Calera, Ala., 1974-83, pres., 1974-79; mem. State Dem. Exec. Com., Birmingham, Ala., 1974-98, County Dem. Exec. Com., Chilton County, 1982-94; del. Dem. Nat. Conv., N.Y.C., 1976; mem. pres. cabinet U. Ala., 2000—. 1st lt. U.S. Army, 1966-67. Mem. Ala. Young Lawyers Sect. (exec. com. 1969-70), Chilton County Bar Assn. (pres. 1969, 74), Ala. State Bar Assn. (bd. bar commrs. 1984-87, 93-99, chmn. adv. com. to bd. bar examiners 1986-87, 19th cir. indigent def. commn. 1983—, chmn. disciplinary panel II 1997-99), Ala. Alumni Assn. (pres. Chilton County chpt. 1978-79), Kiwanis, Phi Alpha Delta. Methodist. Home: Samaria Rd Clanton AL 35045 Office: PO Box 1818 500 2nd Ave S Clanton AL 35046-1818 Home Phone: 205-755-1101; Office Phone: 205-755-2004. Personal E-mail: jhjatty@bellsouth.net.

JACKSON, JOHN HOWARD, lawyer, educator; b. Kansas City, Mo., Apr. 6, 1932; s. Howard Clifford and Lucile (Deischer) J.; m. Joan Leland, Dec. 16, 1962; children: Jeannette, Lee Ann, Michelle. AB, Princeton U., NJ, 1954; JD, U. Mich., 1959. Bar: Wis. 1959, Mo. 1959, Calif. 1964, Mich. 1970. Pvt. practice law, Milw., 1959-61; assoc. prof., prof. law U. Calif., 1961-66; prof. law U. Mich., 1966-97; univ. prof. law Georgetown U., Washington, 1998—, dir. Inst. of Internat. Econ. Law. On leave gen. counsel US Office Spl. Trade Rep., 1973-74, acting deputy spl. rep. for trade, 1974; vis. prof. U. Brussels, 1975-76; vis. fellow Inst. for Internat. Econs., Washington, 1983; Hessel E. Yntema prof. law U. Mich., 1983-97, assoc. v.p. acad. affairs, 1988-89; disting. vis. prof. law Georgetown Law Ctr., Washington, 1986-87, 93; Ford Found. cons. legal edn., vis. prof. U. Delhi, India, 1968-69; Hersch Lauterpacht Meml. lectr. Cambridge U., Eng., 2002. Author: World Trade and the Law of GATT, 1969, Contract Law in Modern Society, 1973, 2d edit., 1980, Legal Problems of International Economic Relations, 1977, 4th edit. (with William Davey and Alan Sykes), 2002; (with Jean-Victor Louis and Mitsuo Matsushita) Implementing the Tokyo Round, 1984; (with Edwin Vermulst) Anti-Dumping Law & Practice: Comparative Study, 1989; The World Trading System, 1989, 2d edit., 1997, Restructuring the GATT System, 1990; (with Alan Sykes) Implementing the Urugauy Round, 1997, World Trade Organization, 1998, The Jurisprudence of GATT and the WTO, 2000, Sovereignty, the WTO, and Changing Fundamentals of International Law, 2006; editor-in-chief Jour. Internat. Econ. Law; bd. editors: Am. Jour. Internat. Law, Jour. Law and Policy in Internat. Bus., others; contbr. articles to profl. jours. With M.I. US Army, 1954-56. Recipient Wolfgang Friedman Memorial award Columbia U., 1992; Rockefeller Found. fellow for study European community law Brussels, 1975-76 Mem. ABA, Am. Soc. Internat. Law (v.p. 1990-92), Am. Law Inst., Council Fgn. Relations, Phi Beta Kappa, Order of Coif. Office: Georgetown U Law Ctr 600 New Jersey Ave NW Washington DC 20001-2022

JACKSON, JOHN WYANT, biotechnology company executive; b. Corpus Christi, May 25, 1944; s. Donald LeGarde and Marion (McNulty) J; m. Susan Gager, Sept. 6, 1969; children: Alexandra C., Kimberly F., Donald M., Jennifer L. BA, Yale U., 1967; MBA, INSEAD, Fontainbleau, France, 1971; diploma, Inst. Political Sci., Paris, 1966. With Merck & Co., Rahway, NJ, 1971-78; various internat. positions, including v.p.-internat. Am. Cyanamid, 1978—86, pres., worldwide med. device divsn., 1986—91; founder, pres. Gemini Med., Warren, NJ, 1991-96; chmn., CEO Celgene Corp., Summit, NJ, 1996—2006. Chmn. Liana Found., 2006—; mem. Yale Internat. Adv. Bd.; bd. dirs. Gordonstoun Am. Found., U.S. Insead Coun. 1st lt. USMCR, 1967—70. Decorated Navy Commendation medal; decorated Purple Heart Mem. Soc. Paper Money Collectors. Republican. Episcopalian.

JACKSON, JON, medical educator, consultant; s. Dale and Marlys Alice Jackson; m. Margaret Ellen Moore, May 1, 1999; children: Maia, Finn. BA, Luther Coll., 1983; PhD, U. ND, 1989. Post-doctoral fellow Vanderbilt U., Nashville, 1990—93; asst. prof. Vanderbilt U. Sch. Medicine, 1993—96, U. ND, Grand Forks, 1998—; prin. med. tech. writer Daedalus Consulting, Oakland, Calif., 1996—98; prin., account exec. Jensen, Ramsey and Jackson, San Ramon, 1996—97; cons. Inst. Natural Resources, Berkeley, 1998—2000, Pearson Christensen, Grand Forks, 2002—04. Med. tech. writer Daedalus Consulting, Grand Forks, 1998—; med. writer MedCo Comm., Evergreen, Colo., 1998—2004. Author: Corpus: A User's Guide to the Human Body; musician: (musical performance, acappella quartet) 4 Blow Zero. Vol. ND Mus. Art, 1999—2005; vol. educator Dakota Sci. Ctr., 2003—05; pres. Grand Forks Master Chorale, 1998—2004; mem. North Valley Arts Coun., 2000—. Scholar, Archibald Bush Found., 2001—02. Mem.: AAAS, Am. Assn. Clin. Anatomists (anatomic svcs. com. 2007—), ND Acad. Sci. (sec., treas. 1999—2006), ND Funeral Dir.'s Assn., Am. Med. Writers Assn., Human Anatomy and Physiology Soc. (co-chair membership 2005—), Am. Assn. Anatomists, Grand Forks C. of C., Sigma Xi. Democrat-Npl. Avocations: music, rugby, travel, running. Office: U ND Dept Anatomy and Cell Biology Grand Forks ND 58202-9037 Home Phone: 701-787-5758; Office Phone: 701-777-2101. Office Fax: 701-777-2477. Personal E-mail: jackson@gra.midco.net. Business E-Mail: jackson@medicine.nodak.edu.

JACKSON, JOSEPH ESSARD, religious organization administrator; b. Negril, Jamaica, May 22, 1951; came to the U.S., 1968; s. Redverse and Edna Artilla (Gordon) J.; m. Elaine Marie Jacintho, July 1, 1978; children: Joseph E. II, Jonathan N. BS, Westfield State Coll., 1975; MAR, Yale U. Div. Sch., 1981; CAS, Harvard U., 1983; DMin, Wesley Theol. Sem., 1993. Ordained to ministry , 1983. Counselor urban edn. program Westfield (Mass.) State Coll., 1972-74, 80; teaching fellow Harvard U., 1982-83; math. tchr. Springfield (Mass.) Pub. Schs., 1983-84; v.p. external rels. Charge, Inc., Glen Ellyn, Ill., 1984; history tchr. Tech. High Sch., Springfield, 1984-86; adj. prof. Ch. of God Sch. Theology, Cleveland, Tenn., 1986-89; sr. pastor Harvest Temple Ch. of God, Forestville, Md., 1989-92; exec. dir. Black ministries Ch. of God Internat. Offices, 1992-98; sr. pastor New Testament Ch. God, Hartford, Conn., 1998—. Asst. prof. religion dept. Bible and Christian Ministries Lee Coll., Cleveland, 1986-89; assoc. min. Ch. of God, Hartford, Conn., 1980-86; keynote speaker many confs. and convs. Author: Reclaiming Our Heritage, 1993; contbr. articles to profl. jours. Active alumni com. Tech. High Sch., 1984-85, Blue Hills Child Care Ctr., Hartford, 1981-86, State Bd. Edn., So. New England, 1984-89, Music Bd., So. New England, 1979-84, State Youth and Christian Edn. Bd. Ch. of God, So. New England; mem. ministerial devel. bd. State of Tenn., 1987-89. Mem. NAACP (bd. dirs. 1984-85), Nat. Assn. Evangelicals (bd. adminstrs. 1993—, mem. exec. com. 1994—, treas. 1995—, World Relief Corp. bd. mem. 1997—). Democrat. Avocations: fishing, writing. Home: 59 Greenlawn St East Hartford CT 06108-2952

JACKSON, JUANITA WALLACE, educational consultant; b. Cin., Mar. 7, 1931; d. William J. and Viola D. (Shively) Wallace; m. John Arter Jackson, Apr. 21, 1967; children: Karon Gibson-Mueller, Blaine Gibson. BS, U. Cin., 1955; MEd, Miami U., Oxford, Ohio, 1963. Cert. elem. tchr., Md., elem. prin., Mass., tchr., shpr., adminstr., Ohio. Sr. supr. Mass. State Dept. Edn.; dir. kindergarten edn. Wilmington (Mass.) Pub. Schs.; coord. reading Cin. Pub. Schs.; exec. dir. Schoharie County Child Devel. Coun., Cobleskill, N.Y.; dir. bus. maintenance orgn. SUNY Rsch. Found., Albany. Cons. in field. Contbr. articles, book revs. to profl. publs. Chmn. N.Y. State Legis. Forum. Recipient cert. of achievement Schenectady County Reps., Schenectady County Community Coll., 1985, Tribute to Women award Albany YWCA, declaration of Mayor Whalen Juanita Wallace Jackson Day, Albany, July 10, 1990. Mem. AAUW (mem. edn. found., past pres. Schenectady br.), Woman's Club McLean (pres. 1994), LINKS Inc. (pres.), Delta Kappa Gamma (past pres. Alpha Kappa chpt.). Home: PO Box 4103 Mc Lean VA 22103

JACKSON, KEITH MACKENZIE, retired sports commentator; b. Carrollton, Ga., Oct. 18, 1928; s. Lucille Polly Perdue Jackson Bragg; m. Turi Ann Johnsen, Aug. 2, 1952; children: Melanie Ann, Lindsey Keith, Christopher Keith. BA in Broadcast Journalism, Wash. State U., 1954. Sports and spl. events dir., assoc. news dir. KOMO Radio-TV, Seattle, 1954-64; news corr. ABC Radio, 1964-69; sports dir. Radio Sta. KABC, 1971-74; sports commentator, writer, producer ABC-TV, NYC, 1964—2006; ret., 2006. Founding mem. vis. com. Wash. State U.; trustee Wash. State U. Found. Served with USMC, 1946-50. Recipient Disting. Alumnus award, 1978, Sylvania award, 1956, Headliners award, 1958, Golden Mike award So. Calif. News Dirs. Assn., 1972, Amos Alonzo Stagg award Am. Football Coaches Assn., 1993, Good Guy award Am. Legion, 1983, Nat. Football Found & Hall of Fame Gold medal, 1999; named Nat. Sportscaster of Yr., 1972-76, Seattle-Puget Sound Sportscaster of Decade, 1978; elected to Hall of Fame, Am. Sportscasters Assn., 1994, Nat. Assn. Sportswriters and Sportscasters, 1995. Mem. AFTRA, SAG, Nat. Football Found. (life), Spanish HIlls Country Club (founding bd.), L.A. Country Club. Presbyterian. Office: ABC Sports 47 W 66th St Rm 800 New York NY 10023-6290 *All any society owes an individual is an opportunity, and the color of a person's skin will never tell you anything about their character nor their potential.*

JACKSON, KENNETH ARTHUR, physicist, researcher; b. Connaught, Ont., Can., Oct. 23, 1930; s. Arthur and Susanna (Vatcher) J.; m. Jacqueline Della Olyan, June 20, 1952 (div.); children: Stacy Margaret, Meredith Suzanne, Stuart Keith; m. Camilla M. Maruszewski, June 21, 1980 (div.); m. Gina Kritchevsky, April 30, 2005. BS, U. Toronto, 1952, MS, 1953; PhD, Harvard U., 1956. Postdoctoral fellow Harvard U., Cambridge, Mass., 1956-58, asst. prof. metallurgy, 1958-62; mem. tech. staff Bell Labs., Murray Hill, NJ, 1962-67, head material physics research dept., 1967-81, head optical materials research dept., 1981-89; prof. materials sci. and engring. U. Ariz., 1989—2003, prof. emeritus, 2004—. Lectr. Welch. Found., 1970, 85; mem. research adv. panel Air Force Office Sci. Research, 1976-82, space application bd. Nat. Acad. Sci., 1974-82. Editor-in-chief Optical Materials, 1999-2003; contbr. articles to profl. jours.; patentee in field. Recipient Mathewson Gold medal AIME, 1966, Crystal growth award AACG, 1993, Frank prize IOCG, 1998, TMS Chalmers award, 2003. Fellow AAAS, The Metall. Soc.-AIME, Am. Phys. Soc.; mem. NAE, Internat. Orgn. Crystal Growth (treas. 1978-86, Frank prize 1998), Am. Assn. Crystal Growth (pres. 1968-75, coun., award 1993), Materials Rsch. Soc. (v.p. 1975-77, pres. 1977-78, coun.), Am. Soc. Metals, Engring. Coun. for Profl. Devel. (mem. coun.), Fedn. Materials Soc. (trustee), Nat. Acad. Engring. E-mail: kaj@aml.arizona.edu.

JACKSON, KENNETH TERRY, historian, academic administrator; b. Memphis, July 27, 1939; s. Kenneth Gordon and Elizabeth Owen (Willins) J.; m. Barbara Ann Bruce, Aug. 25, 1962; children: Kevan Parish, Kenneth Gordon (dec.). BA magna cum laude, U. Memphis, 1961; MA, U. Chgo., 1963, PhD, 1966. Asst. prof. history Columbia U., NYC, 1968-71, assoc. prof., 1971-76, prof., 1976-87, Mellon prof., 1987-90, Jacques Barzun prof. history and soc. sciences, 1990—, chmn. dept. history, 1994-97. Vis. prof. Princeton U., NJ, 1973-74, George Washington U., 1982-83, UCLA, 1986-87; chair Bradley Commn. on History in Schs., 1987-90; chair Nat. Coun. for History Edn., Inc., 1990-92; dir. Herbert H. Lehman Ctr. for Am. History, Columbia U. 2005-. Author: The Ku Klux Klan in the City, 1967, Crabgrass Frontier, 1985 (Bancroft prize 1986, Francis Parkman prize 1986), Silent Cities: The Evolution of the American Cemetery, 1989; co-editor: Cities in American History, 1972, American Vistas, 1971, 7th edit., 1995, Empire City: New York Through the Centuries, 2002, Robert Moses and the Modern City: The Transformation of New York, 2007; editor-in-chief Dictionary of American Biography, 1991-95, Scribner's Encyclopedia of American Lives, 1996-2005; editor Encyclopedia of New York City, 1995; gen. editor Columbia History of Urban Life, 30 vols., 1980—. Trustee Nat. Coun. Hist. Edn., 1990—, South St. Seaport Mus., 1989—2001, Transp. Alternatives, 1995—97, Skyscraper Mus., 1996—2001, NY Hist. Soc., 1996—, vice chmn., 1998—2001, pres., CEO, 2001—04; trustee NY State Hist. Assn., 1996—, Henry Luce Found., 2002—, Regional Plan Assn., 2003—; vestryman Trinity Ch. Wall St., 1997—2004. Capt. USAF, 1965—68. Recipient Mark Van Doren Tchg. award Columbia U., 1989, Outstanding Alumni award U. Memphis, 1989, Great Tchr. award Soc. Columbia Grads. 1999, Nicholas Murray Butler medal Columbia U., 2005; named NY State Scholar of Yr., NY State Coun. on the Humanities, 2001; fellow Woodrow Wilson Found., 1961-62, Guggenheim Found., 1983-84; sr. fellow NEH, 1979-80. Mem. Soc. Am. Historians (pres. 1998-2000), Orgn. Am. Historians (pres. 2000-2001), Am. Hist. Assn., Urban Hist. Assn. (pres. 1994-95), Century Assn.; fellow Am. Acad. Arts & Scis. Episcopalian. Avocations: skiing, tennis, basketball. Home: 44 Kitchel Rd Mount Kisco NY 10549-4516 Office: Columbia U Dept History 603 Fayerweather Hall New York NY 10027 Office Phone: 212-854-2555. Business E-Mail: ktj1@columbia.edu.

JACKSON, KINGSBURY TEMPLE, educational and financial consultant; b. Newton, Mass., May 15, 1917; s. Ralph Temple and Elizabeth Mesarole (Rhodes) J.; m. June Stewart Cooper, July 29, 1950 (dec. Feb. 1976). BS, MIT, 1940; postgrad., NYU, 1949—51; MS, U. Ala., 1964, U. So. Calif., 1969, Pepperdine U., 1975. Registered profl. engr., Calif., Ala.; lic. and bonded tax preparer, IRS and Calif. Commd. 2d lt. U.S. Army, 1940, advanced through grades to lt. col., 1961, ret., 1965; comdr. U.S. Army Depot, also Camp Mercer, Republic of Korea, 1957-58; project officer, indsl. project dir. U.S. Army Saturn Space Vehicle Program and Pershing Missile Sys., 1959-61; dir. U.S. Army Missile Command Engring. Documentation Ctr., Redstone Arsenal, Ala., 1962-63; program coordinator NATO-Hawk Missile System, 1963-65; prin. contracting officer, chief European procurement U.S. Army Ordnance, 1964-65; lectr. mgmt. and engring. Grad. Sch., U. So. Calif., LA, 1965-69; contractual rels. supr. L.A. Bd. Edn., 1969-82; pres. Contract Consultants, LA, 1982—, K.T. Jackson, Gen. Contractors, LA, 1991—. Author: Engineering Documentation Systems Development: Department of Defense and NASA, 1963, Aerospace Propellants and Chemicals: The Manager's Approach, 1968. V.p., mem. bd. dirs. Kingsbury Properties Ltd.; corp. sec., bd. dirs. The Concert Singers, Inc. Mem.: Am. Soc. Automotive Engrs. (rep. to Aerospace gen. stds. divsn. 1962—65), Am. Ordinance Assn. (mem. exec. bd. prodn. technique divsn.,Army rep.to engring. doc. sect. 1962—65), Am. Soc. Mil. Comptrs., Am. Soc. Indsl. Engrs., Nat. Space Soc., Aircraft Owners and Pilots Assn., Calif. Assn. Bus. Ofcls., Ret. Officers Assn. (life), Internat. Assn. Sch. Bus. Ofcls. (emeritus), The Concert Singers Inc., The Planetary Soc., A&E Flying Club, MIT Club (So. and No. Calif.). Home: Ste C302 3400 Paul Sweet Rd Santa Cruz CA 95065-1541 Office: Contract Cons PO Box 402 Capitola CA 95010-0402 Home Phone: 831-464-1547; Office Phone: 831-464-1547. E-mail: kingtempj@sbcglobal.net.

JACKSON, KORY A., lawyer; b. Oxford, Ohio; BA in Eng. Lit., U. Cin., 1997, JD, 2000. Bar: Ohio 2000, US Dist. Ct. Southern Dist. Ohio 2001, US Dist. Ct. Southern Dist. Ind. 2005, US Ct. of Appeals Sixth Cir. 2005. Assoc. Vorys, Sater, Seymour and Pease LLP, Cin. Mem., Conf. Com. Greater Cin. Minority Counsel Prog.; vol. legal cons. Sch. Creative and Performing Arts. Named one of Ohio's Rising Stars, Super Lawyers, 2006. Mem.: ABA, Ohio State Bar Assn., Cin. Bar Assn. Office: Vorys Sater Seymour and Pease LLP Atrium Two Ste 2000 221 E Fourth St PO Box 0236 Cincinnati OH 45201-0236 Office Phone: 513-723-4602. Office Fax: 513-852-7847.

JACKSON, LARRY ARTOPE, retired college president; b. Florence, SC, Feb. 7, 1925; s. Arthur Edward and Rosa (Gilbert) J.; m. Barbara Atwood, June 27, 1953; children: Elizabeth Jackson Eble, Arthur Edward, Barbara Jackson Allen, Charles Rhett. AB, Wofford Coll., 1947, DLitt (hon.), 1976; MDiv, Union Theol. Sem., 1953; MA, U. Pacific, 1973, DD (hon.), 1961; D in Humanities (hon.), Clemson U., 1991. Prin. Santiago (Chile) Coll., 1959-64; provost Callison Coll. of U. Pacific, Stockton, Calif., 1964-70; v.p. for adminstrn. U. Evansville, 1970-73; pres. Lander Univ. (formerly Lander Coll.), Greenwood, SC, 1973-92, ret., 1992. Vis. fellow Wolfson Coll., Cambridge U., 1985; appointed by Gov. to serve as mem. S.C. Commn. on Higher Edn., 2000-2003. Mem. Fulbright Commn. for Chile, 1961-64; mem. Commn. on Black Colls. Related to the Meth. Ch., 1973-76. With USAAF, 1943-45; with Am. Friends Svc. Com., 1948-49. Decorated Air medal with 2 oak leaf clusters. Mem. Rotary. Democrat. Home: 604 Cambridge Ave W Greenwood SC 29649-1967 Personal E-mail: ljack@gogenesis.com. *Love is the law of life and it is by striving to live under the rule of this law that we find authenticity.*

JACKSON, LAUREN, professional basketball player; b. Australia, May 11, 1981; d. Gary and Maree Jackson. Player Seattle Storm, 2001—. Mem. Gems team Jr. World Championships, 1997, WNBL Championship team, 2000; mem. Australian Nat. Team Sydney Olympics, 2000, Athens Olympics, 2004. Named a Peak Performer, WNBA, 2003, 2007; named WNBA MVP, 2003, WNBA Defensive Player of Yr., 2007; named to WNBA Western Conf. All-Star Team, 2001—03, 2005—07, All-WNBA First Team, 2003, 2005, 2006, WNBA All-Defensive Team, 2007; recipient Silver medal, Sydney Olympics, 2000, Espy Award for Best WNBA Player, 2004, 2005. Achievements include being selected first in the 2001 WNBA draft. Office: Seattle Storm 351 Elliott Ave W Ste 500 Seattle WA 98119*

JACKSON, LINDA SHORTER, nutritionist, educator; b. Birmingham, Ala., Feb. 10, 1955; d. Wiley and Mary Russell Shorter; 1 child, Ramikiel L. Jackson-Macon. BS, Jacksonville State U., Ala., 1976; Assoc., U. Md., Baumholder, West Germany, 1991; M in Tchg., Wayne State U., Detroit, Mich., 2005. Cert. tchr. Mich. Food mgr. U. South Ala. Med. Ctr., Mobile, 1976—77, Springhill Meml. Hosp., Mobile, 1980—83; food and nutrition mgr. Colo. Coll., Colorado Springs, Colo., 1983—86; supr. U.S. Army, Baumholden, Germany, 1986—89; food mgr. Detroit Med. Ctr., 1990—2000; tchr. Detroit Pub. Schs., 2000—; direct care worker Metro Staff, Southfield, Mich., 2000—. Coord. singles ministry Seventh Day Adventist, 1992—2000, coord. childrens ministries, 1994—2002. Recipient Plaque for Faithful Svc., Women's Ministries of Seventh Day Adventist, 2002, scholarship, Detroit Fedn. Tchrs., 2004. Mem.: Mich. Coun. Social Studies, Nat. Coun. Tchrs. of English, Delta Sigma Theta. Seventh Day Adventist. Avocations: travel, community work, walking. Home: 20111 Regent Dr Detroit MI 48205 Office Phone: 313-866-2072. Office Fax: 313-866-2074. E-mail: Linderf7@aol.com.

JACKSON, LORI LEE, secondary school educator, elementary school educator; b. Omaha, Nebr., Aug. 24, 1960; d. Lloyd Vernard and Lotus Lee Beckwith; m. Edward John Jackson; children: Aaron Lloyd Neyhart, Tanner John, Isaac Martin. BS, U. Nebr., Lincoln, 1983. Cert. elem. educator SD, 2006. Tchr. Dist. 100, Valentine, Nebr., 1983—85, Todd County Sch. Dist., Mission, SD, 1987—2006, dist. literacy coach, 2006—. Editor: Lit Coach. Mem.: Tchrs. Applying Whole Lang., Internat. Reading Assn., Nat. Coun. Tchrs. English. Democrat. Avocations: reading, travel. Office: Todd County Sch Dist Box 87 Mission SD 57555 Home Phone: 605-856-4706; Office Phone: 605-856-2211 2. Business E-Mail: ljackson@tcsdk12.org.

JACKSON, MARGARET ELIZABETH, science educator; b. Richmond, Va., Mar. 15, 1930; d. Joseph and Bertha Annette Jackson. BS, Va. Union U.; MA in Sci. Edn., Trinity Coll.; postgrad., Oxford U., 1976—78, George Washington U., 1981, Roehampton Inst. Higher Learning, England, 1985. Resource tchr. sci. Garrison Elem. Sch., Washington, 1968—. Tchr. Howard U., Washington, 1984; devel. sci. materials U.S. Dept. Agr., 1970; tchr. English Elem. Schs., Campo De Criptana, Spain, 1987; writer curriculum Elem. Pub. Schs., Washington, 1980—93; mentor Carnegie Acad. Sci. Edn. Carnegie Instn., Washington, 1995—96. Co-author: Addison Wesley Science Textbook for Elementary School, 1987. Named Internat. Educator of Yr., 2003. Mem.: ASCD, Smithsonian Instn., N.Y. Acad. Scis., D.C. Sci. Tchrs. Assn., Nat. Sci. Tchrs. Assn. Home: 2505 -13th St NW Apt 501 Washington DC 20009 Office Phone: 202-673-7263.

JACKSON, MARK JAMES, engineering educator; b. Widnes, Lancashire, Eng., Feb. 14, 1967; arrived in U.S., 2001; s. George and Monica Mary Jackson; m. Joanne Lesly Pinnington, July 20, 1990. MA, Cambridge U., 1998; MS in Engring., Liverpool U., Eng., 1991, PhD, 1995. Chartered engr., Engring. Coun., UK, 1998. Mech. plant engr. I.C.I. Pharmaceuticals, Macclesfield, Cheshire, England, 1988—89, Anglo Blackwells, Widnes, Lancashire, England, 1990—91; tech. mgr. St. Gobain Abrasives Group Unicorn Internat., Gloucester, Gloucestershire, England, 1992—97; rsch. fellow U. of Cambridge, Cambridgeshire, England, 1997—98; lectr. U. of Liverpool, 1998—2002; prof. of engring. Tenn. Technol. U., Cookeville, Tenn., 2002—04; prof. engring Purdue U., West Lafeyette, Ind., 2004—. Cons. tech. mgr. St. Gobain Abrasives Group Unicorn Internat., Gloucester, 1997—99; cons. engr. MIJA Ltd., Cambridge, 1997—2000; v.p., chief tech. officer Vitrified Techs. Inc., Kans. City, 2002—06; dir. rsch. Micromachinists LLC, 2006—. Contbr. chapters to books, articles to profl. jours. Councillor Halton Borough Coun., Widnes, 2001—02. Recipient prize, Imperial Chem. Industries, 1986; fellow, U. of Cambridge, 1997—98; scholar, Royal Acad. of Engring., 2000, Royal Soc. of London, 2000, Engring. and Phys. Scis. Rsch. Coun., 1992—95. Fellow: Liverpool (Eng.) and North Wales Materials Soc. (hon. sec. 1998—2002), Cambridge (Eng.) Philos. Soc. (life), Liverpool (Eng.) Athenaeum; mem.: ASME, Soc. Mfg. Engrs., Am. Soc. of Materials, Inst. of Materials, Minerals, and Mining, Instn. of Mech. Engrs. (scholar 1990). Labor. Roman Catholic. Achievements include design of manufacturing processes at the micro and nanoscale; invention of piezoelectric nanogrinding process and pulsed water drop micro machining center. Avocations: running, reading, travel, history, debating. Office: Purdue U Dept Mech Engring Tech Knoy Hall Tech West Lafayette IN 47907-2021 Home Phone: 765-463-3325; Office Phone: 765-494-0365. Business E-Mail: jacksomj@purdue.edu.

JACKSON, MARVIN DENNIS, journalism educator, writer; b. Jackson, Miss., June 30, 1945; s. Roy Dennis and Margie Emma (Cade) Jackson; m. Anna Jean Ferrell, Aug. 26, 1997 (dec. Mar. 8, 2005); m. Patricia Agnes Lake, Apr. 3, 2006. BA, Belhaven Coll., Jackson, Miss., 1967; MA, U. Ark., 1970, PhD in English, 1978. From asst. to assoc. prof. English U. Del., Newark, 1978—92, prof. English, 1992—, dir. journalism program, 1995—2003. Seminar dir. Bulgarian Mass Media Devel. Program, U.S. Info. Agy., Sofia, Bulgaria, 1994—95; mem. seminar faculty Nat. Writers Workshop, 1991—. Author: A Programmed Study of Accelerated Reading Skills, 1975; mng. editor Irish Renaissance Ann., 1980—83; editor: D.H. Lawrence Review, 1984—94; assoc. editor D.H. Lawrence: An Annotated Bibliography of Writings About Him, Vol. I, 1982, D.H. Lawrence: An Annotated Bibliography of Writings About Him, Vol. II, 1985; co-editor: D.H. Lawrence's Lady, 1985, Critical Essays on D.H. Lawrence, 1988, D.H. Lawrence's Literary Inheritors, 1991, Editing D.H. Lawrence: New Versions of a Modern Author, 1995, The Journalist's Craft, 2002; contbr. chapters to books. Recipient Nat. Teaching Award, Poynter Inst. Media Studies, 1982, Harry T. Moore Disting. Scholar Award for Lifetime Achievement in D.H. Lawrence Studies, D.H. Lawrence Soc. N.Am., 1999, College of Arts and Science Outstanding Advisement Award, U. Del., 2000; fellow Gannett Teaching Fellowship, Assn. Edn. Journalism, 1981; sr. fellow, Nat. Endowment for the Humanities, 1999. Mem.: Modern Language Assn., D.H. Lawrence Soc. N.Am. (sec.-treas. 1979—82, pres. 1985—86), Conf. of Editors of Learned Jours., Nat. Assn. Black Journalists (assoc.), Phi Beta Kappa. Democrat. Home: 814 Bradford Ln Newark DE 19711 Office: U Del Dept English 212 Memorial Newark DE 19716 Business E-Mail: dennisjackso@gmail.edu.

JACKSON, MARY ELLEN, librarian, consultant; b. Oshkosh, Wis., Nov. 20, 1949; d. Lawrence Herbert and Jeanette Lucille Marten; m. Alan Robert Jackson, Sept. 11, 1971. BA, Carroll Coll., Waukesha, Wis., 1971; MLS, Drexel U., 1974. Libr. searching dept. U. Pa. Libr., Phila., 1973-74, head Rosengarten res., 1974-77, head serials dept., 1977-78; head interlibr. loan dept. U. Pa. Librs., Phila., 1978-93; access and delivery svcs. cons. Assn. Rsch. Libr., Washington, 1993-98, sr. program officer access svc., 1998—2003, dir. collections and access programs, 2003—06, dir. collections and access initiatives, 2006, LibQUAL svcs. mgr., 2006; product mgr., resource sharing Auto-Graphics Inc., Pomona, Calif., 2006—. Cons., spkr. in field; adv. bd. Inst. for Sci. Info., Phila., 1993—96; dir. N.Am. Coordinating Com. on Japanese Libr. Resources, 1998—99; adv. bd. Ingenta Libr., 2001—02; governing bd. Internat. Fedn. Libr. Assoc., 2001—03. Author: Measuring the Performance of Interlibrary Loan Ops. in North Amer. Rsch. and Acad. Libraries, 1998, Interlibrary Loan/Resource Sharing Systems, 2000, Assessing ILL/DD Services: New Cost-Effective Alternatives, 2004; editor: AMS Studies in Interlibrary Loan, Document Delivery, Access Svcs., and Resource Sharing (ILL/DD), 2000; editor 5 books, Rsch. Access Through New Technology, 1989, RLG Shared Resources Manual, 1992, Advances in Preservation and Access, 1992, Uses of Document Delivery Svc., 1994, Managing Resource Sharing in the Electronic Age, 1996; contbr. over 120 articles to profl. jour. Recipient cert. of merit Pa. Libr. Assn., 1993. Mem. ALA (Amer. Library Assn., various offices 1978—), Safari Club Internat., Beta Phi Mu. Avocation: sewing. Office: Auto Graphics Inc 3201 Temple Ave Pomona CA 91768

JACKSON, MARY L., health services executive; b. Phila., June 25, 1938; d. John Francis and Helen Catherine (Peranteau) Martin; m. Howard Clark Jackson III, Dec. 17, 1954; children: Michael, Mark, Brian, Bert. Student, Bucks County C.C., 1977-83. Asst. mgr. retail divsn. Sears Roebuck & Co., Bensalem, Pa., 1972-77; educator, adminstr., dir. Trevos Behavior Modification Program, Pa., 1975—, leadership tng. workshops, 1979—. Participant rsch. studies in field; salesman Makefield Real Estate, Morrisville, Pa., 1977-78; mortgage fin. cons. Tom Dunphy Real Estate, Feasterville, Pa., 1978-81; weight loss cons., Hulmeville, Pa., 1984—, also TV and radio appearances on behavior modification for weight loss and maintenance. Co-author: The Official Calorie Book; pub., columnist monthly newsletter The Modifier, 1977—; pub. several studies in weight loss field; pub.

co-author multi-studies in field. Recipient Chapel of Four Chaplain award, 1977. Mem. Assn. Advancement Behavior Therapy, Bucks County Bd. Realtors, Hulmeville Hist. Soc. (founder, charter mem.). Democrat. Presbyterian. Avocations: reading, classical music, speed walking, knitting, fishing. Home: 218 Main St Hulmeville PA 19047-5635

JACKSON, MICHAEL J., automotive retail company executive; Technician Mercedes-Benz dealership, Cherry Hill, N.J.; mng. ptnr. Euro Motorcars, Bethesda, Md.; dist. mgr. Mercedes-Benz N.Am.; sr. mktg. exec. Mercedes-Benz USA, Inc., pres., CEO, responsible for N.Am. bus., until 1999; chmn., CEO AutoNation, Inc., Ft. Lauderdale, Fla., 1999—. Former chmn. Mercedes-Benz Nat. Dealer Coun. Recipient All-Star Dealer award Sports Illustrated, 1990; mem. automotive execs. Dream Team, Automotive News, 2 times; recognized mem. of Mktg. 100, Advt. Age, 4 times; named to Automobile Hall of Fame, 2003; named Automotive Industry Leader of Yr., 2003. Office: AutoNation Inc 110 SE 6th St Fort Lauderdale FL 33301-5000*

JACKSON, MICHAEL JOSEPH, musician; b. Gary, Ind., Aug. 29, 1958; s. Joseph Walter and Katherine Esther (Scruse) Jackson; m. Lisa Marie Presley, May 18, 1994 (div. Jan. 18, 1996); m. Debbie Rowe, Nov. 15, 1996 (div. Oct. 8, 1999); children: Prince Michael, Paris Michael Katherine, Prince Michael II. Student pvt. sch.; LHD (hon.), Fisk U., 1988. Lead singer Jackson-Five (later called The Jacksons), from 1969, recs. for Epic Records, performed at Queen Elizabeth's Silver Jubilee, May 1977; actor: (films) The Wiz, 1978, Moonwalker, 1988, Dangerous the short film, 1993, Men in Black II, 2002; (TV series) The Jacksons, 1976—77; albums with Jackson-Five include Diana Ross Presents the Jackson Five, 1969, ABC, Jackson Five Christmas Album, Third Album, 1970, Goin' Back to Indiana, Greatest Hits, Maybe Tomorrow, 1971, Looking Through the Windows, 1972, Farewell My Summer, Get it Together, Skywriter, 1973, Dancing Machine, 1974, Moving Violation, 1975, Joyful Jukebox Music, 1976, Boogie, 1980, albums with The Jacksons include The Jacksons, 1976, Goin' Places, 1977, Destiny, 1978, Triumph, 1980, The Jacksons Live, 1981, Victory, 1984; musician: (albums) Got To Be There, Ben, 1972, Music and Me, 1973, Forever Michael, The Best of Michael Jackson, 1975, Off the Wall, 1979, Thriller, 1982 (Grammy Award for Best Male Pop Vocal Performance, 1983, Grammy Award for Album of the Yr., 1983, Grammy Award for Best Video Album, 1984), Bad, 1987, Dangerous, 1991, Anthology, 1995, HIStory: Past, Present and Future, Book 1, 1995, Blood on the Dance Floor: HIStory in the Mix, 1997, The Best of Michael Jackson, 2000, HIStory: Greatest Hits, Vol. 1, 2001, Invincible, 2001, Michael Jackson: The Ultimate Collection, 2004; narrator E.T.: The Extra Terrestrial storybook, 1982; author: (autobiography) Moonwalk, 1988, Dancing the Dream Poems and Reflections, 1992; performer: (Sporting Event) Super Bowl XXVII Halftime show, 1993, (TV Special) Michael Jackson: 30th Anniversary TV Special, 2001. Founder Heal the World Found., 1992—2002. Recipient Grammy Award for Best R&B Vocal Performance (Don't Stop 'til You Get Enough), 1979, w/ Quincy Jones, Grammy Award for Producer of the Yr. (Non-Classical), 1983, Grammy Award for Best Recording for Children (E.T. The Extra-Terrestrial), 1983, Grammy Award for Best Rhythm & Blues Song (Billie Jean), 1983, Grammy Award for Best Male R&B Vocal Performance (Billie Jean), 1983, Grammy Award for Best Male Rock Vocal Performance (Beat It), 1983, Grammy Award for Record of the Yr. (Beat It), 1983, w/ Lionel Richie, Grammy Award for Song of the Yr. (We Are The World), 1985, Grammy Award for Best Music Video (Leave Me Alone), 1989, w/ Janet Jackson, Grammy Award for Best Music Video (Scream), 1995, w/ Janet Jackson, MTV Video Music Award for Best Dance Video (Scream), 1995, w/ Janet Jackson, MTV Video Music Award for Best Art Direction (Scream), 1995, w/ Janet Jackson, MTV Video Music Award for Best Choreography (Scream), 1995, Star on Hollywood Walk of Fame, 1984, MTV Vanguard Award, 1988, MTV Movie Award for Best Movie Song (Will You Be There), 1994, Best Selling Male Pop Artist of the Millennium award, World Music Awards, 2000, numerous other awards. Achievements include record for most Grammys won in one year with 8 in 1983; inducted into the Rock and Roll Hall of Fame, mem. Jackson 5, 1997, solo artist, 2001; record for best selling album of all-time (Thriller); record for the three best selling albums of all-time, (Thriller, Dangerous, Bad); brother of Janet, LaToya, Randy, Jermaine, Tito, Marlon, and Jackie; owner 2700-acre Neverland Ranch, Calif.

JACKSON, MICHAEL L., wholesale distribution executive; B in mgmt., Univ. Wis. With Supervalu Inc., Eden Prairie, Minn., 1979—, pres. NW Region, 1995—99, sr. v.p. ops., retail food cos., 1999—2001, exec. v.p., pres. distribution food cos., 2001—05, pres., COO, 2005—. Mem. wholesale adv. bd. Food Mktg. Inst.; bd. dir., mem. exec. com. Nat. Grocers Assn.; bd. dir. IGA. Bd. dir. Metro. Mpls. YMCA. Office: Supervalu Inc 11840 Valley View Rd Eden Prairie MN 55344 Mailing: Supervalu Inc PO Box 990 Minneapolis MN 55440*

JACKSON, MICHAEL LYNN, civil and structural engineer, sales executive; b. Birmingham, Ala., Mar. 27, 1952; s. Marce L. and Mary Joyce (Bean) Ballinger J.; m. Joyce Hay Land, Mar. 30, 1974 (div.); children: William Blake, Jeffrey Craig; m. Phyllis Carol Wood, Sept. 15, 1989; children: Lance, Kendall, Brett. BSCE, Auburn U., 1974; postgrad., U. Houston, 1977. Registered profl. engr., Tex. Structural engr. fed. govt. mktg. Fluor Engrs., Inc., Houston, 1974-81, prin. project engr., 1981-84; pres. exch. exec. U.S. Govt., Washington, 1983-84; prin. project engr. Fluor Engrs., Inc., Houston, 1984-85; indsl. cons. Houston Area Rsch. Ctr., The Woodlands, Tex., 1984-85, govt. sales rep., 1986-90, project dir., 1990-96; sr. project mgr. Bechtel Corp., 1996—. Tech. cons. graphic design aids for structural systems. Elected sch. bd. trustee Alief ISD, 1986—. Mem. Chi Epsilon. Republican. Methodist. Avocations: personal computing, photography, woodworking. Home: 13122 Dogwood Blossom Trl Houston TX 77065-3322 Office: Bechtel Corp 3000 Post Oak Blvd Houston TX 77056-6580

JACKSON, MICHAEL P., federal agency administrator, former engineering company executive; married; 1 child. BA, U. Houston; PhD in Govt. with distinction, Georgetown U., 1985. Reported to sec. edn. Pres. Reagan adminstrn.; spl. asst. to Pres. George H.W. Bush for cabinet liaison The White House; COO IMS transp. sys. and svcs. Lockheed Martin; sr. v.p., counselor to pres. Am. Trucking Assn., 1993—97; chief of staff to sec. US Dept. Transp., Washington, 1992—93, dep. sec., 2001—03; sr. v.p. AECOM Tech. Corp., Fairfax, Va., 2004—05; dep. sec. US Dept. Homeland Security, Washington, 2005—. Rschr. Am. Enterprise Inst.; instr. polit. sci. U. Ga., Georgetown U. Republican. Office: US Dept Homeland Security 3801 Nebraska Ave Washington DC 20528

JACKSON, MIKE, finance company executive; b. NYC, July 6, 1972; s. Michael Dean Hopkins and Donna Marie Field, Phillip Field (Stepfather); life ptnr. Natalie Mackiel. BA in Polit. Sci., Yale U., New Haven, 1994. Analyst mortgage and asset capital Prudential Securities, NYC, 1994—98; assoc. asset fin. JP Morgan Securities, NYC, 1998—2001; assoc. dir. West LB AG, NYC, 2001—05; dir. residential MBS and ABS Hyperion Brookfield Asset Mgmt., NYC, 2005—. Chair Bronx Acad. Letters, NYC, 2002—06; trustee, alumni coun. pres. Williston Northampton Sch., Easthampton, Mass., 2003—06; bd. mem. Harlem Youth Devel. Found., NYC, 1997—2000. Office: Hyperion Brookfield Asset Management 3 World Financial Center 200 Vesey St New York NY 10281-1010 Home Phone: 212-787-2686; Office Phone: 212-549-8409. Personal E-mail: mikejackson@bronxletters.org.

JACKSON, MILES MERRILL, retired university dean; b. Richmond, Va., Apr. 28, 1929; s. Miles Merrill and Thelma Eugertha (Manning) J.; m. Bernice Olivia Roane, Jan. 7, 1954; children: Miles Merrill III, Marsha, Muriel, Melia. BA in English, Va. Union U., 1955; MS, Drexel U., 1956; postgrad., Ind. U., 1961-64; PhD, Syracuse U., 1974. Br. libr. Free Libr., 1955-58; acting libr. C.P. Huntington Meml. Libr., Hampton (Va.) U., 1958-59, libr., 1959-62, asst. prof. libr. sci., 1958-62; territorial libr. Am. Samoa, 1962-64; chief libr. Trevor Arnett Libr., Atlanta U., 1964-69; also lectr. Sch. Libr. Sci.; assoc. prof. State U. N.Y., Geneseo, 1969-75; prof. U. Hawaii, 1975—, dean, 1983-95, chmn. interdisciplinary program in communication and info. scis., 1985-89; cons. in field, 1995—. Fulbright lectr. U. Tehran, Iran, 1968-69; libr., cons. Fiji, Samoa, Papua New Guinea, Micronesia, USIA India, 1993, Pakistan, 1985, Nat. Libr. Edn., 1996, Govt. Am. Samoa, 1997, Hawaii Pub. Libr. Found., 1986-2000; chmn. bd. Hawaii Lit., Inc., 1985-88; commr. Hawaii Libr. Commn., 1996-97. Editor: A Bibliography of Materials on Negro History and Culture for Young People, 1968, Comparative and International Librarianship, 1971, International Handbook of Contemporary Developments in Librarianship, 1981, Pacific Island Studies: Review of the Literature, 1986, Linkages Over Space and Time, 1993, And They Came: A Brief History of Blacks in Hawaii, 2001, They Followed the Trade Winds: African Americans in Hawaii, 2005; mem. editl. bd. Internat. Jour. Info. Mgmt., Internat. Libr. Rev., 1982-87; founder, editor Pacific Info. and Libr. Svcs. Newsletter; columnist Mahogeny: Covering People of Color, 1999—; contbr. articles to profl. jours.; book reviewer. Bd. dirs. Cen. YMCA, 1986-94, Hawaii Gov.'s Coun. on Literacy, 1986-96, Hawaii ACLU, 1990-94, office holder in Dem. party of Hawaii, 1992—. With USNR, 1946-48. Recipient Outstanding Alumnus award Va. Union U., 1987; Rsch. grantee Am. Philos. Soc., 1966; Coun. on Libr. Resources fellow, 1970, vis. fellow Republic of China, 1986; Harold Lancour fgn. travel awardee Beta Phi Mu, 1976 Mem. ALA (chmn. Internat. Rels. Roundtable 1988-89), Assn. for Libr. and Info. Sci. Edn. (pres. 1989-90), Coll. Lang. Assn. (hon. mention poetry 1954, 2d prize award short story 1955) Democrat. Business E-Mail: jackson@hawaii.edu.

JACKSON, NAGLE, stage director, playwright; b. Seattle, Apr. 28, 1936; s. Paul Joseph and Gertrude (Dunn) J.; m. Sandra L. Suter, Sept. 15, 1963; children: Rebecca J., Hillary J. BA, Whitman Coll., 1958, LittD (hon.), 1995. Resident dir. Am. Conservatory Theatre, San Francisco, 1967-70; artistic dir. Milw. Repertory Theatre, 1970-76, McCarter Theatre, Princeton, NJ, 1979-90; stage dir. N.J. Opera Festival, Lawrenceville, 1985-91; currently assoc. artist Denver Center Theatre Co., Denver; prin. dir. Santa Fe Shakespeare Co. Guest dir. Gorky Theatre, Leningrad, 1988, Trøndelag Teatre, Trondheim, Norway, 1990. Playwright: At This Evening's Performance, 1985, Opera Comique, 1988, They Shoot Horses, Don't They?-The Musical (book and lyrics), 1992, This Day and Age, 1994, The Quick-Change Room, 1995, Moliere Plays Paris, 1996, A Hotel on Marvin Gardens, 2002, Taking Leave, 2002. Fulbright fellow, Paris, 1958; recipient Prize Onassis Found. Internat. Playwrights Competition for "The Elevation of Thieves", 1997. Mem. Soc. Stage Dirs. & Choreographers, The Dramatists Guild. Personal E-mail: naglejackson@att.net.

JACKSON, NONA ARMOUR, writer, illustrator; b. Denison, Tex., Sept. 22, 1939; d. Thomas Jefferson and Novella Mae (Binion) A.; m. R.L. Jackson, Jr., Apr. 16, 1966. Supr., illustrator Diaper Jeans, Inc., Denison, 1959-62; clothing pattern maker, designer Srader's Sportswear, Denison, 1963-65; receptionist Glad Tidings Ch., Sherman, Tex., 1981-84, pastor elderly ministry, 1984-87; author Pottsboro, Tex., 1987—. Spkr. in field. Author, illustrator, photographer: The Cotton Mill! Can Anything Good Come from There? Vol. I-IX, 1995, Industries 1873-1981, Vol. I, 1995, Churches 1906-1991, vol. II 1995, Schools 1890-1964, vol. III, 1995, Golden Rule Independent School Extra-Curricular Activities, vol. IV, 1995, Cotton Mill Community, vol. V, 1995, The People: A Biography in Three Volumes, Vols. VI-VIII, 1995, Associates, Vol. IX, Index, Vols. VI-IX, 1995, Vol. X, 2001, Addenda, 1998-2001; author, illustrator: Pioneers of North West Grayson County, Texas Mid to Late 19th Century and Early 20th Century: Delaware Bend, Red Branch/Prairie Valley, Rock Creek with Some Dexter, Texas Data, 1996, Pioneers of Central Grayson County, Texas Mid to Late 19th Century and Early 20th Century: Cherrymound and Ambrose, 1996, Pioneers of Central Grayson County, Texas Mid to Late 19th Century and Early 20th Century: Cedar Community, 1996, Pioneers of South East Grayson County, Texas Mid to Late, 19th Century and Early 20th Century: Pilot Grove, 1996, Series 1 (4000 B.C.-A.D. 1607) The Overseas Connection, Big Oaks from Little Trees Grow, vols. I-III, 2000, Series 2 (A.D. 1607-A.D. 1837) Immigrant & Colonial Ancestors, vols. IV-VIII, 2000, Series 3 (A.D. 1937-A.D. 1987) A Grayson County, Texas Epic-One Hundred and Fifty Years, vols. IX-XV, 2000, Series 4 (A.D. 1855-A.D. 1991), Twentieth Century-Big Oaks-Precious Memories, vols. XVI-XVII, 2000, Series 5-10 The Collective Works of Nona Jackson vols. XVIII-XXXIX, 2000, Series 11, Jesus or Die!, Father, Son & Holy Ghost, Obedience, and Walking With God, vols. XL-XLII, 2000, Yummy, Yummy, Sweets for the Tummy, 2002, Pass the Taters Please, 2002, Me, Myself & I, 2002, My Split Apart, vol. 59, 2002, The Final Chapter-Part I, The Cotton Mill! Can Anything Good Come From There?, 2002, Addenda-Part II, Nona's Family Update: The Last Report, vol. 60, 2002, River of Death: Don't Swim in Polluted Water!, 2005, Revelation/Genesis, 7 vols., 2007; contbr. articles and photographs to publs. Sec., treas., young people's supt. Sunnyside Bapt. Ch., Denison, 1963-65; Sunday sch. tchr. Glad Tidings Ch., Sherman, 1978-83; tour guide, hostess Grayson County Frontier Village, Inc., Denison, 1978-97; active Adopt a Nursing Home, Tex. Dept. Human Resources, 1999— Mem. Grayson County Humane Soc., Nat. Audubon Soc., Nat. Trust Hist. Preservation, Libr. Congress Assoc. (charter). Republican. Avocations: guitar, art, nature, theology, genealogy. Home: 109 Houston St Unit 2 Pottsboro TX 75076-3031

JACKSON, O'SHEA See ICE CUBE

JACKSON, PATRICK JOSEPH, real estate company officer; b. Minn., Mar. 31, 1942; s. Paul Arthur and Lucille Margaret (Cummings) J.; m. Barbara Ann Simpson, July 19, 1964 (div. Apr. 1980); children: Laura Kathleen, Katherine Lucille; m. Shirley Ann Wellman, Sept. 12, 1982 (div. Oct. 1998); m. Kath Jo Holm, Sept. 9, 2001; 1 child, Liza Ann Holm. BS, Portland State U., 1968. Bank loan officer First Nat. Bank of Oreg., Portland, 1964-68; credit mgr. Meier & Frank Corp., Portland, 1968-70; agt., mgr. Aetna Life, San Jose, Calif., 1970-75; dist. mgr. Calif. Casualty, San Jose, 1975-78; gen. agt. Great So. Life, San Jose, 1978-82; account agt., agy. owner Allstate Ins., San Jose, 1982—2001; assoc. broker Home Realty, 2001—; pres. Delta Direct Enterprises, Sequim, Wash., 2001—. Instr. Santa Clara (Calif.) U., 1974-76. Author: (monograph) The Affairs of, 1978; newspaper columnist, 1978-04. Mem. ins. subcom. Calif. State Senate, 1978; officer Los Gatos (Calif.) Police Res., 1970-78, treas., 1974-78; mem. Sch. Site Coun., Saratoga, Calif., 1978-80; mem. City Coun., Discovery Bay, Calif., 1991-95, mayor, 1993-94; mem. port commn. Port Angeles, Wash., 2002-04. Named Man of Yr., Los Gatos Youth Unltd., 1978. Mem. San Jose Life Underwriters (bd. dirs. 1974-76), No. Calif. Tollycraft Assn. (sec. 1995-97), Sequim Bay Yacht Club, Puget Sound Anglers, Jefferson County Sportsman Club. Republican. Lutheran. Avocations: boating, fishing, shooting, reading. Office: Delta Direct Enterprises 325 E Washington St #106 Sequim WA 98382 Business E-Mail: pjackson@olypen.com.

JACKSON, PETER, film director; b. Pukerua Bay, New Zealand, Oct. 31, 1961; s. Bill and Joan Jackson; m. Frances Walsh, 1987; 2 children. Grad. (hon.), Massey U., 2001. Owner WingNut Films, Weta Ltd., Three Foot Six, Nat. Film Unit, New Zealand, 1998—. Dir., actor (films) The Valley, 1976, dir., prodr., writer, actor Bad Taste, 1987, The Frighteners, 1996, Lord of the Rings: The Fellowship of the Ring, 2001 (Nat. Bd. Rev. award for spl. achievement, 2001, Southea. Film Critics Assn. award best dir., best adapted screenplay, 2001, Las Vegas Film Critics Soc. award best dir., 2001, Fla. Film Critics Cir. award best dir., 2001, Am. Film Inst. award movie of yr., 2001, Golden Satellite award best motion picture, 2001, BAFTA award best film, David Lean award best achievement in direction, 2002), Lord of the Rings: The Two Towers, 2002 (Las Vegas Film Critics award best dir., 2002, Online Film Critics Soc. award best dir., 2002, Dallas-Ft. Worth Film Critics award best dir., 2002), Lord of the Rings: The Return of the King, 2003 (Glođen Globe for best dramatic film, 2004, Golden Globe for best dir., 2004, best dir. for 2003, Dir.'s Guild of Am., 2004, Academy Award for best director, 2004, Academy Award for best adapted screenplay, 2004, Academy Award for best picture, 2004), King Kong, 2005, dir., prodr., writer Meet the Feebles, 1989, dir., writer, actor Braindead, 1992, dir., co-prodr., co-writer Heavenly Creatures, 1994, dir., exec. prodr., writer Forgotten Silver, 1995, prodr., writer (films) Jack Brown Genius, 1994, co-prodr. Valley of the Stereos, 1992, exec. prodr., actor The Long and Short of It, 2003, co-exec. prodr. (TV series) Ship to Shore, 1993—94. Named Man of Yr., Australian Empire mag., 2003; named one of 50 Most Powerful People in Hollywood, Premiere mag., 2003—06; recipient Golden Plate award, Acad. Achievement, 2006. Mem.: New Zealand Order of Merit. Office: WingNut Films Ltd PO Box 15 208 Miramar Wellington New Zealand also: Nat Film Unit 23 Frederick St Wellington New Zealand*

JACKSON, PHILIP DOUGLAS, professional basketball coach; b. Deer Lodge, Mont., Sept. 17, 1945; m. June; 5 children. Grad., U. ND, 1967. Player NY Knicks, 1967-78, NJ Nets, 1978-80, asst. coach, 1980-82; head coach Continental Basketball Assn. Albany Patroons, 1982-87; asst. coach Chgo. Bulls, 1987-89, head coach, 1989-98, LA Lakers, 1999—2004, 2005—. Co-author (with Hugh Delehanty): Sacred Hoops: Spiritual Lessons of a Hardwood Warrior, 1996; co-author: (with Charley Rosen) More Than A Game, 2002; author: The Last Season: A Team in Search of Its Soul, 2004. Named NBA Coach of Yr., 1996; named one of NBA Ten Greatest Coaches, 1997; named to Naismith Meml. Basketball Hall of Fame, 2007. Achievements include winning NBA Championships as a member of the Knicks, 1970, 73; led the Bulls to NBA Championships as head coach, 1991, 92, 93, 96, 97, 98; led the Lakers to NBA Championships as head coach, 2000, 01, 02; best winning percentage as an NBA head coach in regular season and playoffs. Office: LA Lakers Staples Ctr 1111 S Figueroa St Los Angeles CA 90015*

JACKSON, PHILLIP ELLIS, marketing executive, writer; b. Kansas City, Mo., June 4, 1952; s. Phillip Anthony and Lois Irene (Seward) J.; m. Dawn Mutolo Jackson, Aug. 9, 1975; 1 child, Emily Mutolo. AA, Mohawk Valley C.C., 1972; BA magna cum laude in Liberal Arts, SUNY, Albany, 1974; MA in Internat. Rels., SUNY, 1975; PhD in Polit. Sci., U. Chgo., 1981. Speech writer; speech writer, issue com. chmn. Steve Bartlett Congl. Campaign, 1982; sr. v.p. pub. affairs Greater Dallas C. of C., 1982-93; exec. dir. Dallas United, 1984-93; dir. Tex. office Cassidy & Assocs., Dallas, 1993-95; v.p. Signal Sites, Dallas, 1995—. Author fiction. Cons. Dallas Charter Rev. Com., 1989; dir. City of Dallas, Dallas C. of C. N.Am. Free Trade Agreement Labor Secretariat Task Force, 1991-93. Recipient Citizens award Chgo. Police Dept., 1978, Presdl. citations Pvt. Sector Initiatives, 1985, 86, 89. Office: 3068 E Sunset Rd Ste 1 Las Vegas NV 89120

JACKSON, RANDY, music producer, television personality, musician; b. Baton Rouge, Feb. 29, 1956; s. Herman and Julia Jackson; m. Elizabeth Jackson (div. 1990); 1 child, Taylor; m. Erika Riker, 1995; children: Zoe, Jordan. BA in Music, So. U., 1979. Bass player Journey, 1983—87; v.p. A&R Columbia Records; sr. v.p. A&R MCA Records. Talent judge (TV series) American Idol, 2002—; prodr.: (albums) Truth About Cats & Dogs soundtrack, 1996, First Wives Club soundtrack, 1996, (various artists) Eddie Money, Trisha Covington, Richard Marx, Rahsaan Patterson, Gladys Knight, Jesse Powell, many others; musician (bass player): (instrn. video) Randy Jackson: Mastering the Groove, 1992, albums, Journey, Patti LaBelle, Michael Bolton, Bon Jovi, Mariah Carey, Tracy Chapman, Cher, Kelly Clarkson, Celine Deon, Bob Dylan, Aretha Franklin, Keeny G, Herbie Hancock, Whitney Houston, Billy Idol, Elton John, Madonna, others; co-writer: songs My Saving Grace (from Mariah Carey album "Charmbracelet", 2003, Irresistible (from Mariah Carey album "Charmbracelet", 2003. Home: 700 N San Vicente Blvd Ste G910 West Hollywood CA 90069-5061

JACKSON, RAYMOND A., federal judge; b. 1949; BA, Norfolk State U., 1970; JD, U. Va., 1973. Capt. U.S. Army JAGC, 1973-77; asst. U.S. atty. Ea. Dist. Va., Norfolk, 1977-93, chief criminal divsn., civil divsn., exec. asst.; judge U.S. Dist. Ct. (ea. dist.) Va., Norfolk, 1993—. Mem. jud. conf. U.S. Ct. Appeals (4th cir.); adj. faculty Marshall Wythe Sch. of Law, Coll. of William and Mary, 1978—93; mem. com. on admistrn. Magistrate Judges Sys., 1998—2004. Active Day Care and Child Devel. Ctr., Tidewater, 1980—86; mem. exec. com. Va. State Bar, 1991—93; bd. dirs. Peninsula Legal Aid Ctr., 1977. Col. Res. USAR, ret. 1998. Fellow: Va. Law Found.; mem.: Am. Inn Ct. (Hoffman-l'Anson chpt. pres. 2000—02), South Hampton Rds. Bar Assn., Norfolk-Portsmouth Bar Assn., Old Dominion Bar Assn. (pres. 1984—86), U.S. Dist. Judges Assn. Office: 600 Granby St Norfolk VA 23510-1915

JACKSON, RAYMOND CARL, cytogeneticist; b. Medora, Ind., May 7, 1928; s. Thornton Comadore and Flossie Oliva (Booker) J.; m. T. June Snyder, Oct. 24, 1947; children: Jeffrey Wayne, Rebecca June. AB, Ind. U., 1952, AM, 1953; PhD, Purdue U., 1955. Instr. to asst. prof. U. N.Mex., Albuquerque, 1955-58; asst. prof. of Botany U. Kans., Lawrence, 1958-60, assoc. prof. of Botany, 1961-64, prof. of Botany, 1964-71, prof. and chmn. Botany, 1969-71; prof. and chmn. biol. scis. Tex. Tech U., Lubbock, 1971-78, Horn prof. of Biol. Scis., 1990—. Chmn. interdepartmental PhD Program in Genetics, U. Kans., chmn. dept. Botany, U. Kans., 1969-71; speaker and presenter in field. Contbr. numerous articles to profl. jours. Staff sgt. USAF, 1946-49. Mem. Genetics Soc. Am., Genetics Soc. of Can., Soc. for the Study of Evolution, Botanical Soc. of Am. (BSA Merit award 1992), Am. Soc. Plant Taxonomists, Internat. Orgn. of Plant Biosystematists, Delta Phi Alpha, Sigma Xi, Phi Sigma. Republican. Achievements include research in pairing control genes and their comparative effects at the diploid and polyploid levels; genetics, cytogenetics, and gametic selection in Haplopappus gracilis, cytogenetics of diploid Triticum species. Home: 7922A Aberdeen Ave Lubbock TX 79424-2808 Office: Dept Biol Scis Tex Tech Univ Lubbock TX 79409 Fax: 806-742-2963.

JACKSON, RAYMOND SIDNEY, JR., lawyer; b. Bklyn., Sept. 17, 1938; s. Raymond Sidney and Mary Frost (McInerney) Van Vranken. BA, William Coll., 1960; JD, Harvard U., 1966. Bar: N.Y. 1967, U.S. Dist. Ct. (so. and ea. dists.) N.Y. 1969, U.S. Ct. Appeals (2d cir.) 1969. Assoc. Thacher, Proffitt & Wood, NYC, 1966-76, ptnr., 1976-94, of counsel, 1994—. Mem. South St. Seaport Mus., N.Y.C., 1974—, Gramercy Neighborhood Assocs., N.Y.C., 1974—, Nat. Assn. Coll. and Univ. Attys., 1972. Mem. ABA (vice chmn. admiralty and maritime law com. sect. of tort and ins. practice 1990-92), N.Y. State Bar Assn. (admiralty and maritime com. internat. law and practice sect. 1989-94), Assn. Bar City N.Y. (admiralty com. 1984-85, 88-91), Maritime Law Assn. U.S. (com. on practice and procedure 1976-91). E-mail: rsjacksonj@aol.com.

JACKSON, REGGIE (REGINALD MARTINEZ JACKSON, MR. OCTOBER), retired professional baseball player; b. Wyncote, Pa., May 18, 1946; s. Martinez Jackson; m. Juanita Campos (div.). Student, Ariz. State U. Outfielder Oakland Athletics (formerly Kans. City Athletics), 1967-75, Balt. Orioles, 1976, NY Yankees, 1977-81; outfielder, designated hitter Calif. Angels, 1982-86, Oakland Athletics, 1987, adv., 1988-93; spl.

adv. to prin. owner N.Y. Yankees, 1993—. Co-author: (with Bill Libby) Reggie, 1975, (with Joel Cohen) Inside Hitting, 1975; actor (films) The Naked Gun: From the Files of Police Squad!, 1988, Richie Rich, 1994, Bad Day on the Block, 1997, BASEketball, 1998, Summer of Sam, 1999, The Benchwarmers, 2006; (TV appearances) The Love Boat, 1979, Diff'rent Strokes, 1979, Archie Bunker's Place, 1982, The Jeffersons, 1985, Mr. Belvedere, 1989, MacGyver, 1990, Blossom, 1991, Suddenly Susan, 1999, Malcolm in the Middle, 2004 Named Am. League Most Valuable Player Am., 1973, The Sporting News Major League Player of Year, 1973, World Series Most Valuable Player, 1973, 1977; Named to Baseball Hall of Fame, 1993, Am. League All-Star Team, 1969, 71-75, 77-82, 84; recipient Am. League Babe Ruth award, 1977, Legend award, Bronx C. of C., 2006 The only non-pitcher to win World Series Most Valuable Player honors twice; hit 3 homeruns in Game 6 of the 1977 World Series; 563 career homeruns. Office: NY Yankees Yankee Stadium 161st St and River Ave Bronx NY 10451*

JACKSON, REGINALD SHERMAN, JR., lawyer, educator; b. Oct. 8, 1946; s. Reginald Sherman and Frances (Holland) J.; m. Joanne Marie Warren, Aug. 31, 1968; children: Reginald Sherman III, Michael W., Adam H. BA, Ohio State U., 1968, JD, 1971. Bar: Ohio 1971, U.S. Supreme Ct. 1976; cert. civil trial advocate Nat. Bd. Trial Advocacy. Mem. Fuller, Henry, Hodge Snyder, Toledo, 1971-76; asst. U.S. atty. no. dist. Ohio U.S. Dept. Justice, 1976-78; ptnr. Connelly, Jackson & Collier, Toledo, 1978—. Adj. prof. trial practice U. Toledo Coll. Law, 1976-89. Fellow Am. Bar Found., Ohio State Bar Found. (trustee 1998—, pres. elect 2007—), Toledo Bar Found. (pres. 1993-98); mem. ABA (ho. of dels. 1996-99, 2001—, exec. com. nat. caucus state bars, litig. sect.), Am. Bd. Trial Advocates, Ohio State Bar Assn. (pres. 2000-01), Toledo Bar Assn. (pres. 1989-90), Toledo Golf Hall of Fame (founder), Toledo Country Club (trustee 1981-93, pres. 1991-93), Rotary (trustee 1994-96, 1st v.p.). Home: 2907 River Rd Maumee OH 43537-3740 Office: Connelly Jackson & Collier 405 Madison Ave Ste 1600 Toledo OH 43604-1226 Home Phone: 419-893-1472; Office Phone: 419-243-2100. Business E-Mail: rjackson@cjc-law.com.

JACKSON, REGINALD W., lawyer; b. Phila., Aug. 24, 1955; BA, Cornell U., 1977; JD, U. Pa., 1980. Bar: OH 1980, US Dist. Ct. (no. and so. dists.), US Ct. Appeals (6th cir.). Mem. Vorys, Sater, Seymour and Pease, Columbus, Ohio; pres. Am. Bankruptcy Inst., 2007—. Exec. editor ABI Jour.; contbr. articles to profl. jours. Named one of Am.'s Top Black Lawyers, Black Enterprise Mag., 2003. Mem. ABA (bus. law com.), Columbus Bar Assn. (chmn. bankruptcy law com. 1990-92), Am. Bankruptcy Inst. (bd. trustees, exec. com. bd., chair environ. subcommittee), Am. Coll. Bankruptcy, OH State Bar Found. (pres. 2001), OH State Bar Assn. (dist. 7 rep., bd. govs., coun. dels. 2002-04). Office: Vorys Sater Seymour and Pease PO Box 1008 52 E Gay St Columbus OH 43215-3161

JACKSON, RICHARD JOSEPH, epidemiologist, educator, pediatrician, preventive medicine physician; b. Newark, Oct. 23, 1945; s. Robert Joseph Jackson and Dorothy C. (Devine) Connolly; m. Joan M. Guilford, June 21, 1975; children: Brendan, Devin, Galen. AB in Biology, St. Peter's Coll., Jersey City, 1969; M in Med. Sci., Rutgers U., 1971; MD, U. Calif. San Francisco, San Francisco, 1973; MPH in Epidemiology, U. Calif. Berkeley, Berkeley, 1979. Diplomate Am. Bd. Pediatrics, Am. Bd. Preventive Medicine; lic. physician, Calif. Intern, resident U. Calif., San Francisco, 1973-74, 77-78, resident San Francisco Gen. Hosp., 1974-75; officer Epidemic Intelligence Svc. U.S. Pub. Health Svc., Albany, N.Y., 1975-77; spl. epidemiologist World Health Orgn., Bihar State, India, 1976; med. officer Epidemiol. Studies Sect. Calif. State Dept. Health Svcs., Berkeley, 1979-88, acting chief Office Environ. Health Aassessment Sacramento, 1988-90, chief hazard identification and risk assessment br. Berkeley, 1990-91; chief hazard identification and risk assessment br. office environ. health hazard assessment Calif. EPA, Berkeley, 1991-92; chief divsn. communicable disease control Calif. State Dept. Health Svcs., 1992-94; dir. Nat. Ctr. Environ. Health, Ctrs. Disease Control and Prevention, Atlanta, 1994—2003; sr. advisor to dir. Ctr. Disease Control, Atlanta, 2003—04; state pub. health officer State of Calif., Sacremento, 2004—. Adj. lectr. U. Calif. San Francisco, 1980—, asst. clin. prof., 1986—; adj. prof. Emory U. Rollins Sch. Pub. Health, 1998—. Lt. comdr. USPHS, 1975-77. Office: Ca Dept Of Health Services PO Box 997413 Sacramento CA 95899-7413 Home Phone: 925-837-7890. E-mail: RJJackson@cdc.gov, rjackso6@dhs.ca.gov.

JACKSON, RICHARD MONTGOMERY, air transportation executive; b. Jacksonville, Fla., Dec. 9, 1920; s. William Kenneth and Katharine (Mitchell) J.; m. Martha Eustis Turner, Sept. 12, 1942; children: Richard Montgomery, Susanne (Mrs. Jeffrey Miller), William Mitchell. B.Sc., Harvard, 1942. With Am. Airlines, Inc., 1945-58; asso. L.S. Rockefeller, 1958-60; with Seaboard World Airlines, Inc., Jamaica, NY, 1960-80, pres., chmn. bd., 1960-80; chmn. exec. com. Flying Tiger Line, Jamaica, 1980-81. Bd. govs., chmn. The Internat. Air Cargo Assn. Trustee Village of Lloyd Harbor, NY, 1960-68; pres. Lloyd Harbor Sch. Bd., 1957-58; trustee, pres. African Wildlife Found.; bd. govs. Huntington (NY) Hosp., 1960-74. Lt. cmmdr. USNR, WWII. Mem.: Piping Rock (Locust Valley, NY); Jupiter Island (Hobe Sound, Fla.); Wings (NYC); Cold Spring Harbor Beach Club (NY). Home: 84 Mallard Ln Greenport NY 11944-3106

JACKSON, ROBERT HOWARD, food company executive, scientist; b. Pitts., Jan. 3, 1932; s. Robert and Anna J.; m. Betty Jean Jackson, June 15, 1957; 1 child, Jay Michael. BS, Penn. State Univ., 1953, MS, 1955; PhD, Mich. State Univ., 1959. Asst. prof. Univ. Mass., Amherst, 1955-57; group leader R.J. Reynolds Industries, Winston-Salem, N.C., 1961-64; tech. dir. Lehigh Valley Dairies, Allentown, Pa., 1964-68; v.p. ops. Marriott Corp., Washington, 1968-79; pres.,COO Marshall Foods, Inc., Marshall, Minn., 1979-82; pres., CEO Nutrisearch Co., Cin., 1982-85; CEO Bioproducts Internat., Inc., Sarasota, Fla., 1985—. Bd. dirs. IDEP, LLC, Chgo., JJ Group, Inc., Chgo.; mem. adv. bd. Einstein Medical, Inc., LaJolla, Calif., 1995-96; dir. bus. devel. Quest Internat. (Unilever), Sydney, Australia, 1991-94. Contbr. articles to profl. jours. With U.S. Army, 1959-61. Mem. Inst. of Food Tech., Soc. Sigma Xi, Food Industry Assocs., Am. Men of Sci. Republican. Episcopalian. Avocations: physical fitness, golf, fishing, bass violinist. E-mail: jubilance@att.net.

JACKSON, ROBERT LEE, mechanical engineer, educator; BS in Mech. Engring., Ga. Inst. Tech., Atlanta, 1994—98, MS in Mech. Engring., 2002, PhD in Mech. Engring., 2004. Engring. intern Raytheon E-Sys. Comm. Divsn., St. Petersburg, Fla., 1996; grad. rsch. asst. Ga. Inst. Tech., 1998—2004; asst. prof. Auburn U., Ala., 2004—. Contbr. scientific papers. Grantee Summer Inst. Surface Engring. & Coatings fellow, NSF, 2004, Rsch. grant, Taiho Kogyo Tribology Rsch. Found., 2006, Summer Inst. Sci. Fundamentals Nano-and Bio-Mechanics Materials fellow, NSF, 2006. Mem.: ASME (tribology divsn. mem. com.), Soc. Tribologists & Lubrication Engrs. (surface engring. tech. com. chair), Gamma Beta Phi, Pi Tau Sigma. Achievements include research in elastoplastic contact mechanics, hydrodynamic lubrication, rough surface contact, thrust washer bearings, thermal and electrical contact resistance. Avocations: swimming, poetry, sailing. Office: Auburn Univ Dept Mech Engring 270 Ross Hall Auburn University AL 36849-5341 Home Phone: 338-826-1349; Office Phone: 334-844-3340. Office Fax: 334-844-3307. Business E-Mail: robert.jackson@eng.auburn.edu.

JACKSON, ROBERT R., lawyer; b. Newark, 1945; BS in Civil Engring., MIT, 1966; JD, Yale U., 1969. Bar: NY 1971, US Dist. Ct. (so. & ea. dist.) NY, US Ct. Appeals (2d & fed. cir.), US Patent & Trademark Office. Assoc. mem. of patent staff Bell Telephone Laboratories.; ptnr. Ropes & Gray (Fish & Neave IP Grp.), NYC. Mem. ABA, Am. Intellectual Property Law Assn., NY Patent, Trademark and Copyright Law Assn., Assn. of Bar of City of NY, Chi Epsilon, Tau Beta Pi, NY Intellectual Property Law Assn., NY Law Inst. Office: Ropes & Gray (Fish & Neave IP Grp) 1211 Ave Of Americas New York NY 10036-8704 Office Phone: 212-596-9022. Office Fax: 646-728-2646. E-mail: robert.jackson@ropesgray.com.

JACKSON, ROBERT ROSCOE, education educator; b. Mather AFB, Rancho Cordova, Calif., Nov. 24, 1970; s. Jimmy Joe Jackson and Susan Florence Robertson; m. Carin Bernice Myers, Jan. 3, 1998; 1 child, William Robert. MEd, Tex. Christian U., 2001; MACE, MABS, Dallas Theol. Sem., 1997; BA in acctg., Cedarville U., 1993. Cert. std. tchr. elem. self contained grades 1-6 State Bd. Educator Cert. Tex., 2001, std. prin. grades EC-12 State Bd. Educator Cert. Tex., 2003, temp. prin. grades EC-12 State Bd. Educator Cert. Tex., 2003, ESL State Bd. Educator Cert. Tex., 2006, spl. edn. (supplemental) State Bd. Educator Cert. Tex., 2006, ednl. adminstrn. Tex. Christian U., 2003. Children's pastor intern Trinity Bapt. Ch., Dallas, 1994—94; instr. Dallas Theol. Sem. Ctr. for Bibl. Studies, 1995—95; field sales assoc., adminstrv. asst. Lifeway Christian Stores, Dallas and Richardson, 1996—98; adminstrv. asst. Holmes Murphy, Dallas, 1998—99, Internat. Solutions, Arlington, 1999—2000; self contained tchr. and dist. ACT tchr. Cockrell Hill Elem. Sch. DeSoto Ind. Sch. Dist., DeSoto, 2000—03; adminstrv. intern Amber Ter. Intermediate Sch. DeSoto Ind. Sch. Dist., 2003—05, math tchr., dept. head and dist. ACT tchr., 2003—05; ednl. mentor Tex. A&M U., Commerce, 2004—05; tchr. lang. arts, math and social studies grade 4 Golden Meadows Elem. Garland Ind. Sch. Dist., Garland, 2005—06; 5th grade self-contained tchr. Grand Prarie Ind. Sch. Dist., 2006—. Ednl. cons. Edn. Svc. Ctr. Region 10, Richardson, Tex., 2004; scope and sequence ednl. cons. Spl. Edn. Dept. DeSoto Ind. Sch. Dist., 2004—05; presenter at profl. confs. Conf. Advancement of Math Tchrs., 2005, Math-A-Rama, 2005, 6th Ann. Coll. Edn. Ednl. Rsch. Exch. U. North Tex., 2006. Author essays; contbr. scientific papers, articles to profl. jours. Edn. chair Lone Star Region NMRA, 2006—; bd. mem. Zula B. Wylie Libr., Cedar Hill, Tex., 1999—2001. Grantee Undoing Checkmate, DeSoto ISD Ednl. Found., 2004-2005, Royal Measurement with the Pharaohs, DeSoto ISD Edn. Found., 2004-2005, Jazzing Up Math Through Reading, 2004-2005, Flying High with Geometric Kites, 2004-2005, DeSoto We Have Lift off from Space Sta. Ctrl., 2004-2005, Sen. Royce West's One Community-One Child Parental Involvement Project Grant for PAT, Edn. Svc. Ctr. Region 10, 2003-2004, Exemplary Exemplars, DeSoto ISD Edn. Found., 2002-2003, Math Manipulatives, 2000-2001, Knights Reading Action, 2005—06; UNT Grad. Sch. Doctoral fellowship, U. North Tex., 2004-2005, Best SW scholarship, Bank of Am., 2004. Mem.: ASCD, Assn. Childhood Edn. Internat., Nat. Assn. Elem. Principals, Assn. Tex. Profl. Educators, Nat. Coun. Tchrs. Math., Nat. Coun. Tchrs. English, Nat. Coun. Social Studies, Tex. Assn. Supervision and Curriculum Devel. (mem. southwest Dallas County modular RR group), Cedarville U. Leadership Team, N.Am. Water Garden Soc., U.S. Chess Fedn., Md. and Pa. R.R. Preservation Soc., Nat. Model Railroader Assn. (mem. divsn. 3 Lone Star region), Md. and Pa. R.R. Preservation Soc., North Tex. Water Garden Soc., Southwest Dallas County Modular RR Group, Southwest Dallas County Train Group, Seguin Silver Knights Chess Club (co-founder), Soc. Descendants of the Schwenkfeldian Exiles (life), Golden Hawk Stock Market Club (founder), Clan Donnachaidh Soc. Scotland (life), Golden Hawk Regiment Chess Club (founder), Phi Kappa Phi, Kappa Delta, Pi Lambda Theta. Conservative. Achievements include research to secure a 5-year $750,000 grant from the Dept. of Edn. for Hispanic Administrators for the U. North Tex. Avocations: chess, gardening, stamp collecting/philately, coin collecting/numismatics. Home: 301 Teakwood Ln Cedar Hill TX 75104 Home Phone: 972-291-5453. Home Fax: 972-291-5475.

JACKSON, ROBERT WILLIAM, retired utilities executive; b. Beaumont, Tex., June 22, 1930; s. Robert and Elizabeth (Watler) J.; m. Theta Ann Watt, Aug. 14, 1959; 1 child, Robert W. Jr. BBA, U. Tex.; MBA, U. Ill. With Gulf States Utilities Co., Beaumont, Tex., 1955-79, sec., chief fin. officer, 1972-74, sec., treas., chief fin. officer, 1974-75, v.p. fin., chief fin. officer, sec., 1975-79, Cen. Ill. Pub. Svc. Co., Springfield, 1979—95, sr. v.p. fin., chief fin. officer, corp. sec., 1980-95, also bd. dirs.; pres., chief exec. officer CIPSCO Investment Co., Springfield, 1990-95, also bd. dirs.; sr. v.p. CIPSCO Inc., Springfield, 1990—95; ret., 1995. Bd. dirs. 1st Bank of Ill. Co., Springfield, 1st Nat. Bank Springfield, Sangamon State U. Found.; bd. govs. Econs. Am. Mem. bus. adv. coun. U. Ill.; bd. dirs. Springfield Symphony Orch., United Way of Sangamon County; adv. bd. St. John's Hosp., Springfield. Served with U.S. Army, 1953-55. Mem. Am. Soc. Corp. Secs., Fin. Execs. Inst., Edison Electric Inst. (fin. exec. com.). Methodist. Office Phone: 936-756-0562.

JACKSON, ROBERTA Q., music educator; d. Donald Robert and Frances Montana McLeod; BA in Music Edn., MacPhail Coll. Music, Mpls., 1964; MA in Music Edn., U. Colo., 1970. Elem. music tchr. Red Wing (Minn.) Pub. Schs., 1964—66; elem. music resource tchr. Mpls. Pub. Schs., 1966—68; choral dir. South H.S., Mpls., 1968—70; music tchr. grades 3-8 Robert Gray Elem., Portland, Oreg., 1972—78, Franklin HS, Portland, Oreg., 1978—80; choral dir. Cedar Park Mid. Sch., Beaverton, Oreg., 1980—85, Five Oaks Mid. Sch., Beaverton, Oreg., 1985—97; founding artistic dir. Portland Symphonic Girlchoir, 1989—. Presenter Internat. Soc. Music Educators Conf., Innsbruck, Austria, 1985. Contbr. articles to profl. jours. Recipient award for adventurous programming, ASCAP/Chorus Am., 2003; Commemorative scholar, Delta Kappa Gamma Internat., 1986, 1990. Mem.: Assn. Choral Music Experience (recording sec. 2000—04, master tchr. diploma 1999, artist tchr. diploma 1997), Internat. Fedn. Choral Music, Am. Choral Dirs. Assn. (pres. Oreg. state 1983—85, repertoire and stds. elem. chair N.W. divsn. 1997—2004, organizing chair children's honor choir N.W. divsn. 1998, 2000, 2002, 2004, presenter nat. conventions 1999, 2001, 03, 05, cert. adjudicator Oreg. 1994—). Avocations: travel, movies, reading, concerts. Office: Portland Symphonic Girlchoir 1898 NW Everett AVe Portland OR 97205 Office Phone: 503-226-6162. E-mail: rjackson@girlchoir.com.

JACKSON, ROGER A., human resources specialist, automotive executive; Various positions Rockwell Internat., 1977—95; v.p. human resources Allen Bradley (subsidiary of Rockwell Internat.), 1991—95; sr. v.p. human resources Lear Corp., Southfield, Mich., 1995—. Office: Lear Corp 21557 Telegraph Rd Southfield MI 48086-5008 Office Phone: 248-447-1500.

JACKSON, RUTH MOORE, university librarian; b. Potecasi, NC, Sept. 27, 1938; d. Jesse Thomas and Ruth Estelle (Futrell) Moore; m. Roderick Earle Jackson, Aug. 14, 1965; 1 child, Eric Roderick. BS in Bus., Hampton Inst., 1960; MSLS, Atlanta U., 1965; PhD in Libr. and Info. Sci., Ind. U., 1976. Asst. edn. libr. Va. State U., Petersburg, Va., 1965-66, head reference dept., 1966-67, asst. prof., 1976-77, assoc. prof., program coord., 1977-84, interim dept. chair, 1978-79; teaching fellow Ind. U., Bloomington, Ind., 1968, vis. lectr., 1971-72; asst. dir. librs. U. N. Fla., Jacksonville, 1984-88; dean univ. librs. W.Va. U., Morgantown, W.Va., 1988—99, asst. to provost libr. outreach programs; dean librs Wichita State U.; univ. libr. U. Calif., Riverside, 2002—. Pers. cons. Va. State U., 1980; archival cons. N.C. Ctrl. U., Durham, N.C., 1984-85; automation cons. W.Va. Acad. Libr. Consortium, 1991—; co-prin. investigator State-Wide Electronic Libr. Network (Project Infomine), 1994-98. Editor: W.Va. U. Press, 1990—; contbr. to books. Active Big Brother/Big Sister of Am., Jacksonville, Fla., 1985-88; den leader Boy Scouts of Am., Petersburg, Va., 1976-78. U.S. Office Edn. fellow, 1968-71, Rsch. fellow So. Fellowships Found., 1973-74; recipient Outstanding Alumni award Hampton Inst., 1980, Non-Italian Woman of Yr. award, 1992, Disting. West Virginian award Gov. W.Va., 1992. Mem. NAFE, ALA, Southeastern Libr. Assn. (mem. standing com.), Assn. Coll. and Rsch. Librs. (mem. standing com., mem. Fla. chpt.), W.Va. Libr. Assn., Libr. Info. Tech. Assn., Coalition for Networked Info., Coun. of State Univ. Librs. (founding mem.), Addison-Wesley Higher Edn. Tech. Bd., Alpha Kappa Alpha. Democrat. Roman Catholic. Avocations: walking, sightseeing, collecting rare coins and artifacts. Home: 5535 Via San Jacinto Riverside CA 92506-3652 Office: U Calif Rivera Libr, 1st Fl 900 University Ave Riverside CA 92521 Office Phone: 951-827-3221. E-mail: ruth.jackson@ucr.edu.*

JACKSON, RUTHA MAE, pastor, military reserve officer, secondary school educator; d. Willie James Porter Sr. and Mattie Ruth Smith; m. Clarence Jackson, Nov. 22, 1971; children: Nikesha Monique, Michelle Shenique, Kimbria None. B, Ft. Valley State U., Ga., 1993; MDiv, Interdenomination Theol. Sem., Atlanta, 2006. Pastor Christian M.E.Ch., Atlanta, 1980—; supt. Air Force Res., Warner Robins, Ga., 1980—; tchr. Houston County Bd. of Edn., Perry, 1993—. Coord. activities NAACP, Warner Robins, 1991—2000. Sr. master sgt. USAR, 1980—. Mem.: Ga. Assn. Educators (assoc.). Home: 302 Athens St Warner Robins GA 31088 Office: Houston County Bd Edn 110 Main St Perry GA 31069 Home Phone: 478-922-2819; Office Phone: 478-929-7832.

JACKSON, SAMUEL L., actor; b. Washington, Dec. 21, 1948; m. LaTanya Richardson, 1980; 1 child, Zoe. Actor: (TV series) Happily Ever After: Fairy Tales for Every Child, 1995-99; (TV movies) The Trial of the Moke, 1978, Uncle Tom's Cabin, 1987, Common Ground, 1990, Dead and Alive: The Race for Gus Farace, 1991, Simple Justice, 1993, Assault at West Point, 1994, Against the Wall, 1994, Honor Deferred, 2006; (films) Together for Days, 1972, Ragtime, 1981, Eddie Murphy Raw, 1987, Coming to America, 1988, School Daze, 1988, Mystery Train (voice only), 1989, Do The Right Thing, 1989, Sea of Love, 1989, A Shock to the System, 1990, Def by Temptation, 1990, Betsy's Wedding, 1990, Mo' Better Blues, 1990, The Exorcist III, 1990, Goodfellas, 1990, Return of Superfly, 1990, Jungle Fever, 1991 (Best Actor award Cannes International Film Festival), Strictly Business, 1991, Juice, 1992, White Sands, 1992, Patriot Games, 1992, Johnny Suede, 1992, Jumpin' at the Boneyard, 1992, Fathers and Sons, 1992, National Lampoon's Loaded Weapon 1, 1993, Amos & Andrew, 1993, Menace II Society, 1993, Jurassic Park, 1993, True Romance, 1993, Hail Caesar, 1994, Fresh, 1994, Hail Caesar, 1994, The New Age, 1994, Pulp Fiction, 1994, Losing Isiah, 1995, Kiss of Death, 1995, Fluke, 1995, Die Hard With a Vengeance, 1995, The Great White Hype, 1996, Trees Lounge, 1996, The Search for One Eye Jimmy, 1996, A Time to Kill, 1996, The Long Kiss Goodnight, 1996, 187, 1997, Jackie Brown, 1997, Hard Eight, 1997, Eve's Bayou, 1997, Sphere, 1998, Out of Sight, 1998, The Negotiator, 1998, Rules of Engagement, 1999, Mefisto in Onyx, 1999, Star Wars Episode I: The Phantom Menace, 1999, Deep Blue Sea, 1999, Shaft, 2000, Unbreakable, 2000, Changing Lanes, 2002, Star Wars: Episode II - Attack of the Clones, 2002, XXX, 2002, Basic, 2003, S.W.A.T., 2003, In My Country, 2004, Twisted, 2004, Kill Bill: Vol. 2, 2004, The Incredibles (voice only), 2004, Coach Carter, 2005 (Outstanding Actor in a Motion Picture, NAACP Image awards, 2006), xXx: State of the Union, 2005, Star Wars: Episode III Revenge of the Sith, 2005, The Man, 2005, Freedomland, 2006, Snakes on a Plane, 2006, Black Snake Moan, 2006, Home of the Brave, 2006, Resurrecting the Champ, 2007, 1408, 2007. Named to Hollywood Walk of Fame, 2006; recipient Achievement in Acting award, Hawaii Internat. Film Festival, 2005, Dream Keeper award, I Have A Dream Found., 2005, Golden Plate award, Acad. Achievement, 2006. Office: c/o Internat Creative Mgmt Agy Agent: Toni Howard 10250 Constellation Blvd Los Angeles CA 90067 Office Phone: 310-550-4000. Office Fax: 310-550-4100.*

JACKSON, SHIRLEY ANN, academic administrator, physicist; b. Washington, Aug. 5, 1946; d. George Hiter and Beatrice (Cosby) Jackson; m. Morris A. Washington; 1 child, Alan. BS in Physics, MIT, 1968, PhD in Theoretical Elementary Particle Physics, 1973; DSc (hon.), Bloomfield Coll., 1991, Fairleigh Dickinson U., 1993; LLD (hon.), Villanova, 1996. Rsch. assoc. Fermi Nat. Accelerator Lab, Batavia, Ill., 1973—76; mem. tech. staff AT&T Bell Labs, Murray Hill, NJ, 1976—91; prof. physics Rutgers U., Piscataway, NJ, 1991—95; chairperson Nuclear Reg. Commn., 1995—99; U.S. Rep. to Gen. Conf. Internat. Atomic Energy Agy., 1995—99; pres. Rensselaer Poly. Inst., Troy, NY, 1999—. Vis. scientist European Orgn. Nuclear Rsch., Geneva, 1974—75; visitor Stanford Linear Accelerator Ctr., 1976, Aspen Ctr. Physics, 1976—77; mem. com. edn. and employment women in sci. and engring. Nat. Rsch. Coun., 1980—95, cons., 1977—91, NSF, 1977; mem. ednl. coun. MIT, 1976—80; chmn. Internat. Nuclear Regulators Assn., 1997—99; bd. trustees Lincoln U., Pa., 1980—92, exec. com., 1985—92; mem. advisory coun. Inst. Nuclear Power Ops.; bd. trustees Rutgers U., 1986—91, bd. gov., mem. ednl. planning and policy com., 1990; bd. trustees Associated U., Inc., 1993, Brookings Instn., 2000—; trustee Georgetown U., Rockefeller U., Emma Willard Sch., Troy, NY; bd. dirs. NY Stock Exch., NYC, 2003—06, NYSE Group, Inc., 2006—, IBM, FedEx Corp., AT&T Corp., Marathon Oil Corp., U.S. Steel Corp., Medtronic, Inc.; mem. Coun. Fgn. Rels.; mem. exec. com. Coun. Competitveness; coun. mem. Govt.-U.-Industry Rsch. Roundtable; life mem. bd. trustees MIT Corp.; mem. Nat. Adv. Coun. Biomedical Imaging and Bioengineering, Nat. Inst. Health (NIH); US Comptroller-Gen. adv. com. Govt. Acctg. Office (GAO). Editl. adv. bd. (jour.) Jour. Sci. Tech. and Human Values, 1982; contbr. articles to physics jours. Mem. NJ Commn. Sci. and Tech., Com. Status Women in Physics, 1986—88. Named one of 50 Most Important Women in Sci., Discover mag., 2002, 50 Most Inspiring African Am., pub. book, ESSENCE, 2002, 50 R&D Stars to Watch, Industry Week mag., 2002; named to Nat. Women's Hall Fame, 1998, Women Tech. Internat. Found. Hall Fame (WITI), 2000; recipient Candace award, Nat. Coalition 100 Black Women, Salute to Policy Makers award, Exec. Women NJ, 1986, Black Achievers in Industry award, Harlem YMCA, 1986, Thomas Alva Edison award (NJ Gov.'s award), 1993, 100 Women Excellence award, Albany-Colonie Regional C. of C. and Women's Bus. Coun., 2000, eLeadership award, Ctrl. NY Tech. Devel. Orgn. and CASE Ctr., Syracuse U., 2000, Golden Torch award for Lifetime Acheivement in Academia, Nat. Soc. Black Engrs., 2000, Richtmyer Meml. Lecture award, Am. Assn. Physics Tchrs., 2001, Immortal award, 15th Annual Black History Makers award, Associated Black Charities, 2001, Black Engr. Yr. award, US Black Engr. and Info. Tech. mag., 2001, Vannevar Bush award, Nat. Sci. Bd., 2007; fellow, Ford Found., 1971—73; grantee, 1974—75; trainee, NSF, 1968—71. Fellow: Am. Acad. Arts and Scis., Am. Phys. Soc. (mem. com. status of women in physics 1986); mem.: AAAS Am. Assn. Advancement Sci. (com. sci., freedom and responsibility, pres. 2004), Nat. Acad. Engring., Nat. Soc. Black Physicists (pres. 1980—82), Nat. Inst. Sci., NY Acad. Scis., MIT Alumni Assn. (v.p. 1986), Delta Sigma Theta, Sigma Xi. Office: Rensselaer Polytechnic, Pres Office 3031 Troy Bldg, 3rd Fl 110 8th St Troy NY 12180-3590 also: NYSE Group Inc c/o Corp Sec 11 Wall St New York NY 10005*

JACKSON, STANLEY EDWARD, retired special education educator; b. Washington, Sept. 3, 1918; s. Eugene Edward and Inez Christine (Booth) Jackson. BS, Miner Tchrs. Coll., Washington, 1939; MA, Columbia U., 1947, diploma, 1948, EdD, 1958; postgrad., Johns Hopkins U., Peabody Inst. Elem. tchr. DC Pub. Schs., 1940-58, elem. sch. prin., 1958-66, dir. spl. edn., 1966-72; gov.-at-large Coun. Exceptional Children, Reston, Va., 1971-72, asst. exec. dir., membership, 1972-82; ret., 1982. Lectr. Cath. U., Washington, 1965—66, asst. prof. edn., 1967; instr. DC Tchrs. Coll., 1971—72, initiator Tchr. Aide Program Spl. Edn. Classes, 1968; founder Juvenile Decency Corps Uplift House, 1964; co-planner Mamie D. Lee Sch. Mentally Retarded, 1968. Author: School Organization for the Mentally Retarded, 1973, Educational Strategies and Services for Exceptional Children, 1976. Pres. Area K Bd. Commrs. Youth Coun., Washington, 1959—65; founder UPLIFT Cmty. House, Washington, 1963, pres.

Chpt. 49, 1962—64, 1st pres. Fedn. 524, 1965—66; bd. dirs. Found. Exceptional Children, 1978. With US Army, 1941—45, WWII. Decorated 4 Battle Stars; named Stanley E. Jackson Scholarship in his honor, Peabody Prep., Johns Hopkins U., 1988, Stanley E. Jackson Scholarship award established in his honor, Found. for Exceptional Children, 1980, Philanthropic Honor Roll, George Washington U., 1949—2001; recipient Yes I Care award, Found. for Exceptional Children, 1992, Plaque for Outstanding Svc., Commr. Coun., Washington, 1963, Outstanding Ret. Tchr. award, Jr. Citizens Corps, 1979, Stanley E. Jackson Spl. Edn. award established in his honor, Bd. Edn. D.C. Pub. Schs., 1973, Cert. of Appreciation, Nat. Fedn. Blind, 2001. Mem.: NAACP, AAUP, NEA, Dept. Elem. Sch. Prins., Coun. Exceptional Children, DC Congress Parents and Tchrs., Johns Hopkins Assoc. Program, Urban League, AMVETS, Phi Delta Kappa, Kappa Delta Pi. Avocations: music, coin collecting/numismatics, writing, philanthropy. Home: Apt 703 One E University Pky Baltimore MD 21218

JACKSON, STU, sports association executive, former university basketball coach; b. Reading, Pa., Dec. 11, 1955; m. Dr. Janet Taylor; four daughters. B in Bus. Adminstrn. and Mgmt., Seattle U., 1978. Grad. asst. coach U. Oreg., 1981-82, asst. coach, 1982—83, Wash. State U., 1983-85; assoc. coach, head recruiting coord. Providence Coll., 1985-87; asst. coach NY Knicks, 1987-89, head coach, 1989-91; dir. basketball ops. NBA, NYC, 1991—92, exec. v.p. basketball ops., chair competition com.; head coach U. Wis., Madison, 1992-94; pres., gen. mgr. basketball ops. Vancouver Grizzlies, Brit. Columbia, Canada, 1994. V.p. sr. men, mem. exec. com. USA Basketball, 2005—. Office: NBA Olympic Tower 645 5th Ave Fl 10 New York NY 10022-5986*

JACKSON, SUSAN MARIE, lawyer; b. Painesville, Ohio, June 17, 1978; d. James Thomas and Gloria Jean Hirsch; m. Thomas Leo Jackson, Aug. 13, 2005. BS in Comm., Ohio U., 2000; JD, Cleve. Marshall Coll. Law, 2006. Paralegal Grant & Grant, Attorneys at Law, Indpls., 2001—02, Novelis Corp., Mayfield Heights, Ohio, 2005—06, atty., 2005—; youth dir. First Presbyn. Ch., 2006—. Author: (copyright) Spy Cat. Sr. high youth leader First Presbyn. Ch. Willoughby, Ohio, 2005—; mem. AIDS Walk Com. AIDS Taskforce Greater Cleve., 2005—; horse leader Fieldstone Farm Therapeutic Riding Ctr., Chagrin Falls, Ohio, 2005—. Mem.: ABA (assoc.; lt. gov. for programming for the 6th cir. 2004—05, law student divsn.), Cuyahoga County Bar Assn., Ohio State Bar Assn. (assoc.). Democrat. Presbyn. Avocations: travel, scrapbooks, films. Home Phone: 440-796-6237; Office Phone: 440-423-6993. Business E-Mail: susan.jackson@novelis.com.

JACKSON, TAMARA NICOLE, lawyer; d. Roby Henry and Linda Fae Jackson. BA in Polit. Sci., Spelman Coll., Atlanta, 1996; JD, U. Wis., 1998. Atty./ptnr. Figueroa & Jackson, LLC, Milw., 2001—. Mem. Felmers Chaney Adv. Bd., Milw., 2005. Mem.: Alpha Kappa Alpha Sorority, Inc. (assoc.). Office: Figueroa & Jackson LLC 2051 W Wisconsin Ave Milwaukee WI 53233 Home Phone: 414-449-2224; Office Phone: 414-342-3580. Office Fax: 414-342-3581. E-mail: tjackson@figueroaandjackson.com.

JACKSON, THELMA HARRISON, educational consultant, researcher; b. Prichard, Ala., Jan. 14, 1946; d. Charles Lillian and Myrtle Christine Harrison; m. Nathaniel Jackson, Sept. 12, 1966; children: Debrena Jackson Gandy, Ericka Devette, Nathaniel Jr. BS in Biochemistry, So. U., Baton Rouge, 1968; EdD in Ednl. Leadership and Change, Fielding Grad. U., Santa Barbara, Calif., 2002. Cert. mgmt. tng. and decision-making Seattle U., Nat. Safety Coun., Key Mgmt. Devel. ProgramSeattle U., career counseling/life planning Evergreen State Coll. Tutor for the blind La. Dept. of Social and Health Svcs., Baton Rouge, 1964—66; substitute tchr. Morehouse Parish Sch., Bastrop, La., 1967; recreation dir. Milw. Pub. Schools Summer Program, 1967; rsch. scientist Battelle Meml. Inst. Pacific N.W. Lab., Richland, Wash., 1968—71; project coord. Work Options for Women YWCA, Olympia, 1975—78; tng. coord. Jackson and Assocs., Inc., Olympia, 1979—85; v.p. mgmt. svcs. divsn. Nat Jackson and Assocs., Inc., Olympia, 1986—92, sr. v.p. edn. svcs. divsn., 1993—97; owner, prin. cons. Foresight Consultants, Olympia, 1997—. Bd. dirs. Thurston Group of Wash. State, Olympia; adj. faculty urban edn. Evergreen State Coll., Tacoma, 2002—03; founder, pres. N.W. Inst. for Leadership and Change, Olympia, 2004—; coun. mem. Fielding Grad. U. Alumni Coun., Santa Barbara, Calif., 2004—. Contbr. articles and rsch. reports to profl. jours. Mem. Wash. State Coordinating Com. for Internat. Women's Yr., Seattle, 1977; founder, chairperson African-Am. Alliance of Thurston County, Olympia, 1997—2006; founder, pres. Black Women's Caucus of Wash. State, Olympia, 1977—83; pres. PTA Lydia Hawk Elem. Sch., Lacey, 1974—76; founder Black Youth Group, Pasco, Wash., 1969—72, African Am. Edn. Think Tank, Olympia, 1998—2006; pres. North Thurston Sch. Dist. Bd. Mem., Lacey, 1976—97; summit convenor African-Am.Leadership Summit, Thurston County, Olympia, 1996; vice-chair, sec./treas. Edn. Renewal Inst., Seattle, 1992; pres., bd. of trustees Evergreen State Coll., Olympia, 1981—86; chairperson State Adv. Coun. on Vocat. Edn., Olympia, 1982; mem. Wash. Women United, Seattle, 1979—85, Thurston County Urban League, Olympia, 1973—90; founding mem. African Am. Think Tank of Wash. State, Olympia, 1997—2006, Multi-Ethnic Think Tank of Wash. State, Olympia, 1997—2006; mem. Black Child Devel. Inst., Wash., 2000—06; conf. planner, state del. Wash. State Women's Conf., Houston, 1977; mem. U.S. Dept. of Labor, Nat. Coun. on Working Women, Washington, 1979; v.p., pres. Wash. State Commn. on African-Am. Affairs, Olympia, 1992—96; cabinet mem. Gov. Mike Lowry's Citizens Cabinet, Olympia, 1992; mem. Gov. Mike Lowry's K-12 Edn. Transition Task Force, Olympia, 1992, Gov. Booth Gardner's Coun. on Edn. Reform and Funding, Olympia, 1990—91; pres. Black Women's Caucus of Wash. State, Thurston County Chpt., Olympia, 1980—83; co-chair White Ho. Conf. on Families, Olympia, 1980; mem. N.W. Conf. of Black Pub. Ofcls., Olympia, 1978—89; bd. dirs. N.W. Regional Ednl. Lab., Portland, Oreg., 1994—96; mem. Cmty. Found., Olympia, 1996—2000; chair Wash. State Legis. Ethics Bd., Olympia, 1994—96; bd. mem. Pacific Mountain Pvt. Industry Coun., Olympia, 1987—91, Wash. Women United Bd. of Dirs., Seattle, 1987—89, Wash. State Sch. Vol. Programs, Olympia, 1986—88; co-chair Lacey Area Youth Task Force, 1994—96; program com. mem. Olympia YWCA, 1974—76; bd. dirs. Pacific Peaks Girl Scout Coun., Olympia, 1972—74; mem. Benton Franklin ARC, Richland, Wash., 1972, Mid-Columbia Girl Scout Coun., Richland, 1969—72, Citizens Edn. Ctr. N.W., Olympia, 1983—89, Thurston Group of Wash. State, Olympia, 2001—06. Named Layperson Contbr. of the Yr., Vocat. Edn., 1984, Outstanding Freshman Student, So. U., 1964; named one of 100 Wash. Women, Supt. of Pub. Instrn., 1984; named to Glimpses into N.W. Lives: Some Outstanding Women, N.W. Regional Ednl. Lab., 1989; recipient Golden Acorn award, Lydia Hawk Elem. Sch. PTA, 1976, Outstanding Contbn. award, Multi-Ethnic Think Tank, 2005, 1st Ann. Breakfast of Champions Honoree, African Am. Cultural Inst., 1995, Cmty. Svc. award, Nat. Assn. of Partners in Edn., 1991, Disting. Svc. and Outstanding Cmty. Achievement award, Martin Luther King, Jr., 1988, Disting. Leader award, Thurston County, 2000, 2002. Mem.: ASCD, NAACP (life), Nat. Caucus of Black Sch. Bd. Mems. (bd. dirs. 1977—97), Nat. Sch. Bds. Assn. (nat. task force on vocat. edn., pres. Pacific region 1990, resolutions com. 1990, pres.'s coun. 1991), Wash. Alliance of Black Sch. Educators (Disting. Svc. in Edn. award 1998), Thurston County Sch. Dirs. Assn. (pres. 1987—97), Wash. State Sch. Dirs. Assn. (pres. 1986—91, 20-Yr. Sch. Bd. Svc. award 1997, Sch. Bd. Mem. of Yr. 1987), Nat. Assn. for Multicultural Edn., Rotary Club of Lacey. Home: 6335 Pacific Ave SE Olympia WA 98503 Office: Foresight Cons Ste 100 6335 Pacific Ave SE Olympia WA 98503 Home Phone: 360-456-1412; Office Phone: 360-491-2306. Office Fax: 360-412-1108; Home Fax: 360-412-1108. Personal E-mail: thelmajackson@comcast.net.

JACKSON, THEODORE MARSHALL, retired oil industry executive; b. Beaumont, Tex., Oct. 18, 1928; s. Robert and Mary Louise (Watler) J.; m. Maria Pierracou-Dobrowolska Countess de Wernicki de Vladis la Goda, June 19, 1954; 1 child, Mark Andrew. BBA in Engring, U. Tex., Austin, 1951. V.p., sec.-treas. Purvin & Gertz, Inc., Dallas, 1955-71; v.p. treasury and strategic planning New Eng. Petroleum Corp., NYC, 1971-75; v.p. fin. Crown Central Petroleum Corp., Balt., 1975-83, sr. v.p., chief fin. officer, 1984-91, also bd. dirs. Emeriti bd. dirs., Bd. of Child Care; emeriti gov. Wesley Theol. Sem. Lt. USNR, 1952-55. Mem. Beta Gamma Sigma, Delta Tau Delta. Republican. Methodist. Home: 8 Wythe Ct Glen Arm MD 21057-9134 E-mail: tmjack8@comcast.net.

JACKSON, THOMAS FRANCIS, III, lawyer; b. Memphis, Oct. 21, 1940; s. Thomas Francis and Sarah Elizabeth (Farris) J.; children: Thomas Francis, Wythe Macrae Bogy. Grad., The Taft Sch.; BA, Rhodes Coll., 1962; LLB, George Washington U., 1967. Bar: Tenn. 1967, U.S. Supreme Ct. 1974. Law clk. to chief judge U.S. Dist. Ct. Western Dist. Tenn., 1967-68; with Armstrong, Allen PLLC, Memphis, 1968-72, Lawler, Humphreys PLLC, Memphis, 1972-83; pvt. practice Memphis, 1983—. Lt. USNR, 1962-67. Mem. ABA, Tenn. Bar Assn., Memphis Bar Assn. Episcopalian. Home: 232 S Highland St Memphis TN 38111-4540 Office: PO Box 111221 Memphis TN 38111-1221 Home Phone: 901-833-1100; Office Phone: 901-324-1100. Office Fax: 901-324-6997. Business E-Mail: tfj@lawtn.com.

JACKSON, THOMAS GENE, lawyer; b. NYC, Mar. 9, 1949; s. Alan Clark and Clare Seena (Werther) J.; m. Beatrice Lafrance Korab, June 11, 1972; children: Sarah Ann, Alan Edward. AB magna cum laude in English, Dartmouth Coll., 1971; JD, U. Va., 1974. Bar: N.Y. 1975, U.S. Dist. Ct. (so. and ea. dists.) N.Y. 1975, U.S. Ct. Appeals (2d cir.) 1975, U.S. Ct. Appeals (5th cir.) 1978, U.S. Supreme Ct. 1978, U.S. Ct. Appeals (D.C. cir.) 1986. Editor The Rsch. Group, Charlottesville, Va., 1973-74; assoc. Phillips Nizer Benjamin Krim & Ballon LLP, NYC, 1974-82; ptnr. Phillips Nizer LLP, NYC, 1982—. Mem. fed. bar coun. com. 2d Cir. Cts., 1997-2000, chmn. subcom. on tech. in the cts., 1997-2000. Contbr. chapters to books. Mem. Village of Irvington Cable TV Adv. Com., N.Y., 1979-91, 95—, chmn. franchise renewal com., 1991-95; sec. Village of Irvington Environ. Conservation Bd., 1983-87, chmn., 1987—; mem. Dartmouth Coll. Alumni Coun., 1986-89. Mem.: ABA (sect. antitrust law, mem. Clayton Act com., computer industry and internet com., intellectual property com., mem. sect. intellectual property, mem. antitrust matters com., computer programs com., mem. litig. sect., mem. antitrust litig., computer and internet litig. sect.), Assn. Bar City N.Y. (antitrust and trade regulation com. 1988—92, mergers acquisitions and joint ventures subcom. 1991—92), Am. Arbitration Assn. (comml. tribunal 1986—, panel of arbitrators), Dartmouth Coll. Class Secs. Assn. (v.p. 1984—85, pres. 1985—86), Dartmouth Club Westchester (sec. 1984—87, pres. 1987—90), Dartmouth Coll. Club Officers Assn. (exec. com. 1988—91). Home: 32 Hamilton Rd Irvington NY 10533-2311 Office Phone: 212-977-9700. Business E-Mail: tjackson@phillipsnizer.com.

JACKSON, THOMAS HUMPHREY, former academic administrator; b. Kalamazoo, June 20, 1950; s. William Humphrey and Louise Longstreth (Cone) Jackson; m. Bonnie Eileen Gelb; children: Richard, Steven. BA, Williams Coll., 1972; JD, Yale U., 1975. Bar: N.Y. 1976, Calif. 1979. Law clk. to judge U.S. Dist. Ct. NY, 1975—76; law clk. to justice U.S. Supreme Ct., Washington, 1976—77; asst. prof., assoc. prof. to prof. Stanford U. Law Sch., Calif., 1977—86; prof. Harvard U. Law Sch., Cambridge, Mass., 1986—88; dean Sch. Law, U. Va., Charlottesville, 1988—91, v.p., provost, 1991—93; pres. U. Rochester, NY, 1994—2005, Disting. Univ. prof., 2005—. Assoc. Heller, Ehrman, White & McAliffe, San Francisco, 1979—81, spl. counsel, 1981—86. Co-author: Secured Transactions, 1982, Secured Transactions, 3d edit., 2000, Bankruptcy, 1985, Bankruptcy, 3d edit., 2000; author: Logic and Limits of Bankruptcy Law, 1986. Trustee George Eastman House. Office: U Rochester 3-110N Carol Simon Hall Rochester NY 14627

JACKSON, THOMAS O., real estate appraiser, urban planner; BA in Polit. Sci. with honors, U. South Fla., 1975; MA in Polit. Sci., Ohio State U., 1979; M in Regional Planning, U. N.C., 1984; PhD in Urban and Regional Sci., Tex. A&M U., 2000. Cert. gen. real estate appraiser, Tex., Fla. Planning dir. City of West Melbourne, Fla., 1978-80; cmty. assistance cons. Fla. Dept. Cmty. Affairs, Tallahassee, 1983-84; sr. rsch. assoc. Econ. Rsch. Svcs., Inc., Tallahassee, 1984-86; project mgr. BHR Planning Group, Inc., Jacksonville, Fla., 1986-87; sr. cons., devel. econ. group Reynolds, Smith and Hills, Inc., Jacksonville, 1987-92; sr. project mgr. Harland Bartholomew & Assocs., Inc., Jacksonville, 1992-93; pres. Planning Rsch. Svcs., Inc., Jacksonville, 1993—95; dir. fin. adv. svcs. Coopers & Lybrand LLP, Houston and Phoenix, 1994-98; sr. cons. Entrix, Inc., Houston, 1998-99; pres. Real Property Analytics, Inc., College Station, Tex., 2000—. Lectr. Coll. Architecture Tex. A&M U., College Station, 1998-99, lectr. Coll. Bus., 2002-04, exec. prof., 2004-05, assoc. prof., 2005—, dir. real estate programs, 2005-06; expert witness, presenter in field. Contbr. articles to profl. jours. Dissertation Rsch. grantee NSF, 1999; Dissertation fellow Lincoln Inst. Land Policy, 1999. Fellow Royal Instn. of Chartered Surveyors; mem. Am. Planning Assn. (bd. dirs. 1993-94, chair legis. com. 1993-94), Am. Real Estate Urban Econ. Assn., Am. Real Estate Soc., Counselors Real Estate (membership devel. com. 1997, edn. com. 1997, pub. policy com. 1997-99, ethics profl. practice com. 1998-2000), Appraisal Inst. (ethics counseling com. 1995-97, mem. task group 1999-2000), Appraisal Found. (mem. appraisal stds. bd. 2001-02), Am. Inst. Cert. Planners, Urban Land Inst. (assoc., reviewer 1993), Houston Assn. Realtors, Am. Mensa, Omicron Delta Kappa, Phi Kappa Phi, Pi Sigma Alpha, Themis. Office: Real Property Analytics Inc 4805 Spearman Dr College Station TX 77845-4412 E-mail: tomjackson@real-analytics.com.

JACKSON, THOMAS PENFIELD, federal judge; b. Washington, Jan. 10, 1937; s. Thomas Searing and May Elizabeth (Jacobs) J. AB in Govt., Dartmouth Coll., 1958; LLB, Harvard U., 1964. Bar: DC 1965, Md. 1966, US Supreme Ct. 1970. Assoc., ptnr. Jackson & Campbell, P.C., Washington, 1964-82; US dist. judge US Dist. Ct. DC, Washington, 1982—2004; ret., 2004. Of counsel Jackson & Campbell, P.C., 2004—. Vestryman All Saints' Episcopal Ch., Washington, 1969-75; trustee Gallaudet U., Washington, 1985-99, St. Marys Coll., Md., 2001—. Lt. (j.g.) USN, 1958-61. Fellow Am. Coll. Trial Lawyers; mem. ABA, Bar Assn. DC (pres. 1982-83), Rotary. Clubs: Chevy Chase, Metropolitan, Lawyers', Barristers. Republican. Office Phone: 202-457-1600. E-mail: tjackson@jackscamp.com.

JACKSON, VALERIE PASCUZZI, radiologist, educator; b. Oakland, Calif., Aug. 25, 1952; d. Chris A. Pascuzzi and Janice (Mayne) Pacuzzi; 1 child, Price Arthur III. AB, Ind. U., 1974, MD, 1978. Diplomate Am. Bd. Radiology. Intern, resident in diagnostic radiology Ind. U. Med. Ctr., 1978-82; from asst. prof. radiology to prof. radiology Ind. U. Sch. Medicine, Indpls., 1982-94, John A. Campbell prof. radiology, 1994—. Dir. residency program in radiology Ind. U. Sch. Medicine, 1994—2003, chair dept. radiology, 2004—; trustee Am. Bd. Radiology. Contbr. over 80 articles to profl. jours., chapters to books. Fellow: Soc. Breast Imaging (pres. 1990—92), Am. Coll. Radiology (bd. chancellors, chair 3 coms., pres. 2002—03); mem.: AMA, Radiol. Soc. N.Am., Am. Roentgen Ray Soc., Am. Inst. Ultrasound in Medicine, Alpha Omega Alpha. Office: Indiana U Sch Med Dept Rad 550 N Univ Blvd Rm 0663 Indianapolis IN 46202-2859

JACKSON, VICTORIA LYNN, actress, comedienne; b. Miami, Fla., Aug. 2, 1959; d. James McCaslin and Marlene Esther (Blackstad) J.; m. Nisan Mark Eventoff, Aug. 5, 1984; 1 child, Scarlet Elizabeth. Student, Fla. Bible Coll., 1976-77, Furman U., 1977-79, Auburn U., 1979-80. Actress Summerfest/Town & Gown, Birmingham, Ala., 1980; stand-up comedienne Variety Arts Ctr., LA, 1982-83, Tonight Show with Jonny Carson, NBC, LA, 1983; actress-comedienne The Half Hour Comedy Hour, Dick Clark, LA, 1983; comedienne Bizarre/John Beiner, Toronto, Can., 1983; actress commls. LA, 1983—; comedienne Bob Munkhouse Show, London, 1983; actress-comedienne Saturday Night Live, NBC, NYC, 1986—. Actress series Half Nelson, NBC, L.A., pilot Walter Fox, L.A. Actress (films) Stoogemania, Double Exposure, The Pick Up Artist, 1986, Baby Boom, 1987, Couch Trip, 1987, Dream a Lil Dream, 1988, Casual Sex, 1988, UHF with Weird Al, 1989, Family Business, 1990, I Love You to Death, 1990. Mem. ASCAP, SAF, AFTRA. Baptist. Avocations: motherhood, photography, gymnastics.

JACKSON, WILLIAM DAVID, research and development company executive; b. Edinburgh, May 20, 1927; came to U.S., 1955, naturalized, 1968; s. Joseph and Margaret (Johnston) Jackson; m. Eleanor Burdeshaw; children from previous marriage: Margaret Eleanor, David Foster. BSc, U. Glasgow, 1947, PhD, 1960; postgrad., U. Strathclyde, 1948. Apprentice English Electric Co., Stafford, 1945—47; rsch. asst. elec. engring. dept. U. Strathclyde, Glasgow, 1948—51; lectr. elec. engring. U. Manchester, England, 1951—55, 1957—58; vis. lectr. dept. elec. engring. MIT, 1955—57, asst. prof., 1958—62, assoc. prof., 1962—66, lectr. elec. engring., 1968—73; vis. prof. Tech. U., Berlin, 1966; prof. elec. engring., dept. energy engring. U. Ill., Chgo., 1966—67; prin. rsch. scientist, dir. tech. edn. Avco-Everett Rsch. Lab., Mass., 1967—72; prof. elec. engring. U. Tenn. Space Inst., Tullahoma, 1972—73; mgr. Electric Power Rsch. Inst., Palo Alto, Calif., 1973—74; mgr. office coal rsch. Interior Dept., Washington, 1974—75; dir. magnetohydrodynamic divsn. ERDA, Washington, 1975—77; dir. tech. analysis divsn. Office Energy Rsch., Dept. Energy, Washington, 1977—79; pres. Energy Cons., Inc., 1979—84, HMJ Corp., 1982—. Professorial lectr. George Washington U., 1979—91, vis. prof., 1986—87, adj. prof., 1991—, faculty in residence Wise program, 2007; bd. dirs. Hexogon Inc., prodn. v.p., 1999—2001; bd. dirs. Clean Energy Combustion, Inc., 2001—03; mem. Internat. Magnetohydrodynamic Liaison Group, 1966—, chmn., 1969—74, sec., 1986—2002; coord. coop. program magnetohydrodynamic power generation U.S.-USSR, 1974—79; mem. numerous govt. and internat. coms. and panels; cons. numerous indsl. firms and govt. agencies, 1948—. Editor: Electricity From MHD, 1968; editl. bd.: Internat. Jour. Elec. Engring. Edn, 1962-70; editor-in-chief Magnetohydrodynamics: An Internat. Jour., 1987-92. U.K. Fulbright scholar, 1955-57; recipient ILG award Internat. Magnetogydrodynamic Liaison Group, 2005 Fellow Instn. Elec. Engrs. (past com. sec., chmn.), IEEE (sec.-treas. prof. group biomed. electronics Boston sect. 1962-63, energy devel. subcom. 1973—, chmn. 1988-98, energy devel. and power gen. com. 1986-99, steering com. intersoc. energy conversion engring. conf. 1988—2002, conf. program chair 1989, conf. gen. chair 1996, 2002), ASME (past chmn. adv. energy sys. divsn., energy com. 1986-90), AIAA (assoc., Energy Sys. award 1995); mem. AAUP, AAAS, Am. Phys. Soc., Am. Soc. Engring. Edn., Sigma Xi. Office: 710 N College St Tullahoma TN 37388 Home Phone: 240-304-7842; Office Phone: 240-304-7842, 931-455-2360. Personal E-mail: hmjcorpwdjackson@aol.com.

JACKSON, WILLIAM ELMER, JR., retired packaging company administrator; b. Washington, Pa., Oct. 25, 1935; s. William Elmer and Hazel Celestine (Moore) Jackson; m. Suzanne P. Jackson; children: Randall Lee, Barry Howard. BS in Indsl. Engring., Okla. U., 1966; MBA in Fin., U. Mo., Kansas City, 1970. With Sealright Co. Inc., Overland Pk., Kans., 1966—98, corp. econ. evaluation engr., 1966—69, process engr. central div, 1969—72, profit evaluation specialist, cen. div., 1972—74, corp. mgr. econ. evaluation, 1974—75, corp. ops. analysis mgr., 1975—78, adminstrv. mgr. cent. div., 1978—81, mfg. and control mgr. cen. div., 1981—83, corp. planning and devel., 1983—91, chmn. eastern div. operational study project, 1976, chmn. corp. mfg. info. requirements study project, 1978, chmn. western div. operational study project, 1984, Kansas City plant relocation project, 1987, mem. bus. profile study team, ea. div. plant rearrangement project, 1989—90, plastics plant operational study, 1990, mfg. mgr. ctrl. divsn., 1991—94; mgr. mfg. tech. transfer sealright flexible packaging group, 1994—98. Mng. dir. Sealright of Australia, Brisbane, 1996—98; sec., treas., dir. Agrl. Tech. Internat. Mktg., Inc., Louisburg, Kans., 1984—85. Com. chmn., merit badge counselor Troop 278 Heart of Am. coun. Boy Scouts Am., 1972—74; adv. Jr. Achievement of Greater Kansas City, 1974—75; mem. Brisbane Christian Cmty. Choir, 1996—97, Johnson County Assn. Retarded Citizens; caravan dir. Overland Park Nazarene Ch., 1968—74, choir, 1968—81, 1989—95, 1998—, ch. bd., 1976—79, 1988—95, 1998—, ch. treas., 1977—78, fin. com., 1976—78, mem. house com., 1978—79, 1990—92, vice chmn. fin. com., 1990—91, chmn. youth ministries bd., 1990—93, mem. pers. com., 1992—95, mem. fin. com., 1993—95, 2000—02, chmn. facility comm., 2002—04; chmn. adv. bd. mid-mgmt. program Penn Valley C.C., Kansas City, Mo., 1980—84, 1987—93. With USAF, 1955—59. Mem.: Inst. Indsl. Engrs. (sr.), Fishing Club Am. Republican. Personal E-mail: jackj@attglobal.net.

JACKSON, WILLIAM J. (BILL JACKSON), lawyer; b. Houston, 1967; BA, U. Tex., Austin, 1989; JD, U. Houston, 1992. Bar: Tex. 1992, US Ct. Appeals (Fifth Cir.), US Dist. Ct. (no., so. and ea. dists. Tex.). Founding ptnr. Connelly, Baker, Maston, Wotring & Jackson, LLP. Assoc. editor: U. Houston Law Rev., 1991—92. Bd. dirs. Justice For Children, U. Houston Law Alumni Assn., 2002—. Named a Rising Star, Tex. Super Lawyers mag., 2006. Fellow: Houston Young Lawyers Found. (mem. bd. trustees 1996—2001, chmn. 1999—2000), Tex. Bar Found.; mem.: Tex. Assn. Def. Counsel, Internat. Assn. Def. Counsel, Tex. Young Lawyers Assn. (bd. dirs. 1997—98), Houston Young Lawyers Assn. (pres. 2001—02, bd. dirs. 1995—2002).*

JACKSON, WILLIAM PAUL, JR., lawyer; b. Bexar, Ala., July 7, 1938; s. William Paul and Evelyn Mabel (Goggans) J.; m. Barbara Anne Seignious, Sept. 30, 1966; children: Jennifer Anne, Susan Barrett, William Paul III. BS in Physics, U. Ala., 1960, JD, 1963. Bar: Ala. 1963, D.C. 1969, Va. 1975. Law clk. to judge Ala. Ct. Appeals, Montgomery, 1965; assoc. Bishop and Carlton, Birmingham, Ala., 1965-68, Todd, Dillon and Sullivan, Washington, 1968-70; founding ptnr. Jackson & Jessup, Washington, 1970-75, Arlington, Va., 1975—76; pres., sr. atty. Jackson & Jessup, PC, Arlington, 1976—2001, McLean, Va., 2002—. Advisor Oren Harris chair of transp. U. Ark., 1974-91. Comments editor U. Ala. Law Rev., 1962, leading articles editor, 1963; conbtr. articles to profl. jours. V.p. McLean Hunt Homeowners Assn., Va., 1974, pres., 1975-76; bd. dirs. McLean Citizens' Assn., 1976-78; pres. McLean Legal Action Fund, Inc., 1977-81; session mem. Lewinsville Presbyn. Ch., 1981-84; v.p. Marjoribanks Family, 1994-96, pres., 1996-98; active The Alexandria Chorale, 1985-94. 1st lt. Signal Corps, U.S. Army, 1963-65. Recipient Pub. Service awards Am. Radio Relay League, 1958, Merit award Armed Forces Comm. and Electronics Assn., 1963; Sigma Delta Kappa scholar, 1963. Mem. ABA, Ala. State Bar, Va. State Bar, DC Bar, Bar Assn. DC (chmn. computer tech. com. 1998-2000, chmn. mem. com. 2000-01, treas. 2001-02, bd. dirs. 2002-03, chmn. website com. 2004, Presdl. award 2000), Transp. Lawyers Assn. (chmn. legis. com. 1989-90), Bar Assn. DC Found. (bd. dirs. 1999-2001), Assn. Transp. Law Profls. (nat. pres. 1991-92, chmn. nominating com. 1992-93, chmn. membership com. 1993-99, chmn. DC chpt. 1989-90, com. govtl. rels. 1975-90, motor editor Assn. Highlights 1992-98, Presdl. award 1994, 99), So. Transp. Logistics Assn. (exec. dir. 1970-99), Ea. Indsl. Traffic League (exec. dir. 1978-88), Bench and Bar Legal Honor Soc. (pres. 1963), Farrah Law Soc. (trustee 2000—, sec.-treas. 2006—), Nat. Soc. DAR (bd. advisors to pres. gen. 2004-07), Omicron Delta Kappa.

Presbyterian (elder). Avocation: amateur radio operator. Home: 1003 Spring Hill Rd Mc Lean VA 22102-1331 Office: Jackson & Jessup PC PO Box 4030 Mc Lean VA 22103 Business E-Mail: wpj@translaw.com.

JACKSON, WILLIAM RICHARD, entrepreneur; b. Nampa, Idaho, Aug. 23, 1936; s. Richard W. and Josie P. (Mulder) J.; m. Marilyn Kay Samp, June 10, 1956 (div. 1975); children: James Lee, Robbi Jo, Jolynn Kay. BA in Secondary Edn., N.W. Nazarene Coll., Nampa, 1957; MA in Secondary Edn. Adminstrn., U. No. Colo., 1961; EdM, U. Denver, 1964, PhD in Higher Edn. Adminstrn. and Rsch., 1991; PhD in, Stanford U., 1991. Owner, operator Janitorial Svc., Walla Walla, Wash., 1950-54; account mgr., collection contractor Montgomery Ward, Walla Walla, Wash., 1953-57; exec. ins. dir. edn. svcs. Idaho Sch. Employment, Boise, 1957-58; sch. tchr., football coach Humanities, Speech & Art, Caldwell, Idaho, 1958-60; tchr. psychology and econs. Englewood (Colo.) Sch. Dist., 1961-64; dir. student coun. Brook Forest Leadership Inst., Evergreen, Colo., 1961-64; co-owner, operator Jackson Bros. Investments, Englewood, 1970-84; co-owner, pres. Internat. Bell Mus., Inc., Evergreen, 1978-86; pres. Jackson Bros. Industries, Evergreen, 1984—, Jackson Internat., Inc., Evergreen, 1984—. Chmn. bd. Petro Silver, Inc., Denver, 1979-83; rsch. cons. in agr., toxic waste remediation and hyperbaric oxygenation medicine; sr. cons. Envrion. Health Found., San Francisco; mem. staff Southwest Rsch. Inst., San Antonio, Tex. Co-author: Brook Forest Leadership Curriculum, 1964, Disciplining Curriculum, 1978; author: Hyperbaric Oxygenation Effects on the Cognitive Function of Memory, Barter, The History, Mystery and Mastery of Mutual Exchange, Humic, Fulvic and Micorbial Balance: Organic Soil Conditioning, Environmental Care & Share, 1995, The Arthritis, Osteoporosis and Silica Link, The Calcium Deception, Fabulous Fulvic Electrolyte, 1995. Co-founder Benevolent Brotherhood Found., Denver, 1971—; bd. dirs. Ch. of the Nazarene, past chmn. bd. edn. Grantee Denver Presbyn. Med. Ctr., 1991, Hyperbaric Oxygen Therapy System, San Diego, 1991, Denver, 1991; recipient 1st Pl. Nat. Self-Publishing award Writer's Digest, 1993. Mem. Internat. Found. Hyperbaric Medicine, Undersea and Hyperbaric Med. Soc. (rsch. cons. 1990—), Stanford U. Alumni Assn., Phi Delta Kappa. Republican. Avocation: bartering. Office: Jackson Internat Rsch Ctr PO Box 1749 Evergreen CO 80437-1749 Personal E-mail: wirjak@jps.net.

JACKSON, WILLIAM VERNON, Latin American studies and library science educator; b. Chgo., May 26, 1926; s. William Olof and Lillian (Scharenberg) J. BA summa cum laude, Northwestern U., Evanston, Ill., 1945; MA, Harvard U., Cambridge, Mass., 1948, PhD, 1952; MLS, U. Ill., 1951; Diploma (hon.), U. Ctrl. Venezuela, 1968. Tchr. York Cmty. HS, Elmhurst, Ill., 1946—47; tchg. fellow Harvard U., 1948—50; spl. recruit Libr. of Congress, 1951—52; libr., asst. prof. libr. sci. U. Ill., Urbana, 1952—58, assoc. prof., 1958—62, U. Wis., Madison, 1963—65, faculty rsch. fellow, summer, 1963, 1964; prof. libr. sci., dir. internat. info. ctr. U. Pitts., 1966—70; prof. libr. sci. George Peabody Coll. for Tchrs., 1970—76; prof. Spanish and Portuguese Vanderbilt U., Nashville, 1970—76; prof. libr. sci. U. Tex. Austin, 1976—86, prof. emeritus, 1986—, assoc. Inst. Latin Am. Studies, 1976—. Vis. lectr. U. Minn. Libr. Sch., summers 1954-56, Columbia U. Sch. Libr. Svc., summers 1960, 90, Syracuse U. Sch. Libr. Sci., summer 1962, Simmons Coll. Sch. Libr. Sci., summer, 1974, 75, Coll. Librarianship, Aberystwyth, Wales, summer 1977, U. Zulia, Maracaibo, Venezuela, summer 1980, Dominican U. Libr. Sci., summers 1981-84, 86, 89-98, 2000, 02-05, Pratt Inst. Sch. Info. and Libr. Sci., summers 1995-98, Coll. St. Catherine, summer 1999, 2001, LI U. Palmer Sch. Libr. and Info. Sci., summer 2001, U. South Fla. 2005; vis. prof. Inter-Am. Libr. Sch., U. Antioquia, Medellín, Colombia, 1960, 68, adviser internat. exec. coun., 1961-63; cons. State Dept., 1956, 59, 61, 62, 67, 77, 2002, 03, 04; Regional AID Office for Ctrl. Am. and Panama, 1965-66, AID Mission to Brazil, 1967-72, AID Mission to Colombia, 1970-71, USIA, 1979-80, 85, 87, 89-92, 94-2000, OAS, 1970-71; Coun. Rectors Brazilian Univs., 1972; cons. rsch. librs. NY Pub. Libr., 1965-70, Hispanic Found., Libr. Congress, Washington, 1964-65; Fulbright rsch. scholar, France, 1956-57; Fulbright lectr. U. Córdoba (Argentina), 1958, adviser, 1970; adviser U. San Marcos, Peru, 1962, 75; external examiner U. West Indies, Jamaica, 1974-78; cons. Bibliothèque Nationale, France, 1979, 81-87; ofcl. rep. 350th anniversary Harvard U., 1986, Libr. of Congress Bicentennial, 2000; sr. fellow Dominican U., 1989—; vis. prof. faculty philosophy and letters U. Buenos Aires, 1991; dir. various activities on the Quin centennial and librs. in Latin Am., 1992; adv. U. Francisco Marroquín, Guatemala, 1992-2005; U. del Norte, Barranquilla, Colombia, 1993, various univs. and librs. in El Salvador, 1994-2003, Nat. Libr. and Archives Sch., Mexico City, 1995; adviser Francisco Marroquin Found., 2002-06, Am. U. Paris, 2005; pres. Coun. Books and Librs. in L.Am., 1993—; adviser Nat. Pedagogical U., Honduras, 2006; lectr. in field Author: Basic Library Techniques, 1955, A Handbook of American Library Resources, 1955, 2d edit., 1962, Studies in Library Resources, 1958, The Foundation Grants Program, 1959, The Libraries of the Associated Colleges of the Midwest, 1960, Aspects of Librarianship in Latin America, 1962, second series, 1992, Library Guide for Brazilian Studies, 1964, The National Textbook Program and Libraries in Brazil, 1967, Resources of Research Libraries, 1969, Steps Toward the Future Development of a National Plan for Library Services in Colombia, 1971, Catalog of Brazilian Acquisitions of Library of Congress, 1964-74, 1977, Resources for Brazilian Studies at the Bibliothèque Nationale, 1980, Library Resources of Harvard University, 1986, Las Megabibliotecas, una Bibliografía Comentada, 1993, Resources of Research Libraries: A Bibliographical Guide to Printed Material, 1998, Nueve Bibliotecarios Distinguidos, 2004; editor: U. Ill. Library Sch. Assn. News Letter, 1954-56, Assn. Coll. Research Libraries Monographs, 1961-66, Latin Am. Collections, 1974, Reference Publications in Latin American Studies, 1977-92, Library and Information Science Education in the Americas: Present and Future, 1981, Library and Information Science in France: A 1983 Overview, 1984, Doce Bibliotecarios Latinoamericanos, 1992; mem. editorial staff Libr. Trends, 1958-62, Ency. Libr. and Info. Sci., 1971-90, Jour. Libr. History, 1976-88, Internat. Jour. Revs. in Libr. and Info. Sci., 1985-88; assoc. editor World Librs., 1990-99, consulting editor, 2000-; contbr. articles to profl. jours. and encys Mem. ALA (chmn. internat. rels. round table 1965-66, trustee endowment funds 1977-86), Ill. Libr. Assn., Assn. Libr. and Info. Sci. Edn., Bibliog. Soc. Am., Assn. Coll. and Rsch. Libraries, MLA, Am. Assn. Tchrs. Spanish and Portuguese, Theatre Libr. Assn., Conf. on Latin Am. History, Latin Am. Studies Assn., Sem. on Acquisition Latin Am. Library Materials (pres. 1977-78), Assn. Caribbean U. and Rsch. Libraries, Asociación Paceña de Bibliotecarios (hon.; La Paz, Bolivia), Henry Wade Rogers Soc., John Harvard Soc., Phi Beta Kappa, Beta Phi Mu (pres. 1955-56), Phi Sigma Iota, Sigma Delta Pi (hon.), Phi Lambda Beta (hon.) Clubs: Harvard (Chgo.), Caxton (Chgo.). Home: 196 W Kathleen Dr Park Ridge IL 60068-2618 Office: Dominican U 7900 W Division St River Forest IL 60305

JACKSON, WILLIE, writer, researcher; b. Lake Providence, La., Dec. 8, 1948; s. Cleophus and Martha Jackson. Student, Grambling Coll., 1967—68. Founder Jackson Book Co. Author more than 60 books, Sweet Desperations, 1973, (poetry) Redemption, 1979, The Ideal Human State, 1980, A Son of Lake Providence, Martha's Only Son, (poetry) From Day to Day, 4 vols., 2001—03, The Evidence of Love, 2001, Servant of Humanity, 2003, Eternal Romantic Love, 2003; recordings: (speechs on oudio cassettes). Founder Jackson Peace Campaign. With US Army, 1969—71. Achievements include research in cell biology, cancer; more than 30 inventions. Home: PO Box 94325 Park Hill Sta North Little Rock AR 72190 Office Phone: 501-340-5151.

JACKSON, YVONNE RUTH, former pharmaceutical executive; b. LA, June 30, 1949; d. Giles B. Jackson and Gwendolyn (Battle); m. Frederic Jackson, Jr., Mar. 24, 1989; children: Cortney, Douglass. BA, Spelman Coll., 1970; MA, Harvard U., 1985. Asst. dept. mgr. to dept. mgr. Sears, Roebuck & Co., Torrance, Calif., 1970—71, asst. buyer, asst. retail sales mgr. NYC, 1972—77, pers. mgr., 1977—79; exec. recruiter employee rels.mgr., dir human resources Avon Products, Inc., 1979—85, dir. mfr., redeployment, fir human resources internat., 1985—87, v.p. internat., v.p. human resources, 1987—93; sr. v.p. worldwide human resources Burger King Corp., 1993—99; sr. v.p. human resources Compaq Computer Corp., Houston, 1999—2002, Pfizer, Inc., NYC, 2003—05; founder, pres. BeecherJackson, Coral Gables, Fla., 2005—. Apptd. Pfizer Leadership Team; bd. trustees Spelman Coll., 1996—, chmn., 2004—; bd. dirs. Inst. Women's Policy Rsch., Girls, Inc., Winn-Dixie Stores, Inc., 2006—; mem. adv. bd. Catalyst, 1993—. Named a Black Achiever, YMCA, 1986, Woman Achiever, YMCA of Greater NY, 1992; recipient Bus. Achievement award, Spelman Coll. Alumnae Assn., 1993. Office: BeecherJackson 13633 Deering Bay Dr Ste 235 Coral Gables FL 33158 Office Phone: 212-733-2323.*

JACKSON LEE, SHEILA, congresswoman; b. Queens, NY, Jan. 12, 1950; d. Erica Shelwyn and Jason Cornelius Bennett; m. Elwyn C. Lee; 2 children. BA with honors in Polit. Sci., Yale U., New Haven, 1972; JD, U. Va. Sch. Law, Charlottesville, 1975. Bar: Tex. Sr. counsel select com. on assassinations US Congress, 1977—78; trial atty. Fulbright and Jaworski, 1978-80; sr. atty. United Energy Resources, Inc., 1980; assoc. judge Mcpl. Ct., Houston, 1987-89; mem. City Coun., Houston, 1990-94, US Congress from 18th Tex. dist., 1995—, mem. judiciary com., ranking mem. immigration, border security and claims subcommittee, mem. sci. com., mem. homeland security com., founder Congl. Children's Caucus. Named one of 100 Most Influential Black Americans, Ebony mag., 2006; recipient Top Women in the Sciences Award, Nat. Tech. Assn. of Scientists and Engrs., 1998, Policy award, Phillip Burton Immigration & Civil Rights Awards, 2006. Mem.: Tex. Mcpl. Judges Assn., State Bar Assn. Justice Com. Democrat. Office: US Ho Reps 2435 Rayburn Ho Office Bldg Washington DC 20515-4318 Office Phone: 202-225-3816.*

JACKSON-LESLIE, LLENDA DIANE, media consultant; b. Oct. 1955; B, Univ. Mich., Ann Arbor. Dir, media, mktg. NAACP, Detroit; staff asst. Hon. John Conyers; dep. dir., pub. info. Detroit; comm. dir. Third Judicial Cir. Ct.; comm. coord. Coalition to Defend Equal Opportunity; press sec. City Council mem. JoAnn Watson, Detroit; now cons. pub. rels., Detroit. V.p., comm Nat. Women's Polit. Caucus, Washington, 1999—2004, pres., 2004—. Named one of 150 Disting. Women of Detroit, Women's Informal Network; recipient Harriet Tubman award, Detroit NOW, Horizon award, Detroit Human Rights Commn., Disting. Leadership award, Cmty. Services Commn., Shirley Chisholm Unbought and Unbossed award, Nat. Polit. Congress of Black Women. Mem.: NAACP.*

JACKSON-TKAC, STEPHANIE ANN, nurse; b. Thomasville, NC, Jan. 2, 1960; d. Ellis Wade and Nancy (Myers) Jackson. BSN, East Carolina U., 1982. RN, cert. case mgr., infusion nurse. Staff nurse Pitt County Meml. Hosp., Greenville, N.C., 1981-83, N.C. Bapt. Hosp., Winston-Salem, N.C., 1983-87, Duke U. Med. Ctr., Durham, N.C., 1987-91, Rex Hosp., Raleigh, 1991—92; nurse clinician Health Infusion, Morrisville, 1992—95, Coram Health Care (formerly Health Infusion), Morrisville, 1992—94, infusion care mgr. Goldsboro and Kinston brs., 1995-96; with Chartwell S.E., 1996-97; per diem case mgr. Columbia Home Care, Raleigh, N.C.; home health per diem clin. nurse U. N.C., Chapel Hill; collections spec. Am. Red Cross; case mgr. Killette and Assocs., Inc., 1999—2004; nurse cons. PPD Med. Comm., Durham, NC, 2004; med. case mgr. Crawford & Co., Raleigh, NC, 2005, Carolina Case Mgmt., Raleigh, NC, 2005—. Mem.: Carolina Case Mgmt., Infusion Nurses Soc., Case Mgr. Soc. Am. Republican.

JACKSON WRIGHT, ADRIENNE A., educational consultant; b. Calif., 1960; d. Harold and Clora (Ellis) J.; m. Kenneth E. Wright, Nov. 2005. BA, Chapman U., Orange, Calif., 1982, MA, 1988; EdD, U. So. Calif., 1997. Teaching and Adminstrv. Svcs. Cert., Calif. Dance instr. Centinela Valley Union High Sch. Dist., Lawndale, Calif., 1987-90; dir. of activities Tustin (Calif.) Unified Sch. Dist., 1990-93; vice prin. Grossmont (Calif.) Union High Sch. Dist., 1993—97; prin. Inglewood Unified Sch. Dist., 1997—2000, Montgomery County Pub. Schs., 2000—05; ednl. cons. Coastline C.C., 2006—. Mem. ASCD, Coalition of One Hundred Black Women (charter mem. San Diego chpt.), Newport Beach C. of C., Phi Delpa Kappa, Delta Gamma. Avocations: choreography, travel, cooking, reading. Office Phone: 949-355-6078. Personal E-mail: jacksal2@sbcglobal.net.

JACO, WILLIAM H., mathematics professor, researcher; b. Grafton, W.Va., July 14, 1940; s. William Howard Sr. and Catherine Virginia (White) J.; children: William, Brent; m. Linda Kanewske, May 6, 1978; children: John, Andrew. BA magna cum laude, Fairmount State U., W.Va., 1962; MA, Pa. State U., 1964; PhD, U. Wis., 1968. Project mathematician Ordinance Rsch. Lab., University Park, Pa., 1962-64; asst. prof. U. Mich., Ann Arbor, 1968-73, Rice U., Houston, 1970-73, assoc. prof., 1973-78, prof., 1978-82; head dept. math. Okla. State U., Stillwater, 1982-87, prof. math., 1982-93; exec. dir. Am. Math. Soc., Providence, 1988-95; Grayce B. Kerr prof. math. Okla. State U., Stillwater, 1993—. Mem. Joint Policy Bd. for Math., Washington, 1988-95, Bd. Math. Scis., Washington, 1987-90, Inst. for Advanced Study, 1971-72, 78-79, 86; vice chmn. R.I. Math. Scis. Edn. Coalition, Providence, 1990; sr. rsch. fellow Math. Scis. Rsch. Inst., 1984-85, Am. Inst. Math., 2000, bd. dirs. 1997-; professorial rsch. fellow U. Melbourne, Australia, 1987-88, 95-96; Gehring vis. chair. U. Mich., 2005-. Author: Lectures on Three-Manifolds, 1977; co-author: Seifert Fibered Manifolds, 1979; editor: Contemporary Math., 1985-88; contbr. articles to profl. jours. Active Bd. Edn. Devel. Fund, Providence, 1991-95; mem. adv. bd. Roger Williams Coll. Sch. Sci. and Math., Bristol, R.I., 1990-95. Graduate fellow NSF, 1964-67, Postdoctoral fellow NSF, 1971-72; Rsch. grantee, NSF, 1968-88, 96—. Fellow AAAS. Office: Okla State Univ Math Dept 401 Math Scis Stillwater OK 74078-0001 Office Phone: 405-744-5688. Business E-Mail: jaco@math.okstate.edu.

JACOB, BERNARD MICHEL, architect; b. Paris; arrived in U.S., 1950, naturalized; s. Paul and Therese (Abase) J.; m. Rosamond Gale Tryon; children: Clara, Paul. Diploma in architecture, Cooper Union; BArch, U. Minn. Registered architect, Minn. Sr. designer Ellerbe Assocs., St. Paul; head design Grover Dimond & Assocs., St. Paul; co-founder Team 70 Architects, St. Paul, 1970—, pres., 1977—83, Bernard Jacob Architects Ltd., Mpls., 1983—. Mem. constrn. panel Am. Arbitration Assn., 1973—; lectr. Sch. Architecture, U. Minn., Mpls., 1982— Editor: Architecture Minn. Mag., Minn. Soc. Architects, 1970-80; archtl. criticism columnist: Mpls. Star and Tribune, 1980-83, Corp. Report Mag., 1983; reviewer: (archtl. books) Choice Mag.; co-author: Skyway Typology/Mpls., Pocket Architecture/A Walking Guide to the Architecture Downtown Mpls. and St. Paul, 2d. rev. edit., 1988, Letters to Palladio, 1999. Founding chmn. Heritage Preservation Commn., St. Paul; past mem. St. Paul Planning Bd.; apptd. mem. Minn. State Designer Selection Bd., 1987-90; bd. dirs. Winslow House, 1995-97; chmn. archtl. subcom. Minn. Gov.'s Residence Coun., 1996-99. Fellow: AIA. Office: 825 Nicollet Mall Ste 1447 Minneapolis MN 55402-2703 Office Phone: 612-332-5517. Business E-Mail: palladio@skypoint.com.

JACOB, BRUCE ROBERT, law educator; b. Chgo., Mar. 26, 1935; s. Edward Carl and Elsie Berthe (Hartmann) J.; m. Ann Wear, Sept. 8, 1962; children: Bruce Ledley, Lee Ann, Brian Edward. BA, Fla. State U., 1957; JD, Stetson U., 1959; LLM, Northwestern U., 1965; SJD, Harvard U., 1980; LLM in Taxation, U. Fla., 1995. Bar: Fla. 1959, Ill. 1965, Mass. 1970, Ohio 1972. Asst. atty. gen. State of Fla., 1960-62; assoc. Holland, Bevis & Smith, Bartow, Fla., 1962-64; asst. to assoc. prof. Emory U. Sch. Law, 1965-69; rsch. assoc. Ctr. for Criminal Justice, Harvard Law Sch., 1969-70; staff atty. Cmty. Legal Assistance Office, Cambridge, Mass., 1970-71; assoc. prof. Coll. Law, Ohio State U., 1971-73, prof., dir. clin. programs, 1973-78; dean, prof. Mercer U. Law Sch., Macon, Ga., 1978-81; v.p., dean, prof. Stetson U. Coll. Law, St. Petersburg, Fla., 1981-94, dean emeritus, prof., 1994—. Contbr. articles to profl. jours. Mem. Fla. Bar, Sigma Chi. Democrat. Home: 1946 Coffee Pot Blvd NE Saint Petersburg FL 33704-4632 Office: Stetson U Coll Law 1401 61st St S Saint Petersburg FL 33707-3246 Office Phone: 727-562-7866. Business E-Mail: jacob@law.stetson.edu.

JACOB, DEIRDRE ANN BRADBURY, manufacturing executive, finance educator, consultant; b. Providence, Mar. 7, 1952; d. John Joseph and Marion Damon (Shute) Bradbury; m. Thomas Keenan, Nov. 15, 1975 (div. Dec. 1980); 1 child: Victoria Irene; m. Robert A. Jacob, June 22, 1996; 1 child, Meggin Rosemary. BA in Govt. and Law, Lafayette Coll., 1973. Supr. Procter & Gamble Mfg. Co., SI, N.Y., 1973-76, mgr. warehouse dept., 1976-79, mgr. shortening and oils, 1979-81, fin. mgr. food plant, 1981-82, mgr. personnel, 1982-86, mgr. total quality and pub. affairs, 1986-91; ptnr. Avraham Y. Goldratt Inst., New Haven, 1991—2005, exec. v.p., 2005—06, mng. ptnr., 2006—; pres. AYG, Inc., 2006—. Cons. Procter & Gamble, SI, 1987—89, Cin., 1989—91. Trustee Lafayette Coll., 1985-90. Mem. Lafayette Coll. Alumni Assn. (pres. 1992-94, Clifton P. Mayfield award), Maroon Club (Easton, Pa., pres. 1987-89). Roman Catholic. Avocation: singing. Office: Avraham Y Goldratt Inst 442 Orange St New Haven CT 06511-6201 E-mail: dee.jacob@goldratt.com.

JACOB, EDWIN J., lawyer; b. Detroit, Aug. 25, 1927; s. A. Aubrey and Estelle R. (Vesell) J.; m. Constance Dorfman, June 15, 1948; children Louise, Beth, Ellen. AB cum laude, Harvard U., 1948, JD cum laude, 1951. Bar: N.Y. 1951, U.S. Dist. Ct. (so. dist.) N.Y. 1953, U.S. Dist. Ct. (ea. dist.) N.Y. 1953, U.S. Ct. Appeals (2d cir.) 1954, U.S. Supreme Ct. 1963, U.S. Ct. Appeals (8th cir.) 1981, U.S. Ct. Appeals (10th cir.) 1987. Assoc. Davis Polk Wardwell Sunderland & Kiendl, NYC, 1951-62; ptnr. Cabell, Medinger, Forsyth & Decker, NYC, 1962-69, Lauterstein & Lauterstein, NYC, 1969-72, Jacob, Medinger & Finnegan, LLP, NYC, 1973—. Bd. advisors Inst. for Health Policy Analysis, Georgetown U., 1987-90. Contbr. articles to profl. jours. Mem. nat. bd. Assn. Ref. Zionists Am., 1991-97; trustee Stephen Wise Free Synagogue, 1991—, pres., 1994-96. With USN, 1945—46. Mem. Am. Law Inst., Am. Judicature Soc., Assn. Bar City N.Y. Clubs: Harvard of N.Y.C. Office: Jacob Medinger Finnegan LLP 1270 Ave of Americas New York NY 10020 Home Phone: 212-757-2425; Office Phone: 212-524-5000. Business E-Mail: ejjacob@jmfnylaw.com.

JACOB, FRANÇOIS, biologist, educator; b. Nancy, France, June 17, 1920; s. Simon and Therese (Franck) Jacob; m. Lysiane Bloch, Nov. 27, 1947 (dec. 1984); children: Pierre, Laurent, Odile, Henri; m. Geneviève Barrier, 1999. MD, Faculty of Medicine, Paris, 1947; DSc, Faculty of Scis., Paris, 1954; DSc (hon.), U. Chgo., 1965; Dr (hon.), various univs. Asst. Pasteur Inst., 1950—56, head dept. cellular genetics, 1960—92, pres., 1982—88; prof. cellular genetics Coll. of France, 1964—92; prof. emeritus Coll. of France and Inst. Pasteur, 1992—. Author: (books) The Logic of Life, 1970, The Possible and the Actual, 1981, The Statue Within, 1987, Of Flies, Mice and Men, 1997. Recipient Charles Leopold Mayer prize, 1962, Nobel prize in physiology and medicine (with A. Lwoff and J. Monod), 1965. Mem.: Royal Acad. Scis. Madrid, Acad. Scis. Hungary, Royal Acad. Medicine Belgique, Royal Soc. (London), Am. Philos Soc., Nat. Acad. Scis., Am. Acad. Arts and Scis. (fgn.), Royal Danish Acad. Scis. and Letters (fgn.), Acad. Française Paris, Acad. Sci. (Paris). Achievements include research in on genetics bacterial cells and viruses; contbr. to mechanisms of information transfer (messenger RNA) and genetic basis of regulatory circuits, early stages of the mouse embryo. Office: Pasteur Inst 25 Rue du Dr Roux 75724 Paris Cedex 15 France Office Phone: 0145688487. Business E-Mail: fjacob@pasteur.fr.

JACOB, MARVIN EUGENE, lawyer; b. NYC, Feb. 4, 1935; s. Sam Jacob and Ann (Garfinkel) Law; m. Atara Binnun, Mar. 27, 1960; children: Shalom J., Aviva, Asher. BA, Bklyn. Coll., 1961; JD cum laude, N.Y. Law Sch., 1964. Bar: N.Y. 1964, U.S. Supreme Ct. 1967. Assoc. regional adminstr. SEC, NYC, 1964-79; ptnr. Weil, Gotshal & Manges, NYC, 1979—. Adj. prof. law N.Y. Law Sch., 1972-97. Editor: Restructurings, 1993, Reorganizing Failing Businesses, 1999. Mem. ABA, N.Y. State Bar Assn. Office: Weil Gotshal & Manges 767 5th Ave Fl 29 New York NY 10153-0023 Business E-Mail: marvin.jacob@weil.com.

JACOB, PAUL BERNARD, JR., electrical engineering educator; b. Columbus, Miss., June 9, 1922; s. Paul Bernard and Sarah Dorsey (Jamison) J.; m. Mildred Evelyn Hammack, Aug. 20, 1946; children: William Boswell, Paul Bernard, III. BS in Elec. Engring., Miss. State U., 1944; MS, Northwestern U., 1948. Registered profl. engr., Miss. Engr., Tenn. Eastman Corp., Oak Ridge, 1944-46; mem. faculty Miss. State U., 1946-88, prof. elec. engring., 1956-88, prof. emeritus, 1988—, assoc. head dept., 1962-88, Paul B. Jacob high voltage lab. and Paul B. Jacob endowed prof. chair elec. and computer engring. dept. Cons. in field; mem. steering com. Internat. Symposium on High Voltage Engring., 1987—. Author articles on high voltage engring. Recipient Alumnus of Yr. award Miss. State U., 1987, UOP Tech. award Instrument Soc. Am., 1988 Mem. IEEE (life), Power Engring. Soc. (chmn. com., Com. Disting. Svc. award), Am. Soc. Engring. Edn., Sigma Xi, Tau Beta Pi, Eta Kappa Nu (dir. 1962-63, nat. v.p. 1982-83, nat. pres. 1983-84), Phi Kappa Phi, Sigma Alpha Epsilon (bd. dirs. 1961-69, nat. pres. 1969-71, Disting. Svc. award 1975, Highest Effort award for profl. accomplishments 1986, Merit Key award, Order of the True Gentleman 1994), Omicron Delta Kappa. Clubs: Rotary (past pres. Starkville, Miss.). Baptist. Home and Office: 102 Kenswick Ct Starkville MS 39759-9493 E-mail: pbj@ece.msstate.edu.

JACOB, STANLEY WALLACE, surgeon, educator; b. Phila., 1924; s. Abraham and Belle (Shulman) J.; m. Marilyn Peters; 1 son, Stephen; m. Beverly Swarts; children: Jeffrey, Darren, Robert; m. Gail Brandis; 1 dau., Elyse. BA, Ohio State U., Columbus, 1945; MD cum laude, Ohio State U. Med. Sch., Columbus, 1948. Diplomate Am. Bd. Surgery. Intern Beth Israel Hosp., Boston, 1948-49, resident surgery, 1949-52, 54-56; chief resident surg. svc. Harvard Med. Sch., 1956-57, instr., 1958-59; assoc. vis. surgeon Boston City Hosp., 1958-59; Kemper Found. rsch. scholar ACS, 1957-60; asst. prof. surgery U. Oreg. Med. Sch., Portland, 1959-66, assoc. prof., 1966—; Gerlinger prof. surgery Oreg. Health Scis. U., 1981—. Author: Structure and Function in Man, 5th edit, 1982, Laboratory Guide for Structure and Function in Man, 1982, Dimethyl Sulfoxide Basic Concepts, 1971, Biological Actions of DMSO, 1975, Elements of Anatomy and Physiology, 1989; contbr.: Ency. Britanica. Served to capt. M.C. AUS, 1952-54; col. Res. ret. Recipient Gov.'s award Outstanding N.W. Scientist, 1965; 1st pl. German Sci. award, 1960; Markle scholar med. scis., 1960. Mem. Phi Beta Kappa, Sigma Xi, Alpha Omega Alpha. Achievements include co-discovery of therapeutic usefulness of dimethyl sulfoxide and MSM. Home: 1055 SW Westwood Ct Portland OR 97239-2708 Office: Oreg Health Scis U Dept Surgery 3181 SW Sam Jackson Park Rd Portland OR 97239 Business E-Mail: jacobs@ohsu.edu.

JACOBI, FREDRICK THOMAS, newspaper publisher; b. Neenah, Wis., July 10, 1953; s. H. Paul and Patricia Mary (Steele) J.; m. Kim Lee Muenchow, Aug. 23, 1980; children: James Paul, Steven Thomas. AA in Bus., U. South Fla., 1973; BBA in Fin., Mktg., U. Wis., 1976; MBA in

Mktg., U. Wis., Whitewater, 1980. Cert. newspaper circulation. City dist. mgr. Madison (Wis.) Newspapers Inc., 1977-79, city circulation mgr., 1979-80, circulation mgr., 1980-81, mktg. mgr., 1981-82, circulation dir., 1982-85, Gannett Co., Inc., Reno, Nev., 1985-88, regional circulation dir. Arlington, Va., 1988-90; pub., pres. Wausau (Wis.) Daily Herald, Gannett Co., Inc., 1990-92, Springfield (Mo.) News-Leader, 1993-96; v.p. Midwest region Gannett Co., Inc., 1993-96; pub., pres. Ft. Myers (Fla.) News-Press, 1996-2000, Rockford (Ill.) Register-Star, 2000—. Bd. dir. Coun. of 100, Rockford Coll., Inland Press Found.; com. chmn. Sales and Mktg. Exec., Madison, Ill., 1985. Editor: Circulation-Central States, 1985. Program chmn. Jr. Achievement of Nev., Reno, 1987—88; pres. Springfield Bus. and Devel. Corp., 1996; bd. dir. Ozarks Press Assn., Make A Wish Mo., Horizon Econ. Devel. , 1997—2000, Lee County Pub. Schs. Found., 1997—2000. Mem.: Newspaper Assn. Am., Inland Press Assn., Ill. Press Assn., Young Pres.'s Orgn., The Exec. Com., Rotary. Republican. Roman Catholic. Avocations: micro-computers, running, gardening. Office: Rockford Register Star 99 E State St Rockford IL 61104 Office Phone: 815-987-1451. E-mail: fjacobi1@rockford.gannett.com.

JACOBI, PETER PAUL, journalism educator, writer; b. Berlin, Mar. 15, 1930; came to U.S., 1938, naturalized, 1944; s. Paul A. and Liesbeth (Kron) J.; m. Harriet Ackley, Dec. 8, 1956 (div. 1979); children: Keith Peter, John Wyn. BS in Journalism, Northwestern U., 1952, MS, 1953. Mem. journalism faculty Northwestern U., Evanston, Ill., 1955-81, profl. lectr., 1955-63, asst. prof., 1963-66, assoc. prof., 1966-69, prof. journalism, 1969-81, assoc. dean, 1966-74; communications cons. NYC, 1980-84, Bloomington, Ind., 1985—; prof. journalism Ind. U., Bloomington, 1985-99, prof. emeritus, 1999—. News assignment editor, newscaster, theatre and music reporter NBC, Chgo., 1955-61; news editor ABC, Chgo., 1951-53; radio commentator on music and opera, 1958-65; theatre and film critic Sta. WTTW, Chgo., 1964-74, arts critic, 1975-77; theatre and film critic Hollister Newspapers Suburban Chgo., 1963-70; music columnist Chicagoan mag., 1973-74; script cons. Goodman Theater, Chgo., 1973-75; syndicated commentator on arts and media N.Am. Radio Alliance, 1978-80; arts corr. Christian Sci. Monitor, 1956-81; music critic, columnist Bloomington (Ind.) Herald-Times, 1985—; columnist Arts Indiana, 1987-2001, Editors Only, 1994—, Editor's Workshop, 1995-98. Author: Writing with Style, The News Story and the Feature, 1982, The Messiah Book-The Life and Times of G.F. Handel's Greatest Hit, 1982, (with Jack Hilton) Straight Talk about Videoconferencing, 1986, The Magazine Article: How to Think It, Plan It, Write It, 1991, (with others) From Budapest to Bloomington, Janos Starker and the Hungarian Cello Tradition, 1999; contbg. essayist Lyric Opera Companion, 1991; editor Chgo. Lyric Opera News, 1958-61, Music Mag./Musical Courier, Chgo., 1961-62; contbr. articles on writing to Folio, Ragan Report, other mags., articles on arts to Sat. Rev., Chgo. Daily News, N.Y. Times, Highlights for Children, World Book, others. Mem. AAUP, NATAS, Assn. Edn. in Journalism, Soc. Profl. Journalists, Ind. Arts Commn. (chmn. 1990-93), Arts Midwest, Bloomington Cmty. Arts Commn. Home: 3003 N Browncliff Ln Bloomington IN 47408-1317 Office: Ind U Sch Journalism Bloomington IN 47405 Office Phone: 812-334-0063.

JACOBOWITZ, ELLEN SUE, curator, museum administrator; b. Detroit, Feb. 21, 1948; d. Theodore Mark and Lois Clairesse (Levy) Jacobowitz. BA, U. Mich., 1969, MA, 1970; postgrad., Bryn Mawr Coll., 1976—83, Wharton Sch., 1997. Curator Phila. Mus. Art, 1972-90; adminstr. Cranbrook Inst. Sci., Bloomfield Hills, Mich., 1991-94; adminstr. Temple Emanu-El, Oak Park, Mich., 1995-96. Cons. ArtServe Mich., 1997; primary caregiver, 1998—2004. Author: The Prints of Lucas Van Leyden, 1983, American Graphics 1860-1940, 1982. Treas. Sat. Luncheon Club, 1995—96, pres., 1999—2000; active Leadership Oakland, Detroit Inst. Arts, 1993—2007; mem. Nat. Coun. Jewish Women, Detroit, 1990—2007; com. mem. Franklin Archives Temple Beth El, 1991—2007; bd. dirs. Print Coun. Am., Balt., Netherlands Am. Amity Trust, Washington, 1982—84, Mich. Mus. Assn., 1993—94. Mem.: Detroit Inst. Arts, U. Mich. Alumni Assn., Am. Jewish Com. Avocations: cooking, gardening, reading, the arts, sports.

JACOBOWITZ, ISRAEL JACOB, cardiothoracic surgeon; b. Lanzberg, Germany, Nov. 8, 1947; came to U.S., 1949; MD, SUNY, Buffalo, 1973. Diplomate Am. Bd. Thoracic Surgery. Attending surgeon in cardiothoracic surgery Maimonides Med. Ctr., Bklyn., 1982—, Brookdale Med. Ctr. SUNY, Downstate Med. Ctr. Prof. surgery SUNY, Bklyn., 1991—. Fellow ACS, Am. Coll. Chest Physicians, Am. Coll. Cardiology. Office: 984 50th St Brooklyn NY 11219

JACOBS, ALAN MARTIN, physicist, researcher; b. NYC, Nov. 14, 1932; s. Samuel J. and Amelia M. (Ziegler) J.; m. Evelyn Lee Banner, Aug. 7, 1955 (dec. Jan. 1977); children: Frederick Ethen, Heidi Joelle; m. Sharon Lynn Auerbach, Oct. 14, 1978; children: Aaron Michael, Seth Joseph. B.Engring. Physics (John McMullen scholar, LeVerne Noyes scholar, Clevite scholar), Cornell U., Ithaca, NY, 1955; postgrad., Oak Ridge Sch. Reactor Tech., 1955-56; MS, in Physics, Pa. State U., 1958, PhD, 1963. Research asso. nuclear reactor facility Pa. State U., 1956-63, mem. faculty, 1963—, prof. nuclear engring., 1968-80; prof. U. Fla., Gainesville, 1980—, chmn. dept. nuclear engring. scis., 1980-82; chief scientist Future Tech, Inc., Gainesville, 1986-87. Cons. to industry. Co-author: Basic Principles of Nuclear Science and Reactors, 1960; patentee dynamic radiography, control of radiation beams by vibrating media, multichannel radiograph, digital x-ray imaging system, snapshot backscatter x-ray imaging system, radiography by selection detection scatter field components. NSF sci. faculty fellow, 1960-61; recipient Glenn Murphy award for nuclear sci. edn. ASEE, 1994. Mem.: Tau Beta Pi, Sigma Xi, Pi Mu Epsilon. Home: 3718 SW 80th Dr Gainesville FL 32608-3662 Office: Dept Nuclear & Radiol Engring U Fla Gainesville FL 32611-8300 E-mail: jacobs@ufl.edu.

JACOBS, ALBERT LIONEL, JR., lawyer; b. Pitts., May 6, 1939; s. Albert Lionel and Sarah Edith (Burns) J.; m. Laurel Elizabeth Moore, Dec. 20, 1960 (div. 1982); children: Laura Jean, Patricia Anne, Albert Lionel III, Robert Charles, Michael Peter; m. Carol S. Fisher, Feb. 6, 1983; children: Daniel Stephen, David Andrew. BA, Harvard U., 1961; JD, Columbia U., 1964. Bar: N.Y. 1964, D.C. 1966, U.S. Dist. Ct. (so., ea., no.), N.Y. 1969, U.S. Dist. Ct. (we. dist.), N.Y. 1978, U.S. Ct. Appeals (D.C. cir., 2d cir.), U.S. Ct. Appeals (1st cir.), 1968, U.S. Ct. Appeals (9th cir.)1982, U.S. Ct. Appeals (10th cir.), U.S. Ct. Appeals (fed. cir.), U.S. Ct. Claims, U.S. Supreme Ct. Ptnr. Jacobs & Jacobs, NYC, 1965-70, pres., chmn. bd. dirs., 1970; pres., ptnr., chmn. intellectual property dept. Rosenman & Colin, NYC, 1991; now shareholder, nat. chair, intellectual property dept. Greenberg Traurig, LLP, NYC. Bd. dirs. A.L.E. Industries, Inc., N.Y.C., Meditech Ltd., Chappaqua, N.Y., Internat. Bioimmune Systems, Inc. Bd. dirs. Chappaqua (N.Y.) Children's Workshop, 1990-93. Mem. ABA, Harvard Club (N.Y.C., mem. bd. ho. com., chmn. athletic com., chmn. food and wine com.), Univ. Club, N.Y. Athletic Club, Met. Squash Rackets Assn. Avocations: food and wine, squash, skiing, tennis. Office: Greenberg Traurig LLP MetLife Bldg 200 Park Ave New York NY 10166 Office Phone: 212-801-9200. Office Fax: 212-801-6400. Business E-Mail: jacobsa@gtlaw.com.

JACOBS, ALONZO, federal agency contracting officer; b. San Diego, Nov. 30, 1949; s. George and Alberta Jacobs; m. Luella Simmons, Dec. 31, 1975 (div. Apr. 15, 1998); m. Sharen Marie Jones, Oct. 11, 1999; 1 child, Kendall Raschid; life ptnr. Bonnie Lee Pyett; 1 child, Emilee Ashley Pyett. BSBA, Grambling State U., La., 1976. Broadcast lic. FCC, 1998. Contract specialist USN Aviation Supply Office, Phila., 1976—79, US Nuc. Regulatory Commn., Washington, 1979—84; contract cost price analyst USAF Plant Rep. Office-Gen. Dynamics, Ft. Worth, 1984—85; staff cost price analyst DCASR Atlanta, Marietta, Ga., 1984—89; USAF contracting officer Air Force Office Sci. Rsch., Washington, 1989—96; procurement cons. Silver Spring, Md., 1996—97; advt. sales profl. CBS Radio, Rockville, Md., 1997—98; procurement cons. JF Kennedy Ctr. Performing Arts, Washington, 1998; cost price analyst DC Govt., Washington, 1998—2002; contract specialist NOAA, Silver Spring, 2002—04; contracting officer USDA, Farm Svcs. Agy., Washington, 2004—. Vol. swim instr. Nat. Capitol YMCA, Washington, 1997—2000. Cpl. USMC, 1968—71, Vietnam. Decorated Viet Nam Svc. medal USMC and Republic of South Vietnam, Vietnam Cross of Gallantry with palm device, Vietnam Campaign medal with device, Nat. Def. Svc. medal. Mem.: Vietnam Vets. Assn. Avocations: travel, swimming, music and sound reproduction and engineering. Office: USDA Farm Svcs Agy 1280 Maryland Ave SW Ste 580A Washington DC 20024 Home Phone: 301-780-5542; Office Phone: 202-205-9471.

JACOBS, ANDREW ROBERT, lawyer; b. Newark, Sept. 18, 1946; s. Seymour B. and Pearle (Flaschen) J.; m. Yardana Steinberg, July 10, 1976; 1 child, Suzanne Michal BA high honors, Rutgers U., 1968; JD, Columbia U., 1971. Bar: NJ 1971, DC 1976, US Dist. Ct. NJ 1971, US Ct. Appeals (3d cir.) 1974, US Supreme Ct. 1979, US Dist. Ct. (ea. and so. Dists.) NY 1980, NY 1980, Pa. 1981, US Ct. Appeals (2d cir.) 1984, US Claims Ct. 1986. Law clk. to chief judge US Dist. Ct., Newark, 1971—72; asst. U.S. atty. US Atty.'s Office, Newark, 1972—76; assoc. Cole Berman & Belsky, Rochelle Park, NJ, 1976, Lanigan O'Connell Jacobs & Chazin, Basking Ridge, N.J. and NYC, 1977—78, ptnr., 1979—82; asst. US atty. (ea. dist.), chief spl. pros., dep. chief criminal divsn. US Atty.'s Office, NYC, 1983—95; ptnr. Horowitz & Jacobs, Hackensack, N.J. and NYC, 1985—89, Gern, Dunetz, Davison & Weinstein, Roseland, N.J. and NYC, 1990—93, Fitzsimmons Ringle & Jacobs, Newark, Hackensack, and NYC, 1993—2000, Epstein, Fitzsimmons, Brown, Gioia, Jacobs and Sprouls, P.C., Chatham, Hackensack, NYC, 2000—07, Ramsey Berman PC, Morristown, NJ, 2007—; arbitrator, mediator Superior Ct. NJ. Faculty Practicing Law Inst., NYC, 1980—82; legal writing instr. N.Y. Law Sch., 1981—82; master Justice William J. Brennan, Jr., Chief Justice Arthur Vanderbilt Inn of Ct., 1995—. Trustee N.J. YM-YWHA Camps, Fairfield, NJ, Milford, Pa., 1985—, pres., 2001—04; trustee Congregation Shomrei Emunah, Montclair, NJ, 1985—96; pres. Rutgers Coll. Alumni Class 1968. Capt. US Army, 1997. Harlan Fiske Stone scholar; recipient US Dept. Justice Spl. commendation award, 1973, 75, US Dept. Treasury ATF cert. of Appreciation, 1976, Jerome Michael prize for Excellence in Trial Advocacy Columbia U Mem.: ATLA, ABA, Million Dollar Advs. Forum, Assn. Fed. Bar NJ, Essex County Bar Assn., Bergen County Bar Assn., Morris County Bar Assn. (trustee 2007—), Assn. Criminal Def. Lawyers NJ, NY State Trial Lawyers Assn., NY County Lawyers Assn. (fed. cts. com.), NJ State Bar Assn., Soc. Loyal Sons and Daus. of Rutgers Coll. (elected), Phi Beta Kappa. Office: Ramsey Berman PC 222 Ridgedale Ave PO Box 2249 Morristown NJ 07962 Home: 47 Haller Dr Cedar Grove NJ 07009 Office Phone: 973-267-9600 ext. 5482. Office Fax: 973-984-1632. Business E-Mail: ajacbos@ramseyberman.com.

JACOBS, ANN ELIZABETH, lawyer; b. Lima, Ohio, July 28, 1950; d. Warren Charles and Virginia Elizabeth (Lewis) J.; m. Mark S. Bush, Nov. 26, 1988; 1 child, Whitney Elizabeth. BA, George Washington U., 1972; JD, Cath. U., 1976. Bar: Ohio 1977, Calif. 1977, SC 2000, US Ct. Appeals (D.C. cir.) 1980, US Dist. Ct. (no. dist.) Ohio 1982. Asst. atty. gen. State of Ohio, Columbus, 1977-78; trial atty. EEOC of Ohio, Miami, Fla., 1978-80; pvt. practice Lima, 1980—. Bd. dirs. Allen County Blackhoof Area Legal Svcs. Assn., Marimor Industries, Inc., Lima, Apollo Career Ctr. V.p. Shawnee Sch. Dist. Bd. Edn., 2006-07, pres., legal liaison, 2007—; fundraiser Lima Symphony Orch., 1985, pres. legis. liaison, 2002-03; trustee Lima Art Assn., YWCA; bd. dirs. Sr. Citizens; bd. elders Market St. Presbyn. Ch., chair mission com., 2001. Recipient Recognition award US Naval Air Sta., Jacksonville, Fla., 1979. Mem. LWV, Ohio Bar Assn., Calif. Bar Assn., DC Bar Assn., Allen County Bar Assn. (chmn. juvenile ct. com. 1993), SC Bar Assn. Avocations: sailing, golf, reading. Home: 1529 Shawnee Rd Lima OH 45805-3801 Office: 558 W Spring St Lima OH 45801-4728 Office Phone: 419-229-9800. Personal E-mail: annjacobs@earthlink.net.

JACOBS, ARNOLD STEPHEN, lawyer; b. NYC, Feb. 26, 1940; s. Charles Edwin and Harriet (Flug) Jacobs; m. Ellen Margaret Kheel, June 10, 1962; children: Beryl Kheel, Arnold Stephen Jr. BME, Cornell U., 1961, MBA, 1963, LLB with distinction, 1964. Bar: NY 1964. Assoc. Hughes, Hubbard & Reed, NYC, 1964-65, 1967-71; ptnr. Shea & Gould, NYC, 1971-94, Proskauer Rose LLP, NYC, 1994—. Adj. prof. NYU Law Sch., NYC, 1977—91. Author: The Impact of Rule 10b-5, 3 vols., 1974, Litig. and Practice Under Rule 10b-5, 6 vols., 1981—2001, Manual of Corp. Forms for Securities Practice, 4 vols., 1981—, Opinion Letters in Securities Matters: Text-Clause-Law, 3 vols., 1980—, Section 16 of the Securities Exchange Act, 1 vol., 1989—, Disclosure and Remedies Under the Securities Laws, 6 vols., 2002—, The Williams Act: Tender Offers and Stock Accumulations, 1vol., 2005—; contbr. articles to profl. jours. Capt. US Army, 1965—67, Korea. Mem.: Assn. Bar City NY (chmn. securities regulation com. 1982—86), Harmonie Club (NYC). Home: 108 E 82nd St Apt 7A New York NY 10028-1136 Office: Proskauer Rose LLP 1585 Broadway New York NY 10036-8299 Office Phone: 212-969-3210. Business E-Mail: ajacobs@proskauer.com.

JACOBS, ARNOLD STEPHEN, writer, commentator; b. NYC, Mar. 20, 1968; s. Arnold Stephen Jacobs Sr. and Ellen Kheel Jacobs; m. Julie Schoenberg Jacobs, Sept. 9, 2000; 1 child, Jasper Kheel. BA, Brown U., 1990. Commentator NPR, NYC; sr. editor Entertainment Weekly, NYC, 1995—2000; editor at large Esquire, NYC, 2003—; columnist Life Mag., NYC, 2004—07, Mental Floss Mag., NYC, 2004—. Editor: What It Feels Like; author: The Know-It-All, America Off-Line, Fractured Fairy Tales, The Two Kings: Jesus and Elvis. Avocations: travel, reading. Office: Esquire 1790 Broadway New York NY 10019 Home Phone: 212-496-1190; Office Phone: 212-649-4256.

JACOBS, ARTHUR DIETRICH, health services executive, educator, researcher; b. Bklyn., Feb. 4, 1933; s. Lambert Dietrich and Paula Sophia (Knissel) Jacobs; m. Viva Jane Sims, Mar. 24, 1952; children: Archie(dec.) , David L., Dwayne C., Dianna K. Hatfield. BBA, Ariz. State U., 1962, MBA, 1966. Enlisted USAF, 1951, commd. 2d lt., 1962, advanced through grades to maj., 1972, ret., 1973; indsl. engr. Motorola, Phoenix, 1973-74; mgmt. cons. State of Ariz., 1974-76, Productivity Internat., Tempe, Ariz., 1976-79; faculty assoc. Coll. Bus. Adminstrn. Ariz. State U., Tempe, 1977-94, sr. lectr., 1995, ret., 1996. Productivity advisor Scottsdale Meml. Health Svcs. Co., Ariz., 1979—84; rschr. U.S. Internment of European-Am. Aliens and Citizens of European Ancestry during World War II. Author: (book) The Prison Called Hohenasperg: An American Boy Betrayed by His Government During World War II, 1999; editor, pub.: Freedom of Information Times; co-editor: The World War Two Experience - The Interment of German-Americans, Documents, vol. IV (now in spl. collections of USAF Acad.); contbr. Bd. dirs. United Way of Tempe, 1979—85. Recipient Meritorious Svc. award, Coll. Ozarks, Mo., 2000. Mem.: Ops. Rsch. Soc. Am., Inst. Indsl. Engrs. (pres.ctrl. Ariz. chpt. 1984—85), Am. Soc. Quality Control, Ariz. State U. Alumni Assn. (bd. dirs. 1973—79), Optimist (life), Delta Sigma Pi, Beta Gamma Sigma, Sigma Iota Epsilon. Achievements include research in the special collections of the United States Air Force Academy. Personal E-mail: adjacobs@cox.net.

JACOBS, BENJAMIN FRANKLIN, cardiologist; b. St. Louis, Oct. 2, 1942; MD, Tulane U., 1968. Intern Barnes Hosp., St. Louis, 1968-69, resident, 1969-70, VA Hosp., St. Louis, 1972-73; fellow in cardiology Ochsner Found. Hosp., New Orleans, 1973-75, staff cardiologist, 1975—78; with East Jefferson Gen. Hosp., Metairie, La. Fellow Am. Coll. Cardiology. Office: 4200 Houma Blvd Metairie LA 70006-2970 Office Phone: 504-454-4102. E-mail: bfj3@aol.com.

JACOBS, BETTY JANE LAZAROFF, communications educator; d. Saul and Rae (deceased) Lazaroff; m. Rabbi Sidney J. Jacobs, July 1, 1971 (dec. 2001). BSc in Comm., U. Ill., Champaign, 1966; MA in Mass. Comm., Calif. State U., Northridge, 1978. Prodn. assoc. Broadcasting Commn., Chgo., 1965—67; dir. broadcasting Chgo. Bd. of Rabbis, 1967—2001; prof, comm. West L.A. Coll., Culver City, Calif., 1972—, chair, lang. arts divsn., 2003—. Media cons. C.C. Consortium, LA, 1973—75. Co-author (non-fiction books) Clues About Jews For People Who Aren't, (book) 122 Clues For Jews Whose Children Intermarry, Jewish Clues to Your Health and Happiness. Bd. dirs. Zero Pet Population Growth, LA, 1979—81. Recipient NISOD Tchg. Excellence award, U. of Tex. at Austin, 1993, Emmy Nomination, Chgo. Acad. of TV Arts and Sci., 1968, Excellence in TV Writing and Prodn. award, Tikvah Inst., 1971, Creative TV Writing award, Hadassah, 1970. Mem.: Alpha Gamma Sigma (Tchg. Excellence award 2000, 2002, Tchg. Excellence award 2000, 2001, 2003, 2006). Jewish. Avocations: running, tennis, dogs, reading, movies. Office: West Los Angeles College 9000 Overland Ave Culver City CA 90230 Home Phone: 310-558-1166; Office Phone: 310-287-4207. Business E-Mail: jacobsbl@wlac.edu.

JACOBS, BRADLEY S., former rental company executive; CEO Amerex Oil Assocs., Inc., 1979-83; chmn., COO Hamilton Resources Ltd., 1984-89; founder, chmn., CEO United Waste Sys., Inc., 1989-97; co-founder, chmn., CEO United Rentals, Greenwich, 1997—2007.*

JACOBS, CARYN LESLIE, lawyer, former prosecutor; b. Chgo., Mar. 3, 1958; d. Edward Jesse and Ann Marie (Paun) J.; m. Daniel Goldman Cedarbaum, Sept. 6, 1987; children: Jacob Jesse, Samuel Goldman. AB with distinction, Stanford U., 1980; JD cum laude, Harvard U., 1983. Bar: Ill., US Dist. Ct. (no. dist. Ill.) 1984, US Ct. Appeals (8th cir.) 1986, US Ct. Appeals (7th cir.) 1987. Law clk. to Hon. Susan Getzendanner US Dist. Ct. (no. dist. Ill.), Chgo., 1983-85; assoc. Mayer, Brown & Platt, Chgo., 1985-88; asst. US atty. Chgo., 1988-93; ptnr. Mayer, Brown, Rowe & Maw, Chgo., 1993—. Mem. ABA, Phi Beta Kappa. Office: Mayer Brown Rowe & Maw 71 S Wacker Dr Chicago IL 60606 Office Phone: 312-701-7621. Office Fax: 312-706-8645. E-mail: cjacobs@mayerbrown.com.*

JACOBS, CHARLES NATHAN, editor, writer; b. Paterson, NJ, July 11, 1930; s. Samuel I. and Beatrice J. (Levine) J.; m. Joan Stearns Weiss, May 30, 1953 (div. 1979); children: Julie Gail, JoDee Winger; m. Rosalind H. Eigenfeld, Feb. 21, 1987. BA in Humanities, Columbia Coll., 1952; MS in Journalism, Columbia U., 1953. Reporter N.Y. Jour. Am., NYC, 1950-53; owner Jacobs Dept. Store, Paterson, 1955-80; pub. Alameda Newspaper Group, San Francisco, 1985-87, Garden State Newspapers, Passaic, NJ, 1985—87; pvt. practice editl. cons. Woodcliff Lake, NJ, 1988—90; editor FOCUS Mag., Totowa, N.J., 1990-92; pres., pvt. practice editl. cons. CJ Enterprises, Woodcliff Lake, 1992—; editor Travel World Internat., 2000—02; travel editor That's Life Mag., 2002; pres. Caros Books. Author: The Business of Writing, 1996, Blood Bond, 2002, The Writer Within You, 2007. Dep. mayor Paterson, 1966-70; campaign mgr. Kramer for Mayor, Paterson, 1966, 70, 74, 78. Sgt. U.S. Army, 1953-55. Recipient Disting. Svc. award Jaycees, Paterson, 1966, Nat. Vol. award Lane Bryant/U.S. Govt., Washington, 1969, various awards Soc. Profl. Journalists, N.Am. Travel Journalists Assn. Mem. N.Am. Travel Journalists Assn. (award winner), N.J. Press Club (award winner), Working Press Assn. (award winner), East West News Bur. (award winner). Jewish. Avocations: skiing, golf, reading, gardening. Home and Office: CJ Enterprises 16 Pinecrest Dr Woodcliff Lake NJ 07677-8220 Office Phone: 201-391-4539. Personal E-mail: charles@retirement-writing.com.

JACOBS, CHARLOTTE DE CROES, oncologist, educator; b. Oak Ridge, Tenn., Jan. 27, 1946; BA, U. Rochester, 1968; MD, Washington U., St. Louis, 1972. Diplomate Am. Bd. Internal Medicine, Am. Bd. Med. Oncology, Nat. Bd. Med. Examiners. Intern, jr. resident dept. medicine Washington U. Sch. Medicine, St. Louis, 1972—74; sr. resident dept. medicine U. Calif., San Francisco, 1974—75; postdoctoral fellow divsn. oncology Stanford (Calif.) U. Med. Sch., 1975—77, acting asst. prof. oncology, 1977-80, asst. prof. medicine and oncology, 1980-86, assoc. prof. clin. medicine, 1986-92, assoc. prof. medicine and oncology, 1992-96, prof., 1996—, sr. assoc. dean. edn. and student affairs, 1990-97, acting dir. Clin. Cancer Ctr., 1994-97; dir. Oncology Day Care Ctr. Stanford Med. Ctr., 1977-90, dir. Clin. Cancer Ctr., 1997—2001. Bd. dirs. Nat. Comprehensive Cancer Network, Rockledge, Pa., 1994-2001. Recipient presdl. citation Am. Soc. for Head and Neck Surgery, 1990, Aphrodite Hofsomner award Washington U., 1993. Mem. AMA, Am. Soc. Clin. Oncology (bd. dirs. 1992-95), Am. Assn. for Cancer Rsch. Office: Clin Cancer Ctr Rm 2241 875 Blake Wilbur Dr Stanford CA 94305-5826 Office Phone: 650-725-8738. Business E-Mail: cjacobs@stanford.edu.

JACOBS, CHRISTOPHER L., real estate developer, former state official; b. Nov. 28, 1966; m. Patti Jacobs. BA, Boston Coll.; MBA, American U.; JD, U. Buffalo. Pres. Avalon Devel., LLC, Buffalo; dep. commr. Office of Planning & Econ. Devel. County of Erie, NY, 2000—02; acting sec. state State of NY, Albany, 2006—07. Mem. bd. edn. City of Buffalo, 2004—; co-founder Buffalo Inner City Scholarship Opportunity Network (B.I.S.O.N.).*

JACOBS, DAVID ERNEST, environmental health scientist; married; 2 children. BA in Polit. Sci., Antioch Coll., 1973; BS in Environ. Health, Oakland U., 1983; MS in Tech. and Sci. Policy, Ga. Inst. Tech., 1988; PhD in Environ. Engring., Kennedy Western U., 1998. Cert. indsl. hygienist. Tchg. asst. quantitative analytical chemistry Oakland U., 1982, lectr., coord. qualitative analytical chemistry, 1983; chemist Nat. Stds. Tech. Inc., 1983; environ. rsch. scientist Ga. Inst. Tech., 1983-87, dir. Ga. State Employee Hazardous Chems. Tng. Program, 1987-88, dir. So. Lead-Based Paint Tng. Consortium, 1989-92; dep. dir. Nat. Ctr. for Lead-Safe Housing, Washington, 1992—95; dir. US Dept. Housing and Urban Devel. Office of Healthy Homes and Lead Hazard Control, Washington, 1995—2004, CPO, 2004—06; rsch. dir. Nat. Ctr. for Healthy Housing, 2006—. Adj. assoc. prof. U. Ill., Chgo., 2005—; faculty assoc. Johns Hopkins U., Balt.; bd. dirs. Nat. Lead Abatement Coun., 1993-95. Author: (Pres.'s task force report) Childhood Lead Poisoning Prevention; contbr. articles to profl. jours. Recipient Spl. Commendation, Dept. Justice, 1999. Mem. APHA, Am. Indsl. Hygiene Assn. (chmn. social concerns com. 1991, nat. nominating com. 1990-92, Ga. sect. sec. 1988, pres. 1989), Am. Acad. Indsl. Hygiene. Office: 5025 Hawthorne Pl NW Washington DC 20016 Home Phone: 202-237-2875; Office Phone: 202-607-0938. Personal E-mail: dejacobs@starpower.net.

JACOBS, DEBORAH L., library director; b. LA, Feb. 28, 1952; d. Morton Daniel and Adrienne (Rimmel) J.; m. Brian Brogan, Mar. 29, 1982 (div. 1985); 1 child, Jacob Brogan. BA in Govt., Mills Coll., 1974; MLS, U. Oreg., 1975. Children's libr. Deschutes Libr., Bend, Oreg., 1976-77; extension svcs. libr. Sacramento City Libr., 1977-78; libr., libr. dir. Corvallis-Benton Pub. Libr., Oreg., 1978-97; city libr. Seattle Pub. Libr., 1997—. Treas. Freedom to Read Found., Chgo., 1994-98. Bd. dirs. NW Sch., Seattle, Boys & Girls Club, Corvallis, 1993-97; chair Commn.

Children & Families, Corvallis, 1992-97; sec., bd. dirs. da Vinci Days, Corvallis, 1993-97. Named Libr. of Yr. Libr. Jour., 1995, Pub. Employee of Yr. Mcpl. League King Couny, Seattle, 1999, Leader of Yr. City of Seattle Mgmt. Assn., 1999, Governing Mag. Pub., Ofcl. of Yr., 2001; named among Top 25 Most Influential People, Seattle Mag., 2004. Mem. ALA (co-chair presdl. initiative 1997-99, v.p. Leroy-Merritt Fund. 1998—, intellectual freedom champion 1995), Oreg. Libr. Assn. (pres. 1992-93), Wash. State Women's Forum, Wash. Libr. Assn., Bertelsmann Founds. Internat. Network Pub. Librs., Rotary. Democrat. Jewish. Avocations: baking, gardening, running, pottery. Office: Seattle Pub Libr 1000 Fourth Ave Seattle WA 98104-1109 Office Phone: 206-386-4147. E-mail: city.librarian@spl.org.*

JACOBS, DENNIS G., federal judge; b. NYC, Feb. 28, 1944; s. Harry N. and Rose J.; m. Judith Weissman. BA, Queens Coll., 1964; MA, NYU, 1965, JD, 1973. Assoc. Simpson Thacher & Bartlett, NYC, 1973—80, ptnr., 1980—92; judge US Ct. Appeals (2d Cir.), NYC, 1992—, chief judge, 2006—. Lectr. Queens Coll., 1967—69; mem. Com. on Judicial Resources, Judicial Conf. of US, 1997—, chmn., 1999—. Office: US Ct Appeals US Courthouse 500 Pearl St Rm 2520 New York NY 10007-1502*

JACOBS, DONALD LOUIS, medical educator; MD, U. Nebr. Assoc. prof. surgery St. Louis U., Mo., 1994—. Dir. vascular surgery tng. program St. Louis U., 2000—. Fellow: ACS (pres. Mo.); mem.: Midwest Vascular Surgery Soc., Soc. Vascular Surgery. Office: St Louis Univ Med Ctr 3635 Vista Ave Saint Louis MO 63110-0250 Home Phone: 314-423-4640; Office Phone: 314-577-8310.

JACOBS, DONALD P., finance educator; b. Chgo., June 22, 1927; s. David and Bertha (Nevod) J.; children: Elizabeth, Ann, David; m. Dinah Nemeroff, May 28, 1978. BA, Roosevelt Coll., 1949; MA, Columbia U., 1951, PhD, 1956. Mem. research staff Nat. Bur. Econ. Research, 1952-57; instr. Coll. City N.Y., 1955-57; mem. faculty to Morrison prof. fin. Northwestern U. Sch. Mgmt., 1970—75, chmn. dept., 1969-75, dean, 1975—2001, Gaylord Freeman Disting. prof. banking, 1978—. Chmn. bd. AMTRAK, 1975-79; bd. dirs. CDW Corp., Prologis Corp., Terex Corp.; co-dir. staff Presdl. Commn. Structure and Regulation, 1970-71; sr. economist banking and currency com. U.S. Ho. of Reps. Contbr. articles to profl. jours. Served with USNR, 1945-46. Ford Found. fellow, 1959-60, 63-64 Mem. Am. Econ. Assn., Am. Statis. Assn., Am. Fin. Assn., Econometrics Soc., Inst. Mgmt. Sci. Office: Northwestern Univ J L Kellogg Sch Mgmt 2001 Sheridan Rd Evanston IL 60208-0814 Office Phone: 847-491-2838.

JACOBS, DONALD PAUL, architect; b. Cleve., Aug. 8, 1942; s. Joseph W. and Minnie Mae (Grieger) J.; m. Sharon Daugherty, Apr. 14, 1963 (dec. Feb. 1992); m. Julie Brinkerhoff, Apr. 24, 1993. BS, U. Cin., 1967. Registered architect, Calif., Tex., Ariz., Nev., Ga., Fla., Colo., Hawaii, N.C., Ill. Draftsman, intern Skidmore, Owings & Merrill, San Francisco, 1967-70; pvt. practice architecture Sea Ranch, 1970-86, chmn. design com., 1975-79; prin. Dorius Archs., Corona del Mar, Calif., 1986-94; pres. JZMK Ptnrs., Irvine, Calif., 1994—. Bd. dirs. Homeaid Am. Prin. works represented to numerous newspapers and magazines. Co-chair Project Playhouse, Homeaid, 1993-95. Mem. AIA (chmn. nat. housing com. 1996, awards 1973-74, 77-78, Bay Area Honor Design Excellence award 1974, Homes for Better Living Merit award 1976, Housing Merit award 1978), Sr. Housing Coun. (bd. dirs. Orange County chpt. 1993-94). Democrat. Avocations: tennis, skiing, hiking. Home: 309 Poppy Ave Corona Del Mar CA 92625-3024 Home Phone: 949-644-7919.

JACOBS, GARY N., lawyer, hotel executive; b. NYC, July 12, 1945; m. Robin Jacobs; children: Melissa, Matthew. BA summa cum laude, Brandeis U., 1966; student, London Sch. Econs.; LLB, Yale U., 1969. Bar: NY 1970, Calif. 1972. Law clk. to Hon. Wilfred Feinberg US Ct. Appeals (2nd cir.), 1969—70; assoc. to ptnr. Wyman, Bautzer, Christensen, Kuchel & Silbert, LA, 1971—88; sr. ptnr. Christensen, Miller, Fink, Jacobs, Glaser, Weil & Shapiro, LLP, LA, 1988—2000, of counsel, 2000—; exec. v.p., gen. counsel MGM Mirage, Las Vegas, 2000—, sec., 2002—. Vis. lectr. UCLA Law Sch., 1982; dir., mem. exec. com. The InterGroup Corp., LA. Bd. govs. Am. Jewish Com.; bd. overseers Brandeis U. Grad. Sch. Internat. Econs. and Fin.; bd. dirs. Nev. Ballet Theatre, Nev. Cancer Inst.; mem. exec. com. Las Vegas Performing Arts Ctr. Mem.: Order of Coif, Phi Beta Kappa. Office: MGM Mirage 3600 Las Vegas Blvd S Las Vegas NV 89109 also: Christensen Miller Fink Jacobs Glaser Weil & Shapiro LLP 10250 Constellation Blvd 19th Fl Los Angeles CA 90067 Office Phone: 702-693-7120. Office Fax: 702-693-8626. E-mail: gary_jacobs@mgmmirage.com.*

JACOBS, GEORGE, broadcast engineering consulting company executive; b. NYC, July 16, 1924; s. Benjamin and Henrietta (Myerson) J.; m. Beatrice Gregerman, May 27, 1947; children: Michele Jacobs Gordon, Joy Jacobs. BEE, Pratt Inst., 1949; MSEE, U. Md., 1960. Registered profl. engr., Md., DC. Govt. exec. Voice of America, USIA, 1949—76; bd. Internat. Broadcasting, Washington, 1976—80; pres. George Jacobs & Assocs., Inc., Silver Spring, Md., 1980—. Commr. Commn. Broadcasting to Cuba, 1983; mem. U.S. Del. major ITU Comm. Confs., 1949-92; sr. advisor to chmn. U.S. Del. ITU Conf. on High Frequency Broadcasting, 1984, 87. Co-author: The Shortwave Propagation Handbook, 1976, 80, rev. edit., 1995; also articles. 2d lt. USAF, 1943-46. Decorated Air medal, 1945; recipient Marconi Gold medal engring. achievement Radio Club of Am., 1977, Superior Honor award U.S. Govt., 1976, Outstanding Performance award 1980; Presdl. Commn. Pres. U.S., 1983; Jack Poppele Broadcast Honor award, 1992, Radio Engring. Achievement award Nat. Assn. Broadcasters, 1997; named to CQ Radio Hall of Fame, 2001. Fellow IEEE, Radio Club of Am.; mem. Assn. Fed. Comms. Cons. Engrs. Avocations: amateur radio, stamp collecting/philately, travel. Office: PO Box 12298 Silver Spring MD 20908-0298 Office Phone: 301-598-1283. E-mail: george@gjainc.com.

JACOBS, GEORGE BRAUN, neurosurgeon; b. Poland, Jan. 9, 1934; naturalized U.S. citizen, 1954; s. Maurice and Lena J.; m. Rosanne Wille, 1980; children: Leigh, Steven, Alec. Jeffrey. Student, NYU, 1952-54; MD, SUNY, Syracuse, 1958; postgrad. in general surgery, Bronx Mcpl. Hosp., 1958-59; postgrad. in neurological surgery, Albert Einstein Coll. of Medicine, 1959-64. Cert. airline transport pilot, flight instr., sr. aviation med. examiner, FAA accident counselor. Attending neurosurgeon Hackensack (N.J.) Med. Ctr., 1965-86, sr. attending neurosurgeon, 1986—, chief neurosurgery sect., 1981-86; attending surgeon Holy Name Hosp., Teaneck, NJ, 1965, chief neurosurgery, 1976-81, 90-94; chief sect. neurosurgery Hackensack U. Med. Ctr., 1970-86, chief spine surgery, 1986—2001, chmn. dept. neurosurgery, chief spine surgery, 1986—2001; dir. spine svcs. Montefiore Med. Ctr. Albert Einstein Coll. Medicine, Bronx, 1992-93; prof. neurological surgery U. Pitts. Sch. Medicine, 1993-94; dir. spine ctr., spine surgery U. Pitts., 1993-94; prof. neurosurgery U. Medicine and Dentistry of N.J., Newark, 1994—. Vis. prof. neurosurgery, U. Saigon, Vietnam, 1965-66; clin. asst. prof. neurosurgery, N.J. Coll. Medicine, Newark, 1970-73; asst. prof. clin. neurosurgery, Albert Einstein Coll. Medicine, 1973-75; assoc. prof. clin. neurosurgery, 1975-89; prof. clin. neurosurgery, 1989-92, prof. neurosurgery, 1992-93; prof. neurosurgery, 1993-1994, prof. surgery N.J. Med. Sch., UMDNJ, 1994-; spkr. numerous convs./cons. in field. Author: (novels) A Simple Twist of Fate, Freedom Quest, (textbooks) Medical Malpractice: A Guide to Medical Issues, 1986, Textbook of Operatives Spine Surgery, 1999; contbr. numerous articles to profl. jours. and publs. Fellow U.S. Public Health Svc., 1959-60; bd. trustees Lehman Coll. Art Gallery, 1986-87; bd. dirs. Hackensack U. Med. Ctr. Found., 1997-2003, gov. bd. govs., 1979-2002; mem. Hillcrest Found. Bd., 1980-2002; bd. dirs. Lehman Coll. Art Gallery, 1986-87; hon. surgeon Police Dept. City of N.Y. Decorated Army Commendation medal for Vietnam Svc., 1966; Disting. Svc. cert. of Merit Bd. of Chosen Freeholders of Bergen County, 1971. Fellow USPHS, Am. Coll. Surgeons, Am. Coll. Angiology, Internat. Coll. Angiology, Internat. Coll. Surgeons, Scoliosis Rsch. Soc., Cervical Spine Rsch. Soc., N.Am. Spine Soc.; mem. AMA, Internat. Soc. Pediatric Neurosurgery, Internat. Health Policy and Mgmt. Inst., Am. Pain Soc., Am. Assn. Neurol. Surgeons (chmn. liaison com. 1976-78), Bergen County Med. Soc. (trustee 1976, mem. judicial com. 1977-82, chmn. legis. com. 1980), Congress of Neurol. Surgeons, Assn. of Mil. Surgeons of U.S., N.Y. Soc. Neurosurgery, Acad. Medicine N.J., N.J. Neurosurg. Soc. (mem. exec. com. 1973, chmn. peer review com., 1974, pres. 1989-90), Fla. Med. Assn., Fla. Physicians Assn., Soc. Surgeons of N.J., Med. Soc. N.J., San Francisco Neurosurg. Soc. (corr.), others. Avocations: golf, aviation, boating, cooking gourmet. Address: PO Box 799 Hampton Bays NY 11946 Home Phone: 201-289-1719, 201-637-9406.

JACOBS, GORDON WALDEMAR, surgeon, educator; b. Cuero, Tex., May 30, 1933; s. Elmer Waldemar and Clara Esther Jacobs; m. Lorraine Maria Maguire, Oct. 24, 1970; children: Mary Lou Baker, Kristen Clara, Damien Gordon, Melanie Anne. BA, U. Iowa, 1955, MD, 1958; diploma in Tropical Medicine and Hygiene, U. Liverpool, 1983; diploma in French, Tng. Inst. for Execs., 1984. Diplomate Am. Bd. Surgery, 1972. Resident in surgery Loma Linda U., Riverside, Calif., 1959; intern U. Calif., Sacramento, 1958—59; locum tenens family practice Santa Barbara County Hosp., Calif., 1962; locum tenens gen. surgery Kaiser Permanente Hosp., Santa Clara, Calif., 1966, 1969; resident gen. surgery U. Calif., Oakland-Martinez, Calif., 1962—66; fellow gen. surgery Lahey Clinic, Boston, 1969—70; gen. surgeon Somerville (Mass.) Surg. Assocs., 1970—75; pvt. practice gen. surgeon Gordon W. Jacobs, Md, Vallejo, Calif., 1975, Berkeley, Calif., 1975—83, Lancaster, SC, 1986—88, Gordon W. Jacobs, Md Facs Pa, Charlotte, NC, 1989—2003, gen. surgeon locum tenens, 2003—. Missionary gen. surgeon Evang. Covenant Mission Hosp., Karawa, 1984—86; missionary gen. surgeon, instr. in surgery Evangelical Covenant Mission Hosp. & N.W. Teams Internat., Karawa, 2005; missionary gen. surgeon, instr. in surgery Bongolo Hosp. Pan African Acad. Christian Surgeons and N.W. Med. Teams Internat., Lebamba, Gabon, 2005; missionary gen. surgeon Luth. Mission Hosp., Madang, Papua New Guinea, 1966—69; missionary surgeon, instr. surgery Haile Selassie U. Med. Sch., Addis Ababa, Ethiopia, 1973—74. Contbr. articles to profl. jours. Pres. Oakland (Calif.) Uptown Toastmasters, 1980—81; active Big Bros., Boston, 1970—73; pres. Trinity Luth. Ch., Oakland, 1979—81; troop physician Boy Scouts Am., Charlotte, Calif., 1995—2006. Maj. med. corp. US Army, 1960—62, Germany. Named one of Notable Americans, Am. Biog. Inst., 1978, Cmty. Leaders & Noteworthy Americans, 1978, Personalities Of West & Midwest, 1978; named to Book Of Honor, 1978, Personalities Of Am., 1978, Men Of Achievement, Internat. Biog. Centre, 1979; recipient Silver Presdl. Svc. award, Northwest Med. Teams, 2007. Fellow: ACS, Am. Soc. Gen. Surgeons, S.E. Surg. Congress; mem.: AMA (chmn. com. medicine and religion Calif. chpt. 1980—81), Mecklenburg County Med. Soc., Charlotte Surg. Soc., N.C. Med. Soc. Republican. Avocations: woodworking, french studies, flying, exercise, gardening. Home and Office: Gordon W Jacobs Md Facs Pa 14920 Wyndham Oaks Drive Charlotte NC 28277 Home Phone: 704-543-8236; Office Phone: 704-543-8236. Business E-Mail: gordonjacobsmd@pol.net.

JACOBS, GRETCHEN HUNTLEY, psychiatrist; b. NYC, July 20, 1941; d. L. Gordon and Gertrude Mary (Eberz) La Pointe; m. Michael Edward Jacobs, Dec. 26, 1965 (div.); children: Dylan Huntley, Danielle La Pointe. BS, Fordham U., NYC, 1963; MD, SUNY, Bklyn., 1968. Diplomate Am. Bd. Psychiatry and Neurology, Am. Bd. Child and Adolescent Psychiatry. Pediatric intern St. Luke's Hosp., NYC, 1968—69; psychiatry resident George Washington U. Hosp., Washington, 1969—71; child psychiatry resident Beth Israel Hosp., Boston, 1972—73, McLean Hosp. Children's Ctr., Waltham, 1973—74; coord. health and human devel. Martha's Vineyard Sch. Sys., 1974—80; pvt. practice adult and adolescent/child psychiatry, 1974—; asst. clin. prof. child psychiatry Tufts U. Med. Sch., Boston, 1974—. Contbr. articles to profl. jours. Cons. Mass. Dept. Pub. Health Svcs. to Multi-Handicapped Children, 1974-75; bd. dirs. Mass. Dept. Social Svcs., 1979-83; founding mem., clin. dir. Vineyard Child Assault Prevention Project, 1986, Com. on Rural Child Psychiatry, 1988-92; mem. Coun. for Young Children. Mem. AMA, NAACP, LWV, Am. Psychiat. Assn., Am. Acad. Child and Adolescent Psychiatry, Mass. Med. Soc. Avocations: music, dance, travel, sailing, theater, basketball.

JACOBS, HARRY MILBURN, JR., advertising executive; b. July 23, 1928; s. Harry Milburn and Nina (Gibbs) J.; m. Barbara Ann Mills; children: Kathryn, Christopher, Letitia. Student, East Carolina U., 1947-49; BFA, Corcoran Coll. Design, 1951. Art dir. The Hecht Co., Washington, 1951-53, Bradham & Co., Greensboro, N.C., 1953-54, sr. art dir., 1956-59; assoc. art dir. Cargill, Wilson & Acree, Richmond, Va., 1959-61, creative dir. Charlotte, N.C., 1961-68, corp. creative dir. Atlanta, 1969-74, pres., 1970-74, Martin Agy., Richmond, Va., 1977-83, 1983-86, chmn. bd., 1993—97, CEO, 1993, chmn. emeritus, 1997. Scoutmaster Boy Scouts Am., 1956—58, mem. exec. coun. Robert E. Lee coun., 1987—89; bd. visitors Sch. Journalism U. N.C., Chapel Hill, Va. Commonwealth U. Found.; bd. visitors East Carolina U., 2001—; bd. overseers Corcoran Coll. Design, Washington; bd. dirs., exec. com. Richmond Renaissance, Tryon Palace Comm.; trustee Woodberry Forest Sch., 1986—2001, St. Mary's Coll., 1986—2001; bd. dirs. Meml. Guidance Clinic, Richmond Children's Mus., Marymount Park, Goodwill Industries, Richmond Sch. Ballet, Virginians in Support of Guard and REs., Downtown Presents. With US Army, 1954—56. Named Advt. Man of Yr. Silver medal, Am. Advt. Fedn., 1972; named to Va. Comm. Hall of Fame, 1986, N.C. Advt. Hall of Fame, 1991, One Club Creative Hall of Fame, N.Y., 2001, Am. Advt. Fedn. Hall of Fame, 2004; recipient numerous advt. awards, Disting. Eagle Scout award, Boy Scouts Am., 1988. Mem. One Club Art & Copy NY, Art Dirs. Club of NY, Commonwealth Club. Republican. Office: Martin Agy One Shockoe Plaza Richmond VA 23219-4132 Office Phone: 804-698-8310. Business E-Mail: harry.jacobs@martinagency.com.

JACOBS, HELEN NICHOLS, artist; b. Kent, Conn., Feb. 16, 1924; d. Spencer Baird and Helen (Mather) Nichols; m. Steven M. Jacobs, Jan. 20, 1950; children: Richard, Barbara. Student, Marot Jr. Coll., Thompson, Conn., 1940-42. Instr. oil painting Ridgewood (N.J.) Art Inst., 1970-96. Fellow Am. Artist Profl. League; mem. Hudson Valley Art Assn., Kent Art Assn., Catharine Lorillard Wolfe Art Club. Democrat. Home: 684 Terrace Dr Paramus NJ 07652-4926 E-mail: sj684t@aol.com.

JACOBS, IRWIN LAWRENCE, diversified corporate executive; b. Mpls., July 15, 1941; s. Samuel and Rose H. Jacobs; m. Alexandra Light, Aug. 26, 1962; children: Mark, Sheila, Melinda, Randi, Trisha. Student pub. schs. Chmn. Watkins Inc., Winona, Minn., 1978—; pres., CEO Minstar, 1982—94; chmn. Genmar Holdings, Inc., Mpls., 1982—; chmn. bd. Genmar Industries, Inc., Mpls.; chmn. Jacobs Trading Co., Mpls.; pres., CEO Jacobs Investors, Inc., Mpls.; pres. Jacobs Realty II, Inc., Mpls., 1993—, Jacobs Mgmt. Corp., 1983—, Gateway S/B, Inc., 1993—; chmn. FLW Outdoors (formerly Operation Bass, Inc.), Gilbersville, Ky., 1996—. Mem.: Mpls., Lafayette Country, Oakridge Country. Office: Genmar Holdings Inc 2900 IDS Ctr 80 S 8th St Minneapolis MN 55402-2100*

JACOBS, IRWIN MARK, communications executive; b. New Bedford, Mass., Oct. 18, 1933; B in Elec. Engring., Cornell U., 1956; MS, MIT, 1957, ScD, 1959; doctorate (hon.), Technion U., 2000, U. Penn., 2002. Rsch. asst. in elec. engring. MIT, Cambridge, Mass., 1958-59, from asst. to assoc. prof., 1959-66; from assoc. to prof. info. and computer sci. U. Calif., San Diego, 1966-72; co-founder, pres., chmn., CEO Linkabit Corp., 1969—85; co-founder, chmn. bd. dirs. Qualcomm Inc., San Diego, 1985—, CEO, 1985—2005. Cons. Applied Rsch. Lab. Sylvania Elect. Products, Inc., 1959—, Lincoln Lab. MIT, 1961—62, Indsl. Tchg. Mpls. Honeywell, Inc., 1963, Bolt Beranek & Newman, Inc., 1965; NASA resident rsch. fellow Jet Propulsion Lab., 1964—65; chmn. sci. adv. group Def. Comm. Agy. and Engring. Adv. Coun. U. Calif.; mem. Coun. on Competitveness; mem. pub. awareness engring. com. Nat. Acad. Engring.; bd. dirs. Bldg. Engring. and Sci. Talent; vis. com. MIT Lab. for Info. and Decision Sys., Calif. Coun. on Sci. and Tech.; past chmn. U. Calif. Pres. Engring. Adv. Coun. Author: Principles of Communication Engineering, 1965. Named Cornell's Entrepreneur, 1994, Entrepreneur Yr., Master Entrepreneur category, RCR, 1996, inductee for significant contbn. to advancement of wireless, Radio Comm. Report (RCR) Wireless Hall Fame, 2000; named one of Forbes' Richest Americans, 2006; recipient Biannual award for outstanding contbn. to aerospace comm., Am. Inst. Aeronautics and Astronautics (AIAA), 1980, elected to, Nat. Acad. Engring., 1982, Disting. Cmty. Svc. award, Anti-Defamation League of B'nai B'rith, 1984, Excel award, Am. Electronics Assn., 1989, Entrepreneur Yr. award, Inst. Am. Entrepreneurs, 1992, San Diego Bus. Leader Yr. award, San Diego Venture Group, 1993, Inventing America's Future award, AEA, 1993, Internat. Citizens award, World Affairs Coun. of San Diego, 1993, Nat. Tech. medal, U.S. Dept. Commerce Tech. Adminstrn., 1994, Albert Einstein award, Am. Soc. Technion, 1996, Person Yr. award, RCR, 1996, Medal Achievement award, Am. Electronics Assn. (AEA), 1998, Ernst & Young Leadership award for Global Integration, Computerworld Smithsonian Award Program, 1999, Golden State award, Bd. Dirs. Calif. Coun. for Internat. Trade, 2000, Dir. Yr. award for Enhancement of Econ. Values, Corp. Dir. Forum, 2000, Scientist Yr. award, Achievement Rewards for Coll. Scientists (ARCS), 2000, Bower award in Bus. Leadership, Franklin Inst., 2001, Innovation award in Comm., The Economist, 2002, Internat. Engring. Consortium Fellow award, 2002, Dr. Morris Chang Exemplary Leadership award, The Fabless Semiconductor Assn. (FSA), 2003; fellow, Am. Acad. Arts and Sci., 2001. Fellow: IEEE (IEEE Alexander Graham Bell Medal 1995); mem.: NAE, Assn. Computing Machinery, Tau Beta Pi (Disting. Alumnus award 2003), Eta Kappa Nu (Eminent Mem. award 2003), Phi Kappa Phi, Sigma Xi. Achievements include patents for several CDMA patents. Office: Qualcomm Inc 5775 Morehouse Dr San Diego CA 92121-1714 also: 10185 Mckellar Ct San Diego CA 92121-4233*

JACOBS, JACK BERNARD, state supreme court justice; b. July 23, 1942; s. Louis K. and Phoebe J.; m. Marion Antiles, Apr. 2, 1967; 1 child, Andrew Seth. AB, U. Chgo., 1964; LLB, Harvard U., 1967. Bar: Del. 1968, U.S. Dist. Ct. Del. 1968, U.S. Ct. Appeals (3d cir.) 1968, U.S. Supreme Ct. 1975. Law clk. Del. Chancery and Superior Cts., 1967-68; assoc. Young, Conaway, Stargatt & Taylor, Wilmington, Del., 1968-71, ptnr., 1971-85; vice chancellor Ct. of Chancery State of Del., 1985—2003; justice Del. Supreme Ct, 2003—. Adj. prof. Widener U. Sch. Law, 1986—, NYU Sch. Law, 2006—; chmn. Bar-Bench-Media Conf., Del., 1992—93; faculty continuing legal edn. programs. Contbr. articles to profl. jours. Vice chmn. Nat. Jewish Cmty. Rels. Adv. Coun., 1985-89; bd. dirs. Jewish Fedn. Del., 1981-87, Del. Symphony Assn., 1991-95, Del. Cmty. Found., 1994-2000, chair grants com., 1998-2000, 02-, chmn. governance com., 2002-2004; pres. Milton & Hattie Kutz Home, 1990-92. Fellow: Am. Bar Found.; mem.: ABA (litigation sect. 1979—, bus. law sect. 1979—, mem. com. corp. laws 1999—2006), Harvard Law Sch. Del. (pres. 1986—87), Del. Bar Assn., Am. Judicature Soc. (bd. dir. 1999—2004), Am. Law Inst. (advisor Restatement (3d) Restitution), Phi Beta Kappa. Democrat. Jewish. Office: Supreme Ct of Del Carvel State Office Bldg 820 N French St PO Box 1997 Wilmington DE 19899 Office Phone: 302-577-8690. Business E-Mail: jack.jacobs@state.de.us.

JACOBS, JANICE LEE, ambassador; b. Dearborn, Mich., Dec. 5, 1946; d. Robert and Oma Lee (Corgan) J.; m. Royce J. Fichte, June 16, 1968 (div. Dec. 1982); children: Eric A. Fichte, Kurt M. Fichte; m. Kenneth B. Friedman, Mar. 21, 1985. BA in French, So. Ill. U., Carbondale, 1968; postgrad., Fla. Internat. U., Miami, 1986; MS in Nat. Security Strategy, Nat. War Coll., 1995. Cert. tchr., Ill. Consular officer, econ. officer Am. Embassy, Lagos, Nigeria, 1980-81, consular chief Addis Ababa, Ethiopia, 1982-83, consular officer Paris, 1983-85; geog. case officer coordination divsn. visa office US Dept. State, Washington, 1987-88, chief coordination divsn., 1988-90, dep. dir. Office of Cuban Affairs, Inter-Am. Affairs Bur., 1995-98, sr. watch officer Ops. Ctr., 1990-91; prin. officer Am. Consulate, Matamoras, Mexico, 1991-94; dep. chief of mission Am. Embassy US Dept. State, Santo Domingo, Dominican Republic, dep. asst. sec. visa services Bur. Consular Affairs Washington, 2002—05, US amb. to Senegal Dakar, 2006—. Mem. Phi Kappa Phi. Methodist. Avocations: running, hiking, civil war history. Office: Am Embassy 2130 Dakar Pl Dulles VA 20189

JACOBS, JEREMY MAURICE, SR., diversified financial services company and professional sports team executive; b. Jan. 21, 1940; m. Margaret Jane Davis; 6 children. BA, SUNY, Buffalo; grad. advancement mgmt. prog., Harvard U.; LHD (hon.), Canisius Coll. Head Dominion Del. North Cos. Sportservice, Ltd., 1961; chmn., CEO Del. North Cos., Buffalo, 1968—; co-owner Cin. Royals Basketball team, 1965—72; owner, gov. Boston Bruins, 1974—; former owner, gov. Boston Garden, 1975—; owner, gov. TD BankNorth Garden (formerly Fleet Ctr.), 1995—. Mem. US Travel & Tourism Promotion adv. bd., 2003—; chmn. bd. govs. NHL, 2007—. Active United Way, NCCJ, Joint Ctr. for Polit. and Econ. Studies, Internat. Tennis Hall of Fame.; founder Boston Bruins Found., 2003. Named one of 400 Richest Ams., Forbes mag., 2006; named to Sports Hall of Fame in Western NY, 2006. Avocation: golf. Office: Del North Cos 40 Fountain Plz Buffalo NY 14202-2229 also: Boston Profl Hockey Assn, Inc TD Banknorth Garden 100 Legends Way Boston MA 02114*

JACOBS, JIM, actor, composer, librettist, playwright; b. Chgo., Oct. 7, 1942; m. Diane Rita Gomez, June 5, 1965 (div. 1974); 1 child, Kristine; m. Denise Nettleton, Apr. 29, 1978 (div. 2003). Student, Chgo. City Coll., 1962-63. Appeared in over 50 cmty. and profl. theatre prodns. including Until the Monkey Comes, 1966, Take Me Along, 1967, Flora, The Red Menace, 1968, Entertaining Mr. Sloane, 1969, The Serpent, 1969, Don't Drink the Water, 1970, Jimmy Shine, 1970, all Chgo., No Place to Be Somebody, nat. touring co., 1971, on Broadway, 1971, The Magnolia Club, Chgo., 1975, The Local Stigmatic, Chgo., 1976; dir. The Ruffian on the Stair, Chgo., 1975; actor: (films) Medium Cool, 1969, Love in a Taxi, 1976, (TV series) Open All Night, 1982; author, lyricist, composer: (with Warren Casey) Grease, Broadway, 1972-80, (Tony award nomination 1972, Grammy award nomination 1972), London-West End, 1973, 77, motion picture, 1979, (revival) Grease, London, 1993— (Olivier award nomination), (revival) Broadway, 1994-98 (Tony award nomination), Grease On Ice (Am. Ice Show Tour), 1998—; author: (with Warren Casey) Island of Lost Coeds, 1979; (with Jim Weston) Bats in the Belfry, 1982; (with Jim Weston) Remember the Night, 1988. Recipient Humanitarian of Yr. award Young Adult Inst., N.Y.C., 1992. Mem. Dramatists Guild, Authors League Am., ASCAP, Actors Equity Assn., Screen Actors Guild., AFTRA. Office: care Ronald Taft PC 18 W 55th St New York NY 10019-5315

JACOBS, JOHN PATRICK, lawyer; b. Chgo., Oct. 27, 1945; s. Anthony N. and Bessie (Montgomery) J.; m. Linda I. Grams, Oct. 6, 1973; 1 child, Christine Margaret. BA cum laude, U. Detroit, 1967, JD magna cum laude, 1970. Bar: Mich. 1970, US Dist. Ct. (ea. dist.), Mich. 1970, US Dist. Ct. (we. dist.), Mich. 2004, US Ct. Appeals (6th cir.) 1974, US Ct. Appeals (DC cir.) 1988, US Ct. Appeals (4th cir.) 2001, US Supreme Ct. 1978, US Ct. Appeals (7th cir.) 2005, US Dist. Ct. (no. dist.), Ind. 2005. Law clk. to chief judge Mich. Ct. Appeals, Detroit, 1970-71; assoc., then ptnr. Plunkett & Cooney PC, Detroit, 1972-92, also bd. dirs.; founding ptnr., prin. mem.

O'Leary, O'Leary, Jacobs, Mattson, Perry & Mason PC, Southfield, Mich., 1992-99; prin., owner John P. Jacobs, PC, 1999—. Investigator Atty. Grievance Com., Detroit, 1975-84; mem. hearing panel Atty. Discipline Bd., Detroit, 1984-87, 94—; adj. prof. law Sch. Law, U. Detroit, 1983-84, faculty advisor, 1984-89, Pres.'s Cabinet, 1982—; elected rep. State Bar Rep. Assembly, Lansing, Mich., 1980-82, 91-92, 93-96; fellow Mich. State Bar Found., 1990-2005; pres., treas., mem. steering com. Mich. Bench-Bar Appellate Conf. Com., 1994—; apptd. mem. Mich. Supreme Ct. Com. on Appellate Fees, 1990, on Delay Docket Reduction, 2003-05; spl. mediator appellate negotiation program Mich. Ct. Appeals, 1995—; mem. exec. com. Mich. Appellate Bench-Bar Conf. Found., 1996—; appellate counsel to State Bar of Mich., mem. profl. ethics com., 1998, mem. multi-disciplinary practice com., 1999. Bd. editors Mich. Lawyers Weekly. Bd. dirs. Holy Cross Childrens Svcs. Mich., Clinton, 1988-95, 99—, chmn. pub. policy com., 1993-95, pub. policy liaison, 1999—; apptd. mem. State Bar Mich. Blue Ribbon Com. Improving Def. Counsel-Insurer Rels., 1998-99, Appellate Delay Reduction Task Force, 2003-05, Supreme Ct. Com. Regarding Case Mgmt., 2003-06. Named Lawyer of Yr., Mich. Lawyers Weekly, 2004, Mgsr. Malloy Cath. Lawyer of Yr., Archdiocese of Detroit, 2001, Lawyer of Yr. Excellence in Def. award, Mich. Def. Trial Counsel, 2004, Mich.'s Best Appellate Lawyer, Super Lawyers, Detroit News, 2006, 2007, Best Lawyers in Detroit, DBus. Mag., 2007; named one of 100 Most Influential Lawyers in Mich., Super Lawyers, Detroit News, 2006, 2007; recipient Robert E. Dice Med. Malpractice Def. Atty. award, Mich. Physicians, 1986, Lawyer of Yr. and Lifetime Achievement award, Mich. Def. Trial Counsel, 2004, Lawyer of Yr.; fellow Reginald Heber Smith fellow, 1971—72. Fellow Am. Acad. Appellate Lawyers, Mich. Std. Jury Instn. (subcom. employment law 1984-87); mem. ABA (litigation sect., appellate subcom., torts and ins. practice), Internat. Assn. Def. Counsel (v.p., amicus curiae com., med. and legal malpractice coms., product liability com.), Fedn. Ins. and Corp. Counsel, Mich. Def. Trial Counsel (chmn. amicus curiae com. 1986-88, chmn. future planning com., bd. dirs. 1989—, treas. 1993-94, sec. 1994-95, v.p. 1995-96, program chair 1990, 94, 95, pres., 1996-97); Def. Rsch. Inst. (state rep. 1997-98, Outstanding Performance Citation 1997, nat. appellate com. steering com. 1997—), Cath. Lawyers Soc. (bd. dirs. 1988-98, emeritus dir. 1998—, pres. 1994-95), Supreme Ct. US Hist. Soc., Supreme Ct. Mich. Hist. Soc., Am. Constitutional Soc. (bd. dirs. 2005), Detroit Athletic Club. Democrat. Roman Catholic. Avocations: collecting antique law books, films.

JACOBS, JONATHAN MARK, parliamentary consultant; s. Rev. William Herbert and Norva Dorothy Jacobs. BS, Pa. State U., 1985. Income maintenance caseworker Phila. County Assistance Office, 1992—98; parliamentary cons. Freelance, 1998—. Author: (textbook) Comparison of Parliamentary Authorities, (reference) Updated Index for Parliamentary Opinions, Updated Index for Parliamentary Opinions II; contbr. articles to profl. jours. including Parliamentary Jour., Nat. Parliamentarian. Fed. census local rev. liaison Borough of Ferndale, Johnstown, Pa., 1989—90; active Westmoreland County Rep. Com., Seward, Pa., 1982—85, voter registration chmn. Greensburg, Pa., 1984—85; coun. mem. Borough of Seward (Pa.), Pa., 1984—86; rsch. coord. Cambria County Rep. Com., Johnstown, Pa., 1987—88; issues/policy analyst Com. to Elect Robert N. Hughes, 71st Pa. State Ho. Dist., Johnstown, 1988; assessor Borough of Ferndale, Pa., 1988—89; sch. dir., region #1 Ferndale Area Sch. Dist., Johnstown, Pa., 1989—92; sec. Ferndale Area Sch. Bd., Johnstown, Pa., 1991—92; campaign mgr. Jean Gaston-McGuire, Richland Twp. Supr., Jonhstown, Pa., 1991; alt. del. Episcopal Diocese of Pa. Conv., Phila., 2005—06; lay reader Calvary Ch. Germantown (Episcopal), Pa., 1999; bd. dirs. Covenant Ho. Health Svcs., Phila., 2001—. Recipient Am. Legion award, Charles Sutton Post #128, Am. Legion, 1980, Order of Silver Trowel, Coun. of Annointed Kings, 1992, Long Term Svc. award, Pa. Assn. of Parliamentarians, 2000. Mem.: Pa. Assn. Ret. State Employees, Commn. on Am. Parliamentary Practice, Am. Inst. of Parliamentarians (cert.), Phila. Unit, Nat. Assn. of Parliamentarians (v.p. 2000—02, sec.-treas. 2002—04, pres. 2004—06, v.p. 2006—), Pa. Assn. of Parliamentarians (parliamentarian 1997—98, sec. 2002—06, parliamentarian 2006—), Nat. Assn. of Parliamentarians (profl. registered parliamentarian), Am. Mensa Soc., Intertel, Pa. State Alumni Assn. (life). R-Consevative. Episcopalian. Achievements include first to develop rules for multi-shift meetings; define the role of custom in meeting procedure. Home: 3346 North Smedley St Philadelphia PA 19140-4901 Office Phone: 215-229-1185. Personal E-mail: jjparlia@juno.com.

JACOBS, JULIAN I., federal judge; b. Balt., Aug. 13, 1937; s. Sidney and Bernice (Kellman) J.; m. Donna Buffenstein; children: Richard S., Jennifer K. BA, U. Md., 1958, JD, 1960; LLM, Georgetown U., 1965. Bar: Md., 1960. Atty. chief counsel's office IRS, Washington, 1961-65, trial atty. regional counsel's office Buffalo, 1965-67; assoc. Weinberg & Green, Balt., 1967-69, Hoffberger & Hollander, Balt., 1969-72, Gordon Feinblatt Rothman Hoffberger & Hollander, Balt., 1972-74, ptnr., 1974-84; judge US Tax Ct., Washington, 1984—99, sr. judge, 1999—. Chmn. study commn. Md. Tax Ct., 1978-79, mem. rules com., 1980; mem. spl. study group Md. Gen. Assembly, 1980; adj. prof. grad. tax prog. U. Balt., 1991-93; adj. prof. law, U. San Diego, 2001; adj. prof. grad. tax prog., U. Denver, 2001—. Mem.: U Md. Law Rev. Bd. Mem. Md. State Bar Assn. (past chmn. taxation sect.), Balt. City Bar Assn. (past chmn. tax legis. subcommittee). Office: US Tax Ct 400 2nd St NW Washington DC 20217-0002 Office Phone: 202-521-0720. E-mail: jjacobs@ustaxcourt.gov.*

JACOBS, LAURA ELIZABETH, school librarian, educator, archivist; b. Duluth, Minn., Dec. 21, 1957; d. Howard Edward Jacobs and Elizabeth Susan (Dodge). BFA, U Minn., 1980; MA in Libr. and Info. Studies, U Wis., 1995; MLS in Liberal Studies, U Minn., 2004. Reference archivist WI State Hist. Soc., Madison, Wis., 1995; pub. svc. libr., archivist SD Sch. of Mines & Tech., Rapid City, 1996—98; info. literacy libr., archivist U Wis., Superior, Wis., 1998—, faculty, libr. sci. program, 1998—. Liaison U. of Wis. Sys. Archives Consortia; mentor Wis. State Hist. Soc., Wis., 2000—02; mem. U. Wis. Sys. Digital Collections Adv. Com., 2001—04; selection com. Millionth Image: U. Wis. Sys. Digital Collections, Madison, 2005; bd. mem. Assn. of Gt. Lakes Maritime History, 2000—. Contbr. digital archives project, PBS TV program. Cons. Lake Superior Marine Mus. Assn., Duluth, 2000—; bd. of dirs., editor Duluth Scottish Heritage Assn., 2003—05; mentor Learning Program, NW H.S., Wis., 2002; chair St. Andrews. Recipient Governor's award for Archival Achievement, State Hist. Soc. of Wis., 2004, Beta Beta Epsilon scholar, Wis.chpt. Beta Phi Mu - Internat. Libr. and Info. Studies Honor Soc., 1995; Liberal Studies Acad. scholar, U Minn., 2000, Libr. Sch. scholar, Sch. of Lib & Info Studies, Madison, 1995, Minn. Acad. scholar, Hunt Scholarship Com., Duluth Minn., 1975—79. Mem.: ALA, Wis. Ednl. Media Assn., Assn. of Coll. Rsch. Librs., Soc. of Am. Archivists. Episcopalian. Avocations: kayaking, sailing, music, art, dance. Home: 219 Mygatt Ave Duluth MN 55803 Office: JDH Libr U Wis Superior Belknap & Catlin Superior WI 54880 Home Phone: 218-728-1325; Office Phone: 715-394-8359. E-mail: ljacobs@uwsuper.edu.

JACOBS, LAWRENCE A., media company executive, lawyer; b. Phila., May 4, 1955; m. Hannah Jacobs; children: Emily, Molly. BA summa cum laude, Temple U., 1978; JD cum laude, Bklyn. Law Sch., 1981. Bar: NY 1982, Pa. 1984. Ptnr. Squadron, Ellenoff, Plesant & Lehrer, 1991—96; sr. v.p., dep. gen. counsel News Corp., Ltd., NYC, 1996—2001, exec. v.p., 2001—04, sr. exec. v.p., group gen. counsel, 2005—. Dir. satellite pay-TV Sky Mex., Sky Brasil. Bd. dirs. Cookie Ctr. Learning and Devel., NYC. Mem.: NY State Bar Assn., Assn. Bar City of NY. Office: News Corp Ltd 1211 Avenue of the Americas New York NY 10036 Office Phone: 212-852-7000. Office Fax: 212-768-2029.*

JACOBS, LESLIE WILLIAM, lawyer; b. Akron, Ohio, Dec. 5, 1944; s. Leslie Wilson and Louise Francis (Walker) J.; m. Laurie Hutchinson, July 12, 1962; children— Leslie James, Andrew Wilson, Walker Fulton. Student, Denison U., 1962-63; BS, Northwestern U., 1965; JD, Harvard U., 1968. Bar: Ohio 1968, D.C. 1980, U.S. Supreme Ct. 1971, Brussels 1996. Law clk. to Chief Justice Kingsley A. Taft Ohio Supreme Ct., 1968-69; assoc. Thompson, Hine and Flory, Cleve., 1969-76, ptnr., 1976—, chmn. antitrust, internat. and regulatory area, 1988-99; chmn. bus. regulation and trade dept. Thompson Hine LLP and predecessor, Cleve., 1999—. Lectr. conf. bd. Ohio Legal Ctr. Insts., Ohio State Bar Assn. Antitrust and Corp. Counsel Insts., Fed. Bar Assn., ABA, Canadian Inst., Internat. Assn. Young Lawyers, others; mem. Ohio Bd. Bar Examiners, 1990-94. Contbr. articles to profl. jours. Chmn. EconomicsAmerica, 1990-93; mem. vis. com. Case Western Res. U. Sch. Law, 1985-91; dir., mem. exec. com., chair audit com. The Holden Arboretum; mem. Leadership Cleve., 1988; mem. exec. bd. Greater Cleve. Coun. Boy Scouts Am. Lt. comdr. USNR, 1967-79. Fellow Am. Bar Found. (life), Ohio State Bar Found. (life, trustee 1985-87, Ritter award 1997); mem. ABA (ho. dels. 1986-2004, antitrust law sect. coun. 1985-88, officer 1991-97, state del. 1995-2001, nominating com. 1995-2001, bd. gov. 2001-2004, task force on corp. responsibility), Ohio State Bar Assn. (pres. 1987, Ohio Bar medal 1990), Cleve. Bar Assn. (chmn. jud. selection com. 1982, chmn. jud. election monitoring comm. 2004—, trustee 1983-85), Am. Law Inst., 6th Cir. Jud. Conf. (life), Nat. Conf. Bar Pres., Harvard Club (N.Y.C.), Chagrin Valley Hunt Club, Union Club (Cleve.), Castalia Trout Club. Republican. Presbyterian. Office: Thompson Hine LLP 3900 Key Ctr 127 Public Sq Cleveland OH 44114-1291 Home Phone: 216-561-5840; Office Phone: 216-566-5675. Business E-Mail: les.jacobs@thompsonhine.com.

JACOBS, LIBBY SWANSON, state official; b. Lincoln, Nebr., Oct. 1, 1956; m. Steven G. Jacobs. BA, U. Nebr.; MPA, Drake U. Dir. pub. rels. Am. Lung Assn., 1983—86; dir. comms. IA Bankers Assn., 1986—88; mgr., ops. mgr. disability income svcs. Prin. Fin. Group, 1989—96, asst dir., 1996—2002, dir. cmty. rels., 2002—; majority whip Iowa Ho. of Reps., 1999—2006, mem. Iowa, 1994—. Mem. adminstrn. and rules com.; mem. appropriations com.; mem. commerce and regulation com.; mem. state govt. com.; mem. judiciary com., 1994. Bd. mem. Drake Univ., Blank Children's Hosp.; co-chair Downtown Cmty. Alliance; past chair Midwestern Legis. Conf.; bd. mem. Choose Des Moines Cmtys., Greater Des Moines Partnership, Greater Des Moines Convenient Vis. Bur. Mem.: PEO. Republican. Office: State Capitol E 12th and Grand Des Moines IA 50319

JACOBS, LLOYD A., vascular surgeon; b. Holland, Mich., 1940; MD, Johns Hopkins U., 1968. Diplomate Am. Bd. Surgery. Intern Johns Hopkins Hosp., Balt., 1969-70, resident, 1970-71, U. Calif., San Diego, 1971-72, Wayne State U., Detroit, 1972-74; prof. surgery U. Mich. Sch. Medicine, Ann Arbor, 1974—2003, sr. assoc. dean, 1996—2003; COO U. Mich. Health Sys., Ann Arbor, 1997—; pres. Med. Coll. Ohio, 2003—. Hosp. appts.: VA Hosp., Ann Arbor, Mich., U. Mich. Hosp., Ann Arbor, chief of staff, VAH Med. Ctr., 1989-96. Fellow ACS; mem. AMA, Internat. Soc. Cardio Vascular Surgeons, Midwest Surgeons Assn. Office: 3045 Arlington Ave ML-213 Toledo OH 43614

JACOBS, LOUIE A., state agency administrator; Commr. banking SC State Bd. Fin. Instns. Office: SC State Bd Fin Instns PO Box 12549 Columbia SC 29211 Office Phone: 803-734-2001. Office Fax: 803-734-2013. E-mail: louie.jacobs@banking.sc.gov.

JACOBS, M. LOUISE, secondary school educator; b. Macon, Miss., Jan. 1, 1947; d. James Wallace and Mary Elizabeth Cade, Virginia Cade (Stepmother); m. Steven Paul Jacobs, May 25, 1969 (div. June 13, 1991); children: Steven Paul Jr., Rachael Mary Jacobs-Geiser, Cade Jourdan, Faith Elizabeth. BS in Edn., U. Memphis, 1979. Cert. tchr. Tenn., 1990. Tchr. Memphis City Schs., 1983—. Sgt. USAF, Vietnam. Recipient Econs. Tchr. of Yr. award, Jr. Achievement, 2000. Mem.: NEA, Tchrs. Edn. Assn., Phi Kappa Phi, Kappa Delta Pi. Republican. Roman Catholic. Avocations: travel, nature, reading. Home: 1090 Cambrain Dr Memphis TN 38134 Office: Memphis City Schs - Cordova HS 1800 Berryhill Dr Cordova TN 38016 Home Phone: 901-826-9875; Office Phone: 901-416-4540. Personal E-mail: louisecadejacobs@midsouth.rr.com.

JACOBS, MADELEINE, professional society administrator, writer; b. Washington; m. Joseph Jacobs; 1 stepchild. BS in Chem., George Washington U., 1968, DSc (hon.), 2003; M course work in Organic Chem. completed, U. Md. Writer, editor Nat. Inst. Allergy and Infectious Disease, 1972—74; with Nat. Bur. of Standards (now Nat. Inst. of Standards & Tech.), 1974—79; head, Smithsonian News Svc. and publications mgr. Smithsonian Inst., 1979—86, dir., public affairs, 1986—93; reporter Chem. and Engring. News, 1969—72, mng. editor, 1993—95, editor-in-chief, 1995—2003; exec. dir., CEO Am. Chem. Soc., 2004—; also bd. dirs. Spkr. in field. Freelanced Physics Today, Smithsonian mag., asst. editor and writer Chemical & Engineering News, Am. Chem. Soc., 1969—72, mng. editor, 1993, editor-in-chief (first women), 1995. Recipient Smithsonian Inst. Secretary's Gold medal, 1993, Exec. Director's award, Am. Chem. Soc., 1999, award for Encouraging Women into Careers in Chemical Sciences, 2003, George Braude Meeml. award (Md. sect.), 2004, award for Exec. Excellence, Comml. Develop. and Mktg. Assn., 2004. Fellow: AAAS; mem.: NY Acad. Scis. (bd. trustee, Women's History Month award 2001), Coun. Advancement Sci. Writing (bd. dirs.), Nat. Assn. Sci. Writers, Phi Beta Kappa. Avocations: cooking, photography, swimming, gardening, writing, weight training. Office: Am Chem Soc 1155 16th St NW Washington DC 20036

JACOBS, MARC, fashion designer; b. NYC, 1963; Student, Parsons Sch. Design, 1981-84. Stock boy Charivari, NYC; designer Ruben Thomas Inc. (under Sketchbook label), NYC, Kashiyama, NYC; debuted his Marc Jacobs label, 1986; v.p., women's Perry Ellis, head designer NYC, 1989—92; creative designer Louis Vuitton, 1997, developed first ready-to-wear line., 1997; designer Mark Jacobs, NYC, 1988—; developed the Marc by Marc Jacobs line, 2001. Recipient Perry Ellis Golden Thimble award, 1984, Women's Designer of the Year award, Council of Fashion Designers Am., 1992; named The Guru of Grunge, Women's Wear Daily. Mem. Coun. of Fashion Designers of Am. (Young Designer 1987, Women's Wear Designer of the Yr. 1992). Democrat. Avocations: films, exercise, music. Office: Marc Jacobs Internat LLC 72 Spring St Fl 9 New York NY 10012-4019 Address: Marc Jacobs 163 Mercer St New York NY 10012 Office Phone: 212-343-0222, 212-343-1490.*

JACOBS, MARIAN, advertising executive; b. Stockton, Calif., Sept. 11, 1927; d. Paul and Rose (Sallah) J. AA, Stockton Coll. With Bottarini Advt., Stockton, 1948-50; pvt. practice Stockton, 1950-64; with Olympius Advt., Stockton, 1964-78; pvt. practice Stockton, 1978—. Pres. Stockton Advt. Club, 1954, Venture Club, Stockton, 1955; founder Stockton Advt. and Mktg. Club, 1981. Founder Stockton Arts Comms., 1976; co-founder Sunflower Entertainment for Institutionalized, 1976, Women Execs., Stockton, 1978; founding dir. Pixie Woods, Stockton; bd. dir. Goodwill Industries, St. Mary's Dining Room, Alan Short Gallery; mem. Calif. Coun. for the Humanities, 1994-95. Named Stocktonian of Yr., Stockton Bd. Realtors, 1978, Outstanding Citizen, Calif. State Senate and Assembly, 1978, Woman of Yr., State of Calif. Assembly, 2002, Woman of Achievement, Kaiser-Permanente Women's Wellness Conf., 2002, Disting. Alumni Vol., U. of the Pacific, 2003, Marian Jacobs Lit. Forum Stockton Arts Commn. established in her honor; recipient Woman of Achievement award, San Joaquin County Women's Coun., Stockton, 1976, Achievement award, San Joaquin Delta Coll., Stockton, 1978, Friend of Edn. award, Calif. Tchrs. Assn., Stockton, 1988, Stanley McCaffrey Disting. Svc. award, U. of the Pacific, Stockton, 1988, Athena award for businesswoman of Yr., Greater Stockton C. of C., 1989, Role Model award, Tierra del Oro Girl Scouts U.S., 1989, Heart of Gold award, Dameron Hosp. Found., 2000, Bravo award, Stockton Civic Theater; Paul Harris fellow, Rotary Club, 1994. Republican. Roman Catholic. Avocations: art, photography. Home and Office: 4350 Mallard Creek Cir Stockton CA 95207-5205

JACOBS, MARILYN ARLENE POTOKER, gifted education educator, consultant, author; b. NYC, Oct. 22, 1940; m. David Jacobs, Dec. 10, 1960. BA in Psychology, Hunter Coll. CUNY, 1961, MS in Edn., 1963; cert. in gifted edn., U. South Fla., 1977. Cert. elem. edn., gifted and early childhood edn., Fla. Tchr. Yonkers (N.Y.) Pub. Schs., 1961-63; dir., tchr. Creative Corners Pre-Sch., Pomona, N.Y., 1971-74; tchr. of gifted, tchr. trainer Pinellas County Schs., Clearwater, Fla., 1975—2004; ret., 2004. Pvt. practice computer edn. cons., 1987—; freelance grant writer, 1976—, freelance curriculum writer, 1993—. Contbr. articles to profl. jours. Recipient numerous county, state and nat. Econs. Edn. Curriculum awards, 1982—. Mem. NEA, ASCD, Coun. for Exceptional Children (Educator of the Yr. 1985), Assn. for Gifted, Fla. Assn. Computer Educators, Phi Delta Kappa, Phi Beta Kappa, Kappa Delta Pi, Psi Chi. Home: 2642 Cedarglen Dr Dunedin FL 34698-6505

JACOBS, MARK, biology professor, dean; b. Princeton, May 19, 1950; s. William Paul and Jane Shaw Jacobs; m. Candace Margaret Clarke, Dec. 29, 1973 (div. June 1998); children: Jeffrey William, Robinson Clarke, Patrick Shaw; m. Ellen Ruth Abelman, Oct. 14, 2000; 1 child, Madeleine Jane. BA magna cum laude, Harvard Coll., 1971; PhD, Stanford U., 1975. Post doctoral fellow NATO, Freiburg, Germany, 1976—77; asst. prof. Swarthmore (Pa.) Coll., 1975—81, assoc. prof., 1981—89, prof., 1989—2003, assoc. provost, 1993—96; prof. Sch. Life Scis., Ariz. State U., Tempe, 2003—, dean Barrett Honors Coll., 2003—. Panel mem. metabolic biology program NSF, Washington, 1984—88; commr., vice chair Mid. States Assn. Commn. Higher Edn., Phila., 1997—2003; mem. com. arts and scis. Franklin Inst., Phila., 1996—2003. Contbr. 23 articles to profl. jours.; editor: Molecular Biology of Plant Growth Control, 1987; assoc. editor-in-chief (sci. jour.) Plant Physiology and Biochemistry, mem. editl. bd. The New Biologist. Named Endowed Chair, Centennial prof. biology, Swarthmore Coll., 1990—2003; fellow, German Acad. Exch. Svc. (DAAD), 1979, Guggenheim Found., 1986—87; grantee, NSF, NIH, USDA, 1976—99. Mem.: Am. Soc. Plant Biologists (nat. treas. 1991—97), Nature Conservancy, Sigma Xi. Office: Barrett Honors Coll Ariz State Univ PO Box 871612 Tempe AZ 85287-1612 Home Phone: 480-705-4665; Office Phone: 480-965-2354. E-mail: mark.jacobs@asu.edu.

JACOBS, MARK M., energy executive; b. 1962; BBA, So. Methodist U.; MBA, Northwestern U. Mng. dir. natural resources group Goldman, Sachs and Co., Houston, 1989—2002; exec. v.p., CFO Reliant Energy, Inc., Houston, 2002—07, pres., CEO, 2007—. Mem. bd. dirs. Theatre Under the Stars. Office: Reliant Energy Inc 1000 Main St Houston TX 77002 Mailing: Reliant Energy Inc PO Box 148 Houston TX 77201-0148*

JACOBS, MARK RANDOLPH, lawyer; b. Columbus, Ohio, June 7, 1953; s. Lee Randolph and Sally Ann (Cummins) J.; m. Linda Beth Rogozinski, Oct. 29, 1983; children: Philip Randolph, Gregory Cummins. BA cum laude with distinction, Yale U., 1979, JD, 1982. Bar: N.Y. 1983, U.S. Dist. Ct. (so. dist.) N.Y. 1983, Conn. 1993. Law clerk Hon. S.W. Kram U.S. Dist. Judge, NYC, 1983-84; ptnr. Pryor, Cashman, Sherman & Flynn, NYC, 1988-90, Cadwalader, Wickersham & Taft, NYC, 1990-92; of counsel Gregory & Adams, Wilton, Conn., 1992-96; ptnr. Jacobs Goldman LLC, Norwalk, Conn., 1997—. Office: Jacobs Goldman LLC Merritt View 383 Main Ave Norwalk CT 06851-1543

JACOBS, MICHAEL ALLEN, lawyer; b. NYC, Mar. 10, 1955; s. Gerson and Marilyn J.; m. Ellen L. Fuerst; children: Rebecca, Jonathan. BA, Stanford U., 1977; JD, Yale U., 1983. Bar: Calif. 1983, US Dist. Ct. (no. dist.) Calif. 1983, US Dist. Ct. (so. dist.) Calif. 1991, US Ct. Appeals (4th cir.) 1988, US Ct. Appeals (9th cir.) 1991, US Ct. Appeals (fed. cir.) 1992, US Dist. Ct. (ctrl. dist.) Calif. 1993. With fgn. svc. State Dept., Washington, 1977-81, Kingston, Jamaica; assoc. Morrison & Foerster, San Francisco, 1983-89, ptnr., co-head intellectual property group, 1990—2000, ptnr. Editor: No. Calif. ABTL newsletter; U.S. editor: Intellectual Property Reports (Australia); co-author: The World Intellectual Property Guidebook - US, Matthew Bender & Co., 1992. Mem. ABA (subcom. chair sect. patent, trademark and copyright law, subcom. on computer software 1990-91), Computer Law Assn., Am. Intellectual Property Law Assn. Office: Morrison & Foerster 425 Market St San Francisco CA 94105 Office Phone: 415-677-7455, 415-268-7000. Office Fax: 415-268-7522. Business E-Mail: mjacobs@mofo.com.

JACOBS, MICHAEL ROY, microbiologist, researcher; arrived in U.S., 1979; s. Philip and Ruth Joan Jacobs; m. Gretta Hazel Jacobs; children: Erica Yvonne, Kevin Bryan, Paul Daniel, David Andrew. MB, BChir, U. Witwatersrand, Johannesburg, 1971, Diploma in Tropical Medicine and Hygiene, 1974, Diploma in Pub. Health, 1976, PhD, 1978. Fellow faculty pathology Coll. Medicine South Africa, 1977, diplomate in Pub. Health and Med. Microbiology Am. Bd. Med. Microbiology, 1980. Microbiologist South African Inst. for Med. Rsch., Johannesburg, 1977—79; dir. clin. microbiology U. Hosps. Cleve., 1979—; asst. prof. dept. pathology Case Western Res. U., Cleve., 1979—86, assoc. prof. dept. pathology, 1986—93, prof. dept. pathology, 1993—. Com. mem. Drug Resistant Streptococcus Pneumoniae Therapeutic Working Group, Atlanta, 1977—2000; com. mem. sinusitis guidelines com. Sinus and Allergy Health Partnership, Washington, 1998—2004. Contbr. chapters to books, articles to profl. jours. Mem.: Am. Soc. for Microbiology, Infectious Disease Soc. Am., Royal Coll. Pathologists. Achievements include discovery of first strains of Streptococcus pneumoniae resistant to multiple groups of antimicrobial agents in South Africa in 1978; development of treatment guidelines for acute otitis media; treatment guidelines for community acquired pneumonia; treatment guidelines for acute bacterial rhinosinusitis; research in antimicrobial susceptibility of respiratory tract pathogens; application of pharmacokinetic and pharmacodynamic parameters to interpretation of antimicrobial susceptibility of bacterial pathogens; detection and prevention of bacterial contamination of platelet products.

JACOBS, NANCY CAROLYN BAKER, writer; b. Milw., Dec. 9, 1944; d. Alvin Donald and Wilma Carolyn (Robertson) Moll; m. James Ross Baker, Aug. 28, 1965 (div. 1979); 1 child, Bradley; m. Jerome Martin Jacobs, June 20, 1981. BA, U. Minn., 1965, MA, 1973; MFA, U. So. Calif., 1977. Reporter St. Paul Dispatch, 1965-66; pub. rels. writer U. Minn., Mpls., 1966-67, Northwest Airlines, St. Paul, 1967-69; TV scriptwriter Control Data Corp., Mpls., 1971-73; dir. news and pub. Met. State U., St. Paul, 1973-75; author, free lance journalist, 1975—; pvt. investigator Spl. Reports, LA, 1986-90; journalism lectr. Calif. State U., Northridge, 1977-92. Author: Deadly Companion, 1986, The Turquoise Tattoo, 1991, A Slash of Scarlet, 1992, See Mommy Run, 1992, The Silver Scalpel, 1993, Cradle and All, 1995, Daddy's Gone A-Hunting, 1995, Rocking the Cradle, 1996, Double or Nothing, 2001, Star Struck, 2002, Flash Point, 2002, Ricochet, 2003 (nominated Mary Higgins Clark award Mystery Writers Am.) , Desperate Journeys, 2004; (as Nancy C. Baker) Babyselling: The Scandal of Black Market Adoption, 1978, Act II: The Mid-Career Job Change and How to Make It, 1980, New Lives for Former Wives: Displaced Homemakers, 1980, Cashing in on Cooking, 1982, The Beauty Trap: Exploring Woman's Greatest Obsession, 1984, Relative Risk: Living with a Family History of Breast Cancer, 1991 (Am. Med. Writers Assn. Rose Kushner award). Mem. Mystery Writers Am., Authors Guild, Sisters in Crime. Personal E-mail: nancy@nancybakerjacobs.com.

JACOBS, NORMAN JOSEPH, publishing executive; b. Chgo., Oct. 28, 1932; s. Herman and Tillie (Chapman) J.; m. Jeri Kolber Rose, Jan. 2, 1977; 1 son, Barry Herman; children by previous marriage: Carey, Murray, Dale. BS in Mktg, U. Ill., 1954. Display salesman Chgo. Daily News, 1954-57; dist. mgr. Davidson Pub. Co., Chgo., 1957-62; v.p. Press-Tech, Inc., Evanston, Ill., 1962-69; pres. Century Pub. Co., Evanston, 1969—. Bd. dirs. Chgo. Bulls. With USNR, 1951—59. Mem. B'nai B'rith, Birchwood Tennis Club, Alpha Delta Sigma, Tau Epsilon Phi. Jewish. Office: Century Pub Co 990 Grove St 3rd Fl Evanston IL 60201-6510 Home Phone: 847-831-0738; Office Phone: 847-491-6440. Business E-Mail: njacobs@centurysports.net.

JACOBS, PAUL, lawyer; b. NYC, Sept. 29, 1946; s. William R. and Sylvia (Wanshel) J.; m. Lisette Simon, Oct. 10, 1979; children: Alexia, Caroline. BA, Colgate U., 1967; JD, Columbia U., 1971. Bar: NY 1971, US Dist. Ct. (so. dist.) NY 1971. Assoc. Reavis & McGrath, NYC, 1971-78, ptnr., 1978-89, Fulbright & Jaworski, NYC, 1989-96, sr. ptnr., 1996—; co-head corp. bus. and banking sect. Fulbright & Jaworski LLP, NYC, 2000—. Mem. adv. com. Grace Ventures Corp., Cupertino, Calif., 1988-98, Euro-Am.-I C.V., San Bruno, Calif., 1988-98; sec. Zygo Corp., Middlefield, Conn., 1992—. Mem. NY Bar Assn., NYC Bar Assn., Phi Beta Kappa, The University Club. Office: Fulbright & Jaworski LLP 666 5th Ave Fl 31 New York NY 10103-3198 Office Phone: 212-318-3348. Office Fax: 212-318-3400. Business E-Mail: pjacobs@fulbright.com.

JACOBS, PAUL A., music educator; b. Washington, Pa., Feb. 1, 1977; s. Mary Jeanne Novi. MusB, Curtis Inst. Music, 2000; MusM, Yale U., 2002. Prin. organist Immaculate Conception Ch., Washington, Pa., 1992—95; organist Wash. Meml. Chapel, Valley Forge, 1995—2000; chair organ dept. The Juilliard Sch., NYC, 2003—, William Schuman Scholars chair, 2007; artist in residence Christ and St. Stephen's Ch., 2003—. Recipient Horatio Parker Meml. award, Yale Sch. Music, 2002, Arthur W. Foote award, Harvard Musical Assn., 2003, Disting. Alumni award, Yale Sch. Music, 2005; scholar, Curtis Inst. Music, 1995—2000, Yale Inst. Sacred Music, 2000—03. Mem.: Am. Guild Organists. Conservative. Roman Catholic. Achievements include Performances across North America, South America, Europe, Australia and Asia. Avocations: hiking, travel. Office: The Juilliard Sch 60 Lincoln Ctr Plz New York NY 10023 Home Phone: 212-496-8725; Office Phone: 212-799-5000. Personal E-mail: pjacobs@juilliard.edu.

JACOBS, PAUL ALAN, lawyer; b. Boston, June 5, 1940; s. Samuel and Sarah (Rodman) J.; m. Carole Ruth Greenstein, Aug. 28, 1962; children: Steven N., Cheryl R., David F., Craig A. BA in Econs. magna cum laude, Tufts U., 1960; JD magna cum laude, U. Denver, 1968. Bar: Colo. 1968, U.S. Dist. Ct. Colo. 1968. Pers. officer First Nat. Bank Denver, 1964-68; assoc. Holme Roberts & Owen, Denver, 1968-73, sr. ptnr., 1973-93; exec. v.p., gen. counsel Colo. Rockies profl. baseball orgn., Denver, 1991-95; ptnr. Jacobs Chase Frick Kleinkopf & Kelley, Denver, 1995—. Bd. dirs. Anti-Defamation League B'nai B'rith, Denver, 1987-95, Colo. Sports Hall of Fame, 2000—, Am. Jewish Com., 2002-. Served to 1st lt. USAF, 1960-63. Recipient Outstanding Alumni award, U. Denver Sturm Coll. Law, 2004. Mem. ABA, Denver Bar Assn., Colo. Bar Assn. Jewish. Avocations: skiing, golf. Home: 4041 S Narcissus Way Denver CO 80237-2025 Office: Independence Plz 1050 17th St Ste 1500 Denver CO 80265-2078 Business E-Mail: pjacobs@jcfkk.com.

JACOBS, PAUL E., communications company executive; b. 1962; s. Irwin Mark and Joan Jacobs; m. Stacy Jacobs; 3 children. BS, U. Calif., Berkeley, 1984, MS, 1986, PhD in Elec. Engring, 1989. Engring. positions QUALCOMM Inc., 1990—95, v.p. & gen. mgr. handset & integrated circuit divsn., 1995, sr. v.p., 1996, pres. QCP, 1997, exec. v.p., 2000—05, group pres. QWI, 2001, mem. exec. com., 1992—, CEO, 2005—. Bd. dirs. Qualcomm Inc., 2005—. Bd. mem. Mus. Contemporary Art, San Diego, Salk Inst. Biol. Studies; mem. adv. bd. U. Calif., Berkeley, Coll. Engring.; chmn. adv. bd. U. Calif., San Diego, Jacobs Sch. Engring. Named one of 50 Who Matter Now, CNNMoney.com Bus. 2.0, 2006, 2007. Mem.: Phi Beta Kappa, Eta Kappa Nu, Tau Beta Pi. Office: QUALCOMM Inc Qualcomm Inc 5775 Morehouse Dr San Diego CA 92121*

JACOBS, RALPH, JR., artist; b. El Centro, Calif., May 22, 1940; s. Ralph and Julia Vahe (Kirkorian) J. Paintings appeared in: Prize Winning Art (3 awards), 1964, 65, 66, and New Woman Mag., 1975; one man shows and exhbns. Villa Montalvo, Calif., Stanford Rsch. Inst., Calif., Fresno Art Ctr., Calif., de Young Meml. Mus., Calif., Rosicrucian Mus., Calif., Cunningham Meml. Gallery, Calif., 40th Ann. Nat. Art Exhibit, Utah, Nat. Exhbn. Coun. of Am. Artists Socs., N.Y.C., Am. Artists Profl. League Show, Armenian Allied Arts, Calif., Monterey Peninsula Mus. Art, Calif. Recipient 1st place award Statewide Ann. Santa Cruz Art League Gallery, 1963, 64; 2d place award Soc. We. Artists Ann. M.H. de Young Mus., 1964; A.E. Klumpkey Meml. award, 1965. Address: PO Box 5906 Carmel CA 93921-5906

JACOBS, RANDALL SCOTT DAVID, lawyer; b. Sept. 6, 1944; s. Irving and Lea Sylvia (Kerner) Jacobs; m. Jill Barbara Weiss, June 20, 1981; children: Evan, Todd. BSBA, NYU, 1967, LLM in Corp. Law, 1971; JD, Temple U., 1970. Bar: N.Y. 1977, U.S. Dist. Ct. (ea. dist.) N.Y. 1979, U.S. Dist. Ct. (so. dist.) N.Y. 1979, U.S. Ct. Appeals (2d cir.) 1980, U.S. Supreme Ct. 1980. Assoc. Coudert Brothers, NYC, 1968; with Comml. Coverage Corp., NYC, 1971—78; assoc. Levy, Tandet, Sohn and Loft, NYC, 1978—82; of counsel Harvis and Zeichner, NYC, 1982—84; ptnr. Rich, Krinsly, Dorman & Jacobs, P.C., NYC, 1984—91, Mintz and Fraade, PC, NYC, 1991—94, Branin Investments, Inc., NYC, 1995—96, Recap. Ptnrs., LLC, NYC, 1996—2000, FMG Acquisitions Fund, LLC, NYC, 2000—, Turnaround Capital, LLC, 2003—; of counsel Bienstock & Michael, P.C., 2004—. Mem. staff Temple Law Quarterly Law Rev., 1969—70. Mem.: Assn. of Bar of City of N.Y., N.Y. State Bar Assn., ABA. Office: 67 Wall St Ste 1901 New York NY 10005 Office Phone: 212-399-0099. E-mail: randall.jacobs@musicesq.com.

JACOBS, RHODA S., state legislator; b. Bklyn. 3 children. BA, Bklyn. Coll. Co-founder, formerly co-dir. Bklyn. Coll. Day Care Ctr.; mem. N.Y. State Assembly, 1978—, asst. spkr., mem. task force New Americans, mem. banks com., higher edn. com., ins. com., health com., women's caucus. Mem. Nat. Assn. Jewish Legislators. Office: NY State Assembly LOB Rm 736 Albany NY 12248-0001 Office Phone: 718-434-0446. Business E-Mail: jacobsr@assembly.state.ny.us.

JACOBS, RICHARD ALBERTO, mechanical engineer; s. Rufus Jacobs and Nelida Cardozo de Jacobs. Degree in mech. engring. cum laude, U. Simon Bolivar, Caracas, 1985; PhD, MIT, 1995. Project engr. Petroleos de Venezuela, S.A, Maracaibo, Venezuela, 1985—91, conceptual design engr., 1995—98, project definition leader, 1998—2001, engring. and constrn. mgr., 2001—03; grad. rsch. asst. MIT, Cambridge, Mass., 1991—95; process engring. supr. Jacobs Engring. Group, Inc., Houston, 2003—. Author: (software) Tricad, solid modeling and visualization (Epson's 2nd Nat. award for Software Devel., 1985). Recipient Productivity award, Petroleos de Venezuela, 1998; Internat. Grad. Studies scholar, 1991—95. Mem.: ASME, Soc. Petroleum Engineers. Achievements include patents for electrode geometry for soil electroremediation; identifying and solving bottlenecks in production flow stations and gathering networks; design of LPG storage, transport and loading facilities; developed and validated a two-dimensional finite element code to describe coupled mass and charge transport in porous media; proposed optimization plan for the engineering and projects organization, adopted at a corporate scale; ensured the design integrity of five offshore production platforms for a total of 600, 000 bpd of added capacity; coordinated taskforce for ISO 9000 certification of an engineering department; development of deferred production and improved equipment design margins through statistical analysis and modeling of oil and gas production data; computer models to simulate and improve oil and gas transport, storage and shipping installations in the Lake Maracaibo area. Personal E-mail: rajacobs@alum.mit.edu.

JACOBS, RICHARD E., real estate company executive, sports team owner; 3 children from previous marriage. Ptnr. Jacobs, Visconsi & Jacobs; former chmn., chief exec. officer Cleve. Indians. Office: Richard E Jacobs Group 25425 Center Ridge Rd Cleveland OH 44145-4122

JACOBS, ROBERT ALAN, lawyer; b. Waco, Tex., June 23, 1937; s. Abe and Ruth (Englander) J.; m. Sue C. Braunstein, Aug. 22, 1961; children: Jacqueline Anne, Michelle Keri. BBA, U. Tex., 1957; LLB cum laude, NYU, 1960, LLM in Taxation, 1963. Bar: N.Y. 1961. Assoc. Greenbaum, Wolff & Ernst, NYC, 1961-63; asst. br. chief, chief counsel IRS, Washington, 1963-67; assoc. Paul, Weiss, Rifkind, Wharton & Garrison, NYC, 1967-69; sr. tax mem. Milgrim Thomajan Jacobs & Lee PC, NYC, 1969-87; tax ptnr. Milbank, Tweed, Hadley & McCloy, LLP, NYC, 1987—2002, cons. ptnr., 2002—03, ret. ptnr., 2003—; head low income tax clinic Benjamin A. Cardozo Sch. Law, 2002; underwriting dir. Gulf Ins. Group, 2002. Adj. prof. law NYU, 1976-85; adj. prof. bus. planning Pace Law Sch., 2005—; vis. sr. lectr. taxation, U. Calif. Davis, 1977; spl. counsel to sec. treas., Washington, 1965-67. Note and comment editor NYU Law Rev.; contbr. articles to profl. jours. Mem. adv. group Senate Fin. Com. Staff on Subchpt. C. Revision, 1983-85; arbitrator Civil Ct. City of N.Y., 1972—; bd. dirs. Community Action Legal Svcs., 1978-82, MFY Legal Svcs., 1991-98, N.Y. County Lawyers, 1990-93, 2004—. With U.S. Army, 1960-61, 61-62. Root-Tilden scholar; recipient commendation medal U.S. Army. Mem. ABA (tax sect., asst. sec. 1987-88, chmn. corp. stockholder relationships 1983-85, chmn. task force on pass-through entities 1986-88), Am. Law Inst., Tax Forum (chmn. 1989-2001), Am. Coll. Tax Counsel, N.Y. State Bar Assn. (tax sect., exec. com. 1980—, chair 2001), Tax Club (chmn. 1987-88). Office: 61 Broadway Ste 1601 New York NY 10006 Home Phone: 212-614-0517; Office Phone: 212-267-2600. Personal E-mail: rajacobs23@aol.com, rjacobs@broadviewnet.net. Business E-Mail: rjacobs@gfrglawfirm.com.

JACOBS, ROLLY WARREN, judge; b. Nashville, Aug. 26, 1946; s. William Clinton Jr. and Eleanor Olive (Warren) J.; m. Karen Lee Ponist, Sept. 16, 1972; children: Collin Wayne, Tyler Warren. BA in Econs., Washington & Lee U., 1968; JD, U. S.C., 1974. Bar: SC 1975, US Dist. Ct. SC 1975. Assoc. Carl R. Reasonover, Camden, S.C., 1975-77; ptnr. Reasonover & Jacobs, Camden, S.C., 1977-80; pvt. practice law Camden, S.C., 1980-99; judge family ct. 5th Jud. Cir., S.C., 1999—. Asst. city judge Mcpl. Ct., Camden, 1976-77; master in equity S.C. Jud. Sys., Camden, 1978-99; mem. Jud. Coun. for S.C., Columbia, 1989-2000; mem. fee dispute panel S.C. Bar Assn., 1986-93. Bd. dirs. ARC, Camden, 1976-78, Am. Cancer Soc., Camden, 1976-78, United Way, Camden, 1978-82; active Boy Scouts Am., Camden, 1984-96. Capt. U.S. Army, 1968-72. Recipient Dist. Award of Merit Indian Waters Coun. Boy Scouts Am., 1991; named Scouting Family of Yr., 1990. Mem. ABA, VFW, S.C. Bar Assn., Am. Legion, Res. Officers Assn., Elks, DAV. Methodist. Home: 418 Lafayette Way Camden SC 29020-1642 Office: Kershaw County Courthouse PO Box 664 Camden SC 29020-0664 Office Phone: 803-425-1500 ext. 5390.

JACOBS, ROXANNE, development director; d. George Warren and Nancy Jane Huff; children: Kenneth Ryan, Dustin Robert. BSBA, Barry U., Miami, Fla., 1999. Cert. fundraising exec. 1997. Sr. bookkeeper Jameson Meml. Hosp., New Castle, 1974—84; dir. ann. fund and spl. events Bethesda Hosp. Found., Boynton Beach, Fla., 1984—98; dir. devel. South Fla. Sci. Mus., West Palm Beach, 1998—2000, Palm Beach Habilitation Ctr., Lake Worth, Fla., 2000—. Mem.: Assn. Fundraising Profls. (treas. 2006—, immediate past pres. 2004—05, pres. 2003, treas. 2001—02). Office: Palm Beach Habilitation Ctr 4522 S Congress Ave Lake Worth FL 33461 Home Phone: 561-969-7425; Office Phone: 561-965-8500. Office Fax: 561-433-2073. Business E-Mail: rjacobs@pbhab.com.

JACOBS, RUTH HARRIET, poet, playwright, sociologist, gerontologist; b. Boston, Nov. 15, 1924; d. Samuel J. and Jane G. Miller; m. Neal Jacobs, Aug. 1948 (div.); children: Eli, Edith. BS, Boston U, 1964; PhD, Brandeis U., 1969. Reporter, feature writer Herald-Traveler, Boston, 1943-49; instr. Mass. Bay CC, Northeastern U., 1961-69; prof. sociology Boston U., 1969-82; prof., chmn. dept. sociology Clark U., Worcester, Mass., 1982-87; rsch. scholar Women's Ctr. Wellesley Coll., Mass., 1985—; prof. human svcs. Springfield Coll., St. Johnsbury, Vt., 1988—; lectr. Regis Coll., Weston, Mass., 1989—2002, instr. lifetime learning, 2006—, Brandeis U., 2000—. Vis. prof. Coll. William and Mary, 1990; vis. rsch. scholar Five Colls. Women's Rsch. Ctr. Mt. Holyoke Coll., 1992; spkr. in field. Author: Life After Youth: Female Forty, What Next, 1979, Button, Button, Who has the Button, 1983, rev. edit., 1996, Older Women Surviving and Thriving, 1987, Out of Their Mouths, 1988, Be an Outrageous Older Woman: A.R.A.S.P., 1991, 2d rev. edit., 1997, We Speak for Peace: An Anthology, 1993, Women Who Touched My Life: A Memoir, 1996, The ABC's of Aging: Mother Ruth Rhymes for Ageing, Sageing and Rageing, 2000, rev. edit., 2005, ABC's for Seniors: Advice from an Outrageous Gerontologist, 2006; co-author: Re-Engagement in Late Life: Re-Employment and Re-Marriage, 1979, (plays) Happy Birthday, 2003; contbr. chapters to books, articles to profl. jours., poetry to anthologies and mags. Recipient Dewing Peace award, Pendle Hill, 1993; NIMH grantee, 1972—75, Faculty fellow, NSF, 1977—78. Mem.: New Eng. Sociol. Assn. (v.p. 1976, Pioneer award 1993, Athena award for mentoring 1998). Mem. Soc. Of Friends. Home and Office: 75 High Ledge Ave Wellesley MA 02482-1042 Home Phone: 781-237-1793; Office Phone: 781-237-1793.

JACOBS, TIMOTHY ANDREW, epidemiologist, consultant; b. St. Petersburg, Fla., Nov. 5, 1944; s. W. Andrew and Virginia (Ott) J.; m. Carolyn Martin, Nov. 4, 1972; 1 child, Jenny Thuy Ha. BSN, U. Fla., 1970; MS, PNP, U. Utah, 1976; PhD, Internat. Inst. Advanced Studies, 1979; C.T.M., Liverpool Sch. Medicine, Eng., 1982; cert. hosp. epidemiology, U. Iowa, 1985; MPH, Yale U., 1991. Nat. design and media cons. Nat. Assn. Pediatric Nurse Assocs. and Practitioners, Cherry Hill, NJ, 1977-83; asst. prof., co-coord. community health nursing U. N.D., Grand Forks, 1980; vol. epidemiologist, pub. health specialist Vinh Children's Hosp., Vinh City, Vietnam, 1989; pediatric staff nurse I U. Fla. Pediatric Svc., Shands Teaching Hosp., Gainesville, 1970; instr. pediatric nursing U. Utah Coll. Nursing, Salt Lake City, 1976-77; pvt. cons. Internat. Cmty. Health and Epidemiology, New Haven, 1990-94; med. supr., health svcs. mgr. Brown & Root Logcap Med. Clinic, Port-au-Prince, Haiti, 1994-95; med. tech. proposal cons. UN, Rwanda, Angola, 1995; specialist Home Health Care, Tampa, Fla., 1996—. Vol. pub. health scientist, cons. Hanoi (Vietnam) Sch. Pub. Health; cons. epidemiologist Vinh and Huong Son, Vietnam, 1993; internat. edn. cons. U. Am., New Orleans, 1994; cons. infectious disease epidemiology, consulate of Nicaragua, Miami, Health for Health Svcs. Hurricane Mitch, 1998; cons. Christian Haitian Outreach Clinics and Orphanages, Jeremie and Mariani, Haiti, 1998—; pediatric clin. planner and designer, Carrafour, Haiti, 2002; prin. designer Ambulatory Primary Care Clinic, Mariani, Haiti, 2002; trustee Burnett Internat. U. Sch. Medicine and Health Scis., Port-au-Prince, 2004. Contbg. editor Episource, 1991, 97, Resources in Epidemiology; contbr. articles to profl. jours.; contbr. to poetry jours.; anthologies Daybreak on the Land, 1997, Audiotape Sounds of Poetry, 1997, Archive of the Vietnam Conflict, Personal Papers Collection, 1999. Donor, contbr. Asian Family and Cmty. Empowerment Ctr., St. Petersburg, Fla., Caribbean Mercy, Mercy Ships, Garden Valley, Tex., 2001, Love a Child Orphanage and Med. Clinic, Fond Parisien, Haiti, 2001-02. Capt. Nurse Corps, U.S. Army, 1968-73, Vietnam. Recipient Cert. of Achievement in HIV-AIDS Edn., AIDS Project, New Haven, Conn., 1994, Editor's Choice award for outstanding achievement in poetry Nat. Libr. Poetry, 1997. Fellow Royal Soc. Tropical Medicine and Hygiene (London), Am. Biog. Inst. (advisor, rsch. adv. bd.); mem. AMA, VFW, Am. Legion, Vietnam Vets. Am., Nat. Assn. Pediatric Nurse Assocs. and Practitioners (com. dir. graphics & logos mil. chpt., former chmn. nat. art and exhibits subcom., former mem. pub. rels. com., Cert. Recognition 1983), Am. Pub. Health Assn. (epidemiology sect., internat. healthsect., mem. caucus pub. health and faith cmty.), Internat. Assn. Med. Assistance to Travellers, Fla. Pub. Health Assn., Nat. Adolescent Health Promotion Network, Assn. Mil. Surgeons U.S., Ret. Army Nurse Corps Assn., Liverpool Tropical Sch. Assn. (Eng.), Assn. Yale Alumni in Pub. Health, Consortium for Internat. Nursing Edn., Rsch. & Practice, U.S.-Vietnam Friendship Assn., Doctorate Assn. N.Y. Educators, Fleet Marine Force Corpsman Assn. (former Conn. rep., charter mem.), U.S. Navy Corpsmen United Assn., Am. Assn. Navy Hosp. Corpsmen, U.S. Army (Vietnam) 24th Evacuation Hosp. Assn. (com. asv. reunion 1993), Vets. Vietnam Restoration Project, U.S. Com. Scientific Cooperation with Vietnam, N.Y. Acad. of Sci., Walter Reed Army Med. Ctr. Soc. (charter), Spl. Ops. Med. Assn., Soaring Soc. Am., Tampa Bay Soaring Soc. (student pvt. pilot), Sigma Xi, Sigma Theta Tau (charter mem. Gamma Rho chpt.), Phi Kappa Phi. Avocations: racewalking, fishing, travel. Home: 11333 Calgary Cir Tampa FL 33624-4804 Home Phone: 813-269-9094; Office Phone: 813-269-9094. Personal E-mail: epidoc91@tampabay.rr.com.

JACOBS, TONYA A., lawyer; b. Yoakum, Tex. BA in History with honors, U. Tex., Austin, 1991; JD cum laude, U. Houston, 1994. Bar: Tex. 1994, US Dist. Ct. (so. dist. Tex.) 1995, US Dist. Ct. (ea. dist. Tex.) 1996, US Dist. Ct. (no. dist. Tex.) 1999. Ptnr. labor and employment grp. Baker Hostetler, Houston. Mng. editor: Houston Law Rev. Named a Rising Star, Tex. Super Lawyers mag., 2006. Mem.: Tex. Bar Assn., Houston Young Lawyers Assn., Houston Mgmt. Lawyer's Forum, ABA, Houston Bar Assn. Office: Baker Hostetler 1000 Louisiana St Ste 2000 Houston TX 77002 Office Phone: 717-646-1358. E-mail: tjacobs@bakerlaw.com.*

JACOBS, TRAVIS BEAL, historian, educator; b. NYC, Apr. 22, 1936; s. Albert Charles and Loretta Field (Beal) J.; m. Eleanor Morison (div. 1982); children: Travis Beal, Holmes Morison. AB, Princeton U., 1958; MA, Columbia U., 1960, PhD, 1971. Mem. faculty Middlebury Coll. (Vt.), 1965—, prof. history, 1978-92, Fletcher D. Proctor prof. Am. history, 1992—, chmn. dept. history, 1976-88, 91-95. Vis. prof. Johannes Gutenburg U., Mainz, Germany, 2006. Editor: Middlebury College General Catalogue: Bicentennial Edition, 2000; co-editor: Navigating The Rapids, 1918-1971, From the Papers of Adolf A. Berle, 1973, Eisenhower at Columbia, 2001, America and the Winter War, 1939-1941, 1981, Dwight D. Eisenhower and the Founding of The American Assembly, 2004. Cons. 20th Century Fund, 1972-73; bd. dirs. Psi Upsilon Found., 1971-98, hon., 1998—; trustee Sheldon Mus., 1984-90, 95-01, pres., 1987-90, hon. trustee, 2003-; pres. Chappaquiddick Island Assn., 1983-86; participant Eisenhower Centennial Programs, 1990. Earhart fellow, 1989-90, 95-96; Fulbright sr. specialists grant, Tunisia, 2004. Mem. Am. Hist. Assn., Ctr. for Study of Presidency, Orgn. Am. Historians, Soc. Historians Fgn. Rels., Vt. Hist. Soc., Princeton Club (N.Y.C.). Episcopalian. Home: 1104 Vt Route 125 Bridport VT 05734-9756 Office: Dept Hist Middlebury Coll Middlebury VT 05753 Home Phone: 802-758-2351; Office Phone: 802-443-5315. E-mail: tjacobs@middlebury.edu.

JACOBS, WENDELL EARLY, JR., lawyer; b. Detroit, Nov. 15, 1945; s. Wendell E. and Mildred P. (Horton) J.; m. Elaine M. Lott (div.); children: Wendell Early III, Damon R. BFA, Denison U., 1969; JD, Wayne State U., 1972. Bar: Mich. 1972, U.S. Dist. Ct. (ea. dist.) Mich. 1973, Fla. 1974. Asst. prosecutor Jackson County, Mich., 1973-76; ptnr. Jacobs & Engle, Jackson, 1977—. Mem. Mich. Coun. on Crime and Delinquency. Mem. Nat. Assn. Criminal Def. Lawyers, Criminal Def. Attys. Mich., Jackson County Bar Assn., Eagles Club, Grotto Club, Elks. Avocations: paddleball, motorcycling. Home: 9281 Greenwood Rd Grass Lake MI 49240-9590 Office: Jacobs & Engle 1104 W Michigan Ave Jackson MI 49202-4123 Office Phone: 517-782-9459.

JACOBS, WENDY, editor, realtor; b. Conn. d. Gerald and Eileen Jacobs. BA with honors, U. Conn., 1974; postgrad., The Russian Sch., Northfield, Vt., 1974, Ind. U., Bloomington, 1975, U. Toronto, 1978—79, Three Schs. Art, Toronto, Ont. Coll. Art. With Jours. divsn. Plenum Pub., NYC, 1974—76, 1976—77; with HIAS, Vienna, 1976, Yorkville Press, Toronto, 1977, Macmillan Can., 1977—78, U. Toronto, 1979—80, Harlequin Books/Torstar Enterprises, 1980—81; cons. and editor, 1981—; realtor Prudential Fla. WCI Realty, Boynton Beach. Recipient Svc. award, Internat. Assn. Bus. Communicators, 1992, Hist. Mus. So. Fla., 2004; fellow, U. Toronto, 1978—79. Mem.: Nat. Assn. Realtors, Hist. Mus. So. Fla., Hadassah. Office: 5645 Lakeview Mews Dr Boynton Beach FL 33437 Office Phone: 561-317-3878. Business E-Mail: wjacobs1@aol.com.

JACOBSEN, DIANE DEMELL, foreign policy specialist; b. NYC, Sept. 21, 1944; d. A. Leonard and Lizette DeMell; m. Thomas H. Jacobsen, June 15, 1985 (dec. July 20, 2002). Bachelors Degree, CUNY, 1965; M in Liberal Arts, Washington U., 1995, M in Internat. Affairs, 2000, PhD in Internat. Affairs, 2003. Sr. exec. Internat. Bus. Machine, Armonk, N.Y., 1965-86; sr. v.p. Bapt. Health Inc., Jacksonville, Fla., 1987-88; pres., CEO Dependable Ins. Group, Jacksonville, 1988-91; pres. DeMell Group, Ponte Vedra Beach, Fla., 1991—2001. Conflict resolution specialist Ctr. for Internat. Understanding, St. Louis; adv. dir. internat. leadership program Washington U., St. Louis, 1998—; adv. group, Coun. Fgn. Rels., 2002-. Commr., trustee St. Louis Art Mus., 1992—; trustee Children's Hosp., St. Louis, 1992—94, Repertory Theater, Webster Grove, Mo., 1992—95; bd. dirs. World Affairs Coun. of Jax. Named Disting. Alumna of Yr., Washington U., 2005; recipient Allison Allas award, Nat. Marrow Donor Program, 2003, JCOC 73, 2007. Mem.: Women's Fgn. Policy Group. Avocations: woodworking, swimming, bicycling, American art.

JACOBSEN, ERIC N., chemistry professor; BS in Chemistry, NYU, 1982; PhD, U. Calif., Berkeley, 1986. Postdoctoral fellow MIT, 1986—88; asst. prof. U. Illinois, 1988—91, assoc. prof., 1991—93; prof. dept. chemistry Harvard U., Cambridge, Mass., 1993—2001, Sheldon Emery prof. dept. chemistry, 2001—. Consultant Sepracor, Mass., 1990—, Merck, NJ, 1994—, Rhodia ChiRex, Mass., 1994—, Versicor, Calif., 1995—; mem. editorial bds. Advanced Synthesis and Catalysis, Sci. of Synthesis, Jour. Organic Chemistry, Organic Letters, Jour of Combinatorial Chemistry, Jour. Molecular Catalysis, Current Opinion in Drug Discovery & Devel. Co-author: (books) Comprehensive Asymmetric Catalysis: Comprehensive Overviews in Chemistry, 1999, Comprehensive Asymmetric Catalysis: Supplement 1, 2003. Recipient Dean Granger Brown award, 1981, NIH Postdoctoral Fellowship, 1986-88, NSF Presidential Young Investigator award, 1990, Packard Fellowship Sci. & Engring., 1991, Eli Lilly Grant, 1991, Merck Faculty Devel. award, 1991, Union Carbide Innovation award, 1992, Alfred P. Sloan Found. Fellowship, 1992, Zeneca Chemistry award, 1993, Fluka prize, 1994, Vant Hoff prize, 1998, Piero Pino prize, 1999, Baekeland award, 1999, NIH Merit award, 2002. Fellow: Am. Acad. Arts & Sci., AAAS; mem.: Am. Chemical Soc. (Creative Work in Organic Synthesis award 2001, Chemical Pioneer award 2004). Office: Harvard U Dept Chemistry 12 Oxford St Cambridge MA 02138

JACOBSEN, HUGH NEWELL, architect; b. Grand Rapids, Mich., Mar. 11, 1929; s. John Edwall and Lucy Ellen (Newell) J.; m. Robin Kearney, Dec. 27, 1952; children: John Edwall, Matthew Christian, Simon

Townsend. BA, U. Md., 1951; cert., Archtl. Assn. Sch. Architecture, London, 1954; BArch., Yale U., New Haven, 1955, MArch, 1955; LHD (hon.), Gettysburg Coll., Pa., 1974, Bradford Coll., 1990; DFA (hon.), U. Md., 1993. Arch. Philip Johnson, New Canaan, Conn., 1955, Keyes, Lethbridge & Condon, Washington, 1957-58; prin. Hugh Newell Jacobsen, FAIA, Washington, 1958—. Lectr. univs.; vis. prof. U. Cairo, Egypt, 1970. Editor: A Guide to the Architecture of Washington, DC, 1965; prin. works include US Embassy, Paris, addition to US Capital, two Smithsonian Mus. (renovations), So. Vt. Art Ctr., Fred Jones Jr. Mus. Art U. Okla., 2005, Samuel Riggs IV Alumni Ctr. U. Md., 2005, Chatham House (Metal Architecture award 2006), A House in Snowmass (Prism award 2006), Boxwood Winery (AIA NOVA Merit award 2007). Mem. adv. bd. Internat. Hassan Fathy Inst.; trustee Corcoran Gallery Art, 1973-81, Washington Gallery Modern Art, 1965-69, Washington Theater Club, 1965-72. Served with USAF, 1955-57. John Fitzgerald Kennedy Meml. fellow New Zealand Govt., 1971, Silver medal for distinction in design Tau Sigma Delta, 1981; named to Hall of Fame U. Md., 2000, Washington Design Hall of Fame, 2003. Fellow AIA (Centennial award 1996, nat. AIA honor awards 1969, 74, 78, 80, 85, 88, numerous AIA chpt. awards, 20 Archtl. Record awards, Outstanding Learning Disabled Achiever award 1990, others); mem. NAD (elected), Cosmos Club (Washington), Century Assn., Yale Club (NYC). Office: Hugh Newell Jacobsen FAIA 2529 P St NW Washington DC 20007-3024 Office Phone: 202-337-5200. E-mail: hughjacobsen@hughjacobsen.com.*

JACOBSEN, JEFFREY SCOTT, environmental scientist; BS in Soil Sci., Calif. Polytech. State U., San Luis Obispo, 1979; MS in Agronomy, Colo. State U., 1982; PhD in Soil Sci. Fertility and Plant Nutrition, Okla. State U., 1985. Rsch asst. dept. agronomy Colo. State U., Fort Collins, 1979-82, technician dept. agronomy, 1982; tchg. asst. dept. agronomy Okla. State U., Stillwater, 1982-86; from asst. prof. to assoc. prof, soil scientist Mont. State U., Bozeman, 1986—, interim head dept. plant, soil and environ. scis., 1994-98, dept. head land resources environ. sci., 1998—. Recipient CIBA-GEIGY award in Agronomy Am. Soc. of Agronomy, 1994. Fellow Am. Soc. Agronomy. Office: Montana State U Dept of Agriculture 202 Linfield Hall PO Box 172860 Bozeman MT 59717-0001

JACOBSEN, KENDRA, health facility administrator; b. Racine, Wis., Mar. 18, 1975; d. Frederick and Karen Kreutz; m. Erik Jacobsen, Feb. 23, 2003; 1 child, Andrew. MusB, U. Wis., Madison, 1998, MS, 2001. Software implementation staff Epic Systems Corp., Madison, 2002—04; exec. dir. Madison Patient Safety Collaborative, 2004—. Freelance musician, tchr. Subcom. mem. Wis. eHealth Quality and Patient Safety Bd., Madison, 2006—07. Mem.: Women in Healthcare Mgmt. Office: Madison Patient Safety Collaborative 202 S Park St Madison WI 53715 Office Phone: 608-417-5889. Office Fax: 608-417-5645. Personal E-mail: kendrajacobsen@tds.net. Business E-Mail: kjacobsen@madisonpatientsafety.org.

JACOBSEN, LAREN, retired programmer; b. Salt Lake City, June 15, 1937; s. Joseph Smith and Marian (Thomas) J.; m. Audrey Bartlett, July 29, 1970 (div.); children: Andrea, Cecily, Julian. BS, U. Utah, 1963. Programmer IBM, 1963-70; sys. programmer Xerox Computer Svcs., 1970-79; pres. Prescient Investment Co., 1975-82; sr. sys. analyst Quotron Sys., LA, 1979-86; programmer, analyst Gt. Western Bank, 1987-92; word processing adminstr. Intex Svcs, Inc., Montebello, Calif., 1993-99; data processing specialist ACC Info. Svcs., LA, 2000—02; ret., 2002. Cons. in field. With USAR, 1961. Mem.: Am. Guild Organists (dean San Jose chpt. 1966—67), Mensa. Home: 10971 Quartz Dr South Jordan UT 84095 Personal E-mail: larenj@yahoo.com.

JACOBSEN, RAYMOND ALFRED, JR., lawyer; b. Wilmington, Del., Dec. 14, 1949; s. Raymond Alfred and Margaret (Walters) J.; m. Marilyn Perry, Aug. 4, 1973; 1 child, Hunter Perry. BA, U. Del., 1971; JD, Georgetown U., 1975. Bar: D.C. 1975, U.S. Supreme Ct. 1982. From assoc. to ptnr. Howrey & Simon, Washington, 1975-97; head antitrust/trade regulation group McDermott, Will & Emery, Washington, 1997—, ptnr., 1997—, chmn. regulatory and govt. affairs dept. and mem. mgmt. com. Adj. prof. internat. anti-trust law Am. U. Law Sch. Spl. projects editor Law & Policy in International Business, 1974-75. Served to capt. U.S. Army, 1975. Mem. ABA (antitrust law sect, litigation sect., internat. law sect., pub. contract law sect.), D.C. Bar Assn., U.S. Supreme Ct. Bar Assn., City Club (Washington), Army and Navy Country Club. Republican. Home: 4205 Maple Tree Ct Alexandria VA 22304-1035 Office: McDermott Will & Emery 600 13th St NW Fl 12 Washington DC 20005-3096 Office Phone: 202-756-8028. Business E-Mail: rayjacobsen@mwe.com.

JACOBSEN, RICHARD T., mechanical engineering educator; b. Pocatello, Idaho, Nov. 12, 1941; s. Thorleif (dec.), and Edith Emily (Gladwin) J. dec.); m. Vicki Belle Hopkins, July 16, 1959 (div. Mar. 1973); children: Pamela Sue, Richard T, Eric Ernest; m. Bonnie Lee Stewart, Oct. 19, 1973; 1 child, Jay Michael; stepchild: Erik David Lustig. BSME, U. Idaho, 1963, MSME, 1965; PhD in Engrng. Sci., Wash. State U., 1972. Registered profl. engr., Idaho. From instr. to prof. emeritus U. Idaho, 1964—2006, prof. emeritus, 2006—, chmn. dept. mech. engrng., 1980-85, assoc. dean engrng., 1985-90, assoc. dir. Ctr. for Applied Thermodynamic Studies, 1975-86, dir., 1986-99, 2005—06, dean engrng., 1990-99; chief scientist Idaho Nat. Engrng. Environ. Lab. Bechtel BWXT Idaho LLC, 1999—2005, from dep. lab. dir. to assoc. lab. dir. Idaho Nat. Engrng. Environ. Lab., 1999—2003; prof., dean engrng. Idaho State U., 2006—. Guest rschr. Nat. Inst. Standards Tech., 1979, 86, 99; mem. annex 18 thermophys. properties environ. acceptable refrigerants com. Internat. Energy Agy., 1991-98; mem. nat. adv. coun. Fed. Lab. Consortium for Tech. Transfer, 2002—; mem. adv. coun Idaho State U. Coll. Engrng., 2000-05; instl. rev. bd. protection human subjects in rsch. Idaho Nat. Engrng. Environ. Lab., 2000-05, chmn., 2001-05 Author: International Union of Pure and Applied Chemistry, Nitrogen-International Thermodynamic Tables of the Fluid State-6, 1979; Oxygen-International Thermodynamic Tables of the Fluid State-9, 1987, Ethylene-International Thermodynamic Tables of the Fluid State-10, 1988, ASHRAE Thermodynamic Properties of Refrigerants (2 vols.), 1986, (monograph series) Thermodynamic Properties of Cryogenic Fluids, 1997; numerous chpts. in books and handbooks, reports on thermodynamic properties of fluids, 1971-; contbr. articles to profl. jours. Recipient Outstanding Engr. award Idaho State U., 2002; NSF sci. faculty fellow, 1968-69; NSF rsch. and travel grantee, 1976-83; Nat. Inst. Stds. and Tech. grantee, 1974-91, 95-98, 2006, Gas Rsch. Inst. grantee, 1986-91, 1992-98, Dept. Energy grantee, 1991-95. Fellow ASME (faculty advisor 1972-75, 78-84, chmn. region VIII dept. heads com. 1983-85, honors and awards chmn. 1985-91, K-7 tech. com. thermophys. properties 1985—, chmn. 1986-89, 92-95, 2001-04, rsch. tech. com. on water and steam in thermal power systems, 1988—, gen. awards com. 1985-91, chmn. 1988-91, com. on honors 1988-99, vice chmn. 1995-99, mem. bd. on profl. practice and ethics, 1991-2004, v.p. profl. practice 1998-2001, v.p. rsch. 2004-05, v.p. fin. ops. 2005-07, chair bd. rsch. and tech. devel. 2007—, Inland Empire Sect. Engr. of Yr. award 1999, Dedicated Svc. award 2003); mem. N.W. Coll. and Univ. Assn. for Sci. (bd. dirs. 1990-93), NSPE (Excellence in Engrng. Educator award Idaho chpt. 2007), Am. Soc. Engrng. Edn., Am. Nuc. Soc., Idaho Rsch. Found. (bd. dirs. 1991-99, 2000-06), Soc. Automotive Engrs. (Ralph R. Teetor Edn. award, Detroit 1968), Bonneville County Hist. Soc. (trustee 2001—), ASHRAE (co-recipient Best Tech. Paper award 1984), Sigma Xi, Tau Beta Pi, Phi Kappa Phi (Disting. Faculty award 1989). Office: Coll of Engring 921 S 8th Ave Stop 8060 Pocatello ID 83209-8060 Home Phone: 208-233-4095. Business E-Mail: jacorich@isu.edu.

JACOBSEN, STINE, veterinarian, educator; b. Odense, Denmark, Nov. 1, 1972; d. Per and Hanne Jacobsen; m. Steen Frantzen, Nov. 1, 2003. DVM, Royal Vet. and Agrl. U., Frederiksberg, Denmark, 1998, PhD, 2003. Asst. prof. U. Copenhagen, Frederiksberg, 2003—. Contbr. articles to profl. jours. Vol. Project Outside, Coepnhagen, 2006—07. Grantee, Danish Rsch. Coun., 2003, 2006. Mem.: Vet. Wound Healing Assn. Achievements include patents pending in field. Home: Amagerbrogade 73 1th Copenhagen 2300 S Denmark Office: Univ Copenhagen Dyrlaegevej 48 Frederiksberg Copenhagen 1870 Denmark Home Phone: 45 35241172; Office Phone: 45 35282873. Office Fax: 45 35282880. Business E-Mail: stj@life.ku.dk.

JACOBSEN, THEODORE H. (TED H. JACOBSEN), labor union administrator, secondary school educator; BS, Fordham U., 1955; postgrad., Hunter Coll., 1957—80, NYU, 1957—80, Columbia U., 1957—80. Cert. HS English tchr. N.Y.C. Tchr. (on leave) N.Y.C. Bd. Edn., 1957—86; editor Labor News and Trade Union Handbook N.Y.C. Ctrl. Labor Coun. AFL-CIO, 1986—. Mem. exec. bd. Jewish Labor Com., NYC, 1977—, Workers Def. League, 1986—, Am. Labor ORT, 1986—; regional v.p. Union Label and Svc. Trades Dept., NY, 1980—96; mem. adv. bd. Harry Van Arsdale Jr. Coll. Labor Studies, Empire State Coll., NYC, 1986—; mem. adv. coun. occupation edn. N.Y.C. Bd. Edn., 1986—2000, vice chmn., 1989—2000; bd. dirs. Nat. Ethnic Coalition Orgns., Inc.; mem. bd. govs. Forum; sec. N.Y.C. Ctrl. Labor Coun. AFL-CIO. Mem. Cmty. Bd. 8, NYC, 1987—93; mem. N.Y.C. Sch. to Work regional coun. Regional Planning Assn.; mem. exec. bd. Friends A. Philip Randolph Campus H.S. City Coll., 1990—; bd. dirs. Cath. Interracial Coun., United Way N.Y., 1988—95, Coun. Environ., NYC, 1988—95, Italian Acad. Found., Nat. Ethnic Coalition Orgns., Inc., Italic Studies Inst.; trustee ARC Greater N.Y., 1989—2001, Italian Hosp. Soc.; mem. exec. bd. Workman's Cir. Home-Geriatric Ctr., 1986—89, treas., 1989—2003; sec. Robert F. Wagner Labor Archives NYU, 1986—; mem. bd. advisors Transition Ctr., N.Y.C. Bd. Edn., Svc. Area Planning Group; mem. Naval War Coll. Found.; mem. N.Y. State coastal mgmt. adv. com. N.Y. Harbor Maritime Industry; charter mem. Battle Normandy Found., 1988—; chmn. N.Y. Trade Union Coun. Histadrut; mem. Asian Pacific Am. Labor Alliance; life mem. Workmen's Cir. Arbeter Ring; patron N.Y.C. Met. Opera. Decorated knight Order of Merit (Italy), comdr. Order Sts. Maurice and Lazarus (Savoy), Order of Merit (Savoy), knight Royal Order Francis I of Bourbon and Two Sicilies; named Man of the Yr., Jewish Heritage Com. and Educators chpt., 1990, June 23, 1993 Theodore 'Ted' Jacobsen Day, Queens Borough Pres., Educator of the Yr., Assn. Tchrs. N.Y., 1986; recipient Cope awards, N.Y. State United Tchrs., 1975, 1978, Best Newsletter award, 1974, 1975, 1979, 1980, 1981, Spl. award educators chpt., Jewish Labor Com., 1986, Roberto Clemente award, Nat. Assn. P.R. Civil Rights, 1988, 75th Anniversary Cert. of Appreciation, U.S. Dept. Labor, 1988, Hurricane Hugo Disaster Relief citation, ARC, 1991, Good Scout award, Greater N.Y. Couns. Boy Scouts Am., 1992, Spl. Recognition award, Hispanic Labor Com., 1992, Leadership Svc. Recognition award, United Way N.Y.C., 1992, Consumer Merit award, N.Y. Consumer Assembly, 1992, Torch of Hope award, Pride Judea, 1993, Congl. Ellis Island medal Honor, 1993, N.Y.C. Coun. citation, 1993, Coalition Labor Union Women award, 1994, John LaFarge award interracial justice, Cath. Interracial Coun. N.Y., 1995, N.Y.C. Nova Ancora Job Tng. Program award of appreciation, N.Y.C. Dept. Probation, 1995, Disting. Svc. award, Internat. Brotherhood Elec. Workers, Local 3, J divsn., 1996, Robert Briscoe award, Emerald Isle Immigration Ctr., 1996, George Meany award, Greater N.Y. Couns. Boy Scouts Am., 1999, Chieftaincy conferment, His Majesty Udumeze of Ohafia, Nigeria. Mem.: NAACP (80th Anniversary Exempler award 1991, golden life heritage), NATAS (bd. govs. N.Y. chpt.), AFTRA, Nat. Italian-Am. Found., TV and Radio Working Press Assn., Internat. Platform Assn., Jewish Heritage Com., Black Trade Unionists Leadership Com., Coalition Labor Union Women, Internat. Labor Comm. Assn., Cath. Tchrs. Assn., Jewish Tchrs. Assn., United Fedn. Tchrs. (P.M. staff 1973—, editor newsletter, chpt. chmn. 1974—86, Eli Trachtenberg award 1966, 1974, 1977, 1981, Albert Lee Smallheiser citation 1976), Actor's Fund (life), Citizens Commn. African Union, United African Congress (coun. elders, adv. bd.), Asia Soc., Lower East Side Tenement (hon. commr. Celebrate Africa Found. 1992—), U.S. Naval Inst., Irish-Am. Studies Com., Irish-Am. Heritage Mus., U.S. Holocaust Meml. Mus. (charter), Masons, Elks, B'nai B'rith (trustee 1989—96, bd. dirs. Adelstein Family Project HOPE Found. Housing Elderly 1992—), Order Sons Italy Am., Loyal League Yiddish Sons Erin (hon.). Avocations: theater, opera, travel. Office: NYC Cen Labor Coun AFL-CIO 31 W 15th St New York NY 10011 E-mail: thjnycusa@aol.com.

JACOBSEN, WILLIAM M., plastic surgeon; MD, U. Ill., Chgo., 1986. Cert. Am. Bd. Plastic Surgery, 1996. Gen. surgery resident Med. Coll. Va. Hosps., Richmond, Va., 1986—87, New Hanover Regional Med. Ctr., Wilmington, NC, 1987—88, Mayo Grad. Sch. Medicine, Rochester, Minn., 1988—92, plastic surgery resident, 1992—94; pvt. practice Phoenix. Named one of Top Doctors, Phoenix Monthly. Mem.: Am. Soc. Aesthetic Plastic Surgeons, Am. Soc. Plastic Surgeons. Office: 2400 E Arizona Biltmore Cir Ste 2450 Phoenix AZ 85016 Office Phone: 602-212-0100. Office Fax: 602-279-1701. E-mail: drj@drjsoffice.com.*

JACOBSON, ALLEN HOWARD, economist; b. NYC, July 5, 1939; s. Jack Joseph and Mary (Laxman) J.; m. Gladys Cecile Safier, Sept. 20, 1970; children: Gennifer Ann, Allison Lindsay. BA, NYU, 1962, postgrad., 1965. Lic. acct. exec. in securities bus., real estate agt., gen. securities prin.; lic. broker/dealer in securities bus. Economist Lional D. Edie & Inc., NYC, 1966-69; sr. economist U.S. Trust Co., NYC, 1969-79; ptnr. Washington Analysis Corp., 1979-87; v.p. NatWest Markets, Washington, 1988-95; sr. v.p. HSBC Securities, Inc., 1995-99; ptnr. Washington Analysis Corp., 1999—; sr. v.p. Xinhua Fin. Corp. Bd. mem. Falls Grove Recreation Assn. Mem. Nat. Economists Club (v.p. 1982-83, 91-92, bd. govs. 1992-93), Nat. Assn. Bus. Economists (coun. nat. chpt. 1985-86), Washington Assn. Money Mgrs., Montgomery County Assn. Realtors, Lakewood Club, Norbeck Club (bd. dirs. 1981-82). Avocations: tennis, aerobics, real estate, golf, dance. Home: 210 Jersey Ln Rockville MD 20850 Office: Washington Analysis Corp 1120 Connecticut Ave NW Ste 400 Washington DC 20036-3939 Office Phone: 202-756-7710. Business E-Mail: ajacobson@washingtonanalysis.com.

JACOBSON, ANTONE GARDNER, retired zoology educator; b. nr. Salt Lake City, May 22, 1929; s. Rufus Ingman and Marvell (Gardner) J.; m. Jacqueline James, July 26, 1962; children: Lauren, Eric. AB, Harvard U., 1951; PhD, Stanford U., 1955. Mem. faculty dept. zoology U. Tex., Austin, 1957—, assoc. prof., 1961-68, prof., 1968-97, prof. emeritus, 1997—; instr. Marine Biol. Lab., Woods Hole, Mass., 1969-70; ret., 1997. Contbr. articles to profl. jours. Harvard Nat. scholar, 1947-51, Henry Newell Honors scholar, 1951-55. Mem. Soc. Devel. Biology, Soc. Integrative & Comparative Biology, Am. Assn. Anatomists, Sigma Xi. Home: 201 Skyline Dr Austin TX 78746-3610 Office: Univ Tex MCDB Pat Labs 1 University Sta C1000 Austin TX 78712-0253 Office Phone: 512-471-5403. Business E-Mail: antone@mail.utexas.edu.

JACOBSON, BARBARA DINGER, music educator; d. Norman Bennetch and Ethel Hickernell Dinger; m. Howard Newman Jacobson, Aug. 20, 1961. MusB, New Eng. Conservatory of Music, 1957—62, MusM, 1972—76. Permanent Professional Certification Music Teacher's Nat. Assn., 2001. Music tchr. various Boston schools, 1961—65; mem. New England Chamber Trio, 1972—74; flutist Basking Ridge Symphony Orch., NJ, 1974—78; adj. flute tchr. U. NC, Chapel Hill, NC, 1979—81; flutist Greensboro Symphony Orch., NC, 1979—83; music tchr. Elon Coll., NC, 1983—86; 1st flute Space Coast Symphony Orch., Brevard County, Fla., 1987—91; adj. faculty-flute Fla. So. Coll., Lakeland, 1988—, dir. summer flute workshop, 1993—2005; performer New Eng. Conservatory Orch. Flutist Quintessence Woodwind Quintet, Boston, 1972—74, Radley Woodwind Quintet, Scotch Plains, NJ, 1974—78; sec., v.p., pres., chair of bd. Fla. Flute Assn., 1987—98. Musician: (holiday concerts) Colorado Flute Orchestra, (exchange concerts) American Flute Orchestra; performer: (master classes) Accademia Chigiana, Ramsgate, Royal Coll. of Music. Mem.: Music Teacher's Nat. Assn., Fla. Bandmaster's Assn., Nat. Flute Assn., Fla. Flute Assn. Avocations: photography, travel, reading, stamp collecting/philately. Office: Florida Southern Coll 111 Lake Hollingsworth Dr Lakeland FL 33801-5698 Home Phone: 813-752-7854; Office Phone: 863-680-4575. E-mail: barbaradjacobson@mac.com.

JACOBSON, BARRY STEPHEN, lawyer, judge; b. Bklyn., Mar. 30, 1955; s. Morris and Sally (Ballaban) J.; m. Andrea Jacobson; children: Faith Blair, Matthew Aaron Jacobson. Cert. in drama, Sch. of Performing Arts, NYC, 1973; BA, CUNY, 1977, MA, 1980; JD, Bklyn. Sch. Law, 1980. Bar: NY, 1981, US Dist. Ct. (ea. and so. dists.) NY 1981, US Dist. Ct. (we. and no. dists.) NY, 1988, US Dist. Ct. DC, 1988, US Ct. Appeals (2d cir.) 1981, US Ct. Appeals (fed. and DC cirs.) 1988, US Supreme Ct. 1984, US Ct. Claims, 1985, US Tax Ct. 1988 and others. Sole practice, Bklyn., 1981; asst. corp. counsel NYC Law Dept., Bklyn., 1981-84; asst. dist. atty. Borough of Queens, Kew Gardens, NY, 1984-85; judge adminstrv. law NY Dept. Motor Vehicles, Bklyn., 1985-86, 87-92; assoc. counsel NY State Dept. Health, NYC, 1986; arbitrator NYC Small Claims Ct., 1986-91; pvt. practice Bklyn., 1992—. Gen. counsel Amersfort Flatlands Devel. Corp., Bklyn., 1981-82; arbitrator NYC Civil Ct. 1987-92; adminstrv. law judge NYC Parking Violators Bur., 1987-93; mem. Indigent Defenders Appeal Panel, 1988-96; sr. adminstrv. law judge NYC Parking Violation Bur., 1989-93; leader Nat. Jud. Coll., NY Mem. Roosevelt Dem. Party, Bklyn., 1984-95, mem. adv. bd., 1989-92, treas., 1990-92; active Kings Hwy. Dem. Party, Bklyn., 1982-95, Dem. com. 1986-95; active King's County Young Dems., 1985-86; gen. counsel Bklyn. Coll. Hillel, Bklyn. Coll. Student Govts., 1980-90, also advisor; treas. local div. dept. mtr. vehicles pub. employees fedn. AFL-CIO; coun. ldr. div. #255 Pub. Employee's Fedn., 1989-92, conv. del. 1989, 90, 91; chmn. Bklyn. Traffic Employee Assistance Prog., 1989-92. Named one of Outstanding Young Men Am., 1983, 85, 86, 87, 88. Mem. ABA (judicial sect., spl. const. judges traffic cts. com.), Am. Judges Assn. (hwy. safety com.), Bklyn. Bar Found. (trustee, bd. dirs.), Am. Arbitration Assn. (forums 1988—), Am. Judicature Soc., Assn. Adminstrv. Law Judges (pres.), NY State Dept. Motor Vehicles (v.p.), NY State Adminstrv. Law Judges Assn. (pres. bd. dirs. parking violation com., v.p.), NY State Bar Assn. (pres. for DMV, spl. com. juvenile justice, adminstrv. law jud. coms., jud. adminstrn. com.), Bklyn. Bar Assn. (family ct. com., chmn. young lawyers sect., trustee 1991, chmn. adminstrn. law com.), NY County Lawyers Assn. (family Ct. Com.), Bklyn. Coll. Alumni Assn. (gen. counsel student govt. affiliate 1983-92, bd. dirs. 1985-92), Jaycees, B'nai B'rith, Hillel (bd. dirs. 1983-91, gen. counsel 1987-91), many others. Jewish. Avocations: motorcycling, drama, theater, target shooting, flying. Home: 342 Coleridge Ln Jericho NY 11753-2605 Office: 26 Court St Ste 810 Brooklyn NY 11242-1108 Office Phone: 718-923-1000. E-mail: ticklaw@aol.com.

JACOBSON, BERNARD, lawyer; b. Hartford, Conn., Feb. 27, 1930; s. Samuel Barnard and Lillian Jacobson; m. Florence Ellen Greenberg, Oct. 7, 1956; children: Daniel John, Alice Lash, Nancy Jacobson-Penn. AB, Amherst Coll., 1951; LLB, Columbia U., 1954. Bar: Conn. 1955, Fla. 1957, U.S. Dist. Ct. (so. dist.) Fla. 1957, U.S. Ct. Appeals (11th cir.) 1961. Pvt. practice, Miami, Fla., 1957-68; ptnr. Fine, Jacobson, Miami, Fla., 1968-94, Holland & Knight LLP, Miami, Fla., 1994—2002, Akerman Senterfitt, Miami, 2002—. Pres., CEO Rep. Mortgage Investors, Miami, 1973-81; presenter in field. Contbr. articles to profl. jours. Chmn. Fla. Congl. Partnership, Miami, 1987; vice chmn. Greater Miami C. of C., 1988-92. With U.S. Army Counter Intelligence Corps, 1955-57. Named a Super Lawyer, 2007; named to Best Lawyers in Am. Mem. ABA, Fla. Bar. Avocations: tennis, boating, skiing. Office: Akerman Senterfitt One SE 3d Ave Ste 2800 Miami FL 33131 Office Phone: 305-982-5655. Business E-Mail: bernard.jacobson@akerman.com.

JACOBSON, CARRIE ISABELLE, lawyer; BA with distinction, U. Wis., Madison, 1995; JD magna cum laude, Hamline U. Sch. Law, 2000. Bar: Minn. 2000, US Dist. Ct. (dist. Minn.) 2001. Atty. adult prosecution divsn. Hennepin County Atty.'s Office, 1998—2000; assoc. atty. workers' compensation def., underinsured and uninsured motorist def., no-fault arbitrations and personal injury def. litig. Hansen, Dordell, Bradt, Odlaug & Bradt, 2000—02; assoc. atty. workers' compensation def., no-fault arbitrations and personal injury def. litig. Brown & Carlson, P.A., Mpls., 2002—. Primary editor, assoc.: Hamline Jour. Pub. Law and Policy. Named a Rising Star, Minn. Super Lawyers mag., 2006. Mem.: Minn. Women Lawyers, ABA, Minn. State Bar Assn., Minn. Def. Lawyers Assn. Office: Brown & Carlson PA 5411 Circle Down Ave Ste 100 Minneapolis MN 55416 Office Phone: 763-591-9950.*

JACOBSON, CLAS A., engineering educator, director; s. Julian and Helena Jacobson; m. Diane S. Skorupski, May 24, 1986; 1 child, Lucie E. BS in Computer Engring., RPI, 1982, M in Elec. Engring., 1984; PhD, Rensselaer Poly. Inst., Troy, NY, 1986. Assoc. prof. elec. engring. Northeastern U., Boston, 1986—95; dir., systems dept. United Techs. Rsch. Ctr., East Hartford, Conn., 1995—. Home: 138 Metcalf Rd Tolland CT 06084 Office: United Techs Rsch Ctr 411 Silver Ln East Hartford CT 06108 Home Phone: 860-875-7577; Office Phone: 860-610-7652.

JACOBSON, DAVID EDWARD, lawyer; b. Port Chester, NY, May 17, 1949; s. Robert Herzel and Ruth Doris (Rosenzweig) J.; m. Debra Ann Denkensohn, Aug. 10, 1975; 1 child, Andrew. BA in Econs., U. Rochester, NY, 1971; JD, SUNY, Buffalo, 1974; LLM in Taxation, Georgetown U., Washington, DC, 1977. Bar: NY 1975, DC 1976, US Tax Ct. 1982, US Ct. Appeals (fed. cir.) 1983. Atty.-advisor Office Chief Counsel, IRS, Washington, 1974-79; tax counsel com. fin. US Senate, Washington, 1979-81; assoc. Reid & Priest, Washington, 1981—86; ptnr. Thelen Reid Brown Raysman & Steiner LLP, Washington, 1986—. Mem. Partnership Coun., 2001-03. Vol. Income Tax Assistance, Arlington, Va., 1977-81; treas. Overlook Townhouse Homeowners Assn., Arlington. Mem. ABA (mem. tax sect. 1982—, vice chmn. regulated utilities com. 1988-90, chmn. 1990-92), NY State Bar Assn. Office: Thelen Reid Brown Raysman & Steiner LLP 701 Eighth St NW Washington DC 20001-3721 Office Phone: 202-508-4300. Business E-Mail: djacobson@thelen.com.

JACOBSON, EDWARD, retired elementary school educator, principal; b. NYC, Apr. 12, 1914; s. Joseph and Kitty Jacobson; children: Mark, Betsy. PhB, U. Vt., 1939, MA, 1940; profl. degree in edn., Columbia U., 1962. Owner, dir. Camp Dunmore for Boys, Salisbury, Vt., 1946—60; tchr., prin. Drum Hill Jr. HS, Peekskill, NY, 1948—74; tchr. Fulbright, Scotland, 1960—61, 1974—75. Mem. regional planning commn., Middlebury, Vt.; mem., chmn. planning commn. Whiting, Vt.; vol. Porter Hosp., Middlebury. Lt. sr. grade USN, 1942—45, ATO, PTO. Mem.: Phi Beta Kappa. Democrat. Jewish. Home: 15 Shoreham Rd PO Box 55 Whiting VT 05778 E-mail: esjvt@shoreham.net.

JACOBSON, EDWIN JAMES, medical educator; b. Chgo., June 27, 1947; s. Edwin Julius and Rose Josephine (Jirinec) J.; m. Martha Shanks; 1 child, Emily. BA, U. So. Calif., 1969; MD, UCLA, 1976. Diplomate Nat. Bd. Med. Examiners, Am. Bd. Internal Medicine; lic. physician, Calif. Intern in medicine UCLA Hosp., 1976-77, resident in medicine, 1977-79, fellow in nephrology, 1979-81, chief resident in medicine, 1979-81; asst. clin. prof. of medicine UCLA, 1981-88, assoc. clin. prof. medicine, 1988-94, clin. prof. medicine, 1994—. Adj. asst. prof. medicine, UCLA,

1980-81; mem. med. sch. admissions com. UCLA, 1981—, med. staff credentials com., 1984—, med.staff exec. com., 1990-94, med. staff/hosp. adminstrn. liaison com. 1991-94, hosp./med. sch. faculty rels. com., 1991—, nat. kidney found., 1991—, med. adv. bd., 1991—; prin. investigator A/M Group Grant, UCLA Med. Ctr., 1993, Peter Langer Meml. Fund Award, 1993; lectr. in field. Author: Medical Diagnosis: An Algorithmic Approach, 1989, rev. edit., 2000; co-author: (with P. Healy) Il Proceso Decisionale nella Diagnosi Medica, 1992; manuscript rev. bd.: Bone Marrow Transplantation, 1988—, Jour. Am. Geriatrics Soc., 1989—; editor: Clin. Controverics; mem. editl. bd. Jour. Drugs; editor for symposia in field; contbr. articles to profl. jours.; editor book chpts. Recipient Upjohn Achievement award, 1977. Mem. ACP, Alpha Omega Alpha. Office: UCLA 100 Ucla Medical Plz Ste 690 Los Angeles CA 90024-6992 Office Phone: 310-209-2033. Business E-Mail: ejacobso@ucla.edu.

JACOBSON, EUGENE DONALD, medical educator, academic administrator, researcher; b. Bridgeport, Conn., Feb. 19, 1930; s. Morris and Mary (Mendelsohn) J.; m. Laura Kathryn Osborn, June 9, 1973; children from previous marriage: Laura Ellen, Susan Ruth, Morris David, Daniel Frederick, Miriam Louise. BA, Wesleyan U., 1951; MD, U. Vt., 1955; MS, SUNY, Syracuse, 1960; DM (hon.), Jagiellonian U., 1996. Assoc. prof. UCLA Sch. Medicine, 1965-66; prof., chmn. U. Okla. Sch. Medicine, Oklahoma City, 1966-71, U. Tex. Med. Sch., Houston, 1971-77; vice dean Coll. Medicine U. Cin., 1977-85; dean Sch. Medicine, U. Kans., Kansas City, 1985-88; dean Sch. Medicine U. Colo., Denver, 1988-90, prof., 1990-99, prof. emeritus, 1999—, acting head divsn. gastroenterology, 1994. Cons. NIH, Bethesda, Md., 1968-72, mem. nat. digestive adv. bd., 1985-87; chmn. Nat. Commn., U.S. Congress, Washington, 1977-79; cons. Upjohn Co., Kalamazoo, 1970-87, G. D. Searle and Co., Chgo., 1984-85. Contbr. 320 articles to profl. jours. Served to maj. U.S. Army, 1956-64. NIH Rsch. grantee, 1967-97. Fellow ACP; mem. AMA (ho. of dels. 1991—2004), Am. Soc. Clin. Investigation, Assn. Am. Physicians, Am. Physiol. Soc., Am. Gastroenterol. Assn. (pres. 1989-90, Friedenwald medal 1998), Am. Digestive Health Found. (bd. dirs., vice chair 1995-98).

JACOBSON, FRANK JOEL, cultural organization administrator; b. Phila., Sept. 14, 1948; s. Leonard and June Anette (Groff) J.; m. Stephanie Lou Savage, July 5, 1970; children: Aaron Jeffery, Adam Michael, Ashley Celeste. BA, U. Wis., 1970; MFA, Boston U., 1973. Mng. dir. Mont. Repertory Theater, Missoula, Mo., 1973-75; asst. prof. drama U. Mont., Missoula, 1973-75; program dir. Western States Arts Found., Denver, 1975-77, dir. programs, 1977-78, gen. mgr. budget/planning, 1978-79; exec. dir. Arvada (Colo.) Ctr. for the Arts & Humanities, 1979-85; dir. theatres and arenas City & County of Denver, 1985-87; pres., CEO Scottsdale (Ariz.) Cultural Coun., 1987—. Bd. dirs. Met. Denver Arts Alliance, pres., 1979-85, Rocky Mountain Arts Consortium, pres., 1979-80. Contbr. articles to profl. jours. Mem. panel theater program Nat. Endowment for the Arts, Washington, 1990-92; bd. dirs. Scottsdale Focus, 1988-93, 93-97, Arizonans for Cultural Devel., 1992-97; bd. dirs. Scottsdale Edn. Found., 1994-99, chmn., 1994-96; bd. dirs. Scottsdale Convention and Visitors Bur., 2001—. Mem.: Assn. for Performing Arts Presenters (bd. dirs. 1984—87), Rocky Mountain Theatre Assn. (bd. dirs., pres. 1976—78), Mont. State Theatre Assn. (bd. dirs., pres. 1974—75), Am. Theatre Assn. (bd. dirs. 1976—78), Scottsdale C. of C. (bd. dirs. 2001—). Office: Scottsdale Cultural Council 7380 E 2nd St Scottsdale AZ 85251-5604

JACOBSON, GARY CHARLES, political science professor; b. Orange, Calif., July 7, 1944; s. Charles William and Ruth Hope (Brown) J.; m. Martha Ellen Blake, June 2, 1979. AB in Polit. Sci., Stanford U., 1966; MPhil, Yale U., 1969, PhD in Polit. Sci., 1972. From instr. to assoc. prof. Trinity Coll., Hartford, Conn., 1970-79; from assoc. prof. to prof. polit. sci. U. Calif., San Diego, 1979—; Woodrow Wilson fellow, 1969. Author: Money in Congressional Elections, 1980, (with Samuel Kernell) Strategy and Choice in Congressional Elections, 1981, The Politics of Congressional Elections, 1983, 87, 91, 97, 2000, 2004, The Electoral Origins of Divided Governments, 1990, The Logic of American Politics (with Samuel Kernell), 2000, 2003, 2006, A Divider, Not a Uniter: George W. Bush and the American People, 2006. Grantee NSF, 1980-82. Mem. Am. Acad. Arts and Scis., Am. Polit. Sci. Assn. (Gladys E. Kammerer award 1981), Western Polit. Sci. Assn., Midwest Polit. Sci. Assn., So. Polit. Sci. Assn. Office: U Calif San Diego Dept Polit Sci # 0521 La Jolla CA 92093

JACOBSON, GARY STEVEN, lawyer; b. Holyoke, Mass., Sept. 4, 1951; s. Rudolph Milton and Frederika Helena (Vanderryn) J.; m. Sharon W. Turkish, June 16, 1974; children: Lowell Daniel, Lee Stuart. BA cum laude, Wesleyan U., Middletown, Conn., 1973; JD, Northwestern U., 1976. Bar: Conn. 1976, N.Y. 1977, N.J. 1977, U.S. Ct. Appeals (3d cir.) 1981, U.S. Ct. Appeals (2d cir.) 1996. Investigative atty. N.Y. State Commn. on Jud. Conduct, NYC, 1976-77; spl. asst. atty. gen. Office Spl. State Prosecutor, NYC, 1977-79; assoc. Hofheimer, Gartlir, Gottlieb & Gross, NYC, 1979-80, Kleinberg, Moroney, Masterson & Schachter, Millburn, NJ, 1980-85, ptnr., 1986-90; of counsel Kelley Drye & Warren, NYC, 1990-91, ptnr., 1992-96, Farer Siegal Fersko, Westfield, NJ, 1996-98; bankruptcy trustee Panel Chpt. 7, 1997—; mem. Gary S. Jacobson, LLC, Mountainside, Springfield, 1998—2002; of counsel Herold and Haines, Warren, NJ, 2002—04, shareholder, 2004—. Co-author: Commercial Litigation in New York State Courts, 1995; editor: Judicial Discipline Reporter, 1976. Republican. Jewish. Home: 99 Susan Dr Chatham NJ 07928-1055 Office: Herold and Haines PA 25 Independence Blvd Warren NJ 07059-6747 Home Phone: 973-635-5027; Office Phone: 908-647-1022. E-mail: gjacobson@heroldhaines.com.

JACOBSON, GILBERT H., lawyer, director; b. Memphis, Feb. 6, 1956; s. Irvin and Edith (Shainberg) J.; m. Shauna Brown, Aug. 23, 1983; children: Yisroel, Esther, Nechama, Mordechai, Avrohom, Doniel. BBA, Memphis State U., 1980; JD, Touro Coll. Sch. Law, Huntington, NY, 1983. Bar: N.Y. 1984, Tenn. 1985, Colo. 1986. Tax cons. Rooney, Pace, Inc., NYC, 1983-84; chief fin. officer Denton Mills, Inc., New Albany, Miss., 1984-85; endowment cons. Coun. of Jewish Fedns., NYC, 1986-90, assoc. dir. endowment devel., 1990-92, assoc. dir. planned giving and found. rels., 1992-95; dir. Endowment Found. UJA Fedn. Bergen County, River Edge, NJ, 1995-99; assoc. exec. dir. planned giving and endowments UJA-Fedn. N.Y., NYC, 1999—2002; mng. dir. Stellar Fin., 2002—06; nat. dir. planned giving Bar-Ilan U., 2006—. Contbr. articles to profl. jours. Founding pres. Torah Comty. Project, Denver, 1985-86; officer Congregation Adas Israel, Passaic, N.J., 1987-99. Carmi Schwartz fellow Coun. Jewish Fedns., 1993. Mem. N.Y. State Bar Assn. Avocation: talmudic study. Office: Bar-Ilan U 235 Park Ave S New York NY 10005 Home Phone: 973-777-9833; Office Phone: 212-573-3460. E-mail: gilj@biuny.com.

JACOBSON, HOWARD NEWMAN, obstetrics and gynecology educator, researcher; b. St. Paul, Aug. 13, 1923; s. Irvin Oliver and Nora Henrietta (Olson) J.; m. Barbara Jane Dinger, Aug. 20,1961. BSc in Medicine, Northwestern U., Chgo., 1947, BM, 1950, MD, 1951. Intern Presbyn. Hosp., Chgo., 1950-51, resident in ob-gyn, 1951-52; fellow, rsch. fellow in obstetrics, mem. family clinic Harvard Sch. Pub. Health, Boston, 1952-55; resident Boston Lying-In Hosp. and Free Hosp. for Women, Brookline, Mass., 1955-58; obstetrician, physiologist Lab. Neuroanat. Scis., Nat. Inst. Nervous Disease and Blindness, NIH, Bethesda, Md., 1958-60; instr., asst. prof. Harvard Med. Sch., Boston, 1960-65; assoc. prof. U. Calif., San Francisco, Berkeley, 1965-69; dir. Macy program Med. Sch. Harvard U., 1969-74; prof. dept. cmty. medicine Coll. Medicine and Dentistry NJ, Piscataway, NJ, 1974-78; dir. Inst. Nutrition, clin. prof. U. NC, Chapel Hill, 1978-88; rsch. prof. Coll. Pub. Health U. So. Fla., 1988—2003; prof. dept. ob-gyn U. South Fla. Med. Sch., Tampa, 1990-96, facilitator spl. programs Health Sci. Ctr., 1996—2003. Cons. Children's Bur., HEW, Washington, 1964-73, GAO, Washington, 1974-83, AMA, 1980-82, 88—; mem. food and nutrition bd. NRC/NAS, Washington, 1971-74; prof. dept. biology and Sch. Home Econs., U. N.C., Greensboro, 1978-88, Ellen Swallow Richards lectr., 1978; cons. pregnancy and nutrition study U. Minn., Mpls., 1979—; adj. prof. dept. food, nutrition and instn. mgmt. East Carolina U. Sch. Home Econs., Greenville, 1981-88; mem. nutrition grad. faculty N.C. State U., Raleigh, 1979-88. Contbr. over 130 articles and abstracts to FMA Today, Jour. Nurse-Midwifery, Clin. Nutrition, Contemporary Internal Medicine, Food and Nutrition News, Nutrition Today, New Eng. Jour. Medicine, chpt. to books. Panel vice chmn. White House Conf. on Food, Nutrition and Health, Washington, 1969; chmn. Quality of Life Conf., Mass. Med. Soc., Boston, 1972; mem. hunger com. Episcopal Ch. S.W. Fla., 1990-94; mem. Fla. Health Start Initiative working Group, 1991—. Lt. (j.g.) USNR, 1943-46, PTO. Recipient Agnes Higgins award March of Dimes and APHA, 1987; recipient Career Devel. award NIH, 1963-65. Fellow Am. Coll. Ob-Gyn (assoc.); mem. Am. Soc. Clin. Nutrition, Am. Physiol. Soc., Mass. Med. Soc. (chmn. commn. 1972-74), Fla. Pub. Health Assn. (chmn. sect. 1990-91), Am. Dietetic Assn. (hon.). Democrat. Achievements include co-develop. of guides for clin. nutrition studies, portable ultrasound for body composition; co-determination of nature of cardiovasc. changes at birth; co-intro. of computer assisted methodology in nutrition; co-initiation of modern nutrition standards for healthy pregnancy. Office: U South Fla Coll Pub Health 13201 Bruce B Downs Blvd Tampa FL 33612-3805

JACOBSON, JAMES BASSETT, retired insurance and financial services company executive; b. San Francisco, Nov. 16, 1922; s. James Peter and Bertha (Bassett) J.; m. Janice Isabel Meilstrup, Aug. 29, 1949 (dec. Dec. 13, 2001); children: Steven Blair, Karen Christine, Richard Barlow; m. Lesley Evans, Apr. 12, 2004. BS, UCLA, 1947; postgrad., U. Pa., 1947-48; MBA, U. So. Calif., 1954. CLU. With Prudential Ins. Co. Am., various cities, 1948-83, v.p. group pension mktg. Newark, 1967-70, sr. v.p. in charge group ins., 1970-73, pres., western ops. LA, 1973-83; exec. v.p. CalFed Inc. and Calif. Fed. Savs. & Loan Assn., LA, 1983-87; chmn., chief exec. officer Beneficial Standard Life Ins. Co., LA, 1987-88, chmn. bd. dirs., 1984-88; ret., 1988. Bd. dirs. Galorath, Inc., El Segundo, Calif.; chmn. bd. dirs. Bonneville Internat. Corp., Salt Lake City. Author: An Analysis of Group Creditors Insurance, 1954. V.p. L.A. Philharm. Assn., 1977-83, bd. dirs., 1975-83; vice chmn. Community TV So. Calif. L.A., 1983, bd. dirs., 1979-83; chmn. bd. dirs. Orthopaedic Hosp., L.A., 1981-84, trustee, 1980-84; chmn. bd. L.A. Ballet, 1974-79, bd. dirs., 1974-83; mem. Calif. Round Table, 1981-83; bd. dirs. Dance Gallery, L.A., 1988-92, NCCJ L.A. Region, 1987-95, co-chair, 1994-96; chmn. bd. trustees Criminal Justice Legal Found., 1993-95, trustee 1990—2004, Sacramento; bd. dirs. v.p. L.A. Area coun. Boy Scouts Am., 1980-85, others. With U.S. Army, 1943-46, 2d lt. res., 1951. Recipient Silver Beaver award Boy Scouts Am., 1984, Cmty. Svc. award UCLA Alumni Assn., 1985. Mem. Am. Coll. CLUs, Calif. C. of C. (bd. dirs. 1974-83), L.A. C. of C. (bd. dirs. 1981-83), Calif. Club, Lochinvars Club (pres. 1981-84).

JACOBSON, JAMES EDMUND, retired newspaper editor; b. Mobile, Ala., Sept. 19, 1934; s. George Frederick and Annie Virginia (Taggart) J.; m. Diana Sue Tremer, Dec. 22, 1956; children— James Edmund, Jr., Jennifer Jo, Jay Alan, Jayna Diane BA, U. Ala., 1958, MA, 1959. Editorial writer The Birmingham News, 1959-66, editorial page editor, 1966-72, asst. mng. editor, 1972-75, mng. editor, 1975-78, editor, 1978-97, contbg. editor, 1997-2000. Mem. steering com. Leadership Birmingham, 1984-94; adv. bd. Salvation Army, 1986-2001; bd. dirs. United Way-Community Chest of Central Ala., 1986-98, chmn., 1997. Served with USAF, 1952-56 Recipient Disting. Alumnus award U. Ala. Journalism Dept., 1968, Sesquicentennial Hon. Prof. award U. Ala., 1981, Presdl. citation U. Ala., 1982. Mem. Am. Soc. Newspaper Editors, Ala. Press Assn. (pres. 1989), Soc. Profl. Journalists (pres. U. Ala. student chpt. 1957-58, pres. Ala. profl. chpt. 1965, 78, 84), Kiwanis. Roman Catholic. Home: 5728 Meadowview Dr Trussville AL 35173-2276 E-mail: jejdsj@aol.com.

JACOBSON, JEFFREY E., lawyer, consultant, educator; b. NYC, Aug. 19, 1956; s. Murray and Adele (Ebert) J.; m. Linda Moel, Aug. 11, 1984; children: Justin Myles, Sari Amanda. BA, Fordham U., 1976; JD, N.Y. Law Sch., 1980. Bar: NY 1982, DC 1982, US Tax Ct. 1982, US Ct. Internat. Trade 1982, US Dist. Ct. (so. and ea. dists.) NY 1982, US Ct. Appeals (2nd cir.) 1988, US Supreme Ct. 1988. Assoc. SESAC, Inc., NYC, 1980-82; sole practice NYC and D.C., 1982-85; sr. ptnr. Jacobson & Colfin, P.C., NYC, Washington, L.I., Nashville, 1985—90, mng. mem., 1991—; exec. v.p., sec. Fifth Ave. Media, Ltd., NYC, 1995—; assoc. prof. Five Towns Coll., N.Y., 1999—. Asst. mgr. Embassy Theatre, NYC, 1975, Victoria Theatre, NYC, 1975; asst. Theatre Confections, Inc., NYC, 1975; mgr. Criterion Theatre, NYC, 1976; mgr., sec. Squirrels Prodns. Ltd., NYC, 1976-78; pres. Aldous Demian Prodns., Ltd., NYC, 1980-82; guest spkr. Ctr. for Media Arts, NYC, 1985, Fordham U., NYC, 1986, NY Law Sch., 1987, 06, Detroit Sch. Law, 1991, 93, Sch. Visual Arts, 2004, 05, St. John's Law Sch., 2006; counsel Box Office Media, NYC, 1982-88, Performance Records, 1988-97, Anamaze Records, 1982-95, Cynthia Entertainment Group, Ltd., 1989-91, ROIR Records, Inc., 1992—, Super Bubble Music Corp., 1992-99, Sergei Artemiev, 1993, New Riders of Purple Sage, 1985—, Mick Taylor Music, 1985—, Best Film and Video Corp., 1988-91, Marty Balin, 1988—, Dope Bros. Record, 2001—, Vega Records, Inc., 2003—, Audrey Tosh, 1990—, Vaneese Y. Thomas Ent. Ltd., 1993—; spkr. CMJ Music Marathon Music Fest, 1995, Phila. Music Confs., 1993, 94, 95, 96, 97; counsel Trump Mag., 2005—. Mem. editl. bd. Mealey's Intellectual Property Litigation Law Report, 1992-93; contbr. articles to profl. jours.; music and internat. promotion mgmt., 1984-85; columnist IMPS Jour., 1990-95; featured columnist: Show Business, 1996, NY Law Jour., 1998, Replication News Medialine, 1998-02; editor-at-large: Rock St. Jour., 2006—; counsel Trump mag., 2005-. Mem. Rep. candidate assembly; v.p. Pelham Pkwy., 1983-88; entertainment arbitrator Am. Arbitration Assn., N.Y.C., 1984-95; counsel Pelham Pkwy. Block Assn., Inc., 1991; panelist Mid-Am. Music Conf., Detroit, 1993, Black Radio Exclusive, Econs. of Music, 1993; league lawyer Hewlett-Woodmere Little League, 1994-00; mem. planning bd. Village of Hewlett Harbor, 2001-04, 06-07. Recipient Cert. of Merit Bronx House, 1973, Nathan Burkan award ASCAP, 1980, Plaque of Appreciation, Am. Arbitration Assn., 1985. Mem. ABA (chmn. subcom. on satellites, chmn. subcom. on copyright compliance, chmn. subcom. on copyright renewal, patent trademark, copyright law sect., forum com. on entertainment and sports law sects., spl. com. on corp. practice 1992-97, chmn. sub. com. on broadcasting and music industry, forum com. on comm. law, young lawyer's divsn., vice chmn. 1992-94, patent, trademark, intellectual property sect. exec. com., 1992-93, media law com., young lawyers divsn., founder Urban Intellectual Property Law seminars 1993-95, dir., 1993-95, spl. com. on atty. opinions 1994—, spl. com. on internet 1997—, chmn. subcom. on internat. copyright 2002-03, com. on databases, com. on atty./client opinions, spl. com. internet usage, internat. trademark treaties and laws com. 2002—, ethics and profl. responsibility com., mem. broadcasting, sound recs. and performing artists com. 1982—), Assn. Bar City N.Y. (entertainment law com. 1992-95, 2001-04, trademark law com. 1997-2000, copyright and lit. property law com. 2005—), Copyright Soc. USA (com. on Bicentennial of copyright, mem. editl. bd. Jour. of Copyright Soc. 1991-93, 97—, trustee 2001-04, exec. bd. 2001-04, exec. com. 2002-04, co-chmn. website com. 2002-04), Nat. Acad. Rec. Arts and Scis. (edn. com., columnist N.Y. chpt. newsletter 1997-2000), Rock and Roll Hall of Fame and Mus. (founding mem.), Internat. Assn. Entertainment Lawyers, B'nai B'rith (v.p. 1988-91), Order of the Arrow Brotherhood (Eagle Scout Hall of Fame induction reunion com. 2003), Sephardic Jewish Brotherhood Am., Masons (officer 1997-2000), Audubon Soc. Inc., Phi Delta Phi. Jewish. Avocations: music, photography, swimming, stereo equipment, travel. Office: Jacobson & Colfin PC 60 Madison Ave Ste 1026 New York NY 10010 Office Phone: 212-691-5630. Business E-Mail: jeffrey@thefirm.com.

JACOBSON, JEROLD DENNIS, lawyer; b. NYC, Oct. 12, 1940; s. Sidney and Lillian D. (Fink) J.; m. Gertraude M.J. Holle-Suppa, May 4, 1998; children: Diana, Lisa, Pamela. AB, U. Vt., 1962; JD, Cornell U., 1965; LLM in Labor Law, NYU, 1966. Bar: N.Y. 1966, U.S. Dist. Ct. (so. and ea. dists.) N.Y. 1968, U.S. Dist. Ct. (no. dist.) N.Y. 1981, U.S. Ct. Appeals (2d cir.) 1979, U.S. Ct. Appeals (5th cir.), 1980, U.S. Ct. Appeals (11th cir.) 1981, U.S. Supreme Ct. 1982. Assoc. to gen. counsel ILGWU, AFL-CIO, NYC, 1966-69; assoc. Rains, Pogrebin and Scher, NYC, Mineola, NY, 1969—70, Guggenheimer & Untermyer, NYC, 1970-74, ptnr., 1975-85, Summit, Rovins & Feldsman, NYC, 1986-89, Patterson, Belknap, Webb & Tyler, NYC, 1989-91, Proskauer Rose LLP, NYC, 1991—. Lectr. in labor and employment relations law Practising Law Inst., Am. Soc. Law and Medicine, Profl. Edn. Systems, Inc. Contbr. articles to profl. jours. Mem. adv. bd. Nassau County chpt. N.Y. State Civil Liberties Union; mem. adv. bd. U. Vt. Holocaust Study Ctr., U. Vt. Coll. Arts and Scis.; bd. dirs. Harlem Day Charter Sch. Mem. ABA, Legal Aid Soc., Am. Arbitration Assn., NY State Bar Assn. (lectr.). Office: Proskauer Rose LLP 1585 Broadway Fl 20 New York NY 10036-8299 Office Phone: 212-969-3885. Business E-Mail: jjacobson@proskauer.com.

JACOBSON, JERRY IRVING, biophysicist, theoretical physicist, medical researcher; b. Bklyn., Jan. 25, 1946; s. Saul Lane and Miriam (Cassin) Jacobson; children: Solomon, Jacqueline, Faith, Maria, Shere. BA, Bklyn. Coll., 1963-66; DDS, DMD, Temple U., 1970; PhD, CUNY, 1983; PhD in Medicine, Bundel Khand U., 2002. Oral surgeon Tremont Med. Group, Bronx, NY, 1972-73, University Ave. Med. Group, Bronx, NY, 1973-77; pvt. practice Westchester and New City, NY, 1972—; pres. Perspectivism Found., Jupiter, Fla., 1980—, Inst. Theoretical Physics & Advanced Studies for Biophys., Jupiter, 1985—, Alzheimers Rsch. Found., Jupiter, 1990—, Jacobson Resonance Inc., Jupiter, 1991—, Magneto Therapeutics Mfg., Inc., 1994—, Jacobson Resonance Machines Inc., 1995—; prof. rsch., founding dir. microgravity and electromagnetics Inst. Molecular Medicine, U. Calif., Irvine, 1996; CEO, pres. Pioneer Svcs. Internat., Ltd., Deerfield Beach, Fla., 1996—; chmn. dept. applied med. physics and neuromagnetics Nat. Med. and Rsch. Inst., Boca Raton, Fla., 1997—; pres. Pioneer Svcs. Internat. Ltd., Juno Beach, Fla., 1996; chmn. bd., CEO Jacobson Resonance Enterprises, Inc., Juno Beach, Fla., 1998—, chmn. bd., pres., CEO Boco Raton, Fla., 1998—2000, also dir. R&D, dir. sci. and tech., chmn. bd., pres., CEO Boynton Beach, 2000—; pres., chief magnetics therapist Magnetic Resonance Therapy Ltd., Bahamas, 2003—04. Mem. adv. bd. Kingdor Nat. Parkinson Found., Nassau, Bahamas, Bahamas Parkinson's Found., Nassau; editl. cons. Ctr. Frontier Scis., Temple U., Phila.; chief sci. officer Applied Magnetics, LLC, Denver, 2006, prin. investigator Idiopathic Parkinson's Disease, 2007—; chief sic. and tech. officer Pico Tesla Magnetic Therapies, LLC, Denver, 2007; spkr. in field. Contbr. articles to profl. jours. Served to capt. Dental Corps US Army, 1970—72. Mem.: Internat. Assn. Biologically Closed Electric Cirs. (mem. internat. adv. bd.), Italian Assn. Biomed. Physics, European Bioelectromagnetics Soc., Bioelectromagnetics Soc., Am. Phys. Soc. Achievements include patents in field of med. and plasma physics, agricultural and dental. Avocations: painting, musical composition, writing, philosophy. Home and Office: 2006 Mainsail Cir Jupiter FL 33477-1418 Office Phone: 561-746-8719. E-mail: drjijacobson@yahoo.com.

JACOBSON, JON L., law educator; BA, Univ. Iowa, 1961, JD, 1963. Bar: Calif. 1964. Atty. Bronson Bronson & McKinnon, San Francisco, 1963—67; Bigelow Fellow Univ. Chgo., 1967—68; Bernard B. Kliks prof. emeritus U. Oreg. Sch. Law, founding dir. Ocean & Coastal Law Ctr. Stockton chair internat. law U.S. Naval War Coll., Newport, RI, 1982—83. Editor (in chief): Ocean Development & Internat. Law, 1990—99. Fulbright Found. scholar, Scandinavian Inst. Maritime Law, U. Oslo, 1976, 1984. Office: University of Oregon School of Law 1515 Agate St Eugene OR 97403 Office Phone: 541-346-3852.*

JACOBSON, JULIUS H., II, vascular surgeon, writer; m. Joan Jacobson. AS, U. Toledo, 1947; MS in Cell Physiology, U. Pa.; MD, John Hopkins Sch. Medicine, 1952. Resident, gen. and thoracic surgery Columbia-Presbyn. Hosp., NY; dir. surg. rsch. U. Vt.; dir. emeritus, vascular surgery Mt. Sinai Med. Ctr., NY, disting. svc. prof. surgery. Established Joan L. and Julius H. Jacobson II Professorship Pub. Health Harvard Sch. Pub. Health. Author: (Book) The Classical Music Experience, 2002. Named in his honor, Julius H. Jacobson, II award, Vascular Disease Found., 2004. Fellow: Am. Coll. Surgeons. Preeminent pioneer in microsurgery; first surgeon to bring a microscope into the operating room for the entire range of surgery beyond the eye and ear; developed the first microscope "diploscope" that allowed the surgeon and first assistant to view the operative field simutaneously (now in a collection at the Smithsonian Institution); widely renowned as the inventor of microsurgery, the technique that accounts for half of all neurosurgeries performed in the US; established professorships in vascular surgery(with wife) at John Hopkins University, Hadassah-Hebrew University School of Medicine, Jerusalem, Mount Sinai Medical Center, NY, and (endowed professorship in Biomedical Research) University of Toledo. Address: 1125 Fifth Ave New York NY 10128 Home Phone: 212-289-1417; Office Phone: 212-289-1417. E-mail: jhjdoc@pipeline.com.

JACOBSON, KATHERINE LOUISE, musician, educator; b. Mpls., Feb. 16, 1948; d. Donald Robert Jacobson and Clarice Adeline Graff; m. Leon Fleisher, Oct. 6, 1982. MusB, St. Olaf Coll., 1970; MusM, Cleve. Inst. Music, 1974. Piano instr. Cleve. Inst. Music, 1970—76, Peabody Inst. Preparatory, Balt., 1976—86; asst. prof. Goucher Coll., Towson, Md., 1980—2005. Piano ensemble coach Peabody Conservatory Music, Balt., 2000—; performer NPR Performance Today, Aspen Summer Music Festival, 2001, 02, 03, Santa Fe Chamber Music Festival, 2005, Fountainebleau Chamber Music Festival, 2005. Performer: Chgo. Symphony, Balt. Symphony, Balt. Chamber Symphony, Gulbenkian Orch. Portugal, Royal Conservatory Orch., Carnegie Hall, Phila. Orch. Pres. Fleisher-Jacobson Internat. Children's Edn. Found., Balt., 1990—2001; bd. mem. Young Audiences Md., Balt., 1988—90. Recipient 1st prize, Nat. Piano Ensemble Competition, 1977; grantee, Mayor's Adv. Com. on Art and Culture, Balt., 1990. Mem.: Daus. of Norway. Democrat. Avocations: ballet, yoga, swimming. Office: Peabody Conservatory Music 1 E Mt Vernon Pl Baltimore MD 21202 Office Phone: 410-659-8100 1135.

JACOBSON, KENNETH ALAN, chemist, researcher; s. Norman Charles and Gail Ruth (Newberger) J.; children: Gabriel A., Dorit S., Mihal R.; m. Cheryl V. Dare, Nov. 3, 2002. BA in Chemistry, Reed Coll., Portland, Oreg., 1976; MS in Chemistry, U. Calif., San Diego, 1978, PhD in Chemistry, 1981. Chemist Nalco Chem. Co., Anaheim, Calif., 1976; grad. rsch. asst. U. Calif., 1976-81; rsch. fellow Weizmann Inst. Sci., Rehovot, Israel, 1981-83; staff fellow Nat. Inst. Diabetes Digestive, Kidney Diseases NIH, Bethesda, Md., 1983-88, rsch. chemist, 1988—2003, chief molecular recognition, 1993—, sect. chief, 1993—2003, sr. investigator, 2003—, dir. chem. biology, 2003—. Sci. adv. bd. Rsch. Biochems., Internat., Natick, Mass., 1990-99; adj. prof. Uniformed Svcs. U., 1997—; lectr. in field. Mem. editl. bd. Drug Devel. Rsch., Med. Chem. Rsch., Bioconjugate Chem, Jour. Med. Chem.; contbr. over 400 articles to profl. jours.; patentee in field. Recipient Fassina award 1996, NIDDK Director's award 2006, Hillebrand prize, Chem. Soc. of Wash., 2003; Kroll scholar, 1974; Bantrell fellow, 1981-83. Mem. Internat. Soc. Nucleosides, Nucleotides, and Nucleic Acids, Am. Chem. Soc. (chair med. chem. divsn. 2004), Am. Soc.

Pharmacology and Exptl. Therapeutics (co-chair symposium 1989), Soc. Neurosci. Jewish. Avocations: hiking, travel. Office: NIH Bldg 8 Rm B1A-19 Bethesda MD 20892-0810 Business E-Mail: kajacobs@helix.nih.gov.

JACOBSON, LOUIS ALAN, journalist; s. Raymond Marvin and Eileen Marion Jacobson; m. Elisabeth Layton, June 23, 2001. BA in Pub. and Internat. Affairs, Princeton U., 1992, cert. in African-Am. studies, 1992. Virginian-pilot, ledger-star, Virginia Beach, Va., 1991; reporting intern Wall St. Jour., NYC, 1992, Nat. Jour., Washington, 1993, Economist, London, 1993—94; assoc. editor Nat. Jour., Washington, 1994—97, staff corr., lobbying, 1997—2004; dep. editor, columnist Roll Call, Washington, 2004—07, contbg. editor, 2007—; editor CongressNow, 2007—. Contbg. writer Wash. City Paper, Washington, 1992—; contbg. editor Congress Daily, Washington, 1994—2004, Govt. Exec., Washington, 1993—2004; freelance contbr. Economist, 1994—, Wash. Post, Washington, 1996—2004, Planning, Chgo., 1994—, Foresight, Tokyo, 2001—, Princeton Alumni Weekly, 1995—; columnist breakaway sect. Wall St. Jour., NYC, 2000—01; state legis. handicapper The Cook Polit. Report, 2002; state legis., ballot initiative handicapper The Rothenberg Polit. Report, 2004—; instr. USDA Grad. Sch., 2005—. Contbtg. writer (book) The Almanac of American Politics 2000, prin. contbg. writer The Almanac of American Politics 2004. Recipient Wash. Dateline award in arts criticism, Soc. Profl. Journalists, Washington chpt., 2002, Capitolbeat Statehouse Reporting award, 2006, 2007. Mem.: Capitolbeat: The Assn. Capitol Reporters and Editors, Nat. Book Critics' Cir., Soc. Am. Baseball Rsch. Office: CongressNow 50 F St NW 700 Washington DC 20001 Office Phone: 202-824-6800. E-mail: ljacobson@rollcall.com.

JACOBSON, MARC STEPHEN, pediatrician, educator; b. June 25, 1947; BA, U. Kans., 1969, MD, 1973. Diplomate Am. Bd. Pediatrics; lic. physician, Kans., Mo., Md., N.Y. Resident in pediatrics U. Kans., Kansas City, 1973-77; fellow in adolescent medicine U. Md., Balt., 1977-79, asst. prof. pediatrics, 1979-85, dir. adolescent ambulatory clinic, 1980-85, asst. dir. adolescent medicine div., 1981-85, dir. nutrition lab., 1981-85; dir. attending physician Schneider Children's Hosp., New Hyde Park, N.Y., 1985—, dir. atherosclerosis prevention ctr., 1986—. Asst. prof. pediat. SUNY, Stony Brook, 1985-89; asst. prof. Albert Einstein Coll. Medicine, Bronx, N.Y., 1989, assoc. prof., 1991—; lectr., cons. in field. Ad hoc reviewer Annals of Internal Medicine, 1992—; contbr. abstracts and articles to profl. jours. Mem. women's, infants and children nutrition adv. bd. Md. Dept. Mental Health and Hygiene, Balt., 1982-84; bd. dirs. L.I. Heart Coun., 1986, mem. exec. com., 1989-92, pres., 1993—. Grantee Bressler Fund, 1983-85, HHS Materna and Child Health, 1984-87, L.I. Jewish Med. Ctr., 1986, 88-92, Am. Heart Asn. Nassau County, 1986-87, S.L.E. Found., 1986-88, Merck Sharpe and Dohme, 1990-91. Fellow Am. Acad. Pediatrics (nutrition com. 1985—, chmn. 1987—); mem. AAAC, Am. Heart Assn., Queens Pediatric Soc., N.Y. Acad. Sci., Soc. Adolescent Medicine (jour. adv. com. 1993—), Nassau County Pediatric Soc., Soc. Pediatric Rsch. Home: 7 Woodcleft Ave Port Washington NY 11050-2736 Office: Schneider Childrens Hosp Atherosclerosis Prevention New Hyde Park NY 11042

JACOBSON, MARIAN SLUTZ, lawyer; b. Cin., Nov. 10, 1945; d. Leonard Doering and Emily Dana (Wells) Slutz; m. Fruman Jacobson, Sept. 21, 1975; 1 child, Lisa Wells. BA cum laude, Ohio Wesleyan U., 1967; JD, U. Chgo., 1972. Bar: Ill. 1972, U.S. Dist. Ct. (no. dist.) Ill. 1972, U.S. Ct. Appeals (7th cir.) 1973. Assoc. Sonnenschein Nath & Rosenthal, Chgo., 1972-79, ptnr., 1979—. Mem. vis. com. U. Chgo. Law Sch., 1992-94, 05-. Mem. ABA, Chgo. Coun. Lawyers, Met. Club Chgo. (bd. govs. 1998—), Hyde Park Neighborhood Club (bd. dirs. 2003-). Office: Sonnenschein Nath & Rosenthal 7800 Sears Tower Chicago IL 60606-6491 Office Phone: 312-876-8167. Business E-Mail: mjacobson@sonnenschein.com.

JACOBSON, MATTHEW FRYE, historian, educator; b. Boulder, Colo., Nov. 8, 1958; s. Jacob and Sarah Jacobson; m. Farncesca Schwartz, Sept. 18, 1993; children: Nicholas, Tess. BA, Evergreen State Coll., Olympia, Wash., 1981; MA, Boston Coll., 1986; PhD, Brown U., Providence, 1992. Asst. prof. History SUNY Stony Brook, 1992—95; prof. Am. Studies Yale U., New Haven, 1995—. Author: (scholarly book) Whiteness of a Different Color: European Immigrants and the Alchemy of Race (John Hope Franklin Prize; Ralph Bunche Prize, 1999), (scholarly work) Special Sorrows, (scholarly) Barbarian Virtues, Roots Too, What Have They Built You to Do?. Fellow, Nat. Endowment for Humanities, 1994. Mem.: Am. Studies Assn. (nat. coun. 2002—05). Home Phone: 212-988-2822.

JACOBSON, MELVIN JOSEPH, mathematician, educator; b. Providence, Nov. 25, 1928; s. Charles and Rose (Chusmir) J.; m. Dorothy Troup, June 8, 1952 (div. Aug. 1985); children: Deborah Lynn, Donald Bruce; m. Gertrude R. Ackerman, Jan. 27, 2002. AB, Brown U., 1950; MS, Carnegie Inst. Tech., Pitts., 1952, PhD, 1954. Instr. Carnegie Inst. Tech., 1953-54; mem. tech. staff Bell Tel. Labs., Whippany, NJ, 1954-56; asst. prof. math. Rensselaer Poly. Inst., Troy, NY, 1956-58, assoc. prof., 1958-63, prof., 1963-90, prof. emeritus, rsch. cons., 1991—; prin. investigator and cons. Office Naval Rsch. Contracts, 1957-96; contract Unisys. Corp., 1985-88; prin. investigator NSF grant, 1962-67; contract Inst. for Naval Oceanography, 1987-91, NASA, 1988-91, U.S. Mil. Acad. (for U.S. Army Atmospheric Sci. Lab.), West Point, NY, 1989-91. Vis. prof. Rosenstiel Sch. Marine and Atmospheric Sci., U. Miami, Fla., 1963-64, adj. prof., 1969-72; cons. to industry, NRC. Contbr. articles to numerous publs. Fellow Acoustical Soc. Am.; mem. AAUP, Sigma Xi, Phi Kappa Phi, Pi Mu Epsilon. Home: 4705 Chandlers Forde Sarasota FL 34235-7120 Personal E-mail: melgeet@comcast.net.

JACOBSON, MICHAEL F., lawyer; b. 1967; Grad., U. Colo., 1989; JD, Detroit Coll. Law., 1992. Bar: Mich. 1992, Fla. Ptnr. Hertz Schram & Saretsky P.C., Bloomfield Hills, Mich., 1999—2005; atty. Jaffe Raitt Heuer & Weiss P.C., Southfield, Mich., 2005—06, ptnr., 2006—. Named one of 40 Under 40, Crain's Detroit Bus., 2006. Office: Jaffe Raitt Heuer & Weiss PC 27777 Franklin Rd Ste 2500 Southfield MI 48034-8214 Office Phone: 248-351-3000. Business E-Mail: mjacobson@jaffelaw.com.

JACOBSON, MICHAEL FARADAY, consumer advocate, writer; b. Chgo., July 29, 1943; s. Larry and Janet (Siegel) J.; m. Donna Ruth Lenhoff; 1 child, Sonya. BA, U. Chgo., 1965; postgrad., U. Calif., San Diego, 1965-67; PhD, MIT, 1969. Research assoc. Salk Inst. for Biol. Studies, 1970-71; cons. Ctr. for Study of Responsive Law, 1970-71; co-founder, exec. dir. Ctr. for Sci. in the Pub. Interest, Washington, 1971—. Founder Ctr. for Study Commercialism, 1990. Author: Nutrition Scoreboard, 1975, Eater's Digest, 1972, The Complete Eater's Digest and Nutrition Scoreboard, 1986; (with others) The Booze Merchants, 1983, Salt: The Brand Name Guide to Sodium, 1983, The Changing American Diet, 1983, The Fast Food Guide, 1986, 2d edit., 1991, Marketing Booze to Blacks, 1987, Tainted Booze, 1987, Marketing Disease to Hispanics, 1989, Kitchen Fun for Kids, 1991, Safe Food, 1991; co-editor: Food for People Not for Profit, 1975, Cooking With the Stars, 1992, What Are We Feeding Our Kids?, 1994, Marketing Madness: A Survival Guide for a Consumer Society, 1995, Restaurant Confidential 2002. Originator, nat. coord. Food Day, 1975-77. Office: Ctr for Sci in the Pub Interest 1875 Connecticut Ave NW Ste 300 Washington DC 20009-5736

JACOBSON, MICHAEL HAROLD, educational administrator; b. La-junta, Colo., Feb. 16, 1945; s. Irving Ralph and Bernice Marie (Rubin) J. BS, Loyola U., Chgo., 1967; LLB, LaSalle U., 1971; MA, Northeastern Ill. U., 1970; PhD, Sussex Coll. (Eng.), 1973; LHD (hon.), 1974, DM, 1976; MBA, Keller Grad. Sch. Mgmt. Tchr., Chgo. Bd. Edn., 1967-71, counselor, 1971-76; pres. Chgo. Counseling Assocs., 1971-74; coordinator Chgo. Region, Effectiveness Tng. Assocs., 1972-73; Ill. state rep. Universal Life Ch., 1975—; prof. psychology Foster G. McGaw Grad. Sch., Nat. Coll. Edn., Chgo., 1975-80; dir. guidance services Orr High Sch., Chgo., 1976-78; assoc. prin. Dunbar Vocat. High Sch., 1978-79, Phillips High Sch., 1979-80; prin. Abbott Elem. Sch., Chgo., 1980-90; assoc. prof. dept. early childhood and elem. edn. Chgo. State U., 1990—. Dist. commr. Boy Scouts Am., Chgo., 1975—, asst. dist. commr., 1973-75, mem. sea exploring com., 1980—; staff officer public edn. USCG Aux., 1979-81, div. staff officer pub. affairs, 1981-82, asst. dist. staff officer communications, 1982-83, vice comdr., 1984, flotilla comdr., 1984, div. staff officer, 1983—, dist. staff officer, 1986—. Served to capt. USNR; Vietnam. Decorated D.S.MLegion of Merit; Vietnamese Cross of Gallantry; Knight Sovereign Order of Lichstenstine; Knight commdr. Order Sursum Corda; Knight Order of Constantine. Mem. U.S. Naval Inst., Am. Assn. Sex Educators Counselors and Therapists (cert. sex educator and sex therapist), Assn. for Supervision and Curriculum Devel., Chgo. Prins. Assn., U.S. Naval League, Spl. Elite Forces Soc., Mensa, Am. Legion, Psi Chi, Phi Delta Kappa, Phi Delta Epsilon, Alpha Phi Omega (nat. exec. alumni com. 1974—). Contbr. articles to profl. jours., also books. Office: 3630 S Wells St Chicago IL 60609-1833

JACOBSON, MICHAEL R., lawyer, Internet company executive; b. 1954; BA in Econs. magna cum laude, Harvard U., 1975; JD, Stanford U., 1981. Bar: Calif. 1981. Ptnr. Cooley Godward LLP; v.p. legal affairs to sr. v.p., gen. counsel, sec. eBay Inc., San Jose, Calif., 1998—. Mem.: Phi Beta Kappa. Office: eBay Inc 2145 Hamilton Ave San Jose CA 95125-5905 Office Phone: 408-558-7400. Office Fax: 408-558-7514.*

JACOBSON, NINA R., film producer and former company executive; b. 1965; life ptnr.; 2 children. AB, Brown Univ., 1987. Doc. rschr. Arnold Shapiro Prodns.; story analyst Disney Sunday Movie, 1987; dir. develop. Silver Pictures; head develop. McDonald/Parkes Prodn.; sr. v.p. prodn. Universal Pictures, 1994—95; sr. film exec. DreamWorks SKG, 1995—98; exec. v.p. prodn. Walt Disney Pictures/Hollywood Pictures, 1998; co-pres. Buena Vista Motion Pictures Group (divsn. The Walt Disney Co.), Burbank, Calif., 1999—2000, pres., 2000—06; prodr. DreamWorks Studios, 2006—. Named one of 100 Most Powerful Women in Entertainment, Hollywood Reporter, 2004, 2005, 100 Most Powerful Women in World, Forbes mag., 2005, 50 Most Powerful People in Hollywood, Premiere mag., 2004—06; recipient Crystal award, Women in Film, 2003. Office: DreamWorks Studios 1000 Flower St Glendale CA 91201

JACOBSON, NORMAN L., retired agricultural educator, researcher; b. Eau Claire, Wis., Sept. 11, 1918; s. Frank R. and Elma E. (Baker) J.; m. Gertrude A. Neff, Aug. 24, 1943; children: Gary, Judy. BS, U. Wis., 1940; MS, Iowa State U., 1941, PhD, 1947. Asst. prof. animal sci. Iowa State U., Ames, 1947-49, assoc. prof., 1949-53, prof., 1953, Disting. prof. agr., 1963-89, assoc. dean Grad. Coll., 1973-88, assoc. v.p. rsch., 1979-88, assoc. provost, 1988-89, dean Grad. Coll. Ames, 1988-89, emeritus disting. prof. agr., 1989—, interim chair dept. food sci. and human nutrition, 1990-92. Contbr. articles to profl. jours., chpts. to books. Served to lt. USN, 1942-46, ETO, PTO. Fellow AAAS, Am. Soc. for Nutritional Scis., Am. Soc. Animal Sci. (Morrison award 1970), Am. Dairy Sci. Assn. (pres. 1972-73, Am. Feed Mfrs. Assn. award 1955, Borden award 1960, award of honor 1978, Disting. Svc. award 1989). Presbyterian. Personal E-mail: nljacob@iastate.edu.

JACOBSON, NORMAN MARON, computer science educator; b. Hollywood, Calif., May 30, 1954; s. Eugene and Sylvia J. BA Math., U. Calif., Irvine, 1976, BS Info. & Computer Sci., 1976. Cert. tchr., Calif. Programmer Office Housing and Transp. U. Calif., Irvine, 1974—85, sr. program analyst Pub. Policy Rsch. Orgn., 1975—84, programmer Office Vice Chancellor, 1977—78, articulation officer Donald Bren Sch. Info. and Computer Scis., 1985—98, 2002—; v.p. Custom Software, Inc., Calif., 1979—85. Instr. summer sessions Sch. Info. and Computer Sci., U. Calif., 1979-2004, asst. chair undergrad. affairs, 1994-98; software cons. Visual Resource Collection, Irvine, 1986—2006; writer, host ednl. TV series The New Literacy, 1984; expert witness in computer-related cases, 1984—. Author: Structured Programming Using Think Pascal on the MacIntosh, 1992 Mem. Assn. Computing Machinery Avocations: hammer dulcimer, stamp collecting/philately. Office Phone: 949-824-7300. Business E-Mail: jacobson@uci.edu.

JACOBSON, PHILLIP LEE, architect, educator; b. Santa Monica, Calif., Aug. 27, 1928; s. Allen Wilhelm and Greta Percy (Rohde) J.; m. Effie Laurel Galbraith, Nov. 6, 1954; children: Rolf Wilhelm, Christina Lee, Erik Mackenzie. B. Archtl. Engring. with honors, Wash. State U., 1952; postgrad. (Fulbright scholar), U. Liverpool, Eng., 1952-53; M.Arch., Finnish Inst. Tech., Helsinki, 1969. Field supr. Gerald C. Field Architect, 1950; designer, draftsman John Maloney Architect, 1951, 53-55; designer, project mgr. Young, Richardson, Carleton & Detlie Architects, 1955-56; designer, project architect John Carl Warnecke Architect, San Francisco, 1956-58; ptnr., design dir. TRA, Seattle, 1958-92; prof. architecture and urban design and planning Coll. Architecture and Urban Planning, U. Wash., Seattle, 1962—2000. Author: Housing and Industrialization in Finland, 1969, The Evolving Architectural Design Process, 1969; contbr. articles to profl. jours.; major archtl. works include Aerospace Research Lab., U. Wash., Seattle, 1969, McCarty Residence Hall, 1960, Highway Adminstrn. Bldg., Olympia, Wash., 1970, Sea-Tac Internat. Airport, 1972, Issaquah (Wash.) High Sch., 1962, State Office Bldg. 2, Olympia, 1976, Sealaska Corporate Hdqrs. Bldg., Juneau, Alaska, 1977, Group Health Hosp., Seattle, 1973, Metro Shelter Program, Seattle, 1977, N.W. Trek Wildlife Preserve, 1976, Rocky Reach/Rock Island Recreation Plan, 1974, master plan mouth of Columbia River, 1976, U. Wash. Biol. Sci. Bldg., 1981, Wegner Hall, Wash. State U., 1982, Wash. Conv. Ctr., 1988, King County Aquatics Ctr., 1990, Albuquerque Airport, 1989, U. Wash. Health Scis. H Wing, 1993, Elegant Explorations The Designs of Phillip Jacobson, 2007. Mem. Seattle Planning and Redevel. Council, 1959-69, v.p., 1966-67; mem. Seattle Landmark Preservation Bd., 1976-81; trustee Pilchuck Sch., 1982-2001, Northwest Trek Found., 1987-94, AIA/Seattle Archtl. Found., 1986-92. With U.S. Army, 1946-47. Fulbright-Hays Sr. Rsch. fellow Finland, 1968-69; named to Order of White Rose Govt. of Finland, 1985; recipient Silver plaque Finnish Soc. Architects, 1992; recipient numerous design awards. Fellow AIA (pres. Wash. state Council 1965, dir. Seattle chpt. 1970-73, sr. council 1970—, Seattle chpt. medal 1994); mem. Am. Inst. Cert. Planners, Phi Kappa Phi, Tau Beta Pi, Tau Sigma Delta, Scarab, Sigma Tau (outstanding alumnus 1967). Office: U Wash PO Box 355720 Seattle WA 98195-5720 Personal E-mail: plj54@msn.com.

JACOBSON, RAYMOND EARL, electronics executive; b. St. Paul, May 25, 1922; s. Albert H. and Gertrude W. (Anderson) J.; m. div. 1986; children: Michael David, Karl Raymond, Christopher Eric. BE with high honors, prize for excellence in mech. engring., Yale U., New Haven, Conn., 1944; MBA with distinction, Harvard U., Cambridge, Mass., 1948; BA in Econ. and Politics (Rhodes Scholar), Oxford U., 1950, MA, 1954. Asst. to gen. mgr. Polytech Rsch and Devel. Co., Inc., Bklyn., 1951-55; sales mgr. Curtiss-Wright Electronics Divsn., Carlstadt, NJ, 1955-57; dir. mktg. TRW Computers Co., LA, 1957—60; v.p. ops. Electro-Sci. Investors, Dallas, 1960-63; pres. Whitehall Electronics, Inc., Dallas, 1961-63; chmn. bd. Gen. Electronic Control, Inc., Mpls., 1961-63, Staco, Inc., Dayton, Ohio, 1961-63; pres. Maxson Electronics Corp., Gt. River, NY, 1963-64, Jacobson Assocs., San Jose, Calif., 1964-67; co-founder, pres., chmn., CEO Anderson Jacobson, Inc., San Jose, Calif., 1967-88. Chmn. Anderson Jacobson, SA, Paris, 1974-88, Anderson Jacobson, Ltd., London, 1975-88, Anderson Jacobson Can., Ltd./Ltée, Toronto, 1975-85, Anderson Jacobson, GmbH, Cologne, 1978-83, CXR Corp., San Jose, 1988-94; bd. dirs. Tamar Electronics, Inc., LA, Rawco Instruments, Inc., Dallas, 1960-63, Micro Radionics, Inc., LA, 1964-67, ComputerMan USA, Inc., Reno, 1997—; lectr. engring., UCLA, 1958-60, lectr. bus. adminstrn. U. Calif. Berkeley, 1965-66; mem. underwriting Lloyd's London, 1975-96. Eagle Scout Boy Scouts Am., 1935, committeeman, 1968-80. Lt. (j.g.) USNR, 1943-46, radar maintenance officer, USS Puget Sound. Mem. Assn. Am. Rhodes Scholars, Oxford Soc., Brasenose Soc., Yale Club, Yale Class 1944 (exec. com.), Harvard Bus. Sch. Assn., Sigma Xi, Tau Beta Pi. Courtside Tennis Club, Seascape Swim and Racquet Club. Republican. Lutheran. Home and Office: 543 Elk River Ct Reno NV 89511 Home Phone: 775-851-3796; Office Phone: 775-851-3796.

JACOBSON, RICHARD JOSEPH, lawyer; b. Ft. Benning, Ga., July 12, 1943; s. Harold Gordon and Ruth Fern (Enenstein) J.; m. Judy Josephine Dunbar, Sept. 17, 1966; 1 child, David Dunbar. AB, Harvard U., 1965, PhD, 1970; JD, U. Va., 1977. Bar: Ill. 1977, Va. 1977, D.C. 1979, U.S. Dist. Ct. (no. dist.) 1977, U.S. Ct. Appeals (7th cir.) 1991. Asst. prof. English U. Va., Charlottesville, 1970-74; assoc. Keck, Mahin & Cate, Chgo., 1977-83, ptnr., 1984-96; prin. Flaherty, Jacobson & Youngerman, P.C., Chgo., 1996—. Adj. prof. Sch. Law Northwestern U., Chgo., 1999—. Author: Hawthorne's Conception of the Creative Process, 1965; contbr. articles to profl. jours. Pres. North Park Condominium assn., Chgo., 1978-80. Woodrow Wilson Nat. fellow, 1965. Fellow Am. Bar Found.; mem. Va. State Bar Assn., DC Bar Assn., Chgo. Bar Assn. (chmn. com. preventing atty. malpractice 2000-01), Assn. Profl. Responsibility Lawyers, Cliff Dwellers Club, Lawyers Club Chgo., Chgo. Lit. Club. Home: 850 W Adams St Apt 3D Chicago IL 60607-3088 Office: Flaherty Jacobson & Youngerman PC 134 N Lasalle St Ste 1600 Chicago IL 60602-1108 Personal E-mail: rjacobson@fjylaw.com.

JACOBSON, RICHARD LEE, lawyer, educator; b. LA, Nov. 2, 1942; s. Joseph and Betty (Koenig) Jacobson; m. Pamela; children: David, Peter, Michael, Jacqueline. S.B., U. Chgo., 1964; JD, U. So. Calif., 1970. Bar: Calif. 1971, U.S. Ct. Appeals (9th cir.) 1971, D.C. 1980, U.S. Ct. Appeals (4th cir.) 1980, U.S. Ct. Appeals (D.C. cir.) 1980, U.S. Supreme Ct. 1980, U.S. Ct. Appeals (6th cir.) 1983. Law clk. Walter Ely, U.S. Ct. Appeals (9th cir.), 1970-71; law clk. to Assoc. Justice William O. Douglas U.S. Supreme Ct., Washington, 1971-72; assoc. Irell & Manella, Los Angeles, 1973-76; mem. trial unit SEC, Washington, 1977-78, spl. counsel to chmn., 1978-79; ptnr. Mayer, Brown & Platt, Washington, 1980-85; spl. counsel Heller, Ehrman, White & McAuliffe, Palo Alto, 1986-88; counsel Fulbright & Jaworski, Washington, 1988-89, ptnr., 1990—2000, sr. coun., 2003—05; sr. v.p., gen. counsel Sorrento Networks Corp., LA and San Diego, Calif., 2000—03; counsel Arnold & Porter LLP, Washington, 2005—. Adj. prof. law Georgetown U. Law Ctr., Washington, 1979-86; mem. bd. advisors, Sec. Reform Act Litig. Reporter, 1998-2000. Exec. editor So. Calif. Law Rev., 1969-70; contbr. articles to profl. jours. Bd. dirs. Washington Lawyers Com. for Civil Rights and Urban Affairs, 1983-2000. Mem. ABA (chmn. subcom. uniformity of local discovery rules 1983-85, chmn. subcom. securities class actions 1995-2003, fed. regulation securities com., securities litigation com.), Am. Law Inst., Washington Coun. Lawyers (bd. dirs. 1982-86, 88-99, pres. 1985-86), D.C. Bar Assn. (nominations com. 1984-85, steering com. computer law divsn. 1985-86), Assn. SEC Alumni (pres. 1995-97, dir. 1998-2000), Order of Coif. Office: Arnold & Porter LLP 555 Twelfth St NW Washington DC 20004-1206 Business E-Mail: Richard.Jacobson@aporter.com.

JACOBSON, ROBERT ANDREW, chemistry professor; b. Waterbury, Conn., Feb. 16, 1932; s. Carl Andrew and Mary Catherine (O'Donnell) J.; m. Margaret Ann McMahan, May 26, 1962; children: Robert Edward, Cheryl Ann BA, U. Conn., 1954; PhD, U. Minn., 1959. Instr. Princeton U., NJ, 1959-62, asst. prof. NJ, 1962-64; assoc. prof. Iowa State U., Ames, 1964-69, full prof., 1969-99, asst. dean Scis. and Humanities, 1982-85, prof. emeritus, 1999—. Chemist Ames Lab, Iowa, 1964-69, sr. chemist, 1969-99. Contbr. articles to profl. jours. Recipient Wilkinson Teaching award Iowa State U., Ames, 1974, 91. Mem. Am. Chem. Soc., Am. Crystallographic Assn. (chmn. apparatus and standards com. 1982-83) Avocations: gardening, painting. Home: 2732 Thompson Dr Ames IA 50010-4759 Office: Iowa State U 1271 Gilman Ames IA 50011-3111 Office Phone: 515-294-1144. E-mail: raj@ameslab.gov.

JACOBSON, ROBERT JULIAN, oncologist, director; b. Johannesburg, Sept. 7, 1943; MD, U. Witwatersrand, Johannesburg, 1966. Cert. in hematology, in hematopathology. Internship internal medicine Johannesburg Gen. Hosp., 1967—68; resident hematology Sinai Hosp., Balt., 1968—70; resident medicine Georgetown U. Hosp., Washington, 1970—72; faculty Georgetown U., prof. medicine and pathology, Vincent T. Lombardi Cancer Ctr., co-dir. hematologic oncology svc.; med. dir. Helen and Harry Gray Cancer Inst. Good Samaritan Med. Ctr., West Palm Beach, Fla., dir. bone marrow and stem cell transplantation program. Interim chmn. dept. medicine Vincent T. Lombardi Cancer Ctr.; cons. prof. dept. medicine Duke U. Med. Ctr., Durham, NC; mem. med. adv. bd. FindCancerExperts.com; bd. dirs. Hospice of Palm Beach County. Contbr. chapters to books, scientific papers to profl. jours. Fellow: ACP, Royal Coll. Physicians and Surgeons Can.; mem.: Leukemia and Lymphoma Soc. Am., Am. Soc. Hematology, Am. Soc. Clin. Pathologists, Am. Soc. Clin. Oncology. Office: Good Samaritan Med Ctr Cancer Inst 1309 N Flagler Dr West Palm Beach FL 33401 Office Phone: 561-366-4150. Office Fax: 561-366-4106.*

JACOBSON, SHELDON HOWARD, engineering educator; b. Montreal, Sept. 9, 1960; BSc, McGill U., 1981, MSc, 1983; PhD, Cornell U., 1988. Asst. prof. Case We. Res. U., Cleve., 1988—93; assoc. prof. Va. Tech., Blacksburg, 1993—99, U. Ill., Urbana, 1999—2002, prof., 2002—, assoc. Ctr. for Advanced Study, 2002—03. Sci. adv. bd. BioPop Inc., Charlotte, NC, 2000—02. Recipient Best Application award, Inst. Indsl. Engring. Ops. Rsch. Divsn., 1998, Aviation Security Rsch. award, Aviation Security Internat., 2002; Willett Faculty scholar, U. Ill., 2002—08, Guggenheim fellow, 2003. Office: Univ Illinois 201 N Goodwin Ave MC-258 Urbana IL 61801-2302

JACOBSON, SIDNEY, editor; b. NYC, Oct. 20, 1929; s. Reuben and Beatrice (Edelman) J.; m. Ruth Allison, July 4, 1957 (div. Feb. 1975); children: Seth, Kathy Battat; m. Maggi Silverstein, Feb. 26, 1975. BA, NYU, 1950. Exec. editor Harvey Comics, NYC, 1952-83, Marvel Comics, NYC, 1983-89; v.p., editor-in-chief Harvey Comics Entertainment, LA, 1989—. Author: Streets of Gold, 1985, Another Time, 1989, Pistol: The Story of Pete Reiser, 2004, The 9/11 Report: A Graphic Adaptation, 2006 (Libr. Jour. Fall Editors' Pick, 2006); writer (comic books) Captain Israel, 1972, The Black Comic Book, 1973, Wally the Wizard, 1985, Labyrinth, 1986, Pinocchio & the Emperor of the Night, 1988, (TV animation series) Johnny Cypher in Dimension Zero, 1975, (TV series) Felix the Cat, 1982, (monthly) You Can't Do That in Comics, 1986; editor (comic books) The Muppets Take Manhattan, 1984, The Get Along Gang, 1985, Ewoks, 1985, Strawberry Shortcake, 1985, Care Bears, 1985, Star Wars: Droids, 1986, Heathcliff's Funhouse, 1987, ALF, 1988, Damage Control, 1989, Monsters in my Pocket, 1991, Beetlejuice in the Neitherworld, 1994; lyricist various popular songs. Mem. Am. Soc. Composers, Authors and Pubs., Am. Guild Authors and Composers, Authors Guild. Home: 435 S Curson Ave Los Angeles CA 90036 Office: 20501 Ventura Blvd Woodland Hills CA 91364 E-mail: sidjacobson2@aol.com.

JACOBSON, TRACEY ANN, ambassador; m. Lars Anders Johansson; 1 stepchild, Emmelie Johansson. BA, MA, John Hopkins U. Dep. exec. sec. Nat. Security Coun., Washington; dep. chief of mission US Embassy, Riga, Latvia, 2000—03; US amb. to Turkmenistan US Dept. State, Ashgabat, 2003—06, US amb. to Tajikistan Dushanbe, 2006—. Recipient Superior Honor award, US Dept. State, Meritorious Honor award. Office: US Embassy 7090 Dushanbe Pl Washington DC 20521

JACOBSON, VAN, computer scientist, researcher; Group leader Network Rsch. Lab., Lawrence Berkeley Lab.; chief scientist Cisco Sys., Packet Design LLC, 2001—. Recipient ACM SIGCOMM Award, 2001. Mem.: IEEE (Koji Kobayashi Computers and Comm. Award 2003), NAE. Office: Packet Design Inc Bldg 3 3400 Hillview Ave Palo Alto CA 94304 Office Phone: 650-739-1850.

JACOBS-QUAM, VIVIEN MARIE, retired music educator; b. Dover, NJ, Apr. 8, 1943; d. Charles Jacobs and Elizabeth Toth; m. Leonard Egil Quam, Jan. 6, 1964; 1 child, Leonard Charles Quam. B in Music Edn., Westminster Choir Coll., 1965; MA, Montclair State U., 1972. Cert. music tchr. K-12 NJ. State Dept. Edn., 1965, elem. sch. tchr. NJ. State Dept. Edn., 1986. Tchr. vocal music Sparta Alpine Sch., 1965—66; catering mgr., owner Viking House Delicatessen, Denville, 1972—91; tchr. vocal music Frelinghuysen Twp. Sch., Newton, 1981—85; organist, choir dir. Union Hill Prebyterian Ch., Denville, NJ, 1982—85; tchr. vocal music Lafayette Twp. Sch., Augusta, NJ, 1982—85, Morris Hills Regional Bd. Edn., Rockaway, NJ, 1986—2002; organist, choir dir. Sparta United Meth. Ch., Sparta, 1989—2001. Cons. tchr. fine and performing arts Morris Hills Regional Bd. Edn., Rockaway, NJ, 1997—2002; coach debate and forensics Morris Hills H.S., N.J. Debate League, N.J. Forensics League. Singer (soprano soloist): (high holy days) Northwestern U. Orch, Lakeland Youth Symphony, Westminster Choir Coll. Alumni; dir.(Morris Hills H.S. vocal students): (performance of music with orchestra) Carnegie, Avery Fisher, and Alice Tully Halls (included 25th Ann. Bklyn. Philharm., 1990). Tennis coach Morris Hills Regional Bd. Edn., Rockaway, NJ, forensics coach, 1988—2000, debate coach, 1988—2002; chair choral procedures NJ Music Edn. Assn., 1998—2002; chair region I choral Performance Region I Sch. Music Assn., 1988—91. Recipient Honor award, Morris Hills Bd. Edn., 1992, Superior Ratings, Madrigal Choir, Music Performance Festivals, 1998—2002, Northwestern N.J. Music Tchr. of Yr., William Paterson U., 2001; fellow, Northwestern U. Sch. Music, 1986. Mem.: N.J. Ret. Educators Assn. Achievements include original design and a refit for new hardware and software used in the teaching of music theory, ear/training and graphic arts in computer labs at Morris Hills Regional District schools; development of general music course in the curriculum at Morris Hills Regional District schools for the non-performance student; an accepted (model) proposal for NJ All- State Women's Chorus which allows many additional talented young NJ women to perform in an honor's choir. Avocations: piano, cross stitch, beading. Home: 41 Rogers Ln Sparta NJ 07871 Office Phone: 973-729-6587. Personal E-mail: vmjq53le@earthlink.net, vivienjacobsquam@mac.com.

JACOBS-SMITH, RUBY EUDORA, retired medical/surgical nurse, public health service officer; b. Georgetown, Guyana, Aug. 13, 1921; arrived in U.S., 1963; d. Eustace LeRoy and Emily Alene (Edey) Skeete; m. Randolph C.F. Jacobs (dec.); 1 child, Seth Noel Jacobs; m. William Spencer Smith (dec.). Degree in nursing, midwifery and pub. health, Georgetown Hosp. U., 1944; degree in pub. health adminstrn., Seton Hall U., 1964; degree in psychology and sociology, Upsala Coll., 1968. Cert. pub. health officer NJ; RN NJ. Pub. health officer, nurse NJU State Dept. Health, Trenton, 1964—; health fisitor Newark Health Dept., 1964—75; nurse in charge Univ. Hosp., Newark, 1975—92; ret., 1998. Contbr. articles to profl. jours. Mem. So. Poverty Law Ctr., Montgomery, Ala., 2004; counselor Caribbean Youth Assn., East Orange, NJ, 1971, NJ Fellowship Units Inc., East Orange, 1971. Named Woman of Yr., NJ Fellowship Forum, 1972, East Orange Record, 1972; recipient award for pub. health nursing, NJ State Dept. Health, 1992, award, Union Twp. City Hall, 1992. Mem.: AAUW, Guyanese Cultural Assn. (founder, fin. sec. 1963, Cmty. Svc. award 1992). Democrat. Episcopalian. Avocations: travel, sports. Home: 213 Hilton Ave Vauxhall NJ 07088 Office: NJ Fellowship Units Inc 213 HIlton Ave Vauxhall NJ 07088 Office Phone: 708-687-7113.

JACOBUS, CHARLES JOSEPH, lawyer, title company executive, writer; b. Ponca City, Okla., Aug. 21, 1947; s. David William and Louise Graham Jacobus; m. Heather Jeanne Jones, June 6, 1970; children: Mary Helen, Charles J. Jr. BS, U. Houston, 1970, JD, 1973. Bar: Tex. 1973; cert. specialist residential and commerical real estate law Tex. Bd. Legal Specialization. Pvt. practice, Houston, 1973-75; staff counsel Tenneco Realty, Inc., Houston, 1975-78, v.p., gen. counsel, 1979—83; chief legal counsel Speedy Muffler King, Deerfield, 1978-79; v.p. Commerce Title Co., Houston, 1983-85; exec. v.p. Charter Title Co., Houston, 1986—; ptnr. Jacobus & Melamed PC, Houston, 1988-97; shareholder Jenkens & Gilchrist, Houston, 1998-99; pvt. practice Bellaire, Tex., 1999—. Adv. dir. Prosperity Bank, Houston; adj. faculty Tex. A&M U., 1986-90; adj. prof. U. Houston Law Ctr., Houston C.C., Champions Sch. Real Estate; course dir. State Bar Tex., 1990; chmn. Tex. Land Title Inst., 2001; mem. broker-lawyer com. Tex. Real Estate Commn. Author: Real Estate Law, 2d edit., 1996, Texas Real Estate Law, 9th edit., 2004; co-author: Mastering Real Estate Titles and Title Insurance in Texas, 1996, Georgia Real Estate, 1995, Ohio Real Estate, 2d edit., 1990, Calif. Real Estate, 1989, Keeping Current with Texas Real Estate, updated annually, Real Estate Principles, 9th edit., 2005, Real Estate, An Introduction to the Profession, 9th edit., 2005, Texas Title Insurance, updated annually, Texas Real Estate Brokerage and the Law of Agency, 2006; co-author: Real Estate Brokerage Law and Practice; editor: Building Blocks of a Commercial Transaction, 1992, Building Blocks of a Residential Real Estate Transaction, 1994, Texas Real Estate Law Deskbook, 1995; editor-in-chief Tex. Forms Manual. Chmn. Planning and Zoning Commn., Bellaire, Tex., 1976-77; bd. dirs. Tax Increment Fin. Dist., Bellaire, 1984-91; chmn. task force on edn. Tex. Real Estate Commn.; chmn. profl. adv. com. dept. urban and regional planning Tex. A&M U., 1988-89; 1st asst. scoutmaster Boy Scout World Jamboree, Holland, 1995, scoutmaster, Chile, 1999; scoutmaster Nat. Boy Scout Jamboree, 1997, 1st asst. scoutmaster, 2001; mayor City of Bellaire, 1998-2000; sec.-treas. Harris County Mayors and Coun. Assn. 1999. Recipient Peggy Hayes Tchg. Excellence award TLTA, 1993, Don Roose award of excellence in real estate edn., 2001. Mem. ABA (acquisitions editor books and pubs. com. 1994-2001, chmn. brokers and brokerage com. 1986-93), Internat. Wine Food Soc. (host Houston chpt. 1993-94), Am. Coll. Real Estate Lawyers, Tex. Land Title Assn. (chmn. forms manual com., TREC earnest money contract task force), State Bar Tex. (mem. coun. of real estate, probate and trust law sect. 2002-06, chmn. title ins. com., mem. Tex. Real Estate Commn. broker-lawyer com. 2005—), Tex. Real Estate Tchrs. Assn. (Outstanding Real Estate Educator 1986, treas. 2007), Houston Real Estate Lawyers Coun., Real Estate Educator's Assn. (pres. 1987-88, Real Estate Educator of Yr. 1986, 2000, Disting. Career award 2004), Houston Bar Assn. (chmn. real estate sect. 1987-88), Internat. Wine and Food Soc. (bd. dirs.), South Ctrl. Educator's Group (pres. 2000-02, treas. 2007), Bellaire/S.W. Houston C. of C. (Outstanding Businessman of Yr. 1990, chmn. Tex. Real Estate Commns. Edn. Task Force, 1999-2000), U. Tex. Mortgage Lending Inst. (faculty), U. Houston Law Alumni Assn. (bd. dirs. 1999-2005), Les Amis Escoffier. Republican. Roman Catholic. Home: 5223 Pine St Bellaire TX 77401-4820 Office: Ste 615 6750 West Loop S Bellaire TX 77401-4525 Office Phone: 713-839-8800. E-mail: jacobusbellaire@aol.com.

JACOBUS, MARY, publishing executive; b. 1957; m. Dean Jacobus; 3 children. BA in English, Le Moyne Coll., Syracuse, NY, 1979. With Buffalo News, NY, Buffalo Courier Express, NY, Long Beach Press-Telegram, NY, 1981—89; dir. sales & mktg. Escondido Times Adv., Calif., 1989—95; v.p. sales & mktg. Colorado Springs Gazette, 1995—98; pres., pub. News Tribune, Duluth, Minn., 1998—2001; pub. News-Sentinel, Ft. Wayne, Ind., 2001—05; CEO Ft. Wayne Newspapers, Inc., Ft. Wayne, Ind., 2001—05; pres., gen. mgr. Boston Globe, 2006; pres., COO Regional Media Group NY Times Co., 2006—. Office: NY Times Regional Media Group 2202 N Westshore Blvd Ste 370 Tampa FL 33607

JACOBY, ERIKA, social worker; b. Miskolc, Hungary, May 1, 1928; came to U.S. 1949; d. Jeno and Malvina (Salamonovits) Engel; m. Emil Jacoby, Sept. 24, 1950; children: Jonathan, Benjamin, Michael. BA, Calif. State U., Northridge, 1971; MSW, U. So. Calif., LA, 1975. LCSW Calif., bd. cert. diplomate in clin. social work. Tchr. Adat Ari El Religious Sch., North Hollywood, Calif., 1961-73; tchr./counselor Camp Ramah, Ojai, Calif., summers 1961-72; clin. social worker Family Svc. of L.A., Van Nuys, 1975-80; psychiatric social worker Kaiser Psychiatry, Van Nuys, 1980—97; pvt. practice Valley Village, Calif., 1975—; ret., 1997. Lectr. in field; conductor workshops in field. Author: I Held the Sun In My Hands, 2004; contbr. articles to profl. jours. Mem. Nat. Assn. Social Workers, Common Cause, Hadassah, Amnesty Internat., Adat Ari El. Democrat. Jewish. Avocations: reading, biking, music, arts. Office Phone: 818-505-1658.

JACOBY, HENRY DONNAN, economist, educator; b. Dallas, June 25, 1935; s. Henry Harris and Margaret Cameron (Miller) J.; m. Martha Hughes Jacoby, Apr. 4, 1959; children— Daniel Donnan, Caroline Hughes. BS in Mech. Engring, U. Tex., Austin, 1957; PhD in Econ, Harvard U., 1967. Systems analyst Tudor Engring. Co., San Francisco, 1959-61; economist Harvard Devel. Adv. Service, Argentina Project, 1963-65; asst. prof. dept. econs. Harvard U., Cambridge, Mass., 1965-69; assoc. prof. polit. economy John F. Kennedy Sch. Govt., 1969-73; prof. mgmt. MIT, Cambridge, 1973—, William. F. Pounds prof. mgmt., 1991—2001, chmn. faculty, 1988-91; dir. global change program, 1991—; dir. Center for Energy Policy Research, 1978-83; vis. scholar London Bus. Sch., 1983-84. Chmn. Mass. Gov.'s Emergy Energy Tech. Adv. Com., 1973-74; mem. Nat. Petroleum Coun., 1975-83 Author: (with F.S. Brooman) Macroeconomics, 1970, (with R. Dorfman and H.A. Thomas, Jr.) Models for Managing Regional Water Quality, 1973, (with J.D. Steinbruner) Clearing The Air, 1973, Analysis of Investment in Electric Power, 1979, (with R. deLucia) Energy Planning for Developing Countries, 1982, (with R.L. Gordon and M.B. Zimmerman) Energy: Markets and Regulation, 1987 Served with USN, 1957-59 Mem. Am. Econ. Assn., Tau Beta Pi. Democrat. Episcopalian. Office: MIT Sloan Sch of Mgmt E40-439 50 Memorial Dr Cambridge MA 02139 Business E-Mail: hjacoby@mit.edu.

JACOBY, IRVING, physician; b. NYC, Sept. 30, 1947; s. Philip Aaron and Sylvia Jacoby; m. Sara Kay Vartanian; children: James Tyler, Kathryn Aaryn. BS magna cum laude, U. Miami, Coral Gables, Fla., 1969; MD, Johns Hopkins U., 1973. Diplomate Am. Bd. Internal Medicine, Am. Bd. Infectious Diseases, Am. Bd. Emergency Medicine, Am. Bd. Preventive Medicine (undersea and hyperbaric medicine). Intern Boston City Hosp., 1973-74, resident in medicine, 1974-75, chief resident, 1978-79; resident in medicine Peter Bent Brigham Hosp., Boston, 1975-76, fellow in infectious diseases, 1976-78; asst. dir. emergency med. svcs. U. Mass. Med. Ctr., Worcester, 1979-84; asst. dir. dept. emergency med. San Diego (Calif.) Med. Ctr. U. Calif., 1984—, assoc. prof. med. surgery San Diego (Calif.) Med. Ctr., 1988-94, hosp. dir. for emergency preparedness and response San Diego (Calif.) Med. Ctr., 2003—, prof. med. surgery San Diego (Calif.) Med. Ctr., 1994—, disaster control officer San Diego (Calif.) Med. Ctr., 1985—. Assoc. dir. Hyperbaric Med. Ctr., 1985—; vis. physician, cons. infectious diseases Soroka Med. Ctr., Ben Gurion U., Beer-Sheva, Israel, 1980; flight physician New Eng. Life Flight, Worcester, 1982-84, Life Flight Aeromed. Program U. Calif., 1984-87. Sect. editor for disaster medicine Jour. Emergency Medicine, 1996—; assoc. editor Undersea and Hyperbaric Medicine, 1996-2002. Comdr. Disaster Med. Assistance Team CA-4, 1991-. Fellow ACP, Am. Coll. Emergency Physicians; mem. Am. Soc. Microbiology, Infectious Diseases Soc. Am., Nat. Assn. Disaster Med. Assistance Teams (vice chair 1999, chmn. 2000-01), Soc. Acad. Emergency Medicine, Undersea and Hyperbaric Med. Soc., World Assn. for Disaster and Emergency Medicine, Disaster Emergency Response Assn., Johns Hopkins Med. and Surg. Assn., Iron Arrow Leadership Soc., Omicron Delta Kappa, Phi Kappa Phi, Alpha Epsilon Delta, Phi Eta Sigma. Office: U Calif Med Ctr 200 W Arbor Dr San Diego CA 92103-8676 Office Phone: 619-543-6216.

JACOBY, JACOB, consumer psychology educator; b. Bklyn., Feb. 17, 1940; s. David and Frances (Berman) Jacoby; m. Francine Crystal Jacoby (div.); children: Robin Ann, Jonathan Scott; m. Renée Berkowitz; 1 child, Dana Eve. BA, Bklyn. Coll., 1961, MS, 1963; PhD, Mich. State U., 1966. Prof. consumer behavior Purdue U., West Lafayette, Ind., 1968-81, NYU, 1981—. Cons. DuPont, Gen. Electric Co., Gen. Motors. Co., Am. Assn. Adv. Agys., Procter and Gamble, Standard Oil, U.S. Senate, FTC, FDA, others Author: Brand Loyalty, 1978, Miscomprehension of Televised Communication, 1980, The Comprehension and Miscomprehension of Print Communications, 1987. Served to 1st lt. USAF, 1965-68 Recipient Outstanding Contbn. to Advt. award Am. Acad. Advt., 1991, Disting. Sci. Contbn. award Soc. for Consumer Psychology, 1996. Fellow APA (pres. divsn. 23 1973-74, Disting. Sci. Rsch. award 1995), Assn. for Consumer Rsch. (pres. 1975); mem. Am. Mktg. Assn. (H.H. Maynard award 1978), Am. Assn. Pub. Opinion Rsch., Advt. Ednl. Found. (bd. dirs.). Jewish. Office: NYU 40 W 4th St New York NY 10012-1106 Office Phone: 212-769-2700. E-mail: jj@jjri.com.

JACOBY, JEFF, journalist, commentator; b. Cleve., Feb. 10, 1959; s. Mark and Arlene Fay (Winograd) J. Student, Hebrew U., Jerusalem, 1977; BA with distinction, George Washington U., 1979; JD cum laude, Boston U. Law Sch., 1983. Bar: Ohio 1983. Atty. Baker and Hostetler, Cleve., 1983-84; exec. dir. Mass. Civic Interest Coun., Boston, 1984-85; asst. to pres. Boston U., 1985-87; chief editorial writer Boston Herald, 1987-94; op-ed columnist Boston Globe, 1994—. Columnist Lowell (Mass.) Sun, 1985-86; polit. analyst Sta. WBUR-FM Nat. Pub. Radio, Boston, 1987—; talk show host Sta. WBZ, Boston, 1990-93; commentator Opinion Page, Monitor Channel, Boston, 1991-92; program host Talk of New Eng., New Eng. Cable News, 1992-96; panelist, WCBB-TV, Five on Five; syndicated columnist, NY Times. Bd. dir. The Concord Review. Exec. com. Cuyahoga County Rep. Party, Cleve., 1983-84; dep. campaign mgr. Ray Shamie for U.S. Senate, Boston, 1984; overseere Huntington Theatre Co. Recipient Breindel award for Excellence in Opinion Journalism, 1999. Jewish. Office: Boston Globe 135 Morrissey Blvd Boston MA 02125-3338 Mailing: PO Box 55819 Boston MA 02205

JACOBY, JOHN PATRICK, lawyer; b. Chgo., Dec. 29, 1957; s. James William and Rose Elizabeth Jacoby; m. Diane G. Gilbert, Oct. 29, 1994; children: Renee Grace, Kyra Jade. BS cum laude, Northwest Mo. State U., 1982; JD, Wash. U. Sch. Law, 1987. Bar: Mo. 1987, Ill. 1988, U.S. Dist. Ct., east. dist., Mo. 1987, U.S. Dist. Ct., so. dist., Ill. 1988, U.S. Dist. Ct., no. dist., Ill. 1994. Atty. Sandberg, Phoenix & Von Gontard, St. Louis, 1987—92; ptnr. Pappas, Jacoby & Marcus, Chgo., 1993—2006, McDonald Hopkins, LLC, 2006—. Lectr. How to Negotiate a Case in Civil Litigation Ill. Inst. on Continuing Legal Edn., 2002—, lectr. Taking The Deposition of the IME Physician, 2007. Pres. Bicycle Homeowner's Assn., Chgo., 1998—2002; chmn. fin. com., mem. sch. bd. South Loop Sch., Chgo., 2002—; treas. Prairie Dist. Owner's Assn., Chgo., 2003—; CEO Friends and Family of South Loop Sch., Inc.; bd. dirs. Idlewind Country Club, 2007—. Recipient Am. Jurisprudence award, Am. Jurisprudence Soc., 1986. Mem.: ATLA, ABA, Def. Rsch. Inst., Chgo. Bar Assn. Avocation: golf. Office: McDonald Hopkins 640 N La Salle St Ste 590 Chicago IL 60610 Office Phone: 312-280-0111. Office Fax: 312-280-8236. Business E-Mail: jjacoby@mcdonaldhopkins.com.

JACOBY, LOWELL EDWIN (JAKE JACOBY), information technology executive, retired military officer; b. Aug. 28, 1945; m. Celia L. Williams, Dec. 9, 1975. Grad., Aviation Officer Cand. Sch., 1969; student, Navy Postgrad. Sch., 1975; BS in Econs., U. Md.; M in Nat. Security Affairs, Naval Postgrad. Sch. Commd. ensign USN, 1969, advanced through grades to rear admiral, 1997, ret., 2005; with fighter sq. 24 USS Hancock (CV-19); intelligence officer seventh fleet detachment Charlie RVN Saigon; intelligence watchstander, briefing officer, 1973-75; intelligence placement officer, jr. officer assignment officer Naval Mil. Personnel Command, 1979-81; head naval ops. br. Navy Field Operational Intelligence Office, dir. Naval Surveillance Info. Ctr.; adminstrv. asst. to dir. naval intelligence, 1983; head, chief naval ops. intelligence plot, 1983; asst. chief of staff, intelligence carrier group eight USS South Carolina, North Atlantic, 1985, USS Nimitz Battle Group, Mediterranean; N2 NATO striking fleet Atlantic, J2 CJTF 120, CJTF 140; head intelligence assignments, placement br. Washington, 1989-90; asst. chief of staff intelligence for comdr. in chief U.S. Pacific fleet, 1990-92; commdg. officer Joint Intelligence Ctr. Pacific, 1992-94; dir. intelligence U.S. Pacific Command, 1994-97; dir. Naval Intelligence; comdr. Office Naval Intelligence, 1997-99; dir. Joint Staff J-2 The Pentagon, Washington, 1999—2002; acting dir. Def. Intelligence Agy., Washington, 2002, dir., 2002—05; exec. v.p. for strategic intelligence opportunities CACI Internat. Inc., Arlington, Va., 2006—. Decorated Def. Disting. Svc. medal, Navy Disting. Svc. medal, Def. Superior Svc. medal, 3 Meritorious Svc. medals, 2 Legion of Merit medals, 2 Navy Commendation medals, Navy Achievement medal, Nat. Intelligence Medal for Achievement Dir. Ctr. Intelligence, Australian Chief of Def. Commendation. Office: CACI Internat 1100 N Glebe Rd Arlington VA 22201

JACOBY, NEIL HERMAN, JR., astronautical scientist, engineer, consultant; b. Chgo., Oct. 20, 1940; s. Neil Herman and Clair (Gruhn) J. BA in Astronomy, UCLA, 1965, MS in Engring., 1969. Sci. guide Griffith Obs., LA, summer 1962; comuter program cons. UCLA Western Data Processing Ctr., 1966-67; tchg. asst. in astrodynamics UCLA Sch. Engring. and Applied Sci., summer 1968; staff scientist Computer Scis. Corp., LA, 1972-76; sys. analyst Sys. Devel. corp., Santa Monica, Calif., 1977-81; cons. in astrodynamics, astronautics LA, 1981—. Ind. property mgr., LA, 1979—. Contbr. articles to sci. and profl. jours. Named Internat. Scientist of Yr., Internat. Biog. Ctr., 2004, Genius Laureate, 2005; recipient Internat. Diploma of Honor Am. Order of Excellence, 500 founders of the 21st Century. Mem. AIAA, AAAS, Am. Astronautical Soc. (sr.), NY Acad. Sci., Planetary Soc., Alpha Gamma Sigma. Achievements include development of time series for rapid and accurate missile trajectory determination; an original solution to determine predictions of closest approaches of near earth objects; a numerical integration method for predicting orbits of potentially hazardous asteroids, including perturbations of all planets in our solar system; novel, accurate methods for interplanetary space travel; a novel method of non-co-planer orbital transfer for a geocentric satellite; determined that 5 observations are better than 3 observations for low to moderate eccentricities of heliocentric orbits; but 3 observations are better than 5 for optimal orbit determination for very high eccentric orbits of comets. Home and Office: 1434 Midvale Ave Los Angeles CA 90024-5406 Personal E-mail: neiljacoby@yahoo.com.

JACOBY, ROBERT HAROLD, management consulting executive; b. NYC, June 9, 1942; s. Harold and Ruth (Johnson) J. BA in Econs., Dartmouth Coll., 1964; MA in Polit. Philosophy, Columbia U., 1998, MPhil, 2001. Cert. mgmt. cons. Prin. Albert Ramond & Assocs. Inc., Chgo., 1968-75; pres. Systemetrics Internat. Inc., Indpls., 1975-77; v.p. Theodore Barry & Assocs., London, 1977-82; ptnr. Deloitte & Touche, NYC, 1982—85; pres. R.H. Jacoby & Assocs. Inc., NYC, 1985—. Contbr. articles to profl. jours. Mem. Acad. Mgmt., Am. Econ. Assn., Nat. Assn. Corp. Dirs., Am. Gas Assn., Strategic Mgmt. Soc., Am. Arbitration Assn. (comml. arbitrator 1982—), The Strategic Leadership Forum. Office: RH Jacoby & Assoc Inc 355 South End Ave New York NY 10280-1005 Office Phone: 212-321-2494.

JACOBY, WILLIAM JEROME, JR., internist, retired military officer; b. Mt. Carmel, Pa., Aug. 9, 1925; s. William Jerome and Florence Marie Jacoby; m. Joeann J. Powroznick, May 5, 1956; children: William Jerome, Teresa Marie. AB, Emory U., 1946; MD, Jefferson Med. Coll., 1950. Diplomate Am. Bd. Internal Medicine. Commd. lt. (j.g.) M.C., USN, 1950, advanced through grades to rear adm., 1972; intern Jefferson Med. Coll. Hosp., Phila., 1950-51, resident in internal medicine, 1951-52, 55-56; Am. Heart Assn. fellow, 1956-57; chmn. dept. medicine U.S. Naval Hosps. Gt. Lakes, Ill., 1964-69, Phila., 1969-72; chmn. dept. medicine, dir. edn. and rsch. Nat. Naval Med. Ctr., Bethesda, Md., 1972-75; comdg. officer Naval Regional Med. Ctr., Portsmouth, Va., 1975-78; dir. med. svcs. VA Cen. Office, Washington, 1978-80, dep. chief med. dir., 1980-83. Assoc. clin. prof. Jefferson Med. Coll., 1969—; prof. medicine George Washington U. Med. Sch., 1972, Eastern Va. Sch. Medicine, Norfolk, 1976-78; mem. adv. coun. Nat. Heart, Lung and Blood Inst., NIH, 1972-75. Contbr. articles to profl. jours. Decorated Legion of Merit, Meritorious Svc. medal. Fellow ACP (Laureate award 1996); mem. Assn. Mil. Surgeons (Founders medal 1974), Alpha Omega Alpha, Phi Beta Pi. Roman Catholic. Home: 737 E Tazewells Way Williamsburg VA 23185-6521

JACOBY HURD, JENNIFER, foundation administrator; b. 1972; m. Timothy Marc Hurd, July 2002. B in Polit. Sci., Princeton U.; M in Pub. Policy, Harvard U. Strategy cons. Bain & Co., Wilkerson Grp.; exec. dir. Arie and Ida Crown Meml., Chgo. Office: Arie and Ida Crown Memorial 222 N LaSalle St Ste 2000 Chicago IL 60601-1109 Office Phone: 312-750-6671. Office Fax: 312-984-1499.*

JACOBY HURD, JENNIFER BETH, not-for-profit executive; b. 1971; d. Mark A. Jacoby; m. Timothy Marc Hurd, July 2002. BS in Polit. Sci., summa cum laude, Princeton Univ.; MPP, Harvard Univ. Strategy consul. Bain & Co., Wilkerson Group; exec. dir. Arie and Ida Crown Meml., 2001—. Named one of 40 Under Forty, Crain's Bus. Chgo., 2005. Office: Arie and Ida Crown Meml Ste 2000 222 N LaSalle St Chicago IL 60601 Office Phone: 312-236-6300. Office Fax: 312-984-1499.*

JACONETTY, THOMAS ANTHONY, lawyer; b. Chgo., May 21, 1953; s. George Bernard and Mary Jane (Sgarioto) J.; m. Judith Hamill; 1 child, Nicole Alicia. AB in History and Polit. Sci. summa cum laude with honors, Loyola U., Chgo., 1975; JD, Northwestern U., 1978. Bar: Ill. 1978, U.S. Dist. Ct. (no. dist.) Ill. 1978, U.S. Ct. Appeals (7th cir.) 1979; cert. rev. appraiser, valuation cons. Adminstrv. asst. Chgo. Dept. Aviation, 1979; asst. corp. counsel Chgo. Dept. Law, 1980; asst. to commr. Cook County Bd. Tax Appeals, Chgo., 1981-83, dep. commr., 1983-87, commr., 1988-89, chief dep. commr., 1989—2006, 1st asst. commr., 2007—; sole practice Chgo. Lectr. Ill. Inst. Continuing Legal Edn.; lectr. and presenter Lorman Edn. Svcs., Lincoln Inst. Land Policy, Internat. Assn. Assessing Officers, Chgo. Chpt. Appraisal Inst., Commerce Clearing House Ill. State Tax Reports Nat. Bus. Inst., Nat. Assn. State and Local Equity Funds, NAHB Multi-Family Housing Credit Group, Inst. Profl. Taxation, Wichita Tax Program. Asst. editor, indexer: Corwin on the Constitution, 1981; author book chpts.; editor: Issues Confronting Properties Affected by Contamination or Environmental Problems, 2002, Valuation of Subsidized Housing,

2003, Illinois Institute Continuing Legal Education, State and Local Taxation, 2004; contbr. articles to profl. jours., property tax policies and adminstr. practices, Can., U.S., 2000. Mem. Cook County Dem. Orgn.; pres., bd. dir. Polish and Am. Citizens Club, 1981—; pres. Italian Am. Cath. Assn., Chgo., 1981—; mem. Old Timers' Baseball Assn., Art Inst. Chgo., Channel 11-PBS, Mus. Sci. and Industry, Ill. Spl. Olympics, Nat. Trust Hist. Preservation, Libr. of Congress, Ill. Alzheimer's Assn., Civic Fedn. Tax Com.; mem. planning com. Nat. Conf. State Tax Judges, 1999—, chair 2002-04; mem. athletic bd. St. Eugene Sch., 2005-06; judge Northwestern U. Moot Ct. and Chgo. Metro History Fair. Named Lawrence Lasser Tax Judge of Yr., Nat. Conf. State Tax Judges, 2005. Mem. ABA, Ill. Bar Assn. (mem. assembly 1988-91, 92-94, state and local taxation sect. coun. and several subcoms., chmn. 1994-95, vice chmn. 1993-94, ad hoc and 4 separate civic fedn. and mayoral coms. on property tax reform, 1994-96, 2000-2001, 05-06), Chgo. Bar Assn. (chmn. election law com., Ill. gov. transition com. 2002), Internat. Assn. Assessing Officers (arbitrator cir. ct. Cook County, 1990-97, various sects., legal coms., chmn. nat. legal com. 1995-2002, 04-06, property tax reform com. 2005-06, children's Christmas party 2004, Donohoo Essay award, 1996, presdl. citations and spl. svc. award, 2002, twice-nominated Barnard award, Charles Plichta Meml. award, 2005, Clifford Allen Most Valuable Mem. award 2006), Justinian Soc. Italian Lawyers, Northwestern Law Sch. Alumni Assn., Loyola U. Alumni Assn., Pi Sigma Alpha, Alpha Sigma Nu. Avocations: travel, reading. Office: Cook County Bd of Review 118 N Clark St Ste 601 Chicago IL 60602-1311 Office Phone: 312-603-5562.

JACONO, ANDREW A., Plastic Surgeon; MD Otorhinolaryngology, Albert Einstein Coll. of Medcine, NYC. Cert. American Bd. of Facial Plastic and Reconstructive Surgery. Intern St. Vincent's Hosp. and Med. Ctr., New York City; surgical resident New York Eye and Ear Infirmary, New York City, chief adminstr. resident. Sect. head facial plastic reconstructive surgery North Shore U. Hosp., Manhasset, NY. Author: (medical lit.) topics including minimal incision eyelid surgery, endoscopic (telescopic) minimally invasive brow lifting, endoscopic midface and face lifting surgery, rhinoplasty and revision rhinoplasty, lip augmentation, orbital reconstruction. Volunteer surgeon Beyond Our Borders; chair About Face: Making Changes, 2003—06. Recipient William H. Turner, excellence in surgical and patient care skills, Ten Leaders in Plastic Surgery in Long Island, The New York Times, One of America's Top Physicians, The Consumer Rsch. Coun. of America, 2005, Good Guy, Ctr. for the Women of New York, 2006; fellow American Academy of Facial Plastic and Reconstructive Surgery, American Coll. of Surgeons. Achievements include He is one of a small group of surgeons that has achieved Dual Board Certifiction in Facial Plastic and Reconstructive Surgery as well as Head and Neck Surgery; has appeared on ABC's Good Morning America, Inside Edition, CNN, CNBC and WB 11 News and he has conducted radio interviews on NPR, 1010 Wins and WCBS Radio. Office: NY Ctr for Facial Plastic and Laser Surgery 900 Northern Blvd Great Neck NY 11020 Office Phone: 516-773-4646.

JACOUD, ADRIANA, art director; Creative dir. Brady Comm., Pitts.; art. dir. CITY Mag., NYC; sr. designer TenUnited, Pitts., 2007—. Bd. dir., Pitts. chpt. Am. Inst. Graphic Arts. Recipient Nat. Mag. award for Photo Portfolio, CITY Mag., Am. Soc. Mag. Editors, 2007. Office: TenUnited 4 Gateway Ctr Pittsburgh PA 15222 E-mail: ajacoud@summa-tech.com.*

JACOVER, JEROLD ALAN, lawyer; b. Chgo., Mar. 20, 1945; s. David Louis and Beverly (Funk) J.; m. Judith Lee Greenwald, June 28, 1970; children: Aric Seth, Evan Michael, Brian Ethan. BSEE, U. Wis., 1967; JD, Georgetown U., 1972. Bar: Ohio 1972, Ill. 1973, U.S. Ct. Appeals (7th cir.) 1974, U.S. Ct. Appeals (Fed. cir.) 1983. Atty. Ralph Nader, Columbus, Ohio, 1972-73, Brinks Hofer, Gilson & Lione, Chgo., 1973—, shareholder, 1977—, pres., 2000—06. Mem. ABA, Am. Intellectual Property Law Assn. (bd. dirs. 1994-98), Decalogue Soc. Lawyers, Intellectual Property Law Assn. Chgo. (bd. dirs. 1993-94, 98-99, pres. 2000), Intellectual Property Law Assn. Chgo. Ednl. Found. (pres. 1990-93), Am. Techion Soc. (pres. 1994-97). Office: Brinks Hofer Gilson & Lione Ste 3600 455 N Cityfront Plaza Dr Chicago IL 60611-5599 E-mail: jjacover@brinkshofer.com.

JACOX, MARILYN ESTHER, chemist; b. Utica, NY, Apr. 26, 1929; d. Grant Burlingame and Mary Elizabeth (Dunn) J. BA, Syracuse U., 1951; PhD, Cornell U., 1956; ScD (hon.), Syracuse U., 1993, U. Waterloo, 2006. Postdoctoral rsch. assoc. U. NC, Chapel Hill, NC, 1956-58; fellow in fundamental rsch. Mellon Inst., Pitts., 1958-62; rsch. chemist Nat. Bur. Std., Washington, 1962—; fellow Nat. Bur. Std. (now Nat. Inst. Std. and Tech.), Gaithersburg, Md., 1986-95, sci. emeritus, 1996—. Mem. editl. bd. Revs. Chem. Intermediates, 1984-89, Jour. Chem. Physics, 1989-91; contbr. numerous articles to profl. jours. Recipient gold medal U.S. Dept. Commerce, 1970, Fed. Women's award, 1973, Lippincott award, 1989, Hillebrand prize Chem. Soc. Washington, 1990, WISE lifetime achievement award, 1991, E. Bright Wilson award in Spectroscopy, Am. Chem. Soc., 2003, George C. Pimentel award advances in matrix isolation spectroscopy, 2005. Fellow AAAS, Am. Phys. Soc., Washington Acad. Scis. (Phys. Sci. award 1968, Disting. Sci. Career award 2007); mem. Am. Chem. Soc. (bd. mgrs. Chem. Soc. Wash. Sect. 2005—), Exec. Women in Govt. (sec. 1981, vice-chmn. 1982), Inter-Am. Photochem. Soc. (exec. com. 1978-79), Sigma Xi (pres. NBS chpt. 1988-89). Office: Nat Inst Standards & Tech Optical Technology Division Gaithersburg MD 20899-8441 Home Phone: 301-948-5047; Office Phone: 301-975-2547. E-mail: marilyn.jacox@nist.gov.

JACQUES, JOSEPH WILLIAM, investment advisor; b. Stroudsburg, Pa., Sept. 26, 1953; s. Joseph Francis and Millie C. (Dave) J.; m. Joy Lynn Turner, Dec. 28, 1974; children: Jeffrey, Justin, Joelle, Jeremy. AA in Acctg., Northampton Community Coll., 1973; BS in Acctg., Bloomsburg U., 1974. CPA, Md.; registerd fin. planner master, Md., investment advisor, Md. Auditor U.S. Gen. Acctg. Office, Washington, 1975-82; pres. Coord. Fin. Svcs., Ltd., Bethesda, Md., 1982-84, Joseph W. Jacques, CPA, PA, Rockville, Md., 1985—. Registered rep. Jacques Fin., LLC, 1990—. Contbr. articles to profl. jours. Pres. Avery Forest Homeowners Assn., Rockville, 1989-90. Mem. Nat. Assn. Life Underwriters, Internat. Assn. Registered Fin. Planners, Internat. Assn. Fin. Planners, Md. Assn. CPA's. Republican. Roman Catholic. Avocations: tennis, golf, children. Home and Office: 15430 Avery Rd Rockville MD 20855-1711 Home Phone: 301-340-6340; Office Phone: 301-738-1303. Business E-Mail: joe@joejacquescpa.com.

JACQUESSON, ALAIN L., librarian; b. Geneva, Nov. 3, 1946; s. Guy and Elisabeth (Giddey) J.; m. Marie-Jose Chanez, Feb. 8, 1975; children: Severine, Mathieu. Responsable Ecole de bibliothecaires, Geneva, 1978—81; project chief U. Geneva, 1981—88; dir. Bibliothèques Municipales, Geneva, 1988—93, Bibliothèque Publique et Universitaire, Geneva, 1993—. Mem. ALA, Assn. Swiss Librs., Assn. French Librs., Am. Soc. Info. Sci. Office: Bibliotheque Publique Univ Parc des Bastions 1211 Geneva 4 Switzerland Home Phone: (022) 751 20 63; Office Phone: (022) 418-2800. Fax: (022) 418-28-01. Personal E-mail: alain.jacquesson@ville-ge.ch.

JACQUETTE, YVONNE HELENE, artist; b. Pitts., Dec. 15, 1934; Student, R.I. Sch. Design, 1952-56; studies with John Frazier, Robert Hamilton, Herman Cherry, Robert Roche. Instr. Moore Coll. Art, Phila., 1972; instr. painting, vis. artist U. Pa., 1972-76, 79-82, instr. Grad. Sch. Fine Arts, 1979-84; instr. Parsons Sch. Design, 1975-78; instr. painting Pa. Acad. Fine Arts Grad. Sch., 1991—. Vis. artist Nova Scotia Coll. Art, 1974; artist in residence Harvard U., 1995; represented by DC Moore Gallery, N.Y.C., Mary Ryan Gallery (Prints) N.Y.C.; instr. in field. One-woman shows include St. Louis Art Mus., 1983-84, Berggruen Gallery, San Francisco, 1984, Yuracho Seibu-Takanawa Art, Tokyo, 1985, Brooke Alexander Inc., 10 shows 1974-88, 90, 92, 95, NY Mus. Art, Bowdoin Coll. Mus. Art, Maine, 1986, D.C. Moore Gallery, 1997, 00, 03, 06, Mary Ryan Gallery, 1997, Huntington (W.Va.) Mus., 1997, Mention: Retrospective, Cantor Arts Ctr., Stanford (Calif.) U., 2002, Colby Coll. Mus., Waterville, Maine, 2002, Utah Mus., Salt Lake City, 2002, Hudson River Mus., Yonkers, NY, 2003, Arrivals and Departures; 2-person show Mary Ryan Gallery, 1997; exhibited at Rutgers U. Art Gallery, 1972, Whitney Mus. Art, 1972, NY Cultural Ctr. and U.S. Travelling Show, 1972-73, Internat. Biennial, Tokyo, 1974, Art Inst. Chgo., 1975, Mus. Modern Art, NY, 1981-82, Weatherspoon Gallery, NC, Met. Mus. Art, Mus. Modern Art, Whitney Mus. Am. Art, NY, Colby Coll. Mus., Libr. Congress, Washington, Staatliche Mus., Berlin, Carnegie Inst. Mus. Art, Pitts., Am. Acad. Inst. Arts and Letters, NY; represented in permanent collections at North Cen. Bronx Hosp., Horace Mann Sch., Riverdale, NY, Fed. Bldg. and Post Office, Bangor Maine; prints commissioned by Provincetown Fine Arts Workcenter, 1992, Zimmerli Mus. Rutgers, 1993, Bus. Com. for the Arts, 1994, Cleve. Print Club, 1999; illustrator Country Rush, Adventures in Poetry, 1982, Aerial, Eyelight Press, 1981, Fast Lanes, 1984, (with Maureen Owen) Erosion's Pull, 2004; film (with Rudy Burckhardt) Night Fantasies, 1992; set designer Sch. Hardknocks, Dance Theatre Workshop, NYC and nat. tour, 1989 Recipient Painting award, Am. Acad. Arts and Letters, 1990, Nat. Acad. Painters award, 1998, Print award, Nat. Acad., 1999; Guggenheim Meml. Found. grantee, 1997-98. Mem.: Am. Acad. Arts and Letters (Painting award 1990), Artists Equity Assn., Nat. Acad. (Painting award 1998, Print award 1999). Office: 50 W 29th St New York NY 10001-4227 Home Phone: 212-679-5519. Personal E-mail: yvonnejb@mymailstation.com.

JACZKO, GREGORY BELA, commissioner, physicist; b. 1970; BS, Cornell U.; Ph.D in Particle Physics, U. Wis.-Madison. Congressional sci. fellow, Office Rep. Edward Markey US Ho. Reps., Washington; appropriations dir. to Senator Harry Reid US Senate, Washington, 2001—05; commr. US Nuclear Regulatory Commn., Rockville, 2005—. Adj. prof. Georgetown U. Office: US Nuclear Regulatory Commn One White Flint N Bldg 11555 Rockville Pike Rm 18G1 Rockville MD 20852

JADVAR, HOSSEIN, nuclear medicine physician, biomedical engineer; b. Tehran, Iran, Apr. 6, 1961; arrived in U.S., 1978, naturalized, 1995; s. Ramezan Ali and Fatemeh (Afzal) Jadvar; m. Mojgan Maher, 1995; children: Donya S., Delara A. BS, Iowa State U., Ames, 1982; MS, U. Wis., Madison, 1984, U. Mich., Ann Arbor, 1986, PhD, 1988; MD, U. Chgo., 1993; MPH, Harvard U., Boston, 2005; MBA, U. So. Calif., LA, 2007; student, U. Cambridge, Eng., 2007. Diplomate Am. Bd. Nuc. Medicine, Bd. Nuc. Cardiology. Rsch. asst. dept. human oncology U. Wis., Madison, 1983-84; rsch. asst. dept. elec. engrng. U. Mich., Ann Arbor, 1984-88; sr. rsch. engr. Arzco Med. Electronics, Inc., Chgo., 1988-89; sr. rsch. assoc. Pritzker Inst., Ill. Inst. Tech., Chgo., 1989-92; med. intern U. Calif., San Francisco, 1993-94; resident in radiology Stanford (Calif.) U., 1994-96, resident in nuclear medicine, 1996-98, chief resident in nucelar medicine, 1997-98; clin. fellow in radiology (positron emission tomography) Harvard Med. Sch., Boston, 1998-99; asst. prof. radiology and biomed. engrng. U. So. Calif., LA, 1999—2005, assoc. prof. radiology and biomed. engrng., 2005—, dir. rsch. radiology, 2006—. Reviewer study sect. small bus innovative rsch. program NIH, 1989, med. imaging, 2005—; vis. assoc. bioengring. Calif. Inst. Tech., Pasadena, 2001—; fellow clin. effectiveness program Sch. Pub. Health Harvard U., Boston, 2003; mem. radioactive drug rsch. com. FDA, 2003—; faculty fellow Ctr. Excellence in Rsch. U. So. Calif., 2007—. Author (with J.A. Parker): Clinical PET and PET-CT, 2005; mem. editl. bd. Clinical Nuclear Medicine, 2007—; contbr. chapters to books, articles to profl. jours. Recipient Resident Rsch. award, NIH, 1994; grantee, Am. Cancer Soc., The Wright Found., NIH/Nat. Cancer Inst. Fellow: Am. Coll. Nuc. Medicine (faculty New Orleans 2000, faculty Tampa 2001, faculty Scottsdale 2002, faculty San Antonio 2006, sci. sessions co-chmn. 2008, bd. reps.), Am. Coll. Nuc. Physicians (bd. regents); mem.: IEEE (sr.), Soc. Molecular Imaging, LA Radiol. Soc. (faculty 2002, pres. nuc. medicine sect. 2007—), Calif. Med. Assn. (nuc. med. sci. com. 2002—05), Computers in Cardiology (local organizing com. 1990), Acad. Molecular Imaging (mem. editl. bd. Molecular Imaging and Biology 2004—), Soc. Nuc. Medicine (mem. editl. bd. Jour. Nuc. Medicine 2006—, mem. pub. and govt. rels. com., Tetalman Young Investigator award 2000, seed grant award 2000), Radiol. Soc. N.Am. (Resident Rsch. award 1997, seed grant award 2002), Eta Kappa Nu, Sigma Xi, Tau Beta Pi. Achievements include patents for for esophgeal catheters and method and apparatus for detection of posterior ischemia. Office: U So Calif Divsn Nuc Medicine Dept Radiology Keck Sch Medicine 2250 Alcazar St CSC Ste 102 Los Angeles CA 90033 Business E-Mail: jadvar@usc.edu.

JAEGER, AL (ALVIN A. JAEGER), state official; b. Beulah, ND, Dec. 10, 1943; m. Naomi Berg, 1969 (dec. 1979), m. Kathy Grangaard Anderson, 1986; children: Todd, Stacy, Heidi. AA, Bismarck State Coll., 1963; BS, Dickinson State U., 1966; postgraduate studies, U. ND, 1968, Mont. State U., 1970. Tchr. Killdeer HS, 1966-69, Kenmare HS, 1969-71; mktg. analyst Mobil Oil Corp., 1971-73; real estate broker, 1973-93; sec. state State of ND, 1993—. Active Charity Luth. Ch., 1966-72. Served in ND Army Nat. Guard, 1980. Named Realtor of Yr. Mem. Nat. Assn. Secs. State (exec. com., com. chmn.), Fargo-Moorhead Area Assn. Realtors (mem. coms. edn., profl. stds., bylaws, multiple listing svc.), ND Assn. Realtors (past chairperson state bylaws), Bismarck Kiwanis Club. Republican. Lutheran. Office: Office Sec of State Dept 108 600 E Boulevard Ave Bismarck ND 58505-0500 Office Phone: 701-328-2900. Business E-Mail: sos@nd.gov.

JAEGER, LESLIE GORDON, academic administrator; b. Southport, Eng., Jan. 28, 1926; s. Henry M. and Beatrice A. (Highton) J.; m. Annie Sylvia Dyson, Apr. 3, 1948; children: Valerie Ann, Hilary Frances.; m. Kathleen Grant, July 24, 1981. BA, Cambridge U., 1946, MA, 1950; PhD, London U., 1955, DSc, 1986; DEng (hon), Carlton U., 1991, Meml. U., 1994, Tech. U. of N.S., 1995; LLD (hon.), Dalhousie U., 2005. With W.P. Thompson & Co., Liverpool, England, 1948-50, Renold Ltd., Manchester, England, 1950-52; mem. faculty Univ. Coll. of Khartoum, 1952-56; Univ. lectr. Cambridge (Eng.) U., 1956-62; prof. civil engrng. and applied mechanics McGill U., Montreal, Que., Canada, 1962-64, 66-70; Regius prof. engrng. U. Edinburgh, Scotland, 1964-66; dean Coll. Engrng., U. N.B., Fredericton, 1970-75, acting v.p., 1972-73; acad. v.p. Acadia U., Wolfville, N.S., Canada, 1975-80; spl. asst. to pres. Tech. U. N.S., Halifax, 1980-85, v.p. rsch., 1986-93; emeritus rsch. prof. tech. U. N.S., 1993—. Cons. structural engrng. Expo '67, Rolls Royce Ltd., Adjeleian & Assos., Ottawa, and others. Author: (with A.W. Hendry) The Analysis of Grid Frameworks and Related Structures, 2nd edit, 1968, Elementary Theory of Elastic Plates, 1962, Cartesian Tensors in Engineering Science, 1964, (with B. Bakht) Bridge Analysis Simplified, 1985, (with B Bakht) Bridge Analysis by Micro Computing, 1988, (with A.A. Mufti and B. Bakht) Bridge Superstructures, New Developments, 1996; contbr. numerous rsch. papers to profl. jours. Mem. Cambridge City Coun., 1961-62; mem. Nat. Coun. Liberal Party U.K., 1960-62; fellow, mem. bd. govs. Magdalene Coll., Cambridge, 1959-62. With Royal Navy, 1945-48. Decorated Order of Can., 2002; recipient Telford premium Instn. Civil Engrs., 1959, Nat. Rsch. Coun. Can. rsch. grantee, 1962-92, A.B. Sanderson award Can. Soc. Civil Engring., 1983; Gzowski medal Engrng. Inst. Can., 1985, cert. of merit Indian Insts. of Engrs., 1989, Assoc. Profl. Engrs. N.S. Engring. award, 1992, P.L. Pratley award, 1993, Julian C. Smith medal Engrng. Insts. Can., 1996, Nova award Constrn. Innovation Forum, Mich., 2000. Fellow Royal Soc. Edinburgh, Can. Acad. Engrng., Engrng. Inst. Can., Can. Soc. for Civil Engrng. (pres. 1992-93, Host Leipholz medal 2007); mem. Assn. Profl. Engrs. N.S. (hon. life), Mason Club (N.S.). Office: Dalhousie Univ Dept Engineering Mathematics 1340 Barrington St Rm K205 Halifax NS Canada B3J 1Y9 Office Phone: 902-494-6029. Office Fax: 902-423-1801. E-mail: leslie.jaeger@ns.sympatico.ca.

JAEGER, PATSY ELAINE, retired secondary school educator, artist; b. Douglas, Ariz., Mar. 18, 1936; d. Thomas Conrad and Cora Maxine Forbes; m. John Walter Jaeger, Aug. 26, 1956 (div. Feb. 1984); children: Sherilee Jaeger Appleby, John Everett. BA in Fine Arts, Chapman U., Orange, Calif., 1961; MA in Art History, Calif. State U., LA, 1970; MA in Edn. Adminstrn., San Francisco State U., 1988. Life gen. secondary credential life gen. jr. h.s. spl. secondry credential, spl. secondary art credential, preliminary adminstrv. credential, Calif. Tchr. adult edn. oil painting Novato Unified Sch. Dis., 1973—78; tchr. art, chmn. fine arts dept. Torrance H.S., Calif., 1962-71; tchr. art and math., chmn. art dept. San Jose Jr. H.S., Novato, Calif., 1974—79; tchr. art and English, chmn. site coun. Hill Jr. H.S., Novato, 1979-83; tchr. English, San Marin H.S., Novato, 1983-95, leadership tchr., 1995-96, tchr. art, 1996-98; semi-ret., 1998; specialist tobacco use edn. Marin County Office Edn., 2000—03, ret., 2003—. Chmn. site rev. team Novato Unified Sch. Dist., 1981; specialist tobacco use edn. Marin County Office Edn., 2000-03. Set designer Cavalleria Rusticana, 1981; cover designer Dimensions III, 1987, Novato United Meth. Ch. Register, 2005; designer stained glass window Novato United Meth. Ch., 2006; contbr. articles to profl. jours. Coord. cmty. vol. program Hill Jr. H.S., 1981-83; chair worship Novato United Meth. Ch., 2005—; co-v.p. Novato United Meth. Women, 2005—; co-chair Lydia Cir. United Meth. Women, 2005-06. Recipient Pub. Svc. award U.S. Postal Svc., Torrance, 1968, Tchr. of Yr. award Parent-Tchr.-Student Assn. Hill Jr. H.S., 1983, Extra Step award Marin Spl. Edn. Adv. Com., 1996. Mem. Nat. Mus. Women in Arts (charter, co-chair 2005-07), Fine Arts Mus. San Francisco, Novato United Meth. Women (co-v.p. 2005-07, designer stained glass window, co-chmn. Lydia cir. 2005-07). Republican. Avocations: book illustration, painting, gardening, singing. Home: 40 Brown Dr Novato CA 94947-7404 Office Phone: 415-892-9896.

JAEGER, RICHARD CHARLES, electrical engineer, educator, science association director; b. NYC, Sept. 2, 1944; s. O. Fred and Mary Jane (Shatzer) J.; m. Joan Carol Hill, Dec. 28, 1964; children: Peter, Stephanie. BSEE with high honors, U. Fla., 1966, M in Elec. Engring., 1966, PhD in Elec. Engring., 1969. Staff engr. IBM Corp., Boca Raton, Fla., 1969—72, adv. engr., 1972-74, 77-79, rsch. staff Yorktown Heights, NY, 1974—76; assoc. prof. Auburn (Ala.) U., 1979—82, prof. elec. engring. dept., 1982—90, alumni prof., 1983—88, disting. prof., 1990—; dir. Ala. Microelectronics Ctr., Auburn, 1984—2000, interim dir. wireless engring., 2001—03. Program com. Internat. Solid State Circuits Conf., San Francisco and N.Y.C., 1978-93, program vice-chmn., 1992, program chmn., 1993; program co-chmn. Internat. VLSI Cirs. Symposium, Kyoto, Japan, 1989, conf. chmn., Honolulu, 1990, exec. comm. chair, 2000-06. Author: Introduction to Microelectronic Fabrication, 1988, 2d edit., 2002, Microelectronic Circuit Design, 1997, 3d edit., 2007, Computerized Circuit Analysis Using SPICE Programs, 1997 (IEEE Edn. Soc. McGraw Hill/Jacob Millman award 1998); editor: IEEE Jour. Solid State Cirs., 1995-98; contbr. over 200 articles to profl. jours.; patentee in field. Grantee NSF, Semicondr. Rsch. Corp., Dept. Def., Ala. Rsch. Inst. Fellow IEEE (pres. solid state cirs. coun. 1990-91, v.p. 1988-89, sec. 1984-87, Undergraduate Tchg. award 2004)); mem. Computer Soc. IEEE (bd. govs. 1985-86, Outstanding Contbn. award 1984, Golden Core award 1996), IEEE Solid-State Cirs. Soc. (adcom mem. 1996—, v.p. 2004-05, pres. 2006-07, Outstanding Contbn. award 1998, Millenium medal 2000, Outstanding Svc. award 2004). Home: 2160 Estate Dr Auburn AL 36830 Office: Auburn U Elec and Computer Engring 200 Broun Hall Auburn AL 36849-5201 Office Phone: 334-844-1871. Business E-Mail: jaeger@eng.auburn.edu.

JAEGERS, DONNA MARIE, securities analyst; b. St. Louis, Jan. 7, 1958; d. Tony R. and Helen C. (Krivi) J. BA in Econs., U. Mo., 1980, MA in Econs., 1981. Chartered fin. analyst. Securities analyst Merc. Bank, St. Louis, 1981-84, Paine Webber, NYC, 1984-87, SeaFirst Bank, Seattle, 1987-91, BA Capital Mgmt., Seattle, 1991, Miss. Valley Advisors, Invesco Funds Group; sr. rsch. analyst telecom services Janco Partners Inc., Greenwood Village, Colo., 2004—. Named one of Top Stock Pickers, Forbes Mag. Mem. Seattle Soc. Fin. Analysts. Office: Janco Partners 5251 DTC Pkwy Greenwood Village CO 80111*

JAENISCH, HOLGER MARCEL, physicist; b. Salt Lake City, Apr. 22, 1963; s. Klaus Peter Reinhardt and Sieglinde Erika (Freimann) J.; m. divorced; children: Falco Alexander, Marcel Fabry, Marcus Antone. MS, Columbia Pacific U., 1989, PhD, 1990. Teaching asst. U. Utah Physics Dept., Salt Lake City, 1979-82; laser engr. Com Tel Inc., Salt Lake City, 1982-85; sr. engr. Odetics Inc., Anaheim, Calif., 1985-88; sr. optical engr. Talandic Rsch. Corp., Irwindale, Calif., 1988-89; sr. rsch. assoc. NASA MSFC, Huntsville, Ala., 1989-90, UAH Ctr. Applied Optics, Huntsville, Ala., 1990-91; sr. scientist Nichols Rsch. Corp., Huntsville, Ala., 1991-92, Tec-Masters Inc., Huntsville, 1992—, program mgr. of level 13 and theater high altitude area defense (THAAD) seeker modeling for (THAAD) ind. validation & verification, 1994—. Assoc. prof. So. Calif. U., West Coast U., U. Ala., Huntsville; owner, pres. Licht Strahl Engring., Madison, Ala., 1989—. Author: Genesis II: Chaos/Fractals, 1989, Laser Analogy Using Video Feedback, 1990; contbr. tech. papers to publs. Founder enterprise squadron U.S. CAP, Salt Lake City; bd. dirs. Huntsville Sr. Citizen Ctr., 1992; mem. Hemsi Rescue Dive Team; scuba instr. Recipient U.S. Army Medal for Excellence in Sci., Harvey Eckenrode award South Eastern Simulation Conf., 1992, 93, Best Paper award, 1994, 95. Mem. IEEE, SPIE, OSA, Astron. League, U.S. Parachute Assn. (instr., Profl. Assn. Diving Instrs. diver, dive master, Cross Country award), Masons, Shriners, Scottish Rite. Independent. Achievements include development of ROSETA & KABA fractal 25 tech. papers, analysis, forecasting and data/image/majqanda/Futura, fractal data modeling, synthesis algorithms; 2 patents; inventor embedded recursive neural network architecture; developed algorithm for equation extraction from neural networks; algorithm for automatic differential equation model generation of orbitary data sets. Home: 29383 Mckee Rd Toney AL 35773-7733 Office: Tec-Masters Inc 1500 Perimeter Pky NW Huntsville AL 35806-3520

JAENISCH, RUDOLF, biologist, educator; b. Wolfeslgrund, Germany, 1942; arrived in U.S.A., 1984; MD, U. Munich, 1967. Postdoctoral fellow Max Planck Inst. Biochemistry, Munich, 1967; vis. fellow Inst. Cancer Rsch., Phila.; from asst. prof. to assoc. prof. Salk Inst., La Jolla, Calif., 1972—77; head Dept. Tumor Virology, Heinrich Pette Inst. Exptl. Virology and Immunology U. Hamburg, Germany, 1977—84; founding mem. Whitehead Inst. Biomedical Rsch. MIT, Cambridge, Mass., 1984—, prof. biology, 1984—. Contbr. articles to profl. jours. Recipient Boehringer Mannheim Molecular Bioanalytics prize, 1996, Award in Genetics, Peter Gruber Found., 2001, Robert Koch prize for excellence in sci. achievement, 2002. Fellow: Am. Acad. Arts and Scis., Am. Acad. Microbiology; mem.: AAAS, NAS. Achievements include creating first transgenic animal model; development of first experiment showing therapeutic cloning could correct genetic defects in mice. Office: Massachusetts Inst Tech 77 Massachusetts Ave 68 132 Cambridge MA 02142 Address: Whitehead Inst Nine Cambridge Center Cambridge MA 02142-1479 Office Phone: 617-258-5186. Office Fax: 617-258-6505. E-mail: jaenisch@wi.mit.edu.*

JAFEK, BRUCE WILLIAM, otolaryngologist, educator; b. Berwyn, Ill., Mar. 4, 1941; s. Robert William and Viola Mabel (Newstrom) J.; m. Mary Bell Kirkpatrick, Sept. 1, 1962; children: Lynette A., Robert K., Timothy

B., Britta C., Kayla E., Kristen M. BS, Coe Coll., 1962; postgrad., U. Omaha, 1962; MD, UCLA, 1966; postgrad., Oxford U., 2002—03. Instr. dept. otology/laryngology Johns Hopkins Sch. Medicine, Balt., 1971-73; asst. prof. dept. otolaryngology U. Pa. Med. Sch., Phila., 1973-76; prof., dept. chmn. dept. otolaryngology/head and neck surgery U. Colo. Med. Sch., Denver, 1976-98, prof., 1998—. With USPHS, 1971—73. Recipient Fowler award Triologic Soc., 1983, Cottle award Am. Rhinol. Soc., 1991. Mem. Triologic Soc. (west region v.p. 1999), Am. Acad. Otolaryngology/Head and Neck Surgery. Republican. Mem. Lds Ch. Office: U Colo Health Sci Ctr 4200 E 9th Ave # B-205 Denver CO 80220-3706 Home Phone: 303-795-9584; Office Phone: 303-315-7988. Business E-Mail: bruce.jafek@uchsc.edu.

JAFFA, AYAD A., medical educator, researcher; Student, Brunel Tech. Coll., Bristol, Eng., 1975—77; BSc in Biol. Chemistry with honors, U. Essex, Colchester, Eng., 1980, PhD in Biol. Chemistry, 1984. Postdoctoral fellow dept. medicine Med. U. S.C., Charleston, 1984—86, rsch. assoc. dept. medicine, 1986—89, asst. prof. medicine dept. medicine, endocrinology-diabetes-metabolism divsn., 1989—96, asst. prof. pharmacology dept. cell and molecular pharmacology and exptl. therapeutics, 1990—96, mem. grad. faculty, 1991—, assoc. prof. to prof., medicine dept. medicine, divsn. endocrinology-diabetes-med. genetics, 1996—, assoc. prof. to prof., pharmacology dept. cell and molecular pharmacology and exptl. therapeutics, 1996—. Mem. rsch. com. endocrinology-diabetes-med. genetics divsn. Med. U. S.C., Charleston, 1986—; grant reviewer Med. U. Rsch. Com. VA; vis. prof. Cath. U. of Chile, Santiago, 1996; lectr. in field. Manuscript reviewer: Am. Jour. Physiology, Kidney Internat., Life Scis., Jour. Pharmacology and Exptl. Therapeutics, Diabetes; contbr. articles to profl. jours. Recipient FIRST award, 1995; grantee, Med. U. S.C., 1991—92, 1992—93, 1995—96, VA, 1993—, NIH, 1995—. Mem.: Am. Fedn. Clin. Rsch. (Henry Christian award 1995), Am. Diabetes Assn. (exec. mem. fund raising com. S.C. affiliate 1992—96, bd. dirs. 1995—, Rsch. and Devel. award 1990, John A. Colwell award 1992, Rsch. award 1996). Achievements include research in pathogenesis of diabetic nephropathy, mechanisms of progressive renal disease, renal kallikrein-kinin system, kallikrein and renin gene regulation and expression, growth factors and signal transductio. Office: Med U SC Dept Medicine Divsn Endocrinology 171 Ashley Ave Charleston SC 29425-0001

JAFFA, HARRY VICTOR, political philosophy educator emeritus; b. NYC, Oct. 7, 1918; s. Arthur Sol and Frances (Landau) J.; m. Marjorie Etta Butler, Apr. 25, 1942; children: Donald Alan, Philip Bertran, Karen Louise Jaffa McGoldrick. BA, Yale U., 1939; PhD summa cum laude, New Sch. for Social Rsch., 1951; LLD (hon.), Marietta Coll., 1979, Ripon Coll., 1987. Instr. Queens Coll., CCNY, New Sch. for Social Rsch., 1945-49, U. Chgo., 1949-51, Ohio State U., 1951-64; faculty Claremont (Calif.) McKenna Coll. and Claremont Grad. Sch., 1964-89, Henry Salvatori Rsch. prof. polit. philosophy, 1971-89, prof. emeritus, 1989—; disting. fellow The Claremont Inst., 1989—. Author: Thomism and Aristotelianism: A Study of the Commentary by Thomas Aquinas on the Nicomachean Ethics, 1952, Crisis of the House Divided: An Interpretation of the Issues in the Lincoln-Douglas Debates, 1959, Equality and Liberty, 1965, The Conditions of Freedom, 1975, How to Think About the American Revolution, 1978, American Conservatism and the American Founding, 1984, Original Intent and the Framers of the Constitution: A Disputed Question, 1994, Storm Over the Constitution, 1999, A New Birth of Freedom: Abraham Lincoln and the Coming of the Civil War, 2000; (with Allan Bloom) Shakespeare's Politics, 1964; contbg. author: Shakespeare As Political Thinker, 1981; editor, contbg. author: Statesmanship: Essays in Honor of Sir Winston Churchill, 1982; general editor: Studies in Statesmanship; co-editor: (with Robert Johannsen) In the Name of the People: Speeches and Writings of Lincoln and Douglas in the Ohio Campaign of 1859, 1959. Organizer/dir. Bicycle Racing Program at Claremont Coll., 1976—. Fellow Ford, Rockefeller, Guggenheim, and Earhart founds. Fellow The Claremont Inst. Study of Statesmanship & Political Philosophy (disting.); mem. Am. Polit. Sci. Assn., Winston S. Churchill Assn. (founding pres. 1969—). Republican. Jewish. Avocation: bicycling. Home: 549 W Baughman Ave Claremont CA 91711-3733 Office: Claremont Inst 937 W Foothill Blvd Claremont CA 91711 Office Phone: 909-621-6825.

JAFFE, AMY MYERS, energy executive, educator; d. Allen and Lois Edna Myers; m. Richard Aaron Jaffe, May 22, 1984; children: Jordan Michael, Rebecca Ann, Daniel Isaac. BA, Princeton U., NJ, 1980. Sr. editor Mideast Report, NY, 1980—84; news mgr. Dow Jones & Co., NY, 1984—88; sr. editor, sr. mid. east analyst Petroleum Intelligence Weekly, NY, 1988—96; Wallace Wilson fellow James A. Baker inst. Rice U, Houston, 1996—. Project dir. Coun. Fgn. Rels., NY, 1999—2002; expert adv. econ. reconstruction Iraq study group Baker-Hamilton, Washington, 2006—07; mem. com. sustainable Iraqi oil industry study US AID, Washington, 2003—04; assoc. dir. energy program Rice U., 2002—07. Editor (author): (book) Geopolitics of Natural Gas 1970-2040; author: Energy Security; editor: Energy in the Caspian Basin; contbr. columns in newspapers, articles to profl. jours. Vol. Houston Pub. Schs., 1994—2004. Named one of Best and Brightest, Esquire Mag., 2005. Mem.: Internat. Assn. Energy Econs. (mem. com. various confs. and awards 1998—2007, Excellence in Writing award 1994), Wellsprings. Office: James A Baker III Inst Pub Policy 6100 Main St MS 40 Rice U Houston TX 77005 Home Phone: 713-348-2148; Office Phone: 713-348-2148. Office Fax: 713-348-5993; Home Fax: 713-348-5993. Business E-Mail: amjaffe@rice.edu.

JAFFE, ARTHUR MICHAEL, mathematician, physicist, educator; b. NYC, Dec. 22, 1937; s. Henry and Clarisse Jaffe; m. Nora Frances Crow, July 24, 1971; 1 child, Margaret Collins; m. Sarah Robbins Warren, Sept. 12, 1992. AB, Princeton U., 1959; BA, Cambridge U., 1961; PhD, Princeton U., 1966; MA, Harvard U., 1970. Acting asst. prof. math. Stanford U., 1966-67; asst. prof. physics Harvard U., Cambridge, Mass., 1967-69, assoc. prof., 1969-70, prof. physics, 1970-77, prof. math. physics, 1977-85, Landon T. Clay prof. math. and theoretical sci., 1985—, chmn. dept. math., 1987-90. Rsch. fellow Princeton U., 1965—66, vis. prof. math. physics, 1971; rsch. fellow Stanford Linear Accelerator Ctr., 1966—67; mem. Inst. Advanced Study, 1967; vis. prof. Eidgenössische Technische Hochschule, Zurich, 1968, 2005, Rockefeller U., 1977, U. Rome, 1993, Boston U., 2001; mem. pres.'s com. Nat. Medal Sci., 1997—2002, acting chair, 2001—02; mem. sci. bd. Santa Fe Inst., 1998—; founding mem., dir., pres. Clay Math. Inst., 1998—2002; bd. dirs. Internat. Math. Olympiad 2001, Inst. Schs. Future, Ctr. Math. Physics U. Hamburg, Germany, Found. Internat. U., Bremen; mem. Math. Scis. Edn. Bd. NRC, 2000—06, mem. exec. com., 2002—06; chmn. bd. Sch. Theoretical Physics Dublin (Ireland) Inst. Advanced Study, 2005—; mem. perspective commn. Internat. U. Bremen, 2005—06; advisor Jour. Comms. Math. Physics, 2000—; mem. US Nat. Com. for Math., 2007—; lectr. in field. Author: Vortices and Monopoles, 1980, Quantum Physics, 1981, 87, Quantum Field Theory and Statistical Mechanics, Expositions, 1985, Constructive Quantum Field Theory, 1985; assoc. editor Jour. Math. Physics, 1970-72; mem. editl. coun. Annals of Physics, 1975-77, asst. editor, 1977-2002; editor Comms. Math. Physics, 1976-2000, chief editor, 1979-2000; mem. adv. bd. Letters in Math. Physics, 1975—; editor Progress in Physics, 1979-86, Selecta Mathematica Sovetica, 1980—, Revs. in Mathematical Physics, 1990; contbr. articles to profl. jours. Alfred P. Sloan Found. fellow, 1968-70; Guggenheim Found. fellow, 1977-78, 92; award Math. and Phys. Scis., N.Y. Acad. Sci., 1979; Dannie Heineman prize for Math. Physics, 1980; NSF fellow, 1961-64; NAS Air Force Office Sci. Rsch. fellow, 1965-67. Fellow: AAAS (chair math. sect. 2001), Am. Acad. Arts and Scis., Am. Phys. Soc.; mem.: Joint Policy Bd. Math. (chair 1998), Coun. Sci. Soc. Presidents (chmn. 2000), Internat. Assn. Math. Physics (pres. 1991—96), Am. Math. Soc. (exec. com. of coun. 1991—95, pres. 1997—98), US Nat. Acad. Scis., Harvard Musical Assn., Cosmos Club (Washington). Home: 27 Lancaster St Cambridge MA 02140-2837 Office Phone: 617-495-4320.

JAFFE, CHARLES J., allergist; b. Phila., Feb. 3, 1946; MD, Duke U., 1971, PhD, 1972. Allergist Scripps Meml. Hosp., Encinitas, Calif. Prof. allergy and immunology U. Calif., San Diego. Mem. Am. Coll. Allergy Asthma and Immunology (chair computer sect.), Am. Acad. Allergy Asthma and Immunology (chair med. informatics), Am. Med. Informatics Assn. (chmn. clin. info. syss.).

JAFFE, ELAINE SARKIN, pathologist; b. NYC, Aug. 27, 1943; d. David and Mona (Shane) Sarkin; m. Michael Evan Jaffe, July 22, 1967; children: Gregory, Caleb. AB, Cornell U., 1965; MD, U. Pa., 1969. Cert. Am. Bd. Pathology. Intern in pathology Georgetown U. Hosp., 1969; resident anatomic pathology Clin. Ctr. NIH, Bethesda, Md., 1970-72; sr. investigator lab. pathology Nat. Cancer Inst., NIH, Bethesda, Md., 1974-80, chief hematopathology sect. lab. pathology, 1980—, dep. chief lab. pathology, 1982—2005; acting chief lab of pathology Nat. Cancer Inst. NIH, Bethesda, Md., 2005—. Med. dir. USPHS, 1970—2000; exec. coun. assembly scientists NIH, 2005—; lectr. in field. Assoc. editor: Cancer Rsch.; mem. editl. bd. Am. Jour. Pathology, Blood; mem. editl. bd.: Clin. Lymphoma; mem. editl. bd. Am. Jour. Surg. Pathology; editor: Surgical Pathology of the Lymph Nodes and Related Organs, 1984, 2d edit., 1996, WHO Classification of Hematopoietic and Lymphoid Neoplasms, 2001; contbr. articles to New Eng. Jour. Medicine, Blood. Recipient Fred W. Stewart award, Meml. Sloan Kettering Cancer Ctr., 2002, Walter Putscher Lectureship, Harvard U., 2003, Dir.'s award, NIH, 2005, Disting. Tchr. award, 2006, Anita B. Roberts Disting. Women Scientist award, 2006. Fellow AAAS (chair med. scis. sect. 2004-2005); mem. Am. Soc. Hematology (exec. coun. 1988-91), U.S.-Can. Acad. Pathology (pres. 1998-99), Am. Soc. Investigative Pathology (Meritorious awards), Soc. for Hematopathology (pres. 1994-96). Office: NCI NIH Lab of Pathology 10 Center Dr MSC-1500 Bethesda MD 20892-1500 Office Phone: 301-496-0183. Business E-Mail: ejaffe@mail.nih.gov.

JAFFÉ, ERNST RICHARD, medical educator, dean; b. Chgo., Jan. 4, 1925; s. Richard Hermann and Berta (Kohn) J.; m. Anne Jane Sylvestre, Aug. 5, 1950; children: Stephanie Anne Green, Richard Sheridan Jaffé. BS, U. Chgo., 1945, MD, 1948, MS in Pathology, 1948; DHL (hon.), Yeshiva U., 1987. Diplomate Am. Bd. Internal Medicine, Hematology, Nat. Bd. Med. Examiners; lic. physician, N.Y. Intern Med. Presbyn. Hosp., NYC, 1948—50, resident, 1953-55; postdoctoral fellow Albert Einstein Coll. of Medicine, Bronx, NY, 1955-57, instr., asst. prof., 1957-62, assoc. prof., 1962-69, prof. medicine, 1969-84, acting dean, 1972-74, 83-84, sr. assoc. dean, 1974-83, 84-91, disting. univ. prof. medicine, 1984-92, disting. univ. prof. medicine emeritus, 1992—. Mem. hematology study sect. Nat. Inst. Health, Bethesda, Md., 1972-82, Hirschl Sci. Adv. Com. I.T. Hirschl Trust, NYC, 1974-92, NY Cmty. Trust Blood Disease Panel, NYC, 1978-97; dir. Belfer Inst. for Advanced Biomed. Studies, 1978-92. Co-editor Seminars in Hematology, 1968-2000, co-editor emeritus, 2000—; editor-in-chief Blood, 1975-77; contbr. articles to profl. jours. Nat. bd. govs. ARC, Washington, 1984-90, chmn. blood svcs. com., 1988-90; bd. dirs. Nat. Marrow Donor Program, 1987-2000; bd. dirs. Henry M. and Lillian Stratton Found., 1985-96, pres., 1989-96; trustee Bergen Cmty. Regional Blood Ctr., 1997-2000. With U.S. Army, 1944-46; capt. USAF, 1951-53. Named Career Scientist, Health Rsch. Coun.; recipient Charles R. Drew award ARC, 1990. Fellow Internat. Soc. Hematology (counselor 1980-88, v.p. 1984-88, historian 1990—); mem. Am. Soc. Hematology (pres. 1983, historian 1993—, Outstanding Achievement award 1998), Assn. Am. Physicians, Am. Fedn. Clin. Rsch., Am. Soc. Clin. Investigation, Am. Physiol. Soc., Assn. Am. Med. Colls. (emeritus), Coun. Acad. Socs. (adminstrv. bd. 1985-90, chmn. 1989), N.Y. Soc. Study Blood (pres. 1978-80), Soc. for Exptl. Biology and Medicine (pres. 1993-95, past pres. 1995-97), U. Chgo. Alumni Assn. (Profl. Achievement citation 1992), U. Chgo. Med. Alumni Assn. (Disting. Svc. award 1981), Phi Beta Kappa, Sigma Xi, Alpha Omega Alpha. Lutheran. Avocations: photography, reading. Office Phone: 516-944-0232. Business E-Mail: ejaffe@pol.net. *Nothing is more satisfying than to have done a good job and to have earned the affection of your colleagues. However, wife and children are paramount!!.*

JAFFE, F. FILMORE, lawyer, retired judge; b. Chgo., May 4, 1918; s. Jacob Isadore and Goldie (Rabinowitz) J.; m. Mary Main, Nov. 7, 1942; children: Jo Anne, Jay. Student, Southwestern U., 1936-39; JD, Pacific Coast U., 1940. Bar: Calif. 1945, U.S. Supreme Ct. 1964. Practiced law, Los Angeles, 1945-91; ptnr. Bernard & Jaffe, Los Angeles, 1947-74, Jaffe & Jaffe, Los Angeles, 1975-91; apptd. referee Superior Ct. of Los Angeles County, 1991-97, apptd. judge pro tem, 1991-97; ret., 1997; atty. in pvt. practice LA, 1997—. Mem. L.A. Traffic Commn., 1947-48; arbitrator Am. Arbitration Assn., 1968-91; chmn. pro bono com. Superior Ct. Calif., County of Los Angeles, 1980-86; lectr. on paternity; chair family law indigent paternity panel L.A. County Supr. Ct., 2001—. Served to capt. inf. AUS, 1942-45. Decorated Purple Heart, Croix de Guerre with Silver Star, Bronze Star with oak leaf cluster; honored Human Rights Commn. Los Angeles, Los Angeles County Bd. Suprs.; recipient Pro Bono award State Bar Calif., commendation State Bar Calif., 1983. Mem.: ABA, Beverly Hills Bar Assn., US Supreme Ct. Bar Assn., LA Criminal Ct. Bar Assn. (charter mem.), Los Angeles County Bar (honored by family law sect. 1983), Shriners, Masons. Office: 433 N Camden Dr Ste 400 Beverly Hills CA 90210-4408 Home Phone: 310-553-3350; Office Phone: 310-859-8921. Personal E-mail: filmorejaffe@sbcglobal.net.

JAFFE, FREDRICK F., surgeon; b. New York City, June 3, 1942; s. David A. and Mildred C. (Leibner) J.; m. Mary E. (Mark), June 14, 1964 (div. Dec. 1994); children: David and Harry; m. Deborah L. (Moody), Nov. 5, 1995. BS, Tufts Univ., 1964, MD, 1968. Diplomate Am. Bd. Orthop. Surgery. Surg. intern NYC Hosp., 1968-69, surg. fellow, 1969-70; orthop. resident Hosp. Joint Diseases, NYC, 1970-73, fellow, 1973-74, attending orthop. surgeon, 1974—, chief adult re-constructive surgeon, 1991-94, dir. joint replacement ctr. NYU Med. Ctr., chief divsn. adult reconstructive surgery, 2006; attending orthop. surgeon Beth Israel Med. Ctr., NYC, 1994—, chief adult reconstructive surgery singer divsn., 1994-96, sect. chief hip svc. singer divsn., 1997—; dir. Insall, Scott, and Kelley Inst. for Orthop. and Sports Medicine, NYC, 1994—2000; clin. prof. of orthop. surgery NYU Sch. Medicine, 2003. Fellow Am. Acad. Orthop. Surgery, ACS, Am. Assn. Hip and Knee Surgeons, NY Acad. Medicine; mem. Orthopaedic Rsch. Soc., Ea. Orthopedic Assn., NY State Orthopedic Assn. Avocations: sailing, skiing, scuba diving, tennis, photography. Office: 301 E 17th St Ste 213 New York NY 10003

JAFFE, HAROLD W., federal agency administrator; b. Newton, Mass. AB, U. Calif., Berkeley; MD, UCLA. Clin. rsch. investigator, venereal disease control program CDC, Atlanta, epidemic intelligence svc. officer, 1981, chief, AIDS epidemiology program, deputy dir. for sci., HIV/AIDS program, dir. AIDS/HIV program, 1992—95, head, HIV, STD and TB lab., acting dir., Nat. Ctr. for HIV, STD and TB prevention, 2001—02, dir., Nat. Ctr. for HIV, STD and TB prevention, 2002; fellow, St. Cross Coll. U. Oxford, England, 2003—, prof., chmn., dept. pub. health. Mem.: Inst. Medicine. Office: 1600 Clifton Rd NE E07 Atlanta GA 30333

JAFFE, HELENE D., lawyer; BA magna cum laude, Barnard Coll., 1976; JD, Columbia U. Sch. Law, 1976; Harlan Fiske Stone Scholar. Bar: NY 1977, US Dist. Ct. (So. and Ea. Districts, NY) 1980, US Ct. Appeals (2nd, 3rd, and 8th Districts) 1982, US Supreme Ct. 1982, US Ct. Internat. Trade 1982. Co-head antitrust/competition practice, trade practices and regulatory law dept. Weil, Gotshal & Manges LLP, NYC. Assoc. asst. prof. to adj. assoc. prof. NY U. Sch. Law, 1983—; faculty mem. Ohio Legal Ctr., 1980—; chair Consumer Protection Com.; lectr. in field. Contbr. articles on antitrust, merger, advertising, and marketing issues to profl. publs. Mem.: Assn. Bar City NY (mem. trade regulation com.), NY County Lawyer Assn. (chair, com. on trade regulation), ABA (mem. council antitrust sect., vice-chair Clayton Act Com., antitrust sect.). Office: Weil Gotshal & Manges LLP 767 Fifth Ave New York NY 10153 Office Phone: 212-310-8572. Office Fax: 212-310-8007. Business E-Mail: helene.jaffe@weil.com.

JAFFE, JEFF HUGH, retired food products executive; b. Washington, Dec. 25, 1920; s. Henry A. Jaffe and Mildred (Loewenberg) Auslander; m. Natalie Rubin, Dec. 31, 1945; children: Bonita Jaffe Berens, Holly Anne. BS in Archtl. Engring., Va. Poly. Inst. and State U., 1943. Chmn. bd. dirs., pres. The Chunky Corp. (now Ward Candy, Inc.), 1950-69; pres., CEO candy, chocolate and biscuit group Ward Foods Inc., 1969-71, pres., COO, 1971-72; also bd. dirs. Ward Foods, Inc., 1972-74; chmn. bd. dirs., pres. Schutter Candy Co., 1958-67, Klotz Confection Co., 1960-67; pres., CEO The Schrafft Candy Co., 1974-78; v.p. consumer products group Gulf and Western Industries, 1974-78; pres., CEO Bernan Foods, Inc., 1980-85, ret., 1985. Bd. dirs. Cmty. Nat. Bank of S.I., N.Y., Ward Foods, Inc., Ward Candy Co., Oxford Energy Co.; guest lectr. Harvard Bus. Sch., 1970-84. Bd. dirs., nat. treas. Young Pres.'s Orgn., Woodmere Acad., Martin County (Fla.) Libr. Found.; bd. dirs. Village Hewlett Bay Park; sponsor and patron Fla. Laws of Life Essay Contest for H.S. Students, Martin County, 1999-. Mem. Assn. Mfrs. of Confectionery and Chocolate (past chmn.), Candy Execs. Club, Property Owners Assn. (Sailfish Point, Fla., pres., chmn. transition com., chmn. emeritus, CEO). Home: 128 Via Mariposa Palm Beach Gardens FL 33418-6211

JAFFE, JONATHAN M., construction executive; Grad., U. Fla., Gainesville; student in Architecture, Ga. Inst. Tech. With Lennar Corp., Miami, Fla., 1983—, regional pres. homebuilding divsn., v.p., 1994—, head Western Region ops. Calif., 1996, bd. dirs., 1997—2004, COO, 2004—. Bd. dirs. HomeAid Am. Named to Calif. Bldg. Industry Found. Hall of Fame. Office: Lennar Corp 700 NW 107th Ave Ste 400 Miami FL 33172 Office Phone: 305-559-4000. Office Fax: 305-226-4158.*

JAFFE, KATHARINE WEISMAN, retired librarian; b. Cambridge, Mass., Apr. 27, 1927; d. Maurice and Esther (Feinberg) W.; m. Myron I. Jaffe, Dec. 18, 1949; children: Stephen Philip, Jane Elizabeth J. Martin, Samuel Morris. AB in Am. Civilization, Colby Coll., 1948; MS in Libr. Sci., Simmons Coll., 1952. Asst. children's libr. Boston Pub. Libr., 1948-51; libr. Mishkan Tefila Synagogue, Newton, Mass., 1955-58, Temple Emmanuel, Newton, 1958-59; reserve libr. Brandeis U., Waltham, Mass., 1960-62; reference libr., archives libr., rare books libr. Boston Coll., 1963-75; vol. libr. and archives libr. Berkshire Hist. Soc., Pittsfield, Mass., 1994-96; chairperson Friends of Libr., New Marlborough, Mass., 1978-94. Libr. rep. to design referenc and Atrium New Libr. Boston Coll., 1973-75; founding chair bookstore Brandeis Women's Com., Noami Lodge, 1950-75; book group leader, organizer, 1955-75; voter edn. chair South and Ctrl. Berkshire chpt. LWV, 1994-96, 97-2001, pres. 1996-97, mem. governing bd.; docent Edith Wharton Home, Mount Lenox, 1988-92; class sec. Colby '48, 1993-98, class agt., 2000—; assoc. editor New Marlborough Hist. Soc. Pictorial Hist. New Marlborough, 2001, sec. New Marlborough Hist. Soc., 2002—; vol. Fairview Hosp., 2006—. Jewish. Avocations: reading, travel. Home: PO Box 113 Mill River MA 01244

JAFFE, LEONARD, orthopedist, surgeon, educator; MD, Chicago Med. Sch. Intern Albert Einstein Coll.-Montefiore Med. Ctr., Bronx, NY; orthopaedic resident NYU Med. Ctr., NYC, fellow sports related injuries; attending orthopaedic surgeon St. Barnabas Med. Ctr., Livingston, NJ. Team physician, orthopedist NJ Devils, 1984—; former assoc. physician NY Islanders, NJ Nets, NJ Pride; clin. instr. U. Medicine and Dentistry of NJ, Newark. Mem.: Am. Med. Soccer Assn., Am. Coll. Sports Medicine, Assn. Profl. Team Physicians (bd. fellows), NHL Team Physicians Assn. (charter mem.), Greater Met. Sports Medicine Soc. (charter mem.). Office: Saint Barnabas Ambulatory Care Ctr Sports Medicine Inst 200 S Orange Ave Livingston NJ 07039 also: 609 Morris Ave Springfield NJ 07081 Office Phone: 973-322-7330, 973-467-9500.*

JAFFE, MORRIS EDWARD, insurance company executive, financial analyst; b. Bklyn., Apr. 24, 1947; s. Eugene Netter and Sabina (Sensor) J.; m. Laurie F. Lucas, Feb. 14, 1986; children by previous marriage: Shelley Lynne Jaffe Venincasa, James Edward. Student, U. Miami, Fla., 1965-67; BS in Math., U. Md., 1970. CLU, ChFC, CFP (investment advisor rep.), LUTC. Sales, ops. mgr. Levitz Furniture, Rockville, Md., 1972-75; agt. and sales mgr. MetLife Ins. Co., Camp Springs, Md., 1975-86; ptnr., ind. ins. agt. Price, Williams, Jaffe & Assocs., Brandywine, Md., 1986-88; ind. ins. agt. So. Md. Ins. Agy., Brandywine, Md., 1988-96; propr. Jaffe Assocs., Brandywine, 1996—. Mem. pres.'s conf. MetLife, Camp Springs, Md., 1977, leader's conf., 1975, 76, 78, 80, pres.'s adv. coun., 1978. Treas., v.p. Gwynn Park High Sch. Parent-Tchr.-Student Assn., Brandywine, 1987-92; mem. Prince Georges Mental Health Assn., Largo, Md., 1988-91, 96—; mem. Regional Inst. for Children and Adolescents-So. Md. Citizens Adv. Bd., Cheltenham, Md., 1988-2002, chmn., 1989-96; mem., treas. Friends of RICA, Cheltenham, 1988—; sponsor Boy Scouts Am. Mem.: Life Underwriters PAC (state treas. 1987—90), Soc. Fin. Svc. Profls., Nat. Assn. Ins. and Fin. Advisers of Prince Georges (dir. 1977—99, sec. 1981—82, treas. 1982—85, pres. 1985—86, state committeeman 1986—99, Agt. of Yr. 1984), Nat. Assn. Ins. and Fin. Advisors of Md. (dir. 1985—2005, sec./treas. 1999—2000, v.p. 2000—01, pres.-elect 2001—02, pres. 2002—03, immediate past pres. 2003—05, sr. regional v.p. 2005—, named Outstanding Local Pres. 1986, elected to Hall of Fame 1997, Paul J. Murphy award 2004), Nat. Assn. Ins. and Fin. Advisors (voting del. to nat. coun. 1986, 2002). Office: Jaffe Assocs PO Box 230 Brandywine MD 20613-0230 Home Phone: 301-782-7966. Personal E-mail: ed.jaffe@verizon.net.

JAFFE, MURRAY SHERWOOD, retired surgeon; b. Sept. 29, 1926; s. Lester A. and Rosa (Shor) J.; m. Margery Blum, Mar. 26, 1951; children—Emily, Margaret, Dan BS, MD, U. Cin., 1948. Diplomate Am. Bd. Surgery. Intern Barnes Hosp., St. Louis, 1948-49; resident Cin. Gen. Hosp., 1949-50, 52-56, Cin. VA Hosp., 1949-50, 52-56, Dayton VA Hosp., Ohio, 1949-50, 52-56; practice medicine specializing in surgery Cin., 1958-98; asst. chief surgery VA Hosp., Cin., 1958-82; pres. med. staff Jewish Hosp., Cin., 1978-80; pres. Medco Peer Rev., 1981-84; retired surgeon, 1996; assoc. clin. prof. surgery emeritus U. Cin. Pres. Ohio div. Am. Cancer Soc., 1970-71. Served with USN, 1945, 50-52 Mem. ACS, Cin. Surg. Soc., U. Cin. Grad. Surg. Soc., Shriners, Phi Beta Kappa, Alpha Omega Alpha Republican. Jewish. Home: 56 Tradd St Charleston SC 29401-2540 Personal E-mail: jaffems@email.uc.edu.

JAFFE, RICHARD S., lawyer; b. NYC, Apr. 14, 1968; s. Stanley Robert and Myra Jacqueline Jaffe; m. Lainie Joy Jaffe, Aug. 4, 2002; children: Brandon, Skylar. BA, SUNY, Binghamton, 1990; JD, Touro Coll., 1994. Bar: N.Y. 1995, N.J. 1995, D.C. 1995, U.S. Dist. Ct. (so. dist.) NY 1995, U.S. Dist. Ct. (ea. dist.) NY 1995. Assoc. Law Office of Stephen M. Cohen, Lake Success, NY, 1995—98, ptnr., 1998—2004, Cohen & Jaffe, Esquire, 2003—, Law Office of Cohen and Jaffe LLP, Lake Success, 2004—. Mediator Supreme Ct. State of N.Y. Firefighter, EMT Jericho Vol. Fire Dept., 2005—; arbitrator Small Claims Ct., Bronx, 2000—. Mem.: ATLA, Nassau County Bar Assn., N.Y. State Trial Lawyers Assn., N.Y. State Bar

Assn., Trial Lawyers Care, Inns Of Ct., West Birchwood Civic Assn., Million Dollar Advocates Forum (life). Office: Law Office of Cohen & Jaffe LLP 2001 Marcus Ave New Hyde Park NY 11042 Office Phone: 516-358-6900.

JAFFE, ROBERT STANLEY, lawyer; b. Walla Walla, Wash., May 16, 1946; BA, U. Wash., 1968, JD, 1972. Bar: Wash. 1972. Ptnr. Preston Gates & Ellis, L.L.P., Seattle, 1986—. Mem. ABA (mem. corp., banking and bus. law sect., mem. small bus. com. 1982-92), Order of Coif. Office: Preston Gates & Ellis 925 4th Ave Ste 2900 Seattle WA 98104-1158 Office Phone: 206-623-7580.

JAFFE, RUSSELL MERRITT, pathologist, research director; b. Albany, NY, Jan. 1, 1947; AB cum laude, Boston U., 1972, MD with honors, 1972, PhD in Biochemistry, 1972. Diplomate Am. Bd. Pathology (clin., chem.), Nat. Bd. Med. Examiners. Med. intern Boston U. Med. Ctr., 1972-73; resident in clin. pathology NIH, Bethesda, Md., 1973-75, sr. staff physician clin. pathology dept., 1973-79, chief resident tng. program clin. chemistry sect., 1976-79; fellow health rsch., practice, policy devel. Health Studies Collegium, 1979—; dir. ELISA/ACT Biotech., Sterling, Va., 1987—, Princeton BioCenter, 1989-92. Prin. faculty Oriental Med. Strategy in Western Med. Practice, HSC, N.Y.C., 1980-85. Assoc. editor The New Physician, 1971-72, sr. assoc. editor, 1972-73. Bd. govs. Light Found., 1980-99. Comdr. USPHS, 1973-79. Recipient Nat. Rsch. award Am. Acad. Med. Preventics, 1979, J.D. Lane award USPHS, 1975, Excellence in Rsch. award Mead Johnson, 1969, Man of Yr. award Hillel Found., 1967. Fellow Am. Coll. Nutrition, Am. In-Vitro Allergy/Immunology Soc., Am. Soc. Clin. Pathologists; mem. APHA, Am. Assn. Clin. Chemists. Achievements include patent in field. Home: 300 Amwell Rd Hopewell NJ 08525-3116 Office: ELISA/ACT Biotech 14 Pidgeon Hill Dr Ste 300 Sterling VA 20165-6133

JAFFE, SETH ROTH, lawyer, retail executive; b. NYC, Mar. 8, 1957; s. Harold and Ruth Jaffe; m. Merrie Fanshel, Oct. 20, 1991. AB, Brown U., 1977; JD, U. Mich., 1980. Bar: Calif. 1980, U.S. Dist. Ct. (no. dist.) Calif., U.S. Ct. Appeals (9th cir.). Assoc. McCutchen, Doyle, Brown & Enersen, San Francisco, 1980-84; chief gen. counsel Levi Strauss & Co., San Francisco, 1984—99; sr. v.p., gen. counsel CareThere, Inc., 2000—01; v.p., dep. gen. counsel Williams-Sonoma, Inc., San Francisco, 2002—03, sr. v.p., gen. counsel, sec., 2003—. Office: Williams Sonoma Inc 3250 Van Ness Ave San Francisco CA 94109 Office Phone: 415-421-7900.*

JAFFE, SUSAN, ballerina; b. Washington, 1962; Student, Md. Sch. Ballet; student, Sch. Am. Ballet, Am. Ballet Theatre Sch. With Am. Ballet Theatre II, 1978-80; with Am. Ballet Theatre, 1980—, soloist, 1981-83, prin., 1983—2002, tchr., advisor. Repertoire includes: Le Corsaire, The Merry Widow (by Ronald Hynd), Apollo, Eugene Onegin (by John Cranko), La Bayadere, Bouree Fantastique, Carmen, Cinderella, Concerto, Duets, Giselle, The Guards of Amager, Push Comes to Shove, Symphonie Concertante, Ballet Imperial, Coppelia, Etudes, Giselle, Jardin auxLilas, Romeo and Juliet, The Sleeping Beauty, Other Dances, Theme and Variations, Swan Lake, La Sylphide, Undertow, Voluntaries, Dim Lustre, Manon, Gala Performance, Don Quioxte, Cruel World, Sextet, The Snow Maiden, Fall River Legend, Grande Pas Classic, Stepping Stones, Without Words (by Nacho Duato), Anastasia, others; created role Lynne Taylor-Corbett's Great Galloping Gottschalk, Bruch Violin Concerto No. 1, Serious Pleasures; appeared Spoleto in An Evening of Jerome Robbins Ballets, 1982, Known by Heart (Twyla Tharp); appeared with Kirov Ballet, 1988; guest appearances with The Royal Swedish Ballet, The Royal Danish Ballet, The English Nat. Ballet, La Scala Ballet, Milan, 1997, 98, The Royal Ballet, 1998, 2000, Stuttgart Ballet, 1998, 2000, The Munich Opera Ballet, The Vienna State Opera Ballet; dir. (movie) Angie, by Martha Koolidge. Recipient N.Y. Woman-Lancome Paris Woman of Yr. award, 1989, Dance Mag. award, 2003 Office: Am Ballet Theatre 890 Broadway 3d Fl New York NY 10003-1211

JAFFEE, ANNETTE WILLIAMS, novelist; b. Abilene, Tex., Jan. 10, 1945; d. Jules Henry and Evelyn June (Witensky) Williams; m. Dwight M. Jaffee, Aug. 16, 1964 (div. May 1991); children: Jonathan, Elizabeth. BS, Boston U., 1966. Author: Adult Education, 1981, Recent History, 1988, The Dangerous Age, 1998. N.J. Arts Coun. grantee State of N.J., 1985-86, Geraldine Dodge fellow Yaddo, 1991. Mem. PEN.

JAFFREY, IRA, oncologist, educator; b. NYC, July 28, 1939; s. Mack and Elaine (Schneider) J.; m. Jane Sharon Friedman, Dec. 26, 1964 (div. Mar. 1979); children: Jonathan David, Marc Jason; m. Sandra Read, June 17, 1979; 1 child, Marc Read. AB, Columbia Coll., NYC, 1960; MD, SUNY, Bklyn., 1965. Intern Jewish Hosp., Bklyn., 1965-66; chief resident Elmhurst Gen. Hosp., NYC, 1970; asst. resident Mt. Sinai Hosp., NYC, 1968-69, resident, 1969-70, chief resident, 1970, ednl. fellow dept. hematology, 1970-71, asst. clin. prof. dept. medicine divsn. neoplastic disease, 1980—99; pres. Palisades Oncology Assocs. P.C., Pomona, 1972—; asst. clin. prof. dept. medicine U. Colo. Health Scis., Denver, 2000—. Lt. USNR, 1961-65. Oak Ridge (Tenn.) Inst. fellow, 1965. Fellow ACP, Am. Cancer Soc. (pres. Rockland City unit 1973-74), Rockland City Med. Soc. (v.p. 1992, pres. 1993-94), Mt. Sopris County Med. Soc. (pres. 2002-03, 2006-), Colo. Med. Soc. (bd. dirs. 2004—). Office: Western SLOPE Oncology Assoc PC 622 19th St Ste 301 Glenwood Springs CO 81601 Office Phone: 970-384-2274. Personal E-mail: dr.jaffrey@aol.com.

JAGDMANN, JUDY (JUDITH WILLIAMS JAGDMANN), commissioner, former state attorney general; b. Norton, Va., Nov. 3, 1958; d. Glen and Jane Williams; m. Joseph V. Jagdmann; children: Emily, Daniel. Grad., U. Va; JD, U. Richmond. Staff atty. Va. State Corp. Commn., 1985—91, asst. gen. counsel, 1991—95, assoc. gen. counsel, 1995—98, commr., 2006—; dep. atty. gen. State of Va., Richmond, 1998—2005, atty. gen., 2005—06. Office: Va State Corp Commn PO Box 1197 Richmond VA 23218

JAGENDORF, ANDRÉ TRIDON, physiologist; b. NYC, Oct. 21, 1926; s. Moritz Adolph and Sophie Sheba (Sokolsky) J.; m. Jean Elizabeth Whitenack, June 12, 1952; children: Suzanne E., Judith C., Daniel Z.S. BA, Cornell U., 1948; PhD, Yale U., 1951. Merck postdoctoral fellow UCLA, 1951-53; from asst. prof. to prof. Johns Hopkins U., 1953-66; prof. plant physiology Cornell U., Ithaca, N.Y., 1966—, Liberty H. Bailey prof. plant physiology, 1981-96, Liberty H. Bailey prof. emeritus, 1997—. Author papers, revs. in field. Recipient Outstanding Young Scientist award Md. Acad. Sci., 1961, Kettering Rsch. award, 1963; Weizmann fellow, 1962 Fellow Am. Acad. Arts and Scis., AAAS; mem. NAS, Am. Soc. Plant Physiologists (hon., life, pres. 1967, C.F. Kettering award in photosynthesis, 1978, Charles Reid Barnes award 1989, Disting. Fellow award 2007), Am. Soc Biol. Chemists, Am. Soc. Photobiology (councilor 1980), Soc. Gen. Physiologists, Am. Soc. Cell Biology, Japanese Soc. Plant Physiologists. Jewish. Office: Cornell U Plant Biology Dept Plant Sci Bldg Ithaca NY 14853 Home Phone: 607-266-0243; Office Phone: 607-255-8940. Business E-Mail: atj1@cornell.edu.

JAGER, MELVIN FRANCIS, lawyer; b. Joliet, Ill., Mar. 23, 1937; s. Melvin Van Zandt and Lucille Marie (Callahan) J.; m. Virginia Sue Maitland, Aug. 15, 1959; children: Lori, Jennifer, Scott, Christy. BSME, JD, U. Ill., 1962. Bar: Ill. 1962, D.C. 1962. Assoc. Iron, Birch, Swindler & McKie, Washington, 1962-65; ptnr. Hume, Clement, Brinks, Willian & Olds Ltd., Chgo., 1965-80, Lee, Smith & Jager, Chgo., 1981-83, Niro, Jager & Scavone, Chgo., 1984-85, Brinks, Hofer, Gilson & Lione Ltd., Chgo., 1985—2004, Ocean Tomo LLC, 2004—06. Editor U. Ill. Law Rev., 1961-62; adj. prof. law No. Ill. U. Sch. Law, 1979-80, John Marshall Law Sch., 1992, U. Ill. Coll. Law, Champaign, 1992-2003; chmn. Practicing Law Inst. Trade Secret Protection Symposium, 1986, 89. Author: Trade Secrets Law, 1984, Licensing Law Handbook, 2005; editor: Worldwide Trade Secrets Law, 2005; contbg. author: Sorting Out the Ownership Rights in Intellectual Property: A Practical Guide to Practical Counseling and Legal Representation, 1980. Mem. bd. edn. Glen Ellyn, Ill., 1974-80; chmn. Civic Betterment Party Nominating Com., Glen Ellyn, 1982-88; chmn. Glen Ellyn Environ. Protection Com., 1971-72; chmn. budget rev. com. Glen Ellyn United Fund, 1972, Glen Ellyn Ednl. Loan Fund trust, 1973. Mem. ABA (chmn. litigation sect. intellectual properties and patents com. 1984-88), Ill. State Bar Assn. (chmn. patent, trademark and copyright, coun. 1982-83, editor newsletter 1979-82), Chgo. Bar Assn., Am. Patent Law Assn., Intellectual Property Law Assn. of Chgo. (pres. 1997), Lic. Execs. Soc. (pres. U.S.A./Can. 1993-94, lic. found. pres., 2001-04, pres., 2003-04), Am. Law Inst., Glen Ellyn Jaycees (life mem., pres. 1972, trustee), Chgo. Law Club, Union League Club, Phi Gamma Delta, Phi Delta Phi. Republican. Roman Catholic. Home: 2302 Walfert Rd Sanibel FL 33957 Office: Ocean Tomo LLC 200 W Adams Chicago IL 60606 Home Phone: 239-472-5706; Office Phone: 312-327-4419. E-mail: mfjager@msn.com.

JAGGER, SIR MICK (MICHAEL PHILIP JAGGER), singer, musician; b. Dartford, Kent, Eng., July 26, 1943; s. Joe and Eva Jagger; m. Bianca Perez Morena de Macias, May 12, 1971 (div. Nov. 1979); children: Jade, Karis; m. Jerry Hall, Nov. 21, 1990 (annulled Aug. 13, 1999); children: Elizabeth Scarlett, James Leroy Augustine, Georgia May Ayeesha, Gabriel Luke Beauregard. Student, London Sch. Econs., 1962-64. Lead singer The Rolling Stones, 1962—. Singer: (albums with The Rolling Stones) England's Newest Hitmakers: The Rolling Stones, 1964, 12 X 5, 1964, The Rolling Stones, Now!, 1965, Out of Our Heads, 1965, December's Children (And Everybody's), 1965, Big Hits, High Tide, & Green Grass, 1966, Aftermath, 1966, Got Live if You Want It!, 1966, Between the Buttons, 1967, Flowers, 1967, Their Satanic Majesties Request, 1967, Beggars Banquet, 1968, Through the Past, Darkly (Big Hits Vol. 2), 1969, Let It Bleed, 1969, Get Yer Ya-Yas Out!: The Rolling Stones in Concert, 1970, Hot Rocks, 1964-1971, 1971, Sticky Fingers, 1971, More Hot Rocks: Big Hits and Fazed Cookies, 1972, Exile on Main Street, 1972, Goats Head Soup, 1973, It's Only Rock and Roll, 1974, Metamorphosis, 1975, Made in the Shade, 1975, Black and Blue, 1976, Love You Live, 1977, Some Girls, 1978, Emotional Rescue, 1980, Sucking in the Seventies, 1981, Tattoo You, 1981, "Still Life" (American Concert, 1981), 1982, Undercover, 1983, Rewind (1971-1984), 1984, Dirty Work, 1986, Singles Collection: The London Years, 1989, Steel Wheels, 1989, Flashpoint, 1990, Jump Back: The Best of the Rolling Stones, 1993, Voodoo Lounge, 1994 (Grammy Award for Best Rock Album, 1994), Stripped, 1995, Bridges to Babylon, 1997, No Security, 1999, Forty Licks, 2002, Singles: 1965-1967, 2004, Live Licks, 2004, A Bigger Bang, 2005, Rarities 1971-2003, 2005, (albums with The Rolling Stones & other artists) Jamming With Edward, 1972, The Rolling Stone's Rock and Roll Circus, 1996, (solo albums) She's The Boss, 1985, Primitive Cool, 1987, Wandering Spirit, 1993, Goddess In the Doorway, 2001, (soundtracks) Alfie, 2004 (with David A. Stewart) Golden Globe award for best original song "Old Habits Die Hard", 2005); performer: (films) Gimme Shelter, 1970, Sympathy for the Devil, 1970, Ladies and Gentlemen: The Rolling Stones, 1974, Let's Spend the Night Together, 1983, 25 X 5: The Continuing Adventures of the Rolling Stones, 1989, At The Max, 1991, Voodoo Lounge, 1995, The Rolling Stones Rock and Roll Circus, 1996, The Rolling Stones Bridges to Babylon Tour '97-98, 1997, Being Mick, 2001; actor: (films) Performance, 1969, Ned Kelly, 1970, Freejack, 1992, Bent, 1997, The Man From Elysian Fields, 2001; prodr.: Enigma, 2001, The Women, 2004. Named Greatest Touring Band of All Time, World Music Awards, 2006; named an Honorary Knight Comdr. of the Most Excellent Order of the British Empire, Queen Elizabeth II, 2003; named to Rock and Roll Hall of Fame (as mem. of The Rolling Stones), 1989. Office: Virgin Records 5750 Wilshire Blvd Ste 300 Los Angeles CA 90036-3640

JAGLOM, ANDRE RICHARD, lawyer; b. NYC, Dec. 23, 1953; s. Jacob and Irene (Moore) J.; m. Janet R. Stampfl, Apr. 12, 1980; children: Peter Stampfl Jaglom, Wendy Stampfl Jaglom. BS in Mgmt., BS in Physics, MIT, 1974; JD, Harvard U., 1977. Bar: N.Y. 1978, U.S. Dist. Ct. (so. and ea. dists.) N.Y. 1978, U.S. Supreme Ct. 1982, U.S. Ct. Appeals (2d cir.) 1987. Assoc. Paul, Weiss, Rifkind, Wharton & Garrison, NYC, 1977-84; mng. ptnr. Stecher Jaglom & Prutzman LLP, NYC, 1984-2000; ptnr. Tannenbaum Helpern Syracuse & Hirschtritt LLP, NYC, 2000—. Bd. dirs. Cmty. Fund of Bronxville, Eastchester and Tuckahoe, Inc., 1988-94; lectr. law and the culinary bus. French Culinary Inst., 2002—, faculty, alcoholic beverage mktg., distbn., 2006-, Am. Conf. Inst. Computer mktg. and distbn. editor Computer Law Reporter, 1984-90; contbr. articles to profl. jours., chpts. to books. Trustee bd. edn. Bronxville Union Free Sch. Dist., 1997—2001. Mem.: ABA (adv. panel on bus. and corp. law 2006—), Bar Assn. City NY (computer law com. 1986—89, sec. 1990—94, com. on tech. and practice of law 1993—96), NY State Bar Assn. (co-chmn. internat. privacy law com. 2003—06, exec. com. internat. law and practice sect. 2003—, co-chmn. internat. distbn. sales and mktg. com. 2006—), Inst. of Masters of Wine N.Am. Inc. (bd. dir.), Am. Inst. Wine and Food (bd. dirs. N.Y. chpt. 1991—99, treas. 1992—99, adv. bd. 2000—, nat. bd. dirs. 2006—), MIT Club of N.Y. (counsel 2001—). Office: 900 3d Ave New York NY 10022-4728 Office Phone: 212-508-6740. Business E-Mail: jaglom@thshlaw.com.

JAGODA, BARRY LIONEL, communications executive, writer; b. Youngstown, Ohio, Feb. 5, 1944; s. Saul S. and Anne (Fradin) Jagoda; m. Karen Bernhardt, 1980. BA, U. Tex., 1966; MS, Columbia U., 1967. Writer, editor NBC News, Washington, 1967-69, NYC; prodr. CBS News, NYC, 1969-75; ptnr. Houston, Ritz, Cohen, Jagoda, NYC, 1975; TV advisor Jimmy Carter presdl. campaign, 1976; spl. asst. Pres., Washington, 1977-79, cons., 1979-80; pres. Am. Info. Exch., 1980—; dir. news and pub. affairs George Washington U., 1983-87; v.p. Stackig, Sanderson and White Advt. and Pub. Rels., 1988-93, Shandwick Pub. Affairs, Washington, 1993-97, IMPAC Corp., 1997-2001; writer Washington Times, 2001—03; dir. comms. U. Calif., San Diego, 2003—. Recipient Emmy award as producer CBS news special, Watergate 1974. Chmn. bd. dirs. Friends of Raoul Wallenberg Found., 1989-96. Ford Found. fellow, 1967 Mem. Nat. Bus. Travel Assn., Sigma Delta Chi. Home: 9302 La Jolla Farms Rd La Jolla CA 92037-2901 Office: Univ Calif 9500 Gilman Dr San Diego CA 92093-0938 Business E-Mail: bjagoda@ucsd.edu.

JAGR, JAROMIR, professional hockey player; b. Kladno, Czech Republic, Feb. 15, 1972; Right wing Poldi Kladno, 1988—90, Pitts. Penguins, 1990—2001, Washington Capitals, 2001—04, NY Rangers, 2004—, capt., 2006—; mem. Czech Republic Olympic Team, Nagano, Japan, 1998, Salt Lake City, 2002, Torino, Italy, 2006. Player NHL All-star game, 1992, 93, 96, 1998—2004. Named Best NHL Player, ESPY awards, 2006; named to All-Rookie Team, NHL, 1991, First All-Star Team, 1995, 1996, 1998—2001, 2006, Second All-Star Team, 1997, Czechoslavakian League All-Star Team, 1989—90; recipient Art Ross Trophy, 1995, 1998—2001, Hart Meml. Trophy, 1999, Lester B. Pearson Award, 1999, 2000, 2006, Golden Stick trophy for Czech Republic player of yr., 1995, 1996, 1999, 2000, 2002, 2005, 2006. Achievements include being a member of Stanley Cup Champion Pitts. Penguins, 1991, 1992; being a member of gold medal winning Czech Republic Hockey Team, Nagano Olympics, 1998, bronze medal team, Torino Olympics, Italy, 2006; set the NY Rangers franchise record for goals in a season, 2006. Office: c/o New York Rangers 2 Pennsylvania Plaza New York NY 10121*

JAHANMIR, SAID, materials scientist, mechanical engineer; b. Mar. 18, 1950; married; 2 children. BSME, U. Wash., 1971; MSME, MIT, 1973, PhD in Mech. Engring., 1976. Instr. mech. engring. MIT, 1975-76; lectr. mech. engring. U. Calif., 1976-77; asst. prof. Sibley Sch. Mech. & Aerospace Engring. Cornell U., 1977-80; sr. staff engr. Exxon Rsch. and Engring. Co., 1980-85; program dir. tribology program NSF, 1985-87; group leader Nat. Inst. Stds. & Tech., 1987—2002; pres., CEO MitiHeart Corp., Gaithersburg, Md., 2002—. Adj. prof. mech. engring. U. Md., 1987-96; adj. prof. U. Del., 1997—; presenter in field. Author: Tribology in Manufacturing Processes, 1994, Friction and Wear of Ceramics, 1994, Machining of Ceramics and Composites, 1999; exec. editor Machining Sci. and Tech. Jour.; contbr. articles to profl. jours., chpts. to books; patentee in field. Mem.: ASME (tribology divsn. exec. com. 1988—90, assoc. editor 1990—93, bd. rsch. and tech. devel. 1995—98, chair tribology divsn. 1997—99, v.p. rsch. 2001—04, others, Disting. Svc. award, Mayo D. Hersey award 2001), Am. Soc. for Artificial Internal Organs, Soc. Tribologists and Lubrication Engrs. (lubrication fundamentals com. 1986—87, ceramics and compositets com. founding chmn. 1987—89, ann. meeting program com. 1987—91, edn. com. 1987—95, fellows com. 1993—99, Internat. award). Office: MitiHeart Corp PO Box 83610 Gaithersburg MD 20883 Office Phone: 301-869-9720. Business E-Mail: sjahanmir@mitiheart.com.

JAHIEL, RENE INO, physician; b. Boulogne, Seine, France, Mar. 29, 1928; s. Richard and Cecile (Lwovsky) J.; m. Deborah Berg, May 8, 1955; children: Abigail, Richard, Beth. BA, NYU, 1946; MD, SUNY, Bklyn., 1950; PhD, Columbia U., 1957. Intern Montefiore Hosp., NYC, 1950-51; resident Mt. Sinai Hosp., NYC, 1951—52, fellow in virology, 1952-55; exptl. immunologist Nat. Jewish Hosp., Denver, 1957-59; asst. attending pathologist, exptl. pathology Mt. Sinai Hosp., 1959-61; asst. prof. pub. health Cornell U. Med. Coll., NYC, 1961-66; rsch. assoc. prof. preventive medicine NYU, NYC, 1967-70, rsch. prof., 1970-76, rsch. prof. medicine, Sch. Medicine, 1976-88. Cons. health svcs. rsch., policy and planning, 1989—; adj. prof. health svcs., rsch. and policy New Sch. for Social Rsch., 1991-96; dean faculty of sci. and pub. health, Ecole Libre des Hautes Etudes of N.Y., 1991-94, v.p. scis., 1994—, acting pres., 2003-06, pres. 2006—; vis. prof. dept. cmty. medicine and healthcare U. Conn. Health Ctr., 1995-98, lectr., 1999—; pres. Internat. Health Policy Rsch. Corp., Hartford, Conn., 1995—; med. dir. Southbury (Conn.) Tng. Sch., 1993-95; med. cons. State of Conn. Dept. Mental Retardation, 1996-97; tchr. met. leadership program, U. Coll., NYU, 1969-73; physician Assn. for Help for Retarded Children, 1982-88, Young Adult Inst., 1984-89, Assn. for Children with Retarded Mental Devel., 1988-93; cons. Nat. Ctr. for Health Svcs. Rsch., 1983-85; bd. dirs. N.Y. Scientists Com. Pub. Info., 1974-79, Physicians Forum, 1975-84; cons. Yale U Primary Care Tng. Program at Waterbury (Conn.) Hosp., 2000-04. Editor: Homelessness: A Prevention-Oriented Approach, 1992; contbr. articles to profl. jours.; mem. editl. bd. European Jour. Disability Rsch., 2007—. Mem. interferon adv. com. Am. Cancer Soc., 1984-93; mem. nat. bd. Com. for Nat. Health Svc., 1976-79, coalition, 1980-85. Lt. USNR, 1955-57. Recipient Daring to Dream award, U. Maine, 2005; grantee, USPHS, 1966—79. Mem.: APHA (chmn. com. health svcs. rsch. 1980—87, governing com. 1983—85, 1999—2007, chmn. homelessness study group 1984—90, chmn. policy com. caucus on disablement 1989—92, founding chmn. caucus on homelessness 1990—91, chmn. membership com. spl. interest group on disability 1993—97, chair 1998—99, edn. bd. 2000—01, Med. Care sect. award 1985), Am. Assn. Psychol. Rehab., Acad. Health, Internat. Soc. for Equity in Health (founding), World Assn. Psychosocial Rehab. (chmn. com. on mental handicaps 1992—94), Assn. Health Svcs. Rsch. (Spl. Recognition award 1986), Internat. Soc. Sys. Sci. Health Care, Physicians for Social Responsibility, Internat. Assn. Health Policy (bd. dirs. 1998—2000). Achievements include research in tissue culture, virology, interferon, preventive medicine, health policy, health svcs. rsch., disability, homelessness, sociology of knowledge. Office: 250 Main St Unit 732 Hartford CT 06106-1875 Business E-Mail: jahiel@nso2.uchc.edu.

JAHNKE, KRISTOPH, internist, hematologist, oncologist, researcher; b. Halle, Germany, Apr. 13, 1973; s. Hans-Otto and Monika Jahnke. RN, Franziskus Hosp., Bielefeld, Germany, 1995; MD, Martin Luther Univ., Halle-Wittenberg, Germany, 2001. Lic. Oreg. Bd. Med. Examiners, 2005. Resident and fellow dept. hematology, oncology and transfusion medicine Charité Univ. Medicine, Berlin, 2002—; rsch. instr. and vis. instr. dept. neurology, blood-brain barrier and neuro-oncology program and dept. medicine Oreg. Health and Sci. U., Portland, 2005—07. Contbr. articles to profl. jours. Mem.: German Soc. Hematology and Oncology, German Soc. Internal Medicine, German Cancer Soc., European Soc. Med. Oncology, Am. Soc. Clin. Oncology, German Child Welfare Orgn. (assoc.), Fedn. for Environment and Nature Protection Germany (assoc.), Marburger Fedn. (assoc.), German Child Def. Assn. (assoc.). Office: Charité Univ Medicine Campus Benjamin Franklin Dept Hematology Oncology and Transfusion Hindenburgdamm 30 D-12200 Berlin Germany Home Phone: 49-5201-2524; Office Phone: 49-30-84452337.

JAHNS, JEFFREY, lawyer; b. Chgo., July 6, 1946; s. Maxim G. and Josephine Barbara (Czernek) J.; m. Jill Metcoff, Sept. 8, 1973; children: Anna Hope, Claire Martine, Elizabeth Grace. AB, Villanova U., 1968; JD, U. Chgo., 1971. Bar: Ill. 1971, U.S. Dist. Ct. (no. dist.) Ill. 1971, U.S. Ct. Appeals (7th cir.) 1973, U.S. Supreme Ct. 1974. Assoc. Roan & Grossman, Chgo., 1971-77, ptnr., 1977-81, Seyfarth Shaw LLP, Chgo., 1981—. Mem. tax mgmt. adv. bd. Bur. Nat. Affairs, Washington, 1981—. Co-author: Corporate Acquisition Debt Interest Deduction, 1973; contbr. numerous articles to legal publs., chpts. to books. Trustee, sec. Chgo. Architecture Found., 1982—; bd. dirs. Prairie Ave. House Mus., 1995-98; trustee, treas. Graham Found., 1998—; bd. dir., treas. Am. Friends of Coubertin Inc., 2007. Ctr. for Urban Studies fellow U. Chgo., 1969-71. Mem. ABA, Chgo. Bar Assn. (chmn. various coms.), Internat. Coun. Shopping Ctrs., Mid-Day Club, Econ. Club Chgo., Lambda Alpha. Office: Seyfarth Shaw LLP 131 S Dearborn St Ste 2400 Chicago IL 60603-5577 Home Phone: 773-728-0994; Office Phone: 312-460-5819. Business E-Mail: jjahns@seyfarth.com.

JAHREN, (A.) HOPE, geochemist, educator; BA, U. Minn., Mpls., 1991; PhD, U. Calif., Berkeley, 1996. Postdoctoral rschr. ecosystem sci. divsn. U. Calif., Berkeley, 1996; asst. prof. geochemistry Ga. Inst. Tech., 1996—99; asst. prof. geobiology Johns Hopkins U., Balt., 1999—2003, assoc. prof., 2003—06, prof., 2006—. Contbr. articles to sci. jours. Named one of Brilliant 10, Popular Sci. mag., 2005; recipient Macelwane medal, Am. Geophys. Union, 2005. Fellow: Geol. Soc. Am. (Donath award 2001). Office: Johns Hopkins U Dept Earth and Planetary Scis 301 Olin Hall 34th and N Charles Sts Baltimore MD 21218 Office Phone: 410-516-7134. Office Fax: 410-516-7933. E-mail: jahren@jhu.edu.*

JAIN, ARCHANA, medical educator; MB, BChir, Maulana Azad Med. Coll., New Delhi, 2001. Diplomate Am. Bd. Internal Medicine, 2006. Internal medicine housestaff St. Francis Hosp., Evanston, Ill., 2003—06, chief med. resident, 2005—06; academic hospitalist U. Ala. Sch. Medicine, Tuscaloosa, 2006—. Mem.: ACP (assoc.), Soc. Gen. Internal Medicine (assoc.). Home Phone: 708-386-3205. Home Fax: 205-348-1770.

JAIN, DIPAK CHAND, dean, marketing educator, consultant; b. Tezpur, India, June 9, 1957; came to U.S., 1983; s. Jagdish C. and Sumitra (Jain) J.; m. Sushant Jain, Dec. 12, 1989; children: Dhwani, Kalash, Muskaan. BS in math. and stats., Gauhati U., Assam, India, 1976, MS in math. stats., 1978; MS in mgmt. sci., U. Tex., Dallas, 1986, PhD in mktg., 1987. Asst. prof. Gauhati U., 1979-83; teaching and rsch. asst. U. Tex., Dallas, 1983-86; asst. prof. mktg. Kellogg Sch. Mgmt., Northwestern U., Evanston, Ill., 1986-89, assoc. prof., 1990-93, prof. mktg., 1993—, Sandy and Morton Goldman prof. entrepreneurial studies, 1994—, assoc. dean for acad. affairs, 1996—2001, dean, 2001—. Vis. prof. mktg., Sasin Grad. Inst. Bus. Adminstrn., Chulalongkorn U., Bangkok, 1989-; mktg. dept. editor, Management Science; bd. dirs. Deere & Co., Hartmarx Corp., Peoples Energy Corp., UAL Corp., No. Trust Corp., 2004-; cons. to pharm. and telecom. firms, consumer goods co. Recipient Outstanding Educator Award, State of Assam, India, 1982, Sidney Levy Award for Excellence in Tchg., Kellogg Sch. Mgmt., 1994—95, Alumni Prof. of Yr. Award, 2002, Pravasi Bharatiya Samman Award, govt. India, 2004. Office: Northwestern U 2001 Sheridan Rd Evanston IL 60208-0814 Office Phone: 847-491-2728. E-mail: d-jain@kellogg.northwestern.edu.*

JAIN, JOHN KUMAR, medical educator, health facility administrator; b. Georgetown, Guyana, June 15, 1962; s. Sat Kumar and Celeste Chandrouti Jain; children: Luke Edward, Kate Evelyn. BA, U. So. Calif., LA, 1986, MS, 1988, MD, 1992. Assoc. prof. U. So. Calif., 1998—; med. dir. Lyan Inst. Fertility Rsch., LA, 2005—. Bd. mem. Excel Nat. Bank, Beverly Hills, Calif., 2005—06. Grantee, NIH, 2002—05. Mem.: Am. Coll. Obstetrics and Gynecology (nat. ethics com. 2004—), Am. Soc. Reproductive Medicine. Avocations: running, horse breeding, wine tasting. Office: Santa Monica Fertility Specialists 2825 Santa Monica Boulevard Santa Monica CA 90404 Home Phone: 213-713-2569; Office Phone: 866-991-1990.

JAIN, MANISH, researcher; b. New Delhi, May 22, 1975; s. Kunth Kumar and Rekha Jain; m. Tracy Lynne Palazzolo, Feb. 10, 2004. B in Engring. Electronics with Optoelectronics, U. Glasgow, Scotland, 1998, PhD, 2003. Lab. demonstrator U. Glasgow, 1998—2002; postdoc. rschr. U. Regensburg, Germany, 2003—05; postdoc. fellow U. Rochester, NY, 2006—. Recipient award for poster presentation, Inst. of Physics Quantum Electronics and Photonics Conf., 2001. Mem.: IEEE (Pa.) (assoc.). Achievements include research in Continuing work on investigating mid-infrared type-II quantum well lasers; Successfully achieved the first colliding pulsed mode-locked operation in broad gain multiple width quantum well material (also referred to as asymmetric wells); Tera-Hertz superlattice oscillators, European Commission project entitled "Interaction". Avocations: travel, photography. Office: U Rochester Inst of Optics Wilmot Bldg 275 Hutchinson Rd Rochester NY 14627 Personal E-mail: manish.jain@ieee.org.

JAIN, PIYARE LAL, physics professor; b. Punjab, India, Dec. 11, 1921; came to U.S., 1949; naturalized, 1961; s. Labh Ch and Maya (Devi) J.; m. Sulakshana Dhawan, Feb. 15, 1966. BA, Punjab U., 1944, MA, 1948; PhD, Mich. State U., 1954. Research assoc. chemistry dept. U. Minn., 1953-54; instr. physics dept. State U. N.Y., Buffalo, 1954-59, asst. prof., 1959-61, assoc. prof., 1961-67, prof., 1967—. Research assoc. U. Chgo., 1959-60, Lawrence Radiation Lab., Berkeley, Calif.; vis. prof., Bristol, Eng., 1961-62, U. Wash., Seattle, summer 1960; Fulbright vis. prof. Rajasthan U., India, 1965-66; Sci. adviser Am. embassy AID, New Delhi, India, summer 1966 Recipient Excellence award State of N.Y. and United Univ. Professions, Hind Ratten award Govt. of India, 1994. Fellow Am. Phys. Soc. Achievements include rsch. in sold state physics, electron and nulcear magnetic reesonance, cosmic radiation and high energy physics, relativistic heavy ion physics. Home: 223 Surrey Run Buffalo NY 14221-3363 Office: Suny At Buffalo Buffalo NY 14260-0001

JAIN, PREM CHAND, mechanical engineer; b. New Delhi, Jan. 26, 1936; s. Kishori Lal and Kapoori Devi Jain; m. Renu Jain, Oct. 3, 1965; 1 child, Payal. BME, Banaras Hindu U., 1957; MSME, U. Minn., 1960, PhD in Mech. Engring., 1967. Trainee engr. Imperial Chemical Industries, Melbourne, Australia, 1956-57; sr. rsch. engr. Carrier Corp. RDC, Syracuse, NY, 1967-69; vis. prof. Indian Inst. Tech., Kanpur, 1970-71; sr. engr. Stein Doshi Bhalla, New Delhi, 1971-79; chmn., mng. dir. Spectral Svc. Cons. Pvt. Ltd., New Delhi, 1980—. Vis. prof. Sch. Planning & Architecture, Delhi U., New Delhi, 1973—; cons. engr. with 45 yrs. experience in design of Heating, Ventilating and Air-Conditioning, elec., pub. health, fire suppression, bld. automation system, security, data and voice transmissions sys. for bldgs. in India and worldwide; convener National Bldg. Codes (section Bldg. Svcs.) Bur. Indian Stds., 2005; designer svs. sys. more than eight hundred super deluxe hotels, state of art med. facilities, instnl. bldgs., large comml. complexes and multiplex theatres all over the country; bd. dirs. Triveni Kala Sangam, New Delhi and Rangu Lal Trust, Delhi; pres. emeritus. Indian Society of Heating, Refrigerating and Air-Conditioning Engrs., 1992; chmn. India Green Bldg. Coun.; chmn. Internat. Green Bldg. Congress, 2006. Recipient Best Faculty award, Sch. Planning and Architecture, Delhi U., 1990, Rashtriya Gaurav award, All-India Achiever's Conf., 1997, Platinum award Godrej Bus. Ctr., Leadership in Energy and Environ. Design, 2003, Platinum award ITC Green Ctr., 2004, Platinum award Wipro Gurgaon, 2005, Lifetime Achievement award, IPA, 2005. Fellow Am. Soc. Heating, Refrigerating and Air-Conditioning Engrs. (founder, pres. India chpt.-at-large 1990, Louise and Bill Holladay Disting. fellow and ASHRAE Highest award 2005), Internat. Inst. Refrigeration London, Instn. Engrs. India, Instn. Energy Engrs. India, Indian Soc. Lighting Engrs., Indian Soc. Heating, Refrigerating and Air Conditioning Engrs. (founding mem., pres. emeritus 1992); mem. ASME, Internat. Solar Energy Soc. (Germany), Nat. Fire Protection Assn., Illuminating Engring. Soc. N.Am., Consulting Engrs. Assn. India. The Spectral organization has the distinct honor of being the only consultanting organization in the world today of having designed the service system for three platinum rated Green Buildings accredited by Leed, USA. Home: S 126 Greater Kailash II New Delhi 110048 India Office: Spectral Svcs Cons Pvt Ltd A-197 sector- 63 Noida 201301 India Home Phone: 91-11-29218059; Office Phone: 91-120-4049000. Office Fax: 91-120-4049001. Business E-Mail: spectraldel2@airtelbroadband.net, info@spectralservices.net.

JAIN, RACHNA D., psychologist, consultant, small business owner; b. Richmond, Va., Oct. 7, 1970; d. Daya and Usha Jain; m. Michael G. Purkis, Apr. 15, 2006. BA in Psychology, George Washington U., 1992; PsyD, U. Denver, 1998. Lic. psychologist Md., 2000. Pvt. practice psychology assoc., Glen Burnie, Md., 1998—2000; owner Excel with Ease Internat., Beltsville, Md., 2000—. V.p. Jain Found., Columbia, Md., 2002—. Author: (book) Get it Done: A Coach's Guide to Dissertation Success, 2002, Get it Done Faster: Secrets of Dissertation Success, 2004, Overcome Rejection: The SMART Way, 2006; contbg. editor: Seventeen Mag., 2004—. Mem.: APA. Avocations: travel, reading, technology, sailing, music. Office Phone: 410-772-3758. Business E-Mail: rachna@rachnajain.com.

JAIN, RAKESH K., chemical engineering and tumor biology educator; b. Lalitpur, India, Dec. 18, 1950; came to U.S., 1972; s. Sanat Kumar and Kailash W. Jain; m. Janet Carrick. BTech in Chem. Engring., Indian Inst. Tech., Kanpur, 1972; MS in Chem. Engring., U. Del., 1974, PhD in Chem. Engring., 1975. Asst. prof. chem. and biomed. engring. Columbia U., NYC, 1976-78; from asst. to assoc. prof. chem. and biomed. engring. Carnegie Mellon U., Pitts., 1978-83, prof., 1983-91; Andrew Werk Cook prof. tumor biology dept. radiation oncology Harvard Med. Sch., Boston, 1991—; dir. Edwin L. Steele Lab. for Tumor Biology MGH Cancer Ctr. Mass. Gen. Hosp., Boston, 1991—; prof. Harvard-MIT divsn. health scis. and tech. MIT, Cambridge, Mass., 1991—. Vis. prof. chem. engring. MIT, 1983; vis. prof. bioengring. U. Calif., San Diego, LaJolla, 1984; vis. prof. radiology Stanford (Calif.) U. Med. Sch., 1984; vis. prof. pathophysiology, U. Mainz, Germany, 1990-91; vis. prof. surg. rsch. U. Munich, 1991; vice chmn. Gordon Conf. Microcirculation, 1993; cons. Lab. Pathophysiology, NCI, 1976-84, DuPont Merck Pharm., Wilmington, Del., 1988-90, Hybritech-Lily, San Diego, 1988-93; mem. adv. bd. Pitts. Biomed. Devel. Corp., 1989-91; mem. radiation study sect. NIH, 1991-94; bd. dirs. Am. Cancer Soc.; B.F. Ruth lectr. Iowa State U., Ames, 1983; Allan P. Colburn lectr. U. Del., Newark, 1983; Hugh C. Muldoon lectr. Duquesne U., Pitts., 1986; Kurt Wohl lectr. U. Del., 1992. Mem. edit. bd. Biotech. Progress, 1985—, Microvascular Rsch., 1985—, CRC Crit. Revs. in Biomed. Engring., 1986-95, Cancer Rsch., 1987—, Drug Targeting and Delivery, 1991—, Microcirculation, 1994-2001, Angiogenesis, 1997-, British Journal of Cancer, 1997-, Internat. Journal of Oncology, 1997-, Journal of Theoretical Medicine, 1997, Molecular Imaging, 2002, Clinical Cancer Rsch., 2003, Nature Reviews Cancer (Highlights Section), 2004-. Recipient Rsch. Career Devel. award Nat. Cancer Inst., 1980-85, Abbott Microcirculation award European Soc. Microcirculation, 1990, Sr. Scientist award Alexander von Humboldt Found., 1990-91, Instrumentation for Physiology and Medicine award Am. Microcirculation Soc., 1993, 94, Disting. Alumnus award Indian Inst. Tech., 1994; Outstanding Investigator grantee Nat. Cancer Inst., 1993—; John Simon Guggenheim Meml. Found. fellow, 1983-84. Fellow Am. Inst. Biol. and Med. Engrs. (founder); mem. AICE (chmn. nat. planning com. area 15e-engring. fundamentals in life scis. 1981-84, chmn. tech. sects. life scis. area 1976-82, 84-86, co-editor AIChE Symposium Series 1983, 86), AAAS, NAE, Am. Assn. Cancer Rsch., N.Am. Soc. Biorheology (chmn. membership com. 1988-90), N.Am. Hyperthermia Soc., N.Y. Acad. Scis. (chmn. thermal characteristics of tumors conf. 1979, guest editor Annals N.Y. Acad. Scis. 1980), Internat. Inst. Microcirculation (bd. dirs. 1987-91, co-chmn. cancer cells and tumor microcirculation conf. 1989, Rsch. award 1984), Microcirculation Soc. (chmn. membership com. 1986-88, nomination com. 1993—), Biomed. Engring. Soc. (conf. chmn. ann. meeting 1987, chmn. meeting programming com. 1987-90), Radiation Rsch. Soc., Sigma Xi, Inst. Medicine. Avocations: swimming, classical music, jazz. Office: Edwin L Steele Lab Dept Radiation Oncology, Cox 7 Mass Gen Hosp Boston MA 02114 Office Phone: 617-724-1819. Office Fax: 617-726-7083. E-mail: jain@steele.mgh.harvard.edu.

JAISI, DEB P., geologist, researcher; MSc in Geology, Tribhuvan U., Kathmandu, 1998; MS in Geotechnical & Geoenviron. Engring., Asian Inst. Tech., Klong Luang, Thailand, 2003; PhD in Geology, Miami U., Oxford, Ohio, 2007. Asst. prof. Tribhuvan U., Kathmandu, Nepal, 1999—2001; rsch. assoc. Asian Inst. Tech., 2002—03, Miami U., 2003—; interdepartmental Bateman scholar Yale U., New Haven, 2007—. Recipient Gold medal award, King Nepal, 1999. Achievements include development of reactive barrier for the immobilization of inorganic contaminants. Office: Yale Univ Dept Geology and Geophysics 210 Whitney Ave New Haven CT 06511 Office Phone: 203-432-3180. Personal E-mail: jaisi72@hotmail.com. Business E-Mail: debjaisi@yale.edu.

JAKAB, IRENE, psychiatrist; b. Oradea, Romania; came to U.S., 1961, naturalized, 1966; d. Odon and Rosa A. (Riedl) J. MD, Ferencz József U., Kolozsvar, Hungary, 1944; lic. in psychology, pedagogy, philosophy cum laude, Hungarian U., Cluj, Rumania, 1947; PhD summa cum laude, Pazmany Peter U., Budapest, 1948; Dr honoris causa, U. Besançon, France, 1982, U. Pécs, Hungary, 1999. Diplomate Am. Bd. Psychiatry, Am. Bd. Pediatric Neuropsychology. Rotating intern Ferencz József U., 1943-44; resident in psychiatry Univ. Hosp., Kolozsvar, 1944-47, resident in neurology, 1947-50; resident internal medicine Univ. Hosp. for Internal Medicine, Pécs, Hungary, 1950-51; chief physician Univ. Hosp. for Neurology and Psychiatry, Pécs, 1951-59; staff neuropathol. rsch. lab. Neurol. Univ. Clinic, Zurich, 1959-61; sect. chief Kans. Neurol. Inst., Topeka, 1961-63; dir. rsch. and edn., 1966; resident psychiatry Topeka State Hosp., 1963-66; asst. psychiatrist McLean Hosp., Belmont, Mass., 1966-67, assoc. psychiatrist, 1967-74; prof. psychiatry U. Pitts. Med. Sch., 1974-89, prof. emerita, 1989—, co-dir. med. student edn. in psychiatry, 1981-89. Dir. John Merck Program, 1974-81; faculty dept. psychiatry Med. Sch., Pecs, 1951-59; asst. Univ. Hosp. Neurology, Zurich, 1959-61; assoc. psychiatry Harvard U., Boston, 1966-69, asst. prof. psychiatry, 1969-74, program dir. grad course mental retardation, 1970-87; lectr. psychiatry, 1974—; editor in chief newsletter Am. Bd. Pediatric Neuropsychiatry. Author: Dessins et Peintures des Aliénés, 1956, Zeichnungen und Gemälde der Geisteskranken, 1956, Pictorial Expression in Psychiatry, 1998; editor: Psychiatry and Art, 1968, Art Interpretation and Art Therapy, 1969, Conscious and Unconscious Expressive Art, 1971, Transcultural Aspects of Psychiatric Art, 1975; co-editor: Dynamische Psychiatrie, 1974; mem. editl. bd. Confinia Psychiatrica, 1975-99; contbr. articles to profl. jours. Recipient 1st prize Benjamin Rush Gold medal award for sci. exhibit, 1980, Bronze Chris plaque Columbus Film Festival, 1980, Leadership award Am. Assn. on Mental Deficiency, 1980; Menninger Sch. Psychiatry fellow, Topeka, 1963-66. Mem. AMA, Am. Psychol. Assn., Am. Psychiat. Assn., Société Medico Psychologique de Paris, Internat. Rorschach Soc., N.Y. Acad. Scis., Internat. Soc. Psychopathology of Expression (v.p. 1959—), Am. Soc. Psychopathology of Expression (chmn. 1965—, Ernst Kris Gold Medal award 1988), Royal Soc. of Medicine (overseas fellow), Internat. Soc. Child Psychiatry and Allied Professions, Internat. Assn. Knowledge Engrs. (v.p. for medicine 1988-95), Deutschsprachige Gesellschaft für Psychopathologie des Ausdruckes (hon. Prinzhorn prize 1967), Hungarian Psychiat. Assn. (hon. 1992), World Psychiat. Assn. (co-chmn. sect. on mass and media and mental health, co-chmn. sect. on psychopathology of expression). Home and Office: 74 Lawton St Brookline MA 02446-5801 Office Phone: 617-738-9821.

JAKES, J. MICHAEL, lawyer; b. Waukegan, Ill., May 28, 1957; s. John William and Rachel (Payne) J.; m. Carolee Taylor, June 16, 1979; children: Nathan Taylor, John Matthew, William Payne. BSEE, Duke U., 1979; MS, Johns Hopkins U., 1983; JD, Georgetown U., 1986. Bar: Va. 1986, D.C. 1988, U.S. Ct. Appeals (fed. cir.) 1988, U.S. Dist. Ct. (eas. dist.) Va. 1993, U.S. Supreme Ct. 1993, U.S. Patent and Trademark Office 1988. Elec. engr. Westinghouse Corp., Balt., 1979—83; law clk. Hon. Giles S. Rich U.S. Ct. Appeals (fed. cir.), Washington, 1986—88; assoc. Finnegan, Henderson, Farabow, Garrett & Dunner, 1988—94, ptnr., 1995—. Lectr. Columbus Sch. Law, Cath. U., Washington, 1993-96. Co-author: Court of Appeals for the Federal Circuit: Practice and Procedure, 1993; mem. editorial bd. Mealy's Litigation Reporter: Intellectual Property, 1992—; contbr. articles to profl. jours. Mem. ABA, D.C. Bar, Va. Bar, Fed. Cir. Bar Assn., Am. Intellectual Property Law Assn., Giles S. Rich Am. Inn of Ct., Order of Coif, Eta Kappa Nu, Tau Beta Pi. Office: Finnegan Henderson et al 901 New York Ave Washington DC 20001 Home Phone: 703-556-0481; Office Phone: 202-408-4045.

JAKES, JOHN, author; b. Chgo., Mar. 31, 1932; s. John Adrian and Bertha (Retz) J.; m. Rachel Ann Payne, June 15, 1951; children: Andrea, Ellen, John Michael, Victoria. AB, DePauw U., 1953, LittD (hon.), 1977; MA, Ohio State U., 1954; LLD (hon.), Wright State U., 1976; LHD (hon.), Winthrop Coll., 1985, U. S.C., 1993, Ohio State U., 1996. With advt. dept. Abbott Labs., 1954-60; with creative dept. various advt. agencies, 1960-69; creative dir. Dancer Fitzgerald Sample Co., Dayton, Ohio, 1969-70. Rsch. fellow dept. history U. S.C., 1989. Author: The Texans Ride North, 1952, A Night for Treason, 1956, Murder He Says, 1958, When the Star Kings Die, 1967, Master of the Dark Gate, 1970, The Kent Family Chronicles: The Bastard, 1974, The Rebels, 1975, The Seekers, 1975, The Furies, 1976, The Titans, 1976, The Warriors, 1977, The Lawless, 1978, The Americans, 1980, North and South Trilogy: North and South, 1982, Love and War, 1984, Heaven and Hell, 1987, California Gold, 1989, Homeland, 1993, In the Big Country, 1993, American Dreams, 1998, On Secret Service, 2000, Charleston, 2002, Savannah (Or) A Gift for Mr. Lincoln, 2004, The Gods of Newport, 2006, (juvenile) Susanna of the Alamo, 1986, (musical) Great Expectations - The Musical, 1999; co-editor anthology: New Trails, 1994; editor: (anthology) A Century of Great Western Stories, 2000. Trustee DePauw U. Recipient Ohio Gov.'s award, 1977, ann. lit. award Friends of Rochester Pub. Libr., 1983, Citizen-Celebrity award for libr. advocacy White House Conf. on Librs., 1995, Disting. Alumni award Ohio State U. Coll. Humanities, 1995, Western Heritage Lit. award Nat. Cowboy Hall of Fame, 1995, Profl. Achievement award Ohio State U. Alumni Assn., 1997, Career Achievement award S.C. Humanities Coun., 1998, Cooper medal Thomas Cooper Libr., U. S.C., 2002, Owen Wister award Western Writers Am., 2007. Mem.: PEN, Century Assn., Writers Guild Am. (East), Authors Guild, Dramatists Guild, S.C. Acad. Authors, Rotary. Office: care Rembar & Curtis Post Box 908 Croton Falls NY 10519 E-mail: jjfiction@aol.com.

JAKES, PETER H., lawyer; b. NYC, July 17, 1946; s. Walter and Liesel (Lilienfield) J.; m. Karen J. Sorkin, Aug. 23, 1970; children: Susan J., Aaron G. AB with honors, Brown U., 1968; JD, Yale U., 1971. Bar: NY 1972, US Dist. Ct. (so., ea. dists.) NY 1975. Assoc. Willkie, Farr & Gallagher, NYC, 1971-79, ptnr., 1979—. Bd. dir. Selfhelp Comty. Svcs. Inc. Mem. ABA, Assn. of Bar of City of N.Y. Office: Willkie Farr & Gallagher 787 7th Ave New York NY 10019-6018 Office Phone: 212-728-8230. Office Fax: 212-728-9230. Business E-Mail: pjakes@willkie.com.

JAKES, T(HOMAS) D(EXTER), bishop; b. So. Charleston, WV, June 9, 1957; s. Ernest Jakes, Odith Jakes; m. Serita Jakes; 5 children. Founder, CEO Potter's House of Dallas, Inc., 1996—; founder Clay School. Host numerous conferences and speaking tours. Author: Can You Stand To Be Blessed?, 1994, So You Call Yourself a Man?, Woman Thou Art Loosed, Loose That Man and Let Him Go, The Lady, Her Lover, and Her Lord, 2000, Anointing Fall On Me, Your Harvest Without Limits, Follow the Star, God's Trophy Woman, Beside Every Good Man, 10 Commandments of Working in a Hostile Environment, God's Leading Lady, 2003, HeMotions: Even Strong Men Struggle, 2004, Mama Made the Difference, 2006 (Quills award religion/spirituality The Quills Literacy Found., 2006, NAACP Image award best instructional book, 2007), Reposition Yourself: Living Life Without Limits, 2007. Recipient Grammy Award, 2004, 100 Most Influential Black Americans, Ebony mag., 2006. Office: The Potter's House PO Box 5390 Dallas TX 75208*

JAKES, WILLIAM BRYAN, III, lawyer; s. William Bryan, Jr. and Una (Moore) Jakes; m. Rita Jane Whitten, Sept. 20, 1986; children: Bryan, Georgia. BS, Mid. Tenn. State U., Murfreesboro, 1979; JD, U. Memphis, 1982. Bar: Tenn. Ptnr. Howell Fisher, PLLC, Nashville, 1983—88, 1991—, North Gideon, Nashville, 1988—91. Bd. dirs. Donelson Christian Acad., Tenn., 1998—2005. Office: Howell Fisher PLLC 300 James Robertson Pky Nashville TN 37201

JAKES, WILLIAM CHESTER, electrical engineer; b. Milw., May 15, 1922; s. William Chester and Eleanor (Knight) J.; m. Mary Elizabeth Bristle, Sept. 3, 1948; children: Robert, Elizabeth. BS in Elec. Engring., Northwestern U., 1944, MS in Elec. Engring, 1947, PhD, 1949. With Bell Tel. Labs., Inc. (various locations), 1949-87, head radio transmission research dept. Holmdel, N.J., 1963-71; dir. Radio Transmission Lab., North Andover, Mass., 1971-87. Mem. sci. adv. bd. Voice of Am., 1957-58 Contbr. articles to profl. jours.; patentee antennas and comm. systems. With USN, 1944-46. Ph.D. (hon.) Iowa Wesleyan U., 1961; recipient Alumni Merit award Northwestern U., 1962 Fellow IEEE (Paper award 1971, co-recipient Alexander Graham Bell medal 1987); mem. Eta Kappa Nu, Pi Mu Epsilon. Home: 58 Wild Rose Dr Andover MA 01810-4620 *Intense dedication to physics and engineering with constant desire for understanding and intellectual honesty, plus the enjoyment of working with others, have been my guiding principles.*

JAKOBSON, MARK JOHN, retired physics professor; b. Carlyle, Mont., May 4, 1923; s. Hans M. and Bessie Mae (Fessenden) J.; m. Marguerite Elizabeth Thomsen, Aug. 17, 1945; children— Kristin Marie, Sandra Lynne. BA, U. Mont., 1944, MA, 1947; PhD (Whiting fellow), U. Calif., Berkeley, 1951. Physicist Lawrence Radiation Lab., 1951-52; instr. U. Wash., 1952-53; prof. U. Mont., Missoula, 1953-93, chmn. physics and astronomy dept., 1969-73. Mem. vis. staff Los Alamos Sci. Lab., 1963-96. Served to lt. (j.g.) USNR, 1944-46. Fellow Am. Phys. Soc.; mem. Sigma Xi, Phi Beta Kappa, Pi Mu Epsilon. Democrat. Lutheran. Home: 3000 Queen St Missoula MT 59801-8651 *A dominant force in my life has been a commitment to the work ethic, a commitment that was nurtured by the Depression. As part of that work ethic I have tried to focus my entire being at any given time on a particular problem. I believe that characteristic, when present in a delineated effort, is what identifies the true professional.*

JAKOPEC, CARL THOMAS, pharmaceutical executive; b. Chgo., May 31, 1945; s. Charles George and Lillian (Seps) Jakopec; m. Elizabeth Todd Dunlap, Aug. 23, 1969 (div. Sept. 1976); m. Carol Coon, Jan. 7, 1977 (dec. July 2006); children: Kimberly Jo, Jeffery Allyn. BS in Pharmacy, Drake U., Des Moines, 1969. Registered pharmacist Iowa. Chief pharmacy Walgreen Drug Co., Des Moines, 1969-77; owner Greeley Pharmacy Corp., Colo., 1977-81; mgr. govt. sales Marion Labs., Inc., Kansas City, Mo., 1981-95; dir. govt. sales Forest Labs., Inc., NYC, 1996—. Mem. nat. commn. future Drake U., 1988, mem. nat. adv. bd. Coll. Pharmacy, 1997—. Bd. dirs. Little League Baseball, Greeley, Colo., 1977—84. Recipient Distinguished Svc. award, Marine Corps League, 1992, Merit award, Uniformed Svc. Acad. Family Physicians, 2006. Mem.: Assn. Mil. Surgeons of US Sustaining Mems. (sec. 2005—, treas. 2005—, vice chmn. 2006, chmn. 2007), Am. Soc. Health Sys. Pharmacists, Am. Pharm. Assn., Am. Soc. Cons. Pharmacists, Nat. Hot Rod Assn., Ferrari Club Am., Sports Car Club Am. (bd. dirs. 1991—92). Avocations: auto racing, travel, golf. Home and Office: Forest Labs Inc 4033 Highland Castle Ct Las Vegas NV 89129-3664 Office Phone: 702-364-8162. Personal E-mail: ctjak@aol.com.

JAKSICH, DANIEL J., controller; V.p. Berkshire Hathaway Fin.; contr. Berkshire Hathaway, Inc., Omaha. Office: Berkshire Hathaway Inc 1440 Kiewit Plz Omaha NE 68131

JAKUBAUSKAS, EDWARD BENEDICT, college president; b. Waterbury, Conn., Apr. 14, 1930; s. Constantine and Barbara (Narstis) J.; m. Ruth Friz, Aug. 29, 1959; children— Carol, Marilyn, Mark, Eric. BA, U. Conn., 1952, MA, 1954; PhD, U. Wis., 1961. Economist FPC, 1956, Dept. Labor, 1956-58; instr. U. Wis., 1961-62, asst. prof. econs., 1962-63; asst. prof. Iowa State U., 1963-65, assoc. prof., 1965-66, prof., 1966-71; dean U. Wyo., 1971-76, prof. econs., 1971-79, v.p. acad. affairs, 1976-79; pres. SUNY, Geneseo, 1979-88, Cen. Mich. U., Mt. Pleasant, 1988-92; cons. in higher edn., 1992—. Author: Manpower Economics, 1971. Served with U.S. Army, 1954-56. Mem. Am. Assn. State Univs. and Colls. Mem. United Chs. of Christ.

JAKUBCZYK, JOHN JOSEPH, lawyer; b. New Britain, Conn., Dec. 21, 1953; s. Stanley Walter and Madeline Regina (Hinchliffe) J.; m. Petra Kunigunda Mead, Jan. 8, 1983; children: Kristan Marie, John Joseph II, Jamie Nicole, Joseph Michael, Michael Thomas, Stanley Walter, Peter Anthony, Samuel Francis, Justin Peter, Anthony Edward, William James. BA in Bus. Adminstrn. and Polit. Sci., U. San Diego, 1976; JD, U. Ariz., 1979. Bar: Ariz. 1979, U.S. Dist. Ct. Ariz. 1979, U.S. Ct. Appeals (9th cir.) 1992, U.S. Supreme Ct. 1989. Atty. pvt. practice, Phoenix, 1979—. Gen. counsel, Ariz. Right to Life, 1990-99, pres. 1999-2006; spkr. in field. Actor in cmty. theater prodns.; author pro-life articles; radio commentator and host Catechist St. Paul's Cath. Ch., 1982-92. Bd. dirs., cons. Ariz. Youth for Life, Phoenix, 1979-82; trustee Ville de Marie Acad., 1991-2005, pres., 1995-99, v.p., 1999-2001, treas. 2002-2005; chmn. polit. action com. Arizonans for Life, 1980-891; pres. Ariz. Right to Life, Phoenix, 1983-85, 99—, bd. dirs. 1983-92, v.p., 1988-89; bd. dirs. Life Ednl. Corp., 1984-90, sec.; founder, pres. S.W. Life and Law Ctr.; bd. advisors Free Speech

Advs.; precinct committeeman Rep. Com., Phoenix, 1982-96; pres. Life Ednl. Corp., 2000—. Recipient Pro-Life Action League Protector award, 1987, Wallace McWhirter award, 1989, Honor Guard award Alliance Defense Fund. Mem. ATLA, Ariz. State Bar Assn., Nat. Lawyers Assn. (bd. dirs. 1994—), Maricopa County Bar Assn., St. Thomas More Soc., Christian Legal Soc., Cardinal Newman Soc., KC (pro-life chmn. 1982-83, 2004-06), Phi Delta Phi. Office: 2711 N 24th St Ste 200 Phoenix AZ 85008-1052 Office Phone: 602-468-0030. E-mail: jakeslaw@lonet.net.

JAKUBOWSKI, JENNIFER SARA, music educator; b. Carpentersville, Ill., Feb. 16, 1973; d. Catherine Anne Andrews; m. Paul Matthew Jakubowski, June 21, 1997; children: Liam Andrew, Logan Daniel. BFA, U. Wis., Milw., 1997. Cert. music edn. Wis., 1997. Yoga instr. Feel Your Best Yoga, Mequon, Wis., 2001—04; instrumental band educator Grafton Sch. Dist., Grafton, Wis., 1997—; elem. music educator Grafton Elem., Wis., 1997—. Pub. rels. Grafton Educators Assn., 1999—2002; wis. listening project mem. Wis. Music Educators Assn., Madison, Wis., 2001—02. Home: W59 N954 Essex Dr Cedarburg WI 53012 Office: Grafton Elem Sch 1800 Washington Ave Grafton WI 53024 Home Phone: 262-546-4555; Office Phone: 262-376-5700. Personal E-mail: jjakubowski@grafton.k12.wi.us.

JAKUBOWSKY, FRANK RAYMOND, religious writer; b. Belfield, ND, Oct. 11, 1931; s. William and Catherine (O'bach) J. Student, U. N.D., 1950—52. Chemist Sherwin-Williams Paint Co., Emeryville, Calif., 1958—85; pres. Bold Books, Oakland, Calif., 1978—. Editor Spiritfest, Berkeley, Calif., 1997—. Author: Creation, 1978, Jesus Was a Leo, 1979, The Psychological Patterns of Jesus Christ, 1982, The Creative Theory of the Universe, 1983, Caldecott, 1985, Frank on a Farm, 1988, Lake Merritt, 1988, Thank God, I Am Alive, 1989, Whitman Revisted, 1989, Spiritual Symbols for the Astrology of the Soul, 1990, This New World; Birth: Sept. 8, 1958, 1990, Perceptive Types, 1993, Father Figure Frank's Stories, 1996, Inspiration Stories, 1998, Universal Mind, 1998, Big Bang Goes Puff, 1999, My Inspirational Stories, 2004, Oakland's Lake Merritt, 2004. Pfc. U.S. Army, 1952-54. Mem. Urantia Fellowship, Inst. Noetic Scis., Nat. Coun. Geocosmic Rsch. Roman Catholic. Avocation: writing songs for children on fraimba. Home: 1565 Madison St Apt 308 Oakland CA 94612-4511 Business E-Mail: boldbooks@sbcglobal.net.

JAKUBS, DEBORAH, university librarian; BA, U. Wis. Madison; MLIS, U. Calif. Berkeley; PhD in Latin Am. History, Stanford U., 1986. With Duke U., Durham, NC, 1983—, previously libr. for Latin Am. & Iberia, head Internat. and Area Studies Dept., dir. Collections Svc., Rita DiGiallonardo Holloway U. Libr. and vice provost Libr. Affairs, 2005—. Assoc. dir. U. NC-Duke U. Consortium in Latin Am. Studies, 1995—97, 2000—02, dir., 1997—99; chair Area Studies Coun. of Ctr. for Rsch. Libr.; mem. steering com. Program for Latin Am. Libr. & Archival Collections Harvard U.; adj. prof. history Duke U. Mem.: Assn. Rsch. Libraries (vis. program officer 1996—2002). Office: Duke U 220 Perkins Libr Durham NC 27708 Office Phone: 919-660-5800. E-mail: deborah.jakubs@duke.edu.*

JALALI, BEHNAZ, psychiatrist, educator; b. Mashad, Iran, Jan. 26, 1944; came to U.S., 1968; d. Badiolah and Bahieh (Shahidi) Samimy; m. Mehrdad Jalali, Sept. 18, 1968. MD, Tehran U., Iran, 1968. Rotating intern Burlington County Meml. Hosp., Mt. Holly, NJ, 1968—69; resident in psychiatry U. Md. Hosp., Balt., 1970—73; asst. prof. psychiatry dept. psychiatry Sch. Medicine Rutgers U., Piscataway, NJ, 1973—76, Yale U., New Haven, 1976—81, assoc. clin. prof. psychiatry, 1981—85; assoc. clin. prof. psychiatry dept. psychiatry UCLA, 1985—94, clin. prof. psychiatry dept. psychiatry Sch. Medicine, 1994—. Dir. psychotherapy Sch. Medicine Rutgers U., Piscataway, 1973-76; dir. family therapy unit dept. psychiatry Yale U., New Haven, 1976-85; chief clin. med. svcs. Mental Health Clinic, 1987-96; coord. med. student edn. in psychiatry West LA VA Hosp., 1985—2000; dir. family therapy clinic W.Va. VA Hosp., 1991—, co-leader Schozophrenia Clinic, Mental Health Clinic, West LA VA Med. Ctr., 1996—; med. dir. Mental Health Clinic, West LA VA Med. Ctr., 2004-. Author: (with others) Ethnicity and Family Therapy, 1982, Clinical Guidlines in Cross-Cultural Mental Health, 1988; contbr. articles to profl. jours. Fellow Am. Psychiatric Assn., Am. Orthopsychiatry Assn., Am. Assn. Social Psychiatry; mem. Am. Family Therapy Assn., So. Calif. Psychiatric Assn. (chair com. for women 1992), World Fedn. Mental Health. Avocations: photography, hiking, cinema, painting. Home: 1203 Roberto Ln Los Angeles CA 90077-2304 Office: UCLA Dept Psychiatry West LA VA Med Ctr B116aa Los Angeles CA 90073-1003 Office Phone: 310-268-4651. Business E-Mail: behnaz.jalali@med.va.gov.

JALBA, MIHAI SERGIU, epidemiologist, pulmonologist, physician, researcher; b. Tecuci, Moldova, Romania, May 28, 1953; arrived in US, 1995; s. Teodor and Olimpia Jalba; children: Theodor Lucian, Heliodor Ioan. MD, Carol Davila U. Medicine, 1980, PhD in Clin. Med. Scis., 2001; MPH in Epidemiology, U. Medicine Dentistry, NJ, 2006. Cert. pulmonologist Ministry of Health, Romania, 1994. Intern Nat. Inst. Endocrinology, Bucharest, 1980—83; gen. practitioner Barlad City Hosp., Perieni, Romania, 1984—87, Ialomitza County Hosp., Milosesti, Romania, 1987—91; sci. rschr. Nat. Inst. Pulmonology, Bucharest, 1991—95; assoc. sci. rschr. Bklyn. Hosp., 1996—2001; epidemiologist Dept. of Health, NYC, 2002—03; postdoctoral rsch. fellow Robert Wood Johnson Med. Sch., New Brunswick, NJ, 2004—. Contbr. articles to profl. jours. Mem.: N. am. Primary Care Rsch. Group, Am. Thoracic Soc., Romanian Soc. Pulmonology (sec. (exec. bd. nat. com.) 1992—95), So. Med. Assn. Achievements include breakthroughs in tuberculosis epidemiology, adult respiratory distress syndrome and asthma research. Avocations: chess, opera, violin. Personal E-mail: drmjalba@netzero.net.

JALBERT, JANELLE JENNIFER, executive recruiter, secondary school educator; d. Gerald Edward and Linda S. Jalbert. AA, Pasadena City Coll., 1995; BA cum laude, Calif. State U. Northridge, 1998; MEd, Nat. U., 2004, MA in Cross Cultural Tchg., 2006. Character edn. cert. U. San Diego Ext., 2004, cert. tchr. AP English lit., composition UCLA, 2005. Tchr. Sun Valley Mid. Sch., Calif., 1999—2000, New Ave. Ednl. Ctr., Monterey Park, Calif., 2000—02; owner, educator Solteria Acad., Monrovia, Calif., 2001—04; prin., owner Jalbert-Thomason Photography, Arcadia, Calif., 2003—04; tchr. English, activities dir. Monrovia HS, 2004—05; tchr. English Bonita HS, La Verne, Calif., 2005—. Bd. dirs., pres., assoc. Delta Dimensions, 2003—05; cons. Hondiat Inc., Arcadia, Calif., 1994—; co-founder, cons. YouCanDo-Travel.com, 2004—; owner, cons. J-Cubed Enterprises, 2007—; presenter in field. Author: Success Skills, 2001, Get Gatsby and Other Greats in Five Minutes a Day, 2006. Fundraiser, mem. crew Calif. AIDS Ride 4 &5, LA, 1997—98; founder Nat. U. Sigma Tau Delta, 2006—; ptnr. Life in the Word, Fenton, Mo., 2001—, World Changers Ministries, College Park, Ga., 2001—, Jesse Duplants Ministries, New Orleans, 2002—; ptnr. Aaron's Army TD Jakes Ministries, Dallas, 2003—04. Grantee Ednl. award, Sunshine Brooks Found., 1994, Sushine Brooks Found., 1995, John Glyes Ednl. Fund, 1997; scholar Collegiate Honor scholar, Nat. U., 2002. Mem.: Jr. C. of C. (com. Kasukabe, Japan Visitation 1999), Soroptimist Internat. (mem.Arcadia/Monrovia chpt. 2003—04, Youth Citizenship award 1991), Pi Lambda Theta (presenter internat. convention 2005), Blue Key (bd. dirs. 1996—98, Cmty. Svc. award 1996), Foothill Panhellenic, Omicron Delta Kappa (pres. 1997—98), Alpha Gamma Sigma (chair fundraising 1994—95), Sigma Kappa Alumnae (1st v.p. membership 2003—05). Avocations: travel, languages, wine, marine activities, photography. Office: Bonita High Sch 3201 D Street La Verne CA 91750 Personal E-mail: booksnmore4u@hotmail.com.

JALENAK, PEGGY EICHENBAUM, volunteer; b. Little Rock, Oct. 14, 1935; d. E. Charles and Helen Lockwood Eichenbaum; m. Leo Richard Jalenak, Jr., Aug. 28, 1955; children: Laurie J. Williamson, Terri J. Mendelson, Jan J. Ordway, E. Charles. Commr., vice chair Tenn. Art Commn., Nashville, 1975—80; bd. dirs., exec. com. Tennesseans for Arts, Nashville, 1981—85; bd. dirs. Tenn. State Mus. Found., Nashville, 1994—2003. Bd. dirs. Nat. Found. Jewish Culture, NYC, 1999—; former bd. dirs. Ballet Memphis, Theatre Memphis, Memphis Arts Coun., Memphis Jewish Fedn., 1997—, Bornblum Solomon Schechter Sch., 2002—; former bd. dirs., sec., treas. Opera Memphis; bd. dirs., past pres., sec. Memphis Jewish Hist. Soc. Memphis & Mid-South, 1998—; bd. dirs. Temple Israel Mus., 2001—; adv. bd. Judaic studies program U. Memphis, 2000—. Named Tenn. Arts Amb., Tenn. Arts Commn., 1985. Home: 6025 River Oaks Rd Memphis TN 38120

JALILI, NADER, mechanical engineer, educator; b. Tehran, Iran, Oct. 26, 1970; came to U.S., 1995; s. Ahmad and Delnaz (Doulat Abadi) J.; m. Jaleh Esmailzadeh, Dec. 5, 1993; children: Paneed Fatemeh, Pouya Mohammad. BSc with 1st class honors, Sharif U. tech., Tehran, 1992, MSc with 1st class honors, 1995; PhD, U. Conn., 1998. Design cons. Iranian truck Mfg., Tehran, 1992-93; tchg. asst. Sharif U. Tech., Tehran, 1993-95; design engr. Iranian Crane Mfg., Tehran, 1993-95; lectr. Azad U. Karaj, Iran, 1994-95; design cons. Indsl. Mixers Mfg. Co., Esfehan, Iran, 1994-95; rsch. asst. U. Conn., Storrs, 1995-98; vis. asst. prof. dept. mech. engring. No. Ill. U., DeKalb, 1999-2000; asst. prof. mech. engring. Clemson U., SC, 2000—06, assoc. prof. mech. engring., 2006—. Computer cons. Sharif U. Tech., 1993-94, U. Conn., 1997-98. Contbr. articles to profl. jours. Recipient Ralph E. Powe Jr. award, Oak Ridge Associated Univs. Dept. Energy, 2002, Career award, NSF, 2003; U. Conn. scholar fellow, 1995—98. Mem. ASME (founding chmn. vibration and control of smart structures tech. com., assoc. tech. editor), IEEE (tech. editor transaction). Muslim. Avocations: volleyball, running, soccer. Home: 108 Shaftsbury Rd Clemson SC 29631 Office Phone: 864-656-5642. Business E-Mail: jalili@clemson.edu.

JALLINS, RICHARD DAVID, lawyer; b. LA, Mar. 21, 1957; s. Walter Joshua and Elaine Beatrice (Youngerman) J.; m. Katherine Sue Pfeiffer, June 12, 1982; children: Stephen David, Rachel Marie. BA, U. Calif., Santa Barbara, 1978; JD, Calif. Western Sch. Law, 1981. Bar: Calif. 1988, U.S. Dist. Ct. (so. dist.) Calif. 1988. Panel atty. Bd. Prison Terms, Sacramento, 1989-96, Appellate Defenders, Inc., San Diego, 1989-91, Calif. Dept. Corrections, Parole Hearings Divsn., Sacramento, 1992-94; dep. commr. Bd. Prison Terms, 1996—2001, assoc. chief dep. commr., 2001—. Mem. ABA, Calif. Bar Assn. (del. Conf. of Dels. 1991, 93—, resolutions com. 2005—), Orange County Bar Assn., Phi Alpha Delta.

JALURIA, YOGESH, mechanical engineering educator, department chairman; came to U.S., 1970; s. Jagdishwar and Maya J.; m. Anuradha Malhotra, Sept. 9, 1975; children: Pratik, Aseem, Ankur. BS, Indian Inst. Tech., Delhi, 1970; MS, Cornell U., 1972, PhD, 1974. Mem. tech. staff Bell Labs., Princeton, NJ, 1974-76; asst. prof. Indian Inst. Tech., Kanpur, 1976-80, Rutgers U., New Brunswick, NJ, 1980-82, assoc. prof., 1982-85, prof. of mech. engring., 1985-91, prof. II, disting. prof., 1991—2001, Bd. Govs. prof., 2001—, chmn. dept. mech. engring., 2005—. Cons. David Sarnoff Lab., SRI, Princeton, 1989-90, Steel Authority, Ranchi, India, 1977-80, others; mem. NSF grants rev. panel, other panels, 1996-98; NSF vis. scientist Indian Inst. Tech., 1988-89; lectr. in field; participant workshop on natural convection NSF, Colo., 1982, Indo-Australian Solar Energy Workshop, New Delhi, 1978, others; spkr. in field. Author: Natural Convection Heat and Mass Transfer, 1980; co-author: Computational Heat Transfer, 1986, 2d edit., 2003, Buoyancy Induced Flows, 1988, Computer Methods for Engineering, 1988, Design and Optimization of Thermal Systems, 1998; contbr. chpts. to books: Natural Convection, 1985, Handbook of Single-Phase Convective Heat Transfer, 1987, Energy Storage Systems, 1989, Handbook of Fire Protection, 1995, numerous others; contbr. more than 300 articles and papers to profl. jours. and confs. including Rev. Sci. Instrum., Jour. Heat Transfer, Jour. Thermophysics Heat Transfer, Numerical Heat Transfer, Jour. Fluid Mech., Jour. Numerical Meth. Engring.; mem. editl. adv. bd. Numerical Heat Transfer, 1987—, Internat. Jour. Heat Mass Transfer; mem. editl. bd. Internat. Jour. Numerical Meth. Heat and Flow, 1990-04, numerous others; reviewer including Applied Mechanics Rev., Jour. Fluid Mechanics, Jour. Heat Transfer, Jour. Solar Energy Engring.; referee numerous articles. NATO Disting. lectr., 1984, 88; recipient cert. of recognition Dept. of Commerce, 1982, Disting. Alumni award IIT, 1994, Max Jakob Meml. award ASME/AIChE, 2002, Thurston lecture award, 2003. Fellow ASME (chmn. nat. heat transfer conf., coord. com. 1991-92, exec. com. heat transfer divsn. 1998-03, editor Jour. Heat Transfer 2005—, Heat Transfer Mem. award 1995, Worcester Reed Warner medal 1999, Freeman scholar 2000), Am. Phys. Soc., Combustion Inst., India Assn. of East Brunswick (pres. 1985, 91, 94-96), Cornell India Assn. (v.p. 1972-73). Democrat. Hindu. Achievements include patents for Methods and apparatus for heating articles, for Methods and apparatus for avoiding undesirable deposits in crystal growing operations; copyrighted computer software in materials processing and electronics cooling; research in thermal processing of materials, fires, computational heat transfer, natural convection, cooling of electronic equipment and environmental flows, flows rising above finite heated bodies, interaction of buoyant flows with surfaces, buoyant jet flows, mixed convection in enclosures, heat removal from heated elements on a vertical surface, thermal stratification and heat rejection problems, solar energy storage in salt-gradient solar ponds, numerical and experimental simulation of thermal processes in manufacturing systems, computer aided design of thermal systems, knowledge based design methodology, and enclosure fire growth processes. Office: chair Rutgers U Mech Engring Dept New Brunswick NJ 08903 Business E-Mail: jaluria@jove.rutgers.edu.

JAMAIL, JOSEPH DAHR, JR., lawyer; b. Houston, Oct. 19, 1925; s. Joseph Dahr and Marie (Anton) J.; m. Lillie Mae Hage, Aug. 28, 1949; children: Joseph Dahr III, Randall Hage, Robert Lee. BA, U. Tex., 1950, JD, 1953. Bar: Tex. 1952. Asst. dist. atty., Harris County, Tex., 1954-55; sole propr. Jamail & Kolius, Houston. Prof. tort law U. Tex., 1981; guest lectr. at law schools throughout the country. Contbr. articles to profl. jours. Served to sgt. USMCR, 1943-46. Named one of top 25 philanthropists in U.S., 1996, The Lawyer of the Century, 1999, King of Torts, Washington Post, Chgo. Tribute, and other publications, Forbes' Richest Americans, 2006; U. Tex. Sch. Law designated Jessie Jones Hall as The Joseph D. Jamail Ctr. for Legal Rsch., U. Tex. Sch. of Law created The Joseph D. Jamail Centennial chair in law and advocacy; recipient Jurisprudence award, Anti-Defamation League B'nai B'rith, 1989, War Horse award, So. Trial Lawyers Assn., 1993, Brotherhood award, Nat. Conf. Christians and Jews, 1993, Houston Tex. Exes award, 1993, U. Tex. Sch. Law Outstanding Alumnus award, 1996, Tex. Appleseed Good Apple award, 2005. Fellow Internat. Acad. Law and Sci., Internat. Soc. Barristers, Internat. Acad. Trial Lawyers, Am. Coll. Trial Lawyers, Coun. Law and Sci.; mem. ABA, Houston Bar Assn., Houston Jr. Bar (dir. 1954-55, treas. 1955-56, v.p. 1956-57, pres. 1957-58), State Bar Tex. (chmn. grievance com. 1963, chmn. town hall task force 1973-74), Inner Circle of Advocates, Assn. Trial Lawyers Am., Am. Judicature Soc., Lawyer-Pilot Bar Assn., World Assn. Lawyers, World Jurist Assn., Philosophical Soc. Tex.; U. Tex. Ex-students' Assn. (life mem.), Order of Barristers, U. Tex. (hon. mem.), Delta Theta Phi; advocate Am. Bd. Trial Advocates. Home: 3682 Willowick Rd Houston TX 77019-1114 Office: Jamail & Kolius One Allen Ctr 500 Dallas St Ste 3434 Houston TX 77002-4793*

JAMAR, STEVEN DWIGHT, law educator; b. Ishpeming, Mich., May 11, 1953; s. Dwight W. and Lorraine (Persgard) J.; m. Shelley June Von Hagen-Jamar, May 19, 1979; children: Alexander S., Eric D. BA, Carleton Coll., 1975; JD, Hamline U., 1979; LLM, Georgetown U., 1994. Bar: Minn. 1979, D.C. 1993, U.S. Supreme Ct. 1985. Jud. clk. Minn. Supreme Ct., St. Paul, 1979-80; pvt. practice law Minn., 1980—89; prof. law U. Balt., 1989-90; prof. Sch. Law, Howard U., Washington, 1991—, dir. legal rsch. and writing program, 1990—2002; co-founder, assoc. dir. Inst. Intellectual Property and Social Justice, 2002—. Cons. on Environ. Legal Info. Sys. project NASA, 1998-2002; cons. on Global Legal Info. Network to Law Libr. of Congress, 1999—. Rsch. fellow Law Libr. Congress, 2000-01. Mem. ABA, ACLU, Legal Writing Inst. (pres. 1997-98), Amnesty Internat., Assn. Legal Writing Dirs. Avocations: canoeing, soccer, camping, photography, guitar. Office: Howard U Sch Law 2900 Van Ness St NW Washington DC 20008-1106 E-mail: stevenjamar@gmail.com.

JAMARIS, JOSEPH KASTYTIS, neurosurgeon; b. Seligenstadt, Germany, June 7, 1946; arrived in US, 1952; s. Josef and Stanislava (Turcinskaite) Jimramovsky; m. Suzann Naasz Gregg, June 17, 1988; children: Benjamin Richard Naasz, Bo James Naasz, Jacqueline Katherine, Joseph Kastytis Jamaris II, Camy Lee Naasz. MD, U. Md., Balt., 1972. Pvt. practice, Glen Burnie, Md., 1980—. Maj. US Army, 1978—80. Mem.: Md. Neurosurg. Soc., Amer. Assn. Neurol. Surgeons. Democrat. Roman Catholic. Avocations: yachting, tennis, travel, soccer. Home: 11005 Wood Elves Way Columbia MD 21044 Office: Dr Joseph K Jamaris LLC 300 Hospital Dr Ste 226 Glen Burnie MD 21061 Home Phone: 410-720-1215; Office Phone: 410-768-4644. Office Fax: 410-768-4648; Home Fax: 410-720-4514. Personal E-mail: jaasz7@comcast.net. Business E-Mail: jamarismd@comcast.net.

JAMBOR, ROBERT VERNON, lawyer; b. Chgo., Aug. 29, 1936; s. Vernon C. and Anne M. Jambor; m. Arlene M. Gale, Nov. 9, 1957 (dec. Aug. 1993); children: Robyn, Cheryl, Steven; m. Terri J. Skyrme, Jan. 11, 1995. BME, Kettering U., 1958; JD, John Marshall Law Sch., Chgo., 1963. Bar: Ill. 1963, U.S. Dist. Ct. Ill. 1963, U.S. Ct. Appeals (7th cir.) 1974, U.S. Ct. Appeals (fed. cir.) 1982, U.S. Supreme Ct. 1983. Product engr. product devel. Electro-Motive div. Gen. Motors Corp., La Grange, Ill., 1958-63; asso. firm Marks & Clerk, Chgo., 1961-63; patent atty. Borg-Warner Corp., Chgo., 1964-69; ptnr. Haight, Hofeldt, Davis & Jambor, Chgo., 1970-87, Dorn, McEachran, Jambor & Keating, Chgo., 1987—2000; counsel Jenner & Block LLP, Chgo., 2001—05, Leydig Voit & Mayer, LTD, Chgo., 2005—. Mem. ABA, Ill. Bar Assn., Fed. Cir. Bar Assn., Am. Intellectual Property Law Assn., Intellectual Property Law Assn. Chgo. Home Phone: 262-245-9209; Office Phone: 815-963-7661. Business E-Mail: rjambor@leydig.com.

JAMES, ALLIX BLEDSOE, retired university president; b. Marshall, Tex., Dec. 17, 1922; s. Samuel Horace and Tannie Etta (Judkins) James; m. Sue Nickens, Feb. 14, 1945; children: Alvan Bosworth, Portia Veann. AB, Va. Union U., 1944, MDiv, 1946; ThM, Union Theol. Sem. Va., 1949, ThD, 1957; postgrad., Boston U., summer 1951, Pa. State U., summer 1957; LLD, U. Richmond, 1970; DD, St. Paul's Coll., 1980. Ordained to ministry Bapt. Ch., 1942. Moderator No. Neck Bapt. Assn., 1950-52; minister Union Zion Bapt. Ch., Gloucester, Va., 1944-53, Mt. Zion Bapt. Ch., Downings, Va., 1945-57, 3d Union Bapt. Ch., King William, Va., 1953-70; dean students Va. Union U., Richmond, Va., 1950-57, dean Sch. Theology, 1957-70, Henderson-Griffith prof. pastoral theology, v.p., 1960-70, pres., 1970-79, ret., 1979, pres. emeritus, 1975—85, chancellor, 1985-93, pres. emeritus, 1993—. Author: Calling a Pastor in a Baptist Church, Threescore and Ten Plus-the Pilgrimage of an African-American Educator, 1922-, 1997; contbg. editor: The Continuing Quest, 1970. Chmn. Richmond City Planning Commn., 1969—75; dir. Va. Electric and Power Co., Dominion Resources, Inc., Consol bank and Trust Co.; mem. Commn. on Ch. Family Fin. Planning; mem. scholarship selection com. Philip Morris, Inc.; mem. Mayor's Commn. on Human Rels., 1963—65; pres. Norrell Sch. PTA, 1963—65; mem. exec. com. Ctrl. Va. Ednl. TV; mem. Richmond Independence Bicentennial Commn., Richmond Downtown econ. and Devel. Commn.; co-chmn. Northside Cmty. assn., 1964—68; chmn. Univ. Ctr. in Va.; mem. State Bd. Edn. Va., 1975—85, pres., 1980—82; bd. dirs. NCCJ, Va. Inst. Pastoral Care, Task Force for Renewal Urban Strategy and Tng., Richmond chpt. ARC, 1974—75, Better Richmond, Inc., Richmond Downtown Devel. Unltd., Am. Coun. on Edn., 1970—72, Richmond renaissance, Inc., Met. Richmond Leadership; mem. adv. bd. Inst. for Bus. and Cmty. Devel. U. Richmond; bd. fellows Interpreters House, Lake Janaluska, NC; trustee Richmond Meml. Hosp., Nat. Assn. for Equal Opportunity in Edn., v.p.; pres. Richmond Gold Bowl Sponsors, Inc., Nat. Conf. Richmond and Jews, Inc., 1987—90; nat. co-chair Nat. Conf. Christians and Jews, Inc., 1994; chmn. bd. dirs. Cosol. Bank and Trust Co., chmn./bd. dirs., 2001—. Named Citizen of Yr., Astoria Beneficial Club, 1971, Omega Psi Phi, 1972, Univ. chapel named Allix B. James Chapel in his honor, 1992; recipient Disting. Svc. award, Links, Inc., 1971, Ednl. Achievement award, 1985, Good Govt. award, Richmond First Club, 1985, Brotherhood award, NCCJ, 1975, Mozelle E. Manuel Outstanding Svc. award, Met. Bus. League, 1991, Exemplary Vision award, Fullwood Foods, Inc., 1992, Flame Bearers Edn. award, United Negro Coll. Fund, 1997, Excellence in Leadership award, Dominion Va. Power, 2000, Disting. Cmty. Svc. award, Sigma Pi Phi, 2003. Mem.: Clergy Assn. Richmond Area (pres.), Bapt. Gen. Conv. Va. (exec. bd.), Soc. for Advancement Continuing Edn. for Mins. (exec. bd.), Am. Bapt. Conv. (pres. coun. on theol. edn. 1969—72), Am. Assn. Theol. Schs. (pres. 1970—72), Greater Richmond C. of C. (bd. dirs.), Kiwanis (honoree Richmond area Appreciation Dinner 1993), Alpha Phi Alpha (Achievement award 1981, 1985), Alpha Kappa Mu.

JAMES, ALTON EVERETTE, JR., radiologist; b. Oxford, NC, Aug. 22, 1938; s. Pattie Royster; children: Everette III, Jeannette, Elizabeth. AB, U. N.C., 1959; MD, Duke U., 1963; MSc, Johns Hopkins Sch. Pub. Health, 1971. Diplomate Am. Bd. Radiology, Am. Bd. Nuc. Medicine. Fellow Harvard Med. Sch., Boston, 1966—69; from asst. to prof. radiology Johns Hopkins Med. Sch., Balt., 1969—74; dir. rsch. radiology Johns Hopkins Hosp., Balt., 1969—74; fellow Royal Soc. Medicine, London, 1974—75; chmn. dept. radiology and radiol. sciences Vanderbilt U. Sch. Medicine, Nashville, 1975—92; founder Vanderbilt Ctr. Med. Imaging Rsch., 1978—; pres. N.C. State U. Sch. Vet. Medicine Found., Raleigh, NC, 1996—98. Vis. scientist Nat. Cancer Inst., 1992—93, NIH, 1992—93; sr. program officer NAS Inst. of Medicine, 1993—94; clin. prof. Georgetown U., 1994—, U. N.C., 1996—; adj. prof., chair emeritus Vanderbilt U. Sch. Medicine, Nashville, 1994—; lectr. Johns Hopkins Med. Sch., Balt., 1993—; bd. visitors U. N.C., 1980; deans coun. Johns Hopkins Bloomberg Sch. Pub. Health, 2002—; founder Russell Morgan Fund, Johns Hopkins, 2002. Author 24 books, 14 monographs; contbr. over 600 articles to profl. jours., 140 chpts. to books. Spl. advisor sci. tech. Office Gov. NC, Raleigh, 1994—96; bd. dirs. Duke U. Med. Sch., 1986—94, N.C. Sch. Vet. Medicine; adv. bd. N.C. Pottery Mus., 2006—, Preservation, N.C., 2004—. Capt. US Army, 1964—66. Picker fellow NRC/NAS, 1969-71, fellow Royal Soc. Medicine, 1974-75; decorated Commendation medal US Army. Mem.: AAMC (mem. adminstrv. bd.), Royal Soc. Health, Am. Roentgen Ray Soc. (pres. 1992, Gold medal 2003), Assn. Univ. Radiologists (pres. 1985, bd. dirs. 1989, Gold medal 2003), Nat. Coun. Radiation Protection, Can. Radiol. Soc. (hon.; radiologist smithsonian), Cosmos Club, Davison Club, Explorers' Club, Pres.'s Club (John Hopkins U.), Chancellors Club (U. N.C.) (bd. visitors), Order Long Leaf Pine (N.C.), Alpha Omega Alpha, Pi Kappa Alpha (Founder's Cir.). Avocations: writing, art, pottery, decoys, quilts. Home: 205 New Castle Pl Chapel Hill NC 27517 Office: St James Place 205 New Castle Place Chapel Hill NC 27514 Personal E-mail: everette@nc.rr.com.

JAMES, ANTHONY AMADÉ, molecular biologist, educator; b. Ypsilanti, Mich., Nov. 16, 1951; s. Bernard Benedict and Florence (Fitzgerald) J. BSc in Biology, U. Calif., Irvine, 1973, PhD in Developmental Genetics, 1979. Postdoctoral fellow in biol. chemistry Harvard U., Boston, 1979-83, asst. prof. Tropical Pub. Health, 1985-89; postdoctoral fellow in biology Brandeis U., Waltham, Mass., 1983-85; asst. prof. molecular biology and biochemistry U. Calif., Irvine, 1989-93, assoc. prof., 1993, prof. Author: (with others) Tropical and Geographical Medicine, 2d edit., 1990; editor Insect Molecular Biology, 1991—; contbr. articles to profl. jours. Fellow Am. Cancer Soc., 1980-81, Med. Found., Inc., 1982-84; recipient Burroughs-Wellcome award, 1994. Fellow Royal Entomol. Soc. (Burroughs-Wellcome Fund scholar award in Molecular Parsitology, 1994), AAAS; mem. Am. Soc. Tropical Medicine and Hygiene, Am. Com. on Vector Entomology, Entomol. Soc. Am., Genetics Soc. Am, Soc. Vector Ecology, NAS. Avocations: music, fishing, sports, cooking. Office: Dept of Molecular Biology and Biochemistry U Calif McGaugh Hall 3205 Irvine CA 92697-3900

JAMES, ANTHONY R., utilities executive; b. 1950; AA in Engring., Polk CC, Winter Haven, Fla., 1970; BSEE, U. South Fla., Tampa, 1973. Elec. and instrumentation mgr. Procter & Gamble, resident engr.; safety and health supr. Ga. Power Southern Co., 1978, asst. plant mgr. Atlanta, human resources mgr. for employee benefits, mgr. Arkwright Plant Manco, Ga., asst. to wholesale mktg. v.p., v.p., sr. prodn. officer Savannah Electric, 2000—01, pres., CEO Savannah Electric, 2001—05, exec. v.p., pres. shared svcs., 2006—. Co-author (with Ken Chapman): The Shoulders of Giants, 2005. Named Black Engr. of Yr., Career Comm., 2004; named one of 50 Most Important Blacks in Tech., 2005. Mem.: 100 Black Men of Savannah, Savannah Rotary. Office: Southern Co 30 Ivan Allen Jr Blvd NW Atlanta GA 30308 Office Phone: 404-506-5000.*

JAMES, BILL, baseball writer, statistician; b. Mayetta, Kans., Oct. 5, 1949; m. Susan McCarthy; children: Rachel, Isaac, Reuben. BA in English, Econs., Univ. Kans., 1973, BE, 1975. Boiler room worker Stokely Van Camp, Lawrence, Kans.; baseball writer/statistician Lawrence, Kans., 1977—; Sr. Baseball Ops. Adv. Boston Red Sox, 2002—. Author: Bill James Baseball Abstract annual edit., 1977—88, The Bill James Historical Baseball Abstrac, 1985, This Time Let's Not Eat the Bones, 1989, The Politics of Glory/Whatever Happened to the Hall of Fame?, 1994, The Bill James Baseball Book annual edits., 1990—92, The Bill James Player Ratings Book annual edits., 1993—96, The Bill James Guide to Baseball Managers, 1997, The New Bill James Historical Baseball Abstract, 2001, Win Shares, 2002; co-author (with Rob Neyer): The Neyer/James Guide to Pitcher, 2004. With US Army, 1971—73, S. Korea. Named one of 100 Most Influential People, Time Mag., 2006. Achievements include development of sabermetrics to use scientific data collection and interpretation methods to explain why teams win and lose; invention of Runs Created stat, and Major League Equivalency, which predicts how a minor league player will perform in the majors; known as Sultan of Stats. Office: care Boston Red Sox 4 Yawkey Way Boston MA 02215-3496

JAMES, BRENT CARL, health care executive, biomedical sciences educator; b. Shelley, Idaho, Dec. 28, 1950; s. John Carl and Barbara Joyce (Hendrickson) J.; m. Karen Anne Stephenson, Nov. 21, 1979 (Sept. 1986); 1 child, Ian Carl. BS in Computer Sci., U. Utah, 1974, BS in Med. Biology, 1975, MD, 1978, M in Statis., 1983. Sr. systems programmer 1st Security Bank, Salt Lake City, 1972-79; asst. dir. cancer dept., dir. computing dept. ACS, Chgo., 1979-83; lectr. Harvard U. Sch. of Pub. Health, Boston, 1984-85, asst. prof., 1985-86; v.p. med. rsch. and continuing med. edn. Intermountain Health Care, Salt Lake City, 1986—; exec. dir. IHC Inst. for Health Care Delivery Rsch., Salt Lake City, 1990—. Pres. Health Care Software, Salt Lake City, 1980—; vis. lectr. dept. biostatis. Harvard U. Sch. of Pub. Health, 1986-95; adj. prof. dept. family and preventive medicine U. Utah, Salt Lake City, 1987—; v.p. Interwest Quality of Care, Inc., Salt Lake City, 1990—; vis. lectr. dept. health policy and mgmt. Harvard Sch. Pub. Health, 1995—. Contbr. numerous articles to profl. jours. Capt. USPHS, 1979-80. Nat. Merit scholar, 1969. Mem. Inst. Medicine, Am. Coll. Physician Execs., Am. Statis. Assn., Am. Assn. for Med. Systems and Informatics, Phi Beta Kappa. Mem. Lds Ch. Avocations: technical rock climbing, stained glass. Office: Intermountain Health Care 21st Fl 36 S State St Salt Lake City UT 84111

JAMES, BRUCE RICHARD, publishing executive; b. Cleve., Oct. 19, 1942; s. George R. and Dorothy B. (Watson) J.; m. Jo Ann Osborn, Feb. 5, 1966 (div. Feb. 1982); children: Michael, Jeffrey, Stephen; m. Nora Ellen Thomas, May 11, 1985. BS, Rochester Inst. Tech., NY, 1964; degree (hon.), Nev. Sys. Higher Edn., 2006. V.p. Keller-Crescent Co., Evansville, Ind., 1964-70, Cardinal Co., San Francisco, 1970-73; pres., CEO Uniplan Corp., San Francisco, 1973-83, Electrographic Corp., San Francisco, 1983-93, Nev. New-Tech, Inc., Incline Village, Nev., 1993—; chmn., CEO Barclays Law Pubs., San Francisco, 1986-94. Mem. dean's adv. coun. U. Nev. Las Vegas, Boyd Sch. Law, 1999-2002; bd. dirs. BIPAC, Washington, 1999-2002; chmn. bd. dirs. Polish-Am. Print Co., Warsaw, 1990-93; pres. Printing Industries Calif., 1989-91; pub. printer, CEO US Govt. Printing Office, 2002-07; mem. Nat. Digital Strategy Adv. Bd., 2004-07; dir. Associated Governing Bds. Univs. and Colls., 2006-, Davidson Acad. Nev., 2006-; commr. Northwest Commn. Colls. and Univs., 2006-; regent Nat. Libr. Medicine, 2007—. Candidate US Senate, 1997-98; chmn. emeritus bd. trustees Rochester Inst. Tech., 1993—, Sierra Nev. Coll., Incline Village, 1997-2005; mem. Bd. Equalization, Reno, 1995-97; trustee U. Nev. Desert Rsch. Inst., 1999-2002; dir. Nev. Test Site Devel. Corp., 1999-2002, Western Folklife Ctr., Elko, Nev., 1999-2002; bd. dirs. Cmty. Found. Western Nev., 1999-2002; fin. chmn. Nev. Rep. Party, 2000-02. Commencement spkr. Rochester Inst. Tech., 1998, named Alumnus of Yr., 1997; recipient Silver Beaver award Boys Scouts Am., 1992; Civilian Exec. of Yr. US Govt., 2006. Mem.: Internat. Wine and Food Soc., No. Nev. Network, Cosmos Club (Washington), Genesee Valley Club (Rochester NY). Republican. Episcopalian. Office Phone: 775-831-9499.

JAMES, CHARLES ALBERT, lawyer, oil industry executive; b. Newark, May 2, 1954; s. Charles Albert and Mary Letitia (Baskerville) J.; 1 child, Kathryn E. BA, Wesleyan U., Middletown, Conn., 1976; JD, George Washington U., Washington, 1979. Bar: D.C. 1979. Atty. FTC, Washington, 1979—85; assoc./ptnr. Jones, Day, Reavis & Pogue, Washington, 1986—91; dep. asst. atty. gen. US Dept. Justice, Washington, 1991, acting asst. atty. gen., 1991—93, asst. atty. gen. Antitrust Divsn., 2001—02; ptnr. Jones, Day, Reavis & Pogue, Washington, 1993—2001; v.p., gen. counsel ChevronTexaco Corp., San Ramon, Calif., 2002—. Recipient Chmn.'s award FTC, 1985, Edmund Randolph award Dept. Justice, 1992. Mem. ABA (sect. of bus. law chmn. com. 1999), Fed. Bar Assn. (chmn. antitrust com. 1990), U.S. C. of C. (mem. antitrust coun. 1993—), Psi Upsilon. Republican. Office: Office Gen Coun Chevron Corp 6001 Bollinger Canyon Rd San Ramon CA 94583 Home Phone: 925-743-4011; Office Phone: 925-842-3232. Personal E-mail: cjae@chevron.com.

JAMES, CHARLES E., JR., lawyer; b. Pontiac, Mich., Sept. 19, 1948; BA, Occidental Coll., 1970; JD with high distinction, U. Ariz. Bar: Ariz. 1973. Ptnr. Gust Rosenfeld, Phoenix, 1979—86, Chapman and Cutler, Phoenix, 1986—92, Snell & Wilmer, Phoenix, 1992—99, Squire, Sanders and Dempsey, Phoenix, 2000—. Mem. ABA, Nat. Assn. Bond Lawyers. Office: Squire Sanders & Dempsey 40 N Central Ave Ste 2700 Phoenix AZ 85004-4498 Office Phone: 602-528-4000. E-mail: cjames@ssd.com.

JAMES, CHARLES FRANKLIN, JR., retired engineering educator; b. Des Arc, Mo., July 16, 1931; s. Charles Franklin and Beulah Frances (Kyte) J.; m. Mollie Keeler, May 18, 1974; children: Thomas Elisha, Matthew Jeremiah. BS, Purdue U., 1958, MS, 1960, PhD, 1963. Registered profl. engr., Wis. Sr. indsl. engr. McDonnel Aircraft Co., 1963; asst. prof. U. RI, Kingston, 1963—66, prof., chmn. dept. indsl. engring., 1967—82, co-founder, mem Robotics Rsch. Ctr., 1980—83; assoc. prof. U. Mass., Amherst, 1966—67; C. Paul Stocker prof. engring. Ohio U., Athens, 1982-83; dean Coll. Engring. and Applied Sci., U. Wis., Milw., 1984—95; academic v.p. Milw. Sch. Engring., 1995—2000; ret., 2000. Cons. Asian Productivity Orgn.; arbitrator Fed. Mediation and Conciliation Svc., Am. Arbitration Assn.; bd. dirs. Badger Meter Co., Milw., 1986-2002; vis. prof. Massey U., New Zealand, 1978-79. Contbr. articles to profl. jours. Bd. dir., v.p. Clay County Water Dist. No. 7, Mo. 2004—; mem. corp. bd. Milw. Sch. Engring., 2000—. With USAF, 1951-55. Recipient Silver medal Tech. U. Budapest, Hungary, 1989. Mem. NSPE, ASME, Wis. Soc. Profl. Engrs. (pres. Milw. chpt. 1993-94, Outstanding Profl. Engr. in Edn. 1993, state-wide treas. 1994-96), Inst. Indsl. Engrs., Am. Soc. Engring. Edn., Soc. Mfg. Engrs., Am. Foundrymen's Soc., Engrs. and Scis. of Milw. (bd. dir. 1988-95, v.p. 1991-93, pres.-elect 1993-94, pres. 1994-95). Office Phone: 816-750-4615. Personal E-mail: cfjames@earthlink.net.

JAMES, CLARITY (CAROLYNE FAYE JAMES), mezzo soprano; b. Wheatland, Wyo., Apr. 27, 1945; d. Ralph Everett and Gladys Charlotte (Johnson) J. Mus.B., U. Wyo., 1964; Mus.M., Ind. U., 1967. Cert. instr. Radiance Technique. Prof. voice Radford (Va.) U., 1990—. Asst. prof. voice U. Iowa, Iowa City, 1968-72 Debut in opera as Madame Flora in: The Medium, St. Paul Opera, 1971; also sang role with Houston Grand Opera, 1972, Opera Theatre St. Louis, 1976, Augusta (Ga.) Opera Co., 1976; N.Y.C. Opera debut as Baroness in: The Young Lord, 1973; N.Y.C. Opera debut as Widow Begbick in Mahogonny, Opera Co. of Boston, 1973; created role Mother Rainey in: The Sweet Bye and Bye, 1973; Mrs. G. in: Captain Jinks, 1976; Mrs. Cratchit in A Christmas Carol (Musgrave), 1979; created Mrs. Doc in world premiere of A Quiet Place (Leonard Bernstein), Houston, 1983; debut Chgo. Lyric Opera, 1983, Vienna Staatsoper, 1986, National Symphony, 1986, Phila. Orch., 1986; numerous appearances with opera cos. throughout U.S. and fgn. countries including, Dallas Civic Opera, Cin. Opera Co., Netherlands Opera, Amsterdam, Florentine Opera. Rec. artist. Martha Baird Rockefeller grantee, Corbett Found. grantee, 1968; Met. Opera Assn. grantee; recipient Lillian Garabedian award Santa Fe Opera, 1967, Exemplary Alumni award U. Wyo., 1994; named Young Artist Nat. Fedn. Music Clubs, 1972. Office: Radford U Dept Music Radford VA 24142 Home Phone: 540-633-2914; Office Phone: 540-831-5296. Business E-Mail: cjames@radford.edu.

JAMES, CRAIG T., former congressman; b. Augusta, Ga., May 5, 1941; m. Kitty Folk. AA, U. Fla., 1961; BS, Stetson U., 1963, JD, 1967. Bar: Fla. 1967, US Dist. Ct. (Mid. Dist. Fla.) 1968, US Supreme Ct. 1976. Commr. De Land Housing Authority, 1971—75; mem. 101st-102nd Congresses from 4th Fla. Dist., 1989—93; ptnr. James, Zimmerman and Paul, 1993—. Served with USAR, served with Nat. Guard. Republican. Baptist. Office: James & Zimmerman PL 431 E New York Ave PO Box 208 Deland FL 32721-0208 Office Phone: 386-734-1200. Office Fax: 386-734-1295.

JAMES, DAVID LEE, lawyer, writer, international advisor; b. Chgo., Aug. 23, 1933; s. Roy L. and Ethel (Wells) J.; m. Sheila Feagley, May 26, 1962; children: Pamela, James, Winifred, Paul, Brian, Adam. AB, Harvard U., 1955; JD, U. Chgo., 1960; grad. exec. program, Stanford U., 1979. Bar: NY 1961, NJ 1967, Hawaii 1976, Ill. 1987. With various law firms, NYC, 1960-67; counsel and asst. gen. counsel, asst. sec. Texasgulf Inc., 1967-75; gen. counsel, sec. Dillingham Corp., Honolulu, 1975-77, v.p., gen. counsel, sec., 1977-84, v.p. legal affairs, sec. San Francisco, 1984-85; asst. gen. counsel, asst. sec. Crown Zellerbach Corp., San Francisco, 1985-86; sr. ptnr., sr. corp. atty. Arnstein & Lehr, Chgo., 1987-90, of counsel, 1990-96; chmn. bus. programs East-West Ctr., Honolulu, 1990-92; chief of party and sr. law devel. advisor USAID and Govt. of Indonesia, Jakarta, Indonesia, 1992-93; pres. Bus. Strategies Internat., San Francisco, Calif., 1993—, www.bsicorp.net, San Francisco, 1993—. Hon. consul of Malaysia, Hawaii, 1977-84; adv. bd. Internat. and Comparative Law Ctr., Southwestern Legal Found., Dallas, 1976-91; adv. com. Law of Sea Inst., Honolulu, 1977-84; lectr. in law Stanford U. Sch. Law, 1996-98. Author: Doing Business in Asia, 1993, The Executive Guide to Asia-Pacific Communications, 1995; contbg. editor TheFeature.com, 2000-2004; contbr. various articles on bus. and legal subjects. Bd. dirs. Chgo. Chamber Orch., 1988-90, pres. 1989-90, Jr. Achievement Hawaii, 1976-84, Hawaii Opera Theatre, 1981-84, Friends of East-West Ctr., 1982-84; mem. Morristown (N.J.) Bd. Edn., 1967-68. Served to lt. (j.g.) USNR, 1955-57. Mem. Outrigger Canoe Club (Honolulu), Harvard Club (N.Y.C.). Office: Bus Strategies Internat 425 Market St Ste 2200 San Francisco CA 94105-2434 E-mail: djames@bsicorp.net.

JAMES, DONALD M., construction materials executive; b. 1949; Pres. so. divsn. Vulcan Materials, 1994-96, sr. v.p. south constrn. materials group, 1995-96, pres., COO, 1996-97, pres., CEO, 1997, chmn., CEO, 1997—; also bd. dir. Bd. dirs. Protective Life Corp., So. Co., SouthTrust Corp. Office: Vulcan Materials 1200 Urban Center Dr Birmingham AL 35242*

JAMES, DOUG L., computer scientist, educator; m. Karen James; 1 child. BSc in Applied Math., U. Western Ont., Can., 1995; MSc in Math., U. Brit. Columbia, Can., 1997, PhD in Math., 2001. Postdoctoral rschr. computer sci. U. Brit. Columbia, Canada, 2001—02; asst. prof. dept. computer sci. and Robotics Inst. Carnegie Mellon U., Pitts., 2002—06; assoc. prof. dept. computer sci. Cornell U., Ithaca, 2006. Contbr. articles to sci. jours. Named one of Brilliant 10, Popular Sci. mag., 2006; recipient CAREER award, NSF, 2004. Office: Dept Computer Sci Cornell U 5146 Upson Hall Ithaca NY 14853-7501 Office Phone: 607-255-9215. Office Fax: 607-255-4428. E-mail: djames@cs.cornell.edu.*

JAMES, EDGERRIN TYREE, professional football player; b. Immokalee, Fla., Aug. 1, 1978; s. Edward German and Julie James; 1 child, Edquisha. Student, U. Miami, 1996—99. Running back Indpls. Colts, 1999—2006, Ariz. Cardinals, 2006—. Guest spkr. DARE prog. various schools; founder Edgerrin James Found. Named NFL Rookie of the Yr., 1999; named to NFL Pro-Bowl, 1999, 2000, 2004—05. Achievements include NFL rushing title, 1999, 2000. Office: Ariz Cardinals PO Box 888 Phoenix AZ 85001-0888

JAMES, ELIZABETH JOAN PLOGSTED, pediatrician, educator; b. Jefferson City, Mo., Jan. 15, 1939; d. Joseph Matthew Plogsted and Maxie Pearl (Manford) Plogsted Acuff; m. Ronald Carney James, Aug. 25, 1962; children: Susan Elizabeth, Jason Michael. BS in Chemistry, Lincoln U., 1960; MD, U. Mo., 1965. Diplomate Am. Bd. Pediat., Am. Bd. Neonatal-Perinatal Medicine. Resident in pediat. U. Mo. Hosps. & Clinics, Columbia, 1965-68, fellow in neonatology, 1968-69, dir. neonatal-perinatal medicine Children's Hosp., 1971—; fellow in neonatal-perinatal medicine U. Colo. Hosps., Denver, 1969-71; from asst. to assoc. prof. pediatrics and obstetrics sch. medicine U. Mo., 1971-83, prof. child health and obstetrics, 1983—. Dir. pediatric edn. program dept. child health sch. medicine U. Mo., Columbia, 1989-98. Mem. editl. bd. Mo. Medicine, 1983—; contbr. chpts. to books and articles to profl. jours. Fellow Am. Acad. Pediat. (sect. neonatal-perinatal medicine); mem. Mo. State Med. Assn., Boone County Med. Soc., Alpha Omega Alpha. Roman Catholic. Avocations: classical music, bicycling, gardening. Office: U Mo Hosps & Clinics Childrens Hosp 1 Hospital Dr Columbia MO 65201-5276 Office Phone: 573-882-7919. Business E-Mail: jamese@health.missouri.edu.

JAMES, ELIZABETH R. (LEE LEE JAMES), bank executive; b. Columbus, Ga., June 11, 1961; m. David M. (Sandy) James Jr.; children: David, Parker. BA in polit. sci., Auburn U., 1983; grad., Cannon Fin. Inst. Trust Sch., 1988; grad, Duke U. Exec. Edn., 1990. Mem. staff Trust Dept. Columbus Bank and Trust Co. Synovus Fin. Corp., Columbus, Ga., 1986—89, dir. training TSYS, 1989—90, v.p., human resources dir. TSYS, 1990—94, sr. v.p., human resources dir. TSYS, 1994—95, sr. v.p., human resources divsn. officer Synovus Svc. Corp., 1995—96, pres. Synovus Svc. Corp., 1996—2000, chief people officer, 1996—, vice chmn., chief info. officer, 2000—, dir., 2001—. Mem. tech. secretariat adv. group Banking Industry. Chmn. staff parish St. Paul United Meth. Ch., mem. adminstrv. bd.; chmn. The Alexis de Tocqueville Soc. of United Way; bd. dir. Columbus (Ga.) Symphony, Ronald McDonald House; mem. YMCA Task Force Com.; chmn. Leadership Devel. Task Force Gov.'s Comm. for a New Ga. Named Woman of Yr. in Tech., Tech. Assn. of Ga., 2002; named one of The 25 Most Powerful Women in Banking, US Banker mag., 2003, 2004. Mem.: Alexis deTocqueville Soc. United Way (past chmn.), Library Found., Fin. Svcs. Roundtable. Office: Synovus Financial Corp PO Box 120 Columbus GA 31902

JAMES, ESTELLE, economist, educator; b. Bronx, NY, Dec. 1, 1935; d. Abraham and Lee (Zeichner) Dinerstein; m. Ralph James (div. 1971); children: Deborah, David; m. Harry Lazer, June 27, 1971 (dec. 1994). BS, Cornell U., Ithaca, NY, 1956; PhD, MIT, Cambridge, 1961. Lectr., econs. dept. U. Calif., Berkeley, 1964—65; acting asst. prof. Stanford U., 1965—67; assoc. prof. SUNY, Stony Brook, 1967—72, prof., 1972—94, provost, div. Social and Behavioral Sci., 1975—79, chmn. dept., 1982—86. Vis. scholar Yale U., Australian Nat. U., Tel Aviv U., Brookings Inst., others; cons. World Bank, Washington, 1986—91, sr. economist, 1991—94, lead economist, 1994—2000, cons., 2000—; vis. fellow Urban Inst., Washington, 2002—04; mem. governing bd. Kosovo Pension Saving Trust, 2001—. Author: (book) Hoffa and the Teamsters, 1964, The Nonprofit Sector in Market Economies, 1986, Pub. Policy and Pvt. Ed. in Japan, 1988, The Nonprofit Sector in Internat. Perspective, 1989, Averting the Old Age Crisis, 1994, The Gender Impact of Social Security Reform, 2008; contbr. articles to profl. jour. Fellow, Woodrow Wilson Internat. Ctr., Washington, 1981—82, Netherlands Inst. Advanced Study, 1986—87, U.S. Dept. Edn., 1988, Sec. of Navy, 1990, AAUW, Soc. Sci. Rsch. Coun.; grantee, Spencer Found., USAID, NEH, Exxon Edn. Found., Mich. Retirement Rsch. Consortium, Smith Richardson Found.; Fulbright awardee, 1979. Mem.: Am. Econs. Assn. Office Phone: 202-338-7108. Business E-Mail: ejames@estellejames.com.

JAMES, ETTA (JAMESETTA HAWKINS), recording artist; b. LA, Jan. 25, 1938; d. Dorothy Leatherwood Hawkins; m. Artis Dee Mills, May 20, 1969; children: Donto, Sametto. Blues singer Johnny Otis, LA, 1954, Bihari Bros. Record Co., LA, 1954, Leonard Chess Record Co., LA, 1960, Warner Bros., LA, 1978, Fantasy Record, LA, 1985, Island Record, LA, 1988. Record Albums include Respect Yourself, 1997, Love's Been Rough on Me, 1997, Come A Little Closer. The Essential Etta, 1993, Etta James Rocks the House, Etta, Red Hot'n Live, Her Greatest Sides, Vol. 1, Live, 1994, Mystery Lady: Songs of Billie Holliday, 1994 (Grammy award 1994), R&B Dynamite, 1987, reissue, 1991, The Right Time, 1992, Rocks the House, 1992, The Second Time Around, 1989, Seven Year Itch, 1988, Sticking to My Guns, 1990, The Sweetest Peaches, 1989, The Sweetest Peaches: Part One, 1989, The Sweetest Peaches: Part Two, 1989, Tell Mama, 1988, These Foolish Things: The Classic Balladry of Etta James, 1995, Time After Time, (with Eddie Cleanhead Vinson) Blues in the Night, Lane Supper Club, 1986, Blues in the Night, Vol. 2, 1987, Twelve Songs of X-mas, 1988, Life, Love & the Blues, 1988, Heart of a Woman, 1999, 20th Century Master: The Best of Etta James, 1999, Platinum Series, 2000, The Chess Box, 2000, Matriarch of the Blues, 2000, Etta James, 2001, Love Songs, 2001, Blue Gardenia, 2001, Blowin' in the Wind, 2002, Live and Ready, 2002, Burnin' Down the House, 2002, Let's Roll, 2003, Rock Me Baby, 2004, Live in New York, 2005. Recipient Lifetime Achievement award Rigby & Blues Assn., 1989, Living Legends award KJLH, 1989, Image award NAACP, 1990 W.C. Handy award, 1989, Blue Soc. Hall of Fame award, 1991; 5th Handy Blues award, 1993, 94, Soul of Am. Music award, 1992; 8 Grammy nominations, Beyond War award, Best Song, 1984; inducted into Rock & Roll Hall of Fame, 1993; sang opening ceremony of 1984 Olympics. Office: Etta James Enterprises 16409 Sally Ln Riverside CA 92504-5629

JAMES, FRANCIS EDWARD, JR., investment advisor; b. Woodville, Miss., Jan. 5, 1931; s. Francis Edwin and Ruth (Phillips) J.; m. Iris Senn, Nov. 3, 1952; children: Francis III, Barry, David. BS, La. State U., 1951; MS, Rensselaer Poly. Inst., 1966, PhD, 1967. Commd. 2d lt. USAF, 1950, advanced through grades to col., 1972; prof. mgmt. and statistics, chmn. dept quantitative studies Air Force Inst. Tech., Wright Patterson AFB, 1967-71, dir. grad. edn. div. mgmt. programs, 1972-74; ret. USAF, 1974; chmn. James Investment Rsch., Inc., Alpha, Ohio, 1972—. Cons. math. modeling. Author: A Matrix Solution for the General Linear Regression Model; contbr. articles to profl. jours. Bd. dirs. James Capital Alliance, Inc. Decorated Legion of Merit, D.F.C., Air medal, Joint Services Commendation medal, Meritorious Service medal; recipient Outstanding Acad. Achievement award Rensselaer Poly. Inst., 1965, first Alumni Fellow appointment Rensselaer Poly. Inst. Mem. Am. Statis. Assn., Mil. Ops. Research Soc., Am. Fin. Assn., Investment Counsel Assn. Am., Mktg. Technicians Assn., Soc. Logistics Engring. (Eckles award 1973, tech. chmn.), Sigma Iota Epsilon, Epsilon Delta Sigma. Lodges: Masons; Rotary. Home: 2604 Lantz Rd Dayton OH 45434-6627 Office: James Investment Rsch Inc PO Box 8 Alpha OH 45301-0008 Personal E-mail: drfrankejames@yahoo.com. *To come up with an outstanding idea is brilliance. To put that idea into action is real genius.*

JAMES, FRANCIS MARSHALL, III, anesthesiologist; b. Phila., Dec. 22, 1935; MD, Hahnemann U., 1961. Intern Phila. Gen. Hosp., 1961—62; resident Hosp. U. Pa., Phila., 1964—67, attending anesthesiologist, 1967—68, NC Bapt. Hosp., Winston-Salem, 1968—2000; assoc. dean grad. med. edn. Wake Forest U., NC, 1999-2000, faculty Sch. Medicine NC, 1968—2000, chair dept. anesthesiology NC, 1983—98, prof. emeritus NC, 2001—. Dir. Am. Bd. Anesthesiology, 1988-2000, pres., 1999-2000. Office: Wake Forest U Sch Medicine Dept Anesthesiology Medical Ctr Blvd Winston Salem NC 27157-1009 Personal E-mail: fmj111@aol.com.

JAMES, GARY DOUGLAS, biological anthropologist, educator, researcher; b. Norwich, Conn., Dec. 6, 1954; s. Godfrey Merchant and Joan (McIlwaine) J.; m. Kathleen Louise Wilson, July 28, 1979. BA, Wake Forest U., 1976; MA, Pa. State U., 1980, PhD, 1984. Part-time instr. Pa. State U., University Park, 1982-84; postdoctoral assoc. Cornell U. Med. Coll., NYC, 1984-86; asst. prof., assoc. rsch. prof. physiology medicine biophysics Med. Coll. Cornell U., NYC, 1991—98; rsch. prof. Decker Sch. Nursing SUNY, Binghamton, 1998—2003, dir. Inst. Primary Preventive Health Care, 1998—, adj. prof. anthropology, 1999—2003, prof. anthropology, 2003—, prof. nursing, 2003—, prof. bioengring., 2006—. Adj. prof. dept. psychology SUNY, Binghampton, NY, 2000—. Contbr. chapters to books, articles to profl. jours. Recipient New Investigator Rsch. award NIH, 1986, Internat. Man of Yr. award Internat. Biog. Ctr., 1993; NIH postdoctoral trainee, 1984. Fellow Human Biol. Assn. (sec.-treas. 1992-96, exec. com. 1996-2000, pres.-elect. 2007—), Soc. Behavioral Medicine; mem. AAAS, Am. Assn. Phys. Anthropologists, Internat. Platform Assn., Soc. Study Social Biology, Am. Soc. Hypertension, Am. Anthrop. Assn., Am. Dermatologlyphics Assn. (exec. com. 1996-98, sec. 1998-99, editor newsletter 2001-07, pres.-elect, pres. 2002-05), Harvey Soc. Lutheran. Office: Decker Sch of Nursing Binghamton Univ SUNY Box 6000 Binghamton NY 13902-6000 Business E-Mail: gdjames@binghamton.edu.

JAMES, GEORGE BARKER, II, financial executive; b. Haverhill, Mass., May 25, 1937; s. Paul Withington and Ruth (Burns) J.; m. Beverly A. Burch, Sept. 22, 1962; children: Alexander, Christopher, Geoffrey, Matthew. AB, Harvard U., 1959; MBA, Stanford U., 1962. Fiscal dir. E.G. & G. Inc., Bedford, Mass., 1963-67; fin. exec. Am. Brands Inc., NYC, 1967-69; v.p. Pepsico, Inc., NYC, 1969-72; sr. v.p., chief fin. officer Arcata Corp., Menlo Park, Calif., 1972-82; exec. v.p. Crown Zellerbach Corp., San Francisco, 1982-85; sr. v.p., chief fin. officer Levi Strauss & Co., San Francisco, 1985-98; sr. ptnr. Pacific States Investors Group LLC, 2002—. Bd. dirs. Pacific States Industries, Inc., Sharper Image, Inc., Callious Software Inc. Author: Industrial Development in the Ohio Valley, 1962. Mem. Andover Town Com., Mass., 1965-67; mem. Select Congl. Com. on World Hunger; mem. adv. coun. Calif. State Employees Pension Fund; chmn. bd. dirs. Towle Trust Fund; trustee Nat. Corp. Fund for the Dance, chmn. Cate Sch., Levi Strauss Found., Stern Grove Festival Assn., Zellerbach Family Fund, San Francisco Ballet Assn., Com. for Econ. Devel.; bd. dirs. Stanford U. Hosp., Calif. Pacific Med. Ctr.; dir. KQED Pub. Broadcasting; chmn. World Affairs Coun.; mem. San Francisco Com. on Fgn. Rels.; overseer Hoover Instn., Standford U.; trustee Grace Cathedral, San Francisco. With US Army, 1960-61. Mem. Pacific Union Club, Bohemian Club, Menlo Circus Club, Harvard Club, N.Y. Athletic Club. Home: 207 Walnut St San Francisco CA 94118-2012

JAMES, GESILLE, librarian; Supervising libr. NY Pub. Libr., Allerton Br., Bronx, NY, 2003—. Recipient NY Times Libr. award, 2006. Mem.: Spl. Librs. Assn. (mem. ITE divsn. 2003—). Office: NY Pub Libr Allerton Br 2740 Barnes Ave Bronx NY 10467 Office Phone: 718-881-4240. E-mail: allerton@nypl.org.

JAMES, GUS JOHN, II, lawyer; b. Koma Yiolou, Cyprus, Dec. 29, 1938; s. John and Salome James; m. Helen Alexion, July 25, 1964; children: Mary Margaret, Nicole. BS in Bus., U. Richmond, 1962; JD, Coll. William and Mary, 1966, LLM in Taxation, 1967. Bar: Va. 1966. Assoc. Kaufman and Oberndorfer, Norfolk, Va., 1966—72, ptnr., 1972—76, mng. ptnr., 1976—81, 1994—; mem. Kaufman & Canoles, Norfolk, 1982—, chmn. exec. com., 1982—84. Editor-in-chief William and Mary Law Rev., 1965—66. Bd. dirs. Med. Ctr. Hosps., Norfolk Symphony, 1978—79, Va. Orch. Group, 1979—81, Old Dominion U. Intercollegiate Found., 1984—88, Old Dominion U. Ednl. Found., Bon Secours DePaul Health Found., 1998—; chmn. Old. Dominion U. Soccer Com.; bd. commrs. Norfolk Airport Authority, 2002—; bd. dirs. Annunciation Greek Orthodox Ch., Norfolk, 1972—80, 1981—84, 1989—92, pres. parish coun., 1973—74, 1984, 1989—92, chmn. Neptune Festival com., 1977—84, 1990—91, chmn. Azalea Festival com., 1976—84, Greek Festival, 1986—2004. With USAR, 1963—68. Mem.: ABA, Norfolk-Portsmouth Bar Assn., Va. Bar Assn., Order Ahepa Club (pres. 1972, 1989), Harbor Club (bd. dirs. 1993—2004, pres. 1995—96), Town Point Club (bd. dirs. 2002—). Home: 1521 Chandon Cres Virginia Beach VA 23454-1367 Office: 150 W Main St Norfolk VA 23510

JAMES, HAMILTON EVANS (TONY JAMES), private equity executive; b. Wyandotte, Mich., Feb. 3, 1951; s. Hamilton Renson and Waleska Bacon (Evans) J.; m. Amabel George Boyce, Aug. 25, 1973; children: Meredith Evans, Rebecca Lee, Hamilton Boyce. BA, Harvard U., 1973, MBA, 1975. Registered rep. N.Y. Stock Exch. From assoc. to sr. v.p. Donaldson, Lufkin & Jenrette, NYC, 1975-87, prin., 1982—, mng. dir., 1987-95, chmn. banking group, 1995—2000, also bd. dirs.; chmn., global investment banking & pvt. equity Credit Suisse First Boston, NYC, 2001—02; pres. Blackstone Group, NYC, 2002—. Bd. dirs. Costo Wholesale, Inc., Kirkland, Wash. Trustee Second Stage Theatre, Choate Rosemary Hall, Trout Unltd. John Harvard scholar, 1973; Baker scholar, 1975 Mem. River Club, Tokeneke Club, Links Club, Wee Burn Country Club, Club Ltd., Little Harbor Club. Republican. Episcopalian. Avocations: fly fishing, paddle tennis. Office: The Blackstone Group 345 Park Ave New York NY 10154 Home Phone: 212-734-6629. Business E-Mail: james@blackstone.com.

JAMES, JAMES FRANKLIN, psychiatrist, educator, academic administrator; b. Liberty, NC, Sept. 2, 1937; married; 7 children. AB in Comparative Lit., U. N.C., 1959; MD, U. Tenn., 1963. Diplomate Am. Bd. Psychiatry and Neurology. Intern Med. Coll. Va., Richmond, 1964—65; resident aerospace medicine U.S. Navy Aerospace Med. Inst., Pensacola, Fla., 1965—66; dir. Lithium project Dorothea Dix Hosp., Raleigh, 1967—69; resident psychiatry U. N.C.-Dorothea Dix Hosp. and Duke U., Raleigh/Durham, 1969; assoc. dep. commr. Ea. Region-N.C., 1969—71; supt. Cherry Hosp., N.C. State Mental Hosp., Goldsboro, 1969—71; part-time pvt. practice gen. and forensic psychiatry, 1969—78; mental health program chief Fresno (Calif.) County Dept. Health, 1971—78, dep. head dir., adult svcs. and mental health program chief, 1974—78; clin. prof. dept. psychiatry U. Okla. Sch. Medicine, 1978—89; chief consultation-liaison psychiatry VA Hosp., Oklahoma City, 1978—89; commr. Okla. Dept. Mental Health, Oklahoma City, 1978—89; attending staff Pitt County Meml. Hosp., 1989—; dir. residency tng. East Carolina U. Sch. Medicine, Greenville, NC, 1989—90, prof., chmn., 1990—2001, asst. dean, dir. personal counseling ctr., prof. dept. psychiat. medicine, 2001—. Founding bd. mem. East Carolina Counseling Ctr., 1998—2001; psychiat. edn. grant rev. cons. Nat. Inst. Mental Health, 1979—85, mem. internal rev. com., 1979—90, state manpower devel. grant rev. cons., 1979—90; examiner Am. Bd. Psychiatry and Neurology, 1985—96; mem. profl. adv. com. Joint Commn. on Accreditation Healthcare Orgns., 1988—89; presenter in field. Mem. editl. bd.: Current Surgery, 1991—, article reviewer: Hosp. and Cmty. Psychiatry, 1978—95, Jour. Medicine and Philosophy, 1991, Psychiat. Svcs., 1995—; contbr. articles to profl. jours. Lt. comdr. USN, 1965—66. Decorated Combat Air medal USN, S.E. Asia Expedition medal, Vietnam Svc. medal, Unit Commendation medal, Comdg. Officers' commendation; recipient Bd. Govs. Excellence in Tchg. award, U. NC, 2005. Fellow: Am. Coll. Mental Health Adminstrs., Am. Coll. Psychiatrists (mem. budget com. 1990—91, mem. nomination com. 1995—96, 2002—03), Am. Psychiat. Assn. (disting. life) (rep. to the assembly 1978, chmn. com. on state svcs. 1982—86, mem. coun. on psychiat. svcs. 1986—90, chmn. coun. on psychiat. svcs. 1988—90, mem. com. to develope a nat. data base for psychiatry 1988—90, mem. joint reference com. 1988—90, mem. budget com. 1990—94, chmn. consortium of chairs of pub. psychiatry components 1990—95, mem. com. on reorganization of fed. agys. 1991—92, mem. search com. for dep. dir. 1993); mem.: AMA, APHA, Pitt County Med. Soc., N.C. Med. Soc., Am. Assn. Mental Health Adminstrs., World Psychiat. Assn., N.C. Psychiat. Assn. (mem. cmty. mental health com. 1989—93, mem. program com. 1991, chmn. program com. 1998). Office: East Carolina Univ Sch Medicine Personal Counseling Ctr Lakeside Annex #3 Greenville NC 27858-2500

JAMES, JEANNETTE ADELINE, state legislator, accountant, small business owner; b. Maquoketa, Iowa, Nov. 19, 1929; d. Forest Claude and Winona Adeline (Meyers) Nims; m. James Arthur James, Feb. 16, 1948; children: James Arthur Jr., Jeannette, Alice Marie. Student, Merritt Davis Sch. Commerce, Salem, Oreg., 1956-57, U. Alaska, 1976—77. Payroll supr. Gen. Foods Corp., Woodburn, Oreg., 1956-66; cost acctg., inventory control clk. Pacific Fence & Wire Co., Portland, Oreg., 1966-67, office mgr., 1968-69; substitute rural carrier U.S. Post Office, Woodburn, 1967-68; owner, mgr., acct. and tax preparer James Bus. Svc., Goldendale, Wash., 1969-75, Anchorage, 1975-77, Fairbanks, Alaska, 1977—83, North Pole, Alaska, 1983—; co-owner, mgr. Jolly Acres Motel, North Pole, 1987—; mem. Alaska Ho. of Reps., Juneau, 1993—2003; chmn. House State Affairs, 1995-2000, jud. com., 1998—2002; vice chmn. Legis. Coun., 1995-96; chmn. joint com. Adminstrv. Regulation Rev., 1997-98, ho. majority leader, 2001—02. Instr. workshop Comm. Dynamics, 1988; railroad advisor to Gov. Murkowski, 2003-. Vice chmn. Klickitat County Dems., Goldendale, 1970-74; bd. dirs. Mus. and Art Inst., Anchorage, 1976-80; pres. Anchorage Internat. Art Inst., 1976-78; chmn. platting bd. Fairbanks North Star Borough, 1980-84, mem. Planning Commn., 1984-87; treas., vice chmn. 18th Dist. Reps., North Pole, Alaska, 1984-92; mem. City of North Pole Econ. Devel. Com., 1992-93; mem. Rep. State Ctrl. Com., 2004—. Named Legislator of Yr., Alaska Farm Bur., 1994, Alaska Outdoor Coun., 2000, Juneau Empire, 2002, Guardian of Small Bus., Nat. Fedn. Ind. Bus., 1998, Friend of Psychology, 2001; recipient Defender of Freedom award, NRA, 1994, Friend of Municipalities award, Alaska Mcpl. League, 1996, Courage in Preserving Equal Access award, Alaska chpt. Safari Club Internat., 2000, Cmty. Svc. award, Arctic Alliance for People, 2001. Mem. Internat. Tng. in Comm. (Alaska State winner speech contest 1981, 86), North Pole C. of C., Emblem Club, Rotary (treas. North Pole 1990, v.p. membership 2004-05, pres. 2006—), Eagles, Women of Moose Presbyterian. Avocations: bowling, dolls, children. Home: 3068 Badger Rd North Pole AK 99705-6117 Home Phone: 907-488-9093; Office Phone: 907-488-9339. Personal E-mail: jamesjeannette@gci.net, usually@acsalaska.net.

JAMES, JENNIFER DUFAULT, lawyer; BA summa cum laude, Rutgers U., 1988; JD cum laude, Harvard U., 1991. Bar: Supreme Ct. of US, US Ct. Appeals (1st. & 3rd. cir.), US Dist. Ct. (ea. dist.) Pa. Ptnr., vice chair Litig. Svcs. Dept. Schnader Harrison Segal & Lewis LLP, Phila. Named one of 40 Under 40, Phila. Bus. Jour., 2006. Mem.: ABA, Phila. Bar Assn., Pa. Bar Assn., Phi Beta Kappa. Office: Schnader Harrison Segal & Lewis LLP 1600 Market St, Ste 3600 Philadelphia PA 19103-7286 Office Phone: 215-751-2446. E-mail: jdjames@schnader.com.

JAMES, JOHN WHITAKER, SR., finance company executive; b. Summit, NJ, Aug. 19, 1942; s. Nathan Whitaker and Dorothy Jane (Laffey) J.; m. Loretta Marie Porter, Dec. 7, 1968; children: John Whitaker Jr., Laurissa Marie, Corinne Helena, Randolph Whitaker. BA in Econs., Princeton U., 1964; MBA in Fin. and Investment cum laude, NYU, 1970. From ofcl. asst., asst. treas. to asst. v.p. Bankers Trust Co., NYC, 1964-72, v.p. equipment leasing, 1972-76; pres., dir. Bankers Trust of Binghamton, NY, 1976-80; v.p., divsn. head Bankers Trust Co., NYC, 1980-82; new bus. strategist E.F. Hutton Credit Corp., Greenwich, Conn., 1983-85; sr. ops. mgr. corp. fin. and equipment leasing Chrysler Capital Corp. (formerly E.F. Hutton Credit Corp.), Greenwich, 1985-91; v.p. Chrysler Capital Corp., Stamford, Conn., 1991-97; pres. MicroGenesis LLC, 1997—; cons. Daimler Chrysler Global Capital Svcs., 1999—. Contbr. articles to profl. jours.; inventor baseball game Diamond Challenge. Campaign chmn. Broome County United Way, Binghamton, 1978; dir., pres. New Canaan chpt. United Way, 1985-90; dir., asst. treas. Family and Children's Svcs., Stamford, 1990-96; dir. New Canaan Cmty. Found., 1991-98, pres., 1998, Family Ctrs. Inc., Greenwich, 1996-97; dir. Christian Cmty. Action, New Haven, Conn., 2000-. With USAR, 1966-70. Mem. Societal Inst. Math. Scis. (bd. dirs., v.p., sec., treas. 1993—2004), David Ackerman Decs. (v.p. 1997-98, pres. 1998—2002), Assn. Blauvelt Desc., Princeton Club New Canaan (treas. 1985—2004). Republican. Presbyterian. Avocations: tennis, genealogy. Home and Office: MicroGenesis LLC 18 Waterbury Ave Madison CT 06443-3205 Office Phone: 203-245-1290. E-mail: jwjsr@aol.com.

JAMES, KATHRYN A., secondary school educator; b. Springfield, Mo., Aug. 1, 1925; d. Joseph Fred and Sybil Mae (Rogers) Giboney; m. Charles Elwyn James, Jan. 24, 1948 (wid. May 1999); children: Kathryne Janette, Jacquelyn Annette, Charles Roger. BSEd, S.W. Mo. State Tchrs. Coll., Springfield, 1945; MA, U. Mo., 1955; postgrad., U. Va., 1968. Cert. tchr. Calif., Kans., Ky., Ind., Mo., Va. Art supr. Mountain Grove (Mo.) Pub. Schs., 1945-47; art instr. Moberly (Mo.) Jr. Coll., 1947-49, Exptl. Sch., Springfield, Mo., 1949-54; art and home econs. instr. Ashland (Ky.) Pub. Schs., 1954-59; itinerant art tchr. Boyd County (Ky.) Pub. Schs., 1960-63; tchr. U. Ky., Lexington, 1963-65; art inst. Fairfax Pub. Schs., Va., 1965-68; art tchr. Terre Haute (Ind.) Pub. Schs., 1968-73, Springfield (Mo.) Pub. Schs., 1973-87. Judge sewing contests Singer Sewing Machine Co., Ashland, 1957-59, tchr. sewing classes pub. schs., adult evening and pub. sch. art classes, Ashland, 1956-58, Springfield, 1982-83. Author curriculum/art dept. Ashland and Terre Haute schs., 1955, 67-68; designer/banner constructor: Richard Ghephardt, Springfield, 1987. Campaigner Mo. State Legislators, Springfield, 1980-81, others. Recipient Gov.'s award Hon. Order of Ky. Cols., Lexington, 1965. Mem. Ky. Cols., Nat. DAR (flag chmn. 1991—2004, art awards 1995-97). Methodist. Avocations: china painting, interior decorating, freelance art work. Home: 1019 Joanne Dr Webb City MO 64870-1778 Personal E-mail: jameswood@joplin.com.

JAMES, KAY COLES, former federal agency administrator; b. Portsmouth, Va., June 1, 1949; d. Susie Armistead Coles; m. Charles Everett James; children: Charles Jr., Elizabeth, Robert III. BS, Hampton Inst., Va., 1971. Traffic svc. advisor C&P Telephone, Roanoke, Va., 1971-72, group supr., 1973, force mgr., 1974; conf. coord. devel. disabilities project State of Va., Richmond, 1978-79; asst. to housing coord. Housing Opportunities Made Equal, Richmond, 1980-81, dir. community edn. and devel., 1981-83; personnel dir. Cir. City Stores, Beltsville, Md., 1983-85; dir. pub. affairs Nat. Right to Life Com., Washington, 1985-88; asst. sec. pub. affairs US Dept. Health & Human Services, Washington, 1989—90; assoc. dir. Office of Nat. Drug Control Policy, 1991—93; sr. v.p. Family Rsch. Coun., 1993—94; sec. Va. Dept. Health & Human Resources, Richmond, 1994—96; dean Sch. of Govt. Regent U., 1996—99; sr. fellow of the Citizenship Project Heritage Found., 1999—2001; dir. US Office of Pers. Mgmt., Washington, 2001—05. Pres. Black Ams. for Life, Washington, D.C., 1985-88; asst. sec. pub. affairs HHS Office of the Sec., Washington, D.C., 1989—; mem. White House Com. on Children, Washington, D.C., 1988, White House Task Force on Blacks, Washington, D.C., 1988, Nat. Coalition on Pro-Family Issues, Washington, D.C., 1988; co-founder Nat. Family Inst., Washington, D.C., 1987; chair, Nat. Gambling Impact Study Com., 1999-2001. Contbr. numerous articles to jours. and newspapers. Recipient Disting. Fed Svc. award, Nat Assn. Hispanic Fed. Executives, 2004. Republican. Presbyterian. Avocations: reading, walking, cooking.

JAMES, KEVIN, actor; b. Stony Brook, NY, Apr. 26, 1965; m. Steffiana de la Cruz, June 19, 2004; children: Sienna-Marie, Shea Joelle. Attended, Cortland U. Actor: (TV series) Candid Camera, 1991, King of Queens, 1998—2007; writer:, 1999—2007; exec. prodr.:, 2000—07; host: Funny Flubs & Screw-Ups, 2000; exec. prodr.: (comedy spl.) Kevin James: Sweat the Small Stuff, 2001; actor: (films) 50 First Dates, 2004, Grilled, 2005, Hitch, 2005, (voice only) Monster House, 2006, Barnyard: The Original Party Animals, 2006, I Now Pronounce You Chuck & Larry, 2007; TV appearances include: Everybody Loves Raymond, 1996—99; Cosby, 1998; Martial Law, 1999; Becker, 1999. Named one of 100 Most Creative People, Entertainment Weekly mag., 2001.*

JAMES, LEBRON, professional basketball player; b. Akron, Ohio, Dec. 30, 1984; s. Gloria James; children: LeBron Jr., Bryce Maximus. Forward Cleve. Cavaliers, 2003—. Mem. US Sr. Men's Nat. Team, 2004—. Co-host: ESPY Awards show, 2007. Named Nat. HS Player of Yr., USA Today, 2003, NBA Rookie of Yr., 2004, NBA All-Star Game MVP, 2006; named one of 100 Most Influential People, Time Mag., 2005; named to Ea. Conf. All-Star Team, NBA, 2005—07, All-NBA 1st Team, 2006; recipient Espy award, Best Breakthrough, 2004, Best Male Athlete award, Black Entertainment TV (BET), 2006, 2007, Espy award, Best NBA Player, 2007. Achievements include being picked number 1 in the 2003 NBA Draft; member of the Bronze Medal-winning 2004 US Olympic Team; youngest player in NBA history to record a triple-double, Jan. 19, 2005; youngest player in NBA history to score 50 points in one game, March 20, 2005; youngest player in NBA history to score 4,000 career points, Nov. 12, 2005; youngest player in NBA history to score 5,000 career points, Jan. 21, 2006. Office: Cleveland Cavaliers 1 Center Ct Cleveland OH 44115-4001*

JAMES, LEE J., agriculture educator; Cert. Nat. Bd. Tchg. Standards. Named Miss. Tchr. of Yr., 2007. Mem.: Miss. Assn. Vocational Agr. Tchrs. (ctrl. dist. v.p. 2002—03), Nat. Assn. Agr. Educators (pres.-elect 2005—06, pres. 2006—07). Office: Choctaw County Career and Tech Ctr 319 E Church St Ackerman MS 39735 Office Phone: 662-285-3205. E-mail: leejjames@yahoo.com.*

JAMES, LINDA COATES, elementary school educator; b. Reno, Nev., Jan. 20, 1954; d. David Allison and Ethel Bluemel Coates; m. Donald Lyle James, Nov. 3, 1977; children: Camille James Bradshaw, Spencer, Laurel, Craig, Janelle. BS in Elem. Edn., Brigham Young U., Provo, Utah, BS in Early Childhood, 1977, diploma in ESL, 2000; postgrad., So. Utah. U., Cedar City. Tchr. Uintah County Sch. Dist., Lyman, Wyo., 1976—77, Provo Sch. Dist., 1977—78, Alpina Sch. Dist., American Fork, Utah, 1978—80; kindergarten tchr. Jordan Sch. Dist., Sandy, Utah, 1980—83, 5th grade tchr., 1994—. ESL specialist Columbia Elem., West Jordan, Utah, 1995—97, Jordan Hills Elem., West Jordan, 1997—2003; team leader Jordan Hills 5th Grade, West Jordan, 2004—. Mem. Women's Relief Soc., 1972—, pres., 1989—2001; Rep. county del. Salt Lake City, 1986—94; Rep. state del., 1994—98. Grantee, Jordan History Acad., 2005—06. Mem. Lds Ch. Avocations: scrapbooks, gardening, sewing, basketball. Office: Jordan Hills Elem 8892 S 4800 W West Jordan UT 84088 Office Phone: 801-565-7163.

JAMES, MARC STEPHEN, brokerage house executive; b. Phila., Apr. 17, 1961; s. Charles and Thelma Janet (Graves) J.; m. Melissa Elizbeth Mask, July 15, 1989. BS in Mech. Engring., Carnegie-Mellon U., 1983; MBA in Fin., U. Chgo., 1988. Engr. IBM, Dayton, Ohio, 1983-84, mktg. rep. Bethesda, Md., 1984-85, regional staff rep., 1985-86; index arbitageur Paine Webber, NYC, 1986-90; derivative products originator Chase Securities, Inc., NYC, 1990—94; mng. dir. fixed-income derivatives Bear Stearns & Co., 1994—2001; head corp. derivative sales (Am.) Commerzbank Securities, NYC, 2001—. Author: (with others) Recent Advances in Interest Rates and Currency Slips, 1992. Vol. counselor N.Y. Cares, 1991—. Avocations: tennis, bicycling, basketball. Home: 120 Prospect Park W Brooklyn NY 11215-4207 Office: Commerzbank Securities 1251 Avenue of the Americas New York NY 10020-1104

JAMES, MARION RAY, retired publishing executive, editor; b. Bellmont, Ill., Dec. 6, 1940; s. Francis Miller and Lorraine A. (Wylie) James; m. Janet Sue Tennis, June 16, 1960; children: Jeffrey Glenn, David Ray, Daniel Scott, Cheryl Lynne. BS, Oakland City Coll., Ind., 1964; MS, St. Francis Coll., Fort Wayne, Ind., 1978. Sports and city editor Daily Clarion, Princeton, Ind., 1963-65; English tchr. Jac-Cen-Del HS, Osgood, Ind., 1965-66; indsl. editor Whirlpool Corp., Evansville and LaPorte, Ind., 1966-68, Magnavox Govt. and Indsl. Electronics Co., Ft. Wayne, Ind., 1968-79; editor, pub., founder Bowhunter mag., Ft. Wayne, 1971-88, editor-in-chief Kalispell, Mont., 1989-2001, editor emeritus, 2001—06. Instr. Purdue U., Ft. Wayne, 1980—88. Author: Bowhunting for Whitetail and Mule Deer, 1975, Successful Bowhunting, 1985, My Place, 1991, The Bowhunter's Handbook, 1997, Of Blind Pigs and Big Bucks, 2002, Unforgettable Bowhunters, 2007; editor: Pope and Young Book of Bowhunting Records, 1975, 1993, 1999, Bowhunting Adventures, 1977. Named Alumnus of the Yr., Oakland City Coll., 1982; named to Hall of Fame, Mt. Carmel HS, Ill., 1983, Archery Hall of Fame, 2003; recipient Best Editl. award, United Cmty. Svc. Publs., 1970—72. Mem.: Ft. Wayne Assn. Bus. Editors (pres. 1975—76, Ft. Wayne Bus. Editor of the Yr. award 1969), Outdoor Writers Assn. Am. (Excellence in Craft Lifetime Achievement award 1999), Toastmasters (Able Toastmaster award), Pope and Young Club (pres. 2006—), Mu Tau Kappa, Alpha Psi Omega, Alpha Phi Gamma. Home: 11631 Blue Grass Rd Evansville IN 47725 Mailing: PO Box 55 Inglefield IN 47618 Personal E-mail: mrjames@cyberport.net, mrjames12640@aol.com. *Read! Being a good reader is the key to good thinking. Develop and expand your mind through active use of the printed word and you will discover a wide world of unlimited possibilities - and ultimate success that comes with self-discovery.*

JAMES, MARK A., lawyer, former state legislator; b. Eugene, Oreg., Oct. 9, 1959; m. Lori M. James; children: Anne A., John S. BS, Lewis and Clark Coll., 1982; JD, U. Ariz., 1985. Bar: U.S. Dist. Ct. Nev., U.S. Dist. Ct. (so. dist.) Tex., U.S. Ct. Appeals (9th and 5th cirs.). Senate judiciary intern Senator Paul Laxalt, Nev., 1981; former mem. Nev. Senate, Dist. 8, Carson City; former Las Vegas County commr.; founder James, Driggs, & Walch; pvt. practice, 2000; of counsel Bullivant Houser Bailey PC. Apptd. Nat. Conf. Commissioners Uniform State Law, Nat. Conf. State Legislators law and justice sect., criminal justice sect., Coun. State Govts. West Trade and Transp. Com., We. Water Policy Com. Articles editor Ariz. Law Rev. Active Clark County Pub. Edn. Found., Boys and Girls Clubs; mem. statewide adv. coun. Water Resources Rsch. of the Desert; bd. dirs. Aquavision, chair water law forum, 1992; bd. dirs. Las Vegas Valley Water Dist., So. Nev. Water Authority, So. Nev. Regional Planning Coalition, Met. Police Dept. Fiscal Affairs Com., Nat. Multiple Sclerosis Soc., Clark County Pub. Edn. Found., statewide adv. coun. water resources rsch. Desert Rsch. Inst., Nev. Earthquake Safety Coun., Family and Child Treatment SW Nev. Named one of Top 40 Lawyers Under 40, Las Vegas Bus. Press, 1994. Mem. ABA, State Bar Nev., State Bar Tex., Nev. Water Resources Assn. Republican. also: Nev State Legis Bldg 401 S Carson St Rm 240 Carson City NV 89701-4747 Office: Bullivant Houser Bailey PC 3980 Howard Hughes Pwy Ste 550 Las Vegas NV 89109 Office Phone: 702-650-6565 708. Office Fax: 702-650-2995. E-mail: mark.james@bullivant.com.

JAMES, MICHAEL THAMES, information technology executive, consultant; b. Gulfport, Miss., Feb. 16, 1949; s. William Denning and Christell (Cruthirds) J.; m. Debra Lynn Bryant, May 21, 1983; children: William Bryant, Shelley Christine. BS, US Naval Acad., Annapolis, Md., 1971; MS, U. So. Calif., LA, 1978. Commd. ensign USN, 1971, advanced through grades to lt., 1975, resigned, 1978; mktg. rep. IBM, South Bend, Ind., 1978-79; cons. Price Waterhouse, Houston, 1979-85; internal cons. Shell Oil, Houston, 1985-86; mgr. systems devel. & support Carolina Power & Light, Raleigh, 1986-91; v.p. Sprint Kansas City, 1991-93; ptnr. KPMG Peat Marwick, Dallas, 1994-96; prin. Scott, Madden & Assocs., Dallas, 1996-98; CEO James Cons. Group, Plano, Tex., 1998—. Guest lectr. N.C. State U., 1989-91; mem. adv. bd. So. Meth. U. Cox Sch. Bus., 1997—. Mem. computer studies adv. bd. Meredith Coll., 1987-91; adv. bd. Kansas City Met. Spl. Olympics, 1993; mem. industry steering com. Sch. Bus., U. Kans., 1993-94. Recipient Duke Vision award, 1998, 1999. Mem. Inst. Mgmt. Cons., U.S. Naval Acad. Alumni Assn., Stonebriar Country Club, Texoma Sailing Club. Republican. Presbyterian. Avocations: golf, tennis, sailing. Home: 4525 Emerson Dr Plano TX 75093-7226 Business E-Mail: mikejames@jamesconsultinggroup.com.

JAMES, PHYLLIS A., lawyer; b. L.I., NY, Mar. 23, 1952; BA magna cum laude in Am. hist. and lit., Harvard U., 1974, JD, 1977. Bar: Calif. 1978, Mich., Fed. Dist. Ct. Calif., US Ct. Appeals (9th cir.). Jud. law clerk Hon. Theodore R. Newman Jr. DC Ct. Appeals, 1977—78; mem. Pillsbury Madison & Sutro, San Francisco, 1979—94; corp. counsel City of Detroit Law Dept., 1994—2001; sr. v.p. and sr. counsel MGM Mirage, Las Vegas, Nev., 2001—. Pursuant State Mich. Trial Ct. Assessment Commn., 1997—98. Recipient Capt. Jonathan Fay prize. Mem.: Mich. Bar Assn., Calif. Bar Assn., Phi Bet Kappa. Office: MGM Mirage 3600 Las Vegas

Blvd S Las Vegas NV 89109 Office Phone: 702-693-7590. Office Fax: 702-693-7591. Business E-Mail: phyllis_james@mgmmirage.com.

JAMES, P(HYLLIS) D(OROTHY) (BARONESS JAMES OF HOLLAND PARK OF SOUTHWOLD IN COUNTY OF SUFFOLK), author; b. Oxford, Eng., Aug. 3, 1920; d. Sidney Victor and Dorothy May Amelia (Hone) J.; m. Connor Bantry White, 1941 (dec. 1964); children: Clare Bantry, Jane Bantry. Student Brit. schs.; LittD (hons.), U. Buckingham, Eng., 1992, U. Hertfordshire, 1994, U. Glasgow, Scotland, 1995, Durham U., 1998, Portsmouth U., 1999; DLitt, U. London, 1993; D, U. Essex, Eng., 1996. Adminstr. Nat. Health Service, 1949-68; apptd. prin. Civil Svc. Home Office, 1968; prin. Police Dept., 1968-72, Criminal Policy Dept., 1972-79. Author: Cover Her Face, 1962, A Mind to Murder, 1963, Unnatural Causes, 1967, Shroud for a Nightingale, 1971; (with T.A. Critchley) The Maul and the Pear Tree, 1971; An Unsuitable Job for a Woman, 1972, The Black Tower, 1975, Death of an Expert Witness, 1977, Innocent Blood, 1980, The Skull Beneath the Skin, 1982, (play) A Private Treason, 1985, A Taste for Death, 1986, Devices and Desires, 1989, The Children of Men, 1992, Original Sin, 1994, A Certain Justice, 1997, Time to be in Earnest, 1999, Death in Holy Orders, 2001, The Murder Room, 2003, The Lighthouse, 2005. Gov. BBC, 1988-93; bd. dirs. Brit. Coun., 1988-93; bd. dirs., chair lit. adv. panel Arts Coun. Gt. Britain, 1988-92. Decorated Order Brit. Empire, 1983; created life peer (Baroness) of U.K., 1991; assoc. fellow Downing Coll., Cambridge, 1986, hon. fellow, 2000; hon. fellow St. Hilda's Coll., Oxford, 1996, Girton Coll., Cambridge, 2000; recipient Grandmaster award Mystery Writers Am., 1999, medal of honor for lit. Nat. Arts Club, 2005. Fellow Royal Soc. Lit., Royal Soc. Arts; mem. Soc. of Authors (chmn. 1984-86, pres. 1997—), Detection Club. Office: Greene & Heaton Ltd 37 Goldhawk Rd London W12 8QQ England

JAMES, RANDALL S., state agency administrator; m. Kathy James; children: Allison Dredla, Amanda Johnson. BA in Econs. and Govt., U. Tex., 1969; grad., So. Meth. U. Grad. Sch. Banking, 1982, Tex. Gov.'s Exec. Devel. Prog., 1994. Bank examiner FDIC, 1970—80, reg. office rev. examiner Dallas, 1980—82; credit rev. mgr. Interfirst Bank (now First Rep. Bank), Austin, Tex., 1982—88; credit examiner Bracewell & Patterson, 1988—89; pvt. practice, 1990—91; dep. banking commr. Tex. Dept. Banking, Austin, 1991—99, acting banking commr., 1999, banking commr., 1999—. Adv. bd. mem. Sch. Cmty. Bank Mgmt. Tex. Tech. U., Lubbock, Bank Ops. Inst. Tex. A&M U., Dept. Fin. Econs. SW Tex. State U., San Marcos; chmn., sec. Conf. State Bank Suprs. Dist. IV; bd. mem. Money Transmitter Regulators' Assn. Recipient Outstanding Fin. Exec. award, Fin. Mgmt. Assn. SW Tex. State U., 2003. Office: Tex Dept Banking 2601 N Lamar Blvd Austin TX 78705 Office Phone: 512-475-1325. Office Fax: 512-475-1313. E-mail: rjames@banking.state.tx.us.*

JAMES, ROBERT LEO, advertising executive, director; b. NYC, Sept. 23, 1936; s. Leo Francis and Mildred Virginia (Schaffa) J.; m. Anne Krapp, Feb. 2, 1968; children: Robert Leo, Victoria, Jeffrey. AB, Colgate U., 1958; MBA, Columbia U., 1961. Field researcher Farm Jour., Inc., Cleve., 1956-57; salesman Procter and Gamble Co., Schenectady, 1958-59, office head sales mgr. Syracuse, NY, 1959—; new product devel. Colgate Palmolive Co., NYC, 1961-64; sr. v.p., mgmt. svc. dir. Ogilvy and Mather, Inc., NYC, 1964-68; sr. v.p., mgmt. service dir. Marschalk Co., Inc., NYC, 1968, dir., 1968-80, exec. v.p., 1970, gen. mgr., 1971, pres., 1974, chmn. bd., chief exec. officer, 1975-80; vice chmn. Interpub. Group of Cos., Inc., 1980-81, also dir.; vice chmn. McCann-Erickson Worldwide, 1981-85, chmn. bd., pres., 1985-95; chmn. emeritus McCann-Erickson, 1995—. Adj. assoc. prof. mktg. Fordham U., 1968-69. Trustee Fordham Prep. Sch., 1977-83, South Street Seaport Mus., 1990-2002, N.Y. Presbyn. Hosp., N.Y.C.; bd. dirs. March of Dimes, N.Y.C., 1981-88; mem. Corp. Woods-hole Oceanographic, 1996, trustee exec. com., 1997—; trustee, v.p. Worldship Trust, 2002—. Mem. NAS (chmn. pres. circle), Am. Assn. Advt. Agys. (chmn. 1992-93), Young Pres. Orgn., Nat. Captioning Inst. (chmn. corp. adv. coun. 1990-94), Internat. Exec. Svc. Corp. (mem. coun. 1988-92, adv. coun. 2000—), The Advt. Coun. (dir. 1992), Smithsonian Inst. (nat. bd. dirs. 1994—), Op Sail (trustee, exec. com. 1994—), N.Y. Yacht Club (trustee, commodore N.Y. Yacht Club 1997-99), Clove Valley Rod and Gun Club (bd. dirs., v.p. 1998-2002), Indian Harbor Yacht Club (bd. dirs. 1986-89), Nat. Air and Space Mus. (chmn. bd. dirs. 1999-2002, bd. dirs.). Home: 68 W Brother Dr Greenwich CT 06830-6751 Office: McCann-Erickson Worldwide New York NY 10017-2798

JAMES, RONALD J., civilian military employee, lawyer; b. Apr. 8, 1937; s. Raymond Babe and Jennie May (Smith) J.; m. Vivian Thelma, June 1961 (div. Sept. 1969); m. Patricia O'Donnell, Oct. 31, 1970; children: Ronald Jr., Kevin, Shannon, Kelly, Catlin. BA, U. Mo., 1959; JD, Am. U., 1966; MA, So. Ill. U., 1971. Bar: Iowa 1966, Ohio 1977, U.S. Supreme Ct. 1972. Legis. aide U.S. Congress, Washington, 1963-64; dir. City of Waterloo, Iowa, 1966-67; asst. county atty. Black Hawk County, Iowa, 1967-69; spl. asst. to counselor to Pres. The White House, Washington, 1970-71; trial atty. US Dept. Transp., Washington, 1971-72; asst. gen. counsel Equal Employment Opportunity Commn., Chgo., 1972-75; adminstr. wage and hour divsn. US Dept. Labor, Washington, 1975-77; ptnr. Squire, Sanders & Dempsey, Cleve., 1977—2003; chief human capital officer US Dept. Homeland Security, Washington, 2003—06; asst. sec for manpower & reserve affairs, Dept. Army US Dept. Def., Washington, 2006—. 1st lt. U.S. Army, 1960-63. Avocations: soccer, skiing, african-american history, buffalo soldiers. Office: US Army 111 Army Pentagon Rm 2E468 Washington DC 20310 Home Phone: 202-360-3097.*

JAMES, SHARON ANN, elementary school educator; b. Bayshore, NY, Sept. 29, 1948; d. John Joseph Melton and Pauline Rita Tranovich; m. Robert Taylor James, July 22, 1978; children: Kelly Ann, Robert John, Kathleen Megan. BA, SUNY, Oneonta, 1970; MS in Edn., SUNY, New Paltz, 1971. Elem. tchr. C.I. Pub. Schs., Central Islip, NY, 1971—. Mem.: Ctrl. Islip Tchrs. Assn. (bldg. com. rep. 2004, math task force mem. 2005, mem. math curriculum writing team 2005, PTA programmer 1975), Alpha Delta. Home: 40 Offenbach St Centereach NY 11720 Office: CI Pub Schs 299 Sycamore Ave Central Islip NY 11722

JAMES, SHARPE, state senator, former mayor; b. Jacksonville, Fla., Feb. 20, 1936; m. Mary Mattison; children John, Elliott, Kevin. Grad., Montclair State Coll.; M, Springfield Coll.; student, Washington State U., Columbia U., Rutgers U.; LLD (hon.), Montclair State U., 1988; PhD (hon.), Drew U., 1991. Tchr. Newark Pub. Sch. Dist.; former mem. faculty Essex County Coll., Newark, from 1968, prof., dept. chair, athletic dir.; councilman, South Ward City of Newark, 1970—82, councilman-at-large, 1982, mayor, 1986—2006; mem. NJ Senate, Dist. 29, Trenton, 1999—; comm. NJ State Redevelopment Authority, 1995—. Head Urban Issues Inst., Essex CC, Newark, 2006—07. Bd. trustees US Conf. Mayors, v.p. NJ chpt. Served with AUS.; v.p. then pres., Garden State Athletic Conf.; past pres. Nat. League of Cities. Named Mayor of Yr., N.J. Conf. Mayors, 2001, The Most Valuable Pub. Ofcl., City and State Mag.; named to N.J. Elected Officials Hall of Fame, 1999; recipient Arts Leadership award, U.S. Conf. Mayors and Ams. for the Arts, 2002. Democrat. Avocation: tennis.

JAMES, SHERMAN ATHONIA, epidemiologist, educator; b. Hartsville, SC, Oct. 25, 1943; s. Jerome and Helen Genese (Bachus) J.; m. Vera Lucia Moura; children: Sherman Alexander, Scott Anthony. AB, Talladega Coll., 1964; PhD, Washington U., 1973. Prof. epidemiology U. N.C., Chapel Hill, 1973-89, U. Mich., Ann Arbor, 1989—2003, assoc. dean acad. affairs Sch. Pub. Health; prof. pub. policy Duke U., Durham, NC, 2003—. Cons. NIMH, NIH, Bethesda, Md., 1979-83, Nat. Heart, Lung and Blood Inst., 1985—, Nat. Inst. Environ. Health Sci., 1990—; cons. NAS, Washington, 1994—. Contbr. articles to profl. jours. Capt. USAF, 1964-69. Fellow Soc. of Fellows, U. Mich., 1993—. Fellow Am. Heart Assn., Acad. Behavioral Medicine Rsch., Soc. Behavioral Medicine, Am. Coll. Epidemiology; mem. Am. Men and Women of Sci. Inst. Medicine. Avocations: travel, photography, tennis, nature walks. Office: Duke Univ 136 Sanford Inst 90245 Durham NC 27708

JAMES, T. KENNETH, school system administrator; BA, Ark. State U.; MA in Ednl. Adminstrn., No. Ariz. U., PhD in Ednl. Adminstrn. and Supervision, US Internat. U., 1992. Asst. supt. for ednl. svcs. Escondido Union HS Dist., Calif.; supt. schs. Fayette County Pub. Schs., Lexington, Ky., Little Rock, Ark., Van Buren, Ark., Batesville, Ark.; commr. Ark. Dept. Edn., 2004—. Mem. U. Ark. Ednl. Adminstrn. Steering Com., State Adv. Bd. on Reforming Edn.; bd. dir. AASA, Coun. Chief State School Officers, Regional Edn. Named Supt. of the Yr., State Ark., 1998. Mem.: Ark. Assn. of Ednl. Adminstrs. Office: Ark Dept Edn 4 Capitol Mall Little Rock AR 72201 Office Phone: 501-682-4475.*

JAMES, THOMAS A., investment company executive; BA magna cum laude, Harvard Coll., 1964; MBA with high distinction, Harvard Bus. Sch., 1966; JD, Stetson Coll. Law, 1969. With Raymond James & Assocs., Raymond James Fin. Inc., St. Petersburg, Fla., 1966—; CEO Raymond James Fin., Inc., St. Petersburg, Fla., 1969—87; chmn., CEO Raymond James & Assocs., Raymond James Fin. Inc., St. Petersburg, Fla., 1987—. Bd. dir. Cora Health Services, 1997—; chmn. Fin. Services Roundtable, 2007—; past. chmn. Securities Industry Assn. Pres. bd. trustees Salvador Dali Mus.; chmn. Fla. Council of 100; mem. bd. Dean's advisors Harvard Bus. Sch.; bd. mem. Internat. Tennis Hall of Fame; chmn. Chi Chi Rodriguez Youth Found. Baker Scholar. Office: Raymond James Fin Inc 880 Carillon Pkwy Saint Petersburg FL 33716-1100*

JAMES, THOMAS LARRY, chemistry professor; b. North Platte, Nebr., Sept. 8, 1944; s. James Jennings and Guinevere (Richards) J.; m. Olga Schmidlin; children: Marc, Tristan. BS, U. N.M., 1965; PhD, U. Wis., 1969. Research chemist Celanese Chem. Co., Corpus Christi, Tex., 1969-71; NIH post-doctorate fellow U. Pa., Phila., 1971-73; prof. chem., pharmaceutical chemistry and radiology U. Calif., San Francisco, 1973—, chair dept. pharm. chemistry, 1995—, dir. Magnetic Resonance Lab., 1975. Author: NMR in Biochemistry, 1975; editor: Biomedical NMR, 1984, Methods in Enzymology, 1989, 5th edit., 2005; mem. editl. bd. Jour. Magnetic Resonance, Jour. Biomolecular NMR, Magnetic Resonance Imaging; editor FEBS Letters; contbr. articles to profl. jours. Mem. Internat. Soc. Magnetic Resonance, Am. Biophys. Soc., Am. Chem. Soc., Am. Biochem. Soc., Soc. Magnetic Resonance in Medicine, Phi Beta Kappa, Phi Kappa Phi, Kappa Mu Epsilon. Mem. Cmty. Of Christ. Avocations: skiing, kayaking, travel, photography. Office: UCSF MC2280 600 16th St San Francisco CA 94158-2517 Business E-Mail: james@picasso.ucsf.edu.

JAMES, THOMAS NAUM, cardiologist, educator; b. Amory, Miss., Oct. 24, 1925; s. Naum and Kata J.; m. Gleaves Elizabeth Tynes, June 22, 1948; children: Thomas Mark, Terrence Fenner, Peter Naum. BS, Tulane U., 1946, MD, 1949. Diplomate Am. Bd. Internal Medicine (mem. bd. govs. 1982-88), Bd. Cardiovasc. Diseases (bd. dirs. 1972-78). Intern Henry Ford Hosp., Detroit, 1949-50, resident in internal medicine and cardiology, 1950-53, staff, 1959-68; instr. medicine Tulane U., New Orleans, 1955-58, asst. prof., 1959; prof. medicine U. Ala. Med. Ctr., Birmingham, 1968-87, prof. pathology, 1968-73, assoc. prof. physiology and biophysics, 1969-73, dir. Cardiovasc. Rsch. and Tng. Ctr., 1970-77, chmn. dept. medicine, dir. divsn. cardiovasc. disease, 1973-81, Mary Gertrude Waters prof. cardiology, 1976-87, Disting. prof., 1981-87; prof. medicine, prof. pathology U. Tex. Med. Br., Galveston, 1987—, pres., 1987-97, dir. WHO Cardiovasc. Ctr., 1988-98, Thomas N. and Gleaves T. James disting. chair cardiol. scis., 1997—. U. Tex. Med. Br., Galveston, 1997—; physician-in-chief U. Ala. Hosps., 1973-81; mem. adv. coun. Nat. Heart Lung and Blood Inst., 1975-79; pres. 10th World Congress Cardiology, 1986; mem. cardiology del. invited by Chinese Med. Assn. to China, 1978; Campbell orator Queens U., Belfast, No. Ireland, 1982; Mikamo lectr. Japan Circulation Soc., 1982; Sir Thomas Lewis lectr. Brit. Cardiac Soc., 1983, Einthoven lectr. U. Leiden, The Netherlands, 1993, Bailey K. Ashford lectr. U. P.R., 1995; hon. lectr. U. Padua, 1998. Author: Anatomy of the Coronary Arteries, 1961, The Etiology of Myocardial Infarction, 1963; Mem. editl. bd. Circulation, 1966-83, Am. Jour. Cardiology, 1968-82, Am. Heart Jour, 1976-79; contbr. articles to profl. jours. Capt. M.C. U.S. Army, 1953-55. Recipient Sesquicentennial Medal of Honor Paul Tulane Coll. Tulane U., 1997, 50-year Lifetime Achievement award Tulane Med. Alumni Assn., 1999, James B. Herrick award Am. Heart Assn., 1999, Disting. Achievement award Soc. Cardiovasc. Pathology, 2005. Fellow ACP (gov. Ala. 1975-79, master 1983); mem. AMA, Am. Clin. and Climatological Assn. (v.p. 1992-93, councillor 1992-93), Assn. Am. Physicians, Am. Soc. Clin. Investigation, Assn. Univ. Cardiologists (pres. 1978-79), Am. Heart Assn. (pres. 1979-80, Herrick award Coun. on Clin. Cardiology 1999), Am. Coll. Cardiology (v.p. 1970-71, trustee 1970-71, 76-81, First Disting. Scientist award 1982, chmn. publs. com. 1994-97), Am. Soc. Pharmacology and Exptl. Therapeutics, Soc. Exptl. Biology of Medicine, Am. Coll. Chest Physicians, Ctrl. Soc. Clin. Rsch., Internat. Soc. and Fedn. Cardiology (pres. 1983-84), WHO (expert adv. panel on cardiovasc. diseases 1988-97), So. Soc. Clin. Investigation, Am. Fedn. Clin. Rsch., Ala. Acad. Honor. Philos. Soc. Tex., Cosmos Club, Mountain Brook Club, Galveston Arty. Club, Phi Beta Kappa, Sigma Xi, Omicron Delta Kappa, Alpha Omega Alpha, Alpha Tau Omega, Phi Chi. Presbyterian. Office: U Tex Med Br 301 University Blvd Galveston TX 77555-0175 Office Phone: 409-747-9645. Business E-Mail: pbbevil@utmb.edu. E-mail: tnj@oakmountain.net.

JAMES, WILLIAM HALL, former state official, educator; b. North Providence, RI, July 20, 1910; s. John William and May (Hall) J.; m. Virginia Stowell, June 24, 1950, 1 child, Hillery Stowell. Student, U. Lausanne, 1928-29; BPhil, Brown U., 1933; MA, Yale U., 1946, PhD, 1955; LLD, U. New Haven, 1976. Tchr. New Canaan (Conn.) Bd. Edn., 1933-36; teaching prin. Easton (Conn.) Bd. Edn., 1936-42, 46-47, supervising prin., 1947-53, supt. schs., 1953-58, Branford (Conn.) Bd. Edn., 1958-66; staff Commn. Higher Edn., Hartford, Conn., 1966-77, dir. accreditation and scholarships, 1966-77; ret., 1977. Cons. Greater New Haven State Tech. Coll., 1977-78, Conn. Commn. Higher Edn., 1980-81; adj. prof. history So. Conn. State Coll., New Haven, 1947-49, adj. prof. econs. and labor-mgmt. rels., 1981-92, adj. prof. labor-mgmt. rels.; adj. prof. internat. rels., Eurasian affairs and history Western Conn. State Coll., Danbury, 1949-58; adj. prof. ednl. adminstrn. U. Bridgeport, Conn., 1958; adj. prof. econs. and indsl. rels. U. New Haven, West Haven, Conn., 1979-90, adj. prof. indls. rels.; adj. prof. labor-mgmt. rels., mgmt. Teikyo Post U., Waterbury, Conn., 1988-93; lectr. in field. Author: The Monetarists and the Current Crisis, 1975. Mem. North Branford (Conn.) Commn. Econ. Devel., 1980-95, chmn., 1981-95; mem. PTA. Maj. USAAF, 1942-46. Recipient Disting. Friend of Greater New Haven State Tech. Coll. award, 1984; Paul Harris fellow Rotary Found; named to Branford's Edn. Hall of Fame. Mem. SAR, NEA, Conn. Edn. Assn., Conn. Assn. Pub. Sch. Supts., Conn. Assn. Advancement Sch. Adminstrn., Am. Assn. Sch. Adminstrs., Yale Post-Doctoral Seminar Group (pres. 1968-69), Conn. State Employees Assn., Conn. Coun. Higher Edn. (treas. 1971-77), Am. Assn. Higher Edn., Royal Can. Geog. Soc., Numerical Control Soc., Rotary, Schoolmasters Rotary U.S. (sec.-treas. 1965-69), Am. Legion (post comdr. Easton 1948-49), China-Burma-India Vets. Assn., Exchange Club. Home: 373 Reeds Gap Rd Northford CT 06472-1106

JAMES, WILLIAM RAMSAY, broadcast executive; b. South Bend, Ind., Oct. 6, 1933; s. William Stubbs and Rose (Ramsay) James; m. Jane Mehrer, Dec. 29, 1955; children: William Harold, Martha Courtney Quay. BS in Mech. Engring., Princeton U., 1955; MBA, Harvard U., 1960. CPA Mich. Plant mgr. N. A. Woodworth Co., Ferndale, Mich., 1960-62; ptnr. Touche Ross & Co., Detroit, 1962-69; v.p., gen. mgr. Sta. WJR, Detroit, 1969-80; exec. v.p. Capital Cities Comm., NYC, 1980-86, pres. Cable TV div. Bloomfield Hills, Mich., 1980-86; pres. James Comm. Inc., 1986-87; mng. ptnr. James Comm. Ptnrs., Bloomfield Hills, 1988—. Trustee, treas. William Beaumont Hosp., Royal Oak, Mich. 1st lt. USAF, 1956—58. Mem.: AICPA, Mich. Assn. CPAs, Everglades Club (Palm Beach, Fla.), Orchard Lake (Mich.) Country Club, Country Club (Bloomfield Hills). Republican. Episcopalian. Office: James Communications Ptnrs 6150 Highland Rd Waterford MI 48327 Office Phone: 248-886-0337. Personal E-mail: wrj@michigan-aviation.com.

JAMES, WILLIAM W., financial consultant; b. Oct. 12, 1931; s. Will and Clyde (Cowdrey) James; m. Carol Ann Muenter, June 17, 1967; children: Sarah James Banks, David William. AB, Harvard U., 1953. Cert. trust and fin. advisor. Asst. to dir. overseas divsn. Becton Dickinson & Co., Rutherford, NJ, 1956-59; stockbroker Merrill Lynch, Pierce, Fenner & Smith, Inc., St. Louis, 1959-62; with trust divsn. Boatmen's Nat. Bank, St. Louis, 1962-90, v.p. in charge estate planning, sr. v.p., 1972-90; sr. v.p. Boatmen's Trust Co., St. Louis, 1989-96, fin., trust mktg. cons., 1996—. Mem. gift and bequest coun. Barnes Hosp., St. Louis, 1963—67, St. Louis U., 1972—78; dir. Mark Twain Summer Inst., St. Louis, 1987—92. With US Army, 1953—55. Mem.: Am. Inst. Banking, Mo. Bankers Assn., Estate Planning Coun. St. Louis, Harvard Alumni Assn. (bd. dirs. 1987—90), Noonday Club (St. Louis), Mo. Athletic Club, Harvard Faculty Club (Cambridge, Mass.), Harvard Club St. Louis (pres. 1972—73). Republican. Home: 1415 Michele Dr Saint Louis MO 63122-1404

JAMESON, DARRELL P., social studies educator; b. Easley, SC, May 20, 1972; s. L. Doyle and Diane S. Jameson. BA in History, Francis Marion U., Florence, SC, 1995, MEd in Social Studies, 2002; MEd in Adminstrn., U. Cin., 2007. Tchr. Simpson Acad., Easley, 1995—97, Marion HS, SC, 1997—. Named Vol. Alumni of the Yr., Francis Marion U., 2005, Tchr. of the Yr., Marion HS, 2005, History Tchr. of the Yr., DAR, 2005. Mem.: SC Coun. Social Studies. Home: 1814 Sun Valley Ct Marion SC 29571 Personal E-mail: nosemaj_delmer@yahoo.com.

JAMESON, JAMES LARRY, medical educator, endocrinologist, internist; b. Fort Benning, Georgia, June 21, 1954; MD, U. North Carolina, Chapel Hill, 1981. Cert. NBME, 1982, Am. Bd. Internal Medicine, 1985, Endocrinology & Metabolism, 1987. Intern Mass. Gen. Hospital, Boston, 1981—82, resident, 1982—83, fellow, 1983—85; rsch. assoc. Howard Hughes Medical Inst., Boston, 1985—87; asst. physician Mass. Gen. Hospital, Boston, 1987—92, chief thyroid unit, 1987—93; asst. prof. Harvard Medical Sch., Boston, 1987—92, assoc. prof., 1992—93; dir. molecular biology Mass. Gen. Hospital, Boston, 1991—93, assoc. physician, 1992—93; dir. endocrinology & metalbolism Northwestern U., 1993, Irving S. Cutter prof. medicine div. endocrinology, metabolism, & molecular medicine, 1993—, chmn. medicine, 1993—. Fellow: Am. Acad. Arts & Sciences; mem.: Inst. Medicine. Office: Northwestern U Galter Pavilion Ste 3-150 251 E Huron St Chicago IL 60611

JAMESON, JENNIFER A., lawyer; BA, U. Minn., 1996, JD cum laude, 1999. Bar: Minn. 1999. Law clk. to Hon. Gary Larson Hennepin County Dist. Ct., 2000; assoc. McGrann, Shea, Anderson, Carnival, Straughn & Lamb, Chartered, Mpls. Vol. Chrysalis Legal Progs., 2001—. Named a Rising Star, Minn. Super Lawyers mag., 2006. Mem.: Minn. Women Lawyers, Minn. State Bar Assn., Collaborative Law Inst. Office: McGrann Shea Anderson Carnival Straughn & Lamb Chartered 2600 US Bancorp Ctr 800 Nicollet Mall Minneapolis MN 55402 Office Phone: 612-338-2525. E-mail: jaj@mcgrannshea.com.*

JAMESON, PATRICIA MARIAN, government agency administrator; b. Pitts., Mar. 17, 1945; d. Vernon L. and Dorothy Leam (Wilson) J. BA, Northwestern U., Evanston, Ill., 1967; MA, Ohio State U., 1969. With HUD, 1970-2000, project mgr. Detroit, 1976-77, acting dir. housing mgmt., 1978, dep. area mgr. Milw. Area Office, 1978-85, acting area mgr., 1979-80, 82, regional dir. adminstrn. Chgo. Regional Office, 1985-95, dir. adminstrv. svc. ctr. Denver, 1995-2000, ret., 2000. Vol. call ctr. ARC; vol. Sierra Club; active Denver World Affairs Coun., Internat. Inst. for Edn.; vol. Habitat for Humanity; vol. tax aide program AARP; vol. Project C.U.R.E.; efile coord. tax aide program AARP. Recipient Quality Performance award HUD, 1973, 75, 80, Outstanding Performance award, 1980, 85, 87, 88, 90, 91, 92, 94, 96, 97, 98, 99, 2000, Disting. Svc. award 1992, 2000, Secs. award for Supervisory Excellence, 1998. Mem. Fed. Execs. Inst. Alumni Assn., Phi Beta Kappa, Pi Sigma Alpha.

JAMGOCHIAN, VICTORIA, interior designer; b. Richmond, Va., Apr. 18, 1922; d. John A. and Azniv (Marsevonian) Jamgochian. BS in Psychology, Coll. William and Mary, 1946; cert. interior design and architecture, Parsons Sch. Design, NYC, France, Italy, 1955. Cert. comml., residential and office interior designer. Asst. interior designer McMillen, Inc., NYC, 1955-56, Lord and Taylor, NYC, 1956-57; interior designer J. Frank Jones Interiors, Richmond, 1957-61, Miller & Rhoads, Richmond, 1961-67, Thalhimer's Indsl. Design, Richmond, 1967-79; exec. dir. design Chasen's Bus. Interiors, Richmond, 1979—2001. Projects pub. in Hospitality Mag., 1967, Interiors Mag., 1968, 69, Va. Record, 1971. Interior designer (prin. works) Country Club of Va., The Woman's Club, Richmond, Va., Busch Gardens Hospitality Ctr., Williamsburg, Va., Pres.'s House, U. Richmond, Richmond Meml. Hosp., Va. Bapt. Hosp., Lynchburg, Engineer's Club, Richmond, Rotunda Club, Hilton Hotel, Wilmington, NC, Wachovia, Richmond, Chemtreat, Inc., Cascades Restaurant and Meeting Ctr., Woodlands, Colonial Williamsburg, Inc. Mem.: William and Mary Alumni Soc., Kappa Delta. Avocations: tennis, travel, horseback riding, piano. Home: 211 Sleepy Hollow Rd Richmond VA 23229-7153

JAMIESON, CYNTHIA KAY, military specialist; b. Warren, Pa., Jan. 6, 1969; d. Richard Charles and Sandra Lee Jamieson. Assoc., Bus. Inst. Pa., Sharon, 2004. Specialised bus. degree Pa., 2004. Ship's serviceman US Navy, Norfolk, Va., 1989—93; mil. guard US Army, Heidelberg, Germany, 2002—03, security specialist Iraq, 2005—06. With USN, 1989—93. Decorated Nat. Def. Svc. medal USN, US Army, Kuwait Liberation medal USN, South West Asia Svc. medal with Bronze Svc. Star, Navy Sea Svc. Deployment, Combat Action ribbon US Army, Army Commendation medal, Army Good Conduct medal, Iraq Campaign medal, Global War on Terrorism Svc. medal, Army Svc. ribbon, Overseas Svc. ribbon, Armed Forces Res. medal with M Device. Mem.: VFW (life). Home: 658 Pennsylvania Ave Renovo PA 17764 Office: Pennsylvania Army NG 66 Armory Rd Lock Haven PA 17754 Home Phone: 570-923-0164; Office Phone: 570-823-2445. Personal E-mail: cindy.jamieson@us.army.mil.

JAMIESON, EDWARD B., investment company executive; BA, Bucknell Univ.; M in fin. & acctg., Univ. Chgo. Dir. internat. treas. Pepsico; treas. Beatrice Consumer Products Inc.; positions through pres. Franklin Advisers Inc., San Mateo, Calif., 1987—; chief investment officer Franklin Equity Group, San Mateo, Calif. Mem. investment adv. com. ARCS Found.; mem. Parents Fund com. Duke Univ. Served USAR, 1971. Office: Franklin Equity Group 1 Franklin Pkwy San Mateo CA 94403*

JAMIESON, GRAHAM A., biochemist, researcher, retired organization official; b. Wellington, New Zealand, Aug. 14, 1929; came to U.S., 1956; s. Andrew Wilson and Nan (Graham) J.; m. Barbara MacLachlan, Feb. 20, 1960; 1 child, Brian. BSc, U. Otago, 1949; MSc with first class honors in Organic Chemistry, U. New Zealand, 1951; PhD Lister Inst. Preventive

Medicine, U. London, 1954, DSc, 1972. Research fellow dept. biochemistry Cornell U., NYC, 1956; research biochemist Am. Nat. Red Cross, Bethesda, Md., 1961-64, asst. dir. research, 1964-69, dir. research, 1969-78, assoc. dir. blood services, 1978-84, sr. scientist, 1984—. Vis. scientist NIH, 1957-61, mem. exptl. hematology study sect., 1978-84; lectr. biochemistry Georgetown U., Washington, 1961, professorial lectr., 1966-74, adj. prof., 1974-96; Winzler Meml. lectr. U. Fla., 1975; mem. adv. com. on blood preservation and substitutes U.S. Army Med. Rsch. and Devel. Command, 1980-92, chmn., 1981-92; vis. prof. U. Sao Paulo, Brazil, 1992, U. Barcelona, Spain, 1993. Editor: (with T.J. Greenwalt) Red Cell Membrane-Structure and Function, 1969, Formation and Destruction of Blood Cells, 1970, Glycoproteins of Blood Cells and Plasma, 1971, The Human Red Cell In Vitro, 1974, Transmissible Disease and Blood Transfusion, 1975, Trace Components of Plasma-Isolation and Clinical Significance, 1976, The Granulocyte: Function and Clinical Utilization, 1977, The Blood Platelet in Transfusion Therapy, 1978, (with D.M. Robinson) Mammalian Cell Membranes, Vol. I, 1978—, Generalizations and Methodology, Vol. II, 1978—, The Diversity of Membranes, Vol. III, 1978—, Surface Membranes of Specific Cell Types, Vol. IV, 1978—, Membranes and Cellular Functions, Vol. V, 1978—, Responses of Plasma Membranes; Interaction of Platelets and Tumor Cells, 1982, Platelet Membrane Receptors: Molecular Biology Immunology, Biochemistry and Pathology, 1988; mem. editorial bds. Thrombosis Rsch., 1978-81, Thrombosis Haemostas, 1989—, Internat. Jour. Hematology, 1989—, Blood, 1996—; contbr. articles to profl. jours. Sir George Grey scholar U. New Zealand., 1951, U. Otago 50; John Edmond fellow. Fellow AAAS; mem. Am. Soc. Biol. Chemists, Am. Chem. Soc., Biochem. Soc. (London), Internat. Soc. Thrombosis and Hemostasis (Shirley Johnson award 1997), N.Y. Acad. Scis., Am. Heart Assn. (exec. com., council on thrombosis), Am. Soc. Hematology, Soc. Exptl. Biology and Medicine, Soc. for Complex Carbohydrates (exec. com.) Home: 5622 Johnson Ave Bethesda MD 20817-3504 E-mail: Jamieson_Graham@msn.com.

JAMIESON, JAMES CHILLES, biochemist, educator; b. Aberdeen, Scotland, May 15, 1939; came to Can., 1967; s. John Munro Jamieson and Margaret Chilles; m. Muriel Margaret Shaw, Aug. 19, 1967. BS, Heriot Watt, Edinburgh, Scotland, 1963; PhD, Aberdeen U., 1967. Chartered chemist. Contbr. articles to profl. jours. Recipient grant NSERC, Manitoba, Can., 1995, IOR grant NSERC/Novopharm Bio., Manitoba, 1995. Fellow Chem. Inst. Can.; mem. Royal Inst. Chemistry. Achievements include research in field of glycobiology. Office: Univ of Manitoba Office Dean of Sci 250 Machray Hall Winnipeg MB Canada R3T 2N2

JAMIESON, JOHN EDWARD, JR., social services administrator, minister; b. Phila., Mar. 5, 1945; s. John Edward and Frances (Hayes) J.; m. Marilyn T. Haws, June 8, 1968; children: Douglas Stuart, Heather Lynn, Mark Stuart. BA, U. Pa., 1967; MDiv, Ref. Episcopal Sem., Phila., 1970; PhD, Christian Bible Coll., Rocky Mount, NC, 1990. Ordained to ministry Ref. Episcopal Ch., 1970, Bapt. Ch., 1978. Pastor Trinity Ref. Episcopal Ch., Phila., 1970-73, St. Mark's Ref. Episcopal Ch., Miami, Fla., 1973-75, Hammonton (N.J.) Bapt. Ch., 1978-81; supr. Nepaug Christian Acad., New Hartford, Conn., 1976-78; coord. ops. emergency med. svcs. div. AID Ambulance Svc., Atlantic City, 1982-83; paramedic mobile ICU, West Jersey Health, Camden, N.J., 1983-88; dir. pastoral care Atlantic City Med. Ctr., 1988—2003, dir. patient support, 2003—. Pastor Grace Bible Chapel, Ocean City, N.J., 1988-95; min. pastoral care Cornerstone Ministries, Ocean City, 2000-02; vice chmn. instnl. med. ethics com. Atlantic City Med. Ctr., 1988-96, co-chair, 1996—. Editor Bibl. Bioethics, 1990. Chaplain Somers Point (N.J.) Vol. Rescue Squad, 1987-96, Ocean City Fire Dept., 1995—; bd. dirs. Atlantic County unit Am. Cancer Soc., Absecon, N.J., 1988-90, program coord. Cansurmount support program, 1988-90; bd. trustees Ctrl. Ocean City Union Chapel; exec. v.p. Reformed Bible Inst. Delaware Valley, 2000-01. Fellow Am. Acad. Experts in Traumatic Stress (bd. cert. expert), mem. Am. Assn. Christian Counselors, So. Jersey Ethics Alliance, Internat. Critical Incident Stress Found., Fedn. Fire Chaplains (mastser chaplain). Republican. Avocations: travel, photography, reading. Office: Atlantic City Med Ctr 1925 Pacific Ave Atlantic City NJ 08401-6713 *When we concentrate our thoughts on that which is true, noble, right, pure, lovely, admirable and excellent we are lifted above the drudgery of life and open ourselves to the possibility of true greatness.*

JAMIESON, LEAH H., engineering educator; BS in Math., MIT, 1972; MA in Elec. Engring. and Computer Sci., MSE in Elec. Engring. and Computer Sci., Princeton U., 1974, PhD in Elec. Engring. and Computer Sci., 1977. Asst. prof., sch. elec. engring. Purdue U., West Lafayette, Ind., 1976—82, assoc. prof., sch. elec. engring., 1982—86, prof., sch. elec. engring./sch. elec. and computer engring., 1986—2002, grad. coord., sch. elec. engring., 1990—94, dir. grad. admissions, sch. elec. engring./sch. elec. engring. and computer engring., 1994—96, co-founder, Ctr. for Engring. Projects in Cmty. Svc. (EPICS), sch. engring., 1995, co-director, Ctr. for Engring. Projects in Cmty. Svc. (EPICS), sch. engring., 1996—2002, Ransburg prof. elec. and comp. engring., 2002—, interim head, sch. elec. and computer engring., 2002, mem., Dean's advisory com., 2002—, dir., EPICS: Engring. Projects in Cmty. Svc., 2003—, assoc. dean for undergraduate edn., coll. engring., 2004—; co-founder, co-director, Nat. EPICS, 1999—; vis. scientist, Computer Sci. lab. SRI Internat., Menlo Park, Calif., 1985, 1986. Chair. elec. engring. grad. com. Purdue U., 1986—89, mem. senate, 1987—90, 1992—95, chair, computer engring. area com., 1991—92, chair, senate steering com., 1992—95, mem., Task Force on Women's Issues, 1995—97, vice-convener, Coun. on the Status of Women, 1999—2000, mem., Neil Armstrong Hall of Engring. Planning Com., 1999—, founding chair, Women Faculty in Engring. Com., 1999—, co-convener, Coun. on the Status of Women, 2000—01, mem. engring. leadership team, 2004—, co-chair, Engring. Curriculum Reform Task Force; workshop organizer for workshops with Girl Scouts, jr. high, and HS girls, part of Expanding Your Horizons in Math and Sci. Program Soc. of Women Engr. and Purdue U. Women in Engring. Career Day; chair Policy Com. on World Wide Web Publishing, 1996—97, Rsch. Computing and Communications Advisory Com., 1997—2001; spkr. in field. Contbr. articles to profl. jours. Co-recipient Chester F. Carlson award for Innovation in Engring. Edn., Am. Soc. for Engring. Edn., 1997, Class of 1922 award for outstanding innovation in helping students learn, Purdue U., 1997; finalist with Edward J. Coyle, Boeing Outstanding Educator award, 1998, with Edward J. Coyle, Thomas Ehrlich Faculty award for Svc. Learning, 2000; named Ind. Prof. Yr., Carnegie Found. and Coun. for the Advancement and Support of Edn., 2002. Fellow: IEEE (assoc. editor, Transactions on Acoustics, Speech and Signal Processing 1986—87, assoc. editor, Transactions on Parallel and Distributed Sys. 1991—94, chair, Jack S. Kilby Signal Processing medal com. 1996—99, pres., Signal Processing Soc. 1998—99, mem. editl. bd., Proceedings of the IEEE 1999—2001, v.p. tech. activities 2003, IEEE bd. dir. and Excom 2003, chair, tech. activities bd. new tech. directions com. 2004—06, v.p. for publ. svcs. and products 2005, IEEE bd. dir. and Excom 2005, chair, Publ. Svcs. and Products Bd. 2005, pres.-elect 2006, pres. 2007, founder, organizer, Women in Signal Processing Lunch 1993—, IEEE Edn. Soc., Harriet B. Rigas, Outstanding Women Engring. Educator award 2000, Third Millennium medal 2000, IEEE Signal Processing Soc., Meritorious Svc. award 2004); mem.: NAE (co-recipient, Bernard M. Gordon prize 2005), NSF (mem. advisory com. for NSF directorate, computer & info. sci. engring. 1997—2000, Director's award for Disting. Teaching Scholars 2001), Computing Rsch. Assn. (editor, Expanding the Pipeline, Computing Research News 1993—96, co-chair, com. on the status of women and computing rsch. 1996—99, bd. dir. 1998—2000, sec. 1999—2000, bd. dir. 2001—07, co-chair, Snowbird Conf. 2002). Office: Sch Elec and Computer Engring Purdue U 465 Northwestern Ave West Lafayette IN 47907-2035 Address: Purdue U 400 Centennial Mall Dr West Lafayette IN 47907-2016 Office Phone: 765-494-4966. Office Fax: 765-496-1180. Business E-Mail: lhj@purdue.edu.

JAMIESON, MARK T., corporate financial executive; BA acctg., Cleve. State Univ. Fin. mgmt. positions GE, 1976—93; CFO European bus. GE Lighting, 1993—95; CFO GE Elec. Distbn. & Control, 1995—98, GE Indsl. Systems, 1998—2004; CEO Elec. Ins. Co. GE, 2004; exec. v.p., CFO Sammons Enterprises Inc., 2005—06, Ryder System Inc., Miami, Fla., 2006—. Office: Ryder System Inc 11690 NW 105th St Miami FL 33178*

JAMIESON, STUART WILLIAM, surgeon, educator; b. Bulawayo, Rhodesia, July 30, 1947; came to U.S., 1977; MB, BS, U. London, 1971. Intern St. Mary's Hosp., London, 1971; resident St. Mary's Hosp., Northwick Park Hosp., Brompton Hosp., London, 1972-77; asst. prof. Stanford U., Calif., 1980-83, assoc. prof. Calif., 1983-86; prof., head cardiac surgery U. Minn., Mpls., 1986-89, U. Calif., San Diego, 1989—. Dir. Minn. Heart and Lung Inst., Mpls., 1986-89; pres. Calif. Heart and Lung Inst., San Diego, 1991-95. Co-author: Heart and Heart-Lung Transplantation, 1989; editor: Heart Surgery, 1987; contbr. over 600 papers to med. jours. Recipient Brit. Heart Found. Fellowship award, 1978, Irvine H. Page award Am. Heart Found., 1979, Silver medal Danish Surg. Soc., 1986. Fellow ACS, Royal Coll. Surgeons, Royal Soc. Medicine, Am. Coll. Chest Physicians, Am. Coll. Cardiology; mem. Royal Coll. Physicians (licentiate), Internat. Soc. for Heart Transplantation (pres. 1986-88), Calif. Heart and Lung Inst. (pres. 1991—), Internat. Soc. Cardiothoracic Surgery (pres. 2003-.). Office: U Calif Divsn Cardiothoracic Surgery 200 W Arbor Dr San Diego CA 92103-8892 Office Phone: 619-543-7777. E-mail: sjamieson@ucsd.edu.

JAMIESON, WENDELL, editor; Reporter Newsday; editor, Portraits of Grief NY Times, 2001, day editor, Met. Desk. Office: NY Times Metropolitan Desk 229 West 43rd St New York NY 10036 Office Phone: 212-556-1533. Office Fax: 212-556-3690. E-mail: wendell@nytimes.com.

JAMIN, MATTHEW DANIEL, lawyer, judge; b. New Brunswick, NJ, Nov. 29, 1947; s. Matthew Bernard and Frances Marie (Newburg) J.; m. Christine Frances Bjorkman, June 28, 1969; children: Rebecca, Erica. BA, Colgate U., 1969; JD, Harvard U., 1974. Bar: Alaska 1974, U.S. Dist. Ct. Alaska 1974, U.S. Ct. Appeals (9th cir.) 1980. Staff atty. Alaska Legal Svcs., Anchorage, 1974-75, supervising atty. Kodiak, Alaska, 1975-81; contract atty. Pub. Defender's Office State of Alaska, Kodiak, 1976-82; prin. Matthew D. Jamin, Atty., Kodiak, 1982; ptnr. Jamin & Bolger, Kodiak, 1982-85, Jamin, Ebell, Bolger & Gentry, Kodiak, 1985-97; part-time magistrate judge U.S. Cts., Kodiak, 1984—; shareholder Jamin, Ebell, Schmitt & Mason, Kodiak, 1998—2005, Jamin Schmitt St. John, St. John, 2006—. Part-time instr. U. Alaska Kodiak Coll., 1975—; active Theshold Svcs., Inc., Kodiak, 1985—, pres., 1985-92, 95-96, 99-2000. Mem. Alaska Bar Assn. (Professionalism award 1988), Kodiak Bar Assn. Office: US Dist Ct 323 Carolyn Ave Kodiak AK 99615-6348 Office Phone: 907-486-6024. Business E-Mail: matt@jesmkod.com.

JAMISON, ANTAWN, professional basketball player; b. June 12, 1976; Attended, UNC. Basketball player Golden State Warriors, 1998—2003, Dallas Mavericks, 2003—04, Wash. Wizards, 2004—. Named to NBA Eastern Conference All-Star Team, 2005; recipient John A. Naismith award Best Coll. Player, 1998, John Wooden award Best Coll. Player, 1998. Office: Washington Wizards MCI Center 601 F St Washington DC 20004

JAMISON, DANIEL OLIVER, lawyer; b. Fresno, Calif., Nov. 28, 1952; s. Oliver Morton and Margaret (Ratcliffe) J.; m. Debra Suzanne Parent, May 23, 1981; 1 child, Holly Elizabeth. Student, Claremont Men's Coll., 1970—72; BA in Philosophy, U. Calif., Berkeley, 1974; JD, U. Calif., Davis, 1977. Bar: Calif. 1977, U.S. Dist. Ct. (ea. dist.) Calif. 1977, U.S. Dist. Ct. (no. dist.) Calif. 1982, U.S. Ct. Appeals (9th cir.) 1987. Law clk. to judge M.D. Crocker U.S. Dist. Ct. (ea. dist.) Calif., Fresno, 1977—78; assoc. Stammer, McKnight, Barnum & Bailey, Fresno, 1978—83, ptnr., 1983—95; shareholder Sagaser, Franson, Jamison & Jones (formerly Sagaser, Hansen, Franson & Jamison), 1995—99; pvt. practice Law Offices of Daniel O. Jamison, P.C., Fresno, 1999—2005; preferred shareholder Dowling, Aaron & Keeler, Inc., 2005—. Vol. atty. Calif. H.S., Fresno, 1983-87; 89-94; mem. Assocs. of Valley Children's Hosp., Fresno, 1980-81; co-chmn. Fresno County Law Day, 1995-96; panelist for CEB Selected Issues in Employment Discrimination and Wrongful Discharge Litigation; panelist on indigent care Calif. Soc. for Healthcare Attys.; panelist Lorman Edn. Svcs. on Health Care Corp. and Physician Compliance Programs in Calif., Pres' Circle, Bulldog Found., Calif. State U., Fresno; sustaining mem. Fresno Met. Mus.; mem. Fresno Hist. Soc. Mem. ABA, Am. Arbitration Assn. (panel of neutrals, panel mem. comml. arbitration), Fed. Bar Assn., Fresno County Bar Assn. (spkr.), East Dist. Hist. Soc. (charter mem.), 9th Jud. Cir. Hist. Soc., Calif. Soc. for Healthcare Attys., Am. Health Lawyers Assn. (panelist Alt. Dispute Resolution credentialing and peer rev., teleconf. ADR in credentialing and peer review). Republican. Avocations: golf, aerobics. Office Phone: 559-432-4500. Business E-Mail: djamison@daklaw.com.

JAMISON, DEAN TECUMSEH, economist; b. Springfield, Mo., Oct. 10, 1943; s. Marshall Verdine and Mary Dell (Temple) J.; m. Joanne Leslie, Sept. 14, 1971 (div. 1995); children: Julian C., Eliot A., Leslie S.; m. Kin Bing Wu, Jan. 19, 1997. AB in Philosophy, Stanford U., 1966, MS in Engring. Sci., 1967; PhD in Econs., Harvard U., 1970. Asst. prof. grad. sch. bus. Stanford U., Palo Alto, Calif., 1970-73; economist World Bank, Washington, 1976-88, dir., 1992-93, advisor, 1993-98; dir. Ctr. for Pacific Rim Studies UCLA, 1993-2000, prof. Sch. Pub. Health, Grad. Sch. Edn. and Info. Studies, 1988—2006; dir. econs. adv. svc. WHO, Geneva, 1998-2000; fellow Fogarty Internat. Ctr., NIH, 2002—06; prof. U. Calif, San Francisco, 2006—. Chmn. ad hoc com. on health R&D for developing countries WHO, Geneva, 1996-97; trustee Drug Strategies, 1994—; chmn. bd. on global health Inst. Medicine NAS, 2000-05; vis. prof. Harvard U., 2006—; chmn. expert group econs., fin., and impact Malaria control programs WHO, 2006—. Author: Farmer Education and Farm Efficiency, 1982, (with L. J. Lau) Disease Control Priorities in Developing Countries, 2006, World Bank World Development Report 1993: Investing in Health, 1993, WHO World Health Report 1999: Making a Difference, 1999; cons. editor AERA Ency. Rsch., 6th edit., 1992. Fellow Woodrow Wilson Found., 1967, NSF, 1968, Bill and Melinda Gates Found. fellow, 2001. Mem. Inst. Medicine Nat. Acad. Scis. Avocation: tennis. Office: UCSF Global Health Sci 50 Beale St 12th Fl San Francisco CA 94105 Business E-Mail: djamison@globalhealth.ucsf.edu.

JAMISON, DOUGLAS W., venture capitalist; b. 1970; BA, Dartmouth Coll., 1992; MS, U. Utah, 1999. Sr. tech. mgr. tech. transfer office U. Utah, 1997—2002; v.p. Harris and Harris Group, Inc., NY, 2002—, mng. dir. NY, 2004—, pres., COO, CFO NY, 2005—. Mem. sci. adv. bd. Chlorogen, Inc., St. Louis; mem. adv. bd. Mass. tech. Collaborative Nanotech. Venture Forum. Mem. adv. bd. Nanotechnology Law & Bus. (Jour. Attys., Entrepreneurs, and Investors small scale techs.). Mem.: IEEE, AAAS, Assn. U. Tech. Mgrs. (mem. survey stats. and metrics com.). Office: Harris & Harris Group Inc 111 W 57th St Ste 1100 New York NY 10019 also: Harris & Harris Group Inc 11150 Santa Monica Blvd Ste 1200 Los Angeles CA 90025 Business E-Mail: admin@tinytechvc.com.

JAMISON, HARRISON CLYDE, retired oil company executive; b. St. Louis, Jan. 15, 1925; s. William Clyde and Katherine Maurice (Fitzgerald) J.; m. Beverly Joy Johnson, June 26, 1946; children: Susan, David, Leslie, Daniel, Dale, Nancy, Sara BA cum laude, UCLA. Geologist Richfield Oil Corp., Bakersfield, Calif., 1950-52, Olympia, Wash., 1952-55, LA, 1955-60, regional exploration supr., 1961-65; Alaska dist. mgr. Atlantic Richfield Co., Anchorage, 1966-69, Alaska coord. Dallas, 1969-70; mgr. govt. rels. Alyeska Pipeline Svc. Co., 1971-72; chief geologist ARCO Oil & Gas Co., Dallas, 1973-80, v.p. dist. mgr. Denver, 1981; pres. ARCO Exploration Co., Dallas, 1981-85; sr. v.p. Atlantic Richfield Co., LA, 1981-85. Contbr. articles to profl. jours. Former bd. dirs. Tex. Rsch. League, Austin, Dallas Citizens Coun., Mex. Am. Legal Def. and Edn. Fund, Resolution Seismic Svcs. Inc., Wilmington, Del., ARCO Alaska Inc., Thomas Wilson Dibblee Jr. Geol. Found., Hospice of Bend. Fellow Geol. Soc. Am. (former chmn. bd. dirs., trustees GSA Found. 1986-88); mem. Am. Assn. Petroleum Geologists. Home and Office: 37615 S Stoney Cliff Ct Tucson AZ 85739-1412

JAMISON, JAYNE, publishing executive; m. Jan Philip Browne, 1986 (div.); 2 children; m. Edward J. Bisno, June 11, 2006. Grad., Penn. St. U., 1978. With Elkman Advt., Phila.; acct. mgr., advt. Family Circle mag.; advt. dir. American Health, pub.; group pub., parenthood group Gruner & Jahr USA Pub., NYC, 1994—97; pub. v.p. Redbook, 1997—2003; pub., v.p. Seventeen, 2003—. Office: Seventeen Mag 1440 Broadway 13th Fl New York NY 10018 Office Phone: 212-204-4300, 917-934-6601. Office Fax: 917-934-6650.*

JAMISON, JOHN CALLISON, business educator, investment banker; b. Lafayette, Ind., July 12, 1934; s. John Ruger and Sara (Callison) J.; m. Carol Ann Sansone, July 7, 1979; children: Kelly Elizabeth Supplee, Deborah Louise Jamison. BS in Indsl. Econs., Purdue U., 1956; MBA, Harvard U., 1961. Assoc. Goldman, Sachs & Co., NYC, 1961-69, ptnr., 1969-82, ltd. ptnr., 1983—99; dean Sch. Bus. Adminstrn., John N. Dalton prof. bus. adminstrn. Coll. William and Mary, Williamsburg, Va., 1983-90; pres. bd., CEO The Mariners' Mus., Newport News, Va., 1991-93, trustee, 1991—2003; pres. Williamsburg Cmty. Trust, 2001—04, chmn., 2005—07. Bd. govs. Purdue Found., West Lafayette, Ind., 1979-83; bd. dirs. Theatre Devel. Fund, N.Y.C., 1979-83; mem. corp. Hurricane Island Outward Bound Sch., Rockland, Maine, 1983-95; mem. vis. com. Harvard Grad. Sch. Edn., 1983-89. Lt. USN, 1956-59, PTO. Recipient Old Master award Purdue U., 1977; recipient Sagamore of Wabash award Gov. of Ind., 1982 Mem. Rotary, Beta Gamma Sigma Episcopalian. E-mail: mallardee@aol.com.

JAMISON, JOHN L., musician, educator; s. Edgar Merritt Jr. and Patricia Jamison. Asst. band dir., percussion dir. Roosevelt HS, Yonkers, NY, 1980—86, Barnstable H.S., Hyannis, Mass., 1996—. Instr. Thom Hannum's Mobile Percussion Seminar, Amherst, Mass., 1996—; artist, mem. edn. team Vic Firth, Inc., Dedham, Mass., 2000—; artist Zildjian Cymbal Co., Norwell, Mass., 2006—; leader, drummer, composer, arranger John Jamison Band-Planet Jazz, Mashpee, Mass., 1983—; adjudicator Cape Cod Music Educator's Assn., Hyannis, 1996—. Arranger: (percussion ensemble show) Asgardstrand, Spring Heeled Jack, To Sleep No More; composer: (jazz ensemble compositions) Skyline Drive, The Truffle Shuffle, New Life. Co-founder Save The Music-Barnstable Sch. Dist., Hyannis, 2001. Finalist, McDonalds All Am. HS Band, 1978; named to Who's Who Among America's Teachers, 2004; recipient All Am. Hall of Fame Band Honors, Purdue U., 1978, certs. of achievement, Barnstable Sch. Com., 1996—2005; Gene Krupa scholar, Local 402, Am. Fedn. Musicians, 1979. Mem.: Broadcast Music Inc., Percussive Arts Soc., Mass. Music Educators Assn., Internat. Assn. Jazz Educators, Music Educators Nat. Conf., Am. Fedn. Musicians. Home: 21 Wilann Rd Mashpee MA 02649-2715 Home Phone: 508-539-0231; Office Phone: 508-274-7345.

JAMISON, JOI NICHOLE, media specialist, performing company executive, educator; b. Portsmouth, Va., Feb. 26, 1981; d. Bruce and Veronica W. Jamison. BS in Mass Comm. cum laude, Norfolk State U., Va., 2003. Promotions coord. Sta. KISS-FM, Clear Channel Radio, Norfolk, 2004—. Artistic co-founder Rythmic Creacion, Va., 2004—; mem. alumni rels. bd. Norfolk State U. Choreographer Virginia Thunder, dancer Norfolk Nighthawks Hawtime Dance Girl (Most Attitude on the Dance Field, 2003). Active mem. Salvation Army, Va., 2004; pub. rels. chair Womens Aux. Salvation Army, Norfolk, 2005—; cardio dance and aerobics trainer YMCA; young adult advisor scholarship com. St. Paul AME Ch., Va. Named Celebrity Reader Day, Pk. View Elem. Sch., 2005. Mem.: Coalition Young Black Profls. (membership chair 2005—), Hampton Rds. Black Media Profls., Delta Sigma Theta. Democrat. Avocations: travel, reading, mentoring to youth, shopping, performing. Home: 4212 Queenswood Dr Apt A Portsmouth VA 23703 Office: Clear Channel Radio Norfolk 1003 Norfolk Sq Norfolk VA 23502 Home Phone: 757-536-2396; Office Phone: 757-466-0009. Personal E-mail: joij99@yahoo.com. Business E-Mail: joijamison@clearchannel.com.

JAMISON, JUDITH, performing company executive, dancer; b. Phila., May 10, 1943; d. John Jamison. Student, Fisk U., Phila., Phila. Dance Acad. (now U. of Arts); studied with, Anthony Tudor, John Hines, Delores Brown, John Jones, Joan Kerr, Madame Swaboda. Dancer Alvin Ailey Am. Dance Theatre, NYC, 1965-80, artistic dir., 1990—; dancer, choreographer touring U.S., Europe, Asia, S.Am., Africa, 1980—; formerly with Maurice Hines Dance Sch., NYC; founder Jamison Project, 1988-91. Vis. disting. prof. U. Arts; guest assoc. artistic dir. 30th ann. tour Alvin Ailey's Am. Dance Theatre, 1990—; guest appearances Harkness Ballet, Am. Ballet Theatre, San Francisco Ballet, Dallas Ballet. Dancer debut Agnes DeMille's The Four Marys, 1965, (Broadway plays) Joseph's Legend, Vienna Opera, Le Spectre de la Rose, Brussels, Paris, N.Y.C., Maskela Language, 1969, Cry, 1971, Choral Dance, 1971, Mary Lou's Mass, 1971, The Lark Ascending, 1972, The Mooche, 1975, Passage, 1978, (Broadway plays) Sophisticated Ladies, 1980, choreographer Divining Hymn for Alvin Ailey Am. Dance Theatre, works for Maurice Bejart, Dancers Unltd., Dallas, Washington Ballet, Jennifer Muller/The Works, Alvin Ailey Repertory Ensemble, Ballet Nuevo Mundo de Caracas, Riverside for Alvin Ailey Am. Dance Theatre, (Operas) Boito's Mefistofele, Opera Co. Phila.; author: Dancing Spirit, 1993. Recipient Dance Mag. award, 1972, Key to City, NYC, 1976, Spirit of Achievement award Nat. Women's Divsn., Yeshiva U. Albert Einstein Coll. Medicine, 1992, Golden Plate award, Am. Acad. Achievement, 1993, Kennedy Ctr. honor, 1999, Nat. Medal of Arts, 2001, Algur H. Meadows award, So. Methodist U., 2001, Making a Difference award, NAACP ACT-SO, 2003, Paul Robeson award, Actors' Equity Assn. Office: Alvin Ailey Dance Theatre 405 W 55th St New York NY 10019-4402*

JAMISON, PHILIP, artist; b. Phila., July 3, 1925; s. Philip Duane and Daisy (McCadden) J.; m. Jane B. Gray, Oct. 11, 1950; children: Philip Duane III, Terry Jane, Linda B. Student, Phila. Mus. Sch. Art, 1946-50. Instr. Phila. Coll. Art, 1961-63. Author: Capturing Nature in Watercolor, 1980, Making Your Paintings Work, 1984, A Painting Without Spirit is Like Flat Beer, 1988, I Hate People Who Refer to Works of Art as "Pieces!", 1995; one-man shows Hirschl & Adler Galleries, N.Y.C., 1959, 63, 65, 67, 69, 71, 74, 76, 80, Sessler Gallery, Phila., 1963, 72, Duke U., 1969, Del. Art Mus., 1973, Janet Fleisher Gallery, Phila., 1977, Grand Gallery, Wilmington, Del., 1977, Whistler's Daughter Gallery, Basking Ridge, N.J., 1981, Newman Galleries, Bryn Mawr, Pa., 1982, 84, 86, 88, 90, 93, Patricia Carega Gallery, Washington, 1985, 87, Ruthven Gallery, Lancaster, Ohio, 1986, Hahn Gallery, Phila., 1998, 2002, Chester County Hist. Soc., 1999; represented in permanent collections Pa. Acad. Fine Arts, NAD, Wilmington Soc. Fine Arts, U. Del., Boston Mus. Fine Arts, Nat. Air and Space

Mus., Washington, Brandywine River Mus., Pa., others; NASA artist for Apollo-Soyuz, for Space Shuttle Mission 51-G, 1985. Served with USNR, 1943-46. Recipient Dawson medal Pa. Acad. Fine Arts, 1959, 77, Dana medal, 1961, first award Nat. Arts Club, N.Y.C., 1961; Lena A. Mason prize NAD, 1962, Samuel Finley Breese Morse medal NAD, 1969, Walter Biggs Meml. award NAD, 1982, William Church Osborn prize Am. Watercolor Soc., 1961, 79, medal of Honor Knickerbocker Artists, N.Y.C., 1961, Bainbridge award Allied Artists Am., 1958, 60, first prize Wilmington Soc. Fine Arts, 1957, 59, 61, M.W. Zimmerman Meml. prize Phila. Watercolor Club, 1963, Gold medal honor Allied Artists Am., 1964, Childe Hassam Fund purchase prize AAAL, 1965; C.F.S. award, 1966, Edgar A. Whitney award, 1971, High Winds award, 1972, Whitney award, 1973; Ted Kautzky Meml. award, 1974, Ranger Fund purchase prize NAD, 1962, prize, 1967, Alfred Easton Poor award, 1999, Zella W. Pike award, 2003, Pike prize, 2003; Adolph and Clara Obrig award, 1974, Thornton Oakley Meml. prize Phila. Watercolor Club, 1967, Gold medal Franklin Mint Gallery Am. Art, 1974, Merit award Nat. Watercolor Exhbn., Springfield (Ill.) Art Assn., 1979, Mem. N.A.D. (academician), Am. Watercolor Soc. (Lily Saportas award 1965, Mary S. Litt medal 1978, Larry Quackenbush Meml. award 1982, Edgar A. Whitney award 1984, Dale Meyers Cooper medal 1985, Bronze medal of honor 1994, Saunders/Waterford award, 1996), Phila. Water Color Club (Dawson Meml. prize 1977, George Gansworth Meml. prize 1981).

JAMISON, ROGER W., pianist, educator; b. Marion, Ohio, June 18, 1937; s. Harold Theodore and Martha Louise (Haas) J.; m. Caroline R. Hansley, Jan. 26, 1957; children: Lisa Renee, Eric Karl. BS, Ohio State U., 1959, MA (scholar), 1961; postgrad. Oberlin Conservatory, Oakland U.; student George Haddad, Columbus, Ohio, Mischa Kottler, Detroit. Piano faculty mem. Detroit Conservatory of Music, 1964-68, Cranbrook Schs., Bloomfield Hills, Mich., 1981-84; performer in one-man mus. presentation Spirits of Great Composers, 1979—; dir. music Birmingham Temple, Farmington Hills, Mich., 1984-95; soloist Brunch with Bach series Detroit Inst. Arts., Detroit Symphony Orch.'s Internat. Brahms Festival; regular soloist Christ Ch., Cranbrook, 1982-95; concert tour of Eng., 1991; condr. All Ohio Piano Ensemble, 1997; cons. Royal Oak Arts Council; adjudicator Am. Coll. Musicians. Mem. Nat. Guild of Piano Tchrs. (past pres. Oakland-Macomb chpt.) Address: 173 W Heffner St Delaware OH 43015-1258

JAMPOL, LEE MERRILL, ophthalmologist, educator; b. Nov. 5, 1944; BA, Yale U., New Haven, 1965, MD, 1969. Diplomate Am. Bd. Ophthalmology. Intern Yale-New Haven Hosp., 1969—70, resident, 1970—73; mem. faculty U. Ill., Chgo., 1974—83; Louis Feinberg prof., chmn. ophthalmology Northwestern U., Chgo., 1983—. Contbr. more than 200 articles to profl. jours. Recipient Sr. Honor award, Am. Acad. Ophthalmology, 1993. Mem.: Macula Soc. (pres., Gass medal), Am. Ophthalmol. Soc. (mem. coun.). Office: 645 N Michigan Ave # 440 Chicago IL 60611

JAMPOLE, MICHAEL, music educator, composer; b. NYC, Jan. 12, 1953; s. Sidney and Anita Prager Jampole; m. Jane Hutten, Dec. 30, 1979; 1 child, Jaime Kikpole. MusB in Edn., Northwestern U., 1973; MS in Edn., No. Ill. U., 1983. Music Teaching, grades K-12 State of Ill., 1973, Classroom Teaching, grades K-9 State of Ill., 1984. Band dir. Wilmette (Ill.) Pub. Schools, 1974—, chair dept. music, 1995—2005; band dir. Rockford (Ill.) Pub. Schools, Rockford, 1973. Condr., musician, Beach Park, Ill., 1969—; composer, arranger, Beach Park, 1970—; clinician, lectr., Beach Park, 1995—. Contbr. First Lessons on Each Instrument, The Instrumentalist, The Creative Band and Orchestra. Vol. Northwestern U. Sch. of Music, Evanston, Ill., 1993—; mem. Waukegan (Ill.) Mcpl. Band. Mem.: NEA, Ill. Edn. Assn., Am. Sch. Band Dirs. Assn., Music Educators Nat. Conf., Ill. Music Educators Assn. (Cert. Outstanding Svc. 2000), Northwestern U. Marching Band Alumni. Democrat. Avocations: guitar, singing, computers. Office: Wilmette Public Schools 569 Hunter Road Wilmette IL 60091 Business E-Mail: jampolem@wilmette39.org.

JAMRICH, JOHN XAVIER, retired university administrator; b. Muskegon Heights, Mich., June 12, 1920; s. John and Mary (Mudry) J.; m. June Ann Hrupka, June 26, 1944; children: June Ann, Marna Mary, Barbara Sue. Student, Milw. State Tchrs. Coll., 1939-40, Ripon Coll., 1940-42; BS, U. Chgo., 1942-43; MS, Marquette U., 1946-48; PhD, Northwestern U., 1951; LHD (hon.), No. Mich. U., 1968. Instr. math. Marquette U., 1946-48; asst. instr. math. U. Wis., 1948-49; asst. dean men Northwestern U., 1949-51; dean students Coe Coll., Cedar Rapids, Iowa, 1951-55; dean faculty, prof. math. Doane Coll., Crete, Nebr., 1955-57; assoc. dir. Legis. Survey Higher Edn. in Mich., 1957-58; prof. higher edn., dir. Center for Study Higher Edn., Mich. State U., 1957-63, assoc. dean Coll. Edn., prof. higher edn., 1963-68; pres. No. Mich. U., 1968-83, adj. prof., 1983—. Cons.-examiner N. Central Assn. Colls. and Secondary Schs., 1962—; cons. in field, 1959—; Ford Found. cons. for devel. U. Nigeria, 1964; cons. higher edn. Govt. of Thailand, 1967; dir. Lake Superior & Ishpeming R.R.; chmn. Nat. Adv. Council Fin. Aid to Students, 1975 Author numerous articles in field; co-author several books; piano and vocal music composer. Apptd. pianist in residence Mayo Clinic, Jacksonville, 2007, vol. pianist, 2004—07; bd. dirs. Mich. Joint Coun. on Econ. Edn., 1977—; trustee Marquette Gen. Hosp., Mich.; bd. dirs. Bay Cliff Health Camp, Marquette; mem. Mich. Coun. for Arts, 1969—73. Served to capt. USAAF, 1942—46. Decorated Order Lion Finland; recipient City of Peace award (Israel), World War II Victory medal Russian Govt., 1997, Disting. Svc. medal U.S. Dept. Army, 1983. Mem.: Newcomen Soc. N.Am. Home: 13971 Croton Ct Jacksonville FL 32224

JAMSHIDIPOUR, YOUSEF, bank executive, economist, financial advisor; b. Arak, Iran, July 7, 1935; came to U.S., 1991; s. Hossein and Kobra (Sohrabi) J.; m. Aghdas Jalaifar, 1938; children: Ramin, Lily, Katia. BA, Tehran U., 1959, MBA, 1961; MA, The Am. U., 1963; MPA, Harvard U., 1973; postgrad., U. Mich., U. Colo. Dir. gen. Bank Markazi Iran, Tehran, 1963-76; v.p. Iranian Inst. of Banking, Tehran, 1973-78; exec. v.p., mem. exec. bd. Bank Melli Iran, Tehran, 1976-80; exec. v.p. D.M.I., Geneva, 1981-88; sr. fin. advisor Hill Samuel Investment Svc., London, 1988-91; fin. cons. 1st Affiliated Securities, Irvine, Calif., 1991-93; fin. planner IDS Fin. Svcs., Irvine, 1993-95; sr. financial advisor Ameriprise Fin., Inc., Irvine, 1995—. Lectr. U. Tehran, 1973-78. Contbr. articles to profl. jours. Office: Ameriprise Fin Inc 2 Park Plz Irvine CA 92614-8561 Office Phone: 949-250-2920 ext. 250. Personal E-mail: y.jam@att.net, yjam@cox.net.

JAN, CHWU-CHING HWANG, environmental chemistry consultant; b. Taipei, Taiwan, July 10, 1956; d. Chau-Ching and Hsiu-Mei (Lin) Huang; m. Deng-Yang Jan; 1 child, Avery. BS, Nat. Cheng-Kung U., 1978; MBA, U. Chgo., 1995; PhD, Ohio State U., 1986. Rsch. asst. Nat. Sci. Found., Taipei, Taiwan, 1978-79; lab. mgr. Nat. Tsing Hua U., Hsinchu, Taiwan, 1979-81; sr. rsch. chemist UOP, Des Plaines, Ill., 1986-92; cons. IRIS DC Inc., Elk Grove Village, Ill., pres., 1993—. Advisor tech. CASDAY Co., Ltd., Hsinchu, Taiwan, 1993—. Contbr. articles to profl. jours. including Jour. Electro.-analytical Chem., Interfacial Electrochem., Analytical Chemistry. Mem.: Am. Chem. Soc. (Internat. Student grant 1985). Achievements include patents for hydrotreating processes for organic and halogenerated organic feedsocks containing undesirable olefinic and/or halogen components and/or organic materials, process for decomposing peroxide impurities in a tertiary butyl alcohol feedstock. Office: IRIS DC Inc 1644 Von Braun Trl Elk Grove Village IL 60007-3100 Home Phone: 847-891-8760. E-mail: dyccjan@aol.com.

JAN, DOMINIQUE MICHEL, surgeon, educator; b. Villeneuve St. Georges, France, Jan. 8, 1953; s. Robert Jan and Yvette Bezou-Jan; m. Claire Anita Marie Guilhamon, June 17, 1986; children: Mathilde, Etienne, Antoine, Lucile. MD, Paris 6 U., France, 1978. Cert. Surgeon Paris 6 U., 1984. Prof. pediat. surgery Necker U. Hosp., Paris, 1984—. Bd. mem. Surgeons of Hope Fund, NYC; prof. clin. surgery Columbia U., NYC, 2003. Rep. pediat. surgeon Chaine de L'espoir, Paris, 1992—2003. Mem.: Intestinal Transplantation Soc., Am. Soc. Pediat. Surgeons, Am. Soc. Transplant Surgeons. Achievements include first to accomplish intestinal transplantation in children. Home: 601 W 113 St New York NY 10025 Office: Columbia Univ Med Ctr 622 W 168 St New York NY 10032 Home Phone: 212-662-4792; Office Phone: 212-305-3000. Business E-Mail: dj2107@columbia.edu.

JAN, GEORGE POKUNG, political science professor; b. Peking, Jan. 6, 1925; arrived in US, 1955; s. Yunan and Tehchieh (Lee) J.; m. Norma Yingchiang Wen, Sept. 28, 1946; children: Gregory, David, Daniel. BA, Nat. Chengchi U., Nanking, China, 1949; MA, So. Ill. U., 1956; PhD, NYU, 1960. Various positions including editor newspaper/mag., tchr., writer, dean, 1949-55; instr. Chinese NYU, NYC, 1959-60; asst. prof. polit. sci. No. Ill. U., DeKalb, 1961; asst. to full prof. of govt. U. S.D., Vermillion, 1961-68, dir. Summer Inst. for Asian Studies, 1964-66; prof. polit. sci. U. Toledo, 1968-93, prof. emeritus, 1993—, chmn. Asian studies program, 1970-93, dir. Inst. for Asian Studies, 1990-93; pres. Am. Inst. Tech., Toledo, 1993-00. Vis. prof. polit. sci. Beijing U., China, 1988; hon. rsch. fellow Rsch. Ctr. for Contemporary China, Beijing U., 1988—; adviser to China U. Geol. Scis., Beijing, 1993—; hon. chmn. bd. Second H.S., Wenzhou Tchr's. Coll., China, 2000—, frequent commentator on Radio Free Asia,2000— Author: The Chinese Commune Experiment, 1964, A Practical English Grammar for Junior Middle Schools, 1953, A Study of English Words, 1955, How to Do Business with China, 1994, Introduction to Political Science, 2000, Understanding Contemporary China, 2004, The Chinese Commune, 2004, others; editor: Government of Communist China, 1966, The International Politics of Asia, 1969, China Bus. Newsletter, 1993-98, International Relations of Asia, 1998, Political Development of China, 1998; mem. editl. bd. Asian Profile Jour., 1983-86, Jour. Econs. and Internat. Rels., 1986—, The New World of Politics, 1991—; contbr. articles to profl. jours., ency. and books. Pres. Chinese Assn. Greater Toledo, 1983-84; bd. dirs. Toledo Coun. on World Affairs, 1969-76; chmn. keynote session, Symposium on Chinese Ams. in the 1990s, Detroit, 1987; hon. chmn. bd. Second H.S. Wenzhou Tchrs. Coll., 2000—. Recipient Outstanding Svc. award The Internat. Inst. of Greater Toledo, 1983, teaching grants Asia Found., Japan Soc., 1964, 65, 66, rsch. grants U. Toledo, U. S.D., U. Mich., U. Chgo. numerous years, Significant Contribution award Pacific Cultural Found., Republic of China, 1988; named Hon. Rsch. Fellow, Rsch. Ctr. for Contemporary China, Beijing U., 1988, others. Mem. AAUP, Am. Polit. Sci. Assn., Midwest Polit. Sci. Assn., Assn. Asian Studies, Ohio Chinese Acad. and Profl. Assn. (bd. dirs. 1991—, pres. 1994-95), Mich. Chinese Acad. and Profl. Assn. (outstanding leadership award 1992), Am. Assn. Chinese Studies, Internat. Studies Assn., Ohio Internat. Edn. Assn. (chmn. planning and program com. 1976-77), Chinese Acad. and Profl. Assn. of Mid-Am. (bd. dirs. 1986-89), Am. Biog. Inst., Inc. (rsch. bd. advisors 1996—), Internat. Biog. Ctr. (hon. adv. coun.), Phi Beta Kappa, Pi Sigma Alpha, Phi Kappa Phi, Pi Gamma Mu, Phi Beta Delta. Avocations: gardening, photography, travel, swimming, chess. Home: 16230 N Edgewater Dr Fountain Hills AZ 85268 Home Phone: 480-837-5478. Personal E-mail: aitje@aol.com. E-mail: gpjan@cox.net.

JAN, LILY YEH, physiology, biochemist; b. China, Jan. 20, 1947; came to U.S. Grad., Nat. Taiwan U., 1968; MSc, Calif. Inst. Tech., 1970, PhD in Biophysics and Physics, 1974. Rsch. fellow Calif. Inst. Tech., 1974-77, Harvard Med. Sch., 1977-79; asst. prof. to prof. physiology U. Calif., San Francisco, 1979-85, prof. physiology and biochemistry, 1985—. Rsch. fellow Alfred P. Sloan, 1977-79; lectr. Columbia U., 1988; faculty lectr. U. Calif., San Francisco, 1995. Recipient Kavots Neuroscience Investor award Nat. Inst. Neurol. and Communicable Diseases and Stroke, 1988—; Klingenstein fellow, 1983-86. Fellow Am. Acad. Arts & Scis.; mem. NAS. Office: Univ Calif Howard Hughes Med Inst 533 Parnassus Ave San Francisco CA 94143-0001*

JAN, YUH NUNG, biochemistry and physiology educator; b. Shanghai, Republic of China, Dec. 20, 1946; m. Lily Yeh, 1971. BS, Nat. Taiwan U., 1967; MS, Calif. Inst. Tech., 1970. Postdoctoral rsch. fellow Calif. Inst. Tech., 1974-77, dept. neurobiology, Harvard U. Sch. Medicine, 1977-79; asst. prof., then assoc. prof. U. Calif., San Francisco, 1979-85, prof. physiology and biochemistry, 1985—. Investigator Howard Hughes Med. Inst., 1984—; fellow Scottish Rite Schizophrenia Rsch. Program, 1974-76, Muscular Dystrophy Assn., 1976-78; W. Alden Spencer lectr., Columbia U., 1988. McKnight scholar, 1978. Fellow Am. Acad. Arts & Scis.; mem. NAS, Genetics Soc. Am., Soc. Chinese Bioscientists Am., Am. Soc. Cell Biology, Soc. Neurosci., Soc. Develop. Biology.*

JANA, SADHAN C., engineering educator, researcher; s. Surendra Nath and Snehalata Jana; m. Soma Dasadhikari, Dec. 11, 1987; children: Subhra Jyoti, Sanhita. B, U. of Calcutta, 1983—86; M, Indian Inst. of Tech., 1986—88; PhD, Northwestern U., 1991—93. Postdoctoral fellow CUNY, 1993—94; sr. engr. Gen. Electric Rsch. Ctr., Schenectady, NY, 1994—98; asst. prof. U. Akron, Ohio, 1998—2004, assoc. prof., chmn. dept., 2004—07, prof., 2007—. Mem. summer faculty NASA Glenn Rsch. Ctr., Cleve., 1999—2005; rsch. asst. U. Mass., Amherst, 1988—91, Northwestern U., Evanston, Ill., 1991—93. Contbr. articles to profl. jours. Named Disting. Young Alumnus, U. Calcutta, 2001, Mentor of Yr., U. Akron, 2005; recipient NSF Career award, 2002—, Gold medal, U. Calcutta, 1986, Chemcon Disting. Spkr. award, Indian Inst. Chem. Engrs., 2005, C.N.R. Rao medal, 2005; fellow, NASA Glenn Rsch. Ctr., 1999, 2005; Nat. Merit scholar, Govt. of India, 1977—86. Mem.: Polymer Processing Soc. (assoc.), Am. Chem. Soc. (assoc.), Soc. Plastics Engrs. (assoc.; mem. bd. dirs. engring. properties and structure divsn. 2005—, mem. new tech. com.). Achievements include patents for process for multi-layer polymeric articles with surface conductivity; on process for making composite materials with thermoplastic and thermosetting polymers; on process for shear isolation of rubber latex particles without chemicals; on design of chaotic single extrusion screws for chastic mixing of immiscible polymers. Office: U Akron 250 S Forge St Akron OH 44325-0301 Office Phone: 330-972-8293. Business E-Mail: janas@uakron.edu.

JANAK, PETER HAROLD, retired automotive company executive; b. Detroit; BS in Aerospace Engring., Miss. State U., 1963; grad. exec. program, Stanford U., 1994. Rsch. fluid amplifiers dept. aerospace engring. Miss. State U., State College, 1962—63; propulsion engr. space disvn. Chrysler Corp., New Orleans, 1963—65; from sr. engr. to chief performance analysis sect. Teledyne-Brown Engring., Hunstville, Ala., 1965—68; head propulsion tech. sect. TRW Def. and Space Sys. Group, Houston, 1968—71, mgr. surveillance sys. engring. McLean, Va., 1972—78, mgr. signal processing sys. dept., 1978—79, mgr. SURTASS engring., 1979—80, mgr. undersea surveillance projects and combat sys., 1980—83, mgr. def. sys. ops. Fairfax, Va., 1987—90, mgr. tax modernization program, 1990—92, dep. gen. mgr. divsn. info svcs., 1992—94, v.p., gen. mgr. divsn. info. svcs., 1994—95; mgr. propulsion sys. dept. Technologieforschung, GmbH, Stuttgart, Germany, 1971—72; v.p., dep. gen. mgr. ea. divsn. PRC Sys. Svcs., McLean, 1983—84, pres., gen. mgr. divsn. sys. engring. and analysis, 1984—87; v.p., chief info. officer TRW Inc., Cleve., 1995—98; chief info. officer Delphi Automotive Sys., Troy, Mich., 1998—99; v.p., chief info. officer Delphi Corp., Troy, 1999—2003. Mem. external rsch. adv. bd. Miss. State U. Mem.: IEEE, Conf. Bd., Working Coun. Chief Info. Officers, Soc. Automotive Engrs., Soc. Mfg. Engrs.

JANAKIRAM, MANI, manufacturing engineer; s. Arunachalam and Leela Janakiram; m. Geetha Rajavelu; 1 child, Ajay. PhD, Ariz. State U., Tempe, 2001. Cert. mfg. engr., Soc. Mfg. Engrs., 1991, quality engr., Am. Soc. for Quality, 1994. Sr. engr. Widia India Ltd., Bangalore, Karnataka, 1985—88; rsch. asst. Ariz. State U., Tempe, 1989—90; sr. engr. Allied Signal Aerospace, Phoenix, 1990—92, Spl. Devices Inc., Mesa, Ariz., 1992—95; sect. mgr., prin. engr. Motorola, Mesa, Ariz., 1995—99; staff mgr., prin. engr. Intel Corp., Chandler, Ariz., 1999—. Recipient Mahboob Khan Mentor award, Semiconductor Rsch. Corp., 1999, 2003, Nation's Brightest Young Engr. award, NAE, 2006. Achievements include patents for composite machining and bonding techniques. Office: Intel Corp 5000 W Chandler Blvd M/S CH2-152 Chandler AZ 85226 Office Phone: 480-554-4324. Business E-Mail: mani.janakiram@intel.com.

JANAVITZ, KURT L., insurance company executive; b. Pitts., Pa., May 18, 1967; s. Carl Max and Gloria Korn Janavitz; m. Kari Vedder Janavitz, May 25, 1997; 1 child, Eve Tobyn. BA summa cum laude, Tufts U., Medford, Mass., 1988; MBA with honors, Northwestern U., Evanston, Ill., 1994. Cons. Ernst & Young, Chgo., 1990—92; mgr. Berkshire Hathaway, Omaha, 1994—95, Tiber Group, Chgo., 1995—98; dir. mktg. solutions Solucient, Evanston, 1998—2000; dir. Dimension Data, Chgo., 2000—03; dir. network mgmt. UnitedHealthcare, Chgo., 2003—04, v.p. network mgmt. Milw., 2004—. Bd. dirs. Am. Heart Assn., Milw., 2004—06. Recipient Anna Quincy Churchill Gen. Biology prize, Tufts U., 1987, Class of 1921 Leonard Carmichael prize, 1987; Austin scholar, Northwestern U. Kellogg Grad. Sch. Mgmt., 1992—94. Mem.: Phi Beta Kappa, Psi Chi, Beta Gamma Sigma. Democrat. Jewish. Avocations: tennis, travel. Home: 1105 Highland Dr Elm Grove WI 53122 Office: UnitedHealth Group 10701 West Rsch Dr Milwaukee WI 53226 Home Phone: 262-784-9975; Office Phone: 414-443-4444. Office Fax: 414-443-4439. Personal E-mail: kjanavitz1994@kellogg.northwestern.edu. Business E-Mail: kurt_janavitz@uhc.com.

JANC, JOHN J., language educator; b. Blue Island, Ill., July 24, 1945; BA in French Lang. and Lit., English Lang. and Lit., U. Wis., Eau Claire, 1967; MA in French Lang. and Lit., U. Mich., 1968; MA in Comparative Lit., U. Wis., Madison, 1974, PhD in French Lang. and Lit., 1981; diplôme de méthodologie audio-visuelle, U. Poitiers, France, 1975; Doctorat, U. La Sorbonne Nouvelle, Paris, 1977; diplôme supérieur de Français des Affaires, C. of C. and Industry Paris, 1981. Instr. French St. Benedict Coll., Ferdinand, Ind., 1968—69, U. Wis. Stout, Menomonie, 1969—72; lectr. English CAREL, Royan, France, 1972—74; prof. French Minn. State U., Mankato, 1979—. Tester Internat. Baccalaureate Exam, Mpls., St. Paul and Owatonna, Minn., 1990—95; spkr. in field. Author: (edit. critique) Les Deux Trouvailles de Gallus, 1983, Victor Hugo: Torquemada, 1989, Victor Hugo: Hernani, 2001, 2006, (series) Que se passe-t-il en France in Minn. Lang. Rev., 1987—, Faisons des progrès: Manuel de conversation, 1997; contbr. articles to profl. jours. Decorated chevalier in l'Ordre des Palmes Académiques, 1986; named CASE Univ. Prof. of Yr., State of Minn., 1988; recipient Founders award, Ctrl. State Conf., 1999; grantee, U. Wis., Madison, 1976, Minn. State U., 1980, 1982, 1987, 2000, NEH, 1990; Woodrow Wilson fellow, 1967—68, E.B. Fred fellow, U. Wis., Madison, 1976—77, Fulbright fellow, 1976—77. Mem.: Ctrl. States Conf. (pub. rels. com. 1990—91, pub. awareness com. 1991—92, leadership mentor 1996—97, state svcs. com. 1997—98, grants and fiscal devel. com. 1998—2002, bd. dirs. 2000—01, rev. bd. ann. report 2001—06, leadership program 2002, bd. dirs. 2002—03, awards and scholarships com. 2002—, local chair ann. conf. 2003), Am. Assn. Tchrs. French (pres. 2001—03, Minn. chpt.), Minn. Coun. Tchg. Langs. and Cultures (v.p. 1987—90, co-chair fall conf. 1990, chair fall conf. 1991, pres. 1991—92, exhibits chair fall conf. 1991—, co-chair fall conf. 1992, campus coord. French lang. contest 1994—96, advt. editor Minn. Lang. Rev. 1997—, Emma Birkmaier award 1994), Soc. des Etudes Romantiques et Dix-Neuvièmistes, Am. Coun. Tchg. Fgn. Langs., Assn. des Amis de Victor Hugo, Sigma Tau Delta, Pi Delta Phi, Phi Kappa Phi, Kappa Delta Pi, Alpha Mu Gamma. Office: Minn State U AH 227 Mankato MN 56001 Business E-Mail: john.janc@mnsu.edu.

JANCZAK, ANDREW ANTHONY, marketing professional; b. Buenos Aires, Feb. 20, 1950; came to U.S., 1955; s. Zygmunt and Gertrude (Sierocki) J.; m. Helen Mary Gimber, Jan. 27, 1973; children: Andrew S., Jeanette M. BS in Aerospace Engring., Polytech. Inst. Bklyn., 1972, MS in Mgmt., 1976. Mktg. dir. Telsonic/Trescott, Inc., L.I. City, NY, 1973-76; pres. Belzona, Inc., Uniondale, 1976-83; pres., owner Molecular Systems, Inc., Edgewood, 1983-90; pres. Enecon Corp., Bethpage, 1990—. Patentee in field. Avocations: golf, boating. Office: Enecon Corp 700 Hicksville Rd Ste 110 Bethpage NY 11714-3496 Home Phone: 516-798-3975; Office Phone: 516-349-0022. Business E-Mail: andy@enecon.com.

JANDA, CHRISTOPHER CRISCO, actor; b. Greenbrae, Calif., July 17, 1955; s. Frank Albert and Christina Teenie Janda; m. Lori Kaye Janda; children: Christina Virginia, Michael Joseph, Matthew Jeremy. Musician, Tiburon, Calif., 1966—; bartender Larkspur, Calif., 1976—; actor San Francisco, 1986—; drummer, ptnr. Ed Earley Band, Tiburon, 1994—; owner Lunamitz Prodns., Tiburon, 2001—. Primary actor in movie Blood in Blood Out, 1991, TV series Jesse Hawks, 1992, also commls. With U.S. Army, 1974-76. Mem. SAG, E. Clampis Vitis, Am. Legion. Avocations: ridng harley's, shooting, pool, camping, travel. Home Phone: 415-789-1014; Office Phone: 415-789-1014. Personal E-mail: cljanda@comcast.net.

JANDA, JOHN MICHAEL, microbiologist; b. Burbank, Calif., Nov. 4, 1949; s. Bernard Frederick and Mary Ellis (Alexopoulos) J.; m. Claudia Beth Kissling, June 2, 1979; children: Michael Jr., Matthew, Jennifer. PhD, UCLA, 1979. Diplomate Am. Bd. Medical Microbiology. Asst. prof. of clin. microbiology, asst. dir. of clin. microbiology Mt. Sinai Med. Ctr., NYC, 1981—84, assoc. prof. of clin. microbiology, assoc. dir. of clin. microbiology, 1984—86; rsch. scientist III Calif. Dept. of Health Svcs., Berkeley, Calif., 1986—98, chief microbial diseases lab. Richmond, Calif., 1998—. Editorial bd. European Jour. Clinical Microbiology and Infectious Diseases, 1990—. Author book chpts.; contbr. articles to profl. jours. Mem. ch. subcoms. St Joseph's Cath. Ch., Pinole, Calif., 1986—2006. Recipient Disting. Alumni award Calif. St. U., 1993. Mem. Am. Soc. Microbiology, Phi Kappa Phi, Am. Philatelic Assn. Avocations: stamp collecting/philately, golf, travel, music. Office: Microbial Diseases Lab 850 Marina Bay Pkwy Richmond CA 94804 Home Phone: 510-222-6367; Office Phone: 510-412-3725.

JANDA, MARK WILLIAM, history educator; s. Charles William and Sharon Alice Janda; m. Kristy Anne Mattox, Oct. 24, 1997. BA in History, U. Mo., Columbia, 1992, BS in Edn., 1992; MAT, Columbia Coll., Mo., 2006. Tchr. history Gateway Inst. Tech., 1993—96, Columbia Pub. Schs., 1996—. Facilitator Let's Talk Columbia, 2001—; cmty. award judge Columbia Values Diversity Breakfast, 2002; group leader EF, 2000—07. Named Vol. Month, City of Columbia, 2002; recipient Catalyst award, U. Mo., 2002. Mem.: Phi Delta Kappa (chpt. pres. 2001—02). Office: David H Hickman HS 1104 North Providence Rd Columbia MO 65202 Home Phone: 573-446-9019; Office Phone: 573-214-3000. Business E-Mail: mjanda@columbia.k12.mo.us.

JANDES, KENNETH MICHAEL, retired superintendent of schools; b. Berwyn, Ill., Aug. 6, 1943; s. George Jerry and Dorothea Frieda Clara (Grabow) J.; m. RoseMary Patricia Klingebiel, June 18, 1966; children: Michael Jon, Kenneth Mark. BS in Edn., Ill. State U., 1966; MEd, Loyola U., Chgo., 1972; EdD, No. Ill. U., 1984. Cert. tchr., chief sch. bus. official, gen. adminstrv., supt., Ill. Math. tchr. Brook Park Sch. Sch. Dist. 95, LaGrange Park, Ill., 1966-69, sci. tchr. Brook Park Sch., 1969-74, acting prin. Brook Park Sch., 1972-74; prin. Waterman Sch. Sch. Dist. 149, South Holland, Ill., 1974-79; prin. Berger-Vandenberg Sch., Dolton, Ill., 1979-95; supt. Lincoln Sch. Dist. # 156, Calumet City, Ill., 1995—2001, Ridgeland Sch. Dist. # 122, Oak Lawn, Ill., 2001—07; ret., 2007. Chmn. dept. applied saxophone Am. Conservatory Music, Chgo., 1968-78; owner, operator Midwest Music Mart, Riverside, Ill., 1968-73; primary sci. cons. Instructor Mag., Dansville, NY, 1969-73; adj. prof. Govs. State U., University Park, Ill., 1985—, Concordia U., River Forest, Ill., 2007-; prof. Am. Coll. Edn., Washinton, 2007-; co-founder Customized Edn. Cons., Oakland, Ill., 2007- Composer of numerous choral, band, and orchestral works, 1961—; performing saxophonist Ken Jandes Dance Orch., Andy Tecson's Chgo. Jazz Ensemble, Pk. Ridge Symphony Orch.; contbr. articles to profl. jours. Bd. dirs. Cmty. Family Svc. and Mental Health Ctr. La Grange, 1968-74; pres. bd. dirs. ECHO Spl. Edn. Coop., 1999-2001; bd. dirs. Thornton Fractional Area Ednl. Coop., v.p., 1998-99, pres. 1999-2001; mem. bd. supts. AERO Spl. Edn. Coop., 2001-07; mem. com., treas. Boy Scouts Am., Woodridge, 1985-96; baseball coach Woodridges Athletic Assn., 1980-89; active com. on youth traffic safety Ill. Sec. of State, 1987-91; chmn. Thornton Twp. Regional Action Planning Project, 1996-99; mem. chancel choir St. Luke Presbyn. Ch., Downers Grove, Ill., 1976-2006, elder, 1980-86, 92-98. Named one of Outstanding Young Men Am. Jaycees, 1970. Mem. ASCD, Am. Assn. Sch. Adminstrs. (mem. govs. task force edn. in Ill., Rsch. award 1986), Ednl. League Ill. (program chmn. 2006, pres. 2007), Ill. Assn. Sch. Adminstrs. (legis. chmn. South Cook County divsn. 1997-2006, pres. 1999-2005, bd. dirs. 2005-06, membership chmn. 2006-07), Ill. Assn. Sch. Bus. Ofcls. (fed. legis. ins. com. 2003-07), Ill. Congress Parents and Tchrs. (hon. life), South Cook County Elem. Sch. Supt.'s Assn. (pres. 1997-98), Oak Lawn and Calumet City C. of C., Bus. Assocs. Calumet City, South Coop. Orgn. Pub. Edn., MENSA, Lions, Kappa Delta Pi, Phi Mu Alpha Sinfonia, Phi Delta Kappa. Avocations: astronomy, tennis, mathematics, computers, scientific reading, wine and fine dining. Home: 6671 Wheatfield St Woodridge IL 60517-1715

JANDREY, BECKY LEE, psychologist; b. Appleton, Wis., Apr. 20, 1951; d. Elton and Eleanor Jandrey; life ptnr. Dean Nelson; stepchildren: Jeremy Nelson, Joshua Nelson. BS, Ariz. State U., Tempe, Ariz., 1974; MA, Fielding U., Santa Barbara, Calif., 1994, PhD, 1998. Licensed Psychologist Calif. Bd. of Psychology, 2000. Corp. real estate broker Dempsey Constrn. Corp., Mammoth Lakes, Calif., 1978—84; regional pers. mgr. Staffing Svcs., LA, Calif., 1984—91; psychol. asst. La Vie Counselling Ctr., Pasadena, Calif., 1992—96; fellow Kaiser-Permanente Outpatient Psychiatry, Santa Rosa, Calif., 1998—99; psychologist Pvt. Practice, Santa Rosa, Calif., 1997—. Tchr. Kaiser Permanent Health Edn., Santa Rosa, Calif., 1999—2000; presenter Kaiser Permanent Women's Health Week, Santa Rosa, Calif., 2000—02. Contbr. scientific papers (Dissertation Recognition Award - Fielding U., 1997). Vol. - counselling, crisis hotline Pasadena Mental Health Ctr., Pasadena, Calif., 1992—93; fin. organizer/contbr. Valley of the Moon Children's Found., Santa Rosa, Calif., 2004, Heifer Internat., Little Rock, 2003; vol. counselor/mentor for amputees Nova-Care Prosthetics, LA, Calif., 1981—96; vol. Veterans Adminstrn. - Geriatric neuropsychiatry, Sepulveda, Calif., 1996. Recipient Frieda Fromm Reichmann Award, Fielding U., 1998; scholar DAR Leadership Scholarship, DAR, 1969, 4-yr. Coll. Leadership Scholarship, Rotary Club, 1969-1973. Mem.: APA (assoc.), Calif. Psychol. Assn. (assoc.). Achievements include First amputee to learn downhill skiing at Mammoth Mountain, Calif. (ski sch. instr. - Jim Northrup). Avocations: writing, amputee skiing, reading, swimming, yoga. Office: Becky L Jandrey PhD 825 College Ave Santa Rosa CA 95404

JANES, BRANDON CHAISON, lawyer; b. Uvalde, Tex., Oct. 9, 1951; s. Brandon Chaison and Phyllis (Collins) J.; children: Margaret, Michael, Brandon. BBA, Baylor U., 1972; JD, U. Tex., 1976. Bar: Tex. 1976, U.S. Dist. Ct. (we. dist.) Tex. 1978, U.S. Tax Ct. 1981, U.S. Ct. Appeals (5th cir.) 1981, U.S. Supreme Ct. 1981. Assoc., then ptnr. Grambling & Mounce, El Paso, Tex., 1976-80; ptnr. Small, Craig & Werkenthin, Austin, Tex., 1981-97, Akin, Gump, Strauss, Haver & Feld, Austin, Tex., 1997; now ptnr. Jackson Walker LLP, Austin, Tex. Contbr. articles to profl. jours. Mem. ABA (taxation sect.), State Bar Tex., Tex. Soc. CPAs. Office: Jackson Walker LLP Ste 1100 100 Congress Ave Austin TX 78701 E-mail: bjanes@akingump.com.

JANES, BRIAN D., electronics specialist; b. Aberdeen, SD, Apr. 4, 1957; s. Wayne L. and Joy A. Janes; m. Donna D. Dilley, Mar. 13, 1982; m. Dawn R. Lehr, Nov. 28, 1975 (div. Mar. 29, 1979); children: Bradley E., Stephanie R. Hanson, Daniel W. Grad. in electronics tech., Control Data Inst., Mpls., 1978. Br. mgr. Scan-Optics, Inc., Crystal Lake, Ill., 1978—2005; customer support specialist Scan-Optics, LLC, Crystal Lake, 2005—. Boy scout leader Boy Scouts Am., Crystal Lake, 1998—2007. Home: 1642 Dogwood Dr Crystal Lake IL 60014 Office: Scan-Optics LLC 1642 Dogwood Dr Crystal Lake IL 60014 Home Phone: 815-455-5004; Office Phone: 815-455-5004.

JANES, JACKSON, research institute executive; b. Washington, Aug. 25, 1947; s. Roth and Lois Janes; m. Marlis Rohwer, Sept. 7, 1979; children: Tanya, Nicolas. BA in Sociology, Colgate U., 1969; MA in Theology, U. Chgo., 1971; PhD in Internat. Studies, Claremont Grad. Sch., 1981. Instr. English and Am. studies U. Giessen, Germany, 1971-74; dir. German-Am. Inst. Tuebingen, Germany, 1977-80; dir. European Office, German Marshall Fund U.S., Bonn, 1980-85; dir. program devel. Univ. Ctr. for Internat. Studies, U. Pitts., 1986-88; dep. dir. Am. Inst. Contemporary German Studies at The Johns Hopkins, Washington, 1989-94, exec. dir., 1994—. Mem. Coun. on Fgn. Rels., 2002—. Author: Mixed Messages: The Study of Contemporary Germany in the United States, 1986, Priming the Pump: The Making of Foreign Area Experts, 1992. Recipient friendship award Fed. Rep. Germany, 1987, Officer's Cross of the Order of Merit Fed. Rep. Germany, 2005. Mem.: Coun. Foreign Rels. Office: Am Inst for Contemporary German Studies at Johns Hop 1755 Massachusetts Ave NW Ste 700 Washington DC 20036-2121 Fax: 202-265-9531. E-mail: jjanes@aicgs.org.

JANES, NORMAN K., lawyer; BA, Earlham Coll.; JD, U. Conn., 1968. Staff atty. Conn. Aging Legal Services, Tolland-Windham Legal Assistance Program, 1968—71, project dir.; task force dir. Elderly/Disabled Task Force Conn. Legal Services, 1975—79, exec. dir., 1980—95, Statewide Legal Services of Conn., 1995. Mem.: Conn. Bar Assn. (chmn. acess to justice task force 1992, chmn. unbundled legal services com. 2003—, mem. pro bono com., mem. pub. svc. com., mem. pub. svc. recognition com., mem. profl. ethics com., mem. edn. law com., mem. com. on long range planning, mem. bill of rights action com., mem. legal svc. steering com., treas. 2001—02, sec. 2002—03, v.p. 2004—05, pres.-elect 2005—06, pres. 2006—07, Charles J. Parker Legal Services award 1995). Office: Statewide Legal Services 62 Washington St Middletown CT 06457

JANES, RAENA, private school educator; b. 1973; m. Craig Janes; children: Chloe, Cole. Founder, superintendent La Paloma Acad., 2002—. Founder Grace Chapel Early Edn. Ctr. Named one of 40 Under 40, Tucson Bus. Edge, 2006; recipient Excellence in Special Edn. Cmty. award, Ariz. Dept. Edn. Mem.: Nat. Assn. Edn. Young Children, Jr. League of Tucson. Office: La Paloma Academy 225 N Country Club Rd Tucson AZ 85716 Office Phone: 520-733-7373.

JANES, ROBERT ROY, museum director, archaeologist, editor; b. Rochester, Minn., Apr. 23, 1948; m. Priscilla Bickel; children: Erica Helen, Peter Bickel. Student, Lawrence U., 1966—68, BA in Anthropology cum laude, 1970; student, U. of the Ams., Mexico City, 1968, U. Calif., Berkeley, 1968—69; PhD in Archaeology, U. Calgary, Alta., Can., 1976. Postdoctoral fellow Arctic Inst. N.Am., U. Calgary, 1981-82; founding dir. Prince of Wales No. Heritage Centre, Yellowknife, N.W.T., 1976-86, project dir. Dealy Island Archaeol. and Conservation Project, 1977-82; founding exec. dir. Sci. Inst. of N.W.T.; sci. advisor Govt. of N.W.T., Yellowknife, 1986-89; exec. dir., pres., CEO Glenbow Mus. Art Gallery Libr. and Archives, Calgary, 1989-2000; fellow Glenbow-Alta. Inst., 2000—. Mus./heritage cons., 2000—; adj. prof. archaeology U. Calgary, 1990—. Author: Preserving Diversity-Ethnoarchaeological Perspectives on Culture Change in the Western Canadian Subarctic, 1991, Museums and the Paradox of Change, 1995, 2d edit., 1997, Looking Reality in the Eye: Museums and Social Responsibility, 2005, (with Gerald Conaty) Museum Management and Marketing, 2007; (with Richard Sandell) The Arctic Institute of North America Technical Paper No. 28, 1983; editor-in-chief Jour. Mus. Mgmt. and Curatorship, 2003—; contbr. articles to profl. jours. Mem. First Nations/CMA Task Force on Mus. and First Peoples, 1989-92, Banff, Kootenay and Yoho Nat. Pks. Devel. Adv. Bd.; nat. adv. bd. Ctr. for Cultural Mgmt., U. Waterloo; chair bd. dirs. Friends of Banff Nat. Park, 2003-05; vice-chair, chair bd. dirs. Biosphere Inst. of Bow Valley, 2003—. Recipient Nat. Parks Centennial award Environ. Can., 1985, Can. Studies Writing award Assn. Can. Studies, 1989, Disting. Alumni award Alumni Assn. of U. Calgary, 1989, L.R. Briggs Disting. Achievement award Lawrence U., 1991, Queen Elizabeth II Golden Jubilee Commemorative medal 2003; Can. Coun. doctoral fellow, 1973-76; rsch. grantee Govt. of Can., 1974, Social Scis. and Humanities Rsch. Coun. Can., 1988-89. Fellow Arctic Inst. N.Am. (bd. dirs. 1983-90, vice chmn. bd. 1985-89, hon. rsch. assoc. 1983-84, chmn. priorities and planning com. 1983-84, exec. com. 1984-86, assoc. editor Arctic jour. 1987-97), Can. Mus. Assn. (hon. life, cert. accreditation 1982, Outstanding award in Mus. Mgmt., Outstanding Achievement award for publ. 1996), Am. Anthrop. Assn. (fgn.); mem. Can. Archaeol. Assn. (v.p. 1980-82, pres. 1984-86, co-chmn. fed. heritage policy com. 1986-88), Can. Art Mus. Dirs. Orgn. (mem.-at-large bd. dirs. 1992-95), Alta. Mus. Assn. (moderator seminars 1990, Merit award 1992, Merit award for Museums and the Paradox of Change 1996), Assn. Cultural Execs. (bd. dirs. 1999--2002, ACE award for Can. Cultural Mgmt. 1998), Sigma Xi. Home: 104 Prendergast Pl Canmore AB Canada T1W 2N5

JANES, WILLIAM SARGENT, real estate company executive; b. Cambridge, Mass., Mar. 24, 1953; s. G. Sargent and Ann (Brown) J.; m. Alice Maxine Rowley, June 19, 1982; children: Pack Sargent, Maxine Cotton. BA, Bowdoin Coll., 1976. Sr. sales cons. Coldwell Banker, Washington, 1976-84; ptnr. Lincoln Property Co., Washington, 1984-89; pres. Rock Creek Ptnrs., Inc., Washington, 1990—; mng. ptnr. Oak Hill Realty, Washington, 1990—. Bd. dirs. Am. Skiing Co., Brazos Asset Mgmt., Inc., Brazos Fund L.P., CapStar Hotel Co., Carr Real Estate Svcs., Inc., First Atlantic Holdings, LLC, Max/FW Mgmt., LLC, Max/FW, LLC, MeriStar Hospitality Corp., MeriStar Investment Ptnrs., Oak Hill REIT Mgmt., LLC, Power Loft, LLC. Trustee Bowdoin Coll., Kennedy Ctr. Circles Bd., Washington Nat. Cathedral Found. Mem. NAREIT, SIOR, Urban Land Inst., Washington Bd. Realtors. Home: PO Box 1204 Middleburg VA 20118-1204 Office: Oak Hill Realty LLC 1133 Connecticut Ave NW Washington DC 20036-4305

JANEWAY, RICHARD, retired academic administrator; b. LA, Feb. 12, 1933; s. VanZandt and Grace Ellen (Bell) Janeway; m. Katherine Esmond Pillsbury, Dec. 23, 1955; children: Susan Kent, David VanZandt, Elizabeth Anne. AB, Colgate U., 1954; MD, U. Pa., 1958. Diplomate Am. Bd. Psychiatry and Neurology. Intern Hosp. U. Pa., 1958—59; resident N.C. Baptist Hosp., Winston-Salem, 1963—66; mem. faculty Bowman Gray Sch. Medicine (now Wake Forest U. Sch. Medicine), Winston-Salem, 1966—; prof. neurology Wake Forest U., Winston-Salem, 1971—2003, prof. medicine and mgmt., 1997—2003, prof. emeritus, 2003—, dir. Cerebral Vascular Rsch. Ctr., Bowman Gray Sch. Medicine, 1969—71; dean Bowman Gray Sch. Medicine, Wake Forest U., Winston-Salem, 1971—85, exec. dean, 1985—94, v.p. health affairs, 1983—90, exec. v.p. health affairs, 1990—97, ret., 1997—. Mem. exec. com. So. Nat. Bank, Winston-Salem, NC, 1982—95; dir. BB&T Corp., 1995—2003, bd. dirs., mem. exec. com., chmn., 2001—03; mem. nat. adv coun. regional med. programs HEW, 1974—77; mem. -at-large Nat. Bd. Med. Examiners, 1979—87; mem. N.C. Joint Conf. Com. on Med. Care, Inc., 1983—2003; dir. N.C. Inst. Medicine. Mem. Winston-Salem Forsyth Co. Bd. Edn., 1970—73; trustee Winston-Salem State U., 1991—95, Colgate U., 1988—95, Sr. Svcs. Inc., 2007—; mem. investment com. Episcopal Diocese NC, 2000—06, chmn., 2004, 2005; bd. dirs. Nat. Assn. for Biomed. Rsch., 1993—96, Ams. for Med. Progress, Inc., 1993—97, Winston-Salem Found., 1994—2002, chmn., 1997, 1998. Capt. USAF, 1959—63, flight surgeon, 1962—63. Recipient fellow, USPHS, 1956, Markle scholar, 1968—73, Medallion of Merit, Wake Forest U., 1998, Maroon citation, Colgate U., 2004. Fellow: ACP, Am. Heart Assn. (coun. on stroke), Am. Acad. Neurology; mem.: AMA, Soc. Med. Adminstrs., Greater Winston-Salem C. of C. (bd. dirs. 1985—89, 1991—95, chmn. 1992), Inst. Medicine of NAS, Am. Clin. and Climatol. Assn., Assn. Am. Med. Colls. (exec. coun. 1977—86, mem. accreditation coun. on grad med. edn. 1981—85, chmn. coun. of deans 1982—83, exec. com. 1982—86, chmn. 1984—85), Am. Neurol. Assn., Rotary (dir. 1977—80, v.p. 1981—82, pres. 1982—83), Alpha Omega Alpha, Sigma Xi, Phi Beta Kappa. Republican. Episcopalian. Avocations: photography, golf, flower arranging, reading, gardening. Personal E-mail: rjaneway@triad.rr.com.

JANG, JEONG, professional golfer; b. Taejeon, Korea, June 11, 1980; Attended, JoongBoo U. Winner Korea Women's Open, 1997, Korea Women's Amateur, 1998, Women's British Open, 2005, Wegmans LPGA, 2006. Mem. Korea Women's Nat. Team, 1997—98, World Amateur Championship Team, 1998. Achievements include five top-ten finishes, 2002; six top-ten finishes, 2003; seven top-ten finishes, 2004. Avocations: skiing, nintendo. Office: c/o LPGA 100 International Golf Dr Daytona Beach FL 32124-1092

JANG, JIN-WOOK, electronics engineer; b. Seoul, Republic of Korea, Dec. 7, 1967; US, 1997; s. Ki-Heung Jang and Kye-Ja Kim. BS in Ceramics Engring., Seoul Nat. U., 1990, MS in Materials Sci. and Engring., 1992, PhD in Materials Sci. and Engring., 1996. Sr. staff engr. semiconductor products sector Motorola, Tempe, Ariz., 1999—2001, tech. staff engr., 2002—05; prin. staff engr. Freescale Semiconductor Inc. (Motorola spinoff), Tempe, 2005—. Contbr. chapters to books, articles to profl. jours. Recipient Best Paper award, Hermes Symposium, 2001, New Product Devel. award, Final Mfg. Orgn., 2001, cert. of excellence, Final Mfg. Orgn., Motorola, 2002. Achievements include patents for semiconductor device with strain relieving bump design; manufacturing method of high frequency; patents pending for gold edge seal backmetal for solder die attach assembly process. Home: 855 N Dobson Rd #2042 Chandler AZ 85224 Office: Freescale Semiconductor Inc MD EL725 2100 E Elliot Rd Tempe AZ 85284 Home Phone: 480-203-5152; Office Phone: 480-413-3068. Office Fax: 480-413-4511; Home Fax: 480-413-4511. E-mail: j.jang@freescale.com.

JANG, SOOCHEONG (SHAWN), education educator; arrived in US, 1998; s. Kilyong Jang and Youngjoo Kim; m. Soyeon Park, Nov. 26, 1993; 1 child, Jiwoong. PhD, Purdue U., West Lafayette, Ind., 2002. Asst. prof. Kans. State U., Manhattan, Kans., 2002—05, Purdue U., West Lafayette, Ind., 2005—. Dep. gen. mgr. LG Mcht. Banking Corp., Seoul, Korea (South), 1995—98. Recipient Best Paper Award, CHRIE, 2004, 2005, Best Travel Grant Award, TTRA, 2003, Best Paper Award, ISTTE, 2002, HTM Grad. Edn., 2002. Achievements include research in Hospitality and Tourism Mgmt. Home: 3358 Putnam St West Lafayette IN 47906 Office: Purdue Univ Stone Hall 700 W State St West Lafayette IN 47907-2059 Home Phone: 765-464-2870; Office Phone: 765-496-3610. Business E-Mail: jang12@purdue.edu.

JANIAK, ANTHONY RICHARD, JR., investment banker; b. Pitts., Sept. 21, 1946; s. Anthony R. and Ann Theresa Janiak; m. Anne Marie McDevitt, Aug. 23, 1969; children: Brian Richard, Carolyn Marie. BS, Pa. State U., 1968; MBA, U. Chgo., 1970. Assoc. Smith Barney & Co., NYC, 1970-74; v.p. Smith Barney Internat., Tokyo, 1974-77, Smith Barney, Harris Upham & Co., NYC, 1977-78, mng. dir., 1980—, Citigroup/Smith Barney, NYC, 1998—; v.p. Smith Barney, Harris Upham Internat., Paris, 1978-80; mng. dir., dir. internat. Smith Barney Inc., NYC, 1995-98. Bd. dirs. Global Wrap Cons. Group, Tokyo, 1997-2001, Soditic Fin., Geneva, 1998-2004, Fubon Securities, Taipei, Taiwan, 2001-03; chmn. bd. dirs. Genesis Energy LLC, 1999-2002; mem. adv. com. bus. coun. UN, 1984-90, N.Y.C.; mem. task force on fin. svcs. U.S.-Japan Businessmen's Coun., 1982-83; mem. adv. com. on pub. affairs Japan Soc., N.Y.C., 1986-88; mem. emerging markets adv. com. SEC, 1991-93; exch. ofcl. Am. Stock Exch., 1992—, NASDAQ listing com., 1999-2000. Bd. dirs. Town and Village Civic Club of Scarsdale, 1992-95, 98-2001, A Better Chance, 2003—; trustee Scarsdale Hist. Soc., 1999-2001. Republican. Roman Catholic. Avocations: tennis, coin collecting/numismatics, music, golf. Home: 172 Woodbrook Rd White Plains NY 10605 Office: Citigroup/Smith Barney 485 Lexington Ave New York NY 10019 Business E-Mail: a.r.janiak@citigroup.com.

JANICAK, PHILIP GREGORY, psychiatrist, educator; b. Chgo., Aug. 2, 1946; s. Edward and Josephine (Raskauskas) J.; m. Mary Judith Cray, Oct. 16, 1976; 1 child, Matthew Cray. BS in Psychology with honors, Loyola U., Chgo., 1969, MD, 1973. Diplomate Am. Bd. Psychiatry and Neurology. Asst. clin. prof. dept. psychiatry Loyola U., Maywood, Ill., 1976-78; rsch. assoc. U. Chgo., 1979-81; asst. prof. U. Ill., Chgo., 1982-85, assoc. prof., 1986-92, prof., 1992—2004, Rush U., 2004—. Chief rsch. unit Ill. State Psychiat. Inst., Chgo., 1984-96; med. dir. psychiat. clin. rsch. ctr. U. Ill., 1996-2004, Rush U., 2004-. First author: Principles and Practice of Psychopharmacotherapy, 1993, 4th edit., 2006. NIMH grant co-investigator, 1986, 91, 93; NIMH grant prin. investigator, 1990; NIH grant assoc. program dir. 2000-2004. Fellow Am. Psychiat. Assn. (disting. fellow). Roman Catholic. Business E-Mail: pjanicak@rush.edu.

JANICKI, ROBERT STEPHEN, retired pharmaceutical executive; b. Manette, Wash., Dec. 7, 1934; s. Stephen Walter and Elizabeth Caroline (Gorman) J.; m. I. Jane Betcher, Aug. 18, 1956; children: Robert, Beth, David. BS, Grove City Coll., 1956; MD, Temple U., 1961. Diplomate Nat. Bd. Med. Examiners. Intern U.S. Naval Hosp., Phila., 1961-62; resident in occupl. medicine USN, 1962-63; assoc. dir. clin. rsch. Dow Pharms., Indpls., 1966-68; assoc. med. dir. Neisler divsn. Union Carbide Corp., Sterling Forest, NY, 1968-69; assoc. med. dir. regulatory affairs Abbott Labs., North Chicago, Ill., 1969-70, dir. clin. rsch. pharm. products divsn., 1970-71, v.p. med. affairs pharm. products divsn., 1971-79, v.p. research pharm. products divsn., 1979-83, corp. v.p. R & D pharm. products divsn., 1983-89, sr. v.p., 1989-90. Bd. dirs. Osprey Pharms., Jacksonville, Fla.; cons. New Drug Devel Contbr. articles to profl. jours. Trustee Grove City (Pa.) Coll., 1995-99. Lt. comdr. M.C., USN, 1961-66. Fellow Am. Coll. Clin. Pharmacology; mem. Am. Soc. Clin. Pharmacology and Therapeutics, Sigma Xi, Alpha Omega Alpha. Home: 138 Anchor Dr Vero Beach FL 32963-2941 Personal E-mail: rsjanicki@aol.com.

JANIGA-PERKINS, CONSTANCE GABRIELLE, language educator; d. Edward John and Margaret (Mihalovic) Janiga; m. Michael Allen Perkins, Mar. 8, 1992; 1 child, Gabrielle Janiga Perkins. PhD, Ind. U., 1987; BA, Douglass Coll., 1977. Assoc. prof. of hispanic lang. and lit. Modern Languages and Classics, Tuscaloosa, Ala., 1987—; asst. prof. Spanish SUNY, Oswego, 1986—87. Co-editor (with Dr. Heitor Martins): (critical edition) Dialogo Entre o Deus Momo e o Censor. VII Anuario do Museu da Inconfidencia e do Grupo de Museus e Casas Historicas de Minas Gerais. Brasilia: Ministerio da Educacao e Cultura, 1985.; contbr. critical articles, studies to profl. publs.; author: (book) Immaterial Transcendence: The Process of the Colonial Writing Subject in Brazil's Letter of Discovery, 2001. V.p. Univ. Pl. Sch. PTA, 1999—2004; active Girl Scouts U.S. Fellow, NEH, 1991, 1992; grantee, Fulbright Found., 1983, U.S. Dept. Edn./Fulbright Found., 1995—97, 1986; Fulbright Rsch./Tchg. grantee, Costa Rica, 1991, Arts & Sciences Tchg. fellow, Coll. of Arts and Scis., 1997—2001. Mem.: South Ea. Coun. on L.Am. Studies, South Ea. MLA, Nat. Fulbright Assn., Parent Tchr. Assn., Phi Beta Kappa, Sigma Delta Pi, Sigma Beta Delta. Avocation: 2d degree blackbelt. Office: Modern Langs and Classics BB Comer 200 Tuscaloosa AL 35487-0246 Office Fax: 205-348-9909. E-mail: cgjaniga@msn.com.

JANIGIAN, BRUCE JASPER, lawyer, educator; b. San Francisco, Oct. 21, 1950; s. Michael D. Janigian and Stella (Minasian) Amerian; m. Susan Elizabeth Frye, Oct. 4, 1986; children: Alan Michael, Alison Elizabeth. AB, U. Calif., Berkeley, 1972; JD, U. Calif., San Francisco, 1975; LLM, George Washington U., 1982. Bar: Calif. 1975, U.S. Supreme Ct. 1979, D.C. 1981. Dir. Hastings Rsch. Svcs., Inc., San Francisco, 1973-75; judge adv. in Spain, 1976-78; commr. U.S. Navy and Marine Corps Ct. Mil. Rev., 1978-79; atty. advisor AID U.S. State Dept., Washington, 1979-84; dep. dir., gen. counsel Calif. Employment Devel. Dept., Sacramento, 1984-89; Fulbright scholar, vis. prof. law U. Salzburg, Austria, 1989-90; chmn. Calif. Agrl. Labor Rels. Bd., 1990-95; v.p. Europe, resident dir. Salzburg (Austria) Seminar, 1995-96; U.S. legate European Acad. Scis. and Art, 1996—; Rapporteur, World Economic Forum, 1996; of counsel Weintraub Genshlea Chediak Sproul, Sacramento, 1998—2001; pvt. practice Sacramento, 2001—; adviser European-Am. C. of C., 2003—; law dean Am. U. Armenia, 2005—06, v.p., 2005—; prof. Golden Gate U. Law Sch., 2004—. Prof. McGeorge Sch. Law, U. Pacific, Sacramento, 1986—, Inst. on Internat. Legal Studies, Salzburg, 1987, London Inst. on Comml. Law, 1989, 1992—93; vis. scholar Hoover Inst. War, Revolution and Peace, Stanford U., 1991—92; dir. Vienna-Budapest East/West Trade Inst., 1993; vis. prof. law U. Salzburg, 1995—96; prof. internat. bus. mgmt., internat. law Golden Gate U., 1998—, prof. internat. litigation law, 2004—; founder, bd. dirs. Global Devel. Ptnrs., San Francisco, London, 2003—; sr. rsch. assoc. South NH U. Applied Rsch. Ctr., 2004—05. Editor: Financing International Trade and Development, 1986-87, 89, International Business Transactions, 1989, 92, International Trade Law, 1993-94. Coord. fund raiser March of Dimes, Sacramento, 1987; adviser European-Am. C. of C., 2003—. Capt. USNR, JAGC, 1976-79, mem. Res. Fulbright scholar, 1989-90; decorated Navy Achievement medal; recipient USAID Meritorious Honor award, Faculty of Yr. award Golden Gate U., 2001. Mem.: Am. Soc. of Internat. Law, Austro-Am. Soc., World Art Forum (v.p. 1996), European Acad. Scis. and Art (U.S. Legate 1996—), Pub. Internat. Law and Policy Group, Anthony M. Kennedy Am. Inn of Ct. (barrister 1998—2001), Sacramento Bar Assn. (exec. com. taxation sect. 1988—89, chair internat. law sect. 1999—2002), D.C. Bar Assn., Calif. Bar Assn., Marine Meml. Assn., Navy League (gen. counsel 1997—), Naval Res. Officers Assn. (life), Knights of Vartan, Sacramento Capitol Club (dir. 1999—2001), Comstock Club (bd. dirs. 1998—99), Sacramento Met C. of C. (award for program cntbns. and cmty. enrichment 1989), Rotary (chair, internat. found. com. 1999—2002), Fulbright Assoc. (life), Phi Beta Kappa. Avocations: cross country skiing, tennis, bicycling. Home: 1631 12th Ave Sacramento CA 95818-4146 Office: 770 L St Ste 950 Sacramento CA 95814 Office Phone: 916-449-3955. Business E-Mail: law@janigian.com.

JANIS, ALLEN IRA, retired physicist, educator; b. Chgo., Sept. 11, 1930; s. David M. and Rosa (Ginsburg) J.; m. Phyllis Meyer, Sept. 6, 1953; children: Stuart, Wynne. BS, Northwestern U., 1951; postgrad., Cornell U., Ithaca, NY, 1951-53; PhD, Syracuse U., 1957. Mem. faculty U. Pitts., 1957-92, assoc. prof. physics, 1963-68, prof., 1968-92, prof. emeritus, 1993—, sr. research assoc. Philos. Sci. Center, 1967-75, assoc. dir. Philos. Sci. Center, 1975-92; fellow emeritus Philos. Sci. Center, 1993—. Mem. Fedn. Am. Scientists (sec. 1964-65), Am. Phys. Soc., Am. Assn. Physics Tchrs., AAAS, AAUP, Philosophy of Sci. Assn. Home: 425 Garden City Dr Monroeville PA 15146-1258 Office: Univ Pitts Dept Physics and Astronomy Pittsburgh PA 15260 E-mail: aij@pitt.edu.

JANIS, CONRAD, actor, musician, art dealer; b. NYC; s. Sidney and Harriet J.; children: Christopher, Carin; m. Maria Grimm, Nov. 30, 1987. Appeared in numerous Broadway plays including Junior Miss, 1942, Dark of the Moon, 1945, The Next Half Hour, 1945, The Brass Ring, 1951 (World Theater award), Time Out for Ginger, 1952, Visit to a Small Planet, 1957, Sunday in New York, 1961, Marathon '33, 1963, The Front Page, 1969, Same Time Next Year, 1975-76; films include Snafu, 1945, Margie, 1946, That Hagen Girl, 1947, Let's Rock, 1958, Airport '75, The Duchess and the Dirtwater Fox, 1976, The Buddy Holly Story, 1977, Roseland, 1977, Oh, God! Book II, 1979, Nothing in Common, 1987, Sonny Boy, 1987, Mr. Saturday Night, 1992, The Gods Must Be Crazy III, 1992; star, dir. The Feminine Touch, 1995, The Cable Guy, 1995, Addams Family Reunion, 1998; actor, dir. The November Conspiracy, 1996, actor, dir., prodr., editor Bad Blood, 2006; appeared in over 350 major network TV shows including Suspense, 1950, Philco Play House, 1951, Studio One, 1952, Armstrong Circle Theater, 1953, Highway to Heaven, 1986, Golden Girls, 1987, 89, Murder, She Wrote, 1988, 91, Baywatch, 1996, The New Rockford Files, 1997, Frasier, 1997, 2000, 02, Diagnosis Murder, 1998, (recurring role) Family Law, 1999-2000; numerous TV movies including Miracle on 34th Street, 1973, The Virginia Hill Story, 1974, The Magnificent Magnet of Santa Mesa, 1977, The Gossip Columnist, 1984, The Red Light Sting, 1984, Asimov's Probe, 1987, Caddie Woodlawn, 1988, Time After Time, 2002; TV series include I Bonino, Quark, Mork and Mindy, 1978-82; spokesperson TV series on modern art, Appreciating Art, 1991; leader jazz group, 1951—; TV appearances with Johnny Carson, Diana Shore, Mike Douglas, The Late Show with Ross Schaeffer, David Letterman Show, spls. include Burt Convy, Juke Box Hits, Jerry Lewis Telethons, others; appeared in major jazz clubs throughout US, jazz festivals, Monterey, Calif., Palm Springs, Calif., Sacramento, L.A. Classic and many others, concerts at N.Y. Carnegie Hall, Town Hall, Phila. Acad. Music, Nugget Jazz Festival, Playboy Jazz Festival, 1997, others; jazz trombonist with various artists including Roy Eldredge, Coleman Hawkins, Buddy Rich, Bobby Hackett, Hot Lips Page, Wild Bill Davison; leader Beverly Hills Unlisted Jazz Band, 1978- (subject of PBS spl. titled That's A Plenty 1981), The Tuxedo Junction, (PBS spl.) This Joint is Jumpin, 1997; writer, producer, star: (with others) (video spl.) This Joint Is Jumpin', 1997, numerous recs. for many jazz labels; co-owner. Sidney Janis Gallery, N.Y.C.; co-founder with Maria Grimm, prodr. Golden Era Pictures (co. now titled MiraCon Pictures), 1988—, ConMar Prodns. LLC, 2005. Recipient Theatre World award, 1952; named to Playboy Jazz Poll, 1960, 61; Silver Theatre award, 1950 Mem. SAG, AFTRA, Acad. Motion Picture Arts and Scis., Actors Equity Assn., Am. Fedn. Musicians, Nautico Club (Bilbao, Spain), Bohemian Club (San Francisco). Home Phone: 310-273-4062; Office Phone: 310-820-9225. Fax: (310) 273-0180. E-mail: traid43@aol.com.

JANIS, ELINOR RAIDEN, artist, educator; b. NYC, Dec. 8, 1934; d. Edward and Lea Raiden; m. Leon Janis, July 14, 1957 (div. Jan. 5, 1970); children: Madeline, Richard, Cheryl. BA in Elem. Edn., UCLA, 1957; MFA, Instituto Allende, 1975. Instr. elem. schs., 1957—66, Woman's Workshop, Granada Hills, Calif., 1971—73; painting instr. Instituto Allende, 1974, 1976—77, Santa Monica Pks. and Recreation, Calif., 1977; instr. L.A. City Schs., 1978—86; profl. artist, 1986—. One-woman shows include Galeria Conde, San Miguel de Allende, Mex., 1974, Beyond Baroque Gallery, Venice, Calif., 1977, Canyon Cafe, Glendale, Calif., 2000—01, exhibited in group shows at Barnsdall Pk., L.A., 1972, Emerson Gallery, 1972, Brentwood (Calif.) Art Ctr., 1973, McCaffery Galleries, L.A., 1973, Ryder Gallery, 1973, Galeria Pintora de Jovenes, Mexico City, 1974, Powerhouse Gallery, Montreal, Can., 1975, Woman's Bldg., L.A., 1975, Woman's Ctr., Ridgefield, Con., 1975, Assn. Humanist Artists, San Francisco, 1975, Museo de Arte Contemporaneo, San Miguel de Allende, 1977, Viva Gallery, Sherman Oaks, Calif., 2000—05, others. Mem. Amnesty Internat., LA, 1995—2001, NOW, 1985—2001, Handgun Control, 1990—2001. Recipient scholarship, Instituto Allende, 1974, 2d prize, Burbank Creative Arts Ctr. Show, 2001. Mem.: Valley Artists Guild, L.A. County Mus. Art. Democrat. Jewish. Avocations: pottery, stone carving, etching. Office: Elinor Janis Studio 14417 Chase St # 298 Panorama City CA 91402 Personal E-mail: erjanis@aol.com.

JANISCHEWSKYJ, WASYL, electrical engineering educator; b. Prague, Czechoslovakia, Jan. 21, 1925; arrived in Can., 1950; s. Ivan and Hanna (Ravych) J.; m. Emilia Miszczuk; children: Roxolana, Marko. Student, Tech. U. Hannover, Fed. Republic of Germany, 1948-50; B of Applied Sci., U. Toronto, 1952, M of Applied Sci., 1954; Hon. Doctor, Natl. Tech. U. of Ukraine Polytechnical Inst., Kyiv, 1998. Registered profl. engr., Ont. Testing engr. Moloney Electric Co., Toronto, Can., summer 1952; demonstrator/instr. U. Toronto, 1952-55, lectr. to prof., 1959-90, prof. emertius, 1990—, asst. dept. head elec. engring., 1964-70, assoc. dean faculty of applied sci. and engring., 1978-82; elec. engr. Aluminium Labs., Kingston, Ont., 1955-59; elect. engr. NRC, Ottawa, Ont., Can., summer 1961, Ont. Hydro, Toronto, Can., summers 1962-65. Contbr. over 100 articles to profl. jours. Fellow IEEE; mem. Internat. Elec. Commn., Internat. Conf. on Large High Vol. Elec. Systems, Can. Elec. Assn., Assn. Profl. Engrs. Ont., Taras Shevchenko Sci. Soc., Ukrainian Free Acad. Scis. Mem. Ukranian Orthodox Ch. Home: 65 Humbercrest Blvd Toronto ON Canada M6S 4K6 Office: Univ Toronto Dept Elec/Computer Engring Toronto ON Canada M5S 3G4 Office Phone: 416-978-3116. Business E-Mail: janisch@ecf.utoronto.ca.

JANJUA, NAVEED ZAFAR, research scientist; s. Zafar-ul Islam and Fahmida Begum. MBBS, Rawalpindi Med. Coll., Pakistan, 1999; MSc, Aga Khan U., Karachi, Pakistan, 2001; DPhil, U. Ala., Birmingham, 2005. Lic. Pakistan Med. and Dental Coun., 1999. Sr. instr. Aga Khan U., Karachi, 2002—05; rschr. U. Ala. Sch. Pub. Health, Birmingham, 2005—. Fellow, Fogarty Internat. Ctr., 2005—; grantee, UNICEF, Pakistan, 2005, Getz Pharma, 2005; Rsch. grant, WHO, Geneva, 2003. Mem.: Pakistan Epidemiology Assn. (pres. 2005—06), Soc. Risk Analysis. Achievements include research in unsafe medical injection that transmit hepatitis B, C and HIV lead to formulation of national policy on injection safety in Pakistan and legislation to regulate quality of syringes. Avocation: travel. Office: Univ Ala 1665 University Blvd RPHB 430 Birmingham AL 35294 Business E-Mail: naveed@uab.edu.

JANKE, JOHN ERIC, secondary school educator; b. Longview, Wash., Mar. 30, 1960; s. John Charles and Rose Kathryn (Albertson) Janke. AA, Lower Columbia Coll., 1982; BA in History, Ctrl. Wash. U., 1984, MEd, 1999; BA in Edn., Western Wash. U., 1986. Cert. tchr. Wash. Jr. sch. high tchr. Bd. Edn., Kelso, Wash., 1986-94, jr. high tchr. Longview, 1986-94, Spannaway, Wash., 1994-2000. Named Alumni of the Yr., Ctrl. Wash. U., 1997. Mem.: NEA, Kelso Edn. Assn., Wash. Edn. Assn. Avocations: golf, stamp collecting/philately, pool. Home: 912 Elizabeth St Kelso WA 98626-2817 E-mail: johnjanke@yahoo.com.

JANKE, KENNETH, investment consultant; b. Ft. William, Ont., Can., May 13, 1934; s. Adolf Earthman and Julianna (Dika) J.; m. Sally Mildred Roach, June 29, 1957; children: Kenneth Stuart, Laura Lynn, Julie Ann. Student, Mich. State U., East Lansing, 1952-56. Asst. mgr. Household Fin. Co., Detroit, 1958—60; gen. mgr. Nat. Assn. Investors, Royal Oak, Mich., 1960—76, pres., CEO, 1976—2002, chmn., CEO, 2002—. Bd. dirs. Investment Edn. Inst., Royal Oak, pres. 1995-2002, chmn., 2002—; bd. dirs. World Fedn. Investors, Brussels, pres., 1995—. Author: Ask Mr. Naic, 1982, Golf Is A Funny Game (But It Wasn't Meant To Be), 1992, Starting and Running a Profitable Investment Club, 1996, Firsts, Facts, Feats and Failures in the World of Golf, 2006; co-author: Wit and Wisdom of Golf, 1997; columnist mag. Better Investing. Chmn. Mich. Golf Hall of Fame, Lake Orion; pres. Am. Cancer Soc.-Oakland Country, Southfield, Mich., 1974-75; pres., bd. dirs. NAIC Growth Fund, Royal Oak; bd. dirs. AFLAC, Inc., Columbus, Ga.; bd. advisors Mich. PGA, West Bloomfield. With U.S. Army, 1956-58, ETO. Recipient Disting. Svc. award Investment Edn. Inst., 1972, Founder award Am. Cancer Soc., 1970; inductee Dearborn Sports Hall of Fame, Mich., 2002. Fellow Fin. Analysts Soc. Detroit (pres. 1984—), Fin. Analysts Fedn.; mem. Nat. Investor Rels. Inst. (pres. Detroit 1985—), We. Golf Assn. (bd. dirs., pres.), Indianwood Golf and Country Club (Lake Orion), Renaissance Club (Detroit), NFL Alumni (Lauderdale, Fla.), Scalawag's Country Club (Mt. Clemens, Mich.), Masons. Republican. Episcopalian. Avocation: golf. Home: 4305 W Maple Rd Bloomfield Hills MI 48301-2901 Office: Nat Assn Investors Corp 711 W 13 Mile Rd Madison Heights MI 48071-1806 Business E-Mail: naicinvest@aol.com.

JANKE, KENNETH S., JR., insurance company executive; BS in Polit. Sci., U. Mich.; MBA, Oakland U., Rochester, Mich. Dir. corp. svcs. Nat. Assn. Investors Corp., chmn. corp. adv. com., bd. dirs. Investment Edn. Inst.; with AFLAC Inc., Columbus, Ga., 1985, sr. v.p. investor rels., chair corp. disclosure com. Mem. sr. investor rels. roundtable Nat. Investor Rels. Inst. Office: AFLAC Inc 1932 Wynnton Rd Columbus GA 31999 Office Phone: 706-323-3431.*

JANKE, NORMA E., legal nursing consultant; b. Chgo. d. Cornel and Sylvia Louise Wohlberg; m. Louis P. Janke. B Univ. Studies in Biology, U. N.Mex., Albuquerque, 1976; BSN, U. Ala., Huntsville, 1979; student in Paralegal Studies, Arapahoe C.C., Littleton, Colo., 1992—93. RN Tex., Colo., Calif., bd. cert., Am. Assn. Legal Nurse Cons. and Am. Bd. Nursing, 2000. Emergency rm. nurse intravenous therapy, radiology Swedish Med. Ctr. & Porter Meml. Hosp., Englewood, Denver, Colo., 1980—90; nurse, med. specialist Am. Family, Englewood, Colo., 1990—94; nurse, asst. mgr. compliance Gt. West Life, Englewood, Colo., 1994—96; nurse, claims med. specialist Nationwide, Englewood, Colo., 1996—2000; nurse, risk mgmt. specialist Exempla Health Care, Wheat Ridge, Colo., 2001—02. Pres. Merevan Legal Nurse Cons. Svcs., Sedalia, Colo. and, Argyle, Tex., 1994—; instr. Am. Heart ACLS & BCLS, Englewood, Colo., 1984—94; freelance writer/reporter, 2005—. Vol. Metroport Meals-On-Wheels, Roanoke, Tex., 2004—05, North Tex. Charities, 2005—. Mem.: Am. Assn. Legal Nurse Cons. (sec. Denver chpt. 2001). Avocations: champion labrador retriever breeder, hiking, photography, silversmithing. Office Phone: 817-308-1960. Personal E-mail: merevan@hughes.net, norma.janke@hughes.net.

JANKE, RONALD ROBERT, lawyer; b. Milw., Mar. 2, 1947; s. Robert Erwin and Elaine Patricia (Wilken) J.; m. Mary Ann Burg, July 3, 1971; children— Jennifer, William, Emily. B.A. cum laude, Wittenberg U., 1969; J.D. with distinction, Duke U., 1974. Bar: Ohio 1974. Assoc. Jones Day, Cleve., 1974-83, ptnr., 1984—. Served with U.S. Army, 1970-71, Vietnam. Mem. ABA (chmn. environ. control com. 1980-83), Ohio Bar Assn., Greater Cleve. Bar Assn., Environ. Law Inst. Office: Jones Day N Point 901 Lakeside Ave E Cleveland OH 44114-1190 Office Phone: 216-586-7279. Business E-Mail: rrjanke@jonesday.com.

JANKI, DANIEL C., corporate financial executive; married; 2 children. BS fin. & acctg., Ohio State Univ., 1990. Fin. mgmt. positions GE, Fairfield, Conn., 1992—99; fin. mgr. E-Bus. GE Capital, 1999—2001; CFO GE Equity, Stamford, Conn., 2001—03; staff exec. corp. fin. GE, Fairfield, Conn., 2003—04; CFO GE Consumer Fin., 2004—06; v.p. investor comm. GE, Fairfield, Conn., 2006—. Office: GE 3135 Easton Tpke Fairfield CT 06431*

JANKLOW, MORTON LLOYD, lawyer, literary agent; b. NYC, May 30, 1930; s. Maurice and Lillian (Levantin) J.; m. Linda Mervyn LeRoy, Nov. 27, 1960; children: Angela LeRoy, Lucas Warner. AB, Syracuse U., 1950; JD, Columbia U., 1953. Bar: NY 1953, DC 1961, U.S. Dist. Ct. (so. and ea. dists) NY, U.S. Ct. Appeals (2d cir.), U.S. Supreme Ct. Chmn., CEO Morton L. Janklow Assocs., Inc., 1977-89; of counsel Janklow & Ashley, LLP, NYC, 1989—; sr. ptnr. Janklow & Nesbit Assocs., 1989—. Trustee Managed Accts. Svcs., PaineWebber PACE funds, 1996-2003; chmn. Janklow & Nesbit (U.K.); bd. dirs. Revlon, Inc., 1997-2000, Orbis Comm., Inc., N.Y.C., 1986-89; bd. dirs., mem. finance com. McCaffrey & McCall, Inc., N.Y.C., 1962-87; chmn. exec. com. Harvey Group, Inc., N.Y.C., 1968-71, Cable Funding Corp., N.Y.C., 1971-73; mem. exec. com. Sloan Commn. Cable Comm., 1970-71. Andrew Wellington Cordier fellow Columbia U. Sch. Internat. Affairs; vis. lectr. Radcliffe Coll., Columbia U. Law Sch., NYU; bus. and fin. adv. bd. NYU Press and NYU Sch. Arts, 1977—; donor, founder Morton L. Janklow Professorship of Lit. and Artistic Property, Columbia U. Sch. Law; life mem., Harlan Fiske Stone fellow of Columbia U. Law Sch.; founder Morton L. Janklow Program for Advocacy in the Arts, Columbia U. Law Sch.; mem. dean's coun. Columbia U. Law Sch., 1992—. Bd. dirs., exec. com., devel. chmn. City Center Music and Drama, 1971-75; bd. dirs. Film Soc., Lincoln Ctr., 1972-75, Am. Cinematheque, 1971-75; bd. govs. Jewish Mus., 1969-75; dir., chmn. Janklow Found.; trustee Mr. and Mrs. Harry M. Warner Found., 1965—, Sidney Sheldon Found.; mem. Council of Friends, Whitney Mus. Am. Art, 1973-82, also mem. com. on paintings and sculptures; ad hoc com. on pub. and merchandising activities Met. Mus. Art, 1998-03; bd. advisors Princeton U. Art. Mus., 1984-89; mem. adv. bd. Guggenheim Mus., 1980-86; adv. council Sch. Arts, NYU; mem. Ind. Com. on Arts Policy; bd. advisors Columbia U. Jour. Art and the Law; assn. of fellows Pierpoint Morgan Libr., NYC; founder Janklow program arts leadership Syracuse U. Served with AUS, 1953-55. Decorated chevalier l'Ordre des Arts et des Lettres de la Republique Française. Mem. ABA, N.Y. Bar Assn., Assn. of Bar of City of N.Y. (membership com. 1967—), N.Y. County Lawyers Assn., Fed. Comms. Bar Assn., Am. Judicature Soc., Coun. on Fgn. Rels., Com. on the Rsch. Librs., N.Y. Pub. Libr: chmn. Arthur Ross Book award Jury. Office: 445 Park Ave New York NY 10022-2606 Home Phone: 212-794-8844; Office Phone: 212-421-1700. E-mail: mjanklow@janklow.com.

JANKO, RICHARD CHARLES MURRAY, humanities educator; b. Weston Underwood, Eng., May 30, 1955; arrived in U.S., 1982; s. Charles Arthur Janko and Helen Murray; m. Michele Ann Hannoosh, May 26, 1984. BA with 1st class honors in Classics, Cambridge U., Eng., 1976; MA, Cambridge U., 1980, PhD in Classics, 1980. Temp. lectr. U. St. Andrews, Scotland, 1978—79; rsch. fellow Trinity Coll., Cambridge, 1979—82; from asst. prof. to assoc. prof. Columbia U., NYC, 1982—87; prof. classics UCLA, 1987—94; prof. greek Univ. Coll. London, 1995—2002; Gerald F. Else collegiate prof., chair classical studies U. Mich., Ann Arbor, 2003—. Editor Ayios Stephanos Excavations, 1989—; co-dir. Philodemus Translation Project, 1992—; mem. Inst. for Advanced Study, 2000. Author: (book) Homer, Hesiod and the Hymns, 1982, Aristotle on Comedy, 1984, Aristotle: Poetics, 1987, The Iliad: A Commentary, Vol. IV, 1992, Philodemus: On Poems Book I, 2000 (Mommsen prize, 2002, Goodwin award, 2002). Guggenheim Found. fellow, 1986—87, Nat. Humanities Ctr. fellow, 1990. Fellow: Am. Acad. Arts and Scis. Avocation: walking. Office: Univ of Michigan Dept Classical Studies Ann Arbor MI 48109

JANKOVIC, JOSEPH, neurologist, educator; b. Teplice, Czechoslovakia, Mar. 1, 1948; came to U.S., 1965; m. Cathy Sue Inselberg, May 26, 1973; children: Jason, Daniel, Zachary. MD, U. Ariz., 1973. Diplomate Am. Bd. Neurology. Med. intern Baylor Coll. Medicine, Houston, 1973-74, asst. prof. neurology, 1977-84, assoc. prof., 1984-88, prof., 1988—; resident in neurology Columbia U., NYC, 1974-76, chief resident in neurology, 1976-77. Dir. Parkinson's Disease Ctr. and Movement Disorder Clinic, Houston, 1977—; sr. attending physician Meth. Hosp., Houston, 1988—. Author over 500 articles and book chpts. in field; editor/co-editor 16 med. books; mem. editorial bd. jours. Movement Disorders, Clin. Neuropharmacology, Neurology Jour., Jour. Neurology Psychiatry. Chmn. sci. adv. bd. Blepharospasm Rsch. Found.; mem. adv. bd. Dystonia Med. Rsch. Found., Internat. Tremor Found., Tourette's Syndrome Med. Adv. Bd. Grantee disease rsch. founds., pharmaceutical cos., NIH Fellow Am. Acad. Neurology; mem. AMA, Am. Neurol. Assn., Soc. for Neurosci., Movement Disorders Soc. (pres.-elect 1991-94, pres. 1994-96). Avocations: tennis, music. Office: Baylor Coll Medicine 6550 Fannin St Ste 1801 Houston TX 77030-2744

JANKOWSKA, MARIA ANNA, school librarian, educator; b. Jarocin, Poland, Aug. 12, 1952; d. Tadeusz and Aleksandra (Ruszkowska) Nocun; m. Piotr L. Jankowski, Jan. 14, 1978; children: Pawel Pat, Marta Maja. MA, Sch. Econs., Poznan, Poland, 1975, PhD, 1983; M Libr. Info. Sci., U. Calif., Berkeley, 1989. Rsch. and tchg. asst. Sch. Econs., Poznan, 1976-83, asst. prof., 1983-85; catalog libr., asst. prof. U. Idaho, Moscow, 1989-94, network resources libr., 1995—, assoc. prof., 1995—2001, prof., 2001—. Author: Electronic Guide to Polish Research and University Libraries, 1996, Idaho Geospatial Data Center, 1998; founding editor Green Libr. Jour., 1991-94; gen. editor Electronic Green Jour., 1994—. Recipient Movers and Shakers award Libr. Jour., 2002; scholar Smithsonian Inst., Woodrow Wilson Internat. Ctr., Washington, 1985; fellow U Calif., Berkeley Sch. Libr. and Info. Studies, 1989, Fulbright Found., 2004-05; grantee Rsch. Coun. Grant, U. Idaho, 1990, 95, 2001, Internat. Rsch. and Exchs. Bd., Washington, 1995, 96 Mem. ALA (chair task force on environ. 1993-95, 98—), Idaho Libr. Assn., Beta Phi Mu. Office: U Idaho Libr PO Box 442350 Moscow ID 83844-2350 Office Phone: 208-885-6631. Office Fax: 208-885-6817. Business E-Mail: majanko@uidaho.edu.

JANKOWSKI, THEODORE ANDREW, artist; b. New Brunswick, NJ, Dec. 14, 1946; s. Theodore Andrew and Lois (Amarescu) J.; m. Rebecca Buck, July 23, 1983; 1 child, Tito Henry. Student, McMurrough Sch. Art, Indialantic, Fla., 1956-58, 74-75, R.I. Sch. Design, 1972, Cape Sch. of Art, Provincetown, Mass., 1975-76, 79-87, Cen. Fla. U., 1976-77. One-man shows include Eye of Horus Gallery, Provincetown, 1985; exhibited in group shows at Provincetown Art Assn. Mus., 1984, Bethlehem (Pa.) City Hall, 1988, Michael Ingbar Gallery, NYC, 1988, 91, Kameakmeaka Golf Course, 2007; represented in permanent collections at State Mus. at Palace of Peter the Gt., Leningrad, USSR, Cigna Mus. and Art Collection, Phila., Mishkan Olemanut Mus. Art, Israel, Novosibirsk (Russia) Picture Gallery, CIGNA Mus., Phila., Johns Hopkins U., Balt., Vassar Coll. portrait collection, Hiroshima Peace Meml. Mus., Hiroshima Japan - Hunter Mus. of Am. Art, Chattanooga, Holyoke (Mass.) Mus. Art, McGill U., Montreal, Que., Can., Downey (Calif.) Mus. Art, Ark. Art Ctr., Little Rock, Muzeum Niepoldlegosi, Warsaw, Poland, Nat. Mus. Bosnia, Sarajevo, Yad Vashem The Holocaust Martyrs and Heroes Art Mus., Jerusalem, Beloit Coll. Wright Mus. Art, Pradd Sch. Design, NYC, Mt. Holyoke Coll. Art Mus., Kokoiki Bapt. Ch. (mural), Hawaiian Royal Family, others Home: PO Box 791 Kapaau HI 96755-0791

JANN, GREGG, counselor, sales executive, consultant; b. Lexington, Nebr., Aug. 10, 1962; s. Donn Gerard and Alice Hartwell Jann; life ptnr. AS in Computer Sci., Santa Rosa Jr. Coll., Calif., 1982; BS in Mgmt. Sci., Calif. State U., Chico, 1986; BA in Bus. Econs., Sonoma State U., Rohnert Park, Calif., 1994. Sr. asst. mgr. F.W. Woolworth Co., San Francisco, 1988—91; coord., counselor Cmty. Support Network, Santa Rosa, Calif., 1999—; counselor Buckelew Programs, 2004—05; customer svc. mgr. Schwans Home Svc., 2005—06; owner, cons. Jann Demystifying Affects, 2005—. Chair Sonoma County Mental Health Bd., 1994—98; liaison Calif. Network Mental Health Clients, Sacramento, 1999—2002. V.p. Piner-Olivet Union Sch. Dist. Governing Bd., Santa Rosa, Calif., 1998—2005; pres. Santa Rosa Dem. Club, 1992—2006; adminstrv. coun. mem. Christ Ch. United Meth., Santa Rosa, 1994—2002; treas. Calif. Parenting Inst., Santa Rosa, 1998—2001. Recipient Redwood award, Sonoma County Office Edn., 1999. Mem.: Nat. Orgn. for Women (assoc.; invited candidate for candidates night), Sierra Club (assoc.). Achievements include design of California's proposition 63 mental health services act; face valve selling as original contribution to business service; creation of lost patents of wordsmith representation on internet and in medicine; patents for trademarks for jann demystifying affects and jannda. Avocations: rock audiophile, movies. Office: Jann Demystifying Affects PO Box 4207 Santa Rosa CA 95402 Home Phone: 707-292-5176; Office Phone: 707-889-0922. Office Fax: 707-237-6071; Home Fax: 707-237-6071.

JANNERS, ERIK NIKOLAS, music educator, conductor; b. Ft. Sam Houston, San Antonio, Jan. 8, 1972; s. Sigurds and Martha Janners. MusB, Alma Coll., 1994; MusM, U. Utah, 1997; D in Musical Arts, U. Ala., 2001. Dir. bands U. Regina, Sask., Canada, 2001—04, St. Xavier U., Chgo., 2004—. Dir. condr.'s workshop St. Xavier U., Chgo., 2004—. Contbr. articles to profl. publs. Mem. at large Sask. Band Assn., Canada, 2002—04. Mem.: World Assn. Symphonic Bands and Ensembles, Coll. Band Dirs. Nat. Assn., Music Educators Nat. Conf. Avocations: hiking, reading, travel, sports, fitness. Office: Saint Xavier U 3700 W 103rd St Chicago IL 60655 Home: 246 Indiana St Park Forest IL 60466 Home Phone: 708-748-0609; Office Phone: 773-298-3422. Personal E-mail: nikolas1972@hotmail.com. Business E-Mail: janners@sxu.edu.

JANNETTA, PETER JOSEPH, neurosurgeon, educator; b. Phila., Apr. 5, 1932; s. Samuel and Frances (Alfano) J.; m. Diana R. Jannetta, Sept. 9, 1989; children: Susan, Carol, Joanne, Peter, Elizabeth, S. Michael. AB, U. Pa., 1953, MD, 1957. Diplomate Am. Bd. Surgery, Am. Bd. Neurol. Surgery. Intern Hosp. U. Pa., 1957-58, resident in surgery, 1958-63; resident in neurosurgery, asso. UCLA Center for Health Scis., 1963-66; asst. instr. U. Pa., 1958-62, instr., 1960-63, instr. surgery, 1962-63; assoc. prof., chmn. surgery La. State U., 1966-71, prof., chmn. neurosurgery, 1971; prof. neurosurgery U. Pitts., 1971-76, Francis Sergeant Cheever Disting. prof., 1976-98, chmn. dept. neurol. surgery, 1976-2000, dir. divsn. neurol. surgery, 1973-2000; active staff Presbyn.-Univ. Hosp., Pitts., Children's Hosp. Pitts.; sr. attending staff Montefiore Hosp., Pitts.; sr. cons. VA Hosp., Pitts.; prof., vice chmn. dept. neurosurgery Allegheny Gen. Hosp. Sec. of health Commonwealth of Pa., 1995-96. Co-editor: The Cranial Nerves, 1981, Trigeminal Neuralgia, 1990; contbr. numerous articles to profl. jours. Mem. A.C.S., AMA, AAAS, Am. Surg. Assn., Allegheny County, Pa. med. socs., Assn. Academic Surgery, Am. Assn. Neurol. Surgeons, Congress Neurol. Surgeons, Fellowship Acad. Neurosurgeons, Internat. Assn. Study Pain, Internat. Soc. Pediatric Neurosurgery, Mid-Atlantic, Pa., Pitts. neurosurg. socs., N.Y. Acad. Scis., Pitts. Acad. Medicine, Pitts. Surg. Soc., Ravdin-Rhoads Surg. Soc., Research Soc. Neurol. Surgeons, Soc. Critical Care Medicine, Soc. Neurol. Surgeons, Soc. Neurosci., Soc. Neurosurg. Anesthesia and Neurol. Supportive Care. Office: Allegheny Gen Hosp Dept Neurosurgery 420 E North Ave Ste 302 Pittsburgh PA 15212

JANNEY, ALLISON, actress; b. Dayton, Ohio, Nov. 19, 1960; BA, Kenyon Coll.; pvt. studies in acting, Neighborhood Playhouse, NYC. Appeared in feature films: Big Night, 1996, Private Parts, 1997, Primary Colors, 1998, Six Days, Seven Nights, 1998, The Ice Storm, 1997, Celebrity, 1998, 10 Things I Hate About You, 1999, Drop Dead Gorgeous, 1999, Nurse Betty, 2000, American Beauty, 1999, Leaving Drew, 2000, Finding Nemo (voiceover), 2003, How to Deal, 2003, Over the Hedge (voice), 2006, Hairspray, 2007; plays (on Broadway) A View From The Bridge (Tony award nominee 1998, Outer Critics Circle award,Drama Desk award); appearances on TV: The West Wing (role C.J. Gregg), 1999-2006, (Emmy award Outstanding Lead Actress in a Drama Series, 2004), A Girl Thing (TV mini), 2000 Recipient Outstanding Featured Actress in a Play for "A View From the Bridge", Drama Desk Award, 1998, Outstanding Supporting Actress in a Drama Series for "The West Wing", Emmy Award, 1999, 2000, Best Actress in a Television Series Drama for "The West Wing", Golden Satellite, 2000, Best Ensemble Cast Performance for "The West Wing", 2000, Outstanding Female Actor in a Drama Series for "The West Wing", The Actor Awards, 2000, Outstanding Ensemble in a Drama Series for "The West Wing", 2000, Outstanding Supporting Actress in a Drama Series for "The West Wing", Emmy Awards, 2001, Outstanding Female Actor in a Drama Series for "The West Wing", The Actor Awards, 2001, Outstanding Ensemble in a Drama Series for "The West Wing", 2001, Outstanding Female Actress in a Drama Series for "The West Wing", Emmy Awards, 2002.*

JANNEY, CHRISTOPHER G., lawyer; b. Bethesda, Md., Feb. 14, 1964; BA summa cum laude, U. Md., 1986; JD cum laude, Harvard U., 1991. Bar: Md. 1991, DC 1993. Analyst Nat. Drug Policy Bd. US Dept. Justice, Washington, 1986—88; assoc. to ptnr. Shaw Pittman LLP, Washington; ptnr., health care group Sonnenschein Nath & Rosenthal LLP, Washington, 2003—. Mem.: ABA (mem. health law sect.), Am. Health Lawyers Assn. Office: Sonnenschein Nath & Rosenthal LLP Ste 600, E Tower 1301 K St NW Washington DC 20005 Office Phone: 202-408-6399, 202-408-9151. Business E-Mail: cjanney@sonnenschein.com.

JANNEY, DANIEL S., health products executive; BA, Georgetown U.; MBA, UCLA. V.p. health care and biotech. investment banking group Montgomery Securities, 1993—96; mng. dir. Alta Ptnrs., 1996—; chmn. bd. dirs. Dynavax Technologies Corp., Berkeley, Calif., 1996—, Corgentech, Inc. Mem. adv. bd. Rebecca and John Moores Cancer Ct., U.C.S.D. Office: Dynavax Technologies Corp 2929 7th St Ste 100 Berkeley CA 94710-2753

JANNEY, DONALD WAYNE, lawyer; b. Clinton, NC, Jan. 9, 1952; s. Wayne Columbus and Bernice (Talley) J.; m. Sydney Louise Rhame, May 28, 1977; children: Taylor Columbus, Camden St. Clair. BA, Furman U., 1974; JD, U. Va., 1978. Bar: Ga. 1978, US Dist. Ct. (no. dist.) Ga. 1978, US Ct. Appeals (11th cir.) 1982. Assoc. Troutman Sanders, Atlanta, 1978-85; ptnr. Troutman Sanders and predecessor firm, Atlanta, 1985—. Bd. dirs. State YMCA Ga., Atlanta, 1980-91. Mem. State Bar of Ga., Atlanta Bar Assn., Phi Beta Kappa. Baptist. Home: 705 E Morningside Dr Atlanta GA 30324-5220 Office: Troutman Sanders Ste 5200 600 Peachtree St NE Atlanta GA 30308-2216 Office Phone: 404-885-3000. E-mail: donald.janney@troutmansanders.com.

JANNEY, KAY PRINT, retired performing arts educator, theater director; b. Cleve., June 22, 1938; d. Walter James and Zenza Mae (Williams) Print; m. Frederick George Janney, Feb. 6, 1960; children: Brooke Hopkins, Eric Matthew, Catherine Marie. BA cum laude, Case We. Res. U., Cleve., 1959, MA, 1962. Copywriter Howard Marks Advt., Cleve., 1958—59; tchr. Speech, drama and English South-Euclid Lyndhurst Pub. Schs., Ohio, 1960—61, Lakewood Pub. Schs., Ohio, 1961—62; tchr. speech and drama, dept. head Berea H.S., Ohio, 1962—65; instr. comm. scis. U. Conn., Storrs, 1966—70, instr. comm. and dramatic arts Avery Point and Groton, 1971—74, asst. prof. comm. and dramatic arts, 1975—80, assoc. prof. comm. and dramatic arts, 1981—89, prof. dramatic arts, 1990—97, prof. emeritus, 1997—. Author: (monographs) A Bibliography on the Mask, 1989, Masks: The Power of Transformation-Put a New Face on Your Curriculum, 1989, Scriptsearch, 1988; book reviewer Speech Communication Teacher, 1990, Black Like My Soul Is Black (Michael Bradford), 1994-95; dir. (theatre prodns.) Mother Hicks, 1992, The Hide 'N Seek Odyssey of Madeline Gimple, 1991, The Angel With The Broken Wing, 1990, In A Room Somewhere, 1990, others; contbr. articles to profl. jours. Adjudicator Cmty. Theatre Coun., New London County, Conn., 1977, 93-97, chair of judges, 1987-89; various appts. P.E.O., 1980-; adjudicator Mass. Drama Guild, 1986-93, Conn. Drama Assn., 1989; state bd. govs. Ballard State Mus. and Inst., 2005—, Mus. Puppetry, 2005—; ch. moderator Mystic Congl. Ch., 2005-. Named to Parma City (Ohio) Schs. Hall of Fame. Mem. AAUW, Am. Alliance for Theatre and Edn. (co-chair, founder mid./jr. H.S. program com. 1972—, chair membership com. 1989, bd. dirs. 1988-91, chair conv. 1993), New Eng. Theatre Conf. (chair children's theatre divsn. 1986-89, judge John Gassner Meml. Playwriting Contest 1989-95, v.p. nat. conf. 1993, coll. fellows 1993—), Conn. Alliance for Arts, Ballard Inst., Mus. of Puppetry (chair 1995-2003, adv. 2003—). Republican. Avocations: music, needlecrafts, travel.

JANNEY, OLIVER JAMES, lawyer; b. NYC, Feb. 11, 1946; s. Walter Coggeshall and Helen Jennings (James) Janney; m. Suzanne Elizabeth Lenz, June 21, 1969; children: Elizabeth Flower, Oliver Burr. BA cum laude, Yale U., 1967; JD, Harvard U., 1970. Bar: Mass. 1970, N.Y. 1971, Fla. 1991. With Walston & Co., Inc., NYC, 1970—73, asst. v.p., 1971-73; assoc. Cleary Gottlieb, Steen & Hamilton, NYC, 1973-76; with RKO Gen., Inc., NYC, 1976-90, asst. sec., 1977-85, asst. gen. atty., 1978-82, asst. gen. counsel, 1982-85, sec., gen. counsel, 1985-89; exec. v.p., gen. counsel, sec. Uniroyal Tech. Corp., Sarasota, Fla., 1990—2003; ptnr. Janney & Curd, LLP, 2005—06; mng. atty. Robbins Equitas, 2006—. 1st lt. USAR, 1969—77. Mem.: ABA, Fla. Bar Assn., Sarasota County Bar Assn., N.Y. State Bar Assn., Am. Corp. Counsel Assn. Republican. Home: 8555 Woodbriar Dr Sarasota FL 34238-5664 Office: Robbins Equitas 2639 Martin Luther King Jr St N Saint Petersburg FL 33704 Office Phone: 941-684-3314, 727-822-8696. Business E-Mail: ojjanney@floridalawyer.com, ojjanney@robbinslaw.org.

JANNEY, STUART SYMINGTON, III, investment company executive; b. Balt., Aug. 30, 1948; s. Stuart Symington and Barbara (Phipps) J.; m. Lynn Mary Buchheit, Oct. 28, 1975; children: Emily, Matthew. BA, U. N.C., 1970; JD, U. Md., 1973. Bar: Md. 1973. Legis. asst. Sen. Charles Mathias U.S. Senate, Washington, 1973-75, fgn. policy asst. Sen. Howard Baker, 1976-77; spl. asst. U.S. Sec. State U.S. State Dept., Washington, 1975-76; ptnr. Niles, Barton & Wilmer, Balt., 1977-86; mng. dir. Alex Brown & Sons, Balt., 1986-94; head Alex. Brown Asset Mgmt., Balt., 1986-93; chmn. bd. Bessemer Trust Co., NYC, 1994—, Bessemer Securities Corp., NYC, 1994—. Bd. dirs. Johns Hopkins U., Balt., 1988—, vice chmn., 1995-2002; chmn. bd. dirs. Johns Hopkins U. Applied Physics Lab., 1991—, Md. Zool. Soc., Balt., 1979—; bd. dirs. Md. Horsebreeders, 1991-98; bd. dirs. Thoroughbred Owners and Breeders Am.; bd. dirs. Keeneland Assocs., Nat. Audubon Soc., N.Y.C., 1982-92; steward Jockey Club U.S. Mem.: NY Racing Assn. (bd. dirs.). Office: Bessemer Trust Co 630 5th Ave New York NY 10111-0100

JANNINI, RALPH HUMBERT, III, electronics executive; b. Boston, Dec. 30, 1932; s. Humbert P. and Marian H. (Roman) J.; m. Pauline T. Occhinto, Feb. 16, 1957; children: Ralph H. IV, Mark L., Lisa M. BS in Acctg., Bentley Coll., 1957. CPA, Mass. Auditor New Eng. Electric System, Westboro, Mass., 1957-68, mgr. rates and statistics, 1968-73; asst. to pres. Gas Inc.-Colonial, Lowell, Mass., 1973-76; v.p. Colonial Gas Co., Lowell, 1976-87; pres. James Millen Electronics, Malden, Mass., 1988—. Cons. Antennas Etc., Andover, Mass., 1980—; prin. Unadilla/Reyco/InLine Products, 1986—, Andover Book and Collaborative, 1995—. Served with U.S. Army, 1952-53, Korea. Republican. Roman Catholic. Office: James Millen Electronics 87 Belmont St North Andover MA 01845-2304

JANNOTTI, GENE PATRICK, business consultant, telecommunications professional; b. Newburgh, NY, Oct. 10, 1946; s. Pellegrino and Anne J BS Math., Siena Coll., 1968; MA Math., St. John's U., 1970; MS Bus. Policy, Columbia U., 1981. Cert. sys. profl. Asst. programmer N.Y. Tel., NYC, 1971—72, mgr. computer ops., 1973—80, staff mgr., 1980—84; programmer Bell Labs., Greensboro, NC, 1972—73; dist. mgr. Bell Comm. Rsch., Piscataway, NJ, 1984—87; staff dir. NYNEX Corp. Comm., NYC, 1987—89, NYNEX Videoteleconferencing, NYC, 1989—91; dir. ops. NYNEX Computer Ops., Pearl River, NY, 1991; dir. NYNEX Software Devel., NYC, 1992—95; founder, pres. Llewellyn Cons. Assocs., Westfield, NJ, 1995—99; prin. cons. Computer Scis. Corp., 1999—; founder Unique Cruise and Travel, 2000—, prin., owner Garwood, NJ, 2000—. Capt. USAR, 1968-74 Mem. Data Processing Mgmt. Assn. (bd. dirs. N.Y. chpt. 1980-84, exec. v.p. 1984), Project Mgmt. Inst., Livingston Lodge # 11, Free and Accepted Masons (past master bd. trustees), Shriners, Tall Cedars Lebanon, Ancient Order Sciots, Ancient Accepted Scottish Rite. Roman Catholic. Avocations: travel, gardening, photography. Home and Office: PO Box 267 Garwood NJ 07027-0267 E-mail: genej@homemail.com.

JANNUZI, BUELL T., astronomer; m. Alison Lowell Jannuzi; 2 children. AB in Astronomy & Astrophysics, Harvard Coll., 1984; PhD in Astronomy & Astrophysics, U. Ariz., 1990. Mem. Inst. Advanced Study, Princeton, NJ, 1990—95; mem. sci. staff Nat. Optical Astronomy Obs., Tucson, 1995, co-prin. investigator Deep Wide-Field Survey; acting dir. Kitt Peak Nat. Obs., Tucson, 2005—07, dir., 2007—. Mem. US Gemini Sci. Adv. Com., 1995—2000, Gemini Sci. Com., 1996—2000, Space Infrared Telescope Facility User's Panel, 1998—; coord. Rsch. Experience for Undergraduates prog. Kitt Peak Nat. Obs., 1997—2000. Contbr. articles to sci. jours. Office: NOAO 950 N Cherry Ave Tucson AZ 85719 Office Phone: 520-318-8283. E-mail: jannuzi@noao.edu.*

JANNUZI, F. TOMASSON, economics professor; b. Pitts., Apr. 23, 1934; s. Frank Humbert and Angela Mary (Tomasson) J.; m. Barbara Lucille Gallagher, Sept. 15, 1957; children: Buell Tomasson, Frank Sampson. AB, Dartmouth Coll., 1955; PhD in Econ., U. London, 1958. Field rep. for So. Asia, E. Africa Found. For Youth and Student Affairs, NYC, 1959-61; asst. rep. The Asia Found., NYC, 1961-62, program officer for So. Asia div. San Francisco, 1962-65, asst. rep. for India, 1965-68; vis. lectr. in econs. U. Tex., Austin, 1968-72, dir. at the Ctr. for Asian Studies, Nat. Resource Ctr. for So. Asia, 1972-86, assoc. prof. of econs., 1973-79, prof. of econs. and Asian studies, 1979-98, assoc. chmn. dept. econs., 1995-97, prof. emeritus econs., 1998—. Pres. Asia Rsch. Assoc. Inc., Austin, Tex., 1985-99; vis. fellow Internat. Devel. Ctr. U. Oxford, Eng., 1989-92; sr. assoc. St. Antony's Coll. Oxford, 1989; vis scholar Ctr. for South Asian Studies, U. Va., 1999—; cons. USAID, Dept. State, Def. Intelligence Coll., World Bank, 1973—. Author: Agrarian Crisis in India: The Case of Bihar, 1974, India in Transition: Issues of Political Economy in a Plural Society, 1988; India's Persistent Dilemma: The Political Economy of Agrarian Reform, 1994; co-author: (with James T. Peach) The Agrarian Structure of Bangladesh, 1980; contbr. articles to profl. jours. Dir. Austin Coun. on Fgn. Affairs Inc., Tex., 1987-98; mem. Inst. of Current World Affairs, Hanover, N.H., 1987—98; trustee Am. Inst. of Indian Studies, Chgo., 1973-87, chmn. 1979-81. Ford Found. fellow. Mem.: Phi Beta Kappa. Democrat. Avocation: travel. Home: 1835 Mountainside Dr Blacksburg VA 24060-9203 Home Phone: 540-961-2904. Personal E-mail: ftjannuzi@msn.com.

JANOLLARI, DAVID, television broadcasting executive, cable and television producer; With Nederlander TV Prodn., NY; dir. comedy devel. Fox Broadcasting; v.p. comedy devel. Warner Bros. TV Network, 1991—93, sr. v.p. comedy devel., 1993—95, exec. v.p. creative affairs, 1995—97, pres. entertainment, 2004—; co-founder, pres. Greenblatt Janollari Studio, 1997—2004. Exec. prodr.: (TV series) The Hughleys, 1998—2002, To Have & to Hold, 1998, Maggie Winters, 1998—99; exec. prodr.: (TV series) OH Grow Up, 1999; exec. prodr.: (TV series) Heat Vision and Jack, 1999, Chicks, 1999, The Chronicle, 2001—02, One on One, 2001—, Definitely Maybe, 2001; exec. prodr.: (TV series) Six Feet Under, 2001—; exec. prodr.: (TV series) American Family, 2002—04, Platinum, 2003, Eve, 2003—. Office: WB Network 4000 Warner Blvd Burbank CA 91522

JANOS, ELLEN L., lawyer; b. 1951; BA with honors, Simmons Coll., 1973; JD magna cum laude, New Eng. Sch. Law, 1977. Bar: Mass. 1977, US Supreme Ct. 1984, US Ct. Appeals (1st Cir.). Adminstrv. counsel Mass. Atty. Gen. Office; asst. atty. gen. Commonwealth of Mass.; ptnr., Health Care Sect. Mintz Levin Cohn Ferris Glovsky & Popeo PC, Boston, coord., Fraud & Abuse &,Corp. Compliance Practice Group. Contbr. editor Health Care Fraud & Abuse Newsletter, NY Law Pub. Co., spkr. in field. Mem. Mass. Bd. Medicine Task Force, 1992. Office: Mintz Levin Cohn Ferris Glovsky & Popeo PC One Financial Ctr Boston MA 02111 Office Phone: 617-348-1662. Office Fax: 202-542-2241. Business E-Mail: ejanos@mintz.com.

JANOS, JAMES See VENTURA, JESSE

JANOSKI, HENRY VALENTINE, investment advisor, former banker; b. Nanticoke, Pa., Feb. 14, 1933; s. Bruce and Marie (Rozmarek) J.; m. Rita Rosemary Ruane, Sept. 27, 1980; children: Maria, Elizabeth. BA magna cum laude, Yale U., 1955; MBA, U. Pa., 1960. CFA, CSA. Sr. credit analyst Nat Bank Detroit, 1960-63; asst. cashier First Nat. Bank, Wilkes-Barre, Pa., 1963-65; sr. v.p. Northeastern Bank, Scranton, Pa., 1965-80; investment counselor, fin. planner Clarks Summit and Scranton, Pa., 1980-92; realtor assoc. Clarks Summit, 1992; chief trust investment officer Penn Security Bank and Trust Co., Scranton, 1992—2001; sr. investment officer Linden Asset Mgmt., Inc., Scranton, Pa., 2002—05; sr. investment advisor Northeastern Fin. Cons., Inc., Clarks Summit, Pa., 2005—07; registed investment advisor Janoski Investment Adv. Svc. LLC, Clarks Summit, 2007—. Instr. fin. Marywood Coll., Scranton, 1983. Bd. dirs. Cmty. Med. Ctr., Scranton, 1974-97, asst. treas., 1976-91; bd. dirs. Emergency Med. Svcs. Northeastern Pa., Pittston, 1976—, pres., 1985-87; bd. dirs. Polish Am. Congress No. Pa. divsn., Scranton, 1972—, v.p., 1972-89, pres., 1989-2004; bd. dirs. Ethics Inst. N.E. Pa., Dallas, 1991-96; bd. dirs. Keystone chpt. Am. Heart Assn., Scranton, 1968-74, treas., 1968-74; chmn. Campaign for Yale U., Northeastern Pa., 1976-78; incorporating dir. Lackawanna County U.S. Constn. Bicentennial Commn., 1987-88; mem. Lackawanna County Commrs. Transition Task Force for Fin./Budget, 2003-04; treas. Grove St. Home Sch. Assn., Clarks Summit, 1987-90; lectr. Christ the King Ch., Dunmore, 1982-87, Our Lady of the Snows Ch., Clarks Summit, 1987—, Ch. of St. Benedict, Newton Twp., 1991—; allocations vol. United Way, 1988-91, 2002-05. 1st lt. AUS, 1955-57. Recipient Assn. U.S. Army award, 1954, Disting. Mil. Student award, 1955, Am. Legion award, 1947, 51, Cert. Leadership Lackawanna, 1989. Mem. CFA Soc. Phila., CFA Inst., Soc. Cert. Sr. Advisors, Estate Planning Coun. Northeastern Pa., Experiment in Internat. Living (France), Le Cercle Francais (treas. 1994-2004), Ecologia/Ekologiya, Luzerne County Hist. Soc., Nanticoke Hist. Soc., Greater Scranton C. of C., Esperanto League for N.Am., Universala Esperanto Asocio, Polish Nat. Alliance, Polish Falcons Am., Polish Am. Hist. Assn., Kosciuszko Found., Assn. Yale Alumni (rep. 1988-91), Aircraft Owners and Pilots Assn., Schultzville Airport Pilots Assn., Westmoreland Club (Wilkes-Barre), Scranton Club, Yale Club of Northeastern Pa. (sec. 1985-88, alumni sch. com. interviewed applicants 1965-98), U. Pa. Alumni Club of Northeastern Pa., Leadership Lackawanna Alumni Assn., Phi Beta Kappa. Republican. Roman Catholic. Avocations: travel, languages. Home: 107 Carteret Dr Clarks Summit PA 18411-1009 Office: Janoski Investment Adv Svc LLC 3 Abington Exec Park Ste 9 Clarks Summit PA 18411 Office Phone: 570-586-1064. Personal E-mail: HJanoski@aol.com.

JANOWITZ, JAMES ARNOLD, lawyer; b. NYC, Sept. 2, 1946; s. Arnold and Erna (Frankel) J.; m. Katherine Eva Sborovy, Aug. 6, 1967; children: Jessie Elizabeth, William Aaron. BA, Haverford Coll., 1967; JD, NYU, 1971. Bar: N.Y. 1972, U.S. Dist Ct. (so. dist.) N.Y. 1972. Tchr. St. David's Sch., NYC, 1968-72; assoc. Guzik & Boukstein, NYC, 1972-73, Reavis & McGrath, NYC, 1973-74, Pryor, Cashman & Sherman, NYC, 1974-76; ptnr. Pryor, Cashman, Sherman & Flynn, NYC, 1977—. Adj. prof. Cardozo Law Sch., Yeshiva U., N.Y.C., 1992; bd. dirs. Avenue Entertainment, 1986-99. Editor NYU Jour. Internat. Law and Politics, 1970-71. Mem. N.Y. State Bar Assn., Assn. of Bar of City of N.Y. Office: Pryor Cashman Sherman & Flynn 410 Park Ave Fl 10 New York NY 10022-4407

JANOWITZ, JEFFREY MARK, management consultant; b. NYC, June 12, 1952; s. Irving and Sabina Janowitz; life ptnr. Arthur Talamantes Zabala, Feb. 27, 2004. BA, CUNY, 1973; MA, U. Birmingham, England, 1974; MSW, U. Md., 1980; PhD, NC State U., 1992. LCSW clin. social worker NC. Therapist Choice Points, Cary, NC, 1983—94; pres. CONDUIT, Cary, 1987—94; vis. asst. prof. psychology Guilford Coll., Greensboro, NC, 1991—94; gen. mgr. Ctr. Profl. Devel., Inc., Santa Cruz, Calif., 1994—2000; practice leader, consullting services Kaiser Found. Health Plan, Inc., Oakland, Calif., 2001—02; sr. cons., global client mgr. Pers. Decisions Internat., San Mateo, Calif., 2003—05; sr. cons., practice leader Hay Group, Walnut Creek, Calif., 2005—. Mem.: NASW, APA. Home: 530 Queens Rd Alameda CA 94501 Home Phone: 510-749-0351; Office Phone: 925-279-3726.

JANSEEN, FAMKE, actress; b. Amsterdam, Noord-Holland, Netherlands, Nov. 5, 1965; m. Tod Williams, 1995 (div. 2000). Actor: (films) Fathers and Sons, 1992, Relentless IV: Ashes to Ashes, 1994, Lord of Illusions, 1995, GoldenEye, 1995, Dead Girl, 1996, City of Industry, 1997, Snitch, 1998, The Gingerbread Man, 1998, Deep Rising, 1998, RPM, 1998, Celebrity, 1998, Rounders, 1998, The Adventures of Sebastian Cole, 1998, The Faculty, 1998, House on Haunted Hill, 1999, Love and Sex, 2000, Circus, 2000, X-Men, 2000, Made, 2001, Don't Say a Word, 2001, I Spy, 2002, X2: X-Men United, 2003, Eulogy, 2004, Family of the Year, 2004, Hide and Seek, 2005; (TV films) Model by Day, 1994; TV appearances include: Star Trek: The Next Generation, 1992; Melrose Place, 1994; The Untouchables, 1994; Ally McBeal, 2000, 2001; Dinner for Five, 2002, 2003; Nip/Tuck, 2004. Office: Creative Artist Agency 9830 Wilshire Blvd Beverly Hills CA 90212-1825

JANSEN, ANGELA BING, artist, educator; b. NYC, Aug. 17, 1929; d. Lester and Jean Bing; m. Gunther Jansen, Mar. 8, 1956; children—Edmund, Douglas. BA, Bklyn. Coll., 1951; MA, NYU, 1953; student, Bklyn. Mus. Art Sch., 1947-50, Atelier 17, NYC, 1950-52. Tchr, art, public schs., NYC, 1954-60. One-man shows: Madison (Wis.) Art Center, 1977, Gimpel & Weitzenhoffer, N.Y.C., 1974, 78, group shows: Bklyn. Mus., 1950, 70, 76, Library of Congress, Washington, 1969, 71, Ljubijana Internat. Print Biennale, Yugoslavia, 1971, 73, 75, 77, Venice Biennale, 1972, Internat. Exhbn. Drawing, Rejeka, Yugoslavia, 1972 (award), Internat. Print Biennale, Cracow, Poland, 1978; represented in permanent collections: Mus. Modern Art, N.Y.C., Met. Mus. Art, N.Y.C., N.Y. Pub. Library, Art Inst. Chgo., Tate Gallery, London, Victoria and Abert Mus., London, Bibliotheque Nationale, Paris, Bklyn. Mus., Phila. Mus. Art, Fonds d'Art Contemporain, Centre de Recherche et d'Etude de la Sculpture Contemporaine, Mauberge, France, Musée du Petit Format, Couvin, Belgium, Bklyn. Mus., Francine Tyler Art Forum, summer, 1979. Nat. Endowment for Arts grantee, 1974—75. Personal E-mail: ghjansen@aol.com.

JANSEN, DANIEL ERVIN, former professional speedskater, marketing professional, former olympic athlete; b. Milw., June 17, 1965; s. Harry William and Geraldine (Grajek) J.; m. Robin Wicker, Apr. 28, 1990 (div.); children: Jane Danielle, Olivia Renee. Student, U. Wis., Milw., 1986, 87, 89. Speed skater U.S. Olympic Com., Colorado Springs, Colo.; pro tour speedskater; sports mktg. profl. Miller Brewing Co., Milw., 1988—; skating coach Chicago Blackhawks, 2005—. Overall World Cup Champion Internat. Skating Union, 1986, 87, 92, 93, 94, World Sprint Champion, 1988, 94; recipient Gold medal for 1000m men's speedskating Lillehammer Winter Olympic Games, 1994. Roman Catholic. Achievements include 46 World Cup victories, 75 World Cup medals, setting world record for 1000m race in 12.43 seconds, Lillehammer Winter Olympic Games, 1994; inducted into US Olympic Hall of Fame, 2004.

JANSEN, DONALD ORVILLE, lawyer; b. Odessa, Tex., Nov. 17, 1939; s. Orville Charles and Dolores Elizabeth J.; m. E. Janice Law; children: Donald Orville, Lauren, Christine, David, Margaret. BBA magna cum laude, Loyola U., New Orleans, 1961, JD cum laude, 1963; LLM, Georgetown U., 1966. Bar: La. 1963, Tex. 1965. Sr. ptnr. Fulbright and Jaworski, Houston, 1966—2005; sr. tax counsel U. Tex. Sys., 2007—. Served to capt. JAGC US Army, 1963—66. Mem. ABA, Fed. Bar Assn. State Bar Tex., La. Bar Assn., Am. Coll. Trust and Estate Counsel, Am. Coll. Tax Coun. Roman Catholic. Home: 5137 Doliver Dr Houston TX 77056 Office: U Tex Sys Office Gen Counsel 201 W 7th St Austin TX 78701 Office Phone: 512-499-4493. Personal E-mail: djansen@fulbright.com.

JANSEN, G. THOMAS, dermatologist; b. Manitowoc, Wis., July 16, 1926; s. Gerald M. and Sarah (Grady) J.; m. Frances Bovick, Sept. 6, 1952; children: Mark, Kurt, Anne, Drew, Fran. BS, U. Wis., Madison, 1948, MD, 1950. Diplomate: Am. Bd. Dermatology (pres. 1985-86). Intern Med. Coll. of Va., 1950-51; resident in dermatology U. Wis., 1953-54, U. Mich., 1954-56; practice medicine specializing in dermatology Little Rock, 1956—2004; pres. Little Rock Dermatology Clinic, 1968—2004; ret., 2004. Mem. faculty U. Ark. Med. Center, 1956—2004, prof. dermatology, 1965—2004, prof. emeritus, 2004—, chmn. dept., 1965-82; mem. staff Doctors Hosp., U. Ark. Hosp., St. Vincent Infirmary, Bapt. Hosp.; pres. Am. Dermatology Found., 1980-81 Served as officer M.C. USNR, 1951-54. Recipient Disting. Svc. award, Am. Bd. Dermatologists, 1987, Finnerud award, 1996, Alumni citation, U. Wis. Med. Sch., 2002. Mem. AMA, Am. Dermatol. Assn. (pres. 1993), Am. Acad. Dermatology (asst. sec.-treas. 1980-83, sec.-treas. 1983-85, pres.-elect 1987, pres. 1988, hon. 1991, Master in Dermatology 1991, Everett C. Fox Lectureship award 1995, Gold medal 1997), Soc. Investigative Dermatology, Nat. Program Dermatology, Am. Coll. Chemosurgery, So. Med. Assn. (pres. 1976-77, Disting. Svc. award 1991), Ark. Med. Soc., Ark. Dermatol. Soc., Pulaski County Med. Soc. (A Lifetime of Outstanding Contbns. to Medicine award 2004), Alpha Omega Alpha. Roman Catholic. Home: 6601 Pleasant Pl Little Rock AR 72205-2868 Office: 500 S University Ave Ste 501 Little Rock AR 72205-5307

JANSEN, JAMES STEVEN, lawyer; b. Marshalltown, Iowa, Mar. 16, 1948; s. Virgil Charles and Virginia Rae (Hiatt) J.; m. Patricia Jean Beard, Nov. 24, 1984; children: Katherine, Emily, Ashley, Kristen. BS in Edn., U. Nebr., 1970; JD, Creighton U., 1973. Bar: Nebr. 1974, U.S. Dist. Ct. Nebr.

1974. Dep. county atty. County of Douglas, Omaha, 1974-78, county atty., 1991—2003; assoc. Naviaux, Kinney, Jansen and Dosek, Omaha, 1979-83; from assoc. to ptnr. Stave, Coffey, Swenson, Jansen and Schatz, Omaha, 1984—90; assoc. atty. McGrath, North, Mullin and Kratz PC LLO, Omaha, 2003—05, ptnr., 2005—. Bd. dirs. Domestic Violence Coord. Coun. Greater Omaha, 1996-2003, co-chair, 1996-97, chmn., 1997-98; bd. dirs. Omaha Cmty. Partnership, 1991-2003, chmn., 2000-01; mem. Nebr. Drug and Violent Crime Policy Bd., Lincoln, 1991-98, bd. dirs. Project Harmony Child Protection Ctr., 1996—, chmn., 1998. Mem. Nebr. State Bar Assn., Omaha Bar Assn., Nebr. County Atty.'s Assn. (bd. dirs. 1991—98, pres. 1997-98). Democrat. Roman Catholic. Avocations: golf, reading. Office: McGrath North Mullin and Kratz PC LLD 3700 First National Tower 1601 Dodge St Omaha NE 68102 Office Phone: 402-341-3070. Business E-Mail: jjansen@mcgrathnorth.com.

JANSEN, LAMBERTUS, retired state agency administrator, judge, criminal justice educator; b. Salt Lake City, Oct. 27, 1934; s. Lambertus Christianus and Cobi Maria (van Ekelenburg) J.; m. Rosemary Van Dyke, Aug. 22, 1958 (div. 1969); children: Jackie Lyn, David Scott; m. LaNita Joyce Lindley, Sept. 10, 1982. AA, Westminster Coll., Salt Lake City, 1954, BS, 1959; JD, U. Utah, 1968. Bar: Utah 1968, NY 1983. Tchr. English Jordan Sch. Dist., Sandy, Utah, 1959-62; fraud investigator Utah Job Svc., Salt Lake City, 1962-65; instr. U. Utah, Salt Lake City, 1965-68; lawyer Jansen Law Office, Salt Lake City, 1968-83, Hyatt Legal Svc., Syracuse, NY, 1983-87, Shanley Law Office, Oswego, NY, 1987-92; city ct. judge Oswego, 1992-2000; hearing officer Utah Dept. Health, Salt Lake City, 2000—05; ret. Adj. prof. criminal justice Salt Lake C.C. Dir. Utah Housing Devel. Agy., Salt Lake City, 1969-71; mem. steering com. Oswego County Anti-Drug Program, 1996-97; mem. Oswego County Drug Ct. Program, 1996-97. Mem. Am. Judges Assn., NY State City Ct. Judges Assn., Am. Trial Lawyers Assn., Utah State Bar, Utah Bar Assn., Salt Lake County Bar. Roman Catholic. Avocations: skiing, hiking, golf, camping. Home: 1382 E 850 N Tooele UT 84074-9026

JANSEN, MICHAEL JOHN, health facility administrator; b. Swannanoa, NC, July 24, 1945; s. Edward John and Mary Bernadette (Haughian) J.; m. Roxanne Shellenberger, June 27, 1970 (div. May 1992); m. Linda Kathryn Hughes, Aug. 21, 1993; children: Kathryn Anne, Victoria Elizabeth. BS in BA, U. S.C., 1967; M. Health Adminstrn., Duke U., 1976. Adminstrv. asst. Watts Hosp., Durham, NC, 1976-77; asst. dir. Durham County Gen. Hosp., 1977-80; asst. adminstr. St. Joseph's Hosp., Atlanta, 1980-83, sr. v.p., COO, 1983-89; group v.p. SunHealth, Charlotte, NC, 1989-90; sr. assoc. adminstr., COO Cape Fear Valley Health Sys., Fayetteville, NC, 1991-2001; CEO MedAccom, Research Triangle Park, NC, 2001—03; adminstr. Breezewood Family Healthcare, Fayetteville, NC, 2003—. Bd. dirs. St. Joseph's Hosp., Atlanta, 1985-89, Fayetteville Symphony Orch., 1993-95, United Way of Cumberland County, Fayetteville, 1993-95; chmn. bd. dirs. Shared Svcs. for So. Hosps., Atlanta, 1986-87. Capt. USAF, 1967-72, Col. USAFR, 1990-96. Recipient Falcon award/Spaatz award Civil Air Patrol, 1967. Fellow Am. Coll. Healthcare Execs. Office: Breezewood Family Healthcare PA PO Box 87448 Fayetteville NC 28304-7448

JANSEN, ROBERT BRUCE, consulting civil engineer; b. Spokane, Wash., Dec. 14, 1922; s. George Martin and Pearl Margaret (Kent) Jansen; m. Barbara Mae Courtney, Sept. 18, 1943. BSCE, U. Denver, 1949; MSCE, U. So. Calif., LA, 1955. Registered profl. engr., Calif., Wash. Chief Calif. Div. Dam Safety, Sacramento, 1965-68; chief of ops. Calif. Dept. Water Resources, Sacramento, 1968-71, dep. dir., 1971-75, chief design and constrn., 1975-77; asst. commr. US Bur. Reclamation, Denver, 1977-80; cons. civil engr., 1980—. Cons. TVA, Chattanooga, 1981—2003, So. Calif. Edison Co., Rosemead, 1982—2002, Pacific Gas and Electric, San Francisco, 1982—93, Hydro-Quebec, Montreal, 1986—98, Ala. Power Co., Birmingham, 1986—2006, Ga. Power Co., 1989—94. Author: Dams and Public Safety, 1983; editor: Safety of Existing Dams, 1983; co-author: Development of Dam Engineering in the United States, 1988; editor, co-author: Advanced Dam Engineering for Design, Construction, and Rehabilitation, 1988. Mem. US Soc. on Dams (chmn.1979-81), ASCE, NAE (elected). Home and Office: 509 Briar Rd Bellingham WA 98225-7811

JANSKY, JEANNETTE JEFFERSON, learning disabilities specialist; b. Urbana, Ill., Nov. 27, 1927; d. Bernard Levi and Irma Nicholson (Williams) Jefferson; m. Curtis Moreau Jansky, Aug. 14, 1949 (div. 1976); 1 child, Matthew Jefferson. BS, U. Ill., Urbana, 1949; MS in Pre-Clinical Psychology, CCNY, 1960; PhD in Edn. Psychology, Columbia U., 1970. Speech therapist Blythedale Convalescent Home, Valhalla, N.Y., 1950-51; clinician Lang. Disorder Clinic Columbia-Presbyn. Med. Ctr., NYC, 1951-57, 65-72, dir. Lang. Disorder Clinic, 1972-74, dir. de Hirsch Robinson Reading Clinic, 1974—. Pvt. practice learning disabilities specialist, N.Y.C., 1951-2005; mem. adv. bd. Fisher-Landau Found., N.Y.C., 1986-91; coun. advisors Internat. Dyslexia Assn., 1993—; cons. Knowledge is Power Program, Charter Sch., 2001-04. Author (with K. de Hirsch): Predicting Reading Failure, 1966, Preventing Reading Failure, 1972; contbr. chpts. to books; assoc. editor Annals of Dyslexia. Recipient N.Y. State award Orton Soc., 1977, Samuel T. Orton award, 1995, Priscilla L. Vail Language award for Lifetime Achievement, 2006; grantee Health Research Council N.Y., 1966, Babies Hosp. Fund, 1966, Bienecke Found., 1974, 82. Fellow Am. Orthopsychiat. Assn.; mem. Am. Psychol. Assn., Internat. Reading Assn., Orton-Dyslexia Soc., Sigma Xi. Clubs: Cosmopolitan (N.Y.C.); Columbia U. Faculty (N.Y.C.). Democrat. Presbyterian. Avocations: travel, bridge. Home and Office: 120 E 89th St New York NY 10128-1516

JANSON, JULIA S., energy executive; m. Chip Janson; children: Jennifer, Rachel. BA in Am. Studies, Georgetown Coll., Ky.; JD, U. Cin., 1988. Bar: Ohio 1988, Ky. Law clk. Adams, Brooking, Stepner, Wolterman & Dusing, Covington, Ky., Cin. Gas & Electric Co., 1987—88, supr. securities processing, transfer agt. common and preferred stock, 1988—93; corp. atty., key mem. legal team responsible for completing merger of Cin. Gas & Electric Co. and PSI Energy Cinergy Corp., 1993—94, mgr. investor rels., 1995—96, counsel, 1996—98, sr. counsel, 1998—2004, corp. sec., 2000—06, chief compliance officer, 2004—06; sr. v.p. ethics and compliance, corp. sec. Duke Energy, Charlotte, NC, 2006—. Bd. dirs. Lighthouse Youth Svcs., 2000—01. Office: Duke Energy 526 S Church St Charlotte NC 28202-1904 Office Phone: 704-594-6200.*

JANSON, PATRICK, vocalist, educator, actor; b. Cleve., Oct. 10, 1967; s. Robert L. and Gloria Ann (Dominguez) J.; m. Christine Marie Fondaw, June 8, 1991; children, Emma Susanne, Madison Ann. MusB, Baldwin-Wallace Coll., 1990. Singer, actor, dir., mus. dir., condr. various theatres and opera cos., 1990—; tchr. music St. Joseph Acad., Cleve., 1990-91, 98—, Univ. Sch., Hunting Valley, Ohio, 1991-92; tchr. Perry-Mansfield Performing Arts Camp, Steamboat Springs, Colo., summer 1993, 95, Usdan Ctr. for the Creative and Performing Arts, LI, NY, summer 1998. Prodn. asst. Broadway musical The Life. Recipient 1st pl. prize Profl. Artists Devel. Competition, 1990. Mem. Actors Equity Assn., Alpha Sigma Phi (pres. interfraternity coun. 1988-89, pres. chpt. 1989-90). Address: 4018 Shelley Dr North Olmsted OH 44070 Home Phone: 440-777-1974. Personal E-mail: pjanson02@aol.com.

JANSON, RICHARD ANTHONY, plastic surgeon; b. Passaic, NJ, Nov. 30, 1945; m. Mary Ann Janson, 1971; children: Sarah, Matthew. BA, Rice U., 1967; MD, Med. Coll. Wis., 1971. Diplomate Am. Bd. Plastic Surgery. Intern St. Joseph Hosp., Denver, 1971-72, resident in gen. surgery, 1972-76; resident in plastic surgery U. Tex. Med. Branch, Galveston, 1976-79; pvt. practice Grand Junction, Colo., 1979—. Fellow ACS, Am. Soc. Plastic & Reconstructive Surgeons; mem. Colo. Soc. Plastic & Reconstructive Surgeons. Office: 1120 Wellington Ave Grand Junction CO 81501-6129 Office Phone: 970-243-6200.

JANSSEN, CARRON JOYCE, music educator; b. Chgo., Aug. 28, 1955; d. Howard Armstrong and Shirley Lois Turpin; m. Uwe Detlof Janssen, June 18, 1983; children: Noel Uwe, Rachel Frances, Erica Heather. AA, William Rainey Harper Coll., 1980; MusB, Elmhurst Coll., 1997; MA in Tchg., Aurora U., 2002. Cert. tchr. State of Ill., 1997. Elem. music specialist Sch. Dist. U-46, Elgin, Ill., 1997—, mem. music/art/spl. edn. task force, 2005—. Music dept. com. Sch. Dist. U-46, Elgin, 1999—, Sunnydale bldg. com., 2004—, dist. stds. and reporting com., 2000—04. Clk. course Hanover Pk. Pk. Dist. Swim Team, Ill., 1998—. Mem.: NEA, Nat. Campaign for Tolerance, Elgin Tchrs. Assn., Ill. Edn. Assn., Ill. Music Educators Assn., Nat. Assn. Music Edn., Omicron Delta Kappa, Lambda Sigma Psi, Kappa Delta Pi, Phi Kappa Phi. Mem. United Church Christ. Avocations: various musical instruments, singing, reading, swimming. Home: 216 Carver Ln Schaumburg IL 60193-1219 Home Phone: 847-352-2622; Office Phone: 630-213-5610. Personal E-mail: carronuwe6183@sbcglobal.net. E-mail: carronjanssen@u-46.org.

JANSSEN, JAMES ROBERT, consulting software engineer; b. Frederick, Md., June 14, 1959; s. Robert James and Kathryn Doris (Randolph) J.; m. Deborah June Dellwo, Mar. 15, 1986 (div. Sept. 20, 1988). BSEE, Stanford U., 1981, MSEE, 1982; student, Calif. Culinary Acad., 2004. Simulation technician Varian Assocs., Palo Alto, Calif., 1981; hardware design engr. Fairchild Test Systems, San Jose, Calif., 1982-86, Factron Test Systems, Latham, NY, 1986-87; software, sys. designer Schlumberger Technologies Labs., Palo Alto, 1988; software engr. Photon Dynamics, Inc., San Jose, 1989-90, ADAC Labs., Milpitas, Calif., 1990-92, software, system designer Aalborg, Denmark, 1992, Milpitas, 1992-94; consulting software engr. self-employed, Sunnyvale, Calif., 1994-96; mem. tech. staff Netscape Comms. Corp., Mountain View, Calif., 1996-99, Am. Online Inc., Mountain View, 1999-2001; pres., founder MouseMine, Inc., Scotts Valley, Calif., 2001—03, Chefnology Software, Santa Cruz, Calif., 2004—. Pres., founder Digital Studio Systems, Inc., Sunnyvale, 1990-93. Patentee multiple timing signal generator. Civic vol. City of Sunnyvale, 1993. Mem. Tau Beta Pi. Avocations: motocross racing, auto race driving, auto race spectating, composing and recording pop music, piano. Home and Office: 721 Wolverine Way Scotts Valley CA 95066-2923 E-mail: jimj@chefnology.com. *I know enough to know how little I know.*

JANSSEN, MARIDITH ANNETTE, recreational therapist, educator; d. Cecil Howard and Janis Lorraine Curfman; m. Timothy Janssen, May 31, 1986. BS, Calif. State U., Sacramento, 1982; MA, Calif. State U., Chico, 1990; EdD in Applied Ednl. Studies, Okla. State U., Stillwater, 1999. Recreational therapist Hillhaven Convalescent Hosp., Modesto, Calif., 1988—90; therapeutic recreation supr. Fresno Cmty. Hosp., Calif., 1990—96; grad. assoc. Okla. State U., Stillwater, 1996—99; assoc. prof., dept. chair Calif. State U., Long Beach, 1999—. Cons. Janssen TR Cons., Fresno, 1990—96. Developer BEACH Symposium, Long Beach, 1996—2007. Named Most Valuable Prof., Calif. State U., Long Beach, 2007; recipient Presdl. Citation, Nat. Therapeutic Recreation Soc., 2003, Outstanding Therapeutic Recreation Educator, Calif. Pk. and Recreation Soc., 2003, Outstanding Faculty Award, Recreation Soc. CSULB, 2000, 2001. Mem.: Nat. Coun. Therapeutic Recreation (cert. therapeutic recreation specialist 1986), Calif. Bd. Recreation and Pk. (educator rep. 2005—, cert. recreation therapist 1986), Nat. Therapeutic Recreation Soc. (mem. stds. hearing com. 2006—), Nat. Recreation and Pk. Assn., Am. Therapeutic Recreation Assn., Calif. Pk. and Recreation Soc., Phi Kappa Phi. Office: Calif State U Long Beach 1250 Bellflower Blvd Long Beach CA 90840-4903 Home Phone: 562-489-2054; Office Phone: 562-985-4079. Business E-Mail: mjanssen@csulb.edu.

JANSSENS, JOE LEE, accountant; b. Alpine, Tex., Apr. 13, 1964; s. Charles Louis Janssens and Sue Ellen (Cheairs) Ticknor; m. Diana Bookout, Sept. 9, 1995; children: Ryan, Stephanie. BBA in Fin., Tex. A&M U., 1986; BA in Spanish, U. Houston, 1996, MA in History, 2004. CPA Tex., cert. mgmt. acct. Staff auditor Price Waterhouse, Houston, 1988-89; consol. acct. Energy Ventures, Inc., Houston, 1989-92; sr. internat. acct. Ashland Exploration, Inc., Houston, 1992-95; contr. Peak Svcs. USA Ltd., Texas City, Tex., 1996-97, Peak USA Energy Svcs., Ltd., Houston, 1997, Tube-Alloy Corp., Houston, 1997-98; fin. dir. Grant Prideco SA de C.V. Veracruz, Mexico, 1998-2000; fin. svcs. rep. IBM (formerly PriceWaterhouseCoopers), Houston, 2001—04; project contr. BP, Houston, 2005—06, NGL team leader, 2007—. Mem.: AICPA, Inst. Mgmt. Accts., Phi Kappa Phi. Roman Catholic. Avocations: western history, linguistics, scuba diving. Home: 7803 Braesdale Ln Houston TX 77071-1303 Office: BP 200 Westlake Pk Blvd Ste 871 Houston TX 77079 Business E-Mail: joe.janssens@bp.com.

JANSSON, JOHN PHILLIP, architect, consultant; b. Phila., Nov. 27, 1918; s. John A. and Isabelle (Ericson) Jansson; m. Ann C. Winter, Apr. 8, 1944 (div. Oct. 1970); children: Linda Ann, Lora Jean; m. Elizabeth Clow Peer, Jan. 21, 1978 (dec. May 1984). BArch, Pratt Inst., 1947; postgrad., SUNY, 1949. Registered arch., N.Y., lic. Nat. Coun. Archtl. Registration Bd.s. Architect various firms, 1949—54; pvt. practice NYC, 1949—; cons. mktg. products, materials and svcs. to bldg. and constrn. industry, 1949—; exec. v.p. Archtl. Aluminum Mfrs. Assn., NYC, 1954—58; mgr. market devel. Olin-Metals Div., NYC, 1958—62; dir. Pope, Evans & Robbins, cons. engrs., 1970—82; ptnr. Morris Ketchum, Jr. and Assocs., Archs., 1964—68; exec. dir. N.Y. State Coun. Architecture, 1968—73; dir. Gruzen & Ptnrs., 1972—74; pres. Bldg. Constrn. Tech., 1975—78; v.p. Ehrenkrantz Group, 1974—82. Cons. N.Y. State Pure Waters Authority, 1968—69; chmn. N.Y. State Architecture-Constrn. Interagency Com., 1968—74; sec. N.Y. State Gov.'s Adv. Com. State Constrn. Programs, 1970—71; dir. U.S. trade mission leader to Nigeria Dept. of Commerce, 1981. Mem. N.Y. State Citizens Com. Pub. Schs., 1952—55; v.p. citizens adv. com. Housing Authority, Town of Oyster Bay, NY, 1966—68; bd. dirs. Bldg. Industry Data Adv. Coun., 1976—78, Park Ten Coop., 1981—82; instr. Outward Bound, Hurrican Island, Rockland, Maine, 1982—; media specialist Image Ctr. Am.'s Cup, 1987. Served to capt. USMCR, 1943—46. Mem.: AIA (mem. archs. govt. com. 1971—77), Soc. Mil. Engrs. Soc. N.Y.C., Am. Mgmt. Assn., Associated Coun. Arts, Nat. Trust Historic Preservation, Soc. Archtl. Historians, N.Y. State Assn. Archs. (dir.), N.Y. Bldg. Congress, Archtl. League N.Y., Nat. Inst. Bldg. Scis., BRAB Bldg. Rsch. Inst., Nat. Inst. Archtl. Edn., Constrn. Specialist Inst., Am. Arbitration Assn., Fleety Res. Assn., Victorian Soc. Am., Mus. Modern Art, U.S. Naval Acad. Officers and Faculty Club, Md. Capital Yacht Club (bd. dirs. 1993—94). Home: 6301 River Crescent Dr Annapolis MD 21401-7721 Personal E-mail: jpjansson@yahoo.com.

JANULIS, THEODORE P., investment company executive; AB, Harvard Univ.; MBA, Columbia Univ. With fixed income div. Lehman Bros. Holdings, NYC, 1985—96, co-head mortgage & asset backed bus., 1996—97, head mortgage & asset backed bus., 1997—2000, co-head fixed income div., 2000—02, mng. dir., mem. exec. com., global head investment mgmt. div., 2002—06, mng. dir., mem. exec. com., global head mortgage capital, 2006—. Bd. mem. Lehman Bros. Found., Ronald McDonald House, Internat. Ctr. Photography. Office: Lehman Bros Holdings 745 Seventh Ave New York NY 10019*

JANURA, JAN AROL, apparel manufacturing executive; b. Chgo., May 12, 1949; s. Cornel Harold Charles and Violet Mary Janura. BS, Colo. State U., 1971; MA, Fuller Theol. Sem., 1973; postgrad., Harvard Bus. Sch., 1997. Area dir. Young Life Campaign, Seattle, 1973-76; CEO, dir. Carol Anderson, Inc., LA, 1977—2002; CFO Fresh Retail Chain, 1988—, Outdoor Videos Inc., 1988—; CEO Old Maui Brand, Rancho Dominguez, Calif., 2000—. Dir. Camp Anderson.Cabi, LLC; pres. LA Electric Motor-car Co., 1979-80; prin., dir. Pheasant Hill Orchards, Connel, Washington; founder, CEO Old Maui Brand; bd. dirs. C.A., Inc., catalog mfg. Nordstrom, Neiman Marcus, Coldwater Creek; prin., owner Feather Chuckers Brand clothing; founder, originator Carol Anderson's By Invitation; founder, Carol Anderson's By Invitation Women's Home Clothing Sales, oldmaui website, cabionline website. Mem. Rep. Nat. Com., 1986, Rep. Presdl. Task Force, 1984-86; trustee Janura Libr., Glendale; founder Smiling Moose Lodge, Cameron, Mont. Weyerhaueser fellow, 1972-73, Glendale Fellowship Found.; bd. dirs. Palos Verdes Leadership Found., We. Leadership Found., Starr Leadership Found., SW Leadership Found., NW Fellowship, Rivergate Fellowship, Crested Butte, Colo., Glendale (Calif.) Young Life Found. Fellowship, bd. mem., Oaks Christian HS, bd. dirs. 2001-06, Westlake Village, Calif.; commence spkrs. Colo. State U., Fort. Collins, 2003. Recipeint Salesman of Yr. award, 1983, 84; Carpenteria fellow, 2002. Mem. Fly Fishermen Am. (life), Trout Unlimited (life), Henrys Fork Found., Calif. Trout, 11-99 Found. (life), Pvt. Aircraft Owners Assn., Beechcraft Owners' Club, Montana and Land Reliance, Friends of Montana Land Reliance, Mammoth Lakes Fly Fisherman, Young Pres.'s Orgn. (LA chpt., Beta Forum), World Pres. Orgn., Friends of Norris Theater, Snowcreek Athletic Club, LA Athletic Club, Wash. Athletic Club, NY Athletic Club, Pres. Pointe Assn. (pres. 1991-96), Juniper Ridge Assn., Admirals Club (life), Solomon Hill Hunt Club, Scootney Farms Hunting Club, High Desert Hunt Club, Ironwood Country Club, Fly Fisherman Club, Virginia Country Club (Long Beach, Calif.; winner 50th Intergalactic Golf Tournament 1999). Office: 18915 S Laurel Park Rd Rancho Dominguez CA 90220-6005 Office Phone: 310-638-3333. Business E-Mail: jjanura@oldmaui.com.

JANVIER, PASCAL PAUL, chef, educator; s. Marcel Victor and Nicole Alice Janvier; m. Nicola Marion Morf, July 11, 1996; children: Cedric Roger Marcel, Claire Marion. MA, CIFAPA, Paris, 1988. Cap Ministere de l Edn. Nationale France, 1979, master of pastry , confection, chocolate and ice-cream Ministere de l'Education Nationale Frannce, 1988. Tech. mgr., sch. dir. Cacao Barry Us, Pennsauken, NJ, 1990—99; chef, owner Fleur de Cocoa, Los Gatos, Calif., 2000—. Cons., lectr. Pascal Janvier, San Jose, Calif., 1999—. Contbr. recipes to mags. and publs. Amb. Barry Callebaut, Vieze, Belgium, 1999. Field sgt. Arty. French Army, 1982—83. Co-recipient Bronze medal Nat. Pastry Team Championship, Carymax, Inc., 1999, 2005, Silver medal Nat. Pastry Tean Championship, 2001; named Nat. Dessert Champion, Paris Gourmet, 2002; named one of Top Ten Pastry Chef, Pastry Arts and Design Mag., Chocolatier mag., 1998; recipient, 1999. Mem.: Societe Culinaire Philanthropique, Academie Culinaire de France. Office: Fleur de Cocoa 39 N Santa Cruz Ave Los Gatos CA 95030 Home Phone: 408-377-3622; Office Phone: 408-354-3574. Personal E-mail: chefpascal@gmail.com.

JANZEN, DONNA LEE (BRICKER), music educator, singer; b. Atwood, Kans., Aug. 19, 1929; d. Don and Anna Linnea (Bergling) Bricker; m. George Vernon Janzen (div.); children: Lori Linnea, Lisa Lynn Hendricks. BMus, U. Denver, 1952. Tchr. music Denver Pub. Schs., 1953—57, 1969—92; instr. voice Met. State Coll., Denver, 1974—2006. Instr. voice Lamont Sch. Music U. Denver, 1953—58; soloist Churches and Synagogues, Operas, Symphonies, Rocky Mountain Region, 1997—2005. Singer: Denver Symphony, Colo. Springs Symphony, Brico Symphony, Golden Symphony, Colo. Chorale, U. N.C. Symphony, Jefferson Symphony, Denver Concert Chorale, El Paso Symphony, Metro State Orch.; singer: (Hansel) Hansel and Gretel; singer: (Dorabella) Cosi fan Tutti; singer: (Dryad) Ariadne auf Naxos; singer: (Alisa) Lucia di Lammermoor; singer: (L'Amica) Amelia Goes to the Ball; singer: (Suzuki) Madama Butterfly; singer: (Vera Boronel) The Consul; singer: (Daisy) Col. Jonathan the Saint; singer: (Maddelena) Rigoletto; singer: (the Page) Salome; singer: (Carmen) Carmen; singer: (Siebel) Faust; singer: (Annina) La Traviata; singer: (Aennchen) Der Freischutz; singer: (Olga) Eugene Onegin; singer: (Gaea) Daphne. Head judge Colo. All-State Choir Auditions, 1986—2005. Recipient Winner, Rocky Mountain Regional Met. Opera, 1959, Outstanding Achievement award, Coalition Pub. Edn., 1990, 1st pl., Rocky Mountain Regional Met. Opera auditions. Mem.: Denver Lyric Opera Guild, Met. Opera Nat. Coun., Nat. Assn. Tchrs. Singing, Lamont Alumni Assn., Lamont Assocs., Alpha Gamma Delta, Sigma Alpha Iota. Avocations: music, golf. Home: 7540 Crested Quail St North Las Vegas NV 89084

JANZEN, NORINE MADELYN QUINLAN, clinical laboratory scientist; b. Fond du Lac, Wis., Feb. 9, 1943; d. Joseph Wesley and Norma Edith (Gustin) Quinlan; m. Douglas Mac Arthur Janzen, July 18, 1970; 1 son, Justin James. BS, Marian Coll., 1965; med. technologist, St. Agnes Sch. Med. Tech., Fond du Lac, 1966; MA, Ctrl. Mich. U., 1980. Med. technologist Mayfair Med. Lab., Wauwatosa, Wis., 1966—69; supr. med. technologist Drs. Mason, Chamberlain, Franke, Klink & Kamper, Milw., 1969—76, Hartford-Parkview Clinic, Ltd., 1976—94; supr. patient svc. ctrs. Med. Sci. Labs., Wauwatosa, 1994—97; supr. patient svc. ctrs. Poole Med. Tech. Med. Sci. Labs, 1997—98; clin. mgr. Planned Parenthood Wis., 1997—99; coord. health in bus. Hartford Parkview Clinic, 1990—91, coord. drug program, 1991—94; lab. outreach coord. Cmty. Meml. Hosp., Menomonee Falls, Wis., 2000—. Co-chair joint mtg. Clin. Lab. Mgrs. Assn. and Wis. Assn. for Clin. Lab. Scientists, 1993-94. Mem. Dem. Nat. Com., 1973—; substitute poll worker Fond du Lac Dem. Com., 1964—65; recognition coord Cmty. League Youth Coll., 2000—; focus team leader Coll. Youth Ministries, Meth. Ch., 2000—07; mem., coord. Post Card Ministry Bd., 1998—2001; lay del. to ann. conf. United Meth. Ch., Menomonee Falls, 2004—; bd. dir. Menomonee Falls Teen Ctr., 2000—07, Iowa State Parents Assn., 2001—04; sr. ctr. com. Village of Germantown, 2007—. Mem.: AAUW (corr. sec. 1994—96, rec. sec. 1996—98, pub. policy chair 1998—2001, chair Evening of Literary Excellence 2001—02, pres. 2001—03, treas. 2003—06, state, dist. 2 coord. 2003—, co-chair ann. meeting 2004—05), Southea. Suprs. Group (co-chmn. 1976—77), Milw. Soc. Clin. Lab. Scientists (pres. 1971—72, bd. dir. 1972—73), Clin. Lab. Mgmt. Assn. (co-chair joint meeting 1993—94), Wis. Assn. Clin. Lab. Scientists (chmn. awards com. 1976—77, treas. 1977—81, dir. 1977—84, pres.-elect 1981—82, pres. 1982—83, chmn. awards com. 1984—85, dir. 1985—87, chmn. awards com. 1986—87, chair ann. meeting 1987—88, exec. sec. 1991—, Mem. of Yr. award 1982, 1995, Svc. award), Nat. Soc. Clin. Lab. Scientists (awards com. chair 1984—87, 1988—91, nominations com. 1989—92), Am. Soc. Clin. Lab. Scientists (people to people clin. lab. scientist del. to People's Rep. China 1989, Mem. of Yr. award 1997), Warhawk Band Boosters (uniform fundraiser chair 1996—98, chair Trysting Place tent party fundraiser 1997—2000), Comm. Wis. (chmn. 1977—79, originator), LWV, Cmty. League, Alpha Mu Tau, Alpha Delta Theta (nat. dist. chmn. 1967—69, nat. alumnae dir. 1969—71). Home: N101 W17383 Tanglewood Dr Germantown WI 53022 Office: Cmty Meml Hosp W180 N 8085 Town Hall Rd Menomonee Falls WI 53051 Personal E-mail: nmjanzen@aol.com.

JANZEN, PETER S., lawyer, food products executive; b. Chgo., Apr. 2, 1959; BA in Polit. Sci., Hamline U., 1981, JD, 1984. Bar: Minn. 1984. With law dept. Land O' Lakes Inc., 1983—, v.p., gen. counsel, 2003—. Mem.: US Trademark Assn., ABA, Minn. State Bar Assn. Office: Land O Lakes Inc 4001 Lexington Ave N Saint Paul MN 55126 Office Phone: 651-481-2222. Office Fax: 651-481-2832.*

JAO, CHIANG, information technology educator; arrived in U.S., 1978; s. T. and L. Jao; m. Li Jao, 1987; children: N., A. BS, Nat. Cheng-kung U., Taiwan, 1977; PhD, Ill. Inst. Tech., 1992, cert. in Med. Informatics, 2005. Software engr. Imagen Corp, Mountain View, Calif., 1984—85; group leader Lockheed Internat. Taiwan, Taipei, 1985—87; sr. specialist ACER Group, Taipei, Taiwan, 1987—89; software programmer U. Ill., Chgo., 1991—92, rsch. asst. prof., 1992—. Author: (computer application) Intelligent Event-Driven Medical Information System. Com. mem. U. Ill., Chgo., 2005. Recipient Best Med. Edn. Program award, U. Ill. Sch. Medicine, 2000. Mem.: IEEE. Office: U Ill 845 S Damen Ave M/C 802 Chicago IL 60612 Business E-Mail: csjao@uic.edu.

JAOUEN, RICHARD MATTHIE, plastic surgeon; MD, U. Autonoma de Guadalajara, Jalisco, Mexico, 1975. Intern St. Joseph Hosp., Denver, 1976-77, surgeon, 1977-81; plastic surgeon Ind. U. Med. Sch., Indpls., 1981-83, North Colo. Med. Ctr., Greeley, Colo., 1983—. Office: 1640 25th Ave Greeley CO 80634-4959

JAQUA, RICHARD ALLEN, pathologist; b. Fort Dodge, Iowa, Apr. 15, 1938; s. John Franklin and Esther J.; m. Mary Joanne Stewart, Dec. 29, 1969 BA magna cum laude, Yale U., 1960; MD, Harvard U., 1965. Diplomate: Am. Bd. Pathology, Am. Bd. Nuclear Medicine. Teaching fellow pathology Harvard Med. Sch., 1965-67; resident clin. pathology NIH, 1967-69; intern pathology Mass. Gen. Hosp., Boston, 1965-66; fellow tumor pathology Meml.-Sloane Kettering Cancer Center, NYC, 1969-70; asst. prof. pathology U. S.D. Sch. Medicine, Vermillion, 1970-73, asso. prof., 1973-74, asso. prof., acting chmn. dept. lab. medicine, 1974-77, prof., chmn. dept. lab. medicine, 1977—2002, dir. Electron Microscopy Lab. and Clin. Virology Lab., 1979—2002; pathologist VA Hosp., Sioux Falls, SD, 1978—2002; physician Lab. Clin. Medicine, Sioux Falls, 1970—2002. Part-time prof. pathology Sch. Medicine U. S.D., 2003—; prof. emeritus U. S.D. Sch. Medicine. Served with USPHS, 1967-69. Recipient Outstanding Prof. awards U. SD Med. Students, 1971, 75, 77, U. SD Faculty Recogition award, 1986, U. SD Sci. Faculty award, Student Am. Med. Assn., 1992, Lifetime Achievement award, 2002, U. SD Centennial Tchg. award, 2007; VA grantee, 1980-82. Fellow Coll. Am. Pathologists, Am. Soc. Clin. Pathologists; mem. AAAS, Sigma Xi, Alpha Omega Alpha. Home: 27546 483rd Ave Canton SD 57013-5511 Office: USD Health Sci Ctr 1400 W 22nd St Sioux Falls SD 57105-1505 Business E-Mail: rjaqua@usd.edu.

JAQUISS, ROBERT DOUGLAS BENJAMIN, pediatric cardiac surgeon; b. Pittsfield, Mass., Sept. 18, 1960; s. Donald Benjamin George and Georgina Mary Stephen Jaquiss; m. Cheryl N. Nephew, June 24, 1983; children: William Donald Francis, Caroline Elizabeth, Audrey Perry. AB, Wabash Coll., Crawfordsville, Ind., 1982; MD, Vanderbilt U. Sch. Medicine, Nashville, 1986. Resident, gen. surgery Washington U., 1986—90, mem. cardiothoracic rsch. lab., 1990—92, resident, cardiothoracic, 1992—94; fellow, cardiothoracic Washington U./St. Louis Children's Pediatric Hosp., 1994—95; asst. prof. surgery U. Miami Sch. Medicine, 1995—97; dir. pediat. cardiac surgery Joe DiMaggio Children's Hosp., Hollywood, Fla., 1997—2000; assoc. prof. pediat. cardiac surgery Children's Hosp. Wis., Milw., 2002—05, cardiac surgeon, 2000—05; prof. surgery, chief pediat. cardiac surgery Ark. Children's Hosp./U. Ark. Med. Sciences, Little Rock, 2005—. Contbr. articles to profl. jours. Fellow: ACS; mem.: Soc. Thoracic Surgeons, Phi Beta Kappa, Alpha Omega Alpha. Office: Ark Childrens Hosp 800 Marshall Slot 677 Little Rock AR 72202 Office Phone: 501-364-5858. Office Fax: 501-364-5869; Home Fax: 501-224-1782. Personal E-mail: rjaquiss@mac.com. Business E-Mail: rjaquiss@uams.edu.*

JAQUITH, GEORGE OAKES, ophthalmologist; b. Caldwell, Idaho, July 29, 1916; s. Gail Belmont and Myrtle (Burch) J., m. Pearl Elizabeth Taylor, Nov. 30, 1939; children: Patricia Ann Jaquith Mueller, George, Michele Eugenie Jaquith Smith. BA, Coll. Idaho, 1938; MB, Northwestern U., 1942, MD, 1943. Intern Wesley Meml. Hosp., Chgo., 1942-43; resident opthalmology U.S. Naval Hosp., San Diego, 1946-48; pvt. practice Brawley, Calif., 1948—83. Pres. Pioneers Meml. Hosp. staff, Brawley, 1953, dir. exec. com. Calif. Med. Eye Coun., 1960—, v.p. Calif. Med. Eye Found., 1976—. Sponsor Anza coun. Boy Scouts Am., 1966—, Gold card holder Rep. Assocs., Imperial County, Calif., 1967-68, PTO. With USMC, USN, 1943-47 Mem. Imperial County (pres. 1961), Calif. Med. Assn. (del. 1961—), Nat., So. Calif. (dir. 1966—, chmn. med. adv. com. 1968-69), Soc. Prevention Blindness, Calif. Assn. Ophthalmology (treas. 1976—), San Diego, LA Ophthal. Soc., LA Rsch. Study Club, Nathan Smith Davis Soc., Coll. Idaho Assocs., Am. Legion, VFW, Res. Officers Assn., Basenji Assn., Nat. Geneal. Soc., Cuyamaca Club (San Diego), Elks, Phi Beta Phi, Lambda Chi Alpha (Hall of Fame). Presbyterian (elder).

JARABAK, PHYLLIS A., music educator; b. St. Louis, Apr. 5, 1950; d. Samuel and Lydia Ann (Boor) Boda; m. Godfrey Paul Jarabak, June 18, 1972; children: Emily Katherine, Betsy Louise. BA, Concordia Tchrs. Coll., Ill., 1971. Cert. tchr. Ill. Home econ. tchr. Walther Luth. HS, Melrose Park, Ill., 1971—72, Grigsby Jr. High, Granite City, Ill., 1972—73, North HS, Granite City, Ill., 1974—75; organist, choir dir. Faith Lutheran Ch., Eldersburg, Md., 1981—91; pvt. piano tchr., 1982—; organist, choir dir. Grace Luth. Ch., Woodbridge, Va., 1991—97, Good Shepherd Luth. Ch., Collinsville, 1997—99; piano tchr. Good Shepherd Luth. Sch., Collinsville, 1997—; organist, choir dir. St. John Luth. Ch., Granite City, Ill., 1999—. Judge piano contests Md. State Piano Tchrs. Fedn., Eldersburg, Md., 1988—90. Mem.: Nat. Guild Piano Tchrs. Lutheran. Avocations: sewing, swimming, reading. Home: 59 Glen Echo Rd Glen Carbon IL 62034-1030

JARAMILLO, ALBA, community educator; b. Mex., 1980; Rschr., cmty. educator Southern Ariz. Ctr. Against Sexual Assault, Tucson. Mem. Tucson Youth Take Back the Night; dir., coordinator cmty. com., V-Day Tucson: The Vagina Monologues; bd. dirs. Borderlands Theatre Co. Named one of 40 Under 40, Tucson Bus. Edge, 2006. Office: Southern Arizona Center Against Sexual Assault 1600 N Country Club Tucson AZ 85716 Office Phone: 520-327-1171. Office Fax: 520-327-2992.

JARAMILLO, CARLOS ALBERTO, civil engineer; b. Medellin, Colombia, Dec. 5, 1952; arrived in US, 1986; s. Alberto and Maria Jaramillo; m. Celeste Jaramillo; children: Daniel J., Nicolas, Diego A., Javier A. BCE, U. Nacional, Medellin, 1978; MS, U. Minn., 1980. Registered profl. engr., Wis., Colobmia. Engr. Integral S.A., Medellin, Colombia, 1977-79, sr. design engr., 1980-86; rsch. asst. St. Anthony Falls Lab., Mpls., 1979-80; civil engr. Mead & Hunt Inc., Madison, 1986-89; sr. geotech. engr. Harza Engrng. Co., Chgo., 1989—2001, jr. ptnr., 1998—2001; sr. geotech. engr. , ptnr. MWH Global, 2001—05; sr. project mgr. URS Corp., Oakland, Calif., 2006—. Prof. Escuela de Ingenieria de Antioquia, Medellin, 1981—86; designer numerous dams & underground structures; cons. to public utilities, various countries, 1994—. Contbr. articles to profl. jours. Mem.: AAAS, ASCE (rock mechanics com.), US Nat. Soc. Soil Mechanics and Found. Engrng., US Soc. Dams, Soc. Mining, Metallurgy and Exploration, Am. Rock Mechanics Soc., Phi Kappa Phi. Avocations: jogging, photography, stamp collecting/philately, astronomy. Office: URS Corp 1333 Broadway Ste 800 Oakland CA 94612 Business E-Mail: carlos_jaramillo@urscorp.com.

JARAMILLO, MARI-LUCI, retired federal agency administrator; b. Las Vegas, N.Mex., June 19, 1928; BA magna cum laude, N.Mex. Highland U., 1955, MA with honors, 1959; PhD, U. N.Mex., 1970. Tchr., Albuquerque and Las Vegas, N.Mex., 1955-65; asst. prof. U. N.Mex., 1965-72, assoc. prof., chmn. dept. elem. edn., 1972-75, assoc. prof. edn., 1976-77, prof., 1977, spl. asst. to pres., 1981-82, assoc. dean Coll. Edn., 1982-85, v.p. for student affairs, 1985-87; amb. to Republic of Honduras U.S. Dept. State, 1977-80, dep. asst. sec. for Inter-Am. affairs Washington, 1980-81; asst. v.p., dir. Ednl. Testing Service, Emeryville, Calif., 1987-93; dep. asst. sec. for Inter-Am. affairs Dept. Def., Washington, 1993-95. Bd. trustees Tomas Rivera Nat. Policy Ctr., Claremont (Calif.) Coll. Grad. Sch., 1985-93; minority recruiter Dept. State, Washington, 1990-2000; commr. Calif. Commn. of Post-Secondary Edn., Sacramento, 1990-93; active Coun. Am. Ambs., Washington, 1983-; bd. dirs. Latin Am. Scholarship Program for Am. Univs., Boston, Children's TV Workshop, N.Y.C.; cons. for curriculum, tchr. tng. and sch. reform, 1960-; vice chair, bd. regents, N.Mex. Highlands U., 2001—. Author: Madame Ambassador; The Shoe Maker's Daughter, 2002; contbr. articles to jours., chpts. to books. Bd. dirs. Internat. House, U. Calif., Berkeley, 1989-93; scholar panelist Nat. Latino Comm. Ctr., L.A., 1990—; active Bay area Network L.Am. Women, San Francisco, 1987-93; regent N.Mex. Highlands U., 2003—, vice chair, 2000—. Decorated Order Francisco Morazan (Honduras), Order of Great Silver Cross (Honduras); recipient Cubberly award Stanford U., 1975, N.Mex. Disting. Svc. award, 1977, Anne Roe award Harvard U. Grad. Sch. Edn., 1986, PRIMERA award Mex. Am. Women's Nat. Assn., 1990; named Outstanding Chicana, 1975, Hon. Honduran Citizen, Govt. of Honduras, 1980, Disting. Woman of Yr., U. N.Mex. Alumni Assn., 1985, Disting. Hispanic lectr. Calif. State U. at Fullerton, 1988, Outstanding Hispanic Educator, 1988, Outstanding Leader in Edn. to Hispanic Cmty., 1991. Mem. Nat. Assn. Bilingual Edn., Latin Am. Assn., Am. Assn. Colls. for Tchr. Edn., Nat. Council La Raza. Home: 10501 Lagrima de Oro NE Apt 342 Albuquerque NM 87111

JARBOE, MARK ALAN, lawyer; b. Flint, Mich., Aug. 19, 1951; s. Lloyd Aloysius and Helen Elizabeth (Frey) J.; m. Patricia Kovel, Aug. 20, 1971; 1 child, Alexander. Student, No. Mich. U., 1968-69; AB with high distinction, U. Mich., 1972; JD magna cum laude, Harvard U., 1975. Bar: Minn. 1975, U.S. Dist. Ct. Minn. 1975, U.S. Ct. Appeals (8th cir.) 1975, U.S. Ct. Appeals (7th cir.) 1993. Law clk. to presiding justice Minn. State Ct., St. Paul, 1975-76; from assoc. to ptnr. Dorsey & Whitney LLP, Mpls., 1976-81, ptnr., 1982—, and chmn., Indian law practice group and Indian & gaming practice group, mem. policy com., 1991, 2005—. Lectr. U. Minn. Law Sch., Hamline U. Sch. Law. Contbr. articles to profl. jours. Pres. parish coun. Ch. of Christ the King, Mpls., 1981-83. Mem. Minn. Am. Indian Bar Assn., Mensa, Phi Beta Kappa. Republican. Roman Catholic. Office: Dorsey & Whitney LLP 50 S 6th St Ste 1500 Minneapolis MN 55402-1498 Office Phone: 612-340-2686. Office Fax: 612-340-2868. Personal E-mail: jarboe.mark@gmail.com. Business E-Mail: jarboe.mark@dorsey.com.

JARDETZKY, OLEG, retired medical educator, researcher; b. Yugoslavia, Feb. 11, 1929; came to U.S., 1949, naturalized, 1955; s. Wenceslas Sigismund and Tatiana (Taranovsky) J.; m. Erika Albensberg, July 21, 1975; children by previous marriage: Alexander, Theodore, Paul. BA, Macalester Coll., 1950, D.Sc. (hon.), 1974; MD, U. Minn., 1954, PhD (Am. Heart Assn. fellow), 1956; postgrad., U. Cambridge, Eng., 1965-66; LL.D. (hon.), Calif. Western U., 1978; MD (hon.), U. Graz, Austria, 1994; Doctorate (hon.), U. Aix-Marseille II, 1998. Rsch. fellow U. Minn., 1954-56; NRC fellow Calif. Inst. Tech., 1956-57; assoc. Harvard U., 1957-59, asst. prof. pharmacology, 1959-66; dir. biophysics and pharmacology Merck & Co., 1966-68, exec. dir., 1968-69; prof. Stanford U., 1969—2006, prof. emeritus, 2006—, dir. Stanford Magnetic Resonance Lab., 1975-97, dir. NMR Ctr. Sch. Medicine, 1983-84, dir. emeritus, 1998—. Vis. fellow Merton Coll., Oxford (Eng.) U., 1976; cons., vis. prof., lectr. in field; chmn. Internat. Coun. on Magnetic Resonance in Biology, 1972-74; dir. Internat Sch. on Magnetic Resonance in Biology, 1993—; mem. adv. bd. Ettore Majorana, 2006—; chmn. biotech. panel World Fedn. Scientists, 1998-2003. Contbr. articles to profl. jours.; mem. editorial bd. Jour. Theoretical Biology, 1961-88, Molecular Pharmacology, 1965-75, Jour. Medicinal Chemsitry, 1970-78, Biochimica Biophypica Acta, 1970-86, Revs. on Bioenergetics, 1972-89, Biomembrane Revs., 1972-80, Jour. Magnetic Resonance in Biology and Medicine, 1986—2000, Jour. Magnetic Resonance, 1993—2000. Recipient Career Devel. award USPHS, 1959-66, Kaiser award, 1973, Von Humboldt award, 1977, Pauling medal, 1984, Grand Gold Honor insignia, Austria, 1993, Founder's Gold medal Internat. Coun. Magnetic Resonance in Biology, 1994, Prix Marianne Dessewffy Internat. Conf. of Genealogy and Heraldry, 1998; grantee NSF, 1957-2001, NIH, 1957-2006; travel fellow Am. Physiol. Soc., 1959. Fellow AAAS; mem. Am. Chem. Soc., Am. Soc. Biol. Chemistry and Molecular Biology, Biophys. Soc., Assn. Advanced Tech. in Biomed. Scis. (pres. 1981-88), Internat. Soc. Magnetic Resonance (chmn. divns. of biology and Medicine 1986-89), Phi Beta Kappa, Sigma Xi, Alpha Omega Alpha. Home: 950 Casanueva Pl Stanford CA 94305-1068 Office: Stanford U CCSR 269 Campus Dr Rm 3155-B Stanford CA 94305-5174 Office Phone: 650-723-6153. Business E-Mail: jardetzky@stanford.edu.

JARDIN, XENI, journalist, blogger; Supr. enterprise web tech. Latham & Watkins law; v.p., sr. writer Rising Tide Studios; tech. weblog co-editor BoingBoing.com. Has made appearances on CNN, ABC, NBC, PBS; contbr. articles to WIRED, Popular Sci., Playboy; host (podcast) Xeni Tech, NPR. Named one of Top 25 Web Celebs, Forbes mag., 2007. Mailing: care of Nick Khan ICM 10250 Constellation Blvd Los Angeles CA 90067 Office Phone: 323-843-9364. Business E-Mail: xeni@xeni.net.*

JAREB, JEROME, history professor, researcher; b. Sepurine, Croatia, May 3, 1922; arrived in U.S., 1952; s. Marko Jareb and Tade Kursar; m. Olga Zlvkovic, Sept. 12, 1959; children: Helena, Anthony, Ivan, Mark. BS, Columbia U., NYC, 1955, MA, 1958, PhD, 1964. Lectr. Rutgers U., New Brunswick, NJ, 1963—66; prof. history St. Francis U., Loretto, Pa., 1966—92, prof. emeritus, 1992—, chair dept. history and polit. sci., 1968—92. Author: Half A Century of Croatian Politics 1895-1945, 1995, Political Recollections and Activities of Dr. Branimir Jelic, 1982, Gold and Money of the Independent State of Croatia Moved Abroad During 1944, and 1945, 1997, State Economic Commission of the Independent State of Croatia from August 1941 to April 1945, 2001; co-editor: Jour. of Croatian Studies, 1960—. Mem.: Am. Cath. Hist. Assn., Am. Hist. Assn., Am. Assn. Advancement Slavic Studies, Croatian Acad. Am. (founding mem., mem. exec. com., pres. 1982—88). Roman Catholic. Home: 169 Kelly Dr Loretto PA 15940 E-mail: helga188@hotmail.com.

JARECKI, HENRY GEORGE, physician, financial planner; b. Stettin, Germany, Apr. 15, 1933; s. Max Jarecki and Gerda Kunstmann; m. Gloria Friedland, 1957; children: Andrew, Thomas, Eugene, Nicholas. MD, U. Heidelberg, Germany, 1957. Diplomate Am. Bd. Psychiatry and Neurology. Dir. Mocatta Metals Corp., NYC, 1970-89, Mocatta & Goldsmid Ltd., London, 1973-89, Mocatta Hong Kong Ltd., 1975-89; chmn. Brody, White & Co. Inc., NYC, 1971-95, Brody White Ltd, London, 1989-95, Guana Island Hotel Corp., British Virgin Islands, 1975—, Falconwood Corp., NYC, 1976—, Gresham Investment Mgmt., Inc., NYC, 1992—, The Programming Corp., NYC, 1999—, MovieFone, Inc., NYC, 1989-99, PsychoGenics, Inc., Tarrytown, NY, 1998—. Bd. dirs. Classical Theatre Harlem; gov. Brit. Virgin Islands CC, 1989—; dir. Caribbean Cellular Telephone, Brit. V.I., 1993-; dir. Tourist Bd. Brit. V.I., 2003-; trustee Inst. Internat. Edn., 2000-, vice-chmn., 2003—; chmn. Scholar Rescue Fund, 2002-; clin. prof. psychiatry Yale U. Sch. Medicine, New Haven, 2007-. Author: Modern Psychiatric Treatment, 1971; dir. (film) Gardeners of Eden, 1997, Cuba, Island of Music, 2000; contbr. articles to profl. jours. Adv. coun. Princeton U., Yale U. Sch. Medicine Dept. Psychiatry, 1992—; trustee Am. Mus. Natural History, 1991-99; bd. dirs. Botanic Soc. Brit. V.I., 1986—, Chgo. Bd. Trade, 1993-96; internat. liaison com. Food Corps Program, 1987-95, Island Resources Found., Tortola, Brit. Virgin Is., 1988— Mem. Nat. Futures Assn. (bd. dirs. 1979-93), Am. Psychiat. Assn. (Presdl. Commendation 1984). Office: Falconwood Corp 67 Irving Pl 12th Fl New York NY 10003 Business E-Mail: hj@falconefone.com.

JARECKIE, STEPHEN BARLOW, museum curator; b. Orange, NJ, Feb. 18, 1929; s. Eugene Albert and Doris Condit (Brittin) J.; m. Gretchen Kinsman Fillmore, Aug. 10, 1959. BA, Lehigh U., 1951; MA, Syracuse U., 1961. Installation asst. Munson-Williams-Proctor Inst., Utica, NY, 1955-60, edn. asst., 1960-61; registrar Worcester (Mass.) Art Mus., 1961-83, assoc. in photography, 1962-69, assoc. curator photography, 1969-73, curator photography, 1973-94, curator of photography emeritus, 1995—; photo. adv. Fitchburg (Mass.) Art Mus., 1996—. Author: WAM catalogue, The Early Republic: Consolidation of Revolutionary Goals, 1976, American Photography: 1840-1900, 1976, Photographers of the Weimar Republic, 1986; contbr. to catalogue, pamphlets, articles to mus. lit. With AUS, 1951-53. Guest Fed. Republic of Germany for study of republic's museums, 1967. Mem. U.S. Naval Inst. (assoc.) Episcopalian. Home: 47 Mount View Dr Holden MA 01520-2137 Office: 185 Elm St Fitchburg MA 01420-7503 Office Phone: 978-345-4207.

JARLES, RUTH SEWELL, education educator; d. Nashville Clyde Sewell and Zetta Marie Hurt; m. Terry Waters Milligan, June 16, 1990; m. Marion Evert Jarles, Dec. 19, 1957 (div. Mar. 1980); children: Leslie Marie Murphy, Eva Colleen Wakeley, Brian Keith. AA, Western Okla. State Coll., 1976; BA magna cum laude, U. Colo., Colorado Springs, 1982; MDiv, Iliff Sch. Theology, 1985; PhD, U. Denver, 1993. Dir. Christian edn. Patrick Henry Village Army Chapel, Heidelberg, Germany, 1973—74; dir. curriculum Grace Child Devel. Ctr., Altus, Okla., 1976—77; dir. Christian edn. First Congl. Ch., Colorado Springs, Colo., 1980—84; asst. to the dir. joint PhD program U. Denver, Iliff Sch. Theology, 1991—92; adj. faculty, tchg. or rsch. asst. U. Denver, Iliff Sch. Theology, Front Range and Auraria C.C., 1983—98; asst. materials sci. br. Nat. Renewable Energy Lab., Golden, Colo., 1994—95; exec. dir. Colo. Libr. Assn., Denver, 1995—98; gen. edn. faculty Art Inst. Colo., Denver, 1998—. Seminar leader Gender Differences in Comm. in the Workplace; session convenor, panel mem. Women in Religion; lectr. in field. Contbr. articles to profl. jours. Student senate Iliff Sch. Theology, Denver, 1984—86; mentor students cmty. svc. projects Art Inst. Colo., Denver, 1997—; chair/mem. South Africa task force, race and religion com., women's com. Iliff Sch.Theology, Denver, 1984—92; mem. publs. com. Colo. Women's Agenda, Denver, 1993—95, 2005; chair/mem. edn., fin., adminstrv. bd., music and fine arts, peace with justice coms. Trinity United Meth. Ch., Denver, 1984—92; mem. exec. com. Nat. Renewable Energy Lab. Women's Network, Golden, 1994—95; active Art Inst. Colo. Christmas project Denver Safe Ho., 2001—. Recipient E. Craig Brandenburg award, United Meth. Ch.; scholar Ea. Star Tng. awards for Religious Leadership, The Grand Chpt. Colo., Order Ea. Star, 1984—86; Oliver Read Whitley scholar, Iliff Sch. Theology, Seminarian scholar, Ctr. for Biblic Studies, Jerusalem, Israel, Ga. Harkness scholar, United Meth. Ch. Mem.: AAUW, Nat. Mus. Women in the Arts. Office: Art Inst Colo 1200 Lincoln St Denver CO 80203 Home: 6240 W 24th Ave Edgewater CO 80214-1034 Office Phone: 303-824-2151. Personal E-mail: r.jarles@gmail.com.

JARMAN, BETH S., former state agency administrator, consultant; d. Wayne David and Jean (Hathaway) Marshall Smith; m. Michael C. Jarman, Mar. 19, 1962 (div. Aug. 1981); children: Joseph Alexander, Michelle; m. George A. Land, Nov. 3, 1986. BA cum laude, U. Utah, 1963, MS, 1970, PhD, 1977. Pub. sch. tchr. Twenty Nine Palms H.S., Twenty Nine Palms, Calif., 1964—65, Davis County Sch. Dist., Bountiful, Utah, 1971—74; dir. Utah Dept. of Commerce, Salt Lake City, 1977—79; mem. Utah State House of Rep., Salt Lake City, 1974—79; chairperson Utah Housing Fin. Agy., Salt Lake City, 1979—80; pres. Site Devel. Corp., Socttsdale, Ariz., 1983—85; asst. dir. dept. health svcs. State of Ariz., Phoenix, 1985—88, dir. dept. of commerce, 1985—88; pres. The Farsight Group, Scottsdale, Ariz., 1988—. Bd. dirs. Leadership 2000, Phoenix, 1980—. Author: (book) You Can Change Your Life by Changing Your Mind, 1985, Breakpoint and Beyond, 1987. Pres. Charter 100; mem. New Vision Toastmasters, 2005—06. Named Woman of the Year Soroptomist of Utah, 1976, Outstanding Woman of Radio and TV, 1986. Mem.: Women Execs. in State Govt., Charter 100 (program chair 2004—05, pres. 2005—06), Phoenix City Club (founding pres. 1987). Avocations: writing, walking, gardening. Office: Farsight Group 6619 N Scottsdale Rd Scottsdale AZ 85250 Home Phone: 480-945-8748; Office Phone: 480-296-2048. Office Fax: 480-945-8765.

JARMAN, MARK FOSTER, language educator; b. Mt. Sterling, Ky., June 5, 1952; s. Donald Ray and Bo Dee (Foster) J.; m. Amy Lynn Kane, Dec. 28, 1974; children: Claire Marie, Zoe Anne. BA, U. Calif., Santa Cruz, 1974; MFA, U. Iowa, 1976. Instr. Ind. State U., Evansville, 1976-78; vis. lectr. U. Calif., Irvine, 1979-80; asst. prof. English Murray State U., Ky., 1980-83, Vanderbilt U., Nashville, 1983-86, assoc. prof. English, 1986-92, prof. English, 1992—2007, Centennial prof. English, 2007—. Mem. Associated Writing Programs, Norfolk, Va., 1980—, Poets' Prize Com., NYC, 1988—2002. Author: Iris, 1992, The Black Riviera, 1990, 2d edit., 1995, Far and Away, 1985, The Rote Walker, 1981, North Sea, 1978, 2d edit., 1989, The Reaper Essays, 1996, Questions for Ecclesiastes, 1997, Unholy Sonnets, 2000, The Secret of Poetry, 2001, Body and Soul: Essays on Poetry, 2002, To the Green Man, 2004, Epistles, 2007; editor: Rebel Angels: 25 Poets of the New Formalism, 1996. Winner Poets' prize, 1991, Lenore Marshall Poetry prize, Acad. of Am. Poets and The Nation Mag.,1998; John Simon Guggenheim Meml. Found. poetry fellow, 1991-92, Robert Frost fellow, Bread Loaf Writer's Conf., 1985: NEA grantee, 1977, 83, 92; recipient Joseph Henry Jackson award SF Found., 1974. Mem.: Nat. Book Critics Cir. Mem. Christian Ch. Office: Vanderbilt U Dept English Nashville TN 37235 Home Phone: 615-353-9895; Office Phone: 615-322-2541. Business E-Mail: mark.jarman@vanderbilt.edu.

JARMON, CHARLES, social sciences educator, dean; b. Kinston, NC, Nov. 22, 1938; s. John Baker and Beatrice Jarmon; m. Faith Patricia Jarmon, Aug. 15, 1965 (dec. Mar. 4, 1984); children: Thad Patrick, Lee Eugene, Faith Kinsetta, Julius Morning. BS, NC Coll., Durham, 1964, MA, 1965; PhD, SUNY, Buffalo, 1972. Asst. prof. So. U., Baton Rouge, 1967—68, acting chmn. dept., 1968—69; instr. SUNY, Buffalo, 1971—72; asst. prof. Va. Commonwealth U., Richmond, Va., 1972—78; assoc. prof. Howard U., Washington, 1978—87, chmn. dept. sociology and anthropology, 1988—91, assoc. dean arts and scis., 1992—. Cons. bur. Africa US Agy. Internat. Devel., 1982—83; cons. African Devel. Fedn. State Dept., 1985—86. Book rev. editor Jour. African Asian Studies, 1985—93, editl. bd. mem. Can. Rev. Studies Nationalism, 1985—2006; author: (book) Nigeria: Reorganization and Development, 1988; co-author: Blackwell Encyclopedia of Sociology, 2007; contbr. chapters to books. Founder Howard U. Student Parent Support Group, 1999—; advisor population undercount US Census Project, 1999; pub. mem. sr. svc. selection bd. US State Dept., 2007; pub. mem. Assn. Foreign Svc. Recipient Svc. award, Howard U., Army ROTC, 1999—; James B. Duke fellow, Duke U., 1965, Travel grant, Reginald Lewis Rsch. Fund, 2006. Mem.: Am. Coun. Deans, Am. Sociol. Assn., Assn. Black Sociologists (life). Avocations: billiards, reading, gardening. Office: Howard Univ Sixth St Washington DC 20059

JARMUSCH, JIM, film director, actor; Actor: (films) American Autobahn, 1984, Straight to Hell, 1987, Helsinki Napoli All Night Long, 1987, Leningrad Cowboys Go to America, 1989, The Golden Boat, 1990, In The Soup, 1992, Iron Horsemen, 1994, Tigrero: A Film That Was Never Made, 1994, Blue in the Face, 1995, Typewriter, the Rifle & the Movie Camera, 1996, Cannes Man, 1996, Sling Blade, 1996, Divine Trash, 1998, (TV series) Fishing With John, 1991, American Cinema, 1994; writer, dir., editor, prodr., composer: Permanent Vacation, 1982 (Joseph von Sternberg prize Mannheim 1980, Internat. Critics prize Figueira da Foz, Portugal 1982); dir., writer, editor: Stranger Than Paradise, 1984 (Camera D'Or Cannes Film Festival 1984, Best Picture of Yr. Nat. Soc. Film Critics 1984), Coffee and Cigarettes, 2003; dir., editor: Coffee and Cigarettes III, 1993 (Golden Palm for short film Cannes Film Festival 1993); dir., writer: Down By Law, 1986 (Best Film award Locarno, Best Fgn. Film Norway, Denmark and Israel), Mystery Train, 1989 (Highest Artistic Achievement prize Cannes Film Festival), Dead Man, 1995 (World Premiere Cannes Film Festival 1995, Felix award Best Non-European Film 1996, Best Cinematography award N.Y. Critics Cir. 1996); dir., writer, prodr.: Night on Earth, 1991 (Grand award Best Feature Film Houston Internat. Film Festival 1992, Ind. Spirit award Best Cinematography 1993), Ghost Dog: The Way of the Samurai, 1999, Broken Flowers, 2005; exec. prodr.: When Pigs Fly, 1993; dir., cinematographer: Year of the Horse, 1997; cinematographer: You Are Not I, 1981.

JAROFF, LEON MORTON, retired magazine editor; b. Detroit, Feb. 27, 1927; s. Abraham and Ruth (Rakita) J.; m. Claire Lynn Fox, Aug. 15, 1954 (div. Nov. 1975); children: Peter, Jill, Susan, Nicholas, Jennifer; m. Mary Katherine Moran, Jan. 10, 1976. BS in Elec. Engring. and Math., U. Mich., Ann Arbor, 1950. Writer Materials and Methods Mag., NYC, 1950-51; researcher, reporter, corr. Life Mag., NYC, Detroit, Chgo., 1951-58; corr., assoc. editor, sr. editor Time Mag., NYC, Detroit, Chgo., 1958-79, scis. editor NYC, 1985-87, contbr., 1988—2006, Time.com columnist, 2002—06; founder, mng. editor Discover Mag., NYC, 1980-84; ret. Co-chair bd. for student publs. U. Mich., 1992-98, 2006-; bd. dirs. Internat. Astron. Union's Working Group on Near-Earth Objects; cons. in field. Author: The New Genetics, 1991, also 44 Time mag. cover stories. Trustee Neurosci. Rsch. Found., La Jolla, Calif.; bd. dirs. Rogosin Inst., NYC; mem. Coun. Media Integrity, 2001-. With USN, 1944-45. Recipient Robert S. Ball Meml. award Aviation Space Writers Assn., 1978, Excellence award, 1989; Sci. Writing award AAAS/Westinghouse Corp., 1978, Sci. Writing award Am. Inst. Physics/US Steel Corp., 1976, 82-83; named Asteroid 7829 Jaroff in his honor Fellow AAAS, Com. for Skeptical Inquiry; mem. Am. Soc. Mag. Editors (exec. com. 1984-85), Am. Inst. Physics (adv. com. 1982—). Jewish. Avocations: tennis, computers, chess. Home: PO Box 1080 East Hampton NY 11937-0901 Personal E-mail: neonleo@aol.com.

JARON, DOV, biomedical engineer, educator; b. Tel Aviv, Oct. 29, 1935; came to U.S., 1958, naturalized, 1972; s. Meir and Sara (Levit) Yarovsky; m. Brooke E. Boberg, Sept. 16, 1978; children: Shulamit, Tamara. BS magna cum laude, U. Denver, 1961; PhD, U. Pa., 1967. Sr. research asso. Maimonides Med. Center, Bklyn., 1967-70; dir. surg. research Sinai Hosp. of Detroit, 1970-73; asso. prof. elec. engring. U. R.I., Kingston, 1973-77, prof., 1977-79, coordinator biomed. engring., 1973-79; prof. biomend. engring. and sci. Drexel U., Phila., 1979—, dir. Biomed. Engring. and Sci. Inst., 1979-96. Calhoun disting. prof., 1998—; vis. prof. elec. engring. Rutgers U., New Brunswick, N.J., 1968-73; adj. prof. biomed. engring. Wayne State U., 1971-73; adj. prof. physiology Temple U. Sch. Medicine, 1980—; adj. prof. radiology Jefferson Med. Coll., 1983—; dir. Div. Biol. and Critical Systems, NSF, 1991-93; assoc. dir. Nat. Ctr. Rsch. Resources, dir. biomedical tech. NIH, 1996-98. Contbr. articles to sci. jours. NSF, NIH, Office Naval Research, pvt. founds. research grantee. Fellow AAAS, IEEE, Am. Inst. for Med. and Biol. Engring., World Acad. Biomed. Tech., Internat. Acad. for Med. and Biol. Engring., Biomed. Engring. Soc.; mem. AAUP, Internat. Fedn. for Med. and Biol. Engring. (pres. 2000-03), Internat. Union for Phys. and Engring. Scis. in Medicine (v.p. 2003-06), Am. Soc. for Engring. Edn., Assn. for Advancement Med. Instrumentation, Internat. Soc. Artificial Organs, Am. Soc. for Artificial Internal Organs, Biophys. Soc., NY Acad. Scis., Engring. in Medicine and Biology of IEEE (pres. 1986-87), Sigma Xi, Tau Beta Pi, Eta Kappa Nu. Achievements include research of cardiac assist devices, cardiovascular dynamics and modeling, microcirculation, biomed. instrumentation. Home: 122 Bethlehem Pike Philadelphia PA 19118-2815 Office: Drexel U Sch Biomed Engring Sci and Health Systems 32nd and Chestnut St Philadelphia PA 19104 Business E-Mail: dov.jaron@drexel.edu.

JAROS, JOHN A., physics professor; BS in Physics, MIT, 1968; PhD in Physics, U. Calif. Berkeley, 1975. Rsch. assoc. Stanford Linear Accelerator Ctr., Stanford, 1975—79, asst. prof., 1979—84, assoc. prof., 1984—90, prof., 1990—, chair HEP faculty, 2001—05. Fellow: Am. Phys. Soc. (W.K.H. Panofsky prize 2006). Office: Stanford Linear Accelerator Ctr 2575 Sand Hill Rd Menlo Park CA 94025 Office Phone: 650-926-2852. Business E-Mail: john@slac.stanford.edu.

JAROSLAWICZ, DAVID, lawyer; b. Paris, Jan. 19, 1947; came to U.S., 1948; s. Moses and Mina (Etner) J.; m. Rena Nadoff, Feb. 3, 1987. BA, NYU, 1968; JD, Bklyn. Law Sch., 1971, LLM, 1974. Bar: N.Y. 1972, Calif. 1972, Fla. 1978, U.S. Supreme Ct. 1986. Pvt. practice, NYC, 1978—; prin. ptnr. Jaroslawicz & Jaros. Office: Jaroslawicz & Jaros 150 William St New York NY 10038-2603 E-mail: DJaroslawicz@lawjaros.com.

JARQUE, CARLOS M., former federal official; b. Mexico City, Oct. 18, 1954; Actuary Degree, U. Anáhuac, 1976; diploma, M in Econs. and Polit. Sci., London Sch. Econs., 1978; postgrad., U. Oslo, 1978; PhD in Econs., Nat. U. Australia, 1982; postgrad., Harvard U., 1984. Pres. Nat. Inst. for Stats., Geography and Informatics; gen. dir. stats. Dept. Programming and Budget; pres. Interdeptmental Pub. Fin. Com.; gen. dir. Internat. Stats. Inst.; world pres. UN Stats. Commn.; pres. UN Cartographic Conf.; sec. of social develop. Govt. of Mexico, 1999—2000; mgr. sustainable develop. Inter-Amer. Develop. Bank, 2001—05. Sec. Nat. Devel. Plan, 1995-2000, InterAm. Devel. Bank; vis. prof. Harvard U. Contbr. articles to profl. jours. Recipient Nat. Sci. and Tech. award, Nat. Actuaries' award, Benito Juárez medal of merit, Henri Willen Methorst medal, Adolf Quetelet medal. Office: 1300 New York Ave NW Washington DC 20577

JARQUIN VALDIVIA, ADRIAN ALBERTO, internist, neurologist, researcher; b. Jinotepe, Nicaragua, June 16, 1966; s. Alberto Jarquin Bonilla and Yolanda Valdivia Quijano; m. Tonya Jarquin Valdivia, May 1, 2004; 1 child, Isabella G. Jarquin-Valdivia. MD, Universidad Nacional Autonoma de Honduras, 1993. Diplomate Am. Bd. Internal Medicine, 1997, Neurology ABPN, 2004, Critical Care Am. Bd. Internal Medicine, 2005, Vascular Neurology ABPN, 2005, ARDMS, 2003, Ct/Mri ASN, 2004, Neurosonology ASN, 2002. Asst. prof. neurology, anesthesiology and internal medicine Vanderbilt U. Med. Ctr., Nashville, 2002—. Dir., neurology clerkship Vanderbilt U. Med. Ctr., Nashville, 2004—. Recipient CANDLE Tchg. Award, Vanderbilt Med. Sch., 2004. Mem.: AMA. Achievements include research in new ultrasound sign for non-invasive intracranial pressure determination - the angle of deceleration. Office: Vanderbilt University Med Ctr Department of Neurology Nashville TN 37232-3375 Home Phone: 615-832-0815; Office Phone: 615-936-1354.

JARRARD, LEONARD EVERETT, psychologist, educator; b. Waco, Tex., Oct. 23, 1930; s. Thomas Ivan and Levis Everett (Lasswell) J.; m. Janet Grier Shoop, Aug. 16, 1958; children: Alice Grier, David Frazier, Hugh Everett. BA, Baylor U., Waco, 1955; MS, Carnegie Inst. Tech., Pitts., 1957, PhD, 1959. Asst. to asso. prof. psychology Washington and Lee U., 1959-66; assoc. prof. to prof. psychology Carnegie-Mellon U., 1966-71; Robert L. Telford prof. psychology Washington and Lee U., Lexington, Va., 1971-2001, prof. emeritus, 2001—. Vis. lectr., prof. exptl. psychology U. Oxford, Eng., 1975-76; interim assoc. prof. anatomy U. Fla., 1965-66; acad. visitor Inst. Psychiatry, U. London, 1988-89. Editor: Cognitive Processes of Nonhuman Primates, 1971; cons. editor: Jour. Comparative and Physiol. Psychology, 1970-75, Behavioral Neurosci. Psychology, 1995-2001. Served with USAF, 1952-54. Fellow AAAS, APA, APS; mem. Soc. for Neurosci., Psychonomics Soc., Va. Acad. Sci. So. Soc. Philosophy and Psychology, Phi Beta Kappa, Omicron Delta Kappa, Sigma Xi. Home: RR 5 Box 1067 Lexington VA 24450-9805 Office: Washington and Lee U Dept Psychology Lexington VA 24450

JARRELL, CHARLES MICHAEL, bishop; b. Opelousas, La., May 15, 1940; Student, Immaculata Minor Sem., Cath. U. Ordained priest Roman Cath. Ch. 1967, bishop 1993. Bishop Diocese of Houma (La.)-Thibodaux, 1993—2002, Diocese of Lafayette, La., 2002—.

JARRETT, ALEXIS, insurance agent, lawyer; b. Independence, Kans., July 2, 1948; d. Robert Patterson and Betty June (Johnson) Jarrett. BS, U. Minn., Duluth, 1970; postgrad., U. Mo., 1974—77; JD, John Marshall Law Sch., 2001. Lic. property and casualty ins. Ind., life and health ins. Ind., cert. Life Underwriting Tng. Coun.; coach Minn. Tchr. Esko Pub. Schs., Minn., 1970—74; asst. dir. athletics, head coach basketball, softball, track U. Mo., Columbia, 1974—77; pvt. practice Schererville, Ind., 1984—; pres., CEO INFINITE Sports and Entertainment, Inc., 2002—. Women's basketball and softball color analyst Regional Radio Sports, N.W. Ind., 1992—94; with Moot Ct. Coun., 1999; jud. extern Cir. Ct. Cook County, Chgo., 1999; coord. women's sports info. dept. U. Mo., 1974—77; v.p. legal affairs Nat. Assn. State Farm Agts., Inc., 1997—2000; contract advisor NFL Players Assn., 2002—, Women's Nat. Basketball Players Assn., 2002—, CFL Players Assn., 2003—. Contbr. articles on sports to newspapers. Sponsor Lake County HS Girls Basketball Banquet, Ind., 1989—99; bd. dirs. Samaritan Counseling Ctr. N.W. Ind., pres., 1994; bd. dirs. VNA Found., sec.-treas., 1994; celebrity Am. Heart Assn. Celebrity Dinner; v.p. S.W. Lake divsn. Am. Heart Assn., 1992—94; mem. bd. advisors Basketball Hall of Fame, 1999—; bd. dirs. Boys and Girls Club N.W. Ind.; mem. adv. bd. indsl. rsch. liaison program Ind. U., Bloomington, 1990—96. Recipient Individual with Vision award, Ind. HS Athletic Assn., 1996. Mem.: ABA (entertainment and sports law forum, labor and law com., ins. law com., sports law subcom.), Sports Lawyers Assn., Chgo. Bar Assn. (labor and employment law com., ins. law com., immigration law com., health law com.), Ind. State Med. Assn. Alliance (chair media rels. 1990—91, treas. 1992—93, chair media rels. 1993—94), Am. Bus. Women's Assn. (pres. New Image chpt. 1983, Woman of the Yr. 1983), Lake County Med. Soc. Alliance (pres. 1992—94), Nat. Life Underwriters (bd. dirs. N.W. Ind. chpt. 1995, 1996, 1997). Address: 2330 Wicker Blvd Schererville IN 46375-2810

JARRETT, CHARLES ELWOOD, lawyer, insurance company executive; b. Abilene, Tex., Apr. 11, 1957; s. Jerry Vernon and Martha (McCabe) J.; m. Stephanie J. Baker, Apr. 16, 1988; 1 child, Megan McCabe. AB, Dartmouth Coll., 1980; JD, U. Mich., 1983. Bar: Mass. 1984, US Dist. Ct. (dist. Mass.) 1984, Ohio 1986, US Dist. Ct. (no. dist. Ohio) 1986, US Ct. Appeals (6th cir.) 1987, US Supreme Ct. 1988. Assoc. Choate, Hall & Stewart, Boston, 1984-86, Baker & Hostetler, Cleve., 1986-90, ptnr., 1990—2000; chief legal officer The Progressive Corp., Ohio, 2000—, sec., v.p. Ohio, 2001—. Office: Progressive Corp 6300 Wilson Mills Rd Mayfield OH 44143*

JARRETT, FREDRIC, surgeon, educator; s. Julian Everett and Melba Jarrett; m. Esther Kathleen Szeolleosy-Toth, June 26, 1972; children: James Alexander, Julia Nicole Reid, Andrew Whitney. AB, Dartmouth Coll., Hanover, NH, 1963, B Med. Sci., 1965; MD cum laude, Harvard U., Boston, 1967. Diplomate Am. Bd. Surgery. Commd. 2d lt. US Army, 1967; intern then resident in surgery Mass. Gen. Hosp., Boston, 1967—71, 1974—75; chief resident Sint Lukas Ziekenheis, Amsterdam, 1971—72; surg. cons. US-UN Forces, Republic of Korea, 1972—74; asst. prof. U. Wis., Madison, 1974—81; advanced through grades to col. US Army, 1990; adj. prof. surgery Temple U. Sch. Medicine, 2000—; clin. prof. surgery U. Pitts., 1981—. Cons. vascular surgery Blue Cross/Blue Shield Pa., Camp Hill, 1983. Editor: (textbook) Vascular Surgery of the Lower Extremity; contbr. numerous sci. papers to profl. publs. (Nat. Leadership award, 2002, Physician of Yr., 2003). Bd. dirs. Three Rivers Shakespeare Festival, Pitts., 1989—95. Col. US Army, 1972—95, Usa. Fellow: ACS (pres. SW Pa. chpt. 2005—06), Royal Soc. Medicine Gt. Britain, Royal Coll. Surgeons Can. (cert.); mem.: Ctrl. Surg. Assn., Soc. Vascular Surgery, Dutch Surg. Soc., Ea. VascularSociety (sec., pres.-elect, pres. 1992—99), Harvard Club Boston. None. Office: Shadyside Med Ctr 5200 Centre Ave Ste 705 Pittsburgh PA 15232 Office Phone: 412-681-8720. Office Fax: 412-681-8713. Business E-Mail: jarrettf@upmc.edu.

JARRETT, JEFFREY D., energy companies association executive, former federal agency administrator; b. W. Va., 1953; s. Leslie and Agatha Jarrett; m. Janet Goodwin; children: Sarah, Tyler. BS in Human Resources Mgmt., Geneva Coll.; AAS in Land Stabilization & Reclamation, Belmont Tech. Coll. Reclamation supr. The Drummond Co.; dir. planning, divsn. mgr., reclamation dir. Cravat Coal Co.; bur. dir. Pa. Dept. Environ. Protection, 1995—2001, dep. sec. mineral resources & mgmt., 2001—02; dep. asst. dir. program ops. Pitts. regional office Office Surface Mining US Dept. Interior, 1988—94, dir. Office Surface Mining Reclamation & Enforcement Washington, 2002—05; asst. sec. for fossil energy US Dept. Energy, Washington, 2006—07; exec. dir. Coal-Based Generation Stakeholders, 2007—.*

JARRETT, POLLY HAWKINS, retired secondary school educator; b. Columbia, SC, May 6, 1929; d. William Harold and Ann Beatrice (Carson) Hawkins; m. Nov. 21, 1953 (dec. Aug. 1984); children: William Guy Jr., Henry Carson. Student, Montreat Coll., 1947-49; BS in Secondary Edn., Longwood Coll., 1951. Tchr. 7th grade McDowell County Schs., Marion, N.C., 1951-52; tchr. 8th grade Marion City Schs., 1952-53, Burke County Schs., Morganton, N.C., 1954-56; tchr. 7th grade Wake County Schs., Raleigh, N.C., 1956-58, Durham (N.C.) County Schs., 1958-59; tchr. 7th and 8th grade Raleigh City and Wake County Schs., Raleigh, 1959-79; tchr. social studies Wake County Pub. Schs., Raleigh, 1979-90, ret., 1990. Adv. bd. State Employees Credit Union, Raleigh, 1988—92, Raleigh, 1994—2000. Mem. United Daus. of the Confederacy (chpt. pres. 1978-81, 91-96, divsn. historian 1981-83, dist. VI dir. 1983-85, divsn. chaplain 1986-90, divns. parliamentarian 1994-96, chmn. bd. trustees 1990-91), Delta Kappa Gamma (chpt. pres. 1988-90, regional dir. 1990-92, state 2d v.p. 1997-99, chmn. N.C. divsn. State Conv. 2001, mem. S.E. regional steering com. 2003), Kappa Delta Pi, Pi Delta Epsilon, Pi Gamma Mu. Democrat. Methodist. Avocations: travel, growing roses, reading, pets. Home: 3405 White Oak Rd Raleigh NC 27609-7620 Personal E-mail: jarretth@bellsouth.net.

JARRETT, VALERIE BOWMAN, real estate company executive, former stock exchange executive; b. Shiraz, Iran, Nov. 14, 1956; d. James Edward and Barbara (Taylor) B.; 1 child, Laura Allison. BA, Stanford U., 1978; JD, U. Mich., 1981. Bar: Ill. 1981, U.S. Dist. Ct. (no. dist.) Ill. 1981. Assoc. Pope, Ballard, Shepard & Fowle Ltd., Chgo., 1981-84, Sonnenschein, Carlin, Nath & Rosenthal, Chgo., 1984—87; dep. corp. counsel for fin. and devel. City of Chgo., 1987—91, dep. chief of staff for Mayor Richard Daley, 1991—95, commr., dept. planning and devel.; chmn. Chgo. Transit Authority, 1995—2003; exec. v.p., mng. dir. The Habitat Co., Chgo., 1995—2007, CEO, 2007—. Bd. dirs. USG Corp., 1998—, Joyce Found., Met. Planning Coun., Chgo. Stock Exch. Inc., 2000—07, chmn., 2004—07, Local Initiative Support Corp.; exec. counsel Chgo. Metropolis 2020. Dir. RREEF Am. II, Navigant Cons., Inc.; pres. Southeast Chgo. Commn., Chicago-land C. of C.; trustee Mus. Sci. and Industry, Windows to the World Comm., U. Chgo.; vice chmn. U. Chgo. Hosps. Leadership Greater Chgo. fellow, 1985-86; recipient Govt. Support award, Women's Bus. Devel. Ctr., 1992 Mem. Econ. Club, Comml. Club. Democrat. Avocation: travel. Office: The Habitat Co 350 West Hubbard St Chicago IL 60610 Office Phone: 312-527-5400.*

JARROW, ROBERT ALAN, economist, educator; b. Hackensack, NY, June 16, 1952; s. Benjamin Charles and Irene Elizabeth (Kozniewski) Jaworowski; m. Gail Dian Goundry; children: Kyle, Tate, Heather. BA, Duke U., 1974; MBA, Dartmouth Coll., 1976; PhD, MIT, 1979. Prof. fin. and econs. Cornell U., Ithaca, NY, 1979—. Cons. Bank of Am., San Francisco, 1987-89, Merrill Lynch, 1994, Kamakura Corp., 1995—, FDIC, 2003—. Magnetar, 2005—. Author: Option Pricing, 1983, Finance Theory, 1988, Modelling Fixed Income Securities and Interest Rate Options, 1996, 2d revised edit., 2002, Derivative Securities, 1996, 2000; editor: Math. Fin., 2001—06; co-editor: Jour. Derivatives, 1999—2002; assoc. editor: Rev. Derivatives Rsch., 1997—; contbr. articles. Recipient Pomerance prize Chgo. Bd. Options Exch., 1982; named Fin. Engr. Yr., 1997; named to Fixed Income Security Analysts Hall of Fame, 2004. Mem. Am. Fin. Assn., Econ. Soc., Ops. Rsch. Soc., Soc. for Promotion Econ. Theory, Math. Assn. Am. Avocations: jogging, soccer, Karate. Office: Cornell U Sage Hall Ithaca NY 14853 Business E-Mail: RAJ15@cornell.edu.

JARSMA, CYNTHIA LYNN, secondary school educator; d. John Truman and Joyce Marilyn Taylor; m. Brian Matthew Jarsma, Aug. 27, 1988. BA in English, Nazareth Coll., Kalamazoo, Mich., 1989; MA in Edn., Saginaw Valley U., Mich., 2000. Cert. tchr. State of Mich., 1990. Tchr. L'Anse Creuse Pub. Schs., Chesterfield, Mich., 1994—99, East China Sch. Dist., Mich., 1999—. Intake worker Macomb St. Clair Pvt. Industry Coun., Mount Clemens, Mich. Avocations: travel, photography, scrapbooks.

JARVEY, JOHN ALFRED, federal judge; b. Mpls., 1956; BS, U. Akron, 1978; JD, Drake U., 1981. Law clk. to Hon. Donald E. O'Brien U.S. Dist. Ct. (no. dist.) Iowa, Cedar Rapids, 1981-83; trial atty. US Dept. Justice, Washington, 1983-87; chief magistrate judge US Dist. Ct. (no. dist.) Iowa, Cedar Rapids, 1987—2007; dist. judge US Dist. Ct. (so. dist.) Iowa, 2007—. Office: US Dist Ct 123 E Walnut St Rm 300 PO Box 9344 Des Moines IA 50306*

JÄRVI, NEEME, conductor, music director; b. Tallinn, Estonia, June 7, 1937; arrived in U.S., 1980; s. August and Elss Jarvi; m. Liilia Jarvi, Sept. 2, 1961; children: Paavo Jarvi, Kristjan Jarvi, Maarika Jarvi. Diploma in Music and Conducting, St. Petersburg State Conservatorium, USSR, 1960; doctorate (hon.), U. Aberdeen, Scotland, Music Conservatory Talinn, Estonia, Gothenberg U., Sweden, U. Mich. Condr. Estonian Radio Symphony Orch., 1960-63, chief condr., 1963-76, Estonian State Opera, 1963-76, Estonian State Symphony, 1976-80; prin. condr. Gothenburg (Sweden) Symphony Orch., 1982—; prin. condr., music dir., condr. laureate Royal Scottish Orch., Glasgow, 1984-88; music dir. Detroit Symphony Orch., 1990—2005, music dir. emeritus, 2005—. Prin. guest condr. Birmingham Symphony Orch., England, 1980—83; guest condr. N.Y. Philharm. Orch., Boston Symphony Orch., Phila. Orch., Chgo. Symphony, Royal Concertgebow, Amsterdam, Philharmonia London, London Symphony, Scandinavian Orch., Met. Opera House, NYC. Rec. artist music of Ellington, Barber, Beach and Ives with DSO, rec. artist Sibelius Symphony, Stenhammar Symphony, Berwald Symphony, Dvorak Symphony, Gade Symphony, Svendsen Symphony, Brahms Symphony, R. Strauss Symphony, Glasounov Symphony, Eduard Tubin Schostakovitch Symphony, Prokoffiev Symphony, Rimski-Korsakov Symphony, Part Symphony. Decorated Knight Comdr. North Star Order Sweden; recipient 1st prize in conducting, Accademia Nazionale di Santa Cecilia, 1971.*

JARVI, PAAVO, conductor, music director; b. Tallinn, Estonia, 1963; U.S., 1980, arrived in US, 1980, naturalized; Studied at, Curtis Inst. of Music, Los Angeles Philharm. Inst. Prin. guest condr. Royal Stochkholm Philharm., City of Birmingham, Eng.; music dir., condr. Cin. Symphony Orch., 2001—. Condr. UBS Verbier Youth Orch. (summer series); artistic adv. Estonian Nat. Symphony Orch., 2002—; guest condr. London Symphony, London Philharm., Orch. of the Age of Enlightenment, BBC Philharm., Atlanta Symphony Orch., Boston Symphony Orch., Cleveland Symphony Orch., Chgo. Symphony Orch., Dallas Symphony Orch., Detroit Symphony Orch., Houston Symphony Orch., LA Symphony Orch., Montreal Symphony Orch., Phila. Symphony Orch., Pitts. Symphony Orch., San Francisco Symphony Orch., Toronto Symphony Orch. Named Editor's Choice, Feb. 2003 edit. of Gramophone; recipient Kultuurkapital award, Estonian Min. of Culture, Spirit of Cin. Queen City Adv. award, 2004. Office: CSO Administrative Offices Music Hall 1241 Elm St Cincinnati OH 45202*

JARVIK, ROBERT KOFFLER, biomedical research scientist; b. Midland, Mich., May 11, 1946; m. Elaine Levin, 1968 (div. 1985); 2 children; m. Marilyn Vos Savant, 1987. BA, Syracuse U., 1968, DSc (hon.), 1983; MA, NYU, 1971; MD, U. Utah, 1976; Dr sc (hon.), Hahnemann U., 1985. Rsch. asst. Div. Artificial Organs U. Utah, Salt Lake City, 1971-76, asst. dir. exptl. labs. Div. Artificial Organs, 1976-82, asst. rsch. prof. surgery, 1979-87; pres. Symbion, Inc., Salt Lake City, 1981-87; pres., CEO Jarvik Heart Inc., NYC, 1987—; mem. nat. selection panel NASA Tchr. in Space Project, Washington, 1985. Sect. editor Internat. Jour. Artificial Organs, 1979-88; inventor repeating hemostatic clip instruments and cartridges, total artificial hearts powered by electrohydraulic energy and Jarvik-7; patentee in field. Named Inventor of Yr. Intellectual Property Owners, 1983, named John W. Hyatt award Soc. Plastics Engrs., 1983; recipient Golden Plate Am. Acad. Achievement, 1983, Gold Heart award Utah Heart Assn., 1983, Nat. Hero award, 1992. Mem. Am. Soc. Artificial Internal Organs The Jarvik-7, the first permanent implantable artificial heart. The first Jarvik-7 was implanted into Barney Clark in 1982 - he survived 112 days; the Jarvik 2000, a thumb sized battery operated pump that fits directly into the left ventricle and pushes oxygenated blood throughout the body; donated one of the newer artificial hearts & the pioneering artificial heart that kept Barney Clark alive for 112 days for the Treasures of American History exhibition, National Air & Space Museum, Smithsonian Institution in 2007. Office: Jarvik Heart Inc 333 W 52d St New York NY 10019

JARVIS, CHARLENE DREW, academic administrator, former scientist; b. Washington, July 31, 1941; 2 children. BA, Oberlin Coll., Ohio, 1962; MS in Psychology, Howard U., 1964; PhD in Neuropsychology, U. Md., 1971; DSc (hon.), Amherst Coll., 1994, George Washington U., 2001. Supr. statis. lab. Howard U., 1965-66, prof. psychol. Washington, 1970-71; rsch. psychologist NIMH, 1971-78; coun. mem. Coun. of the D.C., 1979-2000; chair com. on housing and econ. devel. coun. of the D.C., 1981-2000; chair pro temp Coun. of the D.C., 1994-2000; pres. Southeastern Univ., Washington, 1996—. Chair bd. dirs. Met. Washington Coun. of Govts.; bd. dirs. Pa. Ave. Devel. Corp., Nat. Health Mus., Fed. City Coun., BB&T Regional Bank, Washington office; mem. steering com. Greater Washington Mktg. Partnership of the Greater Washington Bd. of Trade, 1993—; mem. coms. NIMH, adv. coun., 1993—; mem. breast cancer task force, 1993—; mem. Ronald Reagan Ctr. for Emergency Medicine, George Washington U. Hosp., 1993—. Bd. dirs. Girl Scouts Am., Pvt. Industry Coun., 1986—; mem. Leadership Washington, 1991-92; chair transp. subcom. D.C. chpt. ARC; del. Nat. Dem. Conv., 1980, 84, 88, 92; nat. co-chair Mondale for Pres., 1984, Clinton/Gore campaign, 1992; candidate for mayor, D.C., 1982, 90; chair pro tempore Coun. D.C., 1997—; chair cmty. bus. partnership com. Greater Washington Bd. of Trade; chair, bd. dirs. Washington D.C. Conv. and Tourism Corp., 2001—. Recipient Howard U. Alumni award, 1993, over 100 others; Named one of 50 Most Powerful Women in the Washington Area Washington Bus. Jour. , 1985, 100 Most Powerful Women in the Washington Area, Washingtonian Mag., 1989, 94, Washingtonian of Yr. Washingtonian Mag., 1999. Mem. Nat.

Assn. Ind. Colls. and Univs. (bd. dirs.), D.C. C. of C. (pres.-elect). Home: 1789 Sycamore St NW Washington DC 20012-1030 Office: Southeastern Univ 501 I St SW Washington DC 20024-2715 E-mail: president@admin.seu.edu.

JARVIS, DONALD BERTRAM, judge; b. Newark, Dec. 14, 1928; s. Benjamin and Esther (Golden) J.; m. Rosalind C. Chodorcove, June 13, 1954; children: Nancie, Brian, Joanne. BA, Rutgers U., 1949; JD, Stanford U., 1952. Bar: Calif. 1953. Law clk. to justice John W. Shenk Calif. Supreme Ct., 1953-54; assoc. Erskine, Erskine & Tulley, 1955, Aaron N. Cohen, 1955-56; law clk. Dist. Ct. Appeal, 1956; assoc. Carl Hoppe, 1956-57; adminstrv. law judge Calif. Pub. Utilities Commn., San Francisco, 1957-91, U.S. Dept. of Labor, San Francisco, 1992—. Mem. exec. com. Nat. Conf. Adminstrv. Law Judges, 1986-88, sec. 1988-89, vice-chair, 1990-91, chair-elect, 1991-92, chair 1992-93; pres. Calif. Adminstrv. Law Judges Coun., 1978-84; mem. faculty Nat. Jud. Coll., U. Nev., 1977, 78, 80; mem. U.S. Bd. of Alien Labor Cert. Appeals, 1995—. Chmn. pack Boy Scouts Am., 1967-69, chmn. troop 1972; class chmn. Stanford Law Sch. Fund, 1959, mem. nat. com., 1963-65; dir. Forest Hill Assn., 1970-71; patron San Francisco Opera. Served to col. USAF Res., 1949-79. Decorated Legion of Merit. Mem. ABA (mem. ho. of dels. 1993-99, vice chair jud. divsn. 1997-98, chair elect 1998-99, chair 1999-2000), State Bar Calif., Bar Assn. San Francisco, Calif. Conf. Pub. Utility Counsel (pres. 1980-81), Air Force Assn., Res. Officers Assn., Ret. Officers Assn., San Francisco Gem and Mineral Soc., Stanford Alumni Assn., Rutgers Alumni Assn., Phi Beta Kappa (pres. No. Calif. 1973-74), Tau Kappa Alpha, Pi Alpha Theta, Phi Alpha Delta. Home: 530 Dewey Blvd San Francisco CA 94116-1427 Office: 50 Fremont St San Francisco CA 94105-2230

JARVIS, ELBERT, II, (JAY JARVIS), employee benefits specialist; b. Washington, NC, Sept. 20, 1944; s. Elbert J. Sr. and Laura F. (Lilley) J.; m. Anita Kleinfeld, Nov. 28, 1968 (div. Nov. 1983); 1 child, Elbert J. III; m. Audrey H. Liebross, July 28, 1991; 1 child, Benjamin Grover. A of Bus. Adminstrn., No. Va. C.C., 1972; BSBA, George Mason U., 1974. Sales mgr. Baumgarten Co., Washington, 1970-71; sales rep. Mass Mut., Washington, 1974-84; pres. The Pers. Dept., Inc., Annandale, Va., 1983—2001, Jarvis Consulting Ltd., 2001—. Founder No. Va. Group Health Alliance, No. Va. C. of C., 1998. Editor: (student handbook) Focal Point, 1973, Beth El Temple 1995-97, bd. dirs. Directory chair, 1990, 91, 92, 94, v.p., 2003, treas., 2003-2004, web master, 1999-2000, fund chair, 2000—; v.p. Brotherhood, 1999-2001, pres., 2001-2003. Scoutmaster, cubmaster, Webelos leader Boy Scouts Am., Clifton, Annandale and Arlington, Va., 1970-71, 85-86; mem. county com., state del. Arlington Rep. Party, 1975-85; pres., sec. Arlington Jaycees, 1980-82; pres., bd. dirs. Lafayette Village Cmty. Assn., Annandale, Va., 1994-95, 2007; bd. dirs. Beth El Hebrew Congregation, v.p. 2000-01, 1st v.p. Brotherhood Beth El, 1999-2001, Brotherhood pres., 2001-2003, webmaster, 1999-2000, chmn. permanent endowment fund, 2000—, v.p., treas. 2003—; bd. dirs. Annadale Sq. Office Condominium, 1999. Mem. Am. Compensation Assn., Health Underwriters Assn. (sec. No. Va. chpt. 1996-97), Washington chpt. Cert. Employee Benefit Specialist (assoc.), Arlington C. of C. (chmn. comms. com. 1983, bd. dirs. 1988-92, 92-94, chmn. sml. bus. coun. 1990, 92, chmn. expo com. 1991, chmn. awards and small bus. week 1994, Disting. Svc. awards 1989), Soc. Employee Benefits Profls., Alexandria C. of C. (mem. advantage program com. 1993-96), Fairfax County C. of C. (vice chmn. small bus. awards 1993-94, mem. team captain 1996), Northern Va. C. of C. (founder, bd. chair 1998—), Lafayette Village Comm. Assn. (pres.). Jewish. Avocations: canoeing, camping, photography. Home: 7828 Ashley Glen Rd Annandale VA 22003-1556 Office: Jarvis Cons Ltd PO Box 1650 Annandale VA 22003 Office Phone: 571-235-5420. E-mail: jay@jarvisconsulting.org.

JARVIS, ERICH DAVID, neurobiologist, educator; b. NYC, May 6, 1965; s. James Reginald Jarvis and Sasha Valeria (Monk) McCall; m. Miriam Virtudes Rivas, May 1984; children: Electra Riva, Syrus Chaske. BA in Biology and Mathematics, Hunter Coll., 1988; PhD in Molecular Neurobiology & Animal Behavior, Rockefeller U., 1995, postdoc. in Molecular Neurobiology & Animal Behavior, 1995—98. Asst. prof. Rockefeller U., NY, 1998—, Duke U., NC, 1999—. Pres. coun. black affairs Duke U., 1999—2002, grad. students admissions com., 1999—, grad. student steering com., 1999—, dir. minority recruitment, 2000—, mem. steering com. black collective, 2001—, mem. molecular biology com., 2001—. Contbr. genetic rsch. articles in learning and memory to sci. publs. Recipient First Pl. award Excellence in Biomed. Rsch., NIH, 1986, George H. Hitching New Investigator award, Triangle Cmty. Found., 2000—01, award, Esther & Joseph Klingenstien Fund., 2000—03, Whitehall Found., 2000—, Alan T. Waterman award, NSF, 2002—, Dir.'s Pioneer Award, NIH, 2005; grantee, NSF, 2000—03, NIH, 2001—02. Democrat. Avocations: dance, genealogy. Office: Duke U Med Ctr Dept Neurobiology Box 3209 Durham NC 27710

JARVIS, GILBERT ANDREW, humanities educator, writer; b. Chelsea, Mass., Feb. 13, 1941; s. Vernon Owen and Angeline M. (Burkard) J.; m. Carol Jean Ganter, Jan. 26, 1963; children: Vicki Lynn, Mark Christopher. BA, St. Norbert Coll., De Pere, Wis., 1963; MA, Purdue U., 1965, PhD, 1970. Prof. Ohio State U., Columbus, 1970-95, chmn. humanities edn., 1980-83, assoc. chmn. dept. ednl. theory and practice, 1983-87, chmn. dept. ednl. studies, 1987-95, dir. ESL programs, 1994-2000, chmn. prof. emeritus, 1995—. Cons. Internat. Edn. Program, U.S. Dept. Edn., Washington, 1977-84, others. Author: Et Vous?, 1983, 3d edit., 1989; Invitation, 1979, 4th edit., 1993, Y tu?, 1986, 2d edit., 1988, Connaitre et se connaitre, 3d edit., 1986, Invitation Essentials, 1991, 2d edit., 1995, Invitation au monde francophone, 2000, 2d edit., 2005; editor: The Challenge for Excellence, 1984; mem. editl. bd. Modern Lang. Jour., 1979-86; adv. bd. Can. Modern lang. Rev., 1982-2006. Mem. Am. Coun. Tchg. Fgn. Langs. (editor Rev. Fgn. Lang. Edn. 1974, 75, 76, 77), Phi Delta Kappa. Avocations: travel, photography. Home: 8337 Evangeline Dr Columbus OH 43235-1136

JARVIS, JAMES HOWARD, II, judge; b. Knoxville, Tenn., Feb. 28, 1937; s. Howard F. and Eleanor B. J.; m. Martha Stapleton, June 1957 (div. Feb. 1962); children: James Howard III, Leslie; m. Pamela K. Duncan, Aug. 23, 1964 (div. Apr. 1991); children: Ann, Kathryn, Louise; m. Gail Stone, Sept. 4, 1992. BA, U. Tenn., 1958, JD, 1960. Bar: Tenn. 1961, U.S. Dist. Ct. (ea. dist.) Tenn. 1961, U.S. Ct. Appeals (6th cir.) 1965. Assoc. O'Neil, Jarvis, Parker & Williamson, Knoxville, Tenn., 1960-68, mem., 1968-70, Meares, Dungan, Jarvis, Knoxville, Tenn., 1970-72; judge Law & Equity Ct., Blount County, Tenn., 1972-77, 30th Jud. Ct., Blount County, Tenn., 1977-84, U.S. Dist. Ct. (ea. dist.) Tenn., Knoxville, 1984—, chief judge, 1991-98. Bd. dirs. Maryville (Tenn.) Coll., 1991-98; past chmn. fin. com. St. Andrews Episc. Ch.; past bd. dirs. Detoxification Rehab. Inst. Knoxville; past com. codes of conduct Jud. Conf. U.S. Named Trial Judge of Yr., Am. Bd. Trial Advs., 2004. Mem. Tenn. Bar Assn. (bd. govs. 1983-84), Am. Judicature Soc., Tenn. Trial Judges Assn. (pres. exec. com.), Tenn. Jud. Conf. (pres. 1983-84), Blount County Bar Assn., Knoxville Bar Assn. (Judicial Excellence award 2002), Great Smoky Mountains Conservation Assn., Phi Delta Phi, Sigma Chi (significant Sigma Chi). Republican. Home: 6916 Stone Mill Rd Knoxville TN 37919-7431 Office: Howard H Baker Jr US Courthouse 800 Market St Knoxville TN 37902-2327

JARVIS, JEFF, journalist, former critic, news blogger; BS in Journalism, Medill Sch. Journalism, Northwestern U. With Chgo. Sun Times, 1974; former TV critic TV Guide, People; creator, founding mng. editor Entertainment Weekly; Sunday editor, assoc. pub. NY Daily News; columnist San Francisco Examiner; former pres., creative dir. Advance.net; currently editor of news start-up; assoc. prof., dir. interactive journalism program CUNY, Grad. Sch. Journalism, 2006—; creator, blog author Buzzmachine.com. Working with on content develop. and strategy NY Times, About.com; columnist Media Guardian; cons. for Advance and Fairchild. Contbr. articles to NY Post, NY Times, The Nation, Rolling Stone and Money. Named one of Top 25 Web Celebs, Forbes mag., 2007. Office: City Univ of NY Graduate Sch Journalism 535 E 80th St New York NY 10021 E-mail: jeff@buzzmachine.com.*

JARVIS, MARK, information technology executive; Degree in Computer Science, Leeds U., 1982. Tech support Philips Data Systems, Netherlands, 1985; joined as twelfth employee as a software engineer Oracle Corp., Netherlands, 1989, dir. product mgmt. network products divsn. Calif., 1993, v.p. mktg. all Oracle database products, 1995, sr. v.p. mktg. worldwide, 1998, sr. v.p., chief mktg. officer, 2000—03, cons., 2003—07; chief mktg. officer Dell Inc., 2007—. Advisor Oracle Venture Fund. Named a Marketer of the Next Generation, Brandweek, 2002; named Marketer of Yr., Mktg. Computers mag., 2000. Avocations: mountain climbing, rock climbing, movies. Office: Dell Inc 1 Dell Way Dell Computers TX 78682-2222*

JARVIS, PETER R., lawyer; b. NYC, July 19, 1950; BA in Econs. magna cum laude, Harvard U., 1972; MA in Econs., Yale U., 1976, JD, 1976. Bar: Oreg. 1976, U.S. Dist. Ct. Oreg. 1976, U.S. Ct. Appeals (9th cir.) 1977, Wash. 1983, U.S. Dist. Ct. (we. dist.) Wash. 1983, U.S. Dist. Ct. (ea. dist.) Wash. 1985, U.S. Tax Ct. 1991. Assoc. Stoel Rives LLP, Portland, Oreg., 1976—82, ptnr., 1982—2003; ptnr.-in-charge, Portland, legal ethics, risk mgmt. Hinshaw & Culbertson LLP, Portland, Oreg., 2003—. Author: (with others) Oregon Rules of Professional Responsibility (updated annually); editor, author: (with others) The Ethical Oregon Lawyer, 1991, 98; ethics columnists: Oregon Law Jour.; spkr. on legal ethics issues. Mem. ALI (Harrison Tweed Spl. Merit award 1993), Oreg. State Bar (former mem. legal ethics com., Pres.'s Membership Svcs. award 1991), Wash. State Bar (mem. profl. conduct com.), Assn. Profl. Responsibility Lawyers (bd. dir., 1999-,pres. 2005), Phi Beta Kappa. Office: Hinshaw & Culbertson LLP Ste 1950 1000 SW Broadway Portland OR 97205-3078 Office Phone: 503-243-3243. Office Fax: 503-243-3240. Business E-Mail: pjarvis@hinshawlaw.com.

JARVIS, REBECCA, financial reporter; b. Mpls., 1981; Grad., U. Chgo., 2003. Interest rate trader fgn. exchange desk Citigroup, London; investment banking analyst Banc of Am. Securities, Chgo.; fin. journalist Chgo.; assoc. reporter CNBC, 2006—. Pro bono cons. Pivot Consulting. Participant (TV series) The Apprentice 4, 2005. Founder Minn. Alliance with Youth; bd. dirs. Youthrive. Named one of 20 Teens Who Will Change the World, Teen People mag., 2000. Office: CNBC NASDAQ Mkt Site 4 Times Sq 2nd Fl New York NY 10036*

JARVIS, RENEE MARIE, language educator; b. Bloomington, Minn., Aug. 10, 1966; d. Jerry James and Ruth Kathleen Bontrager; 1 child, Rikki Lynn. BA, U. Wis., Eau Claire, 1988; M, Nova U., Las Vegas, Nev., 1994. Cert. Spanish tchr. Las Vegas, 1989, ESL tchr. Las Vegas, 1994. Spanish tchr. Boulder City H.S., Nev., 1989—91, Green Valley H.S., Henderson, Nev., 1991—95, Clark County C.C., Las Vegas, 1999—2001, The Meadows Sch., Las Vegas, 2001—; Spanish/ESL tchr. Virgin Valley H.S., Mesquite, Nev., 1995—97. Cheerleader advisor Boulder City H.S., 1989—90, tennis coach, 1990—91, Green Valley H.S., Las Vegas, 1991—94; advisor Club Sol, Mesquite, 1996—97, Picasso (Jr. Spanish Honor Soc.), Las Vegas, 2005—. Dir. children's choirs The Lakes Luth. Ch., Las Vegas, 1999. Mem.: Am. Coun. Tchrs. Fgn. Lang. Office: The Meadows School 8601 Scholar Ln Las Vegas NV 89128 Home Phone: 702-256-3653; Office Phone: 702-254-1610. Personal E-mail: rjarvis@themeadowsschool.org.

JARVIS, RICHARD S., academic administrator; b. Nottingham, Eng., Feb. 13, 1949; came to U.S., 1974; s. John Leslie and Mary Margaret (Dodman) J. BA in Geography, Cambridge U., Eng., 1970, MA, 1974, PhD in Geography, 1975. Lectr. Durham (Eng.) U., 1973-74; assoc. prof. SUNY, Buffalo, 1975-87, asst. to pres., 1986-87, v.p. acad. Fredonia, 1987-90, prof. geoscis., 1987-90; vice provost SUNY Sys., Albany, 1990-94; chancellor Univ. and C.C. Sys. Nev., Reno and Las Vegas, 1994-99, U.S. Open U., Aurora, Colo., 1999—2002, Oreg. U. Sys., 2002—04; provost U. Tex., El Paso, 2005—. Editor: River Networks, 1983; contbr. articles to profl. jours. Office: U Tex El Paso 500 W University Ave El Paso TX 79968 Home Phone: 915-307-6383; Office Phone: 915-747-7885. Business E-Mail: rsjarvis@utep.edu.

JARVIS, ROBERT MARK, law educator; b. NYC, Oct. 17, 1959; s. Rubin and Ute (Hacklander) J.; m. Judith Anne Mellman, Mar. 3, 1989. BA, Northwestern U., 1980; JD, U. Pa., 1983; LLM, NYU, 1986. Bar: N.Y. 1984, Fla. 1990. Assoc. Haight Gardner Poor & Havens, NYC, 1983-85, Baker & McKenzie, NYC, 1985-87; asst. prof. law ctr. Nova Southeastern U., Ft. Lauderdale, Fla., 1987-90, assoc. prof., 1990-92, prof., 1992—. Chmn. bd. dir. Miami Maritime Arbitration Bd., 1993—94; vice chmn. bd. dir. Miami Internat. Arbitration and Mediation Inst., 1993—94; mem. adv. bd. Carolina Acad. Press, 1996—. Author: Careers in Admiralty and Maritime Law, 1993, An Admiralty Law Anthology, 1995; co-author: AIDS: Cases and Materials, 1989, 3d edit., 2002, AIDS Law in a Nutshell, 1991, 2d edit., 1996, Notary Law and Practice: Cases and Materials, 1997, Travel Law: Cases and Materials, 1998, Sports Law: Cases and Materials, 1999, Art and Museum Law: Cases and Materials, 2002, Gaming Law: Cases and Materials, 2003, Theater Law: Cases and Materials, 2004, Admiralty: Cases and Materials, 2004, Aviation Law: Cases and Materials, 2006; editor: Maritime Arbitration, 1999, Law of Cruise Ships, 2000; co-editor: Prime Time Law: Fictional Television as Legal Narrative, 1998, Bush v. Gore: The Fight for Florida's Vote, 2001, Amicus Humoriae: An Anthology of Legal Humor, 2003; mem. editl. bd. Washington Lawyer, 1988—94, Jour. Maritime Law and Commerce, 1990—92, 2001—, Gaming Law Rev., 2006—, assoc. editor Jour. Maritime Law and Commerce, 1993—95, editor, 1996—2000, Maritime Law Reporter, 1991—99, Hospitality Law, 1999—2001, adv. bd. World Arbitration and Mediation Review, 1990—, Transnat. Lawyer, 1991—2004, U. San Francisco Maritime Law Jour., 1992—95, 2002—06, contbg. editor Preview US Supreme Ct. Cases, 1990—95, 1999—2002. Mem.: ABA (vice chmn. admiralty law com. young lawyers divsn. 1992—93, chair 1993—94), Phi Delta Phi (province pres. 1989—91, coun. 1991—93), Assn. Am. Law Schs. (chmn.-elect maritime law sect. 1991—93, chmn. 1993—94), Maritime Law Assn. U.S., Fla. Bar Assn. (admiralty law com. 1988—95, vice chmn. 1991—92, chmn. 1992—93, exec. coun. internat. law sect. 1992—96), Acacia, Northwestern U. Club South Fla. (v.p. 1992—93, pres. 1993—95), Phi Beta Kappa. Democrat. Jewish. Office: Nova Southeastern U Law Ctr 3305 College Ave Fort Lauderdale FL 33314-7721 Office Phone: 954-262-6172. Business E-Mail: jarvisb@nsu.law.nova.edu.

JARVIS, SCOTT, state agency administrator; Legal counsel Office of State Treas., Wash.; spl. policy and enforcement adminstr. Wash. State Dept. Fin. Instns., dir., 2005—; dep. commr. consumer protection Office of Ins. Commr., Wash., 2001. Office: Wash State Dept Fin Instns PO Box 41200 Olympia WA 98504-1200 Office Phone: 360-902-8707. Office Fax: 360-753-6070. E-mail: sjarvis@dfi.wa.gov.

JARVIS, SUE KAY, science educator; b. Cherokee, Iowa, Feb. 9, 1958; d. Virgil Harry Schlinz; m. Stephen Lee Jarvis (div.); children: Stephanie Cady, Jason Lindsay. BA in Edn., Wayne State Coll., Nebr., 1986; post grad., Marycrest Coll., Davenport, Iowa, 1986—89, U. No. Iowa, Cedar Falls, 1990—96, post grad., 2003, post grad., 2002, Morningside Coll., Sioux City, 1996—98, Iowa State U., Ames, 1997, Iowa Ctrl. Cmty. Coll., Fort Dodge, 1999. Cert. tchr. Iowa, endorsements in biology, anatomy, physiology, gen. sci., chemistry, physics, phys. edn. and coaching Iowa. Tchr. jr. high biology St. John's Cath. Sch., Bancroft, Iowa, 1987—89, Holy Family Schs., Sioux City, 1989—95; tchr. phys. sci., biology, chemistry and physics Albert City- Truesdale Combined Sch. Dist., 1995—99; substitute tchr. Pocahontas Area Combined Sch. Dist., 2000; tchr. biology, chemistry and TAG Schaller- Crestland Combined Sch. Dist., Early, 2000—03; tchr. biology, anatomy and physiology, health Pocahontas Area Combined Sch. Dist., 2003—. Advisor Nat. Honor Soc.; asst. H.S. softball and basketball; head softball and volleyball; jr. high softball and volleyball; jr. high athletic dir.; advisor dist. and state sci. fairs; faculty sponsor Iowa State Bar Assn. Mock Trial State Tournament; volleyball official. Named AEA 12 Demonstration Sci. Classroom. Mem.: NEA, Ia. State Edn. Assn., Nat. Sci. Tchrs. Assn., Iowa Girls HS Athletic Union (volleyball official), Delta Kappa Gammaa Upsilon. Republican. Roman Catholic. Avocations: kayaking, gardening, house remodeling, motorcycling. Office: Pocahontas Area CDS Pocahontas IA 50574 Office Phone: 712-335-4848.

JARVIS, WILLIAM DAVID, pharmacologist, researcher; s. Floyd Eldridge and Pauline Lemon Jarvis. BA in English in Biology, U. Va., Charlottesville, 1984, PhD in Neurosci., 1991; post doctoral, Massey Cancer Ctr. Postdoctoral fellow U. Va., Charlottesville, Va.; rsch. assoc cancer biology Massey Cancer Ctr., Richmond, Va., 1996—99; asst. prof., then assoc prof. integrative biology and pharmacology U. Tex. Health Sci. Ctr., Houston, 1999—2003; chief tech. officer Dominion Diagnostics, Inc., North Kingstown, RI, 2003—. Author over 70 reports, revs., chpts., articles in field. Recipient Howard Temin Rsch. Scientist Devel. award, NIH/Nat. Cancer Inst., 1999—; Individual Nat. Rsch. Svc. fellow, 1993—95, Specialized Program of Excellence in Cancer Rsch. grantee, 2004—. Mem.: Endocrine Soc., Soc. Neuroscience, Am. Soc. Biochemistry and Molecular Biology, Am. Soc. Pharmacology and Exptl. Therapeutics, Am. Cancer Soc. Episcopalian. Achievements include research in pharmaceutical development and mechanistic investigations of multiple anti-neoplastic drugs; discovery of delineation of the ceramide signaling pathway for initiating cell death in human cancers; development of effective drug interactions for more powerful and innovative anti-cancer treatments (Leukemia, Lymphoma); discovery of multiple protective signaling systems that allow cancers to thwart various modern treatment strategies; research in complex and interrelated signaling networks that centrally regulate tumor cell survival. Avocations: historical / architectural rennovation, collecting antiques, rare books, ephemera, travel, writing, photography. Office: Dominion Diagnostics Inc 211 Circuit Dr North Kingstown RI 02852-7440 Home Phone: 401-743-0710; Office Phone: 401-667-0892. E-mail: wdjarvis@dominiondiagnostics.com.

JARVIS, WILLIAM ROBERT, epidemiologist, educator; b. Oakland, Calif., June 2, 1948; s. John James and Mattie Belle (Steele) J.; m. Janine M. Jason, July 4, 1982; children: Danielle Kristin, Ashley Alana. BS in Psychology with honors, U. Calif., Davis, 1970; MD, U. Tex., Houston, 1974. Intern U. Tex. Med. Ctr., Houston, 1974-75; resident in pediat. Children's Hosp., LA, 1975-77; pediatric infectious disease fellow Toronto Hosp. for Sick Children, 1977-78; fellow pediat. infectious diseases, virology, pub. health Yale U. Sch. Med., 1978-80; commd. med. officer USPHS, 1980, advanced through grades to capt., 1990, ret., 2003; asst. chief Nat. Nosocomial Infections Surveillance Systems Ctrs. for Disease Control, Atlanta, 1981-90, asst. chief epidemiology br., 1984-87, chief epidemiology br. hosp. infections program, 1987-91, chief investigation, prevention br. hosp. infections program, 1991-2000, acting dir. hosp. infections program, 1996-98, assoc. dir. program devel. Divsn. Healthcare Quality Promotion, 2001—02; dir. Office Extramural Rsch. Nat. Ctr. for Infectious Diseases, Atlanta, 2002—03. Asst. prof. pediat. infectious disease and immunology Emory U., Atlanta, 1985-96, assoc. prof., 1996—; asst. prof. Rollins Sch. Pub. Health, 1999—, pvt. cons., 2003—; pres Jason & Jarvis Assocs., 2003—. Editor: ICHE, 2004—07, Hosp. Infections Book, 2005—; contbr. articles to profl. jours., chapters to books. Mem. Infectious Diseases Soc. Am., Am. Soc. Microbiology, Soc. Hosp. Epidemiologists Am. (pres. 2001-02). Roman Catholic. Avocations: stock market, gardening, tennis, travel. Office: Jason &Jarvis Assoc 135 Dune Ln Hilton Head Island SC 29928 Address: 4483 23rd St 1 San Francisco CA 94114 Office Phone: 404-512-4777. Personal E-mail: wrjmj@aol.com.

JARY, MARY CANALES, business owner; b. Premont, Tex., Nov. 22, 1936; d. Gus and Ruth (Shively) Canales; m. Lloyd Walker Jary, Apr. 18, 1958; children: Lloyd Walker III, Elisa Jary, Bettina Mathis, Pamela Rosser. Student, Rollins Coll., 1955-56, U. Tex., 1956-58, Incarnate Word Coll., 1959-60, Trinity U., 1966—. Prin., owner Restoration Assocs., San Antonio, 1985—. Pres. San Antonio PTA, 1971; vice chmn. Night in Old San Antonio, 1989—; bd. dirs. San Antonio Conservation Soc., 1972-90, 2d v.p. 1997—. Mem.: AIA (aux. pres. San Antonio chpt. 1970), Assn. of Preservation Tech. (v.p. 2005), Am. Inst. Conservation (assoc.). Republican. Roman Catholic. Avocations: tennis, hunting. Office: Restoration Assn Ltd 3617 Broadway St Ste 302 San Antonio TX 78209-6509 Office Phone: 210-820-3432. Fax: 210-820-3447. E-mail: cisi@prestorationassociates.com.

JASEN, MATTHEW JOSEPH, lawyer, retired judge; b. Buffalo, Dec. 13, 1915; s. Joseph John and Celina (Perlinski) Jasinski; m. Anastasia Gawinski, Oct. 4, 1943 (dec. Aug. 1970); children: Peter M., Mark M., Christine, Carol Ann; m. Gertrude O'Connor Travers, Mar. 25, 1972 (dec. Nov. 1972); m. Grace Yungbluth Frauenheim, Aug. 31, 1973 (dec. Nov. 13, 2003). BA, Canisius Coll., 1937; LLB, U. Buffalo, 1939; postgrad., Harvard U., 1944; LLD (hon.), Union U., 1980, N.Y. Law Sch., 1981. Bar: N.Y. 1940. Ptnr. firm Beyer, Jasen & Boland, Buffalo, 1940-43; pres. U.S. Security Rev. Bd., Wurttemberg-Baden, Germany, 1945-46; judge U.S. Mil. Govt. Ct., Heidelberg, Germany, 1946-49; sr. ptnr. firm Jasen, Manz, Johnson & Bayger, Buffalo, 1949-57; justice N.Y. Supreme Ct. (8th jud. dist.), 1957-67; judge N.Y. Ct. Appeals, 1968-85; U.S. Supreme Ct. spl. master S.C. v. U.S., 1987-88; spl. master Ill. vs. Ky. U.S. Supreme Ct., 1989-95; of counsel Moot & Sprague, Buffalo, 1986-90; counsel Jasen, Jasen & Sampson, P.C., Buffalo, 1990-99, Jasen & Jasen, P.C., Buffalo, 1999—. Mem. N.Y. State Jud. Screening Com., 1996—. Contbr. articles to profl. jours. Mem. council U. Buffalo, 1963-66; trustee Canisius Coll. Chair of Polish Culture, also, Nottingham Acad. Served to capt. AUS, 1943-46, ETO. Fellow Hilbert Coll.; recipient Disting. Alumnus award SUNY-Buffalo Sch. Law, 1969, Disting. Alumnus award Alumni Assn., 1976, Disting. Alumnus award Canisius Coll., 1978, Edwin F. Jaeckle award SUNY-Buffalo Sch. Law, 1982. Mem. Nat. Conf. Appellate Judges, State U. N.Y. at Buffalo Law Sch. Alumni Assn. (pres. 1964-65), Am., N.Y. State, Erie County bar assns., Am. Law Inst., Am. Judicature Soc., Lawyers Club Buffalo (pres. 1961-62), Nat. Advocates Club, Profl. Businessmen's Assn. Western N.Y. (pres. 1952), Phi Alpha Delta, DiGamma Soc. Roman Catholic (mem. Bishop's Bd. Govs., Buffalo diocese 1951—). Clubs: K.C. (4 deg.). Home: 26 Pine Ter Orchard Park NY 14127-3928 Office: Ste 700 69 Delaware Ave Buffalo NY 14202-3805 Office Phone: 716-848-9500. Personal E-mail: jjatts@buffnet.net.

JASHEL, LARRY STEVEN (L. STEVEN ROSE), entrepreneur, media consultant; b. Dayton, Ohio, Jan. 21, 1950; s. Joseph John and Ruth Margarete (Race) Jashel. Student, Harper Coll., Palatine, Ill., 1968—70, Northwest Med. Inst., Arlington Heights, Ill., 1970—71. Pub.'s asst. Pub.'s Devel. Corp., Chgo., 1971-73; pub. rels. dir. Ill. Entertainer/Chgo. Star/Bankers' Guide, Chgo., 1973-76; v.p. Internat. Media Prodns., Inc., Chgo., 1976-78, Microdynamics Corp., Chgo., 1978-80; exec. v.p. Calif. Aqua Tech, Inc., The Solar Generation, LA, 1980-82; pres., CEO Ra-Tel

Comms. Corp., Ra-Tel Entertainment Corp./Cable Radio, Chgo., 1982-88; founder Steven Rose Prodns. and L.S. Jashel Assocs., Chgo., 1988-98; founder, CEO Spuppets, Ltd., 1996, Children's Cultural Network, 2000—; exec. dir. Superior Benefit Solutions, 1998-2000. TV prodr., dir., writer Ind. Broadcasting, Chgo., 1982—; radio prodr., on-air personality Nat. Pub. Radio, Chgo., Washington, 1982—, Sta. WJRC-AM, Chgo., 1987—88; music prodr. ind. rec. artists, Chgo., 1982—; cons. Corp. Pub. Broadcasting, 1982—; spkr. in field. Author: Song of a New Age, 1990, A Bakers Dozen, 1995, The Best Poems of 1997, Planet Medieval, 1998, Mystic Blue and the Z-Generation, 2001, Beyond Dreams, 2002, Discovery of Earf, 2003, (book and TV script) Lovestar--The Exciting Adventures, 1994—95; author: (prodr. and dir.) Spuppets (puppets in space), 1997; author: Sojourns Of A Mystic, 2006; co-author: Morning Song, 1997; musician: (musical acts) The Detours, Sudden, The Amboy Dukes, The Yellow Brick Road, J.J. Lee and the Radiants, 1964—72, Mystic Blues, 2002—; actor: (films) Sore Losers, 2001, Road to Perdition, 2002, Insanity, 2003—. Named del. rep. to Presdl. Inauguration Ball, Washington, D.C., 1980; recipient Blue Ribbon award, Midwest Sports Assn., 1968, award, Chgo. Film Festival, 1984, Am. Svc. award, Am. Svc. Corp., 1988, Award of Distinction, Internat. Comm., 1998, Award of Excellence, Nat. Videographer, 1998, 1st pl. Telly award, 2000, Omni award, 2001, Telly music video award, 2003, Golden Telly award for best in producing, writing, directing and performance of 25 years, 2004. Mem.: NARAS (Grammy awards 1982—), ASCAP (award 1998—99, 2000), Am. Soc. Composers, Artists and Publishers, Children's Entertainment Assn., Internat. Assn. Bus., Nat. Cable TV Assn., Nat. Assn. Pvt. Enterprise, Higher Consciousness Soc., Chgo. C. of C., Smithsonian Instn. (assoc.). Avocations: writing for children, bicycling, camping, hiking. Office: PO Box 435 Willow Springs IL 60480-0435

JASINSKI, KENNETH M., energy executive; Exec. v.p., gen. counsel Energy East Corp., New Gloucester, Maine, 1998—2000, exec. v.p., gen. counsel, sec., 2000—02, exec. v.p., CFO, 2002—. Office: Energy East Corp 52 Farm View Dr New Gloucester ME 04260-5116

JASINSKI-CALDWELL, MARY L., insurance company executive; b. Chester, Pa., May 8, 1959; d. A. Robert and Helen M. Jasinski; m. William A. Caldwell, Aug. 4, 1990; children: Helaina M., Anna L. Student, student, Loyola Coll., Balt., 1980; AS, Goldey Beacom Coll., Wilmington, Del., 1982, BS, 1983. Registered orthotic fitter; cert. sr. pharmacy technician. Gen. mgr. pension plan City Pharmacy of Elkton (Md.), Inc., 1975-96, treas., 1987-96, jr. ptnr., 1994, v.p., 1996—; founder, pres. City Home Health Care, Inc., Elkton, 1997—. Disc jockey, promoter Garfield's Restaurant, Elkton; editl. writer local newspapers; pro-life columnist KC newsletter; nat. bd. advisors McKesson Drug Co., 2001—. Creator ednl. program PARTICIP.A.A.T.E. For Life. Advisor Cecil County Pregnancy Ctr., Cecil County Bd. Edn. Textbook Adoption Policy Com., 1995; pro-life educator City of Elkton, Inc.; varsity I coach Christian Youth Orgn., 2004—06, coach youth volleyball, 2002—; asst. volleyball coach Mason Dixon Volleyball Club, 2005—; chmn. arts and environment com. Immaculate Conception Parish, 2004—; bd. dirs. Cecil County chpt. ARC, 1996—2001, fin. devel. chmn. Cecil County chpt., 2000—01; bd. dirs. Mission Am., Inc., Md. Right to Life, 1993—94, co-chair Cecil County chpt., 1993—94. Recipient J.W. Miller award, Outstanding Achievement in Excellence award K.C., 1994, Ralph and Eleanor Hicks Outstanding Vol. svc. award ARC, Cecil County, Md., 1999-2000; named Family of Yr., 1995, Bus. Person of Yr., Elkton C. of C., 2006; named to Honor Roll of Best 250 Independents in U.S., Drug Topics, 1992, Cecil County Md.'s "Favorite Pharmacy" Cecil Whig's Reader's Poll, 2002, 03, 04, 05, 06; Alpha Chi scholar, Lindback scholar. Mem. NAFE, NRA, Am. Pharmacists Assn. (assoc.), Am. Mgmt. Assn., Nat. Fedn. Ind. Bus., Bd. Orthotic Cert., Am. Assn. Pharm. Technicians, Nat. Right to Life Com., Am. Life League, Internat. Platform Assn., Pro-Life Md., Christian Coalition, Cath. Alliance, Cecil County C. of C., Stopp Internat., Human Life Internat., Concerned Women for Am., Pharmacists for Life, Goldey Beacom Coll. Alumni Assn., Movement for a Better Am., Cath. League, Liberty Alliance, Epic Pharmacies, Inc., Susan B. Anthony List, Alpha Chi. Republican. Roman Catholic. Avocations: gardening, pro-life education, reading, coaching youth volleyball. Office: City Pharmacy Inc 723 N Bridge St Elkton MD 21921-5398 Office Phone: 410-398-4383 ext. 413. Personal E-mail: williamandmarycaldwell@msn.com. Business E-Mail: citypharmacy@dol.net.

JASON, J. JULIE, portfolio manager, writer, lawyer; d. Richard and Grazina Pauliukonis; m. Marius J. Jason, Dec. 19, 1970; children: Ilona, Leila. BA, Baldwin-Wallace Coll., 1971; JD, Cleve. State U., 1974; LLM, Columbia U., 1975. Bar: Ohio 1974, N.Y. 1976, U.S. Dist. Ct. (so. dist.) N.Y. 1976, U.S. Ct. Appeals (2d cir.) 1976, U.S. Supreme Ct. 1978. Pvt. practice, NYC, 1974—78; asst. gen. counsel Paine Webber, NYC, 1978—83; pres. P.W. Trust and Paine Webber Futures Mgmt. Co., NYC, 1983—88; sr. fin. svcs. atty. Donovan, Leisure, Newton & Irvine, NYC, 1988—89; co-founder, pres. Jackson, Grant & Co., Stamford, Conn., 1989—. Arbitrator, mediator NASD; mediator U.S. Bankruptcy Ct., 1997; apptd. mem. Taxpayer Advocacy Panel, 2006—. Author: You and Your 401(K), 1996, The 401(K) Plan Handbook, 1997, Strategic Investing After 50, 2001, Julie Jason's Guide to Connecticut Probate, 2006; columnist: 401-OK, Road to Security. Mem.: AAUW (chair scholarship com. 1992—93), ABA, Investment Co. Inst. (sec. regulation com. 1978—83), Am. Soc. Journalists and Authors, Nat. Assn. Securities Dealers (arbitrator, mediator), Wesfaca, Columbia U. Alumni Club Fairfield County (pres. 1993—94, chair pres.'s coun. 1994—96). Office: Jackson Grant 2 High Ridge Pk Stamford CT 06905-1203 Business E-Mail: julie@jacksongrant.us.

JASON, SONYA, writer; b. Jefferson, Pa. d. Michael and Sophia (Kovac) Negra; m. John J. Jason; children: John Jr., Gary. BA in Journalism, Calif. State U.-Northridge, LA, 1963. Social worker Dept. Pub. Social Svcs., LA, 1964-66; probation officer LA Probation, 1966-76; West Coast editor Ethnic Am. News, LA, 1977-78; freelance writer, 1978—. Spkr. in field. Author: Concomitant Soldier, 1974, Icon of Spring, 1993, Helper, 1994, Professional Angel: A P.O's Story; contbr. articles to profl. jours. Pres. Am. Citizens Together, LA, 1986-90. Recipient award Freedom Found. Valley Forge, Pa., 1987; named to Greenwood Ency. of Multi Ethnic Am. Lit., 2006. Avocations: travel, historical research, golf, bridge. Home: 21165 Escondido St Woodland Hills CA 91364-5904 Office Phone: 818-347-2553.

JASPAN, STANLEY S., lawyer; b. NYC, Apr. 13, 1946; BS, Cornell U., 1968; JD, Yale U., 1971. Bar: Wis. 1971. Mng. ptnr. Foley & Lardner LLP, Milw., 1999—. Lectr. in law, adj. assoc. prof. Marquette U. Law Sch., 1978-88. Mng. editor: Yale Law Jour., 1970-71. Mem. ABA, State Bar Wis., N.Y. State Bar Assn., Milw. Bar Assn. Office: Foley & Lardner LLP Firstar Ctr 777 E Wisconsin Ave Ste 3800 Milwaukee WI 53202-5367 Office Phone: 414-297-5814. Business E-Mail: sjaspan@foley.com.

JASPER, DORIS J. BERRY, nurse; b. Banner, Miss., Sept. 12, 1933; d. William Richard and Lena Martha (Gambill) Berry; m. Lyman W. Jasper, Jan. 8, 1949; children: Richard L., Lynn William. Student, Blytheville (Ark.) Sch. Nursing, 1949, Purdue U., Westville, Ind., 1979-80, Lake Mich. Coll., Benton Harbor, 1980—83. Staff nurse St. Anthony's Hosp., Michigan City, Ind., 1951-66; pvt. duty nurse Michigan City, 1962-68; emergency rm. nurse St. Anthony's Hosp., 1968-74; charge nurse, emergency rm. nurse Meml. Hosp., Michigan City, 1974-75; pvt. duty nurse Three Oaks, Mich., 1972-84, Michigan City, 1981-88; staff nurse Alpha Christiansan Registry, New Buffalo, Mich., 1988—; pvt. practice Three Oaks, 1989-90; owner, practitioner Jaspers Health Care, Three Oaks, 1991—; owner, mgr. D.J.'s Frolick Kennel. Pvt. practice No. Ind., So. Mich.; co-owner, mgr. grain farm. Med. missionary Chiadoc, El Paso, Tex., 2002. Mem. Bus. and Profl. Women's Club, Inc. (legis. chair dist. 2 1987-88, rec. sec. dist. 2, exec. bd. mem.), Mich. Fedn. Bus. Profl. Women USA (legis. chair dist. 9), New Buffalo Area Bus. Profl. Women (legis. chair), Tenn. Walking Horse Assn., Smithsonian Inst. Republican. Baptist. Avocations: reading, horseback riding, travel. Home and Office: 1883 Bethel Church Rd Camden TN 38320 Personal E-mail: jasperdoris@yahoo.com.

JASPER, NORMAN HANS, engineer; b. Detmold, Germany, May 10, 1918; came to U.S., 1932; s. Friedrich and Hannah (Franzmeier) J.; m. Wilma L. Knief, Aug. 1940; children: Norma, Richard. BME, CCNY, 1941; MS, U. Md., 1952; Dr. Engring., Catholic U. Am., 1956. Naval architect Puget Sound Naval Shipyard, Bremerton, Wash., 1941-46; with David Taylor Model Basin U.S. Navy, Washington, 1946-61, spl asst. David Taylor Model Basin, 1960-61, tech. dir. U.S. Navy R&D Lab. Panama City, Fla., 1961-72, sci. adviser comdr. operational test evaluation force Norfolk, Va., 1972-73; pres. Lagoon Investment Co., Tallahassee, 1972—. Mem. U.S. Navy Anti-Submarine Warfare Coun., 1961-68. Author numerous tech. papers and reports. Sloan Inst. Advanced Engring. Studies fellow MIT, 1971-72; recipeint Disting. Civilian Svc. awards U.S. Navy Dept., Def. Dept., 1962. Fellow ASME; mem. Am. Soc. Naval Architects and Marine Engrs. (mem. tech. panels and coms.), Elks, Sigma Xi. Achievements include development of patented explosion-resistant ship design for minesweeping; development and installation of a solution for silencing nuclear submarines, for computing temperature induced stresses i ships, for dynamic slamming loads on high-speed boats. Avocations: tennis, camping, travel, coin collecting/numismatics, art collecting. Personal E-mail: normanjasper@aol.com.

JASPERSEN, FREDERICK ZARR, economist; b. Phila., Sept. 23, 1938; s. Frederick Franklin and Jean Lorraine (Zarr) J.; m. Margie C. Trainor, Oct. 10, 1965. BA in Internat. Relations, Dartmouth Coll., 1961; MA Peace Corps fellow, Ind. U., 1965, PhD in Econs., 1969. Mem. Peace Corps, Colombia, 1961-63; teaching asst. fellow Ind. U., Bloomington, 1964-65; Harvard U. econ. advisor Ministry Fin., Chile, 1968-69; economist Standard Oil N.J., NYC, 1969-70, Am. Embassy Brazil, 1970-71; sr. economist World Bank, Washington, 1978-86, lead economist macroecon. adjustment policy and growth, 1987-91; chief devel. policy rsch. divsn. Inter-Am. Devel. Bank, Washington, 1991-95; sr. advisor Internat. Fin. Corp., Washington, 1995-98; dir. Latin Am. Inst. of Internat. Fin., Washington, 1999—. Lectr. econs. Chile, Brazil, Ind. U. Contbr. author: World Development Report, 1981, Adjustment Experience and Growth Prospects of the Semi-Industrial Countries, 1981; co-editor: Pathways to Growth: Comparing Latin America and East Asia, 1997. V.p. Sidwell Friends Sch. Alumni Assn., 1978-80. Ford Found. Latin Am. teaching fellow Fletcher Sch., Tufts U., 1967-68 Mem. Am. Econ. Assn., World Affairs Coun. Clubs: Dartmouth (Washington), Cosmos (Washington). Home: 5013 Randall Ln Bethesda MD 20816-1959 Office: Ste 8500 2000 Pennsylvania Ave NW Washington DC 20006-1852

JASSO, GUILLERMINA, sociologist, educator; b. Laredo, Tex., July 22, 1942; d. José Jasso-Rodríguez and Guillermina de los Santos-Lozano. BA, Our Lady of the Lake Coll., 1962; MA, U. Notre Dame, 1970; PhD, Johns Hopkins U., 1974. Asst. prof. Barnard Coll. and Columbia U., NYC, 1974-77; spl. asst. to commr. U.S. Immigration and Naturalization Svc., Washington, 1977-79; dir. rsch. U.S. Select Commn. on Immigration and Refugee Policy, Washington, 1979-80; asst. prof. U. Mich., Ann Arbor, 1980-82; assoc. prof. U. Minn., Mpls., 1982-86, prof., 1986-87; prof., dir. theory workshop U. Iowa, Iowa City, 1987-91; prof. NYU, NYC, 1991—, dir. methods workshop, 1991-97. Mem. study sect. on social sci. and population NIH, 1991-95; mem. U.S. Com. for Internat. Inst. for Applied Sys. Analysis, 1993-2001; mem. various programs NSF, 1987-96, 98-99; panel on demographic and econ. impacts of immigration NAS, 1995-97; population rsch. subcom. Nat. Inst. Child Health and Human Devel., NIH, 1998-2002, adv. com. SBE Directorate, NSF, 2003—; mem. com. on redesign of U.S. naturalization test NAS, 2004-05; vis. prof. Zentrum Umfragen, Methoden, und Analysen, Mannheim, Germany, 1995, U. Leipzig, Germany, 1996; core rsch. team bination study on migration between Mex. and US, U.S. Commn. on Immigration Reform, 1995-97; disting. alumni lectr. U. Notre Dame, 1987; pub. lectr. Our Lady of Lake U., 1989; disting. lectr. NSF, 2003; spkr. in field. Author: The New Chosen People, 1990; mem. editl. bd. Social Justice Rsch., 1985—, Jour. Math. Sociology, 1985—, Rationality and Society, 1999—, European Sociological Review, 2000—, Internat. Jour. Comparatine Sociology, 2001-; dep. editor Am. Sociol. Rev., 1996-99, Social Forces, 2004-2007, Contemporary Sociology, 2006-2007; contbr. articles to profl. jours. Grantee Russell Sage Found., 1983-85, Rockefeller Found., 1985-86, NSF, 1994-97, 2000-02, NIH, 1995-99, 2000-, PEW, 2001-; fellow Ctr. for Advanced Study in Behavioral Scis., Stanford, Calif., 1999-2000; rsch. fellow Inst. for the Study of Labor (IZA), Bonn, Germany. Fellow Johns Hopkins Soc. Scholars; mem. Am. Sociol. Assn. (chair internat. migration sect. 1996-99, chair theory sect. 1996-99, chair rational choice sect. 2000-03, chair soc. psychol. sect. 2002-04), Sociol. Rsch. Assn. Office: NYU Dept Sociology 295 Lafayette St New York NY 10012-9605 Home Phone: 212-505-5703; Office Phone: 212-998-8368. E-mail: gj1@nyu.edu.

JASSY, EVERETT LEWIS, lawyer; b. NYC, Feb. 4, 1937; s. David H. and Florence A. (Pollak) J.; m. Margery Ellen Rose; children: Katherine Savitt Lennon, Andrew Ralph, Jonathan Scott. AB, Harvard U., 1957, JD, 1960. Bar: N.Y. 1960, D.C. 1975. Assoc. Dewey Ballantine, NYC, 1960—68, ptnr., 1968—2005, chmn. mgmt. com., 1991—2003, of cousnel, 2005—. Mem. ABA, N.Y. State Bar Assn., Assn. Bar City N.Y., The Tax Club, Fairview Country Club (Greenwich, Conn.), Stockbridge (Mass.) Golf Club. Avocations: golf, travel. Home: 1100 Park Ave New York NY 10128-1202 Office: Dewey Ballantine LLP 1301 Avenue Of The Americas New York NY 10019-6022 Home Phone: 212-410-1745; Office Phone: 212-259-6200. Business E-Mail: ejassy@dbllp.com.

JASTROW, KENNETH M., forest products, real estate and financial company executive; Pres., CEO Lumbermen's Investment Corp.; chmn. Capital Mortgage Bankers; CFO Temple-Inland Inc., Austin, Tex., 1991—99, group v.p., 1995—98, pres., COO, 1998—99, chmn., CEO, 2000—. Bd. dir. MGIC Investment Corp., KB Home. Office: Temple-Inland Corp 1300 S Mopac Expressway Austin TX 78746*

JASZCZAK, RONALD JACK, physicist, researcher, consultant; b. Chicago Heights, Ill., Aug. 23, 1942; s. Jacob and Julia J.; m. Nancy Jane Bober, Apr. 15, 1967; children: John, Monica. BS with highest honors, U. Fla., 1964, PhD, 1968. Staff physicist Oak Ridge Nat., 1969-71, AEC postdoctoral fellow, 1968-69; prin. rsch. scientist Searle Diagnostics, Inc., 1971-73, sr. prin. rsch. scientist, 1973, rsch. group leader, 1973-77, chief scientist, 1977-79; assoc. prof. radiology Duke U. Med. Ctr., Durham, NC, 1979-89, prof., 1989—. assoc. prof. biomed. engring., 1986-91, prof., 1992—. Rsch. prof. Inst. of Stats. and Decision Scis., 1991-93; founder, chmn. bd. dirs. Data Spectrum Corp., Hillsborough, N.C.; investigator Nat. Cancer Inst. Grant, 1983—, Dept. Energy Grant, 1989—. Contbr. articles to profl. jours.; patentee in field. Recipient Outstanding Alumni award U. Fla. Dept. Physics, 2004; NASA fellow, 1964-67, U. Fla. fellow, 1967-68; RCA scholar, 1963-64. Fellow IEEE; mem. IEEE Nuc. and Plasma Scis. Soc. (pres. 1997-98), AAAS, Soc. Nuc. Medicine (Paul C. Aebersold award 2000), Am. Phys. Soc., Am. Assn. Physicists in Medicine, Soc. Photo-Optical Instrumentation Engrs., Sigma Xi, Phi Beta Kappa, Phi Kappa Phi, Tau Sigma, Sigma Pi Sigma. Office: Duke U Med Ctr Dumc 3949 Durham NC 27710-0001

JATLOW, PETER I., pathologist, medical educator, researcher; b. New Brunswick, NJ, Feb. 12, 1936; s. Daniel and Anne (Davis) J.; m. Stephanie Bea Yager, Dec. 22, 1959; children: Allison, Julia. BS, Union Coll., Schenectady, NY, 1957; MD, SUNY Downstate Med. Ctr., Bklyn., 1961; MS (hon.), Yale U., 1976. Cert. in pathology 1967. Intern Montefiore Hosp., Bronx, NY, 1961-62; resident Yale-New Haven Hosp., 1962-66; asst. prof. lab. medicine Yale U., New Haven, 1968-73, assoc. prof. lab. medicine, 1973-76, prof. lab. medicine, 1976—, chmn. dept. lab. medicine, 1984—2006. Cons. FDA, Washington, 1978-82; mem. biomed. rsch. rev. com. USPHS, Nat. Inst. Drug Abuse, Rockville, Md., 1982-86; mem. test material devel. subcom. FLEX Program Nat. Bd. Med. Exam., Phila., 1990-91. Editor: Methodology in Analytical Toxicology, vol. II, 1982; editl. bd. Clin. Chemistry, 1973-83, Selected methods in Clin. Chemistry, 1976-79, Jour. Analytical Toxicology, 1978-79, Therapeutic Drug Monitoring, 1979-86, 90—, Clinica Chimica Acta, 1984-90, Am. Jour. Clin. Pathology, 1988—; co-editor The Yale University School of Medicine Patient's Guide To Medical Tests, 1998; contbr. numerous articles to profl. jours. Served to surgeon USPHS, 1966-68. Recipient Irving Sunshine award in clin. toxicology Internat. Assn. Therapeutic Drug Monitoring and Toxicology, 1993, Jean R. Oliver award/Master Tchr. in Pathology, Alumni Assn., SUNY Health Sci. Ctr., Bklyn., 2001. Fellow AAAS (award for rsch. and leadership in lab. medicine 1997), Coll. Am. Pathologists; mem. Acad. Clin. Lab. Physicians and Scientists (pres. 1983-84, Gerald T. Evans award 1988), Am. Soc. Clin. Pathology, Am. Assn. Clin. Chemistry (award for outstanding contbns. to clin. chemistry in selected area of rsch. 1985, award for outstanding contbns. in edn. 1995). Home: 617 Saddle Ridge Rd Orange CT 06477-2024 Office: Yale U Sch Medicine Dept Lab Medicine PO Box 208035 New Haven CT 06520-8035

JATRAS, JAMES GEORGE, lawyer; b. 1955; m. Kathy Jatras; 2 children. BA, Pa. State U., 1974; JD, Georgetown Univ., 1978. Bar: Pa. 1978. Consular officer US State Dept., Tijuana, Mexico, 1979—81, fgn. svc. officer, Russian affairs, 1981—85; policy analyst US Senate Republican Policy Com., 1985—2002; ptnr., legis. practice Venable LLP, Washington, 2002—. Office: Venable LLP 575 7th St NW Washington DC 20004 Office Phone: 202-344-8308. Office Fax: 202-344-8300. Business E-Mail: jgjatras@venable.com.

JAUDON, VALERIE, artist; b. Greenville, Miss., Aug. 6, 1945; d. Baize R. and Gladys E. (Hill) J.; m. Richard Kalina, Oct. 23, 1979. Student, Miss. State Coll. for Women, 1963—65, Memphis Acad. Art, 1965, U. of Americas, Mexico, 1966—67, St. Martins Sch. Art, London, 1968—69. One-woman shows of paintings include Holly Solomon Gallery, N.Y.C., 1977-79, 81, Pa. Acad. Fine Arts, Phila., 1977, Galerie Bishofberger, Zurich, Switzerland, 1979, Galerie Hans Strelow, Dusseldorf, Fed. Republic Germany, 1980, Corcoran Gallery, L.A., 1981, Sidney Janis Gallery, N.Y.C., 1983, 85, 86, 88, 90, 93, 96, Quadrat Mus., Bottrop, Fed. Republic Germany, 1983, Amerika Haus, Berlin, 1983, Dart Gallery, Chgo., 1983, Fay Gold Gallery, Atlanta, 1985, Macintosh/Drysdale Gallery, Washington, 1985, Barbara Scott Gallery, Bay Harbor Islands, Fla., 1994, Miss. Mus. Art, Jackson, 1996, Betsy Senior Gallery, N.Y.C., 1998, Stadel Mus., Frankfurt, Germany, 1999-2000, Von Lintel Gallery, N.Y.C., 2003, 05; numerous group shows including, Mayor Gallery, London, 1979, Galerie Habermann, Cologne, Germany, 1979, Galerie Hans Strelow, Dusseldorf, 1979, Galerie Modern Art, Vienna, Austria, 1980, Mus. Modern Art, Oxford, Eng., 1980, Greenberg, Gallery, St. Louis, 1980, Sidney Janis Gallery, N.Y.C., 1980, San Francisco Art Inst., 1980, Mus. Modern Art, N.Y.C., 1980, Leo Castelli Gallery, N.Y.C., 1980, Thomas Segal Gallery, Boston, 1980, Venice (Italy) Biennale, 1980, Nat. Gallery of Art, Washington, 1980, Chgo. Art Inst., 1981, Mus. Fine Arts, Boston, 1982, Neuberger Mus., Purchase, N.Y., 1982, Hudson River Mus., Yonkers, N.Y., 1983, Berkshire Mus., Pittsfield, Mass., 1983, La Jolla Mus., Calif., 1983, Margo Leavin Gallery, L.A., 1984, Bronx Mus., 1985, Am. Ctr., Paris, 1986, Dayton Art Inst., 1987, Cin. Art Mus., 1989, Tel Aviv Mus. Art, 1992, Robert McClain Gallery, Houston, 1996, Turner/Runyon Gallery, Dallas, 1997, Kunsthallen Brandts Kaledefabrik, Odense, Denmark, 2001, Angel Row Gallery, Nottingham, England, 2001, Porin Taidemuseo, Eteläranta, Finland, 2002; executed ceramic mural Equitable Bldg., N.Y.C., 1988, brick and granite plaza Police Plaza, N.Y.C., 1989; Blue Pools Courtyard Birmingham (Ala.) Mus. Art, 1993; mosaic floor Washington Nat. Airport, 1997, grass garden Thomas Eagleton Courthouse, St. Louis, 2004; represented in permanent collections including Hirshhorn Mus., Washington, Mus. Modern Art, N.Y.C., Albright-Knox Art Gallery, Buffalo, N.Y., Fogg Art Mus., Cambridge, Mass.,Sammlung-Lugwig Mus., Aachen, Fed. Republic Germany, Dayton (Ohio) Art Inst., Nat. Museum of Women in the Arts, Washington, St. Louis Art Mus., Ludwig Mus., Budapest, Hungary, Miss. Mus. Art, Jackson. Recipient 1st prize award So. Contemporary Arts Festival, 1967, Art award Miss. Inst. Arts and Letters, 1981, 97, Excellence in Design award N.Y.C. Art Commn., 1988, civic Spirit award Women's City Club of N.Y., Merit award Am. Soc. Landscape Architects Ala. chpt., 1994; named Honored Artist from State of Miss. Nat. Mus. Women in Arts, Washington; N.Y. State CAPS grantee for graphics, 1980; Visual Arts Fellowship grant Nat. Endowment Arts, 1988; N.Y. Found. for Arts grantee in painting, 1992. Address: 795A Accabonac Rd East Hampton NY 11937-1807 E-mail: vjaudon@earthlink.net.

JAURON, DICK (RICHARD M. JAURON), professional football coach; b. Peoria, Ill., Oct. 7, 1950; m. Gail Jauron; children: Kacy, Amy. Degree in History, Yale U. Profl. football player Detroit Lions, 1973-77, Cin. Bengal, 1978-80; co-owner health and fitness ctr. Cin.; with Nautilus; secondary coach Buffalo Bills, 1985; defensive backs coach Green Bay Packers, 1986—94; defensive coord. Jacksonville Jaguars, 1995—98; head coach Chgo. Bears, 1999—2003; defensive coord. Detroit Lions, 2004—06, interim head coach, 2005—06; head coach Buffalo Bills, 2006—. Active numerous charities. Named 1974 Pro Bowl selection, NFL Coach of the Yr., 2002 Avocation: golf. Office: c/o Buffalo Bills 1 Bills Dr Orchard Park NY 14127

JAVAHERI, ASHKAN, physician; b. Tehran, Iran, Feb. 19, 1974; s. G. Javaheri and N. Rostami. MD, SBUMS, Tehran, 1998. Rsch. fellow Georgetown U., Washington, 2002—04; resident physician Ea. Va. Med. Sch., Norfolk, 2004, chief resident, 2005—. Grantee, PRIDE, 2006. Mem.: Am. Geriat. Soc. (assoc.). Achievements include research in novel calcium sotre in atrial myocyte. Office: Eastern Va Med Sch 721 Fairfax Ave Norfolk VA 23507 Home Phone: 757-622-0544; Office Phone: 757-446-5983. Personal E-mail: ashkxii@yahoo.com.

JAVAID, HASSAN BILAL, management consultant; b. Peshawar, Pakistan, Oct. 30, 1979; s. Mohammad Aslam and Nayar Javaid; m. Fatima Choudhry, 2006. BS, Rutgers U., New Brunswick, NJ, 2001; MBA, U. Rochester, NY, 2006. Investment mgmt. analyst Aetna Inc, Hartford, Conn., 2005—05; mgmt. cons. IMS Health, Florham Park, NJ, 2006—. Office: IMS Health 200 Park Ave Ste 240D Florham Park NJ 07932 Home Phone: 732-921-7694. Personal E-mail: hassanj@gmail.com.

JAVERBAUM, KENNETH S., lawyer; b. Newark, Feb. 26, 1942; m. Tema Javerbaum; 1 child, Alison Minion; 1 child, David. BA, Rutgers U., 1963; LLB, Rutgers, The State U. of NJ Sch. Law, 1966, Doctor of Judicial Sci., 1968. Admitted to: NJ State Bar 1966, US Supreme Ct.: 1971. Judicial clerk with Hon. Samuel Larner Superior Ct. State NJ; founding ptnr. Javerbaum & Wurgaft (now Javerbaum, Wurgaft, Hicks Kahn Wikstrom & Sinins), Springfield, NJ, 1978—. Lectr. in field; frequent spkr. Inst. Continuing Legal Edn.; instructor in trial practice Seton Hall Law Sch. Named one of Top 10 Super Lawyers, NJ Monthly Mag.; named to People of Yr. List, Union County Voice, 2006. Mem.: Essex County Bar Assn. (chair, professionalism com., Civil Trial Atty. Achievement award 2003),

Union County Med. Soc. (chmn. joint com. 1983—,), Am. Bd. Trial Advocates, Richard J. Hughes Inns of Ct. (pres. 1995—97, founding mem.), Nat. Inst. for Trial Advocacy, Assn. Trial Lawyers Am., Assn. Trial Lawyers Am.-NJ (bd. gov. 1985—, parliamentarian 1988—89, asst. sec. 1989—90), Essex County Bar Assn., NJ State Bar Assn. (trustee 2002—, mem. task force on professionalism 2002—, mem. exec. com. civil trial bas sect.), Am. Arbitration Assn. (mem, nat. panel arbitrators), Nat. Panel of Arbitrators, Union County Bar Assn. (chmn. joint com. 1983—, trustee, mem. judicial and prosecutorial appointments com., chmn. joint com.), Million Dollar Advocates Forum. Office: Park Place Legal Ctr 959 S Springfield Ave Springfield NJ 07081-3555 Office Phone: 973-379-4200. Office Fax: 973-379-7872. Business E-Mail: kenj@jwhz.com.*

JAVERNICK, AMY SUE, special education educator; b. Canon City, Colo., July 19, 1969; d. James Joseph Javernick and Linda Ruth (Dilley) Thrush; 1 child, Nathan Monte. BA History, Western State Coll., Gunnison, Colo., 1991; MA Spl. Edn., U.Colo., Colo. Springs, 1994. Cert. elem. tchr. Colo., 1991, spl.edn. tchr. Colo., 1994. Rsch. asst. U. Colo., Colorado Springs, 1993—96; spl. edn. tchr Mitchell HS, Colorado Springs, 1994—95, Florence Elem. Sch., Colo., 1994—96, Gunnison HS, Colo., 1996—2006; spl. edn. tchr. Grand Junction HS, Colo., 2006—. Resource mem. Colo. State Autism Task Force, Denver, 2000—04; online instr. U. Phoenix, Ariz., 2003—. Mem.: Coun. for Exceptional Children. Republican. Avocations: sewing, cross stitch, hiking, quilting, reading.

JAVID, MANUCHER J., retired neurosurgeon, educator; b. Tehran, Iran, Jan. 11, 1922; came to U.S., 1944, naturalized, 1957; s. Asdolah and Touba (Ahdiyeh) J.; m. Lida Emma Fabbri, Oct. 19, 1951; children— Roxane, Daria, Jeffrey, Claudia. MD, U. Ill., 1946. Diplomate: Am. Bd. Neurosurgery. Intern Augustana Hosp., Chgo., 1946-47, resident gen. surgery, 1947-48, resident neurosurgery, 1948-49; asst. in neuropathology Ill. Neuropsychiat. Inst., Chgo., 1948-49; fellow in neurosurgery Lahey Clinic, Boston, 1949; resident neurosurgery New Eng. Med. Center, Boston, 1950; clin. research fellow neurosurgery Mass. Gen. Hosp., Boston, 1950, asst. resident, 1951, chief resident neurosurgery, 1952; teaching fellow in surgery Harvard, 1952; instr. Med. Sch. U. Wis., Madison, 1953—54, asst. prof., 1954—57, assoc. prof., 1957—62, prof. neurosurgery, 1962—98, chmn. dept. neurosurgery, 1962—95, endowed named prof. neurol. surgery, 1998, emeritus prof., 1998—; ret., 1998. Cons. neurosurgeon VA Hosp., Madison, 1956-98. Contbr. articles profl. jours. Mem. AMA, ACS, AAUP, AAAS, Soc. Neurol. Surgeons, Am. Assn. Neurol. Surgeons, Am. Assn. Med. Colls., Soc. for Neurosci., Central Neurosurg. Soc. (pres. 1964), Internat. Intradiscal Therapy Soc. (hon., treas. 1987-90, pres.-elect 1990—, pres. 1991), NY Acad. Scis., Xeiron, Sigma Xi, Phi Beta Pi, Alpha Omega Alpha. Mem. Baha'i Faith. Club: Rotarian. Achievements include introduction of osmotherapy in neurosurgery and ophthalmology by the clin. use of urea for reduction intracranial and intraocular pressure. Home: 4750 Lafayette Dr Madison WI 53705-4865 Personal E-mail: mjavid@facstaff.wisc.edu. *Since I was a small child, I wanted to be a doctor and help the sick. As I grew older, the Baha'i Faith, served as a guideline to achieve this goal. Its teachings have helped me to appreciate the oneness of God, the oneness of religion, the oneness of humanity, and the sanctity of life.*

JAVID, NIKZAD SABET, dentist, prosthodontist educator; b. May 24, 1934; s. Salam and Pika (Farhang) Javid-S; m. Mahnaz Zolfaghari, Oct. 22, 1942; children: Nikrooz, Behrooz, Farnaz. DMD, U. Tehran, Iran, 1958; cert., U. Chgo., 1970; MSc, Ohio State U., 1971; MEd, U. Fla., 1981. Asst. prof. U. Tehran, 1959-69; prof., dean, 1975-79; asst. prof. Ohio State U., 1971-73; assoc. prof., 1973-74; assoc. prof. removable prosthodontics U. Fla., 1974-75; prof., 1982; pvt. practice dentistry specializing in prosthodontics Gainesville, Fla., 1980—. Cons., lectr. in field. Author books, including: Stress Breaker in partial Denture, 1966, Cleft Palate Prosthetics, 1968, Complete Denture Construction, 1974 (with Sara Nawab) Essentials of Complete Denture Prosthodocntics, 1988; contbr. numerous articles to profl. jours. Named Outstanding Clin. Instr. of Yr., Student Dental Coun., Columbus, Ohio, 1973, Outstanding Tchr. of Yr., 1990, Excellent Clin. Prof., U. Fla., 1994, Most Outstanding Prof. of Yr., 1996, Disting. Prof. of Yr., 1998, 2000, 2001, 2002, Tchr. of Yr., Class of 2001, 2001, Prof. of Yr., Class of 2002, 2002. Fellow Internat. Coll. Dentists, Internat. Coll. Prosthodontics, Am. Coll. Prosthodontics, Am. Acad. Maxillofacial Prosthetics, Royal Soc. Health (Eng.); mem. Iranian Dental Assn. (dir. 1975-78), ADA, Internat. Assn. Dental Rsch. (sec.-treas. Iran div. 1978), Iranian Dental Assn. Calif. (hon. life, award 2000), Lions. Office: U Fla PO Box 100435 Gainesville FL 32610-0435 Home: 143 W Polson Ave Clovis CA 93612-0290

JAVITS, ERIC MOSES, ambassador, lawyer; b. NYC, May 24, 1931; s. Benjamin A. and Lily Javits; m. Margaretha Espersson, May 24, 1979; children from previous marriage: Jocelyn Ingrid, Eric Jr. Student, Stanford U., 1948-49; AB, Columbia U., 1952, JD, 1955. Bar: N.Y. 1955, U.S. Supreme Ct. 1959. Temp. cons. Office Def. Moblzn., Washington, 1951; assoc. firm Javits & Javits, NYC, 1955-58, mem. firm to ptnr., 1958-82; sr. ptnr. Javits, Robinson, Brog, Leinwand & Reich, P.C. (and successor firms), 1984-89; cons. to Dept. State, amb.-designate to Venezuela, 1989-90; sr. counsel Robinson, Brog, Leinwand, Reich, Genovese & Gluck, P.C. (and successor firms), 1993—2001; U.S. perm. rep. & amb. UN Conf. on Disarmament, Geneva, 2002—03, Orgn. Prohibition Chem. Weapons, The Hague, 2003—. Ind. gen. ptnr. ML Venture Ptnrs., 1982-96; spl. dep. to N.Y. Atty. Gen. Elections Frauds Bur., 1958-59; counsel N.Y. Senate Com. on Affairs of City N.Y., 1959; mem. N.Y.C. Commn. for Protocol, 1994-2001; bd. dirs. N.Y. State Conv. Ctr. Oper. Corp., 1995-2001; past dir. N.Y. Stock Exch., Am. Stock Exch., over the counter cos. Author: SOS New York, 1961. Mem. numerous charitable coms.; bd. govs. N.Y. Young Rep. Club, 1955-58, v.p., 1957-58, bd. advisors, 1958-64; trustee French Inst./Alliance Francaise, 1995-2001, Cardozo Law Sch., 1997-2001; mem. exec. com. Jacob K. Javits campaigns, 1954-80; mem. N.Y. Rep. County Com., 1960-64; mem. exec. com. Nat. Rep. Club, 1962-70; exec. sec. U.S. Paper Exporters Coun., Inc., 1964-72; mem. bd. Spain-U.S.A. C. of C., 1993-2001; chmn. emeritus Spanish Inst., N.Y.C.; bd. dir. Fair Return League, Inc., pres., 1975-2006, Erie Janits Famil Fedn., 2006—, pres., 2006—; chmn. Republican Eagles, 1999-2001. Decorated Order of Isabel La Catolica (Spain), 1981, 89; recipient Spanish Inst. Gold medal, 1994. Mem.: Nacoms, U. Club N.Y.C., Phi Alpha Delta, Beta Theta Pi, Phi Beta Kappa. Jewish.

JAVITS, JOAN (ZEEMAN), writer, inventor; b. NYC, Aug. 17, 1928; d. Benjamin Abraham and Lily (Braxton) Javits; m. John Huibert Zeeman III, Mar. 20, 1954; children: Jonathan Huibert, Andrea Zeeman Deane, Eloise Zeeman Scharff, Phoebe Zeeman Fitch, Merrily Margaret Zeeman Bodell. BA, Vassar Coll., Poughkeepsie, NY, 1949; MEd, U. Vt., Burlington, 1976. Pub. rels. exec. Benjamin Sonnenberg, NYC, 1949-51; freelance writer, 1952—; pres. Javits Zeeman Music Assocs., JJZ Realty. Author: The Compleat Child, 1964, lyricist mus. plays Young Abe Lincoln, 1961, Quality St., 1964, Hotel Passionato, 1965; author, lyricist Young Columbus, 1992; song lyricist Santa Baby, 1953; patentee Alphocube. Trustee Theatreworks (formerly Performing Arts Repertory Theatre), N.Y.C., 1953-83, Profl. Childrens Sch., N.Y.C., 1980-89, Palm Beach Sch. Arts Found., 1993-2000, 2006—, Fla. Theatrical Assn., 1994—; bd. dirs. Baroque Srings Quartet, 1996-2000. Mem. ASCAP, Dramatists Guild, Gilbert and Sullivan Soc., Vassar Club (Westchester, N.Y. and Palm Beach, Fla.) (sec. 1978-84, v.p. 1984-86(. Home: 230 Palmo Way Palm Beach FL 33480-3135 Home (Summer): 4331 E Warren Rd Warren VT 05674 Home Phone: 561-844-3182. Personal E-mail: joanjav@aol.com.

JAVITS, JOSHUA MOSES, lawyer; b. NYC, Jan. 2, 1950; s. Jacob Koppel and Marian (Borris) J.; m. Sabina Paula Golding, May 25, 1985. BA, Yale U., 1972; JD, Georgetown U., 1978. Bar: D.C. 1979, Calif. 1983. Trial atty. NLRB, LA, 1978-83; assoc. Mullholland & Hickey, Washington, 1983-85, Cades, Schuttte, Fleming & Wright, Washington, 1985-87; arbitrator Washington, 1985-88; mem., chmn. Nat. Mediation Bd., Wshington, 1988-93; ptnr. Ford & Harrison, Washington, 1993—2001; arbitrator and mediator, 2001—. Mem. ABA, Nat. Acad. Arbitrators, Indsl. Relations Rsch. Assn., Soc. Fed. Labor Relations Profls., Soc. Profls. in Dispute Resolution. Home Phone: 202-363-1499; Office Phone: 202-237-2044. E-mail: jjavits@aol.com.

JAVITT, DANIEL C., psychiatrist, researcher; b. NYC, Nov. 16, 1958; s. Norman and Suzanne Javitt; m. Reba Kizner, Oct. 20, 1957; children: Solomon, Michael, Sarah, Gabriel. BA, Princeton U., 1979; MD, Albert Einstein Coll. of Medicine, 1983, PhD, 1990. Lic. Md., diplomate Am. Bd. of Psychiatry and Neurology. Intern in gen. medicine Albert Einstein Coll. of Medicine, Montefiore Med. Ctr., Bronx, NY, 1983—84; resident in psychiatry Albert Einstein Coll. of Medicine, Bronx, 1984—87, asst. prof., 1990—95; assoc. prof. NYU Sch. of Medicine, NYC, 1995—2000, prof. of psychiatry and neuroscience, 2001—. Dir. schizophrenia rsch. unit Bronx Psychiat. Ctr., 1992—95; dir. program in cognitive neurosci. and schizophrenia Nathan Kline Inst. for Psychiat. Rsch., Orangeburg, NY, 1995—. Contbr. papers to med. jours. (Milton Rosenbaum award, 1986, Hillside Jour. of Psychiatry Resident Rsch. award, 1986, Am. Psychiat. Assn. Kempf Fund award, 1992, MA Brazier award 14th Internat. Congress of EEG and Clin. Neurophysiology, 1997, A.E. Bennet award Soc. for Biol. Psychiatry, 1998, Joel Elkes Rsch. award Am. Coll. of Neuropsychopharmacology, 2002). Recipient Young Investigator award, Internat. Congress of Schizophrenia Rsch., 1987, merit scholarship, N.Y. State, 1979—83, Physician Scientist award, NIMH, 1986—91, FIRST award, 1992—97, Ind. Invesigator award, Nat. Alliance for Rsch. on Schizophrenia and Affective Disorders, 1995—97, Rsch. award, McDonnell-Pew Found., 1995, Nat. Inst. on Drug Abuse, 1998—2006, Clin. Rsch. award, Stanley Found., 2000, Ind. Scientist award, NIMH, 1997—2006, Young Investigator award, Nat. Alliance for Rsch. on Schizophrenia and Affective Disorders, 1990, Lieber Investigator award, 1995, Dozor vis. prof., Ben-Gurion U. of the Negev, 1995, N.Y. State Rsch. Award, N.Y. State Office of Mental Health, 1998, Sr. Investigator award, Winter Workshop of Schizophrenia Rsch., 1998, Clin. Scientist award, Burroughs Wellcome Fund, 2000; fellow Joels vis. prof., Hebrew U. Med. Ctr., 2001. Fellow: Am. Coll. of Neuropsychopharmacology (mem. credentials com. 2004—06); mem.: Soc. for Neuroscience, Soc. for Biol. Psychiatry. Independent. Jewish. Achievements include patents for Treatment of negative and cognitive symptoms of schizophrenia with glycine and its precursors; Treatment of negative and cognitive symptoms of schizophrenia with glycine uptake antagonists; Treatment of negative and cognitive symptoms of schizophrenia with glycine uptake antagonists; Treatment of negative and cognitive symptoms of schizophrenia with D-serine; Glycine substitutes and precursors for treating a psychosis; Assay for D-serine transport antagonist and use for treating psychosis. Avocations: scuba diving, sailing, skiing, hiking, travel. Home Phone: 914-552-6491; Office Phone: 845-398-6545. Office Fax: 834-398-6545. Business E-Mail: javitt@nki.rfmh.org.

JAVITT, JONATHAN C., ophthalmologist; b. NYC, Nov. 7, 1956; s. Norman B. and Suzanne (Markovits) J.; m. Marcia C. Fishman, June 29, 1986; children: Zachary, Matthew, Gabrielle. AB with honors, Princeton U., 1978; MD, Cornell U., 1982; MPH, Harvard U., 1984. Diplomate Am. Bd. Ophthalmology. Intern Lenox Hill Hosp., NYC, 1982-83; resident Wills Eye Hosp., Phila., 1984-87; fellow Johns Hopkins Hosp., Balt., 1988-89; instr. Johns Hopkins U., 1987-90, asst. prof., 1990-99, prof. Balt., 1999—; asst. prof. Georgetown U., Washington, 1990-93, assoc. prof., 1993-96, prof. Sch. Medicine, prof. sch. Pub. Policy, 1996—; founder, chmn. Certitude, Inc., Mpls., 1994—; sr. v.p., nat. med. dir. United Health Care/Applied Health Care Informatics, Mpls., 1997-98; chmn. Health Directions LLC, Bethesda, 1998—; founder, pres., vice chmn. EMEDX, Inc., 1999—. Founder Coderyte, Inc., 2000; bd. dirs. Acad. Homeland Security; expert cons. Health Care Fin. Adminstrn., Balt., 1987—; spl. employee The White House Health Reform Task Force, Washington, 1992; cons. Nat. Eye Inst./NIH, 1990—, Nat. Inst. Diabetes Digestive and Kidney Disease/NIH, 1991—, Agy. for Health Care Policy Rsch., 1994—, The World Bank, Washington, 1993—, Swedish Coun. on Tech. Improvement, 1997, Japanese Min. of Health, 1993, Australia Min. of Health, 1994—; apptd. Pres.'s Info. Tech. Adv. Com., 2003—. Sect. editor Archives of Ophthalmology, 1993—, Ophthalmology Times, 1993—; author more than 200 books, chpts., articles; patentee in field. Com. chair Nat. Health Policy Coun., Washington, 1992—; cmty. spkr. on health care The White House, 1992—; trustee Md. Rep. Party, 2000—; mem. campaign com. Bush for Pres., 2000; mem. Rep. Presdl. Roundtable; bd. dirs. Washington Jewish Fedn., Brookdale Inst., Am. Joint Distbn. Com.; active Johns Hopkins Pres.'s Club, Weill Cornell Med. Coll. Deans Cir., Rep. Senatorial Trust; fin. dir. Erlich for Gov., 2002. Recipient Cert. of Appreciation, USAF, 1991, Physician Scientist award Nat. Eye Inst., 1988; U.S. Presdl. Letter of Appreciation, 1993; Kellogg Found. fellow, 1983, sr. fellow Potomac Inst. for Policy Studies, 2001—; named guest of honor Japanese Glaucoma Soc., 1996, New England Ophthalmologic Soc., 1997. Fellow Am. Acad. Ophthalmology (Honor award 1990, Sr. Recognition award 2000), Am. Glaucoma Soc.; mem. AMA, AOPA, NBAA, Assn. for Rsch. in Vision and Ophthalmology, Assn. for Health Svc. Rsch., Am. Glaucoma Soc., Kehilath Jeshurun, Royal Ocean Racing Club, Princeton Club, Harvard Club, Cosmos Club. Avocations: sailing, aviation. E-mail: jjavitt@healthdirections.net.

JAVITT, NORMAN B., medical educator, researcher; b. NYC, Mar. 9, 1928; s. Bernard and Zara (Hillman) Jakubovitz; m. Suzanne Markovits, June 5, 1955; children: Jonathan Chaim, Daniel Coleman, Joel Israel, Gail Hannah. AB cum laude, Syracuse U., 1947; PhD in Physiology, U. N.C., 1951; MD, Duke U., 1954. Diplomate Am. Bd. Internal Medicine; lic. physician, N.Y. Predoctoral fellow USPHS, Chapel Hill, NC, 1949-51; intern Mt. Sinai Hosp., NYC, 1954-55, asst. resident, 1957-58, chief resident, 1959-60, Sara Welt fellow in medicine, spl. USPHS, 1961-62; asst. physician, advanced fellow Am. Heart Assn. Vanderbilt Clinic, Columbia Coll. Physicians and Surgeons, NYC, 1957-58; instr. dept. medicine NYU Sch. Medicine, 1962-64, asst. prof., 1964-68; assoc. prof. Cornell U.Med. Coll., NYC, 1968-73, prof., 1973-83; assoc. attending physician N.Y. Hosp., NYC, 1968-73, attending physician, 1973-83; prof. medicine, prof. pediatrics NYU Med. Ctr., NYC, 1983—, dir. divsn. hepatic diseases, 1983-2000; guest investigator Nat. Inst. Child Health and Development, Nat. Insts. of Health, Bethesda, Md., 2000—; assoc. dir. clin. rsch. unit NYU Med. Ctr., NYC, 1985-90. Cons. Meml. Sloan-Kettering Cancer Ctr., N.Y.C., 1970-83; vis. prof. Rockefeller U. Hosp., 1970-76; cons. medicine VA Hosp., Bklyn., 1977-83; chief divsn. gastroenterology Cornell-N.Y. Hosp. Med. Ctr., 1973-81, chief divsn. hepatic diseases, acting chief divsn. gastroenterology, 1981-83; cons. Tisch Hosp., NYU Med. Ctr., 1983—; mem. tng. grant study sect. Nat. Inst. Arthritis, Metabolic & Digestive Diseases, NIH, 1978-85; mem. steering com. Nat. Cooperative Gallstone Study, 1973-80, chmn. clin. mgmt. com., 1974-78; gen. medicine study Section A, NIH, 1976-80. Mem. editl. adv. bd. Hosp. Practice, 1969-93; assoc. editor Jour. Lipid Rsch., 1977-78, 86—, editl. bd., 1983—; author, editor 2 books; contbr. articles to profl. jours. Capt., M.C., U.S. Army, 1955-57. Fellow ACP; mem. Am. Physiol. Soc., Am. Soc. Pharmacology and Exptl. Therapeutics, Am. Fedn. Clin. Rsch., Am. Soc. Clin. Investigation, Am. Assn. Study of Liver Disease, Am. Gastroenterol. Assn., Am. Soc. Clin. Pharmacology and Therapeutics, Am. Soc. Biol. Chemists, Am. Pediatric Soc., Am. Soc. Parenteral and Enteral Nutrition, Harvey Soc., Sigma Xi, Alpha Omega Alpha. Jewish. Home: 501 E 79th St New York NY 10021-0735 Office: NYU Med Ctr Divsn Hepatic Disease New York NY 10016 Business E-Mail: norman.javitt@med.nyu.edu.

JAVORE, GARY WILLIAM, lawyer; b. San Antonio, Apr. 3, 1952; s. Fred Walter and Glennice Jean (Gilbert) J. BA, Kent State U., Ohio, 1975; JD, Cleve. State U., 1978. Bar: Tex. 1978, U.S. Dist. Ct. (we. dist.) Tex. 1981, U.S. Ct. Appeals (5th cir.) 1981, U.S. Supreme Ct. 1981. Atty. Bexar County Legal Aid, San Antonio, 1979-81; prin. Johnson, Christopher, Javore & Cochran, San Antonio, 1981—. Author, speaker legal seminars. Mem. Leadership San Antonio Class XXIV. Fellow Tex. Bar Found., San Antonio Bar Found.; mem. San Antonio Trial Lawyers Assn. (bd. dirs. 1986—, treas. 1991, pres. 1993, Outstanding Young Lawyer award 1986), Greater San Antonio Builders Assn. (cons., exec. bd. 1990—, v.p. assoc. coun. 1993), Tex. Trial Lawyers Assn., Order of Barristers. Avocations: wood carving, tennis, scuba diving, underwater videography. Office: Johnson Christopher Javore & Cochran 5802 Northwest Expy San Antonio TX 78201-2851

JAVOREK, RICHARD ALAN, history educator, consultant; b. Cleve., Nov. 16, 1950; s. Sylvester Richard and Elanor Javorek; m. Nancy Ruth Bublo Wagner Javorek, Dec. 23, 1978; children: Maryann Wagner, Carolyn Wagner. B of History, Baldwin Wallace Coll., Berea, Ohio, 1972; M in Curriculum & Instrn., Kent State U., 1998. Social studies tchr. Brunswick City Schs., Ohio, 1974—2006. Mem. planning com., youth for justice Ohio Ctr. for Law Related Edn., Columbus, 1996—; mem. social studies curriculum adv. rev. com. Ohio Grad. Test Stds. Setting Com., Ohio Dept. Edn., 2003—05; chair-elect, chair, past chair Ohio Social Studies Resource Ctr., Columbus, 2004—; adj. prof. Bryant & Stratton Coll., Parma, Ohio, 2006—. Capt. Ohio Hist. Soc., Columbus, 2007—. Recipient Golden Apple Achievement award, Ashland Oil Co., Ohio, 1990, Positive Image award, N.E. Ohio Edn. Assn., 1998. Mem.: NEA (mem. mid atlantic regional dir. NEA Rep. Educators Caucus 1998—2005, mem. resolutions com. representing Ohio 2003—06), N.E. Ohio Edn. Assn. (chair internal polit. action com. 1990—98, mem. exec. com. unit 4 2000—06, chair day com. 2002—06), Ohio Edn. Assn. (chair pres. svc. adv. coun. 1984—98, mem. state coun. fund for children and pub. edn. 1992—2006, mem. awards com. 2000—06, mem. resolutions commn. 2003—06, liaison to legis. commn. 2004—06, chair, regional coord. coun. 2005—06, mem. exec. com. 2000—06). Home: PO Box 295 7410 Lake Rd Chippewa Lake OH 44215

JAW, ANDREW CHUNG-SHIANG, software analyst; b. Tainan, Taiwan, Feb. 10, 1953; came to U.S., 1978; s. Ping-Tsen and Pey-Yuh Jaw; m. Amy Chi, July 30, 1979; children: Andrew, Anfin, Audrey. BS in Mech. Engring., Tatung Inst. Tech., Taipei, Taiwan, 1974; MS in Metall.Engring., Poly. Inst. N.Y., 1981; MSEE, Syracuse U., 1987. Engr. Tatung Co., Taipei, Taiwan, 1976-78; sr. assoc. engr. IBM Corp., Endicott, NY, 1980-89, Rochester, Minn., 1990-91; software cons. A BOC Health Care Co., Madison, Wis., 1991-92; sr. software engr. A Rockwell Internat. Co., Milw., 1992-94; staff software assurance analyst ARDIS Co., Lincolnshire, Ill., 1994-96, lead tech. programmer analyst, 1996-98, Am. Mobile Satellite Corp., Lincolnshire, Ill., 1998-2000; sr. network mgmt. sys. engr. Motient Corp., Lincolnshire, Ill., 2000—03, project mgr., 2004—05; project engr. Dedicated Computing LLC, Waukesha, Wis., 2005—. Adj. prof. info. sys. ITT Tech. Inst., Greenfield, Wis., 2003—04, Concordia U., Mequon, Wis., 2003—. Patentee in field. Recipient Cert. of Merit, Assembly of the State of NY, 1985; rsch. fellow Poly. Inst. NY, 1979. Mem. IEEE Computer Soc. Home Phone: 262-782-3354. Business E-Mail: Andrew.Jaw@Computer.org.

JAWAD, SAID TAYEB (SAID TAYEB DJAWAD), ambassador, commentator, writer; b. Kandahr, Afghanistan, Feb. 27, 1958; came to U.S., 1986; s. Mir Hussain and zakia Shah; m. Shamim Rahman, Nov. 16, 1986; 1 child. Student, Kabul U., Afghanistan, 1976-80, Wilhelms U., Muenster, Germany, 1984-86, Long Island U., 1986; MBA, Golden Gate U., San Francisco, 2001. With Lehnardt & Bauman, NYC, 1988-89, Steefel, Levitt & Weiss, San Francisco, 1989—2002; chief of staff, spokesman Pres. Afghanistan, Kabul, Afghanistan, 2002—03; dir. Office Internat. Rels., 2001—03; Afghan amb. to US, 2004—. Writer, polit. commentator various newspapers, radio and TV stas. including BBC. Columnist OMAID, 1992-95; pub. Substratum of Human Rights Violations in Afghanistan, Modern Dictatorship, The United States and the Afghan Resistance, Soviets Expansion to the South, Fundamentalism in Central Asia; contbr. articles to BBC World Reports (London) and to polit. jours. throughout world. Bd. dirs. Afghanistan Cultural Soc., San Francisco, 1990-92; mem. Internat. Soc. for Human Rights, Frankfort, Germany, 1983-86; mem. nat. adv. bd. Info. Am., Atlanta, 1991-94; active Amnesty Internat., NYC, 1987—. Mem. World Affairs Coun. Office: Embassy of Afganistan 2341 Wyoming Ave NW Washington DC 20008 Office Phone: 202-483-6410. Office Fax: 202-483-6488. E-mail: info@embassyofafghanistan.org.

JAWAHAR, AJAY, neurosurgeon, educator; b. India, Mar. 14, 1965; arrived in U.S., 1997; s. Joseph Hingorani and Saudine Jawahar; m. Lisa Louise Smith, June 21, 2003; children: Dylan Wayne, Stuti Celeste, Eleanor Clarice. MD, U. Rajasthan, Jaipur, India, 1987, M of Surgery, 1992; MS in Med. Physics, Haywood U., London, 2004. Diplomate Nat. Bd. Neurosurgeons India. Leskell fellow in radiosurgery U. Pitts., 1997—99; postdoctoral fellow in radiosurgery La. State U., Shreveport, 2000—01, lectr. in neurosurgery, 2001, asst. prof. neurosurgery, 2004—05; dir. med. rsch. Spine Inst. La., Shreveport, 2005—. Mem. instnl. rev. bd. for human rsch. La. State U., Shreveport, 2004—; cons. on brain tumors Guilford Pharms., Balt., 2003—. Author: Saunder Manual of Neurosurgical Practice, 2003; contbr. articles to profl. med. jours. Mem. Think First, Shreveport, 2003. Recipient Jason Cardelli Award for Exellence in Cancer Rsch., Feist-Weiler Cancer Ctr., 2003, Mahaley Award for Best Clin. Rsch. in Brain Tumors, Nat. Brain Tumor Soc., 2005. Mem.: Internat. Stereotactic Radiosurgery Soc., Am. Assn. Neurol. Surgeons, Congress of Neurol. Surgeons, KC (1st deg.). Roman Catholic. Avocations: reading, music, travel, movies. Office: Dir Med Rsch Spine Inst La 1500 Line Ave 2 Floor Shreveport LA 71101 Office Phone: 318-629-5555.

JAWIDZIK, EDWARD MARK, priest; b. New Brunswick, NJ, Apr. 25, 1954; s. Edward John and Phyllis Jean (Kaczmarek) Jawidzik. BA in Humanities, St. Mary's Sem.Coll., Balt., 1976; MDiv, Immaculate Conception Sem., Mahwah, NJ, 1980. Ordained priest Roman Catholic Church, 1981. Deacon intern Saint Joan of Arc Ch., Marlton, NJ, 1980—81; parochial vicar St. Mary of the Lake Ch., Lakewood, NJ, 1981—86, Our Lady Star of the Sea Ch., Long Branch, NJ, 1986—87, St. Ann's Ch., Keansburg, NJ, 1987—94; pastor Our Lady of Perpetual Help Ch., Highlands, NJ, 1994—95; parochial vicar St. Rose Ch., Belmar, NJ, 1995—2001, St. Robert Bellarmine Ch., Freehold, NJ, 2001—. Mem. liturgy com. Emmaus Program for Priestly Spirituality, 1982—83; Rep. for Bayshore Deanery Priest's Coun., Trenton, NJ, 1992—95; pro-life chaplain Monmouth County, NJ, 1995—; rep. for Coastal Monmouth Deanery Priests' Coun., Trenton, 1995—2001; rep. Western Monmouth Deanery Priests' Coun., 2005—. Co-author: Concise History of Freehold Township Since 1693, 2005. Mem Keansburg Alliance on Substance Abuse, 1987—94; chaplain KC Bayshore Coun., East Keansburg, 1987—92, KC St Catharine's Coun., Spring Lake, NJ, 1999—2001; Faithful Friar assembly KC Monsignor Kivelitz, Freehold, 2004—06; chaplain KC Freehold Coun., 2004—; mem. commemorative book com. Diocese Trenton 125th Ann., 2004—06. Recipient Proclamation of Acclaim, Mayor and Borough Coun., Keansburg, 1991, Proclamation award, 1994, Proclamation of Congratulations, Mayor and Twp. Coun., Freehold, 2006, Guardian of Life award, St. Catharine-St. Margaret Pro-Life Com., 2006.

Mem.: Freehold Twp. Hist. Preservation Commn., Acton Inst. Study of Religion and Liberty, Freehold Interfaith Clergy Assn. Roman Catholic. Achievements include founding mem., Nat. Campaign for Tolerance, 2004. Avocations: baseball, history, music. Home: 61 Woodstock Pl Freehold NJ 07728 Office: St Robert Bellarmine Ch 61 Georgia Rd Freehold NJ 07728 Office Phone: 732-462-7429. Personal E-mail: rfriedmann@optonline.net.

JAWORSKA, TAMARA, artist; b. Archangel, Russia; arrived in Can., 1969; d. Antoni Jankowski; m. Tadeusz Jaworski, 1957; children: Ewa, Piotr. BFA in Painting, State Acad. Fine Arts, Lodz, Poland, 1950, MFA in Design and Weaving Art, 1952; M of Painting (hon.), Accademia Italia, 1982. From asst. prof. to sr. asst. prof., lectr. State Acad. Fine Arts, Poland, 1952-58. One-woman shows include State Gallery of Textiles, Lodz, 1965, State Gallery of Fine Arts, Warsaw, 1965, Pushkin Nat. Mus., Moscow, 1966, Fine Arts Mus., Plymouth, U.K., 1968, Scottish Woolen Gallery, Galashields, 1968, Richard Demarco Gallery, Edinburgh, Scotland, 1968, Rothman's Art Gallery, Stratford, 1970, Merton Gallery, Toronto, 1970, London Art Gallery, 1971, Glendon Art Gallery, Toronto, 1972, Nienkamper Art Gallery, Toronto, 1979, Art Gallery of Hamilton, 1980, Nat. Museums and Art Galleries in Spain, 1980-81, Can. Cultural Ctr., Paris, 1981, Galerie Inard, Paris, 1981, Munich Art Gallery, Germany, 1982, Galerie Inard, Toulouse, France, 1982, 91, Galerie Inard, Paris, 1984, 91, Leo Kamen Gallery, Toronto, 1987, 89, John B. Aird State Gallery, Toronto, 1992, Peak Gallery, Toronto, 1997, Solo Gallery, Toronto, 2003, 04, 05, Toronto Weavers Art Gallery, 2005, Designers Walk Gallery, Toronto, 2006, Weavers Art Gallery, Toronto, also in France, Germany, Belgium, Switzerland, Luxembourg, U.K., Spain, Austria, Poland, Russia, Hungary, U.S., Mex., Can., Paris, Eng., Scotland, Holland, Austria, Spain, Moscow, Poland, Hungary, Can., U.S., others; group exhbns. include Warsaw and Lodz art galleries, Pushkin Mus., European Art Gallery, Moscow, Richard Demarco Gallery, Edinburgh, Fine Art Mus., Plymouth, Eng., Merton Gallery, Toronto, Hermitage Leningrad Mus., USSR, Nat. Art Gallery, Teheran, Mus. Modern Art, Mexico City, Art Gallery of Ont., RCA-Art 2000, Toronto and Stratford, 2000, Weavers Art, Toronto, 2006; exhibited tapestries at New Coll., Galerie Inard, Ctr. Nat. de la Tapisserie d'Abusson, Paris, later in Madrid, Barcelona, Valencia, San Sebastian, Paris, Munich, Zurich, others; works in permanent collections of Pushkin Nat. Mus., European Art Gallery, Moskau, Russia, Nat. Mus., Warsaw, Nat. Mus. of Textile Arts, Lodz, Poland, Nat. Mus. of Home Army, King City, Krakow, Poland, Galashields Art Inst., Scotland, Bank of Montreal, Toronto, Bell Can., Ottawa, Molson Canadian, Toronto, Mut. Ins. of Can., Toronto, First Can. Pl. Main Lobby, Gulf Can. Sq. Main Lobby, and many corp. and pvt. collections in Europe, Am., Mid. East, Centre Nat. de la Tapisserie D'Aubusson Galerie Inard, Paris; subject of articles in art books and mags. Decorated Order of Can.; recipient Gold medal-Triennial di Milano, Interior Design and Architecture, Milan, 1957, award for excellence Wool Gathering, Montreal, 1974, Gold medal Academia Italia delle Arti, 1980, Gold Centaur, Academia Italia delle Arti, 1982, Gold medal and 1st prize Internat. Art Competition, N.Y.C., 1985, Commemorative medal Gov. Gen. Can., 1993, Highest Civilian Recognition for Achievements in Field of Creative Visual Arts, 1994, Golden Jubilee medal Her Majesty Elizabeth II, 2002. Fellow York Univ.; mem. Royal Can. Acad. Arts, Academia Italia delle Arti, Ontario Soc. Artists. Home: 49 Don River Blvd Toronto ON Canada M2N2M8

JAWORSKI, RON, sports analyst; b. Mar. 23, 1951; married; 3 children. Student, Youngstown State U. Football player Youngstate State U., Sr. Bowl, Ohio Shrine Bowl, L.A. Rams, 1973-76, Phila. Eagles, 1977-86, Miami Dolphins, 1977-88, Kansas City Chiefs, 1989; sports commentator Sta. WIP-AM, Phila., Ron Jaworski Show, 1988; co-host Celebrity Sports Talk and Eagles wrap-around shows, 1990, Eagles post-game show Sta. WYSP Radio, 1992; analyst Monday Night Matchup, ESPN, 1990—, Monday Night Football on ESPN, 2006-; mgr. two 18-hole golf courses, several fitness centers, and a restaurant. Host Celebrity Golf Classic; campaign chmn. United Way; co-chmn. Muscular Dystrophy Assn. Recipient Super Bowl XV award Eagles, Top Rated Passer NFC, Pro Bowl, Player of Yr. UPI, 1980; holds Eagles passing records including yardage (27,000) yards and touchdowns (175). Office: c/o ESPN ESPN Pla Bristol CT 06010

JAY, CHRISTOPHER EDWARD, stockbroker; b. Walla Walla, Wash., May 2, 1949; s. Orville Elmo and Juanita Hope (Beckius) J.; m. Mardra Marguerite Jones, July 25, 1981; children: Pohaku Kepano, Hope Lauren, Christopher James. BS, Lewis and Clark Coll., 1972; MA, U. Nev., 1975. 1st v.p. Merrill Lynch & Co., Anchorage, 1975—. Dist. chair Rep. Cen. Com., Anchorage, 1980-81; bd. trustees Lewis and Clark Coll., Portland, Oreg., 1988—; bd. dirs. Anchorage Mus. History and Art Found., 1988-90, KSKA Pub. Radio, Anchorage, 1991-93, Alaska Pub. Broadcasting Inc., Anchorage, Providence Hosp. Found., Anchorage; bd. dirs., treas. Anchorage Symphony Orch.; active 1st Presbyn. Ch., Anchorage, apptd. by Anchorage mayor to sit on the Investment Adv. Bd. for the Mcpl. of Anchorage Endownment Fund, 2003 Named one of nation's top brokers Registered Rep. mag., 1995, 1998 Broker Hall of Fame, Rsch. Mag., 1998; recipient Disting. Alumni award Lewis and Clark Coll., 1996. Mem. Rotary (pres. Anchorage chpt. 1989-90, Paul Harris fellow 1989, co-chmn. dist. conv. 1997, elected del. to Nat. Rep. Conv. 2000, elected aternate to Nat. Rep. Convention). Republican. Presbyterian. Avocations: reading, walking, travel, civic activities. Home: 11060 Hideaway Lake Dr Anchorage AK 99507-6141 Office: Merrill Lynch & Co 3601 C St Fl 14 Anchorage AK 99503-5925

JAY, FRANK PETER, retired writer, lexicographer, educator; b. Bklyn., Feb. 12, 1922; s. Frank G. and Harriet Ann (Niffer) J.; m. Jayne Marie Charles, Aug. 15, 1947; children— Jennifer, Christopher, Alison, Angela, Jonathan, Melissa, Bryan, Nicole, Matthew. AB, Fordham U., 1943; MA, Columbia U., 1946. Mem. faculty Fordham U., 1946-92, prof. English, 1948-92; editor-in-chief reference books Funk & Wagnalls, NYC, 1963-65, exec. editor, 1968-73; editor-in-chief reference books Reader's Digest, NYC, 1965-66; editor-in-chief IEEE Dictionary, 1977, 84, 88. Author: Jack: The Story of a Pretty Good Donkey, 1970, also articles, short stories; editor-in-chief: The New Internat. Year Book, 1963, 64, 65, Internat. Everyman's Ency., 20 vols, 1970. Served with USAAF, 1942-43. Mem. Overseas Press Club (N.Y.C.), Writers' Cir. St. Croix, East Enders Soc. St. Croix, Princeton Club (N.Y.C.), Manhasset Bay Yacht Club, Kappa Delta Pi. Home: 3 Huntington Rd Port Washington NY 11050-3510

JAY, NORMA JOYCE, artist; b. Wichita, Kans., Nov. 11, 1925; d. Albert Hugh and Thelma Ree (Boyd) Braly; m. Laurence Eugene Jay, Sept. 2, 1949; children: Dana Denise, Allison Eden. Student, Wichita State U., 1946-49, Art Inst. Chgo., 1955-56, Calif. State Coll., 1963. Illustrator Boeing Aircraft, Wichita, 1949-51; co-owner Back Door Gallery, Laguna Beach, Calif., 1973-88. Guest artist Coos Art Mus., 2003. Exhibited in group shows at Am. Soc. Marine Artists ann. exhbns., 1978—2004, Peabody Mus., Salem, Mass., 1981, Mystic Seaport Mus. Gallery, Conn., 1992—95, Grand Ctrl. Gallery, NY, 1979—84, The Back Door Gallery, Laguna Beach, 1973—88, Mariners' Mus., Newport News, Va., 1985—86, Nat. Heritage Gallery of Fine Art, Beverly Hills, Calif., 1988—, Md. Hist. Mus., 1989, Kirsten Gallery, Seattle, 1991—97, R.J. Schaefer Gallery Mystic Seaport Mus., Conn., 1992, Vallejo Gallery, Newport Beach, 1992, Caswell Gallery, Troutdale, Oreg., 1994—95, Columbia River Maritime Mus., Astoria, Oreg., 1994, Arnold Art Gallery, Newport, Conn., 1994, Mystic Internat. Exhbn., 1995, Lu Martin Galleries, Laguna Beach, 1996—, Frye Art Mus., Seattle, 1997, Cummer Mus. Art & Gardens, Jacksonville, Fla., 1997—98, Cape Mus. Fine Arts Inc., Dennis, Mass., 2001, Coos Art Mus., Coos Bay, Oreg., 2003, Newport Art Mus., RI, 2003, Maine Maritime Mus., Bath, 2003, Connecticut River Mus., Essex, 2004, Vero Beach Mus. of Art, Fla., 2004, Nat. Gallery Art, DC, 2007, Maritime Mus., San Diego, 2007, one-woman shows include Milcir Gallery, Tiburon, Calif., 1978, Newport Beach City Gallery, 1981, two-person show, Las Vegas Mus. Art, 1977, Represented in permanent collections James Irvine Found., Newport Beach, Niguel Art Assn., Laguna Niguel, Calif., Deloitte, Haskins & Sells, Costa Mesa, Calif., M.J. Brock & Sons Inc., North Hollywood, Calif., others. Recipient Best of Show award Ford Nat. Competition, 1961, First Pl. award Traditional Artists Exhbn., San Bernadino County Mus., 1976, artist award Chriswood Gallery Invitational Exhbn., Rancho California, Calif., 1973, Dirs. Choice award, People's Choice award Coos Art Mus. Marine Exhbn., 1996, featured guest artist, 1998, Coos Art Mus., 2003, 1st Pl. award Maritime Art Exhibit, Newport Harbor Nautical Mus., Newport Beach, 1998-99. Fellow Am. Soc. Marine Artists (charter); mem. Niguel Art Assn. (first pres. 1968, hon. life mem. 1978), Artists Equity, Am. Artists Profl. League. Democrat.

JAYADEVAPPA, RAVISHANKAR, science educator; s. K. S. and Shankaramma Jayadevappa; m. Sumedha Chhatre; 1 child, Roshan Ravishankar. PhD, U. Pa., Phila., 1996; B of Engring., Bangalore U., India. Rsch. asst. prof. U. Pa., 1996—. Office: U Pa 224 3615 Chestnut St Philadelphia PA 19104 Home Phone: 610-325-0995; Office Phone: 215-898-3798. Office Fax: 215-573-8684; Home Fax: 215-573-8684. Business E-Mail: jravi@mail.med.upenn.edu.

JAYANARAYANAN, SANKARAN KARTIK, electrical engineer; s. Panchapagesa and Muthulakshmi Sankaran; m. Usha P. Ramachandran, Dec. 15, 2002. PhD, U. Tex., Austin, 2004. Registered profl. engr., Tex., 2004. Rsch. asst. U. Tex., 1999—2004; process engr. Analog Devices, Inc., Santa Clara, Calif.; sr. device tech. engr. Advanced Micro Devices, Sunnyvale, Calif., 2004—. Contbr. numerous articles to profl. jours. Nat. Talent Search scholar, Govt. India, 1989. Mem.: IEEE. Achievements include development of the 65nm process reliability. Home: 1269 Lakeside Dr Apt 1095 Sunnyvale CA 94085 Office: Advanced Micro Devices One AMD Pl Sunnyvale CA 94088 Home Phone: 408-738-1484; Office Phone: 408-749-4000. Office Fax: 408-849-5585. Personal E-mail: kartik.jayan@gmail.com. Business E-Mail: kartik.j@amd.com.

JAYARAMAN, GANAPATHI SUBRAMANIAM, healthcare industry executive; US, 1997; s. P.S. Jayaraman and J. Seethalakshmi; m. Malathi S. Ganapathi; children: Arvind, Aarthi. BSc in Physics, Madras U., India, 1983; MBA, Bharathidasan U., India, 1998; postgrad. diploma in materials mgmt., Annamalai U., India, 1987. Cert. advanced developer redevelopment tech. NIIT, 1997; cert. pharmacy technician PTCB, 2003; cert. project mgr. Stanford U., Calif., 2006, project mgmt. profl. Project Mgmt. Inst., 2006. Software engr. Specsoft Consulting Inc, San Jose, Calif., 1997—99; tech. advisor Caremark Rx Inc., Scottsdale, Ariz., 1999—. Contbr. articles to profl. publs. and orgns. Mem. Fine Arts Assn. Ariz., Phoenix, 2005—07. Recipient Outstanding Performance award, Caremark IT mgmt., 1999—2005. Mem.: Disaster Recovery Inst., Ariz. Bd. Pharmacists (licentiate), ISACA (assoc.), PMI (assoc.), Fine Arts Assn. Ariz. Avocations: music, cricket. Office: CVS/Caremark Corp 9501 E-Shea Blvd (MC 030) Scottsdale AZ 85255 Office Phone: 480-314-8138. Business E-Mail: ganapathi.jayaraman@caremark.com.

JAYASANKAR, SUBRAMANYAN, orthopaedic surgeon; Grad., Elphinstone Coll., Mumbai, Grant Medical Coll. Gen. surgery & orthopaedic surgery residency Grant Medical Coll. & Sir J.J. Group of Hospitals, Mumbai; orthopedic residency Harvard U. & Mass. Gen. Hosp., Mass., prof. orthopedic surgery, 1974—, New England Baptist Hosp., 1974—. Pres. Boston Medical Library; volunteer consulting orthopaedic surgeon Mass. Dept. of Mental Health & Dept. of Corrections, Eunice Kennedy Shriver Ctr., Fernald State Sch., Monson State Sch., Lemuel Shattuck Hosp. Bd. dirs. Mass. Medical Soc. Charitable Found., Network of Indian Professionals, Internat. Health Org. Mem.: AMA (chair Internat. Medical Grad. Section), Mass. Medical Soc. (chair com. on medical svc., vice chair com. on professional liability), Indian Medical Assn. of New England (former bd. trustees chair), Am. Assn. of Physicians of Indian Origin (former pres.). Office: Harvard Medical Sch 74 Country Dr Weston MA 02493

JAYASINGH, PREETHA, food scientist; BS in Microbiology and Chemistry, Mangalore U., India, 1996; PhD in Nutrition and Food Sci., Utah State U., Logan, 2004. Rsch. asst. Utah State U., Logan, 2000—04; sensory sci. intern Kellogg Co., Battle Creek, Mich., 2003—03; academic coord. Oreg. State U., Corvallis, 2004—05; rsch. assoc. IEH Labs. & Consulting Group, Lake Forest Park, Wash., 2005—06; lead rsch. scientist applications R & D Kalsec Inc., Kalamazoo, 2006—. Contbr. articles to profl. jours. Grantee, E.L. and Inez Waldron Biotech. Endowment Fund, 2000. Mem.: Inst. Food Techs. Office: Kalsec Inc PO Box 50511 Kalamazoo MI 49005 Office Phone: 269-349-1556 ext. 3196. Business E-Mail: pjayasingh@kalsec.com.

JAYCOX, GARY DELMAR, research scientist; b. Poughkeepsie, NY, Jan. 10, 1958; s. Delmar C. and Katherine M. Jaycox; m. Mindy Rachelle Kirshenbaum, June 10, 1990 (dec. Dec. 22, 1998); children: Gray E., Jeffrey D., Jillian R.; m. Julie Anne Ferguson, Oct. 10, 2000. BS in Chemistry (hon.), Syracuse U. and SUNY-Syracuse, 1980; MS in Polymer Sci., U. Mass., Amherst, 1984; PhD in Organic Chemistry, Dartmouth Coll., Hanover, NH, 1988. Rsch. chemist SUNY Polymer Rsch. Inst., Syracuse, 1980—81; NIH postdoctoral rsch. fellow Columbia U., NYC, 1988—90; prin. investigator DuPont Ctrl. Rsch. and Devel., Wilmington, Del., 1990—. Jour. editor Progress in Polymer Sci., 1993—2001, mem. editl. bd., 2002—. Recipient Excellence in Polymer Chemistry award, Soc. Plastics Engrs., Syracuse, NY chpt., 1980, Mktg. Excellence award, E.I. DuPont de Nemours and Co., 2003. Mem.: Am. Chem. Soc. Republican. Achievements include patents for anti-tumor aminoacridines, reactive oligomers for coatings; imine reactive diluents for coatings, electroactive polymers and dental materials. Avocations: rowing, surf-skiing, stereo-photography, writing, hiking. Home: 837 Brintons Bridge Rd West Chester PA 19382 Office: DuPont Ctrl Rsch and Devel Exptl Sta Wilmington DE 19880-0500 Office Phone: 302-695-7138. Office Fax: 302-695-9799. E-mail: gary.d.jaycox@usa.dupont.com.

JAYE, DANIEL, principal; Asst. prin., chmn. Math. Dept. Stuyvesant HS, NYC; dir. academy programs Bergen County Academies, Hackensack, NJ, prin., 2007—. Recipient Outstanding Educator Award, Stuyvesant HS, 2006. Mem.: Math Standards Com. Office: Bergen County Academies 200 Hackensack Ave Hackensack NJ 07601 Office Phone: 201-343-6000. E-mail: djaye@bergen.org.*

JAYNE, EDWARD RANDOLPH, II, executive search consultant; b. Kirksville, Mo., Sept. 24, 1944; s. Edward Randolph and Marietta (Jonas) J.; m. Nancy Elizabeth King, June 18, 1966; children: Kathryn Eden, Matthew Randolph. BS, USAF Acad., 1966; PhD, MIT, 1969. Officer, pilot USAF, 1966-77; staff nat. security coun. The White House, Washington, 1976-77; assoc. dir. nat. security and internat. affairs Office of Mgmt. and Budget The White House, Washington, 1977-80; v.p. Gen. Dynamics Corp., St. Louis, 1980-87; pres. McDonnell Douglas Missile Sys. Co., St. Louis, 1987-93; pres., COO, bd. dirs. Insituform Mid-Am., St. Louis, 1993-94; sr. ptnr. Heidrick & Struggles, McLean, Va., 1996—. Bd. dirs. C.A.E., Inc., Toronto, The Falcon Found., USAF Acad., Colo., Inst. Def. Analysis. Bd. dirs. Smithsonian Nat. Air and Space Mus. Maj. gen. USAF N.G., 1998-2000, ret. NSF fellow, 1966-69, White House fellow, 1973-74. Office: Heidrick & Struggles Inc 1750 Tysons Blvd Ste 300 Mc Lean VA 22102-4243 Office Phone: 703-848-2500. E-mail: rjayne@heidrick.com.

JAYSON, MELINDA GAYLE, lawyer; b. Dallas, Sept. 29, 1956; d. Robert and Louise Adelle (Jacobs) J. BA, U. Tex., 1977, JD, 1980. Bar: Tex. 1980, U.S. Dist. Ct. (no. dist.) Tex. 1980, U.S. Ct. Appeals (5th and 11th cirs.) 1981, U.S. Dist. Ct. (so. dist.) Tex. 1989, U.S. Ct. Appeals (8th cir.) 1990, U.S. Supreme Ct. 1991. Assoc. Akin, Gump, Strauss, Hauer & Feld, Dallas, 1980-86, ptnr., 1987-96, Melinda G. Jayson, P.C., 1996—; gen. counsel Hall Fin. Group, Dallas, 1999—. Comml. arbitrator, large complex case arbitrator Am. Arbitration Assn.; arbitrator, mediator N.Y. Stock Exch., NASD Regulation, Inc., Nat. Arbitration Forum, CPR Inst. Dispute Resolution; mediator U.S. EEO Commn., 1999-2000. Named one of Outstanding Young Women Am., 1983. Mem.: Am. Health Lawyers Assn. (arbitrator, mediator), Dallas Bar Assn., State Bar of Tex. (mem. dist. 6A grievance com. 1997-99, mem. professionalism enhancement com. 1997-99). Office: Ste 2015 5445 Caruth Haven Ln Dallas TX 75225-8166 Home Phone: 214-363-9036; Office Phone: 972-377-1145. Business E-Mail: mjayson@hallfinancial.com.

JAY-Z, (SHAWN COREY CARTER), music company executive, rap artist; b. Bklyn., Dec. 4, 1969; Founder Roc-A-Fella Records, NYC, 1995—, Roc-A-Fella Films, Rocawear, 1999—; prin., owner 40/40 Club, NYC; pres. Def Jam Record Co., 2005—. Co-owner NJ Nets. Singer: (albums) Reasonable Doubt, 1996, In My Lifetime, Vol. I, 1997, Vol. 2: Hard Knock Life, 1998 (Grammy award for Best Rap Album, 1998), Vol. 3: Life and Times of S. Carter, 1999, The Dynasty: Roc la Familia, 2000, MTV Unplugged, 2001, The Blueprint, 2001, The Blueprint, Vol. 2: The Gift & The Curse, 2002, Best of Both Worlds, 2002, Blueprint 2.1, 2003 (nominated 6 Grammy awards, 2003), The Black Album, 2003, Unfinished Business, 2004, Collision Course, 2004, Kingdom Come, 2006, (songs) 99 Problems, 2004 (4 MTV Video Music awards for Best Rap Video, Best Directing, Editing, and Cinematography in a Video, 2004), Crazy in Love, 2003 (2 Grammy awards: Best R&B Song, Best Rap/Sung Collaboration, 2005), Numb/Encore, 2005 (Grammy award for Best Rap/Sung Collaboration, 2006), (TV series) Unplugged Blueprint, 2001, Jay-Z LIVE, 2003; actor, prodr., writer Streets Is Watching, 1998; actor: (films) State Property, 2002, Paper Soldiers, 2002; prodr.: Paid in Full, 2002, Fade to Black, 2004. Founder Team Roc, Shawn Carter Scholarship Fund, Annual Jay-Z Santa Claus Toy Drive. Named Sammy Davis Jr. Entertainer of Yr., Soul Train, 2001, Favorite Male Rap/Hip Hop Artist, Am. Music Awards, 2004; named one of World's 100 Most Influential People, Time Mag., 2005, Barbara Walters-10 Most Fascinating People of 2006; recipient R&B/Soul or Rap Album of Yr. for The Blueprint, Soul Train, 2002, Michael Jackson Music Video award, 2007, Best Rap Video award, MTV Music Video Awards, 1999, Rap Artist of Yr. award, Billboard Music, 1999, Lyricist of Yr., Solo award, Source, 1999, Best Hip Hop Artist, Solo award, 2001, Best Male Hip Hop Artist award, BET, 2001, 2004, Hustler of Yr. award, BET Hip-Hop Awards, 2006. Achievements include creating the urban clothing line "Roca Wear"; first rapper to have his own signature sneaker, the S. Carter by Reebok. It went on to become one of the biggest-selling sneakers of 2003. Office: Roc A Fella Records 825 8th Ave 19th Floor New York NY 10019-7416 also: Def Jam Recording Simmons 89 Bradhurst Ave New York NY 10039-3314*

JEAN, CLAUDETTE R., retired elementary school educator; b. Nashua, NH, Sept. 26, 1930; d. Thomas Noel and Elise Marie (Archambault) J. BA, Rivier Coll., 1952; MA, Fitchburg U., Mass., 1956. Cert. tchr. Elem. tchr. Donald St. Sch., Beford, NH, 1952-53, Arlington St. Sch., Nashua, NH, 1953-56, J.B. Crowley Sch., Nashua, NH, 1956-65, Sunset Heights Sch., Nashua, NH, 1965-91, Nashua; ret. Rep. N.H. Gen. Ctr., Concord, 1992—. Negotiating team Nashua Tchrs. Union, 1969—; state Dem. com. N.H. Dems., Concord, 1992; Hillsborough County com. County Delegation, Manchester, N.H., 1992. Recipient Toland award AFL-CIO, 1991. Mem. Nashua Tchrs. Union (cons. 1991-94), Sr. Citizens Club, Retired Tchrs. Assn., Nashau Coll. Club. Roman Catholic. Avocations: golf, travel, reading.

JEAN, RAYMOND A., manufacturing executive; b. Aug. 23, 1942; BS in Engring. Physics, Univ. Maine; MBA, Univ. Chgo. With Allis Chalmers, 1965—73, Evans Products Co., 1974—75, 1979—83, Gulf & Western, 1976—78, I.C. Industries, 1983—87; group v.p. Varlen Corp., 1988—96, COO, 1993—98, pres., 1997—99, CEO, 1999; corp. v.p. Amsted Industries, 1999—2001; chmn., pres., CEO Quanex Corp., Houston, 2001—. Office: Quanex Ste 1500 1900 W Loop S Houston TX 77027 Office Phone: 713-961-4600. Office Fax: 713-439-1016.*

JEAN, WYCLEF, musician, recording industry executive; b. La Plaine, Haiti, Oct. 17, 1972; m. Marie Claudinette Jean, 1994; 1 adopted child, Angelina Claudinelle. Hon. roving amb. Govt. of Haiti, 2007—; co-founder & owner Platinum Sound Recording Studio, NYC. Rap singer with the Fugees; albums include: Blunted on Reality, 1993, The Score, 1996; music videos include: To All the Girls, Gone Till November, Gon Till November - Remix, Gone Til November (live), Guantanamera, Guantanamera II, We Trying to Stay Alive, Wyclef on Production (English), Wyclef Welcome (Creole); remixes include: Cheated - (To All the Girls), What's Clef Got to Do With It, We Trying to Stay Alive Remix, Gone Till November Remix; songs include: Carnival, Yele, Jaspora, Enter the Carnival (interlude), Gunpowder, We Trying to Stay Alive, Street Jeopardy, Mona Lisa, Fresh Interlude, Son Fezee, Year of the Dragon, Words of Wisdom (interlude), Gone Till November, Anything Can Happen Down Lo Ho (interlude) To All the Girls, Prelude to "To All the Girls" (interlude), Bubblegoose, Pablo Diablo (interlude), Guantanamera, Apocalypse, Intro/Court/Clef/Intro (skit/interlude), (with Shakira) Hips Don't Lie, 2006 (MTV Video Music award for Best Choreography, 2006, Billboard Latin Music award for Hot Latin Duet of Yr. 2007); composer (films) When We Were Kings, 1996, Love Jones, 1997, Life, 1999, Next Friday, 2000, Dr. Dolittle 2, 2001, Shottas, 2002, The Agronomist, 2003, The Manchurian Candidate, 2004, Hotel Rwanda, 2004, Rock the Paint, 2005, Block Party, 2005, Step Up, 2006, 7eventy 5ive, 2006, Ghosts of Cité Soleil, 2006; actor (films) Shottas, 2002, Be Cool, 2005, One Last Thing, 2005, Dirty, 2005, Redline, 2007, (TV series) Wyclef Jean in America, 2006-. Founder, mem. bd. dirs. Yéle Haiti Found., 2005—. Recipient Best Campas/Racine Entertainer, Internat. Reggae & World Music Awards, 2005, Spl. award for Cmty. Svc., 2005, Cmty. Svc. award, 2006. Office: c/o J Records 550 Madison Ave New York NY 10022 also: Platinum Sound Recording Studio 5th Fl 320 W 46th St New York NY 10036*

JEANLOZ, RAYMOND, geophysics educator; b. Winchester, Mass., Aug. 18, 1952; BA, Amherst Coll, 1975; PhD in Geology and Geophysics, Calif. Inst. Tech., 1979. Asst. prof. Harvard U., 1979-81; from asst. prof. to assoc. prof. U. Calif., Berkeley, 1982-85, prof., 1985—. Exec. dir. Miller Inst. for Basic Rsch. in Sci., 1998-2003; chair bd. on earth scis. and resources NRC, 1999-2003; chair internat. security and arms control NAS Com, 2004-. Editor Ann. Rev. Earth and Planetary Sci., 1996—. Recipient Mineral. Soc. Am. award, 1988, life fellow, 1988; MacArthur grantee, 1988. Fellow AAAS, Am. Geophysics Union (J.B. Macelwane award 1984); mem. NAS, Am. Acad. Arts and Scis. Office: U Calif Dept Earth & Planetary Sci Berkeley CA 94720-4767

JEANLOZ, ROGER WILLIAM, biochemist, educator; b. Berne, Switzerland, Nov. 3, 1917; came to U.S., 1947, naturalized, 1953; s. William M. and Rose (Poisat) J.; m. Dorothea A.H. de Passavant, Dec. 20, 1945; children: Patrick Marc (dec.), Claude-André, Raymond François, Danielle Renée, Sylvie Anne. Baccalaureate, Coll. Geneva, Switzerland, 1936; Chem.E., U. Geneva, 1941, D.Sc., 1943; A.M. (hon.), Harvard, 1961; D.Sc. (hon.), U. Paris, 1980. Rsch. assoc. U. Geneva, 1943-45, U. Basel, 1945-46; asst. U. Montreal, 1946-47; sr. research fellow NIH, 1947-48; sr. scientist Worcester Found. Exptl. Biology, 1948-51; assoc. biochemist

Mass. Gen. Hosp., Boston, 1951-61, biochemist, 1961—; rsch. assoc. Harvard Med. Sch., 1951-57, assoc. organic chemistry, 1957-60, asst. prof. biol. chemistry, 1960-61, assoc. prof., 1961-69, prof., 1969-88, emeritus prof. biol. chemistry and molecular pharmacology, 1988—. Mem. bd. tutors biochem. scis. Faculty Arts and Scis., Harvard U., 1960-2007; mem. study sect. physiol. chemistry div. research grants NIH, 1964-68, 69-70; mem. physiol. chemistry B. research study com. Am. Heart Assn., 1971-74. Author (with Balazs): The Amino Sugars, 3 vols., 1965; author: (with Gregory) Glycoconjugate Research, 2 vols., 1979; editor: Carbohydrate Research; mem. editl. bd. Connective Tissue Research, Molecular Biology, Biochemistry and Physics, Biochimie; contbr. articles to profl. jours. Recipient medal Société de Chimie Biologique de France, 1960, medal U. Liege, 1964, Prix Jaubert U. Geneva, 1973, Stratton award Am. Friends of Switzerland, 1981, Alexander von Humboldt Sr. Scientist award, 1983; Guggenheim fellow, 1976-77. Fellow AAAS; mem. Am. Soc. Biol. Chemists, Am. Chem. Soc. (C.S. Hudson prize 1973), Swiss Chem. Soc., Royal Chem. Soc. (London), French Biochem. Soc., Biochem. Soc., Soc. for Glycobiology, Am. Coll. Rheumatology. Home: 42 Ruthven Rd Newton MA 02458-2316 Personal E-mail: jeanloz@fas.harvard.edu.

JEANNE, ROBERT LAWRENCE, entomologist, educator; b. NYC, Jan. 14, 1942; s. Armand Lucien and Ruth (Stuber) Jeanne; m. Louise Grenville Bluhm, Sept. 18, 1976; children: Thomas Lucien, James McClure. BS in Biology, Denison U., 1964; postgrad., Justus-Liebig U., Giessen, Fed. Republic Germany, 1964-65; MA, Harvard U., 1968, PhD in Biology, 1971. Instr. biology U. Va., Charlottesville, 1970-71; asst. prof. biology Boston U., 1971-76; asst. prof. entomology U. Wis., Madison, 1976-79, assoc. prof., 1979-83, prof., 1983—. Rschr.: numerous publs. on social insects. Fellow Rotary Found., 1964—65, Guggenheim Meml., 1986—87. Fellow: AAAS; mem.: Wis. Acad. Scis., Arts and Letters, Animal Behavior Soc., Internat. Union Study Social Insects (chmn. protempore, sec.-treas. 1979—80, pres. western hemisphere sect. 1981, assoc. editor Insectes Sociaux 1986—2002), Assn. Tropical Biology, Phi Beta Kappa, Sigma Xi. Achievements include numerous discoveries relating to nest construction, nest architecture, commmunication, defense, caste polymorphism, polyethism, social organization, and life histories in social wasps. Office: U Wis Dept Entomology 1630 Linden Dr Madison WI 53706-1520 Home Phone: 608-271-9481; Office Phone: 608-262-0899. Business E-Mail: jeanne@entomology.wisc.edu.

JEBEJIAN, SARKIS, lawyer; b. NYC, Nov. 14, 1969; BA, Columbia Univ., 1991, JD, 1994. Bar: NY 1995. Assoc. Cravath Swaine & Moore LLP, NYC, 1994—96, 1998—2002, Hong Kong, 1996—98, ptnr., corp. NYC, 2002—. Prodn. editor Columbia Bus. Law Rev. Mem.: Assn. of Bar of City of NY. Office: Cravath Swaine & Moore LLP Worldwide Plz 825 Eighth Ave New York NY 10019-7475 Office Phone: 212-474-1188. Office Fax: 212-474-3700. Business E-Mail: sjebejian@cravath.com.

JEBSEN, HARRY ALFRED ARTHUR, JR., history educator; b. Chgo., Apr. 8, 1943; s. Harry Alfred Arthur Jebsen; m. Elaine Claire Melchert, Sept. 5, 1964; children— Timothy Paul, Christopher Warren. B.A., Wartburg Coll., Waverly, Iowa, 1965; M.A., U. Cin., 1966, Ph.D., 1971. Prof. history Texas Tech U., Lubbock, 1969-81, dir. urban studies, 1972-81, assoc. dean arts and scis., 1980-81; dean Coll. of Arts and Scis., Capital U., Columbus, Ohio, 1981-88, provost, 1988-95, prof. history, 1995—. Author: History of Dallas, Texas Park System, 1971. Contbr. articles to profl. jours. Bd. dirs. Luth. Coun. for Cmty. Action, Lubbock, 1970-78, U. Ministries of Lubbock, 1971-81, Luth. Social Services of Central Ohio, Columbus, 1984-92. Recipient Fish and Loaves award Luth. Coun. for Cmty. Action, Lubbock, 1977; NDEA fellow, Cin., 1966-69. Mem. Am. Assn. Higher Edn., N.Am. Soc. Sport Historians. Democrat. Avocations: golf, reading. Home: 1397 Goldsmith Dr Westerville OH 43081-4526 Office: Capital U 2199 E Main St Columbus OH 43209-2394 Office Phone: 614-236-6191. Business E-Mail: hjebsen@capital.edu.

JECKLIN, LOIS UNDERWOOD, art corporation executive, consultant; b. Manning, Iowa, Oct. 5, 1934; d. J.R. and Ruth O. (Austin) Underwood; m. Dirk C. Jecklin, June 24, 1955; children: Jennifer Anne, Ivan Peter. BA, U. Iowa, 1992. Residency coord. Quad City Arts Coun., Rock Island, Ill., 1973-78; field rep. Affiliate Artists Inc., NYC, 1975-77; mgr., artist in residence Deere & Co., Moline, Ill., 1977-80; dir. Vis. Artist Series, Davenport, Iowa, 1978-81; pres. Vis. Artists Inc., Davenport, 1981-88; pres., owner Jecklin Assocs., Davenport, 1988—2004; personal mgr. to composer Bright Sheng, 2005—. Asst. to exec. dir. Walter W. Naumburg Found., N.Y.C., 1990-2004; personal mgr., composer Bright Sheng, 2005—; cons. writer's program St. Ambrose Coll., Davenport, 1981, 83, 85; mem. com. Iowa Arts Coun., Des Moines, 1983-84; panelist Chamber Music Am., N.Y.C., 1984, Pub. Art Conf., Cedar Rapids, Iowa, 1984; panelist, mem. com. Lt. Gov.'s Conf. on Iowa's Future, Des Moines, 1984. Trustee Davenport Mus. Art, 1975-98, hon. trustee, 1998-2003; mem. nat. adv. coun. Figge Art Mus., Davenport, 2005; trustee Nature Conservancy Iowa, 1987-88; steering com. Iowa Citizens for Arts, Des Moines, 1970-71; bd. dirs. Tri-City Symphony Orch. Assn., Davenport, 1968-83; founding mem. Urban Design Coun., HOME, City of Davenport Beautification Com., 1970-72; bd. dirs. Mus. Arts and Design, NYC, 1995—; devel. coun. U. Iowa Mus. Art, 1996-2002; mem. Washington chpt. Arttable, 2005—. Recipient numerous awards Izaak Walton League, Davenport Art Gallery, Assn. for Retarded Citizens, Am. Heart Assn., Ill. Bur. Corrections, many others; LaVernes Noyes scholar, 1953-55. Republican. Episcopalian. Home and Office: 1232-27th St NW Washington DC 20007

JEE, WON-HEE, radiologist, educator; b. Seoul, Republic of Korea, Oct. 4, 1960; d. Chung Jee and Hong-Suk Yoon; 1 child, Gyu-Won Eo. BS, Kyung-Hee U., 1986. Intern Kyung-Hee U. Hosp., Seoul, 1986—87; resident radiology, fellow, then instr. to asst. prof. Cath. U. Korea, Seoul, 1989—99, asst. prof., 2000—04; assoc. prof. Kangnam St. Mary's Hosp. Cath. U. Korea, Seoul, 2005—. Vis. assoc. Yale U. Hosp., New Haven, 1999—2000. Contbr. articles to profl. jours. Mem.: Asian Musculoskeletal Soc., Internat. Skeletal Soc., Radiol. Soc. N.Am., Korean Radiol. Soc. Avocations: music, movies, travel. Office: Kangnam St Marys Hosp Cath Univ Korea 505 Banpo-dong Seocho-gu Seoul 137 701 Republic of Korea Office Phone: 82-2-590-2784. Business E-Mail: whjee@catholic.ac.kr.

JEFF, KEVIN IEGA, choreographer, performing company executive; Grad., Julliard Sch. Founder JUBILATION! Dance Co., NYC, 1982; former artistic dir. Joseph Holmes Chgo. Dance Thearer; founder, artistic dir. Deeply Rooted Dance Theatre, Chgo.; artist-in-residence Howard U. dance major prog.; artist-in-residence, choreographer Jahari Dance Troupe, Purdue U. Choreographed for Alvin Ailey Am. Dance Theatre Ensemble, Berkeley, Calif., Cleo Parker Robinson Dance Ensemble, Denver, Williams/Henry Dance Theatre, Kans. City, Dallas Black Dance Theater. Choreographer (films) She's Gotta Have It, Beauty and the Beast, (productions) The Wiz, Porgy and Bess, Deeply Rooted. Named one of 100 Outstanding Alumni, Julliard Sch., 2005; recipient Best Choreography, Black Theater Alliance, 1996, merit award, Nat. Coun. for Culture and Arts, Internat. Conf. of Blacks in Dance; fellow Nat. Endowment for Arts. Office: Deeply Rooted Dance Theater 3712 N Broadway Ste 148 Chicago IL 60613 Office Phone: 312-913-9773. Office Fax: 312-913-9774.*

JEFFCOAT, MARJORIE K., dean, dental educator; Degree, MIT; DMD, Harvard U. Sch. Dental Med., 1976. Faculty mem. Harvard U. Sch. Dental Med.; asst. dean rsch. U. Ala. Sch. Dentistry, prof., chair dept. periodontics, prof. biomedical engring., James Rosen Endowed chair of dental rsch., interim chair dept. oral biology; dean U. Penn. Sch. Dental Med., 2003—. Mem. adv. com. rsch. on women's health Nat. Inst. Dental and Craniofacial Rsch., NIH; dir. Friends of the Nat. Inst. of Dental and Craniofacial Rsch., 2005—. Editor-in-chief: Journal of the American Dental Assoication, 2001—. Recipient President's Achievement award, U. Ala., Birmingham. Mem.: Inst. Medicine, Acad. of Osseointegration (pres.), Am. Acad. Periodontology (Clin. Rsch. award, Gies award), Internat. Assn. Dental Rsch. (past pres.), Am. Assn. Dental Rsch. (past pres.). Office: U Penn Sch Dental Med Robert Shattner Ctr 240 S 40th St Philadelphia PA 19104-6030 Office Phone: 215-898-8941. Office Fax: 215-573-4075. Business E-Mail: jeffcoat@dental.upenn.edu.

JEFFCOTT, JANET BRUHN, statistician, consultant; b. Madison, Wis., Dec. 5, 1939; d. Hjalmar Diehl and Janet H. (Weber) Bruhn; m. Robert Gordon Jeffcott, Apr. 20, 1963. BA, U. Wis., Madison, 1962, MA, 1968. Asst. librarian Madison Area Tech. Coll., 1968-83, dist. librarian, 1983—91, adminstr. instructional media, telecommunications, 1988—91, media tech. adminstr., 1989—91. Pres. and treas. Fidelity & Assocs., Madison, 1982-2005; prin. J.B. Jeffcott & Assocs., Madison, 1989—, Edumetrics, Manistique, Mich., 2003-; sec.-treas. Manistique Mfg. and Tech., Inc., Mich., 1990-99, pres., treas., 1999-02; mem. City Coun., Manistique, 2006, planning and zoning bd., 2006; prosperity team capt. Land Policy Inst., 2007. Home and Office: Edumetrics 711 Oak St Manistique MI 49854 E-mail: jbjeff@chartermi.net.

JEFFE, SIDNEY DAVID, automotive executive, engineer; b. Chgo., May 6, 1927; s. J.I. Jeffe; children: Robert A., Leslie A. BSME with honors, Ill. Inst. Tech., Chgo., 1950; MS in Automotive Engring. with honors, Chrysler Inst. Engring., 1952; postgrad., Carnegie Mellon U., Pitts., 1968. With Chrysler Corp., 1950-80, v.p. engring. and rsch., 1976-80; sr. v.p. ops. Sheller Globe Corp., Detroit, 1982-86; prof. mech. engring. Ohio State U., 1980-82; sr. v.p. internat. bus. and tech. devel. and implementation, head customer and govt. rels. activities Sheller Globe Corp., Detroit, 1986-90; v.p. internat. bus. and tech. devel. Mesnel S.A.- Schlegel Corp., Madison Heights, Mich., 1990-92; internat. bus. and tech. cons., expert witness, 1992—. Exec. dir. Transp. Rsch. Ctr. Ohio, E. Liberty; sec.-treas. Transp. Rsch. Bd. Ohio, 1980-82; sr. v.p. internat. bus. and tech. devel. United Tech. Engineered Sys. Divsn., 1990; bd. dirs. J.L. French Automotive Castings Inc.; engring. and bus. cons. Energy Conversion Devices, Inc., 2000—. Responsible for devel. Chrysler's first front-wheel drive cars-Omni, Horizon, K cars and Minivans, 1976-80; author papers in field. Served with AUS, Korea, 1945-47. Fellow Engring. Soc. Detroit, Soc. Automotive Engrs. (Russell Springer award 1957, Coll. Fellows 1985); mem. Tau Beta Pi (Outstanding New Mem. award 1948), Pi Tau Sigma (Outstanding New Mem. award 1949). Clubs: DC Ranch Country (Scottsdale, Ariz.), Orchard Lake Country, Detroit Athletic, Ren Cen. Unitarian Universalist. Home (Summer): 41120 Fox Run Rd #110 Madison Green Novi MI 48377 Home (Winter): 13500 N Rancho Vistoso Blvd # 262 Tucson AZ 85755 Office Phone: 248-669-1861. E-mail: sjeffe@sbcglobal.net.

JEFFERDS, WILLIAM JOHN, military officer; b. Stockton, Calif., Sept. 26, 1929; s. Wallace Vincent and Margaret (Moreing) J.; m. Patricia Ann, Aug. 16, 1949; children: Jerilyn Ann, Janelle Kay, Mark Christian. BA, San Jose State U., 1952; EdD, U. Calif., Berkeley, 1966; grad., Harvard U., Cambridge, Mass., 1984. Cert. tchr., Calif. Advanced through grades to maj. gen. US Army, 1985, commd., 1964-68, bn. comdr. 2/159 inf. bn., 1974-75, brigade comdr. 49th MP brigade, 1977-82, comdg. gen. 40th CA task force, 1979-82, comdg. gen. 40th mech. ifn. divsn., 1985-88; tchr. Alum Rock Sch. Dist., San Jose, Calif., 1952-56, asst. prin., 1956-58, prin., 1958-62, asst. supt., 1962-68, supt., 1968-87; comdr. Calif. Army Nat. Guard, Sacramento, 1987-89; spl. asst. chief nat. guard bur. Pentagon, Washington, 1990-2000; sr. mil. advisor Gov. of Calif. and Dir. of Office of Mil. Support, 2000—03. Dir. Calif. Dept. Gen. Svcs., 2003—04; apptd. gov. Coun. on Mil. Support, 2005; exec. sec. Southwest Defense Alliance, 2006. Chmn. March of Dimes Walkathon, Santa Clara County, 1972. Decorated DSM, Legion of Merit, Order of Calif. Mem. Nat. Guard Assn. U.S., Nat. Guard Assn. Calif. Republican. Roman Catholic. Home: 124 Gold Rock Ct Folsom CA 95630 Personal E-mail: wjefferds@aol.com.

JEFFERIES, JOHN TREVOR, astrophysicist, director; b. Kellerberrin, Australia, Apr. 2, 1925; came to U.S., 1956, naturalized, 1967; s. John and Vera (Healy) J.; m. Charmian Candy, Sept. 10, 1949; children: Stephen R., Helen C., Trevor R. MA, Cambridge U., Eng., 1949; DSc, U. Western Australia, Nedlands, 1962. Sr. research staff High Altitude Obs., Boulder, Colo., 1957-59, Sacramento Peak Obs., Sunspot, N.Mex., 1957-59; prof. adjoint U. Colo., Boulder, 1961-64; prof. physics and astronomy U. Hawaii, Honolulu, 1964-83, dir., Inst. Astronomy, 1967-83; dir. Nat. Optical Astronomy Obs., Tucson, 1983-87, astronomer, 1987-92. Cons. Nat. Bur. Stds., Boulder, 1960-62; disting. vis. scientist Jet Propulsion Lab., 1991-94. Author: (monograph) Spectral Line Formation, 1968; contbr. articles to profl. jours. Guggenheim fellow, 1970-71. Mem. Internat. Astron. Union, Am. Astron. Soc. Home: 1652 E Camino Cielo Tucson AZ 85718-1105 E-mail: jtjeff@comcast.net.

JEFFERS, BEVERLY MAYNARD, volunteer; b. NYC, Sept. 2, 1923; d. Richard Field and Lorraine Huling Maynard; children: Alexander, Fiona, Alisandra, Ian, James, Sharon. Student, Radcliffe Coll., 1941—44; BA, Bryn Mawr Coll., 1946. Exhibited in group shows at Cookham Arts Club, 1976—80, Maidenhead Libr., 1976—80, Guidhall, London, 1980, Salmagundi Club, N.Y.C., 1990, Mercer County Libr., 1990—2003, West Windsor Town Hall, 2003, Princeton Hyatt, 1990—2003. Com. mem. Art and Cmty. Ctr., Maidenhead, England, 1977—87; initiator, leader play reading group West Windsor (N.J.) Sr. Ctr., 1997—, initiator choral and poetry groups, 2002—03; founding mem. Conn. Playmakers, 1946—47; prodr., emcee entertainments utilizing sr. citizen talent. Recipient 1st prize oil painting, Mercer County, 2004, 3d prize oil painting, N.J., 2006. Mem.: Art Students League N.Y.C. (life), Garden State Watercolor Soc., Maidenhead Painting Club (life; founding mem., exec. sec. 1976—87). Democrat. Unitarian. Avocations: art, writing fiction and poetry, drama, entertaining, photography, family. Home: 37 Wiggins St #2 Princeton NJ 08540 Office Phone: 609-430-1343. Personal E-mail: b.jeffers@worldnet.att.net.

JEFFERS, EVE JIHAN See EVE

JEFFERS, TRELLIE LEE JAMES, language educator, dean; b. Eatonton, Ga., Dec. 12, 1933; d. Charlie and Florence (Paschal) James; m. Lance F. Jeffers, May 26, 1959 (dec. July 1985); children: Valjeanne Jeffers Thompson, Sidonie Jeffers Jones, Honorée F. BA, Spelman Coll., 1955; MA, Calif. State U., 1970; DA, Atlanta U., 1986. Cert. adminstrn. and supervision. Tchr. high schs., Ga., Ill., N.C., Fla., 1955-66; asst. prof. Calif. State U., Long Beach, 1969-71; freelance writer Carolina Times, Durham, NC, 1979-82; coord. Learning Resource Ctr., chmn. Resource Ctr. Clark Coll., Atlanta, 1983-85; prof. English Talladega (Ala.) Coll., 1985—, dean divsn. humananities and fine arts, 1998—. Vis. lectr. N.C. Ctrl. U., Durham, 1975-81, chair English component acad. skills, 1977-78. Author: poems; contbr. article to book. Fellow NEH, 1988, 93. Mem. Libr. Congress, Coll. Lang. Assn., So. Conf. on African Am. Studies (mem. adv. bd. 1992, 99), Ala. League Advancement Edn., George Moses Horton Soc., Pi Lamda Theta, Kappa Delta Pi. Democrat. Roman Catholic. Avocations: sewing, creative writing, cooking, singing, gardening. Home: 219 Edgewood Ave Talladega AL 35160-3021 Office: Talladega Coll 627 Battle St W Talladega AL 35160-2354 E-mail: tjeffers@talladega.edu.

JEFFERSON, CHARLES E., state representative; b. Waco, Tex., Mar. 31, 1945; children: Carl Edward, Curtis Lamar, Charles Jr. Student, Paul Quinn Coll. Mem., 67th dist. Ill. Ho. of Reps., 2001—, chair person, elections & campaign reform, mem., com. of the whole, mem. aging, labor, pub. utilities, agreed labor bills subcommittes. Past v.p. United Way; mem. Winnebago County Bd. With US Army, 1965—71. Mem.: Rockford Sportsmen Golf Assn. (past pres.), Lions (past pres.), Masons. Democrat. Office: 281-S Stratton Office Bldg Springfield IL 62706 Address: EJ Zeke Giorgi Ctr 200 S Wyman # 304 Rockford IL 61101

JEFFERSON, DAISY M., social studies educator; d. George Jefferson and Irene Jefferson-Wiley; children: April J. Carter, James E. Carter Jr., Maya J. Carter. BA in History, U. La., Monroe, 1974; JD, Loyola U., New Orleans, 1979; MS in Edn., U. Memphis, 1999. Staff atty. NE Legal Asst. Corp., Monroe, 1983—85; arts program coord. Memphis Arts Coun., 1985—88; social studies educator Memphis City Schs., 1994—. Dir. Creative Press Works, Memphis, 1988—. Author: Tears for Ashan, 1988. Mem.: Raleigh Conservancy, Sierra Club, Kappa Delta Pi. Avocations: tennis, hiking, travel, reading.

JEFFERSON, DENISE, dance school director; b. Chgo. Studied ballet with, Edna L. McRae; BA, Wheaton Coll.; MA, NYU; Ph.D. (hon.), Wheaton College, 2000. Co-founder, co-dir. Chgo. Dance Ctr.; tchr. dance U. Ill., Chgo.; with Pearl Lang Dance Co.; mem. dance faculty Sch. Arts NYU, Alvin Ailey Dance Ctr., 1975—80; dir. Alvin Ailey Am. Dance Ctr. Scholarship program, 1980-84, Alvin Ailey Dance Sch., 1984—; v.p. Nat. Assoc. of Schools of Dance. Remedial writing tchr. Seek program Hunter Coll.; developed modern dance program Benedict Coll.; guest tchr. U.S., internat.; mem. internat. team dance profls. Dutch govt. to evaluate Dance acads. in Holland, 1990; adjudicator Arts Recognition, Talent Search Confederation Nat. de Danse, Fedn. Interprofl. de la danse, 1992. Mem. adv. bd. Profl. Children's Sch.; mem. adv. com. dance dept. U. Okla.; trustee Elisa Monte Dance Co. Grantee Nat. Endowment Arts and Humanities; scholar Martha Graham Sch. Contemporary Dance. Mem. Nat. Assn. Schs. Dance (bd. dirs. 1989-91, program evaluator, mem. commn. accredation), N.Y. State Coun. Arts (dance panel, appeal panel). Office: Alvin Ailey Dance Theatre 405 W 55th St New York NY 10019-4402

JEFFERSON, HELEN BUTLER, public health service officer; b. Edgefield, SC, Aug. 4, 1954; d. W.D. and Martha H. Butler; m. John H. Jefferson, July 2, 1977; children: Sheldon H., Brandon D. Assoc. Computer Prgramming, Kerr Bus. Coll., Augusta, Ga., 1984; BS in Orgnl. Mgmt. with honors, Voorhees Coll., Denmark, SC, 2006. IBM keypunch operator Piedmont Tech. Coll., Greenwood, SC, 1976; health protection inspector WSRC, Aiken, SC, 1985—. Mem., leader AB Miles Voices of Praise Choir, Aiken; cmty. leader Edgefield County Assn., SC, 2005; Sunday sch. tchr. Friendship Bapt. Ch., Aiken, 2003—. Mem.: Health Physics Soc., Alpha Kappa Mu. Democrat. Baptist. Avocations: reading, cooking, writing, walking. Home: 721 Teague St NW Aiken SC 29801 Office: WSRC PO Box 616 Aiken SC 29801

JEFFERSON, JAMES WALTER, psychiatrist, educator; b. Mineola, NY, Aug. 14, 1937; s. Thomas Hutton and Alice (Withers) J.; m. Susan Mary Cole, June 25, 1965; children: Lara, Shawn, James C. BS, Bucknell U., Lewisburg, Pa., 1958; MD, U. Wis., 1964. Diplomate Am. Bd. Psychiatry and Neurology, Am. Bd. Internal Medicine. Asst. prof. psychiatry U. Wis. Med. Sch., Madison, 1974-78, assoc. prof., 1978-81, prof., 1981-92; disting. sr. scientist Dean Found. for Health, Rsch. and Edn., Madison, 1992-98; clin. prof. psychiatry U. Wis. Med. Sch., Madison, 1992—; disting. sr. scientist Madison Inst. Medicine, 1998—. Pres. Healthcare Tech. Sys., Madison, 1998-2005; co-dir. Lithium Info. Ctr., Madison, 1975—, Obsessive Compulsive Info. Ctr., Madison, 1990—; dir. Ctr. Affective Disorders, Madison, 1983-92. Co-author: Neuropsychiatric Features of Medical Disorders, 1981, Lithium Encyclopedia for Clinical Practice, 1983, 2nd edit., 1987, Depression and Its Treatment, 1984, 2d edit., 1992, Anxiety and Its Treatment, 1986, Handbook of Medical Psychiatry, 1996. Served to maj. US Army, 1968-71. Fellow ACP, Am. Psychiat. Assn.; mem. Collegium Internat. Neuropsychopharmacologium, Am. Soc. Clin. Psychopharmacology (nat. bd. trustees 1996—). Avocations: bicycling, travel. Office: Madison Inst Medicine 7617 Mineral Point Rd Madison WI 53717-1623 Office Phone: 608-827-2451. Business E-Mail: jjefferson@healthtechsys.com.

JEFFERSON, JONATHAN KENNETH, dean; BS in Math., Morehouse Coll., 1982; M in Engring., Cornell U., 1983. Comprehensive cert. coach Ga., cert. behavioral co ns. Ga., behavioral analyst in bus. perspectives Ga., leadership coach Ga. Ptnr. CSC Cons. Sys., Bridgewater, NJ, 1992—94; exec. dir. BellSouth Corp., Atlanta, 1994—96; ptnr. Computer Scis. Corp., Atlanta, 1996—97; v.p. A.T. Kearney, Atlanta, 1997—2004; dean, sch. bus. adminstrn. Clark Atlanta U., 2004—. Internat. treas. Ch. of Our Lord Jesus Christ, NYC. Featured in Article, Black Enterprise Mag., 2002. Mem.: Christian Coaches Network (assoc.), Internat. Coaching Fedn. (assoc.), Beta Kappa Chi, Pi Mu Epsilon. Office: Clark Atlanta Univ Sch Bus 223 James P Brawley Dr Atlanta GA 30314 Home Phone: 404-880-8973.

JEFFERSON, JOSEPH MURRAY, banker; b. Heilwood, Pa., July 9, 1919; s. Ernest Maloy and Edith (Morris) J.; m. Mary Margaret Kerr, May 27, 1943 (dec. Mar. 1991); children: James Murray, Sharon Lee; m. Mary Jo Greenly, Dec. 11, 1999; 1 stepchild, Traci Romedy. BS, Waynesburg Coll., Pa., 1943; postgrad., Ind. U., 1949—51, Dartmouth Coll., 1963—64. Laborer Buckeye Coal Co., Nemacolin, Pa., 1936-41; sec. First Fed. S&L Assn., Waynesburg, Pa., 1945-52; exec. v.p., CEO Provident Fed. S&L Assn., Pitts., 1953-61; v.p. First Fed. S&L Assn. of Pitts., 1961-68; pres., CEO Washington (Pa.) Fed. Savs. Bank, 1968-86, dir. emeritus, 1995—; dir., vice chmn. Fed. Home Loan Bank of Pitts., 1986-91. Bd. dirs. Pa. Indsl. Devel. Agy., Harrisburg, 1963-64, Pa. Econ. League, Harrisburg, 1985-95, YMCA, Washington, 1968-85. With U.S. Army Aircorps, 1941-42, lt. USN, SubPac, 1943-46. Named to Pa. Cmty. Bankers Hall of Fame, 1992. Mem. U.S. S&L League (dir. exec. com. 1968-71), Pa. S&L League (pres. 1963-64), Masons (32 deg.), Lions (Melvin Jones fellow). Avocations: golf, public speaking. Home: 320 Olympia St Pittsburgh PA 15211-1367

JEFFERSON, LETITIA GIBSON, rehabilitation counselor; b. Providence, Dec. 5, 1937; d. Walter J. Vreeland (stepfather) Jr. and Mary Ledore Halton; m. Carl F. Jefferson, Jr., Sept. 13, 1961 (div. 1968); children: Halton Matthew, Nancy, Robert. BA, Wells Coll., 1959; postgrad., Syracuse U., NY, 1966. Sr. employment counselor N.Y. State Dept. Labor, Albany, 1963-67; labor specialist Suffolk County Dept. Labor, Hauppauge, NY, 1967—99, asst. dir.; ret., 1999. Mem. St. Marks Choir, Hampton Coun. of Chs. Ecumenical Choir, Westhampton Beach, N.Y., mem. prayer group, St. Phillip Ch.; lay leader, chalice adminstr., eucharistic min. St. Marks Ch.,; performer Hampton Theatre Co., Quogue, N.Y.; co-founder Eleventh Step Meditation Workshop, St. Marks Ch. Mem. Nat. Rehab. Assn. (co-founder Suffolk chpt.), Suffolk County Rehab. Coun. (past pres.), Southampton Town Rep. Club. Republican. Episcopalian. Avocations: sailing, poetry, theater, art, singing. Home: 8 Majestic Trce Hendersonville NC 28739-8466 Personal E-mail: mamajeff@webtv.net.

JEFFERSON, MARGO L., journalist; b. Chgo., Oct. 17, 1947; BA in English and Am. Lit. cum laude, Brandeis U., 1968; MS, Columbia U., 1971. Editor Newsweek, 1973—78; asst. prof. dept. journalism NYU, 1979—83, 1989—91; contbg. editor Vogue, 1984—89, 7 Days, 1984—89; lectr. Am. Lit., performing arts & criticism Columbia U., NYC, 1991—93; critic culture desk NY Times, 1993—95, Sunday theater critic, 1995—97, cultural corr., 1997—. Recipient Pulitzer Prize for criticism, 1995. Office: NY Times 229 W 43rd St New York NY 10036-3959

JEFFERSON, MARVIN KAZEMBE, actor, theater educator; b. Newark, Sept. 2, 1958; s. Preston and Lorraine Wideman Jefferson; m. Rasheeda Sabrin Sampson-Jefferson, Oct. 8, 1995; children: Omar Bashir, Fatimah Bashir. Student, Rutgers U., New Brunswick, NJ, 1976—81. Paul Robeson Chautauquan N.J., 2004, Bus. Registration Cert. Prodr./artistic dir. Ensemble Theatre Co., Newark, 1981—96; instr. Bloomfield Coll., 1994—; Paul Robeson Chautauquan Bd. Edn., Newark, 1997—. Dir. of controversy Bloomfield Coll., 1991—96; theatre dir. Hudson Guild, NYC, 2001—07. Actor: performed as William Still for Underground Railroad Walk in N.J., performed the Paul Robeson Chautauqua for the High Plains in Colo.,Md., SC, NC. Recipient award, Mayor, Newark, N.J., 1999, Senate & Gen. Assembly, Trenton, N.J., 2002, Sec. of State, Trenton, 2002. Avocations: reading, travel.

JEFFERSON, MONICA LOUISE, neuroscientist, psychologist; b. Augusta, Ga., Oct. 27, 1977; d. Jasper and Annie J. Jefferson. BS, SUNY, Stony Brook, 1999; PhD, Ohio State U., Columbus, 2005. Psychology intern Northport VA Med. Ctr., NY, 2004—05; post doctoral fellow clin. neuropsychology Maplewood, NJ, 2005—07; clin. neuropsychologist War Related Illness and Injury Study Ctr. East Orange VA Med. Ctr., 2007—. Contbr. chapters to books. Recipient Student Excellence award, NY State Chancellor, 1999, SUNY Stony Brook Provost, 1999, Travel award, Ctr. Substance Abuse Treatment, 2000; fellow, NIH, 1997—99, Ohio State U., 1999; scholar, NSF, 1995—99. Mem.: APA (MFP fellow 1999—2002), Internat. Neuropsychological Soc., Nat. Assn. Black Psychologists (chmn. student cir. rsch. com. 2003—05), Psi Chi (dir. undergraduate rsch. conf. 1998—99), Golden Key, Phi Beta Kappa, Phi Kappa Phi. Home Phone: 614-327-8720. Personal E-mail: scorpiamlj@hotmail.com.

JEFFERSON, RICHARD, professional basketball player; b. LA, June 21, 1980; Grad., U. Arizona, 2001. Player NJ Nets, 2001—. Mem. USA Basketball Men's Sr. Nat. Team, 2003, US Olympic Basketball Team, Athens, Greece, 2004. Office: NJ Nets 390 Murray Hill Pkwy East Rutherford NJ 07073

JEFFERSON, SANDRA TRAYLOR, choreographer; b. Tarboro, NC, Feb. 28, 1942; d. Charles Labon and Doris Vivian (Parker) Traylor; m. Milton Franklin Jefferson, July 2, 1960; children: Mark Franklin, Todd Christopher. Student, Parks Sch. Dance, Petersburg, Va., 1947-58, Sch. of the Richmond (Va.) Ballet, 1958-60; diploma, Julia Mildred Harper Sch. Dance, Richmond, 1960; studied with Robert David Brown, Sterling, Va., 1978-80. Soloist Ballet Impromptu, Richmond, 1958-60; freelance dance instr. Chantilly, Va., 1968-70; ballet coach Artistic Skating Club of Sterling, 1980; founder, dir. Ballet for Skaters, Manassas, Va., 1980-89; artistic dir., cons. in choreography No. Va. Artistic Skating Club, Manassas, 1986-89. Artistic dir. Skating Club of Manassas, 1989; founder, dir. Ballet for Skaters, Seabrook, Md., 1989-94; choreographer, ballet coach Nat. Capitol Dance and Figure Club, Seabrook and Washington, 1989-94; founder, dir. Ballet for Figure Skaters, Sterling, Va., 1993-94; students include nat. medalists in the U.S. and Can. and mems. Can. World Team, U.S. Olympic Sports Festival Team; freelance choreographer, ballet coach, Sterling, 1993—. Developer Brosano Technique Vocabulary of Movement, 1986, Free Form Ballet, 1993, co-developer (artistic skating technique) Brosano Technique, 1981. Social dir. Jaycee-ettes, Winchester, Va., 1963—67. Recipient Achievement award Jaycee-ettes, 1963, 64, 65, 66, 67, U.S. S.E. Soc. Roller Skating Tchrs. Am. award, 1988, World Decoration of Excellence award Am. Biog. Inst., 1989. Mem.: Profl. Dance Tchrs. Assn. United Methodist. Avocations: art, music. Home and Office: 507 S Maple Ct Sterling VA 20164-2710 Home Phone: 703-481-0573.

JEFFERSON, WALLACE B., state supreme court chief justice; s. William and Joyce Jefferson; m. Rhonda Jefferson; 3 children. BA in Political Philosophy, 1985, JD U. Tex., 1988. Cert.: Tex. Bd. Legal Specialization (in civil appellate law). With Groce, Locke & Hebdon, San Antonio, 1988—91; ptnr. Crofts, Callaway & Jefferson, San Antonio, 1991—2001; justice Tex. Supreme Ct., Austin, 2001—04, chief justice, 2004—. Mem. Tex. Supreme Ct. Advisory Com., Tex. State Commn. on Jud. Conduct; chair host com. Fifth Circuit Jud. Conference, 2000. Mem. bd. dirs. San Antonio Pub. Libr. Found., Alamo Area Big Bros./Big Sisters.; mem. edn. com. San Antonio Area Found. Named 40 Under 40 Rising Star, San Antonio Bus. Jour., 1996, Texas Lawyer, 2001, Outstanding Young Lawyer, San Antonio Young Lawyers Assn., 1997. Mem.: William S. Sessions Am. Inns of Ct. (past pres.), San Antonio Bar Assn. (pres. 1998—99, President's award 2000). Office: 201 W 14th St Austin TX 78701 also: PO Box 12248 Austin TX 78711*

JEFFERSON, WAYNE, language educator; AA in Liberal Arts, Bronx CC, 1980; BS in Social Sci., Va. State U., Petersburg, 1988, BA in English, 1992; MEd, Queens Coll., NYC, 1999, M in Supervision, 2004; AS in Bus., La Guardia CC, 2006. English tchr. NYC Dept. Edn. With USMC. Home: 11553 114th Pl # 2 Jamaica NY 11420-2302

JEFFERSON, WILLIAM JENNINGS (JEFF JEFFERSON), congressman; b. Lake Providence, La., Mar. 14, 1947; s. Mose and Angeline (Harris) Jefferson; m. Andrea Louise Green, 1970; children: Jamila, Jalila, Jelani, Nailah, Akilah. BA in English & Polit. Sci., Southern U., 1969; JD, Harvard U., 1972; LLM in Taxation, Georgetown U., 1996. Law clk. to Hon. Alvin B. Rubin US Dist. Ct. (Ea. dist.) La, 1972—73; founding ptnr. Jefferson, Bryan and Gray, 1976—90; legis. asst. to Senator J. Bennett Johnston US Senate, 1973—75; mem. La. State Senate, 1979—90, U.S. Congress from 2nd dist. La., 1991—. Former mem. ways and means com., Dem. steering com., subcoms. select revenue and trade. Served AUS, Judge Advocate General Corps., 1969-75 Named Legis. of the Yr., Info. Tech. Industry Coun.; named one of 100 Most Influential Black Americans, Ebony mag., 2006; recipient Sprit of Enterprise award, US C of C, Disting. Svc. award, Washington Internat. Trade Assn. & Wash. Internat. Trade Found., 2002, Iberville award, New Orleans mag., 2002, Salute to Congress award, Propeller Club of the US, 2005. Mem.: DC Bar Assn., LA Bar Assn., ABA, Congl. Black Caucus Found. Inc., New Orleans Urban League, Am. Found. Negro Affairs, NAACP. Democrat. Baptist. Office: US Ho Reps 2113 Rayburn Ho Office Bldg Washington DC 20515-1802*

JEFFERSON, ZANOBIA BRACY, artist, educator; b. Chgo., Sept. 3, 1926; d. Francis Wright and Hattie Ocie (Robinson) Bracy; m. Robert L. Jefferson, June 4, 1950 (dec. Dec. 23, 1983); children: Heidi V. Long, Robyn F. Sims, Ionis M. Swoope, Robert L. Jr., Gisele Z. Mestre. BA, Fisk Univ., Nashville, Tenn., 1948; MEd, Nova Univ., Ft. Lauderdale, Fla., 1987. Tchr. Fla. A & M Univ., Tallahassee, 1948—50; adult educator Ft. Pierce, Fla. Sch., Ft. Pierce, Fla., 1950—70; art tchr. St. Lucie Co. Pub. Sch., Ft. Pierce, Fla., 1960—93; tchr. art edn. Nova Univ., Ft. Pierce, Fla., 1980. Sculpture, 3-4ft. children, St. Anatasia Cath. Ch., 1988, Felix Elem. Sch., 1986. Bd. dirs. Backus Art Gallery; manpower com. Gov. Graham, Tallahassee; bd. Sunrise Theater, St. Pierce, Fla. Recipient 1st Lifetime Arts Achievement award, St. Lucie County Cult. Affairs Coun., 2005. Mem.: Opera Soc., African Am. Exo. for the Arts, Ret. Educators of Fla., Links Inc., Alpha Kappa Alpha. Christian. Achievements include mentor to highwaymen artists group, tchr. of original group, Afred Hair, James Gibson, Rodney Demps, etc. Avocations: art, crafts, travel, gardening, coin collecting/numismatics. Home: 2300 Valencia Ave Fort Pierce FL 34946 Office Phone: 772-461-4109.

JEFFERY, GEOFFREY MARRON, medical parasitologist; b. Dundee, NY, May 13, 1919; s. Joseph Ewart and Augusta (Knapp) J.; m. Jane Wicker, Aug. 16, 1941; children: Janet A. Harrison, Thomas W., Sarah V. Houghton, Susan E. Tosh. AB, Hobart Coll., 1940; MA, Syracuse U., 1942; ScD, Johns Hopkins U., 1944; MPH, Yale U., 1961. Biol. aide health and safety dept. TVA, 1944; commd. officer USPHS, 1944, scientist dir., 1960; tech. aid, cons. malaria control in war areas TVA, 1944-45; assigned divsn. lab. svcs. Communicable Disease Ctr., 1945-46, charge br. lab. Sch. Tropical Medicine San Juan, 1946-47; asst. prof. biology U. Bridgeport, Conn., 1947-48; charge Malaria Rsch. Lab., NIH, Milledgeville, Ga., 1948-54; mem. staff Lab. Tropical Diseases-Lab. Parasite Chemotherapy, NIAID, NIH, Columbia, SC, 1954-63, head sect. epidemiology, 1961-63; asst. chief Lab. Parasite Chemotherapy, NIAID, NIH, Bethesda, 1963-66, acting chief, 1966, chief, 1967-69, C.Am. Malaria Rsch. Sta., San Salvador, El Salvador, 1969-74; asst. dir. Bur. Tropical Diseases, Ctr. Disease Control, Atlanta, 1974-75; dir. vector biology and control div. Bur. Tropical Diseases, 1975-81; asst. dir. divsn. parasitic diseases Ctr. for Infectious Diseases, Ctrs. for Disease Control, 1982-84. Mem. expert adv. panel on malaria WHO, 1963—99; assoc. mem. commn. malaria Armed Forces Epidemiol. Bd., 1965-69, mem., 1969-73; Del. Internat. Congress Tropical Medicine and Malaria, Lisbon, 1958, Rio de Janeiro, 1963, Teheran, Iran, 1968; Del. Internat. Congress Parasitology, Rome, Italy, 1964, Washington, 1969; Del. Internat. Conf. on Protozoology, London, 1965, Latin Am. Congress Parasitology, Medellin, Colombia, 1973; mem. sci. group on chemotherapy of malaria WHO, Geneva, 1967, mem. sci. group on parasitology, Teheran, 1968; cons. on status of malaria in Africa AID, 1979; mem. sci. working group on applied field rsch. in malaria WHO, Geneva, 1979, mem. steering com., 1981-86; cons. on malaria U.S.-China Health Agreement, 1980; del. Asia and Pacific Conf. on Malaria, Honolulu, 1985; temp. advisor meetings WHO, Kuala Lumpur, 1981, Albuquerque, 1982, Nairobi, 1983, Bangkok, 1984; invited participant concerted action 1st plenary meeting on malaria modelling European Union, Tuebingen, Germany, 1998. Contbr. numerous articles to sci. jours. tropical medicine and parasitology. Recipient Pub. Health Svc. Commendation medal, 1966, Dept. Army cert. of appreciation patriotic civilian svc., 1973 Fellow Royal Soc. Tropical Medicine (local sec. 1984-89); mem. Am. Soc. Tropical Medicine and Hygiene (sec.-treas. 1961-67, v.p. 1971, pres. 1975, Bailey K. Ashford award 1959), Am. Soc. Parasitologists, Assn. Southea. Biologists (editor bull. 1959-60, exec. com. 1962-66), Tropical Medicine Assn. Washington, Southea. Soc. Parasitologists, S.C. Acad. Sci. (mem. council 1960, 62, Jefferson award 1952, 56, 60), Commd. Officers Assn. USPHS, Sigma Xi, Kappa Sigma. Presbyterian. Home: 1085 Blackshear Dr Apt B Decatur GA 30033-2626 Office: Center Disease Control Atlanta GA 30333 Personal E-mail: gjeffery2@comcast.net.

JEFFERY, REUBEN, III, federal agency administrator; b. Aug. 21, 1953; BA, Yale U., 1975; MBA, JD, Stanford U., 1981. Atty. Davis, Polk & Wardwell LLP, NYC, 1981—83; with Goldman Sachs & Co., 1983—2001, ptnr., mng. dir. European Fin. Institutions Group, 1992—97, mng. ptnr. Paris, 1997—2001; spl. adv. to the Pres. for Lower Manhattan Develop. Exec. Office of the Pres., Washington, 2002—03; spl. adv. to adminstrn. Coalition Provisional Authority, US Dept. Def., 2003, rep. & exec. dir. Washington, 2003—04; spl. asst. to pres., sr. dir. internat. econ. affairs, Nat. Security Coun. Exec. Office of Pres., Washington, 2004—05; commr., chmn. Commodity Futures Trading Commn., Washington, 2005—07; spl. adv., US Dept. Def.; under sec. for econ. bus. & agrl. affairs US Dept. State, Washington, 2007—. Office: US Dept State Harry S Truman Bldg 2201 C St NW Rm 7256 Washington DC 20520*

JEFFERY, WILLIAM JEREMY, insurance company executive; Grad. in Polit. Sci., Yale U., New Haven. Exec. dir. Fixed Income Instl. Sales Morgan Stanley; sr. v.p. investments, chief investment officer AFLAC Inc., 2005—. Chmn. Annual Fund Rippowam/Cisqua Sch., Bedford, NY; bd. mem. Friends of the John Jay Homestead, NY. Office: AFLAC Inc 1932 Wynnton Rd Columbus GA 31999 Office Phone: 706-323-3431.*

JEFFERY, WILLIAM RICHARD, developmental biology educator, researcher; b. Chgo., June 9, 1944; s. William and Marjorie (Gross) J. BS, U. Ill., Chgo., 1967; PhD, U. Iowa, 1971. Rsch. assoc. U. Wis., Madison, 1971-72, Sch. Medicine, Tufts U., Boston, 1972-74; asst. prof. biophysics U. Houston, 1974-77; asst. prof. zoology U. Tex., Austin, 1977-80, assoc. prof., 1980-85, prof., 1985-87, J.F. Miescher Regents prof., 1987-90; prof. zoology U. Calif., Davis, 1990-93, prof. molecular and cellular biology, 1993-96; prof., head biology Pa. State U., University Park, 1997-99; prof., chair biology U. Md., College Park, 1999—2004. Co-dir. embryology course Marine Biology Lab., Woods Hole, Mass., 1983-87, active, 1975—. Mem. editl. bd. Devel., 1987-98, Jour. Exptl. Zoology, 1989—, Seminars in Devel. Biology, 1990-96, Seminars in Cell and Devel. Biology, 1997—, Biol. Bull., 1985-90, Cell Motility and the Cytoskeleton, 1985-86, Internat. Jour. Devel. Biology, 1989-2002, Animal Biology, 1991—, Internat. Rev. of Cytology, 1999—, Molecular Biol. Evolution, 2000—, Internat. Jour. Devel. Biology, 2002-; N.Am. editor Zygote, 1993-96 Fellow AAAS; mem. Am. Soc. Zoologists (divsn. chmn. 1988-90, Outstanding Svc. award 1990), Soc. Devel. Biologists (trustee 1987-89, 1995-97, pres. 1995-96), Am. Soc. Cell Biology, Sigma Xi. Home: 1530 Thursto Rd Dickerson MD 20842 Office: Univ Md Dept Biology 1200 Bio Psych Bldg College Park MD 20742-0001 E-mail: Jeffery@umd.edu.

JEFFORDS, JAMES MERRILL, former senator; b. Rutland, Vt., May 11, 1934; s. Olin Merrill and Marion (Hausman) J.; m. Elizabeth Daley; children: Leonard Olin, Laura Louise. BS, Yale U., 1956; LLB, Harvard U., 1962. Bar: Vt. 1962. Law clk. to Hon. Ernest Gibson US Dist. Ct. Vt., 1962—63; ptnr. Bishop, Crowley & Jeffords LLP, Rutland, 1963-66, Kenney, Carbine & Jeffords LLP, Rutland, 1966-69; atty. gen. State of Vt., Montpelier, 1969-72; ptnr. George E. Rice, Jr. & James M. Jeffords, 1973-74; mem. US Congress from Vt., 1975—89; mem. agr. com., ranking minority mem. edn. and labor com., chmn. environ. study conf., 1978-79; a founder Congl. solar coalition, mem. Congl. tourism caucus, mem. Nat. Commn. on Employment and Unemployment Stats., 1979-89; US Senator from Vt., 1989—2007; ranking mem. environ. and pub. works, health, edn., labor and pensions com., vet. affairs com., fin. com. Mem. spl. com. on aging; mem. New Eng. Congl. Caucus, N.E.-Midwest Coalition; town agt. Shrewsbury, 1964-68, zoning adminstr., 1966-68; mem. Jud. Selection Bd., 1967-68; chmn. Hwy. Dept. Investigating Com., 1968; mem. Vt. Senate, 1967-68. With USNR, 1956-59; capt. Res. (ret.). Mem. ABA, Vt. Bar Assn., Rutland County Bar Assn., Am. Judicature Soc. (dir. 1973-76), VFW, Lions, Elks. Independent.*

JEFFORDS, KEITH (KELLAND KEITH JEFFORDS JR.), plastic surgeon; b. Nov. 14, 1959; BS in Chemistry and Biology, Lee U., Cleveland, Tenn.; DDS, Emory U., Atlanta; MD, Ea. Va. Med. Sch., Norfolk, 1995. Cert. Am. Bd. Plastic Surgery, 2002. Gen. practice resident Harvard U./Brigham and Women's Hosp.; oral and maxillofacial surgery resident U. Miami/Jackson Meml. Hosp.; resident plastic surgery program U. Pitts.; founder Advantage Plastic Surgery, PC, Smyrna, Ga. Guest host: (TV series) WATC Atlanta Live; guest CNN Presents; Celebration with Marcus and Joni Lamb; Montel Williams Show; Entertainment Tonight; (TV channel) Discovery Health Channel; recurring guest (radio show) 96 Rock with Southside Steve Rickman and Tim Rhodes. Mem. nat. alumni bd. Ea. Va. Med. Sch. Named Alumnus of Yr., Lee U. Dept. Natural Scis. Office: Advantage Plastic Surgery PC 3964 Atlanta Rd Smyrna GA 30080 Office Phone: 678-503-0506.

JEFFRESS, WILLIAM HORACE, JR., lawyer; b. Birmingham, Ala., July 17, 1945; s. William H. and Dorothy (Grubbs) J.; m. Judith Ray Jones; children: Amy, Jonathan, William. BA summa cum laude in Econs., Washington & Lee U., 1967; LLB, Yale U., 1970. Bar: DC 1971, US Dist. Ct. (dist. DC, no. dist. Tex. and ea. dist. Mich.), US Ct. Appeals (2nd, 3rd, 4th, 5th, 6th, 9th and DC cirs.), US Supreme Ct. 1975. Law clk. to Judge Gerhard A. Gesell US Dist. Ct. (dist. DC), Washington, 1970-71; law clk. to Justice Potter Stewart US Supreme Ct., Washington, 1971-72; atty. Miller, Cassidy, Larroca & Lewin, Washington, 1972—2000; ptnr. litig. dept., mem. exec. com. Baker Botts, LLP, Washington, 2001—. Chmn. adv. bd. Am. Criminal Law Rev., 1984-86. Editor-in-chief, Yale Law Jour.; vice-chmn. editl. bd. Criminal Justice Mag., 1986—. Named one of 75 Best Lawyers in Washington, Washingtonian survey mag., 2002. Fellow Am. Coll. Trial Lawyers, Am. Bar Found.; mem. ABA (past chmn. Criminal Justice Stds. Com., mem. standing com. on Ethics and Profl. Responsibility, 1996-2002). Democrat. Office: Baker Botts LLP The Warner 1299 Pennsylvania Ave NW Washington DC 20004-2400 Office Phone: 202-639-7751. Office Fax: 202-585-1087. E-mail: william.jeffress@bakerbotts.com.*

JEFFREY, DAVID LYLE, literature and language professor, writer; b. Ottawa, Ont., Can., June 28, 1941; s. Lyle Elmo Jeffrey and Florence Lucy Brown; m. Wilberta Elisabeth Johnson, June 17, 1961 (div.); children: Bruce, Kirstin, Adrienne; m. Katherine Beth Brown, July 28, 1984; children: Gideon, Joshua. BA, Wheaton Coll., Ill., 1965; PhD, Princeton U., 1968. Asst. prof. English U. Victoria, BC, Canada, 1968—69, prof., chair English dept., 1973—78; from asst. to assoc. prof. U. Rochester, NY, 1969—73; prof. U. Ottawa, Ont., Canada, 1978—2000, chair English dept., 1978—81; disting. prof. lit. and humanities Baylor U., Waco, Tex., 2000—, provost, 2003—05. Reckitt prof. U. Hull, England, 1971—72; vis. prof. grad. sch. U. Notre Dame, Ind., 1995, 2002; guest prof. Peking U., Beijing, 1996—; dir. Can. Fedn. for the Humanities, 1983—86; v.p. Inst. Advanced Christian Studies, Chgo., 1986—87, 1989—93, 1997—2000; del. exec. assembly MLA, NYC, 1978—80; mem. adv. bd. Younger Scholars Program, Pew Charitable Trusts, 1990—92, 1997—2002; Sir Andrew Lang lectr. St. Andrews U., Scotland, 2004. Author: (book) The Early English Lyric and Franciscan Spirituality, 1975 (Conf. on Christianity and Lit. Book of Yr., 1975), (monographs) People of the Book: Christian Identity and Literary Culture, 1996 (Conf. on Christianity and Lit. Book of Yr., 1996), Houses of the Interpreter, 2003; author, editor A Dictionary of Biblical Tradition in English Literature, 1992 (Conf. on Christianity and Lit. Book of Yr., 1993), William Cowper: Selected Poetry and Prose, 2006, The Bible and the Academy, 2007. Bd. dirs. Augustine Coll., Ottawa, 1997—, Augustine Sch., Jackson, Tenn., 2005—. Woodrow Wilson fellow, Princeton U., 1965—68, rsch. grantee, SSHRCC, 1984—87. Fellow: Internat. Assn. Univ. Profs. English, Royal Soc. Can. (adv. coun. 1997—2000). Avocation: fly fishing. Office: Baylor U 1 Bear Pl Waco TX 76798 E-mail: david_jeffrey@baylor.edu.

JEFFREY, JOHN ORVAL, Internet company executive, lawyer; b. Portsmouth, Va., Aug. 6, 1963; s. Orval L. and Mary L. (Coakley) J.; m. Jaimi Jeffrey, children: Logan, Emilie BA, U. Dayton, Ohio, 1985; diploma internat. legal studies, U. San Diego, Paris, 1987; JD, Southwestern U., LA, 1988. Bar: Calif. 1988, U.S. Dist. Ct. (cen. dist.) Calif. 1988. Assoc. Shield & Smith, LA, 1989-90, Hewitt, Kaldor & Prout, LA, 1990-93; mgr. bus. & legal affairs fx subs. Fox TV, 1993—95; v.p. bus. & legal affairs TCI Interactive, 1995—97; sr. counsel, dir. legal affairs Discovery Comms., 1997—99; exec. v.p. corp. strategy gen. counsel Live365.com, 1999—2003; gen. counsel, bd. sec. ICANN (Internet Corp. for Assigned Names & Numbers), 2003—. Campaign worker John Glenn Campaign for Pres., N.H., 1984; vol. Amnesty Internat. Mem. ABA (internat. law sect., litigation sect., entertainment/sports law sect.), Internat. Bar Assn., Los Angeles County Bar Assn. (mem. evaluation profl. standards com., mem. legis. activity com., mem. artists and the law com.), Phi Alpha Delta, Alpha Nu Omega. Democrat. Avocations: tennis, running, languages. Office: ICANN 4676 Admiralty Way Ste 330 Marina Del Rey CA 90292

JEFFREY, JUDY, school system administrator; BA, U. of No. Iowa, 1963; MA, Creighton U., 1981. With Council Bluffs Cmty. Sch. Dist.; adminstr. Early Childhood, Elementary and Secondary Edn. div. Iowa Dept. Edn., 1996—, dir. edn., 2004—. Tchr. Cedar Falls and Goldfield dists., Iowa; instr. Creighton U.; pres. Coun. of Chief State Sch. Officers Dep. Commn., 2001—03, bd. dirs., co-chair, Task Force on Math and Sci. Edn.; serves on Reauthorization Task Force Elementary and Secondary Edn. Act. Office: Iowa Dept Edn Grimes State Office Bldg 400 E 14th and Grand Des Moines IA 50319-0146 Office Phone: 515-281-3436. Office Fax: 515-281-4122. Business E-Mail: judy.jeffrey@iowa.gov.*

JEFFREY, ROBERT (BOB JEFFREY), advertising executive; Grad, Manhattan Coll., Riverdale, NY, 1975. Co-founder Goldsmith/Jeffrey, 1987; exec. v.p., mng. dir. Lowe and Partners (formerly Goldsmith/Jeffrey), 1996—98; pres. J. Walter Thompson NY, 1998—2001, J. Walter Thompson N. Am., 2001—04; CEO JWT USA, Inc. (formerly J. Walter Thompson), 2004—, chmn., 2005—. Office: JWT USA Inc 466 Lexington Ave New York NY 10017*

JEFFREY, ROBERT GEORGE, JR., manufacturing executive; b. Bronx, NY, Oct. 2, 1933; s. Robert George and Ethel Ruth (Rohrbeck) J.; m. Linda L. Nardone; children: Diana, Christine, Jennifer, Joseph. BBA, Pace U., 1959; MBA, NYU, 1966. CPA, N.Y., N.J. Sr. acct. Deloitte & Touche, NYC, 1959-65; asst. mgr. corp. acctg. Union Camp Corp., Wayne, NJ, 1965-66, asst. to comptr., 1966-69, mgr. corp. acctg., 1969-70, dir. fin. planning, 1970-72, corp. comptr., 1972-79; exec. v.p. Huntington Mgmt. Corp., 1980-82; v.p. fin. Rudco Industries Inc., 1982-84, sr. v.p., 1984-87; ptnr. R.G. Jeffrey, CPA, Wayne, 1987—. Adj. prof. taxation William Paterson U., 1993—; bd. dirs. The Corby Group. Trustee Wayne Twp. Bd. Edn., 1975-78. Served with USAF, 1952-56. Mem. AICPA, NY State Soc. CPAs, NJ Soc. CPAs (state trustee 2005—, bd. dirs. Passaic County chpt.), Fin. Execs. Inst. Home: 28 Pelham Rd Wayne NJ 07470-2873 Office: 61 Berdan Ave Wayne NJ 07470-3229 Office Phone: 973-628-0022. E-mail: rgjcpa@optonline.net.

JEFFREY, SHERI, lawyer; BS cum laude, Loyola Marymount U., 1982, JD, 1985; LLM, NYU, 1986. Bar: Calif. 1985. Ptnr. Corp. & Fin. Dept., mem. Entertainment Group Kaye Scholer LLP, LA. Mem.: State Bar Calif. Office: Kaye Scholer LLP Ste 1700 1999 Ave of the Stars Los Angeles CA 90067 Office Phone: 310-788-1270. E-mail: sjeffrey@kayescholer.com.

JEFFREY, WILLIAM ALAN, federal agency administrator, physicist; b. Arlington Heights, Ill., Jan. 13, 1960; s. Lynn Ann Engelking Jeffrey. BSc, MIT, 1982; MA, Harvard U., 1984, PhD, 1988. Rsch. analyst Strategic Planning Assocs., Washington, 1982-83; rsch. staff mem. Inst. for Def. Analyses, Alexandria, Va., 1988-91; sr. rsch. scientist Grumman Aerospace, Herndon, Va.; dep. dir. Advanced Tech. Office, chief scientist Tactical Tech. Office, Def. Advanced Rsch. Projects Agy. US Dept. Def., asst. dep. for tech. Def. Airborne Reconnaissance Office; sr. dir. for homeland & nat. security, asst. dir. for space & aeronatics Office Sci. & Tech. The White House, Washington; dir. Nat. Inst. Standards & Tech, US Dept. Commerce, Gaithersburg, Md., 2005—. Tutor Boston Dept. Edn., 1984, Alexandria Dept. Edn., 1989—. Contbr. articles to profl. jours. Danforth Ct. Excellence in teaching award, 1985, Am. Astron. Soc. Solar Physics studentship, Harvard Grad. Sch. Arts and Sciences award, 1985; NASA fellow, 1985, 86, 87. Mem. Am. Phys. Soc., Am. Astron. Soc., Sigma Xi, Sigma Pi Sigma. Office: Nat Inst Standards & Tech 100 Bureau Dr Stop 1000 Gaithersburg MD 20899 E-mail: william.jeffrey@nist.gov.

JEFFREYS, SIR ALEC JOHN, geneticist, educator; b. Luton in Bedfordshire, Eng., Jan. 9, 1950; married; 2 children. Studied biochemistry and genetics, Oxford Univ., PhD, 1975; DSc, Univ. Leicester. Postdoctoral rsch., dept. med. enzymology and molecular biology Univ. Amsterdam, 1975—77; with Univ. Leicester, 1977—, prof., dept. genetics, 1987—91, Royal Soc. Wolfson Rsch. prof., dept. genetics, 1991—. Spkr. in field.

Contbr. articles to prof. jours. Named Midlander of Yr., 1989, Hon. Freeman, City of Leicester, 1993; named to Nat. Inventors Hall of Fame, 2005; recipient Knighthood for Services to Genetics, 1994, Albert Einstein World of Sci. award, 1996, Australia prize, 1998, Albert Lasker award for Clin. Med. Rsch., Lasker Found., 2005. Fellow: Royal Soc. (Davy medal 1987, Royal medal 2004); mem.: NAS (fgn. assoc. 2005), Am. Acad. Forensic Sciences, Academia Europaea, European Molecular Biology Orgn. (EMBO). Achievements include invention of genetic fingerprinting. Office: Dept Genetics Univ Leicester University Rd Adrian Bldg Rm G19 Leicester LE1 7RH England Office Phone: 44 0 116 252 3435. Office Fax: 44 0 116 252 3378. Business E-Mail: ajj@leicester.ac.uk.

JEFFREYS, ELYSTAN GEOFFREY, petroleum consultant; b. Apr. 26, 1926; s. Geoffrey and Georgene Frances (Littell) Jeffreys; m. Pat Rumage, May 1, 1946 (div. 1967); children: Jeri Lynn, David Powell; m. Peggi Villar, Feb. 28, 1975 (div. 2000); m. Sandra H. Garthwait, Aug. 5, 2002. Geol. Engr., Colo. Sch. Mines, 1951, grad. in Econ. Evaluation and Investment Decision Methods, 1972, grad. in Econ. Evaluation and Investment Decision Methods, 1991. Registered profl. engr., Miss., land surveyor, Miss, profl. geologist, Ala.; cert. sr. appraiser of oil and gas properties Am. Soc. Appraisers, 1993. Ptnr. G. Jeffreys & Son, 1951-53, Jeffreys & Launius, 1953-55; pvt. practice petroleum exploration, 1954-77; exploration mgr. Arrowhead Exploration Co., Mobile and Brewton, Ala., 1977-83; cons. petroleum geologist and appraiser, 1964—. Pres., chmn. bd. dirs., CEO Major Oil Co., Jackson, Miss., 1961—84, v.p., 1984—98, The Jeffreys Co., Inc., Mobile, 1976—96, pres., CEO, 1996—2001; asst. mgr. Kee Energy Co., LLC, 1996—. Vestryman Trinity Episcopal Ch., Mobile, 1989-92, 94-96, sr. warden, 1991-92; bd. trustees The Appraisal Found., 1993-94. With 3d U.S. Army, 1944-46, ETO. Mem. Miss. Geol. Soc., Ala. Geol. Soc., New Orleans Geol. Soc. Am. Assn. Petroleum Geologists (50 Yr. Membership 2001), Fla. Ind. Petroleum Prodrs. Assn., Gulf Coast Assn. Geol. Socs. (treas. 1960, Cert. of Svc. 1971), Miss. Assn. Petroleum Landmen, Assn. Petroleum Landmen of Ala., Am. Geol. Soc., Masons (32 degree), Pi Kappa Alpha. Address: 115 Fairway Dr Daphne AL 36526-7401 Home Phone: 251-621-1850; Office Phone: 251-621-1850. Personal E-mail: EGJeffreys@aol.com.

JEFFREY-SMITH, LILLI ANN, biofeedback specialist, educator, administrator; b. Bedford, Ind., 1944; d. Charles Constantine and Adelai (Malon) Jeffrey-Smith. Grad., Ind. Bus. Coll., 1963; BS, Ind. U., 1973; grad., psychosomatic Med. Clinic, Berkeley, Calif.; PhD in Behavioral Sci., Kennedy-Western U., 1988. Diplomate Am. Bd. Disability Analysis; cert. biofeedback specialist. Project assoc., stress mgmt. clinician City of Indpls., 1973-79; pres., dir. Biofeedback Ctr. of Minn., Edina, 1979—; dir. biofeedback dept. Sister Kenney Inst., Mpls., 1979-81; outreach coord. Abbot-Northwestern Hosp., Mpls., 1981; dir. biofeedback dept. Noran Clinic, Mpls., 1981-83. Mem. faculty Ctr. Spiritually and Healing U. Minn., Mpls., 2000—; cons. in field. Author, narrator health and wellness tape series. Mem. Rep. Presdl. Task Force, 1984—, NCS, 1985; co-chmn. Mayor's Handicapped Task Force, Indpls., 1975; founder, pres. Miss Wheel Chair Ind., Inc.; mem. U. Minn. Cmty. Faculty Ctr. Spirituality and Healing, 2000. Named Hon. Lt. Gov., State of Ind., 1978; given Key to the City of Indpls., 1973, Flag of the City if Indpls., 1975. Mem. ABDA, NAFE, AAUW, AAAS, Am. Inst. Stress, N.Y. Acad. Sci., Edina C. of C., Minn. Women's Network, Biofeedback Soc. Am., Biofeedback Soc. Minn., Am. Assn. Control Tension, Am. Assn. Behavioral Therapists, Am. Assn. Biofeedback Clinicians, Nat. Assn. Bus. Owners, Soc. Open Focus and Tng. Rsch., Assn. Trainers Clin. Hypnosis, Internat. Stress and Tension Control Assn., Minn. Assn. Rehab. Providers, Internat. Platform Assn, Nat. Women's Health Resource Ctr. (bd. mem., 2000). Avocations: music, stamp collecting/philately, poetry. Office: Biofeedback Ctr of Minn 7300 France Ave S Ste 200 Edina MN 55435-4542 Office Phone: 952-893-9400. Personal E-mail: nopills2@aol.com.

JEFFRIES, JOHN CALVIN, JR., dean, law educator; b. 1948; BA, Yale U., 1970; JD, U. Va., 1973. Bar: Va. 1973, D.C. 1974. Law clk. to Hon. Justice Powell U.S. Supreme Ct., 1973-74; asst. prof. U. Va., Charlottesville, 1975-79, assoc. prof., 1979-81, prof. law, 1981—, Emerson Spies prof., 1986—, acad. assoc. dean, 1994—99, Arnold H. Leon prof. law, dean Sch. Law, 2001—. Prof. FBI Acad., Quantico, Va., 1976—; vis. asst. prof. Stanford U., fall 1977; vis. prof. Yale U., 1981-82, So. Calif. U., fall 1986, 89, 93; John V. Ray rsch. prof. 1989-1991; Horace W. Goldsmith rsch. prof. 1992-1995; William L. Matheson and Robert M. Morgenthau disting. prof. 1996-2001. Author: Justice Lewis F. Powell, Jr.: A Biography, 1994, (with Low) Model Penal Code and Commentaries, 3 vols., 1980, (with Karlan, Low and Rutherglen) Civil Rights Actions: Enforcing the Constitution, 2000, Federal Courts and the Law of Federal-State Relations, 4th edit., 1998, (with Low and Bonnie) Cases and Materials on Criminal Law, 1982, 2d edit., 1986; editor-in-chief Va. Law Rev. 2nd lt. gen. US Army. Mem. Am. Law Inst., Va. State Bar (com. for oversight of bar activities). Office: U Va Sch Law Charlottesville VA 22903 Office Phone: 434-924-7343. Business E-Mail: jcj3w@virginia.edu.*

JEFFRIES, MICHAEL S. (MIKE JEFFRIES), apparel executive; b. Elk City, Okla., July 13, 1944; m. Susan Jeffries; 1 child, Andrew. BA in Econs., Claremont McKenna Coll., 1966; MBA, Columbia U., 1968. With Abraham and Straus, 1968; exec. v.p. merchandising Bullock's, 1980-83; pres., CEO Alcott & Andrews, 1983-89; exec. v.p. merchandising Paul Harris, 1990-92; pres., CEO Abercrombie & Fitch Co., New Albany, Ohio, 1992—98, chmn., CEO, 1998—. Office: Abercrombie & Fitch Co 6301 Fitch Path New Albany OH 43054*

JEFFRIES, PAUL FRANKLIN, philosophy professor; s. Alfred Albert and Mary Louise Jeffries; m. Ruth Alice Watts, May 9, 1981. BA, Colo. State U., Ft. Collins, 1980; MAR, Yale U., New Haven, Conn., 1986; MA, U. Minn., Mpls., 1990, PhD, 2000. Ordained elder Presbyn. Ch., 1991. Campus min., team leader InterVarsity Christian Fellowship, Albuquerque, 1980—84; instr., debate coach Bethel Coll., St. Paul, 1986—87; instr. U. of Minn., Mpls., 1990—92, nat. scholarship coord., adviser CLA honors divsn., 1992—95, mem. com. on scholastic standing rep., adviser Coll. Liberal Arts, 1995—97, instr. philosophy dept., 1998—99, coord. Acad. Disting. Tchrs., 1999—2001; assoc. prof. dept. of philosophy and religion U. of Dubuque, Iowa, 2001—05, Wendt Univ. prof., 2004—05; asst. prof. dept. of philosophy Ripon (Wis.) Coll., 2006—. Mem. nat. strategic planning working group Emerging Scholars Network-InterVarsity Christian Fellowship, Madison, Wis., 2002—04; mem. faculty ministries adv. coun InterVarsity Christian Fellowship, Madison, 2004; mem. quality improvement com. Home Instead Sr. Care, Dubuque, 2003—04; adj. prof. U. Dubuque Theol. Sem., 2002—05. Host family for internat. students, 1987—2005. Recipient Bibl. Pedagogy grant, Presbyn. Church-USA, 2003—05, Pew Younger Scholars Summer Seminar Participant, Pew Found., 1998, U. Honors award, Colo. State U., 1980, Christian Practices grant, Valparaiso Project on Edn. and Formation of People of Faith, 2004—06, Faculty/Student Rsch. Project grant, Iowa Coll. Found. McElroy Trust, 2004—05, Philosophy Dept. fellowships, U. of Minn., 1987—88, 1997—99. Mem.: Am. Assn. Univ. Profs., Emerging Scholars Network, Soc. for Ethics Across the Curriculum, Soc. of Christian Philosophers, Am. Philos. Assn. Office: Ripon Coll 300 Steward St Ripon WI 54971 Home Phone: 563-748-2108; Office Phone: 920-748-8377. Business E-Mail: jeffriesp@ripon.edu.

JEFFRIES, ROBERT JOSEPH, retired engineer, information technology executive, educator; b. Norwalk, Conn., Jan. 6, 1923; s. Charles William and Christine (Jacobsen) J.; m. Anna Darling Cumming, Oct. 13, 1945; children: Christine Darling, Bruce Cumming. BS, U. Conn., 1944, MS, 1946; DEng, Johns Hopkins U., 1948. Engr. NACA, 1944-46; instr. Johns Hopkins U., 1946-48; research assoc. N.C. State Coll., 1948-49; assoc. prof. Mich. State U., 1949-54; tech. planning adviser Schlumberger Instrument Co., 1954-55; asst. to pres. Daystrom, Inc., 1955-57; pres., founder Data-Control System, Inc., 1957-66, chmn. bd., 1966-68; prof. U. Bridgeport, Conn., 1968-75, ret.; founder, dir. Ednl. & Tech. Cons., Inc., 1953-57. V.p., dir. TJB Resources Inc., 1972-88; dir. emeritus Evergreen Fund Family; v.p., founder Found. Instrumentation Edn. and Rsch., 1958-66; fellow-in-residence Edgar Cayce Found., Virginia Beach, Va., 1981-88; prof. Atlantic U., 1986-90. Editor Jour. Instrument Soc. Am., 1953-54; contbr. tech. papers. Trustee Am. Unitarian Assn., Cmty. Ch. Coll., Sun City Ctr., Tampa Bay Cmty. Found., SCC coun. Recipient Disting. Alumnus award U. Conn., Disting. Alumnus award John Hopkins U. Fellow NRC; mem. Instrument Soc. Am. (pres. 1957-58), Assn. Rsch. and Enlightenment (trustee), Conn. Commn. for Higher Edn. (vice chmn.), U. Conn. Engring. Alumni Assn. (pres. 1969-71), Sigma Xi, Tau Beta Pi, Eta Kappa Nu. Home: 1010 American Eagle Blvd Apt 502 Sun City Center FL 33573-5284 E-mail: rjjeff@tampabay.rr.com.

JEFFRIES, RUSSELL MORDEN, communications company official; b. Carmel, Calif., July 15, 1935; s. Herman M. and Louise (Morden) J.; m. Barbara Jean Borcovich, Nov. 24, 1962; 1 child, Lynne Louise. AA, Hartnell Coll., 1971. Sr. communications technician AT&T, Salinas, Calif., 1955-91. Mayor City of Salinas, 1987-91. Pres. El Gabilan Sch. PTA, Salinas, 1971-74, Salinas Valley Council PTA, 1975-76; mem. Salinas City Sch. Bd., 1975-81; mem. Salinas City Council, 1981-87; bd. dirs. Community Hosp. Salinas Found., 1987—, Salinas-Kushikino Sister City, 1987—, pres. 1992-93, John Steinbeck Ctr. Found., 1987-96, Food Bank for Monterey County, 1992-96; hon. bd. dirs. Monterey Film Festival, 1987-96, Calif. Rodeo Assn., 1987; mem. ctrl. bd. Calif. Regional Water Quality, 1992—; commr. Moss Landing Harbor, 1996. Recipient hon. service award PTA, Salinas, 1976; cert. of appreciation Calif. Dept. Edn., 1980, Salinas City Sch. Dist., 1981, Calif. Sch. Bds. Assn., 1981, Steinbeck Kiwanis, Salinas, 1987; named hon. mem. Filipino community Salinas Valley, 1988. Mem. Salinas C. of C., Native Sons Golden West, K.C. Republican. Roman Catholic. Avocations: fishing, hunting, bowling, golf. Home: 204 E Curtis St Salinas CA 93906-2804

JEFFRIES, TELVIN, retail executive; With Best Products, 1987—93; various human resources positions including sr. v.p. Kohl's Corp., Menomonee Falls, Wis., 1993—2003, exec. v.p., 2003—. Com. chmn. Holy Redeemer Instl. Ch. of God in Christ Ednl. complex project. Named one of Rising Stars: 40 Under 40, Chain Store Age, 2004. Office: Kohls Corp N56 W17000 Ridgewood Dr Menomonee Falls WI 53051-5660 Office Phone: 262-703-7000. E-mail: telvin.jeffries@kohls.com.*

JEFFS, THOMAS HAMILTON, II, retired bank executive; b. Grosse Pointe Farms, Mich., July 11, 1938; s. Thomas Raymond and Geraldine (Bogan) J.; m. Patricia Lucas, June 20, 1964; children: Leslie, Laura, Caroline BBA in Gen. Bus., U. Mich., 1960, MBA, 1961. With NBD Bank, 1962-99, pres., COO, until 1999; vice chmn., bd. dirs. First Chgo. NBD Corp., 1995-98. Bd. dirs. MCN Energy Group, Inc., Detroit, Intermet Corp., Local Initiatives Support Corp. Bd. dirs. Detroit Symphony, Econ. Club Detroit; chmn. New Detroit, Inc.; dir. Detroit Renaissance, Inc. With U.S. Army, 1960-62. Mem. Bankers Roundtable, Detroit Athletic Club, Detroit Club (pres. 1982), Detroit Country Club, Yondotega Club, Grosse Pointe Club. Republican. Episcopalian. Office: NBD Bank 611 Woodward Ave Detroit MI 48226-3408 Home: PO Box 675 Boca Grande FL 33921-0675

JEGEN, SISTER CAROL FRANCES, religious studies educator; b. Chgo., Oct. 11, 1925; d. Julian Aloysius and Evelyn W. (Bostelmann) J. BS in History, St. Louis U., 1951; MA in Theology, Marquette U., 1958, PhD in Religious Studies, 1968; degree (hon.), St. Mary of the Woods, Terra Haute, Ind., 1977. Elem. tchr. St. Francis Xavier Sch., St. Louis, 1947-51; secondary tchr. Holy Angels Sch., Milw., 1951-57; coll. tchr. Mundelein Coll., Chgo., 1957-91; prof. pastoral studies Loyola U., Chgo., 1991—. Adv. coun. U.S. Cath. Bishops, Washington, 1969-74; trustees Cath. Theol. Union, Chgo., 1974-84. Author: Jesus the Peace Maker, 1986, Restoring Our Friendship with God, 1989, Sharing God's Own Life, 2007; co-author: (with Byron Sherwin) Thank God, 1989; editor: Mary According to Women, 1985. Participant Nat. Farm Worker Ministry, Fresno, Calif., 1977—; mem. Pax Christi, U.S.A., 1979—, Jane Addams Conf., Chgo., 1989. Recipient Loyola Civic award Loyola U., Chgo., 1981, Chgo. medallion for Excellence in Catechesis, 1996, Sor Juana award Hispanic Ministry, 2000; named one of 100 Women to Watch Today's Chgo. Woman, 1989. Mem. Cath. Theol. Soc. Am., Coll. Theology Soc., Cath.-Jewish Scholars Dialog, Liturgical Conf. Democrat. Roman Catholic. Avocations: music, gardening. Home: Wright Hall 6364 N Sheridan Rd Chicago IL 60660-1700

JEGEN, LAWRENCE A., III, law educator; b. Chgo., Nov. 16, 1934; s. Lawrence A. and Katherine M. Jegen; children: Christine M., David L. BA, Beloit Coll., Wis., 1956; JD, U. Mich., 1959, MBA, 1960; LLM, NYU, 1963. Bar: Ill. 1959, US Dist. Ct. (no. dist.) Ill. 1959, US Dist. Ct. (so. dist.) Ind. 1962, Ind. 1966, US Tax Ct. 1966, US Ct. Appeals (7th cir.) 1980, US Supreme Ct. 1980. Tax cons. Coopers & Lybrand, NYC, 1960-62; asst. prof. law Ind. U., Indpls., 1962-64, assoc. prof., 1964-66, prof., 1966—, Thomas F. Sheehan prof. tax law and policy, 1982—, prof. philanthropic studies Ctr. Philanthropy, 1992—, external tax counsel, 1997—. Ind. U. rep. to Nat. Assn. Coll. and Univ. Attys., 1994—; co-founder, co-dir. Ann. Tax Inst. for Colls. and Univs., 1994—; bar rev. lectr., vis. prof. in field; spl. counsel Ind. Dept. Revenue, 1963-65, Gov.'s Commn. on Med. Edn., 1970-72; mem. commr.'s adv. com. IRS, 1981-82; advisor Notre Dame Estate Planning Inst.; mem. Ind. Corp. Law Survey Commn.; State Tax Notes corr. for Tax Analysts; contbg. editor Inst. Bus. Planning's Tax Planning Svc.; bd. dirs., officer Ind. Continuing Legal Edn. Forum; 1st chmn. bd. dirs. Baccalaureate Edn. Sys. Trust of Ind.; mem. Ind. Gen. Assembly Study Commn.-Ind. Gen. Corp. Act; mem. Ind. Corps. Survey Commn., 1965—; commr. Nat. Conf. Uniform State Laws, 1981-91; dir. N.Am. Wildlife Assn., 1981-90. Author: Indiana Will and Trust Manual, 1967-95; Lifetime and Estate, Personal and Business Planning, 1987; Estate Planning and Administration in Indiana, 1979, numerous other books, articles, chpts. Chmn. bd. dirs. Ind. Bar Ednl. Sys. Tchrs., 1988-89; mem. adv. bd. Ind. U. Ctr. on Philanthropy. Named hon. sec. of state, State of Ind., 1967, 1980, hon. dep. atty. gen., 1968, hon. state treas., 1969, Ford fellow, 1963; recipient Spl Alumni Tch. award, Ind. U. Alumni Assn., 1970, 1976, 1980, 1985, Excellence in Taxation award for improvement tax adminstrn., State of Ind. Quality for Ind. Taxpayers, Inc., 1990, The Thomas Hart Benton Mural medallion, 1993, The Thomas Hart Benton Mural medallion, 1994, 3 Sagamore of the Wabash awards, State Ind.; Internat. award, Assn. Continuing Legal Administrators for Excellence in Continuing Legal Edn., Ind. U. Most Outstanding Law Prof. award 6 times, Pres.'s Cir. Commemorative medallion, Ind. U. Disting. Tchg. award, Tchr. of Significance, Ind. U. Fellow Am. Bar Found. (life), Am. Coll. Probate Counsel, Am. Coll. Tax Counsel; mem. ABA, FBA, Mid-West Inst. Estate and Tax Planning (adv. bd.), Ind. Bar Assn. (chmn. taxation sect. 1969-70, presdl. citation 1971), Indpls. Bar Assn. (Dr. Morton Finney Jr. Excellence in Legal Edn. award), Ind. Trial Lawyers Assn. (corp. taxation, estate taxation, state and local taxation). Achievements include having a law professorship created at Indiana University in his honor in 2006. Office: Indiana Univ Sch Law 530 W New York St Indianapolis IN 46202-3225 Office Phone: 317-251-5300. Personal E-mail: profjegen@aol.com.

JEHLE, MICHAEL EDWARD, financial advisor, lawyer; b. Lawrence, Kans., Apr. 2, 1954; s. Edwin Paul and Catherine Claire (Cragoe) J.; m. Kimberly Ellen Davis, Aug. 4, 1979; children: Kathryn Anne, Christine Michelle. BS, S.W. Mo. State U., 1976; JD, Stanford U., 1979. Bar: Calif., Ill., Pa. Atty. The First Nat. Bank of Chgo., 1979-84, sr. atty., 1984-86; v.p., gen. counsel Equibank, Pitts., 1986-87, sr. v.p., gen. counsel, sec., 1987, Equimark Corp., Pitts., 1987-89, exec. v.p., chief fin. officer, 1989-90; pres. Strategic Adv. Group, Pitts., 1990-95, Strategic Healthcare Advisors, Pitts., 1993-95; dir. rsch. MED 3000 Group, Inc., Pitts., 1995-96; pres. THI, Inc., Pitts., 1996—. Co-author: Sovereign Lending, 1984. Mem. ABA, Nat. Health Lawyers Assn., Healthcare Fin. Mgmt. Assn., Sewick Martial Arts Club (head instr.). Republican. Methodist. Avocations: martial arts, wine collecting. Home: 411 Maple Ln Sewickley PA 15143-1021 Office: THI Inc 411 Maple Ln Sewickley PA 15143-1021 Office Phone: 412-749-8959. Personal E-mail: mejehle@hotmail.com.

JEHLEN, PATRICIA D., state legislator; b. Austin, Tex., Oct. 14, 1943; d. Paul Kindred Jr. and Ruth Miller (Zumbrunnen) Deats; m. Alain Peter Jehlen, Aug. 29, 1969; children: Nicholas, Wendy, Peter. BA, Swarthmore Coll., 1965; MA in Teaching, Harvard U., 1969. Rschr. Harvard Sch. Edn., Cambridge, Mass., 1966-67; tchr. history Brookline (Mass.) H.S., 1968-71; mem. Somerville (Mass.) Sch. Com., 1976-91, Mass. Ho. of Reps., Somerville, 1991—. VISTA vol. Cook County Migrant Coun., Chicago Heights, Ill., 1965-66. Democrat. Home: 67 Dane St Somerville MA 02143-3730 Office: Mass Ho of Reps Rm 275 Boston MA 02133 Office Phone: 617-722-2676. Business E-Mail: rep.patricia.jehlen@hon.state.ma.us.

JELALIAN, ALBERT V., electrical engineer; b. Bridgewater, Mass., June 30, 1933; s. Siragan and Zarouhi (Tanelian) J.; m. Mary B. Karoghlanian; children: Alan H., Leslie K. BSEE, Northeastern U., 1957. Reg. profl. engr., Mass. Engr. Raytheon Co., Waltham, Mass., 1957—81, mgr. electro-optics lab Sudbury, 1981—86, asst. dir., 1986—91, asst. mgr. equipment devel. labs. (electro optics), 1991—92; pres. Jelalian Sci. & Engring., Bedford, 1992—. Inventor: holds ten patents relating to aviation safety and mil. products; contbr. articles to profl. jours.; author: Laser Radar Systems, 1992; guest editor IEEE Procs. Spl. Issue on Laser Radar Sys., 1995-96. Recipient Recognition award NASA, Washington, 1974, Group Achievement award, 1975, Disting. Svc. award IRIS, 1993, Nat. Sci. and Tech. award IRIS, 1998; fellow Mil. Sensing Symposium. Mem. IEEE (sr.), Infrared Info. Symposium (vice chmn. active systems 1989-91, nat. chmn. 1991-93), Optical Soc. Am. Office: Jelalian Sci & Engring 3 Reeves Rd Bedford MA 01730-1334 Personal E-mail: jsne@aol.com.

JELINEK, FREDERICK, electrical engineer, educator; b. Prague, Czechoslovakia, Nov. 18, 1932; arrived in U.S., 1949, naturalized, 1955; s. William and Trudy (Kocmanek) J.; m. Milena Tobolova, Feb. 4, 1961; children— Hannah, William. BS, MIT, 1956, MS, 1958, PhD, 1962; DS Math. and Physics (hon.), Charles U., Prague, 2001. Instr. MIT, Cambridge, 1959-62; lectr. Harvard U., Cambridge, 1962; asst. prof. Cornell U., Sch. Elec. Engring., Ithaca, NY, 1962-66, assoc. prof., 1966-72, prof., 1972-74; vis. scientist MIT, Lincoln Lab., 1964, 65, IBM, 1968-69; sr. mgr. continuous speech recognition IBM, T.J. Watson Research Center, Yorktown Heights, NY, 1972-93; prof., dir. Ctr. Lang. and Speech Processing Whiting Sch. Engring. Johns Hopkins U., Balt., 1993—, Julian Sinclair Smith prof. Author: Probabilistic Information Theory, 1968, Statistical Methods for Speech Recognition, 1998; contbr. articles to profl. jours. Chmn. Liberal Party, Ithaca, NY, 1970-72, mem. state exec. com., 1971-73. Recipient Outstanding Achievement in the Field of Speech Comm. European Speech Comm. Assn., 2000; named One of top 100 innovators in speech recognition by Tech. Mag., 1981. Fellow IEEE (life; pres. Info. Theory Group 1977, bd. govs. 1970-79, 81-86, Info. Theory Group best paper award 1971, Soc. award Signal Processing Soc. 1998, Golden Jubilee Paper award Info. Theory Soc. 1998, Third Millennium medal 2000, Computer, Speech and Lang. paper award 2002); mem. NAE. Office: Johns Hopkins U Ctr Lang and Speech Processing Barton Hall 3400 N Charles St Baltimore MD 21218 Office Phone: 410-516-7730. Business E-Mail: jelinek@jhu.edu.

JELINEK, GREGORY M., bank executive; B in Fin., U. Dayton, Ohio, 1985; MBA in Acctg., Cleve. State U., 1992. Trainee retail lending tng. program Nat. City Corp., Cleve., 1986, various positions in mid. market, investment real estate, spl credits and retail divsns., exec. v.p., mgr. dealer fin. Consumer and Small Bus. Fin. Svcs. group, sr. v.p., divsn. mgr. Northcoast Mid. Market Corp. Banking, sr. v.p. bus. banking, 2004—. Mem. St. Frances Xavier Parish of Medina; bd. mem. Western Res. Hist. Soc., Cliffside Artist Collaborative; mem. exec. com. United Way. Mem.: Cleve. Assn. Corp. Growth. Office: Nat City Corp Nat City Ctr 1900 E Ninth St Cleveland OH 44114-3484 Office Phone: 216-222-2000.*

JELINEK, JOHN JOSEPH, public relations executive; b. San Pedro, Calif., Sept. 3, 1955; s. Joseph Francis and Patricia Valerie (Powers) J.; m. Christl Michele Schneider, June 1986 (div. July 1997). BA, Loyola U., 1977; MA, Loyola-Marymount U., 1983; postgrad., Syracuse U. Assoc. editor E-Go Enterprises, Sherman Oaks, Calif., 1976-77; advt. dir. Select Promotions, Irvine, Calif., 1977-78; editor SCORE Internat., Westlake Village, Calif., 1978-79; exec. editor Petersen Pub. Co., LA, 1979-82, editor, 1982-85; pub. rels. account exec. Hill and Knowlton Inc., LA, 1985-87; acct. supr. Freeman/McCue Pub. Rels., Newport Beach, Calif., 1987-88; account supr. tech. div. Fleishman Hillard Inc., LA, 1988-89; rep. pub. affairs corp. news dept. Ford Motor Co., Dearborn, Mich., 1989-90; product info. mgr. Ford of Can., Oakville, 1990-92; car product devel., pub. affairs mgr. Ford Motor Co., Dearborn, Mich., 1993-96, product devel., pub. affairs mgr., 1996-98, dir. car strategy comm., 1998-2001, Ford brand comm. mgr., 2001—02; v.p. pub. affairs Ford of Can., Oakville, Ont., 2002—05. Author: (with others) Consumer's Guide to 1978 Trucks, 1978, Consumer's Guide to 1980 Trucks, 1979, Complete Guide to Used Cars, 1981, How to Buy the Best Compact Truck, 1984; columnist Guns & Ammo Mag., 1980-84, Petersen's Hunting Mag., 1986-87. Capt. Calif. State Mil. Res. 1982-89. Recipient 1st place award Calif. Newspaper Pub. Assn., 1977 Mem. NRA (life), L.A. County Mus. Natural History-Automobile Collection Coun., Aircraft Owners and Pilots Assn., Nat. Aeronautical Assn., Detroit Inst. Art. Republican. Roman Catholic. Avocations: travel, flying, skiing, cooking. E-mail: jjelinek@peoplepc.com.

JELINEK, VERA, dean; b. Kosice, Czechoslovakia, Dec. 16, 1935; came to U.S., 1947; d. Joseph and Margit (Lefkovits) Schnitzer; m. Josef E. Jelinek, June 19, 1960; children: David, Paul. BA in History, CUNY, 1956; MA, Johns Hopkins U., 1958; PhD in Modern European History, NYU, 1977; diploma, Sch. Advanced Internat. Study, Bologna, Italy. Translator Rockefeller Bros. Fund, NYC, 1958-59; exec. dir. US Youth Coun., 1959-63; dir. internat. programs, social and natural scis. NYU, 1985—, dir. Lillian Vernon Ctr. Internat. Affairs, 2000—04, dir. Energy Forum, 2000—05, divisional dean, dir. Ctr. Global Affairs, 2004—. Mem. adv. com. N.Y.C.-Budapest Sister City Program, 1991-94; prin. dir. pilot tng. program for new UN diplomats NYU, 1996-97. Author audio cassette: Before You Go-Italy, 1985. Active Mus. Am. Folk Art, NYC; edn. co-chair The Am. Antiques Show, 2002—03. Recipient fellowship Ford Found., 1960, grant NYU Curriculum Challenge Fund, 1989, 90, 99, Phillip E. Frandson award Nat. Univ. Continuing Edn. Assn., 1991. Mem. Am. Folk Art Soc., Carnegie Coun. on Ethics and Internat. Affairs, Women's Fgn. Policy Group, Phi Beta Kappa. Democrat. Avocations: tennis, jogging, folk art, cooking, travel. Office: Woolworth Bldg 15 Barclay St New York NY 10007

JELKS, GLENN WILLIAM, plastic surgeon; b. South Gate, Calif., Oct. 21, 1943; s. William Harry and Parthena Imogene Jelks; m. Elizabeth Anne Brady, Sept. 4, 1965; children: Jennifer, Deborah, Michael. BA, U. Calif., Berkeley, 1965; MS, Mich. State U. Coll., 1973; MD, Mich. State U. Coll.

Human Medicine, 1973. Diplomate Am. Bd. Ophthalmology, 1979, Am. Bd. Plastic and Reconstructive Surgery, 1982, Nat. Bd. Med. Examiners. With med. edn., mktg. and sales dept. Merck, Sharp and Dohme divsn. Merck and Co., Inc., San Francisco, 1965-69; med. rsch. fellow dept. interdepartmental curriculum Mich. State U.-Biomed. Comm. Ctr., East Lansing, 1971-73; grad. asst., clin. sci. instr. Mich. State U., East Lansing, 1973; intern straight surgery UCLA, 1973-74, resident gen./orthopaedic surgery, 1974-75; resident ophthalmology UCLA-Jules Stein Eye Inst., 1975-78; resident Inst. Reconstructive Plastic Surgery, NYU Med. Ctr., NYC, 1978-80. Assoc. prof. ophthalmology, assoc. prof. plastic surgery NYU Med. Ctr., NYC, 1980-; attending plastic surgeon NYU Med. Ctr., NY, 1980-, Bellevue Hosp., NYC, 1980-, Manhattan Eye, Ear and Throat Hosp., NYC, 1980-, The Valley Hosp., Ridgewood, NJ, 1991-; adj. attending in ophthalmology and plastic surgery NY Eye and Ear Infirmary-Lenox Hill Hosp., NYC, 1995-; examiner Am. Bd. Plastic Surgeons, 1995, 96; mem. continuing med. edn. adv. com., surg. case rev. com., oper. rm. com. NY Eye and Ear Infirmary; mem. laser com. NYU Med. Ctr.; mem. audiovisual com. Manhattan Eye, Ear and Throat Hosp.; vis. prof. Mass. Eye and Ear Infirmary, Boston, 1989, Robert H. Ivy Soc., Phila., 1990, UCLA, 1992, Yale U., New Haven, Conn., 1992. Consulting editor Ophthalmic Plastic and Reconstructive Surgery, Plastic Surgery Outlook, Ophthalmic Plastic and Reconstructive Surgery Jour; assoc. editor Annals of Plastic Surgery, 1995-96. Recipient Rsch. Travel award Am. Coll. Cardiology, 1970, Sci. Exhibit award AMA Conv., San Francisco, 1972, Lester T. Jones award for excellence in surg. anatomy Am. Soc. Ophthalmic Plastic and Reconstructive Plastic Surgeons 1986, Arthur L. Garnes Lectr. award Harlem Hosp., N.Y., 1987; NIH Cardiovas. trainee Mich. State U., 1969; Student Rsch. fellow Mich. Heart Assn., 1970, 71; Plastic Surgery Ednl. Found. traveling prof., 2000-01, named one of Best Doctors in NY, NY mag., 2002, named to The List for eyelid lifts, NY Times mag., 2005. Fellow Am. Acad. Ophthalmology; mem. AMA (Continuing Edn. award 1976, 79, 82, 85, 88), Internat. Soc. Craniofacial Surgeons, European Soc. Opthalmic Plastic and Reconstructive Surgery, Am. Acad. Ophthalmology, Am. Soc. Plastic and Reconstructive Surgeons, Am. Coll. Surgeons, Am. Soc. Maxillofacial Surgeons (mem. continuing med. edn. com. 1995-96), Am. Soc. Aesthetic Plastic and Reconstructive Surgery (mem. edn. commn. 1994, traveling prof. 1995), Am. Assn. Plastic Surgeons (mem. time and place com. 1995-96), Northeastern Soc. Plastic Surgeons (chmn. membership com. 1994-95, mem. nominating com. 1994-95, sec. 1995-99, pres. 1999-2000), NY State Med. Soc., NY County Med. Soc., NY Regional Soc. Plastic and Reconstructive Surgeons, NY Acad. Medicine, NY Orbit Soc. Avocations: boating, fishing, golf, skiing, tennis. Office: 875 Park Ave New York NY 10021-0341 Address: FPT 8 8V 550 First Ave New York NY 10016 Office Phone: 212-263-7300. E-mail: gwj@jelksmedical.com.*

JELKS, MARY LARSON, retired pediatrician; b. Galva, Ill., 1929; MD, U. Nebr., 1955. Diplomate Am. Bd. Pediats., Am. Bd. Allergy and Immunology. Intern Johns Hopkins Hosp., Balt., 1955-56, resident, 1956-57, 58-60, Grace-New Haven Hosp., 1957; fellow U. Fla. Tchg. Hosp., 1960-61; clin. asst. prof. U. South Fla.; ret.; active aerobiology, 1985—. Fellow Am. Acad. Allery and Immunology, Am. Acad. Pediats.; mem. AMA. Achievements include active research in aerobiology. Home: 1930 Clematis St Sarasota FL 34239-3813 E-mail: mjelks99@cs.com.

JELLICORSE, JOHN LEE, communications and theatre educator; b. Bristol, Tenn., Nov. 1, 1937; s. Harold Lee and Kathleen J.; m. Lenah Mary Lawrence, July 21, 1961 (div. 1980); 1 child, Jennifer Lee; m. Delayna Maxine Jordan, June 28, 1992; 1 child, John Adam. AB, U. Tenn., 1959; PhD, Northwestern U., 1967. From instr. to assoc. prof. Northwestern U., Evanston, Ill., 1962-69; assoc. prof. U. Tenn., Knoxville, 1969-74; prof., head dept. communication and theatre U. N.C., Greensboro, 1974-88, dir. theatre divsn., 1988-90, dir. broadcasting/cinema divsn., 1990-91; dean Sch. Comm. Hong Kong Bapt. U., 1991-94; prof. U. N.C., Greensboro, 1994—, head dept. broadcasting and cinema, 2001—06. Cons. Wroclaw Tech. U., Poland. Contbr. chapters to books, articles to profl. jours. Recipient Outstanding Tchr. award Northwestern U., 1968; So. Fellowship Fund fellow, 1959-62. Mem. Assn. for Comm. Adminstrn., Am. Film Inst., Internat. Comm. Assn., Nat. Comm. Assn., Univ. Film and Video Assn. Office: U NC Greensboro 308 McIver PO Box 26170 Greensboro NC 27402 Office Phone: 336-334-3846. Business E-Mail: jljellic@uncg.edu.

JELLINEK, GEORGE, broadcast executive, music educator, writer; b. Budapest, Hungary, Dec. 22, 1919; came to U.S., 1941; s. Daniel and Jolan Jellinek; m. Hedy Dicker, July 29, 1942; 1 child, Nancy Berezin. Student, Lafayette Coll., 1943; MusD (hon.), L.I. U., 1984. Dir. program services SESAC, Inc., NYC, 1955-64; rec. dir. Muzak, Inc., NYC, 1964-68; music dir. Sta. WQXR, NYC, 1968-84; asst. prof. music NYU, NYC, 1976-91. Author: Callas, Portrait of a Prima Donna, 1960, 2d edit. 1986, The Magic Chair, 1966, The Scarlet Mill, 1968, History Through the Opera Glass, 1994; contbg. editor: Stereo Rev. mag., 1958-74, Ovation mag., 1974-88; contbr. articles to the N.Y. Times, Musical America, The Opera Quar.; host (radio show) The Vocal Scene, 1969-2004. Trustee emeritus Bagby Found. Served to 1st lt. M.I., U.S. Army, 1942-46. Recipient Maj. Armstrong Broadcast award, 1978, Ohio State award, 1978, Gabriel award, 1982, George Washington award Am. Hungarian Found., 1986, Gold medal Internat. Radio Festival, 1995, Grammy award, 1996. Mem. ASCAP, AFTRA. Office: Sta WQXR 122 5th Ave New York NY 10011-5605

JELLINEK, MICHAEL STEVEN, psychiatrist, pediatrician; b. NYC, Sept. 30, 1948; s. Kurt and Kate (Jacoby) J.; m. Barbara A. Jellinek, June 14, 1970; children: David M., Abraham R., Isaiah T., Hanna R. BA, Columbia Coll., 1970; MD, Albert Einstein Coll. Medicine, 1973. Diplomate Nat. Bd. Med. Examiners, Am. Bd. Pediatrics; diplomate in psychiatry and child psychiatry Am. Bd. Psychiatry and Neurology. Instr. pediatrics Montefiore Hosp. & Med. Ctr., NYC, 1976—79; chief child psychiat. svcs. Mass. Gen. Hosp., Boston, 1979—, asst. in pediat., 1979—81, asst. pediatrician, 1981—83, dir. outpatient psychiatry, 1984—93, assoc. pediatrician, 1984—86, assoc. psychiatrist, 1984—86, pediatrician, 1986—, psychiatrist, 1986—, asst. gen. dir. ambulatory svcs., 1992—95, sr. v.p. ambulatory svcs., 1994—2001, sr. v.p. adminstrn., 1995—2001; pres. Newton Wellesley Hosp., 2001—; assoc. prof. psychiatry (pediatrics) Harvard U., Boston, 1987—96, prof. psychiatry and pediatrics, 1996—. Asst. instr. Columbia U., NYC, 1970; cons. Shriner Burns Inst., Boston, 1979—; bd. dirs. Bright Futures: Nat. Guideline for Health Supervision Infants, Children and Adolescents, 1999-2006. Dir. Camp Rainbow, Croton-on-Hudson, 1977-81. Named Profl. Person of Yr., Wellesley C. of C., Mass., 2005; recipient Blanche F. Ittleson award, Am. Psychiatric Assn., 1999, Mayor's Medallion award, City Newton, Mass., 2005; Dupont-Warren fellow, Harvard Med. Sch., Dept. Psychiatry, 1978, Laughlin fellow, Am. Coll. Psychiatrists, 1978, Paul Harris fellow, Rotary Found., Rotary Internat., 2004. Fellow Am. Acad. Pediat. (mem. Mass. chpt. mental health task force), Am. Acad. Child Psychiatry (treas. 1991-93, Simon Wile award 1993); mem. Am. Pediat. Soc., Am. Psychiat. Soc., Soc. Prof. Child Psychiatry, New Eng. Coun. Child Psychiatry. Democrat. Jewish. Avocations: running, soccer coach, carpentry. Home: 132 Pleasant St Newton MA 02459-1828 Office: Newton Welesley Hosp 2014 Washington St Newton MA 02462 Office Phone: 617-243-6250. Business E-Mail: mjellinek@partners.org.

JELLISON, BEVERLY IRENE, literature and language educator; d. Edward Robert and Julia Etta Dornoff; m. Walter Thomas Jellison, Mar. 24, 1972 (div.); children: Janet Irene Tait Waugh, Nancy Elizabeth Tait Carrillo. BS in Speech English, U. Ill., 1952—57; MA in Theater Arts, CA State U., 1959—61. English drama tchr. Stephen Decatur H.S., 1957—58, Arcadia H.S., 1958—61; English tchr. Helix Adult Sch., 1968—71; English, AP English, creative writing, Shakespeare, tchr. Santana H.S., 1971—2001, Grossmont Union High Sch. Dist. (GUHSD), 1993—2003. Support provider CA tchr. evaluation program GUHSD, 2001—03, support provider, 2003—, GATE Liaison, 2003—; tng. future tchrs. various, 1975—2002. Profl. adv. comm. GUHSD, 1974—, superintendent's adv. comm., 1983—85, mem. purchasing rev. cmty., 1993, chair, 1993—2001, mem. curriculum master plan steering cmty., 1994—2001, mem., 75th anniversary task force, 1996; literary book adv. Santana H.S., 1975—87, mem. WASC leadership team, 1996—97, coord. adv.; edn. bd. J. Paul Getty Mus., 1983—85; secondary lang. arts adv. cmty. San Diego County, 1993—2001. Recipient Key to the City, City of San Diego, 1969, Tchr. of Year, GUHSD, Golden G award, 1999, 2003. Mem.: Greater San Diego Coun. Tchr. English (presenter conf. 1974—, speaker 1995), Am. Assoc. U. Women, Nat. Coun. Tchr. English (presenter nat. conv. 1988), Calif. Assoc. for the Gifted (presenter state conv. 1985—), Calif. Assoc. Tchr. English (presenter state conv. 1972—), Nat. Edn. Assoc., Calif. Tchrs. Assoc., Grossmont Edn Assoc., Kappa Delta. Avocations: travel, bridge, art history, classical music. Home: 6912 Maury Dr San Diego CA 92119 Personal E-mail: bevejell@cox.net.

JELLISON, BRIAN D., manufacturing executive; BS, Indiana U.; MS, Columbia U. Mgmt. positions with Ingersoll-Rand Co., Woodcliff Lake, NJ, 1985—94, corp. v.p., 1994—98, corp. exec. v.p., 1998—2001; pres., CEO Roper Industries, Sarasota, Fla., 2001—03, chmn., pres., CEO, 2003—. Bd. dir. Champion Enterprises. Office: Roper Industries Ste 200 6901 Professional Pkwy E Sarasota FL 34240*

JELSEMA, JERRY RICHARD, music director; b. Byron Center, Mich., Nov. 27, 1942; s. Richard Jelsema and Katherine Frances Brinks. BA, Ctrl. Coll., Pella, Iowa, 1964; MusM, U. Mich., Ann Arbor, 1970. Purchasing coord. Brunswick Corp, Chgo., 1972—75, market rsch. assoc., 1975—79; organist, choir master Epworth United Meth. Ch., Chgo., 1972—79; min. music Trinity Luth. Ch., Des Plaines, Ill., 1979—99; organist, dir. music First United Meth. Ch., Evanston, Ill., 1997—. Composer organ works. Mem.: Am. Guild Organists (bd. dirs. 1979—94, 2000—04, chair workshops 2006). Avocations: fossil hunting, photography. Home: 5455 N Sheridan Rd Chicago IL 60640

JEMELIAN, JOHN NAZAR, management consultant; b. NYC, May 10, 1933; s. Nazar and Angel (Jizmejian) Jemelian; m. Rose Melkonian, Nov. 22, 1958; children: Sheri, Lori, Brian, Joni. BS, U. So. Calif., 1956. CPA Calif., 1961. Mgr. audit staff Price Waterhouse & Co., LA, 1958-64; treas. The Akron, LA, 1964-82, v.p. fin., 1976, exec. v.p., 1977-82; v.p., gen. mgr., dir. Acromil Corp., City of Industry, Calif., 1982-85; sr. v.p. fin. and adminstrn., CFO, sec., treas. World Vision Inc., 1985-98; pres. Claremont Facilities Corp., 1990—, Pasadena Resources Corp., 1990-94. Dir. D.I. Engring., Inc.; fin. advisor African Enterprises, 1966—68. Bd. dirs. Pasadena Christian Sch., 1965—67, 1969—70, treas., 1965—67; chmn. bd. Donor Automation, 1975—2001; trustee Haigazian Coll., Beirut, 1974—78; deacon Lake Ave. Congl. Ch., 1964—68, trustee, 1970—73, chmn. bd. trustees, 1972—73, chmn. ch. com., 1974; chmn. bd. Media Ministries, Inc., 1975—95; trustee Narramore Christian Found., 1976—93, Met. Ministries, 1979—80; chmn. Christian Bus. Men's Com., 1979—81, 1986—87, Sahag Mesrob Armenian Christian Sch., 1980—85; deacon, elder Ch. on the Way, 1980—95; chmn. bd. dirs. Armenian Gospel Mission, 1999—; bd. dirs. Forest Home Christian Conf. Ctr., 1972—75, 1978—81, 1984—88, 1992—95, 2001—04. With F.A. US Army. Named Boss of Yr. Beverly Hills chpt., Nat. Secs. Assn., 1970. Mem.: AICPA, Retail Contr. Assn. (dir. 1973—74), Calif. Soc. CPA, Toastmasters-Windjammers LA (pres. 1963), LA Athletic Club, Beta Gamma Sigma, Beta Alpha Psi, Delta Sigma Pi. Home: 261 Sharon Rd Arcadia CA 91007-8044 Office: 800 West Chestnut Monrovia CA 91016-3198 Fax: 626-301-1128. E-mail: jjemelia@worldvision.org.

JEMIELITY, THOMAS JOHN, language educator; b. Cleve., Dec. 17, 1933; s. Joseph Henry and Margaret Anne (Wielgus) Jemielity; m. Barbara Gray, Aug. 7, 1965; children: David Christopher, Samuel Andrew, Sarah Margaret. MA, John Carroll U., Cleve., 1958; PhD, Cornell U., 1965. Lectr. English Carleton U., Ottawa, Ont., Canada, 1962-63; instr. U. Notre Dame, Ind., 1963-65, asst. prof. English Ind., 1965-70, assoc. prof. Ind., 1970-90, prof. Ind., 1990—2003, prof. emeritus Ind., 2003—. Vis. lectr. Lancaster (Eng.) U. Author: Satire and the Hebrew Prophets, 1992, Ancient Biblical Satire, 2007; contbr. articles to profl. jours. Summer fellow, Ind. Com. Humanities, 1988. Mem.: Johnson Soc. Ctrl. Region (pres. 1985), Johnson Soc. London, Johnson Soc. (Lichfield, Eng.), Jane Austen Soc. N.Am., Am. Soc. 18th Century Studies. Home: 20408 Kern Rd South Bend IN 46614-5046 Office: U Notre Dame Dept English Notre Dame IN 46556 Business E-Mail: thomas.j.jemielity.1@nd.edu.

JEMISON, MAJOR LEWIS, pastor, religious organization administrator; m. Jacqueline Jemison; 1 child, Master MaKinsley. BA, Bishop Coll., 1977; ThM, Perkins Sch. of Theology, 1982; D of Ministry, Midwestern Baptist Theol. Seminary, 1990. Lic. 1974, ordained pastor 1982. Staff mem. Greater Bethlehem Bapt. Ch., Dallas; sr. pastor St. John Missionary Bapt. Ch., Oklahoma City. Pres., exec. bd. mem. Progressive Nat. Baptist Convention, Inc.; mem. Gov.'s Marriage Initiative Bd., City of Okla. City's Park & Recreation Commn., Governance Bd. of Okla. City Enterprise Cmty., Gov. Bd. of Empowerment Zone. Founder St. John Cmty. Optimist Club. Named an Most Influential Black Americans, Ebony mag., 2006. Mem.: NAACP (life), Urban League (mem. exec. bd. Okla. City branch), Coalition of Civic Leadership, 33rd Degree Mason, Okla. City Rotary Club. Office: St John Missionary Bapt Ch 5700 N Kelley Ave Oklahoma City OK 73111

JEMISON, SANDRA J., educational association administrator, educator; d. James and Virginia Johnson; m. Walter Jemison, Mar. 16, 1974; children: Stephen, Lance. MA, U. Ala., 1975, EdS, 1988, PhD, 2002. Cert. sch. psychologist Ala., instructional leadership Ala., tchr. Spl. edn. tchr. Hale County Bd. Edn., Greensboro, Ala., 1973—74, Tuscaloosa City Schs., Ala., 1974—79, sch. psychometrist, 1979—88, sch. psychologist, 1988—92, chpt. I supr., 1992—96, elem. dir., 1996—2000, fed. programs adminstr., 2000—04; dir. Thumbs Up Svc. Agy., Tuscaloosa, 2005—. Asst. prof. edn. and psychology Stillman Coll., 2005—; mem. Mayor's prekindergarten com.; cons. Rural Dists., Ala. Contbr. articles to profl. jours. Bd. mem. Tombigbee Girl Scouts, Tuscaloosa, 2004—, Skyland SDA Sch., Tuscaloosa, 2004—; personal ministries leader Skyland SDA Ch., 2004. Recipient Breakthrough Literacy award, Nat. Alliance Black Sch. Educators, 2000; grantee Patricia Roberts Harris fellowship, U. Ala., 1994—95. Mem.: NEA, Ala. Assn. Supr. & Curriculum Devel., Nat. Assn. Sch. Psychologists, Phi Delta Kappa. Achievements include established intergenerational preschool programs. Avocations: reading, cooking. Home: 9908 Fieldstone Ln Tuscaloosa AL 35405

JEN, FRANK CHIFENG, finance and management educator; b. Shanghai, May 15, 1931; came to U.S., 1957; s. Seybold E. and Susan (Lin) J.; m. Daisy Chi, Aug. 26, 1962; children: Amy K., Wendy K., Edward K. BS, N. Central Coll., 1959; MBA, U. Wis., 1960, PhD, 1963. Asst. prof. finance SUNY, Buffalo, 1964-66, assoc. prof., 1966-68, prof., 1968-97, chmn. dept. fin., 1967-70, Mfrs. & Traders Trust Co.'s prof. banking/fin. to emeritus, 1972-97, 97—, Univ. rsch. scholar, 2002—, chmn. dept. fin., 1967-70, chmn. dept. operating analysis, 1970-77, dir. bank mgmt. inst. and advanced comml. lending program, 1977-97, co-dir., dir. China MBA program, 1984-91, univ. rsch. scholar, 2002—. Vis. prof. Dalian (China) U. Tech., 1980-04. Contbr. articles to profl. jours. Mem. Am. Fin. Assn., Am. Econ. Assn., Soc. Econ. and Fin. Mgmt. in China (pres. 1985-88), Pi Gamma Mu, Beta Gamma Sigma. Office: SUNY Buffalo Sch Mgmt Jacobs Ctr Amherst NY 14260-0001 Office Phone: 716-645-3297. Business E-Mail: frankjen@buffalo.edu.

JEN, JOSEPH JWU-SHAN, academic administrator, former federal agency administrator; b. Chung King, Sichuan, China, May 8, 1939; arrived in U.S., 1962; s. H.C. and Lucia (Chang) J.; m. Salina Fond, Sept. 4, 1965; children: Joanne Pauline, Jeffrey Jay. BS, Nat. Taiwan U., 1960; MS, Wash. State U., 1964; PhD, U. Calif., Berkeley, 1969; MBA, So. Ill. U., 1986. Asst. prof. Clemson (S.C.) U., 1969-74; rsch. food technologist U.S. Dept. Agr., Beltsville, Md., 1975; assoc. prof. Clemson (S.C.) U., 1974—79, prof., 1979; assoc. prof. Mich. State U., East Lansing, 1979-80; mgr. Campbell Soup Co., Camden, NJ, 1980-83, dir., 1983-86; chmn. divsn. food sci. and tech. U. Ga., Athens, 1986-92; dean Coll. Agr. Calif. Poly. State U., San Luis Obispo, 1992—2001; under sec. rsch., edn. & econ. USDA, Washington, 2001—06; sr. adv. to pres. Calif. Poly. State U., San Luis Obispo, Calif., 2006—. Vis. prof. Nat. Taiwan U., 1976. Editor: Chemistry and Function of Pectin, 1986, Quality Factors of Fruits and Vegetables, 1989; contbr. articles to profl. jours. Recipient Cert. of Merit, Ministry of Econ. Affairs, Rep. of China, 1980, Ministry of Agr., Rep. of China, 1988, Disting. Educator award, Nat. Assn. Coll. Tchrs. Agr., 1999, Grad. Alumni achievement award, Wash. State U., 2002, Leadership Citation, Coun. Sci. Soc. Presidents, 2005, Century Pioneer award, Union Chinese Am. Profl. Orgns., 2006. Fellow Inst. Food Technologists (chmn. fruits and vegetable products 1988-89); mem. Am. Chem. Soc., Chinese Am. Food Soc. (pres. 1977, Profl. Achievement award 1986), Sigma Xi. Achievements include first to use hydrophobic chromatography in food enzyme research; development of high quality dehydrated vegetable pieces; establishment of teaching and research program in food processing in China and Taiwan; established innovative public/private partnership programs at Calif. Poly. State U. Office Fax: 805-756-2334. Business E-Mail: jjen@calpoly.edu.

JENAI, MARILYN, psychotherapist; children: Michael Stover, Dianne Stover. BA in Psychology and Comm., Oakland U., 1973, MA in Counseling Psychology, 1974; MA in Culture and Spirituality, Holy Names Coll., 1990, DMin in Integral Psychology and Spirituality, 2000. Lic. marriage and family therapist Fla., Oreg., 2007, massage therapist Fla., cert. social worker Mich., Nat. Bd. Cert. Clin. Hynosis, compassion fatigue specialist. Group leader, workshop cons. Contiuum Ctr., A First Women's Ctr., Oakland U., Rochester, Mich., 1967—75; psychotherapist, coord. Threshold Ctr. for Drug Studies and Cmty. Mental Health, Hazel Park, Mich., 1970—74; psychotherapist, instr. St. Mary's Hosp., Redford, Mich., 1974—76; psychotherapist Sarasota Guidance Clinic, 1976—78; instr. Manatee C.C., Bradenton, Fla., 1978—81; dir. counseling Safe Place and Rape Crisis Ctr., Sarasota, 1986—88; pvt. practice transpersonal psychotherapy Ctr. Integrative Psychotherapy, Sarasota, Fla., 1979—, pvt. practice psychotherapy Berkeley, Calif., Portland, Oreg. Trainer in transpersonal psychology; workshop leader in healing compassion fatigue. Democrat. Home Phone: 503-206-4741. E-mail: jenaipsy@comcast.net.

JENCKS, CHRISTOPHER SANDYS, sociologist, educator; b. Balt., Oct. 22, 1936; s. Francis Haynes and Elizabeth (Pleasants) J. BA, Harvard U., 1958, M.Ed., 1959; postgrad., London Sch. Econs., 1959-61; LL.D., Kalamazoo Coll., 1969; D.Litt., Columbia Coll., 1983. Assoc. editor New Republic mag., 1961-63; fellow Inst. Policy Studies, Washington, 1963-67; mem. faculty Harvard U., 1967-80, 96—, prof., 1973-80, 96—, Malcolm Wiener prof. social policy, 1998—; John D. MacArthur prof. sociology and urban affairs Northwestern U., Evanston, Ill., 1980-96; vis. prof. U. Chgo., 1994-95. Author: (with David Riesman) The Academic Revolution, 1968, (with others) Inequality, 1972, Who Gets Ahead?, 1979, (with Paul Peterson) The Urban Underclass, 1991, Rethinking Social Policy, 1992, The Homeless, 1994, (with Meredith Phillips) The Black-White Test Score Gap, 1998. Guggenheim fellow, 1967-68, 82-83, Inst. for Advanced Study fellow, 1985-86, Russell Sage Found. fellow, 1991-92, Ctr. for Advanced Study in Behavioral Scis., 1997-98, 2001-02. Mem.: Am. Philos. Soc., Nat. Acad. Scis. Office: Harvard U Kennedy Sch Govt Cambridge MA 02138

JENDRZEJEWSKI, ROXANNE MARIE, social studies educator, language educator; b. Detroit, Oct. 2, 1954; d. Roman and Helen Jablonski; m. James Edmund Jendrzejewski, Apr. 27, 1984. AAS with high honors, Macomb County C.C., Warren, Mich., 1975; BA with distinction, Wayne State U., Detroit, 1979, MAT, 2000. Cert. reading specialist 2006. Tchr. French and social studies St. Florian H.S., Hamtramck, Mich., 1981—85, Regina H.S., Harperwoods, 1985—95, Thomas M. Cooley H.S. Detroit Pub. Schs., 1996—. Coach Social Studies Olympics, Harperwoods, Mich., 1994; adj. prof. inclusive tchg. Wayne State U., 2006—. Recipient Exceptional Accomplishment in Psychology award, Wayne State U., 1979; scholar, Wayne State Social Studies Edn., 1980. Mem.: Nat. Coun. Social Studies, Nat. Coun. Tchrs. of French, Internat. Reading Assn. Avocations: tennis, films. Home: 1972 Los Angeles Warren MI 48091 Office: Thomas M Cooley HS 15055 Hubbell Detroit MI 48227 Office Phone: 313-866-9400.

JENERETTE, JOYCE WILLIAMS, elementary school educator, educational consultant; b. Oct. 29, 1948; d. George Milford Williams and Esther L. Morris-Williams; children: David Duane Williams, Deninne Brittanie Pritchett, DaShanda Nichole Pritchett; m. James E. Jenerette, June 25, 1988. A in Personnel Mgmt., Salem CC, 1982; BS in Bus. Mgmt. & Supervision, Wilmington Coll., 1985; MS, Wilmington Grad. Ctr., 1989; M in Ednl. Adminstrn., Grand Canyon U., 2005. Tchr. Salem Bd. of Edn., NJ, 1990—93; cons. ETS Nat. Bd. Profl. Tchg., Princeton, 1998—2001; tchr., tutor Trenton Bd. Edn., 1993—. Assessor, validator Nat. Bd. for Profl. Tchg. Stds., Tex., 1999—; next generation test team developer Ednl. Testing Svc., Princeton, 2000—; literacy curriculum team mem. Trenton Bd. Edn., 2003—04. Contbg. author Blessed Assurance: Stories of the Heart, 2004. Mem.: Handy-Simmons Scholarship Com. (chair), NJ AME Ministers Spouses (pres. 2002—04), Women's Missionary Soc. (3rd v.p. Phila conf.), NJ Ednl. Assn. Fast Coord. (sch. coord. 2003—). Avocations: reading, public speaking, missionary activities.

JENES, THEODORE GEORGE, JR., retired military officer; b. Portland, Oreg., Feb. 21, 1930; s. Theodore George and Mable Marie (Moon) Jenes; m. Beverly Lorraine Knutson, Jan. 29, 1953; children: Ted, Mark. BS, U. Ga., 1956; MS, Auburn U., 1969; grad., Army Command and Gen. Staff Coll., Armed Forces Staff Coll., Air War Coll.; LLD (hon.), U. Akron, 1986. Enlisted U.S. Army, 1951, commd. 2d lt., 1953, advanced through grades to lt. gen., 1984, various assignments, 1953—75, combat duty Vietnam, 1965—66; comdr. 3d Brigade, 2d Inf. Divsn., Republic of Korea, 1975—76, 172d Inf. Brigade, Ft. Richardson, Alaska, 1978—81; dep. commdg. gen. U.S. Army Tng. Ctr., Ft. Dix, NJ, 1976—78; comdr. 4th Inf. Divsn., Ft. Carson, Colo., 1982—84; dep. commdg. gen. U.S. Army Combined Arms Combat Devel. Activity, Ft. Leavenworth, Kans., 1981—82; commdg. gen. 3d U.S. Army, Ft. McPherson, Ga., 1984—87; comdr. U.S. Army Forces Ctrl. Command, Ft. McPherson, Ga., 1984—87; dep. commdg. gen. hdqrs. U.S. Army Forces Command, Ft. McPherson, 1984—87, ret., 1987; cons. Burdeshaw and Assocs., 1987—88; gen. mgr. Seattle Tennis Club, 1988—94. Decorated D.S.M., Legion of Merit, Bronze Star, Meritorious Sevc. medal, Air medal, Army Commendation medal, Vietnamese Cross of Gallantry with Silver Star, Combat Infantry Badge. Mem.: Am. Hellenic Ednl. Progressive Assn., Assn. U.S. Army, Rotary. Methodist. Avocations: reading Biblical and military history, golf. Home: 809 169th Pl SW Lynnwood WA 98037-3307 Personal E-mail: tedbevjen2@comcast.net.

JENG, JUDY HORNG, librarian; 2 children. BA, Nat. Taiwan U., 1981; MLS, U. Tex., 1984; PhD, Rutgers U., 2006. Tech. svcs. libr. Tex. A&M U., Galveston, Tex., 1985—87; coord. copy cataloging U. Del., Newark, Del., 1987—91; head tech. svcs. Rutgers U., Newark, 1991—98; asst. dir. resource mgmt. William Paterson U., Wayne, NJ, 1999—2000; head collection svcs. NJ City U., Jersey City, 2005—. Cons. in field. Editor: Going Digital: Experiences From East Asia And The Pacific; editor-in-chief: Cala, 2006—, mem. editl. bd.: Jour. Web Librarianship. Bd. dirs. Chinese Am. Libr. Assn., 1996—99. Grantee Instrnl. Computing Initiative, Rutgers U., 1994; SREB Doctoral scholar, So. Regional Edn. Bd., 2004. Mem.: ALA (Olofson Meml. award 1988), Am. Soc. Info. Sci. and Tech., Chinese Am. Libr. Assn. (life; bd. dirs. 1996—99). Achievements include research in usability evaluation of digital library. Office: NJ City U 2039 Kennedy Blvd Jersey City NJ 07305-1597 Office Phone: 201-200-2372.

JENG, TZYY-WEN, biochemist, researcher; b. Taichung, Taiwan, Nov. 2, 1947; came to U.S., 1974; s. Ching-Po and Yu-Ju (Wong) J.; m. Kwan-Yee Sum; children: Howard L., Way A. BS, Nat. Taiwan U., Taipei, 1970; PhD, U. Calif., Berkeley, 1978. Rsch. assoc. U. Ariz., Tucson, 1979-84, rsch. asst. prof., 1984-86, rsch. specialist and rsch. asst. prof., 1986-88; sr. rsch. biochemist Abbott Labs., Abbott Park, Ill., 1988-90, rsch. investigator, 1991-92, assoc. rsch. fellow, 1992—. Author: Natural Toxins, 1980; contbr. articles to Jour. Molecular Biology. Wilhelm Bernard Fund grantee Internat. Congress on Electron Microscopy, 1982. Mem. N.Y. Acad. Scis. Achievements include patents in field. Office: Abbott Labs AP 20 100 Abbott Park Rd Apt 20 Abbott Park IL 60064-3502

JENICEK, ALICIA JOANNE, nursing consultant; d. John Andrew and Alice Jeanette Jenicek; children: James Josef Wong, John Daniel Wong. BS in Biology, Tex. A&M U., 1982; BSN, U. Tex. Med. Br., 1984. Cert. legal nurse cons., Med.-Legal Consulting Inst., Inc., RN Tex.; cert. massage therapist Dept. Health, Tex., massage therapy instr. Dept. of Health, Tex. Staff nurse U. Tex. Med. Br., Galveston, 1984—85, La. State U. Med. Ctr., Shreveport, 1986, Hosp. Corps. Am. Highland Hosp., Shreveport, 1986—87, Highland Clinic, Shreveport, 1987, Schumpert Med. Ctr., Shreveport, 1987—92; tchr. San Jacinto Med. Ctr., Baytown, Tex., 1992—2001; massage therapist Healing With Feeling, Taylor Lake Village, 1997—, massage therapy instr., 1998—; legal nurse cons. Med.-Legal Consulting, Taylor Lake Village, 2001—; paramed. technician Exam One, Houston, 2004—. Instr. European Massage Therapy Inst., Houston, 1999—2001; cons. James M. Andersen, Esquire, Houston, 2002—, Sanes, Matthews and Forester, Houston, 2004—; admission nurse Compassionate Care Hospice, 2006—. Editor: (newsletter) Medical-Legal Consulting. Mem. St. Paul Cath. Cmty., Houston, 1992. Mem.: U. Tex. Med. Br. Aux., Internat. Massage Assn., Healing Arts Network, Am. Specialty Health Networks, Am. Assn. Legal Nurse Cons., Nat. Alliance Cert. Legal Nurse Cons., Bay Area Aggies Former Student Assn. (scholarship reviewer 2003—04), Massage and Bodywork Educators Alliance. Roman Catholic. Avocations: art, crafts, reading. Home and Office: Med-Legal Consulting 1126 Live Oak Ln Taylor Lake Village TX 77586 Home Phone: 281-532-3123; Office Phone: 281-460-8239. Personal E-mail: ajajenicek@cs.com. Business E-Mail: ajenicekwongclnc@cs.com.

JENKIN, JAMES THOMAS, video editor; b. Montclair, NJ, Apr. 28, 1964; s. David Alan and Dolores Ann (Hyland) J.; m. Evelyn Lebron. Student, Raritan Valley Coll., Somerville, NJ, 1987-88; cert. advanced non-linear editing, Avid Sch. Forman Rising Sun Coatings, Flemington, N.J., 1985-89; with dept. videotape playback Picsonic Prodns., NYC, 1989-91, videotape editor, 1991—; sr. editor program Headliners and Legends MSNBC, 1999—2002, sr. editor primetime unit, 2002—; pres. TBM Prodns., Hoboken, NJ, 2005—. Pres. Thought Bubble Media. Contbr. articles to mags. Recipient various Telly awards, 1991, 92, 95, Communicator award, 1997, Videographer award, 1998, Silver medal NY Festival, 2001, Emmy nomination for best editing single camera, 2006. Mem. Internat. TV Soc. Avocations: music composition, softball, tennis, movie research. Office Phone: 201-583-4000. E-mail: jtj909@aol.com.

JENKINS, ADRIENNE, women's health nurse; b. Valentine, Nebr., June 17, 1949; d. William Jay Spelts, Jr. and Sarah Agnes (Digneo) Spelts; children: Angela Marie, Francesca Christine. BSN, U. Colo., 1972, degree in Women's Health Care Nurse Practioner Program, 1981. RN Colo., Nat. Cert. Corp., 1985. Nurse psychiat. divsn. Fort Logan Mental Health Ctr., Denver, 1973—73; nurse Newborn Nursery U. Colo. Med. Ctr., Denver, 1973—74; nurse ob.-gyn. Rose Med. Ctr., Denver, 1977—82; nurse Eating Disorders Unit Harbor View Med. Ctr., San Diego, 1987; nurse practioner U. Calif., San Diego, 1988—89, San Diego (Calif.) State U., 1988—89; nurse practioner ob. Perinatal Program U. Colo., San Diego, 1988—89; nurse practioner womens health Beach Area Cmty. Clinic, San Diego, 1988—89, Reproductive Med. Group, San Diego, 1989—94, Naval Med. Ctr., San Diego, 1994—2002; nurse practioner student health Miramar C.C., San Diego, 2003—. Scholar, Rose Med. Ctr., 1980. Mem.: Calif. Assn. Nurse Practitioners. Democrat. Avocation: writing. Home: 10653 Caminito Memosac San Diego CA 92131 Office: San Diego Community Coll Miramar Coll 10440 Black Mtn Rd San Diego CA 92126

JENKINS, ALBERT FELTON, JR., lawyer; b. Madison, Ga., Jan. 18, 1941; s. A. Felton and Jimmie Lucille (Davis) J.; m. Julie Richardson Green, Apr. 16, 1966; children: A. Felton III, Emily Green, Alan Davis. AB, U. Ga., 1963, LLB, 1965. Bar: Ga. 1965, U.S. Dist. Ct. (no. dist.) Ga. 1965, U.S. Ct. Appeals Ga. 1965, U.S. Ct. Appeals (4th cir.) 1981, U.S. Ct. Appeals (5th cir.) 1966, U.S. Ct. Appeals (11th cir.) 1981, U.S. Ct. Appeals (D.C. cir.) 1987, U.S. Supreme Ct. 1968. Assoc. King & Spalding, Atlanta, 1965-70, ptnr., 1971-92, ret. ptnr., 1992—. Chmn. bd. visitors U. Ga. Law Sch., Athens, 1974; mem. Gov.'s Appellate Jud. Selection Com., Atlanta, 1972-73, Gov.'s Jud. process Rev. Com., Atlanta, 1984-85, Ga. Joint Study Commn. on Revenue Structure, 1992-95, Ga. Agrl. Exposition Authority, 1998-2006. Co-author: (2 vol. treatise) Georgia Civil Procedure Forms-Practice, 1988. Sec. bd. trustees U. Ga. Found., 1979-85; chmn., pres. Atlanta unit Am. Cancer Soc., 1982-83; trustee, vice-chmn. Atlanta Fulton Pub. Libr. Sys., 1995-97; regent Univ. Sys. of Ga., 2006—. Sgt. Air N.G., 1965-71. Fellow Am. Bar Found.; mem. State Bar of Ga. (pres. Young Lawyers 1972-73, bd. govs. 1983-91), Piedmont Driving Club (Atlanta), Phi Beta Kappa, Omicron Delta Kappa. Methodist. Office: King & Spalding 1180 Peachtree St NW Atlanta GA 30309-3521 Office Phone: 706-342-3564.

JENKINS, ALEXANDER, III, consumer products company executive, consultant; b. Weymouth, Mass., Feb. 17, 1934; s. Alexander and Eva Gladys (Price) J.; m. Judith H. Switzer, Jan. 4, 1975; children: Alexander Tuxbury, Edith Garland, Charles Jordan. BS, Yale U., 1956; MBA, Harvard U., 1961. Rsch. asst. Harvard Bus. Sch., Boston, 1961-62; treas. Ocean Rsch. Equip., Inc., Falmouth, Mass., 1962-65, 77-78, Orion Rsch., Inc., Cambridge, Mass., 1962-70, exec. v.p., 1970-71; pvt. practice cons. Cambridge, Mass., 1971-79; v.p. Adcole, Cambridge, Mass., 1972-77; pres. Jenkins Trading, Inc., Chelsea, Mass., 1973-91; prin. Sormani Calendars divsn., Chelsea, 1991—. Treas., dir. Pintek, Inc., 1979-81; div. mgr. Spectra Physics, 1980-81; pres., CEO Orion Rsch., Inc., Cambridge, 1981-88, chmn., chief exec. officer, 1988-89; pvt. cons., 1989—, treas. Jenkins Trading Inc. (dba Sormani Calendars) 1991—. With USN, 1956-59. Episcopalian. Home: 37 Breakwater Dr Chelsea MA 02150-4024 Office: 121 Webster Ave Chelsea MA 02150 Office Phone: 617-889-9300. Personal E-mail: sormani@mindspring.com.

JENKINS, ALYCE MITCHEM, writer, educator; b. Harvard, Ill., Nov. 3, 1935; d. John Foster and Queenie Black Mitchem; m. Reese Valmer Jenkins, Dec. 27, 1962; children: David William, Elizabeth Ann Jenkins Manfredi. BA, U. Colo., 1957; MS, U. Wis., 1961. Cert. tchr. Ill., Wis., Ohio, N.J. English tchr. Crystal Lake (Ill.) H.S., 1957—60; demonstration tchr. No. Ill. U., DeKalb, 1961—62; English, social studies tchr. H. Schenk Jr. H.S., Madison, Wis., 1962—66; homebound tchr. Cleve. Pub. Schs., 1971—76, 1977—78; tchr. social studies Laurel Sch., Shaker Heights, Ohio, 1977—78; English instr. Kean U., Union, NJ, 1980; social studies, English tchr. Middlesex (N.J.) H.S., 1980—85, 1993—94; freelance writer, 1985—. Founder, leader Rainbow Writers, Bridgewater, 1992—95. Author: Lost in a Blizzard, 2001; co-author: College Board Achievement: English Composition, 1988; contbr. over 100 articles to adult and juvenile periodicals. Founder, leader Connected Hearts Adoption Triad Support, North Plainfield, NJ, 1997—2007; instr., mentor Sisters Aftercare, Bridgewater, NJ, 2001—; mem. adv. bd. NJ Adoption Resource Clearing House, 2003—; mem. Presbyn. Women, 1997—; bd. dirs. Friends of New Brunswick Free Pub. Libr., 2005—, v.p., 2007—. Recipient Congl. Angel in Adoption award, Congl. Coalition on Adoption Inst., 2005; Knapp grad. fellow, U. Wis., 1960—61. Mem.: Somerset Children's Writers, Soc. Children's Book Writers and Illustrators (award com., Mag. Merit awards 1999, Mag. Merit award 1996), Pi Lambda Theta, Kappa Delta Pi, Phi Beta Kappa. Democrat. Presbyterian. Avocations: genealogy, reading, gardening, writing. Home: 11 Clifton Ave New Brunswick NJ 08901 Personal E-mail: alycemj@aol.com.

JENKINS, ANTHONY JEROME, prosecutor; BS in Polit. Sci., Troy U., Ala.; JD, Mercer U. Sch. of Law. Chief prosecutor State Atty.'s Office, Clay County Divsn., Green Cove Sprngs, Fla.; dep. dir. Juvenile and Special Assault Divsn., Duval County, Fla.; mng. asst. US atty. US Dept. Justice, St. Thomas, criminal chief, first asst. US atty., US atty. V.I., 2005—. Atty. Organized Crimes Drug Enforcement Task Force. Served in US Army. Decorated Army Commendation medal; recipient Victim Adv. of Yr. award, Mayor of Jacksonville, Fla., Dir.'s award, Exec. Office US Atty., Special Achievement awards. Mem.: Kappa Alpha Psi. Avocation: music. Office: US Attys Office US Courthouse and Fed Bldg 5500 Veterans Dr Ste 260 St Thomas VI 00802-6424 Office Phone: 340-774-5757. Office Fax: 340-776-3474.*

JENKINS, BARBARA ALEXANDER, pastor, overseer; b. Ft. Bragg, NC, Oct. 13, 1942; d. Archie Herman Alexander and Hattie Elizabeth (Thigpen) Truitt; m. Warren Keith Jenkins, Aug. 22, 1964 (div. Sept. 1980); children: Pamela, Eric, Jason. BS, Ea. Mich. U., 1964, postgrad., 1964-66, Duke U., 1978; DD (hon.), Ch. of Christ Bible Coll., Madras, India, 1988. Ordained to ministry, World Faith Clinic Inc., 1983, A.M.E. Zion Ch., 1982. Min. World Faith Clinic Inc., Fayetteville, N.C., 1981-83, A.M.E. Zion Ch., Fayetteville, 1982-84; pastor Noah's Ark Ministry, Fayetteville, 1985-86; founder, pastor Rainbow Tabernacle of Faith Ministries, Inc., Winston-Salem, N.C., 1984—; founder Rainbow Raleigh (N.C.) Outreach Ministries, 1986—, Rainbow Tabernacle of Faith, Charlotte, N.C., 1987—. Dir. Spotlight on Truth Internat. Radio Ministries, Winston-Salem, 1985—, overseer hdqrs. Ogun State, Nigeria, 1992, others; founder Rainbow Internat. Crusade Ministry, Winston-Salem, 1986—; pres. Rainbow Bible Coll., Winston-Salem; dean Rainbow Inst. Commensurate Studies, Winston-Salem, 1985—; mem. Internat. Conv. Faith Ministries, Tulsa, 1989—. Author: Guidelines for Ministers, 1994; contbr. articles to religious jours. Concert vocalist N.C. Black Repertory Co., Winston-Salem, 1987, 88; youth coord. Jerry Lewis Muscular Dystrophy Telethon, Raleigh, 1987, 88; guest speaker Wake Forest U., Winston-Salem, 1991. Recipient Outstanding Svc. award Rainbow Tabernacle Faith, Inc., 1987; scholar March of Dimes-Easter Seals, 1960-64. Mem. NAFE, N.C. Women in Ministry (bd. dirs.), Am. Assn. Christian Counselors, Nat. Assn. Religious Profls., Delta Theta (project coord. 1979-80). Democrat. Office: Rainbow Tabernacle Faith Ministries Inc 4091 New Walkertown Rd Winston Salem NC 27105-9734 Home: 5490 Woodcliff Dr Winston Salem NC 27106-1922 E-mail: elect.lady@excite.com. *Life is the culmination of ascending and descending movements through time and space. A journey to reach the ultimate equilibrium that permits us to control and maintain order as it is perceived. Of course, many fail the Divine Assignment.which is: to share and to enjoy the fullness and richness of this precious experience—regardless of the gains and losses. There is a secret for Peace through it all: To Surrender the Control of it back to God!.*

JENKINS, BENJAMIN P., III, bank executive; b. May 8, 1944; BS in Textile Chemistry, N.C. State U.; MBA, U. Ala. Pres. First Union-Va./Md./D.C., First Union-Fla., 1999; pres. Gen. Bank Wachovia Corp., Charlotte, NC, 1999—, sr. exec. v.p., 2001—05, vice chmn., 2005—. 2002 campaign chmn. Mecklenburg Arts & Sci. Coun.; bd. dirs. Presbyn. Hosp. Healthcare/Novant; trustee Queens U.; bd. advisors N.C. State U., POST; bd. visitors N.C. State U. Office: Wachovia Corp Ste 400 301 S College St Charlotte NC 28288*

JENKINS, BILL (WILLIAM LEWIS JENKINS), former congressman; b. Detroit, Nov. 29, 1936; m. Mary Kathryn Myers; 4 children. BA, Tenn. Technol. U., 1958; JD, U. Tenn. Coll. Law, 1961. Farmer, Rogersville, Tenn.; atty.; mem. Tenn. State Ho. Reps., 1963—71, speaker, 1969—71; bd. dirs. TVA, 1972—78; cir. ct. judge 3rd Jud. Dist., Tenn., 1990-96; mem. US Congress from 1st Tenn. dist., 1997—2007, mem. judiciary com., mem. agr. com., chmn. specialty crops and fgn. agr. progs. subcommittee. Commr. Tenn. Dept. Conservation; policy adv. energy and legis. issues to gov. State of Tenn. 2nd lt. Mil. Police Corps US Army. Mem. Tenn. Bar Assn., Hawkins County Farm Bur., Am. Legion, Masons. Republican. Baptist. Avocations: hunting, fishing.*

JENKINS, BRENDA GWENETTA, pre-school administrator, special education educator; b. Durham, NC, Aug. 11, 1949; d. Brinton Alfred and Ophelia Arden (Eaton) Jenkins. BS, Howard U., 1971, MEd, 1972, cert. advanced grad. studies, 1975; postgrad., Trinity Coll., Am. U., U. DC, Marymount Coll., 1976—. Cert. tchr., Washington; cert. Advanced Grad. Studies Spl. Edn., aerobics instr., Nat. Dance Exercise Instr.'s Tng. Assn. Cheerleading coach Howard U., Washington, 1971—86; tchr. DC Pub. Schs., Washington, 1972—, aerobics instr., 1982—, Goals 2000 English, lang. arts, history writer, 1995—96; v.p. Nerdlihc Corp., Washington, 1985—; ptnr. Jenkins, Trapp-Dukes and Yates Partnership, Washington, 1984; co-owner Fantasia Early Learning Acad., Washington, 1985—98; instr. aerobics Washington Dept. Recreation, Washington, 1988—93; instr. You Fit, Inc. Nat. Children's Ctr. Washington, 1991—93, Anthony Bowen YMCA, Washington, 1992—93; instr. health, nutrition support Rockville, Md., 1992; instr., coach Maryvale PomPom/cheerleaders, Montgomery County, Md., 1992—94, asst. chmn. tchr. collaborative program, 1992—94, co-chair program com. tchr. collaborative, 1995—96; fitness instr. Oxedine Performing Arts Acad., Prince George's County, 1995—96. Aerobic instr. Coun. Exceptional Children, Washington, 1982, recreation svcs., City of Rockville, 1986-2005; developer My Spl. Friend program, 1984, BJ's Thinking Cap, 1991, Learning Creations, 1994, Girlfriends; bldg. rep. Washington Tchrs. Union AFT, AFL-CIO, 1987-89, 91-94, 96-04, asst. bldg. rep., 1990-91, 94-95, 04-05; supr. Foster Grandparent program Sharpe Health Sch., 1988—; trainer AIDS in Workplace, 1990, Early Childhood Substance Abuse Project Tng., 1992-93, Substance Abuse Prevention Edn., 1995, Metro Foster Grandparent Program Adv. Bd., Washington, 1992; mem. preschool adv. bd. DC Pub. Schs., 1992-93, coord. curriculum coun., 1994-96; master tchr. Coop. Tchr. Corp., 1993; curriculum writer, 1993; v.p. spl. edn. Washington Tchrs. Union Local 6, 1994-04; stds. specialist, 1997—; conv. del. Am. Fed. Tchrs., 1998, 04; adv. bd. Supt.'s Tchr. Affairs, 1999-; mem. Spl. Edn. State Adv. Panel, Washington, 1998-00, D.C. Parent Tng. and Info. Ctr., ARC, Inc. Adv. Panel; exec. bd. dirs. Assembly of Petworth, 1998—; DC Pub. Schs. recruiter Nat. Alliance Black Sch. Educators, Nashville, 1999, resident mentor tchr., 1999-04; mem. Disting. Educators Roundtable, 1998-04; supt. search com. D.C. Pub. Schs., 2004; pre-test participant Corp. for Nat. and Cmty. Svc., 2004, mem. Ga. Ave. collaborative, 2005—; aerobic instr. Regent Pk. Cmty. Clubhouse, Prince George's County, Md., 2006; presenter, spkr. in field. Singer: 2000 Voices Lincoln Meml., 2000. Active DC Spl. Edn. State Adv., 1998, Internat. Space Camp, Huntsville, Ala., 1998; mem. Martin Luther King Tribute Choir, 2005—; leadership/anchor stds. team DC Pub. Schs., 2005—, chmn. profl. devel. collaboration team, 2006-07. Recipient Outstanding Svc. award Kappa Delta Pi, 1978-79, 81-82, 84, citation Washington Tchr. Union, 1985, State winner Elem. Level Nat. Citizenship Edn. Tchr.'s award Ladies Aux. VFW, Washington, 2002, 03, Educator Excellence award Masonic Scottish Rite, 2001; named DC Tchr. of Yr., Coun. Chief State Sch. Officers, 1998, U. DC Cooperating Tchr., 2004, Tchr. of Month, DC Pub. Schs., 2006; grantee DC Pub. Sch. State Office, 1993, Citibank, 1994, Washington Post Grants In Arts, 1999-04, 2006; named to Hall of Fame Bison Found. Inc., Howard U., 1995. Mem.: ASCD, Am. Fedn. Tchrs. (presiding officer Wash. Spl. Educator and Svc. Provider Forums 1998—2005, sch. to careers tchr. extern 2001, D.C. Pub. Schs. new tchr. orientation trainer 2001—04, Wash. Tchrs. Union new tchr. coord. 2001—04, Wash. Tchrs. Union Positive Tchr. ad campaign 2004, DCPS stds. facilitator 2005), Howard U. Alumni Cheerleaders Assn. (co-founder 1977, pres. 1990—94, v.p. 1998—, Outstanding Recognition award 1984, Recognition award named Brenda G. Jenkins Outstanding Cheerleader award 1987), DC Parents and Friends of Children with Spl. Needs (critical ptnrs. group/supts. task force 2003, DCPS leadership/anchor stds. team mem. math specialist 2005—, bd. dirs.), Pi Lambda Theta, Kappa Delta Pi (exec. com. Theta Alpha chpt.). Democrat. Avocations: alumni cheerleading, fashion design, cooking, dance, poetry. Office Phone: 202-576-6161.

JENKINS, BRUCE STERLING, federal judge; b. Salt Lake City, May 27, 1927; s. Joseph and Bessie Pearl (Iverson) J.; m. Margaret Watkins, Sept. 19, 1952; children— Judith Margaret, David Bruce, Michael Glen, Carol Alice. BA with high honors, U. Utah, 1949, LLB, JD, U. Utah, 1952. Bar: Utah 1952, U.S. Dist. Ct. 1952, U.S. Supreme Ct. 1962, U.S. Circuit Ct. Appeals 1962. Pvt. practice, Salt Lake City, 1952-59; assoc. firm George McMillan, 1959-65; asst. atty. gen. State of Utah, 1952; dep. county atty. Salt Lake County, 1954-58; bankruptcy judge U.S. Dist. Ct., Utah, 1965-78, judge Utah, 1978—, chief judge Utah, 1984-93. Adj. prof. U. Utah, 1987-88, 95-99. Research, publs. in field; contbr. essays to Law jours.; bd. editors: Utah Law Rev, 1951-52. Mem. Utah Senate, 1959-65, minority leader, 1963, pres. senate, 1965, vice chmn. commn. on orgn. exec. br. of Utah Govt., 1965-66; Mem. adv. com. Utah Tech. Coll., 1967-72; mem. instl. council Utah State U., 1976. Served with USN, 1945-46. Named Alumnus of Yr. award Coll. Law Univ. Utah, 1985; recipient Admiration and Appreciation award Utah State Bar, 1995, Lifetime Svc. award, 2006, Emeritus Merit of Honor award U. Utah Alumni Assn., 1997. Fellow Am. Bar Found.; mem. ABA, Am. Inn Ct., Utah State Bar Assn. (Judge of Yr. 1993), Salt Lake County Bar Assn., Fed. Bar Assn. (Disting. Jud. Svc. awrd Utah chpt. 1993), Order of Coif, Phi Beta Kappa, Phi Kappa Phi, Phi Eta Sigma, Phi Sigma Alpha, Tau Kappa Alpha. Democrat. Mem. Lds Ch. Office: US Dist Ct 462 US Courthouse 350 S Main St Salt Lake City UT 84101-2106

JENKINS, CAROL ANNE, educator; b. Kearny, NJ, Mar. 1, 1945; d. Lawrence Augustine and Sara (Ball) J. BA, Malone Coll., 1968; MA in Religious Edn., Chgo. Grad.Sch. Theology, 1969; MA in Sociology, Western Mich. U., 1972; PhD in Sociology, Kans. State U., 1986. Asst. prof., program dir. various orgns., Grand Rapids and Livonia, Mich., 1970-73; asst. prof. Judson Coll., Elgin, Ill., 1973-74, No. State U., Aberdeen, S.D., 1974-75, Henry Ford Community Coll., Dearborn, Mich., 1975-76, Wheeling Jesuit (W.Va.) Coll., 1976-78, Tabor Coll., Hillsboro, Kans., 1978-82; instr. Kans. State U., Manhattan, 1982-85; assoc. prof. Biola U., La Mirada, Calif., 1985-92; prof. Glendale (Ariz.) C.C., 1992—. Bd. dirs., chairwoman La Mirada, Christian Conciliation Svcs. of Orange County, Calif.; chair Maricopa C. C. Dist. Sociology Instructional Coun., 1992-93; vis. scholar Va. Poly. and State U., 1992, North Cen. Regional Ctr. for Rural Devel., Iowa State U., 1998-99; cons. in field. Author: Thanatology: Discussions On Death & Dying, 1986, Social Problems: Issues and Their Opposing Viewpoints, 1987, Toward An Understanding of Social Thought, 1987, Toward an Understanding of Sociological Theory, 1989, Teaching About the Diversities and Complexities of American Rural Life, 2000; contbr. chpts. to books and articles to profl. jours. Recipient Hans O. Mauksch award for disting. contbns. to undergrad. edn., 2002; Instnl. Rsch. grantee, 1990-91, 91-92, 98-99, 2001-02; MIL fellow Scholarship of Tchg. and Learning, 2005-06. Mem. Am. Sociol. Assn. (exec. coun., awards chair, sect. undergrad. edn. 1993-96, com. on sociology in elem. and sec. schs. 1996—, chair sect. on undergrad. edn. 1998-99), Pacific Sociol. Assn. (program chair 1988), Midwest Sociol. Assn. (undergrad. edn. com. 1982-85, 96-99, com. chair 1998-99), Rural Sociol. Soc. (membership com. 1996-97, task force on futures 1996-97, co-chair subcom. on curriculum transformation 1997-99, chair curriculum and instrn. com. 2000-02, Excellence in Tchg. award 2002)), Assn. Christians Tchg. Sociology (nat. program chair 1981, 92, 90), Religious Edn. Assn., William Lock Singers Players, Alpha Kappa Delta. Mennonite. Avocations: singing, home redecorating, genealogical searches, travel. Home: 19502 N 98th Ave Peoria AZ 85382-4113

JENKINS, CHARLES H., JR., retail company executive; m. Dorothy Chao; children: Jennifer, Anthony. BBA in bus. administrn., Emory U., 1964, MBA in bus. administrn., 1965; PhD, Havard Bus. Sch. Asst. to real estate v.p. Publix, 1969, v.p., 1974, exec. v.p., 1988, chmn. exec. com., 1990—2000, COO, 2000, CEO, 2001—, also mng. chair. Pres. Lakeland C. of C. Mem.: Boston Symphony Orch. Bd. of Overseers.*

JENKINS, DARRELL LEE, librarian; b. Roswell, N.Mex., Aug. 12, 1949; s. Lindon C. and Joyce (King) J.; m. Susan Jenkins. BA, Ea. N.Mex. U., 1971; MLS, U. Okla., 1972; MA, N.Mex. State U., 1976. Asst. edn., psychology, gift libr. N.Mex. State U., Las Cruces, 1972—73, edn. psychology libr., 1973—74, asst. reference libr., 1974—75, asst. catalog libr., 1975—76, asst. serials libr., 1976—77, acting head reference dept., 1977; adminstrv. svcs. libr. So. Ill. U., Carbondale, 1977—82, dir. libr. svcs., 1982—91, head social scis. divsn., 1992—2001. Cons. U.S. Naval Base, So. Ill. U., Groton, Conn., 1985-91; chmn. bd. dirs. CEC Comm., Inc., 1997-99. Author: Specialty Positions in ARL Libraries, 1982; co-author: Library Development and Fund Raising Capabilities, 1988; contbr. articles to profl. jours. Mem. ALA (chmn. libr. orgn. mgmt. sect. 1985-86), Am. Soc Info. Sci., Assn. Christian Librs., Ill. Libr. Computer System Orgn. (pres. 1985-86), Phi Kappa Phi, Beta Phi Mu, Phi Alpha Theta (Outstanding Libr. award 2002). Republican. Mem. Ch. Assembly God. Avocations: tennis, swimming, bicycling. E-mail: dj779@hotmail.com.

JENKINS, DAVID RAY, lawyer; b. Hammond, La., Sept. 6, 1955; s. Harlan Herbert Jenkins and Lilly Ann (Miller) Seitter; m. Francis Ann Radnich Brandenburg, June 11, 1977 (div. Oct. 1988); m. Katrina Lee Weatherson, Dec. 3, 1993; children: Daniel Harlan, Andrew James. BA in Integrated Liberal Arts, St. Mary's Coll. Calif., Moraga, 1977; JD, U. Calif., Davis, 1980. Bar: Calif. 1980, U.S. Dist. Ct. (ea. dist.) Calif. 1980. Staff atty. Alaska Code Revision Project, Davis, 1980-81; law clk. U.S. Bankruptcy Ct., Modesto, Calif., 1981-83; assoc. Rutan & Tucker, Costa Mesa, Calif., 1983-85, Fullerton, Lang, Richert & Patch, Fresno, Calif., 1985-87; shareholder Lang, Richert & Patch, Fresno, 1987-95; ptnr. Motschiedler, Michaelides & Wishon, Fresno, 1995—2004; pres. David R. Jenkins, PC, 2004—. Mem. Calif. Bankruptcy Forum (dir. 2002-03), Ctrl. Calif. Bankruptcy Assn. (dir. 1995-98, 2002-, pres. 2003). Democrat.

Roman Catholic. Avocations: tennis, bicycling, hiking, gardening. Office: David R Jenkins PC 2444 Main St #120 Fresno CA 93721 Home Phone: 559-277-3950; Office Phone: 559-264-5695. Personal E-mail: drjbklawyer@sbcglobal.net.

JENKINS, DAWN PAULA, special education educator, dancer; b. Harrisburg, Pa., Sept. 12, 1955; d. Reese Walls and Catherine Verbos Jenkins. EdB magna cum laude, U. Miami, Fla., 1977, EdM, 1978. Cert. profl. educator Fla., cert. assoc. master tchr. Fla. Tchr. of mentally challenged Holmes Elem. Sch., Miami, 1978—79; tchr. of deaf and hard of hearing Auburndale Elem. Sch., Miami, 1979—80; tchr. elem. deaf and hard of hearing Arcola Lake Elem., Miami, 1980—93; tchr. of deaf and hard of hearing Palm Springs Mid. Sch., Hialeah, Fla., 1993—. Applicant tchr. in space, 1986; choreographer and tchr. South Fla. Theatre of the Deaf, Miami, 1990—96; presenter Very Spl. Arts movement workshop, incorporating dance into curriculum Mid. Sch. Conv., Ft. Lauderdale, Fla., 1997; conf. presenter What's Up in Deaf Education; choreographer, dance tchr. for deaf students Very Spl. Arts program VSA Internat., Brussels; adj. prof. Interpreters Deaf program Miami Dade Coll., 1998—2000; developer deaf dance program MDCPS, 1991. Mem. Homeowners' Assn., Miami Lakes, Fla., 1995—98; founding mem. local club for the deaf Optimist Internat., Miami Lakes, 1996—97; fund raising sponsor Am. Cancer Soc., Miami, 1995—2003. Recipient Outstanding ESE tchr., Miami-Dade County, 1996; grantee, Impact II Com. of Miami Dade Schs., 2000; scholar, U. Miami Marching Band, 1973—77. Mem.: Nat. Dance Edn. Orgn., Fla. Educators of Hearing Impaired, Fla. Registry Interpreters, Nat. Dance Edn. Orgn., Nat. Assn. of the Deaf, Coun. Exceptional Children, Conv. Am. Instrs. Deaf. Presbyterian. Achievements include students performing The Wind That Blew at Internat. Very Spl. Arts Festival, representing Fla., Belgium, 1994. Avocations: dance, exercise, travel, reading, yoga. Office: Palm Springs Mid Sch 1025 W 56th St Hialeah FL 33012 Home Phone: 305-934-3692, 305-825-3692; Office Phone: 305-821-2460. Personal E-mail: dancindawn@bellsouth.net. Business E-Mail: dpjenkins@dadeschools.net.

JENKINS, EDWARD BEYNON, research astronomer; b. San Francisco, Mar. 20, 1939; s. Francis Arthur and Henrietta Beynon (Smith) J.; m. Myrna Dean Stewart, June 29, 1963; children: Brian Francis, Eric Dean. AB, U. Calif., Davis, 1962; PhD, Cornell U., 1966. Rsch. assoc. Princeton (N.J.) U., 1966-67, mem. rsch. staff, 1967-73, rsch. astronomer, 1973-79, sr. rsch. astronomer, 1979—. Mem. mgmt. and ops. working group NASA, Washington, 1976-79, 88-91, mem. astrophysics subcom., 1992-93; mem. com. on space astronomy and astrophysics NAS, Washington, 1986-89; co-investigator Space Telescope Imaging Spectrograph, 1985-2006, Far Ultraviolet Spectroscopic Explorer, 1989-2007; prin. investigator Interstellar Medium Absorption Profile Spectrograph, 1980-2002. Contbr. numerous articles to Astrophys. Jour. Recipient Rsch. award Alexander von Humboldt Found., 1992-93. Mem. Am. Astron. Soc. (v.p. 1996-99), Internat. Astron. Union (pres. Commn. 44, 1988-91). Democrat. Unitarian Universalist. Office: Princeton U Obs Astronomy Dept Princeton NJ 08544-1001 Home Phone: 609-921-7126; Office Phone: 609-258-3826. Business E-Mail: ebj@astro.princeton.edu.

JENKINS, ELAINE, middle school educator; d. Adam and Anne Kolasa; children: Allison, Laura. BA, William Paterson Coll., Wayne, NJ, 1973; MEd, William Paterson Coll., 1977. Cert. elem. sch. tchr. K-8 NJ, reading specialist NJ, tchr. of handicapped NJ. Substitute tchr. Elmwood Pk. Bd. Edn., NJ, 1973—76, compensatory edn. tchr., 1976—82; mid. sch. lang. arts tchr. Hawthorne Bd. Edn., NJ, 1988—89; mid. sch. basic skills lang. arts and math tchr. Paramus Bd. Edn., NJ, 1989—. Office: West Brook Mid Sch 550 Roosevelt Blvd Paramus NJ 07652 Business E-Mail: ejenkins@paramus.k12.nj.us.

JENKINS, ELIZABETH ANN, federal judge; b. 1949; BA, Vanderbilt U., 1971; JD, U. Fla. Coll. Law, 1976. Bars: Fla. 1977, D.C. 1978. Atty. advisor U.S. Dept. of Justice, 1976-78; asst. U.S. atty. Middle Dist. of Fla., Orlando, Fla., 1978-82, Southern Dist. of Fla., West Palm Beach, Fla., 1983-85; magistrate judge U.S. Dist. Ct. (mid. dist.) Fla., 1985—. Office: US Courthouse 801 N Florida Ave Ste 32 Tampa FL 33602-3849 Office Phone: 813-301-5774.

JENKINS, EVAN H., state legislator, medical association administrator, lawyer; married; 2 children. BS, Univ. Fla., 1983; JD, Marshall Univ., 1987. Atty. Jenkins Fenstermaker PLLC, 1987—92; with W. Va. C. of C., 1992—99; exec. dir. W. Va. Med. Assn., 1999—. Del., ho. dels. W. Va., 1994—2000, state senator, 2002—. Pres., bd. dir. Big Brothers/Big Sisters of the Tri-State; bd. dir. Cabell County Comty. Svcs. Orgn., Huntington Main St.; pres. bd. dir. Leadership W. Va., Operation Bus. and Edn. Succeeding Together; bd. dir. Riverview Manor, W. Va.Coun. on Economics in Edn., W. Va. EPSCORE. Recipient Med. Exec. Meritorious Achievement award, AMA, 2006. Mem.: W. Va. Bar Assn., Cabell County Bar Assn., ABA, Dem. Leadership Coun. (adv. bd.). Democrat. Presbyn. Office: W Va Legislature East Bldg 1 Room 216W 1900 Kanawha Blvd Charleston WV 25305 also: W Va Med Assn 4307 MacCorkle Ave SE PO Box 4106 Charleston WV 25364 Office Phone: 304-325-0342.*

JENKINS, EVERETT WILBUR, JR., lawyer, writer, historian; b. Oklahoma City, Nov. 28, 1953; s. Everett Wilbur and Lillie Bell (Ingram) J.; m. Monica Lynn Endsley, June 3, 1978 (div. Aug. 13, 2003); children: Ryan, Camille, Jennifer, Cristina. BA cum laude, Amherst Coll., 1975; JD, U. Calif., Berkeley, 1978. Bar: Calif. 1979. Dep. county counsel Contra Costa County, Martinez, Calif., 1980—81; dep. city atty. City of Richmond, Calif., 1981—84; bd. atty. West County Agy., Richmond, 1981-90; asst. city atty. City of Richmond, 1984—2004; authority atty. West Contra Costa Solid Waste Mgmt. Authority, Richmond, 1985—87, 1988—91; interim city atty. City of Richmond, 2004—05, sr. asst. city atty., 2005—. Legal rep. tech. adv. com. Contra Costa County Solid Waste Commn., Martinez, Calif., 1986-87, pub. mem., 1987-88; adv. atty. West Contra Costa Transp. Adv. Com., San Pablo, 1991-2005; bd. atty. Richmond Housing Authority, 1992-99; bd. dirs. Contra Costa Co. Hazardous Materials Commn., Martinez, 1987-88. Author: Pan-African Chronology, 1996, Pan-African Chronology II, 1998, Pan-African Chronology III, 2001, The Muslim Diaspora, 1999, The Muslim Diaspora, vol. 2, 2000, The Creation, 2003. Bd. dirs. YMCA of the East Bay, Oakland, 1996—; bd. dirs. West Contra Costa YMCA, Richmond, 1987—, chair program com., 1991-92, vice chair bd. dirs. 1992-96, chair bd. dirs., 1996-98, chair cmty. gifts campaign, 1992-94 (named Rita Davis Vol. of the Yr., 1993); umpire Little League Baseball, 1997—, ASA Softball, 1997—. Mem. ABA, State Bar Calif. (exec. bd. pub. law sect. exec. com. 1987-91, editor Pub. Law News 1988-91, liaison to bd. govs. 1991-92), Continuing Edn. Bar (joint adv. com. 1993-96), Contra Costa County Bar Assn., Charles Houston Bar Assn., Nat. Assn. Sports Officials. Independent. Office: City Atty's Office 1401 Marina Way South Richmond CA 94804-1654 Office Phone: 510-620-6509.

JENKINS, GEORGANN KLAUS, librarian; b. Oct. 9, 1950; d. Francis William and Mary Ida (Steingraber) Klaus; m. Robert M. Jenkins, Jr., Aug. 24, 1974; children: Andrew Klaus, Jeffrey Robert. BS in Edn., Edinboro U., Pa., 1972; MLS, U. Pitts., 1977, postgrad. suprs. program, 1986. Cert. sch. libr. Pa. Libr. grades 5-8 Pitts. Pub. Schs., 1972-74; libr. grades K-8, dist. audio-visual coord. Baldwin-Whitehall Sch., Pitts., 1974-87; asst. dir., children's libr. Whitehall Pub. Libr., Pitts., 1987-88; head libr. grades K-6 Whitehall Elem. Sch. Baldwin-Whitehall Sch. Dist., 1988-97; head libr. Harrison Mid. Sch., Pitts., 1997—2004, Baldwin Sr. HS, Pitts., 2004—06; adj. prof. edn. Chatham U. Coll. Women, Pitts., 2007—. Instrnl. materials reviewer Allegheny intermediate unit, Wilkinsburg, Pa.; review coord. Librs. Book Review Program, Allegheny County, Pa., 1991-2004; rec. sec. Pitts. Newspaper Unions Unity Coun. Women's Orgn., 1992-99; guest lectr. Sch. Sociology, U. Pitts., 1982. Contbr. book revs. to profl. jours. Mem. ALA, Pa. Edn. Assn., Am. Assn. Sch. Librs., Coun. Sch. Librs. (S.W. Pitts. chpt.), Pa. Sch. Librs. Assn., Beta Phi Mu. Democrat. Home: 520 Clair Dr Pittsburgh PA 15241-2013 Personal E-mail: georgannjenkins@netscape.net.

JENKINS, HOWARD M., supermarket executive; b. 1951; MBA, Emory U. With Publix Supermarkets, Inc., Lakeland, Fla., 1966—, v.p. rsch., exec. v.p., 1976-90, CEO, 1990—2001, chmn., 1990—. also: 1936 George Jenkins Blvd Lakeland FL 33815-3760*

JENKINS, JAMES ROBERT, lawyer, manufacturing executive; b. Waukegan, Ill., June 10, 1945; s. William Ivy and Louise Elnora (Lampkins) J.; m. Anita Louise Horne, June 29, 1968; children: James R. II, Andrea Louise. AB in Philos., U. Mich., 1967, JD, 1973. Bar: Mich. 1973, Ill. 1974. Law clk. to assoc. Koster & Bullard, Ann Arbor, Mich., 1971-73; law clk. to Justice Seidenfeld Ill. Ct. Appeals (2nd dist.), Waukegan, 1973-74; asst. defender State of Mich. Appellate Defender Office, Detroit, 1974-75; dep. defender Fed. Defender Office, Detroit, 1975-76; v.p., sec., gen. counsel, counsel sec. to corp. bd. dirs., counsel to exec. com., mem. fin. com. Dow Corning Corp., Midland, Mich., 1976—2000; sr. v.p., gen. counsel Deere & Co., Moline, Ill., 2000—. Trustee Alma Coll., 1985—. 1st lt. US Army, 1967—70, Vietnam. Decorated Bronze Star. Fellow Mich. State Bar Found.; mem. Mich. State Bar Assn., Am. Law Inst., Am. Arbtration Assn. (bd. dirs.), Assn. Corp. Counsel (chmn, 2005-, vice chmn. bd. dirs.). Office: Deere Co 1 John Deere Pl Moline IL 61265-8098*

JENKINS, JAMES STEPHEN, internist; b. Little Rock, Jan. 24, 1961; MD, U. Ark., 1987. Diplomate Am. Bd. Internal Medicine. Intern U. Mo. Hosp., Columbia, 1987-88, resident in medicine, 1988-90, fellow in cardiology, 1991-93; fellow in interventional cardiology Oschner Clin., New Orleans, 1993-94; assoc. sect. head, interventional cardiol. Ochsner Med. Inst., New Orleans, and dir. interventional cardiology rsch. Named one of Top Doctors La., La. Life mag., 2007. Fellow Am. Coll. Cardiology (La. chpt.), mem. Coll. Physicians. Office: Ochsner Med Inst 1514 Jefferson Hwy New Orleans LA 70121-2429 Office Phone: 504-842-3786.*

JENKINS, JEFFERY A., mathematics professor; s. Fred and Connie Jenkins; m. Lisa Milligan, May 10, 2001. PhD, U. Ill., Champaign, 1993—98. Asst. prof. Mich. State U., E.Lansing, 1999—2002, Northwestern U., Evanston, Ill., 2002—. Home Phone: 847-570-9260. Business E-Mail: j-jenkins3@northwestern.edu.

JENKINS, JIMMY RAYMOND, academic administrator; b. Selma, NC, Mar. 18, 1943; s. Alma (Street) Jenkins; m. Faleese Moore-Jenkins; children: Lisa, Ginger, Jimmy R. BS, Elizabeth City State U., 1965; MS, Purdue U., PhD in Sci. Edn., 1972. Asst. acad. dean Elizabeth City State U., 1972-73, assoc. prof., 1973-75, vice chancellor, 1977-83, chancellor, 1983-97; pres. Edward Waters Coll., Jacksonville, Fla., 1997—2005, Livingstone Coll., Salisbury, NC, 2006—. Mem. N.C. Bd. Sci. Tech., N.C. State Adv. Team Examiners Coll. Licensing, N.C. Humanities Com. Author: The Mini Patt Approach to Individualized Instruction, 1973, The Ultimate Evidence of Scholarship: The Meaning of a Good Education, 1979, Competency Based Approach Stresses Individualization, 1981 Mem. Am. Assn. Higher Edn., Nat. Sci. Tchr. Assn., Am. Biology Tchrs. Assn., Nat. Alliance Black Sch. Educators, Assn. Supervision and Curriculum Devel., Nat. Caucus Black Aged Mem. Christian Ch. (Disciples Of Christ). Office: Livingstone Coll 701 W Monroe St Salisbury NC 28144

JENKINS, JOHN BALESTER, academic administrator; BS in Polit. Sci., Temple U., Phila.; M in Vocat. Guidance and Counseling, Roosevelt U., Chgo. Pres. Fox Coll., Oak Lawn, Ill., bd. mem.; ops. mgr. Internat. Acad. Design and Tech., Chgo.; commr. Commn. on Human Rels., Chgo.; bd. mem. Taylor Bus. Inst.; pres. Ill. Inst. Art-Chgo., 2005—. Chair Com. on Cmty. Outreach. Office: Ill Inst Art Chgo 350 N Orleans St Chicago IL 60654 Office Phone: 312-280-3500.*

JENKINS, JOHN I., academic administrator; BA, U. Notre Dame, 1976, MPhil, 1978; PhB, Oxford U., 1987, PhD, 1989; MDiv, Jesuit Sch. Theology, Berkeley, 1988; licentiate in Sacred Theology, Jesuit Sch. Theology, Berekeley, 1988. Ordained a priest Basilica of the Sacred Heart, Notre Dame U., 1983. Mem. faculty U. Notre Dame, 1990—, prof. ancient philosophy, medieval philosophy, philosophy of the religion, adj. prof. London program, 1988—89, religious superior of Holy Cross priests, fellow, trustee, 1997—2000, v.p. and assoc. provost, 2001—05, pres., 2005—; dir. Old Coll. program for Notre Dame undergraduate candidates for Congregation of Holy Cross, 1991—93. Author: Knowledge and Faith in Thomas Aquinas, 1997, (articles published in) The Jour. Philosophy, Medieval Philosophy and Theology, The Jour. of Religious Ethics; spkr. Ann. Aquinas Lecture, U. Dallas, 2000. Recipient Lilly Teaching Fellowship, Notre Dame U., 1991—92. Office: Office of the President U Notre Dame 400 Main Bldg Notre Dame IN 46556

JENKINS, JOHN SMITH, retired dean, lawyer; b. Pittston, Pa., Dec. 11, 1932; s. Walter Hershel and Mildred (Lewis) J.; m. Marilyn Lewis, Aug. 23, 1958; 1 child, John Smith Jr. BA, Lafayette Coll., Easton, Pa., 1954; JD with honors, George Washington U., 1961; MA, Am. U., 1967. Bar: Va. 1961, U.S. Ct. Appeals for the Armed Forces, 1964, U.S. Supreme Ct. 1982. Commd. ensign U.S. Navy, 1955, advanced through grades to rear admiral, 1978; stationed at naval communications sta. Pearl Harbor, Hawaii, 1955—56; duty on U.S.S. Rochester, 1956-57; with Bur. Naval Personnel Washington, 1957-62; with Hdqrs. 1st Naval Dist. Boston, 1962-64; staff Office Navy JAG, 1964-65; staff Office Legis. Affairs Washington, 1969-71; staff Office of Asst. Sec., 1971-73; spl. counsel to sec. Office of Sec., 1973-76; asst. civil law JAG, 1976-78; dep. JAG, 1978-80; JAG, 1980-82; asst. dean Nat. Law Ctr. George Washington U., Washington, 1982-86, assoc. dean, 1986-2000, sr. assoc. dean, 2000—01, sr. assoc. dean emeritus, 2001. Decorated D.S.M. Legion of Merit. Fellow Am. Bar Found.; mem. ABA (ho. of dels., 1987-2005, chair standing com. on lawyers in the armed forces 1991-94, standing com. on delivery of legal svcs. 1997-2001, standing com. on legal assistance for mil. pers. 2001-05, chair, 2003-05), FBA, Judge Advs. Assn., Army and Navy Club (gov. 1988-98), George Washington U. Club. Episcopalian. Home: 5809 Helmsdale Ln Alexandria VA 22315-4138 Home Phone: 703-971-5421; Office Phone: 703-971-5421. Personal E-mail: jsjmlj@aol.com.

JENKINS, JUDITH ALEXANDER, bank consultant; b. Fort Sill, Okla., Oct. 14, 1940; d. James Buchanan and Gerry Lee (Gibbs) Permenter; m. Robert Miles Turner, Oct. 28, 1962 (div. 1972); m. Clarence Withers Alexander, Dec. 19, 1975 (div. Jan. 1987); m. David Claude Jenkins, Apr. 23, 1994. Student, U. Okla., 1958-59; BA in English, U. Tulsa, 1962; MBA, U. Okla., 1969; postgrad., U. St. Thomas, 1975-78. Asst. cashier So. Nat. Bank of Houston, 1971-73, asst. contr., 1973-74, asst. v.p. and asst. contr., 1974, v.p., contr., 1974-77, sr. v.p., contr., 1977-79; cons., 1979—. Mem. Beta Gamma Sigma, Gamma Phi Beta. Office: 16218 Wrangler Rd Rosharon TX 77583 Home Phone: 281-595-2030; Office Phone: 281-595-2030. E-mail: calikino@msn.com. *Learning, discipline, and independence are my goals and the major contributors to my success in business and personal life.*

JENKINS, KENNETH VINCENT, literature educator, writer; b. Elizabeth, NJ; s. Thomas Augustus and Rebecca Meredith (Williams) J.; 4 children. AB, MA, Columbia Coll.; postgrad., Columbia U. Tchr. South Side Sr. High Sch., Rockville Centre, NY, 1953-72, chmn. dept. English, 1965-72. Prof. English, Afro-Am. lit. Nassau Community Coll., Garden City, N.Y., 1972—, chmn. Afro Am. studies dept., 1975—, supr. adj. faculty, 1974-82; cons. in English, N.Y. State Dept. Edn., Albany, 1965-72; mem. Regents Question Com. in English, Albany, 1966-71; owner Black Books and Artifacts. Author: Teaching African Literature, 1960, Last Day in Church, 1965; contbr. revs., poems to profl. publs. Chmn. bd. dirs., founder Target Youth Ctrs., Inc., 1973-76, African-Am. Book Ctr., 1982—; hnem. nat. bd. Pacifica Found., 1973-79, chmn., 1975-76, pres., 1976-78; bd. dirs. Sta. WBAI-FM, N.Y.C., 1972-85, Nassau County Youth Bd., 1976-2000, chmn., 1978-99, chair emeritus 1999—; mem. N.Y. Gov.'s Commn. on Youth, 1984-94; bd. dirs. L.I. Cmty. Found., 1989-98, N.Y. State Youth Support, Inc., 1990-93; mem. bd. Schomburg Ctr., N.Y.C., 1990-98. Recipient cmty., county, state awards, M.L. King Award, Celebration Com. Nassau County, 1990, Special Svc. Award One Hundred Black Men, 1994, Nat. Coun. of Negro Women, Inc. Award, 2003; Pennington grantee, 1953. Mem.: Afro-Am. Inst., Assn. Study of Afro-Am. Life and History, Mensa, Phi Delta Kappa. Office: Nassau C C Garden City NY 11530

JENKINS, LAWANNA, elementary school educator; d. Duffie E. and Ree F. Jenkins. BS in Elem. Edn., Delta State U., Cleve., 1975; MEd, Lamar U., 1989. Cert. tchr. Tex. Tchr. Beaumont (Ind.) Ind. Sch. Dist., 1986—90, Dallas Pub. Schools, 1990—98, Pflugerville (Tex.) Ind. Sch. Dist., 1998—2003, Ft. Bend Ind. Sch. Dist., Sugarland, Tex., 2003—. Cons. Coll. Bd., Austin, 1999—. Contbr. curriculum materials to ednl. publs. Tchr. Bapt. chs., Okahoma City, 1884—1986. Named Tchr. of Yr., Beaumont PTA, 1991; recipient Governor's Recognition award, Office of Gov., Tex., 1994, proclamation, Senate of State of Tex., 1997; grantee, Ft. Bend Edn. Found., 2005—06. Mem.: Sci. Teachers Assn. Tex. (assoc.). Home Phone: 281-610-2341; Office Phone: 281-634-3000.

JENKINS, LOREN B., broadcast executive, publisher, writer; b. New Orleans, Oct. 26, 1938; s. Stephen B. Jenkins and Lorena (Lackey) Dabney; m. Nancy Harmon, June 1964 (div. 1985); children: Sara, Nicholas; m. Laura Thorne, Aug. 31, 1996. BA in Polit. Sci., U. Colo., 1961; postgrad., Columbia U., 1963-64. Ski instr. Aspen (Colo.) Ski Sch., 1958-61; tchr. Peace Corps., Sierra Leone, West Africa, 1961-63; reporter Port Chester (N.Y.) Dayly Item, 1964-65; newsman UPI, NY, London, Madrid, Paris, 1965-69; corr. Newsweek, Madrid, Hong Kong, Beirut, Saigon, Rome, 1969-79, The Washington Post, Rome, 1979-89; publisher, editor The Aspen Times, 1992-95; sr. fgn. editor Nat. Pub. Radio, Washington, 1995—. Edward R. Murrow fellow Coun. Fgn. Rels., 1988-89; recipient Pulitzer Prize for Internat. Reporting The Washington Post, 1983, Overseas Press Club award Newsweek, 1976; Overseas Press Club award Nat. Pub. Radio. 1998, Robert F. Kennedy award, 1998, Alfred I. duPont-Columbia U. award for coverage of Iraq, 2007. Avocations: skiing, mountain climbing. Office: National Public Radio 635 Massachusetts Ave NW Washington DC 20001-3753*

JENKINS, LYNN M., state official, former state legislator; b. Topeka, June 10, 1963; m. Scott M. Jenkins; children: Hayley, Hayden. AA, Kans. State U., 1984; BS, Weber State Coll., 1985. CPA. CPA, 1985—; rep. Kans. State Ho. Reps., 1998—2000; mem. Kans. State Senate, 2000—03, mem. gen. govt. budget com., ins. com., post audit com., govt. orgn. and elections com., taxation com.; treas. State of Kans., 2003—. Mem. Pooled Money Investment Bd., Coll. Savings Plan Network. Mem. adv. bd. Ct. Apptd. Spl. Advocate; bd. dirs. YMCA Metro, Family Svc. and Guidance Ctr., Kans. Children's Svc. League; treas., bd. dirs. Prince of Peace Presch.; active Jay Snideler PTO, Susanna Wesley United Meth. Ch.; mem. Kans. Pub. Employee's Retirement Sys., Aspen Inst. Rodel Fellowship in Pub. Leadership Program, Am. Coun. Young Polit. Leaders; mem. hon. bd. gov. Dwight D. Eisenhower Excellence in Pub. Svc.;mem. adv. coun. Kans. State U. Acctg. Dept.; mem. found. bd. Auburn-Washburn Pub. Sch. Mem. Kans. Soc. CPAs, Nat. Assn. Unclaimed Property Adminstr., Nat. Assn. State Treasurers (sr. v.p.) Republican. Methodist. Office: 900 SW Jackson St Ste 201 Topeka KS 66612-1235 Office Phone: 785-296-3171.*

JENKINS, MARC DELANO, music educator; s. John David and Alma Elizabeth Holley Jenkins; 1 child, Marc Delano Jr. MusB in Voice, Temple U., 1978, MusM, 1981. Cert. profl. tchr. Pa. Mem. voice faculty Settlement Music Sch., Phila., 1978—79; baritone soloist Bryn Mawr (Pa.) Presbyn. Ch., 1979—83; mem. adj. voice faculty Temple U., Phila., 1983—87; mem. voice faculty Freedom Theatre, Phila., 1986—88; music tchr. Phila. Sch. Dist., 1988—; min. of music Mother Bethel A.M.E. Ch., Phila., 1989—2005; voice and piano instr. Chestnut Hill (Pa.) Summer Arts Camp, 1991—93. Soloist Pa. Pro Musica, Phila., 1978—87, asst. musical dir., 1982—87; soloist U. Pa. Collegium Musicum, Phila., 1983—86; musical dir. The New Skyliters Jazz Chorale, Phila., 1992—95, Del Art Chorale, Phila., 1996—; dir. Benjamin Franklin Cluster Choir, Phila., 2000—02; artistic dir. W. Russell Johnson Music Guild, Nat. Assn. Negro Musicians, Phila., 2001—04; condr. W. Russell Johnson Music Guild Chorus, Phila., 2003—. Scholar Blossom Festival Vocal Chamber Ensemble, Kent. Ohio, 1980, Berkshire Music Festival, 1997. Mem.: Am. Choral Dirs. Assn., Phi Mu Alpha (life). Home: 6901 Old York Rd A-411 Philadelphia PA 19126 Home Phone: 215-927-3121. Personal E-mail: mdjdac@att.net.

JENKINS, MARGARET BUNTING, human resources executive; b. Warsaw, Va., Aug. 3, 1935; d. John and Irma (Cookman) Bunting; children: Sydney, Jr., Terry L. Student, Coll. William and Mary, 1952, AA in Bus. Adminstrn., 1973; BA in Human Resource Devel., St. Leo Coll., 1979; M in Adminstrn., George Washington U., 1982; PhD in Human Rsch. Mgmt., Columbia Pacific U., 1986. Rehab. counselor, tchr. York County Schs., Yorktown, Va.; mgr. Waterfront Constrn. Co., Seafood Corp., Seaford, Va., 1960—72; labor rels. specialist Naval Weapons Sta., Yorktown, 1974—77, staffing specialist, 1977—78, position classification specialist, supr. shipbuilding, conversion and repair Newport News, Va., 1978-81, supr. pers. mgmt. specialist, supr. shipbuilding, conversion and repair, 1981—90, pers. mgmt. specialist Yorktown and Cheatham, Va., 1990—94. Bd. dirs. various health orgns.; owner Jenkins Consulting. Author: Organizational Impact on Human Behavior, 1996; (poetry) Heron Haven Reflections, 1996; poetry published in Mists of Enchantment, 1995, Treasured Poems of America, 1996, Poets of the 90's, A Celebration of Poets, Showcase Edit., 1998, 99, The Best Poems of Poets award 2001; featured in: Cancer Has Its Privileges, Stories of Hope and Laughter (Christine K. Clifford), 2002 (Best Poets award 2002, 03, 04, 05, 06, Internat. Poetry award 2003, 04, 05). Decorated Meritorious Civilian Svc. award USN Supvr. Shipbuilding, Conversion and Repair, 3 Navy commendations; recipient award Newport News, 1990, Alumni medallion Coll. William and Mary, 1994-2000. Mem.: Chesapeake Writers Assn., Classification and Compensation Soc. (pres. 1984), Soc. for Human Resource Mgmt., Long Ridge Writers Group, Toastmasters Internat. (pres. 1985—87, various offices, award), Nature Conservancy, Audubon Soc., 4-Alumni Assn., Internat. Soc. of Poets (Disting. mem. 1996, 2005, 2006), Sierra Club, Fedn. Women's Clubs. Methodist. Avocations: art, writing, crafts. Home: PO Box 203 Seaford VA 23696-0203 *Excel beyond the norm. Be a risk-taker, and blaze a trail so others may follow. Allow creativity to flourish.*

JENKINS, MELANIE SHUN, dietician, counselor; b. Jackson, Miss., May 11, 1969; Dietary specialist Shaney's, Compton, Calif., 2000, Compton Sch. Bd., Compton, 2002; chef Foundary, Bessemer, Ala., 2007—. Cmty. svc. vol. Foundry, Bessemer, 2006, dorm supr., 07, ministry mem., 07. Author of poetry and music.

JENKINS, MELVIN LEMUEL, lawyer; b. Halifax, NC, Oct. 15, 1947; s. Solomon Green and Minerva (Long) Jenkins; m. Wanda Joyce Holly, May 20, 1972; children: Dawn, Shelley, Melvin, Holly Rae-Ann. BS, NC Agrl. and State U., 1969; JD, U. Kans., 1972. Bar: Nebr. 1973, US. Dist. Ct. Nebr. 1973. Atty. Legal Aid Soc., Kansas City, Mo., 1972, HUD, Kansas City, Mo., 1972—73; regional atty. U.S. Commn. on Civil Rights, Kansas City, Mo., 1973—79, regional dir., 1979—2002; atty. Stennis and Assocs., Omaha, 2002—. Chmn. A.M. Roundtable, Kansas City, 1981—83; mem. Kansas City Human Relations Commn., 1980. Mem. Mo. Black Adoption Adv. Bd., Kansas City, 1981—; bd. dirs. Joan Davis Spl. Sch. Mem.: ACLU, ABA, Fed. Bar Assn., Nat. Bar Assn., Nebr. Bar Assn., Urban League, Masons (master mason for civil rights 1979). Mem. Ame Ch. Home: 8015 Sunset Cir Grandview MO 64030-1461 Office: 300 S 19th St Ste 216 Omaha NE 68102 Office Phone: 402-342-4093.

JENKINS, NORMAN, accountant; m. Cammye Jenkins; children: Nicholas, Alexandra. Undergraduate bus. admin., Howard Univ.; graduate bus. admin., George Washington Univ. Vice-pres. Marriott Internat., Inc.; pres., CEO Nat. Assn. Black Accts. Named one of Most Influential Black Americans, Ebony mag., 2006. Office: Nat Assn Black Accts 7249-A Hanover Pkwy Greenbelt MD 20770 Office Phone: 301-474-6222. Office Fax: 301-474-3114.

JENKINS, PAUL, artist; b. Kansas City, Mo., July 12, 1923; s. William Burris and Nadyne (Fellers) J.; m. Esther Ebenhoe, 1944 (div.); 1 child, Hilarie Paula; m. Alice Baber, 1964 (div.); m. Suzanne Donnelly, 1979. Student, Art Students League, NYC, 1948-52; Hum.D., 1973-96. Author: (plays) Strike the Puma, 1966; co-author: Observations of Michel Tapie, 1956, Shaman to the Prism Seen, 1987, Anatomy of a Cloud, 1983, Seven Aspects of Amadeus and the Others, 1992, Shaman to the Prism Moon, 1994; contbr. articles to profl. jours.; co-author: (films) The Ivory Knife, 1965; exhibitions include Studio Paul Facchetti, Paris, 1954, Gimpel Weitzenhoffer Gallery, N.Y.C., Karl Flinker Gallery, Paris, Georges Fall Gallery, Galerie Patrice Trigano, Galerie Sapone, Nice, Gimpel Fils Gallery, London, Gallery Art Point, Tokyo, Martha Jackson Gallery, N.Y.C., Assoc. Am. Artists, NY, Galerie Proarta, Zurich, Chateau-Musée de Cagnes Sur Mer, Joseph Rickards Gallery, N.Y., Redfern Gallery, London, Jerald Melberg Gallery, Charlotte, NC, Robert Green Fine Art, Mill Valley, Calif., D. Wigmore Fine Art, N.Y.C., one-man shows include Mus. Fine Arts, Houston, San Francisco Mus. Art, Palm Springs Desert Mus., Musée Picasso, Antibes, Mus. Nice, France, Hofstra Mus., Hempstead, N.Y., Butler Inst. Am. Art, Youngstown, Ohio, Basilica Palladiana Vicenza, Centre D'Art Contemporain Bouvet Ladubay, Saumur, Palais des Beaux-Arts, Lille, Ark. Arts Ctr., Little Rock, Represented in permanent collections Mus. Modern Art, Whitney Mus., Guggenheim Mus., NY, Corcoran Gallery, Washington, Fogg Art Mus., Cambridge, Tate Gallery, London, Musee D'Art Moderne, Paris, Centre Georges Pompidou, Fondation Maeght, St-Paul-de-Vence, Musee Picasso, Antibes, Stedelijk Mus., Amsterdam, Netherlands, Mus. Western Art, Tokyo, Hirshhorn Mus. and Sculpture Garden, Nat. Gallery Art. Served with USNR, 1943-45. Decorated Commandeur des Arts et Lettres France; recipient Silver medal Corcoran Gallery Art, 1967, Art Dir.'s award for Anatomy of a Cloud, 1984, Life Achievement award Butler Inst. Am. Art, 1997, medal City of Paris, 1997, medal City of Lille, 2005, Benjamin West Clinedinst medal Artists' Fellowship N.Y., 2000. Mem. Royal Cambrian Acad. (hon.; Wales), Nat. Acad. N.Y. (elected). Studio: Imago Terrae PO Box 6833 Yorkville Sta New York NY 10128

JENKINS, PAUL OWEN, library director, educator; s. Owen and Barbara Jenkins; m. Mary Elizabeth Feick; 1 child, Thomas Owen. BA in Lit., Lawrence U., Appleton, Wis., 1983; MLS, U. Wis., Madison, 1987. Head collection dept. Coll. Mt. St. Joseph, Cin., 1988—95, dir. libr. svcs., 1995—. Contbr. articles to profl. publs.; author: Faculty-Librarian Relationships, 2005. Recipient NY Times Libr. award, 2006. Mem.: ALA, Ohio Libr. and Info. Network (OhioLINK) (mem. pvt. colls. dir. coun. 1995—, mem. collection bldg. task force 2002—05). Democrat. Office: Coll Mt St Joseph Archbishop Alter Libr 5701 Delhi Rd Cincinnati OH 45233 Office Phone: 513-244-4351. Office Fax: 513-244-4355. E-mail: paul_jenkins@mail.msj.edu.

JENKINS, REESE V., historian, educator; b. Muncie, Ind., June 28, 1938; s. John Thomas and Vada Arline Fraze Jenkins; m. Alyce Jeanette Mitchem Jenkins, Dec. 27, 1962; children: David William, Elizabeth Ann Manfredi. BA, U. Rochester, 1960; MS, U. Wis., 1963, PhD, 1966. Tchr. history and math. Madison (Wis.) Ctrl. Univ. H.S., 1963—64; asst. prof. history No. Ill. U., Dekalb, 1966—67; from asst. to assoc. prof. history of sci. and tech. Case Western Res. U., Cleve., 1967—78; dir., editor Thomas A. Edison Papers Rutgers U., New Brunswick, NJ, 1978—95, prof. history, 1978—. Harvard-Newcomen Bus. History fellow Harvard U., Boston, 1969—70; vis. assoc. prof. history U. Rochester, NY, 1976—77; hist. cons. Eastman Kodak Co., Rochester, 1993, Fuji Photofilm Co., Ashagara, Japan, 1995—99; participant PBS-TV programs on Thomas Edison, 1979—95; prin., cons., participant PBS-TV Am. Experience: George Eastman, 2000—01. Author: Images & Enterprise, 1975 (award N.Y. Photo Soc., 1976, Choice award, 1976), Japanese edit., 1998; editor-in-chief Papers of Thomas A. Edison, Vols. 1-3, 1989—94 (award Assn. Am. Pubs., 1989), microfilm edit., 1985—95; contbr. articles to profl. jours.; mem. editl. bd.: N.J. History, 1980—. Trustee Wesley Found., Rutgers U., New Brunswick, 1984—90, chair, 1987—89. Recipient award of recognition, N.J. Hist. Commn., Trenton, 1991; grantee NSF, NEH, NEA, numerous others. Mem.: Soc. for History of Tech. (exec. coun. 1980—82, 1992—94, chair various coms. 1977—, Dexter prize 1978, Spl. Ferguson prize 2005), Assn. for Documentary Editing (chair various coms. 1991—96, commendation 1996), History of Sci. Soc. (pres. Mid-West Junta 1978—79, coun. 1973—75). Democrat. Presbyterian. Avocations: reading, photographica, women's collegiate basketball, walking. Home: 11 Clifton Ave New Brunswick NJ 08901-1503 Office: Dept History Rutgers U College Ave Campus New Brunswick NJ 08903-5059 Personal E-mail: reese638@aol.com.

JENKINS, RICHARD DALE, actor, theater director; b. DeKalb, Ill., Dec. 2, 1953; s. Dale Stevens and M. Elizabeth (Wheeler) J.; m. Sharon R. Friedrick, Aug. 23, 1969; children: Sarah Pamela, Andrew Dale. BFA, Ill. Wesleyan U., 1969, LHD (hon.), 1991. Actor Trinity Repertory Co., Providence, 1970-84, stage dir., 1984-90, artistic dir., 1990-94. Appeared in (plays) The Suicide, The Iceman Cometh, In the Belly of the Beast, American Buffalo, Waiting for Godot, Of Mice and Men, True West, Fool for Love, others, (films) Silverado, 1985, Hannah and Her Sisters, 1986, The Witches of Eastwick, 1987, Stealing Home, 1988, Little Nikita, 1988, Sea of Love, 1989, Blaze, 1989, Blue Steel, 1990, Wolf, 1994, The Indian in the Cupboard, 1995, Flirting With Disaster, 1996, The Imposters, 1998, There's Something About Mary, 1998, The Mod Squad, 1999, Snow Falling on Cedars, 1999, Me, Myself & Irene, 2000, One Night at McCool's, 2001, The Man Who Wasn't There, 2001, Changing Lanes, 2002, Stealing Harvard, 2002, The Mudge Boy, 2003, The Core, 2003, Intolerable Cruelty, 2003, Cheaper by the Dozen, 2003, I Heart Huckabees, 2004, Shall We Dance, 2004, North Country, 2005, Fun with Dick and Jane, 2005, Rumor Has It., 2005, many others (TV movies) Double Crossed, 1991, Afterburn, 1992, And The Band Played On, 1993, Into Thin Air: The Death of Everest, 1997, Sins of the Father, 2002, others, (TV Series) Six Feet Under, 2001-2005. Recipient Spl. Recognition award New Eng. Theatre Conf., 1991, Achievement in Theatre award, 1991; named Best Dir., Boston Theatre Critics, 1982.

JENKINS, RICHARD ERIK, lawyer; b. Newport News, Va., Jan. 12, 1946; s. Willard Erette and Ina Beatrice (Porter) J.; m. Susan Rankin Thurston, Aug. 24, 1968 (div. Nov. 1991); 1 child, Anna; m. Lisa Joanne Weavers, Nov. 11, 2003. BS, N.C. State U., 1968, M in Stats. and Econs., 1971; JD, U. N.C., 1975. Engr. Celanese Corp., Charlotte, NC, 1971-72; assoc. atty. Stevens, Davis, Miller & Mosher, Washington, 1975-76, Bell, Seltzer, Park & Gibson, Charlotte, NC, 1976-78; ptnr. Adams &Jenkins, Charlotte, 1978-80; asst. patent counsel Burlington Industries, Inc., Greensboro, NC, 1980-84; sr. ptnr. Jenkins, Wilson Taylor & Hunt, P.A., Durham, NC, 1984—. Adj. assoc. prof. Duke U., Durham, 1989—, N.C. State U., Raleigh, N.C., 1992-95. Trustee N.C. Ctrl. U., Durham, 1992-95, Peace Coll., Raleigh, 2001—; bd. govs. Univ. Club, Durham, 1994-98; bd. dirs. Coun. Entrepreneurial Devel., 1988-90, N.C. State Found., 2002—; bd. visitors Duke U. Med. Ctr., 2007-. Mem. ABA, N.C. Bar Assn., Rotary, Hope Valley Country Club, Univ. Club, Carolina Club. Republican. Presbyterian. Avocations: yard, reading. Office: Jenkins Wilson Taylor & Hunt 3100 Tower Blvd Ste 1400 Durham NC 27707-2563 Office Phone: 919-493-8000. E-mail: rjenkins@jenkinswilson.com.

JENKINS, RICHARD LEE, manufacturing executive; b. Lynchburg, Va., July 20, 1931; s. Robert Julian and Beulah Vivian (Crews) J.; m. Doris E. Rucker, Dec. 24, 1958; children: Terena M., Richard C. BA, Lynchburg Coll., 1957; MBA, U. Mass., 1970. Various fin. mgmt. positions Gen. Electric Co., Lynchburg, Schenectady, NY, and Pittsfield, Mass., 1957-72; controller, mgr. Mfg. Transformer div. Allis-Chalmers, Pitts., 1972-75; gen. mgr. Indsl. Pump div. Allis-Chalmers, Cin., 1975-79; sr. v.p. Lynchburg Foundry, 1979-81; gen. mgr. service div. Siemens-Allis, Inc., Atlanta, 1981-84; sr. v.p. adminstrn. and internat. ops., chief fin. officer Diversified Products Corp., Opelika, Ala., 1984—. Treas., bd. dirs. Micah Corp. of Berkshire County, Pittsfield, 1968-72; bd. dirs. Va. Nat. Bank, Lynchburg, 1979-81. Auditor ARC, Pittsfield, 1966; bd. dirs., exec. on loan United Community Services, Pittsfield, 1972; campaign chmn. Piedmont Heart Assn., Lynchburg, 1980. Served with USN, 1950-54, Korea. Mem.: Cherokee Country (Atlanta), Saugahatchee Country (Opelika). Home: 2245 Springwood Dr Auburn AL 36830-7231 Office: Diversified Products Corp 309 Williamson Ave Opelika AL 36804-7313 E-mail: richardjenkins@charter.net.

JENKINS, ROBERT BERRYMAN, real estate developer; b. Evanston, Ill., Oct. 11, 1950; s. Clive Ridley and Genevieve (Brown) Crawford J.; m. Carol Lynn Kealey, Sept. 22, 1984; children: Paul Brown, Leighanne Kealey. BEE, Cornell U., 1972; postgrad., U. W. Fla., 1974. Cert. Profl. Solar Technology, 1984. Owner Fothergill's Outdoor Sportsman, Aspen, Colo., 1978-81, Jenkins Timber Properties, LLC, 2004—; owner, engr. Sophisticated Solar, Aspen, 1983-85; owner/pres. Sandhill Devels., Gulf Breeze and Aspen, 1985—; owner, pres. Roaring Fork Liquors, Inc., Glenwood Springs, Colo., 1992-2000. Recipient U.S. Dept. Energy Nat. Award for Energy Innovation, 1987, Gov.'s Energy award Fla. Gov., 1987; named Man of Yr., Gulf Breeze, 1991. Mem. Trout Unltd. (life). Republican. Methodist. Avocations: snowskiing, fly fishing, white-water rafting. Address: PO Box 14 200 Doc Henry Rd Woody Creek CO 81656

JENKINS, ROBERT GORDON, retired military officer, federal official; b. Charlottesville, Va., Dec. 14, 1941; s. Charles Gordon and Rosa Lee (Berry) J.; m. Nicki Jean Mitchell, Aug., 1966; children: Lara Elizabeth, Christopher Scott. BS, Va. Poly. Inst. and State U., 1964; MS, W.Va. U., 1967. Commd. USAF, 1968—, advanced through grades to brig. gen., fighter pilot Vietnam, Thailand, 1968-75; comdr. 22d Tactical Fighter Squadron, Bitberg Air Base, Germany, 1981-82; asst. chief staff AOC Allied Air Forces Ctrl. Europe, Boerlink, Germany, 1982-84; dep. comdr. for ops. Tactical Air Warfare Ctr., Eglin AFB, Fla., 1984-85; comdr. Air Forces Iceland, Keflavik, 1985-87; vice comdr. 354 Tactical Fighter Wing, Myrtle Beach, S.C., 1987-88, comdr., 1988-90; dep. dir. gen. purposes forces HQ USAF, Pentagon, Washington, 1990-92, dep. dir. ops., 1992; comdr. 51st Fighter Wing, Osan Air Base, Korea, 1992-94; vice comdr. 7th Air Force, Osan Air Base, Korea, 1994-95; dir. logistics HQ Pacific Air Force, 1995-97; pres. Exco Techs. Inc., 1997-2000; dir. aviation mgmt. U.S. Dept. Energy, 2000—. Decorated Legion of Merit with cluster, DFC, 2 Meritorious Svc. medals, 12 Air medals, 2 Commendation medals, DFC with cluster, Disting. Svc. medal. Mem. Order of Daedalians. Home: 9853 Hidden Estates Cv Vienna VA 22181-6090 E-mail: RandNJenk@aol.com.

JENKINS, ROBERT NORMAN, reporter, editor; b. Washington, Oct. 22, 1943; s. Jack Julian and Mina Lorraine (Katz) J.; m. Dianne Ruth Lang, June 1966 (div. June 1973); children: Kirsten Rose, Joshua Matthew; m. Dianne Carol Dearmin, Dec. 14, 1974; children: Michael Robert, Ryan Robert. BA in Journalism, Mich. State U., 1965. Newspaper reporter Grand Rapids (Mich.) Press, 1965-67; newspaper reporter, editor Newsday, Garden City, NY, 1967-69, St. Petersburg (Fla.) Times, 1969—. Recipient 1st Place News Section Design, Fla. Soc. Newspaper Editors, 1974. Mem.: Soc. Am. Travel Writers (nat. v.p. 1999—2001, Lowell Thomas Travel award Gold 1996, 2000, Lowell Thomas Travel award Silver 1996, 1999, Lowell Thomas Travel award Bronze 1999, 2000, 2001, 2002), Hon. Coaches Mich. State U. Office: St Petersburg Times 490 1st Ave S Saint Petersburg FL 33701-4204 Business E-Mail: bjenkins@sptimes.com.

JENKINS, RONALD WAYNE, lawyer, mediator, engineer; b. Johnson City, Tenn., Aug. 14, 1950; s. James Herman and Peggy Sue (Hutchison) J.; children: April Chalice, Kimberly Michelle, Robert Herman, Ronald Wayne II. BSEE, U. Tenn., 1972, JD, 1980. Bar: Tenn. 1980, U.S. Supreme Ct. 1986, U.S. Ct. Appeals (6th cir.) 1986, U.S. Dist. Ct. (ea. dist.) Tenn. 1986. Assoc. M. Lacy West, P.C., Kingsport, Tenn., 1980-83, Herndon, Coleman, Brading & McKee, Johnson City, 1984-86, ptnr., 1985—2001, Herrin, Booze, Rambo, Jenkins & Wheeler, Jonesborough, Johnson City, 2001—. Instr. rsch. and writing III U. Tenn. Coll. Law, 1979; mediator Tenn. Supreme Ct. Rule 31. Rsch. editor Tenn. Law Rev., 1978-79, editor-in-chief, 1979. With Ubon Royal AFB, 1972—73, Thailand Eglin AFB, 1973—74, Fla. Hahn AFB, 1974—75, Germany Spangdahlem AFB, 1976—77 Royal AFB, 1977, England Andrews AFB, 1983—84, Md. Mem. ABA, Tenn. Bar Assn., Washington County Bar Assn., Fed. Bar Assn., Nat. Aeronautic Assn., Aircraft Owners and Pilots Assn., Am. Bd. Trial Advs. (assoc. 1999), Tau Beta Pi (Tenn. col., engring. honor), Eta Kappa Nu (electrical engring. honor), Spangdahlem AB Aero Club (pres. 1976-77). Avocations: agriculture, aviation. Office: Herrin Booze Rambo Jenkins & Wheeler PO Box 308 806 E Jackson Blvd Jonesborough TN 37659-0308

JENKINS, RUBEN LEE, chemicals executive; b. Beggs, Okla., Nov. 27, 1929; s. William Arnold and Myrtle (Kimble) J.; m. Sylvia Griffin, July 17, 1956; children: Amy, Kimble Lee, William Griffin. BA, U. Okla., 1952, LLB, 1956; LLM, NYU, 1959. Bar: Okla. 1956. Law clk. to presiding justice U.S. Dist. Ct. (we. dist.) Okla., Oklahoma City, 1956; clk. U.S. Ct., Oklahoma City, 1956-58; research asst. in internat. law NYU, NYC, 1958-59; assoc. Allende & Brea, Buenos Aires, 1959-60; exec. v.p., gen. counsel White Eagle Internat., Midland, Tex., 1960-65; v.p. corp. devel. Plough, Inc., Memphis, 1965-71, dir. 1970, sr. v.p. hdqrs., 1972-73, exec. v.p., 1973-76, pres., 1976-89; dir. Schering-Plough Corp., Madison, NJ, 1971-89, sr. v.p., 1976-80, exec. v.p., 1980-89. Bd. dirs. Chickasaw coun. Boy Scouts Am., Memphis; hon. trustee Memphis U. Sch. Capt. USMC, 1952-54. Mem. ABA, Tenn. Bar Assn., Okla. Bar Assn., Non-Prescription Drug Mfrs. Assn. (bd. dirs. 1976-89), Palm Beach Polo and Country Club. Methodist. Address: 2886 Winding Oaks Ln West Palm Beach FL 33414 Personal E-mail: rljenkins1@comcast.net.

JENKINS, SHARON LEIGH, special education educator; b. Boynton Beach, Fla., Sept. 10, 1975; d. Allan Lee and Candace Esther Barnett; m. Tony Hayes Jenkins. BSc in Edn., Baylor U., 1998; M in Edn., Tex. Christian U., 2004. Spl. edn. tchr. Arlington Ind. Sch. Dist., Tex., 1999, 1999—2001, Mansfield Ind. Sch. Dist., Tex., 2001—. Mentor Mansfield Ind. Sch. Dist., 2003—04. Mem.: United Educators Assn., Coun. for Exceptional Children. Republican. So. Bapt. Avocations: reading, scrapbooks, walking. Home: 4311 Foster Ln Killeen TX 76549 Personal E-mail: tsjenkins@earthlink.net.

JENKINS, SHEILA ALNITA, psychologist; b. Inverness, Fla., Sept. 28, 1963; d. Peggy Ann Gary. BS, U. Houston, 1985, MEd, 1987; PhD, U. Ga., 1992. Psychologist Tex., registered Nat. Register Health Svc. Providers in Psychology. Psychologist Houston Ind. Sch. Dist., 1992—2003; psychologist, owner Sheila A. Jenkins, PhD & Associates, Houston, 1993—. Bd. dirs. Tex. Psychol. Found., 2004—, pres., 2007, Houston Psychol. Found., 2004—; active Delta Academic, Artistic, and Philanthropic Found., Inc., Houston, 2004—. Named Leadership Honoree, Heman Sweat Found., 2004; grad. scholar, U. Ga., 1989. Mem.: APA, Houston Psychol. Assn. (pres. 1999—2000, President's award 1997, 2004), Tex. Psychol. Assn. (trustee 2000—01), Delta Sigma Theta (chpt. pres. 2004—06). Office: Sheila A Jenkins PhD & Associates 2630 Fountain View Dr Ste 350 Houston TX 77057 Home Phone: 281-403-6056; Office Phone: 713-266-9837. Business E-Mail: drjenkins@drsheilajenkins.com.

JENKINS, SPEIGHT, opera company director, writer; b. Dallas, Jan. 31, 1937; s. Speight and Sara (Baird) J.; m. Linda Ann Sands, Sept. 6, 1966; children: Linda Leonie, Speight. BA, U. Tex.-Austin, 1957; LL.B., Columbia U., 1961; DMus (hon.), U. Puget Sound, 1992; HHD, Seattle U., 1992. News and reports editor Opera News, NYC, 1967-73; music critic N.Y. Post, NYC, 1973-81; TV host Live from the Met, Met. Opera, NYC, 1981-83; gen. dir. Seattle Opera, 1983—. Classical music editor Record World, NYC, 1973—81; contbg. editor Ovation Mag., NYC, 1980—87. Served to capt. U.S. Army, 1961-66. Recipient Emmy award for Met. Opera telecast La Boheme TV Acad. Arts and Scis., 1982 Mem. Phi Beta Kappa Assocs. Presbyterian. Office: Seattle Opera PO Box 9248 Seattle WA 98109-0248*

JENKINS, THOMAS H., lawyer; b. Washington, Oct. 25, 1951; BA, Davidson Coll., 1974; MS, Pa. State U., 1976; JD, U. Va., 1979. Bar: NY 1980, DC 1984, lic.: US Dist. Ct. (Ea. Dist.) NY, US Dist. Ct. (So. Dist.) NY, registered: US Patent & Trademark Office. Ptnr. Finnegan, Henderson, Farabow, Garrett & Dunner LLP, Washington, mng. ptnr., 1996—2001, leader, Bio./Pharm. Practice Group. Mem.: Bar Assn. DC, DC Bar Assn. Office: Finnegan Henderson Farabow Garrett & Dunner LLP 901 New York Ave NW Washington DC 20001-3315 Office Phone: 202-408-4000. Office Fax: 202-408-4400. Business E-Mail: tom.jenkins@finnegan.com.

JENKINS, WILLIAM L., former academic administrator; b. South Africa; arrived in US, 1978; m. Peggy Jenkins; children: Sharon, Gwynn, Anthea, Warren. Professional vet. medicine degree, U. Pretoria, South Africa, 1958, vet. specialist credentials, 1968; PhD, U. Missouri, Columbia, Mo., 1970; D (hon.), U. Pretoria, 2004. Various positions over several years to prof. and head, Dept. of Vet. Physiology, Pharmacology and Toxicology U. Pretoria, South Africa, 1971—78; faculty, Dept. of Vet. Physiol. and Pharmacology Texas A&M U., College Station, Tex., 1978—88; dean of Sch. of Vet. Medicine La. State U., Baton Rouge, 1988—93, provost and vice chancellor, 1993—96, chancellor, 1996—99; pres. La. State U. Sys., Baton Rouge, 1999—2007. Mem. NIH's Alcohol Abuse and Misuse on Coll. Campuses Com., La. Blue Ribbon Commn. for Teacher Quality. Pub. more than 60 scientific articles and 15 textbook chapters; co-author of vet. pharmacology textbook. Bd. dir. Greater Baton Rouge C. of C., Baton Rouge Ctr. for World Affairs, Coun. for a Better La., Arts Coun. of Greater Baton Rouge, La. Endowment for the Humanities, Academic Distinction Fund; mem. Baton Rouge board of Nat. Conf. for Cmty. and Justice. Named Communicator of Yr., PublicRelations Assn. of La., 1997, Disting. Alumnus, U. Mo., 1997; recipient Communication and Leadership award, Toastmasters Internat., 1999, Vision of Excellence award, New Orleans Regional C. of C., 2000. Mem.: Am. Academy of Vet. Nutrition, Internat. Assn. of Forensic Toxicologists, World Assn. of Vet. Physiologists, Pharmacologists and Biochemists, Am. Coll. Vet. Clin. Pharmacology, Am. Vet. Medical Assn.

JENKS, BOBBY (ROBERT SCOTT JENKS), professional baseball player; b. Mission Hills, Calif., Mar. 14, 1981; m. Adele Jenks; children: Cuma, Nolan. Draft pick Anaheim Angels, 2000; pitcher Chgo. White Sox, 2005—. Named to Am. League All-Star Team, 2006—07. Mailing: Chgo White Sox 333 W 35th St Chicago IL 60616*

JENKS, CYNTHIA J., research scientist; d. James S. and Carolyn A. Kakalik; m. William S. Jenks, Aug. 16, 1982. PhD, Columbia U., 1992. Assoc. scientist Ames (Iowa) Lab., 1995—2002, scientist, 2002—. Recipient CYtation Award, Iowa State U., 2006, Staff Excellence award, Iowa Bd. Regents, 2006. Mem.: AVS, Materials Rsch. Soc., Assn. for Women in Sci., Am. Chem. Soc., Ames Soccer Club. Achievements include research in Surface Studies of Novel Intermetallics. Office: Ames Lab 221 Spedding Hall Ames IA 50011 Office Phone: 515-294-8486.

JENKS, EILEEN A., academic administrator, real estate agent; b. NYC, Oct. 8, 1951; d. Robert K. and Katherine M. Petrausch; 1 child, Eileen K. Straiton. AB, Grace Inst., NYC, 1982; BA, Mercy Coll., Yonkers, 1984, Coll. New Rochelle, NYC, 1986. Lic. real estate Conn. Adminstrv. asst. Mobil Oil Corp., NYC, 1983—85; bus. mgr. dept. pediatrics Albert Einstein Coll. Medicine, Bronx, 1985—87; bus. mgr./adminstr. N.Y. Med. Coll., Valhalla, 1987—. Mem.: Academic Assn. Univ. Women. Home: 40 Big Trail Sherman CT 06784 Office: NY Med Coll Valhalla NY Office Phone: 914-594-4117. Personal E-mail: Eikedia@aol.com. Business E-Mail: eileen_jenks@nymeikdeic.edu.

JENKS, JONATHAN ALDEN, biologist, educator; BS, Unity Coll., Unity, Maine, 1984; MS, U. Maine, Orono, 1986; PhD, Okla. State U., Stillwater, 1991. Cert. wildlife biologist The Wildlife Soc., 1995. Disting. prof. S.D. State U., Brookings, 1991—. Contbr. articles to profl. jours. Recipient Excellence in Rsch. award, F. O. Butler Found., 2003, Griffith Faculty Rsch. award, S.D. State U., 2003, Rsch. Excellence award, Okla. State U., 1991. Fellow: The Wildlife Soc. (editl. panel 2004—06); mem.: Gt. Plains Natural Sci. Soc. (pres. 2003—04), Am. Soc. Mammalogists. Office: SD State U Box 2140B Brookings SD 57007 Home Phone: 605-693-4854; Office Phone: 605-688-4783. E-mail: jonathan.jenks@sdstate.edu.

JENKS, THOMAS EDWARD, lawyer; b. Dayton, Ohio, May 31, 1929; s. Wilbur L. and Anastasia A. (Ahern); m. Marianna Fischer, Nov. 10, 1961; children: Pamela (dec.), William, David, Christine, Daniel, Douglas Student, Miami U., Oxford, Ohio, 1947-50; JD cum laude, Ohio State U., Columbus, 1953; grad. with honors, US Naval Sch. Justice, Newport, RI, 1953. Bar: Ohio 1953, U.S. Dist. Ct. (so. dist.) Ohio 1961, U.S. Supreme Ct. 1971, U.S. Ct. Appeals (6th cir.) 1984. Pvt. practice, Dayton, 1955—; atty. Jenks, Pyper & Oxley, Dayton. Lectr. in med. malpractice law; mediator. Served to 1st lt. USMC, 1953-55 Named, Ohio Super Lawyer. Fellow Am. Coll. Trial Lawyers, Ohio Bar Found.; mem. ABA (ho. of dels. 1985-88), Am. Bar Found. (life), Dayton Bar Assn. (life, pres. 1978-79), Ohio Bar Assn. (life, bd. govs. litig. sect., 1990-98), Internat. Assn. Def. Counsel, Ohio Assn. Civil Trial Attys., Am. Bd. Trial Advs. (adv.), Kettering C. of C. (past pres.), Kettering Holiday at Home Found. (past pres.), Order of Coif, Dayton Lawyers Club (pres. 1999-2002), Optimist

Club (past pres. Oakwood chpt.), Phi Delta Phi, Sigma Chi. Republican. Roman Catholic. Office: Jenks Pyper & Oxley Courthouse Plz SW 10 N Ludlow St Dayton OH 45402 Office Phone: 937-223-3001. Business E-Mail: tjenks@jpolawyers.com.

JENKYN, ADRIAN JOHN, computer company executive; b. Milford Haven, Wales, July 19, 1939; s. Reginald John Mantell and Alice Thora (Laugharne) J.; m. Elizabeth Jane Hatton, Mar. 11, 1961 (div. 1989); children: David Adrian, Anthony Graham; m. Joyce Faye Brazier, Oct. 27, 2001. Higher nat. cert. in elec. engring., Rugby Coll., Eng., 1960. Supervising engr. ICL Ltd., Worcester, Eng., 1964-68, sr. engr. Cairo and Berlin, 1967-68, field mgr. Norwich, Eng., 1968-72, project mgr. Cairo, 1972-75, engring. mgr. Moscow, 1975-77, sr. mgr. Bracknell, Eng., 1977-82, br. mgr. Tokyo, 1982-88; pres. JAI Computer Tech., Tokyo, 1988-98; Y2K tech. coord. AARP, Washington, 1998—2000; specialist in bus. ETrade Bank, 1999—2001, continuity and disaster prevention and recovery, 1999—2001; bus. continuity mgr. Ill. Dept. Pub. Health, 2003—07. Chmn. St. David's Soc. Wales, Tokyo, 1992. Decorated Most Excellent Order Brit. Empire. Fellow Brit. Computer Soc., Instn. Inc. Elec. Engrs.; mem. Inst. Dirs., Bus. Continuity Inst., Brit. C. of C. in Japan (exec. com. 1992), Tokyo Brit. Club (founder, chmn. 1986). Avocations: contract bridge, photography, community theater. Office Phone: 217-220-0528. E-mail: jenkyn@earthlink.net.

JENNE, SUE OAK, secondary school educator; b. Alexandria, Va., Oct. 7, 1959; d. Jesse Calvin and Betty Ann Oak; 1 child, Jordan Michael. BS, Va. Commonwealth U., 1982; MA, Georgetown Coll., 1985; postgrad., Ind. Wesleyan U., 2002—03. Tchr. Franklin County Pub. Schs., Frankfort, Ky., 1984—98; tchr. spl. edn. Owen County Schs., Owenton, 1982—84; instrnl. coach Jefferson County Pub. Schs., Louisville, 1998—. Mem.: NEA, LWV, Ky. Tchrs. Assn., Jefferson County Tchrs. Assn., Phi Sigma Sigma Sorority (pres. 1981—82). Democrat. Avocations: reading, travel. Home: 9517 Palladio Ct Louisville KY 40299 Office: Jefferson County Pub Schs 3526 W Muhammad Ali Blvd Louisville KY 40212 Home Phone: 502-266-5931; Office Phone: 502-485-8354. Personal E-mail: soj1007@aol.com. E-mail: sue.jenne@jefferson.kyschools.us.

JENNER, JESSE JACOB, lawyer; b. NYC, Sept. 29, 1947; m. Tyler Tragle; children: Lydia, Alec. BSEE, Cornell U., 1969; JD, Harvard U., 1972; postgrad., U. Warwick, Coventry, UK, 1972-73. Bar: NY 1973, US Dist. Ct. (so. & ea. dists.) N.Y. 1973, US Ct. Appeals (2d cir.) 1975, US Ct. of Claims 1979, US Ct. Appeals (Fed. cir.) 1982, US Supreme Ct. 1983, US Patent & Trademark office, Fed. Cir. Bar Assn, US Court of Fed. Claims. Ptnr. Fish & Neave, NYC, 1974—, mng. ptnr, 2000—04; ptnr. Ropes & Gray LLP. Dir. Nat. Neurofibromatosis Found., NYC 1990, bd. dir. Children's Tumor Found. 1989-2005. Captain USAF, 1969—76. Recipient The Best Lawyers in Am. (since inception), America's Leading Lawyers for Bus., Chambers USA, 2003—06, Euromoney's Guide to World's Leading Patent Law Experts, 2003—05, Euromoney's The Best of Best, 2006, Leading Litigators in Am., Lawdragon 500, 2006, Lawdragon 3000, 2006, NY Super Lawyers, 2006; grantee Am. Coll. Trial Lawyers. Mem.: ABA, NY Intellectual Property Law Assn., Internat. Trade Commn. Trial Lawyers Assn., Am. Intellectual Property Law Assn., Assn. Bar NYC (past sec. com. on patents), Am. Arbitration Assn. (arbitrator). Office: Ropes & Gray LLP 1251 Ave of Americas New York NY 10020-1105 Office Fax: 646-728-2581. Business E-Mail: jesse.jenner@ropesgray.com.

JENNERICH, EDWARD JOHN, academic administrator, dean; b. Bklyn., Oct. 22, 1945; s. William James and Anna Johanna (Whicker) J.; m. Elaine Zaremba, May 27, 1972; children— Ethan Edward, Emily Elaine BA, Trenton State Coll., 1967; MSL.S., Drexel U., 1970; PhD, U. Pitts., 1974. Cert. tchr., learning resources specialist. Tchr. U.S. history Rahway High Sch., NJ, 1967-70; librarian Westinghouse High Sch., Pitts. Pub. Sch., 1970-74; adminstrv. intern U. Pitts, 1973; chmn. dept. library sci. Baylor U., Waco, Tex., 1974-83; dean Sch. Library Sci. So. Conn. State U., New Haven, 1983-84; v.p. acad. affairs Va. Intermont Coll., Bristol, 1984-87; grad. dean Seattle U., 1987-89; assoc. provost for acad. adminstrn., dean Grad. Sch., 1989-97; pres. Knowledge N.W. Inc., 1997—. Mem. rev. panel Fulbright Adminstrv. Exch., 1983-86. Co-author: University Administration in Great Britain, 1983, The Reference Interview as a Creative Art, 1981, 2d edit., 1997; contbr. articles to profl. jours. Bd. dirs. Waco Girls Club, Tex., 1977-83 Mem. ALA (office for libr. pers. resources 1980-82), Am. Assn. Univ. Adminstrs. (bd. dirs. 1980-82, 83-86, 89-93, 94—, v.p. 1996—, exec. com. 1982-87, chmn. overseas liaison com. 1982-87, Eileen Tosney Adminstrv. Excellence award 1985), Assn. for Coll. and Rsch. Librs. (exec. bd. dirs. 1984-88), Queen City Yacht Club (rar commodore) Phi Delta Kappa. Republican. Episcopalian. Avocations: model building, reading, travel, sports, sailing. Home: 6935 NE 164th St Kenmore WA 98028-4282 E-mail: jennerich@mindspring.com.

JENNESS, JAMES M., food products executive; b. Chgo., May 15, 1946; m. Sharon Jenness; 3 children. B in Mktg., DePaul U., Chgo., M in Bus. Adminstrn. Vice chmn., COO Leo Burnett Co., mem. exec. com., bd. dirs.; CEO Integrated Merchandising Sys. LLC; chmn., CEO Kellogg Co., Battle Creek, Mich., 2005—06, chmn., 2006—. Co-trustee W.K. Kellogg Found. Trust; bd. dirs. Kellogg Co., 2000—, Grocery Mfrs. Am., Schwarz Paper Co.; guest lectr. DePaul U., Chgo. Bd. dirs. exec. com. mem., chair mktg. com. Children's Meml. Hosp.; bd dirs. Mercy Home for Boys and Girls; bd. trustees DePaul U., Chgo., chmn. coll. commerce advisory coun. Mem.: Econs. Club Chgo. Office: Kellogg Co 1 Kellogg Sq Battle Creek MI 49016-3599*

JENNESS, MURIEL WHITLOCK, reading specialist; d. Hunter Bowles Whitlock, Sr. and Dorothy Lawhorne Knighton; m. Charles Franklin Jenness, III, Dec. 17, 1966; children: Michael Ryan, Brandon Whitlock. BA in English Edn., Coll. William and Mary, 1972; EdM in Spl. Edn., Va. Commonwealth U., 1986. English tchr. grades 10-11 Hanover County Schs., Mechanicsville, Va., 1972—76, learning disabilities tchr. grades K-5, 1985—88; learning disabled substitute Henrico County Schs., Richmond, Va., 1988—89, primary reading and math. instr. grades 3-5, 1990—92, chpt. 1 tchr. grades K-2, 1992—93; lang. fundamentals tchr. New Cmty. Sch., 1989—90; reading specialist grades K-5 Chesterfield County Schs., Va., 1993—. Co-prodr.: (video) Reading at Home: The Magic is You, 1993. Pres. Varina Jr. Woman's Club, Richmond, 1982—83; hostess contestant Tobacco Festival Varina and Richmond Area Woman's Clubs, 1983; mem. PTA adv. bd. Varina Elem., Richmond, 1984—85. Nominee Reading Tchr. of Yr., Richmond Area Reading Coun., 1996; named Tchr. of Yr., Enon Elem. Sch., 2004. Mem.: NEA, Chesterfield Edn. Assn., Va. Edn. Assn. Methodist. Avocations: reading, gardening, furniture refinishing, antiques.

JENNETT, JOSEPH CHARLES, retired academic administrator, engineering educator; b. Dallas, June 11, 1940; s. James C. and Rita (Gavin) Buchanan; m. Linda Ellis, Aug. 2, 1963; children: Erin, Brian. BS in Civil Engring., So. Meth. U., 1963, MS in Civil Engring., 1966; PhD, U. N.Mex., 1969. Registered profl. engr. Mo., NY, SC, Tex., NH, Colo. Field engr. Pitometer Assocs., U.S., Can., 1964-65, 69; instr. civil engring. U. N.Mex., Albuquerque, 1965-66; asst. prof. civil engring. U. Mo., Rolla, 1969-73, assoc. prof. civil engring., 1973-75; assoc. prof., chmn. civil engring. Syracuse (N.Y.) U., 1975-78, prof., chmn. civil engring., 1978-81; prof. environ. systems engring. Clemson (S.C.) U., 1981—, dean engring., 1981—96, provost, v.p. acad. affairs, 1991—96; pres. Tex. A&M U., Laredo, Tex., 1996—2001, pres. emeritus, 2001—. Adj. prof. civil engring. Syracuse U., 1981-87; constr. engr. Dept. of Water Resources, State of Calif., 1963-64, Projects in N. Sydney, New Waterford, Halifax, Can., 1969; cons. Pitometer Assocs., Pa., Ga., Mich., Ky., 1964-65, Calspan Corp., Litton Industries, Schwitzer Corp., Dow Chem., Union Carbide, Martin Marietta, 1969, 85—; bd. dirs. Chgo. Bridge and Iron N.V. Co-author: Lead in the Environment, Geochemistry and the Environment; contbr. articles to profl. jours. Adviser Water and Wastewater Treatment Authorities, Natal, Brazil, Wesley Found.; patron Greenville (SC) Theatre on the Green. Named Outstanding Young Engr. of Yr. Mo. Soc. Profl. Engrs., 1974. Fellow ASCE; mem. NAS, NSPE, Am. Soc. Engring. Edn. (bd. dirs. 1986-89), Am. Acad. Environ. Engrs. (bd. dirs. 1988-91), S.C. Soc. Profl. Engrs. (pres. Piedmont chpt. 1987-88, Outstanding Engr. of Yr. Piedmont chpt. 1990, S.C. Engr. of Yr. 1990), U. N.M. Outstanding Coll. Engring. Alumni, Water Pollution Control Fedn., Nat. Rsch. Coun. Commn. (life scis. com.), Order of Engr. (bd. dirs. 1988-91). Episcopalian. Avocations: photography, travel, camping, fishing, reading, skiing. Home: PO Box 2761 Wimberley TX 78676

JENNETTE, NOBLE STEVENSON, III, lawyer; b. Brunswick, Ga., May 20, 1953; s. Noble Stevenson Jr. and Geraldine Elanor (Emmanuel) J.; m. Linda Lee King, May 13, 1978; children: N. Stevenson IV, Emily King, Nicholas Andrew. BS, Ind. U., 1980; JD cum laude, Harvard U., 1984. Bar: Ind. 1984, US Dist. Ct. Ind. 1984, Mich. 1986, US Dist. Ct. Mich. 1987, US Ct. Appeals (6th and 7th cirs.) 1989, US Supreme Ct. 1990. Assoc. Baker & Daniels, Indpls., 1984-86, Varnum, Riddering, Schmidt & Howlett, Grand Rapids, Mich., 1987-90, ptnr., 1991—. Vice chairperson zoning and land use com. State Bar Mich., Lansing, 1989-92. Author: A Practical Guide to Obtaining Land Use Approvals and Permits, 1989; contbr. articles to profl. publs. Chairperson Children's Trust Fund, 1993-95, Child Abuse and Neglect Prevention, 1995-97. With USN, 1971-74. Mem. ABA (child custody com. family law sect. 1993—), Grand Rapids Hockey Assn. (commr.), Harvard Club Western Mich. Avocations: ice hockey, writing. Home: 1094 Idema Dr SE Grand Rapids MI 49506-3149 Office: Varnum Riddering Schmidt & Howlett PO Box 352 Grand Rapids MI 49501-0352 Home Phone: 616-340-9635; Office Phone: 616-336-6521. Business E-Mail: nsjennette@varnumlaw.com.

JENNEWEIN, JAMES JOSEPH, architect; b. New Rochelle, NY, July 20, 1929; s. Carl Paul and Gina (Pirra) J.; m. Edith Joan Wilson, Nov. 28, 1953; children: James Christopher, Gina Louise, Donald Andrew, Jonathan Paul. BArch, Syracuse U., 1952. Fulbright scholar Stuttgart U. (Technische Hochschule), Federal Republic of Germany, 1955-56; draftsman McCoy & Blair Architects, White Plains, NY, 1956-57; designer Harrison & Abramovitz Architects, NYC, 1957-60; prin./ptnr. Jennewein Architects, NYC, 1961-62; prin. McElvy, Jennewein, Stefany & Howard, Architects, Tampa, Fla., 1962-84, Jennewein, Archtl. Planning, Tampa, 1984; prin., ptnr. Jennewein Schemmer and Assocs., Tampa, 1985-91; ptnr. Ruyle Darby Plus Jennewein, Architects, PA, Tampa, 1992—. Pres. Fla. State Bd. Architecture, 1969-72. Trustee Brookgreen Gardens, Murrells Inlet, S.C., 1983-05, trustee emeritus, 2006—; chmn. Gasparilla Art Show, Tampa, 1977, Tampa C. of C. Environ. Com., 1987; pres. Tampa Bay Art Ctr., 1975, Tampa Mus. Art, 1985. Lt. (j.g.) USN, 1952-55. Recipient House of Yr. award Archtl. Record, N.Y.C., 1963, Ybor Sta. P.O. award Hillsborough County Planning Commn., Tampa. 1989. Fellow AIA; mem. Fla. Assn. AIA (pres. 1985-86, Pullara award 1985), Fla. Cen. Chpt. AIA (pres. 1967-68, Honor medal 1985), Nat. Sculpture Soc. (bd. dirs. 2004—), Tampa Yacht Club, Ye Mystic Krewe of Gasparilla, Tampa. Republican. Episcopalian. Avocations: fishing, sailing. Home: 4710 W Clear Ave Tampa FL 33629-5512 Office: Ruyle Darby Plus Jennewein Archs 3333 W Kennedy Blvd Ste 203 Tampa FL 33609-2959 Office Phone: 813-879-6633. E-mail: rdjmail@rdjarchitects.com.

JENNINGS, BOJAN HAMLIN, chemist, former educator; b. Waukegan, Ill., Apr. 4, 1920; d. Frank M. and Gertrude E. (Miller) Hamlin; m. Addison Llewellyn Jennings, June 12, 1942; children: Hamlin Manson, Nora Lyn, Constance. AB, Bryn Mawr Coll., 1941; MA, Radcliffe Coll., 1943; PhD, Harvard U., 1955. Mem. faculty Wheaton Coll., Norton, Mass., 1944-46, 50-85, A. Howard Meneely prof. chemistry, 1975-78, prof. emerita chemistry, 1985—. Research grantee NIH; Research grantee Petroleum Research Fund; Research grantee Research Corp.; Research grantee NSF Mem. Am. Chem. Soc.(award for encouraging women into careers in chemical sciences, 2007), N.Y. Acad. Scis.*

JENNINGS, BYRON, actor; m. Carolyn McCormick. Actor: (Broadway plays) A Month in the Country, 1995, The Man Who Came to Dinner, 2000, The Invention of Love, 2001, Noises Off, 2001, Dinner at Eight, 2002, Henry IV, 2003, Sight Unseen, 2004, Twelve Angry Men, 2004, Touch of the Poet, 2005, Inherit the Wind, 2007; (plays) Stuff Happens, 2006 (OBIE award Village Voice, 2006); (TV series) Law & Order, 1991, 1994, 1996, Central Park West, 1996, One Life to Live, 1996, Law & Order: Special Victims Unit, 2000, 100 Centre Street, 2001, Judging Amy, 2004; (TV films) An Enemy of the People, 1990, The Cosby Mysteries, 1994, The Man Who Came to Dinner, 2000, Hamlet, 2000; (films) A Simple Twist of Fate, 1994, Quiz Show, 1994, A Time to Kill, 1996, The Ice Storm, 1997, I'm Losing You, 1998, A Civil Action, 1998.*

JENNINGS, DAVID C., library director, educator; B in Am. Studies, Kent State U., Ohio, 1977, MLS, 1981. Asst. dir. Akron-Summit County Pub. Libr., Ohio, 1994—2004, interim dir., 2004—05, dir., 2005—. Adj. faculty mem. Sch. Libr. and Info. Sci. Kent State U., 1987—. Bd. mem. Project LEARN Summit County, Heart to Heart Comm.; mem. coordinating com. This City Reads!; bd. trustees Downtown Akron Partnership. Named Sch. Libr. and Info. Sci. Friend of Yr., Kent State U., 2005; recipient Grad. Applause Tchg. award, 2004. Office: Akron Summit County Pub Libr 60 S High St Akron OH 44326 Office Phone: 330-643-9100. E-mail: djenning@akronlibrary.org.

JENNINGS, DEBORAH E., lawyer; b. Washington, Feb. 8, 1949; BA with honors, U. Md., 1970; JD, Georgetown U., 1974. Bar: Md. 1974, D.C. 1984. Asst. state's atty. Montgomery County, Md., 1975-77; asst. atty. gen. Md., 1977-80; chief Criminal Investigations Divsn., 1978-80; ptnr. Piper & Marbury, Balt., 1983—99, Piper Marbury Rudnick & Wolfe, 1999—2004; ptnr., chmn. Environ. practice group DLA Piper Rudnick Gray Cary, Washington, 1995—. Co-author: Md. Handbook on Environ. Law. Mem. & past pres. Network 2000. Fellow Am. Bar Found. Office: DLA Piper Rudnick Gray Cary 1200 19th St NW Washington DC 20036-2412 Office Phone: 202-861-3842. Office Fax: 202-223-2085. Business E-Mail: deborah.jennings@dlapiper.com.

JENNINGS, FREDERIC BEACH, JR., economist, saltwater flyfishing guide; b. Boston, Dec. 29, 1945; s. Frederic Beach III and Ellen (Osgood) J.; m. Lucille Candace Giglio, Aug. 15, 1975; children: Frederic Beach V, Thomas Chapin. BA magna cum laude, Harvard U., 1968; MA in Econs., Stanford U., 1980, PhD in Econs., 1985. Jr. medicare acct. Blue Cross-Blue Shield, Boston, 1968-69; ind. rsch. fellow Inst. Humane Studies, Menlo Park, Calif., 1969-71, 77-78; asst. mgr. Globe Bag Co., South Boston, 1972-73; rsch. asst. Charles River Assocs., Cambridge, Mass., 1973-74; rsch. and teaching fellow Stanford (Calif.) Dept. Econs., 1974-79; instr. econs. Tufts U., Medford, Mass., 1979-83; asst. prof. Bentley Coll., Waltham, Mass., 1985-87; sr. econ. cons. The Mac Rsch. Group, Cambridge, 1987-88, Charles River Assocs., Boston, 1988-91; sr. mgr. Econ. Analysis Group Office of Fed. Tax Svcs. Arthur Andersen & Co., Washington, 1991-92; pres. EconoLogistics, Ipswich, Mass., 1992—; owner Peak Dawn Anglers, Ipswich, 1996—; founder Ctr. Ecol. Econ. and Ethical Edn., Ipswich, 1998—. Chmn., rep. Stanford Grad. Student Coun., 1974-76; senator Stanford Student Senate, 1975-76; co-pres. Associated Students Stanford U., 1976-77; founder Stanford Grad. Students Assn., 1978-79, Bentley Participants, Waltham, 1986-87, Full Circle Discussion Group Tufts U., Medford, 1981-84; resident assoc. Residential Edn., Stanford, 1978-79. Author: Democracy in Disarray, 1978, Mystical Tides, 1996; co-author Greenpeace Study on Fisheries Mgmt., 1999. Mem. joint Greenpeace Study on Fisheries Mgmt., 1999; bd. dirs. Internat. Network for Econ. Rsch., 2004—. Mem. Am. Econ. Assn., Indsl. Orgn. Soc., Western Econ. Assn., Internat. Soc. for Ecol. Econs., U.S. Soc. for Ecol. Econs., Atlantic Econ. Soc., Harvard Travellers Club, Rotary. Avocations: fly fishing, sailing, skiing, tennis, golf. Home: 261 Argilla Rd Ipswich MA 01938-2615 Office: EconoLogistics PO Box 946 Ipswich MA 01938-2212 also: Peak Dawn Anglers PO Box 946 Ipswich MA 01938-0946 Office Phone: 978-356-2188. Business E-Mail: Fbj@Fohe.zzn.com.

JENNINGS, GEORGE HAROLD, psychology professor; s. Slater Haigler and Alice Jennings. BA, Drew U., Madison, NJ, 1976; MS, Pa. State U., University Park, 1978, PhD, 1981. Prof., staff clin. psychologist Drew U., Madison, 1984—. Author: (book) Passages Beyond the Gate: a Jungian approach to understanding the nature of American psychology at the dawn of the new millennium, 1999. Named one of 100 Positive Men of Color, Coun. of Elders of the Generation Ctr. in Cherry Hill, NJ, 2002; recipient Francis B. Sellers award, Drew U., 2001, EOF Champion award, State of NJ Commn. Higher Edn., 2003; fellow, NIMH, 1976—79, Yale Sch. Medicine, 1979—80. Mem.: APA, Assn. Black Psychologists. Independent. African Methodist Episcopal. Avocations: cooking, travel. Office: Drew Univ 36 Madison Ave Madison NJ 07940 Office Phone: 973-408-3392. Business E-Mail: gjenning@drew.edu.

JENNINGS, GERALD D. (JERRY JENNINGS), mayor; b. Albany, NY, July 31, 1948; 1 child, Gerald Joseph. BA, SUNY, Brockport, 1970; MEd, SUNY, Albany, 1975. Tchr. Philip Schuyler High Sch., Albany, 1971-73, Albany High Sch., 1973-79, vice prin.; mayor City of Albany, 1993—. Former mem. Dem. com.; former alderman Common Coun. City Albany, 1979-93. Recipient City Livability award, US Conf. of Mayors, 1998, Pub. and Private Partnership Outstanding Achievement award, 1999, Pub.-Private Partnership Program award, Nat. Coun. for Urban Economic Develop., 1998. Mem. Ft. Orange Vets. Post, KC. Office: City Hall Rm 102 24 Eagle St Albany NY 12207 Office Phone: 518-434-5100. Office Fax: 518-434-5013.*

JENNINGS, HAMLIN MANSON, materials scientist, educator; b. NYC, Aug. 4, 1946; s. Addison Llewellyn and Bojan Hamlin Jennings; m. Glenys Nell Robinson; 1 child, Ashley. BSc, Tufts U., 1969; PhD, Brown U., 1975. Cert. chartered engr. U.K., 1994. Rsch. fellow U. of Cape Town (South Africa), 1975—76, lectr., 1976; rsch. asst. Imperial Coll., London, 1977—79, lectr., 1979—82, sr. vis. fellow, 1983; phys. scientist Nat. Inst. of Stds. and Tech., Gaithersburg, Md., 1983—87; prof. civil and environ. engring. and materials and sci. engring. Northwestern U., Evanston, Ill., 1987—, chair civil and environ. engring. dept., 2002—06; pres. Evanston Materials Consulting Corp., Wilmette, Ill. Editor Cement and Concrete Rsch., 1998—; assoc. editor Jour. of the Am. Ceramic Soc., 1999—; adv. bd. Jour. of Advanced Concrete Tech., Japan, 2001—. Author over 200 pubs., 12 patents. Fellow: Inst. of Materials, U.K., Am. Ceramic Soc. (Copeland award 2004, Brunauer award 1985); mem.: ASCE, Am. Concrete Inst. Avocations: sailing, squash, outdoors. Office: Northwestern Univ Dept Civil and Environ Engring A236 Tech Inst 2145 Sheridan Rd Evanston IL 60208-3109 Home Phone: 847-256-4387; Office Phone: 847-491-5282. Office Fax: 847-491-4011. Business E-Mail: h-jennings@northwestern.edu.

JENNINGS, HENRY SMITH, III, cardiologist; b. Atlanta, May 16, 1951; s. Henry Smith Jr. and Elizabeth (Martin) J.; m. Polly Cooper; 1 child, Mary Bailey. BS summa cum laude, Davidson Coll., 1973; MD, Vanderbilt U., 1977. Diplomate Am. Bd. Internal Medicine, subspecialty cardiovascular diseases and interventional cardiology, Nat. Bd. Med. Examiners; lic. physician and surgeon, Tenn., Ky. Intern internal medicine Vanderbilt U. Affiliated Hosps., Nashville, 1977-78, resident internal medicine, 1978-80; fellow clin. cardiology divsn. cardiology dept. medicine Vanderbilt U., 1980-82; clin. instr. medicine Vanderbilt U. Sch. Medicine, 1982-89, asst. clin. prof. medicine, 1989-97, assoc. clin. prof. medicine, 1997—2007, asst. prof. medicine, 2007—; med. dir. Cardiac Rehab. Ctr. St. Thomas Hosp., Nashville, 1984—2001, assoc. chief cardiac scis., 2001—05, pres.-elect med. staff, 2005—06; chmn. steering com. St. Thomas Heart Inst., 2002—04. Mem. active staff Vanderbilt U. Med. Ctr.; mem. courtesy staff Centennial Med. Ctr., Nashville, St. Thomas Hosp.; mem. cons. staff Bapt. Hosp., Nashville. Contbr. articles to profl. jours. Bd. dirs. Heart Inst., St. Thomas Hosp., Nashvile, 1992-94, Tenn. Heart Inst., 1989-91. Justin Potter med. scholar Vanderbilt U. Sch. Medicine, Nashville, 1973-77. Fellow ACP, Am. Coll. Cardiology, Am. Coll. Chest Physicians, Coun. Clin. Cardiology Am. Heart Assn., Soc. Cardiac Angiography and Interventions; mem. AMA, Am. Assn. Cardiovasc. and Pulmonary Rehab., Internat. Soc. Heart Transplantation, Am. Heart Assn., So. Med. Assn., Tenn. Med. Assn., Nashville Acad. Medicine, Gottlieb Friesinger Soc. (pres.-elect 2001, pres. 2002). Methodist. Home: Northumberland 3 Castle Rising Nashville TN 37215-4126 Office: Vanderbilt Heart and Vascular Inst Ste 5209 MCE South Tower 1215 21st Ave S Nashville TN 37232-8802 Home Phone: 615-665-0860; Office Phone: 615-322-2318. Office Fax: 615-936-7365. Business E-Mail: henry.jennings@vanderbilt.edu.

JENNINGS, JAMES BURNETT, oil industry executive; b. Temple, Tex., Sept. 20, 1940; s. William Donald and Ruth Imogene (Dodson) J.; m. Sharon Marie Lewis, Aug. 7, 1964 (div. 1982); 1 child, James Christopher; m. Regina Ann Richter, Nov. 5, 1983; 1 child, Michael Thomas. AA, Del Mar Coll., Corpus Christi, Tex., 1961; BS, Trinity U., 1963; MS, Purdue U., 1966; postgrad., Cornell U., 1967. Tchr. Burbank High Sch., San Antonio, 1963-65; tchr., coach Munster (Ind.) High Sch., 1965-69; geophysicist Shell Oil Co., Houston, 1969-74; chief geophysicist Columbia Gas Devel. Corp., Houston, 1974-79; exploration mgr. Hunt Oil Co., Houston, 1979-84, sr. v.p. Dallas, 1984-88, group v.p. worldwide exploration, 1988-91, exec. v.p., dir., 1991—99, pres., 1999—2004, chmn., 2004—. Contbr. articles to mags. Mem. Soc. Exploration Geophysicists, Am. Assn. Petroleum Geologists, Assn. Internat. Petroleum Negotiators. Republican. Office: Hunt Oil Co 1445 Ross Ave Ste 1400 Dallas TX 75202-2739 Business E-Mail: jjennings@huntoil.com.

JENNINGS, JEFFREY SCOTT, government agency administrator; b. Princeton, Ky., Oct. 26, 1977; BA polit. sci., U. of Louisville, 2000. Broadcast journalist WHAS Radio, Louisville; dir. polit. ops. President Bush's Kentucky campaign, 2000, Senator Mitch McConnell's campaign, 2002, Governor Ernie Fletcher's campaign, 2003; mgr. President Bush's campaign in NM, 2004; assoc. dir. Office of Political Affairs, White House, 2004—06; spl. asst. to the Pres., dep dir. of polit. affairs White House, 2006—. Spokesman and sr. adv. Republican Party of Ky.; press sec. Ky. Senate President David L. Williams. Spkr. in field.*

JENNINGS, JIM, architect; Founder, prin. Jim Jennings Architecture, San Francisco, 1975—. Prin. works include Group One Office, 1989, Brush Place, 1990, Pischoff Bldg., 1990, Barclay Simpson Studio, 1992, Oakland Hills House 1, 1993, Oakland Hills House 2, 1994, Telegraph Hill House, 1997, 85 Natoma, 1998, Hillsborough House 1, 1998, Italian Cemetery, 1998, Embarcadero Restaurant, 2000, Soma House, 2001, Visiting Artists House, 2003 (Kirby Ward Fitzpatrick prize, Archtl. Found. San Francisco, 2005, AIA Excellence in Architecture Honor award, 2005, AIA Inst. Honor award, 2006), Napa House, 2004, Hillsborough House 2, 2004. Office: Jim Jennings Architecture 49 Rodgers Alley San Francisco CA 94103 Office Phone: 415-551-0827. Office Fax: 415-551-0829.*

JENNINGS, JOSEPH ASHBY, banker; b. Richmond, Va., Aug. 12, 1920; s. Joseph Ashby and Leone (Bishop) J.; m. Anne Barrow Hatcher, Oct. 29, 1960; children: Joseph Ashby III, Ashby Anne. BS, U. Richmond, 1949, DSc (hon.), 1980; grad. certificate, Rutgers U., 1952; LLD (hon.), Va. Union U., 1991. With United Va. Bank, Richmond, 1949-85, v.p., 1956-66, sr. v.p., 1966-67, exec. v.p., 1967-71, pres., 1971, chmn. bd., 1972-85; also dir.; vice chmn. bd. United Va. Bankshares, Inc., 1972-75, pres., 1975-76, chief adminstrv. officer, 1972-76, chmn. bd., chief exec. officer, 1976-85, chmn. bd., 1985-86. Served with USAAF, 1942-46. Mem. Fin. Analysts Fedn. (past exec. v.p., dir.), Phi Beta Kappa, Omicron Delta Kappa, Phi Delta Theta, Beta Gamma Sigma. Presbyterian.

JENNINGS, KAREN, telecommunications industry executive; b. Mich. BA, U. Ark., Fayetteville. Various positions Southwestern Bell, Ark., 1972—95; chmn. SBC Asset Mgmt, Inc., 1995—96; assoc. v.p. chmn.'s office SBC Comm., Inc., 1995—96; pres. Southwestern Bell, Mo., 1996—97; v.p., gen. mgr. operator svcs. SBC Telecom., Inc., 1997—98; sr. v.p. human resources SBC Comm. Inc., 1998—99, sr. exec. v.p. human resources, 1999—2002, sr. exec. v.p. human resources and comm., 2002—05; sr. exec. v.p. human resources & comm. AT&T Inc., San Antonio, 2005—06, sr. exec. v.p. advt. & corp. comm., 2007—. Bd. mem. Cullen/Frost Bankers, San Antonio Spurs. Bd. dirs. Elizabeth Glaser Pediatric AIDS Found.; bd. mem. AT&T Found., Marion Koogler McNay Art Mus., United Way San Antonio. Mem.: Leaders Forum. Office: AT&T Inc 175 E Houston St PO Box 2933 San Antonio TX 78205 Office Phone: 210-821-4105. Office Fax: 210-351-2071.*

JENNINGS, KRIS, music educator; d. William and Michaelene Simms. BS in Music Edn., Gettysburg Coll., Pa., 1988. Jr. high band dir. Wilson Ctrl. Jr. High, West Lawn, Pa., 1989—90; mid. sch. band dir. Spring-Ford Area Sch. Dist., Royersford, Pa., 1990—. Ch. choir dir. First United Ch. of Christ, Spring City, Pa., 2000—. Mem.: Internat. Assn. of Jazz Educators (assoc.). Office: Spring-Ford Middle School 833 S Lewis Rd Bldg #2 Royersford PA 19468 Office Phone: 610-316-3642. E-mail: krisjen32@aol.com.

JENNINGS, MARCELLA GRADY, rancher, investor; b. Springfield, Ill., Mar. 4, 1920; d. William Francis and Magdalene Mary (Spies) Grady; student pub. schs.; m. Leo J. Jennings, Dec. 16, 1950 (dec.). Pub. relations Econolite Corp., LA, 1958-61; v.p., asst. mgr. LJ Quarter Circle Ranch, Inc., Polson, Mont., 1961-73, pres., gen. mgr., owner, 1973—; dir. Giselle's Travel Inc., Sacramento; fin. advisor Allentown, Inc., Charlo, Mont.; sales cons. Amie's Jumpin' Jacks and Jills, Garland, Tex. Investor. Mem. Internat. Charolais Assn., LA County Apt. Assn. Republican. Roman Catholic. Home and Office: 509 Mount Holyoke Ave Pacific Palisades CA 90272-4328 Office Phone: 310-454-4209.

JENNINGS, MEGHAN YOUNG, music educator; b. Oswego, NY, May 1, 1978; d. Elizabeth Young and Robert Paul Jennings. Bachelor magna cum laude, Syracuse U., 2000, Master, 2002—02. Cert. tchr. N.Y., 2000. Band. chorus, gen. music tchr. Bridgeport Elem. Sch., NY, 2002—; ch. organist Holy Family-St. Michael's Parish, Fulton, NY, 2003—. Piano tchr., Fulton/Bridgeport, NY, 2000—; Irish dance instr. Bridgeport Elem. Sch., NY, 2002—; music dir. Fulton Cmty. Theater, NY, 2003; voice tchr., Fulton, NY, 2003—; youth choir dir. Holy Family-St. Michael's Parish, Fulton, NY, 2004—. Coord. elem. sch. entry in ann. Chittenango Wizard of Oz Parade, Bridgeport Elem. Sch., NY, 2003—04; dir. Bridgeport Chorus, Carrier Dome, Syracuse U., 2006. Recipient Chancellor's scholarship, Syracuse U., 1996-2000, Music award, 1996-2000, Richard J. and Joann Olson Fay scholarship, 1999-2000, Harwood Simmons award, Syracuse U. Wind Ensemble, 2002. Mem.: Pi Eta Sigma, Phi Kappa Phi, Golden Key Nat. Honor Soc., Pi Kappa Lambda, Sigma Alpha Iota. Roman Catholic. Achievements include Established After School Irish Dancing Program at Bridgeport Elementary School; Established School-Wide Piano Recital at Bridgeport Elementary School. Avocations: playing musical instruments, Irish dancing, N.Y. Yankees baseball fan, Syracuse U. basketball fan, researching on the internet. Home: 46 West 4th St Fulton NY 13069 Home Phone: 315-593-7850. Personal E-mail: irishdancer23@yahoo.com.

JENNINGS, PAUL CHRISTIAN, civil engineering educator, academic administrator; b. Brigham City, Utah, May 21, 1936; s. Robert Webb and Elva S. (Simonsen) J.; m. Millicent Marie Bachman, Aug. 28, 1981; m. Barbara Elaine Morgan, Sept. 3, 1960 (div. 1981); children: Kathryn Diane, Margaret Ann. BSCE, Colo. State U., 1958; MSCE, Calif. Inst. Tech., 1960, PhD, 1963. From prof. civil engring., applied mechanics to prof. emeritus Calif. Inst. Tech., Pasadena, 1966—2002, acting v.p. bus. and fin., 1995, 1998—99, prof. emeritus, 2002—, provost, 2004—07. Cons. in field. Author: (with others) Earthquake Design Criteria. Contbr. numerous articles to profl. jours. 1st lt. USAF, 1963-66. Recipient Honor Alumnus award Colo. State U., 1992, Achievement in Academia award Coll. Engring., 1992; Erskine fellow U. Canterbury, New Zealand, 1970, 85. Fellow AAAS, New Zealand Soc. Earthquake Engring.; mem. ASCE (Walter Huber award 1973, Newmark medal 1992), Seismol. Soc. Am. (pres. 1980), Earthquake Engring. Rsch. Inst. (pres. 1981-83), Athenaeum Club. Avocations: fly fishing, hiking. Home: 640 S Grand Ave Pasadena CA 91105-2423 Office: Calif Inst Tech Mail Code 206-31 Pasadena CA 91125-0001 Business E-Mail: pcjenn@caltech.edu.

JENNINGS, RICHARD, communications executive; b. 1969; Worked for Sears, Roebuck and Co.; mgr. Time Warner Cable, Calif., Wis., regional ops. v.p.; v.p., gen. mgr. Comcast Colo.-North Denver Metro. Named one of 40 Executives Under 40, Multichannel News, 2006. Mem.: Nat. Assn. Multi-Ethnicity in Comm. Office: Comcast Corporation 1500 Market St Philadelphia PA 19102-2148

JENNINGS, RICHARD MILBURN, resort developer; b. Washington, Nov. 7, 1927; s. Maurice Edgar J. and Norma Milburn; m. Nini Bjonness, Mar. 21, 1964 (div. 1986); children: Lynn Urban, Stephanie, Jan. Student, Stanford U., 1944-46; BA, Ariz. State U., 1955; MA, Georgetown U., 1968, PhD in Govt., 1975. Commd. 2d lt. U.S. Army, 1947, advanced through grades to brigade comdr., 1969; asst. to Sec. of Def., 1971—72; retired U.S. Army, 1975; pres. Western Colo. Investments, Aspen, 1982-89; sr. v.p. Preferred Resorts, Aspen, 1989-95; pres. Western Resorts Internat., Aspen, 1995-98, chmn., 1998—. Author: U.S./Soviet Arms Competition, 1975; contbr. articles to profl. jours. Pres. Anderson Ranch Arts Ctr., Showmass Village, Colo., 1979-82; nat. coun. mem. Aspen Theater in the Park, 1997-99; bd. mem. World Affairs Coun. Desert. Decorated Legion of Merit with oak leaf cluster, Korean Silver Star, Bronze Star with 3 oak leaf clusters, Air medal with 7 oak leaf clusters, Vietnamese Gallantry Cross. Mem. Nat. Assn. Realtors, Stanford Alumni Assn., Indian Wells Tennis Club, Mil. Officers Assn. Avocations: writing, tennis. Office: Western Resorts Internat 75852 Camino Cielo Indian Wells CA 92210 E-mail: dickjennin@aol.com.

JENNINGS, ROBERT BURGESS, experimental pathologist, medical educator; b. Balt., Dec. 14, 1926; s. Burgess Hill and Etta (Crout) J.; m. Linda Lee Sheffield, June 28, 1952; children: Carol L., Mary G., John B., Anne E., James R. BS, Northwestern U., 1947, MS, B.M., 1949, MD, 1950. Diplomate Am. Bd. Pathology (trustee 1976-87, pres. 1986-87). Intern Passavant Meml. Hosp., Chgo., 1949—50, resident pathology, 1950—51; mem. faculty Northwestern U. Med. Sch., 1953—75, prof. pathology, 1963—75, chmn. dept., 1969—75, Magerstadt prof., 1969—75; prof., chmn. dept. pathology Duke U. Med. Sch., Durham, NC, 1975—89, James B. Duke prof., 1980—2003, prof. emeritus, 2003—. Vis. scientist Middlesex Hosp. Med. Sch., London, 1961-62; cons. VA Rsch. Hosp., Chgo.; mem. attending staff Northwestern Meml. Hosp., Chgo., 1963-75; mem. pathology A Study sect. USPHS, 1960-65; mem. clin. cardiology adv. com. NIH, 1976-80, mem. cardiovasc. and renal study sect., 1992-95. Mem. editl. bd. Lab. Investigation, 1967-95, Archives Pathology, 1970-80, Jour. Molecular and Cellular Cardiology, 1972-89, Exptl. and Molecular Pathology, 1973-99, Circulation, 1988-91, 93-96, Circulation Rsch., 1976-82, Histopathology, 1977-92, Am. Jour. Pathology, 1983-92, Jour. Applied Cardiology, 1986-90, Cardiosci., 1990-95, Trends in Cardiovasc. Medicine, 1991-92, Cardiovasc. Pathology, 1991-95, Heart Failure Revs., 1996-. Served as lt. (j.g.) USNR, 1951—53. Recipient Peter Harris award, Internat. Soc. Heart Rsch., 1992, Disting. Achievement award, Soc. Cardiovasc. Pathology, 1996, Discovery Health Channel Am. Med. Honors award, AHA, 2004, Medal of Merit award, Internat. Acad. Cardiovasc. Scis., 2005, Gold-Headed Cane award, Am. Soc. Investigative Pathology, 2007; Markle scholar med. scis., 1958—63. Office: Duke U Med Ctr Dept Pathology Durham NC 27710-0001 Office Phone: 919-684-3776. Business E-Mail: jenni004@mc.duke.edu.

JENNINGS, ROBERT LEE, retired music educator; b. Whitehall, Mich., Feb. 23, 1928; s. Robert L. Jennings and Mildred Evelyn Bjorkman Jennings; m. Geraldine May French, Aug. 17, 1957; children: Pamela Ann, Lisa Jean, Linda Gail, Brian Lee. B Music Edn., Augustana Coll., 1953; MA in Music Edn., We. Mich. U., 1960; PhD in Music Edn., Mich. State U., 1969. Cert. tchr. Mich. Tchr. voice, dir. choir Whitehall (Mich.) Pub. Schs., 1955—56; dir. choir and voice Muskegon (Mich.) Sr. H.S., 1956—60; grad. asst. Mich. State U., East Lansing, 1960—62; tchr., dir. choral We. Mich. U., Kalamazoo, 1962—63; prof. voice and choral music, dir. opera workshop U. S.D., Vermillion, 1963—66; prof. U. Wis., Whitewater, 1966—92, ret., 1992. Bus. mgr. West Shore Symphony Orch., Muskegon, Mich., 1959—60; founder, dir. Whitewater Singers Chamber Choir, Wis., 1994—2006; leader 5 summer music study tours U. Wis., Whitewater, 1966—92; dir. choir various chs., 1955—84; freelance soloist. Cpl. US Army, 1953—55. Recipient Morris D. Hayes award, Wis. Choral Dirs. Assn., 1994. Mem.: Nat. Assn. Tchrs. Singing (life), Music Educators Nat. Conf. (life), Kiwanis (song leader breakfast club 1978—). Avocations: concerts, travel. Home: 204 N Esterly Ave Whitewater WI 53190-1315 Personal E-mail: grjenmus@idcnet.com.

JENNINGS, STEPHEN GRANT, academic administrator; b. Indpls., Dec. 6, 1946; s. Grant Orville and Helen Zura (MacDonald) J.; m. Sarah Ferguson, Apr. 26, 1969; children: Amy Jennings Bishop, Meredith Jennings Poole. BA, Trinity U., 1968; MS, Miami U., Oxford, Ohio, 1970; PhD, U. Ga., 1976; diploma in ednl. mgmt., Harvard U., 1982; LLD, Coll. Ozarks, Point Lookout, Mo., 1997; LHD, Simpson Coll., 1998. Asst. dean for resident life So. Meth. U., Dallas, 1970-73; asst. dir. housing U. Ga., Athens, 1973-76; assoc. dean students Tulane U., New Orleans, 1976-80; v.p. student svcs. Furman U., Greenville, SC, 1980-83; pres. Coll. of Ozarks, Point Lookout, Mo., 1983-87, Simpson Coll., Indianola, Iowa, 1987-98, Oklahoma City U., 1998-2001, U. Evansville, Ind., 2001—. Instnl. cons. Am. Coll. in London, 1995; bd. dirs. Old Nat. Bank, Nat. Pub. Radio and TV (WNIN). Mem. Coun. Ind. Colls., Nat. Assn. Schs., Colls. and Univs. (bd. dirs. 1993—), Nat. Assn. Intercollegiate Athletics (coun. of pres. 1983-87), So. Assn. Colls. and Schs. (vis. teams 1982—), North Cen. Assn. Colls. and Schs. (vis. teams 1989—), So. Assn. Coll. Student Pers. (pres. 1983), Harvard U. Alumni Assn. (class rep.), Rotary, Evansville Club, Sigma Alpha Epsilon. Avocations: sports, golf, reading. Office: U Evansville Office of President 1800 Lincoln Ave Evansville IN 47722-0001

JENNINGS, THOMAS PARKS, lawyer; b. Alexandria, Va., Nov. 16, 1947; s. George Christian and Ellen (Thompson) J.; m. Shelley Corrine Abernathy, Oct. 30, 1971; 1 child, Kathleen Eayre. BA in History cum laude, Wake Forest U., 1970; JD, U. Va., 1975. Bar: Va. 1975. Assoc. Lewis, Wilson, Lewis & Jones, Arlington, Va., 1975-78; atty. First Va. Banks, Inc., Falls Church, 1978-80, gen. counsel, 1980—2003, sec., 1993-99, sr. v.p., 1995—2003; sr. atty. advisor Fed. Housing Fin. Bd., 2004—. Adj. prof. George Mason U. Sch. Law, Arlington, 1987—88. Trustee Arlington Cmty. Found., 1998-2003, treas., 2001-03; dir. Rixey St. Found., Inc., 1997—; deacon Georgetown Presbyn. Ch., Washington, 1980-82, elder, 1983-85, 95-97, 2006—, trustee, 1988-90, dir. Bd. Pensions, Presbyn. Ch. USA, 2001—. With US Army, 1970—71. Mem.: Va. State Bar Assn. Presbyterian. Avocations: bridge, kayaking. Personal E-mail: stkj123@verizon.net.

JENNINGS, TONI (ANTOINETTE LEE JENNINGS), former lieutenant governor, former state senator; b. Orlando, Fla., May 17, 1949; d. Jack C. and Margaret (Murphy) J. BA, Wesleyan Coll., Macon, Ga., 1971; postgrad., Rollins Coll., 1972-73. Pres. Jack Jennings and Sons, Inc., Gen. Contractors, Orlando, 1973; mem. Fla. Ho. of Reps., 1976-80, Fla. Senate, 1980—2000, pres., 1996—2000; lt. gov. State of Fla., Tallahassee, 2003—07. Republican leader pro tempore, Fla. Senate, 1982-83, 85, 86, Rep. leader, 1984, 86-88; legis. del. Orange County, 1980-82, 86-88; bd. dirs. Brown & Brown, Inc., 1998-2000, 2007-, FPL Group, Inc., 2007- Bd. dirs. Salvation Army; active Rep. Women's Federated Club of Winter Park, Orlando Women's Rep. Club Federated. Recipient Spl. Commendation award Fla. Restaurant Assn., 1979, Meritorious Svc. award Fla. Fedn. Humane Socs., 1979, Disting. Alumni awrd Wesleyan Coll., 1981, Freedom award Women for Responsible Legislation, 1982, Support of Law Enforcement award Fla. Sheriffs Assn., Outstanding Efforts award Tampa Missing Children Help Ctr., 1983, Outstanding Svc. award Grocers' Assn. Fla., 1983, Legis. award Fla., 1983, Legis. award Fla. Chiropractic Assn., 1983, 86, Appreciation award Fla. Med. Assn. and Physicians of Fla., 1983, 2d Ann. Frank J. Fahrenkopf, Jr. Outstanding State Minority Leader award, 1988, Am. Legis. award for Leadership in Econ. Devel. Legislation award Fla. C. of C., 1987; named Legislator of Yr., Orange County Young Rep. Club, 1980-81. Mem. Orlando Area Bd. Realtors (Friend of Realtors award 1989), Builders and Contractors, Ctrl. Fla. Builders Exch., Delta Kappa Gamma, Phi Kappa Phi, Kappa Delta Epsilon. Republican.*

JENNINGS, SISTER VIVIEN, literature and language professor; b. Jersey City; d. Eugene O. and Alice (Smith) J. BA, Caldwell Coll.; MA in English, Cath. U. Am.; MS in Telecommunications, Syracuse U.; PhD in English, Fordham U.; postgrad., Oxford U., Eng., 1994; EdD (hon.), Providence Coll.; LittD (hon.), Caldwell Coll.; DHL (hon.), St. Peter's Coll. Prof. English Caldwell Coll., 1960-69; major supr. Dominican Sisters-Caldwell, 1969-79; instr. broadcasting writing Syracuse U., 1979-80; with community affairs dept. Sta. WIXT TV, Syracuse, NY, 1980; dir. telecommunications Barry U., 1982-83; dir. pub. affairs Cath. Telecommunications Network Am., 1983-84; pres. Caldwell Coll., 1984-94, prof. English, 1995-99; prin. St. Dominic Acad., Jersey City, 1999—. Originator, designer campus TV studios Caldwell Coll., Barry U.; curriculum planner, coord. new grad.-level curriculum in telecommunications Barry U.; lectr. on ednl. and media issues. Producer: Centenary Journey, 1981, Advent Vesper Chorale, 1981, American Immigrant Church, 1982, Las Casas: Ministry of Presence, 1987; co-producer: The Boat People, 1980. Founder, dir. Children's TV Experience; founder Project Link Ednl. Ctr., Newark. Recipient Gov.'s Pride N.J. Albert Einstein award for edn., 1989. Office: St Dominic Acad 2572 Kennedy Blvd Jersey City NJ 07304-2107

JENNISON, BRIAN (LESTER), environmental specialist; b. Chelsea, Mass., June 13, 1950; s. Lewis L. and Myra S. (Piper) J. BA, U. N.H., 1972; PhD, U. Calif., Berkeley, 1977; cert. hazardous materials mgr., U. Calif., Davis, 1986. Tchg., rsch. asst. U. Calif., Berkeley, 1972-77; staff rsch. assoc. Dept. of Molecular Biology, Berkeley, 1978-80; instr. dept. biology Calif. State U., Hayward, 1977; sr. biologist San Francisco Bay Marine Rsch. Ctr., Emeryville, Calif., 1980-81; inspector I Bay Area Air Quality Mgmt.Dist., San Francisco, 1981-83, inspector II, 1983—87; enforcement program specialist Bay Area Air Quality Mgmt. Dist., San Francisco, 1987—92; dir. air quality mgmt. divsn. Washoe County Dist. Health Dept., Reno, 1992-2000; dir. Lane Regional Air Pollution Authority, Springfield, Oreg., 2000—05; planning specialist NH Dept. Environ. Svcs., Air Resources Divsn., 2005—. Cons. U.S. Army C.E., L.A., 1980, San Francisco, 1981; instr. U. Calif., Berkeley, 1990-93, Assoc. Bay Area Govs., 1990-92; adj. prof. U. Nev., Reno, 1994-2003. Contbr. articles to profl. jours. Harbor Br. Found. fellow, 1977-78. Mem.: ABA (assoc.), Assn. Local Air Pollution Control Ofcls. (bd. dirs. 2001—05), Air and Waste Mgmt. Assn. (chmn. Ea. Sierra chpt. 1994—96), Navy League U.S. (life), Phi Beta Kappa. Avocations: railroad history, photography. Office Phone: 603-271-0536. Business E-Mail: bjennison@des.state.nh.us.

JENNY, CAROLE, physician, researcher; b. St. Louis, June 4, 1946; d. Vance Buescher and Alice Emelie Jenny; m. Thomas Allen Roesler, Mar. 16, 1974; children: Laura Alice Roesler, Amelia Martha Roesler. BA, U. Mo., 1968; BMS, Dartmouth Med. Sch., 1970; MD, U. Wash., 1972; MBA, Wharton Sch., U. of Pa, 1976. Pediatrics Am. Bd. of Pediat., NC, 1977. Prof. of pediat. Brown Med. Sch., Providence, 1996—; dir., child protection team Hasbro Children's Hosp., Providence. Chair, com. on child abuse and neglect Am. Acad. of Pediat., Elk Grove Village, Ill. Mem. Am. Profl. Soc. on the Abuse of Children, Chgo., 1991—. Recipient Outstanding Svc. to Maltreated Children, Am. Acad. of Pediat., 1999, Ray Helfer award, Nat. Coalition of Children's Trust Funds, 2002. Achievements include research in child abuse, head trauma, sexual abuse. Office: Brown Medical School 593 Eddy St Potter-005 Providence RI 02903 Home Phone: 401-831-6324; Office Phone: 401-444-3996. Personal E-mail: cjenny@lifspan.org. Business E-Mail: cjenny@brown.edu.

JENRETTE, RICHARD HAMPTON, investment and insurance company executive; b. Raleigh, NC, Apr. 5, 1929; s. Joseph M. and Emma V. (Love) J. BA, U. N.C., 1951; MBA, Harvard U., 1957; LittD (hon.), U. N.C. With Brown Bros. Harriman & Co., NYC, 1957-59, Donaldson, Lufkin & Jenrette, Inc., NYC, 1959—, now chmn. bd., 1986-1995; chmn. bd. dirs. The Equitable Cos. Inc., NYC, 1987-96; ret. Equitable Cos. Inc., NYC, 1996; chmn., chief exec. officer Equitable Cos. Inc. (now Credit Suisse First Boston), 1986-90; sr. advisor Donaldson Lufkin & Jenrette, NYC. Bd. dirs. Bus. Found. N.C., Hist. Hudson Valley, Bus. Roundtable. 2d lt. USAR, 1953-55; trustee Duke Found. Mem. Securities Industry Assn. (bd. dir., exec. com.), Inst. Chartered Fin. Analysts, N.Y. Soc. Security Analysts, Phi Beta Kappa. Clubs: University, Brook, Harvard, Harvard Bus. Sch., Links (N.Y.C.); Carolina Yacht (Charleston, S.C.). Democrat. Episcopalian. Office: Credit Suisse First Boston 11 Madison Ave New York NY 10010-3643

JENRETTE, THOMAS SHEPARD, JR., music educator, choral director; b. Roanoke, Va., Feb. 1, 1946; s. Thomas Shepard and Virginia Catherine (Harris) J. BA, U. N.C., 1968, MusM, 1970; D of Mus. Arts, U. Mich., 1976. Choral dir. Cummings H.S., Burlington, NC, 1969—72; dir. cultural arts Burlington City Schs., NC, 1972—73; dir. choral activities S.W. State U., Marshall, Minn., 1976—79, East Tenn. State U., Johnson City, 1979—. Dir. music First Christian Ch., Johnson City, 1981-84, Covenant Presbyn. Ch., Johnson City, 1991—; dir. East Tenn. State U. Chorale European Tour, 1985, 98, 2001, 06; guest condr. choral festival N.C. High Sch., Raleigh, 1987, 2002, Govs. Sch. for Arts, Murfreesboro, Tenn., 1987, Nat. Seminar of Intercollegiate Men's Choruses, Inc., 1992, 2004; guest condr. N.C. All-State Male Choir, 1997, All-East Tenn. H.S. Male Choir, 1998, Tenn. All-State H.S. Male Choir, 2001, S.C. All-State Male Choir, 2002, Ga. All-State H.S. male choir, 2003, We. Carolina Choral Festival, 2005, Nat. Condrs. Conf., U. So. Miss., 2000. Grantee East Tenn. State U., 1988, 90, 96, 99. Mem. Am. Choral Dirs. Assn. (life; condr. 1986, 88, 94, 2000, 04, so. divsn. convs., 89, 99, 2007, nat. conv., so. divsn. repertoire and stds. chair for male choirs 1999-2005), Tenn. Music Educators Assn. (conductor state convs. 1990, 91, 94, 2000, dir. White House, Christmas 1989, 2001, Canticum Novum Festival, Caracas, Venezuela, 1996), Internat. Fedn. Choral Music, Nat. Assn. Tchrs. Singing, Coll. Music Soc. (life), Music Educators Nat. Conf. (condr. so. divsn. conv. 1997), Phi Mu Alpha (hon.), Omicron Delta Kappa, Pi Kappa Lambda. Home: 2734 E Oakland Ave Apt C-25 Johnson City TN 37601-1887 Office Phone: 423-439-6949. Business E-Mail: jenrette@etsu.edu.

JENSEN, ARTHUR SEIGFRIED, retired engineer, physicist, consultant; b. Trenton, NJ, Dec. 24, 1917; s. Emil Anthony and Emma Anna (Lund) J.; m. Lillian Elizabeth Reed, Aug. 9, 1941; children: Deane Ellsworth, Alan Forrest, Nancy Lorraine. BS, U. Pa., Phila., 1938, MS, 1939, PhD in Physics, 1941; diploma in advanced engring., Westinghouse Sch. Applied Sci., Balt., 1972, diploma in computer sci., 1977. Registered profl. engr., Md. Research physicist U.S. Naval Research Labs., Washington, 1941; research physicist RCA Labs., Princeton, NJ, 1945-57; mgr. spl. electron devices Westinghouse Electronic Tube Div., Balt., 1957-65; sr. adv. physicist Electronics Systems Ctr., Balt., 1965-91; cons. physicist Westinghouse Electronic Systems Ctr., Balt., 1991-94; co-owner, chief engr. Jensen Cons. Engring., Parkville, Md., 1994—2004; ret., 2004. Mem. Md. State Bd. Registration Profl. Engrs., 1979-86, vice chmn., 1983-86; cons. Nat. Acad. Sci., 1970 Author: (novels) Persian Gulf Jeopardy, 2007; contbr. articles to profl. jours. Mem. Endowed Sons of Norway Found., Nancy Lorraine Jensen Meml. Scholarship Fund. Served to capt. USN, 1941-46, USNR, 1946-77, ret., 1977—. Hector Tyndale fellow, 1939, George Lieb Harrison fellow, 1940; recipient Outstanding Svc. award Engrs. Coun. Md., 1986, Gov.'s citation, 1986, Westinghouse spl. patent award, 1972. Fellow IEEE (life), Washington Acad. Scis.; mem. AAAS, AIAA, Res. Officers Assn., Ret. Officers Assn., Naval Res. Assn., Am. Phys. Soc., Am. Assn. Physics Tchrs., Soc. Photo-Optical Instrumentation Engrs., Optical Soc. Am., N.Y. Acad. Scis., Md. Acad. Scis. (chmn. awards com.), Nat. Coun. Engring. Examiners (chmn. internat. rels. com.), Infrared Info. Symposium, Am. Legion, Fleet Res. Assn., Sons of Norway, Nat. Eagle Scout Assn., Vigil Honor Order of Arrow, Sigma Xi, Pi Mu Epsilon, Kappa Phi Kappa. Clubs: U.S. Naval Acad. Officers and Faculty. Achievements include patents in field; invention of practical random access memory (RAM) electron tube (used in early computers, first computerized telephone central office, over-the-horizon radar; airborne moving target radar and DEW line radar analysis); infrared TV camera tube which aided aerodynamic design of SR-71 supersonic plane; micro-mirror matrix TV projection light modulator that projected large, bright, live TV picture display; digital light processing using the same micro-mirror projections; low noise integrated circuit for camera photoplane detector chip; research in conceptual designs of military meteorological satellite sensor sys. Home: Chapel Gate 1104 Oak Crest Village 8820 Walther Blvd Parkville MD 21234-9022

JENSEN, BILL, editor; b. 1973; m. Kendall Jensen; 2 children. Profl. roller hockey player NY Riot; writer & editor Long Island Voice, NY; mng. editor Long Island Press; lead editor Boston Phoenix, 2005—06; dir. new media Village Voice Media LLC, NYC, 2006—. Mem.: Soc. Profl. Journalists (Green Eyeshade award for Feature Reporting 2005). Office: Village Voice Media LLC 36 Cooper Sq New York NY 10003*

JENSEN, CLAYNE R., retired academic administrator; b. Gunnison, Utah, Mar. 17, 1930; s. Alton H. and Arvilla R. Jensen; m. Elouise Henrie, Mar. 14, 1952; children: Craig, Mike, Blake, Chris. BA, U. Utah, 1952, MA, 1956; EdD, Ind. U., 1963. From instr. to assoc. prof. phys. edn., coach Utah State U., 1956-64; assoc. prof. Brigham Young U., Provo, 1965-67, prof. and assoc. dean, 1968-74, dean, 1973-91, v.p., dir. athletics, 1991—95; ret., 1995. Vis. prof. No. Ill. U., DeKalb, 1969 Author: Manual of Kinesiology, 1966, (with Garth Fisher) Scientific Basis of Athletic Conditioning, 1972, 4th edit., 1991 (with Vernon Barney) Conditioning

Exercises to Improve Body Form and Function, 1972, 2d edit., 1981, (with N.P. Nielson) Statistics & Measurements in Education, 1972, 2nd edit., 1980, (with Clarence Robison) Modern Track and Field Coaching Technique, 1974, Recreation and Leisure Time Careers, 1976, 3d edit., 1990, Winter Touring and Mountaineering, 1977, Leisure and Recreation in America, 1977, 2d edit., 1990, (with Clark Thorstenson) Issues in Outdoor Recreation, 1977, 3d edit., 1985, (with Karl Tucker) Skiing, 1977, 4th edit., 1986, Outdoor Recreation in America, 1977, 6th edit., 2006, Applied Kinesiology, 1978, 3d edit., 1985, Adminstration of Physical Education and Athletic Program, 1988, 4th edit., 2003, (with Craig Jensen) Backpacking, 1981; contbr. articles to profl. jours. Exec. dir. Utah Inter-Agy. Coun. for Recreation and Parks, 1962-65; chmn. Nat. Conf. on Inter-Agy. Planning for Parks and Recreation, 1963-64; chmn. Nat. Conf. on Outdoor Recreation, 1966. Capt. USMC, 1952—55. Recipient Breitbrad Athletic Found. award, 1955; spl. citation for outstanding contbns. to recreation and park devel. State of Utah, 1965 Mem. AAHPERD, Utah Assn. Health, Phys. Edn., Recreation and Athletics (pres. 1970), Nat. Coll. Athletic Assn. (mem. governing coun. 1985-89). Mem. Lds Ch. Home: 3131 N Cottonwood Ln Provo UT 84604-4497 Personal E-mail: crjensen@comcast.net. *As a professional educator I have long been devoted to the concept of helping people succeed and not causing them to fail. Success of each individual ought to be the principal objective of education. In my administrative role, I have tried to perpetuate an environment in which people are constantly encouraged and where there is opportunity for professional development and personal improvement.*

JENSEN, D. LOWELL, federal judge; b. Brigham, Utah, June 3, 1928; s. Wendell and Elnora (Hatch) J.; m. Barbara Cowin, Apr. 20, 1951; children: Peter, Marcia, Thomas. AB in Econs, U. Calif.-Berkeley, 1949, LL.B., 1952. Bar: Calif. 1952. Dep. dist. atty., Alameda County, 1955-66; asst. dist. atty., 1966-69; dist. atty., 1969-81; asst. atty. gen. criminal divsn. US Dept. Justice, Washington, 1981-83, assoc. atty. gen., 1983-85, dep. atty. gen., 1985-86; judge US Dist. Ct. (no. dist.) Calif., Oakland, 1986—97, sr. judge, 1997—. Mem. Calif. Coun. on Criminal Justice, 1974—81, US Jud. Panel on Multidistrict Litig., 2000—. Served with U.S. Army, 1952-54. Fellow Am. Coll. Trial Lawyers; mem. Nat. Dist. Atty.'s Assn. (victim/witness commn. 1974-81), Calif. Dist. Atty.'s Assn. (past pres.), Boalt Hall Alumni Assn. (past pres.) Office: US Dist Ct 1301 Clay St Rm 490C Oakland CA 94612-5217

JENSEN, DALLIN W., lawyer; b. Afton, Wyo., June 2, 1932; s. Louis J. and Nellie B. Jensen; m. Barbara J. Bassett, Mar. 22, 1958; children: Brad L., Julie N. BS, Brigham Young U., 1954; JD, U. Utah, 1960. Bar: Utah 1960, U.S. Dist. Ct. Utah 1962, U.S. Supreme Ct. 1971, U.S. Ct. Appeals (10th cir.) 1974, U.S. Ct. Appeals D.C. 1980. Asst. atty. gen. Utah Atty. Gen., Salt Lake City, 1960—83, solicitor gen., 1983—88; shareholder Parsons, Behle & Latimer, Salt Lake City, 1988—. Spl. legal cons. Nat. Water Commn., Washington, 1971—73; mem. Colo. River Basin Salinity Adv. Coun., 1975—2005; alt. commr. Upper Colo. River Commn., 1983—2006; commr. Utah Reclamation Mitigation and Conservation Commn., 2003—. Author (with Wells A. Hutchins): The Utah Law of Water Rights, 1965; mem. editl. bd. Rocky Mountain Mineral Law Found., 1983—85; contbr. articles on water law and water resource mgmt. to profl. jours. With US Army, 1955—57. Mem. Lds Ch. Home: 3565 S 2175 E Salt Lake City UT 84109-2902 Office: PO Box 45898 Salt Lake City UT 84145-0898 Office Phone: 801-532-1234. Business E-Mail: djensen@parsonsbehle.com.

JENSEN, DANIEL, history educator; s. Andrew and Mary Jensen; m. Sheri Jensen, May 30, 1987. BS, Dana Coll., Blair, Nebr., 1984; MA, U. Nebr., Lincoln, 1991. Tchr. Johnson-Brock Jr.-Sr. Pub. H.S., Nebr., 1985—95, Waverly Pub. H.S., 1995—; instr. U. Nebr. Coun. Econ. Edn., Lincoln, 2004—. Mem. literacy team Waverly Pub. H.S., 2003—; mem. tech. com. Sch. Dist. #145, 2004—, mem. curriculum coun., 2003—; mem. faculty adv. team Waverly Pub. H.S., 2002—, chair social edn. area, 2003—. Recipient Tchr. the Yr., Gilder-Lehrman Inst., 2005. Mem.: ASCD. Office: Waverly Public High School 13401 Amberly Road Waverly NE 68462 Home Phone: 402-465-9158; Office Phone: 402-786-2765.

JENSEN, DAVID GRAM, management consultant; b. New Britain, Conn., Jan. 24, 1955; s. Robert and Vera (Ericksen) J. BS, Cen. Conn. State U., 1977; MS, U. Wis., 1979. Assoc. dir. phys. dept. New Britain (Conn.) YMCA, 1975-77; grad. asst. LaCrosse (Wis.) Exercise Program, 1978-79; staff rsch. assoc. U. Calif., San Diego, 1979-81, coord. rsch. cardiology, 1981-83; med. application cons. Med. Data Systems, San Diego, 1983-84; med. sales specialist Siemens Med. Systems, Mission Viejo, Calif., 1984-90; chief adminstrv. officer UCLA, 1990-95; pres. Scientific Selling Systems, LA, 1993—. Cons. Western Imaging, Denver, 1991—. Contbr. articles to profl. jours. Mem. Nat. Speakers Assn., Inst. for Mgmt. Cons. Avocations: pub. speaking, exercise, motivational books and tapes. Home and Office: 3518 Barry Ave Los Angeles CA 90066-2802

JENSEN, DENNIS LOWELL, lawyer; b. Erie, Pa., July 5, 1951; s. Lowell and Roberta (Umbaugh) J. Student, Cornell Coll., 1969-70; BA, Macalester Coll., 1973; JD, U.Houston, 1977. Bar: Tex. 1977, U.S. Dist. Ct. (so. dist.) Tex. 1978, Calif. 1981. Sole practice, Houston, 1977-78; asst. housing coordinator Santa Ana Housing Authority, Calif., 1979; polit. cons. Huntington Beach, Calif., 1980-81; legis. analyst Tosco Corp., Los Angeles, 1981-82; polit. cons. Lynn Wessell Co., 1982-83, George Young & Assocs., 1983-84; legis. aide Los Angeles City Councilman Ernani Bernardi, 1984-86; dep. atty. Los Angeles City Atty.'s Office, 1986-95; pvt. practice Huntington Beach, 1995—. Lectr. in field. Contbr. articles to profl. jours. Campaign mgr. for Congressman Tom Kindness, Hamilton, Ohio, 1978, Initiative to Abolish Inheritance Tax, Bakersfield, Calif., 1980; alumni admissions rep. Macalester Coll., 1984; mem. bd. dirs. Adult Day Svc. Orange County, 1998-2004; instr. Calif. State U. Fullerton Extended Edn. programs gerontology and geriatric care mgmt., 1999—. Mem. Am. Assn. Polit. Cons., Nat. Acad. Elder Law Attys., Orange County Bar Assn. (chmn. elder law sect. 2004), Order of Barons, Phi Delta Phi. Republican. Home: 18801 Gregory Ln Huntington Beach CA 92646-1921 Office: Dennis L Jensen Atty at Law 18377 Beach Blvd Ste 212 Huntington Beach CA 92648-1349 Office Phone: 714-843-0450.

JENSEN, DICK LEROY, lawyer; b. Audubon, Iowa, Oct. 25, 1930; s. A.B. and Bernice (Fancher) J.; m. Nancy Wilson, June 30, 1956; children: Charles F., Sarah R. (dec.). LL.B., U. Iowa, 1954. Bar: Iowa 1954. Practice in, Audubon, Iowa, 1958-60; gen. counsel, sec. Walnut Grove Products, Co., Atlantic, Iowa, 1960-64; legal staff W.R. Grace & Co., Atlantic, 1964-66; gen. counsel, v.p., sec. Spencer Foods, Inc., Iowa, 1966-72, dir., 1968-72; mem. Dreher, Simpson and Jensen, Des Moines, 1972—. Notes and legis. editor Iowa Law Rev., 1953—54. Pres. S.W. Iowa Mental Health Inst., 1964-66. Served to lt. USNR, 1955-58. Mem.: Masons, Phi Delta Phi, Sigma Nu. Republican. Presbyterian. Home: 4823 Cedar Dr West Des Moines IA 50266 Office: Dreher Simpson & Jensen The Equitable Bldg Ste 222 Des Moines IA 50309-3723 Office Phone: 515-288-5000. Business E-Mail: djensen@dreherlaw.com.

JENSEN, ELWOOD VERNON, biochemist; b. Fargo, ND, Jan. 13, 1920; s. Eli A. and Vera (Morris) J.; m. Mary Welmoth Collette, June 17, 1941 (dec. Nov. 1982); children: Karen Collette, Thomas Eli; m. Hiltrud Herborg, Dec. 21, 1983 AB, Wittenberg U., 1940, DSc (hon.), 1963; PhD, U. Chgo., 1944; DSc (hon.), Acadia U., 1976, Med. Coll. Ohio, 1991; MD (hon.), U. Hamburg, 1994, U. Athens, 2005. Faculty U. Chgo., 1947-90, assoc. prof. biochemistry Ben May Inst. Cancer Rsch., 1954-60, prof., 1960-63, Am. Cancer Soc. rsch. prof. physiology, 1963-69, dir. Ben May Inst., 1969-82, dir. Biomed. Ctr. Population Research, 1972-75, prof. physiology, 1969-73, 77-84, prof. biophysics, 1973-84, prof. biochemistry, 1980-90, Charles B. Huggins disting. svc. prof., 1981-90, emeritus prof., 1990—; rsch. dir. Ludwig Inst. for Cancer Rsch., 1983-87; scholar-in-residence Fogarty Internat. Ctr. NIH, 1988, Cornell U. Med. Coll., 1990—91; prof. Inst. for Hormone and Fertility Rsch. U. Hamburg, Germany, 1992—97. Adv. coun., GM Cancer Rsch. Found.; Nobel vis. prof. Karolinska Inst., Huddinge, Sweden, 1998, STINT vis. scientist, 1998-99, prof. emeritus, 1999-2001; John and Gladys Strauss chair for cancer rsch. U. Cin., 2002-03, George and Elizabeth Wile chair in cancer rsch. and disting. prof., 2004—; vis. scientist NICHD/NIH, 2001; vis. prof. Max-Planck-Inst. for Biochemie, Munich, 1958; chemotherapy rev. bd. Nat. Cancer Inst., 1960-62, bd. sci. counselors, 1969-72; mem. Nat. Adv. Coun. Child Health and Human Devel., 1976-80; adv. com. biochemistry and chem. carcinogenesis Am. Cancer Soc., 1968-72, coun. for rsch. and clin. investigation, 1974-77; mem. assembly life scis. NRC, 1975-78; com. on sci., engring. and pub. policy Nat. Acad. Scis., 1981-82; rsch. adv. bd. Clin. Rsch. Inst. of Montreal, 1987-96, Klinik for Tumor Biologie, Freiburg, 1993-2002, Strang Cancer Prevention Ctr., 1994-98; cons. Rockefeller U. Hosp., 1990-92; internat. adv. bd. Fundazione Giovanni Lorenzini, Milan, 2001—. Mem. editl. bd. Perspectives in Biology and Medicine, 1966—, Archives of Biochemistry and Biophysics, 1979-84, Biochemistry, 1969-72, Life Scis., 1973-78, Breast Cancer Rsch. and Treatment, 1980—, Endocrine-Related Cancer, 1994-2004, Jour. Biol. Markers, 1998—, Internat. Jour. Oncology, 2004-; assoc. editor: Jour. Steroid Biochemistry, 1974-94; contbr. articles to profl. jours. Recipient D.R. Edwards medal, 1970, La Madonnina prize, 1973, Pap award, 1975, prix Roussel, 1976, Nat. award Am. Cancer Soc., 1976, Gregory Pincus Meml. award, 1978, Gairdner Found. award, 1979, Lucy Wortham James award, 1980, Charles F. Kettering prize, 1980, Golden Plate award, 1980, Nat. Acad. Clin. Biochemistry award, 1981, Scientist of Yr. award Achievement Rewards for Coll. Scientists Found., 1981, Pharmacia award, 1982, Hubert H. Humphrey award, 1983, Rolf Luft medal, 1983, Renzo Grattarola medal, 1984, Fred C. Koch award, 1984, Axel Munthe award, 1985, Humboldt Sr. Rsch. prize, 1992, Joseph Bolivar DeLee award Chgo. Lying-In Hosp., 1995, Brinker Internat. award for breast cancer rsch. Susan G. Komen Found., 2002, Albert Lasker award for Basic Med. Rsch., Albert and Mary Lasker Found., 2004; Thomson Sci. laureate in physiology/medicine, 2006; citations: Ohio State Senate and Ho. Reps., 2004; Guggenheim fellow, 1946-47. Mem. NAS (coun. 1981-84), AAAS (Amory prize 1977), Am. Soc. Biochemistry and Molecular Biology, Am. Chem. Soc., Am. Assn. Cancer Rsch. (G.H.A. Clowes award 1975, Dorothy P. Landon prize 2002), Endocrine Soc. (pres. 1980-81), Am. Gyn/Ob Soc. (hon.), St. Paul Surg. Soc. (hon.), EORTC Receptor and Biomarker Group (hon.), Honorable Order Ky. Cols. Office: U Cin Dept Cell Biology Vontz Ctr Molecular Studies 3125 Eden Ave Cincinnati OH 45267-0521 Office Phone: 513-558-5750. Business E-Mail: elwood.jensen@uc.edu.

JENSEN, ERIC REINHARD, music educator; s. Ernest Anton and Elsa Minna Jensen. B of Music, U. Colo., 1955; MA, U. Denver, 1956; PhD, Mich. State U., 1970. Tchr. choral, music appreciation Shorewood Pub. Schs., 1960—65; chmn. dept. music Coll. Artesia, 1965—68; dean Milton Coll., 1970—73; assoc. dir. Colegio Americano, Monterrey, Mexico, 1973—77; choral condr. Eunice Pub. Schs., 1977—78; v.p. Am. Home Security Life Ins. Co., 1978—81; faculty Nova U., 1990—95; tchr. piano pvt. practice, 2005—; organist/pianist First Christian Ch., Roswell, N.Mex. Arranger, pianist: Marriage of Figaro, Godspell, condr., pianist: Amahl, condr.: Annie, chorus condr.: Fidelio; composer: Chautauqua; condr.: Bye Bye, Birdie, Music Man, Babes in Arms, Li'l Abner, How to Succeed in Business, Major Oratorios-Sacred Choral Literature, Calamity Jane; contbr. articles to profl. jours. Pres. bd. Artesia Literacy Coun. Scholar, U. London, U. Colo. Mem.: Am. Guild Organists (dean 1999), Coun. Grad. Students Mich. State U. (pres. 1969). Avocations: running, bicycling. Home and Office: 703 W Mann Artesia NM 88210 Office Phone: 505-746-4025. Personal E-mail: ejensen@zianet.com.

JENSEN, EVA MARIE, medical/surgical nurse; b. Santa Maria, Calif., Sept. 2, 1956; d. Paul Cabello and Dolores Margaret Gutierrez; m. Royal George Jensen, Mar. 22, 1986 (div. Mar. 15, 1993). AA, Cuesta Coll., Calif., 1977; lic. vocation nurse, Hartnell Coll., Salinas, Calif., 1980. RN Calif., 1982, cert. psychiat. and mental health nurse, Calif., 1995. Nurse Atascadero State Hosp., Calif., 1986—2003, Twin Cities Hosp., Templeton, 1982—86, 2003—. Participant nurses' health study Harvard Med. Sch., Boston, 1992—. Democrat. Roman Catholic.

JENSEN, HANNE MARGRETE, pathologist, educator; b. Copenhagen, Dec. 9, 1935; came to US, 1957; d. Niels Peter Evald and Else Signe Agnete (Rasmussen) Damgaard; m. July 21, 1957 (div. Apr. 1987); children: Peter Albert, Dorte Marie, Gordon Kristian, Sabrina Elisabeth. Student, U. Copenhagen, 1954—57; MD, U. Wash., 1961. Resident and fellow in pathology U. Wash., Seattle, 1963-68; asst. prof. dept. pathology U. Calif. Sch. Medicine, Davis, 1969-79, assoc. prof., 1979—2001, dir. transfusion svc., 1973—, prof., 2001—. McFarlane prof. exptl. medicine U. Glasgow, Scotland, 1983. Fellow Pacific Coast Ob-Gyn. Soc., Coll. Am. Pathologists; mem. No. Calif. Soc. for Electron Microscopy, U.S. and Can. Acad. Pathology, Am. Cancer Soc., Am. Soc. Clin. Pathologists, AAAS, Am. Assn. Blood Banks, Calif. Blood Bank Sys., People to People Internat., Internat. Platform Assn. Office: U Calif Sch Medicine Dept Pathology Davis CA 95616 Office Phone: 530-752-7229. Business E-Mail: hmjensen@ucdavis.edu.

JENSEN, HAROLD LEROY, medical liability insurance administrator, physician; b. Mpls., Aug. 17, 1926; s. Harold Hans and Nell Irene (Cameron) Jensen; m. Nancy Elizabeth Scharff, Sept. 9, 1950 (div. 1976); children: Eric Richard, Kris Ann, Beth Susan; m. Sandra Lee Steinel, Oct. 18, 1976. BS, U. Ill., 1950, MD, 1955. Intern Ill. Ctrl. Hosp., Chgo., 1955-56, resident, 1956-57; pvt. practice in internal medicine Ill., 1957—87; mem. staff Ingalls Meml. Hosp., Harvey, Ill., dir. continuing med. edn., 1979-87, v.p. med. affairs, 1987-2000, cons. med. affairs, 2000—. Asst. clin. prof. medicine U. Ill.; guest lectr. Gov.'s State U., University Park, Ill.; bd. gov. ISMIE Mut. Ins. Co., 1986—. Mem. editl. bd.: Chgo. Healthcare, 1990—93; contbr. articles to profl. jours. Chmn. Med. Polit. Action Com., 1990—92; pres. bd. dirs. Homewood (Ill.) Pub. Libr., 1970—76; mem. policy bd. Cook County Healthcare Summit, 1990; chmn. Met. Chgo. Health Info. Network, 1995—2000. With US Army, 1944—46. Mem.: AMA (del. 1983—95), Ill. Med. Physicians' Svc. Orgn. (bd. dirs. 1995—96), Am. Coll. Utilization Rev. Physicians (bd. dirs. 1985—89, cert.), ACP Execs., Chgo. Health Econ. Coun. (vice chmn. 1981—85), Ill. Med. Soc. (trustee 1983—86, sec., treas. 1986, chmn. bd. trustees 1988—90, treas. 1988—96), Chgo. Med. Soc. (pres. 1985—86), Flossmoor Country Club (pres. 1972—73). Republican. Office: ISMIE Mutual Ins Co 20 N Michigan Ave Chicago IL 60602-4811

JENSEN, HENRIK WANN, computer graphics designer, educator; MSEE, Tech. U., Denmark, 1993, PhD in Computer Sci., 1996. Unix networking specialist Image Scandinavia ApS, 1995—96; rsch. scientist Mental Images, 1996—98; postdoctoral assoc. MIT, Cambridge, 1998—99; rsch. assoc. Stanford U., Calif., 1999—2002; asst. prof. U. Calif. San Diego, 2002—04, assoc. prof., 2004—. Cons. Pixar Animation Studios, 2001. Contbr. articles to profl. publs.; author: Realistic Image Synthesis using Photon Mapping, 2001. Named one of 10 Brilliant, Popular Sci. mag., 2004; recipient Acad. award, Tech. Achievement, Acad. Motion Picture Arts and Scis., 2004; grantee Sloan Found. fellowship, 2004. Mem.: Assn. Computing Machinery Spl. Interest Grp. on Graphics and Interactive Techniques. Avocations: cooking, bicycling, scuba diving, swimming. Office: Computer Graphics Lab U Calif San Diego CSE 4116 9500 Gilman Dr La Jolla CA 92093-0404 E-mail: henrik@cs.ucsd.edu.*

JENSEN, J. ALAN, lawyer; b. Cedar Falls, Iowa, July 27, 1938; BA, Carleton Coll., 1960; LLB, U. Mich., 1963; LLM in Taxation, NYU, 1967. Bar: Minn. 1963, Calif. 1968, Oreg. 1972. Ptnr. Holland & Knight, LLP, Portland, Oreg. Asst. prof. Lewis and Clark Law Sch., 1970—73, assoc. prof., 1973—74, prof. law, 1974—76, adj. prof. law, 1977, 89, 1999—2001. Mem. planned giving com. Oreg. Humane Soc.; gen. counsel Portland Marathon; bd. dirs., treas. Sister City Assn. Ulsan, Republic of Korea. Named one of Top 100 Attys., Worth mag., 2006. Fellow: Am. Coll. Trust and Estate Counsel; mem.: Oreg. State Bar Assn., Estate Planning Coun. Portland, Calif. State Bar Assn., ABA (mem. tax sect., mem. estate and gift tax com., mem. partnership com., chair subcommittee on life ins.). Office: Holland & Knight LLP 2300 US Bancorp Tower 111 SW 5th Ave Portland OR 97204 Office Phone: 503-243-5867. E-mail: alan.jensen@hklaw.com.*

JENSEN, JESSICA, lawyer; b. Toronto, Ont., Can., Sept. 23, 1974; BA, Univ. Wash., Seattle, 1996; JD, Univ. Wash., 1999. Bar: Wash. 1999. Atty., litig., comml. bus. practice area Ogden, Murphy & Wallace, P.L.L.C., Seattle. Contbr. articles to numerous profl. jours. Named Wash. Rising Star, SuperLawyer Mag., 2006. Mem.: ABA, Wash. State Trial Lawyers Assn., King Co. Bar Assn., Wash. State Bar Assn. Office: Oden Murphy Wallace PLLC Ste 2100 1601 Fifth Ave Seattle WA 98101-1686*

JENSEN, JILL SUSAN, music educator; b. Milw., Aug. 14, 1956; d. Joan and James Jensen. BS Music Edn., U. Wis. Madison, 1979. Cert. Tchr. K-12 Music Edn. Wis., 1980. Music educator Appleton Sch. Dist., Wis., 1980—87, Cudahy Mid. Sch., Wis., 1990—96, Inter-Am. Acad., Guayaquil, Ecuador, 1996—98, Nichols Sch., Monona, Wis., 2003—. Named Tchr. of Yr., Cudahy Sch. Dist., 1995. Office: Nichols School 100 Nichols Road Monona WI 53713 Home Phone: 608-442-9715. E-mail: jill_jensen@mononagrove.org.

JENSEN, JOHN ROBERT, lawyer; b. Rapid City, SD, Aug. 9, 1946; s. Edwin Robert and Roxina Althier (Hollinger) J.; m. Susan McClelland, Aug. 27, 1977; children: Margaret Marie, Jennifer Jo, Edwin Robert II, James Peder. BA, Calif. State U., Northridge, 1971; JD, Baylor U., 1976. Bar: Tex. 1977, U.S. Dist. Ct. (no. dist.) Tex. 1977. Asst. ins. dir. Groesbeck Fin., LA, 1971-73; v.p. Capital Cons., Dallas, 1973-74; assoc. McConnell & Assocs., Arlington, Tex., 1977; sole practice Arlington, Tex., 1984—. Author: Checklist for Texas Lawyers, 1979, 2d edit., 1981. Served with U.S. Army, 1966-68, Vietnam. Decorated Army Commedation medal. Mem.: Tex. Bd. Legal Specialization (cert. personal injury trial law), Baylor Order Barristers, Arlington Bar Assn., Delta Theta Phi (treas. Baylor chpt. 1976). Lutheran. Office: Jensen & Jensen 6025 Interstate 20 W Arlington TX 76017-1077 Office Phone: 817-478-4940.

JENSEN, JUDY DIANNE, psychotherapist, consultant; b. Portland, Oreg., Apr. 8, 1948; d. Clarence Melvin and Charlene Augusta (Young) J.; m. Frank George Cooper, Sept 4, 1983; stepchildren: Pamela Cooper, Brian Cooper. BA in Sociology and Anthropology with honors, Oberlin Coll., 1970; MSW, U. Pitts., 1972; postgrad., U. Wis., 1977. Lic. clin. social worker, marriage and family therapist, Oreg. Social worker Day Hosp. Western Psychiat. Inst. and Clinic, Pitts., 1972-73, South Hills Child Guidance Ctr., Pitts., 1973-74; mem. drug treatment program Umatilla County Mental Health Clinic, Pendleton, Oreg., 1975-77; social worker Children's Services Div. State of Oreg., Pendleton, 1978-80, therapist intensive family services project, 1980—2001, dir. intensive family services project, 1986—2001; pvt. practice Pendleton, 1980—2004, Sandy, Oreg., 2004—; founder Cherryville Heartsongs LLC, 2004—. NIMH grantee, 1970-72; NDEA fellow 1977; Gen. Motors scholar Oberlin Coll., 1966-70 Mem. Am. Assn. Marriage and Family Therapists (clin.), Nat. Assn. Social Workers. Avocations: photography, personal jour. and poetry writing, hiking, dog and miniature horse training. Home: 53755 E Terra Fern Dr Sandy OR 97055 Office: 57355 E Terra Fern Dr Sandy OR 97055 E-mail: aeriejjj@aol.com.

JENSEN, KATHRYN PATRICIA (KIT), broadcast executive; b. Fairbanks, Alaska, June 20, 1950; d. Edward Leroy and Doris Patricia (Fee) Bigelow; 1 child, Alexander Morgan. BA, U. Alaska, 1974. Sta. mgr., program dir. Sta. KUAC-FM, U. Alaska, Fairbanks, 1976-82; gen. mgr. Sta. KUAC-FM-TV, U. Alaska, Fairbanks, 1982-87; pres., gen. mgr. Sta. WCPN-FM, 1987—2001; COO Stas. WVIZ/PBS and 90.3 WCPN Ideastream, Cleve., 2001—. Founding mem. Alaska Pub. Radio Network, 1978-85; bd. dirs. Nat. Pub. Radio, 1983-89, Pub. Radio Internat., 1997—; mentor Civic Innovation Lab, 2007; bd. dirs. Parkworks, 2007. Bd. dirs. United Way, Cleve., 2001—04. Recipient Elaine B. Mitchell award Alaska Pub. Radio Network, 1988, Oebie award, 1992, 95, William H. Kling Innovation and Entrepreneurship award Pub. Radio Internat., 1995, Leadership in Non-profit Mgmt. award Case We. Res. U., Mandel Ctr. Non-Profit Orgns., 1999, No. Ohio Live Rainmakers award, 2002, Cleve. Preservation award, 2006, Arts Prize Cleve. award, 2006; named Pub. Radio Gen. Mgr. of Yr., DEI/PRADO, 1999. Episcopalian. Avocations: reading, gardening. Office: Stas WVIZ & WCPN Ideastream 1375 Euclid Ave Cleveland OH 44115 Office Phone: 216-916-6100.

JENSEN, LESLIE DWIGHT, curator; b. Cin., Feb. 8, 1949; s. Alfred August and Clara Schanner Jensen; m. Juanita Mary Leisch, Feb. 14, 2003. BA in History, Roanoke Coll., Salem, Va., 1971. Curator collections Mus. of Confederacy, Richmond, Va., 1973—91; pvt. practice historian, conservator Williamsburg, Va., 1981—82; curator US Army Transp. Mus., Ft. Eustis, Va., 1982—84; dir. 2d Armored Divsn. Mus., Ft. Hood, Tex., 1984—87, Old Guard Mus., Ft. Myers, Va., 1987—90; curator, chief collections br. US Army Ctr. Mil. History, Washington, 1990—2002; curator arms and armor West Point Mus., NY, 2002—. Drummer, sgt. maj. Colonial Williamsburg Fife and Drum, 1962—66. Author: 32d Virginia Infantry, 1990, Echoes of Glory, 1991. Fellow, Summer Inst., Mus. Early So. Decorative Arts. Mem.: Fed. Interagy. Collections Working Group, Co. Mil. Historians (v.p. publs. 2000—06, pres. 2006—), Armor and Arms Club (sec.). Avocations: southern decorative arts, antiques, historical costumes. Office: West Point Mus 2110 New South Port Rd West Point NY 10996

JENSEN, LYNN EDWARD, retired medical association administrator, economist; b. Rock Springs, Wyo., May 27, 1945; s. Glen and Helen (Anderson) J.; m. Carol Jean Lombard, June 10, 1967 (dec. Dec. 2001); children: Chelsea, Kara; m. Janet Gayle Clash, Jan 24, 2004. BA, Idaho State U., 1967; PhD, U. Utah, 1979. Rsch. assoc. Dept. Commerce, Washington, 1967, U. Utah, 1971-74, Utah State Planning Office, 1971-74; economist AMA Rsch. Ctr., Chgo., 1974-75, dir., 1975-85; v.p. health policy AMA, Chgo., 1985-96, group v.p. strategic mgmt. and devel., 1996-97, COO, 1997-2000, interim exec. v.p., 1998, ret., 2000. Mem. Robert Wood Johnson Found. Adv. Com., Princeton, N.J., 1983-84, Johnson & Johnson Cmty. Health Program, 1985-88; health adv. com. GAO. Editor-in-chief Intermountain Econ. Rev., 1972-73; assoc. editor Jour. Bus. and Econ. Stats., 1981-85; contbr. articles to profl. jours. With U.S. Army, 1968-70. Mem. AMA, Assn. Am. Med. Soc. Execs., Am. Soc. Assn. Execs., Am. Econ. Assn., Nat. Assn. Bus. Economists. Presbyterian. Avocations: reading, computers, swimming, photography, bicycling. Home: 1310 W Francis Dr Arlington Heights IL 60005-2210 Personal E-mail: lejensen@comcast.net.

JENSEN, MARGARET, real estate broker; b. Payson, Utah, Aug. 12, 1948; d. Basil D. Broadbent and V. Merlene Ellsworth; m. Don E. Jensen, Sept. 27, 1997; children: Chad, Troy, Kristin, Dean, Debbie, Sean, Julie. AS, Casper Coll., Wyo., 1968; BS with distinction, Colo. State U., Ft. Collins, 1989, postgrad., 1990. Grad. Realtor Inst., CRB, CRS, EMT. Clk. Colo. 8th Jud. Dept., Loveland; owner, CEO Lil Rascals, Ft. Collins, 1980-96; real estate salesperson Hometown Advantage, Loveland, 1996, Century 21, Ft. Collins, 1996; pres. Home Sweet Home Realty, Inc., Ft. Collins, 1997—; owner Home Sweet Home Bakery, Inc., Home Sweet Home Knitted Creations, Inc. Rental cons. Ft. Collins, 1985-99; tax cons., Ft. Collins, 1975-90; family cons. Ft. Collins, 1990-97; profl. pet groomer. Instr. ARC, Ft. Collins, 1975-85; tax preparer for VITA IRS, Ft. Collins, 1975-90; supr. trip to Russia People to People, 1990. Finalist Miss Am. Pageant, 1968; named Grand Champion Baking Divsn., Larimer County Fair, 2005. Mem. Lions Club Internat., Mortar Bd., Golden Key Nat. Honor Soc., Colo. Assn. of Realtors, Nat. Assn. of Realtors, Omicron Nu, Alpha Gamma Delta, Phi Kappa Phi. Avocations: piano, baking. Home and Office: 2205 Stonecrest Dr Fort Collins CO 80521-1318 Office Phone: 970-227-7884. Personal E-mail: buycolorado@aol.com.

JENSEN, MARK A., lawyer; BA summa cum laude, Ind. Univ., 1994; JD cum laude, Harvard Univ., 1997. Bar: Ill. 1998, D.C. 1999, US Dist. Ct. No. Ill. 1998, US Dist. Ct. So. Ind. 1999, US Ct. Appeals, 7th Cir. 1999. Law clk. Chief Judge Sarah Evans Baker, US Dist. Ct. So. Ind.; ptnr., Spec. Matters & Govt. Investigations, hiring ptnr. Washington King & Spalding LLP, Washington. Office: King & Spalding LLP 1700 Pennsylvania Ave NW Washington DC 20006 Office Phone: 202-626-5526. Office Fax: 202-626-3737. Business E-Mail: mjensen@kslaw.com.

JENSEN, MARVIN ELI, retired agricultural engineer, science administrator; b. Clay County, Minn., Dec. 23, 1926; s. John M. and Inga C. (Haugness) J.; m. Doris A. Lundberg, Sept. 4, 1947; children: Connie, Jeffrey, Eric. BS in Agr., N.D. State U., 1951, MS in Agrl. Engring., 1952, DSc (hon.), 1988; PhD in Civil Engring., Colo. State U., 1965. Instr., asst. prof. N.D. State U., Fargo, 1952-55; agrl. engr. Soil and Water Rsch. divsn. USDA, Bushland, Tex., 1955-58, head irrigation and drain sect. Ft. Collins, Colo., 1959-61, investigation leader Ft. Collins and Kimberly, Idaho, 1961-68; dir. Snake River Conservation Rsch. Ctr. Agrl. Rsch. Service USDA, Kimberly, 1969-78, nat. program leader Ft. Collins and Beltsville, Md., 1979-87; dir. Colo. Inst. for Irrigation Mgmt. Colo. State U., Ft. Collins, 1987—92; ret. Pres. Internat. Commn. Irrigation and Drainage, New Delhi, 1984-87. Editor: (monograph) Design and Operation of Farm Irrigation Systems, 1980; sr. editor: (manual) Evapotranspiration and Irrigation Water Requirements, 1990. Recipient Disting. Svc. award USDA, 1983, W.E. Morgan Alumni Achievement award, 1990, Disting. Svc. award Colo. State U., 1994; named to USDA-ARS Sci. Hall of Fame, 2000. Fellow Am. Soc. Agrl. Engrs. (tech. v.p. 1983-86, John Deere Gold medal 1982); mem. NAE, ASCE (hon., chmn. irrigation and drainage div. 1976-77, Tipton award 1982, Arid Lands Hydraulic Engring. award 1990, State-of-the-Art award, 1992, Lifetime Achievement award 2007). Avocations: golf, photography.

JENSEN, MICHAEL ALLEN, engineering educator; b. Fullerton, Calif., Mar. 27, 1966; s. Paul Allen and Dorothy Carolyn Jensen; m. Angela Evans, June 28, 1991; children: Kamber Nicole, Paige Natalie, Matthew Allen, Andrew Michael. BSEE, Brigham Young U., 1990, MSEE, 1991; PhD, U. Calif., Los Angeles, 1994. Asst. prof. Brigham Young U., Provo, Utah, 1994—2000; v.p. AJ Design Group, Inc., Provo, Utah, 1999—; sr. scientist Wavetronix, LLC, Lindon, Utah, 2000—; assoc. prof. Brigham Young U., 2000—05; pres. RFWare, LLC, Springville, Utah, 2004—; prof. Brigham Young U., 2005—, chair, dept. elec. and computer engring., 2006—. Bd. mem. Wavetronix, LLC, Lindon, 2000—. Contbr. articles to profl. jours., chapters to books. Recipient Karl G. Maeser Rsch. and Creative Arts award, Brigham Young U., 2005, Cert. of Achievement, NASA, 1994; Rsch. award, NSF, 1999—, US Dept. Def., 2000—. Mem.: IEEE (adminstrv. com. mem. 2005—). Lds Ch. Achievements include patents for radar technology for traffic monitoring; patents pending for multi-antenna communications technology; research in multi-antenna communications systems. Office: Brigham Young U 459 Clyde Bldg Provo UT 84602 Office Phone: 801-422-5736.

JENSEN, MICHAEL CHARLES, journalist, lecturer, author; s. Stanley Charles and Billie Jane (Cooke) J.; m. Jane Rice Woodruff, July 23, 1960; children: Heidi, Michael Charles Jr. AB, Harvard U., 1956; MS, Boston U., 1961. Reporter Boston Herald-Traveler, 1960-63, exec. fin. editor, 1963-64; reporter, editor N.Y. Times, NYC, 1970-78; chief. fin. corr. NBC Nightly News, Today program, NYC, 1978-2000. Lectr. in field. Author: The Financiers, 1976; contbg. author: Corporations and Their Critics, 1980; contbr.: articles to Saturday Rev., Harvard Bus. Rev. Served to lt. (j.g.) USNR, 1957-60. Recipient Page One award Newspaper Guild N.Y., 1973, Deadline Club award N.Y.C., 1976, media awards for econ. understanding, 1980, Janus awards for excellence in fin. broadcasting, 1981, 88, Best News Documentary award San Francisco Film Festival, 1984, Gabriel awards, 1988, 89, 93, Disting. Alumnus award Boston U., 1989, Nat. News Emmy, 1993; named best econs. and bus. corr. in Am., TV Guide, 1988; named Luminary, 1999. Mem. Am. Soc. Bus. Press Editors (pres. N.Y. chpt. 1965-66). E-mail: mikejensencom@aol.com.

JENSEN, NANCY DAGGETT, music educator; b. LA, Sept. 10, 1942; d. Daniel Thomas and Louise Helen (Kuljian) Daggett; m. Sven Oxfeldt Jensen, Nov. 19, 1978; children: Lori, Brian. BA, San Jose State U., Calif., 1964, MA, 1967. Cert. master tchr. in music. Pvt. piano tchr., Los Altos, Calif., 1967—. Mem. Music Tchrs. Assn. of Calif. (pres. 1972-74, 82-83, 85-86, 93-94, state chmn. cert. of merit 1974-79), Calif. Assn. of Profl. Music Tchrs., Steinway Soc. (bd. dirs.). Personal E-mail: nanchopin@sbcglobal.net.

JENSEN, PAUL ALLEN, mechanical engineer; b. Chgo., Aug. 27, 1936; BS, U. Ill., 1959; MS, U. Pitts., 1963; PhD in Ops. Rsch. and Indsl. Engring., Johns Hopkins U., 1967. Engr. surface div. Westinghouse Electric Corp., 1959-63, from asst. prof. to assoc. prof., 1967-73; prof. indsl. engring. ops. rsch. U. Tex., Austin, 1973—, Cullen prof. of mech. engring., 1991. Mem. Inst. Ops. Rsch. and Mgmt. Sci. Office: U Tex Dept Mech Engring Austin TX 78712-1063

JENSEN, REUBEN ROLLAND, former automotive company executive; b. Ainsworth, Nebr., Dec. 22, 1921; s. Jens Christian and Amy Caroline (Boyer) J.; m. Janet A. McCann, Oct. 19, 1974; children: Shannon (Mrs. Roger Santora), Bruce. Student, U. Nebr., 1938-41. With Gen. Motors Corp., Detroit, 1946, jr. engr. Hydra-Matic div., 1965-67, gen. mgr. Hydra-Matic div., 1967-70, gen. mgr. Allison div., 1970-72, v.p., group exec., 1972-74, exec. v.p., 1974-84. Mem. adv. bd. Chem. Bank Internat., 1973-86. Served with USNR, 1943-45. Recipient Silver Beaver, Disting. Eagle, Silver Buffalo, Boy Scouts Am., 1973 Mem. Assn. U.S. Army, Navy League U.S., Am. Ordnance Assn., Quail Ridge Country Club (Boynton Beach, Fla.), Meadowbrook Country Club (Northville, Mich.), Masons. Home: 3609 Chinaberry Ter Boynton Beach FL 33436-4528 also: 14016 Eaton Dr Plymouth MI 48170

JENSEN, RICHARD DENNIS, librarian; b. Payson, Utah, Oct. 20, 1944; s. Ruel Whiting and Ethel Josepha (Otte) J.; m. Maxine Swasey, Apr. 21, 1966; children: Shaun, Craig, Todd, Jana, Brad, Kristine, April, Lynne. BS in Zoology, Brigham Young U., 1971, MLS, 1976. From asst. sci. libr. to pub. svc. coord. Brigham Young U., Provo, Utah, 1971—2001, reference svc. coord., 2001—03, life sci. libr., 2003—, chair dept. sci./maps, 2004—. Co-author: Agricultural and Animal Sciences Journals and Serials: An Analytical Guide, 1986, (indexes) Great Basin Naturalist, 50 Year Index, 1991, BYU Geology Studies, Cumulative Index, vol. 1-37, 1954-1991, 1992. Mem. Lds Ch. Avocations: farming, sports, camping. Office: Brigham Young U Libr Sci & Maps Dept 2324 HBLL Provo UT 84602-2734 Home Phone: 801-375-1253; Office Phone: 801-422-6012. Business E-Mail: Richard_Jensen@byu.edu.

JENSEN, RICHARD JORG, biologist, educator; b. Sandusky, Ohio, Jan. 17, 1947; s. Aksel Carl and Margaret (Wolfe) Jensen; m. Faye Robertson, May 30, 1970. BS, Austin Peay State U., 1970, MS, 1972; PhD, Miami U., 1975. Asst. prof. Wright State U., 1975-79; prof. St. Mary's Coll., 1979—. Guest prof. U. Notre Dame, Ind., 1981—, dir. Greene-Nieuwland Herbarium, 1988—; sr. rsch. fellow Ctr. field Biology, Austin Peay State U., 1986—88; vis. scholar dept. botany Miami U., 1987; panelist systematic biology program NSF, 1983—87; exec. com. Am. Midland Maturalist, 1990—. Assoc. editor: Am. Midland Naturalist, 1989—2004; mem. editl. bd. Plant Systematics and Evolution, 1990—96; assoc. editor: Systematic Botany, 1996—2000. Named to Acad. Hall of Fame, Austin Peay State U., 1998; grantee, NSF, 1973, 1979, 1985, 1987, 1995, Rsch. Corp., 1984, Eli Lilly, 1990. Fellow: Ind. Acad. Sci. (co-chair program com. 1988, fellow com., biol. survey com., publ. com., grantee 1983, 1991); mem.: Internat. Oak Soc. (bd. dirs. 1997—, membership chair 1997—, webmaster 2000—06, Spl. Svc. award 2006), Soc. Systematic Biology, Internat. Assn. Plant Taxonomy, Bot. Soc. Am., Am. Soc. Plant Taxonomists (rsch. com. 1987—90, chmn. 1989—90, treas. 1991—96, honors and awards com. 2000—02, coun. mem. at large 2000—03, chair 2001, pres.-elect 2004, pres. 2005, past pres. 2006, Disting. Svc. award 1996), Sigma Xi (grantee 1974). Democrat. Avocations: reading, computing, genealogy. Home: 2044 Carrbridge Ct South Bend IN 46614-3514 Office: St Mary's Coll Dept Biology Notre Dame IN 46556 also: Greene-Nieuwland Herbarium Univ of Notre Dame Dept Biol Scis Notre Dame IN 46556 Office Phone: 574-284-4674. Business E-Mail: rjensen@saintmarys.edu.

JENSEN, ROBERT NEAL, lawyer; b. Elizabeth, NJ, Jan. 5, 1947; s. Christian M. and Marion (Schou) J.; m. Martha Arlene FitzGerald, Sept. 29, 1973; children: Halden F., Katharine M. AB, Dartmouth Coll., 1969; JD, Yale U., 1972. Bar: NJ 1972, DC 1974. Atty. Judge Adv. Gens. Corps USNR, Wash., 1973-74; mil. asst. Office of Sec. of Def., Washington, 1974-76; ptnr. Peabody, Lambert & Meyers, Washington, 1976-84, McDermott, Will & Emery, Washington, 1984—. Author mag. column, 1985-87; contbr. articles to profl. jours. Lt. USN, 1973—76. Mem. Phi Beta Kappa. Office: McDermott Will & Emery LLP 600 13th St N W Washington DC 20005 Office Phone: 202-756-8023. Office Fax: 202-756-8087. Business E-Mail: rjensen@mwe.com.

JENSEN, SAM, lawyer; b. Blair, Nebr., Oct. 30, 1935; s. Soren K. and Frances (Beck) J.; m. Marilyn Heck, June 28, 1959 (div. Jan. 1987); children: Soren R., Eric, Dana; m. Carmen Patton, Apr. 7, 1990. BA, U. Nebr., 1957, JD, 1961. Bar: Nebr. 1961. With Smith Bros., Lexington, Nebr., 1961-63, Swarr, May, Smith and Andersen, Omaha, 1963-83, Erickson & Sederstrom, P.C., Omaha, 1983—2005, Berens and Tate, P.C., L.L.O., Omaha, 2005—. Chmn. bd. dirs., v.p. bd. dirs. Omaha Public Power Dist., 1979-81; chmn. Nebr. Coordinating Commn. for Postsecondary Edn., 1976-78. Del. Nat. Rep. Conv., 1960, mem. Nebr. Rep. Ctrl. Com., 1968-70; mem. Regents Commn. Urban U., U. Nebr., Omaha, chmn. Task Force on Higher Edn.; mem. Hwy Commn. State of Nebr., 1989-95; vice chmn. Opera Omaha, 1992-95, v.p., 1994-96. Recipient Disting. Service award U. Nebr., 1981 Mem. Omaha Bar Assn. (past exec. com.), Nebr. Bar Assn. (chmn. com. public relations 1973-76), Am. Bar Assn., U. Nebr. Alumni Assn. (pres. 1976-78), Rotary Club, Omaha Club, Beta Theta Pi, Phi Delta Phi. Clubs: Rotary, Omaha, Racquet. Office: Berens and Tate PC LLO 10050 Regency Cir Ste 400 Omaha NE 68114 Home Phone: 402-963-9715; Office Phone: 402-391-1991. Personal E-mail: samjensen@cox.net. Business E-Mail: samj@berenstate.com.

JENSEN, THOMAS C., lawyer; b. Pasadena, Calif., 1958; BA, U. So. Calif., 1980; JD, Lewis & Clark Coll., Portland, Oreg., 1983. Bar: Oreg. 1984, DC 1998. Dep. exec. sec. US-Can. Pacific Salmon Commn., 1987—89; majority counsel US Senate Com. on Energy and Natural Resources, Subcom. on Water and Power, 1989—92; exec. dir. Grand Canyon Trust, 1992—95; assoc. dir. natural resources White House Coun. on Environ. Quality, 1995—97; of counsel to ptnr. Troutman Sanders LLP, Washington, 1997—2004, head environ. and natural resources practice; ptnr., environ. & energy group Sonnenschein Nath & Rosenthal LLP, Washington, 2004—. Chair Nat. Environ. Conflict Resolution Adv. Com. US Inst. for Environ. Conflict Resolution, 2002—; mem. leadership coun. Pew Inst. for Oceans Sci. Trustee William D. Ruckelshaus Inst. for Environment and Natural Resources U. Wyo. Named Disting. Environ. Law Grad., Lewis & Clark Coll. Office: Sonnenschein Nath & Rosenthal LLP Ste 600, E Tower 1301 K St NW Washington DC 20005 Office Phone: 202-408-3956. Office Fax: 202-408-6399. Business E-Mail: tjensen@sonnenschein.com.

JENSEN, WALTER EDWARD, retired lawyer, educator; b. Chgo., Oct. 20, 1937. AB, U. Colo., 1959; JD, Ind. U., 1962, MBA, 1964; PhD (Univ. fellow), Duke U., 1972. Bar: Ind. 1962, Ill. 1962, DC 1963, US Tax Ct. 1982, US Supreme Ct. 1967. Asst. prof. bus. law U. Colo., Boulder, 1958-62; assoc. prof. Colo. State U., 1964-66, U. Conn., Storrs, 1966-67, Ill. State U., 1970-72; prof. bus. adminstrn. Va. Poly. Inst. and State U., from 1972, prof. fin., ins. and law, 1972-2005, prof. emeritus, 2005—; with Inst. Advanced Legal Studies, U. London, 1983-84; ret.; prof. US Air Force Grad. Mgmt. Program, Europe, 1977-78, 83-85; Duke U. legal rsch. awardee, rschr., Guyana, Trinidad and Tobago, 1967; vis. lectr. pub. internat. law U. Istanbul, 1988, Roberts Coll. U. Bosporous, Istanbul, Uludag U., Turkey, 1988; rschr. U. London Inst. Advanced Legal Studies, London Sch. Econs. and Inst. Commonwealth Studies, 1969, 71-74, 76; Ford Found. Rsch. fellow Ind. U., 1963-64; faculty rsch. fellow in econs. U. Tex., 1968; Bell Telephone fellow in econs. regulated pub. utilities U. Chgo., 1965. Recipient Dissertation Travel award Duke U. Grad. Sch., 1968; Ind. U. fellow, 1963, 74, scholar, 1963-64. Mem. DC Bar Assn., Ill. Bar Assn., Ind. Bar Assn., ABA, Am. Polit. sci. Assn., Am. Soc. Internat. Law, Am. Judicature Soc., Am. Bus. Law Assn., Alpha Kappa Psi, Phi Alpha Delta, Pi Gamma Mu, Pi Kappa Alpha, Beta Gamma Sigma. Contbr. articles to profl. publs.; staff editor Am. Bus Law Jour., 1973—; vice chmn. assoc. editor for adminstrv. law sect. young lawyers Barrister (Law Notes), 1975-83, ABA Jour.; book rev. and manuscript editor Justice System Jour: A Mgmt. Rev., 1975—; staff editor Bus. Law Rev., 1975—. Home: 3358 Glade Creek Blvd Apt 5 Roanoke VA 24012 Office: Va Poly Inst and State U Blacksburg VA 24060

JENSH, RONALD PAUL, retired anatomist; b. NYC, June 14, 1938; s. Werner G. and Dorothy (Hensle) J.; m. Ruth Eleanor Dobson, Aug. 18, 1962; children: Victoria Lynn, Elizabeth Whitney BA, Bucknell U., 1960, MA, 1962; PhD, Jefferson Med. Coll., 1966. From instr. anatomy to prof. Thomas Jefferson U., Phila., 1966—68, prof. anatomy, 1982—2004, course coord. histology, 1988—2004, emeritus, 2004—. Staff Op. Concern Inc., Cherry Hill, N.J., 1970-72; cons. reproductive biology Bio-Search Inc., Argus Rsch. Lab. Inc., Ortho Rsch. Found. Contbr. articles to sci. jours. Task force com. on comm. S. Jersey Methodist Conf., 1974-80; chmn. Learning Resources Ctr., Haddonfield United Meth. Ch., NJ, 1976-79. Recipient Christian R. and Mary F. Lindback Found. Disting. Teaching award, 1978, Disting. Alumnus award, 1985, Faculty Achievement award Burlington Northern Found., 1989, Jefferson Med. Coll. Portrait, 1994, Award for Disting. Alumnus in a Chosen Profession, Bucknell U., 1997. Mem. AAAS, Am. Soc. Zoologists, N.Y. Acad. Scis., Teratology Soc. (treas. 1989-92), Behavioral Teratology Soc. (pres. 1985-86), Am. Assn. Anatomists, Soc. Am. Mus. Natural History, Inst. Social Ethics and Life Scis., Jefferson Med. Coll. Alumni Assn. (hon. life), Phi Beta Kappa, Sigma Xi, Psi Chi, Phi Sigma. Home: 230 E Park Ave Haddonfield NJ 08033-1835 Personal E-mail: histdoc@verizon.net.

JENSON, JON EBERDT, metal products executive; b. Madison, Wis., Aug. 1934; s. Theodore Joel and Gertrude Beatrice (Eberdt) J.; m. Jeannette Marie Hasman, May 1, 1976; children: James, Peter. BS, U. Wis., 1956; postgrad., Goethe U., Frankfort, Germany, 1956; diploma, U. Cologne, West Germany, 1957. From staff rep. to dir. mktg. and tech. svcs. Forging Industry Assn., Cleve., 1959-75; exec. v.p., sec. Am. Metal Stamping Assn., Cleve., 1975-80; pres. Precision Metalforming Assn., Independence, Ohio, 1980-2000, pres. emeritus, 2000—; interim dir. Precision Machined Products Assn., Brecksville, Ohio, 2001—02. Exec. dir., sec. Forging Industry Ednl. and Rsch. Found., Cleve., 1967-75; lectr. NYU, 1973-75; Ohio bd. advisors Liberty Mut. Ins. Co. Author: Forging Industry Handbook, 1966; editor: Metal Forming mag., 1975-90, pub. 1990-2000. Bd. regents Insts. Orgn. Mgmt., U.S. C. of C., 1977-83, vice chmn., 1982, chmn., 1983; mem. bd. regents Marycrest Sch., Independence, Ohio, 1979-86; bd. dirs. Cleve. Conv. and Visitors Bur., 1988; chmn. Consuming Industries Trade Action Coalition, 1999-; mem. U.S. adv. trade com. With USNR, 1958-59. Rotary Internat. fellow, 1956 Mem. Am. Soc. Assn. Execs. (cert. assn. exec.), Cleve. Soc. Assn. Execs., Rockwell Springs Trout Club. Home: 5700 Brookside Rd Cleveland OH 44131-6013 E-mail: jjenson@pma.org.

JENSON, WILLIAM G., federal agency administrator; b. Hartford, Conn. BA in History, Hobart Coll., 1970; JD, Suffolk U., 1975. Bar: Mass. 1975. Atty. Office Gen. Counsel USDA, Washington, 1976-96, jud. officer, 1996—. Instr. USDA, 1980—, mem. grad. sch.'s paralegal com., 1987. Mil. intelligence specialist1970 US Army, 1970—72, Vietnam. Mem.: ABA (vice chairperson adminstrv. law and regulatory practice-agr. sect. 1996—), Mass. Bar Assn. Office: Dept Agr Office Jud Officer S Bldg Rm 1449 Washington DC 20250-0001 E-mail: william.jenson@usda.gov.

JENSSEN, WARREN DONALD, microbiologist, consultant; b. Woodbridge, NJ, Aug. 23, 1942; s. Joseph and Lillian (Anderson) J.; m. Donna M. Larson; children: Kirsten E., Erik C. BA, Rutgers U., 1965, PhD, 1970; MS, Purdue U., 1966. Diplomate Am. Acad. Microbiology, Am. Bd. Bioanalysis. Tchg. fellow Purdue U., W. Lafayette, Ind., 1965-66; rsch. fellow Rutgers U., New Brunswick, N.J., 1966-70; postdoctoral fellow Rutgers Med. Sch., New Brunswick, N.J., 1983-84; rsch. fellow Robert Wood Johnson Med. Sch., 1984-87; adj. prof. Union County Coll., Cranford, N.J., 1969-70, asst. prof., 1970-74, assoc. prof., 1974-79, prof., 1979-85, sr. prof., 1985—; adj. prof. Kean Coll., Union, N.J., 1972-75. Clin. microbiology cons. JFK Med. Ctr., Edison, N.J., 1973-76, Raritan Bay Med. Ctr., Perth Amboy, N.J., 1976-98, VA Med. Ctr., Lyons, N.J., 1989-96; dir. health svcs. lab. Union County Coll., 1974-82; dir. Union County Pub. Health Lab., 1977-82; pub. health bacteriologist N.J. Dept. Environ. Protection, 1973—; assoc. med. staff Raritan Bay Med. Ctr., 1985—; clin. lab. dir. N.J. Bd. Med. Examiners, 1985—; adj. clin. instr. Robert Wood Johnson Med. Sch., 1985-91; adj. prof. biomed. careers program Univ. Medicine and Dentistry of N.J., 1999—2002; recycling coord., Califon, 1988-92, Hunterdon County Health Adv. Com., 1985-88, Hunterdon County Mcpl. Officers Assn., 1987-89. Contbr. articles to profl. jours. Den leader, asst. scoutmaster Boy Scouts Am., Califon, N.J., 1980-84; vice chmn. Bd. Health, Califon, 1983-89; mem. Environ. Comm., Califon, 1985-89. Mem. Theobald Smith Soc., Am. Soc. Microbiology, N.J. Link for Microbiology (program chair 1983-85), AAUP (exec. bd. 1973-98). Achievements include antibiotic action on membrane-associated polyribosomes of Streptococcus faecalis, photoinduction of sporulation in Trichoderma viride, computerized compilation of antimicrobial susceptibility data, fatal septicemia due to CDC-DF2 in a splenectomized patient, a novel insertion of a resistance transposon in methicillin-resistant Staphylococcus aureus, prevalence of MLS resistance and erm gene classes among clinical strains of staphylococci and streptococci, molecular epidemiology of MLS resistance in staphylococcus aureus and coagulase-negative staphylococci. Home: 83 River Rd Califon NJ 07830-4371 Office: Union County Coll 1033 Springfield Ave Cranford NJ 07016-1528 Office Phone: 908-709-7562. Business E-Mail: jenssen@ucc.edu.

JENTZ, GAYLORD ADAIR, law educator; b. Beloit, Wis., Aug. 7, 1931; s. Merlyn Adair and Delva (Mullen) Jentz; m. JoAnn Mary Hornung, Aug. 6, 1955; children: Katherine Ann, Gary Adair, Loretta Ann, Rory Adair. BA, U. Wis., 1953, JD, 1957, MBA, 1958. Bar: Wis. 1957. Pvt. practice law, Madison, 1957-58; from asst. prof. to assoc. prof. bus. law U. Okla., 1958-65; assoc. prof. U. Tex., Austin, 1965-68, prof., 1968-98, Herbert D. Kelleher prof. bus. law, 1982-98, prof. emeritus, 1998—, chmn. gen. bus. dept., 1968-74, 80-86. From vis. instr. to vis. prof. U. Wis. Law Sch., Wis., 1957—65. Author (with others): Texas Uniform Commercial Code, 1967; author: rev. edit., 1975; author: (with others) Business Law Text and Cases, 1968, Business Law Text, 1978, Legal Environment of Business, 1989, Texas Family Law, 7th edit., 1992, Business Law Today-Alternate Essentials Edition, 4th edit., 1997, Fundamentals of Business Law, 7th edit., 2007, Fundamentals of Business Law, Excerpted Cases, 2007, West's Business Law: Alternate Edition, 10th edit., 2007, West's Business Law: Text and Cases, 10th edit., 2006, Law for E-Commerce, 2002, West's Business Law-Extended Case Approach, 2d edit., 2006, Business Law Today-Interactive Text, 7th edit., 2006, Business Law Today-The Essentials, 7th edit., 2006, Business Law Today-Comprehensive Edition, 7th edit., 2007, Business Law Today-Standard Edition, 7th edit., 2006, Essentials of the Legal Environment. 2nd edit., 2008; dep. editor: Social Sci. Quar., 1966—82, mem. editl. bd.; 1982—94, editor-in-chief: Am. Bus. Law Jour., 1969—74, adv. editor:, 1974—. With US Army, 1953—55. Named to CBA Hall of Fame, U. Tex., 1999; recipient Outstanding Tchr. award, U. Tex. Coll. Bus., 1967, Jack G. Taylor Tchg. Excellence award, 1971, 1989, Joe D. Beasley Grad. Tchg. Excellence award, 1978, CBA Found. Adv. Coun. award, 1979, Grad. Bus. Coun. Outstanding Grad. Bus. Prof. award, 1980, James C. Scorboro Meml. award for outstanding leadership in banking edn., Colo. Grad. Sch. Banking, 1983, Utmost Outstanding Prof. award, 1989, CBA award for excellence in edn., 1994, Banking Leadership award, Western States Sch. Banking, 1995, Civitatis award, U. Tex., 1997. Mem.: So. Bus. Law Assn. (pres. 1967), Wis. Bar Assn., Tex. Assn. Coll. Tchrs. (pres. Austin chpt. 1967—68, mem. exec. com. 1979—80, state pres. 1971—72), Acad. Legal Studies Bus. (pres. 1971—72, mem. exec. com. 1989—94), Am. Arbitration Assn. (nat. panel 1966—96), Southwestern Fedn. Adminstrv. Disciples (v.p. 1979—80, pres. 1980—81), Phi Kappa Phi (pres. 1983—84), Omicron Delta Kappa. Home: 4106 N Hills Dr Austin TX 78731-2826 Office: U Tex IROM Dept B6500 McCombs Sch Bus CBA 5 202 1 U Sta Austin TX 78712

JEON, BYONG-HUN, environmental engineer, educator; b. HongSung, Chungnam-do, Republic of Korea, July 20, 1970; s. Hak-Soo Jeon and Sun-Ja Kim; m. Duk-Ja Lee, June 1, 1997; children: Cha-Rin, Ye-Rin. PhD, Pa. State U., University Park, 2001. Rsch. scientist U. Ala., Tuscaloosa, Ala., 2002—04; rschr. Pacific NW Nat. Lab., Richland, Wash., 2004—05; asst. prof. Yonsei U., Won Ju, Republic of Korea, 2005—. Exhibitor: Environmental Science & Technology (hon. mention, 2001). Sec. Korean Student Assn. Pa. State U., University Park, 1999—2000. With 5th br. Republic of Korea Army, 1990—92. Recipient Best Abstract award, PennState U., 2000. Mem.: Am. Chem. Soc. Achievements include development of oxygen trap. Avocations: travel, tennis. Home: Apt 847-3

Myeongnyun 202-1201 Choeng-Gu Gangwon-do Wonju Republic of Korea Office: Yonsei Univ 234 Maeji Heungup Gangwon-do Wonju 220-710 Republic of Korea Office Phone: 82-33-760-2446. Office Fax: 82-33-763-5224.

JEONG, JI-HOON (RAIN), singer; b. Seoul, Republic of Korea, June 25, 1982; Singer: (albums) Bad Guy, 2002, How to Avoid the Sun, 2003, It's Raining, 2004, Sad Tango, 2006; actor: (TV series) Sangdoo, Let's Go to School, 2003, Full House, 2004 (Best Actor, KBS Acting Awards). Named one of 100 Most Influential People, Time Mag., 2006; recipient Daesang award, KBS, 2004, Favorite Artist from Korea, MTV Asia Awards, 2005, Popular Asian Artist award, Channel V Thailand, 2005, Best Korean Singer, Mandarin Music Honors, 2005. Office: c/o JYP Entertainment JYP Center 123-50 Cheongdam-dong kangnam-ku Seoul 135-995 Republic of Korea Office Phone: 02-3438-2300. Office Fax: 02-3442-7020.

JEONG, JINHO, writer; b. Jinju, June 14, 1973; s. Kyounggue Jeong and Kyesoon Kang; m. Eunjin Choi, May 18, 2002; 1 child, Amy. PhD, Seoul Nat. U., Rep. of Korea, 2004. Post-doctoral scholar U. Calif., La Jolla, 2004—. Grantee, Korea Rsch. Found., 2004—06; scholar, Nongpa Fellowship, Korea, 1993—97. Mem.: IEEE. Achievements include patents for wideband, variable-bandwidth distributed amplifier; research in millimeter-wave fully integrated PLL MMIC; millimeter-wave injection-locking frequency divider; millimeter-wave waveguide based power combining; CMOS power amplifiers using stacked FETs; digital transmitters; envelope tracking power amplifier for base-station.

JEONG, SEONG-IL, aerospace engineer, researcher; b. Kwangju, Republic of Korea, May 9, 1968; s. Doo-Sung and Hyo-Yeon (Oh) Jeong; m. Guk-Hee Kim, June 20, 1998; 1 child, Alexander. BS, Seoul Nat. U., Republic of Korea, 1990, MS, 1992; PhD, Tex. A&M U., 2002. From jr. rsch. engr. to sr. rsch. engr. Samsung Aerospace Industries, Ltd., Seoul, Republic of Korea, 1992—97; commd. rschr. Korea Inst. Sci. & Tech., Seoul, 1997—98; rschr., tchg. asst. Tex. A&M U., College Station, 1998—2002; rsch. assoc. NRC, Washington, 2003—05, U. Md., 2005—06; sr. rschr. Satellite Tech. Rsch. Ctr., Korea Advanced Inst. Sci. Tech., Daejeon, Republic of Korea, 2006—. Contbr. articles to profl. jours. Recipient Innovation and Creativity Prize Paper award, IEEE Industry Application Soc., 2004. Presbyterian. Avocations: golf, soccer. Home: Kukdong Apt 201-1803 Kkotmae-Maul Jukjeon-Dong Kyunggi-Do Yongin OTH Republic of Korea 448 160 Office: Korea Advanced Inst Sci Tech Satellite Tech Rsch Ctr 373-1 Guseong Dong Yuseong Gu Daejeon Republic of Korea 305 701 Office Phone: 82-42-869-8617. Business E-Mail: sijeong@satrec.kaist.ac.kr.

JEPPERSON, THOMAS C., lawyer; b. 1954; JD, Brigham Young U, J. Rueben Clark Law Sch., Provo, Utah, 1981. Bar: Utah 1981, U.S. Dist. Ct., Dist. Utah 1981, U.S. Ct. of Appeals 10th Cir. 1984, U.S. Supreme Ct. 1998. Atty to ptnr. Nielsen & Sr. Attys., 1981—88; sr. atty. Celsius Energy Corp., 1988—91, mng. atty., 1991—2005; gen. counsel Questar Corp., Salt Lake City. Office: Questar Corp 180 E 100 South St Salt Lake City UT 84139-1500

JEPSEN, DAVID ANDREW, retired counselor, educator; b. Dumont, Iowa, Dec. 2, 1938; s. Henry Washington and Clara Elizabeth Jepsen; m. Mary Lovina Marden, June 10, 1967; children: Alyson Claire Olson, Sarah Beth. BA, U. No. Iowa, Cedar Falls, 1960; MA in Counseling and Guidance, U. Wis., Madison, 1963, PhD in Counseling and Guidance, 1970. Cert. tchr. Iowa, 1960, Wis., 1964. Tchr., counselor Orange Twp. Cmty. Schs., Waterloo, Iowa, 1960—62; counselor Waterloo Cmty. Schs., 1964—67; prof. U. Iowa, Iowa City, 1970—2005, U. Md., College Park, 1992; ret., 2005. Grad. asst. U. Wis., Madison, 1962—64, 1967—70. Editor: (jour.) Career Development Quarterly, 1982—88; contbr. articles to profl. jours. Governing bd. mem., co-chair, Des Moines, 1997—2007. Recipient Eminent Career award, Nat. Career Devel. Assn., 1995. Fellow: ACA (governing coun. mem. 1988—91, Extended Rsch. award 2006); mem.: Assn. Assessment Counseling and Edn. (governing bd. 2003—05), Nat. Career Devel. Assn. (pres. 1989—90), Iowa Acad. Edn. (pres. 1998—99). Unitarian-Universalist. Avocations: sports, history. Home: 1014 Marcy St Iowa City IA 52240 Office Fax: 319-338-6160. Business E-Mail: david-jepsen@uiowa.edu.

JEPSEN, GEORGE C., state legislator, lawyer; b. Miss., Nov. 23, 1954; married, two children. BA summa cum laude, Dartmouth Coll., 1976; MPP, Harvard U., 1982, JD cum laude, 1982. Legis. asst. Spkr. James J. Kennelly Conn. Ho. of Reps., 1976-77, campaign mgr. William Ratchford, Dist. 5, 1978; intern U.S. Atty.'s Office, New Haven, 1979; field dir. Senate Campaign of Congressman Christopher Dodd Conn. Senate, 1978; mem. Stamford Bd. Reps., 1985-86; mem. Dist. 148 Conn. Ho. of Reps., 1987-90, asst. majority leader, vice chmn. ins. com., mem. banks com., mem. family and workplace com., fin., rev. and bonding com.; mem. Dist. 27 Conn. Senate, Hartford, 1991—, chmn. jud. com., asst. majority leader, mem. planning and devel. com., majority whip; assoc. Abate & Fox, 1992—; Dem. nominee Lt. Gov., 2002; majority leader State Senate, 1997—2003; state chmn. Conn. Dem. Party, 2003—04; asst. majority leader House of Reps.; chair Judiciary Com.; atty. Shipman & Goodwin LLP; of councel Cowdery, Ecker & Murphy LLC, Hartford, Conn., 2003—. Asst. sr. tutor, dean, resident pre-law adv. Quincy House, tchg. fellow Harvard U. 1980-82, assoc. dir. negotiation project, 1982; gen. counsel Carpenters' Union Local 210, 1982-92. Mem. Phi Beta Kappa. Office: Legis Office Bldg Rm 3300 Hartford CT 06106 Home: Cowdery Ecker & Murphy LLC 750 Main St Hartford CT 06103 Office Phone: 860-278-5555. Office Fax: 860-249-0012. Business E-Mail: gjepsen@cemlaw.com.

JEPSON, HANS GODFREY, investment company executive, director; b. Spencer, W.Va., July 24, 1936; s. Hans G. and Juanita Imogene (Shears) J.; m. Barbara Gayle Keller, Dec. 3, 1966. AB magna cum laude, Princeton U., 1958. Exec. editor Arnold Bernhard & Co., NYC, 1961—68; v.p., rsch. dir. Dominick & Dominick, Inc., NYC, 1968—70; dir., sr. v.p., rsch. dir. Alliance Capital Mgmt. Corp., NYC, 1970—76; exec. v.p., chief investment officer U.S. Trust Co. NY, NYC, 1976—80; pres. Valquest Assocs., Inc., NYC, 1980—, Lafayette Enterprises, Inc., NYC, 1983—, The Stanton Corp., Del., 1994—. Bd. dirs. J. Aron Charitable Found.; trustee Am. Bible Soc. 2d lt. US Army, 1958—59, capt. USAR, 1959—66. Mem. CFA Inst., NY Soc. Security Analysts, Dial, Elm and Cannon Club (Princeton, NJ), Princeton Club (NYC), Econ. Club (NYC), La Boule New York Yorkaise (NYC), Fedn. Petanque USA, Inc. Home: 11 5th Ave New York NY 10003-4342 Office: Lafayette Enterprises Inc 126 E 56th St New York NY 10022-3639

JEPSON, ROBERT SCOTT, JR., bank executive; b. Richmond, Va., July 20, 1942; m. Alice Finch Andrews, Dec. 28, 1964; children: Robert Scott, John Steven. BS, U. Richmond, 1964, M of Commerce, 1975; JD (hon.), Gonzaga U., 1986; DCS (hon.), U. Richmond, 1987; DH (hon.), Hamline U., 1988; LLD (hon.), Tusculum Coll., 1989, Ashland U., 1990, Elmhurst Coll., 1991; DSC in Bus. Adminstrn., Franklin U., 1996; D in Bus. (hon.), Fla. So. Coll., 2006. With Va. Commonwealth Bankshares, Richmond, 1966-68; v.p. corp. fin. Birr Wilson & Co., Inc., San Francisco, 1968-69; pres. Calif. Capital Mgmt. Corp., Irvine, 1970-73; v.p., dir. corp. fin. Cantor Fitzgerald & Co., Beverly Hills, Calif., 1973-75; dir. corp. planning and devel. Campbell Industries, San Diego, 1975-77; v.p., mgr. merger and acquisition divsn. Continental Ill. Bank, Chgo., 1977-82; sr. v.p., group head U.S. Capital Markets Group, 1st Nat. Bank Chgo., 1982-83; chmn., CEO The Jepson Corp., Chgo., 1983-89, Jepson Assoc. Inc., Savannah, Ga., 1989—. Chmn. Jepson Vineyards Ltd., Ukiah, Calif., 1985—, Coburn Optical Industries Inc., Tulsa, 1992-98; chmn., CEO Kuhlman Corp., Savannah, Ga., 1993-99; bd. advisors Jepson Found., Chgo., 1988—; bd. dirs. AGL Resources, Inc., Atlanta, 1999-2003, Dominion Resources, Inc., Richmond, Va.; asst. prof. fin. Nat. U., 1976; lectr. U. Richmond, U. Chgo., Northwestern U., Kansas U., Luther Coll., Wake Forest U Bd. trustees Gonzaga U., Spokane, Wash., 1982—86, Hamline U., St. Paul, 1987—92; bd. trustees, vice rector U. Richmond, 1992—95; mem. bd. advisors Franklin U., Columbus, 1996—; chmn., bd. dirs. Ga. Cancer Coalition, 2004—; chmn., bd. visitors Savannah Coll. of Art and Design, 2001—. 1st lt. US Army, 1964—66. Recipient Citation Honor Founders medal Elmhurst Coll., Ill., 1994, Volunteerism and Philanthropy award Coun. Ind. Colls., 1997. Mem. Commonwealth Club (Richmond), Savannah Yacht Club, Oglethorpe Club (Savannah), Chatham Club (Savannah), Plantation Club (Savannah), Omicron Delta Kappa, Alpha Kappa Psi, Beta Gamma Sigma (Entrepreneur of Yr. medallion 1996), Phi Gamma Delta. Republican.

JEREMIAH, BARBARA S., metal products executive; b. Pitts., Jan. 9, 1952; m. John M. Wilson; 2 children. B in Polit. Sci., Brown U., Providence; JD, U. Va., Charlottesville. Atty. Alcoa, Inc., 1977, gen. atty., mng. gen. atty., sr. mng. atty., 1991—92, asst. gen. counsel, 1992—93, sec., 1993, v.p. corp. devel., 1998—2002, exec. v.p. corp. devel., 2002—. Bd. dirs. Equitable Resources, Inc. Bd. trustees Pitts. Ballet Theatre; mem. bus. adv. coun. U. Va. Sch. Law; mem. women's ctr. nat. coun. U. Va.; bd. dirs. Women's Ctr. and Shelter of Greater Pitts. Office: Alcoa Inc Alcoa Corp Ctr 201 Isabella St Pittsburgh PA 15212-5858 Office Phone: 412-553-4545. Office Fax: 412-553-4498.*

JERGE, MARIE CHARLOTTE, minister; b. Mineola, NY, Dec. 26, 1952; d. Charles Louis and Helen Marie (Scheld) Scharfe; m. James Nelson Jerge, Aug. 27, 1977. AB, Smith Coll., 1974; MDiv, Luth. Theol. Sem. of Phila., 1978. Pastor St. Mark Evang. Luth. Ch., Mayville, NY, 1978-88; co-pastor Zion Evang. Luth. Ch., Silver Creek, 1983-88; asst. to the bishop Upstate NY Synod, Buffalo, 1988—2002; dir., bd. dirs. Acad. of Preachers, Phila., 1995-99; bishop Upstate NY Synod, ELCA, Syracuse, 2002—; v.p. NY State Coun. of Chs., 2003—. Bd. dirs. Acad. Preachers, Phila., 1982-99. Chairperson Chautauqua County Commn. of Family Violence and Neglect, Mayville, 1981-82, bd. dirs., 1978-88. Named one of outstanding Young Women in Am., 1980. Avocations: needlecrafts, aerobics, golf, cross country skiing. Office: Upstate NY Synod 890 E Brighton Ave Syracuse NY 13205

JERGER, EDWARD WILLIAM, engineering educator, dean; b. Milw., Mar. 13, 1922; s. Nickolaus and Ann (Huber) J.; m. Dorothy Marie Post, Aug. 2, 1944 (dec. 1981); children: Betty Ann Murphy, Barbara Lee Smyth; m. Elizabeth Cordiner Sweitzer, Mar. 27, 1982. BS in Mech. Engring, Marquette U., 1946; MS, U. Wis., 1948; PhD, Iowa State U., 1951. Registered profl. engr., Iowa, Ind. Process engr. Wis. Malting Co., Manitowoc, 1946-47; asst. prof. mech. engring. Iowa State U., 1948-55; asso. prof. mech. engring. U. Notre Dame, 1955-61, prof., head mech. engring., 1961-68, asso. dean, 1968-82, prof. mech. engring., 1982-97, prof. emeritus, 1989—. Cons. U. Madre De Maestra Santiago, Dominican Republic, 1965-71 Bd. dirs. Beaufort County Schoolbook Found. Served with USAAF, 1943-46. Mem. ASME, Am. Soc. Engring. Edn., Nat. Soc. Profl. Engrs., Nat. Fire Protection Assn., Sigma Xi, Phi Kappa Phi, Pi Tau Sigma (nat. v.p. 1969-74, pres. 1974-78), Tau Beta Pi. Home: 4 Coburn Ct Bluffton SC 29909-4560 Personal E-mail: profjerger@davtv.com.

JERMIASON, JOHN LYNN, elementary school educator, farmer, investor; b. Rochester, Minn, Jan. 9, 1958; s. Orlyn and Evelyn S. Jermiason; m. Ann M. Gebhardt, June 30, 1990. BA in Music, Psychology, St. Olaf Coll., 1981; AS in Agr., N.D. State U., 1982; BS in Edn., Minot State U., 1990. Computer repair cert. Sales rep. Century 21 Real Estate, Minot, ND, 1989; ind. farmer Minot, 1982—; ind. investor, 2006—. Substitute elem. tchr. Minot Pub. Sch., 1993—2005. Composer: Americana, Etudes. Prin. violist Minot Symphony Orch., 1983—, bd. dir., 1996—; mem. Augustana Luth. Ch. coun., Minot, 1989-91, No. Lights String Quartet, Augustana Luth. Endowment Bd., 2007—. Mem.: Elks, Kappa Delta Pi, Phi Mu Alpha. Republican. Avocation: church choir. Home and Office: PO Box 452 Minot ND 58702-0452 Personal E-mail: jdeere@bigfoot.com.

JERNIGAN, DAVID BRUCE, men's college basketball coach; s. Paul and Virginia Jernigan; m. Camilla Viertel Randrup; 1 child, Christopher. AA, Met. State U., 1990. Basketball player and coach, Fjellhamar, Norway, 1998—99, Innsbruck, Austria, 1999—2000, H.E.I. Denmark, Aarhus, 2000—01; basketball coach Hesser Coll., Manchester, Mass., 2004—; supr. GCA Svcs., Newmarket, NH, 2004—. Recipient Golden Poet award, Worldwide Poetry, 1998, 1999. Home: 3 Bennett Way Apt 212 Newmarket NH 03857-2303 Personal E-mail: dskywalkerj@hotmail.com.

JEROME, JERROLD V., retired insurance company executive; BS, Linfield Coll., 1952; MBA, Stanford U., 1959. V.p. Teledyne, Inc., LA, 1962-90; pres., CEO Unitrin, Inc., Chgo., 1990-92, vice chmn., 1992-94, chmn., 1994-99; ret., 1999. Office: Unitrin Inc 1 E Wacker Dr Chicago IL 60601-1802

JEROME, JOHN JAMES, lawyer; b. NYC, Oct. 17, 1933; s. Eugene George and Gladys Odette (Conterno) J.; children by previous marriage: Christopher J., Jennifer T.; m. Maureen M. Murphy, Sept. 19, 1981; children: Mairin Ashling, Emily Campbell. BBA, St. John's U., NYC, 1958, LLB, 1961. Bar: NY (state and fed. courts), Pa. Assoc. Milbank, Tweed, Hadley & McCloy, NYC, 1962-70, supreme ct. ptnr., 1962—98, ptnr., 1970-98; pres. Jerome Advisors, LLC, NYC, 1999—; ptnr. Saulewing, 2003—. Adj. prof. N.Y. Law Sch., 1978-81; lectr. Am. Law Inst., Corp. Strategies, Inc., N.Y. State Bar Assn., Nat. Law Jour., Oreg. Law Sch., Ky. Law Sch. Mem. ABA, Assn. of Bar of City of N.Y. (chmn. com. on bankruptcy and corp. reorgn. 1990-93), Nat. Bankruptcy Conf. Clubs: N.Y. Athletic, Sharon and Norfolk Country. Home: 1165 5th Ave New York NY 10029-6931 Office: 228 Farnum Rd Lakeville CT 06039

JEROME, JOSEPH WALTER, mathematics professor; b. Phila., June 7, 1939; s. Joseph Walter and Hermena Josephine (Ostertag) J.; m. Sara Tobin, July 2, 1999. BS in Physics, St. Joseph's U., 1961; MS, Purdue U., 1963, PhD, 1966. Vis. asst. prof. U. Wis., Madison, 1966-68; asst. prof. Case Western Res. U., Cleve., 1968-70; faculty Northwestern U., Evanston, Ill., 1970—, assoc. prof., 1972, prof. math., 1976—. Vis. fellow Oxford (Eng.) U., 1974—75; vis. prof. U. Tex. , Austin, 1978—79, Rush Med. Coll., Chgo., 1994—97; cons. Bell Labs., NJ, 1981—87; vis. scientist, 1982—83; vis. scholar U. Chgo.1, 1985; mem. adv. panel Internat. Workshops on Computational Electronics, 1990—; reviewer in field. Author (with S. Fisher): Springer Lecture Series Math. 479, 1975, Approximation of Nonlinear Evolution Systems, 1983, Analysis of Charge Transport, 1995; editor: Modelling and Computation for Applications, 1998; editor: (with G.Q. Chen and G. Gasper) Nonlinear Partial Differential Equations, 2005; mem. editl. bd.: Jour. Nonlinear Analysis, Jour. Computational Electronics; contbr. more than 120 articles to profl. jours. Br. Sci. Coun. Sr. Vis. fellow Oxford, 1974-75; NSF Rsch. grantee, 1970—, Office Naval Rsch. Rsch. grantee, 2005—; recipient Disting. Alumnus award Purdue U. Sch. Sci., 1996. Mem. Am. Math. Soc., Soc. for Indsl. and Applied Math. Roman Catholic. Office: Northwestern U 2033 Sheridan Rd Evanston IL 60208-0830 Office Phone: 847-491-5575. Business E-Mail: jwj@math.northwestern.edu.

JEROME, NORGE WINIFRED, nutritionist, anthropologist, educator; b. Grenada, Nov. 3, 1930; arrived in U.S.A., 1956, naturalized, 1973; d. McManus Israel and Evelyn Mary (Grant) Jerome. BS magna cum laude (hon.), Howard U., 1960; MS, U. Wis., 1962, PhD, 1967. Cert. nutrition splty.; fellow Am. Coll. Nutrition. Asst. prof. U. Kans. Med. Sch., Kans. City, 1967—72, assoc. prof., 1972—78, prof., 1978—95, dir. cmty. nutrition divsn., 1981—95; dir. Office of Nutrition, AID, Washington, 1988—91; sr. rsch. fellow Univ. Ctr., AID, Washington, 1991—92; interim assoc. dean minority affairs U. Kans. Med. Sch., Kans. City, 1996—98, prof. emerita, 1996—. Tech. adv. group The Nat. Ctr. for Minority Health; dir. ednl. resource centers U. Kans. Med. Center, 1974-77, head cmty. nutrition lab., 1978-95; cons. Children's TV Workshop, 1974-77; chair adv. bd. Teenage Parents Ctr., 1971-75; planning and budget coun., children and family svc. United Cmty. Svc., 1971-80; panel on nutrition edn. White House Conf. on Food, Nutrition and Health, 1969; bd. dir., health care com. Prime Health, 1976-79; bd. dir. Coun. on Children, Media and Merchandising; consumer edn. task force Mid Am. Health Systems Agy., 1977-79; commr. N. Am. working group Commn. Anthropology Food and Food Habits, Internat. Union Anthrop. and Ethnol. Sci., 1979-80; chmn. com. nutritional anthropology Internat. Union Nutritional Sci., 1979-80; lipid metabolism adv. com. NIH, 1978-80; nat. adv. panel multi-media campaign to improve children's diet U.S. Dept. Agrl., 1979-81; bd. advisers Am. Coun. on Sci. and Health, 1985-88; cons. in field. Sr. author: Nutritional Anthropology, 1980; asso. editor: Jour. Nutrition Edn., 1971-77; adv. council, 1977-80; editor: Nutritional Anthropology Communicator, 1974-77; mem. editl. bd.: Med. Anthropology: Cross Cultural Studies in Health and Illness, 1976-88, Internat. Jour. Nutrition Planning, 1977-88, Nutrition and Cancer: An Internat. Jour, 1978-2000, Jour. Nutrition and Behavior, 1981-86; contbr. articles to profl. journals. Mem. com. man food sys. NRC, 1980-83; bd. dirs. Kans. City Urban League, 1969-77, Crittenton Ctr., Kans. City, Mo., 1979-80, Johnson County Kans. Libr. Found., 2004—, exec. com., 2005—; mem. awards com. in nutrition edn. Met. Life Found., 1983-85; pres. Assn. for Women in Devel., 1991-93; trustee U. Bridgeport, Conn., 1992—; trustee Child Health Found., 1992-2000, chmn. bd. dirs., 1996-98; v.p., bd. trustees U. Bridgeport, Conn., 1997—; bd. dirs. Black Health Care Coalition of Kansas City, 1993-2002, Solar Cookers Internat., 1992-2000, pres., 1998-2000, Johnson County, Kans. Found. on Aging, 2001-04, Health Care Found. Greater Kansas City, 2004-06; mem. Commn. on Aging, Johnson County, Kans., 1997-2007; bd. dirs., vice chair cmty. adv. com. Kansas City Health Care Found., 2004. Decorated Dau. Brit. Empire; recipient First Higuchi Irvin Youngberg Rsch. Achievement award U. Kans., 1982, Excellence in Academia award Inst. Caribbean Studies, 2002, Disting. Svc. award NAACP, 2005, Johnson County Trailblazer award, 2006. Fellow Am. Soc. for Nutritional Sci., Am. Anthrop. Assn. (chair com. nutritional anthropology 1974-77, founder com. nutritional anthropology 1974), Soc. Applied Anthropology, Am. Coll. Nutrition, Soc. Med. Anthropology, Am. Soc. Nutritional Sci., 1998; mem. Am. Public Health Assn. (food and nutrition coun. 1975-78, governing coun. 1982-85), Am. Inst. Nutrition (program com. 1983-86), Am. Soc. Clin. Nutrition, Am. Men and Women of Sci., Nat. Acad. Sci. (world food and nutrition study panel), N.Y. Acad. Sci., Inst. Food Technologists, Am. Dietetic Assn., Assn. for Women in Devel. (pres. 1991-93), Soc. Behavioral Medicine, Club of Rome (U.S. assoc.). Office: U Kans Med Ctr 3901 Rainbow Blvd Mail Stop 1008 Kansas City KS 66160 Office Phone: 913-588-2770. Business E-Mail: njerome@kumc.edu. *Creative blending appears to have been the key for me--the melding of multiple traditions and styles, the melding of philosophies and strategies, and most importantly, the melding of ancient and modern thought and practices.*

JERPHAGNON, OLIVIER L., telecommunications industry executive; b. Paris, Apr. 21, 1975; s. Jean and Helene Jerphagnon; 1 child, Mia Helene. Diploma in engring., Nat. Poly. Inst., Grenoble, France, 1998; MS, U. of Calif., Santa Barbara, 1998—99. Intern Alcatel Submarine Networks, London, 1996, European Molecular Biology Lab., Heidelberg, Germany, 1997; tchg. asst. U. Calif., Santa Barbara, 1998—99, rsch. asst., 1999; mng. dir. Europe, Calient Networks, Goleta, Calif., 2000—. Sponsor Christian Children's Funds, Brazil, 2006. Fellow, U. Calif., 1998—99; grantee, Region Rhone-Alpes, France, 1997—98; scholar, U. Calif., 1998—99. Mem.: IEEE (sr.). Roman Catholic. Achievements include patents for wavelength selective optical switch; development of 3D-MEMS photonic switches; integration of photonic switches and GMPLS protocols in GRID networks; research in optical sub-carrier multiplexing; optical packet switching. Avocation: basketball. Office: Calient Networks 25 Castilian Dr Goleta CA 93117 Home Phone: 805-886-1375; Office Phone: 805-562-5521. Personal E-mail: jerph2000@yahoo.com.

JERRY, ROBERT HOWARD, II, dean, law educator; b. Lafayette, Ind., July 11, 1953; s. Robert Howard and Marjorie (Collings) J.; m. Lisa Nowak, Sept. 4, 1982; children: John Robert, James Martin, Elizabeth Catherine. BS magna cum laude, Ind. State U., 1974; JD cum laude, U. Mich., 1977. Bar: Ind. 1977, U.S. Ct. Appeals (D.C. cir.) 1978, U.S. Ct. Appeals (7th cir.) 1980, U.S. Ct. Appeals (10th cir.) 1989. Law clk. to Hon. George MacKinnon U.S. Ct. Appeals (D.C. cir.), Washington, 1977-78; assoc. Barnes, Hickam, Pantzer & Boyd, Indpls., 1978-81; assoc. prof. law U. Kans., Lawrence, 1981-85, prof., 1985-94, dean sch. law, 1989-94; prof., Herbert Herff chair of excellence law Cecil C. Humphreys Sch. Law U. Memphis, 1994—98; Floyd R. Gibson Mo. endowed prof. law U. Mo.-Columbia Sch. Law, 1998—2003; dean Levin Coll. Law, U. Fla., 2003—, Levin, Mabie and Levin prof., 2003—. Author: Understanding Insurance Law, 1987, 2d edit., 1996, 3rd edit., 2002; (with Roger C. Henderson) Insurance Law: Cases and Materials, 2d edit., 1996, 3rd edit., 2001; contbr. numerous articles to profl. jours., chpts. to books. Recipient Bodman-Longley Award, Mich. Law Review, 1976, Coblentz Prize, 1977, Disting. Alumnus Award, Ind. State U., 1992, Dean Sina Award, U. Fla., 2005. Fellow Am. Bar Found.; mem. ABA, Am. Law Inst. Democrat. Episcopalian. Office: Levin College of Law PO Box 117620 Gainesville FL 32611 Home Phone: 352-505-6903; Office Phone: 352-273-0600. Office Fax: 352-392-8727. Business E-Mail: jerryr@law.ufl.edu.*

JERRYTONE, SAMUEL JOSEPH, financial property broker; b. Pittston, Pa., Mar. 21, 1947; s. Sebastian and Susan Teresa (Chiampi) J.; children: Sandra, Cheryl, Samuel, Sebastian Assoc. in Bus., Scranton Lackawanna Jr. Coll., Pa., 1966. Mgr. House of Jerrytone Beauty Salon, West Pittston, Pa., 1967—68; regional sales dir. United Republic Life Ins., Harrisburg, Pa., 1970—76; night instr. Wilkes-Barre Vo-Tech H.S., Pa., 1976—78; spl. sales agt. Franklin Life Ins. Co., Wilkes-Barre, 1978—80; instr. Jerrytone Beauty Sch., Pittston, 1968—69, supr., 1969—95, pres., CEO, 1975, Jerrytone Tng. Ctrs., Pittston, 1989, Las Vegas, 1989; fin. broker Exec. Bus. Mgmt. and Property Svcs., Las Vegas, 2001—. Prof. sch. evaluator Nat. Accrediting Com. Arts and Scis., 1974-95; mem. adv. craft com. Wilkes-Barre Vo-Tech H.S., 1988 Mem. com. Rep. Presdl. Task Force, Washington, 1984, mem. parish coun. Guardian Angel Cathedral, Las Vegas, 1997 Mem. Pa. Hairdressers Assn., Nat. Accrediting Com. Cosmetology, Am. Coun. Cosmetology Educators, Masons (3d degree award 1983, 32d degree award Lodge Coun. chpt. consistory 1984), Shriners (Irem temple) Roman Catholic. Avocations: reading, golf, bowling, music, video filming. Personal E-mail: samuellv@earthlink.net.

JERSE, EDWARD, state representative; b. Cleve., Apr. 8, 1958; married; 3 children. BA in Hist., Georgetown U., 1980; JD, Harvard U., 1983. Lawyer Arter & Hadden, Ohio; asst. atty. gen. Office Of Atty. Gen. Ohio; state rep. dist. 7 Ohio Ho. of Reps., Columbus, 1995, ranking minority mem. fin. and appropriations com., mem. criminal justice, health, judiciary, and ways and means coms., mem. transp. and justice subcom.; atty. Moscarino & Treu LLP, Cleveland, Ohio, 1983. Adj. faculty Case Western Res. U. Sch. Law, Cleve., 1990. Sr. assoc. Cleve. Tomorrow, 1984—85;

councilman Euclid (Ohio) City Coun., 1989—93. Mem.: Phi Beta Kappa. Democrat. Office: Moscarino & Treu LLP 1422 Euclid Ave Ste 630 Cleveland OH 44115 Office Phone: 216-621-1000. Office Fax: 216-622-1556.

JERVIS, JANE LISE, academic administrator, historian; b. Newark, June 14, 1938; d. Ernest Robert and Helen Jenny (Roland) J.; m. Kenneth Albert Pruett, June 20, 1959 (div. 1974); children: Holly Jane Pruett, Cynthia Lorraine Pruett; m. Norman Joseph Chonacky, Dec. 26, 1981; children: Philip Joseph Chonacky, Joseph Norman Chonacky. AB, Radcliffe Coll., 1959; MA, Yale U., 1974, MPhil, 1975, PhD in History of Sci., 1978. Freelance sci. editor and writer, 1962-72; lectr. in history Rensselaer Poly. Inst., 1977-78; dean Davenport Coll., lectr. in history of sci. Yale U., 1978-82; dean students., assoc. prof. history Hamilton Coll., 1982-87; dean coll., lectr. in history Bowdoin Coll., 1988-92; pres. Evergreen State Coll., Olympia, Wash., 1992-2000; acad. dean Goddard Coll., 2004—. Cons. in field. Author: Cometary Theory in 15th Century Europe; contbr. articles to profl. jours.; book reviewer; presenter in field. Trustee Maine Hist. Assn., 1991-92, Stonehill Coll., 1996-02, Providence St. Peter's Hosp., 1997-2000; chair Maine selection com. Rhodes Scholarship Trust, 1990-92, chair N.W. selection com., 1992-93; commr. N.W. Assn. Schs. and Colls. Commn. on Colls., 1994-99. Office: Goddard College 123 Pitkin Road Plainfield VT 05667 Business E-Mail: jane.jervis@aya.yale.edu. E-mail: jjervis99@comcast.net.

JERVIS, ROBERT, political science professor; b. NYC, Apr. 30, 1940; s. Herman and Dorothy J.; m. Kathe Weil, June 19, 1967; children: Alexa, Lisa. BA, Oberlin Coll., 1962; MA, U. Calif.-Berkeley, 1963, PhD, 1967. Asst. prof. govt. Harvard U., 1968-73, assoc. prof., 1973-75; vis. assoc. prof. polit. sci. Yale U., 1974-75; prof. polit. sci. UCLA, 1975-80, Columbia U., NYC, 1980—, Adlai E. Stevenson prof. of internat. rels., 1989—, chair exec. com. of faculty arts and scis., 1993-94, acting assoc. v.p. arts and scis. for planning, 1994-95. Lady Davis vis. prof. Hebrew U., Jerusalem, spring 1977 Author: Perception and Misperception in International Politics, 1976, The Illogic of American Nuclear Strategy, 1984, Psychology and Deterrence, 1985, The Logic of Images in International Relations, 2d edit., 1989, The Meaning of the Nuclear Revolution, 1989, System Efects: Complexity in Political and Social Life, 1997, American Foreign Policy in a New Era, 2005; editor: Perspectives on Deterrence, 1989, Dominoes and Bandwagons, 1990, Soviet American Relations after the Cold War, 1991, Coping with Complexity in the International System, 1992; contbr. articles to prof. jours. Guggenheim fellow, 1978-79; recipient Grawemeyer award Ideas Improving World Order, Nevitt Sanford Career Achievement award Internat. Soc. Polit. Psychology, 1992, Lionel Trilling award, 1998, award for Behavior Sci. Relevant to the Prevention of Nuc. War, Nat. Acad. Scis., 2006. Fellow AAAS; mem. Am. Polit. Sci. Assn. (v.p. 1988-89, pres. 2000-01, Best Book in Polit. Psychology award 1998), Internat. Studies Assn. (Security Studies award 1996), Coun. on Fgn. Rels. (fellow 1970-71). Democrat. Home: 1170 5th Ave New York NY 10029-6527 Office: Columbia U Dept Polit Sci New York NY 10027 E-mail: RLJ1@columbia.edu.

JESBERG, ROBERT OTTIS, JR., educational consultant, science educator; b. Springfield, Ill., Nov. 17, 1947; s. Robert O. Sr. and Catharine I. (Patton) J.; m. Ruth Marie Andreas, Aug. 21, 1971; children: Kate Debra, Amy Lyn. BA in Biology, Susquehanna U., Selinsgrove, Pa., 1969; MEd, Temple U., Phila., 1971, secondary prin. cert., 1974. Cert. secondary biology and gen. sci. tchr., secondary sch. prin. Sci. tchr. Centennial Schs., Warminster, Pa., 1969—99, asst. prin., 1979, 85, 88; sci. cons. K'NEX Industries, Inc., Hatfield, Pa., 1994—; sci. coord. Centennial Schs., Warminster, Pa., 1996-98; mem. adv. com. Gov.'s Sci. Inst. Carnegie Mellon U., 1999—. Site dir., instr. Lawrence Hall of Sci., NSF Summer Insts., U. Calif., Berkeley, 1990-92; sci. cons. Singapore Am. Schs., 1993; dir. adult edn. Centennial Schs., Warminster, Pa., 1984-97, staff devel. trainer, 1985-99; instr. Pa. Commonwealth Excellence in Sci. Tchg. Alliance, Franklin Inst. Mus., Phila., 1996-2003. Author: (with others) K'NEX Racer Energy Educator Guide, 1996, K'NEX Bridges Educator Guide, 1996. Elder Lenape Valley Presbyn. Ch., New Britain, Pa., 1988—. Recipient Outstanding Sci. Supr. in Pa. Pa. Sci. Suprs. Assn., 1989; named Outstanding Educator in Bucks County, Pa. Bucks County ASCD, 1987, Outstanding Contbn. and Svc. to Bucks County ASCD, 1987. Mem. Nat. Sci. Tchrs. Assn., Pa. Math/Sci. Eisenhower Consortium (chairperson 1997-98, 2003-2005), Bucks County Sci. Tchrs. Assn. (pres. 1992-99). Republican. Home: 116 Blue Jay Rd Chalfont PA 18914-3104 Office: K'Nex Edn 2990 Bergey Rd Hatfield PA 19440-0700 Office Phone: 215-499-3917. Business E-Mail: rjesberg@knex.com.

JESKE, CHARLES MATTHEW, lawyer; b. Bartlesville, Okla., July 16, 1964; s. Arnold Carl and Maudie Marie (Matthews) J.; m. Pamela Kay Paholek, May 20, 1989. BBA in Fin./Acctg., Tex. A&M U., 1986; JD, South Tex. Coll. Law, Houston, 1989. Bar: Tex. 1989, U.S. Dist. Ct. (so. dist.) Tex. 1990, U.S. Ct. Appeals (5th cir.) 1990. Briefing atty. 14th Dist. Ct. of Appeals Tex., Houston, 1989-90, 90-91; sr. assoc. atty. Renneker & Assocs., Houston, 1991-96; pvt. practice Jeske & Assocs. PLLC, Houston, 1996—, mng. ptnr., 1998—. Contractor, investment analyst Jeske Homes, Bryan, Tex., 1986—. Trustee, officer Meml. Hollow Citizens, Inc., Houston, 1994—. Mem. ABA, Houston Bar Assn., Tex. A&M U. Former Students Assn., Phi Alpha Delta Alumni Assn. Republican. Lutheran. Avocations: photography, travel. Home and Office: 12407 Barryknoll Ln Houston TX 77024-4113 E-mail: cmjeske@usa.net.

JESKE, HOWARD LEIGH, retired insurance company executive, lawyer; b. York, Nebr., Sept. 25, 1917; s. Charles W. and Sina (Hanna) J.; m. Bettyclaire Barton, Nov. 23, 1943; children: Vaughn C., Craig B., Lynn Ellen Braziel, Laurel Claire McFarland. AB, Cornell Coll., Mt. Vernon, Iowa, 1940; LL.B., McGeorge Coll. Law, Sacramento, 1951. Bar: Calif. 1951. Capt. USAAF, 1942-45. Mem. ABA, Calif. Bar Assn., Sutter Club (Sacramento). Republican. Home: 4035 Eagles Nest Auburn CA 95603-5922

JESKY, T. J., pharmaceutical products executive; b. Chgo., Feb. 15, 1947; s. Henry J. and Joan F. (Lalko) J.; m. Jackeline Vasquez, Feb. 28, 2004; 1 child, Julia Alexandra. Lic. in derecho, Nat. U. Autónoma Mexico, Mexico City, 1968—70; BA Mktg. and Retailing, Bradley U., 1969. Field rep. Morton Norwich, Chgo., 1973-76, major account rep., 1976-79; Chgo. dist. mgr. Norwich Eaton Pharms., NY, 1979-80; NYC dist mgr. Norwich Eaton (A Procter & Gamble Co.), NY, 1980-83; mgr. Midwest and P.R. divsn. Norwich Eaton, Oak Brook, Ill., 1983-90; mgr. P.R. divsn. nat. accounts, mgr. nat. hosp. divsn. Procter & Gamble Pharms., Norwich, NY, 1990-93, mgr. divsn. Cin., 1994-95; pres., CEO Studebaker's, Inc., Scottsdale, Ariz., 1995-97, Ionosphere, Inc., Scottsdale, 1997-98, Barrington Labs., Inc., Las Vegas, 1998-2000; CEO Eaton Labs., Inc., Las Vegas, 2000—. Contbr. articles to profl. jours. Mem. Pharm. Mfr. Assn., Am. Mgmt. Assn., Nat. Pharm. Coun. Home: PO Box 8744 Scottsdale AZ 85252-8744

JESSEE, ROY MARK, lawyer; b. Kingsport, Tenn., Feb. 8, 1966; s. Roy Claude and Myrtle Delight (Robinette) J. BA, King Coll., 1988; JD, U. Va., 1991. Bar: Va. 1991, U.S. Dist. Ct. (we. dist.) Va. 1992. Law clk. Ct. of Appeals of Va., Bristol, 1991-92; assoc. atty. Mullins, Thomason & Harris, Norton, Va., 1992-94; shareholder, prin., atty. Mullins, Thomason, Harris & Jessee, Norton, Va., 1995-98; shareholder, prin. Mullins, Harris & Jessee, Norton, Va., 1998—. Panelist Bar Leader's Inst., 2000—03. Contbr. articles to legal jours. Chmn. Scott County Dem. Party, 1994-98. Named one of Outstanding Young Men in Am., 1989. Mem. ABA, Wise County Bar Assn. (pres.-elect 1998, pres. 1999), Am. Judicature Soc., Va. Assn. Def. Attys., Conf. Local Bar Assns. Democrat. Baptist. Avocations: running, weightlifting, reading, poetry. Office: Mullins Harris & Jessee PO Box 1200 30 Seventh St Norton VA 24273 Home: 1736 Main Ave SW Norton VA 24273 Home Phone: 276-679-3360; Office Phone: 276-679-3110. Business E-Mail: rjessee@mhjpc.com.

JESSELL, THOMAS M., medical educator; PhD in Neurobiology, Cambridge U., Eng. Rsch. fellow Trinity Coll., Cambridge U., England; postdoctoral fellow Gerald Fishbach Lab. Harvard Med. Sch., Boston, asst. prof. neurobiology; prof. biochemistry and molecular biophysics and mem. Ctr. for Neurobiology and Behavior Columbia U. Coll. Physicians and Surgeons, 1985—; investigator Howard Hughes Med. Inst. Contbr. articles to profl. jours.; co-editor (with others): Principles of Neural Science; mem. editl. bd. several jours. Co-recipient (with Corey Goodman) March of Dimes prize in developmental biology, March of Dimes, 2001; recipient Bristol-Myers Squibb award for disting. achievement in neurosci. rsch., 2000. Fellow: cad. Arts and Scis., Royal Soc. London; mem.: Inst. of Medicine of NAS. Achievements include research in on early development of the vertebrate central nervous system; the molecular mechanisms that determine the identities of neurons generated in the spinal cord; on the guide the axons of sensory and motor neurons to their targets that permit them to form functional neuronal circuits. Office: Columbia Univ Med Ctr Haener Health Sci Ctr 701 W 168 St 1013 New York NY 10032

JESSELLI, STEVE, journalist; Sports photog. editor New York Times. Office: NY Times Sports Desk 229 W 43rd St New York NY 10036 Office Phone: 212-556-1887. Office Fax: 212-556-5848.

JESSEN, DAVID WAYNE, accountant; b. Albuquerque, Jan. 13, 1950; BBA in Acctg., U. N.Mex., 1972. CPA N.C., N.Mex., S.C. Staff acct. local CPA firm, Albuquerque, 1971-74, jr. ptnr., 1974-75; mgr. in charge Santa Fe office Ernst & Young, 1975-80, prin. in charge Santa Fe office, 1980—86, dir. taxes N.Mex. offices Albuquerque, 1980-86, tax ptnr. N.Mex. offices, 1986, ptnr. Raleigh, NC, 1987-89, mng. ptnr. office, 1987—89. Mem. Arthur Young Nat. Real Estate Com., 1988, mem. nat. hightech com., 1988—94; ptner., dir. entrepreneurial svcs. Ernst & Young, Raliegh, 1989—2002, S.E. region dir. entrepreneurial svcs., 1992—94, dir. tax dept., 1995—, dir. tax entrepreneurial svcs., 1998—2002; bd. dirs. WakeMed Health & Hosps. Asst. scoutmaster Boy Scouts Am.; bd. dirs. St. Joseph Hosp. Health Care Found., 1986—87, NC Mus. Art Found., 1992—, treas., 1994—2001, Kiwanis Found. Eagle Scout, Bus. Friends Coun., NC Soc. Prevent Blindness; chmn. pres.'s cir. Wake Med. Ctr. Found., 1996—2001, bd. dirs., 1996—2006; bd. dirs., chmn. fin. com., exec. com. WakeMed, 2005—06, treas., 2005—; bd. dirs. Food Bank NC, 2001—, chmn. fin. com., treas.; mem. parents coun. U. NC, Chapel Hill, 2000—03; bd. trustees WakeMed Health & Hosp. Sys., 2006—; mem. bus. sch., acctg./MSA adv. bd. U. NC, Wilmington; treas. NC Mus. Art, 1994—2001, bd. dirs., 2002—. Mem.: AICPA, NC Assn. CPAs, N.Mex Soc. CPAs, N.Mex Estate Planning Coun., Nat. Assn. Accts., Coun. Entrepreneurial Devel., Albuquerque Jaycees, Albuquerque C. of C., Santa Fe C. of C., Raleigh C. of C., Santa Fe Jaycees, West Raleigh Rotary, Kiwanis, Elks, Alpha Kappa Psi. Home: 8840 Mariner Dr Raleigh NC 27615 Office Phone: 919-981-2905.

JESSEN, JOEL ANNE, not-for-profit executive, art educator; b. Seattle, Sept. 7, 1940; d. John Paagard and Anne Vilma Jessen. BA, U. Wash., 1962, MFA, 1964. Instr. Cornish Coll. Arts, Seattle, 1965—76; pres., CEO Kappeler Inst., Inc., Seattle, 1975—. Instr. U. Wash., Seattle, 1970—71, Highline Coll., Seattle, 1970—71. Author: The Imperative Step, 1972, The Physical, The Mental, and The Spiritual, 1978, rev. edit., 2007. Recipient Patrick Gavin Meml. prize, Boston Printmakers, 1965. Mem.: U. Wash. Alumni. Avocation: art. Office: Kappeler Inst Inc PO Box 99735 Seattle WA 98139-0735 Business E-Mail: joel@kappelerinstitute.org.

JESSOR, RICHARD, psychologist, educator, director; b. Bklyn., Nov. 24, 1924; s. Thomas and Clara (Merkin) J.; m. Shirley Glasser, Sept. 27, 1948 (div. 1982); children: Kim, Tom; m. Jane Ava Menken, Nov. 13, 1992. Student, CCNY, 1941-43; BA, Yale U., 1946; MA, Columbia U., 1947; PhD, Ohio State U., 1951. Intern, clin. psychology trainee VA, Ohio State U., Columbus, 1947-50; asst. prof. psychology U. Colo., Boulder, 1951-56, assoc. prof., 1956-61, prof., 1961—, disting. prof. behavioral sci., 2005—, dir. rsch. program problem behavior Inst. Behavioral Sci., 1966-97, dir. Inst. Behavioral Sci., 1980—2001, dir. health and soc. program Inst. Behavioral Sci., 2001—. Dir. MacArthur Found. Rsch. Network on Successful Adolescent Devel. Among Youth in High Risk Settings, 1987-96; cons. Nat. Inst. on Drug Abuse, 1975-76, Nat. Inst. on Alcohol Abuse and Alcoholism, 1976-80, WHO, Geneva, 1976-80; cons. in field. Author: (with T.D. Graves, R.C. Hanson & S.L. Jessor) Society, Personality, and Deviant Behavior: A Study of a Tri-Ethnic Community, 1968, (with S.L. Jessor) Problem Behavior and Psychosocial Development: A Longitudinal Study of Youth, 1977, (with J.E. Donovan and F. Costa) Beyond Adolescence: Problem Behavior and Young Adult Development, 1991; co-editor: Contemporary Approaches to Cognition, 1957, Cognition, Personality and Clinical Psychology, 1967, Ethnography and Human Development: Context and Meaning in Social Inquiry, 1996; editor: New Perspectives on Adolescent Risk Behavior, 1998, Perspectives on Behavioral Science: the Colorado Lectures, 1991; cons. editor Jour. Cons. and Clin. Psychology, 1975-77, Cmty. Mental Health Jour., 1974-78, Alcohol Health and Rsch. World, 1981-90, Alcohol, Drugs and Driving, 1985-92, Adolescent Medicine: State of the Art Revs., 1989—; mem. editl. bd. Prevention Sci., 1999—; cons. editor Sociometry, 1964-66, assoc. editor, 1966-69; contbr. articles to profl. jours. Served with USMC, 1943-46, PTO. Decorated Purple Heart; Social Sci. Rsch. Coun. pre-doctoral fellow Ohio State and Yale U., 1950-51; Social Sci. Rsch. Coun. fellow Ohio State U., 1954, Social Sci. Rsch. Coun. postdoctoral fellow U. Calif.-Berkeley, 1956-57, NIMH spl. rsch. fellow Harvard-Florence Rsch. Project, Italy, 1965-66, Ctr. for Advanced Study in the Behavioral Scis. fellow Stanford U., 1995-96; recipient Faculty Rsch. Lectureship award U. Colo., 1981-82; Gallagher lectr. Soc. Adolescent Medicine, 1987, Outstanding Achievement in Adolescent Medicine award, 2005; named Highly Cited Rsch. in Social Scis., Inst. for Sci. Inf., 2003. Fellow APA, Am. Psychol. Soc. (charter fellow); mem. Soc. for Psychol. Study of Social Issues, Soc. for Study of Social Problems. Avocations: mountain climbing, running marathons. Home: 1303 Marshall St Boulder CO 80302-5803 Office: U Colo Inst Behavioral Sci Cb 483 Boulder CO 80309-0001 Home Phone: 303-440-4024; Office Phone: 303-492-8148. Business E-Mail: jessor@colorado.edu.

JESSUP, JAN AMIS, arts volunteer, writer; b. Chgo., Aug. 10, 1927; d. Herman Harvey and Anita (Lincoln) Sinako; m. Everett Orme Amis, Dec. 20, 1970 (dec. Nov. 1981); m. Joe Lee Jessup, Apr. 16, 1989. BA, U. Minn., 1948; postgrad., Rutgers U., 1969-70. Prin., owner, v.p. Leading Edge Design Assocs., LLC, 2004—, sec., treas., 2006—. Bd. dirs., mem. exec. com. Broward Ctr. Performing Arts Pacers, Ft. Lauderdale, Fla., 1985—88, pres., 1987—88; spkr. U. Internat. Bus., Beijing, 1985. Mem. beautification com. Lighthouse Point, Fla., 1978—89, sec. beautification com., 1988—91; bd. govs. Fla. Philharm. Orch., 1981—98, v.p. representing all affiliates, 1985—87, 1992, 1994—96, exec. com., 1989—93, v.p. individual giving, 1991—92, Boca Raton bd. dirs., 1994—2002, chmn. affiliate com., 1994—95; rep. Fla. Art Orgns., 1987—88; bd. dirs. Archways, Ft. Lauderdale, 1987—91, Fla. Grand Opera, 1993—, Symphony of the Ams., 2004—, Master Chorale South Fla., 2004—06; trustee Miami City Ballet, 1991—94, Harid Conservatory, 1997—; adv. bd. Guild of the Palm Beaches, Fla., 1994—95; founding pres. Harid Guild, 1997—99; program com. Boca Raton Ctr. for Arts, 2002—05; bd. advs. Youth Automotive Tng. Corps, 2004—; leadership coun. Boca Raton Philharmonic Symphonia. Mem.: Symphony Am. Soc. (pres. 2004—06), Univ. Club of Washington, Gold Coast Jazz Soc. (bd. dirs. 1992—98, v.p. 1994—98), Royal Dames Cancer Rsch. (trustee 1995—97), Opera Soc. (sec. 1986—87, bd. dirs. 1986—, v.p. pub. rels. 1987—88), The Opus Soc. (chmn. 1981—85, bd. dirs., mem. exec. com. 1981—96, pres. 1989—93), Am. Symphony Orch. League (bd. dirs. 1998—2007, liaison and com. mem. Nat. Youth Orch. Festival 2000 Com. 2000—01), Internat. Game Fish Assn. (adv. coun. 2001—06), Nat. Soc. Arts and Letters, Am. Symphony Orch. League Vol. Coun. (sec. 1986—87, bd. dirs. 1986—92, v.p. 1987—88, vice chmn. 1989—90, pres. 1989—90, advisor 1990—91, assoc. Resource Devel. Inst. 1996—98), Ft. Lauderdale Philharm. (bd. dirs. 1986—2003), Royal Palm Dinner Theatre (bd. dirs. 1998—2000), Harvard Club of NYC, Univ. Club Washington, Harvard Club NYC, Univ. Club DC, Harvard Club NY, Centre For The Arts (program com. 2002—04), Ocean Reef Club, Sea Grape Garden Club (past pres.), Royal Palm Yacht and Country Club Women's Club (mem. yachting com. 2006—), Boca Raton Resort and Club. Republican. Avocations: music, boating, fishing, writing, bridge. Home: 133 Coconut Palm Rd Boca Raton FL 33432-7975 Personal E-mail: janjessup@aol.com. Business E-Mail: amisj@bellsouth.net.

JESSUP, MARIELL, physician, director; d. Mary Badger Jessup; 1 child, Mary Parker. MD, Hanhnemann U., 1972. Med. dir. heart failure/transplant program U. Pa., Phila., 2001—, prof. medicine, 2003—. Office: U Pa 6 Penn Tower 3400 Spruce St Philadelphia PA 19104 Office Phone: 215-615-0808. Office Fax: 215-615-0828. Business E-Mail: jessupm@uphs.upenn.edu.

JESSUP, NANCY JEAN, music educator; d. Gene Frank and Patricia Ann Taylor; m. George Lloyd Jessup, Feb. 6, 1971; 1 child, Jonathan David. Assoc. in Music, Pasadena City Coll., Calif., 1969; BA in Am. Studies, Calif. State U., LA, 1971; MEd, Concordia U., Irvine, Calif., 2003. Tchr. Good Shepherd Luth. Sch., Higland Park, Calif., 1969—72; tchr., handbell dir. Prince of Peace Luth. Sch., Costa Mesa, Calif., 1972—93; handbell editor Nat. Music Pubs., Tustin, Calif., 1983—91; adj. instr. Concordia U., 1993—, univ. supr., 1995—. Handbell cons., Costa Mesa, 1980—. Performer: (nat. debut) John Tarkner's Quartet No. 2, Calingirian String Quartet, 1996. Mem.: Am. Guild English Handbell Ringers (mem. handbell industry coun. 1988—90, membership chmn. 1994—96). Personal E-mail: nanjessup@aol.com.

JESSUP, PAUL FREDERICK, financial economist, educator; b. Evanston, Ill., Apr. 16, 1939; s. Paul S. and Gertrude (Strohmaier) J.; m. Johanna A.M. Friesen, June 27, 1970; children: Christine Marieke, Paul Charles Friesen. BS, Northwestern U., 1960, PhD, 1966; AM, Harvard U., 1963; BA, U. Oxford, Eng., 1963; MA, U. Oxford, 1983. Economist com. banking and currency U.S. Ho. of Reps., Washington, 1963-64; faculty U. Minn., Mpls., 1967-82, prof. fin., 1973-82; with Jessup & Co., Inc., St. Paul, 1982—; William Kahlert prof. mgmt. and econs. Hamline U., St. Paul, 1988—. Dir. Gerbill Inc.; Sabbatical prof. in residence Fed. Res. Bank, Mpls., 1973-74 Author: The Theory and Practice of Nonpar Banking, 1967, (with Roger B. Upson) Returns in Over-the-Counter Stock Markets, 1973, Competing for Stock Market Profits, 1974, Modern Bank Management: A Casebook, 1978, Modern Bank Management, 1980, Invest To Win: A Coach's Guide to Stocks, Bonds and Mutual Funds, 2001; editor: Innovations in Bank Management: Selected Readings, 1969; contbr. articles to profl. jours. Mem. Midwest Fin. Assn. (past pres.), Univ. Club. Home: 1979 Shryer Ave W Saint Paul MN 55113-5414 Office: Hamline U 1536 Hewitt Ave Saint Paul MN 55104-1284

JESSUP, PHILIP CARYL, JR., retired lawyer; b. Utica, NY, Aug. 30, 1926; s. Philip C. and Lois K. (Kellogg) J.; m. Dorothy A. Kerr, Jan. 15, 1951 (div.); children: Timothy, Nancy, Margaret; m. Helen I. Ibbitson, Jan.24, 1969; stepchildren: Genevieve, Lucinda, Francesca, Alexander. BA, Yale Coll., 1949; JD, Harvard U., 1952. Bar: N.Y. 1954. Atty. Whitman, Ransom & Coulson, NYC, 1952-58; legal officer Internat. Nickel Co., Inc., NYC, 1958-63; gen. solicitor internat. Inco Ltd., NYC, 1963-68; chief legal officer, sec., dir. Inco Europe Ltd., London, 1968-72; pres., mng. dir. P.T. Internat. Nickel Indonesia, Jakarta, 1972-78; v.p., gen. counsel and sec. Inco Ltd., NYC, Toronto, Can., 1978-84; sec., gen. counsel Nat. Gallery Art, Washington, 1984—2000. Dir. Biogen N.V., Geneva, 1981-85; chmn. bd. Inco Gulf, E.C., Bahrain, 1980-84; chmn. bd. Am. Friends Nat. Gallery Art Australia, N.Y.C., 2001—; bd. dirs. Norfolk Land Trust, Norfolk, Conn., 2002—, v.p., 2003—. Trustee Obor, Internat. Book Inst. Inc., Phila., 1978—2001, sec.-treas., 1989-96, chmn. bd., 1996-2001; mem. adv. commn. H.H. Humphrey Fellowship Program, 1984-89; trustee Asia Soc., 1991-99, sec., 1993-99, mem. adv. com. Washington Ctr., 1985-2000, chmn. adv. com., 1989-2000, trustee emeritus, 2007—; pres. Friends of Hosp. for Sick Children, Toronto, 1985—; mem. Coun. on Fgn. Rels., N.Y.C., 1972—; pres. West Brooklyn Ind. Dems., 1956-58. Served to staff/sgt. C.E., U.S. Army, 1944-46. Mem. ABA, Assn. of Bar of City of N.Y., Century Assn. (N.Y.C.). Democrat. Home: 97 Gamefield Rd Norfolk CT 06058-1272

JESSUP, STUART DODGE, marine engineer; MS, MIT, 1976; PhD, 1989. Sr. rsch. scientist Carderock Divsn. Navy Surface Warfare Ctr., West Bethesda, Md., 2003—. Author: An Experimental Investigation of Viscous Aspects of Propeller Blade Flow, 1989. Recipient Gold Medal award, Am. Soc. Naval Engrs., 2004. Mem.: NAE. Achievements include being first to explore three-dimensional boundary layers on rotating propeller blades. Office: Carderock Divsn Naval Surface Warfare Ctr 9500 MacArthur Blvd West Bethesda MD 20817-5700 Office Phone: 301-227-5080. E-mail: JessupSD@nswccd.navy.mil.*

JESTRAB, FRANK F., retired lawyer; b. Havre, Mont., Jan. 28, 1914; s. Frank Ferdinand and Anna Sophia Ulrica Jestrab; m. Elvira W. Jestrab (dec.); children: Laurel Ann Lesch, James David. At, No. Mont. Coll., Havre, 1933—35; LLB, U. Mont. Sch. Law, Missoula, 1938; BA, U. Mont., Missoula, 1946; at, Harvard U. Law Sch., Springfield, Mass. Bar: Mont., NY, Tex., ND, Wyo. Legal dept. Anaconda Mining Co., Butte, Mont., 1938—41; solo practice Houston; legal dept. Amerada Pet Corp., 1951; ptnr. Bjella & Jestrab, Williston, ND, 1951—77; mem. fed. mine safety health rev. com, Washington, 1978—84; ret., 1984. Adj. lectr. U. Houston, 1948; pres. State Bar Assn. N.D., 1964—65; cons. in field. Founder Asbury Dem. Club, Gaithersburg, Md., 2003. Capt. inf. US Army, 1941—46, Burma. Decorated Bronze Star. Mem.: Internat. Acad. Trial Lawyers, Am. Law Inst., Soc. Middle Temple London (hon.), Am. Birding Assn. Home: Apt 1118 415 Russell Ave Gaithersburg MD 20879 Personal E-mail: frankjestrab@aol.com.

JESWALD, JOSEPH, artist; b. Leetonia, Ohio, May 17, 1927; s. Philip and Susan Jeswald; m. Hester Parker Jeswald; children: Peter, Paul, Melissa. Founder, first pres. Montserrat Coll. Art, Beverly, Mass. Represented in permanent collections Hirschorn Mus., Wash. DC, Addison Gallery of Am. Art, Andover, Mass., Rockefeller Found., NYC, Simmons Coll., Boston, Cape Ann Hist. Assn., Gloucester, Ma., Roy M. Neuberger Mus., Purchase, NY. Sgt. US Air Corps, 1945—46, ETO. Recipient 1st prize, Northeast Regional Invitational Exhbn., 1962.

JETER, DEREK SANDERSON, professional baseball player; b. Pequannock, NJ, June 26, 1974; s. Charles and Dorothy Jeter. Student, U. Mich., 1992. Draft pick NY Yankees, 1992, shortstop, 1995—. Mem. US Team World Baseball Classic, 2006. Author: Game Day: My Life on and off the Field, 2001; co-author (with Jack Curry): The Life You Imagine: Life Lessons For Achieving Your Dreams, 2001. Founder Turn 2 Found., 1996—. Named Minor League Player of Yr., The Sporting News, 1994, Am. League Rookie of Yr., Baseball Writers Assn. of Am., 1996, World

Series MVP, 2000, All-Star Game MVP, 2000; named to Am. League All-Star Team, 1998—2002, 2004, 2006, 2007; recipient Babe Ruth award, 2000, Am. League Gold Glove award, 2004—06, Hank Aaron award, 2006, Silver Slugger award, 2006. Achievements include being a member of World Series Champions, 1996, 1998-2000; led Am. League in hits (219), 1999; holds Major League Baseball record for post-season hits (123), 2003; appeared as a guest host, Saturday Night Live, 2001. Office: NY Yankees Yankee Stadium E 161st and River Ave Bronx NY 10451*

JETER, WAYBURN STEWART, retired microbiologist, educator; b. Cooper, Tex., Feb. 16, 1926; s. Joseph Plato and Beulah (Stewart) J.; m. Margaret Ann McDonald, May 30, 1947; children— Randall Mark, Monette Ann, Marcus Kent. BS, U. Okla., 1948, MS, 1949; PhD, U. Wis., 1950. Diplomate: Am. Bd. Microbiology. Mem. faculty U. Iowa, 1950-63, assoc. prof., 1958-63; prof. microbiology U. Ariz., Tucson, 1963-89, prof. microbiology emeritus, 1989—, prof. pharmacology and toxicology, 1983-91, prof. pharmacology and toxicology emeritus, 1991—, head dept. microbiology and med. tech., 1967-83, dir. lab. cellular immunology, 1976-91, dir. med. tech. program, 1976-79. Vis. prof. immunology and med. microbiology U. Fla., 1980; pres. Scientific Rels. Svcs., Inc., 1988—99. Contbr. articles profl. jours. Served with USNR, 1943-46. Fellow AAAS; mem. Am. Acad. Microbiology, Am. Assn. Immunologists, Ariz. Acad. Sci., Am. Soc. Microbiology (mem. council 1975-77), Soc. Exptl. Biology and Medicine, Sigma Xi. Democrat. Presbyterian. Home: 5140 N Via Sempreverde Tucson AZ 85750-5966 E-mail: wayburnjeter520@comcast.net.

JETLEY, KARUN, software company executive, consultant; s. Baldev Krishan and Shobhna Jetley. BS, Houston Bapt. U., 1990; MBA, U. Houston, 1992. Dir. software devel. BKI, Houston, 1993—97; data arch. Reliant Energy, Houston, 1998—99; pres. effesoft, Houston, 2000—03; global data arch. BMC Software Inc., Houston, 2002—03, BindView Devel. Corp., Houston, 2004—06; software dir. Symantec Corp., Houston, 2006—. Bd. dirs. CMP Adv. Bd., Houston, BindView Devel. Corp., 2004—06; rsch. panel IDE, Evans Data Corp., 2004—; adv. panel eWeek, 2005—. Founding sponsor Martin Luther King Build the Dream Monument, 2006; founding mem. Nat. Campaign for Tolerance, 2004. Mem.: IEEE (tech. mem. 2005—, adv. panel 2005—), SQL Server Group, Houston Advt. Fedn. (corr.). Achievements include invention of first request/requirements software suite; metadata tool effesoft. Personal E-mail: knvrqut@sbcglobal.net.

JETT, BRENT W., JR., astronaut, military officer; b. Pontiac, Mich., Oct. 5, 1958; m. Janet Leigh Lyon, 1992. BS in Aerospace Engring., U.S. Naval Acad., Annapolis, Md., 1981; MS in Aero. Engring., U.S. Naval Postgrad. Sch., Monerey, Calif., 1989. Commd. ensign USN, Annapolis, Md., 1981, advanced through grades to capt., 2002; naval aviator USN Fighter Squadrons 101 and 74, Naval Air Sta. Oceana, Va. Beach, 1983—86; student Naval Postgrad. Sch., Monterey, Calif., 1986—89; project test pilot USN Strike Aircraft Test Directorate, 1989—91; F-14B pilot USN USS Saratoga, 1991—92; astronaut USN Johnson Space Ctr., Houston, 1992—. NASA dir. ops. Yuri Gagarin Cosmonaut Tng. Ctr., Star City, Russia, 1997—98; crew mem. STS-72 Endeavour, 1996, STS-81 Atlantis, 1997, STS-97 Endeavour, 2000; comdr. STS-115 Atlantis, 2006. Decorated Disting. Flying Cross USN, 3 space flight medals NASA, Dept. Def. Superior Svc. and Meritorious Svc. medals, Navy Commendation medal; recipient NASA Exceptional Svc. medal. Mem.: Soc. Exptl. Test Pilots, U.S. Naval Acad. Alumni Assn., Assn. Space Explorers, Assn. Naval Aviation. Office: Asromaut Office NASA Johnson Space Ctr Houston TX 77058

JETT, CHARLENE M., biologist, researcher; d. Charles W. Harre and Sybel Hodges. BS in Physiology, U. Ill., Champaign, 1972; MS in Biology, Northeastern Ill. U., Chgo., 1980; MS, Lake Forest Grad. Sch. Mgmt., Ill., 1990. Lab. asst. U. Ill., Champaign, 1970—72; sr. rsch. scientist GD Searle/ Pharmacia/Pfizer, Skokie, Ill., 1972—80; sr. clin. rschr. project mgmt. Abbott Labs., North Chgo., 1980—88; prin., owner 3R's Mgmt. and Rsch. Consulting, Vandalia, Ill., 1988—. Presenter in field. Contbr. articles to profl. jours. Cons. ARC, other various businesses; mem. choir United Meth. Ch., Vandalia, 2005—06. Fellow: Sigma Xi (pres. 1987—88); mem.: Regulatory Affairs Assn., Am. Chem. Soc. (assoc.; mem., contbr. 1988—2007), U. Ill. Alumni Club (life; none 1989—2007). Conservative. Methodist. Achievements include invention of various drugs, medical devices, diagnostics and other medical products. Avocations: hiking, travel, singing, dance, reading. Home and Office: 3R's Mgmt and Rsch Consulting 329 S 4th St Vandalia IL 62471 Office Phone: 618-283-1923. Personal E-mail: charlenemjett@yahoo.com.

JETT, ERNEST CARROLL, JR., paper company executive, lawyer; b. Liberty, Tex., July 10, 1945; m. Janene L. Jett. BA cum laude, Baylor U., 1967; MA, La. State U., 1969; JD, U. Tex., 1973. Bar: Tex. 1973, U.S. Dist. (so. dist.) Tex. 1979, U.S. Ct. Appeals (5th cir.) 1979, U.S. Supreme Ct. 1979, Mo. 1980. Mem. legal staff Cooper Industries, Inc., 1973-75, Tenneco, Inc., 1975-79; v.p., gen. counsel, sec. Leggett & Platt, Inc., Carthage, Mo., 1979—. Editor Tex. Internat. Law Jour. 1972-73. Mem. ABA, Am. Corp. Coun. Assn., Am. Soc. Corp. Secs., State Bar Tex., Mo. Bar Assn., Phi Alpha Theta, Alpha Chi, Phi Eta Sigma, Phi Delta Phi, Pi Gamma Mu. Office: Leggett & Platt Inc PO Box 757 1 Leggett Rd Carthage MO 64836-9649 Home: 4702 S Jackson Ave Joplin MO 64804-4837 Office Phone: 417-358-8131. E-mail: ernest.jett@leggett.com.*

JETT, STEPHEN CLINTON, geography and textiles educator, researcher; b. Cleve., Oct. 12, 1938; s. Richard Scudder Jett and Miriam Ida (Horn) Greene; m. Mary Frances Manak, Aug. 7, 1971 (div. 1977); 1 child, Jennifer Frances Heider; m. Lisa Sue Roberts, June 17, 1995. AB, Princeton U., 1960; postgrad., U. Ariz., 1962—63; PhD, Johns Hopkins U., 1964. Instr. geography Ohio State U., Columbus, 1963-64; asst. prof. geography U. Calif., Davis, 1964-72, assoc. prof., 1972-79, prof., 1979—2000, prof. textiles and clothing, 1996—2000, prof. emeritus geography, textiles and clothing, 2000—, chmn. geography dept., 1978-82, 87-89. Author: Navajo Wildlands, 1967 (1 of 50 Books of Yr., Am. Inst. Graphic Arts 1967, 1 of 20 Merit Award Books, Western Book Pubs. Assn. 1969), House of Three Turkeys, 1977, Navajo Architecture, 1981 (1 of Outstanding Acad. Books, Choice mag. ALA 1981), Navajo Placenames and Trails of the Canyon de Chelly System, Arizona, 2001, France, 2004; (monograph) Tourism in the Navajo Country, 1966; editor jour. Pre-Columbiana; curator textile exhbns.; contbr. numerous articles to profl. jours. and chpts. to books. Mem. Hist. and Landmarks Commn., Davis, 1969-73; vice chmn. Gen. Plan Noise Element Study Com., Davis, 1974-76, chmn. ad hoc citizens noise com., 1997-98; mem. exec. coun. Univ. Farms Unit Number 1 Neighborhood Assn., Davis, 1987-90. Fellow: Am. Geog. Soc., Explorers Club; mem.: AAAS, Found. Rsch. Ancient Maritime Explorations (bd. dirs. 2002—, treas. 2006—), Inst. for Study of Am. Cultures (bd. dirs. 1996—), Epigraphic Soc. (bd. dirs. 1996—, v.p. 2005—), Soc. Am. Archaeology, Assn. Am. Geographers (chair Am. Indian splty. group 1989—91). Avocations: travel, photography, textiles and other ethnographic arts, French language and culture. E-mail: scjett@hotmail.com.

JETTE, ERNEST ARTHUR, lawyer; b. Nashua, NH, Apr. 19, 1945; s. Fernand Ernest and Jeannette M. (Thibodeau) J.; m. Bridget Belton, Sept. 4, 1977; 1 child, Alexandra. BA, Boston Coll., 1967, JD, 1970. Bar: N.H. 1970, U.S. Dist. Ct. N.H. 1971, U.S. Tax Ct. 1972; U.S. Ct. Appeals (1st cir.) 2004; diplomate Trial Practice Inst. Mng. atty. N.H. Legal Assistance, Nashua, 1970-72; ptnr. Janelle, Nadeau & Jette, Nashua, 1972-81; dir. Hamblett & Kerrigan, P.A., Nashua, 1981-93; pvt. practice Nashua, 1993—. Lectr. paralegal studies Rivier Coll., Nashua, 1977-78. Chmn. Nashua Regional Planning Commn., 1981-82; mem. Town of Merrimack (N.H.) Master Plan Com., 1981, dir. Nashua Youth Coun., Inc., 1975-80, pres., 1978-79; dir. NEEDS, Inc., 1972-75; chmn. Heart Sunday, N.H. Heart Assn., 1973; mem. pub. affairs com. N.H. Assn. Commerce and Industry, 1983-93; bd. dirs. Cmty. Coun. Nashua, 2002—, sec. 2004—; mem. sch. bd. Bishop Guertin HS, 1994-96; mem. adv. bd. St. Joseph Hosp. Sch. Nursing, Nashua, NH, 2005-. Capt. U.S. Army, 1970. Mem. ABA (state com. disaster legal assistance 1973-75, litigation, tort and ins. practice sects.), N.H. Bar Assn. (past mem. law related edn., coop. with the cts., profl. responsibility coms.), N.H. Bar Found., N.H. Trial Lawyers Assn., Nashua Bar Assn. (pres. 1990-91), Greater Nashua C. of C. (dir. 1985-96), Four Seasons Property Owners' Assn. (pres. 1977-78), Rotary Club Nashua (dir. 1978-79, pres. 1992-93). Home: 9 Westbrook Dr Nashua NH 03060-5314 Office: 187 Main St Nashua NH 03060-2701 E-mail: ejette@ejette.com.

JETTER, ARTHUR CARL, JR., insurance company executive; b. Omaha, Oct. 9, 1947; s. Arthur Carl and Virginia Ann (Turner) J.; m. Jennifer Ann Jochim, Mar. 30, 1974; children: Arthur Carl III, Sarah Ann. BBA, Dana Coll., 1974. Registered health underwriter; CFP, CLU; registered employee benefits cons.; FLMI, LTCP. Sales rep. life ins. Guarantee Mut., Omaha, 1974-81; pres. Art Jetter & Co., Omaha, 1981—, Employers Mut. Acceptance Co., Omaha, 1981—. Capt., helicopter pilot inf. U.S. Army, 1968-72, Vietnam. Fellow Life Mgmt. Inst.; mem. Life and Health Ins. Found. for Edn. (life; dir. 2004-), CLU (cert., edn. chmn. Omaha chpt. 1984-91), Nat. Assn. Ind. Life Brokerage Agencies (chmn. 2000), Nat. Assn. Health Underwriters (pres. 1991-92, Gordon Meml. award 1995, Health Ins. Industry person of yr. 1995), Mass Mktg. Ins. Inst. (Person of Yr. award 1993). Republican. Lutheran. Home: 13624 Parker Cir Omaha NE 68154-3829 Office: Art Jetter and Co 11305 Chicago Cir Omaha NE 68154-2636 Office Phone: 402-330-2900. E-mail: art@jetter.com.

JETTON, C. LORING, JR., lawyer; b. Pitts., Feb. 10, 1943; s. Clyde Loring and Barbara (Lewis) J.; m. Marion Luyken, Feb. 19, 1966; children: Ada Elizabeth, Christopher Loring. AB, Harvard U., 1964; JD, Columbia U., 1969. Bar: N.Y. 1969, D.C. 1970. Law clk. to Hon. W. Feinberg U.S. Ct. Appeals (2d. cir.), 1969-70; assoc. Wilmer, Cutler & Pickering, Washington, 1970-76, ptnr., 1977—. Lt. U.S. Army, 1964-66. Mem. ABA, D.C. Bar.

JETT-PARMER, JONATHAN JACKSON, mechanical engineer; b. Tampa, Fla., June 28, 1965; s. Jackson and Emily Marie (Knecht) Parmer; m. Tamera Elaine Jett, Nov. 3, 1990. Student, Ga. Inst. Tech., 1987-88; BSME, U. South Fla., 1991; MME and Environ. Engring., 1992. Registered intern engr., Fla. Gen. mgr. Sta. WREK-FM, Atlanta, 1983-88; dir. affiliate rels., gen. mgr. Sun Radio Network, Tampa, Fla., 1988-89; project engr. Zephyrhills (Fla.) Bottled Waters, 1989-91, prodn. and maintenance mgr., 1991-92; mgr. engring. VanDenBerg Foods, Balt., 1992—98; mfg. mgr. Lipton, 1998—2003; plant mgr. Unilever, Atlanta, 2004—. Asst. dir. Ga. Renaissance Festival, Fairburn, 1987—; founder, dir. Fla. Fantasy Festival, Tampa, 1989—; recruiter Young Reps., Atlanta, 1988; dir. Md. Renaissance Festival, 1993; Balt. Mayor's task force Greenways, 1993; bd. dirs. Franklintown Land Trust, 1993. Lt. cmdr., commdg. officer USN, 1997. Mem. ASME (recognition award 1990, 91), AIAA, NSPE, Fla. Soc. Profl. Engrs., Diver's Alert Network, Order of Engr., Themis. Avocations: racquetball, hiking, bicycling, reading, writing. Office: Unilever 1591 Murphy Ave Atlanta GA 30310

JEUB, MICHAEL LEONARD, financial consultant; b. Mpls., Mar. 2, 1943; s. Leonard M. and Florence J.; m. Alice Ann Linden (div. 1980); children: Christopher Michael, Annette Michelle; m. Julia Jean Stephenson, Feb. 4, 1983; children: Michael Leonard Jr., Robert. BS in Acctg., Calif. State Poly. U., 1966. CPA, Tex., Calif. Staff acct. Ernst & Whinney, LA, 1966-70; CFO Internat. Clin. Lab., Inc., Nashville, 1970-85, pres. east, 1985-88; pres. August Enterprises, 1988-91; pres., COO, CFO MICA, San Diego, 1991-93; exec. v.p., CFO, treas. Nat. Health Labs., Inc., 1993-94; sr. v.p., CFO Jenny Craig Internat., 1994-2000; fin. cons. La Jolla, Calif., 2000—01; ptnr. Tatum CFO, 2000—; CFO The Immune Response Corp., San Diego, 2002—03, Road Runner Sparts, 2005—. Office: 5549 Copley Dr San Diego CA 92111 Home: 5526 Caminito Exquisito San Diego CA 92130-2822 Personal E-mail: MikeJeub@aol.com.

JEVTOVIC-TODOROVIC, VESNA, physician, researcher; d. Dragomir Jeftimije and Milka Radisav Jevtovic; m. Slobodan Milenko Todorovic, Oct. 6, 1984; children: Marko Slobodan Todorovic, Nikola Slobodan Todorovic, Katarina Vesna Todorovic. MD, U. Belgrade Sch. Medicine, Yugoslavia, 1980—85; PhD, U. Ill. Sch. Medicine, Chgo., 1986—2000. Cert. Mo., 1992, Va., 2001. Asst. prof., anesthesiology Wash. U. Sch. Medicine, St. Louis, 1998—2001; assoc. prof. U. Va., Dept. Anesthesiology, Charlottesville, 2001—. Grantee, NIH, 2000—. Mem.: Va. Soc. Anesthesiology (life), Assn. U. Anesthesiologists (life), Soc. for Neuroscience (life), Mo. Soc. Anesthesiologists (life), Am. Soc. Anesthesiologists (life). Achievements include patents for the role of NMDA antagonists in the management of chronic painful conditions. Avocations: piano, needlepoint, gardening. Office: U Va Dept Anesthesiology PO Box 800710 Charlottesville VA 22908-0710 Business E-Mail: vj3w@virginia.edu.

JEWELL, JASON ERIC, adult education educator; b. Searcy, Ark., Feb. 23, 1973; s. Fred Richard and Alice Joyce Jewell; m. Vickie Lynn Richardson; children: Jonathan Edward, Frederick William. BA, Harding U., Searcy, 1995; MA, Pepperdine U., Malibu, Calif., 1997; PhD, Fla. State U., Tallahassee, 2004. Asst. prof. Faulkner U., Montgomery, Ala., 2004—. Adj. faculty Ludwig von Mises Inst., Auburn, Ala., 2005—. Author: Harding University's Department of Music. Tchr. Vaughn Pk. Ch. of Christ, Montgomery, 2004—07; min. Coy Ch. of Christ, Ark., 2003—04; dir. The Montgomery Christian Endowment for the Arts and Humanities, 2007. Recipient Thomas Campbell award for Excellence in Tchg., Fla. State U., 2002; U. fellow, 1998—2001, Dissertation Rsch. grantee, 2001. Mem.: So. Conf. on Brit. Studies, Oxford Round Table (assoc.), Oxford Club (life), Phi Kappa Phi, Phi Eta Sigma (life), Alpha Chi (life), Phi Alpha Theta (life). American Heritage. Avocations: travel, coin collecting/numismatics. Home: 920 Green Ridge Ct Montgomery AL 36109 Office: Faulkner University 5345 Atlanta Highway Montgomery AL 36109 Home Phone: 334-356-3102; Office Phone: 334-386-7919. Business E-Mail: jjewell@faulkner.edu.

JEWELL, JUDY ANN, funeral director, counselor; b. Seattle, July 15, 1946; d. Orval Arthur and Violet Anna (Altemose) Huntington; m. Crowell (Rocky) Edward Jewell, Sr., Jan. 6, 1996; children: Crystal Paulette Jewell Voelker, Crowell Edward Jr. BA, Ctrl. Wash. U., Ellensburg, 1970; M in Religious Edn., Seattle U., 1983; MDiv, Claremont Sch. Theology, Calif., 1989, D in Ministry, 1990. Tchr. Christ the King Acad., Poulsbo, Wash., 1978—83; tchr., coach St. Anthony HS, Maui, Hawaii, 1983—85; chaplain Tri-Cities Chaplaincy, Kennewick, Wash., 1985—86; min. Christian edn., chaplain First Congl. Ch. & Pilgrim Sch., LA, 1988—90; assoc. pastor Univ. Temple United Meth. Ch., Seattle, 1990—95; dir. pastoral care & counseling Bayview Manor Retirement Res., Seattle, 1995—99; bereavement specialist, funeral dir. Evergreen Funeral Home, Everett, Wash., 1999—. Pastoral counselor NW Pastoral Counseling, Tacoma, 1992—94; chaplain Providence Everett Med. Ctr., Everett, 2002—07. Co-chair edn. sect. discipleship bd., elder United Meth. Ch.; v.p. Serene Alternatives II, Stanwood, Wash., 1996—2007; bd. dirs. Univ. Temple Day Care, Seattle, 1990—95, U. of W. Recommitant DNA, Seattle, 1991—95. Recipient Svc. Driven Excellence award, Alderwoods Group, 2000. Mem.: Am. Assn. Pastoral Counselors (cert.), Assn. Profl. Chaplains (bd. cert. chaplain). Avocations: skiing, boating, tennis, bicycling, guitar. Office: Evergreen Funeral Home 4504 Broadway Everett WA 98203

JEWELL, MARK LAURENCE, plastic surgeon; b. Kansas City, Mo., Oct. 26, 1947; s. James Lemley and Martha (Bullock) Jewell; m. Mary Rita Lind, Nov. 30, 1975; children: Mark II, James, Hillary. BS in Zoology, U. Kans., 1969, MD, 1973; postgrad., UCLA, 1977, U. Tenn., 1979. Cert. Am. Bd. Plastic Surgery, 1981. Resident in surgery UCLA, 1973—76; fellow, burn surgery U. So. Calif., LA, 1976—77; resident, plastic surgery U. Tenn., Chattanooga, 1977—79; practice medicine specializing in plastic surgery Eugene, Oreg., 1979—; plastic surgeon Inamed Aesthetics; asst. clin. prof. plastic surgery Oreg. Health Sci. Univ., Portland. Pres. Aesthetic Surgery Jour.; contbr. articles to profl. jours. Lt. USNR, 1970—79. Recipient Rsch. award, Am. Soc. Clin. Pathologists, 1972, U. Kans. Sch. Medicine, 1973. Mem.: Oreg. Soc. Plastic Surgery, Am. Soc. for Aesthetic Plastic Surgery (v.p., pres., Tiffany award 2003), Am. Med. Joggers Soc., Lane County Med. Soc., Oreg. Med. Assn., Am. Soc. Plastic Surgeons. Episcopalian. Avocations: helicopter skiing, marathons, art, cooking, computers. Office: 630 E 13th Ave Eugene OR 97401-3625 E-mail: mljmd@teleport.com.*

JEWELL, ROBERT V., lawyer; b. Houston, 1954; BBA in Fin., U. Tex., 1975; JD, So. Meth. U., 1978. Bar: Tex. 1978. Ptnr., Corp./Securities Dept. Andrews & Kurth LLP, Houston, mem. mgmt. com. Editor: Southwestern Law Jour., 1978. Mem.: ABA, Tex. Bus. Law Found., State Bar Tex. (corp. law com., Corp. Banking & Bus. Law Sect.), Houston Bar Assn., Phi Delta Phi. Office: Andrews & Kurth LLP 600 Travis St Ste 4200 Houston TX 77002-3090 Office Phone: 713-220-4358. Office Fax: 713-238-7135. Business E-Mail: bjewell@andrewskurth.com.

JEWELL, VANESSA YODER, surgical physician's assistant; b. June 19, 1956; BMS, Alderson Broaddus Coll., Phillipi, W.Va., 1978; MHA, Ctrl. Mich. U., 1986. Physician asst. thoracic surgery Bay Pines VAMC, Fla., 1987—; asst. clin. prof. of health care svc. George Washington P.A. program, Washington, 1996—; surgical preceptor U. Fla. P.A. program, Gainesville, 1990—; asst. clin. prof. physician asst. program South U., Savannah, Ga., 1999—. Instr. water safety ARC, 1972-90; bd. dirs. (event planner) Gifted Assn. Pinellas Co., 1995-98; various dist. level. positions West. Ctrl. Fla. coun. Boy Scouts Am., 1989-98. Office: 10000 Bay Pines Blvd Surg Svc-112 Bay Pines FL 33744 Office Phone: 727-398-6661 ext. 5203. E-mail: Vanessa.Jewell@Med.Va.gov.

JEWETT, GEORGE FREDERICK, forest products company executive; b. Spokane, Wash., Apr. 10, 1927; s. George Frederick and Mary Pelton (Cooper) J.; m. Lucille Winifred McIntyre, July 11, 1953; children: Mary Elizabeth, George Frederick III. BA, Dartmouth Coll., 1950; MBA, Harvard U., 1952. Asst. sec., asst. treas. Potlatch Corp., 1955-62, v.p. adminstrn., 1962-68, corp. v.p. adminstrn., 1968-71, sr. v.p., 1972-77, vice chmn. bd. adminstrn., 1977-78, vice chmn., 1979-99, retired, 1999. Trustee Calif. Pacific Med. Found. Mem.: NY Yacht Club, Pacific Union Club, Bohemian Club, St. Francis Yacht Club. Home: 2990 Broadway St San Francisco CA 94115-1062 Office: 235 Montgomery St Ste 611 San Francisco CA 94104 Office Phone: 415-981-3390.

JEWETT, THOMAS O., science educator, writer; b. Belleville, Ill., Apr. 6, 1949; s. Robert Wayne and Mamie Louise Jewett; m. Laura Lorraine Lloyd, May 20, l995; children: Sean Thomas, Jefferson Travous. BS, So. Ill. U., Edwardsville, 1971, MS, 1976; EdS, St. Louis U., 1984, PhD, 1985. Cert. tchr. K-6 Ill., tchr. 6-12 Ill., gen. adminstr. K-12 Ill., supervisory adminstr. K-12 Ill. Tchr. Wolf Br. Sch. Dist., Belleville, 1971—87, prin. and asst. supt., 1987—92; adj. instr. Southwestern Ill. Coll., Belleville, 1976—86; prof. So. Ill. U., Edwardsville, 1992—2001, emeritus prof., 2001—; prof. McKendree Coll., Lebanon, Ill., 2001—. Curriculum cons. and author Met. Area Urban Resources Partnership, St. Louis, 1995—96; cons. Project Concern-Ill. Dept. Edn., Springfield, 1995—96, Met. Profl. Devel. Sch. Consortium, St. Louis, 1995—97. Author: Outdoor Environmental Learning Activities (Ill. Environ. Conservation Tchr. of the Yr., 1986), First Impressions: 200 Years of St. Clair County History, The Belleville Germans; contbg. author: Prairie For the Prairie State; contbr. articles to numerous profl jours. Bd. dirs. St. Clair County Hist. Soc., Belleville, 1983—86; mem. exec. com. Met. Profl. Devel. Sch. Consortium, St. Louis, 1995—97. Recipient Outstanding Young Educator award, Belleville Jaycees, 1984, Tchr. of Yr. award, Ill. Conservation Dept., 1986, Generations of Success award, Southwestern Ill. Coll., 1996, Sch. of Edn. Gt. Tchr. award, So. Ill. U., Edwardsville, 1996; Sch. of Edn. rsch. grantee, So. Ill. U., 1999 to 2001. Mem.: Ill. Sci. Tchrs. Assn., Nat. Sci. Tchrs. Assn., Ill. State Acad. Sci., Kappa Delta Pi (counselor 1992—96). Avocations: scuba diving, triathlons, fiction writing, gardening. Office: McKendree College 701 College Road Lebanon IL 62254 Home Phone: 618-566-7163. Business E-Mail: tojewett@mckendree.edu.

JEWITT, DAVID, astronomer; b. Eng. m. Jing Li. BS in Astronomy, U. London, 1979; MS in Planetary Sci., Calif. Inst. Tech., 1980; PhD in Planetary Sci. and Astronomy, Calif. Tech. Inst., 1983. Rsch. asst. Calif. Inst. Tech., 1980—83; asst. prof. MIT, 1983—88; assoc. astronomer, Inst. for Astronomy U. Hawaii, Honolulu, 1988—93, astronomer, Inst. for Astronomy, 1993—, assoc. prof. Dept. Physics & Astronomy, 1993—, prof. Dept. Physics & Astronomy, 1993—. Recipient Exceptional Scientific Achievement medal, NASA, 1996. Fellow: Am. Assn. for Advancement of Sci., Am. Acad. Arts and Sciences, U. Coll. London; mem.: NAS. Office: Inst for Astronomy 2680 Woodlawn Dr Honolulu HI 96822 Office Phone: 808-956-7682. Office Fax: 808-956-4532. E-mail: jewitt@hawaii.edu.

JEYAKUMAR, ANITA, pediatrician, otolaryngologist; BS, Belmont U., Nashville, Tenn., 1996; MS, Tenn. State U., Nashville, Tenn., 1999; MD, Meharry Med. Coll., Nashville, Tenn., 2001. Fellow pediatric otolaryngology Cleve. Clinic Found., 2006—. Contbr. articles to profl. jours. Mem.: Am. Otolaryngology Assn. (life; pres. gamma chpt. 1999—2001). Office: Cleve Clinic Found 9500 S Euclid Ave Cleveland OH 44195 Home Phone: 216-444-2200; Office Phone: 216-444-2200.

JEYARETNAM, BENJAMIN S., science administrator; b. Batticaloa, Sri Lanka, Mar. 07; PhD, U. Ga., Athens, 1998. Mgr. Sanofi Pasteur, Swiftwater, Pa., 2002—07. Home Phone: 570-895-3122. Personal E-mail: benjamin.jeyaretnam@sanofipasteur.com.

JEYDEL, RICHARD K., lawyer; b. Livingston, NJ, Jan. 10, 1950; m. Ellen C. Ebert, Aug. 30, 1981; children: Patricia, Peter. AB, Sarah Lawrence Coll., 1972; JD, Harvard U., 1975. Bar: N.J. 1975, N.Y. 1983, U.S. Ct. Appeals (3d and 5th cirs.) 1983. Assoc. McCarter & English, Newark, 1976-79; corp. counsel Kanematsu-Gosho (USA), Inc., NYC, 1979-85, v.p., gen. counsel, 1985-91; sr. v.p., sec., gen. counsel Kanematsu USA Inc., NYC, 1991—. Past mem. ethics com. Supreme Ct. Dist. XIII; mem. panel of arbitrators and mediators, large complex case program arbitrator and pres. panel mediator Am. Arbitration Assn. Capt. U.S. Army, 1975-76. Mem. ABA, Am. Corp. Counsel Assn. (bd. dirs. 1996-2002), N.J. Bar Assn., N.J. Corp. Counsel Assn. (bd. dirs. 1986-90, 93—, past pres.), Am. Arbitration Assn. (panel arbitrators and mediators, bd. dirs. 1996—). Office: Kanematsu USA Inc 75 Rockefeller Plz 22nd Fl New York NY 10019 Office Phone: 212-704-9482. Business E-Mail: rjeydel@kanematsuusa.com.

JEYNES, MARY KAY, college dean; b. Miami, Fla., Oct. 31, 1941; d. Nasrallah and Martha Demetry; m. Paul Jeynes, Sept. 30, 1978. BS, Fla. State U., 1963. Program dir. Orange County YMCA, Orlando, Fla., 1964-69, Ea. Queens YMCA, Belrose, N.Y., 1970-73; regional coord. N.Y. State Park and Recreation Commn., NYC, 1974-77; dir. health, fitness and recreation YWCA of N.Y.C., 1978-79; dean continuing edn., dir. spl. events Marymount Manhattan Coll., NYC, 1980—2005, dir. spl. events, 2005—. Mem.: Manhattan (N.Y.) C. of C. (hon.; pres. 1996—97, chmn. bd. dirs. 1998—2002). Office: Marymount Manhattan Coll 221 E 71st St New York NY 10021-4532

JEYNES, WILLIAM HETTICH, education educator, religious organization administrator, minister; b. NYC, Mar. 27, 1957; s. Paul Hettich and Enid Phillips Jeynes; m. Hyelee Jung Jeynes, June 17, 1986; children: Isaiah, Elisha, Luke. BA, U. Wis., 1979; DMin, Freedom U., 1986; PhD, Freedom Sem., 1992; EdM grad. first in class, Harvard U., 1993; PhD, U. Chgo., 1997. Lectr. Northea. Ill. U., Chgo., 1996—99, U. Chgo., 1996—99, Roosevelt U., Schaumburg, 1999, Nat. Louis U., Evanston, 1999; asst. prof. Hillsdale Coll., Mich., 1999—2001; assoc. prof., prof. Calif. State U., Long Beach, 2001—. Advisor, spkr. Harvard Family Rsch. Project, Cambridge, Mass., 2005—; non resident rsch. fellow Baylor U. Author: Divorce, Family Structure and the Academic Success of Children, 2002, Religion, Education and Academic Success, 2003, A Hand Not Shortened, 2006, American Educational History: School, Society and the Common Good, 2007, Christianity Education and Modern Society, 2007; contbr. articles. Pres. God's Love Ministries, Huntington Beach, Calif., 1978—. Named to Internat. Network Scholars, Johns Hopkins U., 2001; recipient Rosenberger award, U. Chgo., 1994. Mem.: APA, Am. Ednl. Rsch. Assn. (chair religion and edn. spl. interest group 2004—, exec. bd. mem. family, sch. cmty. partnerships spl. interest group 2004—06). Avocations: football, baseball, walking, weightlifting, chess. Office: Calif State U 1250 Bellflower Blvd Long Beach CA 90840 Office Phone: 562-985-5619.

JEZIERSKI, SCOTT, wireless monitoring, security, and surveillance company executive; married. B in Computer Engring., U. Minn. Pres. Wireless Imaging, LLC, Lino Lakes, Minn., 2003—. Achievements include invention of MailboxCam, a wireless security camera that can go months without a change of batteries. Office: Wireless Imaging LLC 1461 Sherman Lake Rd Lino Lakes MN 55038 Office Phone: 651-470-9507. Office Fax: 651-340-1382. Business E-Mail: scott@wirelessimaging.com.

JEZIORSKI, MICHAEL A., social studies educator; b. Plainview, NY, June 30, 1979; s. Anthony Robert and Corinne Joan Jeziorski. BS summa cum laude in Comm., St. John's U., Jamaica, NY, 2001; MS in Tchg. Social Studies, Columbia U., NYC, 2002; MA in History, L.I. U., Brookville, NY, 2006; postgrad., St. John's U., Jamaica, 2006—. Tchr. Commack (N.Y.) H.S. Mem.: L.I. Coun. Social Studies, Nat. Coun. Social Studies, Kappa Delta Pi. Home: 589 Coakley St East Meadow NY 11554

JEZUIT, LESLIE JAMES, manufacturing executive; b. Chgo., Nov. 4, 1945; s. Eugene and Tillie (Fleszewski) Jezuit; m. Janet Diane Bushlus, Oct. 12, 1968; children: Douglas Blake, Kevin Lane. BS in Mech. and Aerospace Engring., Ill. Inst. Tech., 1969, MBA, 1974. Mgr. engring. graphic systems group Rockwell Internat., Chgo., 1968-74, dir. comml. systems Cicero, Ill., 1974-75; v.p. mktg. and sales Mead Digital Sys., Dayton, Ohio, 1975-80; v.p. mktg. and sales Signal divsn. Fed. Signal Corp., University Park, Ill., 1980-81, pres. Signal divsn., 1981-85, v.p. corp. devel. Oak Brook, Ill., 1985-86; div. mgr. power distbn. div. Eaton Corp., Milw., 1986-87, gen. mgr. indsl. control and power distbn. div., 1987-88, v.p., 1988-91; pres., COO Robertshaw Controls Co., Richmond, Va., 1991-95; pres., CEO, chmn. bd dirs. Quixote Inc., Chgo., 1995—; chmn. Transp. Mgmt. Techs., LLC, Chgo., 1998-2001, Quixote Corp., 2001. Instr. Keller Sch. Mgmt., Chgo., 1982—83. Active United Way, Chgo., 1983—85; mem. Chgo. Crime Commn.; bd. dirs. Better Bus. Bur. Milw., 1986, United Performing Arts Found. Milw., 1986, Greater Milw. Com., 1991—92. Mem.: Gas Appliance Mfrs. Assn. (bd. dirs. 1994—96), Am. Hwy. Users Assn. (bd. dirs. 2001—, vice chmn. 2003), Monee C. of C., Will County Local Devel. Co. (v.p. 1984—85, Bus. Man of the Yr. award 1985), S. Surburban C. of C., Met. Club (Chgo.). Republican. Achievements include patents in field. Avocations: boating, fishing, cross country skiing, photography. Home: 26576 Countryside Lake Dr Mundelein IL 60060-3342 Office: Quixote Inc 35 E Wacker Dr Chicago IL 60601-2108 Office Phone: 312-467-6755. Personal E-mail: quixpres@msn.com.

JHA, MANISH, communications executive; b. 1968; B in Philos. and Religion, Colgate U., 1998. Comml. sales analyst ESPN, Inc., 1991, dir., Affiliate Ops. and Planning, v.p., Affiliate Sales Devel. and Ops., 1999, v.p., Broadband and Interactive TV Sales, 2001—03, sr. v.p., gen. mgr., Emerging Media & Data Services, 2003—04, sr. v.p., gen. mgr., Mobile ESPN, 2004—. Named one of 40 Executives Under 40, Multichannel News, 2006. Office: ESPN Inc ESPN Plz 935 Middle St Bristol CT 06010

JHABVALA, FARROKH, lawyer; b. Bombay, May 2, 1945; arrived in U.S., 1972; s. Pheroze and Freny Jhabvala; m. Margarita Gutierrez, Aug. 25, 1978. PhD, Tufts U., 1977; JD, U. Miami, 1988. Bar: Fla. 1988, DC 1989, US Dist. Ct. (so. dist. Fla.) 1989, US Dist. Ct. (mid. dist. Fla.) 2000, US Ct. Appeals (11th cir.) 1996, US Ct. Appeals (5th cir.) 1997, US Ct. Appeals (4th cir.) 2001, US Ct. Appeals (7th cir.) 2002, US Ct. Appeals (8th cir.) 2004. Asst., assoc. prof. Fla. Internat. U., Miami, 1976—84, prof. Internat. Rels., 1984—98; assoc. Jorden Burt LLP, Miami, 1988—97, ptnr., 1997—. Contbr. articles to profl. jours. Recipient Francis Deak prize, Am. Soc. Internat. Law, 1979. Mem.: ABA. Avocations: history, gardening. Office: Jorden Burt LLP 777 Brickell Ave Ste 500 Miami FL 33131 Office Phone: 305-371-2600. Office Fax: 305-372-9928. Business E-Mail: fj@jordenusa.com.

JHABVALA, RUTH PRAWER, writer; b. Cologne, Germany, May 7, 1927; lived in India, 1951-75; came to U.S., 1975; d. Marcus and Eleonora (Cohn) Prawer; m. Cyrus S. H. Jhabvala, 1951; 3 children. MA, London U., 1951, DLitt (hon.), 1986, LHD (hon.), 1995, D Arts (hon.), 1996. Author: To Whom She Will, 1955, The Nature of Passion, 1956, Esmond in India, 1957, The Householder, 1960, Get Ready for Battle, 1962, A Backward Place, 1965, A New Dominion, 1972, Heat and Dust, 1975 (Booker award for fiction Nat. Book League 1975), In Search of Love and Beauty, 1983, Three Continents, 1987, Poet and Dancer, 1993, Shards of Memory, 1995; (short story collections) Like Birds, Like Fishes and Other Stories, 1964, A Stronger Climate: Nine Stories, 1968, An Experience of India, 1971, How I Became a Holy Mother and Other Stories, 1976, Out of India: Selected Stories, 1986, East Into Upper East, 1998, My Nine Lives, 2004; (film scripts) The Householder, 1963; (with James Ivory), Shakespeare Wallah, 1965, The Guru, 1968, Bombay Talkie, 1970, Autobiography of a Princess, 1975, Roseland, 1977, Hullabaloo over Georgie and Bonnie's Pictures, 1978, The Europeans, 1979, Jane Austen in Manhattan, 1980, Quartet, 1981, Heat and Dust, 1983, The Bostonians, 1984, A Room With a View, 1986 (Writers Guild of Am. award for best adapted screeplay 1986, Acad. award for best adapted screenplay 1986); (with John Schlesinger) Madame Sousatzka, 1988, Mr. and Mrs. Bridge, 1990, Howards End, 1992 (Acad. award for best adapted screenplay 1992), Remains of the Day, 1993 (Acad. award nomination for best adapted screenplay 1993), Jefferson in Paris, 1995, Surviving Picasso, 1996; (with James Ivory) A Soldier's Daughter Never Cries, 1998, The Golden Bowl, 2000. Decorated comdr. Brit. Empire; Guggenheim fellow, 1976; Neil Gunn. Internat. fellow, 1979; MacArthur Found. fellow, 1984-89. Home: 400 E 52d St New York NY 10022-6404

JI, TINGTING, mortgage company executive, consultant; PhD, Ohio State U., Columbus, 2002. Sr. quantitative analyst Irwin Home Equity, San Ramon, Calif., 2002—03; mgr. Kpmg, LLP, San Francisco, 2004—. Recipient Standing Ovation award, Kpmg, 2006. Mem.: Am. Econ. Assn. Home: 7203 590 Avocet Dr Redwood City CA 94065 Office: Kpmg LLP 55 2d St San Francisco CA 94105 Personal E-mail: pangtuzi@yahoo.com. Business E-Mail: tji@kpmg.com.

JIA, DONGDONG, nanoscience educator, physics professor; b. Beijing, Dec. 30, 1968; arrived in U.S., 2001; s. Weiyi Jia and Lizhu Lu; m. Yi Wu Jia, Aug. 12, 1999; children: Jessica H., Margaret D. Student, Tsinghua U., Beijing, 1991; BSc in Exptl. Physics with honors, Trinity Coll., Dublin, Ireland, 1993, MA in Laser and Laser Spectroscopy, 1993; PhD in Materials Sci., Ctrl. Iron and Steel Rsch. Inst., Beijing, 2000. Postdoctoral rschr. U. Ga., Athens, 2001—02; asst. prof. U. PR, Mayaguez, 2003—04, Lock Haven U. Pa., 2005—. Contbr. articles to profl. jours., Phosphor Handbook. Grantee, USN, 2004, U.S. Dept. Energy, 2005. Mem.: Am. Electrochem. Soc., Am. Phys. Soc. Achievements include patents pending for two-dimensional nanorings and fabrication methods; sifted sol gel method to synthesize nanophosphoros; three international patents on new phosphors. Avocations: board games, poker. Office: Lock Haven U Pa 401 N Fairview St Lock Haven PA 17745 Personal E-mail: ddjia2002@yahoo.com.

JIABAO, WEN, Chinese government official; b. Tianjin, China, Sept. 1942; m. Zhang Peili; 2 children. B in Geol. Structure, Beijing Inst. Geology, 1965, postgrad., 1968. Technician & polit. instr. geomechanics survey team, head political div. Gansu Provincial Geological Bureau, 1968—78, mem. standing com. of party com. geomechanics survey team, 1978—79, deputy section head & engr., 1979—81, deputy dir.-general, 1981—82; dir. policy & law rsch. office Ministry of Geology & Mineral Resources, 1982—83, vice-minister, 1983—85; deputy dir. gen. office CPC Central Com., 1985—86, dir. gen. office, 1986—87, alt. mem. of secretariat, dir. gen. office, sec. work com., 1987—92, alt. mem. political bureau, mem. secretariat, dir. gen office, sec. work com., 1992—93, alt. mem. political bureau, mem. secretariat, 1993—97, mem. political bureau, mem. secretariat, 1997—98, mem. political bureau, mem. secretariat, vice-premier state council, sec. financial work com., 1998—2002, mem. standing com. of political bureau, 2002—03; vice-premier state council People's Republic of China, 2002—03, mem. standing com. of political bureau, 2003—, premier state council, 2003—. Mem. Communist Party of China, 1965—. Named one of 100 Most Influential People, Time Mag., 2006. Mem.: Leading Party Members' Group. Office: Office of the Premier c/o State Council Secretariat Zhong Nan Beijing China

JIALI, YE, medical researcher; b. Tianjin, Aug. 29, 1973; d. Guodong Ye and Yunzhen Chen; m. Roy Xu, July 3, 2000; children: Andrew Xu, Allison Xu. PhD, Ga. State U., Atlanta, 2006. Rsch. fellow Ga. State U., Atlanta, 2004—06; rsch. coord. Nat. Ctr. Primary Care, Atlanta, 2007—. Recipient Outstanding Academic Achievement in Grad. Studies award, Ga. State U., 2006. Mem.: Internat. Comm. Assn. (assoc.), Nat. Comm. Assn. (assoc. participant doctoral honors seminar 2004, award for top 4 paper in comm. and tech. divsn. 2006). Achievements include research in health communication and public health awareness; health disparity in cardiovascular disease; health information seeking and communication technology. Home: 6200 Crestgate Ln Tucker GA 30084 E-mail: jye@msm.edu.

JIAMBALVO, JAMES, dean; BS, U. Ill., 1970, MAS, 1973; PhD in Acctg., Ohio State U., 1977. Auditor Haskins & Sells, 1970—72; mem. faculty U. Wash. Bus. Sch., Seattle, 1977—, chmn. dept. acctg., 1992—96, faculty dir. e-business, 2000—03, Pricewaterhouse Coopers and Alumni Prof. in Acctg., 1995—, dean, 2005—. Mem. editl. bd. Jour. Mgmt. Acctg. Rsch., 1989—, Contemporary Acctg. Rsch., 1989—; assoc. editor The Acctg. Rev. Author: (textbook) Managerial Accounting. Recipient Andrew V. Smith Award for Svc. to Sch. Bus., Wash. U., 2000, Lex N. Gamble award excellence in field e-commerce. Office: UW Business School Mackenzie Hall Box 353200 Seattle WA 98195-3200 Office Phone: 206-543-4750. Office Fax: 206-685-9392.

JIAN, CHEN, international organization official; b. Feb. 2, 1942; married; 1 child. Attaché Dept Internat. Orgn. and Conf. Fgn Min., 1977—80; asst. Office Exec. Dir. representing China at Internat. Monetary Fund., 1984—85; dir. to counselor to dep. dir-gen Dept. of Internat. Orgn. and Conf. of Fgn Min., 1985—92; dir. - gen. Dept. Info., 1994—96; asst. min. Fgn. Affairs, 1996—98; spokesman Fgn. Min.; amb. extraordinary and plenipotentiary of China to Japan, 1998—2001; dip. Chinese Fgn. Min.; attaché, Chinese Permanent Mission UN, 1972—77, third sec., second sec., and then first sec., 1980—84, amb. extraordinary and plenipotentiary and dep. permanent rep., 1992—94, under sec.-gen. gen. assembly and conf. mgmt., 2001—. Rep. Gen. Assembly, Sec. Coun., Econ. and Soc. Counc., UN Environ. Program, Econ. and Soc. Commn. for Asia and Pacific. Office: UN Dept Gen Assembly and Conf Mgmt First Ave at 46th St New York NY 10017*

JIANG, BIN, mathematician, educator; arrived in U.S., 1995; s. Zhijin Jiang and Guifang Zhang; m. Jinhua Hao, Feb. 19, 1968; 1 child, Jenny. BS in Math., U. Sci. and Tech. of China, 1990; MS in Math., Chinese Acad. Sci., 1993; MS in Computer Sci., U. Calif., Santa Barbara, 1999, PhD in Math., 1999. Rsch. assoc. Chinese Acad. Scis., Beijing, 1993—95; tchg. asst. U. Calif., Santa Barbara, Calif., 1995—99; rsch. assoc. Environ. Sys. Rsch. Inst., Redlands, Calif., 1999—2003; asst. prof. math. Portland State U., Oreg., 2003—. Proposal rev. panelist U.S. Dept. Energy, Washington, 2005—. Contbr. articles to profl. jours. Recipient Outstanding Tchg. award, U. Calif., Santa Barbara, 1998; fellow, 1999; grantee, Portland State U., 2004, 2005; Zhang Zongzhi Scientific fellowship, U. Sci. and Tech. China, 1990. Mem.: Soc. Applied and Indsl. Math., Am. Math. Soc. Achievements include development of an open source parallel sparse matrix solver; invention of a modern automatic window system for advanced passenger trains. Office: Math Dept Portland State University 724 SW Harrison Street Portland OR 97201 Home Phone: 503-520-0305; Office Phone: 503-725-8294. Office Fax: 503-725-3661. Business E-Mail: bjiang@pdx.edu.

JIANG, ERIC Y, research scientist, marketing executive; s. Wenqing Jiang and Yuying Zhu; m. Ning Ma, Aug. 8, 1988; children: David D., Dirk. BS, Wuhan U. Tech., China, 1983, MS, 1986; PhD, Duke U., Durham, NC, 1995. Sr. scientist Bio-Rad Labs. Inc., Cambridge, Mass., 1995—99; rsch. product mgr. Thermo Fisher Sci. Inc., Madison, Wis., 1999—. Recipient Student award, Coblentz Soc., 1994; US Nat. Coun. Rsch. award, 1995. Mem.: Soc. Applied Spectroscopy. Achievements include discovery of development of generalized PAS theory for multilayer materials; first application of global phase 2DCOS in PAS and sample modulation experiment; revealing significant advantage and convenience of 2D global phase methods in analyzing complex data from modulation experiments; applications of G2DCOS in imaging data analysis of concentration varying complex bio-tissue samples; applications of generalized 2DIR in FTIR PAS; first applications of G2DIR in the field of FTIR PAS; theory for converting PM-IRRAS signal to conventional FTIR spectral intensity; this appraoch simplies the conversion of complex spectral intensity to normal spectral intensity; patents for developed new VCD optics and calibration method; invention of new optics produced VCD spectra with shortest data collection time (world record 16 sec); invention beat IR differation limit for tough thin layer material analysis; research in developed phase approach for submicro depth profiling in FTIR PAS. Office: Thermo Fisher Scientific 5225 Verona Rd Madison WI 53711 Business E-Mail: eric.jiang@thermofisher.com.

JIANG, JASON NANCHUN, advertising executive; b. 1974; BA Chinese Language and Lit., Huadong Normal U., 1995. CEO Everease Advertising Corp., 1994—2003; gen mgr. Aiqi Advt. (renamed Focus Media Advt.), 2003; founder, chmn., CEO Focus Media Advt., 2003—. Named a Media Person of the Year, China News Publisher's Media Mag., 2003; named one of 40 under 40, Advt. Age, 2007. Office: Focus Media Holding Ltd #369 Jiangsu Rd Fl 28-30 Shanghai 200050 China Office Phone: 86-21-32124661. Office Fax: 86-21-52400228.

JIANG, SHENGXIANG, electrical engineer, researcher; b. Huang-gang, China, May 11, 1979; arrived in US, 2002; s. Fuyuan Jiang and Guixiang Zhou; m. Zhe Yin, Feb. 9, 2007. B in Engring., U. Sci. and Tech. of China, Anhui, 2002; MS, U. Ill., Urbana, 2004, PhD, 2007. Rsch. asst. U. Sci. and Tech. China, Hefei, China, 2000—02; tchg. asst. U. Ill., Urbana, 2002—03, rsch. asst., 2003—. Contbr. articles to profl. jours. Scholar, U. Sci. and Tech. China, 1998, 1999; Guo Mo-Ruo scholarship, 2001. Mem.: IEEE, Soc. Indsl. and Applied Math. Avocations: travel, music, badminton. Home: 610 W Stoughton St 5 Urbana IL 61801 Office: Univ Illinois 1308 W Main St 164 CSL Urbana IL 61801 Home Phone: 217-344-7406; Office Phone: 217-333-6721. Personal E-mail: sjiang1@uiuc.edu.

JIANG, TIANYI, computer company executive; arrived in US, 1986; s. Guisen Jiang and Cheng Dian Wang. BS, Cornell U., Ithaca, NY, 1996, M in Engring., 1996; PhD, NYU, NYC, 2007. Mem. tech. staff Lucent Techs., Warren, NJ, 1997—99; sr. software cons. Deutsche Bank, NY, 1999—2000, Lehman Bros., NY, 2000—02; sr. software developer Citadel Investment Group, Chgo., 2004—05; COO AvePoint, Jersey City, 2002—. Cons. in field. Contbr. articles to profl. jours. Recipient PhD Tchg. Excellence Stern award, NYU, 2006; fellow, U. Wash., 2005; Kurnow Rsch. fellowship, NYU, 2007. Avocations: travel, swimming. Home Phone: 646-283-7211; Office Phone: 201-793-1111.

JIANG, WEI, adult education educator; b. Xi'an, China; s. Lehua Jiang and Jieping Zhao; m. Chuqian Jiang; 1 child, Xiaobo. PhD, Hong Kong U. Sci. and Tech., 2000. Stats. cons. AT&T, Morristown, NJ, 2000—03; asst. prof. Stevens Inst. Tech., Hoboken, NJ, 2003—. Recipient Career award, NSF, 2006. Mem.: INFORMS.

JIANG, WILLIAM YUYING, business educator, consultant, researcher; b. Hengyang, Hunan Province, China, Jan. 18, 1955; s. Rongguang Jiang and Hongkang Lei; m. Leslie Rongqui Yi, Sept. 5, 1988; children: Cosmo Yi, Cordelia Yi. BA in English, Hunan Normal U., Changsha, China, 1981; MA in English Lexicology, Xiamen U., China, 1984; MA in Comparative Lit., U. Ill., 1985, MS, 1986; MPhil in Bus., PhD in Bus., Columbia U., 1991. Asst. prof. San Jose State U., 1991—94, assoc. prof., 1994—97, prof., 1997—. Mng. dir. JS Cresvale Securities (US) Inc., Cupertino, Calif., 1999—2001; chancellor First Light Acad., Centreville, Va., 2002—. Translator: (novel) The Egoist, To Kill a Mockingbird; contbr. articles to profl. jours. Recipient Acad. Rsch. award, Chinese NSF, 1997, 2000; scholar, Pres. Fellowship, 1984—86, Columbia U., 1987, 1988, 1989, 1990; Marjorie Hope Nicolson scholar, 1987, Provost's Internat. scholar, San Jose State U., 2003. Mem.: Internat. Mgmt. Assn. Human Resource (chmn. mgmt. divsn. 1995—96), The Asian Am. Mfg. Assn., Chinese Economist Soc., Monte Jade Soc. Sci. and Tech., Indsl. Rels. Rsch. Assn., The Am. Econ. Assn., Assn. Chinese Profs. U.S. (dir. bd. 2001—03, dir. mem. 2001—03), Acad. Mgmt. (participation com. chair 1999—2002). Avocations: skiing, travel, foreign languages learning, reading. Home: 19901 La Mar Dr Cupertino CA 95014-3377 Office: San Jose State Univ One Washington Sq San Jose CA 95192-0070 Office Phone: 408-924-3551. Personal E-mail: jiang.w11@gmail.com. Business E-Mail: jiang_w@cob.sjsu.edu.

JIANG, XIAOMO, engineering researcher; b. Lengshuijiang, China, Jan. 18, 1973; s. Weixing Jiang and Manxiu Wu. MS, No. Jiaotong U., Beijing, 1998, Nat. U. Singapore, 2000; PhD in Civil Engring., Ohio State U., Columbus, 2005. Cert. profl. civil engr. Contbr. articles to profl. jours. Mem.: ASCE (corr.), Am. Soc. Engring. Edn. (corr.). Achievements include development of intelligent computational models adroitly integrating neural network, wavelet, chaos theory, & fuzzy logic with applications in structural system identification, healthy monitoring & transp. system. Office: Vanderbilt U Dept Civil Engring 279 Jacobs Hall VU Station B 351831 Nashville TN 37235 Office Phone: 615-322-8633. Personal E-mail: jiangxm2000@yahoo.com.

JIANG, ZHI-GANG, neuroscientist; b. Changchun, Jilin, China; s. Heng Jiang and Zhujun Gao; m. Jie Wang, 1987; 1 child, Hao. MD, Norman Bethune U. Med. Scis., Changchun, China, 1982, MSc, 1987; PhD, U. Glasgow, Scotland, 1994. Rsch. fellow lab. neurotoxicology NIMH, NIH, Bethesda, Md., 1997—2002; acting chief, lab. cell biology China Rehab. Rsch. Ctr., Beijing, 1987—91; postdoctoral rschr. Ohio State U. Med. Ctr., Columbus, 1994—97; postgrad. fellow U. Glasgow, Scotland, 1991—94; dir., neurodegenerative diseases Panacea Pharm., Inc., Gaithersburg, Md., 2002—. Contbr. sci. reports to profl. jours. Recipient Found. award, Henry Lester Trust, 1991, Intramural Rsch. Tng. award, NIMH, NIH, 1997—2000, Spl. Act Svc. award, 2002; grantee, Nat. Inst. Neurol. Disorders and Stroke, NIH, 2004, Nat. Lung, Heart and Blood Inst., NIH, 2006—; scholar, U. Glasgow, 1992—94. Mem.: Chinese Scholar Assn (organizer seminars and celebration activity 1997—98), Soc. Neurosci. Achievements include patents for novel neuroprotectant PAN-811, which efficiently suppress ischemic neurodegeneration; three patens pending in field. Avocations: drawing, music, travel, ping pong/table tennis, martial arts. Home: 15710 Winners Dr Gaithersburg MD 20878 Office: Panacea Pharm Inc 207 Perry Pky Ste 2 Gaithersburg MD 20877 Office Phone: 240-454-8023. Office Fax: 240-465-0450. Personal E-mail: zgjiang2002@yahoo.com. Business E-Mail: zgjiang@panaceapharma.com.

JIH, WEN-JANG, information scientist, educator; b. Chao-Chow, Taiwan, Feb. 2, 1951; arrived in U.S., 1981; s. Sien-Chiau and Moo-Lian Jih; m. Ya-Ling Hsu, June 22, 1992; children: Hsin-Jie children: Tiffany Jill, Melody Joanne, Emily Grace. Degree, Nat. Cen. U., 1974; MBA, Nat. Chengchi U., Taiwan, 1977; PhD in Bus. Adminstrn., U. North Tex., 1985. Mgmt. cons. China Productivity Ctr., Taipei, Taiwan, 1979—81; tchg. fellow North Tex. State U., Denton, 1981—84; vis. asst. So. Meth. U., Dallas, 1984—85; asst. prof. Auburn (Ala.) U., 1985—88; assoc. prof. U. Tenn., Chattanooga, 1988—94, prof. MIS, 1994—97; vis. prof. Chung-Yuan Christian U., Chung-Li, Taiwan, 1994—95; dean Coll. Mgmt. Da-Yeh U., Chang-Hua County, Taiwan, 1997—2001, prof., 1997—2001, Longwood U., Farmville, Va., 2001—03, Mid. Tenn. State U., Murfreesboro, 2003—. Pres. Chattanooga Chinese Assn., 1993—94. Recipient Best Paper award, SE Decision Sci. Inst., 2002, Disting. Alumnus award, Nat. Chau-Chow HS, 2002; grantee Excellent Rschr. award, Nat. Sci. Coun., Taiwan, 1997—2000. Mem.: Info. Resource Mgmt. Assn., Assn. Info. Sys. Office: Mid Tenn State U 1500 Greenland Dr Murfreesboro TN 37132 Office Phone: 615-898-5181. Business E-Mail: kjih@mtsu.edu.

JILES, DAVID COLLINGWOOD, physicist, materials science educator; b. London, Sept. 28, 1953; s. Kenneth Gordon and Vera Ellen (Johnson) J.; m. Helen Elizabeth Graham, Oct. 29, 1979; children: Sarah Jane, Elizabeth Anne, Andrew John, Richard David. BSc, Exeter U., Eng., 1975; MSc, Birmingham U., Eng., 1976, DSc, 1990; PhD, Hull U., Eng., 1979. Registered profl. engr.; chartered engr. Postdoctoral fellow Victoria U., Wellington, New Zealand, 1979-81; rsch. assoc. Queens U., Kingston, Ont., Canada, 1981-84; rsch. fellow Iowa State U., Ames, 1984-86, assoc. physicist, 1986-88, physicist, 1988-90, assoc. prof., 1988-90, sr. physicist,

1990—, prof., 1991—, Anson Marston disting. prof., 2003—; prof. magnetics, dir. Wolfson Ctr. U. Cardiff, Wales, 2005—, dir. Inst. for Advanced Materials and Energy Sys., 2006—. Chmn. Conf. on Properties and Applications of Magnetic Materials, Chgo., 1985-2001; pres. Magnetics Tech. Inc., Ames, 1989—; dir. Magnetics Tech. U.K., Ltd., 2004—; cons. engr. State of Iowa, Des Moines, 1996; sci. advisor Brit. Admiralty, 1991-92, NATO, 1992-2000, U.S. NRC, 1996-97; vis. prof. U. Hull, Eng., 1991, 94, U. Saarland, Germany, 1992, 97, Tech. U. Vienna, 2000, 03, Cardiff (Wales) U., 2004; vis. scientist Czech Acad. Sci., 1999. Author: Introduction to Magnetism and Magnetic Materials, 1991, 2d edit., 1998, Introduction to Electronic Properties of Materials, 1994, 2d edit., 2001; editor: IEEE Transactions on Magnetics, 1992—2004, editor-in-chief, 2004—; editor Nondestructive Testing and Evaluation, 1988-2005, Jour. of Materials Sci. Materials in Electronics, 2002; contbr. more than 450 articles to profl. jours. Recipient Fed. Lab. Consortium award U.S. Dept. Energy, 1994, Magnetics Soc. Disting. Lectr. award, 1997; Royal Soc. rsch. fellow. Fellow IEEE, Inst. Elec. Engrs. U.K., Inst. Physics, Am. Phys. Soc. (chair topical group on magnetism and its applications, 1997-99), Magnetics Soc. (adminstrv. com. 1995-2001, 03-), Inst. Math. and its Applications; mem. AAAS. Achievements include 14 patents; developer of various models relating to non-linear effects and theory of ferromagnetic hysteresis. Home: 9 Evenlode Ave Penorth CF64 3PD Wales Office: Cardiff U Wolfson Ctr Magnetics Cardiff CF24 3AA Wales Office Phone: (44) 292-087-6729. Fax: (44) 292-087-9538.

JILHEWAR, ASHOK, gastroenterologist; b. Nanded, Maharashtra, India, Jan. 30, 1947; arrived in US, 1977, naturalized, 1987; BS, MB, Marathwada U., 1970; MD, Govt. Med. Coll., Aurangabad, 1970. Diplomate Am. Bd. Internal Medicine, Am. Bd. Gastroenterology, Am. Bd. Geriatric Medicine, Am. Bd. Quality Assurance and Utilization Rev. Physicians. Rotating intern Med. Coll. Hosp., Aurangabad, India, 1968—70; resident St. Luke's Hosp. and Royal Infirmary, Huddersfeild, Bolton, England, 1970—72; med. registrar internal medicine Gen. Hosp., Sligo, Ireland, 1973—77; chief resident PG1 and internal medicine U. Health Scis.-Chgo. Med. Sch. and VA Hosp., 1977—79; clin. instr. U. Health Scis.-Chgo. Med. Sch., 1978—79; fellow in gastroenterology Michael Reese Hosp., Chgo., 1980—81; mem. exec. com. Meth. Hosp., Chgo., 1985—90, chmn. med. dept., 1988—90; mem. staff dept. medicine Grant Hosp., Chgo., 1986—. Lectr. preventive and social medicine Med. Coll., Aurangabad, 1970; mem. exec. com. Meth. Hosp. Chgo., 1985-90, v.p. med. staff, 1987-88, treas., sec. 1985-87, chmn. dept. medicine, 1988-90; med. dir. approved home for intermediate care nursing home, 1986-95; med. advisor Office Hearings and Appeals, HHS, 1985—; med. reviewer Ill. Med. Rev. Orgn., 1993—, Crescent Cmty. Found. for Med. Care, 1994—. Fellow Royal Coll. Physicians Can., Am. Coll. Internat. Physicians; mem. AMA, ACP, Am. Headache Soc., Am. Gastroenterol. Assn., Royal Coll. Physicians U.K., Royal Coll. Physicians Ireland, Ill. State Med. Assn., Chgo. Med. Soc. (PRO study com., fee mediation subcom. 1992) Office: North Park Stomach Clinic 5393 N Milwaukee Ave Chicago IL 60630-1251 Office Phone: 773-775-9500. Personal E-mail: ajilhewar@hotmail.com.

JILLETTE, ARTHUR GEORGE, JR., school system administrator, educator; b. Malden, Mass., May 1, 1937; s. Arthur George and Esther Harriett (Peachey) J.; m. Janet Downs White, June 20, 1960 (div. 1973); 1 child, Joseph Arthur; m. Beatrice Miriam Ellis, May 3, 1975; children: Grace Harder, Andrew Hopkins, Timothy Hopkins. BS, Boston U., 1960, MRE, 1964; cert. in audio communicative disability, NYU, 1967. Cert. tchr., N.H., community coll. adminstr., Calif. Assoc. rsch. scientist NYU Deafness Rsch. Ctr., NYC, 1965-67; cons. spl. edn. N.H. Dept. Edn., Concord, 1967-74, 85-88, 1997-99, acting dir. spl. edn., 1974-75; dir. planning and devel. N.H. Div. Vocat. Rehab., Concord, 1975-79; dean spl. svcs. N.H. Tech. Coll., Claremont, 1979-83, dean students, 1983-85; dir. spl. svcs. Sch. Admnstrv. Unit #43, Newport, NH, 1988—91, asst. supt. schs., 1991-94; dir. spl. svcs. Sch. Admnstrv. Unit 32, Lebanon, N.H., 1994-97; dir. spl. edn. Lyme N.H. Sch. Dist., 1999—2000; coord. spl. edn. svcs. Goshen-Lempster Coop. Sch. Dist., 2000—; mem. N.H. Ho. Reps., Concord, 2005—. Dir. Lake Sunapee Mediation Program, Newport, 1990—, pres., 1996—; mem. state adv. coun. Individuals with Disabilities Edn. Act., 1989-94; consumer mem. N.H. State Bd. Hearing Care Providers, 2001-2005; pres., dir. Sullivan County Rehab. Ctr., Claremont, 1980-83. Editor: Denominational Work With the Deaf, 1966. Moderator Town of Goshen, N.H., 1980—, planning bd. chmn., 1985-89, zoning bd. chmn., 1986-89, cemetary commr., 2000—; mem. Goshen-Lempster Coop. Sch. Bd., 1975-80, 95-2000, chmn., 1979-80, 97-2000; mem., sec. Newport Revitalization Com., 2002—; mem. N.H. Ho. Reps., 2005—. Social and Rehab. Svcs. fellow U.S. Dept. Edn., 1964-65. Mem. Nat. Stereoptician Assn., Nat. Assn. Watch and Clock Collectors, N.H. Graveyard Assn. (pres. 2004-2006), Elks, Odd Fellow, Masons. Democrat. Mem. Soc. Of Friends. Avocations: house restoration, stereo photography, cemetary restoration, computers. Home: PO Box 1016 Goshen NH 03752-1016 Office: Legis Office Bldg Rm 204 Concord NH 03301

JILLSON, ANDREW E., lawyer; b. Suffern, NY, Jan. 30, 1954; BA with distinction, Va. Poly. Inst. and State U., 1976; JD, Coll. William and Mary, 1980. Bar: Tex. 1980, U.S. Ct. Appeals (5th cir.), U.S. Dist. Ct. (so. and we. dist.) Tex., U.S. Dist. Ct. (we. dist.) Okla., U.S. Dist. Ct. no., ea. and we. dists.) Tex. Law clk. to Hon. Dean M. Gandy U.S. Bankruptcy Ct., Tex., 1980-81; mem. Jenkens & Gilchrist P.C., Dallas; ptnr. Hunton & Williams LLP, Dallas, 2007—. Assoc. editor William & Mary Law Review, 1979-80; contbr. articles to profl. jours. Mem. ABA, State Bar Tex., Dallas Bar Assn., Phi Delta Phi, Phi Alpha Theta, Phi Kappa Phi. Office: Hunton & Williams LLP Energy Plz 30th Fl 1601 Bryan St Dallas TX 75201-3402

JIMENEZ, DAWN MARIE, judge; b. Mar. 2, 1964; BA, Princeton U., NJ, 1986; JD, Temple U., Phila., 1989. Bar: NY, NJ. Ptnr., assoc. Borah Goldstein Altschuler & Schwartz, NY, 1989—99; judge NY State Office Ct. Admin., Bklyn., 1999—.

JIMENEZ, FRANK R., lawyer, civilian military employee; Grad., U. Miami, 1987; JD, Yale U., 1991; MBA, U. Pa., 2005. Law clk. to Hon. Pamela Ann Rymer US Ct. Appeals (9th cir.), Pasadena, Calif., 1991—92; with Steel Hector and Davis LLP, Miami, 1992—98, ptnr., 1998; staff mem. Office Gov. State of Fla., Tallahasseee, Fla., 1998—2002, dep. chief of staff to Gov. Tallahassee, acting gen. counsel to Gov., dep. gen. counsel to Gov.; chief of staff US Dept. Housing & Urban Devel., Washington, 2002—04; prin. dep. gen. counsel Dept. Navy, US Dept. Def., Washington, dep. gen. counsel, gen. counsel, 2006—. Office: US Dep Def Dept Navy 1000 Navy Pentagon Washington DC 20350*

JIMENEZ, JOSEPH, management executive; b. Dec. 27, 1959; s. Joseph and Catherine (Lucente) J.; m. Denise Lynn Kovach, Mar. 21, 1987. AB, Stanford U., 1982; MBA, U. Calif., Berkeley, 1984. Brand asst., Hidden Valley Ranch Clorox Co., Oakland, Calif., 1984-85, asst. brand mgr., new products, 1985-86, asst. brand mgr., Kingsford, 1986-87, brand mgr., new products, 1987; joined Hunt-Wesson, 1993, various positions including v.p. mktg. La Choy/Rosarita Food Co., v.p to sr. v.p. Orville Redenbacher, pres. Orville Redenbacher Swiss Miss Food Co., 1997—98, pres. Wesson Peter Pan Food Co., 1997—98; pres., CEO Heinz N. Am. H.J. Heinz Co., Pitts., 1998—2002, exec. v.p., 2001—, pres, CEO Heinz Europe, 2002—06, pres., CEO Heinz Asia, Australia, New Zealand, Latin Am., Africa and Middle East, 2006—. Bd. dirs. The Hain Celestial Group, Inc., 1999—2004, Blue Nile, 2000—, AstraZeneca PLC, 2003—. Asst. brand mgr. Kingsford Charcoal, TV, 1987, brand mgr. Kingsford BBQ Bag, TV, 1988.

JIMENEZ, MARCOS DANIEL, former prosecutor; b. Havana, Cuba, Dec. 15, 1959; came to U.S., 1961; s. Frank T. and Daisy (D'Clouet) J.; m. Michelle Ann; 3 children. BA, U. Miami, Fla., 1980, JD, 1983. Bar: Ill. 1983, U.S. Dist. Ct. (no. dist.) Ill. 1983, Fla. 1984, U.S. Dist. Ct. (so. dist.) Fla. 1984, U.S. Ct. Appeals (11th cir.) 1985. Assoc. Phelan, Pope and John, Ltd., Chgo., 1983-84, Greenberg, Traurig et al, Miami, 1984-89; asst. U.S. atty. (So. dist.) Fla. U.S. Dept. Justice, Miami, 1989—92, US atty., 2002—05; ptnr. White & Case LLP, 1992—2002. Contbr. articles to profl. jours. Mem. ABA, Fla. Bar Assn. (com. mem.), Dade County Bar Assn. (com. mem.), Hurricane Club. Republican. Baptist. Avocations: basketball, saxophone.

JIMENEZ, SERGIO A., internist, educator, rheumatologist; b. Cuzco, Peru, Feb. 21, 1942; s. Julio Alexandre and Bertha Margarite (Astete) J. BS, Nat. U. San Marcos, Lima, Peru, 1959, MD, 1964; MS, U. Pa., 1984. Diplomate Am. Bd. Internal Medicine. Asst. prof. dept. medicine U. Pa., Phila., 1974-80, asst. prof. dept. orthop. surgery, 1978-80, assoc. prof. medicine and orthop. surgery, 1980-86, prof., 1986-87; prof. medicine, dir. rheumatology rsch. Thomas Jefferson U., Phila., 1987-92, prof. biochemistry and molecular biology, 1987—, dir. divsn. rheumatology, 1992—, Dorrance H. Hamilton prof. medicine, 1992—, vice-chmn. rsch. dept. medicine, 1999—2003. Hon. adj. fellow Benjamin Franklin Inst., Phila., 1981-85; chmn. med. adv. bd. Scleroderma Rsch. Found., Mid-Atlantic Chpt., 1979—; mem. rsch. scholarships com., Ea. Pa. chpt. Arthritis Found., 1981-84; mem. med./sci. bd. Scleroderma Fedn., 1994—; mem. Nat. Inst. Health Gen. Medicine A Study Sect., 1990-94, mem. spl. rev. com., 1995-2000; mem. NIH Peer Review Oversight Group, 1998-2000; bd. sci. councellors Nat. Inst. Arthritis Musculoskeletal Diseases, NIH, 1999-2000; acting chmn., bd. councellors Nat. Inst. Arthritis Musculoskeletal Diseases NIH, 2000-02; chmn. bd. sci. councellors Nat. Inst. Arthritis Musculoskeletal Disease, NIH, 2002-05. Author over 270 articles to med. jours., 450 abstracts in procs. worldwide sci. jours., 90 editls., revs., and chpts. to jours. and books. Bd. dirs. Washington Square West Civic Assn., Phila., 1978-82, v.p., 1981-82, trustee, 1988—; mem. Phila. Hispanic C. of C., 1990—. Capt. Peruvian Army Res., 1964-65. Recipient Gerald P. Rodnan award for excellence in scleroderma rsch., U. Pitts., 1986, Joseph Lee Hollander award for excellence in rheumatology Ea. Pa. Arthritis Found., 2000,Hero award, Arthritis Found., 2000, Basic Rsch. award, Osteoarthritis Rsch. Internat., 2005; program project for rsch. on osteoarthritis, NIH, 1992-2006. Fellow Soc. for Molecular Medicine; mem. Am. Coll. Rheumatology, Am. Soc. Biol. Chemistry and Molecular Biology, Osteoarthritis Rsch. Soc. (exec. bd. 1994—, pres.-elect 1997-2000, pres. 2000-02), Internat. Soc. for Matrix Biology (founding mem.), Am. Soc. Matrix Biology. Republican. Roman Catholic. Avocations: sculpture, opera, archaeology. Home: 900 Spruce St Philadelphia PA 19107-6131 Office: Thomas Jefferson Univ 233 S 10th St Ste 509 Philadelphia PA 19107-5541

JIN, BYOUNGHO, retail executive, educator; d. Chan Sik Jin and Byung Ki Noh; m. Seungwon Hong, Jan. 8, 1996; 1 child, Jungsu Hong. PhD, Yonsei U., Seoul, 1995. Cert. internat. retailing Mich. State U., 1998. Assoc. prof. Okla. State U., Stillwater, 2001—. Researcher (research paper) The Mediating Role of Excitement in Customer Satisfaction and Repatronage Intention of Discount Store Shoppers in Korea. Rsch. grants, USDA, Rsch. grant, US Dept. Edn., National Textile Center, U.S. Dept. Commerce. Mem.: Korean Soc. Clothing and Textiles, Assn. Consumer Rsch., Internat. Textiles and Apparel Assn., Am. Collegiate Retailing Assn., Phi Beta Delta. Achievements include development of comprehensive China education modules that include both cognitive and experiential learning components; video on China market overview; video on Chinese retail environment; edited photo modules about Chinese market. Office Phone: 405-744-5035.

JIN, DEBORAH, physicist, educator; b. 1969; AB, Princeton U., 1990; PhD, U. of Chgo., 1995. Rsch. assoc. Nat. Inst. of Standards and Tech., 1995—97, physicist, commerce dept., 1997—; fellow, adjoint asst. prof. physics, JILA U. of Colo., Boulder, 1997—. Named Rsch. Leader of Yr. within the "Scientific American 50", Scientific American, 2004; recipient Pres. Early Career for Sci. and Engr., 2000, Maria Goeppert-Meyer prize, Am. Phys. Soc., 2002; fellow MacArthur Found., 2003. Fellow: Am. Acad. Arts & Scis.; mem.: NAS (award for initiatives in rsch. 2002). Office: Univ of Colo JILA 440 UCB Boulder CO 80309-0440 Office Phone: 303-492-0256. Office Fax: 303-492-5235. Business E-Mail: jin@jilau1.colorado.edu.*

JIN, HELENA, research scientist; arrived in US, 1999; d. Gaozhong and Aifang Jin; m. Brian Hu, Jan. 8, 2005; 1 child, Kacie J. Hu. B in Engring., U. Sci. and Tech. China, HeFei, 1999; PhD, U. Md., College Park, 2004. Rsch. scientist Sandia Nat. Lab., Livermore, Calif. Achievements include research in biaxial strain measurement at the nanosc, new metrological techniques for mechanical characterization at the microscale and nanoscale. Business E-Mail: hqjin@yahoo.com.

JIN, HYUN SEUNG, communications educator; b. Sooncheon, Republic of Korea, Feb. 7, 1963; s. Juwha Jin and Jeonja Choi; m. Soontae An; 1 child, Frances. BA, Sogang U., Seoul, Republic of Korea, 1989, MA, 1993; PhD, U. NC, Chapel Hill, 2000. Vis. asst. prof. U. Conn., Stamford, 2000—01; asst. prof. Kans. State U., Manhattan, 2001—. Contbr. articles to profl. jours. Advisor Ad Club, Manhattan, 2007. Recipient Rubinstein Dissertation award, U. NC, Chapel Hill, 2000, Stamy Outstanding Undergraduate Tchg. award, Kans. State U., 2005, President's Faculty Devel. award, 2006, 2006; grantee, Korea Rsch. Found., 2005; Big Twelve fellowship, Kans. State U., 2002. Mem.: Am. Acad. Advt. Home: 1512 Little Kitten Ave Manhattan KS 66503 Office: Kansas State Univ 105 Kedzie Manhattan KS 66506 Home Phone: 785-770-3270; Office Phone: 785-532-3959. Office Fax: 785-532-5484. Business E-Mail: hsjin@ksu.edu.

JIN, JING YI, photographer, film director; b. Shenyang, Liaoning, China, July 29, 1932; s. Shou Shan and Xi Yun (Song) Fu; m. Ming Zhi Cai, Apr. 18, 1958; children: Ge, Jun. BS with honors, Hua Bei U., Zheng Ding, People's Republic of China, 1953. From asst. photographer to photographer, dir. Ctrl. Newsreel and Documentary Film Studio China, Beijing, 1953—93; pvt. practice LA, 1994—. Pres. Internat. New Reel and News Film Assn., 1987—88. Dir.: (documentaries) Great Rejoicing of Tibet, 1959, Cambodia Today, 1960, Royal Ballet, 1960, Golden Phoenix, 1979, Violin and Bee, 1983, Teacher of Ballet, 2003, Gymnastic Coaches, 2003, Mongolia Doctor in LA, 2003, World Basketball Invitational Tournament for Chinese, 2003, Joys of Spring, 2004, Paradise on the Sea, 2004, The Coast Cities of Mexico, 2004, I Love You China, 2004, Kentucky Derby, 2004, Magical Photographer, 2004, At Xmas Eve, 2004, Antique Cars, 2004, The Tournament of Roses Parade, 2005, Celebrate Lunar New Year, 2005, Halloween, 2005, Renaissance Pleasure Faire, 2005, National Date Festival, 2006, Three Brothers Raise Cows, 2006, Dr. Phillips, 2006, Fifteen Years Birthday, 2006, Air Show, 2006, Crossing Guard, 2006, Painting the Town, 2006, Artist Dennis, 2006, Richard's Philatelic Center, 2007. Home: 9316 Claudia Cir Rosemead CA 91770

JIN, TAO, research scientist; s. Shanzhi Jin and Yongmei Wang; m. Meiduo Wu, Dec. 16, 1996; children: Grace, Owen Wu. PhD in Physics, Kent State U., Ohio, 2003. Rsch. asst. Kent State U., 1999—2003; rsch. assoc. U. Pitts., 2003—06, rsch. asst. prof., 2007—. Contbr. articles to profl. jours. Mem.: Internat. Soc. Magnetic Resonance Medicine (assoc.), Sigma Xi. Office: Univ Pitts 3025 E Carson St Rm 156 Pittsburgh PA 15203 Office Fax: 412-383-6799. Business E-Mail: taj6@pitt.edu.

JIN, XIAOYING, electrical engineer, computer engineer, researcher; arrived in U.S., 2000; d. Jingrang and Musen Jin; m. Yuanfang Gao; 1 child, Jason Deli Gao. BS, Wuhan U., Hubei, 1996, MS, 1999; PhD, U. Missouri, Columbia, 2005. Software engr. Huawei Tech. Co. Ltd., Shenzhen, China, 1999—2000; rsch. asst. U. Missouri, Columbia, 2000—05; software engr. ITT Visual Info. Solutions, 2005—. Session chmn. ann. meeting Sensing Photo-Optical Instrumentation Engrs., Denver, 2004; session moderator Imaging Geospacial Soc., Reno, 2006—07. Reviewer: Transactions on Geosci. and Remote Sensing, Geosci. and Remote Sensing Letters, ISPRS Jour. Phogrammetry and Remote Soc.; reviewer Info. Scis.; contbr. articles to profl. jours. Recipient Rsch. Excellence award, SPIE Soc. and Newport, 2004; Gui & Xu acad. scholar, Wuhan U., 1997—98, 1994—95, First-Class scholar, 1992—96. Mem.: IEEE, Internat. Soc. Optical Engring., Am. Soc. Photogrammetry and Remote Sensing, Tau Beta Pi. Achievements include development of registered letter image analysis and database management system; multimedia broadcasting-on-demand system; automatic feature extraction system from remote sensing imagery. Office: 4990 Pearl East Cir Boulder CO 80301 Home Phone: 573-529-3341. Personal E-mail: jinxiaoying@gmail.com. Business E-Mail: xjin@ittvis.com.

JIN, XUEFEI (HA JIN), literature educator, writer; b. Jinxian, China, Feb. 21, 1956; s. Danlin Jin and Yuanfen Zhao; m. Lisha Bian, July 6, 1982; 1 child, Wen. BA, Heliongjiang U., 1981; MA, Shandong U., 1984; PhD, Brandeis U., 1993. Lectr. Boston U., 1992-93, prof. English, 2002—; asst. prof. Emory U., Atlanta, 1993—2002. Author: (poetry collections) Between Silences, 1990, Facing Shadows, 1996, Wreckage, 2001, (short story collections) Ocean of Words: Army Stories, 1996 (PEN/Hemingway Award, 1997), Under the Red Flag, 1997 (Flannery O'Connor Award for Short Fiction, 1997), (novels) In the Pond, 1998, Waiting, 1999 (Nat. Book Award for Fiction, 1999, PEN/Faulkner Award for Fiction, 2000), The Bridegroom, 2000, The Crazed, 2002, War Trash, 2004 (Named one of 10 Best Books of Yr., NY Times Book Rev., 2004, PEN/Faulkner Award for Fiction, 2005). Served People's Liberation Army, China. Guggenheim Fellowship, 1999. Fellow: Am. Acad. Arts & Sciences. Avocations: reading, walking. Office: Boston U Dept English 236 Bay State Rd Boston MA 02215 Business E-Mail: xjin@bu.edu.

JIN, ZHENRONG, electrical engineer, researcher; arrived in U.S., 1999; s. Jiaxi Jin and Shuhua Chao; m. Xue Li, Dec. 18, 2002; 1 child, Alex. BS, SE U., Nanjing, China, 1996, MS, 1999; PhD, Ga. Inst. Tech., 2004. Grad. rsch. asst. Auburn (Ala.) U., Auburn, 1999—2002, Ga. Inst. Tech., Atlanta, 2002—04; adv. engr. IBM Microelectronics, Essex Junction, Vt., 2004—. Contbr. articles to profl. jours. Scholar, BASF, 1999; Presdl. fellow, Auburn U., 1999—2002. Mem.: IEEE, Sigma Xi. Achievements include research in silicon germanium (SiGe) hetero-junction bipolar transistors (HBTs); discovery of small size effects on low-frequency noise in SiGe HBTs; new low-frequency noise mechanisms in SiGe HBTs; development of low-frequency noise model in SiGe HBTs in radiation enviroments; low-frequency noise simulations in SiGe HBTs. Office: IBM Microelectronics 1000 River St MS 972F Essex Junction VT 05452 Office Phone: 802-769-3161. Business E-Mail: zhenrjin@us.ibm.com.

JINDAL, BOBBY PIYUSH, congressman; b. Baton Rouge, La., June 10, 1971; s. Amar Jindal, Raj Jindal; m. Supriya Jolly; children: Selia, Shaan, Slade Ryan. ScB in Biology, Brown U., 1991; MLitt in Politics, Oxford U., England, 1994. Assoc. McKinsey & Co., Washington, 1994—96; sec. La. Dept. of Health and Hosps., Baton Rouge, 1996—98; exec. dir. Nat. Bipartisan Commn. Future of Medicare, Washington, 1998—99; pres. U. La. Sys., Baton Rouge, 1999—2001; asst. sec. Dept H.H.S., Washington, 2001—03; mem. US Congress from 1st Dist. La., 2005—. Bd. dirs. Our Lady of the Lake Hosp., Baton Rouge, 2000—01, Edn. Commn. of States, 2000—01. Bd. dirs. Nat. Conf. Cmty and Justice, Baton Rouge chpt., 2000—01, Teach for Am., Baton Rouge chpt., 1997—98, BBB, Baton Rouge, 1987—88, Salvation Army, Baton Rouge, 1986—87. Named La.'s Most Outstanding Young Man, Junior C. of C., 1995; named to All-USA First Acad. Team, USA Today, 1992; recipient Jefferson award, Nat. Inst. Pub. Svc., 1998; scholar, Rhodes Trust, 1992—94. Mem.: Phi Beta Kappa. Republican. Catholic. Avocation: tennis. Office: 1205 Longworth House Office Bldg Washington DC 20515-1801 Office Phone: 202-225-3015. Office Fax: 202-226-0386.*

JINDRA, CHRISTINE, editor; b. Cleve., Sept. 18, 1947; d. Lad Joseph and Ann Frances (Makar) J.; m. Peter J. Junkin, Aug. 1, 1970 (div. Dec. 1987); children: William Patrick, Michael Lad. BS in Journalsim, Ohio State U., 1969. City reporter Buffalo News, 1969-70; metro reporter Plain Dealer, Cleve., 1970-82, assignment editor, nat. reporter, 1982-84, state editor, 1984-86, metro editor, 1986-88, feature editor, 1988-92, asst. mng. editor, 1992-2001, Sunday editor, 2001—. Mem.: Women's Cmty. Found., Women's City Club. Avocations: skiing, gardening, travel, cooking. Office: Plain Dealer 1801 Superior Ave E Cleveland OH 44114-2198 Home Phone: 440-232-1460; Office Phone: 216-999-4839. E-mail: cjindra@plaind.com.

JINES, MICHAEL L., lawyer, energy executive; JD, U. Houston. Bar: Tex. Joined Reliant Energy, 1982; sr. v.p., gen. counsel Reliant Resources' Wholesale Group; dep. gen. counsel Reliant Energy, Inc.; dep. gen. counsel, gen. counsel wholesale group Reliant Resources, Inc., Houston, sr. v.p., gen. counsel, 2003—. Mem. Pro Bono Coll. State Bar Tex. Editor: Houston Law Rev.; mem. adv. bd.: Houston Jour. Internat. Law. Fellow: Houston Bar Found. (life); mem.: Houston Bar Assn. (co-chair legal line com. 1996—97). Office: Reliant Energy Exec Offices PO Box 1384 Houston TX 77251-1384 Office Phone: 713-497-7465. Business E-Mail: mjines@reliant.com.*

JING, BING, business educator; b. Dezhou, Shandong Province, China; BE, Beijing Info. Tech. Inst., 1992; MBA, Bentley Coll., Mass., 1996; PhD, U. Rochester, NY, 2001. Mis engr. Beijing Automation Rsch. Inst., Beijing, 1992—94; lead sys. analyst Instrumentation La., Lexington, Mass., 1996; asst. prof. info. sys NYU. Stern Sch. Bus., NYC, 2001—. Contbr. articles to profl. jours. Mem.: INFORMS, Mktg. Sci. Soc., Econometric Soc., Beta Gamma Sigma. Office: NYU Stern Sch 44 West 4th St KMC 8-79 New York NY 10012 Office Phone: 212-998-0822.

JING, ZHIGANG, electrical engineer; arrived in US, 2000, naturalized; s. Liangyun Jing and Xianxiu Wang. BSEE, U. Electronic Sci. and Tech. China, 1993, MSEE, 1996, PhD, 1999; postgrad., Columbia U./Poly. U., NYC, 2004. Sr. rsch. assoc. Dept. Elec. Engring. Tsinghua U., Beijing, 1999—2000; rsch. scientist NY State Ctr. for Advanced Tech., 2000—04; sr. staff engr., sys. engring. MeshNetworks Inc., Maitland, Fla., 2004; prin. staff engr. sys. Motorola Inc., Maitland, 2004—06; sr. engr., sys. Qualcomm, Inc., San Diego, 2006—. Spkr. in field. Author: QOS control in high-speed networks, 2001, Broadband Packet Switching Technologies-A Practical Guide to ATM Switches and IP Routers, 2001; contbr. articles to profl. jours. Recipient Best Paper awards, U. Tex., Austin., 2004. Mem.: IEEE (jour. editor). Achievements include design of a packet-switching system, Petastar, which is based on an innovative multi-dimensional multiplexing scheme. Petastar provides as much as 1, 000 times the capacity as traditional switch; MediaFlo system, delivering live TV to handsets; development of MAC, a new class of distributed matching algorithms for a large-dimensional switching system that solves the scheduling and routing problem in much less time than traditional scheme; invention of round robin-based dispatching schemes for a multi-stage switch, which outperform Lucent ATLANTA switch in achieving 100% throughput without an internal bandwidth expansion. Office: Qualcomm Inc 5775 Morehouse Dr San Diego CA 92121

JINKS, ROBERT LARRY, retired newspaper publisher; b. Mt. Pleasant, Tex., Jan. 26, 1929; s. Leon Carlton and Mary (Cunnyngham) J.; m. Anne Claire van Ravesteyn, May 8, 1971; children by previous marriage: Laura Beth, Daniel Carlton, Beau Pottorff. BJ, U. Mo., 1950; MS, Columbia, 1956. News editor Muskogee (Okla.) Times-Democrat, 1950-51; reporter Greensboro (N.C.) Daily News, 1953-55; reporter, city editor Charlotte (N.C) Observer, 1956—60; mem. staff Miami (Fla.) Herald, 1960-77, mng. editor, 1966-72, exec. editor, 1972—76; editor, v.p. San Jose (Calif.) Mercury News, 1977-81; sr. v.p. news and ops. Knight-Ridder Corp., Miami, Fla., 1981-89; pub. San Jose (Calif.) Mercury News, 1989-94, ret., 1994. Pres. AP Mng. Editors, 1975—76, Fla. Soc. Newspaper Editors, 1975; bd. dirs. McClatchy Newspapers, Inc. With AUS, 1951-53. Named to 50th anniversary honors list Columbia Grad. Sch. Journalism, 1963, Disting. Grad., 1983; Disting. Grad. award U. Mo., 1990. Mem. Am. Soc. Newspaper Editors (dir. 1980-86).

JINRIGHT, NOAH FRANKLIN, security firm executive, retired vocational school educator; b. Banks, Ala., Dec. 5, 1936; s. William Carroll and Ila Marie (Garrett) J.; m. Sarah Ann (Graham) Nickolson, Nov. 21, 1959 (dic. Sept. 1974); children: Charlene M., Lisa A., Michael D.; m. Frances Lenora (Gaskins), June 11, 1978; children: Diana Carol, Jonathan Franklin. Attended, Ga. State U., Columbus, 1979, attended, 1981; attended for math., Columbus State U., 1990. Lic. ins. agt., Ga; cert. in sheet metal techniques Ga. Power Co., 1982; cert. profl. security officer, 2004; cert. archtl. and mech. drafting Columbus Tech. Inst., 1969-71; cert. plate and pipe welder Columbus Tech. Inst., 1978, 79, 81, 84; cert. in numerically controlled tech., tools and dies Columbia Tech. Inst., 1983; cert. in pattern making (metal and wood); cert. in constrn.; cert. in sheet metal basics (indsl. plant), 1997-98; Microsoft Cert. Solution Devel. Operator scale Bibb Textiles, Columbus, Ga., 1954-56; operator press and share Columbus Iron Works, 1957-58; ins. agt. Interstate Life, Columbus, 1958-61; operated winder, starter, generator Joe Hooten, Inc., Columbus, 1960; fireman City of Columbus, 1960-66; ins. agt. Murray Meadows Ins. Agy., Columbus, Ga., 1960—67; advt. rep. Jinright Enterprises, Columbus, 1966; ins. agt. Security Life of Ga., Columbus, 1966; operator share and press Pascoe Steel, Columbus, 1966-67; machinist Goldens' Foundry and Machine Works, Columbus, 1967; carpenter, roofer Muscogee County Sch. Dist., Columbus, 1968-72; pattern maker Pekor Iron Works, Columbus, 1972-78; instr. metals tech. Spencer HS, Columbus, 1978-91, Carver HS, Columbus, 1991-94, Kendrick HS, Columbus, 1994-99; security officer Sizemore Security Internat., 1994-95, 97-99; ret., 1999; security officer Sizemore Security Internat., 1999-2001, The Wackenhut Corp. Security Internat., 2001—03, Securitas Security Svc., USA, Inc., 2003—05, Angel Security Co., Inc., 2005—. Past mfg. rep. printing and advtg. specialties; cons. Voc. Tng. and Rsch. Inst., Seoul, Korea, 1989-90; instr., ptnr. with M. Davis; fire protection supr. 9311th A.F.Rescuer Squadron Columbus, Ga., (Tech. Sgt.). Contbg. articles to local newspapers. Sponsor Spencer HS AWS Club, 1979-81; exec. trainer Precision Metalforming Assn., 1996-99; past trustee Epworth United Meth. Ch., ch. usher; active Columbus Confederate Drill Team; adv. bd. Am. Biog. Inst., 1999—. Staff sgt. Ga. Army Nat. Guard, 1954-63; tech. sgt. USAFR, 1963-65. Named one of Top Instrs. Ga. N.G. 560th engring. br. 48th divsn. col., Ga. (1960s). Mem. NEA, Internat. Soc. Welding Educators (1st symposium program adv. bd.), Am. Foundry Soc., Am. Welding Soc. (adv. bd.), Vocat. Indsl. Clubs Am. (advisor, cert. of appreciation region VIII 1996), Trade and Indsl. Educators Ga. (mem. West Ga. Sch. to work-evaluation team 1994-99), Muscogee Edn. Assn., Ga. Assn. Educators, Ga. Vocat. Assn., Am. Vocat. Assn., Precision Metalforming Assn., Am. Foundrymen's Soc., Ga. Tchrs. Union, So. Assn. Colls. and Schs., Ga. Assn. Educators. Methodist. Avocations: fishing, hunting, camping, model building, photography. Mailing: PO Box 63 Columbus GA 31902-0063 Home: 2040 Lee Rd 427 Phenix City AL 36867 Home Fax: 334-297-7545.

JIRAK, SARAH REED, secondary school educator; b. Washington, Iowa, Oct. 21, 1963; d. Cletus Constant and Audrey Jean Reed; m. Donald Myles Jirak, Dec. 29, 1989; 1 child, Shawn Douglas. BA in Religion and World History, U. Iowa, Iowa City, 1987. Lic. secondary edn. Tchr. religion St. Mary's Jr.-Sr. HS, Sleepy Eye, Minn., 1987—. Parish music liturgist St. Mary's Parish, Sleepy Eye, 2003—; mem. worship com. New Ulm Diocese, 2005—. Mem.: Nat. Pastoral Musicians Assn., Phi Beta Kappa. Avocations: music, piano. Office: Saint Marys Jr HS 104 Saint Marys St NW Sleepy Eye MN 56085 Office Phone: 507-794-4121.

JIRAUCH, CHARLES W., lawyer; b. St. Louis, Apr. 27, 1944; m. Sally J. Costello, 1968 (div. Mar. 1977); m. Dana K. Bowen, 1980; children: Melissa, Mathew, Kathleen. BSEE, Washington U., 1966; JD, Georgetown U., 1970. Bar: Ill. 1971, Ariz. 1975, Nev. 1991, , Calif. 1993, Colo. 1993, U.S. Patent Office 1970, U.S. Supreme Ct. 1978. Examiner US Patent Office, 1968—70; atty. Leydig, Voit & Mayer, Chgo., 1970-71, McDermott, Will & Emery, Chgo., 1971-75, Streich Lang, Phoenix, 1975-2000, Quarles & Brady LLP, Phoenix, 2000—. Bd. dirs. Valley Big Bros./Big Sisters, 1980-86, pres. bd. dirs., 1985-86; pres., bd. dirs. Valley Big Bros./Big Sisters Found., 1988-92; mem. Gov.'s Coun. on Workforce Policy, 2004; mem. bd. advisors to dean Ariz. State U. Sch. Engring., 1998-2007; bd. dirs., mem. exec. com., gen. counsel, v.p. Ariz. Bus. and Edn. Coalition, 2002-2006, pres., 2006—; mem. Ariz. Dem. Coun., 2002-07. Named one of Best Lawyers in Am., Intellectual Prop. Litig., 2006—07, Ariz. Super Lawyers, 2007. Mem. ABA, Internat. Bar Assn., Fed. Cir. Bar Assn., Calif. Bar Assn., Ariz. Bar Assn. and Found., Maricopa County Bar Assn. and Found. (tech. law sect. bd. dirs. 2000-04, chmn. 2003-04), Am. Judicature Soc., Am. Intellectual Property Law Assn., Ariz. Civil Liberties Union, Am. Electronic Assn. (exec. com. Ariz. chpt. 1999-2003), Ariz. Tech. Coun. (bd. dirs. 2000—, chair workforce devel. com. 2001-06), Ariz. C. of C. (edn. and tech. comms. 2002—). Democrat. Roman Catholic. Office: Quarles & Brady LLP 2 N Central Ave Phoenix AZ 85004-2345 Home Phone: 602-840-3507; Office Phone: 602-229-5503. Office Fax: 602-420-5103. Business E-Mail: cjirauch@quarles.com.

JIRTLE, RANDY, medical educator, geneticist; b. Kewaunee, Wis., Nov. 9, 1947; s. Vernon and Nettie Jirtle; m. Nancy McGinnis, Oct. 22, 1983; children: James, Bonnie. BS in Nuc. Engring., U. Wis., Madison, 1970, MS in Radiation Biology, 1973, PhD in Radiation Biology, 1976. Prof. radiation oncology Duke U. Med. Ctr., Durham, NC, 1977—. Invited spkr. Nobel Symposium on Epigenetics, 2004. Editor: Liver Regeneration and Carcinogenesis: Cellular and Molecular Mechanisms, 1995; contbr. articles to profl. jours. Recipient Disting. Achievement award, U. Wis.-Madison, 2006; grantee, NIH, 2003, 2004—, DOE, 2005—. Mem.: Soc. Toxicology (assoc.), Fedn. Am. Societies Exptl. Biology (assoc.), Am. Soc. Human Genetics (assoc.), Am. Assn. Cancer Rsch. (assoc.). Presbyterian. Achievements include discovery of imprinted IGF2R as a tumor suppressor gene; CALLIPYGE gene that results in hypertrophy of fast twitch muscles; maternal methyl supplementation during pregnancy can alter adult disease susceptibility of the offspring by methylating the epigenome; development of definition of subsets of imprinted genes in the mouse and human genomes; patents in field. Avocations: gardening, reading, drawing. Home: 4904 Montvale Dr Durham NC 27705 Office: Duke Univ Med Ctr Box 3433 Durham NC 27710 Office Phone: 919-684-2770. Business E-Mail: jirtle@radonc.duke.edu.

JISCHKE, MARTIN C., retired academic administrator; b. Chgo., Aug. 7, 1941; m. Patricia Fowler; 2 children. BS in Physics with honors, Ill. Inst. Tech., 1963, Doctoral Degree (hon.); MS in Aeronautics and Astronautics, MIT, 1964, PhD in Aeronautics and Astronautics, 1968; Doctoral Degree (hon.), Nat. Agrl. U. Ukraine. Engr. Rand Corp., Santa Monica, Calif., 1965; research engr. Battelle N.W. Lab., Richland, Washington, 1970; research fellow Donald W. Douglas Lab., Richland, 1971, Nat. Aeronautics and Space Adminstrn., Moffett Field, Calif., 1973; from asst. prof. to prof. aerospace, mech. and nuclear engring. U. Okla., 1968-75, prof., dir. Sch. Aerospace, Mech. and Nuclear Engring., 1977-81, interim pres., 1985, dean Coll. Engring., 1981-86, mem. various coms., 1985; White House fellow, spl. asst. to sec. of transp. U.S. Dept. Transp., Washington, 1975-76; chancellor U. Mo., Rolla, 1986-91; pres. Iowa State U., Ames, 1991-2000, Purdue U., 2000—07. Bd. dirs. Wabash Nat. Corp., 2002-, chmn. 2007-; bd. dirs. Kerr McGee Corp., Wabash Nat. Corp., Duke Realty Corp., Ctrl. Ind. Corp. Partnership, Assn. Am. Univs., NCAA, Nat. Assn. State Univs. and Land Grant Colls., Mo. Alliance for Sci., 1987-91, The Keystone Found., 1984-90, Mo. Corp. for Sci. and Tech., vice-chmn., 1990-91; participant Japanese Econ. Found. Vis. Leaders Program, 1983; mem. Gov.'s Coun. on Sci. and Tech. State of Okla., 1983-84, Gordon Rsch. Conf. on Geophysics; mem. planning com. for 80's Okla. State Regents for Higher Edn.; mem. organizing com. 14th Midwestern Mechanics Conf.; mem. adv. com. for engring. sci. NSF Engring. Directorate, 1985-88; mem. com. on statewide postsecondary telecomm. policy Mo. Coordinating Bd. for Higher Edn., 1987-91; chmn. Congrl. Aero. Adv. Com., 1987-89; sci. adviser to Gov. of Mo., 1990-91; mem. Am. Coun. on Edn. Com. on Math. and Sci., 1990-91; mem. coun. Nat. Acads. Govt. Univ. Industry Roundtable; chair Big Ten Conf. Coun. Presidents/Chancellors; mem. Pres.'s Coun. of Advisors on Sci. and Tech., 2006-. Contbr. articles and reports to profl. publs. Civilian aide Sec. of Army, State of Mo. East, 1987-91; bd. dirs. Bankers Trust, 1995—, Iowa Spl. Olympics, Am. Coun. on Edn., 1996—, Nat. Merit Scholarship Corp., 1997—99; mem. Kellogg Commn. on the Future of State and Land-Grant U., 1995—2000; founding pres. Global Consortium of Higher Edn. and Rsch. for Agr., 1999. Decorated Ukraine medal of merit; recipient Ralph Teetor award Soc. Automotive Engrs., 1971, Brandon H. Griffith award U. Okla., U. Okla. Regents award for superior teaching, 1975, IIT Prof. Achievement award, 1992, Delta Tau Delta Achievement award, 1992, Engrs. Club St. Louis Achievement award, 1991, Dept. Army Outstanding Civilian Svc. medal, 1991, Justin Smith Morrill award USDA, 2004; NASA fellow, 1966; NSF fellow, 1965; AEC/NORCUS summer faculty fellow, 1970-71, NASA/ASEE fellow, 1973. Fellow AAAS, AIAA (assoc., sec.-treas. Okla. chpt., vice chmn., chmn.); mem. ASME, AAUP (v.p., pres. Okla. chpt.), NSPE, Am. Phys. Soc., Am. Soc. Engring. Edn. (Centennial Medallion 1993), Nat. Assn. State Univs. and Land Grant Colls. (bd. dirs., chair 1997-98), Assn. Big Twelve Univs. (pres. 1994-96), Mo. Soc. Profl. Engrs., Rotary, Phi Beta Kappa, Tau Beta Pi, Sigma Xi, Pi Tau Sigma, Sigma Gamma Tau, Sigma Pi Sigma, Phi Eta Sigma. Home: 500 McCormick Rd West Lafayette IN 47906 Office: Wabash Nat Corp PO Box 6129 Lafayette IN 47905*

JITOMIRSKAYA, SVETLANA, mathematics professor; b. Kharkov, Ukraine, June 4, 1966; US citizen; married; 3 children. BS, MS in Math., summa cum laude, Moscow State U., 1987, PhD in Math., 1991. Researcher Internat. Inst. of Earthquake Prediction Theory and Math. Geophysics, Moscow, 1990—; lectr. U. Calif., Irvine, 1991—92, vis. asst. prof., 1992—94, asst. prof., 1994—97, assoc. prof., 1997—2000, prof., dept. math., 2000—; vis. asst. prof. Caltech, 1996. Invited prof. CPT, CNRS, Marseille, 1998; rsch. prof. Math. Sciences Rsch. Inst., 2003; lectr. in field. Contbr. articles in profl. jours.; reviewer (for several profl. jours.). Alfred P. Sloan Rsch. Fellowship, 1996—2000. Mem.: Am. Math. Soc. (editl. bd. com. 2002—05, Ruth Lyttle Satter prize in Math. 2005). Office: U Calif Dept Math 243 Multipurpose Science and Technology Irvine CA 92697-3221 Office Phone: 949-824-3221. Office Fax: 949-824-7993. Business E-Mail: szhitomi@math.uci.edu.

JIUYONG, SHI, judge; b. Zhejiang, China, Sept. 10, 1926; BA in Govt. and Pub. Law, St. John's U., Shanghai, 1948; MA in Internat. Law, Columbia U., 1951, postgrad., 1951-54. Asst. rsch. fellow Internat. Law Inst. Internat. Rels., Beijing, 1956-58; sr. lectr., assoc. prof. Internat. Law Fgn. Affairs Coll., Beijing, 1958-64; rsch. fellow Internat. Law Inst. Internat. Law, Beijing, 1964-73, 73-80; tchr. Internat. Econ. Law Dept. Law Peking U., 1980-85; prof. Internat. Law Fgn. Affairs Coll., Beijing, 1984-93; prof. Law Fgn. Econ. Law Tng. Ctr. Min. Justice People's Republic China, Beijing, 1987-88; judge Internat. Ct. of Justice, The Hague, Netherlands, 1994—2000, 2006—, v.p., 2000—03, pres., 2003—06. Adviser Chinese Soc. Internat. Law, Beijing, Chinese del. 35th session Gen. Assembly UN, China's Alt. Rep. Sixth Com. to 35th session, Chinese del. to 36th, 37, 38th sessions UN Gen. Assembly and China's del. Sixth Com. at same sessions, 1981-83; legal adviser Ministry Fgn. Affairs People's Republic China, 1980-93, Office Chinese Sr. Rep. Sino-Brit. Joint Liaison Group on Hong Kong plenary sessions, 1985-93, Chinese Ctr. Legal Consultancy, Beijing, 1989-93, Chinese del. 1980 Ann. Meeting Bd. Govs. Internat. Monetary Fund and Internat. Bank Reconstruction and Devel., del. Ministry Fin. People's Republic China Internat Bank Reconstruction and Devel., Chinese del. talks between Govt. China and Asian Devel. Bank, 1986, Chinese side Working Group Sino-Brit. Negotiations regarding Hong Kong, 1984, Chinese del. Disarmament Conf., 1991-92; del. Chinese del. to sessions Asian-African Legal Consultative Com., 1981, 85, 93, Chinese del. legal consultations between Ministry Fgn. Affairs of People's Republic China and Dept. State U.S. Am., 1983, 1984, Chinese del. negotiations between Govt. People's Republic China and Govt. U.S. Am. on Mut. Promotion and Protection of Investment Agreement, 1983, 1984; expert sr. legal experts meeting rev. Montevideo program, UN Environ. Program, Geneva, 1991, Nairobi, 1991; lectr. internat. fin. instns. Nat. Bureau Oceanography, People's Republic China, 1986, protection of private fgn. investment Hague Acad. Internat. Law Regional Program, Beijing, 1987, Grad. Inst. Internat. Studies, Geneva, 1988, autonomy in Internat. Law Sem. UN Office, Geneva, 1988, certain issues relating to legal status of Hong Kong Spl. Adminstrv. Region, internat. trade regulation, 1985-86, others; chmn. panel discussions new internat. econ. order Beijing Conf. Law of the World World Peace through Law, 1990; participant symposium internat. law arms control and disarmament, Geneva, 1991, Seminar Draft Code Crimes and internat. criminal jurisdiction, symposium on tchg., dissemination and rsch. internat. law in devel. countries, Beijing, 1992. Mem. Am. Soc. Internat. Law, Internat. Law Commn. (rep. to 45th session UN gen. Assembly 1990, 30th meeting of Asian-African Legal Consultative Conf. 1991, mem. 1987-93, rapporteur, 1988, chmn. 1990, lectr. 1991), Inst. Hong Kong Law Chinese Law Soc., Standing Com., Beijing Com., Eighth Ann. Com., Chinese People's Polit. Consultative Conf., Fgn. Econ. and Trade Arbitration Commn., China Coun. Promotion Internat. Trade, Steering Com. Office: Internat Ct of Justice Peace Palace 2517 KJ The Hague Netherlands*

JO, MI-YEOUNG, neuropsychologist; d. Bo-Soo Jo and Soon-Ja Park. BS, Duke U., Durham, NC, 1993; MA, Calif. Sch. Profl. Psychology, LA, 1997, PsyD, 1999. Neuropsychologist SUNY Downstate Med. Ctr., Bklyn., 2002—05, Columbia-Presbyn. Med. Ctr., NYC, 2005—06; neuropsychological cons. Neuroscience Assocs., LA, 2006—. Postdoctoral fellow Children's Hosp. of Phila., 1999—2000, Bergen Neuropsychology Group, Hackensack, NJ, 2000—02. Tchr. Teach for Am., South Bronx, NY, 1993—95. Mem.: Nat. Acad. Neuropsychology, Internat. Neuropsychological Soc. Home Phone: 818-647-0105.

JO, SUNGHO, computer scientist, researcher; b. Seoul, Republic of Korea, Dec. 17, 1974; s. Sinhaeng Jo and Chuja Oh. BS in Engring., Seoul Nat. U.; MSME, MIT, Cambridge, Mass., 2001, PhD in Elec. Engring. and Computer Sci., 2006. Rsch. asst. Man Vehicle Lab., MIT, 1999—2001, rsch. asst. artificial intelligence lab., 2001—03, rsch. asst. Lab. for info. sys. and decisions, 2003—06, rsch. asst. computer sci. and artificial intelligence lab., 2003—06; rsch. asst. MIT-Harvard NeuroEngring. Rsch. Collaborative, Cambridge, 2001—06; rsch. fellow MIT Media Lab., 2006—. Contbr. chapters to books, articles to profl. jours. Fellow Presdl. fellow, MIT, 1999, Shillman fellow, 2004, elec. engring. computer sci. grad. alumni fellow, 2005, Harold E. Edgerton fellow, 2005—06, Fernando J Corbato fellow, 2006. Mem.: Soc. Neurosci. Achievements include patents pending for computer-implemented model of the central nervous system. Office: MIT Media Lab 20 Ames St E15-054 Cambridge MA 02139 Office Phone: 617-324-1701. Business E-Mail: shjo@mit.edu.

JO, YOUNG GYUN, nuclear engineer; b. Cheong Ju City, Republic of Korea, June 10, 1961; s. Yijoon and Ohran Jo; m. Miae Jo; children: Eunji, Eunyoung. BS Nuc. Engring., Seoul Nat. U., 1984, MS Nuc. Engring., 1986; PhD Nuc. Engring., U. Tex., Austin, 1998. Level I nuc. engr., Korea, 1984. Rschr. Korea Atomic Energy Rsch. Inst., Taejon, 1986—89, sr. rschr., 1990—94; tchg. asst. U. Tex., Austin, 1994—98; sr. engr. So. Nuc. Oper. Co., Birmingham, Ala., 1998—. Rsch. adviser Korea Atomic Energy Rsch. Inst., Taejon, 2003—. Contbr. numerous articles to profl. confs. and proceedings. Ch. treas. St. Luke Hwang Korean Cath. Ch., Birmingham, 2001—03. Mem.: Am. Nuc. Soc. Roman Catholic. Achievements include designed and developed a thermal neutron imaging system for real time neutron radiography and computed tomography; principal investigator and project mamager of Korea's technical self reliance in the area of probabilistic safety assessment of nuclear power plants; development of procedures to analyse plant specific common cause failures in nuclear power plants. Avocations: gardening, writing poems. Office: So Nuc Operating Co 40 Inverness Ctr Pky Birmingham AL 35242 Home Phone: 205-981-2923; Office Phone: 205-992-7305. E-mail: ygjo@southernco.com.

JOANIDHI, ZHANI, mathematician, educator; b. Tirana, Albania, Sept. 17, 1965; arrived in US, 2000, naturalized; s. Tasho and Meri Joanidhi; m. Ornela Gambeta, Apr. 30, 1995; children: Nei, Patris. BS in Math., State U. Tirana, 1988; MA in Math. Edn., CUNY, 2004. Cert. math. tchr. NY. Shareholder, mktg. mgr. Extra Ltd., Korca, Albania, 1993—2000; math tchr. John Adams H.S., Ozone Park, NY, 2002—; math instr. Interboro Inst., NYC, 2004—. Advisor of math team, chess club John Adams H.S., 2003—; instr. math. State U. Albania, Korca, 1999—2000. Mem. Americorps, 2002—; mem. coun. St. Nicolas Albanian Ch., Jamaica Estates, NY, 2001—05. Tchg. fellow, Americorps, 2002—07. Mem.: Nat. Coun. Tchrs. Math., Math. Assn. Am. Greek Orthodox. Avocations: tennis, chess, travel, gardening, reading. Home: 47-10 188 St Flushing NY 11358 Office: John Adams HS 101-01 Rockaway Blvd Ozone Park NY 11417 Home Phone: 718-423-3047; Office Phone: 718-322-0500. Office Fax: 718-738-9077. Personal E-mail: joanidhizh@msn.com.

JOANNOU, DAKIS, businessman; b. Nicosia, Cyprus, Dec. 29, 1939; s. Stelios and Ellie Ioannou; m. Lietta Stavrakis; children: Maria, Christos, Ellie, Stelios. BCE, Cornell U.; MCE, Columbia U.; D in Architecture, U. Rome. V.p. bd. dir. J&P Ltd., Athens, Greece, 2000—; chmn. J&P Avax SA, Athens, Greece, Athenaeum InterContinental, Athens, YES! Hotels & Restaurants SA, Athens. Pres. DESTE Found. for Contemporary Arts, Athens, Christos Stelios Joannou Found., Nicosia; mem. bd. trustees New Mus. Contemporary Art, NYC; mem. Tate Modern Coun.; mem. internat. dir. coun. Solomon R. Guggenheim Found. Avocation: Collector contemporary art. Office: J&P-Avax SA 9 Fragoklissias St Marousi 15125 Greece Office Phone: 302106185551.

JOANOU, PHILLIP, advertising executive; b. Phoenix, June 5, 1933; s. Paul and Alice (Lukken) J.; m. Michelle Mason, Aug. 18, 1956; children: Janet, Phillip, Jennifer, Kathleen. BS, U. Ariz., 1956; MA, N.Y. Acad. of Art, 1996. Exec. v.p. Galaxy Inc., Los Angeles, 1958-60; sr. account exec. Erwin Wasey Co., 1960-64; account supr. Dancer, Fitzgerald, Sample Co., Los Angeles, 1964-67; v.p. Grey Co., Los Angeles, 1966-68, Doyle, Dane & Bernbach Inc., Los Angeles, 1968-71; exec. v.p., dir. Nov. Group, NYC and Washington, 1971-72; pres., dir. Dailey & Assocs., LA, 1973-83, chmn., chief exec. officer, 1984-95. Instr. mktg. U. So. Calif., 1975-76, dir. inst. advt. studies, 1976-77. Mem. Washington Com. to Re-elect Pres. Nixon, 1971-72; advisor Pres. Ford Election Com., 1976, Pres. Reagan Campaign, 1980; founder, dir. Partnership For A Drug Free Am.; pres. La Canada Ednl. Found. trustee Art Ctr Coll. Served to capt. USAR, 1957-58. Recipient Pvt. Sector Initiative award Pres. Reagan and Bush, 1987; named Advt. Leader of the West, Am. Advt. Fedn., 1992. Mem. Western States Advt. Assn. (dir. 1975— , pres. 1980-81, Advt. Man of Yr. 1983), Am. Assn. Advt. Agencies (gov. 1980-81, bd. dirs. 1981-83). Clubs: California. Republican. Episcopalian.

JOAQUIN, LINTON, lawyer; b. 1950; JD, Univ. Calif., Berkeley. Bar: Calif. 1977. Atty. United Farm Workers, People's Coll., LA; exec. dir. Central Am. Refugee Ctr., Calif.; litigation dir. Nat. Immigration Law Ctr., LA, 1990—2004, exec. dir., 2004—. Adj. faculty Southwestern Univ. Sch. Law, 1991—96, Univ. So. Calif. Law Sch., 1997. Recipient Carol King award, Nat. Immigration Project, Nat. Lawyers Guild. Mem.: Am. Immigration Lawyers Assn. (Jack Wasserman award). Office: National Immigration Law Center Suite 2850 3435 Wilshire Blvd Los Angeles CA 90010 Office Phone: 213-639-3900.

JOBE, FRANK WILSON, orthopedic surgeon; b. Greensboro, NC, July 16, 1925; MD, Loma Linda U., Calif., 1956; PhD (hon.), U. Tokushima, Japan. Diplomate Am. Bd. Orthop. Surgery. Intern LA County Gen. Hosp., 1956-57, resident, orthop. surgery, 1960-64; staff Centinela Hosp. Med. Ctr., Inglewood, Calif., med. dir., bio mechanics; staff LA County U. So. Calif. Med. Ctr., LA; clin. prof. dept. orthopedics U. So. Calif. Sch. Medicine. Orthop. cons. LA Dodgers Baseball Team, PGA Tour, Sr. PGA Tour, LOA Lakers Basketball Team, LA Kings Hockey Team, Calif. Angels Baseball Team; cons. President's Coun. on Phys. Fitness and Sports; mem., sponsor Neufeld Chair, orthop. surgery, Loma. Authored several med. publications, books and chapters to books. With AUS, 1943-46. Fellow ACS, Am. Acad. Orthop. Surgeons (past mem., com. on sports medicine, chmn., com. on shoulder, 1982-87); mem. Western Orthop. Assn., LA Chpt. (program chmn., 1978-79), Internat. Soc. of the Knee (founding mem.), Am. Orthop. Assn., Major League Baseball Physicians Assn. (pres. 1976-77, sec. 1977-79), Am. Shoulder and Elbow Surgeons (founding mem., pres. 1985-86, Charles S. Near award, 1987, 1997), Am. Orthop. Soc. for Sports Medicine (founding mem., chmn. membership com., 1978-79, O'Donohue award, 1984). Achievements include being responsible for the procedure known as Tommy John surgery (LA Dodgers pitcher Tommy John, diagnosed with a career-threatening torn ulnar collateral ligament was repaired by this procedure). Office: Kerlan-Jobe Orthop Clinic Westchester 6801 Park Ter Dr Fl 5 Los Angeles CA 90045 Office Phone: 310-665-7200. Office Fax: 310-665-7242.*

JOBE, LARRY ALTON, finance company executive; b. Knox City, Tex., Jan. 12, 1940; s. Lloyd Alton and Georgia (Swift); m. Suzanne Marie Storch, Aug. 2, 1980; 1 dau., Jennifer Marie; children by previous marriage: Lorrie Aileen, Lezlie Amee, Lowell Alton, Lloyd Alan, Leland Austin, Llewyn. BBA, U. North Tex., 1961, postgrad., 1961-65. CPA, Tex. Joined Grant Thornton, Dallas, 1961, mgr., 1967-69, ptnr., 1968-69, mng. ptnr., mem. exec. com. Dallas, 1973—, S.W. regional mng. ptnr., 1983-91; chmn. Legal Network, Inc., 1991—; pres. PI Resources LLP, 1997—; chmn. Ind. Bank Tex., 2002—; asst. sec. commerce Washington, 1969-72; v.p. fin. Dart Industries, 1972-73. Mem. acctg. adv. bd. U. North Tex., U. Tex.; bd. dirs. Ind. Nat. Bank, US Home Sys., Inc., SWS Group, Inc., Mannatech, Inc. Contbr. articles to profl. jours. Bd. dirs. Dallas Citizens Coun., Eisenhower World Affairs Inst.; chmn. bd. trustees Dallas Theol. Sem.; mem. Chief Execs. Roundtable; chmn. bd. Dallas Alliance for Minority Enterprise, Dallas Minority Bus. Ctr., Profl. Devel. Inst. of U. North Tex.; mem. pres.'s coun. North Tex. State U. Recipient Excellence in Acctg. award Haskins and Sells Found., 1960; Outstanding Alumni award U. North Tex., 1965, Pres.' Svc. award, 1986; U.S. Interagy. Audit Tng. award, 1970, Outstanding Svc. award, 1st Place Author's award Fed. Govt.

Accts. Assn., 1970. Mem. AICPA, Tex. Soc. CPAs, Fed. Govt. Accts. Assn., Dallas C. of C. (dir., vice chmn.), Blue Key, Phi Eta Sigma, Alpha Chi, Alpha Lambda Pi, Beta Alpha Psi. Office: 600 N Pearl St Ste 2100 Dallas TX 75201-2825 E-mail: ljobe@legaljobnet.com.

JOBS, STEVE(N) (PAUL), computer company executive; b. Feb. 24, 1955; adopted s. Paul J. and Clara J. Jobs; m. Laurene Powell, Mar. 18, 1991; 4 children. Student, Reed Coll. With Hewlett-Packard, Palo Alto, Calif.; designer video games Atari Inc., 1974; co-founder Apple Computer Inc., Cupertino, Calif., 1976, chmn. bd., 1976—85, interim CEO, 1997; CEO Apple Inc. (formerly Apple Computer Inc.), Cupertino, Calif., 1998—; pres. NeXT Computer, Redwood City, Calif., 1985—97; CEO NeXT Computer (acquired by Apple Computer Inc.), 1985—97; co-founder Pixar Animation Studios Inc., Emeryville, Calif., 1986, chmn., CEO, 1986—. Bd. dirs. Apple Inc., 1997—, The Walt Disney Co., 2006—. Exec. prodr.: (films) Toy Story, 1995. Nominee Rave award in Business, WIRED, 2005; named one of 50 Most Powerful People in Hollywood, Premiere mag., 2002—06, The World's Most Influential People, Time Mag., 2005—07, Forbes' Richest Americans, 2005—, World's Richest People, 2005—, 50 Who Matter Now, CNNMoney.com Bus. 2.0, 2006, 2007, 25 Most Influential People in Web Music, Powergeek 25, 2007; recipient Nat. Medal Tech., presented by Pres. Ronald Reagan, 1985, Jefferson award for pub. svc., 1987, Entrepreneur of the Decade award, Inc. Mag., 1989, The Steve Jobs Award, WIRED Rave award, 2006. Achievements include co-designer (with Stephan Wozniak) Apple I Computer; development of Apple II computer in 1977; iMac in 1998; iPod portable music player in 2001, iTunes in 2002 and iTunes Music Store, 2003, iPhone, 2007; Apple Computer Inc. celebrated 30th birthday on April 1, 2006. Address: Apple Inc 1 Infinite Loop Cupertino CA 95014 Office Phone: 510-752-3000, 408-996-1010. Office Fax: 510-752-3151, 408-974-2113.*

JOCELYN, MARTHE MARY, writer; b. Toronto, Ont., Can., Feb. 24, 1956; arrived in US, 1980; d. Arthur Gordon and Joy Dorreen Brownscombe (Martyn) Jocelyn; m. Tom Robert Slaughter (div.); children: Hannah May, Nell Marie. Author: A Day With Nellie, 2002, One Some Many, 2004, Mayfly, 2004, Hannah's Collections, 2000, The Invisible Day, 1997, The Invisible Harry, 1998, Hannah and the Seven Dresses, 1999, Earthly Astonishments, 2000, The Invisible Enemy, 2002, ABC x 3 English Espanol, 2005, Mael Riley, 2004, Over Under, 2005, A Home for Foundlings, 2005, Secrets: Stories Selected by Marthe Jocelyn, 2005, How it Happened in Peach Hill, 2007, First Times: Stories Selected by Marthe Jocelyn, 2007, Eats, 2007. Trustee Little Red Elisabeth Irwin Sch., NYC, 2001—. Recipient Children's Lit. award, TD Bank, Toronto, 2005. Personal E-mail: marthe@marthejocelyn.com.

JOCHIM, MICHAEL ALLAN, archaeologist; b. St. Louis, May 31, 1945; s. Kenneth Erwin and Jean MacKenzie (Keith) J.; m. Amy Martha Waugh, Aug. 12, 1967; children: Michael Waugh, Katherine Elizabeth. BS, U. Mich., 1967, MA, 1971, PhD, 1975. Lectr. anthropology U. Calif., Santa Barbara, 1975-77, asst. prof., 1979-81, assoc. prof., 1981-87, prof., 1987—, dept. chmn., 1987-92; asst. prof. Queens Coll. CUNY, Flushing, 1977-79. Mem. archaeology rev. panel NSF, Washington, 1988-90. Author: Hunter-Gatherer Subsistence and Settlement, 1976, Strategies for Survival, 1981, A Hunter-Gatherer Landscape, 1998; editor (series) Interdisciplinary Contributions to Archaeology, 1987—; editor Am. Antiquity, 2004—. Chmn. Community Adv. Com. for Spl. Edn., Santa Barbara County, 1980-82. Grantee NEH, 1976, NSF, 1980, 81, 83, 89, 91, 94, 2002, Nat. Geog. Soc., 1987, 97, Wenner-Gren, 1999. Fellow Am. Anthrop. Assn.; mem. Soc. for Am. Archaeology, Sigma Xi. Office: U Calif Dept Anthropology Santa Barbara CA 93106 Home Phone: 805-964-3667; Office Phone: 805-893-4396. Business E-Mail: jochim@anth.ucsb.edu.

JOCHMANN, FRANK, mathematician; b. Berlin, Oct. 29, 1965; D, Tech. U. Berlin, 1992. Rsch. asst. Humboldt U., Berlin, 1996—2001, U. Leipzig, Germany, 2001—02; rsch., tchg. asst. Tech. U. Berlin, 2002—. Contbr. articles to profl. jours. Office: Tech Univ Berlin Strasse des 17 Juni 136 10623 Berlin Germany

JOCHNER, MICHELE MELINA, lawyer; b. Naperville, Ill., May 19, 1966; BA summa cum laude, Mundelein Coll., 1987; JD with honors, DePaul U., Chgo., 1990, LLM in Taxation Law, 1992. Bar: Ill. 1990, US Dist. Ct. (no. dist.) Ill. 1990, US Ct. Appeals (7th cir.) 1996, US Supreme Ct. 1996. Law clk. US Securities & Exch. Commn., Chgo., 1989; legal rsch. asst. to prof. Marlene Nicholson DePaul U. Sch. Law, Chgo., 1989-91, legal rsch. asst. to assoc. dean Vincent Vitullo, 1989-91; law clk. extern US Dist. Ct. (no. dist.) Ill., Chgo., 1989-90; jud. law clk. Cir. Ct. of Cook County, Chgo., 1991-92, staff atty., 1992-93, sr. staff atty., 1993-95, acting supr. legal rsch. divsn., 1995-96; staff atty. permanency project child protection divsn. Cir. Ct. Cook County, Chgo., 1996-97; jud. law clk. to Chief Justice Mary Ann G. McMorrow Ill. Supreme Ct., Chgo., 1997—2006, jud. law clk. to Justice Charles E. Freeman, 2006—. Adj. prof. law John Marshall Law Sch., Chgo., 1994—, DePaul U. Coll. Law, 1998—, mem. alumni bd., 2005—; mem. subcom. money transfers and adminstrv. regulations Ill. Supreme Ct., 1995—96; judge Herzog Moot Ct. Competition, 1997—; spkr. in field. Contbr. articles to profl. jours. Planning com. Women Everywhere: Ptnrs. in Svc. Project, 2003—, bd. dirs., 2004—; planning com. Chgo. Battered Women's Network Ann. Banquet, 2004—, bd. dirs., 2005—, bd. sec., 2006—; co-chair ednl. seminar Project, 2004—. Named one of Forty Ill. Attys. Under Forty to Watch, Chgo. Daily Law Bull., 2004; recipient Harold A. Shertz award, Film, Air & Package Carriers Conf., 1990. Fellow: Ill. Bar Found.; mem.: ABA, Ill. Govt. Bar Assn. (sec. 2007—), Ill. Appellate Lawyer's Assn., Women's Bar Assn. Ill. (bd. dirs. 2005—, recording sec. 2007—), US Supreme Ct. Hist. Soc., Chgo. Bar Assn. (mem. Alliance Women exec. com., constitutional law com., judiciary com 2005—), Fed. Bar Assn., Ill. State Bar Assn. (elected assembly mem. 2000, bd. govs. 2002—, former chair gen. practice sect. coun. 2003—04, chair planning com. for ann. solo and small firm conf. 2004—, sec. 2006—, chair continuing legal edn. subcom., mem. tradition of excellence award subcom., mem. bench and bar sect. coun., co-editor Bench and Bar Newsletter, mem. spl. com. on minority outreach, mem. jud. evaluations com., bd. govs. com. on scope and correlation, mem. Pres.'s spl. com. on mentoring, mem. spl. com. on implementing mentoring program, Lincoln award 2d pl. 1994, Lincoln award 1st pl. 1996, Lincoln award 2d pl. 1997, Lincoln award 1st pl. 1999, Lincoln award 2d pl. 2000, Lincoln award 1st pl. 2002, 2001), Lawyer's Club Chgo., Order of Coif, Phi Sigma Tau, Kappa Gamma Pi. Avocation: writing fiction, non-fiction.

JOCHUM, JAMES J., lawyer, former federal agency administrator; b. Dubuque, IA, June 16, 1965; BA in Polit. Sci. with high distinction, U. Iowa, 1987, JD, 1990. Atty. Foley & Lardner, Milwaukee, 1990—92; asst. v.p. Brenton Bank, Cedar Rapids, Iowa, 1992—94; internat. trade counsel to Sen. Charles E. Grassley US Senate, 1994—97, legis. dir. to Sen. Charles E. Grassley, 1997—99; majority counsel U.S. Senate Banking Com.; sr. mgr. govt. rels. Accenture L.L.P., 2000—01; asst. sec. for export adminstrn. U.S. Dept. Commerce, Washington, 2001—03, asst. sec. for import adminstrn., 2003—05; ptnr. Mayer, Brown, Rowe & Maw LLP, Washington, 2005—. Recipient William C. Redfield award for Disting. Svc., US Dept. Commerce, 2005. Mem.: Order of Coif. Republican. Office: Mayer Brown Rowe & Maw LLP 1909 K St NW Washington DC 20006

JOCHUM, PAM, state representative; b. Dubuque, Iowa, Sept. 26, 1954; AA, BA, Loras Coll. Pub. info. and mktg. dir. Loras Coll.; instr. N.E. Iowa C.C.; mem. Iowa Ho. Reps., Des Moines, 1993—, mem. various coms. including judiciary, mem. state govt. ways and means com. Chair Alzheimer Memory Walk, CROP Walk; del. Dem. Nat. Conv., 1980, floor whip, 1984; chair Dubuque County Dem. Ctrl. Com., 1982; statewide co-chair U.S. Senator Tom Harkin's Re-Election Com.; former bd. dirs. Dubuque County Assn. for Retarded Citizens, Dubuque County Compensation Bd., Loras Coll. Arts and Lectr. Series, Nat. Cath. Basketball Tournament, Sacred Heart Cath. Ch., Women's Recreation Assn., Mississippi Valley Promise, LWV. Democrat. Office: State Capitol East 12th and Grand Des Moines IA 50319 also: 2368 Jackson St Dubuque IA 52001 E-mail: pam.jochum@legis.state.ia.us.

JOCHUM, VERONICA, pianist; b. Berlin; d. Eugen and Maria (Montz) J.; m. Wilhelm V. von Moltke, Nov. 15, 1961. MusM, Staatliche Musikhochschule, Munich, 1955, Concert Diploma, 1957; pvt. study with, Edwin Fischer, Josef Benvenuti, 1958—59, Rudolf Serkin, Phila., 1959—61. Faculty Settlement Sch. Music, Phila., 1959-61, New Eng. Conservatory Music, Boston, 1965—, Berkshire Music Center, Tanglewood, 1974, Radcliffe Inst., Cambridge, Mass. Recs. with Laurel, Deutsche Grammophon, Philips, Golden Crest, Pro Arte, GM Recs., CRJ, Tahra recs., Tudor; Numerous tours, throughout N. and S. Am., Asia, Europe and, Africa; as soloist with world renowned orchs., including Boston Symphony, Balt. Symphony, London Philharmonic, Los Angeles Chamber Orch., London Symphony, Mpls. Symphony, Berlin, Hamburg and Munich Philharmonics, Bavarian and Bamberg Symphonies, Munich Chamber Orch., radio orchs. of Hamburg, Munich, and Frankfurt, Orch. Maggio Musicale, Florence, La Fenice Orch., Venice, RAI-Orch., Naples, Mozarteum Orch., Salzburg, Concertgebouw Orch., Amsterdam, The Hague Philharmonic, Venezuelan Symphony, Caracas, Jerusalem Symphony, others; appearances on radio, TV, and films, recitals in more than 50 countries on 4 continents; participant, Marlboro Music Festival, Montreux Festival, Bregenz Festival, Mecklenburg Festival, Festival de Vallonie (Belgium), Tanglewood, N.W. Bach Festival, Spokane, Ea. Music Festival, Chambermusic East. Bd. mem. Berkshire Inst. Theology and the Arts. Recipient cross Order of Merit (Germany); Bunting fellow Harvard U., 1996-97. Office: New Eng Conservatory Music 290 Huntington Ave Boston MA 02115-5018

JOCK, PAUL F., II, lawyer; b. Indpls., Jan. 25, 1943; s. Paul F. and Alice (Sheehan) J.; m. Gail A. Webre, Sept. 16, 1967; children: Craig W., Nicole L. BBA, U. Notre Dame, 1965; JD, U. Chgo., 1970. Bar: Ill. 1970, NY 1990. Ptnr. Kirkland & Ellis, Chgo. and NYC, 1970-2001; sr. v.p., gen. counsel GM Asset Mgmt., NYC, 2000—05; ptnr. Jenner & Block LLP, NYC, 2005—. V.p. legal affairs Tribune Co., Chgo., 1981. Assoc. editor U. Chgo. Law Rev., 1969-70. Served to lt. USN, 1965-67. Mem. ABA, Chgo. Bar Assn., Assn. of the Bar of City of NY Office: Jenner & Block LLP 919 3d Ave Ste 3700 New York NY 10022-3908 Business E-Mail: pjock@jenner.com.

JODOCK, DARRELL HARLAND, minister, educator; b. Northwood, ND, Aug. 15, 1941; s. Harry N. and Grace H. (Hansen) J.; m. Janice Marie Swanson, July 8, 1972; children: Erik Thomas, Aren Kristofer. BA summa cum laude, St. Olaf Coll., 1962; BD with honors, Luther Theol. Sem., 1966; postgrad., Union Theol. Sem., NYC, 1966-67; PhD, Yale U., 1969. Ordained to ministry Am. Luth. Ch., 1973, Luth. Ch. in Am., 1978. Instr. Luther Theol. Sem., St. Paul, 1969-70, asst. prof., 1970-73, 75-78; asst. pastor Grace Luth. Ch., Washington, 1973-75; prof. dept. religion Muhlenberg Coll., Allentown, Pa., 1978-99, head dept. of religion, 1978-92, Class of 1932 rsch. prof., 1989; disting. prof. religion Gustavus Adolphus Coll., St. Peter, Minn., 1999—. Chmn. various coms. N.E. Pa. Synod Evang. Luth. Ch. in Am., 1979-99, del. to nat. assembly, 1995, 97, 99, 2005; adv. bd. Berman Ctr. for Jewish Studies, 1985-92; founder, chmn. bd. Inst. for Jewish-Christian Understanding, 1988-99; bd. Inst. for Ecumenical and Cultural Rsch., Collegeville, 1999—; chair Assn. Tchg. Theologians of the Evang. Luth. Ch. Am., 2002-06, Evang. Luth. Ch. Am. Consultative Panel Luth.-Jewish Rels., 2001—, chair, 2005—. Author: The Church's Bible: Its Contemporary Authority, 1989; translator: Luther and the Peasants' War (Hubert Kirchner), 1972; editor and co-author: Ritschl in Retrospect: History, Community and Science, 1995, Catholicism Contending with Modernity: Roman Catholic Modernism and Anti-Modernism in Historical Context, 1999; contbr. articles to profl. jours. Recipient Paul C. Empie Meml. award Muhlenberg Coll., 1987; Danforth Found. fellow 1962-69, Inst. for Ecumenical and Cultural Rsch. fellow, 1982-83. Mem. Am. Acad. Religion (pres. 19th Century theology group 1981-86, 1997-2001), Am. Soc. Ch. History, Soc. for Values in Higher Edn., Internat. Schleiermacher Soc., Internat. Bonhoeffer Soc., Søren Kierkegaard Soc., Phi Beta Kappa, Omicron Delta Kappa (campus leadership 1985—). Office: Gustavus Adolphus Coll Dept Religion 800 W College Ave Saint Peter MN 56082-1485

JODRY, LOUIS FREDERICK, V, music educator; b. Jan. 10, 1962; MusB, New Eng. Conservatory, Boston, 1984, MusM, 1986. Dir. choral activities Brown U., Providence, 1991—; music dir. Trinity Ch., Newport, RI, 1995—2001, 1st Unitarian, Providence, 2001—. Recipient Chadwick medal, NEC, 1984. Mem.: Am. Guild Organists.

JOEL, AMOS EDWARD, JR., telecommunications consultant; b. Phila., Mar. 12, 1918; s. Amos Edward and Anna (Potsdamer) J.; m. Rhoda Ethel Fenton (dec.); children: Jeffrey (dec.), Stephanie, Andrea. BEE, MIT, 1940, MEE, 1942. Registered profl. engr., N.Y. Mem. tech. staff Bell Tel. Labs., N.Y. and N.J., 1940-52, supr. Whippany, N.J., 1952-54, dept. head, 1954-61, dir. Holmdel, N.J., 1961-67, cons., 1967-83, ret., 1983; cons., 1983—. Cons. AT&T Bell Comm. Rsch., GTE, IBM, Contel, Pacific Tel.; lectr. in field of switching sys. Author: Electronic Switching Central Office Systems of the World, 1976, Electronic Switching: Digital Central Office Systems of the World, 1982, History of Science and Technology in the Bell System-Switching Technology, 1982; author: (with others) Fundamentals of Digital Switching, 1983, 2d edit., 1990, Electronics, Computers and Telephone Switching, 1990, Future of the Central Office, 1991; contbr. articles to encys. and profl. jours.; holder more than 70 patents. Co-recipient Outstanding Patent award N.J. R & D Coun., 1972, Stuart Ballantine medal Franklin Inst., 1981, Century prize Internat. Telecom. Union, 1983, Columbian medal City of Genoa, Italy, 1984, Kyoto prize in advanced tech., 1989, Nat. Med. of Tech., 1993; named N.J. Inventor of Yr., 1989. Fellow IEEE (life, co-recipient Alexander Graham Bell medal 1976, IEEE medal of honor 1992, nat. medal tech. 1993, 3d Millennium medal 2000), Am. Acad. Arts and Scis.; mem. NAE, AAAS, Comm. Soc. of IEEE (pres. 1973-75), Sigma Xi, Eta Kappa Nu (Karapetoff eminent members' award 2000). Avocations: organ and keyboard music, railroading. Home: Winchester Gardens One Turnberry Ct Maplewood NJ 07040-2423 E-mail: a.joel@ieee.org.

JOEL, BILLY (WILLIAM MARTIN JOEL), musician; b. Bronx, NY, May 9, 1949; s. Howard and Rosalind (Nyman) Joel; m. Elizabeth Webber, 1972 (div. 1982); m. Christie Brinkley, Mar. 23, 1985 (div. Aug. 1994); 1 child, Alexa Ray; m. Kate Lee, Oct. 2, 2004. LHD (hon.), Fairfield U., 1991; HMD (hon.), Berklee Coll. Music, 1993; LHD (hon.), Hofstra U., 1997; Mus D (hon.), Southampton Coll., 2000; DFA (hon.), Syracuse U., 2006. Joined band The Hassles, LI, 1968, Attila, 1970; solo rec. artist, 1972—; performed in piano bars under name Bill Martin LA, 1973; co-founder LI Boat Co., 1996. Albums: (with The Hassles) The Hassles, 1967, Hour of the Wolf, 1968; (with Attila) Attila, 1970; (solo albums) Cold Spring Harbor, 1971, Piano Man, 1973, Streetlife Serenade, 1974, Turnstiles, 1975, The Stranger, 1977, 52nd Street, 1978 (Grammy Award for album of yr., 1979, Grammy Award for best male pop vocal performance, 1979), Glass Houses, 1980 (Grammy Award for best male rock vocal performance, 1980), Songs in the Attic, 1981, The Nylon Curtain, 1982, An Innocent Man, 1983, Billy Joe's Greatest Hits, Vols. I and II, 1985, The Bridge, 1986, Kohuept: Live from the Soviet Union, 1987, Storm Front, 1989, River of Dreams, 1993, Billy Joe's Greatest Hits, Vol. III, 1997, 2000 Years: Millenium Concert, 2000, Essential Billy Joel, 2001, Fantasies & Delusions: Music For Solo Piano, 2001, My Lives, 2005, 12 Gardens Live, 2006; Author: Goodnight My Angel: A Lullabye, 2005, New York State of Mind, 2005. Established The Rosalind Joel Scholarship CCNY, 1996. Grammy Legend Award, 1990, Humanitarian Award, Cathedral of St. John the Divine, 1990, Billboard Century Music Award, 1994, ASCAP Founder's Award, 1997, Am. Music Awards Award of Merit, 1999, James Smithson Bicentennial Medal of Honor, 2000, Johnny Mercer Award, Songwriter's Hall of Fame, 2001, Music Cares Person of Yr., 2002; inducted into Songwriter's Hall of Fame, 1992, Rock and Roll Hall of Fame, 1999. Achievements include premiering first prodn. tour of the USSR by an Am. popular artist, 1987; inspiring Broadway musical Movin' Out, 2002. Home: 2 E Main St Oyster Bay NY 11771-2406

JOEL, KATIE (KATIE LEE JOEL, KATHERINE LEE), television personality; b. Huntington, W. Va., Sept. 1981; m. Billy Lee, Oct. 2, 2004. B in English and Journalism, Miami U., Ohio; studied a wide range culinary classes including a semester in Florence, Italy. Helped open Jeff and Eddy's Restaurant, Hamptons, 2003. Critic (TV series) George Hirsch: Living It UP! (PBS); contbr. "East End Girl", Hamptons Mag.; co-creater (culinary website) www.oliveandpeach.com, 2005, host (TV series) Top Chef (Bravo), 2006—.

JOEL, RICHARD MARC, academic administrator, law educator, dean; b. NYC, Sept. 9, 1950; s. Avery Joel and Annette (Bloom) Ashwal; m. Esther Duora Ribner, Nov. 11, 1973; children: Penina, Avery, Arielle, Noam. BA, NYU, 1972, JD, 1975. Bar: N.Y. 1976, U.S. Dist. Ct. (ea. dist.) N.Y. 1976. Asst. dist. atty. Borough of Bronx, NY, 1975-78; dir. alumni affairs Yeshiva U., NYC, 1978-80, asst. dean Cardozo Sch. Law, 1980-82, assoc. dean Cardozo Sch. Law, 1982, adj. prof. law, 1985, pres., 2003—. Pres. Hillel, Found. for Jewish Campus Life. Sec. Hebrew Acad. Long Beach, N.Y., 1983—; bd. dirs. Jewish Community Council Oceanside, N.Y., 1977-81, Young Israel Oceanside, 1986—. Root-Tilden scholar NYU, 1972-75. Mem. ABA. Democrat. Jewish. Avocations: music, youth work. Office: Yeshiva U Cardozo Sch Law 55 5th Ave New York NY 10003-4301*

JOEL, WILLIAM LEE, II, interior and lighting designer; b. Richmond, Va., Feb. 23, 1933; s. J. Alton and Dorothy Joel; m. Merry Pick, June 5, 1955; children: Taryn, Dana, Wendy, Holly. Student, R.I. Sch. Design, 1953-55; AB, Brown U., 1955; postgrad., N.Y. Sch. Interior Design, 1956, Pratt Inst., 1958-61. Cert. interior designer Commonwealth of Va. Draftsman Mills Denmark Inc., NYC, 1957-58; with sales and interior design Lord & Taylor's Inc., NYC, 1958-61; pres., interior designer Richmond (Va.) Art Co. Inc. Instr. Va. Commonwealth U. (formerly Richmond Profl. Inst.), 1963-67; set designer Barksdale Theatre, Hanover, Va., 1977-88; mem. adv. bd. interior design program Va. Poly. Inst and State U., 1986-90; speaker numerous orgns., radio and TV programs. Prin. works include Culpepper (Va.) Hosp., The Curles Neck Pl., Richmond, Dominion Nat. Bank, Richmond, Gary, Stoch, Walls offices, Richmond, Gov.'s Exec. Mansion, Commonwealth Va., 1976, Hello Inc., Richmond, Hill Bldg., Richmond, Hunter House Mus., Norfolk, Va., Richmond, Fredericksburg and Potomac R.R. Co. corp. hdqrs., Rolph Clark Stone Packaging Co. offices, Straub and Dalch office complex, Westminster Canterbury House, Richmond, Wickham Valentine House, Willow Oaks Country Club, Continental Cablevision, Richmond, St. Paul Episcopal Ch., Richmond, numerous residences; author: articles published bi-monthly in Rich Art website. Co-chmn. com. for cert. Va. Interior Designers, 1982-90; mem. Downtown Mktg. Com., chmn. subcom. Xmas Sound and Lighting, Richmond, 1988-91, mem. prodn. Richmond Forum sets and lighting design, 1989-95; bd. visitors Found. for Interior Design Edn. and Rsch., 1977-84, mem. accreditation com., 1984-88; mem. Va. Mus. Fine Arts, City of Richmond Christmas Candlelight Com., edn. com. Retail Mchts. Assn., 1980-85; mem. urban design com. Ctrl. Richmond Assn., 1993. 1st lt. USMC, 1952-57. Recipient award Va. Mus. Fine Arts, Richmond, 1970, Cert. Distinction, 1973; named contest winner Richmond Symphony Orch., 1975. Fellow Am. Soc. Interior Designers (cert., pres. Va. chpt. 1970-72, 80-81, mem. nat. bd. 1972-74, 76-77, regional v.p. 1976-77, nat. com. 1976); mem. Nat. Fire Protection Assn. Avocations: sailing, canoeing, electronics, sport cars. Home: 8905 Sierra Rd Richmond VA 23229-7828 Office: Richmond Art Co 530 E Main St Ste 600 Richmond VA 23219-2431 Office Phone: 804-644-0733. Business E-Mail: rich@richartco.com.

JOELSON, MARK RENÉ, lawyer; b. Paris, Oct. 23, 1934; came to U.S., 1941, naturalized, 1947; s. Michael and Helen (Streicher) J.; m. Anastasia Whelan, June 4, 1967; children: Helen, Daniel, Marisa. BA, Harvard U., 1955, LLB, 1958; diploma in law, Oxford U., Eng., 1962. Bar: D.C. 1958, U.S. Supreme Ct. 1959. Atty. U.S. Dept. Justice, Washington, 1958-63; assoc., then ptnr. Arent, Fox, Kintner, Plotkin & Kahn, Washington, 1963-80; ptnr. Wald, Harkrader & Ross, Washington, 1980-85, Morgan, Lewis & Bockius LLP, Washington, 1986-97; pvt. practice, 1998—. Mem. adv. com. internat. investment, tech. and devel. U.S. Dept. State, 1978-87; cons. UN Conf. Trade and Devel., 1977-79; adj. prof. Georgetown U. Law Ctr., Washington; panelist N.Am. Free Trade Agreement, Am. Arbitration Assn., Nat. Arbitration Forum, NASD, mediator US Dist. Ct., DC, 2001-. Author (with Earl W. Kintner): An International Antitrust Primer, 1974; author: An International Antitrust Primer, 3d edit., 2006; editor (with others): Current Legal Aspects of Doing Business in the E.E.C., 1978; editor: Enterprise Law in the 80's, 1980, Joint Ventures in the United States, 1988. Fulbright scholar Oxford U., 1961-62. Mem. ABA (chmn. sect. internat. law and practice 1983-84, del. Internat. Bar Assn. coun. 1984-92), Internat. Bar Assn., Fed. Bar Assn. (pres. D.C. chpt. 1976-77), DC Bar (chmn. internat. dispute resolution com., internat. sect., 2001-03), Washington Inst. Fgn. Affairs, Cosmos Club (Washington), Order of Brit. Empire. Office Phone: 202-626-6815. Personal E-mail: joelsonmr@msn.com.

JOERGER, JAY HERMAN, psychologist, entrepreneur; b. Freeport, NY, Sept. 23, 1957; s. Herman Alexander and Ellen Rose (Becker) J.; m. Diana Botero, Mar. 27, 1993; children: Nicholas Alexander, Richard Andrew. BS, Union U., 1980; MA, Colgate U., 1981; EdD, Columbia U., 1987. Diplomate Am. Bd. Profl. Disability Consultants, Substance Abuse Psychology, Clin. Psychology, Psychology Assessment, Evaluation and Testing, Child Custody Evaluation, lic. psychologist N.Y., Pa., bd. cert. forensic examiner, bd. cert. in forensic medicine, cert. homeland security, registered hypnotherapist, cert. med. examiner. Drug abuse counselor Drug Abuse Coun., Norwich, NY, 1980-81; vocat. rehab. counselor Community Workshop, Glens Falls, NY, 1981-83; assoc. psychologist N.Y. State, Wingdale, NY, 1986-96; pres. Mentors Resource and Devel. Corp., 1991—; mem. group practice Ctr. Stress Reduction, 1993-97, Carmel Psychol. Assocs., 1993-94. Admission and hosp. privileges Four Winds Hosp., Katonah, N.Y., 1995—; cons., Somers, N.Y., 1988—; adj. asst. prof. Iona Coll., 1993-95; adj. prof. Lehman Coll., 1994-97; founding coord. Alcoholism and Drug Abuse Counselor Tng. Program Lehman Coll., 1996; bd. dirs. Rapid Rabbit, Inc.; forensic psychol. cons. and expert witness. Author: A Participant Manual for Mentally Ill Chemical Abusers, 1989, Living Successfully: A Self-Study Guide, 1993; co-author: The Physical, Psychological and Social Effects of Chemical Abuse - A Clinician's Workbook, 1994, 2d edit., 1995, Substance Abuse: Evaluation and Treatment Training Program, 1995; (book, audio tape) Living Successfully: Relax and Enhance Your Life, 1996. Amateur radio operator USAF; mil. affiliate radio operator Westchester Emergency Comm. Assn., Westchester County, 1983-99; bd. dirs. Hudson Valley Fedn., Clintondale, N.Y., 1987-88. Recipient Excellence in Psychology award Med. Staff Orgn., Harlem Valley Psychologists,

1990. Mem. Am. Coll. Forensic Examiners (life), Am. Bd. Profl. Disability Cons., N.Y. State Psychol. Assn. (sec.-treas. addiction divsn. 1993-95, liaison managed care task force 1994-95), Westchester County Psychol. Assn. (pres. indsl. orgn. divsn. 1992-95). Avocation: amateur radio. Home and Office: RR 2 1016C Dingmans Ferry PA 18328-9613 Office: 758 E Main St Middletown NY 10940 Home Phone: 570-828-6664; Office Phone: 570-828-6444. Personal E-mail: mentors@ptd.net.

JOERN, CHARLES EDWARD, JR., lawyer; b. Oak Park, Ill., Apr. 27, 1951; s. Charles Edward and Eleanor Joern; m. Christine Mary Lake, July 28, 1973; children: Jessica, William, Marisa, Angela, Alexandra. BA, Knox Coll., 1973; M in Urban Affairs, U. Colo., 1976; JD, De Paul U., 1980. Bar: Ill. 1980, U.S. Dist. Ct. (no. dist.) Ill. 1980, U.S. Ct. Appeals (7th cir.) 1981, U.S. Supreme Ct. 1995. Asst. to planning cons. J.R. Crowley and Assocs., 1973-74; sys. analyst Aravada, Colo. Bldg. Inspection Divsn., U. Colo. sponsorship, 1974-75; student intern divsn. comprehensive health planning Colo. Dept. Health, 1976; law clk. Cook County Legal Assistance Found., Chgo., 1978; consumer fraud divsn. Office Ill. Atty. Gen., 1979-80; assoc. Pope, Ballard, Shepard & Fowle, Ltd., Chgo., 1980-94, Burke, Weaver & Prell, Chgo., 1994-2000, Holland & Knight, Chgo., 2000—. Panel atty. Chgo. Vol. Legal Svcs. Found. Bd. advisors N.C. Outward Bound Sch., Morgantown, 1983-99; bd. dirs. Richport YMCA, LaGrange, Ill., 1984—, chmn., 1990-93; village trustee LaGrange Park, 1997—. Fellow in pub. affairs U. Colo., 1979. Mem. ABA (litigation sect.), Ill. State Bar Assn., Chgo. Bar Assn. (chmn. child abuse and neglect com. 1985-86), Pi Alpha Alpha. Republican. Roman Catholic. Office: Holland & Knight LLC 131 S Dearborn Chicago IL 60603 E-mail: charles.joern@hklaw.com.

JOERRES, JEFFREY A., employment services executive; BS, Marquette U., Milw., 1983. Various mgmt. positions IBM; v.p. sales and mktg. ARI Network Svcs.; v.p. mktg. Manpower, Inc., Milw., 1993, sr. v.p. European ops. and global account mgmt. and devel., pres., CEO, 1999—, chmn., 2001—. Bd. dirs. Artisan Funds, Johnson Controls, NAM; bd. trustees Comm. Econ. Devel. Bd. trustees Marquette U., 2000—; mem. Commn. Tech. & Adult Learning Nat. Gov. Assn. Mem.: Am. Soc. Tng. & Devel. Office: Manpower Inc 5301 N Ironwood Rd Milwaukee WI 53217-4982 Office Phone: 414-961-1000.*

JOERSZ, FRAN WOODMANSEE, secondary school educator; b. Bismarck, ND, Apr. 29, 1954; d. Joe G. and Winnie (McGillic) Woodmansee; m. Jon D. Joersz; children: Brett, Ben, Courtney. Student, Bismarck State Coll., 1972; BA in Edn., U. Wyo., 1975. Tchr. 3rd grade Deer Trail (Colo.) Pub. Sch., 1975-76; tchr. 8th grade remedial reading Mandan (N.D.) Jr. High Sch., 1976-78; tchr. title I reading Saxvik St. Mary's Grade Sch., Bismarck, 1979; tchr. 8th grade devel. reading Wachter Jr. High Sch., Bismarck, 1979-81; tchr. 7th grade devel. reading written and oral communications Hughes Jr. High Sch., Bismarck, 1981—. Bd. dirs. Rape Victim Adv. Program; founding bd. dirs. Our Kids Need to Know; state bd. dirs. Make A Wish Found. Recipient Milken award, 1994; named Edn. alumna of Yr., U. Wyo., 2003. Mem. PEO, ND Edn. Assn. (Tchr. of Yr. 1991, Profl. Courage award 1994), Internat. Reading Assn., Nat. Assn. Student Activity Advisers. Avocations: walking, reading, volleyball, writing, travel. Home: 520 N Mandan St Bismarck ND 58501-3748 Office: Horizon Mid Sch 500 Ash Coulee Dr Bismarck ND 58503 Office Phone: 701-221-3555. Business E-Mail: fran_joersz@educ8.org.

JOFFE, BARBARA LYNNE, business transformation architect; b. Bklyn., Apr. 12, 1951; d. Lester L. and Julia (Schuelke) J.; 1 child, Nichole. BA, U. Oreg., 1975; MFA, U. Mont., 1982. Cert. project mgr. IBM; cert. project mgmt. profl. Project Mgmt. Inst. Applications engr., software developer So. Pacific Transp., San Francisco, 1986-93; computer fine artist Barbara Joffe Assocs., San Francisco, Englewood, Colo., 1988—; instr. computer graphics Ohlone Coll., Fremont, Calif., 1990-91; adv. programmer, project mgr.-client/server Integrated Sys. Solutions Corp./IBM Global Svcs. So. Pacific/Union Pacific Railroads, Denver, 1994-97; applications sys. mgr. IBM Global Svcs./CoBank, Greenwood Village, Colo., 1997-99; exec. project mgr. IBM/GM Web Hosting, 2000—01, IBM/Cendant, 2001—. Artwork included in exhibits at Calif. Crafts XIII, Crocker Art Mus., Sacramento, 1983, Rara Avis Gallery, Sacramento, 1984, Redding (Calif.) Mus. and Art Ctr., 1985, Euphrat Gallery, Cupertino, Calif., 1988, Computer Mus., Boston, 1989, Siggraph Traveling Art Shown, Europe and Australia, 1990, 91, 4th and 7th Nat. Computer Art Invitational, Cheney, Wash., 1991, 94, Visual Arts Mus., N.Y.C., 1994, 96, IBM Golden Circle, 1996. Recipient IBM Project Mgmt. Excellence award, 1998. Mem. Project Mgmt. Inst. (cert.), Assn. Computing Machinery. Avocations: art, gardening, hiking. Personal E-mail: joffeb@aol.com.

JOFFE, CRAIG P.R., personal care industry executive; b. 1973; s. Stephen N. and Sandra Joffe; m. Lucy Haverland, Aug. 14, 1999; 2 children. BA summa cum laude, Columbia U., NYC, 1994; JD cum laude, Harvard Law Sch., 1997. Corp. fin. atty. Sullivan & Cromwell law firm, London and NYC, 1997—2000; asst. gen. counsel InterActiveCorp, 2000—03; sr. v.p. LCA-Vision, Cincinnati, Ohio, 2003, gen. counsel, sec., 2003, COO, 2005, founder, bd. dir., interim CEO, 2006—. Mem.: Phi Beta Kappa. Office: LCA-Vision Inc 7840 Montgomery Rd Cincinnati OH 45236 Office Phone: 513-792-9292, 513-792-5629. Office Fax: 513-792-5620.*

JOFFE, ROBERT DAVID, lawyer; b. NYC, May 26, 1943; s. Joseph and Bertha (Pashkovsky) Joffe; m. Virginia Ryan, June 20, 1981; stepchildren: Elizabeth DeHaas, Ryan DeHaas;children from previous marriage: Katherine, David. AB, Harvard U., 1964, JD, 1967. Bar: NY 1970, US Dist. Ct. (so. and ea. dists.) NY 1971, US Ct. Appeals (2d cir.) 1972, US Supreme Ct. 1973. Ford Found. fellow Maxwell Sch. Africa Pub. Svc., Malawi, 1967—69; state counsel, 1968—69; assoc. Cravath, Swaine & Moore, NYC, 1969—75; ptnr. Cravath, Swaine & Moore LLP, NYC, 1975—, dep. presiding ptnr., 1998, presiding ptnr., 1999—2006. Apptd. bd. dirs. Pres. Clinton Romanian Am. Enterprise Fund, 1994—2003. Chair Harvard Law Sch. Nat. Fund, 1995—97, dean's adv. bd., 1997—; bd. dirs. Jericho Project, 1985—97, Human Rights First, 1988—, vice chmn., 2005—; bd. dirs. After Sch. Corp., 2001—, chmn., 2006—; bd. trustees, mem. legal com. Met. Mus. Art, 2006—. Named one of 100 Most Influential Lawyers, Nat. Law Jour., 2006; recipient Disting. Leadership Recognition award for helping secure passage of Civil Rights Act of 1991, Lawyers Com. Civil Rights, 1992, Learned Hand award, Am. Jewish Com., 2004, John J. McCloy award, Fund for Modern Courts, 2005, Servant Justice award, Legal Aid Soc., 2006. Mem.: ABA, NY State Jud. Screening Commn., Coun. Fgn. Rels., Assn. Bar City N.Y. (chmn. trade regulation com. 1980—83, mem. exec. com. 1995—99, mem. nominating com. 2001—02, chmn. task force jud. selection 2003, v.p. 2003—04, chmn. task force jud. selection 2006), N.Y. Bar Assn., Human Rights Watch/Africa (mem. adv. com.), Century Assn. Club, Harvard Club. Home: Apt 13A 300 W End Ave New York NY 10023-8156 Office: Cravath Swaine & Moore LLP Worldwide Plz 825 8th Ave Fl 42 New York NY 10019-7475 Office Phone: 212-474-1448. Office Fax: 212-474-3700. Business E-Mail: rjoffe@cravath.com.

JOFFE, RUSSELL T., former dean; BS, U. Witwatersrand, Johannesburg, S. Africa, 1977. Diplomate Am. Bd. Psychiatry and Neurology, 1984. Intern Mount Sinai Hosp., Toronto, Ont., Canada; resident in psychiatry Royal Ottawa Hosp., U. Ottawa, McMaster U.; fellow NIH, Bethesda, Md., 1983—85; mem. dept. psychiatry U. Toronto; chair dept. psychiatry and behavioral neurosciences McMaster U., 1994—97, dean faculty of health scis.; dean U. Medicine and Dentistry NJ - NJ Med. Sch., 2001—05, with clin. office, dept. psychiatry dept. Maplewood, NJ, 2005—. Mem. Expert Adv. Com. on Psychiatric Illness of U.S. Pharmacopoiea, 1990—. Contbr. of more than 250 articles in profl. jours.; author: more than 30 chpts. for med. textbooks about depression. Recipient Award of Excellence, Depressive and Manic Depressive Assn. Ont.; grantee of more than 50 rsch. grants. Fellow: Royal Coll. Physicians and Surgeons Can., Am. Psychiatric Assn. (Gold award for Academically Sponsored Programs). Office: 185 S Orange Ave Newark NJ 07103

JOFFE, STEPHEN NEAL, surgeon, medical educator; b. Springs, Transvaal, Republic of South Africa, Jan. 11, 1943; came to U.S., 1980; s. Hirshy N. and Pearl (Cohen) J.; m. Sandra Noche, Dec. 18, 1966; children: Heidi, Craig. BS, U. Stellenbosch, Cape Province, South Africa, 1963, MD, 1976; B in Medicine and Surgery, U. Witwatersrand, Johannesburg, South Africa, 1967. Fellow Coll. of Surgeons of South Africa, 1972, Royal Coll. Physicians and Surgeons of Glasgow, 1973, Royal Coll. of Surgeons of Edinburgh, 1973, Am. Coll. Surgeons, 1983; Diplomate Am. Bd. Laser Medicine and Surgery, 1986. Rotating registrar surgery Groote Schuur Hosp. Univ. of Capetown (South Africa), 1970-72, sr. registrar in surgery, 1972-73; sr. registrar 3 tutor in surgery dept. of surgery Hammersmith Hosp. and Royal Postgrad. Med. Sch., London, U.K., 1973-75, resident surg. officer, 1974-75; hon. cons. surgeon, sr. lectr. in surgery Univ. of Glasgow (Scotland), 1975-80, Dept. of Surgery Glasgow Royal Infirmary, 1975-80; prof. of surgery U. Cin. Coll. of Medicine, 1980-90; esteemed quondam prof. surgery and medicine U. Cin. Med. Ctr., 1990—. House surgeon, house physician Johannesburg Gen. Hosp., 1968; resident surg. officer Hammersmith Hosp., 1974; courtesy staff and cons. surgeon various U.S. Hosps.; chmn. bd., dir. Surg. Laser Techs. (Japan) Co., Ltd., 1986, 88; pres. Laser Ctrs. Am., Inc., Cin., 1985—. Editor numerous med. books; contbr. articles to numerous publs., mags. and jours. Recipient Nash Meml. Prize, 1966, 1989 Enterprise award Cin. Bus. Courier; Barnes Agranat scholar, 1967. Mem. AAAS, AMA, Internat. Assn. Endocrine Surgeons, Internat. Duodenal Club, Internat Fedn. Surg. Colls., Internat. Nd:Laser Soc. (chmn., founder 1983, co-chmn. 1985), Collegium Internat. Chirurgiae Digestivae, Internat. Soc. Surgery, Internat. Soc. Optical Engring. (co-chmn. Lasers in Medicine 1986, 87), Internat. Hosp. Fedn., European Soc. Surg. Rsch., Assn. Surgeons Great Britain and Ireland, British Soc. Gastroenterology, Pancreatic Soc. Great Britain, Surg. Rsch. Soc. (U.K.), Caledonian Soc. Gastroenterology, Scottish Soc. for Exptl. Medicine, Indian Soc. Gastroenterology, Assn. for Advancement Med. Instrumentation, Assn. for Gnotobiotics, Soc. U. Surgeons, Soc. for Surgery of Alimentary Tract, Royal Soc. Medicine, Endocrine Soc., Assn. Acad. Surgeons, Pancreas Club, Am. Assn. Clin. Anatomists, Am. Assn. Endocrine Surgeons, Am. Bd. Laser Surgery (examiner 1986), Am. Coll. Gastroenterology, Am. Coll. Healthcare Adminstrs., Am. Coll. Healthcare Mktg. Inst., Am. Coll. Med. Staff Affairs Inst., Am. Fedn. Clinic Rsch., Am. Gastroent. Assn., Am. Inst. Physics, Am. Physiol. Soc., Am. Soc. Gastrointestinal Endoscopy, Am. Soc. Laser Medicine and Surgery, N.Y. Acad. Scis., numerous others. Home: 8750 Red Fox Ln Cincinnati OH 45243-3731 Personal E-mail: stephen@sjoffe.com.

JOGLAR, FRANCISCO, academic administrator; Dean U. P.R., Sch. Medicine, San Juan, 1999—. Office: UPR Sch Medicine A-878 Main Bldg Med Sci Campus PO Box 365067 San Juan PR 00936-5067 Office Phone: 787-765-2363. Office Fax: 787-756-8475. Business E-Mail: fjoglar@rcm.upr.edu.

JOGLEKAR, SATISH DINKAR, physicist, educator; b. Junnar, India, Feb. 25, 1949; s. Dinkar Ganesh Joglekar. BSc, U. Poona, India, 1969; MSc, Indian Inst. Tech., Bombay, 1971; PhD, SUNY, Stony Brook, 1975. Postdoctoral rsch. assoc. Fermilab, Batavia, Ill., 1975; mem. Inst. for Advanced Study, Princeton, NJ, 1975-77; postdoctoral rsch. assoc. U. Calif., Berkeley, 1977-79; lectr. physics Indian Inst. Tech., Kanpur, India, 1981-83; asst. prof. IIT Kanpur, India, 1983-91, prof., 1991—. Contbr. over 70 articles to sci. jours. Fellow Nat. Acad. Scis. India, Maharashtra Acad. Scis.; mem. Am. Phys. Soc., NY Acad. Scis., Am. Order of Excellence (founding mem.), Order of Internat. Ambassadors. Avocation: music. Office: Dept Physics Indian Inst Tech Kanpur Kanpur 208016 India Home Phone: 91 512 2598314; Office Phone: 91 512 2597014. Business E-Mail: sdj@iitk.ac.in.

JOHANN, ANNE DOROTHY, visual and graphic artist, painter; b. North Tarrytown, NY, Feb. 24, 1957; d. John Thomas and Elizabeth Keay (Hamilton) Sekelsky; m. Thomas Richard Johann, Aug. 28, 1982. BFA with highest honors, Pratt Inst., 1980. Printer asst. Solo Press, Inc., NYC, 1980—82; tchr. oil painting Croton-Cortlandt Ctr. for Arts, NY, 1994, 1995, 2001—07, tchr. watercolor painting, 1998—2007, tchr. drawing, 2001—07. Summer instr. watercolor painting Putnam Arts Coun., 2003—05, 2007, tchr. oil, acrylic painting, 2004—07. Open edit. print, The Old Mill as seen from the Charles Bridge, Prague, N.Y. Graphic Soc., 2001. Recipient award, NY State Art Tchrs., 1975, award of Excellence, Manhattan Arts Internat. mag., 1999, Vasari Oil Colors award, Art NE USA, Silvermine Guild Galleries, New Canaan, Conn., 2000; grantee residency grant, Vt. Studio Ctr., Johnson, Vt., 2000, artist grant, Vt. Studio Ctr., 2000. Mem.: Garrison Art Ctr., Westchester Arts Coun. (Mcpl. Challenge grant, CCCA/Town Cortland 2001—02, Mcpl. Challenge grant, CCCA/Town Ossining 2006), Croton Coun. on Arts, Nat. Assn. Women Arts (France Lieber Meml. award 2002), New Haven Paint and Clay Club (David T. Langrock Found. prize for landscape 2001, honorable mention active mems. exhibit 2001). Home: 316 Grand St Croton On Hudson NY 10520-3500 Office Phone: 914-806-4067. Personal E-mail: johann@bestweb.net.

JOHANNES, JOHN ROLAND, political science professor, dean; b. Milw., Dec. 15, 1943; s. Jerome Fridolin and Teresa (Stoiber) J.; m. Frances Virginia Slater, Aug. 5, 1967; children: Teresa, Michael, James. BS, Marquette U., 1966; AM, Harvard U., 1968, PhD, 1970. Asst. prof. polit. sci. Marquette U., Milw., 1970-75, assoc. prof., 1975-84, prof., 1984-95, chmn. dept. polit. sci., 1980-88, dean Coll. Arts and Scis., 1988-93; v.p. acad. affairs Villanova (Pa.) U., 1995—. Chmn. Bradley Inst. for Democracy and Pub. Values, 1988-93. Author: Policy Innovation in Congress, 1972, To Serve the People, 1984; co-editor and contbr. editor Money, Elections, and Democracy, 1990; contbr. articles to profl. jours. Am. Philos. Soc. grantee, 1978; Everett Dirksen Ctr. grantee, 1981, 82, NEH grantee, 1972. Mem. Am. Polit. Sci. Assn., Midwest Polit. Sci. Assn., So. Polit. Sci. Assn., Assn. Am. Colls. and Univs. Home: 840 Galer Dr Newtown Square PA 19073-3517 Office: Villanova U Office Acad Affairs 800 E Lancaster Ave Villanova PA 19085-1603 Office Phone: 610-519-4521. E-mail: john.johannes@villanova.edu.

JOHANNES, KAY L., insurance company executive; b. Milw., July 3, 1952; d. James Ben and Evelyn (Horne) J.; m. Thomas A. Rozek, June 13, 1972 (div. Oct. 1975); m. Alexander David Bub, Jan. 5, 1982; 1 child, David A. AAS in Visual Comm., Milw. Area Tech. Coll., 1972; BS in Instrnl. Tech., Rochester Inst. Tech., 1977. Audio visual tech. Nicolet H.S., Glendale, Wis., 1972-75; visual designer, animator Pohlman Studios, Milw., 1977-79; designer multimedia AV Centrum AB, Stockholm, 1979-80; owner, prodr. Johannes, Milw., 1980-82; audio visual prodr. Photography Unltd., Milw., 1982-87; sr. salestrack specialist Northwe. Mut. Life Ins. Co., Milw., 1987—. Chair visual comm. adv. bd. Milw. Area Tech. Coll., 1990—2005; mem., owner Wis. Off-road Adventures, LLC, 2005—. Vol. Big Brothers/Big Sisters, Ozaukee County, Wisc., 1978-91. Mem. order of Amaranth (royal matron), White Shrine Jerusalem (worthy high priestess). Methodist. Avocations: motorcycles, computer web design. Home: W4802 Knuth Rd Random Lake WI 53075 Office: Northwestern Mut Life Ins Co 720 E Wisconsin Ave Milwaukee WI 53202 Personal E-mail: kaylj@myexcel.com.

JOHANNES, RICHARD SCOTT, medical association administrator; b. Rhinelander, Wis., Nov. 10, 1946; s. Russell Frederick and Patricia Jane Johannes; m. Catherine Bishop Bishop, July 14, 1984; children: Caleb William, Claire Lucy. MD, Johns Hopkins Sch. Medicine, Balt., 1972; MS, GWC Whiting Sch. Engring., Balt., 1983. Cert. specialist Am. Bd. Internal Medicine, 1979. V.p. clin. sys. DataMedic Corp., Waltham, Mass., 1989—2000; v.p. clin. rsch. Cardinal Health, Marlborough, Mass., 2000—; assoc. physician Brigham & Women's Hosp., Boston, 2002—; asst. prof. gastroenterology and biomedical engring. Johns Hopkins Sch. Medicine. Spl. asst. dir. NIH, Bethesda, Md., 1980—82. Contbr. scientific papers. Bd. mem. HUB Divsn., Nat. Model RR Assn., Boston, 2001—07. Lt. comdr. Pub. Health Svc., 1973—75, Bethesda, Maryland. Recipient Daniel Baker Jr. Meml. award, Johns Hopkins Sch. Medicine, 1976, Dean's Cert. Excellence in Tchg., 1977. Mem.: Mass. Med. Soc. (licentiate). Achievements include first to a successful 24 hour ambulatory pH Monitor; research in adverse outcomes from hospital-acquired infection in Pennsylvania; a continuous portable intraesophageal pH monitoring system; first to report prescription writer using a personal computer; lead team that developed clinically based risk adjustment methods. Avocations: model railroading, running. Office: Cardinal Health 500 Nickerson Rd Marlborough MA 01752 Home Phone: 617-244-0068; Office Phone: 508-571-5118. Business E-Mail: richard.johannes@cardinal.com.

JOHANNING, GARY LEE, medical educator; b. Boonville, Mo., Sept. 29, 1950; s. Leon Fredrick Johanning and Evelyn Marie Brucks; m. Feng Wang, Apr. 24, 1993; children: Tony Xiao Meng, Emily Marie. BS, U. Mo., Columbia, 1973, MS, 1976; PhD, U. of Mo., Columbia, 1978. Assoc. prof. U. of Ala., Birmingham, 1993—2003, M.D. Anderson Cancer Ctr., Bastrop, Tex., 2003—. Asst. prof. Armstrong Atlantic State U., Savannah, Ga., 1981—86; postdoctoral fellow U. of Mo., Columbia, 1987—89, Case Western Res. U., Cleve., 1989—93; spkr. and lectr. in field; jour. reviewer. Author: (book chpt.) Annual Review of Nutrition, Methods of Molecular Biology; contbr. articles to profl. jours. Recipient Cancer CAM Vitamins and Cancer Chemotherapy Resistance grant, NIH, 2003—06, Vitamins and Prevention of Cancer Progression grant, 2003—06, Epigenetic Changes and Vitamin Status in Breast Cancer grant, 2000—03, HPV Oncoprotein Expression in Cervical Cancer grant, 1999—2001, HPV Oncoprotein Ablation via Single-Chain Antibodies grant, 1998—2000, Folic Acid and Antigen-Specific Cellular Immunity grant, Cattlemen for Cancer Rsch., 2006—07, Acyl Co-A Binding Protein Expression in Cancer grant, 2004—06. Mem.: AAAS, Am. Assn. for Cancer Rsch., Am. Soc. for Nutrition, Sigma Xi. Achievements include patents for animal feedstuffs and process; research in cellular vitamins, DNA methylation and cancer risk; DNA methylation and diet in cancer; Timecourse of Cisplatin Resistance in Tumor Cells; Cellular Vitamins and DNA Methylation in Cancer; HPV 16 Oncogene Variant Expression in Cervical Cancer; Role of Environmental Factors in Epigenetic Cancer Therapy. Home: 128 Musket Dr Bastrop TX 78602 Office: 650 Cool Water Dr Bastrop TX 78602 Office Phone: 512-332-5211. Office Fax: 512-332-5218. Business E-Mail: gljohann@mdanderson.org.

JOHANNS, MICHAEL OWEN, secretary of agriculture, former governor; b. Osage, Iowa, June 18, 1950; s. John Robert Sr. and Adeline Lucy (Royek) J.; m. Constance J. Weiss, June 10, 1972 (div. Dec. 1985); children: Justin Michael, Michaela Susan; m. Stephanie A. Suther, Dec. 24, 1986. BA, St. Mary's Coll., Winona, Minn., 1971; JD, Creighton U., 1974. Law clk. to Hon. Hale McCown Nebr. Supreme Ct., Lincoln, 1974-75; assoc. Cronin & Hannon, O'Neill, Nebr., 1975-76; ptnr. Nelson, Johanns, Morris, Holdeman & Titus, Lincoln, 1976-91; mayor City of Lincoln, 1991-98; gov. State of Nebr., 1999—2005; sec. USDA, Washington, 2005—. Econ. devel & commerce com. chmn. Nat. Govs. Assn., 2000-03 Mem. Lancaster County Bd., Lincoln, 1983-87; mem. City Coun. Lincoln, 1989-91. Mem. Nebr. Bar Assn. Republican. Roman Catholic. Avocations: skiing, biking, reading. Office: Office Sec USDA 1400 Independence Ave SW Washington DC 20250*

JOHANNSEN, CHRIS JAKOB, agronomist, educator, administrator; b. Randolph, Nebr., July 24, 1937; s. Jakob J. and Marie J. (Lorenzsen) J.; m. Joanne B. Rockwell, Aug. 16, 1959; children: Eric C., Peter J. BS, U. Nebr., Lincoln, 1959, MS, 1961; PhD, Purdue U., 1969. Program leader lab. for applications of remote sensing Purdue U., West Lafayette, Ind., 1966—69, from asst. prof. to assoc. prof. agronomy, 1969—77, prof., 1985—2003, dir. ag data network, 1985—87, dir. lab. for applications of remote sensing, 1985—2003, dir. emeritus, prof. emeritus, 2003—; prof. U. Mo., Columbia, 1977-84, dir. geogrpahic resources ctr., 1981-84; dir. Ag Data Network, Purdue U., 1985-87, Nat. Resources Rsch. Inst., 1987-93, Environ. Scis. and Engring. Inst./Purdue U., West Lafayette, 1994-96. Vis. prof. U. Calif., Davis, 1980—81; cons. Lockheed Electronics, Houston, 1975—76, NOAA, Columbia, Mo., 1978—80, FAO UN, Nairobi, Kenya, 1983, 87, Rome, 87, U.S. Agy. Internat. Devel., Ea. Africa, 1983, USDA-Soil Conservation Svc., Washington, 1984—85, IBM, 1991, Ball Aerospace Corp., 1995, Space Imaging Inc., 1996—, Bayer CropSci. Inc., 1998—, RapidEye Corp., 2001—; pres. Ecologistics Ltd., 1996—2002, assoc., 2002—; vis. chief scientist Space Imaging Inc., 1996—97; adj. prof. Katholieke U. Leuven (Belgium), 2000—06. Pres. coun. St. Andrew's Luth. Ch., Columbia, 1975-77; asst. scoutmaster Boy Scouts Am., Gt. Rivers coun., Columbia, 1979-84, West Lafayette, 1985-91; pres. Purdue Luth. Ministry, 1989-95; apptd. mem. West Lafayette Redevel. Authority, 2001-2004; ch. coun. Our Savior Lutheran Ch., West Lafayette, 2005-07. Recipient Tech. Innovation Rsch. award NASA, 1979, Disting. Svc. award Mo. Assn. Soil and Water Conservation Dists., 1982, Agr. Alumni Merit award U. Nebr., 1995, Career award Purdue Coop. Ext. Specialist Assn., 2003, Cert. of Achievement, Agr. Alumni Assn. of Purdue U., 2006. Fellow: Ind. Acad. Scis., Soil and Water Conservation Soc. (pres. 1982—83, HughHammond Burnett award 2005), Am. Soc. Agronomy, Soil Sci. Soc. Am., Am. Soc. Photogrammetry and Remote Sensing (Outstanding Svc. award 1992); mem.: Geosci. and Remote Sensing Soc. of IEEE, Internat. Union Soil Sci., World Assn. Soil and Water, Rotary (Lafayette chpt. bd. dirs. 1995—98), Epsilon Sigma Phi (Internat. award 2000, Global Awareness award 2004, Internat. award 1987). Home: 209 Cedar Hollow Ct West Lafayette IN 47906-1671 Office: Purdue Univ AGRY 915 W State St West Lafayette IN 47907-2054 Home Phone: 765-463-7641; Office Phone: 765-494-4773. Business E-Mail: johan@purdue.edu.

JOHANSEN, ERLING, retired dental educator, dean; b. Overhalla, Norway, Apr. 8, 1923; arrived in US, 1945; s. Trygve Vilmar and Jenny Marie (Gansmo) J.; m. Inger Marie Nordback, July 4, 1952; children: Erling Trygve, Erik Bjarne, Steven Douglas. DMD cum laude, Tufts U., Medford, Mass., 1949; PhD, U. Rochester, NY, 1955; DSc (hon.), Athens U., Greece, 1981; HHD (hon.), New Eng. Sch. Law, 1993. Eastman/Squibb fellow, dental rsch. Rochester U., 1950-55, asst. prof. dentistry, 1955-58, assoc. prof. dentistry, 1958-61, prof. dental rsch., 1961-66, Welcher prof. dental rsch., 1966-78, chair dept. dentistry and dental rsch., 1955-78; prof. general dentistry Tufts U. Sch. Dental Medicine, Boston, 1979-95, acting chmn. oral health svc. dept., 1979-86, dean, 1979-95, dean emeritus, Disting. Prof. emeritus, 1995—. With Norwegian Armed Forces Dental Corps, 1949-50, Norwegian Pub. Health Svc., 1950; cons. Strong Meml. Hosp., Rochester, 1958-79, Eastman Dental Ctr., Rochester, 1967-78, Genesee Hosp., Rochester, 1967-78, Monroe Cmty. Hosp., Rochester, 1968-75; project supr. Rochester Neighborhood Health Ctr., 1965-70, Migrant Dental Program, Rochester, 1965-70; coord. dental program, U. Rochester Cancer Ctr., 1974-78; cons. Highland Hosp., 1975-78; numerous coms. and consultantships, including AMA Coun. on Drugs, USPHS, Bur. Environ. Health, Nat. Inst. Dental Rsch., King Abdulaziz U., Jeddah, Saudi Arabia, Ministry of Health, Kuwait, Union of 11 faculties State of Planalto Ctrl., Brasilia, Brazil, others; internat. lectr. and presenter in field. Contbr.

articles to profl. jours.; editor Jour. Dental Edn., 1974-76, AAAS Symposium 11, 1979, AAAS Symposium on Oral Health of Elderly, 1987; patentee in field of remineralizing solution; reviewer, mem. editl. bds. various jours. Bd. dirs., chair, fundraising com., pres., trustee-advisor Scandinavian Charitable, West Newton, Mass., 1995—, pres., 2003; Gavel lectureship com., Forsyth Inst., Boston, 1997—., chmn. 1998-2003; Lt., Norwegian Army, 1949-50. Disting. Lectr. Pan Am. Health Orgn., WHO, 1973; Dr. Erling Johansen Endowed Professorship, Tufts U., 1994; recipient Leif Erikson Day Citation award Sons of Norway, 2004. Fellow AAAS (coun. mem. 1963-67, 72-77), Am. Coll. Dentists (chmn. We. NY sect., New Eng. sect.), Internat. Coll. Dentists, Pierre Fauchard Dental Honor Soc.; mem. ADA (internat. com., 7th dist., NY, 1969-76, Coun. Scientific Rsch., NY, 1971-78, 83-87; various coms. and task forces; presenter testimony U.S. Ho. of Reps. 1986), Am. Assn. Dental Schs. (chmn. sect. advanced edn. 1968-69, v.p. advanced edn. programs 1970-74, exec. com. 1970-74, adminstrv. bd. coun. deans 1989-93, chair 1992-93, various other coms. and subcoms.), Am. Assn. Dental Rsch. (sec.-treas., bd. dirs. 1976-79), Internat. Assn. Dental Rsch. (coun. mem. 1958-61, 69-76, bd. dirs. 1974-75, various coms. and subcoms.), Greater NY Dental Soc. (Dr. Irving E. Gruber award 1998), Mass. Dental Soc. (rsch. awards com. 1980—), Dental Soc. Norway, Korean Dental Assn. (hon.), Tufts U. Alumni Assn. (Disting. Svc. award 1994), Sigma Xi, Omicron Kappa Upsilon. Avocations: fishing, skiing, photography, historical research. Home: 69 Windsor Rd Needham MA 02492-1440 Office: Tufts U Sch Dental Medicine One Kneeland St Boston MA 02111

JOHANSEN, JOHN MACLANE, architect; b. NYC, June 29, 1916; s. John Christen and Jean (MacLane) J.; m. Beate Gropius; children from previous marriage: Deborah, Christen BS, Harvard U., 1939; MArch, Harvard Grad. Sch. Design, 1942. Draftsman Marcel Breuer; rschr. Nat. Housing Agy., Washington; with Skidmore, Owings, & Merrill, NYC; founder pvt. practice, New Canaan, Conn., 1948; prin. Johansen-Bhavnani, NYC, 1973-89; pvt. practice NYC, 1989—. Co-author: A Life in the Continuum of Modern Architecture, 1996. Fellow AIA (honor award 1972, medal of honor NY 1976); mem. Am. Acad. in Rome, NAD, Am. Acad. Arts and Letters (Brunner award 1968), Archtl. League (NY pres. 1968-70)

JOHANSEN, ROBERT JOSEPH, consulting actuary; b. NYC, May 2, 1922; s. Irving Joseph and Margaret (McKee) J.; m. Mary Carroll Hayes, June 27, 1964; children: Mary Carroll, Robert Hayes, David McKee. BA, Manhattan Coll., 1943; MA, Columbia U., 1974. With Met. Life Ins. Co., NYC, 1947-82, 3d v.p., 1964-68, 2d v.p., 1968-69, v.p. personal ins. adminstrn., 1969-70, v.p., 1970-72, v.p., actuary, 1972-82; cons. actuary, 1982—. Sec. Coun. Profl. Assns. on Fed. Stats., 1980-83, chmn., 1984; vice chmn. exec. com. Ins. Guaranty Corp. NY, 1974-82. Contbr. articles to profl. jours. Trustee Dominican Coll., Blauvelt, NY, 1970-87; former pres. Van Cortlandt Terr. Assn.; mem. Mayor's Com. for Cmty. Rels., Yonkers, NY, 1978-86. Served with USAAF, 1943-46. Fellow Soc. Actuaries (treas. 1980-83, gen. chmn. edn. and exam com. 1970-71, chaired com. that produced the 1983 Table A annuity valuation mortality table, mem. com. on rsch. mgmt. 1998-91, com. on experience studies 1988-91, com. on life ins. rsch. 1993-05, chmn. 1997-05, chmn. task force on mortality guarantees in variable products 1996—, developed Annuity 2000 valuation mortality table; mem. individual life ins. valuation mortality taskforce, 2000-03, com. for internat. symposia on living to 100 and beyond, chmn. 2002-05, chmn. com. on living to 100 rsch. symposium chmn. 2006-, com. on life ins. co. expenses, 2000-, chmn. com. to develop a new basis for individual annuity valuation chmn. 2006-); mem. Am. Acad. Actuaries, Am. Statis. Assn., Internat. Actuarial Assn., NY Actuaries Club (treas. 1978-81), Actuarial Studies in Non-Life Ins., NY Acad. Scis. Roman Catholic. Office: Life Actuarial Svcs 56 Pershing Ave Yonkers NY 10705-3631 Personal E-mail: rjjfsa@aol.com.

JOHANSEN KASTELL, CHRISTINA MARIE, curator; b. Champaign, Ill., May 19, 1961; d. Mary Lou Kringel Johansen and Walter Henry Johansen. B in Anthropology, U. Ill., Urbana, 1987; Grad. Studies in Anthropology, U. Wis., Madison, 1988. Cert. Plastics Preservation Campbell Ctr. for Hist. Preservation Studies, Ill., 2003, Basketry and Plant Material Care Campbell Ctr. for Hist. Preservation Studies, Ill., 2004, Leather Care Campbell Ctr. for Hist. Preservation Studies, Ill., 2005. Archaeological rschr. State Hist. Soc. Wis., Burials Divsn., Madison, 1988; archaeologist, archtl. historian Gt. Lakes Archaeological Rsch. Ctr., Milw., 1988—95; editl. asst., lab. tech. Office the Iowa State Archaeologist, Iowa City, 1995—96; curator history The History Ctr., Cedar Rapids, Iowa, 1997—2002; curator history and anthropology Putnam Mus. History and Natural Sci., Davenport, Iowa, 2002—. Bd. mem. Johnson County Hist. Preservation Commn., Iowa City, 1996—2000, Cedar Rapids Hist. Preservation Commn., 2000—02; bd. dirs. Iowa Conservation and Preservation Consortium, 2001—; cons. African Am. Hist. Mus. and Cultural Ctr. Iowa, Cedar Rapids, 2002—03, Iowa Masonic Libr. and Mus., Cedar Rapids, 2002. Co-author: (book) Cedar Rapids, Iowa, 2001. Mem.: Iowa Conservation and Preservation Consortium (pres. 2004—06), Iowa Mus. Assn. Office: Putnam Mus History and Natural Sci 1717 W 12th St Davenport IA 52804 Home Phone: 563-388-6184; Office Phone: 563-324-1054 222.

JOHANSON, DAVID RICHARD, lawyer; b. St. Paul, Sept. 27, 1957; s. Carol Lyle and Mabel Ruth (Person) J.; m. Anne Ritteri; children: David Richard II, Britta Mae. AA in Liberal Arts, Columbia Coll., 1980; B in Individualized Studies summa cum laude, U. Minn., 1983, JD cum laude, 1986. Bar: Minn. 1986, DC 1989, Md. 1990, Calif. 1993, US Dist. Ct. Minn. 1987, US Dist. Ct. (no. dist.) Calif. 1994, US Dist. Ct. Colo. 2004, US Tax Ct. 1987, US Ct. Appeals (8th cir.) 1987, US Ct. Appeals (11th cir.) 2001, US Ct. Appeals (9th cir.) 2003. Assoc., law clk. Bowman & London, St. Paul, 1984-85, 86-87; tax cons. Ernst & Whinney, Mpls., 1986-87; assoc. Ober, Kaler, Grimes & Shriver, Balt., 1988-93; mem. Ludwig & Jeans, San Francisco, 1993; income ptnr. Keck, Mahin & Cate, San Francisco, 1993-95; equity ptnr. Graham & James LLP, San Francisco, 1995-97; of counsel Case Bigelow & Lombardi, Honolulu, 1997-99, Johanson Berenson LLP, Napa, Calif., 1999—. Author: (introduction) Selling to an ESOP, 1998, Employee Stock Ownership Plans 1996 Yearbook, and subsequent edits.; editor (periodical) ESOP Calif., 1993-2003; bd. editors Jour. Employee Ownership Law and Fin., 1994—, ESOP Report, Legal Update, 1992—, The Stock Options Book, Employee Stock Options and Related Equity Incentives, 1997. Pro bono work Bar Assn. San Francisco, 1993-97, Napa County (Calif.) Pub. Defender's Office, 1994. Sgt. USAF, 1976-80. Mem. The Employee Stock Ownership Plan, Assn. (bd. dirs. 1994-96, chair legis. and regulatory adv. com. 1993-95, 2005-07, chair adv. com. chairs coun. 1994-96, Calif./western states chpt. steering com. 1993-2003, v.p. profl. mems. 1996-98, Outstanding Adv. Com. Chair 1993-94, monthly columnist 1992—), Nat. Ctr. for Employee Ownership (bd. dirs., gen. counsel 1996—, stock options adv. bd. 1997—), Found. for Enterprise Devel. Avocations: running, bicycling, hiking, travel. Business E-Mail: drj@esop-law.com.

JOHANSON, DONALD CARL, physical anthropologist; b. Chgo., June 28, 1943; s. Carl Torsten and Sally Eugenia (Johnson) Johanson; 1 child, Tesfaye Meles. BA, U. Ill., 1966; MA, U. Chgo., 1970, PhD, 1974; DSc (hon.), John Carroll U., University Heights, Ohio, 1979, Coll. of Wooster, Ohio, 1985. Mem. dept. phys. anthropology Cleve. Mus. Natural History, 1972-81, curator, 1974-81; pres. Inst. Human Origins, Berkeley, Calif., 1981-97, dir. Tempe, Ariz., 1997—. Prof. anthropology Stanford U., 1983-89, Ariz. State U., 1997, Virginia M. Ullman chair human origins, 2000; adj. prof. Case Western Res. U., 1978-81, Kent State U., 1978-81. Co-author: (with M.A. Edey) Lucy: The Beginnings of Humankind, 1981 (Am. Book award 1982), Blueprints: Solving the Mystery of Evolution, 1989, (with James Shreeve) Lucy's Child: Discovering a Human Ancestor, 1989, (with Kevin O'Farrell) Journey from the Dawn: Life with the World's First Family, 1990, (with Lenora Johanson and Blake Edgar) Ancestors: In Search of Human Origins, 1994, (with Blake Edgar) From Lucy to Language, 1997, 2d edit., 2006, (with Giancarlo Ligabue) Ecce Homo, 1999, (with W.H. Kimbel and Y. Rak) The Skull of Australopithecus afarensis, 2004; host PBS Natures Series; prodr. (film) Lucy in Disguise, 1982; host, narrator NOVA series In Search of Human Origins, 1994 (Emmy nomination 1995); contbr. numerous articles to profl. jours. Recipient Jared Potter Kirtland award for outstanding sci. achievement Cleve. Mus. Natural History, 1979, Profl. Achievement award U. Chgo., 1980, Gold Mercury Internat. ad personem award Ethiopia, 1982, Humanist Laureate award Acad. of Humanism, 1983, Disting. Svc. award Am. Humanist Assn., 1983, San Francisco Exploratorium award, 1986, Internat. Premio Fregene award, 1987, Alumni Achievement award U. Ill., 1995, Anthropology Media award Am. Anthropol. Assn., 1999, Webby award for best sci. web site, 2002; named Endowed Chair Virginia Ullman Chair in Human Origins, Webby award Internat. Acad. Digital Arts and Scis., 2002; grantee Wenner-Gren Found., NSF, Nat. Geog. Soc., L.S.B. Leakey Found., Cleve. Found., George Gund Found., Roush Found. Fellow AAAS, Calif. Acad. Scis., Rochester (NY) Mus., Royal Geog. Soc.; mem. Am. Assn. Phys. Anthropologists, Internat. Assn. Dental Rsch., Internat. Assn. Human Biologists, Am. Assn. Africanist Archaeologists, Soc. Vertebrate Paleontology, Soc. Study of Human Biology, Societe de l'Anthropologie de Paris, Centro Studi Ricerche Ligabue (Venice), Founders' Coun., Chgo. Field Mus. Natural History (hon.), Accademia Fisiocritici (hon., Sienna), Assn. Internationale pour l'etude de Paleontologie Humaine, Mus. Nat. d'Histoire Naturelle de Paris (corr.), Explorers Club (hon. dir.), Nat. Ctr. Sci. Edn. (supporting scientist). Office: Inst Human Origins Ariz State U PO Box 874101 Tempe AZ 85287-4101 Office Phone: 480-727-6578. Business E-Mail: johanson.iho@asu.edu.

JOHANSON, GREGORY JOHN, psychotherapist, minister; b. Portland, Oreg., Jan. 29, 1947; s. Knut Harry and Liv Angel (Einarsen) J.; m. Cherith Hope Hansen, May 20, 1967; 1 child, Leif Nathan. BA in Psychology and Philosophy, Willamette U., 1969; MDiv Pastoral Care, Emory U., 1972; postgrad., Pacific U. Grad. Sch., 1979—82; MPhil, Drew Grad. Sch., 1994, PhD, 1997. Lic. profl. counselor N.J., clin. counselor N.J. Pastor United Meth. Chs., Oreg. and N.J., 1969—; pvt. practice as pastoral psychotherapist Oreg. and N.J., 1979—; dir. counseling svcs., chaplain Plz. Santa Maria Hosp., Baja, Calif., 1980—81; lectr. in psychology Western State Chiropractic Coll., Portland, Oreg., 1981—82; lectr. Nat. Coll. Naturopathic Medicine, Portland, 1981—82, Mt. Hood C.C., 1981—82; contract therapist Luth. Family Svcs., Klamath Falls, Oreg., 1982—; psychotherapy trainer, founding trainer Hakomi Inst., Boulder, Colo., 1982—, also bd. dirs.; clin. assoc. prof. marriage and family therapy Ctrl. Conn. State U., New Britain, 1998—. Editor Hakomi Forum, Hakomi Inst., Boulder, 1982—; faculty tutor PhD students Union Grad. Sch., Yellow Springs, Ohio, 1989—; book rev. editor pastoral care sect. Pulpit Digest, San Francisco, 1986-91; guest lectr. Western Oreg. State Coll. Psychology Hons. Program, Monmouth, Oreg., 1980, Drew U. DMin Program, Madison, N.J., summer 1996, Columbia Coll. Master's Program, Chgo., 1993, Australian Sch. of Applied Psychology, Sydney, Australia, 1996, counseling masters program Pace U., White Plains, N.Y.; adj. prof. pastoral counseling Drew U., 2001—; bd. dirs. U.S. Assn. for Body Psychotherapy; rsch. faculty Santa Barbara Grad. Inst., 2005; lectr. Loyola U. Chgo. Grad. Sch., 2006; adj. faculty grad. dept. counselor edn. Northeastern Ill. U., adj. faculty Columbia Coll. Chgo. Grad. Sch., 2007. Author: Grace Unfolding, 1991, Sanfte Stärke: Heilung im Geiste des Tao te King, 1993, Revelacion de la Gracia: Psicoterapia en el Espiritu de el Tao-te King, 1994; editor: Feed My Sheep, 1984, Pastoral Care Issues In the Pulpit, 1984; co-editor The Jour. of Self-Leadership; mem. editl. bd. Jour. of Pastoral Care, 2000—; book rev. editor Jour. Spirituality in Mental Health; contbr. numerous articles to books and periodicals. Ordained elder United Meth. Ch., 1974; mem. peer rev. com. U.S. Assn. for Body Psychotherapy, bd. dirs. Lelia S. Bortzmeyer scholar Willamette U., 1966, Dean's award scholar Emory U., 1970, Shirley Sugerman scholar Drew Grad. Sch., 1987; postdoctoral fellowship Princeton U., 1999—. Fellow Am. Assn. Integrative Medicine (diplomate Coll. Pastoral Counselors); clin. mem. Assn. for Clin. Pastoral Edn., Clin. Theology Assn. (profl., Eng.), Am. Assn. Pastoral Counselors, Am. Psychotherapy Assn. (diplomate; editl. rev. bd.), Soc. for Pastoral Theology, Internat. Pastoral Care Network for Social Responsibility, Assn. for Transpersonal Psychology, Am. Acad. Religion, Forge Inst. for Spirituality and Social Change, Integral Inst. of Spirituality, Am. Psychological Assn. (divsn. 24 and 32). Republican. United Methodist. Avocations: stained glass work, sailing, wood construction, sports, Aikido. Home and Office: 2523 W Lunt Chicago IL 60645-3201 Office Phone: 773-338-9606. E-mail: greg@gregjohanson.net.

JOHANSON, PATRICIA MAUREEN, artist, architect; b. NYC, Sept. 8, 1940; d. Alvar Einar and Elizabeth (Deane) J.; m. E.C. Goossen (dec.); children: Alvar Deane, Gerrit Hull, Nathaniel James. Student, Bklyn. Mus. Art Sch., 1958, Art Students League, 1961; AB, Bennington Coll., 1962; MA, Hunter Coll., 1964; BS, BArch, City Coll. Sch. Architecture, 1977; DFA (hon.), Mass. Coll. of Art, 1995. Vis. prof. art SUNY-Albany, 1969; vis. artist MIT, 1974, Oberlin Coll., Ohio, 1974, Alfred U., NY 1974, West Tex. State U., 1988, Yale U., 1989, Mass. Coll. Art, Boston, 1994, Calif. State U., Monterey Bay, 1997, 99, 2006, Wentworth Inst. Tech., Boston, 2006; Southworth lectr. Colby Coll., Waterville, Maine, 1981; cons. Mitchell-Giurgola Assocs., architects, NYC, Phila., 1972—, Oikos, Seoul, South Korea, 1996, Yukong Ltd., Ulsan, South Korea, 1996, Seoul Devel. Inst., Seoul, 1999, Millenium Park, Seoul, 1999, Nat. Endowment for Arts, Washington, 1988, City of Petaluma, Calif., 1999, Carollo Engrs., 2001, The Murie Ctr., Moose, Wyo., 2001—; bd. dirs. Islands Inst. Salt Spring Island B.C.; bd. advisors Hall Farm Ctr. Arts and Edn., Townshend, Vt., 2006, Ctr. Econ. and Environ. Devel. Allegheny Coll., Meadville, Pa., 2007; artist-in-residence NY Found. for Arts, 1987—; del. Survival and the Arts, Sundance Inst., Utah, 1991; del. Global Forum Gen. Assembly, Kyoto, Japan, 1993, Art & Environ., Ankara, 1997, Year 2000 Symposium, Dumbarton Oaks, Washington, keynote spkr. Internat. Fedn. of Landscape Architects, Belem, Brazil, 2002, Wuhan U., China, 2004, Art in Embassies program US Dept. State; mem. grants selection com. NEA, 2000. Solo shows Tibor de Nagy Gallery, NYC, 1967, SUNY at Albany, 1969, Montclair State Coll., NJ, 1974, Rosa Esman Gallery, NYC, 1978, 79, 81, 83, Dallas Mus. Art, 1982, Philippe Bonnafont Gallery, San Francisco, 1984, New Arts Program, Kutztown, Pa., 1987, Albany Acad., 1987, Painted Bride Art Ctr., Phila., 1991; National Museum of Kenya, Nairobi, 1996—, Salina Art Ctr., Kans., 2001, Allegheny Coll., Pa., 2006; retrospectives, Bennington Coll., 1973, 91, Twining Gallery, NYC, 1987, Berkshire Mus., Pittsfield, Mass, 1987, Coll. St. Rose, Albany, NY, 2004; numerous group shows including most recently Gallery Route One, Point Reyes, Calif., 1999, The Presidio, San Francisco, 1999, Villa Medici, Rome, 2000, Mass. Coll. Art, 2000, French Cultural Svcs. Gallery, NYC, 2000, Institut Francais D' Architecture, Paris, 2000, Contemporary Arts Ctr., Cin., 2002, Mus. of Contemporary Art, LA, 2004, Armory Ctr. Arts, Pasadena, Calif., 2004, The Natural World Mus., San Francisco, 2004, Antioch Coll., Ohio, 2006; represented in permanent collections, Detroit Inst. Arts, Dallas Mus. Art, Mus. Modern Art, Met. Mus. Art, NYC, Nat. Mus. Women in Arts, Washington, Herbert F. Johnson Mus., Cornell U., Berkshire Mus., NY State Coun. on Arts Film Collection, Syracuse, Storm King Art Ctr., Mountainville, NY, Crawford and Chester Sts. Park, Cleve., Oberlin Coll., Bennington Coll., Brandeis U., U. Mass., Amherst, Dumbarton Oaks Contemporary Landscape Design Collection, Washington, pvt. collections; films The Art of the Real, USIA, 1968, Stephen Long, CBS-TV, 1968, Patricia Johanson: Cyrus Field, 1974, The City Project: Cleveland, 1977, A Conversation with Patricia Johanson, Heritage Cablevision, 1985, Patricia Johanson, Berks (Pa.) Community TV, 1990, Patricia Johanson: The Leonhardt Lagoon, 1992, Patricia Johanson: A Sense of Place, 1992, Patricia Johanson: Multilevel Designs, Aesthetic, Ecological, Functional, Cedar Arts Forum, Iowa, 1994, Q&A with Patricia Johanson, PBS, 1998, Chicken Scratch with Patricia Johanson, Petaluma, California Cmty. TV, 1999, Johanson interview The Environment Show Nat. Pub. Radio, 2000, Patricia Johanson: Zhang Jia Jie National Forest Park, Wulingyuan-TV, China, 2004; author: Art and Survival: Creative Solutions to Environmental Problems, 1992; co-author: (with Caffyn Kelley) Art and Survival: Patricia Johanson's Environmental Projects, 2006; works include park design, sculpture, ecol. landscapes, street furniture, pavement designs, site planning for Consol. Edison Co., Yale U., Columbus East HS, Ind., House and Garden mag., Internat. Yr. of Child Commn., Fair Park Lagoon, Dallas, Corning Preserve, Albany, Cathedral Sq., Sacramento, Pelham Bay Pk., NYC, Candlestick Pt. State Park, San Francisco, Omame Project, Brasilia, Brazil, Park for the Amazon Rainforest, Brazil, Nairobi River Park, Kenya, Ulsan Dragon Park, Ulsan, Korea, The Rocky Marciano Trail, Brockton, Mass., Millenium Park, Seoul, French Cultural Svcs. Garden, NY, South Ninth St. Corridor, Salina, Kans., Ellis Creek Water Recycling Facility and Tidal Wetlands Park, Petaluma, Calif., Pub. Art Master Plan, Rockland County, NY, 1990, Ecol. Master Plan Greater Boston Met. Region, 1994—, Sugarhouse Pedestrian Crossing, Salt Lake City, Bayfront Stormwater Garden, Duluth, Minn. Bd. dirs. New Arts Program, Pa., 1988—, Islands Inst. Interdisciplinary Studies, Can., 2005; bd. advisors Artists Representing Environ. Arts, Inc., NYC, 1991—. Guggenheim fellow, 1970, 80, NEA fellow, 1975, Olesen fellow Bennington Coll., 1991; Adolph & Esther Gottlieb Found. grantee, 1998; recipient 1st prize Environ. Design Competition, Montclair State Coll., 1974, Internat. Womens Yr. award, 1976, Gold medal Acad. Italia delle Arti, Parma, 1979, Townsend Harris medal CCNY, 1994, Arts and Healing Network award, 2003, Gov.'s Quality Growth Grand Achievement award Envision Utah, 2004; named to Hunter Coll. Hall of Fame, 1987; named to Mepham HS Hall of Fame, 1998. Mem. Global Forum Arts Group. Home: 179 Nickmush Rd Buskirk NY 12028-3202 Personal E-mail: johansonsite@aol.com. *Let problems be your inspiration.*

JOHANSSON, ALICIA BARBARA, musician; b. Warsaw, May 21, 1941; arrived in US, 1986; d. Boleslaw Bielik and Halina Helena Napiorkowska; m. Evert Johansson, May 13, 1972 (div. 1978); m. Kjell Johansson, Jan. 2, 1980 (div. 1986); 1 child, Sandra; m. James McClung, Nov. 29, 1986 (div. 1995). *Daughter Sandra Lillian Johansson graduated in May 2006 with her B.A. in International Studies, a minor in Spanish, with distinction, college honors and magna cum laude honors from the University of Colorado at Denver. She received eight scholarships during her college career including the National Dean's List Scholarship and the CU Alumni Assoc. Scholarship. She is listed in the National Dean's List honoring America's outstanding college students: 2001-2002, 2002-2003, 2003-2004, 2004-2005, 2005-2006. Currently she is studying towards her master's degree at the the University of Uppsala Peace and Conflict Resolution Institute in Uppsala, Sweden. She hopes to work in the field of peace-keeping, arms control and disarmament affairs in sub-Saharan Africa.* BA Piano Solo, Conservatory Warsaw, 1961, MA Musical Sci., 1968; cert. organist, U. Stockholm, 1984. Radio anchor Polish Radio and TV, Warsaw, 1959—63; piano accompanist Royal Opera, Stockholm, 1973—78, Cramer and Cullberg Ballet, Stockholm, 1974—80, Opera Ballet Sch., Stockholm, 1973—86, various concerts, Stockholm, 1978—86, Cleve. Ballet, 1986—90, Colo. Ballet, Denver, 1990—2000; organist various chs., Cleve. and Denver, 1987—; pvt. accompanist; tchr. piano and organ Denver, 1990—; organist, choir dir. Jefferson Ave. United Meth. Ch., Denver, 2003—. Performer: numerous organ and piano concerts; composer ch. music, 1973—. Organizer Royal Opera and Ballet Club, Stockholm, 1975—86. Mem.: Music Tchrs. Assn., Am. Guild Organists, Musicians Union. Democrat. Avocations: investing, hiking, travel, nature. Office Phone: 303-358-3361. Personal E-mail: aliciajohan@ricochet.com.

JOHANSSON, JERKER MATS, investment banker; b. Uppsala, Sweden, May 19, 1956; came to U.S., 1979; s. Mats Erik and Ingrid Margareta (Rosengren) J.; m. Stephanie K. Matthews, Aug. 7, 1982; children: Marika, Tanja, Kirsten. M Econs., Stockholm Sch. Econs., 1979; MBA, Stanford U., 1986. Trainee Bankers Trust, NYC, 1979-80; asst. treas. Chase Manhattan Bank, NYC, 1980-82; investment mgr. Wallenberg Group, NYC, 1982-84; assoc. in equity capital markets Morgan Stanley, NYC, 1985—95, mng. dir., 1995—97, CEO European Instl. Equity div., 1997—2002, head, European Equities, 2002—, co-head, instl. sales & training, 2005—. Sgt. Swedish Marine Corps., 1975-76. Arjay Miller scholar, 1986. Mem. Swedish Am. C. of C., N.Y. Investment Club, Lyford Cay Club. Lutheran. Office: Morgan Stanley 1585 Broadway New York NY 10036-8200

JOHANSSON, SCARLETT, actress; b. NYC, Nov. 22, 1984; d. Karsten and Melanie Johansson. Student, The Lee Strasberg Theatre Inst., NYC; Grad., Profl. Children's School, 2002. Actor: (films) North, 1994, Just Cause, 1995, If Lucy Fell, 1996, Manny & Lo, 1996, Fall, 1997, Home Alone 3, 1997, The Horse Whisperer, 1998, My Brother the Pig, 1999, Ghost World, 2000 (Best Actress award Toronto Film Critics Assn., 2001), The Man Who Wasn't There, 2001, An American Rhapsody, 2001, Eight Legged Freaks, 2002, Lost in Translation, 2003 (Best Actress award Boston Soc. Film Critics, 2003, Upstream prize for best actress Venice Film Festival, 2003, BAFTA Film award, 2004), Girl with a Pearl Earring, 2003, The Perfect Score, 2004, A Love Song for Bobby Long, 2004, A Good Woman, 2004, (voice only) The SpongeBob Squarepants Movie, 2004, In Good Company, 2004, Match Point, 2005, The Island, 2005, Scoop, 2006, The Black Dahlia, 2006, The Prestige, 2006, The Nanny Diaries, 2007; (TV series) Entourage, 2004. Named Woman of Yr., Hasty Pudding Theatricals, Harvard U., 2007; named one of 100 Most Powerful Celebrities, Forbes.com, 2007. Office: Artists Mgmt Group 9465 Wilshire Blvd #519 Beverly Hills CA 90212-2604*

JOHN, CHRISTOPHER CHARLES, lobbyist, former congressman; b. Crowley, Acadia Parish, La., Jan. 5, 1960; m. Payton Smith; children Hays, Harrison BA, La. State U., 1982. Aide to John N. John, Jr. La. Ho. of Reps., 1974—82, mem., 1988—96, U.S. Congress from 7th La. dist., 1997—2005, mem. energy and commerce com.; mng. dir. Federalist Group LLC, Washington, 2006—. Bd. aldermen City of Crawley, 1984—88. Democrat. Roman Catholic. Office: Federalist Group LLC 1331 H St NW Ste 1200 Washington DC 20005

JOHN, SIR ELTON HERCULES (REGINALD KENNETH DWIGHT), musician; b. Pinner, Middlesex, Eng., Mar. 25, 1947; s. Stanley and Sheila Eileen (Farebrother) Dwight; m. Renate Blauel, Feb. 14, 1984 (div. Feb. 20, 1991); life ptnr. David Furnish, Dec. 21, 2005. Attended, Royal Acad. Music, London, 1959—64; PhD with honors, Royal Acad. Music, 2002. Singer, songwriter, musician; began playing piano, 1951; band mem. Bluesology, 1965—67. Composer: (albums) Empty Sky, 1969, Elton John, Tumbleweed Connection, 1970, 11.17.70, Friends, Madman Across the Water, 1971, Honky Chateau, 1972, Don't Shoot Me I'm Only The Piano Player, Goodbye Yellow Brick Road, 1973, Caribou, Greatest Hits, 1974, Captain Fantastic and the Brown Dirt Cowboy, Rock of the Westies, 1975, Here and There, Blue Moves, 1976, Greatest Hits Vol. II, 1977, A Single Man, 1978, Victim of Love, 1979, 21 at 33, 1980, The Fox, 1981, Jump Up, 1982, Too Low for Zero, 1983, Breaking Hearts, 1984, Ice on Fire, 1985, Leather Jackets, 1986, Live in Australia, 1987, Reg Strikes Back, 1988, Sleeping with the Past, 1989, To Be Continued, 1990, The One, 1992, Duets, 1993, Made in England, 1995, Love Songs, 1996, The Big Picture, 1997, Elton John and Tim Rice's Aida, The Muse, 1999, One Night Only, 2000, Songs From the West Coast, 2001, Greatest Hits

1970-2002, 2002, Peachtree Road, 2004, The Captain & The Kid, 2006, (soundtrack) The Lion King, 1994 (Best Original Song Acad. award for Can You Feel the Love Tonight?), (Broadway musical) Aida, 2000 (Tony award for Best Original Score), The Lion King, 1998 (6 Tony awards), Lestat, 2006, (West End musical) Billy Elliot the Musical, 2005; actor: (films) Tommy, 1975, (voice only) The Lion King, 1994, The Road to El Dorado, 2000; appearances Live Aid, 1985, Freddie Mercury Tribute Concert, 1992, Live 8, 2005. Established Elton John Aids Found., 1992—; chmn. Watford Football Club, 1976—90, pres., 1990—. Named an Honorary Knight Comdr. of the Most Excellent Order of the British Empire, Queen Elizabeth II, 1998; named to Rock 'n Roll Hall of Fame, 1994; recipient 11 Ivor Novello awards, 1973—2000, 5 Grammy awards, 1986—2000, Best British Male Artist Brit award, 1991, Grammy Legend award, 2001, Kennedy Ctr. Honor, John F. Kennedy Ctr. Performing Arts, 2004. Fellow: British Acad. Songwriters and Composers. Achievements include since 1969 has toured across the world consistently as a solo performer and with the Elton John band; playing to over 2 million people across 4 continents, 1984-1986; first popular Western singer to perform in USSR, 1979; released biggest selling single of all time, Candle in the Wind, 1997 with over 33,000,000 copies sold; internat. hit songs with Bernie Taupin including Your Song, Rocket Man, Crocodile Rock, Daniel, Goodbye Yellow Brick Road, Candle in the Wind, Don't Let the Sun Go Down on Me, Philadelphia Freedom, Don't Go Breaking My Heart (duet with Kiki Dee); Sorry Seems to be the Hardest Word, The Bitch Back, Song for Guy, I Guess That's Why They Call the Blues, I'm Still Standing, Nikita, Blue Eyes, Sacrifice, Circle of Life, Are You Ready For Love; I Want Love, Electricity. Address: Twenty First Artists Ltd 1 Blythe Rd London W14 OHG England

JOHN, FRANK HERBERT, JR., real estate appraiser, investor, marketing executive; b. Georgetown, Guyana, Mar. 4, 1961; s. Frank Herbert Clement and Doris Marian (Schofield Jones) J.; m. Barbara Jean Stewart, June 1989 (div. Dec. 1999); 1 child, Andre Nicholas John. BBA, Howard U., 1984. Lic. real estate appraiser. Intern IBM, NYC, 1983, account rep. Washington, 1984-92; pres. Washington Appraisal, 1993—, Unity Techs., LLC, 2005—; nat. dir. 5LINX, 2006—. Bd. dirs. Concerned Black Men, Washington, 1990-93, chmn. internat. awareness program, 1990-93. Mem. Nat. Assn. Realtors, D.C. C. of C., Delta Sigma Pi, Beta Gamma Sigma. Baptist. Office: Washington Appraisal 601 Pennsylvania Ave NW Ste 900 Washington DC 20004-3615

JOHN, HUGO HERMAN, natural resources educator; b. Natoma, Kans., Feb. 13, 1929; s. Lorenz Louis and Clara Marie (Doehrmann) J.; m. Prudence Patricia Shuck, Sept. 9, 1950; children: Patrick, Peter, Sarah. BS, U. Minn., 1959, MS, 1961, PhD, 1964. From asst. prof. to assoc. prof. Coll. Forestry U. Minn., St. Paul, 1964-69, prof., 1969-72; prof. Coll. Forestry, Wildlife and Range Scis., assoc. dean U. Idaho, Moscow, 1972-74; dean, prof. Sch. Natural Resources U. Vt., Burlington, 1974-83; dean Coll. Agriculture and Natural Resources, dir. Agrl. Expt. Sta. and Coop. Extension U. Conn., Storrs, 1983-87, prof. natural resources, 1987-94, prof. emeritus, 1994—. Forestry expert UN Food and Agr. Orgn., Puerto Cabezas, Nicaragua, 1965-66, Nat. Univ. Medellin, Colombia, 1969-71; cons. Taconic Found., N.Y.C., 1981-84; sr. cons. UN Devel. Programme, Humane Soc. of U.S., 1993—; devel./planning cons. Internat. Exec. Svcs. Corps., Zimbabwe, 1996, Ukraine, 1998; Minn. conf. moderator UCC, 2002—. Contbr. articles to profl. jours. Mem., treas. bd. dirs. Smokey House Project, Danby, Vt., 1976—; bd. dirs. Merek Forest Found., Rupert, Vt., 1980-83, Ea. States Expn., West Springfield, Mass, 1989—, mem. Conn. trustees, 1984—, chmn., 1989-94. With U.S. Army, 1950-52. Mem. Soc. Am. Foresters (chmn. accreditation com. 1981-84), Am. Forestry Assn. Avocations: gardening, woodworking. Home: Box 732 501 4th Ave SE Mapleton MN 56065-9782 Personal E-mail: hugohoya@hickorytech.net.

JOHN, LEWIS GEORGE, political science educator; b. Waco, Tex., Nov. 25, 1936; s. Lewis Hervin and Margaret Reese J.; m. Annette Louise Church, June 3, 1961; children: Andrew Lewis, Christopher Donald. BA, Washington & Lee U., 1958; M in Pub. Affairs, Princeton U., 1961; PhD, Syracuse U., 1973. Asst. dean students, dir. fin. aid and placement Washington & Lee U., Lexington, Va., 1963-66, assoc. dean students, 1968-69, dean students, prof. politics and adminstrn., 1969-90, prof. politics, 1969—. Leader workshops and seminars, various colls., 1981-85; presenter symposia and confs. Contbr. articles to profl. jours. and chpts. to books. Chmn. Lexington Sch. Bd. 1979-80; pre-law adviser, 1993-2001; rep. NCAA Faculty Athletics, 1998-2001. Served to 1st lt. US Army, 1961-63. Woodrow Wilson fellow Princeton U., 1959-60; Fulbright scholar U. Edinburgh, 1958-59. Mem. ASPA, Nat. Assn. Student Personnel Adminstrs. (bd. dirs. 1977-79, 87-89, region III exec. bd. 1980-85, chmn. career devel. and profl. standards div. 1987-89, Disting. Svc. award 1982), Va. Assn. Student Personnel Adminstrs. (pres. 1975, Outstanding Profl. award 1983), Am. Polit. Sci. Assn., Phi Beta Kappa, Beta Gamma Sigma, Omicron Delta Kappa (faculty sec. Washington and Lee chpt. 1987-90, 98-2001, faculty advisor 1990-98), Omicron Delta Epsilon, Pi Sigma Alpha. Democrat. Presbyterian. Avocation: sports. Home: 8 Edmondson Ave Lexington VA 24450-1904 Office: Washington & Lee U Williams Sch 101B Lexington VA 24450 Home Phone: 540-463-5009; Office Phone: 540-458-8972. E-mail: johnl@wlu.edu.

JOHN, PETER C., lawyer; b. Albany, NY, Dec. 25, 1941; BA, Cornell Univ., 1963; JD, Villanova Univ., 1966. Bar: Ill. 1966, US Dist Ct. (no. dist. Ill.) 1969, US Ct. Appeals (5th, 7th cir.). Atty. Isham Lincoln & Beale, 1966—79; ptnr. Phelan Pope & John, 1979—94, Hedlund Hanley & John, 1994—2000; ptnr., comml. litigation, product liability practices Williams Montgomery & John Ltd., Chgo., 2000—. Mem. adv. council Nat. Judicial Coll.; mem. Ill. Supreme Ct. Com. on Jury Instructions, 1967—76. Contbr. articles to profl. jours. Served USMC, 1966—67, served to comdr. USNR, 1967—76. Named an Ill. Super Lawyer, Chgo. Mag., 2004. Fellow: Am. Coll. Trial Lawyers, Internat. Soc. Barristers; mem.: Internat. Acad. Trial Lawyers (pres. 2001—02), ABA, Am. Bd. Trial Advocates, Soc. Trial Lawyers, Ill. State Bar Assn., Chgo. Bar Assn. Office: Williams Montgomery & John Suite 2100 20 N Wacker Dr Chicago IL 60606 Office Phone: 312-443-3210. Office Fax: 312-630-8510. Business E-Mail: pcj@willmont.com.

JOHN, RICHARD C., enterprise development organization executive; b. Milw., Mar. 17, 1950; s. Richard C. and Mary W. (Widrig) J.; m. Carolyn H. Finn, June 2, 1973; children: Catherine M., Yuri G., Meredith C. BBA, U. Wis., 1972; MBA, Northwestern U., 1982. CPA. Supr. sr. acct. Price Waterhouse, NYC, 1972-78; with Amoco Corp., Chgo., 1978-83; supr. fin. contr. Amoco Prodn. Co. Internat., Chgo., 1983-84; mgr. acctg. Amoco Oil Co., Chgo., 1984-85; staff dir. budgets Amoco Corp., Chgo., 1985-87; mgr. fin. & adminstrn. Amoco Chem. Co., Houston, 1987-89; contr. Amoco Performance Products, Atlanta, 1989-93; mgr. Amoco Corp., Chgo., 1993-96; sr. v.p. fin. and adminstrn., CFO Opportunity Internat., Oak Brook, Ill., 1996—. Bd. dirs., treas. Opportunity Transformation Investments, Oak Brook, Opportunity Microcredit Fund, Oxford, Eng.; bd. dirs. Oportunidad Microfinanzas, Guadalajara, Mexico, 2003—. Bd. dirs., treas. Flagstaff Mission to the Navajos, 1996-2005; deacon 4th Presbyn. Ch., 1979-87; elder, treas. Clear Lake Presbyn. Ch., 1988-89; officer, mem. choir Johnson Ferry Bapt. Ch., 1990-93; missions com. small group leader Wheaton Bible Ch., 1994—, elder, 2003—, treas., 2004—. Mem. AICPA, Fin. Execs. Internat. Office: Opportunity Internat 2122 York Rd Oak Brook IL 60523-1930 Business E-Mail: rjohn@opportunity.org.

JOHN, RICHARD RODDA, transportation executive; b. Berlin, Mar. 31, 1929; came to U.S., 1938; s. Richard R. and Margaret G. (Howard) J.; m. Suzanne L. Heckman, June 7, 1958; children: Richard Rodda, Margaret Louise, Robert Edward. BS in Engring. Physics magna cum laude, Princeton U., 1951, MSME, 1952, MS in Aero. Engring., 1953, PhD in Aero. Engring., 1957. Dir. Aerophysics lab. AVCO Corp., Wilmington, Mass., 1958-70, chief mech. engring. div., 1971-76, dir. Office Energy and Environment, 1976-82, dep. dir., chief scientist, 1982-89; dir. John A. Volpe Nat. Transp. Sys. Ctr., Cambridge, Mass., 1989—2004, dir. emeritus, sr. tech. advisor, 2004—. Mem. adv. com. on space power and electric propulsion, NASA, 1965-70, aero. engring. dept. adv. coun. Princeton U., 1972-78. Contbr. articles to profl. jours. Recipient Presdl. Meritorious Rank award Pres. Reagan, 1987, Presdl. Disting. Rank award from Pres. Bus., 1990, from Pres. Clinton, 2000; Howard C. Phillips fellow Princeton U., 1952, Guggenheim fellow, 1953. Mem. AIAA (assoc., chmn. electric propulsion com. 1965-70); Soc. Automotive Engrs. (rsch. exec. bd. 1978-85), Phi Beta Kappa, Sigma Xi. Congregationalist. Avocations: gardening, golf, print collecting, classical music. Home: 19 Saddle Club Rd Lexington MA 02420-2102 Office: Dept Transp John A Volpe Nat Transp Systems Ctr 55 Broadway-Kendall Sq Cambridge MA 02142 Personal E-mail: richardrjohn@yahoo.com. Business E-Mail: john@volpe.dot.gov.

JOHN, RICKY, state official; b. Chaguanas, Trinidad, May 2, 1957; BSEE, N.J. Inst. Tech., 1981, MS in Mgmt., 1992; PhD in Engring. Mgmt., Kennedy-Western U., 2000. Space shuttle flight test engr. NASA, Kennedy Space Ctr., Fla., 1981-82; lectr. John Donaldson Tech. Inst., Trinidad, West Indies, 1982; systems engr. FAA, NYC, 1983-84; adminstr. divsn. energy N.J. Bd. Pub. Utilities, Newark, 1985-96, tech. adviser, 1996—. Developer space shuttle tech. launch procedures, 1981. Judge and presenter of NASA award, North N.J. Regional Sci. Fair, 1993—; mem. edn. com. N.J. Martin Luther King, Jr. Commn., 1987-90; bd. dir. N.J. Inventor's Hall Fame. Named Energy Mgr. of Yr. N.J. Assn. Energy Engrs., 1994, N.J. Aviation Hall Fame; recipient Nat. Cert. of Recognition U.S. Dept. Energy, 1995. Mem. IEEE (sr.), N.J. Inst. Tech. Alumni Assn. (trustee 1991—, treas. 1994-96, v.p. pub. rels. 1996-98). Home: 350 Davis Ave Kearny NJ 07032-3558

JOHN, ROBERT MCCLINTOCK, lawyer; b. Phila., May 21, 1947; s. Lewis Timothy and Marie (McClintock) J.; m. Barbara Ann Weand, May 10, 1975; children: Jennifer, Ryan. BA, Villanova U., 1969, JD, 1972. Bar: Pa. 1972, U.S. Dist. Ct. (ea. dist.) Pa. 1973, U.S. Ct. of Appeals (3d cir.) 1998. Atty. Schneider, Nixon & John, Hatboro, Pa., 1972-74, ptnr., 1975-93, sole proprietor, 1993—. Prodr.: Pub. Access TV shows, 2001—, Hatboro Holiday Parade, 2001—, Hatboro Coun. Report, 2001—, 2001 Year in Review, 2001—, Hatboro-Horsham HS sports events, 2001—, Science Rocks, 2001, Everybody's Playground, 2001, Horsham Day, 2001—, Blue Light Project (Horsham Police), 2001—. Little Miss & Mr. Hatboro, 2001—05, Borough Ball awards, and others. Scoutmaster Boy Scouts Am., Hatboro, 1972—, long range planning com., 1979; lectr. and student loan com. Hatboro-Horsham High Sch., 1972-95, co-chmn. Tip of the Hat Cavalcade of Bands, 1994, 95, 96; co-prs. Hatters for Music, 1997-99; prodr. multi media banquet show Marching Hatters, 1994-2000; mgr. Little League, Horsham, Pa., 1985-96, girls' sr. tournament coach, 1993; referee Hatboro-Horsham Youth Basketball Assn., 1990-91, mgr., 1991-94. Recipient award Hatboro-Horsham Sch. Bd., 1979, medal Hatboro YMCA Triathlon, 1983, Silver Beaver award Boy Scouts Am., 1981, Scoutmaster's Merit award, 1989, Nat. God and Svc. award, 1991, Hatboro-Horsham HS Prin.'s Golden Apple award, 1997, 03, Martin Luther King Humanitarian award Upper Moreland Mid. Sch., 1997, Cmty. Svc. award Borough of Hatboro, 2002, Outstanding Cmty. Svc. citation Horsham Township, 2007, others; named to Hatboro-Horsham HS Hall of Fame, 2000. Mem. Pa. Bar Assn., Montgomery County Bar Assn., Greater Hatboro C. of C. (pres. 1983, Honored Citizen Svc. to Youth award 1984, judge adv. 1984—, chmn. awards com. and prod. multimedia awards ceremony biannual borough ball, 86, 89, 97, 99, 01, 03, 05, 07), Navy League (sec. southeastern Pa. coun. 1975-89, pres. 1989, judge adv. 1989-99, 04, S.E. Pa. Coun. Svc. to Youth and Cmty. award 1990, Willow Grove Naval Air Sta. Svc. award 1986), Rotary (pres. 1984, Dist. Gov.'s Outstanding Pres.'s award 1984, host family foreign exch. students, Cliff Dochterman Cmty. Svc. award 2007, scouting rotarians internat. fellowship). Republican. Roman Catholic. Avocations: scouting, swimming, bicycling, backpacking. Home: 83 Home Rd Hatboro PA 19040-1830 Office: Schneider Nixon & John 76 Byberry Ave # 698 Hatboro PA 19040-3419 Office Phone: 215-672-7660. Business E-Mail: rmjohnatty@msn.com.

JOHN, SARAH, physicist; b. Trivandrum, India, Feb. 18, 1953; arrived in U.S., 1981; d. Walliaveetil John and Sarah (Thomas) J. BSc, Univ. Coll. Trivandrum, India, 1971, MSc, 1973; MS, Coll. William and Mary, 1984, PhD, 1986. Tchg. asst. Coll. William and Mary, Williamsburg, Va., 1981-86; staff scientist Sci. & Tech. Corp., Hampton, Va., 1988-91, Vigyan, Inc., Hampton, Va., 1991-92; postdoctoral fellow N.Mex. State U., Las Cruces, 2001—02; rsch. assoc. U. Md., College Park, 2003—04; pres. Eloimagnus Advanced Scis. & Techs., Bethesda, Md., 2004—. Vis. asst. prof. U. Mo., Columbia, 1994—97. Contbr. articles to profl. jours. Nat. Sci. Talent Search awardee, India, 1968. Mem.: Am. Phys. Soc. Achievements include development of a novel computational technique for quantum dynamics as a stochastic process and formulating a geometric model for nuclear absorption from microscopic theory; research in image processing and nonlinear optics.

JOHN, SUSAN V., state representative; b. Nov. 20, 1957; BA, George Washington U.; JD, Syracuse U. Bar: N.Y. Assoc. Phillips, Lytle, Hitchcock, Huber and Blaine, 1983—; mem. N.Y. State Assembly, mem. jud. com., edn. com., also mem. energy com., libr. and edn. tech. com., chair labor com. Chair Legis. Commn. on Solid Waste Mgmt., 1995—97, Alcholism and Drug Abuse Com., 1997—99, Govtl. Ops. Com., 1999—2000; served on First Legis. Joint Budget Conf. Com. on Mental Health, 1998, Joint Budget Conf. Com. on Edn., 1999—2000. Chair Majority Steering Com.; serves on Judiciary, Edn., Energy, Libraries and Tech. and Social Svcs. Coms. Mem. Greater Rochester Assn. Women Attys. Office: 840 University Ave Rochester NY 14607 also: NY State Assembly LOB Rm 522 Albany NY 12248-0001 Office Phone: 518-455-4527. Business E-Mail: johns@assembly.state.ny.us.

JOHNNES, DANIEL, chef; Wine dir. Montrachet, Dinex Grp., 2005—; founder Jeroboam Wines. Founder, host La Paulée Burgundy celebrations, NYC, 2000, NYC, 03, NYC, 05, San Francisco, 01, Aspen, 06. Author: Daniel Johnnes's Top 200 Wines, An Expert's Guide to Maximum Enjoyment for Your Dollar, 1996; contbr. articles Food & Wine Mag., Gourmet Mag., Wine & Spirits Mag., Santé Mag.; guest appearances (TV series) CBS This Morning, NBC Today Show, TV Food Network. Named Profl. of Yr., Santé Mag., 2000; recipient Grand award, Wine Spectator, 1994, Outstanding Wine and Spirits Profl. award, James Beard Found., 1995, 2006. Office: The Dinex Group 60 E 65th St New York NY 10021 Office Phone: 212-327-3434. Office Fax: 212-933-5266.

JOHNS, BEVERLEY ANNE HOLDEN, special education administrator; b. New Albany, Ind., Nov. 6, 1946; d. James Edward and Martha Edna (Scharf) Holden; m. Lonnie J. Johns, July 28, 1973. BS, Catherine Spalding Coll., 1968; MS, So. Ill. U., 1970; postgrad., Western Ill. U., 1973—74, postgrad., 1979—80, postgrad., 1982, U. Ill., 1984—85. Cert. adminstr., tchr. Ill. Demonstration tchr. So. Ill. U., Carbondale, 1970-72; instr. MacMurray Coll., Jacksonville, Ill., 1977—79, 1990—93, 2002—; intern Ill. State Bd. Edn., Springfield, 1981; program supr. Four Rivers Spl. Edn. Dist., Jacksonville, 1972—2003; learning and behavior cons., 2003—. Chair Ill. Spl. Edn.; conf. coord. Ill. Alliance, Champaign, 1982-94; lectr., cons. in field. Author: Report on Behavior Analysis in Education, 1972; author: (with V. Carr) Techniques for Managing Verbally and Physically Aggressive Students, 2002, Reduction of School Violence: Alternatives to Suspension, 2005; author: (with B. Johns, E. Crowley & E. Guetzloe) Effective Curriculum for Students with Behavioral Disorders, 2002; author: (with J. Keenan) Techniques for Managing a Safe School, 1997; author: (with E. Paula Crowley) Students with Disabilities & General Education: A Desktop Reference for School Personnel, 2003; author: Getting Behavioral Interventions Right, 2005, Preparing Test-Resistant Students for Assessments: A Staff Training Guide, 2005; author: (with M. McGrath) The Teacher's Reflective Calendar & Planning Journal, 2006; author: (with M. McGrath and S. Mathur) Surviving Internal Politics Within the School, 2006; editor: Position Papers of Ill. Council for Exceptional Children, 1981; contbr. articles to profl. jours. Bd. dirs. Jacksonville Area Assn. Retarded Citizens, v.p., 1993-94, sec. 1996-99; govt. rels. chair Internat. Coun. Exceptional Children, 1984-87; fed. liason Ill. Adminstrs. Spl. Edn., 1985-86. So. Ill. U. fellow, 1968; resolution honoring Beverly H. Johns Internat. Coun. for Exceptional Children Conv., 1982; recipient Recognition cert. Ill. Atty. Gen., 1985, Outstanding Leadership award Internat. Coun. Exceptional Children, 2000; named Jacksonville Woman of Yr., Bus. and Profl. Women, 1988, Unsung Hero Jacksonville Jour.-Courier, 1993. Mem. ASCD, Assn. Retarded Citizens (com. 1982-85), Ill. Coun. for Children with Behavioral Disorders (founder, past pres., pres. Ill. divsn. for learning disabilities 1991-92, Presdl. award 1985), Ill. Alliance for Exceptional Children (v.p. 1982-94), Learning Disabilities Assn. (bd. dirs., pres. 2000-03), Ill. Coun. Exceptional Children (past pres., chair govt. rels. com. 1982-95, 97-98, 2002—, governing bd. 1984-95, Presdl. award 1983, Lifetime Achievement award 1989, First Lady 1993), Internat. Coun. for Children with Behavioral Disorders (pres. 1997), West Ctrl. Assn. for Citizens with Learning Disabilities (founder, com. chair 1997), Internat. Assn. Spl. Edn. (pres.), Internat. Pioneer Press (editor CEC pioneer divsn., pres. internat. pioneers divsn.), Internat. Divsn. Learning Disabilities (exec. bd.), Delta Kappa Gamma (chpt. pres. 1988-90, state exec. bd. 1991—), Internat. Assn. Spl. Edn. (pres. 2006—), Phi Delta Kappa. Roman Catholic. Avocation: world travel. Home: PO Box 340 Jacksonville IL 62651-0340 Office Phone: 217-245-5781. Personal E-mail: bevjohns@juno.com.

JOHNS, CHRISTOPHER GEORGE, editor-in-chief, photojournalist; b. Medford, Oreg., Apr. 15, 1951; s. George Arthur and Joanne Harriet (Utz) J.; m. Pamela Jean Formick, Sept. 11, 1976 (div.); m. Elizbeth Johns, 3 children. BS in Tech. Journalism, minor in Agriculture, Oreg. State U., 1974; M in Photojournalism, U. Minn. Sch. Journalism and Mass Communications, 1975. Staff photographer Albany (Oreg.) Democrat-Herald, 1973-74; teaching asst. U. Minn. Sch. Journalism, Mpls., 1974-75; staff photographer Topeka Capital-Jour., 1975-80, Seattle Times, 1980-84; freelance contract photojournalist Nat. Geog., 1985—95, staff photographer, 1995—2003, assoc. editor, 2003—05, editor-in-chief, 2005—. Photographer/author Valley of Life: Africa's Great Rift, Hawaii's Hidden Treasures, Our Inviting Eastern Parklands, Wild at Heart: Man and Beast in Southern Africa. Named Photographer of Yr., Region 7, Nat. Press Photography Assn., 1977, 1978, Photographer of Yr., Photographer of Yr. Competition, 1978, Nat. Newspaper Photographer of Yr., 1979; named one of world's 25 most important photographers, Am. Photo mag., 2003; recipient 2 Nat. Mag. awards for Gen. Excellence in 2,000,000+ circulation, & for Photography, Am. Soc. Mag. Editors, 2007. Mem.: Nat. Press Photographers Assn., Sigma Delta Chi. Office: Nat Geographic 1145 17th St NW Washington DC 20036-4688*

JOHNS, CHRISTOPHER P., utilities executive; B in Acctg., U. Notre Dame, Ind., 1982. CPA Calif., Fla. Ptnr., assoc. nat. dir. Pub. Utilities KPMG Peat Marwick LLP; v.p., contr. Pacific Gas & Electric Co. PG&E Corp., San Francisco, 1996—97, v.p., 1997—2001, contr., 1997—2005, sr. v.p., 2001—, CFO, 2005—, treas., 2005—, sr. v.p., treas. Pacific Gas & Electric Co. Bd. trustees San Francisco Ballet. Mem.: Fin. Execs. Inst. Office: PG&E Corp One Market Spear Tower Ste 2400 San Francisco CA 94105-1126 Office Phone: 415-267-7070. Office Fax: 415-267-7268.*

JOHNS, DIANA, secondary school educator; BS, Mich. State U.; MS, U. Mich. Jr. high school tchr. Crestwood Dist. Schools, Dearborn Heights, Mich., sr. high sch. tchr., sci. dept. chair. Outstanding Earth-Sci. Tchr. award, 1992, Tchr. of the Year award Crestwood Sch. Dist., Scholarship award Crestwood High Sch. Chpt. NHS. Mem. Nat. Assn. Geology Tchrs., Mich. Earth Sci. Tchrs. Assn. Office: Crestwood Sr High Sch 1501 N Beech Daly Rd Dearborn Heights MI 48127-3403

JOHNS, JASPER, artist; b. Augusta, Ga., May 15, 1930; s. Jasper and Jean (Riley) J. Student, U. S.C., 1947-48. One-man exhbns. include, Leo Castelli Gallery, N.Y.C., 1958, 60, 61, 63, 66, 68, 76, 81, 84, Minami Gallery, Tokyo, 1965, 75, Galerie Rive Droite, Paris, 1959, 61, Galleria D'Arte Del Naviglio, Milan, 1959, Ileana Sonnabend, Paris, 1963, Columbia Mus. Art (S.C.), 1960, Jewish Mus., N.Y.C., 1964, White-chapel Gallery, London, 1964, Pasadena Mus. (Calif.), 1965, Smithsonian Instn. Nat. Collection Fine Arts, 1966, Arts Council Gt. Britain, 1974-75, Whitney Mus. Am. Art, 1977, Kunsthalle, Cologne, 1978, Centre Pompidou, Paris, 1978, Hayward Gallery, London, 1978, Seibu Mus., Tokyo, 1978, San Francisco Mus. Modern Art, 1978, Kunstmuseum, Basel, 1979, Des Moines Art Ctr., 1983, St. Louis Art Mus., 1985, Mus. Modern Art, 1986, Kunsthalle, 1986, Wight Art Gallery UCLA, 1987, Galerie Daniel Templon, Paris, 1987, Mus. Contemporary Art, L.A., 1987, Venice Biennale, 1958, 64, 78, Phila. Mus. Art, 1988, Walker Art Ctr., Mpls., 1990, Mus. Fine Arts, Houston, 1990, Fine Arts Mus. San Francisco, 1990, Montreal Mus. Fine Arts, 1990, Nat. Gallery Art, Washington, 1990, Kunstmus. Basel, 1990, Hayward Gallery, London, 1990, St. Louis Art Mus., 1991, Ctr. for Fine Arts, Miami, 1991, Denver Art Mus., 1991, Brooke Alexander Edits., N.Y.C., 1991, Whitney Mus. Am. Art, N.Y.C., 1991, Harvard U. Art Mus., 1992, San Diego Mus. Art, 1992, Cana Art Gallery, Seoul, 1991, Gagosian Gallery, N.Y., 1992, Palaus de Luppe, La Fondation Vincent Van Gogh, Arles, France, 1992, Milw. Art Mus., 1992, Galeria Weber Alexander Cobo, Madrid, 1992, Nat. Acad. Design, N.Y.C., 1996, Phila. Mus. of Art, 1999, Art Inst. Chgo., 1999, others; represented in permanent collections Mus. Modern Art, Albright-Knox Art Gallery, Buffalo, Tate Gallery, London, Moderna Museet, Stockholm, Stedelijik Mus., Amsterdam, The Netherlands, Whitney Mus., N.Y.C., Kunstmuseum, Basel, Centre Pompidou, Art Inst. Chgo., Balt. Mus. Art, Cleve. Mus. Art, Kunsthaus Zurich, Mpls. Inst. Art, Nat. Gallery Art, San Francisco Mus. Modern Art, Va. Mus. Fine Arts, Richmond, Walker Art Ctr., others; illustrator (book) In Memory of My Feelings, 1967. With US Army, 1949—51, Japan. Recipient 1st prize Print Biennale Ljubljana, Yugoslavia, prize IX Sao Paulo (Brazil) Biennale, Skowhegan medal for painting Skowhegan Sch. of Painting and Sculpture, Skowhegan medal for graphics, Mayors award of Honor for Arts and Culture City of N.Y., Wolf prize for painting, Wolf Found., 1986, Internat. prize Venice Biennale, 1988, Nat. Medal of Arts, The White House; named to S.C. Hall of Fame, 1989. Mem. Am. Acad. Arts and Letters (Gold medal for graphic art), Royal Acad. Arts, Nat. Inst. Arts and Letters, Am. Acad. Arts and Scis. Address: PO Box 642 Sharon CT 06069-0642

JOHNS, JOHN D., insurance company executive, lawyer; BA, U. Ala.; MBA, JD, Harvard U. Ptnr. Cabaniss, Johnston, Gardner, Dumas & O'Neal; founding ptnr. Maynard Cooper & Gale; v.p., gen. counsel Sonat Inc., 1988—93; exec. v.p., CFO Protective Life Corp., Birmingham, Ala., 1993—96, pres., COO, 1996—2001, chmn., pres., CEO, 2001—. Bd. dir. John H. Harland Co., Ala. Nat. Bancorporation, Genuine Parts Co. Office: Protective Life Corp 2801 Hwy 280 S Birmingham AL 35223*

JOHNS, MICHAEL DOUGLAS, healthcare executive, medical device executive, former federal government official; b. Allentown, Pa., Sept. 8, 1964; s. Glenn Franklin and Nancy Louise (Hummel) J.; m. Nicole Denise Miles, Sept. 30, 1995 (div. 1999); 1 child, Michael Douglas Jr. Student, Cambridge U., Eng., 1984; BBA in Econs., U. Miami, 1986. Asst. editor Policy Rev. Mag., Washington, 1986-88; policy analyst The Heritage Found., Washington, 1988-91; spl. asst. to pres. Drew U., Madison, NJ, 1991-92; speechwriter to Pres. of U.S. The White House, Washington, 1992; speechwriter to U.S. Sec. Commerce U.S. Dept. Commerce, Washington, 1992-93; dir. rsch. Internat. Rep. Inst., Washington, 1993-94; mgr. corp. comm., sr. writer Eli Lilly and Co., Indpls., 1994-95; aide to U.S. Senator Olympia J. Snowe U.S. Senate, Washington, 1996-97; sr. assoc. S.R. Wojdak & Assocs., Phila., 1997-2000; v.p. Gentiva Health Svcs., Melville, NY, 2000—02. Fgn. policy group advisor Dole for Pres., Inc., Washington, 1996; sr. advisor to global devel. projects Internat. Rep. Inst., Kuwait, Turkey, other nations, 1993-94; mgr. mktg., promotion and communication strategies cancer, cardiovasc., endocrine, infectious and ctrl. nervous sys. pharm. products Eli Lilly and Co., 1994-95; guest polit. and pub. policy analyst MacNeil/Lehrer News Hour, C-SPAN, CNBC, PBS Nightly Bus. Report, Fox Morning News, Voice of Am., BBC, others; sr. mgmt. and mgr. mktg., comms. and investor rels. for Fortune 1000 health svcs. co., 2000-02; guest lectr. UN, Vassar Coll., U. N.C., Chapel Hill, others. Author: Seventy Years of Evil in the Soviet Union, 1988, U.S. and Africa Statistical Handbook, 1990, U.S. and Africa Statistical Handbook, 2d edit., 1991; co-author: Freedom in the World: The Annual Survey of Political Rights and Civil Liberties, 1993, Finding Our Roots, Facing Our Future: America in the 21st Century, 1997; contbg. editor: USSR Monitor newsletter, The Heritage Found., 1989—91; contbr. articles to Wall St. Jour., Christian Sci. Monitor, Nat. Rev., others. Active Luth. Ch. of the Holy Spirit, Emmaus, Pa. Recipient Century III Leadership award, Shell Oil Co., 1981, Svc. award, Kiwanis, 1982, Cert. appreciation, Spl. Olympics, 1983, award of appreciation, Lao Vets Am., 1995, numerous citations, Congl. Record, U.S. Congress, First Pl. Health and Sci. awards, LI Web, 2001. Mem.: Case Mgmt. Soc. Am., Bush/Quayle Alumni Assn., Reagan Alumni Assn., Nat. Journalism Ctr. Alumni Coun., Am. Assn. Homecare (pub. affairs com.), Am. Med. Writing Assn., Pub. Rels. Soc. Am., Internat. Assn. Bus. Comminicators, Nat. Investor Rels. Inst., Assn. on Third World Affairs, Iron Arrow Honor Soc. of U. Miami, Lambda Chi Alpha (Internat. Hall of Fame 1996). Republican. Lutheran. Home: 219 Cabot Ct Deptford NJ 08096-5114 Office Phone: 856-853-8672. Personal E-mail: mjohns8@aol.com.

JOHNS, MICHAEL MARIEB EDWARD, otolaryngologist, academic administrator; b. Detroit, Jan. 27, 1942; s. Trini Lou DelCampo; children: Christina, Michael. BS, Wayne State U., 1964, Grad. Biol. Sci., 1965; MD with distinction, U. Mich., 1969. Diplomate Am. Bd. Otolaryngology. Intern Univ. Hosp., Ann Arbor, Mich., 1968—70, resident in otolaryngology, 1971—75; resident in gen. surgery St. Joseph's Mercy Hosp., Ann Arbor, 1970—71; asst. prof. U. Va. Med. Ctr., Charlottesville, 1977—79, assoc. prof., 1979—82, prof., 1982—84, Johns Hopkins U. Sch. Medicine, Balt., 1984—96, dean med. faculty, v.p. medicine, 1990—96; exec. v.p. health affairs Emory U., Atlanta, 1996—. Co-chmn. Md. Sci. Week Blue Ribbon Panel, Balt., 1992—; chmn.-elect Coun. of Deans. Co-author: Head and Neck Cancer, 1990; contbr. articles to profl. jours.; editor: Archives of Otolaryngology; contbg. editor: Journal of American Medical Association. Grantee, Robert Wood Johnson Found., 1992, NIH, 1995. Mem.: Inst. of Medicine, Ctr. Club, Cosmos Club. Office: Emory U Robert W Woodruff Health Scis Ctr 1440 Clifton Rd NE Ste 400 Atlanta GA 30322-1053

JOHNS, RICHARD JAMES, physician, educator; b. Pendleton, Oreg., Aug. 19, 1925; s. James Shanard and Pearl (McKenna) Johns; m. Carol Greacen Johnson; children: Richard Clark, Robert Shanard, James Ashmore. BS, U. Oreg., 1947; MD, Johns Hopkins U., 1948. Diplomate Am. Bd. Internal Medicine. Intern Johns Hopkins Hosp., Balt., 1948—49, asst. resident, 1951—53, fellow in medicine, 1953—55, resident, 1955—56, instr., 1955—57, physician, 1956—, asst. prof., 1957—61, assoc. prof., 1961—66, asst. dean admissions, 1962—66, prof. medicine, 1966—, dir. subdept. biomed. engring., 1966—70, mem. adv. bd., prin. profl. staff Applied Physics Lab., 1967—, prof., dir. dept. biomed. engring., 1970—91, disting. svc. prof., 1991—. Bd. dirs. Sparton Corp. Bd. visitors Sch. Engring., Duke U., 1986—; chmn. adv. com. Divsnl. Health Scis. and Tech., Harvard-MIT, 1987—92; mem. com. sci., engring. and pub. policy NAS, 1988—90; mem. sci. adv. com. GM, 1991—97; sec., vice chmn., chmn. med. bd. Myasthenia Gravis Found.; trustee Am. Bd. Clin. Engring., pres., 1976—83; bd. dirs. Whitaker Found., 1991—94. Capt. M.C. US Army, 1949—51. Fellow: Royal Soc. Medicine, Am. Inst. for Biol. and Med. Engring. (founding), AAAS, ACP; mem.: Inst. Medicine-NAS (coun. 1987—90), IEEE (pres. group on engring. in medicine and biology 1970—72), Biomed. Engring. Soc. (bd. dirs. 1972—75, pres. 1978—79), Assn. Am. Physicians, Am. Soc. Clin. Investigation, Am. Clin. and Climatol. Assn. (v.p. 1977—78, sec.-treas. 1979—85, pres. 1986—87), Sparton Corp. (dir. 2002—), Annapolis Yacht Club, Caduceus Club, Elkridge Club, Johns Hopkins Club (v.p. 1969—70), Peripatetic Club, Interurban Clin. Club (pres. 1980—81), Johns Hopkins Med. Soc. (pres. 1968—69), Tau Beta Pi, Nu Sigma Nu, Phi Kappa Psi, Alpha Omega Alpha, Sigma Xi. Home: 203 E Highfield Rd Baltimore MD 21218-1105 Office: Johns Hopkins U Sch Med 1830 E Monument St Ste 501 Baltimore MD 21287 E-mail: rjohns@jhmi.edu.

JOHNS, SARA KELLY, school librarian, library association executive; b. Plattsburgh, NY, July 31, 1949; d. Richard Walter and Lita Vance Lynch Kelly; m. Frank Robert Johns, Aug. 18, 1991; m. Robert Frederick Brenizer, July 10, 1977 (dec. July 23, 1987); children: Anthony Francis, Robin Lynn Brenizer, Robert Douglas Brenizer, Tyler Jacob, Ryan Kelly Brenizer. BA in English, SUNY, Plattsburgh, 1971; MLS, SUNY, Albany, 1972. Cert. sch. libr. media specialist Bd. of Regents, NY State, 1972. Seconday sch. libr. media specialist Beekmantown Mid./Sr. H.S., Plattsburgh, 1972—99; secondary libr. media specialist Lake Placid (NY) Mid./Sr. H.S., 1999—. Adj. prof. for libr. rsch. methods Feinbrug Libr., SUNY, Plattsburgh, 1990—; cons. libr. media program evaluation, 2004—. Mem. capital campaign com. Saranac Lake Free Libr., NY, 2001—05, pres. bd. trustees, 1998—2002. Recipient Excellence in Librarianship, North Country Reference and Rsch. Libr. Resources, 1996; grantee, AASL and 3M® Corp., 2004. Mem.: ALA (councilor-at-large 2001—04), Nat. Bd. for Profl. Tchg. Standards Libr. Media Standards Writing Com. (mem. writing com. 1997—2001), NY Online Virtual Libr., Regents Commn. Libr. Svc. for 21st Century (rep. building-level sch. libr. media specialists 1998—2000), AASL (mem. com. 1994—96, adv. ad hoc task force 1996—97, mentoring ad hoc task force 1996—97, chair leadership forum planning com. 2001—, pres.-elect 2006—07, pres. 2007—), NY Libr. Assn. (bd. dirs., sch. libr. career awareness network sch. libr. media sect. 1985—90, pres. sch. libr. media sect. 1993—94, program dir., summer leadership retreats 1993—, chair ednl. leadership com. 1994, mem. com. co-chair 1994—96, sr. councilor-at- large 2003—05), No. Adirondack Libr. Assn. (charter mem., past pres. 1986), Delta Kappa Gamma (chpt. pres., co-pres.). Baptist. Avocations: travel, reading, needlecrafts. Home: 67 Canaras Ave Saranac Lake NY 12983 Office: Lake Placid Mid/Sr High Sch 34 School St Lake Placid NY 12946 Home Phone: 518-891-2339; Office Phone: 518-523-2474 4132. Office Fax: 518-523-4861. E-mail: sjohns@lakeplacidcsd.net.

JOHNS, TAMMY, employment services executive; MBA, Richard Ivey Bus. Sch., London, Ont., Can. Cert. human resource profl. Can. Country mgr. Can. to chmn. Can. ops. Manpower, Inc., 1992—2002, sr. v.p. global sales, 2002—06, sr. v.p. workforce strategy, 2006—. Office: Manpower Inc 5301 N Ironwood Rd Milwaukee WI 53217 Office Phone: 414-961-1000.*

JOHNS, WARREN LEROI, retired lawyer; b. Nevada, Iowa, June 9, 1929; s. Varner Jay and Ruby Charlene (Morrison) J.; m. Elaine C. Magnuson, July 24, 1955 (div. June 1983); children: Richard Warren, Lynn Cherie Johns-Pence; m. Ruth Page Scott, Sept. 29, 1985. BA, La Sierra U., 1950; MA, Andrews U., 1951; JD, U. So. Calif., 1958. Bar: Calif. 1959, U.S. Dist. Ct. (cen. dist.) Calif. 1959,U.S. Supreme Ct. 1963, Md. 1976, D.C. 1976, U.S. Dist. Ct. Md. 1976, U.S. Dist. Ct. D.C. 1976, U.S. Tax Ct. 1976, U.S. Ct. Appeals (4th cir.) 1976, U.S. Ct. Appeals (10th cir.) 1977, U.S. Ct. Customs and Patent Appeals 1979. Gen. counsel So. Calif. Conf. Seventh-day Adventists, Glendale, 1959-63, Pacific Union Conf. Seventh-day Adventists, Glendale and Sacramento, 1964-69; pvt. practice Sacramento, 1969-75; gen. counsel Gen. Conf. Seventh-day Adventists, Washington, 1975-92, trustee; pvt. practice Brookeville, Md., 1992-98; ret., 1998. Adv. bd. Ctr. for Ch./State Studies, De Paul U. Coll. Chgo., 1987-93, spl. counsel to gen. conf., 1992-95; spl. counsel Adventist HealthCare Corp., Columbia Union HealthCare Corp., 1992-97. Author: Dateline Sunday USA, 1967, Ride to Glory, 1999; editor CreationDigest.com, 2001, Beyond Forever, 2006; founding editor JD, 1978-92 Chmn. bd. dirs., pres. Sacramento Area Econ. Opportunity Coun., 1974; co-founder CH. State Coun., 1963; founder CMT scholarship fund for H.S. srs., 2005. Recipient Frank Yost award Ch. State Coun., Glendale, Alumnus of Achievement award Andrews U., 1981, Alumnus of Yr. award La Sierra U., 1994. Mem. AAAS, ABA (vice-chmn. com. on torts, non-profit, charitable and religious orgns., sect. of tort and ins. practice 1990-91). Democrat. Achievements include design of an aliphatic synthesis chart. Avocations: sports, photography, book collecting. Personal E-mail: wj1929@dtccom.net.

JOHNSEN, DAVID C., dean, dental educator; BS, U. Mich., 1965, DDS, 1970; MS in Pediat. Dentistry, U. Iowa, 1973. Diplomate Am. Bd. Pediat. Dentistry. Pediat. dentistry instr. U. Iowa Coll. of Dentistry, Iowa City, 1972-73, prof. pediat. dentistry, dean, 1995—; from asst. to assoc. prof. W.Va. U. Hosp., 1974-80, Case Western Res. U., Cleve., 1980-95, interim dean, 1993-95, dir. pediat. dentistry residency program, 1990-95. Bd. mem. Am. Dental Edn. Assn. Coun. of Deans, 1998—2001. Contbr. articles to profl. jours. Mem. Head Start, World Vision, QualChoice Managed Health Care, Ctrs. for Disease Control, HHS Bur. Maternal and Child Health. Recipient numerous grants. Mem. Monongalia (Ohio) County Dental Soc., Iowa Pediat. Dentistry Alumni Assn., Am. Assn. for Dental Rsch., Am. Assn. Dental Schs., Am. Acad. Pediat. Dentistry (bd. of dirs. 1988-91), Am. Dental Education Assn. (pres. 2002-03). Office: U Iowa Coll Dentistry Rm 308 Iowa City IA 52242

JOHNSEN, EUGENE CARLYLE, mathematician, educator; b. Mpls., Jan. 27, 1932; s. Bernhardt Thorwald and Esther Elvira (Eklund) J.; m. Marjorie Marie Wacklin, Aug. 31, 1957. BChem, U. Minn., 1954; PhD, Ohio State U., 1961. NAS/NRC Rsch. Assoc. Nat. Bur. Stds., Washington, 1962-63; lectr. math. U. Calif., Santa Barbara, 1963-64, asst. prof., 1964-68, assoc. prof., 1968-74, prof., 1974-94, prof. emeritus, 1994—, dir. summer sessions, 1981-94, 94-97, cons. rschr., 1994—. Vis. lectr. in math. U. Mich., Ann Arbor, 1968-69; vis. scholar in sociology Harvard U., Cambridge, Mass., 1984-85; mathematician Sperry Rand, St. Paul, 1956, 57; instr. chem. and math. U. Minn., 1956-57; instr. math. Ohio State U., Columbus, 1962; organizer and co-organizer of math. social sci. confs.; reviewer NSF. Contbr. numerous articles to profl. jours.; referee numerous profl. jours.; mem. editl. bd. Jour. Math. Sociology. Mem. Los Angeles County Mus. Art, 1985—, L.A. Music Ctr. Opera League, 1986—; mem. Santa Barbara C. of C./U. Calif. Santa Barbara Bus. Adv. Com., 1979-84. Grantee USAFOSR, NSF, Dept. Edn.; Fulbright travel award fellow U. Tübingen, 1969; fellow NSF, 1959. Mem. AAAS, Am. Math. Soc., Math. Assn. Am., Am. Statis. Assn., Soc. Indsl. and Applied Math., Internat. Network for Social Network Analysis, Am. Sociol. Assn. (acting chair, then chair math. sociology sect. 1995-97), U. Calif. Santa Barbara Faculty Club, Channel City Club, Am.-Scandinavian Found. (bd. dirs. Santa Barbara chpt. 2005—), Sons of Norway (pres. Ivar Aasen Lodge 1999-2001, 03—), Phi Beta Kappa, Sigma Xi, Phi Lambda Upsilon, Pi Mu Epsilon, Alpha Chi Sigma. Avocations: music, opera, tennis, travel. Home: 1603 Paterna Rd Santa Barbara CA 93103-1826 Office: U Calif Dept Math Santa Barbara CA 93106-3080 Business E-Mail: johnsen@math.ucsb.edu.

JOHNSEN, KAREN KENNEDY, marketing professional; b. Easton, Pa., June 28, 1939; d. Charles Edward and Gladys Swensen Kennedy; m. Henry Lehmann Johnsen, May 26, 1962; children: Erik Lehmann, Elisa Beth Johnsen Peters. BS in Bus. cum laude, Russell Sage Coll., Troy, NY, 1961; MS in Bus. Edn., SUNY, Albany, 1970. Cert. bus. tchr. N.Y., 1970. With account svc. divsn. McCann-Erickson, Inc., NYC, 1961—62; exec. asst. pub. rels. Johnson & Johnson, New Brunswick, NJ, 1962—65; staff writer investment divsn. Glens Falls Ins. Co., NY, 1965—66; exec. sec. to pres., sec.-treas. Glens Falls Portland Cement Co., 1966—69; dir. devel. (funding and audience) Lake George Opera Festival, Glens Falls, 1970—73; publicity dir. fund raising campaign Glens Falls YMCA; freelance writer, adminstrn./media/mktg. cons., 1974—; exec. asst., media dir., staff writer Kimberly Comm., Inc., Chatham, NJ, 1974—82; sales mgr. Lifelines Gifts & Cards, NYC, 1982—84; entrepreneur mktg., sales and mgmt. KJ Assocs., 1985—; ind. Mary Kay beauty cons., 1994—. Charter sec. pub. relations Scotch Plains Assn. Concerning Environment, 1999—; former bd. dirs. Plainfield Symphony Soc.; charter sec. Lake George Opera Guild, 1970—73; charter sec. adv. bd. Project 2000, Norwegian Immigration Assn. Mem.: AAUW (chpt. treas., comm. chmn.), Vesterheim Norwegian-Am. Mus., Russell Sage Coll. Alumnae Assn. (class agt., alumnae admissions liaison 1995—, class reunion chair 2001, 2006), Am. Scandinavian Found., Vasa Order of Am. (past NJ dist. sec., cultural leader, supr. children's clubs, past local lodge chmn., sec., supr. children's club, past chmn., cultural leader, supr. children's clubs local lodge), Order Ea. Star, Delta Pi Epsilon. Presbyterian. Avocations: skiing, singing, writing, folk-art painting. Home and Office: 109 Glenside Ave Scotch Plains NJ 07076 Office Phone: 908-928-9061. E-mail: kkjohnsen@comcast.net.

JOHNSEN, KEN C., steel products company executive; b. 1958; BA in Fin., Utah State U.; JD, Yale U. Assoc. Parr Waddoups Brown Gee & Loveless, 1986-91; mgr. spl. projects Geneva Steel Holdings Corp., Vineyard, Utah, 1991, v.p., gen. counsel, 1991-97, sec., 1992—, exec. v.p., gen. counsel, 1997—, also bd. dirs., dir., pres. and ceo, 2001—05; bd. mem. Amerityre Corp., Boulder City, Nev., 2005—. Mem. bd. dir. Joy Global, Inc., Milw. Mem. AISI (com. mem.). Office: Amerityre Corp 1501 Industrial Rd Boulder City NV 89005 Office Phone: 800-808-1268. Office Fax: 801-227-9090.

JOHNSEN, WALTER CRAIG, manufacturing executive; b. NYC, Dec. 15, 1950; BS, Cornell U., 1973, MS in Eng., 1974; MBA, Columbia U., 1978. Gen. ptnr. First Century Partnerships, NYC, 1981-85; v.p. Smith Barney, Harris Upham Venture Corp., 1978-85; mng. ptnr. Johnsen Securities, NYC, 1985-95; chmn., CEO Acme United Corp., Fairfield, Conn., 1995—. Bd. dirs. Acme United Corp., Fairfield, Conn. Office: Acme United Corp 60 Round Hill Rd Fairfield CT 06824-5172

JOHNSON, A. PAUL, composer; b. Indpls., Jan. 27, 1955; m. Minda A. Stephens, Feb. 14, 1980. Composer, music dir. Ind. Repertory Theatre, Indpls., 1976-78, Syracuse (N.Y.) Stage, 1978, Palisades Theatre Co., Washington, 1979-81, Royal Palm Theatre, St. Petersburg, Fla., 1982-86, Am. Stage Co., St. Petersburg, 1986-87; artistic dir. Nettle Creek Players, Hagerstown, Ind., 1987—. Pres. Fla. Composers Forum, St. Petersburg, 2001—06; cons. in field. Composer: Flute Sonata, 1980 (Fla. Arts Council fellow), (mime and ballet) Parchman Plays the Game, 1982 (Ind. Arts Commn. fellow), (opera) Dream Child, 1986 (Nat. Inst. for Music Theatre award), Clarinet Concerto, 1986 (Meet the Composer award). Grantee, NEA, 1995, Nat. Inst. Music, Kennedy Ctr., 1985; Indian Artist fellow, Fla. Arts Coun., 1982, 2002. Mem. Am. Composers Alliance, Broadcast Music Inc. Avocations: reading, dogs, walking. Office: Am Composers Edition 170 W 74th St New York NY 10023-2350

JOHNSON, ABIGAIL PIERREPONT, investment company executive; b. Boston, Dec. 19, 1961; d. Edward C. Johnson; m. Christopher J. McKown; 2 children. BA in Art Hist., Hobart and William Smith Coll., 1984; MBA, Harvard U., 1988. Rsch. assoc. Booz, Allen & Hamilton; portfolio mgr. Fidelity Investments, Boston, 1988—, assoc. dir., 1994—, sr. v.p., 1998—, pres. Fidelity Mgmt. & Rsch., 2001—05, pres. Fidelity Employers Svcs., 2005—. Bd. dirs. FMR Corp. Named one of Most Powerful Women, Forbes mag., 2005, Top 50 Women to Watch, Wall St. Jour., 2005, Forbes Richest Ams., 2005, 2006, 50 Most Powerful Women in Bus., Fortune mag., 2006, World's Richest People, Forbes mag., 2007. Office: Fidelity Investments 82 Devonshire St Boston MA 02109-3605*

JOHNSON, ALAN ARTHUR, physicist, educator, consultant; b. Beckenham, Eng., Aug. 18, 1930; arrived in US, 1962; s. Frederick W. and Dorothy (Tew) S.; m. Elizabeth Ann Banks, June 22, 1958 (div. Dec. 1981); children: Stephen Graham, Michael Andrew, David Nicholas, Brian Philip, Susan Christine; m. Barbara Davidson Pinkerton, Mar. 11, 1990. B.Sc. with spl. honours in Physics, Reading U., Eng., 1952; MA in Physics, U. Toronto, 1954; Ph. D. in Metal Physics, U. London, Eng.; diplomate, Imperial Coll., London, 1960. Chartered engr., Coun. Engring. Instns. Sci. officer Royal Naval Sci. Service, England, 1954-56; lectr. metallurgy Imperial Coll. Sci. and Tech., U. London, 1960-62; dir. rsch. Materials Rsch. Corp., Orangeburg, NY, 1963-65; prof. phys. metallurgy Bklyn. Poly. Inst., 1965-71, head dept. phys. and engring., metallurgy, 1967-71; prof. materials sci., chmn. dept. Wash. State U., 1971-75; dean Grad. Sch. U. Louisville, 1975-76, prof. materials sci., 1975—2002. Cons. to govt. and industry, 1960—; pres. Metals Rsch., Inc., 1988—. Recipient Kentuckiana Metroversity award for innovative tchg., 1995, Disting. Citizen of Louisville, 1996, Cmty. Svc. award U. Louisville, 2001. Fellow AAAS, Inst. Materials, Inst. Physics, Am. Soc. Metals (nat. nominating com. 1980-81, chmn. Louisville chpt. 1981-82, 89-90, 96-97, chmn. metals engring. inst. com. 1982-83); Tau Beta Pi, Phi Kappa Phi. Office: Metals Rsch Inc 101 W Chestnut St Louisville KY 40202-0001 E-mail: barbalan@bellsouth.net.

JOHNSON, ALBERT WESLEY, retired political science professor, public official; b. Insinger, Sask., Can., Oct. 18, 1923; s. Thomas William and Louise Lillian J.; m. Ruth Elinor Hardy, June 27, 1946; children: Andrew, Frances, Jane, Geoffrey. BA, U. Sask., 1942; MA, U. Toronto, 1945; MPA (Littauer fellow), Harvard U., 1950, PhD (Littauer fellow), 1963; LLD (hon.), U. Regina, 1977, U. Sask., 1978, Mt. Allison U., 1982, Queen's U., 1992, Carleton U., 1999. Dep. provincial treas. Govt. of Sask., Regina, 1952-64; asst. dep. minister fin. Govt. of Can., Ottawa, Ont., 1964-68, econ. adviser to prime minister on constn., 1968-70, sec. treasury bd., 1970-73, dep. minister nat. welfare, 1973-75; pres. CBC, Ottawa, 1975-82; Skelton-Clark fellow Queens U., 1982-83; prof. polit. sci. U. Toronto, 1983-89; sr. fellow Can. Centre for Mgmt. Devel., Ottawa, 1989-91; prof. emeritus U. Toronto. Cons. on governance IMF, Indonesia, 1988, 91, South Africa, 1992-99; chmn. task force on univ. programs, Sask., 1992-93. Author: Dream No Little Dreams: A Biography of the Douglas Government of Saskatchewan, 1944-1961, 2004; contbr. articles to profl. publs.; editorial bd.: Can. Public Policy, 1974-75. Bd. dirs. Nat. Film Bd., 1970-82, U. Sask. Hosp., 1957-64; mem. Nat. Arts Centre, 1975-82; bd. govs. U. Sask., Saskatoon, 1952-63. Recipient Gold medal Profl. Inst. of Pub. Svc. of Can., 1975; decorated Companion of the Order of Can., 1997; A.W. Johnson Disting. Chair established Sask. Dept. Fin., 2000. Mem. Ottawa Polit. Economy Assn. (pres. 1969-70), Inst. Public Adminstrn. Can. (pres. 1962-63, Vanier medal 1976, nat. council 1951-69), Can. Polit. Sci. Assn. (exec. council 1963-64) Mem. United Ch. of Can. Home Fax: 613-225-6735. Personal E-mail: johnsona@magma.ca.

JOHNSON, ALBERTA CLARK, psychology professor; b. Chattanooga, Apr. 19, 1942; d. William Ross and Helen W. Clark; m. John Burlin Johnson, Mar. 12, 1965; children: Sonya K., Roxanne Johnson Dingman. BA, U. N.C., Greensboro, 1964; MS, U. Ariz., 1979, PhD, 1988. Cert. family life educator, Nat. Coun. Family Rels. Membership dir. Tucson Area Coun. Camp Fire, 1981—83; asst. dir. Ext. Winter Sch., Tucson, 1984—87; human devel. specialist U. Ariz. Coop. Ext. Svc., Tucson, 1983—87; assoc. faculty Pima C.C., Tucson, 1987—88; family life specialist U. Ariz. Coop. Ext. Svc., 1989—92, U. Ark. Coop. Ext. Svc., Little Rock, 1989—92; cons. Little Rock, 1992—93; asst. prof. psychology and edn. Ga. Highlands Coll. (formerly Floyd Coll.), Rome, 1993—97, assoc. prof. psychology, 1997—2002, prof. psychology, 2002—, study abroad coord., 2003—05. Sec., governing state bd. dirs. Parents Anonymous of Ariz., Phoenix, 1983-84; mem. Gov.'s Coun. on Children, Youth and Families, Phoenix, 1983-84; pres. bd. dirs. Pima County chpt. Parents Anonymous, Tucson, 1985-86; v.p. Women's Info. Network, Inc., Rome, 1997-99; bd. dirs. Ga. Breast Cancer Coalition, 2000-03. Named Woman of Excellence, 1998, Women in Mgmt. and Greater Rome C. of C. Mem.: SEPA, APA, AAUP, Coun. Tchrs. of Undergrad. Psychology, Am. Psychol. Soc., Nat. Coun. on Family Rels., Pi Lambda Theta, Kappa Omicron Nu, Psi Beta (nat. pres., pres.-elect). Avocations: photography, hiking, reading, travel. Office: Ga Highlands Coll 3175 Highway 27 N Rome GA 30161 Business E-Mail: ajohnson@highlands.edu.

JOHNSON, ALEX MOORE, dean, law educator; b. Portland, Oreg., Oct. 5, 1953; s. Alex M. and Margaret Johnson; m. Karen J. Anderson. BA, Claremont U., 1975; JD, UCLA, 1978. Bar: Calif. 1978, U.S. Dist. Ct. (cen. and so. dists.) Calif. 1978. Atty. Latham & Watkins, LA, 1978-80, 82-84; assoc. prof. law U. Minn., Mpls., 1980-82, William S. Pattee prof. law, dean, law sch. Mpls., 2002—; asst. prof. U. Va., Charlottesville, 1984—88, prof. law, 1989-93, Mary and Daniel Loughran prof. law, 1993—2002, vice provost for faculty, 1995—2002; chair Law Sch. Admissions Coun., 2001—03. Vis. prof. U. Tex., Austin, 1988-89, Stanford Law Sch., 1991. Contbr. articles to profl. jours. Mem. Law Sch. Admission Coun. (bd. trustees 1994, minority affairs com. 1989-94, chmn. 2001-2003), Assn. Am. Law Schs. (chair curriculum and rsch. com. 1993—), U. Va. Alumni Assn. (chmn. career counseling panel 1987—). Office: U Minn Sch Law Walter F Mondale Hall Rm 381 229-19th Ave S Minneapolis MN 55455 Office Phone: 612-625-4841. E-mail: alexjohn@umn.edu.

JOHNSON, ALEXANDER D., biochemist, molecular biologist, educator; BA in Molecular Biology, Vanderbilt Univ., Nashville, 1974; PhD in Biochemistry, Harvard Univ., 1980; postdoctoral fellow, Univ. Calif., San Francisco, 1981—85. Prof., vice chair, microbiology & immunology Univ. Calif., San Francisco. Fellow: Am. Acad. Arts & Scis. Office: Mission Bay Genentech Hall Suite N372 Box 2200 600 16th St San Francisco CA 94142-2200 Office Phone: 415-476-8789. Business E-Mail: ajohnson@socrates.ucsf.edu.*

JOHNSON, ALLEN HALBERT, surgeon; b. Atascadero, Calif., Jan. 23, 1922; s. Halbert Theodore and Julia Hallock (Kommers) J.; m. Mary Marchant McGee, Oct. 21, 1945 (dec. July 1983); children: Kathryn, Martha, Elizabeth, Kenneth; m. Darlyn Richardson, June 17, 1990. AB, U. Calif., Berkeley, 1943; MD, U. Calif., San Francisco, 1946. Diplomate Am. Bd. Surgery. Intern U. Calif., San Francisco, 1946-47, asst. resident, 1947-48, asst. resident surgery, 1950-54, chief resident, 1954-55; pvt. practice San Jose, Calif., 1955-91; clin. prof. surgery U. Cal., San Francisco, 1991—. Chief of staff Santa Clara (Calif.) Valley Med. Ctr., 1969-72, San Jose (Calif.) Hosp., 1980-82; instr. in field. Contbr. articles to profl. jours. Bd. dirs. Boys & Girls Clubs, San Jose, 1962—, YMCA, San Jose, 1964—, Vis. Nurses Assn., San Jose, 1964-70, ARC, San Jose, 1960-72. Capt. Med. Corps, U.S. Army, 1948-50. Mem. ACS (bd. govs.

1974-80), San Jose Surg. Soc. (pres. 1963-64), U. Calif. Med. Alumni Assn. (pres. 1981-82), Nafziger Surg. Soc. (pres. 1973-74), Pacific Coast Surg. Assn. (sec.-treas. 1980-86, pres. 1990-91), Calif. Acad. Medicine (pres. 1992), San Jose Country Club (bd. dirs. 1975-78). Republican. Avocations: music, photography. Home: 1655 Emory St San Jose CA 95126-1909

JOHNSON, A(LYN) WILLIAM, chemistry professor, writer, researcher, consultant; b. Calgary, Alta, Can., Dec. 16, 1933; arrived in US, 1954, naturalized, 1981; s. Alyn C. and Irene (Johnston) Johnson; m. Joan Auger, July 26, 1956; children: Patricia, Nancy, Robert, Katherine. BS, U. Alta., 1954; PhD, Cornell U., 1957. Research fellow Mellon Inst., Pitts., 1957-60; from asst. to assoc. prof. chemistry U. ND, 1960-65, prof. chemistry Grand Forks, 1988-94, emeritus prof., 1995—, dean Grad. Sch., prof. chemistry, 1967-75, 77-88, dir. R & D, 1967-75; assoc. prof., chmn. dept. chemistry U. Sask. Regina, 1965-67. Dir. ND regional environ. assessment program ND Legis. Coun., Bismark, 1975—77; vis. prof. U. Mass., Amherst, 1989, US Mil. Acad., West Point, NY, 1994—95. Author: Ylid chemistry, 1966, Ylides and Imines of Phosphorus, 1993, Invitation to Organic Chemistry, 1998; contbr. articles to profl. jours. Fellow: AAAS, Chem. Inst. Can.; mem.: Am. Chem. Soc. (cons. C3S program), Rotary. Episcopalian. Home: 9 Tanyard Ln Bella Vista AR 72714-2450

JOHNSON, ANDREA, biologist, researcher; BS, U. Miami, Fla., 1991; MS, U South Fla., 1995; PhD, NC State U., Raleigh, 2004. Rsch. asst. prof. U. Md. Ea. Shore, Princess Anne, 2004—. Mem.: Am. Fisheries Soc., Sigma Xi. Office: Univ Md Eastern Shore 1 Backbone Rd Princess Anne MD 21853 Office Phone: 410-651-8447.

JOHNSON, ANITA LOUISE, artist, art director; b. Silver Creek, NY, Oct. 22, 1931; d. Samuel Joseph and Louisa Veronica (Guarcello) Militello. BFA, Albright Art Sch., Buffalo, 1952. Comml. artist Buffalo Courier Express, 1952—80; art dir. The Buffalo News, 1980—81. One-woman shows include Ground Fl. Gallery, Buffalo, 1972, A.A.O. Gallery, 1976, Erie Art Mus., Pa., 1977, Theodore Roosevelt Site, Buffalo, 1978, Trocaire Coll., 1980, SUNY, 1982, Orchard Park Sci. Fair, NY, 1983, Daemen Coll., Amherst, NY, 1989, Garrett Club, Buffalo, 1995, Studio Arena Theatre, 1995, Upstairs at Sutherlands Gallery, 1995, 1996, Arts Coun., 2001, exhibited in group shows at MacAlpine Religious Exhbn., 1972—76, Barbara Schuller Art Assocs., 1986, A.A.O. Gallery, 1976, 1980—82, 1984—85, 1987, Michael Rockefeller Ctr. State Coll. Fredonia, NY, 1975, Rochester Meml. Art Gallery, 1976—88, 1976—91, New Orleans Nat. Exhbn., 1973, Nina Freudenheim Gallery, Buffalo, 1991, Menorah Campus Invitational, Amherst, 1993—95, Nat. League Am. Pen Women, 2000, Jane Clary-Miner Gallery, Buffalo, 1988—90, Carnegie Cultural Ctr., Tonawanda, NYq, 1997, Broome St. Gallery, NYC, 1999—2000, Big Orbit Gallery, 1994—96, Art Loft Gallery, Lockport, NY, 2001, Art Dialogue Gallery, Buffalo, 1994—2006, Albrigh-Knox Art Gallery, 1970—2005, many others, Represented in permanent collections Bethlehem Steel Co., Buffalo, Buffalo City Hall, Am. Bur. Collections, Buffalo, First Nat. Bank Pa., Erie, Fisher-Price Toys, East Aurora, NY, Automobile Assn. Am., Amherst, Ford Motor Co., Inland Divsn., Dayton, Westwood Pharm., Inc., Buffalo, Empire Am. Savings Bank, Lincoln Chase Bank, Orchard Park, NY, Blue Cross Western NY, Buffalo, Buffalo Gen. Hosp., Roswell Hosp., Buffalo. Recipient Purchase award, Erie Art Ctr., 1974, award, A.A.O. Gallery, Amherst, 1973, 1975, 1981, 1982, 1987, Joan Walton Primerano award, Burchfield Ctr., Buffalo, 1976, award, Wilcox Mansion Gallery, Amherst, 1978, 1979, Lockport Savings Bank award, Kenan Ctr., Buffalo, 1993, award, Nat. League Am. Pen Women, 2000. Mem.: Buffalo Soc. Artists (pres. 1989—90, bd. dirs. 1978—90).

JOHNSON, ANTHONY O'LEARY (ANDY JOHNSON), meteorologist, consultant; b. Tampa, Fla., Apr. 19, 1957; s. Paul Bryan and Katie Hobbs (Nunez) J. BS in Meteorology, Fla. State U., 1979. Courthouse runner Gregory, Cours, et. al., Tampa, 1977; water resources planner S.W. Fla. Water Mgmt. Dist., Brooksville, 1978; staff meteorologist Sta. WTVT-TV, Tampa, 1979-82; systems mgr., 1982-89, weather office mgr., 1989—. Meterol. cons. Gulf Coast Weather Svc.-Weather Vision, Tampa, 1979—; software devel. mgr. TTI Techs. Inc., Tampa, 1989-92; site coord. Space Sci. and Engring. Ctr. U. Wis., Madison, 1989—. Active capital improvements com. Plantation Homeowners Assn., Tampa, 1991; judge Hillsborough Regional Sci. Fair, Tampa, 1990, 91, 92, 96; fundraiser Dunedin Youth Guild, 1992, Northside Mental Health Hosp. Aux., 1993, 94, Children's Home, Pinellas Aux., 1993, 94, 95; vol. Sch. Enrichment Vols. in Edn. (SERVE), 1992. Mem. AAAS, Am. Meteorol. Soc. (Seal of Approval for TV weathercasting 1982—, v.p. West Fla. chpt. 1984-85, pres. 1989-92, 94—, cert. meteorologist), Internat. Platform Assn., Phi Beta Kappa, Pi Mu Epsilon, Chi Epsilon Pi. Republican. Achievements include development of quantitative predictive methods of energy delivery interruption in severe Florida freezes; research on temporal and spatial climatological anomalies on landfalling hurricanes in West Central Florida. Office: Sta WTVT-TV Weather Svc 3213 W Kennedy Blvd Tampa FL 33609-3006 Home: 3912 W Dale Ave Tampa FL 33609-4405 Home Phone: 813-878-2929; Office Phone: 813-870-9696. Personal E-mail: andyccm@aol.com.

JOHNSON, ANTONIA AXSON, food products executive; b. Sept. 6, 1943; d. Axel Axson and Antonia Johnson; m. P. Göran Ennerfelt; children: Alexandra Mörner, Caroline Mörner, Axel Mörner, Sophie Mörner. Student, Radcliffe Coll., 1963-64; MA in Psychology and Econs., U. Stockholm, 1971. With Nordstjernan AB, 1971—79, Axel Johnson AB, Stockholm, 1979—, chair, 1982—. Chmn. bd. Axel Johnson Inc., Stamford, Conn.; bd. dirs. The Axel and Margaret Axson Johnson's Found., NCC Nordic Constrn. Co., World Childhood Found., Axfood AB, Nordstjernan AB, Axel Johnson Internat., Sweden; mem. IVA-Royal Swedish Acad. Engring. Scis. Named Profl. Woman of Yr., 1987, Fin. Woman of Yr., 1988; named one of Am.'s Top 25 Women Bus. Owners (ranked number 1), Nat. Found. for Women Bus. Owners and Working Women, 1992, Am.'s Top 50 Women Bus. Owners, 1993, World's Richest People, Forbes mag., 2001-2007, 100 Most Powerful Women, Forbes mag., 2004-2006. Avocation: horseback riding. Office: Axel Johnson AB Villagatan 6 PO Box 26008 SE-100 41 Stockholm Sweden Office Phone: +46 8 7016100.*

JOHNSON, ARNOLD J., lawyer, energy executive; With ARCO, 1980—89; asst. gen. counsel. Vastar, 1997—2000; sr. counsel BP America, Inc., 2000—01; assoc. gen. counsel, asst. sec. Noble Energy, Inc., Houston, 2001—04, v.p., gen. counsel, sec., 2001—. Office: Noble Energy, Inc 100 Glenborough Dr Ste 100 Houston TX 77067*

JOHNSON, ARTHUR GILBERT, microbiology educator; b. Eveleth, Minn., Feb. 1, 1926; s. Arthur Gilbert and Selma (Niemi) J.; m. Mildred Louise Anderson, June 15, 1951; children: Susan, Sally, Gary, Peter. BA, U. Minn., 1950, M.Sc., 1951; PhD, U. Md., 1955. Biochemist Walter Reed Army Inst. Rsch., Washington, 1952-55; asst. prof. U. Mich., 1956-62, asso. prof., 1962-66, prof. microbiology, 1966-78; prof., head dept. med. microbiology/immunology U. Minn. Sch. Medicine, Duluth, 1978-99, prof. emeritus, 1999—. Mem. pre, postdoctoral and spl. fellowships study sect. NIH, 1968-70; mem. nat. adv. dental rsch. coun. NIH, 1972-75; mem. Nat. Bd. Med. Examiners, 1980-84; mem. bacteriology and mycology study sect. NIH, 1983-87, chmn., 1986-87; cons. microbiology. Editor Infection and Immunity, 1977-86. Served with US Merchant Marine, 1943-46. Mem. Am. Assn. Immunologists, Am. Soc. Microbiology, Infectious Diseases Soc. Am., Soc. Biol. Therapy, Immunocomprised Host Soc., Internat. Endotoxin Soc., Assn. Med. Sch. Microbiology and Immunology Chairs (pres. 1991-92). Achievements include research on immunology. Home: 209 Rockridge Cir Duluth MN 55804-1857 Office: U Minn Sch Medicine Dept Microbiology/Immunology Duluth MN 55812 Office Phone: 218-726-7561.

JOHNSON, ARTHUR WILLIAM, JR., retired research scientist; b. Steubenville, Ohio, Jan. 8, 1949; s. Arthur William and Carol (Gilcrest) J. BMus, U. So. Calif., 1973. Lectr. Griffith Obs. and Planetarium, 1969-73; planetarium writer, lectr. Mt. San Antonio Coll. Planetarium, Walnut, Calif., 1970-73; dir. Fleischmann Planetarium U. Nev., Reno, 1973-2001; ret., 2001. Apptd. Nev. state coord. NSTA/NASA Space Sci. Student Involvement Program, 1994. Writer, prodr. films (with Donald G. Potter) Beautiful Nevada, 1978, Riches: The Story of Nevada Mining, 1984. Organist, choirmaster Trinity Episcopal Ch., Reno, 1980—; bd. dirs. Reno Chamber Orch. Assn., 1981-87, 1st v.p., 1984-85. Nev. Humanities Com., Inc. grantee, 1979-83; Chautauqua scholar, 2007. Mem. Am. Guild Organists (dean No. Nev. chpt. 1984-85, 96-99, 2002-05), Assn. Anglican Musicians, Internat. Planetarium Soc., Cinema 360 (treas. 1985-90, pres. 1990-98), Pacific Planetarium Assn. (pres. 1980), Lions (pres. Reno Host Club 1991-92), Large Format Cinema Assn. (v.p. 1996-99). Republican. Episcopalian. Office Phone: 775-322-9001. Business E-Mail: arthurj@unr.edu.

JOHNSON, ARTIS, educational administrator, clergyman; b. Thomasville, Ga., Oct. 3, 1948; s. Moses and Lillie Ruth (Ross) J.; m. Myrtle Elizabeth Woodruff, Sept. 16, 1969; children: Latoya, Mike, Jamal, Isaac, Solomon, Artis II, Simon, Kelvin, Stephanie, Chad, Alvin. AA, Birdwood Jr. Bapt. Coll., 1968; BS, Albany State Coll., 1970; MEd, MS, Valdosta State Coll., 1971; D Ministry, Bethany Theol. Sem., Dothan, Ala., 1992; PhD, Bethany Theol. Sem., 1993, DBS, 1006. 4th grade tchr. Harper Elem. Sch., Thomasville, Ga., 1971-76, Scott Elem. Sch., Thomasville, 1976-81; tchr., asst. headmaster Vashti Methodist Sch., Thomasville, 1981-82; from tchr. to dean students Howard Mid. Sch., Monticello, Fla., 1982-93; prin. Jefferson County Adult Sch., Monticello, 1993—. Pastor Bethany Congl. Ch., Thomasville, 1971-81, Evergreen Congl. Ch., Beachton, Ga., 1974—. Author: (children's book) Oliver Wants a Pony, 1978. Mem. NAACP (life), Am. Soc. Notaries, Ga. Notaries, Ga.-S.C. Assn. Congl. Mins., Monticello Ministerial Assn., Fla. Assn. Sch. Adminstrs., Literacy Vols. Am., Kiwanis (youth advisor 1994—, Kiwanian of Yr. award 1996), Masons. Democrat. Avocations: fishing, hunting, bicycling, swimming. Home: 3888 Ga Highway 33 Boston GA 31626-4000 Office: Jefferson Co Adult Ctr 575 S Water St Monticello FL 32344-1373

JOHNSON, AUSTON GILBERT, III, auditor; m. Mary Bosworth; 3 children. BS, Utah State U., 1976. CPA, Utah. Auditor State of Utah, Salt Lake City, 1996—. Mem. acctg. adv. bd. U. Utah Sch. Acctg., 1993; mem. sch. accountancy adv. coun. Utah State U., 1994—. With USN, 1969-73. Mem. AICPA (Outstanding Discussion Leader 1993), Utah Assn. CPAs (vice-chmn. state and local govt. com. 1987-88). Office: Office Utah State Auditor Utah State Capitol Complex East Office Bldg Ste 310 Salt Lake City UT 84114-2310 E-mail: austonjohnson@utah.gov.

JOHNSON, AVERY, professional basketball coach, retired professional basketball player; b. Mar. 25, 1965; m. Cassandra, 1991; children: Christianne, Avery Jr. Student, So. U., New Orleans. Player US Basketball League Palm Beach Stingrays, 1988, Seattle SuperSonics, 1988—90, Denver Nuggets, 1990, 2001—02, San Antonio Spurs, 1990—91, 1992—93, 1994—2001, Houston Rockets, 1991—92, Golden State Warriors, 1993—94, 2003—04, Dallas Mavericks, 2002—03, head coach, 2005—; asst. coach, 2004—05. Head coach NBA Western Conf. All-Star Team, 2006. Active Toys for Tots, Kids Now. Named NBA Coach of Yr., 2006; Named to NBA All-Interview First Team, 1997-98, 98-99, 99-2000; recipient Home Team Cmty. Svc. award Fannie Mae Found., NBA Sportsmanship award, 1997-98. Achievements include winning an NBA Championship as a member of the San Antonio Spurs, 1999. Avocations: golf, tennis. Office: Dallas Mavericks The Pavilion 2909 Taylor St Dallas TX 75226*

JOHNSON, BARBARA ELIZABETH, lawyer; b. Des Moines, Aug. 2, 1957; d. William Frederick and Dorothy Jane (Colvin) Spotz; m. Richard Gordon Johnson, Mar. 4, 1984. BS, Grove City Coll., Pa., 1979; JD, Coll. of William and Mary, 1984. Bar: Pa. 1984, U.S. Dist. Ct. (we. dist.) Pa. 1984, U.S. Ct. Appeals (3d and Fed. cirs.) 1984. Patent agt. NASA-Langley Rsch. Ctr., Hampton, Va., 1982-84; assoc. atty. The Webb Law Firm, Pitts., 1984-92, shareholder, dir., 1992—. Mng. dir. The Webb Law Firm, 2001-04; bd. dirs. Precision Staffing Svcs., Inc., Metro Family Practice. Recipient Alumni Achievement award, Grove City Coll., 2004. Mem.: Pitts. Intellectual Property Law Assn. (pres. 2000—01), Am. Chem. Soc. (chmn. Pitts. sect. 1995), Pitts. Chemists Club. Republican. Avocations: piano, writing, figure skating, auto repairing.

JOHNSON, BARBARA JEAN, retired judge, lawyer; b. Detroit, Apr. 9, 1932; d. Clifford Clarence and Orma Cecile (Boring) Barnhouse; m. Ronald Mayo Johnson, June 24, 1965; 1 child, Belinda Etezad. BS, U. So. Calif., 1953, JD, 1970. Bar: Calif. 1971. Ptnr. Angela, Burford, Johnson & Tookay, Pasadena, Calif., 1970-77; judge L.A. Mcpl. Ct., 1977-81, L.A. Superior Ct., 1981-97; ret., 1997. Lectr. U. So. Calif. Law Sch. profl. program; adj. prof. Southwestern U. Law Sch. Recipient Ernestine Stahlhut award, 1981. Mem. Calif. Judges Assn., 1977-98, Nat. Assn. Women Judges, 1980-98, Calif. Women Lawyers Assn. (pres. 1976-77), Women Lawyers Assn. LA (pres. 1975-76), Christian Legal Soc. Home: 1000 Prospect Blvd Pasadena CA 91103-2810

JOHNSON, BENJAMIN F., VI, economist, consultant; b. Kingston, NY, Sept. 17, 1952; s. Benjamin F. and Alice (Terry) J. BA in Econs., U. South Fla., 1974; MS in Econs., Fla. State U., 1977, PhD in Econs., 1982. Sr. utility analyst Office of Pub. Counsel, State of Fla., 1974-77; pres., cons. economist Ben Johnson Assocs., Inc., Tallahassee, Fla., 1977—. Contbr. articles to N.Y. Times, Pub. Utilities Fortnightly, profl. jours. Mem. Am. Econ. Assn. Office Phone: 850-893-8600.

JOHNSON, BERNETTE JOSHUA, state supreme court justice; b. Ascension Parish, La. d. Frank Joshua Jr. and Olivia W. Johnson. BA, Spelman Coll., Atlanta, 1964; JD, La. State U., 1969; LLD (hon.), Spelman Coll., 2001. Bar: La. Law intern Civil Rights divsn. U.S. Dept. Justice; judge La. Civil Dist. Ct., 1984-94, chief judge, 1994; assoc. justice La. Supreme Ct., New Orleans, 1994—. Legal svc. atty. New Orleans Legal Assistance Corp.; community organizer NAACP Legal Defense & Educational Fund, NYC; chair New Orleans Chapter So. Christian Leadership Conference. Bd. dirs. YMCA, New Orleans; chmn. bd. Learning Ctr., Greater St. Stephen Full Gospel Bapt. Ch.; bd. dirs. NOLAC, 1992-99. Named Woman of Yr., LaBelle chpt. Am. Bus. Women's Assn., 1994; Named one of Outstanding Women on Bench New Orleans Assn. Black Women Attorneys; recipient Ernest N. Morial award NOLAC, Daniel Byrd award NAACP, A.P. Tureaud Citizenship award NAACP, Margaret A. Brent Women Lawyers of Achievement award ABA. Office: La Supreme Ct 400 Royal St New Orleans LA 70130*

JOHNSON, BETSEY LEE, fashion designer; b. Hartford, Conn., Aug. 10, 1942; d. John Herman and Lena Virginia J.; m. John Cale, Apr. 4, 1966; 1 child, Lulu; m. Jeffrey Olivier, Feb. 7, 1981. Student, Pratt Inst., NYC, 1960-61; BA, U. Syracuse, 1964. Editorial asst. Mademoiselle mag., 1964-65; prin. designer Paraphernalia (owned by Puritan Fashions, Inc.), 1965—69; ptnr., co-owner Betsey, Bunky & Nini, NYC, 1969; designer Alvin Duskin Co., San Francisco, 1970; head designer Alley Cat by Betsey Johnson (div. LeDamor, Inc.), 1970—74; freelance designer jr. women's div. Butterick Pattern Co., 1971—75; designer Betsey Johnson's Kids Children Wear, Shutterbug, Inc., 1974—77, Jeanette Maternities, Inc., 1974-75, 1974—75; designer first line womens clothing Gant Shirtmakers, Inc., 1974—75; designer Tric-Trac by Betsey Johnson, Womens Knitwear, 1974—76; head designer jr. sportswear Star Ferry by Betsey Johnson and Michael Milea, 1975—77; owner, head designer B.J., Inc., NYC, 1978—; owner retail stores N.Y.C, L.A., San Francisco, Coconut Grove, Fla., Venice, Calif., Boston, Chgo., Seattle, London, Eng., Vancouver, B.C. Hon. chair. Fashion Targets Breast Cancer initiative, CFDA, 2004. Named to Fashion Walk of Fame, 2002; recipient Coty award, 1972, Timeless Talent award, CFDA, 1999, Nat. Breast Cancer Coalition award, 2004, Lifetime Achievement award, Signature Awards and NAWBO-NYC, 2005, Accessories Coun., 2005, Designer of the Yr. award, Am. Apparel and Footwear Assn., 2006. Mem. Coun. Fashion Designers Am., Women's Forum. Office: Betsey Johnson Co 251 E 60th St New York NY 10022*

JOHNSON, BOINE THEODORE, manufacturing executive, mayor; b. NYC, Dec. 17, 1931; s. Boine Theodore and Emma (Hall) J.; children: Boine Theodore III, Marc Ian, Jordan James, Jann Louise; m. Kathleen Piaggesi, July 11, 1992. BA cum laude, Williams Coll., 1953; MBA with high distinction (Baker scholar), Harvard, 1958. Instr. Harvard Bus. Sch., Cambridge, Mass., 1958—59; asst. to dir. corporate planning AMF Corp., NYC, 1959—62; mgr. mgmt. cons. div. Commonwealth Services Inc., NYC, 1962—66; mgr. corporate planning Gen. Electric Co., 1966—68; sr. v.p. corporate devel., gen. mgr. chem. div. Technicon Corp., Tarrytown, NY, 1968—79; v.p. Perkin Elmer Corp., Norwalk, Conn., 1979—81; v.p., gen. mgr. Capintec, Inc., Montvale, NJ, 1981—82; pres. Voland Corp., Hawthorne, NY, 1982—88; chmn. bd. Texture Techs. Corp., Scarsdale, NY, 1988—. Trustee, mayor Village of Scarsdale, N.Y., 1971-77; bd. dirs., vice chmn. Westchester County Assn. Served to lt., C.E. USNR, 1953-56. Mem. Sci. Apparatus Makers Assn., Theta Delta Chi (trustee edn. found. 1968-72, pres. Founders' Corp. 1966-87, pres. grand lodge 1969-71), Williams Club, Amateur Comedy Club (N.Y.C.), Town Club (Scarsdale), St. Botolph Club (Boston). Republican. Presbyterian. Home and Office: 18 Fairview Rd Scarsdale NY 10583-2136

JOHNSON, BRAD, professional football player; b. Marietta, Ga., Sept. 13, 1968; m. Nikkie Johnson. Postgrad in phys. edn., Fla. State Univ. Quarterback Tampa Bay Buccaneers, 2001—04, Wash. Redskins, 1999—2000, Minn. Vikings, 1992—98, 2005—. Involved Muscular Dystrophy Assn., Children's Miracle Net., Children's Hosp., Toys for Tots. Achievements include being a member of Super Bowl XXXVII Champion Tampa Bay Buccaneers, 2002. Office: 9520 Vikings Dr Eden Prairie MN 55344

JOHNSON, BRAD, state official; b. Lake Forest, Ill., Mar. 6, 1952; s. Kenneth A. and Claire Rabe Johnson; m. Lisa Storey. Dist. rep. to Congressman Ron Marlenee US Congress, 1983—84; mgr. Gallatin County Fairgrounds, 1985—89; sec. state State of Mont., Helena, 2005—. Co-chmn. Young Voters for the Pres. (Nixon), Ill., 1972; volunteer John Connally for Pres, Tex., 1980. Mem.: Mont. Rep. Party (exec. bd. 1984—89, 2003—). Republican. Office: Office Sec State State Capitol Rm 260 PO Box 202801 Helena MT 59620-2801 Office Phone: 406-444-2034. Fax: 406-444-3976.*

JOHNSON, BRADFORD MCCLURE, financial consultant, investor; BA in econs., Princeton U., NJ, 1972; MA, Univ. Paris, 1990. With Fed. Res. Bank of Kansas City, 1969—93; pres. Citibank N.A., 1971, Goldman Sachs & Co., 1972—77, Johnson, Lane, Space, Smith & Co., Inc., 1978—81, Sterne, Agee & Leach, Inc., 1991—93, Heron Hill Corp., Shawnee Mission, Kans., 1993—. Dir. First State Ban Corp., Albuquerque, 1994—; adv. dir. Ariz. Bancshare Inc., Flagstaff, 1998—. Co-editor: (book) Takeovers of Banks, 1983. Bd. chair The Children's Place, Kansas City, Mo., 2004—06. Mem.: SAR, N.Y. Soc. Security Analysts, Eagle Scout Assn., Mensa. Office: Heron Hill Corp PO Box 8208 Shawnee Mission KS 66208

JOHNSON, BRENDA L., university librarian; MLS, Rutgers U. Reference libr. Rutgers U., 1979, head interlibrary loan svcs. and NJ reference svcs.; libr. U. Mich., Ann Arbor, 1985—, assoc. univ. libr., 1997—, interim co-univ. libr., 2006—07. Office: Libr Adminstrn U Mich 818 Hatcher S Ann Arbor MI 48109-1205 Office Phone: 734-764-9356. Office Fax: 734-764-5080. E-mail: bljohn@umich.edu.

JOHNSON, BRENDA LAGRANGE, ambassador; BA, Duke U.; MA, Columbia U. Ptnr. BrenMer Industries, 1977—2005; tchr. Operation Head Start, Adminstrn. for Children and Families US Dept. Health & Human Svcs., supr., mem. nat. cancer advisory bd., nat. inst. health, 1989—94; mem. Nat. Fin. Com. Bush-Cheney Presdl. Campaign, 2004; U.S. amb. to Jamaica US Dept. State, Kingston, 2005—. Trustee President's advisory coun. on the arts John F. Kennedy Ctr. for Performing Arts Smithsonian Inst., 2002—.

JOHNSON, BROOKE BAILEY, broadcast executive; b. LA, May 12, 1951; d. Edwin Beauvais and Jeanne (Foote) Bailey; m. Peter Michael Johnson, Sept. 18, 1982; children: Bailey Peter, Lee Keating. BA, Northwestern U., 1973, MS in Journalism, 1974. Promotion dir. Sta. KGUN-TV, Tucson, 1975-77; asst. programming dir. Sta. WLS-TV, Chgo., 1977-82; dir. programming Sta. WABC-TV, NYC, 1982-89; became v.p. programming Arts & Entertainment Network, NYC, 1989, sr. v.p. programming and production, 1989—2000; cons. A&E; sr. v.p. and gen. mgr. The Food Network, NYC, 2003—04, pres., 2004—. Mem. NOW. Mem. Nat. Cable Acad., Cable TV Assn., NATAS, Nat. Assn. TV Program Execs. (Iris award), Kappa Alpha Theta. Office: The Food Network 1180 Avenue of the Americas New York NY 10036

JOHNSON, BRUCE, engineering educator; b. Hawarden, Iowa, Sept. 4, 1932; s. York and Dorothy Ellen (DeBruce) J.; m. Dorothy Jane Rylander, Aug. 27, 1955; children: Sharon Hilgart, Kristen Aiken. BS in Mech. Engring., Iowa State U., 1955; MS in Mech. Engring., Purdue U., 1962, PhD, 1965. Instr. U.S. Naval Acad., Annapolis, Md., 1957-59, assoc. prof., 1964-70, project dir. model basin, 1968-76, prof., 1970-99, Naval Sea Systems Command prof. hydrodynamics, 1975-87, dir. Hydromechanics Lab., 1976-87, dir. ocean engring. program, 1996-99, dir. spl. projects hydromechanics lab., 2000—, prof. emeritus, 2001—. Instr. Purdue U., 1959-64; chmn. 18th Am. Towing Tank Conf., 1977, U.S. Rep. Info. Com. Internat. Towing Tank Conf., 1975-84, chmn. symbols and terminology group, 1985-99, editor, pub. ITTC Symbols and Terminology List, 1996-99. Author: (with T. Gillmer) Introduction to Naval Architecture, 1982, (with D. Newman) Engineering Economic Analysis, 1994, (with J. Womack) A Guide to Fishing Vessel Stability, 2004; editor: (with B. Nehrling) Proc. of 18th Am. Towing Tank Conf, 1977; contbr. articles to profl. publs. Trustee Bauman Bible Telecasts, 1970-93, fin. chmn., 1990-93; mem. Bowie State U. Found., 1995-97. Served with USN, 1955-59. Recipient award for excellence in engring. teaching Western Electric Fund, 1971, Navy Meritorious Civilian Svc. award, 1994, 96, Navy Superior Civilian Svc. award, 1998, 00, Svc. Excellence award Naval Acad. Alumni Assn., 1998, Meritorious Pub. svc. award USCG, 2002; Ford Found. grantee, 1962-64. Fellow Soc. Naval Archs. and Marine Engrs. (chmn. Chesapeake Sailing Yacht Symposium 1985, 87, chmn. electronic media com. 2000-03, exec. com. 2000-03, chmn. fishing vessel ops. and safety panel 2001-05, co-chmn. small working vessel ops. and safety panel 2005-); mem. ASME, Am. Soc. Naval Engrs. (chmn. scholarship com. 1983-89, nat. coun. 1986-88, 89-91), Md. Capital Yacht Club (bd. dirs. 1986-93, commodore

1992), Naval Acad. Sailing Squadron, Chesapeake Bay Yacht Racing Assn. (pres. 1990). Unitarian Universalist. Achievements include rsch. in naval architecture, hydrodynamics. Home: 7101 Bay Front Dr Apt 523 Annapolis MD 21403 Office: Dept Naval Architecture and Ocean Engring US Naval Acad Annapolis MD 21402 E-mail: aronj@verizon.net.

JOHNSON, BRUCE CHR., librarian; Acting asst. chief, cataloging distbn. svc. Libr. of Congress, Washington. Skipper emeritus S.S.S. Columbia Ranger, Ship 361, Columbia, Md.; mem. Nat. Sea Scouting Com.; chair Sea Scout exhibit, Nat. Jamboree, 1989, 1993, 1997. Recipient Nat. Venturing Leadership award. Mem.: Assn. Libr. Collections and Tech. Services (pres. 2006—07, pres.-elect, mem. exec. bd., bd. dirs.), ALA. Achievements include leading Northeast Region Sea Exploring team to World Jamboree in Netherlands, 1995. Office: Libr of Congress Cataloging Distbn Svc 101 Independence Ave SE Washington DC 20540-4911 Office Phone: 202-707-1652. Office Fax: 202-707-3959. Business E-Mail: bjoh@loc.gov.*

JOHNSON, BRUCE E., former lieutenant governor, state legislator; b. Tripoli, Libya, May 25, 1960; m. Kelley Johnson; children Shane, Megan, Connor, Morgan Christine BS, Bowling Green State U., 1982; JD, Capital U., 1985. Mem. Ohio Senate from 3rd dist., Columbus, 1994—2001; chmn. Senate Judiciary Com.; chmn. Ways & Means Com.; mem. counsel Chester, Wilcox & Saxbe, Columbus; dir. OH Dept. Devel., Columbus, 2001—07; lt. gov. State of OH, Columbus, 2005—07. Recipient Watchdog of the Treasury, Crime Victims Witness Assn award for Outstanding Legis. Mem. Columbus Bar Assn., Ohio Bar Assn. Republican.*

JOHNSON, BRUCE EDWARD HUMBLE, lawyer; b. Columbus, Ohio, Jan. 22, 1950; s. Hugo Edward and M. Alice (Humble) J.; children: Marta Noble, Winslow Collins, Russell Scott. AB, Harvard U., 1972; JD, Yale U., 1977; MA, U. Cambridge, Eng., 1978. Bar: Wash. 1977, Calif. 1992. Atty. Davis Wright Tremaine LLP, Seattle, 1977—. Mem. oversight com. King County Gov. Access Channel, 1996—2001. Co-author: Advertising and Commerical Speech, A First Amendment Guide, 2d edit., 2004. Bd. dirs. Seattle Repertory Theatre, 1993—, pres., 1999-2001, chair, 2004-06; bd. dirs. Huntington's Dis. Soc. of Am., N.W. chpt., 2001—; mem. Nat. Coun. for Am. Theatre, 2005—. Mem. ABA (tort and ins. practice sect., media law and defamation torts com. chair 1999-2000). Office: Davis Wright Tremaine LLP 1201 3d Ave Ste 2200 Seattle WA 98101-3045 Office Phone: 206-628-7683, 206-628-7683. Business E-Mail: brucejohnson@dwt.com.

JOHNSON, BRUCE MARVIN, language educator; b. Chgo., Apr. 29, 1933; s. George A. and Elsie L. (Clausing) J.; m. Jean C. Kruger, June 29, 1957 (dec. Mar. 1, 2006); 1 son, Abram. BA, U. Chgo., 1952, Northwestern U., Evanston, Ill., 1954, MA, 1955, PhD, 1959. Instr. English U. Mich., 1958-62; asst. prof. English U. Rochester, NY, 1962-68, assoc. prof., 1968-76, chmn. dept. English, 1981-84, prof., 1976-92, prof. emeritus, 1992—. Author: Conrad's Models of Mind, 1971, True Correspondence: A Phenomenology of Thomas Hardy's Novels, 1983. Sr. fellow NEH, 1974-75; fellow Guggenheim Found., 1977-78 Democrat. Home: Apt 407 16540 Heron Coach Way Fort Myers FL 33908-5523 Office: U Rochester Dept English Rochester NY 14627 Office Phone: 585-275-4092.

JOHNSON, BRUCE ROSS, elementary school educator; b. La Porte, Ind., May 18, 1949; s. Egbert Johannes Daniel and Ruth Elvera (Johnson) J. BS, Ball State U., Muncie, Ind., 1971; ME, Valparaiso U., 1975; postgrad., Nat. Coll. Edn., Evanston, Ill., 1974, Beijing Normal U., 1988, Western Mich. U., U. Va., Ind. U. Purdue, Antioch U., Seattle, Calif State U. Cert. elem. sch. tchr., Ind. Vol. tchr. Peace Corps, St. Vincent, W.I., W.I., 1971-72; tchr. South Ctrl. Sch., Union Mills, Ind., 1972-76, 77—; tchr. gifted and talented Purdue U., 1995—97. Missionary tchr. Luth. Ch., Liberia, West Africa, 1976-77; vis. instr. U. London, 1974, U. Moscow, 1974, U. Paris, 1974; ednl. seminar China, 1988, Japan, 1990, Australia, 1993; guest lectr. dept. edn. Purdue U., 1995-2002. Contbr. articles to newspapers. Pres. People to People Internat., La Porte, Ind., 1981-83, trustee, Kansas City, Mo., 1983-88; bd. dirs. La Porte County Libr. Leasing Corp., 1988—; mem. ch. coun. Bethany Luth. Ch., La Porte, 1983-86, 90-93; LaPorte County Bicentennial Commn., 1975-76; v.p. Friends of La Porte County Libr., 1984-86, pres., 1986-88, 2005-07; chmn. books and coffee meet the author series LaPorte County Pub. Libr., 1985—; trustee La Porte County Hist. Soc., 1985-92, 94—; v.p. N.W. Ind. Geneal. Soc., 1981-82; pres. Cmty. Concert Assn., La Porte, 1984; mem. Pan Am. Games Com., 1986-87; mem. steering com. La Porte County Spelling Bee, 1979-91, chmn., 1981, 85, 90, 99, 04, LaPorte County Leadership, Inc., 1986-87; chmn. Miss. Valley coun. People-to-People, 1983-88; mem. bicentennial com. Bill of Rights, 1989-90; bd. dirs. LaPorte Literacy Coalition, 1997-02. Named Outstanding Young Men Am., 1985, State finalist NASA Tchr.-in-Space project, 1985; Ind. State Tchrs. Assn. scholar, 1970; recipient Dean Earl A. Johnson Outstanding Svc. award Ball State U., 1971, Lifetime Achievement award People to People, 2005, cert. of merit Ind. Dept. Edn., 1985, Samaritan award, 2006. Mem. NEA (life), Ind. State Tchrs. Assn., Amateur Music Club (pres. 1982-83), Little Theater Club (bd. dirs. 1980-83, 89-92), Lions (pres. 2000-01, bd. dirs. 1983-05), Phi Delta Kappa (life). Avocations: performing in musical theater, collecting foreign coins, travel, gardening. Home: 2012 Village Rd La Porte IN 46350-7874 Office: South Cen Community Schs 9808 S 600 W La Porte IN 46382-9600

JOHNSON, BRUCE S., law librarian, educator; married; 3 children. BA, Amherst Coll., 1970; JD, NYU, 1973; MLS, Rutgers U., 1978. Bar: NJ 1973. Assoc. Young, Rose & Millspaugh, Newark, 1973—76; reference libr. Law Libr. Seton Hall U. Sch. Law, Newark, 1977—78; chief reference libr. U. Mich. Sch. Law, Ann Arbor, 1978—84; assoc. prof. law, head Coleman Karesh Law Libr. U. SC Sch. Law, Columbia, 1984—92; prof. law, dir. Law Libr. Moritz Coll. Law, Ohio State U., Columbus, 1992—97, assoc. dean info. svcs., prof. law, 1997—. Contbr. articles to profl. jours. Mem.: ABA, Ohio State Bar Assn., Am. Assn. Law Librs. Office: Ohio State U Moritz Coll Law Drinko Hall 274B 55 W 12th Ave Columbus OH 43210 Home: 1847 Suffolk Rd Columbus OH 43221 Office Phone: 614-292-6691. E-mail: johnson.726@osu.edu.*

JOHNSON, C. NICHOLAS, dance company executive; b. Jan. 15, 1955; MFA in Dance/Drama, U. Ariz.; studied with, Stefan Niedzialkowski, Frank Hatchett, Richard Levi, De Marco, NYC. Assoc. artistic dir. Goldston & Johnson Sch. of Mimes; chief officer Mid-Am. Dance Theatre, Wichita, Kans.; asst. prof., dir. dance, modern dance, jazz, mime Coll. Fine Arts Wichita State U. Freelance tchr., dir., choreographer and performer various U.S. ballet schs. and univs. Performer Marcel Marceau World Ctr. Mime, Invisible People Mime Theatre, Internat. Children's Theatre Festival, Hong Kong. Kans. Arts Commn. fellow, 1999. Office: Wichita State U Sch Performing Arts-Dance PO Box 101 Wichita KS 67260-0001 Home Phone: 316-686-3640; Office Phone: 316-978-3645. Personal E-mail: alltheacreations@cox.net. Business E-Mail: nick.johnson@wichita.edu.

JOHNSON, C. TERRY, lawyer; b. Bridgeport, Conn., Sept. 24, 1937; s. Clifford Gustave and Evelyn Florence (Terry) J.; m. Suzanne Frances Chichy, Aug. 24, 1985; children: Laura Elizabeth, Melissa Lynne, Clifford Terry. AB, Trinity Coll., 1960; LLD, Columbia U., 1963. Bar: Ohio 1964, U.S. Ct. Appeals (6th cir.) 1966, U.S. Dist. Ct. (so. dist.) Ohio 1970. Legal dep. probate ct. Montgomery County, Dayton, Ohio, 1964-67; head probate dept. Coolidge Wall & Wood, Dayton, 1967-79, Smith & Schnacke, Dayton, 1979-89, Thompson, Hine and Flory, Dayton, 1989-92; head estate planning and probate group Dayton office Porter, Wright, Morris & Arthur, Dayton, 1992—. Frequent lectr. on estate planning to various profl. orgns. Contbr. articles to profl. jours. Fellow Am. Coll. Trust and Estate Counsel; mem. Ohio Bar Assn. (bd. govs. estate planning, trust and probate law sect., chmn. 1993-95), Dayton Bar Assn. (chmn. probate com. 1992-94), Ohio State Bar Found. (trustee 1995-2000), Ohio CLE Inst. (trustee 1995-99, chair 1998-99), Dayton Legal Secs. Assn. (hon.), Dayton Bicycle Club. Home: 8307 Rhine Way Centerville OH 45458-3017 Office: Porter Wright Morris & Arthur 1 S Main St Ste 1600 Dayton OH 45402-2028 Office Phone: 937-449-6701. E-mail: cjohnson@porterwright.com.

JOHNSON, CAGE SAUL, hematologist, educator; b. New Orleans, Mar. 31, 1941; s. Cage Spooner and Esther Georgianna (Saul) J.; m. Shirley Lee O'Neal, Feb. 22, 1968; children: Stephanie, Michelle. Student, Creighton U., 1958-61, MD, 1965. Cert. Am. Bd. Internal Medicine, 1972, Am. Bd. Hematology, 1974. Intern U. Cin., 1965-66, resident, 1966-67, U. So. Calif., 1969-71, instr. LA, 1971-74, asst. prof., 1974-80, assoc. prof., 1980-88, dir. Comprehensive Sickle Cell Ctr., 1991—, prof., 1988—. Chmn. adv. com. Calif. Dept. Health Svcs., Sacramento, 1977—; dir. Hemoglobinopathy Lab., L.A., 1976—; bd. dirs. Sicke Cell Self-Help Assn., L.A., 1982-86, Team HEAL, 2002-. Contbr. numerous articles to profl. jours. Dir. Sickle Cell Disease Rsch. Found., L.A., 1986-94; active Nat. Med. Fellowships, Inc., Chgo., 1979—; chmn. rev. com. NIH, Washington, 1986-91; chmn. adv. com., 1995-97, mem. adv. coun., 1997-2002. Major U.S. Army, 1967-69, Vietnam. Fellow N.Y. Acad. Scis., Am. Coll. Angiology; mem. Am. Soc. Hematology, Am. Fedn. Clin. Rsch., Western Soc. Clin. Investigation, Internat. Soc. Biorheology, E.E. Just Soc. (sec.-treas. 1985-93, pres. 1994-95, sec. 1996—). Avocation: restoring antique automobiles. Office: 2025 Zonal Ave Rm R304 Los Angeles CA 90089-0110 Home Phone: 323-294-0187; Office Phone: 323-442-1259. E-mail: cagejohn@usc.edu.

JOHNSON, CALVIN, professional football player; b. Tyrone, Ga., Sept. 25, 1985; s. Calvin and Arica Johnson. Studied, Ga. Inst. Tech., 2003—06. Wide receiver Detroit Lions, 2007—. Named Rookie Yr., ACC, 2004; named to First Team Freshman All-America, AP, 2004, First Team All-American, 2005—06, First Team Atlantic Coast Conf., 2004—06; recipient Beletnikoff award, NCAA, 2006. Achievements include being second overall pick in 2007 NFL Draft. Office: Detroit Lions 222 Republic Dr Allen Park MI 48101*

JOHNSON, CANDICE ELAINE BROWN, pediatrician, educator; b. Cin., Mar. 21, 1946; d. Paul Preston and Naomi Elizabeth Brown; m. Thomas Raymond Johnson, June 30, 1973; children: Andrea Eleanor, Erik Albert. BS, U. Mich., 1968; PhD Microbiology, Case Western Reserve U., 1973, MD, 1976. Diplomate Am. Bd. Pediat., 1981. Intern, resident in pediat. Rainbow Babies and Children's Hosp./Met. Gen. Hosp., Cleve., 1976-78; fellow in ambulatory pediatrics Met. Gen. Hosp., 1978-79; asst. prof. pediat. Case Western Res. U., Cleve., 1980-90, assoc. prof., 1990-97; prof. pediat. U. Colo., Denver, 1997—; pediatrician Children's Hosp., Denver, 1997—. Mem. rev. panel NIH, Washington, 1993; faculty sen. Case Western Res. U., 1988-91; mem. spkrs. bur. Merck, GlaxoSmithKline, Abbott Labs. Contbr. articles profl. jours. Mem. Am. Acad. Pediat., Pediat. Infectious Disease Soc., Infectious Disease Soc. Am., Soc. for Pediat. Rsch., So. Utah Wilderness Alliance, Sierra Club. Home: 2290 Locust St Denver CO 80207-3943

JOHNSON, CARL FREDERICK, marriage and family therapist; b. July 18, 1947; BA in Psychology, Northwestern U., 1969; MA in Clin. Psychology, Ga. State U., 1975. Lic. marriage and family therapist, Ga. Grad. tchg. asst. Ga. State U., Atlanta, 1972-73; family therapist Bridge Family Ctr., Atlanta, 1973-80; pvt. practice The Family Workshop, Atlanta, 1979—. Adj. instr. Dekalb C.C., Clarkston, Ga., 1981-82; appointee Ga. Composite Bd. Profl. Counselors, Social Workers and Marriage and Family Therapists, 1985-93; exec. dir. Ga. Assn. Marriage and Family Therapy, Atlanta, 1997—. Contbr. articles to profl. jours. Fellow: Am. Assn. for Marriage and Family Therapy (Divsnl. Contbn. award 1993, Outstanding Contbn. to Marriage and Family Therapy award 2001); mem.: Assn. Marital and Family Therapy Regulatory Bds. (founder, pres. 1987—91, coord. devel. nat. licensing exam in marital and family therapy 1989—92), Ga. Assn. for Marriage and Family Therapy (chair legis. affairs com. 1980—85, 1993—95, Outstanding Contbn. award 1983, 1985, 1993, Lifetime Achievement/Disting. Svc. award 1996). Home: 751 N Parkwood Rd Decatur GA 30030-5023 Office: Family Workshop Ste 200 2200 Century Pkwy NE Atlanta GA 30345 Office Phone: 404-633-3347.

JOHNSON, CARL RANDOLPH, chemist, educator; b. Charlottesville, Va., Apr. 28, 1937; BS, Med. Coll. Va., 1958; PhD in Chemistry, U. Ill., 1962. NSF rsch. fellow chemistry Harvard U., 1962; from asst. to prof. chemistry Wayne State U., Detroit, 1962—90, Disting. prof., 1990—2001, chair dept. chemistry, 1997—2001, Disting. prof. emeritus, 2002—. Humboldt sr. scientist, 1991; bd. dirs. Organic Syntheses, Inc. Mem. adv. bd.: Jour. Organic Chemistry, 1976—81. Alfred P. Sloan fellow, 1965-68. Mem. Am. Chem. Soc. (assoc. editor jour. 1984-89, Harry and Carol Mosher award 1992, Arthur C. Cope Sr. Scholar award 2002). Achievements include research in organic sulfur chemistry, especially sulfoxides and sulfoximines, exploratory synthetic chemistry, synthesis of compounds of potential medicinal activity, organometallic chemistry, synthesis of natural products, enzymes in synthesis. Home: 118 Wilton Coves Dr Hartfield VA 23071 E-mail: crj@chem.wayne.edu.

JOHNSON, CARLA CONRAD, library dean; b. Cleve., June 10, 1948; d. James Procop and Joanne Graham Conrad; m. Roger Jeffrey Freeman, Mar. 23, 1979 (div. 1995); children: Jason Hale Freeman, Johanna Erica Freeman; m. Jeffery Harry Johnson, 1997. BA, U. Pa., 1969; MLS, SUNY, 1982; MS in Art Edn., Alfred U., 1988. Visual resources asst. Scholes Libr. Ceramics, NYS Coll. Ceramics Alfred U., NY, 1979—85, asst. libr., visual resources & art ref., Scholes Libr. Ceramics, NYS Coll. Ceramics, 1985—90, assoc. libr., visual resources & art ref., Scholes Libr. Ceramics, NYS Coll. Ceramics, 1990—95, dir., Scholes Libr. Ceramics, NYS Coll. Ceramics, 1993—, libr., 1995—, dean librs., 2005—. Cons. Vassar Coll., Art Libr., Poughkeepsie, NY, 1994; evaluator NSF Industry U. Ctr. Glass Rsch., Pa., 1995—2005; evaluator Internat. Mats. Inst. New Functionality in Glasses NSF, 1995—. Editor: (reference book) The Visual Resources Directory: Art Slide and Photograph Collections in the United States and Canada, 1995 (Worldwide Books Publ. award, Art Libraries Soc. N.Am., 1997); contbg. editor: (book) Fusion: A Centennial History of the New York State College of Ceramics, 2003. Recipient Chancellor's award for Excellence in Librarianship, SUNY, 1993; grantee Rsch. and Publ. grant, The Visual Resources Directory, Samuel H. Kress Found., 1992. Mem.: Visual Resources Assn. (pres. 1990—92), Am. Ceramic Soc. (design divsn. chair 1998—99), SUNY Librarians Assn., SUNY Coun. Libr. Directors (sec. 2002—04, chair elect, program chair 2005—06, chair 2006—), Phi Kappa Phi (chpt. pres. 1992—93). D-Liberal. Avocations: book collecting, photography, drawing, painting. Office: Alfred U Scholes Libr 2 Pine St Alfred NY 14802-1297 Home Phone: 607-324-7431.

JOHNSON, CAROLYN ELIZABETH, librarian; b. Oakland, Calif., May 29, 1921; d. Ferdinand Orin and Clara Wells (Humphrey) Hassler; m. Benjamin Alfred Johnson, Feb. 12, 1943; children: Robin Rebecca, Anne Elizabeth, Delia Mary. BA, U. Calif.-Berkeley, 1946; cert. libr., Calif. State U. Fullerton, 1960; MLS, Immaculate Heart Coll., 1968. Cert. libr. Calif. Asst. children's libr. Fullerton Pub. Libr., 1951—59, coord. children's svcs., 1959—81, city libr., 1981—90, ret., 1990, apptd. curator Mary Campbell collection hist. children's lit., 1990. Part-time instr. Rio Hondo City Coll., Whittier, Calif., 1970—72, Calif. State U.-Fullerton, 1972—77; vice chmn. 3d Pacific Rim Conf. Coun., 1983—86; mem. Korczak award com. U.S. Bd. Books for Young People, 1988. Author: (book) The Art of Walter Crane, 1988. Mem. CityLights; founding bd. dirs. Youth Sci. Ctr., Fullerton, 1958; mem. Libr. Tech. Tng. Adv. Com., Fullerton Coll., 1970; chmn. adv. bd. YWCA Child Devel. Ctr., 1992—; bd. dirs. Fullerton Pub. Libr. Found., mem. endowment fund, 1994, sec., 1995; bd. dirs. Friends of the Fullerton Pub. Libr. Named Profl. Woman of Yr., North Orange County YWCA, 1986, Woman of Yr., Fullerton C. of C., 1990, North Orange County YWCA, 2003. Mem.: LWV, AAUW, ALA, PTA (life), So. Calif. Coun. on Lit. for Children and Young People (pres. 1979—81, Dorothy C. McKenzie award 1987), Orange County Libr. Assn. (v.p.), Calif. Libr. Assn. (chmn. children's service div.), Theta Sigma Phi, Phi Beta Kappa. Methodist. Home: 644 Princeton Cir E Fullerton CA 92831-2728

JOHNSON, CARRIE CLEMENTS, executive; b. Atlanta, Jan. 2, 1931; d. Emanuel G. and Lucile Clements; 1 child, Alfia Katherine. BA, Morris Brown Coll., Atlanta, 1951; MA, Columbia U., NYC, 1954; DEd, SUNY Buffalo, 1978. Tchr. Fulton County Schs., Atlanta, 1951—54, 1955; dir. Career Planning Morris Brown Coll., Atlanta, 1961—67; assoc. prof., asst. prof. Buffalo State Coll., 1967—86; dir. affirmative action, staff devel. Fulton County Schs., Atlanta, 1986—95; CEO Johnson & Johnson, Atlanta, 1996—. Author: Career Opportunities for the Minorities, 1974. Bd. dirs. Atlanta br. NAACP; mem. pers. bd. Fulton County Cathechist, Atlanta, 2003—. Named Woman of Yr., Health Bus. League Atlanta, 2005; recipient edn. award, Alpha Kappa Alpha, 1984. Mem.: LWV, Zeta Phi Beta. Avocations: piano, attending plays and concerts. Home: 3965 Old Fairburn Rd SW Atlanta GA 30331

JOHNSON, CARYN ELAINE See GOLDBERG, WHOOPI

JOHNSON, CHAD, professional football player; b. Miami, Fla., Jan. 9, 1978; Student, Langston U., Okla., 1996; grad. in Phys. Ed., Oreg. State U., 2000. Wide receiver Cin. Bengals, 2001—. Named to AFC Pro Bowl Team, 2003—06, All-AFC Team, Pro Football Weekly, 2004, All-Pro 2nd Team, Coll. & Pro Football Weekly, 2004, NFL All-Pro Team, 2005—06. Achievements include leading the AFC in receiving yards in all three seasons from 2003 to 2005; led NFL in receiving yards, 2006. Office: Cin Bengals 1 Paul Brown Stadium Dr Cincinnati OH 45202*

JOHNSON, CHARLES, political blogger; Co-owner software mktg. firm CodeHead Technologies; blog creator, host LittleGreenFootballs.com. Named Best Internat. Blog, Washington Post Reader Poll, 2004, Best Israel Advocacy Blog, Jerusalem Post, 2005; named one of Top 25 Web Celebs, Forbes mag., 2007. Avocation: jazz guitar.*

JOHNSON, CHARLES BARTLETT, corporate financial executive; b. Montclair, NJ, Jan. 6, 1933; s. Rupert Harris and Florence (Endler) J.; m. Ann Demarest Lutes, Mar. 26, 1955; children: Charles E., Holly, Sarah, Gregory, William, Jennifer, Mary (dec.). BA, Yale U., 1954. With R.H. Johnson & Co., NYC, 1954-55; pres. Franklin Distbrs., Inc., 1957-97; chmn. Franklin Resources, Inc., 1969—, CEO, 1969—2004. Bd. dirs. various Franklin and Templeton Mut. Funds; bd. govs. Investment Co. Inst., 1973-88. Trustee Crystal Springs Uplands Sch., 1984-92; bd. dirs. Peninsula Cmty. Found., 1986-96, San Francisco Symphony, 1984-2002; bd. overseers Hoover Instn., 1993—. 1st lt. US Army, 1955—57. Named one of Forbes Richest Americans, 1999—, Forbes Executive Pay, 1999—, World's Richest People, Forbes Mag., 2001—. Mem. Nat. Assn. Securities Dirs. (bd. govs. 1990-92, 95-96, chmn. 1992), Commonwealth Club of Calif. (bd. dirs. 1995-97). Office: Franklin Resources Inc One Franklin Pkwy San Mateo CA 94403-1906

JOHNSON, CHARLES E., federal agency administrator; married; 6 children. BS, Brigham Young U., 1960. CPA. Various positions in public acctg. KPMG; dir. planning and budget Office of Gov., Utah, 1991—92, chief of staff to Gov. Utah, 1992—97; vice chmn. bd. strategic direction Garff-Warner Orgn., 1997—2001; chmn. Utah State Bd. Regents, 1997—2002, mem., 1997—2004; v.p. Huntsman LLC, 2001—04; pres. Huntsman Cancer Found., 2001—04; CFO EPA, 2004—05; asst. sec. budget, tech. and fin. US Dept. Health and Human Svcs., Washington, 2005—. Office: US Dept Health and Human Svcs Hubert H Humphrey Bldg 200 Independence Ave SW Rm 514G Washington DC 20201 Office Phone: 202-690-6396. Office Fax: 202-690-5405. E-mail: Charles.Johnson@hhs.gov.

JOHNSON, CHARLES FOREMAN, architectural firm executive; b. Plainfield, NJ, May 28, 1929; s. Charles E. and E. Lucile Johnson; m. Beverly Jean Hinnendale, Feb. 19, 1961; children: Kevin, David; m. Susie Mills, 2005. Student, Union Jr. Coll., 1947-48; BArch, U. So. Calif., 1958; postgrad., UCLA, 1959-60. Draftsman Wigton-Abbott, P.C., Plainfield, 1945—52; arch., cons. graphic, interior and engring. sys. designer, 1953—; designer, draftsman H.W. Underhill, Arch., LA, 1953—55; tchg. asst. U. So. Calif., LA, 1954—55; designer with Carrington H. Lewis, Arch., Palos Verdes, Calif., 1955—56; grad. arch. Ramo-Wooldridge Corp., LA, 1956—58; tech. dir. Atlas Weapon Sys. Space Tech. Labs., LA, 1958—60; advanced planner and sys. engr. Minuteman Weapon Sys. TRW, LA, 1960—64, dir. staff ops. divsn., 1964—68; cons. N.Mex. Regional Med. Program and N.Mex. State Dept. Hosps., 1968—70; prin. Charles F. Johnson, arch., LA, 1953—68, Santa Fe, 1968—88, Carefree, Ariz., 1988—97, Carpenteria, Calif., 1998—2003, Green Valley, Ariz., 2003—. Founder Keva West LLC, owner and operator Keva Juice Smoothie stores; freelance archtl. photographer, Santa Fe, 1971—; tchr. archtl. apprentice program, 1974—; program writer, workshop leader, keynote spkr. Mich. Archtl. Design Competition, 1993; keynote spkr. Mex. Inst. Tech. y de Estudios Superiores, 1993; lectr., spkr., judge III Bienal Arch. and Urbanism Costa Rica, 1996. Major archtl. works include: residential bldgs. in Calif., 1955-66; Bashein Bldg. at Los Lunas (N.Mex.) Hosp. and Tng. Sch., 1969, various residential bldgs., Santa Fe, 1973—, Kurtz Home, Dillon, Colo., 1981, Whispering Boulders Home, Carefree, 1981, Hedrick House, Santa Fe, 1983, Kole House, Green Valley, Ariz., 1984, Casa Largo, Santa Fe (used for film The Man Who Fell to Earth), 1974, Rubel House, Santa Fe, 1986, Smith House, Carefree, 1987, Klopfer House, Santa Fe, 1988, Janssen House, Carefree, 1988, Art Start Gallery, 1988, Dr. Okun's House, 1990, Luterback House, Carefree, 1992, Phillips House, Carefree, 1992, Balagura House, Santa Fe, 1993, Davis House and Guest House of Rio Rico, AZ, 2004; master plan cons. Sky Ranch devel., N.Mex.; subject mag. articles, projects in books, shown on TV; contbr. articles on facility planning and mgmt. to profl. pubs.; contbr. archtl. photographs to mags. in U.S., Eng., France, Japan and Italy; contbr. articles on facility mgmt., planning info. sys. to profl. jours. Pres. Santa Fe Coalition for the Arts, 1977; set designer Santa Fe Fiesta Melodrama, 1969, 71, 74, 77, 78, 81, Ariz. Audiophile Soc., 1997; designer Jay Miller & Friends Fiesta float, 1970-88 (winner 20 awards); started Keva West LLC, owns and oper. Keva Juice smoothie stores. Named one of Top 100 Archs., Archtl. Digest mag., 1991. Mem. Ariz. Audiophile Soc. (bd. dirs.), Delta Sigma Phi. Avocations: music, photography, architecture. Home: 1130 Placita Cotonia Green Valley AZ 85614

JOHNSON, CHARLES L., II, military officer; BSCE, USAF Acad., 1972; MS in Engring. Adminstrn. and Law, George Washington U., 1976; grad., Air Command and Staff Coll., 1986, Air War Coll., 1991, Def. Sys. Mgmt. Coll., 1993; grad. in Exec. Devel., U. Ill., 1995. Commd. 2d lt. USAF, 1972, advanced through grades to lt. gen., 2006; UH-1N/CH-3E instr. pilot, chief scheduling and tng. 89th Mil. Airlift Wing, Andrews AFB, Md., 1973-78; AB-212 instr. pilot Joint DOD Helicopter Tech. Asst. Field Team Royal Saudi Air Force, Taif Air Base, Saudi Arabia, 1978-79; C-141 flight examiner, chief pilot, chief current ops. 60th Mil. Airlift Wing, Travis

AFB, Calif., 1980-83; chief spl. actions and studies group Airlift and Trainers Sys. Program Office, Wright-Patterson AFB, Ohio, 1983-85; chief C-17 program divsn. Mil. Airlift Command, Scott AFB, Ill., 1986-90; mil. asst. to asst. sec. of Air Force for acquisition The Pentagon, Washington, 1991-92; comdr. 97th Ops. Group 97th Air Mobility Wing, Altus AFB, Okla., 1992-93; dir. C-141 Sys. Program Office Warner Robins Air Logistics Ctr., Robins AFB, Ga., 1993-96; program dir. C-17 Sys. Program Office Aero. Sys. Ctr., Wright-Patterson AFB, Ohio, 1996-99; dir. logistics, Hdqrs. Air Mobility Command Scott AFB, Ill., 1999; dir. plans and programs, Hdqrs. Air Mobility command, 1999-2000; comdr. Oklahoma City Air Logistics Ctr., Tinker AFB, Okla., 2000—03; comdr. Electronic Sys. Ctr. Hanscom AFB, Mass., 2003—. Decorated Legion of Merit with one oak leaf cluster, Meritorious Svc. medal with five oak leaf clusters, Meritorious Svc. medal with six oak leaf clusters, Air Force Commendation medal with one oak leaf cluster, Disting. Svc. medal, Aerial Achievement medal. Office: Hanscom AFB 9 Eglin St Hanscom Afb MA 01731-2109 E-mail: charles.johnson@hanscom.af.mil.

JOHNSON, CHARLES OWEN, retired lawyer; b. Monroe, La., Aug. 18, 1926; s. Clifford U. and Laura (Owen) Johnson. BA, Tulane U., 1946, JD, 1969; LLB, Harvard U., 1948; LLM, Columbia U., 1955. Bar: La. 1949. Pvt. practice, Monroe, 1949-50; mem. law editl. staff West Pub. Co., St. Paul, 1953; atty. Office of Chief Counsel, IRS, Washington, 1955-79, chief Ct. Appeals br. Tax Ct. divsn., 1968-79. Author: (book) The Geneology of Several Allied Famillies, 1961. With AUS, 1950—52. Fellow: Samuel Victor Constant Soc.; mem.: S.R. (past pres. D.C. soc.), SAR (past pres. D.C. soc.), Va. Hist. Soc., Miss. Hist. Soc., Nat. Gavel Soc. (past treas., past pres.), Nat. Lawyers Club, La. Bar Assn., Fed. Bar Assn., Royal Order Scotland, Va. Geneal. Soc., The Mil. and Hospitaller Order St. Lazarus Jerusalem, Soc. King Charles Martyr, New Eng. Ancestry Alliance (pres.), St. Nicholas Soc. City of N.Y., St. David's Soc. of N.Y., Harvard Club NYC, Nat. Hugenot Soc. (genealogist gen.), Plymouth Hereditary Soc. (past gov. gen.), Round Table Club of New Orleans, Nat. Soc. Sons and Daus. of Antebellum Planters 1607-1861 (past pres. gen.), Harvard Club Boston, Army and Navy Club Washington, Order Scions Colonial Cavaliers 1640-1660 (gov., founding gov.), Sons and Daus. Colonial and Antebellum Bench and Bar 1565-1861 (founding pres. gen. 1994—98), Soc. Cin., Mil. Order Stars and Bars (past judge adv. gen.), First Families of Ga. (past chancellor gen.), Soc. Descs. Colonial Clergy (past chancellor gen.), Soc. Descs. Old Plymouth Colony, Jamestowne Soc., Sons and Daus. of Province and Republic of West Fla. 1763-1810 (past gov.), La. Colonials, Soc. Desc. Jersey Settlers, Huguenot Soc. La. (past pres.), Huguenot Soc. S.C., Sons and Daus. Pilgrims (past treas., 2d dep. gov. gen.), Royal Soc. St. George, St. Andrew's Soc. Washington, Sons Union Vets, Nat. Soc. Desc. Early Quakers (past nat. presiding clk.), Soc. Colonial New Eng. (past gov. gen. nat. soc.), SCV, Soc. of 1812 (past pres. D.C. soc.), Soc. Colonial Wars (past dep. gov. D.C. soc., lt. gov., gov.), Order of the First Families of Conn., 1631-1662 (past gov. gen.), Order Descs. Ancient and Honorable Artillery Co. (past gov. gen.), The Hereditary Order of the Families of the Pres. and First Ladies of Am. (founding mem., atty. gen.), Order Descs. Colonial Physicians and Chirurgiens (past. pres. gen.), Order First Families R.I. and Providence Plantations 1636-1647 (past gov. gen.), Hereditary Order First Families of Mass. (past registrar gen., past gov. gen.), Order First Families Miss. 1699-1817 (gov. gen. 1967—69), Order Founders and Patriots of Am. (past gov. D.C., past geneal. gen., past dep. historian gen.), Hereditary Order Descs. Colonial Govs. (past gov. gen.), Order Ams. of Armorial Ancestry (past pres.). Home: Cystal Plz Apt 809 S 2111 Jefferson Davis Hwy Arlington VA 22202-3137 Home (Winter): Patrician Condominiums Apt 223 3450 S Ocean Blvd Palm Beach FL 33480

JOHNSON, CHARLES RICHARD, writer, teacher; b. Evanston, Ill., Apr. 23, 1948; s. Benjamin Lee and Ruby Elizabeth (Jackson) J.; m. Joan New, June 1970; children: Malik, Elizabeth. BA, So. Ill. U., 1971, MA, 1973; postgrad., SUNY, Stony Brook, 1973-76; PhD in Philosophy; ArtsD (hon.), Northwestern U., 1994; LHD (hon.), Southern Ill. U., 1995; LittD (hon.), SUNY, Stony Brook, 1999. Cartoonist, reporter Chgo. Tribune, 1969-70; mem. art staff St. Louis Proud, 1971-72; asst. prof. U. Wash., Seattle, 1976-79, assoc. prof., 1979-82, prof. of English, 1982—, dir. Creative Writing Dept., S. Wilson and Grace M. Pollock Prof.; writer-in-residence Seattle Post Intelligencer, 2007—. Fiction editor Seattle Rev., 1978-98; dir. Assoc. Writing Programs Awards series in short fiction, 1979-81, bd. dirs., 1983—. Author: Faith and the Good Thing, 1974, Oxherding Tale, 1982 (Gov.'s Award Lit. State of Wash. 1983), Being and Race: Black Writing since 1970, 1988 (Gov.'s Award Lit. 1989), The Middle Passage, 1990 (Nat. Book Award 1990), All This and Moonlight, 1990, (with Ron Chernow) In Search of a Voice, 1991, Dreamer, 1998; short story collections: The Sorcerer's Apprentice, 1986; scriptwriter: (PBS series) Charlie's Pad, 1970, Visions ("Charlie Smith and the Fritter Tree"), 1978, Up and Coming, 1981, (with John Alman) Booker, 1983, Y.E.S., Inc., 1983; screenwriter: Booker, 1985 (Internat. Prix Jeunesse Award, 1985, Writers Guild Award, 1985); cartoonist: (collections) Black Humor, 1970, Half-Past Nation Time, 1972; contbr. of cartoons to periodicals including Ebony, Chgo. Tribune, Jet, Black World, Players Named journalism alumus of yr. So. Ill. U., 1981; recipient Callaloo Creative Writing award, 1983, Citation outstanding writers' sect. Puschcart Prize, 1984, Lifetime Achievement in the Arts Award Corp Coun. for Arts, 2000, Achievement Award Pacific Northwest Writers Assn., 2001. Office: care Atheneum Pub Macmillan Pub Co 866 3rd Ave New York NY 10022-6221 also: Dept English Univ Washington A-406 Padelford Seattle WA 98195-4330 Office Phone: 206-543-4233. E-mail: chasjohn@u.washington.edu.*

JOHNSON, CHARLES WILLIAM, state supreme court justice; b. Tacoma, Mar. 16, 1951; m. Dana Johnson. BA in Economics, U. Wash., 1974; JD, U. Puget Sound, 1976. Bar: Wash. 1977. Former atty. priv. practice; justice Wash. Supreme Ct., 1991—, assoc. chief justice. Adjunct prof. Seattle U. Law Sch., 1977—91; co-chair Wash. State Minority and Justice Commn., Equal Civil Justice Funding Task Force. Mem. bd. dirs. Wash. Assn. Children and Parents; mem. vis. com. U. Wash. Sch. Social Work; bd. visitors Seattle U. Sch. Law; liaison ltd. practice bd., co-chair BJA subcom. on juc. svcs.; mem. Am. Inns of Ct., World Affairs Coun. Pierce County. Mem. Wash. State Bar Assn., Tacoma-Pierce County Bar Assn. (Liberty Bell award young lawyers sect. 1994). Avocations: sailing, downhill skiing, bicycling. Office: Wash State Supreme Ct PO Box 40929 Olympia WA 98504-0929*

JOHNSON, CHERLYN ANN, education educator; b. New Orleans, Dec. 27, 1969; d. Isadore and Kathleen Marie Johnson. BA, Dillard U., 1992; MA, U. Akron, 1995; PhD, Syracuse U., 2000. Tchg. asst. U. Akron, 1993—95, English tchr., 1994—95; instr. Syracuse U., 1995—99; tchr. English, summer supr. Syracuse Ednl. Opportunity Ctr.-SUNY, 1999—2000; asst. prof. Va. State U., 2001—. Rev. Multicultural Perspectives Jour., 2002—; author: Guests at an Ivory Tower: The Challenges Black Students Experience While Attending a Predominantly White University, 2005. English Edn. Cultural Diversity grant, Nat. Coun. of Tchrs. of English, 1999. Mem.: Am. Edn. Rsch. Assn., Nat. Coun. of Tchrs. of English, Nat. Assn. of Multicultural Edn. Democrat. Baptist. Avocations: reading, writing, travel. Office: Va State U PO Box 9072 Petersburg VA 23806 Business E-Mail: cajohnso@vsu.edu.

JOHNSON, CHRISTOPHER D., lawyer; b. Little Rock, 1952; BA magna cum laude, Princeton U., 1974; JD, U. Va., 1977. Bar: Ariz. 1977, registered: US Dist. Ct., Ariz. 1977, US Ct. Appeals (9th cir.) 1978. Ptnr. Squire, Sanders & Dempsey LLP, Phoenix, chmn., Corp. Fin. Practice Group. Contbr. articles to profl. jours.; spkr. in field. Bd. dir. Enterprise Network, Ariz. Tech. Incubator. Mem.: Ariz. Software & Internet Assn., State Bar Ariz. (exec. coun. mem. 1979—95, chmn. Securities Regulation Sect. 1994—95), Order of Coif. Office: Squire Sanders & Dempsey LLP Two Renaissance Sq 40 N Central Ave Ste 2700 Phoenix AZ 85004-4498 Office Phone: 602-528-4046. Office Fax: 602-253-8129. Business E-Mail: cjohnson@ssd.com.

JOHNSON, CLARKE COURTNEY, financial consultant, educator; b. Wisconsin Rapids, Wis., July 11, 1936; s. Julius and Esther (Larsen) L. BSEE, U. Wis., 1958; MSIM, Purdue U., 1962, PhD, 1972. Asst. prof., asst. dean U. Wis.-Milw., 1966-72; vis. prof. Boston U. Sch. Mgmt., 1973-75; assoc. prof., assoc. dean DePaul U. Coll. Commerce, Chgo., 1975-77; prof., dean Iona Coll. Sch. Bus., New Rochelle, NY, 1977-79; prof. fin. Pace U. Grad. Sch. Bus., NYC, 1979-98, chmn. dept., 1985-98, chmn. faculty coun. Sch. Bus., 1996-98; ret., 1998; pres. C. Johnson and Assocs., 1998—. Cons. in field Contbr. articles to profl. jours. Served with USAF, 1958-61. Mem. Am. Fin. Assn., Am. Econs. Assn., Fin. Mgmt. Assn., Eta Kappa Nu, Beta Gamma Sigma. Home: 333 E 79th St Apt 20Y New York NY 10021-0961 Home Phone: 212-535-9411; Office Phone: 212-535-9411. E-mail: ckcjohnson@aol.com.

JOHNSON, CLAY, III, federal official; b. Mar. 22, 1946; m. Anne S. Johnson; children: Robert, Weldon. BA, Yale U., 1968; MA, MIT, 1970. Appointments dir. for Gov. State of Tex., Austin, 1995—99, chief of staff to Gov., 1999—2000; exec. dir. Bush-Cheney Transition, Washington, 2000—01; asst. to Pres. for presdl. pers. & dep. to chief of staff The White House, Washington, 2001—03; dep. dir. for mgmt. Office Mgmt. & Budget Exec. Office of the Pres., Washington, 2003—. Dir. mktg. Horchow and Neiman Marcus Mail Order Cos., 1981—82, pres., 1983—91; COO Dallas Mus. of Art, 1992—94; adj. prof. U. Tex. Grad. Sch. Bus. Past pres. bd. trustees St. Marks Sch., Tex.; bd. mem. Equitable Bankshares, Goodwill Industries, Dallas. Mem.: Young Pres. Orgn. (Dallas Chap. bd. mem.). Office: Office Mgmt and Budget 725 17th St, NW Washington DC 20503 Office Fax: 202-395-3888.*

JOHNSON, CLIFTON HERMAN, archivist, retired professional society administrator; b. Griffin, Ga., Sept. 13, 1921; s. John and Pearl (Parrish) Johnson; m. Rosemary Brunst, Aug. 2, 1960; children: Charles, Robert, Virginia. Student, U. Conn., Storrs, 1943—44; BA, U. NC, 1948, PhD, 1959; MA, U. Chgo., 1949; postgrad., U. Wis., 1951. Tutor LeMoyne Coll., Memphis, 1950—53, asst. prof., 1953—56, prof., 1960—61, 1963—66; asst. prof. East Carolina Coll., 1958—59; asst. libr. and archivist Fisk U., 1961—63; exec. dir. Amistad Rsch. Ctr., New Orleans, 1966—92, emeritus, 1992. Author (with Carroll Barber): The American Negro: A Selected and Annotated Bibliography for High Schools and Junior Colleges, 1968; author: A Legacy of La Amistad: Some Twentieth Century Black Leaders, 1989, Abolitionism in the Antislavery Movement, 1997; editor: God Struck Me Dead: Religious Conversions and Experiences and Autobiographies of Ex-Slaves, 1969. Exec. bd. dirs. All Congregations Together, 1997—2002; bd. dirs. La. World Expn., 1980—82, Lillie Carroll Jackson Mus., 1978—89, Countee Cullen Found., 1981—87, Friends of Archives La., 1978—90, La. Folklife Commn., 1982—85, Ctr. for Black Music Rsch., 1986—, New Orleans Urban League, 1994—2001; cons. DreamWorks Prodns., 1997. With AUS, 1940—45. NEH fellow, 1994. Mem.: Am. Cival Liberties Union, Lane Co. Com. for Defense of Bill of Rights, So. Poverty Law Ctr., Beyond War, Amistad Am. Business E-Mail: clifton@peak.org.

JOHNSON, COLLISTER, JR., (TERRY JOHNSON JR.), federal official; m. Elizabeth Kelley Johnson; children: Kelley Muir, Collister Ward. BA, Yale U.; JD, U. Va. Asst. atty., Fairfax County, Va.; dep. pub. counsel U.S. Rail Svcs. Planning Office, Washington; ptnr. Lockie & Johnson; CEO FastShip Atlantic, Inc.; sr. cons. Mercer Mgmt. Cons., Inc.; adminstr. St. Lawrence Seaway Devel. Corp. (SLSDC), 2006—. Named Man of Yr., Hampton Roads Maritime Assn., 1993. Office: SLSDC 400 Seventh St SW Ste 5424 Washington DC 20590*

JOHNSON, CONOR DEANE, mechanical engineer; b. Charlottesville, Va., Apr. 20, 1943; s. Randolph Holaday and Louise Anna (Deane) J.; m. Laura Teague Rogers, Dec. 20, 1966; children: William Drake, Catherine Teague. BS in Engring. Mechanics, Va. Poly. Inst., 1965; MS, Clemson U., 1967, PhD in Engring. Mechanics, 1969. Registered profl. engr., Calif. With Anamet Labs., Inc., 1973-82, sr. structural analyst Dayton, Ohio, 1973-75, prin. engr. San Carlos, Calif., 1975-81, v.p., 1981-82; program mgr. Aerospace Structures Info. and Analysis Ctr., 1975-82; co-founder, pres. CSA Engring., Inc., Mountain View, Calif., 1982—. Tech. dir. damping conf., exec. com. N.Am. Conf. on Smart Materials and Structures. Contbr. articles to profl. jours.; patentee in field. Capt. USAF, 1969-73 Mem. AIAA (structural dynamics tech. com.), ASME (adaptive structures tech. com., structures and materials award 1981), N.Am. Smart Structures and Materials Conf. (mem. exec. com., tech. chmn. Damping confs. 1991, 93, 95, 96), Gourmet Cooking Club, Sigma Xi. Methodist. Home: 3408 Beresford Ave Belmont CA 94002-1302 Office: CSA Engring Inc 2565 Leghorn St Mountain View CA 94043-1613 Home Phone: 650-591-1595; Office Phone: 650-210-9000. Business E-Mail: cjohnson@csaengineering.com.

JOHNSON, CONSTANCE ANN TRILLICH, web site designer; b. Chgo., Apr. 16, 1949; d. Lee and Ruth (Goodhue) Trillich; m. Robert Dale Neal, Dec. 25, 1972 (div. 1988); 1 child, Adam Danforth; m. Lewis W. Johnson Jr., Feb. 14, 1990. BA in French, U. Tenn., 1971; cert., Sorbonne, Paris, 1970; MLn, Emory U., 1979; JD, Mercer Law Sch., 1982; PhD magna cum laude, Internat. Sem., 1995. Bar: Ga. 1982. Reservationist AAA, Tampa, 1971-72; libr. tech. asst. I Mercer U., Macon, Ga., 1973-74, libr. tech. asst. II, 1974-78; tchg. asst. Mercer Law Sch., Macon, 1981; asst. prof. Mercer Med. Sch., Macon, 1980-82; pvt. practice Macon, 1982-86; min. Ch. Tzaddi, 1986-89; writer/rschr.ADC Project 1988-89; min. Alliance of Divine Love, 1988—; co-owner Cntys. OnLine, Winter Park, Fla., 1990—, Christians on the Net, Winter Park, Fla., 1995—; of counsel Read Found., Evansville, Ind., 1989. Mgr. Lifestream Assocs., 1989; freelance editor Page Design Co., 1989; assoc. AA Computer Care, Winter Park, 1989; founder House of the Lord, 1989—; rsch. asst. Ctr. Constnl. Studies, Macon, 1983; instr. bus. Wesleyan Coll., Macon, 1982; web designer Christians on the Net, 1995—; curator Angel Art Gallery, 1995—; internet editor, Discovery Newspaper, Orlando, Fla., 1998—; assoc. prof., libr., Internat. Sem., Plymouth, Fla., 1991; founder Ruth G. Trillich Meml Sch., Flywheeler Park, Ft Meade, Fla. Author: Treasures From Heaven, 1995; editor (periodical) Ray of Sunshine, 1989. Bd. dirs. Unity Ch., Middle, Ga., 1987, sec., 1987; bd. dirs. Macon Coun. World Affairs, 1981-82, Light of Creative Awareness, Northville, Mich., 1989; mem. Friends Emory Librs., Atlanta, 1980-87, Friends Eckerd Coll. Libr., St. Petersburg, Fla., 1980-87. Mem. ABA, AAUW, Am. Soc. Law and Medicine, Am. Judicature Soc., DAR (DuVall chpt.), Mercer U. Women's Club (treas. 1974, pres. 1986, bd. dirs. 1987), Fla. Flywheelers Antique Engine Club (edn. chairperson 2001—, sec., bd. dirs. 2007), Friends of the Libr., Mid. Ga. Gem and Mineral Soc., Macon Mus. Arts and Scis., La Leche League (sec. 1985), Phi Alpha Delta. Republican. Office: Communities OnLine 1416 Pelican Bay Trl Winter Park FL 32792-6131 E-mail: drjphd@yahoo.com.

JOHNSON, CORNELIUS RAYMOND, prosecutor; b. Waco, Tex., Jan. 20, 1963; s. Virgil O. Howard and Beatrice Earline Johnson; m. Gay Lanell Pasley (div. Dec. 1999). AA, Tarrant County Jr. Coll., 1990; BS, Tex. Christian U., 1991; JD, U. Tulsa, 1995. Bar: Okla. 1996, U.S. Ct. Appeals (10th cir.) 1996, U.S. Dist. Ct. (no. and ea. dists.) Okla. 1997, U.S. Dist. Ct. (we. dist.) Okla. 1998, U.S. Supreme Ct. 2000. Assoc. atty. Law Firm of Riggs, Abney, Tulsa, 1996-99; asst. city atty. Tulsa City Atty.'s Office, Tulsa, 1999—. Bd. dirs. Leadership Tulsa, 1999. Maj. USAR. Mem. ABA, Okla. Bar Assn., Spl. Forces Assn., 1st Calvalry Divsn. Assn., 1st Infantry Divsn. Assn., Internat. Churchill Soc., Nat. Black Prosecutors Assn. Democrat. Unitarian Universalist. Avocations: weightlifting, jogging, reading, cooking, horseback riding. Office: Tulsa City Attys Office 200 Civic Ctr Tulsa OK 74103-3856 Office Phone: 918-596-7717. Business E-Mail: crjohnson@ci.tulsa.ok.us.

JOHNSON, CRAIG M., real estate company executive; BS, U. Ill., 1975; MBA, DePaul U., 1977. Sr. v.p. cmty. devel. U.S. Home Corp., Houston, 1997—2000; v.p. cmty. devel. Lennar Corp., Miami, Fla., 2000—05; pres. Strategic Techs., Inc., Miami, Fla., 2002—04; Midwest regional pres. Lennar, 2005—. Office: Lennar Corp 10707 Clay Rd Houston TX 77041-5497 Office Phone: 713-877-2448. Business E-Mail: craig.johnson@lennar.com.

JOHNSON, CRAIG N., management consultant; b. Warren, Pa., Jan. 8, 1942; s. Norman Andrew and Edice (Rieder) J.; m. Sally Van Dusen, May 23, 1969; children: Maria Pepper, Anna Sergeant, Samantha Bennett. BS, U. Pa., 1963, MBA, 1968. Cert. mgmt. cons. Inst. Mgmt. Cons. Prin. William E. Hill & Co. Inc., NYC, 1968-72; v.p. INA Properties, Phila., 1972-75; sr. prin. Hay Assocs., Phila., 1975-80; pres. Lavino Shipping Co., Phila., 1980-90, Maritrans, Inc., Phila., 1990—94; mng. dir., adv. dir. Glenthorne Capital Inc., Phila., 1994—; chmn. Blair Corp., Phila., 2003—07. Bd. dirs. The Phila. Contributorship; bd. trustees Chestnut Hill Healthcare Found. Mem. Com. of Seventy, Phila., 1975-97; bd. dirs. Acad. Natural Scis., Phila.; trustee Springside Sch., 1994-98; assoc. trustee U. Pa., 1990-96. Repubican. Episcopalian. E-mail: craig.johnson74@verizon.net.

JOHNSON, CRAIG THEODORE, portfolio manager; b. Chgo., Oct. 1, 1955; s. C. Theodore and Dorothy (Lind) J.; m. Dianne Lee Eggen, Oct. 12, 1985; children: Juliana, Kyle. BSBA, Drake U., 1977. Asst. mgr., asst. buyer Marshall Field & Co., Chgo., 1977-80; asst. mgr. Wickes Cos., Wheeling, Ill., 1980-82; salesman John Hancock, Des Plaines, Ill., 1982-83; portfolio mgr. Leonetti & Assocs., Inc., Buffalo Grove, Ill., 1983—. Mem. Nat. Assn. Investors, World Future Soc. Republican. Lutheran. Avocations: reading, sports, gardening, astronomy. Office: Leonetti & Assocs Inc 1130 W Lake Cook Rd Ste 300 Buffalo Grove IL 60089-1976 E-mail: cjohnson@leonettiassoc.com.

JOHNSON, CURTIS LEE, publishing executive, editor, writer; b. Mpls., May 26, 1928; s. Hjalmar N. and Gladys (Goring) J.; m. Jo Ann Lekwa, June 30, 1950 (div. 1974); children: Mark Alan, Paula Catherine; m. Rochelle Miller Hickey, Jan. 11, 1975 (div. 1980); m. Betty Axelrod Fox, Aug. 28, 1982 (div. 1990). BA, U. Iowa, 1951, MA, 1952. Mag. and ency. editing and writing, Chgo., 1953-60; textbook and ednl. editing and writing, 1960-66; editor, pub. December Press, 1962—, pres., 1985—; free-lance editing and writing, 1966-72, 78—; mng. editor Aldine Pub. Co., 1972-73; v.p. St. Clair Press, 1973-77; sr. writer Bradford Exchange, 1978-81; mng. editor Regnery Gateway, 1981-82. Author: (with George Uskali) How to Restore Antique and Classic Cars, 1954; Hobbledehoy's Hero, 1959, Nobody's Perfect, 1973, Lace and a Bobbitt, 1976, The Morning Light, 1977, Song for Three Voices, 1984; The Mafia Manager, 1991, (with R. Craig Sautter) Wicked City Chicago, 1994, Thanksgiving in Vegas, 1995, 500 Years of Obscene.and Counting, 1997; editor: (with Jarvis Thurston) Stories from the Literary Magazines, 1970, Best Little Magazine Fiction, 1970, (with Alvin Greenberg), 1971, (with Jack Conroy) Writers in Revolt, 1973, (with Diane Kruchkow) Green Isle in the Sea, 1986, Who's Who in Writers, Editors & Poets, 1985-96; essays The Forbidden Writings of Lee Wallek, 1978; (with R. Craig Sautter) 26 Martyrs, 2004, Little by Little, 2004, Salud: Selected Writings, 2007; contbr. articles to profl. jours.; cons. editor Panache mag, 1967-76. With USN, 1946—48, with USNR, 1948—53. Nat. Endowment Arts writing grantee, 1973, 81 Mem.: Nat. Writers Union, Club d'Ronde, Phi Beta Kappa. Office: 1097 Sandwick Ct Highland Park IL 60035 Home Phone: 847-940-4122; Office Phone: 847-940-4122.

JOHNSON, CYNDA ANN, physician, educator; b. Girard, Kans., July 16, 1951; BA in Biology and German with honors, Stanford U., 1973; MD, UCLA, 1977; MBA, U. Mo., Kansas City, 1999. Diplomate Am. Bd. Family Medicine (bd. dirs., pres. 1999-2000). Tchg. fellow U. N.C., Chapel Hill, 1980-81; intern U. Kans. Med. Ctr., Kansas City, 1977-78, 1978-80, prof., acting chair dept. family medicine, 1998—99; prof., head dept. family medicine U. Iowa Coll. Medicine, Iowa City, 1999—2003; dean Brody Sch. Medicine East Carolina U., Greenville, NC, 2003—06, sr. assoc. vice chancellor for clin. and translational rsch., 2007—. Mem. Am. Acad. Family Physicians, Soc. Tchrs. Family Medicine, N.C. Acad. of Family Physicians, N.C. Med. Soc. Office: East Carolina U Div Rsch and Grad Studies Greenville Centre Rm 1515 2200 S Charles Blvd Greenville NC 27858-4353 Office Phone: 252-328-9478. Office Fax: 252-328-2769. E-mail: johnsoncyn@ecu.edu.

JOHNSON, CYNTHIA ZUCKERNICK, history educator; b. Abilene, Tex., Aug. 28, 1967; d. Joseph H. Zuckernick and Elaine Ware; m. Willard L. Johnson. AAS, Cisco Jr. Coll., Cisco, Tex., 1997; BA in History, Tarleton State U., Stephenville, Tex., 1999, MA in History, 2001. History instr. Cisco Jr. Coll., Tex., 2002—. V.p. Cisco Civic League, Tex., 2004. Mem.: Faculty Senate (assoc.; pres. 2005—), Tex. C.C. Teachers Assn. (assoc.), Phi Theta Kappa (hon.; v.p. 1996—97), Alpha Chi (hon.), Phi Alpha Theta (hon.; pres. 1997—2001). Bapt. Avocations: travel, reading. Office: Cisco Jr Coll 101 College Heights Cisco TX 76437 Home Phone: 254-442-4132; Office Phone: 254-442-5164.

JOHNSON, DANIEL, JR., lawyer; b. Vallejo, Calif., June 17, 1948; s. Daniel Jones and Arletha Mae (Terrell) J.; children: Stacy, Anne, Cameron; m. Jacqueline Luckett, July 23, 1983. BA in Polit. Sci., U. Calif., Berkeley, 1970; JD, Yale U., 1973. Bar: Calif. 1972. Dep. atty. gen. State of Calif., San Francisco, 1973-76; assoc. Cooley Godward Law Firm, Palo Alto, 1976-81, ptnr., 1981, mem. mgmt. com., 1993-97, head of litigation; ptnr. Morgan, Lewis & Bockius LLP, San Francisco. Dir. San Francisco Legal Aid, 1984-86; lawyer del. No. Dist. Calif.; chmn. patent local rules com., mem. local rules com. U.S. Dist. Ct. Contbr. articles to profl. jours. Bd. dirs. St. Paul's Episcopal Sch., 1988-91. Named Am's. Leading Lawyers, by Chambers USA, 2006, No. Calif. Super Lawyer, 2006. Mem. ABA, Nat. Bar Assn., State Bar Calif. (ethnic minorities com.), Inn at Ct. (intellectual property sect.). Democrat. Baptist. Avocations: woodwork, basketball, tennis. Office: Morgan Lewis & Bockius LLP 1 Market Spear St Tower San Francisco CA 94105 Office Phone: 415-442-1392. Office Fax: 415-442-1001. Business E-Mail: djjohnson@morganlewis.com.

JOHNSON, DARRYL NORMAN, former ambassador; b. Chgo., 1938; m. Kathleen Dessa Forance; 3 children. BA cum laude in English lit., U. Wash., 1960; grad. work in English lit., U. Minn., 1961, Princeton U., 1962. With Boeing Co., Seattle, 1962; vol. Peace Corps, Thailand, 1963—65; US Fgn. Svc. Officer, 1965—2005; ConGen Mumbai, 1966—67; Chinese language training, 1968—69; ConGen Hong Kong, 1969—73; Russian language training, 1973—74; US Embassy Moscow, 1974—77; Dept. of State, Officer-in-Charge Yugoslav Affairs, 1977—79; Officer-in-Charge PRC affairs, 1979—81; Pearson Fellow Office Sen,. Clairborne Pell, 1981—82; special asst. Under Sec. Pol. affairs, 1982—84; Counselor for pol. affairs US Embassy Beijing, 1984—87; Dep. Chief of Mission US Embassy Warsaw, 1988—91; US Amb. to Lithuania, 1991—94; Dep. Coord. for asst. to former Soviet Union, 1994—96; Dir. Am. Inst. in Taiwan, 1996—99; pol. adv. to Chief of Naval Ops., 1999—2000; Dep. Asst. Sec. State for East Asian and Pacific Affairs, 2000—01; US Amb. to Thailand, 2001—04; US Charge d'Affairs Philippines, 2005; aux. prof. internat. studies U. of Washington, Seattle, 2005—. Office: U Washington Jackson Sch Internat Studies Seattle WA 98195 Personal E-mail: johnsondarryln@netscape.net.

JOHNSON, DARRYL THOMAS, communications educator; BS in Edn., MS in Edn., NW Mo. State Univ. Cert. Nat. Bd. Tchg. Standards, 2002. Tchr. NE Nodaway County R-V High School, Ravenwood, Mo., 1992—93, Plattsburg (Mo.) H.S., 1993—95, Smithville (Mo.) H.S., 1995—, also chair, English Dept. Adj. instr. Maple Woods Comty. Coll., 2002—04; mem. NW Mo. State Univ. Adv. Coun. in Secondary English Methods. Named Smithville H.S. Tchr. of Yr. (eight times), Mo. Tchr. of Yr., 2007. Office: Smithville High Sch 645 S Commercial Smithville MO 64089 E-mail: djohnson39@kc.rr.com.*

JOHNSON, DARYL DIANE, painter; b. NYC, Aug. 28, 1953; d. Wilbur Henry and Dorothy (Hinton) J.; m. C. Roth Benson, May 8, 1982; children: Sven Hardy Benson, Astrid Posey Benson. BFA, Hope Coll., 1975; postgrad., U. Cin., 1976, Art Student's League, NYC, 1978, Vt. Studio Sch., Johnson, 1988. Paintings in permanent collections of: Aetna Ins. Co., Hartford, Conn., Delta Airlines, Boston, Gen. Electric, Greenwich (Conn.) Hosp., Mariott Hotels, N.Y.C. and St. Louis, Pepsico, Purchase, N.Y., WMUR-TV, Manchester, N.H. One-man shows: Bell Gallery, Stamford, Conn., 1983, Cityarts Gallery, New Haven, 1987, Hatfield Gallery, Manchester, 1989, McGowan Gallery, Concord, N.H., 1990. Author commd. works Mary Immaculate Hosp., 1983, mural "New Hampshire Triptych" WMUR-TV, 1992. Recipient painting award Conn. Painters and Sculptors Show, Stamford Mus., 1981. Mem. N.H. Art Assn. (in juried shows recipient 1st prize 1989, 90, Miriam Sawyer award 1989, Connor award 1990), N.H. Creative Club. Avocation: motorcycling. Home and Office: 31 Storybrook Ln Amherst NH 03031-2604 Office Phone: 603-672-4422.

JOHNSON, DAVID BLACKWELL, safety engineer; b. Annapolis, Md., 1954; s. Charles McCoy and Jane Johnson; m. Jacalyn Benjamin, Aug. 7, 1976; children: Sarah Ingling, Jeffrey Blackwell, Kevin Berington. BA, Drew U., 1976; postgrad., NYU, 1976-78. Cert. safety profl. Am. Bd. Cert. Safety Profls. Rsch. assoc. NYU Med. Ctr., 1978-79; safety engr., indsl. hygienist Burroughs Corp., Plainfield, NJ, 1979-80; mgr. safety and indsl. hygiene Unisys Corp., Plainfield, 1980-81; corp. supr. hazardous materials Revlon, Inc., Edison, NJ, 1981-82, mgr. safety and health, 1982-84; mgr. indsl. hygiene and safety Celanese Engring. Resins, Inc., Chatham, NJ, 1984-87; corp. dir. environ., health and safety affairs Hoechst Celanese Corp., Somerville, NJ, 1987-96; v.p. environ., health and safety affairs Givaudan-Roure Corp., Clifton, NJ, 1996-99, sr. v.p. ops. N.Am. Mt. Olive, 1999—2002; head corp. health & safety Amerada Hess Corp., NYC, 2002—04; dir. global health, safety & environ. Honeywell Internat., Morristown, 2004—. Bd. dirs., Celanese Emergency Brigade Tng. Ctr., Rock Hill, S.C., 1987—. Adviser safety com. City of Summit, N.J., 1985; pres. Summit Regional Bd. Health. Mem. Am. Indsl. Hygiene Assn. (treas. N.J. sect. 1984-85), Am. Soc. Safety Engrs., Nat. Safety Mgmt. Assn., Am. Pub. Health Assn., Kiwanis. Episcopalian. Avocations: baseball, fishing, golf. Home: 25 Waldron Ave Summit NJ 07901-2805 Office: Honeywell Internat 101 Columbia Rd Morristown NJ

JOHNSON, DAVID D., lawyer, game company executive; b. Sioux City, Iowa, Aug. 17, 1951; BA in Polit. Sci., U. Nev., 1975; JD, Creighton U., 1978. Chief dep. atty. gen. Gaming Divsn. Nev. Atty. Gen. Office, 1985—87; ptnr. Schreck, Jones, Bernhard, Woloson & Godfrey, 1987—95; sr. v.p., gen. counsel, sec. Alliance Gaming Corp., 1995—2000; gen. counsel Anchor Gaming, 2000—01; ptnr. Bernhard, Bradley & Johnson, Las Vegas, 2001—03; sr. v.p., gen. counsel, sec. Internat. Game Tech., Reno, 2003—. Office: International Game Tech 9295 Prototype Dr Reno NV 89521*

JOHNSON, DAVID HARROVER, lawyer, music company executive; b. Rochester, NY, Oct. 6, 1946; s. David O. and Elizabeth (Harrover) J.; m. Kathryn Halbower; children: William Warner, Thomas Louis. BA, Yale Univ., 1969; JD, Univ. Pa., 1973; LLM, NYU, 1981. Bar: N.Y. 1974. Atty. CBS, Inc., NYC, 1975-79, sr. atty., 1979, asst. gen. atty., 1980, dir. bus. affairs cable div., 1981-83; assoc. Mayer, Nussbaum, Katz and Baker, NYC, 1983; v.p. business affairs songs div. CBS, Inc., NYC, 1984-85, assoc. gen. counsel, 1985-87; sr. v.p., gen. counsel CBS Records, Inc., NYC, 1988—90, Sony Music Entertainment, 1990—99; exec. v.p., gen. counsel Warner Music Group, NYC & Burbank, Calif., 1999—2006; interim CEO Warner /Chappell, 2006—. Mem.: Nat. Music Publishers' Assn. (bd. dirs. 2007—). Office: Warner Music Group 75 Rockefeller Plz New York NY 10019

JOHNSON, DAVID HORTON, oncologist; b. Dalton, Ga., Apr. 19, 1948; BS in Zoology, U. Kentucky, MS in Physiology; MD, Med. Coll. Ga., 1976. Intern, medicine U. South Ala. Med. Ctr., Mobile, Ala., 1977, resident, medicine, 1977—79; resident Med. Coll. Ga. Hosp., Augusta, Ga., 1979—80, Vanderbilt U. Med. Ctr.; dir. divsn. oncology, hematology Vanderbilt U., Nashville, Cornelius Abernathy Craig Prof. Med. and Surgical Oncology; dep. dir. Vanderbilt-Ingram Cancer Ctr., Nashville. Investigator in field. Contbr. articles to profl. publications. Recipient Frank Moran Clinical Leadership award, U. Mich., 2000. Mem.: Am. Soc. Clinical Oncology (immediate past pres.). Office: Vanderbilt U 777 Preston Research Bldg Hematology/Oncology Nashville TN 37232-6307 also: 1903 The Vanderbilt Clinic Nashville TN 37232-5536 Office Phone: 615-343-9454, 615-322-6053. Office Fax: 615-343-8668.*

JOHNSON, DAVID J., JR., lawyer; b. Huntington, NY, 1956; BA, U. Va., 1979, JD, MBA, U. Va., 1985. Bar: Calif. 1985, US Dist. Ct., Ctrl. Dist. Calif. 1985, DC 2006, NY 2006. Ptnr. corp./securities O'Melveny & Myers LLP, LA, co-head capital market group, ptnr. NYC. Office: O'Melveny & Myers LLP Times Square Tower 7 Times Sq New York NY 10036 also: O'Melveny & Myers LLP 1999 Avenue of the Stars Los Angeles CA 90067 Office Phone: 212-326-2000. Office Fax: 212-326-2601. Business E-Mail: djohnson@omm.com.

JOHNSON, DAVID L., federal agency administrator, retired military officer; m. Elizabeth Johnson. BA in Geography, U. Kans., 1972; MA in Human Rels., Webster U., 1978; Grad., Squadron Officer Sch., 1981, Air Command and Staff Coll., 1983, Air War Coll., 1986, Nat. War Coll., 1990, Maxwell Sch. Citizenship & Pub. Affairs, Syracuse U., 1997, Paul H. Nitze Sch. Advanced Internat. Studies, Johns Hopkins U., 1998. Commd. 2d lt. USAF, 1973, advanced through ranks to brig. gen., 1998, ret., 2003, pilot training Williams AFB, 1973—74, C-130E co-pilot aircraft comdr. & advanced flying training instr. pilot Little Rock AFB, Ark., 1974—78, air staff training program officer Washington, 1978—79; action officer later chief plans, programs, & budgeting systems divsn. Hdqs. Military Airlift Command, Scott AFB, Ill., 1979—82; internat. politico-military affairs officer, Strategy divsn. US European Command, Stuttgart-Vaihingen, Germany, 1983—86; asst. ops. officer later ops. officer, 61st Tactical Airlift Squadron divsn. then comdr. 34th Tactical Training Squadron USAF, Little Rock AFB, Ark., 1986—89, chief NATO policy divsn., later chief Asia branch Joint Chiefs of Staff, 1990—93, comdr. 435th Ops. Group Rhein-Main Air Base, Germany, 1993—94, comdr. 86th Ops. Group Ramstein AFB, Germany, 1994—95, vice comdr. 23rd Wing Pope AFB, NC, 1995—96; asst. dir. ops. Hdqtrs. Air Combat Command, Langley AFB, Va., 1996-97; comdr. 43rd Airlift Wing, Pope AFB, NC, 1997-99; vice-comdr. Air Force Spl. Ops. Command, Hurlburt Field, Fla., 1999—2000; dir. weather, dep. chief of staff for air & space ops. USAF, Washington, 2000—03; asst. adminstr. for weather svcs. NOAA, Silver Spring, Md., 2004—. Dep. comdr. Joint Task Force Operation Support Hope, Rwanda, 1995; served in Operation Support Watch, Rwanda, 1998—99. Decorated Disting. Svc. medal, Legion of Merit with oak leaf cluster, Def. Superior Svc. medal, Legion of Merit with oak leaf cluster, Def. Meritorious Svc. medal with two oak leaf clusters, Meritorious Svc. medal with two oak leaf clusters, Air medal with two oak leaf clusters, Air Force Commendation medal with two oak leaf clusters, Joint Svc. Achievement medal, Humanitarian Svc. medal. Office: Nat Oceanic & Atmospheric Adminstrn Nat Weather Svc 1325 East West HIghway Silver Spring MD 20910

JOHNSON, DAVID LEE, lawyer; b. Thorntown, Ind., Sept. 22, 1959; s. James W. and Lois M. (Stewart) J. BA, Purdue U., 1981; JD, U. Chgo., 1985. Bar: Ind. 1985. Analyst Nat. Rep. Senate Com., Washington, 1985-87; mem. profl. staff Com. Agr., Nutrition & Forestry, U.S. Senate, Washington, 1987—91; dep. dir. legis. affairs Fgn. Agr. Svc., U.S. Dept. Agr., 1991—93; legis. dir. Capitol Assn., Inc., Washington, 1993—94; minority counsel Com. Agr., Nutrition & Forestry, U.S. Senate, 1994—95, chief counsel, 1995—. Mem. ABA, Ind. Bar Assn., Phi Beta Kappa. Republican. Presbyterian. Office: Committee on Agriculture Nutrition & Forestry Room 328A Senate Russell Office Building Washington DC 20510-6000

JOHNSON, DAVID LEE, lawyer; b. Lima, Ohio, Sept. 23, 1946; s. Albert Edward and Vera Loree (Langdon) J.; m. Joanie Elaine Thomas, Jan. 3, 1986. BA in English magna cum laude, Ohio Wesleyan U., 1968; JD cum laude, Harvard U., 1971. Assoc. Taft Stettinius & Hollister, Cin., 1971-72, 1976-81, ptnr., 1981-83, mng. ptnr. Columbus, Ohio, 1983—. Trustee Secret Santa Fund, Columbus, 1983—, Hannah Neill Ctr. for Children, Columbus, 1990—. Lt. JAGC USNR, 1972—75. Named Ohio Super Lawyer, Cin. mag., Best Lawyers in Am. Mem. ABA, Ohio Bar Assn., Columbus Bar Assn., Hawaii Bar Assn., Calif. Bar Assn., Athletic Club Columbus, Hickory Hills Golf Club, Phi Beta Kappa, Omicron Delta Kappa. Office: Taft Stettinius & hollister LLP E State St 12th FL 21 Columbus OH 43215 Office Phone: 614-221-2838, 614-220-0211. Office Fax: 614-221-2007. Business E-Mail: johnson@taftlaw.com.

JOHNSON, DAVID M., insurance company executive; Bachelor's Degree with honors, Harvard U., 1982; M in Econs., Yale U., 1986. Mng. dir. investment banking divsn. Merrill Lynch, Pierce, Fenner and Smith, 1986—98; exec. v.p. fin. Cendant Corp., 1998, sr. v.p., CFO, 1998—2001; exec. v.p., CFO The Hartford Fin. Svcs. Group, Inc, 2001—. Named one of leading U.S. CFO's under age 40, CFO Mag., 2000. Office: The Hartford Fin Svcs Group Inc Hartford Plaza 690 Asylum Ave Hartford CT 06115*

JOHNSON, DAVID RANDALL, radio director; b. Coffeyville, Kans., Apr. 6, 1946; s. George Edward and Evelyn Elsie Johnson; m. Marilyn Elizabeth Durscherl, Aug. 12, 1967. AA, Coffeyville Coll.; BS, U. Tulsa; MEd, U. Ark., Fayetteville. Dir. Ark. Radio Reading for Blind, Conway, 1980—; instr. U. Ark., U. Tulsa. Bd. mem. LIFE Project, Little Rock. Actor: Shepherd of the Hills. Bd. mem. LIFE Project, Little Rock. Recipient Vol. Svc. award, Lions World Svcs. for Blind, 1982, Pub. Svc. award, State Ark., 1998, City Little Rock, 1998, City Maumelle, 1998, Employee of Yr. award, Ark. Divsn. Svcs. for Blind, 2001. Mem.: Mensa. R-Consevative. Office: Airs 350 South Donaghey Conway AR 72034

JOHNSON, DAVID RAYMOND, lawyer; b. Bartlesville, Okla., Sept. 12, 1946; s. Lloyd Theodore and Mary Pauline (Auten) J.; m. Marion Frances Monroe, May 14, 1977 (div. 2006); children: Marc, Meredith. BA, Tulane U., 1968; JD, U. Va., 1971. Bar: Tex. 1971, D.C. 1977, U.S. Dist. Ct. D.C. 1979, U.S. Ct. Appeals (D.C. cir.) 1981, U.S. Supreme Ct. 1982, U.S. Claims Ct. 1984. Assoc. Fulbright & Jaworski, Houston, 1971-72, Washington, 1974-78, ptnr., 1978-87; atty.-advisor Office of Gen. Counsel of Air Force, Washington, 1972-74; ptnr. Gibson, Dunn & Crutcher LLP, Washington, 1987—2003, adv. counsel, 2004—. Trustee Washington Episcopal Sch., 1991-93, McLean Sch. Md., 1994-96. Capt. USAF, 1972-74. Mem. DC Bar Assn., Raven Soc., Congl. Country Club, Petroleum Club Oklahoma City, Order of Coif, Phi Beta Kappa. Office: Gibson Dunn & Crutcher LLP 1050 Connecticut Ave NW Ste 900 Washington DC 20036-5306 Office Phone: 202-955-8662. Business E-Mail: djohnson@gibsondunn.com.

JOHNSON, DAVID TIMOTHY, diplomat; m. Scarlett M. Swan, May 23, 1981; children: Carrie, Rachel, Andrew. BA in Econs., Emory U., 1976; postgrad., Can. Nat. Def. Coll., 1989-90. Asst. nat. trust examiner US Treasury Dept.'s Office of the Comptroller of Currency, prior to 1977; various assignments US Fgn. Svc., 1977—; econs. officer U.S. Embassy in Berlin US Dept. State, 1981-83, desk officer, NATO, 1983—87, dep. dir. ops. ctr., 1987—89, consulate gen., 1990—93, dep. spokesman for dep. asst. sec., 1993-95; dep. press sec. for fgn. affairs, sr. dir. pub. affairs, Nat. Security Coun. The White House, 1995-97; amb. to Orgn. for Security and Cooperation in Europe US Dept. State, Vienna, 1998—2001, Afghan coord., 2001—03; min. US Embassy, London, 2003—04, chargé d'affaires ad interim, 2004—05. Office: 8400 London Pl Washington DC 20521-8400 Office Phone: (44)(20) 7894 0225.*

JOHNSON, DAVID WESLEY, lawyer; b. Rochester, NY, Mar. 13, 1933; BA, U. Rochester, 1954; LLB, Columbia U., 1959. Bar: N.Y. 1961, U.S. Dist. Ct. (so. dist.) N.Y. 1961, U.S. Dist. Ct. (no. dist.) N.Y. 1971. Counsel, sec., v.p. Textile Banking Co., NYC, 1959-68; legis. counsel CIT Fin. Corp., NYC, 1968-70; ptnr. Otterbourg, Steindler, Houston & Rosen, NYC, 1970-71, Palmer & Johnson, Tupper Lake, N.Y., 1971-74; pvt. practice Tupper Lake, 1974—. Bd. dirs. Adirondack Cmty. Trust Trustee, chmn. bd. North Country C.C., Saranac Lake, N.Y., 1973-82; bd. dirs., pres. High Peaks Hospice, Inc., Saranac Lake, 1988-92; bd. dirs., v.p. Lake Placid (N.Y.) Ctr. for Arts, 1989—, Franklin County Children's Legal Svcs., Inc., pres., 1991—; trustee Nat. History Mus. of the Adirondacks, 1998—; bd. dirs. Adirondack Med. Ctr. Found., 2001-04. Mem. Franklin County Bar Assn. (pres. 1979-81), N.Y. State Bar Assn., Lawyers Assn. Textile Industry (bd. dirs., sec.-treas. 1962-71), Assn. Comml. Fin. Attys. (bd. dirs., v.p. 1962-71). Office: 51 Lake St Tupper Lake NY 12986-1624 Home Phone: 518-359-2652; Office Phone: 518-359-3394. Personal E-mail: jnglaw@roadrunner.com.

JOHNSON, DAVID WILFRED, JR., ceramics engineer, researcher; b. Windber, Pa., Sept. 23, 1942; s. David W. Sr. and Vanessa J. (Shoff) Johnson; m. Bonnie Kay Respet, June 20, 1964; children: Analee J., Bradley D. BS in Ceramic Sci., Pa. State U., 1964, PhD in Ceramic Sci., 1968. Tech. staff Bell Tel. Labs., Murray Hill, NJ, 1968-83; supr. advanced ceramic processing AT&T Bell Labs., Murray Hill, 1983-88; dir. metallurgy and ceramics rsch. dept. Bell Labs Lucent Techs., Murray Hill, 1988-2000; dir. materials rsch. dept. Agere Sys., New Providence, NJ, 2001—02; editor Jour. of Am. Ceramic Soc., 2002—. Adj. prof. Stevens Inst. Tech., Hoboken, NJ, 1982—; Taylor lectr. Pa. State U., University Park, 1989. Contbr. articles to profl. jours. Chmn. Bedminster Twp. Zoning Bd. Adjustment, NJ, 1991—94, NJ, 1996—2005. Fellow: Am. Soc. Materials (disting. life mem.), Am. Ceramic Soc. (v.p. 1990—92, treas. 1992, pres. 1994, Ross Coffin Purdy award 1978, Fulrath award 1984, John Jeppson award 1998, Indsl. Rsch. prize 2000, Orton Lecture 2004); mem.: AAAS, NAE, Electrochemical Soc., Acad. Ceramics, Materials Rsch. Soc., The Materials Soc. Achievements include patents in field; research in in ceramic powder processing as applied to ferrites, ceramic substrates, sol-gel silica glass and high temperature superconductors. Business E-Mail: johnsond@stevens.edu.

JOHNSON, DAVID WOLCOTT, psychologist, educator; b. Muncie, Ind., Feb. 7, 1940; s. Roger Winfield and Frances Elizabeth (Pierce) J.; m. Linda Mulholland, July 7, 1973; children: James, David, Catherine, Margaret, Jeremiah. BS, Ball State U., Muncie, Ind., 1962; MA, Columbia U., NYC, 1964, EdD, 1966. Asst. prof. ednl. psychology U. Minn., Mpls., 1966-69, assoc. prof., 1969-73, prof., 1973—, Emma Birkmaier prof. in ednl. leadership, 1994—. Bd. dirs. Infrared Solutions, Inc.; orgnl. cons., psychotherapist. Author: Social Psychology of Education, 1970; (with Goodwin Watson) Social Psychology: Issues and Insights, 1972, Reaching Out, 1972, 9th edit., 2005, Contemporary Social Psychology, 1973; (with F. Johnson) Joining Together, 1975, 9th edit., 2005; (with D. Tjosvold) Porductive Conflict Management, 1983, Circles of Learning, 1984, 4th edit., 2002; (with R. Johnson) Learning Together and Alone, 1975, 5th edit., 1999, Human Relations and Your Career, 1978, 3d Edit., 1991, Educational Psychology, 1979, Structuring Cooperative Learning, 1987, Creative Conflict, 1987, Leading the Cooperative School, 1989, 2d edit., 1994, Cooperation and Competition: Theory and Research, 1989, Teaching Students to be Peacemakers, 1991, 4th edit., 2005, video, 1991, Learning Mathematics and Cooperative Learning, 1991, Creative Controversy, 1992, 3d edit., 1995, Positive Interdependence, 1992, (video) 1992, Meaningful and Manageable Assessment Through Cooperative Learning, 1996, Learning to Lead Teams, 1997, Human Relations: Valuing Diversity, 1999, Meaningful Assessment, 2002, Multicultural Education and Human Relations, 2002, Constructive Controversy, 4th edit., 2007; (with R. Johnson, E. Holubec) Cooperative Learning, 1984, 7th edit., 1998, Cooperation in the Classroom, 1984, 7th edit., 1998, Advanced Cooperative Learning, 1988, 3d edit., 1998, Cooperative Learning: Increasing College Faculty Instructional Productivity, 1991, The Nuts and Bolts of Cooperative Learning, 1994, Academic Controversy, 1997, (with R. Johnson, K. Smith) Active Learning: Cooperative Learning in the College Classroom, 1991, 3d edit., 2006, (with R. Johnson) Assessing Students in Groups, 2004; editor Am. Ednl. Rsch. Jour., 1981-83; contbr. over 500 articles to profl. jours. and edited books Bd. dirs. Walk-In Counseling Ctr., 1971-74. Recipient Gordon Allport award Soc. for Psychol. Study of Social Issues, 1981, Helen Plante award Am. Soc. Engring. Edn., 1984, Outstanding Rsch. award Am. Pers. and Guidance Assn., 1972, Nat. Coun. for the Social Studies Rsch. award, 1986, Outstanding Rsch. award AACD, 1988, award for Outstanding Contbn. Am. Edn. Minn. ASCD, 1990, Outstanding Alumni of Yr. award Ball State U., 1990, Rsch. and Practice award S.W. Ohio Planning Coun. for Insvc. Edn., 1990, Excellence in Tchg. award Dept. Def. Schs., Panama, 1994, Emma Birkmaier Prof. in Ednl. Leadership Coll. Edn. U. Minn., 1994-97, Brock Internat. prize in Edn., 2007. Fellow APA (Disting. Contbns. Applications of Psychology to Edn. and Tng. award 2003); mem. Am. Sociol. Assn., Am. Ednl. Rsch. Assn. (award for Outstanding Contbn. to Coop. Learning 1996, Disting. Scholar award 2001), Am. Mgmt. Assn., Am. Assn. for Counseling and Devel., Nat. Rsch. Coun. Home: 7208 Cornelia Dr Minneapolis MN 55435-4160 Office: U Minn 330 Burton Hall Minneapolis MN 55455 *Success is a combination of focus, perseverance, and pain-endurance.*

JOHNSON, DAWN SUNDENE, chemistry educator; d. John W. Sundene and Marilyn R. Jordan; m. Tracy L. Wahl (div.); children: Christopher J. Wahl, Jeri Lynne Wahl; m. Matthew L. Johnson, July 18, 1992. BS in Sci. Edn., East Carolina U., Greenville, 1995; MA in Ednl. Leadership, Aurora U., Ill., 2003. Cert. sci. tchr. Ill., adminstr. Ill., sci. tchr. NC. Biology tutor Craven County Schs., New Bern, NC, 1991—94; chemistryand physics tchr. New Bern HS, NC, 1995—99; chemistry tchr. Oswego HS, Ill., 1999—2006, chmn. sci. divsn., 2004—. Lab and tchg. asst. Craven CC, New Bern, 1991—94, sci. tutor, 1991—94; guest lectr. Newport Elem. Sch., NC, 1991—94. Contbr. poetry to lit. publs. HS-univ. sci. and math liaison Sci./Math Edn. Ctr., Greenville, NC, 1999. Recipient WGKTC Tech. award, Regional Office Edn., Will, Grundy, Kendall counties, 2005; grantee, Oswego Found. for Excellence, 2005; Prospective Tchr. scholar, NC Dept. Edn., 1992—95, Daryl Thompson scholar, Daryl Thompson Found., 2005. Mem.: ASCD (assoc.), AAAS (assoc.), Gold Key (assoc.), Phi Theta Kappa (assoc.), Phi Kappa Phi (life). Republican. Lutheran. Avocations: Norwegian American genealogy, literature, writing poetry. Office: Oswego HS 4250 Rt 71 Oswego IL 60543 Home Phone: 630-551-3831; Office Phone: 630-636-2025. Personal E-mail: djohnson_308@yahoo.com.

JOHNSON, DEBORAH G., philosopher, educator; b. Detroit, Mar. 25, 1945; d. Edward Zimmerman and Rose Shiovitz; m. Samuel V. Johnson, Sept. 6, 1968; children: Jesse E., Rose M. B, Wayne State U., Detroit, 1966; MA, U. Kans., Lawrence, 1973, MPhil, 1974, PhD, 1976. Asst. prof. Rensselaer Poly. Inst., Troy, NY, 1978—84; assoc. prof. Renssealer Poly. Inst., 1984—91; prof. Rensselaer Poly. Inst., 1991—99, Ga. Inst. Tech., Atlanta, 1998—2001; Anne Shirley Carter Olsson prof. applied ethics U. Va., Charlottesville, 2001—. Author: (book) Computer Ethics, 1985; editor: Ethical Issues in the Use of Computers, 1985, Ethical Issues in Engineering, 1991, Computers, Ethics and Social Values, 1998, Women, Gender, and Technology, 2006. Recipient Making a Difference award, ACM, 2000, Sterling Olmsted award, Liberal Edn. Divsn. Am. Soc. Engring. Edn., 2001, John Barwise prize, Am. Philos. Assn., 2004. Office: Univ Va A237 Thornton Hall 351 McCormick Rd Charlottesville VA 22904 Office Phone: 434-924-7751. Office Fax: 434-924-4306. Business E-Mail: dgj7p@virginia.edu.

JOHNSON, DEBORAH JEAN, director; b. Hudson, NY, Sept. 28, 1951; d. Duane Paul Johnson and Merlyn Harriet Sharts-Johnson; m. Frederick Richard Potts, May 29, 1971 (div. Dec. 13, 1995); children: Kelly Jean Bulich, Kristie Marie Allen. AAS, SUNY, Cobleskill, 1971; BS, Russell Sage Coll., Troy, NY, 1981; MS in Edn., Coll. St. Rose, Albany NY, 1985. Permanent cert. NY, 1985, cert. permanent elem. edn. NY, 1985, permanent spl. edn. NY, 1985, provisional SAS NY, 1998, permanent sch. dist. adminstr. NY, 2000. Tchr. Coxsackie Athens Ctrl. Sch. Dist., NY, 1981—2002; prin. curriculum and instrn. Catskill Ctrl. Sch. Dist., NY, 2002—04, curriculum coord. k-6, 2004—05, dir. curriculum grades k-12, 2005—. Cons. Questar III BOCES, Schodack, NY, 1996—2006. Mem. bd. assessors Village of Catskill, 1988—91. Mem.: ASCD (assoc.), Capital Dist. Coun. Social Studies (assoc.), Nat. Coun. Tchrs. English (assoc.), Internat. Reading Assn. (assoc.), Nat. Coun. Tchrs. Math. (assoc.), Catskill CSD PTA & PTSO (assoc.), Greene County Mental Health (assoc.), Ulster Greene Assn. Retarded Children (assoc.). Home: 97 Cauterskill Ave Catskill NY 12414 Office: Catskill Central School District 435 West Main St Catskill NY 12414 Home Phone: 518-943-6990; Office Phone: 518-943-5665 1318. Personal E-mail: djohnson@mhcable.com. Business E-Mail: djohnson@catskillcsd.org.

JOHNSON, DEBORAH LORRAINE, not-for-profit developer, consultant; b. Chgo., Dec. 13, 1952; d. Everett A. Johnson and Marion O. Wilson. PhD, Stanford U., Palo Alto, Calif., 1995. Cons., dir. internat. children's program Feed the Children, Oklahoma City, 2003—06; cons. Dramatic Results, Long Beach, Calif., 2000—06; CEO Give a Child Life, 2007—. Cons., evaluator Project STEPS, North Hollywood, Calif., 1999—; cons. Hydration Techs. Inc.; cons. early edn. dept. L.A. Unified Sch. Dist. Prodr.(writer): (fundraising TV shows). Pres. Inter-Canyon League, Silverado, Calif., 2001—06; v.p. Silverado Modjeska Recreation and Parks Bd., 2003—. Home Phone: 714-649-2728.

JOHNSON, DEBRA POPE, education educator; b. Denver, Aug. 10, 1958; d. Ural Pope; m. Frank Johnson, Apr. 26, 1982; children: Tolaison Monique, Ashley Michele. BA in Psychology and Adminstrn. of Justice, Columbia Coll., Mo., 1980; MEd, Ga. Southwestern Coll., Americus, 1996; EdD, U. Sarasota, Fla., 2005. Cert. Edn. Profl. Standards Commn., 2005. Instrnl. tech. specialist Ga. Southwestern State U., Americus, Ga.,

1999—2001; 6th grade tchr. Merry Acres Mid. Sch., Albany, Ga., 2004—05; coord. internat. curriculum Doughery Internat. Edn. Mid. Sch., 2005—. Dir. clin. experiences Ga. Southwestern State U., Americus, Ga., 2001—03. 2d v.p. Delta Sigma Theta Sorority, Inc., Albany, Ga., 2000—02; vol. Reach to Recovery, Am. Cancer Soc. Recipient Tchr. of the Yr., Dougherty County Sch. Sys. Radium Mid. Sch., 1998. Mem.: Ga. Assn. of Educators. Home: 2525 Betty's Dr Albany GA 31705 Office: Dougherty Internat Edn Mid Sch 1800 Massey Dr Albany GA 31705 Home Phone: 229-883-3069; Office Phone: 229-431-3328. Personal E-mail: debrapj@prodigy.net. Business E-Mail: debra.johnson@dougherty.k12.ga.us.

JOHNSON, DENISE REINKA, state supreme court justice; b. Wyandotte, Mich., July 13, 1947; Student, Mich. State U., 1965-67; BA, Wayne State U., 1969; postgrad., Cath. U. of Am., 1971-72; JD with honors, U. Conn., 1974; LLM, U. Va., 1995. Bar: Conn. 1974, U.S. Dist. Ct. Conn. 1974, Vt. 1980, U.S. Ct. Appeals (2d cir.) 1983, U.S. Dist. Ct. Vt. 1986. Atty. New Haven (Conn.) Legal Assistance Assn., 1974-78; instr. legal writing Vt. Law Sch., South Royalton, 1978-79; clerk Blodgett & McCarren, Burlington, Vt., 1979-80; chief civil rights divsn. Atty. Gen.'s Office, State of Vt., 1980-82; chief pub. protection divsn. Atty. Gen.'s Office, Montpelier, Vt., 1982-88; pvt. practice Shrewsbury, Vt., 1988-90; assoc. justice Vt. Supreme Ct., Montpelier, 1990—. Chair Vt. Human Rights Commn., 1988-90. Mem. Am. Law Inst., Am. Judicature Soc. Office: Vt Supreme Ct 109 State St Montpelier VT 05609-0001*

JOHNSON, DERRICK M., information technology executive; b. Dayton, Ohio, July 11, 1969; s. Maurice M. and Hazel J. Johnson; m. Patricia F. Johnson, Apr. 13, 1999; children: Michael M., Alexander T., Veronica W. BS, U. Louisville, Ky., 1998. Dir. support tech. Humana, Inc., Louisville, 1998—2001; v.p. info. devel. CorSolutions, Inc., Rosemont, Ill., 2001—06. Ind. cons. UPS Logistics Group, Louisville, 1997—99. Contbr. articles to profl. jours. Asst. dir. Jr. Achievement, Louisville, 1994. Recipient Ky. Col. award, Commonwealth of Ky., 1997. Mem.: Data Warehouse Inst. (assoc.). Achievements include design of implemented the disease management industry's first publically available business intelligence platform. Avocations: tennis, travel, golf. Home: 1105 Roseling Pl Celebration FL 34747 Office: Derrick Johnson Cons Group 1105 Roseling Pl Celebration FL 34747 Home Phone: 321-939-0030; Office Phone: 321-939-0030.

JOHNSON, DEWEY, JR., retired biochemist; b. Sapulpa, Okla., Sept. 23, 1926; s. Dewey and Maude (Hickey) Johnson; m. Patricia R. Rodgers, Feb. 14, 1953 (dec. Mar. 1997); children: Joseph D., Paul D., Mary Ann, Richard E.; m. Carol S. Martin, Sept. 25, 1999. BS, Colo. State U., 1950; MS, U. Conn., 1955; PhD, Rutgers State U., 1958. Nutritionist Limecrest Rsch. Lab., Newton, NJ, 1958-63; biochemist Equitable Life, NYC, 1963-79, Met. Life, NYC, 1980-90, disability underwriter, 1990-92; chemist EPA, Edison, NJ, 1993—2001; ret., 2001—. Contbr. Avocations: gardening, woodworking. Home: 59 Dunnell Rd Maplewood NJ 07040-1333

JOHNSON, DON EDWIN, lawyer; b. Decatur, Ill., Jan. 29, 1939; s. B. Edwin and Mary Louise (Pitzer) J.; m. Suzanne Curtis, Aug. 23, 1959; children: Jennifer, Marc Wade. BA cum laude, Millikin U., 1959; LLB, U. Ill., 1961, JD, 1968. Bar: Ill. 1961, U.S. Dist. Ct. (so. dist.) Ill. 1961, U.S. Tax Ct. 1986. Law clk. Ill. Supreme Ct., Springfield, 1961-63; assoc. Hohlt, House & DeMoss, Pinckneyville, Ill., 1961-66; ptnr. Johnson Seibert & Bigham, Pinckneyville, 1966—; state's atty. Perry County, Ill., Pinckneyville, 1968-72. Bd. dirs. 1st Nat. Bank, Pinckneyville, First Perry Bancorp, Pinckneyville. Contbr. articles to profl. jours. City atty. DuQuoin, Ill., 1965-68, Pinckneyville, 1983-2003; bd. dirs. Rend Lake Coll. Found., Ina, Ill., 1981-90; bd. visitors U. Ill. Coll. Law, 1984-88. Fellow Am. Coll. Trust and Estate Counsel, Am. Bar Found., Ill. Bar Found. (chmn. 1986-87); mem. Ill. State Bar Assn. (chmn. fed. tax sect. 1983-84, chmn. mineral law sect. 1984-86, 94-95, 96-97), Energy and Mineral Law Found. (trustee 1985—), Nat. Acad. Elder Law Attys., Pinckneyville C. of C. (pres. 1968), So. Ill. Golf Assn. (pres. 1997—2006), USGA (sectional affairs com. 1994—), Rotary (pres. 1966, 76), Scottish Rite, Shriners, Red Hawk Country Club, Crab Orchard Golf Club, Kelly Greens Golf and Country Club, Delta Sigma Phi. Republican. Presbyterian. Avocations: golf, travel, stamp and coin collecting. Home: 605 W South St Pinckneyville IL 62274-1236 Office: Johnson Seibert & Bigham One N Main St Pinckneyville IL 62274 Home Phone: 618-357-2919; Office Phone: 618-357-2178. Fax: 618-357-3314. Personal E-mail: jsb@onecliq.net.

JOHNSON, DONALD CLAY, librarian, curator; b. Clintonville, Wis., Aug. 19, 1940; s. Everett Clay and Gertrude Edna Dorthea J. BA, U. Wis., 1962, PhD, 1980; MA, U. Chgo., 1967. Curator S.E. Asia Collection Yale U., New Haven, 1967-70; head reference libr. No. Ariz. U., Flagstaff, 1971-72; asst. libr. reader svcs. Nat. U. Malaysia, Kuala Lumpur, 1972-74; head reader svcs. Coll. William and Mary, Williamsburg, Va., 1980-87; curator Ames Libr. South Asia, U. Minn., Mpls., 1987—. Author: Southeast Asia: A Bibliography, 1970, Guide to Reference Materials on Southeast Asia, 1970, Index to Southeast Asian Journals, 1982, Agile Hands and Creative Minds, a Bibliography of Textile Traditions in Afghanistan, Bangladesh, Bhutan, India, Nepal, Pakistan, and Sri Lanka, 2000, Wedding Dress Across Cultures, 2003. Ford Found. scholar, 1963-64; Rsch. grantee Am. Inst. Indian Studies, 1989-90, 94; Fulbright fellow, 2003-04. Mem. ALA (life), Assn. for Asian Studies (editor Resources for Scholarship series 1997-98). Avocation: textiles in South and Southeast Asia. Office: U Minn Ames Libr South Asia 309 19th Ave S Minneapolis MN 55455-0438 Office Phone: 612-624-5801. Business E-Mail: d-john4@umn.edu.

JOHNSON, DONALD CRANDALL, b. Richmond, Calif., June 26, 1949; s. Edson Johnson Jr. and Sidney L. Crandall; m. Nelda Sabillon; 2 children. BA, JD, Lewis and Clark Coll.; LLM, George Washington U.; MA, U. Okla. With Fgn. Svc., Guatemala City, 1974-76; desk officer for Costa Rica U.S. Dept. of State, 1976-79; asst. gen. svcs. officer, then polit. officer Dept. of State, Moscow, 1979-81, polit. officer Beijing, 1983-86, Madrid, 1986-87, polit. counselor Tegucigalpa, Honduras, 1987-90; dir. Latin affairs Nat. Security Coun., 1990-91; US amb. to Mongolia Dept. of State, 1993, US amb. to Cape Verde, 2002—05, US amb. to Republic of Equatorial Guinea, 2006—. Contbr. articles to profl. jours. With U.S. Army, 1971-73. Mem. Am. Fgn. Svc. Assn., Mongolian Soc. Mailing: DOS Amb 2320 Malabo Pl Washington DC 20521-2320

JOHNSON, DONALD EDWARD, JR., lawyer; b. Denver, Sept. 24, 1942; s. Donald Edward and Miriam Bispham (Chester) J.; m. Charlotte Marie Hassett, Aug. 15, 1964; children: Julie Anna, Jenny Marie. Student, Lewis and Clark Coll., 1960-62; BA in History, U. Ariz., 1968; JD, U. Wyo., 1971. Bar: Wyo. 1971, Colo. 1971, U.S. Dist. Ct. Colo. and Wyo. 1971, U.S. Supreme Ct. 1978. Assoc. Hammond and Chilson, Loveland, Colo., 1971-72; dep. dist. atty. 8th Jud. Dist., Loveland and Fort Collins, Colo., 1972-80, chief dep. dist. atty., 1977-80; assoc. Allen, Rogers, Metcalf and Vahrenwald, Ft. Collins, 1980-82, ptnr., 1982—. Asst. city atty., prosecutor City of Loveland, 1971-72; asst. mcpl. judge, Loveland, 1972; instr. bus. law Ames Coll., 1972-74; lectr. Regional Homocide Sch., 1977. Author: Criminal Conspiracy—The Colorado District Attorney's Evidence Manual, 1976; student editor ABA Law Student Jour. Chmn. 45th Republican House Dist., 1977-82; mem. Colo. Rep. Central Com., 1980-85; mem. Loveland Open Space Adv. Bd., 1977-78; bd. dirs. Loveland United Way, 1977-84, pres., 1981-83; bd. dirs. Loveland Midget Athletic Assn., sec., 1974-78; mem. ctrl. com. Parlimentarian Larimer County Rep., 1992-96; mem. local adv. bd. McKee Med. Ctr., Loveland, 1992—04, pres., 1995—04; mem. adv. bd. Banner Health Sys., Colo., 1996—2004, pres., 1999-2002; treas. 8th Jud. dist. Victims Assistance Law Enforcement Fund, 1990-96 mem. 8th judicial dist. mem. Larimer County Bench-Bar Commn., 1993-95; mem. Loveland adv. bd. Cmty. Found. No. Colo., 2003—, chair, 2006—; mem. McKee Med. Ctr. Found., 2007—. Served to sgt. USMC, 1966-68. Mem. ABA (Gold Key award 1970), Larimer County Bar Assn. (exec. com. 1990-2002, pres. 1995-96), Colo. Bar Assn. (bd. govs. 1997-2002), Colo. Trial Lawyers Assn. Episcopalian. Office: Allen Vahrenwald & Johnson LLC Key Bank Bldg 125 S Howes St 1100 Fort Collins CO 80521 Office Phone: 970-482-5058.

JOHNSON, DONALD LEE, retired agricultural materials processing company executive; b. Aurora, Ill., Mar. 9, 1935; s. Leonard F. and Fern J. (Johnson) J.; m. Virginia A. Wesoloski, Sept. 3, 1960; children: Joyce E., Janis M., Jolene G., Jay R. AS, Joliet Jr. Coll., 1959; BS, U. Ill., 1962; DSc, Washington U., 1966. Devel. engr. Petrolite Corp., Webster Groves, Mo., 1962-64; sr. devel. engr. A.E. Staley Co., Decatur, Ill., 1965-67, rsch. mgr. chem. div., 1967-75, dept. dir. rsch. div., 1975-87; v.p. product and process tech. Grain Processing Corp., Muscatine, Iowa, 1987-2000. Adv. coun. adult vocat. edn. State of Ill., Springfield, 1983—87; mem. organizing com. Ann. Symposium on Biotech. for Fuels and Chems., 1985—97; departmental vis. com. botany dept. U. Tex., Austin, 1986—99; mem. applied sci. adv. coun. Miami U., Oxford, Ohio, 1987—97; chmn. rev. com. Solar Energy Rsch. Inst., Golden, Colo., 1988—89; mem. Sci. and Industry Adv. Bd., Nat. Renewable Energy Lab., Golden, Colo., 1993—99; mem. Bd. on Higher Edn. in the Workforce NRC, 2001—; mem. sci. adv. bd. Mascoma Corp., 2006—. Contbr. sci. papers to profl. jours.; patentee in field. Staff sgt. USAF, 1953-57. Mem. AAAS, AIChE, Am. Chem. Soc., Nat. Acad. Engring., Am. Legion, Rotary. Republican. Avocations: sailboat racing, running. Home: 106 Cape Fear Dr Hertford NC 27944-9239 Office Phone: 252-426-6499. Personal E-mail: virdon@mchsi.com.

JOHNSON, DONALD RAYMOND, lawyer; b. NYC, June 26, 1960; s. Donald Francis and Jacqueline E. (Barnett) J. BA, Liberty U., 1982, MA, 1984; JD, Washington and Lee U., 1989; postgrad., Va. Polytech. Inst., Yale U., U. Va. Bar: Va. 1989, D.C. 1991, N.Y. 1995, U.S. Dist. Ct. (no., so., and ea. dists.) N.Y., U.S. Dist. Ct. (ea. and we. dists.) Va., U.S. Ct. Appeals (fed. cir.), U.S. Supreme Ct., U.S. Ct. Internat. Trade. Pvt. practice, Charlottesville, Va., 1989-96; dir., pres. Internat. Brokerage & Investment Co., Charlottesville, 1991-99; dir., v.p. Internat. Investment Svcs., Inc., Charlottesville, 1991-2000; pvt. practice NYC, 1995—; pres. Real E.S. AG, 2003—. Bd. dirs. Excellence in Edn., Charlottesville, 1990-92, Heritage Soc., Charlottesville, 1990-92, World of Life Internat., 2000—; U.S. del. German-Am. Multiplicitorian Seminars; founder Mission, Inc., 2000—. Named one of Outstanding Young Men of Am., Alumnus of the Yr.; recipient numerous awards and honors for ednl., civic, and social activities. Mem. ABA, ATLA. Republican. Baptist. Avocations: running, sailing, tennis. Home: 777 US Route 9 Schroon Lake NY 12870-2314 Office Fax: 801-340-1789. Business E-Mail: drjohnson@att.net.

JOHNSON, DONN S., communications executive; b. May 9, 1947; AA, St. Louis CC, 1975; BA, Webster Coll., St. Louis, 1977. Anchor, reporter KTVI Fox 2 TV, St. Louis, 1978—98, KMOV-TV, St. Louis, 2000—02; morning talk show host KTRS Radio, St. Louis, 1998—2000; dir. comms. Mo. Hist. Soc., St. Louis, 2002—. Author: (column) Mo. Hist. Soc., 2002—05. Recipient Telly award, 2005. Mem.: Am. Assn. State and Local History. Office: 5700 Lindell Saint Louis MO 63112

JOHNSON, DORIS JEAN, social worker; b. Raymond, Miss., July 16, 1946; AA, Wayne County C.C., Detroit, 1986; BSW, U. Detroit, 1989; MSW, Wayne State U., 1993. Supr. Ren, Detroit, 1993—94; psychiat. social worker Aurora Healthcare, Inc., Detroit, 1994—2001, Detroit Cmty. Health Connection, 2002—; clin. social worker Psychiat. and Behavioral Medicine Profls., 2003—. Author: (novel) A Reflection of Memories, 2003. Pres. Slum Lord Fighters, Detroit, 1981, Human Svcs. Orgn./Wayne County C.C., 1984; v.p. social work orgn./Univ. Detroit, 1988. Named to Wall of Tolerance, Civil Rights Meml. Ctr., 2005; recipient cert. Appreciation, Detroit Police Athletic League, 1989, award of Recognition, Detroit City Coun., 1989, cert. appreciation, 36th Dist. Ct., Detroit, 1997. Mem.: Black Expression Club. E-mail: doris0716@aol.com.

JOHNSON, DOROTHY CURFMAN, elementary school educator; b. Smithsburg, Md., Nov. 21, 1930; d. Paul Frank and Rhoda Pearl (Witmer) Curfman; m. Robert Nelson Johnson, Jan. 24, 1953 (div. Dec. 1965); children: Gregory Nelson, Eric Paul. Student, Gettysburg Coll., 1948-50, Waynesboro Bus. Coll., 1950, Broward C.C., Ft. Lauderdale, Fla., 1967; BS in Edn., Fla. Atlantic U., 1969, postgrad., 1975-76. Cert. tchr., Fla. Sec. to prodn. mgr. Westinghouse Elec. Corp., Sunbury, Pa., 1951-53; sec. to v.p., sales Metal Carbides Corp., Youngstown, Ohio, 1966; tchr. Sch. Bd. of Broward County, Ft. Lauderdale, Ohio, 1969-93, curriculum specialist, 1993-96. Masters in Edn. Prog., 1973-74, team coord. Sanders Park Elem., Pompano Beach, Fla., 1985-96; mem. North Area Adv. Bd., Pompano Beach, 1990-96; sec. Sanders Park PTA, Pompano Beach, 1994-96, Sec.-treas. Georgen Arms Bd. of Dirs., Pompano Beach, 1997—; dir. Georgen Arms Condo, Inc., Pompano Beach, 1974—; active Jr. League, Youngstown. Recipient Master Tchr. award State of Fla., 1981-82. Mem. Alpha Xi Delta. Lutheran. Home: 280 S Cypress Rd Apt 5 Pompano Beach FL 33060-7038

JOHNSON, DOROTHY JEAN, retired secondary school educator; b. Watsonville, Calif. children: Mark L. Johnson, Michele K. Clark. AA, Coll. of Notre Dame, Belmont, Calif., 1949; BA, San Jose State U., 1950, postgrad., 1951. Cert. tchr., Calif. Tchr. Abraham Lincoln High Sch., San Jose, Calif., 1951; tchr. French, Spanish and English Tule Lake (Calif.) High Sch., 1952—93, mentor tchr., 1989-91. Stanford U. scholar; U. Calif. at Berkeley scholar. Mem. Phi Beta Kappa. Avocations: travel, reading, gardening, writing, crafts. Personal E-mail: dotj@charter.net.

JOHNSON, DOUG, advertising and public relations executive; b. Watertown, NY, Aug. 16, 1919; s. H. Douglas and Clare (Lane) J.; m. Geraldine Evans, Aug. 11, 1943; children: Andrew (dec.), Molly E., Faith D. Student pub. schs. Pres. Doug Johnson Assos. (pub. relations), Syracuse, NY, 1949-61, Barlow/Johnson, Inc. (advt. and pub. relations), Syracuse, 1961-80, Johnlow Corp., Fayetteville; chmn. bd. Nowak Barlow Johnson, Fayetteville, 1980-82; v.p. mktg. Edward Joy Co., Inc., Syracuse, 1982-84. Pres. 10 Co. Mktg.; dir. Agway Indemnity Ins. Co., Dewitt, N.Y., Key Bank of Central N.Y., Syracuse, Syracuse Baseball Club, Inc.; chmn. exec. com. Agway Ins. Co., Dewitt. Home sec. to congressman, 1949-65; bd. dirs., v.p. Community Gen. Hosp. Syracuse, N.Y. State Coll. Forestry Found.; bd. dirs., past pres. Syracuse Boys Club; v.p. CNY Assoc. Artists; pres. L.W. Artists Assn., 1997-98; bd. dirs., past pres. USO of CNY, nat. bd. dirs., USO. Served with AUS, 1941-45. Decorated Purple Heart with 3 oak leaf clusters, Bronze Star, Combat Infantry Badge with Silver Star. Mem. Pub. Rels. Soc. Am. (cert. bus. communicator), Syracuse C. of C. (pres. 1968-69) Clubs: Century (gov.). Home and Office: 1444 Leisure World Mesa AZ 85206-2304 E-mail: johnse2@aol.com.

JOHNSON, DOUGLAS BLAIKIE, lawyer; b. Chgo., Sept. 13, 1952; s. Marvin Melrose and Anne Stuart (Campbell) J.; m. Pamela Jane Tomlinson, Aug. 1, 1975; children: Richard Aaron, Lauren Stuart, Diana Blaikie, Scott Nathaniel, Catherine Joan. BSME, U. Nebr., 1974; JD, Seton Hall U., 1980. Bar: Nebr. 1980, U.S. Dist. Ct. Nebr. 1980; registered profl. engr., Nebr., Ark. Project engr. DuPont, Cleve., 1974-75, Exxon Chems., Linden, NJ, 1975-78, cost engr., 1978-80; sr. engr. InterNorth, Inc., Omaha, 1980-82, market planner, 1982-84, corp. planner, 1984-85, bus. mgr., 1985-86; program mgr. Brunswick Corp., Lincoln, Nebr., 1987-95; product devel. mgr. Lincoln Composites, 1995—98, sr. bus. devel. mgr., 1999—2000, dir. oilfield products, 2000—02; mgr. Gen. Dynamics, Lincoln, Nebr., 2003—06, sr. program mgr., 2006—. Mem. ABA, ATLA, Nebr. Bar Assn., Lincoln Bar Assn., Triangle, Sigma Tau, Pi Tau Sigma, Phi Eta Sigma. Republican. Presbyterian. Home: 4600 Birch Hollow Dr Lincoln NE 68516-5107 Office: Gen Dynamics 150 Johnston Rd Marion VA 24354-4324 Office Phone: 276-783-9628. Personal E-mail: djohnson1@neb.rr.com. Business E-Mail: djohnson2@gdatp.com.

JOHNSON, DOUGLAS L., lawyer; BA, U. Southern Calif., 1996; JD, U. of Pacific, 2000. Bar: Calif., US Dist. Ct. Ctrl. & Ea. Calif., US Ct. Appeals Ninth Cir. Sr. assoc., entertainment law & bus. litigation Johnson & Rishwain LLP, Beverly Hills, Calif. Named a Rising Star, So. Calif. Super Lawyers, 2006. Mem.: ABA, Assn. Trial Lawyers Am., Consumer Attorneys Assn. LA. Office: Johnson & Rishwain LLP Ste 200 430 N Canon Dr Beverly Hills CA 90210 Office Phone: 310-975-1080. Office Fax: 310-975-1095. Business E-Mail: djohnson@jrllp.com.

JOHNSON, DOUGLAS WELLS, lawyer; b. May 31, 1949; s. Robert Douglas and Mildred Irene J.; m. Kathryn Ann Hoberg, Oct. 18, 1980. BA, U. Denver, 1971, JD, 1974. Ptnr. Mellman, Mellman & Thorn, Denver, 1974-80; sr. atty. Amoco Corp., Chgo., 1980-91; mgr. real estate Amoco Oil Co., Chgo., 1991-94; sr. atty. Amoco Corp., Chgo., 1994-98; mng. atty. BP Am. Inc., Warrenville, Ill., 1998—. U. Denver Alumni scholar, 1967—71. Mem. ABA, Ill. Bar Assn., D.C. Bar Assn., Chgo. Bar Assn., Kappa Delta Pi. Home: 3040 Indianwood Rd Wilmette IL 60091 Office: BP America Inc 4101 Winfield Rd Warrenville IL 60555 Office Phone: 630-836-3451. Business E-Mail: johnsodw@bp.com.

JOHNSON, DOUGLAS WILLIAM, radiologist; b. Westpoint, NY; s. Andrew Larson and Barbara Joan (Rosborough) J.; m. Susan Mary Friedman, July 23, 1977; children: Danielle, Michael. BS in Biology, Va. Tech., Blacksburg, Va., 1976; MD, Med. Coll. Va., Richmond, 1979. Chmn. radiation oncology David Grant USAF Med. Ctr., Travis AFB, Calif., 1983-87; ptnr. Fla. Radiation Oncology Group, Jacksonville, Fla., 1987—. Asst. prof. radiation-oncology Stanford Med. Ctr., Stanford U., Calif., 1983-87; asst. prof. oncology Mayo Clinic Med. Sch., Rochester, Minn., 1995—; fellow Am. Coll. Radiology, Phila., 1995. Patentee in field. Col. USAF, 1975-. Fellow Am. Coll. Radiology; mem. Am. Soc. Therapeutic Radiology & Oncology. Avocation: aviation. Office: Baptist Cancer Inst 1235 San Marco Blvd Ste 100 Jacksonville FL 32207-8560 Office Phone: 904-202-7020.

JOHNSON, DWAYNE DOUGLAS (THE ROCK), actor, professional wrestler; b. Hayward, Calif., May 2, 1972; s. Rocky and Ata Johnson; m. Dany Garcia, May 3, 1997 (separated June 1, 2007); 1 child, Simone Alexandra. BA in criminology & physiology, U. Miami, 1995. Profl. wrestler, 1996—2004. Actor: (films) The Mummy Returns, 2001, The Scorpion King, 2002, The Rundown, 2003, Walking Tall, 2004, Be Cool, 2005, Doom, 2005, Southland Tales, 2006, Gridiron Gang, 2006; wrestler (TV series) WWF Superstars of Wrestling, 1996, WWF Monday Night Raw, 1996—97, Sunday Night Heat, 1998—2004, Raw is War, 1997—2004, WWF Smackdown, 1999—2002, TV appearances include That 70s Show, 1999, The Net, 1999, Star Trek: Voyager, 2000. Achievements include 7 time World Wrestling Fedn. champion. Office: c/o WWF Titan Tower 1241 E Main St Stamford CT 06902*

JOHNSON, E. PERRY, lawyer; b. Pa., 1943; BA, W.Va. U., 1965, JD, 1968. Bar: W. Va. 1968, D.C. 1981, Mo. 1983. Instr. Boston U. Sch. Law, 1973-74, asst. dir., 1977-79, bur. competition, exec. asst. to chmn., 1979, dep. dir., 1979-80, dir., 1980-81; ptnr. Bryan Cave LLP, St. Louis. Vis. asst. prof. W. Va. U., 1972-73; adj. prof. St. Louis U. Sch. Law, 1985-86. With USN, 1968-72. Mem. ABA. Office: Bryan Cave LLP One Metropolitan Square 211 N Broadway Ste 3600 Saint Louis MO 63102-2733 E-mail: epjohnson@bryancave.com.

JOHNSON, E. SCOTT, lawyer; b. Washington, June 28, 1951; s. William and Dorothy (Young) J.; m. Karen Colaianni, May 15, 1969 (div. 1972); 1 child, Scott Adrian; m. Cindy Ward, Feb. 14, 1986; 1 child, Tracy Elizabeth. BA summa cum laude, U. Md., 1985; JD cum laude, Georgetown U., 1988. Bar: US Ct. Appeals (Md.), US Dist. Ct. (dist. Md.), Md. 1988. Studio musician Blue Seas Studios, Balt., 1973-75; record prodr. Flite III Studios, Balt., 1975-80; atty. Ober, Kaler, Grimes & Shriver, Balt., 1988—, chmn. intellectual property practice group. Legal intern Nat. Assn. Broadcasters, 1987. Editor-in-chief Public Domain Report, 1993—99; contbr. articles to profl. jours.; producer LP's including Portal of Antrim, 1976, Rivers of Memory, 1979, Portraits, 1978; Doncha Hide It, 1978, co-producer North Mountain Velvet, 1978. Pres. Md. Lawyers for the Arts, Balt., 1990—98; pres. Young Audiences Md., Balt., 1994-97; bd. dirs. Creative Alliance, 2004-; mem. Md. State Arts Coun., 2004. Recipient First Prize: Nathan Burkan Copyright Law Competition ASCAP, Georgetown, 1987, Second Prize: Stephen G. Thompson Nat. Writing Competition Comm. Law; named one of 115 Best Lawyers, Balt. Mag., 1995, Top Attys., 2003. Mem. ABA, ASCAP, NARAS, Washington Area Music Assn., Md. Bar Assn., Copyright Soc. U.S.A., Mid-Atlantic Arts Found., Inc. (v.p. 2001-03, pres. 2003-04), Washington Area Music Assn. (bd. dirs. 1993-). Office: Ober Kaler Grimes & Shriver 120 E Baltimore St Ste 800 Baltimore MD 21202 Office Phone: 410-347-7388. Office Fax: 443-263-7588. E-mail: johnson@ober.com.*

JOHNSON, EARL, JR., judge, author; b. Watertown, SD, June 10, 1933; s. Earl Jerome and Doris Melissa (Schwartz) J.; m. Barbara Claire Yanow, Oct. 11, 1970; children: Kelly Ann, Earl Eric, Agaarn Yanovitch. BA in Econs., Northwestern U., 1955, LL.M., 1961; JD, U. Chgo., 1960. Bar: Ill. 1960, US Ct. Appeals (9th cir.) 1964, DC 1965, US Supreme Ct. 1966, Calif. 1972. Trial atty., organized crime sect. Dept. Justice, Washington, Miami, Fla. and Las Vegas, Nev., 1961-64; dep. dir. Neighborhood Legal Svc. Project, 1964-65, OEO Legal Svc. Program, 1965-66, dir., 1966-68; vis. scholar Ctr. for Study of Law and Soc. U. Calif., Berkeley, 1968-69; assoc. prof. U. So. Calif. Law Ctr., LA, 1969-75, dir. clin. programs, 1970-73, prof. law, 1976-82, dir. Program Study Dispute Resolution Policy, Social Sci. Rsch. Inst., 1975-82; assoc. justice Calif. Ct. Appeal, 1982—; co-dir. Access to Justice Project European U. Inst., 1975-79. Vis. scholar Inst. Comparative Law, U. Florence, Italy, 1973, 75; Robert H. Jackson lectr. Nat. Jud. Coll., 1980; adv. panel Legal Svc. Corp., 1976-80; legis. impact panel Nat. Acad. Sci., 1977-80; faculty Asian Workshop on Legal Svcs. to Poor, 1974; mem. Internat. Legal Ctr., Legal Svcs. in Developing Countries, 1972-75; founder, bd. mem. Action for Legal Rights, 1971-74; pres., trustee Western Ctr. on Law and Poverty, 1972-73, 76-80; v.p., chmn. exec. com. Calif. Rural Legal Assistance Corp., 1973-74; exec. com. Nat. Sr. Citizens Law Ctr., 1980-82; sec. Nat. Resource Ctr. for Consumers of Legal Svc., 1974-82; chair Nat. Equal Justice Libr. Com., 1989-92; pres., Consortium for Nat. Equal Justice Libr., Inc., 1992-95, bd. dir., 1995—; chair Calif. Access to Justice Working Group, 1993-96; mem. Calif. Commn. on Access to Justice, 1997—2004, co-chmn., 2002-03; spl. advisor Presdl. Commn. on Access to Justice, 2005-06. Author: Justice and Reform: The Formative Years of the Am. Legal Svc. Program, 1974, 2d edit., 1978, Toward Equal Justice: A Comparative Study of Legal Aid in Modern Soc., 1975, Outside the Courts: A Survey of Diversion Alternatives in Civil Cases, 1977, Dispute Processing Strategies, 1978, Dispute Resolution in Am., 1985, Calif. Trial Guide, 8 vols., 1986, Tex. Trial Guide, 6 vols., 1989, NY Trial Guide, 5 vols., 1990, Fla. Civil Trial Guide, 5 vols., 1990, Ill. Civil Trial Guide, 5 vols., 1991, Fed. Trial Guide, 5 vols., 1992, Ind. Civil Trial Guide, 5 vols., 1992, Calif. Family Law Trial Guide, 5 vols., 1992, Pa. Civil Trial Guide, 5 vols., 1992, Mich. Trial Guide, 5 vols., 1993, NC Civil Trial Guide, 5 vols., 1993, Calif. Criminal Trial Guide, 3 vols., 1994, Murder on Appeal (as Holmes Marshall), 2001, The Firenze

Faction (as Gideon Black), 2004; editor U. Chgo. Law Rev, 1960; mem. editl. bd. Jour. Law and Social Inquiry, 1987-2001; contbr. articles to books and periodicals. Bd. dir. Beverly Hills Bar Found., 1972-73, Nat. Legal Aid and Defenders Assn., 1987-91; trustee LA Legal Aid Found., 1969-71; mem. LA County Regional Planning Commn., 1980-81; bd. visitors U. San Diego Law Sch., 1983-86. Served with USNR, 1955-58. Recipient Dart award for acad. innovation U. So. Calif., 1971, Loren Miller Legal Svc. award Calif. State Bar, 1977, Appellate Justice of the Yr. award LA Trial Lawyers Assn., 1989, Outstanding Jud. Achievement award Calif. Trial Lawyers Assn., 1991, Legal Svc. Pioneer award LA Legal Aid Found., 1999, Appelate Judge of the Yr. award, Consumer Attorneys of Calif., 2003, Aranda Access to Justice award Calif. Jud. Coun. Judges Assn. Bar Assn., 2004, Beacon of Justice award LA County Law Libr., 2006, Outstanding Jurist award LA County Bar Assn., 2007; named So. Calif. Citizen of Week, 1978; Ford Found. fellow, 1960; Dept. State lectr., 1975; grantee Ford Found., Russell Sage Found., Law Enforcement Assistance Adminstrn., NSF. Fellow Am. Bar Found. (rsch. adv. com. 1996-2001, chair 1999-2002); mem. ABA (com. chmn. 1972-75, spl. com. resolution minor disputes 1976-83, coun. sect. of individual rights and responsibilities 1990-91, consortium on legal svc. and the pub. 1991-94, standing com. on legal aid and indigant defendants 2007-), Calif. Bar Assn., LA Bar Assn. (neighborhood justice ctr. com. 1976-81, Outstanding Jurist award 2007), Law and Soc. Assn., Nat. Legal Aid and Defender's Assn. (bd. dir. 1968-74), Am. Acad. Polit. and Social Sci., Calif. Judges Assn. (appellate cts. com. 1983-87, 98-99, ethics com. 1985-89), Internat. Assn. Procedural Law, Internat. Legal Aid Group, Order of Coif. Democrat. Office: Ct Appeals Calif 2d Appellate Dist 300 S Spring St Los Angeles CA 90013-1230 E-mail: justej@aol.com. *I have profound faith in the power of ideas to shape American society and in the special significance of one fundamental concept— equal justice, in its full meaning.*

JOHNSON, EARVIN See JOHNSON, MAGIC

JOHNSON, EDDIE, professional soccer player; b. Palm Coast, Fla., Mar. 31, 1984; Forward Dallas Burn, 2001—05, Kansas City Wizards, 2005—. 18 caps, 9 goals U.S. Nat. Soccer Team, 2004—; mem. U.S. World Cup Team, 2006. Named to FIFA World Youth Championship All-Star team, 2003. Mailing: US Soccer Fedn 1801 S Prairie Ave Chicago IL 60616

JOHNSON, EDDIE BERNICE, congresswoman; b. Waco, Tex., Dec. 3, 1935; d. Lee Edward and Lillie Mae (White) Johnson; m. Lacy Kirk Johnson, July 5, 1956 (div. Oct. 1970); 1 child, Dawrence Kirk. Diploma in Nursing, U. Notre Dame St. Mary's Coll., South Bend, Ind., 1955; BSN, Tex. Christian U., 1967; MPA, So. Meth. U., 1976; LLD (hon.), Bishop Coll., 1979, Jarvis Coll., 1979, Tex. Coll., 1989, Houston-Tillotson Coll., 1993, Paul Quinn Coll., 1993. Chief psychiat. nurse psychotherapist Vets. Adminstrn. Hosp., Dallas, 1956-72; mem. Tex. State Ho. Reps. from Dist. 33-0, Dallas, 1972-77; regional dir. Dept. Health, Edn. and Welfare, Dallas, 1977-79, exec. asst. to adminstr. for primary health care policy Washington, 1979-81; v.p. Vis. Nurse Assn. Tex., Dallas, 1981-87; mem. Tex. State Senate from Dist. 23, 1986-93, US Congress from 30th Tex. dist., 1993—, mem. transp. and infrastructure com., chairwoman water resources and environment subcom., mem. sci. com. Cons. divsn. urban affairs Zales Corpn., Dallas, 1976-77; exec. asst. pers. divsn. Neiman-Marcus, Dallas, 1972-75; pres. Eddie Bernice Johnson & Assocs., Inc., Metroplex News, Dallas-Ft. Worth Airport. Bd. dirs. ARC. Recipient Citizenship award Nat. Conf. Christians and Jews, 1985, Tex. NAACP Heroes award, 2000, Pres.'s award Nat. Conf. Black Mayors, Visonary award Nat. Orgn. Black Elected Legis. Women, 2001, Woman of Yr. award 100 Black Men of Am., Inc., 2001, 25th Anniversary Outstanding Achievement award Nat. Black Caucus State Legislators; named an Outstanding Alumnus St. Mary's Coll. of Nursing, 1986; named one of Most Influential Black Americans, Ebony mag., 2006 Mem. Alpha Kappa Alpha. Democrat. Office: US Ho Reps 1511 Longworth Ho Office Bldg Washington DC 20515-4330 Home Phone: 703-413-1121; Office Phone: 202-225-8885.

JOHNSON, EDGAR MCCARTHY, psychologist; b. Jacksonville, Fla., Oct. 29, 1941; s. James Mack and Dorothy (Vickers) Johnson; m. Fatima Nunes, Sept. 9, 1967; children: Victoria C., David M. BS in Applied Psychology, Ga. Inst. Tech., 1964; MS in Exptl. Psychology, Tufts U., 1967, PhD in Exptl. Psychology, 1969. Rsch. psychologist U.S. Army Rsch. Inst., Alexandria, Va., 1970-78, chief human factors sect., 1978-80, dir. systems rsch. lab., 1980-82, tech. dir., 1982-93, dir., 1993—2002; chief psychologist U.S. Army, 1982—2002; mem. rsch. staff Inst. Def. Analyses, Alexandria, Va., 2002—. Bd. trustees Amelia Island Mus. H"istory. Served to capt. US Army, 1968—70. NDEA fellow, 1965—67. Fellow: APA, Washington Acad. Sci. (Sci. Achievement award 1980), Human Factors and Ergonomics Soc., Am. Psychol. Soc.; mem.: Cosmos Club (Washington), Sigma Xi. Office: Inst for Def Analyses 4850 Mark Ctr Dr Alexandria VA 22311-1882 Home: 1384 Mission San Carlos Dr Amelia Island FL 32034 Personal E-mail: emj1@sigmaxi.net. Business E-Mail: emjohnso@ida.org.

JOHNSON, EDNA RUTH, editor; b. Sturgeon Bay, Wis., Dec. 23, 1918; d. Charles Frederick and Georgina (Knutson) Johnson; m. Al Larson, 1955. BA, U. So. Fla., 1971. With The Churchman, 1950-89; editor The Human Quest (formerly The Churchman), St. Petersburg, Fla., 1958—98. Tchr. ballroom dancing to Eckerd Coll. Students, St. Petersburg, Fla., 1995-96. Co-author (with Antoni Gronowicz): Sergei Rachmaninoff, 1946; editor: Friendship News (USA-USSR), 1975—88; mem. editl. bd. The Humanist, Amherst, N.Y., 1980—. Bd. dirs. ACLU, Nat. Emergency Civil Liberties Com., N.Y.C. Named Fla. Humanist of Yr. Am. Humanist Assn. Fla., 1975, Pres. Soc. of Fine Arts Arts, Pinellas Park, Fla., 1970-90. Mem. Acad. Sr. Profls. at Eckerd Coll. Avocations: ballroom dancing, ballet, painting. Home and Office: 411 First Ave N Princess Martha Apt 901 Saint Petersburg FL 33701 Office Phone: 727-894-0097.

JOHNSON, EDWARD C., literature and language educator, social sciences educator; b. LaCrosse, Wis., Nov. 7, 1954; s. Alfred L. and Debra A. Johnson; m. Rebecca A. Johnson, July 30, 1977; children: Amber, Aubrey. BS in Elem. Edn., U. LaCrosse, Wis., 1977. Mid. sch. tchr. Clintonville Pub. Sch., Wis. Instr. Nat. Ski Patrol, Nordia Mountain, Wash., 2001—. Mem.: Moose (pres. 2007—, scholar chair 2005—, editor 2005—). Democrat. Home: W8638 Adams Beach Dr Clintonville WI 54929

JOHNSON, EDWARD CROSBY, III, (NED JOHNSON), investment company executive; b. Boston, June 29, 1930; s. Edward C. and Elsie (Johnson) J.; m. Elizabeth Bishop Hodges, Oct. 8, 1960; children: Abigail Pierrepont, Elizabeth Livingston, Edward Crosby. AB, Harvard U., 1954. Analyst Fidelity Investments, Boston, 1957, mgr., Trend Fund, 1960, mgr., Fidelity Internat. Fund (renamed Magellan), 1963—72; pres. FMR Corp., Boston, 1972-77, chmn. bd., CEO, 1977—. Bd. dirs. Ctr. for Neurologic Diseases; hon. trustee Mus. Fine Arts, Boston. Served with AUS, 1954-56. Named one of Forbes Richest Americans, 1999—, World's Richest People, Forbes Mag., 2000—07. Fellow Am. Acad. Arts and Scis.; mem. Mass. Hist. Soc. Office: Fidelity Investments 82 Devonshire St Boston MA 02109*

JOHNSON, EDWARD ELEMUEL, psychologist, educator; b. Jamaica, B.W.I., July 25, 1926; came to U.S., 1941, naturalized, 1948; s. Edward and Mary Elizabeth (Blake) J.; m. Beverley Jean Morris, Jan. 26, 1955; children— Edward Elemuel, Lawrence Palmer, Robin Jeannine, Nathan Jerome, Cyril Ulric. BS, Howard U., 1947, MS, 1948; PhD, U. Colo., 1952. Assoc. prof. psychology Grambling Coll., La., 1954-55; prof. So. U., Baton Rouge, 1955-60, prof., head dept. psychology, 1960-69, assoc. dean univ., 1969-72, dir. Regional Head Start Evaluation and Research Ctr.; clin. prof. La. State U. Med. Sch., New Orleans, 1969-72; dir. United Bd. for Coll. Devel., 1972-74; dir. 13 coll. curriculum program So. U., Baton Rouge; clin. prof. psychiatry Emory U. Med. Sch., Atlanta, 1973-74; prof. psychiatry Robert Wood Johnson Med. Sch., Piscataway, NJ, 1974—2003, clin. prof. psychiatry, 2003—; pres. Limited Liability Corp. in Forensic Psychology, 2002—; pvt. practice, 2003—. Cons. collaborative child devel. project; cons. State Indsl. Sch. Scotlandville, La., 1973-74, VA Hosp., Lyons, N.J., 1987; mem. Med. Rev. Panel, State of N.J., 1976-2006, chmn., 1993; vocat. cons. HEW; mem. mental health adv. group Westinghouse Health Systems, 1978-82; region II mental health coordinator Head Start Program, 1978—; mem. gen. research support rev. com. NIH, 1980—; mem. acad. council Thomas A. Edison Coll. NJ, 1978-83; mem. adv. bd. Office Pub. Guardian, State of N.J., 1988—; chmn. minority and cultural concerns com. div. Mental Health and Hosps. State of N.J., 1989—; psychol. evaluator Superior Ct. NJ Middlesex Vicinage, 1996—; lectr. forensic psychology U. V.I., St. Croix; cons. forensic psychology. Contbr. articles to profl. jours. Bd. dir. Crossroads Theatre Co., New Brunswick, N.J. Served to 1st lt. AUS, 1951-53. Fellow AAAS; mem. Am. Psychol. Assn. (com. on adv. svcs. for edn. and tng. 1968-69, task group on faculty devel. for minority and non-minority faculty to implement culturally relevant curriculum 1992), N.Y. Acad. Scis. (life), Masons, Sigma Xi, Sigma Pi Phi, Alpha Phi Alpha, Beta Beta Beta, Pi Gamma Mu, Psi Chi. Home: PO Box 597 East Brunswick NJ 08816-0597 Home Phone: 732-257-4885; Office Phone: 732-254-1541.

JOHNSON, EDWARD MICHAEL, lawyer, small business owner; b. Waco, Tex., July 12, 1944; s. Edward James and Anne Margaret (Stuchly) Johnson; m. Yvonne Margaret Hill, May 7, 1977; children: Hilary Yvonne, Megan Joy, Michael David. BA in Polit. Sci., S.W. Tex. State U., 1967; JD, St. Mary's U., 1970. Bar: Tex. 1971, U.S. Dist. Ct. (we. and so. dist.) Tex. 1972, U.S. Ct. Claims, 1972, U.S. Supreme Ct. 1976. Asst. law libr. Bexar County Law Libr., 1968-69; briefing clk. Judge Preston H. Dial, Jr., 1969-70; briefing atty. U.S. Dist. Judge John H. Wood Jr., San Antonio, 1971-72; asst. U.S. atty. Dept. Justice, San Antonio, 1972-76; sole practice San Antonio, 1976-81; sr. atty. Wiley, Garwood, Hornbuckle, Higdon & Johnson, San Antonio, 1980-81; pres. McCabe Petroleum Corp., San Antonio, 1981; chmn. bd., CEO, gen. counsel Blue Chip Petroleum Corp., San Antonio, 1981-83; pres., CEO Harvest Investments Corp., San Antonio, 1983-87, also dir.; gen. ptrn. Med. Mobility Ltd. IV, San Antonio, 1984-87; mgr. Med. Mobility Joint Venture, San Antonio, 1984-87; exec. cons. Advance Tax Representation, Inc., 1987-88; gen. ptrn. Harvest Venture Capital Ltd. I, San Antonio, 1986-87; pres., gen. counsel Blue Chip Securities Corp., San Antonio, 1984-87; rep. First Investors Corp., 1987-88; pres., CEO Johnson, Curney, & Fields, P.C., 1990-2000; Diamond direct distbr. Amway Corp., 1997—2000; mem. exec. com. EcoQuest Internat., 2002—04; pres., CEO Mangosteen Health Beverages Internat, Inc., 2004—. Host radio program The Christian Lawyer, 1990-91, TV program God's Army, 1990-98; mem. adv. bd. Red McCombs Galleria Imports, 1996-98, Network Mktg. Lifestyles Mag., 1999-2002, Hovey Motorcars, 1999—. Co-chmn. fund raising Am. Heart Assn., San Antonio, 1982-84; bd. dirs. Am. Cancer Soc., San Antonio, 1982-84; chmn. San Fernando Cathedral Endowment Fund, San Antonio, 1986; mem. Gideons Internat., San Antonio, 1982-86, mem. exec. bd. San Antonio Christian Schs., 1983-84, San Antonio Christian Legal Soc., 1991-2000, Fed. Bar Licensing Bd., 1976-78; bd. dirs. Tex. Bible Coll., 1984-87, Christian Businessmen's Com., San Antonio, 1981-88, Cornerstone Christian Schs., San Antonio, 1991-92, mem., spkr., pres. Med. Ctr. chpt. 1988-91, mem. Full Gospel Businessmen's Fellowship, 1981-92, pres. 1985-88, field rep., 1988-92; Rep. precinct chmn., 1988-89; bd. dirs. Assn. Spirit Filled Fellowships, 1991-93; pres. God's Army Internat. Found., Inc., 1990-92; gen. counsel, bd. dirs. Four Winds Ministries, Inc., 1992-93; scoutmaster Alamo coun. Boy Scouts Am., San Antonio, 1973-74; founder, chmn. Christian Businessmen's Focus on the Family, San Antonio, 1984-85. Recipient spl. commendation Dept. Transp. 1973, Dept. Air Force HQ. ATC, 1974, Dept. Treasury, 1974; named Outstanding Asst. U.S. Atty. Dept. Justice, 1974-75, Outstanding Young Texans, 1976. Mem. Fed. Bar Assn. (pres. San Antonio chpt. 1975-76, v.p. 1973-74, sec. 1972-73, treas. 1971-72, Outstanding Chpt. Pres. award 1976), Tex. Bar Assn., San Antonio Bar Assn. (spl. asst. to exec. dir. 1968-69). Republican. Office Phone: 210-877-0855. Personal E-mail: edjohnson@stic.net.

JOHNSON, ELIZABETH, communications executive, interpreter; b. NYC, Apr. 11, 1961; V.p. MEJ Personal Bus. Svcs., Inc., NYC.

JOHNSON, ELIZABETH DIANE LONG, retired lawyer; b. Pasadena, Calif., Nov. 16, 1945; d. Volney Earl and Sylvia Irene (Drury) Long; m. Lynn Douglas Johnson, Oct. 22, 1966; 1 child, Barbara Annette. BA, U. of Houston, 1967; JD, Rutgers U., 1980. Bar: N.J. 1980, U.S. Dist. Ct. N.J. 1980, Pa. 1984, U.S. Supreme Ct. 1986. Pvt. practice, Riverside, NJ, 1980—96; ret., 1996. Pub. defender Riverside Twp., 1988-91; speaker Comprehensive Justice Ctr. Burlington County, 1987-89. Del. Women in Law to Peoples Republic of China Citizen Amb. Program of People to People Internat., 1989; mem. Orchid Found., 1989-97, rec. sec., 1991-97; mem. Tenby Chase Civic Assn., Delran, N.J., 1972-87, treas., 1976, v.p., 1974; trustee Drenk Mental Health Ctr., 1988-95, pres., 1991-94, chair bd. trustees, 1993-94, vice chair bd. trustees, 1995. Mem.: Burlington County Bar Found. (trustee 1988—91, treas. 1988—90, v.p. 1990—91, pres. 1991—92), Burlington County Bar Assn. (chmn. bench and bar com. 1989—91), N.J. Women Lawyers Assn., Mensa, Soc. for Right to Die, Rotary (sec. Riverside 1991—92, v.p. 1992—93, pres.-elect 1993—94, pres. 1994—95, dir. 1995—96, Dist. 7500 area rep. 1995—96, sec. Beverly 2000—01, 2003—, v.p. 2001—02, pres. 2002—03, Dist. 7500 sec. 2004—05, Outstanding Dist. Officer 2004—05), Delta Gamma. Methodist.

JOHNSON, ELIZABETH ERICSON, retired educator; b. Rockford, Ill., Oct. 5, 1927; d. Gunnar Lawrence and Victoria Amelia (Carlson) Ericson; m. Barent Olaf Johnson, June 2, 1951; children: Ann E. Arellano, Susan M. Taber. BA, U. Ill., Champaign-Urbana, 1949; MSEd, No. Ill. U., Dekalb, 1969. Tchr. Sch. Dist. 205, Rockford, Ill., 1949-53, 65-92; ret., 1992. Mem. Ct. Appointed Spl. Advocate, Rockford, 1992—. Mem. AAUW, LWV (bd. dirs. 1994-96, local bd.), Ill. Ret. Tchrs. Assn., Winnebago Ret. Tchrs. Assn. (various bds.), Phi Delta Kappa (emeritus). Avocations: music, viola, musician, violist. Home: 3655 N Alpine Rd A318 Rockford IL 61114 Personal E-mail: evebridge@at&t.net.

JOHNSON, ELIZABETH MISNER, health services executive; b. Lewiston, Idaho, May 16, 1939; d. Gervase Arthur and Blenda N. (Westerlund) Misner; m. Dohn Robert Johnson, Oct. 13, 1962; children: Dohn Robert Jr., Kevin Arthur. BS in Acctg., U. Idaho, 1961. CPA, Calif., Wash. Audit staff Randall, Emery, Campbell & Parker (now Pricewaterhouse Coopers), Spokane, Wash., 1961—62; audit staff, sr. Price Waterhouse, LA, 1962-65; CPA LA, 1966-73; CFO KLP, Inc. dba Call-America, Mesa, Ariz., 1995-98; gen. mgr. Life Line Screening, Phoenix, 2001—02; contbr. Martin Park Ranch Homeowners Assn., Phoenix, 2002—. Treas., pres., hon. life mem. Arts Coun. Calif. State U., Northridge, 1975—; internat. dir. alumnae devel. Alpha Gamma Delta (recipient unusually outstanding svc. award, 1993), U.S. and Can., 1988-98; chmn. bd. trustees Alpha Gamma Delta Found., 1998-2001, trustee, 1998—2004. Pres. Soroptimist Internat., Coeur d'Alene, Idaho, 1991-92, regional nominating com., 1993-94. Mem. Ariz. Soc. of CPAs. Home: 14839 S 47th Way Phoenix AZ 85044-6881 Office: MPR Home Owners Assn 15425 S 40th St Ste 4 Phoenix AZ 85044 Office Phone: 480-704-5000. Personal E-mail: liz@mtparkranch.org.

JOHNSON, ELMER WILLIAM, lawyer; b. Denver, May 2, 1932; s. Elmer William and Lillian Marie (Nelson) J.; m. Constance Dorothy Mahon, June 18, 1955; children: Julianne Marie, Valerie Lynn, Garrett Douglas. BA, Yale U., 1954; JD, U. Chgo., 1957. Bar: Ill. 1957. Assoc. Kirkland & Ellis, Chgo., 1956-62, ptnr., 1962—99; v.p., group exec. gen. counsel Gen. Motors Corp., Detroit, 1983-87, exec. v.p., dir., 1987-88; gen. counsel Internat. Harvester, Chgo., 1982-83; spl. counsel to chmn. of Ameritech Corp., Chgo., 1982-83; pres., CEO Aspen Inst., Washington, 1999—2002; ptnr. Jenner & Block, Chgo., 2002—. Mem. legal adv. com. N.Y. Stock Exch., 1987-91; v.p., dir. The Econ. Club of Chgo.; chmn. bd. govs. Chgo. Lighthouse for Blind. Author: Avoiding the Collision of Cities and Cars, 1993, Chicago Metropolis 2020, 2001. Trustee U. Chgo., 1977-89, Aspen Inst., Colo., 1988-2002, pres. CEO, 1999-2002. Fellow Am. Acad. Arts and Scis.; mem. ABA, Ill. Bar Assn., Chgo. Club, Old Elm. Republican. Presbyterian. Office: Jenner & Block 1 IBM Plaza Chicago IL 60611

JOHNSON, ERIC B., state legislator; b. New Orleans, Aug. 20, 1953; m. Kathryn Johnson; children: Marcus, Righton. Degree in architecture, Tulane U. Architect North Point Real Estate; mem. Ga. Ho. of Reps., 1993-94; senator 1st dist. Ga. State Legislature, 1994—, pres. pro tem, 2003—, mem. appropriations com., ethics com., fin. com, natural resources/environment com., rules com., vice chmn. regulated industries and utilities com. Sponsor, mem. joint senate-house study com. on cert. of need health care facilities Ga. State Senate. Regional dir. former U.S. Senator Mack Mattingly, 1981-83; alumnus Leadership Savannah; active Inner City Night Shelter. Named Ga.'s Young Rep. of Yr., 1980. Mem. AIA, Exec. Assn. of Savannah. Mem. Savannah Christian Ch. Address: 128 Baymeadow Point Savannah GA 31405 Business E-Mail: ejohnson@senate.ga.gov.

JOHNSON, ERIC B., police chief; b. Feb. 1967; 4 children. Patrol officer Santa Fe Police Dept., 1987—92, detective, 1992—2001, sergeant Spl. Investigations Sect., 2001—03, dep. police chief, 2003—06, police chief, 2006—. Office: Chief of Police City of Santa Fe PO Box 909 Santa Fe NM 87504-0909 Office Phone: 505-955-5010. Office Fax: 505-955-5052. E-mail: ebjohnson@ci.santa-fenm.gov.

JOHNSON, ERNIE, JR., sportscaster; b. Milw. s. Ernie and Lois Johnson; m. Cheryl Johnson; 4 children. Grad., U. Ga. News and sports dir. WAGQ-FM, Athens, Ga., 1977—78; news anchor WMAZ-TV, Macon, Ga., 1979—81; news reporter WSPA-TV, Spartanburg, SC, 1981; gen. assignment news reporter WSB-TV, Atlanta, 1982—83, weekend sports anchor, reporter, 1983—89; with Turner Sports, 1989—; studio host NFL coverage TNT, 1990—94, game host NFL coverage, 1995, 1996, hole-by-hole announcer PGA Grand Slam of Golf coverage, 1999, 2000, 2002, 2003, co-host Listen Up, 2002—03, co-host Inside the NBA, host NBA and PGA coverage; host Pacific-10 and Big-12 Coll. Football TBS. Recipient UPI award, Sportscasting, 1984, Ga. Associated Press award, Sports Reporting, 1988, Ga.-area Emmy award, Outstanding Achievement-TV News Excellence/Sports Reporting, 1989, Emmy award, Outstanding Sports Personality - Studio Host, 2001, 2007. Office: Turner Sports One CNN Ctr 13 South Tower Atlanta GA 30303*

JOHNSON, ESTHER R., federal official; BA, Va. Commonwealth U.; MA; doctorate in ednl. adminstrn., Va. Polytech. Inst. Math tchr. Naval Surface Warfare Ctr., Dahlgren, Va., 1976; with Arlington County Pub. Schools; various positions including comptroller, assoc. adminstr., divisn. chief, spl. asst. to dir. unemployment ins. Employment and Training Adminstrn., U.S. Dept. Labor, adminstr. Office Employment and Tech.; nat. dir. Office of Job Corps US Dept. Labor, 2006—. Office: US Dept Labor Frances Perkins Bldg 200 Constitution Ave NW Washington DC 20210*

JOHNSON, EUGENE CLARE, data processing company executive; b. Whitehall, Wis., Nov. 19, 1940; s. Paul Reuben and Clara Theresa (Severson) J.; m. Livia Ann Baynes, Sept. 23, 1967; children: Andrew Paul, Anthony Alexander. Student, Madison Coll., 1959, Pasadena Coll., 1961, Purdue U., 1962, Harvard U., 1974. Vol. Peace Corps, Chile, 1962-64; acct. Am. Ins. Underwriters, NYC, 1964-66; advanceman to Pres. Richard M. Nixon NYC, 1966-68; asst. treas. Bristol-Myers Co., NYC, 1968-69; spl. asst. to Gov. Nelson Rockefeller NYC, 1969—70; mgr. advanced systems div. U.S. Postal Service, Washington, 1971-80; mgr. govt. relations dept. ITT, Washington, 1980-85; exec. v.p., chief operating officer TCom Systems, Inc., Washington, 1985-88; v.p. market devel. Diversified Data and Communications Inc., Washington, 1988-90; pres., chief exec. officer Bus. Mail Express, Inc., Washington, 1990-95, Mail 2000, Washington, 1995—2003; vice-chmn., founder Global Mail Strategies. Founder Electronic Funds Transfer Assocs., Washington, 1977. Patentee performance analyzer. Sr. adviser Reagan Presdl. Transition Team, 1980; presdl. appointee U.S. Archtl. and Transp. Barriers Compliance Bd., 1988-90; adv. bd. Peace Corps., 1990-92. Mem.: Kenwood Golf and Country (Bethesda, Md.) (chmn. bd. dirs. 1987, chmn. bd. rebuilding together). Avocations: tennis, golf, jogging. Home: 5525 Chamberlin Ave Chevy Chase MD 20815-6643 Office: Ste 300 7316 Wisconsin Ave Bethesda MD 20814-2976 Office Phone: 301-718-1006. Personal E-mail: genecjohnson@hotmail.com.

JOHNSON, EUGENE LAURENCE, lawyer; b. Wisconsin Rapids, Wis., Nov. 30, 1936; s. Elmer Hilding and Claribel May Johnson; m. Barbara Dell Braley, June 18, 1960; children: Mark, Ben, Christopher. BSCE, U. Wis., Madison, 1959, JD, 1962. Bar: Minn. 1963, Calif. 1965, US Patent Office 1963. Atty. Pillsbury Co., Mpls., 1962-64; assoc. Mellin, Hanscom & Hursh, San Francisco, 1964-66; ptnr. Dorsey & Whitney, Mpls., 1966-98, Eugene L. Johnson, PA, Wayzata, Minn., 1998—. Program founder, adj. prof. intellectual property law William Mitchell Coll. Law, 1967-75. Capt. USAR. Mem. Minn. Bar Assn. (past bd. govs.), Am. Intellectual Property Law Assn., Minn. Intellectual Property Law Assn. (past pres.), Am. Swedish Inst. (bd. trustees), Mpls. Athletic Club. Republican.

JOHNSON, EUGENE LEE, political scientist, history professor; b. Boone, Iowa, Oct. 6, 1945; s. Robert Mc Gregor and Mabel Davis Johnson; m. Bennie Sue Cook; 1 child, Edward Vernon Cook Jr. BA, Tex. Christian U., Ft. Worth, 1967, MA, 1973. Cert. tchr. Tex., 1967. Adj. instr. Dallas CC Dist., 1973—82, Ozarks Tech. CC, Springfield, Mo., 2002—; mgr. purchasing Detroit Tool and Engring.; supr. traffic Tracker Marine, Lebanon, Mo. Democrat. Lutheran. Avocations: reading, TV news, travel. Home: 28402 Ozark Dr Lebanon MO 65536 Office: Ozarks Tech CC 933 E Central Springfield MO 65802 Home Phone: 417-588-2474; Office Phone: 417-895-7221. Home Fax: 417-588-2474. Personal E-mail: gene@leblink.com. Business E-Mail: johnsone@otc.edu.

JOHNSON, EVA JO, educational consultant; b. Chattanooga, Aug. 9, 1941; d. Joseph Saddler and Wilma (Logue) Scruggs; m. Richard Louis Spence, Apr. 4, 1959 (div. Mar. 1967); children: Gail, Richard, Donald Lamarion, Stephani. BS, So. Conn. State U., 1975, MS, 1978; postgrad., Fairfield U., 1983. Cert. in spl. edn. and adminstrn. and supervision. Tchr. spl. edn. Hamden (Conn.) Pub. Schs., 1975-87, supr. alternative program, 1987-91; instr. psychology South Ctrl. C.C., New Haven, 1988-89; educator spl. edn. resources Hamden Pub. Schs., 1991—. Chairperson Profl. Devel., Hamden, 1984-85; cons. Hamden Pub. Schs., 1976-87, coord. ann. ethnic celebration, 1978-89 Devel. curriculum project Celebration of Excellence, 1990 (Edn. award 1990). Chairperson membership com. N.H. Urban League, New Haven, 1985-88; mem. League Women Voters, Hamden, 1988-91; v.p. Conn. Afro Am. Hist. Soc., New Haven,

1992—; vol. in missions. Recipient Prudence Crandall award Conn. Edn. Assn., 1987, John Rogers Meml. award Conn. Edn. Assn., 1989, Woman in Leadership award YWCA, 1989, Cmty. Svc. award Bus. and Profl. Women, 1992, So. Conn. State U. Alumni Citation award, 2001. Mem. Phi Delta Kappa, Alpha Kappa Alpha (pub. rels. chair 1992—, Svc. award). Mem. United Methodist Ch. Avocations: travel, writing, walking, cooking, interior decorating. Home and Office: 3 Fern Ln Branford CT 06405-3352 E-mail: evajo7@yahoo.com.

JOHNSON, EVA MARIA, retired translator; b. Ludwigshafen, Rhine, Germany, Jan. 19, 1920; came to U.S., 1951; naturalized 1955; d. George and Maria Regina (Wurzel) Lenz; m. Martin L. Johnson, June 8, 1952 (dec. Jan. 1994); 1 child, Michael Andrew. Student, Ludwigshafen, 1938, Vorbeck Lang. Sch., 1940-43. Interpreter, translator German, English and French, Police, Lampertheim, Germany, 1945-46; reporter Deutsche Presse Dienst, Wiesbaden, Germany, 1946-48; editl. specialist U.S. Mil. Govt., Wiesbaden, Germany, 1948-51; bilingual sec. Embassy of Austria, Washington, 1951-53; translator Internat. Affairs Dept. CIO, Washington, 1953—55; translator Combat Ops. Rsch. Group, CDC, Fort Belvoir, Va., 1965-70; freelance translator top secret clearance Dept. Def., Washington, 1970-72; sr. sect., translator Holman & Stern, Patent Law Office, Washington, 1972-85; ret., 1985. Key-note spkr. Surviving POWs VA Hosp., Martinsburg, W.Va., 1996. Anti-Nazi activist, 1943-45. Mem.: The Ret. Mil. Officer Assn. (life). Avocations: photography, writing, eggeury, gardening, reading. Home: 352 Monastery Ridge Rd Stephenson VA 22656

JOHNSON, EVELYN BRYAN, airport terminal executive; b. Corbin, Ky., Nov. 4, 1909; d. Edward William and Myme Estelle (Fox) Stone; m. Wyatt J. Bryan, Mar. 21, 1931 (dec. 1963); m. Morgan N. Johnson, Feb. 25, 1965 (dec. Mar. 1977). Grad., Tenn Wesleyan Jr. Coll., 1929; student, U. Tenn., 1930—32. With Morristown (Tenn.) Flying Svc., Inc., 1947-97, designated pilot examiner, 1952—2005, sec.-treas., 1949-62, pres., 1962-82; mgr. Moore Murrell Airport, 1962—. Gov.'s appointee Tenn. Aero. Commn., 1983—2001, vice-chmn., 1987—89, chmn., 1989—91, 1994—96. Lt. col. CAP, 1949—. Recipient Carnegie Hero medal, 1958, Svc. to Mankind award Morristown Sertoma Club, 1981, Kitty Hawk award, FAA, 1991, Friends of Aviation award Tenn. Aviation Assn., 1992, Stewart G. Potter Aviation Edn. award Aviation Distbrs. and Mfrs. Assn., 1992, Elder Statesman of Aviation award Nat. Aeronautics Assn., 1993, Katherine Wright Meml. award Nat. Aeronautics Assn. and the Ninety Nines, 2002; named Flight Instr. of Yr., Nashville Dist. 1973, 79, So. region 1979, Nat., 1979 (all FAA), Outstanding Alumnus Tenn. Wesleyan Coll., 1981, Tenn. Divsn. Aviation Airport Mgr. of Yr., 2004; named to Women in Aviation Pioneers Hall of Fame, 1994, Hamblen Women Hall of Fame, 1997, Flight Instr. Hall of Fame, EAA Air Venture Mus., Oshkosh, 1997, Ky. Aviation Hall of Fame, 2000, Tenn. Aviation Hall of Fame, 2002, Kathryn Wright Meml. award Nat. Aeronautics Assn., 2002, Nat. Aviation Hall of Fame, Dayton, Ohio, 2007; holder of record most flying time for women pilots Guiness Book of Records 1995— Mem. CAP, Morristown Area C. of C., Nat. Assn. Flight Instrs. (bd. dirs., treas 1987-88, award 1992), Ninety-Nines (Award of Merit 1994), Whirly Girls (plaque 1992, Livingston award 2004, Airport Mgr. of the Yr. 2004, Wright Bros. Master Pilot award 2004), Aircraft Owners and Pilots Assn., Silver Wings (bd. dirs. 1987-2002, Woman of Yr. 1981, Carl Fromhagen award 1992), United Flying Octogenarians. Republican. Baptist. Home: 775 Commanche Dr Jefferson City TN 37760 Office: PO Box 1013 Morristown TN 37816-1013 Office Phone: 423-586-2483.

JOHNSON, FRANCIS SEVERIN, physicist; b. Omak, Wash., July 20, 1918; s. Ralston Severin and Elizabeth (Gruenes) J.; m. Maurine Marie Green, Sept. 12, 1943; 1 dau., Sharan Kaye. B.Sc. with honors in Physics, U. Alta., Can., 1940; MA in Physics and Meteorology, UCLA, 1942, PhD in Meteorology, 1958. Head, high atmosphere research sect. U.S. Naval Research Lab., Washington, 1946-55; mgr. space physics research Lockheed Missiles & Space Co., 1955-62; head, atmospheric and space scis. div. S.W. Center Advanced Studies, Dallas, 1962-64, dir. earth and planetary scis. lab., 1964-69; acting pres. U. Tex. at Dallas, 1969-71; dir. Center for Advanced Studies, 1971-74, Cecil H. and Ida M. Green honors prof. natural sci., 1974-89, prof. emeritus, 1989—2003, exec. dean grad. studies and research, 1976-79; asst. dir. astron., atmosphere, earth and ocean scis. NSF, Washington, 1979-83. Cons. ionospheric physics subcom., space scis. steering com. NASA, 1960-62, mem. planetary atmospheres subcom., space scis. steering com., 1962-67, chmn. lunar atmospheric measurements team, Apollo sci. planning teams, 1964-67, mem. adv. bd. Mars space missions, 1964-67, mem. lunar and planetary missions bd., 1967-71; mem. adv. panel atmospheric scis. NSF, 1962-67; mem. working group IV COSPAR, 1965-80, v.p., 1975-80; mem. Nat. Acad. Scis. panel adv. to central radio propagation lab. Nat. Bur. Standards, 1962-65, mem. panel weather and climate modification Nat. Acad. Scis., 1964-70, mem. space sci. bd., 1969-81, mem. geophysics research bd., 1971-77, mem. bd. on atmospheric scis. and climate, 1984-87, mem. Nat. Acad. Scis. com. adv. to NOAA, 1966-71, mem. climate research bd., 1977-79; mem. adv. com. research to coordinating bd. Tex. Coll. and Univ. System, 1966-67; mem. sci. advisory bd. USAF, 1968-79; mem. nat. adv. com. Oceans and Atmosphere, 1971-73; pres. Spl. Com. on Solar Terrestrial Physics, 1974-77; mem. Aerocibo adv. bd. and vis. com. Nat. Astronomy and Ionsphere Ctr. Cornell U., 1985-88. Author: Satellite Environment Handbook, 1965; also numerous articles. Served with USAAF, 1942-46. Decorated Bronze Star medal; recipient Henryk Arctowski award NAS, 1972, Exceptional Sci. Achievement medal NASA, 1973, Meritorious Civilian Service award USAF, 1979, Disting. Tex. Sci. award Tex. Acad. Scis., 1984, Disting. Alumni award U. Alta., 2001. Fellow Am. Geophys. Union (vice chmn. sect. geomagnetism and aeronomy 1964-68, pres. sect. solar planetary relationships 1970-72, John Adam Fleming award 1977), AAAS (council mem. 1968-72), Am. Meteorol. Soc. (councilor 1976-78), IEEE, AIAA (chmn. tech. com. space and atmospheric physics 1961-64, Space Sci. award 1966); mem. Internat. Assn. Geomagnetism and Aeronomy (exec. com. 1967-71), Internat. Union Radio Sci. (chmn. U.S. Commn. IV 1964-67, sec. U.S. nat. com. 1967-70, vice chmn. 1970-73, chmn. 1973-76), Internat. Union Geodesy and Geophysics (U.S. nat. com. 1973-76).

JOHNSON, FRANK, educator, retired state official; b. Ogden, Utah, Mar. 12, 1928; s. Clarence Budd and Arline (Parry) J.; m. Maralyn Brewer, Aug. 15, 1950; children: Scott, Arline, Laurie, Kelly, Edward. BS, U. Utah, 1955; MS, U. Ill., 1958, PhD, 1960. Instr. U. N.D., Grand Forks, 1955-56; teaching asst. U. Ill., Urbana, 1956-59; rsch. asst. prof. U. Del., Newark, 1959-60; prof. U. Utah, Salt Lake City, 1960-93, assoc. dean, 1970-77; dir. divsn. pub. utilities State of Utah, Salt Lake City, 1989—97. Cons. Gen. Foods, Sears, Magnavox, Albertsons, Zion Bank, Nat. Food Brokers Assn., others; part-owner Seventeenth St. Storage. Legis. Utah House of Reps., Salt Lake City, 1982-88; mem. Humanitarian Svc. Mission, eastern Europe, 1998-99; trainer vols. Salt Lake City Winter Olympics, 2002. Republican. Avocations: mountains, travel, reading, public and church service. Home: 1048 E Fairway Dr North Salt Lake UT 84054-3056

JOHNSON, FRANK EDWARD, surgeon educator; b. Evanston, Ill., Oct. 28, 1943; s. Frank E. and Beryl Madeline (Johnson) J.; m. Tamiko Asato, Jan. 24, 1976; children: Mariko, Michael, Eric, David. BA, U. Minn., 1964, MD, 1967. Diplomate Am. Bd. Surgery. Intern UCLA affiliated hosps., 1967-78; resident in surgery U. Wash., Seattle, 1972-74, U. Colo., 1974-77; rsch. fellow U. Calif., San Francisco, 1975-76; fellow in surg. oncology Meml. Sloan-Kettering Cancer Ctr., NYC, 1977-79; rsch. prof. Guy's Hosp., London, 1986-87; clin. instr. surgery Cornell U., NYC, 1977-79; asst. prof. St. Louis U. Med. Ctr., 1979-84, assoc. prof., 1984-89, prof., 1989—. Editor: Cancer Patient Follow-up, 1997, The Bionic Human, 2005, author 15 med. films; contbr. articles to profl. jours. Co-founder Children's Heart Link, Mpls., 1969. Lt. comdr. USN, 1969-71, Vietnam. Decorated Bronze Star; grantee NIH, Am. Cancer Soc., Royal Coll. Surgeons Found., VA Merit Rev. Mem. ACS, Am. Gastroent. Assn. AMA, Soc. Surg. Oncology, Am. Soc. Clin. Oncology, Am. Assn. Cancer Edn., Am. Paraplegia Soc., Am. Assn. Cancer Rsch., Am. Radium Soc., Am. Soc. Preventive Oncology, Ctrl. Surg. Assn. (grantee), Southwestern Surg. Congress, Am. Head and Neck Soc., Am. Physiol. Soc., Soc. Univ. Surgeons, Soc. Surgery of the Alimentary Tract, Assn. Acad. Surgeons, Assn. Surgeons of Gt. Britain and Ireland. Office Phone: 314-577-8316.

JOHNSON, FRANK WILLIAM, marketing professional; b. Sumter, SC, Sept. 20, 1948; s. John William and Dorothy (Ferrigan) J.; m. Sally Gattshall; Nov. 25, 1970; children: Lauren Elizabeth, Mark William. BA in Polit. Sci., The Citadel, 1970; MS in Ops. Mgmt., U. Ark., 1976. Sales rep. Union Carbide Corp., Dallas, 1976-78, product mgr. NYC, 1979-82; sales mgr. Steelcase Inc., Dallas, 1982-83; dir. mktg. VECTA divsn. Steelcase Inc., Dallas, 1984-86; dir. sales and mktg. Lista Internat., Dallas, 1986-87; v.p. Kewaunee Sci. Corp., Lockhart, Tex., 1987-92; v.p. sales and mktg. McCoy, Inc., Houston, 1992-95; v.p. Contract Specifix, Richmond, VA, 1995-96; pres. Saxton, Inc., Davenport, Iowa, 1996-97; dir. sales Office Furniture USA, Pelham, Ala., 1998—2003; pres., CEO Norus Office Furniture, Inc., Winston-Salem, NC, 2003—. Capt. USAF, 1970-76. Mem.: Sales and Mktg. Club. Republican. Mem. Ch. of God. Home: 1004 Castle Pines Ct Clemmons NC 27012 Office: Box 67 Winston Salem NC 27102 Home Phone: 336-766-0501; Office Phone: 336-721-1717 223. Personal E-mail: bfree6@earthlink.net.

JOHNSON, FRANKLYN ARTHUR, academic administrator; b. Rochester, NY, Nov. 6, 1921; s. Robert Barnes and Olyve Cole (Eckler) J.; m. Emily Bernetta Lingle, Aug. 15, 1945 (div. Aug. 1978); children: Franklyn Arthur Jr.(dec.), Terri A. Cochran, Sandra C. Fox; m. Elena Senese, Sept. 27, 1991. BA, Rutgers U., 1947; MA, Harvard U., 1949, PhD, 1952; LHD (hon.), Jacksonville U., 1961; DLitt (hon.), Mt. Senario Coll., Ladysmith, Wis., 1971; LLD (hon.), Flagler Coll., St. Augustine, Fla., 1976; DCL (hon.), Drury Coll., Springfield, Mo., 1976; HHD (hon.), Mo. Valley Coll., 1978. Intelligence officer CIA, Washington, 1949-51; asst., assoc. prof. govt. Rollins Coll., Winter Park, Fla., 1952-56; pres., prof. govt. Jacksonville U., Fla., 1956-63, Calif. State U., Los Angeles, 1963-65; asst. sec., dir. Job Corps OEO, Washington, 1965-67; pres., chmn., trustee Wm. H. Donner Found., NYC, 1967-70; dir. Arthur Vining Davis Founds., Coral Gables, Fla., 1970-78; prof. adminstrn. Fla. Atlantic U., Boca Raton, 1970-87; pres., prof. mgmt. S.W. Fla. Coll., Naples, 1987—. Trustee Inst. for Am. Univs., Aix-en-Provence, France, 1967—97, Eckerd Coll., St. Petersburg, Fla., 1978—90; chmn. S.E. Coun. Founds., Atlanta, 1975—77. Author: Defence by Committee, 1960, Defence by Ministry, 1980, 81, One More Hill, 1949, rev. edits., 1982, 88, Santori, 1990, Castro: The Last Hurrah, 1992, The Periled Presidency, 1995, Here and There, 1995, After Thoughts, 1996, D. S. Nemenoff, Maestro, 1996, A Chance Encounter, 1996, Odds and Ends, 1996, The Gods That Failed, 1997, Pearls Are a Girl's Best Friend, 1997, The 22nd Amendment, 1998, The Reluctant Presidents, 1999, Santori Island of Evil, 1999, Key West to Cuba, 2000, The Mismated, 2001, Triangle of Terror: Trauma in Everglades City, 2003, Dynasty of Deceit: 2015, The Last of the 3 Castros, 2004, Eyes Only: Countdown to Chaos, 2005; contbr. articles to profl. jours. Mem. U.S. Com. United World Colls., NYC, 1975-85, Fla. Gov.'s Coun. on Indian Affairs, Tallahassee, 1975-80, exec. adv. coun. Fla. Atlantic U., chmn.; bd. dirs. Collier Cultural and Ednl. Ctr., Naples; v.p., dir. Beachwood Assn., Inc., 1992-94; pres. Francobollo Press, 1998-2006. Lt. U.S. Army, 1942-45, ETO. Decorated Disting. Svc. medal, Jubilee of Liberty, Legion of Honor (France), Croix deGuerre, Diplome de la Liberation de Normandie (France); Prisoner of War medal, Silver Star, 5 Bronze Stars, 3 Purple Hearts, Conspicuous Svc. Cross; recipient George Washington honor medal Freedoms Found., Valley Forge, 1956, Profl. Achievement award Barry U., Miami, Fla., Eric Fenby lectr., 1991; named Champion Ind. Higher Edn. in Fla., Ind. Colls. Fla., 1992 Svc. Medallion, N. Fla. Jr. Coll., Madison, Fla. Fellow Inter-U. Seminar on Armed Forces and Soc.; mem. Delius Assn. Am. (life, founding pres.), Can. Inst. Strategic Studies, Phi Beta Kappa, Phi Alpha Theta, Pi Alpha Alpha (pres.), Phi Kappa Phi. Republican. Presbyterian. Avocations: classical music, writing fiction. Home: PO Box 1873 Bonita Springs FL 34133-1873 Home Phone: 239-992-5190.

JOHNSON, FREDA S., financial analyst, consultant; b. NYC, Mar. 17, 1947; m. J. Chester Johnson, May 7, 1989. BA in Polit. Sci., CUNY, 1968; grad. Advanced Mgmt. Program, Harvard U., 1986. Analyst mcpl. div. Dun & Bradstreet Corp., NYC, 1968-71; sr. analyst Moody's Investor Svc., Inc. (subs. Dun & Bradstreet), NYC, 1972, v.p., assoc. dir. mcpl. dept., 1973-79, sr. v.p., dir. mcpl. dept., 1979-81, exec. v.p., 1981-90; pres. Govt. Fin. Assocs., Inc. pub. fin. adv. co., 1992—. Mem. Anthony Commn. for Pub. Fin.; former sr. credit advisor Ecolink, joint Soviet-Am. pub. fin. project; Congl. testifier U.S. Senate Com. on Banking, Housing and Urban Affairs, subcom. fiscal affairs and health U.S. Ho. of Reps., U.S. Senate Com. Govtl. Affairs, Joing Econ. Com. Congress; Nat. Assn. Ind. Pub. Fin. Advisors, 1993-95, Queens Coll. Corp. Adv. Bd., 1994-99; bd. govs. Coun. Mcpl. Performance, 1984-86; instr. New Sch. for Social Rsch., 1982-83; adv. bd. City Almanac, 1982-84; trustee Citizens Budget Com.; adj. prof. Grad. Sch. Bus. Adminstrn. Columbia U., 1991; spkr. in field. Avocations: theater, museums.

JOHNSON, GARRETT BRUCE, lawyer; b. Akron, Ohio, Sept. 15, 1946; s. Vincent Hadar and Elizabeth Irene (Garrett) J.; m. Barbara Peters Silver, May 31, 1969; children: Emily Peters, Adam Garrett. AB, Princeton U., 1968; JD, U. Mich., 1971. Bar: Ill. 1973, US Dist. Ct. (no. dist. Ill.) 1973, US Ct. Appeals (7th cir.) 1979, US Supreme Ct. 1990. Fellow Max Planck Inst. Fgn. and Internat. Criminal Law, Freiburg, Germany, 1971-72; assoc. Kirkland & Ellis, Chgo., 1973-78, ptnr., 1978—. Article and book rev. editor Mich. Law Rev. 1970-71. Humboldt scholar, 1971-72. Office: Kirkland & Ellis 200 E Randolph Dr Fl 58 Chicago IL 60601-6636 Office Phone: 312-861-2268. Office Fax: 312-861-2200. E-mail: gjohnson@kirkland.com.

JOHNSON, GARY M., lawyer; b. 1947; BS, Gustavus Adolphus Coll., 1969; JD, NYU, 1973. Law clk. to justice U.S. Ct. Appeals (3d cir.), Phila., 1973-74; assoc. Dorsey & Whitney, Mpls., 1974-79, ptnr., 1980—. Fellow Am. Coll. Trust and Estate Counsel; mem. Minn. Bar Assn., Hennepin County Bar Assn., Order of Coif. Office: Dorsey & Whitney Ste 1500 50 South Sixth Street Minneapolis MN 55402-1498 Office Phone: 612-340-2774. Business E-Mail: johnson.gary@dorsey.com.

JOHNSON, GARY ROBERT, political scientist; b. Shenandoah, Iowa, June 30, 1949; s. Glen Robert and Norma Jean (Otte) J.; m. Margaret Delaina Maddox, Aug. 30, 1975; children: Samuel Maddox, Katherine Elizabeth. BA, Augustana Coll., Rock Island, Ill., 1972; MA, U. Cin., 1975, PhD, 1979. Teaching asst., rsch. asst. U. Cin., 1972-78; rsch. cons. Frost & Jacobs, Attys.at Law, Cin., 1976; instr., then asst. prof. polit. sci. Lake Superior State U., Sault Ste. Marie, Mich., 1978-84, assoc. prof. polit. sci., 1984-90, head dept. social scis., 1981-89, prof. polit. sci., 1990—. Vis. lectr. Drake U., Des Moines, 1986-87; manuscript referee various jours., pubs., 1986—; mem. faculty workgroup on undergrad. instrnl. quality Gov.'s Commn. on Future of Higher Edn. in Mich., 1984. Bibliography co-editor Politics and the Life Scis. jour., 1986-91, editor, 1991-2001; contbr. articles, book revs. to profl. jours., edited books. Grantee State of Mich., 1987. Mem. Am. Polit. Sci. Assn. (panel discussant, chair 1989—, sect. program chair 1990-91), Assn. Politics and Life Sci. (exec. dir. 1996-2001, conf. chair 1998, 99, 2000), Internat. Soc. Human Ethology, Human Behavior and Evolution Soc. Avocations: genealogy, old books, racquetball. Home: 924 Johnston St Sault Sainte Marie MI 49783-3324 Office: Lake Superior State U 650 W Easterday Ave Dept Polit Sault Sainte Marie MI 49783-1643 Home Phone: 906-635-9415; Office Phone: 906-635-2763. E-mail: gjohnson@lssu.edu.

JOHNSON, GARY THOMAS, cultural organization administrator; b. Chgo., July 26, 1950; s. Thomas G., Jr. and Marcia Johnson; m. Susan Elizabeth Moore, May 28, 1978; children: Christopher Thomas, Timothy Henry, Anna Louisa. AB, Yale U., 1972; Hons. BA, Oxford U., 1974, MA, 1983; JD, Harvard U., 1977. Bar: Ill. 1977, U.S. Dist. Ct. (no. dist.) Ill. 1977, U.S. Ct. Appeals (7th cir.) 1985, U.S. Supreme Ct. 1986, N.Y. 1993, Supreme Ct. Eng. and Wales 2004. Assoc. Mayer, Brown & Platt, Chgo., 1977-84, ptnr., 1985-94, Jones Day, Chgo., 1994—2005; pres., CEO Chgo. (Ill.) History Mus., 2005—. Mem. spl. commn. adminstrn. justice Cook County Ill. Supreme Ct., 1984—88, 1992—94; v.p. Criminal Justice Project Cook County, 1987—91; trustee Lawyer's Com. Civil Rights Under Law, 1992—94, bd. dirs., 1994—, regional co-chair, 1996—2001, mem. exec. com., 1998—, co-chair, 2001—03. Bd. dirs. Chgo. Lawyers' Com. Civil Rights Under Law, 1981—90, Legal Assistance Found., Chgo., 1987—96, pres., 1994—96; bd. dirs. After Sch. Matters, Chgo. Metro History Fair Edn. Ctr. Rhodes scholar, Oxford U., 1972—74. Fellow: Ill. Bar Found. (life), Am. Bar Found. (life; state chair 2003—); mem.: ABA (ho. of dels. 1991—97), Law Soc. Eng. and Wales, Chgo. Coun. Lawyers (pres. 1981—83), Ill. State Bar Assn., Am. Judicature Soc. (bd. dirs. 1987—91), Am. Law Inst., Comml. Club Chgo. Office: Chgo Hist Museum 1601 N Clark St Chicago IL 60614-6071 Personal E-mail: gary.johnson.bk.72@aya.yale.edu.

JOHNSON, GARY WILLIAM, environmental scientist, consultant; b. Warwick, RI, Feb. 23, 1957; s. Donald Milton and Elaine Carin (Soderlund) J.; m. Diane Lynn Farrell, Aug. 1, 1992; children: Danielle Lynn, Kelsey Ann. BA in Biology, U. R.I., 1979; MS in Environ. Sci., U. New Haven, 1987. Cert. instr. Inst. Nuclear Power Operators; OSHA cert. safety trainer. Rschr. Nat. Marine Fisheries Svc., Narragansett, RI, 1978—79; asst. scientist N.E. Utilities, Waterford, Conn., 1979—84, assoc. scientist Berlin, Conn., 1984—86, scientist Rocky Hill, Conn., 1986—97; sr. scientist, environ. coord. N.E. Nuc. Energy Co., Waterford, Conn., 1997—2000; supr. environ. programs Millstone Nuc. Power Sta. Dominion Nuc. Conn., Waterford, 2000—; pres. Sci. Epicenter and DNA Learning Ctr., New London, Conn., 2001—05. Prin. scientist Ecologic Risk Mgmt. Svcs., Monroe, Conn., 1989-94; guest lectr. U. New Haven, 1990-96; lectr. in field. Contbr. articles to profl. jours. Vol. sci. guide East Lyme (Conn.) Jr. High Sch., 1983-96; guide, lectr. Audubon Soc., Jamestown, R.I., 1983-85; chmn. Waterford Conservation Commn., 1997—; v.p. Meadow Green Homeowners Assn., 1999—; mtn. guide Okemo Mtn. Resort, Ludlow, Vt., 1998—. Mem. Edison Electric Power Industry Biologists, Nat. Environ. Tng. Assn. Achievements include obtaining ISO 14001 environmental management systems certification for Millstone Nuclear Power Facility, Waterford, Conn.; development of state of the art computer models to perform quantitative analysis of ecologic and human health risk from exposure to toxic materials; research in condenser biofouling control efforts for the nuclear power industry; coordinated all environmental issues to support the decommissioning of a nuclear power plant. Home: 2 Melanie Dr Waterford CT 06385-1600 Office: Dominion Nuclear Conn Millstone Nuclear Power Sta Rope Ferry Rd Waterford CT 06385-0128 Office Phone: 860-447-1791 ext. 0757. Personal E-mail: gary_william_johnson@yahoo.com.

JOHNSON, GAYLE ANN, cardiology nurse; b. Chgo., Sept. 4, 1946; d. Russell Arthur and Helen Elizabeth (Lawrence) J.; children: Todd Osinski, Jennifer Johnson. ADN with honors, Elgin CC, Ill., 1986; student, Grossmont Coll., 1988. RN, Calif.; bd. cert. med. surg. RN, ANCC, 1998, 03; cert. ACLS, Am. Heart Assn., 2006. Office nurse Dr. Edward J. Kinn, Barrington, Ill.; staff nurse No. Ill. Med. Ctr., McHenry; asst. unit supr. cardiac unit telemetry, staff nurse Scripps Meml. Hosp., La Jolla, Calif., staff nurse, mem. Nursing Futures Task Force, 1987-88; owner, operator State Lic. Assisted Living (Colony Ct.), San Diego, 1993—96; staff RN UCSD, La Jolla, 2002—. Clin. advisor Va. Mason Med. Ctr., Seattle, 1998—2000; staff RN cardiac unit Swedish Med. Ctr., Seattle, 2000; shift mgr. Alvarado Med. Ctr., San Diego, 2000—02; mem. RN Ednl. Competency Com. USCO, LaJolla, Calif., 2002—. William Rainey Harper Coll., Palatine, Ill., McHenry County Coll., Crystal Lake, Ill., McHenry County Coll. Women's Re-entry scholar, 1982-83, Sherman Hosp. Women's Aux. Nursing scholar, 1984-85. Mem.: Calif. Nurses Assn. (staff Internat. Med. U.). Republican. Evangelical Free. Home: 9418 Stargaze Ave San Diego CA 92129-3801 Office: 9300 Campus Point La Jolla CA 92037 Business E-Mail: gjohnson3@san.rr.com.

JOHNSON, GEORGE AXIL, III, television producer; b. Hastings, Mich., Nov. 14, 1974; s. George Axil, Jr. and Judy Lynn Johnson; m. Karen Gwen Hynes, June 26, 1999; children: George Axil IV, Hannah Joy, Grace Alynn. Diploma, Hollywood Scriptwriting Inst., Calif., 1994—96. Videographer, editor Two Legs Prodns., Lake Odessa, Mich., 1998, Alliance Prodns., Grand Rapids, Mich., 1999—2000; program dir. WKTV TV-25, Wyoming, Mich., 1998—2000; news editor WZZM TV-13, Grand Rapids, Mich., 2000; prodn. mgr. WINM TV-63, Edgerton, Ohio, 2000—; pres., founder Allegory Pictures, Waterloo, Ind., 2000—. TV prodn. instr. WKTV TV-25, Wyoming, Mich., 1998—2000; writer WINM TV-63, Edgerton, Ohio, 2000—. Author: (screenplays) Dreamer: The Movie, 2001, The Komet; dir., prodr. (films) Dreamer: The Movie, 2004 (Internat. Film Festival Outstanding Dramatic Comedy, 2005). Recipient Lifetime Achievement award, Hollywood Scriptwriting Inst. Republican. Avocations: writing, films. Office: Allegory Pictures 875 Plank Rd Waterloo IN 46793 Office Phone: 260-908-0733.

JOHNSON, GEORGE H., finance company executive; b. Boston, Aug. 30, 1941; s. Harry G. and Josephine (Grenda) J.; m. Marguerite Anne Harrington, Aug. 12, 1967; 1 child, Heather Diana. BS, Northeastern U., Boston, 1966. CLU, ChFC; cert. internal auditor; enrolled agt. IRS; cert. tax preparer; fellow life office mgmt. Sr. internal auditor U.S. Life Corp., NYC, 1970-76; dir. internal audit, treas. Consumers United Group, Inc., Washington, 1976—, also bd. dirs. Former bd. dirs., chair World Hunger Edn. Svc., Washington. Participant blood bank donor program ARC, Washington, 1977—. Mem. Inst. Internal Auditors, Md. Soc. Accts., Am. Soc. CLU and ChFC, Cert. Tax Preparers, Washington Inst. Internal Auditors. Home: 11805 Bunchberry Ln Gaithersburg MD 20878-2315

JOHNSON, GEORGE LLOYD, education educator, consultant, writer; b. Dunn, NC, Aug. 13, 1955; s. George Loyd Johnson Sr. and Jean Morrison Johnson. BA in history, Campbell U., 1977, MEd, 1978; MA, East Carolina U., 1985; PhD in am. history, U. of SC, 1991. Instr. history U. SC., 1990—91; asst. prof. history Campbell U., Buies Creek, NC, 1991—97, assoc. prof. history, 1997—2005, dir. hist. studies, 2003, prof. history, 2005—. Cons., advanced placement U.S. history Coll. Bd., Ednl. Testing Svc., Princeton, NJ, 1998—. Author: (history book) The Frontier in the Colonial South: South Carolina Backcountry, 1736-1800, 1997; contbr. author of book reviews, articles to profl. jours., chapters to books. Spl. events com. Averasboro Civil War Battlefield Commn., Dunn, NC, 1998—2001. Fellow Summer Inst. fellow, Nat. Endowment for the Humanities, Univ. of Va. and Va. Found. for the Humanities, 1998. Mem.: NC Lit. and Hist. Soc. (corr.), Bapt. History and Heritage Soc. (corr.), NC Assn. of Historians (corr.; pres. 1999—2000), Am. Hist. Assn. (corr.), So. Hist. Assn. (corr.; membership com. 2002—03), SC Hist. Soc. (assoc.), Ormohundro Inst. for the Study of Early Am. History and Culture (assoc.), Hist. Soc. NC (life), Omicron Delta Kappa (life), Phi Alpha Theta (life),

Phi Kappa Phi (life). Democrat. Baptist. Achievements include research in colonial history in the South. Avocations: weightlifting, travel. Home: 203 East K St Erwin NC 28339 Office: Campbell University 211 Judge Taylor Rd D Rich Building Buies Creek NC 27506 Business E-Mail: johnson@campbell.edu.

JOHNSON, GEORGE WARNER, gifted and talented educator, consultant; b. Logan, Ohio, June 16, 1949; s. George Bernard and Martha Ann Johnson; m. Jean Ann Hutchison, Oct. 31, 1971 (dec. Mar. 5, 1988); children: Melissa Renee Johnson-Stokes, George Christopher, Bryan Michael; m. Jeanne Christina Hohman, Sept. 9, 1989; 1 child, Mark Hohman. EdB, Ohio U., Athens, 1971; MEd, Ashland U., Ohio, 2001; EdD, Ashland U., 2007. Cert. secondary edn-history Ohio, elem. edn. grades 1-8 Ohio, gifted edn. K-12 Ohio, elem./mid. sch. prin. Ohio. Elem. tchr. So. Local Sch. Dist., Hemlock, Ohio, 1974—85, tchr., dir. gifted program and svcs., 1986—. Bd. govs. Southea. Ohio Odyssey of the Mind, Athens, 1986—87, Southea. Ohio Regional Scholars, Athens, 1987; dir., coord. sch. trips to Washington and Europe So. Local Schs., Hemlock, 1987—; dir. ednl. svcs. for Ohio Soc. for Creative Anachronism, Inc., Milpitas, Calif., 1989—92, regional v.p. orgnl. devel. Midwestern U.S. and Can., 1989—91, corp. dir., 1992—94, chmn. internat. edn. com., 1994—95; orgnl. pres. for N.Am. Regia Anglorum, Bristol, England, 2000—05; judge Southea. Ohio Power of the Pen Competition, Logan, 2003—; ednl. cons. for staff devel. Literacy Curriculum Alignment Project, Reynoldsburg, Ohio, 2003—05; adj. prof. Ashland U., 2005—. Author: Christmas Ornaments, Lights, and Decorations, Vol. I, 1987, 1990, 1995, 1998, Christmas Ornaments, Lights, and Decorations, Vol. II, 1997, Christmas Ornaments, Lights, and Decorations, Vol. III, 1997, Pictorial Guide to Christmas Ornaments and Collectibles, 2004, 2005; curator (mus. exhibit) Memories of Halloween Past, 2003, Christmas Through the Ages, 2004. Bd. dirs. Bowen Ho. Cultural Arts Ctr., Logan, 2001—05, Acad. Achievement Scholarship Fund, So. Local Schs., Hemlock, 1985—2005. Named Featured Tchr., Ohio Schs. Mag., 1999; named to Gifted Edn. Hall of Fame, Ohio U., 2003; recipient award for outstanding svc. to edn. of children, Soc. for Creative Anachronism, Inc., 1984, 1989, 1990, author's commendation, Ohio State Senate, 1987, Contbns. to Success of Gifted Students award, Southea. Ohio Spl. Edn. Regional Resource Ctr., 1987, 1992, 1996, Excellence in Talented and Gifted Programming award, S.E. region Ohio Sch. Bds. Assn., 1993; Martha Holdings Jennings scholar, 1985—86. Mem.: NEA, ASCD, Ohio Mid. Sch. Assn., Ohio Assn. Elem. Sch. Administrs., Am. Edn. Rsch. Assn., European Coun. on High Achievement, Nat. Assn. Gifted Children, Ohio Assn. Gifted Children, Ohio Edn. Assn., So. Local Edn. Assn. (pres. 1976, 1999), Masons, Order of Ea. Star (patron 1980—82). Avocations: antiques, historical reenactment, old house restoration, European travel, educational presentations. Home: 18 E Hunter St Logan OH 43138 Office: So Local Sch Dist 10397 State Rte 155 SE Hemlock OH 43743 Home Phone: 740-385-4845. Personal E-mail: taly@ohiohills.net.

JOHNSON, GLENDON E., retired insurance company executive; b. 1924; BS, U. Utah, 1948; JD, Harvard U., 1952. In charge Wash. office Am. Life Convention, Washington, 1959-68; pres. Great Southern Life Ins. Co., Houston, 1968-70; pres., chmn. bd. dirs., CEO Am. Nat. Ins. Co. Inc., Galveston, Tex., 1970-77; law ptnr. Routier & Johnson P.C., Washington, 1978-84; CEO Cathend Valley Ranch, LLC, 1979—; pres., CEO John Alden Ins. Co., Inc., 1984-87; chmn. bd., CEO John Alden Fin. Corp., Miami, Fla., 1987-98; pres., chmn. bd., CEO John Alden Life Ins. Co., 1984-98. Mem. nat. bd. Boy Scouts Am., 1971-77, 1981—, nat. exec. com., 1981—, nat. v.p., chmn. audit com., mem. nominating com., 1994—, mem. exec. bd. Fla. coun., chmn. nat. Cub Scout com., 1981-83, chmn. nat. program group, 1983-86, chmn. mktg. and relationships com., 1987-91, chmn. pers. com., 1992-93 (Silver Beaver award 1971, Silver Antelope award 1974, Silver Buffalo award 1993, Good Scout award 1993); regional rep. to quorum LDS Ch., 1971-76.

JOHNSON, GLENN THOMPSON, retired judge; b. Washington, Ark., July 19, 1917; s. Floyd and Reola (Thompson) J.; m. Elaine Bailey, May. 26, 1993; children: Evelyn A., Glenn T. BS, Wilberforce U., 1941; JD, John Marshall Law Sch., 1949, LL.M., 1950; grad., Nat. Coll. State Trial Judges, 1971, Appellate Ct. Judges Seminar, N.Y. U., 1974; LL.D. (hon.), Ark. Bapt. Coll., 1978. Bar: Ill. 1950. Pvt. practice law, 1950-57; asst. atty. gen. Ill., 1957-63; sr. asst. atty. Met. San. Dist. Chgo., 1963-66; assoc. judge Cir. Ct., Cook County, Chgo., 1966-68, judge, 1968-73; justice Ill. Appellate Ct., Chgo., 1973—. Trustee John Marshall Law Sch. Served with AUS, 1942-46. Recipient merit award John Marshall Law Sch., 1970; Merit award Beatrice Caffrey Youth Service, 1976 Mem. Nat. Bar Assn. (merit award 1970), ABA, Ill. Bar Assn., Chgo. Bar Assn., Cook County Bar Assn. (awards 1967, 73, pres. 1964-66), Am. Acad. Matrimonial Lawyers (gov.) Methodist. Home: 5050 S Lake Shore Dr Apt 2517 S Chicago IL 60615-3217

JOHNSON, GOODYEAR See O'CONNOR, KARL

JOHNSON, GORDON GILBERT, theology studies educator, minister; b. St. Paul, Nov. 19, 1919; s. Gilbert Oliver and Myrtle Isabel (Bjorklund) J.; m. Alta Fern Borden, May 21, 1945; children: Gregg A., Gayle E. Johnson Hyames. Cert., Moody Bible Inst., 1941; AA, Bethel Coll., St. Paul, 1943; student, Harvard U., 1944-45; BA, U. Minn., 1945; BD, Bethel Theol. Sem., 1946; ThM, Princeton Theol. Sem., 1950; ThD, No. Bapt. Theol. Sem., 1960. Ordained to ministry Bapt. Gen. Conf., 1946. Pastor 1st Bapt. Ch., Milltown, Wis., 1946-48, Bethel Bapt. Ch., Montclaire, N.J., 1948-51, Central Ave. Bapt. Ch., Chgo., 1951-59; v.p., dean, prof. preaching Bethel Theol. Sem., St. Paul, 1959-84; interim sr. pastor Trinity Bapt. Ch., St. Paul, 1972-73; assoc. pastor, interim sr. pastor College Ave. Bapt. Ch., San Diego, 1984-89; interim dean Bethel Sem. West, San Diego, 1990-91; interim sr. pastor Clairemont Emmanuel Bapt. Ch., San Diego, 1990-91, First Bapt. Ch., Lakewood, Long Beach, Calif., 1991-92, New Life Ch., Woodbury, Minn., 1993, Elim Bapt. Ch., Mpls., 1995-96. Chmn. bd. publ. Bapt. Gen. Conf., Chgo., 1948-53, pres. bd. trustees, 1953-55, chmn. world mission bd., 1955-60, moderator, 1957-58, 85-86; mem. gen. coun. Bapt. World Alliance, Washington, 1965-85; lectr. in field; del. to World Congress on Evangelism, Berlin, 1965; educator for elderhostels for Bethel Coll., Minn., 1992-98; vis. prof. Regent Coll., Vancouver, 1976; pres. Minn. Sem. Consortium, 1979-81. Author: My Church, Making God Known Through Story; contbr. articles to profl. jours. With USN, 1944—45. Rsch. scholar Yale U. Div. Sch., 1969. Mem. Acad. Homileticians, Religious Speech Assn. Personal E-mail: johgor@bethel.edu. *In a capricious and sometimes explosive world an underlying confidence in the gracious providence of a loving God gives peace and wholeness of life. That makes possible an optimism about life.*

JOHNSON, GORDON JAMES, performing company executive, conductor; b. St. Paul, 1949; BS, Bemidji State U., 1971; MS, Northwestern U., 1977; D in Mus. Arts, U. Oreg.; studied with Leonard Bernstein, Erich Leinsdorf, Herbert Blomstedt. Music dir., condr. Great Falls (Mont.) Symphony Assn., 1981—, Glacier Orch. and Chorale, Mont., 1982-97; artistic dir., condr. Flathead Music Festival, Mont., 1987-96; music dir., condr. Mesa (Ariz.) Symphony Orch., 1997—2005. Grad. tchg. fellow U. Oreg., 1979—81; artist in residence Condr's Guild Inst., W.Va. U., 1984; condr. Spokane Symphony at The Festival at Sandpoint; guest condr. St. Paul Chamber Orch., 1971, Spokane Symphony, 1983, 86, Dubuque Symphony, Iowa, 1985, Charlotte Symphony, NC, 1985, Lethbridge Symphony, Alberta, Canada, 1986, Cheyenne Symphony, Wyo., 1986, West Shore Symphony, Mich., 1988, Bozeman Symphony, Mont., 1989, Kumamoto Symphony, Kyshu, Japan, 1991, Kankakee Symphony, Ill., 1993, Toulon Symphonies, France, 1994, Guam Symphony, 1995, Tokyo Lumiere Orch., 1995, Fort Collins Symphony, Colo., 1995, Wilmslow Symphony Orch., England, 1997; guest ballet condr. Alberta Ballet, 1986, Oakland Ballet, Calif., 1988, Eugene Ballet, Oreg., 1993, David Taylor Ballet, Colo., Colo., 1994, St. Petersburg Ballet , Russia, 1995, Western Ballet Theater, Oreg., 1996; spkr. regional conf. Am. Symphony Orch. League, 1987, spkr. nat. conf., 88; mem. adj. faculty U. Great Falls, 1981—, U. Mont., 1996—; lectr. U. Guam, 1995; condr. seminars L.A. Philharmonic Inst., 1983, Condr.'s Guild Inst., 1984, Festival at Sandpoint, Condr.'s Program, 1986, Am. Symphony Orch. League's Am. Condr.'s Program, N.Y. Philharmonic, 1987, Condr.'s Guild "Bruckner Seminar", Chgo. Symphony Orch., 1989, Carnegie Hall Tng. Program for Condrs., Cleve. Orch., 1993. Named to Highland Park High Sch. Hall of Fame, St. Paul, 1997; Philharmonic Condr.'s scholar St. Paul Chamber Orch., 1971, L.A. Philharmonic Inst. fellow, 1983. Mem.: ASCAP. Office: Great Falls Symphony Assn PO Box 1078 Great Falls MT 59403-1078 Office Phone: 406-453-4102. E-mail: gordon@gfsymphony.org.

JOHNSON, GORDON SELBY, consulting electrical engineer; b. Petersburg, Ind., July 25, 1918; s. Basil Orvil and Lillian May (Selby) J.; m. Frances Marie Overstreet, June 15, 1940; children: Lowell, Anne, Judith, Martha, Carol, Gordon, Mary; m. Alice Woods, 2002. BSEE, Purdue U., 1939. Registered profl. engr., Wis. Engr. Sunbeam Electric Mfg. Co., Evansville, Ind., 1939-41, Kohler (Wis.) Co., 1941-48, dept. head, 1948-55, chief engr., 1955-65, mgr. engring., 1965-76, sr. staff engr., 1976-85, cons. engr., 1985-87; pvt. practice cons. Winter Haven, Fla., 1987—. Dir. communications and tech. assistance Elec. Generating Systems Assn., Boca Raton, Fla., 1986-92, tech. dir., 1993-99, pres., 1983-84. Author: Kohler Tech. Series, 1976-85; editor: Elec. Grounding, 1992, On-Site Power Generation, 1990, 2d edit., 1993, 3rd edit., 1998; editor Powerline mag., 1986-92, tech. editor, 1993-99; contbr. numerous articles to profl. jours. Pres. Sheboygan (Wis.) County Coun. of Chs., 1965-67; lay leader N.E. Wis. Dist. United Meth. Ch., 1975-76; chmn. adv. com. Lakeshore Tech. Coll., Sheboygan, 1970-80; adv. high sch. sci. seminars. With U.S. Mcht. Marine, 1944-45, ETO, NATOUSA. Recipient L.H. Carpenter Outstanding Svc. award Elec. Generating Systems Assn., 1973; named Athlete of Yr., Fla. Sr. Games, 1999. Fellow IEEE (sect. chmn. 1953-54); mem. NSPE, Soc. Automotive Engrs., Nat. Fire Protection Assn. Avocations: competitive running, bicycling, gardening. Home and Office: 421 Flagler Rd SE Winter Haven FL 33884 Office Phone: 863-324-3711. E-mail: johnsonjogs@aol.com.

JOHNSON, GREGORY E., diversified financial services company executive; b. Orange, NJ, June 28, 1961; BBA, Washington and Lee U., 1983. CPA. Former sr. acct. Coopers & Lybrand; with Franklin Resources Inc., San Mateo, Calif., 1986—, co-pres., 1999—2003, pres., co-CEO, 2003—04, pres., CEO, 2005—. Bd. dirs. Fiduciary Trust Co. Internat. Office: Franklin Resources Inc 1 Franklin Pky Bldg 970 1st Fl San Mateo CA 94403*

JOHNSON, HANSFORD TILLMAN, former civilian military employee; b. Aiken, SC, Jan. 3, 1936; s. Wade Hansford and Julia Johnson; m. Linda Ann Whittle, June 21, 1959; children: Richard, Elizabeth, David. BS in Thermodynamics and Aerodynamics, U.S. Air Force Acad., 1959; MS in Aeros., Stanford U., 1967; MBA in Bus. Sci., U. Colo., 1970; postgrad., Nat. War Coll., 1975-76. Registered profl. engr., Colo.; lic. Nat. Assn. Securities Dealer Prin. Commd. 2d lt. USAF, 1959, advanced through grades to 4-star gen., 1989; asst. prof. U.S. Air Force Acad., Colorado Springs, Colo., 1968-71; comdr. 22d Bomb Wing USAF, March AFB, Riverside, Calif., 1979-81; plans staff officer USAF Hdqrs., Washington, 1972-75; asst. dep. for plans Strategic Air Commd., Omaha, 1981-82; dir. programs USAF Hdqrs., Washington, 1982-85, dep. ops. Offutt AFB, Neb., 1985-86; vice comdr. in chief Pacific Air Forces USAF, Hickam AFB, Hawaii, 1986-87; dep. comdr. in chief U.S. Cen. Command, MacDill AFB, Fla., 1987-88; dir., moved forces to and from Persian Gulf Joint Chiefs of Staff, Washington, 1988-89; comdr. in chief U.S. Transp. Command, Mil. Airlift Command (now Air Mobility Command), Scott AFB, Ill., 1989-92; ret. USAF, 1992; bd. dirs. USAA, San Antonio, 1987-92, chief of staff, 1993, vice chmn., 1993—95; pres., CEO USAA Capital Corp., 1993—95; v.p., CEO Credit Union Nat. Assoc., Madison, Wis., 1995—2001; asst. sec. USN, Washington, 2001—02, 2003—04, acting sec., 2003. Mem. Tex. Rsch. and Tech. Found., Decorated DFC with 2 oak leaf clusters, Legion of Merit, Silver Star, DSM, Def. DSM with 2 oak leaf clusters, Def. Meritorious Svcs. medal, Meritorious Svc. medal, Air medal with 22 oak leaf clusters, Air Force DSM with oak leaf cluster; Republic of Vietnam Armed Forces Honor medal 1st class with one svc. star, Gallantry Cross with palm. Mem. AIAA, Order of Daedalians (flight capt. 1975, 84, 85), Soc. Mil. Engrs.

JOHNSON, HARDWICK SMITH, JR., school psychologist; b. Millen, Ga., Aug. 13, 1958; s. Hardwick Smith Sr. and Louise (Joiner) J. BA, Atlanta Christian Coll., 1981; MEd, Ga. So. Coll., 1984; EdS, Ga. State U., 1988; DSc (hon.), Holy Trinity Coll.; DD (hon.), St. Ephrem's Inst.; EdD, Nova Southeastern U., 2002. Cert. spl. edn. tchr., Ga.; nat. cert. sch. psychologist. Ga. Spl. edn. resource tchr. Claxton (Ga.) High Sch., 1983-86, sch. psychologist, lead sch. psychologist, 1986—. Genealogist, 1980—; supervising tchr. Author: The History of the Johnson Family and Johnson Church, 1976, The Aaron Family, 1986, Some Descendants of James and Rachel Oglesby, 1785-1991, 1991. Named Tchr. of the Yr., Coun. for Exceptional Children, Claxton, 1985, Hon. Order Ky. Col., 1986, hon. admiral Tex. Navy Gov. of Tex., 1987, lt. col. a.d.c. Gov. of Ga., 1987, citizen State of Okla., citizen of L.A., col. Gov. La., lt. col. Gov. Ala., hon. mem. Coweta Tribal Town of the Creek Indian Nation (now Okla.); recipient Liberty medal with oak lead cluster SAR, Meritorious Svc. award SAR, Silver Good Citizenship medal SAR, medal of honor NSDAR, medal of honor NSDAC, Minuteman medal NSSAR, 1994, Outstanding Young Man of Yr. award. Fellow Am. Coll. Genealogists; mem. SAR (v.p. chpt. 1985-86, pres. Statesboro chpt. 1986-87, state sec. 1987—, Meritorious Service medal Ga. soc. 1987, state pres., v.p. gen. South Atlantic dist. 1991-92), Nat. Soc. Sons of Am. Colonists (nat. v.p. 1986—, gov. Ga. soc. 1987—, gov. gen. 1989-91, Nat. Order of the Blue and Gray), Coun. for Exceptional Children (pres.-elect, v.p. 1985-86), Ga. Assn. Educators (sch. rep. 1985—, pres.-elect 1986-87), NEA (sch. rep.), Ga. Assn. Sch. Psychologists, Continental Soc. Sons Indian Wars (founding gov. gen., nat. pres.), Nat. Gavel Soc. (past rec. sec.), Jamestowne Soc. (hon. gov. First Ga. Co.), Gen. Soc. Colonial Wars, Colonial Order Acorn, First Families Ga. (founding sec./treas. gen., gov. gen. 1993-98), Nat. Huguenot Soc., Gen. Soc. War 1812 (former v.p. gen.), Sons Revolution in Ga., Hereditary Order Descendants Colonial Govs. (gov. gen. 1999—), Nat. Soc. Descs. Early Quakers, Nat. Soc. Ams. of Royal Descent (1st v.p.), Order Indian Wars of US (hon. comdr.), Order Ams. Armorial Ancestry, Hereditary Order Descs. Loyalists and Patriots Am. Revolution (hon. gov. gen.), Order Colonial Lords of Manors in Am., Baronial Order of Magna Charta (surety Class of 2010), Order of The Three Crusades,(1096-1192), Order of Crown of Charlemagne in USA (pres. gen. 2006—), Colonial Soc. Pa., Aztec Club of 1847-Mil. Soc. of the Mex. War (former v.p.), Baronial Order of Magna Charta, Royal Soc. of St. George, Nat. Soc. Sons and Daus. of Pilgrims (gov. gen. 1993-95), Order Scions of Colonial Cavaliers (dep. gov. gen.), Order of Crown in Am. (Ga. councilor), Sons and Daus. of Antebellum Planters, DeMolay (master councilor 1977-78), Am. Priory Most Venerable Order of Hosp. of St. John of Jerusalem (comdr.), Order Merovingian Dynasty (founder mem., founding first v.p.), Descendants of the Illegitimate Sons and Daughters of Kings of Britain, Charlotte Manigalt Soc., Soc. for Preservation of Early Am. Art, Kappa Delta Pi (historian 1983—), Phi Delta Kappa. Democrat. Avocations: heraldry, travel, writing, reading. Home: 1317 Winburn Drive East Point GA 30344

JOHNSON, HARMER FREDERIK, art appraiser; b. Faversham, Kent, England, Jan. 21, 1943; s. Stanley George and Lorna Mary (Clark) J.; m. Judith Rose Fischman, July 14, 1970; children: Jesse, Joanna, Eliza. Dept. asst. Sotheby & Co., London, 1961-66; dept. head, v.p. Sotheby Parke-Bernet Co., NYC, 1966-73; pres. Harmer Johnson Books Ltd., NYC, 1975—, Harmer Johnson Co., NYC, 1973—. Author: (books) American Indian Art Magazine, Guide to the Arts of the Americas: Pre-Columbian, American Indian, 1992. Mem. Appraisers Assn. Am. (pres. 1986-88, cert.). Avocations: music, theater. Office: Harmer Johnson 146 E 84th St New York NY 10028-2026

JOHNSON, HAROLD EARL, human resources specialist; b. Lincoln, Nebr., July 11, 1939; s. Earl W. and Evelyn Jean (Sipp) J.; m. Carol Louise Schmidt, Aug. 17, 1971 (div.); children: Andrew Brian, Daniel Earl; m. Janet Kendall Gaillard, May 30, 2004. BS, U. Nebr., 1961. From indsl. relations trainee to mgr. profl. employment Am. Can Co., 1961—68; dir. recruitment/devel. metal mining div. Kennecott Copper Corp., 1968—73; v.p. personnel Am. Medicorp Inc., 1973—75; v.p. employee relations. devel., then sr. v.p. employee relations and corp. adminstrn. INA Corp., 1975—79; sr. v.p. human resources Federated Dept. Stores, Inc., Cin., 1979—85; sr. v.p. corp. personnel and adminstrn. The Travelers Cos., Hartford, Conn., 1985—89; mng. ptnr. Korn/Ferry Internat., NYC, 1989—92; exec. search and human resources Norman-Broadbent Internat., NYC, 1992—96; sr. ptnr., bd. dirs. The Cabot Group, Washington, 1996—2002; sr. ptnr. TMP Worldwide, 1997—2001; chmn. global human resources practice Heidrick and Struggles, Internat., Denver, 2002—05; mng. dir. Korn/Ferry Internat., NYC, 2005—. Bd. dirs. Snowfly Inc., Laramie, Wyo. Mem. Winged Foot Golf Club (Mamoroneck, N.Y.), Assn. Exec. Search Cons., Ft. Collins Country Club. Republican. Presbyterian. Office: Korn/Ferry Internat 200 Park Ave New York NY 10166 Business E-Mail: hal.johnson@kornferry.com.

JOHNSON, HAROLD GENE, lawyer; b. St. Louis, July 20, 1934; s. Edward Henry Johnson and Betty (Burton) Pallister; m. Susan Ann Giesecke, Oct. 10, 1953; children: H. Mark, Deborah S. Johnson Schnitzer, Michael R., Laura A. Johnson Schwent, Mitchell D. BSBA, Washington U., St. Louis, 1961, LLB, 1962. Bar: Mo. 1962, U.S. Dist. Ct. (ea. dist.) Mo. 1964, U.S. Ct. Appeals (8th cir.) 1981. Assoc. Schomburg, Marshall & Craig, St. Louis, 1962-63, Green & Raymond, St. Louis, 1963-64; ptnr. Johnson & Hayes, St. Louis, 1978-85, Law Offices Mitchell D. Johnson, St. Louis, 1988-93, Johnson & Johnson, 1993—. Judge mcpl. ct. City of Bridgeton, Mo., 1973-85. Served with U.S. Army 1954-56. Recipient Spl. Service award City of Bridgeton, 1985; Honored with ann. presentation of The Judge Harold Johnson award Pro-Life Direct Action League, 1985. Bar: Mo. Bar Assn., Met. Bar St. Louis, St. Louis County Bar Assn. Avocation: woodworking. Office: 500 Northwest Plz Ste 715 Saint Ann MO 63074-2222

JOHNSON, HARRY A., III, lawyer, finance company executive; b. Memphis, Jan. 30, 1949; s. Harry A. Jr. and Penny (Pentecost) J.; m. Patricia Jane Reynolds; children: McKenzie, Kelly. BBA, So. Meth. U., 1971, JD, 1974. Bar: Tenn., 1974, U.S. Dist. Ct. (we. dist.) Tenn. 1974. Counsel First Tenn. Nat. Corp., Memphis, 1974-79, sr. v.p., div. mgr., 1979-84; ptnr. Glankler, Brown, Gilliland, Chase, Robinson & Raines, Memphis, 1984-88; exec. v.p., gen. counsel First Horizon Nat. Corp. (formerly First Tenn. Nat. Corp.), Memphis, 1988—. Bd. dirs. Brooks Mus. Art, Inc., Memphis, 1990—, chmn. bd., 1996—; bd. dirs. LeBonheur Children's Med. Ctr.; chmn. bd. Christ Meth. Day Sch., Memphis, 1989-92; sr. exec. programs Stanford U., 1999. Mem. ABA, Tenn. Bar Assn., Memphis and Shelby County Bar Assn., Fin. Svcs. Roundtable (lawyer's com.). Methodist. Office: First Horizon Nat Corp 165 Madison Ave Memphis TN 38103-2723 Office Phone: 901-523-5624.*

JOHNSON, HARRY STERLING, lawyer; b. Havre de Grace, Md., Nov. 10, 1954; s. Harry Durwood and Sarah Gladys (Rice) J.; m. Janet Amanda Thomas, May 14, 1988; 1 child, Amanda Sterling. BA, U. Md., Catonsville, 1976; JD, U. Md., Balt., 1979. Bar: Md. 1979, U.S. Dist. Ct. Md. 1979, U.S. Dist. Ct. D.C. 1986. Assoc. Whiteford, Taylor & Preston, Balt., 1979-86, ptnr., 1986—. Instr. U. Md., Baltimore County, Catonsville, 1982-87; bd. dirs. Bedco Devel. Corp., The Chapman Funds, The Afro Am. Newspapers; mem. com. Rules of Practice and Procedure, Ct. Appeals Md., Annapolis, 1986—. Mem. exec. bd. Balt. Area coun. Boy Scouts of Am., 1990—; pres., chair New Community Coll. Balt. Found., 1988, Greater Balt. Com., 1989, chair Balt. County Md. Human Relations Commn., 1998-2003; mem. bd. trustees Balt. Ednl. Scholarship Trust, 1993-, Greater Balt. Med. Ctr., 2001-, Center Stage, 2002-. Named to Am.'s Top Black Lawyers, Black Enterprise mag., 2003; recipient Disting. Black Marylander Award, Towson U., 2003, Leadership in Law Award, The Daily Record, 2003. Mem. ABA, Md. State Bar Assn. (bd. govs. 1987-89, 91—, treas. 1999-2002, pres.-elect 2002-03, pres. 2003-04), Bar Assn. Baltimore City, Nat. Bar Assn., Monumental City Bar Assn. (Founder's award 1987), DC Bar Assn. Avocations: music, sports, tennis. Office: Whiteford Taylor & Preston 7 St Paul St Ste 1400 Baltimore MD 21202-1626 E-mail: hjohnson@wtplaw.com.

JOHNSON, HAYNES BONNER, journalist, writer, commentator; b. NYC, July 9, 1931; s. Malcolm Malone and Ludie (Adams) J.; m. Julia Ann Erwin, Sept. 21, 1954 (div.); m. Kathryn A. Oberly, June 29, 2002; children— Katherine Adams, David Malone, Stephen Holmes, Sarah Brooks, Elizabeth Haynes. BJ, U. Mo., 1952; MS, U. Wis., 1956; HHD (hon.), Wheeling Jesuit U., 1997; LHD (hon.), U. Mo., 1999. Reporter Wilmington (Del.) News-Jour., 1956- 57; with Washington Star, 1957-69, reporter, copy editor, to asst. city editor, night city editor to spl. assignments corr.; nat. corr. Washington Post, 1969-73, asst. mng. editor, 1973-77, columnist, 1977-94; prof. polit. comm. and journalism George Washington U., Washington, 1994-96; Knight chair, prof. journalism U. Md., 1998—. Ferris prof. journalism and pub. affairs Princeton U., 1975-78; TV commentator PBS Washington Week in Rev., 1967-94, The News Hour with Jim Lehrer, 1994—2004; guest scholar Brookings Instn., 1987-91; Regents lectr. U. Calif., Berkeley, 1992; lectr. in field. Author: Dusk at the Mountain, 1963, The Bay of Pigs, 1964, (with Bernard M. Gwertzman) Fulbright: The Dissenter, 1968, (with George C. Wilson) Army in Anguish, 1972, (with Nick Kótz) The Unions, 1972, (with Richard Harwood) Lyndon, 1973, The Working White House, 1975, In the Absence of Power, 1980, (with Howard Simons) The Landing, 1986, Sleepwalking Through History, 1991, Divided We Fall, 1994, (with David S. Broder) The System, 1996, The Best of Times, 2001, The Age of Anxiety: McCarthyism to Terrorism, 2005; editor: The Fall of a President, 1974. Bd. dirs. Herbert Block Found. Served to 1st lt. AUS, 1952—55. Recipient Pub. Svc. prize and Grand award for reporting Washington Newspaper Guild, 1962, 68, Interpretive Reporting award, 1965, Nat. Reporting award, 1968, Pulitzer prize for nat. reporting, 1966, Headliners award for nat. reporting, 1968, Sigma Delta Chi gen. reporting award, 1969; fellow in comm. Duke U., 1973-74; profl. in residence Annenberg Sch., 1993. Mem. Nat. Acad. Pub. Adminstrn., Gridiron Club (Washington), Nassau Club (Princeton). Home: 2812 Woodland Dr NW Washington DC 20008-2742 Office: Coll Journalism U Md Journalism Bldg College Park MD 20742-0001 Personal E-mail: haynesjohnson@hotmail.com.

JOHNSON, HAZEL WINIFRED, nurse, retired army officer; b. West Chester, Pa., Oct. 10, 1927; d. Clarence Lemont and Garnett J. RN diploma, Harlem Hosp., NYC, 1950; BSN, Villanova U., 1959; MSN, Tchr.'s Coll., Columbia U., 1963; PhD in Edn. Adminstrn., Cath. U. Am., 1978. 1st lt. U.S. Army Nurse Corps, 1955, advanced through grades to brig. gen., 1979; mem. staff U.S. Army Med. R&D Command, Washington, 1967-73; dir. Walter Reed Army Inst. Nursing, Washington, 1976-78; asst.

for nursing Office of Surgeon Med. Command, Korea, 1979-83; chief Army Nurse Corps Office of Surgeon Gen. Dept. of the Army, Washington, 1983-86; dir. govtl. affairs office Am. Nurses Assn., 1986-96; prof. Coll. Nursing and Health Sci. George Mason U., 1989-96; dir. Ctr. for Health Policy George Mason U., 1996—. Cons. Nursing Edn. Health Policy, Health Adminstrn. Decorated Disting. Svc. medal, Legion of merit, Meritorious Svc. medal, Army Commendation medal; recipient Evangeline G. Bovard Army Nurse of Yr. award Letterman Army Med. Ctr., San Francisco, 1964, Dr. Anita Newcomb McGee award DAR, Washington, 1971. Mem. Assn. Balck Nursing Faculty, Black Women United for Action, Assn. U.S. Army, Nat. Assn. Military Family, Am. Nurses Assn., Nat. League Nursing, Sigma Theta Tau.

JOHNSON, HENRY C. (HANK JOHNSON), congressman, lawyer; b. Washington, DC, Oct. 2, 1954; m. Mereda Davis; children: Randi, Alex. BA, Clark U., 1976; JD, Tex. So. U., 1979. Judge Magistrate Ct, DeKalb County, Ga., State Ct. of Ga.; ptnr. Johnson & Johnson Law Group LLC, Decatur, Ga.; mem. US Congress from 4th Ga. dist., 2007—. Mem. DeKalb County Bd. Commrs., chmn. Budget Com. Mem.: State Bar Ga., Ga. Lawyers Found., Ga. Assn. Criminal Defense Attys., DeKalb County Law Libr. Democrat. Office: 5700 Hillandale Dr, Ste 110 Lithonia GA 30058 also: 1133 Longworth House Office Bldg Washington DC 20515*

JOHNSON, HENRY LOUIS, former federal agency and school system administrator; b. Tuscaloosa, Ala., Mar. 31, 1946; married; 3 children. BS in Biology, Livingston Coll., Salisbury, NC, 1968; MA in Tchg., U. N.C., Chapel Hill., 1975; DEd in Sch. Adminstrn., N.C. State U., 1990. Tchr. Wake County Pub. Schs., 1969—75, prin. elem. sch., 1975—78, middle sch. dir., 1979—81; asst. supt. for curriculum and instrn. Johnston County Schs., 1986—92; assoc. state supt. instruction and accountability svcs. N.C. Dept Edn., 1997—2002; supt. edn. Miss. State Dept. Edn., 2002—05; asst. sec. for elementary & secondary edn. US Dept. Edn., Washington, 2005—06. Named to Livingston Coll. Hall of Fame, 2002; recipient N.C. Disting. Alumnus award, N.C. State U., 1994, Presidl. citation, Livingstone Coll., 1999.

JOHNSON, HERBERT ALAN, historian, lawyer; b. Jersey City, Jan. 10, 1934; s. Harry Oliver and Magdalena Gertrude (Diemer) J.; m. Barbara Arlene (Balcerak), Sept. 24, 1955 (dec. Nov. 1980); children: Amanda Blair, Vanessa Paige.; m. Jane (McCue), June 4, 1983. AB, Columbia U., 1955, MA, 1961, PhD (Schiff fellow), 1965; LLB, N.Y. Law Sch., 1960; postgrad., Luth. Theol. So. Sem., 1981-84. Bar: N.Y. 1960; U.S. Supreme Ct. 1965; D.C. 1967; S.C. 1983; ordained vocat. deacon, The Episcopal Ch., 1991. Jr. clk. First Nat. City Bank of N.Y., NYC, 1955; adminstrv. asst. Chase Manhattan Bank, NYC, 1957—60; practiced law in NYC, 1960—67; rsch. asst. Papers of John Jay, Columbia U., 1961—63; lectr. Hunter Coll., NYC, 1964—65, asst. prof. history, 1965—67; assoc. sem. on history of legal polit. thought Columbia U., 1966—77, assoc. sem. on early Am. history, 1967—77; assoc. editor Papers of John Marshall, Inst. Early Am. History and Culture, Williamsburg, Va., 1967—70, co-editor, 1970—71, editor, 1971—77; prof. law and history U. S.C., Columbia, 1977—90, Ernest F. Hollings prof. constl. law, 1991—2002, disting. prof. law emeritus, 2002—. Lectr. Coll. William and Mary Williamsburg, 1967-77; Bostick vis. rsch. prof. So. studies program U. S. C., 1976, 77; mem. com. rsch., publ. Heritage '76 Com. Am. Revolution Bicentennial Commn., 1972-73; mem. bd. adjustments, appeals, Williamsburg, 1970-77; trustee Fund for Preservation of John Marshall House, 1972-74; Fund Coop. Editl. Rsch. Am. Antiquarian Soc., 1972-76; mem. profl. adv. bd. Angel Home Health & Hospice, 2002-06. Author: The Law Merchant and Negotiable Instruments in Colonial New York, 1664-1730, 1963; John Jay, 1745-1829, 1970; Imported Eighteenth Century Law Treatises in Am. Libraries 1700-1799, 1978; Essays on New York Colonial Legal History, 1981; History of Criminal Justice, 1988, 3d edit., 2002; John Jay: Colonial Lawyer, 1989; The Chief Justiceship of John Marshall, 1997; Wingless Eagle: U.S. Army Aviation Through World War I, 2001; co-author: Historical Courthouses of New York State-18th and 19th Century Halls of Justice Across the Empire State, 1977; Foundations of Power, John Marshall, 1801-15, vol. 2, History of the Supreme Court of the U.S., 1981; editor: The Papers of John Marshall, Vol. 1, 1974, Vol. II, 1977, South Carolina Legal History, 1980; Am. Legal and Constitutional History: Cases and Materials, 1994, 2d edit., 2000; gen. editor Chief Justiceships of the U.S. Supreme Court Series, 1989—; contbg. articles to profl. jour. Chaplain assoc. Bapt. Med. Ctr., Columbia, 1983-2002; hospice legal svc. vol., 1986-2000; chaplain Angel Hospice, Franklin, N.C., 2002-2004; mem. ethics com. S.C. Episcopal Home, Still Hopes, 1989-99; 1st lt. USAF, 1955-57; ret. col., Res. Recipient: William P. Lyons Masters' Essay Award Loyola U., 1962; Paul S. Kerr History prize NY State Hist. Assn., 1970, Rsch. award Faculty Law U. SC, 2001; U. SC Edn. Found. Rsch. Award profl. sch., 2000; Am. Council Learned Soc. Fellow, 1974-75; Inst. Humane Studies Fellow, 1981, 85; vis. fellow Centre for Comparative Constl. Studies, U. Melbourne Law Faculty, 1992; vis. rsch. scholar U. Toronto Law Faculty, 1995; vis. prof. U. Birmingham, Eng., 1998; fellow Gilder-Lehrman Inst. Am. History, 2006. Mem. Am. Hist. Assn. (Littleton-Griswold com. 1976-81, interim com. Bicentennial era 1976-77), Selden Soc. (state corr. for S.C. 1988-2002), Stair Soc., Air Force Assn., Am. Law Inst., Assn. Am. Law Sch. (chmn. legal history sect. 1979), Am. Soc. Legal History (pres. 1974-75, del. Am. Coun. Learned Soc. 1977-80, bd. dirs. 1999-2001), U. South Caroliniana Soc., Res. Officers Assn., Assn. Profl. Chaplains, Nat. Eagle Scout Assn. Episcopalian. Home: 245 Laurel Falls Rd Franklin NC 28734-9527 Home Phone: 828-524-8032; Office Phone: 828-524-8032. Personal E-mail: janeherb@dnet.net.

JOHNSON, H(ERBERT) FISK, manufacturing executive; AB, Cornell U., 1979, ME, 1980, MS, 1982, MBA, 1984, PhD, 1986. With S.C. Johnson & Son, Inc., Racine, Wis., 1987—, pres., gen. mgr. Canada, mng. dir. corp. new products and tech. Racine, Wis., vice chmn., 1999—2000, chmn., 2000—, CEO, 2004—. Mem. Pres. Adv. Com. Trade Policy and Negotiation, 2002—, World Bus. Coun. Sustainable Devel., 2002—; trustee emeritus Cornell U., 2002—; bd. dirs. Conservation Internat., mem. exec. bd. ctr. environ. leadership in bus.; former trustee nat edn. trust Phi Psi. Named one of Forbes' Richest Americans, 2006. Office: SC Johnson & Son Inc 1525 Howe St Racine WI 53403-2236 Office Phone: 262-260-2000. Office Fax: 262-260-6004.*

JOHNSON, HERBERT FREDERICK, sales executive, retired academic administrator, librarian; b. St. Paul, Minn., Aug. 1, 1934; s. Herbert Oscar and Hazel Grace (Otto) J.; m. Delores Elaine Madson, Aug. 21, 1955; children: Steven F., Eric L., Kirsten M. BA, U. Minn., 1957, MA, 1959; postgrad., Kursverksamheten Vid Lunds Universitet, Betyg, 1975. Libr. U.S. Govt., Washington, 1959-61; asst. bus. libr. Columbia U., 1961-64; head libr., assoc. prof. Hamline U., 1964-71; dir. librs., prof. Oberlin Coll., 1971-78; libr. dir. Oberlin Pub. Libr., 1971-78; dir. librs. Emory U., 1978-88, mem. faculty adv. com. Jimmy Carter Ctr. for Policy Studies, 1982-84; sales & svc. rep. Active Mobility of Ga., Marietta, 1988-91; sr. regional mgr. Williams/Howard Assocs., 1989-91; regional v.p. Primerica Fin. Svcs., Marietta, Ga., 1991—2002, sr. regional mgr., 2003—; registered prin. PFS Investments, Inc., 1991—; project dir. Nat. Drug Info. Ctr. Nat. Families in Action Inc., 1989-90. Lectr. U. Minn. Libr. Sch., 1967; vis. prof. Atlanta U. Sch. Libr. Svcs., 1979; charter bd. Cooperating Librs. in Consortium, St. Paul, 1969-71; libr. adv. com. Minn. Higher Edn. Coordinating Commn., 1970-71; mem. com. input standards Ohio Coll. Libr. Ctr., 1972-73, chmn. com. patron input, 1973-75; chmn. Ohio Multitype Interlibr. Cooperation Com., Ohio State Libr. Bd., 1976-78; mem. adv. and steering com. Ohio Pre-White House Conf. on Libr. and Info. Svcs., 1977-78; bd. dirs. Assn. Rsch. Librs., 1983-88, pres., 1987-88; chmn. librs. adv. com. Univ. Ctr. in Ga., Atlanta, 1979-80, 85-86; del. users coun. OCLC Online Computer Libr. Ctr. Inc., 1981-83, 85-88; bd. dirs. Southeastern Libr. Network, 1980-83, chmn. bd., 1981-83; bd. govs. Rsch. Librs. Group, 1986-87. Contbr. articles to profl. jours. Mem. com. on internat. programs Nat. Student YMCAs, 1962—64; mem. adv. com. DeKalb/Rockdale counties Met. Atlanta chpt. ARC, 1981—88, Cobb/Douglas counties, 1988—92, emergency cmty. svcs. com., 1990—94; mem. Vasa Drängar, Atlanta, 2007—, Minn. Rep. Task Force on Edn., 1966; pres., treas. Lord of Life Luth. Ch., Lorain, Ohio, 1972—75; mem. Lorain Coop. Luth. Ministry Bd., 1976—78; v.p. St. Luke Luth. Ch., Atlanta, 1979—80, 1981—82, treas., 2005—; bd. dirs. Nat. Families in Action, 1979—89, 1990—, pres., 1987—88, v.p., 1990—93, mem. Parent Corps USA, 2004—; bd. dirs. Scandinavian Am. Found. Ga., 1983—, v.p., 1993—2000, chmn. bd., 2000—02; bd. dirs. Swedish Coun. Am., 1987—2004, dir. emeritus, 2005—, chair Glenn T. Seaborg Nobel prize travel award com., 1990—2002, jr. achievement classroom cons., 1993—94. Lt. col. USAR, 1957—78. Decorated Army Commendation medal, Meritorious Svc. medal; George Williams fellow, 1957; Coun. on Libr. Resources fellow, 1974-75; NSF grantee, 1967-71. Mem.: ALA, East Cobb (Ga.) Bus. Assn. (bd. dirs. 1996—2000), Minn. Libr. Sch. Alumni Assn. (chmn. 1967), Southea. Libr. Assn., Ga. Libr. Assn., Vasa Order Am. (bd. dirs. Am. Nordic Lodge 708 2003—), Scandinavian Am. Found. Ga., Wildlife Preservation Trust, Chattahoochee Nature Ctr., Nat. Family Caregivers Assn. (nat. caregivers adv. panel 2000—), Am. Scandinavian Found., Am. Swedish Inst., Atlanta Zool. Soc., Common Cause, Nat. Trust Hist. Preservation, Sierra Club, Mil. Officers Assn. Am., High Mus. Art, Rotary (club sec. 1981—82, club pres. 1984—85, dist. 6900 youth exch. com. 1994—97, treas. 1995—97, club dir. North DeKalb, Ga. 1998—2001, Ga. Rotary Internat. student program host family 1998—, group study exch. team leader to dist. 2360 Sweden 2002, club dir. North DeKalb, Ga. 2002—04, dist. group study exch. com. 2003—, chair 2003—06, Svc. Above Self award 2001, Dist. Svc. award 2002, 2004, 2005), Beta Phi Mu. *Too many folks have given up realizing their dreams, yet with the Lord's help, anyone has the capacity to make their dreams a reality. The toughest part of the struggle is winning the battle between the ears- that is in believing in ones self. There is no greater thrill than having helped another win that struggle and having made a difference in that person's life!.*

JOHNSON, HERBERT MICHAEL, publisher; b. Leipzig, Germany, Mar. 19, 1936; came to U.S., 1940; s. Walter J. Johnson; m. Susan Armstrong, July 9, 1960; children: Walter J. II, Matthew G., Herbert M. Jr., Miranda S., George F. BS, Duke U., 1958. Mgr. domestic sales Acad. Press, Inc., NYC, 1958-66; v.p., founder Greenwood Press, Inc., Westport, Conn., 1967-72; pres., pub., founder Johnson Assocs, Inc., Greenwich, Conn., 1972-80; founder, CEO, JAI Press, Inc., Greenwich, 1975-99; founder, pres., pub. Armstrong Pub. Co., 1993-97; pres. Ablex Pub. Co., 1997-99; dir. Nutmeg Investment Ptnrs. LLC, Greenwich, Conn., 1998—; chmn. Info. Age Pub. Inc., 2001—. Mem. council Boy Scouts Am., Greenwich, 1967-80; bd. dirs. Arch St. Teen Ctr., 1999—, United Way Greenwich, 2004— Home: Augustus Ln Greenwich CT 06830-7040 Office: Nutmeg Investment Ptnrs LLC 80 Mason St PO Box 4967 Greenwich CT 06831-0419 E-mail: hmjnutmeg@aol.com.

JOHNSON, HIROKO, art history educator; b. Osaka, Japan; Postgrad., U. Tokyo, 1987-89, 91-93; PhD, U So. Calif., 1994. Adj. prof. Occidental Coll., LA, 1990-95, Pepperdine U., Malibu, Calif., 1989-97, Calif. Polytech. U., Pomona, 1996—, Calif. State U., Long Beach, 1994—. Contbr. articles to profl. jours. Recipient Kajima Art Found. award, 1998, Kagaku Kenkyu Hojokin award Ministry of Edn. in Japan, 1997-98; Japan Soc for Promotion of Scis. fellow, 1997-98. Mem. Coll. Art Assn., Assn. for Asian Study, Japan Art History Soc., Asiatic Soc. Japan. Avocation: painting.

JOHNSON, HOOTIE See JOHNSON, WILLIAM WOODWARD

JOHNSON, HORTON ANTON, pathologist; b. Cheyenne, Wyo., Nov. 12, 1926; s. Horton Antonius and Katharine Mary (Tidball) J.; m. Caryl Abell Daly, Nov. 20, 1970; children by previous marriage: Katherine, Kristin, Margaret, Ann, Gregory, Marjorie. AB, Colo. Coll., 1949; MD, Columbia U., 1953. Diplomate: Am. Bd. Pathology. Intern Univ. Hosp., Ann Arbor, Mich., 1953-54, resident in pathology, 1954-57, Pondville Cancer Hosp., Walpole, Mass., 1957-58; scientist Brookhaven Nat. Lab., 1958-60, 63-70; asst. prof. pathology U. Utah, 1960-63; prof. pathology SUNY, Stony Brook, 1970-72, Ind. U., 1972-75; prof., chmn. dept. pathology Tulane U., New Orleans, 1975-84; prof. pathology Columbia U., NYC, 1984-91; dir. pathology St. Luke's-Roosevelt Hosp. Ctr., NYC, 1984-91. Docent Met. Mus. Art, 1993—. With USNR, 1944—46, USS Atlanta. Recipient Lederle Med. Faculty award, 1961 Fellow: Royal Soc. Medicine, Coll. Am. Pathologists; mem.: Soc. Health and Human Values, Assn. Clin. Scientists, N.Y. Acad. Scis., Radiation Rsch. Soc., Biophys. Soc., Internat. Acad. Pathology, Am. Soc. Exptl. Pathology, Alpha Omega Alpha, Phi Beta Kappa. Achievements include rsch. on radiation injury, aging, theoretical biology. Home: 39 N Cove Rd Old Saybrook CT 06475-2538 Office: 3 Lincoln Ctr Ste 47C New York NY 10023-6566 Office Phone: 212-721-0204. E-mail: horton_johnson@hotmail.com.

JOHNSON, HOWARD ARTHUR, JR., corporate executive, operations analyst, financial officer; b. Indpls., July 25, 1952; s. Howard Arthur Sr. and Joy (Nelson) J.; m. Teresa Thirsk, Aug. 11, 1979; 1 child, Jamie E. BA in Polit. Sci. and Ops. Rsch Analysis, U. Kans., 1974; MA in Internat. Studies and Mgmt., U. Wyo., 1984; MS in Software Engring., U. Md., 2004. Ops. rsch. analyst Armament Systems, Inc., Ft. Walton Beach, Fla., 1980-81, EG&G InterTech, Inc., Arlington, Va., 1981-84; dep. to U.S. Dir. Plans and Budgets, Royal Saudi Navy, Saudi Arabian Ministry Def. and Aviation, Riyadh, 1981-82; ops. rsch. analyst FMC Corp., Mpls., 1984-85, Honeywell, Inc., 1985-92, sr. prin. systems staff engr., systems engring. mgr., 1985-92; co-founder, CFO, sr. cons. software engr., chief security SEER, Inc., Eden Prairie, Minn., 1992—. Cons. USN, Coronado, 1977-78, United Def., 1992-2004, Embassy Suites, 1993, Medtronic, 2004-06, BRE Sys., 2006-; sustaining mem. Nat. Com., Washington, 1984—. Lt. USN, 1974-78. Grad. acad. scholar U. Wyo., 1983-84. Mem. AAAS, IEEE, HL7 Orgn., Ops. Rsch. Soc. Am., Acad. Internat. Bus., Inst. Mgmt. Scis., Fgn. Policy Rsch. Inst., Mil. Ops. Rsch. Soc., Armed Forces Comms. Electronics Assn., Washington Ops. Rsch. Mgmt. Sci. Coun., Tau Kappa Epsilon. Office: SEER Inc 10409 Huntington Dr Ste 200B Eden Prairie MN 55347-4938

JOHNSON, HOWARD WESLEY, retired academic administrator, finance company executive; b. Chgo., July 2, 1922; s. Albert H. and Laura (Hansen) J.; m. Elizabeth J. Weed, Feb. 18, 1950; children: Stephen Andrew, Laura Ann, Bruce Howard. BA, Central Coll., Chgo., 1943; MA, U. Chgo., 1947; cert., Glasgow U., Scotland, 1946; LLD (hon.), Harvard U., U. Miami, 1966, U. Mass., 1969, Oklahoma City U., 1970, U. Cin., 1973, Babson Coll., 1978; ScD (hon.), Lowell Tech. Inst., Tufts U., Bryant Coll., 1967; LHD (hon.), Northea. U., 1966, Roosevelt U., 1969; LittD (hon.), Clarkson Coll. Tech., 1973. From asst. to assoc. prof., dir. mgmt. rsch. U. Chgo., 1948-51, 53-55; asst. to v.p. pers. adminstrn. Gen. Mills, Inc., 1952-53; assoc. prof., dir. exec. programs, assoc. dean Sloan Sch. Mgmt., MIT, 1955-59, prof., dean, 1959-66; pres. MIT, 1966-71; chmn. corp., 1971-83; hon. chmn. corp., 1983-90; life mem. corp., 1983-97; life mem. emeritus, 1997—. Exec. v.p. Federated Dept. Stores, 1966; chmn. Fed. Res. Bank Boston, 1968-69; trustee Putnam Funds, 1961-71; mem. Pres.'s Adv. Com. on Labor-Mgmt. Policy, 1966-68; chmn. Environ. Studies Bd. NAS-NAE, 1973-75; mem. sci. adv. com. Mass. Gen. Hosp., 1968-70; mem. Nat. Manpower Adv. Com., 1967-69, Nat. Commn. on Productivity, 1970-72; trustee Com. Econ. Devel., 1968-71, Wellesley Coll., 1968-86, trustee emeritus 1986—; trustee Radcliffe Coll., 1973-79; hon. trustee Aspen Inst. for Humanistic Studies, Inst. Deaf Analyses, 1971-79; mem. corp. Woods Hole (Mass) Oceanog. Instn. Author: Holding the Center: Memoirs of a Life in Higher Education, 1999. Trustee WGBH Ednl. Found., 1966-71, Henry Francis du Pont Winterthur Mus., 1984-87, Dibner Inst., 1992-97; mem. corp. Mus. Sci., Boston; overseer Boston Symphony Orch, 1968-72; mem.-at-large Boy Scouts Am.; pres. Boston Mus. Fine Arts, 1975-80, trustee 1971-72, chmn. bd. overseers, 1980-83, chmn. exec. com., 1983-87, hon. life trustee 1992—; trustee Alfred P. Sloan Found., 1982-95, chmn. bd. 1988-95; bd. dirs. Nat. Arts Stablzn. Found., 1983-87, Museo de Arte de Ponce, 1983-87. With AUS, 1943-46. Recipient Alumni medal U. Chgo., 1970, Gyorgy Kepes Fellowship prize MIT, 1999. Fellow AAAS, Am. Acad. Arts and Scis.; mem. Coun. Fgn. Rels., Am. Philos. Soc., Nat. Acad. Scis. (Pres.'s Circle), Nat. Acad. Engring. (Pres.'s Cir.), Inst. of Medicine (Pres.'s Cir.), Century Assn. (N.Y.C.), Comml. Club (Boston), Tavern Club (Boston), St. Botolph Club (Boston), Phi Gamma Delta. Office: MIT 77 Massachusetts Ave Cambridge MA 02139-4307 Office Phone: 617-253-0636. Business E-Mail: hwj@mit.edu.

JOHNSON, HUGH JAMES, retired music educator; b. Clarksville, Tex., June 16, 1935; s. Hugh J. Johnson Sr. and Bennie J. Johnson; m. Jacquelyn M. Johnson, July 20, 1992; children: Jeanine, Maria. BA, Wiley Coll., 1963; MEd, U. N. Tex., 1974. Band dir. Ctrl. H.S., Springfield, Ga., 1963—66, McRae, Ga., 1968—69, W. H.S., Hardeville, SC, 1969—70, Ridgeland H.S., SC, 1970—71, Hubert Mid. Sch., Savannah, Ga., 1970—94. Adjudicator All State Band Auditions; cons. State. Dept. Edn., So. Assn. Colls. and Schs. Scout talent show Wesley Cmty. Ctr.; mem. Bacon Park Woods Cmty. Task Force; lay leader Asbury United Meth. Ch., lay spkr., del. to ann. conf., chmn. adminstrv. bd., mem. pastor, parish rels. com., bd. trustees, mem. fin. com., pres. Meth. Men, Sunday Sch. supt. and tchr., mem. edn. com., mem. ch. choirs, mem. worship com., class leader, children's moment tchr., mem. S. Ga. conf. race and religion com.; team capt. United Way. Named to, Wiley Coll. Musicians' Hall of Fame, 1990. Mem.: NEA, Tex. Music Educator's Assn., Ga. Assn. Educators, Chatham Assn. Educators, Am. Fedn. Musicians, Ga. Music Educator's Assn., Music Educator's Conf., Coastal Jazz Assn., U. N. Tex. Alumni Assn., Edgewater Oaks Condominium Owner's Assn., Inc. (bd. dirs.), Wiley Coll. Alumni Assn., Omega Psi Phi. Home: 718 Apple Blossom Dr Pearland TX 77584

JOHNSON, IRVING STANLEY, pharmaceutical executive, research scientist; b. Grand Junction, Colo., June 30, 1925; s. Walter Glen and Frances Lucetta (Tuttle) J.; m. Alwyn Neville Ginther, Jan. 29, 1949; children: Rebecca Lyn, Bryan Glenn, Kirsten Shawn, Kevin Bruce. BS, Washburn U., Topeka, 1948; PhD, U. Kans., Lawrence, 1953. With Lilly Rsch. Labs., Indpls., 1953-88, v.p. rsch., 1973-88; mem. profl. edn. com. Am. Cancer Soc., 1972-82. Rschr. cancer, virus, genetic engring.; mem. UCLA Symposia Bd., 1988-; bd. dirs. Allelix Biopharms., Ligand Pharms.; sci. adv. bd. Elan Corp., 1996-; trustee La Jolla Cancer Rsch. Found., 1990-93; advisor to biomed. rsch. cos., venture capital groups; mem. Recombinant Adv. Com., NIH; indep. biomedical rsch. cons. Editor: Biology and Medicine in the 21st Century, 2007; mem. sci. adv. bd. Biotech., 1986—; mem. editorial bd. Chemico-Biol. Interactions, 1968-73; contbr. articles to profl. publs.; patentee in field. With USNR, 1943—46. Recipient 1st ann. Congl. award for sci. and tech., 1984, Alumni Disting. Achievement award U. Kans., 2005, Disting. Svc. Citation award U. Kans., 2006. Fellow AAAS; mem. Am. Assn. Cancer Rsch. (Cain Meml. award for outstanding preclin. rsch. in cancer chemotherapy 1986), Am. Soc. Cell Biology (mem. pub. policy com.), Environ. Mutagen Soc., Internat. Soc. Chemotherapy, NY Acad. Scis., Soc. Exptl. Biology and Medicine, Am. Soc. Immunologists (mem. sci. adv. bd. biotech), Soc. for Neurosci., Sigma Xi, Phi Sigma. Episcopalian. Achievements include being widely acknowledged for leadership team which led to the production and approval of the first health care product manufactured by recombinant DNA/genetic engineering techniques, ie human insulin.

JOHNSON, IVER CHRISTIAN, retired real estate appraiser; b. NYC, Oct. 21, 1928; s. Rudolph Albert and Mae Sophia (Bernhardt) Johnson; m. Ann E. Wells, May 15, 1954 (div. Apr. 1978); children: Christian Robert, Roberta Dawn, Brad Milton; m. Rochelle Valene Wehrhelm, Dec. 6, 1986. BSME, N.Y.U., 1950; MBA, Northwestern U., 1958. Registered profl. egnr. Engr. Yale & Towne Mfg. Co., Chgo., 1952-54; computer sales engr. GE, Phoenix, 1958-60; comml. broker O'Malley Investment & Realty Co., Phoenix, 1960-64; v.p. Investors Trust & Realty Co., Inc., Phoenix, 1964-66; ptnr. Shuart Bros. Constrn. Co., Phoenix, 1966-69; pres. Iver C. Johnson & Co., Ltd., Phoenix, 1970-95; ret. Del. mem. Citizen Amb. Program Econ. Mgmt. Delegation to Soviet Union, Moscow, Odessa, 1990; adj. instr. Ozarks Tech. Coll. S.W. Bapt. U. Chmn., mem. bd. appeals Ariz. State Land Dept., 1989—95; mem. exec. com. Ariz. Appraiser Coalition, 1989—92; mem. Ash. Grove (Mo.) City Coun., 1997—. 1st lt. USAF, 1954—56. Mem.: Am. Mktg. Assn. (profl.), Inst. Indsl. Engrs., Am. Soc. Appraisers (sr.; pres. 1985—86, ASA award 1981, Outstanding Mem. award 1990), Internat. Right of Way Assn. (SRWA award 1990). Republican. Lutheran. Avocation: freelance writing. Home and Office: 904 E Auburn Dr Ash Grove MO 65604-9100 Personal E-mail: ivercjohns@hotmail.com. Business E-Mail: i.johnson@mchsi.com.

JOHNSON, J. CHESTER, corporate financial executive, consultant, writer; b. Chattanooga, Sept. 28, 1944; m. Freda Stern; children: Juliet Christina, Guilbert Roland Student, Harvard U., 1962-65; BSE, U. Ark., 1967. Sr. analyst Moody's Investors Svc., 1968-71; head pub. fin. rsch. and adv. group The Morgan Bank, 1972-77; dep. asst. sec. U.S. Treasury Dept., Washington, 1977-78; chmn., prin. Govt. Fin. Assocs., Inc., NYC, 1979—. Bd. dirs., chair fin. com. N.Y. State Environ. Facilities Corp., 1991-95; chmn. Fed. Task Force to create Nat. Devel. Bank; chmn. Fed. Inter-agy. Task Force for Improvement Govtl. Fin. Reporting; chmn. Fund to Assure Pub. Infrastructure Fin., Nat. Infrastructure Bond Coalition, 1988-91; interviewed on pub. fin. Cable News Network, ABC Morning News Feature, PBS News Roundup, NBC Nightly News, others Author: (poetry) OH America!, January 12th, 1967, 2d edit., 1975, Family Ties, Internecine Interregnum!, 1981, For Conduct and Innocents, 1982, Shorts: For Fun, Not for Instruction, 1985, It's a Long Way Home, An American Sequence, 1985, Shorts: On Reaching Forty, 1985, Exile/Martin, 1986, The Professional Curiosity of a Martyr, 1987, Freda's Appetite, 1991, Lazarus, Come Forth, 1993, Plain Bob (Unbehaved), 1993, St. Paul's Chapel and Selected Shorter Poems, 2006; (with W.H. Auden) revised psalms in The Book of Common Prayer of The Episcopal Church, 1971-77; co-author: Original Disclosure Guidelines for Securities' Offerings by State and Local Governments, 1976, The Future of Boston's Capital Plant, 1980, Mayor's Financial Management Handbook, 1985; contbr. numerous articles to profl. jours. and poetry to anthologies Mem. vestry Trinity Wall St. Ch., 2001—. Mem. Nat. Assn. Ind. Pub. Fin. Advisors (pres. 1989-91), Nat. Soc. Mcpl. Analysts, Nat. Fedn. Mcpl. Analysts (Disting. Lifetime Contbn. award 1988) Office: Govt Fin Assocs Inc 21st Fl 590 Madison Ave New York NY 10022-1031 Office Phone: 212-521-4090. Personal E-mail: jchester.gfa@prodigy.net.

JOHNSON, J. M. HAMLIN, manufacturing executive; b. Ridgway, Pa., Oct. 10, 1925; s. Manferd H. and Esther (Hallstrom) J.; m. Sara N. Richardson, Sept. 11, 1948; children: Stephanie (Mrs. William G. Cox), Robert H., Elizabeth E., Lara D. (Mrs. Ellwyn A. Reynolds Jr.), David L., Christine M. (Mrs. Thomas Syzmanski), Shawn J. BS, Grove City Coll., 1949; student, Pa. State U., 1969. With Stackpole Corp., St. Mary's, Pa., 1950—, supr. acctg., to 1960, operational auditor, 1960-64, mgr. acctg., 1964-68, asst. treas., 1968-71, treas., asst. sec., 1971-79, v.p., treas., asst. sec., 1979-84, v.p., treas. asst. sec., dir., 1984-88, v.p., treas., sec., dir., 1988; ret., 1990. Bd. dirs. Hamlin Bank & Trust Co., past bd. dirs. Cmty. Nurses of Elk & Cameron Counties Inc., Home Health Svcs. Past mem. Ridgway Area Sch. Bd.; trustee Stackpole-Hall Found., 1983—; past chmn., bd. dirs. St. Marys Regional Med. Ctr.; bd. dirs., past treas., past pres. ELCAM Vocat. Rehab. Ctr.; past bd. dirs. United Fund St. Marys; past bd. dirs. Elk County Regional Med. Ctr.; bd. dirs., treas. Elk County Cmty. Found., 1999—. With USAAF. Mem. Inst. Mgmt. Accts. (pres. 1958-59), Bavarian Hills Club Home: 517 Center St Saint Marys PA 15857-1001

JOHNSON, JAMES A., finance company executive; b. Benson, Minn., Dec. 24, 1943; s. Alfred I. and Adeline (Rasmussen) J.; m. Katherine Marshall, Feb. 15, 1969 (div. 1973); m. Maxine Isaacs, Jan. 12, 1985; 1 child, Alfred Isaacs. BA, U. Minn., 1965; MA, Princeton U., 1968. Spl. asst. to Sen. Walter Mondale U.S. Senate, Washington, 1972; dir. pub. affairs Dayton Hudson Corp., Mpls., 1973-76; exec. asst. to v.p. Walter Mondale The White House, Washington, 1977-81; pres. Pub. Strategies, Washington, 1981-85; mng. dir. Lehman Bros., NYC, 1985-89; vice-chmn. Fannie Mae, Washington, 1990-91, chmn., CEO, 1991-98, chmn. exec. com. bd. dirs., 1999; chmn., CEO Johnson Capital Ptnrs., Washington, 2000-01; vice chmn. Perseus, 2001—. Bd. dirs. Target Corp., Goldman Sachs Inc., Temple-Inland, Gannett, Inc., KB Home, United HealthGroup. Chmn. John F. Kennedy Ctr. for Performing Arts, 1996-2004; chmn. bd. trustees The Brookings Instn., 1994-2003. Democrat. Avocations: tennis, golf, travel. Office: Perseus LLC 2099 Pennsylvania Ave NW Washington DC 20006 Office Phone: 202-752-6790.

JOHNSON, JAMES D., lawyer; b. LeMars, Iowa, Apr. 12, 1943; BS, U. Iowa, 1965, JD, 1967. Bar: Iowa 1967, Ill. 1970, NY 1994. Law clk. to Hon. George C. Edwards U.S. Ct. Appeals (6th cir.), 1967-68; ptnr. corp. and securities law Sidley Austin Brown & Wood LLP, NYC, and mem. exec. com. Note editor U. Iowa Law Review, 1966-67. Mem. ABA, Chgo. Bar Assn., Phi Delta Phi. Office: Sidley Austin Brown & Wood LLP 787 Seventh Ave New York NY 10019 Office Phone: 212-839-7350. Office Fax: 212-839-5599. Business E-Mail: jjohnson@sidley.com.

JOHNSON, JAMES DAVID, concert pianist, organist, educator; b. Greenville, SC, Aug. 7, 1948; s. Theron David and Lucile (Pearson) J.; m. Karen Elizabeth Jacobson, Feb. 1, 1975. MusB, U. Ariz., 1970, MusM, 1972, D of Mus. Arts, 1976; MusM, Westminster Choir Coll., 1986. Concert pianist, organist Pianists Found. Am., Boston Pops Orch., Royal Philharm., Nat. Symphony Orch., Leningrad Philharmonic, Victoria Symphony, others, 1961—; organist, choirmaster St. Paul's Episcopal Ch., Tucson, 1968-74, First United Meth. Ch., Fairbanks, Alaska, 1974-89, All Saints Episc. Ch., Omaha, 1995—; prof. music U. Alaska, Fairbanks, 1974-96, chair music dept., 1991-94; Isaacson prof. of music U. Nebr., Omaha, 1994—2001, chair dept. music, 1999—2001, Robert M. Spire chair in music, 2002—. Recordings include Moszkowski Etudes, 1973, Works of Chaminade Dohnanyi, 1977, Mendelssohn Concerti, 1978, Beethoven First Concerto, 1980, Beethoven, Reinecke, Ireland Trios with Alaska Chamber Ensemble, 1988, Kabalevsky Third Concerto, Muczynski Concerto, Muczynski Suite, 1990, Beethoven Third Concerto, 1993 (2002). Recipient Record of Month award Mus. Heritage Soc., 1979, 80, Excellence in Tchg. award U. Nebr. at Omaha, 2001; named Tchr. of Yr., Nebr. Music Tchrs. Assn., 2005. Fellow Music Tchrs. Nat. Assn.; mem. Am. Guild Organists, Phi Kappa Phi, Pi Kappa Lambda, Omicron Delta Kappa. Episcopalian. Avocations: painting, woodworking, icon writing. Office: U Nebr Dept Music Omaha NE 68182-0001 Office Phone: 402-554-3353. Personal E-mail: jjpiano@cox.net. Business E-Mail: j.djohnson@mail.unomaha.edu.

JOHNSON, JAMES DOUGLAS (JIM JOHNSON), lawyer; b. Crossett, Ark., Aug. 20, 1924; s. Thomas William and Maudie Myrtle (Long) J.; m. Virginia Morris, Dec. 21, 1947; children: Mark Douglas, John David and Joseph Daniel (twins). LL.B., Cumberland U., 1947. Bar: Ark. 1948. Practice in, Crosset, 1948-58; assoc. justice Supreme Ct. Ark., 1958-66; practice law Little Rock, 1966—; Ark. Senate 22d Senatorial Dist., 1950-54. Served with USMCR, World War II. Mem. Ark. Jud. Council, Lamda Chi Alpha. Republican. Christian Scientist. Home and Office: PO Box 1086 Conway AR 72033-1086 Office Phone: 501-329-8383.

JOHNSON, JAMES ERLING, insurance executive; b. Waseca, Minn., May 19, 1942; s. Erling Olaf and Geneva Eleanor (Nyberg) J. BA cum laude, Carleton Coll., 1964; MS, U. Iowa, 1966. Sr. asst. health svcs. officer USPHS, 1966—68; with Minn. Life Ins. Co., St. Paul, 1968—, 2d v.p., actuary, 1976—79, v.p., actuary, 1979—90, sr.v.p., actuary, 1990—2006; exec. v.p. Minn. Life Ins. Co, 2006—; pres. and CEO Minn. Fire & Casualty, Minnetonka, 1984—97, also bd. dirs.; pres., CEO Adjustable Life Ins. Co., St. Paul, 1988—93, also bd. dirs. Mem. alumni bd. Carleton Coll., Northfield, Minn., 1987-90, coun., 1988-89, bd. trustees 1999-2003, alumni ann. fund bd., 2005—; campaign cabinet St. Paul United Way, 1988-89; bd. dirs. Minn. Landmarks, 1988—, treas., 1989-91, chmn., 1991-96; trustee ECH Found., 1989-95, asst. treas., 1990-91, treas., 1991-95; bd. dirs. Alliance Am. Insurers, 1994-95, vice chmn., 1994-95; mem. St. Paul Chamber Orch., 1998—, co-chair indivdual gifts com., 1998-2000, vice chair devel., 2000—; mem. adv. bd. Minn. Ctr. for Ins. Rsch., 1995— U. Iowa fellow, 1964-66; recipient Exceptional Svc. award Carleton Coll., 2004 Fellow Soc. Actuaries; mem. Am. Acad. Actuaries, Twin Cities Actuarial Club (chmn. 1978-79), Mpls. Club, Univ. Club St. Paul, Minn. Assn. of Mut. Ins. Cos. (bd. dirs. 1984-97, pres. 1992-94), Nat. Assn. Secondary Sch. Prins. (trustee Trust to Reach Edn. Excellence 1999—), Am. Coun. Life Ins. (chair group ins. com., 2003-05), Calhoun Beach Club, Phi Beta Kappa, Pi Mu Epsilon Episcopalian. Avocations: travel, reading, running, swimming. Home: 2034 Lower Saint Dennis Rd Saint Paul MN 55116-2833 Office: Minn Life Ins Co 400 Robert St N Saint Paul MN 55101-2015 E-mail: james.johnson@minnesotamutual.com.

JOHNSON, JAMES HARDING, advertising executive; b. Perry, Iowa, Sept. 26, 1940; s. Richard Harding and Dorothy Margarite (Nelson) J.; m. Kathy Novak, Dec. 27, 1980; children: Ann Katherine, Alexander Simon, Elizabeth Ashely; children by previous marriage: Jennifer Lynn, James Harding. BA, U. Wash., 1963; PhD, U. Minn., 1972. Lic. psychologist, Utah, Va., Ill. Asst. prof. psychology U. Utah, Salt Lake City, 1975-77, dir. divsn. psychology Med. Sch., 1976-77; assoc. prof., vice chmn. dept. psychiatry Ea. Va. Med. Sch., Norfolk, 1977-79; chmn. Va. Consortium for Profl. Psychology, Norfolk, 1978-79; prof., dir. clin. psychology Ill. Inst. Tech., Chgo., 1979-83; pres. Human Edge Software, Inc., San Mateo, Calif., 1983-87, Text Generations Techs., San Mateo, 1987-89, Johnson Direct Advt., Palo Alto, Calif., 1988-89; CEO Connected Brands, 1989—. Author: Mental Health in the 21st Century, 1979, Technology in Mental Health Care Delivery Systems, 1980, How to Buy Almost Any Drug Legally Without a Prescription, 1990; co-author: Mind Prober, 1985; mem. editl. bd. Computers in Psychiatry and Psychology, Computers in Human Service, Behavior Rsch. Methods and Instrumentation, 1977, Computers in Psychiatry and Psychology, Computers and Behavioral Sci.; contbr. articles to profl. jours. Recipient Rush bronze medal Am. Psychiat. Assn., 1975. Mem. APA. Office: Connections 220 Twin Dolphin Dr Ste A Redwood City CA 94065-1488

JOHNSON, JAMES J., lawyer; BA, Mich. State U., 1969; JD, Ohio State U., 1972. Bar: Ohio 1972. Atty, legal divsn. Procter & Gamble Co., Cin., 1973—76, counsel, legal divsn., 1976, asst. brand mgr, PS&D, 1976—79, sr. counsel, legal divsn., 1979—81, divsn. counsel, indsl. divsn., 1981—85, divsn. counsel, PS&D and BS&HCP divsn., 1985—88, assoc. gen. counsel, 1988—90, dep. gen. counsel, 1990—91, v.p., gen. counsel, 1991—92, sr. v.p., gen. counsel, 1992—99, chief legal officer, 1999—2004, chief legal officer, sec., 2004—. Mem.: Chief Legal Officer Roundtable (exec. com.), Ohio Legal Assistance Found. (bd. trustees), Nat. Legal Aid and Defender Assn. (corp. adv. com.), Civil Justice Reform Group (steering com.), Assn. of Gen. Counsel (exec. com.), Queen City Club, Camargo Club, Commonwealth Club. Office: Procter & Gamble Co 1 Procter And Gamble Plz Cincinnati OH 45202-3393 Office Phone: 513-983-1100.*

JOHNSON, JAMES JOSEPH SCOFIELD, lawyer, educator, writer, judge; b. Washington, Apr. 28, 1956; s. Richard Carl and Harriette (Benson) J.; m. Sherry Bekki Hall; children: Andrew Joel Schaeffer Johnson. AA with high honors, Montgomery Coll., Germantown, Md., 1980; BA with honors, Wake Forest U., 1982; JD, U. N.C., 1984; ThD with highest honors, Emmanuel Coll. Christian Studies, 1996, DASc with highest honors, 2000; PhD with highest honors, Cambridge Grad. Sch., Springdale, Ark., 1996, MSc, M of Liberal Arts, 1999. Bar: Tex. 1985, U.S. Dist. Ct. (no. dist.) Tex. 1986, U.S. Dist. Ct. (ea. dist.) Tex. 1987, U.S. Ct. Appeals (5th cir.) 1989, U.S. Dist. Ct. (we. and so. dists.) Tex. 1990, U.S. Supreme Ct. 2000; bd. cert. bus. bankruptcy law Tex. Bd. Legal Specialization, 1990, 95, 2000, 2005, Am. Bankruptcy Bd. Cert., 1992; cert. water quality monitor Tex. Natural Resource Conservation Commn., 1994-1997; cert. ind. hearing examiner, Tex. Edn. Agy., 1996—. Assoc. various orgns., Dallas, 1985—; pvt. practice law Dallas, 1993—. Adj. prof., master faculty LeTourneau U., Dallas, 1991—, Dallas Christian Coll., 1995—, Concordia U. at Austin, Ft. Worth, 2006—; lectr. history, geography, ecology, culture, econs. Norwegian Cruise Lines, 1998—; Bibl. langs. instr. Cross Timbers Inst., 2001—. Author: Introduction to Environmental Studies, 1995, 98, Doxological Zoology and Zoogeography, 1998, How Texas is Addressing Administrative Law Issues in School Law Contexts, 2003; sr. editl. staff N.C. Jour. Internat. Law and Comml. Regulation, 1983-84; conf. issue editor Harvard Jour. Law & Pub. Policy, 1984; contbr. articles to profl. jours. Protestant chaplain Boy Scouts Am., Goshen, Va., 1976; cmty. program dir. Southwestern Legal Founds. Conf. on Internat. and Am. Law, 1991-92; scripture chmn. Gideons Internat., North Dallas, Tex., 1993-94. Recipient award for excellence in biblical studies and biblical langs. Am. Bible Soc., 1982. Mem. Near East Archaeology Soc., Sangre de Cristo Mountain Coun., Icelandic Geneal. Soc., Creation Rsch. Soc., Evangel. Theol. Soc., Norwegian Soc. Tex., Orkney Heritage Soc., Sons of Norway (historian). Avocations: reading, writing, birding, travel, hiking. Office: PO Box 2952 Dallas TX 75221-2952

JOHNSON, JAMES MARTIN, state supreme court justice, lawyer; b. Seattle; married; 2 children. BA in Economics, Harvard U., 1967; JD, U. Wash., 1970. Bar: Wash. 1970, U.S. Supreme Ct., Wash. Supreme Ct., Fed. Ct. of Appeals Eighth Circuit, Fed. Ct. of Appeals Ninth Circuit, Fed. Ct. of Appeals D.C. Circuit. Counsel Wash. Legislative Joint Com. on Banking Insurance & Transportation, 1970—71; chief atty. for fisheries/game div. Wash. State, 1973—83; chief special litigation div., sr. asst. atty. gen. fish & wildlife div. Wash. Atty. Gen. Office, 1983—93; atty. priv. practice, 1993—2004; justice Wash. Supreme Ct., 2005—. Lt., chief administrative services Ninth Infantry Div. US Army, 1971—73. Avocations: scuba diving, sailing, fishing, hunting, opera. Office: Wash Supreme Ct 415 12th Ave SW PO Box 40929 Olympia WA 98504-0929*

JOHNSON, JAMES MYRON, psychologist, educator; b. Sauk Centre, Minn., Aug. 4, 1927; s. Wilfred and Sophie Catherine (Koelzer) J.; m. Constance Mary Blodgett, Apr. 15, 1950; children: Kathryn, Peter, Donna, Daniel, Amy, Linda, Eric, Christian. BA, U. Minn., 1948; MA, Clark U., 1950; PhD, Columbia, 1958; ME (hon.), Stevens Inst. Tech., 1986. Staff psychologist Lever Bros. Co., 1955-64; Adj. prof. Grad. Sch. Indsl. Engring., N.Y.U., 1963-66; dep. dir. lab. psychol. studies Stevens Inst. Tech., 1964-67, dir., 1967-73, prof. mgmt. sci. and psychology, 1966-89, prof. emeritus, 1989—, assoc. dean acad. affairs, 1972-76, dir. tech. and soc. curriculum, 1972-75; dir. Center for Mgmt. of Organizational Resources, 1976-81; sr. partner Organizational Scis. Assocs., 1980-88; v.p. G. W. Fotis Assocs., Inc., 1982-88, head, dept. of mgmt., 1988-89. Cons. to industry. Prodr.: (film) The Man Who Revolutionized Management: Frederick Winslow Taylor; co-editor: Parish Life; editor: Lyme Cath. Observer. Pres. Darien (Conn.) Mental Health Assn., 1961-64, 68-70; mem. Darien Democratic Town Com.; bd. dirs. Gateway, Inc., 1979-86. Served with USNR, 1945-46. Mem. Am. Psychol. Soc., Met. N.Y. Assn. Applied Psychology (pres. 1963-64), Sigma Xi (treas. 1984-89), Old Lyme Country Club. Democrat. Roman Catholic. Home: 4 Tantummaheag Rd Old Lyme CT 06371-1137

JOHNSON, JAMES TERENCE, lawyer, educator, writer, minister; b. Springfield, Mo., Oct. 25, 1942; s. Clifford Lester and Margaret Jeanne (Wallace) Johnson; m. Martha Susan Mitchell, May 2, 1964; children: Jennifer Jeanne Clark, Emily Jill Brown. BA, Okla. Christian Coll., 1964; JD, So. Meth. U., 1967; LLD (hon.), Pepperdine U., 1980. Min., Okla., 1961—2000; staff counsel, asst. prof. Okla. Christian Coll., Oklahoma City, 1968-72; pvt. law practice Oklahoma City, 1969—2000; v.p. Okla. Christian U., 1972-73, exec. v.p., 1973-74, pres., 1974-95, chancellor, 1996—2000. Co-founder Enterprise Sq., 1982, Cascade Coll., 1993. Chmn. Highland Lakes Family Crisis Ctr., 2006—07; elder Marble Falls (Tex.) Ch. Christ, 2004. Named to Okla. Higher Edn. Hall of Fame, 2000. Mem.: Okla. Bar Assn., Phi Delta Theta.

JOHNSON, JANE PENELOPE, freelance/self-employed writer; b. Danville, Ky., July 1, 1940; d. Buford Lee Carr and Emma Irene (Coldiron) Sebastian; m. William Evan Johnson, July l5, l958; children: William Evan Jr., Robert Anthony. Grad., Famous Writer's Sch. Fiction, Westport, Conn., 1967; grad. writer's divsn., Newspaper Inst. Am., NYC, 1969; grad., Am. Assn. Christian Counselors, 2001, student; LittD (hon.), The London Inst. Applied Rsch., 1993; student, World Harvest Bible Coll., 2006—. Lay counselor Caring for People God's Way. Author: (poetry book) A Penny For Your Thoughts, numerous poems including Heaven Awaits, What is it?, others, (song lyrics) Everlasting Freedom, Answered Prayer, Glory Bound, Americans Standing Tall; recs. include America, 1997-98, The Light of the World, 1998-99; contbr. Hilltop Gospel Songbook, (songs) to Sing Hosanna. Patron Menninger; pres. Dwight D. Eisenhower Commn. signed by Pres. Ford, Reagan, George H. Bush, George W. Bush for lifetime contbns. Nat. Rep. Party; charter mem. Pres. George Bush & V.P. Dick Cheney Victory Team. Ennobled by Prince John, The Duke of Avram, Tasmania, Australia; semifinalist Internat. Libr. Poetry, N.Am. Poetry Open; recipient 28 Editor's Choice awards for poetry Nat. Libr. of Poetry, 1994, Editor's Choice award Internat. Libr. Poetry, 2000, Coat of Arms, Coll. of Heraldry; named to Internat. Poetry Hall of Fame, 1996, Pres. award, 2002; named World Laureate, Internat. Writer of Yr. Cambridge Gold Medal, Poet of Merit trophy Internat. Soc. Poets, Nobel Laureate Order Internat. Diplomats. Fellow The World Lit. Acad. Eng.; mem. NAFE, Smithsonian Assocs., Peale Ctr. for Christian Living, Sweet Adelines, Internat. Soc. Poets (laureate founder, life, advisor), Internat. Platform Assn., Charles Menniger Soc. (life), Famous Poets Soc., Internat. Order of Merit, Nat. Writer's Club, Nat. Authors' Registry, Poetry Guild NY, Norman Vincent Peale Fellowship (founder). Republican. Avocations: swimming, skating, dance, piano. Office: Gardenside Br PO Box 8013 Lexington KY 40504-8013 Personal E-mail: pennyspoems@yahoo.com.

JOHNSON, JANET HELEN, literature educator; b. Everett, Wash., Dec. 24, 1944; d. Robert A. and Jane N. (Osborn) J.; m. Donald S. Whitcomb, Sept. 2, 1978; children: J.J., Felicia. BA, U. Chgo., 1967, PhD, 1972. Instr. Egyptology U. Chgo., 1971-72, asst. prof., 1972-79, assoc. prof., 1979-81, prof., 1981—; dir. Oriental Inst., 1983-89; research assoc. dept. anthropology Field Mus. of Natural History, 1980-84, 94-99, 2003—; Morton D. Hull disting. svc. prof. U. Chgo., 2003—. Author: Demotic Verbal System, 1977, Thus Wrote Onchsheshonqy, 1986, 3d revised edit., 2000, (with Donald Whitcomb) Quseir al-Qadim, 1978, 80; editor: (with E.F. Wente) Studies in Honor of G.R. Hughes, 1977, Life in a Multi-Cultural Society, 1992. Recipient Morton D. Hall disting. svc., 2003; grantee, Smithsonian Instn., 1977—83, NEH, 1978—81, 1981—85, Nat. Geog. Soc., 1978, 1980, 1982. Mem. Am. Rsch. Ctr. in Egypt (bd. govs. 1979—, exec. com. 1984-87, 90-96, v.p. 1990-93, pres. 1993-96). Office: U Chgo Oriental Inst 1155 E 58th St Chicago IL 60637-1540 Home Phone: 773-493-8685; Office Phone: 773-702-9530. Business E-Mail: j-johnson@uchicago.edu.

JOHNSON, JANET HOVEY, English language educator; b. Estelline, SD, Jan. 11, 1954; d. Rolf N. and Elsie A. Hovey; m. David W. Johnson, Feb. 17, 1979; children: Reid L., Ethan P. BA, Augustana Coll., Sioux Falls, SD, 1975; MA, S.D. State U., 1981. Instr. English Estelline H.S., 1975—2003; tchr. English Watertown (S.D.) H.S., 2003—. Reading specialist Watertown H.S., 2004—; profl. semester cooperating tchr. SD State U., Brookings, 1994—2007. Author: (local history) History of Grace Lutheran Church; contbr. local history; editor: (local history) History of Trinity Lutheran Church, History of Estelline United Church of Christ. Pres. bd. Estelline City Libr., 1985—2003; Sunday sch. supt. Trinity Luth. Ch., Estelline, 1986—2003; dir. Christmas program Luth. Ch. of Our Redeemer, Watertown, 2004—06; mem. audit com. Reliabank, Watertown, SD, 1987—; com. mem. Schools That Work, Watertown, 2003—05; rural schs. mem., grant writer Estelline H.S., 1994—2000. Recipient Founder's Award in Journalism, S.D. H.S. Press Assn., 2004. Mem.: NEA, Watertown Edn. Assn., S.D. Edn. Assn., Phi Kappa Phi, Kappa Delta Pi. Lutheran. Avocations: reading, writing, running, collecting antiques, watching sports. Home Phone: 605-882-8950; Office Phone: 605-882-6316. E-mail: johnsjan@wtn.k12.sd.us.

JOHNSON, J(ANET) SUSAN, psychologist; b. Ramey AFB, PR, Mar. 24, 1948; d. Wesley Roger and Marie Dolores (Stecher) J.; m. Darrel Edwards, June 9, 1991. BA in Psychology, San Diego State U., 1970, Ma in Psychology, 1974. Coord. nat. exec. lab. Navy Nat. Elec. Lab., San Diego, 1970—72; assoc. dir. clin. decisions Navy Health Rsch. Ctr., San Diego, 1972—78; pvt. practice San Diego, 1972—; exec. dir. Edwards Assocs., San Diego, 1978—; clin. intern in clin. psychology TRI Cmty. Svcs. Outpatient Clinic, San Diego, 1978—80; pres. Strategic Vision, San Diego, 1983—. Co-founder Ctr. for Value Centered Life, 1999; key spkr., program coord. for nat. presidencies, prime mins., Fortune 100 CEO's, 1978—; mem. undergraduate mgmt. adv. bd. Marriott Sch. Bus. Brigham Young U., 2006—; guest rschr. in field; cons. in field. Contbr. articles to profl. pubis. Undergraduate adv. bd. mem. BYU Marriott Bus. Sch., 2006. Avocations: skiing, boating, scuba diving, gardening. Office Phone: 858-576-7141. Business E-Mail: susan.johnson@strategicvision.com.

JOHNSON, JAY L., energy executive; b. Great Falls, Mont., 1946; m. Garland Hawthorne; 1 child, Cullen. Grad., US Naval Acad., Annapolis, Md., 1968. Designated naval aviator. Commd. ensign USN, 1968, advanced through grades to adm., served with VF-191 on USS Oriskany, 1971-73, exec. officer VF-101, 1979-80, exec. officer VF-84, 1980-81, commdg. officer VF-84, 1981-83, comdr. Carrier Air Wing One, 1985-86, asst. chief of staff ops., comdr. 6th fleet, 1986-87, sr. comdr., 1988-89, asst. chief naval pers. Bur. Naval Pers., 1990-92, comdr. Carrier Group 8, Theodore Roosevelt Battle Group, 1992-94, comdr. 2nd Fleet, Striking Fleet Atlantic, Joint Task Force 120, 1994-96, vice chief naval ops. to chief naval ops., mem. Joint Chiefs of Staff Washington, 1996—2000; sr. v.p. bus. excellence Dominion, Richmond, Va., 2000—02, exec. v.p., pres. and CEO Dominion Delivery, 2002—. Chief naval ops. strategic study group, 1989-90; bd. dirs. Gen. Dynamics, 2003-. Decorated Def. Dist. Svc. medal, Def. Superior Svc. medal, 4 Legion of Merit awards, Def. Meritorious Svc. medal, 8 Air medals, others. Office: Dominion PO Box 26532 Richmond VA 23261-6532*

JOHNSON, JAY WITHINGTON, former congressman; b. Bessemer, Mich., Sept. 30, 1943; s. Ruben W. and Catherine W. (Withington) J.; m. Jane Sholtz (div.); m. Jo Lee Works, June 26, 1982; stepchildren: Christopher, Joanna AA, Gogebic Community Coll., 1963; BA, No. Mich. U., 1965; MA, Mich. State U., 1970. Disk jockey Sta. WFMK, Lansing, Mich., 1968-69; news anchorman Sta. WILX-TV, Lansing, 1969-70; radio news reporter Sta. WOWO, Ft. Wayne, Ind., 1970-73; news anchorman Sta. WPTV-TV, West Palm Beach, Fla., 1973-76; radio news reporter Sta. WVCG/WLVE-FM, Miami, Fla., 1976; TV producer Sta. WPLG-TV, Miami, 1976; news anchorman, mng. editor Sta. WPEC-TV, West Palm Beach, 1977-80; news anchorman Sta. WOTV-TV, Grand Rapids, Mich., 1980-81, Sta. WFRV-TV, Green Bay, Wis., 1981-87, Sta. WLUK-TV, Green Bay, 1987-96; mem. 105th Congress from 8th Wis dist., 1997-98, mem. agrl., transp. and infrastructure coms.; acting dep. asst. sec. congl. rels. USDA, 1999-2000; dir. U.S. Mint, Washington, 2000-2001. Vol. Big Bros./Big Sisters, Green Bay, 1982-87 (Vol. of Yr. 1985); pres., bd. dirs. Family Violence Ctr., Green Bay, 1982-87; v.p. communications United Way, Green Bay, 1987—; adv. bd. Libertas Alcohol Treatment Ctr., 1989—. With U.S. Army, 1966-68. Recipient Gov's award Gov. Tommy Thompson, 1988; named Citizen of Yr. Masons, 1987.

JOHNSON, JEAN ELAINE, nursing educator; b. Wilsey, Kans., Mar. 11, 1925; d. William H. and Rosa L. (Welty) Irwin. BS, Kans. State U., 1948; MS in Nursing, Yale U., 1965; MS, U. Wis., 1969, PhD, 1971; DS (hon.), Univ. Wis., 1998. Instr. nursing, Iowa, 1948—58; staff nurse Swedish Hosp., Englewood, Colo., 1958—60; in-svc. edn. coord. Gen. Rose Hosp., Denver, 1960—63; rsch. asst. Yale U., New Haven, 1965—67; assoc. prof. nursing Wayne State U., Detroit, 1971—74, prof., 1974—79; dir. Ctr. for Health Rsch., 1974—79; assoc. dir. oncology nursing Cancer Ctr. U. Rochester, NY, 1979—93, prof. nursing, 1979—95, prof. emerita, 1995—. Rosenstadt prof. health rsch. Faculty Nursing, U. Toronto, 1985; vis. prof. U. Utah Coll. Nursing, 1996—97, U. Wis., Madison, 1998. Author: Self-Regulation Theory: Applying Theory to Your Practice, 1997; contbg. author Handbook of Psychology and Health, vol. 5, 1984; contbr. articles to profl. jours. Recipient Bd. Govs. Faculty Recognition award, Wayne State U., 1975, award for disting. contbn. to nursing sci., Am. Nurses Found. and ANA Coun. for Nurse Rschrs., 1983, Grad. Tchg. award, U. Rochester, 1991, Disting. Rschr. award, Oncology Nursing Soc., 1992, Outstanding Contbns. to Nursing and Psychology award, divsn. of health psychology APA, 1993, recognized as a Living Legend, Am. Acad. Nursing, 2005; grantee, NIH, 1972—95. Fellow: AAAS, Am. Psychol. Soc., Acad. for Behavioral Medicine Rsch.; mem.: ANA (chmn. coun. for nurse rschrs. 1976—78, commn. for rsch. 1978—82), Inst. Medicine of NAS (com. on patient injury compensation 1976—77, membership com. 1981—86, gov. coun. 1987—89), Phi Kappa Phi, Omicron Nu, Sigma Xi. Home: 4924 Whitecomb Dr Apt 15 Madison WI 53711-2661 Personal E-mail: jean_joh@msn.com.

JOHNSON, JEANNE JORDAN, music educator, department chairman; d. Lewis Washington and Eunice Whatley Jordan; m. Clinton Roland Johnson, June 20, 1970; children: Brian, Colin. AA, Kilgore Coll., Tex., 1969; B in Music Edn., East Tex. State U., 1971, MusM, 1972; postgrad., U. North Tex. Cert. tchr. Tex. Instr., grad. asst. East Tex. State U., Commerce, 1971—72; instr. East Tex. Bapt. U., Marshall, 1972—76, Kilgore Coll., Kilgore, 1976—. Dir. Grace Notes Children's Choir 1st Presbyn. Ch., 1986—96; bd. dirs. Opera East Tex., 2004—. Named winner, Met. Opera Dist. Auditions, Shreveport Symphony Auditions, Disting. Musician, East Tex. State U., 1971, Outstanding Faculty Mem., Kilgore Coll., 2001—02. Mem.: Nat. Assn. Tchrs. of Singing (bd. dirs. East Tex. chpt., regional auditions advanced divsn. finalist), Tex. Music Educators Assn., Alpha Chi, Phi Theta Kappa. Avocations: reading, interior decorating. Office Phone: 903-983-8121. Office Fax: 903-983-8124. E-mail: jeannej@kilgore.edu.

JOHNSON, JEFFREY DAVID, artist; b. Oakland, Calif., July 30, 1960; s. Ronald Lee Johnson and Joan Carol Sebastian; children: Forest Isaiah,

Austin Euer. Condr. We. Pacific RR, Winnemucca, Nev., 1978—93; condr., owner Neon Art Envy, Reno, 1998—. Neon art, Fish Breath in the Year of the Plague (Best of Reno Visual Artist award, Reno News & Review, 2002), Triennial Exhibition, Battle Born & Breaking Hearts Since 1864, 2005. Master: E. Clampus Vitus (life; noble grand humbug 2007—). Rastafarian. Achievements include development of underwater neon art. Avocations: history, travel, art. Office: Neon Art Envy Box 8313 Reno NV 89507 Personal E-mail: inert@neonartnv.com.

JOHNSON, JEFFREY M., private equity company executive, former publishing executive; b. July 23, 1959; married; 3 children. BS in Accountancy, U. Ill.; M in Ops. Mgmt., U. Chgo. With KPMG Peat Marwick, 1981—84; mem. corp. office staff Tribune Co., Chgo., 1984—86; various ops. positions Chgo. Tribune, 1986—92; v.p. & dir. ops. Orlando Sentinel, 1992—98; exec. v.p., gen. mgr. & COO Landoll Inc., 1998—2000, pres. & CEO, 2000; sr. v.p. & gen. mgr. LA Times, 2000—05, exec. v.p. & gen. mgr., 2005, pub., pres., CEO, 2005—06; principal current media interests Yucaipa Cos. LLC, 2007—. Bd. dirs. YMCA of Met. LA, United Way of Greater LA, Orange County Performing Arts Ctr. Co-recipient Tribune Mgmt. Award, 1992. Office: Yucaipa Cos LLC 9130 W Sunset Blvd Los Angeles CA 90069 Office Phone: 310-789-7200. Office Fax: 310-228-2873.*

JOHNSON, JEH CHARLES, lawyer; b. NYC, Sept. 11, 1957; s. Jeh Vincent and Norma (Edelin) J.; m. Susan M. DiMarco, Mar. 18, 1994. BA, Morehouse Coll., Atlanta, 1979; JD, Columbia U., 1982. Bar: N.Y. 1983, D.C. 1999. Litig. assoc. Sullivan & Cromwell, NYC, 1982—84; assoc. Paul, Weiss, Rifkind, Wharton & Garrison, NYC, 1984-88, 92-93; asst. U.S. atty. So. Dist. N.Y., 1989-91; ptnr. Paul, Weiss, Rifkind, Wharton & Garrison, NYC, 1994-98, 2001—; gen. counsel USAF, Washington, 1998—2001. Adj. lectr. law Columbia U. Law Sch., NYC, 1995—97. Mem.: Coun. Fgn. Rels. Office: Paul Weiss Rifkin Wharton & Garrison 1285 Ave of Americas New York NY 10019 Business E-Mail: jjohnson@paulweiss.com.

JOHNSON, JEH VINCENT, architect; b. Nashville, July 8, 1931; s. Charles Spurgeon and Marie Antoinette (Burguette) J.; m. Norma Edelin, Dec. 28, 1956; children— Jeh Charles, Marguerite Marie. AB, Columbia U., 1953, M.Arch., 1958. Architect/designer Paul R. Williams, Los Angeles, 1956; designer Adams & Woodbridge, NYC, 1957-62; asso. Gindele & Johnson (P.C. Architects and predecessors), Poughkeepsie, NY, 1967-69, partner, 1969-71, pres., 1971-80; ptnr. LeGendre Johnson McNeil Assos., 1980-90; pvt. practice architecture Wappingers Falls, NY, 1990—. Sr. lectr. in art Vassar Coll., 1964—2001, lectr. in urban studies, 1995—2000, lectr. emeritus, 2001-; mem. N.Y. State Bd. for Architecture, 1974-84, chmn., 1980-82; mem. Nat. Commn. Urban Problems, 1967-69; nat. master grader Nat. Coun. Archtl. Registration Bds., 1984-91. Designer: Dutchess County (N.Y.) Mental Health Ctr., 1969, Lagrange (N.Y.) Town Hall, 1969, Newburgh (N.Y.) Houses on the Lake, 1970, Whitney Young Health Ctr., Albany, N.Y., 1973, St. Simeon Apts. for Elderly, Poughkeepsie, 1973, 93, Bedford-Stuyvesant Comml. Ctr., N.Y.C., 1978, Camp of Tomorrow, Girl Scouts U.S.A., Mt. Pleasant, N.Y., 1985, Millbrook (N.Y.) Ch. Alliance Housing, Ctrl. Bapt. Ch., Salt Point, N.Y., Hillcrest House, Poughkeepsie, 1992, The Intercultural Ctr. at Vassar Coll, 1993, St. Anna Apts., Poughkeepsie, 1996. Active Dutchess County Planning Bd., 1988-92. William Kinne Fellows traveling fellow, 1958 Fellow AIA (nat. task force on affordable housing, Students medal 1958); mem. Nat. Orgn. Minority Architects (charter), AAUP, NAACP, Sigma Pi Phi. Clubs: Masons. Home and Office: 14 Edgehill Rd Wappingers Falls NY 12590-1228 Home Phone: 845-297-5309; Office Phone: 845-297-5524.

JOHNSON, JENNIE, chaplain, social worker, poet; b. Houston, Sept. 18, 1952; d. James L.C. and Marilyn Mildred (Frazier) J.; children: Alan, David. BS in Social Work, Tex. Woman's U., 1976; postgrad., Bishop's Sch. Theology, Denver, 1979—81, Samaritan Theol. Sem., LA, 1982—84, Episcopal Theol. Sem., Austin, Tex., 1986—87, Episcopal Theol. Sem., 2004. Cert. social worker, Tex.; oblate Order of St. Benedict, 1998; mem. Daus. of the King, 2003—. Comdr. 94th Ord. Det. USAR, Ft. Carson, Colo., 1978—80, evaluator 1st maneuver tng. command Denver, 1980—81; planner prodn. control Elmo Semiconducter, LA, 1981—83; planner quality control TRW Def. and Space Guidance, LA, 1983—84; dir. chpt. svcs. Greater Amarillo Red Cross, Tex., 1985—86; chaplain Austin State Hosp., 1987—88, Brackenridge Hosp., Austin, 1988—91, Hospice Austin, 1992—95; asst. dir. Centex Chpt. ARC, Austin, 1995—96; chaplain Seaton Med. Ctr., Austin, 1998—. Convener Integrity Austin, 1989-90, 92-94, 96-97; author poetry; conf. presenter Nat. Episcopal AIDS Coalition, Cin., 1990-2005; self-employed musical instrument woodwork, 2005—. Founding bd. dirs. Out Youth Austin/YWCA, 1990-92; mem. Tex. AIDS Network, Austin, 1992-2001; foster parent Casey Family Program, Austin, 1992-94; diocesan del. St. Michael's Episcopal Ch., Austin, 1988—, jr. warden, 1993-95, mem. vestry, 1993-97, mem. divsn. for spiritual devel. of diocese 1997-2000, Mentor Edn. for Ministry, 1980-2000; mem.-at-large Women for Social Witness Network, Nat. Episcopal Ch., 1992-96; mem. Episcopal Womens Caucus, 1993—, Nat. Hospice Orgn., 1993-2000, Tex. Hospice Orgn., 1992-2000, presenter state conf., 1995, Order of St. Luke the Physician, 1984—. 1st lt. U.S. Army, 1975-80. Democrat. Avocations: paleontology, needlecrafts, reading, woodworking, camping. Office Phone: 512-799-1187. E-mail: johnsonjk@austin.rr.com.

JOHNSON, JENNIFER J., federal official; Dep. sec., bd. mems. office Fed. Res. Sys., Washington. Office: Fed Res Sys Bd Mems Office 20th And C Sts NW Ofc Washington DC 20551-0001

JOHNSON, JENNIFER TOBY, military officer; b. Syracuse, NY, May 23, 1976; d. Norman Edward and Barbara Catherine Johnson. BS, U.S. Mil. Acad., 1998; attended, U.S. Army Flight Sch., 1998—2000, U.S. Army Capt. Career course, 2003—04; student, Harvard U., 2005—. Commd. 2d lt. U.S. Army 1st Battalion (Attack), 3d Aviation Regiment, 3d Inf. Divsn. (Mechanized), Ft. Hood, Tex., 2000—01, advanced through grades to capt., 2001—, served at Hunter Army Airfield, Ga., 2000—03, served Iraq, 2003—, Kuwait, 2003—. Decorated Presdl. Unit Citation. Republican. Lutheran. Avocations: golf, skiing, violin. Home: 38 Ellery St Cambridge MA 02138-4205 Home Phone: 912-596-3228; Office Phone: 912-596-3228.

JOHNSON, JEROME LINNÉ, cardiologist, educator; b. Rockford, Ill., June 19, 1929; s. Thomas Arthur and Myrtle Elizabeth (Swanson) J.; m. Molly Ann Rideout, June 27, 1953; children: Susan R. Johnson, William Rideout. BA, U. Chgo., 1951; BS, Northwestern U., 1952, MD, 1955. Diplomate Nat. Bd. Med. Examiners. Intern U. Chgo. Clinics, 1955-56; resident Northwestern U., Chgo., 1958-61; chief resident Chgo. Wesley Meml. Hosp., 1960-61; mem., v.p. Hauch Med. Clinic, Pomona, Calif., 1961-88; pvt. practice cardiology and internal medicine Pomona, 1988—. Clin. assoc. prof. medicine, U. So. Calif., L.A., 1961—; mem. staff Pomona Valley Hosp. Med. Ctr., chmn. coronary care com. 1967-77; mem. staff L.A. County Hosp. Citizen ambassador, People to People; mem. Town Hall of Calif., L.A. World Affairs Coun. Lt. USNR, 1956-58; bd. dirs. Claremont chpt. ARC, 1993-2000; bd. dirs., health com. Mt. San Antonio Gardens Retirement Home, 1993-2000. Fellow: Am. Coll. Cardiology, Am. Geriatrics Soc., Royal Soc. Health; mem.: Galileo Soc., Am. Heart Assn. (bd. dirs. L.A. County div. 1967-84, San Gabriel div. 1963-89), Am. Soc. Internal Medicine, Inland Soc. Internal Medicine, Pomona Host Lions. Avocations: photography, swimming, bicycling, medical and surgical antiques, travel. Home: 648 Delaware Dr Claremont CA 91711-3457 Personal E-mail: linne1@aol.com.

JOHNSON, JERRILYN JENKINS, academic administrator; b. Winston-Salem, NC; d. Frizzell James and Thessalonia Mae Jenkins; 1 child, Tessa Leigh. BS in Edn., Winston-Salem State U., NC; MEd in Edn. and Counseling, Wayne State u., 1978; MEd in Adminstrn., NC A&T State U., 1994. Tchr. Winston-Salem (N.C.) Forsyth County Schs., counselor, coord. homeless liaison; tchr. Detroit Pub. Schs.; prin., owner Land of Learning Tutorial Acad., Southfield, Mich.; tchr. Chapel Hill (N.C.) Carrboro Schs.; guidance counselor Asheboro (N.C.) Pub. Schs.; prin, owner Southland Consultants, Winston-Salem, 2003—. Author: Mommy, Are We Homeless?, 2004. Vice-chmn., chmn. adv. bd. Goodwill Industries Cmty., Winston-Salem, NC, 2002—04. Named Educator of Yr., Phi Beta Sigma, 2001; recipient Blue Ribbon award, Mayor, 1997, Outstanding Cmty. Impact award, N.C. Interagency Coun. Coordinating Homeless Programs, 1998. Mem.: Nat. Assn. Edn. Homeless Children and Youth (bd. dirs. 2000—02), 100 Women of Faith (pres. 2003—05), Advocates for the Poor. Democrat. Baptist. Avocations: reading, writing, travel.

JOHNSON, JESSICA SUSAN, conservator; b. Tucson, Ariz., Apr. 11, 1960; d. Alfred Edwin and Ann Stofer Johnson. BA, U. Kans., Lawrence, 1983; MA, U. Ariz., 1987; BSc with honors, U. Coll. London, 1990. Asst. conservator Tex. Meml. Mus., Austin, 1991—97; conservator mus. mgmt. program Nat. Ctr. for Resource Stewardship and Partnership, Nat. Pk. Svc., Washington, 1997—2000; sr. objects conservator Smithsonian's Nat. Mus. of the Am. Indian, Washington, 2000—. Head conservator Gordion Project, Yassihöyük, Ankara, Turkey, 1992—2001. Fellow: Am. Inst. for Conservation of Hist. and Artistic Works. Office: Nat Mus the Am Indian CRC 4220 Silver Hill Rd Suitland MD 20746 Office Phone: 301-238-1416. Office Fax: 301-238-3201.

JOHNSON, JIMMIE, race car driver; b. El Cajon, Calif., Sept. 17, 1975; s. Gary and Cathy Johnson; m. Chandra Johnson. Racecar driver Herzog Motorsports, 1999, Lowe's Racing Team. Commentator ESPN; spokesperson Chevrolet divsn. GM. Named Pat Schauer Meml. Rookie of the Yr., Am. Speed Assn. ACDelco Challenge Series, 1998, 7th pl., Busch Series The Milw. Mile, 1999, winner, Mickey Thompson Stadium, 1992—94, Am. Speed Assn. Memphis Motorsports Park, 1999, Am. Speed Assn. Orange County Speedway, 1999, Busch Series Hills Bros. Coffee 300, 2001, Daytona 500, 2006, Talladega Superspeedway, 2006. Achievements include winning Nextel Cup Championship, 2006. Office: c/o Hendrick Motorsports 4400 Papa Joe Hendrick Blvd Charlotte NC 28262*

JOHNSON, JIMMY, sports broadcaster, former professional football coach; b. Port Arthur, Tex., July 16, 1943; BA, U. Ark., 1965. Asst. coach Louisiana Tech. U., LA, 1965, Wichita State U., KS, 1967, Iowa State U., IA, 1968-68, U. Oklahoma, Norman, OK, 1970-72, U. Arkansas, AR, 1973-76, U. Pittsburg, 1977-78; head coach Oklahoma State U., OK, 1979-83, U. Miami, Miami, FL, 1983-88, Dallas Cowboys, Dallas, 1989-94; sports commentator, football analyst Fox Network, 1994-95; head coach, gen. mgr. Miami Dolphins, 1996-99; co-host NFL Sunday, Fox, 2002—. Coach NCAA Divsn. I championship team, 1987, Super Bowl (XXVII, XXVIII) championship team, 1992-93; named Coach of Yr. Walter Camp Found., 1986-87, NFL Coach of Yr. Coll. & Pro Football Newsweekly, 1990, UPI, 1990, AP, 1990, Football Digest, 1991; recipient Seattle Gold Helmet award, 1986.

JOHNSON, JOAN BRAY, insurance company consultant; b. Kennett, Mo., Nov. 19, 1926; d. Pleas Green and Mary Scott (Williams) Bray; m. Frank Johnson Jr., Nov. 6, 1955; 1 child, Victor Kent. Student, Drury Coll., Springfield, Mo., 1949-51, Cen. Bible Inst. and Coll., 1946-49. Staff writer Gospel Pub. Co., Springfield, Mo., 1949-51; sec. Kennett Sch. Dist. Bd. Edn., 1951-58; spl. features corr. Memphis Press-Scimitar, 1959-60; sec. to v.p. Cotton Exchange Bank, Kennett, Mo., 1959-60; proposal analyst Aetna Life Ins. Co., El Paso, Tex., 1960-64, pension adminstr., 1964-71, office mgr. Brokerage div. Denver, 1971-78, office adminstr. Life Consol. div. Oakland, Calif., 1979-82, office adminstr. PFSD div. Walnut Creek, Calif., 1983-86, office adminstr. PFSD-Health Mktg. div. Sacramento, 1986-89, regional adminstr. Hartford, Conn., 1989-91, cons. Santa Ana, Calif., 1991—, Met-Life Ins. Co., Dallas, 1998—, Transamerica Life, LA, 1999—, Reliar Star Ins., 1999—. Officer local PTA, 1964-71; pres. Wesley Svc. Guild, 1968-71; den mother Boy Scouts Am.; fin. sec. Green Valley United Meth. Ch., 1992-05, fin. com., 2005—. Recipient Tex. Life Svc. award PTA, 1970. Fellow Life Office Mgmt. Assn. (instr. classes); mem. DAR (regent Silver State Nev. chpt. 1994-96, Nev. state treas. 1998—01, bd. dirs. Nev. 1996—, Nev. state chaplain 2003-2004, Nev. vice regent 2004-06, Nev. corr. sect. 2006—), Assn. Bus. and Profl. Women, Life Underwriters Assn., Clark County Heritage Mus., Last Monday Club, Opti-Mrs., Allied Arts Club. Democrat. Home: 2415 La Estrella St Henderson NV 89014-3608 E-mail: ojbjohnson1@juno.com.

JOHNSON, JOANN MARDELLE, federal agency administrator; b. Massena, Iowa, Feb. 24, 1949; BA in Edn., U. No. Iowa, 1971. Former tchr.; grain and livestock prodr.; mem. Iowa Senate from 39th dist., Des Moines, 1994—2000; mem. appropriations com., mem. commerce com.; chair ways and means com.; chair commerce com.; mem. Nat. Credit Union Admin., Alexandria, Va., 2002—, vice chair, 2003—. Mem. 4-H, Local Devel. Bd.; vol. various cmty. orgns.; campaign mgr. Rep. Dwight Dinkla, 1992, Congressman Jim Lightfoot, 1990, orgn. dir., 1986-88. Mem. Am. Legis. Exch. Coun., Farm Bur., Cattleman's Assn. Republican. Office: Nat Credit Union Admin Off of the Bd 1775 Duke St Alexandria VA 22314-3428 E-mail: boardmember.johnson@ncua.gov.

JOHNSON, JOE MARCUS, professional basketball player; b. Little Rock, June 29, 1981; s. Dianne Johnson. Student, U. Ark., 1999—2001. Guard-forward NBA Boston Celtics, 2001—02, NBA Phoenix Suns, 2002—05, NBA Atlanta Hawks, 2005—. Mem. U.S.A. Men's Sr. Nat. Team, 2006—. Host Joe Johnson Celebrity Golf Tournament. Named to All-Rookie 2nd Team, NBA, 2002, Ea. Conf. All-Star Team, 2007. Achievements include winning the bronze medal as a member of the U.S.A. Men's Sr. Nat. team at the 2006 World Championship. Avocations: bowling, movies. Mailing: Atlanta Hawks Centennial Tower 101 Marietta St NW Ste 1900 Atlanta GA 30303*

JOHNSON, JOHN, broadcast journalist, artist; b. NYC, June 20, 1938; s. John Edward and Irene Elizabeth (Tutt) J. BA, CCNY, 1961, M Art Edn., 1963; DHL (hon.), St. Thomas Aquinas Coll., 1991. Tchr., asst. prin. NYC Bd. Edn., 1960-67; assoc. prof. fine arts Lincoln U., 1967-68; prodr., dir., writer documentary unit ABC News, NYC, 1968-71; corr. ABC Evening News, NYC, 1971-72; reporter WABC-TV News, NYC, 1972-85, sr. corr., anchor, 1985-95; anchor WCBS-TV News, NYC, 1995-96; anchor, sr. corr. WNBC-TV News, NYC, 1996-97; ret., 1997. Essayist: The Black Power Revolt, 1968; author: Only Son: A Memoir, 2002; one-man shows include Walter Wickiser Gallery, Chelsea, NY, 2003, 2004, exhibited in group shows, 2005; appeared in films Copland, 54. Recipient Best Enterprise Reporting award AP, 1977, Emmy award for Best Sports Programming, 1978, Best Documentary award AP, 1979, Emmy award for Best Investigative Reporting, 1983, Emmy award for Best Spot News, 1982, Emmy award for Best Svc. News, 1982, Nat. Broadcast award for Outstanding Spot News, UPI, 1982, Lifetime Achievement award in broadcast journalism NY Assn. Black Journalists, 1997; named to CCNY Comm. Hall of Fame, 2000. Mem. AFTRA, Dirs. Guild Am. Office Phone: 845-638-2898. Personal E-mail: Gaspard2j@aol.com.

JOHNSON, JOHN D., energy and food products executive; b. Rhame, ND, Sept. 24, 1949; m. Shirley Johnson; 3 children. BBA, Black Hills State U., Spearfish, SD, 1970. Feed cons. GTA feeds divsn. Harvest States, Inver Grove Heights, Minn., 1976, regional sales mgr., dir. sales and mktg., gen. mgr. GTA Feeds, group v.p. Farm Mktg. and Supply, 1992, pres., CEO, 1995; pres., gen. mgr. CHS Inc. (merger of Cenex and Harvest States), Inver Grove Heights, Minn., 1998—2000, pres., CEO, 2000—. Bd. dirs. Ventura Foods, LLC, Sparta Foods, Goldkist, Inc., CF Industries. Named CEO Communicator of Yr., Coop. Communicators Assn. Mem. Nat. Coop. Refinery Assn. (bd. dirs.), Nat. Coun. Farmer Coops. (bd. dirs.) Office: CHS Inc PO Box 64089 Saint Paul MN 55164-0089 Office Phone: 651-355-6000.*

JOHNSON, JOHN GEORGE, JR., industrial services executive; b. Phila., Dec. 2, 1940; s. John George and Mary Frances (Alexander) J.; m. Barbara A., June 11, 1966; children: Barbara, Mary, Dawn, Dottie, Janice, Diane. BSCE, Drexel U., 1970, MBA, 1972; PhD, Harvard U., 1978. Tech., planning mgmt. Atlantic Richfield Co., Phila., 1958-81; v.p. internat. corp. Arco Chem. Co., Phila., 1982-83, v.p. internat. chems., 1984-85, sr. v.p. mktg. & splty. bus., 1985-86, pres., chems., 1987-92; pres., COO Safety-Kleen Corp., Elgin, Ill., 1993-94, pres., CEO, 1994-97, Foamex Internat. Inc., Linwood, Pa., 1999—2001, 2007—; chmn. GenTek Inc., Parsippany, NJ, 2003—. Bd. dirs. McWhorter Techs., Carpentersville, Ill., 1995—, Safety Kleen, 1993—, Arco Chem. Co., 1987-92. Bd. trustees Drexel U., Phila., 1990—; mem. tech. adv. com. U. S.C., Columbia, 1989-93. Sgt. USMC, 1962-67. Mem. AIChE, Chem. Mfgs. Assn., Exec. Club Chgo., Monimah Country Club. Republican. Lutheran. Avocations: golf, coin collecting/numismatics. Office: Foamex Internat Inc 1000 Columbia Ave Linwood PA 19061

JOHNSON, JOHN GRAY, retired university chancellor; b. Irwin, Pa., Aug. 8, 1924; s. John Arthur and Elizabeth (Gray) J.; m. L. Jane Wycoop, Aug. 28, 1948; children: Scott Raymond, Lynn. BS, Carnegie Mellon U., Pitts., 1949; LLD (hon.), U. Indpls., 1980. Alumni dir. Carnegie Mellon U., 1955-60; exec. dir. Am. Alumni Coun., Washington, 1960-64; v.p. devel. Butler U., Indpls., 1964-66, pres., 1978-88, chancellor, 1989-90; v.p. for devel. Carnegie Mellon U., Pitts., 1966-78. Mem. adv. bd. Splendido Cmty. With AUS, 1943-46. Decorated Air medal; named Sagamore of the Wabash. Mem. Ind. C. of C. (life, pres.), Phi Kappa Phi, Omicron Delta Kappa. Home: 13500 N Rancho Vistoso Blvd Apt 333 Tucson AZ 85755-5951 Personal E-mail: jjohn48@comcast.net.

JOHNSON, JOHN H., lawyer; b. Raleigh, NC, 1948; BA, Univ. NC, 1970, JD, 1976. Bar: NC 1976, Ga. 1987. Staff atty., legal br., enforcement divsn., region 4 EPA, 1977—80, chief, air and toxics law br., office of regional counsel, region 4, 1980—83, chief, hazardous waste law br., office of regional counsel, region 4, 1983—86; assoc. Troutman Sanders LLP, Atlanta, 1986—90, ptnr., environ., natural resources, 1990—, and practice group leader, environ. and natural resources. Exec. com. bd. dir. Piedmont Park Conservatory. Named a Super Lawyer, Atlanta Mag., 2004, 2005, 2006, 2007; named one of Am.'s Leading Lawyers for Environ. Law, Chambers USA, 2005, 2006, 2007, Best Lawyers in Am. for Environ. Law, 2006, 2007. Mem.: ABA, NC State Bar, State Bar Ga. Office: Troutman Sanders LLP Bank of America Plz Ste 5200 600 Peachtree St NE Atlanta GA 30308-2216 Office Phone: 404-885-3166. Office Fax: 404-962-6594. Business E-Mail: john.johnson@troutmansanders.com.

JOHNSON, JOHN HENRY, film director, producer, photographer, educator; b. Pueblo, Colo., Oct. 31, 1951; s. William Admiral (Buddy) and Matilda Marie (Trabucco) J.; m. Nadine Sue Milosavich, Aug. 24, 1974; children: Rebecca Sue, Thomas William. Student, Colo. State U.-Pueblo, 1970—73; Assoc. of Fine Arts, Rochester Inst. Tech., 1973, BFA summa cum laude, 1975; MFA, Cranbook Acad. Art, 1977. Photographer Colo. Hwy. Dept., Eisenhower Tunnel, 1971; cinematographer, prodn. asst., writer various prodn. co., Colo., 1979—80; prodn. asst. Metro-Goldwyn-Mayer, Canon City, Colo., 1983; studio cameraman, flr. dir. Sta. KOAA-TV, Pueblo, 1970, 1997—2001; dir., cinematographer, editor Humanities divsn. film series Colo. State U.-Pueblo, 1971—72; photographer Pueblo Chieftain & Star Jour., 1975; pres., founder Tamarack Prodn., Inc., Pueblo, 1982—. Grad. tchg. asst. Cranbrook Acad. Art, Bloomfield Hills, Mich., 1977; instr. photography Arapahoe C.C., Littleton, Colo., 1978, C.C. Denver, 1979; instr. filmmaking, photography and design Colo. Inst. Art, Denver, 1978—79, Colo. State U.-Pueblo, 1978, 1980—81, 2001—04; instr. filmmaking Learning Tree U., Chatsworth, Calif., 1992—93; instr. photography, filmmaking and humanities Pueblo C.C., 1994—2002; instr. filmmaking, film appreciation and documentary Colo. Film Sch., 2004—; instr. photography, art appreciation and art history C.C. Aurora, 2004—. Dir., cinematographer, co-writer, co-editor (documentary film) Damon Runyon's Pueblo, 1981 (Golden Eagle award Coun. on Internat. Nontheatrical Events, 1983), dir., writer, prodr., cinematographer, editor Zebulon Pike & The Blue Mountain, 1984 (Golden Eagle award Coun. on Internat. Nontheatrical Events, 1985, Commendation cert. Am. Assn. State and Local History, 1986, DVD Release, 2006), (feature film) Blue Lights, 1988 (invited feature Internat. Sci. Fiction and Fantasy Film Festival, Rome, 1990), photographer represented in books, including: Visual Concepts for Photographers, 1980, Chinese edit., 1998, Photographic Materials & Processes, 1986, also Italian edit., 1993, 2d edit., 2000, View Camera Technique, 5th edit., 1986, 6th edit., 1993, 8th edit., 1999, Orlin Helgoe-Shaman of the Prairie, 1986, Southwest Fine Arts Biennial Catalogue, 1976; contbg. editor: Focal Encyclopedia of Photography, 3d edit., 1993. Recipient Excellence in Arts award Pueblo Arts Coun., 2006; grantee Thatcher Found., 1973-77, Profl. Photographers Am., 1974, Cranbrook/Ford Found., 1977, NEH, 1979, Colo. Endowment for the Humanities, 1979, Colo. State U.-Pueblo, 1979. Avocations: skiing, music, genealogy, movies. Personal E-mail: johnjohnson@mac.com.

JOHNSON, JOHN PAUL, lawyer, judge; b. Omaha, Dec. 4, 1944; s. John and Dorothy (Mullen) J.; m. Suzanne Alice Smiley, July 12, 1974; children: James Thomas, Jennifer Anne. BA, Washburn U., Topeka, 1967; JD, U. Nebr., 1971; postgrad., Fed. Exec. Inst., Charlottesville, Va., 1988. Bar: Nebr. 1972. Claims examiner VA, St. Paul, 1972; staff atty. Bd. Vets. Appeals, Washington, 1973-79, sr. atty., 1979-81; adminstrv. law judge Office of Hearings and Appeals, Des Moines, 1981—, chief adminstrv. law judge, 1988-93. With U.S. Army, 1968-70 (Vietnam). Decorated Bronze Star; recipient Exceptional Svc. award VA, 1974. Mem. Assn. Adminstr. Law Judges, Nebr. State Bar Assn., Kappa Sigma. Episcopalian. Home: 228 39th St West Des Moines IA 50265-3938 Office: Office Hearings and Appeals 4400 Westown Pky West Des Moines IA 50266 Office Phone: 515-223-5038. Business E-Mail: john.johnson@ssa.gov.

JOHNSON, JOHN PHILIP, geneticist, researcher; b. Wabash, Ind., June 6, 1949; s. Melvin Leroy and Cleo Pauline (Aldrich) J.; m. Sheryl Kay Kennedy, June 3, 1978; children: Craig Eric, Lindsay Sara. BS, U. Mich., 1971, MD, 1975. Diplomate Am. Bd. Pediatrics, Am. Bd. Med. Genetics. Intern, 2d-yr. resident Children's Hosp. Los Angeles, 1975-77; 3d yr. resident in pediatrics U. Utah, Salt Lake City, 1977-78, fellow in genetics, 1980-82, asst. prof. pediatrics, 1982-85; pediatrician Family Health Program, Salt Lake City, 1978-80; assoc. dir. med. genetics, attending/active staff physician Children's Hosp. Oakland, Calif., 1985-92; dir. med. genetics, attending/active staff physician Children's Hosp., Oakland, 1992-94; dir. med. genetics Shodair Children's Hosp., Helena, Mont., 1994—, active mem. staff, 1994—. Clinic physician Utah State Tng. Sch., American Fork, 1982-85; attending and staff physician Primary Children's Med. Ctr., Salt Lake City, 1978-80; pres., bd. dirs. Mtn. States Genetics Found., 2001-07, PI Mountain States Regional Collaborative Ctr., 2004-. Assoc. editor Am. Jour. Med. Genetics, 1995-97; contbr. articles to med. jours. Pres. bd. dirs. Mountain States Genetics Found., 2000—07; mem. govs. adv. bd. Fetal Alcohol Spectrum Disorder, 2001—; bd. mem. Parents Let's Unite for Kids, Helena, Mont. Recipient William J. Branstrom award U.

Mich., 1967. Fellow Am. Acad. Pediatrics; mem. Am. Soc. Human Genetics Avocations: skiing, hiking, camping, piano, jazz. Home: 2604 Gold Rush Ave Helena MT 59601-5625 Office: Shodair Childrens Hosp PO Box 5539 Helena MT 59604-5539 Office Phone: 406-444-7530. Business E-Mail: jjohnson@shodair.org.

JOHNSON, JOHN PRESCOTT, retired philosophy educator; b. Tumalo, Oreg., Apr. 24, 1921; s. John Edward and Caroline Prescott (Eaton) J.; m. Mable Alice Dougherty, June 9, 1943; children: Grace Beth Johnson Booth), John Paul, Carol Ruth Johnson Hull. AB, Pitts. State U., 1947, MS, 1948; PhD, Northwestern U., 1959. Asst. prof. philosophy Bethany (Okla.) Nazarene Coll., 1949-57; asst. prof. U. Okla., Norman, 1957-62; assoc. prof. philosophy Monmouth (Ill.) Coll., 1962-69; prof. philosophy Monmouth (Ill.) Coll., 1969-86; chmn. dept. philosophy Monmouth (Ill.) Coll., 1967-86, emeritus prof. philosophy, 1986—; ret., 1986. Vis. asst. prof. Northwestern U., summer 1961; Cons. research project student values U.S. Office Edn., 1967 Author: The Value Philosophy of Wilbur Marshall Urban, 1988, The Reality of Faith, 1996, The Gates of Light, 2000, The More Excellent Way, 2000, The Living Fountain: The Symbolism of Grace, 2003; contbr. articles to philos. jours. Mem. Am. Philos. Assn., Ill. Philos. Assn. (sec.-treas. 1967-69, pres. 1971-73). Personal E-mail: bengtas@dtnspeed.net.

JOHNSON, JOHN WARREN, retired professional society administrator; b. Mpls., Jan. 29, 1929; s. Walter E. and Eileen L. J.; m. Marion Louise Myrland; children: Daniel Warren, Karen Louise, Nancy Marie. BA, U. Minn., Mpls., 1951. CEO Am. Collectors Assn., Inc., Mpls., 1955-96; ret., 1996. Bd. dirs. Western Nat. Ins. Group, Western Nat. Ins. Co., Mpls. and Seattle. Author: Political Christians, 1979, You Can Manage Your Money, 1981, 38 Days to Cape Town, 1981, Credit Guide for Collectors, 1984, The Pearls of Saigon, 1987, The Use of Humor in Public Speaking Is No Joke!, 1991, 53 Days to Beijing, 1991, The Strange Blood of East Africa, 1995. Mem. Mpls. City Coun., 1963-67; mem. Minn. State Ho. of Reps., 1967-74, asst. majority leader, 1972-74; Rep. candidate for Gov. of Minn., 1974-2007. With USNR, 1947-53. Mem. Am. Soc. Assn. Execs. (chmn. bd. 1986-87), U.S. C. of C. (chmn. bd. regents 1973, bd. dirs. 1990-92), Minn. Soc. Assn. Execs. (past pres.). Lutheran. Office: 5108 James Ave S Minneapolis MN 55419

JOHNSON, JOHN WILLIAM, JR., executive recruiter; b. St. Petersburg, Fla., Dec. 10, 1932; s. John William and Elizabeth (Lowitz) J.; m. Cecelia Lynn Wescott, Feb. 6, 1960; children: William Wescott, James Robert, Gayle McCrimmon. AB, Wesleyan U., Middletown, Conn., 1954; postgrad., NYU, 1958-59. With Benton and Bowles, Inc., NYC, 1958-82, v.p., account supr., 1963-70, sr. v.p., mgmt. supr., 1970-82, adminstr. profit sharing plan, 1969-82, dir., 1977-82; with Webb, Johnson Assocs., NYC, 1982—2002, founder, former pres., 1982-95, mng. dir., 1995-2000, sr. mng. dir., 2000—02; co-founder, mng. dir. Johnson & Norinsky Assocs., 2002—. Mem. Scarsdale Planning Bd., 1984-88, Scarsdale Non-Partisan Jud. Qualifications Com., 1987-92, Scarsdale Bd. Ethics, 1995-2000; pres. Rainsford House Assn., N.Y.C., 1964-66, bd. dirs., 1962-70; bd. mgrs. Jacob Riis Settlement, 1963-89; bd. dirs. St. Christopher's Inc., 1965-2000, hon. bd. dirs., 2000—; mem. parents steering com. Coll. William and Mary, 1987-91; warden Ch. St. James the Less, Scarsdale, 1993-95; trustee Healthcare Chaplaincy, 1999-2005. Pilot USNR, 1954-58 Decorated China Def. Ribbon; co-honoree Scarsdale Hist. Soc. award, 1996. Mem. Winged Foot Golf Club, Union League Club, Harbour Ridge Club. Office: 1 Dag Hammarskjold Plaza New York NY 10017 Home: 24 Stonygate Oval New Rochelle NY 10804 Office Phone: 212-224-7477.

JOHNSON, JOHNNY, research psychologist, consultant; b. Clarksdale, Miss., Jan. 10, 1938; s. Eddie B. and Elizabeth (Ousley) J.; children: Tonya, Anita. Student, Coahoma Jr. Coll., 1957, Hunter Coll., 1964, N.Y.U., 1963; BS, Tenn. State U., 1970, MS, 1974; postgrad., Saybrook Inst., 1987-89. Instr. Dept. of the Navy, Millington, Tenn., 1976-80, edn. specialist, 1980-87, curriculum advisor, 1987-88; prof. human resources mgmt. Pepperdine U., LA, 1975-77; prof. psychology Shelby State C.C., Memphis, Tenn., 1985—. Actor: (films) Elvis, 1989, Memphis, 1990, The Firm, 1993, A Family Thing, 1995; recording artist with releases in jazz, blues and Latino. With USN, 1957-63. Mem. APA (assoc.), Am. Psychol. Soc., Soc. Psychol. Study of Social Issues, Assn. Black Psychologists, Soc. Psychol. Study Gay and Lesbian Issues, Internat. Platform Assn. Avocations: golf, dog breeding, music, foreign languages, pocket billiards. Home: 773 Margie Dr Memphis TN 38127-2727 Office Phone: 901-357-5613. E-mail: CoolJuanJohnny@yahoo.com.

JOHNSON, JOHNNY RAY, retired mathematics professor; b. Chatham, La., Dec. 19, 1929; s. Dave Ernest and Bessie (Morris) J.; m. Betty Ann Moore, Oct. 21, 1960 (div. May 1982); children: Todd Michael, John Fitzgerald, Shauna Renee; m. Barbara F. Kennedy, June 1, 1990. BS, La. Tech U., 1951; MS, Auburn U., 1953, PhD, 1959. Registered profl. engr., La. Asst. prof. math. La. Tech U., 1958-62; assoc. prof. math. Appalachian State U., 1962-63; prof. elec. engring. La. State U., Baton Rouge, 1963-83, prof. emeritus, 1983—; prof. math. U. North Ala., 1984-95, prof. emeritus, 1995—. Adj. prof. elec. engring. U. Fla., Gainesville, 1976-77; mem. staff Combat Ops. Research Group, Ft. Monroe, Va., summer 1957; mathematician Boeing Co., New Orleans, summer 1965; engring. specialist Gen. Dynamics, 1983-84 Author: (with David E. Johnson) Mathematical Methods in Engineering and Physics, 1965, Graph Theory with Engineering Applications, 1972, Introductory Electric Circuit Analysis, 1981, Linear Systems Analysis, 1975; (with David E. Johnson and John L. Hilburn) Basic Electric Circuit Analysis, 1978, 3d edit., 1986, 4th edit., 1990, (with David E. Johnson, John L. Hilburn and Peter D. Scott) 5th edit., 1995, (with David E. Johnson and Harry P. Moore) A Handbook of Active Filters, 1980, (with David E. Johnson) A Funny Thing Happened on the Way to the White House, 1983, revised edit., 2004, (with David E. Johnson and John L. Hilburn) Electric Circuit Analysis, 1989, 2d edit., 1991, Introduction to Digital Signal Processing, 1989, (with David E. Johnson, John L. Hilburn & Peter D. Scott) Electric Circuit Analysis, 3d edit., 1997. Pres. Wildwood PTA, 1973-74. Served with AUS, 1954-56. Mem. IEEE (sr. 1968-93, Centennial medal 1984), U. North Ala. Inst. for Learning in Retirement (v.p., chmn. curriculum com. 1997-98, treas. 1998-99), Sigma Xi, Tau Beta Pi, Phi Kappa Phi, Eta Kappa Nu, Pi Mu Epsilon, Kappa Mu Epsilon. Home: 209 Wesley Ct Florence AL 35630-1486 Personal E-mail: jjohnson66@sprynet.com.

JOHNSON, JOLENE CAROLE, music educator; b. Seattle, Jan. 16, 1952; m. Richard D. Johnson; children: Joseph Lee McGinnis, Stacey Lynn Johnson-Christian, Amanda Dawn, Wayne Michael. B in Music Edn., U. Mich., Flint, 1984; M in Art Tchg., Marygrove Coll., Detroit, 2004. Primary and secondary tchg. cert. Mich. 4-12 vocal music dir. Westwood Heights Schs., Flint, 1987—88; vocal gen. music tchr. Bendle Pub. Schs., Burton, Mich., 1988—89; 4 - 12 vocal music dir., gen. music instr. Atherton Cmty. Schs., Burton, 1992—, mem. Atherton Sch. Improvement Team, 2003—. Troop advisor US Girls Scouts, Columbiaville, Mich., 1978—80; adoptive parent, adv. coun. mem. Whaley Childrens Ctr. Foster and Adoptive Children, Flint, 1986—2004; adv. coun. /musician Jobs Daughters Bethel #33, Clio, Mich., 1988—92; performance mem. Sweet Adelines Thumb Area Chorus, Davsion, Mich., 1992—94, Flint Area Chorus, 1999—2002; host family parent Student Travel Services Fgn. Exch. Students, Flint, 1998—2002. Named Tchr. Yr., Atherton HS, 2001, Atherton Mid. Sch., 2002. Mem.: Mich. Sch. Vocal Music Assn., Atherton Edn. Assn. (exec. bd. mem. 2003—), Killarney Pk. Assn. (by-laws chmn. 2000—06), Nesika Order Ea. Star (chpt. 54), Ladies Aux. VFW (life; dept. Mich. jr. girls chmn. 1986—93, Nat. Chmn. of The Yr. 1987, 1988, 1990—93). Presbytarian. Avocations: gardening, swimming, camping, travel. Home: 4427 Killarney Park Dr Burton MI 48529 Office: Atherton Cmty Schs 3354 S Genesee Rd Burton MI 48519 Home Phone: 810-715-3053; Office Phone: 810-591-0400. Business E-Mail: jjohnson@athertonschools.com.

JOHNSON, JONATHAN EDWIN, II, lawyer; b. Whittier, Calif., May 1, 1936; s. Roger Edwin and Louise (Thompson) J.; m. Clare Hardy, June 23, 1963 (dec. 1995); children: Jonathan III, Hardy, Benjamin, Adam, Rufus, Bradford, Roger, Ralph; m. Garnet Kalsched, June 17, 2000. BChemE, Cornell U., 1959, MBA, 1960; JD with honors, George Washington U., 1963. Bar: Calif. 1964; cert. specialist family law, Calif. Assoc. Tuttle & Taylor, LA., 1963-65; pvt. practice LA, 1965-67; ptnr. Johnson & Jarvis, LA, 1967-68, Johnson, Poulson & Coons, LA, 1968—. Instr. paralegal probate U. West L.A. Sch. Law, 1974; mem. clergy adv. com. to supt. edn., City of L.A., 1978-81. Named Outstanding Lawyer, J. Reuben Clark Law Soc.-L.A. Chpt., 2000, a So. Calif. Super Lawyer, 2004—06. Fellow Am. Acad. Matrimonial Lawyers (counsel So. Calif. chpt. 1998-99); mem. Calif. State Bar Assn. (legis. com. family law sect. 1978-88, chmn. 1980), Beverly Hills Bar Assn. (exec. com. family law sect. 1977-82, 86-88, 91—, chmn. 2003-2004), Inter-stake Bus. and Profl. Assn. L.A. (pres. 1974), Cornell Club of So. Calif. (pres. 1966-68), Order of Coif, Sigma Chi, Phi Delta Phi. Mem. Lds Ch. Home: 1094 Acanto Pl Los Angeles CA 90049-1604 Office: Johnson Poulson & Coons 1900 Avenue of the Stars Ste 1900 Los Angeles CA 90067 Office Phone: 310-475-0611.

JOHNSON, JOSEPH CLAYTON, JR., lawyer; b. Vicksburg, Miss., Nov. 15, 1943; s. Joseph Clayton and Rose Butler (Levy) J.; m. Cherrian Frances Turpin, Oct. 24, 1970; children: Mary Clayton, Erik Cole. BS, La. State U., Baton Rouge, 1965; JD, La. State U., 1969. Bar: La. 1969, U.S. Dist. Ct. (ea. and mid. dists.) La. 1969, U.S. Dist. Ct. (we. dist.) La. 1979, U.S. Ct. Appeals (5th cir.) 1982. Ptnr. Taylor, Porter, Brooks & Phillips, Baton Rouge, 1969—. Mem. civil justice reform act com. U.S. Dist. Ct. (mid. dist.) La., 1995-97, chmn. 1996-97; mem. La. Atty. Disciplinary Bd., 1997-99. Bd. editors Oil and Gas Reporter, 1988—2005. Pres. Baton Rouge area Am. Cancer Soc., 1987—88; mem. adv. bd. Ctr. for Energy Law, 2000—05; bd. dirs. Capital Area chpt. Am. Red Cross, 2005—. With US Army, 1969—75. Recipient John Rogers award, 1999, Ctr. for Am. and Internat. Law. Master: Dean Henry George McMahon Am. Inn of Ct.; mem.: Ctr. for Am. and Internat. Law (bd. editors Oil and Gas Reporter 1987—2005), Baton Rouge Bar Assn., La. State Law Inst. (mineral code com.), La. Bar Assn. (mem. ho. of dels. 1979—92, coun. rep. mineral law sect. 1986—94, chmn. mineral law sect. 1992—93). Republican. Methodist. Office: PO Box 2471 Baton Rouge LA 70821-2471 Office Phone: 225-387-3221. Business E-Mail: clay.johnson@taylorporter.com.

JOHNSON, JOSEPH EGGLESTON, III, physician, educator; b. Elberton, Ga., Sept. 17, 1930; s. Joseph Eggleston Jr. and Marie (Williams) J.; m. Judith H. Kemp, Jan. 21, 1956; children: Joseph Eggleston IV, Judith Ann, Julie Marie. BA cum laude, Vanderbilt U., 1951, MD, 1954. Diplomate Am. Bd. Internal Medicine (bd. govs. 1977-83, exec. com. 1981-83), Am. Bd. Allergy and Immunology. Intern Johns Hopkins Hosp., Balt., 1954-55, resident, 1957-61, physician, 1961-66; mem. faculty Johns Hopkins Med. Sch., Balt., 1961-66, asst. dean, 1963-66; chief infectious diseases U. Fla. Coll. Medicine, Gainsville, 1966-72, assoc. dean, 1970-72; prof., chmn. dept. Bowman Gray Sch. Medicine, Winston-Salem, N.C., 1972-85; chief med. service N.C. Baptist Hosp., mem. residency rev. com. internal medicine, 1978-83, chmn. residency rev. com. internal medicine, 1983-85; dean Med. Sch., prof. medicine U. Mich., Ann Arbor, 1985-90, prof. internal medicine, 1985-93; accreditation commn. on grad. med. edn., 1988-93; sr. v.p. membership and spl. advisor to exec. v.p. Am. Coll. Physicians, Phila., 1993—, interim exec. v.p., 1994-95. Adj. prof. of medicine U. Pa., 1994—. Contbr. articles to profl. jours. Served to lt. USNR, 1955-57. John and Mary R. Markle scholar, 1962-67; Mead-Johnson postgrad. scholar, 1960-61 Fellow ACP (sci. program com. 1979-85, chmn. sci. program com. 1982-85, chmn. elect bd. govs. 1985, chmn. bd. govs., bd. regents 1985-93, gov.-elect N.C. 1981-82, gov. N.C. 1982-86, treas. 1991-93, interim exec. v.p. 1994-95), Am. Acad. Allergy, Royal Soc. Medicine (travelling fellow 1970-71); mem. AMA (chmn. Med. Sch. sect. 1990-91, alternate del. 1996-2003), Internat. Soc. Internal Medicine (pres. 2000-02), Am. Fedn. Clin. Rsch., Assn. Am. Physicians, Infectious Diseases Soc. Am., Soc. Exptl. Biology and Medicine, N.Y. Acad. Scis., Am. Assn. Immunologists, So. Soc. Clin. Investigation, Am. Soc. for Microbiology, Assn. Profs. Medicine (sec.-treas. 1978-81, pres.-elect 1981-82, pres. 1982-83), Am. Clin. and Climatol. Assn., Société Française de la Tuberculose et des Maladies Respiratoires, Assn. Program Dirs. in Internal Medicine (exec. coun. 1980-83), Assn. Am. Med. Colls. (exec. coun. 1983-85), Coun. Acad. Socs. (adminstrv. bd. 1978-85), Federated Coun. for Internal Medicine (vice chmn. 1981-82, chmn. 1982-83), Johns Hopkins Soc. Scholars, Phi Beta Kappa, Sigma Alpha Epsilon, Phi Chi, Omicron Delta Kappa, Alpha Omega Alpha. Office: Am Coll Physicians Independence Mall West 6th St at Race Philadelphia PA 19106 E-mail: jjohnson@mail.acponline.org.

JOHNSON, JOSEPH ERLE, mathematician; b. Memphis, Apr. 27, 1951; s. Louis Miller and Harriette Edith (Geiger) J. BS in Applied Math., Ga. Inst. Tech., 1975; BS in Engring., U. Tenn., Chattanooga, 2005. Tax examiner IRS, Atlanta, 1975—77; sec., treas. Louis M. Johnson & Co., Memphis, 1977—82; grad. asst. dept. math. scis. Memphis State U., 1983—84; warehouse adminstr. The Julien Co., 1986—89; with Venture Constrn. Co., 1990—91, Crager Constrn. Co., 1991—92; mgr. data processing Finishing Techs., Inc., Chattanooga, 1993; engring. records clk. TVA, 1994—99, engring. aide, 1999—2000, 2003—05, student intern, 2001—03; surveyor City of Chattanooga Engring. Divsn., 2005. Treas. Memphis Astron. Soc., 1980-81. Mem. Soc. for Indsl. and Applied Math. Home: 2079 N Cabana Cir Apt 9 Memphis TN 38107 Home Phone: 901-276-1899. Personal E-mail: johnsonjoe51@aol.com.

JOHNSON, JOY ANN, diagnostic radiologist; b. New Richmond, Wis., Aug. 16, 1952; d. Howard James and Shirley Maxine (Eidem) J.que BA in Chemistry summa cum laude, U. No. Colo., 1974; D of Medicine, U. Colo., 1978. Diplomate Am. Bd. Radiology, Nat. Bd. Med. Examiners; cert. added qualification pediatric radiology. Resident in radiology U. Colo., 1978-81, fellow in pediat. radiology, 1981-82; asst. prof. diagnostic radiology and pediatrics, chief sect. pediatric radiology Clin. Radiology Found. U. Kans. Med. Ctr., Kansas City, 1982-87; radiologist Radiology Assocs. Ltd., Kansas City, Mo., 1987-92; mem. staff Bapt. Med. Ctr., Kansas City, Mo., 1987-92; radiologist Children's Mercy Hosp., Kansas City, 1992-95, Leavenworth-Kansas City Imaging, 1996—; assoc. prof. U. Mo., Kansas City, 1992—; chief of staff Cushing Mem. Hosp., 2002—04. Speaker Radiol. Soc. Republic of China, 1985, RSNA 2000 panel mem. Contbr. articles to med. jours. Nat. Cancer Inst. fellow, 1982. Mem. AMA, Am. Coll. Radiology, Radiol. Soc. N.Am., Am. Inst. Ultrasound in Medicine (mem. program com. Kansas City 1984), Soc. Pediatric Radiology (mem. com. for cmty. bsed pediat. radiologists 1998-2003), Am. Assn. Women in Radiology, Lambda Sigma Tau. Avocations: horseback riding, physical fitness, sports, reading. Office: Leavenworth-Kansas City Imaging 9201 Parallel Pkwy Kansas City KS 66112-1528

JOHNSON, JOYCE, retired military officer; m. Jim Calderwood; 1 child, James. DO, Mich. State U., 1980; DSc (hon.), Des Moines U., 2002. Commd. into US Pub. Health Svc.; various positions US Food and Drug Adminstrn., Nat. Inst. Mental Health, Substance Abuse and Mental Health Svcs. Adminstrn.; chief med. officer, surgeon gen. US Coast Guard, 1997—2003, dir. health and safety, 1997—2003, ret., 2003; v.p. health scis. Battelle Meml. Inst., Arlington, Va., 2004—. Bd. trustees US Coast Guard Acad. Named Physician Exec. Yr.; recipient Dr. Nathan Davis award for outstanding govt. svc., Am. Med. Assn. Achievements include among the first to do AIDS rsch. with Ctr. Disease Control, Atlanta; first female flag officer with USCG; first woman to serve on bd. trustees Coast Guard Acad. Avocations: cooking, travel.

JOHNSON, JOYCE MARIE, psychiatrist, epidemiologist, public health officer; b. Baton Rouge, Jan. 30, 1952; d. Gene Addison and Helen Marie (Kalcik) J.; m. James Albert Calderwood, Mar. 28, 1987; 1 child, James. BA, Luther Coll., Decorah, Iowa, 1972; MA, U. Iowa, 1974; DO, Mich. State U., 1980; DFA (hon.), NY Inst. Tech., 2001. Cert. in psychiatry, pub. health and preventive medicine, and clin. pharmacology. Cooking instr. Kirkwood C.C., Iowa City, Iowa, 1974-76; health planner Iowa Regional Med. Program, Iowa City, 1974-76; commd. USPHS, advanced through grades to rear adm./asst. surgeon gen.; intern USPHS Hosp., Balt., 1980-81; med. epidemiologist Hepatitis Labs., Ctrs. Disease Control, Phoenix, 1981-83, AIDS, Ctrs. Disease Control, Atlanta, 1983-84; resident in psychiatry NIMH, 1984-87, staff psychiatrist, 1987-88; epidemiologist, divsn. dir. FDA, 1995—2003; dir. divsn. nat. treatment demonstrations, Substance Abuse and Mental Health Svcs. Adminstrn., 1993-97; chief med. officer USCG, 1997-2003; v.p. health scis. Battelle Meml. Inst., 2004—. Med. Perspectives fellow, New Guinea and Thailand, 1978-79; mem. clin. faculty Mich. State U., 1983-93, Georgetown U. Med. Ctr., 1988—, Uniformed Svcs. U. of the Health Scis. Recipient Dr. Nathan Davis award for Outstanding Work in Govt. Svc., 2001. Mem. Explorers Club, Mensa, Cosmos Club. Office: 5518 Western Ave Bethesda MD 20815-7122

JOHNSON, JUDITH A., educational administrator; b. Bklyn., July 17, 1939; d. Charles Washington and Gwendolyn (Allen) Lockley; divorced; children: Pamela Johnson, Paul Johnson. BA, Bklyn. Coll., 1961; MA, NYU, 1966; 6th yr. cert., SUNY, New Paltz, 1981; postgrad., Columbia U., 1984—. Tchr. N.Y.C. Pub. Schs., 1960-62, asst. prin., guidance counselor, 1964-66, coord. guidance, 1971-73; prin. Mamaroneck (N.Y.) Pub. Schs., 1974-79; dir. instrnl. svcs. So. Westchester Bd. Coop. Ednl. Svcs., Portchester, N.Y., 1979-85; dir. curriculum K-12 Nyack (N.Y.) Pub. Schs., 1985-90; asst. supt. for curriculum and instrn. White Plains (N.Y.) Pub. Schs., 1990-97; dep. asst. secy Office of Elementary and Secondary Edn., Washington, DC, 1997—. Co-author curriculum guides. Recipient cert. of appreciation Phi Delta Kappa, 1982, Founder's award Westchester Prins. Ctr., 1988, One of 100 Exec. Educator's N.Am. award Nat. Sch. Bd. Assn., 1990, achievement award Nyack Bd. Edn., 1990; also numerous grants and awards in field. Mem. Assn. for Supervision and Curriculum Devel. (nat. bd. dirs. l986-88), N.Y. State Assn. for Supervision and Curriculum Devel. (sec., bd. dirs. 1986—), Am. Ednl. Rsch. Assn., NAACP. Avocations: theater, concerts, walking, tennis. Home: 48 Fessler Dr Spring Valley NY 10977-2004

JOHNSON, JUDY VAN, minister, educator; b. Whiteville, NC; d. Henry Byrd and Maebell Bellamy Johnson. BS, Fayetteville State U., 1978, MA, 1987; DivM, Moriah Inst. Christian Studies, 2001, D of Ministry, 2003. Pastor Mt. Horeb, 1996—2002, McCormick Chapel AME, Lumberton, NC, 2002—, Evergreen; tchr. Robeson, Lumberton, NC, Bladen Co., Elizabethtown, NC, New Hanover Co., Wilmington, NC, Jefferson Co., Louisville, Ga. Bd. mem. NC Conf. Assn., 2000—; bd. examiners The North Conf., 2000—; dir. Christian edn., so. dist. N.C. Conf. Recipient Black Heritage award, McCormick Chapel, 2004—05, Advisor's award, Sci. Club, Star Tchr. award, Time Warner, 1997—98, Tchr. of the Yr., Bladen Co., 1993—94, Faith Initial grants, 2004—05. Avocations: reading, sports, travel. Home: 86 Edwards Lane Whiteville NC 28472 Office: McCormick Chapel AME Ch 215 Main St Lumberton NC 28358 Office Phone: 910-739-0461. Personal E-mail: belljvj@yahoo.com.

JOHNSON, JULIA MARTY, psychologist, educator; d. Samuel Clinton Jr. and Juliana Griggs Marty; m. William Arthur Johnson, June 2, 1979; children: William A. Jr., Heather N., Bethany Johnson Bowers. BA in Psychology and Religion, U. Redlands, Calif., 1980, MA in Edn. and Counseling, 1983, postgrad., 2005—; cert. sch. psychologist, La Sierra U., Riverside, Calif., 1991; diploma (hon.), Tex. Women's U., Downey, Calif., 2004. Lic. edn. psychologist Calif., 1994, cert. sports psychologist Calif. Counselor, psychologist S.E.D. programs Moreno Valley Unified Sch. Dist., Calif., 1987—92; ednl. psychologist Brea-Olinda Unified Sch. Dist., Brea, Calif., 1992—2002, Santa Maria/Bonita Unified Sch. Dist., Santa Maria, Calif., 2002—04, Pioneer HS, Whittier Union HS Dist., Calif., 2004—. Edn. psychologist cons. State of Calif. Bd. Behavioral Scis., 1994—2005; pvt. practice edn. neuropsychologist, Brea, 1994—; prof. U. Ct. Tchr. Edn., Calif. Poly. State U., San Luis Obispo, 2002—04; spl. edn. parent advocate, Calif., 1992—. Bd. dirs., prayer coord. Lift Renewal Ministries, Whittier, 2004—; mem. United Meth. Women, Whittier, 1980—. Recipient Golden Apple award, Calif. State PTA, Moreno Valley, 1989. Mem.: Am. Bd. Sch. Neuropsychology, Nat. Assn. Sch. Psychologists, Calif.Assn. Sch. Psychologists, Omicron Delta Kappa, Sigma Alpha Iota. Avocations: tennis, skiing, swimming, reading. Home: 920 Joyce Dr Brea CA 92821 Office: Whittier Union HS Dist Pioneer Sch 10800 E Benavon St Whittier CA 90606

JOHNSON, JULIE MARIE, lawyer, lobbyist, judge; b. Aberdeen, SD, Aug. 7, 1953; d. Howard B. and Jerauldine (Dilly) J.; m. Bryan L. Hisel. BA in Govt., Comm., U. S.D., 1974, MA in Polit. Sci., 1976, JD, 1976. Bar: S.D. 1977, U.S. Dist. Ct. S.D. 1977. Assoc. Siegel, Barnett Law Firm, Aberdeen, 1977; law clk. Fifth Judicial Circuit Ct., Aberdeen, 1977-78; ptnr. Maloney, Kolker, Fritz, Hogan & Johnson, Aberdeen, 1978-84; dep. sec. SD Dept. Labor, Aberdeen, Pierre, 1983-84, sec. Gov.'s Cabinet, 1985-87, SD Dept. Revenue, Pierre, 1995; pres. Industry and Commerce Assn. SD, Pierre, 1987-95; exec. dir. SD Rural Devel. Coun., Pierre, 1995—2003; acting exec. dir. SD Math., Sci. and Tech. Coun., 2002—03; adminstrv. law judge SD, 2003—. Adj. faculty SD State U., 1996—; chair Gov.'s Red Tape Task Force, 2004—05; legal counsel SD Vietnam War Meml. Dedication Com., Inc., 2004—07. Treas. SD Cmty. Found., Pierre, 1987-95; mem. Pvt. Industry Coun., 1985-87, SD Coun. on Vocat. Edn., 1985-87; bd. dirs. Mo. Shores Women's Resource Ctr., Pierre, 1988-89; chmn. SD Main St. Adv. Coun., 1987-91; bd. dirs. United Way, 1988-96, chmn., 1991; mem. Shortgrass Arts Coun., 1987—, South Dakotans for Arts, 1981—, Solid Waste Mgmt. Plan Task Force, 1990, SD Citizens Adv. Coun. Hazardous Waste, 1991-92, gov.'s adv. coun. on health care reform, 1992-93, gov.'s Homestate Underground Lab adv. coun., 2002-04; bd. dirs. Hist. SD Found., 1996-99; founding mem., legal counsel Outdoor Women of SD, Inc., 1995—; bd. trustees USD Found., 1992—; trustee, mem. bus. affairs com., 1996—, com. on trustees, Kelley Ctr. for Entrepreneurship adv. bd., presdl. search com. Dakota Wesleyan U., 1999-2000; founding mem., treas. SD Discovery Ctr. and Aquarium, Inc., bd. dirs., 1988-92; mem. SD Water Congress, 1990-97, bd. dirs., 1987-95; bd. dirs. Nyoda Girl Scout Coun., 1997-99; mem. adv. bd. W.O. Farber Ctr. for Excellence in Civic Leadership, 1998—; bd. dirs. Farber Fund, 1987—; founding mem. SD Chambers and Econ. Devel. Coun., 1989—; mem. Network Mgmt. Team Nat. Rural Devel. Partnership, 1998-2001; course leader Leadership Ctrl. SD, 1996—; mem. Children's Care Hosp. and Sch. Found. Bd., 1997—, vice chair, 2005—, investment com., 1999—, joint exec. com., 2003—, devel. com., 2004—, chair governance com., 2005—; mem. Nat. Rural Devel. Partnership Presdl. Transition Team, 2000-01, Agr. and Econ. Devel. Task Force, 2001, SD Habitat for Humanity Bd., 2001—, vice chair, 2005—; bd. dirs. Historic SD Found., 1995-98, Genesis of Innovation, 2000-03; acting exec. dir. SD Math., Sci. and Tech. Coun., 2000-03; vol. chmn. SD WWII Meml. Dedication, 2001; vol. chair SD Korean War Meml. Dedication Com., 2003-04, seating/decorating co-chair, 2003-04; chmn. Govs. Red Tape Task Force, 2004-05, vice chiar, 2005—07; bd. dirs. SD Habitat for Humanity, 2001—07, pro bono lobbyist, 2004-07, vice chair, 2005—07; founder, treas. Friends of Discovery Ctr., SD; trustee, mem. coms. Dakota Wesleyan U., Children's Care Hosp. Found., U. SD Found.; active SD Vietnam War Meml., 2005-06, chair dignitaries, 2005-06, legal counsel dedication com., 2005-06, mem. fundraising com., 2005-06. RJR Nabisco fellow Women Execs. in State Govt., Harvard, 1986; named Outstanding Young Citizen Jaycees, Aberdeen, 1982, S.D. Jaycees, 1983. Mem. S.D. Bar Assn. (chmn. adminstrv. law com. 2001-04, chair adminstrv. law sect., 2004-06, mem. CLE com., Worker's compensation com., chmn. ad law sect. 2004-06), Industry and Commerce Assn. S.D. (bd. dirs. 1985-87), U. S.D. Alumni Assn. (exec. com. 1987-96, pres. 1990-92), AAUW, Bus. and Profl. Women U.S.A. (nat. legis. chmn. 1987-88, 92-94, nat. chmn. issues mgmt. 1991-93, pres. S.D. 1984-85, Woman of Yr. award Aberdeen chpt. 1982), Women Execs. in State Govt. (bd. didrs. 1985-87), Coun. State Mfrs. Assn., S.D. Mining Assn. (bd. dirs. 1991-95, Gold PAC, 1995-), Nat. Indsl. Coun., Coun. State C.'s of C., Ducks Unltd., Rotary, WIG Investment Club, Rocky Mountain Elk Found. Republican. Lutheran. Address: 1100 E Church St Apt 352 Pierre SD 57501-2354 Office: 210 E 4th St Pierre SD 57501 Home: 1414 Sharpstone Dr Mitchell SD 57301-6250 Business E-Mail: juliem.johnson@state.sd.us.

JOHNSON, JUNE ALEXIS, counselor, social worker; b. Cleve., Dec. 8, 1945; d. Alexander Branshaw and Mary Annette Mangrum; divorced; children: Troy DeShon McQueen, Tara Elaine Johnson, Carrie Jean Johnson. AA, Cuyahoga C.C., 1992; BA, Notre Dame Coll. Ohio, 1995; MA, John Carroll U., 1997. Lic. profl. counselor, Ohio. Med. sec. Cuyahoga County, Cleve., 1970-80, social worker, dept. sr. and adult protective svcs., 1995—. Contbr. poetry to anthologies. Ch. usher Zion Chapel Bapt. Ch., Cleve. Recipient Golden Poet award The World of Poetry, 1989, 91, Editor's Choice award Nat. Libr. Poetry, 1994, 97. Avocation: poetry. Office Phone: 216-420-6731.

JOHNSON, KAREN A., legal association administrator; b. Grand Island, Nebr., Aug. 27, 1954; d. Edward C. and Betty M. Johnson. Degree, Grand Island Sch. Bus., Prince George's C.C. Applicant coord. Dept. of Justice, Washington, 1976—77, rsch. analyst, 1977—98, supervisory legal adminstrn. specialist, 1998—. Recipient Incentive award, Dept. of Justice, 2002, 2004, 2006.

JOHNSON, KATHERINE ANNE, health facility administrator, lawyer; b. Medford, Mass., Apr. 20, 1947; d. Lester and Eileen Anne (Henaghan) J. BS, La. State U., 1969; MSA, George Washington U., 1972; JD, Cath. U., 1985. Bar: Md. 1985. Pub. health adviser HHS, Washington, 1970-76; dir. plan implementation SE Colo. Health Sys. Agy., Colorado Springs, 1976-78; sr. mng. assoc. CDP Assocs., Inc., Atlanta, 1978-87, dir. legal affairs, 1986-87; v.p. Cancer CarePoint Inc., Atlanta, 1987; sr. mgr. Salick Health Care, Inc., Bethesda, Md., 1987-89; pvt. practice Potomac, Md., 1989-90; assoc. dir. for adminstrn. San Antonio Cancer Inst., 1990-96; assoc. dir. planning and adminstrn. CTRC Rsch. Found., San Antonio, 1996-97, v.p., 1997-98; COO Inst. Drug Devel., San Antonio, 1997-98; prin. biomed. program devel. consulting, 1998-99; dir. rsch./adminstrn. Am. Coll. Surgeons, 1999—2002; asst. prof., assoc. dir. adminstrn. Massey Cancer Ctr., Richmond, 2002—. Spkr. in field. Contbr. articles to profl. jours. Vol. Ct.-Apptd. Spl. Adv. for Abused Children, Cat Adoption and Rescue Efforts. Mem. Md. Bar Assn., Am. Health Lawyers Assn., Leadership Tex. Class of 1996, Soc. Rsch. Adminstrs. Avocations: skiing, reading, antiques. Office: Po Box 980037 Richmond VA 23298 E-mail: kajohns@earthlink.net.

JOHNSON, KAY DURBAHN, real estate manager, consultant; b. Crookston, Minn., Apr. 4, 1937; d. Wilbert John and Frieda (Johnson) Durbahn; m. Ray Arvin Johnson, May 14, 1960; children: Sherry Kay Johnson Johnston, Diane Rosalind Johnson Peterson, Laura Faye Johnson Gill. BA, U. Minn., 1959. Reference analyst Indsl. Rels. Ctr. U. Minn., Mpls., 1959-61; real estate mgr. Minnetonka, Minn., 1976—; ptnr. Broadmoor Plantation Investors, Fargo, ND, 1976—2005; v.p. D&T Property, Inc., Minnetonka, 1990—, also bd. dirs.; v.p. Comreco, LLC, 2002—, bd. dirs. Tax reduction cons. R.A. Johnson & Assocs., Minnetonka, 1985—; bd. dirs. Empire Aggregate, Inc., 2001—. City of Minnetonka Planning Commn., 1972-74, vice chair, 1973-74; mem. Land Use Task Force, 1972-74; liaison Ridgedale Devel.; mem. choir, various coun. positions Minnehaha Luth. Ch. Mem. Mpls. Inst. Arts. Republican. Avocations: art, music, travel. *For greater happiness try to balance your life by making time for all aspects of living, including activities to meet social, spiritual, physical, family, work, and intellectual needs.*

JOHNSON, KEITH LIDDELL, retired chemicals executive; b. Darlington, Eng., July 22, 1939; came to U.S., 1948, naturalized, 1958; s. Arthur Henry and Beatrice (Liddell) J.; m. Margaret Elaine Meston, Aug. 29, 1959; children: Leslie Margaret, Kevin Liddell, Gregory Norman, Kathleen Elaine; 1 ward, Ann Louise Warwick. BA, U. Mich., 1960. Chem. technician Ajem Labs., Livonia, Mich., 1956—60; rsch. chemist labs. Swift & Co., Chgo., 1960—63, project mgr., 1963—67, group leader R&D ctr. Oak Brook, Ill., 1967—71, adminstrv. asst. to exec. v.p. Chgo., 1971—72, quality assurance dir., 1974—78, group mgr. plant quality assurance, 1978—82; quality assurance mgr. refinery divsn. Swift Edible Oil Co. subs. Swift & Co., Chgo., 1972—73, corp. quality assurance mgr., 1973—74; tech. dir. Norman Fox & Co., LA, 1982—83, br. mgr., 1983—88, gen. mgr., 1988—93, exec. v.p., dir., 1989—2005, pres., 1993—2003, vice chmn., 2003—05; ret., 2005; proprietor KJ Tech. Directions, 2005—. Bd. dirs. Lexard Corp., LA, v.p. 1990-94; bd. dirs. Chem. Distbn. Network, Des Plaines, Ill.; mem. Chgo. Manpower Area Planning Com., 1971; industry adv. bd. South Coast Air Quality Mgmt. Dist., Calif., 1982-84; cons. in field. Contbr. articles to profl. jours. V.p., dir. St. Martha's Sr. Care Ctr., West Covina, Calif., 1993-97, chmn. bd., 1995-99, vestry St. Martha's Episc. Ch., sr. warden 1991-96, 98-2001; mem. vestry St. Ambrose Episc. Ch., Claremont, Calif., 2002-06, sr. warden, 2004-05; bd. dirs. St. Martha's Epsicopal Sch., 1999-2001. Mem. Chgo. Chemists Club, Chem. Art Forum Chgo. (v.p. 1980, pres. 1981), Am. Chem. Soc. (chair elect so. Calif. sect. 2000-01, chair 2001-02, exec. com. 2000-03), Soc. Cosmetic Chemists (membership chmn. Bay area chpt. 1985, chmn. 1987-88), Am. Oil Chemists Soc., Chem. Mktg. Assn. So. Calif., Internat. Union Pure and Applied Chemistry. Episcopalian. Achievements include patents in field. Home: 342 Amberwood Dr Walnut CA 91789-2473 Office Phone: 213-705-4486. Fax: 909-598-5782. Personal E-mail: keithjohnson@prodigy.net.

JOHNSON, KELLY, chef; b. Tecumseh, Mich. With Ritz-Carlton Hotel Co., 1996; chef de partie Ritz-Carlton Naples, 1997; chef de cuisine The Grill, Ritz-Carlton, Double Day, Sydney, Adam's Mark Hotel, Dallas; co-owner, exec. chef Evans Street Station, Tecumseh, Mich., 2001—. Guest chef James Beard House, 2000. Named to Hall of Fame, Chef2Chef.net, 2006. Office: Evans Street Station 1105 Evans St Tecumseh MI 49286 Office Phone: 517-424-5555. Office Fax: 517-424-0555.*

JOHNSON, KELLY A., lawyer, former federal agency administrator; BS in Environ. Mgmt. with high honors, Rutgers U.; MPA in Environ. Mgmt., Ind. U., JD magna cum laude. Assoc. Holland & Hart, 1990—95, of counsel, 2005—; mem. Bush-Cheney transition team, US Dept. Interior; sr. counsel Senate Energy and Natural Resources Com.; primary adv. to asst. atty. gen., Environ. & Natural Resources divsn. US Dept. Justice, Washington, 2001—05, acting asst. atty. gen., Environment & Natural Resources divsn., 2005. Office: Holland & Hart LLP 701 Pennsylvania Ave NW Ste 250 Washington DC 20004 Office Phone: 202-393-6500. Office Fax: 866-711-8048. E-mail: kajohnson@hollandhart.com.*

JOHNSON, KELLY OVERSTREET, lawyer; b. Tallahassee, May 3, 1958; m. Hal Johnson; 2 children. BS in Real Estate and pre-Law, Fla. State Univ., 1979, JD with honors, 1982. Civil litigator Fla. Dept. of Legal Affairs, 1983—85; atty. Ervin, Varn, Jacobs, Odom & Kitchen, 1985—88; pvt. practice, 1988—90; ptnr. Broad and Cassel, Tallahassee, 1990—. Mem.: Am. Bar Assn. (Ho. of Del. 1992—94, 2003—06), Tallahassee Women Lawyers (pres.), Tallahassee Bar Assn. (pres. 1990—91), Fla. Bar (young lawyers divsn. bd. gov. 1986—90, bd. govs. 1997—2004, pres. 2004—05), Leadership Fla. Class XXIV, Guardian Ad Litem Program, Legal Aid Found., Jr. League of Tallahassee. Office: Broad & Cassel 215 S Monroe St Ste 400 PO Box 11300 Tallahassee FL 32302-1300 Office Phone: 850-681-6810. Business E-Mail: kjohnson@broadandcassel.com.

JOHNSON, KENNETH F., lawyer; b. Ft. Bragg, Calif., June 10, 1938; s. Frank W. and Gertrude Johnson; m. Jane Perry Drennan, June 11, 1961; children: Erik, Mark. BSCE, U. Calif., Berkeley, 1962; JD, U. Calif., Hastings, 1969. Bar: Calif. 1970. Atty. Crosby Heafey Roach & May PC, Oakland, Calif., 1969—2003; of counsel ReedSmith LLP, Oakland, 2003—. Note and comment editor: Hastings Law Jour., 1968-69. Officer USNR, 1962—66. Scholar U. Calif. Hastings, 1967-68, 68-69. Mem. Calif. Bar Assn., Alameda County Bar Assn., Contra Costa County Bar Assn., Bar Assn. San Francisco, Assn. Bus. Trial Lawyers Assn., Order of Coif. Office: Reed Smith LLP 1999 Harrison St Fl 24 Oakland CA 94612-3520 Office Phone: 510-466-6724.

JOHNSON, KENNETH HARVEY, veterinary pathologist; b. Hallock, Minn., Feb. 17, 1936; s. Clifford H. and Alma (Anderson) J.; Sept. 17, 1960; children: Jeffrey, Gregory, Sandra. BS, U. Minn., 1958, DVM, 1960, PhD, 1965. Jr. asst. health officer NIH, Bethesda, Md., 1958; practice vet. medicine Edina, Minn., 1960; USPHS-NIH non-service fellow U. Minn., St. Paul, 1960-65, asst. prof. dept. vet. pathology and parasitology, 1965-69, assoc. prof., 1969-73, prof., 1973-98, prof. emeritus dept. vet. pathobiology, 1998—, head, sect. pathology, dept. vet. biology, 1974-76, chmn. dept. vet. pathobiology Coll. Vet Medicine, 1976-83. Cons. Minn. Mining & Mfg. Co., Medtronic Inc., Natural-Y Surg. Specialties; principle and co-investigator several NIH grants, 1965-98. Mem. editl. bd. Amyloid, the Internat. Jour. of Exptl. and Clin. Investigation; contbr. chpts.: Veterinary Clinics of North America, 1971, Spontaneous Animal Models of Human Disease, 1979, Kirk's Current Veterinary Therapy; contbr. articles to sci. jours. Councilman Nativity Lutheran Ch., St. Anthony Village, Minn., 1972-75. Recipient Tchr. of Yr. award, 1968-69, Norden award for disting. tchr. in vet. medicine, 1970, Beecham award for rsch. excellence, 1989, Ralston Purina Small Animal Rsch. award, 1990, Phi Zeta faculty achievement award, 1992, Outstanding Achievement award Bd. of Regents of U. Minn., 2001. Mem.: Am. Coll. Vet. Pathologists (hon.). Home: 3510 Skycroft Dr Minneapolis MN 55418-1780 Business E-Mail: johns049@tc.umn.edu.

JOHNSON, KENNETH PETER, neurologist, researcher; b. Jamestown, NY, Mar. 12, 1932; s. Kenneth Peter and Nina (Bengtson) Johnson; m. Jacquelyn Johnson, June 23, 1956; children: Peter, Thomas, Diane, Douglas. BA, Upsala Coll., East Orange, NJ, 1955; MD, Jefferson Med. Coll., Phila., 1959. Diplomate: Am. Bd. Psychiatry and Neurology. Intern Buffalo Gen. Hosp., 1959-60; resident Hosp. of Cleve., 1963-65; asst. prof. neurology Case Western Res. U., Cleve., 1968-71, assoc. prof., 1971-74; prof. U. Calif., San Francisco, 1974-81; prof., chmn. U. Md., Balt., 1981—, chmn., 1981—2002; chief neurology VA Hosp., Balt., 1981-83. Editor: Neurovirology, 1984; contbr. numerous articles in field to profl. jours. Served to lt. U.S. Navy, 1961-63. Recipient Weil award Am. Assn. Neuropathology, 1967, Research Ctr. Devel. award NIH, 1968-73, John J. Dystal prize, 2000; Zimmerman lectr. Stanford U., 1981 Fellow Am. Neurol. Assn.; mem. Am. Acad. Neurology, Am. Soc. Virology, Am. Congress Rehab. Medicine, Am. Soc. Neurorehab., Internat. Soc. for Neuroimmunology. Lutheran. Office: Md Ctr for MS 11 S Paca St 3d Fl Baltimore MD 21201

JOHNSON, KEVIN, computer software company executive; married; 2 children. BBA, N.Mex. State U. Software developer, systems programmer petroleum and fin. services industries, 1981; with systems integration and consulting bus. units IBM Corp., 1986—92; gen. mgr., enterprise services Microsoft Corp., Redmond, Wash., 1992, v.p., product support services, mem. sr. leadership team and bus. leadership team, sr, v.p., Microsoft Americas, group v.p., worldwide sales, 2003—05, co-pres., platforms products & services divsn., 2005—07, pres., platforms & services div., 2007—. Founding mem. bd. dirs. NPower; bd. advisor, Western region Catalyst. Avocations: running, skiing, golf, roadie for son's rock 'n' roll band.*

JOHNSON, KEVIN BLAINE, lawyer, educator; b. Wichita, Kans., Aug. 28, 1956; s. Howard Blaine and Ruth Signe (Hornlund) Johnson. BA, Wichita State U., 1978; JD, Washburn U., 1981. Bar: Kans. 1982, US Dist. Ct./Kans. 1982, US Ct. Appeals (10th cir.) 1991, US Supreme Ct. 1993. Sole practice, Overland Park, Kans., 1981—82; asst. dist. atty. Wyandotte, County, Kans., 1982—84; assoc. Law Office of A.B. Fletcher, Wichita, Kans., 1984—86, Law Office of Stan R. Singleton, Derby, Kans., 1986—88; pvt. practice Wichita, 1988—; prof. law Kans. Newman Coll., Wichita, 1984—96, Webster U., Wichita, 1995—99; prof. Emporia State U., 1999—. Author: The 11th Kans. Vol. Cavalry, 1986, A Summer Madness, 1988, A Short Practical Guide to Bus. Law With Forms, 1990, (rev. title) Bus. Legal Guide, 1994, At War on the Prairie, 1990, Employer's Legal Guide, 1995, Employee Law Compliance, 2001, Small Bus. Legal Guide, 2002, Office Manager's Legal Guide, 2002, Fed. Law Prohibiting Employment Discrimination, 2002, Tex. Employer's Legal Guide, 2003, OSHA: Compliance Made Simple, 2004; contbr. articles to profl. jours. Mem.: Am. Immigration Lawyers Assn., Kans. Bar Assn., Wichita Bar Assn., Wichita Citizen Participation Orgn. Coun. (mem. 1985—86), High Plains Drum Corps, Inc. (bd. dir. 1987—90), Sky Ryders Drum and Bugle Corps (drum instr., Hutchinson, Kans. 1978—81, bd. dir. 1988—90). Republican. Luth. Office: 200 W Douglas Ste 700 Wichita KS 67202 Home Phone: 316-789-9791; Office Phone: 316-264-0228. Business E-Mail: kbjlaw@onemain.com.

JOHNSON, KEVIN RAYMOND, law educator; b. Culver City, Calif., June 29, 1958; s. Kenneth R. Johnson and Angela J. (Gallardo) McEachron; m. Virginia Salazar, Oct. 17, 1987; children: Teresa, Tomás, Elena. AB in Econs. with great distinction, U. Calif., 1980; JD magna cum laude, Harvard U., 1983. Bar: Calif. 1985, U.S. Dist. Ct. (no., ea. and so. dists.) Calif. 1985, U.S. Ct. Appeals (9th cir.) 1985, U.S. Supreme Ct. 1991. From rsch. asst. to Charles Haar prof. Harvard U., Cambridge, Mass., 1982-83, instr. legal writing, 1982; law clk. to Hon. Stephen Reinhardt, U.S. Ct. Appeals (9th cir.), LA, 1983-84; atty. Heller Ehrman White & McAuliffe, San Francisco, 1984-89; acting prof. law U. Calif., Davis, 1989-92, prof., 1992—, prof. Chicano studies, 2000—, assoc. dean acad. affairs, 1998—, dir. Chicano studies program, 2000—01; chair pub. interest law Mabie-Apallas, 2004. Instr. civil procedure, complex litig., immigration law, refugee law, acting dir. clin. legal edn., 1992; instr. Latinos and Latinas and the law; instr. critical race theory; mem. legal del., El Salvador, 87. Author: (book) How Did You Get To Be Mexican? A White/Brown Man's Search for Identity, 1999, Race, Civil Rights, and the Law: A Multiracial Approach, 2001, Mixed Race America and the Law: A Reader, 2002, The "Huddled Masses" Myth: Immigration and Civil Rights, 2004; editor: Harvard Law Rev., 1981—83; contbr. articles to profl. jours. Bd. dirs. Legal Svcs. No. Calif., 1996—, mem. exec. com., 1997—, v.p., 2001—03, pres., 2003—; bd. dirs. Yolo County ACLU, 1990—93, chmn. legal com., 1991—93; magistrate merit selection panel U.S. Dist. Ct. (ea. dist.) Calif.; vol. Legal Svcs. Program, San Francisco, Sacramento; mem. Lawyers Com. Civil Rights San Francisco Bay Area, 1991—; various pro bono activities; mem. Am. Law Inst., 2003; bd. dirs. Mex.-Am. Legal Def. and Ednl. Fund, 2006—. Named Law Prof. of Yr., Hispanic Nat. Bar Assn., 2006; recipient commendation, Calif. State Bar, 1985—90, Chancellor's Cmty. and Diversity award, 2001. Mem.: ABA (mem. coordinators com. immigration 1998—), Hispanic Nat. Bar Assn., Assn. Am. Law Schs. (Clyde Ferguson award minority group sect. 2004), Calif. Bar Assn. (mem. standing com. legal svcs. for poor 1992—94, mem. gov. com. continuing edn. bar 1993—98, mem. minority affairs com., mem. law sch. admission coun. 1999—2001), U. Calif. Alumni Assn. (class sec. Class of 1980), Phi Beta Kappa. Democrat. Roman Catholic. Office: U Calif Sch Law King Hall Davis CA 95617 Office Phone: 530-752-0243. Business E-Mail: krjohnson@ucdavis.edu.

JOHNSON, KEYSHAWN, sportscaster, retired professional football player; b. LA, July 22, 1972; Student, W. L.A. Coll., U. So. Calif. Wide receiver NY Jets, 1996—2000, Tampa Bay Buccaneers, 2000—03, Dallas Cowboys, 2004—06, Carolina Panthers, 2006—07; sportscaster ESPN, 2007—. Co-author (with Shelley Smith): Just Give Me the Damn Ball!: The Fast Times and Hard Knocks of an NFL Rookie, 1997. Named First Team All-Am., The Sporting News, 1995; named to Am. Football Conf. Pro-Bowl Team, 1998, 1999, 2001. Achievements include being the the first overall selection in the 1996 NFL Draft. Office: ESPN ESPN Plz 935 Middle St Bristol CT 06010*

JOHNSON, KIMBERLY CASSANDRA, psychologist; BA in Psychology, So. Methodist U., Dallas, 1995; MA in Clinical Psychology, Calif. Sch. Profl. Psychology, Fresno, 1999, D in Clinical Psychology, 2001. Lic. specialist in sch. psychology Tex. Bd. Examiners of Psychologists, 2004, clinical psychologist Tex. Bd. Examiners of Psychologists, 2005. Intern Highland Park Ind. Sch. Dist., Dallas, 2001—02; psychology fellow ADD Treatment and Rsch. Ctr., Dallas, 2003—04; clin. psychologist Meier Clinics, Richardson, Tex., 2004—. Mem.: NASP, Christian Assn. Psychologists.

JOHNSON, KRAIG NELSON, lawyer, arbitrator, mediator; b. Landstuhl, Germany, July 8, 1959; arrived in US, 1966; s. Howard Arthur Sr. and Joy Anne (Nelson) J.; m. AmberJade F. Leca, Nov. 13, 1993. BA with honors, Eckerd Coll., 1981; M in Internat. Mgmt., Am. Grad. Sch. Internat. Mgmt., Glendale, Ariz., 1982; JD, Baylor U., 1992. Bar: Fla. 1993; cert. mediator and arbitrator Supreme Ct. of Fla. Mktg. mgr. Jack Eckerd Corp., Clearwater, Fla., 1982-85; mktg. systems mgr. NCS, Inc., Houston, 1985-87; dir. ops. Petro, Inc., El Paso, 1987-90; atty. and shareholder Zimmerman, Shuffield, Kiser & Sutcliffe, P.A., Orlando, Fla., 1992—2003; atty., founding and mng. ptnr. Goodman McGuffey Lindsey & Johnson LLP, Orlando, Fla., 2003—. Editor: Florida Workers' Compensation Practice, 1994; contbr. articles to profl. jours. Mem. internat. trade and investment adv. bd. Econ. Devel. Commn. of Mid-Fla., Orlando, 1997—; mem. Task Force on Title IX, Baylor U. Bd. of Regents, Waco, 1992-93; bd. dirs. Asian-Am. C. of C., Orlando, 1994-95. Fellow Soc. of Antiquaries of Scotland; mem. Am. Immigration Lawyers Assn., St. Andrew's Soc. of Ctrl. Fla. (bd. dirs., v.p. 1996-98, pres. 1998-2000), Fla. Bar Assn. (sect. on internat. law and litig.), Order of Barristers. Avocations: sailing, flying, shooting sports, mandarin chinese and german languages. Home: 509 N Hampton Ave Orlando FL 32803-5516 Office: Goodman McGuffey Lindsey & Johnson LLP Ste 200 1245 W Fairbanks Ave Winter Park FL 32789 Office Phone: 407-478-1247.

JOHNSON, KRISTINA M., dean; b. 1957; BSEE, MSEE, Stanford U., PhD in Elec. Engring. Rschr. IBM, Trinity Coll., Ireland; prof. elec. & computer engring. U. Colo., Boulder, 1985—99; co-founder, dir. Optoelectronics Computing Sys. Ctr., Boulder, 1993—97; dean Edmund T. Pratt, Jr. Sch. Engring. Duke U., Durham, NC, 1999—. Bd. dirs. Minerals Techs. Inc., Boston Scientific Corp., AES Corp., Nortel, 2006; co-founder Colo. Advanced Tech. Inst. Ctr. for Excellence in Optoelectronics, 1994, ColorLink Inc., KAJ LLC. Recipient State of Colo. Tech. Transfer award, 1987, Emmy award nomination, 1991, Internat. Denis Gabor Medal Outstanding Achievement in Modern Optics, 1993, Photronics Spectra Circle of Excellence award, 1994, Achievement award, Soc. of Women Engrs., 2004. Fellow: IEEE, Optical Soc. Am.; mem.: Fulbright Assn. Achievements include patents in field; invention of a new form of liquid crystal display; named to Women in Tech. Hall of Fame, 2003. Office: Duke U Pratt Sch Engring 305 Teer Bldg Box 90271 Durham NC 27708 E-mail: kristina.johnson@duke.edu.*

JOHNSON, KRISTINE, newscaster; b. June 5, 1972; m. Steve Johnson; children: Ava, Burke. BA in Jour., U. Nebr. Reporter various New England areas; reporter, anchor WPRI, Providence; anchor First Look, MSNBC, 2005—06, Early Today, NBC, 2005—06; alternating anchor Weekend Today, 2005—06; co-anchor WCBS-TV, NY, 2006—. Office: CBS Broadcast Center 51 West 52nd St New York NY 10001*

JOHNSON, LAEL FREDERIC, lawyer; b. Yakima, Wash., Jan. 22, 1938; s. Andrew Cabot and Gudney M. (Fredrickson) Johnson; m. Eugenie Rae Call, June 9, 1960; children: Eva Marie, Inga Margaret. AB, Wheaton Coll., 1960; JD, Northwestern U., 1963. Bar: Ill. 1963, U.S. Dist. Ct. (no. dist.) Ill. 1964, U.S. Ct. Appeals (7th cir.) 1966. V.p., gen. counsel Abbott Labs., Abbott Park, Ill., 1981-89, sr. v.p., sec., gen. counsel, 1989-94; of counsel Schiff Hardin LLP, Chgo., 1995—2005. Bd. trustees Santa Fe Art Inst.; mem., past chmn. Law Sch. bd. Northwestern U.; bd. dirs. Music Theater Workshop. Mem.: Assn. Gen. Counsel. Home Phone: 312-379-1938; Office Phone: 312-258-5536.

JOHNSON, LARRY (LARRY ALPHONSO JOHNSON JR.), professional football player; b. Pomfret, Md., Nov. 19, 1979; s. Larry Johnson, Sr and Christine Johnson. BA in Integrative Arts, Pa. State U., 2002. Running back Kans. City Chiefs, 2003—. Vol. coach Jr. Player Devel. Program, Kansas City, Mo.; founder L.J.'s Legacy and Growth Youth Found., 2005. Named to All-Pro 2nd Team, AP, 2005, All-AFC Team, Pro Football Weekly, 2005, AFC Pro Bowl Team, 2005, NFL All Pro Team, 2007; recipient Doak Walker award, 2002, Maxwell award, 2002, Walter Camp award, 2002, Derrick Thomas award, Kans. City Chiefs, 2005. Achievements include rushing for 1,351 yards after November 1st during the 2005 season, which is the highest mark in NFL history; ranked first in rushing in the AFC and third in the NFL, 2005, second in the NFL, 2006. Office: c/o Kansas City Chiefs 1 Arrowhead Dr Kansas City MO 64129*

JOHNSON, LARRY WALTER, lawyer; b. Princeton, Minn., May 21, 1934; s. Alfred Herbert and Lillian Martha (Wetter) J.; m. Mary Ann Lindstrom, June 14, 1958; children: Lawrence W. II, Kristin Jane. BS in Law, U. Minn., 1957, LLB, 1959. Bar: Minn. 1959. Assoc. Dorsey & Whitney, Mpls., 1961-66, ptnr., 1967-95, of counsel, 1996—. Bd. dirs. Remmele Engring., Inc. Co-author, co-editor Minnesota Estate Administration, 1968. Bd. dirs. Minn. Bus. Found. Excellence in Edn., St. Paul. 1981-85, Walker Sponsor's Fund, Mpls., 1987; trustee Walker Meth. Residence and Health Services, Inc., Mpls., 1985-86. Served to 1st lt. U.S. Army, 1959-61. Mem. Minn. Bar Assn., Hennepin County Bar Assn., Mpls. Athletic Club. Republican. Congregationalist. Avocation: handball. Home: 5400 W Highwood Dr Minneapolis MN 55436-1225 Office: Dorsey and Whitney 50 S 6th St Ste 1500 Minneapolis MN 55402-1553

JOHNSON, LAURENCE MICHAEL, lawyer; b. NYC, Feb. 8, 1940; s. Edgar and Eleanor (Kraus) Johnson; m. Margie Serrano, Mar. 15, 2003; children: Mark Steven, Lisa Arienne, Laura Elizabeth, Daniel Milton, Miguel L., Daniel B. AB cum laude, Harvard U., 1961; LL.B. cum laude,

Columbia U., 1964. Bar: Mass. 1964. Research asst. Columbia U., 1962-64; law clk. Supreme Jud. Ct. Mass., 1964-65; from assoc. to ptnr. firm Nutter, McClennen & Fish, Boston, 1965-77; ptnr. firm Newman & Meserve, Boston, 1977-78, Palmer & Dodge, Boston, 1978-83; sole practice law Boston, 1983-85; ptnr. firm Johnson & Polubinski, Boston, 1985-86, Johnson & Schwartzman, Boston, 1986—91; of counsel Fordham & Starrett, Boston, 1991—96; ptnr. Mahoney, Hawkes & Goldings, Boston, 1996—2001, Davis, Malm & D'Agostine, Boston, 2001—. Arbitrator Am. Arbitration Assn., 1976—; tchg. team Harvard Trial Adv. Workshop, 1976—; mem. trial adv. faculty Mass. Contg. Legal Edn. of New Eng. Law Inst., 1979—. Author: 20 Years of Civil Rights: Epilogue and Prologue, Boston Bar Journal, 1988; contbr. articles to profl. jours. Group chmn. larger law firms United Way of Mass. Bay, 1976; mem. Sudbury Human Rights Council, 1964-68, pres., 1965-66, Recipient Patriot award, 1976 Fellow: Am. Coll. Trial Lawyers (complex litigation com. 1994—99), Mass. Bar Found. (life; trustee 2005—); mem.: ABA (jud. adminstrn. divsn., litigation and anti-trust sects.), Mass. Bar Assn., Am. Law Inst., Boston Bar Assn. (steering com. lawyers com. for civil rights under law 1976—), Harvard Varsity Club, Harvard Club N.Y., Harvard Club Boston. Democrat. Home: 11 Northway Rd Randolph MA 02368-2913 Office Phone: 617-367-2500. Personal E-mail: ljohnson@davismalm.com. *The trial lawyer's art requires a combination of knowledge, both specialized and general, experience (and the judgment that comes with it), energy, determination, uncompromising self-appraisal and receptivity to the ideas of others. Its object is effective communication and to achieve it, it draws upon not only the law, but every area of human interest. It provides boundless opportunities for creative achievement, but they are realized only in proportion to the effort actually expended.*

JOHNSON, LAWRENCE ALAN, cereal technologist, educator, administrator; b. Columbus, Ohio, Apr. 30, 1947; s. William and Wyoma (Swift) J.; m. Bernice Ann Miller, June 15, 1969; children: Bradley, David. BS, Ohio State U., 1969; MS, N.C. State U., 1971; PhD, Kans. State U., 1978; doctorate U. Gent (hon.), Belgium, 2007. Rsch. chemist Durkee Foods div. SCM Corp., Strongsville, Ohio, 1973-75; assoc. rsch. chemist Food Protein R&D Ctr. Tex. A&M U., College Station, 1978-85; dir. Ctr. for Crops Utilization Rsch. Iowa State U., Ames, 1991—. Mem. rsch. com. Am. Soybean Assn., St. Louis, 1987-91, Nat. Corn Grower's Assn., St. Louis, 1990-91. Author: (with others) Handbook of Cereals, 1991; editor: (book/procs.) Technologies for Value-Added Products from Proteins and Co-Products, 1989, Corn Chemistry and Technology; contbr. more than 150 articles to profl. jours. 1st lt. U.S. Army, 1971-73, Vietnam. Recipient Rsch. award Corn Refiners Assn., 1998. Mem. Am. Assn. Cereal Chemists (assoc. editor jour. 1982-85, dir. 2002-04), Am. Soc. Agrl. Engrs., Am. Oil Chemists Soc. (assoc. editor jour. 1989—, v.p. 2003-04, pres. 2004-05, Archer Daniels Midland Rsch. award 1986, 92, 99, 2001, 02), Royal Swedish Acad. Agr. and Forestry (fgn. mem. 1999), Inst. Food Techs. Republican. Lutheran. Achievements include 11 patents. Home: 2226 Buchanan Dr Ames IA 50010-4368 Office: Ctr Crops Utilization Rsch Iowa State U Ames IA 50011-0001 Office Phone: 515-294-0160. Business E-Mail: ljohnson@iastate.edu.

JOHNSON, LAWRENCE M., retired bank executive; b. 1940; Student, U. Hawaii. With Bank of Hawaii, Honolulu, 1963-2000, exec. v.p., 1980-84, vice chmn., 1984-89, pres., 1989-2000, now chmn. bd., CEO, until 2000, ret., 2000. Address: Ste # 230 130 Merchant St Honolulu HI 96813 Office Phone: 808-537-8200.

JOHNSON, LAWRENCE WILBUR, JR., lawyer; b. Columbia, SC, Apr. 17, 1955; s. Lawrence Wilbur and Ruth (Cooper) J.; m. Cindy Ann Small, May 26, 1979. BS in Acctg., U. S.C., 1976, JD, 1979. Bar: S.C. 1979, U.S. Dist. Ct. S.C. 1979, U.S. Ct. Appeals (4th cir.) 1980. Jud. clk. 3d Jud. Cir. Ct., Bishopville, S.C., 1979-80; ptnr. Robinson, McFadden, Moore, Pope, Williams, Taylor & Brailsford, P.A., Columbia, 1980-87; shareholder Adams, Quackenbush, Herring & Stuart, P.A., Columbia, 1987-94; ptnr. Young, Clement, Rivers & Tisdale, LLP, Columbia, 1994-96, Johnson Law Firm, Columbia, 1996—. Mem. S.C. Bar Assn., Richland County Bar Assn. (pres. bankruptcy law sect. 1982-85), S.C. Bankruptcy Law Assn. (bd. dirs.), Greater Columbia C. of C. (bd. dirs.), Com. of 100 (chmn.), U. S.C. Alumni Assn. (bd. dirs. 1980-82), Chi Psi, Omicron Delta Kappa. Republican. Presbyterian. Avocation: golf. Home: 713 Harborview Ct Chapin SC 29036-7716 Office: Johnson Law Firm PA 1728 Main St Ste 221 Columbia SC 29201-2844 also: PO Box 883 Columbia SC 29202-0883

JOHNSON, LAYMON, JR., management analyst; b. Jackson, Miss., Sept. 1, 1948; s. Laymon and Bertha (Yarbrough) Johnson; m. Charlene J. Johnson, Nov. 13, 1982. B in Tech., U. Dayton, 1970; MS in Sys. Mgmt., U. So. Calif., 1978. Mem. tech. staff Rockwell Internat., Canoga Park, Calif., 1975-77; sr. dynamics engr. Gen. Dynamics, Pomona, Calif., 1978-83; fin. sys. specialist Northrop Corp., Pico Rivera, Calif., 1983-90; utility budget analyst dept. water and power City of LA, 1991—97; mgmt. analyst LA Police Dept., 1997—. Lt. comdr. USNR, 1970—92. Mem.: Internat. Assn. Crime Analysts, Inst. Safety and Sys. Mgmt. Triumvirate, Internat. Assn. Law Enforcement Intelligence Analysts, Vietnam Vets. Am., Los Angeles County Mus. Art, Am. Philatelic Soc., Trojan Club, Am. Legion, Tau Alpha Pi. Roman Catholic.

JOHNSON, LEE ALAN, state supreme court justice; b. Caldwell, Kans., June 28, 1947; m. Donna L. Johnson; children: Jordan W., Jennifer L. BSBA, U. Kans., Lawrence, 1969; JD summa cum laude, Washburn U., Topeka, 1980. Bar: Kans. 1980. Sole practitioner, Caldwell, 1980—2001; judge Kans. Ct. Appeals, 2001—07; justice Kans. Supreme Ct., Topeka, 2007—. Bd. dirs. Stock Exch. Bank. Contbr. articles to legal jours. Mayor, City of Caldwell, 1975-76; city atty., Caldwell, Kans., 1987-97; bd. dirs. Sumner County Mental Health Ctr., 1984. Served in CE US Army, 1969—71. Mem. Kans. Bar Assn., Sumner County Bar Assn., Masons. Avocations: fishing, golf. Office: Kans Supreme Ct Kans Judicial Ctr 301 SW 10th Topeka KS 66612-1507*

JOHNSON, LENNART INGEMAR, materials engineering consultant; b. Mpls., Dec. 23, 1924; s. Sixten Richard Wilhem and Marie Augusta Johnson; m. Muriel Grant, Oct. 7, 1961; 1 child, Sandra Lee. BS in Chem. Engring., U. Minn., 1948. Petroleum engr. Northwestern Refining Co., New Brighton, Minn., 1948-49; sr. engr. Ordnance Div. Honeywell, Hopkins, Minn., 1949-67, prin. materials engr. Def. Sys. Div., 1967-69, supr. engring. Def. Sys. Div., 1969-87; staff engr. Armament Sys. Div. Honeywell Inc., Hopkins, Minn., 1987-88; cons. Soc. Automotive Engring., Warrandale, Pa., 1989-99. Cons. Ecubed Assocs., Inc., 1993-97; forum leader and presenter, U. Wis. Engring. Inst., Madison, 1965; presenter in field. Author: Handbook of Aerospace Composite Standards, 1992; contbr. numerous articles to profl. jours. Mem. credentials com. Hennepin County Rep. Conv., Minn., 1972, alt. del., 1974. Recipient Prize Paper award, IEEE, 1965. Fellow Am. Inst. Chemists (emeritus); mem. Soc. Automotive Engrs. (sec. aerospace composites com. 1986-87, chmn. 1987-89). Achievements include development of injection molding technology, urethane and epoxy casting resins, and urethane foaming resins.

JOHNSON, LEONA MELISSA, psychology professor, researcher; b. Natchez, Miss., Oct. 15, 1950; d. Leon Matthews and Leona Stevenson Bradley; m. Arthur Johnson, Aug. 8, 1969; children: Sharika Danice, Amira Celeste. BA, Jackson State U., Miss., 1972; MBA, Strayer U., 1995; diploma in program mgmt., Def. Systems Mgmt. Coll., 1995; MEd, Howard U., 1998, PhD, 2003. With IBM Corp., Owego, NY and Manassas, Va, 1973—95; project mgr. Loral Corp., Manassas, 1995—98, Lockheed Martin Corp., Manassas, 1998—2004. Rschr. United Negro Coll. Fund, Arlington, Va., 2001—02, Ednl. Rsch. Svcs., Arlington, 2001—02; adj. prof. Howard U., Washington, 2004. Pres. Circles of First Bapt. Ch., Manassas, 1993—2003; v.p. Howard U. Alumni, Woodbridge, 2001—03; pres. Tea Rose Investment Club, Woodbridge, 1999—2000. Recipient cert., Fairfax Pub. Sch. Sys., 1998, Nat. Women of Color award, Career Group Comm., 2003, Letter of Appreciation, Jr. Achievement of Am., 2004. Mem.: AAUW, APA (assoc.), Nat. Assn. African Am. Studies, Am. Evaluation Assn., Assn. Black Psychologists (assoc.), Alpha Kappa Alpha (assoc.; chpt. pres. 2000—04, Ednl. Advancement Found. Merit scholar 2002). Office: Hampton U Hampton VA 23668 Home: 1401 Marsh Wren Cir Portsmouth VA 23703 Home Phone: 757-838-7048; Office Phone: 757-727-5370. Home Fax: 703-257-4015. Personal E-mail: johnsonleonam@aol.com. Business E-Mail: leona.johnson@hamptonu.edu.

JOHNSON, LEONARD HJALMA, lawyer; b. Thomasville, Ga., May 22, 1957; s. Hjalma Eugene and Laura Nell (McLeod) J.; m. Nancy Louise Brock, Dec. 13, 1981; children: Brock Hjalma, Paige McLeod. BSBA, U. Fla., 1978, JD, 1980. Assoc. Dayton, Sumner, Luckie and McKnight, Dade City, 1981-83, Greenfelder and Mander, Dade City, 1983-84; pres. East Coast Bank Corp., Ormond Beach, Fla., 1983-2000; pvt. practice Dade City, 1984-89; ptnr. Johnson, Auvil, Brock & Wilson, PA, Dade City, 1990—; vice chmn. Bank of Madison (Fla.) County, 1983—88, N. Fla. Bank Corp., Madison, 1983—88, Bank at Ormond By-the-Sea, 1983-2000. Vice chmn. Lake State Bank, 1989-96. Bd. dirs. Downtown Dade City Main St. Inc., 1987-96, East Pasco Habitat for Humanity, 1998-99; trustee Dade City Hosp., 1994-96, chmn., 1996; mem. Leadership Fla.; bd. mem. Pasco Hernando CC Found., 2007-. Mem. ABA, Fla. Bar Assn., Pasco County Bar Assn. (sec. 1982-83), Young Pres. Orgn. (edn. chmn. Fla. chpt. 1997-98, chpt. chmn. 1998-99), World Pres. Orgn., Dade City C. of C., Fla. Blue Key. Republican. Methodist. Office Phone: 352-567-2500.

JOHNSON, LEONARD MORRIS, retired pediatric surgeon; b. Gowanda, NY, June 11, 1931; s. Leonard Brynolf and Helen Berdena (Morris) J.; m. Ann Marie Homer, Mar. 30, 1968; children: H. Leif B. Johnson, Nils A.C. Johnson. BA, Haverford Coll., 1954; MD, U. Pa., 1958; MS in Surgery, U. Minn., Mayo Grad. Sch., Rochester, 1966. Diplomate in surgery and in pediat. surgery Am. Bd. Surgery. Intern Colo. Gen. Hosp., Denver, 1958—59; fellow in gen. surgery Mayo Clinic, Rochester, 1959—63; fellow in pediat. surgery Children's Mercy Hosp., Kansas City, Mo., 1964—65; vis. pediat. surgeon Acad. Hosp., Uppsala, Sweden, 1967; registrar in pediat. urology Alder Hey Children's Hosp., Liverpool, England, 1967—68; gen. surgeon SS Hope (Project Hope), Guayaquil, Ecuador, 1964, gen. and pediat. surgeon Conakry, Guinea, 1965, Nicaragua, Colombia, Sri Lanka, 1965—68; pediat. surgeon Children's Hosp., Oakland, Calif., 1969—97, ret., 1997, chief surgery dept., 1989—92. Bd. dirs. Children's Hosp., Oakland, Calif., 1982-91; trustee Children's Hosp. Found., Oakland, 1986-95; mem. exec. bd. Mt. Diablo-Silverado Coun. Boy Scouts Am., 1996—. Decorated Order Ruben Dario (Nicaragua), 1966; recipient Bronze Bambino award Children's Hosp., Oakland, 1990, Silver Beaver award Boy Scouts Am., 2005. Fellow ACS, Am. Acad. Pediat.; mem. Am. Trauma Soc. (founder), Am. Pediat.-Surg. Assn., Pacific Assn. Pediat. Surgeons, Brit. Assn. Pediat. Surgeons, Alameda-Contra Costa Med. Assn. Avocations: photography, hiking, skiing, travel, music. Personal E-mail: lmj2544219@aol.com.

JOHNSON, LESTER FREDRICK, artist; b. Mpls., Jan. 27, 1919; s. Edwin August and Helma Marie (Holmes) J.; m. Josephine Valenti, Feb. 12, 1949; children: Leslie Maria, Anthony Edwin. Student, Mpls. Art Inst., 1939-41, St. Paul Art Sch., 1939-41, Art Inst. Chgo., 1943. Prof. painting Yale U., 1964—, dir. studies, 1968—. Mem. Milford (Conn.) Fine Arts Council, 1972-73; mem. art adv. com. Housatonic Community Coll., Stratford, Conn., 1969-87 One-man shows, Zabriskei Gallery, N.Y.C., Martha Jackson Gallery, N.Y.C., Donald Morris, Detroit, Walter Moos Gallery, N.Y.C., Toronto, Can., David Barnett Gallery, Milw., Mpls. Art Inst., Dayton Art Inst., Fort Worth Art Inst., Yale Univ. Mus., Gimpel Fils Gallery, London, Gimpel Hanover Gallery, Zurich, Switzerland, Westmoreland Mus. Art. Greenburg, Pa. (traveling), Augustana Coll. Centennial Hall Gallery, Pa. Acad. Fine Arts, Newport Harbor Art Mus., Edward Thorpe Gallery, N.Y.C., Gimpel-Weitzenhofer Gallery, N.Y.C., Peter Findley Gallery, N.Y.C., Denise Dade' Gallery, N.Y.C., Joseph Rickards Gallery, N.Y.C., Jim Goodman Gallery, N.Y.C.; exhibited in numerous group shows; represented in permanent collections, Albright Knox Mus., Dayton Art Inst., Met. Mus. Art, N.Y.C., Mus. Modern Art, New Sch. for Social Research, Phoenix Art Mus., U. Nebr., Walker Art Mus. Recipient Creative Arts award Brandeis U., 1978, Jimmy Ernest award in art Am. Acad. Arts and Letters, 2003; Trumbull Coll. fellow, 1996—; Guggenheim fellow, 1973. Mem. Nat. Acad. Design (coun.), Am. Acad. Letters. Home: PO Box 7582 Greenwich CT 06836-7582 Office: Yale U Sch Art York And Chapel St New Haven CT 06520

JOHNSON, LESTER LARUE, JR., artist, educator; b. Detroit, Sept. 28, 1937; s. Lester L. and Haroldine M. (Stanley) J. BFA, MFA, U. Mich. Prof. Coll. for Creative Studies, Detroit. Exhibitions include Whitney Mus. Art, Nat. Acad. Design, N.Y.C., Kalamazoo Inst. Arts, Mich., Saginaw Art Mus., Detroit Inst. Arts, Univ. Mich. Mus. Art, Ann Arbor, Centro de Memoria e Cultura dos Correios, Salvador, Bahia, Brazil, Detroit Pretty City at G.R. N'Namdi Gallery and the Univ. Cultural Assn., 2003, Klemm Gallery, Siena Heights U., Adrian, 2004, Buckham Gallery, Flint, 2005, Represented in permanent collections Osaka U. Arts, Japan, Mus. Afro-Brasileiro at Fed. U. of Bahia, Salvador, Brazil, Fed. Reserve Bk. Chgo., Detroit, U. Mich. Mus. Art, Ann Arbor, U. Mich. Cardiovascular Ctr., Dana-Farber Cancer Inst., Boston, prin. works include Bishop Internat. Airport, Flint, U. Mich. Mus. Art, Ann Arbor. Recipient John S. Newberry Purchase prize, 54th Exhibit Mich. Artists, Detroit Inst. Arts, 1964, recognition award African-Am. Music Festival; grantee Andrerw W. Mellon Found. Office: Coll for Creative Studies 201 E Kirby St Detroit MI 48202-4034 Office Phone: 313-664-7486. Business E-Mail: ljohnson@ccscad.edu.

JOHNSON, LINDA DIANE, environmental health specialist, biologist; b. Kans. City, Mar. 2, 1962; d. Leroy Thomas and Mary Louise Hargrave; m. John Robert Johnson, Jan. 2, 1990. BS in Biology, William Jewell Coll., Liberty, Mo., 1999; MS in Biology, Ctrl. Mo. State U., Warrensburg, Mo., 2001. Environ. health specialist Clinton County Health Dept., Plattsburg, Mo., 2001—03, Children's Mercy Hosp., Kans. City, 2003—. Cons. Healthy Homes Network, Kans. City, 2003—05. Contbr. articles to profl. jours. Mem.: Nat. Environ. Health Assn. Achievements include development of indoor environmental assessment protocols; intervention strategies for children with asthma. Home: 28216 NE 174th St Lawson MO 64062 Office: Children's Mercy Hosp 2401 Gillham Rd Kansas City MO 64108 Office Phone: 816-346-1301. Personal E-mail: ldjohnson_99_99@yahoo.com. Business E-Mail: ldjohnson@cmh.edu.

JOHNSON, LOLA NORINE, retired advertising and public relations executive, educator; b. Austin, Minn., Dec. 28, 1942; d. Alton E. and Evelyn M. (Quast) Milbrath; m. Dennis D. Johnson, June 15, 1963 (div. July 1973); children: Brenda J., Erik B. Attended, Coll. of St. Thomas. Pub. rels. account rep. Kerker & Assocs. Advt. and Pub. Rels., Bloomington, Minn., 1973-78; comm. mgr. Norwest Bank Mpls., 1978-83; dir. media rels., account supr. Edwin Neuger & Assocs. Pub. Rels., Mpls., 1983-85; v.p., mng. dir. The Richards Group, Mpls., 1985-86; owner, pres. PR Plus, Edina, Minn., 1986-2000; ret., 2000. Mem. cmty. faculty, instr., counselor Met. State U., Mpls., St. Paul, 1980-93. Cons. comm. United Way, Mpls., 1982. Recipient Gold award United Way Mpls., 1982. Home: 7151 York Ave S Apt 807 Minneapolis MN 55435-4435

JOHNSON, LORELEI MARIE, artist; b. Norwalk, Conn. d. Gordon Tingets and Mary Anna Buschbaum; children: Kristin Lorelei, Derosia, Frank. Student, Paier Coll. Art, Hamden, Conn., Post Coll., Waterbury, Conn., U. Conn., Waterbury; cert., Nat. Acad. Hairdressing, Norwalk, Conn. Freelance artist, Waterbury, 1955—2007. Hairdresser Marie's, Norwalk, 1967—2007; supr. Norwalk Factory Outlet, 1967—70; pres. Comprehensive Bus. Svc., Prospect, Conn., 1976—83; videographer Mark Johnson V. Deo, Waterbury, 1988—2000; set designer Briston Civic Theater, Conn., 1975—2004; router US Postal Svc., Waterbury, 1987—2007. Vol. numerous organizations, 1965—2007. Mem.: AFTRA, Nat. Assn. Letter Carriers, Soc. Poets. Roman Catholic. Avocations: dance, sailing, singing, art, theater. Home: 35 Gorman Cir Waterbury CT 06706

JOHNSON, LOUISE STREET, medical/surgical nurse; b. Prospect, Va., Jan. 25, 1934; d. George and Sarah Jane Street; widowed; 1 child, Desiree Dobbins. Student, U. DC, 1970, Prince George's C.C., Largo, Md., 1993—94. Lic. practical nurse, Md. Bd. Nursing. Staff nurse Washington Hosp., 1962—78, Knullwood Nursing Svc., Washington, 1980—94, Jay Bec Nurses Agy., Upper Marlboro, Md., 1994—. Staff nurse DC Human Resource Dept., 2007—. Mem.: Nat. Fedn. LPN Assn., LPN Assn. (life). Avocations: bowling, cooking, gardening, fishing. Home: 1403 Farmingdale Ave Capitol Heights MD 20743

JOHNSON, LOYD, agricultural engineer, researcher; b. Mar. 18, 1927; s. Iley Benford and Ruth (Humphrey) J.; m. Ester Banegas, Dec. 24, 1952; children: Theresa Ann, Thomas Patrick, Loyd Carl. BS, Auburn U., 1950, MS, 1954. Registered profl. engr., Calif. Sr. project engr. United Fruit Co., Tiquisate, Guatemala, La Lima, Honduras, Almirante, Panama, 1951—60; agrl. engr. Rockefeller Found., 1960-82; mem. rsch. staff Internat. Rice Rsch. Inst., Los Banos, Philippines, 1960-68, Centro Internacional de Agricultura Tropical, Cali, Columbia, 1968-77, Internat. Agrl. Devel. Svc., Guayaquil, Ecuador, 1977-81, Internat. Fertilizer Devel. Ctr., Florence, Ala., 1981-82. Cons. agrl. engr. Internat. Agrl. Devel. Svcs., Dhaka, Bangladesh, 1982-83, Bogor, Indonesia, 1984-85, WINROCK, Pyinmana, Myanmar, 1986-88, Islamabad, Pakistan, 1990, 94. With USNR, 1945-46. Mem. Am. Soc. Agrl. Engrs. (Kishida Internat. award), Indian Soc. Agrl. Engrs. (life), Bangladesh Soc. Agrl. Engrs. Roman Catholic. Achievements include development of agricultural experimental station fields and research support facilities. Home: 5371 Highway 67 S Ste 1 Somerville AL 35670-5893 Personal E-mail: stoutox@hiwaay.net.

JOHNSON, LUAN K., disaster management consultant; d. Jack R. and Colleen (Kesler) J. BA, Brigham Young U., 1981, MA, 1984; PhD, U. Wash., 1994. Dir. Tchg. Resource Ctr., Provo, 1980-84; tchg. asst. comms. dept. Brigham Young U., Provo, 1982-83; counselor Master Acad., Salt Lake City, 1985; ednl. designer, program mgr. City of Sunnyvale, 1986-90; tchg. asst., rsch. asst., speech comm. dept. U. Wash., Seattle, 1991-93; program mgr. City of Seattle, 1993—2005; program mgr. state of Wash. emergency mgmt. dir. SPAN disaster, svcs. a non-profit disaster preparedness & response orgn., 2004—; program mgr. Washington State Emergency Mgmt., 2005—. Recipient Best Ednl. Campaign award Internat. Assn. Emergency Mgrs., 1998, Nat. Coord. Coun. of Emergency Mgmt. Best Newsletter award, 1996, 98, 2002, 1st pl.-best ednl. campaign Internat. Assn. Emergency Mgrs., 1998, Outstanding Pub. Svc. award Seattle Police Dept., 1999, 1st pl.-best ednl. video Internat. Assn. Emergency Mgrs., 1999. Mem.: Phi Kappa Phi. Mem. Lds Ch. Avocation: collecting and flying kites. Home: 10018 Nineteenth Ave Ct S Parkland WA 98444

JOHNSON, MADGE RICHARDS, business owner, fundraiser, consultant, recruiter; b. Washington, Oct. 4, 1952; d. Benjamin Ellsworth and Virginia (Oliver) Richards; m. Jeffrey Leonard Johnson, June 25, 1977; children: Jared Benjamin, Jessica Lauren. B.S. in Bus. Mgmt., Strayer Coll., 1973; MBA Columbia Union Coll. 2004, Nat. govt. sales rep. G.F.C. Mfg. Co., Bklyn., 1972-75; ter. sales rep. John H. Breck, Am. Cyanamid, Wayne, N.J.; ter. sales mgr. Drackett Products Co., Cin., 1977-81, E.J. Brach & Sons., Chgo., Annapolis, Md., 1981-87, owner, pres. Madge Johnson Ltd., 1987—2007; sec.-treas. Recreation Environments Co., Annapolis, Md., 1988-90, recruiter, asst. dir. Columbia Union Coll. Takoma Park, Md., 1999—; recruiter Coll. So. Md., 2007—; treas. Martin Barr Sch., 1989-90 Mem. NAFE, Grocery Mfrs. Reps., Women in Consumer Product Sales. Home and Office: 17205 Magruders Ferry Rd Brandywine MD 20613-8358

JOHNSON, MAGIC (EARVIN JOHNSON JR.), professional sports team and development company executive, former professional basketball coach and player; b. Lansing, Mich., Aug. 14, 1959; s. Earvin and Christine Johnson; m. Earleatha "Cookie" Kelly, Sept. 1991; children: Earvin III, Elisa; 1 child, Andre. Student, Mich. State U., 1976-79. Basketball player LA Lakers, 1979—91, 1996, head coach, 1994, v.p., co-owner, 1994—; sportscaster NBC-TV, 1993-94; chmn., CEO Johnson Devel. Corp., 1993—; chmn. Magic Johnson Entertainment, Magic Johnson Productions & Magic Johnson Enterprises, 1997—; co-chmn. exec. steering com. for diversity NASCAR, 2004—; studio analyst TNT. Author: (autobiography) Magic, 1983; (with Roy S. Johnson) Magic's Touch, 1989; What You Can Do to Avoid AIDS, 1992; My Life, 1992. Established the Magic Johnson Found., 1991. Named Most Outstanding Player, NCAA Divsn. I Tournament, 1979, NBA Finals MVP, 1980, 1982, 1987, NBA MVP, 1987, 1989, 1990, NBA All-Star Game MVP, 1990, 1992, Player of Yr., Sporting News, 1987; named one of 50 Greatest Players in NBA History, 1996; named to All-NBA first team, 1983—91, All-NBA Second Team, 1982, NBA All-Rookie Team, 1980, NBA All-Star Team, 1980, 1982—92, Mich. State U. Athletics Hall of Fame, 1992, Naismith Meml. Basketball Hall of Fame, 2002; recipient All-Around Contributions to Team Success Award, IBM, 1984, Schick Pivotal Player Award, 1984, J. Walter Kennedy Citizenship Award, NBA, 1992, Most Influential Black Americans, Ebony mag., 2006. Achievements include being mem. of NCAA Championship Team, 1979, NBA Championship Team, 1980, 82, 85, 87, 88, US Olympic Basketball gold medal winning team, 1992; chosen first overall in 1979 NBA Draft; holder of career record for highest assists-per-game avg. (11.2), career playoff record for most assists (2346), NBA Finals single-series record for highest assists-per-game avg. (14.0), 1985, NBA Finals single-series highest assists-per-game avg. by a rookie (8.7), 1980, NBA Finals single-game record for most points by rookie (42), 1980. Office: Johnson Devel Corp & Magic Johnson Found 9100 Wilshire Blvd Beverly Hills CA 90212-3415

JOHNSON, MANUEL HOLMAN, JR., government official, economics educator, business executive; b. Troy, Ala., Feb. 10, 1949; s. Manuel Holman and Ethel Lorraine (Jordan) J.; m. Mary Lois Wilkerson, June 10, 1972; children: Marshall, Merritt Student, U. Ala., 1967-68; BS in Econ., cum laude, Troy State U., 1973; MS, Fla. State U., 1974, PhD, 1977; doctorate (hon.), Troy State U., 1986. Instr. econs. Fla. State U., Tallahassee, 1975-76; asst. prof. econs. George Mason U., Fairfax, Va., 1977-79, assoc. prof. econs., 1979-81; dep. asst. sec. U.S. Dept. Treasury, Washington, 1981-82, asst. sec., 1982-86; vice chmn. Fed. Res. Bank, Washington, 1986-90; Koch prof. internat. econs., dir. Ctr. Global Market Studies George Mason U., Fairfax, 1990-94; co-chmn., sr. ptnr. Johnson Smick Internat., Inc., Washington, 1990—. Bd. dirs. NASDQ Stock Market, Dean Witter Intercapital Funds Group, Greenwich Capital Markets, Inc., NVR, Inc.; mem. Pres.'s Commn. on Indian Econs., 1983-84; mem. Nunn Domenici Commn. on Strengthening Am., 1993-94. Co-author: Political Economy of Federal Government Growth, 1980, Better Government at Half Price, 1981, Deregulating Labor Relations, 1981; assoc. editor Jour. Labor Rsch., 1979-81; mem. editorial bd. The Internat. Economy mag., 1990—; contbr. articles to profl. jours. Mem. Scholars for Reagan, L.A.,

1980; chmn. treasury United Way Campaign, 1983. Served with U.S. Army, 1968-71. Recipient Alumnus of Yr. award Troy State U., 1982, Alexander Hamilton award U.S. Treasury Dept., 1986; U.S. NRC fellow, 1975, Coll. Soc. Sci. Disting. Alum. award, FSU, 2003. Mem. Am. Econ. Assn., Western Econ. Assn., So. Econ., Assn. Pub. Choice Soc., Regional Sci. Assn., Fin. Acctg. Found. (pres., bd. trustees, 1997-2003) Republican. Presbyterian. Home: 1770 Delaplane Grade Rd Upperville VA 20184-1916

JOHNSON, MARC ROBERT, music educator, director; s. Verne M. and Karen C. Johnson; m. Darcy Lynn Mueller. MusB in Edn., U. Wis., Stevens Point, 1993. Dir. band White Lake Sch. Dist., Wis., 1994—95, Madison LaFollette H.S., Wis., 1995—99, Berlin H.S., Wis., 1999—2005, Wautoma H.S., Wis., 2005—. Dir. stage band tour Kids from Wis., Milw., 1999—2002; coach football White Lake H.S., 1995; coach wrestling Madison LaFollette H.S., 1996—99, coach football, 1998—99, Berlin H.S., 2004, coach wrestling, 2000—05; coach football Wautoma Mid. Sch., Wis., 2005, Wautoma H.S., 2006—. Musician: River Cities Jazz. Avocations: music, hunting, fishing, travel. Home Phone: 920-361-3480; Office Phone: 920-787-3354 1056.

JOHNSON, MARGARET ANDERSON, writer, publishing and agricultural products executive; b. Knoxville, Tenn., Apr. 19, 1927; d. Samuel Waller and Laura Lewis (Lawhon) Anderson; m. Thomas Carlisle Johnson, Jan. 9, 1949; children: James Scott, Wendy, Laura Lynn. Student, U. Tenn. and U. Fla., 1945—49. Writer, artist Water Oak Pub., Tallahassee, pub., 1990—. Author, illustrator: Berber, A Lamb's Tale, 1998, Revelation is Not a Mystery: A Guide for Teaching the Book of Revelation to Youth, 2007. Past pres. Ednl. TV Coun., Tampa, Tampa Jr. Women's Club; past advisor parliamentary procedure Jr. League of Tallahassee; past v.p. Christian Women's Club, Tampa; past pres. PTA; tchr. Sunday sch. First Bapt. Ch., Tampa, Fla.; tchr. Sunday sch. Tallahassee Bible Ch., 1950—2002; tchr. Sunday sch. Grace Ch., Christ Cmty. Ch., Tampa, Bayshore Bapt. Ch., Grace Ch. of Tallahassee, Tallahassee Buible Ch.; writer, illustrator Sunday sch. materials. Named Most Outstanding Sustainer, Jr. League, Tallahassee, 1989. Mem.: Alpha Omicron Pi (alumni chpt. pres., Tampa 1952). Republican. Avocations: painting, writing, horseback riding, providing a haven for needy animals. Home and Office: Water Oak Pub 2984 Water Oak Plantation Rd Tallahassee FL 32312 Personal E-mail: majwopub@yahoo.com.

JOHNSON, MARGARET ANN (PEGGY), library administrator; b. Atlanta, Aug. 11, 1948; d. Odell H. and Virginia (Mathiasen) Johnson; m. Lee J. English, Mar. 4, 1978; children: Carson J., Amelia J. BA, St. Olaf Coll., 1970; MA, U. Chgo., 1972; MBA, Met. State U., 1990. Music cataloger U. Iowa Librs., Iowa City, 1972-73; analyst Control Data Corp., Bloomington, Minn., 1973-75; br. libr. St. Paul Pub. Librs., 1975-77; head tech. svcs. St. Paul Campus Librs., U. Minn., 1977-86; collection devel. officer Univ. Librs., U. Minn., Mpls., 1987-90; asst. dir. St. Paul Campus Librs., U. Minn., 1987-95; planning officer U. Librs. U. Minn., Mpls., 1993-97, asst. univ. libr., 1997—2003, interim univ. libr., 2002, assoc. univ. libr., 2003—. Libr. cons. Mekerere U., Kampala, Uganda, 1990, U. Nat. Rwanda, 1990, Inst. Agr. and Vet. Hassan II, Rabat, Morocco, 1992—2000, Ecole Nat. Agr., Meknes, Morocco, 2000, China Agrl. U., Beijing, 2001—, Xi'an Eurasia U., Xi'an, China, 2005. Author: Automation and Organizational Change in Libraries, 1991, The Searchable Internet, 1996, Fundamentals of Collection Development and Management, 2004; editor: New Directions in Technical Services, 1997; editor Technicalities Jour., 2000—, Libr. Resources and Tech. Svcs., 2003—; editor Guide to Tech. Svcs. Resources, 1994, Recruiting, Educating and Tng. Librarians for Collection Devel., 1994, Collection Mgmt. and Devel., 1994, Virtually Yours, 1998; contbr. articles to profl. jours. Recipient Samuel Lazerow Rsch. fellowship Assn. Coll. and Rsch. Librs., Inst. for Sci. Info., 1987; Blackwell scholar Assn. for Libr. Collections and Tech. Svcs., 2005. Mem. ALA, Internat. Assn. Agrl. Librs. and Documentatists, U.S. Agrl. Info. Network, Assn. for Libr. Collections and Tech. Svcs. (pres. 1999-2000, 50th Ann. Presdl. citation 2007). Office: U of Minn Librs 499 Wilson Libr 309 19th Ave S Minneapolis MN 55455-0438 Office Phone: 612-624-2312. Business E-Mail: m-john@umn.edu.

JOHNSON, MARGARET HELLER, artist, educator; d. Henry and Elsie Heller; children: Kimberly Lauder, Adrienne. BA in Edn., U. Del., Newark, 1965. Cert. tchr. Del. Tchr. Wesley Presch., Dover, Del., 1979—85; art educator Capital Sch. Dist., Dover, 1985—. Contbr. art to profl. publs.; exhibitions include Del. Mus. Contemporary Art, Briggs Mus. Am. Art, Rehobeth Art League, Del. Women's Conf. Handmade paper demonstrator Winterthur Mus., Wilmington, Del., 2005, mem. tchr.'s adv. bd., 1997—; handmade paper demonstrator Lewes Hist. Soc., Del.; pres. Littleton Hosp. Aux., NH, 1974—76; mem. Del. Art Mus., Dover, 1991—2006. Excellence In Edn. grantee, MBNA, 2003. Mem.: Capital Educators Assn. (mem. exec. bd. 2001—). Home Phone: 302-674-4550.

JOHNSON, MARGUERITE ANNIE *See* **ANGELOU, MAYA**

JOHNSON, MARIE-LOUISE TULLY, dermatologist, educator; b. NYC, July 26, 1927; d. James Henry and Mary Frances (Dobbins) Tully; m. Kenneth Gerald Johnson, June 10, 1950. AB, Manhattanville Coll., 1948; PhD, Yale U., 1954, MD, 1956. Intern, then resident Yale-New Haven Med. Ctr., 1956-59; asst. prof. medicine, dermatology Yale U., 1961-67, clin. prof. dermatology, 1980—; chief dermatologist med. svc. Atomic Bomb Casualty Commn., Hiroshima, Japan, 1964-67; assoc. prof. dermatology NYU, 1967-70, 74-76, prof. dermatology, 1976-80; assoc. prof. dermatology, coord. continuing med. edn. Dartmouth Coll., Hanover, NH, 1971-74; chief dermatology Bellevue Hosp., NYC, 1974-80; dir. med. edn. Benedictine Hosp., Kingston, NY, 1980-93. Cons. Health and Nutrition Exam. Survey I, II, Health Stats., Washington, 1967-84. Contbg. author: Cecil's Textbook of Medicine, 15th edit., 1979, 16th edit., 1982, 17th edit., 1985, Dermatology in General Medicine, 2d edit., 1979. Mem. Cardinal Cooke Pro-Life Commn., Albany, N.Y., 1986-87; bd. dirs. Maternity and Early Childhood Found., Albany, 1984-2001, pres., 1987-2001; bd. dirs. Sulzberger Inst. for Dermatologic Edn., 1986-93; pres. Mid-Hudson Consortium for the Advancement of Edn. for Health Professions, 1989-92; bd. govs. Yale U. Alumni Assn., 1991-94; v.p. Assn. Yale U. Alumni in Medicine, 1991-93, pres., 1993-95. Named Disting. Alumna, Manhattanville Coll., 1977, Rose Hirschler award Women's Dermatologic Soc., 1993, Papal Cross Pro Ecclesia et Pontifice Pope John Paul II, 1994, Clark W. Finnerud award Dermatology Found., 1997. Fellow Am. Acad. Dermatology (master 1995, bd. dirs. 1976-80, Presdl. citation 1999); mem. Am. Dermatol. Assn. (bd. dirs. 1986-92, v.p. 1991-92, pres. 2000-01), Inst. Medicine of NAS, Internat. Physicians for Prevention of Nuc. War (del. 1982, 83, 87, 88, 89). Roman Catholic. Home: 15 Strawberry Bank Rd High Falls NY 12440-5128 Office: Kingston Hosp Med Arts Bldg Ste 202 368 Broadway Kingston NY 12401-5159 Home Phone: 845-687-0404; Office Phone: 845-338-7472.

JOHNSON, MARILYN, retired obstetrician, gynecologist; b. Houston, May 7, 1925; d. William Walton and Marilyn (Henderson) J. BA, Rice Inst., 1945; MD, Baylor U., Waco, Tex., 1950. Intern New Eng. Hosp. Women and Children, Boston, 1950—51; resident Meth. Hosp., Houston, 1951—53; fellow in gynecol. pathology Harvard Med. Sch., 1952—53; resident in gynecology M.D. Anderson Tumor Inst., Houston, 1954, fellow, 1955; practice medicine specializing in ob-gyn. Houston, 1954—81, Fredericksburg, Tex., 1981—97; ret., 1997. Mem. staffs St. Joseph's, Meml., Meth., Park Plaza, Hill Country Meml. Rosewood, South Austin Cmty., Comfort Cmty. hosps., Tex.; clin. instr. ob-gyn Coll. Medicine, Baylor U., 1954—, Postgrad. Sch. Medicine, U. Tex., 1954—; gynecologist De Pelchin Faith Home, Houston, 1954—, also Rice U., Richmond State Sch.; med. dirs. Birthright, Inc., Houston, 1973—; chief med. staff Hill Country Meml. Hosp., Fredericksburg, Tex., 1990-92; cons. Tex. bd. Blue Cross Blue Shield; pro-life public spkr. Bd. dirs. Right to Life, Houston, Found. for Life. Grantee Sandoz Labs., 1973, 75, Delbay Pharm. Co., 1977. Fellow Am. Coll. Obstetricians and Gynecologists; mem. AMA, Am. Soc. Colposcopic Pathologists, Tex. Med. Assn., Am. Med. Women's Assn., Internat. Infertility Assn., Harris County Med. Soc., Postgrad. Med. Assembly South Tex., Houston Ob-Gyn. Soc., Tex. Folklore Soc., Zonta, Fredericksburg Rockhounds. Republican. Baptist. Home: 10022 Briar Forest Houston TX 77042

JOHNSON, MARK ALAN, lawyer; b. Marysville, Ohio, June 5, 1960; s. Neil Raymond and Elizabeth Johnson; m. Deborah Anne Hillis, Sept. 21, 1984. BA, Otterbein Coll., 1982; JD, Ohio State U., 1985. Bar: Ohio 1985, U.S. Dist. Ct. (so. dist.) Ohio 1985, U.S. Ct. Appeals (6th cir.) 1987, U.S. Dist. Ct. (no. dist.) Ohio 1991, U.S. Ct. Appeals (5th cir.) 1998. Assoc. Baker and Hostetler LLP, Columbus, Ohio, 1985-92, ptnr., 1993—. Named one of Ohio's Super Lawyers, 2005, 2007. Mem. ABA (litigation sect., mem. bus. torts litigation com., comml. and banking litigation com.), Ohio Bar Assn., Columbus Bar Assn. Office: Baker & Hostetler LLP 65 E State St Ste 2100 Columbus OH 43215-4215 Office Phone: 614-228-1541. Business E-Mail: mjohnson@bakerlaw.com.

JOHNSON, MARK ANDREW, lawyer; b. Plainville, Kans., Feb. 27, 1959; s. Delton Lee and Margaret Ellen (McCracken) J. BA in Chemistry, Reed Coll., 1982; JD, U. Calif., Berkeley, 1987. Bar: Oreg. 1987, U.S. Supreme Ct. 1991. Jud. clk. U.S. Dist. Ct. Oreg., Portland, 1987-88, Oreg. Ct. of Appeals, Salem, 1988-89; assoc. Gevurtz, Menashe, Larson, Kurshner & Yates, PC, Portland, 1989-93; ptnr. Findling & Johnson LLP, Portland, 1993-99; of counsel Bennett Hartman Morris & Kaplan, LLP and predecessor, Portland, 1999—. Mem. ABA, Nat. Lesbian and Gay Law Assn. (co-chmn. 1994-95), Oreg. Gay and Lesbian Law Assn. (co-chair 1990-92), Oreg. State Bar (pres. 1998-99). Home: 516 SE Morrison St Ste 420 Portland OR 97214-2344 E-mail: johnsonm@bennetthartman.com.

JOHNSON, MARK EUGENE, lawyer; b. Independence, Mo., Jan. 8, 1951; s. Russell Eugene and Reatha (Nixon) J.; m. Vicki Ja Lane, June 11, 1983. AB with honors, U. Mo., 1973, JD, 1976. Bar: Mo. 1976, U.S. Dist. Ct. (we. dist.) Mo. 1976, U.S. Ct. Appeals (8th cir.) 1984, U.S. Supreme Ct. 1993. Ptnr. Stinson Morrison Hecker LLP, Kansas City, Mo., 1976—. Editor Mo. Law Rev., 1974-76. Pres. Lido Villas Assn., Inc., Mission, Kans., 1979-81. Mem. ABA, Mo. Bar Assn., Kansas City Bar Assn., Lawyers Assn. Kansas City, Def. Rsch. Inst., Internat. Assn. Def. Counsel, Mo. Orgn. Def. Lawyers, Carriage Club, Order of Coif, Phi Beta Kappa, Phi Eta Sigma, Phi Kappa Phi, Omicron Delta Kappa. Republican. Presbyterian. Home: 4905 Somerset Dr Shawnee Mission KS 66207-2230 Office: Stinson Morrison Hecker LLP 1201 Walnut St Ste 2900 Kansas City MO 64106-2150 Office Phone: 816-691-2724. Office Fax: 816-412-1208. Business E-Mail: mjohnson@stinson.com.

JOHNSON, MARK MATTHEW, museum administrator; b. Dec. 10, 1950; s. Charles Michael Jr. and Jean Lee (Reid) J.; m. Amy Joy Schneider, March 10, 1984; children: Rachel Amelia, Sarah Jean. BA, U. Wis., Whitewater, 1974; cert. Art Mus. Studies, U. Ill., 1976, MA in Art History, 1976. Rsch. assoc. Krannert Art Mus., Champaign, Ill., 1975, asst. dir., curator, 1981-85; lectr. dept. mus. edn. Art Inst. Chgo., 1975-77; curator dept. art history and edn. Cleve. Mus. Art, 1977-81; dir. Muscarelle Mus. Art. Coll. William and Mary, Williamsburg, Va., 1985-94; lect. dept. fine arts Coll. William and Mary, 1985-94; dir. Montgomery (Ala.) Mus. Fine Arts, 1994—. Author: Idea to Image: Preparatory Studies from the Renaissance to Impressionism, 1980, Romeyn de Hooghe, 1989, Literacy Through Art, 1990, Nissan Engel: Nouvelles Dimensions, 1994, Hans Grohs: An Ecstatic Vision, 1996, (English and French edits.) Nissan Engel, 1998, Ginny Ruffner, 2003, American Painting Collection: Montgomery Museum of Fine Arts, 2006, Cappy Thompson, 2006, Sonja Blomdahl, 2007; organized, curated numerous exhbns., 1980—. Rsch. and travel grantee various mus. Mem. Assn. Art Mus. Dirs., Internat. Coun. Mus., Coll. Art Assn., Am. Assn. Mus. (accreditation com.). Office: Montgomery Mus Fine Arts PO Box 230819 One Museum Dr Montgomery AL 36123-0819 Business E-Mail: mjohnson@mmfa.org.

JOHNSON, MARK P., lawyer; b. Billings, Mont., Aug. 14, 1955; BA cum laude, Yale U., 1977; JD, Harvard U., 1980. Bar: Mo. 1980, US Dist. Ct. We. Dist. Mo. 1980, US. Ct. Appeals 10th Cir. 1982, US Ct. Appeals 8th Cir. 1982, US Supreme Ct. 1985. Ptnr. Spencer Fane Britt & Browne, Kansas City, Mo., 1987—94, Sonnenschein Nath & Rosenthal LLP, Kansas City, Mo., 1994—. Counsel Am. Strokes Found. Mem.: ABA, Racial Justice Collaborative, Kansas City Met. Bar Assn., Mo. Bar, Assn. Yale Alumni. Office: Sonnenschein Nath & Rosenthal LLP Ste 1100 4520 Main St Kansas City MO 64111 Office Phone: 816-460-2424. Office Fax: 816-531-7545. Business E-Mail: mjohnson@sonnenschein.com.

JOHNSON, MARLENE M., educational association administrator; b. Braham, Minn., Jan. 11, 1946; d. Beauford and Helen (Nelson) J.; m. Peter Frankel. BA, Macalester Coll., 1968. Founder, pres. Split Infinitive, Inc., St. Paul, 1970—82; pres., bd. dirs. Face to Face Health and Counseling Clinic, 1977—78; with Working Opportunities for Women, 1977—82; lt. gov. State of Minn., St. Paul, 1983—91; sr. fellow Ctr. for Policy Alternative Family Support Project, 1991—93; assoc. adminstr. for adminstrn. GSA, Washington, 1994—95; v.p. people and strategy Rowe Furniture Corp., McLean, Va., 1995—97; exec. dir., CEO NAFSA: Assn. Internat. Educators, Washington, 1998—. Founder, past chmn. Nat. Leadership Conf. Women Execs. in State Govt.; mem. exec. com., midwestern chair Nat. Conf. Lt. Govs.; bd. dirs. AFS-USA, Inc., 1992-98, Nat. Capitol Region coun. Girl Scouts US, 1997-2004, bd. trustees AFS Internat. progs., 1998-2002; mem. adv. bd. Comm. Consortium Media Ctr., 2000-, Ctr. Children in Poverty, Columbia U., 2002. Chmn. Minn. Women's Polit. Caucus, 1973-76, Dem.-Farmer-Labor Small Bus. Task Force, 1978, Child Care Task Force, 1987; dir. membership sect. Nat. Women's Polit. Caucus, 1975-77; vice chmn. Minn. Del. to White House Conf. on Small Bus., 1980; co-founder Minn. Women's Campaign Fund, 1982; bd. dirs. Nat. Child Care Action Campaign; chair Children's 2000 Commn., 1990; candidate for Mayor St. Paul, 1993. Recipient Outstanding Achievement award St. Paul YWCA, 1980, Disting. Svc. award St. Paul Jaycees, 1980, Disting. Citizen citation Macalester Coll., 1982, Disting. Contbns. to Families award Minn. Coun. on Family Rels., 1986, Minn. Sportfishing Congress award, 1986, Royal Order of Polar Star Govt. Sweden, 1988, Children's Champion award Def. Fund, 1989, Jane Preston award Minn. State Coun. Vocat. Tech. Edn., 1989, Legis. Leadership award Am. Fedn. Tchrs., 1991; named One of Ten Outstanding Young Minnesotans, Minn. Jaycees, 1980; Swedish Bicentennial Commn. grantee, 1987. Mem. Nat. Assn. Women Bus. Owners (past pres.). Office: NAFSA Assn Internat Educators 1307 New York Ave NW 8th Fl Washington DC 20005-4701 Office Phone: 202-737-3699 ext. 209. E-mail: marlenej@nafsa.org.*

JOHNSON, MARSHALL HARDY, investment company executive; b. Raleigh, NC, Sept. 7, 1923; s. William Thompson and Evie (Barnes) J.; m. Mary Lynn Lewis, June 24, 1947 (div. 1977); children: Marshall Hardy, Lynn Lewis Johnson-Titchener, Carter Johnson Overton; m. Beverly Ray Johnson, June 2, 1984. Student, U. N.C., 1942—43, student, 1945—46; grad. in banking, U. Pa., 1957. Reporter, analyst Dunn & Bradstreet, Raleigh, 1946-47; chmn., pres., CEO McDaniel Lewis & Co., Greensboro, NC, 1947—; v.p. Scott & Stringfellow, Inc., Richmond, Va., 1993-96. Mem. Midwest Stock Exch., Chgo., 1960-77; chmn., dir. emeritus First Citizen Bank & Trust, Greensboro, Mcpl. Coun., Raleigh; adv. dir. Friends Home, 1985-93; freelance writer. Contbr. articles to profl. jours. Dir. Young Dems., Greensboro, 1962-66, Jr. C. of C., Greensboro, 1964-70; deacon, tchr. First Bapt. Ch., Greensboro. With USNR, 1942-46. Fellow: Fin. Fedn. Am.; mem.: Securities Dealers of Carolinas (pres. 1976), Securities Industries Assn. (Mid-Atlantic exec. com. 1986—93), Nat. Assn. Securities Dealers, Am. Arbitration Assn., Greensboro Country Club, Kiwanis (Hixon award 1998), Odd Fellows, Magna Charta Barons, VFW, Alpha Tau Omega. Avocations: tennis, golf, swimming. Home: 310 Kimberly Dr Greensboro NC 27408-5018 Office: McDaniel Lewis & Co PO Box 9 Greensboro NC 27402-0009 E-mail: zipjohnson@triad.rr.com. *I've learned that our quality of life is largely determined by our own choices.*

JOHNSON, MARTHA (MARTY) JUNK (MARTY JOHNSON), psychology professor; b. Dayton, Ohio, May 10, 1951; d. William Martin and Frances Smith Junk; m. John Morgan Gerhold, Feb. 14, 2001; m. John Charles Nemeth, Nov. 24, 1973 (div. Mar. 1, 1984); children: John Christian Nemeth, Megan Jeannette Nemeth, Ashley Jane Nemeth. BA in Sociology, Denison U., Granville, Ohio, 1973; MS in Counselor Edn., U. Dayton, Ohio, 1993; PhD in Ednl. Psychology, Capella U., Mpls., 2005. Cert. profl. counselor Counselor, Social Worker, Marriage & Family Therapist Bd. Ohio, 2003. Counselor trainee Dublin Counseling Ctr., Ohio, 1993; psychometrist Thelma White & Assocs., Worthington, Ohio, 1997—98; psychology asst. Xavier U., Cin., 1997—98, Cmty. Diagnostic and Treatment Ctr., Cin., 1998—99; adj. prof. psychology Columbus Coll. Art and Design, 2001—. Mem.: ACA. Avocations: running, travel, cooking, reading. Home: 8686 Caldwell Dr Westerville OH 43082 Office: Columbus Coll Art & Design 107 N Ninth St Columbus OH 43215 Home Phone: 614-899-6918; Office Phone: 614-437-2380. E-mail: johnsonmrgn@aol.com.

JOHNSON, MARTIN ALLEN, publishing executive, artist; b. Bklyn., Aug. 20, 1931; s. Ellis A. and Estelle (Rudnick) Johnson; m. Suzanne Cornbleet, Dec. 12, 1964 (div. Feb. 1979); 1 child, Sarah; m. Diane Schlesinger Krull, Aug. 19, 1981. AB, Bard Coll., 1954. Assoc. editor Am. Printer and Lithographer mag., NYC, 1956-57, mng. editor, 1957-58, editor, 1958; mng. editor Printing Impressions mag., Phila., Delaware Valley Printing Impressions, 1958-61; pub. PTM mag., Chgo., 1959-67; v.p. Ednl. Screen and Audio Visual Guide, Chgo., 1962-67; pres. Trade Periodical Co., Chgo., 1967—, Pub. Dynamics, Inc., Stamford, Conn., 1968—, U.S. Indsl. Publs., Inc., Stamford, 1971—, U.S. Graphics Corp., Stamford, 1974—, Landmark Comms. Corp., Stamford. Spl. cor. Sun-Sentinal, Chgo. Tribune. Contbr. articles to profl. jours. With US Army, 1954—56. Recipient Justin P. Allman award, Wallcoverings Assn., 1993. Mem.: ArtSource, Cornell Mus. Art Guild, Fla. Watercolor Soc., Boca Raton Mus. Artist Guild (profl.), Am. Watercolor Soc. (sustaining), Am. Soc. Interior Designers, Typophiles (N.Y.C.), Norton Mus. Art, Am. Music Libr. Israel, Wellington Club (London), Landmark Club (Stamford), Exec. Club (Chgo.), Chgo. Press Club. Jewish. Avocations: poetry, objective biblical history, painting. Office: 9506 Lantern Bay Cir West Palm Beach FL 33411 Office Phone: 561-204-3883. Personal E-mail: mjtalk2me@aol.com.

JOHNSON, MARY ELIZABETH, musician, educator; b. Tyler, Tex., Mar. 29, 1933; d. Robert Edward and Mamie Oberia (Walters) Spaulding; m. George Devereaux Johnson, Mar. 31, 1955; children: Bradford D., Robin Elizabeth. BFA, So. Meth. U., 1955; pvt. studies with Bomar Cramer, Dallas, 1964—69. Music tchr. Dallas Country Day Sch., 1955; tchr. Dayton Pub. Schs., Ohio, 1956—57; pvt. tchr. piano Dallas, 1962—; profl. accompanist, 1985—; duo-pianist, 1965—; sponsor, tchr. creative and performing arts program Dallas Ind. Sch. Dist., 1981—82, 1983, 1984. Sponsor Jr. Melodie and Jr. Harmonie. Named to Hall of Fame, Am. Coll. Musicians, 1981. Mem. Nat. Guild Piano Tchrs. (cert., named to honor roll 1971, chmn. auditions Dallas chpt. 2007—), Tex. Fedn. Music Clubs (historian 1974-76, state chmn. music svc. in cmty. 1971-73, dist. jr. counselor 1971-78, dist. chmn. music svc. in cmty. 1971-78, rec. sec. 5th dist. 1975-76, 1st v.p. 1977-78, jr. festival chmn. 1977-80, dist chmn. Jr. Gold Cup awards 1980, 84, 85, 86, 87, 88, asst. chmn. North Dallas divsn. 5th dist. jr. festival 1981-82), Music Tchrs. Nat. Assn., Jr. Pianists Guild Dallas (chmn. jr. recitals 1983, chmn. sr. recitals 1984, treas. 2003-2005), Tex. Music Tchrs. Assn., Dallas Music Tchrs. Assn., Van Katwijk Club (tchr. mem.), Music Study Club Dallas (chmn. piano program 1981-82), Dallas Fedn. Music Clubs (del. 1969-78, 1st v.p. 1977), Daus. Republic Tex. (1st v.p. Bonham chpt. 1975-76), Melodie Club (pres. 1969-71, 2d v.p. 1977-78, 2007-, 1st v.p. 2003-04, 2005-06, choral accompanist 2005-, counselor jr. club, historian, press sec. 1981-82, 1st v.p. 2003-2004, 2004—), Kalista Club (yearbook chmn. 1983-2000, v.p. 1984-85, pres. 1986-87), Park Cities Club, Tower Club, Kermis Club, Rondo-Carrousel Club, Trippers Club, Steinway Hall's Ptnrs. in Performance, Alpha Delta Pi, Mu Phi Epsilon (patron). Methodist. Home: 3848 Cedarbrush Dr Dallas TX 75229-2701

JOHNSON, MARY ELIZABETH, lawyer; b. Rome, NY, July 2, 1970; d. Stewart William and Helen Anna Richards; m. Ernest John Johnson, Sept. 26, 1998; children: Cassandra Lynn, Connor Alan. BA, SUNY, Geneseo, 1992; JD, Touro Coll., Huntington, NY, 1998. Law clk. Hon. David N. Hurd US Dist. Ct., Utica, NY, 1998—2001; atty. Getnick Law Firm, Utica, NY, 2001—. Coach New Hartford Pop Warner, NY, 2006—07. Mem.: Ctrl. NY Bankruptcy Bar Assn., NY State Bar Assn., Oneida County Bar Assn. Avocations: bicycling, pilates. Home: 3460 Mohawk St Sauquoit NY 13456 Office: Getnick law firm 258 Genesee St Utica NY 13502 Home Phone: 315-737-9859; Office Phone: 315-797-9261. Office Fax: 315-732-0755.

JOHNSON, MARY LOU, lay worker, educator; b. Moline, Ill., July 15, 1923; d. Percy and Hope (Aulgur) Sipes; m. Blaine Eugene Johnson, May 30, 1941 (dec.); children: Vivian Johnson Sweedy Maday, Michael D. (dec.), Amelia Johnson Harms Thomas, James Michael (dec.). From chmn. Christian edn. to dir. 1st Christian Ch., Moline, 1971—88, dir. Christian edn., 1988—93, ret., 1993, chmn. Christian edn., 2001—03. Author: (poem) What Is A Mother?, 1965. Officer various positions PTA, Moline, 1972-75, hon. life mem. State of Ill., 1972; leader, dist. chair Girl Scouts U.S., Moline, 1955-65; skywatcher USAF Ground Observer Corps, Moline, 1955-57; vol. telethon coord. Muscular Dystrophy Assn., Moline, 1971-94; del. lt. gov.'s Commn. on Aging, Springfield, Ill., 1990; historian 1st Christian Ch., Moline, 1996—, libr., 2000—; vol. C.A.R.E. Ministry, 1999-05, Ring for Care Ministry, 1999-05, We. Ill. Area Agy. on Aging, 1998-03; bd. dirs. Wee Care Day Care Ctr., 2003-06; chmn. 100th Birthday Celebration, First Christian Ch., Moline, 2004-06; Bible study tchr., 2001-; Sunday sch. tchr. 1st Christian Ch., Moline, 1958-84; cluster del. Christian Chs. Ill. and Wisc., Moline, 1988-89. Recipient Appreciation award Muscular Dystrophy Assn., 1964-94. Republican. Home: 2014 9th St Moline IL 61265-4779 Personal E-mail: grmalou624@aol.com. *Life hands us many challenges. I find them interesting and always have been willing to accept them. Not all my efforts have been successful; however, each attempt has helped me grow to be a better person.*

JOHNSON, MARY MARGARET DICKENS, governmental and commercial researcher, consultant; b. Ottumwa, Iowa, July 10, 1955; d. Donald Milton and Maxine Margaret Dickens; m. Donald Hampton Johnson, July 30, 1944; children: Laurie Anne Davidson, Donald, Jr. Hampton. M, U. Hawaii, 1979; B, Iowa State U., 1976; M, Johns Hopkins Sch. Advanced Internat. Studies, 1986; postgrad. in pub. admin., Fla. Atlantic U., 2003—. Cert. purchasing mgr., cert. profl. contracts mgr., scuba diver 1974. Lab. asst. dept. entomology Iowa State U., Ames, 1973—74, rsch. asst. dept. sociology & anthropology, 1974—76; rsch. grantee East West Ctr., Honolulu, 1976—78; fgn. affairs specialist US Dept. State/AID, Washington, 1980—81; fed. summer intern Nat. Telecom. and Info. Adminstrn. US

Dept. Commerce, Washington, 1980—80, export adminstrn. specialist, 1982—85; English lang. tchr. INTERAC, Tokyo, 1985; tchr., pub. rels. officer Overseas Devel. Co., Kowloon, Hong Kong, 1986—87; English lang. tchr. Phillips Lang. Learning Systems, Tokyo, 1986; contract specialist US GSA, Washington, 1987—94, Wash. Suburban San. Commn., Laurel, Md., 1996—97; sr. contracts mgr. Systems Flow, Inc., Rockville, Md., 1997—98; with HSI Geotrans, Sterling, Va., 1997; grad. asst. Fla. Atlantic U., Ft. Lauderdale, 2003—04; rsch. fellow Broward Sheriff's Ofrfice, 2005—06. Leader workshops and seminars; presenter in field. Contbr. articles and book revs. to profl. jours. Mem. CARE Women's Group; active St. James Fisherman Episc. Ch., Islamorada, Fla., 2000—; mem. altar guild St. Albans Anglican Ch., Tokyo, 1985; mem. edn. for ministry St. Patrick's Episcopal Ch., Falls Church, Va., 1995—96. Home Fellowship, Truro Episcopal Ch. Fellow: Nat. Contract Mgmt. Assn. (cert. profl. contracts mgr. 2002, cert. assoc. contracts mgr. 2002, pres. South Fla. chpt. 2003—04, cert. fed. contract mgr. 2006, grant to participate in World Congress 2002); mem.: Nat. Assn. Purchasing Mgmt. (workshop leader 2002), Alpha Chi Omega. Avocations: bicycling, walking, needlepoint, cooking, gardening. Home: 1926 NE 2nd St Deerfield Beach FL 33441 Office: Florida Atlantic U 111 East Las Olas Blvd Fort Lauderdale FL 33301 Office Phone: 954-429-9019. Personal E-mail: conchcontracts@aol.com. Business E-Mail: mjohn110@fau.edu.

JOHNSON, MARY PAULINE (POLLY JOHNSON), nursing administrator; b. Ohio, May 23, 1940; BSN summa cum laude, Ohio State U., 1962; MSN, Duke U., 1980. RN NC. Staff nurse psychiatry unit Univ. Hosps., Ohio, 1963-64; pediatric office nurse Gaithersburg, Md., 1971-73; clin. nurse coord. N.C. Meml. Hosp., Chapel Hill, 1973-86; grant coord. N.C. Assn. Home Care, 1988; practice cons. N.C. Bd. Nursing, Raleigh, 1988-96, assoc. dir. practice, 1996-97, exec. dir., 1997—. Mem. bd. trustees N.C. Ctr. for Hosp. quality and Patient Safety. Chair NC Found. for Nursing Excellence, 2002—. Fellow: Am. Acad. Nursing; mem.: ANA, NC Inst. Medicine (bd. dirs.), Nat. Coun. State Bds. Nursing (bd. dirs., v.p. 2002—06), NC Nurses Assn., N.C. Orgn. Nurse Leaders, Sigma Theta Tau. Office: NC Bd of Nursing 3724 National Dr Raleigh NC 27612-4070 Office Phone: 919-782-3211 ext. 250. E-mail: polly@ncbon.com.

JOHNSON, MARYANN ELAINE, educational administrator; b. Franklin Twp., Pa., Nov. 1, 1943; d. Mary I. Sollick; married. BS in Elem. Edn., Mansfield State U., Pa., 1964; MS in Elem. Edn., U. Alaska, College, 1973; EdD, Wash. State U., Pullman, 1981. Tchr. Nayatt Sch., Barrington, R.I., 1964-66, North Sch., North Chicago, Ill., 1966-67, Kodiak (Alaska) On-Base Sch., 1967-71, Eastmont Sch. Dist., 1971-74, reading coord. East Wanatchee, Wash., 1974-77, adminstrv. asst., 1977-82; asst. supt. Sec. Parent Advisory Com., 1982-93, South Kitsap Sch. Dist., Port Orchard, Wash., 1993-95, Clarkston Sch. Dist., Wash., 1995-97; chair Wash. State Discover Card Scholarship, 1993-97; pvt. cons. Reach for the Future, Inc., 1997—, Learning Workshop, 1999—. Shoebox ministry coord., 2001—05. Active Ctrl. Wash. Hosp. Bd., 1991-93, Ctrl. Wash. Hosp. Found. Bd., 1992-93. Named Eastmont Tchr. of the Year, 1973-74. Mem. ASCD (review coun. 1993-99), Wash. State ASCD (bd. dirs. 1986-89, pres. elect 1989-90, pres. 1990-91, Educator of Yr. 1981), NEA, Wash. Assn. Sch. Adminstrs. (bd. dirs., chmn. curriculum and instrn. Job-Alike, profl. devel. com., Project Leadership, pres. elect 1986-87, pres. 1987-88, leadership award, 1986, award of merit 1992, Exec. Educator 100 1988, 93, chmn. WASA 21st century scholarship com. 1988-96, leadership acad. 1993), Am. Assn. Sch. Adminstrs. (resolutions com. 1988-89, com. for advancement of sch. adminstrs. 1989-92), Horace Mann League, East Wenatchee C. of C. (bd. dirs. 1990-93, chair edn. com. 1990-91), Delta Kappa Gamma (pres. 1982-83), Phi Delta Kappa, Phi Kappa Phi. E-mail: mjohnson@i70west.com.

JOHNSON, MARYANNA MORSE, business owner; b. Oxford, Miss., Dec. 21, 1936; d. Hugh McDonald and Anna Sullivan (Virden) Morse; children: Julianna, Hunter, Cynthia, Capp. Student, Miss. U. for Women, 1957; BSN cum laude, Tex. Woman's U., 1986. RN, Tex. Owner MM Johnson Network India, Boulder, Colo., 1968—, MJM Assocs., Boulder, 1990—. Health promotion cons., 1986—. Recipient Lane Zunker Excellence award, 1999. Mem. Sigma Theta Tau. Home: 3102 Bell Dr Boulder CO 80301-2277 E-mail: mjmassociates@bww.com.

JOHNSON, MARYL RAE, cardiologist; b. Fort Dodge, Iowa, Apr. 15, 1951; d. Marvin George and Beryl Evelyn (White) Johnson. BS, Iowa State U., 1973; MD, U. Iowa, 1977. Diplomate Am. Bd. Internal Medicine, Am. Bd. Cardiovasc. Diseases. Intern U. Iowa Hosps., Iowa City, 1977-78, resident, 1978-81, fellow, 1979-82; assoc. in cardiology U. Iowa Hosps. and Clins., Iowa City, 1982-86, asst. prof. medicine cardiovasc. divsn., 1986-88; asst. prof. medicine Med. Ctr. Loyola U., 1988-92, assoc. prof., 1992-94, Rush. U., 1994-97, Northwestern U. Med. Sch., 1998—2002; prof. medicine U. Wis. Med. Sch., Madison, 2002—. Med. dir. cardiac transplantation U. Iowa Hosp., 1986—88; assoc. med. dir. cardiac transplantation Loyola U., 1988—94, assoc. med. dir. Rush Heart Failure and Cardiac Transplant Program, 1994—97; dir. heart failure cardiac transplant program Northwestern U. Med. Sch., 1998—2001, dir. heart failure program, 2001—02; med. dir. heart failure and transplantation U. Wis. Hosp. and Clinics, 2002—. Assoc. editor: Jour. Heart and Lung Transplantation, 1995—99, 2007—, mem. editl. bd.:, 2000—06. Mem. Nat. Heart Lung and Blood Adv. Coun., Bethesda, Md., 1979—83; mem. biomed. rsch. tech. rev. com. NIH, 1990—93, chairperson, 1992—93, chair biomed. rsch. tech. spl. emphasis panel, 1999—2002. Recipient Jane Leinfelder Meml. award, U. Iowa Coll. Medicine, 1977, Clin. Investigator award, NIH, 1981, New Investigator Rsch. award, 1981, 1986; Barry Freeman scholar, 1974. Mem.: ACP, AAAS, AMA, United Network Organ Sharing (thoracic organ com. 2005—, vice chair 2006—), Am. Soc. Transplantation (chair membership com. 2003—04, bd. dirs. 2004—06, sec.-treas. 2006—), Am. Coll. Cardiology (heart failure and cardiac transplant com. 2002—07, chair 2004—07), Am. Heart Assn., Ctrl. Soc. Clin. Rsch., Internat. Soc. Heart and Lung Transplantation (mem. program com. 2005), Order of Rose, Alpha Omega Alpha, Iota Sigma Pi, Phi Kappa Phi, Alpha Lambda Delta. Office: U Wis Madison E5/582D CSC 5710 600 Highland Ave Madison WI 53792 Office Phone: 608-263-0080. Business E-Mail: mrj@medicine.wisc.edu.

JOHNSON, MATILEE HOWARD, retired headmistress; b. Palmetto, Ga., Dec. 9, 1934; d. Amplus Dilworth and Mattie (King) Howard; m. Andrew Emerson Johnson III, Dec. 27, 1977. BS, U. Ga., 1957; MA in Adminstrn., Ga. State U., 1970; postgrad., Colgate U., 1960, postgrad., 1963, Emory U., 1966—67, Oxford U., 1980. Cert. ednl. adminstrn., Ga. Tchr. Everglades Sch. for Girls, Miami, 1957—61, The Hamlin Sch., San Francisco, 1960—61; tchr., dean of students Westminster Girls' Sch., Atlanta, 1961—66, dean of students, 1966—72, head mistress, 1972—77, ret., 1977. Substitute tchr., Dana Hall, Wellesley, Mass., 1990; ednl. cons. Pingry and Kent Place Schs., Elizabeth, N.J., 1972; conf. chmn. Midsouth Assn. Ind. Schs., Atlanta, 1973; conv. com. Nat. Assn. Prins. Schs. for Girls. Adv. bd., convocation chmn., March of Dimes, Atlanta, 1974; mem. Cmty. Coun. Montgomery, 1997-98. mem. spl. acquisition com. Montgomery Mus. Fine Arts, 1997-99; bd. dirs. Landmarks Found., Montgomery, 1996-99, Montgomery Chorale, 1994-98; mem. women's com. Carnegie Mus., Pitts., 1983-98. Methodist. Avocations: creating jewelry, swimming, skiing, decorating, flower arranging. E-mail: mhjinwi@aol.com.

JOHNSON, M(AURICE) GLEN, political science professor; b. Pikeville, Ky., Nov. 18, 1936; s. Marvin Forrest and Norice (Wicker) J.; m. Sipra Bose, July 13, 1963; children: Denise Bose, Robert Alexander. BA, Georgetown Coll., Ky., 1958; MA, U. N.C., Chapel Hill, 1961, PhD, 1966. Instr. polit. sci. U. Ky., Lexington, 1963-64; from instr. to prof. Vassar Coll., Poughkeepsie, NY, 1964—2002, prof. emeritus, 2002—, acting pres., 1997—98, 2003—04; dir. Am. Studies Rsch. Ctr., Hyderabad, India, 1990-93; disting. vis. prof., exec. dir. Prince Alwaleed Bin Talal Bin Abdulaziz Alsaud Ctr. Am. Studies and Rsch. Am. U., Cairo, 2004—06. Author: (with others) Beyond the Water's Edge, 1975, Consensus at the Crossroads, 1972, La Dèclaration Universelle des Droits de l'Homme, 1991, Ah, Columbus! The Indian Discovery of America, 1993, The Universal Declaration of Human Rights 1948-1993, 1994, The Universal Declaration of Human Rights: A History of its Creation and Implementation, 1998; editor Indian Jour. Am. Studies, 1990-1993; contbr. articles to profl. jours. Trustee Poughkeepsie Day Sch., 1968-72, 85-88, 99—2004, pres. bd. trustees, 1986-88; trustee Eleanor Roosevelt Ctr. at Val-Kill, 1986-90, 94-2002, v.p., 1989-90, 95-97, pres., 1997-2000; bd. dir. Friends of Fulbright in India, 1995—, chmn. bd., 2003-04; bd. dir. World Affairs Coun. Mid Hudson Valley, 2003-. Named Sr. Fulbright lectr. U. Poona, India, 1977-78, sr. Fulbright lectr. India, 1990-93. Mem. Am. Polit. Sci. Assn., Assn. for Asian Studies, Internat. Studies Assn. Home: 39 Garfield Pl Poughkeepsie NY 12601-4321 Office: Vassar Coll Box 376 124 Raymond Ave Poughkeepsie NY 12604-0376 Business E-Mail: johnsong@vassar.edu.

JOHNSON, MAURICE VERNER, JR., agricultural research and development executive; b. Duluth, Minn., Sept. 13, 1925; s. Maurice Verner Sr. and Elvira Marie (Westberg) J.; m. Darlene Ruth Durand, June 23, 1944; children: Susan Kay, Steven Dale. BS, U. Calif., 1953. Registered profl. engr. From research engr. to dir. research and devel. Sunkist Growers, Ontario, Calif., 1953-84, v.p. research and devel., 1984-90, ret., 1990—. V.p., dir. Calif. Citrus Quality Council, Claremont. Contbr. articles to profl. pubs.; patentee in field. Sgt. U.S. Army, 1944-46, ETO. Fellow Am. Soc. Agrl. Engrs. (dir. 1969-70); mem. ASME, Am. Inst. Indsl. Engrs., Am. Assn. Advancement Sci., Nat. Soc. Profl. Engrs., Tau Beta Pi. Republican. Avocation: golf.

JOHNSON, MELODY, school system administrator; BS in Sociology, Phillips U.; Masters, TWU; PhD in Ednl. Adminstrn., U. Tex., Austin. Tchr., Okla., Dallas, Selma, San Antonio, 1975—82; asst. prin. Meridith Magnet Sch., Tex., 1983—85; prin. Travis Mid. Sch., Tex., 1985—89; state sr. dir. Mid. Sch. Edn. for Tex., 1992—95; dist. area supt. for San Antonio, 1995—97; assoc. supt. for curriculum, instrn. and student support San Antonio Ind. Sch. Dist., 1997—2000; dep. supt. Providence Schs., 2000—02, supt., 2002—05, Fort Worth Ind. Sch. Dist., 2005—. Pres. Coop. Superintendency Exec. Leadership Program, U. Tex. Named R.I. Woman of the Yr. for Edn., 2004; fellow Broad Found. Nat. Supt.'s Acad., 2002, Coop. Superintency, 1989. Achievements include commended by State Comptr. of Tex. for excellent curriculum frameworks and stds. documents; acknowledged by Carnegie Corp. N.Y. for having served as one of 15 state dirs. of nat. mid. sch. initiative. Office: Fort Worth ISD Office of the Superintendent 100 N University Dr Fort Worth TX 76107-1360 Office Phone: 401-456-9221.*

JOHNSON, MELVIN N., academic administrator, economist; s. William Thomas and Vernedia Rosemary Johnson; m. Marcelite Elaine Dingle, Dec. 22, 1968; children: DeAndra Chanet Martin, Monet Nichelle Bloodworth, Melvin Roschaun. BS in Econs., N.C. Agrl. and Tech. State U., 1968; MA in Econs., Ball State U., 1974; MBA in Bus. Econs., Ind. U., 1979, DBA in Bus. Econs., 1983. Commd. 2d lt. USAF, 1968, advanced through grades to lt. col., officer Soesterberg Air Base, Netherlands, 1968—90; assoc. prof. econs. N.C. Agrl. and Tech. State U., Greensboro, 1990—92, chair bus. adminstrn., 1992—97, interim dean grad. sch., 1997—98, assoc. vice chancellor, 1998—2000; provost, vice chancellor Winston-Salem (N.C.) State U., 2000—05; pres. Tenn. State U., Nashville, 2005—. Bd. dirs., chair strategic planning Piedmont Triad Ctr. Advanced Mfg., Greensboro, NC, 1994—99, Simon Green Atkins Cmty. Devel. Corp., Winston-Salem, NC, 2000—; bd. advisors Harvard Inst. Higher Edn., Cambridge, Mass., 1999—2002; bd. dirs., chair U. N.C. Tchg. and Learning with Tech., Chapel Hill, 1999—2001; commr. NC State Banking Commn., Raleigh, NC, 1999—2002; bd. dirs., chair investments N.C. Bapt. Hosp., Winston-Salem, 2002—; bd. dirs. Carolina Ctr. Internat. Understanding, Winston-Salem Downtown Devel. Corp., IdeAlliance Rsch. Pk. Devel., WINSTONET; co-chair bd. directors Ctr. Cmty. Safety. Co-author: Balance of Payments Adjustment: Macro Facets of International Finance Revisited, Empirical Evidence for the Traditional Approach to the Capital Account, A Monetary Model of the Mexican Balance of Payments; contbr. articles to profl. jours. Bd. dirs., chair planning Multiple Sclerosis Soc., Greensboro, 1999—2002; chair tech. coun. Winston-Salem C. of C., 2000—03. Named Outstanding Young Men of Am., 1975; Millennium Leadership Inst. Protégé fellow, Am. Assn. State Colls. and Univs., 2001, Nissan fellow, Nissan USA, 1993, Ayres fellow, Am. Banking Assn., 1995, NAFEO Kellogg Leadership fellow, Nat. Assn. Equal Opportunity Higher Edn., 2003—04, Future Focus 2020 Sr. fellow, Babcock Sch., Wake Forest U., 2003—. Mem.: Piedmont Club (mem. wine com. 2003—04), Rotary (mem. program com. 2001—04), Golden Key, Alpha Sigma Lambda, Omicron Delta Epsilon, Beta Gamma Sigma, Alpha Phi Alpha (life). Office: Tenn State Univ 3500 John A Merritt Blvd Nashville TN 37209

JOHNSON, MICAH WILLIAM, television newscaster, director; s. William T. and Joann K. (Pierce) J. Student, Indiana U. Pa., 1981-84; AA in Law Enforcement Tech., Rio Solado Coll., 1999. Announcer WLEM-AM/WQKY-FM, Emporium, Pa., 1978-81; news dir., anchorman WIUP-TV, Indiana, Pa., 1981-84; anchorman, reporter WSEE-TV, Erie, Pa., 1984-85; anchorman, mng. editor WVVA-TV, Bluefield, W.Va., 1985-86; news dir., anchorman WKYN-TV, St. Mary's, Pa., 1986-87; anchorman television and radio news Cable News Network, Atlanta, 1987-89; anchorman, corr. NBC-TV News, Washington, 1989-90; sr. producer radio & TV U.S. Senate, Washington, 1990; anchorman, news dir. Sta. KTSM-TV-AM-FM, El Paso, Tex., 1990-93, Sta. WTOV-TV, Steubenville, Ohio, 1993-94; dir. news Sta. WBRE-TV, Wilkes-Barre, Pa., 1994-96; news dir. Sta. WPXI-TV, Pitts., 1996-97; dir. news and prodn. WVIT-TV Paramount Pictures, Hartford, Conn., 1997—; pres., CEO Mediastars Internat., 2001—; v.p. news ops. Meredith Corp., 2001—05; pres. Washington News Network, 2005—. Talk show host Sta. KTSM Newsradio, El Paso, 1990-93; adj. prof. Dekalb Coll., Clarkston, Ga., 1987-89; guest lectr. Ariz. State U., 2000—; bd. dirs. Conn. Assoc. Press. Vol. fireman Morris Twp. Fire Co., Morrisdale, Pa., 1980—, Erie Emergency Med. Svcs., 1984-85; dir. choir Morrisdale United Meth. Ch., 1982-87; bd. dirs. El Paso Humane Soc., El Paso Zool. Soc.; mem. adv. bd. Salvation Army. With Pa. N.G., 1981—. ROTC Pa. Army Nat. Guard. Recipient Presdl. Citation for Cmty. Svc., 1992, Best of the Best award/Cmty. Svc. Nat. Assn. Broadcasters, 1992, AP award, 1985, 86, 87, 90, 91, 92, 93, 94, 95, 96, 97, 98, Nat. Pianist award Am. Coll. Musicians, 1973-79, Ind. U. Disting. Alumni award, 1990, Gold medal award Internat. Radio Festival N.Y. 1990, Gavel award State Bar of Tex., 1992, Tex. Gov.'s award/Cmty. Svc., 1992, Outstanding Contbn. to Law Enforcement award combined law enforcement assns. of Tex., 1991-92, Spl. Recognition award U.S. Marshal's Svc., 1992, Pub. Safety award Pa. Gov., 1996; nominee Emmy award for Best Newscast, 1994, 95, 96, 97, 2004 nominee Emmy award for Outstanding News Operation, 2004; recipient Emmy award for Best Newscast, 1997. Mem. NATAS (bd. govs.), Nat. Press Club, Radio-TV News Dirs. Assn. (Overall Excellence in News award), Conn. Assoc. Press Bd. Dirs. (v.p.), Nat. Radio Broadcasters Assn., El Paso Police Officers Assn. (hon.), White House Corrs. Assn., Radio/TV Galleries, US Senate, House Reps., Nat. Wildlife Fedn. (bd. dirs. Ind. U. mag.), El Paso Humane Soc. (bd. dirs.), El Paso Zool Soc. (bd. dirs.) Nat. Press Club, Frat. Order Police, El Paso Downtown Lions Club, Masons. Methodist. Avocations: fishing, travel, piano, shark diving. Office: Entegy Group Exec Office Cir 7418 E Helm Dr Ste 220 Scottsdale AZ 85260 Office Phone: 602-999-8838. Business E-Mail: ceo@mediastars.tv.

JOHNSON, MICHAEL KENNETH, chemistry professor; b. Tonbridge, Kent, Eng., Mar. 8, 1953; came to U.S., 1980; s. Thomas Sydney and Eileen J.; m. Carole Ann Woodhouse, Aug. 21, 1976; children: Caroline Louise, Thomas Michael. BA, Cambridge U., 1974, MA, 1977; MSc, U. East Anglia, 1975, PhD, 1977. Postdoctoral fellow U. East Anglia, Norwich, 1977-80; postdoctoral rsch. assoc. Princeton (N.J.) U., 1980-82; asst. prof. chemistry La. State U., Baton Rouge, 1982-86; assoc. prof. chemistry U. Ga., Athens, 1987-91, prof. chemistry, 1991-98, disting. rsch. prof. chemistry, 1998—, dir., 1993—. Biophysics grant rev. panel NSF, Washington, 1990-95; study sects. NIH, Washington, 1998, 2000, 2001, 2003, 2005, 06. Editor: Electron Transfer in Biology and the Solid State, 1990; contbr. over 200 articles to profl. jours. Alfred P. Sloan fellow, 1986; Rsch. grantee NIH, 1984, 87, 90, 94, 2000, 04, NSF, 1986, 90, 94, 98. Mem.: Am. Chem. Soc., Phi Kappa Phi. Home: 1100 Double Bridges Rd Winterville GA 30683-4830 Office: U Ga Dept Chemistry Athens GA 30602 Home Phone: 706-548-2201; Office Phone: 706-542-9378. Business E-Mail: johnson@chem.uga.edu.

JOHNSON, MICHAEL PAUL, historian, educator; b. Ponca City, Okla., July 6, 1941; s. Howard W. and Maybelle P. (Fetrow) J.; m. Anne E. Thompson, June 2, 1962; children: Ian Michael, Sarah Elizabeth. AB in Chemistry cum laude, Knox Coll., 1963; MA in History, Stanford U., 1967, PhD in History, 1973. Asst. prof. LeMoyne Coll., Memphis, 1967-68; instr. San Jose (Calif.) State U., 1970-71; asst. prof. history U. Calif., Irvine, 1971-77, assoc. prof., 1977-84, prof., 1984-94, Johns Hopkins U., Balt., 1994—. Author: Toward a Patriarchal Republic, 1977, Black Masters, 1984, No Chariot Let Down, 1984, The American Promise, 1998, Reading the American Past, 2 vols., 1998, Abraham Lincoln, Slavery and the Civil War, 2000. Am. Coun. Learned Socs.fellow, 1977; NEH fellow, 1982; Ctr. for Advanced Study in Behavioral Scis. fellow, 1999-00; Time Mirror Found. disting. rsch. fellow, Huntington Libr., 2004-05. Mem. Am. Hist. Assn., Orgn. Am. Historians (ABC Clio Am. History and Life award 2003), So. Hist. Assn., Am. Antiquarian Soc., Soc. Am. Historians, Phi Beta Kappa. Office: Johns Hopkins U Dept History Baltimore MD 21218 Office Phone: 410-516-7575.

JOHNSON, MICHAEL RANDY, bank executive; b. York, Nebr., Jan. 29, 1946; s. Sheldon Albert and Mary Lynn (Barbur) J.; m. Virginia L. Allgood, Apr. 5, 1975; children: Cory Michael, Scott Alan, Adam Todd. Student, Doane Coll., 1964-66, U. Nebr., 1966-68. Farmer, Geneva, Nebr., 1968-84; field reporter Agrl. Stabilization and Constrn. Svc., Geneva, 1973-80; adjuster Fed. Crop Ins. Corp., Kansas City, Kans., 1979-81, North Ctrl. Crop Ins., Eau Claire, Wis., 1981-84, Acceptance-Redland Ins. Co./Am. Agrisurance-Agrijusters, Council Bluffs, Iowa, 1984-86, field supr., 1986-88, tng. supr., 1988-90, regional claims supr., 1990-92, v.p., asst. claims mgr., 1993-94, claims mgr., sr. v.p., 1994-98, dir. claims and compliance, sr. v.p., 1998-2001; chief field svcs. officer Am. Assurance, 2001—02; agrl. ins. adv. and cert. agrl. arbitrator/mediator, 2003—04; asst. v.p. Peoples Nat. Bank, Missouri Valley, Iowa, 2004; v.p. City State Bank/Cornerstone Bank, Sutton, Nebr., 2004—; owner M.R. Ins. & Eagle Pointe Ins., 2006—. Cons. Segura La Comml., Monterey, Mex., 1988-92, Segures Am., Mexico City, 1988-92; contbg. bd. mem. Code of Ethics Bd. Nat. Crop Ins. Svc., Overland Park, Kans., 1992—; comml. arbitrator Am. Arbitration Assn., 2002—; spkr. in field. Author: (reference handbook) Grop Growth Patterns and Loss Adjustment, Mexico, 1991; editor: Crop Adjusting Manual, 1990, '91, '92. Mem. Masons. Methodist. Avocations: reading, fishing, platform speaking, plant studies. Home: PO Box 426 Sutton NE 68979 Office: PO Box 325 Sutton NE 68979 Business E-Mail: apex@johnson.org.

JOHNSON, MICHAEL WARREN, international relations specialist; b. Mpls., Oct. 2, 1948; s. Warren Redy and Lorraine Agnes (Capistran) Johnson; m. Jeanine Ann Tyldesley, Feb. 6, 1971 (div. 1991); children: Benjamin T., Joseph A., Katherine E.; m. Deborah V. Matthews, July 26, 1991; children: Maximilian N., Scott M. BS, U.S. Mil. Acad., 1970; MA in Internat. Rels., U. So. Calif., 1973; PhD of Polit. Sci., MIT, 1985; postgrad., Harvard U., 1987. Commd. 2d lt. U.S. Army, 1970, advanced through grades to capt., 1974; resigned, 1975; sr. Mid. East analyst U.S. Army Mil. Intelligence, 1975; stockbroker Merrill Lynch, Pierce, Fenner & Smith, Inc., Boston, 1975—81; v.p. Thomson McKinnon Securities Inc., Boston, 1981—82; 1st v.p. Jefferies & Co., Boston, 1982—84; sr. v.p. Moseley, Hallgarten, Estabrook & Weeden, Inc., Boston, 1984—88; internat. rels. cons. Geopolitical Strategist, Inc., 1984—. Fgn. policy adv. to Congl. adv., 1980. Mem.: Assn. Grads. U.S. Mil. Acad.

JOHNSON, MICHELLE L., lawyer; BSBA, U. Calif. Berkeley, 1975; JD, U. Denver, 1985. Bar: Calif. 1986. Ptnr., exec. dir. Thelen Reid & Priest LLP, San Francisco, mng. ptnr. adminstr. Spkr. in field. Mem.: Bar Assn. San Francisco (Bus. Law Sect.), State Bar Calif. (Bus. Law Sect.), ABA (Corp., Banking & Bus. Law Sect.), Order of St. Ives. Office: Thelen Reid & Priest LLP 101 Second St Ste 1800 San Francisco CA 94105-3601 Office Phone: 415-369-7101. Office Fax: 415-371-1211. Business E-Mail: mljohnson@thelenreid.com.

JOHNSON, MILLARD WALLACE, JR., mathematics and engineering professor; b. Racine, Wis., Feb. 1, 1928; s. Millard Wallace and Marian Manilla (Rittman) J.; m. Ruth Pugh Gifford, Dec. 26, 1953; children: Millard Wallace III, Jeannette Marian Brooks, Charles Gifford, Peter Allen. BS in Applied Math. and Mechanics, U. Wis., Madison, 1952, MS, 1953; PhD in Math, MIT, Cambridge, 1957. Rsch. asst. MIT, 1953-57, lectr., 1957-58; mem. staff Math. Rsch. Ctr. U. Wis., Madison, 1958-94, prof. mechanics, 1958-63, prof. mechanics and math., 1964-94, mem. staff Rheology Rsch. Ctr., 1970—, mem. Engine Rsch. Ctr., 1985—, prof. emeritus math. and engring.-physics depts., 1994—. Contbr. articles to profl. jours. Adv. bd. Internat. Math. and Statis. Librs. (IMSL), 1971-92. With USN, 1946-48. Fellow ASME; mem. Soc. Rheology, Soc. Indsl. and Applied Math., Am. Acad. Mechanics, Brit. Soc. Rheology, Wis. Acad. Scis., Arts and Letters, Phi Beta Kappa. Home: 802 Blue Ridge Pkwy Madison WI 53705-1148 Office: U Wis Dept Eng Phys 1500 Engineering Dr Madison WI 53706-1609 Office Phone: 608-263-1646. Business E-Mail: mwjohns1@wisc.edu.

JOHNSON, MURRAY H., optometrist, researcher, consultant, lecturer; b. Montreal, Que., Can., Jan. 29, 1956; arrived in U.S., 1980; s. William and Leah (Bedzowski) J.; m. Linda Fluxman, Apr. 30, 1978; children: Warren Natan, Tanya Yael, Arielle Carly. Diploma in Optometry, Witwatersrand Coll., Johannesburg, 1977; postgrad., U. Montreal, 1980; BS, OD, U. Houston, 1981, MSc in Physiol. Optics and Vision Sci., 1984; postgrad., U. Tex. Health Ctr., 1983. Lic. optometrist, Tex., 1983, therapeutic lic., Tex., 1992; cert. ocular therapeutics for treatment and mgmt. ocular disease U. Houston, 1992; cert. optometric glaucoma specialist, U. Houston, 2002. Clin. instr. U. Houston, 1981-85, postdoct. fellow, 1981-84; researcher Inst. contact Lens Rsch., Houston, 1983-88; pvt. practice optometry specializing in contact lenses Eye & Contact Lens Assocs. North Tex., Dallas, 1985—. Vis. asst. prof. U. Houston, 1984-85, adj. asst. prof., 1985-89; cons., clin. investigator Metro Optics, Inc., Dallas, 1989—; premktg. clin. evaluator, cons. and investigator to various contact lens and pharm. mfrs., 1989—; clin. investigator Paragon Optical, Mesa, Ariz., 1992; cons. Unilens Corp., Largo, Fla., 1989; clin. examiner Nat. Bd. Clin. Skills Exam., Nat. Bd. Examiners in Optometry, 1997—; cons. Johnson & Johnson Vision Care, Inc. Vistakon Divsn., Jacksonville, Fla., 2005—. Contbr. articles to profl. jours. Mem. clin. care com. Global Vision Inst., Global Vision Dallas,

1996; mem. edn. com. Akiba Acad. Dallas, 1986—88, bd. dirs., 1986—97, long range planning com., 1987—88, devel. com., 1993, v.p., treas, 1993—94, budget com., 1993—96, scholarship com, 1994—2002; bd. dirs. Congregation Share Tefilla, Dallas, 1988—92; steering com. B'nai B'rith, 1986—88, treas., 1987—88; mem.-at-large Jewish edn. com. Jewish Fedn. Dallas, 1998—99; mem. Jewish identity and values experiences com. Jewish Edn. Dept., 1999—2003, chair, 2000—01; local beneficiaries subcom., allocations com. Jewish Fedn. Greater Dallas, 1999—2000, mem. renaissance and renewal subcom. planning and allocations com., 2000—03; chair Jewish identity and values experiences subcom. Jewish Edn. Com., 2000—01. Postdoc. fellow U. Houston, 1981-84, grantee 1981, 82; Ezell Rsch. fellow Am. Optometric Found., 1983. Fellow Am. Acad. Optometry; mem. AAAS, Assn. Rsch. in Vision and Ophthalmology, Am. Pub. Health Assn. (vision care sect.), Am. Optometric Assn. (contact lens sect.), Tex. Optometric Assn., Dallas County Optometric Soc., Am. Optometric Found. (Ezell fellows club), Sigma Xi. Jewish. Avocations: walking, swimming, racquetball. Office: Eye & Contact Lens Assocs N Tex 18111 Preston Rd Ste 180 Dallas TX 75252-6009

JOHNSON, MYSTIE L., obstetrician, gynecologist, department chairman; b. Casper, Wyo., Nov. 16, 1968; m. James M. Johnson, Apr. 28, 2001; 1 child, Tyler R. MD, U. Ariz., Tucson, 1998. Ob-gyn. chair Banner Estrella Med. Ctr., Phoenix; pres. West Valley Women's Care, Phoenix, 2002—. Fellow: ACOG. Office: West Valley Women's Care 9305 W Thomas Rd Ste 155 Phoenix AZ 85037 Home Phone: 602-721-8964; Office Phone: 623-936-1780.

JOHNSON, NANCY LEE, former congresswoman; b. Chgo., Jan. 5, 1935; d. Noble Wishard and Gertrude Reid (Smith) Lee; m. Theodore H. Johnson, June 27, 1932; children: Lindsey Lee, Althea Anne, Caroline Reid. BA, Radcliffe Coll., 1957; postgrad., U. London, 1957-58. Vice chmn. Charter Commn. New Britain, Conn., 1976-77; mem. Conn. Senate from 6th dist., 1977-82, US Congress from 5th Conn. dist., Washington, 1983—2007, mem. ways and means com., chmn. health subcom., com. on taxation; mem. fed. pub. policy group Baker, Donelson, Bearman, Caldwell & Berkowitz, PC, Washington, 2007—. Bd. dirs. Magellan Health Services, Inc., 2007—; fellow Inst. Politics, 2007—. Pres. Friends of Libr., New Britain Pub. Libr., 1973-76, Radcliffe Club Northern Conn., 1973-75; bd. dirs., pres. Sheldon Cmty. Guidance Clinic, 1974-75; dir. religious edn. Unitarian Universalist Soc. New Britain, 1967-72; bd. dirs. United Way New Britain, 1976.79. Recipient Outstanding Vol. award United Way, 1976; English Speaking Union grantee, 1958-59 Republican. Office: Baker Donelson Bearman Caldwell & Berkowitz PC Lincoln Sq 555 Eleventh St NW Sixth Fl Washington DC 20004

JOHNSON, NANCY PLATTNER, retired secondary school educator; b. Milw., July 1, 1938; d. Paul and Mary (Kalns) Plattner; m. Orville Johnson, III, July 1, 1978. BS, U. Chgo., 1960; postgrad., Ohio State U., 1965; M, U. Cen. Fla., Orlando, 1974; PhD, U. Wis., 1979. Cert. elem. tchr., secondary math Nat. Bd. Tchr. Harvard Sch. Boys, Chgo., 1960-61; math. tchr. Boone County Schs., Columbia, Mo., 1962-64, Columbus, Ohio, 1964-66; math. instr. U. Wis., Stevens Point, 1966-72; math. educator Orange County, Orlando, Fla., 1972-76; rsch. grad. asst., instr. U. Wis., Madison, 1976-79; vis. assoc. prof. Stetson U., Orlando, 1980-81; math. educator Seminole County Sch. Bd., Sanford, Fla., 1982; ret., 2006. Contbr. articles to profl. jours. Bd. dirs. Crown Oaks Springs Cmty. Assn., 1974—. Named Math. Tchr. of the Yr., 1999—2000; NSF grantee, Ohio State U., 1964—65, NSF fellow, U. Wis., 1976—79. Mem.: NEA, Seminole County Edn. Assn., Seminole County Math. Coun., Fla. Math. Coun., Fla. Tchg. Profl., Nat. Coun. Tchrs. Math., Math. Assn. Am. Avocations: art, music, writing. Home: 212 Jasmine Ln Longwood FL 32779-4908

JOHNSON, NEAL FREDERICK, psychologist, educator; b. Willmar, Minn., May 1, 1934; s. Malcolm Ruben and Helen Laura Johnson; m. Kathleen A. Crimmins, Sept. 9, 1960 (dec. Jan. 2000); children: Neal, Margaret (dec. Sept. 1999), Elizabeth, Michael. BA, U. Minn., 1956, PhD, 1961. Prof. psychology Ohio State U., Columbus, 1961—. Vis. prof. U. Calif., Berkeley, 1965, Berkeley, 74, Berkeley, 75, Berkeley, 77, Berkeley, 78, Berkeley, 83. Contbr. articles to profl. jours.; assoc. editor Jour. Memory and Lang., 1984-88; consulting editor Jour. Verbal Learning and Verbal Behavior, 1965-84, Memory & Cognition, 1972-82, Jour. Exptl. Psychology: Human Perception and Performance, 1978-82, Jour. Exptl. Psychology: Learning, Memory and Cognition, 1982-89, Jour. Memory and Lang., 1988-94, Gen. Psychology Rev., 1996—. Troop com. Boy Scouts Am., Columbus, 1974-81. Rsch. scholar Tozer Found., Stillwater, Minn., 1959; grantee U.S. Office Edn., NIH, NSF. Fellow APA (pres. Soc. Gen. Psychology 1995, pres. divsn. exptl. psychology 1996), AAAS (governing coun. 1998-2000, presiding officer psychology sect. 2002-04); mem. Psychonomic Soc. (pres. 1997), Coun. Sci. Soc. Presidents, Midwestern Psychol. Assn. (pres. 1987). Presbyterian. Avocations: downhill skiing, fencing. Home: 5478 Rockwood Rd Columbus OH 43229-4324 Office: Dept Psychology Ohio State U Columbus OH 43210 Office Phone: 614-202-2250. Business E-Mail: johnson.64@osu.edu.

JOHNSON, NICHOLAS, writer, lawyer, educator; b. Iowa City, Sept. 23, 1934; s. Wendell A.L. and Edna (Bockwoldt) Johnson; m. Karen Mary Chapman, 1952 (div. 1972); children: Julie, Sherman, Gregory, Alexander; m. Mary Eleanor Vasey, 1991. BA, U. Tex., 1956, LL.B., 1958; L.H.D., Windham Coll., 1971. Bar: Tex. 1958, D.C. 1963, U.S. Supreme Ct. 1963, Iowa 1974; lic. radio amateur. Law clk. to judge John R. Brown, U.S. 5th Circuit Ct. Appeals, 1958-59; law clk. to U.S. Supreme Ct. Justice Hugo L. Black, 1959-60; acting assoc. prof. law U. Calif. at Berkeley, 1960-63; assoc. Covington & Burling, Washington, 1963-64; adminstr. Maritime Adminstrn., chmn. Maritime Subsidy Bd. U.S. Dept. Commerce, 1964-66; commr. FCC, 1966-73; adj. prof. law Georgetown U., 1971-73; Poynter fellow Yale U., 1971; vis. prof. U. Ill., Champaign-Urbana, 1976, U. Okla., Norman, 1978, Ill. State U., Normal, 1979, U. Wis., Madison, 1980, Newhouse Sch., Syracuse U., 1980, U. Iowa Coll. Law, 1981—; vis. prof. dept. communications studies U. Iowa, 1982-85; vis. prof. Western Behavioral Scis. Inst., U. Calif., San Diego, 1986-91. Vis. prof. Calif. State U., Los Angeles, 1986, New Sch. Soc. Resource ConnectEd, 1990, U. Iowa dept. theater arts, 1999; regents prof. U. Calif., San Diego, 2000; co-dir. U. Iowa Inst. for Health, Behavior and Environ. Policy, 1990-93; chmn., dir. Nat. Citizens Comm. Lobby, 1975—, Nat. Citizens Com. for Broadcasting, 1974-78; pub. access, 1975-77; commentator Nat. Pub. Radio, 1975-77, 83-86, Sta. WRC-AM, Washington, 1977, Sta. WSUI, Iowa City, 1982-87; presdl. advisor White House Conf. on Libraries and Info. Services, 1979; exec. com. World Acad. Art and Sci., 1993-97. Author: Cases and Materials on Oil and Gas Law, 1962, How to Talk Back to Your Television Set, 1970, Japanese transl., 1971, Life Before Death in the Corporate State, 1971, Test Pattern for Living, 1972, Broadcasting in America, 1973, Cases and Materials on Communications Law and Policy, 1981, 82, 83, 84, 85, 86, Readings for Law of Electronic Media, 1993-94, (with David Loundy) Law of Electronic Media in a Cyberspace Age, 1996; syndicated columnist: Gannett News Service, 1982-84, Register and Tribune Syndicate, 1984, Cowles Syndicate, 1985-86, King Features Syndicate, 1986, Iowa City Press Citizen, 1998-2001; contbr. to legal, gen., internat. publs.; contbg. editor, host PBS The New Tech Times, 1983-84. Dem. candidate for U.S. Ho. of Reps. from 3d Iowa Dist., 1974; bd. dirs. Ctr. for Study Commercialism, 1991-96, Citizens Ind. Pub. Broadcasting, 1999-2002, Common Cause, 1990-96, Internat. Soc. Gen. Semantics, 1960-2000, Iowa City Cmty. Sch. Dist., 1998-2001, Virtual Classroom Project, 1990-91, Vol. in Tech. Assistance, 1994-2000; mem. adv. bd. Ctr. Media Edn., 1993-, Cultural Environ., Movement, 1992-, Fairness and Accuracy in Reporting, 1996—, Inst. Pub. Accuracy, 1997-, Open Soc. Inst. Media Group, 1999-2000, Project Censored, 1976-, U. Iowa Info. Arcade, 1991-92, War and Peace Found., 1988-, Working Assets Long Distance, 1992-96; mem. Broadband and Telecom. Commn., Iowa City, 1981-87. Named One of 10 Outstanding Young Men in U.S., U.S. Jaycees, 1967, recipient New Republic Pub. Defender award, 1970, Civil Liberties Award Ga. ACLU, 1972, DeWitt Carter Reddick award U. Tex., 1977, George Stoney award Nat. Fedn. Local Cable Programmers, 1987; fellow World Acad. Art and Sci., 1991—. Mem. D.C., Iowa Bar Assn. (Citizenship award 1951), State Bar Tex., Golden Key, Order of Coif, Phi Beta Kappa, Phi Delta Phi, Phi Eta Sigma, Pi Sigma Alpha. Democrat. Unitarian Universalist. Home and Office: PO Box 1876 Iowa City IA 52244-1876 Office Phone: 319-337-5555. E-mail: nicholas@nicholasjohnson.org.

JOHNSON, NICHOLE SHARESE, school nurse practitioner, basketball coach; b. NYC, Nov. 13, 1975; d. Lorelei Davis. BSN, Coll. New Rochelle, 1997; MSN, U. Phoenix, 2005. RN. Staff nurse NYU Med. Ctr., NYC, 1997—98; contract nurse Theracare, 1998—99; contract nursing Allcare Nursing, Hicksville, 1999—2000; sch. nursing NYC Dept. Edn., 1999—; homecare nursing Visting Nurse Svc. NY, Bronx, 2002—03. Jr. h.s. head basketball coach Rainbow Basketball Assn., Bronx, 2002—05. Named Coach of Yr., Rainbow Basketball Assn., 2004—05. Mem.: ANA (licentiate), NY State Sch. Nurse Assn. (licentiate), Nat. Assn. Sch. Nurses (licentiate), NY State Nurse Assn. (licentiate), Sigma Theta Tau. Home Phone: 845-344-6139.

JOHNSON, NOBLE MARSHALL, research scientist; b. San Francisco, Feb. 23, 1945; BSEE cum laude, U. Calif., Davis, 1967, MSEE, 1970; PhD, Princeton U., 1974. Rsch. staff SRI Internat., Menlo Park, Calif., 1974—76; from rsch. staff to sr. rsch. staff Xerox Palo Alto Rsch. Ctr., Palo Alto, 1976—87, prin. scientist Electronic Materials lab., 1987—; mgr. Optoelectronic Materials and Devices, 1999—. Vis. lectr. Princeton (NJ) U., 1986, U. Erlangen-Nürnberg, Germany, 1988; presenter in field. Co-editor 5 books; contbr. over 330 articles to profl. jours.; patentee in field. Recipient Disting. Sr. U.S. Scientist award Alexander von Humboldt Found., Germany, 1987; Nat. Def. Grad. fellow, Princeton U., 1969-72. Fellow Am. Phys. Soc., IEEE; mem. Sigma Xi. Office: Palo Alto Rsch Ctr Electronic Materials Devices Lab 3333 Coyote Hill Rd Palo Alto CA 94304-1314 Business E-Mail: njohnson@parc.com.

JOHNSON, NOEL LARS, biomedical engineer; b. Palo Alto, Calif., Nov. 11, 1957; s. LeRoy Franklin and Margaret Louise (Lindsley) J.; children: Margaret Elizabeth, Kent Daniel. BSEE, U. Calif., Berkeley, 1979; M of Engring., U. Va., 1982, PhD, 1990. Mgr. R & D Hosp. Products divsn. Abbott Labs., Mountain View, Calif., 1986-99; founder HealtheTech., Inc., 1999—2004; pres., CEO NovaShunt, Inc., Saratoga, Calif., 2004—; CEO NovaShunt, AG, Zurich, 2006—. Contbr. articles to profl. jours. Fellowship NIH 1980-85; rsch. grantee Abbott Labs. 1989. Mem. IEEE, Biomed. Engring. Soc., Delta Chi (founder, 1st pres. chpt. U. Calif. at Berkeley). Achievements include invention of metabolic monitor, patented automated drug delivery system, pharmacokinetic drug infusion, and critical care disposables. Business E-Mail: njohnson@novashunt.com. E-mail: noeljo@aol.com.

JOHNSON, NORMAN TERRY, public relations executive, writer; s. Samuel and Francis E. (Morse) Johnson; children: Robin, Denise, Lisa. Degree, San Diego Jr. Coll., 1956. Pub. rels. exec. various hotels, Las Vegas, 1967—77; prin., owner Johnson Agy., Las Vegas, 1978—. Author: History of Off-Road Racing, 1976, Magellan's of the Sky, 2004. Sgt. USAF, 1950—53, Korea. Recipient Lifetime Achievement award, Las Vegas (Nev.) Entertainment, 2004. Mem.: C.A.S.T. Achievements include creator of world famous Mint 400 Off-Road Race 1968-93. Avocations: sculpting, auto racing. Office Phone: 702-798-5210, 702-898-6721. Personal E-mail: racenorm@cox.net.

JOHNSON, OMOTUNDE EVAN GEORGE, economist; b. Freetown, Sierra Leone, Mar. 27, 1941; came to U.S., 1961; s. Evan George and Elizabeth O. (Allen) J.; m. Octavia Olayemi John, Oct. 30 1965; children: Olatunde Cheryl, Omoyemi Evan, Olubayo Darryl. BA, UCLA, 1965, MA, 1967, PhD, 1970. Lectr. in econs. Calif. State U., Long Beach, 1967-69; lectr. U. Sierra Leone, Freetown, 1969-73; vis. asst. prof. U. Mich., Ann Arbor, 1973-74; economist IMF, Washington, 1974-79, sr. economist, dep. divsn. chief, 1979-92, advisor, 1992-94, divsn. chief, 1994-98, asst. dir., 1998-2000; econ. rschr. and cons. McLean, Va., 2000—. Vis. rsch. fellow U. Oxford, Eng., 1996-97; resident rep. IMF, Ghana, 1987-90. Author: African Economic Development: Cooperation, Ownership and Leadership, 2007; contbr. numerous articles to profl. jours. Mem. Am. Econ. Assn., U.S. Chess Fedn., Royal Econ. Soc. U.K., Nat. Symphony Orch. Assn., Met. Opera Guild. Episcopalian. Avocations: chess, piano, classical music, reading. Home and Office: 6401 Oak Meadow Way Mc Lean VA 22101-5342 Personal E-mail: oegjohnson@aol.com.

JOHNSON, OWEN C., food products executive; B in Quantitative and Labor Econs., U. Ill. V.p. bank mergers and acquisitions BankAmerica; sr. v.p. adminstrn. Lit-Am. Trading; v.p. human resources, purchasing, transp., corp. comm. and adminstrn. and pres. Greenfuels, Inc. Nisource, Inc., 1990—98; sr. v.p. human resources and adminstrn. ConAgra Foods, Inc., Omaha, 1998—2001, exec. v.p., chief adminstrv. officer, 2001—. Office: ConAgra Foods Inc One ConAgra Dr Omaha NE 68102-5001 Office Phone: 402-595-4000.*

JOHNSON, OWEN VERNE, historian, educator; b. Madison, Wis., Feb. 22, 1946; s. Verner Lalander Johnson and Marianne Virginia (Halvorson) Muse; m. Marta Kucerova, July 17, 1969 (div. Jan. 26, 2001); children: Eva, Hana; m. Ann Coonradt Tyron, May 12, 2001. BA in History with distinction, Wash. State U., Pullman, 1968; MA in History, U. Mich., 1970, cert. in Russian Ea. European studies, 1978, PhD in History, 1978. Reporter Pullman Herald, Wash., 1961-67; reporter, announcer Sta. KWSU Radio-TV, Pullman, 1965-68; reporter, editor, producer Sta. WUOM, Ann Arbor, Mich., 1969-77; adminstrv. asst. Ctr. Russian and Ea. European Studies U. Mich., Ann Arbor, 1978-79; asst. prof. Sch. Journalism So. Ill. U., Carbondale, Ill., 1979-80; asst. prof. Ind. U., Bloomington, 1980-87, assoc. prof., 1987—, dir. grad. studies, 1990-91, acting dir. Polish studies, 1989-90, 2004—05, dir. Russian and Ea. European Inst., 1991-95, USA swimming and Big 10 swim announcer, 1993—; program host WFIU, Bloomington, 2007—. Mem. Modern Sweden Seminar, Uppsala, 1967; mem. Studia Academica Slovaca Comenius U., Bratislava, 1973; field advisor journalism Am. Coun. Tchrs. Russian, 1993—96; adj. prof. history Ind. U., Bloomington, 1996—. Author: Slovakia 1918-38: Education and the Making of a Nation, 1985; co-author: Eastern European Journalism Before, During and After Communism, 1999; contbr. articles to profl. jours.; mem. editl. bd. Slovakia, 1978—89, Journalism Monographs, 1986—88, Kosmas, 1996—, Media Rsch., 2002—; corr. editor: Journalism History, 1985—2000, cons. editor: Slavic Rev., 1985—91, corr.: Slovak Spectator, 2004—. Capt. USAR, 1971—79. Recipient Excellence in Journalism award, Sigma Delta Chi, 1966; grantee, Nat. Coun. Soviet and E. European Rsch., 1988—90, Am. Coun. Learned Socs./Social Sci. Rsch. Coun. Joint Com. Ea. Europe, 1983, Internat. Rsch. and Exchs. Bd., 1973—74, 1982, 1989, 2003—04. Mem.: Slovak Studies Assn. (pres. 1988—91), Orgn. Am. Historians, Czechoslovak Studies Assn. (editor newsletter 1980—84, mem. exec. com. 1988—92, Stanley Pech award 1987—88), Assn. Edn. Journalism and Mass Comm. (head history divsn. 1985—86), Am. Assn. Advancement Slavic Studies (mem. edn. com. 1988—90), Am. Hist. Assn. Democrat. Presbyterian. Office: Ind U Sch Journalism 200 Ernie Pyle Hall Bloomington IN 47405 Office Phone: 812-855-9247. Office Fax: 812-855-0901. Business E-Mail: johnsono@indiana.edu.

JOHNSON, PAM CLARENE, radiographer, bone densitometrist, consultant; d. Clarence and Palma Johnson. Degree, St. Barnabas Sch. Radiologic Tech., 1971; BS in Med. Tech., U. Minn., 1976. Part-time radiographer St. Barnabas Hosp., Mpls., 1972—83, Hennepin County Med. Ctr., Mpls., 1973—74; radiographer U. Minn., Mpls., 1976—2000; radiographer, clin. supr. Health East Osteoporosis Care, St. Paul, 2002—; rsch. assoc. St. Luke's Body Composition Lab., NYC. Radiography instr. Curran Hosp., Zorzor, Liberia, 1982; bone densitometry cons., 2000—; cert. course instr. Internat. Soc. Clin. Densitometry, 2001; spkr. in field. Contbr. articles to profl. jours.; book & book proposal reviewer for major med. book publishers. Mem.: Internat. Soc. Radiographers & Radiologic Technologists, Am. Registry Radiologic Technologists (bone densitometry cert. com. 1999—2002), Am. Soc. Radiologic Technoloigsts (radiography del. 1995—99, nomination com. 1996, chair 1998—99, task force 1999, profl. standards adv. com. 2004—, publ. contrbr., practice stds. com. 2004—), Internat. Soc. Clin. Densitometry (pub. policy com. 1999—, tech. edn. subcom. 2000, liaison ARRT & ASRT 2000—03, bd. trustees 2001—03, interspecialty com. 2001—04, midwest reg. rep. 2001—, cert. exam. com. 2004—05, pub. contrbr., Oscar Gluck Humanitarian award 2005), Minn. Soc. Radiologic Technologists (life; pres., chair 1988—90, state del. to ASRT 1989—90, state jour. edit. 1991—98), Am. Soc. Clin. Lab. Specialists, Minn. Soc. Radiol. Tech. (life). Avocations: music, writing.

JOHNSON, PAMELA, music educator, director; b. South Charleston, W.Va., June 20, 1950; d. James and Marjorie May; m. Parry Johnson, May 26, 1978; children: David, Christopher. BA in Edn., Marshall U., Huntington, W.Va., 1972, MA in Music Edn., 1977. Tchr. W.Va., 1972. Tchr. Spring Hill Jr. HS, South Charleston, 1976—80; elem. music tchr. Kanawha County Schs., St. Albans, W.Va., 1994—2000; mem. adj. faculty music dept. Marshall U., 2000—. Music dir. Riverlawn Presbyn. Ch., St. Albans, 1983—. Mem. local sch. improvement coun. St. Albans HS, 2002—03. Mem.: Am. Guild Organists (co-dean 2006—). Presbyterian. Avocations: cooking, gardening, handbell ringing. Office: Marshall U 1 John Marshall Dr Huntington WV 25755 Home Phone: 304-722-2772; Office Phone: 304-696-3117. Business E-Mail: johnson164@marshall.edu.

JOHNSON, PAUL EDWARD, poet, writer; b. Northfield, Conn., July 30, 1921; s. Philip Edward and Dorothy Marie (Swanson) Johnson; m. Nina Anikienko Zelinsky, Nov. 19, 1961; stepchildren: Eugene Anikienko, Alexander Anikienko, Ludmila Anikienko. Grad. h.s. Ins. salesman Bankers Life & Casualty, Waterbury, Conn., 1949; machine operator Torrington (Conn.) Co., 1966—86; ret., 1986. Inventor Scribendi-Intellect Game; author: numerous poems. Fin. officer Clausson Raught Post, Copake Falls, NY, 1990. With US Army, 1944—48. Recipient Hon. mention, Iliad Lit. Awards, 1996, Editor's Choice award for Outstanding Achievement in Poetry, Nat. Libr. Poetry, 1996. Avocations: antiques, art, music, reading, poetry. Home: 132 Lincoln Rd Copake NY 12516-1022

JOHNSON, PAUL OREN, lawyer; b. Mpls., Feb. 2, 1937; s. Andrew Richard and LaVerne Delores (Slater) J.; children: Scott, Paula, Amy. BA, Carleton Coll., 1958; JD cum laude, U. Minn., 1961. Bar: Minn. 1961. Atty. Briggs & Morgan, St. Paul, 1961-62, Green Giant Co., Le Sueur, Minn., 1961-66, asst. sec., 1967-74, sec., 1975-79, v.p., gen. counsel, 1971-79, v.p. corporate rels., 1973-79, mem. mgmt. com., 1976-79; gen. counsel H.B. Fuller Co., St. Paul, 1979-84, sr. v.p., sec., 1980-90, mem. mgmt. com., 1981-90. Bd. dirs. The Fulcrum Group, chmn. bd. dirs. Bd. dirs. Boy Scouts Am.; bd. dirs. Rep. County Com., 1965; bd. dirs. Minn. State U., 1979-82, v.p., 1980-82; chmn. bd. dirs. Minn. Com. Serving Deaf and Hard of Hearing, 1992-98; bd. dirs. vice chair Minn. Acads.; bd. dirs., mem. exec. com., treas. Self Help for Hard of Hearing. Office: Lexington-Riverside 403-1077 Sibley Meml Hwy Saint Paul MN 55118-3680

JOHNSON, PAULA D., veterinarian; d. Jack D. and Shirley A. Johnson. DVM, Colo. State U., Ft. Collins, 1987; MS, U. Ariz., Tucson, 1992. Veterinarian Buena Pet Clinic, Inc., Tucson, 1987—88; sr. rsch. specialist U. Ariz., Tucson, 1988—97, assoc. vet. specialist, 1997—. Veterinarian USAR, San Diego, 1997—. Pres. So. Ariz. Campfire Girls and Boys, Tucson, 1987—90, SciEnTeK-12 Found., Tucson, 1997—; sci. rev. com. Internat. Sci. and Engring. Fair, Washington, 1999—. Maj. USAR, 1997—2007. Decorated Army Commendation medal, Operation Enduring Freedom, Army Achievement medal. Mem.: S.W. Assn. Edn. in Biomed. Rsch. (exec. dir. 2000—), Am. Soc. Lab. Animal Practitioners. Office: Univ Ariz 1127 E Lowel St Tucson AZ 85721 Office Phone: 520-621-3483. Business E-Mail: pauladj@email.arizona.edu.

JOHNSON, PETER FORBES, transportation executive, business owner; b. Salem, Mass., May 7, 1934; s. William Bennett and Sarah Loraine (Nee) J.; m. Mikell Kraus, Oct. 11, 1958; children: Krista, Todd, Karyn, Jennifer. BS, U.S. Mcht. Marine Acad., 1957. Deck officer Texaco, Port Arthur, Tex., 1958-63; from deck officer to master Reynolds Metals Co., Corpus Christi, Tex., 1963-65, port capt., 1965-68, operating mgr., 1968-71; internat. marine mgr. Gulf Miss. Marine Corp., New Orleans, 1971-72; cons. Peter F. Johnson & Assocs., New Orleans, 1972-73; exec. v.p. Pyramid Marine, Inc., New Orleans, 1973-76; owner, chmn. bd., pres. Pacific-Gulf Marine, Inc., New Orleans, 1976—2006, owner, chmn. bd., 2007—. Trustee U.S. Mcht. Marine Acad., Kings Point, NY. Lt. (j.g.) USNR, 1959-63. Mem. Coun. Am. Master Mariners, Soc. Naval Architects and Marine Engrs., Propeller Club U.S. (Maritime Man of Yr. 1986), U.S. Navy League, English Turn Country Club. Republican. Roman Catholic. Avocations: fly fishing, golf, hunting, sailing. Office: Pacific Gulf Marine Inc PO Box 6479 New Orleans LA 70174-6479 Home Phone: 504-394-9637; Office Phone: 504-362-8121. E-mail: pfj@pac-gulf.biz.

JOHNSON, PETER JAMES, JR., lawyer, legal analyst; b. NYC; BA, JD, Columbia U., 1982. Bar: NY 1987, NJ 1988, US Dist. Ct (so., ea. districts) NY, US Dist. Ct. NJ. Former sr. advisor to Mayor City of NY; former sr. v.p. NY State Urban Devel. Corp.; pres. Leahey & Johnson, PC, NYC; legal analyst FOX news channel; dir. UN Devel. Corp. Chmn. NY Appellate Divsn., Com. on Character & Fitness; mem. NY State Jud. Screening Panel. Mem.: Def. Rsch. Inst., Assn. Trial Lawyers Am., NY County Lawyers Assn., NY State Bar Assn., NJ State Bar Assn., Assn. Bar of the City of NY. Office: Leahey & Johnson PC 120 Wall St Ste 2220 New York NY 10005 Office Phone: 212-269-7308. Business E-Mail: pjohnsonjr@leaheyandjohnson.com.

JOHNSON, PHILIP LESLIE, lawyer; b. Beloit, Wis., Jan. 24, 1939; s. James Philip and Christabel (Williams) J.; m. Kathleen Rose Westover, May 12, 1979; children: Celeste Marie, Nicole Michelle. AB, Princeton U., 1961; JD, U. South Calif., 1973. Bar: Calif. 1973, U.S. Ct. Appeals (9th cir.) 1975, U.S. Ct. Mil. Appeals 1978, U.S. Supreme Ct. 1980. Pilot U.S. Marine Corps., 1961-70; assoc. Law Office Wm. G. Tucker, LA, 1973-78; ptnr. Engstrom, Lipscomb & Lack, LA, 1978-92; judge pro tem Calif. State Bar Ct., 1990-95; ptnr. Lillick & Charles, Long Beach, Calif., 1993-99, Shaw, Terhar & LaMontagne, LA, 2000—. Chmn. aerospace law com. Def. Rsch. Inst. Contbr. articles to profl. jours. Pres., bd. dirs. U. So. Calif. Legion Lex, 1992-93; chmn. com. to nom. alumni trustees Princeton U., 1996-97, exec. com. of alumni coun., 1996-97; chmn. Marine Corps Scholarship Found. LA Ball, 1997-99, bd. dirs. 1999-2005. Mem. ABA, Nat. Bar Assn., Langston Bar Assn., Princeton Club So. Calif. Avocations: flying, skiing, jazz. Home: 5340 Valley View Rd Palos Verdes Peninsula CA 90275-5089 Office: Shaw Terhar & LaMontagne 707 Wilshire Blvd Ste 3060 Los Angeles CA 90017 Office Phone: 213-614-0400. Office Fax: 212-628-4534. Business E-Mail: pjohnson@stl.lawoffices.com. E-mail: avnlawyer@aol.com.

JOHNSON, PHILIP MCBRIDE, lawyer; b. Springfield, Ohio, June 18, 1938; BA with honors, Ind. U., 1959; LLB, Yale U., 1962. Bar: Ill. 1962, DC 1983, NY 1984. Ptnr. Kirkland & Ellis, Chgo., 1962-81; chmn. Commodity Futures Trading Commn., Washington, 1981-83; ptnr. Wiley, Johnson & Rein, Washington, 1983-84; ptnr., now of counsel, commodities, futures and options Skadden, Arps, Slate, Meagher & Flom, Washington, 1984—; lectr. on commodities regulation U. Va. Law Sch., 1993—. Spkr. panelist on Commodity Exch. Act Fed. Bar Assn., others; mem. adv. com. definition and regulation Commodity Futures Trading Commn., adv. com. state jurisdiction and responsibility; adv. com. regulatory coordination, adv. com. fin. products, adv. com. tech., adv. com. global markets Commodity Futures Trading Commn.; chair, Commodity Futures Trading Commn., 1981-83 Author: Derivatives Regulation, 3 vols., 1997, Derivatives: A Manager's Guide to the World's Most Powerful Financial Instruments, 1999; mng. editor Yale U. Law Jour, 1962, Agrl. Law Jour; bd. editors, International Financial Law Review; contbr. articles to legal jours. Mem. ABA (founder, first chmn. com. on regulation of futures and derivative instruments 1976-81, mem. governing coun. sect. on bus. law 1981-83), Futures Industry Assn. (bd. dirs. 1980-81, 86-87), Internat. Bar Assn. (founder, first chmn. subcom. on commodities, futures and options law 1987-90), NY Stock Exch. (mem. regulatory adv. com. 1989—2004). Office: Skadden Arps Slate Meagher & Flom 1440 New York Ave NW Ste 700 Washington DC 20005-2111 Office Phone: 202-371-7340. Office Fax: 202-661-9081. Business E-Mail: pjohnson@skadden.com.

JOHNSON, PHILIP WAYNE, state supreme court justice; b. Greenwood, Ark., Oct. 24, 1944; s. John Luther and Flora (Joyce) J.; m. Carla Jean Newsom, Nov. 6, 1970; children: Betsy, Carl, Jeff, Laura, Philip. BA, Tex. Tech. U., 1965, JD, 1975. Bar: Tex. 1975, U.S. Dist. Ct. (no. and we. dists.) Tex. 1976, U.S. Ct. Appeals (5th cir.) 1984, U.S. Supreme Ct. 1984; cert. in civil trial and personal injury trial law, Tex. Bd. Legal Specialization. Assoc. Crenshaw Dupree & Milam, Lubbock, Tex., 1975-80, ptnr., 1980-98; justice Tex. State Ct. of Appeals (7th dist), Amarillo, 1999—2002, chief justice, 2003—05; justice Tex. Supreme Ct., Austin, Tex., 2005—. Bd. dirs., pres. Lubbock County Legal Aid Soc., Tex., 1977-79; bd. dirs., chmn. Trinity Christian Schs., Lubbock, 1978-83, 85-89; bd. dirs., pres. S.W. Lighthouse for Blind, Lubbock, 1978-85. Served to capt. USAF, 1965-72. Decorated Silver Star, D.F.C.; Cross of Gallantry (Vietnam); Disting. Alumnus award Tex. Tech. U. Fellow: Tex. Bar Found. (life), Am. Bar Found. (life); mem.: Austin (Tex.) Bar Assn., Lubbock County Bar Assn. (pres. 1984—85), Amarillo Bar Assn., Order of Coif, Phi Delta Phi. Mailing: PO Box 12883 Austin TX 78711 Home: 5604 Southwest Pkwy Austin TX 78735 Office: Texas Supreme Ct 201 W 14th St Rm 104 Austin TX 78701

JOHNSON, PHILLIP EDWARD, lawyer; b. Cleve., Mar. 19, 1950; s. Donald Marquis and Jeannette (Tetinek) Johnson; m. Priscilla Dwinnell, Sept. 12, 1981. BA, Miami U., Oxford, Ohio, 1972; JD, Case Western Res. U., Cleve., 1975. Bar: Ohio 75, U.S. Dist. Ct. (no. dist.) Ohio 75, Maine 77, U.S. Dist. Ct. Maine 77, U.S. Supreme Ct. 2004. Assoc. Arter & Harden, Cleve., 1975—77, Pierce Atwood, Augusta and Portland, Maine, 1977—82, ptnr., 1983—92, Johnson & Webbert, LLP, Augusta, 1992—. Vice chmn. Maine Bd. of Property Tax Rev., 1992—96; mem. Maine Profl. Ethics Commn., 2000—, chmn., 2003—. Mem.: ABA, Kennebec County Bar Assn. (pres. 1983—85), Maine Trial Lawyers Assn. (bd. govs. 1993—2003), Maine State Bar Assn., Lawyer-Pilots Bar Assn. Republican. Home: 66 Hemlock Ter Augusta ME 04330-6248 Office: PO Box 79 160 Capitol St Augusta ME 04332-0079 Office Phone: 207-623-5110. Business E-Mail: pjohnson@johnsonwebbert.com.

JOHNSON, PHYLLIS ELAINE, chemist, researcher, federal official; b. Grafton, ND, Feb. 19, 1949; d. Donald Gordon and Evelyn Lorraine (Svaren) Lanes; m. Robert S.T. Johnson (dec. Mar. 2001), Sept. 12, 1969; children: Erik, Sara. BS, U. ND, 1971; PhD in Phys. Chemistry, U. ND, Grand Forks, 1976. Instr. chemistry Mary Coll., Bismarck, ND, 1971-72; postdoctoral rsch. fellow U. ND, Grand Forks, 1975-79, chemist, 1977-79; rsch. chemist USDA Human Nutrition Rsch. Ctr., 1979-87, rsch. leader for nutrition, biochemistry and metabolism, 1987-91; assoc. dir. Pacific West Area USDA-ARS, 1996-97; dir. Beltsville Area USDA, ARS, 1997—. Editor: Stable Isotopes in Nutrition, 1984; mem. editl. bd.: Jour. Micronutrient Analysis, 1988—91, Jour. Nutrition, 1998—2004; contbr. articles to profl. jours., scientific papers to peer-rev. pubs. Co-chair comm. and media Balt. Regional Initiative Developing Genuine Equality, 2003—. Recipient Arthur S. Flemming award Outstanding Sci. Achievement, 1989, Women in Sci. and Engring. award, 1993, Sioux award ND Alumni Found., 1998, Fed. Energy and Water Mgmt. award, 1998, Disting. Chem. Alumni lectr., U. ND, 1998, Presdl. Rank award of Meritorious Exec., Pres. of U.S., 1999, White House Closing the Circle award for Environ. Mgmt. from Pres. Bush, 2002, for Biobased Products Program, 2003, Oustanding Achievement award United Soybean Assn., 2005, Pub. Sector Innovator of Yr., Tech. Coun. Md., 2006. Mem. Am. Soc. Clin. Nutrition, Am. Chem. Soc., Am. Soc. for Nutrition, Sr. Exec. Assn., Rotary, Sons of Norway (dist. v.p. 1984-86, dist. pres. 1986-88, internat. bd. dirs. 1988-92), Phi Beta Kappa, Sigma Xi, Gamma Sigma Delta. Lutheran. Avocations: cooking, needlecrafts. Home: 7868 Manet Way Severn MD 21144-1649 Office: BARC-WestBldg 003 Rm 223 10300 Baltimore Ave Beltsville MD 20705-2350 Office Phone: 301-504-6078. Office Fax: 301-504-5863. Business E-Mail: phyllis.johnson@ars.usda.gov.

JOHNSON, R. MILTON, healthcare executive; b. Dec. 15, 1956; m. Denice Johnson; children: Lindsay, Tyler. B in acctg., Belmont Univ. CPA. Acct. Ernst & Young; tax mgr. HCA Inc., 1982—87; dir. tax HealthTrust, 1987—95; v.p. tax, v.p. controller HCA Inc., 1995-99, sr. v.p., controller, 1999—2004, exec. v.p., CFO, 2004—. Bd. dir. HCA Found., McNeilly Ctr. for Children. Office: HCA Inc 1 Park Plz Nashville TN 37203*

JOHNSON, RANDALL CLYDE, mortgage company executive; b. Tulsa, Okla., Feb. 12, 1949; s. Clyde O. and Barbara Grace Johnson; m. Mary Dan Peck, June 25, 1971 (div. Aug. 1981); 1 child, Paul C.; m. Frances Evelen Wigelious, Oct. 1, 1982; 1 child, Tyler B. BA, U. Miami, Coral Gables, Fla., 1971. V.p. Baker Mortgage Co., Miami, Fla., 1971-75; S.E. U.S. regional mgr. Gen. Electric Credit Corp., Coral Gables, Fla., 1975-77; pres., CEO Equitable Mortgage Resources, Inc., Clearwater, Fla., 1977-89; chmn., CEO Market St. Mortgage Co., Clearwater, 1989—. Mem. adv. bd. Avondale Funding Corp., Chgo., 1998—2000, Residential Funding Corp./GM Acceptance, Bloomington, Minn., 1999, Fannie Mae Corp., Washington, 2000—02. Contbr.: Real Estate Financing Desk Book, 1977. Pres. Mental Health Assn. Pinellas County, Clearwater, 1986-89; participant Leadership Pinellas, Clearwater, 1988-98; dir. Clearwater Marine Sci. Ctr., 1990-91; vice chmn. Mortgage Bankers Polit. Action Com., Washington, 1996-98; hon. chmn. Pinellas County March of Dimes, 2000; mem. pres.'s coun. U. Miami, 1998—, bd. trustees 2005-; bd. trustees All Children's Hosp. Found., 2003. Recipient Schumacher-Bolduc award, 1999; named Outstanding Young Men in Am., JCs Internat., 1979, Floridans to Watch in the Next Ten Years, Fla. Trend Mag., Miami, 1980, Significant Sig, Sigma Chi Nat. Fraternity, Evanston, Ill., 1998; faculty fellow Sch. Mortgage Banking, Washington, 1988. Fellow Soc. Cert. Mortgage Bankers (master CMB, mem. CMB commn. 2001-); mem. Mortgage Bankers Assn. Am. (profl. mem., bd. govs. 1995—, Legion of Honor 1999), Mortgage Bankers Assn. Fla. (profl. mem., pres. 1987-88), Carlouel Yacht Club, Wade Hampton Golf Club, Cypress Run Golf Club. Republican. Episcopalian. Avocations: spending time with my family, golf, fishing. Fax: 727-791-4136. Business E-Mail: randy.johnson@msmcorp.com.

JOHNSON, RANDY (RANDALL DAVID JOHNSON), professional baseball player; b. Walnut Creek, Calif., Sept. 10, 1963; s. Bud and Carol Johnson; m. Lisa Johnson, 1993; children: Sammantha, Tanner, Willow, Alexandria. Student, U. So. Calif. Pitcher Montreal Expos, 1985—89, Seattle Mariners, 1989—98, Houston Astros, 1998, Ariz. Diamondbacks, Phoenix, 1999—2004, 2007—, NY Yankees, 2005—07. Named Pitcher of Yr., Sporting News, 1995, Sportsman of Yr., Sports Illustrated, 2001, Am. League Strikeout Leader, 1992—95, Am. League Earned Runs Average (ERA) Leader, 1995, Nat. League Strikeout Leader, 1999—2002, 2004, Nat. League Earned Run Average (ERA) Leader, 1999, 2001—02, Nat. League Wins Leader, 2002, Co-MVP, World Series, 2001; named to All-Star Team, 1990, 1993—95, 1997, 1999—2002, 2004; recipient Am. League Cy Young award, 1995, Nat. League Cy Young award, 1999—2002. Achievements include mem. World Series Champion Arizona Diamondbacks, 2001; pitched a no-hitter vs. Detroit Tigers, 1990; pitched a perfect game vs. Atlanta Braves, 2004; holds MLB record for career strikeouts by a left-handed pitcher; ranks 3rd all-time for career strikeouts. Office: Ariz Diamondbacks BankOne Ballpark 401 E Jefferson St Phoenix AZ 85004-2438*

JOHNSON, RAYMOND K., information technology manager; b. Texas City, Tex., Jan. 25, 1959; s. Raymond Knight and Gertrude Delores Johnson; m. Sandra D. Meaux, Nov. 7, 1957; 1 child, Matthew Kee. BSEE, U. Houston, 1983. Instrumentation and elec. specialist Brown & Root, Houston, 1978—85; sr. customer svc. rep. Honeywell, Houston, 1985—89; pres., chief sicentist Kingwood (Tex.) Tech. Group, 1989—97; mgr. info. tech. San Jacinto River Authority, Conroe, Tex., 1997—. Contbr.: ANSI Standard, Application of Safety and Instrumentation Systems for the Process Industries, 1996. Leader Boy Scouts Am., Houston, 1991—; mem. Harris County Cmty. Emergency Response Team, Kingwood Cmty. Response Task Force; S. Tex. tech. coord. Am. Radio Relay League. Recipient Excellence in Engring. award, Chevron Chem. Co., 1991, Project award, Chevron Info. Tech. Co., 1992, Comdr.'s award for civilian Svc., U.S. Army, 1993, St. George award, Episcopal Ch., 2000, Cert. of Achievement, FEMA, 2005. Mem.: IEEE, NRA, Instrumentation, Sys. and Automation Soc., U. Houston Alumni (life), Am. Radio Relay League (life). Republican. Avocations: sailing, photography. Office: San Jacinto River Authority 1577 Damsite Rd Conroe TX 77304 Home Phone: 281-359-6375; Office Phone: 281-367-9511. Personal E-mail: w7rkj@rkjtech.com. Business E-Mail: drrayj@sjra.net.

JOHNSON, RAYMOND LEWIS, mathematician; b. Alice, Tex., June 25, 1943; s. Johnnie V. Johnson; m. Claudette Willia Smith, Aug. 28, 1965; 1 child, Malcolm Patrice. BA in Math., U. Tex., Austin, 1963; PhD in Math., Rice U., 1969. Asst. prof. U. Md., College Park, 1968-72, assoc. prof., 1972-80, prof., 1980—, assoc. chair for grad. studies, 1987—90, chair dept. math., 1991—96. Vis. mem. Institut Mittag-Leffler, Djorsholm, Sweden, 1974-75; vis. prof. Howard U., Washington DC, 1976-78, McMaster U., Hamilton, Canada, 1983-84; bg. gov. Math. Assn. Am., Inst. for Math. and its Applications; founding mem. Conf. for African Am. Researchers in Math. Sciences. Contbr. articles to scholarly and profl. jours. Sec. Woodstream Village Homeowners' Assn., Seabrook, Md., 1987-92. Recipient Disting. Minority Faculty award U. Md., College Park, 1986, 2006 AAAS Mentor award for Lifetime Achievement, 2007. Unitarian Universalist. Home: 6916 Woodstream Ln Lanham Seabrook MD 20706-2146 Office: Dept Mathematics U Md Room 2107 Mathematics Bldg College Park MD 20742-4105 Office Phone: 301-405-7061. Office Fax: 301-314-0827. Business E-Mail: rlj@math.umd.edu.*

JOHNSON, REVERDY, lawyer; b. NYC, Aug. 24, 1937; s. Reverdy and Reva (Payne) J.; children: Deborah Ghiselin, Reverdy Payne. AB cum laude, Harvard U., Cambridge, Mass., 1960, LLB, 1963. Bar: Fla. 1963, Calif. 1964, N.Mex. 1997. Assoc. Brobeck, Phleger & Harrison, San Francisco, 1963-66; from assoc. to ptnr. Pettit & Martin, San Francisco, 1966-95; of counsel Steinhart & Falconer LLP, San Francisco, 1995-97, Scheuer Yost & Patterson, Sante Fe, N.Mex., 1996—, Fenwick and West, LLP, Mountain View, Calif., 1999—2003. Co-owner Johnson Turnbull Vineyards, Napa Valley, Calif., 1977-93; tech. adv. com., com. open space lands Calif. Joint Legislature, 1968-69, chmn., 1969-70 Bd. dirs. Planning and Conservation League, 1966—72, League to Save Lake Tahoe, 1972—77, Found. for San Francisco's Archtl. Heritage, 1975—84, San Francisco Devel. Found., 1986—96, Santa Fe Shakespeare Co., 2001—03, pres., 2002—03. Mem. Urban Land Inst. (vice-chmn. recreational devel. council 1975-78, comml. and retail devel. council 1980-99), Napa Valley Vintners Assn. (bd. dir. 1985-88, v.p. 1987, pres. 1988), Am. Coll. Real Estate Lawyers, Lambda Alpha. Office: Scheuer Yost & Patterson 125 Lincoln Ave Ste 223 Santa Fe NM 87501-2053 also: PO Box 145 Pope Valley CA 94567 Office Phone: 707-965-3430. Personal E-mail: reverdyjohnson@earthlink.net. Business E-Mail: reverdyj@santafelawyers.com.

JOHNSON, RICHARD, editor; b. Jan. 1954; m. Nadine Johnson (div.); children: Damon, Jack. Student, U. Colo.; BA in Communications, Empire State Coll. Editor in chief Chelsea Clinton News; gen. assignment NY Post, 1978, Page Six reporter, 1983—85, Page Six editor, 1985—90, 1993—; asst. mng. editor Preview: The Best of the New, 1990; columnist NY Observer, 1991, NY Daily News, 1991—93. Avocation: art. Office: NY Post 1211 Avenue Of The Americas New York NY 10036

JOHNSON, RICHARD A., lawyer; b. Mar. 23, 1950; AB, Brown Univ., 1972; MS, MIT, 1973; JD, Yale Univ., 1976. Bar: Calif. 1977, D.C. 1978. Law clk. Judge Eugene A. Wright, US Ct. Appeals, 9th Cir., Seattle, 1976—77; assoc. gen. counsel, internat. trade US Dept. Commerce, 1980—81; ptnr., Internat. Trade Practice Group Arnold & Porter, Washington. Editor: Yale Law Journal. Chmn., Biotech. Com. & vice chmn., Tech. & Innovation Com. OECD/BIAC; chmn. OECD Intellectual Property Task Force; mem. bd. vis. MIT Corp. Nat. Fellow, Nat. Sci. Found., 1973. Mem.: Am. Soc. of Internat. Law (mem., exec. bd., past chmn., annual meeting), U.S. Council for Internat. Bus., Bus.-Univ. Forum. Office: Arnold & Porter 555 Twelfth St NW Washington DC 20004-1206 Office Phone: 202-942-5550. Office Fax: 202-942-5999. Business E-Mail: richard.johnson@aporter.com.

JOHNSON, RICHARD ARLO, lawyer; b. Vermillion, SD, July 8, 1952; s. Arlo Goodwin and Edna Marie (Styles) J.; m. Diane Marie Zephier, Aug. 18, 1972 (div. Jan. 1979); m. Sheryl Lavonne Mader, June 5, 1981; 1 stepchild, Chadwick O. Wagner; 1 child, Sarah N. BA, U. SD, 1974, JD, 1976. Bar: SD 1977, US Dist. Ct. SD 1977. Ptnr. Pruitt, Matthews, Muilenberg & Strange, Sioux Falls, SD, 1977—92, Strange, Farrell & Johnson, P.C., Sioux Falls, 1992—. Mem. Pub. Defender Adv. Bd., Sioux Falls, 1983-98; mem. SD Dental Peer Rev. Com. S.E. Dist. Fellow Am. Acad. Matrimonial Lawyers; mem. ATLA, ABA, SD Trial Lawyers Assn., State Bar SD (chmn. family law com. 1989-92, Best Lawyers Am. 1995-2007, Super Lawyers Great Plains 2007), Jazz and Blues Soc. (bd. dirs., 1998-2005, pres. 2003), Phi Delta Phi (pres. 1976-77), Masons, Shriners (past potentate). Democrat. Lutheran. Home: 409 E Lotta St Sioux Falls SD 57105-7109 Office: Strange Farrell & Johnson PC 141 N Main Ave Ste 200 Sioux Falls SD 57104-6429 Home Phone: 605-338-2799; Office Phone: 605-339-4500. Business E-Mail: rico@strangelaw.com.

JOHNSON, RICHARD ARNOLD, statistics educator, consultant; b. St. Paul, July 10, 1937; s. Arnold Verner and Florence Dorothy J.; m. Roberta Anne Weinard, Mar. 21, 1964; children— Erik Richard, Thomas Robert B.E.E., U. Minn., Mpls., 1960, MS in Math., 1963, PhD in Stats., 1966. Asst. prof. stats. U. Wis., Madison, 1966-70, assoc. prof., 1970-74, prof. stats, 1974—, chmn. dept. stats., 1981-84; head Greentree Statis. Consulting, Madison, Wis., 1978—. Cons. industry, Dept. Energy; cooperating scientist Dept. Agr.; lectr. in more than 20 countries. Co-author: Statistical Concepts and Methods, 1977, Applied Multivariate Statistical Analysis, 1982, 6th edit., 2007, Probability and Statistics for Engineers, 7th edit., 2005, Statistics-Principles and Methods, 1985, 5th edit., 2006, Business Statistics-Decision Making with Data, 1997, Statistical Reasoning and Methods, 1998; founding editor Stat. and Probability Letters, 1992—. Recipient Frank Wilcoxon prize, 1991; NATO sr. postdoctoral fellow, 1972; numerous grants NSA, NSF, ONR, Air Force, NASA. Fellow Inst. Math. Stats. (program sec. 1980-86, mem. of council 1980-86), Am. Statis. Assn. (sect. rep. to council 1980-82), Royal Statis. Soc.; mem. Internat. Statis. Inst. Lutheran. Avocations: fishing, cross country skiing. Office: Greentree Statis Cons 7122 Valhalla Trl Madison WI 53719-3039 E-mail: rich@stat.wisc.edu.

JOHNSON, RICHARD AUGUST, literature and language professor; b. Washington, Apr. 18, 1937; s. Cecil August and Esther Marie (Nelson) J.; m. Michaela Ann Memelsdorff, Aug. 20, 1960; children— Nicholas, Patrick, Hong, Loeun. BA, Swarthmore Coll., 1959; PhD, Cornell U., 1965. Instr. English U. Va., Charlottesville, 1963-65; asst. prof. Mt. Holyoke Coll., South Hadley, Mass., 1965-71, assoc. prof., 1971-74, prof., chmn. dept., 1974-80, 1988-91, prof. Alumnae Found., 1980-86, Lucia, Ruth and Elizabeth MacGregor prof. English, 1986—2004, emeritus prof., 2004—. Vis. prof. Amherst Coll., 1979, 84-88. Author: Man's Place: An Essay on Auden, 1973; co-author: Common Ground: Personal Writing and Public Discourse, 1992, Finding Common Ground, 1996; contbr. articles to profl. jours. Mem. MLA, AAUP, Phi Beta Kappa Democrat. Episcopalian. Home: 1214 Noyes Dr Silver Spring MD 20910-2717 E-mail: rjohnson@mtholyoke.edu.

JOHNSON, RICHARD DARRELL, management consultant; b. Columbus, Ohio, Aug. 1, 1935; s. Darrell Dean and Gretchen Price (Motz) Johnson; m. Ann Elizabeth Sektnan, Apr. 9, 1960; children: Julie Ann, Jennifer Lynn, Douglas Richard. B in Indsl. Engring., Ohio State U., 1958, MBA, 1962. CPA Ohio, Ill.; cert. in computer processing Inst. Cert. Computer Profls.; registered profl. engr., Ohio. Consulting staff Arthur Andersen & Co., Cleve., 1962-65, consulting mgr., 1965-70, consulting ptnr., 1970, consulting mng. ptnr., 1971-75, cons. retail industry head, 1969-75, chmn. adv. coun., 1976-78, country mng. ptnr. Iran, Afghanistan and Pakistan Tehran, Iran, 1975-77, mng. ptnr. profl. edn. Chgo., 1977-79, mng. ptnr. edn. consulting, 1979-86; mng. ptnr. change mgmt. Andersen Consulting, Chgo., 1986-91, ret. ptnr., 1991; pres. VIA Internat. Ltd., Chgo., 1992-99; chmn. VIA Internat. LLC, Chgo., 1998-99; pres. RDJ Ltd. Mgmt. Conss., 1999—; mgr., mem. Ventures 33 LLC, 2004—. Sec. Ill. Dist. 67 Bd. Edn., Lake Forest, 1984—85, chmn. edn. com., 1987—90, chmn. strategic planning com., 1989—90, v.p., 1989—90; pres. club adv. bd. Ohio State U., 1990—2000, vice chmn., 1995—96, chmn., 1996—98, emeritus mem., 2000—; trustee Ravinia Festival Assn., Highland Pk., Ill., 1988—2004, 2006—, vice chmn., 1999—2002, chmn. devel. com., 1999—2002, long range planning com., 1996—; treas. Lake Forest (Ill.) Symphony Assn., 1979—81, v.p., 1981—83; exec. v.p. Lake Forest Symphony Assn., Ill., 1983—89, adv. bd., 1989—2000; gen. coord. Chgo. campaign Am. Cancer Soc., 1983; dir. United Way Lake Forest, Lake Bluff, Ill., 1981—, treas., 1984—86, pres., 1986—88; Chgo. adv. bd. Coll. Engring., Ohio State U., 1988—91; mem. Alumni Assn. Bd., 1999—2004; alumni adv. coun. Ohio State U., 1996—99; vice chmn. Alumni Assn. Bd., 2001—04; mem. Coll. Bus. Adv. Coun., 1976—83, 1st v.p., 1978—79; mem. Ruth Weimer Mt. Leadership Initiatives Fund, 1997—2001. 1st lt. USAF, 1958—61. Recipient Internat. Disting. Svc. award, Assn. Sys. Mgmt., 1976, Gerlach award, 1998, Alumni Citizenship Award, OSU Alumni Assoc., 1998, Disting. Alumni award, Fisher Coll. of Bus., 2002, Disting. Svc. award, Ohio State U., 2006. Mem.: Chgo. Coun. Global Affairs, Ohio State Univ. Pres. Club (adv. bd. 1990—2000, vice chmn. 1995—96, chmn. 1996—98, emeritus mem. 2000—), Sloane Gardens Club (London) (treas. 1993—94), Pelican Isle Yacht Club (Naples, Fla.), Pelican Marsh Golf Club (Naples), Sigma Chi (Significant Sig award 2002). Avocations: skiing, boating, travel, golf, classical music. Home: 351 Sussex Ln Lake Forest IL 60045-2057 Office: RDJ Ltd 351 Sussex Lane Lake Forest IL 60045-2057 Personal E-mail: rdjltd@earthlink.net.

JOHNSON, RICHARD DAVID, retired librarian; b. Cleve., June 10, 1927; s. Robert Emanuel and Emma (Lindhorst) J.; m. Harriett Herzog, Sept. 8, 1956; children: Ruth Ellen, Royce Emanuel. BA, Yale U., 1949; MA in Internat. Rels., U. Chgo., 1950, MALS, 1957. Libr. Nat. Opinion Rsch. Ctr. U. Chgo., 1956-57; reference libr. Stanford, 1957-59; cataloger Stanford U., 1959-60, 61-62, adminstrv. asst. to dir., 1960-61, head acquisitions, 1962-64, chief undergrad. libr. project, 1964-67, chief libr. tech. svcs., 1967-68; dir. librs. Claremont (Calif.) Colls., 1968-73, SUNY, Oneonta, 1973-94; ret., 1994. Editor: Calif. Libr., 1966-68, Coll. and Rsch. Librs., 1974-80, Choice, 1982, Lexington Books series on librs., 1981-87, N.Y. Libr. Assn. Bull., 1986-91, Assn. Libr. Collections and Tech. Svcs. Newsletter, 1989-91, Glimmerglass Opera Guild Newsletter, 1995—; mng. editor: Jour. Libr. Automation, 1980. Trustee Four County Libr. System, Binghamton, N.Y., 1978-88, South Cen. Rsch.Libr. Coun., Ithaca, 1986-90. With inf. AUS, 1952-54. Decorated Bronze Star; recipient Acad./Rsch. Libr. of Yr. award Assn. Coll. and Rsch. Librs., 1984, Trustees award for outstanding svc. South Ctrl. Rsch. Libr. Coun., 1994, Ptnr. in Excellence award Opera Vols. Internat., 2000. Mem. ALA, Calif. Libr. Assn. (pres. 1972), N.Y. Libr. Assn. (pres. acad. and spl. librs. sect. 1981-82, 2d v.p. 1982, Spirit of Librarianship award 1992), Beta Phi Mu. Presbyterian. Home: 2 Walling Blvd Oneonta NY 13820-1918

JOHNSON, RICHARD DEAN, pharmaceutical consultant, educator; b. DeKalb, Ill., July 8, 1936; s. Arthur Dean Johnson and Evelyn Alice (Telford) Williams; m. Paula Marcellus Jennings, Nov. 3, 1942; children: Janet Telford Bijur, Julie Johnson McVeigh, Richard Dean Jr., Jennings Brodie. *Maternal Grandfather E.D. Telford, AB 1896 McKendree College, LLB 1899 Georgetown U., was a three term Illinois State Senator and Republican candidate for Congress in 1926. Daughter Janet Telford Bijur, AB 1994 Duke U., MBA 2000 Anderson School of Business, University of California Los Angeles, is currently v.p. institutional sales with Friedman, Billings, Ramsey in San Francisco. Daughter Julie Johnson McVeigh, AB summa cum laude 1997 Bowdoin College, Chartered Financial Analyst, 2007, is a portfolio manager with NorthStar Asset Management Incorporated in Boston. Son Richard Dean Johnson Jr., AA 1998 Tacoma Community College, AB 2000 U. Puget Sound, secondary education teacher's certificate 2005 is currently a graduate student at Woodbridge School of Education, Western Washington University and appeared in the 1998 Disney film 10 Things I Hate About You. Son Jennings Brodie Johnson is completing his degree in military history at Kansas State University while working for the Federal Government.* BS, U. Calif., Berkeley, 1960; PharmD, U. Calif., San Francisco, 1961, MS, 1962, PhD, 1965; MBA, Rockhurst U., 1984. Cert. tchr. Calif., lic. pharmacist Calif. Sect. head R&D Allergan Inc., Irvine, Calif., 1965—67; dir. regulatory affairs Syntex Labs., Inc., Palo Alto, Calif., 1967—73; mng. dir. licensing Marion Labs., Inc., Kansas City, Mo., 1973—79, v.p. licensing, 1980—82, v.p. corp. devel., 1983—87, v.p. bus. alliances, 1987—88; corp. v.p. Marion Merrell Dow, Inc., Kansas City, 1989—91, ret., 2003; prin., owner KC Pharma, LLC, Kansas City, 1991—. Adj. prof. Sch. Pharmacy, U. Mo., Kansas City, 1991-95, R&D coun., 1993—, adj. grad. prof., 1995—; bd. dirs. Dey Labs., Inc., Concord, Calif., Tanabe-Marion Labs., Kansas City, U.S. Biosci., Inc., Blue Bell, Pa., ImmunoPharmaceutics, Inc., San Diego, Lovelace Respiratory Rsch. Inst., Albuquerque, Micrologix Biotech Inc., Vancouver, B.C.; comp. and audit coms. Tima Tech., Inc., Kansas City, AusAm Biotech., Inc., Santa Monica, Calif.; comp. and intellectual property coms. Sober Rovers, LLC, Bellingham, Wash.; guest lectr. U. SC

Sch. Bus. Adminstrn., Columbia, 1975-79; pharm. analyst SunTrust Robinson Humphrey, 2002, Cottonwood Capital Mgmt., LLC, 2002-04; med. analyst Reynders, McVeigh Capital Mgmt. LLC, Boston, 2005— *Over 40 years Dr. Johnson has gained executive experience in the U.S. pharmaceutical industry leading to corporate officer status in two Fortune 500 companies as well as numerous company and community board director and trusteeships. A major contribution to U.S. medicine included his patent licensing role in Japan of two major new drugs, a life saving cardiovascular agent and a gastrointestinal antiulcer product, achieving combined annual sales of more than $2.5 billion. He is currently an Adjunct Graduate Professor in the School of Pharmacy, University of Missouri-Kansas City and founder, owner of KC Pharma, LLC, a technology transfer firm in Kansas City, Missouri. During 2005, Dr. Johnson was nominated by the Missouri governor and confirmed by the State Senate to serve a 4-year term on the Missouri Life Science Research Board.* Contbr. articles to profl. jours. Presdl. exch. exec. White House, Washington, 1970-71, U.S. Pharmacopeia Com. of Rev., 1990-2001; trustee U. Mo., Kansas City Pharmacy Found., 1993-07, v.p., 1994-96, pres., 1996-98, fin. com., 1996—2000, pres. emeritus, 1998—, chmn. devel. com., 1994-96, chmn. exec. and fin. coms., 1996-98, dean's adv. bd., 1995—; trustee Johnson Family Fund, Kansas City Cmty. Found., 1993—, U. Kansas City Bd., Mo., 1996-2001, U. Mo., Kansas City, 2001—; fin., real estate and life scis. coms., 1998—; mem. Kansas City Life Sci. Initiative and Undergrad. Rsch. coms., 2001—; dean's adv. bd. Sch. Pharmacy U. Calif., San Francisco, 1994-97, bd. counsellors, 1997-2001; dean's adv. bd. Sch. Pharmacy U. Mo., Kansas City, 1995-2001, 2003—; trustee Conservatory of Music, U. Mo., Kansas City, 1998-2002; Henry W. Bloch Sch. Bus. and Pub. Adminstrn. exec. roundtable U. Mo., Kansas City, 1998-2003; active Internat. Rels. Coun., Kansas City, 1998—; active De La Salle Sch. Devel. Com., 1993-2001, St. Lukes Hosp. Stroke Com., 1993—2006, U.S. Pharmacopeia Drug Nomenclature Com., 1990-2001, vet. drug com., 1998-2001, ARC; mem. State of Mo. Life Sci. Rsch. Bd., Jefferson City, 2005—. Recipient Grad. award Borden Co., 1962; NIH Pub. Health Svc. Tng. grant, 1962-65; Am. Found. for Pharm. Edn. fellow, 1962-65, Sir Henry S. Wellcome Meml. fellow, 1962-63, Am. Inst. Chemists fellow, 1965-70; named to FBI Citizens' Acad., Kansas City, 2007—. Mem.: ACS, AAAS, Licensing Exec. Soc., Fedn. Internat. Pharmacy, Pharm. Mfrs. Assn., N.Y. Acad. Sci., Acad. Pharm. Sci., Am. Pharm. Assn., Am. Assn. Pharm. Scis., Am. Found. for Pharm. Edn. Centurion, ARC Kirkwood Soc., Mission Hills Country Club, La Jolla Country Club, Carriage Club (Kansas City, Mo.), River Club (Kansas City), La Jolla (Calif.) Beach and Tennis Club, Balboa Bay Club (Newport Beach, Calif.), Hallbrook Country Club (Leawood, Kans.), Sigma Xi, Theta Delta Chi, Phi Lambda Sigma, Rho Chi. Home: 5330 Ward Pky Kansas City MO 64112-2369 Office: KC Pharma LLC 222 W Gregory Blvd Kansas City MO 64114-1110 also: 8486 El Paseo Grande La Jolla CA 92037-3013 Address: 4000 N Lake Blvd Tahoe City CA 96145-5303 Office Phone: 816-444-5556. Business E-Mail: kcpharma@webtv.net.

JOHNSON, RICHARD FRED, lawyer; b. July 12, 1944; s. Sylvester Hiram and Naomi Ruth (Jackson) Johnson; m. Sheila Conley, June 26, 1970; children: Brendon, Bridget, Timothy, Laura. BS, Miami U., Oxford, Ohio, 1966; JD cum laude, Northwestern U., 1969. Bar: Ill. 1969, Ind., 2004, U.S. Dist. Ct. (no. dist.) Ill. 1969), U.S. Dist. Ct. (ctrl. dist.) Ill. 2000, U.S. Dist. Ct. (no. dist.) Ind., 2006, U.S. Ct. Appeals (7th cir.) 1977, U.S. Ct. Appeals (2d cir.) 1980, U.S. Ct. Appeals (9th cir.) 1991, U.S. Ct. Appeals (5th cir.) 1993, U.S. Supreme Ct. 1978. Law clk. U.S. Dist. Ct. (no. dist.) Ill., Chgo., 1969-70; assoc. firm Lord, Bissell & Brook, Chgo., 1970-77, ptnr., 1977—2004, Hughes, Socol, Piers, Resnick and Dym, Ltd., Chgo., 2004—. Lectr. legal edn. Contbr. articles to profl. jours. Recipient Am. Jurisprudence award 1968. Mem. Chgo. Bar Assn., Union League. Home: 521 W Roscoe St Chicago IL 60657-3518 Office: Hughes Socol Piers Resnick & Dym Ltd 70 W Madison Chicago IL 60602 Office Phone: 312-604-2618. Business E-Mail: rjohnson@hsplegal.com.

JOHNSON, RICHARD J., lawyer; b. Mpls., Oct. 19, 1950; BS with high distinction, U. Minn., 1972; JD, Harvard U., 1975. Bar: Minn. 1975. With Moss & Barnett PC, Mpls.; atty. Moss & Barnett PC. Contbr. Recipient Energy/Pub. Utility Law Lawyer, Best Lawyers. Mem. ABA, Beta Gamma Sigma, Minn. State Bar Assn., Hennepin County Bar Assn., Fed. Comm. Bar Assn. Office: Moss & Barnett PC 4800 Wells Fargo Center 90 S 7th St Minneapolis MN 55402-4129 Office Phone: 612-877-5275. Office Fax: 612-877-5999. Business E-Mail: johnsonr@moss-barnett.com.

JOHNSON, RICHARD J., bank executive; b. 1958; Pres., CEO J.P. Morgan Svcs., 1999—2002; sr. v.p., dir. fin. PNC Fin. Svcs. Group, Pitts., 2002—05, CFO, 2005—. Office: PNC Fin Svcs Group Inc 1 PNC Plz 249 5th Ave Pittsburgh PA 15222-2707 Office Phone: 412-762-2000. Office Fax: 412-762-7829.*

JOHNSON, RICHARD KENT, publishing executive; b. Moberly, Mo., Mar. 22, 1952; s. Edward and Elizabeth Johnson; m. Susan Fersh, Sept. 4, 1976; children: Alexis, Claire. BA, Am. U., 1974. TV prodn. specialist Smithsonian Inst., Washington, 1974-77; dir. pub. rels. Congl. Info. Svc., Bethesda, Md., 1977-80, dir. advt. and promotion, 1980-83, dir. communications, 1983-89, dir. mktg., 1989-90, v.p. mktg., 1990-96, Univ. Publs. Am., Bethesda, 1990-96; sr. v.p. Congl. Info. Svc. and Univ. Pubs. Am., 1997-98; exec. dir. Scholarly Pub. and Acad. Resources Coalition, Washington, 1998—2005. Bd. dirs. BioOne, 2000—05; mem. steering com. SPARC Europe, 2001—05; mem. adv. bd. Project Euclid Cornell U., 2002—05; mem. nat. adv. com. NIH PubMed Ctr., 2003—05; sr. advisor Scholarly Pub. and Academic Resource Coalition, 2005—, Alliance Taxpayer Access, 2005—. Recipient Echo Leader award Direct Mktg. Assn., 1986, Mktg. Achievement award Info. Industry Assn., 1985, 89, 90. Home: 5622 Lamar Rd Bethesda MD 20816-1350 Office: 21 Dupont Cir NW Ste 800 Washington DC 20036-1543 Business E-Mail: rick@arl.org.

JOHNSON, RICHARD MARC, civics educator; b. Salt Lake City, Dec. 18, 1981; s. Richard Henry and Barbara Claire Johnson, Ronald Eugene Rice (Stepfather) and Jeanie Ricks Johnson (Stepmother). BA in Govt. with honors, Coll. William and Mary, Williamsburg, Va., 2004; MEd, U. Va., Charlottesville, 2007. Dir. youth programs The Sorensen Inst. for Polit. Leadership, Charlottesville, Va., 2004—, asst. to exec. dir., 2005—. Chmn. programs com. Va. Commn. on Nat. and Cmty. Svc., Richmond, 2005; pres. of the bd. Svc. Dogs of Va., Charlottesville, 2005. Recipient James Frederic Carr Meml. Cup, The Coll. of William and Mary, 2004; Koenig-Nimmo Fgn. Svc. scholar, 2004. Mem.: William and Mary Alumni Assn. (pres. chpt. 2004, chmn. young garde coun. 2005), Phi Beta Kappa. Avocations: reading, hiking. Office: The Sorensen Inst PO Box 400206 Charlottesville VA 22904 Office Phone: 434-982-4527. E-mail: rmjohnson@virginia.edu.

JOHNSON, RICHARD TENNEY, lawyer; b. Evanston, Ill., Mar. 24, 1930; s. Ernest Levin and Margaret Abbott (Higgins) J.; m. Marilyn Bliss Meuth, May 1, 1954; children: Ross Tenney, Lenore, Jocelyn. AB with high honors, U. Rochester, 1951; postgrad., Trinity Coll., Dublin, Ireland, 1954-55; LLB, Harvard, 1958. Bar: D.C. 1959. Trainee Office Sec. Def., 1957-59; atty. Office Gen. Counsel. Dept. Def., 1959-63; dep. gen. counsel Dept. Army, 1963-67, Dept. Transp., 1967-70; gen. counsel CAB, 1970-73, mem., 1976-77; gen. counsel NASA, 1973-75, ERDA, 1975-76; chmn. organizational integration Dept. Energy Activation, Exec. Office of Pres., 1977; ptnr. firm Sullivan & Beauregard, 1978-81; gen. counsel Dept. Energy, 1981-83; ptnr. Zuckert, Scoutt, Rasenberger & Johnson, 1983-87; prin. Law Offices of R. Tenney Johnson, Esq., Washington, 1987-2001; gen. counsel Assn. of Univs. for Rsch. in Astronomy, 1987—. Lt. USNR, 1951-54. Mem. ABA, Fed. Bar Assn., Cosmos Club, Phi Beta Kappa, Theta Delta Chi. E-mail: marandten@starpower.net.

JOHNSON, RICHARD TIDBALL, microbiology and neuroscience educator, virologist, researcher; b. Grosse Pointe, Mich., July 16, 1931; s. Horton and Katharine (Tidball) J.; m. Frances W. Johnson, Sept. 18, 1954; children: Carlton, Erica, Matthew, Nathan. AB cum laude, U. Colo., Boulder, 1953; MD, U. Colo., Denver, 1956. Diplomate Am. Bd. of Psychiatry and Neurology. Intern Stanford U. Hosp., San Francisco, 1956-57; clin. pathologist dept. virus diseases Walter Reed Army Inst. of Research, Washington, 1957-58, asst. chief dept. of virus diseases, 1959; asst. resident in neurology Mass. Gen. Hosp., 1959-60, clin. fellow neuropathology, 1959-61, sr. resident neurology, 1961-62; teaching fellow in neurology Harvard Med. Sch., Boston, 1959-60, teaching fellow neuropathology, 1959-61, teaching fellow neurology, 1961-62; exchange teaching fellow, 1st asst. in neurology Med. Sch. of King's Coll., U. Durham, Newcastle-Upon-Tyne, 1962; hon. fellow dept. microbiology Australian Nat. U., Canberra, 1962-64; assoc. neurologist Cleve. Met. Gen. Hosp., 1964-69; asst. prof. neurology Case Western Res. U., Cleve., 1964-68, assoc. prof. neurology, 1968-69; assoc. prof. microbiology Johns Hopkins U. Sch. of Medicine, Balt., 1969-74, Dwight D. Eisenhower prof. neurology, 1969-88, prof. microbiology, 1974—, prof. neurosci., 1983—; joint appointment dept. molecular microbiology & immunology Johns Hopkins U. Bloomberg Sch. Pub. Health, 1984—. Neurologist Johns Hopkins Hosp., Balt., 1969—, neurologist-in-chief, 1988-97, prof., dir. dept. neurology, 1988-97; cons. neurology Balt. City Hosp., 1974; vis. prof. U. Peruana Cayetano Heredia, Lima, Peru, 1971, Imperial Coll. of Health Sci., Teheran, Iran, 1974, Inst. fur Virologie und Immunobiologie, U. Wurzburg, 1976; vis. prof. neurology and neuropathology Mahidol U., Bangkok, 1984; vis. sci. Armed Forces Research Inst. of Med. Sci., Bangkok, Thailand, 1984; founding dir. Nat. Neurosci. Inst., Singapore, 1997-2000. Author (with others): Amotrophic Lateral Sclerosis: Recent Research Trends, 1976; author: Infections of the Nervous System, 1987, Viral Infections and the Developing Nervous System, 1988, Viral Infections of the Nervous System, 1982, 1998, Vol. 2, 1987, Vol. 3, 1990, Vol. 4, 1993, Vol. 5, 1997, Vol. 6, 2001; mem. editl. bd. 10 profl. jours.; editor: Annal. Neurol., 1988—2005. Mem. adv. bd. Nat. Multiple Sclerosis Soc., 1971—, exec. com., 1981—, chmn., 1985—89; spl. cons. to NIH on transmissible spongiform encephalopathis, 2001—05; mem. adv. coun. James A. Baker Inst. for Animal Health, Cornell U., 1977—89; program dir. Pew Neurosci. Program, Pew Charitable Trusts, 1985—91. Decorated comendador Order of Hipolito Unanue; recipient Jean Martin Charcot aard Internat. Fedn. Multiple Sclerosis Soc. 1985, Smadel medal Infectious Disease Soc. Am., 1986, Multiple Sclerosis Soc. medal Assn. Brit. Neurologists, 1986; Pioneer award Int. Soc. Neuroviro, 1999, fellow Royal College Physicians of London (hon.), 2003, numerous others. Mem. Am. Acad. Neurology (2d v.p. 1975-77), Assn. Am. Physicians, Am. Soc. for Virology, Australian Assn. Neurologists (hon.), Interurban Clin. Club, Acad. Brasileira de Neurologia, Assn. for Rsch. in Nervous and Mental Diseases, Internat. Brain Rsch. Orgn., Peripatetic Club, Soc. for Neurosci., Soc. Peruana de Psiquiatria, Johns Hopkins Med. Soc. (pres. 1970-71), Balt. Neurol. Soc. (pres. 1973-74), Am. Soc. for Clin. Investigation, Am. Neurol. Assn. (councillor 1977-81, v.p. 1984-85, pres. 1986-87), Am. Assn. Neuropathologists (assoc.), World Fedn. Neurology (chmn. rsch. group on neuroimmunology and virology 1979—), Am. Soc. for Microbiology, AAAS, Philippine Neurol. Assn. (hon. fellow), Internat. Soc. for Antiviral Rsch., Inst. of Medicine/NAS, Am. Fedn. Clin. Rsch., Alpha Omega Alpha, Phi Beta Kappa. Avocations: photography, travel. Office: Johns Hopkins U Sch Medicine Dept Neurology 600 N Wolfe St Pathology 627 Baltimore MD 21205 E-mail: rtj@jhmi.edu.

JOHNSON, ROBERT ALAN, lawyer; b. Harrisburg, Pa., June 18, 1944; s. Harry Andrew and Minna Melissa (Ebert) J.; m. Selina Braham Pedersen, Aug. 25, 1979; children: Isabella P., Robert A. Jr. BA, Washington and Jefferson Coll., 1966; JD, Harvard U., 1969. Bar: Pa. 1969. Assoc. Buchanan Ingersoll & Rooney, Pitts., 1969-76, ptnr., 1977—. Contbr. legal articles to profl. jours. Pres. Bach Choir Pitts., 1979—81; bd. dirs. Presbyn. Assn. of Chautauqua, 2005—, Pitts. Opera, 1985—94, River City Brass Band, Pitts., 1986—95, Renaissance and Baroque Soc., Pitts., 1994—, Friends of the Music Libr., Carnegie Libr. of Pitts., 1995—, CTC Found., 1999—, River City Brass Band Charitable Endowment, Pitts., 2000—, Early Music Am., 2002—, Chatham Baroque, Pitts., 2004—. Fellow Am. Coll. Tax Counsel, Am. Coll. Employee Benefits Counsel; mem. ABA, Allegheny County Bar Assn., Allegheny Tax Soc. (chmn. 1982-83), Pitts. Tax Club, Duquesne Club. Republican. Presbyterian. Avocation: avid collector classical music recs. Home: 601 St James St Pittsburgh PA 15232-1434 Office: Buchanan Ingersoll & Rooney 301 Grant St Ste 20 Pittsburgh PA 15219-1410 Office Phone: 412-562-8832. Business E-Mail: robert.johnson@bipc.com.

JOHNSON, ROBERT ALLISON, life insurance company executive; b. Canandaigua, NY, Sept. 8, 1928; s. Allison Fisher and Thelma Marie (Beers) J.; m. Suzanne Amundsen Stone, Dec. 18, 1951; children: Pamela Suzanne, Carol Alison, Elizabeth Stone, Cynthia Marie. BA in History, Harvard U., 1950; MBA, Western New Eng. Coll., 1963. With Mass. Mut. Life Ins. Co., Springfield, 1951—, employment mgr., 1958-72, dir. pers., 1972-76, sr. v.p., 1976—. Author: This Violent Land, 2007. Active ARC. Served with U.S. Army, 1951-53. Mem. Life Office Mgmt. Assn., Am. Soc. CLU's. Home: 181 Windjammer Dr Leesville SC 29070 Office: 1295 State St Springfield MA 01111-0001 Personal E-mail: rallisonj@pbtcomm.net.

JOHNSON, ROBERT BRITTEN, geology educator; b. Cortland, NY, Sept. 24, 1924; s. William and Christine (Hofer) J.; m. Garnet Marion Brown, Aug. 30, 1947; children: Robert Britten, Richard Karl, Elizabeth Anne. Student, Wheaton Coll., Ill., 1942-43, 46-47; AB summa cum laude, Syracuse U., NY, 1949, MS, 1950; PhD, U. Ill., 1954. Asst. geologist Ill. Geol. Survey, 1951-54; asst. prof. geology Syracuse U., 1954-55; sr. geologist and geophysicist C.A. Bays & Asso., Urbana, Ill., 1955-56; from asst. prof. to prof. engring. geology Purdue U., 1956-66, head, engring. geology dept., 1964-66; prof. geology DePauw U., 1966-67, head, dept. geology, 1966-67; prof. geology Colo. State U., 1967-88, acting chmn. dept. geology, 1968, chmn. dept., 1969-73, prof. in charge geology programs, dept. earth resources, 1973-77, acting head dept. earth resources, 1979-81, prof. emeritus, 1988—; regional geophysicist U.S. Bur. of Reclamation, 1967-76; geologist U.S. Geol. Survey, 1976-88. Cons. in field, 1957—; instr. Elderhostel programs, 1991-2000. Active local Boy Scouts Am., 4-H Club, Sci. Fair, dist. schs.; VITA vol. Served with USAAF, 1943-46. Fellow Geol. Soc. Am. (sr. fellow, E.B. Burwell Jr. Meml. award 1989), Assn. Engring. Geologists (Claire P. Holdredge Outstanding Publ. award 1990), Phi Beta Kappa. Republican. Home: 2309 Moffett Dr Fort Collins CO 80526-2122 Personal E-mail: arbjohnson@comcast.net.

JOHNSON, ROBERT BRUCE, historic preservationist, director, small business owner; b. Salina, Kans., Dec. 14, 1941; s. Robert Alexander and Virginia Belle (Keen) J.; m. Dora Koundakjian, May 14, 1966 (div. May 1986); children: Martin, Alicia; m. Genevieve Whittemore, Oct. 18, 1986; 1 child, James Trevor Johnson. BA, Wheaton Coll., 1964; JD, Cath. U. Sch. of Law, Washington, 1976. Orgnl. sales leader The Southwestern Co., Nashville, 1963-65; asst. housing mgr. Nat. Capitol Housing Authority Housing Urban Devel., Washington, 1966-67; project dir. Archdiocese of Washington Office of Edn., Washington, 1967-70; dep. dir. Dept. Labor Youth Svcs., Washington, 1970-75; pres. Intown Properties Inc., Washington, 1977-81, Mt. Vernon Realty Inc., Washington, 1981-86, Premier Realty Svcs. Inc., Washington, 1986-90; sr. v.p. AmeriFund Inc., Washington, 1990-95; devel. dir. Patrick Henry Inst., Lynchburg, Va., 1995-98; pres. Monument Real Estate Historic Properties, 1994—. Cons. Nat. Trust for Hist. Preservation, Washington, 1982-83, New Covenant Schs., Lynchburg, Va.; ptnr. Towne Ctr. Assocs., Staunton, Va., 1979-92, Capitol Link Devel. Assocs., Washington, 1986-89, Coolidge House Assocs., Washington, 1987-94; owner Hilton Hotel, 2006. Contbr. articles to profl. jours. Treas., co-founder New City Montessori Sch., Washington, 1969—73; mem. Cmty. Advisors on Equal Employment, Washington, 1967—70; patron Nat. Children's Choir, 1979—89; treas., initiator Bottle Bill Initiative Campaign, Washington, 1985—86; hon. chmn. Bus. Adv. Coun., 2002; commr. Presdl. Bus. Commn., 2002. Recipient Silver Palm Eagle Scout Boy Scouts Am., 1957. Mem. Nat. Trust for Hist. Preservation, Hist. Staunton Found. (ann. preservation award 1982, 83), Victorian Soc. Am., Lynchburg Acad. Music Theatre (co-chmn. bus. adv. coun.). Home: Villa Mozart 517 Washington St Lynchburg VA 24504 Personal E-mail: oscarlilly@verizon.net.

JOHNSON, ROBERT D., aerospace transportation executive; m. DeDe Johnson; 3 children. Grad., Miami U., Oxford, Ohio. Pres., mng. dir. GE Aircraft Engines, Singapore, 1983—93; v.p., gen. mgr., mfg. and svcs. AAR Corp., Chicago, 1993—94; v.p., gen. mgr., global repair and overhaul operations AlliedSignal Aerospace, Phoenix, 1994—96, v.p., gen. mgr., aerospace svcs., 1996—97, pres., CEO, mktg., electronic and avionics systems, 1997—99, pres., CEO, mktg., sales, & svcs., 1997—99, pres., CEO, 1999—2001, Honeywell Aerospace, Phoenix, 2001—04, chmn., 2005—. Bd. trustee Embry-Riddle Aeronautical U., 2002, Ariz. State U. Pres. Club; bd. Aviation Safety Alliance, Entrada Software. Bd. dirs. Scottsdale Home Nat. Bank, The Zanesville, Ohio. Mem.: Aerospace Inductries Assn. (exec. com.), Devel. and Flight Safety Edu. Com., U. Ariz. (adv. bd.), Miami U. of Ohio (adv. bd.), Conquistadores Del Cielo.

JOHNSON, ROBERT GRAHAM, surgeon, educator, researcher; b. Norman, Okla., July 28, 1953; s. William Froman Johnson and Mary Elizabeth Griffin Davison; m. Cindy Snodgrass, Aug. 2, 1975; children: Chase, Rainey. MD, U. Okla., 1978. Diplomate Am. Bd. Surgery, Am. Bd. Thoracic Surgery. Resident in gen. surgery U. Okla., Oklahoma City, 1978-83, resident in cardiothoracic surgery, 1983-85; fellow in cardiac surgery rsch. Mass. Gen. Hosp., Boston, 1980—81; mem. faculty Harvard U. Med. Sch., Boston, 1985—89, assoc. prof., 1989—99; prof., chair dept. surgery St. Louis U., 1999—. Fellow ACS, Am. Coll. Cardiology, Am. Coll. Chest Physicians (pres. 2001); mem. AMA, Soc. Univ. Surgeons, Alpha Omega Alpha. Episcopalian. Office: St Louis U 3635 Vista at Grand Blvd Saint Louis MO 63110 Home Phone: 314-726-0189; Office Phone: 314-577-8352. E-mail: johnsorg@slu.edu.

JOHNSON, ROBERT JAMES, psychology educator; b. Bridgeport, Conn., Apr. 21, 1955; s. Lois Virginia and Virgil Johnson; m. Deborah Lynn Bernardo, July 14, 1989. BA, Ea. Conn. State U., 1977; MA, Fairfield U., 1979, CAS, 1982; EdD, Nova Southeastern U., 2001. Cert. School PsychologIST NASP, 1988, profl. educator Conn. State Dept. of Edn., 1983. Sch. psychologist Norwalk Pub. Schs., Conn., 1980—. Summer reading tutor Horizons, New Canaan, Conn., 2001—03; summer camp careworker YMCA, Trumbull, Conn., 2004—. Mem.: NASP. Roman Catholic. Avocations: cats, sports, travel. Home: 28 Clark Rd Trumbull CT 06611 Office: Norwalk Pub Schs 125 East Ave Norwalk CT 06852-6001 Home Phone: 203-268-2445; Office Phone: 203-854-4130. Personal E-mail: schlpsy@aol.com. E-mail: johnsonr@norwalkpublicschools.net.

JOHNSON, ROBERT LEE, JR., physician, educator, researcher; b. Dallas, Apr. 28, 1926; s. Robert L. and Doris (Miller) J.; m. Aileen Johnson, 1952; children: Stephen Lee, Robert Edward. BS, So. Meth. U., 1947; MD, Northwestern U., 1951. Intern Cook County Hosp., Chgo., 1951-52; resident in internal medicine Parkland Meml. Hosp., Phila., 1952-55; fellow nat. foun. infantile paralysis and clin. instr. U. Tex. Southwestern Med. Ctr., Dallas, 1955-56; fellow dept. physiol. and pharmacology Grad. Sch. Medicine U. Pa., Phila., 1956-57; asst. prof. U. Tex. Southwestern Med. Ctr., Dallas, 1959-65, assoc. prof., 1965-69, prof. medicine, 1969—; John Butler Meml. lectr. U. Wash., Seattle, 2001. Vis. staff Parkland Meml. Hosp., Dallas, 1957—, Zale Lipshy U. Hosp., Dallas, 1989—, St. Paul Hosp., Dallas, 2000-; cons. chest diseases VA Hosp., Dallas, 1966—; dir. sarcoidosis clinic Parkland Meml. Hosp., 1983—; mem. parent rev. com. Nat. Heart, Lung, and Blood Inst. for Spl. Ctrs. of Rsch. proposals, 1983-85; mem. Nat. Heart, Lung, and Blood Rsch. Rev. Com., 1985-89; mem. respiratory and applied physiology study sect. NIH, 1991-94. Mem. editl. bd.: Jour. Clin. Investigation, 1972—77, Jour. Applied Physiology, 1980—82, Circulation, 1996—, guest referee editor: Jour. Applied Physiology, —, Am. Jour. Physiology, —, Chest, —, Circulation, —, Circulation Rsch., —, Am. Jour. Med. Sci., —, Am. Jour. Respiration and Circulation Medicine, —, Jour. Clin. Investigation, —, Early Human Devel., —, Kidney Internat., —. With Naval ROTC, 1945-46; with USNR, 1944-46; maj. USAR, 1962. Mem. Am. Heart Assn. (cardiopulmonary coun. exec. com. mem. 1990-92, nominating com. cardiopulmonary coun. 1989-93, chmn. 1990-92), Am. Thoracic Soc. (planning com. mem. 1987-90, com. proficiency standards 1985-94, Scientific Accomplishment award 1996), Am. Coll. Chest Physicians, Am. Fedn. Clin. Rsch., Am. Physiol. Soc., Am. Soc. Clin. Investigation, Assn. Am. Physicians, Cen. Soc. Clin. Rsch., So. Soc. Clin. Rsch., Soc. Sigma Xi. Office: UT Southwestern Med Ctr 5323 Harry Hines Blvd Stop 9034 Dallas TX 75390-9034

JOHNSON, ROBERT LOUIS, professional sports team owner, former broadcast executive; b. Hickory, Miss., Apr. 8, 1946; s. Archie and Edna Johnson; m. Sheila Crump, Jan. 19, 1969 (div. 2002); 2 children. BA in Hist., U. Ill., 1968; MA in Pub. Affairs, Princeton U., 1972. Press sec. Hon. Walter E. Fauntroy, Congl. del. from Washington, 1973—76; v.p. govt. rels. Nat. Cable TV Assn., 1976—79; founder Black Entertainment TV, Washington, 1979, pres., 1979—93; founder, pres. Dist. Cablevision, Inc., 1980; chmn., pres., CEO BET Holdings, Inc. (formerly Black Entertainment TV sold to Viacom), Washington, 1993—2001; CEO BET Holdings, Inc., 2001—05, chmn., 2005; founder RLJ Cos., 2001—; majority owner NBA Charlotte Bobcats, 2003—; owner Women's NBA Charlotte Sting, 2003—. Bd. dirs. US Airways, Hilton Hotels, Gen. Mills; bd. govs. Rock and Roll Hall of Fame, Cleve.; appointed to social security commn. Pres. Bush, 2001—. Bd. dirs. United Negro Coll. Fund, Am. Film Inst.; bd. govs. The Grammy Found.; bd. dirs. Jazz at Lincoln Ctr., Strayer Edn., Inc., Johns Hopkins U. Named one of Most Influential Black Ams., Ebony mag., 2006, 400 Richest Ams., Forbes mag., 2006; named to Advt. Hall of Fame, 2006; recipient Image award, NAACP, 1982, Bus. of Yr. award, DC C. of C., 1985, Exec. Leadership Coun. award, Turner Broadcasting, 1993, 20/20 Vision award, Cablevision Mag., 1995, Hall of Fame award, Broadcasting and Cable Mag., 1997, Good Guys award, Nat. Women's Polit. Caucus, 1998, Disting. Alumni award, Princeton U., 1998. Democrat. Office: RLJ Cos 3 Bethesda Metro Ctr Ste 1000 Bethesda MD 20814-6347*

JOHNSON, ROBERT MAX, lawyer; b. Thomas, Okla., Aug. 20, 1942; s. Claude L. and Jesse C. (Stimmel) J.; m. Virginia A. LeForce, May 31, 1964; children: Kelli Brook, Brent Matthew. BS, Okla. State U., 1964; JD, U. Okla., 1967; LLD (hon.), Oklahoma City U., 2001. Bar: Okla. 1967. Shareholder Crowe & Dunlevy, Oklahoma City, 1967—, pres., 1985-87, exec. com., 1992—. Spl. lectr. in land fin. and real estate contracts U. Okla. Coll. of Law, Norman, 1973, 84. Mng. editor: Oklahoma Environmental Law Handbook, 1992-96; contbr. to book: The Law of Distressed Real Estate, 1987; case editor Okla. Law Rev., 1966. Bd. dirs. Redbud Found., Oklahoma City, 1987-96, Myriad Gardens Conservatory, Oklahoma City, 1987-89, Myriad Gardens Found., 1993-96, ARC, 1994-96, Arts Coun. Oklahoma City, 1994—, Am. Heart Assn., 1999—; chmn. Oklahoma City

Festival of Arts, 1993-94, Murrah Fed. Bldg. Meml. Task Force, 1995-96, Oklahoma City Nat. Meml. Found., 1996-98, 2004-, Oklahoma City Nat. Meml. Trust, 1998-2001. Capt. U.S. Army, 1968-70. Recipient Dean A. McGee award, Downtown Now, Inc., 1998, Outstanding Svc. to the Pub. award Okla. Bar Assn., 1998, Cmty. Svc. award, 2000, Disting. Svc. award, Oklahoma City/County Hist. Soc., 2000, Robert M. Johnson award, Am. Coll. Mortgage Attys., 2001; named King, Oklahoma City Beaux Arts Ball, 2001. Fellow Am. Coll. Mortgage Attys. (bd. regents, pres. 1994-95, chmn. exec. com. 1995-96); mem. Am. Coll. Real Estate Lawyers, Oklahoma City Golf and Country Club (bd. dirs. 1981-82, sec. 1982), Order of Coif, Phi Delta Phi (magister 1966-67), Lambda Alpha. Avocations: golf, quail hunting, fly fishing. Office: East Wharf Plz Ste 102 9225 Lake Hefner Pkwy Oklahoma City OK 73120 Home: 2533 Pembroke Terr Oklahoma City OK 73116 Home Phone: 405-848-2792; Office Phone: 405-755-1650. Business E-Mail: rmjohnson@coxinet.net.

JOHNSON, ROBERT WAYNE, federal agency administrator; b. Lovelock, Nev., Mar. 6, 1951; s. Dorsey Edward and Geneva Mae (Shearer) J.; m. Mary Lucy Serrano, May 19, 1974; children: Gabriel, Carolynn. BS, U. Nev., 1973, MS, 1977. Rsch. asst. U. Nev., Reno, 1974-75; agrl. economist US Bur. Reclamation, US Dept. Interior, Sacramento, 1975-79, economist Boulder City, Nev., 1979-81, chief econ. resources bd., 1981-87, chief contracts & repayment Washington, 1987-88, regional supr. water, land and power Boulder City, 1988-91, asst. regional dir. lower Colo. region., 1991—95, regional dir., 1995—2006, commr. Washington, 2006—. Instr. Golden Gate U., Las Vegas, Nev., 1981-87; speaker, panel am. Am. Soc. Pub. Adminstrs., Las Vegas, 1991; speaker Ariz. Agribus. Coun., Phoenix, 1991; participant Western States Water Coun. Workshops, Park City, Utah, 1992. Contbg. author: Water Marketing, 1989; also articles. Recipient performance awards U.S. Bur. Reclamation, 1977, 78, 81, 84-86, 88, 90, Professorial Lectr. award Golden Gate U., San Francisco, 1987; fellow U. Nev., 1974-75; profl. water exch. fellow U.S. Bur. Reclamation, Canberra, Australia, 1992. Memm. Colorado River Water Users Assn., Assn. Calif. Water Agys., Nev. Water Resources Assn. (speaker 1989—). Avocations: golf, tennis, travel. Office: US Dept Interior Bur Land Reclamation 1849 C St NW Washington DC 20240*

JOHNSON, RON, information technology executive; BA in Econ., Stanford U.; MBA, Harvard U. Buying and inventory mgr. Mervyn (divsn. of Target Corp.); mgmt. exec. positions Target Corp., 1984—2000; sr. v.p. retail Apple Computer Inc., Cupertino, Calif., 2000—. Office: Apple Computer Inc 1 Infinite Loop Cupertino CA 95014 Office Phone: 408-996-1010.

JOHNSON, RONALD KAY, retail company executive; b. Abilene, Tex., Feb. 26, 1939; s. Vernon Floyd and Mattye Sue (Milburn) J.; m. Sally Ann Fleet, Nov. 22, 1962 (div.); 1 child, Sheri May. AA, Spokane Falls Coll., 1970; BA in Theatre Arts with honors, Eastern Wash. State U., 1971; AS with honors, Portland C.C., 1992. Divsn. mgr. Nutrition Ctrs. Fred Meyer, Inc., Portland, Oreg., 1971—. V.p. Nutrition Ctrs. Divsn., 1979-87; owner, mgr. Valley Mist Farm, San Diego, 1957-65; med. massage therapist, 2003. Actor Lake Oswego Cmty. Theatre, 1979—, Portland Civic Theatre. Recipient Best Supporting Actor award Spokane Civic Theatre, 1967-68, Best Actor award Oreg. Theatre Soc., 1980-81. Avocation: raising show horses. Home: 2319 Old Maypearl Rd Waxahachie TX 75167 Office: 5790 W Hwy 287 Waxahachie TX 76065 Personal E-mail: ronaldkjohnson@hotmail.com.

JOHNSON, (FREDERICK) ROSS, international management advisory company executive; b. Winnipeg, Man., Can., Dec. 13, 1931; s. Frederick Hamilton and Caroline (Green) J.; m. Laurie Ann Graumann (div); children: Bruce, Neil; m. Susan. BComm, U. Manitoba, 1952; MComm, U. Toronto, Ont., Can., 1956; LLD (hon.), St. Francis Xavier U., Antigonish, 1978, Barry U., Fla., 1980, U. Manitoba, 1996. Tchr. U. Toronto, 1962-64; dir. mktg. CGE, Toronto, 1964-66; mgr. mdse. T. Eaton Co., 1966-67; exec. v.p. GSW Ltd., 1967-71; pres. Standard Brands Ltd., Toronto, 1971, pres., chief exec. officer, 1972; v.p. Standard Brands, Inc., NYC, 1973, sr. v.p., dir., 1974, pres., 1975-81, CEO, 1976-81, chmn., 1977-81, chmn., COO, 1981; pres., COO Nabisco Brands, Inc. (formerly Standard Brands, Inc. and Nabisco, Inc.), Parsippany, 1984-85, vice chmn., 1985-86; pres., COO R.J. Reynolds Industries Inc. (known as RJR Nabisco, Inc. as of 1986), Winston-Salem, 1985-87; CEO RJR Nabisco, Inc., Atlanta, 1987-89; chmn., CEO RJM Group, Inc., Atlanta, 1989—; chmn. Bionaire Inc., Montreal, Can., 1992—. Bd. dirs. Am. Express, NYC, Power Corp., Montreal, Archer Daniels Midland, Decatur, Ill., Nat. Svc. Ind., Atlanta, AuthentiDate Holding Corp., 2003-, chmn., 2005-, Edgestone Capital Ptnrs, Bentley Pharm., Inc., Exeter, NH, 2004-; serves on adv. bd. Wachovia Bank, Fla., Bennett Adv. Group, Palm Beach, Quebecor, Ontario, U. Toronto, Black & McDonald Ltd.; bd. dir., Power Corp. Can., 1982-2001, former chmn. compensation com., former mem. exec. com., mem. internat. adv. coun., 1982-. Profiled in the book Barbarians at the Gate: The Fall of RJR Nabisco and in the movie of the same name. Chmn. bd. NYC chpt. Nat. Multiple Sclerosis Soc., 1978-86; trustee Duke U. Lt. Ordance Corps Royal Can. Army. Decorated Officer of the Order of Canada; recipient US Silver Medal of Patriotism, France's Versailles award, Statesman of Yr. award, Am. Mktg. Assn., John F. Kennedy award, Am. Golf Found. Mem. Grocery Mfrs. Assn. (bd. dirs.), Young Pres. Orgn., Brook Club (NYC), Links Club (NYC), Blind Brook Club (NYC), Econ. Club (NYC), Conn. Golf Club (Easton), Atlanta Country Club, Castle Pines Club (Colo.), Deepdale Club (Manhasset, NY), Jupiter Hills Club (Fla.), Loxahatchee Club (Fla.), Mt. Bruno Country Club, U. Toronto President's Internat. Alumni Coun., Phi Delta Theta. Office: RJM Group Inc 200 Galleria Pky NW Ste 970 Atlanta GA 30339-5945*

JOHNSON, ROY RAGNAR, electrical engineer, researcher; b. Chgo., Jan. 23, 1932; s. Ragnar Anders and Ann Viktoria (Lundquist) J.; m. Martha Ann Mattson, June 21, 1963; children: Linnea Marit, Kaisa Ann. BSEE, U. Minn., 1954, MS, 1956, PhD, 1959. Rsch. fellow U. Minn., 1957-59; from rsch. engr. to sr. basic rsch. scientist Boeing Sci. Rsch. Labs., Seattle, 1959-72; prin. scientist KMS Fusion, Inc., Ann Arbor, Mich., 1972-74, dir. fusion expts., 1974-78, tech. dir., 1978-91, dept. head for fusion and plasmas, 1985-88; tech. dir. Innovation Assocs., Inc., Ann Arbor, 1992; Inertial Confinement Fusion classification/records mgr. Lawrence Livermore (Calif.) Nat. Lab., 1992—; scientist Nat. Ignition Facility, 2001—. Vis. lectr. U. Wash., Seattle, 1959-60; vis. scientist Royal Inst. Tech., Stockholm, 1963-64; cons. Dept. Edn., Washington, 1995, 98, 2000, 03, 04, 05. Author: Nonlinear Effects in Plasmas, 1969, Plasma Physics, 1977, Inertial Confinement Fusion, 1992; contbr. articles to profl. jours.; patentee in field. Bd. advisors Rose-Hulman Inst. Tech., 1982-. Decorated chevalier Order of St. George; comdr. Order of Holy Cross of Jerusalem. Fellow: Am. Phys. Soc.; mem.: AIAA, AAAS, IEEE (life), N.Y. Acad. Scis., Nuc. Plasma Scis. Soc. of IEEE (exec. com. 1972—75), Swedish Am. Hist. Soc., Am. Swedish Inst., Swedish Coun. Am., Commonwealth Club Calif., Torpar Riddar Orden, Vasa Order Am. (past chmn. Svea lodge), Gamma Alpha, Eta Kappa Nu. Lutheran. Home: PO Box 166 Livermore CA 94551-0166 Office: Livermore Nat Lab PO Box 808 Livermore CA 94551-0808 Business E-Mail: johnson3@llnl.gov.

JOHNSON, RUPERT HARRIS, JR., diversified financial services company executive; married. BA, Washington and Lee U., 1962. With Franklin Resources, Inc., San Mateo, Calif., 1965—; sr. v.p., asst. sec. Franklin Templeton Distbrs., Inc.; pres. Franklin Advisers, Inc.; exec. v.p., chief investment officer, dir. Franklin Resources, Inc., San Mateo, Calif., vice-chmn. Mem. exec. com., bd. govs. Investment Co. Inst.; trustee Santa Clara U., Washington and Lee U.; chmn. bd. dirs. Franklin Mgmt., Inc.; exec. v.p., sr. investment officer Franklin Trust Co.; dir. various Franklin Templeton funds; portfolio mgr. Franklin DynaTech Fund. With USMC, 1962-65. Named one of Forbes' Richest Americans, 1999—, World's Richest People, Forbes mag., 2001—. Mem. Nat. Assn. Securities Dealers (dist. conduct com.). Office: Franklin Resources Inc One Franklin Pkwy San Mateo CA 94403-1906*

JOHNSON, S. CURTIS, chemicals executive; BA in Econ., Cornell U., 1977; MBA, Northwestern U., 1983. Mgmt. positions S.C. Johnson & Sons, 1983—89, dir. worldwide bus. develop., 1989—93, v.p., mng. dir. Mexican Johnson, 1993—95, v.p., mng. dir. bus. develop., 1995—96; pres. Comml. Markets Inc., 1996—2002; chmn. JohnsonDiversey Inc., Sturtevant, Wis., 2002—. Co-founder Wind Point Partners LP; mem. bd. dir. Cargill, Inc.; bd. dir. Johnson Fin. Group Inc. Named one of Forbes' Richest Americans, 2006. Office: Johnson Diversey PO Box 902 8310 16th St Sturtevant WI 53177-0902*

JOHNSON, S.A. (TONY JOHNSON), automotive executive; Pres., CEO Onan Corp., 1981—85; CEO Pentair Inc., 1985—89; founder Hidden Creek Inustries, Mpls.; mng. ptnr. J2R Partners. Chmn., dir. Automotive Industries Holding, Inc., 1990—95, Tower Automotive, 1993—; dir. Dura Automotive Sys., Inc. Office: Tower Automotive 27175 Haggerty Rd Novi MI 48377-3626*

JOHNSON, SALLY A., nurse, educator; b. Rockford, Ill., Apr. 24, 1923; d. Herbert A. and Aileen (Peyton) Johnson; m. Bert Klackle; children: Ann Elizabeth Scannell, Stacey Aileen Lerager. RN Good Samaritan Hosp., 1945; nurse obstetrics delivery Women's Hosp., NYC, 1947-49, St. Francis Hosp., Evanston, Ill., 1953; charge, head nurse Broward Gen. Hosp., Ft. Lauderdale, Fla., 1968; night supr. Ashbrook Convalescent and Nursing Hosp., Scotch Plains, NJ, 1968—. Owner Thomas A. Edison Brick Co., Sally Johnson Enterprises. Coun. chmn. Betty Merit Tchrs. Scholarship, 1962; area nat. organizer Girl Scouts U.S.A., 1962-65; Westfield (N.J.) Round-Up and Health chmn., 1962-63; pres. Tamaques Sch., 1965, adviser Parent Tchr. Orgn., 1966, fgn. relationship chmn., 1967-68; exec. bd. chmn. Westfield HS PTA Newsletter, 1968-70; chmn. Nat. Space Edn., Westfield, 1964; Westfield chmn. fgn. nurses Overlook Hosp., Summit, N.J., 1964-69. Recipient scholarship to Harvard U. Coll. Bus. Mem. Nat. Assn. Investors Corp., Nat. Dist. Nurses Assn., NOW (N.J. coord. 1967-68), Am. Contract Bridge League, Bridge Tchrs. Assn., Naples Investment Club (sec. 1995-96). Republican. Achievements include patent for marking devices. E-mail: sallyjohnson@comcast.net.

JOHNSON, SAMUEL (SAM JOHNSON), congressman; b. San Antonio, Oct. 11, 1930; m. Shirley L. Melton; children: James R., Gini Mulligan, Beverly Briney. BBA, So. Meth. U., 1951; MA in Internat. Affairs, George Washington U.; grad., Armed Forces Staff Coll., Nat. War Coll. Mem. USAF, 1950—79, fighter pilot, prisoner of war, 1966-73, dir. Air Force Fighter Weapons Sch., mem. Thunderbirds, wing commdr., air divsn. commdr.; founder home bldg. co., 1979; mem. Tex. State Ho. Reps., 1984-91, US Congress from 3rd Tex. dist., 1991—, mem. ways and means com., mem. edn. and the workforce com., chmn. employer-employee rels. subcommittee. Chmn. Conservative Action Team. Decorated 2 Silver Stars, DFC, 4 Air medals, 2 Purple Hearts, 2 Legions of Merit, Bronze Star with Valor, 3 Outstanding Unit awards. Republican. Office: US Ho Reps 1211 Longworth Ho Office Bldg Washington DC 20515-0001 Office Phone: 202-225-4201.*

JOHNSON, SANDRA ANN, counselor, educator; b. Houston, Apr. 27, 1958; d. Johnnie and Area (Bradford) Johnson. AA, Houston C.C., 1991; BBA, Tex. So. U., 1994; MA, Prairie View A&M U., 1998; PhD, Tex. So. U., 2000; PhD in Psychology, Berne U. Lic. profl. counselor. Tchr. computers Houston Sch. Dist., 1981—. Instr. North Harris Coll., Houston, 1996—, Houston C.C.; counselor Houston C.C. Sys.; rsch. resident, Saint Kitts and Nevis. Vol. Herman Hosp., Houston, 1987—88, U. Tex. Health Sci. Ctr.; intern, vol. DePelchin Children Ctr., 1997—98; counselor Vision of Hope Women, Houston, 1996—97, Cmty. Devel. Corp.; contact person Houston Mayor's Camp, 1997; pres., bd. dirs. Vision of Hope; pres. CAP Cmty. Devel.; pro bono counselor Black Ams. in low income areas; summer resident St. Kitts, West Indies. Named Disting. Role Model of Houston, North Main Ch. of God in Christ, 1998; recipient Outstanding Counselor, Houston C.C. Sys. Mem. Chi Sigma Iota. Democrat. Pentecost. Avocations: tennis, golf, jogging, reading, racquetball. Office: Houston Cmty Coll System Southeast Campus Houston TX 77088-7102 Personal E-mail: sondra_johnson@yahoo.co.uk.

JOHNSON, SANDRA HANNEKEN, law educator; b. St. Louis, Jan. 20, 1952; d. Clarence F. and Mary Rose (Uykosky) Hanneken; m. Robert G. Johnson, 1973; children: Emily, Kathleen. AB summa cum laude, St. Louis U., 1973; JD, NYU, 1976; LLM, Yale U., 1977. Bar: N.Y. 1978. Asst. prof. law N.Y. Law Sch., 1977-78, St. Louis U., 1978-81, assoc. prof. law, 1981-84, prof. of law, 1984—, Tenet prof. health care law & ethics, 2000—, assoc. dean, 1979—81, 1985—88, interim dean, 1991—92, provost, 1998—2002; vis. prof. Univ. Houston Law Ctr., 1991, Washington U. Sch. Law, 1995. Dir. Ctr. for Health Law Studies, St. Louis, 1982-85, 88-91; cons. Inst. of Medicine Project on Nursing Homes, N.Y., 1985; mem. Hastings Ctr. Project on Ethics in Nursing Homes, N.Y., 1988-91. Co-author: Nursing Homes and the Law, 1985, Health Law, 1987, 2nd edit., 1991, Health Law Cases Materials & Problems, 4th edit.; mem. bd. editors Law, Medicine and Health Care, 1985—; contbr. articles to profl. jours. Participant St. Louis Leadership Devel. Program, 1980-81; bd. mem. Inst. for Peace & Justice, St. Louis, 1988-90; mem. Instl. Rev. Bd., St. Louis U., 1989-90. Grantee Nat. Inst. of Dispute Resolution, 1985, AARP, 1988; Edmund Pellegrino medal, 2003, HEAL Inst.; Woman of the Year 2002, St. Louis Daily Record; fellow, Hastings Ctr. Mem. ABA, Am. Soc. Law Medicine & Ethics (dir. Mayday Project on Legal & Regulatory Issues in Pain Relief, Disting. Health Law Tchr. award, William J. Curran award), Midwest Bioethics Roundtable, St. Louis Health Lawyers Assn. (chmn.), Phi Beta Kappa, Alpha Sigma Nu. Office: St Louis U Sch of Law 3700 Lindell Blvd Saint Louis MO 63108-3412

JOHNSON, SANDRA K., electrical engineer; b. Fukuoka, Japan, Sept. 19, 1960; arrived in U.S., 1961; d. George Garland and Gloria Dean (Hagger) Johnson. BSEE summa cum laude, So. U., Baton Rouge, La., 1982; MSEE, Stanford U., 1984; PhD, Rice U., 1988. Rsch. staff mem. T.J. Watson Rsch. Ctr. IBM, Yorktown Heights, NY, 1988—2000, mgr. Websphere database devel. Silicon Valley lab. San Jose, 2000—02, mgr. Linux Performance Austin, Tex., 2002—03, sr. tech. staff, 2003—, chief tech. officer global small and med. bus. sys. and tech. group, 2004—06, assurance architect, 2006—. Fellow: IEEE; mem.: Soc. Women Engrs., Nat. Soc. Black Engrs., Computing Rsch. Assn. (com. on status of women in computing sci. 1990—96), Assn. Computing Machinery (Disting. Engr.), IEEE Computer Soc. Office: IBM 11501 Burnett Rd Austin TX 78758 Home Phone: 512-789-1467; Office Phone: 512-838-4983. Business E-Mail: sandrakj@sbcglobal.net.

JOHNSON, SANDRA KAY, music educator; b. Hampton, Va., Aug. 21, 1952; d. Charles Coburn and Anne Bevins Wilson; m. Jimmy Royce Johnson, Mar. 27, 1993; children: Suzanne Kate Oden, Brandy Brooke. Degree in elem. edn., Sam Houston State U., Huntsville, Tex., 1973. Data processor Tex.; kindergarten endorsement Tex., alphphonics Tex. Tchr. remedial math. Hearne Ind. Sch. Dist., Tex., 1973—74; tchr. kindergarten Pickwickian Schs., League City, Tex., 1978—79, Riyadh Internat. Cmty. Sch., Saudi Arabia, 1980—82, Fredericksburg Ind. Sch. Dist., Tex., 1982—83; tchr. gifted and talented math edn. Comfort Ind. Sch. Dist., Tex., 1983—84, tchr. kindergarten, 1984—85; tchr. kindergarten, 1st and 2d grade music Pearland Ind. Sch. Dist., Tex., 1985—. Compiler, presenter gifted and talented math. curriculum Comfort Ind. Sch. Dist., 1983—84; tchr. alphaphonic curriculum Pearland Ind. Sch. Dist., 1987, tchr. adult English as 2d lang., 86, tchr. adult edn. and citizenship, 86; contbr., bd. sec. to various children's singing and dancing prodns. Author: (children's book) The Baby Elephant. Mem.: Tex. Classroom Tchrs. Assn. (assoc.), Order Ea. Star (Worthy Matron). Methodist. Avocations: crafts, scrapbooks, artistry, community work, travel. Home Phone: 281-489-4763; Office Phone: 281-412-1412.

JOHNSON, SCOTT STUART, merchant banker; s. Tod Stuart and Cindy Schwartz Johnson. BA, Columbia U., 1994, M in Internat. Affairs, 1997, MBA, 1997. Equity rsch. assoc. Salomon Smith Barry, Inc., 1997—99; equity rsch. analyst Merrill Lynch & Co., Inc., 1999—2000; CFO, bd. dirs. BrandAid Comm., NYC, 2000; CEO SJ Partners, LLC, NYC, 2001—. Book reviewer Jour. Internat. Affairs. Sit on term mem., advisory com. Coun. on Fgn. Rels., NYC, 2002—. Recipient First Pl. award, Montauk Sprint Relay Triathalon, 2003; Martin Fischbein fellow, Fischbein Found., 1992. Mem.: Atlantic Coun., Am. Enterprise Inst., Assn. for Corp. Growth, Ctrl. Pk. Track Club (life). Republican. Jewish. Avocation: competitive marathon running. Home: 350 W 53rd St Ph E New York NY 10019-5753 Business E-Mail: scott@sjpartners.com.

JOHNSON, SCOTT WILLIAM, lawyer, bank executive, blogger; b. St. Paul, Apr. 10, 1940; s. Clark William and Ruth (McCulloch) J.; m. Marjorie Anne Rex, June 13, 1964; children: Matthew Rex, Katharine Brooke. AB, Harvard U., 1962; JD, U. Minn., 1966. Bar: Colo. 1966, Wis. 1970, Minn. 1976. Tchr. Maumee Valley Country Day Sch., Toledo, 1962-63; atty. Sherman & Howard, Denver, 1966-70; asst. gen. counsel Trane Co., LaCrosse, Wis., 1970-72; gen. counsel, sec. Western Empire Fin., Denver, 1972-75; asst. gen. counsel Bemis Co., Mpls., 1975-78, sr. v.p., gen. counsel, 1988; v.p. gen. counsel Am. Hoist & Derrick Co., St. Paul, 1978-88, sr. v.p., gen. council, sec. Bemis Co., 1988-2003. Blog writer: powerlineblog.com; contbr. articles to Nat. Rev., The Am. Enterprise, American Experiment Quarterly; Active Edina (Minn.) Sch. Bd., 1988-94, chmn., 1990-94; chair Minn. Coalition Ednl. Reform and Accountability, 1994; Edina City Council, 1996-1998. Fellow Claremont Inst.; mem. ABA, Am. Corp. Counsel Assn., Wis. Bar Assn., Colo. Bar Assn., Minn. Bar Assn., Interlachen Country Club (bd. dirs. 1988-94), Mpls. Club. Independent. Personal E-mail: scottmarjjohnson@gmail.com.*

JOHNSON, SHANNON, professional basketball player; b. Aug. 18, 1974; Grad., U.S.C., 1996. Mem. 2 ABL Champion Columbus Quest; profl. basketball player Valencia, Spain, Orlando Miracle (now Conn. Sun), 1999—2002, Conn. Sun, 2003, San Antonio Silver Stars, 2004—06, Detroit Shock, 2007—. Named All-WNBA 2nd Team, 1999, 2000, Inaugural WNBA All-Star Team, 1999, WNBA All-Star Team, 2000, 2002, 2003. Achievements include mem. US Women's Basketball Team, Athens Olympics, 2004. Mailing: Detroit Shock Palace Sports & Entertainment 5 Championship Dr Auburn Hills MI 48326*

JOHNSON, SHEILA CRUMP, entrepreneur; b. Pa. m. Robert L. Johnson (div. 2002); children: Paige, Brett; m. William T. Newman, 2005. Music tchr. Sidwell Friends Sch., Washington, 1973—89; former cultural liaison to Middle East U.S. Info. Agency; co-founder Black Entertainment TV; owner Salamander Farms, Middleberg, Va.; developer Salamander Inn and Spa, Middleberg, Va.; co-owner Lincoln Holdings, LLC; owner, team pres. WNBA Wash. Mystics; designer of luxury linens. Bd. dirs. Parsons Sch. Design; pres. Washington Internat. Horse Show; established first Nat. Music Conservatory, Amman, Jordan. Achievements include first Black female to be certified as billionaire. Avocations: horseback riding, music, violin. Office: c/o Lincoln Holdings LLC 401 9th St NW Washington DC 20004*

JOHNSON, SILAS R., JR., retired military officer; b. Ft. Worth, Jan. 29, 1945; s. Silas Robert and Lucille (Burns) J.; m. Paulette Kamykowski, Apr. 12, 1968; children: Jennifer, Tyler. BBA, U. Miami, Coral Gables, Fla., 1967; MPA, Pepperdine U., 1979; postgrad., Air U., Montgomery, Ala., 1975, 83, 89. Commd. 2d lt. USAF, 1968, advanced through grades to major gen., 1998; co-pilot, aircraft comdr. 416 Bombardment Wing, Griffiss AFB, NY, 1969-74; spotlight officer, chief of tanker assigments Strategic Air Command, Offutt AFB, 1974-77; RF-4C pilot 363d Tactical Reconnaissance Wing, Shaw AFB, SC, 1977-80; co-pilot, aircraft comdr., flight comdr. 60th Bombardment Squadron, Anderson AFB, Guam, 1981-83; air staff action officer to asst. dir. air force issues team USAF Hdqrs./The Pentagon, Washington, 1983-86; comdr. 46th Bombardment Squadron/319th Bombardment Wing, Grand Forks AFB, ND, 1986-88; dir. Joint Flag Officer Warfighting Course, Maxwell AFB, Ala., 1989-90; asst. dep. comdr. maint., later vice comdr. 319th Bombardment Wing, Grand Forks AFB, 1990-91; vice comdr. 4th Wing, Seymour Johnson AFB, NC, 1991-92; comdr. 93d Bomb Wing, Castle AFB, Calif., 1992-94, 552d Air Control Wing, Tinker AFB, Okla., 1994-96; dep. dir. ops. joint chiefs of staff The Pentagon, Washington, 1996-98; vice comdr. 21st Air Force, McGuire AFB, NJ, 1998-99; comdr. Air Mobility Warfare Ctr. USAF, Ft. Dix, NJ, 1999-2000; chief U.S. Mil. Tng. Mission, Riyadh, Saudi Arabia, 2000—02; ret. USAF, 2002; pres. SRJ Cons. Inc., 2002—; v.p. Burdeshaw Assocs., Bethesda, Md., 2002—04; dir. mktg. EADS N.Am., Arlington, Va., 2004—. Decorated Def. Disting. Svc. medal, Def. Superior Svc. medal, Legion of Merit with 2 oak leaf clusters, Air Medal with 2 oak leaf clusters, Air Force Commendation medal, Vietnam Svc. medal; recipient Moeller Trophy for outstanding wing comdr. in air combat command, 1996. Mem. Daedalians (chpt. pres.), Air Force Hist. Found. (bd. dirs.), Army Navy Country Club, Sigma Chi. Avocations: golf, reading.

JOHNSON, STEPHEN L., federal official; b. Washington, Mar. 21, 1951; s. William Arrett and Nell (Easler) J.; m. Deborah Lynn Jones, Aug. 5, 1972; children: Carrie, Matthew, Allison. BA, Taylor U., 1972; MS in Pathology, George Washington U., 1976. Dir. tech. ops. Litton Bionetics, Kensington, Md., 1976-80; sr. sci. advisor EPA, Washington, 1980-84, 86-88, dir. field ops. disvn., 1984-86, dep. dir. hazard evaluation divsn., 1988-90, dir. registration divsn., dep. dir., pesticide programs, 1997—99, asst. adminstr. prevention pesticides & toxic substances, 2000—03, acting dep. adminstr., 2003—04, dep. adminstr., 2004—05, acting adminstr., 2005, adminstr., 2005—. Dir. tech. ops. Hazleton Labs. Corp., Falls Church, Va., 1984-86; chmn. FIFRA sci. adv. panel EPA, Washington, 1988-90; exput cons. WHO, Geneva, 1988-90. Contbr. articles to profl. jours. Bd. dirs. Frederick (Md.) County Crisis Pregnancy Ctr., 1987; deacon Fredricktown Bapt. Ch., Walkerville, Md., 1991; commr. USTA Jr. League, Frederick County, 1993; bd. dirs. Frederick Tennis Patrons. Mem. USTA (bd. dirs., v.p. Md. dist.). Avocation: tennis. Office: EPA Ariel Rios Fed Bldg 1200 Pennsylvania Ave NW Rm 3000 Washington DC 20460 E-mail: johnson.stephen@epa.gov.*

JOHNSON, STEPHEN PATRICK HOWARD, lawyer; b. Holmfirth, England, Feb. 23, 1957; came to U.S., 1982; s. Herbert Edward Johnson; 1 child, Graham Johnson. BA in genetics, Cambridge U., Eng., 1978, MA (hon.), 1993; solicitors final exam. with honors, Coll. of Law, London, 1980; JD with high honors, Ill. Inst. Tech., 1984. Bar: Ill. 1984, N.Y. 1991, Calif. 2002; solicitor Supreme Ct. Eng. 1982. Solicitor, trainee Bird & Bird, London, 1980-82; assoc. Kirkland & Ellis, Chgo., 1982-88, ptnr., 1988-90, NYC, 1990—2003, ptnr., mem. mgmt. San Francisco, 2003—. Contbr. chpt. to book. Office: Kirkland & Ellis LLP 555 California St San Francisco CA 94104 Office Phone: 415-439-1439. Office Fax: 415-439-1500. Business E-Mail: sjohnson@kirkland.com.

JOHNSON, STEWART WILLARD, civil engineer; b. Mitchell, SD, Aug. 17, 1933; s. James Elmer Johnson and Grace Mahala (Erwin) Johnson Parsons; m. Mary Anis Giddings, June 24, 1956; children: Janelle Chiemi, Gregory Stewart, Eric Willard. BSCE, SD State U., 1956; BA in Bus. Adminstrn. and Polit. Sci., U. Md., 1960; MSCE, PhD, U. Ill., 1964. Registered profl. engr., Ohio. Commd. 2d lt. USAF, 1956, advanced through grades to lt. col., prof. mechs. and civil engring. Air Force Inst. Tech. Dayton, Ohio, 1964-75, dir. civil engring. Seoul, Republic of Korea, 1976-77, chief civil engring. research div. Kirtland AFB, N.Mex., 1977-80, ret., 1980; prin. engr. BDM Corp., Albuquerque, 1980-94, Johnson and Assocs., Albuquerque, 1994—; engr. Northrop Grumman, Albuquerque, 2003—04. Cons. in site surveys, found. design, constrn. of ground stas. for satellite comm. sys., 1992-2001; cons. space sci. and lunar basing NASA, U. N.Mex., N.Mex. State U. and Los Alamos Nat. Lab., 1987-92; adj. prof. civil engring. U. N.Mex., 1987-92; prin. investigator devel. concepts for lunar astron. obs. U. N.Mex., N.Mex. State U., NASA, 1987-94; tech. chmn. Space '88, Space '90, Space '94, Space '96, Space '98, Space 2000, Space 2002, Internat. Confs., Albuquerque; vis. lectr. Internat. Space U., Japan, 1992, Huntsville, Ala., 1993, Barcelona, Spain, 1994, Stockholm, 1995; mem. panel on siting lunar base European Space Agy., 1994; gen. chair Space 96 and RCEII Conf., Albuquerque, 1996; gen. chmn. Space Conf., Albuquerque, 1998, 2000, Robotics Conf., Albuquerque, 1998, 2000; mem. steering com Space Exploration 2005, Albuquerque, Space Exploration 2007; v.p., bd. dirs. Space Engring. and Sci. Inst. Editor Engineering, Construction, and Operations in Space, I, 1988. II, 90, V, 96, Space 2000 Procs., Space 2002 Procs.; contbr. articles to profl. jours. Pres. ch. coun. Ch. of Good Shepherd United Ch. of Christ, Albuquerque, 1983-85, chmn. bd. deacons, 1991-93, 2000, moderator, 1996-97, clk., 2002; S.W. Conf. (United Ch. Christ) del. to Gen. Synod XIX, St. Louis, 1993, Gen. Synod XX, Oakland, Calif., 1995, Gen. Synod XXI, Columbus, Ohio, 1997; trustee Lunar Geotech. Inst., 1990—; mem. adv. bd. Lab. for Extraterrestrial Structures Rsch., Rutgers U., 1990—; mem. meml. to Dr. Martin Luther King, Jr. site selection com., Albuquerque, 2005-06. Fellow Nat. Acad. Scis. NRC, 1970-71; recipient World Bar Assn. Space Humanitarian award, 1996. Fellow: ASCE (chmn. exec. com. aerospace divsn. 1979, tech. activities com. 1984, chmn. com. space engring. and constrn. 1987—, mem. nat. space policy com. 1988—96, chmn. 1990—96, Outstanding News Corr. award 1981, Aerospace Scis. and Tech. Applications award 1990, Edmund Friedman Profl. Recognition award 1989); mem.: AAAS, AIAA (space logistics com., Engr. of Yr. Region IV 1990), Nat. Space Soc., Am. Geophys. Union, Soc. Am. Mil. Engrs., Sigma Xi, Pi Sigma Alpha. Republican. Mem. United Ch. Of Christ. Avocations: photography, swimming, walking, gardening, hiking. Personal E-mail: stwjohnson@aol.com.

JOHNSON, SUSAN F., elementary school educator; d. Gregory Peter and Helen Anna (Dingel) Fettes; m. James R. Johnson, Aug. 26, 1966 (dec. Sept. 2005); 1 child, Christopher Russell. BS in Elem. Edn., Drake U., 1962; postgrad., Mankato State U., 1962—66; MS in English, Nova U., 1989. Cert. tchr. Fla. 6th grade tchr. Royal (Iowa) Cmty. Sch., 1954—56; 4th grade tchr. Carroll (Iowa) Pub. Sch., 1956—58; 6th grade tchr. Ames (Iowa) Pub. Schs., Ames, 1959—62, Mankato (Minn.) Pub. Schs., 1962—66; 7th - 8th grade tchr. Eau Claire (Wis.) Pub. Schs., 1966—69; 5-7th grade tchr. Rockbridge County Schs., Lexington, Va., 1969—72; 7-8 grade tchr. St. Francis (S.D.) Indian Sch., 1977—78; 1st grade tchr. Valentine (Nebr.) Pub. Sch., 1978—80; 4-6th grade tchr. Volusia County Schs., Daytona Beach, Fla., 1980—2004, substitute tchr. grades 2-8, 2004—. Adj. instr. Sinte Gleska Coll., 1978—80; adj. instr. English II Daytona Beach C.C., 1990—94; pres. Volusia County Reading Coun., Daytona Beach, 1995. Named Tchr. of Yr., Spruce Creek Elem., 1987—88, Tchr. of Month, 1987, 1990, Reading Tchr. of Yr., Volusia County Reading Coun., 2001. Mem.: LWV (sec. 2004—), Fla. Reading Assn. (bd. mem., dist. 12 rep. 2002—06), Internat. Reading Assn., Daytona Beach Choral Soc. (2nd v.p. 2002—05). Democrat. Roman Catholic. Avocations: reading, singing, piano, writing, cooking. Home: 929 Mill Road Ln Port Orange FL 32127

JOHNSON, SUZANNE NORA, former diversified financial services company executive, lawyer; b. Chgo., June 14, 1957; married. BA magna cum laude, U. So. Calif., 1979; JD, Harvard U. Bar: Calif. 1983. Law clk. to Hon. Francis Murnaghan US Ct. Appeals (4th Cir.), Balt.; atty. Simpson Thacher & Bartlett, 1980—84; with Goldman Sachs Group, NYC, 1985—2007, ptnr., 1992—2007, sr. dir., 2007—. Henry Crown Fellow Aspen Inst.; bd. dirs. Intuit Inc., 2007—, Am. Red Cross. Trustee Brookings Institution, Carnegie Institution, RAND Health, TechnoServe, Univ. So. Calif.; bd. dirs. Children Now, Markle Found., 2006—; mem. adv. bd. of councilors Harvard Med. Sch. Named one of The World's 100 Most Powerful Women, Forbes mag., 2006. Avocations: fly fishing, kayaking.

JOHNSON, SYDNEY, men's college basketball coach, former professional basketball player; b. Apr. 26, 1974; m. Jennifer Johnson; children: Jalen, Julia. AB in Hist., Princeton U., NJ, 1997. Profl. basketball player Gorizia Pallacanestro, Italy, 1998, Reggio Calabria, Italy, Siena, Italy; asst. coach Georgetown U., Washington, 2004—07; head coach Princeton U., 2007—. Achievements include winning the Italian League Championship as a member of Siena, 2004. Office: Mens Basketball Princeton U Jadwin Gymnasium Princeton NJ 08544 Office Phone: 609-258-3512.*

JOHNSON, SYLVESTER, police commissioner; m. Cynthia Johnson; 3 children. Student, Phila. C.C., Temple U., Harvard U. Joined Phila. Police Dept., 1964, dep. commr. ops., 1998—2002, police commr., 2002—. Recipient George Fencl award, Phila. Daily News, 2001, Dirs. award, US Dept. Exec. Office for the Weed & Seed Program, 2001. Office: Phila Police Dept One Franklin Sq Philadelphia PA 19106

JOHNSON, SYLVIA SUE, university administrator, educator; b. Abiline, Tex., Aug. 10, 1940; d. SE Boyd and Margaret MacGillivray (Withington) Smith; m. William Ruel Johnson; children: Margaret Ruth, Laura Jane, Catherine Withington. BA, U. Calif., Riverside, 1962; postgrad., U. Hawaii, 1963. Elem. edn. credential, 1962. Chmn. bd. regents U. Calif., 2000—; co-chmn. U. Calif.-Riverside Med. Sch., 2006-07. Mem. bd. regents U. Calif.; mem. steering com. Citizens Univ. Com., chmn., 1978-79; bd. dirs., charter mem. U. Calif. Riverside Found., chmn. nominating com., 1983—; pres., bd. dirs. Friends of the Mission Inn, 1969-72, 73-76, Mission Inn Found., 1977—, Calif. Bapt. Coll. Citizens Com., 1980—; bd. dirs. Riverside Comty. Hosp., 1980—, Riverside Jr. League, 1976-77, Nat. Charity League, 1984-85; mem. chancellors blue ribbon com., devel. com. Calif. Mus. Photography; state bd. dirs. C. of C., 2003; co-chmn. inlad empire coalition U. Calif. Riverside Med. Sch., 2006-07. Named Woman of Yr., State of Calif. Legislature, 1989, 91, Citizen of Yr., C. of C., 1989; recipient Golden Key award Soroptimist Internat., 2000, Outstanding Woman honoree U. Redlands Town and Gown, 2001, Chancellor's medal U. Calif. Riverside, 2002, Trustees award for extraordinary svc. U. Calif. Riverside, 2004, Silver Raincross medal Jr. League Riverside, 1993, Spirit of Excellence award Calif. Bapt. Coll., 2004, Annual Frank Miller Civic Achievement award, Mission Inn Found., 2005. Mem. U. Calif.-Riverside Alumni Assn. (bd. dirs. 1966-68, v.p. 1968-70), Calif. C. of C. (bd. dirs. 2003—). Business E-Mail: ssj@johnson-machinery.com.

JOHNSON, TESLA FRANCIS, data processing executive, educator; b. Altoona, Fla., Sept. 2, 1934; s. Tesla Farris and Ruby Mae (Shockley) J.; m. Eleanor Mary Riggs, Oct. 17, 1975. BSEE, U. S.C., 1958; MS in Ops. Rsch., Fla. Inst. Tech., 1968; PhD in Adminstrv. Mgmt., Walden U., Mpls., 1989. Machinist apprentice Seaboard Airline Ry., 1952-54; asst. computer engr. So. Ry. System, Washington, 1958-61; sr. sci. programmer NCR, Dayton, Ohio, 1961-66; staff programmer IBM, East Fishkill, N.Y., 1966-72; mgr. Jay Turner Co., Grace, Idaho, 1973-74; programmer, analyst Ccybernetics & Systems, Inc., Jacksonville, Fla., 1974-77; systems analyst lst Nat. Bank Md., Balt., 1977-78; sr. systems analyst GM, Detroit, 1978-80; tech. analyst Sunbank Data Corp., Orlando, Fla., 1980-81; mgr. data adminstrn. dept. Martin Marietta Corp., Orlando, 1981-92; dir. technology Computer Bus. Assocs., 1993-96; program mgr. GTE Through Computer Horizons, 1997-2000; ret., 2000—. Adj. prof. bus. adminstrn. Valencia C.C., Orlando, 1989-94, Orlando Coll., 1990-92, Fla. Inst. Tech., Melbourne; mentor grad. sch. of computer resource mgmt. Webster U., 1993-94. Recipient cert. of appreciation NASA, 1969, Excalibur award. Mem. Tau Beta Pi, Sigma Phi Epsilon. Republican. Baptist. Avocation: playing the organ. Home: 36649 Sundance Dr Grand Island FL 32735

JOHNSON, THEODORE MEBANE, brokerage house executive; b. Denver, Jan. 25, 1934; s. Harold Theodore and Flora Luella (Cunningham) J.; m. Sandra Hall, May 23, 1970 (dec.). BS, U. Denver, 1956; postgrad. Advanced Mgmt. Program, Harvard U. Partner, Hornblower Weeks-Hemphill, Noyes, 1961-78, sr. v.p., dir., exec. com., until 1978; exec. v.p., divsn. dir. PaineWebber, Inc., NYC, 1978—2003; chmn., CEO Authorizer Techs., Inc., 2006—. Chmn. bd. dirs., CEO Cross Match Techs., 1997—. Co-founder, past dir. N.Am. Housing Corp. Served to lt. (j.g.) USNR, 1956-57. Mem. Securities Industry Assn. (govt. rels. com., past chmn. Mid-Atlantic chpt.), Bond Club (Washington), Congl. Country Club (Washington), Univ. Club (Washington), City Tavern Club (Washington), N.Y. Athletic Club, Robert Trent Jones Country Club (Manasas, Va.), Pine Tree Country Club (Boynton Beach, Fla.). Presbyterian. Home: 140 Atlantic Ave Palm Beach FL 33480-3707

JOHNSON, THOMAS DALE, publishing executive; b. DeKalb, Ill., Aug. 9, 1942; s. Orville J. and Dorace G. Johnson; m. Patricia T. Riley, Sept. 6, 1969; children: Christopher, Todd, Shawn, John Scott. BS in Chem. Engring., Purdue U., 1965, MS in Indsl. Adminstrn., 1966. Cons. Price Waterhouse & Co., Washington, 1969-71; adminstrv. mgr. Nat. Coun. Equal Bus. Opportunity, Washington, 1971-73; owner Riley & Johnson, Washington, 1971—. V.p. Washington Mgmt. Group, 1978—83, Wayne Mid-Atlantic, 1980—90; v.p. fed. regulatory products Info. Handling Svcs., 1983—87; pres. Bus. Rsch. Svcs., Inc., 1991—; v.p. mktg., sales and sys. gen. mgr. Asia UPI, 1996—97; pub. Bradford's Internat. Directory Mktg. Rsch. Agys., 1999—; nat. sales mgr. Carroll Pub. Co., 2002—. Pub.: mktg. rsch. directories, govt. adv. newsletter; contbr. articles to profl. jours. Founder Capital Content Network, DC Tech. Coun.; treas. St. Columba's Ch., 1980—82. With Chem. Corps US Army, 1967—68. Episcopalian. Office: Riley & Johnson 7720 Wisconsin Ave Ste 213 Bethesda MD 20814 Business E-Mail: tjohnson@carrollpub.com.

JOHNSON, THOMAS FLOYD, former academic administrator, educator; b. Detroit, June 1, 1943; s. Edward Eugene and Adella Madeline (Norton) J.; m. Michele Elizabeth Myers, Mar. 26, 1965; children: Jason, Amy, Sarah. BPh, Wayne State U., 1965; BD, Fuller Theol. Sem., 1968; ThM, Princeton Sem., 1969; PhD, Duke U., 1979. Pastor Presbyn. Ch. U.S.A., Pa., Mich., 1969-76; asst. prof. U. Sioux Falls, S.D., 1978-83; acad. dean Sioux Falls (S.D.) Coll., 1981-83, pres., 1988-97; prof. N.Am. Baptist Sem., Sioux Falls, 1983-88; dean George Fox Evang. Sem., Portland, Oreg., 1997—2001; interim pres. George Fox U., Newberg, 1997-98, prof. bibl. theol., 1997—. Contbr. 9 articles to Internat. Standard Bible Ency., 1988; author: 1, 2, and 3 John New International Biblical Commentary, 1993. Bd. dirs. Children's Home Soc. S.D., Sioux Falls, 1980-86, S.D. Symphony Orch., 1988-92, Carroll Inst., 1989-93, Coalition Christian Colls. and Univs., 1992-97. Mem. Am. Bapt. Assn. Colls. and Univs. (pres. 1992-94), Soc. Bibl. Lit., Sioux Falls C. of C. (bd. dirs. 1992-95), Rotary (bd. dirs. Downtown Club 1991-95, pres. 1993-94). Office: George Fox Univ 414 N Meridian St Newberg OR 97132 Office Phone: 503-554-2663. Personal E-mail: tmj365@yahoo.com. *Every day, with all its tasks and relationships, is a gift from God. Our response is to live thankfully, in service to God and God's world.*

JOHNSON, THOMAS MOORE, II, curator, lawyer; b. Durham, NC, Oct. 4, 1929; s. Franklin Plotinus and Martha Beshers Johnson; 1 child, Eleanor Ann Farabee. BA with honors, U. Chgo., 1948, JD, 1951; PhD in Econs., Columbia U., NYC, 1967. Bar: Ill. 1951, Mo. 1955, NY 1957, US Supreme Ct. 1958, Mich. 1974. Assoc. White & Case Law Firm, NYC, 1956—58, atty. Osceola, Mo., 1959—62; asst. prof. U. Mo., Columbia, 1962—64; adj. asst. prof. LI U., NYC, 1965; asst. prof. U. Ill., Chgo., 1965—71; assoc. prof. Ea. Mich. U., Ypsilanti, 1971—86; prosecuting atty. St. Clair County, Mo., 1987—91; mayor City of Osceola, 1991—95; prosecuting atty. Hickory County, 1995—98; founder Johnson Libr. and Mus., Osceola, 1999, pres., 1999—. Address: PO Box 375 Osceola MO 64776

JOHNSON, THOMAS S., electronics executive; b. 1946; BS, U. Fla., 1972; MBA, Harvard U., 1976. With IKON (formerly Alco Std. Corp.), 1975-89, v.p. ops. office products group; COO Danka, 1989-90; office imaging industry cons., 1991-94; dir., pres., CEO Global Imaging Sys., Inc., Tampa, Fla., 1994—. also: PO Box 273478 Tampa FL 33688-3478

JOHNSON, THOMAS STEPHEN, banker; b. Racine, Wis., Nov. 19, 1940; s. H. Norman and Jane Agnes (McAvoy) Johnson; m. Margaret Ann Werner, Apr. 18, 1970; children: Thomas Philip, Scott Michael(dec.), Margaret Ann. AB in Econs., Trinity Coll., 1962; MBA, Harvard U., 1964. Instr. Grad. Bus. Sch. Ateneo de Manila U., Philippines, 1964-66; spl. asst. to contr. U.S. Dept. Def., Washington, 1966-69; with Chem. Bank, NYC, 1969-89, pres., dir., 1983-89, Mfrs. Hanover Trust Co., NYC, 1989-91, GreenPoint Fin. Corp., GreenPoint Bank, NYC, 1993—2004, chmn., CEO, dir. Bd. dirs. Alleghany Corp., R.R. Donnelley & Sons, Inc., Phoenix Cos., Inc., Lower Manhattan Devel. Corp., Freddie Mac. Chmn., bd. trustees US Japan Found.; chmn. bd. dirs. Inst. Internat. Edn.; bd. dirs. United Way NYC, World Trade Ctr. Meml. Found.; past chmn., trustee Trinity Coll.; past chmn. bd. dirs. Union Theol. Sem. Mem.: Coun. Fgn. Rels., Everglades Club (Palm Beach), Harvard Club NYC, Links NYC, River Club NYC, Banyan Country Club (Palm Beach), Montclair Golf Club. Roman Catholic. Office: care of North Fork Bank 90 Park Ave Fl 4 New York NY 10016-1301 Business E-Mail: Thomas.Johnson@GreenPrint.com.

JOHNSON, THOMAS STUART, lawyer; b. Rockford, Ill., May 21, 1942; s. Frederick C. and Pauline (Ross) J. BA, Rockford Coll., 1964, LLD, 1989; JD, Harvard U., 1967. Bar: Ill. 1967. Ptnr., past pres. Williams & McCarthy, Rockford, 1967—. Lectr. in field. Contbr. numerous articles to profl. jours. Chmn. bd. trustees Rockford Coll., 1986—89; trustee Eastern Ill. U., 1996—2000, Emanuel Med. Ctr., Turlock, Calif., 1984—86, Swedish Covenant Hosp., Chgo., 1984—86; regent Lincoln Acad. of Ill., 1999—; chmn. bd. dirs. Ill. Inst. Continuing Legal Edn., Chgo., 1984—86; treas. Lawyers Trust Fund of Ill., Chgo., 1984—86; bd. govs. Regent's Coll., London, 1985—89; bd. dirs., mem. benevolence bd. Covenant Ch. Am., Chgo., 1984—86; chmn. Regent's Found. for Internat. Edn., London; chancellor Ill. Acad. Lawyers, 1999—2005. With US Army, 1968—70. Fellow Am. Coll. Trust and Estate Counsel; mem. ABA (ho. of dels. 1982-89, chmn. commn. on advt. 1984-88), Ill. Bar Assn. (bd. govs. 1976-82, sec. 1981-82, medal of honor 1997), Winnebago County Bar Assn. (pres. 1990), Am. Judicature Soc. (bd. dirs. 1986-90), Rotary (pres. Rockford 1992-93), Univ. Club Rockford. Republican. Home: 913 N Main St Rockford IL 61103-7068 Office Phone: 815-987-8920. Business E-Mail: tjohnson@wilmac.com.

JOHNSON, TIMOTHY AUGUSTIN, JR., lawyer; b. Clearwater, Fla., Dec. 17, 1945; s. Timothy Augustin and Ruth (Brown) J.; m. Clair Smith, Aug. 23, 1967; children: Chester Wolcott, Kathryn Elizabeth. BA, U. Fla., 1966, JD, 1969. Bar: Fla. 1969, U.S. Dist. Ct. (mid. dist.) Fla. 1970, U.S. Ct. Appeals (5th cir.) 1972, U.S. Supreme Ct. 1972. Assoc. Carlton, Fields et al., Tampa, Fla., 1969-73; ptnr., shareholder Johnson, Pope, Bokor, Ruppel & Burns LLP, Clearwater, 1973—. Mem. Fla. Bd. Bar Examiners. Pres. PACT, 1986-88; mem. Leadership Fla., 1983-84; chmn. Clearwater Long Range Econ. Devel. Commn., 1988-89; mem. bd. trustees Tampa Prep. Sch., 1985-90; trustee, chmn. investment subcom. U. South Fla. Found.; chmn. Clearwater Charter Rev. Com. Name 1 of 5 Outstanding Young Men, Jr. C. of C., Fla., 1979, Friend of the Arts, Arts Coun., Pinellas County, Fla., 1986. Mem. Fla. Bar (pres. young lawyers sect., bd. govs.). Republican. Avocations: exercise, hiking, boating. Office: Johnson Pope Bokor Ruppel & Burns LLP 911 Chestnut St Clearwater FL 33756-5643 Office Phone: 727-461-1818. Business E-Mail: timj@jpfirm.com.

JOHNSON, TIMOTHY PATRICK, health and social researcher; b. Batavia, NY, July 14, 1954; s. Elmore Thomas and Sara (McKinsey) J.; m. LuEllen Doty, June 20, 1988; children: Sara Elizabeth, Elliott William. BA, Western Ky. U., 1977; MA, U. Wis., Milw., 1978; PhD, U. Ky., 1988. Rsch. analyst dept. medicine U. Ky., Lexington, 1980-82, rsch. coord. survey rsch. ctr., 1982-88; staff assoc. for psychometrics Am. Bd. Family Practice, Lexington, 1988-89; asst. rsch. prof. epidemiology and biostatistics sch. pub. health U. Ill., Chgo., 1991—2002, project coord. survey rsch. lab., 1989-91, asst. dir. survey rsch. lab., 1991-93, assoc. dir., 1993-96, acting dir., 1996-98, dir., 1998—, assoc. prof. pub. adminstrn., 1996—2003, prof. pub. adminstrn., 2003—, assoc. rsch. prof. pub. health, 2002—03, rsch. prof. public health, 2003—. Contbr. chpts. to books, articles to profl. jours. Mem. APHA, AAAS, Am. Sociol. Assn., Am. Assn. Pub. Opinion Rsch., Am. Statis. Assn., Am. Coll. Epidemiology, Am. Assn. for the Advancement of Sci. Roman Catholic. Office: U Ill Survey Rsch Lab 412 S Peoria St Chicago IL 60607-7063 Business E-Mail: timj@uic.edu.

JOHNSON, TIMOTHY PETER, senator; b. Canton, SD, Dec. 28, 1946; s. Vandal Charles and Ruth Jorinda (Ljostveit) J.; m. Barbara Brooks, June 6, 1969; children: Brooks Dwight, Brendan Vandal, Kelsey Marie. BA in Polit. Sci., U. SD, 1969, MA in Polit. Sci., 1970, JD, 1975; postgrad., Mich. State U., 1970-71. Bar: SD 1975, US Dist. Ct. SD 1976. Fiscal analyst Legis. Fiscal Agy., Lansing, Mich., 1971-72; pvt. practice Vermillion, SD, 1975-86; mem. SD Ho. of Reps., 1979—82, SD Senate, 1983—86, US Congress from SD, 1987-97; US Senator from SD, 1997—. Adj. inst. U. SD, Vermillion, 1974-83; mem. SD Code Commn., Pierre, 1982-86; mem. com. appropriations US Senate, com. banking, housing, and urban affairs, com. budget, com. energy and natural resources, com. Indian affairs, select com. ethics. Mem. Vermillion City Planning Commn., 1977-78; treas. Clay County Dem. Com., Vermillion, 1978; del. Dem. Nat. Conv., 1988, 92, 96. NSF grantee, 1969-70; recipient Outstanding Citizen award Vermillion, SD, 1983, Friend of Edn. award SD Edn. Assn., 1983, Billy Sutton award legis. achievement, 1984, Friends of NAFIS award Nat. Assn. Federally Impacted Schools, 1998, Arthur T. Matrix award Retired Officers Assn., 2001, Congressional Leadeship award Nat. Telephone Coop. Assn., 2001, George Buck Gillispie Congressional award meritorious svc. Blinded Veterans Found., 2003. Mem. SD Bar Assn., Clay County Bar Assn., Phi Beta Kappa, Omicron Delta Kappa. Democrat. Lutheran. Office: US Senate 136 Hart Senate Ofc Bldg Washington DC 20510-0001 also: District Office Ste 103 320 S First St Aberdeen SD 57401-1554 Office Phone: 202-224-5842, 605-226-3440. Office Fax: 202-228-5765, 605-226-2439.*

JOHNSON, TIMOTHY R. B., obstetrician, gynecologist, educator; b. Duluth, Jan. 13, 1950; s. Timothy and Myra Johnson; m. Jo Wiese, June 17, 1972; children: Bradley, Clark, Anna. AB, AM, U. Mich., 1971; MD, U. Va., 1975. Diplomate Am. Bd. Ob-gyn., Am. Bd. Maternal-Fetal Medicine. Asst. prof. Uniformed Svcs. U., Bethesda, Md., 1983-85; assoc. prof. gynecol. obstetrics, pediats., dir. pediats. Johns Hopkins U. Hosp., Balt., 1985-93; prof., chair dept. ob-gyn. U. Mich., Ann Arbor, 1993—, prof. women's studies, 1995—, chmn. med. sch. rev., 1997. Bd. dirs. Ann Arbor Art Ctr., 1994—; bd. dirs. S.E. Mich. March of Dimes, 1998—. Fellow Am. Coll. Ob-Gyn. (chair internat. com. 1991-95), West African Coll. Surgeons (hon.); mem. Soc. for Maternal and Fetal Medicine (bd. dirs. 1993-97), Am. Assn. Med. Colls. (com. on advancing women in the acad.), Inst. Medicine NAS, Alpha Omega Alpha. Office: 1500 East Med Ctr Dr Ann Arbor MI 48109 Home Phone: 734-662-4918; Office Phone: 734-764-8123. Business E-Mail: trbj@umich.edu.

JOHNSON, TIMOTHY VINCENT, congressman, lawyer; b. Champaign, Ill., July 23, 1946; 9 children. Attended, US Military Academy, 1964; BA, U. Ill., 1969; JD, U. Ill. Coll. of Law, 1972. Alderman Urbana City Council, 1971—75; atty. priv. practice, 1972—; mem. from 104th Dist. Ill. Ho. of Reps, 1977—2000; mem. U.S. Congress from 15th Ill. dist., Washington, 2001—, mem. agr. com., sci. com., transp. and infrastructure com. Mem. Congressional Fire Services Caucus, Congressional Internet Caucus, Congressional Rural Caucus, Legislative Audit Commn. Mem. US Army, 1964—65. Recipient Order of the Coif. Mem.: Phi Beta Kappa (Bronze tablet). Republican. Assembly Of God. Office: US Ho of Reps 1229 Longworth Ho Office Bldg Washington DC 20515-1315*

JOHNSON, TOD STUART, market research company executive; b. Mpls., June 6, 1944; s. David Z. and Helen R. (Connor) J.; m. Cindy Schwartz, Aug. 28, 1966; children: Scott, Stacey BS, Carnegie Mellon U., 1966, MSIA, 1967. Vice pres. Market Sci. Assocs., Inc., Des Plaines, Ill., 1967-71; pres., chief exec. officer NPD Research, Inc., Port Washington, NY, 1971-89, Home Testing Inst., Inc., Port Washington, NY, 1980-89, OPOC Computing, Inc., Port Washington, NY, 1980-89, NPD Group, Port Washington, NY, 1982—, The NPD Group Inc. (merger of NPD Rsch. Inc., Home Testing Inst. Inc., and OPOC Computing), Port Washington, NY, 1989—; chmn., dir. NPD/Nielsen, Inc., 1987-91; chmn. ISL Internat. Surveys Ltd., Toronto, 1990-98; mng. dir. GFK Mktg. Svcs. Europe GmbH, 1995-99; chmn., CEO Jupiter Media Metrix, NYC, 1998—2001. Bd. dirs. Advt. Rsch. Found., N.Y.C., sec., 1988, vice chmn., 1989, chmn., 1990; founding co-chmn. Coun. Mktg. and Opinion Rsch., 1992-94. Contbr. articles to profl. jours.; patentee in field Trustee Carnegie-Mellon U., Pitts., 1980—, chmn., trustee student affairs com., 1982-85, co-chmn. devel. com., 1993-2000. Mem. Young Pres. Orgn. Republican. Jewish. Home: 10 Heathcote Rd Scarsdale NY 10583-4414 Office: NPD Group 900 W Shore Rd Port Washington NY 11050-4624

JOHNSON, TOM MILROY, dean, physician, educator; b. Northville, Mich., Jan. 16, 1935; s. Waldo Theodore and Ruth Jeanette (Christensen) J.; m. Emily Chapin Rhoads, June 13, 1959 (div. Aug. 1983); children—Glenn C., Heidi R.; m. Jane Susan Robb, June 10, 1987; 1 stepchild, Elizabeth K. BA in Psychology with honors, Coll. of Wooster, 1956; MD, Northwestern U., 1961; postgrad. in health systems mgmt., Harvard U., 1974. Rotating intern Detroit Receiving Hosp., 1961-62; resident in internal medicine U. Mich. Med. Ctr., Ann Arbor, 1962-65, fellow in pulmonary disease, 1967-68; asst. prof. internal medicine Mich. State U., East Lansing, 1968-71, assoc. prof., asst. dean Coll. of Medicine Grand Rapids, 1971-77; prof. medicine, dean Sch. of Medicine U. N.D., Grand Forks, 1977-88; prof., assoc. dean Coll. Human Medicine, Mich. State U., 1988-94; campus dean, CEO Kalamazoo Ctr. for Med. Studies Mich. State U., 1994-98, prof. emeritus medicine East Lansing, 1999—; cons. in med. edn. Fla. State U., 1999—2001. Bd. dirs. No. Mich. Regional Health Svcs., Petosky, 1991—2001. Contbr. articles to profl. jours. Capt. M.C., USAF, 1965-67. A. Blaine Brower Traveling scholar ACP, 1977; Tom M. Johnson lecture hall named in his honor Grand Rapids Med. Ctr., 1982; recipient Physician Leadership award Mich. Hosp. Assn., 1999, Disting. Alumni award Coll. of Wooster, 2003. Fellow ACP (Laureate award Mich. chpt.); mem. AMA, Mich. State Med. Soc., Studebaker Drivers Club, Antique Automobile Club of Am., Alpha Omega Alpha. Avocation: restoration of antique automobiles and older farm houses. Home and Office: 4815 Barton Rd Williamston MI 48895-9305 E-mail: tmilroyjohnson@yahoo.com.

JOHNSON, TRINA LYNN, special education educator; b. Hot Springs, Ark., Apr. 22, 1964; d. Mildred Maridean and William Kiney Couch. BSE, Henderson State U., Arkadelphia, Ark., 1992; MSE, Henderson State U., 2002. Cert. Nursing Asst., Petra Allied Health; TESOL Ark., 2005. Tchr. Malvern Schools, Ark., 2004—; cert. nursing asst. Alliance Home Health, Arkadelphia. Scholar, Fred's Dept. Stores. Mem. Assembly Of God Ch. Avocations: swimming, canoeing, dog breeding, hunting / fishing, concerts. Personal E-mail: trina@ezclick.net. E-mail: tjohnson@wilson1.dsc.k12.ar.us.

JOHNSON, URSULA ANNE, artist; b. St. Louis, Oct. 11, 1927; d. Lorenzo Bates and Ursula Agnes Lea; m. Herbert Crittenden Johnson, June 10, 1951; children: Amelia Anne Bosque, Raymond Brian. Student, Denison U., 1946—48, Ohio State U., 1951. Artist The Columbus Citizen, Ohio, 1951—52; fashion illustrator F & R Lazarus and Co., Columbus, Ohio, 1952—55. Artist's adv. coun. Marin Soc. of Artists, Ross, Calif., 1965—67, v.p., 1970—71, bd. dirs., 1970—72. Printmaking, Lost Words Found, 1980, Twice-told Tales, 1980, The Waiting Game, 1980, Aeon's Ago, 1980, Omen, 1980, Corrosion, 1981, Primitif, 1981, Symbol, 1981, Forgotten Image, 1981, Kehoe, 1983, Represented in permanent collections Bank Am. Corp., Bank San Francisco, juried show, Roseville Arts Show in the Garden, 2007, one-woman shows include Villa Marin, San Rafael, Calif., 2007. Mem. Art Coun. of Placer County, Auburn, Calif., 1992—2007, Smith Gallery, Sacramento, 2003—05, Roseville Arts, 2006, 2007. Avocations: gardening, swimming, hiking, travel. Home and Office: 1203 Overland Ln Lincoln CA 95648 Home Phone: 916-543-9654; Office Phone: 916-543-9654. Personal E-mail: ursart@sbcglobal.net.

JOHNSON, VAHE DUNCAN, lawyer; b. Providence, Dec. 18, 1938; s. Vahe D. and Katharine (Simpson) J.; m. Diana E. Lepow, Apr. 13, 1964; children: Alexandra, Mark Adam. AB, Harvard U., 1960, LLB, 1963. Bar: R.I. 1964. From assoc. to ptnr. Edwards & Angell (now Edwards Angell Palmer & Dodge LLP), Providence, 1963—. Bd. dirs. Fleet Nat. Bank, Fleet Bank of Mass., N.A., Fleet Bank, N.A. Trustee Providence Found., 1985, Providence Pub. Libr, 1988, Miriam Hosp., Providence, 1990, Lifespan Corp., Capitol Ctr. Commn., Tufts Vet. Sch., 1999, R.I. Sch. Design, 2005. Office: Edwards Angell Palmer & Dodge LLP 2800 Fin Plz Providence RI 02903 Home Phone: 401-861-4887; Office Phone: 401-276-6477. Business E-Mail: djohnson@eapdlaw.com.

JOHNSON, VERDIA E., marketing professional; B in Mktg., Howard U.; MBA in Mktg., NYU. With Colgate Palmolive Co., Standard Brands, Nabisco Brands; dir. advt. Black Enterprise Mag.; v.p. bus. devel. and sales Gannett Outdoor; v.p., gen. mgr. Stedman Graham & Ptnrs.; pres., founding ptnr. Footsteps, LLC, NYU, NY, 2000—. Named 25 Most Black Influential Women in Bus., Network Mag.; recipient Outstanding Women in Mktg. and Comm. award, Ebony Mag., 2001, Urban Wheels award, 2002. Office: Footsteps LLC 200 Varick St Rm 610 New York NY 10014-7487 Office Phone: 212-924-6432.

JOHNSON, VICTOR LAWRENCE, banker, director; b. Phila., Feb. 8, 1928; s. Paul J. and Eleanor (Moskowitz) J.; m. Joan Markovitz, Dec. 4, 1955; children: Linda E., Sally A. Grad., Phillips Exeter Acad., 1945; BA, Haverford Coll., 1949; MBA, Wharton Sch. of U. Pa., 1951. Vice pres. Ocean City Mfg. Co., Phila., 1953-58; pres. Johnson Computing Co., Phila., 1958-68, chmn. bd., dir., 1968—; with Provident Nat. Bank, Phila., 1969—, sr. v.p., 1971—; pres., dir. Allen Data Systems, Inc., Phila., 1970; pres. JCI Data Processing Inc., 1976—. Bd. dirs. Sircom Knitting Co., Spring City, Pa., pres., 1980-81; chmn. Wordco Data Systems Inc., 1992. Bd. dirs., mem. budget com. Phila. United Fund, 1954-67; bd. dirs. Nicetown Club Boys and Girls, Phila., 1954-57, Huntingdon Valley (Pa.) Civic Assn., 1956-64; bd. dirs., exec. com. Rydal/Meadowbrook (Pa.) Civic Assn., 1969—; mem. planning and devel. com. Germantown Friends Sch., 1970-73; vol. trustee Not-For-Profit Hosps. Bd., v.p., 1984-87, chmn. planning com., 1987-89; vice chmn., 1989-96, trustee, exec. com. Albert Einstein Med. Ctr., 1973—, vice chmn., 1980, chmn. bd. govs. No. divsn., 1981-84, chmn. bd. dirs., 1987-90; chmn. bd. trustees Health Care Found., 1987-90; dir. Jefferson Health System, 1998; sec., treas. Delaware Valley Hosp. Couns., 1982-95; chmn. bd. Delaware Valley Health, Edn. and Rsch. Found., 1982-85; bd. dirs. Phila. Festival Theatre for New Plays, 1989-94. With U.S. Army, 1951-52. Fellow Coll. Physicians Phila. (trustee 2002—); mem. Pa. Bankers Assn., Bank Automation Assn. Delaware Valley, Am. Hosp. Assn. (coun. governing bds. 1989, del. 2004), Hosp. Trustees Assn. Pa. (vice chmn. bd. 1991-92, chmn. bd. 1992), Locust Club (Phila.), Philmont Country Club (Huntingdon Valley) (bd. dirs., exec. v.p.). Home: Hidden Glen 1585 Warner Rd Meadowbrook PA 19046 Personal E-mail: victorj1@comcast.net.

JOHNSON, VICTORIA L., library director; married; 2 children. B in Speech Comm., U. So. Calif., MLS. Libr. positions City of Pasadena, 1986—95; dir. libraries Sunnyvale Pub. Libr. and Sunnyvale Ctr. for Innovation, Invention and Ideas, 1995—2004; dir. libr. services San Mateo County Libr., 2004—. Adj. faculty mem., grad. sch. edn. and info. services UCLA; bd. trustee Online Computer Libr. Ctr., Inc. (OCLC), Dublin, 2005—. Office: San Mateo County Libr 125 Lessingia Ct San Mateo CA 94402 Address: Online Computer Libr Ctr Inc (OCLC) 6565 Kilgour Place Dublin OH 43017-3395*

JOHNSON, W. CLAYTON, lawyer; b. Roanoke, Va., Sept. 14, 1955; BA, Univ. Va., 1977, JD, 1980. Bar: Calif. 1980, NY 1985. Atty., Calif., 1980—84; assoc. Cravath Swaine & Moore LLP, NYC, 1984—88, ptnr., corp., 1988—, ptnr. Hong Kong, 1994—2003. Mem. Va. Law Rev. Mem.: ABA, NY State Bar Assn.

JOHNSON, WAINE CECIL, dermatologist, educator; b. Mt. Vernon, Tex., Sept. 30, 1928; s. Tulley Bell and Lizzie J.; m. Deanna Glutz, Dec. 1973; children: Susan Lynn, Carol Ann, Sandra Kay. BS, East Tex. State U., 1949; MD, U. Tex., 1953. Intern Brooke Army Hosp., 1953-54; resident in dermatology Walter Reed Army Hosp., 1955-58; fellow in dermal pathology Armed Forces Inst. Pathology, 1960-61; mem. staff Skin and Cancer Hosp., Phila., 1962-78, asst. dir. lab., 1962, dir., 1970-78; mem. faculty Temple U. Med. Sch., Phila., 1962-78, prof. dermatology, 1970-78; clin. prof. U. Pa. Med. Sch., 1978—; chmn. dept. dermatology Grad. Hosp. U. Pa., 1978-98; mng. ptnr. Delaware Valley Dermatopathology LLP, 1998—2000; co-mng. dir. Delaware Valley Dermatopathology divsn. Inst. Dermatopathology, Conshohocken, Pa., 2001—05; with dept. dermatology U. Pa., Phila., 2006—. Author numerous papers in field.; Co-editor: Dermal Pathology, 1974. Served to maj. M.C. USAR, 1953-62. Recipient Gold medal sci. exhibit Am. Soc. Clin. Pathologists-Coll. Am. Pathologists, 1962 Mem.: ACP, AMA, Coll. Physicians of Phila. (chmn. dermatology sect. 1994—97), Atlantic Dermatol. Conf. (pres. 1979—80), Phila. Dermatol. Soc. (pres. 1979—80), Histochem. Soc., Soc. Investigative Dermatology, Am. Soc. Dermatopathology (pres. 1988), Am. Registry Pathology (pres. 2003—05), Internat. Acad. Pathology, Am. Dermatol. Assn., Am. Acad. Dermatology (chmn. pathology com. 1976—80). Home: 744 Crosswicks Rd Rydal PA 19046-3004 Home Phone: 215-884-0664; Office Phone: 215-614-0269. Business E-Mail: johnson.waine@uphs.upenn.edu.

JOHNSON, WALTER EARL, geophysicist; b. Denver, Dec. 16, 1942; s. Earl S. and Helen F. (Llewellyn) J.; m. Ramey Kandice Kayes, Aug. 6, 1967; children: Gretchen, Roger, Aniela. Grad. in Geophys. Engring., Colo. Sch. of Mines, 1966. Registered profl. engr., Colo.; cert. geologist, Colo. Geophysicist Pan Am. Petroleum Corp., 1966-73; seismic processing supr. Amoco Prodn. Co., Denver, 1973-74, marine tech. supr., 1974-76, divsn. processing cons., 1976-79; geophys. supr. No. Thrust Belt, Denver, 1979-80; chief geophysicist Husky Oil Co., Denver, 1981-82; exploration mgr. Rocky Mountain and Gulf Coast divsn., Denver, 1982-84; geophys. mgr. ANR Prodn. Co., Denver, 1985-99; pres. Exploration GeoCons., Inc., Denver, 2000—. Pres. Sch. Lateral Ditch Co.; cons. engr. Bd. dirs. Rocky Mountain Residence. Mem. Denver Geophys. Soc., Soc. Exploration Geophysicists. Republican. Baptist. Office: 1645 Court Pl Ste 309 Denver CO 80202-4507

JOHNSON, WALTER FRANK, JR., lawyer; b. Georgiana, Ala., 1945; s. Walter F. and Marjorie Ellen (Carnathan) J.; m. Emily Waldrep, Nov. 23, 1969; children: Brian W., Stacey E. BS, Auburn U., 1968; JD, Samford U., 1973. Bar: Ala. 1973, Ga. 1974. Acct. Union Camp Corp., 1968-70; assoc. Hatcher, Meyerson, Oxford and Irvin, Atlanta, 1973-74, Thompson and Redmond, Columbus, Ga., 1974-78, pvt. practice, 1978—. Asst. pub. defender, Columbus, 1978. Master: Nat. Assn. Consumer Bankruptcy Attys.; mem.: ABA, Ala. State Bar, State Bar Ga., Columbus Lawyers Club. Methodist. Home: 3235 Flint Dr Columbus GA 31907-2029 Office: PO Box 6507 3006 University Ave Columbus GA 31917 Office Phone: 706-563-3458. E-mail: wfjattorney@knology.net.

JOHNSON, WALTER KLINE, civil engineer; b. Mpls., Aug. 28, 1923; s. Horace Edward and Ida Axelina (Kline) J.; m. Geneva Lorraine Olson, Sept. 2, 1950; children: Kristine Idelle, Karen Margaret, Konstance Louise. BCE, U. Minn., 1948, MS, 1951, PhD, 1963. Registered profl. engr., Minn. With Greeley and Hansen, Chgo., 1948-49, Infilco, Inc., Tucson, 1951-52, Toltz, King, Duvall, Anderson & Assocs., St. Paul, 1952-55; faculty U. Minn., Mpls., 1955—, assoc. prof. civil engring., 1965-74, prof., 1974-75; dir. planning Met. Waste Control Commn., St. Paul, 1975-89; mgmt. cons. in environ. engring. St. Paul, 1989—. Patentee wastewater sampler. Capt. USAAF, 1943-46. EPA rsch. fellow Brit. Water Pollution Rsch. Lab., 1971. Fellow ASCE (pres. N.W. sect. 1972-73), Am. Water Works Assn., Cen. State Water Environment Assn.; mem. Am. Acad. Environ. Engrs. (diplomate). Lutheran. Achievements include rsch. on biol. waste water treatment, sludge bulking, nitrogen removal by denitrification. Home: 5321 29th Ave S Minneapolis MN 55417-2010 E-mail: WKJ1@JUNO.COM.

JOHNSON, WARREN DOUGLAS, infectious diseases physician, researcher; b. Mt. Vernon, NY, Oct. 9, 1937; s. Warren D. and June Marie (Lavezzi) J.; m. Barbara Florence Bean, June 14, 1969; children: Christopher, Sarah, David, Matthew. BS, Carroll Coll., 1958; MD, Columbia U., 1962. Diplomate Am. Bd. Med. Examiners, Am. Bd. Internal Medicine with subspecialty in infectious diseases. Instr. in medicine Cornell U. Med. Coll., NYC, 1967-69, asst. prof., 1969-74, dir. rsch. and tng. program at U. Bahia, 1969-79, assoc. prof. medicine, 1974-81, prof. medicine, 1981, dir. internat. health svcs., 1986—, chief divsn. internat. medicine, 1986, chief divsn. internat. medicine and infectious diseases, 1995—, B.H. Kean prof. tropical medicine, 1990—; from asst. to attending physician N.Y. Hosp., NYC, 1969—. Mem. nat. adv. allergy and infectious diseases coun. NIAID, NIH, Washington, 1995-99, chmn. micro and infectious diseases rsch. coun., 1987-90; chmn. subspecialty bd. infectious diseases Am. Bd. Internal Medicine, 1996-00, bd. dirs. Contbr. over 200 sci. articles to profl. publs., chpts. to books. Mem. Demerest (N.J.) Sch. Bd., 1984-90. Capt. USAF, 1964-66. Recipient Emilio Ribas medal in infectious diseases Brazil Soc. Infectious Diseases, 1992; named Prof. Hon. Fed. U. Bahia, Brazil, 1989. Fellow ACP, N.Y. Acad. Scis., Infectious Disease Soc. Am., Royal Soc. Tropical Medicine; mem. Am. Soc. Tropical Medicine, Am. Clin. Climatology Assn., Assn. Am. Physicians. Lutheran. Avocations: gardening, cooking. Office: Cornell U Med Coll A421 1300 York Ave New York NY 10021-4805

JOHNSON, WAYNE D., gas industry executive; b. Winterset, Iowa, Sept. 20, 1932; s. Leslie E. and Ruth N. J.; m. Lynne Alice Brouwer, June 15, 1963; children: Christopher W., Kevin B. BA, U. Nebr., 1954; LLB, Harvard U., 1959. Bar: Ill. bar 1959. Assoc., then ptnr. Ross, Hardies, O'Keefe, Babcock & Parsons, Chgo., 1959-72; asst. gen. counsel Peoples Gas Co., Chgo., 1972-75; sr. v.p., gen. counsel Entex, Inc., Houston, 1975-78, pres., 1978-86, utility cons., 1986-87; pres. United Tex. Transmission Co., 1987-93, Am. Natural Gas Power, Inc., Houston, 1993-97; utility cons., 1997—. Dir. Simmons & Co., Internat., 1980—. Past chmn. Galveston Bay Found.; treas. Sam Houston Area Coun., Boy Scouts Am.; mem. data integration team and demand task force Nat. Petroleum Coun., Com. on Natural Gas, 1998-2000. With U.S. Army, 1954-56. Woodrow Wilson fellow, 1954 Mem. Am. Gas Assn., So. Gas Assn. (past chmn.), Lawyer's Club (Chgo.). Home: 5517 Cedar Creek Houston TX 77056

JOHNSON, WAYNE HAROLD, librarian, retired municipal official; b. El Paso, Tex., May 2, 1942; s. Earl Harold and Cathryn Louise (Greeno) J.; m. Patricia Ann Froedge, June 15, 1973; children: Meredith Jessica (dec.), Alexandra Noëlle Victoria. BS, Utah State U., 1968; MPA, U. Colo., 1970; MLS, U. Okla., 1972. Circulation libr. Utah State U., Logan, 1968, adminstrv. asst. libr., 1969; with rsch. dept. Okla. Mgmt. and Engring. Cons., Norman, 1972; chief adminstrv. svcs. Wyo. State Libr., Cheyenne, 1973-76, chief bus. officer libr. archives and hist. dept., 1976-78, state libr., 1978-89; county grants mgr. Laramie County, Wyo., 1989-2001. Cons. in field. Trustee Bibliog. Ctr. for Rsch., Denver, pres., 1983-84; active Cheyenne dist. Longs Park coun. Boy Scouts Am., 1982-86; active Cheyenne Frontier Days, 1975—. Leadership Wyo., 2006; admissions and allocation com. United Way, 1991-94; mem. Ho. of Reps., Wyo. Legislature, 1993-2004; mem. senate Wyo. Legis., 2005—; chmn. Transp. Hwys. Com., 1999-2004. With USCG, 1960—64. Mem. Aircraft Owners and Pilots Assn., Cheyenne C. of C. (chmn. transp. com. 1982, 83, mil. affairs com. 1994—), Am. Legion, Masons (Grand Lodge libr. 2001-, master Cheyenne Lodge No. 1, 2005-06), Kiwanis (bd. dirs. 1986-87), No. Colo. Yacht Club. Republican. Presbyterian.

JOHNSON, WEYMAN THOMPSON, JR., lawyer; b. Atlanta, July 13, 1951; s. Weyman Thompson Sr. and Dixie LaNé (Peevy) J.; m. E. Allison Forkner, July 13, 1974; children: Chloe Forkner, Willa Rose. BA, Mercer U., 1973; JD, U. Ga., 1979. Bar: Ga. 1979, U.S. Dist. Ct. (no. dist.) Ga. 1979, U.S. Ct. Appeals (4th and 11th cir.) 1983, U.S. Supreme Ct. 1989. Reporter Columbus (Ga.) Ledger Newspaper, 1973-75; assoc. Fisher & Phillips, Atlanta, 1979-83, ptnr., 1984; assoc. Paul, Hastings, Janofsky & Walker, Atlanta, 1984-88, ptnr., 1988—, mem. policy com. Adj. prof. U. Ga. Sch. Law, Athens, Ga. State U. Coll. Law, Atlanta, Emory Sch. Law, Atlanta. Author: Plant Closing Law, 1989, Negligence in Employment Law, 2002. Chair Governance Com., 2001—05; bd. deacons First Bapt. Ch., Decatur, 1984—, chmn., 1998, 2002; chair Ga. chpt. Nat. Multiple Sclerosis Soc., Atlanta, 1990—94, 2006—, bd. dirs., 1995—; bd. mem. Multiple Sclerosis Internat. Fedn., 2003—, sec. bd., 2005—. Mem. ABA, State Bar Ga. (chair labor sect. 2001-2002), Atlanta Bar Assn. (chmn. labor sect. 1989-90, bd. dirs. 1991-92), Indsl. Rels. Rsch. Assn., Ga. Def. Lawyers Assn. Office: Paul Hastings Janofsky & Walker 600 Peachtree St NE Fl 24 Atlanta GA 30308-2265 Office Phone: 404-815-2209. Business E-Mail: weymanjohnson@paulhastings.com.

JOHNSON, WILLIAM ALEXANDER, clergyman, philosophy and theology educator; b. Bklyn., Aug. 20, 1934; s. Charles Raphael and Ruth Augusta (Anderson) J.; m. Carol Genevieve Lundquist, June 11, 1955; children— Karin Ruth, Karl William, Krister Frederick. BA, Queens Coll., City U. N.Y., 1953; B.D. (Univ. fellow, Morrow Meml. fellow, Daniel Delaplaine fellow), Union Theol. Sem., 1956; Teol. Kand., Lund U., 1957, Teol. Lic., 1958, Teologie Doktor, 1962; MA, Columbia U., 1958, PhD (Univ. fellow, Rockefeller Bros. fellow), 1959. Ordained deacon Meth. Ch., 1955, priest Episcopal Ch., 1968. Profl. baseball player N.Y. Giants, 1949-51; dir. Boys Club, Salvation Army, Jamaica, NY, 1952-54; minister Mt. Hope and Teabo Meth. chs., Wharton, NJ, 1954-56; elder Meth. Ch., 1956; minister Immanuel and Union Meth. chs., Bklyn., 1957-59; asst. in instrn. Columbia U., NYC, 1957, Union Theol. Sem., NYC, 1958; instr., asst. prof. religion Trinity Coll., Hartford, Conn., 1959-63; lectr. philosophy and theology Hartford Sem. Found., 1961-62; assoc. prof. religion, chmn. dept. religion Drew U., Madison, NJ, 1963-66; research prof. religion NYU, NYC, 1966; vis. lectr. Union Theol. Sem., NYC, 1966; vis. prof. religion Princeton (N.J.) U., 1966-68; prof., chmn. dept. religion Manhattanville Coll., Purchase, N.Y., 1967-71; vis. prof. Christian ethics Gen. Theol. Sem., NYC, 1970; Albert V. Danielsen prof. Christian thought, prof. philosophy and history of ideas Brandeis U., Waltham, Mass., 1971—, prof. Near Ea. and Jewish studies, 1988—; canon residentiary Cathedral Ch. of St. John The Divine, NYC, 1973—. Vis. Prof. Protestant theology N.Am. Coll., Vatican City, 1969-75; vis. prof., Tokyo, Stockholm, 1979, U. Gothenburg, Sweden, 1979, U. Copenhagen, 1994-95, Univ. Perth, Australia, 1997, 99, 2001; examining chaplain Diocese of Arctic, 1982; lectr. in field. Author: The Philosophy of Religion of Anders Nygren, 1958, Christopher Polhem: The Father of Swedish Technology, 1963, Nature and the Supernatural in the Theology of Horace Bushnell, 1963, On Religion: A Study of Theological Method in Schleiermacher and Nygren, 1964, Problems in Christian Ethics, 1965 (with Nels F.S. Ferré) Swedish Contributions to Modern Theology, 1966, The Search for Transcendence, 1974, The Christian Way of Death, 1974, Invitation to Theology, 1979, Philosophy and the Gospel, 1979, (with Moorhead Kennedy) Christianity and Terrorism, 1986, O Boundless Salvation, 1987; also articles; debut as Popolo in Aida, Met. Opera, 1989, Tosca, 1990, La Boheme, 1992. Democratic committeeman Hartford, 1960-63; mem. exec. com. Am. Friends Service Com., Coll. Div., 1966-70; bd. dirs. Queens Coll. CUNY; priest-in-charge Korean Episc. Ch., N.Y.C., 1992—. Recipient David F. Swenson-Kierkegaard Meml. award, 1964, Harbison award for Tchr. of Yr. Danforth Found., 1965; named Outstanding Young Man in Am. Jr. C. of C., 1964; Disting. Alumnus Queens Coll., 1980; Scandinavian-Am. Found. fellow, 1956, 85; Fulbright scholar U. Copenhagen, 1957-58; Dempster Grad. fellow Meth. Ch., 1958; Am. Philos. Soc. fellow, 1971, 85. vis. rsch. fellow Princeton, 1972; Guggenheim fellow for study in Rome, Italy, 1972; NSF grantee, 1978; Rockefeller fellow Aspen Inst., 1978, fellow Aspen Inst., Jerusalem, 1982; Nat. Endowment Humanities grantee, 1978, 86; grantee Arthur Vining Davis Found., 1981; grantee Trinity Ch. of N.Y.C., 1982, 84; grantee Tauber Inst. Study of European Jewry; named All-Am. Baseball Player, Amateur Athletic Assn., 1952, 53, All-Am. Soccer Player, Amateur Athletic Assn., 1953. Mem. Am. Acad. Religion, Asia Soc., Japan Soc., Scandinavian-Am. Heritage Soc., Am. Philos. Assn., Danforth Assos., Soc. for Sci. Study Religion, Soc. for Religion in Higher Edn. (Kent fellow 1959), Australian-Am. Assn., Shakespeare Soc. of Am. (academic advisor), Soc. Anglican Theologians, Vasa Order Am., Am. Soc. Christian Ethics, Swedish Pioneer Hist. Soc., Soc. for Scandinavian Study, Danish-Am. Soc., Australian-Am. Soc., Willa Cather Pioneer Meml. Found., Authors Guild, Episcopal Churchmen for South Africa, New Haven Theol. Group, Westchester Inst. Psychiatry and Psychoanalysis (dir.), Ecumenical Found. for Christian Ministry, English Speaking Union, Ch. Soc. for Coll. Work, Paris Am. Club, Columbia University Club, Met. Opera Club, The Pilgrims, Shakespeare Soc. Am. (acad. advisor), The Coffee House, Lotos Club (medal of hon., medal of merit 2004), Century Club, Explorer's Club, Phi Beta Kappa, Pi Gamma Mu, Phi Sigma Tau. Democrat. Episcopalian. Office: 27 Fox Meadow Rd Scarsdale NY 10583-2903 also: 44 Pascal Ave Rockport ME 04856-5918 Office Phone: 914-723-6389. *I have attempted in my life to fulfill the simple prayer of St. Francis: Lord, make me an instrument of your peace/Where there is hatred... let me sow love/Where there is injury... pardon/Where there is doubt... faith/Where there is despair... hope/Where there is darkness... light/Where there is sadness... joy. For it is giving that we receive; it is pardoning that we are pardoned; and it is dying that we are born to eternal life.*

JOHNSON, WILLIAM DAVID, retired academic administrator; b. Bloomington, Ind., Aug. 9, 1924; s. Ben and Ida Grace (Garlock) J.; m. Audrey Aelise Thurston; 1 child, Sheryn Aelise Johnson Peters BS, Ind. U., 1946. Asst. bursar U. Va., Charlottesville, 1947-54; comptroller George Washington U., 1954-69, dir. planning and budgeting, 1969-82, assoc. provost, 1982-84, provost, 1984-89. Served to 1st lt. U.S. Army, 1943-46; ETO Mem. Fin. Exec. Inst. (chpt. pres. 1969-70), Eastern Assn. Coll. and Univ. Bus. Officers, Nat. Assn. Coll. and Univ. Bus. Officers, Omicron Delta Kappa, Delta Chi Republican. Presbyterian. Avocations: woodworking, golf, skeet shooting. Home: 3440 S Jefferson St Apt 705 Falls Church VA 22041-3125

JOHNSON, WILLIAM DEAN, power company executive; b. Pa., Jan. 9, 1954; BA, Duke U., 1978; JD, U. N.C., 1982. Law clk. Hon. J.D. Philips Jr., U.S. Ct. Appeals, 4th Cir., 1982-83; assoc. Hunton & Williams, 1983-90, ptnr., 1990-92; assoc. gen. counsel Carolina Power & Light, Raleigh, 1992-95, v.p., corp. sec., 1995-1999, sr. v.p., corp. sec., 1999-2001; pres., CEO, Progress Energy Svc. Co., Raleigh, 2002—03; exec. v.p., gen. counsel, sec. Progress Energy, Inc., Raleigh, 2001—02, group pres. energy delivery, 2004—05, pres., COO, 2005—. Mem. ABA, N.C. Bar Assn. Office: Progress Energy Inc 411 Fayetteville Street Mall Raleigh NC 27601-1748 Office Phone: 919-546-6463. E-mail: bill.johnson@pgnmail.com.

JOHNSON, WILLIAM G., neurologist, educator; MD, Columbia U., 1967. Diplomate in clin. genetics and clin. biochem. genetics Am. Bd. Med. Genetics. Intern Medicine N.Y. Hosp. Cornell Med. Ctr., NYC, 1967—68, resident medicine, 1968—69; fellow in Biochem. Genetics NIH, Bethesda, Md., 1969—72; physician dept. neurology Robert Wood Johnson U. Med. Group, New Brunswick, NJ, 1991—. Prof. neurology UMDNJ- Robert Wood Johnson Med. Sch., Piscataway, 1991—; dir. lab. neurogenetics, Piscataway, 1991—. Office Phone: 732-235-4508, 732-235-7340. Business E-Mail: wjohnson@umdnj.edu.

JOHNSON, WILLIAM HOWARD, retired agricultural engineer, educator; b. Sidney, Ohio, Sept. 3, 1922; s. Russell Earl and Dollie (Gamble) J.; m. Wyoma Jean Swift, Oct. 2, 1943; children: Lawrence Alan, Cheri Ellen, Dana Sue. BS, Ohio State U., 1948, MS, 1953; PhD, Mich. State U., 1960. Registered profl. engr. Mem. faculty Ohio Agrl. Expt. Sta., Wooster, 1948-64, Ohio Agrl. Rsch. and Devel. Ctr., Wooster, 1964-70, prof., assoc. chmn. dept. agrl. engring., 1959-70; part-time prof. Ohio State U., 1964-70; prof., head dept. agrl. engring. Kans. State U., Manhattan, 1970-81, dir. Engring. Expt. Sta., 1981-87; ret., 1987. Cons. farm equipment cos. Author: (with B.J. Lamp) Principles, Equipment and Systems for Corn Harvesting, 1966; also articles. Recipient Disting. Alumnus award Coll. Engring., Ohio State U., 1974; named to Coll. Engring. Kans. State U. Hall of Fame, 1992. Fellow Am. Soc. Agrl. Engrs. (pres. 1986-87, McCormick-Case Gold Medal award 1994), Kans. Engring. Soc. (pres. 1985-86), Sigma Xi, Tau Beta Pi. Achievements include research on soil-plant-machine relationships, harvesting, design for soiltillers, planters, harvesters. Home: 2121 Meadowlark Rd #131 Manhattan KS 66502 Office: Kans State U Dept Agrl Engring Seaton Hall Manhattan KS 66506 Business E-Mail: wjohnson@ksu.edu.

JOHNSON, WILLIAM LEWIS, materials scientist, educator; b. Bowling Green, Ohio, July 26, 1948; s. Melvin Carl and Martha Maxine (Roller) J.; m. Rachel Marie Newman, Jan. 21, 1984. BA in Physics, Hamilton

Coll., 1970; PhD in Applied Physics, Calif. Inst. Tech., 1974. Mem. staff IBM Thomas J. Watson Rsch. Ctr., Yorktown Heights, NY, 1975-77; asst. prof. materials sci. Calif. Inst. Tech., Pasadena, 1977-80, assoc. prof., 1980-84, prof., 1984—, Ruben and Donna Mettler Prof. materials sci., 1989—. Cons., GM Rsch., Warren, Mich., 1983—, Amorphous Techs. Internat., Laguna,Calif., 1992—. Co-author: Glassy Metals I, 1981, Properties of Amorphous Metals, 1983, Physical Metallurgy, 1983, ASM Metals Handbook-Metallic Glasses, 1990. US Steel fellow, 1971; Alexander von Humboldt fellow, 1988; recipient William-Hume-Rothery award Metals Soc., 1996. Mem. AAAS, Metals Soc. AIME, Am. Phys. Soc., Materials Rsch. Soc. (Medal award 1998), NAE, NAS, Phi Beta Kappa, Sigma Xi. Lutheran. Office: Materials Sci Dept Calif Inst Tech MC 138-78 1200 California Blvd Pasadena CA 91125 Office Phone: 626-395-4433. E-mail: wlj@caltech.edu.*

JOHNSON, WILLIAM MICHAEL, physician; b. Olean, N.Y., Nov. 20, 1940; s. Loren Edward and Ann Elizabeth (Van Dyke) J.; m. Marlene Elsie Brill, June 26, 1965; children: Michael Scott, Susan Kim, Amy Marlene, Linda Marie. AB, Stanford U., 1963, MD, 1968; MPH, Harvard U., 1970, M in Indsl. Health, 1971. Diplomate Am. Bd. Internal Medicine, Am. Bd. Preventive Medicine. Intern, SUNY-Buffalo Hosps., 1968-69; resident in occupational medicine Harvard Sch. Public Health, Boston, 1969-71; acting dep. dir. div. field studies and clin. investigations Nat. Inst. Occupational Safety and Health Cin., 1971-73; resident in internal medicine U. Ariz. Hosps., Tucson, 1973-75, fellow in pulmonary disease, 1975-77; asst. prof. environ. health, adj. asst. prof. medicine U. Wash., Seattle, 1977-80; commd. lt. col. U.S. Army, 1980, advanced through grades to col., 1986; chief pulmonary disease svc. Dwight David Eisenhower Army Med. Ctr., Fort Gordon, Ga., 1983-93, staff, 1980-83; staff physician dept. Vet. Affairs Med. Ctr., Augusta, Ga., 1993-2004; pvt. cons., 2004; asst. clin. prof. medicine Med. Coll. Ga., Augusta, 1981-88, assoc. clin. prof. of medicine, 1988-1993, assoc. prof. medicine, 1995-2004. Contbr. articles on pulmonary disease and occupational cancer to profl. jours. Served as surgeon USPHS, 1971-73. Fellow Am. Coll. Chest Physicians; mem. Am. Thoracic Soc., Soc. Occupl. and Environ. Health. Home: 2948 Foxhall Cir Augusta GA 30907-3647 Office Phone: 706-863-4270. Business E-Mail: wmjohnson@knology.net.

JOHNSON, WILLIAM POTTER, publishing executive, director; b. Peoria, Ill., May 4, 1935; s. William Zweigle and Helen Marr (Potter) J.; m. Pauline Ruth Rowe, May 18, 1968; children: Darragh Elizabeth, William Potter. AB, U. Mich., 1957. Gen. mgr. Bureau County Rep., Inc., Princeton, Ill., 1961-72; pres. Johnson Newspapers, Inc., Sebastopol, Calif., 1972-75, Evergreen, Colo., 1974-86, Canyon Commons Investment, Evergreen, 1974—, Johnson Media, Inc., Granby, Colo., 1987—. Author: How the Michigan Betas Built a $1,000,000 Chapter House in the '80s. Alt. del. Rep. Nat. Conv., 1968. Lt. USNR, 1958-61. Mem.: Vero Beach Yacht Club, Beta Theta Pi.

JOHNSON, WILLIAM R., food products executive; m. Suzie Johnson; children: Brad, Tracy. Grad., UCLA; MBA, U. Tex. Asst. prod. mgr. Behold Furniture Polish, 1974; gen. mgr., new businesses, Heinz USA H.J. Heinz Co., Pitts., 1982—84, v.p., new businesses, Heinz USA, 1984—88, pres., CEO, pet products, 1988—92, head, Starkist, 1992, sr. v.p., pet products, Starkist, Asia/Pacific oper., 1993—96, pres., COO, 1996—98, pres., CEO, 1998—, chmn., 2000—. Bd. dirs. H.J. Heinz Co., 1993—, Clorox Co., Ga.-Pacific Corp., Grocery Mfr. Am. Bd. dirs. Extra Mile Found.; mem. Athena Awards Com.; chair, ann. campaign United Way Western Pa., 2001.*

JOHNSON, WILLIAM STANLEY, metal distribution company executive; b. Elmhurst, Ill., May 11, 1957; s. Raymond J. and Nancy A. (Zinns) J.; m. Lisa Ann Grundy, July 14, 1990; 1 child, William Chase. BS in Bus. and Acctg., Ind. U., 1979; MBA in Fin., Mercer U., 1986. CPA, Calif.; CFP. Auditor, sr. auditor Ernst & Young, CPA's, Indpls., 1979-80; various fin. and acctg. positions Am. Hosp. Supply Co., Evanston, Ill., 1980-86; v.p. fin., dir. acctg. Abbey Med./Beaverbrook Group, Costa Mesa, Calif., 1987-91; corp. fin. mgr. Severin Group, Ivrine, Calif., 1991-94; corp. contr., CFO, Earle M. Jorgensen Co., Brea, Calif., 1994—. Mem. adj. faculty U. Phoenix, Fountain Valley, Calif., 1998—. Mem. FEI, AICPA, Calif. Soc. CPA's. Home: 744 Via Lido Soud Newport Beach CA 92663-5558

JOHNSON, WILLIAM WOODWARD (HOOTIE JOHNSON), bank executive, retired sports association executive; b. Augusta, Ga., Feb. 16, 1931; s. Dewey Hodges and Mabel Marie (Woodward) J.; m. Sarah Pierrine Baker, July 26, 1951; children: Jennifer, Marie, Sally, Jane. BBA, U. S.C.; HHD (hon.), Lander Coll., 1973. With NCNB Nat. Bank S.C., Columbia, 1954—, sr. v.p., 1960-63, exec. v.p., 1963-65, pres., 1965-79, chmn. bd., pres., chief exec. officer, 1979-80, chmn. bd., chief exec. officer, from 1980, now chmn. bd. Bd. dirs. Liberty Corp. Trustee U. S.C. Bus. Partnership Found., Benedict Coll., Converse Coll.; mem. adv. coun. Furman U.; chmn. S.C. State Ports Authority; legislator S.C. Gen. Assembly; campaign chmn. drive for United Fund Lexington, Richland Counties, 1964; chmn. S.C. drive Radio Free Europe; bd. dirs. Nat. Urban League, Columbia Urban League; former chmn. Augusta Nat. Golf Course Recipient Algernon Sydney Sullivan award U. S.C., 1971, Outstanding Citizen award B'nai B'rith, 1975. Office: NCNB Nat Bank SC NCNB Tower 1301 Gervais St # 448 Columbia SC 29201-3326

JOHNSON, WYLIE PIERSON, electric utility executive; b. Montgomery, Ala., Mar. 28, 1919; BSME, Auburn U., 1942; postgrad., Cornell U., 1943, Ga. Inst. Tech., 1959. Registered profl. engr., Ala. Engr. Ala. Power Co., Montgomery, 1946-52, supt. transmission lines Birmingham, 1952-58, supt. transmission, 1958-66, supt. spl. svcs., 1966-74, mgr. gen. svcs., 1974-76, ret., 1976. Chmn. transmission and large substation com. Southeastern Electric Exchange, Atlanta, 1962-66. Contbr. articles to profl. jours. Chief insp. Election Ofcls., Montgomery County, Ala., 1980-93; pres. Pike Rd. Vol. Fire Dept. Bd., 1985-86. Served to lt. USS Grainger, USNR, 1943-46, PTO. Mem. IEEE (chmn. Ala. sect. 1962-63), ASME, Montgomery Geneal. Soc. (v.p.), SAR (pres. Richard Montgomery chpt. 1989-91, pres. Ala. State soc. 1997, nat. trustee 1998), Birmingham Engrs. Club (chmn. budget and fin. 1961), Green Valley Country Club, The Club, Young Men's Bus. Club, Exch. Club (pres. Vestavia Club 1974-75), Capital City Club, Rotary (pres.-elect Tuskegee club 1998), Masons, Shriners, Lambda Chi Alpha. Baptist. Avocation: wild life preservation. Home: 1991 Shades Crest Rd Birmingham AL 35216-1429

JOHNSON, XAN STUART, performing arts educator; b. Kansas City, Mo., Dec. 14, 1944; s. Dean Lowell and Helen Johnson. BA in Theatre, Psychology and Edn., U. Wis., Whitewater, 1967; MA in Modern Theatre and Stage Dir., U. Nebr., Lincoln, 1968; PhD, Northwestern U., Evanston, Ill., 1978. Faculty U. Utah, Salt Lake City, 1982—, prof. dept. theatre, dept. chair, head theatre edn., artistic dir. Pioneer Meml. Theatre's Young People's Theatre, head Child Drama/Young People's Theatre grad. program, 1988—. Lectr. in field; condr. seminars in field; theatre cons. Utah State Office Edn.; scriptwriter Xtreme Dance, Salt Lake City; playwright Ririe-Woodbury Modern Dance Co. Scriptwriter Eagle Flight; dir.: over 130 stage prodns., Amber Waves, First Stage. Head child abuse program U. Utah; founder, artistic dir. Zona Gale Youth Theatre, Portage, Wis. Recipient Disting. Alumni award, U. Wis.-Whitewater, 1990. Home: PO Box 58669 Salt Lake City UT 84158 Office: University of Utah 300 S 1400 E Salt Lake City UT 84112-0660 Business E-Mail: xan.s.johnson@utah.edu.

JOHNSON, YVONNE THOMAS, elementary school educator; b. Kingston, Jamaica, June 5, 1948; arrived in US, 1956; d. George Diaz Thomas and Lucille Adelle (McCurdy) Thomas-McPherson; m. Glenn Jacobs, Nov. 22, 1986 (div.); 1 stepchild, Brian Jacobs; m. Rick Frederick C. Johnson (div.); children: Lance Cabral, Amaris Kai. BA, Simmons Coll., Boston, 1971; EdM, Harvard Grad. Sch. Edn., Cambridge, Mass., 1982; CAGS, Wheelock Coll. and Harvard Edn. Sch., 1992. Tchr. John Marshall Sch., Boston, 1971—73; Chpt. 1 reading tchr. Lucy Stone Sch., 1974—77, first grad tchr., 1978—79; cluster support tchr. ESAA Schs. Without Failure, 1979—81; lang. arts, soc. studies tchr. Graham and Parks Alternative Schs., Cambridge, Mass., 1982—86; kindergarten tchr. Daniel A. Haggerty Sch., 1986—2002; ret. Mem. Meeting House Hill Neighborhood Assn., 2003—, Friends of Ronan Park, 2004—. Conant fellow, Harvard Edn. Sch. for CAGS Studies. Mem.: Cambridge Tchrs. Assn., Mass. Tchrs. Assn., Dorchester YMCA. Democrat. Baptist. Avocations: art, swimming, singing, reading, cooking.

JOHNSON, ZACH (ZACHARY HARRIS JOHNSON), professional golfer; b. Iowa City, Iowa, Feb. 24, 1976; s. Dave Johnson; m. Kimala Barclay, Feb. 8, 2003. Grad. in Bus. Mgmt. and Mktg., Drake U., Des Moines, 1998. Profl. golfer, 1998—; mem. Prairie Golf Tour, 1998, PGA Tour, 2004—. Mem. US Team Ryder Cup, 2006. Named Hooters Tour Player of Yr., 2001, Nationwide Tour Player of Yr., 2003. Achievements include winning The Masters Tournament, 2007; won the BellSouth Classic, 2004, AT&T Classic, 2007, on the PGA Tour; won the Rheem Classic, 2003, Envirocare Utah Classic, 2003, on the Nationwide Tour; finished at the top of the money list on the Hooters Tour, 2001. Mailing: PGA Tour 112 PGA TOUR Blvd Ponte Vedra Beach FL 32082*

JOHNSON-LAIRD, PHILIP NICHOLAS, psychologist; b. Rothwell, Eng., Oct. 12, 1936; s. Frederick Ryberg and Dorothy (Blackett) J.-L.; m. Maureen Mary Sullivan, Aug. 1, 1959; children: Ben, Dorothy. BA with honors, Univ. Coll., London, 1964; PhD, Univ. Coll., 1967; Doctorate (hon.), U. Gothenburg, Sweden, 1983, Padau U., Italy, 1997, Trinity Coll., Dublin, Ireland, 2000, Nat. U. Distance Edn., Madrid, Spain, 2000, U. Ghent, Belgium, 2002, U. Palermo, Sicily, 2005. Asst. lectr., then lectr. psychology Univ. Coll., London, 1966-73; vis. mem. Inst. for Advanced Study, Princeton, N.J., 1971-72; reader, prof., chair exptl. psychology Sussex U., Brighton, Eng., 1973-82; spl. appointment, asst. dir. Med. Rsch. Coun. Applied Psychology Unit, Cambridge, Eng., 1982-89; prof., Stuart prof. psychology Princeton U., 1989—. Vis. prof. cognitive sci. Stanford (Calif.) U., 1980, vis. prof. psychology, 1985; vis. prof. Trieste (Italy) U., 1990, Univ. Coll., 1992, NYU, 1996, Padua, 2000. Author: Mental Models, 1983, The Computer and the Mind, 1988, (with Ruth Byrne) Deduction, 1991, How We Reason, 2006, 7 others; contbr. over 200 articles to profl. jours. Mem. Campaign for Disarmament, London, 1959-82. Recipient Medaglia D'Onore, U. Florence, Italy, 1989, Fyssen Internat. Prize, 2003, Mind and Brain Prize, U. Turin, 2004. Fellow: Royal Soc. U.K., Brit. Acad.; mem.: NAS, Am. Philos. Soc., Soc. Exptl. Psychologists, Brit. Psychol. Soc. (Spearman medal 1974, Pres.'s award 1985), Am. Psychol. Soc. Avocation: piano. Office: Princeton U Dept Psychology Princeton NJ 08544-0001 E-mail: phil@princeton.edu.

JOHNSON-LEIPOLD, HELEN P., outdoor recreation company executive; b. Dec. 1956; d. Samuel Curtis and Imogene (Powers) Johnson; m. Craig L. Leipold; children: Kyle, Connor, Curtis, Bradford, Chris. BA in Psychology, Cornell U., 1978. With Foote, Cone & Belding, Chgo., 1979—85; v.p. consumer mktg. svcs. worldwide SC Johnson, 1992-95, exec. v.p. N.Am. businesses, 1995-97, v.p. personal and home care products, 1997-98, v.p. worldwide consumer products-mktg., 1998—99; chmn., CEO Johnson Outdoors Inc. (formerly Johnson Worldwide Assocs. Inc.), Racine, Wis., 1999—; chmn. Johnson Fin. Group, 2004—. Co-owner Nashville Predators, NHL, 1997—; bd. dirs. The Home Depot, 2006—, SC Johnson & Co., JohnsonDiversey, Inc.; founder, chmn. Next Generation Now. Named one of Forbes' Richest Americans, 2006. Office: Johnson Outdoors Inc 555 Main St Racine WI 53403 Office Fax: 262-631-6601.

JOHNSON-MARQUART, WINNIE, consumer products company executive; married; 4 children. Attended, Vassar Coll., Cornell U. Project coord. corp. pub. affairs SC Johnson, 1986—. Pres. Johnson Family Found.; mem. bd. dirs. Johnson Fin. Group. Bd. trustees Norfolk Acad. Named one of Forbes' Richest Americans, 2006. Office: SC Johnson 1525 Howe St Racine WI 53403-5011

JOHNSON-MORAN, KELLY KATHLEEN, health facility administrator, writer; b. Milw., Wis., Sept. 10, 1977; d. Clay Phillip Johnson; m. Darren Michael Moran, Aug. 17, 2002. Cert. CNA, Aurora Health Care, 1999. Asst. mgr. CNA Brotoloc Health Care Sys., Muskego, Wis., 1999—2001; caregiver CNA Luth. Soc. Svcs., Waukesha, Wis., 2002—03; resident coord. Creative living Environ., Milw., 2003—. Author: Forty-Second Street, 2002, An Insomniac's Dream, 2005, When the Leaves Stop Falling, 2005. Vol. Big Brothers/Big Sisters, Milw., 2002—, Spl. Olympics, Milw., 2004—. Recipient Editor's Choice award, Nat. Libr. of Poetry, 1993. Democrat. Roman Cath. Avocations: reading, writing, crafts, films, volunteer work. E-mail: authorkellymoran@aol.com.

JOHNSON-WOLFF, CHRISTINA MARIE, retail executive; b. Gulfport, Miss., July 30, 1950; d. William Fredrick and Marian Susan (Varriano) Johnson; m. Richard Karl Wolff; children: Kathlyn Marie. BA, Loyola U., Chgo., 1972. Buyer Carson Pirie Scott, Chgo., 1976-81; sr. buyer Marshall Field & Co., Chgo., 1981-83, div. merchandise mgr., 1982-83, v.p. direct response, 1983-87, sr. v.p., gen. mgr. home store and direct response, 1987—91; positions up to sr. v.p. and regional dir. stores/east Saks Fifth Ave., 1991—99, vice chmn., COO, 1999—2000, pres., CEO, 2000—03; ptnr., mng. dir. retail and consumer investments NRDC Equity Ptnrs., L.L.C., Purchase, NY, 2006—. Bd. dirs. Credit Union, Marshall Fields, Chgo., Lord and Taylor. Bd. dirs. Grant A Wish Found., Chgo., 1987, Women in Need; trustee bd. dirs. Loyola U. Chgo. Office: NRDC Equity Ptnrs LLC 3 Manhattanville Rd Purchase NY 10577 Office Phone: 914-272-8080. E-mail: christina.johnson@nrdc.com.*

JOHNSRUD, BRIAN C., literature educator, scholar; s. Steve Johnsrud and Kimberly Taylor. Student in Anglo Saxon and Old Norse lit., Univ. Oslo, Norway; BA in English Lit., Mont. State Univ., 2006; MPhil. student in Medieval Lit., Oxford Univ., 2007—. English tchr. charter sch., Bozeman, Mont., 2006—07. Planner, organizer Make a Difference Day, Great Falls, Mont. Rhodes Scholar. Achievements include presenting at academic conferences in Europe and US on topics in medieval lit.; doing rsch. at archaeological dig in Jerusalem, 2007.*

JOHNSTON, BERNARD FOX, foundation executive, writer; b. Taft, Calif., Nov. 19, 1934; s. Bernard Lowe and Georgia Victoria (Fox) Johnston; m. Audrey Rhoades, June 9, 1956 (div. Sept. 1963); 1 child, Sheldon Bernard. BA in Creative Arts, San Francisco State U., 1957, MA in World Lit., 1959. Lectr. philosophy Coll. Marin, Kentfield, Calif., 1957—58; lectr. humanities San Francisco State U., 1957—58, 1967—68; instr. English Contra Costa Coll., San Pablo, Calif., 1958—63, Knowles Found. philosophy fellow, 1962; fellow Syracuse U., 1964—66; freelance writer Piedmont, Calif., 1968—77; pres. Cinema Repertory, Inc., Point Richmond, Calif., 1978—89; pres., exec. dir. Athena Found., Tiburon, Calif., 1990—, Incline Village, Nev., 1990—. CEO Athena Found., Inc., 1997, Mahler Festival, U. Colo., Boulder, 1998; guest lectr. Sierra Nev. Coll., 2005; lectr. in field. Author: (screenplays) Point Exeter, 1979, Ascent Allowed, 1988 (award); author, editor: Issues in Education: An Anthology of Controversy, 1964, The Literature of Learning, 1971; musician: (resident pianist) Tahoe-Chrysler Corp., 1988, (festival pianist) Lake Tahoe Internat. Film Festival, 1998, (featured pianist) Lake Tahoe Hebrew Assn. Concert, 2001, Tahoe Forest Hosp. benefit, Lake Tahoe, Lake Tahoe Wildlife Benefit, 2003, Lake Tahoe Summer Music Series, 2000, Thunderbird Lodge, 2003 (North Tahoe Jury Arts award, 2004), Roseville Art Exhibit, 2004, Athena Reform Syllabus, 2006 (Smallwood Family Found. award, 2007), (piano soloist) Sierra Nevada Coll. Presdl. Dinner, 2000, (albums) Time Remembered; musical dir. (albums) Time Remembered; musician: (pianist) San Francisco State U. Athletic Awards Ceremony, 2001, Squaw Creek Resort, Lake Tahoe Forest Benefit, concert; contbr. articles pub. to profl. jour.; exec. prodr.: (TV series) The Heroes of Time; (documentaries) The Shudder of Awe. Recipient Bell-Brook Talent TV award, 1950, TV Arts award, Kirsch Found., 2001; Arts grantee, Silicon Valley Cmty. Found., 1998, Athena Reform Ednl. Project, 2005, Smallwood Fedn. grantee, 2006. Mem.: Calif. Assn. Scholars, Nat. Assn. Scholars, Assn. Lit. Scholars and Critics, Wilson Ctr. Assocs., Coun. Basic Edn., Writers Guild Am., Dirs. Guild Am., San Francisco State Alumni Assn., Donner Land Trust, Smithsonian Instn., Commonwealth Club Calif. Avocations: classical music, backpacking, softball. Office: 845 Southwood Blvd Ste 50 Incline Village NV 89451-9463 Personal E-mail: athenaprods@peoplepc.com.

JOHNSTON, CARDEN, emergency physician, pediatrician, educator; b. Birmingham, Ala., Nov. 23, 1936; MD, U. Ala., 1957. Intern Wilford Hall Meml. Hosp., Lackland AFB, Tex., 1961-62; resident Charity Hosps. La., New Orleans, 1964-66; resident pediat. Hosp. Sick Children, London, 1966-67; with Kaiser Permanente, Honolulu, 1967—70; pvt. practice Gunthersville, Ala., 1970—74; mem. staff Children's Hosp. Ala., Birmingham, 1975—. Prof. pediat. U. Ala., Birmingham, 1992-95, emeritus prof., 1995—. Fellow Royal Coll. Physicians; mem. AMA, Am. Acad. Pediat. (pres. 2003-04), Am. Coll. Emergency Physicians. Office: Childrens Hosp Ala 1600 7th Ave S Ste 1 Birmingham AL 35233-1785

JOHNSTON, CAROLYN S., elementary school educator, reading specialist; AA, Marymount U., 1969; BA, George Washington U., 1971; MEd, Salisbury State U.; EdD, U. Md. Cert. elem. tchr. through supt., Md. Adminstr. Wicomico County Pub. Schs., reading supervisor, pre-K to 12. Mem. Wicomico County Mentoring Program, 2007; sponsor Fruitland Cmty. Ctr. Summer Camp, 2005, 2006, 2007, Reading Rally Program Middle Sch. Students, Wicomico County, 2007. Named one of Maryland's Top 100 Women, 2007; recipient Celebrate Literacy award, Internat. Reading Assn., Eastern Shore Reading Coun., 2003, Presdl. award, Md. Internat. Reading Assn. Coun., 2003, Citation of Merit, 2006, Md. Nat. Disting. Prin. award, NAESP, 2004. Mem.: ASCD, Md. Assn. Elem. Prins., Nat. Assn. Elem. Sch. Prins., State Md. Internat. Reading Assn. Coun. (Presdl. award 2003), Internat. Reading Assn. (Celebrate Literacy award), Kappa Alpha Theta, Phi Delta Kappa.

JOHNSTON, CATHERINE VISCARDI, former magazine publisher; Grad., Manhattanville Coll., 1975. With House & Garden mag., 1977; acct. exec. GQ mag., 1980; former pub. Mirabella mag., NYC; pub. Mademoiselle mag., NYC, 1995-96; sr. v.p. sales & mktg. Conde Nast Publs., 1996—97, exec. v.p. sales & mktg. NYC, 1997—99. Recipient Disting. Alumni award, Manhattanville Coll., 2000.

JOHNSTON, CYRUS CONRAD, JR., medical educator; b. Statesville, NC, July 16, 1929; m. Marjorie Tarkington, Feb. 20, 1960; 2 children. BA, Duke U., 1951, MD, 1955. Diplomate Am. Bd. Internal Medicine. Intern Duke Hosp., Durham, NC, 1955-56; resident in medicine Barnes Hosp., St. Louis, 1956-57; rsch. fellow in endocrinology and metabolism Ind. U., Indpls., 1959-61, instr. medicine, 1961-63, asst. prof., 1963-67, assoc. prof., 1967-69, prof. medicine, 1969-97, disting. prof. medicine, 1997—2002, disting. prof. emeritus, 2002—; assoc. dir. Gen. Clin. Rsch. Ctr. Ind. U. Med. Ctr., Indpls., 1962-67, program dir., 1967-72, prin. investigator, 1968-88, dir. divsn. endocrinology and metabolism, 1968-94. Mem. aging rev. com. Nat. Inst. Aging, 1982-85, chmn. geriatrics rev. com., 1985-86; mem. nursing sci. rev. com. NIH, 1988-89; mem. com. for protection of human subjects Ind. U.-Purdue U., Indpls., 1966—, chmn., 1978—; chmn. Nat. Osteoporosis Found. Sci. Adv. Bd., 1992-96; med. adv. panel Paget's Disease Found., 1989—; bd. trustees Nat. Osteoporosis Found., 1992—, pres., 1996-2001; mem. Nat. Adv. Coun. on Aging, 1992-95. Assoc. editor Bone and Mineral, 1985-94, Bone, 1995-2004; editl. bd. Jour. Bone and Mineral Rsch., Jour. Clin. Endocrinology and Metabolism, 1988-91. Capt. USAF, 1957-59. Recipient Career Rsch. Devel. award USPHS, 1963-68, Sandoz prize Internat. Assn. Gerontology, 1993, Experience Excellence Recognition award Glenn W. Irwin, Jr., MD, 2001. Mem. ACP, AAAS, AMA, Am. Assn. Clin. Endocrinologists (Yank D. Coble, Jr. M.D. Disting. Svc. award 1998), Am. Fedn. Clin. Rsch., Am. Soc. for Bone and Mineral Rsch. (Frederic C. Bartter award 1996), Am. Clin. and Climatological Soc., Ctrl. Soc. for Clin. Rsch., Endocrine Soc. Office: Indiana Univ Dept Medicine 541 N Clinical Dr CL 459 Indianapolis IN 46202-5124 E-mail: cjohnsto@iupui.edu.

JOHNSTON, DAVID CAY BOYLE, journalist; b. San Francisco, Dec. 24, 1948; s. Leslie Jules and Gretchen Elizabeth (Taylor) J.; m. Sharon Snider, July 8, 1966 (div. Dec. 1979); children: Leslie Ann, Susan, Mark, Amy and Andy (twins), Steven; m. Mary Regina Ryan, Jan. 1, 1980 (div. Sept. 1980); m. Jennifer Leonard, May 1, 1982; children: Molly Claire Leonard, Kathleen Taylor Leonard. Student, Foothill Coll., 1968-72, San Francisco State U., 1972, U. Chgo., 1973, Mich. State U., 1973-75. Reporter, photographer County News, Aptos, Calif., 1966-68, Valley Press, Felton, Calif., 1968; staff writer San Jose Mercury and News, Los Altos, Calif., 1968-73, Detroit Free Press, Lansing, Mich., 1973-76, Los Angeles Times, 1976-88, Phila. Inquirer, 1988—95; tax reporter NY Times, NYC, 1995—. Sr. lectr. U. So. Calif., Los Angeles, 1980-88; instr. journalism UCLA, 1986. Author Temples of Chance, 1992, Perfectly Legal: The Covert Campaign to Rig Our Tax System to Benefit the Super Rich - and Cheat Everybody Else, 2003; contbg. editor Feedback, The Calif. Journalism Rev., 1976-86, The Non Profit Times, 1987-89; contbr. articles to newspapers, mags. including The Columbia Journalism Rev., Washington Journalism Rev., others. Urban journalism fellow U. Chgo., 1973, recipient Edward J. Meeman award Scripps Howard Found., 1974, George Polk award L.I. U., 1982, Best Story award Detroit Press Club, 1974, Best Story award UPI Calif. News Editors, 1983, Pulitzer prize for Beat Reporting, 2001. Mem. Investigative Reporters and Editors. Clubs: Los Angeles Athletic, Atlantic City Press Club. Office: NY Times 229 W 43rd St New York NY 10036

JOHNSTON, DAVID FREDERICK, lawyer; b. Tiffin, Ohio, Sept. 9, 1943; s. Frederick Walter and Aleta Marguerite (Ruehle) Johnston; m. Ona Lee Graham, June 18, 1966; children: Matthew, Rebecca, Elisabeth, Benjamin. BA in Chemistry, Oreg. State U., 1965; JD, Golden Gate U., 1971. Bar: Calif. 1972, Oreg. 1973, US Ct. Mil. Appeals 1974, US Supreme Ct. 1983. Commd. officer USCG, 1965; sea duty USCG Cutter Magnolia, 1966-67; staff atty. USCG, 1971-79; dept. chief USCG Marine Safety Office, Norfolk, Va., 1979-82; appeal decision supr. USCG Hdqrs., Washington, 1982-85; pvt. practice Portland, Oreg., 1985-86; workers compensation ins. EBI Ins., Portland, Oreg., 1986-95. Author: Suspension and Revocation of Mariner's Licenses, Certificates and Documents, 1984. Com. chmn. Clermont Sch., Fairfax County, Va., 1963, bd. co-chair Va., 1996—99; land use co-chair Collins View Neighborhood Assn., Portland, 1999—; elder Presbyn. Ch., Green Acres Ch., Portsmouth, Va., 1979; Multnomah Ch., Portland, 1986, St. Andrews Ch., Portland, 2004. Mem.: Oreg. State Bar, Phi Lambda Upsilon, Phi Kappa Phi. Home and Office: 0550 SW Palatine Hill Rd Portland OR 97219-7830

JOHNSTON, DONALD JAMES, lawyer, educator; b. Ottawa, Ont., Can., June 26, 1936; s. Wilbur Austin and Florence Jean Moffat Tucker J.; m. Heather Bell Maclaren, Dec. 11, 1965; children: Kristina, Allison, Rachel, Sara. BA, BCL, McGill U., 1958. Created Queen's counsel. Assoc. Stikeman & Elliott, 1961; founder Johnston, Heenan & Blaikie; lectr. fiscal law McGill U. Faculty Law, 1964-77; mem. Can. Ho. of Commons, Ottawa, 1978-88; pres. Treasury Bd. Can., 1989-82; min. of state for sci. and tech. Econ. and Regional Devel., 1982; min. Justice Atty. Gen. of Can., 1984; pres. Liberal Party Can., 1990-94; sec.-gen. Orgn. Coop. and Devel., Paris, 1996—2006. Vis. prof. Yonsei U., Seoul, Republic of Korea. Contbr. articles to profl. jours.; editor, author three books on public policy. Recipient Highest honor, Govts. Hungary, Belgium, Slovakia, Japan. Mem. Mt. Royal Club, Montreal Indoor Tennis Club. Avocations: writing, tennis, piano. Home: 537 Courser Rd Glen Sutton PQ Canada Office: 1250 Rene Levesque W Ste 2500 Montreal H3B 4V1 Canada Personal E-mail: donaldjames.johnston@gmail.com. Business E-Mail: djohnston@heenan.ca.

JOHNSTON, EDWARD ALLAN, lawyer; b. Balt., Sept. 25, 1921; s. William Henry and Hattie Frisby (Sanner) J.; m. Dorothy Janet Swart, June 23, 1951 (dec. Jan. 1994); children: Elizabeth Janet, Jean Taylor; m. Mary Ellen Kinnaird, Apr. 15, 1995. BBA, U. Balt., 1942, BS, 1947, LLB, 1949, LLM, 1957. Bar: Md. 1949; CPA, Md. Assoc. Whiteford, Taylor & Preston, Balt., 1954-62, ptnr., 1962—. Lectr. taxes U. Balt., 1948-65; bd. dirs. Dunbar Armored Express Inc. Pres. Dickeyville Assn., 1960; bd. dirs. Contact-Balt., 1974-80, chmn. bd., 1976-80; trustee Asbury Found., 1970—; trustee The Wesley Home, Inc., 1985-92; v.p., gen. counsel Soc. of Srs., 1983—; gen. counsel Ea. Srs. Golf Assn., Inc., 1988—; chmn. of adminstrv. bd. Meth. Ch., 1965-69, 88-90, trustee, chmn. bd., 1977-87. Recipient Alumnus of Yr. award U. Balt., 1980; named into Athletic Hall Fame, U. Balt., 2004. Mem. U. Balt. Alumni Assn. (pres. 1975-76), Md. Golf Assn. (v.p. 1960-67, pres. 1968), Mid. Atlantic Golf Assn. (v.p. 1978-81, pres. 1982, gen. counsel 1983—), Balt. Country Club (golf com., house commn., bd. govs. 1989-95, exec. com., treas. fin. com. 1991-95, v.p. 1992-93, pres. 1993-95). Home: 4104 Ravenhurst Cir Glen Arm MD 21057-9767 Office: Whiteford Taylor & Preston 210 W Pennsylvania Ave Ste 400 Baltimore MD 21204-5332 Home Phone: 410-592-3815; Office Phone: 410-832-2029. Business E-Mail: ejohnston@wtplaw.com.

JOHNSTON, FRANCIS CLAIBORNE, JR., lawyer; b. Richmond, Va., Jan. 6, 1943; s. Francis Claiborne and Virginia (Williams) J.; m. Carolyn Satterfield, Dec. 5, 1970; children: Angier Williams, Francis Claiborne III. AB magna cum laude, Princeton U., 1964; LLB, U. Va., 1967. Bar: Va. 1967, U.S. Dist. Ct. (ea. dist.) Va. 1968, U.S. Ct. Appeals (4th cir.) 1968. Assoc. Mays & Valentine, Richmond, 1968-72, mng. ptnr., 1987-91; ptnr. Troutman Sanders LLP (formerly Mays & Valentine LLP), 1972—. Adj. asst. prof. T.C. Williams Sch. Law, U. Richmond, 1974-76. Mem. session and diaconate 1st Presbyn. Ch., Richmond; bd. dirs. 1st Presbyn. Ch. Endowment Fund, Inc., 1972—, pres., 1993—; bd. dirs. Westham Civic Assn., 1984-86, Westminster-Canterbury Found., 1986-91, Westminster-Canterbury Corp., 1996-2000, vice-chmn. 1999; bd. dirs. Va. Post-Conviction Assistance Project, 1991-2000, pres., 1996-98; bd. dirs. Libr. of Va., 1997—, vice-chmn., 2000; trustee Valentine Mus., Richmond, 1980-89; bd. dirs. Westminster Presbyn. Homes Inc., 2000-03. Fellow Am. Bar Found., Va. Law Found. (bd. dirs. 1991-94); mem. ABA (Ho. Dels. 1992-98), Va. Bar Assn. (chmn. exec. com. 1988, pres. 1990), Richmond Bar Assn., Assn. of Bar of City of N.Y., Am. Law Inst., Commonwealth Club, Country Club Va., Forum Club, Farmington Country Club. Home: 7009 Lakewood Dr Richmond VA 23229-6933 Office: Troutman Sanders LLP 1002 Haxell Point Richmond VA 23219-3531 also: PO Box 1122 Richmond VA 23218-1122

JOHNSTON, FRANK C., psychologist; b. West Hartford, Conn., June 21, 1955; s. Frank C. and Chris (Butler) J.; m. Susan H. Leffert, July 26, 1981; 1 child, Daniel Frank. BA, Fairfield U., 1977; MEd, MA, Columbia U., 1979; PhD, SUNY, Albany, 1984. Sch. psychologist bd. coop. ednl. svcs. Herkimer, NY, 1979—80; intern Counseling Ctr., SUNY, Buffalo, 1983—84; psychologist Family Svc. Rochester, NY, 1985—87, Child and Youth divsn. Rochester Mental Health Ctr., 1988; pvt. practice Rochester, 1988—. Cons. Brockport (N.Y.) Day Care Ctr., 1989-90, Learning Devel. Ctr., Rochester Inst. Tech., 1989-90; co-founder Behavioral Health Consortium Rochester, 1993-96. Mem. APA, N.Y. State Psychol. Assn., Genesee Valley Psychol. Assn. (mem. legal legis com. 1988-90, mem. ins. com. 1990-92, chmn. ins. com. 1990-93, pres. 1994, past pres. 1995), Rochester Cmty. Individual Practice Assn. (mem. psychology subcom. 1988-98, mem. mental health task force Preferred Care 1999-2000), Rochester Area Assn. Clin. Psychologists, Nat. Register Health Svc. Providers in Psychology. Office: 480 White Spruce Blvd Rochester NY 14623-1608 Home Phone: 585-442-4992; Office Phone: 585-427-7800. Personal E-mail: jpsych2@frontiernet.net.

JOHNSTON, GEORGE W., lawyer; b. Syracuse, NY, Aug. 8, 1950; s. Norman Fero and Mary Jane (Innes) J. BA, Johns Hopkins U., 1972; JD, Georgetown U., 1975. Bar: Md. 1975. Law clerk U.S. Dist. Ct., Balt., 1975-76; atty. Venable, Baetjer & Howard, Balt., 1976—; chief oper. officer Venable, Baetjer & Howard, LLP, 1999—2001. Lectr. in field. Author: BNA Aids Guide, 1990, Affirmative Action Workbook, 1992, Maryland Employer's Guide, 1991; contbr. articles to profl. jours. Chmn. Md. Citizens for the Arts; bd. dirs. Walters Art Mus. Mem. ABA, FBA, Md. Bar Assn., Balt. City Bar Assn. Office: Venable LLP 1800 Mercantile Bank 2 Hopkins Plz Ste 1800 Baltimore MD 21201-2982 Office Phone: 410-244-7585. Business E-Mail: gwjohnston@venable.com.

JOHNSTON, GLADYS STYLES, university official; b. St. Petersburg, Fla., Dec. 23, 1942; d. John Edward and Rosa (Moses) Styles; m. Hubert Seward Johnston, July 30, 1966. BS in Social Sci., Cheney U., 1963; MEd in Ednl. Adminstrn., Temple U., 1969; PhD in Ednl. Adminstrn.-Orgnl. Theory, Cornell U., 1974. Tchr. Chester (Pa.) Sch. Dist., 1963-66, West Chester (Pa.) Sch. Dist., 1966-67, asst. prin., elem. prin., dir. Summer Sch., 1968-71; dir. Head Start Chester County Bd. Edn., West Chester, 1967-69; teaching asst., rsch. asst. Cornell U., Ithaca, N.Y., 1971-74; asst. prof. ednl. adminstr. and supervision Rutgers U., New Brunswick, N.J., 1974-79, assoc. prof., chmn. dept. Grad. Sch. Edn., 1979-83, chmn. dept. mgmt. Sch. Bus., 1983-85; dean, prof. Coll. Edn., Ariz. State U., Tempe, 1985-91; provost, v.p. for acad. affairs DePaul U., Chgo., 1991-93, chancellor, 1993—. Disting. Commonwealth vis. prof. Coll. William and Mary Sch. Edn., Williamsburg, Va., 1982-83; manuscript reviewer Jour. Higher Edn., Jour. Ednl. Leadership, Prentice Hall Pub. Co., Englewood Cliffs, N.J.; speaker and conf. presenter in field; cons. AT&T, Ednl. Testing Svc., Prentice-Hall Pub. Co.; cons. to coordinating bd. Tex. Coll. and Univ. System. Author: Research and Thought in Administration Theory, 1986; mem. editorial bd. Ednl. Evaluation and Policy Analysis, Ednl. Adminstrn. Quar., Ednl. and Psychol. Rsch. Jour.; contbr. articles and book revs. to profl. jours., chpts. to books. Bd. dirs. Edn. Law Ctr., 1979-86, Sta. KAET-TV, Phoenix, 1987—, Found. for Sr. Living, 1990-91; mem. adv. coun. to bd. trustees Cornell U., 1981-86; trustee Middlesex Gen. Univ. Hosp., 1983-86. Recipient Outstanding Alumni award Temple U.; Andrew D. White fellow Cornell U. Mem. ASCD, Am. Assn. Colls. for Tchr. Edn., Nat. Conf. Profs. Ednl. Adminstrn., Am. Ednl. Rsch. Assn. (proposal reviewer 1979—, chmn. task force for participation and membership 1981—, chmn. E.F. Linquist award com. 1985, mem. govt. rels. com. 1986—, publ. com. 1986—), Phi Kappa Phi, Phi Delta Kappa, Alpha Phi Sigma. Office: U of Nebraska at Kearney Office of Chancellor 905 W 25th St Kearney NE 68845-4238

JOHNSTON, HUGH FRANCIS, corporate development manager; b. Jersey City, Aug. 16, 1961; s. Donald Frederick and Janet Ann (Franey) J.; m. Marianne Lee Trenti, June 18, 1988. BS, Syracuse U., NY, 1983; MBA, U. Chgo., 1987. Acct. GE, Schnectady, NY, 1983-84, fin. analyst, 1984-85; bus. planning & fin. mgmt. positions Pepsico, Somers, NY, 1987—99; v.p. retail Merck & Co., 1999—2002; sr. v.p. mergers & acquisitions Pepsico, Purchase, NY, 2002, sr. v.p. & CFO beverages & foods, 2002—05, sr. v.p. transformation, 2005—06, exec. v.p. ops., 2006—. Office: Pepsico 700 Anderson Hill Rd Purchase NY 10577*

JOHNSTON, JAMES ROBERT, library director; b. Wheaton, Ill., June 3, 1947; s. Robert W. and Elizabeth S. (Townsend) J.; m. Carol Ann Trezza, June 14, 1969; children: Steven J., Julie M. BA, U. Notre Dame, 1969; MLS, Fla. State U., 1973. Head librarian Grande Prairie Library Dist., Hazel Crest, Ill., 1973-76; chief librarian Joliet (Ill.) Pub. Library, 1976—; pres. bd. dirs. Ill. Library Employees Benefit Plan. Mem. automation com. Heritage Trail Libr. Sys., Shorewood, Ill.; pres. Ill. Libr. Employees Benefit Plan, Joliet; bldg. cons. Co-author: Illinois Library Trustees Association Booklet "Selecting Consultants", 1986; contbr. speeches and articles in field. V.p. Joliet/Will County Project Pride; mem. events com. C. of C. Mem. Ill. Libr. Assn. (pub. libr. sect. 1977-78, legis. devel. com. 1977-82, jr. mems. roundtable 1976-77, regional planning com. 1996, Title III rev. com. 1996—, interlibr. coop. subcom., intellectual freedom com.), Kiwanis, Beta Phi Mu. Avocations: model building, softball, bowling, golf. Home: 2208 Graystone Dr Joliet IL 60431-8785 Office: Joliet Pub Library 150 N Ottawa St Joliet IL 60432-4192 Home Phone: 815-436-6154; Office Phone: 815-740-2670. Business E-Mail: jrjohnston@joliet.lib.il.us.

JOHNSTON, JAMES WESLEY, retired consumer products company executive; b. Chgo., Apr. 11, 1946; s. Ted and Irma (Hacker) J.; m. Angela Johnston; children: Amanda E., Emily S. BS in Accountancy, U. Ill., 1967; MBA, Northwestern U., 1971. C.P.A., Ill. Fin. analyst Ford Motor Co., 1967-69; with N.W. Industries, 1969-79, dir. corp. devel., 1973-75, v.p. mktg., 1975-79; exec. v.p. Asia/Pacific R.J. Reynolds Tobacco Internat. Inc., 1979, pres., chief exec. officer Asia/Pacific Hong Kong, 1979-81; exec. v.p. R.J. Reynolds Tobacco Co., 1981-84; divsn. exec. consumer banking N.E. U.S. Citicorp, NYC, 1984-89; chmn. CEO R.J. Reynolds Tobacco Co., Winston-Salem, NC, 1989-95; chmn. R.J. Reynolds Tobacco Worldwide, Winston-Salem, NC, 1993-96; vice chmn. RJR Nabisco, Inc., 1995-96, ret., 1996. Bd. dirs. Sealy Corp., Trinity, NC. Treas., trustee, pres. Village of Bolingbrook, Ill., 1973-75; bd. dirs. Winston-Salem Bus. Inc., 1989—96; active N.C. Bus. Coun. Mgmt. and Devel., Raleigh, 1989—96; trustee Wake Forest U., Winston-Salem, 1991—; mem. bd. visitors Wake Forest U. Bapt. Med. Ctr., Winston-Salem, 1991—. Mem.: Old Town Club. Office: 115 Eastbend Ct Mooresville NC 28117 Office Phone: 704-660-5466.

JOHNSTON, JANIS L., law librarian, educator; MLS, U. Ill.; JD cum laude, Ind. U. Dir. Marion County Law Libr., Indpls.; rural devel. coord. Indian Inst. Cultural Affairs, Bombay; assoc. dir. Kresge Libr. Notre Dame Law Sch., lectr. legal rsch. & Am. legal sys., dir. London Law Ctr.; dir. Albert E. Jenner, Jr. Meml. Law Libr. U. Ill. Coll. Law, Champaign, 1999—, assoc. prof law, assoc. prof. libr. adminstrn., Richard W. and Marie L. Corman scholar in law. Contbr. articles to profl. jours. Office: U Ill Coll Law 504 E Pennsylvania Ave Champaign IL 61820 Office Phone: 217-333-2914.*

JOHNSTON, JOCELYN STANWELL, paralegal; b. Evanston, Ill., Feb. 16, 1954; d. Gerald and Dorothy Jeanne (Schoenfield) Stanwell; m. Thomas Patrick Johnston, Nov. 28, 1986. BA, U. Minn., 1981; cert., Phila. Inst. Paralegal Tng., Phila., 1986. Paralegal Fredrikson & Byron PA, Mpls., 1981-84, Reed, Smith, Shaw and McClay, Phila., 1984-85, McCausland, Keen & Buckman, PC, Radnor, Pa., 1985-86, Harris, Guenzel, Meier & Nichols, PC, Ann Arbor, Mich., 1986-87, Conner & Bentley, PC, Ann Arbor, 1987-88, Cichocki & Armstrong, Ltd., Oak Park, Ill., 1988-90, Bishop and Bishop, Oak Brook, Ill., 1994-95, Martin, Breen & Merrick, Oak Park, 1994-95, Saitlin, Patzik, Frank & Samotny, Ltd., Chgo., 1995, Bryson R. Cloon, Esquire, Leawood, Kans., 1996—, Barry R. Grissom Esq., Overland Pk., Kans., 2004—, Law Offices C. Alberto Herdoiza, Kansas City, Kans. Democrat. Home: 14501 Marty St Overland Park KS 66223-2300 Office Phone: 913-432-4484, 913-661-9600. Personal E-mail: johnstont@umkc.edu.

JOHNSTON, JOHN DEVEREAUX, JR., retired law educator; b. Asheville, NC, Oct. 1, 1932; s. John D. and Marion R. (Green) J.; m. Beryl R. Watson, Dec. 21, 1952; m. Diana Armatage, June 10, 1972; children: Catherine, Patricia, Sharon, Laura, Jackie, John. AB, Duke U., 1954, LL.B., 1956. Bar: N.C. 1956, U.S. Ct. Appeals (4th cir.) 1969, U.S. Supreme Ct. 1969. Mgmt. trainee J.P. Morgan & Co., 1956-58; pvt. practice Asheville, 1959-62; asst. prof. Duke U. Law Sch., Durham, NC, 1963-64, asst. dean, 1963-65, assoc. prof., 1965-67, prof., 1968-69; prof. law NYU Law Sch., NYC, 1969-89, prof. law emeritus, 1990—. Vis. prof. Vanderbilt U., 1972, UCLA, 1975, Washington U., St. Louis, 1981, Hastings Coll. Law U. Calif., San Francisco, 1984. Author: (with G. Johnson) Land Use Control, 1977; contbr. articles to profl. jours. Personal E-mail: jdjjr@worldnet.att.net. *As a young law teacher, I was mentored by two wise elders. One emphasized preparation: Don't ever go into class without knowing where you intend to take it. The other counselled flexibility: Be prepared for anything, and let student input determine how the class will unfold. A third elder provided a synthesis: Never overestimate what your students already know, nor underestimate what they are capable of learning.Applying that maxim, I determined to introduce new subjects slowly and carefully, even spoon-feeding the students for a while. Thereafter, development of the topic proceeded at their speed. After they reached a level of sophistication well beyond my expectations, I concluded that the third elder was the wisest.*

JOHNSTON, JOHN STEVEN, lawyer; b. Kansas City, Mo., Dec. 5, 1948; s. Herschel Wayne and Dixie June J.; m. Deb Neal, Feb. 19, 1977; children: Benjamin, Will. BA in Math., William Jewel Coll., 1970; MA in Psychology, U. Mo., 1975, JD, 1980; postgrad. in clin. psychology, U. Minn., 1975—77. Bar: Mo., 1980, US Dist. Ct. Kans., 1999. Assoc. Linde, Thomson, Fairchild, Langworthy & Kohn, Kansas City, 1980-81, Shook, Hardy & Bacon LLP, Kansas City, 1981-85, ptnr., 1986—, chmn. tort law sect., 1998—2002. Bd. dirs. Lawyers Encouraging Acad. Performance. Author (contbg.): Missouri Methods of Practice-Litigation Guide, 1991; contbr. articles articles to profl. jours. Bd. dirs. Big Bros. and Big Sisters, Kansas City, 1989—, Ozanam Home for Boys, Kansas City, 1990-2002, Lawyers Encouraging Acad. Progress, 2002-2006. Recipient Outstanding Contbn. to Cmty Health award S. Kansas City Mental Health Resource Network, 1975, Michael Coburn award for cmty. svc. Legal Aid of We. Mo., 1999; named to William Jewell Coll. Hall of Fame, 1999. Mem.: Kansas City Met. Bar Assn. (chmn. civil law and procedure com. 1991—92, bd. dirs. 1993—2005, pres. 1998, 7th Ann. Pres. award for bar svc. 1993), Mo. Bar Assn. (bd. govs. 1999—), Kansas City Met. Bar Found. (bd. dirs./exec. com. 1995—2006, chair lawyers for children com. 1998—2002, v.p. 2001—03, pres. 2003—04, 1st Ann. Pres.'s award for bar svc. 2001), Ross T. Roberts Inn of Ct. (master 1995—2006). Home: 25004 Timberlake Trl Greenwood MO 64034 Office: Shook Hardy Bacon LLP 2555 Grand Blvd Kansas City MO 64108-2613 Office Phone: 816-474-6550. Office Fax: 816-421-4066. Business E-Mail: jjohnston@shb.com.

JOHNSTON, KRISTEN, actress; b. Washington, Sept. 20, 1967; BFA, NYU, 1989. Mem. Atlantic Theatre Co., Chelsea, N.Y. Actor: (films) The Orkly Kid, 1985, The Debt, 1993, Backfire!, 1995, Colin Fitz, 1997, Austin Powers: The Spy Who Shagged Me, 1999, The Flintstones in Viva Rock Vegas, 2000, Austin Powers in Goldmember, 2002, Nobody Knows Anything!, 2003, Duane Incarnate, 2004, Strangers with Candy, 2005, Music and Lyrics, 2007, (TV films) London Suite, 1996, Stage on Screen: The Women, 2002, Don't Ask, 2005, (TV series) Third Rock from the Sun, 1996-2001, (guest appearances) Chicago Hope, 1994, The Five Mrs. Buchanans, 1994, Heart's Afire, 1995, ER, 2005; appeared in numerous stage productions.*

JOHNSTON, KURT MALCOLM, pharmaceutical company executive; b. Peoria, Ill., Jan. 25, 1954; s. Harold M. and Anne Marie (Grantham) J. BS, Mass. Coll. Pharmacy, 1976; MBA, Fordham U., 1980. Registered pharmacist, Maine. Head dept. tablets Lederle Labs., Pearl River, N.Y., 1977-80, fed. sales mgr. Washington, 1980-82, hosp. sales mgr. Denver, 1982-84, mgr. new products Wayne, N.J., 1984-86; pres. Johnston Enterprises, Lake Forest, Ill., 1986-87, Jerome Labs., Des Plaines, Ill., 1987-90; chief exec. officer Hydrotech Labs., LP, Des Plaines, Ill., 1990—. Mem. Soc. Cosmetic Chemists, Cosmetics, Toiletries and Fragrances Assn., U.S. Yacht Racing Union, Lake Forest Yacht Club, Chgo. Yacht Club. Republican. Avocations: bobsledding, nordic & alpine skiing, ballooning. Home: 520 Linden Ave Lake Forest IL 60045-3924 Office: Hydro Tech Labs LP 95 Bradrock Dr Des Plaines IL 60018-1937

JOHNSTON, LAURANCE SCOTT, foundation director, healthcare educator; b. St. Paul, Aug. 4, 1950; s. Scott D. and Laura L. (Wallace) J. BS, Hamline U., 1972; MS, Northwestern U., 1973, PhD, 1976; MBA, George Mason U., 1985. Postdoctoral fellow Chgo. Med. Sch., 1977-78; regulatory scientist Bur. Foods, FDA, Washington, 1978-81; exec. sec. NIH, Bethesda, Md., 1981-86; dir. div. sci. rev. Nat. Inst. Child Health and Human Devel., NIH, Bethesda, 1986-92; dir. spinal cord rsch. and edn. founds. Paralyzed Vets. of Am., 1992-97; health educator, grantee, writer and nat. and internat. speaker in biomed. and disability rsch., 1997—. Author: Alternative Medicine & Spinal Cord Injury, 2005; contbr. articles to mags. and profl. jours. Damon Runyon/Walter Winchell Cancer Found. fellow, 1978.

JOHNSTON, LAWRENCE R., former food products executive; b. Corning, NY, Aug. 29, 1948; married; 2 children. BA in Bus. Adminstrn., Stetson U., Deland, FL, 1972. Merchandising mgr. GE Appliances; region mgr. GE; gen. mgr. Eastern Sales & Distbn. Opers., GE Appliances; pres. Internat. GE Puerto Rico; gen. mgr. Domestic Sales Opers., GE; v.p. sales & distbn. GE Appliances, 1989; pres. & CEO GE Med. Sys., Europe, Paris, 1997; sr. v.p. GE, 1999; pres. & CEO GE Appliances, 1999—2001; chmn. bd., pres., CEO Albertson's, Inc., 2001—06. Chmn. GE's European Exec. Coun.; bd. mem. Food Mktg. Inst., Washington, CIES World Food Forum, Paris; co. officer GE, 1989.*

JOHNSTON, LLOYD DOUGLAS, social sciences educator; b. Boston, Apr. 18, 1940; s. Leslie D. and Madeline B. (Irvin) Johnston; m. Janet Wilson, Nov. 13, 2004; 1 stepchild, Leah Wilson Brown; 1 child from previous marriage, Douglas Leslie. BA in Econs., Williams Coll., 1962; MBA, Harvard U., 1965, postgrad., 1965—66; MA in Social Psychology, U. Mich., 1971, PhD, 1973. Research asst. Grad. Sch. Bus. Adminstrn., Harvard U., Boston, 1965-66; asst. study dir. Inst. Social Research, U. Mich., Ann Arbor, 1966-73, asst. research scientist, 1973-75, assoc. rsch. scientist, 1975-78, sr. rsch. scientist and program dir., 1978-98; disting. sr. rsch. scientist, rsch. prof. Inst. Social Rsch., U. Mich., Ann Arbor, 1998—; chmn. exec. com. U. Mich. Substance Abuse Rsch. Ctr. Excellence, 1990-95, acting dir., 1994-95. Prin. investigator Monitoring the Future: A Continuing Study of Lifestyles and Values of Am. Youth, 1975—, Youth, Education and Society, 1996—, also other nat. and internat. survey studies; cons. to WHO, UN, EEC, Coun. of Europe, Pan Am. Health Orgn., White House, U.S. Congress, various founds., numerous fgn. govts., fed. agys., univs., rsch. insts., TV networks, Nat. Partnership for Drug Free Am., 1978—; chmn. tech. planning group; mem. Resource Group for Goal Seven, Nat. Ednl. Goals Panel, 1991-2002; mem. extramural sci. adv. bd. Nat. Inst. on Drug Abuse, 1990-94; mem., also chmn. prevention subcom., Nat. Adv. Coun. on Drug Abuse, 1982-86, Presdl. appointee White House Conf. for a Drug-Free Am., 1987-88, Presdl. appointee Nat. Commn. for Drug Free Schs., 1989-90; chmn. drug epidemiology sect. Internat. Coun. on Alcohol and Addictions, 1982-2002; mem. Com. on Problems of Drug Dependence, 1982-86; mem. or chmn. various adv. coms. various univs., founds.; mem. various working groups NAS; mem. various coms. and adv. groups Nat. Inst. Drug Abuse, 1975—; mem. or chmn. 7 working groups WHO, 1975—; invited lectr. nat. and internat. confs. and convs.; testimony before Congress and fed. regulatory agys. Author: Drugs and American Youth, 1973, Student Drug Use in America, 1975-81, 82, Monitoring the Future Nat. Survey Results on Drug Use 1975-2006, vol. 1 and 2, 2007, over 60 other books and monographs on drug use and lifestyles of Am. secondary sch. students and young adults, 1972—, 31 reference vols.; editor: Conducting Follow Up Research on Drug Treatment Programs, 1977; contbr. more than 130 chpts. to books, articles to profl. jours. Recipient Nat. Pacesetter award in rsch. Nat. Inst. on Drug Abuse, 1982, 1st Sr. Rsch. Scientist award and lectureship U. Mich., 1987, Regents award for disting. pub. svc., 1998, Disting. Rsch. Scientist award, 1998. Fellow Coll. on Problems of Drug Dependence; mem. APA, Soc. for Psychol. Study Social Issues (sec.-treas. 1976-79), Am. Sociol. Assn., Am. Pub. Health Assn. Home: 5538 Lawrence Ct Pinckney MI 48169-9257 Office: U Mich Inst Social Rsch Ann Arbor MI 48109 Business E-Mail: lloydj@umich.edu.

JOHNSTON, LOGAN TRUAX, III, lawyer; b. New Haven, Dec. 9, 1947; s. Logan Truax Jr. and Elizabeth (Josey) J.; m. Celeste Linguere; children: Charlotte Hathaway, Logan Truax IV, Owen Conrad, Oritse J., Gboyega P. BA, Yale U., 1969; JD, Harvard U., 1973. Bar: Ill. 1973, Ariz. 1984, U.S. Ct. Appeals (2d cir.) 1982, U.S. Ct. Appeals (7th cir.) 1973, U.S. Ct. Appeals (9th cir.) 1986, U.S. Ct. Appeals (fed. cir.) 1990, U.S. Supreme Ct. 1991. Assoc. Winston & Strawn, Chgo., 1973-79, ptnr., 1979-83, Phoenix, 1983-89; mng. ptnr. Johnston Maynard Grant & Parker, Phoenix, 1989-97, Johnston & Kelly, Phoenix, 1997—2003. Spl. asst. state's atty. Du Page County, Ill., Wheaton, 1976-77; cons. Community Legal Svcs., Phoenix, 1984—. Contbg author: Arizona Appellate Handbook, Vol. III. Served with U.S. Army N.G., 1970-76. Mem. ABA, Maricopa County Bar Found., Maricopa County Bar Assn., Ariz. Bar Found., Ariz. State Bar Assn., Phoenix Heroes Endowment Fund. Presbyterian. Avocations: books, movies, golf, hiking, travel. Office: Johnston Law Offices PLC 1 N 1st St Phoenix AZ 85004-2357 Home Phone: 602-997-5429; Office Phone: 602-452-0615. Personal E-mail: ltjohnston@qwest.net.

JOHNSTON, MARGARET SCHUSTER, volunteer, retired language educator; b. Corvallis, Oreg., July 17, 1927; d. Carl Ephraim and Agnes Ryder Schuster; m. Lee Robert Johnston, Aug. 20, 1949 (dec. 1998); children: Laurie Anne(dec.) , Caryn Lee Johnston Leahy, Lee Robert Jr. BA in Secretarial Sci., Oreg. State Coll., Corvallis, 1950; MA in Spanish, U. Va., Charlottesville, 1974; postgrad., Oslo U., Norway, 1974—75, U. of the South, 1984—88. Sec. Open Forum Spkrs. Bur., Boston, 1950—52, AF ROTC, Harvard U., Cambridge, Mass., 1952—53; pub. stenographer Boston, 1952—53; Spanish tchr. Tandem Sch., Charlottesville, 1979—83; ret. Accompanist Corvallis Men's Chorus. Bd. dirs. Tuesday Evening Concert Series, 1971—74, 1977—79; vol. Piedmont Environ. Coun., 1989; mem. Save the Children, Natural Resources Def. Coun., ARC, United Way, Nat. Com. to Preserve Social Security and Medicare, Alzheimer's Assn., Am. Brain Tumor Assn., Nat. Trust Hist. Preservation, Nat. Women's History Mus.; bd. dirs., libr. chmn., mem. coun. Greenbrier Elem. Sch. PTA, 1963—67; vol. Opportunity Shop, Univ. League, 1960—70; active Sr. Ctr., Charlottesville, Va.; election officer Batesville, Va., 1989—95; mem. Coop. Am., Focus Women's Resource Ctr., Conductor's Cir.,

Charlottesville Symphony, Friends of Ash Lawn-Highland, Va. Farm Bur., Ctr. Sci. in Pub. Interest, Cmty. Idea Stations; Sunday sch. tchr., mem. vestry, various coms. Episcopal Ch. Mem.: AAUW, U. Va. Alumni Assn., Am. Assn. Retired Persons, Paramount Theater (assoc.), Ret. Faculty Assn., Belleek Collectors Soc., U. Va. Club Charlottesville, Colonnade Club (emeritus mem.), U. Va. Women's Club, Club Hispanoamericano (co-founder), Wednesday Music Club (co-founder Piano Group I), Pi Beta Phi Alumnae Club. Democrat. Episcopalian. Avocations: reading, genealogy, piano. Home: 1314 Barclay Hill Charlottesville VA 22901 Personal E-mail: margjpiano@earthlink.net.

JOHNSTON, MELISSA, school librarian; BA, U. Ga., MEd Inst Tech, 1993. Media specialist Eastside Primary Sch., Calhoun, Ga., 1996—98, Addison Elem. Sch., Cobb County, Ga., 1998—2000, Vickery Creek Elem. Sch., Forsyth County, Ga., 2001—06, Silver City Elem. Sch., Cumming, Ga., 2006—. Named VCE Tchr. of Yr., 2004, Ga. Media Specialist of Yr., 2006, N.E. Ga. Dist. Media Specialist of Yr., 2006; named one of the Movers & Shakers, Libr. Jour., 2007; recipient Exemplary Elem. Media Program award, Ga. Dept. Edn., 2006. Mem.: AASL (dir. elect Intellectual Freedom com. 2002—03, dir. elect Ga. Book Award Selection com. 2003, Editl. Resources com. 2004, Intellectual Freedom com. 2004—06, Region V dir. 2004—06, Collaborative Media Award chair 2005—06, Instrnl. Classification Task Force 2006, By-Laws com. 2006—07, Nat. Standards Task Force 2006—07), Ga. Libr. Media Assn. (pres. 2001, Intellectual Freedom chair 2004—05, Intellectual Freedom com. 2006, AASL liason 2006). Office: Silver City Elem Sch 6200 Dahlonega Hwy Cumming GA 30040 Office Phone: 678-965-5020 ext. 350205. Office Fax: 678-965-5021. E-mail: mjohnston@forsyth.k12.ga.us.

JOHNSTON, MICHAEL (WILLIAM), political science educator, university administrator; b. Omaha, Nov. 1, 1949; s. William M. and Margaret Mary (Ryan) J.; m. Bette Bennett, 1976; children: Michael Joseph, Patrick Brendan Ryan. BA in Polit. Sci summa cum laude, Macalester Coll., St. Paul, 1971; MPhil in Polit. Sci., Yale U., 1974, PhD in Polit. Sci., 1977. Teaching fellow, acting instr. Yale U., 1972-76; instr. U. Pitts., 1976-77, asst. prof., 1977-82, assoc. prof., 1982-86; from assoc. prof. to prof. Colgate U., Hamilton, NY, 1986—2003, Charles A. Dana prof. polit. sci., 2003—, divsn. dir. social sci., 2004—. NEH fellow and mem. Sch. Social Sci. Inst. Advanced Study, Princeton, NJ, 2002—03; vis. lectr. politics, vis. fellow Ctr. Urban and Regional Rsch. U. Glasgow, Scotland, 1983—84; vis. fellow dept. politics and Inst. Rsch. in Social Scis. U. York, England, 1991; vis. fellow St. Aidan's Coll., 1997; vis. fellow dept. politics U. Durham, England, 1997; rsch. assoc. Cogen, Holt and Assocs., New Haven, 1974—75; cons. to numerous U.S. govt. and internat. orgns., 1992—; spkr., cons., presenter in field. Author: Political Corruption and Public Policy in America, 1982, Fraud, Waste and Abuse in Government, 1986, Syndromes of Corruption: Wealth, Power and Democracy, 2005; author: (and co-editor) Political Corruption: A Handbook, 1989; author: Syndromes of Corruption, 2005; co-editor: Political Corruption, 2002; editor: Civil Society and Corruption, 2005; contbr. articles to profl. jours. NSF fellow, 1972-76; grantee U. Pitts., 1983, Nuffield Found., 1984, Fulbright/British Coun. Higher Edn., 1984, Colgate U. Rsch. Coun. Maj. Grants com., 1987, New Liberal Arts program Colgate U./Sloan Found., 1988, 90, Leverhulme Trust/Social and Cmty. Planning Rsch., 1998, NEH fellow 2002-03, Fulbright sr. specialist, 2007. Mem. Phi Beta Kappa, Pi Sigma Alpha Democrat. Roman Catholic. Avocations: computing, baseball, trains. Home: 41 W Main St Earlville NY 13332-1900 Office: Colgate U Dept Polit Sci 13 Oak Dr Hamilton NY 13346-1383 Office Phone: 315-228-7756. Office Fax: 315-228-7883. Business E-Mail: mjohnston@mail.colgate.edu.

JOHNSTON, MICHAEL FRANCIS, auto parts company executive; b. Concord, Mass., May 21, 1947; s. Harold William and Julia Theresa (May) J.; children: Scott, Evon, Meghan. BS, Lowell U., 1969; MBA, Mich. State U., Troy, 1987. Asst. mgr. ops. analysis Western Union, NYC, 1969-71; fin. analyst Microdot, Greenwich, Conn., 1971-72, asst. to gen. mgr. Detroit Diamond div. Wyandotte, Mich., 1972-73, asst. to gen. mgr. Wittek Mfg. div. La Grange Park, Ill., 1973-75, plant mgr. Detroit Diamond div. Wyandotte, 1976-78, v.p., gen. mgr. Internat. div. Mt. Clemens, Mich., 1978-87; v.p., gen. mgr. Kaynar div. Microdot, Fullerton, Calif., 1987-89; fin. analyst United Tech.-Otis, NYC, 1975-76; v.p., gen. mgr. SLI div. Johnson Controls Inc., Milw., 1989-93, v.p. and gen. mgr. battery group, 1993—96, pres., North America/Asia Pacific, 1997—99; pres., COO Visteon Corp., 2000—04, bd. dir., 2002—, CEO, 2004—05, chmn., CEO, 2005—. Mem. bd. dir. Flowserve Corp., Dallas, Whirlpool Corp., Mich. Office: Visteon Corp 17000 Rotunda Dr Dearborn MI 48120*

JOHNSTON, NEIL CHUNN, lawyer; b. Mobile, Ala., Feb. 23, 1953; s. Vivian Gaines and Sara Niel (Chunn) J.; m. Ashley Monroe Hocklander, Dec. 20, 1980; children: Katie, Neil Jr. BA, Southwestern at Memphis (name changed to Rhodes Coll.), 1975; JD, U. Ala., 1978. Atty. Hand, Arendall L.L.C., Mobile, Ala., 1978—. Practice group leader, land use and environment Contbr. articles to profl. jours. Pres. Project CATE Found, Inc., Mobile, 1987—; trustee Nature Conservancy, Ala., 1990-96; bd. dirs. Am. Jr. Miss Program, 1996-2003; bd. dirs., (pres. 2003—),Ala. Coastal Found. Recipient Ala. Gov.'s award-Water Conservationist, Ala. Wildlife Fedn., 1987, EPA Region IV Wetlands Recognition award, 2000, Nat. Wetlands award Environ. Law Inst., 2003, EPA Gulf Guardian award, 2006. Mem. ABA (vice-chair forestry com. sect. environment, energy, resc.), Ala. State Bar Assn. (chmn. environ. law sect. 1984-91, corp. banking, bus. law sect. 1993), Mobile Bar Assn., Ala. Forestry Assn., Ala. Law Inst., Rotary (pres. Mobile 1996-97). Office: Hand Arendall LLC 3000 FNB Bldg 107 St Francis St Mobile AL 36602 Office Phone: 251-432-5511. Business E-Mail: njohnston@handarendall.com.

JOHNSTON, NICKLETT ROSE, research nurse, clinical perfusionist; d. Robert Nick Moriana and Melba Grohe, Roger E. Grohe (Stepfather); m. Roy Edwin Johnston, Aug. 5, 1995; m. Michael Minnella, 1979 (div. 1992); children: Michael Paul Minnella, Anita Marie Minnella. ADN, Cochise Coll., Douglas, AZ, 1979; BSN, U. Phoenix, 2002; MSN, Graceland U., 2005. Cert. clin. perfusionist Tex., 1989, ACLS, Tex., 2002. RN Tucson Med. Ctr., 1982—87; clin. perfusionist, RN, Cardiovasc. Support Svcs., Dallas, 1988—89; clin. perfusionist, RN dept. cardiovascular and thoracic surgery U. Tex. Southwestern Med. Ctr., Dallas, 1989—2003, sr. rsch. nurse dept. cardiovascular and thoracic surgery, 2003—. Mem. ANA, Washington, 1979—90, Am. Soc. for Extra Corporeal Tech., Hattiesburg, Miss., 1989—, knowledge base com., 1999—2000; instr. Am. Heart Assn., Dallas, 1994—95. Author: The Emergency use of Recombinant Hirudin in Cardiopulmonary Bypass (Am. Soc. for Extra Corporeal Tech. Case Report award, 2000), Argatroban in Adult Extracorporeal Membrane Oxygenation, Simplified Solution to Eliminating Electrical Noise During Cardiac Surgery. Mem.: Am. Bd. Perfusionists, Am. Bd. Nursing (licentiate), Theta Tau. Home: 324 Harbor Landing Dr Rockwall TX 75032 Office Phone: 214-645-7728. Personal E-mail: johnstonr@sbcglobal.net.

JOHNSTON, OLIVER MARTIN, JR., (OLLIE JOHNSTON), animator; b. Palo Alto, Calif, Oct. 31, 1912; s. Oliver Martin and Arclissa Florence (Boggs) J.; m. Marie Estelle Worthey, Jan. 23, 1943 (dec. May 27, 2005); children: Richard Oliver, Kenneth Andrew. Student, Stanford U., 1931-34, U. Calif., Berkeley, 1932, Chouinard Art Inst., 1934-35. Directing animator Walt Disney Co., Burbank, Calif., 1935-78. Lectr., spkr. in field. Asst. animator Snow White and the Seven Dwarfs, 1937; animation supr. Fantasia, 1940, Bambi, 1942; animator Pinnochio, 1940, The Fox and the Hound, 1981, Victory Through Air Power, 1943, The Three Caballeros, 1945, Make Mine Music, 1946; directing animator Song of the South, 1946, Melody Time, 1948, The Adventures of Ichabod and Mr. Toad, 1949, Cinderella, 1950, Alice in Wonderland, 1951, Peter Pan, 1953, Lady and the Tramp, 1955, Sleeping Beauty, 1959, 101 Dalmatians, 1961, Sword in the Stone, 1963, Mary Poppins, 1964, The Jungle Book, 1967, The Aristocats, 1970, Robin Hood, 1973, Rescuers, 1977, also shorts and TV cartoons; author: Disney Animation -- The Illusion of Life, 1981, Too Funny For Words, 1987, Bambi-the Story and the Film, 1990, Jungle Book Portfolio, 1992, The Disney Villain, English edit., 1993, French edit., 1995; contbg. editor sketch book series; subject of documentary Frank and Ollie; drawings exhibited in Whitney Mus., NYC, 1981. Guest spkr. Russian Govt. and Soyuzmultifilm, 1976, other East European Countries, US Info. Agy. Cultural Exch. Program, 1986. Recipient Pioneer in Film award Delta Kappa Allpha, 1978, honor award Mus. Modern Art, 1978, Annie award Internat. Animated Film Soc., 1980, Disney Legend award, 1989, Grand Prix of the Am., 1995; Academy Tribute to Ollie Johnston & Frank Thomas, The 8th Marc Davis Lecture on Animation presented by the Acad. of Motion Picture Arts and Sci. and the Academy Found., 2003, Nat. Medal of Arts Nat. Endowment for the Arts, 2005. Avocations: trains, reading, studying, sports.

JOHNSTON, OSCAR BLACK, III, lawyer; b. Tulsa, Oct. 1, 1941; s. Oscar Black Jr. and Carol (VanDerwiele) J.; m. Ruth Archdeacon Darrough; children: Eric Oscar, David Darrough. BBA, Baylor U., Waco, Tex., 1963; JD, U. Tulsa, 1966. Bar: Okla. 1966, US Dist. Ct. (no., ea., we. dists.) Okla., US Ct. Claims, US Ct. Appeals (10th cir.), US Supreme Ct. Asst. U.S. attorney U.S. Dist. Ct. (we. dist.) Okla., 1970-76; ptnr. Logan & Lowry, L.L.P., Vinita, Okla., 1979—. Assoc. editor Tulsa Law Review, 1964-66. Presiding judge divsn. 54 Okla. Temp. Ct. Appeals, 1980-81, judge divsn. XIV, 1991-93; presiding judge panel VI Lawyer-Staffed Ct. Appeals, 1992. Capt. JAGC, U.S. Army, 1966-70. Fellow Am. Bar Found. (state chair 2001-03), Okla. Bar Found. (trustee 1988-96, pres. 1995); mem. ABA (sects. litigation, family law and criminal), Fed. Bar Assn. (pres. Oklahoma City chpt. 1975), Craig County Bar Assn. (pres. 1986-88), Okla. Bar Assn. (mem. fin. com. 2003—, assoc. editor, mem. bd. editors Okla. Bar Jour. 2000-05), Okla. Trial Lawyers Assn., Rotary (pres. Vinita 1983-84), Phi Alpha Delta. Republican. Methodist. Office: Logan & Lowry PO Box 558 Vinita OK 74301-0558 Home: 116 Westwood Ave Vinita OK 74301-2703 Business E-Mail: objohnston@loganlowry.com.

JOHNSTON, PAUL WARREN, retired surgeon; b. Kingsburg, Calif. s. Karl Gunnar and Ester Matilda Johnston; m. Lillian Ruby Rogstad, Nov. 25, 1949; children: Mark, Anne, Gail. BA, U. So. Calif., LA, 1944, MD, 1947. Intern LA County Hosp., LA, 1947; resident VA Hosp., Long Beach, Calif., 1949—53, surgeon, 1953—56; pvt. practice surgeon Burbank and Pasadena, Calif., 1957—95; ret., 1995. Pres. med. staff Huntington Hosp., Pasadena, 1979, chair instnl. rev. bd., 1985—2000, dir. surg. residency program, 1990—95. Contbr. articles to profl. jours. Lt. (j.g.) USNR, 1947—49. Mem.: ACS, Western Surg. Assn., Pacific Coast Surg. Assn. Avocations: golf, reading, travel.

JOHNSTON, PHILIP CONNELLY, lawyer; b. NYC, June 6, 1968; s. John Martin and Suzanne (Shephardson) J. AB, U. Mich., 1990; MA in Internat. Studies, Johns Hopkins U., 1994; JD, Columbia U., 2000. Corr. UPI, Moscow, 1995-97; law clk. to Hon. Joan A. Lenard, U.S. Dist. Ct. for So. Dist. Fla., Miami, Fla., 2000—02; assoc. Skadden, Arps, Slate, Meagher & Flom, NYC, 2002—. Avocations: languages, travel. Office: US Dist Ct for So Dist Fla 301 N Miami Ave 7th Fl Miami FL 33121

JOHNSTON, RICHARD ALAN, lawyer; b. Buffalo, Mar. 18, 1950; s. Richard W. and Virginia (Holmes) J.; m. Patricia Downing, Aug. 28, 1971; children: Matthew, Sarah, Elizabeth, Michael. BA, Cornell U., 1972; JD, Harvard U., 1976. Bar: Mass. 1977, U.S. Dist. Ct. Mass. 1977, U.S. Ct. Appeals (1st cir.) 1977. Law clk. to presiding justice Mass. Ct. Appeals, Boston, 1976-77; assoc. Hale and Dorr LLP, Boston, 1977-82, sr. ptnr., 1982—. Co-chmn. North Area Task Force, Charlestown, Mass., 1981—; trustee Dennis (Mass.) Conservation Trust, 1988—, pres., 1995—; mem. transition team Mass. Gov. William Weld, 1990-91; internat. election observer Internat. Human Rights Law Group, Nepal, 1991; dir. Friends of City Square Park, 1993—2001; trustee Hockey Humanitarian Award Found., 1997—; pres. Friends of Tanzanias Schs., Inc., 1997—, Compact of Cape Cod Conservation Trusts, 2001—; mem. adv. bd. Mass. Correctional Legal Svcs., 2005-; mem. Nat. Coun. Arts and Scis. George Washington U. Mem. ABA, Internat. Bar Assn., Boston Bar Assn., Nat. Health Lawyers Assn., Mass. Bar Assn. Home: 43 Monument Ave Charlestown MA 02129-3323 Office: Wilmer Cutler Pickering Hale and Dorr LLP 60 State St Boston MA 02109-1816 Home Phone: 617-241-7716; Office Phone: 617-526-6282. Business E-Mail: richardjohnston@wilmerhale.com.

JOHNSTON, RICHARD BOLES, JR., pediatrician, educator, biomedical researcher; b. Atlanta, Aug. 23, 1935; s. Richard Boles and Jane (Dillon) Johnston; m. Mary Anne Claiborne, Aug. 13, 1960; children: Richard B. III, S. Claiborne, Kristin M. BA, Vanderbilt U., 1957, MD, 1961; MS (hon.), U. Pa., 1986. Diplomate Am. Bd. Pediat., Am. Bd. Pediat. Infectious Disease. Resident in pediat. Vanderbilt U., 1961-63, Harvard U., 1963-64, fellow pediat. immunology, 1967-70; asst. prof., assoc. prof. depts. pediat. and microbiology U. Ala. Med. Ctr., Birmingham, 1970-76; vis. assoc. prof. Rockefeller U., NYC, 1976-77, vis. prof., 1983-84; prof. pediat. U. Colo. Sch. Medicine, Denver, 1977-86; chmn. dept. pediat. Nat. Jewish Ctr. Immunology and Respiratory Medicine, Denver, 1977-86, U. Pa. Sch. Medicine, Phila., 1986-90, Wm. H. Bennett prof. pediat., 1986-92; physician-in-chief Children's Hosp. of Phila., 1986—90; med. dir. March of Dimes Birth Defects Found., White Plains, NY, 1992-98. Adj. prof. pediat., chief sec. pediat. immunology Yale U. Sch. Medicine, 1992—98; prof. pediat. Sch. Medicine U. Colo., Denver, 1999—, assoc. dean rsch. devel., 2001—; exec. v.p. acad. affairs Nat. Jewish Med. & Rsch. Ctr., 2004—07; trustee Internat. Pediat. Rsch. Found., 1983—87, 1995—98, chmn., 1984—87, 1997—98; chmn. adv. bd. for vaccines and related biols. FDA, Bethesda, Md., 1990—93, chmn. com. vaccine safety, Inst. Medicine, 1992—93, chmn. com. new rsch. in vaccines, 1993—94, chmn. forum vaccine safety, 1995—98, chmn. com. asthma and indoor air, 1998—99, bd. health promotion disease prevention, 1994—2001, chmn. com. rsch. in multiple sclerosis, 1999—2001, chmn. com. health implications of perchlorate, 2003—05, chmn. com. tng. physicians for pub. health careers, 2006—07. Mem. editl. bd. 7 profl. jours., 1978—; contbr. 265 scholarly publs.; editor Current Opinion in Pediatrics, 1997—. Capt. M.C., U.S. Army, 1964-66. Faculty scholar Josiah Macy Jr. Found., 1976-77; recipient Commr. citation and Wiley medal FDA, 1994. Fellow AAAS; mem. Inst. Medicine NAS, Am. Soc. Clin. Investigation, Am. Pediat. Soc. (pres. 1996-97), Assn. Am. Physicians, Soc. Pediat. Rsch. (pres. 1980-81). Office: Office of Dean C-290 U Colo Sch Medicine 4200 E 9th Ave Denver CO 80262 Office Phone: 303-315-6792. Business E-Mail: richard.johnston@uchsc.edu.

JOHNSTON, RICHARD FOURNESS, biologist, educator; b. Oakland, Calif., July 27, 1925; s. Arthur Nathaniel and Marie (Johnson) J.; m. Lora Lee Bliler, Feb. 7, 1948; children: Regan, Janet, Cassandra. BA, U. Calif., Berkeley, 1950, MA, 1953, PhD, 1955. Asst. prof. dept. biology N.Mex. State U., 1956-58; mem. faculty depts. zoology and ecology U. Kans., Lawrence, 1958—, prof., 1968-92, prof. emeritus, 1992—, chmn., 1979-82, editor mus. publs., 1974-76, 86-91; program dir. systematic biology NSF, Washington, 1968-69; editor Ann. Rev. Ecology and Systematics, 1968-92, Current Ornithology, 1981-87. Mem. adv. panel biol. scis. Smithsonian Fgn. Currency Program, 1969-71 Served with AUS, 1943-46. Am. Acad. Arts and Scis. grantee, 1957; nat. Acad. Sci. grantee, 1959; NSF grantee, 1959-83. Fellow Am. Ornithol. Union (Coues award 1975), AAAS, mem. Ecol. Soc. Am., Soc. Systematic Zoology (editor jour. 1967-70, pres. 1977), Soc. Study Evolution. Home: 615 Louisiana St Lawrence KS 66044-2337 Business E-Mail: rfj@ku.edu. *Variability or heterogeneity or pluralism is present in nearly everything humans do or to which they are exposed.*

JOHNSTON, ROBERT FOWLER, venture capitalist; b. Phila., Aug. 15, 1936; s. William S. and Elinor (Fowler) J.; m. Lynn Dixon, Feb. 5, 1972; children: William McCord, Bradford Dixon, Alexandra Fowler. BA, Princeton U., 1958; MBA, NYU, 1964. With F.S. Smithers & Co., NYC, 1960-61, Smith Barney & Co., NYC, 1963-67; pres. Johnston Assocs. Inc., Princeton, NJ, 1967—. Bd. dirs. ExSAR Corp., Princeton, Ctr. for Edn. Reform, Washington, 2004—. Co-author: Entrepreneural Science: New Links Between Corporations, Universities and Government. Mem. adv. coun. Princeton U. Dept. Molecular biology, 1983—; mem. exec. com. Friends of Inst. Advanced Study, Princeton, 1992—, chmn., 1998—2002; founder Edn. Ventures Found. With USAF, 1961-62. Mem. Univ. Club of N.Y.C. Avocations: archaeology, art. Home: 10 Aurora Way Hanover NH 03755 Office: Johnson Assocs Inc 358 Wendover Dr Princeton NJ 08540 Office Phone: 609-924-2575.

JOHNSTON, STANLEY HOWARD, JR., curator; b. Cleve., Apr. 28, 1946; m. Carol Ann Lewis, June 19, 1976. BA, Columbia Coll., 1968; MA, U. Western Ont., London, Can., 1970, PhD, 1977; MS in LS, Case Western Res. U., Cleve., 1979. Tchg. asst. U. Western Ont., London, 1971-72; asst. to editors Spenser Newsletter, London, Ont., 1972-73; bibliographer Cleve. Herbals Project, Cleve, 1984-90; curator of rare books Holden Arboretum, Kirtland, Ohio, 1990—. Internet columnist Coun. on Bot. and Hort. Librs., 1995—; libr. adv. com. The Herb Soc. Am., Kirtland, Ohio, 1997-99. Author: The Cleveland Herbal, Botanical and Horticultural Collections, 1992, Cleveland's Treasures from the World of Botanical Literature, 1998; contbr. articles to profl. jours.; internet columnist. Mem. libr. subcom. of edn. com. Cleve. Botanical Gardens, 2006—. Recipient Charles Robert Long award of Extraordinary Merit, 2005. Mem. MLA, Bibliog. Soc. Am., Soc. for History of Natural History, ALA (rare books and manuscripts sect.), The Bibliog. Soc., Coun. on Bot. and Hort. Librs. (mem. publs. com., electronic comm. com., 1996—, documentation strategy com. 1996-2001, long term planning com., 1997-2001, preservation and access com. 2001—, steering com. 2001-06), Medieval Acad. Am., Am. Philatelic Soc., No. Ohio Bibliophilic Soc. Republican. Presbyterian. Avocations: philately, collecting mystery, science-fiction and fantasy books. Home: 7226 Grant St Mentor OH 44060-4704 Office: The Holden Arboretum 9500 Sperry Rd Kirtland OH 44094-5149 Office Phone: 440-602-3829. Personal E-mail: stanley177@aol.com.

JOHNSTON, STEPHEN C., lawyer; b. Ft. Worth, May 6, 1970; BS cum laude in Wildlife and Fishery Scis., Tex. A&M U., 1993; JD cum laude, Tex. Tech U., 1996. Bar: Tex. 1996. Atty. water contamination litig. sect. Baron & Budd, P.C., Dallas, 1997—. Named a Rising Star, Tex. Super Lawyers mag., 2006. Mem.: Dallas Bar Assn., Tex. Trial Lawyers Assn., Am. Trial Lawyers Assn., ABA, Dallas Trial Lawyers Assn., Trial Lawyers for Pub. Justice, Assn. Trial Lawyers of Am. Office: Baron & Budd PC 3102 Oak Lawn Ave Ste 1100 Dallas TX 75219 Office Phone: 214-521-3605.*

JOHNSTON, SUSAN A., lawyer; b. Dec. 16, 1953; BA, Wellesley Coll., 1975; JD, Harvard Univ., 1978. Bar: Mass. 1978. Assoc. Ropes & Gray, Boston, 1978—87, ptnr., 1987—, immediate past head tax & benefits dept. Co-author: Taxation of Regulated Investment Companies and Their Shareholders, 1999; contbr. articles to profl. jours. Mem. Tax Adv. Bd. Investment Co. Inst., 1988—. Mem.: ABA (chmn. Com. Regulated Investment Cos. 1987—89), Boston Bar Assn. (chmn. tax sect. 1985—87, chmn. Internat. Tax Com. 1985—87, chmn. State Tax Com. 1987—89). Office: Ropes & Gray 1 International Pl Boston MA 02110-2624 Office Phone: 617-951-7301. Office Fax: 617-951-7050. Business E-Mail: susan.johnston@ropesgray.com.

JOHNSTON, THOMAS E., judge; b. 1967; BA, JD, W.Va. U. Atty. Schrader, Byrd and Companion, 1994—96; assoc. Flaherty, Sensabaugh and Bonasso, 1996—98; ptnr. Bailey, Riley, Buch and Harmon, Wheeling, W.Va., 1998—2001; US atty. (no. dist.) W.Va. US Dept. Justice, Wheeling, W.Va., 2001—06; judge US Dist. Ct. (so. dist.) W.Va., Wheeling, 2006—. Office: PO Box 591 Wheeling WV 26003-0011*

JOHNSTON, THOMAS MCELREE, JR., retired church administrator; b. Coral Gables, Fla., June 10, 1934; s. Thomas McElree and Lorine (Davis) J.; m. Anna Youel Armstrong, July 2, 1960; children: Kathryn Armstrong, Timothy Armstrong, Sara Helen. BA, Amherst Coll., 1956; MDiv, Yale U., 1959; ThM, Princeton Theol. Sem., 1963; D of Ministry, San Francisco Theol. Sem., 1978. Ordained to ministry Presbyn. Ch., 1959. Assoc. coord. religious affairs NC State U., Raleigh, NC, 1959-62; min. community svc. Tabernacle Presbyn. Ch., Phila., 1963-66; organizer, head of staff Ch. of the Reconciler, Clearwater, Fla., 1966-78; assoc. Presbytery devel. Synod of the Covenant, Columbus, Ohio, 1978-85, assoc. exec., 1985-88; exec. Synod of the Trinity, Camp Hill, Pa., 1988-2000; ret. Pres. Pa. Coun. Chs., Harrisburg, 1995-98; chair Synod Exec. Forum, 1997; chmn. gen. assembly Synod Staff Forum, 1997; corr. mem. Gen. Assembly Coun., Louisville, 1993-94. Publisher: (newspaper) Trinitarian. Pres., organizer Religious Cmty. Svcs., Inc. Clearwater, 1968-70; pres. Pinellas County Head Start, Inc., Clearwater, 1968-72; mem. Pinellas County Sch. Bd., Pinellas County Coun., Clearwater, 1972-76; bd. dirs. Cmty. Svc. Found., Largo, Fla., 1969-78, Drug Free Pa., Inc., 1999-2002. Named Vol. of Yr., Civic Coun., Pinellas County, Fla., 1972; recipient Humanitarian award Lions Club, 1975. Mem. Rotary Internat. (club. pres. 2003-04, pres. Harrisburg Rotary Found. 2004-05) Presbyterian. Home: 1041 Country Club Rd Camp Hill PA 17011-1049 E-mail: tom.johnston@paonline.com.

JOHNSTON, VIRGINIA EVELYN, retired editor; b. Spokane, Wash., Apr. 26, 1933; d. Edwin and Emma Lucile (Munroe) Rowe; m. Alan Paul Beckley, Dec. 26, 1974; children: Chris, Denise, Rex. Student, Portland C.C., 1964, Portland State U., 1966, 78-79. Proofreader the Oregonian, Portland, 1960—62, teletypesetter operator, 1962—66, operator Photon 200, 1966—68, copy editor, asst. women's editor, 1968—80, spl. sects. editor, 1981—83, editor FOOD day, 1982—2001; ret., 2002. Pres. Matrix Assocs., Inc., Portland, 1975—, chmn. bd., 1979—; past pres. Bones & Brew, Inc. Editor Principles of Computer Systems for Newspaper Mgmt., 1975-76. Cons. Portland Sch. Dist. No. 1, 1978, Dem. Party Oreg., 1969. Democrat. Home: 4140 NE 137th Ave Portland OR 97230-2624 E-mail: ginger1933@comcast.net.

JOHNSTON, WILLIAM DAVID, lawyer; b. Aberdeen, Md., Jan. 31, 1957; s. David Irvine and Nancy (Smith) J.; m. Mary Teresa Miller, May 29, 1983; children: Ellen Christine, Amy Elizabeth. AB, Colgate U., 1979; JD, Washington and Lee U., 1982. Bar: Del. 1982, U.S. Dist. Ct. Del. 1983, U.S. Ct. Appeals (3rd cir.) 1991, U.S. Supreme Ct. 1991. Judicial law clk. to chief justice Daniel L. Herrmann Del. Supreme Ct., Wilmington, 1982-83; assoc. Potter, Anderson and Corroon, Wilmington, 1983-85, Young, Conaway, Stargatt and Taylor, Wilmington, 1985-89, ptnr., 1990—. Contbr. articles to profl. jours. Mem. choir, adminstrv. bd. lay leadership Aldersgate United Meth. Ch., Wilmington, 1970—, chmn. religion and race commn., 1987-89; com. chmn. Boy Scouts of U.S. troop 67, 1982-85, Del. Human Rels. Commn., 1986—; trustee The Pilot Sch., 1995—. Best Brief Worldwide award Am. Soc. Internat. Law, Washington, 1980. Mem. ABA (chmn. indemnification and ins. subcom. 1997-2005, Am. Judicature Soc. (bd. dirs. 2002—), Del. State Bar Assn. (award for pub. svc. 1991, 93,

99, pres.-elect 2000-01, pres. 2001-02), Sigma Chi (pres. Colgate U. chpt. 1984-88), Phi Delta Phi, Univ. and Whist Club (bd. govs. 1990-95), Lincoln (Del.) Club, Wilmington Country Club. Methodist. Avocations: running, squash, reading, travel, golf. Office: Young Conaway Stargatt and Taylor The Brandywine Bldg 1100 West St PO Box 391 Wilmington DE 19899-0391 Office Phone: 302-571-6679. Business E-Mail: wjohnston@ycst.com.

JOHNSTON, WILLIAM DAVID, biotechnologist, director; b. Chgo., Nov. 5, 1944; s. Samuel David and Jeanne (Williams) J.; m. Susan Diane Ward, Aug. 19, 1966; children: Kimberly Dawn Sites, Kirk David, Tiffany Dee Hansen, Kyle Donald, Ryan Daryl. BS in Chemistry, Brigham Young U., 1969, PhD in Organic Chemistry, 1974. V.p. Parish Chem. Co., 1973-75; mgr. materials control Baxter Healthcare Corp., 1975-80; group mgr., polymer rsch. and material control Travenol Labs., Inc., 1980-84, v.p. Material and Membrane Tech. Ctr., 1984-86, v.p. applied scis., 1987-93; v.p., gen. mgr. gene therapy div. Baxter Healthcare Corp., Round Lake, Ill., 1993-97; pres., CEO Inhibitex, Inc., Atlanta, 1997—2006; pres. BioBus. Stategies, Inc., 2007—. Adv. bd. Ill. Jr. Acad. Sci., Springfield, 1984-86; bd. dirs. Ga. Biomed. Ptnrs., vice chmn., 2005—06; emerging co. sect. governing bd. Biotech. Industry Orgn., 2002-07, bd. dirs.; chair BioSci. Coun. Metro Atlanta C. of C., 2005; adv. bd. Coll. Engring., U. Ill., Chgo., 1988-92, dept. chem. engring. Northwestern U., Evanston, Ill., 1989-98. Contbr. articles to profl. jours.; patentee in field. Stake pres. LDS Ch., Buffalo Grove, Ill., 1988-97; exec. coun. N.E. Ill. coun. Boy Scouts Am., 1989-97; chmn. bd. LDS Social Svcs., Naperville, Ill., 1990-97; bd. trustees Emory Johns Creek Hosp., 2006—. Brigham Young U. scholarship. Mem. AAAS, Am. Chem. Soc., Sigma Xi. Home: 1422 Spyglass Hill Dr Duluth GA 30097-5948 Business E-Mail: bjohnston@inhibitex.com.

JOHNSTON, WILLIAM P., health facility administrator; BA, Vanderbilt Univ., 1966, JD, 1969. Ptnr. Waller Landsden Dortch & Davis; mng. dir., mem. bd. dir., CEO Equitable Securities Corp., 1986—97; vice-chmn. SunTrust Capital Markets, Inc., 1998—2001, CEO, 1998—2000; mng. dir. SunTrust Robinson Humphrey, 2001—02; mem. bd. dir. Renal Care Group, 2002—, also chmn., 2003—06. Bd. dirs. Hartford Mut. Funds, MultiPlan, Inc.; mem. supervising bd. Fresenius Med. Care, 2006; sr. advisor The Carlyle Group, 2006. Office: Renal Care Group One American Ctr 3100 West End Ave Ste 875 Nashville TN 37203 Office Phone: 615-345-5500. Office Fax: 615-345-5665.

JOHNSTON, WILLIAM WEBB, pathologist, educator; b. Statesville, NC, Aug. 26, 1933; s. Jesse Clyde and Pauline Elizabeth (Massey) J. BS, Davidson Coll., 1954; MD, Duke U., 1959. Diplomate Am. Bd. Pathology, Am. Bd. Cytopathology, Internat. Bd. Cytopathology. Intern Duke U., 1959-60, resident in pathology, 1960-63, mem. faculty, 1963—, prof. pathology, 1972-97, dir. div. cytopathology and cytotechnology tng. program, 1966—; ret., 1996. Bd. dirs. Anatomical Pathology Svc.; cons. pathologist Durham VA Hosp., Duncan County Hosp.; chmn. Internat. Bd. Cytopathology, 1992-98. Author: (with W.J. Frable) Respiratory Cytopathology, 1974; Diagnostic Respiratory Cytopathology, 1979; (with S.H. Bigner) The Cytopathology of the Central Nervous System, 1981, 2d edit., 1994, Pulmonary Cytology (with James Linder), 1992; assoc. editor Acta Cytologica, 1978—, sr. mem. editorial bd., 1992; editor: Masson Monographs in Cytopathology; mem. editorial bd. Am. Jour. Clin. Pathology, 1986; editorial cons. Masson Publs., N.Y.C.; mem. editorial adv. bd. Jour. Nat. Cancer Inst. Fellow Internat. Acad. Cytology (Maurice Goldblatt award 1995), Am. Soc. Clin. Pathologists, Coll. Am. Pathologists, Royal Soc. Medicine; mem. AMA (del. 1982-96), Am. Soc. Cytology (rev. bd., pres. 1981-82, Papanicolaou award 1986), Am. Assn. Pathologists, Arthur Purdy Stout Soc. Surg. Pathology, Internat. Acad. Pathology, Am. Assn. for Cancer Rsch. Republican. Presbyterian (organist). Home: 8200 Bromley Rd Hillsborough NC 27278-9709

JOHNSTON, YNEZ, artist, educator; b. Berkeley, Calif., May 12, 1920; BFA, U. Calif., Berkeley, 1941, MFA, 1946. Lectr. art U. Calif., Berkeley, 1950—51, Colorado Springs Fine Arts Ctr., 1954—55, Chouinard Art Inst., 1956, Calif. State U., LA, 1966—67, U. Judaism Sch. Fine Arts, LA, 1967, Otis Art Inst., LA, 1978—81; artist-in-residence Fullerton Coll., Calif., 1982. One-man exhbns. include: San Francisco Mus. Art, 1943, Redlands U., 1947, Santa Barbara (Calif.) Mus. Art, 1952, 57, Pasadena (Calif.) Mus. Art, 1955, 62, Colorado Springs (Colo.) Fine Arts Center, 1955, Calif. Palace Legion of Honor, 1956, The O'Hana Gallery, London, 1958, Paul Kantor Gallery, Los Angeles, 1952, 53, 55, 57, 58, 61-62, 63, Beloit (Wis.) Coll., 1961, Barbara Cecil Gallery, New Orleans, 1963, Mex., 1959, Occidental Coll., L.A., 1955, Esther Bear Gallery, 1967, Ball State U., 1967, Stewart-Verde Galleries, San Francisco, 1966, San Francisco Mus. Art, 1967, Mekler Gallery, L.A., 1970-82, 84, 89, Tokyo Shoten Gallery, N.Y.C., 1976, Mitsukoshi Gallery, Tokyo, 1977, Wiener Gallery, N.Y.C., 1977, Worthington Gallery, Chgo., 1982, 85, 88, Mekler Gallery, 1987, 89, Tomlyn Gallery, Fla., 1990-99, 2003, Fresno Mus. Art, 1992, Tortue Gallery, Santa Monica, 1994-96, Tobey Moss Gallery, L.A., 1994, 2003, 05, Kennedy Mus., Athens, Ohio, 1997, Lyman Allyn Mus., New London, Conn., 1998, Schmidt-Bingham Gallery, N.Y.C., 1998, 99, 2001, Santa Cruz Mus., Calif. 1998, Norton-Simon Mus., Pasadena, Calif., 2004, 05; also exhibited numerous group shows including: Whitney Mus. Am. Art, 1953-56, Mus. Modern Art, 1952, 54, Carnegie Inst., 1951, 55, I.F.A. Gallery, Washington, 1963, 100 Prints of the Year, N.Y.C., 1963, Bklyn. Mus., 1966, Vancouver (B.C., Can.) Print Internat., World Print Competition, San Francisco, 1977, Met. Mus., 1978, L.A. County Mus., 1980-81, Drawings from Their Collection, Nat. Gallery Smithsonian, Washington, Wight Gallery UCLA, 1988, Nat. Gallery Modern Art, New Delhi, 1988, Memory Gallery, Nagoya, Japan, 1990, Gallery IV, L.A., 1990, Worcester Art Mus., 1991, Amon Carter Mus., 1991, Women's Art Mus., Washington, 1994, Met. Mus. Fresno, Calif., 1994, Brigitie Haasner Gallery, Wiesbaden, Germany, Norton-Simon Mus., 1999, Traveling Show in China, Macao, Municipal Gallery, Rio Honda Coll., L.A., Taiwan, 2001, Norton Simon Johnston Collection, 2005, Metrospective Show, Worthington Gallery, Chgo., 2005, others; represented in permanent collections numerous museums including, Santa Barbara Mus. Art, Mus. Modern Art, Philbrook Art Center, Los Angeles County Mus., City Art Mus. St. Louis, Whitney Mus. Am. Art, Phila. Mus. Art, San Diego Mus. Art, U. Ill., Met. Mus. Art, Hirshhorn Collection, Herbert F. Johnson Collection (Cornell U.), San Francisco Mus. Art, Otis Art Inst., Milw. Art Center, Worcester Art Mus. (travelling print exhbn. to Terra Mus., Chgo., Amon Carter Mus., Ft. Worth, 1990), Santa Fe Mus. of Fine Art, The Nat. Mus. Israel, Jerusalem, Gift Gardens Bot./Sculpture Pk., Fla., Norton-Simon Mus., numerous schs. and colls., other museums, also pvt. collections. Recipient San Francisco Mus. Art award oil painting, 1946; awards Calif. State Fair, 1951, 61, 62; award etching Los Angeles County Mus., 1950; exhbn. first award Met. Mus. Art, 1952; purchase award Exhbn. Fgn. Artists, Rome, Italy, 1952; purchase award Otis Art Inst., 1963; purchase award Los Angeles Municipal Art Dept., 1967; also commns.; John Simon Guggenheim Found. grantee, 1952; Louis Comfort Tiffany grantee, 1955, 56; Huntington Hartford grantee, 1957; James Phelan grantee, 1958; MacDowell Colony grantee, 1959; Tamarind workshop fellow, 1966; Nat. Endowment Arts painting grantee, 1976, 85 Home and Studio: 579 Crane Blvd Los Angeles CA 90065-5019

JOHNSTONE, D. BRUCE, education educator, academic administrator; b. Mpls., Jan. 13, 1941; s. D. Bruce and Florence Morton (Elliott) J.; m. Gail Eberhardt, July 30, 1965; children: Duncan Bruce, Cameron. BA, Harvard U., 1963, M.A.T., 1964; PhD, U. Minn., 1969; D (hon.), Towson St U., 1995, D'Youville Coll., 1995, Calif. State U., San Diego, 1997. Tchr. econs. and history, Westport, Conn., 1964-65; asst. dir. U. Minn. Center for Econ. Edn., 1966-69; adminstrv. asst. to Sen. Walter F. Mondale, 1969-71; project specialist Ford Found., 1971-72; exec. asst. to pres. U. Pa., 1972-77, assoc. prof. edn., 1976-79, v.p. for adminstrn., 1977-79; pres. State U. Coll. at Buffalo, 1979-88; chancellor SUNY Sys. Office SUNY, Albany, 1988-94, prof. Buffalo, 1994—2005, disting svc. prof. higher and comparative edn., 2006—. Author: New Patterns for College Lending, 1973, Sharing the Costs of Higher Education, 1986, Financing Higher Education: Cost-Sharing in International Perspective, 2006; co-editor: The Funding of Higher Education: International Perspectives, 1993, In Defense of American Higher Education, 2001; contbr. articles to profl. jours. Bd. trustees D'Youville Coll. Democrat. Episcopalian. Office Phone: 716-645-2471 x1092.

JOHNSTONE, DOUGLAS INGE, retired state supreme court justice, lawyer; b. Mobile, Ala., Nov. 15, 1941; s. Harry Inge and Kathleen (Yerger) J.; m. Mary Frances Jayne (div.); 1 child, Francis Inge. BA, Rice U., 1963; JD, Tulane U., 1966. Bar: Ala. 1966, U.S. Dist. Ct. Ala. 1966, U.S. Ct. Appeals (5th cir.) 1968, U.S. Supreme Ct. 1969. Pvt. practice, Mobile, 1966—84, 2005—; dist. judge Ala. Dist. Ct., Mobile, 1984—85, presiding dist. judge, 1985, cir. judge, 1985—99; justice Supreme Ct. Ala., Montgomery, 1999—2005; ret., 2005. Mem. House of Reps. State of Ala., 1974-78. Mem. bd. advisors Salvation Army, Mobile, 1989—; bd. dirs. Mental Health Assn., Mobile, 1990-92. Capt. U.S. Army, 1963-72. Elected Outstanding Freshman Rep., Capital Prses Corps., 1975; recipient Meritorious Svc. award Mobile County Bd. of Health, 1968, Humanitarian Svc. award Mobile Cerebral Palsy Assn., 1973. Mem. Am. Judges Assn., Ala. Bar Assn., Mobile Bar Assn., Internat. Acad. Trial Judges, Exptl. Aircraft Assn. Democrat. Episcopalian. Avocations: hunting, boating, flying. Office Phone: 251-973-1947.

JOHNSTONE, GREGG MARTIN, communications executive; b. San Diego, Apr. 6, 1947; s. Ralph E. and Maxine Ann O'Dell J.; m. Jane Marie Sammon, Jan. 20, 1973; children: Erik Michael, Katie Marie, Kevin Matthew. BS in Physics, Va. Polytechnic Inst., 1970. Application engr. Video Engring. Co., Washington, 1970-73; field svc. engr. Internat. Video Co., Sunnyvale, Calif., 1973-77; pres. Nat. Video Svcs., Inc., Newtown, Ct., 1977—, Intermed Video Technologies Inc., Newtown, Conn., 1991—, Foresight Designs Inc. Ptnr. Tech. Investments, Inc., 1991—, J & J Investments. Patentee in field. Mem. Soc. Motion Picture and TV Engrs., IEEE, Internat. TV Assn., Am. Radio Relay League. Avocation: amateur radio operator (n1gfh). Office: Nat Video Svcs Inc 18 Commerce Rd Newtown CT 06470-1607

JOHNSTONE, IAIN MURRAY, statistician, educator, consultant; b. Melbourne, Victoria, Australia, Dec. 10, 1956; s. Samuel Thomas Murray and Pamela Beatrice (Kriegel) J. BS with honors, Australian Nat. U., Canberra, 1978, MS, 1979; PhD, Cornell U., 1981. Asst. prof. stats. Stanford U., Calif., 1981—85, assoc prof. stats., 1986—92, assoc. prof. biostatis., 1987—92, prof. stats., biostats., 1992—, dept. chmn., 1994—97, sr. assoc. dean natural scis., 2003—, vice dean acad. planning Sch. Humanities and Scis., 2005—. Contbr. articles to profl. jours. Bd. dirs. Bd. on Math. Scis. and its Applications, Washington, 1999—2002; pres. Inst. Math. Stats., 2001—02. Recipient Presdl. Young Investigator award, NSF, 1985—91; Alfred P. Sloan Rsch. fellow, Sloan Found., 1988—90, Guggenheim fellow, John Simon Guggenheim Found., 1997—98. Fellow: AAAS; mem.: NAS.

JOHNSTONE, JOHN WILLIAM, JR., retired chemical company executive; b. Bklyn., Nov. 19, 1932; s. John William and Sarah J. (Singleton) J.; m. Claire Lundberg, Apr. 14, 1956; children: Thomas Edward, James Robert, Robert Andrew. BA, Hartwick Coll., Oneonta, NY, 1954; DSc (hon.), Hartwick Coll., 1990; grad. advanced mgmt. program, Harvard U., 1970. With Hooker Chem. Corp., 1954-75, group v.p., 1973-75; pres. Airco Alloys divsn. Airco, Inc., 1976-79; v.p., gen. mgr. indsl. products, then sr. v.p. chems. group Olin Corp., 1979-80, corp. v.p., pres. chems. group Norwalk, Conn., 1980-85, pres., 1985-87, chief operating officer, 1986-87, chmn., pres., CEO, 1988-96, chmn. of bd., 1996, bd. dirs., ret., 2005. Bd. dirs. Arch Chem. Inc. Trustee Hartwick Coll., 1983-91, 92, ret., 2005. Mem. Chem. Mfrs. Assn. (chmn. bd. dirs. 1991), Woodway Country Club, Blind Brook Club. Episcopalian.

JOHNSTONE, MARTIN E., retired state supreme court justice; b. Louisville, 1949; BA, Western Ky. U.; JD, U. Louisville. Bar: Ky. Judge 3d Magisterial Dist., Ky., 1976-78; dist. judge Jefferson County, Ky., 1978-83; chief judge, 1987-93; circuit judge, 1985-87; justice Ky. Ct. Appeals, 1993-96, chief judge pro tem, 1996; justice Ky. Supreme Ct., 1996—2006, dep. chief justice, 1998—2006. Recipient Outstanding Trial Judge award Ky. Acad. Trial Attys., 1991, Laurence Grauman award, Brandeis Law Alumni Coun., 2005, Spl. Recognition award, Louisville Bar Assn., 2006, Outstanding Judge award, Ky Bar Assn., 2006; Named Judge of the Yr., Louisville Bar Assn., 1981, 1999 Mem. Louisville Bar Assn.*

JOHNSTONE, PHILIP MACLAREN, lawyer; b. Sharon, Conn., Mar. 24, 1961; s. Rodney Stuart and Frances Louise (Davis) J.; m. Elizabeth Laird McGovern, Sept. 10, 1988. BA in Econs. magna cum laude, Duke U., Durham, NC, 1983; JD, U. Pa., Phila., 1986. Bar: Mass. 1986, Conn. 1987, US Dist. Ct. Conn. 1988, RI 1998. Ptnr. Waller, Smith & Palmer, PC, New London, Conn., 1997—. Bd. dirs. J Boats, Inc., Newport, RI, 1987—. Trustee Denison Pequotsepos Nature Ctr., Mystic, Conn., 1998-2002, Pine Point Sch., Stonington, Conn., 2000-03, Stonington Hist. Soc., 2006—. Mem. ABA, Mass. Bar Assn., Conn. Bar Assn., RI Bar Assn. Republican. Episcopalian. Avocations: tennis, golf. Home: 17 Cliff St Stonington CT 06378-1249 Office: Waller Smith and Palmer PC 52 Eugene Oneill Dr New London CT 06320-6324 Office Phone: 860-442-0367. Business E-Mail: pmjohnstone@wallersmithpalmer.com.

JOHNSTONE, QUINTIN, law educator; b. Chgo., Mar. 29, 1915; s. Quintin and Wegia (Metsker) Johnstone; m. Nancy McMullen; children: Robert Dale, Katherine Mary. AB, U. Chgo., 1936, JD, 1938; LLM, Cornell U., 1941; JSD, Yale U., 1951; DHL, Quinnipiac Coll., 1993. Bar: Ill. 1939, Oreg. 1948. Pvt. practice, Chgo., 1939-41; atty. OPA, 1941-47; mem. law faculty Willamette U., 1947—49, U. Kans., 1950-55, Yale U., New Haven, 1955—, Justus S. Hotchkiss prof., 1969-85, prof. emeritus, 1985—; dean law, prof. Haile Selassie I U., Ethiopia, 1967-69. Prof. NY Law Sch., 1985—2000. Author (with D. Hopson): Lawyers and Their Work, 1967; author: (with M. Wenglinsky) Paralegals, 1985; author: (with C. Berger and M. Tracht) Land Transfer and Finance, 5th edit., 2007; contbr. articles to profl. jours. Mem.: ABA, Oreg. Bar Assn., Conn. Bar Assn. Home: 22 Morris St Hamden CT 06517-3423 Office: Yale Law Sch PO Box 208215 New Haven CT 06520-8215 Office Phone: 203-432-4931. Business E-Mail: quintin.johnstone@yale.edu.

JOHNSTONE, ROBERT PHILIP, retired lawyer; b. Bellefonte, Pa., Dec. 1, 1943; s. B. Kenneth and Helene (Hetzel) J.; m. Susan Alice Hardy, June 22, 1968; children: Natalie, Nancy. BS with honors, Denison U., 1966; JD magna cum laude, U. Mich., 1969. Bar: Ind. 1969. Assoc. Barnes, Hickam, Pantzer & Boyd, Indpls., 1969-75, ptnr., 1976-82, Barnes & Thornburg, Indpls., 1982—2004; ret., 2004. Chmn. litigation dept. Barnes & Thornburg, 1988-89, mem. mgmt. com., 1988-89; bd. dirs. Protective Order Pro Bono Porject, 2004—; lectr., panelist legal seminars and trial advocacy programs. Sec.-treas. Contemporary Art Soc. of Indpls. Mus. Art, 1983—84; v.p., bd. dirs. Friends of Herron Gallery, Herron Sch. Art, 1981—85; bd. dirs. Eagle Creek Park Found., 2001—04. Fellow Am. Coll. Trial Lawyers (state com. 1992-97, state chair 1995-96); mem. Ind. Bar Assn., Order of the Coif, Woodstock Club (Indpls., bd. dirs. 1988-90, v.p. 1989, pres. 1990), Indpls. Art Ctr. (bd. dirs. 1991-97), Dramatic Club (Indpls.), Phi Beta Kappa, Omicron Delta Kappa. Home: 1065 W 52nd St Indianapolis IN 46228-2463 Office: Barnes & Thornburg 11 S Meridian St Indianapolis IN 46204-3535

JOHNSTONE, ROSE MAMELAK, biochemistry educator; b. Lodz, Poland, May 14, 1928; d. Jacob Shea and Esther (Rotholz) Mamelak; m. Douglas Johnstone, Aug. 9, 1953; children: Michael, Eric. BSc, McGill U., 1950, PhD, 1953. Nat. Cancer Inst. of Can. fellow Nat. Inst. for Med. Rsch., London, Strangeway Rsch. Lab., Cambridge, England, 1954-56; rsch. assoc. McGill-Montreal Gen. Hosp. Rsch. Inst., 1956-60; faculty McGill U., Montreal, 1961-97, assoc. prof. biochemistry, 1967-76, prof., 1977-97, prof. emeritus, 1997—, chmn. dept., 1980-90. Gilman Cheney chair biochemistry McGill U., Montreal, 1997—. Contbr. articles to profl. jours. Grantee Nat. Cancer Inst. Can., 1965-67, Med. Rsch. Coun. of Can., 1965-2001, NIH, 1987-90, 92-96. Fellow Royal Soc. Can. (treas. 1991-94); mem. McGill Assn. U. Tchrs. (membership sec. 1967-70, treas. 1995-96), Biol. Chemists Am., Can. Biochem. Soc. (pres. 1985-86), Internat. Assn. Women Bioscientists (sec. 1985-88). Home: 4064 Oxford Montreal PQ Canada H4A 2Y4 Office: McGill U McIntyre Med Sci 3655 Sir Wm Osler Promenade #804 Montreal PQ Canada H3G 1Y6 Office Phone: 514-398-7264. Business E-Mail: rose.johnstone@mcgill.ca.

JOHNSTONE, SALLY MAC, educational association administrator, psychology educator; b. Macon, Ga., Dec. 8, 1949; d. Ralph E. and Maxine A. J.; m. Stephen R. Tilson, 1977; 1 child, Emma. BS, Va. Poly. Inst., 1974, MS, 1976; PhD, U. N.C., 1982. Lectr. European div. U. Md., Heidelberg, Germany, 1982-84, instr. psychology College Park, 1984-89, asst. dean, 1984-86, dir. Ctr. for Instructional Telecom., 1986-89; dir. Western Coop. for Ednl. Telecom., Boulder, Colo., 1989—. Cons. Northwest Legis. Leadership Forum, Seattle, 1990, Pacific Northwest Econ. Region, Whistler, B.C., 1991, Calif. State U. System, 1993, UN Ednl., Sci. and Cultural Orgn., 2001, 02, 05, N.Mex. Higher Edn. Commn., 2002, Coun. Regional Commn., 2003, U. Alaska, 2004, 05; invited panelist U.S. Dept. Edn., Washington, 1990, 97, Aspen Inst., Washington, 1990, Pacific Northwest Econ. Region, 1991-92; presenter Pacific Rim Pub. U. Pres. Conf. Asia Found., Bangkok, Thailand, 1990, Workshops Pacific Telecom Coun., Honolulu, 1991, 99; spkr. edn. commn. states' Legislator's Workshop, Cin., 1992; meeting Nat. Assn. State Univs. & Land Grant Colls. Distance Edn. & Telecomm. Working Group, and numerous others; witness U.S. Senate Subcom. Edn., Humanities and Arts, Washington, 1991; study advisor Corp. Pub. Broadcasting, 1993; spkr. So. Assn. Schs. and Colls., 1997, Nat. Assn. State Univs. and Land Grant Colls., 1997, Asia Pacific Learning Forum, 2000-01, Hispanic Assn. Colls. and Univs., 2004, UNESCO, 2002, 2004, LearnTec, Germany, 2005; council Regional Accrediting Commns., 2000, Higher Edn. Accrediting, 2003; internat. coun. for Open & Distance Learning, 2000, 01; advisor Western Govs. U., 1996-98 Author: Lessons on Accommodations for Colleges and Rural High Schools Linking Electronically, 1996, Paring Down and Revving Up: A Companion for Campus Leaders in the Digital Era, 2006; co-author: (with Witherspoon and Wasem) Rural TeleHealth: Telemedicine, Distance Education and Informatics, 1993; editor: Learner's Guide, 2005; co-editor: (with Markwood) New Pathways to a Degree: Technology Opens the College, 1994, Distance Learner's Guide, 2005, (with Farrell and Lopes) The Role of Technology in Higher Education in North American, 1996, (with Ewell and Paulson) STUDENT Learning as Academic Currency, 2002; columnist: Syllabus, 2001-2004; editl. bd. Open Learning Journal, 2001—, Americal Journal of Distance Education Judge sci. fair U. Hills Elem. Sch., Md., 1986-89; mem. adv. com. Boulder Valley Sch. Bd., 1999; bd. trustees US Open Univ., 1998-2002; adv. com. Nat. Info. Ctr. Hispanic Edn., 1999, Consortium Advancement Pvt. Higher Edn., 1998-2001; com. co-chair Nat. Postsecondary Edn. Coop., 1998-99. Grantee Annenberg/CPB Project, 1988, 91-96, U.S. Dept. Edn., 1991, 99, Ford Found., 1991, Fund for Improvement of Postsecondary Edn., 1993, 96, Dept. Commerce Nat. Telecomms. and Info. Adminstrn., 1994, Western Assn. Schs. and Colls., 1997, Hewlett Found., 2001, 02, Lumina Found., 2004; recipient Disting. Rsch. award Nat. U. Continuing Edn. Assn., 1989, Dist. Svc. award NUTN, 2000, Lifetime Achievement award, Nat. U. Telecomms. Network, 2003 Mem. APA, Am. Assn. Higher Edn. (bd. dirs. 1998-2002). Home: 4876 10th St Boulder CO 80304-4319 Office: WICHE PO Box 9752 Boulder CO 80301 Office Phone: 303-541-0232. Business E-Mail: sjohnstone@wcet.info.

JOHNSTONE, STOWELL, former state agency administrator; Grad., U. Idaho, 1953, MA in Edn./Adminstrn., 1960. Tchr. Moscow (Idaho) High Sch., 1956-58; tchr., dir. driver edn. Moscow Sch. Dist. # 28, 1957-66; acting prin. Moscow Mid. Sch., 1958-59; prin. Moscow Jr. High, 1959-61; dir. secondary curriculum Moscow Sch. Dist., 1961-62, adminstrv. asst. to supt. schs., 1962-64; prin. Moscow High Sch., 1964-67, West Anchorage (Alaska) High Sch., 1967-70; dir. audio-visual svcs., libr. processing and TV prodn. Anchorage Sch. Dist., 1970-71, dir. secondary edn., 1971-78, asst. dep. supt. secondary sch. mgmt., 1978-81, asst. dep. supt. ednl. planning, 1981-82; chair Alaska Bd. Edn., Juneau, 1994-98; pres. Stowell and Assoc., 1982; ret. Instr. U. Idaho, 1958-60; part time supr. maintenance pers. Moscow Sch. Dist., 1963-67; part time instr. U. Alaska, Anchorage, 1956-85, Anchorage C.C.; trustee Alaska Coun. Econ. Edn., 1977-85. Active exec. com. Jr. Achievement of Alaska, 1966-85; chmn. Alaska Pub. Broadcasting Commn., 1969-83; bd. dirs. Alaskan of Yr. Com., 1979-82; v.p., mem. Alaska Repertory Theatre Statewide Bd., 1979-85; v.p. Alaska March of Dimes Bd., 1988-89. With USAF, 1953-56, col. Res. ret. Recipient Outstanding Young Men of America award, Disting. Svc. award, Moscow, 1966, Gov.'s award for Outstanding Svc. to Alaska, 1979, Disting. Svc. award Alaska Assn. Secondary Sch. Prins., 1980, Exec. of Yr. award City of Anchorage, 1980. Mem. Northwest Assn. Schs. and Colls. (chmn. Alaska com. 1973-78, pres. commn. schs. 1978-82, sec. 1983—, pres. 1991-94), Northwest Assn. of Schs. and Colls. Office Fax: 907-349-2636. E-mail: stowell@alaska.com.

JOHSON, MICHAEL PENNINGTON, finance educator, consultant; b. Chgo., Feb. 24, 1964; s. Michael Pennington Johnson and Ruth Susan Motley; m. Karen Marie Sampson, June 8, 1991; children: Langston, Devon. BS, Morehouse Coll., 1987; MS, Ga. Inst. Tech., 1987, U. Calif., Berkley, Calif., 1990; PhD, Northwestern U., 1997. Tchg. and rsch. asst. U. Calif., Berkeley, 1990; assoc. Cleve. Consulting Assocs., Mayfield Heights, Ohio, 1990—93; intern Anderson Consulting, Chgo., 1993—95; tchg. asst. Northwestern U., Evanston, Ill., 1995—96; intern Argonne (Ill.) Nat. Lab., 1996; cons. Strategic Sys. Internat., Evanston, 1996—97; assoc. prof. Carnegie Mellon U., Pitts., 1997—. Rschr. Joint Ctr. Poverty Rsch., 1999—2003; pres., v.p. location analysis sect. Informs, Hanover, Md., 2000—05; mem. alumni rev. bd. Dept. Info. Mgmt. Sys. Northwestern U., Evanston, 2004—; cons. in field. Contbr. articles to profl. jours. Bd. dirs. Highland Pk. Cmty. Devel. Corp., Pitts., 1999—2005; dir. Highland Pk. Cmty. Plan, Pitts., 2002—04. Fellow, U.S. Dept. Housing and Urban Devel., 2001—03; grantee, NSF, 2002—; scholar, AT&T, 1982—87. Mem.: Assn. Pub. Policy Analysis in Mgmt., Inst. Ops. and Rsch. Mgmt. Scis. Democrat. Avocations: jazz, reading. Office: Heinz School Carnegie Mellon Univ 5000 Forbes Ave Pittsburgh PA 15213

JOINER, JAMIE A., lawyer; BA, Westminster Coll., 1996; JD, La. State U. Law Ctr., 2000. Bar: Tex. 2000, US Dist. Ct. (so. dist. Tex.) 2001, US Supreme Ct. 2002, US Ct. Internat. Trade 2003, US Dist. Ct. (we. dist. Tex.) 2006. Assoc. Baker Hostetler, Houston. Local coord. Export Legal Assistance Network; mem. Dist. Export Coun. Named a Rising Star, Tex. Super Lawyers mag., 2006. Office: Baker Hostetler 1000 Louisiana St Ste 2000 Houston TX 77002 Office Phone: 713-646-1359. E-mail: jjoiner@bakerlaw.com.

JOINES, SHARON MELISSA BENNETT, design educator, researcher; b. Raleigh, May 5, 1970; d. Sandra Lee and Richard Archer Bennett; m. Jeffrey Allen Joines; children: Thomas Allen, Melissa Lauren. BS in Indsl. Engring., NCSU, Raleigh, 1992, MS in Indsl. Engring., 1996, PhD in Indsl. Engring., 2002. Dir. rsch. The Ergonomics Ctr. NC, Raleigh, 2002—05; asst. prof. Dept. Indsl. Design, NCSU, Raleigh, 2006—. Recipient Order Thirty and Three, NCSU; fellow. Achievements include patents pending for ergonomic interventions for sonographers. Home Phone: 919-851-9396; Office Phone: 919-513-0825. Business E-Mail: sharon_joiens@ncsu.edu.

JOISHY, SURESH K., oncologist; b. Udupi, India, Mar. 12, 1944; s. Keshav K. and Sushila K. Joishy; m. Muktha S. Joishy, June 12, 1944; children: Mahima S., Mahanth S. BS in Post Grad. Med. Edn. Rsch., U. Madras, India, 1970; Masters, Jawaharlal Inst., Pondicherry, 1970. Diplomate internal medicine, hematology, palliative medicine, oncology U. London. Rsch. asst. U. Calif., San Francisco, 1978—80; clin. assoc. prof. Ind. U., Bloomington, 1980—87; assoc. prof. King Saud U., Abha, Saudi Arabia, 1987—91; honorary lectr. radiation Royal Marsden Cancer Hosp., London, 1991—92; staff oncology dept. Cleve. Clinic Found., 1994—97; chief palliative medicine oncology dept. Kaiser Permanente, Fresno, Calif., 2000—. Editl. bd. Modern Medicine Asia, Auaza Lumpur, Malaysia, 1978—80; vis. oncologist Thames Cancer Registry, London, 1991—92. Author: Palliative Medicne Secrets, 1999. Chmn. Am. Cancer Soc., Bloomington, Ind., 1982—85; adv. mem. Bloomington City Arts Coun., 1986—87. Travel grant, Asian Pacific Congress Gastroenterology, 1980. Fellow: Am. Coll. Physicians; mem.: Am. Acad. Hospice and Palliative Medicine, Am. Soc. Oncology. Achievements include invention of two-in-one bone marrow aspiration and biopsy needle; built in assembly for stabilizing and securing intravascular needle. Avocations: Chinese brush painting, medical graphic art, poster design. Home: 165 W Athens Ave Clovis CA 93611 Office: Kaiser Permanente Med Ctr 7300 N Fresno St Fresno CA 93720 Business E-Mail: sureshk.joishy@kp.org.

JOKLIK, WOLFGANG KARL, biochemist, virologist, educator; b. Vienna, Nov. 16, 1926; s. Karl F. and Helene (Giessl) J.; m. Judith Vivien Nicholas, Apr. 9, 1955 (dec. Apr. 1975); children: Richard G., Vivien H.; m. Patricia Hunter Downey, Apr. 23, 1977. B.Sc. with 1st class honors, U. Sydney, Australia, 1948, M.Sc., 1949; D.Phil. (Australian Nat. U. scholar), U. Oxford, Eng., 1952. Australian Nat. U. research fellow, Copenhagen, 1953, Canberra, Australia, 1954-56; fellow, 1957-62; assoc. prof. cell biology Albert Einstein Coll. Medicine, Bronx, NY, 1962-65, prof. cell biology, 1965-68, Siegfried Ullmann prof. biochem. virology, 1966-68; prof., chmn. dept. microbiology and immunology Duke U. Med. Ctr., Durham, NC, 1968-92, James B. Duke Disting. prof. microbiology and immunology, 1972-92, James B. Duke prof. microbiology, 1992-96, James B. Duke prof. emeritus, 1996—. Sr. author: Zinsser Microbiology, 15th, 16th, 17th, 18th, 19th, 20th edits.; editor-in-chief Virology, 1975-93, Microbiological Rev., 1991-95; contbr. articles to profl. jours. Recipient Sr. U.S. award Alexander Humboldt Found., 1985, ICN Internat. prize for virology, 1991. Mem. NAS, Inst. Medicine of NAS, Am. Soc. Virology (pres. 1982-83), Am. Soc. Microbiology, Am. Soc. Biol. Chemists. Address: Duke U Med Ctr Dept Molecular Genetics and Microbiology PO Box 3020 Durham NC 27710-0001 Office Fax: 919-489-4433. Personal E-mail: joklikb@aol.com.

JOLAS, BETSY, composer, educator; b. Paris, Aug. 5, 1926; d. Eugene and Maria (MacDonald) J.; m. Gabriel Illouz, Aug. 27, 1949; children: Frederic, Claire, Antoine. BA, Bennington Coll., 1946; student, Conservatoire Nat. Paris, 1946. Replaced Olivier Messiaen Paris Conservatory, 1971-74, prof. advanced analysis and composition, 1975—. Prof. composition Tanglewood, 1976-77, 2006, SUNY, Buffalo, 1976, Yale U., 1979, 82, Boston U., 1985, Darius Milhaud prof. Mills Colls., Fromm prof. Harvard, 1994; resident Am. Acad. Rome, 1999; Berlin Prize fellow Am. Acad. Berlin, 2000; vis. prof. composition U. Mich., 2003-05, 05-06. Compositions include Points d'or for one saxophonist playing four saxophones and ensemble, 1982, Episode Sixiéme pour alto, 1983; Trois Duos Pour Tuba et Piano, 1983; O Wall, for wind quintet, 1976; Well Met, for ensemble, 1973; Tales of a Summer Sea, for orch., 1977, Stances, for piano and orch., 1978, Points D'Aube, for ensemble and viola solo, 1968; Preludes Fanfares Interludes Sonneries, for wind orch. and percussion, 1983; Trois Rencontres, for string trio solo and orch., 1973, Sonate á 12, for 12 voice soloists a capella, 1970; Motet II, for choir and orch., 1965; Caprice á deux voix, for soloists without accompaniment, 1978; Quatuor II for solo voice and string trio, 1964; Le pavillon au bord de la riviére, chamber opera in 4 acts, 1975; Le Cyclope, chamber opera in one act, 1986; Schliemann opera in 3 acts, 1989; Frauenleben 9 Lieder for viola and orch., 1992, Sigrancia Ballade for baritone and orch., 1995, Lumor 7 sacred lieder for saxophone and orch., 1996, Petite Symphonie Concertante for violin and orch., 1997, Quatvor VI avec clarinette, 1997, Sonate ä 8, for cello octet, 1998, Motet III, for 5 soloists, chorus and baroque orch., 1999, Trio Sopra, for clarinet, violin and piano, 2000, Concerto-Fantaisie, for piano and mixed chorus, 2001, Motet IV for soprano, flute, clarinet, violin, cello and harp, 2002; Wanderlied for cello and ensemble, 2003, others; many recs.; contbr. articles to profl. jours. Performer French Radio, Paris, 1955-65. Decorated Chevalier de la Legion d'Honneur, Officier de l'Ordre Nat. du Mérite, Commandeur des Arts et Lettres; recipient Internat. Conducting Competition prize, Besançon, 1953, Copley Found. Chgo. award, 1954, ORTF award, 1961, Am. Acad. Arts award, 1973, Grand Prix de la Music, 1974, Grand Prix de la Ville de Paris, 1981, Grand Prix de la SACEM, 1982, Koussevitsky Found. award, 1974, Prix Internat. Maurice Ravel, 1992, Personnalité de l'année, 1993, Prix SACEM de la Meilleure Création, 1994. Mem. Am. Acad. Arts and Letters, Am. Acad. Arts and Scis. Office: Conservatoire Nat Supérieur de Musique 209 Ave Jean Jaurés 75019 Paris France E-mail: betsyjolas@noos.fr.

JOLAS, PAUL M., lawyer, diversified financial services company executive; BA, Northwestern U.; JD, Duke U. Mem. Corp. Securities Group Haynes and Boone, LLP; exec. v.p., gen. counsel, corp. sec. Radiologix, Inc.; sr. regional counsel Tex. Div. KB Home; dep. gen. counsel corp. and transactions Trinity Industries, Inc., Dallas, 2006—, corp. sec., 2007—. Office: Trinity Industries, Inc 2525 Stemmons Freeway Dallas TX 75207*

JOLEY, LISA ANNETTE, lawyer, brewery company executive; b. Centralia, Ill., Mar. 30, 1958; BS magna cum laude, Murray State U., Ky., 1980; JD magna cum laude, So. Ill. U., 1983. Bar: Ill. 1983, Mo. 1984. Sr. assoc. gen. counsel litig. Anheuser-Busch Cos. Inc., St. Louis, v.p., dep. gen. counsel litig., 2000—02, v.p., dep. gen. counsel, 2002—04, v.p., gen. counsel, 2004—. Mem.: Mo. Bar Assn., Ill. State Bar Assn., St. Clair County Bar Assn., Bar Assn. Met. St. Louis, ABA, Pi Sigma Alpha. Office: Anheuser-Busch Cos Inc One Busch Pl Saint Louis MO 63118 Office Phone: 314-577-2000.*

JOLIBOIS, MARCUS, professional sports team executive; m. Diane Jolibois; children: Andrew, Connor, Scott, Luke. Grad., Gonzaga U., Spokane, Wash., 1981. Acct. Peterson, Sullivan and Co., Seattle, 1981—84; operational and fin. auditor San Diego, 1984—86; audit mgr. Levitz, Zacks and Ciceric, San Diego, 1986—94; CFO, mem. sr. exec. com. Houston Rockets, 1994—. Office: Houston Rockets Toyota Ctr 1510 Polk St Houston TX 77002*

JOLICOEUR, PAUL, molecular biologist; b. Beauceville, Que., Can., Jan. 4, 1945; s. Philippe Jolicoeur and Eva Rodrigue; m. Claudine Tremblay, Apr. 10, 1976. BA, Laval U., Que., 1964, MD, 1968, PhD, 1973. Intern Royal Victoria Hosp., Montreal, Canada, 1968—69; med. dir Lama-Kara Hosp. (SUCO), Togo, 1969—70; pvt. practice Gaspésie, Canada, 1970; postdoctoral fellow MIT, Cambridge, 1973-76; dir. lab. molecular biology Clin. Rsch. Inst. Montreal, 1976—. Contbr. articles to profl. jours. Recipient medal Lt. Gov. of Que., 1964. Mem. Med. Rsch. Coun. (study sect. 1978-81, Centennial fellow 1975-76), Nat. Cancer Inst. (study sect. 1982-84, 96-98, adv. com. on rsch. 1984-88), Royal Soc. Can. (Can.'s chair 2000). Home: 5296 Durocher Outremont PQ Canada H2V 3Y1 Office: Montreal Inst Clin Rsch 110 W Ave des Pins Montreal PQ Canada H2W 1R7 Office Phone: 514-987-5569. Office Fax: 514-987-5794. Business E-Mail: jolicop@ircm.qc.ca.

JOLIE, ANGELINA, actress; b. LA, June 4, 1975; d. Jon Voight and Marcheline Bertrand (dec. Jan. 27, 2007); m. Jonny Lee Miller, Mar. 3, 1996 (div. Feb. 3, 1999); m. Billy Bob Thorton, May 5, 2000 (div. May 27, 2003); children: (adopted) Maddox Jolie-Pitt, Zahara Marley Jolie-Pitt, Pax Thien Jolie-Pitt; (one child with Brad Pitt) Shiloh Nouvel Jolie-Pitt Student, Strasberg Theatre Inst.; Grad. in Film, NYU. Former profl. model, London, NYC, LA; good will amb. UN High Commr. for Refugees, Geneva, 2001—. Actor: (films) Lookin' to Get Out, 1982, Cyborg 2, 1993, Angela & Viril, 1993, Hackers, 1995, Without Evidence, 1995, Foxfire, 1996, Mojave Moon, 1996, Love Is All There Is, 1996, True Women, 1997, George Wallace, 1997 (Goldon Globe award for best supporting actress, 1998, nominated Emmy award outstanding supporting actress, 1998), Playing God, 1997, Gia, 1998 (Grand Jury Award for best actress, 1998, Outfest award for outstanding actress, 1998, nominated Emmy award outstanding lead actress, 1998, SAG award for best actress, 1999, Golden Globe for best actress, 1999, Golden Satellite award for best actress, 1999), Hell's Kitchen, 1998, Playing by Heart, 1998 (Nat. Bd. of Rev. award for breakthrough performance, 1998), Pushing Tin, 1999, The Bone Collector, 1999, Girl, Interrupted, 1999 (Academy Award for best supporting actress, 2000, Golden Globe award for best supporting actress, 2000, SAG Award for best supporting actress, 2000, Broadcast Film Critics award for best supporting actress, 2000), Dancing in the Dark, 2000, Gone in Sixty Seconds, 2000, Original Sin, 2001, Life or Something Like It, 2002, Lara Croft Tomb Raider: The Cradle of Life, 2003, Beyond Borders, 2003, Taking Lives, 2004, Shark Tale (voice), 2004, Sky Captain and the World of Tomorrow, 2004, Alexander, 2004, Mr. and Mrs. Smith, 2005, The Good Shepherd, 2006, A Mighty Heart, 2007, (music videos) Meat Loaf, Lenny Kravits, Antonello Venditti, The Lemonheads. Named one of 50 Most Powerful People in Hollywood, Premiere mag., 2006, 100 Most Influential People, Time Mag., 2006, Barbara Walters-10 Most Fascinating People of 2006, 100 Most Powerful Celebrities, Forbes.com, 2007; recipient ShoWest Award for supporting actress of yr., 2000, Cambodian citizenship for conservation work, King Norodom Sihamoni, 2005, Global Humanitarian award, UN Assn. USA, 2005. Office: Creative Artists Agy 9830 Wilshire Blvd Beverly Hills CA 90212*

JOLIVET, JOSELYN DEVEZ, music company executive; b. Houston, June 14, 1962; d. Joseph Lynell Jolivet and Naomi Idella Brass. BA, Tex. So. U., Houston, 1988; MA, U. Akron, Ohio, 1992. Tchg. asst. U. Akron, 1989—91; instr. Houston C.C., 1994—95; CEO, pres. Tommy Ray Prodns., Houston, 2001—. Author: When The River Rises, I Fall, 1996, Finally: My Soul Settled, 1996, Last Leaves, 2007; prodr.: Mizunderstanding, 1997, The Equation, 2000. Vol. Americorps, Houston, 1999—2000; musician, singer Chances/Red Cat Club, Houston, 2001—06. Fellow, Ohio U., 1991. Democrat. Avocations: singing, movies, travel. Home: PO Box 21264 Houston TX 77226 Office Phone: 713-222-8560.

JOLLES, BERNARD, lawyer; b. NYC, Oct. 5, 1928; s. Harry and Dora (Hirschorn) J.; m. Lenore Madison Jolles, Oct. 11, 1953 (div. Jan. 1984); children: Abbe, Jacqueline, Caroline. BA, N.Y.U., 1951; LLB, Lewis & Clark Coll., 1961. Bar: Oreg. 1963, U.S. Dist. Ct. Oreg. 1964, U.S. Dist. Ct. (no. dist.) Miss. 1968, U.S. Ct. Appeals (9th cir.) 1965, U.S. Supreme Ct. 1979. Assoc. Anderson Franklin Jones & Olsen, Portland, Oreg., 1963-68; ptnr. Franklin Olsen Bennett & Desbarsay, Portland, Oreg., 1968-79, Jolles, Sokol & Bernstein and successor firms, Portland, Oreg., 1979—, Jolles Bernstein & Garone and predecessor firms Jolles Sokol & Bernstein, Portland, Oreg., 1979—. Editor: Damages, 1974. Bd. dirs. ACLU, Portland, Oreg., 1975—. Fellow Am. Coll. Trial Lawyers; mem. Oreg. State Bar Assn. (pres. 1986-87), Am. Inns of Ct. (sr. barrister 1985—). Avocations: cooking, reading. Office: Jolles & Bernstein 721 SW Oak St Fl 2 Portland OR 97205-3712 Office Phone: 503-228-6474. E-mail: berniej@jollesbernstein.com.

JOLLES, JANET K. PILLING, lawyer; b. Akron, Ohio, Sept. 5, 1951; d. Paul and Marjorie (Logue) Kavanaugh; m. Martin Jolles, Mar. 6, 1987; children: Madeleine Sloan Langdon Jolles, Jameson Samuel Rhys Jolles. BA, Ohio Wesleyan U., 1973; JD, U. Mo., 1976; LLM, Villanova U., 1985. Bar: Pa. 1976, U.S. Tax Ct. 1976, U.S. Dist. Ct. (ea. dist.) Pa. 1976, Ohio 1996. Atty. Schnader, Harrison, Segal & Lewis, Phila., 1976-83; gen. counsel Kistler-Tiffany Cos., Wayne, Pa., 1983-95; lawyer Janet Kavanaugh Pilling Jolles & Assocs., Berea, Ohio, 1996-99; v.p. First Union Trust Co., Wilmington, Del., 1999—2002, Wachovia Trust Co., Wilmington, 2002—. Mem. Estate Planning Coun. Del., Wilmington Tax Group, Phila. Estate Planning Coun., Estate Planning Coun. Cleve., De Bankers Assn., Estate Planning Coun. Del. Mem.: ABA, Wilmington Women in Bus., Pa. Bar Assn., Phila. Bar Assn. (probate sect., tax sect.), Cuyahoga County Bar Assn., Cleve. Bar Assn., Ohio State Bar Assn., Berea Women's League, Phi Beta Kappa, Phi Delta Phi. Office: 505 Carr Rd 2d Fl Wilmington DE 19809 Home Phone: 302-594-0878. Business E-Mail: janet.jolles@wachovia.com.

JOLLEY, SAMUEL DELANOR, JR., academic administrator; b. Fort Valley, Ga., Feb. 1, 1941; s. Samuel Delanor Sr. and Mary Louise (Breazele) J.; m. Jimmye Christine Hambry, Dec. 24, 1963; children: Terena, Samuel III. BS, Ft. Valley State Coll., 1962; MS, Atlanta U., 1965; EdD, Ind. U., 1974. Tchr. math. Ballard Hudson Sr. H.S., Macon, Ga., 1962-67; instr. math. Ft. Valley (Ga.) State Coll., 1967-70, asst. prof. math., 1970-75, assoc. prof. math., 1975-82, coord. student teaching, 1980-83, chmn. divsn. edn., 1983-85; prof. math. Fort Valley (Ga.) State Coll., 1982-93, dean Sch. Arts and Scis., 1985-93; exec. dir., CEO, Atlanta Univ. Ctr., Inc., 1998—2004; pres. Morris Brown Coll., Atlanta, 1993—97, 2004—. Mem. adv. bd. Salvation Army, Atlanta, 1995-97; bd. dirs. AUC Coun. Pres.'s, Atlanta, 1993—, Atlanta Paralympics Organizing Com., 1994-97, Univ. Ctr. Ga., Atlanta, 1993—97, Univ. Cmty. Devel. Corp., Atlanta, 1993—2004; nat. bd. dirs. Fund for Improvement of Post Secondary Edn. Mem. NAACP, Am. Assn. Higher Edn., Omega Psi Phi, Sigma Pi Phi. Democrat. Methodist. Avocations: chess, swimming, tennis. Office: Morris Brown Coll 643 Martin Luther King Jr Dr N Atlanta GA 30314-4140 Office Phone: 404-739-1010. E-mail: sjolleyjr@aol.com.

JOLLIE, SUSAN BARBARA, lawyer; b. Milw., May 23, 1950; d. Harry William and Dolores Eleanor (Schlueter) J. BA, Marquette U., Milw., 1972; JD, Georgetown U., Washington, DC, 1976. Bar: DC 1976; US Ct. Appeals (DC cir.) 1985, US Ct. Appeals (8th cir.) 1991. From trial atty. to assoc. gen. counsel antitrust, litigation Civil Aeronautics Bd., Washington, 1977-83; gen. counsel SMC Internat., Washington, 1984-85; assoc. Galland, Kharasch, Morse & Garfinkle pc, Washington, 1985-87, ptnr., 1987—96; pvt. practice law Annandale, Va., 1996—. Rep. McLean Civic Assn., Va., 1991-92; pres. Nat. Women's History Mus., 2001—. Mem. Wisc. State Soc. (v.p. 1980—), Hummer Woods Civic Assn. (v.p. 2006-07, pres. 2007-), Internat. Aviation Club, Aero Club. Home: 7503 Walton Ln Annandale VA 22003-2558 Office Phone: 703-354-8450. Personal E-mail: sjollie@verizon.net.

JOLLIMORE, TROY, philosophy professor, poet; Student in Philosophy, Dalhousie U., Halifax, Nova Scotia; BA, U. King's Coll.; PhD, Princeton U., 1999. Former asst. prof. dept. Philosophy Georgetown U.; former assoc. prof., dept. Philosophy U. Cal. Davis; external faculty fell., Humanities Ctr. Stanford U., 2006—. Author: (book of poetry) Tom Thomson in Purgatory, 2006 (Nat. Book Critics Circle award for Poetry, 2006); contbr. articles to numerous profl. jours. Office: Stanford Humanities Ctr Stanford U 424 Santa Teresa Street Stanford CA 94305-4015 E-mail: tjollimore@csuchico.edu.*

JOLLOFF, NILDA ELIZABETH, artist, educator; b. Bronx, Sept. 2, 1952; d. Frank Martinez, Jr. and Carmen (Del Arroyo) Martinez; m. William F. Jolloff, Jr., Aug. 30, 1969; children: Sandra Buckland, William F. III, Katherine Wagoner. A in Arts & Scis. cum laude, Blue Ridge CC, 2001; BA with distinction, Mary Baldwin Coll., 2003. Owner Frame It Yourself/You're the Framer, Matawan, NJ, 1979—92; art instr. Staunton/Augusta Fine Art Ctr., Va., 1995—2001, Blue Ridge CC, Weyers Cave, 1998—; art tchr. Shelburne Mid. Sch., Staunton, 2003—; after sch. site dir. Augusta County Parks & Recreation, Verona, 1995—2002; tchr. asst. Mary Baldwin Coll., Staunton, 2003. Art cons. L&S Framing & Stained Glass, Staunton, 1992—. Solo exhibition, Magical Realism, Augusty County Library, Fishersville, 2001, Blue Ridge CC, Weyers Cave, 2001, Works on Paper/Cultural Absorption, Hunt Gallery, Staunton, 2003, exhibited in group shows at The Virtual Art Gallery, Blue Ridge C.C., Weyers Cave, Va., 2000, The Anthem Project: Remembrance of 9/11, U. Va., 2002, Print Making Art Exch., U. Va./Mary Baldwin Coll., 2003, Art in the Park, Staunton, 2005, Transitions: Seeds of Change, 2005, juried show, Hunt Gallery, Staunton, 2002, 2003. Sec. Student Fine Art Assn. Mary Baldwin Coll., Staunton, 2002—03; advisor Talented & Gifted Programs Staunton City Schs., Staunton, 2003—, found. Art For Humanity, 2004—. Recipient Honors Scholar award, Phi Theta Kappa, Cath. U. Am., 1999, Best Show Mixed Media, Augusta County, Fishersville, 2003, Best Show Oils, 2004, 1st Place Mixed Media, 2004. Mem.: Nat. Mus. Women Arts, Nat. Mus. Am. Indian, Nat. Edn. Assn., Staunton Augusta Art Ctr., Phi Theta Kappa Internat. Honor Soc. (Three Star Chpt. award 2000). Avocations: painting, drawing, printmaking, reading, writing. Home: 301 Thompson St Staunton VA 24401

JOLLS, CHRISTINE MARGARET, law educator; b. White Plains, NY, Oct. 1, 1967; d. Robert Talcott and Cecelia (Thurmaier) Jolls; m. Ranier Gavlilk; 2 children. BA in English & Quantitative Economics, Stanford U., 1989; JD, Harvard U., 1993; PhD in Economics, MIT, 1995. Bar: Mass. 1997. Jud. clk. to Judge Stephen F. Williams U.S. Ct. Appeals DC Cir., 1995—96; jud. clk. to Justice Antonin Scalia US Supreme Ct., 1996—97; asst prof. law Harvard Law Sch., Cambridge, Mass., 1994—95, 1997—2001, prof., 2001—, named vice dean scholarship & intellectual life, 2003; prof. of law Yale Law Sch., New Haven, 2006. Contbr. articles to univ. law reviews Stanford U., Harvard U., U. Chicago, 1998—2001; mem. editl. bd. Am. Law and Economics Rev., New Haven, 1999—; reporter Restatement of Employment Law, Phila., 2001—; fellow Mind/Brain/Behavior Interfaculty Initiative Harvard U.; vice dean Harvard Law Sch's for Scholarship and Intellectual Life, 2003—04. Dir. Prog. in Law and Economics Nat. Bureau of Economic Rsch. 2006-, (co-dir. 2003-2006). Dean's teaching award 2003, John M. Olin Prize in Law and Economics. Fellow: Nat. Bur. Econ. Rsch.; mem.: Phi Beta Kappa. Office: Yale Law Sch 127 Wall St New Haven CT 06520 Office Phone: 617-496-4643, 203-432-1958. Office Fax: 617-495-4299. Business E-Mail: christine.jolls@yale.edu.*

JOLLY, BRUCE DWIGHT, manufacturing executive; b. Wheeling, W.Va., Aug. 27, 1943; s. Edward and Martha Elizabeth (Glass) J.; m. Alice Marie O'Beirne, May 25, 1974 (div. Sept. 1997); children— Mara O'Beirne, Brock Thomas; m. Anne Caroline Rist, Dec. 22, 2001. AB, Dartmouth Coll., 1965; MBA, U. Va., 1967. Systems engr. IBM Corp., Richmond, Va., 1967-68; fin. analyst Keystone Consol. Industries, Peoria, Ill., 1970-73; contr. HON Industries, Inc., Muscatine, Iowa, 1973-76, sec., treas., 1976-79; v.p. fin. Hawkeye Steel Products, Inc., Waterloo, Iowa, 1979-83, Cosco, Inc., Columbus, Ind., 1983-90; chief fin. officer Kiel Bros. Oil Co. Inc., Columbus, Ind., 1990-96; v.p. fin. Riverton Investment Corp., Winchester, Va., 1996—2004; ptnr. Tatum, LLC, Charlottesville, 2004—. With AUS, 1968-70, Vietnam. Decorated Bronze Star. Mem. Rotary, Phi Kappa Psi. Republican. Presbyterian. Office: Tatum LLC 977 Seminole Trl PMB 335 Charlottesville VA 22901-2824

JOLLY, BRUCE O., lawyer; BA, Univ. NC, 1969, JD, 1973. Bar: NC 1973, Va. 1974, DC 1976, Md. 1988. Washington counsel Credit Union Nat. Assn.; fed. regulatory counsel Independent Bankers Assn.; atty. Shook, Hardy & Bacon LLP, Washington; ptnr., banking, fin. svcs. practice Venable LLP, Washington, 2003—. Contbr. articles in field. Mem.: ABA, Md. Bar Assn., DC Bar Assn., Va. Bar Assn., NC Bar Assn. Office: Venable LLP 575 7th St NW Washington DC 20004 Office Phone: 202-344-4818. Office Fax: 202-344-8300. Business E-Mail: bojolly@venable.com.

JOLLY, DANIEL EHS, dental educator; b. St. Louis, Aug. 25, 1952; s. Melvin Joseph and Betty Ehs (Koehler) Jolly; m. Paula Kay Haas, 1972 (div.); 1 child, Farrell. BA in Biology and Chemistry, U. Mo., Kansas City, 1974, DDS, 1977. Diplomate Am. Bd. Special Care Dentistry. Resident in hosp. dentistry VA Med. Ctr., Leavenworth, Kans., 1977-78; pvt. practice Newcastle, Wyo., 1978-79; asst. prof. U. Mo., Kansas City, 1979-87; chief restorative dentistry Truman Med. Ctr., Kansas City, 1979-87; dir. dental oncology Trinity Luth. Hosp., 1982-87; assoc. prof., dir. gen. practice residency program Ohio State U., Columbus, 1987—, prof., dir. gen. practice residency program, 1993—. Dir. Honduras Clinic Project, 1992—; bd. dirs. Rinehart Found. U. Mo. Dental Sch., Kansas City, 1985—87; cons. Lee's Summit (Mo.) Care Ctr., 1984—87, Longview Nursing Ctr., Grandview, 1986—87; sec. Combined Hosp. Dental Staff, Columbus, 1989—90, v.p., 1990—91, pres., 1991—92. Author: (manual) Hospital Dental Hygiene, 1984, Hospital Dentistry, 1985, OSU Manual Hospital Dentistry, 1989—, (booklet) Nursing Home Dentistry, 1986, Dental Oncology, 1986. Mem. profl. adv. coun. Easter Seal Soc., 1986—92, sec. bd. dirs. Easter Seal Rehab. Ctr. Columbus, 1990—93, mem. regional coun. Kansas City, 1985—87; pres. Health Profls. Serving Humanity. With U.S. Naval Sea Cadet Corps, 1998—99. Recipient Alumni Achievement award in dentistry, U. Mo., Kansas City, 1995. Fellow: Pierre Fauchard Acad., Am. Coll. Dentistry, Acad. Dentistry Handicapped (pres. 1992), Acad. Gen. Dentistry, Acad. Dentistry Internat., Am. Soc. Dentistry Children, Am. Assn. Hosp. Dentists (regional v.p. 1993—, sec., pres.-elect 2002—03, pres. 2003—), Am. Soc. Geriatric Dentistry; mem.: ADA, Am. Bd. Special Care Dentistry (pres. 2004—, diplomate 2004), Ohio Dental Assn. (Humanitarian award 1998), Internat. Soc. Oral Oncology, S.W. Oncology Group, Fedn. Spl Care Orgns. Dentistry (chmn. 1992—93), Greater Kansas City Dental Soc., Internat. Assn. Dentistry handicapped (pres. 1994—96, past pres. 1996—98, editor 1998—), Magna Charta Barons Club. Avocations: photography, skiing, scuba diving, swimming, horses. Home: 1601 W Fifth Ave 118 Columbus OH 43212-2310 Office: Ohio State U Coll Dentistry PO Box 182357 305 W 12th Ave Columbus OH 43218-2357 Home Phone: 614-329-4178. E-mail: djolly82552@cs.com.

JOLLY, E. GRADY, federal judge; b. Oct. 3, 1937; BA, U. Miss., 1959, LLB, 1962. Trial atty. NLRB, Winston-Salem, NC, 1962—64; asst. U.S. atty. No. Dist. Miss., 1964—67; trial atty. Dept. Justice Tax Div., Washington, 1967—69; pvt. practice Jolly, Miller & Milam, Jackson, Miss., 1969—82; judge US Ct. Appeals (5th cir.), Jackson, 1982—. Office: James O Eastland US Courthouse 245 E Capitol St Rm 202 Jackson MS 39201*

JOLLY, JEFFREY RUSSELL, musician, educator; b. Amarillo, Tex., Oct. 19, 1953; s. M Russell and Joyce Doctor Jolly; m. Diane Marie Knobl, July 6, 1974; children: Joshua Russell, Rebecca Anne. MusB in Classical

Guitar Performance, U. So. Calif., 1978; MusM in Edn., U. N.Mex, 1988. Cert. K- 12 music tchr. N.Mex. Dept. Edn., 1981. Dir. bands Belen H.S. and Mid. Sch., N.Mex., 1981—; dir. music Covenant Presbyn. Ch., Albuquerque, 1981—. Clinician, music ensembles, N.Mex., 1987—; guitar and vocal performer, 1973—; coord. participatory murder mysteries St. James Hotel, Cimarron, 1987—; workshop clinician Presbyn. Assn. Musicians, Albuquerque, 1996—99; tchr., clinician Hummingbird Music Camp, Jemez Springs, 1987—; guitar accompanist De Profundis Men's A Cappella Choral Ensemble, Albuquerque, 2000—03. Composer: (stage musical) Earthstar, (incidental music) See Mommy Cry, (choral anthem) A Word to the Wise, And Ransom Captive Israel, (choral setting) Be Thou My Vision, (incidental music) A Company of Pilgrims; author: (play) The Winter People, The Wrong Game, All That Glitters, The Ace of Hearts, A Murderous Past Time; composer: (choral) The Birth of God (A Service of Carols); musician: (compact disc) Reverberations, Vol. 1, Reverberations, Vol. 2; composer: (incidental music) Frontiers of Faith (Commn., Gen. Assembly of the Presbyn. Ch. (USA), 1994, 1994); musician: (compact disc) The Green Man; composer: (incidental music) Dandelion Wine, (stage musical) Posada de Amor, (choral anthem) Hymn to the Holy Spirit, (incidental music) The Boys Next Door, (television theme music) News 101, News 101Nambe Award Show (Rocky Mountain Emmy Award, 1993), Adventure Rio. Advocate, fund raiser Health Care for Homeless, Albuquerque; various coms. Presbyn. Ch., 1979—2005. Recipient Tchr. of the Yr., Belen Consolidated Schs., 1991—92, N.Mex. Quality in Edn. award, N.Mex. Rsch. and Study Coun., U. N.Mex., 2001; grantee, McCune Found., 1993; Composers Fellowship with Alice Parker, 2005. Mem.: Presbyn. Assn. Musicians, N.Mex. Music Educators Assn. Dist. 6 (band v.p. 2005—), Music Educators Nat. Conf., Phi Kappa Phi (Quality in Edn. award 2001). Presbyterian. Avocations: beer brewing, fly fishing, travel, gardening. Home: 100 Vissing Pl Los Lunas NM 87031 Office: Belen Consolidated Sch Dist 520 N Main Belen NM 87002 Home Phone: 505-865-6177; Office Phone: 505-966-1619. Office Fax: 505-966-1650; Home Fax: 505-865-6177. Personal E-mail: vonjolly@netzero.com. E-mail: jollyj@belen.k12.nm.us.

JOLLY, MEENAKSHI, rheumatologist; arrived in U.S., 1994; m. Neeraj Jolly. MBBS, Med. Coun. of India, India, 1991; MS in clin. profl., U. Chgo., 2004. Cert. Am. Bd. Internal Medicine (cert. in rheumatology), Clin. rsch. trng. program U. Chgo., 2003. Sect. chief, rheumatology Christ Med. Ctr., Chgo., 2003—06; asst. prof. clin. medicine U. Ill., Chgo.; asst. prof. Rush U. Med. Ctr., Chgo., 2006—. Cons., tchg., clin. rsch., mentoring Christ Med. Ctr., Oaklawn, Ill., 2003—. Mem.: Arthritis Found., Lupus Found., Am. Coll. of Rheumatology. Achievements include research in rheumatic issues; quality of life in lupus. Home Phone: 773-288-2605; Office Phone: 312-563-2924. Personal E-mail: meenakshijolly_1@hotmail.com. E-mail: meenaksh_jolly@rush.com.

JOLLY, THOMAS ALAN, journalist; b. Massena, NY, Mar. 26, 1955; s. Thomas Daniel and Betty Ruth (Christensen) J.; m. Linda Klein; children: Sarah, Rachel, Claire, Russell Nitzberg, Joelle Nitzberg. BA in Journalism, Ohio Wesleyan U., 1977. Legis. asst. Ohio State Senator Charles Butts, Columbus, 1977-78; social worker Columbus Met. Cmty. Action Orgn., 1978-79; reporter The Delawre (Ohio) Gazette, 1979-82; reporter/copy editor The Annapolis (Md.) Capital, 1982-86; copy editor/dep. sports editor The Pitts. Press, 1986-92; assoc. sports editor The Pitts. Post-Gazette, 1993; copy editor/asst. sports editor The New York Times, NYC, 1993—2000, asst. sports editor, 2000—03, sports editor, 2003—. Presbyterian. Avocations: photography, bicycling. Office: New York Times 229 W 43rd St New York NY 10036 Office Fax: 212-556-5848. Business E-Mail: jolly@nytimes.com.

JOLOWSKY, CHRISTENE MARIE, pharmaceutical executive, director; m. Michael R. Stenger, Aug. 20, 1983; children: Claire N., Nora C. BS, MS, U. Minn., Mpls. Sys. dir. pharmacy HealthEast Care Sys., St. Paul, 2006—; dir. pharmacy United Hosp., St. Paul, 1998—2006. Scout leader Girl Scouts, Eagan, Minn., 2002—. Mem.: Minn. Soc. Health Sys. Pharmacists (pres. 1999—2000, bd. dirs. 2004—, Hallie Bruce Meml. award 2005). Home Phone: 651-326-7657; Office Phone: 651-326-7657.

JONAS, GARY FRED, healthcare executive; b. NYC, Apr. 26, 1945; s. Otto and Hilde (Levy) Jonas; m. Rosalyn Ethel Levy; children: Lauren, Rachel. BS in Ops. Rsch., Columbia U., 1966; MBA, Harvard U., 1968. Mgmt. cons. Fry Cons., Washington, 1968-69; divsn. dir. Univ. Rsch. Corp. Ctr. Human Svcs., Chevy Chase, Md., 1970-73, exec. v.p., 1973-75, pres., CEO, 1975-85, chmn., CEO, 1985-88, also bd. dirs.; pres., COO The Earle Palmer Brown Cos., Bethesda, Md., 1988-93, also bd. dirs.; pres., CEO 20/20 Laser Ctrs., Inc., Bethesda, 1993-97, also bd. dirs.; exec. v.p., dir. TLC Laser Eye Ctrs., Inc., Bethesda, 1997-2000; mng. ptnr. Venture Philanthropy Ptnrs., Inc., Reston, Va., 2000—02; CEO Strategic Planning Advisors, Inc., 2002—; pres. Alase Laser Hair Removal Ctrs., 2002—05; CEO Med. Body Sculpting, 2006—. Faculty assoc. Johns Hopkins U., 1999—; adj. faculty Am. U., Washington. Contbr. articles to profl. jours. Mem.: Young Pres.'s Orgn. (exec. com., chmn. Washington metro chpt. 1987—88), Washington Bd. Trade, Am. Soc. Tng. and Devel., Conf. Bd., Nat. Contract Mgmt. Assn., Profl. Svcs. Coun. (past bd. dirs., v.p.), Inst. Mgmt. Cons. (cert.), Woodmont Country Club, Harvard Club. Home: 6716 Melody Ln Bethesda MD 20817-3115 Office Phone: 301-469-1945. E-mail: gary@jonas.com.

JONAS, HARRY S., medical education consultant; b. Kirksville, Mo., Dec. 3, 1926; s. Harry S. and Sarah (Laird) J.; m. Connie Kirby, Aug. 6, 1949; children— Harry S., III, William Reed, Sarah Elizabeth. BA, Washington U., St. Louis, 1949, MD, 1952. Intern St. Luke's Hosp., St. Louis, 1952-53; resident Barnes Hosp., St. Louis, 1952-56; practiced medicine specializing in ob-gyn., Independence, Mo., 1956-74; prof. ob-gyn, chmn. dept. ob-gyn Truman Med. Center; asst. dean U. Mo-Kansas City Sch. Medicine, 1975-78, dean, 1978-87, med. edn. cons., 2000—, spl. cons. to the dean; asst. v.p. med. edn. AMA, Chgo., 1987-2000; sr. ptnr. DJW Assocs., LLC, 2003—. Mem. Independence City Council, 1964-68; mem. Jackson County (Mo.) Legislature, 1973-74. Mem. ACOG (pres. 1986-87), Ctrl. Assn. Obstetricians and Gynecologists, Assn. Profs. Gynecology and Obstetrics, Assn. Am. Med. Colls., A.C.S., AMA, Mo. Med. Assn., Jackson County Med. Soc., Kansas City Gynecol. Soc., Chgo. Gynecol. Soc. Home: 207 NW Spruce St Lees Summit MO 64064-1430 Office: U Mo-Kansas City Sch Medicine 2411 Holmes St Kansas City MO 64108-2741 also: 838 E High St Ste 261 Lexington KY 40502 Business E-Mail: jonash@umkc.edu. E-mail: hsj@djwassociates.com.

JONAS, HOWARD S., communications executive; BA economics, Harvard U. Founder, pres. Jonas Publishing Corp, 1979—; founder, chmn. IDT Corp., Newark, 1990—, treas., 1990—2002, pres., 1991—96, CEO, 1991—2001; chmn. IDT Telecom., 1999—2002; co-chmn. IDT Media, 2002—; chmn. Net2Phone, 2001—04, vice-chmn., 2004—06, chmn., 2006—. Bd. dir. Starz Media LLC, Starz Media Holdings LLC, Starz Fgn. Holdings LLC, 2006—. Office: c/o IDT Corp 520 Broad St Newark NJ 07102*

JONAS, JIRI, chemist, educator; b. Prague, Czechoslovakia, Apr. 1, 1932; arrived in US, 1963; s. Frantisek and Jirlna (Vondrak) Jonas; m. Ana M. Masiulis, June 1, 1968. BSc, Tech. U. Prague, 1956; PhD, Czechoslovak Acad Sci., 1960; D honoris causa (hon.), U. Rio de Janeiro, 2003. Research assoc. Inst. Organic Chemistry, Czechoslovak Acad. Sci., Prague, 1960-63; vis. scientist, dept. chemistry U. Ill., Urbana, 1963-65, from asst. to assoc. prof., 1966-72, prof., 1972—2001, prof. Ctr. for Advanced Study, 1996-2001, prof. emeritus, 2001—, sr. staff mem. Materials Research Lab., 1970-93, dir. sch. chem. scis., 1983-93, dir. Beckman Inst. Advanced Sci. and Tech., 1993—2001, dir. emeritus, 2001—. Mem. editl. bd. Jour. Magnetic Resonance, 1975—2000, Jour. Chem., 1980—83, Jour. Chem. Physics, 1986—89, Accts. Chem. Rsch., 1990—93, Ann. Rev. Phys. Chemistry, 1991—95; contbr. articles to profl. jours. Recipient U.S. Sr. Scientist award, Alexander von Humboldt Found., 1988; Alfred P. Sloan fellow, 1967—69, J. S. Guggenheim fellow, 1972—73, Sr. scholar, U. Ill., 1985—88. Fellow: AAAS, Am. Phys. Soc., Am. Acad. Arts and Scis.; mem.: NAS, Materials Rsch. Soc., Am. Chem. Soc. (assoc. editor. Jour. Am. Chem. Soc., Joel Henry Hildebrand award 1983), Am. Philos. Soc., NBTC Club (Naples, Fla.). Office: Univ of Ill 166 Roger Adams Lab 600 S Mathews Urbana IL 61801 Business E-Mail: j-jonas@uiuc.edu.

JONAS, JOAN (JOAN AMERMAN EDWARDS), artist; b. NYC, July 13, 1936; m. Gerald Jonas, 1959. BA in art history, Mt. Holyoke Coll., 1958; studied sculpture, Boston Mus. Fine Arts, 1958—61; MFA in sculpture, Columbia U., 1965. Joined faculty MIT, Cambridge, Mass., 2000, prof. dept. architecture, prof., acting dir. visual arts program. Exhibitions include Aspects de l'art actuel presentes par la Galerie Sonnabend, Musee Galliera, Paris, 1973, Stage Sets, Inst. Contemporary Art, U. Pa., Phila., 1976, Three Tales, Documenta 6, Kassel, Germany, 1977, Joan Jonas: The Juniper Tree, Stedelijk Mus., Amsterdam, 1979, Whitechapel Art Gallery, London, 1979, Music, Sound, Language Theater, Stedelijk Mus., Amsterdam, 1981, Double Lunar Dogs, Contemporary Arts Mus., Houston, 1981, Other Realities - Installations for Performance, 1981, Upside Down and Backwards, Documenta 7, Kassel, Germany, 1982, He Saw Her Burning, DAAD Galerie, Berlin, 1984, Revolted by the thought of known places.Sweeney Astray, Kunst-Werke, Berlin, 1992, Joan Jonas: Works 1968-1994, Stedelijk Mus., Amsterdam, 1994, Props: Works 1994-1997, Pat Hearn Gallery, NYC, 1997, In the Shadow a Shadow, 1999, Drawings, Reinhard Hauff Gallery, Stuttgart, Germany, 2000, Joan Jonas: Film and Video Work, 1968-76, Dia Ctr. for Arts, NYC, 2000, Joan Jonas: Performance, Video, Installation, 1968-2000, Galerie der Stadt, Stuttgart, Germany, 2000—01, Neue Galerie fur Bilden Kunst, Berlin, 2003, Joan Jonas: Video Retrospective, Mus. Carillo Gil, Mex. City, 2003, Joan Jonas: Five Works, Queens Mus. Art, NYC, 2003 (Award for Best Exhbn. of Time Based Art, Internat. Assn. Art Critics/USA, 2005), Lines in the Sand, Rosamund Felsen Gallery, Santa Monica, 2003, The Renaissance Soc., Chgo., 2004, The Shape, the Scent, the Feel of Things, 2004, film and videography, Wind, 1968, Paul Revere, 1971, Mirror Check, 1971, Vertical Roll, 1972, Organic Honey's Visual Telepathy, 1972, Duet, 1972, Left Side Right Side, 1972, Songdelay, 1973, Three Returns, 1973, Barking, 1973, Two Women, 1973, Disturbances, 1974, Merlo, 1974, Glass Puzzle, 1974, May Windows, 1976, Good Night, Good Morning, 1976, I Want to Live in the Country (And Other Romances), 1977, Upside Down and Backwards, 1981, Double Lunar Dogs, 1983, He Saw Her Burning, 1983, Big Market, 1984, Brooklyn Bridge, 1988, Volcano Saga, 1989. Recipient Polaroid Award for Video, 1987, Maya Deren Award for Video, Am. Film Inst., 1988, Hyogo Prefecture Mus. Modern Art Prize, Japan Internat. Video Art Festival, Anonymous Was a Woman Award, 1998. Office: MIT Visual Arts Program 265 Massachusetts Ave N51-315 Cambridge MA 02139

JONAS, JOHN FRANCIS, lawyer; b. St. John's, Que., Can., May 3, 1950; s. Hans and Lora Jonas; m. Sheila Coplan, Sept. 26, 1977; children: Benjamin, David. BA, Clark U., 1972; JD, Cornell U., 1976. Bar: D.C. 1976. Atty. HHS, Washington, 1976-78; legis. asst. Office Congresswoman Liz Holtzman, Washington, 1978-80; legis. dir. Office Congressman Bob Shomansky, Washington, 1980-81; tax counsel Com. on Ways and Means U.S. Congress, Washington, 1981-86; ptnr. Patton Boggs LLP, Washington, 1986—, chmn. Public Policy dept. & Regulatory dept. Office: Patton Boggs LLP 2550 M St NW Washington DC 20037-1350 Office Phone: 202-457-5624. Office Fax: 202-457-6315. Business E-Mail: jjonas@pattonboggs.com.

JONAS, RICHARD ANDREW, medical educator; b. Adelaide, South Australia, Nov. 28, 1951; came to US, 1982; s. Lyall Richard Jonas; m. Dianne E. Wearne, Apr. 12, 1980 (div. May 1996); children: Andrew William, Michael Richard; m. Katherine Vernot, Nov. 6, 1999; 1 child, Nicole Sofia. MBBS with honors, U. Adelaide, 1974; MA, Harvard U., 1994. Gen. surgery resident Royal Melbourne Hosp., Australia, 1975-79; cardiac surgery resident Green Ln. Hosp., Auckland, New Zealand, 1980-82; resident in cardiac surgery Brigham & Women's Hosp., Boston; surg. fellow Brigham and Women's Hosp., Boston, 1982-83; chief resident in cardiac surgery Children's Hosp., Boston, 1983-84; prof. surgery Harvard Med. Sch., Boston, 1994—; chief of cardiac surgery Children's Hosp., Boston, 1994—2004; chief cardiovasc. surgery, co-dir. Congenital Heart Inst., Children's Nat. Med Ctr., Washington, 2004—. Author: Cardiopulmonary Bypass in Neonates and Infants, 1994, Comprehensive Surgical Management of Congenital Heart Disease, 2004. Fellow ACS, Soc. of Neurosci.; mem. Am. Assn. of Thoracic Surgery v.p., Soc. of Thoracic Surgery, Am. Surg. Assn. Episcopalian. Avocations: skiing, mountain trekking. Office: Children's Nat Med Ctr 111 Michigan Ave NW Washington DC 20010 E-mail: rjonas@cnmc.org.

JONAS, SARAN, neurologist, educator; b. NYC, June 24, 1931; s. Myron and Margaret (Wurmfeld) J.; m. Ruth Haber, Sept. 16, 1956; children: Elizabeth Ann, Frederick Jonathan. BS, Yale U., 1952; MD, Columbia U., 1956. Diplomate Am. Bd. Psychiatry and Neurology, Am. Bd. Internal Medicine. Intern Bellevue Hosp., NYC, 1956-57, resident and fellow in medicine and neurology, 1957-62; practice medicine specializing in neurology NYC, 1964—; from clin. instr. to assoc. prof. clin. neurology NYU Sch. Medicine, 1964-77, prof. clin. neurology, 1977—, acting chmn. dept. neurology, 1987-91. Assoc. dir. neurology NYU Hosp., 1970-87, dir., 1987-91, dir. electroencephalography, 1969-94; acting dir. neurology Bellevue Hosp., N.Y.C., 1987-91, assoc. dir., 1991—, dir. electroencephalography, 1994—. Served with USN, 1962-64. N.Y. State fellow in rheumatic diseases, 1962-64 Mem. Am. Acad. Neurology, Assn. for Rsch. in Nervous and Mental Diseases, Am. Heart Assn. (Stroke Coun., Epidemiology Coun.), Am. Epilepsy Soc. Office: 530 1st Ave New York NY 10016-6402

JONAS, STEVEN, preventive medicine physician, author; b. NYC, Nov. 22, 1936; s. Harold Jacob and Florence Jane (Kyzor) J.; m. Josephine Gear, June 19, 1964 (div.); m. Linda Sue Friedman, Nov. 23, 1971 (div.); children: Jacob Henry, Lillian Sara. BA cum laude, Columbia Coll., 1958; MD, Harvard U., 1962; MPH, Yale U., 1967; MS, NYU, 1997. Diplomate Am. Bd. Preventive Medicine-Pub. Health. Intern Lenox Hill Hosp., NYC, 1962—63; postdoctoral rschr. Univ. Coll. London and London Sch. Econs., 1963—65, resident in preventive medicine and pub. health, 1965—67; dist. health officer NYC Dept. Health, 1967—68, dir. ambulatory care planning and devel., 1969; dir. dept. social medicine Morrisania City Hosp., Bronx, NY, 1969—71; asst. prof. Albert Einstein Coll. Medicine, Bronx, 1969—71; lectr. Mt. Sinai Sch. Medicine, NYC, 1969—89, asst. prof. dept. cmty. medicine, 1971—74; coord. ambulatory svcs. Univ. Hosp., 1971—74, assoc. prof. dept. cmty. and preventive medicine, 1974—83, prof. dept. preventive medicine, 1983—; prof. grad. program in pub. health Stony Brook U. Sch. Medicine, NY, 2004—; attending physician Nassau County Med. Ctr., East Meadow, NY, 1973—86. Adj. assoc. prof. Columbia U. Sch. Architecture, 1977-79; cons. dept. medicine Winthrop-U. Hosp., Mineola, N.Y., 1979-93; mem. N.Y. State Bd. Medicine, 1979-88; adj. assoc. prof. med. edn. Tex. Coll. Osteo. Medicine, Ft. Worth, 1980-85; adj. prof. legal edn. Touro Coll. Sch. of Law, Huntington, N.Y., 1998—. Author: Quality Control of Ambulatory Care: A Task for Health Departments, 1977, Medical Mystery: The Training of Doctors in the United States, 1978, Triathloning for Ordinary Mortals, 1986, rev., 1999, 2d edit. 2006, An Introduction to the U.S. Health Care System, 5th edit., 2003, The New Americanism, 1992, Take Control of Your Weight, 1993, Regular Exercise: A Handbook for Clinical Practice, 1995, The Essential Triathlete, 1996, Talking About Health and Wellness with Patients, 2000; editor, co-author: Health Care Delivery in the United States, 1977, 2d edit. 1981 (Book of Yr. award Am. Jour. Nursing 1982), 3rd edit., 1986, co-editor, 1999, 2002, Health Promotion and Disease Prevention in Clinical Practice, 1996; co-author: Pacewalking: The Balanced Way to Aerobic Health, 1988, The "I Don't Eat (But I Can't Lose)" Weight-Loss Program, 1989, Just the Weigh You Are, 1997, Help Your Man Get Healthy, 1999, 30 Secrets of the World's Healthiest Cuisines, 2000; chief editor: (Springer series) Health Care and Society, 1976-79, Medical Education, 1978-2000; assoc. editor Preventive Medicine, 1983-2005; mem. editl. bd. ACSM's Health & Fitness Jour., 1999—, Am. Jour. Preventive Medicine, 1987-99; book rev. editor Am. Jour. Preventive Medicine, 1991-92; mem. editl. bd. Am. Med. Athletic Assn. Quarterly, 1988—, columnist, 1999—, editor-in-chief (J), 2002—; staff writer, Am. TRI, 2002-04; columnist USA Triathlon Life, 2006—; contbr. articles to profl. jours.; reviewer in field. Sr. advisor U.S. Preventive Svcs. Task Force, 1984-89. Recipient Duncan Clark Lifetime Achievement award, Assn. Prevention Tchg. and Rsch., 2006. Fellow APHA, Am. Coll. Preventive Medicine (com. chmn. 1979-82), N.Y. Acad. Medicine (med. edn. com. 1983-92), N.Y. Acad. Scis. (elected); mem. AMA, Am. Hosp. Assn. (life), Profl. Ski Instrs. Am. (cert. level I), Assn. Tchrs. Preventive Medicine (pres. 1977-78), Am. Mensa, Phi Beta Kappa. Democrat. Jewish. Avocations: bicycling, pacewalking and running, weightlifting, triathlon competition, skiing. Home: 105 Washington Ave Port Jefferson Station NY 11777-2003 Office: Stony Brook U Sch Med Stony Brook NY 11794 Office Phone: 631-444-2147. Business E-Mail: steven.jonas@stonybrook.edu.

JONAS, TINA WESTBY, federal agency administrator; BA, Ariz. State U.; MA, Georgetown U. Sr. budget examiner, intelligence br. nat. security divsn. U.S. Dept. Def., Washington, 1991—95, dep. under sec. fin. mgmt., 2001—02; mem. appropriations com., def. subcom. U.S. Ho. Reps., Washington, 1995—2001; asst. dir. fin., CFO FBI, Washington, 2002—04; under sec. (comptr) , CFO U.S. Dept. Def., Washington, 2004—. Recipient Disting. Pub. Service medal, US Dept. Def. Office: US Dept Def 1100 Defense Pentagon Washington DC 20301

JONASON, WILLIAM A., lawyer; b. 1958; BA in Econ. with honors, St. Olaf Coll., 1980; JD with distinction, Univ. Iowa, 1983. Bar: Minn. 1983. Law clk., Chief Judge Donald Lay US Ct. of Appeals (8th cir.), 1983—84; ptnr., corp. group; co-chair, closely held businesses group Dorsey & Whitney LLP, Mpls., and mem., policy com. Adj. prof. law Hamline Law Sch., 1988—89, St. Thomas Law Sch., 2004. Sr. articles editor Iowa Law Rev., 1982—83. Bd. dir. Volunteer Connection, Rochester Pub. Libr. Found., Rochester Pub. Sch. Found., YMCA Camp Olson. Mem.: Minn. Bar Assn., Hennepin Co. Bar Assn. Office: Dorsey & Whitney LLP Ste 1500 50 S Sixth St Minneapolis MN 55402-1498 Office Phone: 612-340-2600, 612-492-6111. Office Fax: 612-340-7800. Business E-Mail: jonason.bill@dorsey.com.

JONASSEN, JAMES O., architect; b. Aberdeen, Wash., July 23, 1940; s. James E. and Marjorie E. (Smith) J.; m. Patricia E. Glen, June 9, 1958 (div. Oct. 1975); m. Marilyn Joan Kampa, June 11, 1977; children: Christian A., Steven E. BArch, U. Wash., 1964; MS in Architecture, Columbia U., 1965. Registered architect Ala., Alaska, Ariz., Calif., Colo., Fla., Ga., Idaho, Ill., Kans., La., Minn., Mo., Mont., Nebr., Nev., N.Mex., N.C., N.C., Ohio, Okla., Oreg., S.D., Tex. Wash., Utah., Wis., D.C., Del. Mass. Miss., N.H., N.Y., R.I., Vt., P.R., British Columbia, Can. Designer NBBJ Group, Seattle, 1965-70, ptnr., 1970—; CEO NBBJ West, 1983-96, mng. ptnr., 1997—. Bd. dirs. Health Insights Found; assoc. prof. Sch. Architecture U. Hawaii. Prin works include Bettelle Meml. Lab., Richland, Wash., 1965 (lab of yr. award 1968), Heath Profl. Bldg., 1970, Children's Orthopedic Hosp., Seattle, 1972 (AIA Honor award 1976), St. Mary's Hosp., Surg. Pavilion, Rochester, Minn., 1982, St. Vincent Med. Office Bldg., Portland, Oreg., 1983, Scottsdale Meml. Hosp. N., Ariz., 1984, Seattle VA Hosp., 1985, Stanford U. Hosp., 1986, St. Joseph Host. Med. Ctr., 1988, Providence Med./ Ctr., Seattle, 1990 (AIA Merit award), David Grant Med. Ctr., Fairfield, Calif., 1986 (USAF Honor award 1989, Spl. citation DOD 1988, Type i Honor award USAF 1989, Excellence in Design award DOD 1991), Alaska Native Med. Ctr., 1997, Kangbuk Med. Ctr., Seoul, Korea, 1998, Capital Coast Health Med. Ctr., Wellington, New Zealand, 2000. Bd. dirs. Sch. Zone Inst., 1990—94, Health Facilities Rsch. and Edn. Project, 1991—98, Swedish Med. Ctr. Found., 1993—2003; pres.bd. Architecture and Children project, 1990; mem. vis. com. U. Washington Sch. Medicine, 2001—; mem. bd. dirs. Seattle Architectural Found, 1986, 2000—05. Recipient Seattle Newsmaker Tomorrow award, Time Mag., 1978, Modern Health Care award, Swedish Med. Ctr., 1997—2000, Seattle Archtl. Found. Bd., 2000—; fellow, Naramore Found., 1969; scholar Columbia U. scholar, 1964. Fellow AIA (chmn. steering com. 1983-85, nat. com. architecture for health, mem. Nat. Life Cycle Task Force 1977, bd. dirs. Seattle chpt. 1985-87, Modern Healthcare award 1998); mem. Sr. Coun. Archs. (pres. 1999, 2000), Wash. Athletic Club, Columbia Tower Club, Rotary. Office: NBBJ 223 Yale Ave N Seattle WA 98109 Business E-Mail: jjonassen@nbbj.com.

JONASSON, RALPH GEORGE, chemist, researcher; b. Hamilton, Ont., Can., July 8, 1957; s. Werner and Cecilia (Liedtke) Jonasson. BSc, McMaster U., Hamilton, 1980; PhD, U. Western Ont., London, Can., 1986. Postdoctoral fellow McMaster U., Hamilton, 1986-87, rsch. assoc., 1987-88; rsch. officer Alta. Rsch. Coun., Edmonton, Can., 1989-98; rsch. chemist Vulcan Performance Chems., Columbus, Ga., 1998—2002. Author: (book chpt.) Advances in Lignocellulosics Characterization, 1999; inventor in field; contbr. articles to profl. jours. Mem. AAAS, Internat. Assn. Water Quality (reviewer 1998-2001), Chem. Inst. Can. (chair Edmonton local sect. 1996, past chair Edmonton local sect. 1997), Am. Chem. Soc., Geochem. Soc. Avocations: history, philosophy, silviculture, wine appreciation. Home: 62 Juanita Dr Hamilton ON Canada L9C 2G3

JONCKHEERE, ALAN MATHEW, physicist; b. Howell, Mich., Feb. 12, 1947; s. August Peter and Elizabeth Gertrude (Nash) Jonckheere; m. Barbara Jean Minter, Aug. 16, 1969; children: Jessica Susan, Laura Jean and Amanda Jean (twins). BS, Mich. State U., 1969; MS, U. Wash., 1970, PhD, 1976. Instr. physics dept. Fermi Nat. Accelerator Lab., Batavia, Ill., 1976—78, staff physicist, 1978—, assoc. dept. head meson dept., 1981—83, assoc. dept. head exptl. areas, 1983—84, coord. Beams group, 1984—85, accelerator divsn. exptl. support dept., 1985—88, rschr. divsn. D0 dept., 1989—. Researcher elem. particle physics Stanford Linear Accelerator Ctr., Lawrence Berkeley Lab., Calif. Contbr. papers to physics publs. Office: Fermi Natl Accelerator Lab PO Box 500 Batavia IL 60510-0500 Business E-Mail: Jonckheere@fnal.gov.

JONDAHL, TERRI ELISE, importing and distribution company executive; b. Ukiah, Calif., May 6, 1959; d. Thomas William and Rebecca (Stewart) J. AA in Bus. Adminstrn., Mendocino Coll., 1981; BA in Adminstrn. and Mgmt., Columbia Pacific U., 1993. Office systems analyst County of Mendocino, Ukiah, 1980-83; micro systems analyst Computerland of Annapolis, Md., 1983-84; controller Continental Mfg. Inc., Nacogdoches, Tex., 1984-87, mktg. mgr., 1987-89, dir. sales and mktg., 1989-95; exec. v.p., chief oper. officer CAB Inc., Oakwood, Ga., 1995—2002; CEO Cab Inc., 2002—. Co-author: National Federation of Business & Professional Women Local Organization Revitalization Plan, 1989. Mem. adv. bd. Gwinnett County Tax Commn. Mem.: NAFE, Am. Bus. Women's Assn., Ukiah Bus. and Profl. Women (pres. 1981—82), Nacogdoches Bus. and Profl. Women (pres. 1987—88), Tex. Fedn. Bus. and Profl. Women (state pres. 1994—95), Com. of 200 Orgns., Gwinnett Chamber Chmn.'s

Club (bd. dirs. 2002—), Leadership Gwinnett, Hall County C. of C., Nacogdoches County C. of C. Home: 6009 Lanier Heights Cir Buford GA 30518 Office: CAB Inc 4161 Chamblee Rd Oakwood GA 30566-3518

JONES, A. ELIZABETH, corporate communications specialist, former federal agency administrator; b. Munich, May 6, 1948; d. William Charles Jones and Sara Demarest (Ferris); m. Thomas Anthony Homan, 1977 (div.); m. Donald Andrew Ruschman, 2000; 2 children. BA in history, Swarthmore Coll., 1970; studied Arabic, in Beirut, Tunis and Cairo, 1975—77; in Internat. Rels., Boston U., 1986. Joined Fgn. Svc., 1970; fgn. svc. post Kabul, Afghanistan, 1971—72; pub. affairs officer Near East and South Asia Bur., 1972—73; polit. officer Cairo, 1973—75, Amman, Jordan, 1977—79; dep. prin. officer U.S. Interests Sect., Baghdad, Iraq, 1979—80; dep. chief mission Islamabad, Pakistan, 1988—92; Lebanon desk officer, 1981—83; dep. dir. for Lebanon, Jordan, Syria, and Iraq, 1983—84; head econ./comml. sect. US Mission, West Berlin, 1985—88; dep. chief mission US Embassy, Bonn, Germany, 1992—93; exec. asst. to sec. US Dept. State, Washington, 1993—94, US amb. to Rep. of Kazakhstan, 1995—98, prin. dep. asst. sec. Bur. Near Eastern Affairs Washington, 1998—2000; sr. advisor Caspian Basin Energy Diplomacy, 2000—01; asst. sec. for European & Eurasian affairs US Dept. State, Washington, 2001—05; exec. v.p. APCO Worldwide, Washington, 2005—. Bd. dirs. AE Jones LLC, 2005—. Office: APCO Worldwide 700 12th St NW Ste 800 Washington DC 20005 Office Phone: 202-478-3559. Business E-Mail: bjones@apcoworldwide.com.

JONES, ABBOTT C., investment company executive; b. Lexington, Ky., Aug. 14, 1934; s. John Catron and Lois (Sauters) J.; m. Carol Donahue, June 29, 1957; children: Cynthia, Alison, Hilary. BA, Principia Coll., 1956; MBA, Harvard U., 1958. Salesman Carnation Co., 1959-60; account exec. Benton & Bowles, NYC, 1960-63; with Ogilvy & Mather, NYC, 1963-77, sr. v.p., dir., 1973-77; sr. v.p., gen. mgr. Foote, Cone & Belding, NYC, 1977-82; pres. Foote, Cone & Belding, Associated Communications Cos., NYC, 1982-86; pres., chief operating officer Foote, Cone, Belding Communications, Inc., NYC, 1986-89; pvt. cons. practice Greenwich, Conn., 1989-90; founder, mng. dir. AdMedia Ptnrs. Inc., NYC, 1990—. Served with U.S. Army, 1958-59. Mem.: Boca Grande, Belle Haven. Office: 19th Flr 444 Madison Ave New York NY 10022-6903 Business E-Mail: ajones@admediapartners.com.

JONES, AIDAN DREXEL, lawyer; b. Wilmington, Del., Dec. 17, 1945; s. Richard Leonard and Dorothy Drexel (Walsh) J.; m. Kathleen Dellert, Aug. 19, 1972; 4 children. BA, Wesleyan U., 1967; JD, Georgetown U., 1974. Bar: D.C. 1975, U.S. Supreme Ct. 1984, Md. 1996. Law clk. U.S. Dist. Ct., Washington, 1974—75; assoc. Edward Greensfelder Jr. P.C., Washington, 1975—77, Haight, Gardner, Poor & Havens, Washington, 1977—83; ptnr. Finley, Kumble, Wagner, Heine, Underberg, Manley, Myerson & Casey, Washington, 1983—87, Laxalt, Washington, Perito & Dubuc, Washington, 1988—90, Washington, Perito & Dubuc, Washington, 1990—91, Graham & James, Washington, 1991—95; pvt. practice, 1995—. Contbr. articles to profl. jours. Mem. nat. alumni com. Wesleyan U., Middletown, Conn., 1987-89, 1967 class agt., 1985-92; trustee River Road Unitarian Ch., 1992-94; co-treas. Sidwell Friends Sch. Parents Assn., 1995-97, v.p., 1997-98, pres. 1998-99. Lt. USN, 1968-71. Mem. ABA (vice chmn. aviation and space law com. 1985-91, mem. DC estate planning coun.). Office: 1320 19th St NW Ste 300 Washington DC 20036 Office Phone: 202-293-2386. Personal E-mail: ajones2506@aol.com.

JONES, ALAN KENT, investment company executive; b. Plainfield, NJ, July 5, 1961; s. Horatio Gates and Audrey Irma Jones; m. Ashley Anne Garrett, Sept. 26, 1992; children: Megan, Caitlin. AB, Harvard U., Cambridge, Mass., 1983; MBA, Harvard U., Boston, 1987. Banker high yield 1st Boston, NYC, 1987—93; coverage officer fin. sponsors Morgan Stanley, NYC, 1993—96, head European leveraged fin. London, 1997—2000, head global leveraged fin. NYC, 2000—02, head global fin. sponsor group, 2002—04, head corp. fin., 2004—06, co-head pvt. equity, 2006—. Pres. bd. trustees Brearley Sch., NYC, 2006—; bd. dirs. Cmtys. in Schs., Alexandria, Va., 2003—, Franklin & Eleanor Roosevelt Inst., Hyde Park, NY, 2003—. Mem.: Phi Beta Kappa. Avocations: reading, music, art, wine, travel. Home: 90 East End Ave 21A New York NY 10028 Office: Morgan Stanley 1585 Broadway New York NY 10028

JONES, ALAN PORTER, JR., food manufacturing executive; b. Milw., Feb. 27, 1925; s. Alan Porter and Eleanor Pratt (Bright) J.; m. Jean Drummond, Sept. 12, 1953; children: Richard, Susan, Cynthia, Alexandra. BA cum laude, Harvard U., 1948, MBA, 1950. With Jones Dairy Farm, Ft. Atkinson, Wis., 1950—, asst. treas., 1953-61, treas., 1961-74, v.p., treas., 1974-93, bd. dirs. Pres. Uncle Josh Bait Co., 1978—2002; bd. dirs. Johnson Bank. Bd. dir. Dwight Foster Pub. Libr., 1952-87, PDQ Corp., 1967-94, Wis. Livestock and Meat Coun., 1981-97, Ft. Atkinson C. of C., 1985-88; mem. Ft. Atkinson Sch. Bd., 1968-69, Wis. Gov.'s Adv. Com. on Internat. Trade, 1981-97, Wis. Internat. Trade Coun., 1997-2003, Wis. Citizens Environ. Coun., 1980-84, Wis. Radioactive Waste Policy Coun., 1984-87; trustee Ripon Coll., Wis., 1974-77; bd. dirs. Wis. Nature Conservancy, 1992-95. With inf. U.S. Army, 1943-45. Decorated Bronze Star, Combat Inf. badge. Mem.: Internat. Crane Found., Nat. Audubon Soc., Nature Conservancy. Republican. Home: 433 Adams St Fort Atkinson WI 53538-1401 Office: Jones Dairy Farm PO Box 808 Fort Atkinson WI 53538-0808

JONES, ALEX S., reporter, writer; b. Greeneville, Tenn., Nov. 19, 1946; m. Susan E. Tifft, Sept. 21, 1985. BA, Washington and Lee U., 1968. Editor Greeneville (Tenn.) Sun, 1978-83; press reporter N.Y. Times, 1983-92; host On the Media Nat. Pub. Radio, 1993-97; host, exec. editor Media Matters PBS, 1995—; Eugene C. Patterson prof. Practice Journalism Duke U., 1998—2000. Sr. fellow Media Studies Ctr., 1996-97; dir. Joan Shorenstein Ctr. on the Press, Politics, and Pub. Policy, Harvard U., 2000—. Author: (with Susan E. Tifft) The Patriarch: The Rise and Fall of the Bingham Dynasty, 1991, The Trust: The Private and Powerful Family Behind The New York Times, 1999. Recipient Pulitzer prize for specialized reporting, 1987; Nieman fellow, 1981-82. Home: Apt 61 1 Waterhouse St Cambridge MA 02138-3612 Business E-Mail: alex.jones@harvard.edu.

JONES, ALICE SAMUELS, elementary education educator, reading specialist; b. Fayetteville, NC, Mar. 20, 1931; d. Jerry Meyer and Maggie Lee (Graham) Samuels; m. Thomas Roosevelt Jones, Jr., Oct. 29, 1954; children: Michelle S. Jones, Thomas R. III. BS in Elem. Edn., Hampton U., Va., 1952; MEd in Reading, Boston U., 1958. Elem. tchr. Carver Elem. Sch., Richmond, Va., 1952-56, Charles Houston Elem. Sch., Alexandria, Va., 1956-58, Greenleaf Elem. Sch., Washington, 1958-60, Blow Elem. Sch., Washington, 1961-65; reading specialist Reading Clinic, Eaton Sch., Washington, 1965-67, Langdon, Plummer, Bacchus, Janney Elem. Sch., Washington, 1967-71, Green Elem. Sch., Washington, 1971-93. Writer: Competency Based Curriculum Guide K-12, 1982-93; editor Silver Tongues, 1985-86, Green Sch. News, 1990-93; assoc. editor Ten Talks, 1988-89. Docent Nat. Mus. Am. History. Named Tchr. of Yr. Edn. Inst., Washington, 1975; recipient Competency Based Curriculum Exemplary award D.C. Pub. Schs., 1979, Plaque D.C. Reading Coun. Internat. Reading Coun., Washington, 1990, Grant, D.C. Pub. Schs., 1985. Mem. ASCD, NAACP, Am. Assn. Ret. Persons, African Am. Women's Assn., Internat. Reading Assn., Internat. Comm. In Reading (pres. 1992-93), DC Columbia Reading Coun. (rec. sec. 1992-93), Silver Tongues Club (pres.), Pi Lambda Theta (pres. 1984-85, plaque 1984). Democrat. Mem. Plymouth Congregation. Avocations: swimming, reading, gardening, travel. Home: 824 Kennedy St NE Washington DC 20011-2731

JONES, ALLAN, medical research organization executive; BS in Biology, Duke Univ.; PhD in Genetics and Develop. Biology, Washington Univ. Sch. Medicine. Post-doctoral tng. U. Pa.; various scientific and mgmt. positions Avitech Diagnostics, Rosetta Inpharmatics, Merck and Co.; with Allen Inst. for Brain Sci., Seattle, 2003—, dir., Allen Brain Atlas project, 2004—06, chief scientific officer, 2006—. Office: Allen Inst for Brain Sci 551 N 34th St Seattle WA 98103 Office Fax: 206-548-7000.*

JONES, ALLEN, history educator, archivist; b. Andalusia, Ala., Aug. 14, 1930; s. Arthur G. and Pearl Fryar Jones; m. Grace Humphrey Preiss, Apr. 25, 1953; children: Allen W., Pamela Gail Saia, Jeffrey Preiss. BS, Auburn U., Montgomery, Ala., 1951, MA, 1953; PhD, U. Ala., University, 1964. Instr. Ala. Polytechnic Inst., Auburn, Ala., 1952—53, U. Md., Crailshim, Germany, 1954—56; grad. tchg. asst. U. Ala., Toscaloosa, 1957—59, asst. prof. Montgomery, 1959—60, Furman U., Greenville, SC, 1960—66; prof., archivist Auburn U., Montgomery, 1966—91; ret., 1991. Author: (book) Auburn U. Through the Years 1856-1977, 1977; contbr. articles. Bd. dirs. Auburn U. Fed. Credit Union, 1970—73; mem. Ala. Records Commn., 1958—91, Ala. Hist. Commn., 1966—70, Auburn Housing Authority, 1980—82. Col. US Army, 1953—56, Germany. Grant, Nat. Endowment for Humanities, 1969. Democrat. Bapt. Avocations: fishing, boating. Home: 602 Homewood Dr Auburn AL 36830

JONES, ANDREW ZIMMERMAN, editor, writer; s. Donnie Ray Jones and Nancy Jo Zimmerman. BA in Physics, Wabash Coll., Crawfordsville, Ind., 1999. Math. specialist Project SEED, Detroit, 1999—2004; math content devel. editor CTB/McGraw-Hill, Indpls., 2004—; physics guide About.com, Anderson, Ind., 2006—. Sr. patrol leader Boy Scouts of Am., Troop 273, 1992—93. Recipient Harold Q. Fuller Prize in Physics, Wabash Coll. Physics Dept., 1998. Mem.: Calvin W. Prather Masonic Lodge #717, Mensa (treas. 2001—02). Avocations: literature, gaming. Home Phone: 765-606-5894; Office Phone: 317-205-0579. Personal E-mail: azj@azjones.info.

JONES, ANDRUW RUDOLF, professional baseball player; b. Willemstad, Curacao, The Netherlands, Apr. 23, 1977; Outfielder Atlanta Braves, 1996—. Named to Nat. League All-Star Team, 2000, 2002—03; recipient Nat. League Gold Glove Award, 1998—2005, Gold Glove award, 1998—2004, 2006, Hank Aaron award, 2005, Silver Slugger award, 2005. Office: Atlanta Braves PO Box 4064 Atlanta GA 30302 Fax: 404-614-1391.

JONES, ANITA KATHERINE, computer scientist, educator; b. Ft. Worth, Mar. 10, 1942; d. Park Joel and Helene Louise (Voigt) Jones; m. William A. Wulf, July 1, 1977; children: Karin, Ellen. AB in Math., Rice U., Houston, 1964; MA in English, U. Tex., 1966; PhD in Computer Sci., Carnegie Mellon U., Pitts., 1973, PhD (hon.) in Sci. and Tech., 2000, DSc (hon.), Duke U. Programmer IBM, Boston, Washington, 1966-69; assoc. prof. computer sci. Carnegie-Mellon U., Pitts., 1973-81; founder, v.p. Tartan Labs. Inc., Pitts., 1981-87; freelance cons. Pitts., 1987-88; prof., head computer sci. dept. U. Va., Charlottesville, 1988-93, prof., 1997—, univ. prof., 1998—, Lawrence A. Quarles prof. engring. and applied sci., 1999; dir. def. rsch. and engring. Dept. Def., Washington, 1993-97. Mem. Def. Sci. Bd., Dept. Def., 1985-93, 98—; mem. sci. adv. bd. USAF, 1980-85; governing bd. NSF, vice-chair governing bd., 1998-2004; bd. dirs. Sci. Applications Internat. Corp., InQTel; trustee Mitre Corp., 1989-93, chair Va. Rsch. and Tech. Adv. Commn., 1999-2002, Commonwealth of Va. Advs. Commn.; mem. corp. Charles Stark Draper Labs., 1999—; bd. dirs. BBN Techs. Editor: Perspectives on Computer Science, 1977, Foundations of Secure Computation, 1971. Recipient Air Force Meritorious Civilian Svc. award, 1985, Medal for Disting. Pub. Svc. Dept. of Def., 1996, Disting. Svc. award Computing Rsch. Assn., 1997, Augusta Ada Lovelace award, Assn. Women in Computing, 2004. Fellow IEEE (Founders medal 2007), AAAS, Assn. Computing Machinery (editor-in-chief Transactions on Computer Sys. 1983-91), Am. Acad. Arts and Scis.; mem. NAE, MIT Corp., Sci. Found. Ireland (bd. dirs. 2000-03), Sci. Found. Ariz. (bd. dirs. 2006—), Sigma Xi. Avocation: gardening. Office Phone: 434-982-2224. Business E-Mail: jones@virginia.edu.

JONES, ARTHUR FREDERICK, art university administrator, educator; b. Queens, NY, Dec. 20, 1945; s. Arthur and Theresa (Schnabel) Jones; m. Crystal Hui-Shu Yang, Oct. 4, 2000; children: Mark Bennett, Meredith Lynn, Leo Wen-Shu. BA, SUNY, New Paltz, 1967; MA, Case-Western Res. U., 1970, PhD, 1974. Lectr. dept. art history Case-Western Res. U., Cleve., 1970; lectr. fine arts dept. John Carroll U., University Heights, Ohio, 1970—71; lectr. Cleve. State U., 1970; lectr. dept. art history and edn. Cleve. Mus. Art, 1971; instr., asst. prof., assoc. prof. dept. art U. Ky., Lexington, 1971—93; dir. U. Ky. Ctr. Contemporary Art, 1984—93, Art Other Side St. Gallery, Cin., 1987—90; chair, prof. dept. art Radford U., Va., 1993—2003; curator modern and contemporary art, co-curator Kolla Landwehr Found. collection Huichol art Radford U. Art Mus., 1998—2003; chair, prof. dept. art U. ND, Grand Forks, 2003—, dir. u., art collections, 2005—. Humanities cons. Ky. Humanities Coun., Frankfort, 1978; mem., bd. dirs. Endowment Appalachian Artists, Lexington, 1983—86; traveling scholar Appalachian Ctr. Traveling Scholars Program, Lexington, 1983—87; v.p. Folk Art Soc. Ky., Lexington, 1983—92; assoc. Appalachian Studies Ctr. U. Ky., Lexington, 1990—93; scholar in residence Pollock-Krasner Ho. and Study Ctr., East Hampton, NY, 1992—93; mem. com. to establish guidelines for coll. and univ. galleries and museums Southeastern Coll. Art Conf., 1999—2000; nominating com. Coll. Art Assn., 2007—. Author: The Art of Paul Sawyer, 1976, Audrey Flack: Love Conquers All, 1996, Adolf Dehn: Works on Paper from the Radford University Art Museum Collection, 2003, Kentucky Tradition in American Landscape Painting, 1983, Introduction to Art, 1992; co-author: Ibram Lassaw: Deep Space and Beyond, 2002, Radford University Art Museum: Selections from the Permanent Collection, 1999, The Kentucky Painter: From the Frontier Era to the Great War, 1981; regional editor Ky., New Art Examiner, Chgo., 1990—93; exhibitions include NOTORO Internat. Art Symposium, Gniew Castle, Poland, 1995, Elaine Benson Gallery, Bridgehampton, NY, 1994, Huntington Mus. Art, WV (Exhbn. award, 1992), Chautauqua Art Assn. Galleries, Chautauqua Instn., NY (Exhbn. award, 1991); curator (exhibitions) U. Ky. Art Mus., 1981, Owensboro Mus. Fine Art, 1983, Art Mus. Western Va., Roanoke, 1996. Mem. Greater Grand Forks Marketing Svcs. Partnership Adv. Bd., 2003—07; bd. dirs. Ibram Lassaw Found., 2006. Radford U. Found. award for Creative scholar, 2002, Project grantee, Ky. Arts Commn., 1980, Spl. Exhibitions grantee, Nat. Endowment Arts, 1980, Pub. Humanities Program grantee, Ky. Humanities Coun., 1985, Project grantee, Ky. Arts Coun., 1992. Mem.: Nat. Coun. Art Adminstrs., Nat. Assn. Schs. Art and Design, Southeastern Coll. Art Assn., Nat. Art Edn. Assn., Mid. Am. Coll. Art Assn., Coll. Art Assn. Avocations: travel, collecting art. Home: 6525 Woodcrest Rd Grand Forks ND 58201 Office: U ND PO Box 7099 Grand Forks ND 58202 Home Phone: 701-772-0692; Office Phone: 701-777-2907. Office Fax: 701-777-2903. Business E-Mail: art.jones@und.nodak.edu.

JONES, BARBARA ELLEN, neurologist, educator; b. Phila., Dec. 19, 1944; d. Charles and Ella (Yeager) J.; m. John Gordon Galaty, Aug. 12, 1972; 1 child, James Gordon. BA, U. Del., 1966, MA, 1969, PhD, 1971. Rsch. assoc., asst. prof. U. Chgo., 1972-77; assoc. prof. dept. neurology and neurosurgery McGill U., Montreal, 1977-82, assoc. prof., 1982-88, prof., 1989—. Vis. lectr. U. Nairobi, Kenya, 1974-75; vis. scientist Oxford U., Eng., 1984-85; vis. prof. U. Geneva, 1991-92, 98-99. Contbr. articles to profl. jours. Postdoctoral fellow Coll. de France, Paris, 1970-72. Mem.: Am. Neurosci. Soc., Sleep Rsch. Soc. Avocations: horseback riding, skiing. Home: 97 Arlington Ave Westmount PQ Canada H3Y 2W5 Office: McGill Univ 3801 Univ St Montreal PQ Canada H3A 2B4 Office Phone: 514-398-1913. Business E-Mail: barbara.jones@mcgill.ca.

JONES, BENJAMIN ANGUS, JR., retired agricultural engineering educator, science administrator; b. Mahomet, Ill., Apr. 16, 1926; s. Benjamin Angus and Grace Lucile (Morr) J.; m. Georgeann Hall, Sept. 11, 1949; children: Nancy Kay Jones-Kepple, Ruth Ann Jones-Sommers. BS, U. Ill., 1949, MS, 1950, PhD, 1958. Registered profl. engr., Ill. Asst. prof., asst. ext. engr. U. Vt., Burlington, 1950-52; instr., agrl. engr. U. Ill., Urbana, 1952-54, asst. prof., agrl. engr., 1954-58, assoc. prof., agrl. engr., 1958-64, prof., agrl. engr., 1964-92, prof. emeritus, 1992—, assoc. dir., agrl. exptl. sta., 1973-92; assoc. dir. emeritus, 1992—, U. Ill., Urbana, 1992. Cons. various Ill. Drainage Dists., 1958—. Co-author: (textbook) Engineering Application in Agriculture, 1973; contbr. articles to Jour. Soil & Water Conservation, Encyclopedia Britannica, Agrl. Engring., Transactions of ASAE, Proceedings of ASCE, Soil Sci. Soc. Am. Proceedings, Crops and Soils, Jour. Hydrology, Water Resources Bulletin. Merit badge examiner Boy Scouts Am., Burlington, 1950-52; lay mem. Cen. Ill. Con. United Meth. Ch., 1978-81. With USN, 1944-46. NSF fellow. Fellow Am. Soc. Agrl. Engrs. (bd. dirs., trustee); mem. Soil and Water Conservation Soc., Am. Soc. for Engring. Edn., Sigma Xi, Gamma Sigma Delta, Alpha Epsilon. Home: 2012B Eagle Ridge Ct Urbana IL 61802-8617

JONES, BEVERLY ANN MILLER, nursing administrator, retired patient services administrator; b. Bklyn., July 14, 1927; d. Hayman Edward and Eleanor Virginia (Doyle) Miller; m. Kenneth Lonzo Jones, Sept. 5, 1953 (dec.); children: Steven Kenneth, Lonnie Cord. BSN, Adelphi U., 1949. Chief nurse regional blood program ARC, NYC, 1951-54; asst. dir., acting DON M.D. Anderson Hosp. and Tumor Inst., Houston, 1954-55; asst. DON Sibley Meml. Hosp., Washington, 1959-61; assoc. dir. nursing svc. Anne Arundel Gen. Hosp., Annapolis, Md., 1966-70; asst. adminstr. nursing Alexandria Hosp., Va., 1972-73; v.p. patient care svc. Longmont United Hosp., Colo., 1977-93; pvt. cons., 1993-99; ret. Instr. ARC, 1953-57, chmn. nurse enrollment com. D.C. chpt., 1959-61; mem. adv. bd. Boulder Valley Vo.-Tech. Health Occupations Program, 1977-80; del. nursing adminstrs. good will trip to Poland, Hungary, Sweden and Eng., 1980. Contbr. articles to profl. jours. Mem.-at-large exec. com. nursing svc. adminstrs. sect. Md. Nurses' Assn., 1966-69; bd. dir. Meals on Wheels, Longmont, 1978-80, Longmont Coalition for Women in Crisis, Applewood Living Ctr., Longmont; mem. utilization com. Boulder (Colo.) Hospice, 1979-83; mem. task force on nat. commn. on nursing Colo. Hosp. Assn., 1982, mem. coun. labor rels., 1982-87; mem. U. Colo. Task Force on Nursing, 1990; vol. Champs program St. Vrain Valley Sch. Dist., 1986—, Prestige Plus program Longmont United Hosp., 1999—. Named Outstanding Vol. of Yr., St. Vrain Valley Sch. Dist., 1986—2004. Mem. Am. Orgn. Nurse Exec. (chmn. com. membership svc. and promotions, nominee recognition of excellence in nursing adminstrn.), Colo. Soc. Nurse Exec. (dir. 1978-80, 84-86, pres. 1980-81, mem. com. on nominations 1985-86, Outstanding Vol. of Yr. 2002). Home: 853 Wade Rd Longmont CO 80503-7017

JONES, BILL T., dancer, choreographer; b. Bunnell, Fla., Feb. 15, 1952; life ptnr. Arnie Zane (dec. 1988). Student, SUNY, Binghampton, 1970; PhD (hon.), Bard Coll., 1996; PhD (hon.), Art Inst. of Chicago, Bard Coll., Columbia Coll., The Juilliard Sch., Swarthmore Coll., SUNY Binghamton. Co-founder Am. Dance Asylum, 1973; co-founder, artistic dir. Bill T. Jones/Arnie Zane Dance Co., 1982—. Author: Last Night on Earth, 1995; choreographer, soloist Negroes for Sale, 1973, Track Dance, 1974, Pas de Deux for Two, 1974, Across the Street, 1975, Everybody Works/All Beasts Count, 1976, WhosedebabedoIlabedoll, 1977, De Sweet Streak to Loveland, 1977, The Runner Dreams, 1978, Stories, Steps and Stomps, 1978, Progresso, 1979, Echo, 1979, Naming Things Is Only the Intention to Make Things, 1979, Floating the Tongue, 1979, Monkey Run Road, 1979, Blauvelt Mountain, 1980, Sisyphus, Act I and II, 1980, Open Spaces, 1980, Secret Pastures, 1984, History of Collage, 1988, D-Man in the Waters, 1989, Dances, 1989, Last Supper at Uncle Tom's Cabin/The Promised Land, 1991, Love Defined, 1991, Aria, 1992, Last Night on Earth, 1992, Fête, 1992, Achilles Loved Patroclus, 1993, War Between the States, 1993, Still/Here, 1994, We Set Out Early.Visibility Was Poor, 1997, Spring Awakening, 2006 (Tony award best choreography, 2007), dir., choreographer (Operas) New Year, 1990, Mother of Three Sons, Lost in the Stars; dir.(with Rhodessa Jones): Perfect Courage, 1990. Named an Irreplaceable Dance Treasure, Dance Heritage Coalition, 2000; recipient Creative Artists Public Svc. award, 1979, NY Dance and Performance award, choreographer/creator, 1986, Dorothy B. Chandler Performing Arts award, 1991, Izzy award, 2001, Dorothy & Lillian Gish prize, 2003, Wexner Prize, Wexner Ctr. for Arts, 2005, Lucille Lortel award, outstanding choreographer, 2006, OBIE award for sustained excellence in music, 2007; MacArthur fellowship, 1994. Office: Bill T Jones/Arnie Zane Co 27 W 120th St #1 New York NY 10027 Office Phone: 212-426-6655. Office Fax: 212-426-5883. Business E-Mail: info@billtjones.org.*

JONES, BLAIR ANTHONY, lawyer; b. Ponape, Micronesia, Nov. 17, 1965; s. Charles William and Martha Ann Jones; m. Jones Marisela Ana, Oct. 16, 2004. BA, Franklin & Marshall Coll., Lancaster, Pa., 1988; JD, Lewis & Clark Coll., Portland, Oreg., 1992. Bar: Kans. 1992, Maine 1996, Mass. 2004, US Dist. Ct. (Kans.) 1992, US Dist. Ct. (Maine) 1996. Ptnr. Caffey, Kieffer & Jones, Manhattan, Kans., 1992—93, Jones & Bernstein, Augusta, Maine, 1997—99, Friedman Gaythwaite Wolf & Leavitt, Portland, 2001—; staff atty. Regional Pub. Defender's Office, Junction City, Kans., 1993—95; assoc. Weary, Davis, Henry, Streubing & Troup, Junction City, Kans., 1996, O'Donnell & Lee, Waterville, Maine, 1999—2001; atty., pvt. practice Jones Law Office, Lewiston, Maine, 1996—97. Mem.: ATLA, ABA (vice chair comml. transp. com. 2004—), Def. Rsch. Inst. Avocations: music, guitar, singing. Office: Friedman Gaythwaite Wolf Leavitt 6 City Ctr Portland ME 04112 Office Phone: 207-761-0900. Office Fax: 207-761-0186. Business E-Mail: bjones@fgwl-law.com.

JONES, BOB, III, academic administrator; b. 1939; m. Beneth Jones; 3 children. BA, MA, Bob Jones U.; D (hon.), Pillsbury Bapt. Bible Coll., San Francisco Bapt. Theological Seminary, Maranatha Bapt. Bible Coll. Various positions with Bob Jones U., pres. Greenville, SD, 1971—. Mem. exec. com., bd. trustees Bob Jones U.; v.p. bd. dirs. Gospel Fellowship Assn. Office: Bob Jones U Office Of Pres Greenville SC 29614-0001

JONES, BOISFEUILLET, JR., (BO JONES), publishing executive; b. Atlanta, Nov. 14, 1946; s. Boisfeuillet and Laura (Coit) J.; m. Barbara Frost Pendleton, Sept. 13, 1969; children: Lindsay Pendleton, Theodore Boisfeuillet. AB, Harvard U., 1968, JD, 1974; D.Phil., Oxford U., 1981. Bar: Mass. 1974, D.C. 1979. Law clk. Judge Levin H. Campbell, US Ct. Appeals (1st cir.), Boston, 1974-75; atty. Hill and Barlow, Boston, 1975-80; v.p., counsel Washington Post, Washington, 1980-95, pres., gen. mgr., 1995-2000, pub., CEO, 2000—. Dir. Bowater Mersey Paper Co., Ltd., N.S., Assoc. Press, NY, Robinson Terminal Warehouse Corp., Alexandria, Va., Fed. City Coun., Washington, Newspaper Assn. Am. Rhodes scholar Rhodes Trust, 1968. Episcopalian. Office: Washington Post 1150 15th St NW Washington DC 20071-0002 Office Phone: 202-334-7141.

JONES, C. PAUL, lawyer, educator; b. Grand Forks, ND, Jan. 7, 1927; s. Walter M. and Sophie J. (Thorton) J.; m. Helen M. Fredel, Sept. 7, 1957; children: Katherine, Sara H. BBA, JD, U. Minn., 1950; LLM, William Mitchell Coll. of Law, 1955. Assoc. Lewis, Hammer, Heaney, Weyl & Halverson, Duluth, Minn., 1950-51; asst., chief dep. Hennepin County Atty., Mpls., 1952-58; asst. US atty. US Atty's. Office, St. Paul, 1959-60; assoc. Maun & Hazel, St. Paul, 1960-61; ptnr. Dorfman, Rudquist, Jones, & Ramstead, Mpls., 1961-65; state pub. defender Minn. State Pub. Defender's Office, Mpls., 1966-90. Adj. prof. law William Mitchell Coll. of Law, St. Paul, 1953-70, prof. law, 1970—2001, prof. emeritus, 2001-. assoc. dean for acad. affairs, 1991-95; adj. prof. U. Minn., Mpls., 1970-90; mem. adv. com. on rules of criminal procedure Minn. Supreme Ct.,

1970—. Author: Criminal Procedure from Police Detention to Final Disposition, 1981; Jones on Minnesota Criminal Procedure, 1955, 64, 70, 75; Minnesota Police Law Manual, 1955, 67, 70, 76 Mem. Minn. Gov.'s Crime Commn., St. Paul, 1970s, Minn. Fair Trial-Free Press Assn., Mpls., 1970s, Citizens League, Mpls., 1955—, Mpls. Aquatennial Assn., Mpls., 1955-60, Minn. Coun. on Crime and Justice, 1991—. Recipient Reginald Heber Smith award Nat. Legal Aid and Defender Assn., 1969 Fellow Am. Coll. Trial Lawyers; mem. Am. Bd. Trial Advs., ABA, Minn. State Bar Assn., Hennepin County Bar Assn., Ramsey County Bar Assn., Nat. Legal Aid & Defender Assn. Clubs: Suburban Gyro of Mpls. Lodges: Rotary. Democrat. Lutheran. Avocations: fishing, hunting, golf, desert watching. Home: 5501 Dewey Hill Rd Edina MN 55439-1906 Office: William Mitchell Coll Law 875 Summit Ave Saint Paul MN 55105-3030

JONES, CARLETON SHAW, information technology executive, lawyer; b. NYC, Sept. 8, 1942; s. Carlyle Herman and Virginia Ann (Sloat) J.; m. Dona Baker VanArsdale, July 15, 1972; children: Emily Baker, Timothy Dustin. BA, Denison U., Granville, Ohio, 1964; LLB, Yale U., New Haven, Conn., 1967. Bar: Ohio 1967, Fla. 1971, DC 1973. Law clk. to chief judge US Ct Appeals (6th cir.), Akron, Ohio, 1967; dep. gen. counsel Price Commn., Exec. Office of Pres., Washington, 1971-73; assoc. Shaw, Pittman Potts & Trowbridge, Washington, 1973-77, ptnr., 1978-91; sr. v.p., counsel Sysorex Info. Sys., Fairfax, Va., 1992, pres., 1992-97, also bd. dirs.; pres. Vanstar Govt. Sys. (formerly Sysorex Info. Sys.), Fairfax, 1997-99, Info Ops Govt. Solutions, Arnold, Md., 2000—01; pres., COO Multimax, Inc., Herndon, Va., 2001—06, CEO, 2006—07, mgmt. cons., 2007—. Spkr. on fed. high-tech. procurement issues. Lt. (j.g.) USNR, 1967-71. Mem. ABA, Chevy Chase Club, Met. Club. Personal E-mail: carleton.505@gmail.com.

JONES, CAROL A., nutritionist, artist; d. John H. and Emma C. Jones. BS in Dietetics, U. So. Miss., Hattiesburg, 1975; MA in Nutrition Edn., U. Miss., Oxford, 1989; postgrad., Miss. State U., Statesville, 2000—. Registered dietitian ADA, lic. dietition Miss. Dietary dept. supr. Miss. Valley Food Scv., Kosoinsko; nutritionist supr. Miss. Dept. Health, Jackson, 1983—. Cons. in field. Exhibitions include Market Ctrl. Gallery, Memphis, Mid-Town Galleries, exhibitions include various local galleries. Deacon First Presbyn. Ch. Columbus; bd. dirs. Pilot Club of Columbus, 2004—06. Democrat. Presbyterian. Home: 616 N Browder St Columbus MS 39702 Office: Mississippi Dept Health 400A Wilkins Rd Columbus MS

JONES, CAROLYN, dean, law educator; 1 child, Alison. BA, U. Iowa, 1976, JD, 1979; LLM, Yale U., 1982. Bar: Iowa. Asst. city atty. Sioux City, 1979—80; assoc. Klass, Whicher and Mishne, 1981—82; prof. St. Louis U. Sch. Law, 1982—90, U. Conn. Law Sch., 1990—2004, assoc. dean academic affairs; dean U. Iowa Coll Law, 2004—. Vis. prof. law U. Exeter, Washington U., U. Iowa, 1986—87, 1989, Moritz Coll. Law, Ohio State U., 2004. Recipient Sanxay Prize, Order of Coif. Office: U Iowa Coll Law 276 Boyd Law Building Iowa City IA 52242 E-mail: carolyn-jones@uiowa.edu.*

JONES, CARTER RUTHVEN, JR., sculptor, educator; b. Mt. Kisco, NY, Mar. 6, 1945; s. Carter R. and Sally Field Jones; m. Carol J. Steen, Sept. 26, 1988. Hon. Degree in Sculpture (hon.), Boston Mus. Sch., 1969. Bd. dirs. Nat. Sculpture Soc., NYC, 2004—. Sculpture of George Balanchine, 1983, medallion, River Otters, 2004, pvt. collections, British Mus., Smithsonian Inst., Am. Numismatic Soc., Brookgreen Garden Mus. Recipient Youth prize, Nat. Sculpture Soc., Art Dirs. award, Illustrators Club NY, 1984. Fellow: Nat. Sculpture Soc.; mem.: Am. Medallic Sculpture Soc. (pres. 1983—85). Personal E-mail: crj3d1@gmail.com.

JONES, CATHERINE CLARISSA, retired secondary school educator; b. Iowa City, Iowa, May 10, 1949; d. Dale E. and Clarissa T. Watt; m. Lawrence Lee Jones, Dec. 7, 1968; children: Christopher Ruppert, Katherine Anna. BA, U. of Iowa, Iowa City, 1971, MA, 1980. HS English tchr., dept. chair Coll. Cmty. Schs., Cedar Rapids, Iowa, 1971—2006, ret., 2006. Tchg. asst. U. of Iowa, Iowa City, 1981—82; instr. Kirkwood Coll., Cedar Rapids, Iowa. Tutor Right to Read. Named Prairie H.S. Tchr. of the Yr., Coll. Cmty. Schs., 2005; recipient Paul C. Packer award for Outstanding Grad. Student Coll. of Edn., U. of Iowa, 1981, Tchr. of the Yr. award, Cedar Rapids Rotary, 2003, 2006. Mem.: Pi Lambda Theta, Phi Delta Kappa. Home: 3197 Dubuque St NE Iowa City IA 52240 Home Phone: 319-351-6722.

JONES, CHARLES CALHOUN, estate and business planning consultant; b. Bedford, Pa., Jan. 12, 1940; s. Charles Stauffer and Marjorie Vesta (Calhoun) J.; m. Patricia Jean Diehl, Aug. 12, 1960; children: Kathryn Lynn, Suzanne Elizabeth, Christopher Andrew. BS in Econs., Widener U., 1961. CLU, chartered fin. cons., Am. Coll., 2000; accredited estate planner Nat. Assn. Estate Planners and Couns., 2001, chartered adv. sr. living Am. Coll., 2005. Field dir. Bus. Men's Assurance, Kansas City, Mo., 1970—76; pres. Agrl. Bus. Adminstrn., Kansas City, 1976—78; br. mgr. E.F. Hutton, Raytown, Mo., 1978—79; pres. C.C.J. Inc., Kansas City, 1979—90; chmn. coun. John Hancock Mut. Life Ins. Co., 1992—98, mem. agts. adv. com., mktg. chmn., 1992—99. Chmn. bd. dirs. Pentrust LLC; advisor Nat. Cattleman's Assn., Denver, 1976-79. Author: Financial Management Pentrust, 1987; contbr. articles to profl. jours. Gov. Am. Royal, Kansas City, 1981; bd. dirs. Povidence/ St. John Hosp. Found., 1999—, Endowment Found. The Am. Coll. Investment and Pension Com., Bryn Mawr, Pa.; found. bd. dirs. Am. Coll. Bryn Mawr, 2005—, treas. Mem. Lees Summit C. of C. (econ. devel. com. 1982-85), Soc. Fin. Svc. Profls. (bd. dirs. 1998-2002), Assn. Internat Fin. Planners (bd. dirs. 1976-80), Planned Giving Coun. (charter), Rotary Internat., Soc. of Fin. Svc. Profls., Blue Hills Country Club, Reynolds Plantation Nat.Golf Club. Avocation: golf. Office: Pentrust LLC PO Box 481993 Kansas City MO 64148-1993 Home Phone: 816-941-2988; Office Phone: 816-941-0513. Business E-Mail: chuck@pentrust.com.

JONES, CHARLES E., retired state supreme court chief justice; b. June 12, 1935; BA, Brigham Young U., 1959; JD, Stanford U., 1962. Bar: Calif. 1963, Ariz. 1964, US Dist. Ct. Ariz. 1964, US Ct. Appeals (9th cir.) 1963, US Ct. Appeals (10th cir.) 1974, US Supreme Ct. 1979. Law clk. to Hon. Richard H. Chambers U.S. Ct. Appeals (9th cir.), 1962-63; assoc., ptnr. Jennings, Strouss & Salmon, Phoenix, 1963-96; apptd. justice Ariz. Supreme Ct., Phoenix, 1996, vice chief justice, 1997—2002, chief justice, 2002—05; ret., 2005—. Bd. visitors Brigham Young U. Law Sch., 1973-81, chmn., 1978-81, Univ. Arizona Coll. Law, 2003—. Named Avocat du Consulat-Gen. de France, 1981—; Alumni Dist. Svc. award Brigham Young U., 1982; recipient Aaron Feuerstein award U. Ariz., 1998, Pub. Svc. award Ariz. Alumni Assn., 2005, Career Achievement award State Bar Ariz., 2005, Chapman award Ariz. League of Women Voters, 2005, Pub. Svc. award, U. Ariz. Fellow Am. Bar Found., Ariz. Bar Found.; mem. ABA, State Bar Ariz. (Career award, 2005), Fed. Bar Assn. (pres. Ariz. chpt. 1971-73), J. Reuben Clark Law Soc. (nat. chmn. 1994-97), Maricopa County Bar Assn., Am. Coll. Labor and Employment Lawyers (former dir.), Pi Sigma Alpha. Office: Phoenix Sch Law 4041 N Central Ave Phoenix AZ 85012 Home Phone: 602-952-0993.

JONES, CHARLES HILL, JR., banker; b. July 14, 1933; s. Charles Hill and Susan Roy (Johnston) J.; m. Hope Haskell, Jan. 28, 1961; children: Hope H., Charles Hill III, Henry M.T. Grad., Groton Sch., Mass., 1952; BA in Econs., U. Va., 1956. With Wood, Struthers & Winthrop, Inc., NYC, 1956-73, gen. ptnr., 1968-69, v.p., dir., dir. rsch., 1969-73; sr. v.p., chief investment officer Midlantic Nat. Bank, Edison, 1974-87; gen. ptnr. Edge Ptnrs., 1987—. Bd. dirs. NJT Holdings. Author: (with Joseph D. Davis) Toll Road Bonds, 1959, The Growth Rate Appraiser, 1968. Treas. N.Y. chpt. R.E. Lee Meml. Found., 1964-69; trustee, chmn. fin. com. Monmouth Med. Ctr., 1975-81; pres. bd. trustees Rumson (N.J.) Country Day Sch., 1982-85; trustee Hampden-Sydney Coll., 1995-99, 2002-03. Mem. Inst. Chartered Fin. Analysts, Bond Club, City Midday Club (trustee, treas. 1965-71, v.p. 1972-74). Office Phone: 732-389-3600 ext 219.

JONES, CHARLES IRVING, bishop; b. El Paso, Tex., Sept. 13, 1943; s. Charles I. Jr. and Helen A. (Heyward) J.; m. Ashby MacArthur, June 18, 1966; children: Charles I. IV, Courtney M., Frederic M., Keith A. BS, The Citadel, 1965; MBA, U. N.C., 1966; MDiv, U. of the South, 1977, DD, 1989. CPA. Pub. acctg. D.E. Gatewood and Co., Winston-Salem, NC, 1966-72; dir. devel. Chatham (Va.) Hall, 1972-74; instr. acctg. U. of the South, Sewanee, Tenn., 1974-77; coll. chaplain Western Ky. U., Bowling Green, 1977-81; vicar Trinity Episcopal Ch., Russelville, Ky., 1977-85; archdeacon Diocese of Ky., Louisville, 1981-86; bishop Episcopal Diocese of Mont., Helena, 1986-2001. Bd. dirs. New Directions Ministries, Inc., N.Y.C.; mem. standing com. Joint Commn. on Chs. in Small Communities, 1988-91, Program, Budget and Fin., 1991-94; v.p. province VI Episcopal Ch., 1991-94, mem. Presiding Bishop's Coun. Advice, 1991-94. Author: Mission Strategy in the 21st Century, 1989, Total Ministry: A Practical Approach, 1993; bd. editors Grass Roots, Luling, Tex., 1985-90; contbr. articles to profl. jours. Founder Concerned Citizens for Children, Russelville, 1981; bd. dirs. St. Peter's Hosp., Helena, 1986-2001; bd. dirs. Christian Ministry in Nat. Parks, 1992—2001. With USMCR, 1961-65. Mem. AICPA, Mont. Soc. CPAs. Episcopalian. Avocations: running, flying, writing, skiing. Office: PO Box 4926 Helena MT 59604 Office Phone: 406-442-0345. E-mail: bpci@aol.com.

JONES, CHARLES W., labor union executive; b. Gary, Ind., Apr. 29, 1923; s. Charles Browning and Inez (Teegarden) J.; m. Ursula M. Wilden, Aug. 25, 1950; children: Charles Alan, Newton Browning, Donna Ruth, Doris Ursula. Grad. high sch., Gary. Boilermaker various constrn. contractors; organizer, then staff rep., rsch. & edn. dir., internat. v.p. Internat. Brotherhood of Boilermakers, Iron Ship Builders, Blacksmiths, Forgers and Helpers, Kansas City, Kans., now internat. pres.; ret. Chmn. bd. dirs. BB&T Co.; v.p. bldg. constrn. trades dept., v.p. metal trade dept. AFL-CIO. Office: Internat Brotherhood Boilermaker Iron Ship Bldrs Blacksmiths 753 State Ave Ste 570 Kansas City KS 66101-2511

JONES, CHERRY, actress; b. Paris, TN, Nov. 21, 1956; Founder Amer. Rep. Theatre, Cambridge, Mass., 1980—; guest artist Arena Stage, Washington, 1983-84. Stage appearances include: (with Amer. Rep. Theatre) King Lear, Twelfth Night, Major Barbara, Caucasian Chalk Circle, The Serpent Woman, Platonov, Life Is a Dream, The School for Scandal, The Three Sisters, As You Like It, Baby with the Bathwater, A Midsummer Night's Dream, Journey of the Fifth Horse, (Off Broadway) Desdemona, Goodnight Desdemona, Baltimore Waltz (Obie award), And Baby Makes Seven, Light Shining in Buckinghamshire, Big Time, Ballad of Soapy Smith, I Am a Camera, The Philanthropist, The Importance of Being Earnest, (Broadway) Angels in America, Our Country's Good, Macbeth, Stepping Out, The Heiress (Tony award Best Actress 1995), The Night of the Iguana, 1996, Doubt, 2005 (Outer Critics Cir. award, outstanding actress in a play, 2005, Lucille Lortel award, outstanding lead actress, 2005, Tony award, best performance by a leading actress in a play, 2005, Drama Desk award, outstanding actress in a play, 2005, Obie award, The Village Voice, 2005), Faith Healer, 2006; television appearances include: (movies) Alex: The Life of a Child, 1986; film appearances include: The Big Town, 1987, Light of Day, 1987, Housesitter, 1992, The Tears of Julian Po, 1997, (voice) Out of the Past, 1998, The Horse Whisperer, 1998, Murder in a Small Town, 1999, Cradle Will Rock, 1999, The Perfect Storm, 2000, Erin Brockovich, 2000, Signs, 2002. Office: The William Morris Agy 151 S El Camino Dr Beverly Hills CA 90212-2775

JONES, CHIPPER (LARRY WAYNE JONES JR.), professional baseball player; b. De Land, Fla., Apr. 24, 1972; s. Larry Wayne and Lynne Jones; m. Karin Fulford, 1992 (div. 1999); m. Sharon Jones, Mar. 26, 2000; 2 children. Student, Stetson U. Shortstop Jacksonville Jaguars, 1990—95; third base Atlanta Braves, 1995—2001, 2004—, leftfield, 2002—03. Mem. Team USA, World Baseball Classic, 2006. Founder Chipper Jones Family Found., 2001—. Named Atlanta Brave's Team MVP, 1996, Nat. League MVP, 1999; named to Nat. League All Star team, 1996—98, 2000—01; recipient Florida High Sch. baseball player of the year, 1990, Nat. League Silver Slugger award, 1999. Achievements include first Round MLB pick, Atlanta Braves, 1990; member of World Series Champion Atlanta Braves team, 1995; reached 2,000 hits on June 17, 2007 against the Cleveland Indians. Avocation: hunting. Office: Turner Field PO Box 4064 Atlanta GA 30302-4064*

JONES, CHRISTINE MASSEY, retired furniture company executive; b. Columbus, Ga., Nov. 7, 1929; d. Louis Everett and Donia (Spivey) Massey; divorced; children— James Raymond, Jr., James David. Student, Ga. Southwestern Coll., 1947-48. With Muscogee Mfg. Co., Columbus, Ga., 1948-56, Haverty Furniture Cos., Atlanta, 1956—97, v.p., corp. sec., 1978—97; ret., 1997. Deacon First Presbyn. Ch., Columbus, Ga., 2004—. Mem. Am. Soc. Corp. Secs. (securities industry com.)

JONES, CHRISTINE REGINA, secondary school educator; d. Edward and Jewett Holland; m. Cliff Jones, June 9, 1990; 1 child, Derek. BA, Auburn U., Ala., 1987. Cert. tchr. Ala., 1986. Tchr. Westlawn Mid. Sch., Huntsville, Ala., 1987—93, Liberty Mid. Sch., Madison, Ala., 2002—04, Discovery Mid. Sch., Madison, 2004—. Named one of Top 15 Preserve America's History Contest, History Channel, 2005; recipient Golden Apple award, Huntsville (Ala.) Times, 2003, World Class Educator's award, Ala., 2004. Mem.: Nat. Coun. Social Studies. Avocations: skiing, swimming, reading. Office: Dixcovery Middle School 1304 Hughes Road Madison AL 35758 Home Phone: 256-464-0104; Office Phone: 256-837-3735. Business E-Mail: cjones@madisoncity.k12.al.us.

JONES, CHRISTOPHER PRESTIGE, classicist, educator, historian, consultant; b. Kent, U.K., 1940; s. William Prestige and Irene May (McCreddie) J. BA, Oxford U., 1962; PhD Classical Philology, Harvard U., 1965. From lectr. to prof. U. Toronto, Can., 1965-92, chair dept. classics, 1986-90; prof. classics and history Harvard U., Cambridge, 1992-97, George Martin Lane prof. classics and history, 1997—. Vis. lectr. Harvard U., 1968; assoc. prof. Ecole Normale Supérieure de Jeunes Filles, Paris, 1979, Ecole Normale Supérieure, Paris, 1992; acting vice dean Faculty Arts and Scis., U. Toronto, 1985-86. Author: Philostratus: Life of Apollonius of Tyana, 1971, Plutarch and Rome, 1971, The Roman World of Dio Chrysostom, 1978, Culture and Society in Lucian, 1986, Kinship Diplomacy in the Ancient World, 1999; co-editor: Le Martyre de Pionios, prêtre de Smyrne, 1994; editor, translator: Philostratus: Life of Apollonius, 2 vols., 2005, Apollonius of Tyana: Letters, 2006; contbr. numerous articles to profl. jours. Fellow Royal Soc. Can., Am. Numismatic Soc.; mem. Am. Philol. Assn. (chair subcom. epigraphical bibliog. 1981-89, subcom. cartography 1986-90), Am. Acad. Arts and Scis., German Archeol. Inst. (corr. mem. 1992—), Am. Philos. Soc. Home: 130 Mount Auburn St Apt 107 Cambridge MA 02138-5757 Office: Harvard U Boylston Hall Cambridge MA 02138 Office Phone: 617-496-3823. Business E-Mail: cjones@fas.harvard.edu.

JONES, CLAIRE BURTCHAELL, artist, educator, writer; b. Oakland, Calif. d. Clarence Samuel and Florence Mallett (Hinchman) Burtchaell; m. E.C. Jones; children: Holland Mallett, Lela Claire, S. Evan. AB, Stanford U.; postgrad., Laguna Beach Sch. Art, 1972-73, San Diego Art Acad., 1980-82. Freelance art tchr., Park Ridge, Ill., 1967; tchr. Jade Fon Group, Pacific Grove, Calif., 1972-73, Merced Coll., Sierra Mountains, Calif., 1973; freelance pvt. workshop, painting for commns. and galleries Calif., 1973—. Bd. reviewers Dorland Mountain Arts Colony, 1990—2004. Author: First The Blade (ann. collection), 1939, Arrows in the Air, 1947-51, Utah Sings, 1953; editor: Watercolor West Newsletter, 1978-83; contbr. articles to profl. jours. Bd. reviewers Dorland Mountain Arts Colony, Temecula, Calif., 1985—. Recipient numerous awards for artwork. Founding mem. Nat. Mus. Women in the Arts, Assn. Western Artists (bd. dirs. 1970-71), Watercolor West (bd. dirs. 1978-81, 86—, membership chmn. 1988-96), Stanford Alumni Assn., Literati West (founder, sec.-treas. 1994—).

JONES, CLAYTON M., computer and electronics company executive; b. Nashville; BS, U. Tenn.; MS, George Washington U. Former fighter pilot USAF; various exec.-level positions aerospace industry; with Rockwell Collins Corp., Cedar Rapids, Iowa, 1995—, sr. v.p., 1999—2001, pres, CEO, 2001—, chmn., 2002—. Mem. AIAA (bd. dirs.), Gen. Aviation Mfrs. Assn. Office: Rockwell Internat Corp 400 Collin Rd NE Cedar Rapids IA 52498-0001*

JONES, CLEOPATRA CELESTE, retired gerontologist, sociologist, educator; d. Dock Thomas and Georgia Ann Davis; m. Julian Thomas Jones, Aug. 19, 1939 (dec. 2001); children: Camille Jeannette Jones-Hanna, Brenda (Naima) Carol Jones-Shamborguer. MA, U. Mich., Ann Arbor, 1976; PhD, Mich. State U., Lansing, 1991; postgrad., U. North Tex., Denton, 1996. Cert. specialist in gerontology U. Mich., 1976, specialist in curiculum devel. adult edn. Wayne State U., 1990. Procurement analyst Fed. Govt., Detroit, 1953—71; tchr. adult edn. Detroit Pub. Schs., 1977—96; adult edn. tchr. Ferndale Adult Edn., 1977—96; prof. sociology Wayne County C.C., Detroit, 2005—06; ret. Adv. coun. on aging State of Mich., Lansing, 1996—2006; adv. bd. Wayne County C.C., Detroit, 1993—96; minority tng. program adminstrn. on aging Fed. Govt., Washington, 1987—88. Author: Special Women On The Move, 1999. Active People's Cmty. Ch., Detroit; parliamentarion Zeta Phi Beta, Detroit, 1989—90. Recipient Howard Mc Clusky award, Howard McClusky Symposium Kansas City, Mo., 1995, Intergenerational Edn. for Aging award, Citizens Amb. Com. Washington, 1995; grantee, U. North Tex., 1996. Mem.: NAACP, Decendents of Black Soldiers who Fought in the Civil War 1861-1865, Daughters of the Civil War, Nat. Soc. Union Heritage (life; vice regent 1998—2006). Home Phone: 313-861-5553.

JONES, CLYDE ADAM, artist, educator; b. Cobleskill, NY, Nov. 10, 1924; s. Lester L. and Myra (Karker) Jones. BFA, Syracuse U., 1948, MA, 1954; EdD, Pa. State U., 1961. Tchr. art North H.S., Binghamton, NY, 1948—49, 1950—56; instr. ceramics Jr. League of Binghamton, 1950—53; guest instr. ceramics Rehab. Guild, Saranac Lake, NY, 1951—54; asst. prof. art edn. Edinboro (Pa.) State Coll., 1956—58; instr., summer creative arts workshop Cornell U., Ithaca, NY, 1958; asst. prof. child devel. U. Conn., Storrs, 1961—66, asst. dean Sch. Home Econs. and Family Studies, 1976—79, assoc. prof. huyman devel. and family rels., 1966—85, prof. emeritus, 1985—; trustee Syracuse U. Libr. Assocs., 1970. Cons. Head Start program, Conn., 1965—66. One-man shows include Rehab. Guild, Saranac Lake, Windham Hosp., Willimantic, Conn., Art Bldg., Pa. State U., Student Union, U. Conn., exhibited in group shows at Roberson Meml., Binghamton, N.Y., Erie (Pa.) Art Mus., Munson-Williams-Proctor Inst., Utica, N.Y., Mus. Fine Arts, Syracuse, Norwich (Conn.) Art Mus., Schoharie County Arts Coun., Albany Inst. History and Art, Essex (Conn.) Art Assn., Rochester (N.Y.) Meml. Art Gallery, illustrations for history vols. of Sch. of Home Econs. and Family Studies and Sch., U. Conn. Mem. Gov.'s Commn. on Status of Women, Conn., 1965—67; governing bd. Nat. Assn. Creative Children and Adults, 1986—; bd. dirs. Greater Mansfield Arts Coun., 1986—, adv. bd., 1989—; dir., bd. dirs. Cobleskill Hist. Soc. Served US Army, 1943—45. Recipient Hon. mention, Ceramic Nat. Exhbn., 1954. Mem.: Conn. Home Econs. Assn. (del., dir. 1978—82, newsletter editor 1984—, named Home Economist of Yr. 1992), Assn. for Childhood Edn. Internat., Internat. Soc. Edn. thru Art, Nat. Art Edn. Assn. (rsch. trainee 1965), Nat. Soc. Study of Edn., Soc. Rsch. in Child Devel., Nat. Assn. Edn. of Young Children, Hartford Assn. Edn. of Young Children (pres. 1967—69), New Eng. Assn. Edn. of Young Children (editor newsletter 1963—65, publs. com. 1980—, fin. com. 1999—), Conn. Assn. Edn. of Young Children (v.p. 1970—72), Phi Delta Kappa. Office: U Conn Sch Family Studies Storrs Mansfield CT 06269-0001 Home: 100 Warren Cir Storrs Mansfield CT 06268

JONES, COBI, professional soccer player; b. Detroit, June 16, 1970; Student, UCLA. Midfielder Coventry City, 1994—95, Vasco da Gama, 1995—96, L.A. Galaxy, 1996—, U.S. Nat. Team, 1996—. With gold medal U.S. team Pan Am. Games, 1991; with U.S. Olympic Team, 1992, U.S. Nat. Team, 1992—95, including victory over Ivory Coast, 1992. Host (TV series) Megadose (MTV), guest appearance Beverly Hills 90210, 1994. Achievements include tied for all-time assist lead, with 11. Office: c/o US Soccer Fedn 1801-1811 S Prairie Ave Chicago IL 60616

JONES, COLETTA L., senior pastor; d. Raymond Jones, Sr. and Burnetta T. Jones; m. Ronald P. Jones, June 27, 1964; children: Phillip A., Catrina M., Michael R., David P. Attended, Morgan State U., 1992—96, Columbia Union Coll., 1998—99. Equal employment specialist US Dept. oEnergy, DC, 1970—82; sch. adminstr. Sunshine Christian Acad., Colmar Manor, Md., 1982—92; bus. adminstr., asst. pastor New Mt. Carmel Holiness Ch. Christ, DC, 1993—96; sr. pastor Mt. Carmel Christian Faith Ctr., DC, 1997—. Bd. mem. Collective Banking Group, Riverdale, Md., 2000—; mem. Jobs Coalition, DC, 2002—; sec., bd. dirs. Faith Based Cmty. Action Partnership, Inc., 2003—; instr. Jobs Partnership Inc., 2004—. Mem.: NW Clergy Assn. Non-Denomination. Avocations: traveling, reading, cooking. Office: Mount Carme Christian Faith Ctr 4100 Illinois Ave NW Washington DC 20011 Home Phone: 301-352-7283; Office Phone: 202-545-0230. Office Fax: 202-545-0230. Personal E-mail: ronaldandcoletta@aol.com.

JONES, CONSTANCE CORALIE, retired music educator; b. Bowling Green, Ky., July 5, 1921; d. Loton Brodie Jones and Constance Coralie Barrington; m. Harold E. Runyon, June 23, 1943 (dec.); children: Randolph Runyon, Constance Ford; m. Earle D. Jones, Dec. 26, 1979 (dec.). AB, Western Ky. State Coll., 1941, MA, 1944. Music tchr. Orangeburg HS, Mason County, Ky., 1941—42, Maysville City Schs., Maysville, Ky., 1942—46, Ripley Sch. Dist., Ohio, 1955—60, Mason County Schs., Ky., 1960—82, Maysville CC, 1968—92. Mem. Lexington Symphony Orch.; guest condr., vis. tchr. Dana Hall Sch., Wellesley, Mass. Founder, conductor Maysville Civic Chorus; musical dir. Maysville Players Prodns.; conductor Limestone Chorale & Limestone Chamber Orchestra; dir. music Maysville Christian Ch., 1942—82. Named a Ky. Col., 1974, 1979; recipient Outstanding Woman Ky., U. Ky. Women's Assn., 1971, Lady of Yr., Maysville, 1979, Ky. Tchr. of Yr., 1982. Mem.: Am. String Tchrs. Assn., Am. Choral Dirs. Assn. (past pres., past. pres.). Achievements include conducting concerts in northern England, Vienna, Innsbruck, Neustadt, Neuremberg, Germany, Monaco and Brussels, Belgium; choir students have had records of superior ratings at the state contest-festival competitions for 32 years; establishing The Coralie Runyon-Jones Music Libr. wing of Maysville Pub. Libr., 2005. Personal E-mail: coralie@maysvilleky.net.

JONES, CRAIG WARD, retired lawyer; b. Pitts., June 14, 1947; s. Curtis Edison and Margaret (McFarland) Jones; m. Sarah Dowding; children: Laura McFarland, Rebecca Long, Nancy Harper. BA, Carleton Coll., 1969; JD, U. Pitts., 1976. Bar: Pa. 1976, U.S. Dist. Ct. (we. dist.) Pa. 1976, U.S. Ct. Appeals (3d cir.) 1981. Ptnr. Reed Smith LLP, Pitts., 1976—2004; ret.,

2004. Served to lt. USNR, 1969—73. Mem.: Allegheny County Bar Assn. Presbyterian. Home: 208 Cornwall Dr Pittsburgh PA 15238-2639 Personal E-mail: cwjones8214@netscape.net.

JONES, D. PAUL, JR., bank executive, lawyer; b. Birmingham, Ala., Sept. 26, 1942; s. D. Paul and Virginia Lee (Mount) J.; m. Charlene Dale Angelich, Aug. 1964; children: Holly, Allison, Paul, III. BS, U. Ala., 1964, JD, 1967; LL.M., N.Y. U., 1968. Bar: Ala. Mem. firm Balch, Bingham, Baker, Hawthorne, Williams & Ward, Birmingham, 1970-78, of counsel, 1978-86; exec. v.p., gen. counsel, dir. Compass Bancshares, Inc., Birmingham, 1978-84, vice chmn., 1984-89, pres., COO, 1989-91, chmn., CEO, 1991—. Bd. dirs. Compass Bank, Russell Lands Co., Bus. Coun. Ala., Compass Bancshares, Inc.; exec. com. Pub. Affairs Rsch. Coun. Ala.; mem. Internat. Fin. Conf. Chmn. Ala. Bus. Charitable Trust Fund; mem. adv. bd. Better Bus. Bur. Birmingham; adv. bd. Salvation Army, Birmingham; bd. visitors Sch. Commerce and Bus. Adminstrn., U. Ala.; mem. pres.'s coun. U. Ala., Birmingham, Ala. Inst. Deaf and Blind; ptnr. Econ. Devel. Partnership Ala.; grad. bd. trustees Leadership Birmingham; grad. Leadership Ala.; mem. adv. bd. Juvenile Diabetes Found., Ala., corp. chmn. Walk to Cure Diabetes, 1999; co-chmn. Advantage 21 Leadership Coun.; mem. adv. coun. Nat. Multiple Sclerosis Soc.; bd. dirs. Region 2020, Inc., Fed. Res. Bank Atlanta; dinner chmn. 32d ann. awards dinner Nat. Conf. for Cmty. and Justice, 2000; adv. bd. Svc. Corp. Ret. Execs. Mem. ABA, Ala. Bar Assn. (chmn. sect. corp., banking and bus. law 1973-75, bd. bar examiners 1975-78), Birmingham Bar Assn., Am. Bankers Assn. (mem. govt. rels. coun. 1985-88), Ala. Bankers Assn. (pres. 1989-90, chmn. fin. com. 1990-91, exec. coun.), Fin. Svcs. Roundtable (bd. dirs., banking and fin. markets com.), Soc. Internat. Bus. Fellows, Newcomen, Birmingham C. of C., Birmingham C. of C. Found., Birmingham Bus. Leadership Group, Svc. Corps Ret. Execs. (adv. bd.), The Club, Old Overton, Country Club Birmingham, Willow Point Golf and Country Club (Alexander City), Rotary. Home: 2010 Garden Pl Birmingham AL 35223-1156 Office: Compass Bancshares Inc PO Box 10566 Birmingham AL 35296-0001 also: Compass Bancshares Inc 15 20th St S Birmingham AL 35233-2000*

JONES, DALE EDWIN, public defender; b. Rahway, NJ, Oct. 22, 1948; s. Horatio Gates and Audrey Irma (Morgan) J.; m. Karen Anne Woodhall, June 19, 1971; children: Sharon, Michael, Stephan; m. Maria D. Noto, Aug. 2, 1987 (div. 1989); m. Joan E. DiTullio, Oct. 18, 1991; 1 child, Trevor. BA, Rutgers U., 1970, JD, 1973. Bar: N.J. 1973, U.S. Dist. Ct. N.J. 1973, U.S. Supreme Ct. 1977, N.Y. 1983. 1st asst. pub. defender Office Pub. Defender, Newark, 1974-84, dep. pub. defender in charge of capital litigation, 1984-87; asst. pub. defender, dir. of policy Office of Pub. Defender, Trenton, NJ, 1987—, dir. policy, 1987—. Mem. model jury charge com., N.J. Supreme Ct., 1983-88, criminal practice com., Trenton, 1983—, com. media rels., 1987-89, strategic planning com., 1996-98, rules of evidence com., 1998-2002. Mem. ACDL-N.J., Nat. Assn. Criminal Def. Lawyers (cert. criminal atty.), Amnesty Internat. Democrat. Office: Pub Defender Office PO Box 850 Trenton NJ 08625-0850 Office Phone: 609-292-9736. Personal E-mail: djones2411@yahoo.com. Business E-Mail: Dale.Jones@opd.state.nj.us.

JONES, DAN LEWIS, psychologist; b. Halifax, Va., Oct. 8, 1951; s. Ernest Lewis and Mary Elizabeth (Francis) J.; m. Temple Kiger Jones, Aug. 17, 1974; children: Natalie Temple, Layla Michelle. BA, Appalachian State U., 1974; MA, West Ga. Coll., 1976; PhD, U. Kans., 1986. Lic. psychologist, N.C., Calif., Va.; diplomate in counseling psychology Am. Bd. Profl. Psychology; cert. treatment of alcohol and other psychoactive substance use disorders, APA Coll. of Profl. Psychology. Instr. psychology N.C. Ctrl. U., Durham, 1976-79; counselor Adult Life Resource Ctr., U. Kans., Lawrence, 1979-84; psychology intern Counseling Ctr. U. Calif., Irvine, 1984-85; acting dir. adult life resource ctr. U. Kans., 1985-86; staff psychologist Counseling Ctr. Utah State U., Logan, 1986-88; psychologist Counseling Ctr. East Tenn. State U., Johnson City, 1988-89; sr. psychologist, dir. tng., asst. dir. Counseling and Psychol. Svcs., Appalachian State U., Boone, NC, 1989-97, dir., 1996—; part-time pvt. practice. Cons. IRS, 1985, Bristol (Tenn.) Mental Health Ctr., 1989, N.C. Ct. Counseling Svcs., 1979. Author: (with others) Counseling Adults, 1985, editor; author (manual) The Stress management Workshop, 1985, (with others) AACD Stress Workshop Manual, 1985; ad hoc reviewer Jour. Psychotherapy Integration, Jour. Coll. Student Devel., Jour. of Am. Coll. Health, others. Fellow Acad. of Counseling Psychology; mem. APA (chmn. spl. interest group on coll. counseling ctrs. divsn. 17, mem. program com. divsn. 29), ACA, Am. Coll. Counseling Assn., NC Psychol. Assn., Am. Coll. Pers. Assn. (directorate commn. VII), Internat. Assn. Counseling Svcs. (bd. dirs., pres.); Assn. Univ. and Coll. Counseling Ctrs. (governing bd.). Democrat. Avocation: racquetball. Home: 357 Fawn Dr Boone NC 28607-8461 Office Phone: 828-262-3180.

JONES, DANIEL BOUGERE, surgeon; naturalized; AB, Cornell U., NYC, 1986, MD, 1990. Lic. surgeon N.Y., 1990. Intern Wash. U. Barnes Hosp., St Louis, 1990, gen. surgeon, 1990—97, resident, 1991—97; dir. Southwestern Ctr. Minimally Invasive Surgery U. Tex. Southwestern, Dallas, 1997—2002; chief Minimally Invasive Surgery Beth Israel Deaconess Med. Ctr., Boston, 2002—, dir. Simulation and Skills Ctr., 2005—. Assoc. prof. Harvard U. Med. Sch., Boston, 2003—. Author (editor): Atlas of Minimally Invasive Surgery, 2006; contbr. chapters to books, articles to profl. jours. Fellow: ACS; mem.: SAGES (Young Investigator award 2003, Gold Laparoscope award 2003). Office: Beth Israel Deaconess Medical Center 330 Brookline Ave Boston MA 02215 Home Phone: 617-667-5101; Office Phone: 617-667-5100. Office Fax: 617-667-5125.

JONES, DANIEL HARE, librarian, consultant; b. Charleston, SC, Jan. 18, 1949; s. Daniel Hare and Maria Clare (Duffy) J.; m. Rajia Christina Tobia, Dec. 15, 1979; children: Andrew Duffy, Patrick Joseph. BS, Clemson U., 1971; MLS, Emory U., 1977. Tchr. pub. schs., Blackville, S.C., 1971-73; tchr. Peace Corps., Malaysia, 1973-74; libr. Biomed. Libr. U. So. Ala., Mobile, 1977-79; libr. Briscoe Library U. Tex. Health Sci. Ctr., San Antonio, 1979-98; pres. Libr. Cons. NA, Inc., Mobile, Ala., 1998—2003; dir. R&D for N.Am. representing Otto Harrassowitz, Wiesbaden, Germany, 1998—2003; dir. P.G. Northrup Meml. Lib. S.W. Found. Biomedical Rsch., San Antonio, 2003—. Indexer publs. Nat. Inst. Arthritis, Metabolism and Digestive Diseases, 1978; cons. Georgetown U. Med. Ctr. Libr., Washington, 1985-87, S.W. Found. for Biomed. Rsch., 1994-95; mem. libr. adv. coun. Springer-Verlag Pub. Co., 1992-96. Mem. editl. bd. Serials Rev., 1991-97, Newsletter on Serial Pricing Issues, 1990-98, Library Collections, Acquisitions, and Tech. Svcs., 1999-2002. Mem. ALA, Acad. Health Info. Profls. (disting.), Med. Libr. Assn., Tex. Libr. Assn. Roman Catholic. Avocations: swimming, gardening. Home: 223 Clearview Dr San Antonio TX 78228-1940 Office: PG Northrup Meml Lib SW Found Biomedical Rsch PO Box 760549 San Antonio TX 78245-0549 Office Phone: 210-258-9426. Personal E-mail: djones@sfbr.org.

JONES, DANIEL W., construction executive; Pres., cheif operating officer Zaring Nat. Corp., Cin., 1989—. Office: Zaring National Corp 625 Eden Park Dr #1250 Cincinnati OH 45202-6024

JONES, DAVID, advertising executive; Bd. dirs. AMV/BBDO, Ltd., England; varoius positions Lowe Europe, J. Walter Thompson, BDH/TBWA; mng. dir. Euro RSCG, Australia, 1998—99, CEO, 1999—2003, exec. v.p. global bus. London, 2003—04; global CEO Euro RSCG Worldwide, NYC, 2004—. Named one of Australia's Top 20 Businessmen Under 40, GQ mag., 40 Under 40, Meadia and Mktg. Europe, 2003, Crain's NY Bus. Journal, 2006. Office: Euro RSCG Worldwide 350 Hudson St New York NY 10014*

JONES, DAVID A., former consumer products company executive; Mgmt. positions GE; exec. v.p. Electrolux Corp., 1985—89; pres., CEO The Regina Co., 1989—94; chmn., CEO, COO Thermoscan, Inc., 1995—96; chmn., pres., CEO Spectrum Brands Inc., Atlanta, 1996—98, chmn., CEO, 1998—2007, chmn., 2007. Bd. dir. Pentair Inc., Simmons Bedding Co.*

JONES, DAVID A., JR., insurance company executive; BA in History magna cum laude, Yale U., 1980, JD, 1988. English tchr. Hunan Med. Coll., Changsha, China; with internat. divsn. First Nat. Bank Boston; atty.-adviser Bur. East Asian and Pacific Affairs U.S. Dept. State, 1988-92; assoc. Hirn Reed & Harper, Louisville; chmn., mng. dir. Chrysalis Ventures, LLC, Louisville, 1993—; vice chmn. Humana, Louisville, 1996—2005, chmn., 2005—. Adj. prof. Georgetown U. Law Ctr., Washington; former chmn. Greater Louisville Health Enterprises Network; mem. adv. com. Brookings Ctr. on Health Policy; bd. mem. Nat. Com. on US-China Relations. Office: Humana Inc 500 W Main St Louisville KY 40202 also: Chrysalis Ventures LLC 1650 Nat City Tower 101 S Fifth St Louisville KY 40202*

JONES, DAVID ALLEN, retired health benefits company executive; b. Louisville, Aug. 1931; m. Betty L. Ashbury, July 24, 1954. BS, U. Louisville, 1954; JD, Yale U., 1960. Bar: Ky. 1960. Founder Humana Inc. (formerly Extendicare Inc.), Louisville, 1961, CEO, 1961—97, chmn., dir. Louisville, 1997—; ptnr. Greenebaum, Doll and McDonald and predecessor, Louisville, 1965—69, of counsel, 1969—74; ret. Lt. (j.g.) USN, 1954—57.

JONES, DAVID CHARLES, retired air force officer, former chairman Joint Chiefs of Staff; b. Aberdeen, SD, July 9, 1921; s. Maurice and Helen Alice (Meade) J.; m. Lois M. Tarbell, Jan. 23, 1942; children: Susan Jones Coffin, Kathy Jones Franklin, David Curtis. Student, U. N.D., Minot State Coll.; grad., Flying Sch., Roswell, N.Mex., 1943, Nat. War Coll., Washington, 1960; H.L.D., U. Nebr., 1974, La. Tech. U., 1975, Minot State Coll., 1979, Boston U., 1980, Troy State U. Commd. 2d lt. U.S. Air Force, 1943, advanced through grades to gen., 1971; dep. comdr. ops. Vietnam; vice comdr. 7th Air Force; comdr.-in-chief U.S. Air Force Europe; comdr. 4th Allied Tactical Air Force; chief of staff U.S. Air Force, Washington, 1974-78; chmn. Joint Chiefs of Staff, Dept. Def., Washington, 1978-82, ret., 1982. Chmn. Nat. Edn. Corp., Hay Sys. Decorated Def. D.S.M., Air Force D.S.M., Navy D.S.M., Army D.S.M., Legion of Merit, D.F.C., Bronze star, Air medal, numerous others. Mem.: Air Force Assn., Falcon Found., Mgmt. Execs. Soc., Coun. on Fgn. Rels., Alfalfa Club. E-mail: dcji@aol.com.

JONES, DAVID M., zoological park administrator; b. Cheshire, Eng., Aug. 14, 1944; arrived in U.S., 1994; m. Janet Jones; 3 children. BSc in Zoology, Royal Vet. Coll., London, 1966; B in Vet. Medicine, Royal Veterinary Coll., London, 1969. 1st resident vet. surgeon Whipsnade pk. Zool. Soc. London, 1969-75, sr. vet. officer, 1975, responsible for animal collection London and Whipsnade, 1981, dir. zoos London and Whipsnade, 1984, CEO, 1991; dir. conservation and consultancy London and Whipsnade, 1993; dir. N.C. Zool. Pk., Asheboro, 1994—, Dept. Environ. Natural Resources State of N.C., 1994—. Chmn. Fauna and Flora Internat., London, 1987—94; chmn. conservation com. World Wide Fund Nature UK, 1988—94, trustee, Brooke Hosp. Animals, 1972—, chmn., Pakistan, 1990—98, India, 2000—02, Yadkin Pee-Dee Lakes Project, 1998—; mem. coun. World Wildlife Fund U.S., 1996—2002; bd. mem. Nat. Audubon NC, 2002—07, Environ. Def. NC, 2003—, Pfeiffer Univ., 2003—. Contbr. articles to profl. jours. Fellow: Inst. of Biology; mem.: Royal Coll. Vet. Surgeons. Home: 1688 Sylvan Way Asheboro NC 27205-2546 Office: 4401 Zoo Pkwy Asheboro NC 27205-1425 Home Phone: 336-626-3528; Office Phone: 336-879-7102. Personal E-mail: david.m.jones@nczoo.org.

JONES, DAVID MILTON, economist, educator; b. Newton, Iowa, June 22, 1938; s. Charles Raymond and Mary Evelyn (Corrough) J.; m. Becky Ann Jones Strait, Aug. 4, 1962; children: David, Jennifer, Stephen. BA with honors, Coe Coll., 1960; MA, U. Pa., 1961, PhD, 1969. Economist Fed. Res. Bank N.Y., NYC, 1963-68; v.p., fin. economist Irving Trust Co., NYC, 1968-72; vice-chmn., chief economist, bd. dirs. Aubrey G. Lanston & Co., Inc., NYC, 1972-2000; owner DMJ Advisors LLC, Denver, 2000—, Crystal Lake Resort, Pine, Colo. Advisor panel Fed. Res. Bank N.Y., 1982-93, cons. bd. govs., 1996—; mem. bd. vis. U. Pa.; former dir. pub. interest Suffolk County Savs. and Loan, Centerreach, N.Y.; bd. dirs. Aubrey G. Lanston & Co., Inc., Coe Coll., Union Theol. Sem.; lectr. CFA security analysts seminar, Northwestern U.; chmn. bd. Investors' Security Trust Co., Ft. Myers, Fla., 2004—; adj. prof. econs., fin. Fla. Gulf Coast U., 2007-. Author: Fed Watching and Interest Rate Projections: A Practical Guide, 1986, The Politics of Money: The Fed under Alan Greenspan, 1991, The Buck Starts Here: How the Federal Reserve Can Make or Break Your Financial Future, 1995, Unlocking the Secrets of the Fed: How Monetary Policy Affects the Economy and Your Wealth Creation Potential, 2002. Chmn. fin. and investment com. United Ch. Bd. for World Ministries, N.Y.C., 1975-86; mem. bond com. Twp. of Montclair, 1982-83. Woodrow Wilson Found. fellow, 1960; NDEA fellow, 1960 Mem. Nat. Assn. Bus. Economists, Econ. Club of N.Y., Nat. Econ. Club (bd. dirs.). Office: PO Box 529 Pine CO 80470 Personal E-mail: dmj@allabouttrust.com.

JONES, DAVID R., not-for-profit executive; b. Bklyn., Apr. 30, 1948; s. Thomas Russell and Bertha Jones; m. Valerie King, June 2, 1978; children: Russell King-Jones, Vanessa King-Jones. BA, Wesleyan U., 1970, MA (hon.), 1983; JD, Yale U., 1974; DHL (hon.), CUNY, 1999. Bar: NY 1975. Law clk. to Judge Constance Baker Motley Fed. Dist. Ct., So. Dist. NY; litig. assoc. Cravath, Swaine & Moore, NYC, 1975-79; spl. advisor to Mayor of NYC, 1979-83; exec. dir. NYC Youth Bur., 1983-86; pres., CEO Cmty. Svc. Soc., NYC, 1986—. Chmn. bd. dirs. Carver Fed. Savs. Bank, NYC, 1989-2000; bd. dirs. Jobs For the Future, Boston, 1990-98; chair Nat. Com. on Responsive Philanthropy, 2000; vice chair NYC Ind. Budget Office; mem. transition com. of mayor-elect Michael Bloomberg. Columnist NY Amsterdam News, 1992—. Bd. dirs. Health & Hosps. Corp., NYC, 1993-98, NY Found., 1996—; vice chair Primary Health Care Devel. Corp., NYC, 1993-95; trustee Wesleyan U., Middletown, Conn., 1984-96 Seherman Found., Nation Inst.; bd. dirs., mem. exec. com., Upper Manhattan Empowerment Zon, NYC, 1996-2000—; bd. dirs. N.Y. Hist. Soc.; trustee emeritus Wesleyan U., 1996—. Thomas J. Watson fellow, 1970. Mem. Black Agy. Execs. (pres. 1987-94). Avocations: bike riding, travel, reading, carpentry. Office: Cmty Svc Soc NY 105 E 22d St New York NY 10010 Personal E-mail: djones@cssny.org.

JONES, DAVID RHODES, editor, consultant; b. Connellsville, Pa., Sept. 13, 1932; s. David Rhodes and Ruth Elizabeth (Dillon) J.; m. Mary Lee Lauffer, Oct. 8, 1955; 1 dau., Elizabeth Lee. BA, Pa. State U., 1954; MA, N.Y. U., 1961. Reporter Wall Street Jour., NYC, 1957-61, bur. chief Pitts., 1961-63; with N.Y. Times, 1963—97, corr., Detroit, 1963-65, nat. labor reporter, Washington, 1965-68, asst. nat. editor, N.Y.C., 1969-72, nat. editor, 1972-87, editor nat. editions, 1987-97; asst. mng. editor, 1989-97. Trustee Pa. State U. Served to 1st lt. USAF, 1955-57. Mem.Tau Kappa Epsilon.

JONES, DAVID ROBERT, retired zoology educator; arrived in Can., 1969; s. William Arnold and Gladys Margery Jones; m. Valerie Iris Gibson, Sept. 15, 1962; children: Melanie Ann, Vivienne Samantha. BSc, Southampton U., 1962; PhD, U. East Anglia, Norwich, Eng., 1965. Rsch. fellow U. East Anglia, 1965-66; lectr. zoology U. Bristol, 1966-69; prof. zoology U. BC, Vancouver, Canada, 1969—, Disting. U. scholar, 2004—, Killam Univ. prof., 2005—06, prof. emeritus, 2006—. Lectr. in field. Contbr. numerous articles to profl. jours. Decorated Order of Can.; recipient Killam Rsch. prize, 1993, Murry A. Newman award significant achievement aquatic rsch., Vancouver Pub. Aquarium and Marine Scis. Ctr., 2004; fellow, Killam Found., Can., 1973, 1989; scholar, Peter Wall Inst. Advanced Studies, Vancouver, 2002. Fellow Royal Soc. Can. (Flavelle medal 2000); mem. Soc. Exptl. Biology, Am. Physiol. Soc. (Scholander Lecture 2006, Krogh Lecture 2007), Can. Zool. Soc. (Fry medal 1992). Avocations: opera, music, theater, English cathedrals. Office: Zoology Animal Care U BC 6199 S Campus Rd Vancouver BC Canada V6T 1W5 Business E-Mail: jones@zoology.ubc.ca.

JONES, DEBBIE JO, finance educator; d. Johnny Albert and Ruby Jones. Assoc. degree, Massey Bus. Coll., Atlanta, 1982. Tchr. Debbie Jones Ministries, Decatur, Ga., 2003—. Dir., tchr. Ruby Jones Leadership Acad. Editor: (monthly letters) LOV Ministries. Office: Debbie Jones Ministries PO Box 2106 Decatur GA 30031-2106 Home Phone: 404-687-8668; Office Phone: 404-376-1709. Business E-Mail: djjkmr02@yahoo.com.

JONES, DENECIA, insurance agent; d. Ed Jones and Alice Lakes. BSBA, U. Phoenix, Las Vegas, Nev., 2003. Cert.: Citadel, Calif. (estate planner) 2005; minority bus. enterprise Calif., 2005, women bus. enterprise Calif., 2005, small bus. enterprise Calif., 2005. Fin. advisor AIG, Orange, Calif., 2002—03; client fin. analyst Citibank, Santa Monica and Pacific Palisades, Calif., 2003—04; pres. D.A. Jones Ins. Svcs., LA, 2004—. Named to Prodr. Rewards Club, Blue Shield Calif., 2005; recipient Top Prodr. award, Word and Brown, 2005. Mem.: LA C. of C., Nat. Assn. of Life and Health Underwriters (assoc.), Nat. Assn. Life and Fin. Advisors (assoc.), Nat. Assn. Women Bus. Owners (assoc.), Rotary. Office: DA Jones Ins Svcs 6080 Center Dr 6th Fl Los Angeles CA 90045 Home Phone: 310-281-6029; Office Phone: 310-281-6029. Business E-Mail: denecia@dajonesinsurance.org.

JONES, DIANA WYNNE, writer; b. London, Aug. 16, 1934; d. Richard Aneurin Jones and Marjorie (Jackson) Hughes; m. John Anthony Burrow, Dec. 22, 1956; children: Richard, Michael, Colin. BA, St. Anne's Coll. U. Oxford, Eng., 1956; DLitt (hon.), Bristol U., Eng., 2006. Free-lance writer part-time, Essex, Oxford, Eng., 1944-70; full-time writer Oxford, Bristol, Eng., 1970—. Panel judge Guardian Award for Children's Books, London, 1979-83, Whitbread Prize for Lit., Children's Sect., London, 1988; judge World Fantasy Awards, 2001. Author: Wilkins' Tooth (in U.S. Witch's Business), 1973, The Ogre Downstairs, 1974, Eight Days of Luke, 1975, Cart and Cwidder, 1975, Dogsbody, 1975, Power the Three, 1976, Drowned Ammet, 1977, Charmed Life, 1977 (Guardian award 1978), Who Got Rid of Angus Flint, 1978, The Spellcoats, 1979, The Magicians of Caprona, 1980, The Homeward Bounders, 1981, The Time of the Ghost, 1981, Witch Week, 1982, Warlock at the Wheel, 1984, Archer's Goon, 1984 (Boston Globe/Horn Book award), Fire and Hemlock, 1985 (Phoenix award, 2005), Howl's Moving Castle, 1986 (Boston Globe/Horn Book award), A Tale of Time City, 1987, The Lives of Christopher Chant, 1988, Chair Person, 1989, Wild Robert, 1989, Hidden Turnings, 1989, Castle in the Air, 1990, Black Maria, 1991, A Sudden Wild Magic, 1992, The Crown of Dalemark, 1993, Stopping for a Spell, 1993, Hexwood, 1993, Fantasy Stories, 1994, Everard's Ride, 1995, The Tough Guide to Fantasyland, 1996, Minor Arcana, 1996, Deep Secret, 1997, Dark Lord of Derkholm, 1998, (retelling of) Puss n' Boots, 1999, Mixed Magics, Year of the Griffin, 2000, The Merlin Conspiracy, 2003, Unexpected Magic, 2004, Changeover, 2004, Conrad's Fate, 2005, The Pinhoe Egg, 2006, The Game, 2007; animated film: Howl's Moving Castle, 2004. Recipient, Mythopoaic Soc. award, 1995, 99, Joseph Wagner award Brit. Fantasy Soc., 1999. Mem. Soc. of Authors, Brit. Fantasy Soc. Avocations: cooking, owning a cat. Home: 9 The Polygon Bristol BS8 4PW England Office: care Greenwillow Books 105 Madison Ave New York NY 10016-7418

JONES, DIANE AUER, government education association administrator; b. Balt. BS, Salisbury State U.; MS Applied Molecular Biology, U. of Md., 1988. Assoc. prof. Cmty. Coll. of Balt. County; program dir. Divsn. of Undergraduate Edn. NSF; acting majority staff dir. Rsch. Subcommittee, Com. on Sci., US Ho. of Reps.; dir. Govt. Affairs, Princeton U., 2003; dep. to the assoc. dir. for sci. Office of Sci. and Tech. Policy, Exec. Office of the Pres.; prin. dep. asst. sec. Office of Postsecondary Edn., US Dept. of Edn., 2007, asst. sec., 2007—. Founder Upper Chesapeake Bay Water Quality Assessment Ctr., The Cmty. Coll. of Baltimore County; co-founder Athena Environ. Sciences, Inc. Office: US Dept of Edn Sec for Postsecondary Edn 1990 K St NW Washington DC 20006 Office Phone: 202-502-7950. Office Fax: 202-502-7875. E-mail: diane.jones@ed.gov.*

JONES, DONALD LEIGH, retired music educator; b. St. Louis, July 2, 1935; s. Norman R.D. and Esther Hamilton Jones; m. Pamela Smith, Aug. 12, 1961; children: Carole Anne, Patricia Annette Doerr, Donna Leigh Ashmore. AB in Music, Monmouth Coll., 1957; EdM in Music, U. Mo., Columbia, 1961. Cert. tchr. Ill. Dir. band Warren County Grade Sch. Dist. #222, Monmouth, Ill., 1956—57; asst. dir. band Monmouth Coll., 1957; tchr. band and vocal music grades 1-12 Stronghurst Cmty. Grade and HS, Ill., 1957—58; dir. vocal music Belleville Twp. HS and Jr. Coll. (now Belleville West HS, Ill., 1961—90; ret., 1990. Music dir. Theta Chi Fraternity Monmouth Coll., Ill., 1953—57; dir. US Army Warner Kaserne Protestant Chapel Choir, Munich, 1959—60; minister of music and chancel choir Hillcrest Christian Ch., Belleville, Ill., 1961—72; substitute tchr. music dept. Belleville West HS, 1990—98. Performer (All Am. Festival Choir): Carnegie Hall, NYC, 1991, Trybonyn Hall, Moscow, 1991, Glinka Amolney Sabor Hall, St. Petersburg, 1991; composer: (songs) Oh Belleville West, Born for Us This Day, Alleluia Christ Lives, Glory Hallelu; arranger and lyricist: And Then There Was Song; author: (software) Music Contest Aids program, 1986—97. Mem. cmty. chorus So. Ill. U., Edwardsville, Ill., 1992—93; dir. chancel choir Stronghurst Presbyn. Ch., Stronghurst, Ill., 1957—58, St. Matthew United Meth. Ch., 1972—80, mem. With US Army, 1958—60. Mem.: St. Clair County Ret. Tchrs. Assn. (life), Ill. Ret. Tchrs. Assn. (life), Am. Choral Dirs. Assn. (life). Republican. Home: 1737 W Belle St Belleville IL 62226-6109

JONES, DONNIE, men's college basketball coach; b. July 7, 1966; m. Michelle Gibson; children: Madisyn Michelle, Donald Isaac. B in Bus. Edn., Pikeville Coll., Ky., 1988; M in Sports Mgmt., Marshall U., Huntington, W.Va., 1992. Asst. coach Pikeville Coll., 1988—90; grad. asst. Marshall U., 1990—92, asst. coach, 1992—96, head coach, 2007—; asst. coach U. Fla., Gainesville, 1996—2006, assoc. head coach, 2006—07. Named to Pikeville Hall of Fame, 2004. Office: Marshall U Mens Basketball Athletic Dept PO Box 1360 Huntington WV 25715*

JONES, DONYA, elementary school educator; d. Deborah Jones-Mayes. BS, NC Ctrl., Durham, 1999, MS, 2006. Tchr. Durham Pub. Sch. Sys., 2000—. Ednl. tutor Delta Sigma Theta Sorority, Durham, 2002—. Home Phone: 919-544-2682.

JONES, DOUGLAS GORDON, retired literature educator; b. Bancroft, Ont., Can., Jan. 1, 1929; s. Gordon Wilfred and Arlene (Ford) Jones; m. Betty Jane Kimbark, Sept. 23, 1950 (div.); children: Stephen, Skyler, Tory Joanne, North; m. Monique Baril, Dec. 1, 1976; 1 stepchild, Nicolas Grandmangin. BA in English, McGill U., 1952; MA in English, Queen's U., 1954; DLitt (hon.), Guelph U., 1982. Instr. Royal Milit. Coll., Kingston, Ont., 1954-55, Ont. Agrl. Coll., Guelph, 1955-61, Bishop's U., Lennoxville, 1961-63; prof. dept. letters and comm. U. Sherbrooke, Que., Canada, 1963-94. Vis prof Univ Victoria, BC, Canada, 1978, Univ Canadienne en France, Villefranche-sur-Mer, 1987; mem arts adv panel, juries Can Coun.

Author: (poetry) Frost on the Sun, 1957, The Sun is Axeman, 1961, Phrases from Orpheus, 1967, Under the Thunder the Flowers Light Up the Earth, 1977 (Gov Gen Award for Poetry, 1977, A J M Smith Award for Poetry, 1977), A Throw of Particles: New and Selected Poems, 1983, Balthazar and Other Poems, 1988 (QSPELL Prize for Poetry, 1989), A Thousand Hooded Eyes, 1991, The Floating Garden, 1995 (QSPELL Prize for Poetry, 1995), Wild Asterisks in Cloud, 1997, Grounding Sight, 1999; translator: The Terror of the Snows: Selected Poems of Paul-Marie Lapointe, 1976, The Fifth Season: Poems by Paul Marie Lapointe, 1995, Normand de Bellefeuille Categorics, One, Two & Three, 1993 (Gov Gen Award for Translation, 1993), Emile Martel, For Orchestra and Solo Poet, 1996; ed, contbg translator: poetry The March to Love: Selected Poems of Gaston Miron, 1986, Esprit de Corps: Quebec Poetry of the Late Twentieth Century in Translation, 1997; contbr. articles to profl jours. Mem.: League Canadian Poets, Royal Soc Can. Home and Office: 120 Houghton St North Hatley PQ Canada J0B 2C0 E-mail: dgjones@abacom.com.

JONES, E. STEWART, JR., lawyer; b. Troy, NY, Dec. 4, 1941; s. E. Stewart and Louise (Farley) J.; m. Constance M., Dec. 28, 1968; children: Christopher, Brady, Erin. BA, Williams Coll., 1963; JD, Albany Law Sch., 1966. Bar: NY 1966, US Dist. Ct. (no. dist.) NY 1966, US Ct. Appeals (2d cir.) 1976, US Supreme Ct. 1976, US Dist. Ct. (we. dist.) NY 1987, US Claims Ct. 1991, US Dist. Ct. (so. and ea. dist.) NY 1994, US Dist. Ct. Vt. 2004. Asst. dist. atty. Rensselaer County, NY, 1968-70, spl. prosecutor, 1974; ptnr. E. Stewart Jones, Troy, 1974—. Mem. com. on profl. stds. of 3d jud. dept. State of NY, 1977-80; mem. 3d jud. screening com. Albany County; mem. merit selection panel for selection and appointment of US magistrate for No. Dist. NY, 1981, 91, 3d jud. dept. jud. hearing officer selection com., 2003-, chmn., 2005-; lectr. in field. Contbr. numerous articles to profl. jours. Trustee Fort Orange Club, Our Lady of Hope/Little Sisters of Poor; trustee Saratoga Performing Arts Ctr., vice chmn. 2005-; trustee Albany Law Sch., chmn. 2002, 07; trustee Albany Acad., chmn. bd. overseers 2007; active Nat. Alumni Coun. Albany Law Sch. With USNG. Named to Best Lawyers in Am. (5 categories); recipient The Teresian House Found. Disting. Alumnus award, Albany Acad., 2002, Trustee Gold medal, Albany Law Sch., 2003. Fellow: Am. Bd. Criminal Lawyers, Am. Bar Found., NY Bar Found., Inner Circle Advs., Am. Bd. Trial Lawyers, Am. Inns. of Ct., Internat. Acad. Trial Lawyers, Am. Coll. Trial Lawyers, Am. Bd. Profl. Liability Attys. (diplomate), Internat. Soc. Barristers (chmn. Upstate NY 1988—); mem.: ABA (numerous coms.), Legal Aid Soc. Northeastern NY (chmn. Campaign for Equal Justice), Acad. Trial Profls., Fed. Ct. Bar Assn., Coll. Master Advs. and Barristers (sr. counsel), Saratoga County Bar Assn., Am. Coll. Barristers (sr. counsel), Internat. Acad. Litigators (diplomate), Civil Justice Found. (founding sponsor), Trial Lawyers for Pub. Justice (founder), Inst. Injury Reduction (founder), Am. Bd. Trial Advs. (adv.), NY State Assn. Criminal Def. Lawyers, Nat. Assn. Criminal Def. Lawyers, Nat. Bd. Trial Advocacy (diplomate), Fed. Bar Coun., Dispute Resolutions, Inc. (nat. panel of arbitrators), Am. Arbitration Assn. (nat. panel of arbitrators), NY State Defenders Assn., Albany County Bar Assn., Am. Soc. Law and Medicine, Rensselaer County Bar Assn., Am. Judicature Soc. (sustaining), Practising Law Inst., Capital Dist. Trial Lawyers Assn. (bd. dirs. 1973—76, Charter Pres. award 2006), NY State Trial Lawyers Assn. (bd. dirs. 1982—91, dir. emeritus 1991), NY State Bar Assn. (mem. exec. com. trial lawyers sect. 1977—90, 1981—94, mem. spl. com. med. malpractice, other coms., Outstanding Practitioner award 1980, Legal Aid Soc. Northeastern NY and Legal Project Svc. award 2005), Williams Club (NYC), Stone Horse Yacht Club (Harwich Port, Mass.), Ft. Orange Club, Schuyler Meadows Club. Home: 46 Schuyler Rd Loudonville NY 12211-1447 Office: 28 2nd St Troy NY 12180-3986 Office Phone: 518-274-5820. Business E-Mail: info@esjlaw.com.

JONES, E. THOMAS, lawyer; b. Buffalo, July 19, 1950; s. Thomas Kenneth and Marian Arlene (Turk) J.; m. Jennifer Dee Lowery, Oct. 19, 1974; children: Evan Thomas III, Courtney Bree. BA, SUNY Coll., Buffalo, 1972; JD, Cleve. State U., 1981. Bar: N.Y. 1982, U.S. Dist. Ct. (we. dist.) N.Y. 1982, U.S. Ct. Appeals (2d cir.) 1987. Mem. mgmt. staff Marine Midland Bank, Buffalo, 1971-76, M&T Bank, Buffalo, 1976-78, 81-82, Nat. City Bank, Cleve., 1978-81; sole practice Buffalo, 1982—. Hearing officer Buffalo City Ct., 1997—. Committeeman Amherst Rep. Party, N.Y., 1984-2004; fire fighter Getzville Fire Co., Inc., Amherst, 1988-91; town councilman, Amherst, 1990-91; coach, bd. dirs. Amherst Youth Hockey Assn.; dep. town atty. Town Amherst, N.Y., 1996-2001, town atty., 2002—. Mem.: Erie County Bar Assn., NY State Bar Assn. (exec. com., mcpl. law com.). Home: 1375 N French Rd Amherst NY 14228-1908 Office Phone: 716-200-1355. Business E-Mail: tom@etjlaw.com.

JONES, EDDIE, architect; m. Lisa Johnson. Founder, prin. Jones Studio Inc., Phoenix, 1979—. Prin. works include Halas Residence, 1985, Ariz. Cardinals Tng. Facility, 1988, Karsten Golf Course Clubhouse, 1994, Japan Eco House, 1996, Walner Residence, 1997, Ariz. State U. Soccer & Softball Stadiums, 1999, Johnson Carlier Office Bldg., 2000, House of 5 Dreams, 2004. Co-recipient Melvin R. Lohmann medal, Okla. State U., 2004. Mem.: AIA. Office: Jones Studio Inc 4450 N 12th St Ste 104 Phoenix AZ 85014 Office Phone: 602-264-2941. Office Fax: 602-264-3440.*

JONES, EDITH HOLLAN, federal judge; b. Phila., Apr. 7, 1949; m. Sherwood (Woody) Jones; 2 children. BA Cornell U., 1971; JD with honors, U. Tex., 1974. Bar: Tex. 1974, US Supreme Ct. 1979, US Ct. Appeals (5th and 11th cirs.), US Dist. (so. and no. dists.) Tex. Assoc. Andrews & Kurth, Houston, 1974—82, ptnr., 1982—85; judge US Ct. Appeals (5th Cir.), Houston, 1985—, chief judge, 2006—. Gen. counsel Rep. Party of Tex., 1981—83. Mem. bd. dir. Boy Scouts of Am. Master: ABA; mem.: Garland Walker Am. Inns of Ct., Houston Bar Assn., State Bar Tex. Presbyterian.*

JONES, EDITH IRBY, internist; b. Conway, Ark., Dec. 23, 1927; d. Robert and Mattie (Buice) Irby; m. James Beauregard Jones, Apr. 16, 1950 (dec. Oct. 1989); children: Gary Ivan, Myra Vonceil Jones Romain, Keith Irby. BS, Knoxville Coll., 1948; MD, U. Ark., 1952; Doctorate (hon.), Mo. Valley Coll., Mary Holmes Coll., Knoxville Coll. Intern Univ. Hosp., Little Rock, 1952-53; gen. practice medicine Hot Springs, Ark., 1953-59; resident in internal medicine Baylor Coll. Medicine, Houston, 1959-62; pvt. practice medicine specializing in internal medicine Houston, 1962—; mem. staff Meth. Hosp., Houston, Hermann Hosp., Houston, St. Elizabeth Hosp., Houston, St. Anthony Ctr., Houston, St. Joseph Hosp., Houston, Thomas Care Ctr., Houston, Town Pk., Houston, chief of staff; chief med. staff Riverside Gen. Hosp., Houston, 2006—. Clin. asst. prof. medicine Baylor Coll. Medicine, U. Tex. Sch. Medicine, Houston; dir. Prospect Med. Lab.; bd. dirs., sec. Mercy Hosp. Comprehensive Health Care Group; ptnr. Jones, Coleman and Whitfield; grad. med. examiner Ct. Calanthe Jurisdiction, Tex.; cons. Social Security Agy., Tex. Pub. Welfare Dept., Vocat. Rehab. Assn., Tex. Rehab. Commn.; bd. dirs. Std. Savs. Assn., others. Contbr. articles to profl. jours. Bd. dirs. Drug Addiction Rehab. Enterprise, March of Dimes, Houston, Odessey House, Houston; adv. bd. Houston Coun. Alcoholism; mem. com. revising justice code Harris County, Tex.; impartial hearing officer Houston Ind. Sch. Dist.; mem. Cmty. Welfare Planning Assn., Friends of Youth, Human Svcs. Adv. Coun., Houston, PTA, YMCA; founder Edith Irby Jones Found.; bd. dirs. Houston Internat. U.; chmn. bd. trustees Knoxville Coll.; trustee Must. Assn. Profl. Svc.; bd. visitors U. Houston, others. Named Dr. Edith Irby Jones Day in her honor, State of Ark., 1985, NYC, 1986, Disting. Alumna, J. William Fulbright Coll. Arts and Scis., 2005, a clinic in her honor, Veracruz, Mex., Most Influential People of 1986, Ebony mag.; named one of 30 Most Influential Black Women Houston, 1984, 100 Leading Black Physicians, Black Enterprise mag., 2001; named to Tex. Black Women's Hall of Fame, 1986, Hall of Fame, U. Ark. Sch. Med. Scis., 2004; recipient proclamation, Houston City Coun., 1985, Mayor of Houston, 1986, cert. of citation, Tex. Ho. of Reps., 1986, commendation, Calif. Senate, 1989, Volunteerism and Cmty. Svc. award, Tex. Acad. internal Medicine, 2000, Scroll of Merit award, Nat. Med. Assn., 2001, Silas Hunt Legacy award, U. Ark., Fayetteville, 2006. Fellow: ACP, Am. Soc. Internal Medicine (Oscar E. Edward award 2001), Am. Coll. Medicine; mem.: NAACP, AMA, Physicians for Human Rights, Bus. and Profl. Women, Tex. Assn. Disability Examiners, Houston Med. Forum, Harris County Med. Assn., Lone Star Med. Assn., Nat. Med. Assn. (first female past pres., Scroll of Merit 2001, Living Legend), Am. Med. Women's Assn. (v.p. Houston chpt.), Nat. Coun. Negro Women (v.p. Dorothy Height chpt.), Women of Achievement (Hall of Fame 1985), Girl Friends, Tops Ladies of Distinction, Links, Order Eastern Star, Eta Phi Beta, Delta Sigma Theta, Alpha Kappa Mu. Democrat. Achievements include African American to graduate from the University of Arkansas School for Medicine Sciences; first African American woman resident at an all white school, the Baylor College of Medicine Affiliated Hospitals. Avocations: travel, walking, swimming. Home: 3402 S Parkwood Houston TX 77021 Office: 2601 Prospect St Houston TX 77004-7737 Home Phone: 713-747-5116; Office Phone: 713-529-3145. Business E-Mail: eijones@advmed.com.

JONES, EDWARD GEORGE, neuroscientist, educator; b. Upper Hutt, Wellington, NZ, Mar. 26, 1939; came to U.S., 1972; s. Frank Ian and Theresa Agnes (Riordan) J.; m. Elizabeth Suzanne Oldham, Apr. 27, 1963; children: Philippa Emilie, Christopher Edward. MD, U. Otago, Dunedin, New Zealand, 1962; PhD, U. Oxford, Eng., 1968. Med. and surg. intern Tauranga Hosp., New Zealand, 1963; demonstrator to assoc. prof. dept. anatomy U. Otago Med. Sch., Dunedin, New Zealand, 1964-72; Nuffield Dominions demonstrator and lectr. Balliol Coll., U. of Oxford, England, 1964-72; assoc. prof. to prof., dept. anatomy and neurobiology Washington U. Sch. Medicine, St. Louis, 1972-84, George H. and Ethel Ronzini Bishop scholar, 1981-84, dir. divsn. exptl. neurology, 1981-84; prof. and chmn. dept. anatomy and neurobiology U. Calif., Irvine, 1984-98, dir. Ctr. Neurosci. Davis, 1998—, prof. psychiatry, 1998—, Disting. prof. psychiatry, 2003—. Cons. NIH, 1972—; dir. Neural Systems Lab., Frontier Rsch. Program in Neural Mechanisms of Mind and Behavior, Riken, Japan, 1988-96; vis. sr. rsch. fellow St. John's Coll. at U. Oxford, Eng., 1989-90. Author: The Thalamus, 1984, 2d edit. 2005; co-author: Thalamus, 1997, The Thalamus and Basal Telencephalon, 1982; co-editor: (book series) Cerebral Cortex, 1984-2001; author, reviewer numerous sci. and hist. articles, chpts. in books, 1964—. Mem. Pres.'s Adv. Bd. Calif. State U., Long Beach, 1986-90. Named one of 100 most cited biol. scientists, Sci. Citation Index, 1982, 151 Thompson scientific highly cited scientist database, 2001; recipient Rolleston Meml. prize, U. Oxford, 1970, Lashley award, Am. Philos. Soc., 2001; grantee rsch. grantee, NIH, 1971—. Fellow: AAAS; mem.: NAS, Anat. Soc. Gt. Britain and Ireland (Symington Meml. prize 1968), Am. Assn. Anatomists (Cajal medal 1999, Henry Gray award 2001), Soc. Neurosci. (com. chair 1978—81, 1988—89, pres.-elect 1997—98, pres. 1998—99). Democrat. Avocations: reading, writing, carpentry. Office: U Calif Ctr Neurosci 1544 Newton Ct Davis CA 95616-4859

JONES, EDWARD PAUL, writer, editor; b. Washington, Oct. 5, 1950; s. Aloysius and Jeanette Majors Jones. BA, Holy Cross Coll., 1972; MFA, U. Va., 1981. Editor, columnist Tax Analysts, Arlington, Va., 1983—2002; prof. Princeton U., George Mason U., U. of Maryland. Author: Lost in the City, 1992 (PEN/Hemingway award for fiction, 1993), The Known World, 2003 (Nat. Book Critics Cir. award for fiction, 2004, Pulitzer Prize for fiction, 2004, Internat. IMPAC Dublin Literary award, 2005). Recipient Lannan Literary award Lannan Found., 1995, Nat. Endowment for the Arts fellowship, MacArthur Fellow, 2004. Mem. PEN Avocation: stamp collecting/philately.

JONES, EDWIN CHANNING, JR., retired electrical and computer engineering educator; b. Parkersburg, W.Va., June 27, 1934; s. Edwin Channing and Helen M. J.; m. Ruth Carol Miller, Aug. 14, 1960; children: Charles, Cathleen, Helene. BSEE, W.Va. U., 1955; Diploma, U. London, 1956; PhD, U. Ill., 1962. Engr. GE, Syracuse, NY and Bloomington, Ill., 1955, 62, Westinghouse Electric Co., Balt., 1959; asst. prof. elec. engring. U. Ill., Urbana, 1962-66; asst. prof. Iowa State U., Ames, 1966-67, assoc. prof., 1967-72, prof., 1972—2001, univ. prof., 1995—2001, assoc. chair dept., 1997—2001, univ. prof. emeritus, 2001—. Mem. Accreditation Bd. Engring. Tech., N.Y.C., 1984-87. Author handbook chpts. on electronic engring. Lt. US Army, 1956—58. Recipient Linton F. Grinter Disting. Svc. award, Accreditation Bd. Engring. Tech., 2001. Fellow AAAS, IEEE (pres. edn. soc. 1975-76, mem. ednl. activities bd. 1975-76, 78-81, 84-87, accreditation activity award), Am. Soc. Engring. Edn.; mem. Soc. History of Tech., Sigma Xi, Tau Beta Pi, Eta Kappa Nu, Phi Kappa Phi, Phi Beta Delta. Avocations: photography, slide rule collecting. Mailing: 5289 Nolan Pkwy Oak Park Heights MN 55082

JONES, ELAINE F., psychologist, educator; b. Phila., Aug. 10, 1961; d. Percy Edward and Frances Louise Jones. BS, U. Pitts., 1983, MS, 1988, PhD, 1991. Asst. prof. U. N.C., Chapel Hill, 1990—95, St. Louis U., 1995—2002; rsch. analyst Parents as Tchrs., Inc., St. Louis, 2002—03; asst. prof. Arcadia U., Glenside, Pa., 2003—05. Cons. editor Jour. Psychology, Washington, 1999—; advisor Naked Eye Prodns., NYC, 1997; project rschr. Dateline NBC/Discovery Channel, NYC, 2000. Panel mem. Youth Aid Panel, Montgomery County, Pa., 2004—. Fellow Minority Program fellow, APA, 1988—99, Tchg. fellow, Eli Lilly Endowment and U. N.C., 1992—93; grantee Lindback Found. Jr. Faculty grantee, Christian R. and Mary F. Lindback Found., 2004—05. Mem.: APA, Soc. for Rsch. in Child Devel., Delta Sigma Theta. Democrat. Avocations: travel, reading, films, music. Office: Arcadia Univ Dept Psychology 450 S Easton Rd Glenside PA 19038

JONES, ELAINE HANCOCK, humanities educator; b. Niagara Falls, NY, Feb. 17, 1946; d. Roy Elmer and June Edna (Clark) Hancock; m. Ralph Jones III, Oct. 9, 1971 (div. June 1981). AAS in Comml. Design, U. Buffalo, 1962; BFA, SUNY, Buffalo, 1971, MFA in Painting, 1975; postgrad., Fla. State U., 1993—. Med. illustrator Roswell Park Meml. Inst., Buffalo, 1967—70; designer, animator Acad. McLarty Film Prodns., Buffalo, 1970—73; publs. designer Buffalo/Erie County Hist. Soc., 1974—78; dir. publs. Daemen Coll., Amherst, NY, 1978—80; owner, art dir. Plop Art Prodns., Melbourne, Fla., 1981—86; instr. humanities Brevard C.C., Melbourne, 1986—; prof. humanities Brevard campus Rollins Coll., Melbourne, 1995—2004. One-woman shows include SUNY, Buffalo, 1974, Upton Gallery, N.Y., 1975, Gallery Wilde, Buffalo, 1978; exhibited in group shows at Fredonia Coll., N.Y., 1975, Upton Gallery, 1975, Brevard Art Mus., Melbourne, Fla., 1987. Mem. docent program Art Mus./Sci. Ctr., Melbourne, 1983-84, mem. edn. com., 1995—; officer Platinum Coast chpt. Sweet Adelines Internat., 1984-90. Nat. Merit scholar, 1971-75; recipient cert. of merit Curtis Paper Co., 1977; N.Y. State Coun. on Arts grantee, 1975. Republican. Home: 2240 Sea Ave Indialantic FL 32903-2524 Office: Brevard CC Liberal Arts Dept 3865 N Wickham Rd Melbourne FL 32935-2310 Office Phone: 321-632-1111 x5744.

JONES, ELAINE R., former legal association administrator, civil rights advocate; b. Norfolk, Va., Mar. 2, 1944; AB, Howard U., 1965; LLB, U. Va., 1970. Spl. asst. to sec. William T. Coleman Jr. US Dept. Trans., Washington, 1975—77; pres., dir.-counsel, atty. NAACP Legal Def. and Ednl. Fund, Washington, 1993—2004. Mem. panel arbitration Am. Stock Exch. Recipient Recognition award Black Am. Law Student Assn, 1974, Spl. Achievement award Nat. Assn. Black Women Attys., 1975, Olender Found. Peacemaker award, 2000, Lamplighter Award for Equity and Justice, Black Leadership Forum, 2003, Lifetime Achievement award, Am. Law mag., 2005 Mem. Nat. Bar Assn., Internat. Fedn. Women Lawyers, Old Dominion Bar Assn., Va. trial Lawyers Assn., Delta Sigma Theta.

JONES, ELIZABETH HARDING, real estate agent, retired elementary school educator; b. Oahu, Hawaii, Feb. 8, 1954; d. Robert Trumbull and Joan Carol (Jenkins) Harding; divorced; children: Colin James Fisher-Jones, Ryan Matthew BA Art Edn., Georgian Ct. Coll., Lakewood, NJ, 1980; cert. elem. edn., Georgian Ct. Coll., 1983, MA Severely Multiple Handicapped, 1999. Cert. K-12 art tchr., tchr. of the handicapped, N.J., 1996. Secondary tchr. art Freehold Regional H.S. Dist., Englishtown, NJ, 1980—81; mid. sch. tchr. art Neptune Bd. Edn., NJ, 1984; elem. tchr. art Howell Twp. Bd. Edn., NJ, 1980, 1982—83, 1984. Adj. instr. Brookdale C.C., Lincroft, NJ; agt. real estate, Manasquan, NJ. Instr. lifeguard tng., water safety instr. trainer, adapted water safety, water safety, stds. first aid, CPR, AED instr., 1988 Mem. Nat. Art Edn. Assn., Art Educators N.J., N.J. Edn. Assn. (women in edn. com. 1991), Monmouth County Edn. Assn. (rep. 1990), Howell Twp. Edn. Assn. (rep. 1989—) Roman Catholic. Avocations: swimming, reading, sewing. Home: 37 N Farragut Ave Manasquan NJ 08736-3127 Office: Diane Turton Realtors Rt 34 S Manasquan NJ 08736

JONES, ELIZABETH WINIFRED, biology professor; b. Seattle, Mar. 8, 1939; d. Kenneth Clifford Harris and Dorothea (Dowty) J. BS, U. Wash., 1960, PhD, 1964. Postdoctoral fellow MIT, Cambridge, 1964-67, instr. in biology, 1967-69; asst. prof. Case Western Res. U., Cleve., 1969-74; assoc. prof. Carnegie Mellon U., Pitts., 1974-82, prof., 1982—, dept. head, 2000—, Frederick A. Schwertz Disting. Prof. of Life Scis., 2000—. Vis. scientist Sch. Medicine Wash. U., 1981-82; adj. prof. in psychiatry U. Pitts., 1985—; mem. genetics tng. com. NIH, Bethesda, Md., 1972-73, mem. genetics study sect., 1976-80, 84-86, chair, 1990-93. Co-author: (with D.L. Hartl) Genetics: Principles and Analysis, 1998, (with D.L. Hartl) Essential Genetics, 1999, Genetics: An Analysis of Genes and Genomes, 2000, 04; editor: Molecular Biology of the Yeast Saccaromyces, 2 vols., 1981, 82, Molecular and Cellular Biology of the Yeast Saccaromyces, 3 vols., 1991, 92, 97; assoc. editor Genetics, 1980-96, editor-in-chief 1997—; assoc. editor Yeast, 1984—, Ann. Rev. of Genetics, 1990—; mem. editl. bd. Molecular Biology of the Cell, 1992-2000. Recipient Rsch. Career Devel. Award, NIH, 1971—74, 1975—77; grantee professorship, Howard Hughes Med. Inst., 2002—. Fellow AAAS; mem. Am. Soc. Microbiology, Am. Acad. of Microbiology, Am. Soc. Cell Biology (coun. 1992-95), Genetics Soc. Am. (pres. 1987), Am. Soc. Human Genetics. Office: Carnegie Mellon U 4400 5th Ave Pittsburgh PA 15213-2617 Business E-Mail: ej09@andrew.cmu.edu.

JONES, ELLEN, elementary school educator; b. Lithonia, Ga., Apr. 16, 1954; d. Bobby and Margaret (Harper) Jackson; children: Gretchen Nichole, Mindy Tissie Antonia. AS in Edn., DeKalb C.C., Decatur, Ga., 1974; BS in Edn., Ga. State U., 1976; MEd, Clark U., 1987; Math. and Sci. specialist degree, Wynbrooke Theme Sch., Minn., 1995. Cert. K-8 tchr., Ga. Tchr. math. DeKalb County Bd. Edn., Decatur, 1980—. Spkr. Rock Eagle Math. Conf., Eaton, Ga., 1991—, Columbus (Ga.) Math. Conf., 1993, NCTM Conf., St. Paul, 2004; radio announcer WY2E. Tutor reading and math. God Life and Living Holiness Ch. of Jesus Christ, Ellenwood, Ga., 1991—, rep. N.Am. Russian Math. Conf., St. Petersburg, Russia, 1998; assoc. min. Big Miller Grove Missionary Bapt. Ch., Lithonia, Ga. Named Tchr. of Yr., Sky Haven Sch., 1990, 91. Mem. Nat. Coun. Tchrs. Math. Home: 1036 Chapman Cir Stone Mountain GA 30088-2558

JONES, EMIL, JR., state legislator; b. Chgo., Oct. 18, 1935; s. Emil Sr. and Marilla (Mims) J.; children: Debra, Renee, John, Emil III; m. Lorrie Stone, Nov. 19, 2005. A in Bus. Adminstrn., City Coll. Chgo., 1970. Mem. Ill. Ho. Reps., Springfield, 1972-82, Ill. Senate, Springfield, 1982—, Senate Dem. leader, 1992—2002, mem. exec. com., pres., 2002—05, senate pres., 2003—, bd. dirs. pres.' forum, 2004—. Active Task Force on Long Term Care, Morgan Pk. Civic League, Chgo. Named one of 100 Most Influential Black Americans, Ebony mag., 2006; named to Hall of Fame, Tilden Tech. Inst., 2004; recipient Legis. of the Yr. award, Keep Chgo. Beautiful, 2002, Outstanding Legis. award, Chgo. Prin. & Adminstr. Assn., 2003, Small Victories award, Chgo. Assn. for Retarded Citizens, 2003, Legis. of the Yr., Ill. Assn. of Minorities in Govt., 2003, Humanitarian of the Yr., Abraham Lincoln Ctr., 2003, Social Action award, Nat. Assn. of Black Social Workers, 2003, Dem. Legis. of the Yr., Ill. State Crime Commn., 2003, Champion Justice award, Ill. Equal Justice Coalition, 2003, Nat. Winn Newman Econ. Equity award, Svc. Employee Internat. Union, 2003, Person of the Yr. award, United Food & comml., 2003, Person of Yr., United Food & Comml. Workers, 2003, Mark Excellence award, Nat. Forum Black Pub. Adminstrs., 2004, LifeSaver award, Save-A-Life Found., 2004, Impact award, Chgo. Minority Bus. Devel. Coun., 2004, Paul Simon Pub. Svc. award, Ill. Hunger Coalition, 2004, Man of Yr. award, Best Buddies, 2005, Let Talent Shine award, Coll. Summit, Chgo., 2005, John R. Hammell award, Chgo. Chpt. ACLU, 2005, Friends of Africa award, Continental Africa C. of C., 2006, Dave Peteron award, Chgo. Tchr. Union, 2006, Lifeline award, Cmty. Mental Health Coun., 2006. Mem. Nat. Black Caucus State Legislators, Nat. Conf. State Legislators, Knights of St. Peter Claver, Shriners. Democrat. Roman Catholic. Home: 11357 S Lowe Ave Chicago IL 60628-4714 Office: 507 W 111th St Chicago IL 60628-4019 also: James R Thompson Ctr 100 W Randolph St Ste 16 600 Chicago IL 60601-3220 Office: 327 State Capitol Springfield IL 62706

JONES, ERVIN E., physician, educator; b. Emerson, Ark., May 10, 1943; s. William McKinley and Charity L. Jones; m. Elaine A. Jones, June 19, 1982; 1 child, Mark Rojette. BS, U. Ark., 1966; PhD, U. Ill., 1971; MD, U. Calif., Irvine, 1977. Diplomate Am. Bd. Reproductive Medicine. Fellow in pathology U. Claif., Irvine, 1976, resident in ob-gyn., 1977-81; rsch. assoc. Yale U. Sch. Medicine, New Haven, 1982-83, instr., 1983-85, asst. prof., 1985-90, assoc. prof., 1991-99, prof., 1999—. Cons. NIH/Alcohol, Drug Abuse and Mental Health Adminstrn. USPHS, 1995—; dir. assisted reprodn. dept. ob-gyn. Yale U. Med. Sch., New Haven. Contbr. articles to profl. jours. Advisor assisted reprodn. Conn. State Legislature, Hartford, 1999—. Mellon fellow, 1982-83, NIH fellow, 1971-73, 1991. Fellow: ACOG; mem.: AAUP, Soc. for Gynecol. Investigation, Soc. Assisted Reproductive Tech., Nat. Med. Assn., Assn. Profs. Gynecology (Excellence in Tchg. award 1992), Am. Soc. Reproductive Medicine. Avocation: outdoor activities.

JONES, EUGENE GORDON, pharmaceutical company executive; b. Lookout, W.Va., June 26, 1929; s. Alphus Raymond and Mona Blanche (Bobbitt) J.; m. Nancy Lee Hall, Aug. 19, 1951; children: Gene Douglas, Michael Gordon, Rebecca Lee, Jody Lynn. BS, Va. Tech. U., 1951. Med. rep. The Upjohn Co., Charlottesville, Va., 1956-60, profl. svcs. mgr. Washington, 1960-63, sr. med. rep. Roanoke, Va., 1963-68, hosp. med. rep. Richmond, Va., 1968-70, dist. sales mgr. Va., 1970-73, tng. specialist Kalamazoo, Mich., 1973-76, tng. mgr., 1976-87, nat. tng. dir., 1987-90; pres., owner Global Meeting Planners, 1991—. Bd. dirs. Kalamazoo Specialty Plants. Author: (self instrn. course) Managed Health Care, 1985, Arthritis Primer, 1976. Founder, pres. Am. Diabetes Assn., Roanoke chpt., 1967, Richmond chpt., 1971, state del. ADA, 1970; bd. dirs. United Way, Kalamazoo, 1990-91, Mich. Diabetes Assn., Detroit, 1979; deacon River Rd. Presbyn. Ch.; mem. Rep. Presdl. Task Force. Lt. U.S. Army, 1951-53, Korea, capt. USAR, 1953-60. Mem. Korean War Vets. Assn. (founder of the Kalamazoo Mi Korea War chpt., life), Nat. Soc. Pharm. Sales Trainers (hon., pres. Western chpt. 1980-81, pres. nat. orgn. 1987-88, dir. 1985-90, founder newsletter 1987), Meeting Planners Internat., Internat. Meeting Planners, Mil. Order World Wars (treas. 1964-68), Kalamazoo Aviation

History Mus., Charles Garfield Group (hon.), Korean War Vets. Assn, Res. Officers Assn. of U.S. (life), PGA Assocs. (life), Am. Legion, Vets. of Fgn. Wars. Avocations: volunteering, golf, reading, walking, travel.

JONES, EVERETT RILEY, JR., oil industry executive; b. Leitchfield, Ky., July 28, 1918; s. Everett Riley and Margie (Hatfield) J.; m. Lois Gibbins, July 15, 1950; children: Stacey Rae, Rande Leigh. Student, Spencerian C.C., 1936-37, U. Louisville, 1946-47. Lic. pub. acct., Ky. Sec. treas., dir. Lafitte Oil Corp., Louisville, 1947-49; ptnr. Fryer & Hanson Drilling Co., Dallas, 1950-58; pres., dir. Bengal Producing Co., Dallas, 1959—. Dir. Dallas County Small Bus. Devel. Ctr., Inc. Contbr. articles/stories to newspapers, publs. Trustee S.W. Engring. Found. Served to capt. USAAF, 1942-45. Decorated D.F.C., Air medal with 4 oak leaf clusters. Mem. Engrs. Club Dallas (past pres.) Dallas Petroleum Club (past pres.), Royal Air Force Club in London, Northwood Country Club Dallas. Episcopalian. Office: 8080 N Central Expy Dallas TX 75206-1838

JONES, FLORENCE M., music educator; b. West Columbia, Tex., Apr. 11, 1939; d. Isaiah and Lu Ethel (Baldridge) McNeil; m. Waldo D. Jones, May 29, 1965; children: Ricky, Wanda, Erna. BS, Prairie View A&M U., 1961, MEd, 1968; postgrad., U. Houston, 1980, Rice U., 1988. Cert. tchr. elem. edn., math. Tchr. English and typing Lincoln H.S., Port Arthur, Tex., 1961-62; tchr. grades three and four Houston Ind. Sch. Dist., 1963-90, tchr. gifted and talented, 1990-94; tchr. piano Windsor Village Liberal Arts Acad., Houston, 1994—. Dist. tchr. trainer Houston Ind. Sch. Dist., 1985-90; shared decision mem. Sch. decision Making Team, 1993-94; coord. gifted/talented program, Petersen Elem. Sch., Houston, 1990-94; participant piano Recital Hartzog Studio, 1985-88; film previewer Houston Media Ctr. Curriculum writer Modules to Improve Science Teaching, 1985; author sci. pop-up book, 1980, gifted/talented program, 1994; contbr. poems to lit. jours. Youth camp counselor numerous non-denominational ch. camps, US, 1961-89; active restoration of Statue of Liberty, Ellis Island Found., NYC, 1983-85; charter founder People Am. Ctr. Ellis Island, 2007; lay min. Ch. of God, 1961-94; charter founder The Am. Family History Immigration Ctr., Ellis Island, NYC; charter mem. Wall of Tolerance, honoree, 2005; co-chair Rosa Parks Commn.; founding sponsor Martin Luther King Jr. Nat. Meml. Project Found. Inc., 2006 Recipient Letter of Recognition Outstanding Progress in Edn., Pres. Bill Clinton, 1994, Congresswoman Sheilia Jackson Lee, Tex. Gov. George Bush, State Rep. Harold V. Sutton Jr., Houston Mayor Bob Lanier, Tex. Gov. Ann Richards; Gold Cup/Highest Music award Hartzog Music Studio, 1987, Diamond Key award Nat. Women of Achievement, 1995, Editors Choice award Nat. Libr. Poetry, 1995, cert. recognition Quaker Oats Co., 1999, Youth Advisors trophy and New Millennium Leader plaque Nat. Women Achievement, 2001, Humanitarian trophy, 2005; named Grandparent of Yr. Nat. Women of Achievement Youth Divsn., 2003; named to The Internat. Poetry Hall of Fame. Mem. NEA, Houston Assn. Childhood Edn. (v.p. 1985-88), Assn. for Childhood Edn. (bd. dir. 1979-91), Houston Zool. Soc., World Wildllife Fund, Nat. Storytelling Assn., Tejas Storytelling Assn. (life), Soc. Children's Book Writers and Illustrators, Nat. Audubon Soc., Am. Mus. Natural History, Tex. Ret. Tchrs. Assn. (life), Internat. Soc. Poets (life, Silver Cup award for outstanding poetry achievement 2003), Smithsonian Instn., Nat. Mus. Am. Indian, Nat. Mus. Women in Arts, Nat. Women's History Mus.(charter mem.) Democrat. Avocations: writing, reading, storytelling, collecting sea shells, crafts. Home: 3310 Dalmatian Dr Houston TX 77045-6520

JONES, FRANCES MARY, law librarian; b. Little Rock, Dec. 27, 1942; d. Henry George and Ruth O'Donnell Nachtsheim; m. Ronald Benjamin Jones, May 6, 1967 (dec. Nov. 22, 1986). BA, Coll. St. Catherine, 1964; MA, U. Minn., 1982; JD, William Mitchell Coll. Law, 1988. Bar: Minn. 1989. With Calif. State Libr., Sacramento, 1995—99; dir. Maricopa County Law Libr., Phoenix, 1991—94; sr. tax cons. Deloitte & Touche, Mpls., 1987—90; libr. U. Minn. Law Libr., 1990—91; dir. Calif. Jud. Ctr. Libr./Calif. Supreme Ct., San Francisco, 1999—. Mem. State Govt. Adv. Group, WestGroup, Eagan, 2002—. Author: (monograph) Defusing Censorship: The Librarian's Guide to Managing Censorship Conflict, (directory) Directory of Library Staff Organizations. Mem.: Ariz. Assn. Law Librs. (pres. 1994), Women Lawyers Sacramento, Minn. State Bar Assn., No. Calif. Assn. Law Librs., Am. Assn. Law Librs., Phi Kappa Phi. Conservative. Catholic. Avocations: music, ice skating, walking. Office: Calif Judicial Center Libr 455 Golden Gate Ave Rm 4617 San Francisco CA 94102 Office Phone: 415-865-7170. Personal E-mail: francesmjones@yahoo.com. E-mail: fran.jones@jud.ca.gov.

JONES, FRANK A., JR., psychiatrist, educator; MD, Case Western U., Cleve., 1972. Diplomate Am. Bd. Psychiatry and Neurology, 1977. Psychiatry intern Boston State Hosp., Dorchester, Mass., 1972—73; resident in psychiatry Worcester State Hosp., 1973—75; physician dept. psychiatry Univ. Behavioral Health Ctr., Piscataway, NJ, 1977—2002. Prof. psychiatry Robert Wood Johnson Med. Sch., 1977—. Office: 2186 Rt 27 Ste 2A North Brunswick NJ 08902 Office Phone: 732-422-0800.

JONES, FRANK CATER, retired lawyer; b. Macon, Ga., June 19, 1925; s. Charles Baxter and Carolyn (Cater) J.; m. Annie Gantt Anderson, Mar. 31, 1951; children: Eugenia Anderson Henderson, Annie Gantt Blattner, Carolyn Corley, Frank Cater. BBA, Emory U., 1947; LLB, Mercer U., 1950, LLD (hon.), 1996. Bar: Ga. 1950. Pvt. practice, Macon, 1950—77; mem. firm Jones, Cork & Miller (and predecessor), 1950—77, King & Spalding, Atlanta, 1977—2001; of counsel Jones, Cork & Miller, Macon, Ga., 2005—. Bd. dirs. So. Trust Corp. Trustee Wesleyan Coll., Macon, 1966-2005, trustee emeritus, 2005—, chmn. bd. dirs., 1981-86; pres. Atlanta Symphony Orch. League, 1982-84; chmn. Ga. Gt. Park Authority, 1980-83, Ga. Pub. Telecom. Commn., 1983-98, Met. Atlanta chpt. ARC, 1987-88; bd. dirs. Carter Ctr., Emory U., 1987—; chmn. Michael C. Carlos Mus., 1991-96; trustee Emory U., Atlanta, 1991-95, trustee emeritus, 1995—. Fellow: ACTL (bd. regents 1986—, sec. 1990—92, pres. 1993—94); mem.: ABA (ho. of dels. 1972—94), U.S. Supreme Ct. Hist. Soc. (pres. 2002—), State Bar of Ga. (pres. 1968—69), Ga. Bar Assn. (pres. young lawyers sect. 1956—57), Macon Bar Assn. (pres. 1954), Greater Macon C. of C. (pres. 1965), Rotary. Home: 4957 Wellington Dr Macon GA 31210-4427 Office: Jones Cork & Miller PO Box 6437 435 Second St Macon GA 31208-6437 Home Phone: 478-474-7807; Office Phone: 478-745-2821. Business E-Mail: frank.jones@jonescork.com.

JONES, FRANK GRIFFITH, lawyer; b. Houston, Sept. 11, 1941; s. A. Gordon and Grace (Griffith) Jones; m. Deborah Ann Young, July 5, 1969; children: Russell G., Sarah G., Christopher Y. BS, Rice U., 1963; JD, U. Tex., 1966. Bar: Tex. 1966, U.S. Dist. Ct. (so., no. and ea. dists.) Tex., U.S. Ct. Appeals (5th and 8th cirs.), cert.: (civil trial specialist). Counsel Fulbright & Jaworski, LLP, Houston, 1966, co-ptnr. in charge Houston office, 2001—06. Chmn. Fulbright & Jaworski Employment Commn., 1988—92. Chmn. troop com. Boy Scouts Am., Houston, 1986—88; chair Environ. Adv. Com., 2004—05, Govtl. Rels. Com., 2005—06; bd. dirs. exec. com. Greater Houston Partnership, 2004—06; bd. dirs. Friends Fondren LIbr.; bd. mem. Friends of Harn's County Court House; bd. dirs., chmn. Houston Forum; cmty. adv. bd. mem. Edn. Found. Houston; mem. Rice U. Fund Coun., Houston, 1987—93; pres. Baker Coll. Rice U., 1962—63. Lt. (j.g.) USNR, 1967—72. Keeton Fellow, U. Tex. Law Sch., 1993—. Fellow: Internat. Acad. Trial Lawyers, Am. Coll. Trial Lawyers (ADR com. 1986—96, chmn. 1992—94, ethics com. 1996—2001, nat. moot ct. competition com. 2004—, chmn. 2005—); mem.: ABA (moot ct. com. 2003—, chmn. 2004—), Chartered Inst. Arbitrators, Def. Rsch. Inst., Tex. Assn. Def. Counsel, Am. Bar Found., Houston Bar Found. (chmn. 2003), Tex. Bar Found., Tex. Bar Assn., Houston Young Lawyers Assn. (pres. 1972—73), Internat. Assn. Def. Counsel, Am. Bd. Trial Advs., Rotary, Phi Delta Phi (past pres.). Avocations: tennis, travel. Office: Fulbright & Jaworski LLP Fulbright Twr 1301 Mckinney St Ste 5100 Houston TX 77010-3095 Home Phone: 713-621-3340; Office Phone: 713-651-5473.

JONES, FRANK JOSEPH, securities exchange executive; BA, U. Notre Dame, 1960, BS, 1961; MS in Nuc. Engring., Cornell U., Ithaca, NY, 1963; MBA, U. Pitts., 1964; PhD in Econs., Stanford U., Calif., 1971. Sr. economist US Gen. Acctg. Office/Office Prog. Analysis, Washington, 1975-76, various to expert cons., 1976-78; sr. economist SRI Internat., Menlo Park, Calif., 1976-78; v.p. rsch., chief economist Chgo. Merc. Exch., 1978-79; exec. v.p., COO NY Futures Exch., 1979-82; sr. v.p., mgr. Index and Options Products Divsn. NY Stock Exch., 1982-83; mng. dir. Fin. Dept. Kidder, Peabody, & Co., Inc., NYC, 1983-88; dir. Barclays de Zoete Wedd Gov. Securities, Inc., NYC, 1988-89; assoc. dir. Global Securities Rsch., dir. Fixed Income Rsch. Merrill Lynch & Co., NYC, 1989-91; exec. v.p., chief investment officer Guardian Life Ins. Co. of Am., NYC, 1991—2002; chmn. Internat. Securities Exch., NYC, 2006—. Bd. dirs. Internat. Securities Exch., NYC, 2000-; assoc. prof. Sch. of Bus., San Jose U., 1973-78; fin. faculty Stern Sch. Bus., NYU, 1995—; prof. acctg. and bus. dept., San Jose State U., 2003-; spkr. in field. Author several books including: Global Government Bonds, 1992, The Futures Game: Who Wins, Who Loses and Why?, 1987, Marco Finance-The Financial System and the Economy, 1978, (with Frank J. Fabozzi, Franco Modigliani and Michael Ferri) Foundations of Financial Markets and Institutions, 3rd edit., 2002; contbr. articles and book chpts. to profl. publs. Office: Internat Securities Exch Holdings Inc 60 Broad St New York NY 10004*

JONES, FRANK WYMAN, management consultant, director, mechanical engineer; b. Ironton, Ohio, Jan. 20, 1940; s. Kylius and Kathleen (McDonald) J.; m. Margaret Kwitek, Sept. 1, 1962; children: Kelly, Connie, Katie, Colleen, Carolyn. BSME, U. Cin., 1963; MBA, Ind. U., 1965. V.p., gen. mgr. G & L Machine Tool Divsn., Fond du Lac, Wis., 1976-80; exec. v.p. Giddings & Lewis Inc., Fond du Lac, Wis., 1980-81, pres., CEO, 1982-86; mgmt. cons. Tucson, 1987—. Bd. dirs. Modine, Racine, Wis., Star Cutter Co., Farmington Hills, Mich., Gardner Publs., Inc., Cin. Gen. Tool Co., Cin. Mem. Am. Mgmt. Assn., Nat. Assn. Corp. Dirs. Republican. Roman Catholic. Home: 6740 N Saint Andrews Dr Tucson AZ 85718-2619

JONES, FRANKLIN CHARLES, judge; b. Hanover, NH, July 2, 1948; s. Laurence Harry and Dorothy Selma (Covey) J. BA, U. NH, 1970; JD, Boston U., 1973. Bar: NH 1973, US Dist. Ct. NH 1978, US Ct. Appeals (1st cir.) 1978, US Supreme Ct. 1979. Atty. Michael & Wallace, Rochester, NH, 1973-76; ptnr. Michael & Jones, Rochester, 1976-78, Michael Jones & Wensley, 1979-1992, Jones, Wensley, Wirth & Azarian, 1992-2001; presiding justice Rochester Dist. Ct., 2001—. Office: Rochester Dist Ct 76 N Main St Rochester NH 03867

JONES, FRANKLIN ROSS, education educator; b. Charlotte, NC, Jan. 3, 1920; s. William Morton and Olive Ruth (Moser) J.; divorced; children: Franklin Ross, C. Morton, Susan Noel. AB, Lenoir Rhyne Coll., 1941; MA, U. NC, 1951; DEd, Duke U., 1960. Tchr., NC, 1944-48; prin. Jr. HS, Henderson, NC, 1948-54; dist. sch. prin. Wake County, NC, 1954-56; dist. supt. Roxboro schs., NC, 1956-58; chmn. dept. edn. Randolph-Macon Coll., Ashland, Va., 1959-64; interim dean U. Richmond, Va., 1962; dean Sch. Edn. Old Dominion U., 1964-69, Eminent prof., 1974-94; founder Child Study Ctr., 1965, disting. prof., 1969—, social founds. program leader, 1973-77, doctoral program liaison rep., 1974-77, faculty chmn., 1981—. Dir. Forest Ridge Corp., 1985; vis. rsch. scholar Duke U., 1967; cons. HEW, State Sch. Sys. and Colls.; lectr. in field; mem. com. White house Conf. Children and Youth, 1968-71, Ea. regional chmn., 1968-71; mem. Va. Gov.'s Com. Implementation, 1971-73; spkr. 25th Internat. Congress of Psychology, Brussels, 1992; symposium chmn. European Congress of Psychology, Athens, Greece, 1995; cons. to dean on test score stats., Old Dominion U., 1995—; adj. prof. U. Va., 1959-64. Author: Psychology of Human Development, 1969, 3d edit. 1992, Handbook on Testing, 1972, Understanding the Middlescent Years, 1978, Theory of Adult Development, 1980, Jack, 2002, How to Survive Middle Age, 2005; Radio series Sta. WTAR, Norfolk, 1973-75; test item writer for NY Regency exams, 1987, Ednl. Testing Svc., 1989; guest editor Education, 1990—, Jack, 2002, How to Survive Middle Age, 2005. Mem. Norfolk Urban Coalition, 1969-73; chmn. March of Dimes, Person County, NC, 1956-57; mem. adv. bd. Tidewater Rehab. Ctr., 1967-69; chmn. Hull Scholarship Fund, 1983-85; coord. U. Joy Fund Drive, 1974-95; univ. chmn. United Fund, 1982, 84; chmn. assessment com. Va. Reading to Learn Program, 1990-91; cons. to sch. systems, ETS, HEW, Coll. 1966—; dir. Praxis Ctr., 1965-2005; adminstr. Nat. Bd. for Cert. Counselors Ctr., Nat. Lang. and Music Bd. of Certification; chmn. scholarship fund Brewton Parker Coll., Mt. Vernon, Ga., 1999-2004; chmn. drive for low-paid faculty Old Dominion U., 2002-. Recipient Heritage Found. award, 1996, Football recognition and scholar Brewton Parker Coll., Ga., 1999, Hon. Chmn., 2007, Hon. Alumnus, 2007; Va. Golden Olymnpics tennis doubles champion, 1982-84, 880 meter run Gold medal, 1983, 100 meter dash Silver medal, 1984. Mem. Am. Psychol. Soc. (charter), S.E. Psychol. Assn., Va. Assn. U. Profs. (dir. 1962-64), South Atlantic Philosophy Edn. Soc. (pres. 1966-69, dir. 1969—), Va. Assn. Rsch. in Edn. (Disting. Rsch. awards 1972, 73, 78), NC Edn. Assn. (pres. North Ctrl. chpt. 1951, pres. North Ctrl. Prins. 1956), Ea. Ednl. Rsch. Assn., Nat. Urban Edn. Assn., Alpha Tau Kappa, Kappa Delta Pi, Phi Delta Kappa, Phi Kappa Phi, Pi Gamma Mu (sec. 1962-64), Harbor Club (Norfolk), Lions, Rotary. Achievements include being member of Bicycle Relay Jr. Marathon World's Record team, 1933; organizing the the 1st off-campus courses for college and teaching the 1st television course at Old Dominion U. Home: 9810 Woodbay Dr Tampa FL 33626-2425

JONES, GAIL, elementary school educator; b. Hibbing, Minn., June 12, 1952; d. Richard David and Anne Jones; 1 child, Robert Williams Jr. AA, Itasca C.C., Grand Rapids, Minn., 1972; BS in Elem. Edn., Bemidji State U., Minn., 1974. Elem. tchr. Greenway Schs., Coleraine, Minn., 1975—. Mem.: NEA. Office: Vandyke Elem Sch 300 Cole Ave Coleraine MN 55722 Office Phone: 218-245-2510. Business E-Mail: gailjones@greenway.k12.mn.us.

JONES, GENIA KAY, critical care nurse, consultant; b. Dallas, Dec. 21, 1954; d. Joe and Juanita Sue (White) Self; m. Paul L. Jones, June 1, 1986. ADN, Tarrant County Jr. Coll., 1976; mgmt. cert., Cedar Valley Coll., 1980; postgrad., Mountain View Coll., Dallas, 1984—85; BSN, Regent's U., 2001. RN; cert. emergency nurse; cert. BLS, ACLS, pediat. advanced life support, trauma nurse core curriculum, ACLS instr. Instr. Steven's Pk. Hosp., Dallas, 1972-77; asst. dir. nursing svcs. Four Season's Conv. Ctr., Dallas, 1977-78; nurse surgery dept. Dallas/Ft. Worth Med. Ctr., 1978-80; dir. nursing Med. Staffing Svcs., Dallas, 1980, Reproductive Svcs., Inc., Dallas, 1981; adminstrv. supr. Dallas Family Hosp., 1982-85; patient care coord., emergency dept. Dallas S.W. Med. Ctr., 1985-90, staff nurse, emergency dept., 1990-99; medical consultant Needham, Johnson, Lovelace, and Johnson, 1992—2002; emergency nurse dir. Rockwall Minor Emergency Ctr., 1999—2001; emergency nurse Virtual Healthcare Svcs. Meth. Med. Ctrs. Dallas, 2001—03; emergency nurse Virtual Healthcare Svcs. emergency dept. Med. Ctr. Arlington, 2002—. Internat. flight nurse Air Ambulance Network, Inc., Dallas, 1987—92; instr. intravenous therapy, 1980—; cons., adv., 1980—; medico-legal cons., 1990—; clin. instr. Edn. Am., 1999—2001. Recipient Citizens award, Certs. Apprecition, HOSA Nat. Leadership Conf., Silver medal of Honor; Internat. Biog. Assn. fellow, 1990. Mem. NAFE, Am. Heart Assnb., Nurses' Svc. Orgn., Tex. Nurses' Assn., Emergency Nurses' Assn. Home: 108 Burkett Ln Red Oak TX 75154-7602 Home Phone: 972-617-3618; Office Phone: 214-803-4903. Personal E-mail: jgeniak@aol.com. E-mail: genia.jones@worldnet.att.net.

JONES, GEOFFREY MELVILL, physiology research educator; b. Cambridge, Eng., Jan. 14, 1923; s. Benett and Dorothy Laxton (Jotham) J.; m. Jenny Marigold Burnaby, June 21, 1953; children: Katharine, Francis, Andrew, Dorothy. BA, Cambridge U., 1944, MA, 1947, MB, BCh, 1949. House surgeon Middlesex Hosp., London, 1949-50; sr. house surgeon Addenbrookes Hosp., Cambridge, England, 1950-51; sci. med. officer Royal Air Force Inst. Aviation Medicine, Farnborough, England, 1951-55; sci. officer Med. Rsch. Coun., England, 1955-61; assoc. prof. physiology, dir. aviation med. rsch. unit McGill U., Montreal, Que., Canada, 1961-68, prof., dir., 1968-88, Hosmer rsch. prof., 1978-91, emeritus prof. physiology, 1991—. Rsch. prof. clin. neuroscis. U. Calgary, Alta., Can., 1991—, Coll. France, 1979, 95; vis. prof. Stanford U., 1971-72. Author: (with another) mammalian Vestibular Physiology, 1979; editor: (with another) Adaptive Mechanisms in Gaze Control, 1985; contbr. numerous articles to profl. jours. Served to squadron leader Royal Air Force, 1951-55. Sr. rsch. assoc. Nat. Acad. Sci., 1971-72; recipient Skylab Achievement award NASA, 1974, 1st recipient Dohlman medal Dohlman Soc. Toronto U., 1987, Quinquennial Gold medal Barany Soc. Internat., 1988, Ashton Graybiel award U.S. Naval Aerospace Labs., 1989, Wilbur Franks Annual award Can. Soc. Aerospace Medicine, Buchanan-Barbour award Royal Aeronautical Soc., 1991, Mc Laughlin Medal, 1991, Royal Soc. Can. Fellow Can. Aeronautics and Space Inst., Aerospace Med. Assn. (Harry Armstrong award 1968, Arnold D. Tuttle award 1971), Royal Soc. Can. (McLaughlin medal 1991), Royal Soc. London, Royal Aeronautical Soc. London (Stewart Meml. award 1989, Buchanan Barbour award 1990); mem. U.K. Physiol. Soc., Can. Physiol. Soc., Can. Soc. Aerospace Med. Soc., Internat. Collegium Otolaryngology, Soc. Neurosci. Avocations: tennis, sailing, outdoor activities, reading, piano and violin playing/composition. Office: U Calgary Dept Clin Neuroscis 3330 Hospital Dr NW Calgary AB Canada T2N 4N1

JONES, GEORGE, country music singer, songwriter; b. Saratoga, Tex., Sept. 12, 1931; s. George Washington and Clara J.; m. Tammy Wynette, 1968 (div. 1975); 1 child, Georgette; m. Nancy Sepulvado, Mar. 4, 1983. Co-founder Bandit Records, Nashville, 2001—. Played guitar and sang professionally from age 16; first rec. Why Baby, Why, 1955; first No. 1 record White Lightning, 1959; propr.: Jones Country Music Park, 1983; sang duets with Tammy Wynette; composer songs including The Race Is On; recent albums include: I Am What I Am, Rockin' the Country, 1985, Best of George Jones, 1986, Country By George!, 1986, Wine Colored Roses, 1986, Too Wild Too Long, 1988, One Woman Man, 1989, You Oughta Be Here With Me, 1990, Friends in High Places, 1991, Walls Can Fall, 1992, (with Sammy Kershaw) Hi-Tech Redneck, 1993, Salutes Hank Williams, 1994, The New Favorites of George Jones, 1995, Like the Dickens, 1995, (with James Taylor) Bartender's Blues, 1996 The George Jones Collection, 1999, Live With The Possum, 1999, The Rock: Stone Cold Country 2001, Higs I Missed.And One I Didn't, 2005, Kickin' Out the Footlights Again, 2006; songs include He Stopped Loving Her Today (Country Music Assn. Song of Yr. 1980, 81, Music City News Single of Yr. 1981, All Time Country Song, 1992), I Don't Need Your Rocking Chair, 1992 (Country Music Assn. Vocal Event of Yr., 1993), Choices, 1999 (Grammy award for Best Male Country Vocal Performance). Served with USMC, 1950-53. Named Most Pronising New Country Vocalist, Billboard, 1956, Male Vocalist of Yr., Country Music Trade Assn., 1962, 63; named Country Singer of Yr., Rolling Stone, 1976; Best Male Vocalist, Country Music Assn., 1980, 81 Male Artist of Yr., Music City News, 1981; named to Country Music Hall of Fame, 1992; recipient Grammy award for Best Male Country Vocal Performace, 1980, 1999, Nat. Acad. Rec. Arts and Sciences, 1980, Grammy nomination, Best Country Male Vocal; Video award, Country Music Assn., 1986, Living Legend award TNN Music City News, 1987, Favorite Male Video Artist award Am. Music Country Video Awards, 1987, Pioneer award, Acad. Country Music, 1993. Office: Bandit Records 635 West Iris Dr Nashville TN 37204 Office Phone: 615-242-1234. Office Fax: 615-242-2134.*

JONES, GEORGE FLEMING, international consultant; b. San Angelo, Tex., June 27, 1935; s. George Fleming and Cora (Brewer) J.; m. Maria Rosario Correa, Apr. 23, 1960; children: George III, Robert, Michael, Mary Louise. AB magna cum laude, Wabash Coll., 1955; AM, Tufts U., 1956; MA, Stanford U., 1967; LLD, Wabash Coll., 2000. Joined Fgn. Svc., Dept. State, 1956; with Econ. Bur., Dept. State, Washington, 1956-58; with Am. Embassy Ecuador, 1958-60, Ghana, 1961-63, Venezuela, 1963-66; officer in charge Venezuelan affairs Dept. State, Washington, 1967-69, officer in charge Colombian affairs, 1969-71; polit. advisor U.S. Mission to IAEA, Vienna, 1971-74; counselor for polit. affairs Am. Embassy, Guatemala, 1974-77; student Nat. War Coll., Washington, 1977-78; Latin Am. adviser U.S. del. U.S.-Soviet Conventional Arms Talks, 1978; dep. dir. office Latin Am. regional polit. affairs Dept. State, 1978-80, dir., 1980-82; dep. chief of mission Am. Embassy Costa Rica, 1982-85, Chile, 1985-89; sr. adviser for Latin Am. and Caribbean affairs U.S. del. UN Gen. Assembly, NYC, 1990, 95; amb. to Republic of Guyana, 1991-95; dir. programs for the Ams., Internat. Found. for Election Sys., Washington, 1996-99. Dir. Democracy and Governance Ctr. Devel. Assocs., Inc., 2000-05; mem. editl. bd. Fgn. Svc. Jour., 2007-. Mem. editl. bd.: Fgn. Svc. Jour., 2007—. Recipient Superior Honor award Dept. State, 1987. Mem. Am. Fgn. Svc. Assn. (v.p. 1989-90, 2003-05, bd. dirs. 1999-2001), Sr. Fgn. Svc. Assn. (bd. dirs. 1990-92), Washington Inst. Fgn. Affairs. Home: 3804 Acosta Rd Fairfax VA 22031-3804 E-mail: georgejones@cox.net.

JONES, GEORGE L., retail executive; b. Little Rock, Oct. 25, 1950; s. George L. Jones and Gwendolyn (Grissom) Whitehead; m. Marion A. Hartwick May 23, 1972 (div. May 1978); 1 child, Keeshan; m. Judy M. Cowan, Nov. 12, 1988; children: Dylan, Bailey. BSBA, Henderson State U., 1972. Gen. mgr. Gold's, Little Rock, 1975-78; buyer Dillard Dept. Store, Little Rock, 1978-80, mgr. divisional mdse., 1980-82; v.p., mgr. gen. mdse. Diamond's Dept. Store, Phoenix, 1982-84; v.p. ready-to-wear Target Stores, Mpls., 1985-86, sr. v.p. merchandising, 1986-87, exec. v.p., 1988-91; chmn., CEO Monica Scott Inc., Mpls., 1987-88; pres., CEO Rose's Stores Inc., Henderson, NC, 1991-94; pres., worldwide licensing & retail Warner Bros. Inc., 1994—2001; pres., CEO Saks Dept. Store Group Saks Inc., 2001—05; pres., CEO Borders Group, Inc., Ann Arbor, Mich., 2006—. Mem. N.C. Retail Merchants Assn. (bd. dirs.), Henderson-Vance County C. of C., 1991, CEO Roundtable. Office: Borders Group Inc 100 Phoenix Dr Ann Arbor MI 48108*

JONES, GEORGE WASHINGTON, JR., lawyer; b. Balt., July 27, 1953; s. George W. and Mattie Alice (Reed) Jones; m. Loretta Phylis Pleasant, Aug. 5, 1978; children: Melissa Grace, George Charles, Jessica Michelle. BA, U. Chgo., 1975; JD, Yale U., 1980. Bar: DC 1980, US Dist. Ct. DC 1980, US Ct. Appeals (DC cir.) 1983, US Supreme Ct. 1986. Law clk. to judge Philip W Tone U.S. Ct. Appeals (7th Cir.), Chgo., 1978-79; assoc. O'Melveny & Myers, Washington, 1979-80; asst. to solicitor gen. U.S. Dept. Justice, Washington, 1980-83; assoc. Sidley & Austin, Washington, 1983-87, ptnr., 1988—2001, Sidley Austin Brown & Wood LLP, Washington, 2001—05, Sidley Austin LLP, Washington, 2006—. Mem.: ABA, DC Bar (pres. 2002—03, bd. gov., gen. counsel). Office: Sidley Austin LLP 1501 K St NW Washington DC 20005 Office Phone: 202-736-8158. Office Fax: 202-736-8711. Business E-Mail: gjones@sidley.com.

JONES, GEORGE YOVICIC, civil engineer; b. Belgrade, Yugoslavia, June 2, 1927; m. Sofia Jones, 1960; 1 child, Appta. BSCE, Northwestern U., 1951, MSCE, 1956, PhD Bus. Adminstrn., 1958; PhD (hon.), Hamilton

State U., U. Fla., 1972. Civil engr. Hollabird & Root, Chgo., 1956—57; profl. engr., gen. mgr. Arcadia Engring. Internat., Inc., 1956—70, chmn. bd., 1970—. Civil engr. U.S. Civil Engrs., 1951—54; prof. structural engring. Northwestern U., Evanston, Ill.; chmn. dept. econs. U. Ill., Chgo.; legis. asst. Gen. Assembly, Ill.; pres. Tetrakear & Assocs., Inc.; bd. dirs. 1st Nat. Bank Chgo., Skokie Cmty. Hosp., Ill. Author: The Pneumatic Tube Goes Modern, 1958, Opportunities in Construction, 1960, Management and Labor, 1962; contbr. articles to profl. jours. Bd. chmn. Oakton Coll.; pres. Hamilton State U. Maj. US Army. Mem.: NSPE, ASCE. Avocation: swimming. Address: Box 462 Osprey FL 34229 Office Phone: 941-926-0964. Personal E-mail: geoyo27@aol.com.

JONES, GERALDINE ANN JOHNSON, secondary school educator; b. Seaford, Del., July 30, 1939; d. Thomas E. and Marion Frances (Walker) Johnson; 1 child, Monica. BA, Del. State Coll., 1961; MBA, Cen. Mich. U., 1978; postgrad., Temple U., 1986—; PhD in Edn., Capella U., 1999; MDiv, Ea. Bapt. Theol. Seminary, 2005. Caseworker Div. Social Services, Dover, Del., 1962-64; tchr. English William C. Jason Sch., Georgetown, Del., 1966-67; vis. tchr. Capital Sch. Dist., Dover, 1967—. Home and sch. coord. migrant edn. program, Dover, 1967; paraprofl. Title I, Dover, 1964, 65; supr. Head Start Program, Camden, Del., 1970; speaker in field Active local polit. coms.; lay leader; pres. United Meth. Women, Whatcoat, pres. Peninsula conf., gen. bd. global ministries Peninsula-Del. conf., bd. laity, Dover dist. nominating com., com. on episcopacy/superintendency, coun. on ministries., del. to gen. conf. and jurisdicitonal conf., 1992; mem. nominating com. Upper Atlantic regional sch., dir. summer day camp, asst. dean; mem. Yesterdays Youth Choir, Seaford; min. Outreach Ministries United Meth. Ch.; pastor Union Wesley Unites Meth. Ch., Claresville, Del., 2005; pastor Union Wesley United Meth. Ch., Clarksville, Del., 2005— Named Woman of Yr., Whatcoat Ch., 1986; recipient Young award 2003. Mem. NEA, Internat. Assn. Pupil Pers. Workers, Del. Assn. Cert. Vis. Tchrs. (sec.-treas. 1984), Capital Educators Assn., Del. State Coll. Alumni Assn. (pres. Kent County chpt., Alumni of Yr. 1985, Ms. Alumni 1986-87), Nat. Alumni Assn. (pres.), William C. Jason Alumni Club (treas.), Delta Sigma Theta, Sigma Iota Epsilon. Democrat. Avocations: singing, writing, sewing, cooking, piano. Office: Capital Sch Dist 945 Forest St Dover DE 19904-3498 E-mail: gerryej@aol.com, gjones@capital.k12.de.us.

JONES, GILBERT LEED, retired law enforcement officer, coroner, author, educator; b. Inglewood, Calif., Mar. 22, 1947; s. Vernal and Gwendolyn Helen J.; m. JoAnne Lynn Stang-Jones, June 4, 1966; children: Natalie Lynn Jones-Henderson, Dean Leed Jones. AS, Mt. San Antonio Coll., Walnut, Calif., 1978. Advanced cert. for peace officer stds. in tng., Calif. Dep. sheriff Los Angeles County Sheriff's Dept., LA, 1969-80; dep. sheriff, coroner Mendocino County Sheriff's Dept., Ukiah, Calif., 1980-2000. Search and rescue mem. mounted posse Mendocino County Sheriff's Dept., 1981-96, mounted enforcement officer, 1994-2000, critical incident negotiator, 1995-2000, property mgmt. officer, 1996-2000; adj. instr. Western Nev. C.C., 2002—. Author: (novels) Journey to Horse Heaven, 1997, A Case of Corruption, 1997, Eleven Ninety-Nine! Officer Down!, 1998, In The Company of Their Own Kind, 1998. Sgt. U.S. Army, 1966-69. Avocations: fishing, writing. Office: Word Craft Tech Svcs 1266 Soda Lake Rd Fallon NV 89406-6322 Business E-Mail: wordcraft@cccomm.net.

JONES, GLENN EARLE, property management executive; b. Greensboro, NC, May 11, 1946; s. Harold Clifford and AnnaBelle (Goodwin) Jones. BS in Hotel and Restaurant Mgmt., Cornell U., 1968. Asst. to gen. mgr. Warwick Hotel, Houston, 1968—69; Northwestern Ohio sales rep. L.G. Balfour Co., Attleboro, Mass., 1969—72; resident mgr. Chase Park Plaza Hotel, St. Louis, 1972—74; gen. mgr. Holiday Inn, Steamboat Springs, Colo., 1974, Santa Fe Hilton Inn, 1975, Sheraton Inn, New Orleans, 1976—79; pres. Landmark Systems Inc., New Orleans, 1979—. Chmn. Sheraton So. Regional Owners and Mgrs. Coun., 1981—. Mem. com. memberships Greater New Orelans Tourist and Conv. Commn.; mem. dist. com. United Fund. Mem.: Am. Hotel Mgmt. Assn. (cert., mem. fund devel. com. Ednl. Inst.), Cornell Soc. Hotelmen, New Orelans Hotel and Motel Assn. (treas.). Episcopalian. Home: 3101 Rue Parc Fontaine # 1408 New Orleans LA 70131-

JONES, GLOWER WHITEHEAD, lawyer; b. Atlanta, May 4, 1936; s. Samuel L. and Alma (Powell) Jones; m. Joanna Dayvault, Apr. 5, 1980; children: Jeff, Tom, Frank, Michael, Mark. Grad., Dartmouth Coll., Hanover, NH, 1958; JD, Emory U., Atlanta, 1963. Bar: Ga. 1962, US Dist. Ct. Ga. 1963, US Ct. Appeals (5th and 11th cirs.), US Ct. Claims, US Supreme Ct. Assoc. Smith, Swift, Currie, McGhee & Hancock, Atlanta, 1963—65; ptnr. Smith Currie & Hancock, Atlanta, 1967—99, of counsel, 2000—. Author: Legal Aspects of Doing Business in North America and Canada, 1987, Alternative Clauses to Standard Construction Contracts, 1990; editor: 2d edit., Construction Subcontracting: A Legal Guide for Industry Professionals, 1991, Wiley Construction Law Update, 1992, 1993, 1994, Construction Contractors: The Right To Stop Work, 1992, Remedies for International Sellers of Goods, 1993; mem. editl. bd. Ga. State Bar Jour.; contbr. articles to profl. jours. Exec. bd. Met. Atlanta Boys' & Girls' Clubs, Inc., asst. sec., 1973—80, sec., 1980—83; trustee, past pres. Atlanta Florence Crittendon Svcs., Inc.; trustee IBA Found.; bd. dirs. Samuel L. Jones Boys' & Girls' Club, Inc., So. Region Boys Clubs Am., Carrie Steele Pitts Home, Gate City Day Nursery Assn. Named Ga. Superlawyer in Constrn. Law, 2004; recipient Golden Boy award, Met. Atlanta Boys' Club, 1971. Fellow: Chartered Inst. Arbitrators; mem.: ABA, Fed. Bar Assn., Internat. Bar Assn. (chmn. internat. sales com., chmn. UNCITRAL subcom., chmn. membership com., mem. governing coun. sect. bus. law), Ga. Bar Assn. (elected Ga. Superlawyer for Constrn. Law 2004), State Bar Ga., Atlanta Bar Assn. (former chmn. prepaid legal svcs. com., engr. lawyers rels. com.), Lawyers Club Atlanta, Am. Judicature Soc., Assn. Trial Attys. Am., Ga. Assn. Trial Lawyers, Dartmouth Coll. Alumni Club, Emory U. Alumni Club, Ansley Park Golf Club, World Trade Club, Dartmouth Club, Atlanta Athletic Club, Baylor Alumni Club, Phi Delta Theta. Home: 195 14th St PH401 Atlanta GA 30309 Office: Smith Currie & Hancock 2700 Marquis One Tower 245 Peachtree Center Ave Atlanta GA 30303-1227

JONES, GORDON KEMPTON, dentist, retired military officer; b. Rochester, NY, July 22, 1946; s. Joseph Kempton and Eunice (Patten)J.; m. Kathleen Anne FitzSimmons, July 24, 1971; children: Bryan Kempton, Brendan Austin, Graeme Meghan, Michael Cameron, Meredith Hunter, Mallory Sterling. BA in Chemistry, U. N.C., 1968, DDS, 1976; MS in Restorative Dentistry, U. Mich., 1984. Lic. dentist, Ill., N.C. Commd. lt. USN, 1976, advanced through ranks to capt., 1993—2006, ret., 2006, resident, Naval Regional Med. Ctr. Camp Pendleton, Calif., 1977, dentist, U.S.S. Holland Holy Loch, Scotland, 1977-80, dentist regional med. ctr. Great Lakes, Ill., 1980-82, head dept. operative dentistry, Naval Dental Clinic, 1984—90, 1993—97, cons. operative dentistry, Naval Dental Clinic, 2000—05, head dept. operative dentistry, Naval Dental Ctr. Norfolk, Va., 1990-93, dir. managed care, Naval Dental Ctr. Great Lakes, 1993-97, clinic dir., Naval Dental Ctr., 1996-97, comdg. officer, Naval Dental Rsch. Inst., 1997-99, splty. leader for dental rsch., 1997-2000, program mgr. mercury abatement Great Lakes, 2001—03, head comprehensive dentistry, 2003—06, contract dentist, 2006—07; pvt. practice, 1990—; fed. civil svc. dentist, 2007—. Cons. Naval Hosp. Great Lakes, 1984—86, 1993—2002, asst. dir. advanced edn. in gen. dentistry, 2002—04, USN Surgeon Gen.'s area coord. for rsch. integrity, 2003—05, mem. exec. com. med. staff, 2004—, naval medicine dep. spl. asst. human subjects protection, 2003—05; asst. clin. prof. Northwestern U. Dental Sch., Chgo., 1985—90, Chgo., 1995—98; quality assurance coord., head advanced clin. program in gen. dentistry, Norfolk, 1990—93; com. chmn. Am. Bd. Operative Dentistry, 1987—, pres., 1996—2000, exec. coun., 1996—2002, chair exam. com., 2000—; cons. ADA Commn. Accreditation, 2003—; Hines rsch. com. US VA, 1998—. Contbr. articles to profl. jours.; speaker in field. Course dir. ARC, Great Lakes, 1984-90. Legion of Merit, Meritorious Svc. Medal, Navy Commendation medal (three awards), Navy Achievement medal. Fellow Internat. Coll. Dentists; mem. ADA, Acad. Operative Dentistry (mem. jour. editl. bd. 1993-95, 96—), Am. Assn. Dental Rsch. (pres. Chgo. sect. 2000-01, chair local organizing com. 2000-01), Am. Dental Edn. Assn., Internat. Assn. Dental Rsch., Acad. Gen. Dentistry, Am. Assn. Dental Schs., Am. Legion, Omicron Kappa Upsilon, Alpha Phi Omega, Delta Sigma Delta. Avocations: computer science, reading, walking. Home: 1541 N McKinley Rd Lake Forest IL 60045-1377 Office Phone: 847-688-4560 ext. 3783. Personal E-mail: gjones1541@sbcglobal.net. Business E-Mail: gordon.jones@nhgl.med.navy.mil.

JONES, GRANT RICHARD, landscape architect; b. Seattle, Aug. 29, 1938; s. Victor Noble and Iona Belle (Thomas) J.; m. Ilze Grinbergs, 1965 (div. 1983); 1 child, Kaija. Student in liberal arts, Colo. Coll., 1956-58; BArch, U. Wash., 1962; M in Landscape Arch., Harvard U., 1966, postgrad. (Frederick Sheldon fellow), 1967-68. Draftsman Jones Lovegren Helms & Archs., Seattle, 1958-59; designer Landscape Archs., Seattle, 1961-65, state conservation planner Honolulu, 1968-69; rsch. assoc. landscape architecture rsch. office Harvard U., 1966-67; prin. Archs. and Landscape Archs., Ltd., Seattle, 1969—. Instr., vis. critic U. Oregon, U. Washington, U. Calif. at Berkeley, CSN Calpoly, U. Va., Harvard U.; lectr. and spkr. in field 30 univs., U.S.; chmn. landscape archtl. registration bd., State of Wash., 1974-79; mem. coun. Harvard U. Grad. Sch. Design, 1978-82, 91-96; vis. com. Harvard U. Grad. Sch., 1993—; bd. visitors U. Oregon Sch. Arch. and Allied Artists; bd. dirs. Scenic Am., Stewardship Ptnrs., Landscape Arch. Found. Author: The Nooksack Plan: An Approach to the Investigation and Evaluation of a River System, 1973; (with B. Gray and J. Burnham) A Method for the Quantification of Aesthetic Values for Environmental Decision Making, 1975, Design as Ecogram, 1975; (with J. Coe and D. Paulson) Woodland Park Zoo: Long Range Plan, Development Guidelines and Exhibit Scenarios, 1976, Landscape Assessment.Where Logic and Feelings Meet, 1978, Design Principles for Presentation of Animals and Nature, 1982, What Are Zoos?, 1984, An Arboretum on a Landfill, 1984, Beyond Landscape Immersion to Cultural Resonance, 1989, Some Thoughts on Power and Influence, 1993; prin. works include Nooksack River Plan, Bellingham, Wash.; Yakima (Wash.) River Regional Greenway, Union Bay Teaching and Research Arboretum, U. Wash., Seattle, Newhalem Campground, North Cascades Nat. Park, Woodland Park Zool. Gardens, Seattle, Washington Park Arboretum, U. Wash., Seattle, zoo master plans for Kansas City, Roanoke, Va., Detroit and Honolulu, Dallas Arboretum and Bot. Garden, Dublin and Fota, Ireland, 2005, Thai Elephant Forest at Woodland Park Zoo, Singapore Bot. Gardens, Paris Pike Hist. Hwy, Denver Commons Park, others. Recipient Nat. award Am. Zoo Assn., 1981-84. Fellow Am. Soc. Landscape Architects (chmn. Wash. chpt. 1972-73, trustee 1979—, v.p., 1988-90, Merit award in community design 1972, Honor award in regional planning 1974, Merit award in regional planning 1977, Merit award in park planning 1977, Merit award in instnl. planning 1977, Pres.'s award of excellence 1980, merit awards in landscape planning), Nature Conservancy, Am. Hort. Soc., Am. Assn. Bot. Gardens and Arboreta, Audobon, Sierrra Club, Phi Gamma Delta, Diet, Rainier Club. Office: Jones & Jones Archs and Landscape Archs Ltd 105 S Main St Ste 300 Seattle WA 98104-2578

JONES, GREGORY R., theater educator; b. Miami, Fla., June 28, 1950; s. Merle Jerome Jones and Ethel Marguerite Anderson; m. Dena Thue, May 29, 1976; children: Are Thue-Jones, Dylan Thue-Jones. BA, Eckerd Coll., St. Petersburg, Fla., 1972. Profl. actor Hippodrome State Theatre, Gainesville, Fla., 1978—; theatre educator Santa Fe CC, Gainesville, Fla., 1988—. Dir. Leadership Devel. Inst., Gainesville, 2002—. Author: (plays) The Faux King, 2005. Recipient Superior Commendation Certificates, Fla. CC Activities Assn., 1998—2006. Fellow: Am. Coll. Theatre Festival (assoc.); mem.: SAG, Theatre Comm. Group, Actors Equity Assn. Independent. Achievements include development of and direction of five world premiers of new dramatic works. Avocations: guitar, playwriting, travel, exercise. Office: Santa Fe CC 3000 NW 83 St Gainesville FL 32606 Home Phone: 352-395-5004; Office Phone: 352-395-5004. Office Fax: 352-395-4432; Home Fax: 352-395-4432. Business E-Mail: gregg.jones@sfcc.edu.

JONES, HAROLD ANTONY, retired banker; b. Bklyn., Nov. 5, 1943; s. Harold Edward and Marie Albertine (Schwietering) J.; m. Jo Ann T. Titone, Oct. 8, 1966; children: Christopher, Gregory. BA, Pace Coll., 1968; postgrad., Am. Inst. Banking, 1970; AAS., Grad. Sch. Savs. Banking, Brown U., 1975; grad., Exec. Mgmt. Program, U. Mass., 1977. With Mfrs. Trust Co., NYC, 1961-64, Lincoln Savs. Bank, NYC, 1964—90, dir. mktg., 1978-79, sr. v.p., corp. sec., 1979-81, dir. retail banking div., 1980-90; sr. v.p. bank adminstrn. Ridgewood Savs. Bank, NYC, 1990—2006; ret., 2006. Guest lectr. money and banking NYU; guest lectr. corp. social responsibility Columbia U.; pres. N.Y. Savs. Banks Life Ins. Council, 1985 Decorated knight comdr. Holy Sepulchre of Jerusalem; named Outstanding Banker in Cmty. Revitalization Brighton Beach Neighborhood Assn., 1978, Banker of Yr. Manhattan C. of C., 1990. Mem. Fin. Advt. and Mktg. Assn. N.Y. (dir.), Bank Mktg. Assn., Cmty. Bankers Assn. NY State (com. on pub. info.), Thrift Inst. Mktg. (chmn. exec. com.), Harbour Green Assn. (pres. 1992). Personal E-mail: haj152@patmedia.net.

JONES, H(AROLD) GILBERT, JR., lawyer; b. Fargo, ND, Nov. 2, 1927; s. Harold Gilbert and Charlotte Viola (Chambers) J.; m. Julie Squier, Feb. 15, 1964; children: Lenna Lettice Mills Jones Carroll, Thomas Squier, Christopher Lee. B of Engring., Yale U., 1947; postgrad., Mich. U., 1948-49; JD, UCLA, 1956. Bar: Calif. 1957. Mem., ptnr. Overton, Lyman & Prince, LA, 1956—61; founding ptnr. Bonne, Jones, Bridges, Mueller & O'Keefe, LA, 1961—89, of counsel, 1990—92, Lewis, Brisbois, Bisgaard & Smith, 1992—; pvt. practice, 2001—. Bd. dirs. Wilshire YMCA, 1969-75. With U.S. Army, 1950-52. Fellow Am. Coll. Trial Lawyers, Am. Bd. Trial Advs. (nat. pres. 1988-89, nat. exec. com. 1990, 92, 96, nat. bd. dirs. 1977—, pres. L.A. chpt. 1980, Calif. Trial Lawyer of Yr. 1999), Internat. Acad. Trial Lawyers: mem. ABA, Calif. Bar Assn., Los Angeles County Bar Assn. (past. chmn. legal-med. rels. com.), Orange County Bar Assn., So. Calif. Assn. Def. Counsel, Jonathan Club, Transpacific Yacht Club (commodore 1996-98), Newport Harbor Yacht Club (commodore 1998), Cruising Club Am., L.A. Yacht Club (Blue Water Cruising award, 1985), Univ. Athletic Club. Home: 818 Harbor Island Dr Newport Beach CA 92660-7228 Office: 650 Town Center Dr Ste 1400 Costa Mesa CA 92626-7020 Home Phone: 949-673-3645; Office Phone: 714-668-5516. Personal E-mail: hg5150@aol.com. Business E-Mail: gjones@lbbslaw.com.

JONES, HARRY EDWARD, diplomat, writer; b. Phila., Feb. 19, 1938; s. Harry Edward and Helen Jean (Spoon) Jones; m. Patricia Anne Pascoe, Oct. 13, 1964; children: Michael Sumner, Christopher Steven, Anne Pelton. BS, Pa. State U., 1959, MPA, 1975. Sr. fgn. svc. officer. min. counselor US Dept. of State, Washington, 1965—2002; advisor CIA, McLean (Langley), Va., 2002—. Polit. econ. min. Consul Gen. Author: (novel) Shadow In A Weary Land. With US Army, 1960—62. Mem.: Am. Foreign Svc. Assn., Diplomatic and Consular Officers Ret. Episcopalian. Avocations: gardening, painting. Home: 208 Caroline St Fredericksburg VA 22401 Home Phone: 540-372-9968.

JONES, HARRY GORDON, electronics executive; b. New Orleans, Nov. 1, 1950; s. Harry G. and Jessie Mae (Alexis) J.; m. Judith D. Pitts, April 16, 1971 (dec. Feb. 1982); children: Kristina, Kimberly. AA, Pensacola Jr. Coll., 1981; student, Southeast La. U., 1975-78. Engr. Xerox Corp., New Orleans, 1975-78, Lear Siegler, Inc., Denver, 1978-81; pres., chief exec. officer Spectrum Systems, Inc., Pensacola, Fla., 1981—. Mem. engring. adv. coun. U. West Fla. Past chmn. adv. bd. Small Bus. Devel. Ctr., U. West Fla. Coll. Bus. Mem. Instrument Soc. Am. (emissions monitoring stds. com.), Air Pollution Control Assn., Am. Mgmt. Assn., Pensacola C. of C. (cluster industry task force). Republican. Assembly of God. Office: Spectrum Systems Inc 3410 W Nine Mile Rd Pensacola FL 32526-7808

JONES, HARVEY ROYDEN, JR., neurologist; b. Plainfield, NJ, Nov. 18, 1936; m. Mary Elizabeth Norman, Mar. 18, 1961; children: Roy, Kathryn, Frederick, David. BS, Tufts U., 1958; MD, Northwestern U., 1962. Diplomate in neurology, clin. neurophysiology and neuromuscular medicine Am. Bd. Psychiatry and Neurology, bd. dirs., 1997-2004 Am. Bd. Psychiatry and Neurology, diplomate Am. Bd. Electroencephalography, Am. Bd. Electrodiagnostic Medicine. Intern Phila. Gen. Hosp., 1962-63; resident in internal medicine Mayo Grad. Sch. Medicine, Rochester, Minn., 1963-65; resident in neurology Mayo Grad. Sch. medicine, Rochester, Minn., 1965-66; chief neurology svc. U.S. Army Hosp., Bad Cannstatt, Germany, 1966-70; resident in neurology/clin. neurophysiology Mayo Grad. Sch. medicine, Rochester, Minn., 1970-72; from clin. instr. to clin. prof. neurology Harvard Med. Sch., Boston, 1973—; staff neurologist, Jaime Ortiz-Patino chair neurology, chair divsn. of med. specialties, emeritus chair Lahey Clinic, Burlington, Mass., 1972—; assoc. in neurology, assoc. divsn. neurophysiology, dir. electromygraphy lab. Children's Hosp. Med. Ctr., Boston, 1977—; assoc. in neurology, assoc. divsn. neurophysiology Brigham Women's Hosp., Boston, 2001—. Editor, author: CIBA Collection, Nervous System Part II, 1986, Pediatric Clinical Electromyography, 1996, Neuromuscular Disorders of Infancy, Childhood and Adolescence, A Clinician's Approach, 2003, Netter's Neurology, 2005, CLinical Neurophysiology of Infancy, Childhood & Adolscence, 2006; contbr. numerous articles to profl. jours. Fellow Am. Acad. Neurology; mem. Am. Neurol. Assn. Office: Lahey Clinic 41 Mall Rd Burlington MA 01805-0002 Office Phone: 781-744-5126. E-mail: royden.jones@lahey.org.

JONES, HENDREE EVELYN, research scientist, psychologist; b. Richmond, Mar. 11, 1972; d. Clinton Edward Jones and Hendree Fitzgerald Mason; m. Erik Matthew Lensch, June 28, 1997; children: Ashley Carter Lensch, Davis M Lensch. BA, Randolph-Macon Coll., 1992; MA, U. Richmond, 1994; PhD, Va. Commonwealth U., 1997. From postdoctoral fellow to assoc. prof. Johns Hopkins U., Behavioral Pharm. Rsch. Unit, Balt., 1997—2004; assoc. prof. behavioral biology Dept. Psychiat. Johns Hopkins U., 2004—, dir. Ctr. Addiction and Pregnancy, 1998—, program dir. cornerstone, 2000—. Rsch. panel mem. Ctr. for Substance Abuse Treatment, Chevy Chase, Va., 2000; grant reviewer Nat. Inst. Drug Abuse, Washington, 2002, standing reviewer, 2004—; reviewer Nat. Registry for Effective Treatment Programs, Washington, 2003—. Contbr. articles various profl. jours. Vol. Hopkins House, Alexandria, Va., 2000—. Recipient Young Psychopharmacologist award, 1999. Fellow: APA (Early Career Contbn. to Applied Psychology award), Md. Psychol. Assn. (Career Contbn. to Sci. 2005); mem.: Coll. on Problems of Drug Dependence, Phi Beta Kappa. Achievements include development of animal model of abused inhalants during pregnancy; behavioral therapy for treating drug abusing partners of pregnant drug dependent women; research in pharmacotherapies for pregnant women. Avocations: reading, scuba diving, exercising, scrapbooks. Office: Johns Hopkins Bayview Med Ctr 4940 Eastern Ave D 3 E Baltimore MD 21224 Office Phone: 410-917-9084. Business E-Mail: hejones@jhmi.edu.

JONES, HOUSTON GWYNNE, archivist, history professor; b. Yanceyville, NC, Jan. 7, 1924; s. Paul Hosier and Lemma Sue (Fowlkes) J. BS, Appalachian State Coll., Boone, NC, 1949; MA, George Peabody Coll., Nashville, 1950; postgrad., NYU, 1951—52; cert. archival adminstrn., Am. U., Washington, 1957; PhD, Duke U., Durham, NC, 1965. Prof. history Oak Ridge Mil. Inst., NC, 1950-53; chmn. div. soc. scis. West Ga. Coll., Carrollton, 1955-56; state archivist of N.C. State Dept. Archives & Hist., Raleigh, NC, 1956-68; dir. State Dept. Archives & History, Raleigh, NC, 1968-74; adj. prof. history U. NC, Chapel Hill, 1974-94, dir. NC Coll., 1974-94, Thomas W. Davis rsch. historian, 1994—. Mem. Nat. Hist. Publs. and Records Commn., Washington, 1978—86, NC Hist. Commn., Raleigh, 1977—. Author: Books For History's Sake, 1966, The Records of a Nation, 1969, Local Government Records, 1980, North Carolina Illustrated, 1983, North Carolina History: An Annotated Bibliography, 1995, Historical Consciousness in the Early Republic, 1995, Scoundrels, Rogues and Heroes of the Old North State, 2004; editor-in-chief NC Hist. Rev., 1968-74; gen. editor: North Caroliniana Society Imprints, 1978—. Chmn. Am's. 400th Anniversary Com., Raleigh, 1978-80; founder, sec.-treas. North Caroliniana Soc., Chapel Hill, 1975—; sec. Joint Commn. on Status of Nat. Archives, Washington, 1967-68. With USN, 1942—46. Recipient Disting. Alumnus award Appalachian State U., 1971, Cannon Cup hist. preservation NC Soc. for Preservation of Antiquities, 1971, Univ. Svc. award U. NC Gen. Alumni Assn., 1990, Disting. Svc. award in documentary publ. and preservation Nat. Hist. Publs. and Records Commn., Washington, 1990, John Tyler Caldwell award in humanities NC Humanities Coun., 2001, NC awrd State of NC, 2002. Fellow Soc. Am. Archivists (pres. 1968-69, Waldo G. Leland prize 1967, 81), Soc. North Caroliniana (sec. 1975-, Soc. award 1994); mem. NC Literary and Hist. Assn. (sec. 1969-75, pres. 1975-76, Crittenden Meml. award 1977), NC Writers Conf. (chmn. 1982, Conf. award 1994), Am. Assn. for State and Local History (sec. 1978-82, award of merit 1968, award of distinction 1989), Nat. Assn. State Hist. Preservation Officers (com. chmn. 1972-74), Hist. Soc. NC (pres. 1979-80, R.D.W. Connor award 1956), Soc. History Discoveries (coun. 2003-05), Carolina Club. Office: U NC Libr NC Collection Chapel Hill NC 27599-3930 Home: 3000 Galloway Ridge C-307 Pittsboro NC 27312-8662

JONES, IRVIN R., engineering educator; BSEE, Stanford U., Calif.; MS in Computer Sci., U. Calif., Santa Barbara; MS in Computer Engring., U. Calif.; PhD in Elec. Engring., U. Colo., Boulder. Devel. engring. Sony Tech. Ctr., Palo Alto, Calif., 1982—84; sr. software engr. Hewlett-Packard Corp., Sunnyvale, Calif., 1988—93; asst. prof. engring. tech. U. NC, Charlotte, 1998—2000; asst. prof. engring. U. Denver, 2000—. Contbr. articles to profl. jours., scientific papers in field. Mem.: IEEE (chpt. chair 2007—, chpt. sec. 2005—07), Assn. Computing Machinery. Achievements include patents pending for state space neural network system and method; patents for system memory initialization with presence detect encoding; system and method for shadowing and re-mapping reserved memory in a microcomputer. Avocations: golf, ballroom dancing, music, exercise. Office: Univ Denver 2390 S York St Denver CO 80208 Business E-Mail: irjones@du.edu.

JONES, J. GILBERT, private investigator; b. San Francisco, June 1, 1922; s. Enoch Roscoe (L.) Jones, Sr. and Remedios (Ponce de Leon) Jones. Student, U.S. Mcht. Marine Acad., 1942—44, San Francisco City Coll., 1941—42, student, 1946—47; AB, U. Calif., Berkeley, 1949, MA, 1952. Pvt. investigator. Ins. insp. Ins. Cos. Insp. Bur., San Francisco, 1959—62; pub. rels. cons. San Francisco, 1962—67; ins. insp. Am. Svc. Bur., San Francisco, 1967—72; propr., mgr. Dawn Universal Internat., San Francisco, 1972—, Dawn Universal Security Svc., San Francisco, 1983—. Mem.: SAR, Libr. Congress Assocs., U. Calif. Alumni Assn., World Affairs Coun. N. Calif., Commonwealth Club of Calif., Sons Spanish-Am. War Vets. Soc. Republican. Office: PO Box 424057 San Francisco CA 94142-4057

JONES, JACK BRISTOL, education educator; b. Las Cruces, N.Mex., Apr. 16, 1931; s. John Keith and Elsie Dean (Bristol) J.; m. Joy Elaine Moffett, Dec. 18, 1954; children: Sherri E. Callinan, Candi Marie, Craig Britol. BA, U. Calif., Santa Barbara, 1957, MA, 1965; EdD, U. Ariz., Tucson, 1970; PhD, Calif. Western U., 1979. Cert. elem. and secondary tchr., adminstr., reading specialist. Sgt. Santa Barbara Police Dept., 1955-61; elem. tchr. Goleta (Calif.) Sch. Dist., 1962-66; grad. asst. U. Ariz., Tucson, 1966-68; instr. Ventura (Calif.) Community Coll., 1968-69; prof. education Calif. Poly. State U., San Luis Obispo, 1969-91, prof. emeritus, 1991—. Author: Tips for Tutors, 1980, ON The Trail of The Presidents, 1994; editor Calif. Reader, 1975-80. Vice-comdr. San Luis Obispo County Sheriff's Aero Squadron, 1977-80; comdr. sheriff's res. San Luis Obispo County, 1980-85, past chmn. sheriff's adv. coun. Lst lt. US Army, 1950—53, col. res. US Army, 1964—87, ret. US Army, 1990. Decorated Legion of Merit, US Army, Meritorious Svc. medal US Army, Commendation medal US Army. Mem. Internat. Reading Assn., Calif. Prof. Reading (pres. 1975-76), Calif. Reading Assn. (pres. 1981-82, Margaret Lynch Svc. award 1984), Orgn. Tchr. Educators in Reading (pres. 1987-88), Retired Officers Assoc., US Army Ranger Assn., Res. Officers Assn., Mil. Order World Wars (nat. comdr. in chief 2005-06), San Luis Obispo Hist. Arms Soc. (founder, prs. 1983-86), Rotary (pres. 1994-95), Elks, Phi Delta Kappa. Republican. Episcopalian. Avocations: flying, hist. arms collecting.

JONES, JACQUELINE ELEANOR, otolaryngologist; b. NYC, Mar. 11, 1958; d. Farrell and Audrey Jones; m. John Wilfred Gassett, Sept. 20, 1986; children: David Scott Gassett, Peter Wilfred Gassett. BA in Biochemistry, Smith Coll., Northampton, Mass., 1980; MD, Cornell U. Med. Coll., NYC, 1984. Lic. physician Pa., 1985, Mass., 1989, NY, 1990, cert. Am. Bd. Otolaryngology, 1989, diplomate Nat. Bd. Med. Examiners, 1985. Intern surgery U. Pa., Phila., 1984—85, resident surgery, 1985—86, resident otolaryngology, 1986—89; asst. instr. otorhinolaryngology, human comm. U. Pa. Sch. Medicine, Phila., 1986—89; fellow pediatric otolaryngology Harvard Med. Sch. Children's Hosp. Boston, 1989—90; asst. prof. clin. otolaryngology Cornell U. Med. Coll., NYC, 1990—96, assoc. prof. clin. otolaryngology, 1996—; pvt. practice Park Ave. ENT, NYC, 2003—. Clin. instr. Harvard U. Med. Coll., Boston U., 1989—90; attending physician otolaryngologist dept. otolaryngology NY Hosp., NYC, 1990—; attending dept. otolaryngology Lenox Hill Hosp., NYC, 1990—, Manhattan Eye, Ear and Throat Hosp., NYC, 1990—; mem. clearinghouse adv. bd. Nat. Inst. Deafness Other Communicative Disorders NIH, Washington, 1991—94, mem. voice, voice disorders panel, 1992—98, panel mem. consensus conf. on cochlear implants, 1995; alt. rep. med. bd., exec. faculty coun. NY Hosp., Cornell U. Med. Coll., NYC, 1992—2003; participant shadow program minority pre-med. students Cornell U. Med. Coll., NYC, 1991—2003, mem. curriculum com., 1992—, mem. admissions com., 1992—2003, mem. affirmative action com., 1994—2003, chair affirmative action com., 1997—2000, resident coord. dept. otolaryngology, 1996—2000; dir. pediat. otolaryngology NY Hosp., NYC, 1996—2003; chair phenylephrine adv. panel NY State Dept. Health, 1997—98; mem. nat. deafness and other communicative disorders adv. coun. NIH, Bethesda, Md., 1998—2002; cons. health and human svcs. NY Presbyn. Hosp., NYC, 2002—03; mem. joint com. physician health NY State Med. Soc, NY State Bd. Profl. Conduct, 2002—07; spr., lectr. in field. Contbr. scientific papers, chapters to books, articles to profl. jours. Participant Mentor Program NY Pub. Schs., NYC, 1982—84, Health Alert Seminars Lenox Hill Hosp., NYC, 1991—; recruiter Smith Coll. Minority Recruitment Program, 1991—; participant quality assurance com. Blue Cross-Blue Shield of NY, 1992—2003; bd. trustees The Episcopal Sch., NYC, 1998—2004; pres. St. Bernard's Sch. Parents Assn., NYC, 2003—04; bd. trustees Kieve Affective Edn., Nobleboro, Maine, 2004—. Named Tchr. of Yr., Dept. Otolaryngology Cornell U. Med. Coll., 1998; named an Top 100 Black Doctors Am.; named one of Best Doctors in NY, Castle Connolly Med., Inc., 1999—2007. Fellow: ACS, Am. Acad. Otolaryngology (head and neck surgery - pediat. otolaryngology com. 1992—99), Am. Acad. Pediat. (exec. com. broncheosophagolgy sect. 1995—97); mem.: AMA, NY Bronchoscopic Soc., Soc. Ear, Nose and Throat Advances in Children, Am. Acad. Facial Plastic and Reconstructive Surgery, Am. Soc. Pediat. Otolaryngology (exec. bd. 2000—04). Office: Park Ave ENT Ste 1A 1175 Park Ave New York NY 10128-1211 Office Phone: 212-996-2559.

JONES, JAMES A., III, lawyer; b. Miami, Fla., June 16, 1944; BA, Yale U., 1966; JD, U. Va., 1973. Bar: Va. 1973, N.Y. 1984. Mem. Hunton & Williams LLP, Richmond, Va., ptnr., head, bus. practice group NYC. With USN, 1966—70. Mem. ABA (com. on devel. in bus. fin. corp. banking and bus. law sect. 1978—), N.Y. State Bar Assn., Va. State Bar Assn. Office: Hunton & Williams LLP 43rd Fl 200 Park Ave New York NY 10166-0136 Office Phone: 212-309-1140. Office Fax: 212-309-1100. Business E-Mail: jjones@hunton.com.

JONES, JAMES ALLEN, secondary school educator; b. Detroit, May 2, 1925; s. David and Cornelia (Lula) J. BS, Wayne State U., 1946; MA, Oakland U., 1949; PhD in Bibl. Studies, Am. Coll. Metaphysical Theology, Mpls., 1998. Tchr. Detroit Pub. Schs., 1949-87; prin., tchr. Roman Catholic Archdiocese, Detroit, 1987-93; supervisor student tchrs. Wayne State U., Detroit, 1993-97; tchr. Loyola Jesuit H.s., Detroit, 1997-2000; lectr., supr. student tchrs. Ea. Mich. U., Ypsilanti, 2000—. Instr. U. Mich., Dearborn, 1981—; ind. distributor seminar workshop in wellness Nikken, 1999. Author: A Guide to Teens Who Take Their Own Lives, 1987. Mem. English Speaking Union, Mich. Assn. Mid. Sch. Educators. Office: PO Box 2097 Detroit MI 48202-0097 Fax: 313-873-2299.

JONES, JAMES ALTON, lawyer; b. Palestine, Tex., Feb. 26, 1956; s. Ralph A. and Jo Nell (Broadway) J. JD magna cum laude, Tulane U., 1983. Bar: Tex. 1985, U.S. Dist. Ct. (so. dist.) Tex. 1985, U.S. Dist. Ct. (no. and eas. dists.) Tex. 1986, U.S. Dist. Ct. (we. dist.) Tex. 1988, U.S. Ct. Appeals (5th cir.) 1985, Minn. 1993, U.S. Dist. Ct. Minn. 1993, U.S. Ct. Appeals (8th cir.) 1993. Law clk. U.S. Ct. Appeals (5th cir.), Houston, 1983-84; assoc. Holtzman & Urquhart, Houston, 1984-86, Johnson & Swanson, Dallas, 1986, Figari & Davenport, Dallas, 1986-89; ptnr. Doke & Riley, Dallas, 1989-92, Sprenger & Lang, Mpls., 1992-95; shareholder Jones & Assocs. P.C., Dallas, 1995—2004, Gillespie, Rozen, Watsky, Motley & Jones, P.C., 2005—. Instr. legal rsch. and writing Tulane U., 1983. Mem. ABA, State Bar Tex., Dallas Bar Assn., Nat. Employment Lawyers Assn., Tex. Employment Lawyers Assn., Order of Coif. Avocations: tennis, skiing. Office: Gillespie Rozen Watsky Motley & Jones P C 3402 Oak Grove Ave Ste 200 Dallas TX 75204-3400 Office Phone: 214-720-2009. Office Fax: 214-720-2291. Business E-Mail: jaj@grlawfirm.com.

JONES, JAMES EARL, actor; b. Arkabutla, Miss., Jan. 17, 1931; s. Robert Earl and Ruth (Williams) J.; m. Cecilia Hart, Mar. 15, 1982; 1 child, Flynn Earl. BA, U. Mich., 1953, LHD (hon.), 1970; diploma, Am. Theatre Wing, 1957; studied with Lee Strasburg, Ted Danielewsky; DFA (hon.), Princeton U., 1980, Yale U., 1982; LHD (hon.), Columbia Coll., 1982; ArtsD (hon.), NYU, 1994. Appeared in plays: Much Ado About Nothing, 1955-59, 1961, Stalag 17, 1955-59, The Caine Mutiny, 1955-59, Arsenic and Old Lace, 1955-59, The Desperate Hours, 1955-59, Othello numerous appearances (Drama Desk award for best performance, 1964, Vernon Rice award, 1965), Egghead (Broadway debut), Sunrise at Campobello, 1958, The Big Knife, 1959, King Henry V, 1960, Measure for Measure, 1960, Richard II, 1961, A Midsummer Night's Dream, 1961, The Apple (Obie award best actor) 1961, Clandestine on the Morning Line (Obie award best actor) 1961, Richard III, 1961, Taming of the Shrew, 1961, Moon on a Rainbow Shawl (Obie award best actor) 1962, The Merchant of Venice, 1962, The Tempest, 1962, Toys in the Attic, 1962, Macbeth, 1962, The Winter's Tale, 1963, The Emperor Jones, 1964, 1967, Baal (Obie award best performance) 1965, Coriolanus, 1965, Troilus & Cressida, 1965, The Great White Hope, 1969 (Drama Desk award outstanding performance 1969, Golden Globe award new male star of yr. 1971, Tony award for best actor, Antoinette Perry award best actor in a dramatic play, 1969), Les Blancs (Drama Desk award outstanding performance) 1970, Hamlet (Drama Desk award outstanding performance) 1973, King Lear, 1973, The Cherry Orchard (Drama Desk award outstanding performance) 1973, The Iceman Cometh, 1973, Of Mice and Men, 1974, Paul Robeson, 1977, Hedda Gabler, 1980, Master Harold and The Boys, 1982-83, Fences, 1985-87 (Drama Desk award, Antoinette Perry award, Outer Critics Circle award for Best Actor, 1987, Tony award for Best Actor, Drama Critics award), On Golden Pond, 2005; appeared in movies: Dr. Strangelove, 1963, The Great White Hope, 1970 (Acad. Award nom. best actor 1970, Golden Globe award new male star of 1971), King: A Filmed Record Montgomery to Memphis, 1970, The Man, 1972, Malcolm X, 1972, Claudine, 1973 (Image award best actor NAACP, 1974, Golden Glove award non. best actor in a musical or comedy, 1974) The River Niger, 1975, The Bingo Long Traveling All-Stars and Motor Kings, 1976, Star Wars, 1977 (voice of Darth Vader), The Greatest, 1977, A Piece of the Action, 1978, The Empire Strikes Back, 1980 (voice of Darth Vader), Conan the Barbarian, 1982, Return of the Jedi, 1983 (voice of Darth Vader), Soul Man, 1986, Allan Quartermain & the Lost City of Gold, 1987, Matewan, 1987, Gardens of Stone, 1987, Coming to America, 1988, Field of Dreams, 1989, The Hunt For Red October, 1990, Sneakers, 1991, Patriot Games, 1992, Meteor Man, 1993, Sommersby, 1993, The Sandlot, 1993, (voice) The Lion King, 1994, Clear and Present Danger, 1994, Cry The Beloved Country, 1995, A Family Thing, 1996, Looking for Richard, 1996, Gang Related, 1997, Summer's End, 1998, (voice) The Lion King II: Simba's Pride, 1998, Undercover Angel, 1999, On the Q.T., 1999, Finder's Fee, 2001, (voice) Recess Christmas: Miracle on Third Street, 2001, (cameo in trailer) The Spongebob Squarepants Movie, 2004, (voice) Robots, 2005, The Sandlot 2, 2005, Star Wars: Episode III Revenge of the Sith, 2005 (voice of Darth Vader), Scary Movie 4, 2006; TV movies include: The Cay, 1974 (Golden Gate award, Golden Hugo award, Gabriel award, 1975), King Lear, 1974, Jesus of Nazareth, 1977, Roots: The Next Generation, 1979, Guyana Tragedy: The Story of Jim Jones, 1980, The Atlanta Child Murders, 1985, The Last Elephant (Ace nomination) 1990, Heatwave, 1990 (Ace award, best actor in a supporting role, Emmy award best supporting actor in a spl. or mini-series 1991), By Dawn's Early Light, 1990 (Emmy award nomination outstanding supporting actor 1991), The Vernon Johns Story, 1993, What the Deaf Man Heard, 1997, Summer's End, 1999, Santa and Pete, 1999, (voice) 2004: A Light Knight's Odyssey, 2004; TV series: (narrator) Malcolm X, 1972, (host) Black Omnibus, 1973, (host) Vegetable Soup, 1975, Sojourner, 1975, Third and Oak (Ace award), Business World News, 2003-; star TV series Paris, 1979-80, Gabriel's Fire, 1990 (Outstanding Lead Actor in Dramatic Series Emmy award 1991), Pros & Cons, 1991 (Emmy award bestactor in a drama series, Best Actor NAACP), Under One Roof, 1995; appeared on TV shows GuidingLight, As The World Turns, The Defenders, East Side, West Side, Dr. Kildare, Tarzan, Highway to Heaven, L.A.Law, Homicide: Life onthe Street, Lois & Clark: The New Adventures of Superman, Frasier, Law & Order, Touched by an Angel, Picket Fences, (voice) The Simpsons, Garfield and Friends; appeared, narrated TV specials including Black Omnibus: Negro in the Arts, 1973, (narrator) Beauty & The Beast CBS Library Misunderstood Monsters, 1981, Aladdin & His Wonderful Lamp Fairie Tale Theatre, 1986, Wonderworks, 1986, Soldier Boys CBS Schoolbreak Special, 1987, The 41st Annual Tony Awards, 1987, Square One Television, 1987, America Picks The All-Time Favorite Movies, 1988, Teach 109 American Playhouse, 1988, (narrator) A Hard Road to Glory: The Black Athlete, 1988, (narrator) Michael Jackson: Motown on Showtime, 1988, (host, narrator) The Way We Hear Smithsonian World, 1988, (host narrator) Who Lives Who Dies, 1988, Saturday Night with Connie Chung, 1989, Third and Oak: The Pool Hall American Playwrights Theatre, 1989, The 43rd Annual Tony Awards, 1989, Reflections on the Silver Screen with Prof. Richard Brown, 1990, America's All Star Tribute to Oprah Winfrey, 1990, World Series, 1990, 44th Annual Tony Awards, 1990, Golden Glove awards, 1990, Nat. Meml. Day Concert, 1990, 42d Annual Primetime Emmy Awards, 1991, A Party for Richard Pryor, 1991, 17th Annual People's Choice Awards, 1991, 12th Annual Ace Awards, 1991, (narrator) Visitors from the Unknown, 1991, Muhammad Ali, Biography, 1991, Portrait of Castro's Cuba, 1991, Twenty-Third Annual NAACP Image Awards, 1991, When It Was A Game, 1991, (narrator) The Creative Spirit, 1992, AFI Salute to Sidney Poitier, 1992, Shelly Duvall's Bedtime Stories, 1992, (narrator) Ivory Wars: Lincoln Memorial Day Concert, 1993, 47th Annual Tony Awards, 1993, The Second Civil War, 1996, Alone, 1997, Lincoln Memorial Day Concert, 1997; recordings include: Great American Documents (with Orsen Welles, Henry Fonda, Helen Hayes), 1976, The People Could Fly, Oedipus Rex, To be Young, Gifted and Black, Poems from Black Africa, The Emperor Jones, Native Son, The Great White Hope, John Henry, The New Testament, Portraits of Freedom; appeared in Bell Atlantic Commercials; the voice behind CNN Lincoln Portrait, 1993; vocal introduction 3rd Rock from the Sun; co-author: (with Penelope Niven) James Earl Jones: Voices and Silences, 1993. Recipient The Village Voice Off-Broadway award, 1962, Theatre World award, 1962, Hon. Doctoral Degree Black Am. Culture Festival, 1969, Grammy award, 1976, medal for spoken lang. Am. Acad. Arts and Letters, 1981, Office of Black Ministries Toussaint medallion, 1982, Theater Hall of Fame award, 1985, Emmy award for performance in children's programming, Soldier Boys, CBS Schoolbreak Spl., 1987-88, L.A. Film Tchrs. Assn. Jean Renoir award, 1990, Commonwealth award Disting. Svc. in the Dramatic Arts, Bank of Del., 1991, Nat. Medal of Arts for outstanding contbn. to cultural life of country, 1992, Hall of Fame Image award for great contbn. to arts, NAACP, 1992, UCLA medal, 1993; named Disting. Artist, L.A. Music Ctr. Club, 1994, John Houseman award The Acting Co., 1995; numerous other acting awards, nominations-Obie, Drama Desk, Tony, Golden Globe, Outer Critics Cir., ACE, others. Mem. Nat. Council of Arts (Presdl. appt. to adv. bd. 1962, presdl. appointee 1970-76), Actors' Equity Assn., SAG, Am. Fedn. TV and Radio Artists, Theatre Comm. Group (bd. dirs. 1962). Can commonly be seen on TV commericals for Verizon (formerly Bell Atlantic). Address: Horatio Prodns PO Box 610 Pawling NY 12564-0610

JONES, JAMES FLEMING, JR., academic administrator, language educator; b. Atlanta, Apr. 9, 1947; s. James F. and Sarah Kate (Smith) J.; m. Jan Sheets, Nov. 15, 1969; children:Jennifer, Justin, Jason BA, U. Va., 1969; MA, Emory U., 1972; cert., U. Paris-Sorbonne, 1972; MPhil, Columbia U., 1974, PhD, 1975. Tchr., chmn. dept. fgn. langs. Woodward Acad., College Park, Ga., 1969-72; preceptor Columbia U., 1973-75; prof. Romance langs. and lit. Washington U., St. Louis, 1975-91, chmn. dept. Romance langs., 1982-91; vice provost, dean Dedman Coll., So. Meth. U., Dallas, 1991-96; pres. Kalamazoo Coll., 1996—2004, Trinity College, 2004—. Sr. visitor for Hilary term, Oxford, 1987. Precentor, Ch. of St. Michael and St. George, Clayton, Mo., 1978-91. Decorated chevalier Ordre des Palmes Académiques; recipient Avis Blewett award Am. Guild Organists, 1989, Faculty award Washington U., 1990, Disting. Alumnus award Ga. Mil. Acad.-Woodward Acad. Alumni Assn., 1990; NEH fellow, 1976, Folger Inst. fellow, 1982. Mem. MLA, Am. Assn. Tchrs. of French, Am. Soc. 18th Century Studies, Soc. Rousseau Studies, Soc. Prévost d'Exiles Office: Trinity Coll 300 Summit St Hartford CT 06106 Office Phone: 860-297-2087. E-mail: James.Jones@trincoll.edu.*

JONES, JAMES M., lawyer; b. Chgo. AB magna cum laude, Miami Univ., Ohio, 1983; JD with honors, Ohio State Univ., 1986. Atty. Jones Day, Columbus, Ohio, adminstrv. ptnr. Pitts. Named Nation's Urban Pro Bono Publico Atty. of Yr., Legal Services Corp., 1992; named one of Columbus' Ten Outstanding Young Citizens, Columbus Jr. C. of C.; recipient Cmty. Svc. award, Columbus Bar Assn. Fellow: Columbus Bar Found.; mem.: ABA, Allegheny County Bar Assn., Pa. Bar Assn., Order of Coif, Phi Beta Kappa. Office: Jones Day One Mellon Bank Ctr 31st Fl 500 Grant St Pittsburgh PA 15219 Office Phone: 412-394-7230. Office Fax: 412-394-7959. Business E-Mail: jmjones@jonesday.com.

JONES, JAMES PARKER, federal judge; b. Tampa, Fla., July 3, 1940; s. Edmund Leroy and Nellie (Parker) J.; m. Mary Duke Trent, June 24, 1964; children: J. Trent, Benjamin P., Jonathan E. AB, Duke U., 1962; LLB, U. Va., 1965. Bar: Va. 1965. Asst. atty. gen. Va. Atty. Gen., Richmond, 1965-66; law clk. US Ct. Appeals, Richmond, 1966-68; atty. Penn, Stuart, Eskridge & Jones, Abingdon and Bristol, Va., 1968-96; judge US Dist. Ct. (We. Dist.) Va., Abingdon, 1996—2004, chief judge, 2004—. Bd. dirs. Va. Ctr. for Innovative Tech., Reston, Va., 1987-90. State senator Commonwealth of Va., 1983-88; mem. Dem. Nat. Com., 1982-92; mem. State Bd. Edn., 1990-96, pres., 1992-96. Fellow Am. Coll. Trial Lawyers (mem. Va. state com. 1995-96); mem. The Nature Conservancy (trustee Va. chpt. 1988-96). Democrat. Espicopalian. Office: US Dist Ct 180 W Main St Abingdon VA 24210-2844 Business E-Mail: jamesj@vawd.uscourts.gov.

JONES, JAMES RICHARD, business administration educator; b. Saginaw, Mich., May 25, 1940; s. George B. and Rena Jones; m. Sheila I. Jones; children: Kimme Ann, Kriste Gay, Kelle Lyn, Karme Jill. BA, Mich. State U., 1962, MBA, 1964; PhD, Ariz. State U., 1969. Research analyst Mich. Public Service Commn., Lansing, 1962; systems analyst Allis-Chalmers Mfg. Co., West Allis, Wis., 1964-65; asst. prof. transp. U. Houston, 1967-70; asso. prof. mktg. U. Ga., Athens, 197— 72; spl. asst. Dept. Transp., Washington, 1972-74, transp. economist, 1974-76; Disting. prof. transp. Memphis State U., 1976-81; George R. Brown Disting. prof. bus. Trinity U., San Antonio, 1981—. Cons. in field. Author books in field; contbr. articles to profl. jours.; bd. editors: Jour. Mktg. Theory and Practice, 1992—. Keeshin fellow, 1963. Mem. Am. Soc. Traffic and Transp., Am. Mktg. Assn., Council Logistics Mgmt., Transp. Research Forum, Transp. Research Bd., So. Mktg. Assn., Assn. Mktg. Theory and Practice, Am. Inst. Decision Scis. Home: 1711 Brush Creek Dr San Antonio TX 78248-2003 Office: Trinity U One Trinity Pl San Antonio TX 78212-3104 Office Phone: 210-999-7230. Business E-Mail: jjones@trinity.edu.

JONES, JAMES ROBERT, ambassador, retired congressman, lawyer; b. Muskogee, Okla., May 5, 1939; m. Olivia Barclay, 1968; children: Geoffrey Gardner, Adam Winston. AB in Journalism and Govt., U. Okla., 1961; LLB, Georgetown U., 1964. Bar: Okla. 1964, D.C. 1964. Legis. asst. Congressman Ed Edmondson, 1961-64; spl. asst. Pres. Lyndon Johnson, 1965-69; mem. 93d-99th congresses from 1st Dist. Okla., Washington, 1973-87; chmn. budget com. 97th and 98th Congress, Washington; chmn. social security subcom. 99th Congress, Washington; ptnr. Dickstein, Shapiro & Morin, Washington, 1987-89; chmn. bd., chief exec. officer Am. Stock Exch., NYC, 1989-93; U.S. amb. to Mexico, 1993-97; pres. Warnaco Internat., 1997-98; CEO Manatt, Jones Global Strategies, Washington. Bd. dirs. Kaiser Family Found., Grupo Modelo, Kansas City So. Ind., Anheuser Busch, Keyspan, Inc.; co-chmn. U.S.-Mex. Bus. Com.; chmn. Meridian Internat. Ctr., World Affairs Couns. of Am. Served to capt. CIC AUS, 1964—65. Mem.: D.C. Bar Assn., Okla. Bar Assn. Office: 700 12th St NW Ste 1100 Washington DC 20005 Home Phone: 202-548-2664; Office Phone: 202-585-6560. E-mail: jjones@manatt.com. *In essence, I try to follow the admonition of Thomas Aquinas, "To work as if everything depends upon you, and pray as if everything depends on God.*

JONES, JAMES THOMAS, state supreme court justice, former state attorney general; b. Twin Falls, Idaho, May 13, 1942; s. Henry C. and Eunice Jones; m. Mary Kelleen Florence, Aug. 12, 1994; 1 child, Katherine A. Montgomery. Studied, Idaho State U., 1960—61; BA, U. Oreg., 1964; JD, Northwestern U., 1967. Bar: Idaho 1967. Legis. asst. to U.S. Senator, Washington, 1970-72; law practice Jerome, Idaho, 1973-82; atty. gen. State of Idaho, Boise, 1983—91; pvt. practice law Boise, 1991—2005; justice Idaho Supreme Ct., Boise, 2005—. Capt. US Army, 1967—69, Vietnam. Decorated Bronze Star, Air medal with 4 oak leaf clusters, Cross of Gallantry (Vietnam), Army Commendation medal. Mem.: Idaho Bar Assn., VFW, Am. Legion. Lutheran. Office: Idaho Supreme Ct PO Box 83720 Boise ID 83720-0101 Office Phone: 208-334-3186.

JONES, JAY ROBERT, music educator; b. Richmond, Mo., Jan. 28, 1968; s. J. W. and Paula Jones. B in Music Edn., Ctrl. Meth. Coll., Fayette, Mo., 1990; MS in Edn., N.W. Mo. State U., 1997; EdD in Edn., U. Mo., Columbia, 2006. Tchg. cert. Mo. Dir. bands So. Boone County, Ashland, Mo., 1990—92, Stewartsville (Mo.) C-II Schs., 1992—98, Platte County R-3 Sch. Dist., Platte City, Mo., 1998—. Condr., clinician Mid Mo. Ednl. Music Festivals, 1996—; condr., band dir. N.W. Mo. State U. Music Camp, 1997—2001, 2005; coord. Wilson Ctr. Performing Arts Platte County Sch. Dist., 2002—; adminstrv. asst. Platte County HS, 2004—05. Co-editor: Building Better Bands, 2002; contbg. author: Mo. Sch. Music Mag., 2002—06. Asst. scoutmaster Stewartsville troop 222 Boy Scouts Am., 1993—98. Recipient proclamation, Gov. Mo., 2001. Mem.: Nat. Band Assn., N. Ctrl. Mo. Bandmasters Assn. (pres. 2000—01), Music Educators Nat. Conf., Mo. State Tchrs. Assn., Mo. Music Educators Assn. (v.p. N.W. dist. 2000—02, pres. N.W. dist. 2002—06), Mo. Bandmasters Assn. (membership chmn. 2000—), Phi Mu Alpha, Phi Beta Mu. Avocations: travel, photography. Office: Platte County R3 Schs 1501 Branch Platte City MO 64079 Home: 7416 NW 85th Terr Kansas City MO 64153

JONES, JEANNE PITTS, pre-school administrator; b. Richmond, Va., Oct. 19, 1938; d. Howard Talliaferro and Anne Elizabeth Pitts; children: Jack Hunter Jr., Judith Anne, James Howard, Jon Martain. BA, Marshall U., 1961, postgrad., 1962, Presbyn. Sch. Christian Edn., Richmond, 1974—94; MEd in Early Childhood Edn., Va. Commonwealth U., 2000. Cert. tchr. Va. Tchr. Richmond Pub. Schs., 1961-65; founder Bon View Sch. Early Childhood Edn., Richmond, 1971, tchr., 1971-91, dir., 1971—. Acad. affairs chmn. Good Shepherd Episcopal Sch. Bd., Ricmond, 1985—88; mentor Ecumenical Child Care Network Nat. Coun. Chs., Washington, 1990—92; ednl. cons., mentor Success By Six, 2002. Chmn. rm. parents Crestwood Sch. PTA Bd., Richmond, 1974—80; children's coord. Bon Air United Meth. Ch., Richmond, 1985—93; v.p. Bon Air United Meth. Ch. Women, Richmond, 1991—94; dir. Camp Friendship Bon Air United Meth. Ch., Richmond, 1992—2002; rep. Va. Conf. United Meth. Ch., 1993—95, weekday com., 1992—94; publicity chmn. Va. Swimming, Richmond, 1978—88; rep. Va. Children's Action Network. Recipient Spl. Mission recognition, Bon Air United Meth. Women, 1987. Mem.: Nat. Assn. Edn. for Young Children (validator 1993—2005, mentor 1994—98), Va. Assn. for Early Childhood Edn. (affiliate pres. 2002—04, 3d v.p. liaisons 2004—05, accreditation chair 2005—06), Chesterfield Coalition Early Childhood Educators (bd. dirs. 1993—97), Presch. Assn. Ch. Ednl. Dirs. (pres. 1993—95), Richmond Early Childhood Assn. (mem.-at-large 1994—96, rec. sec. 1996—98, 1998—2000, v.p. membership 2000—02, pres.-elect 2001—02, pres. 2002—04, past pres. 2004—06, accreditation chair 2006—, Richmond Early Childhood Adv. of the Yr. 2002). Republican. Avocations: aerobics, reading. Home: 9103 Whitaker Cir Richmond VA 23235-4053 Office: Bon View Sch Early Childhood Edn 1645 Buford Rd Richmond VA 23235-4274 Office Phone: 804-320-7043. Personal E-mail: bonviewschool@aol.com.

JONES, JEFFREY A., lawyer; b. Shelbyville, Ind., Dec. 6, 1969; BS, Gustavus Adolphus Coll., St. Peter, Minn., 1992; JD, William Mitchell Coll. Law, 1995. Bar: Minn. 1995. Atty. Jeffrey A. Jones & Assocs., P.A., Mpls. Named a Rising Star, Minn. Super Lawyers mag., 2006. Mem.:

Hennepin County Bar Assn., Minn. Trial Lawyers Assn., Am. Trial Lawyers Assn. Office: Jeffrey Jones & Assocs PA 33 S 6th St Ste 4530 Minneapolis MN 55402 Office Phone: 612-335-9975. E-mail: jeffjoneslaw@yahoo.com.*

JONES, JEFFREY FOSTER, lawyer; b. Phila., Apr. 24, 1944; s. Richard L. and Dorothy A. (Shaw) Jones; m. Susan Craft, Aug. 22, 1970; children: Amanda, Michael. BA, Williams Coll., 1966; JD, Harvard U., 1973. Bar: Mass. 1973, US Dist. Ct. Mass. 1974, US Dist. Ct. Appeals (1st cir.) 1974. Law clk. Supreme Jud. Ct., Boston, 1973-74; assoc. Palmer & Dodge, Boston, 1974-80, ptnr., 1980-88, mng. ptnr., 1998—2005, Edwards Angell Palmer & Dodge, Boston, 2002—. Chmn. bd. dirs. Law Firm Resources Project, 1981—96; bd. dirs. Mass Inc., Mass. Bus. Roundtable. Overseer Boys and Girls Clubs, Boston, 1974—93, sec., bd. dirs., 1993—2000, chair, bd. dirs., 2002—05; trustee Sterling and Francine Clark Art Inst., 1995—98; bd. dirs. Willow Hill Sch., 1991—; trustee Radcliffe Coll., 1995—99. Lt. USN, 1966—70. Mem.: ABA, Mass. Bar Assn., Boston Bar Assn., Nat. Assn. Coll. and Univ. Attys., Greater Boston C. of C. (bd. dirs. 1998—). Democrat. Avocations: golf, reading. Office: Edwards Angell Palmer and Dodge LLP 111 Huntington Ave 19th Fl Boston MA 02199-7613 Office Phone: 617-239-0246. Business E-Mail: jjones@eapdlaw.com.

JONES, JENIVER JAMES, lawyer; b. Sutton, W.Va., Sept. 24, 1915; s. Lee Jackson J. and Mary Ida (Lewis) J.; m. Maxine Hickman, Oct. 3, 1939 (dec. Dec. 1993); children: Gary Keith, Glendon Kent, Ronnie Dale; m. Mary Frame, July 30, 1994; stepchildren: Debra Frame Brady, Joseph Frame. Student, Glenville Coll., W.Va., 1938; JD, W. Va. U., 1947. Bar: W. Va. 1947. Tchr. Braxton County Bd. Edn., Sutton, W. Va., 1936-43, attendance dir., 1947-48; aircraft inspector Glen L. Martin, Middle River, Md., 1943-45; pvt. practice Sutton, 1948-91, Gassaway, 1991—. W. Va. Rep. Supreme Ct. nominee, 1988. Mem. Lions Club Internat. (dist. gov. 1963-64, Sutton, W.Va.). Methodist. Avocations: reading, tennis, baseball, golf. Office: Law Offices of Jeniver J Jones HC 62 Box 75 Gassaway WV 26624-9405 Office Phone: 304-364-5467.

JONES, JERRY (JERRAL WAYNE JONES), professional sports team executive; b. LA, Oct. 13, 1942; m. Gene Jones; children: Stephen, Charlotte, Jerry Jr. Grad., U. Ark., 1965, MBA, 1970. Exec. v.p. Modern Security Life, Springfield, Mo., 1965-69; prin. oil and gas bus., 1970—; pres., gen. mgr. Dallas Cowboys, 1989—. Nat. Paralysis Assn.; Boys Clubs Am.; Salvation Army. Named one of Forbes Richest Ams., 2006; recipient Evangeline Booth award, 1999. Avocations: hunting, fishing, tennis, water-skiing, skiing. Office: Dallas Cowboys 1 Cowboys Pky Irving TX 75063-4999*

JONES, JERRY LEE, computer educator; b. Glade Spring, Va., Nov. 24, 1947; s. William and Mary (Waugh) Jones. BS, Va. State U., Petersburg, 1969, MEd, 1973; EdD, Va. Poly. Inst. and State U., Blacksburg, 1979; postgrad., East Tenn. State U., Johnson City, 1969—71, Morgan State U., Balt., 1970—71, U. Memphis, 1982—86, Va. Commonwealth U., Richmond, 1974, Purdue U., West Lafayette, Ind., 1995—2005, Ind. U., Bloomington, 2006—07. Tchr. H.S. Balt. City Pub. Schs., 1969—74; prof. J. Sargeant Reynolds C.C., Richmond, Va., 1974—2001. Part-time instr. Marymount Cath. HS, Richmond, Va., 1987—89; vis. prof. Emory and Henry Coll., Va., 2001—; adj. prof. Va. Highlands C.C., Abingdon, Va., 2001—02. Author: (textbook) Structured Programming Logic, 1985. Mem. Glade Spring Town Coun., Va., 2006—. Methodist. Avocations: piano, organ. Office: Emory and Henry College PO Box 947 Emory VA 24327-0947 Home: PO Box 183 Glade Spring VA 24340-0183 Home Phone: 276-429-5104; Office Phone: 276-944-6697. Business E-Mail: jjones@ehc.edu.

JONES, JERRY W., protective services official, investor; b. Heidelberg, Germany, Nov. 24, 1971; s. Jerry Wayne and Lori Jones. AA, Aiken Tech. Coll., SC, 2000; BS, U. SC, Aiken, 2002. Cert. law enforcement Ga. POST, 2004. Engring. supr. Radisson Riverfront Hotel, Augusta, Ga., 2002—04; dep. marshal Richmond County Marshal's Office, Airport Divsn., Augusta, 2004—. Pres. Brandon Wilde Retirement Comm. Employee Assn., Evans, Ga., 1997—99, Alzheimers Assn. for U. and St. Joseph Hosps., Augusta, 1998—99. Asst. spl. events coord. U./St. Joseph/Walton Rehab. Hosps. Fund Raising Orgn., Augusta, 1998—2001. Col Beebe Edn. scholar, Col. Beebe Found., 1998—2000. Mem.: Ga. Tactical Officers Assn., Nat. Tactical Officers Assn. Republican. Avocations: scuba diving, travel, rock climbing, kayaking. Home: 110 Sugarcreek Ct Grovetown GA 30813 Home Phone: 706-231-8536. Personal E-mail: arlieghburkeddg51@yahoo.com.

JONES, JEWEL, social services administrator; b. Oklahoma City, Dec. 7, 1941; d. Joseph Samuel and Jewell (Hathyel) Fisher; m. Maurice Jones, July 17, 1976; children: Anthony, Carmen. BA in Sociology, Langston U., Okla., 1962; MA in Pub. Adminstrn., U. Alaska, Anchorage, 1974. Tchr. Seidman Sch., LA, 1962; correctional oifcer State of Calif. Dept. Corrections, Corona, 1963-65; probation officer County of San Bernardino, Calif., 1965-67; dep. exec. dir. Cmty. Action Agy., Anchorage, 1967-70; social svcs. dir. City of Anchorage, 1970-87; social svcs. mgr. Municipality of Anchorage, 1987-2000, dir. health & human svcs., 2000—. Chmn. bd. Alaska Housing Fin. Corp., Anchorage, 1995—; pres. Anchorage KidsPlace Project, 1994-95; chair Alaskan of the Yr. Scholarship Com., 1985—; chmn. bd. Janet Helen Tolan Gamble and Toby Gamble Ednl. Trust, 1998—. Mem. adv. bd. Salvation Army, Anchorage, 1982-87, Alaska R.R., Anchorage, 1990—; trustee United Way of Anchorage, 1990-97; bd. dirs Alaska Ctr. for Performing Arts, 1987-97. Recipient Pres.'s award Alaska Black Caucus, 1984, Employment of Handicapped award Mayor of Anchorage, 1979, Execs. in Profile award Region X Blacks in Govt. award, 1998. Mem. NAACP (Harambe award 1973), Alaska Black Leadership Conf. (Cmty. Svc. award 1979-80), Links Inc., Quota Club Intenrat., Valli Vue Homeowners Assn. (v.p.), Zeta Phi Beta. Democrat. Avocations: cooking, reading, gardening. Office: Municipality Anchorage PO Box 196650 Anchorage AK 99519-6650

JONES, JOE KENLEY, journalist; b. Greenville, SC, Feb. 24, 1935; s. J. Clyde and Mildred Idel (Smith) J.; m. Margaret Jean McPherson, Dec. 11, 1965; children— Stephanie, Jason, Eleanor. Student, Furman U., 1953-55; BS in Speech, Northwestern U., 1957, MS in Journalism, 1963; postgrad., Columbia U., 1964-65. Reporter City News Bur. of Chgo., 1962; reporter, cameraman KRNT-TV, Des Moines, 1963-64, WSB-TV, Atlanta, 1965-69; fgn. corr. NBC News, Asia, 1969-72; corr. NBC News (Southeast Bur.), Atlanta, 1972-98. Served with USNR, 1958-61. Recipient Overseas Press Club award for best television reporting from abroad, 1970 Mem. AFTRA, Nat. Acad. Television Arts and Scis. Presbyterian. Home Phone: 770-934-2170.

JONES, JOEL MACKEY, academic administrator; b. Millersburg, Ohio, Aug. 11, 1937; s. Theodore R. and Edna Mae (Mackey) Jones; children: Carolyn Mae, Jocelyn Corinne. BA, Yale U., 1960; MA, Miami U., Oxford, Ohio, 1962; PhD, U. N.Mex., 1966. Dir. Am. studies U. Md., Balt., 1966-69; chmn. Am. studies U. N.Mex., Albuquerque, 1969-73, asst. v.p. acad. affairs, 1973-77, dean faculties, assoc. provost, prof. Am. studies, 1977-85, v.p. adminstrn., 1985-88; pres. Ft. Lewis Coll., Durango, Colo., 1988-99, pres. emeritus, 1999—; interim supr. of schs. Durango Pub. Schs., 1999; interim pres. Salisbury State U., 1999—2000. Bd. dirs. 1st Nat. Bank; pres. Durango Sch. Bd., 2001-2006. Contbr. numerous essays, articles and chpts. to books. Founder Rio Grande Nature Preserve Soc., Albuquerque, 1974—; bd. dirs., mem. exec. com. United Way, Albuquerque, 1980-83; na. bd. cons. NEH, 1978—; bd. dirs. Mercy Hosp., 1990-94; mem. ACE Commn. on Leadership. Farwell scholar Yale U., New Haven, 1960; sr. fellow NEH, 1972; adminstrv. fellow Am. Coun. Edn., Washington, 1972-73. Mem. Am. Studies Assn., Am. Assn. Higher Edn., Am. Assn. State Colls. and Univs. (chair com. on cultural diversity, Colo. state rep. 1994—).

JONES, JOHN ARTHUR, lawyer; b. San Antonio, Fla., Oct. 9, 1921; s. Charles Garfield and Catherine Magdalene (Smith) J.; m. Margarette Lorraine (Sally) Johnson, Sept. 17, 1949; children: Matthew, Lisa, Malcolm, Darby. AA, U. Fla., 1947, JD with honors, 1949. Bar: Fla. 1949, U.S. Dist. Ct. (so. dist.) Fla. 1952, U.S. Ct. Appeals (5th cir.) () 1959, U.S. Ct. Appeals (11th cir.) 1982, U.S. Supreme Ct. () 1978. Assoc. Holland & Knight and predecessors, Tampa, Fla., 1949-54, ptnr., 1954—. Faculty Fla. Sch. of Banking, 1969-81. Editor, contbr.: How to Live and Die with Florida Probate, 1972, Practice Under Florida Probate Code, 1976-2002; co-author Lawgic Served in U.S. Army, 1940-46; lt. col. USAR. Decorated Bronze Star; recipient Robert C. Scott Meml. award, Fla. Bar Assn., William S. Belcher Lifetime Professionalism award, 2003. Fellow Am. Coll. Trust and Estate Counsel, Am. Coll. Real Estate Lawyers; mem. ABA, Fla Bar Assn. (cert. wills, trusts and estates, chmn. real property probate and trust law sect. 1980-81), Hillsborough County (Fla.) Bar Assn., Internat. Acad. Estate and Trust Lawyers, Am. Bar Found., Masons, Shriners, Tampa Club, Univ. Club. Home: 5027 W San Miguel St Tampa FL 33629-5428 Office: Holland & Knight LLP PO Box 1288 100 N Tampa St Ste 4100 Tampa FL 33602 E-mail: jajones@hklaw.com.

JONES, JOHN E., III, judge; b. Pottsville, Pa., June 13, 1955; s. John E. II and Maryalyce (Schultz) Schulze; m. Beth Ann Feryo, Nov. 27, 1982; 2 children: Meghan Elizabeth, John. BA in Polit. Sci., Dickinson Coll., 1977, JD, 1980. Bar: Pa. 1980, U.S. Dist. Ct. Pa. 1980. Law clk. to presiding justice Schuylkill County, Pottsville, 1980-83; ptnr. Dolbin, Cori & Jones P.C., Pottsville, 1980—86; v.p., sec., counsel, dir. Phoenix Contracting Co., 1980—2002; asst. pub. defender Schuylkill County, Pa., 1983—95; sole practice John Jones & Assocs., Pottsville, 1986—2002; counsel Roland & Schlegel, P.C., Reading, Pa., 1992—2002; solicitor City of Pottsville, 1994—96; judge US Dist. Ct. (mid. dist.) Pa., 2002—. Instr. bus. law Pa. State U., Haven, 1982—; bd. dirs. Union Bank and Trust Co., Pottsville, 1993-2002 Organizer, bd. dirs. vocal scholarship competition St. David's Soc. Schuylkill and Carbon Counties, 1985—, Schuylkill County Jr. Golf Scholarship, 1985—; chmn. Pa. Liquor Control Bd., 1995-2002; bd. dirs., pres. Nat. Alcohol Beverage Control Assn; state atty. Drug Abuse Resistance Edn. (D.A.R.E.). Named one of 100 Most Influential People, Time mag., 2006; recipient Govt. Leadership award, Nat. Commn. Against Drunk Driving, 2000, Disting. Alumnus award, Dickinson Sch. Law, Welsh Citizen of Yr. award, St. David's Soc. Schuylkill & Carbon Counties, Rave award, for decision on intelligent design, Wired Mag., 2006. Mem. ABA, Pa. Bar Assn., Pa. Trial Lawyers Assn., Schuylkill County Bar, Fed. Judges' Assn. Clubs: Schuylkill Country (Orwigaburg, Pa.); Pottsville. Republican. Avocations: golf, reading, sports. Home: 1433 Mahantongo St Pottsville PA 17901-3307 Office: District Judge US Dist Ct (Mid Dist) PA Ste 406 240 W 3rd St Williamsport PA 17701 E-mail: chambers_of_judge_john_e._jones@pamd.uscourts.gov.

JONES, JOHN FRANK, retired lawyer; b. Feb. 24, 1922; s. Dwight Frank and Veronica Esther (Sheehy) Jones; m. Sally Oppegard; children: Janna Jones Bellwin, John M., Jeramy Ridder, Jill Jones Nester, Julie, Jeffrey, J. David. BS, U. N.D., 1946; MS in Organic Chemistry, U. Wis., 1953; JD, U. Akron, 1956. Bar: Ohio 1956, U.S. Patent Office, U.S. Ct. Appeals. Patent atty. B.F. Goodrich Co., Akron, Ohio, 1956—62; sr. patent atty. Standard Oil Co., Cleve., 1962—70, patent counsel, 1970—81, food and drug atty. Vistron Corp. subs., 1968—81; ret., 1981. Cons. Standard Oil Co., Cleve., 1981—95, Ashland Chem. Co. (div. Ashland Oil Co.), Columbus, Ohio, 1981—95, B.F. Goodrich Co. Contbr. articles to profl. jours. With USAAF, 1943—46. Decorated D.F.C., Air medal. Mem.: ABA, Cleve. Intellectual Property Law Assn., Ohio Bar Assn., Am. Chem. Soc., CBI Hump Pilots Assn. Republican. Achievements include patents in the fields of chemical and polymer sciences. Home and Office: 2724 Cedar Hill Rd Cuyahoga Falls OH 44223-1226

JONES, JOHN FRANKLIN, JR., (JACK F. JONES), federal agency administrator; b. Detroit, Dec. 2, 1945; s. John Franklin and Mary Elizabeth (Gallup) J.; m. Shirley Anne Sandoz, July 15, 1970 (div. 1980); m. Sharon Kaye Gibson, Sept. 13, 1986; children: Christopher David, Lauren Elaine. BSME, Case Inst. Tech., Cleve., 1967; MS in Aeronautics, Stanford U., Palo Alto, Calif., 1969, PhD in Aeronautics and Astronautics, 1977. Mem. tech. staff Sandia Nat. Laboratories, Livermore, Calif., 1977-81, supr., 1981-84, Albuquerque, 1984, dir. info. processes, 1993; sr. advisor for cybersecurity to US Sec. Energy; chief IT architect Ctr. Info. Tech., NIH, Bethesda, 2001—05, acting dir., 2005—; acting chief info. officer NIH, 2005—. Lt. USN, 1969-73. Recipient Cert. of Appreciation, Nat. Bur. Standards, Dept. Commerce, Washington. Mem. ASME (dir. 1982-84), IEEE, AIAA. Achievements include first use of initial graphics exchange specification for transmission of CAD/CAM data between two commercial enterprises. Office: NIH Ctr Info Tech Bldg 12A Rm 3033 12 South Dr Bethesda MD 20892 Office Phone: 301-496-5703. E-mail: jonesjf@mail.nih.gov.

JONES, JOHN HARDING, photographer; b. Pitts., Apr. 28, 1923; s. John F. and Emma Eleanor (West) Jones; 1 child , Blair Harding. BFA, Rochester Inst. Tech., 1949; MBA, Pepperdine U., 1978; PhD, U. London, 1983; M Photography (hon.), Brantridge Forest, Eng.; DLitt (hon.), Ky. Christian U.; EdD (hon.), St. John's U. Seaman U.S. Naval Air, 1940, advanced through grades to comdr., 1948; ret., 1963; chief photographer U.S. Steel Corp., Pitts.; mgr. art & photo dept. Magnavox Corp., Urbana, Ill.; chief photographer rehab. medicine sect. U.S. VA, LA; coord. rehab. medicine domiciliary sect. Wadsworth VA Hosp., LA. Tchr. Carnegie Mellon Inst., Pitts., Earl Wheeler Schs., Pitts., Seattle U., Art Inst. Pitts.; dir., owner The Little Studio, Panorama City, Calif., 1989—, The Little Studio West, Panorama City, 1994—, The Little Studio, Pitts., The Little Studio West, The Howling Publ Author: Photography, 1972, The Correspondence Educational Directory, 1976, 79, 84, 94, Correspondence Courses for High School Credit & GED Preparation, 1994 Recipient award Writers Guild, 1977, Merit award Cooking, 1986; elected to Am. Police Hall of Fame, 1996 Mem. Profl. Photographers Am., Masons, Shriners, Order Ea. Star (worthy patron 1986) Presbyterian. Avocations: bowling, writing, travel, civic activities, stamp collecting/philately, publishing. Personal E-mail: jonesusn@verizon.net.

JONES, JOHN HARRIS, retired lawyer; b. New Blaine, Ark., Apr. 9, 1922; s. Ira Burton and Byrd (Harris); m. Marjorie Crosby Hart, 1983. AB, U. Central Ark., 1941; postgrad., George Washington U. Law Sch., 1941-42; LL.B., Yale, 1947. Bar: Ark. 1946, U.S. Supreme Ct. 1963. Comms. clk. FBI, 1941-42; atty. pvt. practice, Pine Bluff, 1947—2005; spl. judge Circuit Ct., 1950; spl. chief justice Ark. Supreme Ct., 1997; ret., 2005. Chmn. bd. Pine Bluff Nat. Bank, 1964-77, pres., 1966-76; Mem. Ark. Bd. Law Examiners, 1953-59; Republican nominee for U.S. Senate, 1974; Rep. presdl. elector, 1980; v.p., dir. John Rust Found., 1953-60. Served to 1st lt. USAAF, 1943-45. Decorated Purple Heart, Air medal. Mem. Ark. Bar Assn., Jefferson County Bar Assn. (pres. 1959-60). Mem. Christian Ch. (elder 1963-65, trustee 1965-71, 78-84). Home: 4001 S Cherry St Pine Bluff AR 71603-7156

JONES, JOHN MARTIN, JR., lawyer; b. Balt., Dec. 31, 1928; s. John Martin and Nannalee (Rogers) J.; m. Dayle Fort Nesbitt, July 27, 1969; children: David Mallory, Kelly Anne, Jeffrey Wallace Arthur, Kathleen Celeste; stepchildren: Martha Nesbitt Dewey, William Fort Nesbitt, Howard Scott Nesbitt. AB, U. Md., 1951, LLB, 1953. Bar: Md. 1953, US Dist. Ct. Md. 1953, US Ct. Appeals (4th cir.) 1954, US Supreme Ct. 1959. Assoc. Piper & Marbury, Balt., 1954-59, ptnr., 1960-86; pvt. practice, 1986-99; asst. atty. gen. State of Md., 1959-60; counsel Wilmer, Cutler & Pickering, Balt., 2000-01; legal cons. to law firms, 2001—02; of counsel Kirkland & Ellis, 2003—. Mem. Md. Gov.'s Commn. to Study Tax Laws. Mem. Balt. Area council Boy Scouts Am.; publ. adv. Regional Planning Council, Greater Balt., 1977. Mem. ABA, Md. Bar Assn., Bar Assn. Balt. City, Am. Judicature Soc. (life), Am. Law Inst. (life), Center Club, Yale Club of NYC, Order of Coif, Delta Theta Phi, Delta Kappa Epsilon. Clubs: Center, Yale of NYC, DKE of NYC Achievements include being a mem. adv. com. in drafting and preparation of Am. Law Inst.'s Model Land Development Code, 1970-77. Office: 200 Saint Paul Pl Ste 2121 Baltimore MD 21202-2004 Office Phone: 410-539-2700. Business E-Mail: jjones@kirkland.com. E-mail: johnmartinjo1967@aol.com. *Palma Non Sine Pulvere.*

JONES, JOHN P., III, chemicals executive; b. 1950; With Air Products and Chem. Inc., Allentown, Pa., 1972—, v.p. and gen. mgr. Environ. & Energy Divsn., 1988—92, group v.p. Process Sys. Group, 1992—93; pres. Air Products Europe Inc., 1993—96; exec. v.p. Gases & Equipment Air Products and Chem. Inc., 1996—98, pres., COO, 1998—2000, chmn., pres., CEO, 2000—06, chmn., CEO, 2006—07, chmn., 2007—. Dir. ADP Inc., Am. Chemistry Coun.; exec. com. Soc. Chem. Industry Am. Sect. Office: Corp Secretary's Office Air Products & Chemicals Inc 7201 Hamilton Blvd Allentown PA 18195-1501*

JONES, JOHN PAUL, probation officer, psychologist; b. Blanchard, Mich., July 23, 1944; s. Lawrence John and Thelma Blanche (Eldred) J.; m. Joan Margaret Bruder, Aug. 18, 1972; children: Jason John, Justin John, Jessica Joan-Margaret. BS, Ctrl. Mich. U., Mount Pleasant, 1970, MA, 1974; PhD, Wayne State U., Detroit, 1980. Diplomate Am. Bd. Forensic Medicine, Am. Bd. Cert. Forensic Examiners, Am. Bd. Psychol. Specialties, Am. Acad. of Experts in Traumatic Stress; diplomate in psychotherapy; cert. addictions counselor. Mgr. F. W. Woolworth Co., Bay City, Mich., 1970; probation officer Oakland County Cir. Ct., Pontiac, Mich., 1970-74, probation officer supr., 1974-78, dir. spl. probation program, 1978-80; chief probation officer County of Oakland, Pontiac, 1980-93; outpatient clin. dir. Auro Med. Ctr., Bloomfield Hills, 1993—. Lectr. Oakland U., Rochester, Mich., 1978-82; lic. psychologist Psychol. Svcs. of Bloomfield Hills, Mich., 1980-82, Family Treatment Ctr., Pontiac, Mich., 1983-84, Associated Profls., Bloomfield Hills, 1984-85, Auro Med. Ctr., Bloomfield Hills, 1985—. Pres. Pontiac Lions Club, 1986-87; study subcom. Oakland County Jail, 1982-84; mem. Oakland County Child Sexual Abuse Task Force, 1982-83. With US Army, 1966-68. Mem. APA (bd. govs.), Internat. Neuropsychol. Assn., Am. Correctional Psychologist Assn., Am. Acad. Experts in Traumatic Stress, Am. Coll. Forensic Examiners (BCFE, BCFM), Am. Psychotherapy Assn., Mich. Corrections Assn., Mich. Assn. Probation Officers Svcs., Mich. Psychol. Assn., Fraternal Order of Police, Cen. Mich. U. Alumni Assn. (bd. dirs. Mt. Pleasant chpt. 1989-93), Mich. Neuropsychol. Soc., Am. Psychol. Assn. Republican. Avocations: travel, horseback riding, reading, fencing. Home: 5199 Greenview Dr Gaylord MI 49735 Office: John Paul Jones PhD 651 N Otsego Ave Gaylord MI 49735

JONES, JOHN WESLEY, entrepreneur; b. Wenatchee, Wash., Nov. 15, 1942; s. Richard F. and Hazel F. (Hendrix) J.; m. Melissa L. Meyer, June 22, 1968 (div. 1982); children: John E., Jennifer L.; m. Deborah G. Matthews, Apr. 24, 1993. BA in Bus./Econs., Western Wash. U., Bellingham, 1966. Trainee Jones Bldg., Seattle, 1967-69, mgr., 1969-78; owner/mgr. N.W. Inboards, Bellevue, Wash., 1974-78, Jones Bldg., Seattle, 1978-86; pvt. investor Bellevue, 1987—; owner/mgr. J. Jones Enterprises, 1994—. Trustee BOMA Health & Welfare Trust, 1982-86, chmn. 1986; mem. Seattle Fire Code Adv. Bd., 1979-86. With USMCR, 1966-72. Mem. Seattle Bldg. Owners Mgrs. Assn. (trustee 1979-86), Bldg. Owners Mgrs. Internat., N.W. Marine Trade Assn., Am. Assn. Individual Investors, Composite Fabricators Assn., Soc. Naval Architects Marine Engrs., Boat US, Seattle Yacht Club, NRA, Internat. Show Car Assn., Nat. Street Rod Assn., Specialty Equipment Mktg. Assn. Republican. Avocations: boating, water-skiing, skiing, automobiles, photography. Home and Office: PO Box 2088 Port Townsend WA 98368

JONES, JOIE PIERCE, entrepreneur, acoustician, writer, educator; b. Brownwood, Tex., Mar. 4, 1941; s. Aubrey M. and Mildred K. (Pierce) J.; m. Kay Becknell, June 12, 1965. BA, U. Tex., 1963, MA, 1965; PhD, Brown U., 1970. Sr. scientist Bolt Beranek & Newman, Inc., Cambridge, Mass., 1970-75; assoc. prof., dir. ultrasonics rsch. lab. Case Western Res. U. Sch. Medicine, Cleve., 1975-77; prof., chief med. imaging, dir. grad. studies, dept. radiol. scis. U. Calif., Irvine, 1977—. Cons. acoustics; pres. Computer Sci. Systems, 1978—; founding gen. ptnr. Of Food and Wine, 1982—, Meditherm Assocs., Ltd., 1983-85, Spar Techs., 1987-90, Surgisonics Inc., 1991—, Dermasonics, Inc., 2002-; proposal reviewer NSF/NIH, 1974—; appointee sci. and tech. adv. com. Pres. Carter, 1977-81. Author: Acoustical Imaging, 1995, Acoustics and Society: Applications of Ultrasound in Medicine, 1972; co-author (with Z.H. Cho, M. Singh): Foundations of Medical Imaging, 1993; mem. editl. bd. Ultrasound in Medicine and Biology, 1976—; contbr. more than 300 articles to profl. jours. Active vol. local govt. Jr. fellow, U Tex., Austin, 1961—63. Fellow Am. Inst. Ultrasound in Medicine, IEEE, Acoustical Soc. Am., Am. Phys. Soc.; mem. AAAS, Am. Assn. Physicists in Medicine, Calif. Wine and Food Soc., Phi Beta Kappa. Democrat. Achievements include more than 50 patents in field. Home: 2094 San Remo Dr Laguna Beach CA 92651-2628 Office: U Calif Dept Radiol Sci Irvine CA 92697-5000 Home Phone: 949-494-6687; Office Phone: 949-824-6147. Business E-Mail: jpjones@uci.edu.

JONES, JOLENE REBECCA, medical transcriptionist, educator; b. Rush City, Minn., Nov. 2, 1947; d. Adrian Moses Sr. and Norma Mae Sauer; m. Gary Luverne Kerg, Aug. 6, 1966 (div. May 31, 1969); m. Orie Austin Jones, Aug. 29, 1999; children: Todd Michael Kerg, Marie Norma Jane Kerg-Frazier. BS in English, History, Ea. N. Mex U., 1999. Lic. Techg. N. Mex, 1999. Tchr. Clovis (N.Mex.) HS, 1999—2000; instr. English Ea. N.Mex U., Portales, N.Mex., 2000—02; med. transcriptionist Sparrow Family Med. Clinic, Portales, N.Mex., 2002—; owner Mo-Mac Enterprises Typing Svc., The Kitchen Table Baking and Crafts. Author: A Christmas Collection, 1978, Simply Poetic, 1982, Expressions, 1993, True? Texas Tales, 1994, Hearts Entwined, 1994, Credit for an Angel: A Collection of Christmas Stories and Poems, 2004, Santa's Christmas Miracle, 1992; Winter in Minnesota (Third Pl., 1998), El Portal, Enmu Arts Mag. Mem. Ladies Aux. VFW, Isle, Minn., 1990—. Named Bus. Woman of Yr., NRCC, 2006; recipient Poet of Merit, Internat. Soc. of Poets, 2002—07, Am. Poetry Assn., 1987, 1989, 1990, Third Pl. poetry, El Portal, 1997, Cert. of Appreciation, Gov. Raul H. Castro, Ariz., 1976, Parker Women's Civic Club, Ariz., 1976, Outstanding Acheivement in English Undergrad. Studies, Outstanding Acheivement in History and Social Studies. Mem.: Portales C. of C. (assoc.), VFW Ladies Aux., Parker Women's Civic Club (assoc.; arts chairperson 1976—77), Friends of the Libr. (assoc.), History Guild (assoc.; sec./treas. 1998—99), Phi Alpha Theta (assoc.; sec./treas. 1998—99), Blue Key Honor Frat. (life). Independent. Presbyterian. Avocations: writing, crocheting, jewelry making/design, cake decorating, sewing. Office Phone: 505-226-0177. Business E-Mail: jolene@yucca.net.

JONES, JOSEPH LOUIS, retired manufacturing executive; b. Farmville, Va., Feb. 27, 1923; s. Joseph Louis and Edna (Elcan) J.; m. Dorothy Jeanne Jennings, June 21, 1949; children: Joseph, Catherine, Carolyn. BA, Va.

Poly Inst., 1947. With Armstrong World Industries, Lancaster, Pa., 1947-88, prodn. mgr., 1961-66, v.p. carpet ops., 1966-74, exec. v.p., dir., 1974-83, chmn., pres., chief exec. officer, 1983-88, bd. dirs. Bd. dirs. Carpenter Technology, Reading, Pa., Armstrong World Industries. Trustee Lancaster Gen. Hosp. Served to capt., inf. AUS, 1943-46. Decorated Bronze Star. Mem. Lancaster C. of C., NAM (dir.), The Club Pelican Bay (Naples, Fla.). Republican. Presbyterian (trustee). Club: Lancaster Country. Home (Summer): 618 Willow Valley Lakes Dr Willow Street PA 17584-9648 Home (Winter): 8420 Abbington Cir Apt B31 Naples FL 34108

JONES, JOSEPH SEYMOUR, small business owner, poet; b. Gadsden, Ala., July 4, 1962; s. Jimmie and Sallie Carstarphen Jones. AS in Bus., Bishop State Jr. Coll., Mobile, Ala., 1983; BS in Bus., U. Mobile, 1986; MA in Tchg., Spring Hill Coll., 1994. Cert. elem. tchr. Ala. Dept. Edn. Acctg./engring. support staff U.S. Army Corps Engrs., Mobile, 1979—87; parts clk. Mobile County Pub. Schs., 1988—90, fuel specialist, 1990—94, cert. elem. tchr., 1994—98; owner, mng. founder Believe Enterprises, LLC, Mobile, 2001—. Author: A Poet's Poetic Expressions: Mustard Seeds, 2001, Lady! The World Forever Thanks You!, 1998, Lady! Le Monde à Jamais Vous Remercie!, 1999, numerous poems. Recipient Poet of Merit awards, Internat. Soc. Poets, Washington, 1998—2000. Avocations: restoring classic cars and antique homes, fishing, photography. Office: Believe Enterprises LLC PO Box 40216 Mobile AL 36640-0216

JONES, JUDITH, editor; Editor Alfred A. Knopf, NYC, 1957—. Editor: Mastering the Art of French Cooking, 1961, A Book of Middle Eastern Food, 1972, An Invitation to Indian Cooking, 1975, The Classic Italian Cook Book, 1976, The Key to Chinese Cooking, 1977, Italian Cooking, 1978, The Book of Latin American Food, At Home with Japanese Cooking; co-author: Evan Jones: The Book of Bread: Knead It, Punch It, Bake It!, The L.L. Bean Book of New England Cookery. Recipient Lifetime Achievement award, James Beard Found., 2006, Internat. Assn. Culinary Professionals, 2007. Office: c/o Knopf Publishing Grp 1745 Broadway New York NY 10019*

JONES, JUDITH MILLER, director; BA, George Washington U., 1965; student, Georgetown U., 1965—67; MA in Edn. Tech., Cath. U., 1969. With IBM, 1965—69; legis. asst. Sen. Winston L. Prouty Vt., 1969—71; spl. asst. Office Dep. Asst. Sec. Legis. Dept. HEW, Washington, 1971—72; dir. Nat. Health Policy Forum The George Washington U., Washington, 1972—. Mem. Nat. Com. Vital and Health Stats., 1988—91, chmn., 1991—96; profl. lectr. health policy The George Washington U.; chmn. Ctr. for Advancement of Health. Office: National Health Policy Forum 2131 K Street NW Ste 500 Washington DC 20037 Office Phone: 202-872-1469. Business E-Mail: jmjones@gwu.edu.

JONES, JULIE ANN, elementary school educator, choreographer; b. New Brunswick, NJ, May 1, 1974; d. Timothy Paul and Ann Nealon Farrell; m. Brian Jones, July 10, 2004. BS magna cum laude, Univ. Scranton, Pa., 1996. Cert. K-6 Tchr. Pa., registered artist Keystone Coll., 2005. 2nd grade tchr. Scranton Sch. Dist., Pa., 1996—97, 5th grade tchr., 1997—; dance instr. ballet mistress Ballet Theatre of Scranton, 1996—2003; choregrapher Regional HS plays, Scranton, 1996—; registered artist Keystone Coll., La Plume, Pa., 2005—. Dist. coord. elem. Spanish instrn. Bancroft Sch., Scranton, 1998—, cheerleading coach, 2005—; registered artist Keystone Coll., LaPlume, Pa., 2005—. Contbg. author (ednl. curriculum guides). Mem. Ballet Theatre of Scranton, Pa., 1982—2003. Recipient Blue Ribbon award, Nat. Dept. of Edn., Washington, 2004. Mem.: Nat. Coun. of Pa. Tchrs. of Math., Scranton Fedn. of Tchrs., Am. Fedn. of Tchrs., Alpha Mu Gamma, Kappa Delta Pi. Democrat. Roman Catholic. Avocations: writing, art, piano, dance.

JONES, JULIUS, professional football player; b. Big Stone Gap, Va., Aug. 14, 1981; BA in Soc., Univ. Notre Dame, So. Bend, Ind., 2003. Running Back Dallas Cowboys, 2004—. Recipient All-American Honors, NCAA, 2003. Achievements include ranking in top four among Univ. Notre Dame Running backs for rushing attempts; holds sch. records for kick return yards and kickoff return yards. Office: Dallas Cowboys 1 Cowboys Pkwy Irving TX 75063-4999

JONES, KAREN ANNETTE, civic volunteer; b. Breckenridge, Tex., Feb. 16, 1941; d. Ballard Dorsie and Iris Alvern (Hampton) Hutchison; m. Jerry Raymond Jones, Mar. 16, 1963; children: Lisa Rene Jones Story, Karen DeAnn Jones. BS, McMurry U., Abilene, Tex., 1963. Sec. McMurry Coll., Abilene, 1959-63, Continental Oil Co., Abilene, 1963; substitute tchr. Abilene Pub. Schs., 1967-68; tchr. continuing edn. Mountainview Community Coll., Dallas, 1974; floral designer/sec. Christopher Design, Dallas, 1978-80. Bd. dirs., sec. Wesley Rankin Community Ctr., Dallas, 1989-97; adminstrv. bd. Inglewood United Meth. Ch., Grand Prairie, Tex., 1986—, Breckenridge (Tex.) United Meth. Ch., 2001—; bd. dirs., Brighter Tomorrows Abused Women's Shelter, Grand Prairie, 1994-97; mentor, Breckenridge Jr. H.S., 2001—; regional dir., liaison Guillain-Barre Syndrome Found. Internat., 1999—. Mem. AAUW (sec. 1988—), Grand Prairie Women's Club (bd. dirs. 1986-88). Democrat. Methodist. Address: 10101 County Road 197 Breckenridge TX 76424-7005 E-mail: jerann@bitstreet.com.

JONES, KEITH ALDEN, lawyer; b. Tulsa, July 11, 1941; s. Leonard Virgil and Bernadine (Hutchison) J.; m. Renata Skuta, June 15, 1974; children: Emily Isobel, Alden Rivendale. BA, Harvard U., 1963, LLB, 1966. Bar: Mass. 1966, D.C. 1978, U.S. Supreme Ct. 1972. Asst. prof. Boston U. Law Sch., 1966-67; lectr. Harvard U. Law Sch., 1967-68; assoc. Ropes & Gray, Boston, 1968-70; minority counsel U.S. Senate Select Com. on Small Bus., 1970-72; asst. to Solicitor Gen. of U.S., 1972-75; dep. solicitor gen., 1975-78; ptnr. Fulbright & Jaworski, Washington, 1978-94; of counsel Beck, Redden & Secrest, Houston, 1995—. Mem. ABA, Am. Law Inst.

JONES, KELSEY A., law educator, law administrator; b. Holly Springs, Miss., July 15, 1933; m. Virginia Bethel Ford; children: Cheryl Darlene Jones Campbell-Smith, Eric Andre, Claude Anthony, Kelsey A. Jr. MS, Indsl. Coll.; AB magna cum laude, Miss. Indsl. Coll., 1955, D.D., 1969; MDiv, Garrett Theol. Seminary Northwestern U., 1959; postgrad. in clin. pastoral care and counseling, U. Mich., 1960; post grad. cert., Wesley Med. Ctr., Wichita, Kans., 1967. Cert. Nat. Parole Inst., Nat Council of Crime and Deliquency SUNY, Albany, 1970, George Mason U., 1984. Vis. lectr. black history Fed. City Coll. (UDC Mt. Vernon Campus), 1973—75; INTER/MET, dir. Bacc & Liason Consult, 1973—77; assoc. prof. social sci. U. DC (Van Ness Campus), 1972—77, chmn. dept. social/behavioral sci., 1977—78, prof. criminal justice dept., 1978—79, assoc. prof. dept. criminal justice, 1978—82, chmn., 1979—91, prof., 1982—94, pres. spl. asst. environ. health occupational safety & insit security, 1984—86, justice prof. emeritus; resident facilitator Think Tank Emeritus Manor, Takoma Park, Md. Nationally in demand pub. spkr. and lectr.; contbr. articles to profl. jours. Dean leadership edn. Episcopal Dist.; sec. KS/MO Annual Conf., 1962—70, NY/WA Ann. Conf. Vis. Chapel Meth. Pop Cook County Jail, 1956—58; apptd. staff Recep-Diag Ctr. MI Correct Commn., 1961; delegate Gen. Conf. Christ Meth. Episc. Ch., 1966, Centennial Session Gen. Conf., 1970; chmn. Kans. State Bd. of Probation and Parole, 1967; v.p. Wichita Urban League; bd. dirs. Bros. Inc. Recipient Presdl. citation, Nat. Assn. Equal Opportunities in Higher Edn., 1979, Alumnus of Yr. Disting. Svc. award, Howard U., Washington, 1980, Disting. Svc. award, Lorton Student Govt. Assn. U. DC, 1980, cert. for workshop on crime prevention for coll. and univ., Campus Crime Prevention Programs, 1985. Mem.: Am. Assn. Higher Edn., Am. Soc. Pub. Adminstrn., Nat. Assn. Chiefs of Police, Am. Soc. Indsl. Security, Northeastern Assn. Criminal Justice Educators, Nat. Criminal Justice Assn., Inst. Criminal Justice Ethics, North Atlan Conf. Criminal Just Educators, Acad. Criminal Justice Sci., Alpha Phi Alpha. Achievements include development of published curriculum at the pre-college, undergraduate and graduate levels; participated in dispute resolutions; conducted workshops and seminars on juvenile violence, and fashioned paradigms of adolescent aggression. Office: Justice Prof Emeritus Resident Facilitator Think Tank at Emeritus Manor Takoma Park PO Box 60379-0379 Washington DC 20039-0379

JONES, KENNETH B., JR., surgeon; b. Shreveport, La., 1940; MD, Tulane U., 1966. Diplomate Am. Bd. Surgery. Intern Confederate Meml. Med. Ctr., Shreveport, 1966—67; resident gen. surgery La. State U. and affiliated Hosp., Shreveport, 1969—73; fellow pediat. surgery Ala. Children's Hosp., 1973; chief staff Christus Schumpert Med. Ctr., Shreveport, 1999—2001; clin. asst. prof. surgery La. State U. Med. Ctr., 1984—. Presenter, lectr. in field. Contbr. more than 50 articles to profl. jours., chpts. to books. Fellow: ACS; mem.: AMA, Internat. Fedn. Surgery Obesity, Surg. Assn. La., Am. Soc. Gen. Surgeons (nomination com. 2004), Am. Soc. Metabolic and Bariatric Surgery (chmn. surg. access com. 1997—2000, sec. treas. 1998—2000, pres. 2001—02, chmn. surg. access com. 2002—06), Southeastern Surg. Congress, Brazilian Soc. Bariatric Surgery (hon.). Achievements include research in bariatric surgery. Office: 1801 Fairfield Ave Ste 408 Shreveport LA 71101-4468 Home: 950 McCormick St Shreveport LA 71104 Home Phone: 318-868-5518; Office Phone: 318-222-7584. Personal E-mail: pbsurgkj@aol.com.

JONES, KENNETH BRUCE, surgeon; b. Scottsville, Ky., Apr. 17, 1953; s. Kenneth C. and Betty (Miller) J.; m. Carol Jean Munger, June 28, 1980; children: Daniel, Christopher, Elizabeth. BS, U. Ky., 1974; MD, Vanderbilt U., Nashville, 1978. Diplomate Am. Bd. Surgery; cert. advanced trauma life saving. Surg. intern and resident U. Louisville Med. Sch., 1978-80; resident in surgery East Tenn. U. Med. Sch., Johnson City, 1980-82, chief resident, 1983; surgeon Claiborne Surg. Group, Tazewell, Tenn., 1983-84, N.E. Ark. Surg. Clinic, Jonesboro, Ark., 1984—; sec. med. staff Meth. Hosp., 1986-87, chief of surgery, 1988-90, vice chief of staff, 1989-91, chief of staff, 1992-94; chief of surgery St. Bernard's Regional Med. Ctr., 1996-97; mem. hosp. bd. Regional Med. Ctr. N.E., 1997. Asst. clin. prof. surgery U. Ark. Area Health Edn. Ctr., Jonesboro, 1985—; cancer liaison of ACS Commn. on Cancer to St. Bernard's, 1996-2006; alumni bd. Vanderbilt Med. Sch., 2005—; cons. Am. Bd. Surgery. Contbr. articles to profl. jours. Active sch. bd., 1993-98; deacon So. Bapt. Ch.; bd. dirs. N.E. Ark. Clinc Found. Justin Potter med. scholar, 1974-78. Fellow: ACS; mem.: NRA, Am. Soc. Bariatric Surgery, Soc. Am. Gastrointestinal Endoscopic Surgeons, Am. Soc. Gen. Surgery, Am. Cancer Soc. (pres. Craighead County unit 2000—01), Nat. Wild Turkey Fedn., Dove Sportsman Soc., Ducks Unltd., Phi Beta Kappa. Baptist. Avocations: hunting, jogging, toy trains. Home: 2600 Nix Lake Dr Jonesboro AR 72404-0917 Office: NE Ark Surg Clinic 800 S Church St Ste 104 Jonesboro AR 72401-4154 Home Phone: 870-972-6895; Office Phone: 870-932-4875.

JONES, KENSINGER, advertising executive, educator; b. St. Louis, Oct. 18, 1919; s. Walter C. and Anna (Kensinger) Jones; m. Alice May Guseman, Oct. 7, 1944; children: Jeffrey, Janice A. Jones Geary. Student, Washington U., St. Louis, 1938-39. Lectr. radio writing Wash. U., 1947—52; TV writer, advt. agy. supr. Leo Burnett Co., 1952-57; exec. v.p., creative dir. Campbell-Ewald Co., Detroit, 1957-68; sr. v.p., creative dir. D.P. Brother & Co., Detroit, 1968-70; sr. v.p., exec. creative dir. Leo Burnett Co., Inc., Chgo., 1970-73; regional creative dir. Leo Burnett Pty. Ltd., Sydney, Australia, 1973-75, Leo Burnett, SE Asia, 1975-77; creative supr. Biggs/Gilmore, 1981-83; lectr. Mich. State U., 1982-95; emeritus, 1996. Vis. lectr., China, 1988, Taipei, Taiwan, Jakarta, Indonesia, 90, Dalhousie U., N.S., 1992. Author: Enter Singapore, 1974, Looking for the Best, 1994; author: (as R. N. Lake) Not Guilty, Just Dead, 1999; co-author: Cable Advertising-New Ways to New Business, 1986, A Call From the Country, 1989, Love Poems of a Business Man, 1997, Case Histories in Co-operation, 1999; author: (radio series) Land We Live In, 1945—52, numerous poems; contbr. articles to profl. jours.; exhibitions include Detroit Hist. Mus., 2004, Represented in permanent collections Hartman Collection, Duke U. Bd. dir. World Med. Relief, Inc., 1961—92, dir. emeritus, 1993; mem. comm. com. Nat. Coun. Boy Scouts Am., 1966—92; mem. Econ. Devel. Action Group, 1988—96; chmn. Barry County Planning and Zoning Commn., Pks. and Recreation Commn.; county grants coord. Barry County, 1977—78, mem. futuring steering com., 1988—, mem. natural resources action team, 2002—06; mem. dean's cmty. coun. arts Mich. State U., 1993—96, mem. coop. ext. adv. coun., 1993—95. With US Army, 1940—44. Named Barry County Sr. Citizen of the Yr., 1999; recipient Silver Beaver award, Boy Scouts Am.; Silver salute, Mich. State U., 1982, award, Freedoms Found., 1984, Positive Action for Tomorrow award, Barry County, 1995. Mem.: Adcraft Club Detroit, Circumnavigators Club, Players Club. Home: 425 Pritchardville Rd Hastings MI 49058-9328 *The opportunity to absorb, examine, synthesize and then utilize facts and experience is what makes creative endeavor fascinating. Somehow the individual mind finds new and meaningful relationships between previously unrelated data. An idea is born. It becomes an advertising campaign, a book or movie, a new product. Trying to find those new relationships makes life rewarding in so many ways. Dissatisfaction with the status quo is the prod toward all progress. Use your talents broadly. Not just to make a living, but to improve your life, your environment, your society. By doing so you'll improve your talents.*

JONES, L. Q. See MCQUEEN, JUSTICE

JONES, LAUREN EVANS, lawyer; b. Lawrence, Kans., Jan. 10, 1952; s. Kevin Rice and Marcia Jo Ann (Peterson) J.; m. Vivien Craig Long, Mar. 26, 1978; children: Dylan Tyler, Hayden Blake, Carson Reed. BA in History, U. Mich., 1973; JD, Duke U., 1977. Bar: R.I. 1978, U.S. Dist. Ct. R.I. 1978, U.S. Ct. Appeals (1st cir.) 1985, U.S. Ct. Appeals (9th cir.) 1994, U.S. Supreme Ct. 1991. Assoc. Lovett, Morgera, Schefrin & Gallogly, Providence, R.I., 1979-83; ptnr. Jones & Aisenberg, Providence, 1983-89; owner Jones Assocs., Providence, 1990—. Mem. Jud. Performance Eval. Commn., 1993—; mem. R.I. Supreme Ct. Com. on Profl. and Civility, 1995-96. Editor R.I. Bar Jour., 1989-95, 2002-06; contbr. articles to profl. jours. Nominee R.I. Supreme Ct., 1993, 95, 96, 97. Fellow Am. Acad. Appellate Lawyers; mem. RI Bar Assn. (exec. com. 1989-2000, 2002-06, 2006—, sec. 1995, v.p. 1996, pres. elect 1997, pres. 1998-99). Office: Jones Assocs 72 S Main St Providence RI 02903-2907 Office Phone: 401-274-4446. E-mail: ljones@appeallaw.com.

JONES, LAUREN PATRICIA, psychologist, not-for-profit developer; b. Cambridge, Mass., Sept. 20, 1961; d. Hubert Eugene and Katherine Elizabeth Jones; m. John Martin Van Buren. BA, Wesleyan U., Middletown, Conn., 1983; MA, U. Calif., Berkeley, 1989, PhD, 1994. Asst. rsch. analyst, rsch. analyst Mass. Gen. Hosp., Boston, 1983—86; clearinghouse dir. Children's Def. Fund, Washington, 1994—95; rsch. dir. Howard U., Washington, 1995—97; psychologist DC Pub. Schs., Washington, 1998—; pres., founder No Offense, Washington, 2005—. Grant reviewer Corp. Nat. Svc., Washington, 1998; psychol. examiner Harcourt, San Antonio, 2005; cons. in field. Founding sponsor Martin Luther King Jr. Nat. Meml., Washington, 2006—. Named Wall of Tolerance honoree, Nat. Campaign Tolerance, 2005; recipient mental health clin. traineeship, Dept. HHS, 1992—94; minority dissertation fellow, U. Calif., Berkeley, 1991—92, psychology fellow, Yale U., New Haven, 1992—94, No Offense Program grant, NASP Children's Fund, Inc., 2005—06. Mem.: APA, Nat. Assn. Sch. Psychologists, Phillips Collection, So. Poverty Law Ctr., Underwater Adventure Seekers. Avocations: photography, singing, tai chi, snorkeling, soccer. Office: No Offense 4401-A Connecticut Ave NW # 184 Washington DC 20008

JONES, LAURIE LYNN, magazine editor; b. Kerrville, Tex., Sept. 2, 1947; d. Charles Clinton and Jean Laurie (Davidson) J.; m. C. Frederick Childs, June 26, 1976; children: Charles Newell (Clancy), Cyrus Trevor; 1 stepchild, Ariel Childs. BA, U. Tex., 1969. Asst. to dir. coll. admissions Columbia U., NYC, 1969-70; asst. to dir. Office Alumni-Columbia U., NYC, 1970-71; asst. advt. mgr. Book World, 1971-72, Washington Post-Chgo. Tribune, 1971-72; editl. asst. N.Y. Mag., NYC, 1972-74, asst. editor, 1974, sr. editor, 1974-76, mng. editor, 1976-92, Vogue Mag., 1992—; exec. mng. editor Men's Vogue, 2005—. Mem. Am. Soc. Mag. Editors, Women in Coummunication, Advt. Women N.Y. Republican. Methodist. Home: 40 Great Jones St New York NY 10012-1109 Also: 62 Giles Hill Rd Redding Ridge CT 06876 Office: Vogue Magazine 4 Times Sq New York NY 10036-6561 Home Phone: 212-473-2399; Office Phone: 212-286-6910. Business E-Mail: Laurie_Jones@condenast.com.

JONES, LAWRENCE ANDREW, research scientist, retired military officer; b. Escondido, Calif., Nov. 8, 1961; s. Harry Jay Jones, Jr. and Darlene Gloria Jones-Saxton; m. Diane Marie Smitley, May 11, 1985; children: Stephen Joshua, Christopher Andrew. Attended, U. Mo., St. Louis, 1986—87; AA, Mohegan CC, Norwich, Conn., 1989; BS in Sociology and Polit. Sci., SUNY, Albany, 1994; MA in Orgnl. Mgmt., U. Phoenix-Hawaii, Honolulu, 1998; PhD in Human Resource Mgmt., Capella U., Mpls., 2004. Cert. subspecialist in resource mgmt. & analysis US Navy, 1999, subspecialist in manpower sys. analysis mgmt. US Navy, 2004, sr. profl. in human resources Soc. Human Resource Mgmt., 2004, instl. review board profl. Coun. for Cert. Instl. Review Bd. Profls., 2006. Asst. material officer Destroyer Squadron Eight, Mayport, Fla., 1991—92; main propulsion asst. USS Jack Williams (FFG 24), Pascagoula, Miss., 1992—96; occupl. safety & health adminstr., command safety officer Afloat Tng. Group Mid. Pacific, Pearl Harbor, Hawaii, 1996—98; elec. officer USS Williamette (AO 180), Pearl Harbor, 1998—99; chief engr. USS Inchon (MCS 12), Ingelside, Tex., 1999—2001; repair officer, dept. head Shore Intermediate Maintenance Activity, Pascagoula, Miss., 2001—02, interim exec. officer, 2002—02; enlisted surface engring. ratings assignments bd. head Navy Pers. Command, Bur. Naval Pers., Millington, Tenn., 2003—04; pers. rsch. scientist Navy Pers. Rsch., Studies & Tech. Divsn., Bur. Naval Pers., Millington, 2004—, dir. tech. programs office, 2004—05, interim dep. dir., 2005—05, chair human rsch. protections bd., 2006—. Divemaster Profl. Assn. Diving Instructors, Honolulu, 1996—99. Lt. comdr. USN, 1980—2005, worldwide. Decorated Navy & Marine Corps Achievement medal US Navy, Navy & Marine Corps Commendation medal, Meritorious Svc. medal; recipient Sta. of Yr. award, US Navy Recruiting Command, 1986, Sec. of Navy award for achievement in shore safety, Sec. of Navy, 1997, Rsch. Excellence award, Bur. Naval Pers., 2006. Mem.: USS Inchon LDO/CWO Assn. (pres. 2000—01), Am. Soc. Naval Engrs., Dept. Def. Interlab. Com. Editing & Pub., Applied Rsch. Ethics Nat. Assn., Pub. Responsibility in Medicine & Rsch., Am. Mgmt. Assn., Acad. Mgmt., Soc. Human Resource Mgmt., Navy Selection & Classification Adv. Panel, Navy League of US, Fleet Adm. Chester Nimitz Found. Achievements include creation of a job matching algorithim; creation of a vocational interest test; research in assessment of multitasking performance. Avocations: scuba diving, genealogy. Home: 4101 Blackheath Dr Bartlett TN 38135 Office: Navy Personnel Rsch Studies & Tech 5720 Integrity Dr Millington TN 38055-1300 Business E-Mail: andy.jones@navy.mil.

JONES, LAWRENCE WILLIAM, retired physicist; b. Evanston, Ill., Nov. 16, 1925; s. Charles Herbert and Fern (Storm) J.; m. Ruth Reavley Drummond, June 24, 1950; children: Douglas Warren, Carol Anne, Ellen Louise. BS, Northwestern U., 1948, MS, 1949; PhD, U. Calif. at Berkeley, 1952. Research asst. U. Calif. Radiation Lab., Berkeley, 1950-52; mem. faculty U. Mich., Ann Arbor, 1952—, prof. physics, 1963-98, chmn. dept. physics, 1982-87, prof. emeritus, 1998—. Physicist Midwestern U. Rsch. Assn., 1956-57; vis. physicist Lawrence Radiation Lab., Berkeley, 1959—, cons., 1964-66; vis. scientist CERN, Geneva, Switzerland, 1961-62, 65, 85—, assoc., 1988—; vis. physicist Brookhaven Nat. Lab., Upton, N.Y., 1963—, Fermi Nat. Accelerator Lab., Batavia, Ill., 1971—; vis. prof. Tata Inst. Fundamental Rsch., Bombay, India, 1979, U. Sydney Australia, 1991; elem. particle physics panel of physics survey com. NRC, 1984; cons. ctrl. design group Superconducting Super Collider Nat. Lab., 1985-87, vis. physicist, 1991-94; cons. NASA, 1974-81, 2002; trustee Univs. Rsch. Assn., 1982-87; disting. vis. scholar U. Adelaide, 1991; vis. scientist U. Auckland, 1991; co-chmn. sci. adv. com. Mich. Environ. Coun., 2000—; mem. internat. adv. com. Bolivian Obs. of Mt. Chacaltaya, 2001—. Mem. adv. panel for Cosmic Rays Jour. of Physics G., 1991-95. Guggenheim fellow, 1965; Sci. Rsch. Coun. fellow, 1977. Fellow Am. Phys. Soc. Home: 2666 Parkridge Dr Ann Arbor MI 48103-1731 Office: U Mich Dept Physics Ann Arbor MI 48109-1040 Business E-Mail: lwjones@umich.edu.

JONES, LEE BENNETT, chemistry professor, academic administrator; b. Memphis, Mar. 14, 1938; s. Harold S. and Martha B. J.; m. Vera Kramar, Feb. 8, 1964; children: David B., Michael B. BA magna cum laude, Wabash Coll, 1960; PhD, M.I.T., 1964; DSC (hon.), Wabash Coll., 1992. Faculty U. Ariz., Tucson, 1964-85, prof. chemistry, 1972-85, asst. head dept. chemistry, 1971-73, head dept., 1973-77, dean Grad. Coll., 1977-79, provost Grad. Studies and Health Scis., 1979-82, v.p. rsch., 1982-85; prof. chemistry, exec. v.p., provost U. Nebr., Lincoln, 1985—2002, exec. v.p., provost emeritus, 2002—. Chmn. bd. dirs. Coun. Grad. Schs., 1986; mem. Grad. Records Exam. Bd., 1986-91; mem. Midwest Higher Edn. Commn., 1995—. Mem. editl. bd. Jour. Chem. Edn, 1975-79; contbr. numreous articles to sci. jours. Mem. Nebr. R&D Authority, 1985—, Midwest Higher Edn. Commn.; vice chmn. Nebr. Ednl. Telecomm. Commn., 1987-88, 91-92. NSF fellow, 1961-63, 64— Mem. AAAS, AAUP, Am. Chem. Soc., Chem. Soc. (London), N.Y. Acad. Scis., Phi Beta Kappa. Office: U Nebr 106 Varner Hall 3835 Holdrege St Lincoln NE 68503-1435 Home: 5645 E Towner St Tucson AZ 85712 Personal E-mail: LBJones@nebraska.edu.

JONES, LEONADE DIANE, media publishing company executive; b. Bethesda, Md., Nov. 27, 1947; d. Leon Adger and Landonia Randolph Jones. BA with distinction, Simmons Coll., 1969; JD, MBA, Stanford U., 1973. Bar: Calif. 1973, DC 1979. Summer assoc. Davis Polk & Wardwell, NYC, 1972; securities analyst Capital Rsch. Co., LA, 1973-75; asst. treas. Washington Post Co., 1975-79, 86-87, treas., 1987-96; dir. fin. svcs. Post-Newsweek Stas., Inc., Washington, 1979-84, v.p. bus. affairs, 1984-86; ind. mgmt. cons., pvt. equity investor, 1997-99, 2001—; CFO, sec. VentureThink, LLC, 1999-2001; exec. v.p., CFO Versura, Inc., 2000-01. Bd. ind. chmn. Am. Balanced Fund, Inc., Income Fund Am., Inc.; bd. dirs. Fundamental Investors, Growth Fund Am., Inc., The New Economy Fund, Smallcap World Fund, Inc.; mem. investment mgmt. subcom. of benefit plans com. Am. Stores Co., 1992—99; mem. investment adv. com. NY State Tchrs. Retirement Sys., 1999—; mem. investment mgmt. subcom. Albertson's Inc., 1999—2007. Bd. dirs. The Women's Found., 2000—03, Access Group, Inc., 2005—. Named to D.C. Women's Hall of Fame, 1992; recipient Candace award for bus., 1992, Serwa award, 1993. Mem.: DC Bar Assn., Calif. Bar Assn., Nat. Bar Assn., Stanford U. Bus. Sch. Alumni Assn. (bd. dirs. 1986—88, pres. Washington-Balt. chpts. 1984—85). Personal E-mail: leonade@att.net.

JONES, LEWIS ARNOLD, JR., physician, radiologist, consultant; b. Detroit, Sept. 16, 1950; s. Lewis Arnold, Sr. and Berlene (Irish) J.; m. Pamela Denise Jennings, Nov. 14, 1992; children: Jennifer Tiffany, Alicia

Dawn, Lewis Alexander. Student, Highland Park Coll., 1968-69, Wayne State U., 1969-72; MD, U. Mich., 1978. Diplomate Am. Bd. Radiology. Radiology residency Providence Hosp., Southfield, Mich., 1978-82; diagnostic radiologist Tri-County Radiology, P.C., West Bloomfield, Mich., 1983-84; clin. instr. of radiology Wayne State U. Sch. of Medicine, Detroit, 1984-91, clin. asst. prof. radiology, 1991-97; physician cons. Mich. Dept. Cmty. Health, Lansing, 1997-2000; radiologist Henry Ford Hosp., Detroit, 2000—02, Genesys Physicians Integrated Diagnostics, Burton, Mich., 2002—04; breast radiologist Karmanos Cancer Inst., Detroit, 2004—. Mem. cmty. adv. com. Karmanos Cancer Inst., Detroit, 1994-97; adv. bd. African Am. anti-platelet stroke prevention Wayne State U., 1996-97; co-investigator Women's Health Initiative, Detroit, 1996-97; co-chmn. 1997 Mich.'s Year of Women's Health, Mich. Dept. Cmty. Health, Lansing, 1997-98. Vol. spkr. Am. Cancer Soc., 1986—. Co-creator, co-presenter seminars Ptnrs. for Life, A women's health empowerment program, Mich., 1996—; bd. dirs. Oakland County Am. Cancer Soc., 1988—. Recipient Life Saver award Am. Cancer Soc., Southfield, Mich., 1990, Frederick Douglass award Nat. Assn. Negro Bus. and Profl. Women's Clubs, New Met. Detroit Club, 1996; winner "What a Man" contest, Essence Mag./ Preferred Stock Cologne, N.Y.C., 1995. Mem. AMA, Mich. State Med. Soc., Wayne County Med. Soc., Am. Coll. Radiology, Assn. Univ. Radiologists, Soc. Breast Imaging. Avocation: jazz and classical music collector. Home: 4951 Champlain Cir West Bloomfield MI 48323-3529

JONES, LINCOLN, III, military officer; b. Ft. Benning, Ga., Jan. 23, 1933; s. Lincoln and Doris G. (Baltz) J.; m. Alexandra Ann Archbald, June 21, 1958; children: Peter L., Patricia A. BS, U.S. Mil. Acad., 1958; MS, Auburn U., 1969. Commd. 2d lt. U.S. Army, 1958; advanced through grades to maj. gen.; brigade comdr. 9th Inf. Div., 1978-79, chief staff div. and Ft. Lewis, 1980, asst. div. comdr., 1980-82; dep. chief of staff LANDSOUTH, Verona, Italy, 1982-85; dep. comdg. gen. V Corps, Frankfurt, Germany, 1985-87; comdg. gen. USASETAF, Vicenza, Italy, 1987-90; pres., CEO ENRON Power Corp., Houston, 1991—98; pres. ENRON Engring. and Constrn. Co., Houston, 1994-96; vice chmn. ENRON Europe Ltd., London, 1996-98; pres. Lincoln Assocs. Inc., Houston, 1999—, Internat. Bus. and Energy Devel. Corp. for Pakistan; chmn. World Wide Strategic Ptnrs. Corp., Houston, 2003—, Internat. Spectrum Develop. Corp. Inc., Houston, 2005—. Exec. prof. U. Houston. Mem. Com. on Fgn. Rels., Houston; bd. dirs. World Coun. Fgn. Affairs; bd. dirs. Nat. Def. U. Found., 1998—, vice-chmn., 2005. Decorated D.S.M. with oak leaf cluster, Def. Superior Svc. Medal, Legion of Merit with oak leaf cluster, D.F.C., Bronze Star for valor with oak leaf cluster, others. Mem. Assn. U.S. Army (vice-chmn.), Assn. Grads. U.S. Mil. Acad. Episcopalian. Home: 9 Fernglen Dr The Woodlands TX 77380-3957

JONES, LINDA, communications educator; BA in English, U. Mich., 1972; MS in Journalism with distinction, Northwestern U., 1985. Reporter The Chelsea (Mich.) Standard, 1973-75; county govt., police reporter The Marshall (Mich.) Evening Chronicle, 1975-77; edn. reporter The Bay City (Mich.) Times, 1977--79, asst. met. editor, 1979-81, met. editor, 1981-86; vis. asst. prof. dept. journalism Roosevelt U., 1986-88; asst. prof. Medill Sch. Journalism Northwestern U., 1988-92, dir. tchg. newspaper program, 1992—; assoc. prof. journalism Roosevelt U., Chgo., 1992—, dir. Sch. Comm., 1995—. Acting dir. Multicultural Journalism Ctr., Urban Journalism Ctr.; tchr. workshop sessions Journalism Edn. Assn./Nat. Scholastic Press Assn. convs., 1992-96, chair Multicultural Scholarship Com., 1996. Contbr. articles to profl. jours.; judge and lectr. in field. Office: Roosevelt Univ 505 E Ctr for Profl Advancement 430 S Michigan Ave Chicago IL 60605-1394 E-mail: ljones@roosevelt.edu.

JONES, LINDA MAY, tour guide, writer; b. El Dorado, Kans., Nov. 9, 1937; d. Forrest Edward and Edith May Carlson; m. William Stanley Conard, Sept. 1, 1957 (div. Nov. 1970); children: Chris Dale Conard, Carin Dene Lockhart, Curtis Dean Conard; m. Verl Ray Jones, Nov. 6, 1982. Student, U. Kans., 1955-57, U. Colo., 1970-71. Tour guide Queen City Tours, Denver, 1976-84, tour guide coord., 1977-84, Am. Travel Brokers, Denver, 1977-84; owner Columbine Tours, Denver, 1984-92; tour dir. Backyard Tours, Englewood, Colo., 1993—2002, Mountains and More Tour Co., Golden, Colo., 1993—, Colo. Conv. Assocs., 1998—. Tourism adv. com. Metro Denver Conv. and Visitors Bur., 1990; staff writer Colo. Gambler, 1994-, Gilpin County News; presenter in field. Co-author: Mile High Denver, A Guide to the Queen City, 1981, Up the Gulch-Historic Walking Tours of Black Hawk, Central City and Nevadaville, 2005; contbr. articles to mags. V.p. Rep. Ctrl. Com., Gilpin County, Colo., 1983-93; v.p. Gilpin County Hist. Soc., Central City, Colo., v.p. 1988-90, pres., 1990—; chmn. Gilpin County Hist. Adv. Commn., 2006—. Mem. Mt. Lookout DAR, Rotary (pres. 2006-07), Intertel, Alpha Phi. Methodist. Avocations: hiking, snowshoeing. Home: PO Box 615 Black Hawk CO 80422 Office Phone: 303-582-3858. Personal E-mail: fairburnmt@surfbest.net.

JONES, LINDA R. WOLF, consulting company executive; b. Jersey City, Sept. 4, 1943; d. Eugene Leon and Lottie (Pinkowitz) Rubin; m. Frank Paul Jones, Oct. 21, 1973 (div. Nov. 1987); 1 child, Elisabeth Noel. AB, Bryn Mawr Coll., 1964; MA, Yale U., 1968; DSW, Yeshiva U., NYC, 1985; MDiv, Wesley Theol. Sem., Washington, 2007. Dir. planning and tng. N.Y.C. Dept. Employment, 1971-77; dir. legislation N.Y.C. Community Devel. Agy., 1977-78; supervisory legis. analyst N.Y.C. Human Resources Adminstrn., 1978; sr. policy analyst Community Svc. Soc. N.Y., 1978-85; dir. pub. policy YMCA Greater N.Y., 1985-89; dir. spl. projects Phoenix House, NYC, 1990-92; dir. income security policy Community Svc. Soc., NYC, 1992-94; exec. dir. Therapeutic Communities Am., Washington, 1994—2002; dir. internat. ops. Conwal divsn. Axiom Resource Mgmt., Falls Church, Va., 2002—. Adj. extension faculty Cornell U./NY State Sch. Indsl. and Labor Rels., NYC, 1975-80; dir. Nonprofit Coord. Com. NY, NYC, 1986-94, Govt. Affairs Profls., NYC, 1989-94. Author: Eveline M. Burns and the American Social Security System 1935-60, 1991; mem. editl. bd. New Eng. Jour. Human Svcs., 1981—; contbr. articles to profl. jours. Active Civic Affairs Forum, NYC, 1985-94; legis. task force NY State Gov.'s Office Vol. Svc., NYC, 1987-90. Mem. Women in Govt. Rels., Am. Pub. Welfare Assn. (dir. 1982), Bryn Mawr Club Westchester (bd. dirs., past pres. 1974-94), Bryn Mawr Club Washington. Home: 6621 7th Pl NW Washington DC 20012 Office: Conwal Divsn Axiom Resource Mgmt Inc Ste 703 5111 Leesburg Pike Falls Church VA 22041

JONES, LINDY DON, lawyer; b. Vernon, Tex., Aug. 20, 1949; s. Earl Irven Jones and Avis June (Koontz) McDowell; m. M. Kathryn Sanders, June 6, 1969; children: Brandi Kim, Megan Dawn, Ty Jeffrey. BBA in Mgmt. with honors, U. Tex., Arlington, 1971; JD, So. Meth. U., 1974. Bar: Tex. 1974, U.S. Ct. Appeals (5th cir.) 1974, U.S. Dist. Ct. (we. dist.) Tex. 1977, U.S. Dist. Ct. (ea. dist.) Tex. 1978, U.S. Dist. Ct. (so. dist.) Tex. 1979. Ptnr. Moseley, Jones, Enoch & Martin and predecessors, Dallas, 1974—81, Moseley, Jones, Allen & Fuquay, Dallas, 1981—86, Jones, Allen & Fuquay, LLP, Dallas, 1986—. Pres. Highland Park United Meth. Ch. Mens Club, Dallas, 1979; chmn. bd. dirs. Dickinson Pl. Charitable Corp., Dallas, 1984-86. Recipient hon. life membership Highland Park United Meth. Ch. Mens Club, 1980. Mem. ABA, Dallas Bar Assn. (com. mem. 1974—), State Bar Tex., Delta Theta Phi. Republican. Home: 8068 Moss Meadows Dr Dallas TX 75231-3915 Office: Jones Allen & Fuquay LLP 8828 Greenville Ave Dallas TX 75243-7160 E-mail: ljones@jonesallen.com.

JONES, LISA MARIA DRAPER, counselor; b. San Francisco, Nov. 7, 1966; d. Ponce DeLeon and Cosima (Zanzarelli) Draper; m. Reginald Joseph Jones, Dec. 29, 1990; children: Lauren Elizabeth, Ryan Joseph. BA, UCLA, 1989; MA Clin. Psychology, Antioch U., 2004; post grad., Alliant U., Calif. Trainee children's social worker Dept Children and Family Svcs., LA, 1990; primary counselor Sasha Bruce Youthwork, Inc, Washington, 1991—92; family therapist The Family Connection, Landover Hills, Md., 1992—94; counselor in-home outreach Youth Intervention Program, LA, 1994—2000, co- program mgr., 2000—02; sch. counselor Outreach Concern, Santa Ana, Calif., 2003—04. Democrat. Roman Catholic. Avocations: travel, reading, fundraising. Home Phone: 562-421-5181; Office Phone: 323-804-3768. Personal E-mail: rllj3@aol.com.

JONES, LOUIS, JR., (BUCKY JONES), academic administrator; Dir. Fayetteville (Ark.) regional campus Webster U. Mem. Ark. Bar Assn. (pres. 1999—).

JONES, LUCIAN COX, lawyer; b. Kew Gardens, NY, Dec. 22, 1942; m. Ann Waters, Aug. 22, 1964; children— L. Rustin, Norman W., Warren R. AB, Davidson Coll., 1964; JD, Columbia U., 1967. Bar: N.Y. 1967. Assoc. Shearman & Sterling, NYC, 1967-68, 70-76, ptnr., 1976-98; lectr.Cameron Sch. Bus. U. N.C., Wilmington, 1998—. Served to capt. U.S. Army, 1968-70 Mem. ABA, N.C. State Bar Assn., Assn. Bar City N.Y. Office: U NC Cameron Sch Bus 601 S College Rd Wilmington NC 28403-3297

JONES, LUPE SIRENA, insurance agent; b. Pasadena, Calif., Jan. 12, 1970; d. Luis Prado and Antonia Diaz Ixta; m. Anthony Jones-Carroll, June 13, 1992 (div. Aug. 1999). Personal E-mail: snoopiejones@yahoo.com.

JONES, LYLE VINCENT, psychologist, educator; b. Grandview, Wash., Mar. 11, 1924; s. Vincent F. and Matilda M. (Abraham) Jones; m. Patricia Edison Powers, Dec. 17, 1949 (div. 1979); children: Christopher V., Susan E., Tad W. Student, Reed Coll., 1942—43; BS, U. Wash., 1947, MS, 1948; PhD, Stanford U., 1950. Nat. Research fellow, 1950—51; asst. prof. psychology U. Chgo., 1951—57; vis. assoc. prof. U. Tex., 1956—57; assoc. prof. U. N.C., 1957—60, prof., 1960—69, Alumni disting. prof., 1969—92, rsch. prof., 1992—, dir. L.L. Thurstone Psychometric Lab., 1957—74, 1979—92, vice chancellor, dean Grad. Sch., 1969—79. Pres. Assn. Grad. Schs., 1976—77; cons. in field. Author: Studies in Aphasia: An Approach to Testing, 1961, The Measurement and Prediction of Judgment and Choice, 1968, An Assessment of Research-Doctorate Programs in the United States, 5 vols., 1982, Indicators of Precollege Education in Science and Methematics, 1985, The Nation's Report Card: Evolution and Perspectives, 2004; Psychometrika, 1956—61, mem. editl. com. for psychology Mc-Graw-Hill, 1965—77; contbr. articles to profl. jours. Mng. trustee J. McKeen Cattell Fund, 1974—2006. With Air Corps US Army, 1943—46. Recipient Thomas Jefferson award, U. N.C., 1979; fellow, Ctr. Advanced Study in Behavioral Scis., 1964—65, 1982—83; grantee, NIH, 1957—63, NSF, 1960—63, 1971—74, 1982—84, 1993—97, NIMH, 1963—74, 1979—87. Fellow: AAAS, APA (pres. divsn. 1963—64), Am. Statis. Assn., Am. Psychol. Soc., Am. Acad. Arts and Scis.; mem.: Psychometric Soc. (pres. 1962—63), Inst. Medicine, Nat. Coun. Measurement Edn., Am. Ednl. Rsch. Assn. Home: 6578 US Highway 15 501 N Pittsboro NC 27312-7793 Office: U NC CB 3270 Davie Hl Chapel Hill NC 27599-0001 E-mail: lvjones@email.unc.edu.

JONES, M. DOUGLAS, JR., pediatrician, educator; b. San Antonio, Apr. 22, 1943; BA, Rice U., 1964; MD, U. Tex., 1968. Diplomate Am. Bd. Pediat. Intern U. Colo. Sch. Medicine, Denver, 1968-69, resident, 1969-71, fellow neonatal-perinatal medicine, 1973-75, prof. pediatrics, 1990—. Mem. Am. Bd. Pediat., Am. Acad. Pediat., Am. Pediat. Soc., Soc. for Pediat. Rsch. Office: Childrens Hosp 1056 E 19th Ave Denver CO 80218-1088

JONES, MALLORY See DANAHER, MALLORY

JONES, MARIAN C., music educator; d. Kenneth E. and Barbara M. Jones; children: Shayla, Brooke, Amber. BS in Music Edn., W. Chester State U., Pa., 1976. Cert. tchr., music edn. K-12 Pa. Dept. Edn., NJ Dept. Edn. Music tchr. Willingboro Bd. Edn., NJ, 1976—78, Lawnside Bd. Edn., 1978—79; music tchr./mentor Downingtown I & A Sch., Pa., 1980—83; admin. asst. USN, Phila., 1983—89; music tchr. Ewing Twp. Bd. Edn., NJ, 1989—90, Mt. Laurel Twp. Bd. Edn., 1990—. Coop. tchr. for sr. music students U. Fine Arts, Phila., 2004, Rowan U., Glassboro, NJ, 2002, 07; dir., various youth choruses in cmty., NJ & Pa., 1980—. Mem.: NEA, Mt. Laurel Edn. Assn., NJ Edn. Assn. Mem. Christian Ch. Avocations: reading, cooking, swimming, travel. Home: 4730 Hawthorne St Philadelphia PA 19124 Office: Larchmont Sch 301 Larchmont Blvd Mount Laurel NJ 08054 Business E-Mail: mcjones@mountlaurel.k12.nj.us.

JONES, MARION, track and field athlete; b. LA, Oct. 12, 1975; d. George and Marion Jones; m. C.J. Hunter, 1998 (div. 2001); 1 child, Timothy Montgomery. Graduate, U. NC. Named Women's Athlete of Yr., Track and Field News, 1997, 1998, 2000, Athlete of Yr., ESPN, Reuters, and the IAAF, 2000, Female Athlete of Yr., AP, 2000; recipient AP and USOC Female Athlete of Yr. award, 2000, Jesse Owens award, U.S.A. Track & Field, 1997, 1998, 2002. Achievements include winning 100m gold, World Championships, 1997, 99; world 4x100m champion, 1997, 2001; ranked #1 in the world at 100m & 200m by Track and Field News, 1997-2002; won 100m, 200m, World Cup, 1998; USA Outdoor 200m champ US title in the event, 1998-2001, 100m and long jump, 1997; USA Outdoor 100m champion, 2006; undefeated in every competition until her last one of the year, 35 of 36 total, 1998; won Goodwill Games 100m, 1998, 2001, 200m, 1998; ran anchor on 4x200m USA team that set the world record (1:27.46) at USA vs. THE WORLD at the Penn Relays, 2000; ran anchor in gold medal winning 4x100m relay at Worlds, 2001; World 200m champion, 2001; 100m, 200m champion, USA, 2002; won World Cup 100m, which completed the first undefeated season of her career, 2002; won 3 gold medals for 100m, 200m , 4x400m, Sydney Games, 2000; won 100m at Reebok Grand Prix, 2006, Meeting Gaz de France Paris Saint-Denis, 2006, Athletissima, 2006. Office: c/o USA Track & Field 1 Rca Dome Ste 140 Indianapolis IN 46225-1023

JONES, MARK LOGAN, educational association executive, educator; b. Provo, Utah, Dec. 16, 1950; s. Edward Evans and Doris (Logan) J.; m. Catherine A. Bailey. BS, Ea. Mont. Coll., 1975; postgrad. in labor rels., Cornell U.; postgrad., SUNY, Buffalo. Narcotics detective Yellowstone County Sheriff's Dept., Billings, Mont., 1972-74; math tchr. Billings (Mont.) Pub. Schs., 1975-87; rep. Nat. Edn. Assn. of N.Y., Buffalo, Jamestown, 1987-91, Nat. Edn. Assn. Alaska, Anchorage, 1991—. Mem. Alaska Tchr. Licensure Task Force, Tchr. Edn. Adv. Coun., Adv. Com. on Tchr. Stds., Alaska Partnership Tchr. Enhancement; bd. mem. Alaska staff Devel. Network; mem. various coms. Alaska Dept. Edn. Photographs featured in 1991 N.Y. Art Rev. and Am. Artist. Committeeman Yellowstone Dem. Party, Billings, 1984-87; exec. com. Dem. Cen. Com., Billings, 1985-87; bd. dirs. Billings Community Ctr., 1975-87; concert chmn. Billings Community Concert Assn., 1980-87; bd. dirs. Chautauqua County Arts Coun.; bd. dirs. Big Brothers and Big Sisters Anchorage. With U.S. Army, 1970-72. Recipient Distinguished Svc. award, Billings Edn. Assn., 1985, Mont. Edn. Assn., 1987. Mem. ACLU, Billings Edn. Assn. (bd. dirs. 1980-82, negotiator 1981-87, pres. 1982-87), Mont. Edn. Assn. (bd. dirs. 1982-87), Ea. Mont. Coll. Tchr. Edn. Project, Accreditation Reviewer Team Mont. Office Pub. Edn., Big Sky Orchard, Masonic, Scottish Rite. Avocations: bonsai, photography, reading, classical and jazz music, hunting, fishing. Home: PO Box 102904 Anchorage AK 99510-2904 Office: 4100 Spenard Rd Anchorage AK 99510 Home Phone: 907-562-0329. Personal E-mail: mark.jones@neaalaska.org. E-mail: cabaileymljones@gci.net.

JONES, MARSHALL BUSH, education educator, researcher; b. Portchester, NY, Jan. 25, 1928; s. Donald and Muriel Marshall Jones; m. Beverly Ratner, Mar. 7, 1952; children: Donald Ratner, Susan Story Marshall. BA, Yale U., 1946—49; PhD, Univ. of Calif. at LA, 1950—53. Lt. j.g. (med. svc. corps) U.S. Naval Sch. of Aviation Medicine, Pensacola, Fla., 1953—55, rsch. psychologist, 1956—62; asst. prof. of psychiatry U. of Fla., 1962—68; assoc. prof. of behavioral sci. Penn State Coll. of Medicine, Hershey, Pa., 1968—72, prof. of behavioral sci., 1973—2003, prof. and chair of behavioral sci., 1979—2003. Contbr. articles to profl. jours. Pres. ACLU of Fla., Gainesville, Fla., 1966—68. Lt. j.g. Navy Med. Svc. Corps, 1956—62, Pensacola, Fla. Recipient McLaughlin Vis. Prof., McMaster U., 1985. Mem.: AAAS (assoc.). D-Liberal. Achievements include development of isoperformance methodology; the theory of behavioral contagion; the risk-factor model of complex genetic diseases. Office: Penn State Coll of Medicine 500 University Dr Hershey PA 17033 Home Phone: 361-837-9799. Business E-Mail: mbj1@psu.edu.

JONES, MARSHALL DAVID, musician, minister; b. Cleve., Apr. 11, 1978; s. David and Linda Jones. MusB in Edn., Coll. Wooster, Ohio, 2000. Dir. of music First United Meth. Ch., Elizabeth City, NC, 2002—05; min. music St. Timothy Luth. Ch., Tarpon Springs, Fla., 2005—. Composer handbell music, choral music. Pres. Elizabeth City Music Club, 2003—05. Maxine R. Loehr Piano scholar, Coll. Wooster, 1998—99. Mem.: Am. Guild Organists, Am. Guild English Handbell Ringers (chmn. youth repertoire com. area III 2004). Avocations: movies, ultimate frisbee. Office: St Timothy Lutheran Ch 812 E Tarpon Ave Tarpon Springs FL 34689 Home Phone: 727-967-3437; Office Phone: 727-937-3503 15. Personal E-mail: mjones755@tampabay.rr.com. Business E-Mail: music@mylutheran.com.

JONES, MARVIN LAMAR, histologist; b. Cleve., Miss., June 8, 1953; s. James Marvin Jones and Margaret Lee Carroll; m. Wanda Lynn Grace, July 9, 1994; children: Kerry Hines Bradford, Robert Kyle Grace. BS, U. Ky., Lexington, 1983—90. Lic. in Histotechnology ASCP, Chgo., 1977. Dir. labs. La. State U., Shreveport, 2002—05; mgr. anatomic pathology Wake Forest U. Bapt. Med. Ctr., Winston-Salem, NC, 2005—. Clin. instr. Davidson County Comm Coll., Thomasville, NC, 2005—; educational workshop dir. medical morkshops; program dir. U. Ky., So. U., Shreveport, Davidson County CC. Asst. editor (medical jour.) Jour. Histotechnology, editor (newsletter) My History News; editor: (scientific newsletter) Lab Leader, (newsletter) Kentucky Society for Histotechnology; co-author (self-assessment books) Histotechnology; contbr. chapters to books, articles to profl. jours. Spkr. ho. del.; bldg. and grounds chmn. Westwood Bapt. Ch., Alabaster, Ala., 1998—2001; trustee biol. stain commission. Recipient Danforth Leadership award, 1972, Rsch. award, Humble Oil Co., 1972, Glynton Hammond Newsletter award, 1986, William J. Hacker award, 1987, Harold E. Resinger, MD award, 1989, Newsletter of Yr. award, Slice of Life, 1989, Lee G. Luna Fgn. Scholarship, 1993, Glass Slide award, 1995, J. B. McCormick, MD award, 1995, Histologist of Yr. award, 1999. Mem.: Ky. Soc. Histotechnology (pres. 1985—87, Histologist of Yr. award 1988), Biol. Stain Commn. (trustee 2005), NC Soc. Histotechnology, Nat. Soc. Histotechnology (spkr. ho. del. 1988—96, v.p. 1996—98, regional dir. 2004—05), Am. Soc. Clin. Pathologists (assoc.), Beta Beta Beta. Achievements include research in osage orange dye for tissue specimens; fat stain for paraffin tissue sections; design of scientific instruments; development of automation of special staining techniques; stain for molecular apoptosis, automated. Home Phone: 336-716-2644.

JONES, MARY CUNNINGHAM, music educator; d. Jesse Clark Cunningham and Mary Lillian Puckett; m. James Sherman Jones, Dec. 25, 1980. BA, Asbury Coll., 1944; Counterpoint with Lewis Henry Horton, U. Ky., 1945, MA in Piano Pedagogy, Music Edn., 1949, Master Classes with John Jacob Niles, 1946—50; Master Classes with Guy Maier, Santa Monica, Calif., 1953; Master Classes with John Crown, Modesto, Calif., 1965; Master Classes with June Weybright, Oakland, Calif., 1969; Master Classes with Istvan Nadas, San Francisco, 1969—71, Master Classes with William Gillock, 1971. Cert. piano tchr. Am. Coll. of Musicians, 1997. Choir dir. Cavalier H.S., ND, 1945—46; elem. music supr. Baker City Schs., Baker City, Oreg., 1947—50; music tchr. Modesto City Schs., Calif., 1951—53, Ripon Christian Sch., Calif., 1954—61; pvt. piano tchr. Modesto, Calif., 1954—; adjudicator Nat. Guild of Piano Tchrs., Austin, 1960—; arts critic The Modesto Bee, Calif., 1970—71. Chmn. Modesto area Berkeley Jr. Bach Festival, Calif., 1961—64. Bd. mem, /asst. to dean, dir. of childrens'activities Calif. Redwood Christian Pk. Assn., Boulder Creek, 1959—74; lay mem. Calif./Nev. Ann. Conf., United Meth. Ch., Ceres, Calif., 1960—64; mem., dir. of publicity Modesto Cmty. Concerts Assn., Calif., 1967—71. Recipient Profl. Alumna of Yr. award, Asbury Coll. Alumni Assn., 1971. Mem.: Maier Mus. Assn., Music Tchrs.' Assn. Calif. (numerous positions 1959—71, Citation for 50 Yrs. of Meritorious Svc. 2004, State Public Relations trophy 1971), Nat. Guild of Piano Tchrs. (life; founder, chmn. Modesto Ctr. 1959—80, Stanislaus County Br., Nat. Honor Roll, Hall of Fame). Methodist. Avocations: crocheting, attending concerts, attending dramatic performances. Home: 1047 Harvard Way Modesto CA 95350-5915

JONES, MARY EMMA B., psychologist; b. Izmir, Turkey, Nov. 10, 1944; came to U.S., 1946; d. Lawrence Hartwell Brown and Erma Marie (Carl) Macfie; m. Robin Dee Jones, Sept. 11, 1966; children: Darcy Marie, Samuel Evan. BA in English, Campbell U., 1967; MEd in Mid. Grades, North Ga. Coll., 1984; EdS in Sch. Counseling, U. Ga., 1990, PhD in Counseling Psychology, 1997. lic. psychologist, Ga. Tchr. high sch. Harnett County Schs., Lillington and Buies Creek, N.C., 1967-69; craftsperson (weaver) Jugtown Pottery, Seagrove, N.C., 1969-70; designer, weaver Wolf Pen Crafts, Young Harris, Ga., 1970-78; instr. weaving Campbell Folk Sch., Brasstown, N.C., 1977-78; tchr. Union County Mid. Sch., Blairsville, Ga., 1978-90; sch. counselor St. Joseph Sch., Athens, Ga., 1990-94; intern in counseling psychology Park Ctr., Ft. Wayne, Ind., 1994-95; therapist Laurelwood Mental Health/Substance Abuse divsn. Northeast Ga. Med. Ctr., Gainesville, 1995-97; dir. Laurelwood Partial Hospitalization Program, Blairsville, Ga., 1997-98; pvt. practice lic. psychologist Blairsville, 1998—. Active PTA, Harnett County, N.C., 1967-69, Union County, 1978-90; active St. Joseph Sch. PTA, Athens, 1990-94. Named STAR Tchr., Union County Schs., C. of C. and Bus. Coun. Ga., 1984. Mem. APA, Ga. Psychol. Assn. Avocations: camping, swimming, hiking, sketching, tennis. Home: PO Box 141 Young Harris GA 30582-0141 Office: PO Box 881 Blairsville GA 30514-0881 Business E-Mail: mebjones@alltel.net.

JONES, MARY LAURA, not-for-profit developer; b. Mpls., 1946; d. William Ray and Emily H. Jones; children: Donald Aaron, Justin David, Mark Joseph Bushman. BA in English, U. S.C., 1968; MA in History, Northwestern U., 2004. Vol. U.S. Peace Corps, 1968—71; assoc. dir. funding and devel. The Inst. of Cultural Affairs, Chgo., 1971-75, dir. Cleve. region, 1975-79, dir. Pacific and Oceania region Apia, Western Samoa, 1979-83, co-creator Cmty. Devel. Tng. Curriculum Chgo., 1984—85, dir. Uptown Cmty. Resource Ctr., 1987—2006; prin. Jones-Otto Neighborhood Devel. Co., Chgo., 2006—. Bd. dirs. Ebenezer Luth. Ch. Mem. Uptown C. of C. (bd. dirs.). Home: 4750 N Sheridan Rd Chicago IL 60640-5042 Office Phone: 773-636-2022. E-mail: mljones@rcn.com.

JONES, MARY TRENT, endowment fund trustee; b. Durham, NC, July 15, 1940; d. Josiah Charles Trent and Mary Duke (Biddle) Semans; m. James Parker Jones, June 27, 1964; children: James Trent, Benjamin Parker, Jonathan Edmund. AB, Duke U., 1963. Trustee The Duke Endowment, Charlotte, N.C., 1988—. Chmn. Josiah Charles Trent Found., Durham, 1978-83; bd. dirs. Mary Duke Biddle Found., Durham, 1983—, chmn. 2004, Concert Artists Guild, N.Y.C., 1996-00. Mem. Va. Perinatal

Svcs. Adv. Bd., Richmond, 1986-91; sec. Va. Arts Commn., Richmond, 1989-92, bd. dirs., 1984-92; trustee Va. Intermont Coll., Bristol, Va., 1986-91, 98-2001; mem. State Coun. Higher Edn. Va., Richmond, 1991-95; trustee Va. Mu. of Fine Arts, Richmond, 1992-97; mem. bd. Washington County Pub. Libr. Found., 1997—; trustee William King Regional Arts Ctr., 1998-2004, Emory and Henry Coll., 1999-, Va. Hist. Soc., 2005-; bd. dirs. Blue Ridge Pub. TV, 2004-06. Recipient outstanding alumni award Durham Acad., 1991. Mem. Va. Highlands Festival Bd., 1997-2001 Episcopalian. Avocations: reading, walking, hiking. Home: 107 Hillside Dr NE Abingdon VA 24210-2013 E-mail: jjones107@embarqmail.com.

JONES, MAURICE D., lawyer; b. 1959; BS, Brigham Young U.; JD, U. Ill. Bar: 1988. Ptnr. Davis & Kuelthau, S.C.; legal counsel Banta Corp.; sec., gen. counsel Manitowoc Co., Manitowoc, Wis., 1999—2002, v.p., gen. counsel, sec., 2002—04, sr. v.p., gen. counsel, sec., 2004—. Office: Manitowoc Co Inc 2400 S 44th St Manitowoc WI 54221-0066 Office Phone: 920-652-1741. Office Fax: 920-652-9777. Business E-Mail: mjones@manitowoc.com.

JONES, MICHAEL A., mathematics professor; BS in Math. (magna cum laude), Santa Clara U., 1989; PhD in Math., Northwestern U., Evanston, Ill., 1994. Asst. prof., dept. math. sciences US Military Acad., West Point, NY, 1994—97, Montclair State U., Upper Montclair, NJ, 1998—2003, assoc. prof., dept. math. sciences, 2004—. Adj. asst. prof., bus. divsn., MBA level Mt. Saint Mary Coll., Newburgh, NY, 1996; vis. asst. prof., dept. math. sciences Loyola U., Chgo., 1997—98; vis. scholar, dept. politics NYU, 2001—04; spkr. in field. Contbr. articles to profl. jours.; mem. editl. adv. bd. The College Mathematics Journal, 2003—. Mem.: Soc. for Chaos Theory in Psychology and the Life Sciences, Am. Math. Soc., Math. Assn. Am. (pub. info. officer, NJ sect. 2003—), Game Theory Soc., Phi Beta Kappa, Sigma Xi, Pi Mu Epsilon. Office: Dept Math Sciences Montclair State Univ Room Number RI-206 Montclair NJ 07043 Office Phone: 973-655-5448. Office Fax: 973-655-7686. Business E-Mail: jonesm@mail.montclair.edu.

JONES, MICHAEL D., lawyer; BA summa cum laude, Dillard U., 1982; JD cum laude, Georgetown U., 1985. Bar: Ga. 1986, DC 1989. Law clk. Eleventh Cir. Ct. Appeals, 1985—86; ptnr., co-chair firm diversity com. Kirkland & Ellis LLP, Washington. Bd. dirs. Legal Aid Soc. Contbr. articles to profl. jours. Named one of Top 10 Trial Attys. in the Nation, Nat. Law Jour., 2001, 75 Best Lawyers in Washington, Washington Mag., 2002, America's Top Black Litigators, Black Enterprise, 2003; recipient Thurgood Marshall award. Office: Kirkand & Ellis LLP 655 Fifteenth St NW Washington DC 20005 Office Phone: 202-879-5294. Office Fax: 202-879-5200. E-mail: mjones@kirkland.com.

JONES, MILTON BENNION, retired agronomist; b. Cedar City, Utah, Jan. 15, 1926; s. William Lunt and Claire (Bennion) Jones; m. Grace Elaine Guymon, Sept. 8, 1951; children: Milton B., Jr., Richard W., Jo Layne, Tamera, Sherilee, Karolyn. BS, Utah State U., 1951; PhD, Ohio State U., 1955. Successively jr. agronomist, asst. agronomist, assoc. agronomist, agronomist, lectr. emeritus U. Calif., Hopland, Davis, 1955—91; ret., 1991. Cons. IRI Rsch. Inst., Campinas, Brazil, 1963—65, CSIRO, Australia, 1974, BLM, Ukiah, Calif., 1970—77, Sulphur Inst., Washington, 1967—88, AID U., Evora, Portugal, 1984, Basque Govt., Bilbao, Spain, 1987, MAF, Invernay, New Zealand, 1990. Contbr. articles to profl. jours. Humanitarian mission, Scotland, 1991—93, Georgia, 1997—2000; mem. sch. bd. Ukiah Elem. Sch. Dist., 1962—63; scout leader local chpt. Boy Scouts Am., Ukiah, 1962—70. With USN, 1944—47. Fellow: Soil Sci. Soc., Agronomy Soc. Office: U Calif 4070 University Rd Hopland CA 95449-9717 Home: 1501 East 1500 N Provo UT 84604 Personal E-mail: gracegjones@yahoo.com.

JONES, MILTON H., JR., bank executive; BS in Acctg., U. Notre Dame, Ind. Sr. planning analyst Bank Am. Corp., various positions, fin. group, 1977—90, exec. v.p., group mgr., fin. and adminstrn. of the Ga. bank, 1990—97, chmn., diversity adv. coun., mem., mgmt. ops. com., group exec., tech. & ops., tech. solutions exec., quality and productivity exec., consumer and comml. bank, quality and productivity exec., 2003, pres. Ga., fin. svcs. exec., pres. NC and Charlotte Market, 2007—; fin. exec. NationsBanc Svcs., Greensboro, NC, 1994—97, pres., dealer fin. svc. group, 1997. Mem. Leadership Atlanta, Leadership Ga.; mem. exec. com. YMCA of Metro. Atlanta, Charlotte YMCA, Metro. Atlanta C. of C., Charlotte Ctr. City Ptnrs.; mem. bd. trustees Meharry Med. Coll., Nashville; bd. dirs. First Tee Charlotte. Recipient Career Achievement award, Nat. Assn. of Black Accts., Corp. Trailblazer award, Dollars and Sense Mag., Best and Brightest award, Pioneer award, Atlanta Urban Banker's Assn. Office: Bank of Am Corp 100 N Tryon St Charlotte NC 28255*

JONES, MILTON WAKEFIELD, publisher; b. Burbank, Calif., Apr. 18, 1930; s. Franklin M. and Lydia (Sinclair) J.; m. Rita Strong, May 4, 1959; 1 son, Franklin Wayne. AA, Santa Monica City Coll., 1950; BS, U. So. Calif., 1952. V.p. mktg. Sav-Ink Co., Newport Beach, Calif., 1956-58; account exec. KDES-Radio, Palm Springs, Calif., 1958-60; pres. Milton W. Jones Advt. & Pub. Rels. Agy., Palm Springs, 1960—, Desert Publs., Inc., Palm Springs, 1965—, Riverside Color Press, Inc., Palm Springs, Olman Travel Svc., Palm Springs, 1979-84. Pres. Franklin Comms. (Sta. KPSL-Radio), 1987-98, Airport Displays Ltd., 1972—; vice chmn. Palm Springs Savings Bank, 1981-96; bd. dirs., treas. Canyon Nat. Bank. Pub. Palm Springs Life Mag., 1965—, Wheeler Bus. Letter, Palm Springs, 1969-77, San Francisco mag., 1973-79, Guest Life, Orange County, N.Mex., Carmel/Monterey, St. Petersburg/Clearwater, Vancouver, Can., El Paso, Houston, 1978—, Orange County mag., 1987-89, McCallum Theatre Program, 1989—, Ofcl. Guide to Houston, 1993, El Paso Guest Life, 1993, Pebble Beach, The Magazine, 2002, Pub. Record newspaper, 1996-2006, Official Guide to Ontario, 2001-06, Official Guide to Galveston Island, 2003-05, Official Guide to Newport Beach, 2007. Mem. Desert Press Club (pres. 1965). Home: 422 N Farrell Dr Palm Springs CA 92262-6559 also: 206 Abalone Ave Newport Beach CA 92662-1304 Office: 303 N Indian Canyon Dr Palm Springs CA 92262-6015 E-mail: milt@palmspringslife.com.

JONES, MONTY P., science administrator; b. Sierra Leone, 1951; Grad., U. Sierra Leone; MSc in Plant Genetic Resources, U. Birmingham, Eng., 1979, PhD in Plant Biology, 1983, PhD (hon.) in Sci., 2005. Mem. staff Mangrove Swamp Rice Rsch. Project West Africa Rice Devel. Agy., Sierra Leone, 1975—91, head Upland Rice Breeding Prog. Cote d'Ivoire, 1991—2002; exec. sec. Forum for Agrl. Rsch. in Africa, Accra, Ghana, 2002—. Contbr. articles to sci. jours. Co-recipient World Food prize, 2004; named one of The World's Most Influential People, TIME Mag., 2007. Mem.: NAS (fgn. assoc.). Office: FARA Secretariat PMB CT 173 Cantonments Accra Ghana E-mail: MJones@fara-africa.org.

JONES, NANCY LANGDON, financial planner, writer; b. Chgo., Mar. 24, 1939; d. Lewis Valentine and Margaret (Seese) Russell; m. Lawrence Elmer Langdon, June 30, 1962 (div. 1970); children: Laura Kimberley, Elizabeth Ann; m. Claude Earl Jones, Jan. 1, 1972. BA, U. Redlands, Calif., 1962; MS, Coll. for Fin. Planning, 1991. CFP; cert. sr. advisor. Bookkeeper Russell Sales Co., Santa Fe Springs, Calif., 1962-70; office mgr. Reardon, McCallum & Co., Upland, Calif., 1970-77; broker, assoc. ERA Property Ctr., Upland, 1977-84; registered rep. Fin. Network Investment Corp., Pasadena, Calif., 1984-92; pvt. practice Upland, 1984—; ptnr. Jones, Graham & Assocs., Registered Investment Advisors, Upland, Calif., 1994; pres. NLJones, Inc., 2000—. Mem. adj. faculty Coll. Fin. Planning, Denver, 1986-94; mem. nat. comprehensive exam. question writing com. CFP Bd. Stds., 1994-98; del. US fin. and investment leaders study mission to China and Hong Kong, 1993; industry spkr. N.Am. Securities Adminstrs. Assn. Investment Advisor Workshop, 1999; panelist LA Times Annual Investment Strategies Conf., 1999, 2000; featured planner LA Times Money Makeover, 1999, 2001, 02. Author: (textbook for UCLA Course) So You Want to Be a Financial Planner: Your Guide to a New Career, 2001. Leader Spanish Trails coun. Girl Scouts US, 1974-81; exec. com. Corp. 2000 Coun., San Antonio Cmty. Hosp.; planned giving adv. bd. Goodwill Industries of the Inland Counties, 1997-98; planned giving roundtable Inland Empire. Recipient Hon. Svc. award Valencia Elem. Sch., 1978, Top Ten, Am. Bus. Womens Assn., 2003, Pioneer award Nat. Assn. Women Bus. Owners, 2005; named one of Top 100 Women Owned Businesses in Inland Empire, Bus. Press, 1996, one of the Most Influential People in the Fin. Planning Profession, readers of Fin. Planning Mag., 2002 Mem. N.Am. Securities Adminstrs. Assn., Inc. (investment adv. coun. 2000—), Internat. Assn. Fin. Planners (pres. San Gabriel Valley chpt. 1987-88, mem. exec. bd. So. Calif. conf. 1992-98, chmn. So. Calif. Conf., 1996-97), Am. Bus. Women's Assn. (pres. Upland chpt. 1989-90, gen. chmn. 1995, Pacific Spring Conf. Woman of Yr. award 1988), Fin. Planning Assn., Inst. CFP San Gabriel Valley Soc. (pres. 1992-93, chmn. 1993-94, bd. dirs. 1990-97), Inst. CFPs (nat. practice mgmt. and tech. com. 1996), Nat. Coun. Exchangers (sec. 1986-87), Fin. Planning Assn., Estate Planning Coun. Pomona Valley (bd. dirs. 1995—, pres. 1998-99). Avocations: travel, acting. Home and Office: 103 Cornell Ave Claremont CA 91711 Business E-Mail: nancy@nljones.com.

JONES, NATHAN JEROME, farm machinery manufacturing company executive; b. Marion, Ind., 1957; BBA in Acctg., U. Wis., Eau Claire, 1979; MBA in Fin., Mktg., U. Chgo., 1983. From acct. to various fin. assignments Deere & Co., Moline, Ill., 1978-91, asst. treas., 1991-94, treas., 1994-98, v.p., 1996-98, sr. v.p., fin., acctg., CFO, 1998—. Office: Deere & Co 1 John Deere Pl Moline IL 61265-8098

JONES, NICHOLAS PATRICK, civil engineering educator; b. New Zealand; BCE with honors, U. Auckland, New Zealand, 1980; MCE, Calif. Inst. Tech., 1981, PhD in civil engring., 1986. Engr. Edwards, Clendon & Partners, New Zealand, 1979—80; asst. prof. civil engring. Johns Hopkins U., Balt., 1986—91, assoc. prof., 1991—95, prof., 1995—2002, 2004—, chair dept. civil engring., 1999—2002, dean Whiting Sch. Engring., 2004—; prof., head dept. civil and environ. engring. U. Ill., Urbana-Champaign, 2002—04. Internat. editor Jour. Wind Engring. and Indsl. Aerodyns., 1998—2005. Named a Presdl. Young Investigator, NSF, 1989; named Young Engr. of Yr., Md. Soc. Profl. Engineers, 1988; recipient George Owen Tchg. Award, Johns Hopkins U., 1987, Robert Pond Tchg. Award, 1991, Excellence in Teaching Award, Johns Hopkins U. Alumni Assn., 2001; Erskine Fellow, U. Canterbury, New Zealand, 1999. Mem.: Internat. Assn. Bridge Aerodynamics (founding exec. sec.), Earthquake Engring. Rsch. Inst., Am. Assn. Wind Engring., ASCE (nat. infrastructure policy com. 2000—03, dir. Md. sect. 1995-97, Walter Huber Civil Engring. Rsch. prize 1997), Sigma Xi, Tau Beta Pi. Office: The Johns Hopkins U Whiting Sch Engring 3400 N Charles St Baltimore MD 21218-2681 Business E-Mail: npjones@jhu.edu, nick@jhu.edu.

JONES, NORAH (GEETHALI NORAH JONES SHANKAR), singer; b. NYC, Mar. 30, 1979; d. Ravi Shankar and Sue Jones. Student, U. North Tex. Singer: (albums) First Sessions, 2001, Come Away With Me, 2002 (Grammy awards: Album of Yr., Record of Yr., Best Female Pop Vocal Performance, Best Pop Vocal Album, 2003), Feels Like Home, 2004 (Grammy award: Best Female Pop Vocal Performance for Sunrise, 2005), Not Too Late, 2007; singer: (with Ray Charles) Genius Loves Company, 2004 (Grammy awards: Record of Yr. & Best Pop Collaboration with Vocal for Here We Go Again, 2005); singer: (with The Little Willies) The Little Willies, 2006; singer: (with others) A Very Special Acoustic Christmas, Where We Live: Stand For What You Stand On, Remembering Patsy Cline, Just Because I'm a Woman (tribute to Dolly Parton); actor: (films) My Blueberry Nights. Named Best Young Female Singer, VH1, 2002; recipient 8 Grammy awards, including Best New Artist, 2003, 3 Grammy awards, 2005. Office: Macklam Feldman Mgmt Ste 200 1505 W 2d Ave Vancouver BC V6H 3Y4 Canada*

JONES, OLIVER HASTINGS, consulting economist; b. Altoona, Pa., Dec. 9, 1922; s. Oliver Hastings and and Mary (Herman) J.; m. Margaret Ann Vogel, July 4, 1942; children: Thomas, William, David, Robert, Richard. BA, St. Francis Coll., Loretto, Pa., 1948; MA, Pa. State U., 1949, PhD, 1961. Analyst, divsn. bank ops., bd. govs. Fed. Res. System, 1951-55; sr. economist, rsch. dept. Fed. Res. Bank, Cleve., 1955-59; assoc. rsch. economist, real estate rsch. program Grad. Sch. Bus. Adminstrn., U. Calif., LA, 1959-61; economist Stanford Rsch. Inst., 1961-62; dir. rsch. Mortgage Bankers Assn. Am., 1962—68, exec. v.p., 1968—77; cons. economist Oliver Jones & Assocs., 1977—. Professorial lectr. Am. U., 1967—Author: (with Leo Grebler) The Secondary Mortgage Market, 1961, Financial Futures Market, 1983. Served with AUS, 1942-45. Mem. Am. Statis. Assn., Am. Econ. Assn., Am. Finance Assn., Nat. Assn. Bus. Economists, Conf. Bus. Economists, Lambda Alpha. (internat. pres. 1976-77) Clubs: Cosmos (Washington), Metropolitan (Washington). Home: 67 Greenfield Dr Carlisle PA 17013-7682

JONES, ORLO DOW, retired lawyer, retired pharmaceutical executive; b. Logan, Utah, June 10, 1938; s. Orlo Elijah and Joyce (Lewis) Jones; m. Ilarene Balls, July 9, 1958; children: Monica, Orlo Courtney. BS, Utah State U., 1960; LL.B., U. Calif., Berkeley, 1963. Bar: Calif. 1964. Atty. Carlson, Collins & Bold, Richmond, Calif., 1968-69, AT&T, San Francisco, 1969-71, Longs Drug Stores, Inc., Walnut Creek, Calif., 1971-76, sec., gen. counsel, 1976—, v.p., 1979-87, sr. v.p., 1987—. Lectr. comml. leases Continuing Edn. Bar U. Ext., U. Calif., Berkeley. Served to capt. JAGC US Army, 1964—68. Republican. Mem. Lds Ch. Home: 156 Santiago Dr Danville CA 94526-1941

JONES, PAUL TUDOR, II, investment executive; b. Memphis, 1954; m. Sonia Jones; 4 children. BA in Economics, U. Va., 1976. Acct. exec. Dunavant Commondity Co., Inc., NYC, 1977; with E.F. Hutton and Co., Inc., NYC, 1976-77, acct. exec., 1978-80, v.p., 1980-82; formed Tudor Investment Corp., NYC, 1983—; founder, chmn. bd. Bellwether Ptnrs., Inc., NYC, 1986. Chmn, NY Cotton Exchange (NYCE), 1992—95, bd. dirs., 1992—99, NY Bd. of Trade, 1992—99. Co-founder (with Jann Wenner) Robin Hood Found., 1988; bd. dirs. Everglads Found., Nat. Fish and Wildlife Found.; co-chair Save Our Everglades Campaign; sponsor I Have a Dream program, Bedford-Stuyvesant Sch.Sys., 1986—. Named one of Forbes' Richest Americans, 2006, New York's Influentials, New York Mag., 2006. Achievements include Instrumental in the creation of FINEX, the fin. futures div. of the NY Cotton Exchange, and the devel. of the US Dollar Index futures contract; designed and implemented the first ethnics training course that became standard for exchange membership on all future exchanges in the US in 1989; sponsored Bedford-Stuyvesant students in the I Have a Dream program by pledging to further the education of the students with fin. and other support. Over 100 students received a college education; organizer of the Madison Square Garden concert raising $33 million for victims of the September 11th attacks. Office: Tudor Investments 1275 King St Greenwich CT 06831 Office Phone: 203-552-8220.*

JONES, PAUL W., manufacturing executive; BSE, Univ. Evansville. Mgmt. positions GE; pres. Greenfield Industries Inc., 1989—92, pres., CEO, 1993—98; chmn., pres., CEO U.S. Can Co., 1998—2002; pres., COO A.O. Smith Corp., Milw., 2004—05, bd. dir., 2004—, chmn., CEO, 2005—. Bd. dir. Fed. Signal Corp. Office: AO Smith Corp 11270 W Park Pl Milwaukee WI 53224*

JONES, PENNY LEE, elementary school educator; b. Blackwell, Okla., May 13, 1969; d. Dennis LeRoy and Bonnie Lee Jones. AA in English, Richland Cmty. Coll., Decatur, Ill., 1989; BA in English, Ea. Ill. U., Charleston, 1991. Lang. arts & history tchr. Eisenhower HS, Decatur, 1996—98, 2000—03, Stephen Decatur HS, 1998—2000; 7th grade social studies tchr. Thomas Jefferson Mid. Sch., Decatur, 2003—. Pom ponm advisor Thomas Jefferson Mid. Sch., Decatur, 1994—; head softball coach Stephen Decatur HS, 1999—2000; girls track coach Thomas Jefferson Mid. Sch., 2004—, volleyball coach, 2005—; tutor local sch. svc. sys., Decatur, 2006—. Mem.: Nat. Coun. Social Studies. Home: 742 N Carolina Decatur IL 62522 Office: Thomas Jefferson Mid Sch 4735 E Cantrell St Decatur IL 62521 Business E-Mail: pjones@dps61.org.

JONES, PETER D'ALROY, historian, writer, retired educator; b. Hull, England, June 9, 1931; arrived in U.S., 1959, naturalized, 1968; s. Alfred and Madge (Rutter) D'Alroy; m. Johanna Maria Hartinger, Feb. 20, 1987; 1 child, Heather Marie; children from previous marriage: Kathryn Beauchamp Fly Ebert, Barbara Collier Rosenberg. BA, Manchester U., Eng., 1952, MA, 1953; postgrad. rsch. in collective bargaining, Inst. Solvay U. Brussels, 1954; PhD, London U. Sch. Econ., 1963. Freelance editor, London, 1953-56; linguist RAF, 1956—57; lectr. U.S. history dept. Am. studies Manchester U., 1957-58; vis. asst. prof. econs. Tulane U., 1959-60; from asst. to full prof. Smith Coll., 1960-68; William R. Kenan Jr. prof. Am. instns. and values Trinity Coll., Hartford, 1980—81; prof. history U. Ill., Chgo., 1968-98, prof. emeritus, 1998—. Vis. prof. Columbia U., U. Mass., U. Hawaii, U. Düsseldorf, Fed. Republic Germany; Fulbright prof. U. Warsaw, Poland, UNAM, Mexico City, U. Salzburg, Austria; mem. com. examiners Grad. Record Exams. Ednl. Testing Svc., Princeton, N.J., 1966-70; mem. Am. studies com. Am. Coun. Learned Socs., 1973-75; lectr. cultural affairs U.S. Dept. State, Bur. Cultural Affairs and USIA, 1973-87; adv. to publs. Author: Economic History of U.S.A. Since 1783, 1956, 2nd edit., 1965, The Story of the Saw, 1961, America's Wealth, 1963, The Consumer Society, 1965, 2d edit., 1967, The Christian Socialist Revival, 1968, The Robber Barons Revisited, 1968, Robert Hunter's Poverty: Social Conscience in the Progressive Era, 1965, La Sociedad Consumidora, 1968, Since Columbus: Poverty and Pluralism in the History of the Americas, 1975, The U.S.A.: A History of Its People and Society, 2 vols., 1976, Henry George and British Socialism, 1991; co-editor: Biographical Dictionary of American Mayors, 1820-1980, 1981, Ethnic Chicago, 1981, rev. and enlarged edit., 1984, 4th edit., 1995; contbr. several entries to Ency. World Biography, 1988, 94; contbr. numerous articles and book revs. to profl. jours., popular newspapers. R.W. Emerson prize com Phi Beta Kappa, 1991—94. Mem. London Sch. Econs. Soc. (life). Personal E-mail: verdi1901@aol.com.

JONES, PHILIP HOWARD, broadcast journalist; b. Marion, Ind., Apr. 27, 1937; s. Thomas Howard and Charline (Shugart) J.; m. Paricia Ann Powell, June 4, 1961. BS in Arts and Scis., Ind. U., 1959. Dir. news Sta. WTHI-TV, Terre Haute, Ind., 1960-61; polit. corr. Sta. WCCO-TV, Mpls., 1961-69; White House corr. CBS News, Washington, 1974-76, Capitol Hill corr., 1977-89, nat. corr., 1989-90; corr. 48Hrs. Broadcast, 1990-95; Washington corr. CBS News, 1995—2001, Washington polit. corr., 1996—2001; contbg. corr. PBS Religion Ethics News Weekly, 2001—. Lectr. in field. Recipient Internat. News award Radio-TV News Dirs. Assn., 1965, award for Vietnam war reporting, 1966, Emmy award for CBS Indochina air war coverage NATAS, 1971, (6) Emmy awards CBS News 48 Hours Broadcast Coverage, 1992. Home: 9117 Terrabella Ct Naples FL 34109 Personal E-mail: jonesgroup@gmail.com.

JONES, PHILIP KIRKPATRICK, JR., lawyer; b. Baton Rouge, June 26, 1949; s. Philip Kirkpatrick and Mary Jane (Kincade) J.; m. Serena Catherine Cockayne, Apr. 5, 1980; children: Veronica Cockayne, Nicola Kincade, Clare Kirkpatrick, Philip Carruth Elliot. BA in Govt., Dartmouth Coll., 1971; JD, La. State U., 1974; LLB, diploma in legal studies, Cambridge U., Eng., 1976. Bar: La. 1974, U.S. Dist. Ct. (ea. and we. dist.) La. 1980, U.S. Ct. Appeals (5th and 11th cirs.) 1981, U.S. Dist. Ct. (mid. dist.) La. 1987, U.S. Supreme Ct. 1992. Law clk. to John A. Dixon Jr. Supreme Ct. La., New Orleans, 1974-75; staff atty. Presdl. Clemency Bd., Washington, 1975; lectr. U. Singapore, 1977-79; from assoc. to ptnr. Liskow & Lewis PC, New Orleans, 1980—. 1st lt. USAFR, 1975. Republican. Presbyterian. Office: Liskow & Lewis PC 50th Fl One Shell Square New Orleans LA 70139 Home Phone: 504-861-0672; Office Phone: 504-556-4132. Business E-Mail: pkjones@liskow.com.

JONES, PHILLIP JOHN, librarian; b. Inglewood, Calif., May 27, 1968; s. John Luther Jones and Shirley Ann Sharp. BA, Univ. Calif., Santa Barbara, 1990; MA, Univ. Calif., Irvine, 1991; MS, Univ. Ill., 1994. Reference libr. Baylor U., Wao, Tex., 1994—2003; head reference, assoc. libr. U. Ark., Fayetteville, 2003—. Contbr. articles pub. to profl. jour. Mem.: ALA (life), Assn. Coll. and Rsch. Librs., Phi Beta Kappa. Roman Catholic. Avocation: travel. Home: 4406 W Cheyenne Dr Fayetteville AR 72704-5549 Office: Univ Ark Librs 365 N McIlroy Ave Fayetteville AR 72701-4002 Office Phone: 479-575-3081.

JONES, PHYLLIS GENE, judge; b. Fargo, ND, May 29, 1923; d. Joseph C. and Rosina Belle (Pinkham) Bambusch; m. Dwight Bangs Jones, May 29, 1945 (dec.); children: Stephanie Martineau, Jacqueline Ridge, Kent Carroll; m. David D. Norman, Oct. 9, 1970 (dec.). BA, Macalester Coll., 1944; JD, William Mitchell Coll. Law, 1960. Bar: Minn. 1960. Wirephoto operator AP, St. Paul, 1943-45; reporter St. Paul Pioneer Press, 1945—46; asst. county atty. Ramsey County, St. Paul, 1960-71; gen. counsel Minn. Urban County Attys. Bd./Minn. County Attys. Coun., St. Paul, 1971-75; pvt. practice St. Paul, Cottage Grove, Minn., 1975-84; judge Minn. Dist Ct. 10th Jud. Dist., Anoka, 1984-93. Mem. Minn. Adv. Coun. to State Investment Bd., 1983-84; mem. Washington County Pers. Com., Stillwater, Minn., 1982-84. Supr. Grey Cloud Town Bd., Minn., 1971—75. Mem. ABA, Minn. State Bar Assn. (chmn. victimless crimes com. 1974-75, co-chair sr. lawyers com. 1997-99), Ramsey County Bar Assn. (exec. com. 1982-83), Washington County Hist. Soc. (dir. 2000-07).

JONES, QUINCY, producer, composer, arranger, conductor, trumpeter; b. Chgo., Mar. 14, 1933; s. Quincy Delight and Sarah J.; children: Kidada, Rashida, Jolie, Martina-Lisa, Quincy III, Rachelle, Kenya. Student, Seattle U., Berklee Coll. Music; studied with Nadia Boulanger; student, Boston Conservatory; degree (hon.), Berklee Coll. Music, 1983, Howard U., 1985, Seattle U., 1990, Wesleyan U., 1991, Loyola U., 1992, Brandeis U., 1992, Clark U., 1993. Head Quincy Jones Entertainment. Trumpeter, arranger Lionel Hampton Orch., 1950-53; arranger for orchs., singers including Frank Sinatra, Dinah Washington, Count Basie, Sarah Vaughan, Peggy Lee, USA For Africa; organizer, trumpeter Dizzy Gillespie Orch. for Dept. of State tour of Near East, Mid. East, S.Am., 1956; music dir. Barchlay Disques, Paris; leader own orch. European tour, concerts, TV, radio, 1960; music dir., Mercury Records, 1961, v.p., 1964; composer: background scores The Boy in the Tree, 1964; condr. (film music) The Pawnbroker, Mirage, The Slender Thread, 1965, Walk Don't Run, Made in Paris, 1966, Banning (Acad. awd. nom. best song 1967), The Deadly Affair, Enter Laughing, In Cold Blood (Acad. awd. nom. best score 1967), In the Heat of the Night, 1967, For the Love of Ivy (Acad. awd. nom. best song 1968), The Split, Mirage, A Dandy in Aspic, The Hell with Heroes, Jigsaw, 1968,

Bob and Carol and Ted and Alice, Cactus Flower, John and Mary, The Italian Job, The Lost Man, MacKenna's Gold, 1969, Eggs, Of Men and Demons, The Out-Of-Towners, Up Your Teddy Bear, The Last of the Mobile Hotshots, They Call Me Mr. Tibbs, 1970, The Anderson Tapes, Brother John, Honky, 1971, Come Back Charleston Blue, The Hot Rock, 1972, The New Centurions, 1972, The Getaway, 1972, Mother, Jugs, and Speed, 1976, The Wiz, 1978, (also co-producer) The Color Purple (Acad. awd. noms., best picture, best song 1985), Fever Pitch, (exec. music producer) The Slugger's Wife, 1985, Listen Up: The Lives of Quincy Jones, 1990; composer, actor (film) Blues for Trumpet and Koto, Life Goes On; rec. artist numerous platinum albums including Body Heat, 1974, Mellow Madness, 1975, I Heard That, 1976, The Dude, 1981, Back on the Block, 1989, Snackwater Jack, 1991; producer videotape Portrait of An Album: Frank Sinatra with Quincy Jones and Orchestra, 1986 (platinum); producer recordings Michael Jackson's Off the Wall, 1980, Thriller, 1982 (world's best selling record), Bad; producer (with Steven Spielberg) The E.T. Storybook, (TV series) Fresh Prince of Bel Air, 1990—; composer (television) Hey Landlord, 1966-67, Ironside, 1967-75, The Bill Cosby Show, 1969-71, The New Bill Cosby Show, 1972-73, Sanford and Son, 1972-77, Sanford Arms, 1977, The Cosby Show, 1984-92, The Oprah Winfrey Show, 1989—; mini-series Roots (Emmy awd., best music composition, 1977), 1977; founder Vibe Magazine, 1992, exec. prodr. A Call for Reunion concert Lincoln Meml. for Clinton Inauguration, 1993. Recipient 76 Grammy nominations, 26 Grammy awards, numerous Readers Poll awards Downbeat Mag., Trendsetters awards Billboard Mag., Golden Note award ASCAP, 1982, Image award NAACP, 1974, 80, 81, 83, 90, 91, Hollywood Walk of Fame, 1980, Man of the Yr. award City of Hope, 1982, Whitney Young Jr. award Urban League, 1986, Humanitarian of Yr. award T.J. Martell Found., 1986, Lifetime Achievement award Nat. Acad. Songwriters, 1989, Grammy Living Legend award, 1990, Grammy award for Best Jazz instrumental, individual or group 1994 for "Miles and Quincy Live ath Montreux". Scopus award Hebrew U., 1991, Spirit of Liberty award People for the Am. Way, 1992, Ivor Novello Spl. Internat. award, Brit. Acad. Composers & Songwriters, 2007; named Entrepreneur of the Yr. USA Today/Fin. News Network, 1991; film biography: Listen Up: The Lives of Quincy Jones, 1990; Named one of 100 Most Influential Black Americans, Ebony mag., 2006. Office: Quincy Jones Music 6671 W Sunset Blvd Ste 1574a Los Angeles CA 90028-7123

JONES, RANDAL R., lawyer; b. 1961; BBA magna cum laude, Pacific Lutheran Univ., 1983; JD with honors, Duke Univ., 1987. Bar: Wash. 1987. Atty., corp. fin. securities practice group Bogle & Gates PLLC, 1987—95, ptnr., corp. fin., securities practice group, 1995—99; co-chair, ptnr., corp. group Dorsey & Whitney LLP, Seattle, 1999—, mem. mgmt. com. Mem.: ABA, Wash. State Bar Assn., King Co. Bar Assn., Phi Delta Phi, Beta Gamma Sigma. Office: Dorsey & Whitney LLP Ste 3400 US Bank Ctr 1420 Fifth Ave Seattle WA 98101-4010 Office Phone: 206-903-8814. Office Fax: 206-903-8820. Business E-Mail: jones.randal@dorsey.com.

JONES, RAYFORD SCOTT, surgeon, educator; b. Dallas, Aug. 24, 1936; MD, U. Tex., Galveston, 1961. Diplomate Am. Bd. Surgery. Intern U. Tex., 1961-62; resident U. Pa. Hosp., Phila., 1962-67; mem. staff Duke U. and VA Hosp., Durham, NC; former prof. surgery Duke U.; now S. Hurt Watts prof. surgery U. Va., Charlottesville. Mem. ACS (pres. 2001-2002), Am. Surg. Assn. (pres. 2003-2004), Soc. Clin. Surgery, So. Surg. Assn., Soc. Univ. Surgeons. Office: U Va Hosps Dept Surgery -Jefferson Park Ave PO Box 800709 Charlottesville VA 22908-0709 Office Phone: 434-924-2000.

JONES, REBA (BECKI) PESTUN, elementary school and music educator; b. Logan, W.Va., Apr. 30, 1949; d. John Rohac and Carolyn Kelly Pestun; m. Edgar Roger Jones, Aug. 22, 1968; 1 child, Karaleah Sabina Reichart. MusB in Edn., W.Va. U., 1970; EdM in Music Edn., U. Md., 1986; DMA, Shenandoah U., 2003. Cert. postgrad. prof. in music edn. grades K-12 Va., 1986, tchr. Am. Orff Schulwerk Assn., 1986. Choir dir. Asbury United Meth. Ch., Charles Town, W.Va., 1976—86; music tchr. grades K-5 Columbia Elem. Sch. - Fairfax County Pub. Schs., Annandale, Va., 1986—2002; music tchr. grades K-6 Herndon (Va.) Elem. - Fairfax County Pub. Schs., 2002—. Musician (composer/educator): (creative musical unit) A Musical Physical Fitness Workout (Semi-Finalist for the Nat. Music Found., 2000), (creative music units for grades k-3) Rabbit on My Mind (Winner of Impact II Nat. Grant and Va. Commn. for the Arts Grant for Outstanding Achievement, 1999), (original musical for grades k-6) Coal Mining Musical (Impact II Nat. Award Winner, 2001), (original musical unit for grades k-3) Sea Turtle Rhapsody (Impact II Nat. Award Winner, 2002), (original music unit for grades k-6) A True Whale Story (Winner Outstanding Achievement from the Va. Commn. for the Arts, 1998), (original musical with appalachian songs) Journey From the Mountain to the Sky (Hon. Mention from Nat. Music Found., 1999), (original music teaching unit) Musical Manatees (Impact II Nat. Grant Award Winner, 2003), (musical teaching unit and performance) Forever Free (Wash. Post Grant in Edn. Winner, 1998); musician: The Bully Butterfly, 2004 (winner Va. Commn. of Arts Grant, 2004). Mem.: Music Educator's Nat. Conf., Appalachian Studies Assn., Am. Orff Schulwerk Assn., Fairfax Gen. Music Educators Assn., Fairfax Edn. Assn. Office: Herndon Elem Sch 630 Dranesville Rd Herndon VA 20170 Office Phone: 703-326-3162. Business E-Mail: becki.jones@fcps.edu.

JONES, RENEE KAUERAUF, health facility administrator; b. Duncan, Okla., Nov. 3, 1949; d. Delbert Owen and Betty Jean (Marsh) Kauerauf; m. Dan Elkins Jones, Aug. 3, 1972. BS, Okla. State U., 1972, MS, 1975; PhD, Okla. U., 1989. Diplomate Am. Bd. Sleep Medicine. Statis. analyst Okla. State Dept. Mental Health, Okla. City, 1978-80, divisional chief, 1980-83, adminstr., 1983-84; assoc. dir. HCA Presbyn. Hosp., Oklahoma City, 1984-2000; mng. ptnr. Sleep Assocs., LLC, Oklahoma City, 2000—, Sleep REMedies, LLC, Okalhoma City, 2003—. Adj. instr. Okla. U. Health Sci. Ctr., 1979—; assoc. staff scientist Okla. Ctr. for Alcohol and Drug-Related Studies, Okla. City, 1979—; cons. in field. Assoc. editor Alcohol Tech. Reports jour., 1979-84; contbr. articles to profl. jours. Mem. assoc. bd. Hist. Preservation, Inc., treas. 1994. Mem. Am. Acad. Sleep Medicine, Assn. Health Svcs. Rsch., Alcohol and Drug Problems Assn. N.Am., Am. Sleep Disorders Assn., N.Y. Acad. Scis., So. Sleep Soc. (sec.-treas. 1989-91), Phi Kappa Phi. Democrat. Methodist. Avocations: skiing, scuba diving, race-walking, bicycling, painting. Home: 810 NW 15th St Oklahoma City OK 73106 Office: The Sleep Clinic 5530 N Francis Ave Oklahoma City OK 73118 Home Phone: 405-521-0853; Office Phone: 405-767-6970. Personal E-mail: sleepdr1@cox.net. Business E-Mail: sleepdr1@thesleepclinic.net.

JONES, RICHARD HENRY, ambassador; b. Shreveport, La., Aug. 26, 1950; m. Joan Wiener; 4 children. BS in Math., Harvey Mudd Coll., 1972; MS in Bus., U. Wis., 1976, PhD in Bus. and Stats., 1980. With US Fgn. Svc., 1976—, mem. US mission Orgn. for Econ. Cooperation and Devel. Paris, 1980—83, petroleum attache, econ. adv. Riyadh, Saudi Arabia, 1984—86, counselor polit. affairs, 1989—92; dir. Office of Developed Country Trade, Bur. Econ. & Bus. Affairs US Dept. State, Washington, 1987—89, dir. office Egyptian affairs, 1993—95, US amb. to Lebanon Beirut, 1996—98, US amb. to Kazakhstan Almaty, 1998—2001, US amb. to Kuwait Kuwait City, 2001—04; chief policy officer, dep. adminstr. Coalition Provisional Authority, Baghdad, Iraq, 2003—04; sr. adv. and policy coord. on Iraq, Office of Sec. of State US Dept. State, Washington, 2005, U.S. amb. to Israel Tel Aviv, 2005—. Office: DOS Amb 9700 Tel Aviv Pl Washington DC 20521-9700 Office Phone: 011-972-03-519-7583. Business E-Mail: ambtelaviv@state.gov.*

JONES, RICHARD K., information technology executive; Student in Computer sci., U. of Waterloo, Ontario, Can. Sr. cons. ptnr. JNL EFT Cons. Inc.; pres. & CEO Bethany Computer Sys. Inc.; dir. computing and comm. & CTO Technicolor Inc.; joined Countrywide Financial Corp., Calabasas, Calif., 1995—, sr. v.p., infrastructure, IT divsn., exec. v.p. of enterprise arch., IT, sr. mng. dir. & chief info. officer. Office: Sr Mng Dir & CIO Countrywide Fin Corp 4500 Park Granada Calabasas CA 91302-1613

JONES, RICHARD LAMAR, entomology educator; b. Charleston, Miss., May 31, 1939; s. Raymond Lee and Tyna Louise (Holland) J.; m. Anne Marchman, June 6, 1964; children: Katherine Mathis, Margaret Holland; m. Joan Marie Wood, Nov. 29, 1997. BS, Miss. State U., 1963, MS, 1965; PhD, U. Calif., Riverside, 1968. Rsch. entomologist Agrl. Rsch. Svc., USDA, Tifton, Ga., 1968-77; assoc. prof. entomology U. Minn., St. Paul, 1977-84, prof., head dept., 1984-91, dean Coll. Agr., 1991-95; dean of rsch., dir. Fla. Agrl. Expt. Sta. U. Fla., Gainesville, Fla., 1995—2005. Editor, author: Semiochemicals, 1974; also over 70 articles. With USN, 1958-60. Scholar NIH, 1965-68, Fulbright scholar, Leiden, The Netherlands, 1980. Mem. AAAS, Entomol. Soc. Am. (fin. com. 1989-96), Am. Chem. Soc. Avocations: golf, fishing. Office: U Fla PO Box 110810 Gainesville FL 32611-0180 Office Phone: 352-284-3315. E-mail: rlj@ifas.ufl.edu.

JONES, RICHARD M., broadcast executive; m. Robin Jones; children: Barbara, Rhys. BS summa cum laude, Syracuse U., NY, bus. degree with honors, law degree; LLM in Taxation, Boston U. Bar: NY, Conn., DC, US Supreme Ct., US Tax Ct. Law clk. Appellate Divsn. NY State Supreme Ct.; with media and entertainment and trans. adv. svcs. practices Ernst & Young; positions up to v.p. tax, asst. treas., tax counsel NBC Universal, 2003—05; sr. v.p., gen. tax counsel CBS Corp. Non-commd. officer 75th Ranger Rgt. US Army. Mem.: ABA, AICPA, Am. Assn. Atty.-CPAs, NY State Bar Assn. (mem. corp. and partnership taxation coms.), NY Soc. CPAs, Am. Legion, Disabled Am. Vets. (life). Office: CBS Corp 51 W 52nd St New York NY 10019-6188 Office Phone: 212-975-4321.*

JONES, RICHARD MELVIN, bank executive, director, former retail executive; b. Eldon, Mo., Nov. 26, 1926; m. Sylvia A. Richardson, 1950; 3 children. BSBA, Olivet Nazarene Coll., 1950, LLD (hon.), 1983; grad. advanced mgmt. program, Harvard U., 1973. With Sears, Roebuck & Co., 1950-89, store mgr., 1963-68, gen. mgr. Washington and Balt., 1974, exec. v.p.-East, 1974-80, corp. v.p., 1980, vice-chmn., CFO, 1980-85, pres., CFO, 1986-88; chmn., CEO Guaranty Fed. Savs. Bank, Dallas, 1989-91. Trustee Field Mus. Natural History, Northwestern Univ. Assocs., Chgo.; adv. coun. J.L. Kellogg Grad. Sch. Mgmt. Northwestern U.

JONES, RICHARD MICHAEL, lawyer; b. Chgo., Jan. 16, 1952; s. Richard Anthony and Shirley Mae (Wilhelm) J.; m. Catherine Leona Ford, May 25, 1974. BS, U. Ill., 1974; JD, Harvard U., 1977. Bar: Colo. 1977, U.S. Dist. Ct. Colo. 1977. Assoc. Davis, Graham & Stubbs, Denver, 1977-81; corp. counsel Tosco Corp., Denver, 1981-82; asst. gen. counsel Anschutz Corp., Denver, 1982-88, gen. counsel, v.p., 1989—. Mem. ABA, Colo. Bar Assn., Denver Bar Assn. Office: Anschutz Corp 555 17th St Ste 2400 Denver CO 80202-3987

JONES, RICHARD SHEFFIELD, veterans service officer; b. Columbus, Ohio, Dec. 11, 1944; s. John David and Margery (Kibler) Jones; m. Pamela Kay Goad, May 27, 1974; children: Sarah, Anna. BA with honors, Hanover Coll., Ind., 1974; MS, Miami U., Oxford, Ohio, 1977. Career counselor Grinnel Coll., Iowa, 1977—78; dir. career edn. placement Findlay Coll., Ohio, 1978—80; coll. union dir. Hanover Coll., 1980—87, career svcs. dir., 1987—91, registrar, 1991—96; vets. svc. officer State Ind., Madison, 2001—. Svc. officer VFW, Madison, 2002—, DAV, Madison, 2004—; chair Jefferson County Vets. Coun., Madison, 2005—. Treas. Cornerstone Soc., Madison, 1987—88; treas., fundraising chair Ulster Project Madison, Madison, 1998—2001; adj. VFW Post 1969, Madison, 2004—; treas., sr. warden Christ Episc. Ch., Madison, 1990—93. Chief warrant officer 2nd grade US Army, 1967—70, Vietnam. Decorated Dist. Flying Cross; named Outstanding Young Man Am., Outstanding Young Ams., 1979, Ind. State Svc. Officer Yr., Disabled Am. Vets., 2003; recipient 21 air medals for meritorious svc., 2 air medals with valor, 2 Army Commendation medals. Mem.: Vietnam Helicopter Pilots Assn. Democrat. Episcopalian. Avocations: gardening, reading, cooking. Office: Vets Affairs Jefferson County 300 E Main Rm 103 Madison IN 47250

JONES, ROBERT ALFRED, retired clergyman; b. Buffalo, July 19, 1930; s. Ralph A. and Edna Mae (Carver) J.; m. Helen T. Webster, July 20, 1957; children: Marc E., Paul R., Nancy L. BA, Houghton Coll., 1953; MA, Alfred U., 1959. Ordained to ministry United Meth. Ch., 1959. Assoc. pastor University United Meth. Ch., Buffalo, 1959-63; campus min. SUNY, Buffalo, 1963-67; pastor Woodside United Meth. Ch., Buffalo, 1967-74; sr. pastor Baker Meml. United Meth. Ch., East Aurora, NY, 1974-80; supr. Rochester dist United Meth. Ch., 1980-86; sr. pastor Ctrl. Park United Meth. Ch., 1986-89; asst. to bishop N.Y. west area United Meth. Ch., Syracuse, 1989-91; sr. pastor Williamsville (N.Y.) United Meth. Ch., 1991—99. Home: 146 Farber Ln Williamsville NY 14221-5754

JONES, ROBERT ALONZO, economist; b. Evanston, Ill., Mar. 15, 1937; s. Robert Vernon and Elsie Pierce (Brown) J.; m. Ina Turner Jones; children: Lindsay Rae, Robert Pierce, Gregory Alan, William Kenneth. AB, Middlebury Coll., 1959, LLD, 1992; MBA, Northwestern U., 1961. Economist Hahn, Wise & Assocs., San Carlos, Calif., 1966-69; sr. rsch. officer Bank of Am., San Francisco, 1969-74; v.p., dir. fin. forecasting Chase Econometrics, San Francisco, 1974-76; chmn. bd. Money Market Svcs., Inc., Belmont, Calif., 1974-86, MMS Internat., Redwood City, Calif., 1986-89, chmn. emeritus, 1989-2000; chmn. bd. dirs. Market News Internat., NYC; chmn. emeritus Geonomics Inst., Middlebury, Vt., 1995—, chmn. bd., 1986-95, Jones Interant., 1990—, Digital Integrator, Inc., Incline Village, Nev., 1993—. Chmn. bd. Jones Fin. Network, Inc., Incline VIllage; dean coun. Harvard U. Div. Sch., Cambridge, Mass., 1991—; mem. Kellogg Alumni Adv. Bd., Northwestern U., 1993—; trustee Middlebury Coll., 1998—; instr. money and banking Am. Inst. Banking, San Francisco, 1971, 72. Author: U.S. Financial System and the Federal Reserve, 2974, Power of Coinage, 1987. Councilman, City of Belmont, Calif., 1970-77, mayor, 1971, 72, 75, 76; dir. San Mateo County Transit Dist., 1975-77; chmn. San Mateo County Coun. Mayors, 1975-76; trustee Incline Village Gen. Improvement Dist., 1984-85, Carlmont United Meth. Ch., 1978-81. 1st lt. USAR, 1961-68. Recipient Ernst & Young Entrepreneur of the Yr. award, 1986, Stanton Recognition award North Shore Country Day Sch., 1996; named Hon. life mem. Calif. PTA, ordo honorum Kappa Delta Rho Nat. Frat.; John Harvard fellow Harvard U., 1996. Mem. Nat. Assn. Bu. Economists, San Francisco Bond Club. Republican. Methodist. Office: Jones Internat Inc PO Box 7498 Incline Village NV 89452-7498 *The entrepreneurial spirit is distinguished by passion, creativity, and the fulfillment of mission through other people.*

JONES, ROBERT CLAIR, middle school educator; b. Norfolk, Va., Apr. 9, 1949; s. Leon Herbert and Barbara Dean (Jones) J.; children: Adam, Matthew, Aaron, Lee. BS, Old Dominion U., 1971, MS, 1981. Tchr. Virginia Beach (Va.) Jr. High Sch., 1971-73, Kempsville Jr. High Sch., Virginia Beach, 1973—. Adj. faculty Old Dominion U., Norfolk, Va., 1990—; co-chmn. faculty coun. Kempsville Mid. Sch., 1992-93, curriculum coord., grade level chair, 1993—; program devel. com. for mid. schs., Virginia Beach City Schs., 1990-91, chmn. social studies curriculum adv. com., 1990-91, instr. staff devel., 1989-91; speaker in field. Contbr. articles to profl. jours.; musician: Stingrays Band. Baseball coach Pony Colt League, Virginia Beach, 1991-92; vol. Make A Wish Found., Virginia Beach, 1990-92. Named Tchr. of Yr., Va. Coun. Social Studies, 1987—. Mem. ASCD, NEA, Nat. Coun. Social Studies, Va. Edn. Assn., Va. Coun. Social Studies, Virginia Beach Edn. Assn. Avocations: collecting records, collecting Beatles memorobilia, writing, songwriting. Home: 812 Yearling Ct Virginia Beach VA 23464-3214 Office: Kempsville Mid Sch 260 Churchill Dr Virginia Beach VA 23456

JONES, ROBERT EDWARD, federal judge; b. Portland, Oreg., July 5, 1927; s. Howard C. and Leita (Hendricks) J.; m. Pearl F. Jensen, May 29, 1948; children— Jeffrey Scott, Julie Lynn BA, U. Hawaii, 1949; JD, Lewis and Clark Coll., 1953, LHD (hon.), 1995; LLD (hon.), City U., Seattle, 1984. Bar: Oreg. Trial atty., Portland, Oreg., 1953-63; judge Oreg. Circuit Ct., Portland, 1963-83; justice Oreg. Supreme Ct., Salem, 1983-90; judge U.S. Dist. Ct. Oreg., Portland, 1990—. Mem. faculty Nat. Jud. Coll., Am. Acad. Jud. Edn., ABA Appellate Judges Seminars; former mem. Oreg. Evidence Revision Commn., Oreg. Ho. of Reps.; former chmn. Oreg. Commn. Prison Terms and Parole Stds.; adj. prof. Northwestern Sch. Law, Lewis and Clark Coll., 1963—, Willamette Law Sch., 1988-90. Author: Rutter Group Practice Guide Federal Civil Trials and Evidence, 1999—. Mem. bd. overseers Lewis and Clark Coll., mem. bd. visitors to Northwestern Sch. Law. Served to capt. JAGC, USNR. Recipient merit award Multnomah Bar Assn., 1979; Citizen award NCCJ, Legal Citizen of the Yr. award Law Related Edn. Project, 1988; Service to Mankind award Sertoma Club Oreg.; James Madison award Sigma Delta Chi; named Disting. Grad., Northwestern Sch. Law; Outstanding Profl. Achievement Alumnus award, U.S. Merchant Marine Acad., 1998; Judge Robert E. Jones Oreg. Justice award, Am. Judicature Soc., 1999, Lifetime Commitment to Jury Trial Sys. award Am. Bd. Trial Advs., 2004. Mem. Am. Judicature Soc. (bd. dirs. 1997-2001), State Bar Oreg. (past chmn. Continuing Legal Edn.), Oreg. Circuit Judges Assn. (pres. 1967-1968), Oreg. Trial Lawyers Assn. (pres. 1959, chair 9th cir. edn. com. 1996-97). Office: US Dist Ct House 1000 SW 3rd Ave Ste 1007 Portland OR 97204-2944 Home Phone: 503-636-2810; Office Phone: 503-326-8340. Business E-Mail: robert_jones@ord.uscourts.gov.

JONES, ROBERT GEAN, religion educator; b. Magnolia, Ark., Feb. 17, 1925; s. Emless Bunyan and Eunice (Gean) J.; m. Marian Laverne Alexander, July 23, 1946; 1 dau., Carolyn Ann. BA cum laude, Baylor U., 1947; B.D. cum laude, Yale, 1950, MA, 1957, PhD, 1959. Ordained to ministry Bapt. Ch., 1946; minister Deep River (Conn.) Bapt. Ch. and; First Bapt. Ch. of, Saybrook, 1950-59; asst. prof. religion George Washington U., Washington, 1959-61, asso. prof., 1961-64, prof., 1964-91, prof. emeritus, 1991—, chmn. dept. religion, 1963-79, univ. marshal, 1969-89. Adj. prof. U. Tenn., Chattanooga, 1991-93, Maryville Coll., 1993-95. Author: The Rules for the War of the Sons of Light With the Sons of Darkness, 1957, The Manual of Discipline (1QS), The Old Testament and Persian Religion, 1964. Mem. Soc. Bibl. Lit. and Exegesis, Am. Acad. Religion, Alpha Chi, Omicron Delta Kappa. Home: 307 Amohi Ln Loudon TN 37774-3013 Personal E-mail: robgjones@aol.com.

JONES, ROBERT GERARD, lawyer; b. Latrobe, Pa., Nov. 13, 1956; BSME, W. Va. U., 1979; JD, St. Louis U., 1987. Bar: Mo. 1987, DC 1988. Sr. engr. Exxon Coal U.S., 1979—84; assoc. Crowell & Moring, Washington, 1987—91; of counsel Arch Mineral Corp., 1991—94; sr. counsel Arch Coal, Inc., St. Louis, 1994—2000, v.p. law, gen. counsel, 2000—. Office: Arch Coal Inc One City Place Dr Ste 300 Saint Louis MO 63141 Office Phone: 314-994-2700.

JONES, ROBERT GRIFFITH, law educator, mayor; b. State Coll., Pa., Mar. 25, 1936; s. Edward H. and Dorothy (Griffiths) J.; m. Carolyn E. Hazard, Aug. 29, 1959; Robert Griffith Jr., Chester H. AB, Davidson Coll., NC, 1958; MDiv, Yale U., 1961; PhD, Duke U., 1966; JD, U. Va., 1974. Bar: Va. 1974, U.S. Supreme Ct. 1977. Asst. prof. Davidson (N.C.) Coll., 1964-65; assoc. prof. Lehigh U., Bethlehem, Pa., 1965-71; prof. U. Va., Charlottesville, 1971-74; mayor City Va. Beach, Va., 1986-88; chmn. Jones & Walker, P.C., Va. Beach, 1991—. Adv. bd. mem. Soc. Trust Bank, 1997-05. Vice-chmn. Tidewater Transp. Dist. Commn., 1987-88, chmn., 1988; councilman City Coun. Va. Beach, 1982-88, chmn. Va. Beach Econ. Devel. Authority, 2001-05. Mem. Va. State Bar. Democrat. Presbyterian. Home: 2716 Robin Dr Virginia Beach VA 23454-1814 Office: 128 S Lynnhaven Rd Virginia Beach VA 23452-7417 Office Phone: 757-486-0333. Personal E-mail: rgjvbva@aol.com. Business E-Mail: rjones@jonesandwalker.com.

JONES, ROBERT HENRY, automotive distribution executive; b. Willow Springs, NC, Dec. 31, 1935; s. Kenneth Tomas and China Christiana (Blalock) J.; m. Margaret Ann Page; children: Julie Beth, Jeffrey Bert, Jay Brent. AA in Acctg., Kings Coll., 1960. Acct. Jones & Guerrero Co., Inc., Agana, Guam, 1961-63, gen. mgr., 1963-67, v.p., 1967-73, exec. v.p., 1973-84; pres., chief exec. officer Triple J Enterprises, Tamuning, Guam, 1984—. Chmn. bd. Guam Visitors Bur., 1974-76, bd. dirs., 1968-89; chmn. Pacific Asia Travel Assn., Micronesia chpt., 1988-89; v.p. Boy Scouts Am., Hawaii, 1968—. Served with U.S. Army, 1957-59. Recipient Silver Beaver award Boy Scouts Am., 1975, Silver Antelope award, 1991; Mr. Tourism award Guam Visitors Bur., 1976. Mem. Guam C. of C. (chmn. 1980, Bus. Man of Yr. award 1983); Guam Hotel and Restaurant Assn. (pres., founder 1969-71). Lodges: Rotary (bd. dirs. Guam). Republican. Presbyterian. Avocations: skiing, dirt bike riding, travel. Home Phone: 671-632-7231; Office Phone: 671-646-9126. Business E-Mail: rhjones@triplejsaipan.com.

JONES, ROBERT JEFFRIES, lawyer; b. Atlantic City, Sept. 7, 1939; s. Robert Louis and Mildred Laura (Jeffries) J.; m. Joan Mary Feichtner, Aug. 17, 1963; children: Christopher, Kendall, Stephen. BA, Colgate U., 1961; LLB with honors, U. Pa., 1964. Bar: Pa. 1965, U.S. Dist. Ct. (ea. dist.) Pa. 1965, U.S. Ct. Appeals (3d cir.) 1965. Assoc. Saul, Ewing LLP, Phila., 1964-71, ptnr., 1971—. Steering com. Bond Atty.'s Workshop, Chgo., 1980. Mem. Montgomery County Rep. Com., Norristown, Pa., 1967-71; chmn. Whitpain Twp. Park and Recreation Bd., Blue Bell, Pa., 1980-84; bd. dirs. Phila. YMCA Camps, 1970-76; trustee Colgate U., 1999-2005; mem. gen. counsel alumni corp., 1993-99, pres. Phila. chpt., 1980-84. Fellow Am. Coll. Bond Counsel (founder); mem. ABA, Phila. Bar Assn. (chmn. tax exempt fin. com. 1985-86), Pa. Bond Lawyers Assn. (founder Harrisburg, Pa. 1987), Pa. Economy League (bd. dirs. 1994—). Avocations: golf, history. Office: Saul Ewing LLP 3800 Centre Sq W Philadelphia PA 19102 Office Phone: 215-972-7802. E-mail: rjjboilerplate@aol.com, rjones@saul.com.

JONES, ROBERT RUSSELL, retired magazine editor; b. Topeka, Oct. 19, 1927; s. Russell Alonzo and and Marie (Carter) J.; m. Dorothy Jean Vincent, Sept. 3, 1947; children— Daniel Robert, Mark Alan. AB in Polit. Sci. and History, Washburn U., Topeka, 1949; MS in Tech. Journalism, Kans. State U., Manhattan, 1959. Expt. sta. editor, asst. prof. agrl. econs. Kans. State U., 1957-60; asst. editor Agrl. Pubs. Inc., Milw., 1960-67; sci. editor, asst. prof. expt. sta. U. Mo., Columbia, 1967-72; assoc. editor Indsl. Research mag., Chgo., 1972-74, editor, 1974-78; editorial dir. Indsl. Research & Devel. mag., Barrington, Ill., 1978-83; editor, editorial dir. Research & Devel. Mag., Barrington, 1984-89, exec. editor Des Plaines, Ill., 1989-91; editorial dir. Chromatography Forum Mag., Barrington, 1986, Chromatography Mag., Barrington, 1987; ret., 1991. Chmn. R & D Scientist of Yr. award ann. program, 1974-91, I-R 100 new products awards ann. program, 1974-87, R & D 100 new product awards ann. program, 1988-91; pres., CEO, editl. dir. Applied Sci. Communications, 1991—. Editor: The Unsettled Earth, 1975, Foresight mag., 1991-93, First Notes mag., 1991-95, The Spire mag., 1995—. Served with USNR, 1945-46. Mem. AAAS, Am. Bus. Press (Jesse H. Neal Editorial Achievement award 1976), Am. Soc. Bus. Press Editors, Nat. Assn. Sci. Writers. Democrat. Baptist. Home: 1213 Main St Evanston IL 60202-1650 Office Phone: 847-328-8133.

JONES, ROBERT THADDUES, retired principal; b. Manhattan, NY, Jan. 11, 1938; s. Monte Jones and Adelle (Brown) Ousmane; m. Geneva Alafair Thomas, Nov. 24, 1957; 1 child, Terry David. BA, Claflin Coll., Orangeburg, SC, 1961; postgrad., SC State U., Orangeburg, 1962-67, U. SC, Greenville, 1967-68; MEd, LaVerne Coll., Calif., 1977. Cert. guidance, elem. and secondary supr., elem. and secondary prin., art. Art tchr., guidance counselor Bryson H.S., Fountain Inn, SC, 1960-69; 1st and 5th grade tchr. Hayne Elem. Sch., Greenville, SC, 1969-70; art tchr., biracial coord. Northwood Mid. Sch., Taylors, SC, 1970-71; guidance counselor Berea Mid. Sch., Greenville, SC, 1971-79, asst. prin., 1982-83, Woodmont H.S., Piedmont, SC, 1979-82, N.W. Mid. Sch., Travelers Rest, SC, 1983-84; prin. Cone Elem. Sch., Greenville, 1984-88, Alexander Elem. Sch., Greenville, 1988—2000; ret., 2000. Asst. formulator model for S.C. schs. Guidance By Objectives, 1977. Vice chmn. Freetown Crime Watch Com., Greenville, 1986—; chmn. Parker Sewer & Fire Subdist., Greenville, (elected 1988 & 1999-), vice-chmn. commn., 1998; precinct pres. Tanglewood Dem. Precinct, Greenville, 1990; vice chmn. Greenville County Planning Commn., 1994; sec.-treas. N.W. Area Coun. Chamber, Greenville, 1994 (plaque 1994); v.p. for membership Blue Ridge Coun. Boy Scouts Am., Greenville, 1992; mem. Greenville Marchers Against Drugs, 1993-94 (plaque 1993); sec. Salvation Army of Greenville County, 2000-; pres. United Meth. Men of John Wesley United Meth. Ch., 2004-. Recipient Silver Beaver award Boy Scouts Am., Greenville, 1988; named Ben E. Craig Outstanding Educator First Union Bank, Greenville, 1991, N.W. Area Bus. Edn. Partnership Prin. of Yr., Greenville, 1993. Mem. Palmetto State Law Enforcement Officers Assn. (sec. 1979-94, Plaque 1988), SC Law Enforcement Officers Assn., Masons. Methodist. Avocations: photography, tennis computer technology. Home: 202 Hollywood Dr Greenville SC 29611-7320 Office: Parker Sewer & Fire Subdistrict 117 Smythe St Greenville SC 29611 Home Phone: 864-269-2749; Office Phone: 864-467-4025. Personal E-mail: rtotojones@aol.com.

JONES, RONALD DAVID, retired lawyer; b. Oneida, NY, Jan. 2, 1930; s. Keith Walton and Winnie (Thomas) J.; children: Susan D., Stephen T.; m. Hildegard Vetter, June 9, 1984. BS, Yale U., 1951; JD cum laude, Harvard U., 1958. Bar: N.Y. 1958, U.S. Ct. Appeals (1st, 2nd, 4th, 5th, 6th and D.C. cirs.), U.S. Supreme Ct. 1980. Assoc. LeBoeuf, Lamb, Leiby & MacRae, NYC, 1958-64, ptnr., 1965-89, of counsel, 1990—2002. Pres. Coun. Econ. Regulation, 1988-92; chmn. United Distbn. Cos., 1990-97; chmn. Upper Housatonic Valley Nat. Heritage Area, Inc., 2000—. Served to lt. USNR, 1951-55 Mem. ABA (chmn. sect. on pub. utilities law 1986-87), Univ. Club (N.Y.C.). Avocations: running, writing, history. Office: 27 Woodcrest Ln PO Box 1942 Lakeville CT 06039 Personal E-mail: rdj655@sbcglobal.net.

JONES, RONALD LEE, lawyer, writer; b. Ames, Iowa, Apr. 11, 1942; s. L. Meyer and Mary Elizabeth (Homer) J.; m. Cynthia Jane Spitzer, Oct. 1, 1994. BA, Ill. Wesleyan U., 1965; cert., Naval Justice Sch., Camp Pendleton, Calif., 1968; JD, Calif. Western Sch. Law, 1972. Bar: Nebr. 1973, U.S. Ct. Appeals (8th cir.) 1973, U.S. Supreme Ct. 1979. Corp. counsel Gene Fuller, Inc., San Diego, 1972-73; asst. gen. counsel Daniel Internat. Corp., Greenville, S.C., 1974-79; v.p., gen. counsel, sec. Royster Co., Norfolk, Va., 1979-83; writer Virginia Beach, Va., 1983—; counsel Peter Kiewit Sons, Inc., Omaha, 1984-87, Occidental Chem. Corp., Dallas, 1988—, The Williams Cos., 1997, Hall Estill Law Firm, Tulsa, Okla., 2002—. Chmn. lawyers coordinating com. Fla. Phosphate Council, Tampa, 1980. Author: Practice Preventive Corporat Law, 1985, How to Counsel Corporate Clients: Ten Reasons Business People Don't Take Legal Advice (And What You Can Do About It), ALI-ABA, 2000; editor (newsletter) Corp. Counsel Reporter, 1985—; contbr. articles to profl. jours. Capt. USMC, 1965-69. Mem. ABA (corp., banking and bus. law sect., constrn. law forum com.), Fertilizer Inst., Am. Mfrs. Assn. Home: 1 Royal Dublin Ln Broken Arrow OK 74011-1127 Office Phone: 918-594-0424. Business E-Mail: rjones@hallestill.com.

JONES, ROSLYN JOYCE, secondary school educator; b. NYC, Apr. 4, 1951; d. Murray and Edith P. Bodofsky; m. Jay Marcus Jones, Aug. 17, 1973; children: Maurissa R., Aimee D. BA, SUNY, Binghamton, 1972; MA, U. Calif., Riverside, 1976. Cert. tchr. Calif. Tchr. Orange (Calif.) Unified Sch. Dist., 1974—90, Riverside (Calif.) Unified Sch. Dist., 1990—. Dir. social action Temple Beth-el, Riverside, 2001—06. Recipient We Honor Ours award, Calif. Teachers Assn., 1983, 2000, 2006. Mem.: Riverside City Tchrs. Assn. (exec. officer 1991—). Democrat. Jewish. Avocations: travel, reading. Home Phone: 951-780-2305. Personal E-mail: buffjones@aol.com.

JONES, RUDOLPH, minister; b. Emporia, Va., Nov. 23, 1937; s. Ralph and Esther Jones; m. Annie Ruth Jones, Dec. 28, 1963; children: Rudolph Jr., Celeste. BTh, Berea Coll. Sem., 1970, MA, 1972, D in Sacred Theology, 1973, DD, 1974; BS, Kensington U., 1986; D in Philosophy, Andersonville Bapt. Sem., 1990, D in Ministry, 1998. Pastor Solid Rock Bapt. Ch. Mem. adminstrv. bd. Am. Bapt., NYC, 1978—84, mem. ordination com., 1981. Mem. Solid Rock Pantry, 1986—, 79th Precinct Coun., 1975—, Cerous Attucks, Bklyn., 1973—74. Named to 2000 Outstanding Scholars 20th Century in religion, Cambridge, Eng., 1999. Mem.: Am. Law Enforcement Assn., Scottish Rite. Democrat. Avocation: travel. Home: 120 Tompkins Ave Brooklyn NY 11206 Office Phone: 718-388-5952.

JONES, RUSSEL CAMERON, civil engineer, educator; b. Tarentum, Pa., Oct. 18, 1935; s. Frederick Russel and Helena Doris (Elliot) Jones; m. Bethany S. Jones; children: Amy Sue, Kimberly Nicole, Tamara Melissa. BS, Carnegie Inst. Tech., 1957, MS, 1960, PhD, 1963; MALS, U. Del., 1994. Structural engr. Hunting, Larsen & Dunnels, Pitts., 1957-59; asst. prof. civil engring. MIT, 1963-66, assoc. prof., 1966-71; prof., chmn. dept. civil engring. Ohio State U., Columbus, 1971-76; dean Sch. Engring., U. Mass., Amherst, 1977-81; v.p. acad. affairs Boston U., 1981-87, v.p. acad. devel., 1985-87; pres. U. Del., Newark, 1987-88, univ. rsch. prof., 1988-95; exec. dir. NSPE, Alexandria, Va., 1995-98; mng. ptnr. World Expertise LLC, Falls Church, Va., 1998—. Named Del. Engr. of Yr., 1994; recipient Collingwood prize, ASCE, 1966, Edmund Friedman profl. recognition award, 1981, Internat. medal for disting. contbns. to engring. edn., Australasian Assn. Engring. Edn., 1993, Chair's award, Am. Assn. Engring. Socs., 2005; fellow, NDEA, 1959—62, ASCE, 1962—63. Fellow AAAS, ASCE (hon.; bd. dirs. 1969-71, 72-75, v.p. 1976-77), NSPE, Am. Soc. Engring. Edn., Accreditation Bd. Engring. and Tech. (bd. dirs. 1983-86, pres. 1987-88), Royal Soc. for Encouragement of Arts, Mfrs. and Commerce, Instn. of Engrs. of Ireland; mem. IEEE, Am. Assn. Higher Edn., Nat. Assn. for Sci., Tech. and Soc. (bd. dirs. 1992-95), Sigma Xi, Tau Beta Pi, Phi Kappa Ph, Chi Epsilon, Sigma Nu. Office: 2001 Mayfair Mclean Ct Falls Church VA 22043-1761 Personal E-mail: rcjonespe@aol.com.

JONES, RUTH A., secondary school educator; b. Quantico, Md., July 7, 1946; d. William Tolbert and Ruth L. (Winder) J. BS, U. Md. at Eastern Shore, 1970; APC, Salisbury State U., 1982. Cert. leadership Salisbury Univ. Athletic dir. sch. curriculum devel. Woodson Middle Sch.; tchr. Somerset County Bd. Edn., Princess Anne, Md.; acting vice prin. Crisfield Acad. H.S., 2004—05. SIT team mem. Woodson Mid. Sch., wellness chairperson, unified arts chairperson, field chairperson, acting vice prin., Md., 2002—03. Participant Rally at Annapolis for Thornton Bill; playground dir. Recipient Coach's award Mid. Sch. Champions, Boys's Basketball Team, 1986—87, Tchr. of the Yr. Rep., Woodson Mid. Sch., 1995, 2004. Mem. NEA, Tchrs. Assn. Somerset County, Md. State Tchrs. Assn., Middle Sch. Rules Com.

JONES, SALLY DAVIESS PICKRELL, writer; b. St. Louis, June 4, 1923; d. Claude Dildine Pickrell and Marie Daviess (Pittman) Pickrell; m. Charles William Jones, Sept. 2, 1943 (dec.); 1 child, Matthew Charles (dec.). Student, Mills Coll., Oakland, Calif., 1941-43, U. Calif.-Berkeley, 1945, Columbia U., 1955-58. Author: (novels) Lights Burn Blue, 1947. Mem. Met. Mus. Art, Nat. Coun. Women, Asia Soc., Fgn. Policy Assn., UN Assn. Episcopalian. Address: 1525 Pelican Point Dr Apt HA101 Sarasota FL 34231-6774

JONES, SANDRA YVONNE, lawyer; b. Chgo., July 13, 1952; d. Fred Alexander and Luenettie (Joiner) J. B.S., U. Ill., 1975; J.D., Valparaiso U., 1977; diploma Nat. Jud. Coll., 1981. Bar: Ill. 1978, U.S. Dist. Ct. (no. dist.) Ill., U.S. Supreme Ct. 1983. Legal asst. Porter County Prosecutor's Office, Valparaiso, Ind., 1977; legal counsel Cook County Legal Asst.'s Office, Maywood, Ill., 1978-81; adminstrv. law judge Human Rights Commn., Chgo., 1981-85; asst. regional civil rights counsel Office Civil Rights, U.S. Dept. Edn., Chgo., 1985—, supervising atty. Office Pub. Guardian, Chgo., 1987-94, adminstrv. hearing officer expedited child support divsn. Cir. Ct. Cook County, Chgo., 1994—. Author: Tenant's Guide to Self-Help, 1981. Mem. ABA, Ill. Assn. Adminstrv. Law Judges (v.p. 1984—), Ill. Assn. Trial Lawyers, Chgo. Bar Assn., Ill. Bar Assn. Home: 3316 S Calumet Ave Chicago IL 60616-3992 Office: Human Rights Commn 32 W Randolph St Chicago IL 60601-3423

JONES, SARA SUE FISHER, librarian; b. Rupert, Idaho, May 2, 1962; d. Richard Sherman and Dana Louise Fisher; m. Martin R. Jones, Jan. 7, 1984; children: Russel, Elaine. BA in Comms., Boise State U., 1983; MLS, Syracuse U., 1999; postgrad., U. North Tex. Libr. dir. Stanley (Idaho) Cmty. Libr., 1984-86; English tchr. Minidoka County Schs., Rupert, Idaho, 1986-88; children's librarian Elko (Nev.) County Libr., 1988-95, libr. dir., 1995-2000; state libr., divsn. adminstr. Nev. State Libr. and Archives, 2000—. Commr. State Nev. Commn. on Edni. Tech. Elko County Libr. Bd. scholar, 1997-99; IMLS scholar Mem. Nev. Libr. Assn. (pres. 2000—, pub. trustee, chair, Dorothy McAlindin award 1995, scholar 1997-98), Nev. Libr. Orgn. (chair N.E. dist.), Philanthropic Edn. Orgn., Soroptimist Internat. (pres. 1995-96). Avocations: reading, camping, golf. Office: 100 N Stewart St Carson City NV 89701

JONES, SARAH, actress, playwright, poet; Attended, UN Internat. Sch., Bryn Mawr Coll. Writer, performer (plays) Waking the American Dream, Women Can't Wait, Surface Transit, actress (films) Bamboozled, (plays) Vagina Monologues, poet Def Poetry Jam, HBO, writer, performer (solo show Broadway plays) Bridge and Tunnel, 2006— (Spl. Tony award, 2006). Recipient Helen Hayes award, Best One Person Show award, HBO's Aspen Comedy Arts Festival, Obie award, Village Voice. Mailing: 302 A West 12th St #121 New York NY 10014 Office Phone: 212-633-2433. Office Fax: 212-627-6659.

JONES, SARAH B., psychologist; b. Corpus Christi, Tex., May 4, 1977; d. Vincent and Claudia Gagliardi; m. Warren C. Jones, Mar. 15, 2003. BA, U. Incarnate Word, 2000; MA, Tex. State U., 2003. Lic. specialist in sch. psychology Tex. State Bd. Examiners Psychology, 2003. Case magr. Communities in Schs., San Antonio, 1999—2000; specialist in sch. psychology Dallas Ind. Sch. Dist., 2002—. Mem.: NASP, Tex. Assn. Sch. Psychologists. Home Phone: 469-964-4219. Personal E-mail: princessbee77@sbcglobal.net.

JONES, SCHUYLER, museum director, anthropologist; b. Wichita, Kans., Feb. 7, 1930; s. Schuyler and Ignace (Mead) J.; m. Lis Margit Søndergaard Rasmussen, Dec. 20, 1955; children: Peter R., Hannah L.; m. Lorraine da'Luz Vieira, Aug. 4, 1998. MA in Anthropology with honors, Edinburgh U., Scotland; MA in Anthropology, DPhil in Anthropology, Oxford U., Eng. Asst. curator Pitt Rivers Mus., U. Oxford, 1970-71, asst. curator, univ. lectr. ethnology, 1971-85, dir., 1985-97; fellow Linacre Coll., Oxford U., 1970-97, prof. emeritus, 1997—. Anthropol. expdns. to Atlas Mountains, So. Algeria, French West Africa, 1951-52, Belgian, Congo, 1952-53, Morocco High Atlas, Algeria, Sahara, Niger River, 1954, East Africa, 1953, Turkey, Iran, Afghanistan, Pakistan, India, Nepal, 1958-59; ten expdns. to Nuristan in the Hindu Kush, 1960-70, Chinese Turkestan, 1985, Tibet and Gobi Desert, 1986, So. China, Xinjiang and Pakistan, 1988, Western Greenland, 1991, Greenland and East Africa, 1993; mem. coun. Royal Anthropol. Inst., 1986-89. Author: Sous le Soleil Africain, 1955, Under the African Sun (revised French version), 1956, Annotated Bibliography of Nuristan (Kafiristan) and the Kalash Kafirs of Chitral, part 1, 1966, part 2, 1969, The Political Organization of the Kam Kafirs, 1967, Men of Influence in Nuristan, 1974, Tibetan Nomads: Environment, Pastoral Economy & Material Culture, 1996; co-author: Nuristan, 1979, Afghanistan, 1992; contbr. numerous articles to profl. jours. Trustee Horniman Mus., 1989—95; bd. govs. Kans. State Hist. Soc., 2004—. Decorated comdr. Brit. Empire. Avocations: travel in remote areas, browsing in second-hand bookstores. Address: 1570 N Ridgewood Wichita KS 67208 E-mail: drschuylerjones@cs.com.

JONES, SCOTT NELSON, psychologist; b. Covington, Ky., Apr. 6, 1959; s. Nelson Gaylord and Dorothy Ann Jones; m. Ellen Marie Roinestad, Oct. 28, 2000; children: Holly Amelia, Drew William. BA, U. Ky., Lexington, 1981; PhD, Miami U., Oxford, Ohio, 1989. Staff geropsychologist Bangor Mental Health Inst., Bangor, Maine, 1988—91; staff geropsychologist, neuropsychologist VA Md. Health Care Sys., Perry Point, Md., 1991—. Clin. asst. prof. U. Md. Med. Sch., Balt., 2004—. Mem.: Am. Psychol. Assn., Phi Beta Kappa. Democrat. Avocations: bicycling, backpacking, archery, target shooting, guitar. Home: 134 Long Ln Kirkwood PA 17536 Office: VA Md Health Care Sys Office 129A Bldg 80 Perry Point MD 21902 Home Phone: 717-529-4031.

JONES, SHARON ELAINE, lawyer; b. Chgo., Aug. 3, 1955; d. Raymond L. and Lillian (Taylor) J. BA, Harvard U., 1977, JD, 1982. Bar: Ill. 1982, US Dist. Ct. (no. dist.) Ill. 1982, Calif. 1990, US Dist. Ct. (cen. dist.) Calif. 1990, US Ct. Appeals (7th cir. and 9th cir.) 1985, 1990. Assoc. Lord, Bissell & Brook, Chgo., 1982-85; asst. U.S. atty. no. dist. Ill. U.S. Atty.'s Office, Chgo., 1985-89; of counsel Orrick, Herrington & Sutcliffe, LA, 1989-91; ptnr. Bird, Marella, Boxer, Wolpert & Matz, LA, 1991-95; sr. counsel Abbott Labs., Abbott Park, Ill., 1995, SBC Comm.; pres. Jones Diversity Grp LLC, Chgo. Adj. prof. Northwestern Law Sch., Nat. Inst. for Trial Advocacy; cons. ABA Gen. Counsel Steering Com. Contbr. articles to profl. jour. Bd. dir. Harvard Club of Chgo., Harvard Law Soc., Ill, Just the Beginning Found., Housing Opportunities for Women; co-chair Harvard Law Sch. (celebration of black alumni); bd. mem. Fellows Assn. of Leadership Greater Chgo.; bd. mem. & vice chair YWCA of Met. Chgo. Mem.: Black Women Lawyers Assn. of Chgo. (pres. 2004—05), ABA (vice chair Pvt. Antitrust Litig. com. 1994—95, vice chair West Coast Com. of White Collar Crimes.). Office: Jones Diversity Grp LLC 225 W Washington St Ste 2200 Chicago IL 60606 Office Phone: 312-924-2824. Office Fax: 312-924-0201. Business E-Mail: Sharon@jonesdiversity.com.

JONES, SHELDON ATWELL, retired lawyer; b. Melrose, Mass., Apr. 20, 1938; s. Sheldon Atwell and Hannah Margaret (Andrews) J.; m. Priscilla Ann Hatch, Sept. 10, 1966; children: Sarah Percy, Abigail Atwell. BA, Yale U., 1959; LLB, Harvard U., 1965. Bar: Mass. 1965, U.S. Dist. Ct. Mass. 1967, Calif. 2001. Assoc. Gaston, Snow, Motley & Holt, Boston, 1965-72; ptnr. Gaston Snow & Ely Bartlett, Boston, 1972-87, Dechert LLP, Boston, Newport Beach, 1987—2003, ret., 2003. Past sec. H&Q Healthcare Investors, Boston. Contbr. articles to profl. jours. Lt. (j.g.) USN, 1959-62. Mem. Calif. State Bar Assn., Harvard Club. Avocations: skiing, sailing. Office: Dechert LLP 200 Clarendon St Boston MA 02116 Home: PO Box 692 Wolfeboro NH 03894-0692 Home Phone: 603-569-7818; Office Phone: 617-728-7123. E-mail: sheldon.jones@dechert.com.

JONES, SHERMAN J., cultural organization administrator, financial consultant, educator; b. Newport News, Va., Jan. 12, 1946; s. Sherman Edward and Leola Mae (Pryer) J.; children: Kimberly, Sherman Edward. BA in Am. Studies with honors, Williams Coll., 1968; MBA, Harvard U., 1970, EdD, 1978. Woodrow Wilson adminstrv. intern, asst. to pres. Cen. State U., Ohio, 1970-71; asst. dir. Office Coop. Acad. Planning Inst. for Svc. to Edn., Washington, 1971-72; mgmt. cons. Cresap, McCormick & Paget, Inc., Washington, 1972-75; mgmt. cons. mgmt. div. Acad. for Ednl. Devel., Inc., Washington, 1975-77; v.p. for adminstrn. Fisk U., Nashville, 1977-80, v.p., acting dean, 1980-82; exec. v.p., prof. mgmt. Tuskegee (Ala.) U., 1982-84, prof. mgmt., exec. v.p., provost, 1984-91; prof. mgmt., provost, v.p. for acad. affairs Clark Atlanta U., 1991-93; pres., headmaster So. Normal Sch., Brewton, Ala., 1993-96; investment rep. Edward D. Jones & Co., 1996-99; fin. advisor Prudential Securities, Inc., Atlanta, 1999—2002; v.p. devel. Knoxville Coll., Tenn., 2000—03; prin., owner Jones Fin. Svcs., Knoxville, 1996—2002; assoc. prof. bus. adminstrn. Tenn. Wesleyan Coll., Athens, 2005—06; v.p. Knoxville Area Urban League, 2007. Bd. dirs. Better Bus. Bur. Nashville/Middle Tenn., 1978-82; mgmt. bd. John A. Andrew Community Hosp., 1982-85; adv. bd. St. Andrews Sewanee Sch., Tenn., 1986-92, bd. trustees, 1993-97; mem. Nashville Coun. on Fgn. Rels., Kiwanis, 1997-.; bd. trustees YMCA, Brewton, Ala., 1995—97. Harvard Grad. Sch. Edn. teaching fellow in edn., 1976-77. Mem. Alumni Coun. Harvard Grad. Sch. Edn., Williams Coll. Exec. Coun. Alumni Soc, Leadership Knoxville, Kiwanis. Republican. Episcopalian. Avocations: sports, reading, tennis, weightlifting, cooking. Office: Knoxville Area Urban League 1514 E 5th Ave Knoxville TN 37917

JONES, SHIRLEY, actress, singer; b. Smithtown, Pa., Mar. 31, 1934; d. Paul and Marjorie (Williams) J.; m. Jack Cassidy, Aug. 5, 1956 (div. 1975); children: Shaun, Patrick, Ryan; m. Marty Ingels, 1977. Grad. high sch., 1952; student, Pitts. Playhouse. Appeared with chorus South Pacific, 1953, in Broadway prodn. Me and Juliet, 1954; other state appearences include The Beggar's Opera, 1957, The Red Mill, 1958, Maggie Flynn, 1968, On a Clear Day, 1975, Show Boat, 1976, Bitter Suite, 1983; films include role of Laurey in Oklahoma, 1954, later stage tour Paris and Rome, sponsorship U.S. Dept. State, Carousel, 1956, April Love, 1957, Never Steal Anything Small, 1959, Bobbikins, 1959, Elmer Gantry, 1960 (Acad. Best Supporting Actress award 1961), Pepe, 1960, The Two Rode Together, 1961, The Music Man, 1962, The Courtship of Eddie's Father, 1963, A Ticklish Affair, 1963, Bedtime Story, 1964, The Secret of My Success, 1965, Fluffy, 1965, The Happy Ending, 1969, The Cheyenne Social Club, 1970, Beyond the Poseidon Adventure, 1979, Tank, 1984, There Were Times, Dear, 1985; night club tour with husband, 1958, later TV and summer stock; star TV series The Partridge Family, 1970-74, Shirley, 1979; guest star: TV series McMillan, 1976; starred with Patrick Cassidy (Broadway): 42nd Street; Silent Night, Lonely Night, 1969, But I Don't Want To Get Married!, 1970, The Girls of Huntington House, 1973, The Family Nobody Wanted, 1975, The Lives of Jenny Dolan, 1975, Winner Take All, 1975, Yesterday's Child, 1977, Evening in Byzantium, 1978, Who'll Save Our Children, 1978, A Last Cry for Help, 1979, The Children Of An Lac, 1980, Inmates: A Love Story, 1981, There Were Times Dear, 1987, Carousel, 2005; one-woman concert: TV series Shirley Jones' America 1981; author: Shirley and Marty: An Unlikely Love Story, 1990. Nat. chairwoman Leukemia Found. Named Mother of Yr. by Women's Found., 1978. Office Phone: 818-728-9505. Business E-Mail: martyingels@msn.com.

JONES, SOPHIA LASHAWN, architect; b. Mt. Holly, NJ, Apr. 24, 1979; d. Stanley Roosevelt and Cynthia Ann Jones. BA in Architecture, U. Miami, 2003; MS in Hist. Preservation, U. Pa., 2005. Draftsman Teletronics Tech. Corp., Bristol, 2000, Clear Choice Windows and Doors, Miami, 2002—03; preservation intern Eastern State Penitentiary, Phila., 2003—04; program asst. N.J. Hist. Preservation Office, Trenton, NJ, 2004—05. Bd. dirs. N.J. Hist. Sites Coun. Recipient scholarship, Nat. Trust Hist. Preservation, 2004; grantee Illona English Travel fellowship, U. Pa., 2004. Mem.: AIA (assoc.), Black Grad. Profl. Student Assn. (recording sec. 2004—05), Pa. Student Preservation Assn. (v.p. 2004—05), Nat. Trust for Hist. Preservation. Avocations: travel, cooking. Office: Hist Bldg Arch 312 W State St Trenton NJ 08618 Home: 10 Garrett Ln Willingboro NJ 08046 E-mail: sj@hba-llc.com.

JONES, STANLEY BOYD, retired researcher; b. Balt., July 27, 1938; s. Arthur Boyd and Lillian Ailene (Powell) J.; m. Judith K. Miller, Mar. 9, 1981; children— Andrew, Jeffrey, Lisa, Julia. BA, Dartmouth Coll., 1960; postgrad., Yale U., 1960-63. Ordained Episc. priest., 1992. Mem. profl. staff Subcom. on Health, U.S. Senate, Washington, 1970-76; program devel. officer Inst. of Medicine, Nat. Acad. Scis., Washington, 1976-78; v.p. Fullerton, Jones & Wollkstein (Health Policy Alternatives), Washington, 1978-80; v.p. for Washington representation Nat. Assns. Blue Cross and Blue Shield Plans, 1980-83; prin. Health Policy Alternatives, 1983-86; pres. Consol. Healthcare, 1986-89; ind. cons. on health policy Washington, 1989—; clergyman Diocese of W.Va., 1992—2004; dir. Health Ins. Reform Project George Washington U., 1994-99. Commr. D.C. Gen. Hosp. Mem. Inst. of Medicine of Nat. Acad. Scis. Office: 2021 K St NW Washington DC 20006-1003 Personal E-mail: stan@stanjudyjones.com.

JONES, STANTON WILLIAM, management consultant; b. New Orleans, May 24, 1939; s. Albert DeWitt and Clara Arimenta (Stanton) J.; m. Gladys Marina Caceres, Aug. 22, 1990; children: Hazel Nathalye, Albert Stanton, 1 child from a previous marriage, Ellen Marie. BS, Embry-Riddle Aero. U., Daytona Beach, Fla., 1973; MBA, Syracuse U., NY, 1977. Cert. internal auditor. Commd. 2d lt. U.S. Army, 1963, advanced through grades to lt. col., 1979, fixed wing pilot Ft. Rucker, Ala., 1965-72, rotary wing pilot, 1972; mgmt. cons. Stanton W. Jones & Assocs., San Francisco, 1987—. Joint venture ptnr. Budget Analyst to Bd. Suprs., San Francisco, 1988—. Decorated Meritorious Svc. medal. Mem. Alpha Phi Alpha (pres. 1988-90). Roman Catholic. Avocations: chess, reading, jogging. Home: 1948 Cortereal Ave Oakland CA 94611-2632 Office: Stanton W Jones & Assocs 57 Post St Ste 713 San Francisco CA 94104-5025 Home Phone: 510-339-8738; Office Phone: 415-399-1013. Personal E-mail: stantonj@aol.com.

JONES, STEPHANIE TUBBS, congresswoman, lawyer, prosecutor; b. Cleve., Sept. 10, 1949; m. Mervyn L. Jones, Sr. (dec.); 1 child. BA in Sociology, Case Western Res. U. Flora Mather Coll., 1971; JD, Case Western Res. U. Sch. Law, 1974; D (hon.), Myers U., Notre Dame Coll., Ctrl. State U. Bar: Ohio 1974, US Dist. Ct. (no. dist.) Ohio 1975, US Ct. Appeals (6th cir.) 1981, US Supreme Ct. 1981. Asst. gen. counsel, EEO adminstr. N.E. Ohio Regional Sewer Dist., 1974-76; asst. prosecutor Cuyahoga County Prosecutor's Office, 1976-79; trial atty. Cleve. dist. office EEO, 1979-81; judge Cleve. Mcpl. Ct., 1982-83, Cuyahoga County Ct. of Common Pleas, 1983-91; prosecutor Cuyahoga County, Cleve., 1991-98; mem. US Congress from 11th Ohio dist., 1999—, mem. small bus. com., 1999—2002, mem. banking and fin. svcs. com., 1999—2002, mem. ways and means com., 2003—, chairwoman stds. of official conduct com. Vis. com. bd. overseers Franklin Thomas Backus Sch. Law, Case Western Res. U. Bd. trustees Cmty. Re-entry Prog.; bd. trustees class of 1984 Leadership Cleve. Alumnae; mem. Task Force on Violent Crime, Substance Abuse Initiative; trustee Cleve. Police Hist. Soc.; bd. trustees

Bethany Bapt. Ch. Recipient Outstanding Vol. Svcs. in Law and Justice award Urban League Greater Cleve., 1986, Women of Yr. award Cleve. chpt. Nat. Assn. Negro Bus. and Profl. Women's Clubs, Inc., 1987, award in recognition of outstanding svc. to judiciary and black cmty. Midwest region Nat. Black Am. Law Student Assn., 1988, Career Women of Achievement award YWCA, 1991, Disting. Svc. award Cleve. chpt. NAACP, 1997; named Black Profl. of Yr., Black Profl. Assn. Cleve., 1995, 1994; named one of Most Influential Black Americans, Ebony mag., 2006; Ohio Dem. of Yr., Ohio Dem. Party, 1995; inductee Collinwood HS Hall of Fame, 1994, Soc. Benchers of Case Western Res. U. Sch. Law, 1996. Mem. ABA, Nat. Black Prosecutor's Assn., Nat. Dist. Atty.'s Assn. (met. prosecutor's com.), Nat. Coun. Negro Women, Nat. Coll. Dist. Attys. (bd. regents), Ohio State Bar Assn. (Nettie Cronise Lutes award 1997), Ohio Prosecuting Attys. Assn. (exec. com.), Cleve. Bar Assn. (trustee), Norman S. Miner Bar Assn. (past treas.), Cuyahoga Women's Polit. Caucus, Delta Sigma Theta (Greater Cleve. Alumnae chpt., Althea Simmons award 1993). Democrat. Baptist. Office: US House Reps 1009 Longworth House Office Bldg Washington DC 20515-3511 Office Phone: 202-225-7032. Office Fax: 202-225-1339. E-mail: Stephanie.Tubbs.Jones@mail.house.gov.*

JONES, STEPHEN, lawyer; b. Lafayette, La., July 1, 1940; s. Leslie William and Gladys A. (Williams) J.; m. Virginia Hadden (dec.); 1 child, John Chapman; m. Sherrel Alice Stephens, Dec. 27, 1973; children: Stephen Mark, Leslie Rachael, Edward St. Andrew. Student, U. Tex., 1960—63; LLB, U. Okla., 1966. Sec. Rep. Minority Conf., Tex. Ho. of Reps., 1963; personal asst. to Richard M. Nixon NYC, 1964; adminstrv. asst. to Congressman Paul Findley, 1966-69; legal counsel to gov. of Okla., 1967; spl. asst. U.S. Senator Charles H. Percy and U.S. Rep. Donald Rumsfeld, 1968; mem. U.S. del. to North Atlantic Assembly NATO, 1968; staff counsel censure task force Ho. of Reps. Impeachment Inquiry, 1974; spl. U.S. atty. No. Dist. Okla., 1979; spl. prosecutor, spl. asst. dist. atty. State of Okla., 1977; judge Okla. Ct. Appeals, 1982; civil jury instrn. com. Okla. Supreme Ct., 1979—81; adv. com. ct. rules Okla. Ct. Criminal Appeals, 1980; now mng. ptnr. Stephen Jones & Assoc., Enid, Okla. Adj. prof. U. Okla., 1973—76; instr. Phillips U., 1982—90; bd. dirs. Coun. on the Nat. Interest Found. Author: Oklahoma and Politics in State and Nation, 1907-62, 1974, Others Unknown: The Oklahoma City Bombing Case and Conspiracy, 1998; co-author: France and China, The First Ten Years, 1964-74, 1991, Vernon's Oklahoma Forms 2d Criminal Practice & Procedure Vols. I, II, 1999; contbr. articles to profl. jours. Bd. dirs., coun. mem. Nat. Interest Found.; acting chmn. Rep. State Com., Okla., 1982; Rep. nominee Okla. atty. gen., 1974, U.S. Senate, 1990; mem. Rep. State Fin. Com., 2006—; spl. counsel to Gov. Okla., 1995; apptd. chief def. counsel by U.S. Dist. Ct., Oklahoma City, U.S. vs. Tim McVeigh, Oklahoma City Bombing Case, 1995-97; mem. vestry St. Matthews Episc. Ch., 1974, sr. warden, 1983-84, 89-90. Mem.: Okla. Bar Assn., Garfield County Bar Assn., Beacon Club. Office: PO Box 472 Enid OK 73702-0472 Office Phone: 580-242-5500. Business E-Mail: sjones@stephenjoneslaw.com.

JONES, STEPHEN B., academic administrator; m. Judy Jones; 2 children. BS, SUNY, Syracuse, PhD in Resources Mgmt. Dir. Ala. Coop. Ext. Sys., 1997—2001; vice chancellor ext. and engagement, prof. Coll. Nat. Resources NC State U., 2001—04; chancellor U. Alaska, Fairbanks, 2004—. Office: University of Alaska Chancellor's Office PO Box 757500 Fairbanks AK 99775

JONES, STEPHEN WITSELL, lawyer; b. Honolulu, Aug. 12, 1947; s. Allen Newton Jr. and Maude Estelle (Witsell) J.; m. Judy Kaye Mason, Aug. 13, 1977; children: MaryAnn, Adam, Kathleen. Student, Hendrix Coll., 1965—66; AB with high honors, U. Ill., 1969; JD with highest honors, U. Ark., Little Rock, 1978. Bar: Ark. 1978, U.S. Dist. Ct. (ea. and we. dists.) Ark. 1978, U.S. Ct. Appeals (7th and 8th cirs.) 1978, U.S. Supreme Ct. 1984. Rsch. statistician Ark. Dept. Parks and Tourism, Little Rock, 1971—72, dir. tourist info. ctr., 1972—74; affirmative action specialist Office of the Gov., Little Rock, 1974—75; dir. pers. Ark. Social Svcs. Div., Little Rock, 1975—77; mgmt. info. specialist Ark. Health Dept., Little Rock, 1977—78; assoc. House, Holmes & Jewell, Little Rock, 1978—84; ptnr. House, Wallace, Nelson & Jewell, Little Rock, 1984—86; ptnr., founding mem. Jack, Lyon & Jones, P.A., Little Rock, 1986—2007, Jack, Jones, Fink, Jiles & Gregory P.A., Little Rock, 2007—. Adj. instr. div. lifelong edn. U. Ark., Little Rock, 1992-95. Co-author: Employment Law Deskbook for Arkansas Employers, 1997; editor-in-chief U. Ark. Little Rock Law Rev., 1977; editor Ark. Employment Law Letter, 1996—; contbr. chpt.: Employment Discrimination Law, 2d edit., 1983. Bd. dirs. United Cerebral Palsy of Ctrl. Ark., Little Rock, 1978-2005. With U.S. Army, 1969-71 Recipient Svc. Recognition award United Cerebral Palsy of Ctrl. Ark., 1986, 95. Fellow Coll. Labor and Employment Lawyers, Greater Little Rock C. of C.; mem. ABA (labor/litigation law practice mgmt. sect.), Ark. Bar Assn., Def. Rsch. Inst., Ark. State C. of C. (bd. dirs., chair health com.). Episcopalian. Avocations: photography, golf. Home: 1724 S Arch St Little Rock AR 72206-1215 Office: Jack Jones Fink Jiles & Gregory PA 425 W Capitol Ave Ste 3400 Little Rock AR 72201-3405 Home Phone: 501-374-8101; Office Phone: 501-375-1122. Personal E-mail: swj010@hotmail.com.

JONES, STEVEN EARL, physics educator, researcher; b. Pocatello, Idaho, Mar. 25, 1949; s. Leroy Earl and Adren (Keller) J., m. Lezlee Danelle Chapman, Jan. 22, 1975; children: Seth, David, Danelle, Rebecca, Nathan, Rachel, Michelle. BS, Brigham Young U., 1973; PhD, Vanderbilt U., 1978. Postdoctoral fellowship U. Wyo., Laramie, 1978-79; sr. rschr. Idaho Nat. Engring. Lab., Idaho Falls, 1979-1985; assoc. prof. physics Brigham Young U., Provo, Utah, 1985, prof. Dept. of Physics and Astronomy. Spokesperson, Los Alamos (N. Mex.) Meson Physics Facility experiments, 1982-1990; prin. investigator muon-catalyzed fusion, U.S. Dept. Energy, Provo, 1982-1990, cold fusion, 1986—; cons., Lawrence Livermore Nat. Lab., Livermore, Calif., 1985-1988; Electric Power Rsch. Inst., Palo Alto, Calif., 1987-88, 1990—; assoc. dir. Ctr. for Fusion Studies Brigham Young U., 1989—; founder, co-chair Scholars for 9/11 Truth Editor: Fla. Muon-Catalyzing Fusion Workshop, 1988, Provo Anomalous Nuclear Effects in Deuterium/Solid Systems Conf., 1990; contbr. articles to profl. jours. Coord. Boy Scouts Am., Provo, 1987—. David O. MacKay scholar, Brigham Young U., 1968, Rsch. Fellowship scholar, Vanderbilt U., 1973; grantee U.S. Dept. Energy, 1982, 1985, 1987, 1990. Mem. Am. Phys. Soc., Sigma Pi Sigma, Phi Kappa Phi. Mem. Lds Ch. Avocations: playing piano, hiking, mountain climbing. Home: 190 E 4680 N Provo UT 84604-5448 Office Phone: 801-378-2749. E-mail: stevejones@byu.edu.*

JONES, SUSAN DORFMAN, real estate broker, writer; b. NYC, Oct. 4, 1939; d. Joseph and Sarah (Sorrin) Dorfman; m. William Harry Jones, Sept. 18, 1960; children: Jeffrey Scott, Eric David, Timothy Mark BA, Syracuse U., 1961. Pres., owner Antiques Corp. Am., 1972—77, Susan & Sons Antiques, 1977—; comm. officer Riggs Bank, Washington, 1978—81; mgr. publs. Potomac Electric Power Co., Washington, 1981—82; sr. mgr. corp. comm. MCI Corp., Washington, 1982—83; dir. corp. comm. Sears World Trade, Washington, 1983—85; dir. corp. comm. and govt. rels. Oxford Devel. Corp., Bethesda, Md., 1985—87; comm. expert pub. health svc./health and human svcs. U.S. Alcohol, Drug Abuse, Mental Health Adminstrn., Rockville, Md., 1989—91; real estate broker Weichert Realtors, Washington, 1991—. Vol. staff Cleve. Clinics, Cleve. Jewish Cmty. Ctr. Book Fair, Cleve. HS of Arts, 2003-; free-lance writer, cons., Washington, 1975-92; radio personality Sta. 4KQ, Brisbane, Australia, 1962; adj. prof. comms. Am. U., Washington, 1978-82. Author, editor, project mgr. corp. ann. reports. Recipient 1st pl. award for columns N.Y. Press Assn., 1961, Gold Quill award Internat. Assn. Bus. Communicators, 1980. Mem.: Greater Capital Area Assn. Realtors, Nat. Assn. Realtors, Pub. Rels. Soc. Am., Women in Telecommunications, Nat. Assn. Bank Women, Internat. Assn. Bus. Communicators, Jewish Cmty. Ctr. Cleve., Nat. Press Club. Democrat. Jewish. Avocations: tai chi, sewing, knitting, reading. Home and Office: 30650 Jackson Rd Chagrin Falls OH 44022-1731 Office: 5035 Wisconsin Ave NW Washington DC 20016-4113 Office Phone: 216-375-5554. Personal E-mail: suebillj@yahoo.com.

JONES, SUSAN EMILY, fashion educator, administrator, educator emeritus; b. NYC, Sept. 9, 1948; d. David and Emily Helen (Welke) J.; m. Henry J. Titone, Jr., Oct. 21, 1974 (div. 1980); m. Douglas S. Robbins, Aug. 21, 1985. BFA, Pratt Inst., Bklyn., 1970. Designer Sue Brett, NYC, 1970-74, St. Tropez, 1975; prof. fashion Pratt Inst., Bklyn., 1972-2000, chairperson fashion dept., 1981-2000, chairperson merchandising and design programs fashion dept., 1983-2000; computer software cons., 1988-89; owner, designer Sej Wearable Artworks, 1992—. Internat. observer Jeunes Createurs de Mode, Paris, 1987, judge, 1988; U.S. rep. SAGA Internat. Design Ctr., Copenhagen, 1992, serdesigns, Hawaii, 2001—. Tech. book reviewer, 1994—. Recipient Young Am. Designer award Internat. Ladies Garment Workers Union, 1970, Ptnr. in Edn. award N.Y.C. Pub. Sch. Sys. Chancellor, 1992-93. Mem. Fashion Group (regional com. 1983-87, mem. com. 1990-93, ednl. com. 1995-96, co-chair ednl. com. 1996-98), Nat. Retail Fedn., Under Fashion Assn. Office: Pratt Inst Dept of Fashion Design 200 Willoughby Ave Brooklyn NY 11205-3899 Personal E-mail: sejpratt@aol.com. Business E-Mail: sjones@pratt.edu, serdesigns@aol.com.

JONES, SYLVANUS BENSON, legal association administrator, consultant; b. Southport, NC, Nov. 21, 1928; s. Thomas Henry and Katie Mable J.; m. Karen Ann Charbonneau, Aug. 10, 1970 (div. May 1975); 1 child, Donovan; m. Brenda Castleyoung-Jones, Sept. 9, 1999. Student, Howard U., 1945-48; AD in Fin., Peter's Bus. Coll., Washington, 1955; postgrad., Fgn. Svc. Inst., Arlington, Va., 1956, George Washington U., 1959-60, Bibliothèque de la Sorbonne U. de Paris, Paris, 1962, Georgetown U., Washington, 1962, Am. U., 1966-68. Lic. real estate agt.; lic. gen. contractor, Md.; lic. ins. agt., Md., D.C. Enumerator, IBM computer operator U.S. Census Bur., Suitland, Md., 1950-51; clk. typist, claims divsn. VA, Washington, 1951-52; rsch. clk. Bur. Security and Consular Affairs, U.S. Dept. State, Washington, 1952-53, supr. passport processing sect., 1953-56, from jr. to sr. adjudicator domestic adjudication divsn., 1956-61, consular affairs officer adv. opinions divsn., 1961-63, chief pvt. bill staff, office of dep. dir. for ops., 1963-68, chief fraud and investigation unit, 1968-72; adjudicator, gen. cons., 1972—. Editor-in-chief The Washington Press, 1957-63; founder, dir. Mut. Fund Investment Program for Govt. Employees, Washington, 1969-73; instr. Tennis U. Puebla (Mex.), 1973-75; editor-in-chief The Annapolis (Md.) Press, 1989—; chmn. ad hoc com. to repeal the utilities tax, Annapolis, 1992—. Contbr. articles to profl. jours; grantee hub cap locking device. Treas. Annapolis City Dem. Ctrl. Com., 1992, 97; Dem. candidate for mayor, Annapolis, 1993, 97, 2001; chmn. trans. adv. bd., Annapolis, 1992-98. Recipient Cert. of Disting. Citizenship, City of Annapolis, 1987, 97, 99, Gov.'s Citation for Outstanding Svc. to Citizens, State of Md., 1997, 99, Red Cross Citizenship award, Trailblazer award U.S. Dept. State, 1998; numerous meritorious svc. awards; Howard U. scholar.

JONES, SYLVIA CALPURNIA, investment company executive; b. Race Course Clarendon, Jamaica, Aug. 16, 1936; d. Aldron Benjamin and Vera Gwendolyn Taylor; m. Walter Gerald Jones, Feb. 7, 1959; children: Gerald, Ashford, Sean, Chester Rhoan, Desiree. BSc, Agrl. State U., Greensboro, NC, 1967; MA, Montclair State U., NJ, 1969; postgrad., U. Mass., Amherst. Tchr. Ministry of Edn., Kingston, Jamaica, 1958—64; tchr. home econs. Newark Bd. Edn., 1967—92; owner S&J Investment, Montclair, 1979—. Examiner Mid. States Accreditation Com., Trenton Ctrl. HS, NJ, West Babylon HS, NY. Recipient Key to City of Montclair, 1988. Mem.: NAACP, Am. Inst. Cancer Rsch., Am. Cancer Soc., Am. Diabetic Assn., So. Poverty Law Ctr. Home: 257 Orange Rd Montclair NJ 07042

JONES, TAD, state representative; b. Tucson, Oct. 23, 1972; s. Ted and Corky (Burkert) Jones; m. Samantha Hamilton Jones; children: Logan Benjamin, Blake Alexander. BS in Mktg., U. Tulsa, 1996. Intern Senator Don Nickles; co-founder Miket Ads Sign Corp.; mem. Okla. Ho. of Reps., 1999—, chair appropriations and budget subcommittee edn., asst. majority floor leader. Mem.: Am. Legis. Action Coun., Fellowship Christian Athletes, Oologah Sch. Found., Rotary (sgt. at arms). Republican. Office: State Capitol 2300 N Lincoln Blvd Rm 301 A Oklahoma City OK 73105

JONES, TERRENCE DALE, foundation executive, consultant; b. Kansas City, Mo., Jan. 11, 1948; s. Bobby J. and Ida Lorene (Overstreet) Jones; m. Polly Nell McDowell, 1992; 1 child, Eryn. BS, U. Kans., 1970, MA, 1972; MFA, U. Ga., 1971. Mgr., dir. Bradford Repertory Theatre, Vt., 1970-71; designer, instr. Miami-Dade CC, Fla., 1972-74; designer, asst. prof. Grinnell Coll., Iowa, 1974-76; mng. dir., asst. prof. Kirkland Fine Arts Ctr., Millikin U., Decatur, Ill., 1976-81; gen. mgr., asst. dean Clowes Meml. Hall/Jordal Coll. Fine Arts, Butler U., Indpls., 1981-86; dir. Krannert Ctr. for Performing Arts U. Ill., Urbana, 1986-96; pres., CEO Wolf Trap Found. Performing Arts, Vienna, Va., 1996—. Arts cons., Ohio, Tex., Wis., Ind., Ill., N.Mex., Australia, Greece, Turkey; mem. panel NEA, end. conf. chmn.; mem. theater and film. profl. adv. bd. U. Kans.; spkr., panel leader Renaissance Weekend, 1998—2005; facilitator Western Arts Alliance Leadership Inst., 2005. Prodr.: (plays) Achilles: A Kabuki Play, 1991. Mem. panel performing arts touring program Va. Commn. Arts; bd. dirs. Cultural Alliance Greater Washington, 1997—; bd. dirs., exec. com. Ill. Arts Alliance, Ill. Presenters Network. Recipient Best Lighting Design award, Unvi. Theatre, U. Kans., Lawrence, 1970, Dawson Arts Mgmt. award, 1989. Mem.: Assn. Performing Arts Presenters (bd. dirs. 1986—88, Fan Taylor Disting. Svc. award 2005), Am. Arts Alliance, Internat. Soc. Performing Arts (mem. edn. com. 1997—), Internat. Assn. Auditorium Mgrs., Fairfax County C. of C. (bd. dirs., U. Kans. Disting. Achievement award 2004), Nat. Press Club (guest spkr. 2001—06). Methodist. Avocations: golf, historical novels, classic films, welsh heritage. Office: Wolf Trap Found for Performing Arts 1645 Trap Rd Vienna VA 22182-2063 Office Phone: 703-255-1900.

JONES, THEODORE T., JR., judge; b. Bklyn., 1944; m. Joan Hogans; children: Theodore III, Wesley. Grad. in Edn. and Polit. Sci., Hampton U., Va.; JD, St. John's, Queens, NY, 1972. Bar: NY 1973. Law sec. for Judge Howard A. Jones NY State Ct. of Claims; pvt. practice atty.; justice NY State Supreme Ct., Kings County, 1990—2007; assoc. judge NY State Ct. Appeals, Poughkeepsie, NY, 2007—. Tchr. NYC Pub. Schs.; criminal def. lawyer Legal Aid Soc.; adminstrv. judge civil term NY State Supreme Ct., Kings County, 2006—07. Capt. US Army, 1967—69, Vietnam. Recipient Jud. Excellence award, Bklyn. Bar Assn. Office: State NY Ct Appeals 20 Eagle St Albany NY 12207-1095 Office Phone: 347-296-1483.*

JONES, THOMAS CLABURN, poet, educator; s. Thomas and Margaret Jones; m. Karin K. Krueger, Nov. 29, 1980; children: Thomas Claburn, Caroline Hollingsworth, Elizabeth Phillips, Drew Bartholomew Vandervelde, Margaret Alfaretta; m. Catherine Schlumberger, Aug. 29, 1964 (div. 1980). BA, Harvard U., Cambridge, Mass., 1964; diploma of French Civilization Studies, Sorbonne U. Paris, 1962; diploma of German Lang. and Lit.-Oberstufe, Goethe Inst., 1963; JD, Columbia U., NYC, 1968; MFA in Creative Writing, George Mason U., Fairfax, Va., 1992. Bar: State Bar Wis. 1980. Rep. Amnesty Internat., Washington, 1972—79; tchr. Greyhills Acad. H.S., Tuba City, Ariz., 1994—98, dean, lang. arts dept., 1997—98; tchr., lang. arts Tuba City H.S., 1998—. Mission del. Egypt Amnesty Internat., London, 1979, mission del. Malaysia, Singapore, Brunei, 78, mission del. Philippines, 75, mission del. Spain, 75; vis. prof. poetry Visva Bharati U., Santiniketan, India, 1992; adj. prof. Navajo C.C., Tuba City, 1993—94; featured spkr. Amnesty Internat. Human Rights Week, Weber State U., 2006. Writer (collections of poems) No Prisoners, 1976, Footbridge to India, 1990, Madmen and Bassoons, 1992, Green Lake, 1996, (collections of poems) Rez Dreamtime, 2001, Writing on Horseback, 2004, India Poems: Songs of Sarasvati, 2004; translator: (collections of poems) Book of Fragments, poems by Rei Berroa, co-translated with the author, Songbook of Absences, poems by Miguel Hernandez; featured writer: Rocky Mountain Writers Festival, 2006. Dist. atty. Green Lake County, Wis., 1983—84.

JONES, THOMAS OWEN, computer company executive; b. Phila., Apr. 6, 1932; s. Paul John and Katharine (McCahey) J.; m. Mary Louise Russell, Sept. 19, 1959 (div. Aug. 1979); children: SusanR., Thomas H., Andrew S. BS in Engring., U. Pa., 1954, MBA, 1958. Account mgr. IBM Corp., Phila., 1958-66; asst. to sec. HEW, Washington, 1966-67; v.p. Donaldson, Lufkin & Jenrette, Inc., NYC, 1967-72; pres. Jones/Hosplex Sys., NYC, 1973-84, Carnegie-Madison Inc., NYC, 1984-87, Fifth Generation Computer Corp., NYC, 1987—, Golden Enterprises, Inc., Melbourne, Fla., 1999. Lectr. fin. Temple U. Evening Sch. Bus., 1959-66; cons. to sec. HEW, Washington, 1967-68; mem. Edn. Commr.'s Adv. Coun. on Copyright Policy, Washington, 1967-70. Mem. N.Y. State Adv. Coun. on Edn., Albany, 1970-75; mem. N.Y.C. #4 Cmty. Planning Bd., 1973-75. With U.S. Army, 1954-56. White House fellow U.S. Commn. on White House Fellows, Washington, 1966-67; named Outstanding Young Man of the Main Line, Jr. C. of C., Bryn Mawr, Pa., 1966. Mem.: IEEE, NY Acad. Scis., Wharton Alumni Assocs. (exec. bd. 1993—2000), Am. Legion, Union League Club Phila., NY Athletic Club. Avocations: tennis, travel. Home Phone: 800-707-0342; Office Phone: 212-756-0964. Personal E-mail: tojones@aol.com. Business E-Mail: tojones@fifthgen.com.

JONES, THOMAS OWEN, JR., finance educator, military officer; b. Washington, June 24, 1935; s. Thomas Owen Jones and Annie May Bell; m. Jasie Barringer, Nov., 1982 (div. Nov. 1989); m. Phyllis Stepp Cage, Oct. 10, 1990; stepchildren: Rebecca Lynn, Julie Gayle Cage. BSME, U. Pa., 1957; BSBA, U. Southwestern La., 1966; MBA, George Washington U., 1968, D of Bus. Adminstrn., 1972. Lic. comml. pilot, bldg. contractor, N.C.; cert. flight instr. Officer (ret.), naval aviator USN, 1958-2000; asst. and acting dean Coll. Bus. Loyola U., New Orleans, 1971-74; dean Sch. Bus., Eastern Ill. U., 1974-78; pres., CEO, Galleries One, NYC, 1978-85; founder, chmn. TJA Consulting, Washington, 1976-85; founder, CEO, chmn. BillPayers, Inc., Greensboro, NC, 1985-99; chmn. divsn. bus. Greensboro Coll., 1986—2005, Fred L. Proctor Sr. prof. bus., emeritus, 2005; vis. prof. bus. Meredith Coll., 2005—. Founding ptnr. Boston Consulting Group, Cambridge, Mass., 1966. Bd. dirs. Prison Ministry of N.C., 1998-2000. Rear admiral USNR, 1958-2000, ret. Recipient Gold medal Pan Am. Games, Mexico City, 1955, Gold medal Am. Canoeing Assn., 1957, Silver medal Olympic Games, Melbourne, Australia, 1956; 12 rowing championships Am. Rowing Assn., 1952-61., Fellow Acad. Mgmt.; mem. Assn. Exptl. Test Pilots, Greensboro City Club, Kiwanis, Beta Gamma Sigma. Republican. Presbyterian. Avocations: home building, teaching sunday school, demonstration piloting, coaching rowing. Home: 1221 Edenham Way Greensboro NC 27410 Home Phone: 336-288-7570. Personal E-mail: billpayers@aol.com.

JONES, THORNTON KEITH, chemist, researcher; b. Brawley, Calif., Dec. 17, 1923; s. Alfred George and Madge Jones; m. Evalee Vestal, July 4, 1965; children: Brian Keith, Donna Eileen. BS, U. Calif., Berkeley, 1949, postgrad., 1951-52. Research chemist Griffin Chem. Co., Richmond, Calif., 1949-55; western product devel. and improvement mgr. Nopco Chem. Co., Richmond, Calif., 1955; research chemist Chevron Research Co., Richmond, 1956-65, research chemist in spl. products research and devel., 1965-1982; product quality mgr. Chevron USA, Inc., San Francisco, 1982-87, ret. Vol. fireman and officer, Terra Linda, Calif., 1957-64; mem. adv. com. Terra Linda Dixie Elem. Sch. Dist., 1960-64. Served with Signal Corps, U.S. Army, 1943-46. Mem. Am. Chem. Soc., Forest Products Research Soc., Am. Wood Preservers Assn., Alpha Chi Sigma. Republican. Presbyterian. Achievements include patents in field. Avocations: music, gardening.

JONES, TIMOTHY R., plastic surgeon, director; b. Shawnee, Okla., Aug. 24, 1958; Grad. with distinction, U. Okla., MD, 1983. Cert. in plastic and reconstructive surgery, in otolaryngology. Internship otolaryngical head and neck surgery U. Va., Charlottesville, 1983—84, resident plastic surgery, 1984—88; resident U. Pitts., 1989—91; asst. prof. plastic and reconstructive surgery Washington U. Sch. Medicine, 1991—98; founder, CEO Genesis Cosmetic Surgery Ctr. and Med. Spa, St. Louis, 1998—. Dir. Cosmetic Surgery and Laser Ctr.; with Missouri-Baptist Med. Ctr., Barnes-Jewish West County Hosp., HealthSouth Surgery Ctrs. Fellow: Am. Coll. Surgeons; mem.: AMA, Am. Acad. Facial Plastic & Reconstructive Surgeons, Am. Soc. Plastic and Reconstruction Surgeons, Am. Soc. Aesthetic Plastic Surgery, Alpha Omega Alpha. Office: 456 N New Ballas Rd Ste 290 Saint Louis MO 63141*

JONES, SIR TOM (THOMAS JONES WOODWARD), singer; b. Pontypridd, Wales, June 7, 1940; s. Thomas and Freda (Jones) Woodward; m. Melinda Trenchard, 1956; 1 son, Mark. Student, Treforrest Secondary Modern Sch. Bricklayer, factory and constrn. laborer. Pub. singing debut at age 3 in village stores of Wales; sang in local pubs; changed name to Tom Jones, 1963; organized backup group the Playboys to sing in London clubs; first hit record was It's Not Unusual, 1964; appeared on Brit. radio and TV; toured U.S. in 1965, 68; appeared on Ed Sullivan Show; star of TV show This is Tom Jones, 1969-71; regular appearances in nightclubs, concert halls and on TV; songs recorded include What's New Pussycat, 1965, Thunderball, 1965, Green Green Grass of Home, 1966, Delilah, 1968, Love Me Tonight, 1969, Can't Stop Loving You, 1970, She's A Lady, 1971, Letter to Lucille, 1973, Say You'll Stay Until Tomorrow, 1976; albums Darlin, 1981, Move Closer, 1989, Carrying A Torch, 1990 (includes collaborations with Van Morrison); sang score for mus. play Matador; hit single A Boy From Nowhere, 1987, Kiss (in collaboration with Art of Noise), 1988, The Complete Tom Jones, 1993, Reload, 1999 (multi-platinum worldwide), Best of Tom Jones, 2000; film appearances include Mars Attacks, 1996, Agnes Brown, 1999, The Emperor's New Groove, 2000; TV appearances include Here, There and Everywhere: a Concert for Linda, 1999, Jerry Springer on Sunday, 1999, An Audience with Tom Jones, 2000, Millenium Celebrations at the White House, 2000, Queen's Jubilee Concert, 2002; TV series The Morecambe & Wise Show, The Sonny and Cher Show, (voice) The Simpsons, The Fresh Prince of Bel-Air, Russell Gilbert Live, The Panel, 20/20. Recipient Grammy award as Best New Artist, 1965, Brit. Best Male Vocalist award, 2003, Brit. Outstanding Contbn. award, 2003, Order Brit. Empire (OBE), 2006. Office: Tom Jones Enterprises 1801 Avenue Of The Stars Ste 200 Los Angeles CA 90067-5904

JONES, TONY, academic administrator; Dir. Glasgow Sch. Arts, 1980—86; pres. Sch. Art Inst. Chgo., 1986—92; dir. Royal Coll. Art, London, 1992—96; pres. & co-CEO Sch. Art Inst. Chgo., 1996—. Named Hon. Dir. Bd., Osaka U. Arts (Japan), 2000, Hon. Prof., U. Wales, 1995; recipient Scotland's Newbery Medal, 1986. Fellow: Royal Coll. Art (sr.); mem.: Am. Inst. Architects (hon.). Office: School of Art Institute of Chicago Office of the President 37 S Wabash Ave Ste 821 Chicago IL 60603 Office Phone: 312-899-5136. Office Fax: 312-263-5629. E-mail: tonyjones@saic.edu.*

JONES, TRACEY KIRK, JR., retired minister, educator; b. Boston, Mar. 16, 1917; s. Tracey Kirk and Marion (Flowers) J.; m. Martha Clayton, Sept.

12, 1942 (dec. June 1975); children: Judith Grace Watson, Tracey Kirk Jones, III, Deborah Anita Jones Breitenbach; m. Junia K. Moss, July 1, 1978. BA, D.D., Ohio Wesleyan U.; B.D., Yale Div. Sch., 1942. Ordained to ministry Meth. Church, 1945; missionary Meth. Ch., China, 1946-50, Malaya, 1952-55, exec. bd. mission, 1955; exec. sec. S.E. Asia, 1955-62; assoc. gen. sec. div. world missions, 1962-64; assoc. gen. sec. world div., 1964-68; gen. sec. bd. missions, 1968-72; gen. sec. bd. global ministries, 1972-80. Adj. prof. Drew Theol. Sch., Madison, N.J., 1980-89; mem. governing bd. Nat. Coun. Chs., 1st v.p., 1978-80. Author: Our Mission Today, 1963. Home: 700 John Ringling Blvd Apt W308 Sarasota FL 34236-1588

JONES, TREVOR OWEN, biomedical industry executive, management consultant; b. Maidstone, Kent, Eng., Nov. 3, 1930; came to U.S., 1957, naturalized, 1971; s. Richard Owen and Ruby Edith (Martin) J.; m. Jennie Lou Singleton, Sept. 12, 1959; children: Pembroke Robinson (dec.), Bronwyn Elizabeth. Higher Nat. Cert. in Elec. Engring., Aston Tech. Coll., Birmingham, Eng., 1952; Ordinary Nat. Cert. in Mech. Engring., Liverpool Tech. Coll., Eng., 1957; DSc (hon.), Cleve. State U., 2006. Registered profl. engr., Wis.; chartered engr., U.K. Student engr., elec. machine design engr. Brit. Gen. Electric Co., 1950-57; project engr., project mgr. Nuc. Ship Savannah, Allis-Chalmers Mfg. Co., 1957-59; with GM, 1959-78, staff engr. in charge Apollo computers, 1967, dir. electronic control sys., 1970-72, dir. advanced product engring., 1972-74; dir. GM Proving Grounds, 1974-78; v.p. engring., automotive worldwide TRW Inc., Cleve., 1978-80, v.p. transp. electronics group, 1980-87; chmn. bd. dirs. Libbey-Owens-Ford Inc., 1987-94; chmn., CEO Internat. Devel. Corp., 1987—; from vice chmn. to chmn. Echlin Inc., 1995-98, chmn. bd. dir., interim pres. and CEO, 1997; chmn., founder, CEO Biomec Inc., 1998—2007; chmn. Electrosonics Med., Inc., 2007—, CEO, 2007—. Chmn. emeritus Ohio Fuel Cell Coalition; vice chmn. Motor Vehicle Safety Adv. Coun., 1971; chmn. Nat. Hwy. Safety Adv. Com., 1976; assoc. NRC, 2002. Author, patentee automotive safety and electronics. Trustee Lawrence Inst. Tech., 1973-76; exec. bd. Clinton Valley coun. Boy Scouts Am., 1975; bd. govs. Cranbrook Inst. Sci., 1977; mem. Sec. of Def. Def. Sci. Bd. Task Force on Internat. Arms Devel. Cooperation, 1995-98; chmn. Nat. Rsch. Coun. Com. Partnership for a New Generation Vehicle, 1994-2001; vice chair bd. trustees Cleve. State U., 2001-06, mem., 2007; trustee Cleve. Orch., 2003—. Officer Brit. Army, 1955-57. Recipient Safety award, US Dept. Transp., 1978. Fellow Brit. Instn. Mechanical Engrs. (hon.), Brit. Instn. Elec. Engrs. (Hooper Mem. prize 1950), IEEE (life, exec. com. vehicle tech. soc. 1977-81), Royal Soc. of the Arts, Mfg. and Commerce, Soc. Automotive Engrs. (Arch T. Colwell paper award 1974-75, Vincent Bendix Automotive Electronics award 1976, Edward N. Cole award 1988), Engring. Soc. Detroit, Engring. Soc. Cleve., Instn. Mech. Engrs. (hon.); mem. NAE, Union Club, Royal Poinciana Country Club (Naples, Fla.) Republican. Episcopalian. Home: Two Bratenahl Pl Ste 9EF Bratenahl OH 44108 also: Ste 2001 4151 Gulf Shore Blvd N Naples FL 34103 Home Phone: 216-681-5621; Office Phone: 216-937-2800 ext. 222. Business E-Mail: tojones@elecsonmed.com. *Innovation and the acceptance of change are fundamental seeds of progress, and only hard work and an open mind will permit you to harvest its fruits.*

JONES, VAUGHAN FREDERICK RANDAL, mathematician, educator; b. Gisborne, New Zealand, Dec. 31, 1952; m. Martha Weare Myers, Apr. 7, 1979; children: Bethany Martha, Ian Randal, Alice Collins. BSc, U. Auckland, New Zealand, 1972, MSc with first class honors, 1973; DSc in Math., Ecoles Mathematiques, Geneva, 1979; DSc (hon.), U. Auckland, 1992, U. Wales, 1993. Asst. lectr. U. Auckland, New Zealand, 1974; asst. U. Geneva, 1975—80; E.R. Hedrick asst. prof. math. UCLA, 1980—81; asst. prof. U. Pa., Phila., 1981—84, assoc. prof., 1984—85; prof. math. U. Calif., Berkeley, 1985—. Vis. lectr. U. Pa., Phila., 1981—82; dir. New Zealand Math. Rsch. Inst. Recipient F W W Rhodes Meml. Scholarship, Swiss Govt. Scholarship, 1973, Vacheron Constantin Prize, 1980, Guggenhein fellowship, 1986, Fields medal Internat. Congress, Kyoto, Japan, 1990, New Zealand Govt. Sci. medal, 1991, Onsager medal, Trondheim U., 2000. Fellow: Royal Soc.; mem.: Norwegian Royal Soc. Letters & Scis., U.S. Nat. Acad. Scis., London Math. Soc. (hon.), Am. Acad. Arts & Scis. Achievements include index theorem for von Neumann algebras; discovery of a new polynomial invariant for knots which led to surprising connections between apparently quite different areas of mathematics. Office: U Calif Berkeley Dept Math 970 Evans Hall Berkeley CA 94720-3841

JONES, VERONNIE FAYE, medical educator, dean; d. Omega Alpha and Stella Mae Jones; m. Leroy Cockroft, Mar. 23, 1991; children: Lauren T. Cockroft, Bryan L. Cockroft, Eric J. Cockroft, Madison R. Cockroft, Courtney L. Cockroft. BS, Western Ky. U., Bowling Green, 1985; MD, U. Louisville, 1985, MS in Pub. Health, 2001, PhD, 2006. Diplomate Am. Bd. Pediat., 1988. Asst. prof. pediat. U. Louisville, assoc. prof. of pediat., 1996—2006, assoc. dean minority and rural affairs, 2005—, prof. pediat., 2006—. Med. dir. Univ. Child Health Specialists U. Louisville, 2005—, dir. Ky. state AHEC program, 2005—. Mem. Bookstart, Louisville, 2002. Named to Who's Who in Black Louisville, 2007; recipient cert. appreciation, Dept. Pediat., U. Louisville, 2002, Thomas H. Pinkstaff Advocacy award, 2004, Academic Acheivement award, Sch. Pub. Health, U. Louisville, 2005, cert. appreciation, Diversity award, Sch. Medicine, U. Louisville, 2005; grantee PEPP Program, Ky. Coun. Postsecondary Edn., 2006—07, AHEC Regional Funds, HRSA, 2006—07, AHEC for GEAR UP, Coun. Postsecondary Edn., 2007—. Mem.: Am. Acad. Pediat. (exec. com., early childhood devel., adoption 2006—). Office: U Louisville 323 E Chestnut St Louisville KY 40202 Home Phone: 502-615-2146; Office Phone: 502-852-7159. Business E-Mail: vfjone01@louisville.edu.

JONES, VICTOR THOMAS, JR., librarian; b. New Bern, NC, Nov. 22, 1966; s. Victor Thomas and Mary Toler Jones. BA in History, Mt. Olive Coll., 1989; MLS, East Carolina U., 1998. Cert. NC Pub. Libr. Certification Commn. Spl. collections libr. New Bern (NC)-Craven County Pub. Libr., 1992—. Author: The Descendants of James and Rebecca Toler, 1992, The Whitford Family of Eastern North Carolina, 2002. Mem.: NC Libr. Assn., ALA (mem. genealogy com. 2002—04), NC Geneal. Soc. (dir. at large 2003—05, 2d v.p. 2006, 1st v.p. 2007—), Craven County Geneal. Soc. (hon.), So. Hist. Assn., Lions (pres. Twin Rivers club 2000—01, sec. Twin Rivers club 2003—, zone chmn. 2005—07). Baptist. Home: 2905 Aurora Rd Ernul NC 28527 Office: New Bern-Craven County Public Library 400 Johnson St New Bern NC 28560 Home Phone: 252-637-6719; Office Phone: 252-638-7800. Office Fax: 252-638-7817.

JONES, VILLIE, music educator; b. NYC, Mar. 3, 1973; s. Willie and Jacqueline Diane Jones; m. Dawn Linette Jones; 1 child, Villie II. BA in Music with Edn. Cert., Savannah State U., 1997. Lic. tchr. N.C., cert. educator Ga. Dir. choral Red Springs Mid. Sch., NC, 1998—99, Reid Ross Classical Sch., Fayetteville, NC, 1999—2000; dir. bands S.W. Mid. Sch., Savannah, Ga., 2000—01, Westover Mid. Sch., Fayetteville, 2001—03, Westover H.S., Fayetteville, 2003—. Named New Tchr. of Yr., S.W. Mid. Sch., 2001. Mem.: N.C. Music Educators Assn., Music Educators Nat. Conf., Southea. Dist. Bandmasters Assn., Alpha Phi Alpha (cmty. svc. advisor 1997—98, Outstanding Cmty. Svc. award 1998). Avocations: travel, cultural outings, exercise, dining out, mentoring. Office: Westover HS 277 Bonanza Dr Fayetteville NC 28303 Home: 2910 Coachway Dr Fayetteville NC 28306 Home Phone: 910-261-5454; Office Phone: 910-864-0190. Personal E-mail: vjones_apa1@hotmail.com. E-mail: villiejones@ccs.k12.nc.us.

JONES, VIRGINIA MCCLURKIN, retired social worker; b. Anniston, Ala., Mar. 13, 1935; d. Louie Walter and Virginia Keith (Beaver) McClurkin; m. Charles Miller Jones, Jr., Mar. 16, 1957; children: Charles Miller III, V. Grace. BA, Agnes Scott Coll., 1957; MA, U. Tenn., 1965, MSSW, 1979. English instr. U. Tenn., Knoxville, 1967-71; religious edn. dir. Oak Ridge Unitarian Ch., 1972-73, 76-78; co-owner, mgr. The Bookstore, 1973-76; English instr. Roane State C.C., 1975-80; pvt. practice clin. social work Oak Ridge, 1980-98. Cons. Mountain Cmty. Health Ctr., Coalfield, Tenn., 1980-83, Valley Ridge Hospice, 1987-89. Contbr. articles to newspapers. Mem.: NASW, Concord Yacht Club, Rotary. Democrat. Episcopalian. Office: 969 Oak Ridge Turnpike Oak Ridge TN 37830-6554

JONES, VIVIAN EILENE, music educator; b. Tulsa, Okla., Oct. 13, 1948; d. Lucius and Vivian Dotson Jones. BS in Music Edn., Morgan State U., Balt., 1970; EdM in Spl. Edn., Coppin State Coll., Balt., 1974. Cert. educator S.C., tchr. Mo. Tchr. Balt. City Pub. Schs., 1970—74, St. Louis Pub. Schs., 1974—84, Oakland (Calif.) Unified Sch. Dist., 1984—90, Kirkwood (Mo.) R-7 Sch. Dist., 1990—94, Charleston (S.C.) County Sch. Dist., 1994—2000, 2004—, Dorchester Dist. 2, Summerville, SC, 2000—04. Dir. Charleston Symphony Orch. Gospel Choir, 2000—; music coord. Charleston Devel. Acad. Charter Sch., 2004—; choral clinician B.E.A.C.H. Gifted and Talented Program, Georgetown, SC, 1999—. Composer: (radio comml.) It's Cajun Delight, (program theme song) If You Gear Up; arranger (Negro spirituals). Scholarship grantor Coastal Cmty. Found., Charleston, 2001—05. Recipient Key to the City, Jefferson City, Mo., 1989, Outstanding Contbn. in the Arts award, Moja Arts Festival Com., 2002. Mem.: Music Educators Nat. Conf., Am. Choral Dirs. Assn., Alpha Kappa Alpha (Neophyte of Yr. 1968). Avocations: travel, puzzles, swimming. Home: 8093 Shadow Oak Dr Charleston SC 29406 Office: Burke HS 244 President St Charleston SC 29403 Home Phone: 843-824-5412; Office Phone: 843-724-7757. Office Fax: 843-720-2359. E-mail: vivian_jones@charleston.k12.sc.us.

JONES, W. S. (STEVE JONES), dean; b. Elkin, NC; m. Lisa Jones; 4 children. BA in Economics, U. NC, 1974; MBA, Harvard Bus. Sch., 1978; PhD (hon.), Queensland U. Tech., 2002. Worked in drive systems divsn. GE; mgmt. cons. McKinsey & Co., Atlanta, 1984—88, Melbourne, Australia, 1988—90; joined as cons. ANZ Banking Group, Australia, 1990, mng. dir. retail ops., 1993—95, New Zealand mng. dir., 1995—96; CEO Suncorp Metway Ltd., Brisbane, Queensland, Australia, 1996—2002; dean Kenan-Flagler Bus. Sch., U. NC, Chapel Hill, 2003—, prof. mgmt., 2003—. Named one of Top 50 CEOs in Australia, The Bulletin mag., 2001; recipient Centenary Medal for svc. to bus. and commerce through banking and fin, Australian Govt., 2003. Office: Kenan-Flagler Bus Sch U NC Chapel Hill Campus Box 3490 McColl 4300 Chapel Hill NC 27599-3490 Office Phone: 919-962-3232. E-mail: deanjones@kenan-flagler.unc.edu.*

JONES, WALTER BEAMAN, JR., congressman; b. Pitt County, NC, Feb. 10, 1943; s. Walter Beaman Jones; m. Joe Anne Jones; 1 child. BA in Hist., Atlantic Christian Coll., Wilson, NC, 1967. Mgr. Walter B. Jones Office Supply Co., 1967-73; salesman Dunn Assoc., 1973-82; pres. Benefit Reserves, Inc., 1989-94, Judson Co., 1990-94; mem. NC Gen. Assembly, 1983-92, US Congress from 3rd NC dist., 1994—, mem. armed svcs. com., mem. fin. svcs. com. With NC Nat. Guard, 1967—71; mem. adv. bd. Disabled Children's Relief Fund. Named a Friend of the Family, Christian Coalition, Friend of the Farmer, Am. Farm Bur. Fedn.; named Taxpayer Hero, Coun. Citizens against Govt. Waste, Guardian of Small Bus., Nat. Fedn. Ind. Bus.; recipient George (Buck) Gillispie Congl. award, Meritorious Svc., Blinded Am. Vets. Found., 2004, George L. Murphy award, United Seniors Assn., Golden Bulldog award, Watchdogs of the Treasury, Inc., Pro-Nat. Security award, Ctr. Security Policy, Spirit of Enterprise award, US C. of C. Republican. Roman Catholic. Office: 1105-C Corporate Dr Greenville NC 27858-4211 Office Phone: 202-225-3415, 252-931-1003. Office Fax: 252-931-1002.*

JONES, WALTON LINTON, internist, retired government agency administrator; b. McCaysville, Ga., Dec. 4, 1918; s. Walton Linton and Pearl Josephine (Gilliam) J.; m. Caroline Wells Schachte, June 5, 1943; children— Walton Linton III, Francis Stephen, Kathleen Caroline BS, Emory U., 1939, MD, 1942. Diplomate Am. Bd. Preventive Medicine. Commd. lt. (j.g.) U.S. Navy, 1942, advanced through grades to capt., 1956; rotating intern U.S. Naval Hosp., Charleston, SC, 1942-43, aerospace medicine, 1944; flight surgeon USMC Aircraft Squadrons, 1944-47; head aero. med. safety Navy Dept., 1947-53; sr. med. officer U.S.S. Randolph, 1953-55; dir. aero. med. ops. and equipment Bur. Medicine and Surgery, Navy Dept., 1955-64; dir. biotech. and human research div. NASA, 1964-66; ret. U.S. Navy, 1966; civilian dir. biotech and human research div. NASA, Washington, 1966-70, dep., dir. life scis., 1970-75, dir. occupational medicine, 1975-82, dir. occupational health, 1982-85; cons. aerospace medicine, 1985—. Mem. exec. com. hearing and bioacoustics Nat. Acad. Scis., 1964-85, chmn., 1970, mem. exec. com. on vision, 1964-85; Kober lectr. Georgetown U., 1968 Leader, mem. com. Nat. Capital Area council Boy Scouts Am., Falls Church, Va., 1956-64 Decorated Legion of Merit; recipient Exceptional Service medal NASA, 1979, Outstanding Leadership medal NASA, 1985. Fellow Aerospace Medicine Assn. (Bauer award 1970, pres. 1980), AIAA (assoc., recipient John Jeffries award 1970), Royal Soc. Health; mem. Internat. Astronatics Acad., Assn. Mil. Surgeons (Founders award 1956), Internat. Acad. Aerospace Medicine.

JONES, WARREN EUGENE, state supreme court justice; b. Montpelier, Idaho, Oct. 19, 1943; m. Karen Jones; 2 stepchildren. BA magna cum laude, Albertson Coll. Idaho, Caldwell, 1965; JD, U. Chgo., 1968. Bar: Idaho 1968. Law clk. for Chief Justice Joseph J. McFadden Idaho Supreme Ct., Boise, 1968—70, justice, 2007—; atty. to sr. litigator Eberle Berlin, Kading, Turnbow, McKlveen and Jones, Boise, 1970—2007. Mem.: ABA, Assn. Def. Trial Attys., Idaho Assn. Def. Counsel, Def. Rsch. Inst., Am. Bd. Trial Advs., Boise Bar Assn. Office: Idaho Supreme Ct PO Box 83720 Boise ID 83720-0101*

JONES, WAYNE ALLEN, psychotherapist, publisher; b. Bisbee, Ariz., Feb. 10, 1945; s. Earl Wayne and Mary Elizabeth Brown Jones; m. Susheel Dheer, Dec. 30, 1967; children: Sangita (Bete) Adrienne Pfister, Alexander Subhash. AB in Biology, Harvard Coll., 1967; MA in English, U. Mich., 1969; AM in English, Harvard U., 1970, PhD in English and Am. Lit. and Lang., 1974; MA in Clin. Profl. Psychology, Roosevelt U., 2005. Lectr., asst. prof. U. Ill., Chgo., 1972—76; asst. prof. U. Miami, Coral Gables, Fla., 1976—80, adj. asst. prof., 1980—89; documentation specialist and other positions Digital Equipment Corp., Maynard, Mass., 1980—98; alliance mgr. Compaq Computer Corp., Marlborough, Mass., 1998—2002; global alliance mgr. Hewlett-Packard Co., Littleton, Mass., 2002—03; pub. Fractal Edge Press, Chgo., 2002—. Adv. bd. Nathaniel Hawthorne Soc., Bloomfield Hill, Mich., 1974—77; founder, co-dir. The Snarks - A Miami Writer Workshop, 1978—80; clin. psychotherapist Autumn Healthcare Ill., Elite Commn. Mental Health Ctr. Contbr. The Nathaniel Hawthorne Calendar, editor, collaborator (three-act play) The Shift by Bernard McCabe, assoc. editor Nathaniel Hawthorne Jour., 1977—80; contbg. editor: Nathaniel Hawthorne Soc. Newsletter, 1975—76; mem. adv. bd., contbr. First Printings of Am. Authors, 1974—80; author: Stone Works, 2002, Decades of Rehearsal, 2003; author: (with Barnard McCabe) The A Poems, 2003. Juried poet Houston Poetry Fest, 2000, 2002, 2003, Chgo. Poetry Fest, 2003—05; pres. bd. dirs. Studio Potter, Dunbarton, NH, 2000—03. Named to Greybeard - DTR-SIG Hall of Fame, Datatrieve Spl. Interest Group, 1982; recipient award of merit, Soc. Tech. Comm., 1981, 1991, Recognition for Outstanding Partnering and Customer Presentations, Platinum Technologies Corp., 1998; fellow, U. Ill., Chgo., 1975, Huntington Libr., San Marino, CA, 1976, Am. Coun. Learned Socs., 1977; grantee, U. Ill., Chgo., 1974; Max Orovitz Summer fellow in arts and humanities, U. of Miami, 1979. Mem.: Phi Kappa Phi (chpt. sec.-tras. 1979—80). Independent. Taoist. Achievements include discovery of Nathaniel Hawthorne's first review of another author; Hawthorne's means of funding Fanshawe, his first novel; Hawthorne's income from The Token and Twice-Told Tales; a previously unknown Hawthorne love letter; 2 volumes of Manning Estate records in Nathaniel Hawthorne's hand. Avocation: photography. Personal E-mail: wayne.jones@att.net.

JONES, WAYNE ELFED, JR., chemist, researcher; b. Springfield, Mass., June 25, 1965; s. Wayne E. Sr. and Elaine Marie (Benoit) J.; m. Michele Louise Brault, Aug. 20, 1988; children: Meghan Elizabeth, Erin Michele, Kathleen Emily, Eric Wayne. BS, St. Michael's Coll., Winooski, Vt., 1987; Phd, U. N.C., 1991. Postdoctoral rschr. U. Tex., Austin, 1992-93; asst. prof. chemistry SUNY, Binghamton, 1993—. Cons. Photoprotective Techs., Arlington, Tex., 1993-94, Universal Instruments, Kirkwood, N.Y., 1998—; cons. reviewer John Wiley and Sons, N.Y.C., 1994—. Cons. editor Chemistry Interactive, 1996; contbr. articles to profl. jours. Merit badge counselor Boy Scouts Am., Binghamton, 1996—; judge Sci. Olympiad, Binghamton, 1994—. SUNY Binghamton rsch. grantee, 1996. Mem. AAAS, Am. Chem. Soc., Phi Eta Sigma. Achievements include patent for Transition Metal AgX Sensitizers; design new polymer materials for electro-optics applications. Home: 1433 Carnegie Dr Vestal NY 13850-4006 Office: SUNY Binghamton Vestal Pkwy E Binghamton NY 13902-6016

JONES, WELLINGTON DOWNING, III, banker; b. Topeka, Feb. 16, 1945; s. Wellington Downing Jr. and Nancy (Neiswanger) J.; m. Andrea Loftus, May 2, 1970; children: Wellington Downing IV, Heather, Lindsey. BSBA, Northwestern U., 1967; postgrad., Grad. Sch. Banking, Madison, Wis., 1980, Harvard U., 1987. Mktg. rep. IBM, Chgo., 1969-76; v.p. data processing 1st Bank & Trust (name 1st Source Bank 1981), South Bend, Ind., 1976-79, v.p. retail banking, 1979-81; sr. v.p. 1st Source Bank, South Bend, 1981-88; pres. 1st Nat. Bank Mishawaka (acquired by 1st Source Bank 1983), Ind., 1983; exec. v.p. 1st Source Corp., South Bend, 1988—98, pres., 1998—. Bd. dirs. Trustcorp Mortgage, South Bend. Bd. dirs. Neighborhood Housing Svcs., South Bend, 1986—, Entertainment Dist. Bd., South Bend, 1991—, United Way St. Joseph County, South Bend, 1991—; chmn. South Bend Mayor's Housing Forum, 1991—; pres. No. Ind. Hist. Soc., South Bend, 1991—. Sgt. USMCR, 1967-73. Mem. Signal Point Club (Niles, Mich.), Morris Park Country Club. Presbyterian. Avocations: golf, platform tennis, reading, investments. Office: 1st Source Bank 100 N Michigan St South Bend IN 46601-1630

JONES, WES, architect; b. 1958; Disting. cadet, US Mil. Acad., West Point, NY, 1978; AB with highest honors in Architecture, U. Calif., Berkeley, 1980; MArch with distinction, Harvard U., 1983. Lic. Calif., NY. With ELS Design Group, Berkeley, Calif., 1980—83, Eisenman/Robertson, Archs., NYC, 1983—87; design ptnr. Holt Hinshaw Pfau Jones, San Francisco, 1987—93; prin. Jones, Ptnrs.: Architecture, LA and San Francisco, 1993—. Vis. prof. Harvard U. Sch. Architecture, Princeton U., NJ, Ill. Inst. Tech., Columbia U., NYC, UCLA, Ohio State U.; studio tchr. So. Calif. Inst. Architecture. Recipient Rome prize, Architecture, Architecture award, AAAL, 2007. Mem.: Phi Beta Kappa. Office: Jones Ptnrs Architecture 141 Nevada St El Segundo CA 90245 Office Phone: 310-414-0761. Office Fax: 310-414-0765. E-mail: info@jonespartners.com.*

JONES, WILLIAM ADRIAN, musician, educator, program developer; b. Princeton, Ind., Feb. 27, 1962; s. Rene Ardell McCormick. BS in Music Mgmt., U. Evansville, Ind., 1985, BA in Spanish, 1986; MusB in Music Performance with distinction, U. Ky., Lexington, 1990, MusM in Performance, 1993. Cert. tchr. Fla., 2003. Instr., composer, arranger various marching band programs, Ind., Ky., 1982—86; percussionist Owensboro Symphony Orchestra, Ky., 1981—83, Evansville Philharmonic Orchestra, 1981—83, Evansville Symphonic Band, 1983—85, Tales and Scales Performing Arts Troupe, Evansville, 1986—87, Encore Dinner Theatre, Evansville, 1986—87; edn. program coord. Lexington Children's Mus., Ky., 1992—94; children's summer program coord. Lexington CC, 1994; camp counselor, percussion instr. Culver Summer Camps, Ind., 1996; asst. band dir., asst. counselor Culver Military Acad., 1996; freelance percussionist Evansville, 1999—2004; percussion instr., arranger Ctrl. HS, Evansville, 1999—2000; co-founder, mgr., percussionist, co-arranger La Mezcla Musical Group, Evansville, 2000—01; developer, instr. After Sch. Percussion Program, Del. Elem. Sch., Evansville, 2000—01; founder, drum circle and drum facilitator Deaconess Hosp. Resource Ctr. for Healthy Living, Evansville, 2000—03; pvt. instr. Moore Music Guitar and Drum Ctr., Evansville, 2000—03; founder, mgr., percussionist, composer NVISION World Drumming Ensemble, Evansville, 2003—04; percussion instr., composer, arranger Princeton Cmty. HS, Ind., 2002—03; freelance percussionist Miami, Fla., 2004—; developer K-6 music program, tchr. Downtown Miami Charter Sch., Fla., 2004—07. Contbr. articles to profl. jours.

JONES, WILLIAM ALLEN, lawyer; b. Phila., Dec. 13, 1941; s. Roland Emmett and Gloria (Miller) J.; m. Margaret Smith, Sept. 24, 1965 (div. 1972); m. Dorothea S. Whitson, June 15, 1973; children— Darlene, Rebecca, Gloria, David. BA, Temple U., 1967; MBA, JD, Harvard U., 1972. Bar: Calif. 1974. Atty. Walt Disney Prodns., Burbank, Calif., 1973-77, treas., 1977-81; atty. Wyman Bautzer et al, LA, 1981-83, MGM/UA Entertainment Co., Culver City, 1983, v.p., gen. counsel, 1983-86; sr. v.p., corp. gen. counsel, sec. MGM/UA Communications Co., Culver City, Calif., 1986-91; exec. v.p., gen. counsel, sec. Metro-Goldwyn-Mayer Inc., Santa Monica, Calif., 1991-95, exec. v.p. corp. affairs, 1995-97, sr. exec. v.p., 1997—. Bus. mgr. L.A. Bar Jour., 1974-75; bd. dirs. The Nostalgia Network Inc.; mem. bd. of govs. Inst. for Corp. Counsel, 1990-93. Charter mem. L.A. Philharm. Men's Com., 1974-80; trustee Marlborough Sch., 1988-93, Flintridge Preparatory Sch., 1993-96. With USAF, 1960-64. President's scholar Temple U., 1972 Mem. Harvard Bus. Sch. Assn. So. Calif. (bd. dirs. 1985-88). Home: 1557 Colina Dr Glendale CA 91208-2412 Office: Metro Goldwyn Mayer Inc 2500 Broadway Santa Monica CA 90404-3065

JONES, WILLIAM AUGUSTUS, JR., retired bishop; b. Memphis, Jan. 24, 1927; s. William Augustus and Martha (Jones) J.; m. Margaret Loaring-Clark, Aug. 26, 1949; 4 children. BA, Southwestern at Memphis, 1948; B.D., Yale U., 1951. Ordained priest Episcopal Ch., 1952; priest in charge Messiah Ch., Pulaski, Tenn., 1952-57; curate Christ Ch., Nashville, 1957-58; rector St. Mark Ch., LaGrange, Ga., 1958-65; asso. rector St. Luke Ch., Mountainbrook, Ala., 1965-66; dir. research So. region Assn. Christian Tng. and Service, Memphis, 1966-67; exec. dir. Assn. Christian Tng. and Service, 1968-72; rector St. John's, Johnson City, Tenn., 1972-75; bishop of Mo. St. Louis, 1975-93. Adj. staff Christ Ch., Wilmington, Del., 2001. Episcopalian.

JONES, WILLIAM BENJAMIN, JR., retired electrical engineering educator; b. Fairburn, Ga., Sept. 17, 1924; s. William Benjamin and Katherine (Davenport) J.; m. Mary Pierce Hammond, Sept. 8, 1948; children: William Benjamin III, Katherine P., Joseph L. BS, Ga. Inst. Tech., 1945, MS, 1948, PhD, 1953. Mem. tech. staff Hughes Aircraft Co., Culver City, Calif., 1954-58; prof. elec. engring. Ga. Inst. Tech., 1958-67; prof. Tex. A&M U., 1967-90, head dept. elec. engring., 1967-84. Vis. prof. U. Fla., 1984-85 Author: Introduction to Optical Fiber Communication Systems, 1987. Served with USNR, 1943-46. Mem. IEEE (sr. mem., editor transactions on communication systems 1960-61, chmn. communication tech. group 1966-67, mem. tech. activities bd. 1966-69, v.p. communications soc. 1972-73, chmn. elec. engring. dept. heads assn. 1983-84), Sigma Xi, Tau Beta Pi, Eta Kappa Nu. Home: Apt 1125 3801 Village View Dr Gainesville GA 30506 Personal E-mail: wjones1125@charter.net.

JONES, WILLIAM HENRY, retired military officer; b. Black Diamond, Wash., Apr. 1, 1924; s. Stanley Ernest Jones and Lena Ellenor Nott; m. Barbara Ann Liestman, May 17, 1960; 1 child, Denise; m. Shirley Ann Williams, Jan. 27, 1946 (div. May 12, 1960); 1 child, Robert. Grad. summa cum laude, Naval Sch. Hosp. Adminstrn., 1950; AA, San Diego City Coll., 1963; BA, San Diego State Coll., 1964; grad., Fed. Health Care Execs. Inst., Chgo., 1972. Apprentice seaman USN, 1942, advanced through grades to capt., combat hosp. corpsman various WWII battles, 1942—45, various enlisted assignments, 1945—50, commissioned ensign med. svc. corps, 1950, asst. fin. officer Naval Hosp. Mare Island Vallejo, Calif., 1950—54, adminstrv. officer med. dept. USS Hancock, 1954—56, asst. adminstrv. officer Naval Hosp. Bethesda, Md., 1956—58, adminstrv. officer Naval Hosp. Corps Sch. San Diego, 1958—60, dir. Amphibious Med. Indoctrination Coronado, Calif., 1960—64, chief patient affairs Naval Hosp. Oakland, Calif., 1964—66, med. adminstrn. officer Hosp. Ship USS Repose - Vietnam War, 1966—67, adminstrv. officer Naval Hosp. St. Albans, NY, 1967—69, Yokosuka, Japan, 1969—71, dir. Health Care Adminstrn. Naval Regional Med. Ctr. Long Beach, Calif., 1971—73, exec. officer Nat. Naval Med. Ctr. Bethesda, Md., 1973—74, commanding officer Field Med. Svc. Sch. Camp Pendleton, Calif., 1974—79, officers selection bd., 1974—79, ret., 1979. Decorated Meritorious Svc. medal (2), Navy Commendation medal, Legion of Merit; recipient Poet of the Year, Famous Poet Soc., 2003. Mem.: Fleet Res. Assn., Fed. Health Care Execs., Am. Coll. Hosp. Adminstrs., Internat. Poetry Hall of Fame, Internat. Poets Soc. (disting.). Avocations: reading, walking, writing. Home: 947 San Pablo Way San Marcos CA 92078 Personal E-mail: banbjones484@msn.com.

JONES, WILLIAM KINZY, materials engineering educator; b. Miami, Fla., July 23, 1946; s. Harold Grover and Josephine (Kinzy) Jones; m. Sharon Mattingly, June 6, 1981; children: Kelli, Kinzy, Brent. BS, Fla. State U., 1967, MS, 1968; PhD, MIT, 1972. Mgr. engring. Cordis Corp., Miami, 1977-87; group head C.S. Draper Lab., Cambridge, Mass., 1972-77; assoc. prof. engring. Fla. Internat. U., Miami, 1987-91, prof., assoc. dean for rsch. Miami, 1991—. Dir. Fla. Mfg. Extension Partnership, Advanced Material Rsch. and Engring. Inst.; chmn. advanced rsch. workshop NATO, 1994-95; gen. chair Internat. Microelectronics Conf., 1992, Multi-Chip Module Conf., 1995; tech. co-chair Electronic Packaging Conf., China, 1996, 98; comm. cons. in field. Contbr. articles to profl. jours.; patentee in field. Recipient Rsch. award Fla. Internat. U., 1991, 2001. Fellow Internat. Microelectronic and Packaging Soc.(pres. 1992-93, v.p. membership 1998, trustee Ednl. Found., Tech. Achievement Wagnon award 1991, Hughes award 1996); mem. IEEE (sr.). Republican. Home: 75560 Overseas Hwy # 534 Islamorada FL 33036-4005 Office: Fla Internat U University Pk Campus Coll of Engineering Eas 3442 Miami FL 33199-0001 E-mail: jones@fiu.edu.

JONES, WILLIAM LEE, JR., psychologist, educator; b. Electra, Tex., Jan. 4, 1944; s. William Lee Jones Sr. and Mamie Kathryn Baker. BA, U. Ariz., Tucson, 1966; cert., Def. Lang. Inst./Yale U., Monterey, Calif./New Haven, 1969; MA, Ariz. State U., Tempe, 1986; MA cum laude, U. Sorbonne, 1974. Psychologist, outpatient coord. St. Luke's Hosp., Phoenix, 1985—91; psychologist Tex. State Hosp., Wichita Falls, 1991—96; pvt. practice psychologist, psychotherapist Hemet, Calif., 1995—; psychology clin. cons. Riverside County, Riverside and Hemet, 1996—2004. Instr. Phoenix Coll., 1988, Rio Sala de Coll., Ariz., 1989—91, Midwestern State Coll., Wichita Falls, Tex., 1993, Mt. San Jacinto Coll., Calif., 2002—03; family advocate Valley Wide Svcs., Hemet and San Jacinto, Calif., 2002—. Author: Rites of Passage, 1996, Group Therapy: Manual for Clinicians, 1987. Mem.: Mensa (1st pl. regional award for fiction 1993), Phi Delta Theta. Mailing: PO Box 3556 Idyllwild CA 92549 E-mail: wljones4@verizon.net.

JONES, WILLIAM O., not-for-profit fundraiser; Pres. Conf. Grand Masters Prince Hall Masons. Office: Prince Hall Masons 1630 N 4th Ave Birmingham AL 35203 Office Phone: 205-328-9078, 334-727-5416.

JONES, WILLIAM OSBORNE, II, physician assistant, nephrologist; b. Corbin, Ky., May 30, 1951; s. William Osborne and Rebecca Marie (Grover) Jones; m. Patsy Jean Jones; children: Anastasia Marie Rising, William Osborne III, Thomas Adam. BS, George Washington U., 1985; MA, Webster U., 1988. Cert. Nat. Commn. Physician Assts., Calif. Coll. Instr. Cert. Enlisted USN, 1970, advanced through grades to lt., hosp. corpsman, technician, physician asst., 1970-94, ret., 1994; pvt. practice physician asst. family medicine, orthopaedics Gaffney, SC, 1994; pvt. practice nephrology Spartanburg, SC, 1994—. Med. lectr. nephrology. Contbr. articles to profl. jours. Founding v.p. Am. Acad. Nephrology Physician Assts.; physician asst. rep. SC State Bd. Med. Examiners. Named to Hon. Order Ky. Cols. Fellow: Am. Acad. Physician Assts.; mem.: Naval Assn. Physician Assts., S.C. Acad. Physician Assts. (pres., v.p. 1996—99), Am. Acad. Nephrology Physician Assts. (v.p. 1997—98, sec. 1998—99), Mensa. Republican. Evangelical Christian. Avocations: motorcycling, travel. Office: Foothills Nephrology 126 Dillon Dr Spartanburg SC 29307 Home: 37 Dorchester Dr Chesnee SC 29323 Office Phone: 864-327-1212. Business E-Mail: kidneypa@chesnet.net.

JONES, WILLIAM REX, law educator; b. Murphysboro, Ill., Oct. 20, 1922; s. Claude E. and Ivy P. (McCormick) J.; m. Miriam R. Lamy, Mar. 27, 1944; m. Gerri L. Haun, June 30, 1972; children: Michael Kimber, Jeanne Keats, Patricia Combs, Sally Horowitz, Kevin. BS, U. Louisville, 1950; JD, U. Ky., 1968; LLM, U. Mich., 1970. Bar: Ky. 1969, Ind. 1971, U.S. Supreme Ct. 1976. Exec. v.p. Paul Miller Ford, Inc., Lexington, Ky., 1951-64; pres. Bill's Seat Cover Ctr., Inc., Lexington, Ky., 1952-65, Bill Jones Real Estate, Inc., Lexington, Ky., 1965-70; asst. prof. law Ind. U., Indpls., 1970-73, assoc. prof., 1973-75, prof., 1975-80; dean Salmon P. Chase Coll. Law. No. Ky. U., Highland Heights, 1980-85, prof., 1980-93, prof. emeritus, 1993—. Vis. prof. Shepard Broad Law Ctr., Nova Southeastern U., Ft. Lauderdale, Fla., 1994-95; mem. Ky. Pub. Advocacy Commn., 1982-93, 97-2000, chmn., 1986-93; chmn. Existing Structures Appeal Bd., City of Newport, Ky., 2002—. Author: Kentucky Criminal Trial Practice, 3d edit., 2001, Kentucky Criminal Trial Practice Forms, 3d edit., 2000. 1st sgt. U.S. Army, 1940-44. Cook fellow U. Mich., 1969-70, W.G. Hart fellow Queen Mary Coll. U. London, 1985. Mem. Order of Coif. Personal E-mail: wrexjones@zoomtown.com. Business E-Mail: jonesw@exchange.nku.edu.

JONES, WINONA NIGELS, retired media specialist; b. Feb. 24, 1928; d. Eugene Arthur and Bertha Lillian (Dixon) Nigels; m. Charles Albert Jones, Nov. 26, 1944; children: Charles Eugene, Sharon Ann Jones Allworth, Caroline Winona Jones Pandorf. AA, St. Petersburg Jr. Coll., 1965; BS, U. So. Fla., 1967, MS, 1968; advanced MS, Fla. State U., 1980. Libr. media specialist Dunedin Comprehensive H.S., Fla., 1967-76; libr. media specialist, chmn. dept. Fitzgerald Mid. Sch., Largo, 1976—87; dir. media svcs. East Lake H.S., Tarpon Springs, 1987—93; ret., 1993. Author: Around Palm Harbor, 2005. Dir. and vol. North Pinellas Hist. Mus.; active Palm Harbor Hist. Soc., Pinellas County Hist. Soc.; del. White Ho. Conf. Libr. and Info. Svcs. Named Educator Yr. Pinellas County Sch. Bd. and Suncoast C. of C., 1983, 88, Palm Harbor Woman Yr. Palm Harbor Jr. Women's club, 1989, Palm Harbor Citizen Yr., Palm Harbor C. of C., 2002. Mem. ALA (coun. 1988-92), NEA, AAUW, ASCD, Assn. Ednl. Comm. and Tech. (divsn. sch. media specialist, coms.), Am. Assn. Sch. Librs. (com., pres.-elect 1989, pres. 1990-91, mem. exec. bd. 1991-92), Southeastern Libr. Assn., Fla. Libr. Assn., Fla. Assn. Media Edn. (pres.), U. So. Fla. Alumni Assn., Fla. State Libr. Sci. Alumni Assn., U. So. Fla. Libr. Sci. Alumni Assn. (pres. 1991-92, 92-93), Phi Theta Kappa, Phi Rho Pi, Beta Phi Mu, Kappa Delta Pi, Delta Kappa Gamma (parliamentarian 1989-90, legis. chmn. 1990, sec. 1994-96), Inner Wheel Club, Pilot Club, Civic Club, Order Ea. Star (Palm Harbor, past worthy matron). Democrat. Home: 911 Manning Rd Palm Harbor FL 34683-6344 Office Phone: 727-724-3054.

JONES-GREGORY, PATRICIA, art educator; b. La Grange, Ga., Apr. 15, 1944; d. Eddie Burrel Jones (dec.), Samuel Lee (stepfather) and Mildred Jones (Johnson) Turrentine; m. Bernard Gregory, Oct. 12, 1985. BFA in Art Edn., Pratt Inst., 1966; MS in Photography, Ill. Inst. Tech., 1970; postgrad. in African Studies and Rsch., Howard U., 1970—74; EdD in Ednl. Adminstrn. and Supervision, Seton Hall U., 1994. Cert. prin./supr., supr., ednl. adminstrn. and supervision, art tchr. grades K-12. Tchr. art Westfield Sch. Dist., NJ, 1966—68; instr. art Howard U., Washington, 1970—71; tchr. art Newark Sch. Dist., 1974—79, Irvington Sch. Dist., NJ, 1979—80, South Orange-Maplewood Sch. Dist., NJ, 1980—81, Montclair Sch. Dist., NJ, 1981—82; instr. art, docent Newark Mus., 1982—84; tchr. art Weequahic H.S., Newark, 1983—98. Mem. com. textbook evaluation curriculum svcs. Bd. Edn., Newark, 1983—; art dir. Ergo-Weequahic H.S., Newark, 1984-93, founder, advisor Kuumba Art Club, 1989-94, PB Graphics Design, liasion, City Without Walls Art Reach mentor program, 1997-98. Author: Many Moods of the Afro-American Woman, 1971, Multicultural Arts Exhibition Catalog, 1992, Pathways to Empowerment, 1997; editor (and pub.): The Harvester, 1979—83, The Beauty of Holiness, 1997, The Clarion: The Voices That Lead to Righteousness, 1999—2000, Friendship With the World, 2000, Metamorphosis of the Christian, 2002, Intermèzzo in l'Italia, 2002, A Good Wife is Without Price, 2005, Ode to Sam Torrentine, 2007. Rschr. Goldman and Kennedy The New York Urban Athlete, Simon and Schuster, N.Y., 1983; vol. tchr., counselor local ch. Recipient cert. of recognition, Gov.'s Tchr. Recognition Program, NJ, 1993, Outstanding Dissertation award, Seton Hall U., 1994; Grace B. Monroe grantee, Pratt Inst., Bklyn., 1964, grad. scholar, Ill. Inst. Tech., Chgo., 1968—70, rsch. fellow, Howard U., Washington, 1972—73. Mem.: ASCD, Nat. Assn. Art Educators, Nat. Assn. for Multicultural Edn., Com. to Eliminate Media Offensive to African People, Studio Mus. in Harlem, Newark Mus., Newark Art Coun., Bklyn. Mus. Art, Schomburg Ctr. Rsch. in Black Culture, Kappa Delta Pi. Avocations: art, travel, discussion, reading, writing. Home: 78 Woodland Ave East Orange NJ 07017-2006

JONES-KETNER, ELIZABETH BROWN, writer; b. Kansas City, Mo., Sept. 27, 1907; d. James Riley and Agnes Julia (Gammage) Brown; m. Clare Hartley Jones, June 4, 1929 (dec. July 3, 1981), m. Francis D. Ketner, Dec. 27, 1982 (dec. Nov. 2, 1990); children— Elizabeth Ann, Sara Denise, David Hartley, Phyllis Elaine. Student U. Mo., Kansas City, 1946, Mid-Am. Nazarene Coll., 1981. Free-lance writer, 1940-62, 78—; author numerous books, including: Teaching Primaries Today, 1974; Because God Made Me, 1975; Stories of Jesus, 1977; When We Share the Bible with Children, 1977; Let the Children Come, 1978; contbr. numerous stories, poems to children's publs.; author song lyrics; editor, curriculum planner, writer Nazarene Pub. House, Kansas City, Mo., 1962-78; workshop leader; speaker at writers' confs.; mem. nat. com. for planning Sunday sch. curriculum; book reviewer; speaker at parent's groups. Mem. Ch. of the Nazarene.

JONES-LUKÁCS, ELIZABETH LUCILLE, physician; b. Norfolk, Va. d. Oliver C. and Gertrude (Layden) Jones; m. Michel J. Lukacs (dec.); children: Amanda, Laurel, Angelique, Klara. BS, Oglethorpe U., 1955; MD, Downstate Med. Ctr., 1964. Diplomate Am. Bd. Family Practice. Intern Beth Israel Hosp., NYC, 1964-65; family practice medicine Goshen, NY, 1965-73, Buckingham, Va., 1973-78; commd. maj. U.S. Air Force, 1978; flight surgeon Andrews AFB, Md., 1978-85, chief exec. med. program Md., 1991-2000; med. dir. Armed Forces Benefit Assn., Alexandria, Va., 2000—04. Unit charge physician Student Health Ctr., U. Md., College Park, 1985—91; bd. dirs. Falcon's Landing Mil. Officers Retirement Home. Author: The Curies Radium & Radioactivity, 1962, The Golden Stamp Book of Flying Animals, 1963. Col. USAFR, commd. 459th USAF Clinic. Mem. Am. Med. Womens Assn. (pres. Br. I), Md. Connemara Breeders. Episcopalian. Home: 15430 Mount Calvert Rd Upper Marlboro MD 20772-9616 Personal E-mail: ejlukacs@verizon.net.

JONES REYNOLDS, STAR (STARLET MARIE JONES), television host, lawyer, former prosecutor; b. Badin, NC, Mar. 24, 1962; m. Al Reynolds, Nov. 13, 2004. BA, Am. U.; JD, U. Houston. Bar: NY. Lawyer; sr. asst. dist. atty. Bklyn. Dist. Atty.'s Office, 1991; studio commentator Court TV, 1991; legal corrs. NBC's Today, Nightly News; host syndicated tv show Jones and Jury, 1994; former sr. corr., chief legal analyst Inside Edition, 1995; co-host ABC Daytime's The View, 1997—2006; nat. spokesperson Payless ShoeSource; host Live from the Red Carpet!, 2004; guest host The Michael Eric Dyson Show, 2006—. Notable guest appearances The Tonight Show with Jay Leno, Bravo's Celebrity Poker, Celebrity Jeopardy, The Daily Show with Jon Stewart, and The Late Show with David Letterman., honored as a subject of Lifetime TV: Intimate Portrait, 2000, host It's All About You With Star Jones on ShopNBC, E! Entertainment Television's Live Red Carpet Arrivals of the Primetime Emmy Awards, 2004, Star Jones, Court TV, 2007—, developer of own website, featured personality for Kohl's Target, and Salon Z of Saks Fifth Avenue, featured on numerous mags. such as: Newsweek, TV Guide, Essence, Black Enterprise, and New York; author: You Have to Stand for Something, or You'll Fall for Anything, 1998; guest appearance (TV series) Strong Medicine, 2001, Soul Food, 2002, Less Than Perfect, 2005; actor: Relative Strangers, 2006; author: Shine: A Physical, Emotional, and Spiritual Journey to Finding Love, 2006. Bd. dir. East Harlem Sch. at Exodus House, Dress for Success, God's Love We Deliver, Girls, Inc.; launched The Starlet Fund, 2002—. Named Chief of Consumer Style, 2002; honored for work in improving the educational opportunities for low income children in East Harlem, East Harlem Sch. at Exodus House; co-recipient with co-host from "The View", Safe Horizon Champion award, 2001. Achievements include launching signature line of shoes, Starlet by Star Jones, sold exclusively at Payless ShoeSource. Office: 320 W 66th St New York NY 10023-6304*

JONES TERGEOGLOU, BEVERLY GLORIA, special education services professional; d. Robert George and Gloria Sarafina (Castelvetere) Jones; children: Timothy Jon Tergeoglou, Nicolas Patrick Tergeoglou, Marc Tergeoglou, Paulina Klein. Attended, U. Conn., Langston Bible Coll., Catherdal Bible Coll.; student, Cmty. Bible Inst. and Sem., Breward City, Fla.; BA in Theology, Lighthouse Christian Coll., 2006. Cert. hospice, infection control, body mechanics & lupus erythematosus Timmonsville Area Vocat. Ctr., hospice McLeod Regional Med. Ctr., children & family svcs. Dist. 7, adminstrn., supervision adminstrn. medication, Fla. Children & Family Svcs. People Choice, in-house trng. van safety ARC, 1999, individual edn. plan ARC, 2004, Ctr. Disease Control HIV/AIDS, 1999, body mechanics & transfer trng. Easter Seals, 2001, devel. disabilities 2002, analysis trng. 2002, adminstrn. medications Fla. Devel. Disabilities Program, 2002, full life ahead trng. Brevard Sch. Dist., 2004, lic. devel. disabilities foster home Dist. 7, Fla., 2005. Instr. Indian River CC, Vero Beach, Fla., 1998—2000; assoc. dir. vocat. svcs., consumer svcs. mgr. Easter Seals, Fla., 2000—02; foster parent Devereux Therapeutic Foster Care Group Home, Palm Bay, Fla., 2002—; instr. Brevard Sch. Dist., Learner Empowerment Through Agency Partnerships Trng. Program, Melbourne, Fla., 2002—. Apptd. mem. Tree Adv., Sebastian; vol. Hospice, Florence, SC, Red Cross, St. John, US Virgin Islands, Town's First Festival, Pamplico, SC, Nat. Pks. and Forest, St. John, US Virgin Islands, Hosanna Book and Gift Shop, St. Croix, US Virgin Islands, Spl. Olympics, Vero Beach, Fla., 1998, soccer vol. Palm Bay, 2005; substitute tchr. Am. Sch. Mallorca, Spain, libr. vol.; mem. Woman's Coalition of Spouse Abuse, St. Croix, US Virgin Islands; stringer TV sta. Florence; reading instr. 2nd and 3rd grades Julius Sprave Sch., St. John, US Virgin Islands; vol. spl. and challenged needs kids, 2005; softball vol. spl. and challenged needs kids, 2005; spl. and challenged needs vol. Spotlight Theater, 2005; vol. Girl Scouts, 2004—, 2004—, Spl. Olympics, Brevard County, Fla., 2004—; vol. children's ch. Zion's Ch., Palm Bay, 2002—05; mem. Our Lady of Grace Ch., Palm Bay, 2005; tchg. asst. St. Ann's RC, Florence, SC; bazaar vol. Our Lady of Mt. Carmel Ch., St. John, US Virgin Islands; mem. PTA, Pamplico, SC. Recipient Fla. Appreciation award, Tree and Landscape Adv. Bd., City of Sebastian, 2002, Learner Empowerment through Agency Partnerships Tng. award, Brevard County Offices of Exceptional Student Edn. and Adult Cmty. Edn., 2003, Cert. of Recognition, Devereux, 2003, Cert. Continued Dedication and Commitment to Helping Children That You Serve, 2003, Cert. Vol. Svc., PTA, Pamplico. Mem.: Coun. Exceptional Children, Newcomer's Club, Elks Lodge Palm Bay. Avocations: swimming, walking, bicycling, reading, history. Home Phone: 321-728-8497. Personal E-mail: inletjetty@aol.com.

JONES-WILSON, FAUSTINE CLARISSE, retired education educator; b. Little Rock, Dec. 3, 1927; d. James Edward and Perrine Marie (Childress) Thomas; m. James T. Jones, June 20, 1948 (div. 1977); children: Yvonne Dianne, Brian Vincent; m. Edwin L. Wilson, July 10, 1981. AB, Ark. A.M.&N. Coll., 1948; AM, U. Ill., 1951, EdD, 1967; LLD, U. Ark., Pine Bluff, 2003. Tchr., sch. libr. Gary (Ind.) Pub. Schs., 1955-62, 1964-67; asst. prof. Coll. Edn., U. Ill., Chgo., 1967-69; assoc. prof. adult edn. Fed. City Coll., Washington, 1970-71; prof. edn., grad. prof. Howard U., Washington, 1969-70, 71-93, acting dean Sch. Edn., 1991-92, prof. emeritus, 1993—. Author: The Changing Mood in America; Eroding Commitment, 1977, A Traditional Model of Educational Excellence: Dunbar High School of Little Rock, Arkansas, 1981; co-author: Paul Laurence Dunbar High School of Little Rock, Arkansas: Take From Our Lips a Song, Dunbar to Thee, 2003; editor Jour. Negro Edn., 1978-91, 92-93; co-editor: Encyclopedia of African-American Education, 1996; assoc. editor Jour. of Edn. for Students Placed at Risk, 1996-2000. Chmn. East Coast steering com. Nat. Coun. on Educating Black Children, 1986—88, 1990—92, 3d v.p., 1992—94, bd. dirs., 1994—98. Recipient Frederick Douglass award Nat. Assn. Black Journalists, 1979, Disting. Scholar-Tchr. award Howard U., 1985, Exemplary Leadership award Am. Assn. Higher Edn. Black Caucus, 1988, Gertrude E. Rush award Nat. Bar Assn., 1990, Disting. Career award V.P. for Acad. Affairs, Howard U., 1993, Disting. Alumni award Coll. Edn. U. Ill., 1997; Phelps Stokes Fund sr. fellow, 1993-2000. Mem.: Soc. Profs. of Edn. (Mary Anne Raywid award 2002), Am. Ednl. Studies Assn. (pres. 1984—85), John Dewey Soc., Phi Delta Kappa (pres. Howard U. chpt. 1986—87, Svc. key 1990). Democrat. Methodist. Home: 6605 Allview Dr Columbia MD 21046-1005

JONES-WOOLFOLK, JERALD MAXINE, dean, educator; b. Leland, Miss., May 21, 1959; d. Robert Lee Jr. and Bessie Mae Jones; m. Lee A. Woolfolk, June 28, 1986 (div. Apr. 1998); 1 child, Brandon. BS, Jackson State U., 1981; MS, Iowa State U., 1984. Assoc. dean of students U. Ark., Pine Bluff, 1989—, instr., counselor, 1984-89. Bd. dirs. ACCESS, Pine Bluff, 1998. Mem. S.W. Assn. of Coll. and Univs. Housing Officers (Ark. dir. 1992-96). Office: U Ark at Pine Bluff PO Box 4933 Pine Bluff AR 71611-4933 Home: 1823 Debra Dr Greenville MS 38703-7832

JONG, ERICA MANN, writer; b. NYC, Mar. 26, 1942; d. Seymour and Eda (Mirsky) Mann; m. Michael Werthman, 1963 (div. 1965); m. Allan Jong (div. Sept. 1975); m. Jonathan Fast, Dec. 1977 (div. Jan. 1983); 1 child, Molly; m. Kenneth David Burrows, Aug. 5, 1989. BA, Barnard Coll., 1963; MA, Columbia U., 1965; PhD honoris causa, CUNY, 2005. Faculty, English dept. CUNY, 1964-65, 69-70, overseas div. U. Md., 1967-69; mem. lit. panel N.Y. State Council on Arts, 1972-74; faculty Breadloaf Writers Conf. Middlebury, Vt., 1982; mem. faculty Saltzburg Seminar, Saltzburg, Austria, 1993, 98. Author: (poems) Fruits and Vegetables, 1971, reissued edit., 1997, Half Lives, 1973, Loveroot, 1975, At the Edge of the Body, 1979, Ordinary Miracles, 1983, Becoming Light: Poems New and Selected, 1992; (novels) Fear of Flying, 1973, How to Save Your Own Life, 1977, Fanny: Being the True History of the Adventures of Fanny Hackabout-Jones, 1980, Parachutes and Kisses, 1984, Serenissima, 1987 (reissued as Shylock's Daughter, 1995), Any Woman's Blues, 1990, Inventing Memory, 1998, Sappho's Leap, 2003, (poetry and non-fiction) Witches, 1981, reissued edit., 1997, (juvenile) Megan's Book of Divorce, 1984 (reissued as Megan's Two Houses, 1995), (memoir) The Devil at Large, 1993, What Do Women Want?, 1998, Seducing the Demon: Writing for My Life, 2006; (autobiography) Fear of Fifty, 1994; composer lyrics: Zipless: Songs of Abandon from the Erotic Poetry of Erica Jong, 1995, (fiction) Inventing Memory, 1997. Recipient Bess Hokin prize Poetry mag., 1971, Prix Literaire, Deauville Film Festival, 1997; named Mother of Yr., 1982; Woodrow Wilson fellow; Nat. Endowment Arts grantee, 1973. Mem. PEN, Authors Guild U.S.A. (coun. 1975—, pres. 1991-93), Poets and Writers Bd., Writers Guild Am.-West, Poetry Soc. Am. (Alice Faye di Castagnola award 1972), Phi Beta Kappa. Office: Erica Jong Prodns c/o Kenneth David Burrows 451 Park Ave S FL 8 New York NY 10016-7390

JONG, SHUNG-CHANG, mycologist; b. Taipei, Taiwan, Nov. 12, 1936; came to U.S., 1965; m. Chiu-Hwa Kou, Apr. 20, 1965; children: Maria, Cynthia, Victoria. MS, Western Ill. U., 1966; PhD, Washington State U., 1969. Plant pathologist Taiwan Agrl. Rsch. Inst., Taipei, 1961—63; instr. Nat. Taiwan U., Taipei, 1963—65; tchg. asst. Western Ill. U., Macomb, 1965—66; rsch. asst. Wash. State U., Pullman, 1966—69; sr. mycologist Am. Type Culture Collection, Rockville, Md., 1969—71, curator, 1971—89, head mycology dept., 1973—, sr. staff scientist, 1989—, dir. mycology and protistology program, 1993—, dir. microbiology divsn., 1997—. Dir. Yeast Genetic Stock Ctr., 1998—; dissertation dir. George Washington U., Washington, 1975-79; tech. advisor Yamazaki Baking Co., Tokyo, Japan, 1984—; exec. bd. World Fedn. for Culture Collection, 1988-92. Contbr. articles to profl. jours. Recipient Internat. Sci. and Tech. award Ministry of Agr., 1988, Brown Hazen grant Rsch. Corp., 1974-76, J. Roger Porter award ASM/ASFCC, 1997; NSF grantee, 1975-80, 80-85, 85-90, 90-95, 95-2000, 2000—. Fellow Am. Acad. Microbiology, Washington Acad. Scis.; mem. World Fedn. for Culture Collections, Internat. Mycol. Assn. (exec. com. 1983-90), Internat. Commn. on Taxonomy of Fungi, Mycol. Soc. of Am. (com. on culture collection 1986-91). Office: Am Type Culture Collection 10801 University Blvd Manassas VA 20110-2204 Office Phone: 703-365-2742. Office Fax: 703-365-2770. Business E-Mail: sjong@atcc.org.

JONGEWARD, GEORGE RONALD, retired systems analyst; b. Yakima, Wash., Aug. 9, 1934; s. George Ira and Dorothy Marjorie (Cronk) J.; m. Janet Jeanne Williams, July 15, 1955; children: Mary Jeanne, Dona Lee, Karen Anne. BA, Whitworth Coll., 1957; postgrad., Utah State U., 1961. Sr. systems analyst Computer Scis. Corp., Honolulu, 1969-71; cons. in field Honolulu, 1972-76; prin. The Hobby Co., Honolulu, 1977-81; sr. systems analyst Computer Systems Internat., Honolulu, 1981-96, asst. v.p., 1994-96; instr. EDP Hawaii Pacific U., Honolulu, 1982-90. Mem. car show com. Easter Seal Soc., Honolulu. 1977-82; active Variety Club, Honolulu, 1978-81. Mem. Mensa (Hawaii pres. 1967-69), Triple-9. Presbyterian. Avocations: travel, professional pianist, theater, classic cars. Home: 4108 Avalanche Ave Yakima WA 98908-2915

JONKER, ROBERT JAMES, federal judge; b. Holland, Mich., Mar. 9, 1960; s. Jerry and Delia (Roels) J.; m. Nancy Grevengoed, Aug. 11, 1984. BA with honors, Calvin Coll., 1982; JD summa cum laude, U. Mich. Law Sch., 1985. Bar: Mich. 1985, U.S. Dist. Ct. (ea. and we. dists.) Mich. 1987. Law clk. to chief judge US Dist. Ct. (ea. dist.) Mich., Detroit, 1985-87; assoc. Warner, Norcross & Judd, Grand Rapids, Mich., 1987—93, ptnr., 1994—2007; judge US Dist. Ct. (we. dist.) Mich., 2007—. Recipient Am.

Jurisprudence award, 1983, 84, 85. Mem. ABA, Mich. Bar Assn. (com. civil procedure), Grand Rapids Bar Assn., Order of Coif. Office: US Dist Ct 399 Fed Bldg 110 Michigan St NW Grand Rapids MI 49503*

JONSEN, ALBERT R(UPERT), retired medical ethics educator; b. San Francisco, Apr. 4, 1931; s. Albert R. and Helen (Sweigert) Jonsen; m. Mary Elizabeth Carolan. BA, Gonzaga U., 1955, MA, 1956; STM, U. Santa Clara, 1963; PhD, Yale U., 1967. Mem. S.J., 1949—76; ordained priest Roman Cath. Ch.; instr. philosophy Loyola U., LA, 1956—59; asst. in instrn. Yale Div. Sch., 1966—67; asst. prof. theology and philosophy U. San Francisco, 1967—72, pres., 1969—72; prof. med. ethics Sch. Medicine, U. Calif.-San Francisco, 1972—87; adj. assoc. prof. dept. community medicine and internat. health Sch. Medicine, Georgetown U., 1977; prof. med. ethics, chmn. dept. med. history and ethics Sch. Medicine U. Wash., Seattle, 1987—99, prof. emeritus; faculty Fromm Inst. for Life-Long Learning, U. San Francisco, 2000—; co-dir. Ctr. for Medicine and Human Values, Calif. Pacific Med. Ctr., San Francisco, 2004—. Vis. prof. Yale U., 1999—2000; mem. artificial heart assessment panel Nat. Heart and Lung Inst., 1972—73, 1984—86; mem. Am. Bd. Med. Spltys., 1978—81; cons. Am. Bd. Internal Medicine, 1978—82, ACOG, 1983—88; mem. Pres.'s Commn. for Study of Ethical Problems in Medicine, 1979—82, Nat. Commn. for Protection Human Subjects of Biomed. and Behavioral Rsch., HEW, 1974—78, Nat. Bd. Med. Examiners, 1985—87, Commn. on AIDS Rsch., NRC, 1986—92, Panel on Social Impact of AIDS (chmn.), 1989—91; chmn. nat. adv. bd. Ethics and Reprodn., 1991—96; mem. ethics adv. bd. GERON Corp., 2000—; vis. prof. Stanford U. Sch. Medicine, 2002, U. Va. Law Sch., 2002; vis. prof. dept. surgery U. Calif., San Francisco, 2004. Author: Responsibility in Modern Religious Ethics, 1968, Patterns of Moral Responsibility, 1969, Christian Decision and Action, 1970, Ethics of Newborn Intensive Care, 1976, Clin. Ethics, 1982, 6th edit., 2005, The Abuse of Casuistry: A History of Moral Reasoning, 1987, The New Medicine and the Old Ethics, 1990, The Social Impact of AIDS in the United States, 1993, Bioethics, 1997, The Birth of Bioethics, 1998, A Short History of Medical Ethics, 2000, Bioethics Beyond the Headlines, 2005; mem. editl. bd. Jour. Philosophy and Medicine, Jour. Clin. Ethics. Bd. trustees Inst. Ednl. Mgmt., Harvard U., 1971—74, Ploughshares Found., 1980—84; mem. San Francisco Crime Com., 1969—71; bd. dirs. Found. Critical Care Medicine, 1983—86, Sierra Health Found., 1987—. Fellow, Guggenheim, 1995—96. Fellow: The Hastings Ctr.; mem.: Am. Osler Soc. (McGovern award 1986), Am. Coll. Cardiology (Convocation Medal 1996), Am. Soc. for Bioethics and Humanities (Lifetime Achievement award 1999), Blue Cross and Blue Shield Assn. (tech. assessment program 1985—2003, med. adv. panel), Instituto de Bioetica (Madrid), Inst. Medicine (com. human values 1973, coun. 1983—85, 1990—92), Soc. Christian Ethics, Am. Soc. Law and Medicine (bd. dirs. 1986—88), Soc. Health and Human Values (pres. 1986—87). Home: 1333 Jones St # 502 San Francisco CA 94109 E-mail: arjonsen@aol.com.

JONTZ, DENNIS EUGENE, lawyer; b. Kewanee, Ill., Feb. 25, 1948; s. Lowell Milton and Maxine Alice (Bitting) J.; m. Mary Ann DeBasio, Jan. 18, 1974; children: Ashlee, Charles. BA in Econs., Drake U., 1970, JD, 1973, MBA, 1974. Bar: Iowa 1973, U.S. Ct. Mil. Appeals 1974, N.Mex. 1977, U.S. Dist. Ct. N.Mex. 1977, U.S. Ct. Appeals (10th cir.) 1979, U.S. Supreme Ct. 1979, U.S. Claims Ct. 1979. Asst. atty. gen. State of Iowa, Des Moines, 1973-74; pres. Civerolo, Hansen & Wolf, Albuquerque, 1978, also bd. dirs.; ptnr. Lewis & Roca LLP, Albuquerque. Bd. dirs. Albuquerque Econ. Develop.; mem. N. Mex Bd. Bar Commissioners; chmn. bd. Oso Grande Technologies Inc.; founding bd. mem. Explora Sci. Ctr. & Children's Mus., N. Mex Natural History Mus. Found. Lt. col. USAF, 1974, judge adv. USAF. Mem. N.Mex. State Bar Assn. (chmn. tech. utilization com. 1986-91, pres. 2006-07; Outstanding Contbn. 1987-88, Pioneer award 1989), Am. Arbitration Assn., Nat. Contract Mgmt. Assn.; Rotary (v.p. Alb Charitable Found.). Lutheran. Avocation: golf. Office: Lewis & Roca LLP Ste 1950 201 Third St NW Albuquerque NM 87102 Office Phone: 505-764-5405. Office Fax: 505-764-5469. E-mail: DJontz@LRLaw.com.

JONTZ, JEFFRY ROBERT, lawyer; b. Stuart, Iowa, May 28, 1944; s. John Leo Jontz and Leora Burnette (Pittman) Myers; m. Sharyn Sue Kopriva, June 8, 1968; 1 child, Eric Barrett. BA, Drake U., 1966; JD with distinction, U. Iowa, 1969. Bar: Iowa 1969, Fla. 1971, U.S. Dist. Ct. (mid. dist.) Fla. 1971, Ohio 1972, U.S. Ct. Appeals (5th cir.) 1972, U.S. Ct. Appeals (11th cir.) 1981, U.S. Tax Ct. 1983. Law clk. to Hon. Charles R. Scott U.S. Dist. Ct. (mid. dist.) Fla., Jacksonville, 1969-70; to Hon. Bryan Simpson U.S. Ct. Appeals (5th cir.), Jacksonville, 1970-71; assoc. Jones, Day, Cockley & Reavis, Cleve., 1971-72; asst. U.S. atty. U.S. Dist. Ct. (mid. dist.) Fla., Orlando, 1972-74; pvt. practice Orlando, 1974—; ptnr. Young, Turnbull & Linscott, Orlando, 1974-79, Baker & Hostetler, Orlando, 1979, DeWolf, Ward & Morris, Orlando, 1979-84, Jontz, Russell & Hull, Orlando, 1985-86, Holland & Knight, 1986-96, Carlton Fields, Orlando, 1996—2005, Swann & Hadley, Winter Pk., Fla., 2005—. Contbr. articles to profl. jours.; mem. editl. bd. Iowa Law Rev., 1968. Chmn. Fed. Jud. Rels. Com., 2001—04; past bd. dirs. Door Drug Rehab. Ctr. Ctrl. Fla.; bd. dirs. Fla. Symphony Orch., 1985—93, Jr. Achievement Ctrl. Fla., 1997—2005; mem. Rollins Coll. Tar Boosters; mem. code enforcement bd. City of Maitland, Fla., 1990—92; chmn bd. adjustment City of Winter Park, Fla., 1995—; mem. parents com. Dartmouth Coll., 1995—99; mem. long range planning com. , former county commiteeman Orange County Reps., Fla.; past chmn. bd. trustees First Congl. Ch., Winter Park. Recipient Outstanding Individual Cmty. Leadership award, Vol. Ctr. Ctrl. Fla., 1991. Mem.: ABA (mem. comml. transactions litig. com., others), Am. Arbitration Assn. (comml. arbitrator 2005—), Orange County Bar Assn. (chmn. jud. rels. com. 1995—, mem. bankruptcy com.), Iowa State Bar Assn., Fla. Bar (mem. 9th cir. grievance com. 1979—82, chmn. comml. litig. com. 1981—82, mem. com. jud. adminstrn., selection and tenure 1985—86, mem. jud. nominating procedures com. 1995—96, mem. bankruptcy and creator's rights com., lectr. seminars), Ctrl. Fla. Bankruptcy Lawyers Assn., Am. Bankruptcy Inst., U. Iowa Alumni Assn. (bd. dirs. 2003—), Drake U. Nat. Alumni Assn. (bd. dirs. 1981—93, past chmn. ctrl. Fla. chpt., pres.'s cir. coun.), Citrus Club, Winter Park Racquet Club (pres. 1989—94, 1996—98, bd. govs., sec., v.p.), Tiger Bay Club Orlando, Order of Coif, Phi Delta Phi, Tau Kappa Epsilon, Omicron Delta Kappa. Office: PO Box 1870 Winter Park FL 32790-1870 also: 1031 W Morse Blvd Winter Park FL 32789 Office Phone: 407-647-2777. Personal E-mail: jontz@earthlink.net. Business E-Mail: jjontz@swannhadley.com.

JOO, DOUGLAS D.M., newspaper and video production and aviation executive; b. Hamheung, Korea, July 14, 1945; came to U.S., 1985; s. Soo Jang and Syn Duk (Choi) J.; m. Myung Mi, Oct. 21, 1970; children: Hoon Hwi, Hoon Pal, Hoon Chul. BS, Seoul Nat. U., 1967; MA, Kyung Hee U., Seoul, 1979; MPhil, George Washington U., 1993; DPolit Sci (hon.), Sun Moon U., Korea, 2005. Pres. Washington Times Corp., 1991—2005, News World Comms., Washington, 1992—2003, Washington Times LLC, 2005—07, chmn., 2007—; pres. Noticias PanAm Corp., 1996—2003; chmn., CEO Atlantic Video, Inc., 1991—2005; pres. U.S. Property Devel. Corp., 1991—2005, Nat. Hospitality Corp., 2000—05; chmn., CEO UPI, 2000—03. Pres. Concept Comms., Washington, 1992-2005; chmn., CEO, AmericanLife TV Network, 1992-2005; pres. Washington Times Aviation, 1997—, WTA Korea, Inc., 2004—. Trustee U. Bridgeport, Conn., 1991—; chmn. bd. dir. Internat. Coalition for Religious Freedom, Washington, 1998-2003;chmn. Am. Freedom Coalition, 1992-2000, Am. Family Coalition, 2000-02; pres. Unification Ch. Internat., 1991-2005. Mem. World Media Assn. (pres. 1992—), Washington Times Found. (pres. 1992—). Office: Washington Times LLC 3600 New York Ave NE Washington DC 20002-1996 Office Phone: 202-636-4841.

JOO, MICHAEL, artist, educator; b. Ithaca, NY, 1966; BFA, Washington U., 1989; MFA, Yale U., 1991. Adj. instr. The Cooper Union Sch. Art, NYC, 1996, guest artist, 2000—. Adj. instr. The Cooper Union Sch. Art, NYC, 1996, guest artist, 2000—. One-man shows include Nordanstad-Skarstedt, N.Y., 1992, Thomas Nordanstad Gallery, 1994—96, Stedelijk Mus., Amsterdam, 1995, Galerie Anne de Villepoix, Paris, 1995, Anthony D'Offay Gallery, London, 1995, Anton Kern Gallery, N.Y., 1997, exhibited in group shows at Ctr. Arts at Yerba Buena, San Francisco, 1993, Queens (N.Y.) Mus. Art, 1993, New Mus. Contemporary Art, N.Y., 1993, The Interart Ctr., 1994, Kumho Mus., Seoul, 1994, Cohen Gallery, N.Y., 1994, Serpentine Gallery, London, 1994, Inst. Contemporary Art, 1995, Randolph St. Gallery, Chgo., 1995, Mus. Contemporary Art, 1995, Kwangju Contemporary Mus., Sydkorea, 1995, Bloom Gallery, Amsterdam, 1996, The Post Office, London, 1996, Mus. Africa, Johannesburg, 1997, Anton Kern Gallery, N.Y., 1997, P.S. 1, 1998, others. Achievements include Represented Korea Venice Art Biennial, 2001. Office: care Cooper Union Sch Art 30 Cooper Sq New York NY 10003-7120

JOOHI, LEE, early childhood educator; b. Seoul, Jan. 15, 1971; d. Soonwong and Eunboon Lee. PhD, Ind. State U., 2004. Asst. prof. U. Tex., Arlington, 2004—. Elizabeth Breathwaite Mini-grant, Assn. for Childhood Edn. Internat., 2003. Office: Univ Tex 701 S College St Arlington TX 76019-022 Home: 8041 N MacArthur Blvd 1175 Irving TX 75063 Office Phone: 817-272-2264. Office Fax: 817-272-1281. Business E-Mail: joohilee@uta.edu.

JOOS, DAVID W., energy executive; BS in Engring. Sci., Iowa State U., 1975, MS in Nuc. Engring., 1976. With CMS Energy Corp., 1976—; pres., CEO elec. Consumers Energy Corp., 1997—2000; exec. v.p., COO elec. CMS Energy Corp., 2000—01, pres. and COO, 2001—04, pres. and CEO, 2004—. Mem.: Assn. Edison Illuminating Co., Mich. Coll. Found., Mich. Mfg. Assn. Office: CMS Energy One Energy Plz Jackson MI 49201*

JOOS, FELIPE MIGUEL, mechanical engineer, researcher; b. Montevideo, Uruguay, Sept. 4, 1952; arrived in U.S., 1973, naturalized, 2003; s. Carlos Jose and Alma Elena Joos; children: Carolina Lucia, Catrina Aneliese, Celina Maria. BS in Engring. and Applied Sci., Calif. Inst. Tech., 1976; MSME, MIT, 1978, PhDME, 1983. Cert. engr., Uruguay. Engr. Ingenieros Consultores Latinoamericanos Limitada, Montevideo, Uruguay, 1978-79; mech. engr. research and devel. div. Gen. Electric Corp., Schenectady, NY, 1982-85; project engr. Creare, Inc., Hanover, NH, 1985-87; tech. assoc. Eastman Kodak Co., Rochester, NY, 1987—2007. Indsl. fellow Ctr. for Interfacial Engring., U. Minn., Mpls., 1991-92; presenter in field. Contbr. articles to profl. jours.; patentee in field. Mem.: ASME, Soc. Hispanic Profl. Engrs. (v.p. 1989—90, treas. 1990—92, treas. Ea. Tech. and Career conf. 1991, award 1993), Internat. Soc. Coating Sci. and Tech. (tech. session chair 1994, 1996, 2000, symposium co-chair 2006), Tau Beta Pi. Avocations: scuba diving, community affairs. Home: 75 Wood Creek Dr Pittsford NY 14534-4415 Personal E-mail: joos@alum.mit.edu.

JOOSTEN, KATHRYN (KATHRYN JOOSTYN), actress; b. Dec. 20, 1939; Actor: (films) Grandview, U.S.A., 1984, The Package, 1989, Best Man, 1997, Phoenix, 1998, Kiss Toledo Goodbye, 1999, Lehi's Wife, 2002, Cojones, 2002, Halfway Decent, 2003, Red Rose and Petrol, 2003, Breaking Dawn, 2004, Win a Date with Tad Hamilton, 2004, Fathers and Sons, 2005, Hostage, 2005, Taking Your Life, 2005, Wedding Crashers, 2005; (TV films) Lady Blue, 1985, The Stranger Beside Me, 1995, The Making of a Hollywood Madam, 1996, Combustion (Silent Killer), 2004, McBride: It's Murder, Madam, 2005; (TV series) Secret Santa, 2003, Highway to Oblivion, 2003; performer: (stage) Ladies of the Corridor; actor: (video) Hellraiser:Inferno, 2000; guest appearences include General Hospital, Grace Under Fire, 1995, Roseanne, 1996, Third Rock from the Sun, 1996, ER, 1996, The West Wing (several episodes), 1996—2001, Murphy Brown, 1996, Boston Common, 1996, Frasier, 1997, Men Behaving Badly, 1997, NYPD Blue, 1997, Brooklyn South, 1997, Dharma & Greg, 1998, Dharma & Greg (several episodes), 2000—01, Just Shoot Me!, 1998, The Nanny, 1998, The Drew Carey Show, 1998, 2003, Providence, 1999, 2001, Home Improvement, 1999, Tracey Takes On, 1999, Buffy the Vampire Slayer, 2000, Becker, 2000, Ally McBeal, 2001, Scrubs, 2001, Spin City, 2001, The X Files, 2002, Judging Amy, 2003, Monk, 2003, Hope & Faith, 2003, Joan of Arcadia (several episodes), 2003—05, Charmed, 2003, Less Than Perfect, 2003, Strong Medicine, 2003, The King of Queens, 2003, A.U.S.A., 2003, Curb Your Enthusiasm, 2004, Will & Grace, 2004, Yes, Dear, 2004, Life with Bonnie, 2004, Everwood, 2004, Gilmore Girls, 2004, Desperate Housewives, 2005 (Creative Arts Primetime Emmy award for guest actress in a comedy series, 2005), Grey's Anatomy, 2005. Mem.: SAG, AFTRA, AEA.

JORAPUR, VINOD, physician, researcher; arrived in U.S, 2001; s. Pandurang Bhimarao and Nirmala Pandurang Jorapur; m. Kshamaya Badarinarayan Panchamukhi, Feb. 4, 1999. MBBS, Sri Venkateswara Med. Coll., Tirupati, Ap, India, 1990; MD, Postgraduate Inst. Of Med. Edn. And Rsch., Chandigarh, 1994; MD in Cardiology, Sanjay Gandhi Post Grad. Inst. Of Med. Sci., Lucknow, Up, India, 1998; MD, Our Lady Of Mercy U. Hosp., Bronx, NY, 2002. Lic. Unrestricted Med. Med. Coun. Of India, 1990, Dm, Cardiology Sanjay Gandhi Postgraduate Inst. Of Med. Sci., Lucknow, 1998, Electrophysiology Training Course Bard South Asia Electrophysiology Tng. Program, 2001. Intern Sri Venkataramana Ruia Hosp., Tirupati, Andhra Pradesh, India, 1989—90; jr. resident in internal medicine Postgraduate Inst. Of Med. Edn. And Rsch., Chandigarh, India, 1991—94; chief resident in cardiology Sri Venkateswara Inst. Of Med. Sci., Tirupati, Andhra Pradesh, India, 1994—95; sr. resident in cardiology Sanjay Gandhi Postgraduate Inst. Of Med. Sci., Lucknow, Uttar Pradesh, India, 1995—98; attending cardiologist St. Stephen's Hosp., Delhi, Delhi, India, 1998—98; asst. prof. of cardiology Ms Ramaiah Inst. Of Cardiology, Rajeev Gandhi U., Bangalore, Karnataka, India, 1998—2001; sr. housestaff Our Lady Of Mercy U. Hosp., Bronx, NY, 2002—. Cons. physician St. Stephen's Hosp., Delhi, India, 1998—98; co-dir. interventional cardiology and cardiac catheterization lab. Ms Ramaiah Inst. Of Cardiology, Rajeev Gandhi U., Bangalore, Karnataka, India, 1998—2001; co-investigator Hero-2 Internat. Multicenter Randomized Control Trial, Bangalore, Karnataka, India, 2000—01; cardiovasc. clin. rsch. fellow NYU Sch. Med., 2005. Author: (post doctoral dissertation) Transbronchial lung biopsy in sarcoidosis and relationship of histological changes to pulmonary function, (chpt.) Vascular Heart Disease, 2005; contbr. articles pub. to profl. jour. Recipient First prize in quiz contest, Indian Acad. of Pediat., 1988, Indian Coun. of Med. Rsch. award; fellow Fellowship In Cardiology, Sanjay Gandhi Postgraduate Inst. Of Med. Sci., 1995-1998; grantee Indian Coun. Of Med. Rsch. Grant, Indian Coun. Of Med. Rsch., 1987; scholar Nat. Talent Search Scholarship, Nat. Coun. of Ednl. Rsch. and Tng., India, 1982. Mem.: ACP (assoc.; assoc. mem. 2002), Am. Assn. Advancement of Sci., Med. Soc. State N.Y. (mem. heart lung cancer com. 2004—), Am. Heart. Assn., A,. Med. Assn., Indian Med. Assn. (life; life mem. 1990), Cardiol. Soc. Of India (life; life mem. 1998). Achievements include research in echocardiographic quantification of annular dilatation and papillary muscle separation in patients of functional mitral regurgitation — role of anterior mitral leaflet length as reference; the effect of percutaneous coronary intervention on QT dispersion in acute coronary syndromes; immunosuppressive therapy in active Takayasu's arteritis — clinical immunological and angiographic study; clinical echocardiographic and angiographic characteristics and outcome in diabetics with acute myocardial infarction; the effect of renal transplantation on left ventricular function in chronic renal failure; immunosuppressive therapy in aortoarteritis — clinical and angiographic follow up; pulmonary sarcoidosis: spirometric correlation with transbronchial lung biopsy; epidemiological study of hypertension and coronary artery disease in urban and rural South India; mitral leaflet coaptation morphology identifies mechanism of functional mitral regurgitation in heart failure: in-vitro insights for surgical strategy; differential scallop reserve and failure mode of leaflet compensatory mechanisms in papillary displacement cardiomyopathy; the role of immunosuppressive therapy on clinical immunological and angiographic outcome in active Takayasu's Arteritis; in-vitro quantification of factors that overwhelm leaflet compensatory mechanisms for mitral regurgitation in heart failure; the influence of inter-papillary distance on mitral regurgitation in normal and myopathic hearts: implications for ventricular geometry restoration; leaflet compensatory mechanisms for functional mitral regurgitation in papillary displacement model of heart failure; the absence of typically described electrocardiographic changes in a patient of hyperkalemia who had preexisting electrocardiographic changes; increased intraventricular velocities — a surrogate marker for left ventricular hypertrophy in patients of hypertension; epidemiological study of ischemic heart disease; the longitudinal study of the morphologic determinants of functional mitral regurgitation in patients with post-infarction left ventricular remodeling. Avocations: travel, reading, photography. Home Phone: 718-696-2060. Personal E-mail: vjorapur@yahoo.com.

JORDA, MERCE MARIA, pathologist; d. Josep Jorda and Rosa Heras; life ptnr. Gustavo Fernandez; children: Arnau Josep Hanly-Jorda, Fiona Maura Hanly-Jorda. MD, U. Barcelona, Spain, 1983; PhD, U. Seville, Barcelona, 1988. Lic. pathologist Fla., 1996. Clin. dir. lab. svcs. sylvester comprehensive cancer ctr. U. Miami, Fla., 1998—. Med. U. Miami, 1998—. Achievements include development of clinical and anatomic laboratory. Home Phone: 305-669-0062; Office Phone: 305-243-6560. Office Fax: 305-243-5134. Business E-Mail: mjorda@med.miami.edu.

JORDAK, JOHN A., JR., lawyer; b. Saginaw, Mich., Dec. 9, 1967; AB cum laude, Duke Univ., 1990; JD with distinction, Emory Univ., Atlanta, 1993. Bar: Ga. 1993. Ptnr., chmn., securities litig. group Alston & Bird LLP, Atlanta. Writes and lectures frequently on securities litig. and regulation. Alumni Admissions Adv. Com. Duke Univ. Named a Ga. Super Lawyer, Atlanta Mag., 2006; recipient NC Scholars Scholarship, Duke U., Am. Jurisprudence award in Contracts. Office: Alston & Bird LLP One Atlantic Ctr 1201 W Peachtree St Atlanta GA 30309-3424 Office Phone: 404-881-7868. Office Fax: 404-253-8358. Business E-Mail: john.jordak@alston.com.*

JORDAN, ALEXANDER JOSEPH, JR., lawyer; b. New London, Conn., Oct. 11, 1938; s. Alexander Joseph and Alice Elizabeth (Mugovero) J.; m. Mary Carolyn Miller, Aug. 8, 1964; children: Jennifer, Michael, Stephanie. BS, U.S. Naval Acad., 1960; LLB, Harvard U., 1968. Ptnr. Gaston & Snow, Boston, 1968-91, Bingham, Dana & Gould, Boston, 1991-93, Nixon Peabody LLP, Boston, 1994—2006. Chmn. adv. com. Town of Hingham, Mass., 1989-95, govt. study com., 2000-01. With USN, 1960-65, capt. USNR, 1965-94, ret. Mem. ABA, Mass. Bar Assn., Boston Bar Assn., U.S. Naval Inst., Naval Res. Assn., Harvard Alumni Assn. (regional dir. 1998-2001), U.S. Naval Acad. Alumni Assn., Harvard Club Hingham (trustee, chmn. com. schs. and scholarships, past pres.), Harvard Club of Boston. Office: Nixon Peabody LLP 100 Summer St Boston MA 02110-2131 Home Phone: 781-749-6549; Office Phone: 617-345-1103. Business E-Mail: ajordan@nixonpeabody.com.

JORDAN, AMOS AZARIAH, JR., foreign affairs educator, retired military officer; b. Twin Falls, Idaho, Feb. 11, 1922; s. Amos Azariah and Olive (Fisher) J.; m. MarDeane Carver, June 5, 1946; children: Peggy Jordan Hughes, Diana Jordan Paxton, Keith, David, Linda Jordan Mabey, Kent. BS, US Mil. Acad., 1946; BA, Oxford U., Eng., 1950, MA, 1955; PhD, Columbia U., NYC, 1961. Commd. 2d lt. US Army, 1946, advanced through grades to brig. gen., 1972; instr. US Mil. Acad., 1950-53, prof. social scis., 1955-72; arty. battery comdr. US Army, Republic of Korea, 1954-55; asst. S-3 7th Divsn. Arty. Korea, 1955; adviser econ. and fiscal policy US Econ. Mission to Korea, 1955; ret. US Army, 1972; dir. Aspen Inst., 1972-74; prin. dep. asst. sec. for internat. security affairs Dept. Def., Washington, 1974-76; dep. undersec. and acting undersec. for security assistance Dept. State, Washington, 1976-77; with Ctr. for Strategic and Internat. Studies, Washington, 1977-94, pres, chief exec. officer, 1983-88, vice chmn., 1988-94, pres. Pacific Forum Honolulu, 1990-94, sr. adviser, 1994—; counselor Pacific Forum, CSIS, 1994—. Mem. staff Pres.'s Com. to Study Fgn. Assistance Program, 1959; staff dir. Adv. Com. to Sec. Def. on Non-Mil. Instrn., 1962; spl. polit. advisor to U.S. amb. to India, 1963-64; cons. NSC, 1979; mem. Nat. Com. on Security and Econ. Assistance, 1983; Henry Kissinger rsch. chair in nat. security policy CSIS, 1988-92; mem. Pres.'s Intelligence Oversight Bd., 1989-93; internat. co-chmn. Coun. on Sec. Coop. in the Asia Pacific, 1993-96, chmn. U.S. com., 1993-98; co-chmn. Korean-Am. Wisemen Coun., 1991-98; Asia area adminstr. Latter Day Saint Charities, 1998-99; spl. asst. to pres. Brigham Young U., Hawaii, 2001-02; bd. dirs. Pacific Forum, Ctr. for Strategic and Internat. Studies, Jackson Hole Ctr. for Global Affairs. Author: Foreign Aid and the Defense of Southeast Asia, 1962, Issues of National Security in the 1970's, 1967; co-author: American National Security Policy and Process, 1981, 5th edit., 1999; contbr. chpts. to books and articles to profl. jours. Decorated D.S.M., Legion of Merit with oak leaf cluster, Disting. Civilian Svc. medal Dept. Def. Mem.: Assn. Am. Rhodes Scholars. Office: Pacific Forum CSIS Pauahi Tower 1001 Bishop St Ste 1150 Honolulu HI 96813-3407 Office Phone: 808-521-6745.

JORDAN, ANGEL GONI, electrical and computer engineering educator; b. Pamplona, Spain, Sept. 19, 1930; came to U.S., 1956, naturalized, 1966; s. Hilario and Perpetua (Goni) J.; m. Nieves Alfonso Cuartero, July 8, 1956; children: Xavier, Edward, Arthur. MS, PhD, Carnegie Inst. Tech., 1959; PhD (hon.), Poly. U. Madrid, Spain, 1985, U. Publica de Navarra, 2001, U. Carlos III, Madrid, 2007. With Naval Ordnance Lab., Madrid, 1952-56; instr. elec. engring. Carnegie-Mellon U., 1956-58, asst. prof. elec. engring., 1959-62, assoc. prof., 1962-65, prof., 1965-90, univ. prof., 1990-97, U.A. and Helen Whitaker prof., 1972-80, head dept., 1969-79, dean engring. Carnegie Inst. Tech., 1979-83, provost, 1983-91, J.F and N.P. Keithley univ. prof. elec., computer engring., 1997-99, univ. prof. emeritus, 1999—. Rsch. fellow Mellon Inst. Indsl. Rsch., 1958—59; bd. dirs. Magnascreen Corp., Mirror Sys., Inc., 1990—2003, SOCINTEC, 1990—2005; cons. in field. Contbr. articles to profl. jours. Dir. Pitts. High Tech. Coun., 1983-; bd. dirs. Pa. Sci. and Engring. Found, 1981-83. Recipient Enterprise award Pitts. Bus. Times, 1985; NATO sr. scientist fellow, 1976; Fulbright Disting. scholar, 1988; named Edn. Man of the Yr., Pitts., 1987. Fellow IEEE, AAAS; mem. Am. Phys. Soc., NAE, Acad. Engring. Spain, Sigma Xi, Eta Kappa Nu, Phi Kappa Phi, Tau Beta Pi. Home: 5874 Aylesboro Ave Pittsburgh PA 15217-1446 Office: Carnegie-Mellon U Wean Hall # 4618 Pittsburgh PA 15213 Office Phone: 412-268-2590. Business E-Mail: ajordan@cs.cmu.edu.

JORDAN, BONNIE, television producer; b. Dayton, Ohio, Mar. 9, 1948; d. Theodore and Faye Annette (Fields) Sampson; divorced; 1 son, Brett Anthony. Student, Habor Jr. Coll., Wilmington, Calif., 1966-68. Assoc. producer Dick Clark Prodns., Hollywood, Calif., 1972-73; assoc. producer, producer, writer Sta. KNBC-TV, LA, 1973-75; account exec. Ameron Co., Monterey Park, Calif., 1976; prodn. coord. Paramount Studios, Hollywood, Calif., 1977-78; asst. to producer Glen Larson Prodns., Film TV Devel. and Casting 20th Century Fox, Beverly Hills, Calif., 1978-84; prodn. coord. Universal Studios, 1986, 1989, 1993, New World TV, 1986—88, 1990—91, Show Time TV, 1991, ABC Productions, 1990—92, Castle Rock, 1992, Universal Studios, 1993, Kushner-Locke Prodns., 1994, Paramount Studios, Dennis Prager Prodns., 1996, Warner Bros., 1996, Triage Entertainment, 1998, Columbia Pictures, 1999—2000, Disney Co.,

2001—02; freelance, 2002—. Co-chairperson, United High Blood Pressure Telethon, CBS-TV, 1977. Mem. exec. bd., 1975-78; congl. record, Ho. of Reps, 1974, co-exec. producer California Magic Fundraiser for Jesse Jackson '88 Presdl. Campaign, 1988. Recipient cert. achievement City of L.A. and UCLA Mardi Gras, 1974. Mem. Women in Film, Nat. Assn. Media Women (corr. rec. sec. 1974-75). Mailing: PO Box 57973 Sherman Oaks CA 91413 Home Phone: 818-795-0027; Office Phone: 818-795-0027. Personal E-mail: zbonz007@sprintpcs.com.

JORDAN, BRYCE, retired university president; b. Clovis, N.Mex., Sept. 22, 1924; s. W. Joseph and Kittie (Cole) J.; children: Julia Cole, Christopher Joseph; m. Barbara E. Brueggebors, Oct. 28, 2000. Student, Hardin-Simmons U., 1941-42; MusB, U. Tex., 1948, MusM, 1949; PhD, U. N.C., 1956; LLD, Juniata Coll., 1985, Milliken U., 1990. Asst. prof. music Hardin-Simmons U., 1949-51; from asst. prof. to prof. music U. Md., 1954-63; prof. music, chmn. dept. U. Ky., 1963-65, U. Tex., 1965-68, v.p. student affairs Austin, 1968-70, pres. ad interim, 1970-71, pres. Dallas, 1971-81; exec. vice chancellor for acad. affairs U. Tex. System, 1981-83; pres. Pa. State U., 1983-90. Mem. faculty Salzburg (Austria) Seminar Am. Studies, 1960, 62, 98; occasional lectr. Fgn. Svc. Inst., Dept. State, 1962-63; mem. Yale Coun. on Music, 1971-73, Nat. Commn. on Higher Edn. Issues, 1982-83; expert witness in field. Author: (with Homer Ulrich) Student Manual for Music: A Design for Listening, 1957, Designed for Listening, 1962, also articles, revs.; assoc. editor: Coll. Music Symposium, 1961-66. Bd. dirs. Dallas Grand Opera Assn., 1973-75, Pa. Econ. Devel. Ptnrship, 1987-90; trustee St. Marks Sch. Tex., 1973-81, Dallas Symphony Assn., 1972-81, Presbyn. Hosp., Dallas, 1976-83; v.p. Dallas Civic Music Assn., 1978-79, pres., 1979-80, exec. com. 1980-81; bd. dirs. Dallas County chpt. ARC, 1976-79; divsn. chmn. United Way Met. Dallas, 1979; Pa. state chmn. Am. Heart Assn., 1983-84; trustee Com. on Econ. Devel. 1988-90; adv. bd. comml. programs NASA, 1988-90; nat. chmn. higher edn. U.S. Treasury Savs. Bond Programs, 1988-89, 89-90; presiding elder Presbyn. Ch.; chmn. Austin Lyric Opera, 1991-94; vis. com. Eastman Sch. Music U. Rochester, 1991-94; chmn. fine arts adv. coun. U. Tex., Austin, 1994-96; chmn. adv. bd. U. Tex. Press, 1997-99; mem. Knight Found. Commn. on Intercollegiate Athletics, 1991-93, 2000-01, mem. oversight com. Knight vs. Ala., 1995-2006. Recipient Hon. Alumni award Pa. State U., 1987, medal, 1990, Doty medal U. Tex., 1996, Presdl. citation U. Tex., 2002; named Disting. Alumnus, U. N.C., 1985, Hardin-Simmons U., 1987, U. Tex., Austin, 1991. Mem. Coll. Music Soc. (v.p. 1963-65, coun. mem. 1968-70), Am. Musicol. Soc. (chmn. greater Washington chpt. 1958-60), Music Educators Nat. Conf. (pres. Md. br. 1963), Music Tchrs. Nat. Assn., Philos. Soc. Tex., Dallas C. of C. (dir. 1979-82), So. Assn. Colls. and Schs. (commn. on colls. 1981-83), Pa. Assn. Colls. and Univs. (chmn. 1988-89), Phi Kappa Phi, Pi Kappa Lambda, Phi Mu Alpha, Golden Key. Home: 5809 Tom Wooten Cove Austin TX 78731-6512 Personal E-mail: bigbendboy@austin.rr.com.

JORDAN, CARRIE GRAYSON (CARRIE GRAYSON-JORDAN), writer, poet, drama designer; b. Laurel, Miss. children: Rickson Vancouver, Corichey Robert. AA in Liberal Arts with honors, Kennedy-King Coll., 1990. With Girl Scouts USA, Chgo., 1966—70, Operation Ish, 1970—71; admissions fgn. student specialist Kennedy-King Coll.; modeling group mgmt. Noir Fashions, 1976—78. Author: (book) Dear Butterflies; (plays) Grandpa's Stocking, Mr. Big Egg, Joy, Cassie, Curtains, Sky, Plays of Faith, Fun and Family, Black Barber Shop; columnist KKC Press; poet World of Poetry, 1991, Sparrowgrass forum, 1991, Crysopoets, 1997. Bd. dirs. S.E. Little League, Chgo., 1986-89; judge Act-SO Contest, NAACP, Chgo., 1996—, annually. Recipient Golden Poet award, World of Poetry, 1990. Mem. Chrysopoets, Renowned Poetry Club, Lyric Opera. Avocations: composing songs, writing, designing clothes, clown collecting, producing and directing own plays.

JORDAN, CHARLENE HANSON, writer; b. Elgin, Tex., Dec. 26, 1937; d. John Herbert Hanson and Ruth Linnea Swenson; m. Henry Goetz Jordan, Sept. 22, 1962 (dec.); 1 child, Andre Christopher; 1 child, Travis Christopher. BA, U. Houston, 1960. Travel cons. Harvey Travel, Houston, 1957—60; fgn. svc. staff U.S. Dept. State, Wash., DC, 1960—61; passport adjudicator U.S. Passport Office, NYC, 1961—62; sec. sales and tours Scandinavian Airlines, NYC, 1962—65; travel cons. Schiller Coll., Ingersheim, Germany, 1972—73; asst. to dir. German Convention Bur., Frankfurt, 1973—75; co-owner, mgr. of groups Longhorn Travelers/Jordan Groups, Austin, Tex., 1975—87; owner, mgr. Ancestral-Home Tours, Elgin, Tex., 1998—2006, Emigrant-Home Tours. Hist. rschr., grant writer, op geneal. hist. tours Ancestral Home and Emigrant Home Tours, Elgin, 1998—2006; founder Vasa Lodge, Waco, Tex., Type, Tex. Author: Crossroads Elgin, 2004, Twelve Swedish Quarterlies, 1998, (quarterly jour.) Tex. Swedish Pioneer and Swedish Texan, 1995—2002. Chair grants com. Coupland Civic Orgn. Cmty. Ctr.; planning com. Elgin Depot Mus., Elgin; grant writer Yegua Creek Evang. Free Ch., 1997. Named Cmty. Builder of Yr., Post Oak Is. Masonic Lodge, 1997, Hon. Raven #67, Korpagillet (Order of the Raven), Uddevalla, Sweden, 1999; recipient Award of Merit, Swedish Coun. of Am., 1998. Mem.: Internat. Orgn. Swedish Speaking Women, Elgin Hist. Assn., Vasa Order of Am. (Cert. Commendation), Am. Assn. State and Local History, Williamson County Hist. Commn. (assoc.). Avocations: travel, genealogy. Home: 1361 County Rd 464 Elgin TX 78621 Office: Ancestral-Home Tours Emigrant-Home Tours 1361 County Rd 464 Elgin TX 78621 Personal E-mail: charlenehansonjordan@yahoo.com.

JORDAN, CHARLES C., lawyer; b. Dallas, Mar. 3, 1952; BA summa cum laude, Emory U., 1974; JD, Harvard U., 1978. Bar: Tex. 1978. Ptnr. Carrington, Coleman, Sloman & Bumenthal, L.L.P., Dallas, Carrington Coleman, Dallas. Contbr. articles to profl. jour. Chmn., bd. dir. Uptown Pub. Improvement Dist., 2003—04. Named The Best Lawyers in Am., 2005—06. Mem. ABA (natural resources, energy, environ., real property, probate and trust law sect.), Tex. Bar Assn. (chair environ. and natural resources law sect., 2001, real estate, probate and trust law sect.), Dallas Bar Assn. (chair environ. law sect. and real property sect., 2005), Phi Beta Kappa. Office: Carrington Coleman 901 Main St Ste 5500 Dallas TX 75202 Office Phone: 214-855-3021. Office Fax: 214-758-3721. Business E-Mail: cjordan@ccsb.com.

JORDAN, CHARLES MILTON, lawyer; b. Houston, Apr. 3, 1949; m. Jeanette Jordan; children: Nicole, John, Rebecca. BBA, U. Tex., 1971, JD, 1975. Bar: Tex. 75, U.S. Dist. Ct. (so. dist.) Tex. 76, U.S. Supreme Ct. 78, U.S. Ct. Appeals (5th cir.) 79, U.S. Dist. Ct. (no. dist.) Tex. 82, U.S. Dist. Ct. (we. and ea. dists.) Tex. 83. Assoc. Troutman, Earle & Hill, Austin, 1975, Simpson & Burwell, Texas City, 1976—78, Smith & Herz, Galveston, Tex., 1978—80; ptnr. Dibrell & Greer, Galveston, 1980—85, Barlow, Todd, Crews & Jordan PC, Houston, 1986—88, Barlow, Todd, Jordan & Oliver, LLP, Houston, 1988—99, Barlow, Todd, Jordan & Jones, LLP, Houston, 1999—2002, Daughtry & Jordan, P.C., Houston, 2003—. Commr. Commn. Texas City/Galveston Ports, 1984. 1st lt. USAF, 1971—77. Recipient Outstanding Young Man Am. award, U.S. Jaycees, 1980. Mem. Tex. Bar Assn., Galveston County Bar Assn. (pres. 1981-82, bd. dirs. 1985-88), Tex. Young Lawyers Assn (bd. dirs. 1982-85, Outstanding Dir. award 1983-84), Galveston County Young Lawyers Assn. (pres. 1979-80, Outstanding Young Lawyer award 1981). Office: Daughtry & Jordan PC 17044 El Camino Real Houston TX 77058-2630 Home Phone: 281-482-3663; Office Phone: 281-480-6888. Business E-Mail: cmjordan@daughtryjordan.com.

JORDAN, CHARLES MORRELL, retired automotive designer; b. Whittier, Calif., Oct. 21, 1927; s. Charles L. and Bernice May (Letts) J.; m. Sally Irene Mericle, Mar. 8, 1951; children: Debra, Mark, Melissa. BS, MIT, 1949; grad. advanced mgmt. program, Harvard U., 1979; Doctorate (hon.), Art Ctr. Coll. Design, 1992, Ctr. for Creative Studies, 2001. With GM, Warren, Mich., 1949—, chief designer Cadillac Studio, 1957-61, group chief designer, 1961-62, exec. in charge automotive design, 1962-67, dir. styling Adam Opel A.G., 1967-70, exec. in charge Cadillac, Oldsmobile, Buick Studios, 1970-73, exec. in charge Chevrolet, Pontiac and Comml. Vehicle Studios, 1973-77, dir. design, 1977-86, v.p. design staff, 1986-92; retired, 1992. 1st lt. USAF, 1952-53. Recipient First Nat. award Fisher Body Craftsman's Guild, 1947, disting. svc. citation Automotive Hall of Fame, 1990, Wally B. Ford award Ctr. for Creative Studies, 1992; named Hon. Judge, Pebble Beach Concours d'Elegance, 1970—. Mem. Calif. Scholastic Fedn. (life), Ferrari Club Am. Address: PO Box 8330 Rancho Santa Fe CA 92067-8330 E-mail: cmjdesign@aol.com.

JORDAN, CHARLES WESLEY, retired bishop; b. Dayton, Ohio, May 28, 1933; s. David Morris and Naomi Azelia (Harper) J.; m. Margaret May Crawford, Aug. 2, 1959; children: Diana, Susan. BA, Roosevelt U., 1956; MDiv, Garrett Evangel. Theol. Sem., Evanston, Ill., 1960; LHD (hon.), Morningside Coll., 1994; DD (hon.), Rust Coll., 1995, Simpson Coll., 2000. Ordained to ministry United Meth. Ch., 1960. Pastor Woodlawn United Meth. Ch., Chgo., 1960-66; dir. of urban ministries Rockford, Ill., 1966-71; prog. staff No. Ill. Con./United Meth. Ch., Chgo., 1971-82; dist. supt. Chgo./So. Dist. United Meth. Ch., 1982-87; sr. pastor St. Mark United Meth. Ch., Chgo., 1987-92; bishop Iowa Area United Meth. Ch., Des Moines, 1992-2000; ret., 2000. Del. United Meth. Gen. Conf., 1976, 80, 84, 88, 92, Gen. Bd. Global Ministries, 1972-80, Gen. Coun. on Ministries, 1980-88; trustee Garrett Evangel. Theol. Sem., 1982-97. Commnr. Rockford Housing Authority, 1969-71; bd. dirs. Cmty. Mental Health Coun., Chgo., 1989-91, Project Image, Inc., Chgo., 1987-92, Cen. Iowa Health System, 1993-2000, Mid-Iowa coun. Boy Scouts Am., 1995-2000; pres. United Meth. Gen. Bd. Ch. and Society, 1996-2000, Ecumenical Ministries Iowa, 1999, Progressive Christians Uniting, LA area, 2002-, pres. Progressive Christians Uniting, 2005-. Named to Hall of Fame Wendell Phillips High Sch., Chgo., 1989. Mem. NAACP (life, chmn. religious affairs 1990-92), Kappa Alpha Psi (life, Achievement in Religion award Chgo. Alumni Chpt., 1986), Sigma Pi Phi. Avocations: politics, church history, sports. Home: 1014 Deborah St Upland CA 91784-1206

JORDAN, DANIEL PORTER, JR., foundation administrator, historian, educator; b. Phila., Miss., July 22, 1938; s. Daniel Porter and Mildred M. (Dobbs) J.; m. Lewellyn Lee Schmelzer, Dec. 18, 1961; children: Daniel P., Grace Dobbs, Katherine Lewellyn. BA, U. Miss., 1960, MA, 1962; PhD, U. Va., Charlottesville, 1970; PhD (hon.), Drake U., Des Moines, Iowa, 2005. Various tchg. positions overseas divsn. U. Md., 1962-65, Richmond, Va., 1968-69, U. Va., summers 1970-72; prof. history Va. Commonwealth U., Richmond, 1969-84, Ariz. State, 1995; dir. Stratford Hall Summer Sem., 1981-91; exec. dir. Thomas Jefferson Found. (Monticello), 1985—, pres., 1994—. Scholar in residence U. Va., 1985—. Author: Political Leadership in Jefferson's Virginia, 1983, A Richmond Reader, 1733-1983, 1983, Tobacco Merchant: The Story of Universal Leaf Tobacco Company, 1995. Mem. adv. com. Papers of Thomas Jefferson, Princeton U.; mem. Sec. of Interior's adv. bd. Nat. Pk. Sys., 1984-88, chmn., 1987-88; mem. Jeffersonian Restoration Adv. Bd., U. Va., 1985—; mem. rev. bd. Va. Hist. Landmarks Commn., 1981-92, chmn., 1989-92; mem. Nat. Pks. and Conservation Bd., 1989-92, Ea. Nat. Bd., 1991-2001; pres. Richmond Civil War Roundtable, 1983; trustee Nat. Trust for Hist. Preservation, 1999—; bd. dirs. Fund for the U.S. Capitol Visitor Ctr., 2000—; mem. adv. bd. Freedom Forum Mus., 2002—, Eudona Welty Found., 2002—; mem. curatorial adv. bd. US Senate, 2004—. Served with inf. US Army, 1962-65. Thomas Jefferson Found. fellow, 1965-68; recipient award of merit Am. Assn. for State and Local History, 1977, 88, Pub. Svc. award US Dept. of Interior, 1990, Medal for Va. Svc., AIA, 1993; named Outstanding Virginian, 2006. Mem. Am. Antiquarian Soc., Va. Hist. Soc. (bd. dirs. 1986-91), Mass. Hist. Soc., So. Hist. Assn. (life), Orgn. Am. Historians (life), Walpole Soc., Phi Beta Kappa (pres. Alpha of Va. 1995-98), Omicron Delta Kappa, Sigma Chi. Methodist. Home and Office: Monticello Home of Thomas Jefferson PO Box 316 Charlottesville VA 22902-0316 Office Phone: 434-984-9801. Business E-Mail: djordan@monticello.org.

JORDAN, DANIEL PORTER, III, federal judge; b. Ft. Bragg, NC, 1964; BBA, U. Miss., 1987; JD, U. Va., 1993. Bar: Miss. 1993. Assoc. Butler, Snow, O'Mara, Stevens & Cannada, PLLC, 1993—99, equity mem., 2000—06; judge US Dist. Ct. (So. dist.) Miss., 2006—.*

JORDAN, DEOVINA NASIS, nursing administrator; b. Bangued, Abra, Philippines, May 7, 1960; d. Demetrio Villamor Nacis and Francisca Bicarme Baptista; m. James Lowell Jordan, July 25, 1992. BS in Nursing, U. Perpetual Help, Rizal, Philippines, 1980; MD in Surgery, U. Santo Tomas, Philippines, 1985; M in Pub. Health, Loma Linda U., 2001; MS in Nursing, UCLA, 2004. Cert. Ednl. Comm. for Foreign Med. Grads. Phila., Pa.; Ped. Nursing, Am. Nursing Credentialing Ctr., Wash. DC. Clin. nurse Hosp. for Joint Dis. Ortho. Inst., NYC, 1987—88; clin. nurse III Mattel Children's Hosp, UCLA, LA, 1988—; admin. nurse IV UCLA Med. Ctr., LA, 2002—; v.p., founder Jordan Rsch. Inst., Murietta, Calif., 1994—; pres Fil-Am Assoc., Murietta, 1994—. Rsch. adv. bd. Am. Biographical Inst., 2002—. Contbr. articles various prof. jours. Recipient Outstanding Profl. Woman award, Am. Biographical Inst., 2001. Mem.: Philippine Nurses Assn. Am., Philippine Nurses Assn. So. Calif., Assn. Calif. Nurse Leaders, Am. Assn. Critical Care Nurses, Calif. Nurses Asn., Am. Coll. Healthcare Execs., Alpha Tau Delta, Sigma Theta Tau. Office Phone: 310-612-4898. Personal E-mail: djjord@verizon.net.

JORDAN, EDDIE, professional basketball coach; b. Washington; m. Charrisse Jordan; children: Jackson, Skylar; children: Justin, Eddie II, Paul. Grad. in Health and Phys. Edn., Rutgers U., 1977. Basketball player Cleve. Cavaliers, 1977, NJ Nets, 1977-80, asst. coach, 1999—2003; basketball player LA Lakers, 1980—83, Portland Trail Blazers, 1983—84; vol. asst. Rutgers U., asst. coach, 1988; part-time asst. Old Dominion; asst. coach Boston Coll., 1986; mem. coaching staff Sacramento Kings, 1992, head coach, 1996-99, Washington Wizards, 2003—. Named Ea. Conf. All-Star Head Coach, NBA, 2007. Office: Washington Wizards 601 F St NW Washington DC 20004*

JORDAN, GILBERT FRED, geophysicist, physicist; b. Salt Lake City, Jan. 27, 1940; s. Frederick and Emily C. (Peukert) Jordan; m. Minnie Irene Flowers, Mar. 1965 (dec.); children: Russell(dec.) , Christian, Marian, Cynthia, Crystal; m. Christine Gunn, Apr. 1979; 1 child, Michael. BS in Physics, Brigham Young U., 1966; studied applied physics and metall. engring., Colo. Sch. Mines; MEA, U. Utah, 1974; HScD, U. Md., 1976; HDD (hon.), Unification Ch. Theol. Sem., NYC, 1987. Registered profl. engr., Calif., cert. energy mgr. Geophysicist Pan Am. Petroleum, Denver, 1964-65; physicist, systems engr., contract tech. requirements Martin Marietta, Denver, 1965-66; sr. project ceramic engr. Honeywell Ordinance Divsn., Golden Valley, Minn., 1966-67; sr. project reliability engr. Univac FSD, Salt Lake City, 1968-70; with U.S. Tech. Spec Inc., 1970—72; base indsl. engr. Edwards AFB, Calif., 1972; sr. mfg. engr. Litton DSD, Van Nuys, Calif., 1972-73; various engring. positions Jordan Assocs., 1973—78; gen. mgr. Specialty Enterprise, Inc., Los Gatos, Calif., 1979—86; sr. staff project cons., gen. mgr., geophysicist J'nA Enterprises, Willow Springs, Mo., 1991—. Cons. in energy issues; contbr. rsch. in areas of ozonation, magnetic water conditioning, water filtration, earthquake prediction and control, coal gasification, detecting gravitational radiation; specialist in plant/facility layout and design and ops. rsch.; lectr. in various local colls./univs. in geology, physics, math, chemistry, and bus. admin.; circ. lectr. on earthquake prediction and control; cons. Inst. of New Energy, Salt Lake City, Mus. of the Unexplained, Reed Springs, Mo. Contbr. articles to profl. jours. Scoutmaster, com. chair Boy Scouts Am., Mpls., 1965-67, den leader, coach, Willow Springs, 1987-92, asst. scoutmaster, 1993; co-founder Interdenominational Minister's Ministry of Restored Chs. of Jesus Christ Assn.; active missions for LDS ch.; leader Girl Scouts Am., 1995-2000. With U.S. Army Nat. Guard, 1957—63. Mem.: AIAA, Toastmasters, Soc. Mfg. Engrs., Am. Soc. Plant Engrs., Am. Ceramic Soc., Am. Soc. Quality Control (chpt. sec.), Nat. Eagle Scout Assn., Inst. Indsl. Engrs. (sr.; chpt. pres. 1974—79, PIN award 1976), Sigma Pi Sigma. Achievements include the design of subsystems for: Apollo experiments pallet, planetary parachute program, Titan Manned Orbital Laboratory, Titan IIIDC, and other subsystems associated with and several aerospace/defense systems; invention of GRASER, an explosively pulsed nitro methane chemical laser, and piezo-electric devices; helped develop slurry AN explosives and shape charges for Nobel Prize winner Dr. Melvin A. Cook (IMER/IRECO); nominated as a candidate for the Physics Nobel Prize with others for work accomplished and related to predicting the existence of gravitons and neutrinos having weight, preliminary meas. of gravity waves, and a relationship between gravitons, photons, neutrinos, gravitinos, photinos, glutinos-based upon Feynman QED, Heisenberg World formula, gage theory and string theory. Office: J'nA Enterprises 319 S Harris St Willow Springs MO 65793-1620

JORDAN, GLENN, film, television and theater director; b. San Antonio, Apr. 5, 1936; BA, Harvard U., 1957; postgrad., Yale U. Sch. Drama, 1957—58. Dir. regional and stock theatre, including Cafe La Mama, late 1950s; N.Y. directorial debut with Another Evening With Harry Stoones, 1961; other plays include A Taste of Honey, 1968; Rosencrantz and Guildenstern Are Dead, 1969, A Streetcar Named Desire at Cin. Playhouse in the Park, 1973, All My Sons at Huntington Hartford Theatre, 1975; founder, N.Y. TV Theater, 1965, dir. various plays, including Paradise Lost and Hogan's Goat; dir. mini-series Benjamin Franklin, CBS, 1974 (Emmy award 1975, Peabody award); Family, ABC-TV series, 1976-77, including segment Rights of Friendship (Dirs. Guild Am. award); numerous TV plays for public TV, including Eccentricities of a Nightingale, 1976; The Displaced Person, 1976; TV movies including Shell Game, 1975, One Of My Wives Is Missing, 1975, Delta County U.S.A, 1977, In The Matter of Karen Ann Quinlan, 1977, Sunshine Christmas, 1977, Les Miserables, 1978, Son-Rise, A Miracle of Love, 1979, The Family Man, 1979, The Women's Room, 1980, Lois Gibbs and the Love Canal, 1982, Heartsounds, 1984 (Peabody award), Toughlove, 1985, Dress Gray, 1986, Something in Common, 1986, Promise, 1986 (2 Emmy awards for producing, directing, Peabody award, Golden Globe award), Echoes in the Darkness, 1987, Jesse, 1988, Home Fires Burning, 1988, Challenger, 1989, The Boys, 1990, Sarah Plain and Tall, 1990, Aftermath, 1990, O Pioneers!, 1991, Barbarians at the Gate, 1992 (Emmy award Outstanding Made for TV Movie, 1993, Golden Globe award, Best Mini-series or movie made for TV, 1994), To Dance with the White Dog, 1994, Jane's House, 1994, My Brother's Keeper, 1994, A Streetcar Named Desire, 1995, Jake's Women (Neil Simon), 1996, After Jimmy, 1996, Mary and Tim, 1996, A Christmas Memory, 1997, The Long Way Home, 1998, Legalese, 1998, Night Ride Home, 1999, Winter's End: Sarah Plain & Tall III, 1999, Midwives, 2000, Lucy, 2003; dir: feature film Only When I Laugh (Neil Simon), 1981, The Buddy System, 1983, Mass Appeal, 1984. Recipient Emmy awards for N.Y. TV Theater Plays, 1970, Actors Choice award, 1970. also: 9401 Wilshire Blvd Ste 700 Beverly Hills CA 90212-2920

JORDAN, GRACE CAROL, music educator; b. Fernandina Beach, Fla., June 15, 1956; d. Benson Henry and Annie Dee Riggin; m. David Howell Jordan, July 2, 1983; children: David Benson, Rebecca Grace. B Music Edn., La. State U., MusM, 1984. Cert. tchr. Fla. Music tchr. Azalea Pk. Elem. Sch., Orlando, Fla., 1983—89, Arbor Ridge Sch., Orlando, 1989—. Sect. leader, soloist All Saints Episcopal Ch., Winter Park, Fla., 1983—; dir. various honor choirs, Fla. Named Tchr. of Yr., Azalea Pk. Elem. Sch., 1986, Arbor Ridge Sch., 2001. Mem.: Orff Assn. (pres. Fla. chpt. 1990—92, Disney Teacherrific Award 1993). Democrat. Episcopalian. Avocations: singing, travel. Home: 825 Hickory Hill Ct Orlando FL 32828 Office: Arbor Ridge Sch 2900 Logandale Dr Orlando FL 32817 Home Phone: 407-380-2408; Office Phone: 407-672-3110. Office Fax: 407-672-1310.

JORDAN, GREGORY B., lawyer; b. Wheeling, W.Va., Aug. 10, 1959; m. Ellen Jordan; 2 children. BA magna cum laude, Bethany Coll., 1981; JD cum laude, U. Pitts., 1984. Bar: Pa. 1984, W.Va. With Reed Smith LLP, Pitts., 1984—, former dir. legal pers., former dir. practice devel., mng. ptnr., chmn. sr. mgmt. team & exec. com., 2001—. Contbr. articles to profl. journals. Bd trustees Bethany Coll., Carnegie Sci. Ctr. Named one of the top 45 lawyers in Am. under age 45, Am. Lawyer, 2003; named to The Best Lawyers in Am., 1995—. Mem.: Order of Coif, Duquesne Club. Office: Reed Smith LLP 435 Sixth Ave Pittsburgh PA 15219 Office Phone: 412-288-4124. Office Fax: 412-288-3063. Business E-Mail: gjordan@reedsmith.com.

JORDAN, HOWARD EMERSON, retired engineering executive, consultant; b. State College, N.Mex., May 14, 1926; s. Howard E. and Elizabeth (Bruden) J.; children: Blair, Julie. BSEE, U. Wis., 1946; MS, Case Western Res. U., 1958, PhD, 1962. With Rayovac Co., Madison, Wis., 1946-52, Reliance Elec., Cleve., 1954-93, dir. corp. R & D, 1993—; pvt. cons.; rsch. scientist U. Tex. Author: Energy Efficient Electric Motors and Their Application, 1983, 2d edit., 1994; contbg. author: Handbook of Electric Machines, 1987. Served to 1st lt. USAF, 1952-54. Recipient Disting. Svc. citation U. Wis., 1989. Fellow IEEE (sr.); mem. Nat. Electrical Mfrs. Assn. (chmn. motor and generator sect. 1979). Methodist.

JORDAN, I(RVING) KING, former academic administrator; m. Linda Jordan; children: I. King III, Heidi. BA, Gallaudet U., 1970; MA in psychology, U. Tenn., 1971, PhD in psychology, 1973. Faculty mem. Gallaudet U., Washington, 1973, chair Dept. Psychology, 1983, dean Coll. Arts and Scis., 1986—88, pres., 1988—2006. Rsch. fellow Donaldson's Sch. for Deaf, Edinburgh; vice chair President's Com. on Employment of People with Disabilities, 1990, 93. Recipient Presdl. Citizen's Medal, Washingtonian of Yr. Award, James L. Fisher Award, Coun. for Advancement and Support of Edn., Larry Stewart Award, American Psychol. Assn., Disting. Leadership Award, Nat. Assn. for Cmty. Leadership.*

JORDAN, JANINE, interior designer, consultant, small business owner; b. Oct. 12, 1932; d. Frank Bertram Jordan, Jr. and Barbara Elizabeth (Schwinn) Jordan; m. C. Roger Williams, May 28, 1956 (div. Sept. 8, 1966); children: Jennifer Anne Williams-Porto, Pamela Nan Williams-Bowen, Ian Clifford Williams; m. George C. Newlin, Dec. 21, 1967 (div. 1991); 1 child, Nicholas Chauncey Christian Newlin. Student in English, Columbia U., 1953—54; BA in English, Chatham Coll., Pitts., 1955; studied painting with Amy Jones, Anthony Toney, 1960—64; studied continuing edn., CC, 1960—70; diploma, Am. Inst. Kitchen Designers, 1980. Cert. Boarman Sch. Kitchen Design Techs., 1977, kitchen designer Am. Inst. Kitchen Dealers, 1980, kitchen specialist Am. Inst. Kitchen Dealers, 1980, Am. Inst. Kitchen Dealers and Nat. Kitchen and Bath Assn. cert. Soc. Cert. Kitchen Designers, 1982. Illustrator's model jr. fashion, 1938—58; copy chief's asst. J. Walter Thompson Agy., 1955—56; four times Cover Girl model Eng. Publs., 1955—56; founder, pres. Internat. Editl. Arts Co., 1956—64; ptnr. Schwinn-Jordan, 1956—59; prin. J.J. Newlin Interiors, Chappaqua, NY, 1969—89; v.p., dir. Braintree Mgmt. Ltd., 1976—88; owner JJ Interiors, Kitchen and Bath Design by Janine, Chapel Hill, NC, 1990—; wholesale owner JanSig-Mirrored Bath Cabinets, 1994—. Panelist, spkr. Bergdorf Goodman's Dept. Store, Westchester County, NY, 1978—88, YMCA, NYC, 1978—88; owner JanSig.-Mirrored Bath Cabinets, 1994—. Interior designer Nestwork's Dreamhouse,

1986—87, coord. design Universal Design Sch. seminars, Raleigh, NC, 1997, interior design projects (featured in) House Beautiful, Home, Perfect Home, Family Circle, Better Homes & Garden, Decorating Remodeling, Home Mechanix, Looking Into Houses, Kitchen & Bath Concepts, Rodale Press, Gannett Newspapers, Westchester Illus.; jazz pianist: The Friends of the Westchester Conservatory of Music, 1986, The Mt. Kisco Concert Assn. Season Kick-off Party, 1990. Fund raiser Pitts. Symphony, 1951—55, NY Philharm., 1951—55, Am. Nat. Theatre and Acad., 1951—55, Nat. Urban League, 1951—55, Katonah Art Gallery, NYC, Speech and Hearing Clinic, No. Westchester, NY; English tchr. Grasslands County Woman's Jail with Jr. League Mt. Kisco, NYC, 1967—69, vol., 1967—69; co-chmn. Friends of Friends Com. to Raise Funds Preservation of Chappaqua Quaker Meeting House, 1976—77; com. mem. Yorkville Youth Project, NYC, 1951; mem. NY Jr. League, 1951—68. Recipient Water Color award, Soc. Illustrators Children's Art Show: 1960-88, 1945, Cmty. Svc. award, Westchester, 1974, Cert. of Appreciation, New Castle Twp., NY, 1980, Profl. Acknowledgements and Honors, 1980—88. Mem.: UN Assn. West Triangle, The Interior Design Soc., Nat. Kitchen and Bath Assn. (guest and radio show panelist, conv. spkr. 1978—88), Soc. Cert. Kitchen Designers/Nat. Kitchen and Bath Assn., Internat. Soc. Interior Designers, The Allied Bd. of Trade, Gov.'s Club Realty, Custom Home Program. Democrat. Soc. Of Friends. Avocations: jazz piano, sailing, sketching, cartooning, gardening.

JORDAN, JEFF, Internet company executive; BA in Polit. Sci. and Psychology, Amherst Coll.; MBA, Stanford U. From mgr. strategic planning Consumer Products Divsn. to CEO The Disney Store Worldwide The Walt Disney Corp.; exec. v.p., CFO Hollywood Entertainment; pres. website; sr. v.p. eBay U.S. eBay Inc., San Jose, Calif., gen. mgr. eBay U.S., sr. v.p. U.S. Bus., 2000—05; pres. PayPal Inc. (subs. eBay Inc.), 2005—. Office: PayPal Inc eBay Inc 2145 Hamilton Ave San Jose CA 95125

JORDAN, JERRY DALE, lawyer, gas industry executive; b. Duncan, Okla., Nov. 27, 1934; s. W.F. and Leona B. (Kile) J.; m. Sally Melton, July 5, 1958; children— Mark, Anne, Whitney. B.S. in Geology, Denison U.; postgrad. U. Okla., 1960; J.D. U. Mich., 1963. Bar: Ohio 1963. Former ptnr., Vorys, Sater, Seymour & Pease, Columbus, Ohio; chmn., chief exec. officer Clinton Gas Systems Inc., 1988-98; mem. nominating com. State Ohio Pub. Utilities Commn., 1998—; mem. tech. adv. coun. Ohio Dept. Natural Resources, 2005—; bd. dirs. Nat. Petroleum Coun., Mountain States Legal Found.; dir. Knox Energy, Inc., 1989—. Chmn. Gov.'s Com. on Self-Help Natural Gas, 1976-81; mem. Franklin County (Ohio) Zoning Commn., 1985-89; adj. prof. Capital U. Law Sch., 1987-92. Mem. Ind. Petroleum Assn. Am. (vice chmn. 1997-99, chmn. 1999-2001), Ohio Oil and Gas Assn. (trustee, pres.), Eastern Mineral Law Found. (founding trustee), Columbus Bar Assn., Ohio Bar Assn., Athletic Club of Columbus (bd. dirs. 1986-92). Home Phone: 614-885-0772; Office Phone: 614-885-4828. E-mail: jjmaw@yahoo.com.

JORDAN, JIM (JAMES D. JORDAN), congressman, former state legislator; b. Troy, Ohio, Feb. 17, 1964; m. Polly Jordan; children: Rachel, Benjamin, Jessie, Isaac. BS in Econ., U. Wis., 1986; MA in Edn., Ohio State U., 1991; JD, Capital U., 2001. Asst. wrestling coach Ohio State U., Columbus; mem. Ohio Ho. of Reps. from 85th dist., Columbus, 1995—2000, Ohio State Senate from 12th dist., Columbus, 2001—07, US Congress from 4th Ohio dist., 2007—, mem. judiciary com., small bus. com., oversight and govt. reform com. Mem. Champaign County Rep. Exec. Com., Mad River Valley Young Rep. Club, Citizens Against Govt. Waste, Right to Life Orgns. Big Ten and NCAA wrestling champion, 1985, 86; recipient: Outstanding Legis. award, 2004, "Defender of Life award Ohio Right to Life Soc., Leadership in Govt. award Ohio Roudtable & freedom Forum, 2001; named Watchdog of the Treasury, 1996, 2000, 2004, Friend of the Taxpayer, 1997, Pro-life Legis. of Yr. United Conservatives of Ohio, 1998 Republican. Evangelical. Office: US House Reps 515 Cannon House Office Bldg Washington DC 20515 also: 24 W Third St Rm 314 Mansfield OH 44902 Office Phone: 419-522-5757. Office Fax: 419-525-2805.*

JORDAN, JOE J., architect; b. Phila., May 5, 1923; s. Edmund F. and Elizabeth N. (Jungkurth) Jordan; m. Sarah Jeanne Connolly, Nov. 1, 1974. BS in Architecture, U. Ill., 1949. Prin. Joe J. Jordan, FAIA, Phila., 1961-81; ptnr. Delta Group, Phila., 1972-74; prin., pres. Jordan, Mitchell Inc., Phila., 1981-93. UN tech. assistance expert Mid. E. Tech. U., Ankara, Turkey, 1958—60, acting head dept. architecture, 1959, archtl. advisor to univ. pres., 60; mem. faculty dept. architecture Drexel U., Phila., 1962, adj. prof., 64, head dept., 1965—77. Author: Senior Center Facilities, 1975, Senior Center Design, 1978, Cape May Point - The Illustrated History, 2003, Cape May Point-Three Walking Tours, 2004; contbr. articles to profl. jours. Mem. citizens coun. city planning, Phila., 1956—70; bd. dirs. Phila. Sr. Ctr., 1964—70, Reed St. Neighborhood Ho., Phila., 1968—69; mem. mayor's com. housing Phila., 1973—76; mem. Gov. Task Force Multi-Svc. Sr. Ctrs. Pa., 1975—77, N.J. Assisted Living Facilities Task Force, 1995—96; v.p. Greater Cape May Hist. Soc., 1998—2000; Cape May Point Hist. Preservation Com., 2004—. Recipient numerous archtl. awards, award of excellence, Urban Design Mag.; Fulbright fellow, 1954—55. Fellow: AIA (emeritus, Citation for Excellence, Phila. chpt. Honor award, others). Home: PO Box 22 Cape May Point NJ 08212-0022 Office Phone: 215-523-7681. Personal E-mail: joejordan@comcast.net.

JORDAN, JOHN FREDERICK, farmer, consultant; b. Mpls., Dec. 20, 1948; s. John Bernard Jordan and Maude Geraldine Hughes; m. Marianne Zerbe, Oct. 6, 0985; m. Judith Kaye Kendrick (div.); children: Patrick, Bridgit. BA, St. Mary's U., Winona, Minn., 1971, MA, 1979. Tchr. Brady H.S., West St. Paul, Minn., 1971—74; residential adminstr. St. Michael's Home Children, Lacrosse, Wis., 1976—78; farmer Ralph's Pretty Good Dairy, Houston, Minn., 1985—. Bd. mem. networks, Caledonia, Minn., 1983—90, Able, Inc., Caledonia, 1990—96; chair Region 10 Shareholders, Rochester, Minn., 1997—2006, Quality Assurance Co., Rochester, 1997—2003. Recipient Ann Fergeson award, ARC S.E. Minn., Rochester, 1999, Betty Hubbard award, ARC, St. Paul, 2000. Avocations: reading, woodworking.

JORDAN, JUDITH VICTORIA, clinical psychologist, educator; b. Milw., July 28, 1943; d. Claus and Charlotte (Backus) J.; m. William M. Redpath, Aug. 11, 1973. AB, Brown U., 1965; MA, Harvard U., 1968, PhD, 1973; DHL (hon.) (hon.), New Eng. Coll., 2001. Diplomate Am. Bd. Profl. Psychology. Psychologist Human Relations Service, Wellesley, Mass., 1971-73; assoc. psychologist McLean Hosp., Belmont, Mass., 1978-93, psychologist, 1993—, dir. women's treatment program, 1988—, dir. tng. in psychology, 1991, dir. Women's Treatment Network, 1992—. Vis. scholar Stone Ctr. Wellesley Coll., 1985—; asst. prof. psychiatry Harvard Med. Sch., 1988—; co-dir. Jean Baker Miller Tng. Inst., dir., 2006, Wellesley Coll. 1998; adv. bd Fox TV Network, Women First healthcare., 1998; disting. prof. Menninger Clinic, 1999; dir. Jean Baker Miller Tng. Inst., 2006. Author: Empathy and Self Boundries, 1984, Women's Growth in Connection, 1991, (with others) The Self in Relation, 1986; editor, author: Relational Self in Women; editor: Women's Growth in Diversity, 1997; editor: The Complexity of Connection, 2004. Recipient Outstanding Contbn. award, Feminist Therapy Inst., 2002. Fellow Am. Psychol. Assn.; mem. Mass. Psychol. Assn. (bd. dirs. 1983-85, Career Achievement award for outstanding contbns. to advancement of psychology as a sci. and a profession), Phi Beta Kappa. Office: McLean Hosp 114 Waltham St Lexington MA 02421-5415

JORDAN, KARLA SALGE, retired primary school educator; b. Berlin, July 4, 1943; came to U.S. 1965; d. Hubert Ernst Richard and Irmgard Klara Salge; m. William Jackson Jordan, May 28, 1963 (div. 1980); 1 child, Michael Bond. BA, Berlin Tchrs. Coll., 1964, Meth. Coll., Fayetteville, NC, 1974; MA, Fayetteville State U., 1986. Cert. tchr., N.C., ednl. supr., 1995, cert. early childhood generalist Nat. Bd. Edn., 2000. Tchr. Eastover Elem. Sch., Fayetteville, 1974-75, Montclair Elem. Sch., Fayetteville, 1975—2005; ret., 2005. Workshop presenter Cumberland County Sch., Fayetteville, spring 1983, 92-95; mem. bldg. leadership team Montclair Elem. Sch., 1992-93, chair, 1994-95, grade chair, 1980-90, 1999-2001, 2002-2003, 2003-2004, sch. improvement team chair, 1995-98, 2001-03. Treas. Montclair PTA, 1987-88, sec., 1988-90, pres. 1985, 86; youth choir dir. Eureka Bapt. Ch., Fayetteville, 1990—, min. of music, 1995—; mem., bible study leader for German fellowship Walstone Bapt. Ch., Fayetteville, German fellowship coord., 1999—. Fayetteville Jr. League mini grantee, 1991; named Tchr. of the Yr. Montclair Elem. Sch., 1987-88; recipient Fayetteville Tchr. of the Week Jr. League and the Huntington Learning Ctr., 1997. Mem. Cross Creek Reading Coun. (rec. sec. 1990), Fayetteville Assn. for Edn. of Young Children, N.C. Assn. of Edn. (bldg. rep. 1981-83), Pi Lambda Theta. Republican. Baptist. Avocations: sewing, crafts, gardening, travel, reading. Home: 845 Mary Jordan Ln Fayetteville NC 28311-7075 Home Phone: 910-822-3766. Personal E-mail: karla-sjs@msn.com.

JORDAN, KATHERINE D. (KATE JORDAN), lawyer; BA with honors, Emory U.; JD, Vanderbilt U. Law clk. to Judge Ewing Werlein Jr. US Dist Ct., Tex.; atty. Vinson & Elkins LLP, Tex., Powell, Goldstein, Frazer and Murphy, Atlanta, 2001—03; law clk. to Chief US Magistrate Judge Gerrilyn Brill No. Dist. Ga., 2003—05; sr. counsel Southeastern Legal Found., Atlanta, 2005—. Rsch. editor Vanderbilt Jour. Transnational Law. Republican.

JORDAN, KENNETH D., chemistry professor; b. Norwood, Mass., Feb. 25, 1948; BA, Northeastern U., Boston, 1970; PhD, MIT, 1974. Gibbs instr. Yale U., New Haven, 1974-76, asst. prof., 1976-78, U. Pitts., 1978-80, assoc. prof., 1980-85, prof., 1985—. Program dir. NSF, Washington, 1984-85; adj. prof. Carnegie Mellon U., 1988—. Contbr. articles to profl. jours. Guggenheim fellow Guggenheim Found., 1981; Dreyfus Tchr. scholar Camille and Henry Dreyfus Found., 1977-82; fellow Alfred P. Sloan Found., 1977-79. Fellow Am Phys. Soc.; mem. Am. Chem. Soc. (chmn. theoretical chemistry subdiv. 1990-91, officer 1988-91, sec.-treas. phys. chemistry divsn. 2001—06), Sigma Xi. Achievements include rsch. in methods to elucidate the role of through-bond interactions in long-range intramolecular interactions; development of techniques for theoretical studies of temporary anions, theoretical methods to characterize hydrogen bonded clusters.

JORDAN, KENT A., federal judge; b. West Point, NY, Oct. 24, 1957; s. Amos Azariah and MarDeane (Carver) J.; m. Michelle Weaver, Apr. 25, 1981. BA in Econs. with high honors, Brigham Young U., 1981; JD cum laude, Georgetown U., 1984. Bar: Del. 1984, US Dist. Ct. Del. 1985, US Ct. Appeals (3d cir.) 1988, US Supreme Ct. 1994, US Ct. Appeals (fed. cir.) 1995, DC Ct. Appeals 1996. Law clk. to Hon. James L. Latchum US Dist. Ct., Wilmington, Del., 1984-85; assoc. Potter Anderson & Corroon, Wilmington, Del., 1985-87; asst. U.S. atty. Del. US Dept. Justice, Wilmington, Del., 1987—92, chief civil divsn., 1991-92; assoc. Morris, James, Hitchens & Williams, Wilmington, Del., 1992-93, ptnr., 1993—97; v.p., gen. counsel Corp. Svc. Co., Wilmington, Del., 1997—2002; judge US Dist. Ct. Del., 2002—06, US Ct. Appeals (3rd cir.), 2006—. Adj. prof. Widener U. Law Sch., Wilmington, 1995-96, Vanderbilt U., 2003-, U. Penn., 2005-; mem. adv. com. US Dist. Ct. Del., 1995-98, ombudsman, 1995-2002; sec. Bd. of Bar Examiners, Del. Supreme Ct., Wilmington, 1997, mem., 2000-02. Contbr. articles to profl. jours. Mem. Greater Hockessin Area Devel. Assn., 1991—, also past pres.; bd. dirs. Cmty. Legal Aid Soc., Wilmington, 1994-97. Mem. Am. Intellectual Property Law Assn., Del. State Bar Assn. (coun. mem. intellectual property sect. 1996-98), Fed. Bar Assn. (Del. chpt.), Richard S. Rodney Am. Inn of Ct. (sec.-treas. 1994-96, counselor 1996-98, pres. 2005-07). Office: US Ct Appeals 21400 US Courthouse 601 Market St Philadelphia PA 19106*

JORDAN, LAMONT, professional football player; b. Forestville, Maryland, Nov. 11, 1978; Grad., U. of MD, 2000. Running back New York Jets, 2001—05, Oakland Raiders, 2005—. Office: c/o Oakland Raiders 1220 Harbor Bay Pkwy Alameda CA 94502

JORDAN, LEO JOHN, lawyer; b. Pittston, Pa., Nov. 24, 1931; s. Joseph Thomas and Agnes (Granahan) J.; children: Leo John, Michael, Paul, Mary Terese; m. Carla Temple. AB in Econ., King's Coll., 1953; JD, U. Md., 1960. Bar: Md. 1960, Tex. 1965, Ill. 1990, N.Y. 1997. Claim supr. Ins. Co. N.AM., Phila., 1956-62; atty. State Farm Ins. Cos., Bloomington, Ill., 1962-96; ret., 1996—. Contbr. articles to profl. jours. Commr. Richardson City Planning Commn., Tex., 1964-68. With USN, 1954-56. Mem. ABA (ho. of dels., chair tort and ins. practice sect. 1992-93), Chgo. Bar Assn., Nat. Com. Property Ins. (chmn. bd. dirs. 1978-79), N.Y. State Bar Assn., Assn. Bar City N.Y., Fedn. Def. and Corp. Counsel, Def. Rsch. Inst., Md. State Bar Assn., Tex. State Bar Assn., Ill. State Bar Assn. Democrat. Catholic. Avocations: tennis, reading, marathon running. Home: 50 Whalen Ct West Orange NJ 07052

JORDAN, LILLIAN B., judge; b. Asheboro, NC, May 19, 1939; d. Obert Charles and Lilly Irene Burrow; m. Thomas Andrew Jordan, Apr. 24, 1999; m. Thomas Lorenzo O'Briant, Sept. 5, 1959 (dec. May 31, 1995); children: Thomas Lorenzo O'Briant, Jr., Patrick Marvin O'Briant, Michael Heilig O'Briant, John Curt O'Briant. BA, Guilford Coll., Greensboro, NC, 1961; JD, Wake Forest U., Winston Salem, 1979. Bar: N.C. 1979, U.S. Dist. Ct. (mid. dist.) N.C. 1979, U.S. Supreme Ct. 2001, cert.: (specialist in family law) 1995, Adminstrv. Office of the Courts, NC (juvenile ct. judge) 1998, (family law mediator) 2003. Ptnr. O'Briant, O'Briant, Bunch and Robins, Asheboro, NC, 1979—97; dist. ct. judge State of N.C., Asheboro, Troy, Carthage, NC, 1997—2002, emergency dist. ct. judge, 2002—. Bd. of trustees IOLTA N.C. State Bar, Raleigh, 1985—92, bd. of law examiners, 1992—97, bd. of law examiners, emeritus mem., mem. adv. coun. juvenile justice, 2007—. Pres. Guilford Coll. Nat. Alumni Assn., Greensboro, NC, 1982—83; mem., bd. of dirs. Merce Clinic, Asheboro, NC, 2000—; mem., bd. dirs. Randolph County Day Reporting Ctr., Asheboro, NC, 1999—; mem., bd. of dirs. United Way of Randolph County, Asheboro, NC, 1981—93, Asheboro/Randolph C. of C., Asheboro, NC, 1986—89, Women's Aid, Inc., Asheboro, NC, 1980—83; chairperson Randolph County Coun. on the Status of Women, Asheboro, NC, 1975—76; mem. N.C. Cts. Commn., Raleigh, NC, 1987—91, Revenue Laws Study Commn. of the N.C. Legis., Raleigh, NC, 1991—95; mem., bd. of dirs. Randolph Hosp. Cmty. Health Found., Asheboro, NC, 1996—2002; bd. trustees Randolph Cmty. Coll., Asheboro, NC, 2004—08; del. Dem. Nat. Conv., NYC, 1980—80. Recipient Athena award, Asheboro/Randolph C. of C., 1994, Paul Harris fellow, Asheboro Rotary Club, 1997, Alumni Excellence award, Guilford Coll., 1998. Mem.: N.C. Ctr. for Justice and Cmty. Devel. (mem. of directors 1997—2005), 19B Jud. Bar Assn. (former pres.), Randolph Bar Assn. (former pres.), N.C. Bar Assn. (bd. of governors 1985—88), N.C. Assn. of Women Attys. (pres. 1995—96), N.C. State Bar (licentiate). Democrat-Npl. Episcopalian. Avocations: travel, reading, gardening. Home: 645 Holly Grove Dr Randleman NC 27317 Personal E-mail: lilliob@yahoo.com.

JORDAN, LISA ANNE, dancer, educator; d. Clement Joseph Zumpella and Nancy Lou DeForest-Mancino; m. John Samuel Jordan, Jan. 4, 1999. Grad., Liberty H.S., Youngstown, Ohio, 1986. Dancer, tchr. Cleve. Ballet, 1993—97; dancer, singer Busch Gardens, Williamsburg, Va., 1987—88; prin. dancer Ballet Mich., Flint. Tchr. Akron U. and Inst., Ohio, 1997—99; guest ballerina Cleve. Orch., 2002; profesional dancer Pointe Of Departure, 2003; children's dir. Moscow Ballet, Youngstown, Ohio, 2004; dir. fine arts program Windham Pub. Sch. Sys., Ohio, 1995—2005; tchr./coach/choreograhper numerous pvt. schs., Youngstown and Cleve.

JORDAN, LYNDON KIRKMAN, physician; b. Mount Olive, NC, Jan. 6, 1935; s. Lyndon Kirkman and Rachael Loucille (Hazelton) J.; m. Beverly Hayes Brooks, Aug. 19, 1961; children: Lyndon III, Christopher, Patrick. BA, Duke U., 1957, MD, 1961. Diplomate Am. Bd. Family Practice. Intern Watts Hosp., Durham, NC, 1961—62; flight surgeon Beale AFB, Marysville, Calif., 1962—64; pvt. practice Smithfield, NC, 1964—2001; dir. family medicine residency program Duke U. Sch. Medicine, Durham, 1972—74. Cons. Roche Biomed. Labs., Burlington, NC, 1987-92, Pfizer Pharms. Co., Mahwah, NJ, 1994-92; bd. dirs. Bank of Four Oaks of Smithfield, NC; chmn. bd. dirs. Millennium Healthczre Network of N.C. and S.C., 1997-99; chmn. Johnston County Bd. Health, Smithfield, 1998-2000; lectr. in field. Capt. USAF, 1962-64. Named family physician of Yr. N.C. Acad. Family Physicians, 1982, N.C. Tarheel of the Week, News & Observer Newspaper, Raleigh, 1983; Paul Harris fellow Rotary Internat., 1989. Fellow Am. Acad. Family Physicians. Episcopalian. Avocations: flying, hunting, fishing, painting. Home: 105 Mariah Dr Four Oaks NC 27524-8433

JORDAN, MARTHA B., lawyer; m. David Lee; children: Stacy, Kristen. BS, Pa. State U., 1976; MBA, U. Cin., 1978; JD, U. Calif., Berkeley, 1983. Bar: Calif. 1983. With Latham & Watkins, LLP, LA, 1983—90, ptnr., 1990—98, 2005—, mng. ptnr., 1998—2004. Named Top US Lawyer, Law Dragon 500, 2005, 2006; named one of Calif.'s Top 100 Most Influential Lawyers, Calif. Law Bus., 1999. Office: Latham and Watkins LLP Ste 4000 633 W Fifth St Los Angeles CA 90071 Home Phone: 213-891-8716; Office Phone: 213-485-1234.

JORDAN, MARVIN EVANS, JR., record company executive, vocalist, actor, composer; b. Muskogee, Okla., Aug. 13, 1944; s. Marvin Evans and May Elizabeth (Williams) J.; m. Suonja Summirs, Aug. 23, 1969 (div. 1983); m. Kristine Lynn Johnson, Nov. 8, 1984; children: Marvin Edwin, Mary Elizabeth, Michael Evans-Lyman; stepchildren: Daniel Noah Winger, David Paul Winger, Karen LaVohn Winger Van Hofer, Cory Brent Winger, Jay Martin Winger, Aaron Thomas Jones, Benjamin Arthur Jones Jordan, Seth Ailean Jones, Sarah Jean Jones Jordan Cottrell. BS, City U., Bellevue, Wash., 1981, MBA, 1983. Prodr., promoter Natures Green Oratory Presents, Seattle, 1966—67; v.p. North Hollywood Releasing, Seattle, 1967-68; prin. Jordan Assocs., Seattle, 1969-89, Lifestyle Design Svc., 1975—; chmn. bd. Western-Internat. Artists, Inc., 1976-78, owner, 1993—; pres. Standard Record Co., Spokane, Wash., 1989—; mem. agy. mktg. network Star Power, 1991-93; pres. Millenial Entertainment Network, 2000—; sr. ptnr., CEO Aztec Mgmt. Sys., Spokane, Wash., 2000—; owner, pres., CEO Music Mountain Studios, Spokane, 2005—; owner Our Hearthside Online Trading Post, 2006—; CEO Hearthside Heritage Homes, 2002—. Artistic dir. Concerts Nimbus, Seattle, 1981-84; co-dir. Kids Khorus Klub, Olympia, Wash., 1985-87. Composer, lyricist, collaborator (song) Heart Songs, 1994; vocalist (album) After All, 1994; numerous unpub. songs. Asst. dist. commr. Whatcom dist. Mount Baker coun. Boy Scouts Am., 1987-91, 94-98, chmn. coun. exploring svc. team, 1993-94, membership chair Thunderbird dist. Inland N.W. Coun., 2001-2003, unit commr., 2003—04; steering com. Adult Attention Deficit Disorder Assn., 1993-94; bd. dirs. nonprofit assn. Nimbus Project, 2006—. With US Army, 1963—66. Named Disting. Commr. Boy Scouts Am., 1992, recipient Wood Badge, 1990. Mem.: N.W. Area Music Assn. Mem. Lds Ch. Avocations: residential design, computer programming, reading. Personal E-mail: jordanmejr@gmail.com.

JORDAN, MICHAEL B., lawyer; b. Ft. Worth, June 8, 1949; BA, Mich. State U., 1971; JD, Harvard U., 1974. Bar: Pa. 1974. Ptnr. Drinker, Biddle & Reath, Phila., 1974. Office: Drinker Biddle & Reath LLP 1 Logan Sq 18th & Cherry St Philadelphia PA 19103 Office Phone: 215-988-2802. Office Fax: 215-988-2757. Business E-Mail: michael.jordan@dbr.com.

JORDAN, MICHAEL HUGH, information technology executive; b. Kansas City, Mo., June 15, 1936; m. Kathryn Hiett, Apr. 8, 1961 (div.); children: Kathryn, Stephen; m. Hilary Cecil, Mar. 4, 2000. BSChemE, Yale U., 1957; MSChemE, Princeton U., 1959. Cons., prin. McKinsey & Co., Toronto, London and Cleve., 1964—74; dir. fin. planning PepsiCo, Purchase, NY, 1974—76, sr. v.p. planning and devel., 1976—77; sr. v.p. mfg. ops. Frito-Lay divsn. PepsiCo Internat., Dallas, 1977—82, pres., CEO Frito-Lay divsn., 1983—85; pres. PepsiCo Foods Internat., 1982—83; exec. v.p., CFO PepsiCo Inc., Purchase, 1985—86, pres., 1986; pres., CEO PepsiCo Worldwide, Dallas, 1987—92; ptnr. Clayton, Dubilier and Rice, NYC, 1992—93; chmn., CEO Westinghouse Electric Corp./CBS, Pitts., 1993—98; ptnr. Beta Capital Group LLC; gen. ptnr. Global Asset Capital, LLC; chmn., CEO Electronic Data Systems Corp., Plano, Tex., 2003—07, chmn., 2007—. Bd. dirs. Aetna, eOriginal Inc.; chmn. Nat. Fgn. Trade Coun.; trustee Brookings Instn. Bd. dirs., former chmn. United Negro Coll. Fund, 1986—; bd. dirs. Ctr. for Excellence in Edn., Washington, 1988—92; mem., former chmn. US -Japan Bus. Coun.; mem. Bus. Coun.; mem. bd. trustees US Coun. for Internat. Bus.; mem. Bus. Roundtable; dir. Viventures. With USN. Recipient cert. nuclear engring., Bettis Labs. Atomic Power Labs., Pitts. Office Phone: 972-605-6000.*

JORDAN, MICHAEL JEFFREY, professional sports team executive, retired professional basketball player, professional baseball player; b. Bklyn., Feb. 17, 1963; s. James and Deloris Jordan; m. Juanita Vanoy, Sept. 2, 1989 (div. Dec. 29, 2006); children: Jeffrey Michael, Marcus James, Jasmine. Student, U. NC, 1981—84. Basketball player Chgo. Bulls, 1984—93, 1995—98, Washington Wizards, 2001—03, pres. basketball ops., 1999—2000; baseball player Chgo. White Sox AA Team, 1994-95; part owner, mng. mem. basketball ops. Charlotte Bobcats, 2006—. Owner Michael Jordan's: The Restaurant, 1993—; founder Jordan Brand Clothing, 1997—. Author: RareAir: Michael on Michael, 1993; author: (with Tinker Hatfield) Driven From Within, 2005; actor: (films) Space Jam, 1996, He Got Game, 1998. Named NBA Rookie of Yr., 1985, Seagram's NBA Player of Yr., 1987, Slam-Dunk Championship winner, 1987, 1988, NBA All-Star Game MVP, 1988, 1996, 1998, NBA Def. Player of Yr., 1988, NBA MVP, 1988, 1991, 1992, 1996, 1998, Male Athlete of Yr., AP, 1991, 1992, 1993, NBA Finals MVP, 1991—93, 1996—98; named to Sporting News All-Am. first team, 1983—84, NBA All-Star team, 1985—93, 1996—98, 2002—03, All NBA First Team, 1987—93, 1996—98, NBA All-Def. Team, 1988—93, 1996—98; recipient Naismith award, 1984, Wooden award, 1984, IBM award, 1985, 1989, Schick Pivotal Player award, 1985, 1989. Achievements include holding record for most points in an NBA playoff game (63); member of NCAA Divsn. I championship team, 1982, NBA champion Chgo. Bulls, 1991, 92, 93, 96, 97, 98, US Olympic basketball gold medal team, 1984, 92. Office: Charlotte Bobcats 333 E Trade St Charlotte NC 28202*

JORDAN, MICHELLE DENISE, judge; b. Chgo., Oct. 29, 1954; d. John A. and Margaret (O'Dood) J. BA in Polit. Sci., Loyola U, Chgo., 1974; JD, U. Mich., 1977. Bar. Ill. 1977, U.S. Dist. Ct. (no. dist.) Ill. 1978. Asst. state's atty. State's Attys. Office, Chgo., 1977-82; pvt. practice Chgo., 1983-84; with Ill. Atty. Gen.'s Office, Chgo., 1984-90, chief environ. control div., 1988-90; ptnr. Hopkins & Sutter, Chgo., 1991-93; apptd. dep. regional adminstr. region 5 U.S. EPA, Chgo., 1994—. Active Operation Push, Chgo., 1971—. Recipient Kizzy Image Achievement and Svc. award, 1990, Suzanne E. Olive Nat. EEO award 1996, Rainbow-PUSH Seed Sower award, 2004; named in Am.'s Top 100 Bus. and Profl. Women, Dollars and SenseMag., Chgo., 1988. Mem. Ill. Bar Assn., Chgo. Bar Assn. (bd. mgrs., chmn. criminal law com. 1987-88, mem. hearing divsn., jud.

evaluation com. 1987-88, exec. coun. 1987-88), Cook County Bar Assn., Nat. Bar Assn., Alpha Sigma Nu. Democrat. Baptist.

JORDAN, MILDRED RICE LORETTA, education educator; b. Chgo. d. Walter Henry Rice and Winnie Beatrice Smith; m. John Richard Medley, July 26, 1997; 1 child, Allison Monique Jordan. BS, Temple U., 1966, DEd, 1989; MEd, Arcadia U., 1977; DHL (hon.), Ea. N.C. Theol. Inst., 2001. Cert. elem. tchr./reading specilist, Pa. Tchr. Phila. Sch. Dist., 1966-72, Abington (Pa.) Sch. Dist., 1972—91; assoc. prof. Rider U., Lawrenceville, NJ, 1991—2006, prof. emerita, 2006—. Dir. Rider U., 1992—; founder, advisor scholarship fund, 1999—; presenter in field Contbr. articles to profl. jours. Amb. People to People Internat., 1997, 2003, 04; adv. bd. minding our bus. mentoring program Rider U., St. Mary Med. Ctr. Found., Langhorne, Pa. Named Ziegler Gee Woman of Yr., Rider U., 2002; recipient Dr. Selma H. Burke Positive Image award, NAACP, 2002. Mem. ASCD (assoc.), NAACP (Dr. Selma H. Burke Svc. award 2000), Phi Delta Kappa Avocation: travel. Office: Rider U 2083 Lawrenceville Rd Lawrenceville NJ 08648 Home: 12 Captiva Ct Hamilton NJ 08691 E-mail: ricejordan@rider.edu.

JORDAN, MOSINA H., federal agency administrator; b. Bklyn., Dec. 14, 1943; 3 children. B, NYU; JD, Am. U. With Cmty. Svcs. Adminstrn., 1973—81; with subcommittee on labor, health, human svcs. and edn. US Senate Appropriations Com.; dep. dir. Office Ctrl. African Affairs for Bur. Africa US Agy. Internat. Devel., dir. Office Equal Opportunity Progs., dep. mission dir. in Cameroon, mission dir. Jamaica, Barbados and Guyana, rep. in Belize, sr. dep. asst. adminstr. Bur. L.Am. and the Caribbean; US amb. to Ctrl. African Republic US Dept. State, Bangui, 1995—97; counselor US Agy. Internat. Devel., 2005—. Recipient Presdl. Meritorious Svc. Rank award, 1991. Mem.: ABA, Am. Fgn. Svc. Assn. Office: RRB 6 08-029 US Agy Internat Devel 1300 Pennsylvania Ave NW Washington DC 20523-6800 Office Phone: 202-712-5010. Office Fax: 202-216-3455.

JORDAN, NEIL PATRICK, film director, writer; b. County Sligo, Ireland, Feb. 25, 1950; m. Vivienne Shields (div.); 2 children; m. Brenda Rawb, June 30, 2004; 2 children. BA, Univ. Coll., Dublin, Ireland, 1968. Dir. (films) Angel, 1982 (Best Film and Best Dir. awards London Critics Circle), Company of Wolves, 1984, Mona Lisa, 1986 (nomiated Best Screenplay-Motion Picture Golden Globe 1987, nominated Best Direction, Best Film, Best Original Screenplay BAFTA 1987), High Spirits, 1988, We're No Angels, 1989, The Miracle, 1991, The Crying Game, 1992 (Alexander Korda award Best British Film, NY Film Critics Cir. award Best Screenplay, 1992, Writers Guild Am. Screen award Best Screenplay Written Directly for Screen, 1993, L.A. Film Critics award, Best Fgn. Film, 1993, Oscar Best Writing, Screenplay Written Directly for Screen 1993, nominated Oscar Best Dir. 1993, nominated Best Original Screenplay, BAFTA 1993, nominated Edgar award Best Motion Picture Edgar Allen Poe Awards 1993), Interview with the Vampire, 1994, Michael Collins, 1996 (Golden Lion award Venice Film Festival 1996), The Butcher Boy, 1997 (nominated CFCA award Best Dir., Best Picture, Chgo. Film Critics Assn. Awards 1999, Silver Bear award Best Dir., Berlin Film Festival 1997), In Dreams, 1999 (Silver Raven award Brussels Internat. Festival Fantasy Film 1999), The End of the Affair, 1999 (award Best Adapted Screenplay, Brit. Acad. Film and TV Arts 2000, nominated Best Film, Best Dir., Golden Globes 2000, BAFTA 2000), Not I, 2000; writer, dir., prodr.: The Good Thief, 2002, Breakfast on Pluto, 2005; author: A Night in Tunisia, 1976 (Guardian Fiction prize 1979), The Past, 1979, The Dream of a Beast, 1983, Sunrise With Sea Monster, 1994, Shade, 2004. Recipient Crystal Isis award Brussels Internat. Film Festival, 1998. Office: c/o Dave Wirtschafter William Morris Agency 1 William Morris Pl Beverly Hills CA 90212 also: Jenne Casarotto Casarotto Co Ltd Nat House 60 66 Wardour St London WIV 3HP England

JORDAN, PATRICIA COLGAN, physical education educator; b. Stamford, Conn., Oct. 18, 1932; d. Thomas Leo Colgan and Alice Peters Hershfelt; m. Michael Alexander Jordan, May 15, 1981; m. John Elwood Losinger (div. Jan. 18, 1978); children: Thomas John Losinger, Patti Losinger Clark. BPE, Pa. State U., 1954; MEd, U. Ctrl. Fla., Orlando, 1973. Tchr. Laurelton State Village, Pa., 1954—55, Bellefonte Area Sch., Bellefonte, Pa., 1955—58, Mt. Vernon Sch., Fortville, Ind., 1965—66; tchr., coach, adminstr. Brevard County Sch., Titusville, Fla., 1966—80; adj. instr. Brevard Cmty. Coll., 1979—80; tchr., coach Irving Ind. Sch., Tex., 1981—94; ret., 1994. Pres. Brevard County PE Edn. Assn., 1970—72; co-chmn. Sch. Health Adv. Coun., 1971—72; chmn., task force com. PE Curriculum Guide, 1970, Adapted PE, 1971, Health Edn. Curriculum, 1972, 74, 75; spkr. in field. Author: The Community and School Health, 1972, Title IX and Physical Education, 1976; editor: Fla. Coaches Manual. Troop leader Girl Scouts, Greenfield, Wis., 1959—65; mem. aquatic bd., water safety instr. Red Cross; CPR instr. Am. Heart Assn.; bd. dirs., program com., coach swim team YMCA, Titusville, Fla., 1966—80; 1st v.p. Palm Harbor Newcomers Club, 1995—96, pres. elect, 1996—97, pres., 1997—98, adv., 1988—99. Recipient Citizen of Yr., Greenfield C. of C., 1965. Mem.: Nat. Soc. of Arts and Letters, Dunedin Fine Arts Soc., Fine Arts Soc., Leading Ladies of PAC Found., Inc. (rec. sec. 1997—99, pres.-elect 1999—2003, pres. 2002—04, advisor 2004—06, parliamentarian exec.com. 2006), Fla. Athletic Coaches Assn. (coord. girls sports clin. 1975, vice chmn., athletic dir. 1975—77), Fla. Assn. for Health, PE, Recreation and Dance, Abilities Found., Palm Harbor Garden Club. Avocations: gardening, bridge. Home: 3817 Muirfield Ct Palm Harbor FL 34685

JORDAN, RICKEY WOODROW, retired automobile manufacturer technician; b. Camden, Tenn., May 10, 1944; s. Woodrow and Elease (Cook) Jordan; m. Mary Margaret Chalmers (div.); children: David Woodrow, Michael Scott. Assembler Chrysler Corp., Trenton, Mich., 1964—69, inspector, 1970—74, tear down dept., 1974—78, tool crib dept., 1979—80, repair dept., 1981—85, ctrl. maintenance dept., 1986—94; ret. Author: Poetry in the Words of Rick Jordan, 2004, Poems to Ponder, 2005, Poems With Rhythm and Rhyme, 2006. E-4 N.G. US Army, 1963—71, Tenn., Mich. Mem.: Internat. Libr. Poetry, United Auto Workers, Internat. Soc. Poets. Democrat. Baptist. Avocations: poetry, bicycling, gardening.

JORDAN, ROBERT ELIJAH, III, lawyer; b. South Boston, Va., June 20, 1936; s. Robert Elijah and Lucy (Webb) J.; m. Deborah A. Jordan; children: Janet Elizabeth, Jennifer Anne, Robert Elijah IV. SB, MIT, 1958; JD magna cum laude, Harvard U., 1961. Bar: D.C. 1962, Va. 1964, Calif. 1998. Spl. asst. civil rights Office Sec. Def., Washington, 1963-64; asst. U.S. atty. for D.C., 1964-65; exec. asst. for enforcement Office Sec. Treasury, 1965-67; dep. gen. counsel Dept. Army, 1967, acting gen. counsel, 1967-68; gen. counsel of Army, spl. asst. for civil functions to Sec. Army, 1968-71; ptnr. Steptoe & Johnson, Washington, 1971—2007, mng. ptnr., 1988-90. Mem. bd. cert. U.S. Cir. Cts. of Appeals Cir. Execs., 1987-88; pres. Langley Sch., 1981-82; mem. civil pro bono com. U.S. Dist. Ct., 1991-92. Contbr. articles to profl. jours. Mem. bd. dirs. Washington Humane Soc., 2000-03. Served to 1st lt. AUS, 1961-63. Recipient Karl Taylor Compton award, 1958, Arthur S. Flemming award, 1970, award for exceptional civilian svc. Dept. Army, 1971; Sloan Found. scholar; Edward J. Noble Found. fellow. Mem. Va. State Bar, D.C. Bar (chmn. ethics com. 1978-83, spl. com. on model rules profl conduct 1983-89, pres. 1987-88), Calif. State Bar, D.C. Bar Found. (pres. 1993-94, 97-98), Atlantic Coun. (bd. dirs. 1993—, exec. com. 1994—2001, chmn. nominating com. 1997-2001), Tau Beta Pi, Tau Kappa Alpha. Democrat. Office: 1330 Connecticut Ave NW Washington DC 20036-1795 Office Phone: 202-429-6290. Personal E-mail: rjordan@steptoe.com.

JORDAN, ROBERT (JAY) L., computer library service and research organization executive; BA in Eng. Lit., Cogate U., 1965. Top mgmt. positions, including pres. engring. Info. Handling Services, 1974—98; pres., CEO Online Computer Libr. Ctr., Inc., Dublin, Ohio, 1998—, bd. trustee. Officer US Army, Germany. Fellow: Standards Engring. Soc.; mem.: Spl. Libraries Assn., ALA. Office: Online Computer Libr Ctr Inc 6565 Kilgour Pl Dublin OH 43017-3395 Office Phone: 614-764-6000. Office Fax: 614-764-6096.*

JORDAN, ROBERT LEON, lawyer, educator; b. Reading, Pa., Feb. 27, 1928; s. Anthony and Carmela (Votto) J.; m. Evelyn Allen Willard, Feb. 15, 1958 (dec. Nov. 1996); children: John Willard, David Anthony BA, Pa. State U., 1948; LLB, Harvard U., 1951. Bar: N.Y. 1952. Assoc. White & Case, NYC, 1953-59; prof. law UCLA, 1959-70, 75-91, prof. law emeritus, 1991—, assoc. dean Sch. Law, 1968-69. Vis. prof. law Cornell U., Ithaca, N.Y., 1962-63; co-reporter Uniform Consumer Credit Code, 1964-70, Uniform Comml. Code Articles 3, 4, 4A, 1985-90; Fulbright lectr. U. Pisa, Italy, 1967-68 Co-author: (with W.D. Warren) Commercial Law, 1983, 5th edit., 2000, Bankruptcy, 1985, 5th edit., 1999. Lt. USAF, 1951-53. Office: UCLA Sch Law 405 Hilgard Ave Los Angeles CA 90095-9000

JORDAN, ROBERT LEON, judge; b. Woodlawn, Tenn., June 28, 1934; s. James Richard and Josephine (Broadbent) J.; m. Dorothy Rueter, Sept. 8, 1956; children: Robert, Margaret, Daniel. BS in Fin., U. Tenn., 1958, JD, 1960. Atty. Goodpasture, Carpenter, Dale & Woods, Nashville, 1960-61; mgr. Frontier Refining Co., Denver, 1961-64; atty. Green and Green, Johnson City, Tenn., 1964-66; trust officer 1st Peoples Bank, Johnson City, 1966-69; v.p., trust officer Comml. Nat. Bank, Pensacola, Fla., 1969-71; atty. Bryant, Price, Brandt & Jordan, Johnson City, 1971-80; chancellor 1st Jud. Dist., Johnson City, 1980-88; dist. judge U.S. Dist. Ct. (ea. dist.) Tenn., Knoxville, 1988—2001, sr. dist. judge, 2001—. Mem. adv. com. U. Tenn. Law Alumni, 1978-80; sec. Tenn. Jud. Conf., 1987-88, mem. exec. com., 1988; del. Tenn. State-Fed. Judicial Coun., 1993—. Bd. dirs., v.p. Tri-Cities estate Planning Coun., Johnson City, 1969; bd. dirs. Washington County Tb Assn., Rocky Mount Hist. Assn., High Rock Camp, Johnson City, Jr. Achievement of Pensacola Inc.; bd. dirs., treas. N.W. Fla. Crippled Children's Assn., Pensacola; chancellor's assoc. U. Tenn. With U.S. Army, 1954-56. Named Boss of Yr. Legal Secs. Assn., Washington, Carter County, Tenn., 1982. Mem. Tenn. Bar Assn., Tenn. Bar Found., Knoxville Bar Assn. (bd. govs. 1999), Washington County Bar Assn. (pres.-elect 1980), Johnson City C. of C., Hamilton Burnett Am. Inn of Ct. (pres. 1993-94), 6th Cir. Dist. Judges Assn. (pres. 2005), Kiwanis (pres. Met. Johnson City Club 1969, Kiwanian of Yr. award 1986-87). Republican. Mem. Ch. Of Christ. Office: Howard H Baker US Courthouse 800 Market St Ste 141 Knoxville TN 37902-2303 Office Phone: 423-545-4224.

JORDAN, ROBERT RANDY, music educator; b. Tulia, Tex., June 18, 1952; s. Louise Wood; m. Debbie Duncan, Jan. 8, 1951; children: Jason Robert, Tiffani Holli Shipman, Travis English, Lacey Franklin. B in Music Edn., Tex. Tech U., 1975; M in Music Edn., U. North Tex., 1981. Cert. secondary choral music edn. Tex., 1975, secondary music supervision Tex., 1996. Choral dir. Azle (Tex.) H.S., 1975—82; choral dir./fine arts dept. chair Martin H.S., Arlington, Tex., 1982—2005; choral dir. St. Barnabas United Meth. Ch., Arlington, 1984—99, Arlington Master Chorale, 2004—. Named Sponsor of the Yr., U. Interscholastic League, 1998. Mem.: PTA (life), Tex. Music Adjudicators Assn., Am. Choral Directors Assn. (Honor Choir, Nat. Conv. San Diego 1997, Honor Choir, Nat. Conv. L.A. 2005), Tex. Choral Directors Assn., Tex. Music Educators Assn. (region V vocal divsn. chair 1993—94, Honor Choir, State Conv. San Antonio 1995, 2005), Phi Mu Alpha Sinfonia. Avocations: golf, reading. Home: 2316 Starlight Ct Arlington TX 76016 Office: Arlington Master Chorale 2316 Starlight Ct Arlington TX 76016 Home Phone: 817-861-2552. Personal E-mail: muzakmn@sbcglobal.net.

JORDAN, ROBERT REED, retired geologist, educator; b. NYC, June 5, 1937; s. Herbert and Irene (Reed) J.; m. Jane H. Jordan, June 28, 1958; children: Richard P., Judith H. AB, Hunter Coll., NYC, 1958; MA, Bryn Mawr Coll., Pa., 1962, PhD, 1964. Cert. profl. geologist, Del.; lic. geologist, N.C., profl. geoscientist, Tex. Geologist Del. Geol. Survey, Newark, 1958-64, asst. state geologist, 1964-69, state geologist, dir., 1969—2003; state geologist emeritus, 2003—; instr. U. Del., Newark, 1962-64, asst. prof., 1964-68, assoc. prof., 1968-88, prof., 1988—2005; prof. emeritus, 2005—. Mem. Del. Air and Water Commn., Dover, 1966-73; chmn. Del. State Boundary Commn., Newark, 1971-2003; mem. Del. State Bd. Registration of Geologists, 1972-2003; mem. Outer Continental Shelf policy com. U.S. Dept. Interior, 1974-77, 85-2003, chmn., 1993-94; mem. N.Am. Commn. on Stratigraphic Nomenclature, 1978—, chmn., 1984, 92; mem. U.S. Nat. Com. on Geology, 1990-96; co-convenor Internat. Geol. Congress, Florence, Italy, 2004; mem. US Nat. Com. Internat. Yr. of Planet Earth, 2007-. Contbr. numerous articles to profl. jours. Recipient tributes Del. Gen. Assembly, 2003; named Hon. Mountaineer, State of W.Va., 1997, Ky. col., 1997. Fellow Geol. Soc. Am.; mem. Del. Acad. Sci. (pres. 1990, 2002), Am. Inst. Profl. Geologists (editor 1989-90, hon. mem. award 1996, Galey Mem. Pub. Svc. award 1992, Ben H. Parker Meml. medal 2006), Am. Geol. Inst. (fin. com. 1992—2000, treas., exec. com. 1992-93, Outstanding Svc. award 1992, 93, Ian Campbell award 1996,), Assn. Am. State Geologists (hon.; pres. 1983-84, Achievement award, Disting. Svc. award, 2007), Am. Assn. Petroleum Geologists (hon. mem. award 1993, Disting. Svc. award 1988, Cohee Pub. Svc. Ea. award 1990, Galey award Ea. 1995, John T. Galey Sr. meml. medal 1998, Pres.'s award divsn. environ. geology 2001, sr. advisor, corp. registration agt., mem. US nat. com. Internat. Yr. of Planet Earth, del.).

JORDAN, ROBERT SANDS, electrical engineer; b. Washington, Sept. 16, 1947; s. Louis and Ethyl Marion (Horen) Jordan; m. Cheryl Ann Adams-Jordan, July 29, 1972. Student in elec. engring., U. Maine, Orono, 1965—67; A. Engring. Elec. Engring. Tech. with highest honors, Wentworth Inst. Tech., Boston, 1969; BSEE with high honors, Northeastern U., Boston, 1972; postgrad. in biomedical engring., Calif. Inst. Tech., Pasadena. Lic. profl. engr. NY, 1989. Supt. elec. maintenance Internat. Paper Co., Livermore Falls, Maine, 1973—78; maintenance engr. Jay, Maine, 1978—79; chief elec. engr. Finch, Pruyn & Co., Inc., Glens Falls, NY, 1979—88; sr. prin. elec. engr. Stone & Webster, Portland, Maine, 1988—90; project elect engr. Rist Frost & Assocs., Laconia, NH, 1990—91, Glens Falls, NY, 1991—94; mgr. elect, controls engring. Williamette Industries, Inc., Charlotte, NC, 1994—2002; sr. elec. engr. Weyerhaeuser Co., 2002—07; elec. engr. Shaw Group, 2007—. Mem. Evergreen Homeowners Assn., 1979—89, elect bd. dirs., 1980—82; mem. Queensbury Ctrl. Vol. Fire Dept., NY, 1980—88, NY, 1992—94, elect v.p. NY, 1984—88; elect chmn. Bylaws Com.; mem. Wilshire Homeowners Assn., Charlotte, 1995—, chmn. archl. rev. com., 1996—97; mem. St. Ann Ch., 1995—2006, fin. com., usher, extra, ordin. min. of eucharist; mem. St. Matthew Ch., 2006—. Mem.: Nat. Fire Protection Assn., IEEE (sr.), Phi Kappa Phi, Eta Kappa Nu, Tau Beta Pi, Tau Alpha Pi. Republican. Roman Catholic. Avocations: history, numismatics, philately, car restoration, architecture. Home: 7140 Broadford Ct Charlotte NC 28277 Office: The Shaw Group 128 S Tryon St Ste 400 Charlotte NC 28202 Office Phone: 704-343-7627. Business E-Mail: robert.jordan@shawgrp.com.

JORDAN, ROBERT SMITH, political science professor, civilian military employee; b. LA, Calif, June 11, 1929; s. Ralph Burdette and Mary Wright (Smith) J.; m. Sara Jane Hatch, Sept. 19, 1961; children: Sara Jane, Mary Rebecca Leming, Robert Hatch, David Thomas. AB, UCLA, 1951; MS, U. Utah, 1955; MA, Princeton U., 1957, PhD, 1960; PhD (Fulbright scholar), St. Antony's Coll., Oxford U., Eng., 1960; Henry P. DuBois fellow, Princeton U., 1956—57. Instr. dept. politics Princeton U., 1956—57; asst. prof. pub. and internat. affairs, exec. asst. to dean Grad. Sch. Pub. and Internat. Affairs, U. Pitts., 1959—60; assoc. professorial lectr. George Washington U., 1960—62; asst. dir. Army War Coll. Center, 1960—61; dir. Air U. Center, 1961—62, assoc. prof. polit. sci. and internat. affairs, 1962—70, asst. to pres., 1962—64; dir. Ford Found. Fgn. Affairs Intern Program, Sch. Pub. and Internat. Affairs, 1968—70; dean faculty econ. and social studies, head dept. polit. sci. Fourah Bay Coll., U. Sierra Leone, 1965—67; prof. polit. sci. State U. NY at Binghamton, 1970—76, chmn. dept., 1970—74; dir. rsch. UN Inst. for Tng. and Rsch., NYC, 1975—79; Dag Hammarskold vis. prof. internat. rels. U. SC, Columbia, 1979—80; prof. polit. sci., rsch. prof. U. New Orleans, 1980—2002, dean Grad. Sch., 1980—82; rsch. prof. Coll. Urban Affairs, 2002—04, emeritus, 2004—. Disting. vis. prof. Naval War Coll., 1984-86; Fulbright prof. Cen. Study of Arms Control and Internat. Security, U. Lancaster, Eng., Jan.-June, 1988; vis. prof. internat. rels. US Air War Coll., 1992-94, U. Wis. sys., 2007-. Author: The NATO International Staff/Secretariat, 1967, Government and Power in West Africa, 1970, rev. edit., 1977, Political Leadership in NATO, 1979, Norstad: Cold War NATO Supreme Commander, 2000, A Mormon's Cold War Odyssey: Early Travails and Travels, 1929-1962, 2007; co-author: Europe and the Superpowers, 1971, rev. edit., 1990, The World Food Conference and Global Problem Solving, 1976, Changing Role and Concepts in the International Civil Service, 1980, Dag Hammarskjold Revisited: The UN Secretary-General as a Force in World Politics, 1983, Europe in the Balance: The Changing Context of European International Politics, 1986, International Organizations: A Comparative Approach of the Management of Cooperation, 2001; editor and contbr.: International Administration, 1971, Multinational Cooperation, 1972, Generals in International Politics: NATO's Supreme Allied Commander, Europe, 1987, co-editor and contbr.: Maritime Strategy and the Balance of Power: Britain and America in the Twentieth Century, 1989. With USAF, 1951—53. Decorated Bronze Star; named Disting. Alumnus, Hinckley Inst., U. Utah, 1964; NATO rsch. fellow, 1969—70, 1990, Hooper postdoctoral fellow, U.S. Naval Hist. Ctr., 1987, 1997. Mem. ASPA (chmn. sect. on internat. and comp. adminstrn.), Assn. Princeton Grad. Alumni (pres.), Internat. Studies Assn. (v.p., chmn. sect. internat. orgn.), Acad. Coun. UN, Internat. Inst. Strategic Studies (London), Royal Inst. Internat. Affairs (London), Cosmos Club (Washington), Plimsoll Club (New Orleans), Sigma Chi (UCLA and Utah). Democrat. Mem. Lds Ch. Personal E-mail: smitty1929@charter.net.

JORDAN, RUTH ANN, retired physician; b. Oct. 12, 1928; d. Willard and Esther (Fouts) J.; children: Diane J., Linda J. AB, Ind. U., 1950; MD, Columbia U., 1957. Intern St. Luke's Hosp., NYC, 1957—58, asst. resident, 1958—59; physician Met. Life Ins. Co., NYC, 1960—62, Standard Oil Co. of N.J., NYC, 1962, MIT, Cambridge, Mass., 1963—71, New Eng. Mut. Life Ins. Co., Boston, 1963—66, asst. med. dir., 1971—74; fellow internal medicine Mass. Gen. Hosp., Boston, 1974—75; physician Simmons Coll., Boston, 1975—78, Northeastern U., Boston, 1976—78; assoc. med. dir. New Eng. Telephone Co., Boston, 1978, med. dir. clin. svcs., 1978—86; dir. occupl. medicine Gen. Med. Assn./Harvard Cmty. Health Plan, Boston, 1986—91; assoc. med. dir. Allmerica, Worcester, Mass., 1991—97; plant med. dir. GM, Westwood, Mass., 1995—2005; physician Health Resource, Woburn, Mass., 1996—2005; ret., 2005. Therapeutic dietitian Meth. Hosp., Indpls., 1951-53, Presbyn. Hosp., N.Y.C., part-time 1954-57; nat. coord. com. on cholesterol, 1986-2005, Mass. Adv. Coun. for Workers Compensation, 1986-89; bd. Coll. Arts and Sci., Ind. U., 2003—. Dean's advisory coun. Ind. U. Coll. Arts and Scis., 2004—. Fellow: Am. Coll. Occupl. and Environ. Medicine (health edn. com. 1984—, membership com. 1985—88, bd. dirs. 1986—92); mem.: PEO, DAR, AMA, Mass. Med. Soc. (ho. of dels. 1984—2005, chmn. environ. and occupl. health com. 1985—88, interspIty. com. 1985—88, nutrition com. 2001—05, bylaws com. 2001—05, bd. trustees 2003—05, nominating com. 2003—05), Norfolk Dist. Med. Soc. (v.p. 1998—99, edn. com. 1998—2005, exec. com. 1998—2005, pres. 1999—2001, alt. rep. to Mass. Med. Soc. nominating com. 2000—03, alt. bd. trustees 2000—03), New Eng. Occupl. Med. Assn. (bd. dirs. 1980—89, pres. 1981—84), The Country Club, Columbia U. Club of New Eng. (v.p. 1981—84, bd. dirs. 1981—91, pres. 1989—91), Alpha Chi Omega. Home: 2618 N Terrace Ave Milwaukee WI 53211

JORDAN, SHANNON COLLEN, medical/surgical nurse; b. Espanola, N.Mex., Dec. 5, 1952; d. William Harrison Roach and Ethel Louise (Hartsfield) Burns; m. Harweda Bruce Jordan, July 9, 1971 (div. 1991); children: Dominic, Peter, Sabian, Simon. BSN with highest honors, U. Tex., El Paso, 1992. Cert. med. surgical nurse ANCC, 1995, ANCC, 2000, ANCC, 2005. Profl. singer, writer The Jordans, Sunrise Creations, 1971-89; staff nurse III R.E. Thomason Hosp., El Paso, Tex., 1992—2002, infection control practitioner, 2002—. Author, lyricist, composer Sunrise, 1978. Bd. dirs. Westside YMCA, El Paso, Tex., 1993-95, Hot Line of El Paso, 1992-93; vol. Reach to Recovery Am. Cancer Soc., El Paso, 1994-99. Recipient Nat. Collegiate Nursing award U.S. Achievement Acad., 1992, Outstanding Nursing award U.S. Air Force, 1992, Women of Mines award U. Tex., 1992; U. Tex. scholar, 1989-92, Teen Expo scholar, 1992, All Am. scholar U.S. Achievement Acad., 1992; Pell grantee U.S. Govt., 1989-92, Marian Meaker Aptekar grantee, 1994. Mem. Assn. Profl. Infection Control Practitioners, Sigma Theta Tau Internat., U. Tex. Alumni Assn., Golden Key Nat. Honor Soc. Alphi Chi. Republican. Protestant. Avocations: composing, writing, walking, photography, gardening. Home: 825 Somerset Dr El Paso TX 79912-4916

JORDAN, STEPHEN M., academic administrator; m. Ruth Kinnie; 3 children. BA in Polit. Sci., U. No. Colo., 1971; MPA in Fin. Adminstrn., U. Colo., Denver, 1979, PhD in Pub. Adminstrn./Policy Analysis, 1990. Vice chancellor for budgets and facilities U. Colo. Health Scis. Ctr., 1985—, asst. sec. bd. regents, 1985—; dep. exec. dir. fin. and planning, Bd. Regents Ariz. State U., 1989—; exec. dir. Kans. Bd. Regents, 1994—; pres. Ea. Wash. U., Cheney, 1998—2005, Met. State Coll. of Denver, 2005—. Mem. edn. subcom. Inland N.W. Tech. Edn. Ctr.; mem. commn. on internat. edn. Am. Coun. of Edn.; mem. com. on econ. and workforce devel. Am. Assn. State Colls. and Univs.; mem. Nat. Collaborative Adv. Group, N.W. Commn. on Colls. and Univs. Bd. dirs. Wash. Tech. Ctr., Wash. State Inst. for Pub. Policy, Coun. of Presidents; mem. exec. bd. Spokane Alliance Med. Rsch., 2003, Providence Health Svcs. Ea. Wash., Wash. Campus Compact, Air Edn. and Tng. Command, Health Industry Devel. Group, Higher Edn. Leadership Group. Mem. NCAA (mem. presdl. adv. group), Spokane Area C. of C. (bd. dirs. 2000 exec. com. 2004), Phi Kappa Phi. Office: Metropolitan State Coll of Denver PO Box 173362 Denver CO 80217-3362 Office Phone: 303-556-2070.

JORDAN, THOMAS FREDRICK, physics professor; b. Duluth, Minn., June 4, 1936; s. Thomas Vincent and Mildred (Nystrom) J. BA, U. Minn., 1958; PhD, U. Rochester, 1962. Rsch. assoc. U. Rochester, 1961-62, instr., 1962-63; NSF postdoctoral fellow U. Bern, Switzerland, 1963-64; asst. prof. U. Pitts., 1964-67, assoc. prof., 1967-70; prof. U. Minn., Duluth, 1970—. Vis. prof., workshop participant U. Wis., 1965, Aspen (Colo.) Inst. for Humanistic Studies, 1966, Summer Inst. for Theoretical Physics, U. Colo., 1967, Internat. Ctr. for Theoretical Physics, Trieste, Italy, 1968, U. Rochester, 1976-77, Syracuse U., Nat. Inst. for Nuclear Rsch., Firenze, Italy, U. Geneva., U. Paris 1982, Internat. Ctr. for Theoretical Physics, Trieste, workshop on early universe, Erice, Italy, Geneva, U. Bern, 1986, U. Calif. at Santa Barbara, 1988, U. Tex., 1990, 94, 2003, 04, 05. Author: Linear Operators for Quantum Mechanics, 1969, Quantum Mechanics in Simple Matrix Form, 1985; contbr. numerous article to profl. jours. Rsch. fellow Alfred P. Sloan Found., 1965-67, Temple U., 1984, Bush Found. fellow U. Tex., 1994; Fulbright Rsch. grantee U. Göttingen, Fed. Republic of Germany, 1991-92, 2003.

JORDAN, V. CRAIG, endocrine pharmacologist, educator; b. New Braunfels, Tex., July 25, 1947; s. Geoffrey Webster and Sybil Cynthia (Mottram) J.; children: Helen Melissa Yvonne, Alexandra Katherine Louise; m. Monica Morrow. B.Sc. with honors, U. Leeds (Eng.), 1969, Ph.D. in Pharmacology, 1972; D.Sc. in Pharmacology, 1985, hon. MD, 2001; hon. DSc, U. Mass., 2001, U. Brad, Eng., 2005. Rsch. assoc. Worcester Found. Exptl. Biology, Shrewsbury, Mass., 1972-73, vis. scientist, 1973-74; lectr. pharmacology U. Leeds, 1973-79; head endocrinology unit Ludwig Inst. Cancer Rsch., U. Berne, Switzerland, 1979-80; asst. prof. human oncology and pharmacology U. Wis., Madison, 1980-81, assoc. prof., 1981-85, prof., 1985-93, visting prof. human oncology, 1993-95, leader pharmacology group dept. human oncology; dir. Breast Cancer Research Program, Wis. Comprehensive Cancer Ctr.; prof. Cancer Pharmacology Northwestern U. Cancer Ctr., 1993-2004, assoc. dir. cancer control, 1993-96, dir. Lynn Sage breast cancer rsch. program, Robert H. Lurie Comprehensive Ctr.Northwestern U., Chgo., 1993-2004, prof. Molecular Pharmacology and Biol. Chemistry, Northwestern U. Feinberg Sch. Medicine, 1994-2004, Diana Princess of Wales Prof. of Cancer Rsch., 1999-2004; v.p., scientific dir., medical sci. divsn. and Alfred G. Knudson Jr., M.D., Ph.D., chair cancer rsch., Fox Chase Cancer Ctr., 2004-; adj. prof. cancer cell biology, U. Pa., 2004-; hon. prof. Leeds Inst. Mol. Medicine, Eng., 2007. Mem. editl. bd. Breast Cancer Rsch. Treatment, Clin. Cancer Rsch., Cancer Letters (mng. editor), Endocrine Related Cancer (assoc. editor), European Jour. Cancer, Jour. Steroid Biochemistry, Jour. Nat. Cancer Inst., Molecular Cell Endocrinology, Receptor, Molecular Aspects Med., assoc. editor; contbr. more than 400 articles to profl. jours. Served to capt., Intelligence Corps, Brit. Army, 1971-76; Served to capt. Spl. Air Svc., 1976-79. Med. Rsch. Coun. scholar, 1969-72; co-recipient Boston Obstet. Soc. prize, 1974; UICC Internat. Cancer Research Tech. Transfer grantee, 1981; Romnes Faculty fellow, 1984-85; recipient Brinker Internat. Breast Cancer award Susan G. Komen Found., 1992, Cameron prize U. Edinburgh, 1993, WL McGuire Meml. award 1994, Herbert J. Block Meml. award Dist. Achievement in Cancer, Ohio State U., 1996, Strang award, Cornell Med. Sch., 2000, hon. fellowship award and medal, Univ. Coll., Dublin, Ireland, 2000, Bristol Myers Squibb award and medal Disting. Achievement in Cancer Rsch., 2001, Third Annual Breast Cancer award, European Inst. Oncology, Milan, Italy, 2001, Vivian and Meyer P. Potamkin found. award Breast Cancer Rsch., Pa. Breast Cancer Coalition, 2001, Avon Med. Advancement award, Avon Found. 2002, Am. Cancer Soc. Medal of Honor, 2002, Officer Most Excellent Order of the British Empire for Services to Internat. Breast Cancer Rsch., Queen Elizabeth II, 2002, Charles F. Kettering award, GM Cancer Rsch. Found, 2003, Miami Breast Cancer Conf. award of Excellence, 2003, 3rd George & Christine Sosnovsky award in Cancer Therapy, 2003-04, N. Am. Menopause Soc./Eli Lilly SERM Rsch. award, 2003, Gregory Pincus award U. Mass. Worcester Found. Exptl. Biology, 2007; hon. prof. Iguca U., Brazil, 2005. Fellow Am. Inst. Chemists, Royal Soc. Chemistry (Sosnovsky award, 2004), Am. Soc. Clin. Oncology (Am. Cancer Soc. award, 2006), Brit. Pharm. Soc. (Sir John Gaddum Meml. award 1993); mem. Am. Assn. Cancer Rsch. (chair Pres. Cir. 2004—, bd. dirs. 2007—, bd. trustees AACR Found., 8th Cain Meml. award 1989, Inaugural Dorothy P. Landon prize Translational Rsch. 2002), Am. Soc. Pharmacology and Exptl. Therapeutics (ASPET award 1993), Endocrine Soc., Biochem. Soc., Pharm. Soc. GB (hon.), Y-ME Chgo. (hon. nat. bd. dir.). Office: Fox Chase Cancer Ctr 333 Cottman Ave Philadelphia PA 19111-2497 Office Phone: 215-728-7410. Office Fax: 215-728-7034. Business E-Mail: V.Craig.Jordan@fccc.edu.

JORDAN, VERNON EULION, JR., lawyer; b. Atlanta, Aug. 15, 1935; s. Vernon Eulion and Mary (Griggs) J.; m. Shirley M. Yarbrough, Dec. 13, 1958 (dec. Dec. 29, 1985); 1 child, Vickee; m. Ann Dibble Cook, Nov. 22, 1986. BA, DePauw U., 1957; JD, Howard U., 1960; degree (hon.), DePauw U., Howard U., Boston Coll., Brandeis U., CUNY, U. Ill., Duke U., U. Mass., NYU, Princeton U., Tulane U., Rutgers U., Yale U., Notre Dame U., Harvard U. Bar: Ga. 1960, Ark. 1964. Practice law, Atlanta, 1960-61, Pine Bluff, Ark., 1964-65; Ga. field dir. NAACP, 1961-63; dir. Voter Edn. Project So. Regional Council, 1964-68; atty. OEO, Atlanta, 1969; exec. dir. United Negro Coll. Fund, NYC, 1970-71; pres. Nat. Urban League, 1972-81; sr. ptnr. firm Akin, Gump, Strauss, Hauer & Feld, LLP, Washington, of counsel, 2000—; sr. mng. dir. Lazard Freres & Co., LLC, NYC, 2000—. Bd. dirs. Am. Express Co., Asbury Automotive Group, Inc., Lazard Ltd., Xerox Corp.; chmn. Clinton Presdl. Transition Bd.; apptd. to Pres.'s adv. com. Points of Light Initiative Found., 1989; mem. Iraq Study Group, 2006 Mem. Nat. Adv. Commn. on Selective Svcs., 1966-67, Am. Revolution Bi-Centennial Commn., 1972—, Presdl. Clemency Bd., 1974; adv. coun. Social Security, 1974; trustee Ford Found., LBJ Found., Urban Inst. (life), Howard U.; mem. steering com. Bilderberg Meetings; mem. Coun. on Fgn. Rels.; adv. trustee DePauw U., bd. dirs. NAACP Legal Def. and Ednl. Fund; hon. mem. Ralph Bunche Inst. on the UN. Fellow 2Met. Applied Research Center, 1968; Fellow Harvard Inst. Politics, 1969; recipient Alexis de Tocqueville award United Way Am., 1977. Mem. ABA, DC Bar Assn., Nat. Bar Assn., Nat. Conf. Black Lawyers, Am. Law Inst., University Club, Board Room, Council on Fgn. Relations, Century Assn. Mem. A.M.E. Ch. Office: Lazard Freres & Co LLC 30 Rockefeller Plz New York NY 10112-0002 Office Phone: 212-632-6000.

JORDAN, W. CARL, lawyer; b. Mobile, Ala., Apr. 7, 1949; s. William Cecil and Lois Elizabeth (Smith) J.; m. Lisa Anne Gagne, Aug. 17, 1974; children: Kimberly Gardner, Hillary Elizabeth, William Christopher, Clement Nicholas. BA, Baylor U., 1971; JD, Harvard U., 1974. Bar: US Dist. Ct. (so., no. and ea. dists.) Tex. 1975, US Ct. Appeals (5th cir.) 1975, US Ct. Appeals (9th cir.), Tex. 1984, US Supreme Ct. 1984. Assoc. Vinson & Elkins, LLP, Houston, 1974-81, ptnr., 1981—, co-head Employment Litig. and Labor Sect. Gen. counsel Tex. Employment Law Coun., Austin, 1984—. Author: Developing and Enforcing Drug and Alcohol Work Rules: A Primer for Tex. Employers, 1986; editor: Employment Discrimination Law, supplement, 1998; contbr. articles to profl. jours. Mem. ABA (labor and employment law sect., equal employment opportunity law com., subcom. chmn. 1983-86). Home: 3722 Farber St Houston TX 77005-3714 Office: Vinson & Elkins 1st City Tower 1001 Fannin St Ste 2300 Houston TX 77002-6706 Business E-Mail: cjordan@velaw.com.

JORDAN, WILLIAM CHESTER, historian, educator; b. Chgo., Apr. 7, 1948; s. Johnnie Parker and Marguerite Jane (Mays) Jordan; m. Christine Kenyon Hershey, May 30, 1970; children: Victoria Marie, John Mark, Clare Kenyon, Lorna Janice. AB, Ripon Coll., 1969; PhD, Princeton U., 1973. Instr. Princeton U., 1973-74, lectr., 1974-75, asst. to assoc. prof. history, 1975-86, prof. history, 1986—, Behrman sr. fellow in humanities, 1990—94, Dayton-Stockton prof., 2005—; dir. Shelby Cullom Davis Ctr. for Hist. Studies, 1994-99. Vis. lectr. U. Pa., Phila., 1981-82; vis. assoc. prof. history Swarthmore (Pa.) Coll., 1985; mem. adv. com. history Grad. Records Exam, 1976-86, chmn., 1980-86; Morgan lectr. Dickinson Coll., Carlisle, Pa., 1985. Co-editor: Order and Innovation in the Middle Ages, 1976; author: Louis IX and the Challenge of the Crusade, 1979, From Servitude to Freedom, 1986, The French Monarchy and the Jews, 1989, Women and Credit, 1993, The Great Famine, 1996, The Middle Ages: An Encyclopedia for Students, 1996, The Middle Ages: A Watts Guide for Children, 2000, Europe in the High Middle Ages, 2001, Ideology and Royal Power in Medieval France, 2001, Dictionary of the Middle Ages; Supplement 1, 2004, Unceasing Strife, Unending Fear, 2005; contbr. articles to profl. jours. Recipient Behrman award Princeton U., 2003; fellow Woodrow Wilson Found., Ford Found., Danforth Found, Mellon Found., Rockefeller Found., Annenberg Rsch. Inst. Fellow Medieval Acad. Am. (Haskins medal 2000); mem. Am. Hist. Assn. (co-chair program com. 1985), Am. Coun. Learned Socs. (sec. 1986-95, bd. dirs. 1982-95), Am. Philos. Soc. (elected), Soc. French Hist. Studies, Soc. Study of the Crusades and Latin East, Haskins Soc. Office: Dept of History Princeton U Princeton NJ 08544-0001 Home Phone: 609-924-8784; Office Phone: 609-258-4165. Business E-Mail: wchester@princeton.edu.

JORDAN, WILLIAM DAVIS, lawyer; b. Palestine, Tex., Aug. 5, 1940; s. Henry Latimer and Evelyn (Davis) J.; m. Toby Stall Feb. 8, 1964; children: Russell Stall Jordan, Stephen Monnig Jordan. BBA with honors, U. Tex., 1963, LLB with honors, 1964. Bar: Tex. 1964; cert. estate planning and probate law Tex. Bd. Legal Specialization. Assoc., then ptnr. Jackson and Walker, Dallas, 1964—97; shareholder Johnson, Jordan, Nipper & Monk, P.C., Dallas, 1997—. Chmn. U. Tex. Tax Conf., 1977, also planning com.; spkr. in field. Contbr. articles to profl. jours. Active Dallas Estate Planning Coun.; chmn. Southwestern Legal Found. Oil and Gas Tax Inst., 1981-86, planning com.; dir., past chmn. Dallas Met. YMCA; past dir. Baylor U. Med. Ctr. Found., YMCA Rockies, Colo.; chmn. YMCA Found.; adv. dir. Cmtys. Found. Tex., Dallas Found.; past mem. Rotary, found. trustee Dallas, 1985-91. Mem. Tex. Bar Assn. (co-chmn. peer com. 1967-68), Dallas Bar Assn. (chmn. tax sect. 1977), Dallas Estate Planning Coun. (past bd. dirs.), Dallas Country Club, Beta Theta Pi. Presbyterian. Office: Johnson Jordan Nipper & Monk PC 13155 Noel Rd Ste 1050 LB3 Dallas TX 75240-1531 Office Phone: 972-392-1123.

JORDAN, WILLIAM REYNIER, SR., retired therapist, poet; s. Russell Clinger and Lois Eleanor (Van Evera) J.; children: William (dec. 2001), Michael, Paul. BS in Journalism cum laude, U. Fla., 1956; South Asia area specialist, U. Pa., 1960-62; grad., Strategic Intelligence Sch., 1962, Gen. Staff Coll., 1968, Def. Lang. Inst., 1970; MA in Psychology, U. No. Colo., 1979; postgrad., U. So. Fla., 1986-87; PhD in Psychology, Calif. Coast U., 1989. Cpl. U.S. Army, 1947-48, with Mil. Intelligence Res., 1948-51, to 1st lt. inf., 1951-54, re-entered, 1957, advanced through grades to lt. col., 1968; chief of plans and analysis psychol. ops. divsn. Mil. Assistance Command, Vietnam, 1970-71; group ops. officer, later spl. asst. to comdg. officer 902d Mil. Intelligence Group, Washington, 1971-72; ret., 1972; vol. psychotherapist Juvenile Detention, Pensacola, Fla., 1976-77, Colorado Springs (Colo.) Social Svcs. Dept., 1977-78; psychotherapist Med. Clinic, St. Petersburg, Fla., 1980-84, Epilepsy Found., St. Petersburg, 1984-88; vol. VA Mental Health Clinic, Bay Pines, Fla., 1985-99; ret., 1999. Author: Darkness and Shadows, 1975, More Than Friends, 1978, Heat Lightning, 1984. Leader Rawalpindi coun. Boy Scouts Am., Pakistan, 1960-62, also troops at Ft. Bragg, N.C., Ft. Leavenworth, Kans., Ft. Holabird, Md., 1964-70; bd. dirs. YMCA, Dundalk, Md., 1969-71, Epilepsy Assn., Pensacola, 1975-77. Decorated Legion of Merit with oak leaf cluster, Cross of Gallantry with Palm (Republic of Vietnam); named Vol. of Yr., Colorado Springs Social Svcs. Dept., 1978. Mem. APA (assoc.), DAV, Epilepsy Assn. Am. (pres.'s club), Am. Assn. Counseling and Devel. Democrat. Congregationalist. Avocation: photography. Address: 1051 79th Ave N Apt 111 Saint Petersburg FL 33702-1127

JORDE, TERRY J., bank executive; b. 1958; married; 3 children. BA in Fin., U. Ill. Champaign-Urbana. Pres. Ind. Cmty. Banks of ND; pres., CEO CountryBank USA, Cando, ND. Mem. Fed. Reserve Bd. Consumer Adv. Coun., Nat. Adv. Coun., Fannie Mae; bd. mem. ND Dept. Fin. Institutions; chmn., Agr.-Rural Am. Com. Ind. Cmty. Bankers of Am., chmn., Securities Corp., chmn., Services Network, treasurer, vice chmn., chmn. Bd. mem. Towner County Econ. Devel. Corp., Towner County Med. Ctr., ND Devel. Fund. Named one of 25 Women to Watch, US Banker, 2006. Office: CountryBank USA PO Box 549 Cando ND 58324 Office Phone: 701-968-4421.*

JORDE, THOMAS, law educator; b. 1947; BA, Yale U., 1969, JD, 1972. Bar: Calif. 1975. Law clk. to presiding justice U.S. Dist. Ct. (no. dist.) Calif., San Francisco, 1972-73; law clk. to Justice William Brennan Jr. U.S. Supreme Ct., D.C., 1973-74; spl. asst. to dir. of Bur. of Competition Fed. Trade Commn., Wash., DC; spl. master for Judge Thelton Henderson US Dist. Ct., San Francisco; pvt. practice law San Francisco, 1974-78; acting prof. law U. Calif., Berkeley, 1978-82, assoc. dean, 1982-85, prof. of law, 1985—. Contbr. articles to profl. jours. Office: U Calif Sch Law 894 Simon Hall Berkeley CA 94720 Office Phone: 510-642-0340. Office Fax: 510-642-3856. E-mail: tjorde@law.berkeley.edu.

JORDEN, DOUGLAS ALLEN, lawyer, municipal official; b. Ft. Smith, Ark., July 17, 1950; s. James Roy and Gordon P. J.; m. Mary Zoe Arendt, Apr. 23, 1983; children: Michael, Willie, Julia. BA, U. Ark., 1972, JD, 1976. Bar: Ark. 1976, Ariz. 1976, US Dist. Ct. Ariz. 1976, US Ct. Appeals (9th cir.) 1977, Calif. 1992, Colo. 1992, US Supreme Ct. 1996. Assoc. Harold Mott Esq., Phoenix, 1976-78; town atty. Town of Paradise Valley, Ariz., 1978-82; assoc. Fennemore Craig, Phoenix, 1982-84; ptnr. Slavin, Kane & Paterson, Phoenix, 1984-88, Lancy, Scult, McVey, Phoenix, 1988-90, Jorden Law Firm, Phoenix, 1990-92, Kane, Jorden, von Oppenfeld, Phoenix, 1992-98, Jorden Bischoff & Hiser, PLC, Phoenix, 1998—. Co-author: Arizona Land Use Law, 1988, 4th rev. edit., 2004. Mem. Paradise Valley Village Planning Com. 1988-90; chmn. Phoenix Environ. Quality Commn., 1988-95. Mem. State Bar Ariz. (continuing legal edn. com. 1990-94), Rocky Mt. Land Use Inst. (regional adv. bd. 1992—). Democrat. Methodist. Avocation: hiking. Office: Jorden Bischoff & Hiser PLC Ste 360 7272 E Indian Sch Rd Scottsdale AZ 85251-6268 E-mail: djorden@jordenbischoff.com.

JORDEN, ELEANOR HARZ, linguist, educator; b. NYC; d. William George and Eleanor (Funk) Harz; m. William J. Jorden, Mar. 3, 1944 (div.); children: William Temple, Eleanor Harz, Marion Telva. AB, Bryn Mawr Coll., 1942; MA, Yale U., 1943, PhD, 1950; D.Litt. (hon.), Williams Coll., 1982; D.H.L. (hon.), Knox Coll., 1985; D. Langs. (hon.), Middlebury Coll., 1991; D. Univ. (hon.), U. Stirling, Scotland, 1993. Instr. Japanese Yale U., 1943-46, 47-48; dir. Japanese lang. program and Fgn. Service Inst. Lang. Sch., Am. Embassy, Tokyo, 1950-55; sci. linguist Fgn. Service Inst., Dept. State, Washington, 1959-69; acting head Far East langs., 1961-64; chmn., 1964-67, 69; chmn. Vietnamese lang. div., 1967-69; vis. prof. linguistics Cornell U., 1969-70, prof., 1970-87, Mary Donlon Alger prof. linguistics, 1974-87, prof. emeritus, 1987—. Bernhard disting. vis. prof. Williams Coll., 1985—86, vis. prof., 1986—87, adj. prof., 1987—92; dir. Japanese FALCON program, 1972—87; prof., Disting. fellow Nat. Fgn. Lang. Ctr. Sch. Advanced Internat. Studies Johns Hopkins U., 1987—91; acad. dir. Exchange: Japan, 1988—2004; sr. cons. prep. framework Japanese lang. curriculum and Japanese coll. bd. exam, 1991—93; sr. cons. Japanese multi-media project U. Md., 1995—97; cons. Part 2 Ohio State U., 2002—06; dir. SPENG Program, 1980—; co-dir. Survey on Japanese Lang. Study, 1988—92; guest scholar Wilson Ctr. Smithsonian Instn., 1982; cons., permanent disting. dir. Nat. Assn. Self-Instrnl. Lang. Programs, pres., 1977—78, 1984—85; mem. Fulbright-Hays Com. on Internat. Exch. Scholars, 1972—75; mem. area adv. com. for East Asia, 1972—76; chmn. Social Sci. Rsch. Coun. Task Force on Japanese Lang. Tng., 1976—78; mem. adv. com. Japan Found., 1979—81; mem. Lang. Attrition Project, 1981—87; advisor Ctr. for Japanese Studies, Stirling U., Scotland, 1988—92; coun. com. langs. and lit. Yale U., 1990—98; acad. dir. Alliance for Lang. Learning and Ednl. Exch., 2004—. Author: (with Bernard Bloch) Spoken Japanese, 1945, Syntax of Modern Colloquial Japanese, 1955, Gateway to Russian, 1961, Beginning Japanese, Part 1, 1962, Part 2, 1963, (with Sheehan, Quang and others) Basic Vietnamese, vols. I, II, 1965, (with Quang) Vietnamese Familiarization Course, 1969, (with Hamako Chaplin) Reading Japanese, 1976, (with Mari Noda) Japanese: The Spoken Language, part 1, 1987, part 2, 1988, part 3, 1990, (with Richard Lambert) Japanese Language Instruction in the U.S.: Resources, Practice and Investment Strategy, 1992, (with Mari Noda) Japanese: The Written Language, Part 1, Vol. 1, 2005 Decorated Order of Precious Crown Emperor of Japan, 1985; recipient Superior Svc. award Dept. State, 1965, Japan Found. and Social Sci. Rsch. Coun. sr. fellow, 1976, Toyota award Twentieth Anniversary Fund grantee, 1978; Japan Found. award, 1985, Papalia award for Excellence Tchr. Tng., 1993, N.E. Conf. award Disting. Svc. and Leadership in Profession, 1994; honoree Eleanor Harz Jorden Festival, Portland State U., 1995. Mem. ALLEX (bd. dirs. 2004—), Assn. Asian Studies (v.p. 1979-80, pres. 1980-81), Linguistic Soc. Am., Am. Coun. Tchrs. Fgn. Langs., Nat. Assn. Self-Instrnl. Lang. Programs (pres. 1978, 85, permanent disting. dir. 1991—), Assn. Tchrs. Japanese (exec. com., pres. 1978-84), Japan Soc. N.Y. (bd. dirs. 1982-88), Exchange: Japan (bd. dirs., v.p., sec. 1998-2004). Office: 3300 Darby Rd Apt 1302 Haverford PA 19041-1067 Office Phone: 610-649-2409. Fax: 610-658-2563. Business E-Mail: ejorden@brynmawr.edu.

JORDEN, JAMES ROY, oil industry executive, consultant; b. Oklahoma City, Apr. 16, 1934; s. James Roy and Gordon (Peeler) J.; m. Shirley Ann Swan, Nov. 17, 1956; children: Philip Taylor, David Emerson. BS in Petroleum Engring., U. Tulsa, 1957; MA in Theol. Studies, Austin Presbyn. Theol. Sem., 2004. Engr. Shell Oil Co., various locations, 1957, 1960-81, petrophys. engr. advisor Houston, 1981-85; mgr. petroleum engring. rsch. Shell Devel. Co., Houston, 1985-88, mgr. head office prodn., tech. tng., 1988-93; mgr. CPI tng. Shell Oil Co., Houston, 1993-95; retired, 1995; cons. Quicksilver Resources, Inc., 1998—. Mem. industry adv. bd. petroleum engring. U. Tulsa, 1987-92, chmn., 1988; vis. com. petroleum engring. Colo. Sch. Mines, Golden, 1988-95. Co-author: Well Logging I., 1984, Well Logging II, 1986; co-inventor in field. 1st lt. USAF, 1957—60. Named to Hall of Fame, Petroleum Engring. Dept. U. Tulsa, 1985. Mem. Am. Inst. Mining, Metall. and Petroleum Engrs. (trustee 1983-85, 2000-02, 2004-, pres., 2006-07), Soc. Petroleum Engrs. (hon., pres. 1984, Disting. Svc. award 1988, DeGolyer Disting. Svc. medal 1991, bd. dirs. 1975-85, dir. svc. corps. 1984-90, life trustee found., treas. found. 1991-92, sr. v.p. found. 1993-95, pres. found. 1995-97), United Engring. Found. (trustee, 2005-), Kappa Alpha. Republican. Presbyterian. Avocations: golf, reading, wine. Home: PO Box 8111 Horseshoe Bay TX 78657-8111

JORDEN, WILLIAM JOHN, writer, retired diplomat; b. Bridger, Mont., May 3, 1923; s. Hugh G. and Jane Ann (Temple) J.; m. Eleanor Harz, 1944 (div.); children: William Temple, Eleanor Harz, Marion Telva; m. V. Mildred Xiarhos, 1972. BA with honors, Yale, 1947; MS, Columbia, 1948. Instr. Japanese Yale, 1945—46; reporter Vineyard Gazette, Edgartown, Mass., 1947; radio news writer N.Y. Herald Tribune, 1948; fgn. corr. A.P., Japan and Korea, 1948—52, N.Y. Times, Japan and Korea, 1952—55, chief of bur. Moscow, 1956—58; diplomatic corr. N.Y. Times (Washington bur.), 1958-61; mem. Policy Planning Coun., State Dept., 1961-62, spl. asst. to under sec. polit. affairs, 1962-65, dep. asst. sec. state pub. affairs, 1965-66; sr. mem. staff NSC, 1966-68, 72-74; mem., spokesman Am. del. Vietnam Peace Talks, Paris, 1968-69; asst. to former Pres. Lyndon B. Johnson, 1969-72; U.S. ambassador to Panama, 1974-78. Scholar-in-residence LBJ Libr.; adj. prof. LBJ Sch. Pub. Affairs, U. Tex., 1978-80; U.S. chmn. U.S.-Panama Consultative com., 1992-95. Author: Panama Odyssey; co-author: Japan Between East and West. Served with AUS, 1943-45. Shared Pulitzer prize for internat. corr., 1958; Recipient Disting. Honor award Dept. State, 1978; Pulitzer traveling fellow, 1948-49; Council Fgn. Relations fellow, 1955-56; Decorated order of Vasco Nunez de Balboa (Republic of Panama) Mem. Coun. Fgn. Rels., Acad. Polit. Sci., Author's Guild. Clubs: Yale of Washington, Fgn. Corrs. Japan (pres. 1952-53).

JORDON, ROBERT EARL, physician; b. Buffalo, May 7, 1938; s. James Wallace and Helen Viola (Sampson) J.; m. Mary Ann Michels, July 12, 1969; children: James H., Kathryn L., Marie H. BA, Hamilton Coll., 1960; MD, SUNY-Buffalo, 1965; MS, U. Minn., 1970. Diplomate: Am. Bd. Dermatology, Dermatological Immunology Diagnostic and Laboratory Immunology. Intern straight medicine Buffalo Gen. Hosp., 1965-66; resident, fellow in dermatology Mayo Clinic and Mayo Found., Rochester, Minn., 1966-69, asso. cons., 1971-73, cons. dermatology, 1973-77; instr. pathology U. Minn. Hosps., Mpls., 1971-73; Nat. Inst. Arthritis and Metabolic Diseases spl. research fellow U. Minn., Mpls., 1972-73; asst. prof. dermatology Mayo Grad. Sch. Medicine, Rochester, 1971-73, Mayo Sch. Medicine, Rochester, 1973-76, asst. prof. immunology, 1974-77, asso. prof. dermatology, 1976-77; prof. medicine, chmn. dermatology Med. Coll. Wis., Milw., 1977-82; med. career investigator VA, 1978-82; chief dermatology Froedtert Meml. Luth. Hosp., Milw., 1980-82; chmn. dept. dermatology U. Tex. Health Sci. Ctr., Houston, prof., 1983—; chief dermatology Hermann Hosp., Houston, 1983—2003; mem. study sect. NIH, 1983-86. Mem. nat. arthritis adv. bd. Nat. Inst. aRthritis and Metabolic Diseases, NIH; mem. nat. adv. bd. Arthritis, Musculoskeletal and Skin Diseases, 1989-91, chmn. 1992-93. Mem. editl. bd. Jour. Investigative Dermatology, 1977-82, Jour. Clin. and Lab. Immunology, 1977—, Archives of Dermatology, 1978-87, sect. editor Am. Jour. Dermatopathology, 1981-83, Clin. Aspects Autoimmunity, 1989-92. Elder Grace Presbyn. Ch., Houston, 1987—; bd. dirs. CAnCare of Houston, 1991-2001, pres. bd. dirs., 1997-99, chmn. bd., 1999-2001. Lt. comdr. M.C., USN, 1965-71. Recipient Bacelli Research award SUNY, Buffalo, 1965, Med. Spltys. Outstanding Achievement award Mayo Found., 1969, Marion B. Sulzberger award Am. Soc. Dermatologic Allergy and Immunology, 1983, award Am. Skin Assn., 1999, JB & Blanche Earthman award 2002. Mem. AAAS, AMA, Soc. Investigative Dermatology (com. nominations 1986—, dir. 1977-82, v.p. 1993-94), Am. Acad. Dermatology (co-chmn. com. lab. proficiency and quality control in immunodermatology 1980-83, dir. Immunopathology Symposium 1981-86, bd. dirs. 1993-98), Am. Assn. Immunologists, Am. Dermatol. Assn., Am. Fedn. Clin. Research, Am. Soc. Clin. Investigation, Assn. Profs. Dermatology (bd. dirs. 1987-89), Central Soc. Clin. Research, Dermatology Found. (chmn. med. and sci. com. 1980-81, trustee 1993-98, discovery award 2000), Soc. Exptl. Biology and Medicine, Lupus Erythematosus Soc. Wis. (mem. med. adv. bd. 1977-83), Wis. Dermatol. Soc. (pres. 1979-80), Wis. State Med. Soc., Chgo. Dermatol. Soc., Tex. Med. Assn., Houston Dermatol. Soc., Lupus Soc. Houston (adv. bd. 1986—90), Sigma Xi. Home: 376 Green Cove Dr Montgomery TX 77356-8267 Office: U Tex Health Sci Ctr Houston TX 77030 Office Phone: 713-500-8336. Business E-Mail: robertejordon@uth.tmc.edu.

JORGENSEN, ALFRED H., retired information technology educator; b. South Gate, Calif., May 1, 1934; s. Peter Hansen and Anna Christine (Nielsen) J.; m. Carole Jean Scott, Sept. 3, 1959; children: Mark Alan, Lora Jean. AA, El Camino Coll., 1958; student, UCLA, 1958-60. Assoc. engr. Litton Industries, Beverly Hills, Calif., 1957-60; engr. Daystrom, Inc., 1960-64; with control sys. divsn. Foxboro Co., Pitts., 1964-67, dist. and regional mgr., 1967-69; founder Interactive Scis., Pitts., 1969—70, v.p., 1970-71, Computeria Inc., 1971, pres., 1971-72; v.p. Interactive Scis. Corp., Braintree, Mass., 1972-77, pres., CEO, 1977-80; exec. v.p. Nat. Data Corp., Atlanta, 1980-83; v.p. nat. sales Cullinet Software Inc., 1983-85; v.p., gen. mgr. Sys. and Computer Tech., 1985-87; pres., COO Infosafe Corp., Atlanta, 1987-88; pres. Corp. Playmakers, 1988-90; dir. bus. alliances Sprint Comm., Atlanta, 1990-95; gen. mgr. Applied Tech. Ctr., 1995—2000; ret., 2000. Bd. dirs. Process Corp., Pitts., Chestatee State Bank; adj. prof. Emory U., 1998—2000. Chmn., Relay for Life Am. Cancer Soc., 2001; bd. dirs. Mass. Assn. Mental Health, 1977—79, v.p., 1978—79; bd. dirs. Dawson Humane Soc., 2003—06, Satisfy (Drug Rehab. Program). Mem. IEEE, Data Processing Mgmt. Assn., Assn. Iron and Steel Engrs., Instrument Soc. Am., Cash Mgmt. Assn., Am. Mgmt. Assn., Nat. Platform Assn., Pearson Yacht Club (commodore 1984). Achievements include design of one of solid state computers to control the first nuclear reactors at Chipping, Pa. Home: 927 Liberty Church Rd Dawsonville GA 30534-7354 Personal E-mail: aljorgy@aol.com.

JORGENSEN, BLAKE J., Internet company executive; b. 1959; m. Debra Jorgensen. BA with honors, Stanford U., 1982; MBA, Harvard U. Mgmt. cons. MAC Group/Gemini Consulting, Marakon Assocs.; mng. dir., prin. Corp. Fin. Dept. Montgomery Securities, 1996—98; co-founder Thomas Weisel Ptnrs., San Francisco, 1998, ptnr., dir. pvt. placements, 1998—2002, co-dir. investment banking, COO, mem. exec. com., 2002—07; CFO Yahoo! Inc., Sunnyvale, Calif., 2007—. Former chmn. Empower Am.; founder, pres. Montgomery Sports (now Tailwind Sports). Bd. mem. Mus. Modern Art, NYC, San Francisco Mus. Modern Art, Stanford Endowment Mgmt. Com. Mem.: US Ski & Snowboard Found. (former chmn.), USA Cycling Devel. Found. (former bd. mem.). Office: Yahoo! 701 First Ave Sunnyvale CA 94086*

JORGENSEN, GERALD THOMAS, psychologist, educator, lawyer; b. Mason City, Iowa, Jan. 15, 1947; s. Harry Grover and Mary Jo (Kollasch) J.; m. Mary Ann Reiter, Aug. 30, 1969; children: Amy Lynn, Sarah Kay, Jill Kathryn. BA maxima cum laude with honors, Loras Coll., 1969; MS in Psychology, Colo. State U., 1970, PhD in Psychology, 1973; JCL in Canon Law, Cath. U. Am., 1998. Lic. psychologist, Iowa; lic. canonist Cath. Ch.; cert. health svc. provider Nat. Register, Iowa; ordained to ministry Roman Cath. Ch. as deacon, 1979. Psychology intern Counseling Ctr., Colo. State U., Ft. Collins, 1971—72, VA Hosp., Palo Alto, Calif., 1972—73; psychologist Loras Coll., Clarke Coll., Dubuque, Iowa, 1973—76; asst. prof. psychology Loras Coll., 1976—80, assoc. prof., 1981—93, dir. Ctr. for Counseling and Student Devel., 1977—86, assoc. dean of students, 1985—86, dean students, v.p. student devel., 1986—93; cons., supervising psychologist Gannon Ctr. for Cmty. Mental Health, 1977—2006. Assoc. med. staff Mercy Med. Ctr., 1989—, mem. credentials com., 1992—; asst. dir. for formation Office of Permanent Diaconate, Archdiocese of Dubuque, 1979-93, 96—, dir., 1993-96; auditor Met. Tribunal, 1993-98, cons. psychologist, 1993—, judge, 1998—; mem. Iowa Bd. Psychology Examiners, Des Moines, chair, 1984-90, coord. continuing edn., 1983, mem., 2003—, vice chmn., 2005—; sec.-gen. First Internat. Congress on Licensure, Certification and Credentialing of Psychologists, New Orleans, 1995. Contbr. articles to profl. jours. Treas. Dubuque County Assn. Mental Health Inc., 1975-82, v.p., 2002—. NDEA fellow, 1969-72. Fellow Assn. State and Provincial Psychology Bds. (exec. com. 1986-89, pres. 1989-92, Morton Berger award 1996); mem. APA, ACA, Am. Coll. Pers. Assn. (chmn. com. VII 1980-82), Iowa Psychol. Assn. (treas. 1976-80, exec. coun. 1980-83, highest honors 1990), Nat. Assn. Diaconate Dirs. (sec. 1983-85, treas. 1985-90, award 1991), Canon Law Soc. Am. (sec. 2002—04), Iowa Student Pers. Assn., Fedn. Assns. Reg. Bds. (v.p. 1993-94, 96-97, pres. 1994-96), Delta Epsilon Sigma, Phi Kappa Phi, Sigma Tau Phi. Democrat. Roman Catholic. Avocations: walking, reading. Office: Archdiocesan Ctr 1229 Mount Loretta Ave Dubuque IA 52003-7826 Home: 480 Woodland Ridge Dubuque IA 52003-6723 Home Phone: 563-556-7239; Office Phone: 563-556-2580. Business E-Mail: dbqcmtaud@arch.pvt.k12.ia.us.

JORGENSEN, GORDON DAVID, retired engineering company executive; b. Chgo., Apr. 29, 1921; s. Jacob and Marie (Jensen) J.; m. Nadina Anita Peters, Dec. 17, 1948 (div. Aug. 1971); children: Karen Ann, David William, Susan Marie; m. Barbara Noel, Feb. 10, 1972 (div. July 1976); m. Ruth Barnes Chalmers, June 15, 1990. BSEE, U. Wash., 1948, postgrad. in bus. and mgmt., 1956-59. Registered profl. engr., Alaska, Ariz., Calif., Colo., Nev., N.Mex., N.D., Utah, Wash., Wyo. With R.W. Beck & Assocs., Cons. Engrs., Phoenix, 1948—, ptnr., 1954-86; pres. Beck Internat., Phoenix, 1971—; ret. Project mgr. for mgmt., operation studies and reorgn. study Honduras power sys., 1969-70. Served to lt. (j.g.) U.S. Maritime Svc., 1942-45. Recipient Outstanding Svc. award Phoenix Tennis Assn., 1967, Commendation, Govt. Honduras, 1970. Mem. IEEE (chmn. Wash.-Alaska sect. 1959-60), NSPE, Am. Soc. Appraisers (sr. mem.), Ariz. Cons. Engrs. Assn., Ariz. Soc. Profl. Engrs., Internat. Assn. Assessing Officers, Southwestern Tennis Assn. (past pres.), U.S. Tennis Assn. (pres. 1987-88, chmn. U.S. Open com.), chmn. U.S. Davis Cup com., chmn. Internat. Tennis Fed., Davis Cup com.). Presbyterian (elder). Home: 74-578 Palo Verde Dr Indian Wells CA 92210-7314 Personal E-mail: gordon@jorgensens.us.

JORGENSEN, JENS ERIK, mechanical engineer, educator; b. Oslo, July 2, 1936; m. Glenda Faye Walton; children: Karin Suzanne, Kristin Lora. BSME, MIT, 1959, MSME, 1963, DSc in Mech. Engring., 1969. Rsch. asst. MIT, 1961-65, instr., 1965-68; asst. prof. U. Wash., Seattle, 1968-73, assoc. prof., adj. assoc. prof. of forest engring., 1973-81, prof., adj. prof. of forest and indsl. engring., 1981—, Boeing prof. of mfg., 1987—2001, prof. emeritus, 2000—. Adj. prof. Indsl. Engring., 1988; cons. numerous corps. in Seattle area, 1969-;dir. Learning Factory, U. Wash. Patents in field; contbr. articles to profl. jours. Recipient Bernard M. Gordon prize, NAE, 2006. Mem. ASME, Sigma Xi. Home: 5015 44th Ave NE Seattle WA 98105 Office Phone: 206-543-5449. Office Fax: 206-685-8047. Business E-Mail: jorgen@u.washington.edu.

JORGENSEN, PALLE E.T., mathematician, educator; b. Copenhagen, Oct. 8, 1947; came to U.S., 1973, naturalized, 1979; s. Soren A.W. and Gyrit D. (Baden) J.; m. Soon-Min Park, Jan. 4, 1975; children: Anton Y., Greta S., Tina S. AB, U. Aarhus, Denmark, 1968, MS, 1970, PhD, 1973. Asst. prof. math. Stanford (Calif.) U., 1977-79; assoc. prof. U. Aarhus, 1979-83; prof. U. Iowa, Iowa City, 1983—. Vis. assoc. prof. U. Pa., Phila., 1982-84; mem. internat. faculty Danish Govt. Rsch. Acad. Author: Operator Commutation Relations, 1984, other books on advanced math.; editor Acta Applicandae Mathematicae, 1983—, Proceedings of the Am. Math. Soc., Wavelets Through A Looking Glass, 2002, Analysis and Probability, Wavelets, Signals, Fractals, 2006; contbr. articles to profl. jours. Grantee Danish Rsch. Coun., 1976-77, NSF, 1977-79, 82—; U. Iowa faculty scholar, 1992—. Mem. Am. Math. Soc., Danish Math. Soc., Math. Assn. Am., Danish Acad. Sci. (internat. faculty), Soc. Indsl. and Applied Math. Office: U Iowa Dept Math Mlh Iowa City IA 52242 Office Phone: 319-335-0782. Business E-Mail: jorgen@math.uiowa.edu.

JORGENSEN, RALPH GUBLER, lawyer, accountant; b. NYC, Mar. 12, 1937; s. Thorvald W. and Florence (Gubler) J.; m. Patricia June Spivey, June 21, 1971 (dec. Oct. 1997); 1 child, Misty AB, George Washington U., 1960, LLB, 1962. Bar: D.C. 1963, Md. 1963, N.C. 1972, U.S. Dist. Ct. D.C. 1963, U.S. Ct. Appeals (D.C. cir.) 1963, U.S. Dist. Ct. Md. 1964, U.S. Dist. Ct. (ea. dist.) N.C. 1972, U.S. Dist. Ct. (mid. dist.) N.C. 1977, U.S. Ct. Appeals (4th cir.) 1974, U.S. Tax Ct. 1976, U.S. Ct. Claims 1979, U.S. Supreme Ct. 1971; CPA, Md., Nev., N.C. Sole practice, Washington, Silver Spring, Md., 1963-71, Tabor City, NC, 1971—. Bd. dirs. Columbus County ARC, N.C., 1974 Mem. Alpha Kappa Psi Democrat. Baptist. Home: 101 Pireway Rd Tabor City NC 28463-2021 Office: 116 W 4th St PO Box 248 Tabor City NC 28463-0248 Office Phone: 910-653-2018. E-mail: R.G.Jorgensen@weblink.net.

JORGENSEN, ROBERT WILLIAM, aerospace engineer; b. Allegan, Mich., Jan. 8, 1946; m. Deborah Ann Geiger; children: Linda, Eric, Laura, Lisa. BS in Aerospace Engring., U. Mich., 1969; AS, Radio Electronics Tech. Sch., South Bend, Ind., 1971. Engr. Kawneer Corp., Niles, Mich., 1970-80; tech. dir. Raco, Inc., South Bend, Ind., 1980—. Mem. adv. coun. Underwriter's Assn. Mem. Underwriters Labs., Nat. Elec. Mfrs. Assn., Nat. Fire Protection Assn., Internat. Assn. Elec. Insps., Can. Stds. Assn. Achievements include 64 patents for electrical boxes, fittings, and electronic controls. Avocations: private pilot, amateur radio, gardening. Home: 1353 Thomson Rd Niles MI 49120-9332 Office: Raco Inc PO Box 4002 South Bend IN 46634-4002 Home Phone: 269-684-5443; Office Phone: 574-283-4233. E-mail: inventorQ1@cs.com, rjorgens@hep.hubbell.com.

JORGENSEN, WILLIAM L., chemistry educator; b. NYC, Oct. 5, 1949; s. Axel V. and Alice C. (Lane) J. AB, Princeton U., 1970; PhD, Harvard U., 1975; MA (hon.), Yale U., 1991. Asst. prof. Purdue U., West Lafayette, Ind., 1975-78, assoc. prof., 1979-81, prof. chemistry, 1982-85, H.C. Brown prof., 1985-90; Whitehead prof. Yale U., New Haven, 1990—. Sci. advisor Ariad Pharms., Inc., 1991—, Combichem, Inc., 1995—. Contbr. several articles to sci. jours. Recipient ann. medal Internat. Acad. Quantum Molecular Sci., 1986, Sato Internat. Award 2004, ISQBP award in Computational Biology, 2004. Fellow Am. Acad. Arts & Scis.; mem. FAAAS, Am. Chem. Soc. (Cope Scholar 1990, award for Computers in Chem. and Pharm. Rsch., 1998). Office: Yale U Dept Chemistry 225 Prospect Ave New Haven CT 06520-8107 Office Phone: 203-432-6288. Business E-Mail: william.jorgensen@yale.edu.*

JORGENSON, DALE WELDEAU, economist, educator; b. Bozeman, Mont., May 7, 1933; s. Emmett B. and Jewell (Torkelson) J.; m. Linda Ann Mabus, July 24, 1971; children: Eric Mabus, Kari Ann. BA, Reed Coll., 1955; AM, Harvard U., 1957, PhD, 1959; PhD (hon.), Uppsala U., 1991, Oslo U., 1991, Keio U., 2003, U. Mannheim, 2004, U. Rome, 2006, Stockholm Sch. Econ., 2007. Mem. faculty U. Calif., Berkeley, 1959-69, prof. econs., 1963-69, Harvard U., 1969-80, Frederic Eaton Abbe prof. econs., 1980—2002, Frank William Taussig rsch. prof. econs., 1992-94, Samuel W. Morris. univ. prof., 2002—. Ford research prof. econs. U. Chgo., 1962-63 Author (with J.J. McCall and R. Radner): Optimal Replacement Policy, 1967, Econometric Studies of U.S. Energy Policy, 1975; author: (with R. Landau) Technology and Economic Policy, 1988, Technology and Capital Formation, 1989, Tax Reform and the Cost of Capital: An International Comparison, 1993; author: (with F.M. Gollop and B.M. Fraumeni) Productivity and U.S. Economic Growth, 1987; author: (with Lars Bergman, Emo Zalal) General Equilibrium Modeling and Economic Policy Analysis, 1990; author: (with Kun-Young Yun) Tax Reform and the Cost of Capital, 1991, Lifting the Burden: Tax Reform, the Cost of Capital, and U.S. Economic Growth, 2001; author: (with Li Jingwen, Zhang Youjing and Masahiro Kuroda) Productivity and Economic Growth in China, USA and Japan, 1993; author: Postwar U.S. Economic Growth, 1995, International Comparisons of Economic Growth, 1995, Capital Theory and Investment Behavior, 1996, Tax Policy and the Cost of Capital, 1996; author: (with E. Hanushek) Improving America's Schools, 1996; author: Aggregate Consumer Behavior, 1997, Measuring Social Welfare, 1997, Econometric General Equilibrium Modeling, 1996, Energy, The Environment and Economic Growth, 1996, Econometric Modeling of Producer Behavior, 2000; author: (with Charles Wessner) Measuring and Sustaining the New Economy, 2002; author: Economic Growth in the Information Age, 2002; author: (with Frank Lee) Industry-Level Productivity and International Competitiveness Between Canada and the United States; author: Economic Growth in Canada and the United States in the Information Age, 2004; author: (with Charles Wessner) Productivity and Cyclicality in Semiconductors, 2004; author: (with Mun S. Ho and Kevin J. Stiroh) Information Technology and The American Growth Resurgence, 2005; author: (with Wessner) Deconstructing the Computer, 2005, Software, Growth, and the Future of the U.S. Economy, 2006, Enhancing Productivity Growth in the Information Age, 2007; author: (with J. Steven Laudefeld and William D. Nordhaus) A New Architecture for the U.S. National Accounts, 2006. Fellow AAAS, NAS (chair sect. 54 Econ. Scis. 2000-03), Am. Philos. Soc., Econometric Soc. (pres. 1987), Am. Statis. Assn., Am. Acad. Arts and Scis.; mem. Am. Econ. Assn. (John Bates Clark medal 1971, pres. 2000), Royal Swedish Acad. Scis. Home: 1010 Memorial Dr Cambridge MA 02138-4859 Office: Harvard U Littauer 122 Cambridge MA 02138-3001 Home Phone: 617-491-4069; Office Phone: 617-495-4661. Business E-Mail: djorgenson@harvard.edu.

JORGENSON, JAMES WALLACE, chromatographer, educator; b. Kenosha, Wis., Sept. 9, 1952; BS, No. Ill. U., 1974; PhD in Chemistry, Ind. U., 1979. From asst. to assoc. prof. U. NC, Chapel Hill, 1979-87, prof. chemistry, 1987-94, Venable prof., 1994-99, W.R. Kenan, Jr. prof. chemistry, 1999—. Fellow Am. Acad. Arts & Sciences; mem. AAAS, Am. Chem. Soc. (Chromatography award 1993, award in analytical chemistry, 2007). Achievements include research in chemical separations, fundamental studies of liquid chromatography, electrophoresis. Office: Univ NC at Chapel Hill Dept Chemistry Campus Box 3290 Caudill and Kenan Labs C240 Chapel Hill NC 27599-3290 Office Phone: 919-966-5071. Office Fax: 919-962-2388. Business E-Mail: jj@unc.edu.*

JORGENSON, MARY ANN, lawyer; b. Gallipolis, Ohio, 1941; BA, Agnes Scott Coll., 1963; MA, Harvard U., 1964; JD, Case Western Res. U., 1975. Bar: Ohio 1975, N.Y. 1982. Ptnr., chair firm's corp. practice Squire, Sanders & Dempsey LLP, Cleve., 1990—2004. Office: Squire Sanders & Dempsey LLP 127 Public Sq Ste 4900 Cleveland OH 44114-1284 Office Phone: 216-479-8654. Business E-Mail: mjorgenson@ssd.com.

JORION, PHILIPPE, education educator; b. Ixelles, Belgium, July 15, 1955; Ingénieur, Université Libre de Bruxelles, Brussels, Belgium, 1975—78; MBA, U. Chgo., Ill., 1980, PhD, 1983. Assoc. prof. Columbia U., NYC, 1987—92; chancellor's prof. U. Calif., Irvine, 1992—; mng. dir. Pacific Alternative Asset Mgmt. Co., 2006—. Editor Jour. of Risk, London, 1998—2006. Author: (books) Big Bets Gone Bad: Derivatives and Bankruptcy in Orange County, 1995, Value at Risk, 2006, Financial Risk Manager Handbook, 2007. Recipient Smith Breeden prize, Am. Fin. Assn., 1999, William Sharpe award, Jour. Fin. and Quantitative Analysis, 1999, Best Paper, European Fin. Mgmt., 2000, Graham and Dodd Scroll award, CFA Inst., 2004. Office: Univ Calif Sch Business Irvine CA 92697-3125 Office Phone: 949-824-5245.

JORTNER, JOSHUA, physical chemist, educator; b. Poland, Mar. 14, 1933; s. Arthur and Regina Jortner; m. Ruth Sanger, Jan. 26, 1960; 2 children. PhD, Hebrew U. Jerusalem; D (hon.), Ben Gurion U. Negev, Israel, 1985, Pierre and Marie Curie U., Paris, 1986; DSc (hon.), Tech. U. Munich, 1996, The Technion, Israel Inst. Tech., 2005; D honoris causa, The Weizmann Inst. Sci., Rehovot, Israel, 2005; D rerum naturalium honoris causa, Free U. Berlin, 2005, The Humboldt U. Berlin, 2005. Instr. dept. phys. chemistry Hebrew U. Jerusalem, 1961-62, sr. lectr., 1963-65; assoc. prof. Tel Aviv U., 1965-66, prof., 1966—2002, emeritus, 2002—, head Sch. Chemistry, 1966—72, dep. rector, 1966-69, v.p., 1970-72. Rsch. assoc. U. Chgo., 1962—64, vis. prof., 1965—71, H.C. Orsted Inst., U. Copenhagen, 1974, 78, U. Calif., Berkeley, 1975; Sherman Fairchild disting. scholar, vis. prof. Calif. Inst. Tech., 1977; Hinshelwood lectr. Oxford U., 1995; Blaise Pascal prof. Ecole Normale Supérieure, Paris, 1999—2000. Author, editor: 24 books; contbr. over 700 articles to profl. jours. Recipient award, Internat. Acad. Quantum Sci., 1972, Weizmann prize, 1973, Rothschild prize, 1976, Kolthof prize, 1976, Israel prize in Chemistry, 1982, Wolf prize, Wolf Found., Israel, 1988, Hon. J. Heyrovsky Gold medal, 1993, August-Wilhelm-von-Hofmann medal, 1995, R.S. Mulliken medal, 1998, J.O. Hirschfelder prize, 1999, Maria Sklodowska-Curie medal, 2003, medal, Israeli Chem. Soc., 2004. Mem.: AAAS, Internat. Union Pure and Applied Chemistry (past pres. 2000—01, v.p. 1996—97, pres. 1998—99), Am. Acad. Arts and Scis., Royal Netherlands Acad. Arts and Scis. (fgn.), Learned Soc. of Czech Repub., U.S. Nat. Acad. Scis. (fgn. assoc.), Indian Acad. Sci., German Acad. Scis. Leopoldina, Romanian Acad. Scis., European Acad. Scis. and Arts, Russian Acad. Scis. (fgn.), Polish Acad. Scis., Danish Acad. Scis. and Letters (fgn. mem.), Am. Philos. Soc., Internat. Acad. Quantum Molecular Scis, Israel Acad. Scis. and Humanities (v.p. 1980—86, pres. 1986—95). Avocation: science policy. Office: Tel Aviv U Sch Chemistry Ramat-Aviv 69978 Tel Aviv Israel also: Israel Acad Scis-Humanities Einstein Sq PO Box 4040 91040 Jerusalem Israel Office Phone: +972-3-6408322. Business E-Mail: jortner@chemsg1.tau.ac.il.

JOSCELYN, KENT BUCKLEY, lawyer; b. Binghamton, Dec. 18, 1936; s. Raymond Miles and Gwen Buckley (Smith) J.; children: Kathryn Anne, Jennifer Sheldon. BS, Union Coll., 1957; JD, Albany Law Sch., NY, 1960. Bar: N.Y. 1961, U.S. Ct. Mil. Appeals 1962, D.C., 1967, Mich. 1979. Atty. adviser hdqts. USAF, Washington, 1965-67; assoc. prof. forensic studies U. Ind., Bloomington, 1967-76; dir. Inst. Rsch. in Pub. Safety, 1970-75; head policy analysis divsn. Highway Safety Rsch. Inst. U. Mich., Ann Arbor, 1976-81; dir. transp. planning and policy Urban Tech. Environ. Planning Program, Ann Arbor, 1981-84; prin. Joscelyn and Treat P.C., Ann Arbor, 1981—93, Joscelyn, McNair & Jeffrey P.C., Ann Arbor, 1993-2001; pvt. practice Ann Arbor, 2001—. Cons. Law Enforcement Assistance Adminstrn., U.S. Dept. Justice, 1969-72; Gov.'s appointee as regional dir. Ind. Criminal Justice Planning Agy., 1969-72; vice chmn. Ind. Organized Crime Prevention Coun., 1969-72; commr. pub. safety City of Bloomington, Ind., 1974-76. Editor Internat. Jour. Criminal Justice, 1972-. Capt. Judge Advocate USAF, 1961—64. Mem. ABA, D.C. Bar Assn., NY State Bar Assn., Mich. State Bar Assn., Transp. Rsch. Bd. (chmn. motor vehicle and traffic law com. 1979-82), Am. Soc. Criminology (life), Assn. for Advancement Automotive Medicine (life), Acad. Criminal Justice Scis. (life), Assn. Chiefs Police (assoc.), Nat. Safety Coun., Assn. Former Intelligence Officers (life), Product Liability Adv. Coun., Sigma Xi, Theta Delta Chi Office: Kent B Joscelyn PC PO Box 130589 Ann Arbor MI 48113-0589 Office Phone: 734-662-7904. Business E-Mail: kbjpc@earthlink.net.

JOSE, PEDRO A., physician; b. Dingras, Ilocos Norte, Philippines, Dec. 6, 1942; s. Urbano Llanes Jose, Filomena Andres Jose; m. Nora Doctor Doctor; children: Kristina, Maria. MD magna cum laude, U. Santo Tomas, Manila, Philippines, 1965; PhD, Georgetown U., 1976. Cert. pediatrics 1970, pediatric nephrology 1974, hypertension 1999. Prof. pediatrics, physiology and biophysics Georgetown U. Sch. Medicine, Washington, 1983—. Chair cardiovascular and renal study sect. B NIH, Bethesda, 1996—98; vis. prof. cardiovascular sci. Sun Yatsen U. Med. Scis., Guangzhou, China, 2002—; adj. prof. pediatrics George Washington U. Sch. Medicine, Washington, 2002—; dir. MD/PhD program Georgetown U., 1997—99, chair radiation safety com., 1997—; Louis K. Dahl meml. lectr. Am. Heart Assn., 2003. Contbr. scientific papers to profl. jours. Profl. and pub edn. com. Am. Heart Assn., Dallas, 2000—02; chair edn. com. Nat.Kidney Found. Capital Area, Washington. Recipient Interstate Postgrad. Med. Society award, 1972, Apolinario Mabini award, 1990, Ernest H. Starling Lectr. award, Water , Electrolyte Homeostasis sect. Am. Physiological Soc., 2007. Fellow: Council High Blood Pressure Rsch.; mem.: Am. Soc. Hypertension, Am. Soc. Nephrology, Am. Heart Assn. (coun. high blood pressure rsch.), Am. Soc. Pediatric Nephrology (pres. 1990—91). Roman Catholic. Avocation: violin. Office: Georgetown U Med Ctr 3800 Reservoir Rd NW Washington DC 20007-2197 Office Phone: 202-444-8675.

JOSEFF, JOAN CASTLE, manufacturing executive; b. Alta., Can., Aug. 12, 1922; naturalized U.S. citizen, 1945; d. Edgar W. and Lottie (Coates) Castle; BA in Psychology, UCLA; widowed; 1 child, Jeffrey Rene. With Joseff-Hollywood, jewelry manufacture and rental and aircraft components and missiles, Burbank, Calif., 1939—, chmn. bd., pres., sec.-treas. TV appearances include CBS This Morning, Australia This Morning, Am. Movie Channel. Active Burbank Salary Task Force, 1979—, LA County Earthquake Fact-Finding Commn., 1981—; bd. dirs. San Fernando Valley area chpt. Am. Cancer Soc., treas., Genesis Energy Systems, Inc., 1993—; mem. Rep. Cen. Com.; del. Rep. Nat. Conv., 1980, 84, 88, 92, 96, 2000; active Beautiful People Award Com. Honoring John Wayne Carcer Clinic; appointed by Gov. Wilson to Barber and Cosmotology Bd; appointed br Pres. Clinton to Selective Svc. System. Recipient Women in Achievement award Soroptimist Internat., 1988, Rep. Congl. Com. award, 2004, Bus. Woman of Yr. award Nat. Rep. Congl. Com., 2004. Mem. Women of Motion Picture Industry (hon. life), Nat. Fedn. Rep. Women (bd. dir., Caring for Am. award 1986), Calif. Rep. Women (bd. dir., treas. 1986-90), North Hollywood Rep. Women (pres. 1981-82, parliamentarian), Nat. Fedn. of Rep (voting mem., program chair, 1994—, bylaws chair 1998—), Calif. Fedn. of Rep. Women (chaplain, Americanism chmn. so. div., regent chmn. Women of Achievement award 1988), L.A. County Fedn. of Rep. Women (scholarship chmn.). Home: 10060 Toluca Lake Ave Toluca Lake CA 91602-2924 Office: 129 E Providencia Ave Burbank CA 91502-1922 Office Phone: 323-849-2306. Personal E-mail: joseff-hollywood@sbcglobal.net.

JOSELL, JESSICA (WECHSLER), public relations executive; b. Balt., June 17, 1943; d. Maury J. and Rose E. (Lodin) Snyder; m. Neil B. Josell, Apr. 30, 1965 (dec. Nov. 1967); m. Steven James Wechsler, Jan. 12, 1980. BA, U. Fla., 1965. V.p., gen. mgr. Morton Dennis Wax & Assocs., NYC, 1976-81; v.p. Raleigh Group, Ltd., NYC, 1981-87; pres. Josell Comm., Inc., NYC, 1981—. Exec. officer, bd. dirs. Bridge, Inc., NYC. Mem.: NY Women in Film and TV. Home and Office: Josell Comm Inc 185 W End Ave Ste 22C New York NY 10023-5549 Office Phone: 212-877-5560. Business E-Mail: jessica@josellpr.com.

JOSELYN, JO ANN, space scientist; b. St. Francis, Kans., Oct. 5, 1943; d. James Jacob and Josephine Felzien (Firkins) Cram. BS in Applied Math., U. Colo., 1965, MS in Astro Geophysics, 1967, PhD in Astro Geophysics, 1978. Research asst. NASA-Manned Space Ctr., Houston, 1966; physicist NOAA-Space Environ. Lab., Boulder, Colo., 1967-78; space scientist NOAA-Space Environ. Ctr., Boulder, 1978-99; chief Geospace Branch, 1992-95; sec.-gen. Internat. Union Geodesy and Geophysics, 1999—. U.S. del. study group 6 Consultive Com. for Ionospheric Radio, 1981, 83; mem. com. on data mgmt. and computation NASA Space Sci. Bd., 1988. Mem. U. Colo. Grad. Sch. Alumni Coun., 1986-90, U. Colo. Engring. Devel. Coun., 1991-99, U. Colo. Adv. Coun. for the Women in Engring. Program, 1992-98, Grad. Sch. Adv. Coun.; bd. trustees U. Colo. Found., 2002-. Recipient unit citation NOAA, 1971, 80, 85, 86, sustained superior performance award 1985, 87-90, 92, 94; group achievement award NASA, 1983, Disting. Engring. Alumnus award U. Colo., 1987, Dir.'s award Space Environ. Lab., 1991, 95, Pacesetter award Boulder County, 1994, Sec. Commerce award for Customer Svc. Excellence, 1994, George Norlin award U. Colo. Alumni Assn., 2000; elected to U. Colo. Disting. Alumni Gallery, 1995; named Woman of Achievement, Zonta Club, Boulder, 1996; named to Colo. Women's Hall of Fame, 2002; fellow Sci. and Tech. Agy. Japan, 1990-91. Mem. AAAS, AAUW, PEO, Am. Women in Sci., Am. Geophys. Union, Union Radio Sci. Internat. (commns. G and H, membership chair of commn. H 1993-96), Internat. Assn. Geomagnetism and Aeronomy (co-chair Divsn. V on observatories, instruments, indices and data 1991-95, sec.-gen. 1995-99), Internat. Astron. Union (commns. 10 and 49), Rotary Internat., Ikebana Internat., Sigma Xi, Tau Beta Pi, Sigma Tau. Republican. Methodist. Office: Univ Colo CIRES Campus Box 216 Boulder CO 80309-0216 Business E-Mail: jjoselyn@cires.colorado.edu.

JOSEPH, ALLAN JAY, lawyer; b. Chgo., Feb. 4, 1938; s. George S. and Emily (Miller) Cohen; m. Phyllis L. Freedman, Sept. 1, 1958; children—Elizabeth, Susan, Katherine. BBA, U. Wis., Madison, 1959; JD cum laude, 1962. Bar: Wis. bar 1962, Calif. bar 1964. Ptnr. Pettit & Martin, San Francisco, 1965-80; ptnr., co-chmn., govt. contracts practice group Rogers, Joseph, O'Donnell & Phillips, San Francisco, 1981—. Editor: (prof. journal) Wis. Law Rev., author articles law jours. Served to capt. JACG AUS, 1962-65. Am. Bar Found. fellow, 1978— Mem.ABA (treas. 2002-05, nat. chmn. pub. contract law sect. 1977-78, ho. of dels. 1980-84, 1995—, bd. govs. 1995-98, chair fin. com. 1997-98), FBA, Am. Bar Retirement Assn. (trustee 1984-92, pres. 1989-90), State Bar Calif., Nat. Contract Mgmt. Assn., Order of Coif. Home: 2461 Washington St San Francisco CA 94115-1816 Office: 311 California St Fl 10 San Francisco CA 94104-2614*

JOSEPH, ANTHONY BARNETT, psychiatrist; b. Bristol, England, Feb. 11, 1955; came to U.S., 1965; s. Bertram Leon and Ada Emilie (Goldschmidt) J.; m. Karen Beverly Spinks, June 20, 1980; m. James Edward, Oliver Charles. BA, MA, CUNY, 1975; BA, U. Oxford, Oxford, England, 1978; M.B., B. Chir., U. Cambridge, Cambridge, England, 1980. Diplomate Am. Bd. Psychiatry and Neurology. House surgeon Hillingdon Hosp., London, 1981; house physician Ashford Hosp., London, 1981-82; resident in psychiatry St. Elizabeth's Hosp., Boston, 1982-85; Asst. pschiatrist Inst. Law and Psychiatry, McLean Hosp., Belmont, Mass., 1985-86; dir. neuropsychiatry clinic Mass. Mental Health Ctr., Boston, 1985-89; clin. instr. psychiatry Harvard Med. Sch., Boston, 1986-88; assoc. med. dir. Medfield State Hosp., Medfield, Mass., 1986-90; sr. cons. forensic psychiatrist Mass. Dept. Mental Health, Boston, 1988-91; asst. clin. prof. psychiatry Harvard Med. Sch., Boston, 1988-95, assoc. clin. prof., 1995—, mem. continuing med. edn. faculty, 1988—; med. dir. Core Mgmt., Inc., Lexington, Mass., 1989-93; dir. neurorehab. unit N.E. Specialty Hosp., Stoughton, Mass., 1990—. Profl. adv. bd. neurobehavioral unit McLean Hosp., Belmont, Mass., 1987-90, Venture Mentoring Svc., MIT, 2000—. Contbr. articles to profl. jours.; reviewer Jour. Clin. Psychiatry, 1987—. Fellow Royal Soc. Medicine; mem. Royal Soc. Chemistry, Am. Psychiat. Assn., Boston Soc. Neurology and Psychiatry, Am. Neuropsychiat. Assn. Office: NE Specialty Hosp Neurorehab Unit 909 Sumner St Stoughton MA 02072

JOSEPH, ANTOINE L., sociologist, educator; s. Antoine L. and Lorraine F. Joseph. BA, Swarthmore Coll., Pa., 1973; PhD, U. Chgo., 1983. Asst. prof. U. Pa., Phila., 1982—87; rschr. U. Ill., Chgo., 1988—92; assoc. prof. Bryant U., Smithfield, RI, 1992—2003, prof., 2003—. Author: (books) Skilled Workers Solidarity: The American Experience in Comparative Perspective, 2000, The Dynamics of Racial Progress: Economic Inequality and Race Relations Since Reconstruction, 2005; contbr. articles to profl. jours. Exec. bd. mem. So. New Eng. Consortium on Race and Ethnicity, Providence, 1999—2006. Mem.: Am. Sociol. Assn. Office: Bryant Univ 1150 Douglas Rd Smithfield RI 02917 Office Phone: 401-232-6099. Business E-Mail: ajoseph@bryant.edu.

JOSEPH, DANIEL DONALD, aeronautical engineer, educator; b. Chgo., Mar. 26, 1929; s. Samuel and Mary (Simon) J.; m. Ellen Broida, Dec. 18, 1949 (div. 1979); children: Karen, Michael, Charles; m. Kay Jaglo, Feb. 9, 1990. MA in Sociology, U. Chgo., 1950; BS in Mech. Engring, Ill. Inst. Tech., 1959, MS, 1960, PhD, 1963. Asst. prof. mech. engring. Ill. Inst. Tech., 1962-63; mem. faculty U. Minn., 1963—, assoc. prof. fluid mechanics, 1965-69, prof. aerospace engring. and mechanics, 1969-90, Russell J. Penrose prof. Mpls., 1990—. Author 4 books on stability and bifurcation theory and fluid dynamics; editor 3 books; editorial bd. SIAM Jour. Applied Math, Jour. Applied Mechanics, Jour. Non-Newtonian Fluid Mechanics, others; contbr. articles to sci. jours. Guggenheim fellow, 1969-70, Timoshenko medal Am. Soc. of Mechanical Engineers, 1995. Mem. NAS, ASME, NAE, Am. Phys. Soc., Am. Acad. Arts and Scis., Soc. Engring. Sci. (G.I. Taylor medal 1990, Bingham medal Soc. of Rheology). Achievements include contbns. to math. theory of hydrodynamic stability; rheology of viscoelastic fluids. Home: 1920 S 1st St Apt 2302 Minneapolis MN 55454-1279 Office: U Minn Dept Aerospace Engring 110 Union St SE Minneapolis MN 55455-0153 Office Phone: 612-625-0309. Business E-Mail: joseph@aem.umn.edu.

JOSEPH, ELEANOR ANN, retired health science association administrator, consultant; b. Cleve., Mar. 6, 1944; d. Emil and Eleanor (Leelais) Dienes; m. Abraham Albert Joseph, Oct. 28, 1984 (dec.). BS in Math. cum laude, Cleve. State U., 1978, MPA in Health Care Adminstrn., 1991. Cert. profl. healthcare quality, coding specialist, accredited records technician, in healthcare privacy, med. coder 2005, registered record adminstr., health info. adminstr. Asst. dir. med. records Suburban Hosp., Warrensville Heights, Ohio, 1963-77; coder Shaker Med. Ctr., Shaker Heights, Ohio, 1965, Huron Rd. Hosp., Cleve., 1965; instr. Cuyahoga C.C., Cleve., 1970-72; dir. med. records Hillcrest Hosp., Mayfield Heights, Ohio, 1977-84; med. records technician Vis. Nurse Assn., Cleve., 1985; coord. med. record svcs. Ctr. for Health Affairs Greater Cleve. Hosp. Assn., 1985-88, dir. coding svcs. Ctr. Health Affairs, 1988-89, dir. health record svcs. Ctr. Health Affairs, 1989-98; v.p. health info. mgmt. svcs. Greater Cleve. Healthcare Assn., 1999—2004, privacy officer Ctr. Health Affairs, 2001—04, v.p. revenue cycle mgmt. Ctr. Health Affairs, 2004; ind. health info. mgmt. cons., 2004—. Coding instr. cmty. edn. dept. Cleve. State U., 1998—2006; instr. cmty. edn. Lakeland C.C., adv. task force cert. program med. office mgmt., 1992—96, coding tchr., 1999; spkrs. bur. Hillcrest Hosp., Mayfield Heights, 1978—84; adv. com. Cuyahoga C.C., 1973—80, 1994—, faculty, 1999—2003; tech. adv. AHIMA Publ., 2004—05; seminar creator, presenter Corp. Coll., 2005—07; coord. seminars in field; cons. in field. Co-author: (manual) Quality Assurance Program for Medical Records Department, 1981, Dollars and Sense: A Reference Guide to Coding and Prospective Payment System Reimbursement Issues, 1988; co-editor: Care and Management of Health Care Records, 1988, 1992. Active Holden Arboretum, Kirtland, Ohio, 1975—, Ohio Hist. Soc., Columbus, 1975—. Recipient Outstanding Svc. award, Ctr. Health Affairs/Greater Cleve. Healthcare Assn., 1997. Mem.: N.E. Ohio Health Info. Mgmt. Assn. (chmn. coding roundtable 1993—), Ohio Health Info. Mgmt. Assn. (project leader alliances 1992—94, data quality reimbursement coun. 1992—2006, liaison to ambulatory sect. 1994—96, project leader developing coding seminars 1996—97, co-chmn. data quality and reimbursement coun. 1996—98, pres.-elect 1998—99, pres. 1999—2000, dir. and del. coord. 2000—01, del. to Am. Health Info. Mgmt. Assn. 2002—03, Disting. Mem. award 1997, Profl. Achievement award 2003), Ohio Assn. Healthcare Quality, Ohio Med. Record Assn. (alt. del. 1982, med. record coun. 1985—92, del. for state assn. mem. at nat. ann. mtg. 1989, legis. com. 1989—90, del. for state assn. mem. at nat. ann. mtg. 1990), N.E. Ohio Med. Record Assn. (treas. 1979, v.p. 1980, pres. 1982—83, counselor 1983, ednl. com. 1984, chmn. nominating com. 1986, ednl. com. 1987, cons. com. 1987—91, audit com., membership com., bylaws com., pub. rels. com.), East Ohio Med. Record Assn., Nat. Assn. Healthcare Quality, Am. Guild Patient Accts. Mgrs., Am. Health Info. Mgmt. Assn. (quality assurance and long term care sects., ambulatory records sec. 1992—2001, del. 1997—2000, item writing panel for cert. coding exams 1997—2003, accredited record tech. practitioner 2000—02, co-chmn. coun. cert. 2001, chair coun. on cert. 2002, nominating com. 2002—03, book reviewer, tech. adv. 2004—05), Am. Med. Record Assn. (cons. roster 1976, charter mem. assembly on edn. 1989), Am. Acad. Profl. Coders (treas. local chpt. 1994, endorsed as tchr. for profl. med. coder curriculum, cert.), Data Quality and Reimbursement Coun. (hon.), Holden Arboretum, Northeastern Ohio Assn. for Healthcare Quality, Cleve. City Club. Lutheran. Avocations: cultural events, nature walks, music.

JOSEPH, ELLA, artist; b. Iasi, Romania, Aug. 21, 1966; d. Alecu and Ileana Visinescu; m. Robert Joseph, Sept. 8, 2003. BS, U. Iasi, Romania, 1989; MFA, U. BC, Vancouver, Can., 2000; MA, Ctrl. St. Martins Sch. Art and Design, London, Eng., 2001. Creative dir. I2i Concepts, 2003—; video encoding specialist Synacor, Buffalo, 2006—. Bd. dirs. YYZ Artists' Outlet, Toronto, Ont., Canada. Video/performance/installation, Theatre of Truth(s). Mem.: Coll. Art Assn. (assoc.), Buffalo Soc. Artists (life). Home: 464 Norwood Ave Buffalo NY 14222 Home Phone: 716-882-0890. Personal E-mail: ellajoseph@i2iconcepts.net.

JOSEPH, GEORGE, insurance company executive; b. 1921; BS, Harvard U., 1949. CLU, CPCU. Sys. analyst, salesman Occidental Ins., 1949—54; ins. agy. owner, 1954—62; founder, chmn. Mercury Gen. Corp., LA, 1961—, CEO, 1961—2007. B-17 navigator USAAF, WWII. Named one of 400 Richest Ams., Forbes mag., 2006. Office: Mercury Ins Grp 4484 Wilshire Blvd Los Angeles CA 90010*

JOSEPH, GEORGE FOSTER, JR., elementary school educator, historian; b. New Bedford, Mass., June 18, 1943; s. George Foster and Ruth Greenwood Joseph; m. Germaine Gagne, June 23, 1966 (div. Jan. 1979); 1 child, Brian Scott Joseph; m. Geraldine Marilyn Simons, Feb. 15, 1980; stepdaus.: Jodi Pacheco, Christine Pacheco. BS in Edn., Bridgewater State Coll., 1965; MA, U. R.I., 1973. Licensed principal, superintendant, Mass. Elem. tchr. Pottersville Sch., Somerset, Mass., 1965-67; tchr. Somerset (Mass.) Jr. High, 1966-94; ops. mgr. Tin Can Sailors Veterans Org., Somerset, 1994-98; prin. Wilbur Elem. Sch., Somerset, 1994—; CPI instr. Contbr. over 70 articles to profl. jours. Founder Summer Accelerated Reading Program Town of Somerset, 1998; mem. reading program planning com. Town of Somerset, 1998; chair Parish Devel. com. Ch. of our Savior, Somerset, 1998; co-chair Speaking of Kids Parenting Conference, Somerset, 1994—; chair Kindergarten Transition, 1999—. Mem. Nat. Council of Elem. Sch. Adminstrs., Mass. Council for Social Studies, Elem. Social Studies com. Somerset Sch. Dept. (chair 1994—), Multi-cultural com. Somerset Sch. Dept. (chair 1994—). Democrat. Episcopalian. Avocations: military history, naval history, model railroading, travel. Home: 10 Dumont Ave Somerset MA 02726-4617 Office: Wilbur School 816 Brayton Point Rd Somerset MA 02725-1907 E-mail: josephg1@somerset.k12.ma.us.

JOSEPH, GREGORY NELSON, media critic, writer, actor, advocate; b. Kansas City, Mo., Aug. 25, 1946; s. Theodore Leopold and Marcella Kathryn (Nelson) J.; m. Mary Martha Stahler, July 21, 1973; children: John, Jacqueline, Caroline. AA, Met. C.C., Kansas City, 1967; BA with honors, U. Mo., Kansas City, 1969. Intern, cub reporter Kansas City Star-Times, 1965-67; feature writer, asst. city editor The Pasadena (Calif.) Union, 1971-73; investigative reporter The Pasadena Star-News, 1973-75; bus. writer The Riverside (Calif.) Press Enterprise, 1975-76; reporter, consumer writer, feature writer, TV critic The San Diego Tribune, 1976-90; TV columnist The Ariz. Republic, Phoenix, 1990-94; writer, media critic, advocate, 1994—; profl. actor Ford-Robert Black Agy., 2007—. Alt. mem. Ariz. Film and Media Coalition. Recipient various writing awards Copley Newspapers, Pasadena and San Diego, 1971-73, 83, Pub. Awareness award San Diego Psychiat. Physicians, cert. of appreciation Epilepsy Soc. San Diego County, 1989. Mem.: NATAS (bd. govs. 1990—92), SAG (Ariz. br. coun. 2004—07, nat. performers with disabilities com.), Ariz. Film and Media Coalition, Phi Kappa Phi. Independent. Roman Catholic. Avocations: reading, writing about Hollywood history, politics, current events and the disabled. Home: 4864 W Alice Ave Glendale AZ 85302-5107 Office: Ford-Robert Black Agy 4032 N Miller Rd Ste 104 Scottsdale AZ 85251 Office Phone: 480-966-2537, 480-966-2537.

JOSEPH, GREGORY PAUL, lawyer; b. Mpls., Jan. 18, 1951; s. George Phillip and Josephine Sheha (Nofel) J.; m. Barbara, Jan. 19, 1979. BA summa cum laude, U. Minn., 1972, JD cum laude, 1975. Bar: Minn. 1975, N.Y. 1979, U.S. Dist. Ct. Minn. 1975, U.S. Dist. Ct. (so. and ea. dist.) N.Y. 1979, U.S. Ct. Appeals (8th cir.) 1976, U.S. Ct. Appeals (2d cir.) 1979, U.S. Ct. Appeals (D.C. cir.) 1980, U.S. Supreme Ct. 1983, U.S. Tax Ct. 1987, U.S. Ct. Appeals (7th cir.) 1989, (5th cir.) 1992, (6th cir.) 1999, (11th cir.) 2002. Pvt. practice, Mpls., 1975-79; assoc. Fried, Frank, Harris, Shriver & Jacobson, NYC, 1979-82, ptnr., 1982-01, chair litigation dept., 2000-01; chmn. Gregory P. Joseph Law Offices, LLC, NYC, 2001—. Asst. U.S. spl. prosecutor N.Y.C., 1981—82, Washington, 1981—82; mem. adv. com. on fed. rules of evidence U.S. Judicial Conf, 1993—99; co-chair 3d Circuit Task Force on Selection of Class Counsel, 2001; chair com. of lawyers to enhance the jury process N.Y. State Cts., 1998—99, mem. adv. com. on civil practice, 1999—2002. Author: Modern Visual Evidence, 1984, Sanctions: The Federal Law of Litigation Abuse, 1989, 3rd edit., 2000, Civil RICO: A Definitive Guide, 1992, 2nd edit., 2000; co-author: Evidence in America, 1987; editor: Emerging Problems Under the Federal Rules of Evidence, 1983, reporter 2d edit., 1991; co-editor: Sanctions: Rule 11 and Other Powers, 1986, 2d rev. edit., 1988; editorial bd. Moore's Fed. Practice, 1995—; contbr. articles to profl. jours. Trustee U.S. Supreme Ct. Hist. Soc., 2005—. Fellow Am. Bar Found., Am. Coll. Trial Lawyers (chmn. fed. rules of civil procedure com. 2000-02, regent 2002-2006); mem. ABA (chmn. litig. sect. 1997-98), Am. Law Inst., N.Y. Bar Assn. (chair trial evidence com. 1988-94), Minn. Bar Assn., N.Y. County Lawyers Assn., Assn. of Bar of City of N.Y. (chmn. profl. responsibility com. 1993-96, mem. exec. com. 1999-2003), U.S. Supreme Ct. Hist. Soc. (trustee 2005—). Home: 845 United Nations Plz Apt 55D New York NY 10017-3536 Office: Gregory P Joseph Law Offices 485 Lexington Ave 30th Fl New York NY 10017 Home Phone: 212-755-5531; Office Phone: 212-407-1210. Personal E-mail: gjoseph@josephnyc.com.

JOSEPH, J. JONATHAN, interior designer; b. Gloucester, Mass., Jan. 14, 1932; s. George Stephen and Maryann (Lattof) Joseph. Cert., Vesper George Sch. Art, Boston, 1952; student theater design, Boston Conservatory Music, 1951. Assoc. designer Reva Lewitt, Boston, 1952-67, Peter Schifando & Co., LA, 1995—; owner interior design bus. Boston, 1967—; pres. Seraphim Galleries, Inc., LA, 1998—. Cons. in fine arts; spl. rschr. 19th century glass in Am., Tiffany glass; curator Tiffany glass collection Mus. Fine Art, Boston, 1965, Worcester Art Mus., Mass., 1968; co-curator Jane Peterson: An Impression Hickory Mus. Art, NC, 1987. Prin. works include restoration of Plaza Hotel, NYC, Ronald Reagan Presdl. Libr., Simi Valley, Calif., 1991; author: Jane Petersen, An American Artist, 1981; co-author: Nancy Reagan Entertaining at the White House, 2007; contbg. editor: William Haines Legendary Hollywood Decorator; contbr. revs. and articles to profl. publs. Recipient award, Internat. V'Soske Rug Design. Mem.: Am. Soc. Interior Designers (chmn. bd. dirs. New Eng. chpt. 1965—66, chpt. v.p. 1969—71, pres. 1971—72, bd. dirs. 1986—87), Nat. Early Am. Glass Club (1st v.p. 1967—69). Home Phone: 310-595-4600; Office Phone: 310-276-9594.

JOSEPH, JAMES WILLIAM, political scientist, consultant, educator; b. Gilroy, Calif., Jan. 1, 1960; s. William A. and Carmina M. J.; m. Mildred P. Maxwell, July 9, 2000. BA in Polit. Sci., Calif. State U., Fresno, 1982; D, U. Calif., Riverside, 1990; MA in Internat. Rels., Calif. State U., Fresno, 1984. Calif. lifetime tchg. credential. Asst. prof. polit. sci. U. Tex., Tyler, 1993—99; prof. polit. sci., dir. model UN programs Fresno (Calif.) City Coll., 1999—. Fgn. policy case reviewer; Am. govt. textbook reviewer. Author: Between Realism and Reality: The Reagan Administration and International Debt, 1994; polit. commentator Sta. KFSN-TV, KSEE-TV, KMPH-TV, KGPE-TV, Fresno; contbr. articles to profl. jours. Recipient Disting. Faculty Member award, Associated Student Govt., Fresno City Coll., 2005—06. Mem.: Nat. Social Sci. Assn., Am. Polit. Sci. Assn., Internat. Studies Assn. Republican. Avocations: bicycling, reading, running. Office: Fresno City Coll 1101 E University Ave Fresno CA 93741 Home: 1871 N Hornet Ave Clovis CA 93619 Office Phone: 559-442-4600. Personal E-mail: jjospolsci@aol.com. Business E-Mail: james.joseph@fresnocitycollege.edu.

JOSEPH, LEONARD, lawyer; b. Phila., June 8, 1919; s. Harry L. and Mary (Pollock) J.; m. Norma Hamberg, 1942; children: Gilbert M., Stuart A., Janet H. Fitzgerald. BA, U. Pa., 1941; LLB, Harvard U., 1947. Bar: N.Y. 1949. Law clk. to chief judge U.S. Ct. Appeals, Boston, 1947-48; since practiced in NYC; ptnr. and of counsel Dewey Ballantine, 1957—. Bd. dirs., exec. com. Legal Aid Soc. N.Y., 1986-89; mem. panel of disting. neutrals CPR Inst. for Dispute Resolution. Bd. editors Harvard Law Rev., 1946-47. Served with AUS, 1943-46. Fellow Am. Bar Found., Am. Coll. Trial Lawyers Office: Dewey Ballantine 1301 Avenue Of The Americas New York NY 10019-6022 Office Phone: 212-259-7180.

JOSEPH, MARC ALTER, philosopher, educator; BA, U. Pa., Phila.; PhD, Columbia U., NYC. Post-doctoral fellow Boston U.; assoc. prof. Mills Coll., Oakland, Calif., 1999—. Author: Donald Davidson; contbr. articles to profl. jours. Summer Seminar Scholar in Residence at San Diego State U., NEH, 2003. Mem.: Am. Philos. Assn., Inst. for Oriental Philosophy (hon.). Office: Mills College 5000 MacArthur Blvd Oakland CA 94613

JOSEPH, MARILYN SUSAN, gynecologist; b. Aug. 18, 1946; BA, Smith Coll., 1968; MD cum laude, SUNY Downstate Med. Ctr., Bklyn., 1972. Diplomate Am. Bd. Ob-Gyn, Nat. Bd. Med. Examiners. Intern U. Minn. Hosps., 1972-73, resident in ob-gyn, 1972-76; med. fellow specialist U. Minn., 1972-76, asst. prof. ob-gyn, 1976—, dir. women's clinic, 1984—. Med. dir. Boynton Health Svc., 1993—. Author: Differential Diagnosis Obstetrics, 1978. Fellow Am. Coll. Ob-Gyn (best paper dist. VI meeting 1981); mem. Hennepin County Med. Soc., Minn. State Med. Assn., Minn. State Ob-Gyn Soc. Avocations: cooking, bird watching, travel. Office: Boynton Health Svc 410 Church St SE Minneapolis MN 55455-0346 E-mail: mjoseph@bhs.umn.edu.

JOSEPH, MICHAEL SARKIES, accountant; b. Peoria, Ill., Dec. 10, 1950; s. Sarkas M. and Theresa I. (Kelch) J.; m. Christine L., June 28, 1975; children: Brian, Christopher, Patrick. BS, No. Ill. U., 1972. CPA. Ptnr. Ernst & Young, Cleve. and Chgo., 1972-89, ptnr. NYC, 1989—; profl. acct. fellow Fed. Home Loan Bank Bd., Washington, 1981-83. Roman Catholic. Avocations: golf, swimming, youth athletic programs. Office: Ernst & Young LLP 5 Times Sq New York NY 10036 Home: 16708 Flying Jib Rd Cornelius NC 28031-7788

JOSEPH, MICHAEL THOMAS, broadcast consultant; b. Youngstown, Ohio, Nov. 23, 1927; s. Thomas A. and Martha (McCarius) J.; m. Eva Ursula Boerger, June 21, 1952. BA, Case Western Res. U., 1949. Program dir. Fetzer Broadcasting, Grand Rapids, Mich., 1952-55; nat. program dir. Founders Corp., NYC, 1955-57; program cons. to ABC, CBS, NBC, Capital Cities, Entercom, Cox, Greater Media, Gannett, Tribune, Telemundo, N.Y. Times, 1958—; v.p. radio Capital Cities, NYC, 1959—60; v.p. owned radio stas. NBC, NYC, 1963—65. Mem. Internat. Radio and TV Soc., Nat. Assn. Broadcasters

JOSEPH, PAMELA A., bank executive; BBA, U. Ill., Urbana-Champaign. Sr. sales and mktg. positions Wells Fargo Bank; dir. new market devel. VISA Internat., 1991—94; pres. mktg. Nova Info. Systems, 1994—95, sr. v.p. bus. devel., 1995—97, chief info. officer, 1997—2001, pres. and COO, 2001, chmn. and CEO, 2004—; vice-chair US Bankcorp, 2004—. Bd. dirs. Paychex, 2005—; adv. bd. mem. Electronic Transfer Assn. Hon. chair Gift for a Child. Named one of 25 Most Powerful Women in Banking, US Banker, 2006. Avocation: golf. Office: Nova Info Systems 73 Chapman Highway Knoxville TN 37920-6609*

JOSEPH, RAMON RAFAEL, internist, educator; b. NYC, May 17, 1930; s. Felix R. and Helen Joseph; m. Mary Ann Kowalchik, June 16, 1956; children: Ricardo George, Maria Ann Thompson, Lisa Marie Benson. BS, Manhattan Coll., 1952; MD, Cornell U., 1956. Diplomate Nat. Bd. Med. Examiners, Am. Bd. Internal Medicine. Intern Meadowbrook Hosp., Hempstead, NY, 1956-57, resident, 1957, Wayne County Gen. Hosp., Westland, Mich., 1959-62, dir. gastroenterology, 1962-84, asst. dir. internal medicine, 1964-73, dir., chmn., 1973-84, pres. med. staff, 1971-72; cons. internal medicine and gastroenterology Annapolis Hosp., 1962-87; from instr. internal medicine to prof. U. Mich., 1962-85, prof. emeritus, 1998—; asst. dean U. Mich. Med. Sch., 1973-84; 1st v.p., dir. Univ. Med. Affiliates PC, 1981-84; pres., CEO Univ. Med. Affiliates (P.C.), 1985-87; med. dir. Henry Ford Hosp. Westland (Mich.) Ctr., 1987-94; sr. attending physician Henry Ford Hosp., Detroit, 1987-95. Cons. gastroenterology St. Mary Hosp., Livonia, Mich., 1966—, chmn. divsn. of gastroenterology, 1987-93. Contbr. articles to profl. jours. Mem. Community Commn. on Drug Abuse, Livonia and Westland, Mich., 1970-73; mem. Mich. Dept. Edn. Council on Drug Abuse, cons. on drug abuse public schs., Livonia, 1968-74; pres. Livonia Sch. Bd. Adv. Council, 1970-71. Capt. US Army, 1957—59. Fellow ACP; mem. Am. Fedn. Clin. Research, Am. Gastroent. Assn., AAAS, Assn. Am. Med. Colls., AMA, N.Y. Acad. Sci., Detroit Gastroent. Soc. (pres. 1969-70), Mich., Wayne County Med. Socs., Am. Assn. Lab. Animal Sci., Am. Soc. Gastrointestinal Endoscopy, Am. Soc. Internal Medicine, Mich. Soc. Gastrointestinal Endoscopy (pres. 1982-86), Mich. Soc. Internal Medicine, Assn. Program Dirs. in Internal Medicine. Personal E-mail: rjoseph514@aol.com.

JOSEPH, ROBERT G., former federal agency administrator; b. Williston, ND, 1949; BA, St. Louis U., 1971; MA, U. Chgo., 1973; PhD, Columbia U., 1978. Asst. for negotiations, Office Asst. Sec. for Internat. Security Affairs US Dept. Def., Washington, 1978; asst. for gen. purpose forces, 1979, asst. for nuclear policy Office Under Sec., 1980—81, chief nuclear policy/plans section, 1982—84, acting prin. dep. asst. sec. for internat. security policy, 1987, prin. dep. asst. sec. for internat. security policy, 1987—89, dep. asst. sec. nuclear forces & arms control policy, 1989—91, amb. U.S.-Russian consultative commn. nuclear testing; prof. nat. security studies Nat. Def. U., Washington, 1992—2001, founder, dir., Ctr. Counterproliferation Rsch., 1992—2001; spl. asst. to Pres., sr. dir. proliferation strategy, counterproliferation and homeland def. NSC, Washington, 2001—05; under sec. for arms control & internat. security US Dept. State, Washington, 2005—07; dir. theater nuclear forces policy, US Mission NATO, Brussels, 1985—87. Sr. scholar, dir. of studies Nat. Inst. Pub. Policy, 2004—05. Recipient Pres. Award for Individual Achievement, Nat. Def. U., 2004, Gold Medal for Disting. Svc., Nat. Nuclear Security Adminstrn., 2004, Medal for Disting. Civilian Svc., US Dept. Def.*

JOSEPH, ROBERT THOMAS, lawyer; b. June 12, 1946; s. Joseph Alexander and Clara Barbara (Francis) J.; m. Sarah Granger, May 22, 1971; children: Paul, Timothy. AB, Xavier U., 1968; JD, U. Mich., 1971. Bar: Mich. 1971, Ill. 1976, US Dist. Ct. (no. dist.) Ill. 1976, US Ct. Appeals (7th cir.) 1983. Staff atty. FTC Bur. Competition, Washington, 1971-76, asst. to dir., 1972-74; atty. Sonnenschein Nath & Rosenthal, LLP, Chgo., 1976—, ptnr., 1978—. Trustee Northbrook Libr. Bd., Ill., 1979-89, pres., 1983-85. Recipient Disting. Svc. award FTC, 1976. Mem. ABA (chair franchising com. of antitrust law sect. 1984-87, chair videotapes com. 1987-90, chair publs. com. 1991-94, coun. 1994-97, program officer 1997-99, com. officer 1999-2000, vice-chair 2000-2001, chair 2002-03, mem. governing bd. forum on franchising 1997-2003), Met. Club. Roman Catholic. Office: Sonnenschein Nath Rosenthal LLP 233 S Wacker Dr Ste 7800 Chicago IL 60606-6491

JOSEPH, RODNEY RANDY, art association administrator; b. Providence, July 13, 1945; s. Sidney Wilson and Philomena Joseph; m. Rumiko Antoinette Joseph, Jan. 29, 1971; children: Randy P., Reiner Scott. Student, Sch. Practical Art, Boston, 1964-67, Boston Conservatory Music, 1972—73; BFA, Art Inst. Boston, 1994. With Joseph Art Studio, Plymouth, Mass., 1973—76; arbitrator Better Bus. Bur., Fair Haven, Mass., 1977—79; prodr. Cape 11-Cable, Yarmouth, Mass., 1980—81; pres. Creative Life for Humanitary Arts Soc., Plymouth, 1992—. Pres. Creative Life Inc., Plymouth, 1976-92; cons. Creative Life Rsch., 1979—; program designer Office for Children of Boston, Plymouth, 1978-79; legal rsch.

pres., 1976; cons., presenter in field. Prodr.: (video) Captain Randy and Scott Terrific Adventures; author: (video) Saga of Old Plimoth Indians Cat the First Thanksgiving, 1999. Designed programs and campaigned for revitalization policies, talent laws; authored Act Naturally Talented Children, Mass., Nat. Campaign Joseph Universal Welfare Act, proposal for Resolution Article to cover local real estate tax cost and protection of hist. lands, Old Plymouth/Plymouth, Ma., Program of the Joseph Univ. Welfare Act proposal for constnl. programs for U.S. Sec. of Interior and Pres. Clinton Joint Social Pilot Project, Mass. State Senate established Nov. 13 as Massasoit Compact Day, 1997; campaign for World Peace by C-Life Inc. Recognized by Pres. Reagan Pvt. Sector Initiatives, 1982; named Man of Yr., Internat. Bio Ctr. Eng., 1992-94; recognized by House of Commons, London, Prime Min. John Major, Social Security divsn., leader of the opposition Tony Blair for the Joseph Universal Welfare Act, 1995. Mem. Internat. Platform Assn., Boston Social Libr. (life), Sandwich Hist. Soc. Republican. Avocations: painting, antiques, art. Home: 558 Wareham Rd Plymouth MA 02360-3239

JOSEPH, STEVEN JAY, lawyer; b. Baker, Oreg., Sept. 7, 1950; s. Jay Hyrum and Patricia Jean (Cahill) J.; m. Melissa Davis Joseph, Jan. 1, 1978; children: Lindsey Joseph, Logan Joseph. BS, Ea. Oreg. State Coll., 1972; JD, U. Oreg., 1975. Bar: Oreg. 1975, U.S. Dist. Ct. Oreg. 1975. Assoc. Willard K. Carey P.C., LaGrande, Oreg., 1975-76; ptnr. Carey & Joseph P.C., LaGrande, Oreg., 1976-88, Carey, Joseph & Mendiguren, LaGrande, Oreg., 1988-95, Joseph & Mendiguren P.C., LaGrande, 1995-96; atty. pvt. practice, LaGrande, 1997—. Pres. La Grande Indsl. Devel. Corp., 1999—. Councilor City of LaGrande, Oreg. 1990-94, 97-98; adv. bd. Salvation Army, 1995-2001; trustee E.O.S.C. Found., 1980-95, pres. 1988-90, East Oreg. U.-East Oreg. U. Found., 2000—, La Grande Sch. Dist. Bd., 2001-07, chmn., 2004-2005 Mem.: LaGrande-Union County C. of C. (bd. dirs. 1982—84), Rotary (pres. 2005—06), Elks. Republican. Avocations: polo, racquetball, skiing, hunting, golf. Home: 806 Highland Pl La Grande OR 97850-3216 Office: PO Box 3230 La Grande OR 97850-7230 Office Phone: 541-963-4901. Personal E-mail: sjoseph@uwtc.net.

JOSEPH, TODD M., lawyer; b. Buffalo, Mar. 18, 1950; AB magna cum laude, Harvard U., 1971, JD cum laude, 1975. Bar: N.Y. 1975, D.C. 1976, U.S. Ct. Appeals (9th cir.) 1977, U.S. Ct. Appeals (D.C. cir.) 1978. Law clk. U.S. Dist. Ct. D.C., 1975-76; asst. gen. counsel EPA, Washington, 1976-82; atty. Hodgson, Russ, Andrews, Woods & Goodyear, Buffalo; ptnr. Hodgson Russ LLP, Buffalo. Mem.: ABA, DC Bar Assn., Erie County Bar Assn. Office: Hodgson Russ LLP 1 M&T Plz Ste 2000 Buffalo NY 14203 Office Phone: 716-848-1404. Office Fax: 716-849-0349. E-mail: tjoseph@hodgsonruss.com.

JOSEPHS, BABETTE, legislator; b. NYC, Aug. 4, 1940; d. Eugene and Myra A. Josephs; children: Lee Aaron Newberg, Elizabeth Master. BA, Queens Coll., 1962; JD, Rutgers U., 1976. Sole practice, Phila., 1976-78; exec. dir. Nat. Abortion Rights Action League of Pa., Phila., 1978-80, Citizens Coalition for Energy Efficiency, Phila., 1980-81; pvt. practice cons., fundraiser Phila., 1981-84; mem. Pa. Ho. of Reps., Phila., 1984—. Mem. Profl. Licensure Com., 1985—86, Ho. Health and Human Services Com., 1985—92, 1995—2002, Ho. Judiciary Com., 1987—94, 1997—2002, Ho. Appropriations Com., 1993—2002, Ho. Urban Affairs Com., 1997—98, Children and Youth Com., 2001—02, Dem. Policy Com., Common Sense Firearms Safety Caucus, Firefighters and Emergency Services Caucus, Autism Caucus, Campaign Fin. Reform Caucus, others, Pa. Commn. on Crime and Delinquency, Joint Selection Com. to Examine Election Issues, 2001—02, Agrl. and Rural Affairs Com., 2003—; mem. adv. bd. Statewide Uniform Registry of Elections, 2001—02; chair State Govt. Com., 2001—. Mem. Women's Internat. League for Peace and Freedom, LWV; hon. chair Jewish Family & Children's Services of Greater Phila.; co-founder, mem. Nat. Abortion and Reproductive Rights Action League; coord. Nat. Orgn. Women Legislators, Pa.; mem. Clean Air Coun.; Am. Jewish Com.; mem. Martin Luther King Task Force, Rebuild the Del. Valley Steering Com., Nuclear Freeze Campaign; super del. Dem. Nat. Conv., 1992; bd. dirs. ACLU; bd. mem. Save the Boyd, Franklin Paine's Skate Park. Named Legislator of Yr., Citizen Action, 1996, Dem. Woman Rep. of Yr., Capitol Area Dem. Woman's Club, 2001, Leader of Yr., Bella Vista United Civic Assn., 2004; recipient Cert. of Appreciation, AIDS WALK, 1996, President's award, Pa. Fedn. Mus. and Hist. Orgns., 1998, Disting. Pub. Svc. award, Concerned Citizens of Del. Valley, 1999, Legislator of Yr. award, Pa. Consumer Action Network, 1999, Cert. of Appreciation award, Statewide Pa. Rights Coalition, 2002, Women of Distinction award, Phila. Bus. Jour. and Nat. Assn. Women Bus. Owners, 2003, Cert. of Appreciation, Phila. 17th Police Dist., 2003, Leadership award, 2003, Disting. Achievement award, Smokefree, Pa., 2003, Spirit of Leadership award, Pathways Pa., 2004. Mem.: Center City Residents Assn., Phila. Bar Assn. (com. on civil and women's rights), Liberty City Gay and Lesbian Dem. Club. Democrat. Jewish. Office: 1528 Walnut St Philadelphia PA 19102-3604

JOSEPHSON, JORDAN STUART, otolaryngologist; b. Dec. 15, 1957; BS in Chemistry, SUNY, Albany, 1979; MD, SUNY Downstate Med. Sch., Bklyn., 1983. Intern gen. surgery Long Island Jewish Hosp., 1983-84, chief resident otolaygoly, 1984-88; fellow in endoscopic sinus surgery Johns Hopkins Med. Sch., Balt., 1989; otolaryngologist N.Y. Nasal and Sinus Ctr., NYC, 1994—. Author, editor: Medical Clinics of North America, 1991, 2d edit., 1993; contbr. articles to profl. jours., chpt. to book. Recipient Functional Endoscopic Sinus Surgery Tchg. award, 1989, NIH Recognition for Svc. and Dedication award, 1989-94, cert. of recognition Best Drs. N.Y. Metro Area, 1994—, N.Y. Magazine Best Doctors in N.Y. Mem. AMA, Am. Rhinologic Soc., Am. Acad. Otolaryngology, Head and Neck Surgery, N.Y. State County Med. Soc. Avocations: skiing, music, reading, writing. Office: NY Nasal and Sinus Ctr 111 E 77th St New York NY 10021-1802 Office Phone: 212-717-1773.

JOSEPHSON, KENNETH BRADLEY, artist, retired educator; b. Detroit, July 1, 1932; s. Ernest Gustav and Hilda Christine (Wick) J.; m. Carol A. Compeau, Feb. 1954 (dec. Apr. 1958); m. Sherill A. Petro, Oct. 28, 1960 (div. 1973); children: Matthew W. (dec.), Bradley J., Anissa C.; m. Sally D. Garen, Jan. 30, 1973 (div. 1978); m. Katherine R. Bateman, June 7, 1991 (div. 1998). BFA, Rochester Inst. Tech., 1957; MS, Inst. Design Ill. Inst. Tech., 1960. Photographer Chrysler Corp., Detroit, 1957-58; exch. tchr. Konstfackskolan, Stockholm, 1966-67; assoc. prof. U. Hawaii, Honolulu, 1967-68; vis. prof. Tyler Sch. Art, Temple U., Phila., 1975, UCLA, 1981-82; prof. Sch. Art Inst. Chgo., 1960-97. Fellowship panelist Nat. Endowment Arts, Washington, 1975; vis. artist Ecole Régionale des Beaux Arts De Saint-Etienne, France, fall 1995. One-man shows include Visual Studies Workshop, Rochester, NY, 1971, U. Iowa Mus. Art, Iowa City, 1974, 291 Galery, Milan, 1974, Cameraworks Gallery, L.A., 1976, Reicher Gallery Barat Coll., Lake Forest, Ill., 1977, Fotoforum, Kassel, Germany, 1978, Photographer's Gallery, London, 1979, Delpire Galerie, Paris, 1981, Young Hoffman Gallery, Chgo., 1981, Swen Parson Gallery No. Ill. U., 1983, Vision Gallery, Boston, 1983, Mus. Contemporary Art, Chgo., 1983, Friends of Photography, Carmel, Calif, 1984, Rhona Hoffman Gallery, Chgo., 1991, 99, La Serre Gallery, Beaux-Arts de Saint Etienne, France, 1996, Art Inst. Chgo., 1999, Whitney Mus. Art, NY, 2001, Yancey Richardson Gallery, NY, 2001-02, Priebe Art Gallery, U. Wis., Oshkosh, 2001, Kenneth Josephson Ctr. Photography, Lectoure, France, 2003, 2007, La Filature, Mulhouse, France, 2004, Cal Solway Gallery, Cin., 2004, Rona Hoffman Gallery, Chgo., 2004; exhibited in group shows at Fla. State Mus., Gainesville, 1965, Sheldon Meml. Art Gallery, Lincoln, 1968, Fogg Art Mus., Harvard U., 1967, Eastman House, Rochester and Nat. Gallery of Can., Ottawa, 1967, Mus. Contemporary Crafts, NYC, 1971, Corcoran Gallery, 1972, Art Inst. Chgo., 1973, 90, 93, 02, 04, 06, Walker Art Ctr., Mpls., 1973, Madison Art Ctr., 1973, Mus. Art, Indpls., 1973, Incontri Internat. d'Arte Precheggio di Villa Borghese, Rome, 1973-74, Atkins Art Gallery, 1974, Kunsthaus, Zurich, 1977, Mus. Contemporary Art, Chgo., 1977, 96, Leslie Tonkonow Art Works and Projects, NYC, 1998, Carol Ehlers Gallery, Chgo., 1999, Tokyo Met. Mus. Photography, 2005, Norton Simon Mus., Pasadena, 2006, La Filature, 2006, Mus. Modern Art, NYC, 2006, Whitney Mus. Art, NYC, 2006, The Art Inst. Chgo., 2006; Mus. Art. R.I. Sch. Design, 1978, Mus. Modern Art, NYC, 1978, 2006, Light Gallery, NYC, 1980, Photokina, Koln, Germany, 1980, Seibu Mus. Art, Tokyo, 1982, Barbican Art Gallery, London, 1985, LA County Mus. Art, Nat. Mus. Modern Art, 1989, State of Ill. Art Gallery, 1989, U. Hawaii Art Gallery, 1990, Rockford Coll. Art Gallery, 1990, Catherine Edelman Gallery, Chgo., 1991, Davenport Mus. Art, 1992, Seagram Bldg. Gallery, 1992, Renaissance Soc., Chgo., Montreal Mus. Fine Arts, 1993, Chgo. Cultural Ctr., 1994, U. Ariz., 1994, Mus. Modern Art, 1995, Laurence Miller Gallery, 1995, Ehlers Caudill Gallery, Chgo., 1996, Gallery 312, Chgo., 1996, Mus. Contemporary Photography, Columbia Coll., Chgo., 1996, VIII Fotobienal Vigo (Spain), 1998, Whitney Mus. Am. Art, NY, 2002, 04, San Francisco Mus. Modern Art, 2002, Phila. Mus. Art, 2002, Stephen Daiter Gallery, Chgo., 2002, Mus. Contemporary Art, Chgo., 2002, Carl Solway Gallery, Cin., 2002, Book Light Ctr. for Book and Paper Arts, Columbia Coll., Chgo., 2004, Cin. Art Mus., 2004, Yancey Richardson Gallery, NYC, 2005, Mus. Fine Arts, Houston, 2006, Norton Simon Mus., 2006, Art Inst. Chgo., 2007, Rhona Hoffman Gallery, Chgo., 2007, others; permanent collections include Mus. Modern Art., NYC, Contemporary Arts Mus., Houston, Addison Gallery Am. Art, Art Inst. Chgo., Bibliothéque Nationale, Paris, Ctr. for Creative Photography, U. Ariz., Fotografiska Museet, Stockholm, Hallmark Collections, Kansas City, Mo., Mpls. Inst. Arts, Mus. Fine Arts, Boston, Grunwald Ctr. Graphic Arts, UCLA, Nat. Mus. Art Smithsonian Instn., Washington, Nat. Mus. Modern Art, Kyoto, LA County Mus. Art, San Francisco Mus. Modern Art, Cartier Internat. Found., Paris, U.S. Trust Co., Art. Inst. of Chgo., Hunter Mus., Chattanooga, Tenn., Deloitte and Louche, Chgo., John D. and Catherine T. MacArthur Found., Seagram Collection, High Mus. Art., Libr. Congress, Internat. Ctr. Photography, N.Y., Cleve. Mus. Art, Tokyo Met. Mus. Photography, Whitney Mus. Am. Art., N.Y., Spencer Mus. Art, U. Kans., Norton Simon Mus., Pasadena, Calif., Tokyo Met. Mus. Photography, Centrede Photographie, France, Nelson-Atkins Mus. Art, La Galerie De LA Filature, Mulhouse, France, 2006. Served with U.S. Army, 1953-55. Guggenheim fellow, 1972, Nat. Endowment for Arts fellow, 1975, 79, Ruttenberg Arts Found. grantee, 1983, Ill. Acad. of Fine Arts Photographer award, 1993. Mem. Soc. for Photog. Edn. (founding mem.)

JOSEPHSON, MARVIN, literary agent; b. Atlantic City, Mar. 6, 1927; s. Joseph and Eva (Rounick) J.; m. Tina Tann Chen, Apr. 12, 1973; children: Celia M., Claire A., Nancy A., Joseph T. Josephson; YiLing L.T. and YiPei R.T. Chen-Josephson. BA, Cornell U., 1949; LL.B., N.Y. U., 1952. Atty. CBS, NYC, 1952-55; pres., then chmn. ICM Holdings Inc. (and predecessors), NYC, 1955—. Served with USN, 1945-46. Office: ICM Holdings Inc 40 W 57th St 17th Fl New York NY 10019-4098 Fax: 212-556-6886. E-mail: mjosephson@icmtalent.com.

JOSEPHSON, NANCY, talent agency executive; d. Marvin J.; m. Larry Sanitsky; 3 children. BA in Economics, Brown U., 1980; JD, Harvard Law Sch., 1982. Atty. Loeb & Loeb, NY, 1982-86, Internat. Creative Mgmt., Beverly Hills, 1986, head N.Y. TV dept.; various positions as an agent, 1979-87; head TV lit. dept. Internat. Creative Mgmt., LA, 1991—95, exec. v.p. TV, 1995—2006, co-pres., 1998—2006; ptnr. The Endeavor Agy., Beverly Hills, Calif., 2006—. Developer (TV shows) Friends, Nash Bridges, Caroline in the City, The Simpsons. Named one of top twenty-five most important women in entertainment Hollywood's Reporter, 2005, 100 Most Powerful Women in Entertainment, 2006. Mem.: Hollywood Radio & Television Soc. (pres.). Office: The Endeavor Agy 9601 Wilshire Blvd 10th Fl Beverly Hills CA 90212*

JOSEPHSON, RICHARD CARL, lawyer; b. Washington, Nov. 20, 1947; s. Horace Richard and Margaret Louise (Loeffler) J.; m. Jean Carol Attridge, Aug. 1, 1970; children: Lee Margaret, Amy Dorothy. AB, Case Western Res. U., 1969; JD, Coll. of William and Mary, 1972. Bar: Oreg. 1973. Law clk. Hon. John D. Butzner, Jr., U.S. Ct. Appeals, 4th Cir., Richmond, Va., 1972-73; mem. Stoel Rives LLP, Portland, Oreg., 1973—2006; v.p., gen. counsel Schnitzer Steel Industries, Inc., Portland, Oreg., 2006—. Bd. dirs. Tucker-Maxon Oral Sch., Portland, 1987-2006, Vis. Nurse Assn., Portland, 1978-89, Healthlink, Portland, 1984-89, St. Mary's Acad., Portland, 1998-2001, Portland Arena Mgmt., LLC, 2006-07. 1st lt. U.S. Army, 1973-79. Fellow Am. Coll. Bankruptcy, Am. Coll. Comml. Fin. Lawyers; mem. ABA, Am. Bankruptcy Inst., Oreg. Bar Assn. (chmn. debtor-creditor sect. 1980-81). Avocations: skiing, white-water rafting, running, bicycling, theater. Office: Schnitzer Steel Industries Inc 3200 NW Yeon Ave Portland OR 97210 Office Phone: 503-224-9900. Office Fax: 503-299-2277. Business E-Mail: rjosephson@schn.com.

JOSEPHSON, WILLIAM HOWARD, retired lawyer; b. Newark, Mar. 22, 1934; s. Maurice and Gertrude (Brooks) J.; m. Barbara Beth Haws, June 18, 1995. AB, U. Chgo., 1952; JD, Columbia, 1955; commoner, St. Antony's Coll., Oxford U., Eng., 1958-59. Bar: NY 1956, DC 1966, US Supreme Ct. 1959. Assoc. Paul, Weiss, Rifkind, Wharton & Garrison, NYC, 1955—58, Joseph L. Rauh, Jr., Washington, 1959; Far East regional counsel ICA, 1959—61; from spl. asst. to dir. to gen. counsel Peace Corps, 1961—66; from assoc. to ptnr. to counsel Fried, Frank, Harris, Shriver & Jacobson, NYC, 1966—99; asst. atty. gen. in charge charities bur. NY State Law Dept., NY, 1999—2004, ret., 2004. Adj. law tchr. George Washington U. Law Sch., 1960-61, Cardozo Law Sch., 2001, NYU Heyman Ctr., 2002—; spl. counsel NYC Human Resources Adminstrn., 1966-67, City Univ. Constrn. Fund, 1967-96, NYC Bd. Edn., 1968-71, NYC Employees' Retirement Sys., 1975-86; Nat. Dem. vice presdl. campaign coord., 1972; pres. Peace Corps Inst., 1980—; mem. NY State Gov. Task Force Pension and Investment, 1987-89, NY State Hist. Records Adv. Bd., 1990-96, NY State Archives Preservation Trust, 1994-96 Bd. editors: Columbia Law Rev, 1953-55; contbr. numerous legal publs. Trustee, advisor various nonprofit orgns. Recipient William A. Jump award exemplary achievement pub. adminstrn., 1965, Disting. Svc. award, Valerie Kantor award, Corp. Social Responsibility award Mex. Am. Legal Def. and Edn. Fund, 1980, 81, 93, Pub. Svc. award U. Chgo., 2007. Mem. Assn. Bar City N.Y. (spl. com. on Congl. ethics 1968-70), Council on Fgn. Relations. Jewish. Home: 58 S Oxford St Brooklyn NY 11217-1305 Office Phone: 212-859-8220.

JOSEY, E(LONNIE) J(UNIUS), librarian, retired state agency administrator; b. Norfolk, Va., Jan. 20, 1924; s. Willie and Frances (Bailey) J.; m. Dorothy Johnson, Sept. 11, 1954 (div. Dec. 1961); 1 dau., Elaine Jacqueline. AB, Howard U., 1949; MA, Columbia U., 1950; MLS, SUNY, Albany, 1953; LHD, Shaw U., 1973; DPS, U. Wis., Milw., 1987; HHD, N.C. Cen. U., 1989; LittD, Clark Atlanta U., 1995; LHD (hon.), Clarion Univ. of Pa., 2001. Desk asst. Columbia U. Libraries, 1950-52; libr. tech. asst. central br. N.Y. Pub. Libr., NYC, 1952; libr. I Free Libr., Phila., 1953-54; instr. social scis. Savannah State Coll., 1954-55, libr., assoc. prof., 1959-66; libr., asst. prof. Del. State Coll., 1955-59; assoc. divsn. libr. devel. N.Y. State Edn. Dept., Albany, 1966-68; chief Bur. Acad. and Rsch. Libraries, 1968-76, Bur. Specialist Libr. Svcs., 1976-86; prof. U. Pitts. Sch. Libr. and Info. Scis., 1986-95, prof. emeritus, 1995—. Mem. bd. advisors Children's Book Rev. Service, Bklyn., 1972— Editor, contbg. author: The Black Librarian in America, 1970, What Black Librarians Are Saying, 1972, New Dimensions for Academic Library Service, 1975; co-compiler, co-editor: Handbook of Black Librarianship, 1977; co-editor: A Century of Service: Librarianship in the United States and Canada, 1976, Opportunities for Minorities in Librarianship, 1977, The Information Society: Issues and Answers, 1978, Libraries in the Political Process, 1980, Ethnic Collections in Libraries, 1983, Libraries, Coalitions, And the Public Good, 1987, Politics and the Support of Libraries, 1990, Festchaift E.J. Josey: an Activist Librarian, 1992, The Black Librarian in America Revisited, 1994, Handbook of Black Librarianship, 2001; mem. editl. bd. Dictionary of Am. Library History, 1974—; mem. editl. adv. bd. ALA Yearbook, 1975-83; spl. advisor: World Ency. Black People, 1974-80; contbr. numerous articles to profl. jours. Mem. Albany Interracial Coun., 1972—86; state youth advisor Ga. Conf., 1962—66, 1st v.p., 1981—82, pres., 1982—86, life mem., 1971—, chmn. program, 1972—76, trustee; mem. tech. task force Econ. Opportunity Authority of Savannah, 1964—66; mem. adv. coun. Sch. Libr. Sci. N.C. Ctrl. U.; mem. adv. coun. Sch. Libr. and Info. Sci. SUNY, Albany, Sch. Libr. and Info. Sci. Queen's Coll. CUNY; mem. exec. bd. Savannah (Ga.) br. NAACP, 1960—66; mem. exec. bd. Albany br. Ga. Conf., 1970—72; mem. exec. bd. Albany Opportunity Authority; bd. dirs. Freedom to Read Found., 1987—91. With AUS, 1943—46. Recipient cert. of Appreciation Savannah br. NAACP, 1963, NAACP award Savannah State Coll. chpt., 1964, Merit award for work on econ. opportunity task force Savannah Chatham County, 1966, award for disting. service to librarianship Savannah State Coll. Library, 1967, Jour. Library History award, 1970, N.Y. Black Librarians Inc. award, 1979, N.J. Black Librarians Network award, 1984, Joseph W. Lippincott award, 1980, Disting. Alumnus of Yr. award SUNY Albany Sch. Library and Info. Sci. and Policy, 1981, 89, Disting. Service award Library Assn. of CUNY, 1982, Martin Luther King Jr. award for disting. community leadership SUNY, Albany, 1984, award for contbns. to librarianship D.C. Assn. Sch. Librarians, 1984, award Kenyan Library Assn., 1984, Disting. Service award Afro-Caribbean Library Assn., Eng., 1984; ALA Hon. Mem. Award, 2002. Mem.: ACLU, AAUP, ALA (hon.; founder, chmn. Black Caucus 1970—71, mem. coun. 1970—, mem. exec. bd. 1979—86, v.p./pres.-elect 1983—84, pres. 1984—85, John Cotton Dana award 1962, 1964, Black Caucus award 1979, ALA Equality award 1991, Black Caucus Demco award for disting. svc. to librarianship 1994, Wash. office award 1996—, Humphrey/OCLC/Forest Press award for contbns. to internat. librarianship 1998), Am. Soc. Info. Scis., Internat. Platform Assn., N.Y. Libr. Assn. (Disting. Svc. award 1985), Am. Acad. Polit. and Social Sci., Assn. Study Afro-Am. Life and History, Pa. Libr. Assn. (Disting. Svc. award 1996), N.Y. Libr. Club, Kappa Phi Kappa, Alpha Phi Omega. Democrat. Home: 5 Bayard Rd Unit 505 Pittsburgh PA 15213-1905 Office: U Pitts Sch Info Scis Bldg Pittsburgh PA 15260 E-mail: ejjosey@mail.sis.pitt.edu.

JOSHI, MADHUKAR, statistician, consultant; s. Vishvanath and Manorama Joshi; m. Jyoti Deodhar, Oct. 13, 1946; children: Swati, Chitra Baylis. BSc, D.G. Ruparel Coll., Mumbai, 1958; MSc, U. Bombay, India, 1960; PhD, Case Western Res. U., Cleve., 1965. Statistician Digital Equipment Corp., Hudson, Mass., 1982—98, Tex. Instruments, Sherman, 1998—2006; ret., 2006; statis. cons., 2007—. Author: (text book) Management Sciences, 31 tech. papers in field. Founder and pres. New Eng. Marathi Mandal, Boston, 1978—79. Fellow, IBM Corp., 1963—65. Hindu. Achievements include patents for web-based mining of statistical information and early warning system for semiconductor parametric tests to improve fab processes. Avocations: bicycling, mountain climbing, travel. Office Phone: 508-622-0240. Personal E-mail: jyotijoshi@comcast.net.

JOSHI, SURESH MEGHASHYAM, engineer, researcher; b. Poona, India; arrived in US, 1969, naturalized, 1982; BS, Banaras U., India, 1967; MS, Indian Inst. Tech., Kanpur, 1969; PhD, Rensselaer Poly. Inst., Troy, NY, 1973. Engr. Stone & Webster Corp., Boston, 1972—73; rsch. assoc. NASA, Hampton, Va., 1973—75, sr. scientist, 1983—; rsch. prof. Old Dominion U. Rsch. Found., Norfolk, Va., 1975—83. Vis. prof. U. Va., Charlottesville, 1992—93. Author: Control of Large Flexible Space Structures, 1989, Adaptive Control of Systems with Actuator Failures, 2004; co-author: Control of Nonlinear Multibody Flexibles Space Structures, 1996; contbr. articles to profl. jours. Recipient Allen B. DuMont prize, Rensselaer Poly. Inst., 1973, Group Achievement award, NASA, 1977, cert. of Recognition, 1981, Quality award, 1984, 1988, 1990, 1991, Spl. Achievement award, 1987, 1989, 1994, 1995, Outstanding Tech. Contbns. award, 1989, 1990, 1992, Floyd Thompson award, 1992, Dual Career Ladder award, 1992. Fellow: ASME (Charles S. Draper award 2006), IEEE (Control Sys. Tech. award 1995, Judith A. Resnik award 2003, Region 3 Outstanding Engr. award 2007), AIAA. Avocation: cartooning. Office: NASA Langley Rsch Ctr Mail Stop 308 Hampton VA 23681

JOSHI, VYOMESH I., computer company executive; MSEE, Ohio State U. Rsch. and devel. engring. Hewlett-Packard Co., Palo Alto, Calif., 1980—84, project mgr., 1984—89, sect. mgr., 1989—94, ops. mgr., San Diego Imaging Operation, 1994—95, digital copier bus., 1995—97, gen. mgr., 1997—99, v.p., gen. mgr., 1999—2002, exec. v.p. imaging & printing grp., 2002—, exec. v.p. imaging & personal systems grp., 2005. Mem. bd. dirs. Yahoo!, Inc., Sunnyvale, Calif., 2005—. Office: Hewlett-Packard Co 3000 Hanover Rd Palo Alto CA 94304*

JOSKOW, JULES, economic research company executive; b. NYC; s. Abraham and Mollie (Neuberg) J.; m. Charlotte Epstein, June 24, 1945; children: Paul, Margaret, Andrew. BS, CCNY, 1941; MA, Columbia U., 1942, PhD, 1953. Mem. faculty dept. econs. CCNY, 1941-60; dir. rsch. Boni, Watkins, Jason & Co., NYC, 1952-61; v.p. Nat. Econ. Rsch. Assocs., NYC, 1961-70, sr. v.p., 1970-76, exec. v.p., 1976-85, pres., 1985-91, spl. cons., 1991—. Contbr. articles to profl. jours. Mem. nat. governing coun. Am. Jewish Congress, N.Y.C., 1968-71; v.p. Temple Emanuel, Great Neck, N.Y., 1974-77. Mem. Glen Head Country Club L.I. (pres. 1988-91). Home: 7503 Rexford Rd Boca Raton FL 33434 Office Phone: 212-345-3000. Business E-Mail: Jules.Joskow@nera.com.

JOSKOW, PAUL LEWIS, economist, educator; b. Bklyn., June 30, 1947; s. Jules and Charlotte Joan (Epstein) J.; m. Barbara Zita Chasen, Sept. 10, 1978; 1 child, Suzanne Zoe. BA, Cornell U., 1968; M.Phil., Yale U., 1971, PhD, 1972. Asst. prof. econs. MIT, Cambridge, 1972-75, assoc. prof. econs., 1975-78, prof. econs., 1978—, Mitsui prof., 1989-96, Elizabeth and James Killian chair, 1996—, head dept. econs., 1994-98, dir. Ctr. for Energy and Environ. Policy Rsch., 1999—. Vis. prof. J.F.K. Sch. Govt., Harvard U., Cambridge, Mass., 1979-80; rsch. assoc. Nat. Bur. Econ. Rsch., 1988—; Joel Dean meml. lectr. Oberlin Coll., Ohio, 1983; cons. NERA, White Plains, N.Y., 1972-97, The World Bank, 1991-92, Rand Corp., Santa Monica, Calif., 1972-87; pub. mem. Adminstrv. Conf. U.S., Washington, 1980-82; mem. adv. coun. EPRI, Palo Alto, Calif., 1980-84; mem. acid rain adv. com. EPA, 1990-93, mem. sci. adv. bd., 1998-2002; chmn. rsch. adv. bd. Com. for Econ. Devel., 1991-94, sci. adv. bd. Inst. d'Organization Industrielle, Toulouse, France, 1991—; bd. dirs. Trans Can. Corp., Exelor Corp.; trustee Putnam Mutual Funds, Boston, 1997—; bd. of overseers Boston Symphony Orch., 2005—. Co-author: Electric Power in the U.S., 1979, Markets For Power, 1983, Markets For Clean Air, 2000, Empirical Industrial Organization, 2003; also author: Controlling Hospital Costs, 1981, Economic Regulation, 2000; also numerous articles, chpts.; co-editor, then assoc. editor Bell Jour. Econs., 1976-85; co-editor Jour. of Law, Econs. and Orgn., 1992-95; bd. editors Am. Econ. Review, 1993-98. Pres. Yale U. Coun., 1993-06; mem. bd. overseers Boston Symphony Orch., 2005—. Fellow Am. Acad. Arts and Scis., Econometric Soc., Indsl. Orgn. Soc.; mem. ABA (assoc.), Am. Econ. Assn., Econometric Soc., Internat. Assn. for Energy Econs.(Best Paper award, 1994), Outstanding Contbns. to the Profession award 2004, Internat. Soc. for New Instnl. Econs. (v.p. 2000-2001, pres.2002-03, Yale medal 2005). Home: 7 Chilton St Brookline MA 02446-3902 Office: MIT Dept Econs 50 Memorial Dr Cambridge MA 02142-1347 Office Phone: 617-253-6664. Business E-Mail: pjoskow@mit.edu.

JOSLIN, ANN, state librarian; With Idaho State Libr., Boise, 1979—, assoc. state libr., state libr., 2005—. Mem.: Idaho Libr. Assn. (officer, Libr. of Yr. award 1992, 2003). Office: Idaho Commn for Libraries 325 W State St Boise ID 83702 Office Phone: 208-334-2150. Office Fax: 208-334-4016. Business E-Mail: ann.joslin@libraries.idaho.gov.*

JOSLIN, JANINE ELIZABETH, preservationist, consultant; b. Kansas City, Mo., Mar. 16, 1948; d. James Bryce and Isabel Quezon (Carr) Traner; m. Jack Leslie Joslin, Dec. 4, 1971; children: Jaclyn, Aaron, Amanda. BA in History, U. Mo., Kansas City, 1971; MA in Heritage Preserevation, Ga. State U., 1992. Pvt. practice cons., Rome, Ga., 1989—92; dir. Chieftains Mus., Rome, 1992—94; pres. Gaia Walkers Inc., Leawood, Kans., 1996—99; pvt. practice cons. Leawood, 1999—. Bd. mem. Women Vision Internat., Overland Park, Kans., 1996—; pres. bd. Donnelly Internat., Kansas City, Kans., 1997—98; team leader Sci. City Mus., Kansas City, Mo., 1998—99. Contbr. articles to mags. Mem. Leawood Hist. Commn., 1998—; bd. dirs. Kans. Preservation Alliance, Topeka, 2001—, pres., 2003—05, exec. dir., 2005; co-founder, pres. bd. Sharing a Vision for Generations, 2005—. Grantee, IMS, 1994, Ga. Heritage 2000, 1995, Kans. Why 150, 1999. Avocations: kayaking, hiking, rowing. Home: 12508 Catalina Leawood KS 66209 E-mail: jjoslin1@kc.rr.com.

JOSLIN, RODNEY DEAN, lawyer; b. Moline, Ill., May 18, 1944; s. Melvin Seth and Dorothy Ruth (Skaggs) J.; m. Ruth Anne Moody, Aug. 21, 1965 (div. July 1985); children: Amy Brooke, Eliot Dean; m. Jeanne Nowaczewski, Nov. 30, 1985; children: Benjamin Case, Cecelia Louise, Frank Augustus. AB, Augustana Coll., 1966; JD, U. Iowa, 1969. Bar: Iowa 1969, Ill. 1969, U.S. Dist. Ct. (no. dist.) Ill. 1970, U.S. Ct. Appeals (7th cir.) 1970, U.S. Supreme Ct. 1975. Assoc. Jenner & Block, Chgo., 1970-76, ptnr., 1976—2002, McGuirewoods, 2002—04; CEO AsleTip, 2004—05; dir. Navigant Consulting Inc., 2006—. Bd. dirs. United Cerebral Palsy Assn., Chgo., 1988-2006, pres., 1992-2002; bd. dirs. Northwestern Libr. Coun., Chgo., 1988—, Augustana Coll., 1996-2002; chmn. Perspectives Charter Sch., 1998—. Address: 706 WHutchinson St Chicago IL 60613-1520

JOSLYN, ROBERT BRUCE, lawyer; b. Detroit, Jan. 9, 1945; s. Lee Everett, Jr. and Juanita Constance Joslyn; m. Karen Sue Glenny, July 8, 1967; children: Gwendolyn Constance, Robert Bruce. BA, Fla. State U., 1967; JD, Emory U., 1970. Bar: Mich. 1970. Law clk. Gurney, Gurney & Handley, Orlando, Fla., summer 1969; assoc. Joslyn & Keydel, Detroit, 1970-74; ptnr. Joslyn, Keydel & Wallace, 1975-95; pvt. practice Robert B. Joslyn, PC, St. Clair Shores, Mich., 1996—. Vis. instr. Oakland U., Rochester, Mich., 1974-75; faculty Inst. Continuing Legal Edn., Ann Arbor, Michl, 1975—; guest instr. U. Mich. Law Sch. Co-author: Manual for Lawyers and Legal Assistants: Probate and Trust Administration, 1977, Manual for Lawyers and Legal Assistants: Taxation of Trusts and Estates, 1977, 3d edit., 1980. Active U.S. All Am. Prep. Sch. Swim Team, 1963. Mem. ABA, Detroit Bar Assn. (chmn. taxation com. 1985-87), State Bar Mich. (chairperson probate and estate planning sect. 1992-93), Am. Coll. of Trust and Estate Counsel (state chmn. 1987-92, bd. regents 1994-2001), Internat. Acad. Estate and Trust Law, Fin. and Estate Planning Coun. Detroit (bd. dirs. 1988-92, pres. 1992), Grosse Pointe Yacht Club (bd. dirs. 2004-), Phi Delta Phi, Phi Kappa Psi. Home: 11 Waverly Ln Grosse Pointe Farms MI 48236-3123 Office: 200 Maple Park Blvd Ste 201 Saint Clair Shores MI 48081-2211

JOSS, PAUL CHRISTOPHER, astrophysicist, atmospheric physicist, educator; b. Bklyn., May 7, 1945; s. Everett Henry and Magda Anna (Hohorst) J.; m. Marjorie Jean Axton, Jan. 24, 1970 (div.); 1 child, Susan Elizabeth; m. Karen Elizabeth Murray, July 3, 1992 (div.); 1 child, Matthew Albert Henry. BA, Cornell U., 1966, PhD, 1971. Mem. Inst. for Advanced Study, Princeton, NJ, 1971—73; asst. prof. MIT, Cambridge, 1973—78, assoc. prof., 1978—83, prof., 1983—, mem. Ctr. for Theoretical Physics, 1973—, mem. Ctr. for Space Rsch., 1973—2005, assoc. head astrophysics divsn., 1983—88, mem. Kavli Inst. for Astrophysics and Space Rsch., 2005—. Vis. scientist Aspen Ctr. for Physics, 1972—, Weizmann Inst. Sci., Rehovot, Israel, 1974—75, 1978, Inst. Astronomy, Cambridge, England, 1977, 93; vis. staff mem. Los Alamos (N.Mex.) Sci. Lab., 1979—80, cons., 1980—92, Visidyne Inc., Burlington, Mass., 1979—82, 1992—93, spl. asst. to pres., 1993—; mem. adv. com. Inst. Geophysics and Planetary Physics Los Alamos Nat. Lab., 1987—92; mem. High Energy Astrophysics Mgmt. Ops. Working Group NASA, 1988—91; mem. Astronomy and Space Physics Sci. Coun. Univs. Space Rsch. Assn., 1988—92; mem. Inst. for Theoretical Physics U. Calif., Santa Barbara, 1991; pres. Joss Consulting Assocs., 1992—. Contbr. 165 articles to profl. jours. Woodrow Wilson Found. fellow, 1966; NSF fellow, 1970; Alfred P. Sloan Found. fellow, 1976. Mem. Am. Astron. Soc. (Helen B. Warner Prize 1980, exec. com. High Energy Astrophysics div. 1983-85), Am. Phys. Soc., Internat. Astron. Union, Phi Beta Kappa. Avocations: classical music, chess. Office: MIT Dept Of Physics Rm 37-607 Cambridge MA 02139 Business E-Mail: joss@space.mit.edu.

JOSS, ROBERT L., dean; m. Betty Badger Joss; children: Randall, Jennifer Joss Bradley. BA in Economics, magna cum laude, U. Wash., 1963; MBA, Stanford U., 1967, PhD, 1970. Fellow The White House, Washington; dep. to asst. sec. for econ. policy US Treas. Dept., Washington, 1968—71; asst. v.p. Wells Fargo Bank, San Francisco, 1971—72, v.p., 1972—75, sr. v.p., 1975—81, exec. v.p., 1981—86, vice chmn., 1986—93, bd. dirs., 1999—; CEO, mng. dir. Westpac Banking Corp., Australia, 1993—99; Philip H. Knight prof. and dean Stanford Grad. Sch. Bus., 1999—. Bd. dirs. Student Loan Mktg. Assn., 1990—93, Bus. Coun. Australia, 1998—99, Shanghai Comml. Bank, Hong Kong, 1978—93, 2002—, Agilent Tech. Inc., 2003—, Epiphany Inc., Makena Capital; chmn. Australian Bankers Assn., 1997—99. Co-author (with Frank Blount): (book) Managing in Australia, 1999. Office: Stanford U Stanford Grad Sch Bus 518 Memorial Way Stanford CA 94305-5015 Office Phone: 650-723-3951. E-mail: joss_robert@gsb.stanford.edu.*

JOSSEL, LAURENCE, chef; Grad., Culinary Acad., San Francisco. Chef La Folie, The Dinning Room, San Francisco; exec. chef Kokkari, Chez Nous, Chow; owner, exec. chef Nopa, San Francisco. Named one of San Francisco's Rising Stars, StarChefs.com, 2007. Office: Nopa 560 Divisadero San Francisco CA 94117 Office Phone: 415-864-8643.*

JOST, LAWRENCE JOHN, lawyer; b. Alma, Wis., Oct. 9, 1944; s. Lester J. and Hazel L. (Johnson) J.; m. Anne E. Fisher, June 10, 1967; children— Peter, Katherine, Susan. BSCE, U. Wis., 1968, JD, 1969. Bar: Wis. 1969, U.S. Dist. Ct. (ea. dist.) Wis. 1969, U.S. Ct. Appeals (7th cir.) 1969, U.S. Supreme Ct. 1980. Law clk. to judge U.S. Dist. Ct., Milw., 1969-70; assoc. firm Brady, Tyrrell, Cotter & Cutler, 1970-74; assoc. Quarles & Brady, 1974-76, ptnr., 1976—, chair real estate group, 1985—, chair real property sect., 2002—. Vis. tchr. gen. practice Wis. Law Sch. Bd. dirs. Milw. Chamber Theatre, 1998-2001, Marcus Ctr. for the Performing Arts, 2003—; pres. Vis. Nurse Assn. Milw., 1982-85, VNA, Corp., 1982-86; bd. dirs. Wis. Heritage Inc., 1980-82, Vis. Nurse Found., 1986-95, pres., 1993-94; bd. dirs. Milw. Repertory Theater, 1987-95, 2001—, pres., 1990-92; bd. dirs. United Performing Arts Fund, 1989-93. Mem. ABA, Wis. Bar Assn. (lectr. seminars), Milw. Bar Assn., Am. Coll. Real Estate Lawyers, Am. Coll. Mortgage Attys. (state chair), Nat. Assn. Indsl. and Office Properties (bd. dirs. Wis. chpt. 2003—). Mem. Plymouth United Ch. of Christ Office: Quarles & Brady LLP 411 E Wisconsin Ave Ste 2550 Milwaukee WI 53202-4497 Office Phone: 414-277-5000. Business E-Mail: ljj@quarles.com.

JOST, RICHARD FREDERIC, III, lawyer; b. NYC, Sept. 25, 1947; s. Richard Frederic Jr. and Gertrude (Holoch) J.; m. Sally Ann Galvin, July 29, 1972; children: Jennifer, Richard IV. BA, Dickinson Coll., 1969; JD, Syracuse U., 1975. Bar: N.Y. 1976, Nev. 1978, U.S. Dist. Ct. Nev. 1979, U.S. Supreme Ct. 1984. Dep. dist. atty. Elko (Nev.) County Dist. Atty.'s Office, 1976-80; dep. atty. gen. Nev. Atty. Gen.'s Office, Carson City, 1980-83; ptnr. Jones & Vargas, Las Vegas, Nev., 1983—. Trustee United Meth. Ch., Carson City, Nev., 1982-83; bd. dirs. Ormsby Assn. Retarded Citizens, Carson City, 1982-83. Served to lt. USNR, 1970-74. Mem. ABA (urban, state and local govt. law sect.), Clark County Bar Assn., Nat. Assn. Bond Lawyers, Med. Liability Assn. Nev. (bd. dirs. 2002—. Democrat. Home: 2840 S Monte Cristo Way Las Vegas NV 89117-2951 Office: Jones & Vargas 3773 Howard Hughes Pkwy Las Vegas NV 89109-0949 Office Phone: 702-862-3383. E-mail: rfj@jonesvargas.com.

JOSTEN, KATHERINE A., artist; b. Dayton, Ohio, Feb. 27, 1949; d. George and Norma Horstman. BSEd in English, Ohio U., Athens, 1971; BFA in Painting and Drawing, Atlanta Coll. Art, 1981; MFA in Painting and Drawing, U. Wis., Madison, 1986. Assoc. faculty mem. Pima Coll., Tucson, 1988—2000; art instr. U. Ariz., Tucson, 1990—91; founder, dir. Global Art Project for Peace, Tucson, 1993—. Mem. art and culture commn. World Summit on Peace and Time, U. Peace, Costa Rica, 1999; spkr. in field. One-woman shows include Ariz. Mus. Art, 1987, exhibitions include Tucson Mus. Art, 1999, Nat. Inst. Arts, Taipei, Taiwan, 1998, Represented in permanent collections Tucson Mus. Art, Ariz. State U., Tempe; editor: Visions of Global Unity: Inspired Images FromThe Global Art Project, 1996. Mem. Brazilian percussion ensemble Batucare. Grantee, Pollock-Krasner Found., NYC, 1994, Tucson Pima Arts Coun., 2003, Cultural Exch. Coun., Tucson, 2005; Flow Fund grantee, Rockefeller Found., 1998. Mem.: Ariz. State U. Mus. Art, Tucson Mus. Art. Avocations: hiking, travel.

JOTCHAM, THOMAS DENIS, marketing communications consultant; b. Llandudno, Wales, Feb. 21, 1918; s. George James and Marion (Brand) J.; m. Margaret Jean Thirlwell, Aug. 10, 1940 (dec.); children: Patricia, Douglas, Joy, Candace (dec.), m. Thelma M. Archer, April 29, 2002. Student, Lower Can. Coll., 1929-36, McGill U., 1937-39. Sales rep. Montreal Lithographing Co., Ltd., Montreal, 1945—47; sales mgr. Wesco Waterpaints Can., Ltd., Montreal, 1947—48; advt. mgr. Pepsi-Cola Co. Can., Ltd., Montreal, 1948—52, mgr., 1952—54; asst. advt. mgr. Reader's Digest Assn., Ltd., Montreal, 1954—56; mgr., v.p. Foster Advt. Ltd., Montreal, 1956—73, exec. v.p., 1973—75, pres., 1977—81, vice chmn., 1981—83; pres. Sherwood Communications Group Ltd., Toronto, 1977—81, vice chmn., 1981—83. Mem. coun. Montreal Bd. Trade, 1973-75, v.p., 1977-78, pres., 1979, hon. chmn., 1980-81. Bd. dirs. Grace Dart Hosp., 1973-83, pres., 1979-83; bd. dirs. Can.Coun. Christians and Jews, 1978-81, Les Grands Ballets Canadien, 1976-77; mem. Venetion Condominium, Inc., pres. 1984, 88-92; treas. Freedom Found.-Broward, 1999-2000. Maj. Can. Army, 1940-45. Recipient ACA Gold medal, 1978; charter recipient McGill Mgmt. Achievement award, 1981. Fellow: Inst. Can. Advt. (pres. 1976—77); mem.: Advt. Agy. Coun. Que. (pres. 1975—76), Advt. and Sales Assocs. Montreal (pres. 1948—49), Advt. and Sales Execs. Club (pres. 1956—58), Can. Advt. and Sales Assn. (pres. 1960—61), Can.- South African Soc. (bd. dirs. 1980—89, chmn. 1983—86), Internat. Swimming Hall of Fame (chmn. 1998—99), Coral Ridge Country Club, Ont. Club, St. James Club (com. chmn. 1979—81), Mt. Stephen Club (pres. 1967—68), Royal Montreal Golf Club, Thistle Curling Club (pres. 1977—78), Highlands Fall Country Club, Coral Ridge Yacht Club (gov. 1993—97, commodore 1997), Ft. Lauderdale Golf and Country Club (bd. dirs. 1990—92), Psi Upsilon. Home and Office: 2000 S Ocean Dr #1510 Fort Lauderdale FL 33316-3813 Office Phone: 954-522-5252.

JOTHEN, MICHAEL JON, music educator, composer, conductor; b. Abington, Pa., Jan. 11, 1944; s. Marvin Carlyle and Judith Agnes Jothen; m. Gail Kristine Peterson, Aug. 19, 1967; children: Peder Joshua, Nels Matthew, Kaarn Agnes. BA, St. Olaf Coll., 1967; MA, Case-Western Res. U., 1972; PhD, Ohio State U., 1978. Tchr. k-12-vocal/gen. music Newaygo (Mich.) Pub. Schs., 1967—69; tchr. 7-9-vocal/gen. music Ashland (Ohio) City Schs., 1969—74; grad. tchg. asst. Ohio State U., Columbus, 1974—77, instr. music Newark, 1977—78; prof. music U. No. Colo., Greeley, 1978—84; supr. vocal/gen. music Balt. County Pub. Schs., Towson, Md., 1984—93; prof. music Towson U., 1993—. Cons. various pub. schs., 1985—; presenter in field. Author: (textbook) Music and You, 1987, Share the Music, 1994, Experiencing Choral Music, 2005, Spotlight on Music, 2005, Master Strategies for Choir, 2005, composer choral compositions for varied voicings; contbr. articles to profl. jours. Musical dir. Greeley (Colo.) Chorale, 1978—85; music dir. St. Michael Luth. Ch., Balt., 1986—; bd. mem. Md. Music Educators Assn., Md., 1995—99. Recipient Std. award, ASCAP, 1992—2006. Mem.: Choristers Guild (bd. dirs. 1991—92, pres. bd. dirs. 1994—96, chair anniversary organizing com. 1997—98), Md. Music Educators Assn. (chair-student membership 1995—99), Music Educators Nat. Conf. (chairperson various coms.), Am. Choral Dirs. Assn. (life). Independent. Lutheran. Avocations: designing houses, museums, travel, sports. Home: 14206 Sawmill Ct Phoenix MD 21131 Office: Towson University 8000 York Rd Towson MD 21252 Home Phone: 410-592-2626. Business E-Mail: mjothen@towson.edu.

JOUBERT, RAYMOND ERNEST, retired electrical engineer; b. Waltham, Mass., Dec. 14, 1926; s. William and Rose Huard Joubert; m. Shizue Sumino; children: James, Anna. Student, Army Extension Sch., Okinawa, Japan, 1952—53. Elec. engr. technician US Army Corps Engrs., 1950—86; constrn. supr. Mass. Dept. Pub. Works, 1997—. With USN, 1944—47, sgt. US Army, 1947—50. Recipient suggestion cert., US Army Corps Engrs., 1967, 1987. Roman Catholic. Avocations: writing poetry, drawing cartoons and caricatures. Home: 245 Bennett Rd Hampden MA 01036-9102

JOUKOWSKY, ARTEMIS A. W., private investor; b. Shanghai, Dec. 26, 1930; s. Artemis M.W. and Helen (Skvorzov) J.; m. Martha Content Sharp, June 9, 1956; children: Nina Lydia Koprulu, Artemis W. III, Michael A. AB, Brown U., 1955, LLD (hon.), 1985. Dep. to dir. Am. Internat. Underwriters, Milan, 1960-66, dep. to regional dir. for Europe, 1963-66, regional v.p. for Middle East, North Africa Beirut, 1966-72, pres., regional dir. S.E. Asia Hong Kong, 1972-74, v.p. NYC, 1974-77; mng. dir. Middle East Assurance and Reinsurance Co., Beirut, 1966-72; dir. Tam Sigorta, Istanbul, Turkey, 1967-72, Union Atlantique de Reassurance SA, Brussels, 1979-88, European Am. Underwriters, Vienna, 1979-87; dir., shareholder's rep. AIG Joint Ventures with Govt. Agencies, NYC, 1979-87, pres. socialist countries div. and spl. world markets div., 1977-87. Founder, chmn. Brown U. Sports Found., 1983—; trustee Brown U., Providence, 1985—, vice chancellor 1988-97, chancellor, 1997-98, chancellor emeritus, 1998—, mem. bd. fellows, 1998—; chmn. campaign for rising generation for Brown U., 1991-96, chmn. campaign for Brown Med. Sch., 1997-2002; mem. bd. overseers Thomas J. Watson Inst. for Internat. Studies, 1981—; mem. vis. com. Ctr. for Old World Archaeology and Art, 1981-92; vice chmn. bd. govs. John Carter Brown Libr., 1988—; trustee Lawrenceville Sch., N.J., 1984—, pres. bd. trustees, 1997-2001; chmn. Archaeol Inst. Am., 1992—; pres. bd. trustees Am. Ctr. Oriental Rsch., Amman, Jordan, 1992—; mem. vis. com. Boston Mus. Fine Arts, 1985-92; dir. Clear Pool Camp, 1976-85; co-founder Am. Sch. Milan, 1962, bd. govs., 1961-65, pres. 1963-64, fin. com. 1962-65; trustee St. Croix Landmark Soc., Fredericksted, U.S. V.I., 1995—; trustee Internat. Rsch. and Exchs. Bd., 1998—. Decorated Order of the Cedars Govt. Lebanon, Order of Independence medal Jordan. Mem. U.S. C. of C. (gov. Hong Kong chpt.), U.S.-USSR Trade and Econ. Coun. (tourist and travel com. 1974-77), Hungarian-Am. Trade and Econ. Coun. (vce chmn. 1984-87), Exploreer's Club (N.Y.C.), India House (N.Y.C.), Hong Kong Club (life), Brown Club (N.Y.C.), Larchmont (N.Y.) Yacht Club, St. Croix Yacht Club (U.S. V.I.) Univ. Club (Providence), Hope Club (Providence), Knickerbocker Club (N.Y.C.). Office: Brown U 5 Benevolent St Providence RI 02912-9018

JOURDAN, TONI CHRISTINA, small business owner, actress, writer; b. Springfield, Oreg., Dec. 29, 1961; d. Jack Eugene and Sharon Rose Frisk; m. Charlie Nelson Jourdan, Jan. 17, 1998; 1 child, Nicholas Dawson; m. Louis Eugene Beery, Feb. 14, 1988 (div. Feb. 2, 1996). BFA, U. Idaho, 1982. Prin., owner Xanadu Theatre Co., Mesa, Ariz., 1990—, Whimsicals Character Parties, 2004—. Drama coach Ventura Pk. and Recreation, Thousand Oaks, Calif., 1995—99, Phoenix Pks. and Recreation, 1999—2002, Copper Canyon Elem. Sch., Scottsdale, Ariz., 2001—04, Washington Elem. Sch., Phoenix, 2004—05. Author: (books on tape) Little Women, Secret Garden, Dracula, Golden Bowl, Cinderella, Peter Pan, Alice in Wonderland, Moby Dick, Wizard of Oz, Huckleberry Finn, Legend of Sleepy Hollow, Joan of Arc, Anne of Green Gables, Captains Courageous; performer: Little Woman, 1998, Secret Garden, 1998, Wizard of Oz, 1998, Dracula, 1998, Cinderella, 1999, Peter Pan, 1999, Alice in Wonderland, 1999, Moby Dick, 1999, Legend of Sleepy Hollow, 1999, Joan of Arc, 1999, Captains Courageous, 1999, Huckleberry Finn, 2000, Golden Bowl, 2000, Gift of the Magi, Anne of Green Gables, 2001. Named Book Pal of Yr., SAG, Ariz., 2004. Mem.: Soc. Children's Book Writers and Illustrators. Democrat. Buddhist. Personal E-mail: empowertivity@aol.com.

JOURDREN, MARC HENRI, investment banking company executive; b. Paris, Dec. 28, 1960; s. Pierre Auguste Jourdren and Berthe Augustine Dubois. Diploma in econs. and fin., Essec, Paris, 1983; MBA, Harvard U., 1987. Pres., founder Essec Enterprises Internat., Paris, 1982-83; attache French Ministry of Economy and Fin., NYC, 1983-85; assoc. Goldman Sachs & Co., NYC and Tokyo, 1987-88, Goldman Sachs Internat., London, 1988—2003, v.p., exec. dir., 1991—2000, head Japanese equities, 1996-99, head global products group, 1999—2003, mng. dir., 2000—03, Lehman Bros., 2003—, mng. dir., head instnl. client group, 2003—. Fgn. advisor Harvard U., Cambridge, Mass., 1989—. Mem. Wigmore Hall London, Soc. Couserans Pyrenees, Brit. Mensa Ltd. Avocations: piano, russian art, gastronomy, nature, skiing. Home: 48-49 Macready House Crawford St London W1H 5LP England Office: Lehman Bros 25 Bank St 29th Fl London E14 5LE England Personal E-mail: m@couzeranes.com.

JOURNEY, G. EDWARD, art educator; b. Ft. Benning, Ga., Feb. 9, 1955; s. Grover E. and Jean Harbison Journey. BA, U. Ala., Tuscaloosa, 1977, MFA, 1988. Resident dir. Birmingham Children's Theatre, Ala., 1990—93; assoc. prof. U. So. Ind., Evansville, 1994—96; dir. edn. Lone Star Performing Arts, Galveston, Tex., 1996—98; dir. theatre Galveston Coll., 1996—98; mng. dir. New Stage Theatre, Jackson, Miss., 1998—99; mgr., casting assoc. Ala. Shakespeare Festival, Montgomery, 1999—2002; asst. prof. Ala. A&M U., Normal, 2002—. Mem.: Theatre Comm. Group, Southeastern Theatre Conf., Actors' Equity Assn. Home: 8331 Whitesburg Way SE #1512 Huntsville AL 35802 Office: Ala A&M U PO Box 333 Normal AL 35762

JOVANOVIC, LOIS, medical researcher; b. Mpls. BS in Biology, Columbia U., 1969; B in Hebrew Lit., Jewish Theol. Seminary, 1968, M in Hebrew Lit., 1970; MD, Albert Einstein Coll. Medicine, 1973. Intern and resident NY Hosp. Cornell U. Med. Coll., 1973—76; fellow in endocrinology and metabolism Cornell U. Med. Coll., 1976—78, instr., asst to assoc. prof., 1978—86; asst. attending physician NY Hosp., 1978—85; asst. adj. prof. and physician Rockefeller U. and Rockefeller U. Hosp., 1979—85; assoc. adj. prof. U. Calif., Irvine, 1986—88; sr. scientist Sansum Med. Rsch. Found., 1985—96; dir. and chief sci. officer Sansum Diabetes Rsch. Inst., 1996—; clin. assoc. prof. medicine U. SC- LA Med. Ctr., 1986—89, prof., 1989—; rsch. biologist U. Calif., Santa Barbara, 1990—. Author numerous books and articles on diabetes and women's health. Fellow: NY Acad. Medicine, Am. Coll. Endocrinology, Am. Coll. Nutrition, ACP. Office: Sansum Diabetes Rsch Inst 2219 Bath St Santa Barbara CA 93105

JOVOVICH, MILLA (NATASHA MILITZA JOVOVICH), model, actress; b. Kiev, Ukraine, Dec. 17, 1975; d. Bogdanovitch and Galina Loginova Jovovich; m. Shawn Andrews, Oct. 2, 1992 (annulled Nov. 25, 1992); m. Luc Besson, Dec. 14, 1997 (div. June 12, 1999). Appeared on mag. covers including Lei, 1987, Mademoiselle, Aerna, Harper's Bazaar, Vogue, Face, i-D, Vanity Fair, W, Marie Claire; internat. spokesmodel L'Oreal; launched line of clothing with Carmen Hawk called Jovovich-Hawk, 2003. Composer: (songs in films) Gentleman Who Fell, 1993, The Rules of Attraction, 2002, The Prince & Me, 2004; costume designer: (films) Mona Lisa Smile, 2003; actor: Two Moon Junction, 1988, Return to the Blue Lagoon, 1991, Kuffs, 1992, Chaplin, 1992, Dazed and Confused, 1993, The Fifth Element, 1997, He Got Game, 1998, The Messenger: The Story of Joan of Arc, 1999, The Million Dollar Hotel, 2000, The Claim, 2000, Zoolander, 2001, Dummy, 2002, Resident Evil, 2002, The House on Turk Street, 2002, You Stupid Man, 2002, Resident Evil: Apocalypse, 2004, Ultraviolet, 2006; (TV films) The Night Train to Kathmandu, 1988; singer: (albums) The Divine Comedy, 1994. Office: c/o Spanky Taylor 3727 W Magnolia Burbank CA 91505

JOY, ALEXA, small business owner, artist, educator; d. Ken Sklar and Wendy Wilson. BS in Nutrition, Clayton Coll., Brimingham, Ala., 1998. V.p., gen. mgr. HMK Corp., Valencia, Calif., 1997—2003; prin., owner A Joy by Design, Valencia, Calif., 1998—, tchr. art, 2001—; designer T2G Prodns., Valencia, Calif., 2005—. Host, designer (films) Quick & Easy Crafting - Mini Books, 2006, Quick & Easy Crafting - Cardmaking, 2006, Quick & Easy Crafting - Christmas, 2006, Down & Dirty Workshops Blooming Flowers, 2007, Down & Dirty Workshops Kids Crafts, 2007, Down & Dirty Workshops Jewelry, 2007, Down & Dirty Workshops H2O Watercolors, 2007; exhibitions include City Hall Bridge Gallery, Calif., 1988—90, Art in Public Places Program Commd. Artist, City of Santa Clarita, 2006, one-woman shows include Canyon Theater Guild, 2007. Co-coord. The Domestic Violence Shelter Benefit Event, Valencia, 2004, Am. Cancer Soc. Benefit Event, 2000. Recipient 2nd Best Profl. Hand Crafter award, AV Fair, 2005, 2006, 1st Pl. Sculpture award, AFL-CIO Union Artist Exhibit, 1990, Humanitarian award, Character Counts, Santa Clarita, Calif., 2006, Best Profl. Rubber Stamp Artist, Creativa Living, 2006; grantee, Creative Living, 1997—2005. Mem.: Hollywood Arts Coun., Santa Clarita Artist Assn. (Art Classic Silver medal 2005). Republican. Jewish Episcopalian. Avocations: singing, acting, travel, music, crafts. Office: A Joy by Design 27023 Mc Bean Pkwy Ste 122 Valencia CA 91355 Office Phone: 661-755-3452. Business E-Mail: alexa@alexajoy.com.

JOY, BILL (WILLIAM NELSON JOY), venture capitalist, former computer software company executive; b. Detroit, Nov. 8, 1954; s. William C. Joy; m. Sara Joy; 4 children. BSEE, U. Mich., 1975; MSEE and Computer Sci., U. Calif. Berkeley, 1982; PhD in Engring. (hon.), U. Mich. Co-founder Sun Microsystems Inc., Mountain View, Calif., 1982, v.p. rsch., 1996—98, chief scientist, 1998—2003; co-founder HighBar Ventures, 2003; ptnr. Kleiner Perkins Caulfield & Byers, Menlo Park, Calif., 2005—. Bd. dirs. SpikeSource Inc., Redwood City, Calif., 2005—. Recipient Grace Murray Hopper award, Assn. for Computing Machinery, 1986, Lifetime Achievement Award, USENIX Assoc., 1993. Mem. NAE, Am. Acad. Arts & Sciences; bd. trustees, Aspen Inst.; co-chmn., Presidential Info. Tech. Adv. Com., 1997. Prin. designer University of California (Berkeley) version of UNIX operating system; co-designer Java technology, SPARC microprocessor architecture; key designer Sun Technologies including Solaris and chip architectures and pipelines; installed the first city-wide WiFi network, 1995; several patents in the field. Office: Kleiner Perkins Caulfield & Byers 2750 Sand Hill Rd Menlo Park CA 94025 Business E-Mail: billj@kpcb.com.

JOY, EDWARD BENNETT, electrical engineer, educator, consultant; b. Troy, NY, Nov. 15, 1941; s. Herman Johnson and Elizabeth (Bennett) J.; m. Patricia Marie Huddleston, Aug. 27, 1966; children: Frederick Huddleston, Rebecca Elizabeth. BEE, Ga. Inst. Tech., 1963, MSEE, 1967, PhD in Elec. Engring., 1970. Asst. prof. elec. engring. Ga. Inst. Tech., Atlanta, 1970-75, assoc. prof., 1975-80, prof., 1980-98, prof. emeritus, 1998—; pres. Joy Engring. Co., Boulder, Colo., 1981—. Cons. in field. Contbr. articles to profl. jours. Lt. USNR, 1963—65, Vietnam. Recipient Continuing Edn. award, Ga. Tech., 1997. Fellow IEEE (life); mem. Antenna Measurements Techniques Assn. (Disting. Achievement award 1999). Republican. Presbyterian. Achievements include patents in field. Avocations: amateur radio, electronics, hiking. Home and Office: 1450 Rembrandt Rd Boulder CO 80302-9478 Home Phone: 303-545-5566; Office Phone: 303-545-5566. Business E-Mail: ed.joy@gatech.edu.

JOY, ROBERT JOHN THOMAS, medical educator; b. South Kingstown, RI, Apr. 5, 1929; s. Angelo Francois and Mary Frances (Egan) Joy; m. Beverly June Boxer, July 5, 1952 (div. May 1984); children: Robert L.F., Lisa; m. Janet Lucille Brady, July 12, 1985. BS, U. RI, Kingston, 1950; MD, Yale U., New Haven, Conn., 1954; MA, Harvard Coll., Cambridge, Mass., 1965; cert., Armed Forces Staff Coll., 1968. Commd. 1st lt. US Army, 1954, advanced through grades to col., 1970; intern, resident Walter Reed Army Med. Ctr., Washington, 1954-58; asst. dir. environ. medicine USA Med. Rsch. Lab., Fort Knox, Ky., 1959-61; comdr. USA Rsch. Inst. Environ. Medicine, Natick, Mass., 1961-62; chief comdr. USA Med. Rsch. Team, Saigon, Vietnam, 1965-66; chief med. rsch. div. Office Surgeon Gen., US Army, Washington, 1968-69; dep. med. life scis. Office Dir. Def. Rsch. Engring., Washington, 1969-71; dep. dir., dir. Walter Reed Inst. Rsch., Washington, 1971-76; prof., chmn. mil. medicine Uniformed Svcs. U. Health Scis., Washington, 1976-81, prof., chmn. med. history, 1981-96, prof. emeritus, 1996—; ret. US Army, 1981. Hon. mem. faculty Indsl. Coll. Armed Forces, Washington, 1990; faculty mem. USAF Sch. Aerospace Medicine, 1992—. Editor: Jour. History Medicine and Allied Scis., 1983—87; contbr. articles to profl. jours. Decorated DSM, Legion Merit (4); recipient John Shaw Billings award, Am. Mil. Surgeons of US, 1986, William P. Clements award Uniformed Svcs., U. Health Scis., 1980. Fellow: Coll. Physicians Phila., AAAS, ACP (Davies award Med. Humanism 2002); mem.: Am. Physiol. Soc., Am. Assn. History Medicine (coun. 1979-81) (William Osler medal 1954), Osler Soc. (bd. govs. 1986-89). Home: 5821 Highland Dr Bethesda MD 20815-5531 Office: Uniformed Svcs U Dept Med History 4301 Jones Bridge Rd Bethesda MD 20814-4712 Office Phone: 301-295-3168.

JOYCE, ANNE RAINE, editor; b. South Bend, Ind., Oct. 2, 1942; d. James Agee and Marjorie Elizabeth (Gilstrap) Raine; m. Glenn Russell Joyce, Aug. 19, 1962; 1 child, Adam Russell. AB, Cen. Meth. Coll., 1962; MA in French, U. Mo., 1966; MA in Linguistics, U. Iowa, 1979. Cert. tchr., Mo. Tchr. Centralia (Mo.) High Sch., 1962-64; instr. Coe Coll., Cedar Rapids, Iowa, 1978-79, Georgetown U., Washington, 1980-83; asst. editor Am.-Arab Affairs, Washington, 1983-84; editor, dir. publs. Mid. East Policy, Washington, 1984—; gen. sec. Mid. East Policy Coun., Washington, 1991—, v.p., 1993—. Mem. edn. com. Fairfax County (Va.) PTA Bd., 1986-88; bd. dirs. Ams. for Middle East Understanding. U.S. Dept. Def. fellow, 1964-66; recipient Recognition award Am.-Arab Affairs Coun., 1988, Disting. Alumni award. Cen. Meth. Coll., 1990. Mem. Middle East Studies Assn., LWV (fin. chair Fairfax county chpt. 1981—). Home: 6916 Tulsa Ct Alexandria VA 22307-1730 Office: Middle East Policy Coun 1730 M St NW Ste 512 Washington DC 20036-4516 E-mail: ajoyce@mepc.org.

JOYCE, BERNITA ANNE, retired federal agency administrator; d. Albert A. and Margaret C. Joyce; m. Kenneth B. Lucas, Aug. 2, 1975. BA, Duchesne Coll.; MBA, U. Santa Clara, PhD, 1974. With Wolfe & Co. CPAs, Washington, 1971-72; fin. dir. Nat. Forest Products Assn., Washington, 1972-74; budget and fiscal officer ICC, Washington, 1974-77, Office Mgmt. and Budget, 1977-80; asst. dir. mgmt. svcs. Bur. Mines, Dept. Interior, 1980-85; asst. dir. Office Policy Analysis, Dept. Interior, 1985-96, asst. spl. trustee Am. Indians, 1996—99; asst. adminstr. S.J. Cmty. Georgetown U., 2000—05; pres. Rogers Sys., Inc., Bethesda, Md., 2005—. Author: Financial Viability of Private Elementary Schools. Mem. AICPA, Sr. Execs. Assn., Assn. Govt. Accts., Cosmos Club, Beta Gamma Sigma. Home: 6001 Bradley Blvd Bethesda MD 20817-3807

JOYCE, FREDERICK MARK (RICK), lawyer; b. Pompton Plains, NJ, Apr. 18, 1958; s. Thomas Francis and Josephine (Kiechle) J.; m. Judy Frances Sledge, Jan. 17, 1955. BA in Polit. Sci. magna cum laude, George Washington U., 1980; JD, Georgetown U., 1984. Bar: Md. 1984, D.C. 1985, Va. 1990, U.S. Dist. Ct. Md. 1992. Assoc. Lukas McGowan, Washington, Reboul MAcMurray, Washington, Ginsburg, Feldman & Bress, Washington; ptnr. Joyce & Jacobs, Washington; ptnr., head telecom. practice group Alston & Bird, Washington; ptnr., chair, telecom. practice group Venable LLP, Washington, 2003—. Precinct capt. Fairfax (Va.) County Den. Coun., 1992—; bd. dirs. Friends of Mt. Vernon, Alexandria, Va., 1993—, vol. Washington Area Lawyers for the Arts. Recipient Leahy prize Georgetown U., 1983. Mem. ABA (litigation sect., comm. forum), D.C. Bar Assn., Alexandria C. of C. Democrat. Avocations: rowing, hiking, beer making, reading. Office: Venable LLP 575 7th St NW Washington DC 20004 Office Phone: 202-344-4653. Office Fax: 404-344-8300. Business E-Mail: rjoyce@venable.com.

JOYCE, JAMES DANIEL, clergyman; b. Spencer, Va., Jan. 12, 1921; s. James Garfield and Mary (Taylor) J.; m. Dorothy Beatrice Campbell, Aug. 2, 1946; 1 son, Kevin Campbell. AB in Religion, Johnson Bible Coll., 1945, Lynchburg Coll., 1946; BD, Butler U., 1949; MA in Biblical Theology, Yale U., 1952, PhD, 1958. Ordained to ministry Disciples of Christ Ch., 1943. Pastor Hanover Ave. Christian Ch., Richmond, Va., 1954-59; sr. student leader ecumenical inst. World Council Chs., Geneva, 1960; prof. New Testament and Bible theology Christian Theol. Sem., Indpls., 1961-62; dean grad. sem. Phillips U., Enid, Okla., 1962-74; pastor Bethany Christian Ch., Houston, 1974-80, Covenant Christian Ch., Houston, 1980—. W.E. Garrison lectr. Disciple students Yale U., 1963; Jesse M. Bader lectr. evangelism Drake U., 1968; columnist Christian Jour., 1962-80; bass soloist rec. Joy-ce Sounds, 1977; pres. World Conv. Chrs. of Christ, 1970-74, mem. exec. com., 1974—; lectr. for armed forces in Far East, 1968; adj. prof. speech and creative writing U. Houston and Houston Community Coll., 1981-82; prof. speech and writing Houston Community Coll., 1982—, also head dept. speech; mem. bd. mgrs. Pension Fund Disciples of Christ. Author: The Living Christ in Our Changing World, 1962, The Place of the Sacraments in Worship, 1967. Recipient cert. of merit Methodist Bishop of Korea, 1972. Mem. Am. Assn. Theol. Schs. (exec. com. 1966-72), Theta Phi. Home: 5211 Carew St Houston TX 77096-1319 Personal E-mail: danbeal@sbcglobal.net.

JOYCE, JEFFREY, research scientist, consultant; b. Columbus, Ohio, Dec. 19, 1951; s. James Neal and Maxine Peterbourg Joyce; m. Sandra H. Jakobs, Feb. 15, 1997; m. Cathleen Gonzales, 1986 (div. 1995); children: Sasha Aitan, Elisabeth Allison, Dmitry Nathan. BS, U. Ill., 1977; PhD, U. Fla., 1983. Postdoctoral fellow dept. psychobiology U. Calif., Irvine, 1983—86; rsch. asst. prof. pharmacology U. Pa. Sch. Medicine, Phila., 1986—89, rsch. assoc. prof. pharmacology, 1989—95, rsch. assoc. prof. psychology and neuroscience in psychiatry, 1989—95; head and sr. scientists T.H. Christopher Ctr. for Parkinson's Disease Rsch., SHRI, Sun City, Ariz., 1995; assoc. dir. Sun Health Rsch. Inst., Sun City, 1995—. Dir. Pharm. Cons., CNS Drug Discovery and Target Devel., Scottsdale, Ariz., 1995—; bd. mem., fin. com. chair Ann. Spring Brain Conf., Gainesville, Fla., 1997—2000; adj. prof. psychology Ariz. State U., Tempe, 1998—, adj. prof. molecular and cellular biology grad. group, 1998—. Contbr. chapters to books, articles to profl. jours. Fellow: Internat. Behavioral Neuroscience Soc. (chair fin. com.), Am. Coll. Neuropsychopharmacology (fin. com. 2001—04); mem.: Internat. Soc. for Devel. Neuroscience, Soc. for Biol. Psychiatry (Ziskind-Somerfeld Research award 1997), Soc. for Neuroscience, The Movement Disorders Soc., European Coll. Neuropsychopharmacology, Collegium Internationale Neuro-Psychopharmacolgicum, Am. Soc. for Pharmacology and Exptl. Therapeutics. Jewish. Office: Sun Health Research Institute 10515 West Santa Fe Dr Sun City AZ 85351 Office Phone: 623-876-5439. Business E-Mail: jeff.joyce@sunhealth.org.

JOYCE, JOSEPH JAMES, lawyer, food products executive; b. Chgo., Sept. 28, 1943; s. Edward R. and Mary E. (Jordan) J.; m. Suzanne M. Sheridan, Aug. 26, 1967; children: Joseph, Michael, Peter, Kevin, Edward. BS, Xavier U., 1965; JD, Loyola U., 1968. Bar: Ill. 1968. Mem. Hill, Sherman, Meroni, Gross & Simpson, Chgo., 1968-72; atty. Pepsico, Inc., Purchase, NY, 1972-74, trademark counsel, 1974-77, asst. gen. counsel, 1977-86, v.p., asst. gen. counsel, 1986-98, v.p., assoc. gen. counsel, 1998—. Contbr. articles to profl. jours. Bd. mgrs. Lincoln Hall Found., Inc., 1989—. Mem. ABA, ATLA, Ill. Bar Assn., U.S. Trade Assn., Assn. Internationale pour la Protection de la Propieté Industrielle (bd. dirs.), Licensing Execs. Soc., Westchester-Fairfield Corp. Counsel Assn., Inc., Assn. Inter-Am. de la Propriedad Industrial, IIPA (exec. com. 1989—, bd. dirs.). Roman Catholic.

JOYCE, JOSEPH M., lawyer, retail executive; b. Mpls., 1951; BSBA, U. Minn., 1973; JD, William Mitchell Coll. Law, 1977. Bar: Minn. 1977. Legal counsel Tonka Corp., Minnetonka, Minn., 1977-81, sec., gen. counsel, 1981-87, v.p., sec., gen. counsel, 1987—91; v.p. human resources, gen. counsel Best Buy Co. Inc., Mpls., 1991—97, v.p., gen. counsel, 1997—2000, sr. v.p., gen. counsel, sec., 2000—. Sec. bd. dir. Best Buy Children's Found. Office: Best Buy Co Inc PO Box 9312 Minneapolis MN 55440-9312*

JOYCE, JUDITH MARIE, radiologist; d. William Charles and Janet Margaret Hugenberg; m. Edward James Joyce, Aug. 16, 1975; children: Janet Margaret, Molly Sandra. BSN, U. Tex., San Antonio, 1977, MD, 1983. Bd. cert. radiologist Am. Bd. Radiology, 1987, bd. cert. in nuc. medicine Am. Bd. Nuc. Medicine, 1988; RN Ohio, 1974. Asst. prof. U. Ky., Lexington, 1988—89; chief and assoc. chief nuc. medicine The Western Pa. Hosp., Pitts., 1989—2003; assoc. prof. Temple Med. Sch., Pitts., 2001—03, U. Pitts. Med. Ctr., 2003—. Radiology residency program dir. The Western Pa. Hosp., Pittsburgh, Pa., 2002—03. Contbr. articles to profl. jours. Recipient Radiology Resident Tchg. award, Western Pa. Hosp. Radiology Residents, 2000—01, Ronald J. Hoy Excellence in Tchg. award, U. Piits. Med. Ctr. Radiology Residents, 2004—05. Mem.: Am. Coll. Radiology, Soc. Nuc. Medicine (pres. Pitts. chpt. 1995—2002). Home: 103 Downing Dr Pittsburgh PA 15238 Office: Univ Pitts Med Ctr 200 Lothrop St Pittsburgh PA 15213 Home Phone: 412-963-1205; Office Phone: 412-623-2282. Business E-Mail: joycejm@upmc.edu.

JOYCE, MICHAEL PATRICK, lawyer; b. Omaha, Oct. 3, 1960; s. Thomas Hunt and Joan Clare (Berigan) J. Student, Miami U., Oxford, Ohio, 1978-79; BSBA, Creighton U., 1982; JD, U. Houston, 1988. Bar: Mo., Kans., U.S. Dist. Ct. (we. dist.) Mo. 1988, U.S. Dist. Ct. Kans. 1989, U.S. Ct. Appeals (8th and 10th cirs.) 1988, U.S. Supreme Ct. 1994. Assoc. mgr. Avco Fin. Svcs. Internat., Inc., Omaha, 1983-85; assoc. Wyrsch, Atwell, Mirakian, Lee & Hobbs, P.C. (formerly Koenigsdorf & Wyrsch, P.C.), Kansas City, Mo., 1988-94; shareholder Wyrsch, Hobbs, Mirakian, & Lee, PC, Kansas City, Mo., 1995-97; pvt. practice, 1997-98; pres. The Joyce Law Firm, LLC, Kansas City, Mo., 1998-2000; shareholder Van Osdol, Magruder Erickson & Redmond, PC, Kansas City, 2000—. Adj. prof. U. Mo. Kansas City Sch. Law, 1997-2001. Asst. editor (newsletter State Bar Tex.) Caveat Vendor, 1987-88. Grad. NITA, 1992; bd. dirs. Creighton U., 1997-99. Mem. ABA, Nat. Assn. Criminal Def. Lawyers, Mo. Bar Assn., Mo. Assn. Criminal Def. Lawyers, Kans. Bar Assn., Kansas City Metro Bar Assn. (bd. dirs. 2007), Johnson County Bar Assn., Creighton U. Alumni Assn. (dir. region IV nat. alumni bd. dirs. 1994-96, pres. 1997-99), Creighton U. Alumni Club (pres. Kansas City area 1992-94). Roman Catholic. Avocations: golf, basketball, community service, coaching youth sports. Office: 2400 Commerce Tower 911 Main St Kansas City MO 64105-2009 Office Phone: 816-421-0644. E-mail: mpjoyce@vomer.com.

JOYCE, ROSEMARY ALEXANDRIA, anthropology educator, department chairman; b. Lackawanna, NY, Apr. 7, 1956; d. Thomas Robert and Joanne Hannah (Poth) J.; m. Russell Nicholas Sheptak, Jan. 7, 1984. BA, Cornell U., 1978; PhD, U. Ill., 1985. Instr. Jackson (Mich.) Community Coll., 1983; lectr. U. Ill., Urbana, 1984-85; asst. curator Peabody Mus., Harvard U., Cambridge, Mass., 1985-86, asst. dir., 1986-89; asst. prof. anthropology Harvard U., Cambridge, Mass., 1989-91, assoc. prof. anthropology, 1991-94, U. Calif., Berkeley, 1994—2001, prof., 2001—, chair, 2006—. Author: Cerro Palenque, 1991, Encounters with the Americas, 1995, Gender and Power in Prehispanic Mesoamerica, 2001, The Languages of Archeology, 2002, Embodied Lives, 2003; editor: Maya History, 1993, Women in Prehistory, 1997, Social Patterns in Preclassic Mesoamerica, 1999, Beyond Kinship, 2000, Mesoamerican Archeology, 2003; contbr. articles to profl. jours. NEH grantee, 1985, 86, NSF grantee, 1989, 98, 2001, Famsi grantee, 1996, Heinz Found., Wenner-Gren Found. grantee, 1997; Fulbright fellow, 1981-82. Mem. Soc. for Am. Archaeology, Am. Anthropol. Assn., Archeol. Inst. Am. Office: U Calif Anthropology Dept 232 Kroeber Hall # 3710 Berkeley CA 94720-3710 Business E-Mail: rajoyce@berkeley.edu.

JOYCE, WILLIAM GEORGE, JR., transportation executive; b. Oswego, NY, Nov. 24, 1949; s. William George and Nannette Davies J.; m. Patricia L., July 1, 1983; children: Tara, Kendra, Andrew. Student, SUNY, Oswego, 1967-71. Ops. mgr. Lake Shore Transp. Lines, Oswego, 1971-96; pres., CEO N.Y. State Motor Truck Assn., Inc., Albany, 1997—. Gen. chmn., treas. Maintenance Coun., Alexandria, Va., 1994-95; chmn. bd. dirs. N.Y. Motor Truck, Albany, 1994-96; first v.p. N.Y. Motor Carrier Conf., Buffalo, 1993-95. Mem. Am. Trucking Assn. (v.p. 1994-97), Am. Soc. Assn. Execs., Trucking Assns. (exec. coun., regional vice chair), N.Y. State Soc. Assn. Execs. Republican. Roman Catholic. Office: NYS MTA 828 Washington Ave Albany NY 12203 E-mail: bjoyce@nytrucks.org.

JOYCE, WILLIAM H., engineering company executive, chemical engineer; b. 1935; BS, Pa. State U., 1957; MBA, NYU, 1971, PhD, 1984. With Union Carbide Corp., Danbury, Conn., 1957—2001, past exec. v.p. ops., pres., COO, 1993—95, CEO, 1995; chmn., pres., CEO Union Carbide Corp. (merged with Dow Chemical Co.), Danbury, Conn., 1996—2001; vice chmn. bd. The Dow Chem. Co., Danbury, 2001; chmn., CEO Hercules, Inc., Willmington, Del., 2001—03, Nalco Co., Naperville, Ill., 2003—. Bd. dirs. CVS Corp., El Paso. Trustee U. Rsch. Assn. Inc. Recipient Nat. medal of Tech., NSF, 1993, Industry Achievement award, Plastics Acad., 1994, Lifetime Achievement award, 1997, Perkin award, Soc. Chemical Industry, 2003. Mem.: NAE, NAS (co-chmn., Gov.-Univ.-Industry Rsch. Roundtable), Am. Plastics Coun. (bd. dirs.), Soc. Chem. Industry (treas., bd. dirs.). Office: Nalco Co 1601 W Diehl Rd Naperville IL 60563-1198 Office Phone: 877-813-3523. Office Fax: 630-305-2900.*

JOYCE, WILLIAM LEONARD, librarian; b. Rockville Centre, NY, Mar. 29, 1942; s. John Francis and Mabel Clare (Leonard) Joyce; m. Carol Gail Bertani, Aug. 13, 1967; children: Susan, Michael. BA, Providence Coll., 1964; MA, St. John's U., 1966; PhD, U. Mich., 1974. Manuscripts libr. William L. Clements Libr. U. Mich., Ann Arbor, 1968-72; curator manuscripts Am. Antiquarian Soc., Worcester, Mass., 1972-81, edn. officer, 1977-81; asst. dir. rare books and manuscripts N.Y. Pub. Libr., NYC, 1981-86; assoc. univ. libr. rare books and spl. collections Princeton U., 1986-2000; Dorothy Foehr Huck chair spl. collections, prof. history Pa. State U., State College, 2000—. Lectr. Clark U., 1975—77; cons. Nat. Hist. Publs. and Records Commn., Washington, 1982, others; adj. faculty Sch. Libr. Svc., Columbia U., NYC, 1984—92; vis. prof. Grad. Sch. Libr. & Info. Sci., UCLA, 1994. Author: Editors and Ethnicity: A History of the Irish-American Press, 1848-1883, 1976; editor: Catalog of Manuscripts Collections of the American Antiquarian Society, 4 vols., 1979; co-author: Evaluation of Archival Institutions, 1982, Documenting America: Assessing the Condition of Historical Records in the States, 1984; co-editor: Printing and Society in Early America, 1983; contbr. articles, revs. to profl. jours. Bd. dirs. Conservation Ctr. Art and Hist. Artifacts, 1992—2000, chmn., 1995—98; mem. J.F.K. Assassination Records Rev. Bd., 1994—98; mem. adv. com. Ctr. Jewish History, 2000—05, chmn., 2001—05. Fellow: Soc. Am. Archivists (coun. mem. 1981—85, pres. 1986—87); mem.: ALA (mem. publs. com. 1985—88, chmn. 1987—88, rare books and manuscripts sect.), Internat. Coun. Archives (mem. com. lit. and art 1993—97), Assn. Rsch. Librs. (mem. spl. collections task force 2000—06), Am. Antiquarian Soc., Orgn. Am. Historians, Bibliog. Soc. Am. (chmn. fellowship com. 1982—85), Am. Hist. Assn. (mem. profl. divsn. com. 1979—81), Grolier Club (coun. 1990—92). Office: Pa State Librs 110 Paterno Library University Park PA 16802-1808 Office Phone: 814-865-1793. Business E-Mail: wlj2@psu.edu.

JOYCE, WILLIAM ROBERT, textile machinery company executive; b. Springfield, Ohio, Mar. 18, 1936; s. Robert Emmet and Christel Beatrice (Beekman) J.; m. Betty Arlene Provonsha, Aug. 29, 1959; children: Jennifer Lynn, Janet Cathleen. BA in Bus., Calif. We. U., 1982. Cert. mfg. engring. tech., Soc. Mfg. Engrs.; registered investment securities rep. Mfg. engring. Heinicke Instruments, Hollywood, Fla., 1964—68; div. mgr. Jensen Corp., Pompano Beach, Fla., 1969—72; pres. Textiles Supply, Inc., Gerton, NC, 1972—82; v.p., gen. mgr. Tex-Fab, Inc., Gerton, 1980—82; pres. Tex-nology Sys., Inc., Gerton, 1982—90, Corrib Enterprises Ltd., Automation Cons., Dana , NC, 1981—; owner The Silver Hammer Jewelry Store Chain, NC. Co-founder Assoc. Woodland Owners N.C.; mem. Hickory Nut Gorge Vol. Fire Dept., Gerton. With USAF, 1958—64. Recipient Innovative Devel. award, 1985, award, Optimist Club, 1953—54. Mem.: NSPE, Handmade in Am. Craft Orgn., We. Carolina Entrepreneurial Coun., Mountain Comml. Lending Consortium, Am. Inst. Design and Drafting, Soc. Mfg. Engrs., Guild Master Craftsmen (internat. mem.), Profl. Engrs. N.C., NRA. Republican. Baptist. Achievements include patents in field. Home Phone: 828-685-2440; Office Phone: 828-698-5595. Business E-Mail: wrj_keystone@bellsouth.net.

JOYCE-BRADY, MARTIN FRANCIS, medical educator; b. Wilmington, Del., Sept. 25, 1953; s. Robert Lawrence and Marjorie Theresa (Martin) Brady; m. Jean Marie Joyce Brady, Sept. 17, 1977; children: Jessica, Erin, Emily. BA in Arts & Scis., U. Del., 1975; MD, U. Md., Balt., 1979. Medicine intern Boston City Hosp., 1979-80, medicine resident, 1980-82, chief med. resident, 1982-83; pulmonary fellow Pulmonary Ctr., Boston U. Sch. Medicine, 1982-87, asst. prof. medicine, 1987-96, assoc. prof. medicine, 1997—; dir. pulmonary function lab. Boston City Hosp., 1987-96; dir. ventilator care unit Jewish Meml. Hosp., Boston, 1988—, dir. pulmonary and respiratory therapy, 1996—. Contbr. articles to profl. jours.; peer reviewer articles to profl. jours. H. Fletcher Brown scholar Bank of Del., Wilmington, 1975, E.L. Trudeau scholar Am. Lung Assn., 1990-92; program project grantee on lung devel. NIH, 1991-96, 97-2002, 02—. Mem. AAAS, Am. Soc. Cell Biology, Mass. Med. Soc., Am. Thoracic Soc., Mass. Thoracic Soc. (chmn. rsch. grant com. 2003—), Am. Physiol. Soc. Democrat. Roman Catholic. Achievements include research in alternative pathway hypothesis for type I alveolar epithelial cell differentiation during lung development; lung surfactant in distributing amphipathic signal anchor proteins throughout the gas exchange surface of the lung; gamma-glutamyl-transferase and its protein isoform in an endoplasmic reticulum stress response; gamma glutamyl transferase-mediated glutathione metabolism in lung alveolar epithelial cell biology and lung redox homeostasis at the gas exchange surface of the lung; oxidant stress at birth exerts selective pressure on the expression of genes required for postnatal lung development; lung lining fluid glutathione attenuates asthma. Office: Pulmonary Ctr 80 E Concord St Boston MA 02118-2307 Office Phone: 617-638-4860. Business E-Mail: mjbrady@bu.edu.

JOYCE-NORRIS, ELAINE ROZELLE, elementary school educator; b. Chgo., Jan. 17, 1947; d. Ernest Chester Joyce and Margie Whitlock Joyce-Ziglor. BS in Elem. Edn., Winston-Salem State U., NC, 1970. Tchr. early literacy Miller Elem. Sch., Huntington, W.Va., 1970—2003. Chairperson inclusion team Miller Sch., Huntington, W.Va., 1997—2003, curriculum team, 1998—2003, local sch. improvement com., 1999—2003, coord. accelerated reader, 2000—03. Mem. Walnut Hills Cmty. Action Team, Huntington, W.Va., 2005—06; mem., rschr. African Am. History and Geneal. Soc., Mt. Airy, NC, 2004—06; U.S. literacy amb. People to People Internat., 1995—2000; mem., soloist sr. choir Bethel Temple AG Ch., Huntington, W.Va., 1984—2006, mem. missions team, 2002—06. Recipient Golden Apple Tchr.'s award, Ashland Oil Co., 1993. Mem.: ASCD, Internat. Reading Assn., People to People Internat., Pro Literacy for Adults. Avocations: interior decorating, reading, genealogy, gardening, walking. Home: 190 Baer St Huntington WV 25705-1163

JOYNER, ALEXANDRA LEIGH, cell biologist; Prof., med., molecular genetics Univ. Toronto, 1986—94; and sr. scientist, Samuel Lunenfeld Rsch. Inst. Mt. Sinai Hosp., Toronto, 1986—94; prof. cell biology, physiology, neuroscience NY Univ. Sch. Medicine; and Skirball Found. prof. genetics, and co-coordinator, developmental genetics program Skirball Inst. Biomolecular Medicine, NYU, 1994—2007; investigator Howard Hughes Med. Inst., NYU, 1997—2007; Courtney Steel chair, pediatric cancer rsch. Meml.l Sloan Kettering Cancer Ctr., NYC, 2007—. Fellow: Am. Acad. Arts & Scis. Office: Memorial Sloan-Kettering Cancer Ctr 1275 York Ave New York NY 10021 Office Phone: 212-639-3962. Business E-Mail: joynera@mskcc.org.*

JOYNER, CHRISTOPHER CLAYTON, international relations educator; b. Aberdeen, Md., May 16, 1948; s. Houston Clay Joyner and Besse Hyde Sowers; m. Nancy Douglas, Dec. 27, 1972; children: Kristin Elizabeth, Clayton Douglas. BA magna cum laude, Fla. State U., 1970, MA, 1972, MA, 1973; PhD, U. Va., 1977. Co-dir. Ctr. for Peace and Environ. Studies Fla. State U., 1971-73, instr. dept. govt., 1972-73; asst. prof. polit. sci. Muhlenberg Coll., 1977-80; vis. prof. dept. govt. and fgn. affairs U. Va., 1980-81; asst. prof. polit. sci. George Washington U., Washington, 1981-85, assoc. prof., 1985-90, prof. dept. polit. sci. and Elliott Sch. Internat. Affairs, 1991-94; prof. dept. govt. sch. fgn. svc. Georgetown U., Washington, 1995—, dir. Inst. Internat. Law and Politics, 2003—. Editl. advisor Internat. Legal Materials, 1988-90; vis. prof. government, Dartmouth Coll., 1989, 91, 93, 95, 97; profl. lectr. Sch. Advanced Internat. Studies Johns Hopkins U., 1991, 92; editl. adv. bd. Rowman & Littlefield Pub., Prentice Hall Internat. Relations series, Transnat. Pubs.; editl. adv. coun. U. Tasmania Antarctic and So. Oceans Law and Policy Paper Series. Author: Antarctica and the Law of Sea, 1992, Eagle Over the Ice: The U.S. in the Antarctic, 1997, Teaching International Law, 1997, Governing the Frozen Commons: The Antarctic Regime and

Environmental Protection, 1998, International Law in the 21st Century: Rules for Global Governance, 2005; editor: International Law of the Sea and the Future of Deep Seabed Mining, 1975, The Antarctic Legal Regime, 1988, The Persian Gulf War: Lessons for Strategy, Law and Diplomacy, 1990, United Nations Legal Order, 1995, The United Nations and International Law, 1997, Reining in Impunity for International Crimes and Serious Violations of Fundamental Human Rights, 1998, Governing the Frozen Commons: The Antarctic Regime and Environmental Protection, 1998, International Law in the 21st Century: Rules for Global Goverance, 2005; sr. editor Va. Jour. Internat. Law, 1973-77; mem. editl. bd. Internat. Studies Rev., Ocean Yearbook Internat. Law, Va. Jour. Internat. Law, Internat. Studies Notes, Internat. Studies Quarterly, Global Governance, Case Western Res. Jour. Internat. Law, Ocean Devel. and Internat. Law, Terrorism: An Internat. Jour., 1988-92, Internat. Jour. Marine and Coastal Law, Polar Record; contbr. articles to profl. jours Governing bd., bd. dirs. Acad. Coun. on the UN Sys., 1999-2002, vice-chmn. governing bd., 2001. With USAR, 1970-76. Grantee Inst. World Order, Inc., 1971-73, Ford Found., 1989-94, , Nansen Inst./Tinker Found., 1992-94, Fridtjof Nansen Inst., 1995—; rsch. fellow Antarctic Ctr. for Rsch. and Cooperation, U. Tasmania, 1994, U. Canterbury, 2001, sr. rsch. fellow Woods Hole Oceanog. Instn., 1986-87. Mem. Am. Polit. Sci. Assn., Am. Soc. Internat. Law (life, exec. com. 1984-87, 1997-2000), Antarctican Soc. (bd. dirs. 1984-87), Internat. Studies Assn. (pres. internat. law sect. 1985-86, 1997-98, mem. governing coun. 1985-86, 96-97, nat. v.p. 2004-06), Internat. Law Assn., Law of Sea Inst., Nat. Eagle Scout Assn., UN Assn., Golden Key Hon. Soc., Raven Soc. Hon., Phi Beta Kappa, Omicron Delta Kappa, Phi Kappa Phi, Pi Sigma Alpha, Phi Theta Kappa, Phi Alpha Theta. Democrat. Methodist. Avocations: jogging; autograph collecting, writing. Home: 3151 Borge St Oakton VA 22124 Office: Georgetown U Dept Govt Washington DC 20057-1034 Office Phone: 202-687-5112. Business E-Mail: joynerc@georgetown.edu.

JOYNER, DEE ANN, bank executive; b. Alton, Ill., Feb. 26, 1947; d. T. Claxton and Dorothy M. (Troeckler) Burroughs; m. Orville Joyner, Mar. 15, 1973; 1 child, Dawn L. Kotva. BA in Govt., So. Ill. U., 1971, MS in Govt., 1973; MBA, St. Louis U., 1985. Adminstrv. asst. So. Ill. U., Edwardsville, 1970-72; staff assoc. Marshall Kaplan, Gans and Kahn, Washington, 1972-73; dir. community affairs East-West Gateway Coordinating Council, St. Louis, 1973-78; exec. dir. Coro Found., St. Louis, 1978-80, St. Louis County Econ. Council, Clayton, Mo., 1985-89; planning dir. St. Louis County, 1980-84, chief of staff to county exec. Clayton, Mo., 1989-90; sr. v.p. Commerce Bank St. Louis, 1990—. Active Civil Svc. Bd., University City, Mo., 1984—93, Better Bus. Bur., 1991—93, Tax Increment Financing Commn./Indsl. Devel. Authority, University City, Mo., 1993—97, Alzheimers Assn., 1992—99, Girl Scout Coun. of Greater St. Louis, 1993—96, St. Louis Boundary Commn., 1999—2002; bd. dirs. Boys and Girls Town, 1994—2005, bd. trustees Mo., 2005—; bd. dirs. St. John's Mercy Med. Ctr., 1997—2000, Deaconess Found., 2002—, pres., 2007; trustee Thomas Aquinas Inst. Theology, 2003—; bd. dirs. Metro. Assn. Philanthropy, 2005—06, Confluence, St. Louis, 1983—89, Focus St. Louis, 1996—2002, 2003—, exec. com., 2006—, bd. chmn., 1996—98; bd. dirs. Forest Park Forever, 2003, Free Cournt, 2006—; active Delta Dental Mo., 1998—. Recipient Joseph E. Boland Meml. Outstanding Alumnus award St. Louis U., 1992, Spl. Leadership award YWCA, St. Louis, 1987, Janet Roede Ashcroft award, Alzheimers Assn., 1999, Above and Beyond Cmty. Svc. award St. Louis Bus. Jour., 2002, Harry Neill Founder's award Boys and Girls Town Mo., 2006, Chancellor's award U. Mo., St. Louis, 2006, Disting. Svc. award, 2006. Mem. Leadership St. Louis, So. Ill. U. Alumni Assn. (Alumnus of Yr. 1994), Mo Women's Forum (bd. dirs. 1989-90, 2000-02), Univ. Club (bd. dirs. 1994-97), Met. Assn. Philanthropists (bd. dirs. 2005—), Automobile Club of Mo. (exec. com. 2003—) Office: 8000 Forsyth Blvd Saint Louis MO 63105-1707 Office Phone: 314-746-7326. Business E-Mail: dee.joyner@commercebank.com.

JOYNER, J(AMES) CURTIS, judge; b. Newberry, SC, Apr. 18, 1948; s. George C. and Joan C. (Glenn) J.; m. Mildred Ann Carter, Apr. 5, 1975; children: Jennifer Christine, Nicole Marie, Jacqlyn Ann. Student, Peirce Jr. Coll., Phila., 1967; BS in Acctg., Ctrl. State U., Wilberforce, Ohio, 1971; JD, Howard U., 1974. Bar: Pa. 1975, U.S. Dist. Ct. (ea. dist.) Pa. 1981. Contr. D.C. Project, Washington, 1972-73; legal publ. specialist Fed. Register, Washington, 1974-75; asst. dist. atty. Dist. Atty. Office Chester County, West Chester, Pa., 1975-80, chief dep. dist. atty., 1980-84, 1st asst. dist. atty., 1984-87; judge Ct. of Common Pleas, 15th Jud. Dist., West Chester, 1987-92, U.S. Dist. Ct. (ea. dist.) Pa., Phila., 1992—. Mem. coun. trustees West Chester U., 1983-2000, trustee emeritus, 2001. Named Trailblazer in Law Enforcement Gov. Thornburgh, 1986; recipient Outstanding Svc. award to law enforcement Pa. Criminal Investigators, 1987, Disting. Law and Justice award County and State Detectives Assn., 1988, Donald K. Anthony Alumni Achievement Hall of Fame Ctrl. State U., 1994, Pres.' Medallion for Svc. West Chester U., 2001. Mem. Fed. Bar Assn. (hon.), Chester County Bar Assn. Avocations: sports, jazz, golf. Office: US Dist Ct Rm 8613 601 Market St Philadelphia PA 19106-1714 Office Phone: 215-597-1537.

JOYNER, JEFFREY K., lawyer; b. Lawton, Okla., May 27, 1967; BA, George Washington Univ., 1989; JD cum laude, Southwestern Univ., 1995. Bar: Calif. 1995, US Dist. Ct. Ctrl., So. & No. Calif. Assoc. Baker & Hostetler, 1994—99; ptnr., intellectual property & entertainment law practice Keats McFarland & Wilson LLP, Beverly Hills, Calif., 1999—. Contbr. articles to law jours.; editor: Southwestern Univ. Law Rev., 1994—95. Named a Rising Star, So. Calif. Super Lawyers, 2004—06; named one of America's Premier Lawyers, Forbes mag., 2006; recipient Am. Jurisprudence Book award. Mem.: State Bar Calif., Beverly Hills Bar Assn., Internat. Anti-Counterfeiting Assn. Home: Keats McFarland & Wilson LLP 9720 Wilshire Blvd Beverly Hills CA 90212 Office Phone: 310-777-3725. Office Fax: 310-860-0363. Business E-Mail: jjoyner@kmwlaw.com.

JOYNER, TOM, radio personality; b. Tuskegee, Ala., 1949; m. Donna Richardson; children from previous marriage: Thomas Jr., Oscar. BA, Tuskegee Inst. Disc jockey WRMA, Montgomery, WLOK, Memphis, KWK, St. Louis, KKDA, Dallas, morning disc jockey; afternoon disc jockey WGCI, Chgo.; host The Tom Joyner Morning Show ABC Radio Networks, 1994—. Original mem. The Commodores. Co-author: I'm Just a DJ but... It Makes Sense to Me, 2005. Founder Tom Joyner Found., HBCU Scholarship Relief Fund, 1998. Recipient Joe Loris Award, Impact Mag., Best Urban Contemporary Air Personality award, Billboard, Most Influential Black Americans, Ebony mag., 2006. Office: Tom Joyner Found 13760 Noel Rd Dallas TX 75240

JOYNER, WALTON KITCHIN, lawyer; b. Raleigh, NC, Apr. 1, 1933; s. William Thomas and Sue (Kitchin) J.; m. Lucy Holmes Graves, Sept. 23, 1955; children: Sue Carson Clark, Walton K. Jr., James Y. II. AB in Polit. Sci., U. N.C., 1955, JD with honors, 1960. Bar: N.C., cert. mediator:; lic. comml. pilot. Ptnr. Joyner & Howison, Raleigh, 1960-80, Hunton & Williams, Raleigh, 1980—. Sec., treas. N.C. R.R. Co., Raleigh, 1966; bd. dirs. United Title Ins. Co., Raleigh; bd. mgrs. Wachovia Bank, N.C., 1969-98; bd. govs. U.S. Power Squadrons, 1974-81. Assoc. editor U. N.C. Law Rev. Pres. Rehab. and Cerebral Palsy Ctr. Wake County, Raleigh, 1974; trustee St. Mary's Coll., 1990-91; bd. dirs. Peace Coll. Found., 2001—. Mem.: Law Alumni Assn. U. N.C. (bd. dirs.), Wake County Bar Assn. (chmn., bd. dirs. 1977), N.C. Bar Assn. (treas. probate sect. 1983), Carolina Country Club (pres. 1983—84, 2000—01), Order of Coif, Phi Beta Kappa. Presbyterian. Avocation: flying. Home: 815 Marlowe Rd Raleigh NC 27609-7022 Office: Hunton & Williams 1 Hannover Sq PO Box 109 Fl 14 Raleigh NC 27602-0109

JOYNER KERSEE, JACKIE (JACQUELINE JOYNER KERSEE), retired track and field athlete; b. East St. Louis, Ill., Mar. 3, 1962; d. Alfred and Mary Joyner; m. Bob Kersee, Jan. 11, 1986. BA in History, UCLA, 1985; LLD (hon.), Washington U., St. Louis, 1992, Iona Coll., 1994; DHL (hon.), Harris-Stowe State Coll., 1993, Fontbonne Coll., St. Louis, 1998, Spelman Coll., 1998, Howard U., 1999, George Washington U., St. Louis, 1999. Basketball player Richmond Rage, ABL, 1996; mem. USA Track & Field Olympic Team, 1984, 1988, 1992, 1996; ret., 2001. Pres., founder JJK & Associates., Inc. Author: (autobiography) A Kind of Grace: The Autobiography of the World's Greatest Female Athlete, 1997; co-author: A Woman's Place Is Everywhere, 1994. Founder JJK Cmty. Found., 1989 (now JJK Youth Ctr. Found., 1997-), Jackie Joyner Kersee Boys & Girls Club; chmn. St. Louis Sports Commn., 1996-2000, chmn. emeritus, 2001—. Recipient Broderick Cup, 1985, James E. Sullivan Award, 1986, Jesse Owens Award, 1986, 87, Am. Black Achievement Award, Ebony mag., 1987, 1st Female Athlete of Yr. Award, Sporting News, 1988, Jim Thorpe Award, 1993, Jackie Robinson "Robie" Award, 1994, Parenting Leader Award, Parenting Mag., Jesse Owens Humanitarian Award, 1999, Humanitarian Award, Women Sports and Fitness, Pres.'s Award, Nat. Conf. Black Mayors; named Athlete of Yr., Track & Field News, 1986, Female Athlete of Yr., AP, 1987, Female of Yr., Internat. Assn. Athletics Federations, 1994, St. Louis Ambassadors Sportswoman of Yr., Hon. Harlem Globetrotter, Woman Athlete of Century, Sports Illustrated, 1999; inductee Nat. Boys and Girls Club Hall of Fame. Achievements include winner of 4 consecutive Nat. Jr. Pentathlon Championships; winner long jump, World Championships, Rome, 1987; winner Mobil Indoor Grand Prix, 1987; winner long jump, Pan Am. Games, 1987; winner heptathlon, World Championships, Stuttgart, Germany, 1993; winner hepthathlon, Goodwill Games, NYC, 1998; winner silver medal for heptathlon, LA Olympic Games, 1984; winner gold medal for heptathlon, Seoul Olympic Games, 1988; winner gold medal for long jump, Seoul Olympic Games, 1988; winner gold medal for heptathlon, Barcelona Olympic Games, 1992; winner bronze medal for long jump, Barcelona Olympic Games, 1992; winner bronze medal for long jump, Atlanta Olympic Games, 1996; set and still holds World Record for heptathlon, Seoul Olympic Games, 9/23/1988.

JOYNES, BARBARA COLE, marketing executive; b. Rahway, NJ, Sept. 4, 1960; d. Clayton Eugene and Margaret (Fitzgerald) Cole; m. Matthew Thomas Thornhill, Oct. 15, 1983 (div. 1996); children: Allison, Clark; m. Stanley Knight Joynes III, June 24, 2000; stepchildren: Elizabeth, Alexandra. BBA in Mktg., Coll. of William and Mary, 1982. Asst. account exec. March Direct/McCann Direct, NYC, 1983-84, account exec., 1984-86, account supr., 1986-87; dir. comml. client divsn. Huntsinger & Jeffer Direct, Richmond, Va., 1987-89; v.p., account supr. The Stenrich Group, Richmond, 1989-90, sr. v.p., dir. account mgmt., 1990-92, exec. v.p., dir. account mgmt., bd. dirs., 1992-95; exec. v.p. for integrated mktg. comm., mem. exec. com. The Martin Agy., Richmond, 1995-96, exec. v.p., chief adminstrv. officer, 1996—99, pnr. integrated svcs., 2000—. Mem. profit sharing com. The Martin Agy., Richmond, 1993—2003, chair mgmt. com., 1999—2002. Exec. com. bd. trustees Richmond Children's Mus., 1992-99, dir. bd. trustees, 1991-92; area coord. William and Mary Alum Admissions Network, Richmond, 1988-98; co-chair William and Mary Class of 82 Reunion com., 1997; mem. Leadership Metro Richmond Class of 1997; book fair chair Maybeury Elem. Sch., 1997—2000; cookie chair Brownie Troop #292, Girl Scouts U.S., 1996-98, bd. dirs. Commonwealth Girl Scouts Coun., 1999-2002; bd. dirs. Arts Coun. Richmond, 1998-2002; bd. dirs. Leadership Metro Richmond, 1998—2004, mem. exec. com., 1999-2004, chair devel. com., chair mem. programs com., sec. awareness/pub. rels. com., mem. recruitment com.; bd. dirs. YWCA of Richmond, 2001-, v.p., 2003-05, pres. 2005-; mem. Direct Mktg. Agy. Leaders Coun. Recipient Silver Echo award Direct Mktg. Assn., 1991, 94, Gold Echo award, 2003, 05, Richmond Area Marketer of Yr. award Am. Mktg. Assn., 1992, 93, 94, Gold Effie award, 1992, Silver Effie award, 2000, YWCA Outstanding Woman award, 1999. Mem. Greater Richmond C. of C. (mem. exec. com. 2002-04, bd. dirs. 2000—), Willow Oaks Country Club, Farmington Country Club. Avocations: travel, reading, golf. Office: The Martin Agy One Shockoe Plz Richmond VA 23219-4132

JOYNT, ROBERT JAMES, academic administrator, physician; b. Le Mars, Iowa, Dec. 22, 1925; MD, 1952, PhD, 1963. Diplomate Am. Bd. Psychiatry and Neurology. Intern Royal Victoria Hosp., Montreal, Que., Canada, 1952—53; chief neurology Strong Meml. Hosp., Rochester, NY, 1966—84; assoc. U. Iowa, Iowa City, 1957—58, asst. prof. neurology, 1958—61, assoc. prof., 1961-66; prof. neurology U. Rochester, 1966—, chmn. dept., 1966—84, Disting. Univ. prof., 1997; dean U. Rochester Sch. Medicine and Dentistry, 1984—89, v.p., vice provost for health affairs, 1989—94. Fulbright scholar, Cambridge U., 1953—54, USPHS fellow, 1954—57. Fellow: AAAS; mem.: AMA (chief editor Arch Neurology 1982—97), Am. Bd. Psychiatry and Neurology (dir. 1973—80, v.p. 1978, pres. 1979), Am. Acad. Neurology (past pres.), Am. Neurol. Assn. (past pres.), Inst. Medicine, Royal Soc. Medicine, Am. Electroencephalographic Soc. Office: U Rochester Sch Medicine and Dentistry PO Box 673 Rochester NY 14642-0001 Business E-Mail: robert_joynt@urmc.rochester.edu.

JOYNT, STEPHEN W., financial services company executive; BBA, U. Ariz. Joined Fitch, 1989; pres., COO Fitch IBCA, 1997; pres., CEO Fitch Ratings, 2002—; CEO Fitch Group, Inc., Algorithmics. Office: Fitch Ratings 1 State Street Plz New York NY 10004 Office Phone: 212-908-0500. Office Fax: 212-480-4435.*

JU, JIANN-WEN (WOODY JU), mechanics educator, researcher; b. Taiwan, 1958; s. Jiang and Kwai J.; m. Mali J., 1985; children: Derek, Tiffany. BS, Nat. (Taipei) Taiwan U., 1980; MS, U. Calif., Berkeley, 1983, PhD, 1986. Registered profl. engr., Calif., Ariz. Teaching asst. U. Calif., Berkeley, 1983-84, rsch. asst., 1984-86, lectr., 1986, postdoctoral rsch. engr., 1986-87; asst. prof. Princeton (NJ) U., 1987-93; assoc. prof. UCLA, 1993-98, prof., 1998—, chmn., 1999—2002, chmn., structural engr., 2001—. Cons. Air Force Engrng. and Svcs. Ctr., Panama City, Fla., 1990—, Titan R&T, Chatsworth, Calif., Kasdan and Simonds, Irvine, Calif., Karagozian and Case, LA, Miller Law, Irvine, Calif.; rev. panel NSF, Washington, 1991—; conf. co-chair 7th World Congress Computational Mechanics, LA, 2006; sci. program com. 9th Nat. Congress Computational Mechanics, San Francisco, 2007; chmn., organizer of 40 symposia; lectr., presenter in field. Author, editor: Damage Mechanics in Engineering Materials, 1990, Recent Advances in Damage Mechanics and Plasticity, 1992, Damage Mechanics and Localization, 1992, Homogenization and Constitutive Modeling, 1993, Micromechanics and Inelasticity of Metal Matrix Composites, 1994, Damage Mechanics in Composites, 1994, Numerical Methods in Structural Mechanics, 1995, Damage Mechanics in Engineering Materials, 1998; mem. editl. bd. Internat. Jour. Damage Mechanics, 1992; editor: Internat. Jour. Damage Mechanics, 2006; contbr. articles to profl. jours. Fed. and indsl. rsch. grantee U.S. Govt., U.S. cos., Japanese cos., 1987—; recipient Presdl. Young Investigator award NSF, 1991. Fellow: ASME (com. mem. 1989—, assoc. editor Jour. Engrng. Materials Tech., Jour. Applied Mechanics 1995—), ASCE (control group 1989-93, Walter L. Huber Civil Engring. Rsch. prize 1997), US Assn. Computational Mechanics (at-large mem., exec. com. 2006-); mem: Am. Acad. Mechanics, Am. Concrete Inst. (chmn. com. 446 fracture mechanics 2004—), Soc. Engring. Sci., Internat. Assn. Computational Mechanics. Office: UCLA Dept Civil Engring Los Angeles CA 90095-1593 Business E-Mail: juj@ucla.edu.

JU, SE-JONG, research scientist; s. Jae-Won Ju and Jung-Ja Park Ju; m. Na Young Kim, Jan. 6, 1996; children: Harrie, Ji-Sue, Elizabeth Lee-Ae. PhD, U. Md., College Park, Md., 2000. Rsch. scientist Chesapeake Biol. Lab., Solomons, Md., 2000—; lectr. Coll. So. Md., La Plata, Md., 2006; invited scientist Korean Ocean Rsch. and Devel. Inst., Seoul, Republic of Korea, 2006—. Reviewer (manuscripts) Marine Ecology Progress Series. Grantee, NOAA, 2000. Mem.: Am. Geophys. Union (assoc.). Achievements include research in biochemical methods to estimate age of crustaceans biochemical approches. Office: Kordi Ansan PO Box 29 Seoul 425-600 Republic of Korea Home Phone: 82-31-458-4282; Office Phone: 82-31-400-7684. Office Fax: 82-31-418-8772. Personal E-mail: sejong-ju@gmail.com. Business E-Mail: sjju@kordi.re.kr.

JUANG, FRED (BIING-HWANG JUANG), engineering educator; With Speech Comms. Rsch. Lab., Signal Technology, Inc.; mem. Acoustics Rsch. Dept. Bell Labs., dir. acoustics and speech rsch., 1996—2001; dir. multimedia technologies rsch. Avaya Labs., 2001—02; joined Sch. Elec. and Computer Engring., Ga. Inst. Tech., Atlanta, 2002, Motorola Found. chair prof., Ga, Rsch. Alliance Eminent Scholar. Contbr. articles to profl. jours. Fellow: IEEE (Third Millennium Medal 2000); mem.: NAE. Office: Sch Elec & Computer Engrig Ga Inst Tech 250 14th St, NW, Rm 341 Atlanta GA 30318 Office Phone: 404-894-6618. Office Fax: 404-894-8363. E-mail: juang@ece.gatech.edu.

JUAREZ, ANTONIO, psychotherapist, consultant, counselor, educator; b. El Paso, Tex., Nov. 6, 1952; s. Juan Antonio and Amelia (Rivas) J. BS in Psychology, U. Tex.-El Paso, 1976, MA in Clin. Psychology, 1982; postgrad., N.Mex. State U., 1987—, Calif. Coast U., 1990—. Cert. counselor; cert. diplomate, Am. Psychotherapy Assn., lic. profl. counselor, Tex., PhD of Martial Arts, Ea. USA Internat. Coll. Martial Arts, Pittsburgh, 2000. Caseworker asst. El Paso Mental Health Ctr., 1978-79, caseworker III, 1982-83; clin. specialist S.W. Mental Health Ctr., Las Cruces, N.Mex., 1979-80; therapist, trainer S.W. Cmty. House, El Paso, 1980-81; psychol. cons. El Paso Guidance Ctr., 1981-82, psychotherapist, 1983—, dir. N.E. svcs.; pvt. practice El Paso, 1987—. Mem. Nat. Bd. for Cert. Counselors; dir. Cross-Cultural Counseling Ctr., 1988-04; asst. prof. psychology El Paso C.C., 1988-90, faculty coord. social scis., counselor, cons.; cons. Citizens and Students Together, El Paso, 1983—; group facilitator, Tai Chi Chuan instr. Sun Valley Regional Hosp., El Paso, Tex., 1988; psychotherapist, treatment team coord. El Paso State Ctr., 1997—; adj. prof. counseling Webster U., Ft. Bliss, Tex., 1995—. Mem. Latin Am. com. N.Mex. State U., 1985. Served with USAF, 1972-76. Recipient Faculty Achievement award, El Paso CC, 2007. Fellow Am. Assn. Integrative Medicine, US-Mex. Border Health Assn., El Paso Psychol. Assn., Tex. Assn. Counseling and Devel., Tex. Assn. Children of Alcoholics, Nat. Acad. Clin. Mental Health Counselors, Nat. Istn. Staff and Orgnl. Devel, Ea. US Martial Arts Assn. (Black Belt Hall of Fame 1996, Master of Wushu 2000), Ea. US Internat. Martial Arts Assn. (named Man of Yr. 2003, Black Belt Hall of Fame 2003), Golden Key. Democrat. Roman Catholic. Avocations: martial arts, playing stringed instruments. Home: PO Box 1493 Santa Teresa NM 88008-1493 Office: Cross-Cultural Counseling Ctr 2112 Trawood Dr # 3B El Paso TX 79935-3318 Office Phone: 915-831-4066. Business E-Mail: antonioj@epcc.edu.

JUBINSKA, PATRICIA ANN, ballet instructor, choreographer, artist, anthropologist, archaeologist; b. Norfolk, Va. d. Joseph John and Lucy (Babey) Topping; children: Vanessa Meredith, Courtney Hilary. Student, Md. State Ballet Sch., Sch. Am. Ballet, NYC; BA, R.I. Coll.; MA, Wesleyan U.; PhD, Union Inst., 1999. Mem. N.Y.C. Ballet; freelance artist Chamber Ballet of L.A., San Antonio Ballet, Md. State Ballet; artistic dir. Blackstone Valley Ballet, Harrisville, RI, 1983, Am. Ballet, Pascoag, RI, 1984—92; asst. artistic dir. Odessa Ukrainian Dancers, Woonsocket, RI, 1991—92; freelance guest artist, 1992—; mem. Mandrivka Dancers of Boston, 1993—; mem. faculty Fine Arts West Warwick Sch., 1995—; mem. faculty Roger Williams U., 2000—. Avocation: equestrian. Home: 110 Gold Mine Rd Chepachet RI 02814 Personal E-mail: pajubinska@aol.com.

JUCEAM, ROBERT E., lawyer; b. NYC, June 16, 1940; s. Benjamin T. and Amelia B. (Spatz) Juceam; m. Eleanor Pam, May 24, 1970; children: Daniel, Jacquelyn, Gregory. AB cum laude, Columbia U., 1961, LLB, 1964, JD, 1972; LLM, NYU, 1966. Bar: NY 1965, US Dist. Ct. (so. and ea. dists.) NY 1966, US Tax Ct. 1968, US Ct. Appeals (2d cir.) 1967, US Supreme Ct. 1971, US Ct. Appeals (5th cir.) 1978, US Ct. Appeals (DC cir.) 1980, US Ct. Appeals (7th cir.) 1989, US Ct. Appeals (9th cir.) 1999. Law clk. US Dist. Ct., NY, 1964-66; assoc. Fried, Frank, Harris, Shriver & Jacobson, NYC, 1966-73, ptnr., 1974—2006, of counsel, 2006—. Bd. dirs. Nat. Network Def. Right to Counsel, Inc., 1985—89, Lawyers Com. Human Rights, 1986—94, Bar Assurance and Reins. Ltd., 1991—2006, Am. Immigration Law Found., 1987—, pres., 1991—2000, treas., 2000—03, sec., 2004—; gen. counsel US Supreme Ct. Hist. Soc., 1995—, trustee, 1999—; mem. arbitration panel US Dist. Ct. (ea. dist.) NY, 1986—; mem. comml. and constrn. panels Am. Arbitration Assn., 1972—94; dir. civil rights Washington Lawyers Com., 1996—99; bd. advisors DC Bar Found., 1996—2001; treas., bd. dirs. Pro Bono Inst., 1997—. Contbr. articles to profl. jours. Trustee Mex.-Am. Legal Def. and Edn. Fund, 1986—90, chmn. program and planning com., 1988—90; mem. adv. com. task force racial, gender and minority discrimination US Ct. Appeals (2d cir.), 1994—96; bd. dirs. Appleseed Found., Inc., 1997—99; bd. advisors Atlantic Legal Found., 2001—05, bd. dirs., 2005—; mem. Immigration Coalition Leadership Coun. NY, 2007—. Recipient Lester Zazuly medal, James Madison HS, 1958, Alumni Achievement award, Columbia Coll., 1961, Edward Foxx prize, 1961, Maldef Corp. Responsibility award, 1993, Valerie J. Kantor award for Extraordinary Achievement, 1997, Am. Immigration Law Found. hon. fellow and Founder's award, 1989, Lifetime Achievement award, Ctr. Human Rights and Constl. Law, 1993, Pro Bono Svc. award, Legal Aid Soc. NY, 2003—04, 2004—05. Fellow: ABA (mem. com. environ. controls sect. banking 1983—86, ho. dels. 1983—, coord. com. immigration law 1984—87, chmn. com. immigration sect. litig. 1985—90, vice chmn. com. constrn., sec. gen. practice 1989—90, chmn. 1989—92, immigration pro bono adv. task force 1992—98, mem. standing com. lawyers pub. svc. responsibility 1993—98, coun. fund justice and edn. 1994—2000, vice chmn. 1995—96, chmn. major gifts com. 1997—98, adv. mem. 2000—02, coun. fund justice and edn. 2003—06, mem. com. Ctr. Profl. Responsibility 2004—06, Pro Bono award 1992), NY Star Bar Found., Am. Bar Found. (life), Royal Philatelic Soc. New Zealand; mem.: German Philatelic Soc., Assn. Fed. Def. Lawyers, Def. Rsch. Inst., NY County Lawyers Assn. (reporter NY Equitable Distgn. Law Proposals 1968, bd. dirs. 1996—98), Am. Immigration Lawyers Assn. (chmn. NY chpt. 1971—72, bd. gov. 1971—, pres. 1982—83, editor Ann. Symposium Handbook 1985—88, gen. counsel 1986—91, assoc. editor 1989—90, liaison to ABA commn. nonlawyer practice 1993—94, Edith Lowenstein Meml. award 1981, Pro Bono award 1992), Am. Bar Endowment, Nat. Assn. Criminal Def. Lawyers (co-chmn. com. immigration 1988—90), Am. Judicature Soc. (life), Nat. Conf. Bar Pres. (assoc.), Assn. Bar City of NY (mem. com. trademarks and unfair competition 1983—86, mem. com. immigration 1986—89, mem. com. profl. and jud. ethics 1989—92, mem. com. Human Rights Law 1994—96), NY State Bar Assn., City Bar Fund Justice (bd. dirs. 2004—), City Bar Justice Ctr. (formerly Assn. Bar NYC Fund) (bd. dirs. 2004—), Internat. Bar Assn. (chmn. sect. gen. practice com. bus. migration 1987—88), Soc. Sachems Columbia Coll., Italy and Colonies Philat. Soc. Gt. Britain (life), Cow Neck Peninsula Hist. Soc. (life), Internat. Fedn. Postcard Dealers, Am. Philatelic Congress, Austrian Philatelic Soc., Am. Helvetia Philatelic Soc. (life), Am. Philat. Soc. (life), India House Club, Jack Knight Soc. (life), Alpha Epsilon Pi.

Home: 106 Hemlock Rd Manhasset NY 11030-1214 Office: Fried Frank Harris Shriver & Jacobson 1 New York Plz Ste 2500 New York NY 10004-1901 Office Phone: 212-859-8040. Business E-Mail: jucearo@ffhsj.com.

JUCKEM, WILFRED PHILIP, manufacturing executive; b. Sheboygan, Wis., Apr. 27, 1915; s. Arvin M. and Martha (Henning) J.; m. Dorothy Iris Dean, Dec. 8, 1941; children— Jean Audrey, Philip Dean. Grad., Sheboygan Bus. Coll., 1934. With Jenkins Machine Co., Sheboygan Falls, Wis., 1933-34, Kohler of Kohler, Wis., 1934-42, Rock Island (Ill.) Arsenal, 1942-45; with Eagle Signal Corp., Moline, Ill., 1947-63, v.p. mfg., 1958-63; asst. to pres. E.W. Bliss Co., Canton, Ohio, 1963-64, adminstrv. v.p., 1964-66, v.p. press div., 1966-67, v.p. corporate devel., 1967-68; v.p., div. mgr. E.W. Bliss Co. (Eagle Signal div.), 1968-77; chmn. bd. Sears Mfg. Co., Davenport, Iowa, 1977-86. Bd. dirs. Long Mfg. Chmn. bd. dirs. Davenport Osteo. Hosp., 1979-80, chmn., 1980-82; bd. dirs. Ridgecrest Retirement Village. Recipient Honorary Alumnus award St. Ambrose Coll., Davenport. Mem. Nat. Elec. Mfrs. Assn. (chmn. emeritus traffic control systems sect. 1972-77), Am. Ordnance Assn. (pres. Iowa-Ill. chpt. 1975-76), Assn. Employers Quad Cities (dir., past pres.). Lutheran. Home: Ridgecrest Village Apt E130 4130 Northwest Blvd Davenport IA 52806-4243

JUDD, ASHLEY, actress; b. Granada Hills, Calif., Apr. 19, 1968; d. Michael Ciminella and Naomi Judd; m. Dario Franchitti, Dec. 12, 2001. BA in French, U. Ky., 2007. Actor: (films) Kuffs, 1992, Ruby in Paradise, 1993, Smoke, 1995, Heat, 1995, The Passion of Darkly Noon, 1996, A Time To Kill, 1996, Normal Life, 1996, The Locusts, 1997, Kiss the Girls, 1997, Simon Birch, 1998, Eye of the Beholder, 1999, Double Jeopardy, 1999, Where the Heart Is, 2000, Someone Like You, 2001, High Crimes, 2002, Divine Secrets of the Ya-Ya Sisterhood, 2002, Frida, 2002, Twisted, 2004, De-Lovely, 2004, Come Early Mornings, 2006, Bug, 2006; (TV films) Till Death Us Do Part, 1992, Norma Jean & Marilyn, 1996, The Ryan Interview, 2000; (TV series) Sisters, 1991—93, Star Trek: The Next Generation, 1991. Spokesperson Youth Aids Internat. Named One of the 50 Most Beautiful People In The World, People Magazine, 1996. Mem.: Phi Beta Kappa. Office: William Morris Agy 1 William Morris Pl Beverly Hills CA 90212-2775

JUDD, BARBARA ANNE, history educator, counselor; b. Howell, Mich., May 6, 1932; d. Francis Glen and Margaret Charlotte Wessinger; m. Bernard Hulett Judd; children: Stephen O., Sarah A. Lavy. BA, Mich. State U., East Lansing, 1955; MA, Mich. State U., 1959; Dr.Arts, Carnegie Mellon U., Pitts., 1972. Cert. tchr. Mo. Grad. asst. Mich. State U., East Lansing, 1955—57; tchr. history Haslatt (Mich.) Pub. Schs., 1957—59, Madison (Wis.) Pub. Schs., 1959—64, Pitts. Pub. Schs., 1965—66; rschr., writer, cons. Carnegie Mellon U., Pitts., 1967—71; tchr., dept. chair Loretto in Kansas City, Mo., 1972—77; tchr. history, coll. counselor Pembroke Hill Sch., Kansas City, 1977—. Mem. legal bd. Loretto in Kansas City, 1978—81. Co-author: Living in Urban America, 1974; co-editor: Meanings of History, 1971; contbr. articles to profl. jours.; co-editor: Women in American History, 1975. Fellow, Johnson Found., Madison, 1962; grantee Curriculum grantee, Sunset Hill Sch., Kansas City, 1980. Mem.: Ind. Schs. Assn. Ctrl. States (bd. dirs. 1980—83), Nat. Coun. Social Studies, Phi Alpha Theta, Tau Sigma, Kappa Delta Pi, Phi Kappa Phi. Avocations: gardening, reading. Home: 7115 Summit Kansas City MO Office: Pembroke Hill school 5121 State Line Rd Kansas City MO 64114-1184 Business E-Mail: bjudd1@kc.rr.com.

JUDD, BRIAN RAYMOND, physicist; b. Chelmsford, Eng., Feb. 13, 1931; s. Harry and Edith (Saltmarsh) J. BA, Brasenose Coll., Oxford U., 1952, MA, D.Phil., Brasenose Coll., Oxford U., 1955. Fellow Magdalen Coll., Oxford U., 1955-62; instr. U. Chgo., 1957-58; assoc. prof. U. Paris, 1962-64; staff mem. Lawrence Radiation Lab., Berkeley, Calif., 1964-66; prof. physics Johns Hopkins U., Balt., 1966-96, chmn. dept., 1979-84, Gerhard H. Dieke prof., 1992-96, prof. emeritus, 1997-98, Gerhard H. Dieke prof. emeritus, 1998—. Vis. Erskine fellow U. Canterbury, Christchurch, New Zealand, 1968; vis. fellow Australian Nat. U., Canberra, 1975; hon. fellow Brasenose Coll., Oxford U., 1983—. Author: Operator Techniques in Atomic Spectroscopy, 1963, reprinted, 1998, Second Quantization and Atomic Spectroscopy, 1967, (with J.P. Elliott) Topics in Atomic and Nuclear Theory, 1970, Angular Momentum Theory For Diatomic Molecules, 1975. Recipient Spedding award for rare-earth rsch. Rhone-Poulenc, Inc., 1988. Fellow Am. Phys. Soc. Office: Johns Hopkins U Dept Physics and Astronomy Baltimore MD 21218

JUDD, BRUCE DIVEN, architect; b. Pasadena, Calif., Sept. 28, 1947; s. David Lockhart and Martha Leah (Brown) J.; m. Diane Reinbolt, Feb. 4, 1976 (div. Oct. 1985); 1 child, Ian David. BArch, U. Calif., Berkeley, 1970, MArch, 1971. Registered arch., Calif., Nev.; cert. Nat. Coun. Archtl. Registration Bds. Designer Ribera and Sue Landscape Archs., Oakland, Calif., 1968-70, Page Clowdsley & Baleix, San Francisco, 1971-75; v.p. Charles Hall Page Assocs., San Francisco, 1975-80; prin. Archtl. Resources Group, San Francisco, 1980—. Mem. adv. bd. fed. rehab. guidelines program Nat. Inst. Bldg. Scis., HUD, 1979-80; mem. city-wide survey planning com. City of Oakland, Calif., 1979-80; cons. Nat. Main St. Program, Washington. Bd. dirs., co-founder Oakland Heritage Alliance, 1980-85; mem. Calif. Hist. Resources Commn., 1982-86, chmn., 1983-85; bd. dirs. Preservation Action, Washington, 1982-85, 90—, Friends of Terra Cotta, 1981-86, Berkeley Archtl. Heritage Assn., 1993—; mem. bd. advisors Nat. Trust for Hist. Preservation, Washington, 1981-90, advisor emeritus, 1990—; bd. trustees Calif. Preservation Found., San Francisco, 1985—, v.p., 1990-92, trustee, 1990—; active Calif. State Hist. Bldg. Safety Bd., 1991-93, also others. Recipient Excellence Honor award State of Calif., Excellence award in archtl. conservation, Spl. Restoration award Sunset Mag.; named Preservationist of Yr., Calif. Preservation Found., 1993. Fellow AIA (preservation officer No. Calif. chpt. 1978-81, hist. resources com. Calif. coun. 1979-80, nat. hist. resources com. 1981—, chmn. 1981-82); mem. Internat. Assn. for Preservation Tech. (bd. dirs. 1983-85), Park Hills Homes Assn. (chmn. archtl. com. 1992—), U.S./Internat. Coun. Monuments and Sites. Office: Archtl Resources Group Pier 9 The Embarcadero San Francisco CA 94111

JUDD, DENNIS L., lawyer; b. Provo, Utah, June 27, 1954; s. Derrel Wesley and Leila (Lundquist) J.; m. Carol Lynne Chilberg, May 6, 1977; children: Lynne Marie, Amy Jo, Tiffany Ann, Andrew, Jacquelyn Nicole. BA in Polit. Sci. summa cum laude, Brigham Young U., 1978, JD, 1981. Bar: Utah 1981, U.S. Dist. Ct. Utah 1981. Assoc. Nielson & Senior, Salt Lake City and Vernal, Utah, 1981-83; dep. county atty. Uintah County, Vernal, 1982-84; ptnr. Bennett & Judd, Vernal, 1983-88; county atty. Daggett County, Utah, 1985-89, 91-99, 2000—07; pvt. practice Vernal, 1988—; prosecutor City of Naples, Naples, 1996-99; legal counsel Uintah County Sch. Dist., 1996—2007; city atty. Naples City, Utah, 1999—, Vernal City, Utah, 2000—; atty. City of Vernal, 2000—; legal counsel Uintah County Econ. Devel. Dist., 2007—. Mem. governing bd. Uintah Basin applied Tech. Ctr., 1991-95, v.p., 1993-94, pres., 1994-95. Chmn. bd. adjustment Zoning and Planning Bd., Naples, 1982-91, 94—; mem. Naples City Coun., 1982-91; mayor pro tem City of Naples, 1983-91; legis. v.p. Naples PTA, 1988-90; sec. Friends of Utah Field House of Natural History, 2000—; v.p. Uintah Dist. PTA Coun., 1990-92; mem. resolution com. Utah League Cities and Towns, 1985-86, small cities com., 1985-86; trustee Uintah Sch. Dist. Found., 1988-97, 2005-, vice chmn., 1991-93; mem. Uintah County Sch. Dist. Bd. Edn., 1991-95, v.p., 1991-92, pres., 1992-95; chmn. Uintah County Rep. Conv., 1998. Hinkley scholar Brigham Young U., 1977; named Oustanding County Atty. Utah, 2003. Mem. Utah Bar Assn., Uintah Basin Bar Assn., Statewide Assn. Prosecutors, Vernal C. of C. Republican. Mem. Lds Ch. Avocations: hunting, photography, lapidary. Home: 460 E 1555 S Naples UT 84078 Office: 497 S Vernal Ave Vernal UT 84078 Office Phone: 435-789-7038. Personal E-mail: judd@easilink.com.

JUDD, GEORGE R., wholesale distribution executive; B mktg., We. Conn. State Univ., 1984. V.p. sw region Georgia-Pacific Corp., 1999—2000, v.p. no. & midwest regions, dist. div., 2000—02, v.p. sales & ea. region ops., 2002—04; pres., COO BlueLinx Holdings, Atlanta, 2004—. Past chmn. Nat. Lumber & Bldg. Materials Dealers Assn. Office: BlueLinx Holdings 4300 Wildwood Pkwy Atlanta GA 30339*

JUDD, JOEL STANTON, lawyer; b. Denver, Sept. 10, 1951; s. E. James and Eleanore Judd. BA, New Coll., 1973; JD, U. Denver, 1976. Bar: Colo. 1976, U.S. Dist. Ct. Colo. 1976, U.S. Ct. Appeals (10th cir.) 1976, U.S. Supreme Ct. 1980. Assoc. Feder & Morris, Denver, 1976-77, Reckseen & Lau, Northglenn, Colo., 1977-82; pvt. practice Denver, 1982—; state rep. Ho. Dist. 5, Colo., 2003—, chmn. fin. com., mem. appropriations Com. Mem. Colo. Bar Assn., Denver Bar Assn. (chair intraprofl. com. 1985-90), Colo. Trial Lawyers Assn., Allied Jewish Fedn. (chair young profls. div. 1984-86, chair Denver Jewish cmty. Israel Independence Day celebration 1987), Optimists (pres. 1980-83). Democrat. Avocations: skiing, river rafting. Home: 2904 W 24th Ave Denver CO 80211-4702 Office: # 100 2222 S Albion St Denver CO 80222-4928

JUDD, O'DEAN P., physicist; b. Austin, Minn., May 26, 1937; MS in Physics, UCLA, 1961, PhD in Physics, 1968. Staff physicist and project dir. Hughes Rsch. Lab., Malibu, Calif., 1959-67; postdoctoral fellow UCLA Dept. Physics, 1968-69; researcher Hughes Rsch. Lab., Malibu, Calif., 1969-72; researcher, group leader Los Alamos (N.Mex.) Nat. Lab., 1972-82, chief scientist for def. rsch. and applications, 1981-87, energy and environ. chief scientist, lab. fellow, 1990-93, ind. tech. advisor and cons., 1995—; chief scientist Strategic Def. Initiative Orgn., Washington, 1987-90; nat. intelligence officer for sci. and tech. Nat. Intelligence Coun., Washington, 1993-94. Mem. numerous govt. coms. related to sci. and tech., def. and nat. security policy; adj. prof. physics U. N.Mex., Albuquerque; mem. sci. adv. bd. USAF, 1999-2003. Patentee in sci. and tech.; contbr. numerous articles to sci. and def.-related jours. Fellow IEEE, AAAS, Los Alamos Nat. Lab. Inst. Advanced Engring.; mem. Am. Phys. Soc. Office: Los Alamos Nat Lab B241 Los Alamos NM 87544-2648

JUDD, SCOTT RANDALL, information technology manager; s. John Franklin Judd and Glenda Jean Campbell; m. Kathleen D'Arcy, Mar. 17, 2001; children: Darcy Isabelle, Mikayla Kathleen. BA in Econs., Va. Inst. Tech. and State U., Blacksburg, 1995; MBA, Goldey Beacom Coll., Wilmington, Del., 2005. Sr. bus. systems analyst MBNA Am., Wilmington, 1997—2006; info. sys. cons. JPMorgan Chase, Wilmington, 2006—. Clk. Bd. Election, Middletown, Del., 2000—05; advisor KC, Middletown, 2006—06. Mem.: Am. Mensa (assoc.). Democrat. Roman Catholic. Home Phone: 302-593-1490. Personal E-mail: vtjudd@atlanticbb.net.

JUDD, WILLIAM ROBERT, engineering geologist, educator; b. Denver, Aug. 16, 1917; s. Samuel and Lillian (Israelske) J.; m. Rachel Elizabeth Douglas, Apr. 18, 1942; children: Stephanie (Mrs. Chris Wadley), Judith (Mrs. John Soden), Dayna (Mrs. Erick Grandmason), Pamela, Connie. AB, U. Colo., 1941, postgrad., 1941-50. Registered profl. engr., Colo., engring. geologist, Oreg. Engring. geologist Colo. Water Conservation Bd., 1941-42; supervisory engring. geologist Denver & Rio Grande Western R.R., Colo. and Utah, 1942-44; head geology sect. No. 1, acting dist. geologist-Alaska U.S. Bur. Reclamation, Office of Chief Engr., Denver, 1945-60; head basing tech. group RAND Corp., Santa Monica, Calif., 1960—66; prof. rock mechanics Purdue U., Lafayette, Ind., 1966-87, head geotech. engring., 1976-86; tech. dir. Purdue U. Underground Excavation and Rock Properties Info. Center, 1972-79, prof. emeritus civil engring., 1988—. Geotech. cons., U.S., Mexico, Cuba, Honduras, Greece, 1950-; geoscience editor Am. Elsevier Pub. Co., 1967-71; chmn. panel on ocean scis. Com. on Instl. Cooperation, 1971-85; founder and chmn. Nat. Acad. Sci. U.S. Nat. Com. on Rock Mechanics, 1963-69, co-chmn. panel on rsch. requirements, 1977-81, chmn. panel on awards, 1972-82; mem. U.S. Army Adv. Bd. on Mountain and Arctic Warfare, 1956-62, USAF Sci. Adv. Bd. Geophysics Panel Study Group, 1964-67; com. on safety dams NRC, 1977-78, 82-83; Nat. dir. Nat. Ski Patrol System, Inc., 1956-62; Alex du Toit Meml. lectr., S.Africa and Rhodesia, 1967; owner Rayanbill Galleries, 1986—2007. Author: (with E.F. Taylor) Ski Patrol Manual, 1956, (with D. Krynine) Principles of Engineering Geology and Geotechnics, 1957, Sitzmarks or Safety, 1960; editor: Rock Mechanics Research, 1966, State of Stress in the Earth's Crust, 1964; co-editor: Physical Properties of Rocks and Minerals, 1981; editor-in-chief: Engring. Geology, 1972-92, hon. editor, 1996—. Recipient Merit award U.S. Bur. Reclamation, 1957, Spl. Rsch. award NRC, 1982; named to Colo. Ski Hall of Fame, 1983; named hon. life mem. Nat. Ski Patrol System, Inc., 1988. Fellow ASCE, Geol. Soc. Am. (Disting. Practice award engring. geology divsn. 1989), South African Inst. Mining and Metallurgy; mem. Assn. Engring. Geologists (hon.), Internat. Assn. Engring. Geologists (Hans Cloos medal 1994), India Soc. Engring. Geology (life), Ind. Acad. Scis., U.S. Com. on Large Dams (exec. coun. 1977-83, com. on earthquakes 1976-90), U.S. Ski Assn. (hon. life), U.S. Recreational Ski Assn. (hon. life). Home and Office: 1051 Cumberland Ave West Lafayette IN 47906 Office Phone: 765-464-2255. Personal E-mail: williamjudd@verizon.net.

JUDD, WYNONNA ELLEN (CHRISTINA CLAIRE CIMINELLA), vocalist, musician; b. Ashland, Ky., May 30, 1964; d. Larry and Naomi Judd, Michael Ciminella (Stepmother); m. Arch Kelly, 1996 (div. 1998); children: Elijah, Grace; m. Dan R. Roach, Nov. 2003 (separated Feb. 2007); 1 child, Zac Roach. Vocalist, musician, entertainer (country duo) The Judds, 1979-1991, signed with RCA, 1984; songs include Had a Dream, 1983, Mama, He's Crazy, 1984, Why Not Me, 1984, Girls Night Out, 1985, Love Is Alive, 1985, Have Mercy, 1985, Rockin' with the Rhythm, 1986, Grandpa, 1986, Let Me Tell You About Love, 1989, She Is His Only Need, 1992, No One Else on Earth, 1992, and many others; albums include Wynonna & Naomi, 1983, Why Not Me, 1984, Rockin' With the Rhythm, 1986, Heartland, 1987, Greatest Hits, 1988, River of Time, 1989, Love Can Build a Bridge, 1990, Greatest Hits Vol. 2, 1991, (video) Their Final Concert, 1992, The Judds Collection, 1983-1990, 1992, Classic Gold, 1992, This Country's Rockin', 1993, (video) Naomi & Wynonna-The Farewell Tour, 1993, Christmas With The Judds & Alabama, 1994, In Concert, 1995, The Judds Reunion: Live, 2000, Number One Hits, 2000, Christmas Time with the Judds, 2003; (solo albums) Wynonna, 1992, Tell Me Why, 1993, Revelations, 1996, Collection, 1997, The Other Side, 1997, New Day Dawning, 2000 (also co-prodr.), What the World Needs Now Is Love, 2003, (CD and DVD) Her Story: Scences From a Lifetime, 2005, A Classic Christmas, 2006; solo duet (with Clint Black) A Bad Goodbye, 1993; co-author: (with Naomi Judd) Love Can Build a Bridge, 1993 (NY Times Best Seller)(also TV movie, 1995), Coming Home to Myself: A Memoir, 2005 (NY Times Best Seller); host Am. Music Awards, 1993, CBS TV Spl., 1996, Nashville Star, 2006-; guest appearances Oprah Winfrey, Touched By An Angel, 1999, Hope & Faith, 2005; performer for the Pope, 1993, Superbowl, 1994, Daytona 500, 1998, MTV-Music In High Places, Italy, 2000, Opening Ceremonies 2002 Paralympic Games, Salt Lake City, MusiCares Person of Yr, 2004, Predident Bush, 2001, The White House and Pentagon, 2004, Good Morning Am. Songs for Tsunami, 2005; (voice-soundtrack) Prince of Egypt (song Freedom), 1998, Lilo & Stitch (Burnin' Love), 2002; co-writer, prodr., recorder (motion picture soundtrack) Someone Like You (song-You Are), 2001; recorded song with others, Heart of America, Habitat for Humanity, 2005 Charitable efforts for Nashville Oasis Ctr., St. Jude Children's Hosp., Am. Red Cross, and Habitat for Humanity; chair, celebrity auction Am. Liver Found., 1998; amb. YouthAIDS, 2003—; nat. spokesperson Power to Change Program, 2000; spokesperson Kmart Corp., 2000. Recipient (with Naomi Judd) Horizon award, Country Music Assn., 1984, five Grammy awards, nine Country Music Assn. awards and eight Billboard Music awards; named with Naomi Judd 40 Greatest Women of Country Music, Country Music TV (CMT), 2002; recipient Female Vocalist of the Yr. award, Acad. of Country Music, 1994, Connie B. Gay award, Country Music Assn., 2004, USO Merit award, 2005; co-recipient with husband Dan R Roach, Turn for Peace award, ANASAZI Found., 2005; nominee for Humanitarian of Yr., Academy of Country Music, 2003; named Grand Marshall, Indy 500 Festival and Race (first country artist), 2003.; named to Nashville Music City Walk of Fame, 2007. Avocation: racquetball. Address: Mercury Nashville 66 Music Sq W Nashville TN 37203-3208*

JUDELL, HAROLD BENN, lawyer; b. Milw., Mar. 9, 1915; s. Philip Fox and Lena Florence (Krause) J.; m. Maria Violeta van Ronzelen, May 5, 1951 (div.); m. Celeste Seymour Grulich, June 24, 1986. BA, U. Wis., 1936, JD, 1938; LLB, Tulane U., 1950. Bar: Wis. 1938, La. 1950. Mem. Scheinfeld Collins Durant & Winter, Milw., 1938; spl. agt., adminstrv. asst. to dir. FBI, 1939-44; legal attache U.S. Embassy Peru, 1942-44; ptnr. Foley & Judell, LLP, New Orleans, 1950—2005, spl. counsel, 2006—; v.p., dir. Dauphine Orleans Hotel Corp., New Orleans, 1970—98, chmn. bd., 1999—2006, pres., 2005—06. Mem. Tulane U. Bus. Sch. Coun.; trustee Greater New Orleans YMCA, 1981—. Fellow Am. Coll. Bond Counsel (founding); mem. ABA, La. Bar Assn., Nat. Assn. Bond Lawyers (bd. dirs., pres. 1984-85), New Orleans Country Club, New Orleans Lawn Tennis Club, Met. Club (N.Y.C.). Office: Foley & Judell LLP 365 Canal St New Orleans LA 70130-1112 Office Phone: 504-568-1249. Business E-Mail: hjudell@foleyjudell.com.

JUDGE, BERNARD MARTIN, editor, publishing executive; b. Chgo., Jan. 6, 1940; s. Bernard A. and Catherine Elizabeth (Halloran) J.; m. Kimbeth A. Wehrli, July 9, 1966; children: Kelly, Bernard R., Jessica. Reporter City News Bur., Chgo., 1965-66; reporter Chgo. Tribune, 1966-70, city editor, 1974-79, asst. mng. editor met. news, 1979-83; editor, gen. mgr. City News Bur. Chgo., 1983-84; assoc. editor Chgo. Sun-Times, 1984-88; from editor to pub. Chgo. Daily Law Bull., 1988—; pub. Chgo. Lawyer, 1989—; v.p. Law Bull. Pub. Co., Chgo., 1988—. Bd. dir. Constnl. Rights Found., Chgo., 1992—, chmn. bd. dir., 1995-97; trustee Fenwick Cath. Prep. HS, Oak Park, Ill., 1989—; bd. dir. Abraham Lincoln Presdl. Libr. and Mus., 2004-06. Named to Chgo. Journalism Hall of Fame, 2000. Mem. Sigma Delta Chi. Home: 360 E Randolph St Apt 1905 Chicago IL 60601-7335 Office: Law Bull Pub Co 415 N State St Chicago IL 60610-4631 Office Phone: 312-644-7006.

JUDGE, JONATHAN J., financial services company executive; BA, Harvard Univ. Sales, mktg. & ops. mgmt. positions IBM, 1976—98, mgr. sales, svc. & support, personal computing div., mem. mgmt. com., 1998—2001, gen. mgr. personal computing div., 2001—02; pres., CEO Crystal Decisions Inc., Vancouver, BC, 2002—03, Paychex Inc., Rochester, NY, 2004—. Bd. dir. PMC-Sierra Inc. Office: Paychex Inc 911 Panorama Trl S Rochester NY 14625*

JUDGE, MIKE, animator; b. Guayaquil, Ecuador, Oct. 17, 1962; m. Francesca Morocco, 1989; 2 children. BA in Phys. Sci., U. Calif., San Diego, 1985. Writer, dir., prodr. (TV series) Beavis and Butt-head, 1993-1997, King of the Hill, 1997—, Monsignor Martinez, 2000; (films) Beavis and Butt-head Do America, 1996, Office Space, 1999; actor (films) Inbred Jed (voice), 1991, King of the Hill (voice), 1997—, Mene Tekel (voice), 1997, Spy Kids, 2001, Spy Kids 2:Island of Lost Dreams, 2002, Serving Sara, 2002, Spy Kids 3-D:Game Over, 2003.

JUDGE, NANCY ELIZABETH, obstetrician, gynecologist; b. Holyoke, Mass., May 21, 1951; d. Martin P. and Barbara Judge; m. David B. Wood, Oct. 30, 1982; children: David, William, Elizabeth, Meredith. AB, Smith Coll., 1973; MD, U. Mass., 1977. Intern Case Western Res. U./MetroHealth Med. Ctr., Cleve., 1977-78, resident, 1978-81; staff physician MetroHealth Med. Ctr. Case Western Res. U. Hosps., Cleve., 1981-90; dir. reproductive imaging ctr. Case Western Res. U. Hosps., 1990—, maternal-fetal medicine cons., 1990—. Asst. prof. reproductive biology Case Western Res. U., 1981—. Contbr. articles to profl. jours. Active Cleve. Art Mus., Playhouse Sq. Assn., Cleve. Garden Ctr. Fellow ACOG; mem. Cleve. Ob.-Gyn. Soc. (pres.).

JUDGE, PATTY JEAN, lieutenant governor, nurse; b. Fort Madison, Iowa, Nov. 2, 1943; m. John Judge; 3 children. Attended, U. Iowa; RN, Iowa Meth. Sch. Nursing, 1965. Lic. Real Estate Broker. Mediator Iowa Farmer Creditor Mediation Svc.; mem. Iowa State Senate, 1992—98, majority leader, 1994—98; sec. agr. State of Iowa, 1998—2007, lt. gov., 2007—. Agr. sec. US Home Land Security, Agrl. Sector Govt. Coordinating Coun.; mem. Senate Natural Resources Com., Ways and Means Com., Appropriations Com., Small Bus. and Econ. Devel. Com., Human Services Com. Mem., bd. dirs. Albia Area Chamber of Commerce; leader 4-H; mem. PEO, Iowa State Fair Bd.; parliamentarian Dem. Nat. Conv., 2000. Mem.: Nat. Assn. State Departments of Agr. (sec., chair, standing com. on agrl. security), Future Farmers of Am. Democrat. Office: Lieutenant Governor State Capitol Rm 9 Des Moines IA 50319 Office Phone: 515-281-0225. Office Fax: 515-281-6611.*

JUDGE, PAUL, information technology executive; b. 1977; BS in Computer Sci., Morehouse Coll.; MS, Georgia Inst. Tech., PhD in Network Security. With NASA, IBM; co-founder CipherTrust (sold to Secure Computing), 2000—06; chief tech. officer Secure Computing, San Jose, Calif., 2006—. Founder Anti-Spam Rsch. Group Internet Rsch. Task Force. Named one of 100 Top Young Innovators, MIT Tech. Rev., 2003, Top 25 Chief Tech. Officers, InfoWorld mag., 2007. Achievements include being lead inventor on 18 patent-pending security technologies. Office: Secure Computing 4810 Harwood Rd San Jose CA 95124-5206 Office Phone: 408-979-6100. Office Fax: 408-979-6501.

JUDGE, RAJINDER, psychiatrist; b. Jullundur, India, Mar. 22, 1961; arrived in Eng., 1964, arrived in US, 1996; d. Sadhu and Parkash Judge. MD, U. Birmingham, Eng., 1984. Intern Wordsley Hosp. and Russells Hall Hosp., Dudley, England, 1984—85; sr. house officer psychiatry Midland Nerve Hosp., Birmingham, 1985—86; physician Riyadh, Saudi Arabia, 1986—87; psychiatry registrar North Worcester, England, 1987—89; assoc. med. dir. Smith Kline Beecham, England, 1991—96; dir., global physician for Prozac, Lilly & Co., Indpls., 1997—2000; psychiatrist Nat. Health Svc., 1991—94; registrar, sr. registrar London Charing Cross Rotation, 1989—91; v.p. neurosci. Novartis, East Hanover, NJ, 2000—03; pharm. cons., 2003—. Forensic med. examiner London Met. Police Force, 1991—. Contbr. articles to profl. jours. Mem.: European Coll. Psychiatry, European Network Cmty. Psychologists, Royal Coll. Psychiatrists. Achievements include research in depression and anxiety disorders. World leader in research studies of Prozac. Responsible for establishing diagnosis of PMDD with FDA. Avocations: automobiles, movies, travel.

JUDICE, MARC WAYNE, lawyer; b. Lafayette, La., Oct. 22, 1946; s. Marc and Gladys B. Judice; m. Michelle Regan; 1 child, Renee. BS, U. La., Lafayette, 1969; MBA, U. Utah, Salt Lake City, 1974; JD, La. State U., Baton Rouge, 1977. Bar: La. 1977, bd. cert. civil trial law, civil trial advocacy: Nat. Bd. Trial Advocacy 2000, 2005. Ptnr. Voorhies & Labbe, Lafayette, 1977-85, Juneau, Judice, Hill & Adley, Lafayette, 1985-93, Judice & Adley, Lafayette, 1993—. Bd. dirs. U. Med. Ctr., Lafayette, 1991, chmn.; bd. dirs. Home Savs. Bank, Lafayette, 1996—, Women's &

Childrens Hosp., Lafayette, 1992-94; bd. trustees Med. Ctr. Southwest La., 1998-2001, chmn. bd. dirs., 1999-2005. Named one of La. Super Lawyers, 2007. Republican. Office: Judice & Adley 926 Coolidge Blvd Lafayette LA 70503-2434 Office Phone: 337-235-2405. Business E-Mail: mwj@judice-adley.com.

JUDSON, ARNOLD SIDNEY, management consultant; b. Brockton, Mass., Mar. 29, 1927; s. Moses Joel and Fanny (Becker) J.; m. June Brenner, June 19, 1949; children: Pamela F., Jill E. BS in Chem. Engring., MIT, 1947, MS in Orgnl. Behavior, 1948. Prodn. foreman U.S. Rubber Co., Providence, 1948-50; pers. mgr., mfg. mgr., then dir. tng. and devel. Polaroid Corp., Cambridge, Mass., 1950-62; mgmt. cons. The Emerson Cons., Ltd., London, 1962-66; sr. mgmt. cons. Arthur D.Little, Inc., Cambridge, 1966-76; dir., mgmt. cons. The Berwick Group, Inc., Boston, 1976-81; pres., CEO Gray-Judson-Howard, Inc., Cambridge, 1981-90, chmn., 1990-94; pres. The Judson Co., Inc., 1994-2001. Cons. Exec. Svc. Corps. Author: A Manager's Guide to Making Changes, 1966, Making Strategy Happen, 1990, 2nd edit., 1996, Changing Behavior in Organizations, 1991, True Success, 2007; contbr. articles to bus. publs.; composer orchestral and chamber music. Chmn. bd. dirs. Greater Boston Rehab. Svcs., Cambridge, 1984-2001. With USN, 1945-46. Mem.: Univ. Club Boston. Office: The Judson Co Inc 364 Del Pond Dr Canton MA 02021 Business E-Mail: ajudson@gis.net.

JUDSON, C(HARLES) JAMES (JIM JUDSON), lawyer; b. Oregon City, Oreg., Oct. 24, 1944; s. Charles James and Barbara (Busch) Judson; m. Diana L. Gerlach, Sept. 11, 1965; children: Kevin, Nicole. BA cum laude, Stanford U., 1966, LLB with honors, 1969. Bar: Wash. 1969, U.S. Tax Ct. 1970, DC 1981. Ptnr. Davis Wright Tremaine, Seattle, 1969—. Bd. dirs. Port Blakely Tree Farms, Garrett and Ring, Joshua Green Corp., Lumera, Sonata Capital, Airbiquity, Welco Lumber; spkr. in field. Author: State Taxation of Financial Intitutions, 1981; contbr. articles to profl. jours. Trustee Wash. State Internat. Trade Fair, Seattle, 1981—86; mem. Assn. Wash. Bus. Tax Com., 1978—, Seattle Tax Group, 1983—; chmn. lawyers divsn. United Way, Seattle, 1986, 1987, chmn. commerce and industry divsn., 1989—91; chmn. Bus. Tax Coalition, Seattle, 1987; bd. dirs. Pacific N.W. Ballet, Pacific Sci. Ctr., Olympic Pk. Inst., 1988—, Yosemite Nat. Insts., 1993—; advisor Wash. State Dept. Revenue; tax advisor Wash. State House Reps. Dem. Caucus. Fellow: Am. Coll. Tax Counsel; mem.: ABA (chmn. com. fin. orgns. tax sect. 1978—82, chmn. excise tax com. 1983—90, interorganization coordination com. 1985—, chmn. environ. tax com. 1991—), Seattle-King County Bar Assn. (mem. tax sect. 1973—86), Wash. State Bar Assn. (chmn. tax sect. 1984—86, chmn. western region IRS/bar liaison com. 1987—88, mem. rules com. 1991—), Seattle C. of C. (mem. tax. com. 1982—), Broadmoor Golf Club (Seattle), Wash. Athletic Club (Seattle) (bd. dirs. 2006—). Avocations: skiing, golf, basketball, woodworking, hiking. Office: Davis Wright Tremaine 2600 Century Sq 1501 4th Ave Seattle WA 98101-1688 Office Phone: 206-628-7686. Business E-Mail: jimjudson@dwt.com.

JUDSON, HORACE AUGUSTUS, academic administrator, chemistry educator; b. Miami, Fla., Aug. 7, 1941; s. Charles Olidge Judson and Louella Edmond; m. Beatrice Gail Shorter, Apr. 13, 1974; children: Tamara Reneé, Sonya Anita, Sojourner Maria, Jessica Gail. AB, Lincoln U., 1963, DSc (hon.), 1994; PhD, Cornell U., 1969. Asst. prof. Bethune-Cookman Coll., Daytona, Fla., 1969, Morgan State U., Balt., 1969-72, assoc. prof., 1972-74, assoc. dean, 1973-74, v.p. acad. affairs, prof., 1974-79, chmn. dept. chemistry, 1982—86; dean arts, letters and scis., prof. chemistry Calif. State U. Stanislaus, Turlock, 1986-90, provost, v.p. acad. affairs, 1991—94; pres. SUNY, Plattsburgh, 1994—2003; sr. fellow Am. Assn. State Colls. and Univs., 2003—04; pres. Grambling State U., La., 2004—. Cons. migrant edn. Md. Dept. Edn., 1977-79; evaluator sci. program Dept. Edn., Lincoln U,. Pa., 1980-82; curriculum cons. several univs., Md. and Pa., 1982-86. Author: (monograph) Reflections of a Former Migrant, 1978; contbr. articles to profl. jours. Civilian aide to Sec. US Army, Md., 1975-79; mem. segmental adv. bd. Md. Bd. for Higher Edn., Annapolis, 1977-79; mem. sci. coun. Md. Acad. Scis., Balt., 1983-86; bd. dirs. Nat. Orgn. for Migrant Children, 1981-84. Recipient Outstanding Cmty. Svc. award Morgan U. Nat. Alumni Assn., 1983, Alumni Achievement award Lincoln U. Alumni Assn., 1983, Profl. Excellence award Nat. Tech. Assn., 1984, Lectureship award Fulbright Sr. Scholar Program, 1984, Disting. Citizen award, Adirondack Coun. Boy Scouts, 1999. Mem. Am. Chem. Soc., Am. Assn. for Higher Edn., Am. Assn. State Colls. and Univs. (mem. black caucus, 1995-, bd. dirs., 2003), Am. Coun. Edn., Sigma Xi. Republican. Baptist. Avocations: golf, gardening, cooking. Office: Grambling State U PO Box 607 Grambling LA 71245 Home Phone: 318-274-6370; Office Phone: 318-274-6117. Business E-Mail: judsonha@gram.edu.*

JUDSON, HORACE FREELAND, history professor, writer; b. NYC, Apr. 21, 1931; s. Freeland and Harriet Louise (Babcock) J.; m. Ann Schramm, 1953 (div.); children: Grace Louise Judson, Thomas Alexander; m. Penelope Sylvia Jones, Jan. 11, 1969 (dec. May 1993); children: Olivia Phoebe, Nicholas Matthew Freeland. AB, U. Chgo., 1948, postgrad., 1949-52, Columbia U., 1962-63. Reports writer Office of Mil. Gov. U.S., Berlin, 1948-49; various editing, advt., polit. positions NYC, N.J., 1952-62; staff writer, book reviewer Time mag., NYC, 1963-65; arts and scis. corr. Time-Life News Svc., London, 1965-69, Paris, 1969-72, corr. NYC, 1972-73; free-lance writer Cambridge, Eng., 1973-80, Balt., 1981—; Henry R. Luce prof. writing seminars, prof. history sci. Johns Hopkins U., Balt., 1981-90; vis. prof. Stanford U., Calif., 1990-94; rsch. prof. History George Washington U., 1994—2003; dir. Ctr. for History of Recent Sci., 1995—2003. Cons. Philbrook Mus. Art, Tulsa, 1983-87, PBS Sta. WHYY-TV, Phila., 1985-88, Henry Luce Found., 1988-89, Harvard U. Press, 1990-95; Fred Friendly Seminars, 1999—, WNET13, NYC, 2000-02; panelist and cons. Office Tech. Assessment, Washington, 1985, 86-87; lectr. US and Europe; keynote spkr. 25th ann. meeting Am. Soc. Cell Biology, Atlanta, Nov. 1985, ann. meeting Pew Scholars, Feb. 1987, symposium on Genetic Experimentation and Evolutionary Change, com. on genetic experimentation Internat. Coun. Sci. Unions, U. Basel, Jan. 1988, DNA Double Helix 40 Yrs. Symposium NY Acad. Scis., 1993, Am. Soc. Human Genetics, 1995; Colin Syme vis. fellow, lectr. Walter and Eliza Hall Inst. Med. Rsch., Royal Melbourne (Australia) Hosp., 1990. Author: The Techniques of Reading, 1954, 3d edit. 1971, Heroin Addiction in Britain, 1974 (Overseas Press Club prize, 1974, Med. Journalists Assn. Great Britain award, 1975), The Eighth Day of Creation, 1979 (transls. in Japanese, German, Spanish, Italian, Chinese, nominated for Nat. Book award 1980), expanded edit. 1996, 25th anniversary edit., 2004, The Search for Solutions, 1980 (transls. in Japanese, German, Dutch), The Great Betrayal:Fraud in Science, 2004; contbg. editor The Sciences, 1982-89; mem. faculty adv. bd. Johns Hopkins U. Press, 1982-84, editl. bd. The Am. Scholar, 1983-86, bd. editors Science Book Program of NY Acad. Scis., 1985-90; editl. cons. various pubs. including Stanford U. Press, 1981, W.H. Freeman, 1988; author articles in The New Yorker, The Sciences, The New Republic, Harper's, The NY Times Book Rev., The Spectator (London), Nature, The Lancet, Jour. AMA, Gene, Science 80, 83, 84, 85, Life, Minerva, New Eng. Jour. Med., Cell, Smithsonian, MIT Tech. Rev.; cons. editor The Eloquent Object, 1987; prodn. cons., scenarist TV films: All My Loving, BBC, 1967, Plague!, PBS, 1987-88, Our Games Our Choices, 1990-92. John Simon Guggenheim Meml. Found. fellow, 1979-80, Ctr. for Advanced Study in Behavioral Scis. (fell.), 1980-81, Prize fellow John D. and Catherine T. MacArthur Found., 1987-92, Wissenschaftskolleg zu Berlin fellow, 1987-88. Fellow AAAS; mem. Lansdowne Club (London), Century Assn. (NY), 14 W. Hamilton St. Club (Balt.), Nat. Press Club (Washington). Democrat. Avocation: cooking. Home: 807 W University Pky Baltimore MD 21210-2911 Personal E-mail: hfjudson@speakeasy.net.

JUDSON, PATRICIA LYNN, obstetrician, gynecologist, oncologist; d. Jayne Jennings; m. Gary James Judson, Sept. 27, 1990; children: Julia, Evan. BS, Hamline U., St. Paul, 1987; MD, U. Minn., 1998. Asst. prof. U. Minn., Mpls., 1999—, fellowship coord., 2003—; dir. gyn. oncology North Meml. Med. Ctr., Robbinsdale, Minn., 1999—. Med. adv. bd. Minn. Ovarian Cancer Alliance, St. Louis Park, 1999—. Reviewer: Jour. Ob-Gyn., 1987—, Jour. Gyn. Oncology, 2000—; contbr. articles to profl. jours., chapters to books. Sci. adv. com. Gyn. Oncology Group, 2005—06. Named one of America's Top Obstetricians and Gynecologists, Consumers' Rsch. Coun. of Am., 2004, Top Twin Cities Doctors for Women, Minn. Monthly Mag., 2006. Fellow: ACS (life); mem.: Soc. Gynecol. Oncologist (edn. com. 2006), Minn. Women Physicians, Minn. Soc. Clin. Oncology, Deborah E. Powell Ctr. for Women's Health, Am. Coll. Ob-Gyn. (life; program com. 2001—05). Lutheran. Office: Univf Minn 420 Delaware St SE MMC 395 Minneapolis MN 55455 Home Phone: 952-285-4447.

JUDSON, PHILIP LIVINGSTON, retired lawyer, consultant; b. Palo Alto, Calif., Oct. 25, 1941; s. Philip MacGregor and Elizabeth Stuart (Peck) Judson; m. Dorothy Louisa Lebohner, Sept. 6, 1963 (div. Jan. 1996); children: Wendy Patricia, Philip Lebohner, Michael Lee; m. Danielle DuPuis Kane, May 18, 1996. BA, Stanford U., 1963; JD, U. Calif., Hastings, 1969. Bar: Calif. 1970, Tex. 1999, U.S. Dist. Ct. (no. dist.) Calif. 1970, U.S. Ct. Appeals (9th cir.) 1970, U.S. Dist. Ct. (ctrl. dist.) Calif. 1984, U.S. Dist. Ct. (ea. dist.) Calif. 1985, U.S. Supreme Ct. 1987, DC 1988, U.S. Dist. Ct. (so. dist.) Calif. 1989, Tex. 1999, U.S. Dist. Ct. (no. and we. dists.) Tex. 2000, U.S. Dist. Ct. (ea. dist.) Tex. 2002. Assoc. Pillsbury, Madison & Sutro, San Francisco, 1969-76, ptnr., 1977-99, Skjerven Morrill MacPherson, LLP, San Jose, Calif., 1999, Austin, Tex., 1999—2002; shareholder Winstead Sechrest & Minick, P.C., Austin, 2002—04, ret., 2004; cons. in field. Lectr. Practicing Law Inst., U. Tex. Advanced Intellectual Property Law Inst., Inst. Am. and Internat. Law Intellectual Property Law Program. Founding mem. trustee St. Mark's Sch., San Rafael, 1980—86, pres., 1983—85; trustee Marin Acad., San Rafael, 1985—91. 1st lt. US Army, 1963—65. Mem.: ABA (mem. antitrust and litig. sects.), Austin Bar Assn., Austin Intellectual Property Law Assn., Am. Judicature Soc., San Francisco Bar Assn., Order of Coif, Phi Delta Theta. Republican. Episcopalian. Home: 9662 Mountain Daisy Way Highlands Ranch CO 80129

JUDY, CHERYL D., art educator, artist; d. Melvin L. and Irene R. Judy. AA, Art Inst. Pitts., 1978; BA, U. Charleston, WV, 1992. Cert. profl. tchg. W.Va. Dept. Edn., 1992. Substitute tchr. Kanawha County Schs., Charleston, 1992—98, art tchr., 1998—99, Boone County Schs., Madison, W.Va., 2002—. Coun. mem. Kanawha Valley Labor Coun. - AFL-CIO, Charleston, 2005; sec. Boone County Fedn. Tchrs., Madison, 2005. Home Phone: 304-949-1657; Office Phone: 304-369-4464.

JUE, JAN-FONG, materials scientist; b. Taipei, Taiwan, May 8, 1961; s. Hsi and Chen Chiu-Hong Jue; m. Fu-Jen Pan; children: Hannah children: Andrew. BS, Nat. Tsing Hua U., Taiwan, 1983; PhD, U. Utah, Salt Lake City, 1991. Post-doctoral fellow U. Utah, 1991—94, adj. asst. prof., 1994—2000; sr. rsch. scientist Materials and Sys. Rsch., Inc., Salt Lake City, 1992—2000; materials scientist Argonne Nat. Lab. West, Idaho Falls, 2001—05, Idaho Nat. Lab., 2005—. Mem.: ASM Internat., Am. Nuc. Soc., Am. Ceramic Soc., Phi Kappa Phi Honor Soc. Achievements include patents for Five US patents on ceramic materials. Home: 4155 Colonial Way Idaho Falls ID 83404 Office: Idaho Nat Lab PO Box 1625 Idaho Falls ID 83415 Home Phone: 208-552-9461; Office Phone: 208-533-7491. Personal E-mail: janfongjue@msn.com.

JUERGENS, GEORGE IVAR, history professor; b. Bklyn., Mar. 20, 1932; s. George Odegaard and Magnhild (Julin) J.; m. Bonnie Jeanne Brownlee; children: Steven Erik, Paul Magnus. BA, Columbia Coll., 1953; BA, MA, Oxford U., 1956; PhD, Columbia U., 1965. Instr. Dartmouth Coll., Hanover, NH, 1962-65; asst. prof. Amherst (Mass.) Coll., 1965-67; assoc. prof. Ind. U., Bloomington, 1967-80, prof. history, 1980—. Cons. Nat. Endowment Humanities, Washington, 1971— Author: Joseph Pulitzer and the New York World, 1966, News From The White House, 1981; assoc. editor: Jour. Am. History, 1968-69. With U.S. Army, 1956-58. Recipient Disting. Teaching award Amoco Found., 1982; Kellett fellow Columbia U., 1954-56; sr. faculty fellow Nat. Endowment Humanities, 1971-72; fellow Rockefeller Found., 1981-82 Mem. AAUP, Orgn. Am. Historians, Phi Beta Kappa Home: 2111 E Meadow Bluff Ct Bloomington IN 47401-6885 Office: Ind U Dept History Bloomington IN 47405 Business E-Mail: juergens@indiana.edu.

JUGENHEIMER, DONALD WAYNE, advertising executive, communications educator, academic administrator; b. Manhattan, Kans., Sept. 22, 1943; s. Robert William and Mabel Clara (Hobert) J.; m. Bonnie Jeanne Scamehorn, Aug. 30, 1970 (dec. 1983); 1 child, Beth Carrie; m. Kaleen B. Brown, July 25, 1987. BS in Advt., U. Ill.-Urbana, 1965, MS in Advt., 1968, PhD in Communications, 1972. Advt. copywriter Fillman & Assocs, Champaign, Ill., 1963-64, 66; media buyer Leo Burnett Co., Chgo., 1965-66; asst., assoc. prof. U. Kans., Lawrence, 1971-80, prof. jounralism, dir. grad. studies and rsch., 1980-85; Manship prof. journalism La. State U., Baton Rouge, 1985-87; prof., chmn. dept. communications and speech Fairleigh Dickinson U., Teaneck, NJ, 1987-89, 92-95, dean coll. liberal arts, 1989-92; chair dept. English, lang. and philosphy, 1995; prof. Sch. Journalism So. Ill. U., Carbondale, 1995—2005; prof., chair dept. advt. Coll. Mass Comm. Tex. Tech U., 2005—. Dir. Sch. Journalism So. Ill. U., Carbondale, 1995-2002; adj. faculty Turku (Finland) Sch. Econs., 1999—; adv. cons. U.S. Army, Fort Sheridan, Ill., Pentagon, Washington, 1981-90, Am. Airlines, 1989-91, IBM Corp., 1989—, U.S. Dept. Def.; cons. editor Grid Publ., Columbus, Ohio, 1974-84; grad. and rsch. dir. U. Kans., 1978-84, adv. chmn., 1974-78; adj. prof. Turku (Finland) Sch. Econs. and Bus. Adminstrn., 1998—. Author: Advertising Media Sourcebook and Workbook, 1975, 3d edit., 1989, 4th edit. 1996, Strategic Advertising Decisions, 1976, Basic Advertising, 1979, 2d edit., 1991, Advertising Media, 1980, Problems and Practices in Advertising Research, 1982, Advertising Media: Strategy and Tactics, 1992, Advertising Media Planning: A Brand Management Approach, 2004, Advertising Media Workbook and Sourcebook, 2005, Advertising Account Planning: A Practical Approach, 2006; bd. editors Jour. Advt., 1985-89, Jour. Interactive Advt., 2000—, Jour. Current Issues and Rsch. in Advt., 1990—. Subscription mgr. Jour. of Advt., 1971-74, bus. mgr., 1974-79; chmn. Univ. divsn. United Fund, Lawrence, 1971-72; pres. Sch.-Cmty. Rels. Coun., Lawrence, 1974-75. Recipient Hope Tchg. award U. Kans, 1977, 78, Kellogg Nat. fellow W.K. Kellogg Found., 1984-88; named Outstanding Young Men in Am. Nat. Jaycees, 1978. Mem. AAUP, Am. Acad. Advt. (pres. 1984-86, exec. dir. 2005-), Assn. Edn. in Journalism (head advt. divsn. 1977-78), Kappa Tau Alpha, Alpha Delta Sigma. Presbyterian. Avocations: skiing, sailing, writing, travel, reading. Office: Coll Mass Comm Tex Tech Univ Box 43082 Lubbock TX 79409-3082 Home: 4015 69t St Lubbock TX 79413 Home Phone: 806-788-0607; Office Phone: 806-742-3385 276. Business E-Mail: donald.jugenheimer@ttu.edu.

JUGULUM, RAJESH, engineer, researcher; s. Sarala Bai and Gopala Char Jugulum; m. Rekha Shripati Koimattur; 1 child, Aaroh. BTech., SV U. Coll. Engring., Tirupathi, India, 1985—89; MTech., Indian Statis. Inst., Kolkata, 1989—91; PhD, Wayne State U., 1996—2000. IS0-9000 Lead Assessor, Briti. Stds. Inst., 1995. Rschr. MIT, Cambridge, 2003—; v.p. global wealth and investment mgmt. divsn. Bank Am., Boston, 2006—. Rsch. affiliate MIT, 2003—. Contbr. scientific papers numerous papers to profl. jours. and pubs., two books; author: The Mahalamobis-Taguchi-Strategy: A Pattern Technology System, 2002, Computer Based Robust Engineering: Essentials for DFSS, 2004. Sponsor Compassion Internat., Colorado Springs. Recipient Feigenbaum medal, Am. Soc. For Quality, 2002, Rockwell medal, Internat. Tech. Inst., 2006, Inducted into Hall of Fame for Engring., Sci. and Tech., 2006; grantee Merit fellowship, Indian Govt., 1989—91, fellowship, Indian Statis. Inst., 1991—92, Ford, 1996—2000, Richard Freund Internat. scholarship, Am. Soc. For Quality, 2000, Ford-MIT grant, 2001. Fellow: Royal Statis. Soc. (assoc.); mem.: Am. Soc. for Quality, Internat. Tech. Inst. (hon. Lifetime award 2006). Achievements include patents for multivariate data analysis method and uses thereof. Avocations: travel, reading, jogging, walking. Personal E-mail: rajesh_jugulum@yahoo.com. Business E-Mail: rajesh.jugulum@bankofame.com.

JUHANI, ERMA, lawyer, former stock exchange executive; b. Tampere, Finland, Nov. 29, 1946; LLM, U. Helsinki, Finland, 1969, Lic. Laws, 1977. Asst. Heikki Haapaniemi Law Office, 1969; lawyer legal affairs dept. Enso-Gutzeit Oy, 1972; legal ops. mgr. Union Bank of Finland, Ltd., 1979, asst. gen. mgr. sect. for investment banking and legal ops., 1981, branch mgr. Helsinki-Eteläsatama branch, 1982; mng. dir. Unitas Ltd., 1983, Indsl. Bank Finland, Ltd., 1988; pres., CEO The Helsinki Stock Exch., 1989-97; CEO HEX Helsinki Exchs., 1997—2000; sr. advisor Borenius & Kemppinen Ltd., Helsinki, Finland, 2002—. Mem. bd. dirs. The Helsinki Stock Exchg., 1986, 88, The Finnish Found. for Share Promotion, 1989-99; chmn., mem. bd. dirs. of several Finnish Co. Office: Borenius & Kemppinen Ltd Yrjönkatu 13A FIN-00120 Helsinki Finland Office Phone: +358(0)9 615333. Business E-Mail: juhani.erma@borenius.com.

JUHL, STACY MARIE, music educator, director; b. Iron Mountain, Mich., Jan. 23, 1976; d. Russell and Mary Dieckman; m. Aaron Dale Juhl, June 27, 1999; 1 child, Karin Elizabeth. BA in Music with Ed. Certification, Gustavus Adolphus Coll., St. Peter, Minn., 1998; MS in Instrumental Pedagogy, So. Oreg. U., Ashland, 2002. Cert. tchr. Wis., 1998. Band dir. Hortonville Mid. Sch., Hortonville, Wis., 1998—. Pvt. tchr. instrumental music, Appleton, Wis., 1998—. Contbr. articles to profl. jours. Blanketeer Project Linus, Fox Cities, Wis., 2006; musician Prince Peace Luth. Ch., Appleton, 1999—2006. Mem.: Wis. State Music Assn. (adjudicator music contest 1998—2006). Lutheran. Avocations: quilting, scrapbooks, reading, travel. Home: 1809 Angela Dr Appleton WI 54915 Office: Hortonville Mid Sch 220 Warner St Hortonville WI 54944 Home Phone: 920-954-9323; Office Phone: 920-779-7922. Personal E-mail: ajuhl@athenet.net. Business E-Mail: stacyjuhl@hasd.org.

JUKNELIS, NICK, music educator; b. Melrose Park, Ill., Apr. 24, 1979; s. Vito and Karen Juknelis; m. Amy Ann Hultgren, July 19, 2003. BA, Augustana Coll., 2001; MA, U. Iowa, 2002. Dir. vocal music Lake Zurich H.S., Ill., 2003—. Mem.: Nat. Opera Assn., Ill. Music Educator's Assn., Music Educator's Nat. Conf., Am. Choral Dirs. Assn. Office: Lake Zurich High Sch 300 Church St Lake Zurich IL 60047 Home Phone: 847-438-1574; Office Phone: 847-540-4249. Business E-Mail: nick.juknelis@lz95.org.

JULANDER, PAULA FOIL, retired foundation administrator; b. Charlotte, NC, Jan. 21, 1939; d. Paul Baxter and Esther Irene (Earnhardt) Foil; m. Roydon Odell Julander, Dec. 21, 1985; 1 child, Julie McMahan Shipman. Diploma, Presbyn. Sch. Nursing, Charlotte, NC, 1960; BS magna cum laude, U. Utah, 1984; MS in Nursing Adminstrn., Brigham Young U., 1990. RN, Utah. Nurse various positions, Fla. and S.C., 1960-66; co-founder Am. Laser Corp., 1970-79; tchg. asst. U. Utah, Salt Lake City; exec. dir. Utah Nurses Assn., 1987—89; mem. Utah Ho. of Reps., Salt Lake City, 1989-92; Dem. nominee lt. gov. State of Utah, 1992; minority whip Utah State Senate, Dist. 1, Salt Lake City, 1998—2000; health care/polit. cons. Salt Lake City, 1992—98. Mem. adj. faculty Brigham Young U. Coll. Nursing, 1987—95; bd. dirs. Block Fin. Svcs.; mem. Utah state exec. bd U.S. West Comm., 1993—96; bd. regents Calif. Luth. U., 1994—97; 2003 trustee KUED TV, 2000—03; trustee Intermountain Health Care Hosps., 2000—. Co-author (cookbook): Utah State Fare, 1995. Pres. Utah Nurses Found., 1986—88; mem. Nat. Conf. of State Legis. Com. on Families and Children, 1999—2001, The Coun. of State Govt. Com. on Health and Aging, 1999—2001, Women's Polit.Caucus, Statewide Abortion Task Force, 1990; bd. dirs. Cmty. Nursing Svc. Home Health Plus, 1992—94; mem. Planned Parenthood Assn. Utah, 1994—2991, Utahns for Choice, 1995—2002; trustee Westminster Coll., 1994—2002, HCA-St. Mark's Hosp., 1994—95; elected sen. State of Utah, 1998—2005; hon. chair Komem Race for Cure, 2007. Recipient Utah pub. health hero award, 2000, Legislator of Yr. awrd, YWCA, 2001, Jacquelyn Erbin MD award, Planned Parenthood Action Coun., 2002, Disting. Alumni award, Coll. Nursing, U. Utah, 2002, Legislator of Yr. award, Nat. Assn. Social Workers, 2002, Eleanor Roosevelt award, Utah State Dem. Com., 2004, Women's Achievement award, Utah Commn. for Women and Families, 2005, Lucy Beth Rampton award, Utah Women's Dem. Club, 2005, Outstanding Achievement award in Govt. and Polit. Svc., YWCA, 2005, Honored Alumni award, Brigham Young U. Coll. Nursing, 2005; honored by, Govt. Commn. on Women and Families, 2005. Mem.: ANA, Women in Govt. (chair 2004), Nat Orgn. Women Legislators, Utah Nurses Assn. (legis. rep. 1987—88, Lifetime Achievement award), Phi Kappa Phi (Susan Young Gates award 1991), Sigma Theta Tau. Home: 476 B St Salt Lake City UT 84103-2544 Office Phone: 801-887-2337. Personal E-mail: paula@ulcu.com.

JULIAN, ALEXANDER, II, menswear designer; b. Chapel Hill, NC, Feb. 8, 1948; s. Maurice S. and Mary L. (Brady) J.; m. Meagan Mannell; 1 child, William; children from previous marriage: Alystyre, Claire. Operator Alexander's Ambition (splty. store), Chapel Hill, 1969-73; designer men's clothing for Baker Clothes, Phila., 1973-76; dir. market research and devel. Trimingham Bros., Bermuda, from 1974; designer sweater collections for Pringle of Scotland, from 1975; pres., chief exec. officer Alexander Julian, Inc., NYC, 1975—. Guest lectr. Fashion Inst. Tech. Costume designer for feature film The Player, 1992. Mem. Chapel Hill Appearance Commn. Recipient Coty award, 1977, 79, 80, 83, 84; named to Coty Hall of Fame, 1980; Cutty Sark award as Outstanding U.S. Designer, 1980, 85. Mem. Council Fashion Designers Am. (dir., award for outstanding U.S. men's wear), Men's Fashion Assn. Clubs: Burke's (London), Alibi, Chelsea Arts. Office: Alexander Julian Inc PO Box 60 Georgetown CT 06829-0060 *To be successful you must liken your endeavours to "defensive driving." You have to be more concerned with what others are doing wrong around you than what you're doing right to really get where you're going.*

JULIAN, JIM LEE, lawyer; b. Osceola, Ark., Dec. 14, 1954; s. John Roland and Lucille Angela (Potts) J.; m. Patricia Lynn Roberts, Jan. 26, 1980; 1 child, Kathryn Elizabeth. BA, Ark. State U., 1976; JD, U. Ark., 1979. Bar: Ark. 1979, U.S. Dist. Ct. (ea. and we. dists.) Ark. 1979, U.S. Ct. Appeals (8th cir.). Assoc. Skillman & Durrett, West Memphis, Ark., 1979-82; staff atty. Ark. Power and Light Co., Little Rock, 1982-84; assoc. House, Wallace & Jewell, Little Rock, 1984-85, ptnr., 1986-89, Chisenhall, Nestrud & Julian, Little Rock, 1989—. Pres. Crittenden County (Ark.) Young Dems., 1980-82; chmn. bd. dirs. Northside YMCA, 1992-96, North Little Rock Boys and Girls Club, 1998—. Mem. ABA, Internat. Assn. Def. Counsel, Ark. Bar Assn., Pulaski County Bar Assn., Ark. Assn. Def. Counsel, Major Sports Assn., North Hills Country Club. Avocation: golf. Home: 3711 Lochridge Rd North Little Rock AR 72116-8328 Office: Chisenhall Nestrud & Julian 400 W Capitol Ave Ste 2840 Little Rock AR 72201-3467 Office Phone: 501-372-5800.

JULIAN, MICHAEL, grocery company executive; b. 1950; With Human Sys. Inc., Florham Pk., NJ, 1975-85, Richfood Inc., Mechanicsville, Va., 1985-87; COO, exec. v.p. Farm Fresh Inc., 1987—, chmn., CEO, 1988—; pres., CEO Jitney Jungle, Jackson, Miss., 1997-1999. Office: Jitney Jungle 1855 Lakeland Dr Ste D20 Jackson MS 39216-4947

JULIAN, PAUL C., health products executive; BS, Salem State Coll., Mass., 1978. Corp. officer Owens & Minor; sales mgr. to grp. v.p., COO Stuart Med., Inc.; dist. mgr. Ivac Corp.; dist. regional mgr. U.S. Surg.; exec. v.p. health systems McKesson Corp., San Francisco, 1996—97, pres. med.-surgical bus., 1997—2000, pres. distbn., retail automation, pharmacy outsourcing and svcs. for payors, 2000—04, grp. pres., 2004—. Bd. mem. GS1 US, NADRO, Parata Systems. Mem.: Internat. Fedn. Pharm. Wholesalers (chmn. bd.), Healthcare Distbn. Mgmt. Assn. (bd. mem.). Office: McKesson Corpn One Post St San Francisco CA 94104*

JULIANO, JOHN LOUIS, lawyer; b. Oct. 21, 1944; s. John Carmine and Jeannette Helen (Ciotti) J.; m. Maryjane Theresa Groccia, July 4, 1966 (dec.); children: Jennifer, Jonathan; m. Edith Helen Martuscello, Aug. 21, 2004. BBA, St. John's U., 1966; JD, Bklyn. Law Sch., 1969. Bar: N.Y. 1970, U.S. Dist. Ct. (ea. and so. dists.) N.Y., U.S. Ct. Appeals (2d cir.), U.S. Supreme Ct. Ptnr. Juliano, Karlson, Weisberg, 1970-72; pvt. practice East Northport, NY, 1972—. Pres., dir. Hillside United Van Lines, Inc.; chair N.Y. State 10th Jud. Grievance Com., 2004—; lectr. Suffolk Acad. Law. Mem. ATLA, N.Y. State Bar Assn., Suffolk County Bar Assn. (pres. 1996-97, v.p. 1995-96, treas. 1994-95, sec. 1993-94, bd. dirs. 1998-2001), N.Y. State Trial Lawyers Assn., Criminal Bar Assn., Columbian Lawyers Assn. (sec. 1972, treas. 1973, pres. 1974-75), Am. Inns of Ct. Address: 39 Doyle Ct East Northport NY 11731-6404 Office Phone: 631-499-9300. Business E-Mail: jlj@johnljulianopc.com.

JULIANO, MARK J., hotel and gaming company executive; b. 1954; m. Jacqueline Juliano; 5 children. BA, LaSalle U., 1976. Pres. Boardwalk Regency Corp., 1994—99, Mirage Atlantic City Corp., 1999—2001; chmn. Atlantic City Convention and Visitors Authority, 2001—03; pres. Desert Palace, Inc., 2003—05; COO Trump Entertainment Resorts, Inc., 2005—07, interim CEO, 2007—. Mem. dinner com. Rock for the Cure, Nev. Cancer Inst.; chair Black and White Ball, Nev. Ballet Theatre; bd. dirs. Alex's Lemonade Stand, Opportunity Village, Las Vegas. Recipient Pinnacle Award for Excellence, NJ Gov.'s Conf. on Tourism, Humanitarian Award, Nat. Conf. for Cmty. and Justice, NJ Bus. Award, AFL-CIO, Man of Yr. Award, UNICO, FDR Cmty. Svc. Award, March of Dimes, Atlantic County chpt., Bus. Man of Yr. Award, Greater Atlantic City C. of C. Office: Trump Entertainment Resorts Inc 1000 Boardwalk at Virginia Ave Atlantic City NJ 08401 Office Phone: 609-449-6515. Office Fax: 605-449-6586.*

JULIBER, LOIS D., manufacturing executive; b. 1949; m. John Adams. BA, Wellesley Coll.; MBA, Harvard U. Former v.p. Gen. Foods Corp.; from gen. mgr. to pres. Far East/Can. divsn. Colgate-Palmolive Co., NYC, 1988-92, chief tech. officer, 1992-94, pres. Colgate—N.Am. divsn., 1994—97, exec. v.p. , chief ops. developed markets, 1997—2000, COO internat. ops., 2000—02, COO L. Am. and growth functions, 2002—, vice chmn., 2004—. Bd. dirs. DuPont Corp., 1995- Bd. trustees Brookdale Found., Wellesley Coll., Girls Inc. Recipient Luminary Award, Corp. Innovator Category, Com. 200, 2002. Mem. Harvard Bus. Sch. Club N.Y. (bd. dirs.) Avocations: tennis, gardening, cooking. Office: Colgate Palmolive Co 300 Park Ave Fl 8 New York NY 10022-7499

JULICH, NANCY C., secondary school educator; d. Robert E. and Fay Presley Conner; m. Marvin Milam Julich, June 4, 1966; children: Marvin Milam Julich, Jr., Rebecca Fay Patterson. BA in English, Music, History, U. Ala., 1966; BSE in English, Music, History, Athens State U., Ala., 1982; MA in Secondary Edn., U. North Ala., 1989; EdS in Secondary Edn., U. Ala., 2003. Tchr. Horizon HS, Decatur. Bd. dirs. Morgan County Adv. Bd. For At Risk Youth, Decatur, Ala.; adj. instr. English Calhoun CC, 1989—. Child abuse prevention specialist PACT, 1984—93; bd. dirs. Decatur (Ala.) Civic Chorus, 1968—80; pres. bd. HANDS, 1992—2000. Mem.: NEA (assoc.), Ala. Million Dollar Band, Decatur Ednl. Assn., Tchrs. English Jr. Coll. (assoc.), Nat. Coll. Tchrs. English (assoc.), Ala. Edn. Assn. (assoc.), Sigma Tau Delta (assoc.), Jr. League. Office: Horizon HS 809 Church St NE Decatur AL 35601 Home Phone: 256-355-7520; Office Phone: 256-552-3054.

JULIEN, CATHERINE, history professor; b. Palo Alto, Calif., May 19, 1950; d. Robert K. and Jean (Blaine) Julien; 1 child, Clara E.P. BA in Anthropology, U. Calif., Berkeley, 1971, MA in Anthropology, 1975, PhD in Anthropology, 1978. Dir. mus. programs Courthouse Mus., Merced, Calif.; lectr. and internat. study tour leader Smithsonian's Am. Mus. Natural History and Calif. Alumni Assn.; instr. Calif. State U., U. Bonn (Germany), U. Calif., Berkeley; assoc. prof. history We. Mich. U., Kalamazoo, 1996—. Author: Reading Inca History (Erminie Wheeler-Voegelin prize, 2000, Katherine Singer Kovacs prize MLA); contbr. articles to profl. jours. Fellow, John Simon Guggenheim Meml. Found., 2003. Mem.: Phi Beta Kappa. Office: We Mich U Dept History 4354 Friedmann Hall Kalamazoo MI 49008-5334 Office Phone: 269-387-4632. Office Fax: 269-387-4651. E-mail: catherine.julien@wmich.edu.*

JULIEN, CLAUDE, professional hockey coach; b. Blind River, Ont., Can., Apr. 23, 1960; m. Karen Julien; 1 child, Katryna Chanel. Profl. hockey player Oshawa Generals, 1977—78, Windsor Spitfires, 1979—80, Port Huron Flags, 1980—81, Salt Lake Golden Eagles, 1981—83, Milw. Admirals, 1983—84, Fredericton Express, 1984, 1986—87, Que. Nordiques, 1984—85, Balt. Skipjacks, 1987—88, Halifax Citadels, 1988—90, Kans. City Blades, 1990—91, Moncton Hawks, 1991—92; head coach Hull Olympiques, 1996—2000, Hamilton Bulldogs, 2000—03, Montreal Canadians, 2003—06, NJ Devils, 2006—07, Boston Bruins, 2007—. Recipient Louis A.R. Pieri Meml. Award, 2003. Office: Boston Bruins TD Banknorth Garden 100 Legends Way Boston MA 02114*

JULIEN, ROBERT MICHAEL, anesthesiologist, writer; b. Port Townsend, Wash., Mar. 24, 1942; s. Frank Felton and Mary Grace (Powers) J.; m. Judith Dianne DeChenne, Feb. 26, 1963; children: Robert Michael, Scott M. BS in Pharmacy, U. Wash., 1965, MS in Pharmacology, 1968, PhD, 1970; MD, U. Calif.-Irvine, 1977. Intern Good Samaritan Hosp., Portland, Oreg., 1977—78; resident Oreg. Health Scis. U., 1978—80; asst. prof. pharmacology U. Calif.-Irvine, 1970—74, asst. clin. prof., 1974—77; assoc. prof. anesthesiology and pharmacology U. Oreg., Portland, 1980—83; staff anesthesiologist St. Vincent Hosp., Portland, 1983—2005. Author: Primer of Drug Action, 1975, 10th edit., 2005, Understanding Anesthesiology, 1984, Drugs and the Body, 1987. Recipient Svc. award Am. Epilepsy Soc., 1975. Mem. Am. Soc. Anesthesiologists, Am. Assn. Pharmacology and Exptl. Therapeutics, Soc. Neurosci., Oreg. Med. Assn., Western Pharmacology Soc. Roman Catholic. Home: 23 Becket Lake Oswego OR 97035 Office Phone: 503-636-3180. Personal E-mail: drsjulien@comcast.net.

JULIEN, THOMAS THEODORE, religious denomination administrator; b. Arcanum, Ohio, June 27, 1931; s. Russel Ray and Clara (Cassel) J.; m. Doris Mardella Briner, Aug. 21, 1953; children: Becky Jean, Terry Lee, Jacqueline Sue. BA, Bob Jones U., 1953; MDiv, Grace Theol. Sem., Winona Lake, Ind., 1957, DD (hon.), 1996; cert. French lang., U. Grenoble, France, 1960. Ordained to ministry Fellowship of Grace Brethren Chs., 1956. Pastor Grace Brethren Ch., Ft. Wayne, Ind., 1955-58; missionary Grace Brethren Fgn. Missions, Grenoble, 1959-64, field supt. Macon, France, 1964-78, dir. for Europe, 1964-86; exec. dir. Grace Brethren Internat. Missions, Winona Lake, 1986-2000. Author: Handbook for Young Christians, 1959, Inherited Wealth, 1976, Spiritual Greatness, 1979, Seize the Moment, 2000, Antioch Revisited, 2006. Decorated chevalier de Republique (Ctrl. African Republic). Home: 545 S Circle Dr Warsaw IN 46580 Office: Grace Brethren Internat Missions PO Box 588 Winona Lake IN 46590-0588 Office Phone: 574-268-1888. Personal E-mail: tjulien@gbim.org.

JULIUS, DAVID, biochemist; BS in Life Scis., MIT, 1977; PhD in Biochemistry, U. Calif., Berkeley, 1984; postdoctoral rsch., Inst. Cancer Rsch., Columbia U., 1984—89. Asst. prof. U. Calif., San Francisco, 1989—96, assoc. prof., 1996—99, prof. dept. cellular and molecular pharmacology, 1999—. Mem. sci. adv. bd. Senomyx, Inc., Hydra Biosciences, Inc. Recipient First-Perl Neuroscience prize, UNC, Scholar award, McKnight Neuroscience Found., 1990, Investigator award, 1997, Syntex prize, 1997. Mem.: NAS. Office: UCSF Genentech Hall 600 16th St Box 2140 San Francisco CA 94143-2140 Business E-Mail: julius@cmp.ucsf.edu.

JULIUS, SCOTT DAVID, music educator; b. Sioux Falls, SD, Mar. 30, 1973; s. David Dale and LeAnn Julius; m. Nicole Marie Lieven; children: Abigail Lorraine, Ethan Miles. BA, U. Wis., Whitewater, 1997. Cert. tchr. Wis., 1999. Tchr. elem. instrumental music New Berlin Pub. Schs., Wis., 2000—01; dir. bands Delavan-Darien H.S., Wis., 2001—. Composer: (songs) Flintstones Got Rhythm. Office: Delavan-Darien High Sch 150 Cummings St Delavan WI 53115 Home Phone: 414-475-1730; Office Phone: 262-728-2642 4472.

JULSON, AMANDA PALMER, science educator; d. James Edward and Dorothy Ann Palmer; m. Bradley DeFlon Julson, Nov. 25, 1988; children: Benjamin Franklin, Evan Palmer, Dannika Brianne, Dale Adam. BS in Geology, U. Del., Newark, 1979; PhD, Princeton U., NJ, 1984. Staff scientist Ocean Drilling Program, College Station, Tex., 1984—91; instr. geology and oceanography Blinn Coll., Bryan, 1996—. Fellow, NSF, 1980—84. Mem.: Am. Geophys. Union, Phi Beta Kappa, Sigma Xi. Achievements include research in Cenozoic Radiolarians. Avocations: fossil collecting, gardening. Office: Blinn College 2423 Blinn Blvd Bryan TX 77805 Home Phone: 979-776-8501; Office Phone: 979-209-7503. E-mail: ajulson@blinn.edu.

JUMA, CALESTOUS, international development educator; b. Busia, Kenya, June 9, 1953; s. John Juma Kwada and Clementina Okhubedo Juma; m. Alison Thornycroft Field, Sept. 9, 1987; 1 child, Eric Kwada Field. MSc, U. Sussex, Falmer, Brighton, UK, 1983, DPhil, 1986. Sch. tchr., Mombasa, 1974-78; rschr., editor Environment Liaison Ctr., Nairobi, 1979-82; exec. dir., founder African Ctr. for Tech. Studies, Nairobi, 1988-95; exec. sec. UN Conv. on Biol. Diversity, Geneva and Montreal, 1995-98; rsch. fellow Kennedy Sch. Govt. Harvard U., Cambridge, Mass., 1999-2000, sr. rsch. fellow, program dir. Kennedy Sch. Govt., 2000—01; prof. practice internat. devel. Kennedy Sch. Govt. Harvard U., 2002—, dir. Sci., Tech. and Globalization Project; chancellor U. Guyana, 2002—. Author: Long Run Economics, 1987, The Gene Hunters, 1989, The Adaptive Economy, 1993, Open the Social Sciences, 1996. Recipient Pew Scholars award Pew Charitable Trusts, 1991, UN Global 500 Roll of Honor, UN Environ. Program, 1993, Henry Shaw medal Mo. Bot. Garden, 2001. Fellow Kenyan Nat. Acad. Scis., N.Y. Acad. Scis., World Acad. Art and Sci.; mem. AAAS, NAS (bd. agr. and natural resources), Internat. Soc. for Study of Time. Avocations: hiking, bicycling. Office: Belfer Ctr Sci and Internat Affairs Littauer 356 79 JFK St Cambridge MA 02138 Office Phone: 617-496-8127. Office Fax: 617-495-8963. E-mail: calestous_juma@harvard.edu.

JUMONVILLE, FELIX JOSEPH, JR., physical education educator, real estate company officer; b. Crowley, La., Nov. 20, 1920; s. Felix Joseph and Mabel (Rogers) J.; m. Mary Louise Hoke, Jan. 11, 1952; children: Carol, Susan. BS, La. State U., 1942; MS, U. So. Calif., 1948, EdD, 1952. Assoc. prof. phys. edn. L.A. State Coll., 1948-60; prof. phys. edn. Calif. State U., Northridge, 1960-87, emeritus prof. phys. edn., 1987—. Owner Felix Jumonville Realty, Northridge, 1974-82, Big Valley Realty, Inc., 1982-83, Century 21 Lamb Realtors, 1983-86, Cardinal Realtors, 1986-87; varsity track and cross-country head coach LA State Coll., 1952-60, Calif. State U., Northridge, 1960-71. With USCGR, 1942—46. Named to, Baton Rouge H.S. Hall of Fame; recipient U.S. Commendation medal. Mem.: Assn. Calif. State Univ. Profs., Pi Tau Pi, Kappa Sigma, Phi Epsilon Kappa. Home: 18427 Vincennes #36 Northridge CA 91325

JUMP, CHESTER JACKSON, JR., clergyman, church official; b. Covington, Ky., Mar. 31, 1918; s. Chester Jackson and Inez (Moore) J.; m. Margaret Elizabeth Savidge, Sept. 5, 1942; children— Karen Jane, Richard Alan, Catherine Louise, Robert Jon. AB, Albright Coll., 1938; MA, Columbia U., 1940; BD, Union Theol. Sem. N.Y.C., 1943; postgrad., Ecole Coloniale, Brussels, Belgium, 1950-51; DD, Eastern Bapt. Theol. Sem., 1965. Ordained to ministry Bapt. Ch., 1943. Pastor N.E. Larger Parish, Lyndon Center, Vt., 1943-44; missionary Belgian Congo, Republic of Congo, 1945-62; regional rep. Am. Bapt. Fgn. Mission Socs., Valley Forge, Pa., 1961-64, exec. dir., 1965-83; assoc. gen. sec. Am. Bapt. Chs., 1965-83, dir. world relief, 1983-88, interim gen. sec., 1987-88; mem. gen. bd. Nat. Council Chs., 1965-75, mem. program bd., exec. com. div. overseas ministries, 1965-83, mem. gov. bd., 1965-75, 87-88; mem. exec. com. Bapt. World Alliance, 1965-85, 87-88, v.p., 1980-85; bd. dirs., exec. com. Am. Bapt. Chs., Pa., Del., 1987-89; chmn., budget commn. Commn. on New Ch. Planting and Adminstrv. Svcs., 1989-99. Trustee Eastern Bapt. Theol. Sem.; mem. Ch. World Service Commn., 1983-88, fin. com., 1983-88; mem. Bapt. World Aid, 1970-85; mem. bd. personnel com. IMPACT. Author: (with wife) Congo Diary, 1950, Coming, Ready or Not, 1959. Mem. Pi Gamma Mu. Home and Office: 240 Applewood Dr Apt 2 Lewisburg PA 17837 E-mail: cjmsjump@ptd.net.

JUMPER, JOHN PHILLIP, retired military officer; b. Paris, Tex., Feb. 4, 1945; s. Jimmy Jumper and Maree Loretta (Jumper) J.; m. Ellen Elizabeth McGhee, Mar. 29, 1969; children: Catherine, Janet, Melissa. BSEE, Va. Mil. Inst., 1966; MBA, Golden Gate U., 1978; postgrad., Air Command and Staff Coll., Maxwell AFB, Ala., 1977-78, Nat. War Coll., Washington, 1981-82. Commd. 2d lt. USAF, 1966, advanced through grades to gen., 1997, ret., 2005; instr. pilot 414th Fighter Weapons Squadron, Nellis AFB, Nev., 1974-77; action officer Directorate for Ops. and Tng., Washington, 1978-81; comdr. 430th Tactical Fighter Squadron, Nellis AFB, Nev., 1983; exec. officer to comdr. Hdqrs. Tactical Air Command, Langley AFB, Va., 1983-86; comdr. 33d Tactical Fighter Wing, Eglin AFB, Fla., 1986-87, 1987-88, 57th Fighter Weapons Wing, Nellis AFB, 1988-90; dep. dir. politico-mil. affairs Joint Staff, Washington, 1990-92; sr. mil. asst. for sec. def. Office Sec. Def., Washington, 1992-94; comdr. 9th AF, Shaw AFB, 1994-96; dep. chief of staff, air & space HAF, Washington, 1996-97; commdr. Allied Air Forces Ctrl. Europe, Ramstein AB, Germany, 1997-2000, HQ Air Combat Command, Langley AFB, 2000—01; chief of staff, USAF US Dept. Def., Washington, 2001—05. Adv. bd. PlatinumSolutions, Reston, Va.; bd. dirs. Goodrich Corp., Rolls-Royce North Am. Holdings, Inc., TechTeam Global, Inc., Jacobs Engring. Group Inc. Contbr. articles to mil. pub. Decorated Def. DSM with oak leaf cluster, Legion of Merit DSM with oak leaf cluster, DFC with 2 oak leaf clusters, Air medal with 17 oak leaf clusters. Mem. Air Force Assn., Air Force Village Charitable Found. Roman Catholic. Avocations: racquet ball, jogging, piano, guitar, golf, sports cars.*

JUN, HEESOON, psychology professor; b. Seoul, Korea (South); d. Yongduck Jun and Whangwool Kang; children: Gabriel J Aust, Eliot P Aust. PhD, U. of Wash., 1979—82. Washington State Licensed Psychologist Health Dept., State of Wash., 1987. Psychology prof. Evergreen State Coll., Olympia, Wash., 1996—. Part-time pvt. practice and consulting, Olympia, Wash. Recipient Exceptional Faculty award, Centalia Coll., 1996, NISOD Excellence award, U. of Tex. at Austin, 1996; Bilingual fellowship, U.S. Dept. of Edn., 1980—82. Mem.: APA, Deschutes Psychol. Assn. Office: Evergreen State Coll 2700 Pkwy Olympia WA 98505 Office Phone: 360-867-6855.

JUN, INSOO, nuclear scientist, researcher; b. Inchon, Republic of Korea, Oct. 3, 1963; arrived in U.S., 1983; s. Si-Won and Chan-Bok Jun; m. Seung-Ah Lee. BS, U. Mass., 1986; PhD, UCLA, 1991. Post-doctoal fellow UCLA, LA, 1992—95; scientist Hughes Space and Comm. Co., El Segundo, Calif., 1996—2000; sr. tech. staff Jet Propulsion Lab., Pasadena, Calif., 2001—. Contbr. articles to profl. jours. Mem.: Am. Geophys. Union, Americal Nuc. Soc. Office: Jet Propulsion Laboratory 4800 Oak Grove Drive Pasadena CA 91109

JUNEK, JOHN C., lawyer, finance company executive; BA, Yale U.; JD, U. Va. Bar: Calif., NY. Regulatory staff lawyer Fed. Reserve Bank of NY, 1973—78; staff atty. Am. Express Co., 1978—82; v.p., mng. counsel regulation and compliance Crocker Nat. Bank, San Francisco, 1982—85; gen. counsel Am. Express Ltd.; dep. gen. counsel Am. Express Travel Related Svcs., 1990—2000; sr. v.p., gen. counsel Am. Express Fin. Corp., 2000; exec. v.p., gen. counsel Ameriprise Financial, Inc., Mpls., 2005—. Bd. dirs., exec. com. Guthrie Theater. Mem.: NY State Bar Assn., State Bar Calif. Office: Ameriprise Fin, Inc 55 Ameriprise Fin Ctr Minneapolis MN 55474 Office Phone: 612-671-3131.*

JUNEWICZ, JAMES J., lawyer; b. Oct. 1, 1950; s. John and Genevieve J.; m. Virginia Bornyas. BS, Georgetown U., 1972; JD, Duquesne U., 1976; LLM, NYU, 1978. Bar: Pa. 1977, D.C. 1978, Ill. 1984. Asst. gen. counsel SEC, Washington, 1982—84; ptnr. Mayer, Brown, Rowe & Maw LLP, Chgo., 1987—2007, Winston & Strawn LLP, Chgo., 2007—. Office: Winston & Strawn LLP 35 W Wacker Dr Chicago IL 60601 Office Phone: 312-782-0600.

JUNG, ANDREA, cosmetics company executive; b. Toronto, Sept. 18, 1958; m. Michael Gould, 1993 (div.); 2 children. BA magna cum laude in English Lit., Princeton U., 1979. With Bloomingdale's; sr. v.p., gen. mdse. mgr. J.W. Robinson; sr. v.p. gen. mdse. I. Magnin, San Francisco, 1987—91; exec. v.p. women's merchandising Neiman Marcus, 1991—92; cons. Avon Products, Inc., NYC, 1993, pres. product mktg. group, 1994—96, pres. global mktg., 1996—97, exec. v.p., pres. global mktg. & new bus., 1997—98, COO, 1998—99, pres., 1998—2001, CEO, 1999—, chmn., 2001—. Chmn. Cosmetic, Toiletry & Fragrance Found., 2001—05; bd. dirs. GE Co., 1998—, Avon Products Inc., 1998—, Cosmetic Exec. Women. Sale Corp., Donna Karan Internat., Catalyst; mem. internat. advisory bd. Solomon Smith Barney. Mem. bd. trustees NY Presbyn. Hosp. Named one of the 50 Most Powerful Women in Bus., Fortune mag., 1998, Most Powerful Women, Forbes mag., 2005, Top 50 Women to Watch, Wall St. Jour., 2005, 2006, 50 Most Powerful Women in Bus., Fortune mag., 2006. Achievements include fluent in Chinese (Mandarin). Office: Avon Products Inc 1345 Ave Americas New York NY 10105-0302*

JUNG, BETTY CHIN, epidemiologist, educator, nurse; b. Bklyn., Nov. 28, 1948; d. Han You and Bo Ngan (Moy) Chin; m. Lee Jung, Oct. 1, 1972; children: Daniel, Stephanie. AA, King's Coll., Briarcliff Manor, NY, 1968; BS, Columbia U., NYC, 1971; MPH, So. Conn. State U., New Haven, 1993. RN, Conn., Miss., N.Y.; cert. health edn. specialist; credentialed health info. web site rater; notary pub., Conn., 2004. Adminstrv. asst. Columbia U., NYC, 1968-69; practical nurse Babies Hosp., NYC, 1969-70, charge nurse, 1974-76; staff nurse Columbia-Presbyn. Hosp., NYC, 1971-73; sch. nurse Nassau County Sch. System, Long Island, NY, 1984-85; grad. asst. So. Conn. State U., New Haven, 1991-92; coop. edn. intern Conn. Dept. Health Svcs., Hartford, 1991-92; intern North Ctrl. Dist. Health Dept., Enfield, Conn., 1992; epidemiologist Conn. Dept. Pub. Health, Hartford, Conn., 1992-98, health program assoc., 1998-2001, cardiovascular epidemiologist, 2003—05, cardiovascular and diabetes epidemiologist, 2005—, hepatitis program evaluator, 2007; staff nurse Quinnipiac Coll. Student Health Svcs., 1998; mem. multicultural adv. coun. Conn. Dept. Children and Families, assoc. rsch. analyst, 2001—03. Instr. Albertus Magnus Coll., 1995—96; health columnist Baldwin Newcomers Club, NY, 1977—78; coord. Dept. Pub. Health and Svcs./Conn. EPI Info. Network, Hartford, 1994—2001; mem. Nat. Lead Info. Ctr. Spkrs. Bur., 1997—98; vol. scientist Sci.-By-Mail, 1997—98; mem. Nat. Safety Coun. Environ. Health Ctr. Spkrs. Referral Bur., 1998—2001; mem. affirmative action employee adv. com. Conn. Dept. Pub. Health, 1998—2001, mem. genetics planning com., 2004—, mem. genetics edn. and workforce devel. work group, 2006—, mem. connectifit adv. com., 2006—07, mem. connectifit survey subcommittee, 2006—07; mem. Permanent Commn. Status of Women Talent Network, 1996—, chair news subcom., editor affirmative action newsletter, 2001; apptd. mem. multicultural adv. coun. Conn. Dept. Children and Families, 2002—03; pilot reviewer CDC Pub. Health Tng. Network, 2002—; assoc. NIH, 2004—; mem. functions workgroup EPI; dir.'s coun. pub. reps. NIH, 2004—; mem. CDC CVH Inst. planning com. Conn. Dept. Pub. Health, 2005—, lead cardiovasc. epidemiology work group, 2005—, mem. genetics edn. nurse edn. subcom., 2006—, lead diabetes data and surveillance work group, 2007—; numerous positions So. Conn. State U., 1991—, adj. prof., 1998—, apptd. CDC cardiovascular health and bus. work group, 2005—; cons. in field; mem. grants and contracts working group Status of Women Talent Network, 2005, mem. cardiovascular state plan exec. com., 2005—; mem. adv. coun. So. Conn. State U. Dept. Pub. Health, 2007—; book proposal reviewer in field. Mem. editl. bd.: Data Quality, 1994—98, mem. manuscript rev. bd.: Jour. Clin. Outcomes Mgmt., 1995—, Pub. Health Reports, 1997—98; contbg. editor: Episource, A Guide to Resources in Epidemiology, 1998—99; editor/web pub.: SCSU Pub. Health E-News Bull., 2000—01, Public Health E-news, 2001—, Public Health Jobs Electronic Newsletter, 2000—; contbr. articles to profl. jours. Vol. nurse health educator, coord. Chinatown's First Ann. Health Fair, 1971-72; treas. Tenant Assn., Bronx, N.Y., 1976-77; pre-confirmation tchr. Bethlehem Luth. Ch., Baldwin, N.Y., 1981-85. Grantee, USPHS, 1992—98, Fed. HUD, 1995—98, U.S. Preventive Health and Health Svcs., 1998, CDC Cardiovasc. Health Program, 2003—07, CDC Diabetes Prevention and Control Program, 2005—, others; Merit scholar, Kings Coll., 1968, Columbia U. scholar, 1968—69, Women's Florist Assn. scholar, 1968, Bessie Lee Gambrill scholar, So. Alumni Assn., 1992, block grantee, Maternal Child Health, 1998—2001, Adult Blood Lead Epidemiology and Surveillance Program grantee, CDC/Nat. Inst. Occupl. Safety and Health, 1992—98. Fellow: Soc. for Pub. Health Edn.; mem.: APHA (health care reform activist network, peer assistance the model stds. project), Nat. Assn. Chronic Disease Dirs., Sci. and Epidemiology (com. mem. 2007—), Pub. Health Expertise Network of Mentors (program dir. 2002—), Internat. Assn. Webmasters and Designers (web site rater Health Improvement Inst. 2006—), Boston Mus. Sci., Nat. Acad. Sci. (mentor career planning ctr. beginning scientists & engrs. 1997—98), Columbia U. Sch. Nursing Alumni Assn. (survey cons. 1994—95), Internat. Assn. IT Trainers (assoc.), So. Conn. State U. Alumni Assn. (founder pub. health chpt. 1994, interim pres, then pres. 1994—98, founder, coord. pub. health alumni mentor program 1994—2002, chair coms. 1994—, numerous other positions 1994—, editor MPH Alumni Record 1995—, founder, dir., coord. pub. health alumni spkrs. bur. 1997—, founder, program dir. pub. health expertise network of mentors 2002—, alumni surveys program dir. 2007—,

Alumni Appreciation award 1998), Conn. Pub. Health Assn., Nat. Lead Info. Ctr. Spkrs. Bur., Conn. State and Territorial Epidemiologists (alternate cons. 1996—, co-leader Healthy People 2010 1999—2001, lead cardiovasc. disease 2002—), Am. Statis. Assn. (OSPA media experts list 1997—). Avocations: reading, writing, research, web development and design, bicycling. Home: 25 Driftwood Ln Guilford CT 06437-1929 Office: Conn Dept Pub Health 410 Capitol Ave Hartford CT 06106 Office Phone: 860-509-7711. Personal E-mail: bettycjung@yahoo.com.

JUNG, CRAIG D., food products executive; Grad., US Mil. Acad., West Point, NY, 1975; MPA, Harvard U., Cambridge, Mass., 2004. Various sr. exec. positions in gen. mgmt., mktg. and sales PepsiCo; founding COO Pepsi Bottling Group; CEO Panamerican Beverages; CEO, bd. dirs. Interstate Bakeries Corp., 2007—. Office: Interstate Bakeries Corp 12 E Armour Blvd Kansas City MO 64111 Office Phone: 816-502-4000.*

JUNG, DORIS, soprano; b. Centralia, Ill., Jan. 5, 1924; d. John Jay and May (Middleton) Crittenden; m. Felix Popper, Nov. 3, 1951; 1 son, Richard Dorian. Student, U. Ill., Mannes Coll. Music, Vienna Acad. Performing Arts; student of Julius Cohen, student of Emma Zador, student of Luise Helletsgruber, student of Winifred Cecil. Voice tchr., NYC, 1970—. Debut as Vitellia in: Clemenza di Tito, Zurich Opera, Switzerland, 1955, other appearances with Hamburg State Opera, Munich State Opera, Vienna State Opera, Royal Opera Copenhagen, Royal Opera Stockholm, Marseille and Strasbourg, France, Naples Opera Co., Italy, Catania Opera Co., Italy, NYC Opera, Met. Opera; soloist: Wagner concert conducted by Leopold Stokowski, 1971; with Syracuse Symphony, NY, 1981; translator Birgit Nilsson Autobiography, 2007. Home: 40 W 84th St New York NY 10024-4749 Office Phone: 212-873-3147. *Whether performing as a singer or teaching, attempting to understand the voice is tremendously daunting. As with life itself, the human voice defies understanding with its day to day differences and one's everchanging points of view. The secret of unflagging devotion to this life's work lies in accepting its elusiveness.*

JUNG, KWAN YEE, artist; b. Toisun, Guang Dong, China, Nov. 25, 1932; came to U.S., 1963; s. Fred Hing and Shun Tong (Lee) J.; m. Yee Wah Yip, Sept. 10, 1962; children: Jeanne, Kathy, Laura. BA, New Asia Coll., Hong Kong, 1961. Comml. artist advt. dept. Hong Kong Soy Bean Products Co., 1961-63; owner Jung's Gallery, La Jolla, Calif., 1976-78; freelance artist, instr., demonstrator San Diego, 1978—. Exhibited in group shows including NAD annuals, 1999, AWS, NWS; one-man shows at Kim Art Gallery, Rowland Heights, Calif., 1981, Co-art Internat. Gallery, Vancouver, B.C., Can., 1996, Kruglak Gallery, Mira Costa Coll., Oceanside, Calif., 1997, San Diego Chinese Hist. Mus., 1997, The Earl and Birdie Taylor Libr., San Diego, 1998; author, Chinese Brush Painting Step By Step, 2003. Recipient First Place award San Diego Watercolor Soc., 1973, Best of Show award Sumi-E Soc. Am., 1974, Purchase award Springville Mus. Art, 1974. Mem. Nat. Acad. Design (Merit award 1992, nat. academician), Am. Watercolor Soc., Nat. Watercolor Soc. E-mail: kjung1@san.rr.com.

JUNG, PETER MICHAEL, lawyer; b. Ossining, NY, May 12, 1955; s. Peter Joseph and Paula June (Moyer) J.; m. Gretchen Lee Megowen, June 19, 1976. SB in (math., earth and planetary scis.), MIT, 1975; JD magna cum laude, Harvard U., 1979. Bar: Tex. 1979, US Dist. Ct. (no. dist.) Tex. 1979, US Ct. Appeals (5th cir.) 1980, US Dist. Ct. (ea. dist.) Tex. 1981, US Ct. Appeals (10th cir.) 1984, S Ct. Appeals (6th cir.) 1992, US Supreme Ct. 1988, US Dist. Ct. (so. and we. dists.) Tex. 1989; cert. civil appellate law Tex. Bd. Legal Specialization, US Cts. of Appeals (8th, 9th, & 11th cirs.). Tech. staff C.S. Draper Lab., Cambridge, Mass., 1975-76; law clk. to hon. Patrick E. Higginbotham US Dist. Ct. (no. dist.) Tex., Dallas, 1979-80; assoc. Strasburger & Price, Dallas, 1980-85, ptnr., 1986—. Lectr. El Centro Cmty. Coll., Dallas, 1980-82; instr. So. Meth. U., Dallas, 1984-86, com. Qualified Judiciary 1992-, Dallas Ethics Rev. Task Force 1999, Dallas Charter Rev. Commn. 2002-03, adv. com. Dallas Comprehensive Plan 2004-06. Co-author: An Alternative Entry-Through-Landing Guidance Scheme for the Space Shuttle Orbital Flight Test, 1976, Introduction to the American Legal System, Texas Edition, 1982; contbg. editor Legal Asst. Today Mag., 1983-88. Sec. Dallas Homeowners League, 1984-86, 1st v.p., 1986-87, pres., 1987-88, treas., 1988-89, 92—, bd. dirs. 1984-90, 91—; pres. White Rock Neighborhood Assn., Dallaas, 1984-85, v.p., 1994—; mem. adv. com. Dallas Zoning Ordinance, 1985-2005, Leadership Dallas, 1985-86, Dallas City Plan and Zoning Commn., 1987-89, 91; bd. dirs. Friends of Fair Park, 1990—, mem. exec. com., 1991—; bd. dirs. Tex. Neighborhoods Together, 1989-95, sec., 1989-91, pres. 1991-95, Harvard Law Sch. Assn. Recipient Pres.'s award, 1992—97, Super Lawyers, Tex. Monthly's top 100, Best Lawyers in Dallas, D Mag.'s, Best Lawyers in Am., 2007. Mem. Tex. Bar Assn. (com.) 1995-1996, Dallas Bar Assn.(chmn.) 1995,2003, Bar Assn. 5th Fed. Cir., Tex. Assn. Def. Counsel (vice-chmn. 1985-87, chmn. amicus curiae com. 1991-1997, regional v.p. 1993-95, adminstrv. v.p. 1995-97), (nominating com., 1998, 2000, 2001), chair Strasburger's Appellate and Zoning & Land Use practices ,mem. Govtl. Law practice grp., fellow Am. Acad. Appellate Lawyer, Supreme Ct.Tex. Task Force Jury Charge 1991-94. Republican. Lutheran. Avocations: theater, travel. Office: Strasburger & Price 901 Main St Ste 4400 Dallas TX 75202 Office Phone: 214-651-4724. Office Fax: 214-659-4022. Business E-Mail: michael.jung@strasburger.com.

JUNG, REX EUGENE, psychologist, researcher; b. Middletown, Ohio, May 4, 1964; s. Sandra Lynn Jung; m. Ann Moore Jung, Dec. 31, 1999; children: Stevan Gutierrez, Mia Gutierrez. BS in Bus., U. Colo., 1986; MS in Clin. Psychology, U. N.Mex., 1996, PhD in Clin. Psychology, 2001. Rsch. asst. Nat. Inst. Aging, Gerontology Rsch. Ctr., Baltimore, Md., 1992—93; neuropsychology intern, dept. neurosurgery MIEMS, Baltimore, Md., 1993; psychometrist U. N.Mex. Mental Health Services, Albuqueque, N.Mex., 1993—94; neuropsychology assoc. Neuropsychology Assocs. PC, Albuquerque, 1994—2003; rsch. asst. Clin. & Magnetic Resonance Rsch. Ctr., Albuquerque, 1996—2000; clin. neuropsychology intern, dept. psychiatry and behavioral medicine Baylor Coll. Medicine, Houston, 2000—01; postdoctoral fellow, psychiatry rsch. U. N.Mex, Albuquerque, 2001—03, asst. rsch. prof., dept. neurology, 2003—; rsch. scientist The Mental Illness and Neuroscience Discovery (MIND) Imaging Ctr., Albuquerque, 2003—. Spkr. in field. Contbr. articles to profl. jours., chapters to books; ad hoc reviewer Am. Jour. Epidemiology, Am. Jour. Psychiatry, Biol. Psychiatry, Human Brain Mapping, and Neuropsychopharmacology. Named to Student Summer Internship Program in Biomedical Rsch., NIH, 1993; recipient Award for Excellence in Rsch., Mensa Edn. and Rsch. Found., 2000; fellow Arts and Scis. Grad. fellow, U. N.Mex., 2000, Gina Finzi Meml. Student Summer fellow, Lupus Found. Am., 1998; scholar Benjamin Franklin Haught revolving scholar in psychology, U. N.Mex., 1999. Mem.: APA (assoc.), Orgn. for Human Brain Mapping, Internat. Soc. for Intelligence Rsch.; Internat. Neuropsychological Soc., Internat. Soc. Magnetic Resonance in Medicine. Achievements include patents in field. Office: Univ New Mexico (CMRRC) 1201 Yale NE Albuquerque NM 87131 also: The MIND Inst The Pete and Nancy Domenici Hall 1101 Yale Blvd NE Albuquerque NM 87106 Address: Dept Neurology MSC10 5620 Health Sci Ctr 1 University of New Mexico Albuquerque NM 87131-0001 Personal E-mail: rexjung@yahoo.com. Business E-Mail: rjung@lizard.unm.edu.

JUNG, SANGWOOK, neurobiologist; arrived in U.S., 2000; s. S.D. Jung and S.J. Kim; m. Seungkyung Yang, Oct. 15, 1997. PhD, U. Tex., Austin, 2005; BS, Korea U., Seoul, 1992. Grad. rsch. asst. KAIST, Daejon, Republic of Korea, 1993—95; rsch. scientist LG Chem. R & D Ctr., Daejon, Republic of Korea, 1995—2000; grad. rsch. asst. Cell and Molecular Biology Program U. Tex., Austin, 2000—05; sr. postdoctroal fellow dept. neurology U. Wash., Seattle, 2005—. Fred Murphy Jones fellowship, Waggoner Ctr. for Alcohol and Addiction Rsch., 2001, 2002. Business E-Mail: swjungf@u.washington.edu.

JUNG, TIMOTHY TAE KUN, otolaryngologist; b. Seoul, Korea, Dec. 1, 1943; came to U.S., 1969; s. Yoon Yong and Helen Chung-Hyuk (Im) J.; m. Lucy Moon Young, Sept. 10, 1972; children: David, Michael, Karen. BS, Seoul Nat. U., 1966, Loma Linda U., 1971, MD, 1974; PhD, U. Minn., 1980. Diplomate Am. Bd. Otolaryngology. Med. intern Loma Linda U. Med. Ctr., Calif., 1974—75; resident in surgery U. Minn. Med. Sch., Mpls., 1975—76, resident in otolaryngology, 1976—80, asst. prof. otolaryngology, 1980—84, clin. asst. prof., dir. prostaglandin lab., 1984—85; assoc. prof., dir. otolaryngology rsch. Loma Linda U., 1985—90, prof., dir. otolaryngology rsch., 1990—92, clin. prof., dir. otolaryngology rsch., 1992—. Mem. deafness and communications disroders rev. com. Nat. Inst. Deafness and Communications, NIH, 1989-92. Mem. editl. bd. Annals of Otology, Rhinology & Laryngology, 1994-2004, Acta Otolaryngologica, 1999—; contbr. chpts. to books, over 100 articles to profl. jours. Sec. gen. Korean-Am. Otolaryngcology Soc., 1990—. Sgt. Korean Army, 1966—69. Recipient Edmund Price Fowler award. Fellow ACS, Triological Soc., Am. Acad. Otolaryngology (honor award 1990), Am. Acad. Surgeons; mem. AMA, Am. Otol. Soc., Am. Neurotol. Soc., Assn. Rsch. in Otolaryngology, Centurions, Collegium Otorhinolaryngogicum Amicetiae Sacrum, Korean-Am. Otolaryngology Soc. (sec. gen. 1990--), Alpha Omega Alpha. Seventh-day Adventist. Avocations: horticulture, photography, hiking, running. Home: 11790 Pecan Way Loma Linda CA 92354-3452 Office: 3975 Jackson St Ste 202 Riverside CA 92503-3947 Home Phone: 909-799-3595; Office Phone: 951-352-7920. Personal E-mail: tjung1790@aol.com.

JUNGBLUTH, CONNIE CARLSON, private banker; b. Cheyenne, Wyo., June 20, 1955; d. Charles Marion and Janice Yvonne (Keldsen) Carlson; m. Kirk E. Jungbluth, Feb. 5, 1977; children: Tyler, Ryan. BS, Colo. State U., 1976. CPA, Colo., Ariz. Sr. acct. Rhode Scripter & Assoc., Boulder, Colo., 1977-81; mng. acct. Arthur Young, Denver, 1981-85; asst. v.p. Dain Bosworth, Denver, 1985-87; v.p. George K. Baum & Co., Denver, 1987-91; acct. Ariz. Luth. Acad., 1994-95; sr. tax acct. Ernst & Young, LLP, Phoenix, 1995-96; nat. tax mgr. personal wealth mgmt. RSM McGladrey, Inc., Phoenix, 1996-2000; mgr. pvt. client svcs. Arthur Andersen, Phoenix, 2000—01; sr. v.p. Bank of Am. Pvt. Bank, Phoenix, 2002—06; dir. Citigroup Pvt. Bank, 2006—. Mem. adv. bd. Ariz. Cmty. Found., 2002—, chair profl. edn. com., 2007—; mem. adv. bd. Jewish Cmty. Found., 2002—, Ariz. State U. Found., 2004—05, Children's Hosp., Phoenix, 2004—, chmn., prof. adv. bd., 2006—. Active Denver Estate Planning Coun., 1981-85, Ctrl. Ariz. Estate Planning Coun., 1997-98, S. Nev. Estate Planning Coun., 2003-4; organizer Little People Am., Rocky Mountain Med. Clinic and Symposium, Denver, 1986; mem. adv. bd. Children's Home Health, Denver, 1986-89, chmn. profl. adv. bd., 2006—; fin. adv. bd. Gail Shoettler for State Treas., Denver, 1986; campaign chmn. Kathi Williams for Colo. State Legislature, 1986; mem. Sch. dist. 12 Colo. Edn. Found. Bd., 1991, Napa Sch. Dist. Elem. Site com., 1992-94; apptd. Ariz. Gov.'s Coun. Devel. Disabilities, 1998-99, chmn. planning com., 1998-99; mem. profl. adv. bd., editor Charitable Giving Guide, Ariz. Cmty. Found., 2002—; dir. Phoenix Symphony, 2007—. Named one of 50 to watch, Denver mag., 1988. Mem. AICPA, Colo. Soc. CPAs (strategic planning com. 1987-89, instr. bank 1983, trustee 1984-87, pres. bd. trustees 1986-87, bd. dir. 1987-89, chmn. career edn. com. 1982-83, pub. svc. award 1985-87), Little People of Am., Colo. Mcpl. Bond Dealers, Ariz. Herb Assn., Metro North C. of C. (bd. dir. 1987-90), Denver City Club (bd. dir. 1987-88), Phi Beta Phi. Avocations: faith, horticulture, philanthropy, gourmet cooking, reading.

JUNGBLUTH, KIRK E., real estate appraiser; b. Lima, Ohio, Apr. 5, 1949; s. Harold A. and Marjorie J. (Brown) Jungbluth; m. Connie Carlson, Feb. 5, 1977; children: Tyler, Ryan. Student, Mesa Coll., Grand Junction, Colo., Regis Coll., Denver. Cert. gen. real estate appraiser Ariz. Loan officer, real estate appraiser Home Fed. Savs. & Loan, Ft. Collins, Colo., 1973-76; real estate appraiser Jungbluth & Assocs., Ft. Collins, 1976-83; pres., bd. dirs. Security Diamond Corp., Denver, 1982-90; nat. sales dir. InfoAm. Computers, Denver, 1982-90; chmn. bd. dirs., CEO U.S. Capital Lending Corp., Denver, 1987-91; ct.-appointed receiver Dist. Ct. State of Colo., 1990; mgr. real estate appraisal World Savs. & Loan Assn., Walnut Creek, 1992-93, Pleasanton, Calif., 1993—94, Phoenix, 1994—2000; pres., CEO Real Estate Rsch. Corp., Phoenix, 2000—. Sgt. USMC, 1969—71. Republican. Avocations: golf, skiing, scuba diving. Office: PO Box 28382 Tempe AZ 85285 Home: 3835 E Minton Pl Mesa AZ 85215 Office Phone: 602-291-0255. Business E-Mail: kj@realestateresearchcorp.com.

JUNGEBERG, THOMAS DONALD, lawyer; b. Berea, Ohio, June 12, 1950; s. Wilbert Donald and Carolyn Francis (Gaube) J.; m. Kathleen Ann Killmer, Oct. 5, 1973; children: Kimberlee Ann, Allison Lynn, Zebulun Thomas, Nathan Aaron. BA, Kent State U., 1972; JD, Cleve. State U., 1976. Bar: Ohio 1976, Mass. 2001, U.S. Dist. Ct. (no. dist.) Ohio 1977, U.S. Tax Ct. 1980, U.S. Supreme Ct. 1980. Tchr. Berea City Schs., Ohio, 1972-75; staff atty. Palmquist & Palmquist, Medina, Ohio, 1977-80, Gibbs & Craze, Parma Heights, Ohio, 1980-81; sole practice Medina, 1981-87; v.p., gen. counsel, corp. sec. Shelby (Ohio) Ins. Co., 1987-95; prin. Lexington (Ohio) Ins. Cons., 1995-96; sole practice Lexington, 1995-96; v.p. legal Reliance Nat., Cleve., 1996-98; asst. v.p., asst. gen. counsel Commerce Ins. Group, Webster, Mass., 1999—2005; v.p., asst. sec. Am. Commerce Ins. Co., Columbus, Ohio, 2005—. Tchr. First Bapt. Christian Sch., Medina, 1981-84; elder, sec. First Bapt. Ch. of Medina, 1979-86, chmn. First Bapt. Christian Sch., Medina, 1984; bd. govs. Ohio Med. Profl. Liability Underwriting Assn., 1993-95; dir. Inst. Inst. Ind., 1994-95. Mem. Ohio State Bar Assn., Am. Corp. Counsel Assn., Aircrafts Owners & Pilots Assn., Experimental Aircraft Assn. Republican. Avocations: piano, gospel music composition, flying. Home: 4181 Goldenseal Way Hilliard OH 43026-3007 Business E-Mail: tdjungeberg@aol.com, tjungeb@commerceinsurance.com.

JUNGER, MIGUEL CHAPERO, retired acoustics researcher; b. Dresden, Germany, Jan. 29, 1923; came to U.S., 1941, naturalized, 1946; s. José and Adrienne (Junger) Chapiro; m. Ellen Sinclair, 1960; children: M. Sebastian, A. Carlotta. BS, MIT, 1944, SM, 1946; ScD (Gordon McKay scholar), Harvard U., 1951. Postdoctoral rsch. fellow in acoustics Harvard U., 1951-55; partner Cambridge Acoustical Assocs., Inc., 1955-59, pres., 1959-89, chmn. bd. dirs., 1989-97; ret. Sr. vis. lectr. ocean enging. dept. MIT, Cambridge, 1968-78; vis. prof. U. Technologie de Compiègne, 1975, 77-82 Author: Sound, Structures and Their Interaction, 1972, 2d edit., 1986, rev. edit., 1993, Eléments d'Acoustique Physique, 1978, Handbook of Acoustic Characteristics of Turbomachinery Cavities, 1997; guest editor, author: Structural Acoustics, 1997; contbr. articles to profl. jours. Fellow ASME (Rayleigh lectr., Per Bruel Noise Control and Acoustics Gold medal 1992), Acoustical Soc. Am. (Trent-Crede medal 1987). Achievements include patents in field. Home: 32 Lake St Arlington MA 02474 Personal E-mail: ellenandmiguel@earthlink.net.

JUNGERMAN, JOHN ALBERT, physics professor; b. Modesto, Calif., Dec. 28, 1921; s. Albert Augustus and Freda (Durst) J.; m. Nancy Lee Kidwell, Oct. 23, 1948; children: Mark, Eric, Roger, Anne. AB, U. Calif., Berkeley, 1943, PhD, 1949. Research physicist Manhattan Project, Oak Ridge, Tenn. and Berkeley, 1944-45, Los Alamos, N.Mex., 1945-46, Lawrence Berkeley Lab., Berkeley, 1946-49, 50-51; asst. prof. physics U. Calif., Davis, 1951, prof. physics, 1960-91, prof. emeritus, 1991, founding dir. Crocker Nuclear Lab., 1965-80, chmn. physics dept., 1981-82, 83-87; assoc. mem. faculty Starr King Sch. for Ministry, Berkeley, Calif., 1992-93. Vis. prof. U. Grenoble, France, 1972; prin. investigator nuclear physics Atomic Energy Commn., U. Calif., Davis, 1956-71; cons. OAS U. Chile, Santiago, 1982, OAS, 1971, Internat. Atomic Energy Agy., 1982. Author: Nuclear Arms Race: Technology and Society, 1986, 2d edit., 1990, World in Process, 2000. Organizer, instr. Davis Summer Insts. on Nuclear Age Edn. for Secondary Sch. Instrs., 1986-93. NSF Nuclear Physics grantee, 1971-73, NSF Sci. Edn. grantee, 1990-93. Fellow Am. Physical Soc.; mem. Am. Solar Soc., Sigma Xi. Democrat. Avocations: piano, sailing, bicycling, painting. Office: U Calif Dept Physics Davis CA 95616 E-mail: jajungerman@ucdavis.edu.

JUNKER, BOBBY RAY, research and development company executive, physicist; b. San Antonio, Tex., Aug. 29, 1943; s. Richard Eugene and Alice Emma (Gruetzmacher) J.; m. Judith Lynne Combs, Sept. 12, 1968 (div. Aug. 1974); 1 child, Bryce Allyn; m. Sheryl Ann Watson, Oct. 8, 1976 (div. July 1995); children: Melissa Sheryl, Evan Ryan; m. Virginia C. Katt, July 13, 1996. BS, U. Southwestern La., 1965; MA, U. Tex., 1967, PhD in Chemistry, 1969. Instr. chemistry U. Tex., Austin, 1969-70; rsch. assoc. physics U. Pitts., 1970-72; asst. prof. physics U. Ga., Athens, 1972-76; sci. officer Office Naval Rsch., Arlington, Va., 1977-84, dir. physic. divsn., 1983-86, dir. math. and phys. scis. dept., 1986-93, head electronics, info. and surveillance dept., 1993—2005, head C4I3R dept., 2006—. Contbr. chpts. to books. Treas. PTA, Fairfax, Va., 1988-89, county rep., 1990-92; treas. Fairfax Christian Ch., 1982-87, 92-95. Recipient Presdl. Meritorious Rank award U.S. Govt., 1989, 99, Presdl. Disting Rank award U.S. Govt., 2003. Mem. AAAS, Am. Phys. Soc., Sigma Xi. Achievements include rsch. theoretical atomic physics, including electron-atom and ion-atom collisions. Office: Office Naval Rsch Info Electronics and Surveillance Dept 800 N Quincy St Arlington VA 22203

JUNKER, ULRICH, computer scientist, researcher; b. Homburg, Saarland, Germany, May 13, 1963; s. Alfred and Rita Junker; m. Isabelle Noufel, Aug. 6, 1994; children: Kevin, Celine, Dylan, Chloe. Abitur, Helmholtz-Gymnasium Zweibruecken, Zweibruecken, Germany, 1973—82; MSc. in Computer Sci., U. of Kaiserslautern, Kaiserslautern, Germany, 1988, PhD. in Computer Sci., 1992. Jr. rschr. GMD, Sankt Augustin, North Rhine Westfalia, Germany, 1988—93; postdoctoral rschr. IFP, Rueil-Malmaison, Ile de France, France, 1993—94; sr. cons. ILOG, Gentilly, Ile de France, France (incl. Monaco), 1995—97, software engr. Valbonne, Provence Alpes Cotes d'Azur, France, 1998—2001, disting. scientist, 2001—. Guest editor (special issue on preferences) Computational Intelligence, Volume 20: Issue 2, May 2004, (special issue on integrating Constraint Programming, Artificial Intelligence, and Operations Research) Annals of Operations Research, Volume 115, 2002. Mem.: Assn. Advancement Artificial Intelligence. Achievements include research in Study of preferences for automated problem solving; organization of events on preference handling. Office: ILOG 1681 rte de Dolines 06560 Valbonne France Business E-Mail: ujunker@ilog.fr.

JUNOT, LORELEI See BELL, LORI

JUNZ, HELEN B., economist; d. Samson and Dobra Bachner. BA, PhD, U. Amsterdam; MA, New Sch. Social Rsch. Acting chief consumer price sect. Nat. Indsl. Conf. Bd., NYC, 1953-58; research officer Nat. Inst. Econ. and Social Research, London, 1958-60; economist Bur. Econ. Analysis, Dept. Commerce, Washington, 1960-62; adviser div. internat. fin. bd. govs. Fed. Res. System, Washington, 1962-77; dep. asst. sec. Office of Asst. Sec. for Internat. Affairs, Dept. Treasury, Washington, 1977-79; v.p., sr. advisor 1st Nat. Bank Chgo., 1979-80; v.p. Townsend Greenspan & Co., Inc., NYC, 1980-82; sr. advisor European dept. IMF, 1982-87, dep. dir. exch. and trade rels. dept., 1987-89, spl. trade rep., dir. Geneva office, 1989-94; dir. gold econs. svc. World Gold Coun., Geneva, Switzerland, 1994-96; pres. HBJ Internat., London, 1996—. Adviser OECD, Paris, 1967-69; sr. internat. economist Council of Econ. Advisers, The White House, Washington, 1975-77. Author: Where did all the money go?, 2002; contbr. articles to profl. jours. Mem. Am. Econ. Assn., Coun. Fgn. Rels., Cosmos Club, Reform Club. Office: HBJ Intnat 39 Chalcot Sq London NW1 8YP England

JUO, JAMES, lawyer; b. Peekskill, NY, Nov. 10, 1967; BSEE, Clarkson Univ., 1989; JD, George Washington Univ., 1993. Bar: Va. 1993, Calif. 1997, US Dist Ct. No. & Ctrl. Calif., US Ct. Appeals Fourth & Fed. Cir., registered: US Patent & Trademark Office. Patent examiner U.S. Patent & Trademark Office, 1989—90; ptnr. patent, trademark, copyright litigation practice Fulwider Patton LLP, LA. Named Rising Star, So. Calif. Super Lawyers, 2006. Mem.: Am. Intellectual Property Law Assn., So. Calif. Chinese Lawyers Assn. Office: Fulwider Patton LLP 10 th Fl Howard Hughes Ctr 6060 Center Dr Los Angeles CA 90045 Office Phone: 310-824-5555. Office Fax: 310-824-9696.

JURA, JAMES J., electric utility executive; b. Creston, Nebr., Dec. 9, 1942; s. Joseph James and Edna Helena (Mackenstadt) J.; m. Sylvia; children: Joseph, James, John, Fredericka. BA, U. Wash., Seattle, 1967; MBA, Seattle U., 1971; postgrad., Harvard U., 1985. With indsl. rels. staff Boeing Co., Seattle, 1968-71; with policy devel. staff OSHA, Washington, 1971-73; legis. and budget analyst Office Mgmt. and Budget, Washington, 1973-78; asst. adminstr. Bonneville Power Adminstrn., U.S. Dept. Energy, Washington, 1978-80, from exec. asst. adminstr. to adminstr. Portland, Oreg., 1980-91; CEO, gen. mgr. Assoc. Electric Coop. Inc., Springfield, Mo., 1991—. Bd. dirs. Assn. Mo. Elec. Coops., Mo. Employers Mut. Ins. Co. With US Army, 1963-65. Republican. Office: Associated Electric Coop PO Box 754 Springfield MO 65801-0754 Office Phone: 417-881-1204. Business E-Mail: jjura@aeci.org.

JURAFSKY, DANIEL, linguist; b. Yonkers, NY, 1962; BA in Linguistics, U. Calif., Berkeley, 1983, PhD in Computer Sci., 1992. Software engr.; postdoc. rschr. Internat. Computer Sci. Inst., 1992—96; assoc. prof. U. Colo., 1996—; assoc. prof. linguistics Stanford U. Drummer Too Many Notes. Mem. editl. bd.: Computer Speech Lang.; co-author: Speech and Language Processing. Recipient CAREER award, NSF; fellow MacArthur Found. fellow, 2002. Office: Stanford Univ Dept Linguistics Bldg 460 Stanford CA 94305-2150 Office Phone: 650-723-4284. E-mail: jurafsky@stanford.edu.

JURAN, SYLVIA LOUISE, retired editor; b. Chgo. d. Joseph Moses and Sadie (Shapiro) J. BA, U. Minn.; MA, Columbia U., 1960; PhD, Harvard U., 1975. Project editor Macmillan Pub. Co., NYC, 1981-91; editor Ralph Appelbaum Assocs. Inc., NYC, 1991—2005; ret. Faculty The New Sch., N.Y.C., 1980-82. Project editor: Ency. of the Holocaust, 1990 (Dartmouth medal ALA, 1990), Ency. of the Third Reich, 1991; editor scripts for mus. exhbns.; contbr. articles to profl. jours. Nat. Def. fgn. lang. fellow, 1960-61, 62-63. Mem. Harvard Club of N.Y.C., Harvard Grad. Sch. Alumni Assn. (N.Y. exec. com. 1984—). Home Phone: 212-253-7783.

JURASEK, JOHN PAUL, mathematics professor, counselor; b. Flushing, NY, June 23, 1959; s. John Steven and Eleanor Rita Jurasek; m. Gale Marie Abrahamsen, May 22, 1993; 1 child, John IV. BS, Fairleigh Dickinson U., 1982; BA, SUNY, New Paltz, 1991; MS, Iona Coll., 1995. Cert. pub. sch. math. tchr., N.Y., N.J. Acct. Sony Corp., Park Ridge, NJ, 1982-85; learning ctr. coord. Rockland C.C., Suffern, NY, 1985-91; math. instr. Collegiate Sch., Passaic, NJ, 1991-92, Ridgefield Park (N.J.) Schs., 1992—99, Cresskill (NJ) Schs., 2000—. Map chair NY/NJ Trail Conf. Contbr. articles to profl. jours. Mem. Town Dem. Com., Piermont, N.Y., 1980. Recipient Above and Beyond award RAMAQUOIS, Pomona, 1990, Counselor of Yr.

award 1990. Mem. Internat. Soc. Technology in Edn., Math. Assn. Am., Nat. Coun. Tchrs. Math., N.J. Edn. Assn., Northvale Rifle and Pistol Club, Am. Mensa, Brit. Mensa, Appalachian Mountain Club (pub. svcs. exec.). Democrat. Roman Catholic. Avocations: model rocketry, target shooting, computer programming, hiking. Home: 193 Howard Ave Orangeburg NY 10962-2314 Office: Cresskill Schs 1 Lincoln Dr Cresskill NJ 07626 E-mail: jjurasek@optonline.net.

JURBALA, BRIAN MICHAEL, orthopedic surgeon; Studied Biomedical Engring. and Chemistry, Pa. State U.; MD, Temple U. Cert. Am. Bd. Orthop. Surgeons, Surgery of the Hand. Intern, gen. surgery East Carolina U.; resident, orthop. and sports medicine Orlando Regional Med. Ctr.; fellow, disorders of the hand, wrist, shoulder and elbow U. Pitts.; founder, pres., orthop. surgeon Highland Ctr. for Orthopedics, Lakeland, Fla., 1995—. Team physician Southeastern Coll., George Jenkins HS, Lakeland Christian HS; assoc. team physician Florida State Coll.; presenter in the field. Contbr. articles to profl. jours., chapters to books. Fellow: Am. Acad. Orthop. Surgery; mem.: Fla. Med. Assn., Fla. Orthop. Assn., Polk County Med. Soc. (sec., treas.), Internat. Cartilage Repair Soc., Am. Orthop. Soc. for Sports Medicine, Arthroscopy Assn. N.Am. Achievements include being considered one of the best orthopedic surgeons near Tampa and in the Central Florida area, special interest in athletics and sports medicine; has performed over 3000 orthopedic surgical procedures during professional career. Office: Highland Ctr for Orthopedics 2161 CR 540A #286 Lakeland FL 33813 Address: Highland Ctr for Orthopedics 3317 US Hwy 98 S Ste 9 Lakeland FL 33803 Office Fax: 863-709-8777.*

JUREVICIUS, JOE, professional football player; b. Cleve., Ohio, Mar. 23, 1974; m. Meagan Jurevicius; 1 child, Michael William (dec.). Attended, Penn State Univ., 1993—97. Wide receiver NY Giants, 1998—2001, Tampa Bay Bucaneers, 2002—04, Seattle Seahawks, 2005—. Recipient Ed Block Courage award, NFL, 2003. Achievements include being mem. of Tampa Bay Bucaneers 2002-2003 Superbowl Team. Office: Seattle Seahawks Qwest Field 800 Occidental Ave So Seattle WA 98134

JURGENS, JULIE GRAHAM, mathematics professor; b. Washta, Iowa, Mar. 8, 1950; d. Albert Harm and Thelma Ann (Johnson) Haenfler; m. Dennis Dean Graham, Mar. 16, 1969 (div. Oct. 17, 1988); children: Tracy Ann Graham-Lester, Tricia Jean Graham-Banta; m. David Dallas Jurgens, Apr. 17, 1998. Undergrad., Morningside Coll., Sioux City, Iowa, 1968—69; BA in Math. Edn./Phys. Edn., Wayne State Coll., 1969—72; MS, Marycrest Coll., Davenport, Iowa, 1985; PhD, U. Iowa, 1997. Prof. math. and computer sci. Marycrest U., 1985—97; dept. chair math., sci., and tech. Flagler Coll., St. Augustine, Fla., 1997—. Mem.: AAUP, Fla. Coun. Tchrs. Math., Fla. Assn. Computer in Edn., Nat. Coun. Tchrs. Math., Math. Assn. Am., Phi Delta Kappa. Home: 138 Creekside Rd Satsuma FL 32189 Office: Flagler Coll Saint Augustine FL 32085 Office Phone: 904-819-6267.

JURGENSEN, WILLIAM G., insurance company executive; BS in Fin., Creighton U., Omaha, Nebr., MBA. Exec. v.p. Norwest Corp.; corp. banking officer Norwest Investment Svcs., pres., CEO; mgmt. First Chicago NBD Corp.; exec. v.p. Bank One Corp.; CEO Nationwide Mutual Ins., 2000—, Nationwide Fin. Svcs., 2000—. Fin. Svcs. Roundtable; Ohio Bus. Roundtable; Columbus Downtown Develop. Corp.; Columbus Partnership; vice chmn., trustee Loyola U., Chgo.; trustee Newberry Libr.; bd. dir. Greater Columbus C. of C., Law Enforcement Found. Ohio, Columbus Children's Hosp.; chair Governor's Commn. on Teaching Success, 2001—03. Office: Nationwide Ins 1 Nationwide Plz Columbus OH 43215*

JURICIC, DAVOR, engineering educator; b. Split, Croatia, Aug. 2, 1928; arrived in U.S., 1968; s. Mate and Slavka (Franceschi) J.; m. Milesa L. Harris, Mar. 10, 1984; 1 child, Ivanna Albertin. Dipl.Ing., U. Belgrade, Yugoslavia, 1952, DSc, 1964. Stress analyst Icarus Aircraft Industries, Zemun, Yugoslavia, 1953-58; rsch. engr. Inst. Aeronautics, Belgrade, 1958-63; asst. prof. U. Belgrade, 1963-65, assoc. prof., 1965-68, S.D. State U., Brookings, 1968-73, prof., 1973-75; vis. prof. Stanford (Calif.) U., 1975-78; prof. mech. engring. U. Tex., Austin, 1978-98, prof. emeritus, 1998—. Contbr. numerous articles to profl. jours. Rsch. grantee various agencies, 1962—. Mem. ASME, Am. Soc. Engring. Edn. (Chester F. Carlson award 1993), Sigma Xi. Achievements include research in a suspension system for railway vehicles; patent in field. Business E-Mail: juricic@mail.utexas.edu.

JURKA, EDITH MILA, psychiatrist, researcher; b. NYC, Dec. 4, 1915; d. Charles Anton and Edith Dorothy (Schevcik) J. BA, Smith Coll., Northampton, Mass., 1936; postgrad., Charles U., Prague, Czechoslovakia, 1936-38; MD, Yale U., New Haven, Conn., 1944. Diplomate Am. Bd. Psychiatry and Neurology. Intern in children's med. svc. Bellevue Hosp., NYC, 1944-45, asst. alienist, 1947-49; rotating intern Gallinger Hosp., Washington, 1945-46; intern NY State Psychiat. Inst., NYC, 1946-47; asst. psychiatrist Mt. Sinai Hosp., NYC, 1949-51; pvt. practice NYC, 1949—; asst. psychiatrist Roosevelt Hosp., NYC, 1954-57; chief psychiatrist Pleasantville Cottage Sch., NY, 1961-74. Bd. dirs. intuition network Inst. Noetic Scis.; founder Wind Song Inst. Sec. Jane Coffin Childs Fund, 1938—41. Fellow Am. Orthopsychiat. Assn.; mem. Am. Psychiat. Assn., NY Coun. Child and Adolescent Psychiatry, NY County Med. Soc., NY State Med. Soc. (psychiat. medicine com.), Westchester Psychiat. Soc. Avocations: architecture, parapsychology, travel, gardening, theater. Home: 16 Apple Bee Farm Ln Croton On Hudson NY 10520-3612 Office: 116 E 66th St New York NY 10065-6547 Office Phone: 212-737-0591.

JURKIEWICZ, CAROLE LYNN, education educator; b. Flint, Mich., Oct. 8, 1958; children: Spencer Alexander, Crosby Mead. PhD, U. Mo., Kansas City, 1994. Prof. La. State U., Baton Rouge, 2000—. Mem.: IIAS, ASPA (chair sect. ethics 1998—2004), La. State U. Faculty Club (life; pres., mem. bd. govs. 2002—). Independent. Avocations: travel, gardening, gourmet cooking, kickboxing, design/art. Home Phone: 225-578-9079; Office Phone: 225-578-9079.

JURKIEWICZ, MAURICE JOHN, surgeon, educator; b. Claremont, NH, Sept. 24, 1923; s. Charles B. and Mary (Ostrowska) J.; m. Mary de Forest Freeman, July 7, 1951; children— Elizabeth de Forest, John Christopher. D.D.S. magna cum laude, U. Md., 1946; MD, Harvard U., 1952. Diplomate: Am. Bd. Surgery, Am. Bd. Plastic Surgery (mem. bd. 1971-77, chmn. 1977-78). Intern Barnes Hosp., Washington U., St. Louis, 1952-53, resident, 1953-58, clin. fellow, 1958-59, instr. surgery, 1957-59; mem. staff U. Fla. Hosp., Gainesville; asst. prof. surgery U. Fla., 1959-64, assoc. prof., 1964-67, prof., 1967-71, chief div. plastic and reconstructive surgery, 1959-71; chief of surgery VA Hosp., Gainesville, 1968-71; prof. surgery, chief of plastic and reconstructive surgery Emory Affiliated Hosps., Atlanta, 1971-92; chief surg. services Grady Meml. Hosp., Atlanta, 1972-77; chief of surgery VAMC, Atlanta, 1989-93. Cons. plastic surgery Walter Reed Gen. Hosp., Washington, 1971-91; sci. counselor Nat. Inst. Dental Rsch., 1966-71; chmn. com. on study of evaluation procedures Am. Bd. Med. Spltys., 1979-81; mem. at large Nat. Bd. Med. Exams., 1985-93; commr. Joint Commn. on Accreditation of Health Care Orgns., 1985-94 (sec. 1989-90, treas. 1990-91, vice chmn. 1991-92); nat. Ccns. plastic surgery Shriners Hosp., 1995-2000. Editor: Operative Techniques in Plastic Surgery, 1994-99; assoc. editor: Plastic and Reconstructive Surgery, 1972-78, 79-83, co-editor, 1985-89; assoc. editor Am. Surgeon, 1977-87. Served to lt. (j.g.) USNR, 1946-48. Fellow Royal Australasian Coll. Surgeons (hon.); mem. AMA, Am. Cancer Soc., Am. Cleft Palate Assn., ACS (bd. regents 1979-88, vice chmn. 1985-88, pres.-elect 1988, pres. 1989-90), Am. Soc. Plastic and Reconstructive Surgeons, Southeastern Soc. Plastic and Reconstructive Surgeons, Ga. Soc. Plastic and Reconstructive Surgeons, Southeastern Surg. Congress (hon. fellow), Am. Soc. Head and Neck Surgeons (pres. 1989), Ednl. Founds. Plastic Surgery Coun., Am. Assn. Plastic Surgeons (pres. 1980, dist. fellow), Am. So. Surg Assns. (1st v.p. 1993-94, hon. fellow), Med. Assn. Ga. Home: 715 Old Post Rd NW Atlanta GA 30328-4758 Office: Emory U Clinic 550 Peachtree St 8th Fl Ste 4300 Atlanta GA 30308 Office Phone: 404-686-8143.

JURKOWSKI, ODIN LECH, education educator; s. Donald Eugene and Bonnie Jean Jurkowski; m. Deanna Lynn Jurkowski, Oct. 21, 1995; children: Kalina Mai, Byron Tyr, Acacia Jade, Amelia Blythe, Cordelia Rae, Valen Thor. BS in Sci. and Tech. in Context, Ill. Inst. Tech., Chgo., 1992, MS in Tech. Comm. and Info. Design, 1997; MS in Libr. and Info. Sci., Dominican U., River Forest, Ill., 1994; EdD in Instrnl. Tech., No. Ill. U., DeKalb, 2003. Access svcs. libr. Ill. Inst. Tech., Chgo., 1994—97, head libr. Rice Campus br. Wheaton, Ill., 1997—98; libr. dir. St. Anthony Coll. Nursing, Rockford, Ill., 1998—2002; assoc. prof. ednl. leadership and human devel. U. Ctrl. Mo., Warrensburg, 2002—. Mem.: ALA, AAUP, Mo. Assn. of Sch. Librarians, Assn. for Libr. and Info. Sci. Edn., Kappa Delta Pi, Alpha Sigma Phi. Avocations: swimming, martial arts, reading. Office: U Ctrl Mo Ednl Leadership and Human Devel Lovinger 4200B Warrensburg MO 64093 Office Phone: 660-543-8387. Business E-Mail: jurkowski@ucmo.edu.

JURS, PETER B., lawyer; b. Toledo, Aug. 8, 1972; BA, Miami U., 1994; JD, U. Cin., 1997. Bar: Ohio 1997, US Ct. of Appeals Sixth Cir. 1998, US Dist. Ct. Southern Dist. Ohio 1999, Ky. 2000. Law clerk Hon. James G. Carr, US Dist. Judge, Western Divsn., Northern Dist. Ohio, 1997—98; assoc. Rendigs, Fry, Kiely & Dennis L.L.P, Cin. Named one of Ohio's Rising Stars, Super Lawyers, 2006. Mem.: Ohio Assn. Civil Trial Attorneys, Def. Rsch. Inst., Northern Ky. Bar Assn., ABA, Ky. Bar Assn., Ohio State Bar Assn., Cin. Bar Assn. Office: Rendigs Fry Kiely & Dennis LLP 1 W Fourth St Ste 900 Cincinnati OH 45202 Office Phone: 513-381-9369. Office Fax: 513-381-9206.

JURTSHUK, PETER, JR., microbiologist, educator; b. NYC, July 28, 1929; s. Peter and Mary (Ferens) J.; m. Rebecca Jones, Jan. 2, 1971; children: Peter, Larissa. AB, NYU, 1951; MS, Creighton U., 1953; PhD, U. Md., 1957. Asst. prof. pharmacology Bklyn. Coll. Pharmacy, L.I. U., 1957-59; asst. prof. enzyme chemistry U. Wis.-Madison, 1962-63; asst. prof. microbiology U. Tex., Austin, 1963-69; assoc. prof. biology and biochemistry U. Houston, 1970-76, prof., 1976—, undergrad. chmn., 1976—80, dir. program in microbiology, 1990—2004. Mem. vis. biol. program Am. Inst. Biol. Scis., 1969-72. Contbr. chpts. to books. Recipient Disting. Svc. award Tex. br. Am. Soc. Microbiology, 1982; NIH grantee, 1964-75; NSF grantee, 1986-89. Fellow Am. Acad. Microbiology; mem. Am. Soc. Microbiology (pres. Tex. br. 1972-74), N.Y. Acad. Scis., Am. Soc. Biochemistry and Molecular Biology, Am. Chem. Soc., Sigma Xi (pres. U. Houston chpt. 1979-80). Russian Orthodox. Home: 879 Ramada Dr Houston TX 77062-5607 Office: U Houston Biology and Biochemistry Dept Houston TX 77204-5001 Office Phone: 713-743-2668. Business E-Mail: jurtshuk@uh.edu.

JUSKOWIAK, TERRY EUGENE, career military officer, computer company executive; s. Joe Leon and Betty; m. Susan K. Renn, Sept. 15, 1974; children: John, Christopher, Jennifer. BA, The Citadel, Charleston, SC, 1973; MS, Fla. Inst. Technology, Melbourne, 1981. Commd. 2d lt. U.S. Army, 1973, advanced through ranks to major gen., 1999, contract cost mgmt. analyst Army Mat. Ctr. Alexandria, Va., 1980-84, aide-de-camp Sec. Army Washington, 1984-85, dep. V Corps logistics officer Frankfurt, Germany, 1986-88, exec. officer 122 Main 3d Armored Divsn. Hanau, Germany, 1988-89, from divsn. staff to battalion cmdr. 82d Airborne Divsn. Ft. Bragg, NC, 1989-92, spl. asst. to chief of Staff Washington, 1992-94, brigade cmdr. 10th Mtn. Divsn. Ft. Drum, NY, 1994-96, asst. divsn. cmdr. support 10th Mtn. Divsn., 1996—; dep. comdg. gen. NATO SFOR Spt Cmd, 1996-98; dir. logistics I4 U.S. Atlantic comd. Norfolk, Va., 1997-98; comdr. 1st Corps Support Command (Airborne), Ft. Bragg, NC, 1998-2000; dir. logistics U.S. Forces Command, Ft. McPherson, Ga., 2000-01; quartermaster gen., comdt. Quartermaster Sch., 2001—02; comdr. Combined Arms Support Command, 2002—04; lead ptnr. Army acct. IBM Global Svcs., 2004—. Decorated DSM, Def. Superior Svc. medal, Legion of Merit, Bronze Star, Def. Meritorious Svc. medal. Mem. Assn. Citadel Men, Assn. U.S. Army, Quartermaster Assn., 82d Airborne Assn., 10th Mtn. Divsn. Assn. Presbyterian. Avocations: reading, running, skiing. Office Phone: 678-546-6407. Personal E-mail: tjuskowiak@aol.com. Business E-Mail: tjuskowiak@us.ibm.com.

JUSSAUME, RAYMOND ADELARD, political science professor; b. Fall River, Mass., June 16, 1954; s. Raymond Adelard and Janet Anna Jussaume; m. Atsuko Yamashita Jussaume, Aug. 28, 1982; children: Kenneth Yamashita, Michael Yamashita, Katherine Yamashita. BA in Polit. Sci., S.E. Mass. U., North Dartmouth, 1976; MA in Polit. Sci., U. Ga., Athens, 1980; PhD in Devel. Psychology, Cornell U., Ithaca, NY, 1987. Prof. and chair Wash. State U., Pullman, 1987—. Author: (book) Japanese Part-Time Farming. Home: 140 NW Thomas St Pullman WA 99163 Office: Wash State Univ Washington State University Pullman WA 99163 Home Phone: 509-332-8981; Office Phone: 509 335-7626. Office Fax: 509 335-2125. Personal E-mail: rayatsuko@pullman.com. Business E-Mail: rajussaume@wsu.edu.

JUST, DAVID RYAN, economist; b. Stillwater, Okla., Dec. 16, 1974; s. Richard Eugene Just and Jane Ann Hardie; m. Lisa Ann Carr, Mar. 28, 1976; children: Vibeka Kristine, William Lloyd, Edward Alexander. BA in Econs., Brigham Young U., Provo, Utah, 1998; MS in Agrl. Econs., U. Calif., Berkeley, 1999, PhD in Agrl. Econs., 2001. Asst. prof. Cornell U., Ithaca, NY, 2002—. Presenter in field. Contbr. articles to profl. jours. Elders quorum pres. LDS Ch., Ithaca, NY, 2003. Mem.: Northeastern Agrl. and Resource Econs. Assn. (bd. mem. 2006), Am. Agrl. Econs. Assn. (teller com. co-chair 2005—07). Republican. Home: 20 Marcy Ct Ithaca NY 14850 Office: Cornell University 254 Warren Hall Ithaca NY 14853 Office Phone: 607-255-2086. Personal E-mail: justspam@twcny.rr.com. Business E-Mail: drj3@cornell.edu.

JUST, GEMMA RIVOLI, retired advertising executive; b. NYC, Nov. 29, 1921; d. Philip and Brigida (Consolo) Rivoli; m. Victor Just, Jan. 29, 1955. BA, Hunter Coll., NYC, 1943. Copy group head McCann Erickson, NYC, 1958-62; copy supr. Morse Internat., NYC, 1962-67; v.p., dir. creative svcs. Deltakos divsn. J. Walter Thompson, NYC, 1967-75; v.p., copy dir. Sudler & Hennessey divsn. Young & Rubicam, NYC, 1980-87, sr. v.p., assoc. creative dir. copy, 1987-88, ret., 1989. Active Episcopal Ch. Women of Ch. of Incarnation, NYC, ch. altar guild pres. and acolyte. Recipient Aesculapius awards Modern Medicine mag., 1980-88; named Best Writer, Art Dirs. Club NY, 1979, Best Writer Young & Rubicam, 1981. Mem. Coun. Comms. Soc., Pharm. Advt. Coun., Am. Med. Writers Assn. (exec. com. 1973). Home: 155 E 38th St Apt 5D New York NY 10016-2663

JUST, RICHARD EUGENE, economist, consultant, agriculturist, educator; b. Tulsa, Feb. 18, 1948; s. William and Leah (Flaming) J.; m. Janet Lee Humphries, Aug. 26, 1989; children: Angela K. Eisinger, David R., Ronald L. Mower BS, Okla. State U., 1969; MA, U. Calif., Berkeley, 1971, PhD, 1972. Prof. agrl. econs. and stats. Okla. State U., Stillwater, 1972-75; prof. agrl. and resource econs. U. Calif., Berkeley, 1975-85, U. Md., College Park, 1985-92, chmn. dept., 1992-95, U Md., College Park, 2003—04; disting. univ. prof. U. Md., College Park, 1995—. Cons. The World Bank, Washington, 1976-93, Oak Ridge Nat. Lab., 1976-81, Winrock Internat., 1979-81, Electric Power Rsch. Inst., 1981-83, Stanford Rsch. Inst., 1981, Safeway Stores, Inc., Oakland, Calif., 1983-86, Price Waterhouse, 1987-91, The Pillsbury Co., Mpls., 1988-89, U.S. Gen. Acctg. Office, Washington, 1978-79, 90-95, U.S. Dept. Justice, 1999, others; prin. Law and Econs. Consulting Group, 1993-2000; vis. prof. Ben Gurion U. Negev, 1977, Brigham Young U., 1977, 79-80, 94; sr. rsch. fellow The Inst. for Policy Reform, 1991—; sr. cons. Charles River Assocs., 2001- Author: A Comprehensive Assessment of the Role of Risk in U.S. Agriculture, 2002, Applied Welfare Economics and Public Policy, 1982, Commodity and Resource Policies in Agricultural Systems, 1991, Conflict and Cooperation on Trans-Boundary Water Resources, 1998, (monographs) Econometric Analysis of Production Decisions, 1975, Econometric Analysis of Processing Tomatoes, 1978, The Welfare Economics of Public Policy: A Practical Approach to Project and Policy Evaluation, 2004, Economics of Regulation of Agricultural Biotechnologies, 2006, Readings in Applied Welfare Economics, 2007; editor Am. Jour. Agrl. Econs., 1984-86, mem. editl. com., 1978-80; mem. editl. bd. Jour. Devel. Planning Lit., 1985—90, Springer-Verlag, 1989—95; mem. editl. coun. We. Jour. Agrl. Econs., 1982-84; also articles to jours Mem. task force on economy Calif. Dem. Com., 1981-83; mem. agrl. policy task force for speaker Calif. Assembly, 1983-84; bishop LDS Ch., 1993-97, stake pres., 1997-2006. Internat. Inst. Ecol. Econs. fellow, 1991- Fellow Am. Agrl. Econs. Assn. (dissertation awards com. 1976-78, selected papers com. 1981-93, com. on jour. pub. 1986, fellows election com. 1991-96, 2005—, mem. pub. enduring quality com. 1998-02, pres. 2007, Quality of Rsch. Discovery award 1977, 80, 83, 89, 90, 96, 2002, Outstanding Jour. Article award 1981, 93, Enduring Quality award 1992, 94, 98, 2003, 05, Quality Comm. award 2007); mem. Western Agrl. Econs. Assn. (editl. coun. 1982-84, Outstanding Pub. Rsch. award 1974, 83, 96, 2003, 05), Am. Econ. Assn., Royal Econ. Soc., Econometric Soc., Atlantic Econ. Soc., Alpha Zeta Office: Agrl/Resource Econs U Md College Park MD 20742-0001

JUST, WARD SWIFT, author; b. Michigan City, Ind., Sept. 5, 1935; s. F. Ward and Elizabeth (Swift) J. Student, Cranbrook Sch., Mich., 1951-53, Trinity Coll., Hartford, Conn., 1953-57. Reporter Waukegan (Ill.) News-Sun, 1957-59, Newsweek, 1959-61, Reporter mag., 1962-63; corr. Newsweek, 1963-65, Washington Post, 1965-70; writer Vineyard Haven, Mass., 1970—. Author: To What End, 1968, A Soldier of the Revolution, 1970, Military Men, 1970, The Congressman Who Loved Flaubert and Other Washington Stories, 1973, Stringer, 1974, Nicholson at Large, 1975, A Family Trust, 1978, Honor, Power, Riches, Fame, and the Love of Women, 1979, In the City of Fear, 1982, The American Blues, 1984, The American Ambassador, 1987, Jack Gance, 1989 (Heartland prize for Fiction, Chgo. Tribune, 1989), Twenty-One Selected Stories, 1990, The Translator, 1991, Ambition & Love, 1994, Echo House, 1997, A Dangerous Friend, 1999 (Cooper prize for Fiction, Soc. Am. Historians); (play) Lowell Limpett, 2000, The Weather in Berlin, 2002, An Unfinished Season, 2004 (Heartland prize for Fiction), Forgetfulness, 2006; contbr. Best Am. Short Stories, 1972-73, 76. Recipient O. Henry award, 1985, 86. Mem.: AAAS.

JUSTER, KENNETH IAN, lawyer; b. NYC, Nov. 24, 1954; s. Howard H. and Muriel (Uchitelle) J. BA, Harvard U., 1976, MA in Pub. Policy, 1980, JD, 1980. Bar: DC and US Dist. Ct. DC 1981, US Ct. Appeals (DC cir.) 1982, US Ct. Internat. Trade 1984, US Ct. Appeals (Fed. cir.) 1985, US Supreme Ct. 1985. Staff Nat. Security Coun., 1978; law clk. to judge US Ct. Appeals (2d cir.), Brattleboro, Vt., 1980—81; assoc. Arnold and Porter, Washington, 1981—87, ptnr., 1988—89; dep., sr. adviser to the dep. Sec. of State, Washington, 1989—92; acting counselor US Dept. State, Washington, 1992—93; ptnr. Arnold and Porter, Washington, 1993—97, sr. ptnr., 1998—2001; under sec. export admin. US Dept. Commerce, Washington, 2001—02, under sec. industry & security, 2002—05; exec. v.p. law, policy and corp. strategy Salesforce.com, San Francisco, 2005—. Faculty Internat. Law Inst., 1987-89, 93-95; vis. fellow Coun. Fgn. Rels., Washington, 1993; bd. dirs. US-India Bus. Coun., US-Panama Bus. Coun. Editor Harvard U. Internat. Law Jour., 1979-80; contbg. articles to profl. jours. Recipient Sec. of State's Disting. Svc. award and Medal, 1993, US-Panama Bus. Coun. Friendship award, 2002, 2004, US-India Bus. Coun. Blackwill award, 2004, Pres. of Panama's Vasco Nunez de Balboa en el Grado de Gran Cruz decoration and medal, 2004, Sec. of Commerce's William C. Redfield award and medal, 2005. Mem. ABA (internat. law sect., chair internat. investment and devel. com. 1994-96, coun. mem. 1996-99, chair tech. legal assistance bd. 2000-01, coun. mem. 2003-04), DC Bar Assn. (internat. law sect., mem. faculty continuing legal edn. program 1987-89), Am. Coun. on Germany, Coun. on Fgn. Rels., US, Phi Beta Kappa. Office: Salesforce.com Ste 300 One Market Plaza San Francisco CA 94105 Office Phone: 415-536-8004. Business E-Mail: kjuster@salesforce.com.

JUSTESEN, TROY RALPH, federal agency administrator; b. Utah, Sept. 17, 1968; BS cum laude, Utah State U., Logan, 1989, MS with honors, 1994; EdD, Vanderbilt U., Nashville, 2001. Civil rights program dir. Utah State U., U.S. Dept. Justice; assoc. dir. domestic policy coun. Exec. Office of Pres.; dep. commr. rehab. svcs. adminstrn. U.S. Dept. Edn., dep. asst. sec. office spl. edn. and rehabilitative svcs., dir. office spl. edn. programs, asst. sec. office vocation and adult edn., 2006—. Gov. apptd. mem. Utah State Bd. Human Svcs., 1994—96; commr. Medicaid Commn. U.S. Dept. Health and Human Svcs., 2005—. Recipient Superior Performance of Duty award, U.S. Atty. Gen. Janet Reno, 1999, Honors, Gov. Bob Taft, OH, 2003, OH State House Reps., 2003, OH State Senate, 2003, Utah State Office Rehab., 2004, Am. Coun. Rural Spl. Edn., 2004, Coun. Adminstrs. Native Ams., 2005, Future Farmers Am., 2006, Joseph H. Owens Exemplary Nat. Advocacy award, 2004, Nat. Honor, Nat. Tourette Syndrome Assn., 2007. Republican. Mem. Lds Ch. Office: US Dept Edn Potomac Ctr Plz 550 12th St SW Rm 11140 Washington DC 20202-7110 Office Phone: 202-245-7595, 202-245-7700. Office Fax: 202-245-7837.

JUSTICE, (DAVID) BLAIR, psychology educator, writer; b. Dallas, July 2, 1927; s. Sam Hugh and Lou-Reine (Hunter) J.; m. Rita Norwood, July 26, 1972; children: Cynthia, David, Elizabeth (dec.). BA, U. Tex., Austin, 1948; MS, Columbia U., 1949; MA, Tex. Christian U., 1963; PhD, Rice U., 1966. Diplomate Am. Bd. Med. Psychotherapists; cert. expert in traumatic stress. Reporter Ft. Worth Star-Telegram, 1952-55; sci. writer N.Y. Daily News, 1955-56, Ft. Worth Star-Telegram, 1956-64; sci. editor, columnist Houston Post, 1964-73; exec. asst. to Mayor Houston, 1966-72; prof. psychology Sch. Pub. Health, U. Tex., Houston, 1968—2001, prof. emeritus, 2001—; assoc. dean for acad. affairs U. Tex., Sch. Pub. Health, Houston, 1994-2000; dir. Project Support, Imagery & Immune Function in Breast Cancer, 1993-99; co-investigator Alt. Medicine Ctr. for Cancer Rsch. U. Tex. Sch. Pub. Health, Houston, 1995-98; patient advocate M.D. Anderson Cancer Ctr., Houston, 2000—. Co-investigator U. Tex. Ctr. for Alternative Med. Cancer Rsch.; sr. psychologist, group therapist, psychiat. residency faculty Tex. Rsch. Inst. Mental Scis., 1973-85; cmty. assoc. Rice U., Lovett Coll.; cons. child abuse Tex. Dept. Human Resources; faculty assoc. Ctr. for Health Promotion, R & D, U. Tex. Health Sci. Ctr., mem. inter-faculty coun., 1991-92; dir. Ctr. for Prevention of Violence and Injury, 1987-89, chmn. faculty Sch. of Pub. Health, 1990-91, chmn. faculty policy com., 1989-90, faculty marshal, 1990, mem. exec. com., 1991-93, vice chair interfaculty coun., 1992-93; vis. scholar U. Colo., 1990—; founding assoc. Blaffer Gallery U. Houston. Author: Violence in the City, 1969, Detection of Potential Community Violence, 1967, (with Rita Justice) The Abusing Family, 1976, The Broken Taboo: Sex in the Family, 1979, Perspectives in Public Mental Health, 1982, Who Gets Sick: Thinking and Health, 1987, Who Gets Sick: How Beliefs, Moods and Thoughts Affect Your Health, 1988, revised edit., 2000, The Abusing Family, rev. edit., 1990, A Different Kind of Health: Finding Well-Being Despite Illness, 1998; Visits with Violet: Lessons on How to Be Happy 100 Years, 1999; editor: Your Child's Behavior, 1972; editorial bd.: Internat. Jour Mental

Health, 1980—. Gen. chmn. Houston Job Fair, 1967-73; chmn. Houston Manpower Area Planning Council, 1972-74; mem. Tex. Urban Devel. Commn., 1970-72; bd. dirs. Houston Housing Devel. Corp., Tex. Citizens Human Devel., 1979-84, Greater Houston Com. Prevention of Child Abuse, 1982-88; sec. bd. mgrs. Tarrant County Hosp., Dist., 1961-64; pres. Greater Houston Youth Council, 1978-79, Houston Area Council on Sudden Infant Death Syndrome, 1977-78; mem. nat. adv. com. Marine Biomed. Inst., U. Tex. Med. Br., 1971-84; mem. Office of Minority Affairs, Resource Persons Network, HHS, 1988—; mem. community bd. Tex. Youth Council; vestry, chmn. adult edn. St. John The Divine Episc. Ch., 1984-88. Served with USNR, 1945-46. Recipient most outstanding book award Tex. Writers Roundup, 1970, award of recognition City of Houston, 1973, Benjamin Franklin Book award Pubs. Mktg. Assn. Am., 1988, Excellence in Media award APA, 1988, Friends of Fondren Libr. book award Rice U., 1989, 91, Heritage award for child abuse rsch. Child Abuse Prevention Coun., 1989, award for outstanding contbn. to sci. Tex. Psychol. Assn., 2001, Living Principles award Internat. Assn. Transactional Analysis, 1999; named One of Five Outstanding Young Men of Tex., 1962; recipient numerous awards for sci. writing; grantee NIH. Fellow Am. Coll. Psychology, Am. Inst. Stress, Phi Beta Kappa (dir. Houston chpt. 1979-89, pres. Houston chpt. 1982-83); mem. APHA (chmn. mental health sect. 1980-81, governing coun. 1983-85, action bd. 1985-87, mental health sect. award 1989), Nat. Assn. Sci. Writers (life; exec. com. 1965-67), Houston Psychol. Assn. (pres. 1975, Lifetime Achievement award for contbn. to psychology 2002)), Knights of the Vine. Home: 6416 Sewanee St Houston TX 77005-3760 Office: 1200 Hermann Pressler Dr Houston TX 77030-3900 Office Phone: 713-500-9157. E-mail: bjustice@sph.uth.tmc.edu.

JUSTICE, CHRISTOPHER, communications and language educator; b. New Brunswick, NJ, Nov. 18, 1970; BA, Rutgers U., New Brunswick, 1993; M of Modern Studies, Loyola Coll., Balt., 2000. Cert. tchr. secondary English edn. U. N.Mex, 1996, online journalism U. Mass., Amherst, 2007. Tech. editor, info. specialist Cmty. Sci., Inc., Balt., 1998—2001; asst. prof., English & mass comm. CC Balt. County, Balt., 2002—. Tchr. Albuquerque Pub. Schs., Albuquerque, 1995—97; staff writer Greater Media Newspapers, Morganville, NJ, 1994. Author: (film revs.) Classic-Horror, Senses of Cinema, (columnist and blog contributor) PopMatters; editor: (book) Untying the Knots That Tie Up Your Life; author: (creative non-fiction) Bay Weekly, Balt. Sun. Office: CC Balt County 800 S Rolling Rd Baltimore MD 21228 Office Phone: 410-922-1630. Business E-Mail: cjustice@ccbcmd.edu.

JUSTICE, FRANKLIN PIERCE, JR., oil industry executive; b. Wanego, W.Va., May 5, 1938; s. Franklin Pierce and Jeneta Ruth (Cooley) J.; m. Eva Mae Hartley, June 8, 1960; children: Kerry, Kelly, Kevin. BSBA, W.Va. State Coll., 1967; MBA in Fin., Marshall U., 1977; postgrad., U. Louisville, 1971—72. Reporter Dun & Bradstreet, Inc., Charleston, W.Va., 1960-63, reporting mgr., 1963-65, office mgr., Huntington, W.Va., 1966-68; domestic trade specialist U.S. Dept. Commerce, Charleston, 1968—70; pres., investment mgr. Equal Opportunity Fin., Inc., Ashland, Ky., 1970-93; adminstrv. asst. to v.p. personnel Ashland Oil, Inc., 1973-74, adminstrv. asst. to v.p. external affairs, 1974-75, mgr. spl. projects, 1975-76, dir. pub. affairs, 1976-78, v.p. pub. rels., 1978-82, v.p., 1985-93; v.p. ops. support Ashland Services Co., 1982-85; pres. Marshall U. Rsch. Corp., 1993-98; exec. dir. Rsch. and Econ. Devel. Ctr. Marshall U., Huntington, W.Va., 1993-95, v.p. devel., 1995-99, dir. major gifts, 2002—03; assoc. dean Southeastern CC, 1999—2000; ret. Cons. in field. Vice chmn. Ky. Ctr. for Arts, Louisville, 1982-92; bd. dirs. Ky. Coun. Econ. Edn., 1978-90, chmn. bd., 1980-83; dir. Marshall U. Bus. Adv. Bd., 1982—2006; exec. com. bd. dirs. W.Va. State Coll. Found., Inc., 1988-95; bd. dirs. Delta Dental of Ky. Mem. W.Va. C. of C. (life; chmn. bd. dirs. 1992-94), Ashland Area C. of C. (1st v.p. 1978-79, pres. 1980, bd. dirs. 1978-98), Ky. C. of C. (chmn. bd. dirs. 1983, life). Republican. Home: 4413 Indigo Ln Murrells Inlet SC 29576

JUSTICE, JACK BURTON, retired lawyer, writer; b. Hardy, Ky., Aug. 2, 1931; s. George Edward and Goldia (Alley) J.; m. Martha Monser, Dec. 28, 1957 (dec. Feb. 1974); m. Judith Farquhar Lang, Apr. 26, 1975; children—Jonathan Burton, George Lewis, Paul Williamson. AB in Polit. Sci, W.Va. U., 1952, postgrad. in law, 1954-55; BA in Jurisprudence, Oxford U., Eng., 1954, MA, 1960. Bar: Pa. 1956. Assoc. firm Drinker Biddle & Reath, Phila., 1956-62, ptnr., 1962-82, White & Williams, Phila., 1982-96. Bus. mgr. Am. Oxonian, 1967-86; pres. Franklin Inn, Phila., 1991-93; lectr. in field. Contbr. articles to profl. and lit. jours. Pres. Youth Svc., Phila., 1962-65; chmn. Phila. Com. on City Policy, 1966-67, Southeastern Pa. chpt. Ams. for Democratic Action, 1968-70; bd. overseers William Penn Charter Sch., Phila., 1978-91, clk., 1986-89. Rhodes scholar, 1952-54. Mem. Assn. Am. Rhodes Scholars (sec. 1967-86, pres. 1986-94), Rancho Viejo North Cmty. Assn. (pres. 2003-04), ACLU (No. N.Mex. chpt. bd. dirs. Santa Fe br. 2007—). Democrat. Home: 10 Coyote Pass Rd Santa Fe NM 87508

JUSTICE, MADELINE CAROL, education educator; b. Beaumont, Tex., Nov. 5, 1950; d. Frank and Rosie Lee Molo; m. James Henry Justice, June 29. BA, Tex. Woman's U., 1972, MA, 1977; EdD, East Tex. State U., 1987. Cert. tchr. English, history, education, mid-mgmt. Tex. English tchr. Plano (Tex.) Ind. Sch. Dist., 1972—92; prof., asst. dept. chair Coll. Edn. Tex. A&M U., Commerce, 1992—. Proposal reviewer S.W. Ednl. Rsch. Conf., 2000—02; chpt. reviewer Wadsworth-Thomson Learning, 2003; grant proposal reviewer Fund for the Improvement of Postsecondary Edn., 2004; presenter and cons. in field. Contbr. articles to profl. jours.; mem. editl. bd.: Contemporary Issues in Technology and Teacher Education: Current Practices, 2000—. Recipient Neil Humfield Disting. Faculty award, Tex. A&M U., 1999. Mem.: Am. Assn. Colls. for Tchr. Edn., Soc. for Info. Tech. and Tchr. Edn. (mem. program com. 1999—), Phi Delta Kappa (Pres. award 1996, 1998). Democrat. Avocations: singing, reading, research. Office: Tex A&M Univ Commerce PO Box 5011 Commerce TX

JUSTICE, PATRICIA, academic administrator, educator; b. Evanston, Ill., Sept. 20, 1950; d. Stephen Walter and Rosella Majorie Szymczak; m. Richard William Justice, Apr. 5, 1986; 1 child, Stephen William. BA, Northeastern Ill. U., Chgo., 1972; MA, Northwestern U., Evanston, 1974; PhD, U. Ill., Champaign, 1990. Dir. alumni affairs Northeastern Ill. U., Chgo., 1972—85; dir. campus rels. U. Ill., Champaign, 1985—88, asst. chancellor, 1988—91, asst. chancellor devel., 1991—. Sec. Case Dist. V, Chgo., 1985. Bd. mem. Downtown Urbana Promotions Com., Ill., 1985—91, Crisis Nursery Champaign County, 1998—2004. Recipient Joan Chad Skinner award, Farmhouse Frat. Internat., Kansas City, Mo., 1996, Medallion Honor award, U. Ill. Mother's Assn., 2003. Mem.: Assn. Fundraising Profls., Coun. Advancement and Support Edn., Sigma Kappa (corp. bd. mem. 2003—). Office: Univ Ill 601 E John St Champaign IL 61821

JUSTICE, PHILLIP HOWARD, marketing professional; b. Pikeville, Ky., Aug. 29, 1948; s. Howard and Opal Fanny (Hatfield) J.; children: Phillip Wayne, Benjamin Howard. Student, Pikeville Coll., 1966-67, Free Will Bapt. Coll., 1972; DD (hon.), Welcome Bapt. Inst., 1987; AS, Vincennes U., 2001. Sales rep. Reynolds and Reynolds, Evansville, Ind., 1978-81; account exec. Merrill Lynch, Evansville, 1981-83, E.F. Hutton, Evansville, 1983-88; assoc. v.p. investments Dean Witter Reynolds, Inc., Evansville, 1988-91, Prudential Securities, Evansville, 1991-95, Citizen's Nat. Bank, Evansville, 1995, Advantage Payroll Svcs., 1995—2002; area mgr. Dale Carnegie Tng., Evansville, 2002—. Bd. dirs. Evansville unit Am. Heart Assn., 1990, 91, Paduah Symphony Orch., 2005-. Mem. Rockport Area C. of C. (v.p. 1990, pres. 1991), Rotary Club (bd. dirs. 1995—). Republican. Home: 17 Meadow Links Dr Paducah KY 42001-9738 Office: 1601 Broadway Paducah KY 42001 Office Phone: 270-217-6022. Personal E-mail: philjustice@yahoo.com.

JUSTICE, WILLIAM WAYNE, federal judge; b. Athens, Tex., Feb. 25, 1920; s. William Davis and Jackie May (Hanson) Justice; m. Sue Tom Ellen Rowan, Mar. 16, 1947; 1 child, Ellen Rowan. LLB, U. Tex., 1942; LLD (hon.), So. Meth. U., 2001. Bar: Tex. 1942. Ptnr. Justice & Justice, Athens, 1946-61; part-time atty. City of Athens, 1948-50, 52-58; U.S. atty. U.S. Dist. Ct. (ea. dist.) Tex., Tyler, 1961-68, judge, 1968-80, chief judge, 1980-90, sr. judge, 1998—. Subject William Wayne Justice, Judicial Biography (Frank R. Kemerer), 1991. Adv. coun. Dem. Nat. Com., 1954; alt. del. Dem. Nat. Conv., 1956, presdl. elector, 1960; v.p. Young Dems. Tex., 1948. 1st lt. US Army, 1942—46, CBI. Named William Wayne Justice Fund for Pub. Svc. in his honor, U. Tex. Sch. Law, 2004; recipient Nat. Outstanding Fed. Judge award, ATLA, 1982, Outstanding Civil Libertarian award, Tex. Civil Liberties Union, 1986, Lifetime Achievement award, NACDL, 1996, Thurgood Marshall award, ABA, 2001, Morris Dees Justice award, U. Ala. Sch. Law & Skadden, 2006. Episcopalian. Office: 903 San Jacinto Blvd Ste 316 Austin TX 78701-2450 Office Phone: 512-916-5283.

JUSTINIANI, FEDERICO ROBERTO, internist, educator; b. Havana, Cuba, Aug. 15, 1929; came to U.S., 1964, naturalized, 1969; s. Federico Luis and Margarita (Longa) J.; m. Maria Suarez, Nov. 29, 1955. BS, De La Salle Coll., Havana, 1947; MD, Havana U., 1954. Diplomate Am. Bd. Internal Medicine (recognized for advanced achievement 1987). Intern, resident in internal medicine Havana U. Hosp., 1955-61; practice medicine Havana, 1961-64; intern St. Francis Hosp., Miami Beach, Fla., 1965; resident in internal medicine Mt. Sinai Hosp., Miami Beach, 1966-69, program coord. residency in internal medicine, 1969-74; dir. med. edn. Mt. Sinai Med. Ctr., Miami Beach, 1974—2002; instr. medicine U. Miami, 1969-72, asst. prof., 1972-82, assoc. prof., 1982-90, prof., 1990—. Contbr. articles to profl. jours. Master ACP; mem. AMA (Physicians Recognition awards), Fla. Med. Assn., So. Med. Assn., Dade County Med. Assn., Am. Geriatrics Soc., Cuban Med. Assn. in Exile, Nat. Assn. Cuban-Am. Educators (pres. 2004—). Office: Ste 900 4302 Alton Rd Miami Beach FL 33140-2800 Home Phone: 305-444-6845; Office Phone: 305-674-2242. E-mail: fjustiniani@bellsouth.net.

JUSTINO, HENRI, pediatric cardiologist; b. Montreal, Quebec, Canada; MD, McGill U., Montreal, Can., 1994. Lic. Cardiology Am. Bd. Pediat., 2000. Cardiology fellow Hosp. for Sick Children, U. Toronto, 1997—2000; dir. cardiac catheterization lab. Children's Hosp. Ea. Ont., U. Ottawa, 2001—03; interventional pediatric cardiologist Tex. Children's Hosp., Baylor Coll. Medicine, Houston, 2003—. Fellow, Royal Coll. Physicians Can., 1998, Am. Coll. Cardiology, 2002. Mem.: Soc. for Cardiovasc. Angiography and Interventions, Am. Heart Assn. Office: Texas Childrens Hosp 6621 Fannin Houston TX 77030 Office Phone: 832-826-5600. Business E-Mail: hjustino@bcm.edu.

JUSZCZYK, JAMES JOSEPH, artist; b. Chgo., Jan. 30, 1943; s. Joseph Peter and Pauline (Polak) J.; m. Phyllis Ann Pozar, May 30, 1965 (dec. Jan. 1992). BFA, Cleve. Inst. of Art, 1966; MFA, U. Pa., 1969. Artist pvt. practice, Zurich, 1986-92; lectr., cons. Binney & Smith Liquitex Paints, Easton, Pa., 1992-94, Lascaux Colours & Restauro, Alois Diethelm AG, Zürich, Switzerland, 1995-98; lectr. Daler-Rowney USA, Cranbury, NJ, 1998—. Adj. prof. art CCNY, 1996—; presented master class workshops in acrylic techniques in the Benelux countries (Amsterdam, DeHaag, Antwerp, Brussels), 1996-99; presenter in field. One-man shows include Phila. Coll. Textiles and Sci., 1970, Rosa Esman Gallery, NYC, 1974, 76, 1978-79, Gimpel-Hanover Galerie, Zurich, 1975, 82, Galerie Christel, Stockholm, 1980, Jan Cicero Gallery, Chgo., 1980, 83, 92, Galerie S65, Aalst, Belgium, 1981, Andre Emmerich Galerie, Zurich, 1982, Galerie Konstructiv Tendens, Stockholm, 1982, Galerie Storrer, Zurich, 1987, Galerie Meissner Edition, Hamburg, 1987, Merril Lynch Internat., Zurich, 1987, ACP Viviane Ehrli Galerie, Zurich, 1988, 93-94, 97, 2000, Galerie Bruno Bucher, Poitiers, France, 1992, Galerie Vromans, Amsterdam, 1995, Fine Arts Gallery L.I. U., Southampton, 1997, Found. for Concrete and Constructivist Art, Zurich, 1991, Galerie Albergo Giardino, Ascona, Switzerland, Ann Reid Art Gallery, Princeton, NJ, 1998, Pearl Conard Gallery, Ohio State U., Mansfield, Ohio, 1999, Bohem Press Galerie Moderne Kunst, Zurich, 2001, Bohem Press, 2003, Galerie Stuker, Zurich, 2004, Look Gallery, Chgo., 2004; group exhbns. include Mondrian House Gallery, Amersfoort, Netherlands, 1999, 16 Young Artists, Inst. Contemporary Art, Phila., 1969, Eight Abstract Painters, 1978, Andre Zarre Gallery, NY, Geometry of Color, 1977, Cleve. Mus. Art, 1982, Bronx Mus. of the Arts, Editions Fanal, Basel, Paris, Saga 93, 96-2003, ACP Viviane Ehrli Gallerie Art-Frankfurt, 1994-96, Noyes Mus., Oceanville, NJ, 1994, Mus. Coopmanhus, Franeker, Netherlands, 1995, DePaul U. Art Gallery, Chgo., 1997; Forum Konkrete Kunst, Erfurt, Germany, 1998, Mus. for Moderne Kunst, Hiebuell, Germany, 1999, Hunter Coll. Times Sq. Gallery, NYC, 2001, 03, Nat. Mus. Szezecin, Poland, 2002; represented in corp. and pub. collections, AT&T, NYC, Arco. Internat.-Anaconda Aluminum, Chgo., Art Inst. Chgo., Chase Manhattan Bank, NYC, Citicorp, NYC, Lehman Bros, NYC, Madison (Wis.) Art Ctr., Merrill Lynch Internat., Zurich, Prudential Life Ins., Newark, Shearson Am. Express, NYC, Svenska Handelsbanken, Stockholm, Swiss Bank Corp., NYC, NJ State Mus., Whitney Mus. Am. Art., Mondrian House Found., Amersfoort, Netherlands, Nat. Mus. Szezecin, Poland. Student Work scholar Cleve. Inst. Art, Angel Fund award U. Pa.; Ford Found. Undergrad. grantee Cleve. Inst. Art, 1965, Pollock-Krasner Found., 1995; 50th Aniversary Print Portfolio, Am. Abstract Artist, 1987, 60th, 1997. Mem. Am. Abstract Artists. Home: 6601 Broadway #6-L Bronx NY 10471-2075 Personal E-mail: james4j@earthlink.net.

JUSZKIEWICZ, HENRY EDWARD, musical instrument company executive; b. San Nicolas, Argentina, Mar. 3, 1953; s. Edward and Irene Juszkiewicz; m. Patricia Ann Arns; children: Alexander, Zachary. BSME, GM Inst.; MBA, Harvard U., 1979. Project mgr. Delco Products div. GM, Rochester, NY; exec. v.p. Niederhoffer, Cross & Zeckhauser, NYC; owner, mgr. Phi Techs., Oklahoma City, 1981—86; chmn., chief exec. officer Gibson Guitar Corp., Nashville, 1986—; chmn. & CEO Gibson Musical Instruments, 1995—. Exec. v.p. Guitar & Accessories Mktg. Assn.; chmn. & CEO Gibson Musical Instruments, 1995—; pres. Gibson Found. Co-founder Music Rising, 2005; T.J. Martin Fund for Leukemia Rsch.; former leader explorer post Boy Scouts Am., Rochester, NY; hon. bd. mem. Nordoff-Robbins music therapy found.; bd. mem. Rainforest Alliance, Country Music Hall of Fame, Beale St. Blues Company, Inc. Office: 309 Plus Park Blvd Nashville TN 37217-1005

JUVET, RICHARD SPALDING, JR., chemistry professor; b. LA, Aug. 8, 1930; s. Richard Spalding and Marion Elizabeth (Dalton) J.; m. Martha Joy Myers, Jan. 29, 1955 (div. Nov. 1978); children: Victoria, David, Stephen, Richard P.; m. Evelyn Raeburn Elthon, July 1, 1984. BS, UCLA, 1952, PhD, 1955. Rsch. chemist Dupont, 1955; instr. U. Ill., 1955-57, asst. prof., 1957-61, assoc. prof., 1961-70; prof. analytical chemistry Ariz. State U., Tempe, 1970-95, prof. emeritus, 1995—. Founding mem. Emeritus Coll., Ariz. State U., Tempe, 2005—; vis. prof. UCLA, 1960, U. Cambridge, Eng., 1964-65, Nat. Taiwan U., 1968, Ecole Polytechnique, France, 1976-77, U. Vienna, Austria, 1989-90; air pollution chemistry and physics adv. com. EPA, HEW, 1969-72; adv. panel on advanced chem. alarm tech., devel. and engring. directorate, def. sys. divsn. Edgewood Arsenal, 1975; adv. panel on postdoctoral associateships NAS-NRC, 1991-94; mem. George C. Marshall Inst., 1998—. Author: Gas-Liquid Chromatography, Theory and Practice, 1962, Russian edit., 1966; editl. advisor Jour. Chromatographic Sci., 1969-85, Jour. Gas Chromatography, 1963-68, Analytica Chimica Acta, 1972-74, Analytical Chemistry, 1974-77; biennial reviewer for gas chromatography lit. Analytical Chemistry, 1962-76. Deacon Presbyn. Ch., 1960—, ruling elder, 1972—, commr. Grand Canyon Presbytery, 1974-76; moderator, communion com. Valley Presbyn. Ch., Scottsdale, Ariz., 1999-2001. NSF sr. postdoctoral fellow, 1964-65; recipient Sci. Exch. Agreement award to Czechoslovakia, Hungary, Romania and Yugoslavia, 1977. Fellow Am. Inst. Chemists; mem. AAAS, Am. Chem. Soc. (nat. chmn. divsn. analytical chemistry 1972-73, nat. sec.-treas. 1969-71, divsn. com. on chem. edn., subcom. on grad. edn. 1988—, councilor 1978-89, coun. com. analytical reagents 1985-95, co-author Reagent Chemicals, 7th edit. 1986, 8th edit. 1993, 9th edit. 2000, chmn. U. Ill. sect. 1968-69, sec. 1962-63, directorate divsn. officers' caucus 1987-90), Internat. Union Pure and Applied Chemistry, Internat. Platform Assn., Am. Radio Relay League (Amateur-Extra lic.), Sigma Xi, Phi Lambda Upsilon, Alpha Chi Sigma (faculty adv. U. Ill. 1958-64, Ariz. State U. 1975-95, profl. rep.-at-large 1989-94, chmn. expansion com. 1990-92, nat. v.p. grand collegiate alchemist 1994-96, trustee ednl. found. 1994-2004). Achievements include research on gas and liquid chromatography, instrumental analysis, computer interfacing, plasma desorption mass spectroscopy. Home: 4821 E Calle Tuberia Phoenix AZ 85018-2932 Office: Ariz State U Dept Chem and Biochem Tempe AZ 85287-1604 Personal E-mail: rsjuvet@juno.com.

JUVILER, PETER HENRY, political scientist, educator; b. London, Mar. 26, 1926; s. Adolphe Adam and Katie (Henry) J.; m. Anne C. Stephens, June 20, 1982; children: Gregory, Geoffry. BE, Yale U., 1948, ME, 1949; PhD, Columbia U., 1960. Project engr. Sperry Gyroscope Co., 1949-52; tchr. polit. sci. Princeton U., 1957-58, Columbia U., 1959-60, Hunter Coll., CUNY, 1960-64; prof. Barnard Coll., 1974—, prof. emeritus, sr. scholar, 2001—. Co-dir. Columbia U. Ctr. for Study Human Rights, 1986—2007; dir. human rights studies Barnard Coll., 2001—05. Author: Revolutionary Law and Order, 1976, Freedom's Ordeal: The Struggle for Human Rights and Democracy in Post-Soviet States, 1998; co-editor, contbr. Gorbachev's Reforms: U.S. and Japanese Assessments, 1988, Human Rights for the 21st Century, 1993, Religion and Human Rights: Competing Claims?, 1999, Non State Actors in the Human Rights Universe, 2006; contbr. numerous articles to profl. jours. With USN, 1944-46. Business E-Mail: pjuviler@barnard.edu.

JYOTHIBHAVAN, JOSEROSE S., chemistry educator; b. India; arrived in Am. Samoa, 1999; m. Bisha Jyothibhavan; 1 child, Charu. BS in Zoology, Kerala Univ., India, 1984; MS in Zoology, Entomology, Bhopal Univ., India, 1987; PhD, Barkatullah Viswavidayalaya Univ., India, 1993. Asst. prof. zoology Sree Narayana Coll., Univ. Kerala; chemistry, physics tchr. Tafuna H.S., Pago Pago, Am. Samoa, 1999—. Named Am. Samoa Tchr. of Yr., 2007. Mem.: Entomological Soc. Am. Office: Tafuna High Sch Dept Education Pago Pago AS 96799 Business E-Mail: joserose@gmail.com.*

KAAKE, NORMAN BRADFORD, quality assurance professional; b. Upper Darby, Pa., July 5, 1954; s. Norman Howard and Dorothy (Harris) K.; m. Kathy May Alexander, Dec. 27, 1983; 1 child, Mikeala Alexandra. BA in Polit. Sci., U. Maine, 1976. Restaurant mgr. That Seafood Place, Virginia Beach, Va., 1981; assoc. Conn. Gen. Life Ins. Co., 1981—82; import/boarding mgr. Containership Agy., Inc., Norfolk, Va., 1982-84, equipment mgr., 1984-86; ops. cost. control mgr. Tricom Shipping Agys., Inc., Norfolk, 1986-87; examiner asset based comml. lending Casco No. Bank, Portland, Maine, 1987-88, sr. examiner, 1988-90, comml. lender, credit officer, 1991-95; mgr. distbn. and quality sys. Merrill Industries, Inc., 1995—98; quality assurance engr. DOCdata New Eng., 1998-99; credit officer, lender Pepperell Bank and Trust, Biddeford, Maine, 2000—04; sr. construction loan specialist Butler Bank, Kennebunk, 2004—. Mem. 20th Maine Honor Brigade, 1975—; com. mem. Hampton Roads Steamship Trade Com., Norfolk, 1982-87; asst. scoutmaster troop 323 Boy Scouts Am., Hollis, Maine, 1987-95, merit badge counselor, York County, 1987—; mem. Hollis Planning Bd. and Comprehensive Planning Com., 1990-98, 2002—, Hollis Budget Com., 1991-94; Pheresis donor ARC, 1988—; active United Way Campaigns, 1987—; vice chmn. Hollis Planning Bd., 1992-93, chmn., 1993-98; vol. So. Maine Agy. on Aging; bd. dirs. Hollis Ctr. Libr. Served to capt. U.S. Army, 1976-80, USAR, 1980-87. Mem. Am. Inst. Banking, Internat. Register Cert. Auditors (cert. auditor quality sys.), Internat. Platform Assn., Hampton Roads Traffic Club, York County Riders, Inc. (v.p. 1990-91, bd. dirs. 1991-92), York County Vets. Alliance, Nat. Eagle Scout Assn., So. Maine Vets. Assn. (bd. dirs.), No. York County Family YMCA Steering Com. Republican. Avocations: antiques, boating, camping, skiing, photography. Home and Office: 15 History Ln Hollis Center ME 04042-3236 E-mail: kaake@sacoriver.net.

KAAKI, BILAL, obstetrician, gynecologist; s. Rafic Kaaki and Tannir Nadwa. BSc, Am. U. Beirut, 1996, MD, 2000. Ob-gyn. physician Allen Meml. Hosp., Waterloo, Iowa. Presenter in field. Contbr. articles to profl. jours. Recipient Mortimer Rosen award, Cleve. Ob-Gyn. Soc., 2003, 2005, 2006, 2d Pl. Rsch. award, Macdonald Women's Hosp., 2005, Best Tchr. award, 2005. Fellow: ACOG; mem.: AMA, Am. Assn. Gynecologic Laparoscopists (Excellence in Laparoscopy 2006). Achievements include research in music therapy in gynecologic office procedures. Office: Allen Meml Hosp Ob-Gyn Dept 1825 Logan Ave Waterloo IA 50703 Home Phone: 319-830-8969; Office Phone: 319-235-5050.

KAASHOEK, M. FRANS, computer science and engineering educator; PhD, Vrije Universiteit, Amsterdam, 1992. Prof. computer sci. and engring. MIT, Cambridge, mem. Computer Sci. and Artificial Intelligence Lab., 1993—. Co-founder Sightpath Inc., 1998; bd. mem. Mazu Networks Inc. Contbr. articles to profl. jours. Fellow: ACM; mem.: NAE. Office: MIT 32-G992 77 Massachusetts Ave Cambridge MA 02139 Office Phone: 617-253-7149. Office Fax: 617-258-8607. E-mail: kaashoek@csail.mit.edu.

KAATZ, FORREST H., physicist, educator; s. Gerald and Ella Kaatz. BS, U. Wis., Madison, 1984; PhD, U. Pa., Phila., 1991. Faculty Mesalands C.C., 1999—2002; with Sandia Nat. Labs., 2003—04; adj. faculty Owens CC, Toledo, 2004—. Rsch. assoc. Northwestern U., Evanston, 1995—98. Finalist Grad. Student awards, Materials Rsch. Soc., 1989; postdoctoral fellow, Am. Soc. Engring. Edn./Naval Rsch. Lab., 1991—93. Mem.: Math. Assn. Am. (assoc.), Am. Phys. Soc. (assoc.). Achievements include patents for oxidation resistant copper. Office: Owens CC 10000 Oregon Rd Toledo OH 43699 Home Phone: 419-388-8485; Office Phone: 567-661-7000. E-mail: forrest-kaatz@owens.edu.

KABACK, KEITH ROSS, emergency physician, educator; b. Middletown, NY, Apr. 21, 1953; m. Debora Kaback, Jan. 26, 1985. BA, Colgate U., Hamilton, NY, 1975; MD, Johns Hopkins U., Balt., 1979. Diplomate Am. Bd. Emergency Medicine. Intern in internal medicine U. Mo., Kansas City, 1979—80, resident in emergency medicine, 1980—82; emergency physician Tucson Med. Ctr., 1986—, med. dir. emergency svcs., 1989—98. Clin. lectr. U. Ariz., Tucson, 1986—; mem. Tobacco Revenue Use Spending and Tracking Commn. Dept. Health Svcs., Ariz., 2005—06; mem. adv. bd. Smokefree Ariz., 2005—06. Pres. MADD Pima County, Ariz., 1992—93; co-chair Clearing the Air, Tucson, 1997—; bd. dirs. Planned Parenthood So. Ariz., Tucson, 2001—; mem. exec. com. Coalition for Tobacco Free Ariz., 2005—; chmn. bd. Tucson divsn. Am. Lung Assn., 2006—. Recipient Spkrs. award, Am. Cancer Soc., 2001, Cmty. Action award, Am. Lung Assn. Ariz., 2003. Fellow: Am. Coll. Emergency Physicians.

KABACK, MICHAEL, medical educator; b. Phila., Sept. 1, 1938; BA, Haverford Coll., Pa., 1959; MD, U. Pa., Phila., 1963. Diplomate Am. Bd. Med. Genetics, Am. Bd. Pediatrics. Intern Johns Hopkins Hosp., Balt., 1963—64, resident pediatrics, 1966—68; fellow molecular biology and genetics NIH, Bethesda, Md., 1964—66; mem. staff Children's Hosp., San Diego; prof. pediatrics and reproductive medicine U. Calif., San Diego. Recipient William Allan Meml. award, Am. Soc. Human Genetics, 1993, Harland Sanders award, March of Dimes, 2000. Fellow: AAAS; mem.: Inst. of Medicine-Nat. Acad. Scis., AMA, Soc. for Pediatric Rsch., Am. Soc. Human Genetics, Am. Coll. Med. Genetics, Am. Pediatric Soc., Am. Acad. Pediatrics. Office: Univ Calif San Diego Sch Medicine 9500 Gilman Dr La Jolla CA 92093-0930 Home Phone: 858-259-6801; Office Phone: 858-822-6400. Business E-Mail: mkaback@ucsd.edu.

KABAKOV, ILYA, artist; b. Dnepropetrovsk, Russia, Sept. 30, 1933; arrived in US, 1988; s. Joseph and Bertha Kabakov; m. Emilia Kabakov. Attended, Leningrad Inst. of Painting, Sculpture & Architecture; grad., Moscow Art Sch., 1951, Surikov Art Inst., 1957. Illustrator Children's Literature, 1956—, Little One, 1956—. Installations include Ten Characters, 1988, The Red Wagon, 1991, The Bridge, 1991, We Are Leaving Here Forever, 1991, The Life of Flies, 1992, The Boat 1993, We Live Here, 1995, One the Roof, 1996, Golden Apples, 1997, The Antenna, 1997, The Palace of Projects, 1998; public projects include The Toilet, 1992, The Blue Dish, 1992, Life With an Idiot, 1992, An Extraordinary Incident, 1995, The Fallen Sky, 1995, Wings, 1996, The Fallen Chandelier, 1997, The Old Bridge, 1998, We Are Free!, 1998, They Are Looking Down, 1999, The Fountain, 2000, The Rice Fields, 2000, The Egg, 2001, Drinking Fountain, 2003, Pianist and Musa, 2003, The Shining Circus and its Spectators, 2004; one-man shows include 10 Characters, 2003, House of Photography, 2003, Center of Cosmic Energy, 2003, Empty Mus., 2004, others. Recipient Best Show award, Internat. Art Critic Assn., 1997.

KABALIN, JOHN NICHOLAS, urologist; b. LA, Dec. 23, 1958; s. Nicholas Augustin and Mary Jane (Engleman) Kabalin; m. Pamela Grace White, July 11, 1981. BS, Stanford U., 1980; MD, Johns Hopkins U., 1984. Diplomate Am. Bd. Urology. Intern in surgery Stanford U. Med. Ctr., 1984-85, resident in surgery, 1985-86, resident in urology, 1986-90, chief resident in urology, 1989-90; chief urology sect. Va Med. Ctr., Palo Alto, Calif., 1990-97; asst. prof. urology Stanford (Calif.) U., 1990-97; asst. prof. surgery U. Nebr. Coll. Medicine, 1999—. Contbr. over 100 articles to profl. jours., over 20 chpts. in books. Fellow: ACS, Am. Coll. Forensic Examiners, Sexual Medicine Soc. of N. Am., Internat. Coll. Surgeons, Am. Soc. for Laser Medicine and Surgery; mem.: AAAS, AMA, Am. Coll. Forensic Examiners, Am. Bd. Forensic Medicine, N.Y. Acad. Scis., Internat. Soc. Urology, Biomed. Optics Soc., Am. Lithotripsy Soc., Endourol. Soc., Soc. Univ. Urologists, Soc. Urol. Oncology, Am. Soc. Clin. Oncology, Am. Urol. Assn., Am. Assn. Clin. Urologists, Alpha Omega Alpha, Phi Beta Kappa. Roman Catholic. Achievements include adaptation and clinical development of Holmium laser sources for soft tissue and prostatic surgery. Office: Ste 2200 3911 Ave B Scottsbluff NE 69361-4669 Home Phone: 308-632-2552; Office Phone: 308-632-5315. E-mail: kabalij@rwmc.net.

KABALKIN, BARRY E., lawyer; b. Providence, May 3, 1955; AB, Brown U., 1977; JD, MBA, Harvard U., 1981. Bar: D.C. Assoc. Covington & Burling, Washington, 1981-88, ptnr. Wash., DC, 1988—96; exec. v.p. Bacardi Ltd., 1996—2000; prin. Pitts Bay Partners LLC, Wash., DC, 2000—. Office: Pitts Bay Partners LLC 1201 Pennsylvania Ave NW Ste 615 Washington DC 20004 Office Phone: 202-662-5730. Office Fax: 202-662-5998. Business E-Mail: principals@pittsbay.com.

KABAT, KEVIN THOMAS, bank executive; b. Huntington, NY, Feb. 15, 1957; s. Harry and Gena (Lorenzetti) Kabat; m. Patricia Lorraine Bullis, Aug. 18, 1979; children: Matthew Kevin, Jennifer Patricia. BA, Johns Hopkins U., 1979; MS, Purdue U., 1981. Cons. orgnl. devel. Mchts. Nat. Bank, Indpls., 1980—82; officer personnel Old Kent Bank, Grand Rapids, Mich., 1982—83, asst. v.p., 1984, v.p. employment, 1986, sr. v.p., dir. corp. operations, 1990, exec. v.p. retail admin. and corp. tech., 1995, sr. exec. v.p., COO, 1997, pres., 1997; sr. exec. v.p. Old Kent Financial Corp., 1997, vice chmn., 1998—2001; pres., CEO Western Mich. Fifth Third Bank, 2001—04; exec. v.p. Fifth Third Bancorp, 2003, exec. v.p. retail banking, affiliate admin. and mktg., 2004—06, pres., 2006—07, pres., CEO, 2007—. Adj. prof. Purdue U., Indpls., 1980—82, Grand Valley State Coll., Allendale, Mich., 1982, Davenport Coll., Grand Rapids, Mich., 1983. Mem.: Assn. Personnel Professionals. Office: Fifth Third Bancorp Fifth Third Ctr 38 Fountain Sq Plaza Cincinnati OH 45263*

KABDEBO, THOMAS GEORGE, library director; b. Budapest, Hungary, Feb. 5, 1934; arrived in U.K., 1956; s. Bela and Klara (Kelen) K.; m. Agnes Wohl, June 29, 1959 (div. 1984); children: Lilian, Andrea; m. Anna Kane, Dec. 22, 1986; 1 child, Istvan. BA, U. Wales, 1959; diploma in Libr., U. London, 1960, MPhil, 1968; PhD in History, U. Manchester, 1983. Asst. libr. U. Wales, 1959, U. London, 1960-69; libr. U. Guyana, 1969-72, U. Westminster, 1973-74; sublibr. U. Manchester, 1975-82; libr. Nat. U. Ireland, Maynooth, 1983—. Author 43 books in English, Hungarian and Welsh including Amonnan, 1993 (quality prize 1994), The Danube Trilogy, 1992-97 (award 1995), Dictionary of Dictionaries, 1992, Attila Jozsef (Fust Prize award), 1997. Decorated Order of Merit (Hungary); recipient Rakoczi essay prize, Hungarians of N.Am., Ottawa, Pro Patria Hungarica, Hungarian Republic, Budapest, 1992, Arany Janos prize for Lit., 1998, Nagy Imre plaque for 1956 Activities, 1999, Arany Janos prize for Lit., 2000, Attila Jozsef prize for Lit., 2001, Peterfy prize, 2006. Fellow Libr. Assn.; mem. P.E.N. Roman Catholic. Avocations: fishing, swimming, chess. Home: 92 Aylmer Rd Newcastle Co Dublin Ireland Office: Nat U Ireland Maynooth County Kildare Ireland Office Phone: 003531-4587100. Personal E-mail: tkabdebo@hotmail.com.

KABEL, ROBERT JAMES, lawyer; b. Burbank, Calif., Nov. 30, 1946; s. Herman James and Margaret Elizabeth (Doyle) K. BA, Denison U., 1969; JD, Vanderbilt U., 1972; LL.M. in Taxation, Georgetown U., 1979. Bar: D.C., Tenn., Ohio, U.S. Supreme Ct. Adminstrv. asst. to Gov. Winfield Dunn of Tenn., Nashville, 1972-75; legis. asst. to Senator Paul Fannin, Washington, 1975-77; legis. dir. Senator Richard G. Lugar of Ind., Washington, 1977-82; spl. asst. to pres. White House, Washington, 1982-84; ptnr. Manatt, Phelps & Phillips and precedessor firm, Washington, 1985—2002; of counsel Baker & Daniels, Washington, 2002—; sr. cons. B & D Cons., Washington, 2002—; DC Republican State Chmn. GOP, 2005—. Part-time mem. Fgn. Claims Settlement Commn., 1987-91. Mem. Vanderbilt Law Sch. Alumni Bd., 1997-00; bd. trustees Denison U., 1999-05; chmn. bd. dirs. Log Cabin Reps., 1994-99; chmn. Liberty Edn., 1999-05; mem. D.C. Rep. Com. 2004—; chmn. AIDS Responsibility Project 2004-05; mem. Rep. Nat. Com. Recipient citation Denison U. Alumni. Mem. ABA, Rep. Lawyers Assn., Denison U. Alumni Soc. (pres. 1994-96), Met. Club Washington, The Federalist Soc. Republican. Presbyterian. Office: Baker & Daniels 805 15th St NW Ste 700 Washington DC 20005 Office Phone: 202-312-7408. E-mail: Robert.Kabel@bakerd.com.

KABEL, ROBERT LYNN, chemical engineering professor; b. Champaign, Ill., Apr. 3, 1932; s. Myron Charles and Marietta Louise (Lynn) K.; m. Barbara Jean Robb, June 8, 1958; children: Joseph Robb, Douglas Alan. BS, U. Ill., 1955; PhD, U. Wash., 1961. Registered profl. engr., Pa. Engr. Conoco, Ponca City, Okla., 1954, Sun Oil Co., Marcus Hook, Pa., 1955, Chevron Rsch. Co., LaHabra and Richmond, Calif., 1967, 68; rsch. scientist NASA Ames Rsch. Ctr., Palo Alto, Calif., 1969; engr. Exxon, Linden, N.J., 1976-78; prof. chem. engring. Pa. State U., University Park, 1963—. Invitational prof. chem. and bioengring. Ariz. State U., Tempe, 1984-85; vis. prof. Tech. U. Norway, Trondheim, 1971-72, Pahlavi U., Shiraz, Iran, 1978, U. N.S.W., Sydney, Australia, 1988, 89, U. Canterbury, Christchurch, New Zealand, 1989, Chulalongkorn U., Bangkok, 1989; co-editor/author: Scaleup of Chemical Processes, 1985; cons. in field. Co-author: Sources and Control of Air Pollution, 1998. Bd. dirs. Oreg.-Calif. Trails Assn., 1999-2002. With USAF, 1961-63. Decorated Air Force Commendation medal; recipient Outstanding Tchg. award Amoco Found., 1983, award for Excellence in Instrn., Western Electric, 1983, Nat. Catalyst award for Excellence in Chem. Tchg., Chem. Mfrs. Assn., 1984, Disting. Achievement award Ariz. State U., 1985, Corcoran award ASEE, 1989, Disting. Vol. award Oreg.-Calif. Trials Assn., 2003; ASEE fellow, 1969, Royal Norwegian Coun. for Sci. and Indsl. Rsch. fellow, 1971-72, NATO fellow, 1974, Erskine fellow, 1989. Fellow AIChE (editl. bd. 1980-85); mem. Am. Chem. Soc., Sigma Xi, Phi Lambda Upsilon, Alpha Chi Sigma, Tau Beta Pi, Phi Eta Sigma. Republican. Presbyterian. Office: 130 Fenske Lab University Park PA 16802-4400 Home Phone: 814-237-6447. Business E-Mail: r8k@psu.edu.

KABOUB, FADHEL, economics professor, consultant; b. Madinah, Saudi Arabia, May 7, 1977; BS in Econs., Faculté des Sciences Economiques et de Gestion de Tunis, Tunis, Tunisia, 1999; MA in Econs., U. Mo., Kansas City, 2001, PhD in Econs., 2006. Lectr. U. of Mo., Kansas City, 2001—04; faculty in econs. Simon's Rock Coll. Bard, Great Barrington, Mass., 2004—05; vis. asst. prof. econs. Denison U., Granville, Ohio, 2005—06; asst. prof. of econs. Drew U., Madison, NJ, 2006—, co=dir. Wall St. semester program. Contbr. articles to profl. jours, ency. entires. Exec. mem. UN Assn.-USA, Kansas City, 2004—05. Recipient Faculty and Staff Appreciation award, U. Mo. Kansas City, 2002, Ilus W. Davis Writing Competition award, Ilus W. Davis Fund, 2002, Outstanding Leadership award, Omicron Delta Epsilon, 2003—04; fellow, Ctr. of Full Employment and Equity, 2002. Mem.: Rev. of Radical Polit. Econs. (editl. bd. 2006—), Assn. for Instl. Thought, Assn. for Evolutionary Econs., Phi Beta Delta (life; v.p. 2002—03), Omicron Delta Epsilon (life; treas. 2002—04). Independent. Muslim. Avocations: internat. currency collector, travel. Office: Drew U Dept Econs 36 Madison Ave Madison NJ 07940 Office Phone: 973-408-3764. Business E-Mail: fkaboubf@drew.edu.

KAC, VICTOR G., mathematician, educator; b. Buguruslan, USSR, Dec. 19, 1943; came to U.S., 1977; s. Gersh and Clara (Landman) K.; m. Elena Bourdenko; children: Luba, Marianne. Diploma, Moscow State U., 1965, cand. of sci., 1968. Asst. Moscow Inst. Electronic Machine Bldg., 1968-71; sr. tchr. MIEM, Moscow, 1971-76; assoc. prof. MIT, Cambridge, Mass., 1977-81, prof., 1981—. Author two books on infinite-dimensional Lie algebras, a book on vertex algebra and a book on quantum calculus; contbr. numerous articles to profl. jours. Recipient Medal Coll. de France, 1981, Wigner medal Group Theory Found., 1994; Guggenheim fellow, 1985, Sloan fellow, 1981. Mem. Am. Acad. Arts & Scis., Am. Math. Soc., Moscow Math. Soc. (hon.). Achievements include structure and representation theory of infinite-dimensional groups and algebras that arise in mathematics and physics. Home: 273 Mason Ter Brookline MA 02446 Office: MIT Math Dept 77 Massachusetts Ave Cambridge MA 02139-4307 Office Phone: 617-253-2945. Business E-Mail: kac@math.mit.edu.

KACHERGIS, JOYCE W., book designer; b. Omaha, Feb. 9, 1925; d. Lawrence Benjamin Webster and Olga Agnes Olsen; m. George J. Kachergis, July 6, 1946 (dec. Aug. 1974); children: Peter W., Karl George, Anne Olga; m. Jess G. Bell, 1986 (dec. Apr. 2001). AA, Stephens Coll., 1945; BFA, Sch. of the Art Inst., Chgo., 1947. Prodn. design mgr. U. N.C. Press, Chapel Hill, 1963-77; prodn. and design mgr. Stanford U. Press, Palo Alto, Calif., 1977-80; founder, pres., designer Kachergis Book Design, Pittsboro, NC, 1980—. Vis. prof. Radcliffe Sch. Pub., Cambridge, Mass., 1979-82. Grantee, Kresge Found., 1974. Mem. Am. Assn. Univ. Presses (bd. dirs. 1978-80). Office: Kachergis Book Design 14 Small St N Pittsboro NC 27312-5453 Personal E-mail: jwkb@mindspring.com.

KACULI, XHEMAL T., oil industry analysis/design engineer; B in Mech. Engring., Poly. U. Albania, Tirana, 1995; M in Engring. Sci., Lamar U., 1999, D in Engring., 2002. Registered profl. engr., Tex. Rschr. Lamar U., Beaumont, Tex., 1997—2003; engring. analysis and design, product devel. dept. Dril-Quip, Inc., Houston, 2001. Contbr. articles to profl. jours. Pres. Albanian Am. Assn., Houston, 2002—04. Fellow, Lamar U., 2001—02; scholar, 1998, 1999, 2000. Mem.: ASME, Nanotechnology Inst., Am. Soc. Metals, Am. Soc. Petroleum Engrs. Achievements include research in effect of mechanical alloying and bulk shear processing on the quality of Tungsten Carbide Tool products; microstructure and properties of mechanical alloyed and equal channel angular extruded Tungsten Carbide; integration of mechanical alloying and equal channel angular extrusion for production of nanostructured materials; application of mechanical alloying and bulk shear processing to produce superior quality oil field tool products; use of mechanical alloying and ECAE for production of nanostructured titanium silicide; patents for ball valve assembly. Office Phone: 281-216-7644. Personal E-mail: kaculi@gmail.com.

KACZMARCZYK, JEFFREY ALLEN, journalist, music and dance critic; b. Patuxent River Naval Air Base, Md., Jan. 7, 1963; s. Frank Joseph and Diane Catherine Kaczmarczyk; m. Cynthia L. Shimmel, Aug. 13, 1988; children: Jessica, Michael, David. BA, Western Mich. U., 1986; postgrad., Calif. State U. Editor-in-chief Western Herald, Kalamazoo, Mich., 1986-87; staff writer, acting editor Albion (Mich.) Recorder, 1987; staff writer, columnist Hastings (Mich.) Banner, 1987-92; arts writer, classical music critic The Grand Rapids (Mich.) Press., 1992—. Freelance arts writer, critic Kalamazoo (Mich.) Gazette, 1990-93; editor The Weekender, Hastings, 1991-93. Dir., sec. Thornapple Arts Coun., Hastings, 1992-97; dir. Grand Rapids Area Coun. for Humanities, 1995-2001; vestryman Emmanuel Episcopal Ch., Hastings, 1997-99, sr. warden, 1999. Episcopalian. Office: The Grand Rapids Press 155 Michigan St NW Grand Rapids MI 49503-2353 Home: 819 E Grant St Hastings MI 49058-1323 Home Phone: 269-945-3871; Office Phone: 616-222-5585. Business E-Mail: jkaczmarczyk@grpress.com.

KACZMAREK, JANE, actress; b. Milw., Dec. 21, 1955; d. Edward and Evelyn Kaczmarek; m. Bradley Whitford, Aug. 15, 1992; 3 children. BFA in Theatre, U. Wis.; MFA, Yale Sch. Drama, 1982. Actor: (TV series) Hometown, 1985, Equal Justice, 1990—91, Big Wave Dave's, 1993, Felicity, 1999—2000, Malcolm in the Middle, 2000— (nominated for 3 Golden Globe awards for best performance actress tv series, nominated for 4 Emmy awards for outstanding lead actress comedy series, Am. Comedy award, Family Friendly award, 2 Individual Achievement in a Comedy awards, TV Critics Assn., nominated best actress quality comedy, Viewers for Quality TV), Help Me Help You, 2006, (guest appearances) Touched by an Angel, Picket Fences, L.A. Law, Hollywood Division, St. Elsewhere, Party of Five, Frasier, Cybill, The Practice,; (TV films) All's Fair, 1989, Apollo 11, 1996, Educating Mom, 1996, Jenifer, 2001, The Deception, Boys Will Be Boys, I'll Take Manhattan, Something About Amelia, The Christmas Story, The Three Kings; (films) The Chamber, 1996, The Spittin' Image, 1997, Pleasantville, 1998, Wildly Available, 1999, Vice Versa, Uncommon Valor, D.O.A., The Heavenly Kid, Falling in Love; (plays, Broadway) Lost in Yonkers; (plays) Kindertransport, Raised in Captivity, Wasp, Escape from Happiness, Eve's Diary, Pride and Prejudice, The Legends of Oedipus, Loose Ends, Ice Cream/Hot Fudge, Better Living, Hands of Its Enemy. Co-founder charity Clothes off our Back.*

KACZOR, DIANE L., marketing professional, researcher; d. Cheslaw and Virginia Grace Kaczor. BA in Comm. minor in Bus., Northwestern U., 1997. Cert. museology U. Ill., Chgo., 1992, project mgmt. Am. Mgmt. Assn., Ill., 1999. Various sales and circulation positions SRDS, Des Plaines, Ill., 1988—2000, internat. & interactive specialist, 2000—01, listing enhancement cons. interactive, internat. media guides & newspaper Des Plaines, Ill., 2001—03, data analysis quality specialist Des Plaines, Ill., 2003—. Mem.: Soc. Am. Archivists. Avocations: performance, art, sculpting. Office: SRDS 1700 Higgins Rd Des Plaines IL 60018 Home Phone: 1-847-473-1009; Office Phone: 1-847-375-5116. Office Fax: 1-847-375-5316. Business E-Mail: dkacz@srds.com.

KACZOROWSKI, GREGORY JOHN, biochemist, researcher, science administrator; b. South Bend, Ind., Nov. 20, 1949; s. John Walter and Jean (Bankowski) K.; m. Maria L. Garcia, June 21, 1982. BS in Chemistry summa cum laude, U. Notre Dame, 1972; PhD in Biochemistry, MIT, 1977. Helen Hay Whitney postdoctoral rsch. fellow Roche Inst. Molecular Biology, 1977-80; sr. rsch. biochemist Merck Inst. for Therapeutic Rsch., Rahway, NJ, 1980-84, assoc. dir. dept. membrane biochemistry and biophysics, 1986-88, dir., 1988-96, sr. dir., 1996—2000, sr. dir. ion channels, 2001—; rsch. fellow Biochemistry, Fundamental and Exploratory Rsch., Rahway, 1984-86. Reviewer NIH, NSF, U.S.-Israel Binational Sci. Found.; invited speaker, presenter papers at various profl. meetings; adj. prof. dept. pharmacology and physiology U. Medicine and Dentistry N.J., 1995—, dept. physiology and biophysics Robert Wood Johnson Med. Sch., 2005—. Contbr. numerous articles, revs. to profl. jours.; patentee in field. Hoosier scholar, 1968-72, Notre Dame scholar, 1968-72. Mem. AAAS, Am. Chem. Soc., Am. Soc. Biol. Chemists, Am. Physiol. Soc., Biophys. Soc., N.Y. Acad. Sci., Phi Beta Kappa. Home: 5 Ashbrook Dr Edison NJ 08820-4318 Office: Merck Sharp & Dohme Rsch Labs PO Box 2000 Rahway NJ 07065-0900 Home Phone: 732-388-8299; Office Phone: 732-594-7565. Business E-Mail: gregory_kaczorowski@merck.com.

KADAK, ANDREW C., engineering educator, former company executive; b. 1945; BSME, Union Coll., 1967; MS in Numerical Methods, MIT, 1970, PhD in Reactor Physics, 1972; MBA, Northeastern U., 1983. With Combustion Engring., Windsor, Conn., 1972-75; mgr. nuc. info. New Eng. Power Co., Westboro, Mass., 1975-79; with Yankee Atomic Electric Co., Bolton, Mass., 1979—, v.p., 1986-89, pres., COO, 1989, CEO, 1989—97; prof. nuclear engring. MIT, Cambridge. Bd. advisors Mars Found.; lectr. in field. Office: MIT Dept Nuclear Sci and Engring 77 Massachusetts Ave, 24-202 Cambridge MA 02139-4307 Office Phone: 617-253-0166. Office Fax: 617-258-8863. E-mail: kadak@mit.edu, kadak@earthlink.net.*

KADANOFF, LEO PHILIP, physicist, educator; b. NYC, Jan. 14, 1937; s. Abraham and Celia (Kibrick) Kadanoff; children: Marcia, Felice, Betsy. AB, Harvard U., 1957, MA, 1958, PhD, 1960. Fellow Neils Bohr Inst., Copenhagen, 1960—61; from asst. prof. to prof. physics U. Ill., Urbana, 1961—69; prof. physics and engring., univ. prof. Brown U., Providence, 1969—78; prof. physics U. Chgo., 1978—82, John D. MacArthur Disting. Service prof., 1982—2004, prof. emeritus, 2004—. Mem. tech. com. R.I. Planning Program, 1972—78, mem. human svcs. rev. com., 1977—78; pres. Urban Obs. R.I., 1972—78. Author: Electricity Magnetism and Heat, 1967; co-author: Quantum Statistical Mechanics, 1963; adv. bd. Sci. Year, 1975—79, editl. bd. Statis. Physics, 1972—79, Nuc. Physics, 1980—. Recipient Wolf prize in physics, Wolf Found., Israel, 1980, Boltzmann medal, Internat. Union Pure and Applied Physics, 1990, Grande Medaille d'Or, Acad. Scis. Inst. France, 1998, Nat. Medal Sci., 1999; fellow NSF, 1957—61, Sloan Found., 1963—67. Fellow: AAAS, Am. Acad. Arts and Scis., Am. Phys. Soc. (Buckley prize 1977, Onsager prize 1998); mem.: NAS, Am. Philosophical Soc. Home: 5421 S Cornell Ave Apt 15 Chicago IL 60615-5678 Office: U Chgo James Franck Inst 5640 S Ellis Ave Chicago IL 60637-1433

KADAR, KARIN PATRICIA, librarian; b. Oil City, Pa., May 30, 1951; d. Michael Joseph and Bette Lee (Painter) Kadar; divorced; 1 child, Michael L. BS, Clarion U., 1973; MLS, U. Pitts., 1975; postgrad., U. S.C. Lic. instrnl. II in libr. sci. and elem. edn., pub. libr. lic. Substitute tchr. McKeesport (Pa.) Area Schs., 1973, elem. sch. libr., 1973-75, 3d grade tchr., 1975-78, elem. sch. libr., 1978-81; adj. prof. Pa. State U., McKeesport, 1988; periodicals libr. Seton Hill Coll., Greensburg, Pa., 1986-89; dir. Penn Twp. Pub. Libr., Level Green, Pa., 1989-90; grade sch. libr. substitute St. Agnes Sch., North Huntington, Pa., 1992; mid. sch. libr. substitute Belle Vernon (Pa.) Area Sch. Dist., 1993-95; dir. West Newton (Pa.) Pub. Libr., 1993-95, Highland Cmty. Libr., Richland, Pa., 1996; libr. Ridgeland (S.C.) Elem. Sch., 1996-98; spl. orders coord. Barnes and Noble, Hilton Head Island, SC, 1998-99; mgr. Bluffton (S.C.) Cmty. Libr., 1998-99; media specialist Jasper (S.C.) County H.S., 1999—2001, dist. libr./ media specialist coord., 1999—; sch. tech. coord. West Hardeeville Sch., 2001—, media specialist, 2002—. Mem. consumer appeals bd. Ford Motor Co., 1989-92, coord. Sch. Dist. Libr. Media Svcs., 2000—; staff writer Current Diversions. Author: (booklet) Sammy the Smokeless Dragon, 1976; mem. adv. panel Pa. mag., 1992—94, staff writer Current Diversions, 1999—2000, mem. editl. bd. SCASL Media Messenger, mem. editl. bd. and SC Reading List com. Media Messenger. Panelist Scan Trak Shoppers, 1984—, Nat. Family Opinion, 1984—; vol. Am. Cancer Soc., 1969-94, pub. edn. chmn., 1974-80, cancer prevention study II chmn., 1982-88, pub. affairs chmn., 1984-86, residential area crusade chmn., 1984-85. Named Vol. of Yr. Am. Cancer Soc. Mon Yough Unit, 1983-84; recipient Crusade award Am. Cancer Soc., Mon Yough unit, 1985-86. Mem. ALA, Pa. Libr. Assn., Parent-Tchr. Guild, Pa. State Edn. Assn., Low Country Reading Assn. (pres.), S.C. Assn. Sch. Librs. (regional rep. Jasper County, writer and mem. editl. bd. Messenger), Westmoreland County Hist. Soc., McKeesport Coll. Club, Heritage Hist. Assn. (Hilton Head, S.C.). Avocations: writing, collecting books, genealogy. Office: West Hardeeville Sch Hwy 46 Hardeeville SC 29927 Office Phone: 843-717-1251. E-mail: akawindy@hargray.com.

KADDEN, JACK, editor; BA, U. Conn., MA in English. Editor Hartford Courant, Conn.; reporter, editor Waterbury Rep., Conn.; editor Met., Nat., and Foreign desks NY Times, dep. edn. editor Nat. Edn. Dept., contbr. column about riding commuter trains. Office: NY Times 229 W 43rd St New York NY 10036 Office Phone: 212-556-4122. Office Fax: 212-556-3758. E-mail: kadden@nytimes.com.

KADEL, LEE A., information technology manager, systems analyst; s. Lee A. and Billie R. Kadel; m. Patricia M. Pond, Feb. 19, 1947; children: Elizabeth, Melody. BS in Mgmt. Info. Sys., Kennedy-Western U., 2004, MS in Mgmt. Tech., 2005; MS in Exec. Bus. Adminstrn., Warren Nat. U., 2007. MCSE 1998, CCSA Checkpoint 2001, NT-CIP Lanop 2001, CCA Citrix 2003, GSEC GIAC 2004, GHSC GIAC HIPAA 2006. Pres., CEO B.I.R.T. Systems Inc., Lake Geneva, Wis., 1986—95; v.p. Custom Indsl. Sales, Inc., Elkhorn, Wis., 1995—98; cons. Teksystems, Inc., Brookfield, Wis., 1998—2002; sr. network analyst Covenant Healthcare, Milw., 2002—04; sr. infosec analyst WFSI, Milw., 2004—. Mem. curriculum adv. bd. Milw. Area Tech. Coll. Mem.: IEEE, Healthcare Info. and Mgmt. Sys. Soc., Computer Security Inst., Info. Sys. Security Assn., Assn. Info. Tech. Profls. (bd. dirs. 2003—). Republican. Achievements include development of computer application testing methodology. Office Phone: 414-465-4449. Personal E-mail: lakadel@yahoo.com.

KADEN, ELLEN ORAN, lawyer, consumer products company executive; b. NYC, Oct. 1, 1951; m. Lewis Kaden; 2 children. AB, Cornell U., 1972; MA, U. Chgo., 1973; JD, Columbia U., 1977. Bar: NY, 1978. Law clk. to Judge Marvin E. Frankel US Dist. Ct. (so. dist. NY), 1977-78; asst. prof. Columbia U. Sch. Law, 1978-82, assoc. prof., 1982-84; exec. v.p., gen. counsel, sec. CBS Inc., NYC, 1991-98; sr. v.p. law and govt. affairs Campbell Soup Co., Camden, NJ, 1998—. Reporter jud. coun. 2nd Cir. Adv. Comm. on Planning for Dist. Cts., 1979-81; assoc. Cravath, Swaine & Moore, 1981-86. Trustee Columbia U., 1996—. Mem.: Fed. Bar

Counsel, ABA (mem. corp. gen. counsel sect.). Office: Campbell Soup Co One Campbell Pl Camden NJ 08103*

KADEN, LEWIS B., bank executive, lawyer, educator; b. 1942; AB, Harvard U., 1963, LLB, 1967. Bar: NY 1970, NJ 1974. Harvard scholar Emmanuel Coll., Cambridge U., 1963-64; law clk. US Ct. Appeals, 1967; legis. asst. Senator Robert F. Kennedy, 1968; ptnr. Battle, Fowler, Stokes & Kheel, 1969-73; chief counsel to gov. State of NJ, 1974-76; assoc. prof. Columbia U., 1976-79, prof., 1979-84, adj. prof., 1984—, dir. Ctr. for Law and Econ. Studies, 1979-83; ptnr. Davis, Polk & Wardwell, NYC, 1984—2005; vice chmn., chief adminstrv. officer Citigroup, Inc., 2005—. Chmn. US Govt. Overseas Presence Adv. Panel, 1999; bd. dirs. Mittal Steel Co. N.V. Chmn. NY State Indsl. Coop. Coun., 1986—92. Office: Citigroup Inc 399 Park Ave 2nd Fl New York NY 10022 Home Phone: 212-769-3047; Office Phone: 212-793-8045. Business E-Mail: kadenl@citigroup.com.

KADER, NANCY STOWE, nursing consultant, bioethicist, philosopher; b. Ogden, Utah, May 29, 1945; d. William Hessel and Mildred (Madsen) Stowe; m. Omar Kader, Jan. 25, 1967; children: Tarik, Gabriel, Aron, Jacob. BSN, Brigham Young U., 1967; PhD, U. Md., 2005. RN. Nurse ICU Glendale (Calif.) Adventist Hosp., 1970-75, Utah Valley Hosp., Provo, 1975-83; campaign coord. Matheson for Gov., Salt Lake City, 1976-85, Wilson for Senate, Salt Lake City, 1980; nurse cons. MESA Corp., Reston, Va., 1984—85; mgr. cost containment Health Mgmt. Strategies, Washington, 1985-88; nurse cons. Birch & Davis, Washington, 1988-90; cons. Inst. Medicine NAS, Washington, 1990-92; cons. Pal-Tech Inc., Arlington, Va., 1992—. Vice chmn. Utah State Bd. Nursing, Salt Lake City, 1977—83; adj. prof. Hood Coll., Md., 2000; ethics cons. to Healthcare Systems, Washington; cons. in field. Contbr. articles various profl. jours. Dem. county chmn., Utah, 1977-79; del. Dem. Nat. Conv., 1980, Va. State Dem. Conv., 1984-95; vice chmn. Gov.'s Commn. on Status of Women, Salt Lake City, 1975-78; bd. dirs. Health Sys. Agy. No. Va., 2000-. Democrat. Home: 10301 Dunfries Rd Vienna VA 22181 Business E-Mail: nkader@cox.net.

KADHIM, ESTELLE BEVERLY, retired librarian; b. Rock Island, Ill., June 16, 1933; d. George and Rose (Zaretsky) Buder; m. Abdul Wahhab Kadhim, 1955; children: Temma, Janon, Muna, Affifa, Dina. BA in Liberal Arts and Sci., U. Ill., 1955, MS in Libr. Sci., 1959. Libr., dept. oceanography and meteorology Tex. A&M Coll., College Station, 1956-59; libr. Scott County Libr., Eldridge, Iowa, 1959—60; gifts and exch. libr. Kans. State U. Libr., Manhattan, 1960, asst. to dir., 1960-61, head circulation dept., 1961-62; serials cataloger U. Calif.-San Diego, La Jolla, 1962-63; head, periodicals and documents Calif. State U., Fullerton, 1964-65; sch. libr. Am. Cmty. Ctr., Baghdad, Iraq, 1966-67; libr., head media ctr. Baghdad Internat. Sch., 1967-93; head children's dept. McAllen Meml. Libr., Tex., 1994—2006; ret., 2006. Tchr. Internat. Children's Ctr., 1968-69, Baghdad Internat. Sch., 1970-75. Mem. Tex. Libr. Assn. Avocations: needlecrafts, storytelling. Personal E-mail: bkadhim@hotmail.com.

KADIN, HEATHER, broadcast executive; b. Aug. 7, 1972; Grad., U. Mich., 1994. Asst. to prodr. Lynda Obst; asst. to Kevin Misher TriStar and Universal Pictures; asst. to dir. Tom Shadyac; devel. exec. to Tom Shadyac; with longform dept. ABC, with drama dept.; v.p. drama devel. Warner Bros. TV, Burbank, Calif. Achievements include working on the TV shows Alias, Lost, Grey's Anatomy, Desperate Housewives, The Closer, Invasion, Traveler, Supernatural and Studio 60 on the Sunset Strip. Office: Warner Bros TV 4000 Warner Blvd Burbank CA 91522*

KADIR, DJELAL, literature educator; b. St. Theodoros, Larnaca, Cyprus, Jan. 21, 1946; m. Juana Celia Cohen, May 24, 1969; 1 child, Aixé. BA, Yale U., 1969; PhD, U. N.M., 1972. Prof., chair comparative lit. Purdue U., West Lafayette, Ind., 1973-91; Disting. prof. lit. U. Okla., Norman, 1991-95, Neustadt prof. comparative lit., 1995-97; E.E. Sparks prof. of comparative lit. Pa. State U., 1998—; dir. Internat. Sch. Theory in Humanities, 1999—2001; founding pres. Internat. Am. Studies Assn., 2000. Editor World Literature Today, U. Okla., Norman, 1991-96; cons. Libr. Congress, Washington, 1975—; vis. scholar Russian Acad. Scis., Moscow, 1992; lectr. in field; sr. rsch. assoc. U. Leipzig, 1994—, Borges Ctr., Aarhus U. Denmark; bd. dirs. Coun. on Nat. Lits., Internat. Writers Ctr.; sr. rsch. fellow, mem. exec. bd. Internat. Sch. of Theory in the Humanities, Santiago, Spain, 1997-99; sr. fellow, mem. internat. bd. Synapsis: European Sch. Comparative Studies, 2000—. Author: Juan Carlos Onetti, 1977, Questing Fictions, 1986, Columbus and the Ends of the Earth, 1992, The Other Writing, 1993; editor, translator selected poetry of Joao Cabral de Melo Neto, 1994; editor: Longman Anthology of World Literature, 2003, Oxford History of Latin American Literature, 2004; mem. editl. bd. PMLA 1998-2002. Mem. State Arts Coun. Okla., Oklahoma City, 1991-96; cons. Indpls. Mus. Art.; v.p. UNESCO Commn. for Ency. Life Support Sys., 2005-. Resident fellow Rockefeller Found., Bellagio, Italy, 1993, 2000. Mem. MLA (chmn. Del. Assembly 1999-2000), Internat. Comparative Lit. Assn. (exec. bd. com. Lit. Histories, 1992—, chmn. com. on theory 1998—), Am. Comparative Lit. Assn., Internat. Found. Global Studies (sec. 1998-2000), Internat. Coll. Global Studies (v.p. 1998-2000). Avocations: music (cello), hiking, horseback riding, polo. Office: Dept Comparative Lit PA State U 311 Burrowes Bldg University Park PA 16802-6203 Business E-Mail: dxk50@psu.edu.

KADISH, RICHARD L., lawyer; b. Newark, Dec. 1, 1943; s. Irving Jerome and Henrietta (Appleblatt) K.; m. Bethany Tortis, Aug. 6, 1972; children: Jennifer, Andrew, Jill. BA, U. Pa., 1965; MA, Rutgers U., 1968, JD, 1970. Deputy atty. gen. N.J. Atty Gen., Trenton, NJ, 1971-74; deputy exec. dir. N.J. Housing Fin. Agy., Trenton, NJ, 1974-77; sr. v.p. CRI Inc., Rockville, Md., 1978-87, exec. v.p., 1987-94; pres. Capital Apt. Properties, Inc., Rockville, Md., 1994-97, CAPREIT, Inc., Rockville, Md., 1998—. Dir. Nat. Multifamily Housing Coun. Mem. ABA, N.J. Bar Assn. Office: CAPREIT Ste 100 11200 Rockville Pike Rockville MD 20852-3154 Business E-Mail: dkadish@capreit.com.

KADISH, SANFORD HAROLD, law educator; b. NYC, Sept. 7, 1921; s. Samuel J. and Frances R. (Klein) K.; m. June Kurtin, Sept. 29, 1942; children: Joshua, Peter. B Social Scis, CCNY, 1942; LLB, Columbia U., 1948; JD (hon.), U. Cologne, 1983; LLD (hon.), CUNY, 1985, Southwestern U., 1993. Bar: N.Y. 1948, Utah 1954. Pvt. practice law, NYC, 1948-51; prof. law U. Utah, 1951-60, U. Mich., 1961-64, U. Calif., Berkeley, 1964-91, dean Law Sch., 1975-82, Morrison prof., 1973-91, prof. emeritus, 1991—. Fulbright lectr. Melbourne (Australia) U., 1956; vis. prof. Harvard U., 1960-61, Freiburg U., 1967; lectr. Salzburg Seminar Am. Studies, 1965; Fulbright vis. lectr. Kyoto (Japan) U., 1975; vis. fellow Inst. Criminology, Cambridge (Eng.) U., 1968. Author: (with M.R. Kadish) Discretion to Disobey— A Study of Lawful Departures from Legal Rules, 1973, (with Schulhofer) Criminal Law and Its Processes, 6th edit., 1995, Blame and Punishment—Essays in the Criminal Law, 1987; editor-in-chief Ency. Crime and Justice, 1983; contbr. articles to profl. jours. Reporter Calif. Legis. Penal Code Project, 1964-68; pub. mem. Wage Stblzn. Bd., region XII, 1951-53; cons. Pres.'s Commn. Adminstrn. of Justice, 1966; mem. Calif. Coun. Criminal Justice, 1968-69. Lt. USNR, 1943-46. Fellow, Ctr. Advanced Study Behavioral Scis., 1967—68, Guggenheim fellow, Oxford U., 1974—75, vis. fellow, All Souls Coll. Oxford U., 1983. Fellow AAAS (v.p. 1984-86), Brit. Acad. (corr.); mem. AAUP (nat. pres. 1970-72), Am. Assn. Law Schs. (exec. com. 1960, pres. 1982), Order of Coif (exec. com. 1966-67, 74-75), Phi Beta Kappa. Home: 774 Hilldale Ave Berkeley CA 94708-1318 E-mail: shk@law.berkeley.edu.

KADISON, RICHARD VINCENT, mathematician, educator; b. NYC, July 25, 1925; married, 1956; 1 child. MS, U. Chgo., 1947, PhD, 1950; doctorate (hon.), U. d'Aix-Marseille, 1986, U. Copenhagen, 1987. NRC fellow math. Inst. Advanced Study, 1950-52; from asst. prof. to prof. Columbia U., 1952-64; Kuemmerle prof. math. U. Pa., 1964—. Fulbright rsch. grantee, Denmark, 1954-55; Sloan fellow, 1958-62; Guggenheim fellow, 1969-70. Mem. NAS (chmn. math. sect. 2003—06), Am. Math. Soc. (Steele prize for lifetime achievement 1999), Royal Danish Acad. Sci. and Letters (fgn. mem.), Norwegian Acad. Sci. and Letters (fgn. mem.), Sigma Xi. Office: U Pa Dept Math Philadelphia PA 19104-6395

KADLEC, KIM, media executive; b. NYC; Assoc. media dir. Backer Spielvogel Bates; mgr. KK Media, 1995; sr. v.p., dir. client svcs. Zenith Media Svcs./NY; sr. v.p. Universal McCann, 2002; v.p. branded entertainment NBC Universal; v.p. worldwide media, chief media officer Johnson & Johnson, New Brunswick, NJ, 2005—. Office: Johnson & Johnson One Johnson & Johnson Plaza New Brunswick NJ 08933 Office Phone: 732-524-3376. Office Fax: 732-214-0332.*

KADONAGA, JAMES TAKURO, biochemist; b. Ft. Bragg, NC, Aug. 24, 1958; s. Tadashi and Alice Ayako K.; m. Anne Kadonaga, Sept. 15, 1984; children: William, Natalie. SB, MIT, 1980; AM, Harvard U., 1982, PhD, 1984. Fellow U. Calif., Berkeley, 1984-88, asst. prof. molecular biology San Diego, 1988-92, assoc. prof., 1992-94, prof., 1994—, vice chmn., 2000—03, chmn. Molecular Biology, 2003—07. Mem. editl. bd. Molecular Cell Jour., 1997—, Genes and Devel. Jour., 1994—, Molecular and Cellular Biology, 1993-2001, Protein Expression and Purification, 1990—, Pub. Libr. of Sci., 2005—; contbr. articles to profl. jours. Recipient Biochemistry grant award Eli Lilly, 1989-91, Am. Inst. of Chemists/MIT award, 1980, prize Alpha Chi Sigma/MIT, 1980; named to Hall of Fame, East Side Union H.S. Dist., San Jose, Calif., 1991; DuPont fellow Harvard U., 1983-84, Miller fellow, 1984-86, sr. fellow Am. Cancer Soc. (Calif. divsn.), 1986-87, Presdl. Faculty fellow Pres. George Bush, 1992-97; Lucille P. Markey scholar, 1987-93. Fellow AAAS, Am. Acad. Microbiology; mem. Am. Chem. Soc., Am. Soc. Microbiology. Office: U Calif San Diego 2212B Pacific Hall 9500 Gilman Dr La Jolla CA 92093-0347 Office Phone: 858-534-4608.

KADONSKY, CHRISTINE ELAINE, historian, educator; b. Columbia, Md., Nov. 13, 1977; d. Carol Jean and William Kadonsky. BA in Social Studies, U. Wis., Eau Claire, 2001, MA in History, 2006. Tchr. U.S. history Wausau West H.S., Wis., 2001—. Vol. camp counselor Rainbow's End Camp for children with spl. needs, Wausau, Wis., 1992—; mem. and pres. U. Wis. - Cir. K Internat., Eau Claire, 1996—99; H.S. faculty advisor Wausau West chpt. of Key Club Internat., Wis., 2001—05; H.S. advisor Wausau West Nat. History Day, Wis., 2003—. Recipient Helen X. Sampson award for undergrad. rsch., U. Wis., Eau Claire, 2001, Outstanding Faculty Advisor, Wis.-Upper Mich. Dist. Key Club Internat., 2005, Participant award, NEH, 2006; fellow History Tchg. fellowship, Learning by Doing Tchg., Am. History Fellowship Program, 2003-2005; Wis. Sr. fellow, James Madison Meml. Fellowship Found., 2004-2006, Jamestown and the Legacy of Settlement Tchr. Inst. scholarship, Nat. History Day, 2006, Tchr. Inst. scholarship, Colonial Williamsburg, 2006. Mem.: Marathon County History Tchg. Alliance, Nat. Coun. for the Social Studies (vice chair govtl. rels. com. 2002—04), Wis. Coun. for the Social Studies (exec. bd. rep. 2002—). Avocations: travel, music, reading. Home Phone: 715-842-5367.

KADOTA, TAKASHI THEODORE, mathematician, electrical engineer; b. Omogo, Ehime-Ken, Japan, Nov. 14, 1930; s. Shigeru and Kikuko (Tominaga) K.; m. Helena Littau, Dec. 21, 1956 (div.); children: Mari, Amy, Kimberley; m. Charlie Frances Hampton. BSEE, Yokkohama U., Japan, 1953; MSEE, U. Calif., Berkeley, 1956, PhDEE, 1960. Mem. tech. staff AT&T Bell Labs., Whippany, NJ, 1960-66, Murray Hill, NJ, 1966-94; ret., 1994. Vis. prof. U. Hawaii, Honolulu, 1978, U. Calif., Berkeley, 1975, Stanford U., 1974. Fellow IEEE (assoc. editor 1977-80).

KADOW, JOSEPH J., lawyer; b. Scranton, Pa., 1956; BS in Acctg., U. Scranton, 1978; JD, Pa. State U. Dickinson Sch. of Law, 1981. Bar: Pa. 1981, Fla. 1983. Ptnr. Baker & Hostetler; v.p., gen. counsel, sec. OSI Restaurant Ptnrs., Inc. (formerly Outback Steakhouse, Inc.), Tampa, Fla., 1994—2001, sr. v.p., gen. counsel, sec., 2001—05, exec. v.p., chief officer legal and corp. affairs, 2005—. Trustee Florida TaxWatch, 2000. Office: OSI Restaurant Ptnrs, Inc 5th Fl 2202 N West Shore Blvd Tampa FL 33607

KADOYAMA, MARGARET, museum educator, management consultant; b. 1955; d. Charles and Mary Anne Convis; m. Robert Kadoyama, 1977; children: Hana, Marie. BS in Anthropology, U. Calif., Davis, 1978. Assoc. curator Navajo Tribal Mus., Window Rock, 1978—82; dir. Mus. Oriental Cultures, Corpus Christi, 1982—83; asst. curator Art Mus. South Tex., Corpus Christi, 1983—85; pub. programs, coord. new audiences Calif. Acad. Scis., San Francisco, 1987—95; prin. Margaret Kadoyama Cons., Fairfax, Calif., 1996—; adj. prof. John F. Kennedy U., Berkeley, Calif., 1997—. Co-author: (exhibit book) The Land, The People; contbr. articles and papers to profl. jours. and pubs. Com. planner Ross Valley Sch. Dist., San Anselmo, Calif., 1999—2003; program chair Cultural Connections, San Francisco, 1989—99; bd. mem. Sci. Interchange, San Rafael, Calif., 1997—2003, Marin Human Rights Roundtable on Hate Violence, San Rafael, 1996—2007; program com. mem. Angel Island Immigration Sta. Found., San Francisco, 2007. Mem.: Japanese Am. Citizens League, Marin Human Rights Roundtable on Hate Violence, Mus. Edn. Roundtable, We. Mus. Assn. (nat. program co-chair 1999), Am. Assn. Mus. (nat. program chair, edn. com. 1996—97, edn., evaluation and diversity coms.). Office: Margaret Kadoyama Cons 7 Shemran Ct Fairfax CA 94930 Home Phone: 415-454-7344; Office Phone: 415-454-7344. Office Fax: 415-454-7344. Personal E-mail: mkadoyama@earthlink.net.

KADZ, BRUCE B., plastic surgeon; b. Tehran, Iran, Jan. 14, 1966; s. Soloman Kadkhodazadeh and Shooshana Hakakian. BA, UCLA, 1987; MD, Med. Coll. Wis., Milw., 1991. Diplomate Am. Bd. Plastic Surgery, 1999. Gen. surgery resident Med. Coll. Affiliated Hosps., Milw., 1991—94; plastic surgery sr. house officer Frenchay Hosp., Bristol, England, 1994; plastic surgery resident Jackson U. Miami Hosp., 1995, 1996, aesthetic surgery fellowship, 1997; plastic surgery Pvt. Practice, Miami Beach, 1997—2001, Beverly Hills, 2001—. Cons. Physician Adv. Bd., Washington, 2005, Washington, 06. Fellow, ACS, 2000. Mem.: D. Ralph Millard Plastic Surgery Soc., Am. Soc. Hair Restoration Surgery, Am. Soc. Laser Medicine Surgery. Home: 10724 Wilshire Blvd #502 Los Angeles CA 90024 Office: 416 N Bedford Dr #406 Beverly Hills CA 90210

KAEGI, WALTER EMIL, history professor; b. New Albany, Ind., Nov. 8, 1937; s. Walter Emil and Ruth Ann (Mergell) K.; m. Louise Polk Mullikin, June 9, 1969; children: Frederick George, Christian Emil. AB, Haverford Coll., 1959; AM, Harvard U., 1960, PhD, 1965. Tchg. fellow Harvard U., Cambridge, Mass., 1961-63; fellow Ctr. for Byzantine Studies Dumbarton Oaks Rsch. Libr., Washington, 1963—65, 1980; asst. prof. history U. Chgo., 1965-69, assoc. prof. history, 1969-74, prof. history, 1974—, voting mem. Oriental Inst., 1997—. Co-founder Byzantine Studies Conf., 1975; co-editor Byzantinische Forschungen, Amsterdam, Las Palmas, 1981—. Author: Byzantium and the Decline of Rome, 1968, Byzantine Military Unrest, 1981, Army, Society and Religion in Byzantium, 1982, Byzantium and the Early Islamic Conquests, 1992, Heraclius Emperor of Byzantium, 2003; editor: The Southern Star, 1947-50; mem. editl. bd. The Shenandoah, 1955-56; co-editor: Byzantinische Forschungen, 1980—; contbr. articles to profl. jours. Recipient Highest Hons. in History, Haverford Coll., 1959, fellow Inst. for Advanced Study, Princeton U., 1971, 85, Am. Coun. Learned Socs., 1978-79, Am. Rsch. Ctr. in Egypt, 1979, Dumbarton Oaks, 1980, Fulbright fellow in Islamic Civilization, Syria, Jordan, 1984, to Iraq, 1988, NEH, 1988-89, 90-91, John Simon Guggenheim Found., 1996-97, Nat. Humanities Ctr. Rsch., Triangle Pk., N.C., 1996-97, Social Sci. Rsch. Coun., N.Y.C., 1996-97; recipient travel grants to Internat. Byzantine Congresses, 1977, 91, travel grant to Southeastern European Studies Internat. Congress, Athens, 1970, U. Jordan grant to participate in Fourth Internat. Conf. on History of Bilad al-Sham, 1983, 85, 87, IREX grant to visit USSR, 1991; Fulbright-Hays fellow Tunisia, Moroccco, Algeria, 2004. Mem. Am. Hist. Assn., Am. Philol. Assn., Byzantine Studies Conf. (governing bd. dirs. 1994-98), Soc. for Studies and Rsch. on the Ancient Aures, US Nat. Com. for Byzantine Studies, Medieval Acad. Am., Swiss-Am. Hist. Soc., Mid. East Medievalists, Phi Beta Kappa. Avocations: gardening, travel, walking. Office: Univ of Chicago Dept of History 1126 E 59th St Dept Of Chicago IL 60637-1580 Office Phone: 773-702-8346. Business E-Mail: kwal@uchicago.edu.

KAEHELE, BETTIE LOUISE, accountant; b. Sherwood, Tenn., Oct. 29, 1950; d. James Henry and Ruby Katherine (Clark) Shetters; divorced; children: Josiah Dean, Dana Marie. AAS, Albuquerque Tech. Vocat. Inst., 1990; BSBA, Nat. Coll., Albuquerque, 1991. Acctg. clk. Am. Auto Assn., Albuquerque, 1980—81, Ryder Truck Rental, Inc., Albuquerque, 1981—82; owner Sherwood Svcs., 1982—86; bookkeeper, sec. Grants Steel Sash & Hardware, Albuquerque, 1986—87; acctg. specialist Burton & Co., Albuquerque, 1987—91, Neff & Co., Albuquerque, 1991—92; acctg. tech. U. N.Mex. Found., Albuquerque, 1992—97; acct. II dept. family and cmty. medicine U. N.Mex., Albuquerque, 1997—2002, acct. III dept. family and cmty. medicine, 2002—. Mem. Light and Liberty Jail Ministry. Mem.: Light and Liberty Jail Ministry. Republican. Avocations: reading, dance, theater, poetry, writing. Home: 7408 Desert Canyon Pl SW Albuquerque NM 87121-6424

KAELIN, DARRYL LOUIS, medical educator; b. Louisville, Feb. 25, 1965; BA, Notre Dame U.; MD, U. Louisville, 1991. Cert. in phys. medicine and rehab.; bd. cert. Am. Assn. Electrodiagnostic Medicine. Intern Kettering Med. Ctr., Ohio, 1991-92; resident Med. Ctr. Va., Richmond, 1992-95; asst. clin. prof. Ind. U. Med. Ctr., Indpls., 1995—2005, Wishard Hosp., Indpls., 1995—2005, Comty. Hosp., Indpls., 1995—2005; med. dir. Hook Rehab. Ctr., Indpls., 1995—2005, Acquired Brain Injury Program, Shepherd Ctr., Atlanta, 2005—. Fellow Am. Acad. Phys. Medicine and Rehab.; mem. Assn. Acad. Physiatrists. Office: Medical Director of Brain Injury Services Shepherd Center 2020 Peachtree Road NW Atlanta GA 30309-1465 Office Phone: 404-350-7353. Office Fax: 404-350-7381.*

KAELIN, EUGENE FRANCIS, retired philosophy educator; b. St. Louis, Oct. 14, 1926; s. Albert Aloysius and Bertha (Earni) K.; m. Pierrette Nicole Demartini, Dec. 30, 1952; children: Valérie Chantal, Carolyne Pascale, Martine Laurence. BA with distinction, U. Mo., 1949, MA, 1950; diploma of higher studies, U. Bordeaux, France, 1951; PhD, U. Ill., 1954. Instr. philosophy U. Mo., 1952-53; fellow philosophy U. Ill., 1953-54, post-doctoral fellow, 1954-55; instr. philosophy U. Wis., 1955-57, asst. prof., 1957-61, assoc. prof., 1961-65, Fla. State U., 1965-67, prof., 1967-96, ret., 1996. Mem. nat. adv. bd. aesthetic edn. program Central Midwestern Regional Ednl. Lab., 1968-76. Author: An Existentialist Aesthetic, 1962, Art and Existence, 1970, The Unhappy Consciousness, 1981, Heidegger's Being and Time: A Reading for Readers, 1988, An Aesthetics for Art Educators, 1989, Texts on Texts and Textuality, 1999. With USMC, 1945-46. Recipient William Henry Kiekhofer Meml. Teaching award U. Wis., 1959. Mem. Am. Philos. Assn., Am. Soc. Aesthetics, Am. Soc. Phenomenology and Existential Philosophy, Fla. Philos. Assn. (pres. 1977-78). Home: 1910 Atapha Nene Tallahassee FL 32301-5851 Personal E-mail: eugkael@comcast.net.

KAEMPEN, CHARLES EDWARD, manufacturing executive; b. Quincy, Ill., Mar. 10, 1927; s. Charles Herman and Margo (Gochicoa) K.; m. Inger Margareta Nystrom, Aug. 5, 1951; children: Charles Robert, Donald Michael, Annette Earline, Laura Inger. BS in Aeron. Engring., U. Ill., Urbana, 1950; DSc in Astronautics, Internat. Acad. Astronautics, Paris, 1964. Registered profl. engr., Calif., Conn. Sr. designer Saab Aircraft Co., Linköping, Sweden, 1950-52; design analyst Sikorsky Helicopter United Aircraft, Stratford, Conn., 1952-56; space mission analyst Missle div. N.Am. Rockwell, Downey, Calif., 1957-60; staff scientist Hughes Aircraft, Fullerton, Calif., 1961-63; lunar systems analyst Northrop Space Lab., Hawthorne, Calif., 1963-64; pres. Am. Space Transport Co., Tustin, Calif., 1964-66; transport systems analyst Dashaveyor Co., Venice, Calif., 1966-67; pres. Kaempen & Assocs., Orange, Calif., 1967-68; sr. rsch. engr. Baker Oil Tools Inc., LA, 1968-69; pres. Kaempen Industries, Inc., Santa Ana, Calif., 1969-82, Kaempen & Assocs., 1982—; pres., CEO Kaempen Composite Products, Inc., 1996-2000; pres. Kaempen Corp., Inc., 2000—. Author papers on fiberglass composites and filament winding; patentee in field. With U.S. Army, 1944-47. Fellow AIAA; mem. ASME, ASTM, NSPE, Soc. Aerospace Materials and Process Engring., Soc. Plastics Industry, Masons. Republican. Lutheran. Home: 3202 E Larkstone Dr Orange CA 92869-5546 Office: Kaempen Composite Products Inc 681 S Tustin St Ste 110 Orange CA 92866-3345 Home Phone: 714-639-3686; Office Phone: 714-493-4105. E-mail: cekaempen@aol.com.

KAEMPER, LAURA JEAN, medical transcriptionist; b. St. Louis, July 26, 1971; d. Charles Leonard and Ada Estell Norris; m. Lee Wayne Kaemper, Aug. 13, 1994; 1 child, Aleksey Lorien. BS, Hannibal-LaGrange Coll., Mo., 1993. Med. transcriptionist Transolutions, Inc., Lake Bluff, Ill., 1999—. Mem.: Am. Assn. Med. Transcriptionists. Home Phone: 660-829-1285; Office Phone: 800-766-3469.

KAEN, NAIDA, state representative; b. Frankenmuth, Mich., May 12, 1946; m. Fred R. Kaen; two children. BEd, U. Mich., 1968; MBA, U. N.H., 1977. Realtor; state rep. N.H. Ho. of Reps., 1995—. Mem. sci., tech. and energy com. N.H. Ho. Reps. Office: NH State Legis State House Concord NH 03301 Address: 22 Toon Ln Lee NH 03824-6507 E-mail: naidakaen@hotmail.com.

KAESBERG, PAUL JOSEPH, virology researcher; b. Engers, Germany, Sept. 26, 1923; came to U.S., 1926, naturalized, 1933; s. Peter Ernst and Gertrude (Mueller) K.; m. Marian Lavon Hanneman, June 13, 1953; children— Paul Richard, James Kevin, Peter Roy. BS in Engring, U. Wis., Madison, 1945, PhD in Physics, 1949; D. Natural Scis. (hon.), U. Leiden, The Netherlands, 1975. Instr. biometry and physics U. Wis., 1949-51, asst. prof. biochemistry, 1956-58, assoc. prof., 1958-60, prof., 1960-63, prof. biophysics and biochemistry, 1963—, Beeman prof. biophysics and biochemistry, 1983-87, chmn. Biophysics Lab., 1970-88, Wis. Alumni Research Found. prof., 1981—, Beeman prof. molecular virology and biochemistry, 1987-90, prof. emeritus, 1990. Cons. in field. Contbr. chapts. to books and articles to profl. jours. Mem. NAS, Am. Soc. Virology (pres. 1987-88). Office: U Wis Inst Molecular Virology 1525 Linden Dr Madison WI 53706-1534 Home: 6205 Mineral Pt Rd Apt 803 Madison WI 53705-4581 Personal E-mail: pjkaes@aol.com.

KAESLER, ROGER L., paleontologist, educator; Grad. in Geol. Engring., Colo. Sch. Mines, 1959; MS in Geology, U. Kans., 1962; spl. student, U. Hull, Eng., 1964; PhD in Paleontology, U. Kans., 1965. Staff US Army Corps Engrs., 1959—60, Seistech Geophys. Co., Wichita, Kans., 1960; tchg. asst. to rsch. asst. to grad. fellow dept. geology U. Kans., 1960—65, asst. prof. geology, asst. curator, 1965—69, assoc. prof., assoc. curator, 1969—73, prof., assoc. curator, 1973—81, prof., dir., sr. curator,

curator-in-charge divsn. invertebrate paleontology Natural Hist. Mus., 1981—; dir. Paleontol. Inst., 1986—. Summer rsch. assoc. Kans. Geol. Survey, 1967, 69, 70, 74, 80, 81, 84, 85, 86; vis. assoc. prof. biology Va. Poly. Inst. and State U., 1972—73. Contbr. articles to sci. jours.; assoc. editor: U. Kans. Paleontol. Contbns., 1965—86; editor, 1986—; assoc. editor: Paleobiology, 1974—79, Palaeontologia Electronica, 1997—, mng. editor: Kans. Acad. Sci., 1969—70; editor: Treatise on Invertebrate Paleontology, 1986—. Fellow: Geol. Soc. Am. (Disting. Svc. award 2006); mem.: Soc. Econ. Paleontologists and Mineralogists, Internat. Paleontol. Assn. (treas. 1989—), Systematics Assn. (life), Paleontol. Soc. (treas. 1981—87, pres. 1991—92), AAAS, Sigma Xi, Sigma Gamma Epsilon Earth Sci. Hon. Soc., Tau Beta Pi Engring. Hon. Soc. Office: U Kans Dept Geology Lindley Hall Rm 121 1475 Jayhawk Blvd Lawrence KS 66045-7613 E-mail: kaesler@ku.edu.

KAESTNER, KLAUS H., genetics educator; BS in Biology and Chemistry, U. Bremen, 1984; MS, U. Md., Coll. Park, 1986; PhD, John Hopkins U. Med. Sch., 1990. Postdoctoral fellow John Hopkins U. Med. Sch., Balt., 1990—91, German Cancer Rsch. Ctr., Heidelberg, 1991—96; asst. prof. genetics U. Pa. Sch. Medicine, 1997—2002, assoc. prof., genetics, 2002—; assoc. dir., molecular biology core, Penn Ctr. for Molecular Studies in Digestive and Liver Diseases U. Pa., 2001—, dir., functional genomics core, Penn Diabetes Ctr., 2001—. Mem. external adv. com. NIH-funded Conti-Ctr., Tufts Med. Sch., Boston, 1999—2005; mem. Cancer Ctr., Diabetes Ctr., Ctr. for Molecular Studies in Digestive and Liver Diseases U. Pa., 1997—, mem. exec. com., Ctr. for Molecular Studies in Digestive and Liver Diseases, 2000—, mem. Cell Ctr. adv. com., 2000—, mem., transgenic core adv. com., sch. medicine, 2001—, chair, Expression Profiling Oversight Com., 2003—, mem., sch. medicine rsch. core com., 2003—, mem. animal program adv. com., 2004—, mem., sch. medicine animal rsch. com., 2004—, mem., diabetes and endocrinology rsch. ctr., exec. com., sch. medicine, 2005—; expert reviewer Juvenile Diabetes Rsch. Found. Internat., 2003—; mem. NIH Initial Review Group, Gastrointestinal Cell and Molecular Biology Study Sect., 2005—; invited lectr. in field. Mem. editl. bd. Diabetes, 2005—, Molecular Endocrinology, 2006—; contbr. articles to profl. jours.; ad hoc reviewer for several profl. publications, 1997—, ad hoc reviewer NIH Initial Review Group, Gastrointestinal Cell and Molecular Biology Study Sect., 2004, NIH Initial Review Group, Cellular Aspects of Diabetes and Obesity, 2005. Mil. svc., Sch. for Handicapped Children, 1979—81, Heiligenberg, Germany. Recipient Paul Ehrlich Grad. Student award, John Hopkins Med. Sch., 1990; Jr. Rsch. Fellowship award, German Cancer Rsch. Ctr., 1992—94. Mem.: Am. Assn. for the Study Liver Diseases, AAAS, Am. Diabetes Assn., Am. Gastroenterological Assn. Office: U Pa Sch Medicine Dept Genetics 560 Clinical Bldg 415 Curie Blvd Philadelphia PA 19104-6145 Office Phone: 215-898-8759. Office Fax: 215-573-5892. Business E-Mail: kaestner@mail.med.upenn.edu.*

KAFARSKI, MITCHELL I., chemical processing company executive; b. Detroit, Dec. 15, 1917; s. Ignacy A. and Anastasia (Drzazgowski) Kafarski; m. Zofia Drozdowska, July 11, 1967; children: Erik Michael, Konrad Christian. Student, U. Detroit, 1939-41, Shrivenham Am. U., Eng., 1946. Process engr. Packard Motor Car Co., Detroit, 1941-44; organizer, dir. Artist and Craftsman Sch., Esslingen, Germany, 1945-46; with Nat. Bank of Detroit, 1946-50; founder, pres. Chem. Processing Inc., Detroit, 1950-65, also bd. dirs.; chmn. bd., pres., treas. Aactron Inc., Madison Heights, Mich., 1965—; chmn. bd., pres. Imtech of Mich., Inc., 1988-92. Treas. Detroit Magnetic Insp. Co., 1960-65; also dir.; v.p. KMH Inc., Detroit, 1960-64; also dir.; treas. Packard Plating Inc., Detroit, 1962-67, also dir. Commr. Mich. State Fair, 1965-72; mem. com. devel. and planning to build Municipal Stadium State of Mich., 1965-88; benefactor, mem. Founders Soc., Detroit Inst. Arts, 1965—; trustee Founders' Soc., Detroit Inst. Arts, 1982-90; sponsor, host world celebrity for World Preview Mich., 1965-66; mem. dist. adv. council SBA, 1971-73; del. White House Conf. on Aging, 1971; organizer, treas. Mich. Reagan for Pres. Com., 1980; treas. Straith Meml. Hosp., Southfield, Mich., 1972— , chmn. bd., 1976; trustee Mich. Opera Theater, 1982—; bd. dirs. Gilbert and Sullivan Light Opera Soc., Palm Beach, Fla., 1985—; White House rep. to opening of first U.S. Trade Center, Warsaw, Poland, 1972; chmn. fund-raising Bloomfield Arts Assn., Birmingham, Mich., 1973-74; mem. Space Theatre Consortium, Inc., Seattle, 1981-83; bd. regents Orchard Lake (Mich.) Schs., 1981-83; Vice chmn. Republican State Nationalities Council Mich., 1969-73; bd. dirs. Bloomfield Arts Assn., 1973-84, Friends of Kresge Library, Oakland U., 1973-86; presdl. appointee bd. dirs. U.S.A. Pennsylvania Ave. Devel. Corp., Washington, 1973-81; chmn. bd. Straith Meml. Hosp., Detroit, 1971— , Detroit Sci. Center, 1972—, corp. dir.; mem. Internat. Soc. Palm Beach; trustee Greater Palm Beach Symphony, 1986; mem. Citizen's Commn. to Improve Mich. Cts., 1986-88; contbr. Kravis Ctr. for Performing Arts, West Palm Beach, 1989; mem. Bus. Com. for the Arts, Palm Beacvh, 1991—. Served with AUS, 1944-46, ETO. Recipient Nat. award for war prodn. invention War Prodn. Bd., 1943; decorated knight's Cross Order of Poland's Rebirth Restituta, 1975, chevalier Chaine des Rotisseurs, 1982, Knight of Malta Order of St. John. Mem. Nat. Assn. Metal Finishers, Mich. Assn. Metal Finishers (dir., chmn. bd. 1976), N.A.M., Am. Electroplaters Soc., Cranbrook Acad. Arts, Am.-Polish Action Coun. (chmn. 1971-76), Am. Assn. Mus. (treas. Detroit), Poinciana Club, Village Club. Clubs: Capitol Hill (Washington); Detroit Athletic. Home: 21 Kingsley Manor Ct Bloomfield Hills MI 48304-3520 Office: Aactron Inc 29306 Stephenson Hwy Madison Heights MI 48071-2394 Office Phone: 248-642-2730. *A basic ingredient to success usually is determined by special events in one's life. In the course of my experiences, a sprinkling of tribulations were a must. From these were gleaned the principles, goals and conduct in attaining success. During the course of my life's pursuit, the ability to help others ensured a complete fulfillment of my goals.*

KAFENTZIS, JOHN CHARLES, journalist, educator; b. Butte, Mont., Aug. 18, 1953; s. Christian and Betty Ann (Gaston) K.; m. Teresa Marie Nokleby, June 5, 1976; children: Kathryn Anne, Christian John. BA in Journalism, U. Mont., 1975. Reporter The Missoulian, Missoula, Mont., 1974-76, The Hardin (Mont.) Herald, 1976, The Spokesman-Rev., Spokane, Wash., 1976-80, copy editor, 1980-83, chief copy desk, 1983-89, news editor, 1989-94, news designer, 1994—2003, design editor, 2003—. Adj. faculty Ea. Wash. U., Cheney, 1982—, Whitworth Coll., 1998, Gonzaga U. 2004-. Greek Orthodox. Avocation: swimming. Office: The Spokesman Rev 999 W Riverside Ave Spokane WA 99201-1098

KAFF, ALBERT ERNEST, reporter, writer; b. Atchison, Kans., June 14, 1920; s. John and Ethel Mae (Worley) K.; m. Lee Chuan Diana Fong, Oct. 15, 1960; children: Arthur Fong, Alban Fong. BA in Econs., U. Colo., 1942. Reporter Atchison Globe, summers 1939-41, Ponca City (Okla.) News, 1946-48, Daily Oklahoman, Oklahoma City, 1948-50; fgn. corr. U.P.I., Korea and Japan, 1952-56, bur. mgr. Saigon Vietnam, 1956—58, bur. mgr. Taipei, Taiwan, 1958—61, Manila, Philippines, 1961—63, news editor Tokyo, 1963-72, dir. Asian svcs. Hong Kong, 1972-75, asst. dir., dir. pers. rels. NYC, 1975-78, v.p., gen. mgr. Asia-Pacific Hong Kong, 1978-84, v.p., mgr. N.Y., 1984-85; media cons., 1985; bus. internat. editor Cornell U. News Svc., 1986-93. Freelance journalist Stamford, Conn., Alexandria, Va., Fairfield, Conn., 1993—; columnist Overseas Press Club Bull. Contbg. author: How I Got That Story, 1967, Eyewitness on Asia, 1997, Foreign Correspondents in Japan: Covering a Half Century of Upheavals from 1945 to the Present, 1998; author: (with Avner Arbel) Crash: Ten Days in October. Will It Strike Again?, 1989. Served with AUS, 1943-46, 50-52. Decorated Bronze Star Mem. Fgn. Corrs. Club Japan (pres. 1967-68), Fgn. Corrs. Club Hong Kong (pres. 1974-75), Overseas Press Club Am. (v.p. 1984-86, bd. dirs. 1988-92, trustee Found. 1992—), Ithaca Press Club (vice chmn. 1987-88) Sigma Chi. Episcopalian. Home and Office: 393 Unquowa Rd Fairfield CT 06824-5028 Home Phone: 203-259-3324; Office Phone: 203-259-3324. E-mail: albertkaff@aol.com. *During 65 years of reporting, writing and editing the news, I missed several opportunities because I ignored a basic rule: If you can accomplish the assignment today or tomorrow, do it today. Tomorrow will bring new demands.*

KAFFER, ROGER LOUIS, bishop; b. Joliet, Ill., Aug. 14, 1927; s. Earl Louis and Helen Ruth (McManus) K. BA, St. Mary of the Lake, Mundelein, Ill., 1950, STB, 1952, MA, 1953, licentiate in sacred theology, 1954; licentiate of canon law, Pontifical Gregorian U., Rome, 1958; D of Pastoral Ministry, St. Mary of the Lake, Mundelein, Ill., 1983; MEd, DePaul U., 1965; LHD (hon.), Felician Coll., 1986; DHL (hon.), Coll. St. Francis, 1990; doctorate (hon.), Lewis U., 1990. Ordained priest Roman Cath. Ch., 1954; cert. K-14 supr. Ill. Eccles. notary Roman Cath. Diocese of Joliet, 1954—56; asst. chancellor Roman Cath. Diocese Joliet, 1958—65; aux. bishop Roman Cath. Diocese of Joliet, 1985—, vicar gen., vicar for clergy, 1985—2004; rector St. Charles Borromeo Sem., Lockport, Ill., 1965—70; prin. Providence High Sch., New Lenox, Ill., 1970—85; rector Cathedral of St. Raymond, Joliet, 1985; consecrated bishop, 1985; ret., 2002. Past. mem. Marriage Tribunal, Diocesan Sem. Bd., Diocesan Bd. Religious Edn. Named Cleric of Yr., KC, 1973, Citizen of Yr., New Lenox Assn. Commerce, 1976, Man of Yr., Joliet Cath. High Alumni Assn., 1978, Citizen of Yr., UNICO, Joliet, 1996; recipient DeLa Salle medallion, Lewis U., 1984, Lifetime Achievement award, Joliet C. of C., 1999, award, Paluch Family Found., 2002. Mem.: Nat. Conf. Cath. Bishops Conf. Ill., KC (Ill. state chaplain 1993—). Roman Catholic. Avocations: youth work, retreat work. Address: 425 Summit St Joliet IL 60435-7155

KAFIN, ROBERT JOSEPH, lawyer; b. Phila., Jan. 1, 1942; s. Jacob A. and Anna C. (Cohen) K.; m. Carol A. Friedman, June 20, 1965; children: Tammy Ellen, Peter Douglas. AB magna cum laude, Franklin & Marshall Coll., 1963; JD cum laude, Harvard U., 1966. Bar: N.Y. 1967, U.S. Dist. Ct. (so. dist.) N.Y. 1968, U.S. Dist. Ct. (no. dist.) N.Y. 1971, U.S. Dist. Ct. (we. dist.) N.Y. 1974, U.S. Ct. Appeals (2d cir.) 1971, U.S. Supreme Ct. 1972, D.C. 1997. Ptnr. Kafin and Needleman, Glens Falls, NY, 1971-78; prin. Miller, Mannix, Lemery & Kafin, Glens Falls, NY, 1978-87; assoc. Proskauer Rose LLP, NYC, 1967-71, ptnr., 1987-91, chief operating ptnr., 1991—. Trustee Adirondack Conservancy Com., Elizabethtown, N.Y., 1980-87; judge Glens Falls City Ct., 1976; counsel N.Y. State Senate, Albany, N.Y., 1973-87. Editor: N.Y. Environmental Law Handbook, 1988, 92. Bd. dirs. Environ. Planning Lobby, Albany, 1977-88; active Manhattan Solid Waste Adv. Bd., N.Y.C., 1987—; dir. Park & Trails NY, 1995—, chmn., 1999; trustee Preservation League N.Y. State, 1997—; dir. Times Square Alliance, 2004—; dir. Adirondack Coun., 2004—. Mem. N.Y. Bar Assn. (sec. environ. law sect. 1988, treas. 1989, 1st vice chmn. 1991, chair 1992-93), Assn. Bar City N.Y. (environ. law com. 1987-89). Democrat. Jewish. Home: 340 E 72d St Apt 3-SE New York NY 10021

KAFKA, BARBARA POSES, writer, chef; b. NYC, Aug. 6, 1933; d. Jack and Lillian (Shapiro) Poses; m. Ernest Kafka, June 19, 1959; children: Nicole, Michael. AB cum laude, Radcliffe Coll., 1954. Cons. in field. Author: American Food California Wine, 1981, 94, (Tastemaker award), Microwave Gourmet, 1987 (N.Y. Times Best Seller), Food for Friends, 1987, 93, Microwave Gourmet Healthstyle Cookbook, 1989, (Tastemaker award), Party Food, 1992, Roasting A Simple Art, 1995 (Julia Child Cookbook award), Soup, A Way of Life, 1998, Vegetable Love2006 (Internat. Assn. Culinary Professionals award, 2006); compiler, editor pro bono: The James Beard Celebration Cookbook, 1990; editor: The Four Seasons, 1980, The Cook's Catalogue, (mags.) Cooking, The Pleasures of Cooking; contbg. editor Vogue, 1981-89, Gourmet, 1988-96; contbg. columnist N.Y. Times, 1987—; contbr. articles to profl. jours. Mem. Internat. Assn. Culinary Profls., Am. Inst. Wine and Food, Culinary Historians Boston, James Beard. Home and Office: 23 E 92nd St New York NY 10128-0607*

KAFKA, GERALD ANDREW, lawyer; b. Martins Ferry, Ohio, Sept. 9, 1951; s. Andrew and Mary (Spustek) K.; m. Rita A. Cavanagh; children: Andrea, Sarah, Justin. BA, Wheeling Jesuit Coll., 1972; JD, U. Cin., 1975; LLM in Taxation, Georgetown U., 1979. Bar: Ohio 1975, D.C. 1982, Md. 1984, U.S. Tax Ct. 1977, U.S. Claims Ct. 1978, U.S. Supreme Ct. 1979, D.C. 1982, U.S. Dist. Ct. (D.C. dist.) 1983, U.S. Ct. Appeals (D.C., fed., 3d, 4th, 5th, 6th, 7th 8th and 9th cirs.). Trial atty. honors program tax div. U.S. Dept. Justice, Washington, 1975-79; ptnr. Scribner, Hall & Thompson, Washington, 1979-84, Steptoe & Johnson, Washington, 1984-92, Dewey Ballantine, Washington, 1992-2000, Mokee Nelson, LLP, Washington, 2000—03, Latham & Watkins, 2003—. Mem. adj. faculty Georgetown U. Law Ctr., Washington, 1979—; master J. Edgar Murdoch Am. Inn of Ct., U.S. Tax Ct., 1989—. Author: Litigation of Federal Tax Civil Controversies, 1996; editor procedure dept. Jour. Taxation; contbr. articles to profl. jours. Named Outstanding Atty., Tax Divsn. US Dept. Justice, 1977. Fellow Am. Coll. Tax Counsel; mem. ABA (chair ct. procedure com. tax sect. 1993-95, chmn. task force civil tax litigation process 1989-90, task force on large case audits and litigation 1990-91, ad hoc joint com. tax ct. jurisdiction 1987, task force on taxpayer bill of rights legis 1987-88, chair tax ct. appts. com. 2003-05), D.C. Bar Assn. (steering com. tax sect. 1986-91, chmn. com. audits and litigation tax sect. 1987). Office: 555 Eleventh St NW Washington DC 20004 Office Phone: 202-637-2198. E-mail: jerry.kafka@lw.com.

KAFOURE, MICHAEL D., food products executive; married; 3 children. BS in Mgmt. and Adminstrn., Ind. U. Joined Campbell Taggart, 1967, pres., COO bakery ops., 1990; pres. Merico, Inc.; sr. v.p. Interstate Bakeries Corp., Kansas City, Mo., 1995, pres., COO, 1995—. Office: Interstate Bakeries Corp 12 E Armour Blvd Kansas City MO 64111

KAGAN, DONALD, historian, educator; b. Kurshan, Lithuania, May 1, 1932; arrived in US, 1934, naturalized, 1940; s. Max and Leah (Benjamin) K.; m. Myrna Dabrusky, Jan. 13, 1955; children: Robert William, Frederick Walter. AB, Bklyn. Coll., 1954; MA, Brown U., 1955; PhD, Ohio State U., 1958. Instr. history Pa. State U., University Park, 1959-60; asst. prof. ancient history Cornell U., 1960-64, assoc. prof., 1964-67, prof., 1967; sterling prof. classics and history Yale U., 1969—2002, master Timothy Dwight Coll., 1976-78, acting dir. athletics, 1987-88, dean Yale Coll., 1989-92. Jefferson lectr. NEH, Washington, 2005. Author: The Great Dialogue, 1965, The Outbreak of the Peloponnesian War, 1969, The Archidamian War, 1974, The Western Heritage, 1979, (with Frank Turner and Steven Ozment) The Peace of Nicias and the Sicilian Expedition, 1981, The Fall of the Athenian Empire, 1987, Pericles of Athens and the Birth of Democracy, 1991, On the Origins of War and the Perservation of Peace, 1995, (with Frederick W. Kagan) While America Sleeps, 2000; The Peloponnesian War, 2003. Named Jefferson lectr., 2005; recipient Nat. Humanity medal, 2002. Home: 37 Woodstock Rd Hamden CT 06517-2949

KAGAN, ELENA, dean, law educator; b. 1960; BA summa cum laude, Princeton U., 1981; MPhil, Worchester Coll., Oxford, 1983; JD magna cum laude, Harvard Law School, 1986. Law clk. US Ct. of Appeals for Judge Abner Mikva of the US Supreme Ct. for the DC Circuit, 1986—87, US Ct. of Appeals for Justice Thurgood Marshall of the US Supreme Ct., 1987—88; assoc. Williams & Connolly, Wash., DC, 1989—91; faculty mem. Univ. of Chgo. Law Sch., Chgo., 1991—99; nominated to serve as judge US Supreme Ct. of Appeals, Wash., DC, 1999; asst. prof. Univ. of Chgo. Law Sch., 1991, prof. of law tenure Chgo., 1995; assoc. counsel to the Pres. White House, Wash., DC, 1995—96, dep. asst. to the Pres. for Domestic Policy, 1997—99, dep. dir. of the Domestic Policy Coun., 1997—99; vis. prof. Harvard Law Sch., Cambridge, Mass., 1999, prof., 2001—, dean, 2003—, Charles Hamilton Houston prof. of law, 2003—. Author: (article) Harvard Law Rev. Article, Pres. Admin., 2001 (honored as the year's top scholarly article by the Am. Bar Assoc. Section on Admin. Law and Reg. Pract., 2001). Kagan has also written on a range of First Amendment issues, including the role of governmental motive in different facets of First Amendment doctrine, and the interplay of libel law and the First Amendment. Mem.: Harvard Law Sch. faculty appt. comm., Harvard Law Sch. Locational options comm. (chair 2001—02). Kagan is a prof. of law at Harvard Law Sch. where she teaches admin. law, constitutional law, and civil procedure. Her recent sholarship focuses primarily on the role of the Pres. of the US in formulating and influencing fed. admin. and regulatory law. Office: Harvard Law Sch Griswold 200 1525 Mass Ave Cambridge MA 02138 Office Phone: 617-495-4601. Office Fax: 617-495-5115. E-mail: ekagan@law.harvard.edu.*

KAGAN, ILSE ECHT, librarian, researcher, historian; b. Free City of Danzig, Sept. 23, 1927; d. Samuel and Hella Echt; m. Robert A. Kagan, Aug. 26, 1951 (dec. Oct. 1994); children: Jonathan, Miki. BA (hon.), Oxford U., MA, 1954; MLS, Columbia U., 1960. With Pira Energy, NYC, 1987—; village historian Village of Gt. Neck (N.Y.) Estates, 1996—. Founding mem. Gt. Neck Hist. Soc. Past pres. Gt. Neck Estates Civic Assn., sec., 2000—; past pres. Gt. Neck chpt. Hadassah; bd. dirs. Am. Jewish Com. Mem.: Oxford U. Club, Brit. Schs. Univ. Club, Harvard Club. Avocations: tennis, theater, music. Home: 25 Elm St Great Neck NY 11021 Office: Pira Energy 3 Park Ave New York NY 10016 Office Phone: 212-686-6808. E-mail: piraiek@concentric.net.

KAGAN, JEROME, psychologist, educator; b. Newark, Feb. 25, 1929; s. Joseph and Myrtle (Liebermann) K. BS, Rutgers U., 1950; PhD, Yale, 1954. Instr. psychology Ohio State U., 1954-55; research assoc. Fels Research Inst., Yellow Springs, Ohio, 1957-59, chmn. dept. psychology, 1959-64; assoc. prof. psychology Antioch Coll., 1959-64; rsch. prof. psychology Harvard U., 1964-2000, dir. Mind Brain Behavior Initiative, 1996-2000, rsch. prof., 2000—05, prof. emeritus, 2005—. Adv. com. Nat. Inst. Child Health and Devel. Author (with G.S. Lesser): Contemporary Issues in Thematic Apperceptive Methods, 1961; author: (with Moss) Birth to Maturity, 1962; author: (with Mussen, Conger and Huston) Child Development and Personality, 7th edit., 1990; author: (with Segal) Psychology, 7th edit., 1991; author: (with Janis, Mahl and Holt) Personality, 1969, Understanding Children, 1971, Change and Continuity in Infancy, 1971; author: (with Kearsley and Zelazo) Infancy, 1978; author: (with Brim) Constancy and Change, 1980, The Second Year, 1981, The Nature of the Child, 1984; author: Unstable Ideas, 1989, Galen's Prophecy, 1994, Three Seductive Ideas, 1998, Surprise, Uncertainty and Mental Structures, 2002; author: (with Snidman) The Long Shadow of Temperament, 2004; author: (with Norbert Herschkovitz) A Young Mind in a Growing Brain, 2005; author: An Argument for Mind, 2006, What is Emotion?, 2007. Served with AUS, 1955-57. Recipient Lucius Cross medal Yale U., 1981; Phi Beta Kappa scholar, 1988-89. Fellow AAAS, APA (Disting. Sci. Contbn. award 1987, G. Stanley Hall award 1995), Am. Acad. Arts and Scis., Soc. Rsch. Child Devel. (Disting. Sci. Contbn. award 1989); mem. NAS, Inst. Medicine, Ea. Psychol. Assn. Home: 210 Clifton St Belmont MA 02478-2605 Office: Harvard U Dept Psychology William James Hall 33 Kirkland Hl Cambridge MA 02138 Business E-Mail: jk@wjh.harvard.edu. *My success has been aided by a combination of hard work, openess to new ideas, a readiness to discard beliefs that are proven invalid; a desire to nurture the growth of others; and belief in the beauty of ideas and the perfectibility of man.*

KAGAN, JULIA LEE, magazine editor; b. Nurnberg, Fed. Republic Germany, Nov. 25, 1948; d. Saul and Elizabeth J. Kagan. AB, Bryn Mawr Coll., 1970. Rschr. Look Mag., NYC, 1970-71; editl. asst., asst. editor McCall's mag., NYC, 1971-74, assoc. editor, 1974-78, sr. editor, 1978-79; articles editor Working Woman mag., NYC, 1979-85, exec. editor, 1985-88; editor Psychology Today, 1988-90; sr. editor McCalls, 1990-91; contbg. editor Working Woman, 1991-93; editor-in-chief Lamaze Parents' Mag., 1992-93, Lamaze Baby Mag., 1993; spl. projects dir. Child Mag., 1993-94; sr. v.p. EDK Assocs., NYC, 1994; psychology/health dir. Fitness Mag., NYC, 1995-96; dep. editor Consumer Reports Mag., Yonkers, NY, 1996, editor, 1996-2000; v.p. and editl. dir. Consumers Union, 2000—03; v.p. content Zagat Survey, 2003—04; nat. editor-in-chief Back Stage, 2005; health dir. Ladies' Home Jour., 2005—. Vis. J. Stewart Riley prof. journalism Ind. U., 1991-93. Co-author: Manworks: A Guide to Style, 1980; contbg. author: The Working Woman Success Book, 1981, The Working Woman Report, 1984. Pres. Appleby Found., N.Y.C., 1982-84; trustee Bryn Mawr Coll., 2000-06 Recipient 2d Ann. Advt. Journalism award Compton Advt., 1983 Mem. Am. Soc. Mag. Editors, Womens Media Group (bd. dirs.), Journalism and Women Symposium (treas. 1993-94, pres. 1995-96), Princeton Club (N.Y.C.), Cosmopolitan Club (N.Y.C.). Office: Ladies Home Jour 125 Park Ave New York NY 10017-5529 E-mail: jlkagan@aol.com.

KAGAN, ROBERT ALLEN, law educator; b. Newark, June 13, 1938; s. George and Sylvia K. AB, Harvard U., 1959; LLB, Columbia U., 1962; PhD, Yale U., 1974. Now prof. polit. sci. and law U. Calif., Berkeley. Office: U Calif Sch Law Boalt Hall Berkeley CA 94720

KAGAN, STEPHEN BRUCE (SANDY KAGAN), corporate financial executive; b. Elizabeth, NJ, Apr. 27, 1944; s. Herman and Ida (Nadel) K.; m. Susan D. Kaltman, July 3, 1966; children: Sheryl, Rachel BS in Econs., U. Pa., 1966; MBA in Fin., Bernard Baruch Coll., 1969. Chartered fin. analyst. CPA security analyst Merrill Lynch Pierce Fenner & Smith, NYC, 1966-68; dir. rsch. Deutschmann & Co., NYC, 1968-70; v.p. Equity Sponsors, Inc., NYC, 1970-72; v.p., investment counselor Daniel H. Renberg & Assocs., Inc., LA, 1972—78; CFO, COO Carlson Travel Network, Van Nuys, Calif., 1978—95; rep. Excel Telecomms., Van Nuys, Calif., 1995—2000; CFO, ptnr. Tatum LLC, San Marcos, Calif., 2000—. Vice pres. bd. Temple Beth Hillel, North Hollywood, Calif., 1976-83 Mem. Inst. Cert. Fin. Analysts, Beta Gamma Sigma Avocations: golf, skiing, poker, travel. Home and Office: Tatum LLC 941 Bridgeport Ct San Marcos CA 92078

KAGEN, STEVEN L., congressman, physician; b. Appleton, Wis., Dec. 12, 1949; s. Marv Kagen; m. Gayle Kagen; 4 children. BS with honors in Molecular Biology, U. Wis., Madison, 1972, MD, 1976. Cert. Am. Bd. Internal Medicine, 1979, Am. Bd. Allergy & Immunology, 1981, diagnostic lab. immunology Am. Bd. Allergy & Immunology, 1988. Teamster Foremost Dairy; intern to resident internal medicine Northwestern U. Sch. Medicine, Chgo., 1976—79; fellow allergy/immunology Med. Coll. Wis., Milw., 1979—81; founder Kagen Allergy Clinics, Appleton, Wis., 1981—, Oshkosh, Wis., 1981—, Green Bay, Wis., 1986—, Fond du Lac, Wis., 1990—; consulting staff HCA Med. Ctr., Port St. Lucie, Fla., 1986—93; asst. clin. prof. allergy & clin. immunology dept. medicine Med. Coll. Wis., Milw.; active staff dept. medicine Mercy Med. Ctr., Oshkosh, Appleton Med. Ctr., Wis.; affiliate staff dept. medicine Bellin Hosp., Green Bay, Wis.; mem. US Congress from 8th Wis. dist., 2007—, mem. agr. com., transp. & infrastructure com. Bd. dirs. Joint Coun. Allergy, Asthma and Immunology 1988-1992, 1988—92; allergy cons. CNN, 1995—2002; dir. Nat. Pollen Network. Contbr. articles to med. jours. Named one of Best Drs. in Am., 1996—97; recipient Founder's award, Fox Cities Children's Mus., 1996, Children's Environ. Health Recognition award, EPA, 2005. Mem.: AMA, State Med. Soc. Wis., Wis. Allergy Soc., Am. Coll. Allergy, Asthma & Immunology, Am. Acad. Allergy, Asthma & Immunology (Pub. Outreach award 2004), Am. Meteorol. Soc. (assoc.). Democrat. Jewish. Achievements include patents in field. Office: 1232 Longworth House Office Bldg Washington DC 20515 also: 700 E Walnut St Green Bay WI 54301 Office Phone: 920-432-8800, 920-437-1954, 202-225-5665. Office Fax: 202-225-5729.*

KAGEYAMA, MARIKO, collections manager; Came to U.S., 2001. d. Yousuke and Mikiko Kageyama. BAS, Nagoya U., Japan, 1997; MS, Kyoto U., Japan, 1999; MA, Tex. Tech U., Lubbock, 2003. Rsch. asst. Natural Sci. Rsch. Lab., Mus. Tex. Tech U., Lubbock, 2001—03; digital imaging specialist divsn. vertebrate zoology Am. Mus. Natural Hist., N.Y.C., 2004—05; collections mgr. vertebrate zoology U. Colo. Mus., Boulder, 2005—. Recipient RC-AAM Young Profl. award, 2006; scholar, Morishita-Jintan Found., 1993, Japan Am. Women of Kansai, 1998, Coll. Women's Assn. Japan, 2001, Tex. Assn. Mus., 2002; ICOM Anniversary travel grantee, 2007. Mem.: Am. Soc. Mammalogists, Mammalogical Soc. Japan, Japanese Soc. Systematic Zoology, Internat. Coun. Mus., Natural Sci. Collections Alliance, Soc. for Preservation of Natural History Collections, Am. Assn. Mus. Office Phone: 303-492-0160. E-mail: mariko.kageyama@colorado.edu.

KAGGEN, LOIS SHEILA, non-profit organization executive, advocate; b. NYC, Jan. 2, 1944; d. Elias and Sylvia (Muntner) K.; m. Harold Jay Burns, June 29, 1969 (dec. June 1975); 1 child, David Henry (dec.); m. Michael Francis McCann, Sept. 26, 1984 (div. Apr. 2007). BS in Fine Arts, Skidmore Coll., 1964; postgrad., Cooper Union, 1967-70; MA in Art Edn., CCNY, 1973; PhD in Art Edn., NYU, 1997. Tchr. fine arts grades 7-9 Jr. HS 149, Bronx, NY, 1967-74; founder, pres. Resources for Artists With Disabilities, NYC, 1987—. Traumatic Brain Injury Consumer Adv., 1977—; adv. bd. com. Art in Edn. Project, NY State Coun. on the Arts, Ctr. for Safety in the Arts, NYC, 1987; cons. Ea. Paralyzed Vets. Assn., Guggenheim Mus. Art, NYC, 1990; bd. advisors Ind. Arts Gallery, Queens Ind. Living Ctr., Jamaica, NY, 1987-98; steering com. Ann. Disability Independence Day March, 1992-93, mem. Media Outreach, 1992; provider written and oral testimony in field to orgns.; bd. dirs. Ctr. for Independence of the Disabled of NY, Inc., NYC, 1996—, Gov.'s appt. to Traumatic Brain Injury Svcs. Coordinating Coun., Albany, 1997-2001, others; presenter NIH Consensus Devel. Conf. on Rehab. of Persons with Traumatic Brain Injury, Bethesda, Md., 1998, 5th Ann. Conf., Traumatic Brain Injury Program, NY State Dept. Health, Albany, 1998, Info. and Comm. Com. TBISEC (TBI Coun.) NYS-DOH, Delmar, NY, 2001, NY State Assembly task force on people with disabilites: pub. hearing City U. NY Grad. Ctr., NY, 2001, Am. Coun. Edn. conf. The Student with a Brain Injury: Achieving Goals for Higher Edn., DC, 2001; originator, conf. com. co-organizer, consumer panelist NYU Moses Ctr. for Students with Disabilities and Ctr. for Independence of Disabled of NY, Loeb Student Ctr., NYU, NYC, 1998; panel organizer, moderator, presenter Inst. for Rsch. on Women's 16th Ann. Celebration of Our Work Conf., Douglass Coll., Rutgers U., New Brunswick, NJ, 1998; search com. for dir. Tang Tchg. Mus. and Art Gallery, Skidmore Coll., Saratoga Springs, NY, 2004; gave testimony Taxi and Limousine Commn., 2004; art presenter in field. Photography exhbns. include 80 Washington Sq. East Galleries, NYC, 1977, Soho Photo Gallery, NYC, 1978, 4th St. Photo Gallery, NYC, 1979, Womanart Gallery, NYC, 1979, Leslie-Lohman Gallery, NYC, 1980, 81, Window Gallery, Met. Savs. Bank, NYC, 1980, Cathedral St. John-the-Devine Gallery, NYC, 1980, Donnell Libr. Gallery, 1981; originator, organizer various exhbns. African-Am. Artists with Disabilities, Artists with Phys. Disabilities; contbr. articles, photographs to profl. jours. Mem. Nat. Inst. Disability and Rehab. Rsch.; mem. Office Spl. Edn. and Rehab. Svcs. US Dept. Edn., Washington, mem. per rev. registry, 1995—; active Disabled in Action of Greater N.Y., 1989—, Manhattan Borough Pres. Disability Adv. Coun., 1988—98, 1999—; access subcom. 504 Dem. Club for Persons with Disabilities, 2000—; mem. Mayor's Adv. Com. on People with Disabilities, NYC, 1991—93, Citywide Coalition on Disability, NYC, 1994—95; active in assistive signage needs Planning Meeting NYC Coun./Dept. Disabled, 2000; mem. info. subcom. NYC Coun. Planning Com. Dept. Disabled, 2000—; mem. Disabilities Network of NYC, 2000—; mem. disability rights steering com. 504 Dem. Club for Persons with Disabilities, 1987—88, mem. exec. com., 1990—2002; mem. NY County Dem. Com. 102ED/95 ED, 1995—; exec. com. The Village Independent Democrats, NYC, 2003—, v.p., 2005—; mem. The Village Independent Dems. Turns 50 com. The Village Independent Democrats 50th Anniversary Reception, 2007. Grantee Whitney Mus. Am. Art and the Smithsonian Instn., summer 1967, summer film inst. Stanford U., 1968; Cooper Union scholar, 1967-70; recipient Appreciation cert. Manhattan Borough Pres., 1991, Dean's Disting. Alumni Achievement award NYU, NYC, 1998. Mem. Coll. Art Assn. (com. mems. with disabilities for accessible programs and places 1990—), NYC Coun. dept. for disabled. Office: Resources for Artists with Disabilities 77 7th Ave Ste PH-H New York NY 10011-6645 Personal E-mail: LoisKaggen@att.net.

KAGIWADA, REYNOLD SHIGERU, electronics executive; b. LA, July 8, 1938; s. Harry Yoshifusa and Helen Kinue (Imura) K.; children: Julia, Conan. BS in Physics, UCLA, 1960, MS in Physics, 1962, PhD in Physics, 1966. Asst. prof. in residence physics UCLA, 1966-69; asst. prof. physics U. So. Calif., 1969-72; mem. tech. staff TRW (now NGST), Redondo Beach, Calif., 1972-75; scientist, sect. head TRW (now NGST), 1975-77, sr. scientist, dept. mgr., 1977-83, lab. mgr., 1984-87, project mgr., 1987-88, MIMIC chief scientist, 1988-89, asst. program mgr., 1989-90, advanced technology mgr., 1990—2001, dir. advanced electronics, 2002—. Presenter in field. Contbr. articles to profl. jours. Recipient Gold Medal award TRW, 1985, Ramo Tech. award, 1985, Transfer award, IEEE MTT-S N. Walter Cox award, 1997. Fellow IEEE (v.p. IEEE MTT-S adminstrn. com. 1991, pres. 1992, Disting. Svc. award 2001); mem. Assn. Old Crows, Sigma Xi, Sigma Pi Sigma. Achievements include patents for solid state devices. Home: 3117 Malcolm Ave Los Angeles CA 90034-3406 Office: NGST Bldg M5 Rm 1492 One Space Park Bldg Redondo Beach CA 90278 Personal E-mail: reynold.kagiwada@ngst.com.

KAGLE, JOSEPH LOUIS, JR., artist, arts administrator, historian and educator; b. Pitts., May 2, 1932; s. Joseph Louis and Edith (Marcellus) K.; m. Anne Cornelia Schiller, Jan. 19, 1957; children: Samantha Anne, Christopher Yung Wook. Student, Carnegie Mus. Sch. Art, 1938-51; BA in English, Dartmouth Coll., 1955; MFA in Art and Art History, U. Colo., 1958; MEd in Gifted and Talented Edn., U. Ark., Little Rock, 1984. Instr. Wis. State U., Whitewater, 1958-60; head dept. art, asst. prof. Washington and Jefferson Coll., Pa., 1960-64; head dept. art, assoc. prof. Keuka Coll., 1964-68; artist in residence Chapman Coll., World Campus Afloat, 1968-69; prof., head dept. fine arts, visual arts, dance, music and theatre U. Guam, 1970-76; prof. art Community Coll. Finger Lakes, 1976-78; exec. dir. S.E. Ark. Arts and Sci. Center, Pine Bluff, 1978-84; dir. Brockton (Mass.) Art Mus., 1984-86, The Art Ctr., Waco, Tex., 1987—2000, Bridgewater State Coll., 1986-87. Artist in residence Wash. State U., Spokane, 1965—66, Naples Mill Sch., 1976—2001, Internat. Plentary of Artists, Kutaisi, Georgia, 2001; bd. contbrs. Waco Tribune-Herald Opinion Editls.; lectr. USIS, Taiwan, 1970—76; critic Pine Bluff (Ark.) News; prof. McLennan CC, 1987—2005, Kingwood Coll., 2006—. Work exhibited in over 700 nat. and internat. exhbns. including Nat. Gallery, Washington, Nat. Mus., Tiblisi, Georgia; dir. 50 TV shows on art; muralist, Hafa Adai Theatre, Bank of Guam, Fine Arts Bldg. U. Guam; author: Death Is All the Time, 1976; curator for world tour exhibition, My Peace Journey by Ryofu Pussel, Japan, 2007-; author of 100 essays and two major works on Peace, Rotary Global History Fellowship, 2006-2007. Mem. planning bd. Pine Bluff Com. Gifted and Talented, 1979-80; mem. adv. bd. Sta. KCTF, 1989-92; bd. dirs. Greater Waco Coun. on the Arts, 1989—; bd. dirs. Assn. for Retarded Citizens., chmn., 1990-92, 93-94. Named Fulbright scholar, Taiwan, 1965, Georgia, 2001—02, Fulbright specialist, Mongolia, 2004, Smithsonian Instn. Kellog Found. Project scholar, 1983, artist of yr., Pacific chpt. AIA, 1976—77; recipient Fulbright specialist, Mongolia, 2003, Darmouth Coll. Alumni award for Outstanding Svc., Class of 1955, 2006. Mem. Am. Mus. Assn., Coll. Art Assn., Tex. Assn. Mus., Coll. Art Assn., Am. Assn. Mus., Waco Assn. Mus. (chmn. bd. dirs. 1995-97), Waco C. of C. (bd. dirs. 1994-97), Rotary, eClub of Southwest, USA, Rotary Global History Fellowship (pres. 2007—), Rotarians on the Internet. Democrat. Avocations: travel, art, writing. Home: 3758 Glade Forest Dr Houston TX 77339-1739 Home Phone: 281-360-7355; Office Phone: 281-360-7355. Personal E-mail: joe_kagle@hotmail.com.

KAHAI, JUGTA, pediatrician; State commr. NC Health & Wellness Trust Fund, 2003—; founder TRY (Tsunami Relief & You); cofounder (with Deepa Bhojwani) Seenigama Rainbow Clinic, Sri Lanka, 2005—; med. dir. Carousel Ctr.; pres., pediatrician Oak Island Pediatrics; pres. & founder AWAKEN (A Working Alliance for Kids with Exceptional Needs). Recipient Leadership award (Young Physicians), AMA Found., 2005. Mem.: NC Med. Soc. Office: Oak Island Pediatrics PA 4734 Long Beach Rd SE Southport NC 28461 also: The Carousel Center 2714 Market St Wilmington NC 28403-1218

KAHAN, BARRY DONALD, surgeon, educator; b. Cleve., July 25, 1939; s. Jacob Marvin and Pearl (Schultz) Kahan; m. Rochelle Liebling, Sept. 22, 1963 (dec.); 1 child, Kara; m. Marsha Capen, Dec. 3, 2005. BS, U. Chgo., 1960, PhD, 1964, MD, 1965. Intern Mass. Gen. Hosp., Boston, 1965-66, resident in surgery, 1968-72; staff asso. in immunology NIH, 1966-68; asst. prof. surgery and physiology Northwestern U. Sch. Medicine, Chgo., 1972-74, asso. prof., 1975-76; prof. surgery U. Tex. Med. Sch., Houston, 1977—, also dir. divs. organ transplantation dept. surgery, dir. program immunology, grad. sch. Bd. dirs. Ill. Kidney Found., 1974—76. Mem. ACS, AAAS, Soc. Univ. Surgeons, Am. Soc. Clin. Investigation, Am. Soc. Transplant Surgeons (pres. 1989—), Am. Surg. Assn., Internat. Transplantation Soc. (charter, treas. 1990—), Am. Surg. Assn., Am. Assn. Immunologists, Am. Assn. Cancer Rsch., Am. Physiol. Soc. Office: U Tex Houston MSB 6-240 6431 Fannin St Houston TX 77030

KAHAN, JAMES S., telecommunications industry executive; BSEE, Purdue U., 1969; MBA, U. NC, 1972. Engring. positions with Western Elec. Co., St. Louis, 1967—72, Bell Labs., Piscataway, NJ, 1972—75, So. Ctrl. Bell, Birmingham, Ala., 1975—81, AT&T Corp., Basking Ridge, NJ, 1981—82, Southwestern Bell Tel., 1983—84; with corp. devel. grp. SBC Comm., 1984—88, mng. dir. corp. devel., 1988—92, sr. v.p. corp. devel., 1992—99, sr. exec. v.p. corp. devel., 1999—2005, AT&T Inc. (merger of SBC Comm with AT&T Corp.), San Antonio, 2005—. Mem. bus. adv. bd. U. Tex., San Antonio; bd. mem. Chase Comm., AMDOCS. Mailing: AT&T Inc 175 E Houston St PO Box 2933 San Antonio TX 78299-2933*

KAHAN, JONATHAN SETH, lawyer; b. NYC, Apr. 5, 1948; s. Paul Herbert and Henrietta Kahan; m. Barbara Kahan, Apr. 28, 1984; children: Rachel, Paul, David, Adam. BA, George Washington U., 1970, JD, 1973. Bar: D.C. 1974, U.S. Dist. Ct. D.C. 1974, U.S. Ct. Appeals (D.C. cir.) 1974. Law clk. to hon. judge Oliver Gasch U.S. Dist. Ct. D.C., Washington, 1973-74; assoc. Hogan & Hartson LLP, Washington, 1974-82, ptnr., 1982—. Contbg. editor Med. Devices and Diagnostics indsl. mag., 1987—, mem. bd. editors, 1989—; mem. bd. editors Food Drug Cosmetic Law Jour., 1989-92. Mem. Fed. Bar Assn. (chmn. fed. bar assn. sect. on health and human svcs. Washington chpt. 1985-90, co-chmn. D.C. Bar sect. on adminstrv. law and agy. practice 1988-93). Office: Hogan & Hartson LLP 555 13th St NW Ste 800E Washington DC 20004-1161 Office Phone: 202-637-5794. Office Fax: 202-637-5910. Business E-Mail: jskahan@hhlaw.com.

KAHAN, MARLENE, professional association executive; b. Bronx, NY, June 10, 1952; d. Meyer and Ruth (Baroth) Schmulewitz. BA in Psychology, CUNY, 1973. Tchr. elem. sch., Bronx, 1974-75; asst. to pres. Mag. Pubs. Am., NYC, 1976-83; asst. dir. Am. Soc. Mag. Editors, NYC, 1983-90, exec. dir., 1990—. Recipient Gold Key award PR News, 1991. Mem. Am. Soc. Assn. Execs., N.Y. Soc. Assn. Execs. (bd. dirs. 2000—03), Women in Comms. (program com. N.Y.C. 1991-93, bd. dirs. 1993-95, v.p. programs 1993-95). Avocations: ballet, jazz dance and music. Office: Am Soc Mag Editors c/o Mag Publishers Am 810 7th Ave 24th Fl New York NY 10019 Office Phone: 212-872-3735. E-mail: mkahan@magazine.org.*

KAHAN, MITCHELL DOUGLAS, museum director; BA, U. Va., 1973; MA, Columbia U., 1975; M of Philosophy, CUNY, 1978, PhD, 1983. Mus. aide Nat. Mus. Am. Art, Washington, 1978; curator Montgomery Mus. Fine Art, Ala., 1978-82, N.C. Mus. Art, Raleigh, 1982-86; dir. Akron Art Mus., Ohio, 1986—. Cons. La. World's Exposition, New Orleans, 1983-84. Author: Art Inc.: American Paintings in Corporate Collections, 1979, Roger Brown, 1981, Minnie Evans, 1986, Art Since 1850-Akron Art Museum, 2001. Columbia U. fellow, 1973, Smithsonian Inst. fellow, 1976-78, CUNY grad. research fellow, 1978, Nat. Endowment for Arts fellow, 1987. Mem. Coll. Art Assn., Intermus Conservation Assn. (trustee 1986-95, pres. 1990-92, 95), Assn. Art Mus. Dirs. (trustee, 2004—), Akron Area Arts Alliance (pres. 2003-2004), Akron Roundtable (pres. 2001). Office: Akron Art Mus One South High Akron OH 44308

KAHANA, EVA FROST, sociology educator; b. Budapest, Hungary, Mar. 21, 1941; came to U.S., 1957; d. Jacob and Sari Frost; m. Boaz Kahana, Apr. 15, 1962; children: Jeffrey, Michael. BA, Stern Coll., Yeshiva U., 1962; MA, CCNY, CUNY, 1965; PhD, U. Chgo., 1968; HLD (hon.), Yeshiva U., 1991. Nat. Inst. on Aging predoctoral fellow U. Chgo. Com. on Human Devel., 1963-66; postdoctoral fellow Midwest Council Social Research, 1968; with dept. sociology Washington U., St. Louis, 1967-71, successively research asst., research assoc., asst. prof.; with dept. sociology Wayne State U., Detroit, 1971-84, from assoc. prof. to prof., dir. Elderly Care Research Ctr., 1971-84; prof. Case Western Res. U., Cleve., 1984—, Armington Prof., 1989-90, chmn. dept. sociology, 1985—2005, dir. Elderly Care Research Ctr., 1984—, Pierce and Elizabeth Robson prof. humanities, 1990—. Cons. Nat. Inst. on Aging, Washington, 1976-80, NIMH, Washington, 1971-75. Co-author: (with E. Midlarsky) Altruism in Later Life, 1994, (with B. Kahous & L. Harel) Survivors of the Holocoust: Late Life Adaptation; editor: (with others) Family Caregiving Across the Lifespan, 1994; mem. edit. bd. Gerontologist, 1975-79, Psychology of Aging, 1984-90, Jour. Gerontology, 1990-94, Applied Behavioral Sci. Rev., 1992—, Annals Family Medicine, 2004-; contbr. articles to profl. jours., chpts. to books (recipient Pub.'s prize 1969). Bd. dirs. com. on aging Jewish Community Fedn., Cleve.; bd. dirs. Jewish Family and Children's Svc.; vol. cons. Alzheimer's Disease and Related Disorders Assn., Cleve. NIMH Career Devel. grantee, 1974-79, Nat. Inst. Aging Merit award grantee, 1989—; Mary E. Switzer Disting. fellow Nat. Inst. Rehab., 1992-93; recipient Arnold Heller award excellence in geriatrics and gerontology Menorah Park Ctr. for Aged, 1992, Diekhoff awrd for disting. grad. tchg., 2002; named Outstanding Gerontological Rschr. in Ohio, 1993, 2003, Outstanding Gerontol. Educator in Ohio, 2004. Fellow Assn. for Gerontology in Higher Edn., Gerontol. Soc. Am. (chair behavioral social sci. com. 1984-85, Disting. Mentorship award 1987, Polisher award 1997); mem. Am. Sociol. Assn. (coun. sect. on aging 1985-87, Disting. Scholar award sect. on aging and life course 1997, chair sect. on aging and life course, 2000-2001), Am. Social Assn., Soc. for Traumatic Stress, Wayne State U. Acad. Scholars (life), Sigma Xi. Avocations: reading, antiques, travel.

KAHANE, JEFFREY, conductor, pianist; b. LA, Sept. 12, 1956; BMus, San Francisco Conservatory, 1977. Prof. piano Eastman Sch. Music, 1988-95; music dir. Santa Rosa (Calif.) Symphony, 1995—2005, LA Chamber Orch., 1996—, Green Music Festival, 2001, Colo. Symphony Orch., 2005—. Office: Colo Symphony Assn Boettcher Concert Hall Denver Performing Arts 1000 14th St #15 Denver CO 80202-2333 E-mail: artistsny@imgworld.com.*

KAHARICK, JEROME JOHN, lawyer; b. Johnstown, Pa., Apr. 15, 1955; s. Stanley Joseph and Emily (Solic) K.; m. Carolyn Marie Safko, Aug. 7, 1977; children: Natalie, Allison. BA summa cum laude, U. Pitts., 1977; JD, Duquesne U., 1991. Bar: Pa. 1991, N.Y. 2000, U.S. Dist. Ct. (we. dist.) Pa. 1991, U.S. Dist. Ct. (we. dist.) Mich. 1998, U.S. Dist. Ct. (no. dist.) N.Y. 1998, U.S. Ct. Appeals (3d cir.) 1992, U.S. Supreme Ct., 1997. Sales rep. Met. Life, Johnstown, Pa., 1977-84; owner, stockholder Planned Fin. Svcs., Johnstown, Pa., 1984-88; law clk. Wayman, Irvin & McAuley, Pitts., 1988-89; legal analyst Elliott Co., Jeannette, Pa., 1989-92; pvt. practice Johnstown, 1992-95, 97—; asst. pub. defender Cambria County, Pa., 1993-99; ptnr. Weaver and Kaharick, 1995-97; atty. in pvt. practice Johnstown, Pa., 1997—. Exec. production editor Duquesne Law Rev., 1990-91. Mem. ABA, ATLA, N.Y. Bar Assn., Nat. Assn. Criminal Def. Lawyers, Pa. Bar Assn., N.Y. State Bar Assn., Order of Barristers. Republican. Roman Catholic. Office: Wallace Bldg 406 Main St Ste 301-302 Johnstown PA 15901-1906 Home Phone: 814-255-1525; Office Phone: 814-539-6789. Personal E-mail: jkaharick@verizon.net.

KAHIN, BRIAN, lawyer, computer industry professional, consultant; b. Torrington, Conn., July 23, 1947; s. George McTurnan and Margaret McFarlan (Baker) K.; m. Julia Campbell Royall, Sept. 21, 1986; children: Angeline DuPré, Owen Low. BA, Harvard U., 1969, JD, 1976. Exec. dir. Ind. Cinema Artists and Producers, NYC, 1981-82; coord. rsch. program on comms. policy MIT, Cambridge, Mass., 1983-85; atty. and cons. in pvt. practice Dubois, Wyo., 1976-91; gen. counsel Interactive Multimedia Assn., Annapolis, Md., 1988—; dir. info. infrastructure project John F. Kennedy Sch. Govt., Harvard U., Cambridge, 1990—, adj. lectr. pub. policy, 1990—; sr. fellow Computer & Comm. Industry Assn., Wash., DC. Mem. organizing com. Telecomms. Policy Rsch. Conf., Wash., 1990-92, 93-94; mem. adv. bd. Ctr. Electronic Texts in Humanities, Rutgers U., New Brunswick, NJ, 1993—, Software Patent Inst., Ann Arbor, Mich., 1992—; cons. EDUCOM, Coun. Libr. Resources, US Congress Office of Tech. Assessment; prin. counsel FARNET, Internat. Interactive Comm. Soc., adj. prof. U. Mich. Sch. of Info. 2003-2005, spl. adv. to Provost's Office, dir. Ctr. for Info. Policy, vis. prof. Coll. of Info. Studies U. Md., sr. Policy Analyst White House Office of Sci. and Tech. Policy 1997-2000, vice chair OECD Working Party on Info. Economy, adj. lectr. in Pub. Policy at Kennedy Sch., chaired US Adv. Com. on Internat. Comms. and Info. Policy 1995. Editor: Building Information Infrastructure, 1992, Information Infrastructure Sourcebook, 1993; co-editor: Public Access to the Internet, 1995, Info. Infrastructure and Policy, 1994-96, Standards Development and Information Infrastructure, 1995; mem. editl. adv. bd. Multimedia Law Strategist, Cyberspace Lawyer. Bd. Pub. Patent Found.; adv. bd. Found. Free Info. Infrastructure. Recipient Bernard M. Fry prize Pergamon Press, 1992. Mem. ABA (chair subcom. on users rights 1987-91), Wyo. State Bar, Internet Soc., mem. Am. U. Task Force Nat. Strategy Mang. Sci. and Tech. Info. 1992-94, bd. Telecom. Policy Rsch. Conf., adv. bd. Ctr. for Electronic Texts Humanities. Office: Computer & Comm Industry Assn 666 11th St NW Washington DC 20001 Office Phone: 202-783-0070. Office Fax: 202-783-0534. Business E-Mail: bkahin@ccianet.org.

KAHL, WILLIAM FREDERICK, retired academic administrator; b. May 23, 1922; s. William Frederick and Bessie (Glading) K.; m. Mary Carson, Jan. 25, 1964; children: Frederick Glading, Sarah Hartwell. BA, Brown U., 1945; MA, Harvard U., 1947, PhD, 1955, LHD, 1993. Lectr. history Boston U., 1947-48, 50; from instr. to prof. Simmons Coll., Boston, 1948-76, provost, 1965-76; pres. Russell Sage Coll., Troy, NY, 1976-88. Bd. dir. Norstar. Author: The London Livery Companies: An essay and bibliography, 1960; contbr. articles to profl. jours. Vice-chmn. Hudson River Valley Assn.; bd. dirs. Albany Symphony Orch., Lower East Side Conservancy; chmn. bd. Tenement Mus., N.Y. State Nature Conservancy, Albany Inst. History and Art, Friends of the Hudson River Valley, Hudson River Valley Coordinating Coun., Russell Sage Pres. Adv. Coun.; pres., trustee, Albany Acad., Wildwood Sch., Albany C. of C. Found. Social Sci. Coun. rsch. grantee, 1957-58. Mem. Am. Hist. Assn., Anglo-Am. Hist. Conf. Episcopalian. Home: 21 Dalton Ct Delmar NY 12054 Office: Russell Sage Coll Troy NY 12180

KAHLER, HERBERT FREDERICK, manufacturing executive; b. St. Augustine, Fla., Sept. 20, 1936; s. Herbert E. and Marie (Strieter) K.; m. Erika Rozsypal, May 16, 1964; children: Erik, Stephen, Christopher, Michael, Craig. AB, Johns Hopkins, 1958; LLB, Harvard U., 1961. Bar: N.Y. bar 1962. With Simpson, Thacher & Bartlett, NYC, 1961-65; sec., gen. counsel Insilco Corp., Meriden, Conn., 1965-70; pres., CEO W.H. Hutchinson & Son, Inc., Chgo., 1970-73, Miles Homes Co., Mpls., 1973-86; v.p., dir. Insilco Corp., 1979-88; pres. Kahler & Assocs., 1988—; pres., CEO Crown Fixtures, Inc., Plymouth, Minn., 1990—, Power Generation Svc., Inc., 1990—97, chmn., 1997—; pres., CEO Crown Tonka Calif., Inc., 2000—. Hon. consul Republic of Austria, 1998—. Bd. corporators Meriden Hosp., 1965-70, Harvard, 1970; bd. govs. Meriden/Wallingford Hosp., 1987; bd. dirs. St. Paul Chamber Orch., 1974-87, St. Paul Opera Assn., 1975-77, Minn. Opera Co., 1977-87. Lt., arty. AUS, 1962-64. Mem. ABA, Mpls. Club, Phi Beta Kappa. Office: Crown Fixtures Inc 10700 Highway 55 Ste 300 Plymouth MN 55441-6134 Office Phone: 763-541-1410.

KAHLES, CHERYL MARY, elementary school educator; b. Bklyn., Aug. 5, 1950; d. Thomas and Cornelia Mary Dickson; m. B. Antonio Cherot (div.); children: Nicole Marie Cherot, Jason Anthony Cherot; m. James Francis Kahles, June 6, 1998. BS in Edn., U. Ill., 1973; MEd, Coll. Mt. St. Joseph, 1987. Tchr. Oakwood (Ill.) Elem. Sch., 1972—74, Diamond Elem. Sch., Danville, Ill., 1974—78, Monee (Ill.) Elem. Sch., 1978—79, Amelia Elem. Sch., Ohio, 1979—. Active The St. John Passion Play, Cinn., 1999—, Immaculate Heart of Mary Roman Cath. Ch., Cinn., 1979—. Mem.: NEA, Nat. PTA, Ohio Edn. Assn. Roman Catholic. Avocations: travel, sailing, celtic and renaissance festivals. Office: Amelia Elem Sch 5 E Main St Amelia OH 45102 Business E-Mail: kahles_c@westcler.org.

KAHLOW, BARBARA FENVESSY, statistician; b. Chgo., June 26, 1946; d. Stanley John and Doris (Goodman) Fenvessy; m. Lloyd Fitch Reese, Dec. 6, 1969 (div. 1977); m. Allan Howard Young, Mar. 31, 1979 (div. 1982); m. Ronald Arthur Kahlow, Sept. 28, 1985 (div. 1990). BA, Vassar Coll., 1968. Analytical statistician US Govt./Dept. HEW, Nat. Ctr. Health Stats., 1968-70, Nat. Ctr. Ednl. Stats., 1970-72, Exec. Office Pres. Office Mgmt. and Budget, Washington, 1972-98. Staff dir. subcom. on energy policy, natural resources and regulatory affairs House Govt. Reform Com., 1998-2005; bd. mem. Dress For Success. Author: Motor Vehicle Accident Deaths in the U.S.: 1950-69, 1970; contbr. articles to profl. jours. Bd. mem. Dress for Success. N.Y. State Regents scholar, 1964-68. Mem. Foggy Bottom Assn., West End Citizens Assn., League of Rep. Women of DC, Friends of Kennedy Ctr., Friends of Corcoran, Friends of Phillips Gallery, Smithsonian Assocs., Washington Vassar Club. Republican. Episcopalian. Home: Apt 704 800 25th St NW Washington DC 20037 Home Phone: 202-965-1083. Personal E-mail: barbara.kahlow@verizon.net.

KAHMANN, SARAH STUBER, retired foundation administrator; b. Clay, Pa., Jan. 18, 1928; d. Harry Miles and Mamie (Stauffer) Stuber; children from previous marriage: Lynne Einhaus, Ed III, Susan Hasty,

Barbara Amato. V.p. Nat. Coalition Protection Children and Families, Cin., 1989-93; ret., 1993. Bd. mem. St. Luke Found.; founder Enough is Enough Bd., 1996—2002, Forward Quest Governance T.F.; apptd. by gov. Ky. Commn. Women, 1998—; grad. Leadership Ky., 2000; bd. dirs. Women's Crisis Ctr., 2003—05, mem. bd., 2003—05; apptd. vice chair Ky. Commn. Women, 2003—. Named Woman of the Yr., Cin. Enquirer, 1997. Avocations: community service, art, travel. *My experience has been a willingness to risk, along with the belief that set-backs are not failures but an opportunity to learn and grow--these principles have led me to risk much, and thus accomplish much and enriched my life tremendously.*

KAHN, ALAN EDWIN, lawyer; b. NYC, Aug. 9, 1929; s. Joseph and Harriet Rose (Rubel) K.; m. Regina Wolf, Aug. 7, 1960 (div. Jan. 1978); 1 child, Jolie Galen; m. Patricia Ann Dugan, June 4, 1978. BBA, CCNY, 1950; JD, Bklyn. Law Sch., 1956. Bar: N.Y. 1956, U.S. Dist. Ct. (so. and ea. dists.) N.Y. 1978, U.S. Tax Ct. 1978; CPA, N.Y. Staff asst.-acct. Feinberg, Jacobs & Furman, NYC, 1956-57; pvt. practice NYC, 1957-96, 98—; prin. Law Office of Alan E. Kahn, NYC, 1957—; sr. ptnr. Kahn, Boyd, Levychin CPAs, NYC, 1993—2003; pvt. practice, 2003—. Tax cons. to various nonprofit orgns., N.Y.C., 1977—. Cons. Vol. Lawyers for the Arts, N.Y.C., 1978—. Sgt. U.S. Army, 1951-52. Mem. ATLA (mem. com. 1990—), N.Y. State Bar Assn. (elder law com.), N.Y. State Trial Lawyers Assn. (chmn. subcom. on legis. estate and trusts 1979, spkr. bd. 1990—, mem. com. 1991—, chair 2000—), N.Y. County Lawyers Assn. (taxation com. 1988—, sec. com. on taxation 1996-2000, chair com. on taxation 2000—), Spkr.'s Bur., Assn. Trial Lawyers City N.Y., Jewish Lawyers Guild, N.Y. State Soc. CPAs, Nat. Sculpture Soc. (patron mem.), Odd Fellows (grand adv. bd. N.Y. chpt. 1979-80, gen. counsel grand lodge 1989-99), Mchts. Club (bd. govs., asst. treas., treas. and gov. 1992—, award chmn. legal com. 1995—). Democrat. Avocations: collecting prints, paintings and oriental ceramics. Home: 370 1st Ave New York NY 10010-4923 Office: 17 Battery Pl New York NY 10004 Home Phone: 212-254-8423; Office Phone: 212-271-4345, 212-271-4308. Personal E-mail: aekwacs@aol.com.

KAHN, ALFRED EDWARD, economist, educator, government official; b. Paterson, NJ, Oct. 17, 1917; s. Jacob and Bertha (Orlean) K.; m. Mary Simmons, Oct. 10, 1943; children: Joel, Rachel, Hannah. AB, NYU, 1936, MA, 1937; postgrad., U. Mo., 1937-38; PhD, Yale U., 1942; LLD (hon.), Colby Coll., 1978, U. Mass., 1979, Ripon Coll., 1980, Northwestern U., 1982, Colgate U., 1983; DHL (hon.), SUNY, Albany, 1985. Mem. staff Brookings Inst., 1940, 51-52; with anti-trust div. Dept. Justice, 1941-42, Dept. Commerce, 1942, WPB, 1943; economist on Palestine surveys, 1943-44, Twentieth Century Fund, 1944-45; asst. prof., chmn. dept. econs. Ripon Coll., 1945-47; asst. prof. Cornell U., 1947-50, asso. prof., 1950-55, prof., 1955-89, chmn. dept. econs., 1958-63, Robert Julius Thorne prof. econs., 1967-89, emeritus, 1989—, dean Coll. Arts and Scis., 1969-74; chmn. N.Y. State Pub. Service Commn., 1974-77, CAB, 1977-78, Council on Wage and Price Stability (adviser to Pres. on inflation), 1978-80. Mem. atty. gen.'s nat. com. to study anti-trust laws, 1953-55; sr. staff U.S. Coun. Econ. Advisers, 1955-57; spl. cons. Boni, Watkins, Jason & Co., N.Y.C., 1957-61, Nat. Econ. Rsch. Assocs., 1961-74, 80—, U.S. Fgn. Agrl. Svc., Israel, 1960-61, Dept. Justice, 1963-64, FTC, 1965, Ford Found., 1967; econ. adv. coun. AT&T, 1968-74; econ. adv. com. U.S. C. of C., 1964-66; mem. environ. adv. com. Fed. Energy Adminstrn., 1974-77; mem. rev. com. sulfur emissions from power plants Nat. Acad. Scis., 1974-75; adv. bd. Electric Power Rsch. Inst., 1974-77; mem. Nat. Antitrust Law Rev. Com., 1978-79; adv. to N.Y. gov. on comm. regulation, 1980-81; mem. usage panel Am. Heritage Dictionary, 1982—; mem. N.Y. Gov.'s Adv. Com. on Pub. Power for L.I., 1986, N.Y. Gov.'s Fact-Finding Panel on Shoreham Nuclear Plant, 1983, N.Y. State Coun. on Fiscal and Econ. Priorities, 1983-89; chmn. adv. com. on price reform and competition in the USSR Internat. Inst. for Applied Systems Analysis, 1990-92; econ. commentator Nightly Bus. Report (pub. TV), 1981-97; mem. Ohio Blue Ribbon Panel Telecomm. Regulation, 1992-93; mem. N.Y. State Telecomm. Exch., 1992-94; Ct.-apptd. expert U.S. Dist. Ct., 1993-94; com. study of competition U.S. airline industry Nat. Rsch. Coun., 1999—; mem. adv. com. Digital Age Comms. Act Project, 2005—. Author: Great Britain in the World Economy, 1946; co-author (with J.B. Diriam): Fair Competition, The Law and Economics of Anti-Trust Policy, 1954; co-author: (with M.G. de Chazeau) Integration and Competition in the Petroleum Industry, 1959; author: The Economics of Regulation, 2 vols., 1970, 71, reprinted/new intro., 1988, Letting Go: Deregulating The Process of Deregulation, 1998, Whom the Gods Would Destroy, Or How Not to Deregulate, 2001, Lessons From Deregulation: Telecommunications and Airlines After the Crunch, 2004. Trustee Cornell U., 1964-69; mem. nat. governing bd. Common Cause, 1982-85; chmn. Blue Ribbon Panel to Investigate Pricing of Electricity in Calif., 2000. Fulbright Rsch. fellow Italy, 1954-55; recipient Wilbur Cross medal for outstanding achievement Yale U., 1995, L. Welch Pogue award for Lifetime Contbn. to Aviation, 1997, Soverign Fund award 1997, J. Rhoads Foster award, 1999. Mem. Am. Econ. Assn. (v.p. 1981-82), Nat. Assn. Regulatory Utility Commrs. (exec. com., chmn. com. on electricity 1975-77), Am. Acad. Arts and Scis., Phi Beta Kappa. Office: 221 Savage Farm DR Ithaca NY 14850-6501 Home Phone: 607-266-8340; Office Phone: 607-277-3007. E-mail: alfred.kahn@nera.com.

KAHN, ALFRED JOSEPH, social services researcher, educator; b. NYC, Feb. 8, 1919; s. Meyer and Sophie (Levine) K.; m. Miriam Kadin, Sept. 3, 1949 (div. 1980); 1 child, Nancy Valerie. B in Social Sci., CCNY, 1939; B in Hebrew Lit., Sem. Coll. Jewish Studies, NYC, 1940; MS, Columbia U., 1946, D in Social Welfare, 1952; DHL (hon.), Adelphi U., 1984; DSc (hon.), U Md., 1989; Dr. (hon.), York U., Eng., 1998. Psychiat. social worker Jewish Bd. Guardians, NYC, 1946-47; mem. faculty Sch. Social Work Columbia U., 1947-89, prof. Sch. Social Work, 1954-89, prof. emeritus, 1989; co-dir. Cross Nat. Studies Rsch. Program, 1973—2005; Disting. vis. prof. Grad. Sch. Social Svc., Fordham U., 1990-2001. Staff cons. Citizens Com. for Children, N.Y.C., 1948-72; mem. summer faculty Smith Coll. Sch. Social Work, 1949-54; cons. govts., founds., vol. agys., 1949-2004; mem. numerous adv. coms.; mem. adv. com. child devel. NRC-Nat. Acad. Scis., 1971-76, mem. com. child devel. rsch. and pub. policy, Acad. Scis., 1977-83, chmn., 1980-83; mem. adv. bd. Inst. Rsch. Poverty, U. Wis., 1967-2002. Author: A Court for Children, 1953, Planning Community Services for Children in Trouble, 1963, Neighborhood Information Centers, 1966, (with Anna Mayer) Day Care as a Social Instrument, 1966, Theory and Practice of Social Planning, 1969, Studies in Social Policy and Planning, 1969, Social Policy and Social Services, 1973; co-author: Not for the Poor Alone, 1975, Social Service in the U.S., 1976, Social Services in International Perspective, 1977, Child Care, Family Benefits and Working Parents, 1981, Helping America's Families, 1982, Maternity Policies and Working Women, 1983, Income Transfers for Families With Children, 1983, Child Care: Facing the Hard Choices, 1987, The Responsive Workplace, 1987, Mothers Alone, 1988, Social Services for Children, Youth and Families in the United States, 1989, Social Services for Children, Youth and Families: The New York City Study, 1990, A Welcome for Every Child, 1994, Social Policy and the Under 3s, 1994, Starting Right, 1995, Big Cities in the Welfare Transition, 1998, Contracting for Child and Family Services, 2000; contbr. monographs, articles to profl. jours., chpts. to books; editor: Issues in American Social Work, 1959, Shaping The New Social Work, 1973; co-editor: Family Policy: Government and Famlies in Fourteen Countries, 1978, Child Support, From Debt Collection to Social Policy, 1988, Privatization and the Welfare State, 1989, Child Care, Parental Leaves and The Under 3s: Policy Innovation in Europe, 1991, Children and Their Families in Big Cities, 1996, Family Change and Family Policies in Great Britain, Canada, New Zealand, and the United States, 1997, Beyond Child Poverty: The Social Exclusion of Children, 2002. With USAAF, 1942-46. Mem. AAUP, Nat. Assn. Social Workers (chmn. div. practice and knowledge 1963-66, bd. dirs. 1967-70), Council Social Work Edn., Assn. for Policy Analysis and Mgmt.

KAHN, ANTHONY F., lawyer; b. Washington, Apr. 29, 1954; s. Henry and Claudia F.; m. Cynthia Marie Farhart, Aug. 11, 1979; children: Brian, Andrew, Stephen. BA, Wake Forest U., 1976; MBA summa cum laude, U. Notre Dame, 1980, JD magna cum laude, 1980. Bar: N.Y. 1981. Ptnr. White & Case LLP, NYC, 1980—. Office: White & Case LLP 1155 Avenue of the Americas New York NY 10036-2711 Home Phone: 914-235-2884; Office Phone: 212-819-8338. Business E-Mail: akahn@whitecase.com.

KAHN, BARBARA B., endocrinologist; BA, Stanford U., 1972; MS, U. Calif. Berkeley, 1975; MD, Stanford U. Sch. Med., 1977. Internal medicine intern, resident U. Calif. Davis Med. Ctr., Sacramento, 1977—80, clin. fellow, 1980—82; endocrine fellow, cellular metabolism & obesity sect. Nat. Inst. Arthritis, Diabetes, Digestive & Kidney Diseases, NIH, Bethesda, Md., 1982—85, sr. staff fellow, experimental diabetes, metabolism & nutrition sect., molecular, cellular & nutritional endocrinology branch, 1985—86; chief, div. endocrinology, diabetes, & metabolism Beth Israel Deaconess Med. Ctr., Boston; prof. medicine Harvard Med. Sch., Boston, dir. endocrinology, diabetes & metabolism fellowship program; assoc. dir. Boston Obesity Nutrition Rsch. Ctr. Vis. prof. Karolinska Inst., Stockholm, 2000; Pfizer vis. prof. U. Washington, 2001; Burroughs Wellcome vis. prof. Univ. NC, 2002; NHLB/NI working group on the pathophysiology of obesity-associated cardiovascular disease, 01; com. on diabetes Am. Heart Assn., 2001—; publications com. Am. Diabetes Assn., 2002—, steering com., 2000—02, NIH, 2002; editorial bd. Am. Jour. Physiology: Endocrinology & Metabolism, 2001—04, Jour. Biological Chemistry, 2002—. Mem.: AAP, Inst. Medicine, Interurban Clin. Club. Office: Div Endocrinology, Diabetes & Metabolism RN 380-C 330 Brookline Ave Boston MA 02215 Office Phone: 617-667-5422. Office Fax: 617-667-2927. E-mail: bkahn@bidmc.harvard.edu.

KAHN, BARBARA E., dean, marketing educator; BA in English Lit., U. Rochester, 1974; MBA, Columbia U., 1982, MPhil, PhD, Columbia U., 1984. Reader Doubleday/Lit. Guild, 1974; writer, rschr. Stimpson Assocs., 1975—78; pub. affairs dir. No. Tier Pipeline Co., 1978—80; lectr. Pace U., NYC, 1983; asst. prof. John E. Anderson Grad. Sch. Mgmt., UCLA, 1984—88, acting assoc. prof., 1989—90; vis. asst. prof. The Wharton Sch., U. Pa., Phila., 1988—89, Stephen M. Peck term assoc. prof., 1990—95, prof., 1995—99, Dorothy Silberberg prof. mktg., 1999—2007, vice dean, dir. undergraduate program, 2003—07; faculty mem. Psychology Grad. Group U. Pa., Phila., 1998—2007; dean Sch. Bus. Adminstrn., U. Miami, Coral Gables, 2007—. Hakuhodo vis. scholar U. Tokyo, 1993; vis. academic Mktg. Dept. U. Sydney, Australia, 1993; cons. Independence Blue Cross, SmithKline Beecham, State Farm Insurance, Intel, Givaudan, Expert Witness, Greensfelder, Hemker & Gale, PC. Co-author: Grocery Revolution: The New Focus on the Consumer, 1997; contbr. articles to profl. jours.; editl. bd. mem. Jour. Consumer Rsch., 1996—, Review Mktg. Rsch., 2003—, Jour. Behavioral Decision Making, 2004—. Recipient David W. Hauck Award for Outstanding Tchg., 1999. Mem.: Assn. Consumer Rsch. (pres. 2006). Office: U Miami Sch Bus Adminstrn PO Box 248505 Miami FL 33124-6524 Office Phone: 305-284-4607.*

KAHN, BERND, radiochemist, educator; b. Pforzheim, Baden, Germany, Aug. 16, 1928; US1938; s. Eric Herman and Alice Dora (Meyer) K.; m. Gail Pressman, Aug. 6, 1961; children: Jennifer, Elizabeth. BSChemE, N.J. Inst. Tech., 1950; MS in Physics, Vanderbilt U., 1952; PhD in Chemistry, MIT, 1960. Commd. officer USPHS, 1954, advanced through grades to capt., 1970, health physicist, radiochemist, Oak Ridge (Tenn.) Nat. Lab., 1951-54, engr. various facilities Tenn., Mass., Ala., Ohio, 1954-74, ret. Tenn., Mass., Ala., Ohio, 1974; prof. nuc. enging. and health physics Ga. Inst. Tech., Atlanta, 1974-96, prof. emeritus, 1996—, dir. Environ. Resources Ctr., 1974—. Editor: Radioanalytical Chemistry, 2006; co-editor: Management of Low-Level Radioactive Waste, 1979. Mem. Nat. Coun. Radiation Protection and Measurments (hon.), Am. Chem. Soc., Am. Phys. Soc., Health Physics Soc. Achievements include research in radiochemistry and environmental radioactivity; co-inventor recovery of magnesium salts from sea water. Office: Ga Tech Rsch Inst Atlanta GA 30332-0841 Business E-Mail: bernd.kahn@gtri.gatech.edu.

KAHN, C. RONALD, research laboratory administrator; b. Louisville, Jan. 14, 1944; s. David L. and Reva W. (Waldman) K.; m. Susan Becker; children: Stacy, Jeffrey. BA, U. Louisville, 1964, MD, 1968, MS, 1984; MA (hon.), Harvard U., 1984; DSc (honoris causa), U. Louisville, 1984, U. Paris-Pierre and Marie Curie, 1990, U. Geneva, 2000. Diplomate Am. Bd. Internal Medicine, Am. Bd. Endocrinology and Metabolism. Intern and resident in ward medicine Barnes Hosp., St. Louis, 1968-70; clin. assoc., sr. clin. assoc., clin. endocrinology br. Nat. Inst. Arthritis, Metabolism and Digestive Diseases, NIH, Bethesda, Md., 1970-73; sr. investigator Diabetes Br. NIH, Bethesda, Md., 1973-78, chief diabetes br., 1979-81; rsch. dir Joslin Diabetes Ctr., Boston, 1981-2000, dir., 1997-99, exec. v.p., dir., 1997-99; assoc. prof. Harvard Med. Sch., Boston, 1981-84, prof. medicine, 1984—, Mary K. Iacocca prof. medicine, 1986—; pres. Joslin Diabetes Ctr., 2000—. Lectr. symposia, meetings, thesis supr., course dir. and devel. numerous med. instns.; admitting and attending physician NIH Clin. Ctr., 1972-81; physician Brigham and Women's Hosp., Boston, 1981, chief div. Diabetes and Metabolism, 1981-92; assoc. staff Endocrinology/Internal Medicine, New Eng. Deaconess Hospital, Boston, 1982, active staff, 1986; clin. assoc. prof. medicine, Uniformed Svcs. U. Health Scis, Bethesda, Md., 1979-81; vis. scientist Centre de Moleculaire, Centre National de la Recherche Scientifique, Gif-sur-Yvette, France, 1979-80; adj. prof. genetics George Washington U., 1980-81; overseas vis. prof. Royal Melbourne Hosp., Australia, 1985; vis. prof. Royal Postgrad. Hosp., London, 1985; Rosemary Sarver vis. prof. in endocrinology and metabolism, The Hosp. of the Good Samaritan, L.A., 1985. Author or co-author over 430 publs. in field; mem. editl. bds. Jour. Clin. Endocrinology and Metabolism, 1977-80, Diabetes, 1977-84, Am. Jour. Medicine, 1979-84, Jour. Clin. Investigation, 1979-84, Jour. Receptor Rsch., 1980-83, Hormone and Metabolic Rsch., 1980-83, Endocrinology, 1981-85, Jour. Biol. Chemistry, 1983-88, Diabetes and Metabolism Revs., 1984, Receptor, 1989—; exec. editor Trends in Endocrinology and Metabolism, 1989-90; cons. editor Jour. Clin. Investigation; assoc. editor Diabetes, 1996-2001. Mem. Nat. Diabetes Adv. Bd., 1981-85, co-chmn. rsch. com., 1982-85. Recipient David Rumbough Meml award for Sci. Achievement Juvenile Diabetes Found., 1977, CIBA-Geigy Drew award for biochem. rsch., 1981, Mary Jane Kugel award Juvenile Diabetes Found., 1982, AFCR award for Outstanding Clin. Rsch. under Age 40, 1983; Sol Berson Meml. lectureship NIH, 1983, Hehnemann Lectr. in Pharmacology U. Calif.,1984, Pfizer Biomed. Rsch. award, Pfizer inc., 1986, Cristobal Diaz award Internat. Diabetes Fedn., 1988, Banting award Am. Diabetes Assn., 1993, Nat. Acad. Scis. award, 1999, Inst. Medicine, 1999, Hamden award U.A.E., 2000, Lawson-Wilkins Lectr. Pediatric Endocrine Soc., 2001, Freedom to Discover Achievement Award for Metabolic Disease, Bristol-Myers Squibb, 2004, others. Fellow AAAS; mem. Nat. Acad. Scis., Am. Acad. Arts & Scis., Am. Fedn. Clin. Rsch., The Endocrine Soc. (Edwin B. Astwood lectr. 1987, Kocl award 2000), Am. Diabetes Assn. (Eli Lilly award for rsch. 1980, Otto Brandman award N.J. affiliate 1989, Elliott P. Joslin medal Mass. affiliate, Albert Renold award 1998), Am. Soc. Clin. Investigation (nat. coun. 1986—, pres. elect 1987-88, pres. 1988-89), Am. Soc. Biol. Chemistry, Assn. Am. Physicians, Sigma Xi, Alpha Epsilon Delta, Phi Kappa Phi, Alpha Omega Alpha. Achievements include rsch. in insulin receptors and insulin action, insulin-like growth factors, diabetes mellitus, hypoglycemia, immunity, autoimmunity and viruses in endocrine disorders. Office: Joslin Diabetes Ctr One Joslin Pl Boston MA 02215 E-mail: c.ronald.kahn@joshn.harvard.edu.

KAHN, CHARLES N., III, (CHIP KAHN), medical association administrator; BA, Johns Hopkins U.; MPH, Tulane U., 1980. Adminstrv. resident with Tchg. Hosp. Dept. Assn. Am. Med. Colls.; former dir. Office Fin. Mgmt. Edn. Assn. Univ. Programs in Health Adminstrn.; former sr. health policy advisor Sen. David Durenberger; former legis. asst. of health Sen. Dan Quayle; minority health counsel Ho. Ways and Means Health Subcom., Washington, 1986—93; exec. v.p. Health Ins. Assn. Am., Washington, 1993—94; pres., 1998—2001; staff dir. health subcom. Ho. Ways and Means Com.; pres. Fedn. Am. Hosps., Washington, 2001—. Chmn. Econ. Rsch. Initiative on the Uninsured U. Mich.; mem. adv. com. Ctr. for Studying Health Sys. Change; mem. program adv. bd. Robert Wood Johnson Health Fellowships Program; mem. Medicare Competetive Pricing Adv. Com.; instr. health policy Johns Hopkins U., George Washington U., Tulane U.; adj. clin. prof. Tulane U. Sch. Pub. Health and Tropical Medicine; bd. dirs. Zix Corp.; commr. Am. Health Info. Cmty.; prin. Hosp. Quality Alliance. Contbr. articles to profl. jours. Mem.: Delta Omega. Office: Fedn Am Hosps Ste 245 801 Pennsylvania Ave NW Washington DC 20004-2604 Office Phone: 202-624-1500. Business E-Mail: ckahn@fah.org.

KAHN, DAVID, editor, author; b. NYC, Feb. 7, 1930; s. Jesse and Florence (Abraham) K.; m. Susanne Monika Fiedler, Oct. 22, 1969 (div. Jan. 1995); children: Oliver, Michael. AB, Bucknell U., 1951; DPhil, Oxford U., Eng., 1974. Reporter Jersey Jour., Jersey City, 1952-53; copyboy N.Y. Daily News, 1953-55; reporter Newsday, Garden City, NY, 1955-63; freelance writer, 1963-65, 67-74; news desk editor Internat. Herald Tribune, Paris, 1965-67; prof. journalism NYU, 1974-79; asst. viewpoints editor Newsday, Melville, NY, 1979-94, mem. editorial bd., 1988-94; scholar in residence Nat. Security Agy., 1995; asst. editor features Newsday, Melville, NY, 1996-98; ret., 1999; freelance author, 1999—. Adj. prof. modern polit. and mil. intelligence Yale U., New Haven, 1985, Columbia U., N.Y.C., 1986-88; founding co-editor Cryptologia mag., 1977—; mem. editorial bd. Intelligence and Nat. Security, 1986—, Internat. Jour. Intelligence and Counterintelligence, 1986—, Jour. Cryptology, 1991-2001, Jour. Intelligence History, 2001-; witness Congl. coms.; adj. prof. journalism SUNY, Stony Brook, 1991-94. Author: Two Soviet Spy Ciphers, 1960, Plaintext in the New Unabridged, 1963; The Codebreakers, 1967, Hitler's Spies, 1978, Seizing the Enigma, 1991 (named Notable Naval Book of 1991 U.S. Naval Inst.), The Reader of Gentlemen's Mail, 2004; editor: Kahn on Codes, 1983; editor, translator: Clandestine Operations, 1983; cons. on cryptology to Oxford English Dictionary; contbr. articles to profl. jours. and encys. Bd. trustees St. Antony's Coll. Trust, ret., 2000; bd. dirs. Nat. Cryptologic Mus. Found.; sr. assoc. mem. St. Antony's Coll., Oxford U., 1972-74; bd. dirs. Great Neck Libr., 2002—, pres., 2006—; patron Bletchley Park (U.K.) Trust. Recipient spl. award, Nat. Security Agy., 1991, 2004, Nat. Intelligence Study Ctr., 1992. Mem. Am. Cryptogram Assn. (pres. 1965-67), World War II Studies Assn. (bd. dirs. 1987—), Internat. Intelligence History Assn., Internat. Spy Mus. (mem. adv. bd. dirs.), Internat. Assn. for Cryptologic Rsch. (bd. dirs. 1980-90), Century Assn., Phi Beta Kappa. Democrat. Jewish. Avocation: tennis. Home and Office: 120 Wooleys Ln Great Neck NY 11023-2301 Office Phone: 516-487-7181. Personal E-mail: davidkahn1@aol.com.

KAHN, DAVID MILLER, lawyer, educator; b. Port Chester, NY, Apr. 21, 1925; m. Barbara Heller, May 9, 1952; children: William, James, Caroline. BA, U. Ky., 1947; LLB cum laude, N.Y. Law Sch., 1950. Bar: N.Y. 1951, U.S. Dist. Ct. (ea. and so. dists.) N.Y. 1953, U.S. Supreme Ct. 1958. Sole practice, White Plains, N.Y., 1951-60; ptnr. Kahn & Rubin, White Plains, 1960-66, Kahn & Goldman, White Plains, 1967-80; sr. ptnr. Kahn & Landau, White Plains, Palm Beach, Fla., 1980-88, Kahn and Kahn, Fla., N.Y., 1988-95, Kahn, Kahn & Scutieri Esq., Palm Beach Gardens, 1995—. Lectr. N.Y. Law Sch., 1982—; spl. counsel Village Port Chester, N.Y., 1960-63; commr. of appraisal Westchester County Supreme Ct., 1973-77; counsel Chemplex Industries, Inc., BIS Communications Corp., Bilbar Realty Co. Chmn. Westchester County Citizens for Eisenhower, 1950-52; pres. Westchester County Young Reps. Clubs, 1958-60; founder, chmn. bd. dirs. Port Chester-Rye Town Vol. Ambulance Corps, 1968-77; pres. Driftwood Corp., Amagansette, L.I., N.Y., 1984-91. Served with Counter Intelligence Corps USAF, 1942-46. Recipient lifetime achievement award, Westchester County Bar Assn., 2001; John Marshall Harlan fellow, N.Y. Law Sch., 1990—93. Fellow Am. Acad. Matrimonial Lawyers (bd. govs. N.Y. chpt. 1976-79); mem. ABA, N.Y. State Bar Assn., Westchester County Bar Assn., White Plains Bar Assn., N.Y. Law Sch. Alumni Assn. (bd. dirs. 1970-80), Elmwood C.C. (legal counsel), Eastpointe Country Club. Home and Office: 6419 Eastpointe Pines St Palm Beach Gardens FL 33418 also: 175 Main St White Plains NY 10601-3105 Office Phone: 561-627-4433, 914-761-1800. Personal E-mail: dmkahnesq@adelphia.net.

KAHN, DOUGLAS ALLEN, law educator; b. Spartanburg, SC, Nov. 7, 1934; s. Max Leonard and Julia (Rich) K.; m. Judith Bleich, Sept. 24, 1959; m. Mary Briscoe, June 12, 1970; children— Margery Ellen, Jeffrey Hodges. BA, U. N.C., 1955; JD with honors, George Washington U., 1958. Bar: D.C. 1958, Mich. 1965, U.S. Ct. Appeals (D.C. cir.) 1958, U.S. Ct. Appeals (5th and 9th cirs.) 1959, U.S. Ct. Appeals (3d, 4th and 6th cirs.) 1960, U.S. Supreme Ct. 1963. Atty. Civil and Tax div. U.S. Dept. Justice, 1958-62; assoc. Sachs and Jacobs, Washington, 1962-64; prof. law U. Mich., Ann Arbor, 1964—, Paul G. Kauper Disting. prof., 1984—. Vis. prof. Stanford Law Sch., 1973, Duke Law Sch., 1977, Fordham Law Sch., 1980-81, U. Cambridge, 1996. Author: (with Gann) Corporate Taxation, 1989, (with Waggoner and Pennell) Federal Taxation of Gifts, Trusts and Estates, 1997, (with Lehman) Corporate Income Taxation, 2001, (with J. Kahn) Federal Income Tax, 2005; comment editor George Washington U. Law Rev., 1956-58; contbr. articles to profl. jours. Recipient Emil Brown Found. prize, 1969 Mem. ABA, Order of Coif. Republican. Jewish. Office: U Mich Law Sch 625 S State St Ann Arbor MI 48109-1215 Home Phone: 734-944-5546; Office Phone: 734-764-9341. Business E-Mail: dougkahn@umich.edu.

KAHN, EDWIN LEONARD, retired lawyer; b. NYC, Aug. 1, 1918; s. Max L. and Julia (Rich) K.; m. Myra J. Green, Oct. 20, 1946 (dec. 1994); children: Martha L., Deborah K. Spiliotopoulos. AB, U. N.C., 1937; LLB cum laude, Harvard U., 1940. Bar: N.C. 1940, D.C. 1949. Atty., asst. head legislation and regulations div. Office Chief Counsel IRS, 1940-52, dir. tech. planning div., 1952-55; ptnr. Arent, Fox, Kintner, Plotkin & Kahn (now Arent Fox PLLC), Washington, 1955—86, of counsel, 1986—2007; ret., 2007. Lectr. NYU Tax Inst., mem. adv. bd., 1959-70; lectr. tax insts. Coll. William and Mary, U. Chgo., U. Tex. Editor: Harvard Law Rev, 1939-40; mem. editl. adv. bd. Tax Advisor of Am. Inst. CPA's, 1974-86. Bd. dirs. Jewish Community Ctr. Greater Washington, 1972-78; trustee Cosmos Club Found., 1989-93, chmn., 1989-91. With U.S. Army, 1943-46, ETO. Decorated Bronze Star. Fellow Am. Bar Found. (life); mem. ABA (coun. 1963-66, vice chmn. sect. taxation 1965-66), Fed. Bar Assn. (chmn. taxation com. 1967-68), D.C. Bar Assn., Nat. Tax Assn.-Tax Inst. Am. (adv. coun. 1967-69, bd. dirs. 1969-73), Am. Law Inst. (life), Am. Coll. Tax Counsel, J. Edgar Murdock Am. Inn Ct. (master bencher 1988-91), Phi Beta Kappa (life mem. fellows). Jewish. Home: 4104 40th St N Arlington VA 22207-4805 Office: 1050 Connecticut Ave NW Washington DC 20036-5303 Personal E-mail: edwinkahn@comcast.net.

KAHN, EDWIN SAM, lawyer; b. NYC, Jan. 22, 1938; m. Cynthia Chutter, May 30, 1966; children: David, Jonathan, Jennifer. BA, U. Colo., 1958; JD, Harvard U., 1965. Bar: Colo. 1965, U.S. Dist. Ct. (Colo.) 1965,

U.S. Ct. Appeals (10th cir.) 1965, U.S. Supreme Ct. 1968. Assoc. Holland & Hart, Denver, 1965-70, ptnr., 1970-77; ptnr., shareholder Kelly, Haglund, Garnsey & Kahn, LLC, Denver, 1978—. Spl. coun. Colo. Ctr. Law and Policies, 2004—. 1st lt. USAF, 1959-62. Fellow Am. Coll. Trial Lawyers; mem. Denver Bar Assn. (pres. 1984-85). Home: 2345 Leyden St Denver CO 80207-3441 Office: Kelly Haglund Garnsey & Kahn LLC 1441 18th St Ste 300 Denver CO 80202-1255 E-mail: edkahn@4dv.net.

KAHN, ELIZABETH, language educator, department chairman; d. Jack H. and Sue Upchurch Kahn; m. Larry R. Johannessen, June 20, 1981. BA, Wake Forest U., Winston-Salem, NC, 1975; MA in Tchg., U. Chgo., 1976, PhD, 1999. Nat. bd. cert. tchr. 2004. English tchr. James B. Conant H.S., Hoffman Estates, Ill., 1978—, chair dept. English, 2000—. Co-author: (book) Talking in Class: Using Discussion to Enhance Teaching and Learning, (monograph) Writing About Literature; contbr. chapters to books. Grantee Rsch. Tng. grant, Spencer Found., 1995. Mem.: Am. Ednl. Rsch. Assn., Conf. on English Edn. (vice chair 1998—2000), Conf. on English Leadership, Ill. Assn. of Tchrs. of English (2d v.p. 2006—07), Nat. Coun. of Tchrs. of English (secondary sect. steering com. 2004—). Avocations: walking, gardening. Home: 1253 Reading Ct Wheaton IL 60187 Office: James B Conant HS 700 East Cougar Trail Hoffman Estates IL 60194 Home Phone: 630-682-1913; Office Phone: 847-755-3716. Office Fax: 847-755-3623. Personal E-mail: ekahn@d211.org.

KAHN, ELLIS IRVIN, lawyer; b. Charleston, SC, Jan. 18, 1936; s. Robert and Estelle Harriet (Kaminski) Kahn; m. Janice Weinstein, Aug. 11, 1963; children: Justin Simon, David Israel, Cynthia Kahn Nirenblatt. AB in Polit. Sci., Citadel, 1958; JD, U. S.C., 1961. Bar: S.C. 1961, U.S. Ct. Appeals (5th cir.) 1963, U.S. Ct. Appeals (4th cir.) 1964, U.S. Supreme Ct. 1970, DC 1978, U.S. Claims Ct. 1988, diplomate: Nat. Bd. Trial Advocacy, Am. Bd. Profl. Liability Attys., cert.: (civil ct. mediator). Law clk. U.S. Dist. Ct. S.C., 1964—66; prin. Kahn Law Firm, Charleston. Adj. prof. med.-legal jurisprudence Med. U. S.C., 1978—87; mem. rules com. U.S. Dist. Ct., 1984—96. Mem. nat. coun. Am. Israel Pub. Affairs Com., 1982—88, Hebrew Benevolent Soc., pres., 1994—96; mem. Hebrew Orphan Soc., S.C. Organ Procurement Agy., 1989—94; chmn. campaign Charleston Jewish Fedn., 1986—87, pres., 1988—90. Capt. USAF, 1961—64. Fellow: Internat. Soc. Barristers; mem.: ATLA (state committeeman 1970—74), ABA, Am. Bd. Profl. Liability Attys. (trustee 1989—, treas. 2006—), S.C. Trial Lawyers Assn. (pres. 1976—77), 4th Cir. Jud. Conf. (life), S.C. Bar. Home: 316 Confederate Cir Charleston SC 29407-7431 Office: PO Box 31397 Charleston SC 29417-1397 Office Phone: 843-577-2128.

KAHN, FREDRICK HENRY, retired internist; b. LA, Aug. 26, 1925; s. Julius and Josephine Leone (Langdon) K.; m. Barbara Ruth Visscher, Feb. 14, 1952; children: Susan, Kathryn, William. AB, Stanford U., 1947, MD, 1951. Diplomate Am. Bd. Internal Medicine. Rotating intern San Francisco Gen. Hosp., 1950-51, fellow pathology, 1951-52; resident medicine Los Angeles VA Hosp., 1954-57, sr. resident, 1956-57; asst. clin. prof. medicine UCLA Sch. Medicine, 1957—2005; attending physician Cedars Sinai Med. Ctr., LA, 1957-96, attending physician emeritus, 1996—2005; attending physician UCLA, 1957-95; ret. Med. advisor Vis. Nurse Assn., Los Angeles, 1957-87. Contbr. articles to med. jours.; inventor blow-through high altitude chamber; promoter iodine method of personal water disinfection for travelers and hikers. Served with USNR, 1943-46; lt. (M.C.), USNR, 1952-54. Fellow ACP; mem. AMA, Microscope Soc. So. Calif, Am. Handel Soc., Sierra Club. Home: 3309 Corinth Ave Los Angeles CA 90066-1312 Personal E-mail: fredandbarbara@ca.rr.com.

KAHN, HERTA HESS (MRS. HOWARD KAHN), retired investment company executive; b. Wuerzburg, Germany; naturalized, U.S. d. Ferdinand and Lilly (Suesser) Hess; m. Herbert Levy (dec.); 1 child, Linda Levy; m. Howard Kahn (dec.). Student, Northwestern U. Sch. Commerce. Joined Paine, Webber, Jackson & Curtis, Inc., Chgo., 1941; registered rep. Paine, Webber Inc. (now UBS Fin. Svcs. Inc.), acct. v.p., v.p. investments; mktg. cons., 1995—. Author: (book) What Every Woman Should Know About Investing Her Money, 1968. Hon. life mem. nat. commn., hon. life. mem. Chgo. exec. com. Anti-Defamation League B;nai B'rith; bd. dirs. Found. Hearing and Speech Rehab. , Chgo. Mem.: Chgo. Crime Commn., Chgo. Fin. Exch., CFA Inst., Investment Analysts Soc. Chgo., NY Soc. Security Analysts, Execs. Club (Chgo.), Econ. Club, Std. Club (Chgo.), Northmoor Country Club (Highland Park, Ill.).

KAHN, JACK MERRILL, television producer; b. Boston, Nov. 25, 1952; s. David Lowell and Shirley Florence Kahn; m. Diana Burlant; 2 children. B of Hebrew Lit., Hebrew Coll., 1974; BS, Boston U., 1974; MA, Am. U., 1975. Reporter James Srodes News Svc., Washington, 1975-76, WCIX-TV, Miami, Fla., 1976-78, exec. prodr., 1978-79; prodr. Nightly Bus. Report WPBT-TV, Miami, 1979-90; sr. prodr. spl. projects NBR Enterprises/WPBT, Miami, 1990-95, dir. program devel., 1996—. Prodr.: (videotapes) How Wall Street Works, 1991 (AFVA 1991), NBR Guides to Retirement Planning, Buying Insurance, 1992 (AFVA 1992), Stock Market Strategies, 1992, 2003 (WorldFest Houston Platinum award 2003), How to Find the Right College, 1992, 2001 (NY Festivals award 1992, WorldFest Houston Gold award 2001), How to Plan Your Estate, 1993 (N.Y. Festivals award 1993, Silver Gavel award ABA 1994), How to Invest in Mutual Funds (N.Y. Festivals award 1994, Gold award Worldfest Houston, 2006), How to Find The Right Franchise (Silver Cindy award 1997), Making Your Company a Better Place for Employees (Silver Cindy award 1999), Careers for the 21st Century (Bronze Cindy award 1999), NBR Guide to Buying Bonds (WorldFest Houston Platinum award 2002), (CD-Rom) Encyclopedia of Personal Finance, NBR Edition (Dalton Comms. award Multi-media 2005, Grand award Worldfest Houston, 2006). Bd. dirs. Beth David Congregation, Miami, 1980-2002; pres. Young Israel Adventura, 2006-07. Recipient Excellence in Fin. Writing award Pannell Kerr Forster, 1989, Excellence in Fin. Journalism award N.Y. State Soc. CPA's, 1991, 2002, Journalism award for excellence in personal fin. reporting Investment Co. Inst. Edn. Found., The Am. U., 1992, Gracie Allen award Am. Women Radio TV, 1998, Silver award, Platinum, Gold Remi award World Fest, Houston, 2005, 06. Mem. Soc. Am. Bus. Editors and Writers Inc., Young Israeli Adventura (pres. 2006-07). Jewish. Office: NBR Enterprises/WPBT 14901 NE 20th Ave Miami FL 33181-1121 Personal E-mail: jsharjoel@aol.com.

KAHN, JAMES ROBERT, lawyer; b. Indpls., Apr. 11, 1953; s. Robert D. and Rose Doris (Hyman) K.; m. Debra Amper, Oct. 21, 1984; children: Adam Joshua, Aliza Toby. BA, U. Pa., 1974; JD, Harvard U., 1978. Bar: Pa. 1978, US Dist. Ct. (ea. dist.) Pa. 1978, US Ct. Appeals (3d cir.) 1982, N.J. 1985, US Dist. Ct. NJ 1985, US Dist. Ct. (ea. and so. dists.) N.Y. 1988, US Supreme Ct. 2007. Jud. clk. U.S. Dist. Ct. Dist. N.J., Camden, 1978-79; assoc. Blank, Rome, Comisky & McCauley, Phila., 1979-88, ptnr., 1988-95, Margolis Edelstein, 1995—. Chair Phila. Bar state civil cts. com., 1994; mem. Gov.'s Task Force on Med. Malpractice, 2002-2003. Bd. dirs., chair, v.p., sec. Jewish Family and Children's Svcs., Phila., 1988—; bd. dirs. Phila. Pride, Inc., 1994-97; bd. dirs., sec. Schylkill River Devel. Coun., Inc., 1993-2002; trustee Jewish Fedn. Greater Phila., 1993—; mem. United Jewish Appeal Young Leadership Cabinet, 1992-96. Recipient Young Leadership award Jewish Fedn. of Greater Phila., 1993, Stella Moore award for contbns. to dance in Phila., 1994. Mem. Pa. Bar Assn., Phila. Bar Assn., Assn. Trial Lawyers Am., Pa. Trial Lawyers Assn., Phila. Trial Lawyers Assn., Phila. Bicycle Club. Avocation: biking. Home: 2420 Fitlers Walk Philadelphia PA 19103-5562 Office: Margolis Edelstein Curtis Ctr 4th Fl Independence Sq W Philadelphia PA 19106-3304 Home Phone: 215-587-9004; Office Phone: 215-931-5887. Business E-Mail: jkahn@mangolisedelstein.com.

KAHN, JAMES STEVEN, retired museum director; b. NYC, Oct. 14, 1931; 3 children. BS in Geology, CCNY, 1952; MS in Mineralogy, Pa. State U., 1954; PhD in Geol. Sci., U. Chgo., 1956. Instr. U. R.I., Kingston, 1957, asst. prof., 1958-60, research assoc. Narragansett Marine Lab., 1957-60; group leader U. Calif., Livermore, 1960-70; dept. head Physics Internat. Co., San Leandro, Calif., 1970-71; div. head geophysics U. Calif., Livermore, 1972—74, dep. assoc. dir. human resources, 1975-78, assoc. dir. nuclear testing, 1978-80, dep. dir. lab., 1980-87; pres., chief exec. officer, dir. Mus. Sci. and Industry, Chgo., 1987-97; retired, emeritus. Trustee Mus. Sci. and Industry; mem. math. scis. edn. bd. NAS, 1991-94; chmn. sci. adv. com. Gov. Ill., 1994-98; IMAX Corp. Co-author: Statistical Analysis in Geological Sciences, 1962; contbg. author: Microstructure, 1968; contbr. articles to sci. jours. Trustee Geol. Soc. Am. Found., 1997—, fellow Geol. Soc. Am.; bd. dirs. Franklin and Eleanor Roosevelt Inst., 1994-2001, Dubuque (Iowa) Art Inst., 1999-02, emeritus trustee Dubuque Mus. Art; rector sci. and medicine Lincoln Acad. Ill., 1994-2002; mem., vice-chmn. Bd. Natural Resources and Conservation, State of Ill. Centennial fellow Pa. State U. Coll. Earth and Mineral Scis., 1996. Mem.: Sigma Xi. Personal E-mail: jbkahn@mac.com.

KAHN, JEFFRY, mathematics professor; Prof. math. dept. Rutgers U., New Brunswick, NJ. Recipient George Polya prize Soc. Indsl. & Applied Math., 1996. Office: Math Dept-Hill Ctr-Busch Campus Rutgers U New Brunswick NJ 08903

KAHN, JOSEPH F., journalist; b. Boston, Aug. 19, 1964; BA in Am. History, Harvard U., 1987, M in East Asian Studies, 1990. City desk reporter, fgn. corr. Dallas Morning News, Tex.; fgn. corr. Wall St. Jour., China, 1994—98; with NY Times, 1998—, Wall St. corr. NYC, Washington bur. reporter, reporter Shanghai, bur. chief Beijing, 2003—. Co-recipient Pulitzer Prize for internat. reporting (with reporters from Dallas Morning News), 1994, Harry Chapin Media award (with Jim Yardley), 2005, Pulitzer Prize for internat. reporting (with Jim Yardley), 2006; recipient Robert F. Kennedy Journalism award for internat. reporting, 2004, citation, Overseas Press Club, 2004. Office: NY Times 229 W 43rd St New York NY 10036

KAHN, LAURENCE MICHAEL, lawyer, management consultant; b. Chgo., May 15, 1947; s. Ernest Newman and Louise (Schoenberg) K.; m. Geraldine Marie Hirsch, July 31, 1971 (div. Oct. 1985); children: Eric M., Melissa M.; m. Candace L. Ross, Sept. 7, 1991. BA magna cum laude, U. Pa., Phila., 1969, MS in Edn., 1971; JD cum laude, U. Mich., 1977. Bar: Mich. 1977, DC 1980, Md. 1981, US Dist. Ct. Md. 1981, US Dist. Ct. DC 1981, US Ct. Claims 1989, US Ct. Appeals (DC cir.) 1992, Calif. 1994. Tchr. Northbrook Sch. Dist. 27, Ill., 1969-70, Abington Sch. Dist., Pa., 1971-73, Phila. Sch. Dist., 1973-74; staff atty. FTC, Washington, 1977-81; from assoc. to ptnr. Sherman Meehan & Curtin, PC, Washington, 1981-91; pres. Negotiated Solutions, Washington, 1991—93, San Diego, 1993—2001, Jacksonville, Oreg., 2001—03; dep. city atty. San Diego City Atty.'s Office, 1994-95; bus. cons. The Thomas Group, Medford, Oreg., 2001—03; exec. dir. Help Now! Advocacy Ctr., Medford, Oreg., 2004—. Adj. prof. U. Md., College Park, 1981, Nat. U., San Diego, 1997, San Diego State U., 1999-2001. Mem. Mental Health Adv. Com. Jackson Co., Oreg.; bd. dirs. San Diego Urban League, San Diego Civic Light Opera Assn. Mem. ATLA, Phi Beta Kappa. Avocations: jogging, participating in team sports, canoeing, hiking, ornithology. Office Phone: 541-732-1911 ext. 14.

KAHN, MARC LESLIE, orthopedic surgeon; b. Phila., Mar. 12, 1956; s. Sigmund and Joanne (Pokras) K.; m. Cynthia Petrowsky; 5 children. AB, Lafayette Coll., 1978; MD, Hahnemann Med. Coll., 1982. Resident in orthopedics Monmouth Med. Ctr., Long Branch, NJ, 1987; surgeon, maj. U.S. Army, Ft. Dix, NJ, 1987-91; orthopedic surgeon Garden State Orthopedics, Cherry Hill, NJ, 1991—. Clin. instr. N.J. Sch. Osteo. Medicine. Contbr. articles to profl. jours. Decorated Army Achievement medal with 2 oak leaf clusters, Meritorious Svc. medal. Fellow: Arthroscopy Assn. N.Am., Am. Acad. Orthop. Surgeons; mem.: AMA, N.J. Med. Soc., Camden County Med. Soc, Orthop. Surgeons of N.J. (bd. dirs., vice chmn.), N.J. Orthop. Soc. (bd. dirs., pres.), N.J. Med. Soc. Home: 455 Rte 70 West Cherry Hill NJ 08002 Office: Garden Hill Orthopedics 455 Rte 70 W Cherry Hill NJ 08002

KAHN, MARK LEO, arbitrator, educator; b. NYC, Dec. 16, 1921; s. Augustus and Manya (Fertig) K.; m. Ruth Elizabeth Wecker, Dec. 21, 1947 (div. Jan. 1972); children: Ann Mariam, Peter David, James Allan, Jean Sarah; m. Elaine Johnson Morris, Feb. 12, 1988 (dec. July 2004). BA, Columbia U., NYC, 1942; MA, Harvard U., Cambridge, Mass., 1948, PhD in Econs., 1950. Asst. economist US OSS, Washington, 1942-43; tchg. fellow Harvard U., 1947-49; dir. case analysis US WSB, Region 6-B Mich., 1952-53; mem. faculty Wayne State U., Detroit, 1949-85, prof. econs., 1960-85, prof. emeritus, 1985—, dept. chmn., 1961-68, dir. indsl. rels. M.A. program, 1978-85. Co-author: Collective Bargaining and Technological Change in American Transportation, 1971; mem. editl. bd. Employee Responsibilities and Rights Jour., 1988-96; contbr. articles to profl. jours. Bd. govs. Jewish Welfare Fedn. Detroit, 1976-82; bd. dirs. Jewish Home for Aged, Detroit, 1978-93, Lyric Chamber Ensemble, Southfield, Mich., 1995-97, Detroit Empowerment Zone Devel. Corp., 1996-99. Pvt. to Capt. AUS, 1943-46. Decorated Bronze Star; recipient Disting. Svc. award US Nat. Mediation Bd., 1987, Am. Arbitration Assn., 1992. Mem. AAUP (past chpt. pres.), Nat. Acad. Arbitrators (hon. life, bd. govs. 1960-62, v.p. 1976-78, chmn. membership com. 1979-82, pres. 1983-84, chmn. nominating com. 1995-96), Indsl. Rels. Rsch. Assn. (pres. Detroit chpt. 1956, exec. sec. 1979-89, nat. exec. bd. 1985-88), Soc. Profls. in Dispute Resolution (v.p. 1982-83, pres. 1986-87). Home and Office: 15151 Ford Rd Apt 321 Dearborn MI 48126-5027 Office Phone: 313-584-0007. Personal E-mail: mleokahn@aol.com.

KAHN, MATT, marketing executive; Sr. brand mgr. Sprite, The Coca-Cola Co.; mktg. dir. Energy Brands Inc. Named one of 40 under 40, Advt. Age, 2007. Office: Energy Brands Inc 1720 Whitestone Expy #202 Whitestone NY 11357-3000 Office Phone: 718-746-0087.*

KAHN, MICHAEL, stage director; b. NYC; s. Frederick J. and Adele (Gaberman) K. BA, Columbia U.; DHL (hon.), U. S.C., 1994, Kean Coll., 1974, The Juilliard Sch., 2005, Am. U., 2005. Artistic dir. Am. Shakespeare Theatre, Stratford, Conn., 1969-77, The Acting Co., 1978-88, Chautauqua Conservatory Theatre Co., 1985-88, Shakespeare Theatre, Washington, 1986—; dir. Chautauqua Inst. Theatre Sch., 1983-88; dir. drama divsn. Juilliard Sch., NYC, 1992—2006, dir. emeritus, 2006—; acad. chmn. Brit. Am. Drama Acad., Oxford, Eng., 1992-96; artistic dir. The Shakespeare Theatre Acad. for Classical Acting George Washington U., Washington, 2000—. Mem. faculty Circle in the Square, N.Y.C., Princeton U.; mem. faculty grad. program Sch. Arts, NYU; mem. panel League of Profl. Theatre Tng. Programs; bd. dirs. Theatre Comm. Group, Theatre Panel, N.Y. State Coun. of Arts; mem. theatre panel Nat. Endowment for Arts; panel mem. D.C. Commn. on Humanities and the Arts; artistic dir. Shakespeare Theater, 2000—. Dir. Romeo and Juliet (Helen Hayes nomination), The Winter's Tale, Macbeth (Helen Hayes nomination), All's Well that Ends Well (Helen Hayes nomination), Anthony and Cleopatra, As You Like It, Twelfth Night (Helen Hayes award 1989), Merry Wives of Windsor (Helen Hayes nomination), Richard III, 1990 (Helen Hayes nomination), King Lear, 1991, Much Ado About Nothing, 1992, Measure for Measure, 1992, Hamlet, 1993 (Helen Hayes award 1993), Mother Courage (Helen Hayes award), 1993, Richard II, 1993, The Doctor's Dilemma, 1994, Henry IV, 1994 (Helen Hayes award), Henry V (Helen Hayes nomination), Volpone, 1996, Henry VI (Helen Hayes award), 1996, Mourning Becomes Electra, (Helen Hayes Award) 1997; Peer Gynt (1997), Sweet Bird of Youth, 1998, A Woman of No Importance, 1998, King John, 1999, The Merchant of Venice, 1999, King Lear, 1999, Coriolanus, 1999, Camino Real, 2000, Timon of Athena, 2000, Don Carlos, 2001 (Helen Hayes nomination), The Oedipus Playe, 2001, The Duchess of Malfi, 2002, Hedda Gabler, 2001, The Winters' Tale, 2002, The Silent Woman, 2003, Five by Tenn at the Kennedy Ctr., 2004, Manhattan Theatre Club, 2004, Cyrano de Bergerac, 2004 (Helen Hayes award, Outstanding Dir., 2005), Macbeth, 2004, Lorenzaccio, 2005, Othello, 2005, Love's Labours Lost, 2006 (Helen Hayes award outstanding dir., 2007), The Beaux Strategem, 2006, Richard III, 2007, Hamlet, 2007; producing dir. McCarter Theater, Princeton, NJ; plays including Beyond The Horizon, Mother Courage, Grave Undertaking, The Heiress, Angel City, The Torchbearers, A Month in the Country, Put Them All Together, 1974—; dir. Broadway prodns. The Death of Bessie Smith, 1967, Here's Where I Belong, 1968, Cat On A Hot Tin Roof, 1974, Night of the Tribades, 1977, Whodunnit, 1983, Showboat, 1983 (Tony nomination); off-Broadway prodns. Funnyhouse of A Negro, 1966, Rimers of Eldritch, 1967, Thorton Wilder plays, 1967, NY Shakespeare Festival's Measure for Measure, 1966, Grand Magic, Manhattan Theatre Club, 1978, A Month in the Country, Roundabout, 1980, Hedda Gabler, Roundabout, 1981, Flux, 1982, Something Different, 1983, Ten By Tennessee, 1986, Sleep Deprivation Chamber, 1996, Goodman Theatre, Chgo., Old Times, 1972, Tooth of Crime, 1973, Tis Pity She's a Whore, 1974, Showboat, Cairo, Egypt, 1987, Five By Tennessee, 1989, Moscow, Leningrad, Vilmius Warsaw, Belgrade, 1990, Signature Theatre Otabenga, Va., 1994, The Oedipus Plays, Athens Festival, 2003, Five by Tenn, Manhattan Theater Club, 2005, Loves Labours Lost Swan Theatre, Stratford-Upon-Avon, Eng., 2006; TV prodn. Beyond the Horizon, WNET, 1975; San Francisco Opera Julio Cesare, 1978, The Acting Co., 1978—, A New Way to Pay Old Debts, 1984, The White Devil, 1979, Carmen, Houston Grand Opera, 1981, Carmen, Washington Opera, 1982, The Glass Menagerie, Chautauqua Conservatory Theatre, 1985, Tis Pity She's Whore (Am. Repertory Theatre), 1988, Much Ado About Nothing, McCarter Theatre, 1993, Vanessa, Dallas Opera, 1994, Washington Opera, 1995, Lysistrata (world premiere) Houston Grand Opera, 2006, Lysistrata NYC Opera, 2006; curator Shakespeare In Washington Festival, 2007. Recipient Best Dir. Revival award Saturday Rev., 1966, Charles MacArthur award for best dir. Old Times, 1973, Joseph Jefferson award, 1974, Washington Post award, 1989; named Best Dir. NJ Drama Critics, 1974, 76, Washingtonian of Yr. Washingtonian mag., 1989, Nat. Theater Conf. award, 2005; nominated for 4 Vernon Rice awards, 1967, John Houseman award, Globe Theater award, Bravo award Opera Music Theatre Internat., 1997, DC Mayor's Art award, 1997, 2007, Champs Cmty. award, 2000, William Shakespeare award for Classical Theatre, 2002, Univ. Club Cultural award of Yr., 2002, Gay and Lesbian Capitol Area award, 2002, Lifetime Achivement award Southeastern Theater Conf., 2003, Arts Founder award DC Cultural Alliance, 2005, John Gielaud award English Speaking Union, 2007. Home: 1 W 72nd St New York NY 10023-3486 Office: The Shakespeare Theatre 301 E Capitol St SE Washington DC 20003-3808 Home Phone: 212-873-8148; Office Phone: 202-547-3230. E-mail: mkahn@shakespearetheatre.org.

KAHN, NORMAN, dental educator, pharmacologist; b. NYC, Dec. 28, 1932; s. Louis Meyer and Dorothy (Simon) Kohn; m. Dale Krasnow, Mar. 30, 1958 AB, Columbia U., 1954, D.D.S., 1958, PhD, 1964. Lic. dentist, N.Y. State. Dental intern Montefiore Hosp., Bronx, NY, 1958-59; instr. Coll. Physicians and Surgeons, Columbia U., NYC, 1962-65, asst. prof., 1965-72, assoc. prof., 1972-80, prof. pharmacology, 1980-99, prof. dentistry, 1980-92, Edwin S. Robinson prof. dentistry, 1992-99; assoc. dean acad. affairs Sch. Dental and Oral Surgery, Columbia U., 1989-94, acting dean, 1994-95; attending dentist Presbyn. Hosp., NYC, 1985-99, Robinson prof. dentistry & pharm. emeritus, spl. lectr., 1999—, cons. dentist, 1999—. Vis. assoc. prof. UCLA, 1978; chair instl. rev. bd. Columbia-Presbyn. Med. Ctr., N.Y.C., 1981-91; cons. pharmcologist Harlem Hosp., N.Y.C., 1966-80; vis. scientist U. Pisa, Italy, 1965-66. Contbr. chpts. to books, articles to profl. jours. NIH grantee, 1969-75, Nat. Fund Med. Edn. grantee, 1973; recipient Outstanding Contbn. to Teaching award Columbia U. Coll. Physicians and Surgeons, 1980, Physicians & surgeons Disting. Svc. award in Pre-Clinical Yrs., 2001; hon. research fellow Univ. Coll., London, 1986. Mem. Am. Physiol. Soc., ADA, Am. Assn. Dental Schs., Confrerie des Chevaliers du Tastevin, Alpha Omega Alpha, Omicron Kappa Upsilon Jewish. Avocation: oenology. Office: Columbia U 630 W 168th St New York NY 10032-3795

KAHN, PHILIPPE, telecommunications industry executive, entrepreneur; b. Mar. 16, 1952; m. Sonia Lee; children: Laura, Estelle, Samuel, Sophie. Educated, ETH Zurich (Swiss Fed. Polytechnic Inst.), Switzerland; M in Math., U. Nice, France; studied musicology and classical flute, Zurich Music Conservatory, Switzerland. Founder, pres. CEO, chmn. Borland, 1982—94; co-founder with Sonia Lee, CEO Starfish Software 9acquired by Motorola in 1998), Scotts Valley, Calif., 1994—98, LightSurf Technologies (acquired by VeriSign in 2005), 1998—2004; co-founder with Sonia Lee, CEO, chmn. Fullpower Technologies Inc., Santa Cruz, Calif., 2004—. Bd. dir. Borland, 1982—96. Musician: (albums) Pacific High, 1990, Walking on the Moon, 1991, Paradiso, 1992. Co-founder with Sonia Lee, trustee Lee-Kahn Found., 1998—. Named one of Top 20 Most Important People in the history of the computer industry, BYTE Mag.; named to Computer History Mus. for three decade of innovation, 2003; recipient Leadership of Yr, award, Intern, Imaging Industry Assn., 2002. Achievements include development of as a student, developed the software for the MICRAL, the earliest non-kit personal computer based on a microprocessor; the vision for the first camera-phone was formed in 1997. Worked with Motorola to build the first camera-phone; patents in field. Avocations: sailing racing and leads a sailing team, Pegasus Racing., flute, jazz, martial arts, snowboarding, dirt biking, surfing, yoga. Office: Fullpower Technolgies Inc 1200 Pacific Ave Ste 300 Santa Cruz CA 95060*

KAHN, RICHARD, lawyer; AB magna cum laude, Hobart Coll., 1961; LLB, Rutgers U., NJ, 1964; LLM in Taxation, NYU, 1973. Bar: NJ 1965. Law sec. to Assoc. Justice Haydn Proctor NJ Supreme Ct., 1964—65; atty. Pitney Hardin, Morristown, NJ; ptnr. Day Pitney, LLP (following merger of Pitney Hardin and Day, Berry & Howard), Florham Park, NJ, 2007—. Mem. civil practice com. NJ Supreme Ct. Contbr. articles to profl. publs.; bd. editors: Rutgers Law Rev., 1963—64. Named one of Top 100 Attys., Worth mag., 2005. Fellow: Am. Coll. Trust and Estate Counsel; mem.: Estate Planning Coun. No. NJ, Internat. Acad. Estate and Trust Law, ABA, NJ State Bar Assn. (mem. bd. consultors real property, probate and trust law sect. 1984—, chmn. 1989—90), Morris County Bar Assn., Phi Beta Kappa. Office: Day Pitney LLP 200 Campus Dr Florham Park NJ 07932 Office Fax: 973-966-1015. Business E-Mail: rkahn@daypitney.com.

KAHN, RICHARD DREYFUS, lawyer; b. NYC, Apr. 25, 1931; s. David Effrian and Lucille Kahn; m. Judith Raff, Sept. 10, 1961 (div. 1977); children: Jason, Adam, Alexander; m. Elaine H. Peterson, July 21, 1983. AB, Harvard U., 1952, JD, 1955. Bar: NY 1955. Assoc. Debevoise & Plimpton, NYC, 1955-62, ptnr., 1963-90, of counsel, 1991-93. Editor: Harvard Law Rev., 1953—55. Bd. dirs. Emerson Sch., NYC, 1968—71, J. M. R. Barker Found., NYC, 1968—, C. G. Jung Found. Analytical Psychology, 1984—90, Concerned Citizens Montauk, 1991—, Group for South Fork, 1993—, Found. Child Devel., NYC, 1970—88, coun. vice chmn., 1996—2000; mem. Montauk Citizens Adv. Com., 1992—; trustee Am. Soc. Psychical Rsch., NYC, 1966—73. Mem.: Assn. Bar City of NY (chmn. com. atomic energy 1965—68), Harvard Club NYC (bd. mgrs. 1991—93), Phi Beta Kappa. Home: 224 W Lake Dr Montauk NY 11954-5235 Personal E-mail: arcon@optonline.net.

KAHN, ROBERT E., electrical engineer; b. Bklyn., Dec. 23, 1938; BEE, CCNY, 1960; MA, Princeton U., 1962, PhD in Elec. Engring., 1964; degree (hon.), Princeton U., U. Pavia, ETH Zurich, U. Md., George Mason U., U. Ctrl. Fla. Mem. tech. staff Bell Telephone Labs.; asst. prof. elec. engring. MIT, Cambridge; sr. scientist Bolt, Beranek & Newman; dir. info. processing techniques U.S. Defense Advanced Rsch. Projects Agy. (DARPA), 1972—86; founder Corp. Nat. Research Initiatives (CNRI), Reston, Va., 1986, pres., chmn., CEO, 2006—. Former mem. bd. regents Nat. Libr. Medicine; former mem. President's Adv. Coun. on the Nat. Info. Infrastructure. Named to Nat. Inventors Hall of Fame, 2006; recipient Harry Goode Meml. award, Am. Fedn. Info. Processing Soc., Computerworld/Smithsonian award, ASIS Spl. award, Pub. Svc. award, Computing Rsch. Bd., Marconi award, Internet Soc., 1994, (twice) Sec. Def. Civilian Svc. award, Nat. Medal of Tech., U.S. Dept. of Commerce, 1997, Prince Asturias award, 2002, Digital ID World award, Digital Object Architecture, 2003, Townsend Harris medal, Alumni Assn., CCNY, 2005, Presdl. Medal of Freedom, The White House, 2005, C&C prize, Tokyo Japan, 2005, Webby Lifetime Achievement, Internat. Acad. Digital Arts and Sciences, 2006; Hon. Fellow, U. Coll., London, 2003. Fellow: AAAS, Assn. Computing Machinery (SIGCOMM award 1993, A.M. Turning award 2004, Software Systems award, Spl. Interest Group on Data Commn. award, Software Sys. award, President's award 1985), Am. Assn. Artificial Intelligence, IEEE (Koji Kobayashi Computer and Communications award, Alexander Graham Bell medal, Third Millennium medal); mem.: NAE (former mem. computer science and technology bd., Charles Stark Draper prize 2001). Achievements include invention of the TCP/IP Protocol with Vinton G. Cerf, the technology used to transmit information on the Internet. Office: Corp for Nat Rsch Initiatives 1895 Preston White Dr Ste 100 Reston VA 20191-5434

KAHN, SANDRA S., psychotherapist; b. Chgo., June 24, 1942; d. Chester and Ruth Sutker; m. Jack Murry Kahn, June 1, 1965; children: Erick, Jennifer. BA, U. Miami, 1964; MA, Roosevelt U., 1976. Tchr. Chgo. Pub. Schs., 1965-67; pvt. practice psychotherapy, Northbrook, Ill., 1976—. Host Shared Feelings, Sta. WEEF-AM, Highland Park, Ill., 1983—; author: The Kahn Report on Sexual Preferences, 1981, The Ex Wife Syndrome Cutting The Cord and Breaking Free After The Marriage Is Over, 1990; columnist Single Again mag. Mem. Ill. Psychol. Assn., Chgo. Psychol. Assn. (past pres. 1990). Jewish. Office: 801 Skokie Blvd Northbrook IL 60062-4039 Office Phone: 847-272-2228.

KAHN, SIGMUND BENHAM, retired internist, dean; b. Phila., May 18, 1933; s. Maxwell Louis and Clara (Parris) K.; m. Joanne Pokras, June 11, 1955; children: Marc L., Elissa Kahn Petrosky, Hillary Kahn Roth, Lauren B. Westlake. BA, U. Pa., Phila., 1954, MD, 1958. Diplomate Am. Bd. Internal Medicine; cert. hematology and med. oncology. Rotating intern Albert Einstein Med. Ctr., Phila., 1958-59; resident in internal medicine Hosp. of U. Pa., Phila., 1959-61, fellow in hematology, 1961-62, USPHS rsch. fellow dept. hematology, 1962-63; assoc. in hematology medicine Hahnemann U. Hosp., Phila., 1963-66, asst., assoc., then prof. medicine, 1966-99; prof. dept. neoplastic disease Hahnemann Univ. Hosp., Phila., 1978-99, dir. edn., vice chmn. dept., 1978-94; assoc. dean Hahnemann U., Phila., 1986-94; prof. emeritus, 1999—2002; prof. dept. medicine divsn. hematology/ med. oncology Med. Coll. Pa./Hahnemann U., Phila., 1992-94, assoc. dean edn., 1992-94, prof. emeritus, 1999—2002, Drexel U. Coll. of Med., 2002—. Cons., chmn. dean's com. Wilkes-Barre (Pa.) VA Hosp., 1987-92. Mem. editl. bd. Jour. Cancer Edn., 1985-95, Am. Jour. Clin. Oncology; contbr. articles to profl. jours. Instl. rep. Boy Scouts Am., 1970-75; pres. Temple Beth Sholom, Cherry Hill, N.J., 1977-80; mem. med. bd. Lupus Found., Delaware Valley, 1977-79. Mem. AMA, ACP, Phila. County Med. Soc., Phila. Hematology Soc., Pa. Med. Soc., Am. Fedn. Clin. Rsch., Am. Hematology Soc., Am. Assn. Cancer Rsch., Am. Soc. Clin. Oncology, Am. Assn. Cancer Edn., Am. Cancer Soc. (chmn. patient svc. com. Phila. divsn. 1981-83, chmn. med. subcom. profl. edn. com. 1979-81, fin. com. 1981), Phi beta Kappa, Alpha Omega Alpha. Jewish. Home: 2307 Sagemore Dr Marlton NJ 08053-4315 Personal E-mail: kahnsb@msn.com.

KAHN, STEVEN EMANUEL, medical educator; b. Durban, South Africa, July 28, 1955; m. Stephanie Berk Kahn; 2 children. MB, ChB, U. Cape Town, South Africa, 1978. Diplomate Am. Bd. Internal Medicine. Intern depts. ob./gyn. and medicine Somerset Hosp., Cape Town, South Africa, 1979; resident dept. ob./gyn. 2 Mil. Hosp., Wynberg, South Africa, 1980, resident and coord. dept. ob./gyn., 1981; resident dept. medicine divsn. endocrinology Groote Schuur Hosp., Cape Town, 1982; rsch. fellow diabetes and endocrine rsch. group U. Cape Town, 1983; resident dept. medicine Albert Einstein Med. Ctr., Phila., 1983—86; sr. rsch. fellow divsn. metabolism, endocrinology and nutrition Dept. Medicine U. Wash. Sch. of Medicine, VA Med. Ctr., Seattle, 1986—88; assoc. investigator, staff physician divsn. endocrinology and metabolism Dept. Medicine VA Med. Ctr., Seattle, 1988—91, rsch. assoc., staff physician divsn. endocrinology and metabolism Dept. Medicine, 1991—95; acting instr. divsn. metabolism, endocrinology and nutrition Dept. Medicine U. Wash. Sch. of Medicine, Seattle, 1988—92, asst. prof. divsn. metabolism, endocrinology and nutrition Dept. Medicine, 1992—95, assoc. prof. divsn. metabolism, endocrinology and nutrition Dept. Medicine, 1995—2001, prof. divsn. metabolism, endocrinology and nutrition, 2001—; dir. R&D VA Puget Sound Health Care Sys., 2001—. Prizer vis. prof. Case Western Res. U., 1999. Mem. editl. bd.: Jour. Clin. Endocrinology and Metabolism, 1995—98, Diabetes Care, 1997—99; contbr. articles to profl. jours. Named Assoc. Investigator, Dept. VA, 1988, Rsch. Assoc., 1991; recipient Career Devel. award, Juvenile Diabetes Found., 1988, NIH, 1999, Feasibility award, Dana Found., 1989, Clin. Investigator award, NIH, 1991, New Investigator award, Diabetes Rsch. Coun., 1992—94, rsch. award, NIH, 1997, Novartis Young Investigator award in diabetes rsch., 2001; scholar Amelia Schenkman, 1973—75. Mem.: ACP, Gen. Med. Coun. (U.K.), Western Soc. Clin. Investigation (councillor 1998—), Endocrine Soc., Am. Soc. for Clin. Investigation, Am. Fedn. Clin. Rsch. (chair program com. for metabolism 1994, 1996, councillor western sect. 1994—96, pres.-elect western sect. 1996, pres. western sect. 1997, nat. councillor 1996), Am. Diabetes Assn. (bd. dirs. Wash. affiliate 1993—94, exec. bd. dirs. 1994—98, rsch. grant rev. panel 1994—97, rsch. award 1996, mentor award 1999). Office: VA Puget Sound Health Cr Dept Medicine 151 1660 S Columbian Way Seattle WA 98108-1532

KAHN, SUSAN, artist; b. NYC, Aug. 26, 1924; d. Jesse B. and Jenny Carol (Peshkin) Cohen; m. Joseph Kahn, Sept. 15, 1946 (dec.); m. Richard Rosenkranz, Feb. 1, 1981. Grad., Parsons Sch. Design, 1945; student, Moses Soyer, 1950-57. Subject of: book Susan Kahn, with an essay by Lincoln Rothschild, 1980; One-woman shows include Sagittarius Gallery, 1960, A.C.A., Galleries, 1964, 68, 71, 76, 80, Charles B. Goddard Art Center, Ardmore, Okla., 1973, Albrecht Gallery Mus. Art, St. Joseph, Mo., 1974, N.Y. Cultural Center, N.Y.C., 1974, St. Peter's Coll., Jersey City, 1978, Heidi Neuhoff Gallery, N.Y.C., 1989, Sindin Galleries, 1996; exhibited in group shows Audubon Artists, N.Y.C., Nat. Acad., N.Y.C., Springfield (Mass.) Mus., City Center, N.Y.C., A.C.A., Galleries, N.Y.C., Nat. Arts Club, N.Y.C., Butler Inst., Youngstown, Ohio, Islip Art Mus., East Islip, N.Y., 1989, Fine Arts Mus. of S., Mobile, Ala., 1989, Chatanooga Regional History Mus, 1989, Longview (Tex.) Mus. Art, 1990; represented in permanent collections, Tyler (Tex.) Mus., St. Lawrence U. Mus., Canton, N.Y., Fairleigh Dickinson U. Mus., Rutherford, N.J., Syracuse U. Mus., Sheldon Swope Gallery, Terre Haute, Ind., Montclair (N.J.) Mus. Fine Arts, Butler Inst. Am. Art, Youngstown, Ohio, Reading (Pa.) Mus., Albrecht Gallery Mus. Art, St. Joseph(Mo.), Cedar Rapids (Iowa) Art Center, N.Y. Cultural Center, N.Y.C., Edwin A. Ulrich Mus., Wichita, Kans., Wichita State U., Johns Hopkins Sch. Advanced Internat. Studies, Washington, Joslyn Mus., Omaha, U. Wyo., Laramie. Recipient Knickerbocker prize for best religious painting, 1956; Edith Lehman award Nat. Assn. Women Artists, 1958; Simmons award, 1961; Knickerbocker Artists award, 1961; Nat. Arts Club award, 1967; Knickerbocker Medal of Honor, 1964; Famous Artists Sch. award, 1967 Mem. Nat. Assn. Women Artists (Anne Barnett Meml. prize 1981, Solveig Stromsoe Palmer Meml. award 1987, Dorothy Schweitzer award 1990,Audrey Hope Shirk Meml. award 2006), Artists Equity, Met. Mus., Mus. Modern Art, Nat. Assn. Women Artists. *I choose to be a realist and humanist in my work. The most important objects of my concern are people, their lives and times. I believe that art is a way of communicating, subject matter translated into color, form and line, so that the work will express the idea convincingly.*

KAHN, THOMAS, medical educator; b. Offenburg, Germany, June 23, 1938; s. Ludwig and Ellen (Kaufman) K.; m. Si Mi Pak, Nov. 7, 1968; children: Diana, David, Philip. BA, NYU, 1958, MD, 1962. Intern medicine Balt. City Hosps., 1962-63, U. Pitts. Hosps., 1963-64, Mt. Sinai, NYC, 1964-65, resident in nephrology, 1965-67; chief renal sect. Bronx VA Med. Ctr., 1979-96; prof. medicine Mt. Sinai Sch. Medicine, NYC, 1988—. Maj. US Army, 1967—69. Office: VA Med Ctr 130 W Kingsbridge Rd Bronx NY 10468-3904 Office Phone: 718-584-9000.

KAHN, THOMAS S., lawyer; Atty. Sullivan & Cromwell, NYC; staffer Dem. policy com. US Ho. of Reps, chief counsel to John M. Spratt, Jr., chief counsel, acting staff dir., subcom. Trade and Banking, chief counsel, staff dir., Budget Com., 2007—. Office: Committee on Budget 207 Cannon HOB Washington DC 20515-6065 Office Phone: 202-226-7200. Office Fax: 202-225-9905.

KAHN, VICTORIA ELAINE HOPKINS, special education educator; b. Grand Junction, Colo., Dec. 11, 1953; d. William Stanley Hopkins, Jr. and Bernice Irene (Porter) Hopkins; m. James Michael Humphrey, Sept. 17, 1982 (div. June 1986); m. Jerome Isidor Kahn, May 1, 1988 (div. June 2004). AA in Theatre Arts, Santa Ana Coll., 1974; BA with distinction in psychology, San Diego State U., 1985. Cert. edn. specialist Calif. State U., 2001. Owner, freelance photographer Victoria Vincent Photography, San Diego and Vista, Calif., 1984—94, Glendale, Ariz., 1993—94; enrichment instr. Felicita Found. for the Arts, Escondido, Calif., 1990—91; photographer, artist Vista (Calif.) Initiative for the Visual Arts, 1990—93; sub. tchr. and aide spl. edn. grades K-14 Orange County Dept. Edn., Costa Mesa, Calif., 1996—98; sub. tchr. spl. edn. grades K-6 Garden Grove (Calif.) Unified Sch. Dist., 1997—2002; resource specialist tchr. grades 1-5 Long Beach (Calif.) Unified Sch. Dist., 2002—03; sub. spl. edn. tchr. grades K-6 North County Coastal Consortium Encinitas (Calif.) Union Sch. Dist., 2003—04; owner, designer Curriculum Creations, San Diego, 2003—05; cmty. trainer United Cerebral Palsy Assn.-Networks, Escondido, Calif., 2005—. Charter mem., artist Gallery Vista (Calif.) Artists' Assn., 1989—91; artist, photographer Holman Gallery, Scottsdale, Ariz., 1993—94. Editor: (book of poetry) Autumn Meditations, 1994, The Complete Poems of James L.O. Porter, 2002, (novella) The Chance, 2002. Vol. genealogy rsch. rm. Nat. Archives and Records Adminstrn., Laguna Niguel, Calif., 1998—2001; vol. South Coast Repertory Theatre, Costa Mesa, Calif., 1978—79; vol. summer stock The Magic Theatre, Berkeley, Calif., 1972. Recipient Achievement award, Nat. Archives and Records Adminstrn., 2000, 2001. Mem.: DAR (chmn. conservation com. Los Cerritos chpt. 2002—04, vol. lineage rsch. look up com. 2004—, chmn. conservation com. Rancho Buena Vista chpt. 2006—, mem. lineage rsch. com. Calif. state soc.), Know Thyself as Soul Found. S.W., Nat. Campaign for Tolerance, Dubois Family Assn., Tchrs. Assn. Long Beach, Coun. for Exceptional Children, Humane Farming Assn., Phi Kappa Phi, Pi Lambda Theta. Achievements include patents pending for a scenario method of teaching multiplication and division concepts (Cowboy Tim); a multisensory method of motivating students to read and write (The Reading Drum). Avocations: historial and geneaological research, writing, art, educational manipulatives and methods design, bird and nature watching. Home Phone: 760-804-0146. E-mail: kahnv@msn.com.

KAHN, WOLF, artist; b. Stuttgart, Germany, Oct. 4, 1927; came to U.S., 1940, naturalized, 1946; s. Emil and Nellie (Budge) K.; m. Emily Mason, Mar. 2, 1957; children: Cecily, Melany. Student, Hans Hofmann Sch., 1948-49; BA, U. Chgo., 1951; degree (hon.), Wheaton Coll., 2002, Union Coll., Schenectady, 2004. Vis. prof. painting U. Calif., Berkeley, 1960; adj. assoc. prof. Cooper Union Art Sch., 1961-77; jury mem. numerous regional art shows; artist-in-residence Dartmouth Coll., 1984. One-man shows include Borgenicht Gallery, NYC, 1957-95, Beadleston Gallery, NYC, 1998, 00, Thomas Segal Gallery, Balt., 2000, Jerald Melberg Gallery, Charlotte, NC, 1993-00, Ft. Lauderdale Mus. Art, 1991, Boca Raton Mus. Art, 1997, NAD, 2004, Addison Ripley Gallery, Wash. DC, 2005; group shows include Whitney Mus., NYC, 1960, 77, Met. Mus., NYC, 1975-76, Ameringder/Yohe Gallery, NYC, Neptune Fine Art, NY, Provincetown Art Assn., Mass., 2006, Melberg Gallery, Charlotte, NC, 2005, others; represented in permanent collections Mus. Modern Art, NYC, Whitney Mus., Houston Mus. Fine Arts, Chase Manhattan Coll., Va. Mus., Met. Mus., NYC, LA County Mus., Hirschhorn Mus., Washington; author: Pastel Light, 1983, Wolf Kahn Pastels, 2000, Wolf Kahn's America, 2003; contbr. articles to profl. jours. Trustee Brattleboro Mus. Vt., 1979—, Vt. Studio Ctr.,1988—; apptd. NYC Art Commn., 1993-95, Marlboro Coll., 2005-. With USNR, 1945—46. Recipient award for art Am. Acad. Arts and Letters, 1979; Fulbright fellow Italy, 1964-65; Guggenheim fellow, 1967-68; Ford Found. grantee, 1969. Mem. Nat. Acad. Design (academician, 1980-, coun. mem. 1982-96, curator 1994), Am. Acad. Arts and Letters (treas. 2005—). Democrat. Jewish. Office: c/o Ameringer Yohe Gallery 20 W 57th St New York NY 10019

KAHNE, KASEY, race car driver; b. Enumclaw, Wash., Apr. 10, 1980; Profl. race car driver NASCAR, 2002—. Achievements include winner Chevy American Revolution 400, 2004, Atlanta Golden Corral 500, 2006, Texas Cup, 2006, 3M Performance 400, Mich. Internat. Speedway, 2006. Office: c/o Evernham Motorsports 320 Aviation Dr Statesville NC 28677

KAHNE, STEPHEN JAMES, systems engineering educator, engineering company executive, academic administrator; b. NYC, Apr. 5, 1937; s. Arnold W. and Janet (Weatherlow) Kahne; m. Irena Nowacka, Dec. 11, 1970; children: Christopher, Kasia. BEE, Cornell U., Ithaca, NY, 1960; MS, U. Ill., Urbana-Champaign, 1961, PhD, 1963. Asst. prof. elec. engring. U. Minn., Mpls., 1966-69, assoc. prof., 1969-76; dir. Hybrid Computer Lab., 1968-76; founder, dir., cons. InterDesign Inc., Mpls., 1968-76; prof. dept. sys. engring. Case Western Res. U., Cleve., 1976-83, chmn. dept., 1976-80; dir. divsn. elec., computer and sys. engring. NSF, Washington, 1980-82; prof. Poly Inst. N.Y., 1983-85, dean engring., 1983-84; pres. Oreg. Grad. Ctr., Beaverton, 1985-86, prof. dept. applied physics and elec. engring., 1985-89; chief engr. civil systems divsn. MITRE Corp., McLean, Va., 1989-90, chief scientist Washington Group, 1990-91, cons. engr. Ctr. for Advanced Aviation Sys. Devel., 1991-94; exec. dir., CEO Triangle Coalition for Sci. and Tech. Edn., 1994; chancellor, v.p. Embry-Riddle Aeronautical U., Prescott, Ariz., 1995-97, prof. engring., 1995—. Cons. in field; exchange scientist NAS, 1968, 75 Contbr. articles to sci. jours. Active Mpls. Citizens League, 1968-75; regent L.I. Coll. Hosp., Bklyn., 1984-85; trustee Yavapai Regional Med. Ctr., 1999-2004; chmn. Beaverton Sister Cities Found., 1986-89; ct. appointed spl. adv. Superior Ct. Ariz., 2005—; bd. dirs. West Yavapai Guidance Clinic, 2005-, No. Ariz. Regional Behavioral Health Authority, 2006-. Served with USAF, 1963-66. Recipient Amicus Poloniae award POLAND Mag., 1975, John A. Curtis award Am. Soc. Engring. Edn., Outstanding Svc. award Internat. Fedn. Automatic Control, 1990; Case Centennial scholar, 1980 Fellow: AAAS, IEEE (life; editor Transactions on Automatic Control 1975—79, mem. editl. bd. Spectrum 1979—82, pres. Control Sys. Soc. 1981, bd. dirs. 1982—86, v.p. tech. activities 1984—85, Centennial medal 1984, Disting Mem. award 1983, Richard Emberson award 1991, Disting. Lectr. 1998—2000), Internat. Fedn. of Automatic Control (hon. editor 1975—81, dep. chmn. mng. bd. publs. 1976—87, v.p. 1987—90, pres.-elect 1990—93, pres. 1993—96, adv. 1999—, chmn. 1999—, mem. publs. mgmt. bd.); mem.: Ea. Fedn. Automatic Control (trustee found.), Air Traffic Control Assn., Am. Soc. Engring. Edn., Eta Kappa Nu. Office: Embry Riddle Aero U 3700 Willow Creek Rd Prescott AZ 86301-3721 Home Phone: 928-541-1293; Office Phone: 928-777-3779. Personal E-mail: s.kahne@ieee.org.

KAHNEMAN, DANIEL, psychology professor; b. Tel Aviv, 1934; BA in Psychology and Math., The Hebrew U., Jerusalem, Israel, 1954; PhD in Psychology, U. Calif., 1961; DSc (hon.), U. Pa., 2001; degree (hon.), U. Trento, 2002, Ben-Gurion U., 2003, New Sch., 2003, Univ. Brit. Columbia, 2004, Harvard Univ., 2004, Univ. East Anglia, 2004, Univ. Wurzburg, 2004. Lectr. in psychology The Hebrew U., Jerusalem, 1961—66, sr. lectr. in psychology, 1966—70, assoc. prof., 1970—73, prof., 1973—78, fellow Ctr. for Rationality, 2000—; prof. psychology U. B.C., Canada, 1978—86, U. Calif., Berkeley, 1986—94; Eugene Higgins prof. psychology, prof. pub. affairs Princeton U. Woodrow Wilson Sch., NJ, 1993—. Vis. scientist dept. psychology U. Mich., 1965—66; fellow, Ctr. for Cognitive Studies, lectr. in psychology Harvard U., 1966—67; vis. scientist Applied Psychol. Rsch. Unit, Cambridge, England, 1968—69; fellow Ctr. for Advanced Studies in the Behavioral Scis., 1977—78; assoc. fellow Canadian Inst. Advanced Rsch., 1984—86; vis. scholar Russell Sage Found., 1991—92; fellow, Ctr. for Rationality Hebrew Univ., Jerusalem, 2000—. Mem. editl. bd. Jour. Risk and Uncertainty, Thinking and Reasoning, Econs. and Philosophy. Second lt. to lt. Israel Defence Forces, 1954. Named Katz-Newcomb lectr. in social psychology, 1979; recipient Fitts Lectures, U. Mich., 1987, Disting. Scientific Contbn. award, Soc. Consumer Psychology, 1992, Tanner Lecture on Human Values, U. Mich., 1994, Bartlett Lecture, Exptl. Psychology Soc., Eng., 1995, Hilgard award lifetime contbn. to gen. psychology, 1995, Nobel Prize in econ. scis., 2002, Grawemeyer Prize in Psychology, 2002, Career Achievement Award, Soc. Med. Decision Making, 2002. Fellow: Econometric Soc., Canadian Psychol. Assn., Am. Psychol. Assn., Am. Psychol. Soc. (William James Fellow, Disting. Scientific Contbn. award 1982), Am. Acad. Arts and Scis.; mem.: NAS, Soc. Judgment and Decision Making (pres. 1992—93), Soc. Econ. Sci., Psychonomic Soc., Soc. Exptl. Psychologists (pres. 1992—93, Warren medal 1995). Office: Princeton U 3-S-3 Green Hall Dept Psychology Princeton NJ 08544-1010*

KAHNWEILER, DAVID R., real estate company executive; BA, U. Mich. Chmn. and CEO Colliers Bennett & Kahnweiler Inc.; chmn. bd. dirs. Colliers USA, 2005—. Bd. dirs. Chgo. Devel. Coun., Chicagoland C. of C. Named Chgo.'s Indsl. Broker of Yr., 1996, 1997; recipient Award for Excellence, Nat. Assn. Indsl. & Office Parks, 1998, Spl. Achievement of Yr. award, 1999, City of Chgo. Indsl. Transaction of Yr., 2000. Mem.: Assn. Indsl. Real Estate Brokers, Soc. Indsl. and Office Realtors (Largest Intercity Transaction award 1997), Young President's Orgn. (Chgo. chpt.). Office: Colliers International USA 200 S Wacker Drive Chicago IL 60606 Office Phone: 847-698-8201. Office Fax: 847-698-8401. E-mail: dkahnweiler@colliersbk.com.*

KAHOL, KANAV, researcher; b. Jammu, Kashmir, India, June 26, 1979; s. Ashok and Renu Kahol. B in Tech. Elec. and Comm. Engring., Guru Nanak Dev Engring. Coll., Ludhiana, India; MS in Computer Sci., Ariz. State U.; PhD in Computer Sci., Ariz. State U., Tempe, 2005. Rsch. assoc. CUbiC (Ctr. Cognitive Ubiquitous Computing), Ariz. State U., Tempe, 2001—. Scholar Ariz. Regents Scholarship, Ariz. State U., 2001-2005. Mem.: IEEE (assoc.). Achievements include research in haptic user interfaces for individuals who are blind; multimodal systems for stroke rehabilitation; human motion analysis for complex motion sequences; psychological basis for haptic perception. Home Phone: 480-332-0919; Office Phone: 480-727-3612. Office Fax: 480-965-3190; Home Fax: 480-965-3190. Business E-Mail: kanav@asu.edu.

KAHOLOKULA, JOSEPH KEAWEAIMOKU, psychologist, researcher; b. Honolulu, Nov. 11, 1969; s. Lawrence Pauahi and Beverly Leilani Lyons Kaholokula. BA in Psychology, U. Hawaii, 1996, MA in Psychology, 2001, PhD in Psychology, 2003. Rsch. specialist Native Hawaiian Health Rsch. Project, Honolulu, 1994—2001; resident dept. psychology Tripler Army Med. Ctr., 2002—03, postdoc. fellow in behavioral medicine, 2003—04; assoc. chmn., asst. rschr., faculty dept. Native Hawaiian health John A. Burns Sch. Medicine, Honolulu, 2004—. Instl. rev. bd. mem. Native Hawaiian Health Care Sys., Honolulu, 2005—. Sr. mem. and protocol com. mem. Halemua o Kuali'i, Honolulu, 1999—2005, Halemua o Mauiloa, Kahului, 1999—2005. Named Outstanding New Program Vol., Am. Diabetes Assn., Hawaii, 2002; recipient Student Rsch. award, Hawaii Psychol. Assn., 2001;, APA Minority fellow, 1998—2001, Kamehameha Schools/Bishop Estate scholar, 1994—2001, U.S. Achievement Acad. scholar, 1995, Honolulu Hawaiian Civic Club scholar, 1996, NIMH-COR scholar, 1996, J. Watumull scholar, Sch. Social Scis., U. Hawaii at Manoa, 1996, Pacific-Asian scholar, U. Hawaii, Manoa, 1998—2001, Dr. Hans & Clara Zimmerman Found. scholar, Hawaii Cmty. Found., 1999—2003, Native Hawaiian Leadership Project, U. Hawaii scholar, 2000—03, Na Liko Noelo scholar, 'Imi Hale, Native Hawaiian Cancer Network, 2002—05. Mem.: APA, Golden Key Nat. Honor Soc. (life). Achievements include research in biological and psychosocial models in predicting depression in people with type 2 diabetes; ethnic-by-gender interactions in cigarette smoking behavior among Asian and Pacific Islanders; the relationship between acculturation and depression among Native Hawaiians; the relationship between cigarette smoking and depression among Native Hawaiians; ethnic differences in the relationship between health-related quality of life and depression in people with type 2 diabetes; diabetes care issues in a state psychiatric hospital. Avocations: Native Hawaiian cultural activities, travel, volleyball, wood carving. Office: Dept Native Hawaiian Health 651 Ilalo St MEB 307H Honolulu HI 96813 Home Phone: 808-221-2481; Office Phone: 808-692-1047. Office Fax: 808-587-8565. E-mail: kaholoku@hawaii.edu.

KAHRILAS, PETER JAMES, medical educator, researcher; b. Culver City, Calif., June 9, 1953; s. Peter Jerome and Leticia (Llorett) K.; m. Elyse Anne Lambiase, Mar. 30, 1984; children: Genevieve Anne, Ian James, Miranda Elyse. Student, Yale U., 1971-75, U. Rochester, NYC, 1975-79. Resident in medicine U. Hosp. of Cleve., 1979-82; fellow in gastroenterology Northwestern U., Chgo., 1982-84; rsch. fellow Med. Coll. of Wis., Milw., 1984-86; asst. prof. medicine Med. Coll. Wis., Milw., 1986—90, assoc. prof. medicine, 1990—95, prof. medicine, 1995—; chief gastroenterology Northwestrn U. Feinberg Sch. Medicine, Chgo., 1999—2006. Contbr. articles to profl. jours. NIH grantee, 1990—. Fellow ACP, Ctrl. Soc. for Clin. Rsch., Am. Coll. Gastroenterology; mem. Am. Gastroenterol. Assn., Am. Fedn. for Clin. Rsch., Am. Soc. for Clin. Investigation, Am. Motility Soc. Democrat. Home: 203 Columbia Ave Park Ridge IL 60068-4923 Office: Northwestern U 676 N St Clair Ste 1400 Chicago IL 60611 Home Phone: 847-823-4799; Office Phone: 312-695-4016. Business E-Mail: p-kahrilas@northwestern.edu.

KAHRL, ROBERT CONLEY, lawyer; b. Mt. Vernon, Ohio, June 2, 1946; s. K. Allin and Evelyn Sperry (Conley) K.; m. LaVonne Elaine Rutherford, July 12, 1969; children: Kurt Freeland, Eric Allin, Heidi Elizabeth. AB, Princeton U., 1968; MBA, JD, Ohio State U., 1975. Bar: Ohio 1975, U.S. Ct. Appeals (6th cir.) 1976, U.S. Dist. Ct. (no. dist.) Ohio 1977, U.S. Ct. Appeals (9th cir.) 1979, U.S. Ct. Appeals (fed. cir.) 1984, U.S. Ct. Appeals (D.C. cir.) 1986. Law clk. to presiding judge U.S. Ct.

Appeals (6th cir.), Cleve., 1975—76; assoc. Jones, Day, Reavis & Pogue, Cleve., 1976—84, ptnr., 1985—; ptnr., practice leader intellectual property practice area Jones Day (formerly Jones, Day, Reavis & Pogue), Cleve., 1991—. Author: Patent Claim Construction, 2001—06. With USN, 1968—72. Mem. Ohio State Bar Assn. (chmn. emeritus intellectual property sect.), Am. Intellectual Property Law Assn., Order of Coif. Republican. Presbyterian. Home: 7624 Red Fox Trl Hudson OH 44236-1926 Office: Jones Day North Point 901 Lakeside Ave E Cleveland OH 44114-1190 Office Phone: 216-586-3939. E-mail: rckahrl@jonesday.com.

KAHWASH, EIAD B., medical educator, poet; s. Badie Kahwash and Anoinette Saada; m. Hala R. Fadlalah, May 28, 2000; children: Nabeel Gabriel, Noor Sophia. MD, Med Sch. Aleppo, Syria, 1990. With Ohio State U., Columbus, 1999—2003, U. Louisville, 2003—04. Med. head hematology and blood bank labs. Queen Elizabeth Hosp., Charlottetown, Prince Edward Island, Canada, 2004—. Contbr. articles to profl. jours.;, author of poems. Recipient A travel award, U. Pitts., 2001. Master: Transfusion Medicine Com. Prince Edward Island (assoc.); fellow: Am. Soc. Clin. Pathology (assoc.); mem.: Med. Soc. Prince Edward Island (assoc.). Independent Thinkers. Avocations: travel, reading, writing, computers. Personal E-mail: ekahwash@earthlink.ca.

KAIDY, MITCHELL, retired journalist, legislative staff member; b. Bklyn., Mar. 23, 1925; s. Murad Abdallah and Asma Araman Kaldy; m. Jean Harris Kaldy; children: Kristen, Mark. Student, U. Miss., 1943—44, Clemson A&M Coll., SC, 1944; BS in Journalism, NYU, 1948. Reporter, editor Monticello Evening News, NY, 1948—49, Middletown Times Herald, NY, 1949—50, Rochester Dem. Chronicle, NY, 1950—65; legis. aide and speech writer NY State Legis., Albany, 1966—83; freelance TV comml. prodr. Rochester, 1983—90; freelance writer, 1983—. Dir. rsch. N.Y. State Joint Legis. Com. on Conservation, 1967; legis. aide NY State Senate Com. on Labor, Albany, 1966; pres., sec. Rochester (N.Y.) Newspaper Guild, 1953—60, N.Y. State Newspaper Guild. Manuscript editor Becoming American: The Early Arab Immigrant Experience, by Alixa Naff, 1985; contbr. columns in newspapers, articles to profl. jours. (Project Censored award, 1993), articles to series (Pulitzer Prize citation, 1963). Founder Peace and Justice Edn. Ctr., Rochester, 1962; founder, pres. Genesee Valley chpt. Vets. of Battle of the Bulge; founder Rochester chpt. Amnesty Internat.; historian 87th Inf. Divsn.; candidate Monroe County, 1963, NY Legis., 1968, Congress, 1982—84; founder Genesee Valley chpt. NY Civil Liberties Union. Cpl. US Army, 1943—45, ETO. Decorated Bronze Star medal, Combat Infantry Badge, European theater ribbon with three battle stars, Army of Occupation medal, Good Conduct medal US Army, WWII Victory medal, Comdr.'s award 87th Inf. Divsn.; named Journalist of Yr., Utica, NY, 1966;, Am. Newspaper Guild fellow, 1963. Democrat. Achievements include design of and writing of four plaques in Belgium, commemorating 87th Infantry Divsn. engagements during Battle of the Bulge, 1995; plaque in Oswego, NY honoring S/Sgt. Curtis F. Shoup, Medal of Honor winner, Battle of the Bulge; 87th Infantry division highway signs, I-390, South of Rochester, NY. Avocations: travel, journalism, writing. Home: 921 Crittenden Rd Rochester NY 14623-1157 Office Phone: 585-424-4746. Personal E-mail: mkaldy@rochester.rr.com.

KAIER, EDWARD JOHN, lawyer; b. Sewickley, Pa, Sept. 23, 1945; s. Edward Anthony and Mary Patricia (Crimmins) K.; m. Annette Thomas, July 31, 1976; children: Elizabeth Anne, Charles Crimmins, Thomas Edward. AB, Harvard U., 1967; JD, U. Pa., 1970. Bar: DC 1970, Pa. 1970, US Dist. Ct. (ea. dist.) Pa. 1971, US Ct. Appeals (3rd and DC cir.) 1971, US Dist. Ct. DC, 1971. Law clk. to presiding justice US Dist. Ct. for DC, Washington, 1970-71; assoc. Dechert Price & Rhoads, Phila., 1971-74; ptnr. Kaier and Kaier, Phila., 1974-77, Hepburn Willcox Hamilton & Putnam, Phila., 1977—2007, Teeters Harvey Gilboy & Kaier, Phila., 2007—. Pres. Savoy Co., Phila., 1978-80; bd. dir. Mgr. Funds, Norwalk, Conn., Mgr. AMG Funds, Boston, Third Avenue Funds, NY Vice chmn. Rosemont (Pa.) Sch. of Holy Child, 1981-90. Mem.: ABA, Phila. Bar Assn. (chmn. office practice com. probate sect. 1987—90, exec. com. 1990—92, 2002—04), Harvard-Radcliffe Club (Phila.) (sec. 1989—2004), Avalon Yacht Club (trustee 1987—90, 1992—93, treas. 1990—92), Phila. Country Club, Phila. Club, Merion Cricket Club. Republican. Roman Catholic. Avocations: sailing, golf. Home: 111 N Lowrys Ln Bryn Mawr PA 19010-1408 Office: Teeters Harvey Gilboy & Kaier 1835 Market St Philadelphia PA 19103 Personal E-mail: ejkaier@gmail.com.

KAIGLER, DENISE, communications executive; m. Joseph Kaigler; children: Danielle, Joseph Jr. B in Journalism, Emerson Coll. Dir. comm. Boys & Girls Clubs of Boston; various positions Reebok Internat. Ltd., Canton, Mass., sr. v.p. corp. rels., chief comm. officer, chief spokesperson, comm. strategist, primary speechwriter for Pres. and CEO, sr. v.p. global pub. rels. and comm. Mem.: Boston Assn. of Black Communicators, Pub. Rels. Soc. Am. Office: Reebok Internat Ltd 1895 JW Foster Blvd Canton MA 02021 Office Phone: 781-401-5000. Office Fax: 781-401-7402.*

KAIL, FLOYD MICHAEL, lawyer; b. Boston, June 19, 1945; s. Nathan and Harriett (Lenox) Kail; m. Wendy Green, June 23, 1968; children: Nicole, Thomas, Kathryn. BA magna cum laude, Yale U., 1967, LLB, 1970; cert. in edn., Oxford U., Eng., 1971. Bar: Conn. 1972, DC 1973, US Ct. Appeals (DC Cir.). From assoc. to ptnr. Steptoe & Johnson LLP, Washington, 1972—, various mgmt positions on exec. & compensation & partnership com., co-chmn. hiring com., chmn. associates com., vice chmn. Author: What Washington Said, Administration, Rhetoric, and the Vietnam War, 1949-69, 1973. Campaign ofcl. Tsongas Presdl. Campaign, Washington, 1992-93. Mem. Yale Club (bd. dirs. Washington, program chair, pres.). Avocations: carpentry, racquetball, reading. Office: Steptoe & Johnson LLP 1330 Connecticut Ave NW Washington DC 20036-1704 Office Phone: 202-429-6327. Office Fax: 202-429-3902. Business E-Mail: mkail@steptoe.com.

KAILAS, LEO GEORGE, lawyer; b. NYC, May 28, 1949; s. George and Evanthia (Skoulikas) K.; m. Merle S. Duskin; children: Arianne, George, Shirley. AB, Columbia U., 1970, JD, 1973. Bar: N.Y. 1974. Assoc. Olwine, Connelly, Chase, O'Donnell and Weyher, NYC, 1973-77; ptnr. specializing in internat., comml.-admiralty litigation Milgrim Thomajan Jacobs & Lee, PC (now Piper Rudnick LLP), NYC, 1977-2000, mem. internat. trade and litigation group, until 2000; ptnr. Reitler Brown & Rosenblatt LLC, NYC, 2000—. Mem. ABA, Assn. Bar City N.Y. (chmn. admiralty com. 1985-88). Office: Reitler Brown Rosenblatt LLC 800 3d Ave 21st Fl New York NY 10022 Office Phone: 212-209-3012. E-mail: lkailas@reitlerbrown.com.

KAILATH, THOMAS, electrical engineer, educator; b. Poona, India, June 7, 1935; arrived in US, 1957, naturalized, 1976; s. Mamman and Kunjamma (George) Kailath; m. Sarah Jacob, June 11, 1962; children: Ann, Paul, Priya, Ryan. BE, U. Poona, 1956; SM, MIT, 1959, ScD, 1961; Dr. Tek (hon.), Linkoping U., Sweden, 1990; D honoris causa (hon.), Strathclyde U., Scotland, 1992; D (hon.), U. Carlos III, Madrid, 1999; D honoris causa (hon.), U. Bordeaux, France, 2003. Comm. rschr. Jet Propulsion Labs., Pasadena, Calif., 1961-62; mem. faculty Stanford U., Calif., 1963—, prof. elec. engring., 1968—, Hitachi Am. prof. engring., 1988—2001, Hitachi Am. prof. emeritus, 2001—; dir. Info. Systems Lab., 1971-81, assoc. chmn. dept., 1981-87. Vis. prof., cons. univs., industry, govt. Author: Linear Systems, 1980, Least-Squares Estimation, 2nd edit, 1981, Linear Estimation, 2000; mem. editl. bd. various jours.; contbr. articles to profl. jours. Recipient Edn. award Am. Control Coun., 1986, Tech. Achievement and Soc. awards Signal Processing Soc. IEEE, 1989, 91, Donald G. Fink Prize award, 1996, Shannon award, 2000; Sr. Vinton Hayes fellow MIT, 1992, Guggenheim fellow, 1970, Churchill fellow, 1977, Michael fellow Weizmann Inst., Israel, 1984, Royal Soc. guest rsch. fellow, 1989, Alexander Humboldt fellow, 2003; named to Silcon Valley Engring. Hall of Fame, 2006. Fellow: IEEE (life Edn. medal 1995, Jack S. Kilby medal 2006, Medal of Honor 2007), Am. Acad. Arts and Scis., Inst. Math. Stats.; mem.: NAS, Royal Spanish Acad. Engring., Third World Acad. Scis., Soc. Indsl. and Applied Math., Am. Math. Soc., Indian Nat. Acad. Engring., Sigma Xi. Office: Info Systems Lab Stanford U 350 Serra Mall Packard Bldg 276 Stanford CA 94305-9510 Business E-Mail: kailath@stanford.edu. E-mail: profkailath@yahoo.com.

KAIM, SAMUEL C., retired psychiatrist; b. NYC, Nov. 24, 1911; s. Adolph and Nettie Kaim; m. Joan P. Kaim, Jan. 25, 1992; 1 child, Edward H. BA, Case We. U., Cleve., 1928—31; MD, U. Zwrich, Switzerland, 1931—37. Resident in psychiatry U. Zurich, Switzerland, 1937—38; pvt. practice Rock Island, Ill., 1938—50. Med. dir. Nat. Pharm. Coun., DC, 1972—75; dir. Nat. Acad. Sci., DC, 1975—80. Contbr. articles to profl. jours. Maj.1946 US Army, 1942. Mem.: NIH (mem. study sections), Am. Coll. Neuropsycho Pharmacology, Am. Psychiat. Assn. Avocation: golf.

KAIMAN, SARAH, retired physician; b. Omaha, June 10, 1915; d. Morris and Bertha Kaiman; children: Eric Koscove, Kristine Koscove. BS, U. Iowa, 1938, MD, 1940; LLB, Denver Sch. of Law, 1962. Bar: Colo. 1963, U.S. Dist. Ct. Colo. 1963, Ill. 1968; diplomate Am. Bd. Med. Examiners. Intern BethEl Hosp., Colorado Springs, Colo., 1941; pvt. practice family practice Denver, 1941—67, Thousand Oaks, Westlake Village and Ventura, Calif., 1973—84; med. officer Continental Assurance Co., Chgo., 1967—68, FDA, Washington, 1968—71, Dept. Health Svc., State of Calif., 1980—93; county physician Merced County, Calif., 1971; ret., 1993. Mem. staff Children's Meml. Hosp., St. Joseph's Hosp., Beth Israel Hosp, Gen. Rose Meml. Hosp., Denver Gen. County Hosp., Park Ave. Hosp., 1942—67, Merced Gen. Hosp., 1971—72, Westlake Cmty. Hosp., Westlake Village, 1972—73, Los Robles Hosp., Thousand Oaks, 1972—73, Simi (Calif.) Dr.'s Hosp., 1974—76, Simi Adventist Hosp., 1974—; cons. rsch. panel Med. World News, 1978; lectr., cons. in field; asst. med. dir. Continental Assurance Co., Chgo., 1967—68; med. examiner Cancer Detection Ctr., Chgo., 1969. Contbr. poems to lit. publs. Fellow: Am. Geriatrics Soc., Am. Acad. Family Physicians; mem.: AMA, LA Med. Assn., Cook County Med. Soc., Denver Med. Soc., Ill. Med. Assn., Colo. Med. Assn., Internat. Soc. Poets. Home: 6162 Calle Bodega Camarillo CA 93012 Personal E-mail: sktrust@aol.com.

KAIMOWITZ, GABE HILLEL, lawyer; b. NYC, May 5, 1935; s. Abraham and Esther (Bialogursky) K.; children: David, Beth. BS, U. Wis., 1955; MA, U. Cen. Fla., 1988; LLB, NYU, 1967. Bar: N.Y. 1969, Mich. 1971, Fla., 1987, U.S. Dist. Ct. (mid. dist.) Fla., 1987, U.S. Ct. Appeals (6th cir.) 1971, U.S. Ct. Appeals (3d cir.) 1982, U.S. Ct. Appeals (2d cir.) 1983, U.S. Ct. Appeals (11th cir.), 1989 U.S. Ct. Appeals (7th cir.) 1990, U.S. Ct. Appeals (D.C. cir.) 1998. Atty. Ctr. Social Welfare, Politics and Law, NYC, 1967-70; sr. atty. Mich. Legal Services, Detroit, 1971-79; assoc. counsel P.R. Legal Def., NYC, 1980-84; exec. dir. Greater Orlando (Fla.) Legal Svcs., 1985-86; equal opportunity investigator Alachua County, Fla., 1999—2002; pvt. practice. Atty. Civil Rights Movement Vets. Orgn.; lect., adj. prof. various univs. Contbr. articles to books; author poems. Served with US Army, 1956-57, Res. 1958-62. Smith fellow, 1970-71, Legal Services Corp. fellow, 1979-80. Mem. N.Y. State Bar Assn., Fla. Bar Assn. Jewish. Home: 4411 SW 34th St Gainesville FL 32608-2562 Office: PO Box 140119 Gainesville FL 32614-0119 Office Phone: 352-375-2670. Personal E-mail: gabehk@aol.com.

KAIMOWITZ, JEFFREY HUGH, librarian; b. NYC, Nov. 3, 1942; AB, Johns Hopkins U., 1964; PhD in Classics, U. Cin., 1970; MS in Libr. Svc., Columbia U., 1976. Asst. prof. Miami U. Ohio, Oxford, 1969—73; libr. trainee N.Y. Pub. Libr., NYC, 1973—77; curator Watkinson Libr. Trinity Coll., Hartford, Conn., 1977—2001, curator Enders Ornithology Collection, 1994—, head libr., 2001—. Home: 27 Stoneham Dr West Hartford CT 06117 Office: Trinity College Watkinson Library 300 Summit St Hartford CT 06106-3186 Office Phone: 860-297-2266.

KAIMSTHORN, LORD RENFREW OF See RENFREW, ANDREW

KAIN, KAREN ALEXANDRIA, ballet dancer; b. Hamilton, Ont., Can., Mar. 28, 1951; d. Charles Alexander and Winifred (Kelly) K.; m. Ross Petty, May, 1983. Student, Nat. Ballet Sch., Toronto; Litt.D. (hon.), York U., Toronto, 1977; other hon. degrees, U. B.C., McMaster U., Trent U. Mem. corps de ballet Nat. Ballet Can., Toronto, 1969-70, prin. dancer, 1970—2004, artistic dir., 2005—. Pres. Canada's Dancer Transition Ctr. Repertoire includes (debut with Nat. Ballet of Can.) Swan Lake, 1970, La Fille Mal Gardée, Giselle, Sleeping Beauty; Glen Tetley's Alice, La Ronde, Daphnis and Chlöe, Tagore; Eliot Feld's Echo; Roland Petit's Nana, Coppelia, Tales of Hoffman; James Kudelka's Musings, The Miraculous Mandarin, The Actress; John Neumeier's Now and Then; Frederick Ashston's Month in the Country; guest artist with Bolshoi Ballet, London Festival Ballet, Feld Ballet, Stuttgart Ballet, Vienna State Opera Ballet, Ballet National de Marseille, others; ptnrs. with Rudolf Nureyev, Frank Augustyn; TV appearances include The Karen Kain Super Spl., CBCV, 1978; author: (with Stephen Godfrey and Penelope Doob Reid) Movement Never Lies: An Autobiography, 1994. Decorated Order Can., 1977; recipient Silver medal Internat. Competition, Moscow, 1973 Mem. Canadian Actors Equity Assn., Assn. Radio and TV Artists. Office: National Ballet of Canada 470 Queens Quay W Toronto ON Canada M5V 3K4*

KAINE, TIMOTHY MICHAEL, governor; b. St. Paul, Feb. 26, 1958; s. Al and Kathleen Kaine; m. Anne Holton; children: Annella, Woody, Nat. AB summa cum laude, U. Mo., 1979; JD cum laude, Harvard U., 1983. Law clk. to judge R. Lanier Anderson III U.S. Ct. Appeals (11th cir.); mem. law firm; mem. city council City of Richmond, 1994—98, mayor, 1998—2001; lt. gov. State of Va., 2002—06, gov., 2006—. Mem. local and state govt. adv. com. FCC. Contbr. articles to profl. jours. Bd. dirs. Historic Jackson Ward Found. Recipient Pro Bono Public award, Richmond Bar Assn., 1995. Mem. ABA, Va. Bar Assn., Richmond Bar Assn. Democrat. Roman Catholic. Office: Office of Gov PO Box 1475 Richmond VA 23218 also: Patrick Henry Bldg 3rd Fl 111 E Broad St Richmond VA 23219 Office Phone: 804-786-2211. Office Fax: 804-371-6351.*

KAINEN, MICHAEL ROLAND, lawyer, state representative; b. Simsbury, Conn., Dec. 25, 1965; m. Michelle M. Newman; 2 children. BA, U. Conn., 1988; JD, MSL, U. Vt., 1992. Bar: Vt. 1993, NH. Atty.; ranking mem., House Judiciary vice-chair, judicial rules and judicial retention coms. Vt. State Ho. Reps., 1999—. Mem. Hartford Housing Authority. Mem.: ABA, Vt. Bar Assn., N.H. Bar Assn., Am. Inns of Ct. Republican. Episcopalian. Home: PO Box 919 51 Marsh Family Rd White River Junction VT 05001 Office Phone: 802-296-2100.

KAISCH, KENNETH BURTON, psychologist, priest; b. Detroit, Aug. 29, 1948; s. Kenneth R. Kaisch and Marjorie F. (Howe) Bourke; m. Suzanne Carol LePrevost, Aug. 31, 1969 (div. May 21, 2004); 1 child, Samuel; m. Julia Ellen Emerson, Feb. 4, 2006. BA, San Francisco State U., 1972; MDiv, Ch. Divinity Sch. Pacific, 1976; MS, Utah State U., 1983, PhD in Clin. Psychology, 1986. Ordained deacon Episcopal Ch., 1976, priest, 1977; lic. clin. psychologist, Calif.; diplomate Nat. Inst. Sports Psychologists. Intern local parish, 1973-76; ordinand tng. program Ch. of the Good Shepherd, Ogden, Utah, 1976-77; pastor St. Francis' Episc. Ch., Moab, Utah, 1977-80, St. John's Episc. Ch., Logan, Utah, 1980-84; psychol. asst. Peter Ebersole, Ph.D., Fullerton, Calif., 1984-86; intern in clin. psychology Patton State Hosp., Calif., 1985-86; psychol. asst. Ronald Wong Jue, Ph.D., Fullerton and Newport Beach, Calif., 1986-88; pvt. practice clin. psychologist Calif., 1988—; clin. dir. Anxiety Clinic, Fullerton, 1993—2003, Consultants for Change, 1994—. Exec. dir. Contemplative Congress, Fullerton, 1988-91, Inner Peace Conf., 1995-97; founder, pres. OneHeart, 1986-98, Contemplative Visions, Fullerton, 1990-2000; supply priest Episc. Diocese of L.A.; invited lectr. Acad. Sch. Profl. Psychology, Moscow, 1992, 93, Moscow Med. Acad., 1998; sports psychologist UCLA Men's and Women's Golf Teams, 2004-2005. Co-author: Fundamentals of Psychotherapy, 1984, Developing Your Feel for Golf, 1998; author: Finding God: A Handbook of Christian Meditation, 1994, The Mental Golf Inventory, 1998, Hit it With Your Best Shot: How to Play Golf in the Zone, 2000; co-editor: God in Russia: The Challenge of Freedom, 1999, Turning the Heart to God, 2001; contbr. articles to profl. jours. Active St. Andrew's Episc. Ch., Fullerton. Mem. APA, Calif. Psychol. Assn., Anxiety Disorders Assn. Am., Nat. Register of Health Svc. Providers in Psychology, Phi Kappa Phi, Rotary (past bd. dirs., past officer). Episcopalian. Office: 733 E Chapman Fullerton CA 92831 Home Phone: 714-390-0601; Office Phone: 714-992-4656.

KAISER, ALBERT FARR, manufacturing executive; b. NYC, May 14, 1933; s. Albert Louis and Lucille (Daggett) K.; m. Joy E. White, Sept. 16, 1961; children— Elizabeth Ann, Albert Farr. BA, Hamilton Coll., Clinton, NY, 1955; MBA, Harvard U., 1960. With acquisitons dept. AMF Inc., 1960-61; with data processing div. IBM Corp., 1961-84; with Sperry and Hutchinson Co., 1974-82; pres. The Gunlocke Co., Inc., 1977-79, pres. promotional services div., also chmn. motivation and travel div., 1979-80; corp. exec. v.p. Sperry and Hutchinson, Inc., NYC, 1980-82; investment banker J.J. Lowrey & Co., NYC, 1983-84; pres. ABB Power Distbn. Inc., 1984-92; ret., 1992—. Served to lt. (j.g.) USNR, 1955-58. Mem.: Hamilton Coll. Alumni Assn. (former pres. Westchester County chpt.), Key Royale Club (Holmes Beach, Fla.), Champlain Country Club (St. Albans, Vt.), Bradenton Country Club, Fox Meadow Tennis Club (Scarsdale). Republican. Mem. Reformed Ch. Am. Home: 105 Sunset Ln Holmes Beach FL 34217 Home (Summer): 25 Camp Rich Rd Milton VT 05468

KAISER, ALLEN BERNARD, health facility administrator; b. Columbia, SC, 1942; BA, MD, Vanderbilt U., 1967. Intern Johns Hopkins Hosp., Balt., 1967—68, resident internal medicine, 1968—69, Vanderbilt U. Hosp., 1971—72, fellow, 1972—74; (former) hosp. epidemiologist St. Thomas Hosp., chief divsn. infectious diseases, chief dept. medicine; vice-chmn. clin. affairs Vanderbilt U. Hosp., prof. medicine, chief of staff, 2004—; chief med. officer Vanderbilt U. Med. Ctr., 2004—. Mem.: Soc. Healthcare Epidemiology Am. (past pres.). Office: Vanderbilt Med Ctr D 3100 Med Ctr N Nashville TN 37232

KAISER, ANN CHRISTINE, magazine editor; b. Milw., Apr. 7, 1947; d. Herbert Walter and Annette G. (Werych) Gohlke; m. Louis Dan Kaiser; children: Richard L., Michael D. BS in Journalism, Northwestern U., 1969. Reporter Waco (Tex.) Tribune-Herald, 1969-71; editor Country Woman, Greendale, Wis., 1971—, Taste of Home, Greendale, 1993—. Named among People of the Yr., Milw. Mag., 1998. Lutheran. Avocations: sailing, tennis, golf, travel. Office: Reiman Media Group 5400 S 60th St Greendale WI 53129-1404

KAISER, FRAN ELIZABETH, endocrinologist, gerontologist; b. NYC, Dec. 6, 1949; d. Philip Francis and Bronia (Weiss) K. BS, CCNY, 1970; MD, N.Y. Med. Coll., NYC, 1974. Diplomate Am. Bd. Internal Medicine, Am. Bd. Geriat. Intern Beth Israel Med. Ctr., NYC, 1974-75, resident to chief resident, 1975-78; fellow in endocrinology and metabolism U. Minn., Mpls., 1978-81, instr. dept. medicine, 1980-81, asst. prof., 1981-86; asst. prof. in residence UCLA Sch. Medicine, 1986-89; assoc. prof. medicine St. Louis U., 1989-94, prof., 1994-97, assoc. dir. divsn. geriatric medicine, 1989-97, prof., 1994-97; sr. regional med. dir. Merck & Co., Inc., Irving, Tex., 1997—2003, exec. med. dir., 2003, 2005—; CEO, Kaiser and Assocs. Cons., 2004—05. Adj. prof. medicine St. Louis U, 1997-; chief sect. endocrinology and metabolism Dept. Internal Medicine, St. Paul Ramsey Med. Ctr./U. Minn. Hosps., St. Paul, 1981-86; John A. Hartford Geriatric Faculty Devel. award scholar Hartford Found., NYC/UCLA Sch. Medicine, 1986-87; chief geriatric medicine Olive View Med. Ctr./UCLA San Fernando Valley Program, Sylmar, Calif., 1987-89; med. dir. Hosp. Based Home Care, VA Med. Ctr., Sepulveda, 1987-89; clin. prof. medicine U. Tex. Southwestern Med. Sch., Dallas, 1999-. Former mem. editl. bd.: Jour. Clin. Endocrinology and Metabolism, ad hoc reviewer: Endocrinology, Jour. AMA, Jour. Am. Geriatrics Soc., past mem. editl. bd.: Am. Geriatric Soc., Internat. Medicine Bull., cons. editor: Am. Health Mag.; contbr. articles to profl. jours. Grantee NIH, 1980-81, 97, Genetech, 1987-89, Syntex Corp. 1990-92, Hoechst-Roussel, 1992-94, Bur. Health Professions, 1991-97, VIVUS, 1993-97, Merck, 1994-97, Upjohn, 1995-97. Fellow: Am. Geriatrics Soc. (past mem. editl. bd. Internal Medicine Bull. , Jour. Geriatric Nephrology & Urology), Gerontol. Soc. Am.; mem.: AAAS, Am. Assn. Home Care Physicians, N.Y. Acad. Sci., Am. Fedn.Clin. Rsch., Endocrine Soc. (mem. women in endocrinology group), Am. Diabetes Assn., Alpha Omega Alpha. Achievements include research in hormonal changes with aging, studies of therapy of erectile dysfunction, testosterone, estrogen and frailty and women's health and sexuality. Office: 3510 Edgewater Dr Dallas TX 75205 Office Phone: 214-686-6008. Personal E-mail: Kaiserf@sbcglobal.net.

KAISER, GEORGE B., corporate financial executive; b. 1943; s. Herman George Kaiser; m. Betty Eudene, 1965 (dec. 2002); 3 children; m. Myra Kaiser. BS, MBA, Harvard U. Chmn. BOK Fin., Tulsa; prin. owner Kaiser-Francis Oil Co., 1969—, Fountains Continuum of Care, Inc. Founder Tulsa Cmty. Found., 1998, George Kaiser Family Found. Named one of Forbes Richest Americans, 1995—, World's Richest People, Forbes Mag., 2001—. Office: Bok Fin Bank of Okla Tower PO Box 2300 Tulsa OK 74192*

KAISER, LARRY ROBERT, thoracic surgeon; b. St. Louis, Aug. 31, 1952; s. Patricia Glaser; m. Lindy Snider; children: Jonathan, Jeffrey, Daniel. BS, Tulane U., 1973, MD, 1977. Diplomate Am. Bd. Thoracic Surgery, Am. Bd. Surgery. Resident in surgery UCLA, 1977—83, fellow in surg. oncology, 1979—81; resident in thoracic and cardiovasc. surgery U. Toronto, Ont., Canada, 1983—85; asst. attending surgeon Meml. Sloan-Kettering Cancer Ctr., 1985—88; asst. and assoc. prof. surgery Washington U. Sch. Medicine, 1988—91; prof. and chief thoracic surgery U. Pa. Sch. Medicine, Phila., 1991—2001, John Rhea Barton prof. and chmn. dept. surgery, 2001—; surgeon-in-chief U. Pa. Health Sys., Phila., 2006—. Elected mem. Inst. Medicine, Nat. Acad. Sci., 2005. Bd. dir. Thoracic Surgery Found. for Edn. and Rsch. Fellow: Am. Coll. Surgeons; mem.: Am. Bd. Thoracic Surgery (dir.), Am. Bd. Surgery (dir.,), Soc. Thoracic Surgeons, Am. Assn. for Thoracic Surgery, Soc. Clinical Surgery, Halsted Soc., Fleischner Soc., Soc. Univ. Surgeons, Am. Surgical Assn. Home: 408 Barbara Lane Bryn Mawr PA 19010 Office: Hosp of U of Pa 3400 Spruce St 4 Silverstein Philadelphia PA 19104 Home Phone: 610-527-0394; Office Phone: 215-662-7539. Business E-Mail: larry.kaiser@uphs.upenn.edu.

KAISER, LOUISE MARTIN, elementary school educator; b. Anderson, SC, Nov. 1, 1948; d. Charles Luther Martin and Helen Brown Whitaker; m. Paul Kaiser III, June 15, 1968; children: Paul IV, Ashley. AA, Anderson U., SC, 1968; BA in Elem. Edn., Clemson U., SC, 1976, M in Elem. Edn., 1992. Assoc. caseworker S.C. Dept. Social Svcs., Anderson, SC, 1968—71; math, lang. arts tchr. Anderson Sch. Dist. #5, SC, 1977—79, third grade tchr., 1980—85, fourth grade tchr., 1986—98, third grade tchr., 1999—. Grade chairperson South Font Sch., Anderson, SC, 1983—88, advisory chairperson, 1985—88; advisory com. McLees Elem., Anderson, SC, 2000—. Nominating com. First Bapt. Ch., Anderson, SC, 1986—89. Mem.: United Daughters of Confederacy (chaplain 1970—), DAR (good citizens chairperson 1987—89), S.C. Edn. Assn., NEA, Anderson Music Club. Baptist. Avocations: writing, travel, plays, sports. Home: 101 Roxbury Ct Anderson SC 29625 Office: McLees Elem Sch 4900 Dobbins Bridge Rd Anderson SC 29626 Personal E-mail: louisekaiser@anderson5.net.

KAISER, MARTIN, editor-in-chief; b. Milw., Oct. 11, 1950; Sports editor Chicago Sun-Times; assoc. mng. editor Baltimore Sun; v.p. & mng. editor Milw. Journal Sentinel, 1994—97, sr. v.p. & editor, 1997—. Mem.: Am. Soc. Newspaper Editors (chmn. readership issues com. 2003—, treas. designate 2005—06, treas. 2006—07, bd. dir., sec. 2007—08). Office: Milwaukee Journal Sentinel PO Box 371 Milwaukee WI 53201-0371 Office Phone: 414-224-2345. E-mail: mkaiser@journalsentinel.com.*

KAISER, MICHAEL M., performing company executive; b. NYC, 1953; s. Harold and Marion Kaiser. B magna cum laude, Brandeis U.; M in Mgmt., MIT. Rsch. economist for Wassily Leontief; past. owner Kaiser Assoc.; past gen. mgr. Kansas City Ballet, 1985; past. exec. dir. Ailvin Ailey Dance Theater Found.; past assoc. dir. Pierpont Morgan Libr.; past exec. dir. Am. Ballet Theatre, Royal Opera House, 1999—2001; pres. John F. Kennedy Ctr. for Performing Arts, Washington, 2001—. Cons. arts orgn.; adj. prof. arts adminstrn. NYU; lectr. U. Witwatersrand, Johannesburg. Author: Understanding the Competition: A Practical Guide of Competitive Analysis, 1981, Developing Industry Strategies: A Practical Guide of Industry Analysis, 1983, Strategic Planning in the Arts: A Practical Guide, 1995. Achievements include arranged, in conjunction with the U.S. State Dept., the historic concert of the Iraqi Nati. Symphony Orch. with the Nat. Symphony Orch., Kennedy Ctr., Dec. 2003. Office: John F Kennedy Ctr Performing Arts 2700 F St NW Washington DC 20566

KAISER, NINA IRENE, healthcare consultant; b. San Diego, Nov. 29, 1953; d. Louis Frederick and Mary Elizabeth (Wright) K.; children: Kellen Anne Kaiser, Ethan Andrew Kaiser-Klimist. BSN, BA in Women Studies, San Francisco State U., 1980; MBA, U. Phoenix, 2001. RN, Calif. RN Calif. Pacific Med. Ctr., San Francisco, 1980-81, Ralph K. Davies Med. Ctr., San Francisco, 1982-85, Planned Parenthood, San Francisco, 1985-86, Visiting Nurses and Hospice, San Francisco, 1986-88; RN supr. St. Mary's Home Care, San Francisco, 1991-93; RN dir. St. Vincent's Homecare and Hospice, Fremont, Calif., 1993-94; aux. dir. Home Health Link, San Leandro, Calif., 1994-99; mgmt. cons. Kaiser Home Health, Oakland, Calif., 1999—2002, mgr., 2003—. Regional coun. chair San Francisco Bay Area, 1999. Pres. Daus. of Bilitis, San Francisco, 1977-78; founding mem. Buena Vista Lesbian and Gay Parents Assn., San Francisco, 1985; treas., bd. dirs. Holladay Ave. Homeowners Assn., San Francisco, 1984-96; bd. dirs. Midrasha High Sch., Berkeley, Calif., 1996. With USN, 1971-74. Personal E-mail: missnynak@aol.com.

KAISER, ROBERT A., telecommunications industry executive; CFO Mobile Sys. Southwestern Bell, 1987—96; CFO SkyTel, 1996—99, CEO, CFO, 2000; CEO WorldCom Broadband Solutions Group, 2000—01, MobileStar Network Corp., 2001; sr. v.p. CellStar Corp, Carrollton, Tex., 2001—, CFO, 2001—, treas., 2001—, pres., 2003—, chmn., CEO, 2004—.

KAISER, ROBERT LEE, retired engineering executive; b. Louisville, June 28, 1935; s. Harlan K. and LaVerne (Peterson) K.; m. Margaret Siler; children: Robin Lee, Robert Lee. Student, U. Louisville, 1953—54, U. Ky., 1958—61; BSME, Ashbourne U., 1977, MSME, 1979. Registered profl. engr., Fla., Ky., 1965. Draftsman, designer E.R. Ronald & Assocs., Louisville, 1953-54, Thompson-Kissell Co., 1954-56; estimator, engr. George Pridemore & Son, Lexington, Ky., 1956-58; designer, engr., supr. Frankel & Curtis, Lexington, 1958-61; engr. Hugh Dillehay & Assocs., 1961-65; owenr, engr., operator K-Svc., Inc., 1965-74; project engr. Mason & Hanger, Silas Mason Co., Inc., 1974-77; v.p. Webb-Dillehay Design Group, 1977-81; pres. Kaiser-Taulbee Assocs., Inc., Lexington, Louisville, Orlando, Fla., ret., 2000. Past chmn., pres. and bd. dirs. Opportunity Workshop Lexington; vis. lectr. mech. engring. and Coll. Architecture, U. Ky.; mem., past chmn. Ky. State Bd. of Registration for Engrs, and Land Surveyors, Ky. Task Force to Develop New Engring. and Surveying Laws; charter commn. merger Lexington-Fayette County govts.; mem. Ky. Airport Zoning Comsn., mem. Gov.'s Task Force on Ednl. Constrn. Criteria; past trustee, chmn. Humana Hosp., Lexington, Aviation Mus. Ky. Chmn. storm water task force Lake County Water Authority, Fla.; mem. Harris Chain of Lake Restoration Coun.; mem., chmn. adv. com. Cmty. Redevelopment Adminstrn. Mem. ASME, NSPE, ASHRAE (past pres. local chpt.), Ky. Soc. Profl. Engrs. (life), Fla. Engring. Soc. (v.p.), Mt. Dora C. of C. (bd. dirs.), Rotary Club Mt. Dora (pres. 2007—). Episcopalian. Home: 1380 Skyline Dr Tavares FL 32778-2533 Office Phone: 352-787-1322. Personal E-mail: rmk22578@earthlink.net. Business E-Mail: RLK62835@aol.com.

KAISER, ROY, performing company executive; b. Perth Amboy, NJ; Studied ballet with, Karen Irvin; student, San Francisco Ballet Sch., Sch. Pa. Ballet. With Pa. Ballet, 1979, prin. dancer, 1980-92, asst. ballet master, 1987-92, ballet master, 1992, assoc. artistic dir., 1993, interim artistic dir., 1994-95, Ruth and A. Morris Williams, Jr. artistic dir., 1995—. Featured artists (with brothers) N.Y. World's Fair and throughout the U.S.; performer on TV with Wayne Newton Music Carnival, Cleve.; performer on TV NBC-TV's Kraft Music Hall. Leading classical roles include Siegfried in Swan Lake, Franz in Coppelia, the Cavalier in The Nutcracker, Bolero, Symphonic Etudes, A Musical Offering, other prin. roles include George Balanchine's Symphony in C, Western Symphony, Symphony in Three Movements, Iago in The Moor's Pavane, Franklin Ct. Office: Pennsylvania Ballet 1101 S Broad St Philadelphia PA 19147-4410 E-mail: rkaiser@paballet.org.*

KAISER, SUZANNE BILLO, investment banker, writer; b. Bronxville, NY, Apr. 9, 1948; d. Otto Emile and Barbara (Leggett) Billo; divorced; 1 child, Kate. Student, U. Lausanne, Switzerland, 1968, U. Paris, 1969; BA in Politics with honors, Hollins Coll., 1971; MBA, Georgetown U., 1997; MS, Columbia U. Sch Journalism, 1999. Staff mem. U.S. Congresswoman Margaret Heckler, Washington, 1971-72; adminstrv. officer internat. divsn. Kidder, Peabody & Co., Inc., NYC, 1980-86; v.p., corp. sec. Concord Internat. Investments, NYC, 1986—2004; fin. advisor Morgan Stanley, Rutland, Vt., 2004—06; v.p., portfolio mgr. K.A. MacGuire and Co., LLC, Darien, Conn., 2006. Bd. dirs. Coun. Jr. Leagues Westchester, 1976-77, Bronxville (N.Y.) Mid. Sch. Coun., 1989-90, Bronxville Pub. Libr., 1990-95; trustee, Vt. Hist. Soc., 2005—; mem. H.S. Coun., Bronxville Sch., 1992-93; mem. coun. Women N.Y. Bot. Garden, 2002—. Mem. Soc. Profl. Journalists, Pen and Brush, Hollins Club of N.Y., Georgetown U. Club (N.Y.C.).

KAISER, WALTER, language educator; b. Bellevue, Ohio, May 31, 1931; AB magna cum laude, Harvard Coll., 1954; PhD, Harvard U., 1960. Allston Burr sr. tutor Eliot House Harvard U., 1957-58, from instr. to assoc. prof. English, comparative lit. Cambridge, Mass., 1960-62, prof. English, comparative lit., 1969—, chmn. dept., 1969-75, 82-85. Mem. coms. degrees in history and lit. Harvard U., 1960—, Faculty coun., 1971-74, libr. com., 1971-74; dep. dir. Villa I Tatti, Florence, 1971-86, dir. 1988-2002. Author: Praisers of Folly: Erasmus, Rabelais, Shakespeare, 1964, Essays of Montaigne, 1964; co-author Program in Literature and the Arts for the Core Curriculum, 1977; transl.: (with intro.) Three Secret Poems, (George Seferis), 1969, Alexis (Marguerite Yourcenar), 1984, Two Lives and a Dream (Marguerite Yourcenar), That Mighty Sculptor, Time (Marguerite Yourcenar), 1992; mem. edit. bd. Studies in English Lit., 1977-88; editor-in-chief I Tatti Studies: Essays in the Renaissance, 1988-2002; editor (with M. Mallon) On Artists and Art Historians: Selected Book Reviews of John Pope Hennessy, 1994; author numerous poems; contbr. articles to profl. jours Chmn. ad hoc vis. com. to Addison Gallery Am. Art, 1978; trustee Michael Rockefeller Meml. Fellowship, 1965-68, 69-70, Rockefeller Family Fund, 1973-79, Mus. Fine Arts, Boston, 1978-88, Bogliasco Found., 2001-07; v.p. Somerset House Art History Found.; bd. dirs. Philip H. Rosenbach Found., 1974-78. Fulbright fellow U. Paris, 1954-55; Tower fellow Ecole Normale Supérieure Paris, 1955-56; fellow to Rome Am. Coun. Learned Socs., 1964-65; Walter Channing Cabot fellow Fac. Arts. and Scis., 1977-78. Mem. PEN, Boston Athenaeum, Am. Comparative Lit. Assn., Renaissance Soc. Am., Signet Soc. (assoc.), Modern Greek Studies Assn., Shakespeare Assn. Am., Coun. Fgn. Rels., Knickerbocker Club, Somerset Club, Harvard Club, Old Salopian, Boston Libr. Soc., Century Assn., Phi Beta Kappa. Home and Office: 25 Sutton Pl S Apt 20M New York NY 10022 Personal E-mail: walter_kaiser@harvard.edu.

KAISERLIAN, PENELOPE JANE, publishing executive; b. Paisley, Scotland, Oct. 19, 1943; came to U.S., 1956; d. W. Norman and Magdalene Jeanette (Houlder) Hewson; m. Arthur Kaiserlian, June 29, 1968; 1 child, Christian. BA, U. Exeter, Eng., 1965. Copywriter, sales rep. Pergamon Press, Elmsford, NY, 1965-68; exhibits mgr. Plenum Pub., NYC, 1968-69; asst. mktg. mgr. U. Chgo. Press, 1969-76, mktg. mgr., 1976-83, assoc. dir., 1983-2001; dir. U. Va. Press, 2001—. Mem. Soc. for Scholarly Pub., Assn. Am. Univ. Presses (pres. 2006—07), Soc. History Early Am. Republic, Assn. for Documentary Editing, Colonnade Club. Office: Univ Va Press PO Box 400318 Charlottesville VA 22904-4318

KAISH, LUISE CLAYBORN, sculptor, painter, educator; b. Atlanta, Sept. 8, 1925; d. Harry and Elsa Meyers; m. Morton Kaish, Aug. 15, 1948; 1 child, Melissa. BFA magna cum laude, Syracuse U., 1946, MFA, 1951; student, Escuela de Pintura y Escultura, Escuela de las Artes del Libro, Taller Grafico, Mexico, 1946-47. Artist-in-residence Dartmouth Coll., 1974; prof. sculpture and painting, 1980-93, chmn. div. painting and sculpture Columbia U., 1980-86, prof. emerita, 1993; vis. artist U. Wash., Seattle, Battelle seminars and study program, Seattle, 1979; artist-in-residence U. Haifa, Israel, 1985. One-man shows include Meml. Art Gallery, Rochester, N.Y., 1954, Sculpture Ctr., N.Y.C., 1955, 58, Staempfli Gallery, N.Y.C., 1968, 81, 84, 87, 88, Minn. Mus. Art, St. Paul, 1969, Jewish Mus., N.Y.C., 1973, U. Ark., 1990, The Century Assn., 1998; exhibited (with Morton Kaish), Rochester Meml. Art Gallery, 1958, USIS, Rome, 1973, Dartmouth Coll., 1974, Oxford Gallery, Rochester, 1988; represented in permanent collections Whitney Mus. Am. Art, N.Y.C., Met. Mus. Art, N.Y.C., Jewish Mus., N.Y.C., Export Khleb, Moscow, Minn. Mus. Art, Gen. Mills Corp., Minn., Rochester Meml. Art Gallery, Smithsonian Instn., Nat. Mus. Am. Art, Washington, also numerous pvt. collections, commns., Syracuse U., Temple B'rith Kodesh, Rochester, Temple Israel, Westport, Conn., Holy Trinity Mission Sem., Silver Springs, Md., Temple Beth Shalom, Wilmington, Del., Beth-El Synagogue Ctr., New Rochelle, N.Y., Temple B'nai Abraham, Essex City, N.J., Continental Grain Co., N.Y. Trustee Am. Acad. in Rome, 1973-81, mem. exec. com., 1975-81, trustee emerita, 1994; trustee St. Gaudens Found., 1978-90, mem. exec. com., 1980-90. Recipient awards Everson Mus., Syracuse, 1947, awards Rochester Meml. Art Gallery, 1951, awards Ball State U., 1963, awards Ch. World Service, 1960, awards Council for Arts in Westchester, 1974, Emily Lowe award, 1956, Audubon Artists gold medal, 1963, Honor award AIA, 1975, Arents Pioneer medal, Syracuse U., 1989; Louis Comfort Tiffany grantee, 1951; Guggenheim fellow, 1959; Rome prize fellow Am. Acad. in Rome, 1970-72 Mem. Nat. Acad. Design, The Century Assn., Eta Pi Upsilon. Address: Kaish Studios 610 W End Ave # 9-a New York NY 10024-1605 Office Phone: 212-595-6815. Business E-Mail: lk4@columbia.edu.

KAISH, MORTON, artist, educator; b. Newark, Jan. 8, 1927; s. Morris and Sophie K.; m. Luise H. Meyers, Aug. 15, 1948; 1 dau., Melissa. BFA, Syracuse U., 1949; postgrad., Academie de la Grande Chaumiere, Paris, 1951, Istituto d' Arte, Florence, Italy, 1952, Accademia delle Belle Arti, Rome, 1957. Vis. critic Parsons Sch. Design, NYC, 1966-70, Phila. Coll. Art, 1983; mem. faculty Art Students League, NYC, 1974—; guest critic Sch. Visual Arts, NYC, 1967; vis. prof. Queens Coll., Flushing, NY, 1979; vis. artist U. Wash., Seattle, 1979; fellow MacDowell Colony, 1976; artist-in-residence Dartmouth Coll., 1974, U. Haifa, Israel, 1985; prof. Fashion Inst. Tech., SUNY, NYC, 1973—; vis. artist Susquehanna U., 1985; dir. Carl Fischer Mus. Instrument Co., 1964-70. Vis. artist Columbia U., N.Y.C., 1986, Boston U., 1987. One-man shows include Manhattanville Coll., Purchase, N.Y., 1955, Rochester (N.Y.) Meml. Art Gallery, 1955, Guild Hall, Easthampton, L.I., 1969, U.S. Info. Service, Rome, 1973, Dartmouth Coll., Hanover, N.H., 1974, Staempfli Gallery, N.Y.C., 1964, 67, 71, 73, 79, 83, 86, 89, Oxford Gallery, Rochester, N.Y., 1989, Century Assn., N.Y., 1989, Hollis Taggart Galleries, Washington, 1993, N.Y.C., 1996; group shows Mus. Galleria 11 Torcoliere, Rome, 1957, Barone Gallery, N.Y.C., 1959, Art Inst. Chgo., 1964, Sheldon Meml. Art Gallery, Lincoln, Nebr., 1964, U. Nebr., Lincoln, 1964, Krannert Art Mus., U. Ill., Urbana, 1965, 68, Herron Mus. Art, Indpls., 1965, Mary Washington Coll., Fredericksburg, Va., 1965, Am. Acad. Arts and Letters, N.Y.C., 1966, Pa. Acad. Fine Arts, Phila., 1966, Ark. Art Ctr., Little Rock, 1966, Whitney Mus. Am. Art, N.Y.C., 1966, Finch Coll. Mus. Art, N.Y.C., 1966, N.J. State Mus., Trenton, 1966, Krannert Art Mus., 1968, Kent (Ohio) State U., 1970, U.S. Info. Service, Rome, 1972, New Sch. Social Research, N.Y.C., 1973, Child Hassam Purchase Fund Exhbn., N.Y.C., 1973; invitational exhbns. Child Hassam Purchase Fund, 1975, Am. Acad. Arts and Letters, 1975, Drawings U.S.A., 1975, Minn. Mus. Art, St. Paul, 1975, Springfield Art Mus., 1975, Springfield Mus. Art, Mo., 1975, Galerie Brusberg, Berlin, W.Ger., 1980, Taft Mus., Cin., 1981, NAD, N.Y.C., 1983, 85, 89, 91; represented in permanent collections Met. Mus. Art, N.Y.C., Whitney Mus. Am. Art, N.Y.C., Bklyn. Mus., Nat. Mus. Art, Smithsonian Instn., Washington, Brit. Mus., London, The Fitzwilliam Mus., Cambridge, Guild Hall, Easthampton, N.Y., Williams Coll., Williamstown. Mass., Syracuse U., N.Y., Swarthmore Coll., Indpls. Mus. Art, U. Mich. Mus. Art., Guilford Coll., Greensboro, N.C., Rochester (N.Y.) Meml. Art Gallery, Bates Coll., Lewiston, Maine, New Britain (Conn.) Mus. Am. Art, Newark Mus., N.J., Butler Inst. Am. Art, Youngstown, Ohio. Recipient SUNY Rsch. Found. award, 1983, William Ward Ranger Fund purchase award, 1983, 85, Gervasi award, 1985, Disting. Alumni award for Achievement in the Visual Arts Syracuse U., 1989, Benjamin Altman prize, 1989, Andrew Carnegie prize, 1992, Adolph and Clara Obrig prize, 2003, Benjamin West Clinedinst medal achievement of exceptional artistic merit, 2006, Alfred Easton Poor award, 2007; Faculty Exch. scholar SUNY, 1987. Mem. NAD (corr. sec., William A. Paton prize 1983), Century Assn., Artists' Choice Mus. (bd. artists), Artists' Fellowship (trustee, v.p.). Address: 610 W End Ave New York NY 10024-1605 Office Phone: 212-595-6815. Business E-Mail: lk4@columbia.edu.

KAJI, AKIRA, microbiology scientist, educator; b. Tokyo, Jan. 13, 1930; arrived in U.S., 1954; s. Kiichi and Chiyo (Hanai) K.; m. Hideko Katayama, Aug. 22, 1958; children: Kenneth, Eugene, Naomi, Amy. BS, Tokyo U., 1953; PhD, Johns Hopkins U., 1958; MS (hon.), U. Pa., 1973. Rsch. fellow Johns Hopkins Hosp., Balt., 1958-59; guest investigator Rockefeller U., NYC, 1959; rsch. assoc. microbiology Vanderbilt Med. Sch., Nashville, 1959-62; vis. scientist Oak Ridge (Tenn.) Nat. Lab., 1962-63; assoc. U. Pa. Med. Sch., Phila., 1963-64, asst. prof. microbiology, 1964-67, assoc. prof., 1967-72, prof., 1972—. Permanent mem. bd. sci. councilors Nat. Eye Inst., Bethesda, Md., 1987-92; prof., chair Tokyo U. Faculty Pharm. Scis., 1972-73; vis. prof. Kyoto U. Virus Rsch. Inst., 1985. Contbr. scientific papers over 200 articles to profl. jours. Recipient Fulbright-Smith-Mundt award, 1954, Helen Hay Whitney award, 1964-69, John Simmon Guggenheim award, 1972-73, Fogarty Internat. Sr. award, 1985-86. Mem. Am. Soc. Biol. Chemistry and Molecular Biology, Am. Soc. Cell Biology, Am. Soc. Microbiology, Am. Soc. Chemistry. Avocations: ice dancing, swimming. Office: U Pa Sch Medicine Dept Microbiology Johnson Pavilion Philadelphia PA 19104 Business E-Mail: kaji@mail.med.upenn.edu.

KAJITANI, MOTOHISA, sociology educator; b. Kamioka, Gifu, Japan, May 8, 1937; s. Miyokichi and Nui (Taguchi) K.; m. Yoko Shimizu, Nov. 1969; 1 child, Kuri BA, Tokyo U. & Sch. Journalism, 1961; Diploma in Social Sci., U. Tokyo, 1961; MA, Kyoto U., Japan, 1964. Lectr. Meijo U., Nagoya, Japan, 1964-69, prof., 1976—, chmn. libr., 1991-2001, univ. prof. grad. sch., 2002—; joint lectr. Tokyo U. Fgn. Studies, 1965—72, 1975—82. Vis. prof. dept. sociology UCLA, 1990; non-resident mem. Queen Elizabeth House, Oxford, 1972-74; guest prof. U. Klagenfurt, Austria, 1996, U. Marburg, Germany, 2007. Assoc. editor History of Sociology, 1981-87; author: Kokusai Shakaigaku to Nippon, A Step to International Sociology, 2005; Press and Empire, 1981; author, editor: Shakaigaku no Rekishi: A History of Sociology, 1982, 89; editor: (with Hisao Naka) Sociologie Globale, 1987; editor: (with J. Langer) Shakaigatu to Europa, 1994; contbr. articles to Global, 1984-87. Recipient prize of social thought Akegarasu Fund, Tokyo and Kanazawa Univs., 1964, Outstanding Achievement award in edn., Cambridge, Eng., 1999; over 10 grants in Japan. Mem.: others, Japanese Sociol. Assn., Internat. Sociol. Assn. (life). Avocations: opera, concerts. Office: Meijo U 1-501 Shiogamaguchi Nagoya 468 Japan Home Phone: +81 52 585 2511; Office Phone: +81 52 832 1151. Fax: (52) 838-7249.

KAKADIARIS, IOANNIS, computer science educator; b. Athens, Greece, May 16, 1966; m. Maria Gasi, Jan. 13, 1996; children: Eugenia, Alexandra. PhD in Computer Sci., U. Pa., 1997. Tchg. asst. Northeastern U., Boston, 1990—90, rsch. asst., 1990—91; rsch. fellow U. Pa., Phila., 1991—96, post-doctoral fellow, 1996—97; asst. prof. U. Houston, 1997—, dir. visual computing lab, 1997—2002, coord. external rels. Virtual Environments Rsch. Inst., 1998—2000, mem. Tex. Learning and Computation Ctr., 1999—, thrust leader bioimaging and biocomputation Virtual Environments Rsch. Inst, 2000—02, interim dir. Virtual Environments Rsch. Inst, 2000—02, co-dir. Visual Computing Lab., 2002—, dir. divsn. bioimaging and biocomputation Inst. for Digital Informatics and Analysis, 2002—. Adj. asst. prof. dept. health informatics Health Info. Scis. U. Tex., Houston, 1999—; adj. asst. prof. dept. plastic surgery U. Tex. M.D. Anderson Cancer Ctr., Houston, 2000—; mem. The W.M. Keck Ctr. for Computational and Structural Biology, 2002—. Editor: Proceedings of the IEEE Human motion analysis and synthesis workshop; contbr. chapters to books, articles to profl. jours. Recipient award, Schlumberger Tech. Found., 1998—99, SHELL Interdisciplinary award, 1999; fellow, Bodosakis Found., 1989—91, Gerondelis Found., 1991—92; grantee, SGI Inc., 1998, NSF, 1998, U. Houston Internat. Space Systems Ops., 2000—02, NSF, 2000—, Tex. Higher Edn. Coordinating Bd., 2000—03, Am. Honda R&D, Inc., 2000—01, MD Anderson Cancer Ctr., 2000—, NSF, 2001—02, Sun Microsystems, 2001—, Tex. Higher Edn. Coordinating Bd., 2001, Keck Ctr. for Computational Biology, 2002—03, Juvenile Diabetes Rsch. Found., 2002—, U. of Houston Faculty Devel. Initiative Program, 2002—03, U. Houston, 2002, Real Time Innovations Inc., 2002. Mem.: IEEE (Disting. Visitor 2002—), Brit. Machine Vision Assn., Internat. Soc. for Computer Aided Surgery, Hellenic Soc. Scientists in Computer and Info. Sci., Assn. for Computing Machinery, Am. Heart Assn., Sigma Xi (pres. 2002—03). Achievements include research in understanding diagrams in technical documents; data interrogation in visual computing; adaptive fuzzy connectedness-based medical image segmentation; automatic hybrid segmentation of dual contrast cardiac MR data; g-HDAF multiresolution deformable models for shape modeling and reconstruction; teleoperating robonaut; m-HDAF multiresolution deformable models; automatic computation of the ejection fraction using dual contrast short-axis cardia MR images; estimating the motion of the LAD; tracking methods for medical augemented reality; multi-sensory investigation of geoscientific data; application of virtual reality in surgery; improvement of anthropometry and pose estimation from a single uncalibrated image; numerous others. Office: Univ Houston 4800 Calhoun MS CSC 3010 Houston TX 77204-3010 E-mail: ioannisk@uh.edu.

KAKU, MICHIO, theoretical nuclear physicist, educator; b. San Jose, Calif., Jan. 24, 1947; s. Toshio and Hideko Kaku. BA, Harvard U., 1968; PhD, U. Calif., Berkeley, 1972; PhD (hon.), Hofstra U., 1997, SUNY, Old Westbury, 1997. Rsch. assoc. Princeton U., NJ, 1972—73; assoc. prof. CCNY and Grad. Ctr., 1973—83, prof., 1983—. Vis. prof. NYU, 1988, Inst. for Advanced Studies at Princeton U., 1990. Author: Nuclear Power: Both Sides, 1983, Beyond Einstein, the Cosmic Quest for The Theory of the Universe, 1986, Introduction to Superstrings, 1988, Strings, Conformal Fields and Topology, 1991, Quarks, Symmetries and Strings, 1991, Quantum Field Theory: A Modern Introduction, 1993, Hyperspace: A Scientific Odyssey Through Parallel Universes, Time Warps and the 10th Dimension, 1994, Frontiers in Quantum Field theory, 1996, Visions: How Science Will Revolutionize the 21st Century, 1997, Einstein's Cosmos, 2004, Parallel Worlds, 2005; contbr. 70 articles to profl. jours.; host nat. syndicated radio show, frequent appearances BBC-TV, PBS-TV, Discovery Channel, Sci. Channel, Nat. Geog. Channel. Fellow: Am. Phys. Soc. Avocation: nuclear arms control. Office: CCNY Physics Dept 138th St at Convent Ave New York NY 10031 Personal E-mail: mkaku@aol.com.

KAKUTANI, MICHIKO, critic; b. New Haven, Jan. 9, 1955; BA in English, Yale Univ., 1976. Reporter Washington Post, 1976—77; staff writer Time mag., 1977—79; reporter, cultural news NY Times, NYC, 1979—83, book critic, 1983—, now chief book critic. Recipient Pulitzer prize for criticism, 1998. Office: c/o NY Times Culture News 229 W 43d St New York NY 10036 Office Phone: 212-556-4874. Office Fax: 212-556-1516.

KALAFUT, GEORGE WENDELL, retired distribution company executive, retired naval officer; b. Chgo., Feb. 21, 1934; s. George Andrew and Ann Catherine (Panak) K.; m. Alice Quinn, Nov. 9, 1957; children: Katherine, Tracy. AB in Econs., St. Joseph's Coll., Rensselaer, Ind., 1955; MBA, Harvard U., 1969. Commd. USN, 1956, advanced through grades to capt., 1976; asst dir. air equipment purchasing divsn. Naval Air Systems Command, Washington, 1969-71, dep. dir. F14/Grumman rev. team Washington and Bethpage, NY, 1971, dir. airframes purchasing div. Washington, 1972-73; supply officer USS Ranger CV61, San Francisco, 1973-75; dir. plans and budget Naval Supply Systems Command, Washington, 1976-78; retired USN, 1978; dir. inventories Motion Industries, Birmingham, Ala., 1979, v.p., 1980-83, v.p. fin., chief fin. officer, 1983-85, sr. v.p., 1985-89, also bd. dirs.; sr. v.p. fin. and adminstrn. Genuine Parts Co., Atlanta, 1989-91, exec. v.p. fin. and adminstrn., chief fin. officer, 1991—2001, exec. v.p., 2001—04; ret., 2004. Baker scholar Harvard Bus. Sch., 1969. Home: 1755 Spalding Dr Atlanta GA 30350-4321

KALAI, EHUD, economist, researcher, educator; b. Tel Aviv, Dec. 7, 1942; arrived in U.S., 1963; s. Meir and Elisheva (Rabinovitch) Kalai; m. Marilyn Lott, Aug. 24, 1967; children: Kerren, Adam. AB with distinction, U. Calif., Berkeley, 1967; MS, Cornell U., 1971, PhD in Applied Math., 1972. Asst. prof. dept. stats. Tel Aviv U., 1972-75; vis. asst. prof. decision scis. J. L. Kellogg Grad. Sch. Mgmt. Northwestern U., Evanston, Ill., 1975-76, assoc. prof., 1976-78, prof. managerial econs. and decision scis., 1978-82, Charles E. Morrison Chair prof. decision scis., 1982-2001, prof. math., 1990—, James J. O'Connor disting. prof. decision and game scis., 2001—, IBM rsch. chair managerial econs., 1980-81, J. L. Kellogg rsch. chair in decision theory, 1981-82, chmn. meds. dept., 1983-85, dir. Ctr. Strategic Decision-Making, 1995—. Expert testimony in ct. cases, 1982—;

Oskar Morgenstern rsch. prof. game theory NYU, NYC, 1991; cons. Israeli Def. Forces, 1974—75, 1st Nat. Bank, Chgo., 1987, Arthur Anderson, 1990, Kaiser Permanente, 1995, Nath Sonnenschein and Rosenthal, 1999, Baxter Healthcare Corp., 1999—. Founder, editor Games and Econ. Behavior Jour., 1988—, mem. editl. bd. Math. Social Scis., 1980—90, Jour. Econ. Theory, 1980—88, Internat. Jour. Game Theory, 1984—; contbr. articles to profl. jours. Sgt. Israeli Def. Forces, 1960—63. Grantee, NSF, 1979—; Sherman Fairchild Disting. scholar, Calif. Inst. Tech., 1994—95. Fellow: Econometric Soc.; mem.: Game Theory Soc. (founder, exec. v.p. 1998—2003, pres. 2003—06), Pub. Choice Soc., Am. Math. Soc., Beta Gamma Sigma. Office: Kellogg Grad Sch of Mgmt Northwestern Univ Evanston IL 60208-0001 Home: 800 Elgin Rd 1003 Evanston IL 60201 Office Phone: 847-491-7017. Business E-Mail: kalai@kellogg.northwestern.edu.

KALAINOV, SAM CHARLES, insurance company executive; b. Steele, ND, May 11, 1930; s. George and Celia Mae (Makedonsky) K.; m. Delores L. Holm., Aug. 10, 1957; children: John Charles, David Mark. BS, N.D. State U., 1956. CLU. Life ins. agt. Am. Mut. Life Ins. Co., Fargo, N.D., 1956-60, supt. agys. Des Moines, 1960-70, sr. v.p. mktg., 1972-80, pres., chmn., CEO, 1980-95; v.p. agy. Western States Life Ins. Co., Fargo, 1970-72; chmn. bd. dirs. Am. Mut. Holding Corp., Amerus Life, 1995-2000. Bd. dirs. Am. Coun. Life Ins., Washington, Bankers Trust, Des Moines; past chmn. Des Moines Devel. Corp. Bd. dirs. Luth. Health Sys., Fargo, 1974-91, City Corp., Des Moines, 1981-95, Civic Ctr. Ct., 1981-95, Iowa Luth. Hosp., 1982-91; trustee Drake U.; past chmn. Des Moines Conv. and Visitors Bur.; civilian aide to Sec. Army at Large, 1991; past state dir. Selective Svc. Sys.; bd. mem. N.D. State U. Devel. Found. With inf. AUS, 1947-49, lt., 1952-55. Decorated Bronze Star; recipient Alumni Achievement award N.D. State U., 1983, Patrick Henry award Army Nat. Guard, 1998. Mem. Nat. Assn. Life Underwriters, Greater Des Moines C. of C. (past chmn., Nat. Leadership award 1978), Corp. for Internat. Trade (chmn.), Alexis de Tocqueville Soc., Am. Legion, Rotary (past pres. Des Moines chpt.), Grand Lodge Iowa, Royal Order of Jesters, Za-Ga-Zig Temple. Office: AmerUs Group 699 Walnut St Des Moines IA 50309-3929

KALAJIAN-LAGANI, DONNA, publishing executive; b. Mountainside, NJ, Feb. 8, 1955; d. Jack and Analid Kalajian; m. Ron Galotti, Oct. 14, 1981. BS, Penn State U., 1975. Internat. credit analyst Irving Trust Co., NYC, 1976—77; ad sales rep. BMT Pub., NYC, 1977—79, Woman's Day Mag., NYC, 1979—81, cosmetics mgr., 1981—83, ea. mgr., 1984—87; v.p., advt. dir. Ladies' Home Jour., NYC, 1987—89, v.p., pub., 1989—95; pub./sr. v.p. Cosmopolitan Mag., 1996—99; publ. dir. Cosmopolitan Group, NYC, 1999—, sr. v.p., 1999—. Home: 100 Park Ave New York NY 10017-5516 Office: Cosmopolitan Hearst Magazines 300 W 57th St New York NY 10019-3299 Office Phone: 212-649-3282. Office Fax: 212-397-7581.*

KALAMOTOUSAKIS, GEORGE JOHN, economist, merchant banker, educator; b. Chios, Greece, July 26, 1936; came to U.S., 1953; s. John S. and Marika (Nikolaides) K.; 1 child, Yannis. BA, CUNY, 1956, MA, 1958; PhD, NYU, 1966. Instr. Fairleigh Dickinson, U., Teaneck, N.J., 1958-59; asst. prof. Ithaca (N.Y.) Coll., 1959-62; chief economist Brown Engr., NYC, 1963-64; instr. Washington Sq. Coll., NYU, 1963-65; econ. cons. N.Y. State Office Regional Devel., Albany, 1964-66; adv. economist IBM, Armonk, N.Y., 1969-73; internat. economist Am. Standard, Inc., NYC, 1973-76; prof. finance Grad. Sch. Bus., NYU, 1971-77. External dir. Rank-Xerox, Hellas, Greece, Atlantic Union Ins. Co., Athens, Greece; vis. prof. U. Md. European divsn. USAF, 1960, 67-68; head dept. pub. fin. Ctr. of Planning and Econ. Rsch., Athens, Greece; dir. econ. rsch. Bank of Greece, 1977-79; chief exec. officer, vice-chmn. bd. Bank of Crete, Athens, 1979-84; exec. dir., country head, gen. mgr. Greece, head Middle Ea. region Am. Express Bank Ltd., N.Y.C., 1985-94, fin. svcs. cons., 1995—; mem. William J. Fulbright Scholarship com., 1990-95, Athens; bd. dirs. Egyptian Am. Bank, Cairo, 1989-94. Contbr. articles to profl. jours.; Author books on internat. fin., Cyprus and self determination, common market and econ. devel. Greece. Bd. dirs., trustee Hellenic Theatre Found., bd. dirs. Aegian U., Greece, 1982-94 Am. Ford Found. Faculty Research fellow, 1962 Mem. Am. Econ. Assn., AAUP (v.p. chpt. 1961), Omicron Delta Epsilon. Home: 124 Lakeview Ave Lynbrook NY 11563-1755 Office: 43 Diamantidou Ave Paleo Psychico 15452 Athens Greece Business E-Mail: gkl@pr-davari-group.gr.

KALANTARINIA, KAMBIZ, medical educator; b. Tehran, Iran, Mar. 28, 1965; s. Hooshang Kalantarinia; m. Carolyn Clark, June 10, 2006. MD, Shiraz U., Iran. Faculty Prince George's Hosp., Internal Medicine Residency Program, Cheverly, Md., 1999—2000; asst. prof. medicine U. Va. Health Sys., Charlottesville, 2002—. Dir. hemodialysis vascular access program U. Va., Divsn. Nephrology, Charlottesville, 2005—, assoc. dir. nephrology clin. rsch. ctr., 2002—; co-dir. high risk diabetes and kidney disease clinic U. Va. Health Sys., 2002—04; dir. multispecialty clinic U. Va., Augusta Med. Ctr., Fishersville. Physician Charlottesville Free Clinic, Va., 2005. Mem.: Nat. Kidney Found. (assoc.), Internat. Soc. Nephrology (assoc.), Am. Diabetes Assn. (assoc.), Am. Heart Assn. (assoc.), Am. Soc. Nephrology (assoc.). Office: University of Virginia Health System Division of Nephrology Box 800133 Charlottesville VA 22908 Office Phone: 434-924-5125. Office Fax: 434-924-5848. E-mail: kk6c@virginia.edu.

KALAS, FRANK JOSEPH, JR., financial, information systems consultant; b. Stafford Springs, Conn., Dec. 31, 1943; s. Frank Joseph and Margaret Mary (LaPanne) K.; m. Minh Tran, June 24, 1972; children: Jennifer Ann, Joanne Catherine. BBA, U. N.Mex., 1966; MS, U. Ark., London, Eng., 1974. Sr. auditor Knox & Scott, CPAs, Albuquerque, 1963-66; commd. officer USN, 1967, advanced through grades to capt., 1987; dir. fin. mgmt. office Naval Sea Systems Command, Washington, 1988-93; ret., 1993; mgr. material and prodn. svcs. Intermarine USA, Savannah, Ga., 1993-95; sr. prin. Am. Mgmt. Systems, Inc., Fairfax, Va., 1995—2001; program mgr. Enterprise Solutions, Inc., Arlington, Va. Adj. prof. acctg. R.I. Coll., 1978-80, Far East divsn. U. Md., 1980-82. Author: Food Service Operations and Contracting, 1987. Decorated Meritorious Svc. medal, Legion of Merit. Mem. Am. Soc. Naval Engrs., Soc. Logistics Engrs. (pres. 1979-80), Profl. Picture Framer's Assn. (cert.), Am. Soc. Mil. Comptrs. (Outstanding Mem. award 1985), Nat. Amateur Press Assn., Inst. of Mgmt. Accts., Am. Prodn. and Inventory Control Soc., Soc. Maintenance and Reliability Profls. (cert.). Roman Catholic. Achievements include invention of automated data capture system for engineering inspections. Avocations: amateur journalism, clocks, russian history, competition dancing, WW II history. Office: CACI Enterprise Solutions Inc 8357 Dix Ellis Tr Jacksonville FL 32256 Business E-Mail: fkalas@caci.com.

KALAVADE, ASA, telecommunications industry executive; MSEE and Computer Sci., U. Calif., Berkeley, PhD in Electrical Engring. and Computer Sci. With Bell Labs; v.p. tech. Savos (acquired by Infospace); founder, chief tech. officer Tatara Systems, Mass., 2001—. Invited spkr. in field. Contbr. chapters to books, articles to jours. Named one of Women to Watch, Mass. High Tech, 2007. Achievements include patents in field. Office: Tatara Systems 35 Nagog Park Acton MA 01720 Office Phone: 978-206-0800. Office Fax: 978-206-0888.

KALAWSKI, EVA, lawyer; BA in Polit. Sci. and French, Mount Holyoke Coll., 1977; JD, Georgetown Univ., 1981. V.p. human resources, gen. counsel, sec. Pilot Software Inc.; exec. v.p., gen. counsel, sec. Platinum Equity Inc., 1997—. Office: Platinum Equity 360 N Crescent Dr Beverly Hills CA 90210 Office Phone: 310-712-1850. Office Fax: 310-712-1848.

KALB, CHESTER H., mathematics professor; b. Cin., Nov. 12, 1945; s. Chester H. and Marie Elizabeth Kalb; m. Gerda C. Rodriguez, Oct. 6, 2000; m. Gale Partee, July 31, 1983 (div. Jan. 30, 1997); children: Cynthia Denise, Deanna Renay. BS in Math. with honors, U. Cin., 1963—68, BS, 1963—68; MS in Math., Xavier U., Cin., 1972—74. Tchr. math. Cin. Pub. Schs., 1967—83; math. tchr. Cleve. Pub. Schs., 1983—98; tchr. math. upward bound Case Western Res. U., Cleve., 1984—98; prof., math. Fla. Keys C.C., Key West, 1998—; tchr. math. Key West H.S., Fla., 1999—. Math. dept. chmn. Woodward H.S., Cin., 1976—83, Lincoln West H.S., Cleve., 1995—98. Recipient Disting. Tchr. Svc. Award, Cin. Pub. Schs., 1979. Mem.: Math. Assn. Am., Nat. Coun. Tchr. Math. Avocations: competitive race walking, fishing, photography, travel. Home: 3930 S Roosevelt Blvd E-105 Key West FL 33040 Office: Florida Keys CC 5901 College Rd Key West FL 33040 Home Phone: 305-294-2551; Office Phone: 305-296-9081 221. Personal E-mail: chester-h-kalb-ii@msn.com. E-mail: kalb_c@firn.edu.

KALB, JOHANNES ANDREAS, research scientist; b. Neuss, Germany, June 21, 1976; Student, U. Edinburgh, 1998—99; M in Physics with honors, Rheinisch-Westfälische Technische Hochschule, Aachen, Germany, 2002, PhD in Physics with honors, 2006. Undergrad. rschr. Sch. Engring. and Applied Scis. Harvard U., Cambridge, Mass., 2001, vis. scholar, rschr., 2003—04; rsch. scientist dept. materials sci. and engring. MIT, Cambridge, 2006—. Recipient Friedrich-Wilhem award, Rheinisch Wesfälische Technische Hochschule Aachen, 2002, Springorum medal, Rheinisch Wesfälische Technische Hochschule, 2003, Borchers medal, 2007; fellow, Heinrich Hertz Found., 2001, German Acad. Exch. Svc., 2003, German Nat. Acad. Found., 2003—06, Alexander von Humboldt Found., 2006—. Office: MIT Rm 13-5005 77 Mass Ave Cambridge MA 02139 Office Phone: 617-253-2802. Business E-Mail: mwwa@kalb.eu.

KALBAUGH, COREY ANDREW, bioengineering researcher; b. Rochester, Pa., Oct. 15, 1977; s. Kevin Joe and Judith Ann Kalbaugh; m. Julianne Marie Ohms. BS, Clemson U., SC, 2000, MS in Bioengineering, 2003. Rsch. bioengineer Greenville Hosp. Sys. U. Med. Ctr., SC, 2002—; adj. instr. Clemson U., 2005—; GHS instr. clin. surgery U. SC, Columbia, 2006—. Contbr. articles profl. jours. Office: GHSUMC 890 W Faris Rd Ste 320 Greenville SC 29605 Office Phone: 864-455-5204. Office Fax: 864-455-8980. Business E-Mail: ckalbaugh@ghs.org.

KALBFLEISCH, JOHN DAVID, statistics educator; b. Grand Valley, Ont., Can., July 16, 1943; s. Claude Elwyn and Janet Marjorie (Agnew) Kalbfleisch; m. Catherine Sharon Allen; children: Michael Allen, Heidi Kathryn, Kirby Ann. BSc in Math. and Physics, U. Waterloo, 1966, M of Math in Stats., 1967, PhD in Stats., 1969. Rsch. assoc. dept. stats. Univ. Coll., London, 1969-70; asst. prof. dept. stats. SUNY, Buffalo, 1970-73; assoc. prof. dept. stats. U. Waterloo, 1973-79, prof. dept. stats. and actuarial sci., 1979—2002, chmn. dept. stats. and actuarial sci., 1984-90, dean faculty of math., 1990-98; prof., chair dept. biostats. U. Mich., Ann Arbor, 2002—. Vis. prof. dept. biostats. U. Wash., 1979-80, dept. biostats. U. Mich., 1987, dept. epidemiology U. Calif., San Francisco, 1988, dept. statistics U. Auckland, 1998, Nat. U. Singapore, 1999. Author: (with R.L. Prentice) The Statistical Analysis of Failure Time Data, 1980, 2d edit., 2002; assoc. editor Can. Jour. Stats., 1981-89, 1998-2004, Annals of Stats., 1980-83, Biometrics, 2003—; contbr. articles to profl. jours. Recipient Gold medal, Statis. Soc. Can., 1994, COPSS Fisher award, 1999; fellow, Royal Soc. Can., 1994, Am. Statis. Assn., Inst. Math. Stats. Mem.: Internat. Statis. Inst., Royal Statis. Soc., Inst. Biomedical Soc., Statis. Soc. Canada, Internat. Statis. Inst. Office: U Mich Dept Biostatistics Ann Arbor MI 48109 Home Phone: 734-332-6082; Office Phone: 734-615-7067. Business E-Mail: jdkalbfl@umich.edu.

KALBFLEISCH, JOHN MCDOWELL, cardiologist, educator; b. Lawton, Okla., Nov. 15, 1930; s. George and Etta Lillian (McDowell) K.; m. Jolie Harper, Dec. 30, 1961. AS, Cameron A&M U., Lawton, 1950; BS, U. Okla., 1952, MD, 1957. Diplomate Am. Bd. Internal Medicine, Am. Bd. Cardiovascular Disease. Intern U. Va. Hosp., 1957-58; resident and fellow U. Okla. Med. Ctr., 1958-62, instr. medicine, 1964-66, asst. prof., 1966-69, assoc. clin. prof., 1970-78, clin. prof. Tulsa br., 1978—; pvt. practice Tulsa, 1969—; founder, chmn. bd., CEO Cardiology of Tulsa, Inc., 1969—; dir. cardiovascular svcs. St. Francis Hosp., Tulsa, 1975—2005. Physician adv. bd. City of Tulsa, 1978-81; bd. dirs. St. Francis Hosp., exec. com., 1987-97, 2001-06; exec. v.p., chief med. officer St. Francis Health Sys., 1998-99; treas. Tulsa Med. Edn. Found., 1988-89, v.p., 1990-92, pres., 1992-94; med. dir., chmn. bd. Warren Clinics, 1990-97; mem. Okla. Ctr. for Advancement of Sci. and Tech., 1989-95; mem. adv. com. Ctr. for Lasser Devel. and Applications, Okla. State U. Contbr. articles to profl. jours. With USPHS, 1962-64. Named Okla. Profl. Health Care Champion, Partnership Blue Cross Blue Shield Okla., 2005; named to, St. Francis Health Sys. Hall of Fame, 2003; recipient Lifelong Svc. award, Tulsa Med. Edn. Found./U. Okla. Coll. Medicine, 2002. Fellow ACP (gov.-elect Okla. 1990-91, gov. 1991-95, Okla. Laureate award 1995), Am. Coll. Cardiology (gov. Okla. 1978-81); mem. AMA, AAAS, Tulsa County Med. Soc., Okla. State Med. Assn., Am. Heart Assn. (Fellow coun. on clin. cardiology), tchg. scholar 1967-69), Okla. Soc. Internal Medicine v.p., pres.-elect 1983-84, pres. 1985-86), Am. Soc. Internal Medicine, Am. Fedn. Clin. Rsch., Am. Inst. Nutrition, U. Okla. Med. Alumni Assn. (Physician of Yr. in Pvt. Practice 1999), Okla. State Dept. Health, Okla. Hosp. Assn., Okla. Osteopathic Assn., Delta Upsilon. Republican. Presbyterian. Office: 6151 S Yale Ave Ste 400 Tulsa OK 74136-1933 Office Phone: 918-307-5500. Business E-Mail: jkalbfleisch@cotheart.com.

KALDHUSDAL, TERRY LEE, elementary school educator; b. Calif. m. Janet Kaldhusdal; 3 children. BA in journalism, Calif. State Polytechnic Univ., San Luis Obispo; MS in Tech. in Edn., Lesley Coll., Cambridge, Mass. Tchg. cert. Chapman Coll., Calif. Tchr. LA Sch. Sys., Calif., 1991—93, Wales Elem. Sch., 1993—99, Magee Elem. Sch., Genesee Depot, Wis., 1999—. Named Wis. Elem. Sch. Tchr. of Yr., 2006, Wis. Tchr. of Yr., 2007. Mem.: Internat. Reading Assn. Office: Magee Elem Sch PO Box 37 Genesee Depot WI 53127 Business E-Mail: kaldhust@kmsd.edu.*

KALER, ERIC WILLIAM, chemical engineer, educator; b. Burlington, Vt., Sept. 23, 1956; s. Ronald Maurice and Mary Elizabeth (Kindred) K.; m. Karen Fults, Dec. 30, 1979. BS, Calif. Inst. Tech., 1978; PhD, U. Minn., 1982. Asst. prof. chem. engring. U. Wash., Seattle, 1982-87, assoc. prof., 1987-89; assoc. prof. chem. engring. U. Del., Newark, 1989-91, prof., 1991-98, chair dept. chem. engring., 1996-2000, Elizabeth Inez Kelley prof., 1998—, dean Coll. Engring., 2000—. Vis. prof. U. Graz, Austria; cons. DuPont, P&G, numerous other companies. Conbr. numerous articles to profl. jours. Elder Andrew Riverside Presbyn. Ch., Mpls., 1980-82, Northminster Presbyn. Ch., Seattle, 1984-88. Named Presdl. Young Investigator, NSF, Washington, 1984; Presdl. scholar Dept. Edn., Washington, 1978. Fellow AAAS; mem. AIChE (Chilton award, 2002), Am. Chem. Soc. (Award in Colloid or Surface Chemistry, 1998, Del. Sect. Award, 1998), Am. Soc. Engring. Edn. (Gordon W. McGraw Rsch. Award, 1995), Am. Crystallographic Assn.

KALES, PAUL ALBERT, engineering educator, cartoonist; b. Boston, Dec. 8, 1937; s. Maurice H. and Eleanor (Kopp) K.; m. Judith Freund, Feb. 27, 1977. BS, Northeastern U., Boston, 1960, MS, 1965. Registered profl. engr., Mass. Engr. GE Co., Lynn, Mass., 1960-64; sr. engr. Avco Corp., Wilmington, Mass., 1964-68, Raytheon Co., Wayland, Mass., 1968-82, C.S. Draper Lab., Cambridge, Mass., 1982-85; assoc. prof. engring. tech. U. Mass., Lowell, 1985-99. Cons., trainer Statis. Process Control and Reliability/Maintainability Engring.; lectr. engring. Northeastern U. Boston, 1979-84; instr. cartooning Cambridge Ctr. for Adult Edn., 1973-83. Author: Reliability for Technology, Engineering and Management, 1998, Betty and Jenn, 2002; cartoons published in Wall St. Jour., Reader's Digest, Saturday Evening Post, Moment, Parkhurst Exchange, Union Communications Services, Boston Globe, Eat and Run, Stitches Jour., Women's World, First for Women, Good Housekeeping, others; contbr. articles to profl. jours. Originator, awards com. Mass. Coun. for Quality, Lowell, 1990-91. Mem. NSPE, Profl. Engrs. in Edn., Mass. Soc. Profl. Engrs., Nat. Asst. Indsl. Tech., Am. Soc. Quality Control (founding mem., sec. edn. divsn. 1994). Democrat. Jewish. Office: PO Box 179 Nantucket MA 02554 Office Phone: 508-280-8761. Personal E-mail: pkales@comcast.net.

KALET, IRA JOSEPH, medical computer scientist; b. Stamford, Conn., Apr. 27, 1944; s. Bernard and Miriam Kalet; m. Teresa Lynn Kalet, Apr. 7, 1973; children: Nathan, Alan, Brian. AB in Physics, Cornell U., 1965; MA in Physics, Princeton U., 1967, PhD in Theoretical Physics, 1968. Rsch. assoc. physics U. Wash., Seattle, 1968-69; asst. prof. Sonoma State Coll., Rohnert Park, Calif., 1969-70; lectr. math. edn. U. Pa., Phila., 1974-75; sr. fellow med. physics U. Wash., Seattle, 1978-80, rsch. assoc., 1980-82, asst. prof. radiation oncology, 1982-88, adj. asst. prof. computer sci., 1982-88, assoc. prof. radiation oncology, 1988—2004, adj. assoc. prof. computer sci., bioengring./biol. structure, 1988—2004, prof. radiation oncology, prof. med. edn. and biomedical informatics, adj. prof. computer sci., 2004—. Mem. adv. bd. program in health info. mgmt. U. Wash., Seattle, 1993—; ad hoc grant reviewer NIH, Bethesda, Md., 1987—; Dozor vis. prof. Ben Gurion U., Israel, 1996; Disting. lectr. computer sci. Dalhousie U., N.S., Can., 2002. Assoc. editor Computerized Med. Imaging and Graphics, 1988—; contbr. articles to profl. jours. Recipient Nat. Rsch. Svc. award NIH, U. Wash., 1978-80, Best Paper award Am. Assn. Med. Sys. and Informatics, 1985, Biomed. and Health Informatics Excellence in Tchg. award U. Wsh., 2003; rsch. grantee NIH, U. Wash., 1984—. Mem. Assn. Computing Machinery, Am. Assn. Physicists in Medicine, Am. Assn. Artificial Intelligence, Am. Assn. Physics Tchrs. Jewish. Achievements include breakthroughs in design of software for radiation treatment planning for cancer; prodn. of the first commercially available three-dimensional radiation treatment planning software. Office: U Wash Radiation Oncology Dept PO Box 356043 Seattle WA 98195-6043

KALETA, PAUL J., lawyer, utilities executive; b. Queens, NY, Aug. 18, 1955; AB in Philosophy and English cum laude, Hamilton Coll., 1978; JD cum laude, Georgetown U., 1981. Bar: DC 1982, NY 1993, US Supreme Ct. 1987. Assoc. Skadden, Arps, Slate, Meagher & Flom, Washington, 1982—84; ptnr. Swidler & Berlin, Washington, 1985-91; v.p., gen. counsel Niagara Mohawk Power Corp., Syracuse, NY, 1991-98; v.p., gen. counsel, sec. Koch Industries, Inc., Wichita, Kans., 1998—2005; sr. v.p., gen. counsel, corp. sec. Sierra Pacific Resources, Reno, 2006—. Vice chmn. Utility Law Commn. Mem. ABA, NY State Bar Assn. Office: Sierra Pacific Resources 6100 Neil Rd Reno NV 89511*

KALFATOVIC, MARTIN ROBERT, librarian, writer; b. San Jose, Calif., Apr. 20, 1961; s. Martin John Kalfatovic and Theresa Ressler; m. Mary Clare Corkery, Nov. 6, 1987; 1 child, Grace. BA in English, Catholic U. Am., 1983, MLS, 1990. Interlibr. loan libr. Nat. Mus. Am. Art/Nat. Portrait Gallery Libr., Washington, 1986-93; info. access coord. Smithsonian Instn. Librs., Washington, 1993-99, digital projects libr., 1999—2001, head new media office, 2001—. Adj. prof. Catholic U., 1996-2001. Author: Nile Notes of a Howadji, 1992, New Deal Fine Arts Projects, 1994, Creating a Winning Online Exhibition, 2002; editor Libr. Info. Tech. Assn. Newsletter, 1997-2000; contbr. articles to profl. jours. including Am. Nat. Biography, Jour. Popular Culture; reviewer Libr. Jour., RQ, Art Documentation, others. 5em. ALA, Assn. for the Study of Travel in Egypt and the Near East, Catholic U. Am. Sch. Libr. and Info. Sci. Alumni Bd. (bd. dirs.s 1994-95, v.p. 1995-96, pres. 1996-98). Roman Catholic. Office: Smithsonian Instn Librs 10th & Constitution Ave NW Washington DC 20560-0001 Business E-Mail: kalfatovicm@si.edu.

KALICKI, JAN H., economist, political scientist, energy executive; b. London, Aug. 5, 1948; s. Jan and Mireya (Jaimes-Freyre) Kalicki; m. Jean Ellen Engelmayer, Oct. 22, 1989; children: Jan Harlan, Alexander Van, Peter Daniel. AB with honors, Columbia Coll., 1968; PhD, London Sch. Econ., 1971. Rsch. assoc., lectr. Princeton U., NJ, 1971—72, Harvard U., Cambridge, Mass., 1972; Fgn. Svc. officer U.S. Dept. State, Washington, 1972—75, policy planning staff, 1974—77; chief fgn. policy advisor to Senator Edward Kennedy U.S. Senate, Washington, 1977—84; adj. prof. Georgetown U., Washington, 1983—85; adj. prof., asst. to pres. Brown U., Providence, 1985—88, exec. dir. Ctr. Fgn. Policy Devel., 1985—88; sr. advisor Watson Inst. Internat. Studies/Brown U., 1988—94, sr. fellow, 1994—99; v.p. Lehman Bros., 1984—88, sr. v.p., 1988—93; U.S. ombudsman for energy and comml. coop. NIS, Washington, 1994—2001; counselor U.S. Dept. Commerce, 1994—2001; pub. policy scholar Woodrow Wilson Internat. Ctr., Smithsonian Instn., 2001—06, sr. scholar, 2006—; internat. policy scholar EastWest Inst., 2002—03. Counselor internat. strategy Chevron Corp., San Francisco, 2001—; mem. Coun. Fgn. Rels. Internat. Inst. Strategic Studies, Royal Inst. Internat. Affairs, London; trustee Eurasia Found., World Affairs Coun. No. Calif. Author: The Pattern of Sino-American Crises, 1975; editor: Russian-Eurasian Renaissance?, 2003, Energy and Security: Towards a New Foreign Policy Strategy, 2005; contbr. numerous chpts. to books and articles to profl. jours. Recipient Superior Honor award, US Dept. State, 1977, Silver medal, US Dept. Com., 2000. Office: Chevron Corp 6001 Bollinger Canyon Rd San Ramon CA 94583

KALIHER, MICHAEL DENNIS, historian, librarian; b. Santa Monica, Calif., Nov. 7, 1947; s. Eugene Charles and Phyllis Joan (McCrary) K. Student, Calif. State Coll., Hayward, 1969—70; BA, U. Ariz., 1990. Bookseller B. Dalton Bookseller, Newport Beach, Calif., 1991—94; correctional officer Ariz. Dept. Corrections, Winslow, 1994—97, libr., 1997—2001; eligibility specialist Ariz. Long-Term Care Sys., Flagstaff, Ariz., 2001—02; libr. II State of Ariz., 2002—. Pres. Klamath County (Oreg.) Hist. Soc., 1985; founder Native Am. History Week, Klamath County Mus., 1985-86. Contbr. articles to profl. jours. Mem. Ariz. Libr. Assn., Flagstaff Friends of Traditional Music, Pi Lambda Theta. Avocations: backpacking, fishing. Home: 1910 W Thatcher Blvd PMB # 222 Safford AZ 85546-3318

KALIK, MILDRED, lawyer; b. NYC, Dec. 4, 1947; BA, U. Wis., 1969; JD, George Washington U. Law Ctr., 1972; LLM in taxation, NYU, 1982. Bar: N.Y. 1973, registered: U.S. Tax Ct. 1973, U.S. Dist. Ct., so. dist. N.Y. 1974, U.S. Ct. Appeals, second cir. 1975. Ptnr. Simpson Thacher & Bartlett LLP, NYC. Mem.: New York State Bar Assn., Internat. Acad. Estate & Trust law, Assn. Bar City N.Y. (surrogates ct. 1999—2003), Am. coll. Trust & Estate Counsel, ABA (chmn. generation skipping tax planning 1981—88, asst. sec., probate & trust law sect. 1988—90, coun. 1990—97). Office: Simpson Thacher & Bartlett LLP 425 Lexington Ave New York NY 10017-3954 Office Phone: 212-455-2778. Office Fax: 212-455-2502. Business E-Mail: mkalik@stblaw.com.

KALIKOW, PETER STEPHEN, real estate developer, former transportation and publishing executive; b. NYC, Dec. 1, 1942; s. Harold J. and Juliet K.; m. Mary T. Jacobatos; children: Nicholas, Kathryn. BSBA, Hofstra U., 1965, LLD (hon.), 1986. With H.J. Kalikow & Co., LLC, NYC, 1966—, pres., 1973—; owner NY Post, 1988-93. Chmn. ins. com. N.Y. State Mortgage Agy., 1981-86; bd. mem., Met. Transp. Authority, 1994-95, vice chmn., 1999-2001, chmn., 2001-07; commr., Port Authority of NY & NJ, 1995 Gov. N.Y. Presbyn. Hosp.; trustee Hofstra U., Mus. Jewish Heritage; gen. chmn. real estate and constrn. divsn. Israel Bonds Recipient Israel Peace medal, Israeli Govt. 1982; named Alumnus of Yr., Hofstra U.,

1988. Mem. N.Y. Athletic Club, Palm Beach Country Club, Fenway Club (Scarsdale, N.Y.), Royal Automobile Club (London). Office: H J Kalikow & Co LLC 101 Park Ave Fl 25 New York NY 10178-0002

KALIKOW, THEODORA JUNE, academic administrator; d. Irving and Rose Kalikow. AB, Wellesley Coll., 1962; ScM, MIT, 1970; PhD, Boston U., 1974. From instr. to prof. Southeastern Mass. U., North Dartmouth, 1968-84; dean Coll. Arts and Scis., U. No. Colo., Greeley, 1984-87; dean of the coll. Plymouth (N.H.) State Coll., 1987-94, interim pres., 1992-93; pres. U. Maine, Farmington, 1994—. Contbr. articles to profl. jours. Chair steering com. Maine ACE/NIP, 1995—; chair Coun. Pub. Liberal Arts Colls., 1997-99; bd. dirs. Maine Humanities Coun., 1999—2006, Fin. Authority Maine, 2000—, Ctr. for the Prevention of Hate Violence, 2004-06, Maine Econ. Growth CouN., 2005—. Named to, Maine Women's Hall of Fame, 2002; recipient Mary Ann Hartman award, 2000, Deborah Morton award, 2006;, NSF grantee, 1978, Am. Coun. on Edn. fellow, Brown U., 1983—84. Mem.: Assn. Am. Colls. and Univs. (bd. dirs. 2000—03), Western Mountains Alliance (chmn. 2000—03), Am. Coun. on Edn. (commn. on women 1994—97, 2000—03), Soc. Values in Higher Edn. (bd. dirs. 1991—94). Office: U Maine at Farmington Office of the Pres 224 Main St Farmington ME 04938-1911 Office Phone: 207-778-7256.

KALIL, CHARLES JAMES, lawyer, chemicals executive; b. 1951; BA, Mich. State U.; JD, Georgetown U. Law Ctr. Asst. US atty. US Dept. Justice (ea. dist. Mich.), 1976—80; atty. environ. law Dow Chem. Co., Midland, Mich., 1980—82; gen. counsel Petrokemyia (joint venture of Dow and SABIC), Rotterdam, Netherlands, 1982—83, regional counsel to Mid. East/Africa Geneva, 1983—86; various litig. and fin. roles Dow Chem. Co., Midland, Mich., 1986—92, gen. counsel and area dir. govt. and pub. affairs Dow L.Am., 1992—97, mgr. global litig. INSITE tech., 1997, asst. gen. counsel corp. fin. law Midland, Mich., 2000—03, assoc. gen. counsel, dir. corp. legal affairs, 2003—04, corp. v.p., gen. counsel, 2004—, corp. sec., mem. Office of the Chief Exec., 2005—. Office: Dow Chem Co 2030 Dow Ctr Midland MI 48674*

KALIL, JAMES, SR., investment executive; b. Buffalo, Oct. 22, 1919; s. Harry and Nazira (Owens) Rossi; m. Claire Homsey, May 5, 1947; children: Donald, Janice, Laura, James Jr. BSChemE, CCNY, 1941; M in ChemE, Poly. U., Bklyn., 1947, PhDChemE, 1951. Rsch. engr. DuPont Co., Wilmington, Del., 1951-80; investment mgr., chmn. bd. dirs. Affinity Wealth Mgmt., Inc., Wilmington, 1974—. Contbr. articles to newspapers; patentee chem products and processes. Fellow Poly. U., 1989. Avocations: reading, travel, writing. Office: Affinity Wealth Mgmt Inc 1702 Lovering Ave Wilmington DE 19806-2120

KALIMI, ROBERT, cardiovascular surgeon; b. Tehran, Iran; BA magna cum laude, NYU; MD, Sackler Sch. Medicine, NYC, 1996. Cert. Am. Bd. Surgery, 2002, Am. Bd. Thoracic Surgery, 2004. Intern LI Jewish Med. Ctr., New Hyde Park, NY, 1996—97, resident, 1997—2001; fellow Rush-Presbyn. St. Luke's Med. Ctr., Chgo., 2001—03; clin. instr. surgery Columbia-Presbyn. Coll. Physicians and Surgeons, NYC, 2003—04; surgeon North Shore Univ. Hosp., Manhasset, NY, 2004—. Presenter in field. Contbr. articles to profl. jours.; co-editor: Clin. Scenarios in Thoracic Surgery, 2004. Office: North Shore Univ Hosp 300 Community Dr Manhasset NY 11030 Office Phone: 516-562-4970. Office Fax: 516-562-3786. E-mail: rkalimi@hotmail.com.*

KALIN, D. JEAN (DOROTHY JEAN KALIN), artist, educator; b. Kansas City, Mo., Feb. 11, 1932; d. William Warner and Esther Dorothy (Peterson) Johnson; m. John Baptist Kalin, Jr., Jan. 5, 1952; children: Jean Loraine, Debra Ann, Diana Yvonne AA, St. Joseph Jr. Coll., Mo., 1951. Artist Hallmark Cards, Inc., Kansas City, 1952—53, 1973—93; freelance artist Kansas City, 1953—72; owner Portraits of Life, Kansas City, 1986—, art tchr., 1988—. Illustrator article Directory of Am. Portrait Artists, 1985; featured in Rockport Pubs. Best of Watercolor 2 and Painting Light and Shadow, 1997, Am. Artist Mag., 1998, 2000, Splash 5, 1998, Best of Collected Watercolor, 2002, Midwest Art, 2003, The Artists' Mag., 2003, Acrylic Highlights Mag., 2004, Watercolor Mag., 2005 Kansas City Art Inst. scholar, 1951-52 Mem. Nat. Oil and Acrylic Painters Soc. (signature), Internat. Soc. Acrylic Painters (signature), Kans. Watercolor Soc. (signature), Women Artists of West (signature), Am. Watercolor Soc. (assoc.), Nat. Watercolor Soc. (assoc.), Transparent Watercolor Soc. Am. (assoc.), Nat. Mus. Women in Arts (charter), Mo. Watercolor Soc. (signature, bd. dir.), We. Colo. Watercolor Soc. (signature), Internat. Platform Assn Avocations: gardening, travel. Address: 20650 State Rt 371 Platte City MO 64079-9344 Office Phone: 816-992-3744.

KALIN, ROBERT, retired mathematics professor; b. Everett, Mass., Dec. 11, 1921; s. Benjamin and Celia (Kraff) K.; m. Shirley Sharney, Oct. 22, 1944; children: Susan Leslie, John Benjamin; m. 2d Madelyn Pildish, Aug. 17, 1962; 1 child, Richard Dean. Student, Northeastern U., 1940-43; BS, U. Chgo., 1947; MAT, Harvard U., 1948; PhD, Fla. State U., 1961. Tchr. math. Holten H.S., Danvers, Mass., 1948-49, Beaumont H.S., Hadley Tech. Sch., Soldan-Blewitt H.S., St. Louis, 1949-52; ednl. statistician Naval Air Tech. Tng. Ctr., Norman, Okla., 1952-53; test specialist, assoc. in research Ednl. Testing Svc., Princeton, NJ, 1953-55; exec. asst. Commn. on Math. of Coll. Entrance Exam. Bd., 1955-56; instr. dept. math. edn. Fla. State U., Tallahassee, 1956-61, asst. prof., 1961-63, assoc. prof., 1963-65, prof., 1965-90, prof. emeritus Tallahassee, 1990, assoc. dept. head, 1968-73, program chmn., 1975-78. Co-author: Elementary Mathematics, Patterns and Structure, 11 vols., 1966, (with George Green) Modern Mathematics for the Elementary School Teacher, 1966, (with E.D. Nichols) Analytic Geometry, 1973, Holt School Mathematics, 9 vols., 1974, rev. 1978, Holt Mathematics, 9 vols., 1981, rev., 1985, (with M.K. Corbitt) Prentice Hall Geometry, 1990, rev. edit., 1993. Mem., treas. Brownsville-Haywood County Libr. Bd., 1991-95, chmn., 1995-97; bd. dirs. Friends of Tenn. Librs., 1995-2002, sec., 1996-97, pres.-elect, 1997-99, pres., 1999-2000, past pres., 2000-02; pres. Temple Adas Israel, 1992-94, treas., 1994-2000; bd. dirs. Jewish Hist. Soc. of Memphis and the Mid-South, 1998-2001, sec., 2000-01. Mem. Math. Assn. Am. (sec.-treas. Fla. sect. 1985-91, Svc. award Fla. sect. 1991), Fla. Coun. Tchrs. Math. (pres. 1960-61), Fla. Assn. Math. Educators (pres. 1984-86), Nat. Coun. Tchrs. Math. (chmn. external affairs com. 1972-73), Nat. High Sch. and Jr. Coll. Math. Clubs (gov. 1972-75, pres. 1978-80). Home: 7 Stoneleigh Pl Brownsville TN 38012-2463 Personal E-mail: r_kalin@bellsouth.net.

KALINA, JOHN, auto parts company executive; Chief info. officer Walbro Corp., 1995—96; exec. info. tech. cons. IBM, 1997—99; c.p., chief info. officer BorgWarner Inc., Chgo., 1999—. Office: Borgwarner 3850 Hamlin Rd Auburn Hills MI 48326-2872

KALINA, RICHARD, artist; b. NYC, May 21, 1946; s. Jacob Wilbert and Helen Ruth (Weinberg) K.; m. Valerie Jaudon, Oct. 23, 1979. BA, U. Pa., 1966. Prof. studio art, art history Fordham U., NYC, 1990—. Chair dept. theatre and visual arts Fordham U.; sr. critic Yale U. One-man shows include Jack Glenn Gallery, L.A., 1970, Okla. Harris Gallery, 1970, Tibor de Nagy Gallery, N.Y.C., 1979, 80, 82, 84, Piezo Electric Gallery, N.Y.C., 1986, 87, L.A., 1986, Elizabeth McDonald Gallery, 1988, 89, Diane Brown Gallery, N.Y.C., 1992, Ledisflam Gallery, N.Y.C., 1992, Lennon, Weinberg Gallery, N.Y.C., 1993, 95, 98, 2001, 03, 06; group shows include Morris Gallery, Toronto, 1970, Lunn Gallery, Washington, 1970, Inst. Contemporary Arts, Boston, 1970, U. Ala. 1971, Jack Glenn Gallery, 1970, 71, NYU, 1972, Indpls. Mus. Art, 1971, 74, Walker Art Ctr., Mpls., 1974, Cas Thomas Jefferson, Brasilia, Brazil, 1975, Lehigh U., 1975, Norton Gallery, Palm Beach, Fla., 1975, Mus. Am. Found. Arts, Miami, 1977, Sewall Gallery, 1978, 80, Nobe Gallery, 1978, Rutgers U., 1978, Weatherspoon Art Gallery, Greensboro, N.C., 1978, Ill. Wesleyan U., 1980, Aldrich Mus., Ridgefield, Conn., 1970, 80, Sidney Janis Gallery, N.Y.C., 1981, McIntosh-Drysdale Gallery, Washington, 1981, Ericson Gallery, N.Y.C., 1982, Mus. Fine Art, Ft. Lauderdale, Fla., 1982, Okla. Mus. Art, Oklahoma City, 1982, Santa Barbara Mus. Art, Calif., 1982, Grand Rapids Art Mus., Mich., 1982, Hudson River Mus., Yonkers, N.Y., 1983, U. Tex., Austin, 1983, Kalamazoo Inst. Art, 1983, Madison (Wis.) Art Ctr., U. Chgo., 1983, Loch Haven Art Ctr., Fla., 1983, Jacksonville (Fla.) Art Mus., 1983, Haber-Theodore Gallery, N.Y.C., 1983, Tibor de Nagy Gallery, 1984, Monmouth Mus., N.J., 1984, Steinbaum Gallery, N.Y.C., 1985, Bass Mus., Miami Beach, Fla., 1985, New Orleans Mus., Contemporary Art, 1985, Anchorage Mus. Fine Arts, 1985, Piezo Electric Gallery, L.A., N.Y.C., 1987, Barbara Mathes Gallery, 1987, R.C. ERPF Gallery, N.Y.C., 1987, Elizabeth McDonald Gallery, 1987, 89, Tower Gallery, N.Y.C., 1988, White Columns, N.Y., 1988, Hunter Coll. Gallery, 1988, John Good Gallery, N.Y.C., 1988, 91, John Davis Gallery, N.Y.C., 1988, Gallerie Rahmel, Cologne, Germany, 1989, J.B. Speed Art Mus., Louisville, 1989, Shea Beker Gallery, N.Y.C., 1989, Scott Hanson Gallery, N.Y.C., 1990, Fay Gold Gallery, Atlanta, 1991, Trenkman Gallery, N.Y.C., Bennington Coll., Vt., 1991, Pamela Auchincloss Gallery, N.Y.C., 1991, Diane Brown Gallery, 1982, Lennon, Weinberg Gallery, N.Y., 1992, 93, 95, 04, 05, 06, Max Protetch Gallery, N.Y.C., 1992, Sergio Tossi Arte Contemporaneo, Prato, Italy, 1992, Stark Gallery, N.Y., 1993, 95, Addison Ripley Fine Art Mus., Washington, D.C., 1993, Guild Hall Mus., East Hampton, N.Y., 1993, Arco Gallery, Turin, Italy, 1994, U. South Fla. Contemporary Art Mus., Tampa, 1995, The Century Assn., N.Y., 1996, McNay Art Mus., San Antonio, Lennon Weinberg, Inc., 1998, Lennon Weinberg Gallery, N.Y., 1998, 99, 01, Katonah Mus., N.Y., 1998, U. N.H., Durham, 1999, N.Y. Studio Sch. Hofstra U., 2000, Wadsworth Atheneum, Hartford, Conn., 2000, Parrish Mus. Art, Southampton, NY, Ark. Arts Ctr., U. Fla., Gainesville, 2003, Miss. Mus. Art, Jackson, 2003, Ark. Mus. Art, Little Rock, 2003, U. N.Mex. Art Mus., 2004, Alex Raben Gallery, NYC, Plattsburgh State Art Mus., SUNY, Plattsburgh; represented in permanent colelctions Indpls. Mus. Art, Norton Gallery Art, Palm Beach, NYU Aldrich Mus., Nat. Mus. Am. Art, Washington, Ind. U. Mus., Rutgers U. Mus.; numerous pvt. collections; contbg. editor Art in Am.; author: Imagining The Present: Context, Content, And The Role Of The Critic, 2006. Nat. Endowment for Arts grantee. Mem. Internat. Assn. of Art Critics (bd. dirs., v.p.).

KALING, MINDY, actress, scriptwriter, television producer; b. Cambridge, Mass., 1979; Grad., Dartmouth Coll., Hanover, NH. Co-writer, actor (plays) Matt & Ben, 2003 (NY Internat. Fringe Festival's Best Play prize, 2003, featured at 2003 US Comedy Arts Festival, Aspen, Named one of Top Ten Theatrical Events of 2003, Time Mag.); actor: (films) The 40 Year Old Virgin, 2005, Unaccompanied Minors, 2006; (TV series) Curb Your Enthusiasm, 2005; actor, co-prodr.: (TV series) The Office, 2005 (Outstanding Performance by an Ensemble in a Comedy Series, SAG, 2007).*

KALINSKE, THOMAS J., education, video game and toy company executive; b. 1944; married. BS, U. Wisconsin, 1966; MBA, U. Arizona, 1968. Acct. rep. Strauss Broadcasting Co., 1966-68, J. Walter Thompson, 1968, sr. acct. rep., 1969; sr. acct. rep., acct. supr. Case & Krone Inc., 1970-72; product mgr. Mattel Toys Mattel Inc., 1972-73, dir. product planning, 1973-77, dir. mktg., 1977-78, v.p. mktg., 1978-79, sr. v.p. mktg., 1979-82, sr. v.p. domestic, worldwide mktg., 1982-83, sr. v.p., gen. mgr. mktg., 1983-84, pres. Mattel USA, 1984-85, pres., CEO, 1985-87; pres., chief oper. officer Universal Matchbox Group, NYC, 1987-90; pres., CEO Sega of Am., Redwood City, Calif., 1990-96; CEO Knowledge Universe (now Krest LLC), Menlo Park, Calif., 1996—2004, LeapFrog Enterprises, 1997—2002, 2004—06, vice chmn., 2006—. Office: LeapFrog Enterprises 6401 Hollis St Ste 100 Emeryville CA 94608-1071

KALINSKY, MICHAEL, management consultant; Co-founder, pres., CEO Empyrean Mgmt. Group, Blue Bell, Pa., 2001—. Vol. fire chief Harleysville Area EMS. Named one of 40 Under 40 To Watch in the Delaware Valley, 2006, 40 Under 40, Phila. Bus. Jour., 2006. Office: Empyrean Mgmt Group Ste 206 1717 Swede Rd Blue Bell PA 19422 Office Phone: 610-275-4400. Office Fax: 610-275-4550.

KALINSKY, ROBERT A., lawyer; b. Cedar Rapids, Iowa, Aug. 24, 1973; BS in Biomedical Engring., U. Iowa, 1996, JD with distinction, 2001. Bar: Minn. 2001, US Dist. Ct. (dist. Minn.) 2001, US Patent and Trademark Office 2001. Software engr. MCI Telecom.; assoc. Merchant & Gould, P.C., Mpls. Named a Rising Star, Minn. Super Lawyers mag., 2006. Mem.: Minn. Intellectual Property Law Assn., ABA, Minn. State Bar Assn. Office: Merchant & Gould PC 3200 IDS Ctr 80 S 8th St Minneapolis MN 55402 Office Phone: 612-336-4771. E-mail: rkalinsky@merchant-gould.com.*

KALIS, MURRAY, advertising agency executive, writer; s. Bernard and Bernis Kalis. BS in Comm., U. Ill.; MFA in Printmaking, Drake U., U. Iowa. Past chmn. art dept. Midwestern Coll., Denison, Iowa; creative dir., v.p. Leo Burnett Advt., Chgo.; creative dir., sr. v.p. Young & Rubicam Advt. Joint Ventures, LA; pres. Coen/Kalis Advt., LA, 1989—95; chmn. Kalis & Savage Advt., 1995—2001; pres. Kalis and Assocs., 2001—06; ptnr., creative dir. Riester-Kalis Advt., 2006—. Chmn. Worldwide Ptnrs. Inc., 2003—04; mgr. Kalis Racing LLC. Author: Candida by Amy Voltaire, 1979, Love in Paris, 1980, Are You Experienced? The Jimi Hendrix Story, 1984, (play) Single Scene, 1989, (play) Mating Dance (Best of Fest, Fresh Faces Festival, NYC, 2002). Juror Baltic Ad Golden Hammer award, Riga, Latvia. 1st lt. US Army. Recipient cert. of merit NY Art Dirs. One Show, Bronze Lion, Cannes Festival, Gold medal Chgo. Film Festival, Clio award, Best in West, Belding, Spl. award for pub. svc. advt. UN; intaglio art in permanent collection Phila. Mus. Art. Mem.: Acad. TV Arts and Sci., Think LA, Creative Club. Office: Riester Kalis 11833 Mississippi Ste 101 Los Angeles CA 90025

KALIS, PETER JOHN, lawyer; b. Detroit, Feb. 20, 1950; s. Michael P. and Helen (Karageorge) K.; m. Beverly A. Poling, Feb. 1, 1976. BA, W.Va. U., 1972; PhD, Oxford U., 1976; JD, Yale U., 1978. Bar: Pa. 1980, U.S. Dist. Ct. (we. dist.) Pa. 1980, U.S. Ct. Appeals (3d cir.) 1983, U.S. Supreme Ct. 1985. Law clk. to presiding justice U.S. Ct. Appeals (D.C. cir.), Washington, 1978-79; law clk. to Justice Byron R. White U.S. Supreme Ct., Washington, 1979-80; assoc. Kirkpatrick & Lockhart, Pitts., 1980-85, ptnr., 1985—2004; ptnr. & chmn. mgmt. com. Kirkpatrick & Lockhart Nicholson Graham LLP, Pitts., 2005—. Adj. prof. law U. Pitts., 1981—. Editor-in-chief Yale Law Jour., 1978; contbr. articles to profl. jours. Bd. dir., mem. exec. com., & chmn. fin. & investment com. Blanchette Rockefeller Neurosciences Inst.; bd. dir. Nat. Pancreas Found. Rhodes scholar, Oxford, Eng., 1973. Mem. ABA, Am. Law Inst., Pa. Bar Assn., Allegheny County Bar Assn. Clubs: Rivers (Pitts.), Shannupin Country. Avocations: theater, literature, sports. Office: Kirkpatrick & Lockhart Nicholson Graham LLP Henry W Oliver Bldg 535 Smithfield St Pittsburgh PA 15222-2312 Office Phone: 412-355-6562. Office Fax: 412-355-6501. Business E-Mail: pkalis@klng.com.

KALISH, ARTHUR, lawyer; b. Bklyn., Mar. 6, 1930; s. Jack and Rebecca (Biniamofsky) K.; m. Janet J. Wiener, Mar. 7, 1953; children: Philip, Pamela. BA, Cornell U., 1951; JD, Columbia U., 1956. Bar: N.Y. 1956, D.C. 1970. Assoc. Paul, Weiss, Rifkind, Wharton & Garrison, NYC, 1956-64, ptnr., 1965-95, of counsel, 1996—. Lectr. NYU Inst. Fed. Taxation, Hawaii Tax Inst., Law Jour. Seminars Contbr. articles to legal jours. Assoc. trustee L.I. Jewish Med. Ctr., New Hyde Park, N.Y., 1978-82, trustee, 1982-95, hon. trustee, 1995-97; trustee emeritus North Shore - L.I. Jewish Health Sys., 1997-98, life trustee, 1998-2003, trustee, 2003—; trustee S.I. U. Hosp., 2004—; bd. dirs. Cmty. Health Program of Queens Nassau Inc., New Hyde Park, 1978-94, pres., 1981-89, chmn. emeritus, 1994-97; bd. dirs. Managed Health, Inc., New Hyde Park, 1990-98, chmn., 1994-95. Advanced from ensign to lt. (j.g.) USN, 1951—53. Fellow Am. Coll. Tax Counsel; mem. ABA, N.Y. State Bar Assn., Assn. Bar City N.Y., Columbia Law Sch. Assn. (bd. dirs. 1990-94). Home: 2 Bass Pond Dr Old Westbury NY 11568-1307 Office: Paul Weiss Rifkind Wharton & Garrison LLP 1285 Avenue Of The Americas New York NY 10019-6064 Home Phone: 516-626-0667; Office Phone: 212-373-3095. Personal E-mail: arthurk767@aol.com. Business E-Mail: akalish@paulweiss.com.

KALISH, BOB, lawyer; JD, South Tex. Coll. Law, Houston. Bar: Tex. 1983. Atty. Kalish Law Offices, The Woodlands, Tex., 1984—. Recipient Houston Top Family Lawyers, H Tex. mag., 2006, Houston Top Lawyers for the People, 2007. Office: Kalish Law Offices 5 Grogans Park Drive The Woodlands TX 77380 Office Phone: 281-363-3700. Office Fax: 281-367-7340. E-mail: bob@kalishlawtexas.com.

KALISH, HEATHER RACHEL, chemist, researcher; d. Lawrence and Gail Penn; m. Michael A. Kalish, June 28, 1998; children: Logan, Ari. BA, Colgate U., Hamilton, NY, 1995; PhD, U. Calif., Davis, 2001. Postdoctoral rschr. lab. diagnostic radiology and rsch. NIH, Bethesda, Md., 2001—04, staff scientist, dept. bioengring. and phys. scis., 2004—. Mem.: Am. Chem. Soc. (assoc.), Sigma Xi (assoc.). Avocation: scuba diving. Office: NIH Bldg 13 Room 3E42 9000 Rockville Pike Bethesda MD 20892 Office Phone: 301-435-5498. Business E-Mail: KalishH@mail.nih.gov.

KALISH, MYRON, lawyer; b. NYC, Dec. 3, 1919; s. Louis and Bertha (Nacht) K.; m. Evelyn J. Zobler, Apr. 1, 1944; children— Nita Jane, Pamela Sue. BS in Social Sci., CCNY, 1940; LLB cum laude, Harvard U., 1943. Bar: N.Y. bar 1944. Since practiced in, NYC; sr. ptnr. Arthur, Dry & Kalish and predecessor firms, 1961-84; gen. counsel UNIROYAL, Inc., 1961-84; spl. ptnr. Shea & Gould, NYC, 1985-91, of counsel, 1992-94, Parker Duryee Rosoff & Haft, NYC, 1994—2002; sole practice, 2002—. Editor: Harvard Law Rev, 1942-43. Adv. bd. Southwestern Legal Found. Lt. USNR, 1943-46. Mem. ABA, N.Y. State Bar Assn., Assn. Bar City N.Y., NAM (mem. lawyers adv. com. to gen. cousnel), Harvard Club, Bellport Country Club, Rockefeller Ctr. Luncheon Club, Westhampton Yacht Squadron. Home: 40 Halsey Rd Remsenburg NY 11960 Office: 50 E 79th St New York NY 10021-0232 Office Phone: 212-737-8142. Office Fax: 212-288-6102. Personal E-mail: mikekalish@hotmail.com.

KALISHER, SIMPSON, photographer; b. Bronx, NY, July 27, 1926; s. Benjamin and Sheva Rusholenker Kalisher; children: Jesse, Amy Simpson, David Colby, Allon Brownell. BA in History, Ind. U., Bloomington, 1948. Freelance photographer Scope Assocs., NYC, 1951—57, NYC, 1957—71, 2005—, Roxbury, Conn., 1971—98, Greenwich, Conn., 1998—2005. Home: 395 S End Ave Apt 33J New York NY 10280-1053 Personal E-mail: simpson@simpsonkalisher.com.

KALISKI, MARY, psychologist; b. Bratislava, Czechoslovakia, Dec. 9, 1938; came to U.S., 1950; d. Frank and Margaret (Fleischman) Reichenthal; m. Thomas Kaliski, Sept. 21, 1957; children: Karen, Kenneth. BS summa cum laude, C.W. Post Coll., 1978; MS, profl. diploma, St. John's U., 1980, PhD, 1987. Psychologist North Shore Schs., L.I., 1977-79, Herricks Schs., L.I., 1979—. Chief psychologist Stepfamily Found., L.I., 1987—92; spkr. in field. Bd. dirs. Nassau Psychol. Svcs. Inst., 1989—. Mem. Am. Psychol. Assn., Nassau County Psychol. Assn. E-mail: tmkaliski@aol.com.

KALISKI, STEPHAN FELIX, economics professor; b. Warsaw, Nov. 4, 1928; emigrated to Can., 1941, naturalized, 1947; s. Jacob and Ludwika (Romanus) K.; m. Marian Ieleen Nelson, Oct. 6, 1960; 1 dau., Susan Maria. BA, U. B.C., 1951; MA, U. Toronto, 1953, postgrad., 1953-54; PhD, U. Cambridge, Eng., 1959. Statistician I Dominion Bur. Statistics, 1951-52; Alexander Mackenzie Research fellow U. Toronto, 1953-54; lectr. Queen's U., Kingston, Ont., 1954-56, prof. econs., 1969-94; chmn. div II Queen's U. (Grad. Sch.), 1971-73; prof. emeritus, 1994—; research fellow in econ. statistics Manchester (Eng.) U., 1958-59; asst. prof. Carleton U., Ottawa, Ont., 1959-62, asso. prof., 1962-65, prof., 1965-69, cmn. dept. econs., 1962-63, 64-66; research supr. Royal Commn. Taxation, 1963-64; Can. Council Sr. fellow, Dept. Labour-Univs. Research Com. research grantee, research asso. U. Calif., Berkeley, 1966-67; Can. Council leave fellow, 1973-74; hon. research asso. in econs. Harvard U., 1973-74. Social Sci. and Humanities Research Council Can. leave fellow, 1980-81, research grantee, 1978, 81; bd. dirs. Nat. Bur. Econ. Research, 1978-84; cons. Royal Commn. on Econ. Union, 1984-85, Commn. of Inquiry on Unemployment Ins., 1985-86. Author: Adjustment Assistance under the U.S. Trade Expansion Act, 1963, The Tradeoff Between Inflation and Unemployment, Some Explorations of Recent Evidence for Canada, 1972; editor, author: Canadian Economic Policy since the War, a Series of Six Public Lectures in Commemoration of the Twentieth Anniversary of the White Paper on Employment and Income of 1945, 1966; mng. editor: Can. Jour. Econs, 1976-79; contbr. articles to profl. publs. Can. Council research grantee, 1969, 77-81; Social Sci. Research Council research fellow, 1956-57 Fellow Royal Soc. Can.; mem. Can. Econs. Assn. (v.p. 1984-85, pres.-elect 1985-86, pres. 1986-87, past pres. 1987-88), Queen's Univ. Club. Home: 649 Fernmoor Dr Kingston ON Canada K7M 8K5 Office: Queen's U Dept Econs Kingston ON Canada K7L 3N6 Business E-Mail: kaliskis@qed.econ.queensu.ca.

KALIYAN, NALLADURAI, research scientist; arrived in US, 2001; s. Kaliyan Rengan and Sellam Perumal. B Engring., Tamil Nadu Agrl. U., 1998; MS, U. Minn., St. Paul, 2004, PhD, 2007. Jr. rsch. fellow Tamil Nadu Agrl. U., India, 1999—2001; rsch. asst. U. Minn., 2001—. Presenter in field. Mem.: Am. Soc. Agrl. and Biol. Engrs. (Hon. Mention Paper award 2006), Alpha Epsilon, Sigma Xi (Merit Poster award 2006). Office: U Minn 1390 Eckles Ave Saint Paul MN 55108 Office Phone: 612-625-9722.

KALKSTEIN, JOSHUA ADAM, lawyer; b. Phila., Oct. 1, 1943; s. Abraham and Helen (Ponemone) K.; children: Aleta K., Trevor W., Maxim J. AB, Brown U., 1965; JD, U. Pa., 1968. Bar: N.Y. 1968, N.J. 1971, Mass. 1978, U.S. Dist. Ct. N.Y. 1968, U.S. Dist. Ct., N.J. 1971, U.S. Dist. Ct., Mass. 1978, U.S. Ct. of Appeals (3d cir.) 1973, U.S. Ct. Mil. Appeals 1969. Asst. gen. counsel Pfizer Inc., Groton, Conn., 1978—2004; assoc. Hellring, Lindeman & Landau, Newark, 1972-75; corp. counsel Hooper Holmes Inc., Basking Ridge, NJ, 1975-78; counsel Hanify & King, Boston, 2004—06, Robinson & Cole, Boston, 2006—. Vis. counsel Harvard U., MIT Ctr. for Exptl. Pharmacology and Therapeutics, Cambridge, 1995—. Bd. dirs. Howland Art Ctr., Beacon, N.Y., 1987-91, Congregation Beth El, New London, Conn., 1995-96, Main Street New London, 2000—03; mem. Waterfront Redevel. Commn., Beacon, 1990-91. Lt. USNR, 1969-72. Mem. N.Y. State Bar Assn., N.J. Bar Assn., Mass. Bar Assn. Jewish. Avocations: art collecting, book collecting, golf. Home: 76 Library St Mystic CT 06355-2420 Office: Robinson & Cole LLP 1 Boston Pl Boston MA 02108-4404 Home Phone: 860-572-2026; Office Phone: 617-557-5964. Business E-Mail: jkalkstein@rc.com.

KALKUS, STANLEY, librarian, administrator, consultant; b. Prague, Czechoslovakia, Apr. 27, 1931; came to U.S., 1952; s. Frank and Zdenka (Hynkova) K.; m. Marta J. Pokorna, Jan. 12, 1952; children: Michaela Z., Olen A., Hynek P. Abitur, Classical Gymnasium, Prague, 1950; Cert. in Germanistics, Charles U., Prague, 1951; MA, U. Chgo., 1959. Librarian, audio-visual coordinator Chgo. Bd. Edn., 1960-62; base librarian U.S. Air Force, Sidi Slimane, Morocco, 1962-63, Hahn AFB, Fed. Republic

Germany, 1963-68; slavic bibliographer U. N.C., Chapel Hill, 1968-69; head library dept. Naval Underwater Systems Ctr., Newport, R.I., 1969-77; dir. U.S. Dept. Navy Library, Washington, 1977-86, coord., 1986-89, libr. of Navy, 1990-92; asst. prof. Charles U., Prague, Czech Republic, 1992—. Lectr. U. N.C., Chapel Hill, 1968-69; participant tech. info. panel AGARD (NATO), Brussels, 1974, Copenhagen, 1975, Washington, 1976, Oslo, 1977; adv. com. Intergovtl. Libr. Cooperation, 1981-82; exec. adv. com. Fedlink, 1986-88; rep. Dept. of Navy on Fed. Libr. and Info. Ctrs. com., 1991-92; chmn. libr. com. Ctrl. European Rsch. and Grad. Edn., 1998-2003, Econ. Inst., Acad. Scis., Prague, 1994-2000; mem. libr. com. Parliament of Czech Republic, 1997-99; adv. bd. U. Koblenz (Germany) Exernal LS Studies, 1998-2000. Editor Navy Libraries in 1980s, 1976; contbr. articles to profl. jours. Mem. core com. R.I. Gov.'s Conf. on Libraries, 1976-77. Served with U.S. Army, 1953-55 Fellow U. Chgo., 1957-58 Mem. ALA (pres. Armed Forces sect. 1974), Spl. Libr. Assn. (chmn. mil. librs. div. 1978-79, rep. for Czech Republic), Internat. Fedn. Libr. Assns. (mem. standing com. on social librs. 1986-96, mem. standing com. edn. and tng. 1996-2000), Am. Translators Assn., Czech Libr. and Info. Profl. Assn. (mem. exec. bd. 1999—), Assn. Americans Residing Overseas, Newport Ski Club, Czech-Am. Club (pres. 2003—), Friends of Newport Pub. Libr., Lions Internat. (pres. 2003-04). Roman Catholic. Avocations: skiing, tennis. Office: Charles U Prague FF UISK U Krize 8 150 00 Prague Czech Republic also: 7009 Dreams Way Ct Alexandria VA 22315-4245 Home Phone: (+420) 251 811 178; Office Phone: +420 2 51 080 368. Fax: +420 2 510 80 413. E-mail: skalkus@yahoo.com, kalkus@cuni.cz.

KALKWARF, KENNETH LEE, dean, dental educator; b. Lincoln, Nebr., Apr. 12, 1946; s. Robert G. and Grace L. (Beck) K.; m. Sharon R. Moore, July 6, 1974; children: Kyle J., Kevin J. Student, U. Nebr., 1964-66, DDS, 1970, MS, 1973. Diplomate Am. Bd. Periodontology. Asst. prof. U. Nebr., Lincoln, 1973-78, prof., 1980-87; assoc. prof. U. Okla., Oklahoma City, 1978-80; prof., assoc. dean U. Tex. Health Sci. Ctr. Dental Sch., San Antonio, 1987-88, prof., dean, 1988—. Cons. Cen. Regional Dental Testing, Topeka, Kans., 1980-87, VA, Nebr., 1981-87, ADA, Chgo., 1982—; vis. prof. Svc. U. Autonoma de Guadalajara/Mexico, 1980-82. Contbg. author textbooks, 1978—; contbr. articles to profl. jours., rsch. abstracts. Bd. dirs. McAllister Park Little League, San Antonio, 1990-94, mem. Leadership San Antonio, 1989-90. Recipient Alumni Achievement award U. Nebr., 1990, Outstanding Tchr. award U. Okla., 1980. Fellow Internat. Coll. Dentists, Am. Coll. Dentists; mem. ADA (chmn. Commn. Dental Accreditation, 2003-04), San Antonio Dist. Dental Soc. (bd. dirs. 1988-93), Am. Acad. Periodontology, S.W. Soc. Periodontology (bd. dirs. 1984-97, pres. 1993-94), Tex. Soc. Periodontists (bd. dirs. 1988-95), Internat. Assn. for Dental Rsch, Am. Dental Edn. Assn. (pres-elect 2005-06). Republican. Methodist. Avocations: spectator sports, jogging, reading. Office: Univ Tex Health Sci Ctr 7703 Floyd Curl Dr San Antonio TX 78284-6200 Office Phone: 210-567-3166. Office Fax: 210-567-6721. Business E-Mail: kalkwarf@uthscsa.edu.

KALKWARF, LEONARD V., minister; b. Parkersburg, Iowa, Mar. 17, 1928; s. John Jr. and Helen Kalkwarf; m. Beverly Jane Hardy, May 22, 1954; children— Deborah Joy, Cynthia Sue, Scott Craig BA, Ctrl. Coll., Pella, Iowa, 1950; BD, New Brunswick Sem., 1953; MA, NYU, 1957; STM, Luth. Sem., Phila., 1973; DMin, Princeton Sem., 1980; DD (hon.), Ctrl. Coll., 1983. Ordained to ministry Ref. Ch. in Am., 1953. Assoc. pastor Bellevue Ref. Ch., Schenectady, NY, 1953—55, Levittown Cmty. Ch., NY, 1955—57; pastor Ref. Ch., Willow Grove, Pa., 1957—64, 1965—91, Nat. Evang. Ch., Kuwait, 1964—65; pastoral asst. Presbyn. Ch., Abington, Pa., 1998—2004. Pres. Particular Synod N.J., 1969-70, 70-71, Gen. Synod Ref. Ch. in Am., 1983-84 Author: History, 1st Reformed Church of Philadelphia, 1960, God Loves His World, Book I, 1963, Book II, 1964, Maundy Thursday Drama, 2007; contbr. articles to religious jours. Served as Chaplain Civil Air Patrol, 1960-62 Mem.: Pa. Rotary (pres. Glenside chpt.). Democrat. Avocations: bowling, horseshoes, ping pong/table tennis, billiards. Home: 7450 Spring Village Dr Apt 509 Springfield VA 22150-4944 Office Phone: 703-451-4129. Business E-Mail: kalkway@aeitv.net.

KALLAHER, MICHAEL JOSEPH, mathematics professor; b. Cin., Sept. 4, 1940; s. Martin Henry and Lou Will (Huff) K.; m. Donalyn May Laraway, Aug. 17, 1963; children: Jay, Michael, Christopher, Daniel, Raymond. BS, Xavier U., 1961; MS, Syracuse U., 1963, PhD, 1967. Postdoctoral fellow U. Man., Winnipeg, Can., 1967-69; from asst. prof. prof. math. Wash. State U., Pullman, 1969—, assoc. dean scis., 1979-84, acting dean scis., 1982, chmn. math dept., 1984-92; vis. prof. Auckland U., New Zealand, 1988. Author: Affine Planes with Transitive Collineation Groups; contbg. editor Finite Geometries, 1982; contbr. articles to profl. jours. Grantee NSF; Fulbright Research scholar, Kaiserslautern, Fed. Republic Germany, 1975-76. Fellow Inst. Combinatories and Its Application (founding); mem. Am. Math. Soc., Math. Assn. Am., N.Y. Acad. of Scis., Assn. of Research Profs. (pres. 1986-87), Sigma Xi. Home: 235 NW Joe St Pullman WA 99163-3410 Office: Wash State U Dept Of Math Pullman WA 99163 Business E-Mail: mkallaher@pullman.com.

KALLAKIS, HIS EXCELLENCY ACHILLEAS MICHALIS S. (HIS EXCELLENCY AMBASSADOR ACHILLEAS M. KALLAKIS OF THE REPUBLIC OF SAN MARINO TO THE SULTANE OF BRUNEI), transportation executive, real estate company executive; b. London, Sept. 3, 1968; s. Michalis and Erinoula (Angelinakis) K.; m. Pamela Anne Stachowsky, Sept. 1995; children: Erinoula, Michalis and Aristotelis (twins), Dionysios. BSc in Econs. with honors, London U., 1989. Dir. Global Transport, Del. and NY, 1989—91; chmn., CEO Pacific Group of Cos., London, NYC, 1991—, Pacific Risk Corp., London, 2000—. Dir. U.S. C. of C., London, 1997—, Ocean Group USA, 1989—, Pacific Maritime, N.Y., 1991—, Bernouli Trust Corp., NY, 1994—, South Pacific Adv. Bd., Sydney, 1994—2000, Brit. Am. Bus., Inc.; chmn., CEO Pacific Coffee Corp., Hellenic Capital Mgmt., Pacific Real Estate Corp., 2000—, Atlas Alliance Group, 2000—, Atlas E-Risk, 2000—01; chmn. Pacific Vending Group; mem. devel. bd. Nat. Portrait Gallery, London, 2000—; amb. of Republic of San Marino to Sultanate of Brunei, 2007—. Author: Maritime Registers of the World, 1994, Transport Economics, 1996; co-editor: The Wonders of Italy, 1996. Pres. Youth Anglo-Hellenic Soc. U.K., London, 1986-88; dir. Friends of Florence, Italy, 1997—, Duke of Edinburgh Special Projects; mem. com. Youth Enterprise Initiative, London, 1989-92; mem. Royal Opera, London, Navy League; patron English Nat. Ballet. Recipient Churchill award for Excellence Churchill Enterprise Foundation, 1993, Pres.'s Golden Honor award South Pacific Action, Foru, 1995, Prime Min.'s award South Pacific Action Forum, 1996, Outstanding Emerging Leader award Office of Maritime Affairs, 1997; fellow Duke of Edinburgh Internat., 2003-. Fellow Inst. Dirs., Inst. Transport and Tourism; mem. Friends of Conservation, Queen's Club, Met. Opera Guild (N.Y.C.), Met. Club (N.Y.C.), Nat. Trust (London), Soc. for Protection of Ancient Bldgs. (London), Landmark Trust (Eng.). Greek Orthodox. Avocations: travel, italian studies, back-gammon, fencing, tennis, antiques, poker. Office: Pacific Group Cos 8 Carlos Pl Mayfair London W1K 3AS England

KALLAS, HANI R., lawyer; b. Kettering, Ohio, Dec. 30, 1968; BS, Miami U., 1991; JD, U. Cin. Coll. Law, 1994. Bar: Ohio 1994. Ptnr. Vorys, Sater, Seymour and Pease LLP, Cin., 1994—. Named one of Ohio's Rising Star, Super Lawyers, 2006. Mem.: Order of Coif. Office: Vorys Sater Seymour and Pease LLP Atrium Two Ste 2000 221 E Fourth St PO Box 0236 Cincinnati OH 45201-0236 Office Phone: 513-723-4615. Office Fax: 513-852-7864.

KALLAY, MICHAEL FRANK, II, medical products executive; b. Painesville, Ohio, Aug. 24, 1944; s. Michael Frank and Marie Francis (Sage) K.; m. Irma Yolanda Corona, Aug. 30, 1975; 1 son, William Albert. BBA, Ohio U., 1967. Salesman Howmedica, Inc., Rutherford, NJ, 1972-75, Biochem Procedures/Metpath, North Hollywood, Calif., 1975-76; surg. specialist USCI divsn. C.R. Bard, Inc., Billerica, Mass., 1976-78; mgr. We. and Ctrl. Region ARCO Med. Products Co., Phila., 1978-80; midwest reigonal mgr. Intermedics, Inc., Freeport, Tex., 1980-82; area mgr. Minntech Renal Systems, Mpls., 1982—. Pres. Kall-Med, Inc., Anaheim Hills, Calif., 1982—. Mem. Am. Mgmt. Assn., Phi Kappa Sigma. Office Phone: 714-397-3617. Personal E-mail: mfkii@att.net.

KALLENBERG, JOHN KENNETH, retired librarian; b. Anderson, Ind., June 10, 1942; s. Herbert A. and Helen S. K.; m. Ruth Barrett, Aug. 19, 1965; children: Jennifer Anne, Gregory John. AB, Ind. U., 1964, M.L.S., 1969. With Fresno County Library, Fresno, Calif., 1965-70, dir., 1976—2003; librarian Fig Garden Pub. Library br., 1968-70; asst. dir. Santa Barbara Pub. Library, Calif., 1970-76; ret. Mem. Calif. Libr. Svcs. bd., 1990—99, v.p., 1992—95, pres., 1996—98; mem. Libr. of Calif. Bd., 1999—2003, pres., 2003; Beth Ann Harnish lectr. com., 1988—91; mem. adv. bd. Pacific S.W. Regional Med. Libr., 1999—; mem. Heartland Regional Libr. Network Bd., 2000—04; bd. mem. Fresno County Retired Employees Assn., 2006—07. Mem. editl. bd.: Past and Present, Fresno City and County Hist. Soc., 1980—. Mem.: ALA, Fresno County Employees Retirement Assn. (mem. bd. 2006—07), William Saroyan Soc. (bd. dirs. 1984—, chmn. 2004—), Am. Soc. Pub. Adminstrn., Libr. Adminstrn. and Mgmt. Assn., Calif. Libr. Authority for Sys. and Svcs. (chmn. authority adv. coun. 1978—80), Calif. County Librs. Assn. (pres. 1977), Calif. Libr. Assn. (councilor 1976—77, v.p., pres. 1987), Pub. Libr. Assn., Kiwanis (pres. Fresno 1981—82, lt. gov. divsn. 5 1991—92, co-editor Cal-Nev-Ha News 1993—94, 1995—96, bd. dirs. 1999—2001, 2002—04, editor Kiwaniscape 2004—05, co-editor 2005—06, 2005—07). Presbyterian. E-mail: jkk59@cvip.net.

KALLEWAARD, SUSAN L., elementary school educator; d. Lloyd MacDonald Braithwaite and Ann Marie Barranti; m. Dan E. Kallewaard, Sept. 22, 1979; 1 child, Hannah Marie. Bachelors, Western Mich. U., Kalamazoo, 2000; Masters, Mary Grove Coll., Detroit, 2002. 5th grade tchr. Portage Pub. Schs., Mich., 2000—05, 4th grade tchr., 2005—. Sci. fair coun. dir. Haverhill Sci. Fair, Portage, Mich., 2005—; student council advisor Haverhill Elem., Portage, 2005—. Mem.: Portage Ednl. Assn. (exec. bd., bldg. rep. 2003—), Mich. Coun. Tchrs. Math. Avocation: photography.

KALLFELZ, FRANCIS A., veterinary medicine educator; b. Syracuse, NY, July 17, 1938; s. Alois Joseph and Josephine Marie (Honold) Kallfelz; m. Leonie Heidi Gantner, June 26, 1965; children: Andrew F., Susan E., Douglas P. Student, Lemoyne Coll., 1956-58; DVM, Cornell U., 1962, PhD, 1966. Diplomate Am. Coll. Vet. Nutrition (charter). Asst. prof. vet. medicine Cornell U., Ithaca, NY, 1966-73, assoc. prof., 1973-80, prof., 1980—; dir. Vet. Med. Tchg. Hosp., 1990-98, James Law prof. medicine (nutrition), 1997—. Sr. Fulbright lectr., Zagreb, Croatia, 1978; cons. FAO/IAEA, Vienna, 1977—78, Indonesia, 1980—83; vis. prof. Johns Hopkins U. Sch. Medicine, 1999; mem. subcom. nutrient requirements dogs and cats NAS NRC, 2000—04. Contbr. articles to profl. jours. Mem.: AVMA (coun. rsch. 1983—89, Am. Bd. Vet. Specialties 1988—2000, chmn. 1999—2000, coun. edn. 2004—), NY State Bd. Vet. Medicine (chmn. 2007—), NY State Commn. Animal Health Issues, NY State Vet. Med. Soc., Soc. Exptl. Biology and Medicine, Soc. Nuc. Medicine, Am. Soc. Nutrition. Republican. Roman Catholic. Avocations: handball, stamp collecting/philately, camping. Home: 11 Bean Hill Ln Ithaca NY 14850-9775 Office: Cornell Univ Coll Vet Medicine Dept Clin Sci Ithaca NY 14853 Office Phone: 607-253-3031. Business E-Mail: fak1@cornell.edu.

KALLICK, DAVID A., lawyer; b. Chgo., Nov. 7, 1945; s. Joseph N. and Elizabeth A. (Just) K.; m. Arline E. Chizewer, Nov. 26, 1972; children: Michelle, Robert. AB in History, Princeton U., 1967; JD, Northwestern U., 1971. Bar: Ill. 1971, Calif. 1972. Law clk. to presiding justice Ill. Appellate Ct., Chgo., 1971-72; assoc. McCutchen, Doyle, Brown & Enersen, San Francisco, 1972-74; asst. dean U. So. Calif. Law Ctr., LA, 1974-76, Ill. Inst. Tech.-Kent Coll. Law, Chgo., 1976-79; ptnr. Hurley Kallick & Schiller, Ltd., Deerfield, Ill., 1979-92, Tishler & Wald, Ltd., Chgo., 1992—. Past bd. dirs. Congregation Solel, Highland Park, Ill., Birchwood Club, Highland Park; past bd. mem., pres. Sch. Dist. 107, Highland Park; former trustee Legacy 107 Edn. Found., Highland Park. With USAR, 1968-74. Mem. ABA, Calif. Bar Assn., Ill. Bar Assn., Chgo. Bar Assn., Princeton Univ. Club. Home: 1887 Spruce Ave Highland Park IL 60035-2150 Office: 200 S Wacker Dr Ste 3000 Chicago IL 60606-5807 Office Phone: 312-876-3800. Business E-Mail: dkallick@tishlerandwald.com.

KALLIR, JANE KATHERINE, art gallery director, author; b. NYC; d. John Otto and Joyce (Ruben) Kallir. BA, Brown U., Providence, RI, 1976. Asst. to dir. Lefebre Gallery, NYC, 1977, Galerie St. Etienne, NYC, 1977-78, co-dir., 1979—. Guest lectr. NYU, 1982—85, 1999, Mus. Am. Folk Art, NYC, 1982—85, Nat. Gallery Art, 1994, guest curator, 94; guest lectr. Ft. Lauderdale Mus. Art, 1996, guest curator, Fla., 96; guest lectr. Mus. Modern Art, 1997, Internat. Found. for Art Rsch., 1998, Wexner Ctr., Columbus, Ohio, 1999, San Diego Mus., 2001, Columbus Mus. of Art, 2002, Clark Art Inst., 2002, Van Gogh Mus., 2005; guest curator NY State Mus., Albany, 1983, Internat. Exhbn. Found., Washington, 1984—85, Mus. of City of Vienna, 1986, Austrian Nat. Gallery, 1990, Indpls. Mus. Art, 1994, San Diego Mus. Art, 1994, Nat. Mus. of Women in the Arts, 2001, Orlando Mus. of Art, Fla., 2001, Museo del Vittoriano, Rome, 2001, San Diego Mus. Art, 2001, Van Gogh Mus., 2005. Author: Gustav Klimt-Egon Schiele, 1980, Austria's Expressionism, 1981, The Folk Art Tradition, 1981, Grandma Moses, The Artist Behind the Myth, 1982, Arnold Schoenberg's Vienna, 1984, Viennese Design and the Wiener Werkstaette, 1986, Gustav Klimt: 25 Masterworks, 1989, Egon Schiele: The Complete Works, 1990, rev., 1998, Richard Gerstl/Oskar Kokoschka, 1992, Egon Schiele, 1994, Egon Schiele: 27 Masterworks, 1996, Grandma Moses, 25 Masterworks, 1997, Grandma Moses in the 21st Century, 2001, The Essential Grandma Moses, 2001, Egon Schiele, Watercolors and Drawings, 2003, Egon Schiele: Love and Death, 2005. Mem.: Art Dealers Assn. Am. (bd. dir. 1994—97, chmn. pub. rels. com. 2001—07, v.p. 2003—06). Democrat. Office: Galerie St Etienne 24 W 57th St New York NY 10019-3918 Office Phone: 212-245-6734. E-mail: gallery@gse.art.com.

KALLMAN, CRAIG, music company executive; b. 1966; BA, Brown U., 1987. Former DJ, NYC; CBS Records coll. rep. Brown U.; program dir. WBRU-FM, Providence; founder Big Beat music label (acquired by Atlantic Records, 1991), NYC, 1987—91; v.p. & asst. to co-chmn., exec. v.p. A&R Atlantic Records, NYC, 1991—2002, co-pres., 2002—04; co-chmn. & COO Atlantic Records Group, NYC, 2004—05, chmn. & CEO, 2005—. Office: Atlantic Records Group 75 Rockefeller Plaza New York NY 10019*

KALLMANN, HELMUT MAX, musicologist, retired librarian; b. Berlin, Aug. 7, 1922; emigrated to Can., 1940, naturalized, 1946; s. Arthur and Fanny (Paradies) K.; m. Ruth Singer, Dec. 31, 1955 (dec. July 1993); 1 stepdaughter, Lynn Liora Salter. MusB, U. Toronto, Ont., Can., 1949, LLD, 1971. With CBC Music Libr., Toronto, 1950-70, supr., 1962-70; chief music divsn. Nat. Libr. Can., Ottawa, Ont., 1970-87, ret., 1987. Can. del. Internat. Assn. Music Librs., 1959-71. Author: A History of Music in Canada, 1534-1914, 1960; editor; Catalogue of Canadian Composers, 1952, Music for Orchestra I, Vol. 8, 1990, (with Gilles Potvin and Kenneth Winters) Ency. of Music in Canada, 1981, French edit., 1983, (with Potvin) 2nd edit., 1992, French 2nd edit., 1993, Music for Piano III, vol. 22, 1998; contbr. articles to profl. publs. Chmn. Can. Music Heritage Soc., 1982—2000. Decorated Order of Can., 1986; dedicatee Musical Can., Words and Music Honouring Helmut Kallmann, 1988; recipient medal Can. Music Coun., 1977, Award of Merit Assn. for Can. Studies, 1998. Mem. Can. Assn. Music Librs. (co-founder 1956, past chmn.), Faculty Music Alumni Assn. U. Toronto (pres. 1963-64), Order of Can. Home: 1 Thorncliffe Pl Apt 115 Nepean ON K2H 9N9 Canada Home Phone: 613-596-3853. Personal E-mail: drkallmann@yahoo.ca, hkallmann@rogers.com.

KALLMANN, STANLEY WALTER, lawyer; b. Bklyn., June 6, 1943; s. Silve and Erna Kallmann; m. Carolee A. McDonald, Aug. 23, 1969; children: Alexander, Andrew. BA, Rutgers U., New Brunswick, 1964; LLB, Rutgers U., Newark, 1967. Bar: NJ 1967, US Dist. Ct. NJ 1967, NY 1984. Law clk. to judge U.S. Dist. Ct. N.J., Newark, 1967-69; assoc. Stryker, Tams & Dill, Newark, 1969-71; asst. U.S. atty. U.S. Atty.'s Office, Newark, 1971-75; ptnr. Gennet, Kallmann, Antin & Robinson, Parsippany, N.J., 1975—. Mem. ABA, NJ Bar Assn. Office: Gennet Kallmann Antin & Robinson 6 Campus Dr Parsippany NJ 07054-4406 Business E-Mail: skallmann@gkar-law.com.

KALLSTROM, JAMES K., state official; b. Worcester, Mass., May 6, 1943; m. Susan Auer; children: Erika, Kristel. Grad., U. Mass., 1966. Spl. agent, various positions FBI, 1971—93, spl. agent in charge spl. ops. divsn. NYC, 1993—95, asst. dir. in charge, 1995—97, ret., 1997; with MBNA Am., 1997—2001, sr. exec. v.p., mgmt. com. mem., dir. govt. affairs, 2002—05; dir. NY State Office Pub. Security, 2001—02, sr. adv. to Gov. for counter-terrorism, 2002—. Bd. dirs. Lower Manhattan Devel. Corp. Advanced through grades to capt. USMC, Vietnam War. Office: Office Homeland Security State of NY 633 Third Ave New York NY 10017*

KALMAN, ANDREW, manufacturing executive, director; b. Hungary, Aug. 14, 1919; came to U.S., 1922, naturalized, 1935; s. Louis and Julia (Bognar) K.; m. Violet Margaret Kish, June 11, 1949; children: Andrew Joseph, Richard Louis, Laurie Ann. With Detroit Engring. & Machine Co., 1947-66, exec. v.p., gen. mgr., 1952-66; exec. v.p. and dir. Indian Head, Inc., 1966-75, also dir. Dir. Acme Precision Products, 1959-80, Reef Energy Corp., 1980-84. Trustee emeritus Alma (Mich.) Coll.; bd. dirs. Am. Hungarian Found., New Brunswick, N.J.; mem. adv. coun., mem. exec. com., U. Mich. Ctr. for Communication Disorders. Home: 708 S Military St Dearborn MI 48124-2108 Office: The Buhl Bldg 535 Griswold Ste 1900 Detroit MI 48226 Office Phone: 313-965-4182.

KALMAN, LAURA, history professor; b. LA, Mar. 19, 1955; d. Newton and Elizabeth Kalman; m. W. Randall Garr, Dec. 23, 1984. BA, Pomona Coll., Claremont, Calif., 1977; JD, U. Calif., LA, 1977; PhD, Yale U., New Haven, Conn., 1982. Bar: Calif. 1977. Asst. prof. to prof. U. Calif., Santa Barbara, 1982—. Fulbright rsch. prof. Tel Aviv U. Law Sch., 2001—02. Author: Legal Realism at Yale: 1927-1960, 1986, Abe Fortas: A Biography, 1990 (Littleton-Griswold prize Am. Hist. Assn., 1991), The Strange Career Of Legal Liberalism, 1996, Yale Law School And The Sixties: Revolt And Reverberations, 2005. Fellow: Am. Soc. Legal History (pres. 1998—99). Democrat. Jewish. Home: 901 West Campus Ln Goleta CA 93117 Office: Univ Calif Dept History Santa Barbara CA 93106 Home Phone: 805-453-8673; Office Phone: 805-893-3691. Home Fax: 805-893-8795. Business E-Mail: kalman@history.ucsb.edu.

KALMANSON, STEVEN R., health products executive; b. Johannesburg, 1952; m. Karen Kalmanson; 2 children. B in Commerce, U. Witwatersrand, Johannesburg, MBA. Project mgmt. specialist Kimberly-Clark Corp., Neenah, Wis., 1977, mktg. dir. Home Health Care, 1984, mktg. dir. Infant Care, 1988—90, v.p. Adult Care, 1990, pres. Adult Care, 1990—91, pres. Child Care, 1991—94, pres. Family Care, 1994—95, group pres. North Am. Family Care, 1995, group pres. North Atlantic Personal Care, 2004—05, group pres. North Atlantic Consumer Products Neenah, 2005—. Office: Kimberly Clark Corp PO Box 2020 Neenah WI 54957-2020*

KALMAR, CARLOS, conductor, music director; b. 1958; m. Britta Kalmar; children: Svenja, Katja. Condr. Vienna Volksoper, Vienna, 1987; music dir. Hamburg Symphony, 1987—91, Stuttgart Philharmonic, 1991—95, Anhaltisches Theater Dessau and Philharmonie Dessau, 1996—2000, Vienna Niederosterreichisches Tonkunstlevorchester, Vienna, 2000—03, Oreg. Symphony, 2003—. Prin. condr. Grant Park Music Festival, Chgo.; guest condr. numerous symphonies and orch., guest appearance. Avocations: hiking, cooking. Office: Oregon Symphony 921 SW Washington Ste 200 Portland OR 97205*

KALMYKOV, SERGUEI, physicist; b. Miass, Russia, June 15, 1972; s. Youri Kalmykov and Antonina Kalmykova. MS in Applied Math. and Physics summa cum laude, Moscow Inst. Physics and Tech., 1995; PhD, Russian Acad. Scis., Moscow, 2001. Rsch. fellow laser plasma lab. Inst. for High Energy Densities of Associated Inst. for High Temperatures, Russian Acad. Scis., Moscow, 1995—2001; postdoctoral fellow Centre de Physique Théorique, École Polytechnique, Palaiseau, France, 2001—03; postdoctoral fellow theory divsn. Max-Planck-Inst. for Quantenoptik, Garching-bei-München, Germany, 2003; postdoctoral fellow Ill. Inst. Tech., Chgo., 2003—04; rsch. assoc. dept. physics Inst. for Fusion Studies, U. Tex., Austin, 2004—. Contbr. articles to profl. jours. Scholar, Internat. Soros Sci. Ednl. Program Open Soc. Inst., 1995—96, 1998. Mem.: Optical Soc. Am., Am. Phys. Soc., European Phys. Soc. Russian Orthodox. Achievements include research in holographical imaging of laser wakefield in plasmas, laser wakefield electron acceleration using ultrashort petawatt laser pulses, laser pulse compression in plasmas relying on electromagnetic cascading effect; stimulated Raman scattering of ultrashort laser pulses in bounded plasmas, plasma channels and plasma-filled capillaries. Avocation: photography. Office: Univ Tex 1 University Station C1500 Austin TX 78712 Office Phone: 512-471-6121. Office Fax: 512-471-6715.

KALNES, DONNA M. SIMONDET, retired principal, alcohol and drug abuse education program director; b. North Redwood, Minn., Jan. 24, 1934; d. Oscar Walter and Alma Mae Simondet; m. Rasmus B.A. Kalnes, Aug. 21, 1954; children: David Michael(dec.) , Stephanie Kae, Eric Peter. BA in Elem. Edn., Luther Coll., Decorah, Iowa, 1953; MS in Tchg., U. Wis., Whitewater, 1979; splty. degree in ednl. adminstrn., U. Wis., Madison, 1995. Tchr. 2d grade Jackson Sch. Dist., Minn., 1953—54; 1st and 2d grade tchr. Hayfield Sch. Disst., Minn., 1954—56, Nichols Sch. Dist., Monona, Wis., 1956—57, Madison Sch. Dist., 1961; tchg. grades 1-8 Mukwonego Sch. Dist., Wis., 1966—68; tchr. grades 4, 7, 8 Palmyra-Eagle Sch. Dist., Wis., 1968—83, prin., 1978—94. Alcohol and other drug abuse coun. dir. K-12 Palmyra-Eagle Sch. Dist., 1983—94; alcohol and other drug abuse program grant reader Wis. Dept. Pub. Instrn., 1985—94, alcohol and other drug abuse prrogram coun. mem., 1988—94; pres. Four Lakes Prins. Assn., 1991; presenter in field. Bd. dirs., bd. curators Wis. Hist. Soc., Madison, 1999—2001; adult leader 4-H, Eagle, 1967—93; cookbook com. Friends of Old World Wis., 1988; vol. holiday fair Waukesha County Hist. Soc., 1990—; edn. com. Eagle Hist. Soc., 2005—; state del. Rep. Party of Wis., Madison, 1975—; co-author 100-yr. history St. John's Luth. Ch., North Prairie, Wis., adult Bible study leader; edn. officer Luth. Brotherhood Prairie Br. # 8146, 1987—95; bd. dirs. Friends of Wis. Hist. Soc., Madison, 1976—, pres., 1999—2001; bd. dirs. Palmyra-Eagle Scholarship and Ednl. Found., 2003—. Named Mother of Yr. for Wis., Mother of the Yr. Program, 1980, Citizen of Yr., Eagle Lioness, 1986; named one of Outstanding Elem. Tchrs. of Am., 1974, 1975, 1976;

recipient Disting. Svc. award, Luther Coll., 1988, US Mcht. Marine Acad., 1992, Assn. Wis. Sch. Adminstrs., 1998. Mem.: Assn. Wis. Sch. Adminstrs. (pres., chair exec. dir. search com. 1995, 1998, bd. dirs. 1991—97, region 2 dir. 1991—93, pub. rels. com. 1993—97, chair regional profl. conf. 1994—95, co-chair exec. dirs. retirement celebration 1995), Nat. Assn. Elem. Sch. Prins., Phi Delta Kappa (nat. fellows program 1989). Lutheran. Avocations: Bible study, rosemaling, gardening, piano, crossword puzzles. Home: 520 E Waukesha Rd Eagle WI 53119 E-mail: dmkalnes@execpc.com.

KALNICKI, SHALOM, radiologist, educator; b. Tel Aviv, July 18, 1951; s. Samuel and Dina K.; m. Rachel Leia Cukier, May 20, 1975; children: Miriam, Michael, Dina Eva. MD, U. Sao Paulo, 1974. Resident Montefiore Hosp. Med. Ctr., Bronx, 1975-78, chief resident, 1978-79; med. instr. U. Sao Paulo Med. Sch., Brazil, 1979-83; asst. prof., dir. radiotherapy dept. Hosp. of Albert Einstein Coll. Medicine, Bronx, 1983-84; asst. prof. clin. radiotherapy Mt. Sinai Med. Ctr., NYC, 1984-88; assoc. prof. Magee Women's Hosp., oncologist dept. radiation oncology, U. Pitts., 1988—; chmn. dept. radiation oncology Allegheny Gen. Hosp., Pitts., 1993-2000; vice chmn. for clin. affairs, dept. radiation oncology U. Pitts. Med. Ctr., 2000—; vice chmn. clin. affairs U. Pitts. Cancer Inst., 2000—; prof. radiation oncology U. Pitts., 2000—; prof., chmn. Albert Einstein Coll. Medicine., Mark Fiore Med. Ctr., Bronx, NY. Contbr. articles to profl. jours. Named Outstanding House Officer, Montefiore Hosp. Med. Ctr. Alumni Assn., 1979; Sao Paulo Rsch. Found. grantee, 1972. Mem. Am. Soc. Therapeutic Radiologists, Am. Soc. Clin. Oncology, N.Y. Acad. Sci., N.Y. Cancer Soc., N.Y. Roentgen Ray Soc. Home: 3636 Waldo Ave Apt 3j Bronx NY 10463-2256 Office: Albert Einsten Coll Medicine Mark Fiore Med Ctr 111 East 210th St Bronx NY 10467 Office Phone: 718-980-5280.

KALOF, ALEXANDRA N., pathologist, educator; d. Daryll D. Major and Linda Henry Kalof; m. John M. Wright, Aug. 7, 1999; 1 child, Elizabeth L. Wright. BA, U. Va., Charlottesville, 1995; MD, U. Vt., Burlington, 2000. Diplomate Am. Bd. Pathology, 2005. Surg. pathology fellow Stanford U., Calif., 2004—05; asst. prof. pathology U. Vt., Burlington, 2005—. Dir. histology lab. UVM/Fletcher Allen Health Care, Burlington, 2006—. Fellow: Coll. Am. Pathologists (assoc.). Office Phone: 802-847-6868.

KALOGJERA, IKAR JAKSA, psychiatrist, educator; b. Zagreb, Croatia, Aug. 30, 1945; arrived in U.S., 1972; s. Jaksa Jakov and Biserka Erak Kalogjera; m. Araceli Colina Cabaron, July 15, 1976; 1 child, Liliana Marie. MD, U. Zagreb, Croatia, 1970. Diplomate in psychiatry and child and adolescent psychiatry Am. Bd. Psychiatry and Neurology. Intern U. Zagreb, 1970—71; resident in psychiatry Med. Coll. Wis., Wauwatosa, 1972—74; fellow in child and adolescent psychiatry U. Cin., 1974—76; pvt. practice Rockford, Ill., 1976—79; dir. adolescent in-patient unit Med. Coll. Wis., 1979—80, dir. adolescent in-patient svc., 1980—81; pvt. practice adult, child and adolescent psychiatry Wauwatosa, 1981—. Asst. clin. prof. Med. Coll. Wis., 1981—87, assoc. clin. prof., 1987—2001, clin. prof. psychiatry, 2001—; mem. hon. staff Aurora Psychiat. Hosp., Wauwatosa, 1999—; founder, leader Milw. Group for the Advancement of Self Psychology, 1991—. Co-author: (article) Am. Jour. Psychotherapy, 1988; author: Hosp. and Cmty. Psychiatry, 1989, (book chpt.) Disordered Couple, 1998. Cons. Family Svc., Milw., 1982—89, Lutheran Social Svcs., Milw., 1984—90, Jewish Family Svc., Milw., 1979—; contbr. Croatian Cmty., Milw., 1979—. Named one of America's Top Psychiatrists, Consumer Rsch. Coun. Am., 2002, 2003, 2004, 2005, 2006, 2007; named to Top Psychiatrists, Psychotherapists, Milw. Mag., 1994; recipient Outstanding Therapists, Town and Country Mag., 1988, Tchg. award, Dept. Psychiatry and Behavioral Medicine, Med. Coll. Wis., 1992, award for Excellence in Tchg., 1992, Top Psychiatrists, Psychotherapists, Milw. Mag., 1996, 2001, Marvin Wagner Clin. Preceptor award, Med. Coll. Wis., 1999, Golden Apple Tchg. award, 1996, 2000, Give a Damn award, 1991, 2003, Cmty. Svc. honor, Jewish Family Svcs. Milw., 2003. Fellow: Acad. Cognitive Therapy, Am. Psychiat. Assn. (Irma Bland award 2006), Am. Acad. Child Psychiatry; mem.: Wisc. Psychoanalytic Soc. (spl. mem.), Med. Soc. Milw. County, Alumni Assn. of Family Inst. Northwestern U., Am. Soc. Addiction Medicine, Am. Group Psychotherapy Assn., Wis. Psychiat. Assn., AMA, Wis. State Med. Soc. Avocations: boating, photography, movies, theater, travel. Office: 1220 Dewey Ave Wauwatosa WI 53213 Office Phone: 414-454-6630.

KALOOSDIAN, ROBERT ARAM, lawyer; b. Watertown, Mass., Oct. 29, 1930; s. Paul and Grace (Mugrditchian) K.; m. Marianne Kaloosdian, June 30, 1957; children: Paul, Lori, Sonia. AB, Clark U., Worcester, Mass., 1952; JD, Boston U., 1957, LLM, 1962. Bar: Mass. 1957, US Dist. Ct., US Supreme Ct. 1962. Assoc. Miles, Curran & Malkasian, Boston, 1958-60; pvt. practice Watertown, 1960—; assoc. Kaloosdian, Ciccarelli & Lerman, Watertown, 1982-99; law offices Robert A. Kaloosdian, 1999—. Corporator Watertown Savs. Bank, 1972—2003, trustee, 1976—2003, mem. cmty. reinvestment com. Corporator Mt. Auburn Hosp., Cambridge, Mass., 1978—2002; pres. Armenian Nat. Inst., Washington, 1996—, Kaloosdian/Mugar Chair of Genocide and History Clark U., 2002. Bd. dirs. Armenian Assembly of Am., 1972-2000, co-chmn., 1974-83, chmn., 1990-92; assoc. dir. State Dept. AID Grant to Lebanon, 1978—; mem. Gov.'s Task Force on Ethinic Heritage, Boston, 1976. With U.S. Army, 1952-54. Recipient Prince of Cilicia award, Catholosate of Antelias, Beirut, 1980, Dist. Svc. award Armenian Assembly, 2000. Mem. ATLA, Middlesex Bar Assn., Mass. Bar Assn. (spl. asst. to pres. 2000), Rotary (pres. 1975-76), Delta Theta Phi. Democrat. Mem. Armenian Apostolic Ch. Home: 25 Fletcher Rd Belmont MA 02478-2014 Office: 43 Mount Auburn St Watertown MA 02472-3924 Office Phone: 617-926-1616.

KALPANA, GANJAM V., biomedical researcher; d. Ganjam P. Venkataramana and Ganjam V. Indira; m. Vinayaka R. Prasad, Aug. 3, 1983; 1 child, Apoorva Ganjam Talanki. PhD, Albert Einstein Coll. of Medicine, Bronx, 1991. Asst. prof. Albert Einstein Coll. of Medicine, Bronx, 1995—2000, assoc. prof., 2000—05, prof., 2005—. Mem. rev. bd. study sect. NIH, 2005—. Contbr. articles to profl. jours. Recipient Irma T. Hirschl scholar for biomed. rsch., Irma T. Hirschl Found., 2004—, Gold Medalist for securing first position in masters degree, U. of Mysore, India, 1983; fellow Helen Hay Whitney Postdoctoral fellow, Helen Hay Whitney Found., 1992—95; grantee Sasha Mehler Rsch. award, Children's Brain Tumor Found., 1998—2000; scholar Mark Trauner Faculty scholar in neuro-oncology, Mark Trauner Found. Mem.: AAAS. Democrat-Npl. Achievements include discovery of INI1 as an intercting partner for integrase; research in INI1 fragmnet as a dominant negative inhibitor of HIV-1 replciation; identification of c-Myc as interacting partner for INI1; Cyclin D1 is required for genesis of rhabdoid tumors resulting from INI1 loss; patents for INI1 as a target for drug develoment against HIV-1 replication. Office: Aecom 1300 Morris Park Ave Ull 821 Bronx NY 10461 Home Phone: 914-779-5583; Office Phone: 718-430-2354. Office Fax: 718-430-2354. E-mail: kalpana@aecom.yu.edu.

KALSNER, STANLEY, pharmacologist, physiologist, educator; b. NYC, Aug. 21, 1936; s. William Louis and Sadie (Feldman) K.; m. Jenny Book, Aug. 4, 1963; children— Lydia, Pamela, Louisa. AB, NYU, 1958; postgrad., SUNY Downstate Med. Ctr., 1959—62; PhD, U. Man., Can., 1966; postgrad., Cambridge U., Eng., 1966—67. Asst. prof. pharmacology U. Ottawa, Ont., Canada, 1967-72, assoc. prof. Ont., 1972-77, prof. Ont., 1977-85; prof., chmn. joint dept. physiology and pharmacology CUNY, 1985—2003. Med. rsch. scientist on heart disease and blood vessel function; sci. referee Med. Rsch. Coun. Can., Can. Heart Found. Editor, contbr. chpts. to books, articles to jours.; asso. editor Can. Jour. Physiology and Pharmacology, until 1985; mem. editorial bd.: Jour. Autonomic Pharmacology, Blood Vessels. USPHS fellow, 1960-67; Med. Rsch. Coun.-NRC and Ont. Heart Found. grantee; Am. Heart Assn. grantee, 1987—. Mem. AAAS, AAUP, Can. Pharmacology Soc., Am. Soc. Pharmacology and Therapeutics. Home: 21 Hillcrest Rd Suffern NY 10901-6834 Office: CUNY Med Sch 138th St and Convent Ave New York NY 10031 Personal E-mail: jskalsner@optonline.net. *I believe that the greatest mystery of all is life and that it is worth devoting oneself to its solution.*

KALSNER-SILVER, LYDIA, psychologist; b. Winnipeg, Can., May 26, 1964; d. Stanley and Jenny Kalsner; m. Jay Silver, Aug. 20, 1994; children: Dylan, Chloe. BS in Psychology, U. Toronto, 1987; MA, EdM, Columbia U., 1992; EdD in Counseling Psychology, Rutgers U., 2000. Dir. clin. assessment dept. psychiatry SUNY, Bklyn., 1992—97; psychology resident Jackson Meml. Hosp., Miami, 1997—98, post-doctoral fellow Juvenile Gun Offender Program, 2000—01; sch. psychologist Temple Beth Am Day Sch., Miami, 2001—02; psychologist Divsn. Alternative Outreach Miami (Fla.) Dade Country Pub. Schs., 2002—; pvt. practice psychotherapist Miami, 2002—. Grant reviewer crime prevention com. Miami (Fla.) Dade Criminal Justice Counsel, Miami, 1997; adj. faculty U. Miami, 1997—98; rsch. writer Higher Edn. Ext. Svc. Columbia U., NYC, 1991—92; instr. Rutgers U., New Brunswick, NJ. Contbr. articles to profl. jours. Scholar, Tchrs. Coll. Columbia U., 1990. Mem.: APA, Soc. Personal Assessment, Fla. Psychol. Assn. Avocations: cooking, travel. Home: 5151 Collins Ave Miami Beach FL 33140 Office: 5151 Collins Ave Ste 223 Miami Beach FL 33140 Home Phone: 305-864-6392; Office Phone: 305-866-3579. Personal E-mail: kalsner@aol.com.

KALT, DAVID, diversified financial services company executive; b. 1967; MS, DePaul U., 1995. Chief tech. officer TRAMS, Inc., 1998—2000; pres., founder Third Party Solutions, 1994—98; CEO OptionsXpress Holdings, Inc., Chgo., 2000—, also pres., chief tech. officer, 2000—. Named one of 40 Under Forty, Crain's Bus. Chgo., 2005. Avocation: collecting vintage Gibson guitars. Office: OptionsXpress Inc Ste 220 39 S LaSalle St Chicago IL 60690 Office Fax: 312-629-5256.*

KALTENBACH, C(ARL) COLIN, dean, educator; b. Buffalo, Wyo., Mar. 22, 1939; s. Carl H. and Mary Colleen (McKeag) K.; m. Ruth Helene Johnson, Aug. 22, 1964; children: James Earl, John Edward. BSc, U. Wyo., 1961; MSc, U. Nebr., 1963; PhD, U. Ill., 1967. Postdoctoral fellow U. Melbourne, Australia, 1967-69; from asst. prof. to prof. U. Wyo., Laramie, 1969-89, assoc. dean, dir. Agrl. Expt. Sta., 1980-89; vice dean, dir. Agrl. Expt. Sta. U. Ariz., Tucson, 1989—2007, dean, dir. Agrl. Expt. Sta., 2007—. Contbr. 200 articles to profl. publs. Named Outstanding Alumnus Coll. Agriculture U. Wyo., 1991; named to USDA Hall Fame, 2005. Mem. Nat. Assn. State Univs. and Land Grant Colls. (mem. policy bd. dirs. 2002-05), Soc. for Study Reprodn. (treas. 1979-82), Am. Soc. Animal Sci., Civitan (officer 1972-85), Agrl. Experiment State Dirs. (chair 1996-97). Office: U Ariz Coll Agr and Life Scis Tucson AZ 85721-0001 E-mail: kltnbch@ag.arizona.edu.

KALTENBACH, JAMES ALBERT, neurobiologist, educator; b. Balt., Jan. 31, 1952; s. Albert Bossyns and Margaret Dorsey Kaltenbach; m. Katarina Cerny, June 26, 1986; children: Rachel, Brenden. BS, George Washington U., 1975; MS, Towson State U., 1980; PhD, U. Pa., 1984. Rsch. fellow Smithsonian Instn., Washington, 1971-72; phys. sci. aide U.S. Geol. Survey, Washington, 1973-76; rsch. asst. Johns Hopkins U., Balt., 1978-80; lectr. U. Pa., Phila., 1986; asst. prof. Wayne State U., Detroit, 1987-93, assoc. prof., 1994-99, prof., 2000—, co-dir. rsch, dept. otolaryngology. Cons. GM Corp., Millford, Mich., 1994-96, NIH, Bethesda, 1997; mem. sci. adv. bd. Am. Tinnitus Assn., 2001—. Mem. editl. bd. Hearing Rsch. Jour., The Netherlands, 1999—. Grantee NIH, 1996—, Am. Tinnitus Assn., 1994-95, Nat. Orgn. for Hearing Rsch., 1992-93, Deafness Rsch. Found., 1989-94. Mem. AAAS, Assn. for Rsch. in Otolaryngology, Soc. for Neurosci., Internat. Brain Rsch. Orgn. Home: 30359 Lincolnshire Dr Beverly Hills MI 48025 Office: Wayne State U Dept Otolaryngology 5E-UHC Detroit MI 48201 Business E-Mail: jkalten@med.wayne.edu.

KALTER, ALAN, advertising agency executive; m. Chris Lezotte. With W.B. Doner & Co., Southfield, Mich., 1967—, exec. v.p., dir. retail divsn., 1990, vice chmn. account mgmt., 1990-92, pres., COO, 1992-95; CEO, chmn. W. B. Doner & Co. (dba Doner), Southfield, Mich., 1995—. Office: W B Doner & Co 25900 Northwestern Hwy Southfield MI 48075-1067

KALTER, ALBERT, lawyer, educator; s. Morris and Goldie Kalter; m. Brenda Kahane Kalter. BBA, CCNY, NYC, 1958; JD, NY Law Sch., NYC, 1961; LLM, NYU, NYC, 1964. CPA NY, 1961; bar: NY 1961. Pvt. practice law, NYC, 1965—; prof., chmn. grad. tax dept. Pace U., NYC, 1965—. Co-author (with Newman): Postmortem Estate Planning. Fellow: Am. Coun. Trust and Estate Counsel. Office: 225 Broadway New York NY 10007

KALTSOS, ANGELO JOHN, electronics executive, educator, photographer; b. Aug. 19, 1930; s. John Angelo and Rita Thomas (Goudas) K.; m. Verna Kay Wilson, June 30, 1952 (dec. Jan. 1973); children: Pamela, Elaine, Gregory, Stephanie, Lenora, Demetra, Dana. Student, Mass. Radio and TV Sch., Boston, 1955—57, Harvard Coll. Extension, Cambridge, 1964, Boston State Coll., 1965—67, U. N.M., Albuquerque, 1976, Fitchburg State Coll., 1977. Clk. U.S. Postal Svc., Boston, 1954-57; electronic rsch. technician Crosley div. Avco, Cin., 1957; electronic rsch. production technician Raytheon Mfg. Co., Waltham, Mass., 1957-63; educator Cambridge (Mass.) Sch. Dept., 1961-81; ind. ethnology rsch. N.Mex., 1969—; mgr. Pampas, Inc., Boston, 1987-90. Bd. dirs. Expansion Dance Co., Boston; cons. 5 P.I.E., Albuquerque, 1976—, Indian Tribal Group, N.Mex.; lectr. S.W. Indian Culture in Boston, Cambridge area, 1990—; pres., treas. Spartan Enterprises, Inc., 1965-69. Author: Southwest Indian, 1986, (non-fiction) Music You Will Never Hear, 2005, (poetry) Unfurling Leaves of the Mind, 2005; one-man shows include Christmas Tree Gallery, Manteo, N.C., 1977, 4th St. Photo Gallery, N.Y.C., 1980, Cambride Rindge and Latin Sch., Mass., 1981, Jay's, Cambridge, Mass., 1983, Here Today Gallery, Boston, 1984, Andover (Maine) Town Hall, 1984, 86, Piedmont Art Assn., Martinsville, Va., 1985-86, Cambalache Gallery, Boston, 1986-87, The 4th St. Gallery, N.Y.C., 1990, Andover (Maine) Pub. Libr., 1997-98; contbg. journalist in field Chmn. No Thank Q Hydro Quebec, Andover, Maine, 1988-91, coord., Dryden, Maine, 1991-2001; regional and media coord. N.E. Alliance to Protect James Bay, 1990-91, exec. bd., adv. bd., treas., 1991-2001, project dir., 1995-2001; project dir., treas. Hydro Electric Watch, 2001—; senate faculty Cambridge Sch. Dept., 1980-81; sec. New Eng. Model Car Assn. of Raceways, 1966-69; educator Cambridge Adult Ctr., 1990-97, Paulist Ctr., Boston, 1991-92; judge Andover amateur photo contest, 1996-99, coord., judge, 2001—. Recipient Robert Sweeney award Rindge Alumni Assn., 1996. Mem. Appalachian Mountain Club (life). Greek Orthodox. Avocations: ethnography, entomology, cooking, gardening, hiking. Home: PO Box 33 Andover ME 04216-0033

KALUDIS, GEORGE, management consultant, publishing executive, educator; b. Balt., Oct. 7, 1938; s. Steven George and Theresa (Topal) K.; m. Eugenia Leone Mihalakis, July 21, 1962; children: Stephen George, Michele Maria, William Michael, Kirk Jamie. BA, U. Md., 1960, MEd, 1965; PhD, Fla. State U., 1968. Asst. dean student life U. Md., 1960-65; resident instr. U. S. Fla., 1965-66; dir. divsn. planning and evaluation State Univ. Sys. Fla., 1966-70; vice chancellor ops. and fin. planning, assoc. prof. mgmt. Vanderbilt U., Nashville, 1970-76, adj. assoc. prof. mgmt., 1976-78; exec. v.p. Ingram Book Co., 1976-78; chmn., pres. Kaludis Consulting, Washington, 1978—. Mem. tech. coun. Nat. Ctr. Higher Edn. Mgmt. Sys., 1970—72, bd. dirs., 1972—76, chmn. bd., 1975—76; pres., bd. dirs. Frat. Advisors Group, Inc., Tallahassee, 1968—70; mem. com. chmn. Nat. Com. on Financing Postsecondary Edn., 1972—74. Editor: Strategies for Budgeting, New Directions in Higher Education, 1973; mem. editl. bd.: On the Horizon, 1996—2001, contbg. author: Mission Management a New Synthesis, vol. 1, Dollars, Distance and Online Education, The University and It's Academic Health Center: New Strategic Contexts, 2005. Bd. dirs. NCCJ, Nashville, St. Photios Nat. Shrine, 1986-87; 1st v.p. Family and Children's Svcs., Inc., 1978-80; chmn. Spl. Com. on Cable TV, Nashville, 1982-95; parish coun. Holy Trinity Greek Orthodox Ch., 1971-94, pres., 1972-78, 81-83, 92-94; stewardship commn. Greek Orthodox Archdiocese, 1993-95, archdiocesan coun., 1994-98, 2000—, co-chmn. com. on strategic and long range planning, 1994-97, metropolis coun., NJ, 1999—, v.p., 2000-06; parish coun. St. George Greek Orthodox Ch., Bethesda, 1998-2001, sec., chair stewardship com., 2000, pres.; del. World Clergy-Laity Congress, Greek Orthodox Ch., Istanbul, 2000, active Leadership 100, 2001; nat. capital campaign com. Fla. State U., 2001-05; trustee Internat. Orthodox Christian Charities, 2003—; arena seating planning com. U. Md.; Ecumenical patriarch Order of St. Andrew, 2003—, chair strategic planning com. Nat. Coun., 2005—; trustee Hellenic Coll./Holy Cross Greek Orthodox Sch. Theology, 2006—. With U.S. Army, 1962-64. Recipient Medal of St. Paul award Greek Orthodox Archdiocese, 1992, Disting. Alumnus award U. Md. Coll. Edn., 1995 Mem. Nat. Assn. Coll. and Univ. Bus. Officers, Soc. for Coll. and Univ. Planning, Fin. Execs. Inst. (pres. Nashville chpt. 1975), Nashville Area C. of C. (gov.), Am. Hellenic Ednl. Progressive Assn., U. Md. Alumni Ctr. (cabinet), Omicron Delta Kappa, Pi Sigma Alpha, Sigma Phi Epsilon (chmn. commn. on univ. rels. 1992-93). Republican. Greek Orthodox. Office: 1730 M St NW Ste 600 Washington DC 20030 Office Phone: 202-349-3631. Business E-Mail: gkaludis@kaludisconsulting.com.

KALWARA, JOSEPH JOHN, engineer; b. Syracuse, NY, June 4, 1953; s. Stanley W. and M. Bonita (Caraglin) K; m. Edith Ann Doust, 1980; children: John C., Joseph S., James V. BS in Forestry, Syracuse U., 1977; BS in Wood Products Engring., SUNY, Syracuse, 1977; AAAS in Archtl. Tech., Onondaga County C.C., 1980. Asst. engr. Firestone Bldg. Products, Indpls., 1983-84, regional tech. coord., 1984-86, product assurance engr., 1986-88, sr. engr., 1988—. Contbr. articles to profl. jours. Mem. Single-Ply Roofing Inst., Riviera Club (Indpls.). Achievements include research in the development and engineering of building products, insulations and adhesives, sealants, and tapes relative to single-ply roofing membranes and systems; patentee in field. Home: 6050 Broadway St Indianapolis IN 46220-1808 Office: Firestone Bldg Products 310 E 96th St Indianapolis IN 46240 Office Phone: 317-575-7015. Business E-Mail: kalwarajoe@firestonebp.com.

KALYANPUR, ARJUN, radiologist; b. Beijing, June 27, 1965; s. Bhaskar Ramkrishna and Leela Rao Kalyanpurkar; m. Sunita Maheshwari, Sept. 24, 1994; children: Alisha, Adil Bharat. MBBS, All India Inst. Med. Scis., New Delhi, 1983—88, MD, 1989—92. Diplomate Am. Bd. Radiology, 1998. Asst. clin. prof. Yale U. Sch. Medicine, New Haven, 1998—. Contbr. articles to profl. jours. Trustee People for People, Bangalore, India, 2003—04. Mem.: Radiologic Soc. N.Am. Avocations: travel, reading, music, theater. Home: Villa 19 Regent Pl Whitefield Mn Rd Bangalore 560066 India Office: Teleradiology Solutions 205 Church St 3rd Fl New Haven CT 06510 Home Phone: 91 80 41693165; Office Phone: 877-295-1705. Office Fax: 775-860-2508; Home Fax: 91 80 41103411. E-mail: arjun.kalyanpur@telradsol.com.

KAMAL, ABU HENA M., electrical engineer, researcher; s. Abdul Hannan and Golenoor Begum; m. Shamima M. Shimu, Sept. 14, 1989; 1 child, Ishmam A. Nawar. BS in Elec. and Electronic Engring., Bangladesh U. of Engring. and Tech., Dhaka, Bangladesh, 1988; MS in Elec. and Electronic Engring., Muroran Inst. of Tech., Japan, 1993; PhD in Elec. Engring., Ariz. State U., 1997. Lectr. Bangladesh U. of Engring. and Tech., Dhaka, 1988—90; sr. process engr. Nat. Semiconductor Corp., Santa Clara, Calif., 1997—99, team leader of cobalt silicide group, 1997—99, sr. circuit design rschr., 1999—2001, staff circuit design engr., 2001—05, prin. engr., design team lead, 2005. Mng. dir. Imdad-Sitara Khan Kidney Ctrs., Bangladesh. Dir., writer 4 Bengali dramas, Phoenix and San Jose, Calif., 1995—2003; bur. chief: Exec. Times; reviewer IEEE, 2000—; contbr. articles to profl. publs. Dir., founder drama group BiNa, Santa Clara; co-founder ORCA-USA, Santa Clara, Calif.; founding mem. SpaandanB, Sunnyvale, Calif., 1998—. Monboshu scholar, Ministry of Edn., Japan, 1990—93. Mem.: IEEE (assoc.), Inst. of Electrochem. Soc. (assoc.). Achievements include patents for Low power analog equalizer with current mode digital to analog converter; Method for the formation of a boron-doped silicon gate layer underlying a cobalt silicide layer; Process for the formation of cobalt salicide layers employing a sputter etch surface preparation step; Method for the formation of a poly silicon layer with a controlled, small silicon grain size during semiconductor device fabrication; Apparatus and method for employing gain dependent biasing to reduce offset and noise in a current conveyer type amplifier; Low power analog equalizer with current mode digital to analog converter; Operational amplifier circuit with improved feedback factor. Avocations: writing mag. articles, novels, travel, reading history, music. Home: 3351 Tracy Dr Santa Clara CA 95051 Office: Nat Semiconductor Corp 2900 Semiconductor Dr M/S-E-170 Santa Clara CA 95052 Personal E-mail: ShimaKamal@aol.com. Business E-Mail: abu.kamal@nsc.com.

KAMALASADAN, SUKUMAR, electrical and computer engineering educator, researcher; s. Krishna Warrier and Kamaladevi Kamalasadan; m. Manya Warrier, July 5, 2000. BTech in Elec. Engring., U. Calicut, Kerala, India, 1991; MEng in Elec. Engring., Asian Inst. Tech., Bangkok, Thailand, 1999; PhD in Elec. Engring., U. Toledo, 2004. Project site engr. Tata Electric Companies, Bombay, Maharashtra, 1991—92; project and devel. engr. Excel Industries Ltd., 1992—94; assoc. mgr., asst. mgr. Reliance Industries Ltd., 1994—97; rsch. assoc. Asian Inst. Tech., Bangkok, 1999—2000; rsch. asst., tchg. asst. U. Toledo, 2000—04; asst. prof. U. West Fla., Pensacola, 2004—. Tech. reviewer Taylor and Francis Group, Abingdon, Oxfordshire, England, 2005—; undergraduate coord. U. West Fla.; ad hoc reviewer NSF; presenter in field. Contbr. articles to profl. jours. Adv. bd. West Fla. Tech. H.S., 2004; student advisor U. West Fla., mem. planning com., 2005—, mem. scholarly and creative activities com., 2005—, program coord. elec. engring. tech., 2004—. Recipient Performance award, Reliance Industries Ltd., 1997, Outstanding Tchg. Asst. award, U. Toledo, 2002—03, Travel award, U. West Fla., 2004—05, Summer Rsch. award, 2005, Faculty Summer award, 2005; scholar, Kerala State Govt., 1987—91, Govt. of Norway, 1998—99, U. Toledo, 2000—04. Mem.: IEEE (tech. reviewer 2004—, session chair, judge southeastern conf. 2006—), Internat. Assn. Engrs., Internat. Soc. Computers and Applications (tech. reviewer 2004). Achievements include research in intelligent agent supervisory loop based adaptive controllers; renewable energy and control; multi-agent based controllers; development of an intelligent supervisory loop based controller; design of an intelligent adaptive controller based on self tuning regulator; fuzzy logic based model reference adaptive controller for multi modal systems; a neural network approach to voltage stability assessment and improvement; online neural network algorithm based adaptive neuro-controller; patents pending for algorithms for intelligent control based on supervisory loop approach. Avocations: chess, travel, reading, music. Home Phone: 850-478-6707; Office Phone: 850-857-6451.

KAMALI, NORMA, fashion designer; b. NYC, June 27, 1945; d. Sam and Estelle (Mariategui) Arraez. Grad., Fashion Inst. of Tech., 1965. Established Kamali Ltd., NYC, 1967-78; owner, designer On My Own Norma Kamali, NYC, 1978—. Designer costumes for Emerald City in The

Wiz, 1978; for Twyla Tharp dance In the Upper Room, 1986; Parachute Designs displayed Met. Mus. of Art, N.Y.C., 1977; prodr., dir. (video) Fall Fantasy; dir. (video) Fashion Aid, 1985. Recipient Coun. Fashion Designers Am. award, 1982, 1985, Coty award, 1981, 82, 83, Ernie awards Earnshaw Rev., 1983, Fashion Inst. Design and Merchandising award, 1983, Annual Interiors award Interiors Mag., 1985, Salute to Women award N.Y. Fashion Group, 1986, Disting. Arch. award N.Y. chpt. AIA, 1986, Outstanding Grad. award Pub. Edn. Assn. N.Y., 1988, Award of Merit, Internat. Video Culture Competition, 1988, Am. Success award Fashion Inst. Tech., 1989, Youth Friends award Sch. Art League, 1997, Pencil award, 1999, Willow award Lower East Side Girls Club, 1999, Fashion Outreach Style award, 1999, Bus. Outreach award Manhattan C. of C., 2002, Entrepreneur award Fashion Group, 2002, Women's History Month award N.Y.C. Controllers Office, 2002, Bd. Director's Spl. Tribute award Coun. Fashion Designers Am., 2005; featured exhibit Met. Mus. Exhibit, 2001; inducted into Fashion Walk of Fame Fashion Ctr. Bus. Improvement Dist. Office: 11 W 56th St New York NY 10019-3902

KAMAN, HELEN S., retired aerospace engineer, artist; b. Coraopolis, Pa., Jan. 5, 1918; d. Nels Sylvander and Myrtel McKee; m. Charles H. Kaman, Oct. 20, 1945; children: Charles William II, Cathleen, Steven. BS in Art, Edinboro U., Pa., 1940; MA in Am. Studies, Trinity Coll., Hartford, 1982. Cert. aero. engring. Penn State U., 1944. Co-founder Kaman Corp. Helicopter Mfg., Bloomfield, Conn., 1946—50; engring. draftsman Sikorsky Aircraft, E. Hartford, Conn., 1944—45; ret. Solo and group shows. Bd. mem. Hartford Art Sch., 1983—89, Watkinson Sch., 1980—90. Mem.: Pen Women. Avocations: painting, skiing, travel. Home: 11 Sonrisa Ct Santa Fe NM 87506

KAMANGAR, NADER, physician, director, researcher, pulmonologist, educator; b. Tehran, Iran, June 21, 1970; s. Fereidoun and Fari Kamangar; m. Goli Khodadad, Dec. 22, 2001; 1 child, Maya. MD, St.George's U., 1997. Diplomate Am. Bd. Internal Medicine, 2001, Am. Bd. Internal Medicine-Pulmonary Disease, 2002, Am. Bd. Internal Medicine-Critical Care, 2003, Am. Bd. Sleep Medicine, 2005. Resident in internal medicine Highland Gen. Hosp., Oakalnd, Calif., 1997—2000; pulmonary, critical care and sleep medicine fellow Cedars-Sinai Med. Ctr., LA, 2000—03; asst. clin. prof. UCLA Sch. Medicine, 2003—; co-dir. Olive View-UCLA Med. Ctr. Sleep Medicine Lab., dir., intensivist hospitalist program, site dir., pulmonary/critical care fellowship program. Edn. dir. pulmonary/critical care medicine Olive View-UCLA Med. Ctr., Sylmar, 2003—; dir. Hospitalist/Intensivist program, 2007—. Contbr. articles to profl. publ., chapters to books. Recipient Golden Apple award Best Sub-Specialist, UCLA, 2003, 2004, 2005. Fellow: Am. Acad. Sleep Medicine, Am. Coll. Physicians, Am. Coll. of Chest Physicians; mem.: Golden Key Nat. Honor Soc. Home: 15506 Moorpark St 323 Encino CA 91436 Office: Olive View-UCLA Med Ctr Sleep Medicine Lab 14445 Olive View Dr 2B-182 Sylmar CA 91342-1495 Home Phone: 818-788-8160; Office Phone: 818-364-3205. Office Fax: 818-364-4573. Business E-Mail: kamangar@ucla.edu.

KAMANU, UCHEMADU CHEE, chemist; b. Umunteke, Asa, Abia, Nigeria, Aug. 8, 1946; s. Lazarus Kamanu Wokaru and Victoria Obiakwa Ogibe Okpor; m. Mgbechi Philomena Nwagboso, Apr. 19, 1984; children: Chihurum Anyatoha, Omumeoma Nneoma, Sowechi Chizuruoke, Chizim Oluomachi. BS, U. Lagos, Nigeria, 1979; MBA, U. Nigeria, Enugu, Nigeria, 1983. Lectr. Oyo State Coll. Arts & Sci., Ile-Ife, Nigeria, 1979—80; sci. tchr. Anambra State Ministry of Edn., Enugu, Nigeria, 1981—82; bus. ops. and mktg. rsch. exec., dep. circulation mgr. Guardian Newspapers Ltd., Lagos, Nigeria, 1983—88; circulation mgr. Prime Publs. Ltd., Lagos, Nigeria, 1988—91; sales mgr. mag. The Daily Times of Nigeria PLC, Lagos, 1992—94; contr. bus. ops. Sentinel Pub. Ltd, Kaduna, Nigeria, 1994—95; substitute tchr. Balt. City Pub. Schs., 1996—97; chemist Balt. City Wastewater Lab., Patapsco, Md., 1997—. Mktg. cons. Kache Cons., Lagos, 1995—96. Author: (poem) Symphonies Of Words (Editor's award, 2001), The Best Poems & Poets Of 2001 (Editor's award, 2002), Poetry.com, The Colors of Life, 2003 (Editor's award, 2003), The Best Poems and Poets of 2003, 2003, Theatre of the Mind. Dir. personal ministries Pikesville S.D.A. Ch., Balt., 2004—. Mem.: Acad. Am. Poets, Internat. Soc. Poets (hon.). Avocations: writing, preaching, bible teaching. E-mail: kamanu3@juno.com, tkflash1@hotmail.com.

KAMBER, VICTOR SAMUEL, political consultant; b. Chgo., May 7, 1943; s. Samuel J. and Cordelia A. Kamber. BA, U. Ill., 1965; MA, U. N.Mex., 1966; JD, Am. U., 1969; LLM, George Washington U., 1971. Adminstrv. asst. Congressman Seymour Halpern, Washington, 1969-72; asst. to pres. Bldg. & Constrn. Trades Dept., Washington, 1974-78; dir. AFL-CIO Labor Law Reform Task Force, Washington, 1978-80; pres., chief exec. officer The Kamber Group, Washington, 1980—2005; pres. Carmen Group Comms., Washington, 2006—. Nat. v.p. Ams. for Dem. Action, Washington; bd. dirs. BB&T Bank, Washington; sr. adv. bd. Am. League Lobbyists, Washington; bd. trustees The Nat. Theatre. Mem. Nat. Dem. Club. With U.S. Army, 1972-74. Mem. ACLU, NOW, Internat. Assn. Polit. Cons., Am. Assn. Polit. Cons. (bd. dirs. 1987-92, treas. 1991-92), Coalition Labor Union Women, Indsl. Rels. Rsch. Assn., Nat. Press Club, Local 35 Newspaper Guild, Phi Gamma Delta. Democrat. Presbyterian. Office: Carmen Group Comms 1301 K St NW Washington DC 20005 Home: 4527 29th St NW Washington DC 20008 Home Phone: 202-244-1608; Office Phone: 202-218-4156. Business E-Mail: kamberv@carmengroup.com.

KAMBHAMPATI, SUBBARAO, computer scientist, educator; s. Gowripathi Sastry and Sitaratnam Kambhampati; m. Chaitali Chakrabarti, Dec. 21, 1990; 1 child, Soumya. BSEE, Indian Inst. Tech., Madras, India, 1983; PhD in Computer Sci., U. Md., 1989. Prof. Ariz. State U., Tempe, Ariz., 1991—. Recipient Young Investigator award, NSF, 1994, Tchg. Excellence award, Coll. Engring., Ariz. State U., 2002, Faculty award, IBM, 2004. Fellow: Am. Assn. Artificial Intelligence (co-chmn. nat. conf. on artificial intelligence 2005); mem.: Intl. Conf. Automated Planning and Scheduling (mem. exec. coun. 2000—06). Office: Dept of Computer Science & Engineering Arizona State University Tempe AZ 85287 Office Phone: 480-965-0113. Business E-Mail: rao@asu.edu.

KAMBOUR, ANNALIESE SPOFFORD, lawyer, media company executive; b. Schenectady, NY, Nov. 19, 1961; d. Roger Peabody and Virginia Louise (Dyer) K. BA, Harvard U., 1983, JD, 1986. Bar: Mass. 1986, N.Y. 1987, U.S. Tax Ct. 1987. Assoc. Paul, Weiss, Rifkind, Wharton & Garrison, NYC, 1986—96, ptnr., 1996—2001; sr. v.p. tax Time Warner Inc., NYC, 2001—. Mem. NOW, N.Y. State Bar Assn. Office: Paul Weiss Rifkind Wharton & Garrison Ste 4A 1285 Avenue Of The Americas Fl 21 New York NY 10019-6028

KAMBOUR, ROGER PEABODY, retired polymer physical chemist, researcher; b. Wilmington, Mass., Apr. 1, 1932; s. George Constantine and Ada Grace (Mattraw) K.; m. Virginia L. Dyer, Oct. 4, 1958 (div. Dec. 1982); children— Annaliese S., Christian R.; m. Barbara Jean Vivier, June 23, 1984; 1 child, Joshua V. BA cum laude, Amherst Coll., 1954; PhD in Chemistry, U. N.H., 1960. Rschr. GE R & D Ctr., Schenectady, NY, 1960-94, U. Mass. rsch. prof., 1994-99. Vis. prof. MIT, 1991; vis. scientist Nat. Inst. Standards & Tech., Washington, 1993. Mem. editl. bd. Polymer Engring. and Sci., 1968-87, Ann. Revs. of Materials Sci., 1985-89; contbr. articles on polymer physics and phys. chemistry to profl. publs.; patentee in field Supr. 1st ward Schenectady County Bd. Suprs., N.Y., 1964-65; mem. Schenectady County Charter Commn., 1964-65; mem. Schenectady City Hist. Dist. Commn., 1975-81; mem. art com. Schenectady Mus., 1975-82; mem. Nat. Ski Patrol, 1988-93; chmn. Freedom Forum, 1975-76. Fellow Am. Phys. Soc. (Ford High Polymer Physics prize 1985); mem. NAE, Am. Chem. Soc. (Union Carbide Chems. award 1968) Democrat. Unitarian Universalist. Avocations: choral singing, skiing, sailing. Home: 2572 Rosendale Rd Niskayuna NY 12309-1312 E-mail: kamviv@nycap.rr.com.

KAMBUTU, JOHN, adult education educator; PhD, U. Wyo., Laramie, 1998. Lectr. U. Wyo., Laramie, 1994—2002; asst. prof. U. Wyo. Casper Ctr., 2003—. Mem., chair Wyo. Humanities Coun., Laramie, 2003—07. Recipient The John P. Ellbogen Meritorious Classroom Tchg. award, U. Wyo., 2006. Mem.: Mountain Plains Adult Edn. Office Phone: 307-268-2584.

KAMEIR, CHRISTIAN, marketing executive; m. Janice Kameir. CEO Colizer Inc., San Diego, 2004—. Home and Office: Colizer Inc 11777 Sorrento Valley Road San Diego CA 92121 Home Phone: 858-205-4122; Office Phone: 866-690-8755. Office Fax: 866-500-0536. E-mail: support@colizer.com.

KAMEL, HOSAM KAMAL, medical educator, researcher, geriatrician; b. Cairo, May 18, 1965; married; 1 child. MB, BChir, Kuwait U., 1989; MPH, Med. Coll. Wis., 2004. Cert. Am. Bd. Internal Medicine, Am. Bd. Geriatric Medicine, Cert. Bd. Nutrition Specialists, Nat. Bd. Wound Mgmt. Asst. prof. medicine SUNY, Stony Brook, 1998—99; chief divsn. geriatric medicine Nassau U. Med. Ctr., East Meadow, NY, 1999—2001; asst. prof. medicine St. Louis U. Sch. Medicine, 1999—; asst. prof. geriatrics Med. Coll. Wis., 2001—03; dir. geriatrics and extended care St. Joseph's Mercy Health Ctr., Hot Springs, Ark., 2003—; asst., assoc. clin. prof. geriatric U. Ark. Med. Sci., 2004—. Dir. edn. and rsch., geriatrics Nassau U. Med. Ctr., East Meadow, 1999; mem. physician adv. panel Divsn. Aging, Dept. Social Svcs., Jefferson City, Mo., 2000—; pres. Ark. Med. Dirs. Assn., 2006—; bd. dirs. Mo. Assn. Long-Term Physicians, Mo. Fellow: Am. Coll. Nutrition; mem.: ACP, Gerontol. Soc. Am., Am. Geriatric Soc., Ctrl. Soc. for Clin. Rsch. Democrat. Muslim. Home: 162 Trabecca Cir Hot Springs AR 71913-8149 Office: Mission Clin Svc 1 Mecy Ln Ste 405 Hot Springs AR 71913 Personal E-mail: kamel@pol.net.

KAMEMOTO, FRED ISAMU, retired zoologist; b. Honolulu, Mar. 8, 1928; s. Shuichi and Matsu (Murase) K.; m. Alice Takeyo Asayama, July 20, 1963; children: Kenneth, Garett, Janice. Student, U. Hawaii, 1946-48; AB, George Washington U., 1950, MS, 1951; PhD, Purdue U., 1954. Research assoc., acting instr. Wash. State U., 1957-59; asst. prof. zoology U. Mo., 1959-62; asst. prof. U. Hawaii, Honolulu, 1962-64, assoc. prof., 1964-69, prof. zoology, 1969-94, prof. emeritus, 1995—, chmn. dept., 1964-65, 71-80, 81-90, dir. biology program, 1992-94. Vis. rsch. scholar Ocean Rsch. Inst., U. Tokyo, Biol. Lab., Fukuoka U., 1968-69; vis. prof. Coll. Agr. and Vet. Medicine, Nihon U., Tokyo, summer 1973, 1979; vis. scholar dept. biology Conn. Wesleyan U., 1975-76; sr. scientist dept. fisheries Nihon U., Tokyo, 1986; vis. fgn. rschr. Tropical Biosphere Rsch. Ctr. U. of Ryukyus Okinawa, Japan, 1994. Contbr. articles to profl. jours. Chmn. Hawaii State Natural Areas Reserve System Commn., 1985-88. Served with AUS, 1954-57. NSF grantee, 1960-79; National Oceanic and Atmospheric Administration grantee, 1985-89. Fellow AAAS; mem. Sigma Xi. Buddhist. Home: 3664 Waaloa Way Honolulu HI 96822-1151 Office: U Hawaii Dept Zoology Honolulu HI 96822

KAMEN, PAULA, journalist, playwright; b. Chgo., 1967; B in Journalism, Univ. Ill., 1989. Former reporter Kenosha (Wis.) News. Vis. rsch. scholar, gender studies program Northwestern Univ., Chgo., 1994—. Author: (books) Feminist Fatale: Voices from the Twentysomething Generation Explore the Future of the Women's Movement, 1991, Her Way: The Report on Young Women's Evolving Sexual Choices, 1999, All in My Head, 2005; contributor: books Shiny Adidas Track Suits and the Death of Camp: The Best of Might Magazine, 1998; playwright: Seven Dates with Seven Writers; (plays) Jane: Abortion and the Underground, 1999; commentaries, book reviews: in NY Times, Washington Post, Salon, Ms. Chicago Tribune, In These Times. Named one of Chicago's 100 Most Influential Women, Crain's Chicago Business mag., 2004.

KAMENSKY, MARVIN, lawyer; b. Chgo., Aug. 16, 1939; s. Frank and Fannie (Kagan) K.; m. Judy N. Ellis, Oct. 7, 1961; children: Todd, Robert, Daniel. BS, U. Ill., 1961; JD, DePaul U., 1966. Bar: Ill. 1966, U.S. Dist. Ct. (no. dist.) Ill. 1966, U.S. Tax Ct. 1969; CPA, Ill. Assoc. Altman, Kurlanner & Weiss, Chgo., 1967-70; ptnr. Kamensky, Rubinstein, Hochman & Delott LLP and predecessor firms Kamensky & Rubinstein, Kamensky & Landan, and Carlins & Kamensky, Chgo., 1970—. Mem. adv. bd. Small Bus. Coun. Am., Washington, 1980—, Pension Cons. Mag., NJ, 1982-89; spkr. in field; bd. dirs. Children's Care Found., Chgo. Author: Formation of Partnerships in Illinois and Tax Aspects, 1977, The Age of Reason for Qualified Plans, 1993, The Changing Healthcare Environment, 1997, MSO Formation, 1998, Mergers and Acquisitions of Medical Practices, 1999, Legal Aspects of Practice Entry and/or Change, 2000, Formation of General and Limited Partnerships in Illinois and Income Tax Aspects, 2005, Physicians and Hospitals: Competitors Working Together to Share in Financial Success, Recent Developments in Tax and Related Areas of Law Affecting Physicians, 2005; editl. cons. Med. Econs., 1975—90. Treas. Northfield Twp. (Ill.) Rep. Orgn., 1981-82; bd. dirs. West Northfield Twp. Bd. Edn., Northbrook, Ill., 1976-80, 82-84, Parents Adv. Coun. Glenbrook Twp. High Sch., Northbrook, 1985, Congregation Beth Shalom, Northbrook, 1979-85, speaker at Ill. Assn. Hlthcare Attys. 22nd Ann. Hlth. Law Symp. Mem. ABA (subcom. chmn.), Ill. Bar Assn., Chgo. Bar Assn., Am. Assn. Pension Actuaries, Am. Health Lawyers Assn. Avocation: golf. Office: Kamensky Rubinstein Hochman & Delott LLP 7250 N Cicero Ave Ste 200 Lincolnwood IL 60712-1693 Office Phone: 847-982-1776. Business E-Mail: mkamensky@kr-law.com.

KAMENTSKY, LOUIS AARON, biophysicist; b. Newark, July 28, 1930; s. Harry and Etta (Brodsky) K.; m. Marcia Alpern, Aug. 28, 1955; children: Lee, Howard, Ellen. BSEE, N.J. Inst. Tech., 1952; PhD, Cornell U., 1956. Mem. staff Columbia U. ERL, NYC, 1954-55, Bell Telephone Labs., Murray Hill, NJ, 1956-60, IBM Research, NYC, 1960-68; pres. Biophysics Systems, Mahopac, NY, 1968-76; v.p. rsch. Ortho Diagnostics Systems, Cambridge, Mass., 1976-88; chmn. CompuCyte Corp., Cambridge, Mass., 1988—. Vis. scientist Karolinska Inst., Stockholm, 1966; sr. rsch. scientist MIT, Cambridge, 1981-88. Patentee in field; contbr. articles to profl. jours. Home: 180 Beacon St Boston MA 02116-1408 Office: Compucyte Corp 12 Emily St Cambridge MA 02139-4507 E-mail: lakam@verizon.net.

KAMER, GREGORY JAY, lawyer; b. Bklyn., Feb. 14, 1955; s. Michael and Fay Kamer; m. Helen Ann Smith, July 11, 1996; children: Michael Seth, Foster Ethan. BA, Washington U., St. Louis, 1975; JD, Emory U., Ga., 1979; LLM, Georgetown U., DC, 1982. Bar: DC 1979, Nev. 1985, NY 1991. Office gen. counsel Nat. Labor Rels. Bd., Washington, 1980—82, field atty. Las Vegas, 1982—83; labor counsel Nev. Resort Assn., Las Vegas, 1983—86; founding ptnr., pres. Kamer Zucker Abbott, Las Vegas, 1986—; adj. prof. U. Nev., 1983—91; vis. faculty U. Reno, 1991—2002. Adv. bd. Am. Arbitration Assn., Phoenix, 1992—; alternate comm. Nev. Judicial Discipline Com., 2003—04; standing com. mem. Judicial Ethics & Election Practices, Nev., 2001—03, Southern Nev. Disciplinary Comm., 1990—99. Contbr. articles various profl. jours. Gov. bd. govs. State Bar Nev., 2004—; bd. dirs. Nev. ACLU, 2007—. Named Rated #1 Firm in Nev. Labor & Employ., Chambers U.S.A., 2005—; named one of Nev. Best Atty. Labor & Employment, Nev. Bus. Jour., 2006; recipient Highest Rating Best Lawyers in Am., Woodward White, 1989—. Mem.: Nev. Am. Inn of Court. Avocations: chess, piano, reading. Office: Kamer Zucker Abbott 3000 W Charleston Blvd Ste 3 Las Vegas NV 89102 Office Phone: 702-259-8640. Business E-Mail: gkamer@kzalaw.com.

KAMERICK, EILEEN ANN, corporate financial executive, lawyer; b. Ravenna, Ohio, July 22, 1958; d. John Joseph and Elaine Elizabeth (Lenney) K.; m. Victor J. Heckler, Sept. 1, 1990; 1 child, Connor Joseph Heckler. AB in English summa cum laude, Boston Coll., 1980; postgrad., Exeter Coll., Oxford, Eng., 1981; JD, U. Chgo., 1984, MBA in Finance and Internat. Bus. with honors, 1993. Bar: Ill. 1984, U.S. Dist. Ct. (no. dist.) Ill. 1985, Mass. 1986, U.S. Ct. Appeals (7th cir.) 1988, U.S. Supreme Ct. 1993. Assoc. Reuben & Proctor, Chgo., 1984—86, Skadden, Arps et al, Chgo., 1986—89; atty. internat. Amoco Corp., Chgo., 1989—93, sr. fin. mgr. corp. fin., 1993—96, dir. banking and fin. svcs., 1996—97, v.p., treas., 1998—99, Whirlpool Corp., Benton Harbor, Mich., 1997; v.p., gen. counsel GE Capital Auto Fin. Svcs., Barrington, Ill., 1997—98; v.p., CFO BP Am., 1998—2000; exec. v.p., CFO United Stationers Inc., Des Plaines, Ill., 2000—01, Bcom3, Chgo., 2001—03; exec v.p., CFO, chief adminstrv. officer Heidrick & Struggles Internat., Inc., Chgo., 2004—. Advisor fin. com. Am. Petroleum Inst., 1992; bd. dirs. Heartland Alliance, ServiceMaster, Westell Tech., Associated Banc-Corp. Vol. adv. 7th Cir. Bar Assn., Chgo., 1987—; bd. dirs. Boys & Girls Clubs of Chgo., Ceve Sch. Mem. Phi Beta Kappa. Roman Catholic. Office: Heidrick & Struggles Internat Inc 233 S Wacker Dr Ste 4200 Chicago IL 60660 Office Phone: 312-496-1557. Personal E-mail: eakesq@aol.com.

KAMERIN, KIM K., music educator; b. Las Vegas, Sept. 1, 1967; s. Kris Kim Kamerin and Mary Louise Browder; m. Elizabeth A. Emmett, May 28, 1993; children: Benjamin Sebastian, Christopher Jameson. MusB, U. Nev., 1993, MusM, 1998. Cert. Tchr. K-12 Music Nev., 1994, Calif., 2001. Organist St. Joan Arc Cath. Ch., Las Vegas, 1989—96; instr. piano Las Vegas Acad. Performing Arts H.S., 1993—95, choir dir., instr. music, 1996—2001; choir dir. Swainston Mid. Sch., 1994—96; choir dir. varsity men's glee club U. Nev., 1998—2000; instr. comml. music Coll. Sequoias, Visalia, Calif., 2001—, Bakersfield C.C., 2001—02, Reedley Coll., 2003—. Rec. engr. Coll. Sequoias, 2001—; propr. Monsterfingers Studios, Dinuba, Calif., 2003—; pianist Spiritual Awareness Ctr., Visalia; accompanist, asst. choir dir. children's choir Nev. Sch. Arts, Las Vegas. Composer: Go, Lovely Rose, The Children's Hair Turned White (Regional U. Theater Competition Hon. Mention, 1991), Gloria (Am. Choral Director's Assn. Composer's of the Future, 1994). Music ministry Spiritual Awareness Ctr., Visalia, 2004. Named Concerto Contest Winner, U. Musical Soc., 1987, Mid. Sch. Tchr. of Yr., Clark County, Alexis Pk. Hotel and Gov. Bob Miller, 1996; recipient Presser award Acad. Excellence, U. Nev., Music Dept., 1990; grantee, Coll. Sequoias Found., 2004; Devos scholar, U. Nev., Music Dept., 1987. Mem.: Music Educators Nat. Conv., Am. Soc. Composers and Pubs., Calif. Music Educators Assn., Calif. Edn. Assn., Am. Choral Dirs. Assn. (nev. state repertoire and std. chmn., women's choir 1997—2001, conv. steering com. 2003—04), Phi Kappa Phi. Home Phone: 559-595-9907; Office Phone: 559-730-3754. Personal E-mail: kimk@cos.edu.

KAMERMAN, SHEILA BRODY, social work educator; b. Jan. 7, 1928; d. S. Lawrence and Helen (Golding) Brody; m. Morton Kamerman, Sept. 11, 1947; children: Nathan Brody, Elliot Herbert, Laura Kamerman-Katz. BA, NYU, 1946; MSW, Hunter Coll., 1966; D in Social Welfare, Columbia U., 1973; PhD (hon.), York U., Eng., 1998. Social worker N.Y.C. Dept. Social Svcs. , 1966-68; social work supr. Bellevue Psychiat. Hosp., 1968-69; assoc. prof. social work Hunter Coll., 1977-79; from rsch. assoc. to sr. rsch. assoc. Columbia U. Sch. Social Work, 1971-79, assoc. prof. social policy and planning, 1979-81; prof. Sch. Social Work Columbia U., 1981—, Compton Found. Centennial prof., 1996—, interim dean Sch. Social Work, 2001—02. Dir. Columbia U. Inst. for Child and Family Policy, 1998—; chair NAS-NRC panel on work, family and cmty., 1980-82; mem. Com. Child Devel. Rsch. and Pub. Policy, 1983-88; mem. com. on prenatal care Inst. Medicine, 1986-88; cons. in field; mem. Gov. Cuomo's Task Force on Poverty and Welfare Reform, 1986-87, adv. com. on Work and Family, 1987-88, UN Expert groups on social welfare and family policies; mem. Inst. Medicine/Nat. Rsch. Coun. bd. on children and families, 1998—. Author: (with Alfred J. Kahn) Not for the Poor Alone, 1975, Social Services in the United States, 1976, Social Services in International Perspective, 1977, Family Policy: Government and Families in Fourteen Countries, 1978, Child Care, Family Benefits and Working Parents, 1981, Parenting in an Unresponsive Society, 1980, Maternity and Parental Benefits and Leaves, 1980, Helping America's Families, 1982, Maternity Policies and Working Women, 1983, Income Transfers for Families with Children, 1983, Child Care: Facing the Hard Choices, 1987, The Responsive Work Place, 1987, Child Support: From Debt Collection to Social Policy, 1988, Mothers Alone: Strategies for a Time of Change, 1988, Privatization and the Welfare State, 1989, Social Services for Children, Youth and Families in the United States, 1990, Child Care, Parental Leave, and the Under 3's, 1991, A Welcome for Every Child, 1994, Starting Right: How America Neglects Its Youngest Children and What We Can Do About It, 1995, Children in big Cities, 1996, Confronting the New Politics of Child and Family Policies, (series of 6 reports), 1997, Family Change and Family Policies in Britain, Canada, New Zealand and the United States, 1998, Big Cities in the Welfare Transition, 1998, Contracting for Child and Family Services, 2000; editor: Early Childhood Education and Care, 2001; co-editor: (with Ronald A. Feldman) The Columbia University School of Social Work, 2001; (with Alfred J. Kahn) Beyond Child Poverty, the Social Exclusion of Children, 2002; contbr. articles to profl. jours. Fellow Ctr. Advanced Study in Behavioral Scis., 1983-84; recipient Hexter award Hunter Coll. Sch. Social Work, 1977, Nat. Leadership award in Social Policy, Heller Sch. Brandeis U., 1989, Lifetime Achievement award Social Welfare Policy and Practice, 2002, Significant Lifetime Achievement award Coun. on Social Work Edn., 2005; named to Hunt Coll. Hall of Fame, 1981, Columbia U Sch. Social Work Hall of Fame, 2003. Mem. NASW, Am. Pub. Human Svcs. Assn., Assn. Policy Analysis and Mgmt., Nat. Acad. Social Ins., Phi Beta Kappa. Home: 1125 Park Ave New York NY 10128-1243 Office: Columbia U Sch Social Work Mail Code 4600 1255 Amsterdam Ave New York NY 10027 Home Phone: 212-348-2505; Office Phone: 212-851-2270. Business E-Mail: sbk2@columbia.edu.

KAMERSCHEN, ROBERT JEROME, retired business executive, private investor, consultant; b. Laurium, Mich., Feb. 16, 1936; s. Robert Raymond and Elsie D (Barsanti) Kamerschen; m. Judith A Campbell, July 26, 1958; children: Kathryn, Carol, Jean. BS, Miami U., Oxford, Ohio, 1957, MBA, 1958. Exec. sales trainee Nat. Cash Register, Gary, Ind., 1958—59; mgmt. trainee Foote Cone & Belding, Chgo., 1959—60; dir. consumer mktg. Scott Paper Co., Phila., 1960—71; v.p. mktg. Revlon Inc., NYC, 1971—73; sr. v.p. mktg. ops. Dunkin Donuts Inc., Randolph, Mass., 1973—77; pres., COO Chanel Inc. and Christian Dior Parfums Inc., NYC, 1977—79; pres., CEO Max Factor & Co., Hollywood, Calif., 1979—83; exec. v.p., office of chmn. sector exec. Norton Simon Inc., 1981—83; pres., COO Mktg. Corp. of Am., 1984-87; pres., CEO RKO Six Flags Entertainment, Inc. div. Wesray Capital Corp., NYC, 1987—88; chmn., CEO ADVO Inc., Windsor, Conn., 1988—99; CEO Dimac Mktg. Corp, Windsor, 1999—2002, pvt. investor, strategic adv., 2002—; chmn. Survey Sampling Internat., 2005—. Disting. practitioner, lectr. U. Ga., Coll. Bus. Adminstrn., 1979—81; guest lectr. various univs. and trade assns.; presiding dir. R.H. Donnelley Corp., MDC Ptnrs. Inc., 1998—; chair nominating and governance com. IMS Health Inc., 2004—, Vertrue, Inc., 2006—, chmn., chmn. comp. com., 2002—05; mem. bus. adv. coun., exec.-in-residence Miami U., 1979—82; dir. various former pub. and pvt. cos. Trustee, 1st vice chmn. Emerson Coll., 1984—89; trustee Columbia Coll., 1993—96, trustee Bushnell Hall, 1995—2002; trustee Wadsworth Atheneum, 1990—; regent

U. Hartford, 1998—2005. Mem.: Metropolitan Club, NY Athletic Club, Sigma Alpha Epsilon, Delta Sigma Pi, Beta Gamma Sigma. Home: 204 Parade Hill Rd New Canaan CT 06840-4132 Personal E-mail: RKamerschen@msn.com.

KAMIENSKA-CARTER, EVA HANNA, designer, artist; b. Warsaw, Feb. 19, 1960; came to U.S., 1987; d. Witold and Kamilla (Karwowska) K.; m. Bernard Owen Carter, July 25, 1992; children: Lisa Camille, Maya Lee, Olav Bernard, Nina Eve Eric. MArch, Warsaw Tech. U., 1983; grad. with honors, Art Inst. Pitts., 1991. Certificate to practice art Ministry of Culture. Freelance artist, design cons., Warsaw, 1983-87, NYC, Detroit, Boston, Pitts., 1987-92; design cons., ptnr. Carter-Kamienska Design, Pitts., 1992—. Freelance set designer in motion picture prodn., Pitts., 1994—; art tchr. Carnegie Mus. Art, Pitts., 1991-92, Pitts. Ctr. Arts, 1991-92. Storyboard illustrator: (software) The Ripper, 1995; one woman shows include Zdzisiaj Gallery, Warsaw, Poland, 1981, Na Brechta Gallery, Warsaw, 1984. At 700 PArker, Detroit, 1988; group exbhns. include Manfred Schuller Gallery, Zurich, 1985, Zdzisiaj Gallery, 1985, Tripoli Gallery, Phila., 1987, Pitts. Ctr. Arts, 1989. Birmingham Loft, Pitts., 1989, Mendelson Gallery, Pitts., 1989, Monroeville (Pa.) Libr. Gallery, 1989, IUP Gallery, Indiana, Pa., 1998, Carnegie (Pa.) Libr., 1992, Associated Artists Pitts. Gallery, 1993, ZPAP Gallery, Warsaw, 1998. Mem. Assoc. Artists Pitts., Pitts. Soc. Artists, Pitts. Ctr. Arts. Avocations: attending cultural and social events, hiking, canoeing, computers. Home and Office: Carter-Kamienska Design 1 Simplon St Pittsburgh PA 15202

KAMIL, ELAINE SCHEINER, pediatric nephrologist, educator; b. Cleve., Jan. 26, 1947; d. James Frank and Maud Lily (Severn) Scheiner; m. Ivan Jeffery Kamil, Aug. 29, 1970; children: Jeremy, Adam, Megan. BS magna cum laude, U. Pitts., 1969, MD, 1973. Diplomate Am. Bd. Pediat., Am. Bd. Pediatric Nephrology. Intern in pediat. Children's Hosp. Pitts., 1973-74, resident in pediat., 1974-76; clin. fellow in pediatric nephrology Sch. Medicine, UCLA, 1976-79, acting asst. prof. pediat., 1979-80, asst. clin. prof. pediat., 1988-91, assoc. clin. prof. pediat., 1991-97, clin. prof. pediat., 1997—; rsch. fellow in nephrology Harbor-UCLA Med. Ctr., Torrance, Calif., 1980-82; med. dir. The Children's Clinic of Long Beach, Calif., 1984-87; med. dir. pediat. nurse practitioner program Calif. State U., Long Beach, 1984-87; assoc. dir. pediatric nephrology and transplant immunology Cedars-Sinai Med. Ctr., LA, 1990—2001, clin. dir. pediatric nephrology, 2001—. Adj. asst. prof. pediat. Harbor-UCLA, Torrance, Calif., 1983-87, UCLA, 1987-88; cons. in pediatric nephrology Hawthorne Cmty. Med. Group, Calif., 1981-2000. Author chpts. to books; contbr. articles to profl. jours. Pres.-elect med. adv. bd. Nat. Kidney Found. So. Calif., 2000-02, pres. med. adv. bd., 2002-04. Recipient Vol. Svc. award Nat. Kidney Found., 1998. Mem. AAUW, Am. Soc. Nephrology, Am. Soc. Pediatric Nephrology (co-chair workforce com. 2003-05, chair 2006—, mem. coun. 2006—), Internat. Soc. Nephrology, Internat. Soc. Pediatric Nephrology, So. Calif. Pediatric Nephrology Assn. (chair steering com. 1998—), Nat. Kidney Found. So. Calif. (med. adv. bd. 1987-96, rsch. com. 1987-90, chmn. pub. info. med. adv. bd. 1988-92, handbook com. 1988, co-chair med. adv. bd. cmty. svcs. com. 1992-93, chair-elect patient svcs. and cmty. edn. com. 1993-94, chair patients svcs. and cmty. edn. com. 1994-95, kidney camp summer vol. physician 1988-91, 93, 94, 97, 99-2005, Arthur Gordon award 1991, Exceptional Svc. award 1992, Exceptional Leadership and Support award 1995, Sprit of Nephrology award, 2007; bd. dirs. 1995-96, 2002—), Alpha Omega Alpha, Phi Beta Kappa. Office: Cedars Sinai Med Ctr 1165 WT 8700 Beverly Blvd Los Angeles CA 90048-1865 Home Phone: 310-202-1307; Office Phone: 310-423-4747. Business E-Mail: elaine.kamil@cshs.org.

KAMIL, MICHAEL, education educator; BA, Tulane U., 1964; MA, U. Wis., 1967, PhD, 1969. Faculty assoc. U. Tex., 1969—71; faculty assoc., dir. Reading Clini Ariz. State U., 1971—72; asst. prof. psychology U. Minn., Duluth, 1972—74; asst. prof. edn., dir. Reading Clinic Purdue U., West Lafayette, Ind., 1978—80; asst. prof. edn. U. Ill., Chgo., 1980—89; assoc. prof. ednl. theory and practice Ohio State U., 1990—92, prof. ednl. theory and practice, 1992—96; prof. edn. Stanford (Calif.) U., 1997—. Vis. prof. ednl. theory and practice Ohio State U., 1989—90; mem. Rand Reading Study Group, 2000—, Nat. Inst. Child Health and Devel. Nat. Reading Panel, 1998—2000; chair tech. com. Nat. Reading Conf., 1998—2001; mem. nat. lit. panel Ctr. Applied Linguistics and SRI, 2002—04; chair reading framework com. Nat. Assessment Edn. Progress, 2003—04; chair nat. adv. bd. Pacific Resources Edn. and Learning, Honolulu, 2004—05; mem. adv. coun. advancing adolescent lit. Carnegie Corp., 2004—. Co-author: Methods of Literacy Research: The Methodology Chapters From the Handbook of Reading Research, Volume III, 2002 (Ed Fry Book award, 2004); editor: Successful Reading Instruction, 2002, Professional Development for Teaching Reading, 2004, Multidisciplinary Perspectives on Literary Research 2nd edit., 2005, Teaching and Learning Vocabulary, 2005; mem. edit. adv. bd.: Jour. Literacy Rsch., 1996—, Jour. Ednl. Psychology, —, Reading Rsch. Quarterly, Lit. Tchg. and Learning. Mem.: APA, Nat. Reading Conf. (Albert J. Kingston award 1989, Oscar B. Causey award 2006), Nat. Conf. Rsch. in Lang. and Lit., Internat. Reading Assn. (Milton Jacobson Readability Rsch. award 1983), Am. Ednl. Rsch. Assn., Sigma Xi. Office: Stanford U Sch Edn 485 Lasuen Mall Stanford CA 94305-3096

KAMIN, BLAIR DOUGLASS, architecture critic; b. Red Bank, NJ, Aug. 6, 1957; s. Arthur Z. and Virginia P. Kamin. BA, Amherst Coll., 1979; M in Environ. Design, Yale U., 1984; HHD (hon.), Monmouth U., 2003. Reporter Des Moines Register, 1984-87; suburban reporter Chgo. Tribune, 1987—91; culture news reporter, 1992; architecture critic, 1992—. Nominating juror Pulitzer Prize, 2000, 02, Gabriel Prize, 2007; adj. prof. art North Ctrl. Coll., 2005—; instr. Graham Sch. Continuing Edn., U. Chgo., 2006. Author: Why Architecture Matters: Lessons from Chicago, 2001, contbr. articles to profl. jours. Recipient Nat. Edn. Reporting award Edn. Writers Assn., 1985, Edward Scott Beck award Chgo. Tribune, 1990, George Polk award for Criticism, 1996, Pulitzer Prize for Criticism, 1999, Inst. Honor for Collaborative Achievement, AIA, 1999, Peter Lisagor award for Exemplary Journalism, 1993-98, 2001, 03, 06, Engring. Journalism award Am. Assn. Engring. Socs. and Engring. Found., 1996, Richard Driehaus Found. Preservation award Landmarks Preservation Coun. Ill., 1997, Wright Spirit award Frank Lloyd Wright Bldg. Conservancy, 2001, Presdl. citation AIA, 2004; named to Chgo. Media Elite, Crains Chgo. Bus., 2005. Jewish. Office Phone: 312-222-4138. Business E-Mail: bkamin@tribune.com.

KAMIN, SHERWIN, retired lawyer; b. NYC, Feb. 5, 1927; s. Theodore and Esther K.; children: Lawrence O., Samuel N., Janet C., David W., Julia E.; m. S. Jeanne Hall, Oct. 1, 1993. BBA, CCNY, 1948; LLB, Harvard U., 1951. Bar: NY 1953. Asst. reporter Fed. Income Tax Project, Am. Law Inst., Cambridge, Mass., 1951—52; assoc. Botein, Hays, Sklar & Herzberg, NYC, 1952—62, ptnr., 1962—68, Kramer, Levin, Naftalis & Frankel, NYC, 1968—93, of counsel, 1993—2001, Fulton, Rowe & Hart and predecessors, NYC, 2002—06. Served with USN, 1945-46. Mem. ABA, Assn. Bar City NY, NY State Bar Assn., Am. Law Inst., Am. Coll. Tax Counsel. Home: 163 W 76th St New York NY 10023-8325 E-mail: sherwink@aol.com.

KAMIN, WILLIAM STEPHEN, food products executive, photographer; b. Chgo., Feb. 3, 1930; s. Emil Zola and Berta Magid; m. Adrienne Bloomberg, Aug. 28, 1955 (dec. June 15, 2001); children: Steven B., Andrew G. PhB, U. Chgo., 1947; BS, U. Ill., 1952. CPA, Ill. Staff acct. D. Himmelblau & Co., Chgo., 1955-57; budget analyst Westinghouse Electric Co., West Mifflin, Pa., 1957-63; contr. Std. Fruit Co., La Ceiba, Honduras, 1963-68, gen. mgr. Guayaquil, Ecuador, 1968-70; v.p. fin. Dole Fruit Co., Honolulu, 1970-72; v.p. ops. Castle & Cooke, Inc., San Francisco, 1972-78, v.p. strategic planning, 1978-82; pvt. practice photography Menlo Park, Calif., 1985—. Cons. William S. Kamin Cons., Atherton, Calif., 1982-85; adj. prof. Coll. Notre Dame, Belmont, Calif., 1984-85, U. Santa Clara, Calif., 1986, Golden Gate U., San Francisco, 1987. Author, photographer: Tenderloin, 1989. Bd. dirs., fin. cons. Valley Inst. of Theatre Arts, Saratoga, Calif., 1986-87; docent Coyote Point Mus., San Mateo, 1992-95, Fitzgerald Marine Res., Pacifica, Calif., 1995-97. Mem. Sons in Retirement. Avocations: tennis, travel. Home and Office: 169 Stone Pine Ln Menlo Park CA 94025-3050 Office Phone: 650-322-4300. E-mail: billkamin@comcast.net.

KAMINE, BERNARD S., lawyer; b. Dec. 5, 1943; m. Marcia Phyllis Haber; children: Jorge H., Benjamin H., Tovy H. BA, U. Denver, 1965; JD, Harvard U., 1968. Bar: Calif. 1969, Colo. 1969. Dep. atty. gen. Calif. Dept. Justice, LA, 1969-72; asst. atty. gen. Colo. Dept. Law, Denver, 1972-74; assoc. Shapiro & Maguire, Beverly Hills, Calif., 1974-76; ptnr. Kamine Ungerer LLP and predecessors, LA, 1976—. Bd. dirs., sec. Pub. Works Stds., Inc., 1996—; mem. adv. com. legal forms Calif. Jud. Coun., 1978—82; bd. dirs. Constrn. Industry Rsch. Bd., 2000—02. Author: Public Works Construction Manual: A Legal Guide for California, 1996; contbr. chpts. to legal texts and articles to profl. jours. Mem. L.A. County Dem. Ctrl. Com., 1982-85; mem. Pacific S.W. regional bd. Anti-Defamation League, 1982—, pres. bd., 1998-2000, assoc. nat. commr., 1995—. Col. USAR, 1969-2003. Decorated Meritorious Svc. medal, Joint Svcs. Commendation medal, Army Commendation medal, Expert Infantryman badge. Mem. ABA, Calif. State Bar (chair conf. dels. calendar coordinating com. 1991-92), L.A. County Bar Assn. (chair Superior Cts. com. 1977-79, chair constrn. law subsect. of real property sect. 1981-83), Engring. Contractors' Assn. (bd. dirs. 1985—, affiliate chair 1992-93, affiliate DIG award 1996, Polit Action Com. Disting. Svc. Medal 2004), Assoc. Gen. Contractors Calif. (L.A. dist. bd. dirs. 1995-00), Am. Constrn. Insps. Assn. (bd. registered constrn. inspectors 1990-97), Beavers, Res. Officers Assn. (pres. chpt. 1977-78), Omicron Delta Kappa. Office: 350 S Figueroa St Ste 250 Los Angeles CA 90071-1201 Office Phone: 213-972-0119.

KAMINER, ARIEL, editor; Editor NY mag.; with NY Times & NY Times mag., 1996—2004; Arts & Leisure sect. dep. editor Sunday Times, 2005—05, editor Arts & Leisure sect., 2005—07; dep. editor online journalism NY Times, 2007—. Contbr. (articles) NY mag., NY Times, NY Times mag. Office: NY Times Sunday Times 229 W 43rd St New York NY 10036 Office Phone: 212-556-1238.

KAMINKER, MARCIA KAHN, physical therapist; b. Phila., Mar. 11, 1955; d. Alan and Norma Bernstein Kahn; m. Martin Alan Kaminker, Dec. 28, 1975; children: Jacob, David, Eva. BS in Phys. Therapy, U. Pa., 1976; MS in Pediat. Phys. Therapy, with distinction, Drexel U., Phila., 2003; D in Phys. Therapy, with distinction, Drexel U., 2007. Cert. sch. based therapy MCP Hahnemann U., 2000, pediat. specialist Am. Bd. Phys. Therapy Specialties, 2004. Phys. therapist Moss Rehab. Hosp., Phila., 1976—79, Cleve. Met. Gen. Hosp., 1979—80, John F. Kennedy Med. Ctr., Edison, NJ, 1984—85, Bayshore Cmty. Hosp., Holmdel, NJ, 1990—91, Robert Wood Johnson U. Hosp., New Brunswick, NJ, 1990—96, Piscataway Regional Day Sch., NJ, 1993—96, South Brunswick Twp. Pub. Schs., Monmouth Junction, NJ, 1995—. Mentor entry-level doctors of phys. therapy students Drexel U., Phila., 2003—04, NY Med. Coll., Valhalla, 2004—06. Contbr. articles to profl. jours. Pres. South Brunswick Bd. Edn., Monmouth Junction, NJ, 1993—95, v.p., 1991—93, bd. mem., 1989—95; leader Girl Scouts of Am., South Brunswick, NJ, 1993—97. Recipient Class of 1958 Award for Scholarship and Svc., U. of Pa., 1976, Evelyn B. Noyovitz award, 2004; grantee Maternal and Child Health Leadership Tng. grantee, US Dept. of Edn., 1998—2000. Mem.: Am. Acad. for Cerebral Palsy and Devel. Medicine, Am. Phys. Therapy Assn., Phila. HS for Girls Alumnae Assn. (life), Alpha Eta Soc., Friars Sr. Honor Soc. (life). Home: 81 Davidson's Mill Rd North Brunswick NJ 08902 Office: South Brunswick Pub Schs PO Box 181 Monmouth Junction NJ 08852 Office Phone: 732-297-7800 3146. Office Fax: 732-297-1997. Personal E-mail: mkkaminker@aol.com. E-mail: marcia.kaminker@sbschools.org.

KAMINS, BARRY MICHAEL, lawyer; b. Oct. 3, 1943; s. Abe and Evelyn Bertha (Goffen) K.; m. Fern Louise Kamins, Mar. 30, 1968; 1 child, Allyson. BA, Columbia U., NYC, 1965; JD, Rutgers U., Newark, 1968. Bar: NY 1969, US Dist. Ct. (ea. and so. dists.) NY 1973, US Supreme Ct. 1974. Asst. dist. atty., 1969-73; dep. chief Criminal Ct. Bur., 1971-73; ptnr. Flamhaft, Levy, Kamins & Hirsch, 1973—. Chmn. grievance com. 2d and 11th Jud. Dist., 1994-98; adj. prof. Fordham Law Sch., Bklyn. Law Sch., Bklyn. Law Sch.; adj. prof. criminal law NY Tech. Coll.; apptd. spl. prosecutor, Kings County, 1990-92; chmn. oversight com. Criminal Def. Orgn. 2d Appellate Divsn., 1997—. Author: The Social Studies Student Investigates the Criminal Justice System, 1978, New York Search and Seizure, 1991; contbr. numerous articles on criminal law to profl. jours. Mem. ABA, NY State Bar Assn. (v.p., chair com. prof. discipline 1999-2004), Bklyn. Bar Assn. (past pres., chair jud. com. 1994-98, v.p.), Kings County Criminal Bar Assn. (past pres.), Assn. Bar City N.Y. (pres, v.p. chair jud. com. 1998-2001, exec. com. 2001-2005, chair exec. commn., 2004-2005, v.p. 2005—, mem. continuing legal edn. bd., bd. editors N.Y. Law Jour.). Office: 16 Court St Brooklyn NY 11241-0102 Office Phone: 718-237-1900. Business E-Mail: b.kamins@flkhlaw.com.

KAMINS, EDWARD, electronics executive; 2 children. BSEE with honors, Stevens Inst. Tech., Hoboken, NJ; MBA in Mktg., C.W. Post Ctr., LI U. Various positions up to v.p. channels Digital Equipment Corp.; sr. v.p. bus. devel. Avnet Computer Mktg. Avnet, Inc., 1996—99, sr. v.p., 1999—, pres. Avnet Applied Computing, 1999—2003, chief info. officer, 2003—05, chief operational excellence officer, 2005—. Bd. dirs. InterDigital Comm. Corp, 2003—, Calence, LLC, 2006—. Bd. dirs. Lupus Found. of Am. Recipient Altruism award, Lupus Found. of Am., 2002. Office: Avnet Inc 2211 S 47th St Phoenix AZ 85034-6403 Office Phone: 480-643-2000.*

KAMINS, JOHN MARK, lawyer; b. Chgo., Feb. 7, 1947; s. David and Beulah (Block) K.; m. Judith Joan Sperling, May 5, 1968; children: Robert, Heather. AB with high honors and distinction, U. Mich., 1968, JD, 1970. Bar: Mich. 1971, Fla. 1991. Assoc., Honigman Miller Schwartz and Cohn, Detroit, 1971-75, ptnr., 1976—; lectr. Inst. on Continuing Legal Edn. Pres. Mich. chpt. Leukemia and Lymphoma Soc., 1991-92, 93-96, nat. trustee, 1996—2004, nat. exec. com., 1997—, chmn. nat. bd. trustees, 2004—, chmn. nat bd. dirs., 2005-06; pres. Goodwill Industries of Greater Detroit Found., 2001-03; pres. Temple Beth El, Bloomfield Hills, Mich., 1994-96. Mem. Nat. Assn. Bond Lawyers (vice chmn. com. on opinions 1985-86), Mich. Bar Assn. (chairperson, pub. corp. law sect. 1992-93). Jewish. Home: 1315 Stuyvessant Rd Bloomfield Hills MI 48301-2144 Office: Honigman Miller Schwartz & Cohn llp 2290 First National Bldg Detroit MI 48226 Office Phone: 313-465-7436.

KAMINSHINE, STEVEN J., dean, law educator; BA summa cum laude, NYU; JD, DePaul U. Ptnr. labor and employment law practice, NYC; atty. Nat. Labor Rels. Bd., Washington, DC; mem. law faculty Ga. State U., Coll. Law, 1985—, assoc. prof., assoc. dean academic affairs, interim dean, 2004—. Contbr. articles to law jours. Mem.: Atlanta Bar Assn. (chair Labor and Employment Sec.), Ga. Bar Assn. Office: Ga State U College of Law 140 Decatur St Rm 422 Atlanta GA 30303 Office Phone: 404-651-2035. Office Fax: 404-651-2570. E-mail: skaminshine@gsu.edu.

KAMINSKI, DONALD LEON, surgeon, gastroenterologist, educator; b. Elba, Nebr., Nov. 9, 1940; s. Edwin and Irene (Syntek) K.; m. Maureen M. Cudmore, Nov. 28, 1964; children: Christian, Julie, Jane, Kathryn. BS, Creighton U., 1962, MD, 1966. Diplomate: Am. Bd. Surgery. Intern. St. Louis U., 1966-67, resident in surgery, 1967-71; attending surgeon St. Louis U. Hosp., 1972—, dir. gen. surgery, 1982—. Mem. Soc. Univ. Surgeons, Am. Surg. Assn., Central Surg. Soc., Alpha Omega Alpha Republican. Roman Catholic. Home: 1025 Joanna Ave Saint Louis MO 63122-1821 Office: St Louis U 3635 Vista at Grand PO Box 15250 Saint Louis MO 63110-0250

KAMINSKI, LEON R., lawyer; b. LaPorte, Ind., Nov. 21, 1924; s. Stanley A. and Stephanie L. Kaminski; m. Norma Jean Lynn Kaminski, Oct. 28, 1950; children: Daniel, Anne, Lynn, Paul, James, William. AB, Ind. U., 1946; JD, Ind. U., Indpls., 1950. Bar: Ind. 1950, U.S. Dist. Ct. (no. and so. dists.) Ind. 1950, U.S. Ct. Appeals (7th cir.) 1967, U.S. Supreme Ct. 1980. Pvt. practice, LaPorte, 1950—57; dep. pros. atty. Prosecutor's Office, LaPorte, 1953—58; ptnr. Newby, Lewis, Kaminski & Jones, LaPorte, 1958—94, sr. counsel, 1995—. Pres. LaPorte City Bar Assn., 1967, LaPorte County Bar Assn., 1972, Ind. State Bar Assn., 1982—83; mem. Ind. Supreme Ct. Bd. Bar Examiners, 1971—75, Ind. Supreme Ct. Character and Fitness Com., 1991—. Charter mem. LaPorte County Sheriff's Merit Bd., 1970—81; chmn. LaPorte City March of Dimes Dr., 1960; v.p. men's coun. Roman Cath. Diocese Gary, Ind., 1968—76. Named diplomat, Def. Trial Counsel Ind., 1982; recipient Disting. Alumni Svc. award, Ind. U. Sch. Law, Indpls., 1988, Sagamore of the Wabash, 1999. Fellow: Ind. Bar Found. (fellows chair 1991—92, 50 Yr. award 2000), Am. Bar Found., Internat. Soc. Barristers (state chair 1985), Am. Coll. Trial Lawyers (state chair 1981—82). Roman Catholic. Avocations: golf, tennis, travel. Office: Newby Lewis Kaminski & Jones 916 Lincolnway La Porte IN 46350 Office Phone: 219-362-1577.

KAMINSKI, PAUL GARRETT, former federal agency administrator, investment banker; b. Cleve., Sept. 16, 1942; s. Theodore Albert and Eleanor Marie (Dobranski) K.; m. Julia Kent Crafts, Oct. 8, 1966; children: Laura Denise, Garrett Kent. BS, USAF Acad., 1964; MS in Aerospace and Astronautics, MIT, 1966, MSEE, 1966; PhD in Aeronautics and Astronautics, Stanford U., 1971. Commd. 2d lt. USAF, 1964, advanced through grades to col., 1979, spl. asst. to under sec. of def. Washington, 1977-81; dir. low observables tech. Office Dep. Chief Staff for R&D, Dept. Air Force, 1981-84; ret., 1984; pres., COO, Tech. Strategies & Alliances, Burke, Va., 1985-93, chmn., CEO, 1993-94; under sec. of def. for acquisition and tech. Dept. Def., Washington, 1994-97; chmn., CEO Technovation, Inc., 1997—; sr. ptnr. Global Tech. Ptnrs. LLC, 1998—. Chmn. Def. Sci. Bd., Washington, 1993-94; dir., Anteon Internat. Corp., Atlantic Coun. US, Charles Stark Draper Lab., Inc., Dyncorp., Eagle-Picher Technologies, General Dynamics, Pacific Sierra Rsch.; mem. Senate Select Com. on Intelligence Technical Adv. Group, Nat. Reconnaissance Office Adv. Coun., Procurement Roundtable; bd. trustee RAND; cons. Office of Sec. Def./Def. Sci. Bd.; mem. strategic adv. bd., MILCOM. Contbr. articles to sci. jours. Dir. Spl. Olympics, Palos Verdes (Calif.) H.S., 1971-73; hon. trustee, Am. Tech. Alliances. Decorated Legion of Merit, D.S.M. Office Sec. Def., Disting. Pub. Svc. medal, , Medal of Merit in gold Netherlands Ministry Def.; named 2006 Nat. Medal Tech. Laureate. Fellow: IEEE, AIAA (assoc.); mem.: NAE, AAAS, Sigma Gamma Tau, Tau Beta Pi, Sigma Xi. Avocations: golf, tennis, jogging, cross country skiing. Office: Technovation Inc 6691 Rutledge Dr Fairfax Station VA 22039-1733*

KAMINSKY, ALAN, lawyer; b. Jersey City, Feb. 2, 1958; BA, NYU, 1980; JD, Hofstra U., 1983. Bar: NY 1983, NJ 1983, US Dist. Ct. Ea. Dist. NY, US Dist. Ct. So. Dist. NY. Ptnr. Wilson, Elser, Moskowitz, Edelman & Dicker LLP, NYC, chmn. gen. liability/toxic tort practice team. Author: A Complete Guide to Premises Security Litigation, 1995, A Complete Guide to Lead Paint Poisoning Litigation, 1998. Mem.: ABA, Am. Trial Lawyers Assn., Def. Rsch. Inst., NY State Bar Assn., Bronx County Bar Assn. (mem. judiciary com.), NY State Trial Lawyers Assn. Office: Wilson Elser Moskowitz Edelman & Dicker LLP 23rd Fl 150 E 42nd St New York NY 10017-5639 Office Phone: 212-490-3000 ext. 2370. Office Fax: 212-490-3038. Business E-Mail: kaminskya@wemed.com.

KAMINSKY, ALICE RICHKIN, retired literature educator; b. NYC; d. Morris and Ida (Spivak) Richkin; m. Jack Kaminsky (dec.); 1 son, Eric (dec.). BA, NYU, 1946, MA, 1947, PhD, 1952. Mem. faculty dept. English NYU, 1947-49, Hunter Coll., 1952-53, Cornell U., 1954-57, Broome Community Coll., 1958-59, Cornell U., 1959-63, SUNY, Cortland, 1963—, prof., 1968-91, prof. emerita, 1991—; faculty exch. scholar State U. NY. Author: George Henry Lewes as Critic, 1968, Logic: A Philosophical Introduction, 1974; editor: Literary Criticism of George Henry Lewes, 1964, Chaucer's Troilus and Criseyde and the Critics, 1980, The Victim's Song, 1985; contbr. more than 75 articles and revs. to numerous jours. Mem.: MLA, Chaucer Soc. *At a very early age I learned that life is fragile, that many loved and lovely things die or disappear. My way of coping with that knowledge was to latch on to the work ethic. This meant working to achieve some end, even during the retirement years.*

KAMINSKY, ARTHUR CHARLES, lawyer; b. Bronx, N.Y., Dec. 29, 1946; s. Daniel and Claire (Sternberg) K.; m. Andrea Lynn Polin, Dec. 28, 1969; children: Alexis Kate, Thomas Suradet, Eric Vorapong. BA cum laude with distinction, Cornell U., 1968; JD, Yale U., 1971. Bar: N.Y. 1974, U.S. Dist. Ct. (so. dist.) N.Y. 1975, U.S. Tax Ct. 1977, U.S. Supreme Ct. 1984. Assoc. Paul Weiss Rikfind Wharton & Garrison, 1973-74; ptnr. Taft & Kaminsky, N.Y.C., 1974-81; pres. A.C.K. Sports, Inc., N.Y.C., 1977-95, Profl. Sports Investors, Inc., N.Y.C., 1982-89; exec. v.p. Tha Marquee Group, Inc. 1995-2000; pres. Athletes and Artists, 2002—; mem. selection com. U.S. Olympic Hockey Team, Mpls., 1980. Co-author: One Goal; A Chronicle of the 1980 U.S. Olympic Hockey Team, 1984; weekly columnist N.Y. Times, 1973-77; analyst H.S. and coll. sports broadcasts Telecare TV, 2001—. Intern for 3d congl. dist. N.Y. Adlai E. Stevenson Meml., 1967. Dep. campaign mgr. Lindsay for Pres., N.Y.C., 1972; del. credentials com. Dem. Nat. Conv., Miami, 1972; adminstrv. asst. Rep. Michael Harrington, Washington, 1972-73; pres. Plandome Civic Assn., 1981-82; trustee African-Am. Athletic Assn., 1992-99. Recipient Outstanding Sr. award Cornell U., 1968, Friends of Edn. award N.Y. State Teachers Union, 1988; named one of the 100 Most Powerful Poeple in Sports, The Sporting News, 1991-92; finalist Thurman Arnold Moot Ct. competition, 1970; inducted charter mem. Jericho H.S. Hall of Fame, 1991. Mem. N.Y. State Bar Assn., Assn. of Bar of City of N.Y., Com. Entertainment and Sports, ABA, New Sch. Soc. Research (lectr.), Sports Lawyers Assn. (lectr.), Quill and Dagger, Friars Club (bd. govs. 2000-05), Plandome Country Club, Phi Beta Kappa (hon.). Democrat. Jewish. Home: 157 Colonial Pky Manhasset NY 11030-1414

KAMINSKY, MANFRED STEPHAN, physicist; b. Koenigsberg, Germany, June 4, 1929; came to U.S., 1958; s. Stephan and Kaethe (Gieger) K.; m. Elisabeth Moellering, May 1, 1957; children: Cornelia K.B., Mark-Peter. First diploma in physics, U. Rostock, Germany, 1951; PhD in Physics magna cum laude, U. Marburg, Germany, 1957. German Research Soc. fellow and grad. asst. in physics U. Rostock, 1950-52; lectr. Rostock Med. Tech. Sch., 1952; German Research Soc. fellow and research asst. Phys. Inst., U. Marburg, 1953-57, sr. asst., 1957-58; research asso. Argonne (Ill.) Nat. Lab., 1958-59, asst. physicist, 1959-62, assoc., 1962-70, sr. physicist, 1970-86, dir. Surface Sci. Center-CTR Program, 1974-80, dir. Tribology Program, 1984-86; sole propr. Surface Treatment Sci. Internat., Hinsdale, Ill., 1986—. Cons. Office Tech. Assessment U.S. Congress, 1986, NRC com. on tribology, 1986-88; guest prof. Inst. Energy, U. Que.,

Montreal-Varennes, 1976-82; E.W. Mueller lectr. U. Wis., Milw., 1978; symposium chmn. Internat. Conf. Metall. Coatings, 1985-93. Author: Atomic and Ionic Impact Phenomena on Metal Surfaces, 1965; contbr. articles to profl. jours.; editor: Radiation Effects on Solid Surfaces, 1976; co-editor: Surface Effects on Controlled Fusion, 1974, Surface Effects in Controlled Fusion Devices, 1976, Dictionary of Terms for Vacuum Science and Technology, 1980; patentee in field. Bd. dirs. Com. 100, Hinsdale, 1970-75, 90-92, pres., 1973-74; pres. St. Vincent de Paul Soc., Hinsdale, 1972-73. Named Outstanding New Citizen of Year Citizenship Council Chgo., 1968; Japanese Soc. Promotion of Sci. fellow, 1982. Fellow Am. Phys. Soc.; mem. Am. Chem. Soc., Scientific Research Soc., Research Soc. Am., AAAS, Union German Phys. Socs., Am. Vacuum Soc. (sr., trustee 1982-84, chmn. Midwest sect. 1967-68, co-founder Gt. Lakes chpt., dir. 1968-70, chmn. fusion tech. div. 1980-81, editorial bd. jour. 1978-83, hon. 1986), Internat. Union Vacuum Sci., Techs. and Applications (chmn. fusion div. 1984-86), Sigma Xi. also: 300 Galen Dr Apt 506 Key Biscayne FL 33149-2177 Office: 906 S Park Ave Hinsdale IL 60521-4519

KAMINSKY, RICHARD ALAN, lawyer; b. Toledo, Nov. 15, 1951; s. Jack and Sally (Kale) K. BA, Johns Hopkins U., 1973; JD, U. Mich., 1975. Bar: Ill. 1976, U.S. Dist. Ct. (no. dist.) Ill. 1976. Assoc. Vedder, Price, Kaufman & Kammholz, Chgo., 1976-83; atty. Borg-Warner Corp., Chgo., 1983-89; v.p., assoc. gen. counsel CNA Ins. Cos., Chgo., 1989—. Contbr. chpt. to book. Mem.: ABA, Chgo. Bar Assn. Home: 47 Williamsburg Rd Evanston IL 60203-1813 Office: CNA Ins Cos Cna Pla Chicago IL 60685-0001 Office Phone: 312-822-5493. Business E-Mail: richard.kaminsky@cna.com.

KAMIONKOWSKI, MARC PAUL, astrophysicist, educator; b. Cleve., July 27, 1965; s. Mario David and Lelia (Sircovich) K. BA, Washington U., St. Louis, 1987; PhD, U. Chgo., 1991. Mem. Inst. Advanced Study, Princeton, NJ, 1991-94; asst. prof. Columbia U., NYC, 1994—99; prof. theoretical physics and astrophysics Calif. Inst. Tech., Pasadena, 1999—, Robinson prof. theoretical physics and astrophysics, 2006—. Contbr. articles to profl. jours. Recipient Ernest Orlando Lawrence award in Physics, Dept. Energy, 2007. Mem. Am. Phys. Soc., Am. Astron. Soc. (Helen B. Warner prize 1998). Office: Calif Inst Tech Mail Code 130-33 Pasadena CA 91125 Office Phone: 626-395-2563. Office Fax: 626-796-5675. E-mail: kamion@tapir.caltech.edu.

KAMISAR, YALE, lawyer, educator; b. NYC, Aug. 29, 1929; s. Samuel and Mollie (Levine) K.; m. Esther Englander, Sept. 7, 1953 (div. Oct. 1973); children: David Graham, Gordon, Jonathan; m. Christine Keller, May 10, 1974 (dec. 1997); m. Joan Russell, Feb. 28, 1999. AB, NYU, 1950; LLB, Columbia U., 1954; LLD, CUNY, 1978. Bar: D.C. 1955. Rsch. assoc. Am. Law Inst., NYC, 1953; assoc. Covington & Burling, Washington, 1955-57; assoc. prof., then prof. law U. Minn., Mpls., 1957-64; prof. law U. Mich., Ann Arbor, 1965-92, Clarence Darrow disting. univ. prof., 1992—2004; prof. San Diego U., 2004—. Vis. prof. law Harvard U., 1964-65, San Diego U., 2000-02; disting. vis. prof. law Coll. William and Mary, 1988; cons. Nat. Adv. Commn. Civil Disorders, 1967-68, Nat. Commn. Causes and Prevention Violence, 1968-69; mem. adv. com. model code pre-arraignment procedure Am. Law Inst., 1965-75. Reporter-draftsman: Uniform Rules of Criminal Procedure, 1971-73; author: (with J.H. Choper, S. Shiffrin and R.H. Fallon), Constitutional Law: Cases, Comments and Questions, 10th edit., 2006; (with W. LaFave, J. Israel and N. King) Modern Criminal Procedure: Cases and Commentaries, 11th edit., 2005, Criminal Procedure and the Constitution: Leading Cases and Introductory Text, 2002; (with F. Inbau and T. Arnold) Criminal Justice in Our Time, 1965; (with J. Grano and J. Haddad) Sum and Substance of Criminal Procedure, 1977, Police Interrogation and Confessions: Essays in Law and Policy, 1980; contbr. articles to profl. jours. Served to 1st lt. AUS, 1951-52. Recipient Am. Bar Found. Rsch. award, 1996. Office: U Mich Law Sch 625 S State St Ann Arbor MI 48109-1215 Business E-Mail: ykamisar@umich.edu.

KAMLER, KENNETH MARK, microsurgeon; b. NYC, Oct. 4, 1947; s. William and Ethel Kamler; children: Jonathan, Jennifer. BA in Biology, CUNY, NYC, 1968; MD, U. Marseille, France, 1975. Resident orthoped. surgery L.I. Jewish Med. Ctr., NYC, 1980; fellow hand and microsurgery Columbia-Presbyn. Med. Ctr., NYC, 1981; microsurgeon specializing in hand surgery New Hyde Park, N.Y., 1981—. Mt. Everest (Nepal) expdn. doctor Nat. Geog., 1992-93, 95-96; chief high altitude physician NASA/Yale Comml. Space Ctr., Mt. Everest, 1998, 99; expdn. doctor Andes, Amazon, Arctic, Galapagos, Antarctica, Peru, Ecuador, 1981, 87-89; tech. advisor IMAX Movie Everest, 1997; lectr. in field. Author: Doctor on Everest, 2000, Surviving the Extremes, 2004; contbg. author: Everest: Mountain Without Mercy, 1997; columnist Nat. Geographic Adventure, Popular Mechanics Fellow Explorers Club (dir. 1995-2001, 2003—, sci. adv. bd. 1996—, v.p. membership 1996-99, v.p. rsch. and edn. 1999—, heroism and altruism on Everest award 1999, Sci. Achievement award 2002); mem. Sigma Xi Jewish. Avocations: sailing, scuba diving, mountain climbing, drawing. Office: 410 Lakeville Rd New Hyde Park NY 11042-1101 Home Phone: 516-728-4308, 516-728-4308; Office Phone: 516-326-8810. E-mail: kenkamler@yahoo.com.

KAMLOT, ROBERT, performing arts executive; b. Vienna, Nov. 28, 1926; came to U.S., 1938, naturalized, 1943; s. Paul and Elsa (Wilhelm) K.; m. Jayne Bullard, Sept. 18, 1948. Student, CCNY, Syracuse U., Hunter Coll., NYC. Freelance mgr. Broadway prodns., 1964-71; prodn. exec. Zev Bufman Prodns., NYC, 1969-71; co.-mgr. Much Ado About Nothing, NYC, 1972, Two Gentlemen From Verona (nat. co.), Los Angeles, 1973. Gen. mgr. N.Y. Shakespeare Festival, 1973-83; gen. mgr. The Real Thing, Sunday in the Park With George, Biloxi Blues, The Odd Couple, Moon for the Misbegotten, Whoopi Goldberg, Social Security, Long Day's Journey Into Night, 1983-86, (nat. tour) Catskills on Broadway, Fool Moon, Wrong Turn at Lungfish; prodr. Hayfever, 1986; gen. mgr. Carole Shorenstein Hays Enterprises; prodr. Fences, 1987; gen. mgr. Martin Starger/The Really Useful Co. Lend Me a Tenor, 1988, Cates Films-Elmer Gantry, 1991-92, Martin Starger The Red Shoes, 1992, Fool Moon (European prodn.), 1994, BIG The Musical, 1995. Served with AUS, 1944. Mem. Assn. Theatrical Press Agts. and Mgrs., Tony Nominating Commn. Home: 175 W 93rd St New York NY 10025-9313 Office Phone: 212-840-8400. Personal E-mail: jaybob175@aol.com.

KAMM, JOHN, non-profit organization administrator, human rights activist; BA, Princeton U., 1972; MA, Harvard U., 1975. Founded chem. co., Hong Kong and China, 1979; Hong Kong rep. Nat. Coun. U.S.-China Trade, 1976—81; pres. Am. C. of C., Hong Kong, 1990; dir. Nat. Com. U.S.-China Rels.; founder, chmn., exec. dir. Dui Hua Found., San Francisco, 1999—. Dir. rsch. project in human rights diplomacy Stanford U. Named MacArthur Fellow, 2004; recipient Best Global Practices award, U.S. Govt., 1997, Eleanor Roosevelt Human Rights award, 2001. Office: Dui Hua Found 450 Sutter St Ste 900 San Francisco CA 94108 Office Phone: 415-986-0536. Office Fax: 415-986-0579. E-mail: duihua@duihua.org.

KAMM, LINDA HELLER, lawyer; b. NYC, Aug. 25, 1939; d. Seymour A. and Mary Heller; children: Lisa, Oliver. BA in History, Brandeis U., 1961; LLB, Boston Coll., 1967. Bar: Mass. 1967, D.C. 1978, U.S. Supreme Ct. 1985. Counsel Dem. Study Group, Washington, 1968-71; counsel select com. on coms. U.S. Ho. of Reps., Washington, 1973-75, gen. counsel budget com., 1975-77; gen. counsel U.S. Dept. Transp., Washington, 1977-80; ptnr. Foley and Lardner, Washington, 1980-84, of counsel, 1984-95; pvt. practice, 1995—; of counsel Boies, Schiller & Flexner, 2001—. Address: 188 E 70th St Apt 24C New York NY 10021-5170

KAMM, SOLOMON M., lawyer; b. Chgo., Jan. 4, 1938; BS, Univ. Ill., 1959; JD, NYU, 1962. CPA Ill., 1959; bar: Calif. 1963. V.p., gen. counsel, sec. Capital Group Companies. Editor (note & comment): NYU Law Rev., 1961—62. Mem.: ABA, Am. Coll. Trust & Estate Counsel, Am. Corp. Counsel Assn., Calif. State Bar, LA County Bar Assn. (chmn. probate & trust law sect. 1976—77, mem. exec. com. corp. law dept. sect.), Order of the Coif. Office: Capital Group Companies 55th Fl 333 S Hope St Los Angeles CA 90071 Office Phone: 213-486-9200. Office Fax: 213-486-4217.

KAMMAN, ALAN BERTRAM, communications consulting company executive; b. Phila., Jan. 25, 1931; s. Daniel Lawrence and Sara Belle K.; m. Madeleine Marguerite Pin, Feb. 15, 1960; children: Alan Daniel, Neil Charles. BCE, Swarthmore Coll., 1952. With Bell Tel. Co. Pa., Phila., 1952-69, Arthur D. Little, Inc., Cambridge, Mass., 1969-85, v.p. telecommunications scis., 1977-81, v.p. corp. staff, 1981-86; nat. dir. telecommunications markets KPMG Peat Marwick, Lexington, Mass., 1987-91; mng. dir. Global Consulting Group, St. Helena, Calif., 1991—; dir. Cambridge (Mass.) Strategic Mgmt. Group, 1992—; v.p. Symmetrix, Lexington, Mass., 1994-96; exec. dir. Vt. Telecomm. Application Ctr., 1998—. Chmn. adv. bd. grad. program telecommunications U. San Francisco, Intelevent, Europe, Telecom 75, Telecom 79, Telecom 83, Telecom 91, Telecommunications Mag.; world rep. KPMG Peat Marwick to Internat. Telecommunications Union, UN. Contbr. articles to jours. in field. Bd. dirs. U.S. Coun. World Comms. Yr.; dir., sec. Vt. Coun. World Affairs, 2005—; dir., chmn. Vt. Symphony Orch., 1999—, bd. region one. Mem. Appalachian Club (v.p. ops., bd. dirs.). Home: 26 Plantation Dr Apt 203 Vero Beach FL 32966-8277

KAMMAN, CURTIS WARREN, retired ambassador; b. Chgo., Jan. 15, 1939; s. Glenn Forrest and Mildred Isabel (Merry) Kamman; m. Mary Glasgow Curtis, Feb. 10, 1962; children: Edward, John, W Stephen. BA, Yale U., 1959; postgrad., U. Washington, 1964-65. Joined Fgn. Service, U.S. Dept. State, 1960-2000; various diplomatic positions Am. embassies, Washington, Mexico City, Hong Kong, Moscow, Nairobi, 1960-80; dir. East African Affairs, Washington, 1980-82; polit. counselor Am. embassy, Moscow, 1982-84, minister, counselor, 1984-85; prin. officer U.S. Interests sect. Swiss embassy, Havana, Cuba, 1985-87; dep. asst. sec. U.S. Dept. State, Washington, 1987-91; amb. to Chile Santiago, 1991-94; amb. to Bolivia, 1994-97; amb. to Colombia, 1997-2000; ret., 2000. Vis. instr. Univ. Notre Dame, 2001—04, adj. instr., 2004—06. Mem. vestry All Saints Ch., Saugatuck, Mich., 2002—05; bd. dirs. Fgn. Students Sch., Havana, 1985—87. Mem.: Am. Acad. Diplomacy, Phi Beta Kappa. Episcopalian. Avocation: choral singing. Address: 2236 Lakeshore Dr Fennville MI 49408-9715

KAMMER, JERRY, reporter; BA, U. Notre Dame; MA, U. N.Mex. Reporter Navajo Times, Window Rock, Ariz., 1974; Northern Mex. corr. Ariz. Republic, investigative reporter Phoenix, 1998—2000, Washington corr., 2000—02; immigration & border issues corr., Washington bur. Copley News Svc., 2002—. Mem. adj. faculty, English & Am. Studies Depts. U. N.Mex. Author: The Second Long Walk. Recipient Nat. Headliner award for investigative reporting, Don Bolles award, Ariz. Press Club, 1989, 2000, Edgar A. Poe award, White House Corrs. Assn., 2006, George Polk award, polit. reporting, 2006, Pulitzer Prize for nat. reporting, 2006. Office: Copley News Svc Washington Bur 1100 Nat Press Bldg Washington DC 20004 Office Phone: 202-737-7681. E-mail: jerry.kammer@copleydc.com.

KAMMERER, KELLY CHRISTIAN, lawyer; b. NYC, Nov. 29, 1941; s. William Henry and Edith (Langley) K.; m. Nancy Davis Frame, Oct. 2, 1999. BA, U. Notre Dame, 1963; LLB, U. Va., 1968. Bar: Va. 1968, N.Y. 1969, D.C. 1969, Fla. 1969. Peace Corps vol., Colombia, 1963-65; Reginald Heber Smith atty./fellow U. Pa., Washington, 1968-70; atty.-advisor, dep. gen. counsel Peace Corps, Washington, 1970-74; atty.-advisor AID, Dept. State, Washington, 1975-76, asst. gen. counsel, 1976-78, sr. dep. gen. counsel, 1978-82, legal counselor, 1981-82, dir. congl. rels., 1983-89; mission dir. Kathmandu, Nepal, 1989-93, counselor to the agy., 1994-99; vice chmn., U.S. rep. OECD/DAC, Paris, 1999—. Recipient Disting. Honor award AID, 1979, 83, Equal Opportunity award, 1982; presdl. rank of Disting. Sr. Exec., 1984, 89, Meritorious Sr. Exec., 1997. Mem. Inter-Am. Bar Assn., Soc. Internat. Law. also: 11 bis Blvd Jules Sandeau 75016 Paris France

KAMNIK, JOSEPH P., lawyer; b. Bristol, Pa., July 16, 1977; s. Joseph W. and Lucy D. Kamnik; m. Lauren C. Casper, May 20, 2006. BA, Susquehanna U., Selinsgrove, Pa., 1999; JD, U. Pa., Phila., 2002. Bar: NJ 2002, Pa. 2002, DC 2003. Atty. Akin Gump Strauss Hauer & Feld, LLP, Washington, 2002—05; spl. counsel US SEC, Washington, 2005—. Mem.: Mensa. Independent. Avocations: poker, writing. Home: 2807 11th St N Arlington VA 22201 Office: US Securities & Exchange Commission 100 F St NE Washington DC 20549 Home Phone: 703-242-4492; Office Phone: 202-551-5714. Personal E-mail: jkamnik@gmail.com.

KAMOIE, LAURA CROGHAN, history professor; b. Hagerstown, Md., Aug. 27, 1970; d. Joseph William and Ann Teresa Croghan; m. Brian Edward Kamoie, Oct. 5, 1996; children: Cara Amelia, Julia Grace. PhD, Coll. William and Mary, Williamsburg, Va., 1999. Vis. asst. prof. history Am. U., Washington, 2000—05; asst. prof. history U.S. Naval Acad., Annapolis, Md., 2005—. Hist. archaeologist Colonial Williamsburg Found., James River Inst. for Archaeology, Jamestown Discovery, Va., 1992—97; sr. editor Washington History mag. Hist. Soc. Washington, 2001—05; project coord., historian Adams Morgan Heritage Trail, Washington, 2001—05. Author: Irons in the Fire: The Business History of the Tayloe Family and Virginia's Gentry, 1700-1860, Neabsco and Occoquan: The Tayloe Iron Plantations, 1730-1830 (Prince William County Hist. Commn. Dissertation award, 1998), (booklet) Roads to Diversity: The Adams Morgan Heritage Trail. Alumni vol. Dickinson Coll., Carlisle, Pa., 1992—2006. Fellow, NEH, 2004. Mem.: Oral History Assn. Mid-Atlantic Region (bd. mem. 2005—), Va. Hist. Soc., Omohundro Inst. for Early Am. History and Culture, Am. Hist. Assn. Liberal. Office: US Naval Academy 107 Maryland Ave Annapolis MD 21402 Home Phone: 410-626-7625; Office Phone: 410-293-6276. Business E-Mail: kamoie@usna.edu.

KAMP, ARTHUR JOSEPH, JR., lawyer; b. July 22, 1945; s. Arthur Joseph and Irene Catherine (Ehrstein) K.; m. Barbara Hays, Aug. 24, 1968; children: Sara, Nathaniel. BA, SUNY, 1968, JD, 1970. Bar: N.Y. 1971, U.S. Dist. Ct. (we. dist.) N.Y. 1971, Va. 1973, U.S. Dist. Ct. (ea. dist.) Va. 1973. Atty. Neighborhood Legal Svcs., Buffalo, 1971; assoc. Diamonstein & Drucker, Newport News, 1972-77; ptnr. Diamonstein, Drucker & Kamp, Newport News, 1977-84, Kamp & Kamp, Newport News, 1984-87, Kaufman & Canoles, 1987-96, David, Kamp & Frank, L.L.C., 1996—; v.p. Peninsula Legal Aid Ctr., Inc., 1978-92. Active Newport News Planning Commn., 1990-97, chmn., 1994-96; mem. bd. visitors Ea. Va. Med. Sch., 1997-2003, vice rector, 2001, rector, 2002; trustee Ea. Va. Med. Sch. Found., 2004—; mem. local bd. dirs. Thomas Nelson C.C., 2005-. Lt. USAF, 1971-72. Mem. Va. State Bar Assn., Newport News Bar Assn. (past bd. dirs., chmn. legal aid com.), Va. Bar Assn., Va. Peninsula C. of C. (bd. dirs., exec. com., chmn. 1997, gen. counsel 1999-2001). Democrat. Office: David Kamp & Frank LLC 739 Thimble Shoals Blvd Ste 105 Newport News VA 23606 Office Phone: 757-595-4500. Business E-Mail: ajkamp@davidkampfrank.com.

KAMP, R. STEPHEN, finance educator; b. Phila., Nov. 9, 1942; s. Robert Shindel and Elizabeth Jackson Kamp; m. Terry Ellen Weingrow, Aug. 25, 1968 (div. 1983); m. Barbara D. Mueller, May 5, 1985; children: Jennifer Jackson Neren, Jonathan David, Courtney Nicole. BBA with honors, George Washington, Washington, 1967; MBA, Harvard U., Cambridge, Mass., 1969. Dir. instnl. syndicate mktg. Merrill Lynch, NYC, 1979—82; v.p. corp. fin. Paine Webber, NYC, 1982—90; dir. corp. fin. Price Waterhouse, Phila., 1990—92; cons. Fin. Directions Inc., NYC, 1993—95, Globecon Group, Ltd., NYC, 1995—96; founder, mng. dir. Montgomery Assocs., Haverford, Pa., 1996—99; sr. cons. Strategic Mgmt. Group, Phila., 1999—2002; asst. prof. fin. Fox Sch. Bus. and Mgmt. Temple U., Phila., 2003—. Acting CFO Every Penny Counts, Inc., Cape Coral, Fla., 1991—. Pres. Guild Ho. West, Phila., 1999—2006; bd. dirs. rehab. program Religious Soc. Friends, Phila., 1999—2006, mem. fin. oversight group Phila. yearly meeting, 2000—06; membership-chair Phila. Skating Club and Humane Soc., Ardmore, Pa., 2006. With US Army, 1962—64. Mem.: Phila. Skating Club and Humane Soc. (bd. govs., Charles Fetter trophy for ice dancing 1998, 2003, 2006), Harvard Bus. Club Phila. Avocations: ice dancing, downhill skiing, photography, bicycling, hiking. Home: 429 Montgomery Ave C-304 Haverford PA 19041 Office: Temple U Fox Sch Bus 1810 N 13th St 205-E Philadelphia PA Home Phone: 610-642-4008; Office Phone: 215-204-7016. Personal E-mail: kamprs@comcast.net. Business E-Mail: kamp@temple.edu.

KAMPE, CAROLYN JEAN, elementary school educator, special education educator, art educator; b. Chicago Heights, Ill., July 8, 1943; d. Fred H. and Harriet (Bobrowski) K. Student, Mt. St. Clare Jr. Coll., Clinton, Iowa, 1966-68; BA in Art, St. Ambrose U., 1970; MA in Cultural Studies, Gov. State U., 1974; EdD in Art Edn., Ill. State U., 1990. Cert. art tchr.; cert. spl. edn.; cert. K-12 specialist. Art supr., coord., and elem. art tchr. Dist. 170, Chicago Heights, 1970-87; grad. asst. art dept. Ill. State U., Normal, 1987-90; spl. edn. tchr. Hugh Jr. H.S., Matteson, Ill., 1990-91, Burr Oak, Calumet Park, Ill., 1991-92; homebound tchr. Dist. 162, Matteson, 1991-98; art edn. for spl. edn. Dist. 170, Chicago Heights, 1992—; art tchr. Field Sch. Dist. 152, Harvey, Ill., 1994, Vogt Visual Art Ctr., Tinley Park, Ill., 1996—2003; spl. edn. tchr. Hufford Jr. H.S., Joliet, Ill., 1996-98; with South Suburban Spl. Edn. Recreation Assn., Frankfort, Ill., 2000—02; spl. edn. tchr. Homewood-Flossmoor Park Dist., 2002. Vis. faculty and adaptive art specialist St. Norbert Coll., DePere, Wis., 1990-92; active in Put Your Heart Illinois Youth Art Month, 1985-86 and 1993-94, spl. edn. "Earth Day" Art Exhbn. (200 works on display); homebound tchr. Dist. 162 and 227, 1991-98; bd. dirs. Very Spl. Arts, Ill. State U., Normal, 1992-96. Group exhbns. include Chicago Heights Libr., Chicago Heights Mcpl. Bldg., 1993-94, Wash. Jr. H.S., Chicago Heights, 1994; contbr. articles to profl. jours. Bd. dirs. Very Spl. Arts Ill., Ill. State U., Normal, 1992-94; Ill. Coalition for Disabilities, Normal, 1985-86; pres. Self Help for Hard of Hearing, Ill., 1984-86; mem. White House Exhbn. Com., Chgo., 1992-93; vol. Chgo. Pub. Libr., 1993; mem. Put Your Heart in Month, Ill. Youth Art Month, 1985-86; art judge Girl Scout Art Contest, 1982, Chicago Heights Jaycees, 1982-83. Named One of 5 Best and Brightest Outstanding Disabled Coll. Grads., Mainstream Mag. and Am. Bus. Women's Assn., 1990, to Hall of Fame for Outstanding Achievement, Mt. St. Clare Coll., 1996, to Hall of Fame for Fine Art, Marian Cath. H.S. Alumni Assn., 1997; recipient Kohl Internat. Tchg. award 1993. Mem. Nat. Assn. Art Edn., Ill. Art Edn. Assn. (Best Art Tchr. award 1984), South Surburban Spl. Recreation Assn., Lincolnway Spl. Recreation Assn. Roman Catholic. Achievements include: first deaf female doctoral graduate from Ill. State Univ.

KAMPHEFNER, PIUS, minister; b. Platte City, Mo., Dec. 22, 1929; s. Ray J. Kamphefner and Ileen Sewell. BS, St. Mary U. of Minn., 1950, MA, 1960. Joined Christian Bros. H.S. tchr. Christian Bros., Ill., 1950—63, H.S. prin. Ill. and Mo., 1963—70; program dir. St. Louis County Juvenile Ct., Mo., 1970—79; house parent Mercy Boys Home, Chgo., 1979—91; resident pastor, min. St. Gabriel Parish, Mound Bayou, Miss., 1991—. Democrat. Roman Catholic. Home: 501 M L King St Mound Bayou MS 38762 Office: St Gabriel Parish 501 M L King St Mound Bayou MS 38762

KAMPINE, JOHN P., anesthesiology and physiology educator; MD, Marquette U. Med. Sch., Milwaukee, WI, 1961, PhD in Physiology, 1965. Intern Med. Coll. of Wis., Milwaukee, 1961—62, Milw. Cty. Gen. Hosp.; fellow, neurosciences NIH, Bethesda, Md., 1965—67; US Pub. Health Svc. postdoctoral rsch. fellow Marquette Sch. Medicine; rsch. assoc. Nat. Inst. Neurological Diseases and Blindness Lab. of Neurochemistry; instr. physiology Med. Coll. of Wis., Milw., 1962—67, asst. prof. physiology and anesthesiology, 1967—71, assoc. prof., 1971—74, prof., chair dept. anesthesiology, 1979—2005, prof. physiology, 1979—2005, prof. anesthesiology and physiology, 1974—. Pres. Assn. for U. Anesthesiologists; mem., surgery, anesthesia, and trauma study sect. NIH. Mem.: Am. Physiological Soc. (chmn., circulation group), Soc. Academic Anesthesia (pres., chmn.), Inst. Medicine-NAS. Office: Froedtert Meml Hosp PO Box 26099 9200 W Wisconsin Ave Milwaukee WI 53226-3596

KAMPMEIER, CURT, management consultant; b. Evanston, Ill., Aug. 15, 1941; s. Carlos Otto and Neva Lou (Brown) K.; m. Susan Brooks, Dec. 30, 1961; children: Rand, Elizabeth, Paul, John. BA with honors, Coll. of Wooster, Ohio, 1964; cert. in bus., Alexander Hamilton Inst., NYC, 1967. Cert. mgmt. cons. Sales rep. Westminster Press, Phila., 1964-67, Random House, Inc., NYC, 1967-73; founder, chmn. The Kampmeier Group, LLC, Columbus, Ohio, 1973—. Former mem. editl. bd. Jour. Mgmt. Cons., Consulting to Mgmt.; reviewer in field:. Trustee Ohio Presbyn. Retirement Svcs., Columbus, 1984-87, Westminster Thurber Community, Columbus, 1984-87; commencement speaker Shawnee State Coll., Portsmouth, Ohio. Fellow: Inst. Mgmt. Cons. Office Phone: 614-488-4401. Personal E-mail: curtkampmeier@tkgp.us.

KAMPMEIER, JACK AUGUST CARLOS, chemist, educator; b. Cedar Rapids, Iowa, June 11, 1935; s. Carlos and Nevalou (Brown) K.; m. Anne Margaret Derk, June 14, 1958; children— Scott, Margaret, Stephen. AB, Amherst Coll., 1957; PhD (NSF fellow), U. Ill., 1960. From instr. to prof. chemistry U. Rochester, NY, 1960-71, prof., 1971—2005, chmn. dept. chemistry, 1975-79, assoc. dean grad. studies Coll. Arts and Sci., 1982-88, dean Coll. Arts and Sci., 1988-91, prof. emeritus, 2005—. Co-author: Peer-Led Team Learning, A Guidebook, 2001, Peer-Led Team Learning, Organic Chemistry, 2001, student edit., 2006; contbr. sci. and pedagogical articles to profl. jours. Recipient Nat. Catalyst award Chem. Mfrs. Assn., 1999; NSF sci. faculty fellow U. Calif., Berkeley, 1971-72; Fulbright Hays sr. rsch. scholar U. Freiburg, Germany, 1979-80; NATO sr. scientist, 1979-80. Mem. Am. Chem. Soc., Sigma Xi. Home: 86 Reservoir Ave Rochester NY 14620-2754 Office: U Rochester Dept Chemistry Box 270216 Rochester NY 14627 Office Phone: 585-275-4441. Business E-Mail: kamp@chem.rochester.edu.

KAMPOURIS, EMMANUEL ANDREW, retired corporate executive; b. Alexandria, Egypt, Dec. 14, 1934; arrived in US, 1979; s. Andrew George and Euridice Ann (Caralli) Kampouris; m. Myrto Stellatos, July 4, 1959 (dec.); children: Andrew, Alexander. Student, King's Sch., Bruton, Somerset, UK, 1953; MA in Law, Oxford U., 1957; cert. in ceramic tech., North Staffordshire Coll. of Tech., UK, 1962. Plant mgr., dir. "KEREM", Athens, Greece, 1962-64; dir. "HELLENIT", Athens, Greece, 1962-65; mng. dir. Ideal Standard, Athens, 1966-79; v.p., group exec. internat. and export Am. Standard Inc., New Brunswick, NJ, 1979-84, sr. v.p. bldg. products, 1984-89; pres., chief exec. officer Am. Standard Inc., Am. Standard Cos. Inc., NYC, 1989-99, now chmn.; bd. dirs. Click Commerce Inc, Chgo., Horizon Blue Cross Blue Shields, Stanley Works, Alticor Inc. Bd. dirs. Ideal Refractories SAI, Athens; bd. dirs. Ideal Standard Mexico, Am.

Standard Sanitaryware (Thailand) Ltd., INCESA, San Jose, Costa Rica, Hoxan Corp., Sapporo, Japan. Bd. dirs. Greek Mgmt. Assn., Athens, 1975—77, Fedn. of Greek Industries, Athens. Mem.: Young Pres. Orgn., Chief Execs. Orgn., Econ. Club of N.Y., Oxford Union, Oxford Law Soc., Am. Hellenic C. of C. (gen. sec. 1975—79), Spring Brook Country (Morristown, N.J.); Quogue Field, Quogue Beach (L.I., N.Y.)., Chemists Club, Laurel Valley Golf Club. Greek Orthodox. Avocations: golf, tennis, classical music.

KAMRAS, JASON, mathematics educator; BS, Princeton U., 1995; MA in Edn., Harvard U., 2000. With Israel Democracy Inst., Jerusalem; mem. Teach For Am., 1996; tchr. math. & social studies John Philip Sousa Middle Sch., Washington, DC, 1996—99, 2000—, co-founder, dir. EXPOSE Program, 1999—; nat. and internat. spokesperson for edn., 2005—06. Named Exemplary After School for All Instr., DC Pub. Schs., 2003, Exemplary Resident Mentor Tchr., 2003, Ward 7 Tchr. of Yr., 2003, Agnes Meyer Outstanding Tchr., Washington Post, 2003, Tchr. Yr., DC Pub. Schs., 2005, Nat. Tchr. of Yr., Coun. of Chief State Sch. Officers, 2005; recipient Mayor's Art Award, 2001. Mailing: Coun Chief State Sch Officers Ste 700 One Massachusetts Ave, NW Washington DC 20001-1431 Office: John Philip Sousa Middle Sch 3650 Ely Pl, SE Washington DC 20019*

KAMRIN, MICHAEL ARNOLD, toxicology educator; b. Bklyn., Aug. 5, 1940; s. Benjamin Barnett and Bessie (Bloom) K.; m. Ritva Anneli Nieminen, July 19, 1964 (dec. Oct. 2002); children: Kari and Edward (twins); m. Katherine O'Sullivan See, Nov 6, 2004. BA in Chemistry, Cornell U., 1960; MS in Biophys. Chemistry, Yale, 1962, PhD in Biophys. Chemistry, 1965. Teaching asst. then rsch. asst. dept. chemistry Yale U., New Haven, 1960-63; rsch. assoc. biology div. Oak Ridge (Tenn.) Nat. Lab., 1963-66; NIH postdoctoral trainee Hopkins Marine Sta. Stanford (Calif.) U., 1966-67; asst. prof. natural sci. Mich. State U., East Lansing, 1967-72, assoc. prof., 1972-79, prof., 1979-89, prof. Inst. for Environ. Toxicology, 1982-2000, prof. resource devel., 1990-2000, prof. emeritus, 2000—. Vis. lectr. dept. zoology U. Turku, Finland, 1973-74, docent, 1996—; vis. scientist Legis. Office Sci. Advisor, State of Mich., 1980-81; participant numerous confs. and workshops, 1965—; mem. internat. evaluation team on environ. toxicology Acad. Finland, Helsinki, 1988; expert Media Resource Ctr., Scientists' Inst. for Pub. Info.; mem. risk comm. project planning group, grant reviewer USDA; peer reviewer for agy.-sponsored rsch. projects Agy. for Toxic Substances and Disease Registry, HHS; numerous others. Author: Toxicology: A Primer on Toxicology Principles and Applications, 1988, (with D.J. Katz and M.L. Walter) Reporting on Risk: A Journalist's Handbook, 1995; also other; editor: (with F.M. D'Itri) PCBs: Human and Environmental Hazards, 1983, (with P. Rodgers) Dioxins inthe Environment, 1985; editor: Pesticide Profiles, 1997, Environmental Risk Harmonization, 1997; contbr. numerous articles and abstracts to sci. jours. Numerous presentations to Rotary, Consumers Coun., LWV, county commrs., Ch. Women United, sch. dists., Mich. Med. Soc.; participant in news broadcasts, radio call-in shows and interview programs. Recipient Meml. medal U. Turku, 1974; grantee USDA, 1983-84, 86-87, 88-89, 91-98, All-Univ. Rsch. Initation grantee, 1989, All-Univ. Outreach grantee, 1995-96, EPA, 1992-95, Agy. for Toxic Substances and Disease Registry, 1992-2000, Nat. Food Safety and Toxicology Ctr., 1993-94, grantee Nat. Inst. Environ. Health Scis., 1995-2000. Fellow AAAS; mem. Am. Chem. Soc., Soc. Toxicology (editor newsletter Mich. chpt. 1984-87, chmn. nominating com. 1986, pres.-elect 1992-93, pres. 1993-94; nat. pub. comm. com. 1987-90, Nat. Pub. Comm. award 1994), Soc. Environ. Toxicology and Chemistry (bd. dirs. Ctrl. Gt. Lakes chpt. 1985-87, v.p. 1988, pres. 1989-90, Disting. Svc. award 1993; nat. govt. affairs com. 1986-2000), Soc. for Risk Analysis. Office Phone: 517-655-1896. Business E-Mail: kamrin@msu.edu.

KAMSICKAS, JAMES, automotive executive; b. Saginaw, Mich., 1967; B in Prodn. and Ops. Mgmt., Mich. State U., 1989. V.p. Lear Corp., Southfield, Mich., 1999—2004, v.p., North Am. Ops., interior systems divsn., 2004—. Named one of 40 Under 40, Crain's Detroit Bus., 2006. Office: Lear Corporation Corporate Headquarters PO Box 5008 21557 Telegraph Rd Southfield MI 48086 Office Phone: 248-447-1500. Office Fax: 248-447-1722.

KAMYSZEW, CHRISTOPHER D., film executive, educator, curator; b. Warsaw, May 7, 1958; came to U.S., 1982; s. Mieczyslaw and Zofia K.; children: Oliver G., Samuel, Jacob. BA, U. Warsaw, 1982, MA in Polish Lit. and Lang., 1984. Freelance writer and translator, Poland, 1977-81; freelance theatre dir. Dearborn Theatre Co., Chgo., 1982-83, Ossetynski Actors Lab., LA, 1982-83; head lit. sect. Krag-Underground Publishers, Warsaw, 1980-83; head archives dept. Polish Mus. Am., Chgo., 1985-88, dir., curator, 1988-93; pres. Soc. for the Arts, Chgo., 1993—. Bd. dirs. Gallery 58, Chgo.; pres. Inst. Symbological Rsch., Chgo., 1986-95, Internat. Ind. Theatre Found., Washington, 1985-86; exec. dir. Polish TV-USA, 1994-97. Co-author, editor: Collective Works of L.-F Celine, 1983, Literary Essays by L. Tyrmand, 1983; curated more than 200 exhbns. in U.S. Dir., chmn., CEO Polish Film Festival, 1988—, Europe Film Festival, 1996—; founder, pres. Chgo. Internat. Documentary Festival, 2003-. Recipient Zycie Warszawy award, 1977, Audience award Edinburgh Theatre Festival, 1980, award for disting. translation Assn. Polish Translators, 1990, award Found. of Friends of Polish Mus., 1991, award Ministry Fgn. Affairs of Poland, 1993, Laterna Magica award disting. achievements in film, 1994, Copernican award, 2002, Warsaw Gold medal Acad. Fine Arts, 2004; Wiehmann Found. scholar, 1982, Golden Cross of Merit, 2001. Avocations: reading, classical music, map collecting, cross country skiing. Office: Society for Arts 1112 N Milwaukee Ave Chicago IL 60622-4017 Office Phone: 773-486-9612. Personal E-mail: christopherkamyszew@msn.com.

KAN, DIANA ARTEMIS MANN SHU, painter, art educator, writer; b. Hong Kong, Mar. 3, 1926; came to U.S., 1949, naturalized, 1964; d. Kam Shek and Sing-Ying (Hong) K.; m. Paul Schwartz, May 24, 1952; 1 son, Kan Martin Meyer Sing-Si. Student, Art Students League, 1949—51, Beaux Arts, Paris, 1951—52, Grande Chaumiere, 1951—52, Ecole Beau Arts, 1952—54. Instr. watercolor Phila. Mus. Art, 1972, Sumi-e Soc., 1974—2003, Art Students League of NY, 1985, The Nat. Acad. Design, 2001, The Smithsonian Inst., Wash., DC. Fgn. corr., city editor Cosmorama Pictorial Mag., Hong Kong, 1968; art reviewer Villager, N.Y.C., 1960-69; lectr. Birmingham So. U., N.Y. U., Mills Coll., St. Joseph's Coll., Phila. Mus., Smithsonian Instn; keynote spkr. Wellsley's Coll. Asia Week, MA, 1993. Author: White Cloud, 1938, The How and Why of Chinese Painting, 1974, Am. Artist Magazine, 1974, 86; One-man shows, London, 1949, 63, 64, Paris, 1949, Hong Kong, 1937, 39, 41, 47, 48, 52, Shanghai, 1935, 37, 39, Nanking, 1936, 38, Macao, 1947, 48, Bankok, 1947, Casablanca, 1951, 52, San Francisco, 1950, 67, N.Y.C., 1950, 54, 59, 67, 71, 72, 74, 78, Naples, 1971, Elliot Mus., Stuart, Fla., 1967, 73, Bruce Mus., Greenwich, Conn., 1969, Nat. Hist. Mus., Taipei, Taiwan, 1971, N.Y. Cultural Center Mus., 1972, Galerie Barbarella, Palm Beach, Fla., 1972, Hobe Sound (Fla.) Galleries, 1976, 81, Nat. Arts Club, 1979, Dyansen Galleries, 1987-Shenchen Mus., China, 1996, Hong Kong Art Ctr., 1996, 90 others; exhibited in group shows Allied Artists of Am., 1957-90, Royal Acad. Fine Arts, London, 1963-64, Royal Soc. Painters, London, 1964, Nat. Arts Club, N.Y.C., 1964-90, Am. Water Color Soc., N.Y.C., 1966-90, Nat. Acad. Design, N.Y.C., 1967-2003, Charles and Emma Frye Mus., Seattle, 1968, Willamette U., Salem, Oreg., 1968, Columbia (S.C.) Mus. Art, 1969, Audubon Artist, 1974-90, Evansville (Ind.) Mus., 1991, Dyansen Gallery, Boston, 1991; represented permanent collections, Met. Mus. Art, Phila. Mus. Art, Nelson Gallery, Elliot Mus., Fla., Bruce Mus., Dalhousie U., Atkin Mus., Kansas City, Nat. Hist. Mus., Taipei, The Government House, Vancouver, BC, Can., Midtown Payson Galleries, China 2000 Fine Art Gallery; subject of film Eastern Spirit, Western World—A Profile of Diana Kan; paintings were published by UNICEF (christmas cards): Four Children Going Fishing, 1996, Lantern Festival, 1999, Flower Drum Song, 2002, Snow Mountain, 2002. Recipient Summer Festival award N.Y.C., 1959, 1st Prize Nat. Art Club, 1982; named most Outstanding Profl. Woman of the Yr., Washington Sq. chpt. N.Y. League Bus. and Profl. Women's Club, 1971, 79, Gold medal of honor Knickerbocker Artists, 1990, Gold medal of honor Audubon Artists, 1991, 2000, Salmagundi Club, Pres. Gold medal of honor, 1998, Audobon Artists Gold Medal of Honor; Diana Kan Appreciation Day proclaimed by Mayor of Boston, 1991, Diana Kan Day proclaimed by Mayor of NY, 2000; offl. citation proclaimed by Pres. Senate of Mass., 1991. Fellow Royal Soc. Arts; mem. Pen and Brush Club (dir. 1968, Brush Fund award 1968, Alice S. Buell Meml. award 1969, Margaret Sussman award 1991), Nat. Acad. Design (assoc., John Pike Meml. award 1987, cert. of merit 1991), Am. Watercolor Soc. (traveling award 1968, Marthe T. McKinnon award 1978, dir. 1975-77), Art Students League, Nat. League Pen Women, Audubon Artists (v.p. 1983), Allied Artists Am. (Barbara Vassilieff Meml. award 1969, Ralph Fabri Meml. award 1975, corr. sec. 1975-78), Catharine Lorillard Wolf Art Club (Anna Hyatt Huntington bronze medal 1970, 74, Gold medal of honor 1982), NYC Cultural Affairs Adv. Commn., 1999. Clubs: Overseas Press Am., Lotos, The Nat. Arts (NYC), The Salamagundi. Mailing: The Nat Arts Club 15 Gramercy Park S New York NY 10003-1705 E-mail: dianakan@dianakan.com. *Failure is the mother of success.*

KAN, KEVIN S., automotive executive; b. Hong Kong; BS, Georgetown U. Exec. Am. Internat. Group (AIG), 1994—99; joined Am. Auto Wash Inc., 1999, CFO, pres., CEO, 2003—. Named one of 40 Under 40, Phila. Bus. Jour., 2006. Avocation: jazz. Office: Am Auto Wash Inc 440 W Street Rd Warminster PA 18974 Office Phone: 215-957-3390.

KAN, YUE-SAI, journalist, writer, television personality, entrepreneur, humanitarian; b. Guilin, China; d. Wing-Lin Kan. Studied for a degree in music, Hawaii. Began career as asst. to casting agent in an advertising agy.; creator, founder, chmn. Yue-Sai Kan Cosmetics Ltd. (formed joint venture with Coty Divsn. in 1996-Yue-Sai Kan-Coty Cosmetics Shanghai Ltd., cosmetics and brand name sold to L'Oreal in May, 2004), Shanghai, 1992—2004; hon. vice-chmn. L'Oreal China, 2004—; founded Yue-Sai Kan Production Co., 1978—, Shanghai, 2005—. Host (TV show) Looking East (First weekly TV show in the US that introduced Eastern Cultures and Customs to the American Audience, last two years broadcasted on the Discovery Channel), 1978—90, First Five Broadcasts from China of the 35th Anniversary of the People's Republic of China (PBS), 1984, host, prodr. (TV series) One World (First TV series ever produced and hosted by an American on China's nat. network, CCTV; First TV series that introduced the outside world to China), China, 1985, exec. prodr. (TV Series (syndicated nationally) and printed column in China's Harper's Bazaar) Yue-Sai's World, 2004—, exec. prodr., host (TV series) Yue-Sai Kan's People in a Changing China, 2005—, host (TV program) Half of Sky, Journey Through a Changing China (syndicated nationwide), 1989, Doing Business in Asia (PBS and worldwide; used by multi-national companies and bus. schools; featuring Japan, South Korea, Hong Kong, and Taiwan), 1991, Doing Business in China, 1999; prodr.: (documentary) China-Walls and Bridges (ABC), 1998 (Emmy award); author: One World, Yue-Sai's Guide to Beauty, Etiquette for the Modern Chinese, 2000, Celebrating Asian Beauty, 2002, How to be a Beautiful, Healthy and Successful Modern Women, 2004. Supports ednl. and humanitarian efforts; established scholarship fund to major Chinese Universities and Hunter Coll. (NYC); involved with Orbis, AIDS, and Mus. of the Chinese Americans. Named Queen of the Middle Kingdom, Time Mag., Modern Day Marco Polo, Money Mag., True Citizen Ambassador, US Congressional Record, the first and only Global Chinese-Say Yes Amb., UNICEF; named one of Most Famous Women in China, People Mag., Most Influential Women in China in the Last 20 Years, Xinhua News Agy.; recipient Exceptional Achievement award, UN, World's Leading Women Entrepreneur award, Star Group, 1999. Mem.: Com. of 100. Achievements include Created the first doll of Asian descent, the Yue-Sai Wa Wa doll in 1999; lead to a weekly cartoon series in the newspaper, Yue-Sai's Adventures, this was the first female cartoon heroine for China.

KAN, YUET WAI, hematologist, educator; b. Hong Kong, China, June 11, 1936; arrived in U.S., 1960; s. Tong-Po and Lai-Wan (Li) Kan; m. Alvera Lorraine Limauro, May 10, 1964; children: Susan Jennifer, Deborah Ann. BS, MB, U. Hong Kong, China, 1958, DSc, 1980, DSc (hon.), 1987, Chinese U., Hong Kong, 1981; MD (hon.), U. Cagliari, Sardinia, Italy, 1981; degree (hon.), Open U. Hong Kong. Investigator Howard Hughes Med. Inst., San Francisco, 1976—2003; prof. lab. medicine U. Calif., San Francisco, 1977—, Louis K. Diamond prof. hematology, 1991—. Mem. NIDDK adv. coun. NIH, 1991—95; trustee Croucher Found., Hong Kong, 1992—, chmn., 1997—; mem. bd. adjudicators The Shaw Prize, Hong Kong, 2005—, chmn. selection com., life sci. and medicine, 2005—. Contbr. chapters to books, over 250 articles to med. jours. Recipient Dameshek award, Am. Soc. Hematology, 1980, George Thorn award, Howard Hughes Med. Inst., 1980, Gairdner Found. Internat. award, 1984, Allan award, Am. Soc. Human Genetics, 1984, Lita Annenberg Hazen award for Excellence in Clin. Rsch., 1984, Waterford award, 1987, ACP's award, 1988, Genetic Rsch. award, Sanremo Internat., 1989, Warren Alpert Found. prize, 1989, Albert Lasker Clin. Med. Rsch. award, 1991, Christopher Columbus Discovery award, 1992, City of Medicine award, 1992, Excellence 200 award, 1993, Helmut Horten Rsch. award, 1995, Shaw prize, Shaw Found., Hong Kong, 2004. Fellow: AAAS, Am. Acad. Arts and Scis., Third World Acad. Scis., Royal Soc. (London) (London), Royal Coll. Physicians (London); mem.: NAS (coun. mem.), Soc. Chinese Bioscientists in Am. (pres. 1998—99), Am. Soc. Hematology (pres. 1990), Assn. Am. Physicians, Chinese Acad. Scis. (fgn. mem.), Acad. Sinica (Taiwan). Office: U Calif 513 Parnassus Ave HSW 901 San Francisco CA 94143-0793 Office Phone: 415-476-5841. Business E-Mail: yw.kan@ucsf.edu.

KANAGY, STEVEN ALBERT, foundation administrator; b. Chgo., Sept. 26, 1956; s. John West and Hazel Elizibeth (Montgomery) K. Student, Kendall Coll., Evanston, Ill., 1974—76, W. Carey Coll., Hattiesburg, Miss., 1980, U. So. Miss. Staff worker Longbeach Pub. Libr., Miss., 1978; mgr. Kanagy Art Found., Inc., Longbeach, Miss., 1982—, lead dir., 1997—; distbr. IBO Quixtar, 1984—; cmty. devel. explorer Harbour Dist., Gulfport, Miss., 1985-89, mng. ptnr., 1989—, Kanagg Industries. Mng. ptnr. Archival Restorations, 1992-2001; candidate U.S. State Dept foreign svc. officer, 2004, 05; exec. Archival Restorations, 2001 Contbr. article to mag. Kendall Coll. scholar. Mem. Am. Mgmt. Assn., Nat. Trust for Hist. Preservation, Internat. Platform Assn., N.Am. Hunting Club (life). Republican. Roman Catholic. Avocations: building restoration, archery, photography. Personal E-mail: friendly20@cableone.net.

KANAKAREDES, MELINA, actress; b. Akron, Ohio, Apr. 23, 1967; m. Peter Constantinades, Sept. 6, 1992; children: Zoe, Karina Eleni. Attended, Ohio State U.; BFA, Point Park Coll. Spokesperson Maybelline NY. Actor: (Broadway plays) Caberet; (films) Carts, 1987, Bleeding Hearts, 1994, The Long Kiss Goodnight, 1996, Dangerous Beauty, 1998, Rounders, 1998, 15 Minutes, 2001, Into the Fire, 2005; (TV films) Saint Maybe, 1998; (TV series) The More You Know, 1989—, The Guiding Light, 1991—95, New York News, 1995, Leaving LA, 1997, Providence, 1999—2002, CSI: NY, 2004—, (TV appearances) NYPD Blue, 1995, Due South, 1995, The Practice, 1997, Oz, 1998, CSI: Miami, 2004. Office: c/o Gersh Agency NY 41 Madison Ave 33rd Fl New York NY 10010

KANAMORI, HIROO, geophysicist, professor emeritus; b. Tokyo, Oct. 17, 1936; BS in Physics, Tokyo U., 1959, MS in Geophysics, 1961, PhD in Geophysics, 1964. Rsch. assoc., Geophysics Inst. U. Tokyo, 1962—66, assoc. prof., Earthquake Rsch. Inst., 1966—70, prof., Earthquake Rsch. Inst., 1970-72; rsch. fellow Calif. Inst. Tech., Pasadena, 1965—66, prof., 1972-89, John E. and Hazel S. prof. geophysics, 1989—2005, John E. and Hazel S. prof. geophysics emeritus, 2005—, dir. Seismological Lab. Vis. prof. MIT, 1969—70; chmn., com. on seismology NRC, NAS, 1986—89; invited eminent scientist of Japan Soc. for Promotion of Sci. Award for Eminent Scientists Disaster Prevention Rsch. Inst., Kyoto U., 2005—06; vis. prof. Nagoya U., 2006—. Contbr. articles to profl. publications, scientific papers. Recipient Arthur L. Day prize and lectureship NAS, 1993; California Scientist of the Year, Calif. Museum of Science and Industry, 1993, Asahi prize, Asahi Shimbun, 1994, Japan Acad. prize, 2004, Person of Cultural Merit award, Japan, 2006, Kyoto prize, Basic Scis. Category, Earth and Planetary Scis., Astronomy and Astrophysics, Inamori Found., 2007. Fellow Am. Geophys. Union (Walter H. Bucher medal 1996); mem. Seismol. Soc. Am. (pres. 1985-86, Harry Fielding Reid medal, 1992), Seimol. Soc. Japan., Earthquake Engring. Rsch. Inst., Am. Acad. Arts & Scis. one of the world's best earthquake scientists. Office: Calif Inst Tech Seismological Lab So Mudd Bldg Rm 361 1200 E California Blvd MS 252-21 Pasadena CA 91125 Office Phone: 626-395-6914. Office Fax: 626-564-0715. Business E-Mail: hiroo@gps.caltech.edu.*

KANARKOWSKI, EDWARD JOSEPH, data processing company executive; b. Jersey City, May 5, 1947; s. Joseph Anthony and Lillian Dorothy (Pietrowicz) K.; m. Carol Ann Miller, Sept. 14, 1969; children: Edward, Kelly, Paul, Karen, Kevin, Casey Michael. BA, St. Peter Coll., 1969; grad., US Army Command and Gen. Staff Coll., 1985. Cons. corp. comm., NJ, 1973—75; staff writer Daily and Sunday Register, Shrewsbury, NJ, 1975—77; corp. staff writer ADP, Roseland, NJ, 1977, dir. corp. comm., 1983—88, v.p. corp. comm., 1988—93; cons. comm., 1993—. Adj. vis. prof. comm. St. Peter's Coll., 1985—. Author: The ADP Story, 1999. Capt. US Army, 1971—73, maj. N.J. Nat. Guard. Decorated Army Commendation medal (3); named Hon. Ky. Col. Commonwealth Ky., 1988. Mem. Internat. Assn. Bus. Communicators, 3d US Inf. Divsn. Assn., NJ Mil. Acad. (assoc.), VFW (life), Nat. Railroad Mus., US Golf Assn., U.S.O. Orgn. (contbr.), 114th Inf. Regiment Assn. Roman Catholic. Home: 132 Yellowbank Rd Toms River NJ 08753-3167 Personal E-mail: k6base@aol.com.

KANAS, JOHN ADAM, bank executive; b. Southampton, NY, Nov. 16, 1946; s. George and Barbara K.; m. Elaine; children: Melissa, Allison, Adam, John. BA in History, Southampton Coll., 1968; postgraduate student, C.W. Post Coll. LI U., 1970, Rutgers U., NJ, 1976. Mgmt. trainee North Fork Bank & Trust Co., Mattituck, NY, 1971, various sr. mgmt. positions, 1971—77, chmn., pres., CEO, 1977—2006, North Fork Bancorporation, Inc., Melville, NY, 1987—2006; pres. banking Capital One Fin. Corp., McLean, Va., 2006—. Recipient Tree of Life award, Jewish Nat. Fund, 2003. Mem. NY State Ind. Bankers Assn. (chmn., pres. 1980-81), LI Bankers Assn. (pres., dir. 1980), NY State Bankers Assn. (pres.). Office: Capital One Fin Corp 1680 Capital One Dr Mc Lean VA 22102-3491*

KANDARIAN, STEVEN A., insurance company executive; BA in Econs., Clark U., 1974; JD, Georgetown U. Law Ctr., 1978; MBA, Harvard Bus. Sch., 1980. Investment banker Rotan Mosle, Inc., Houston; with LCB Holdings, Inc., State St. Bank; mng. dir. Lee Capital Holdings, Boston, 1984—90; pres., founder Eagle Capital Holdings, 1990—93; founder, mng. ptnr. Orion Ptnrs., LP; exec. dir. Pension Benefit Guaranty Corp., 2001—04; exec. v.p., chief investment officer MetLife, Inc., 2005—. Bd. trustees MassMutual Corp. Investors, MassMutual Participation Investors, MassMutual Premier Funds. Office: MetLife Inc 200 Park Ave New York NY 10166

KANDEL, ALAN HAROLD, lawyer; b. St. Louis, Mar. 8, 1955; AB universali cum honore, Washington U., St. Louis, 1983; JD cum laude, St. Louis U., 1986. Bar: Mo. 1986. Assoc. Popkin & Stern, St. Louis, 1986-91, Lewis, Rice & Fingersh, St. Louis, 1991-95; of counsel Farnam Law Firm, St. Louis, 1995-96; sr. atty. Peper, Martin, Jensen, Maichel & Hetlage, St. Louis, 1996-97; ptnr. Blackwell Sanders Peper Martin LLP, St. Louis, 1998—; instr. Fontbonne U., 2000—. Sr. v.p. H.F. Epstein Hebrew Acad., St. Louis, 1999-2001, pres. 2001-2003; pres. Tpheris Israel Chevra Kadisha Congregation, Chesterfield, Mo., 1997-98, Vaad Hoeir of St. Louis, 1998-2000. Mem. Mo. Bar (chmn. employee benefits com. 1991-93), Bar Assn. Met. St. Louis (chmn. employee benefits law com. 1995-96). Office: Blackwell Sanders Peper Martin LLP 720 Olive St Fl 24 Saint Louis MO 63101-2338 E-mail: akandel@blackwellsanders.com.

KANDEL, DENISE BYSTRYN, sociologist; b. Paris, Feb. 27, 1933; came to U.S. 1949; d. Iser and Sara (Wolsky) Bystryn; m. Eric R. Kandel, June 10, 1956; children: Paul, Minouche. BA in French, Acad. Paris, 1950; BA, Bryn Mawr Coll., 1952; MA, Columbia U., 1953, PhD, 1960. Social scientist NIMH, Bethesda, Md., 1959-60; postdoctoral rsch. fellow Harvard Med. Sch., Boston, 1960-62; rsch. assoc. Harvard Sch. Edn., Cambridge, Mass., 1964-69; rsch. scientist VII N.Y. State Psychiatric Inst., NYC, 1969—; from asst. prof. to prof. dept. psychiatry, dept. sociomed. scis. Columbia U. Sch. of Pub. Health, NYC, 1973—. Cons. Nat. Inst. on Drug Abuse, Rockville, 1973—; editl. bd. Jour. Rsch. on Adolescence, 1990—, extramural sci. adv. bd, 1990—93; etiology sci. adv. panel Am. Legacy Found., Ont., Canada, 2000—04. Author (with G. Lesser): (Book) Youth in Two Worlds., 1972; contbg. author: Parental Influences on Adolescent Marijuana Use and the Baby Boom Generation: Findings from the 1979-1996 National Household Surveys on Drug Abuse, 2001; editor: Longitudinal Research on Drug Use, 1978, Stages and Pathways of Drug Involvement: Examining the Gateway Hypothesis, 2002; assoc. editor: Jour. Health and Social Behavior, 1975—78, consulting editor: Am. Jour. Sociology, 1981—83; contbr. articles to profl. jours. Active Nat. Adv. Coun. on Drug Abuse, 1986—90; etiology sci. adv. panel Am. Legacy Found., 2000—04; H. David Archibald lectr. Addiction Rsch. Found., Ctr. for Addiction and Mental Health, Ont., Canada, 2002. Recipient Pacesetter award, Nat. Inst. on Drug Abuse, 1979, Rsch. Scientist award, 1981—, Ann. Norman E. Zinberg Meml. Lectr. award, Cambridge Hosp./ Harvard Med. Sch., 1993, R. Brinkley Smithers Disting. Scientist award, Am. Soc. Addiction Medicine, 2002, Prevention Sci. award, Soc. for Prevention Rsch., 2003; grantee, Addiction Rsch. Found. Ctr. for Addiction and Mental Health, 2002. Mem.: Soc. for Life History Rsch., Internat. Sociol. Assn., Am. Sociol. Assn., Sociol. Rsch. Assn., Soc. for Rsch. on Adolescence (chmn. pubs. 1990—92). Democrat. Jewish. Avocation: collecting art nouveau furniture and glass. Office: Columbia Univ Dept of Psychiatry 1051 Riverside Dr Unit 20 New York NY 10032 Home Phone: 718-884-5447; Office Phone: 212-304-7080. Business E-Mail: dbk2@columbia.edu.

KANDEL, ERIC RICHARD, neuroscience educator; b. Vienna, Nov. 7, 1929; arrived in U.S., 1939; s. Herman and Charlotte (Zimels) Kandel; 2 children. BA, Harvard Coll., 1952; MD, NYU, 1956. Intern Montefiore Hosp., NYC, 1956—57; rsch. assoc. neurophysiology lab. NIH, Washington, 1957—60; psychiatrist Mass Mental Health Ctr. Harvard Med. Sch., 1960—62, 1963—64; dir. Mass. Mental Health Ctr., Boston, 1960—65; assoc. prof. physiology and psychiatry NYU Sch. Medicine, 1965—74; prof. physiology, biochemistry and psychiatry, dir. Ctr. Neurology and Behavior Columbia U. Coll. Physicians and Surgeons, NYC, 1974—83, univ. prof., physiology and cell biophysics, psychiatry, biochemistry and molecular biophysics, 1983—; sr. investigator Howard Hughes Med. Inst., 1984—. Author: Cellular Basis of Behavior: An Introduction to Behavioral Neurobiology, 1976, Cellular Biology of Neurons, 1977, A Cell Biological Approach to Learning, 1978, Behavioral Biology of Aplysia: A Contribution to the Comparative Study of Opisthobranch Molluscs, 1979, Essentials of Neural Science Value Pack, 1995, Psychiatry, Psychoanalysis, and the New Biology of Mind, 2005, In Search of Memory: The Emergence of a New Science of Mind, 2006; co-author (with James H. Schwartz & Thomas M. Jessell): Essentials of Neural Science and Behavior, 1995; editor: Molecular Neurobiology in Neurology and Pschiatry, 1987; co-editor: Molecular Aspects of Neurobiology, 1986, Principles of Neural Science, 2000. Co-recipient Albert Lasker Basic Med. Rsch. award, 1983, Lewis S. Rosentiel award for Disting. Work, 1984, Charles A. Dana award for Pioneering Achievement in Health, 1997; recipient Henry L. Moses award, Montefiore Hosp., 1959, Lester N. Hofheimer prize for Rsch., 1977, Lucy G. Moses prise for Rsch. in Basic Neurology, 1977, Solomon A. Berson Med. Alumni Achievement award, 1979, Karl Spencer Lashley prize in Neurobiology, 1981, Dickson prize in Biology and Medicine, 1982, Howard Crosby Warren medal, 1984, Am. Assn. Med. Colleges award, 1985, Gairdner Internat. award for Outstanding Achievement in med. Sci., Gairdner Found., 1987, Nat. Medal Sci., 1988, Gold medal for Scientific Merit, 1988, Disting. Svc. award, Am. Psychiatric Assn., 1989, Award in Basic Sci., Am. Coll. Physicians, 1989, Robert J. and Clarie Pasarow Found. award in Neurosciece, 1989, Diploma Internat. Cajal, 1990, Bristol-Myers Squibb award for Disting. Achievement in Neuroscience Rsch., 1991, Warren Triennial prize, 1992, Jean-Louis Signoret's prize in Memory, 1992, Harvey prize, Technion, 1993, FO Schmitt Medal and Prize in Neuroscience, 1993, Gerard prize for Outstanding Achievement in Neuroscience, 1997, Wolf prize in Biology and Medicine, Israel, 1999, Nobel prize in physiology or medicine, 2000, Heineken prize, 2000. Fellow: AAAS; mem.: NAS, Acad. Scis. France, Order of Merit for Arts and Scis. Germany, Am. Philos. Soc., N.Y. Acad. of Scis. (Mayor award excellence in sci. and tech. 1994), Internat. Brain Rsch. Orgn., Soc. Neuroscis. (pres. 1980—81). Office: Howard Hughes Med Inst 4000 Jones Bridge Rd Chevy Chase MD 20815-6789 also: Physiology & Biophysics Nyspi-Unit 25 Columbia U 1051 Riverside Dr New York NY 10032 Office Phone: 212-543-5202. Office Fax: 212-543-5474. Business E-Mail: erk5@columbia.edu.

KANDEL, MYRON, newscaster, columnist; m. Thelma Esan. Bachelor's Degree, Bklyn. Coll., 1952; Master's Degree, Columbia U., 1953; LLD (hon.), Washington and Jefferson Coll., 2005, Bethany Coll., W.Va., 2006; DHL (hon.), Franklin Pierce Coll., Rindge, NH, 2006. From copy boy to fin. reporter The N.Y. Times, 1951-63; bus. editor Washington Star; fgn. corr. N.Y. Herald Tribune, Bonn, Germany; fin. editor Herald Tribune; editor, pres. The N.Y. Law Jour.; founder, fin. editor, anchor CNN, 1980—2005. Journalism educator Columbia U., CCNY. Author: How to Cash in on the Coming Stock Market Boom, 1982; co-author (syndicated fin. column) The Greer/Kandel Report, 1976-82; fin. editor N.Y. Post, 1977-79; founding editor, pub. (newsletters) The Wall Street Letter, Rev. of the Fin. Press, The Corp. Shareholder; contbr. articles to profl. jours. Pres. Initiative for Corporate Responsibility and Investor Protection, Concord, NH, 2005—. Recipient Columbia Journalism Alumni award, 1985, Presdl. medal Bklyn. Coll., 2002, Lifetime Achievement award, Loeb Found., 2006. Mem. Soc. Am. Bus. Editors and Writers (past pres., Disting. Achievement award 1994), Soc. Profl. Journalists (past pres. NY chpt.), NY Fin. Writers' Assn. (past pres., Elliot V. Bell award 1988, Fin. Journalism Hall of Fame 2005), Alumni Assn. Columbia Grad. Sch. Journalism (past pres.). Office: 1 Time Warner Ctr New York NY 10019 E-mail: myron.kandel@turner.com.

KANDEL, NELSON ROBERT, lawyer; b. Balt., Sept. 15, 1929; m. Brigitte Kleemaier, Feb. 28, 1957; children: Katrin, Christopher, Peter. BA, U. Md., 1951, LLB, 1954. Bar: Md. 1954, U.S. Supreme Ct. 1964, DC 1980. Pres. Kandel & Assocs. P.A., Balt., 1957—. With U.S. Army. Mem. Md. Bar Assn., Balt. Bar Assn. Democrat. Lutheran. Office: The World Trade Ctr Ste 1252 401 E Pratt St Baltimore MD 21202 Office Phone: 410-837-0646.

KANDEL, WILLIAM LLOYD, lawyer, arbitrator, mediator, educator, writer; b. NYC, Apr. 25, 1939; s. Morton H. and Lottie S. (Smith) K.; m. Joyce Roland, Jan. 27, 1974; 1 child, Aron Daniel (Ari). AB cum laude, Dartmouth Coll., 1961; JD, Yale U., 1964; LLM in Labor Law, NYU, 1967. Bar: N.Y. 1965, U.S. Dist. Ct. (ea. dist.) N.Y. 1978, U.S. Dist. Ct. (so. dist) N.Y. 1980, U.S. Dist. Ct. (no. dist.) N.Y. 1988, U.S. Ct. Appeals (2d cir.) 1982, U.S. Ct. Appeals (3d cir.) 1997, U.S. Ct. Appeals (5th cir.) 2000. Assoc. Lorenz, Finn & Giardino, NYC, 1964-66; labor atty. NAM, NYC, 1966-68; with Singer Co., NYC, 1968-79, asst. v.p. pers. dept., 1973-76, mng. counsel pers. office of gen. counsel, 1976-79; assoc. Skadden, Arps, Slate, Meagher & Flom, NYC, 1979-85; ptnr. Finley, Kumble, Wagner, Heine, Underberg, Manley, Myerson & Casey, NYC, 1985-87, Myerson & Kuhn, NYC, 1987-89, McDermott Will & Emery, 1989-97, Orrick, Herrington & Sutcliffe, 1997-2000; full-time mediator and arbitrator, 2000—; mediator U.S. Dist. Ct. (so. and ea. dists.), Supreme Ct. N.Y., 2001—; pvt. mediator and arbitrator, 2000—. Adj. prof. employment law Fordham U., 1983-86; lectr. Practising Law Inst.'s Ann. Inst. on Employment Law, 1980—, co-chair, 1995, chair, 1996-2002; vol. mediator U.S. EEO Commn., 2000—, NYU Lawyering Program, 2003—, U.S. Ct. Appeals (2d cir.), 2004—; spl. master Appellate Divsn. of Supreme Ct., N.Y., 2002—; panelist comml. and employment, Am. Arbitration Assn., 2002—; arbitrator, mediator Nat. Assn. Securities Dealers, 2002—. Contbg. editor: Employee Rels. Law Jour., 1975—2004; contbr. over 100 articles to profl. jours. V.p., bd. dirs. Assn. for Integration Mgmt., 1979-85; bd. dirs. NY chpt. Am. Jewish Com., 1980-82; human resources com. N.Y. YMCA, 1994-2004. Recipient award of Merit, Nat. Urban Coalition, 1979. Mem.: Assn. Conflict Resolution Greater N.Y., Am. Arbitration Assn. (comml. and employment panels 2001—), Bar Assn. of City of N.Y. (ADR com. 2003—05, arbitration com. 2005—), University Club. Democrat. Jewish. Home and Office: Mediator/Arbitrator 880 Fifth Ave New York NY 10021 Office Phone: 212-570-9064. Personal E-mail: wlkandel@hotmail.com.

KANDER, JOHN HAROLD, composer; b. Kansas City, Mo., Mar. 18, 1927; s. Harold S. and Bernice (Aaron) K. BA, Oberlin Coll., 1951, D (hon.), 1988; MA, Columbia U., 1953. Composer for theatrical prodns. (with James and William Goldman) A Family Affair, 1961, (with Fred Ebb) Flora, the Red Menace, 1964, Cabaret, 1966 (Tony award, N.Y. Drama Critic's Circle award), The Happy Time, 1967, Zorba, 1968, 70 Girls 70, 1971, Chicago, 1975, rev., 1996, 2004 (Touring Broadway award, best musical score, League of Am. Theatres & Producers, 2005), The Act, 1977, Woman of the Year, 1981 (Tony award), The Rink, 1984, Kiss of the Spider Woman, 1990 (Best Mus. Score Tony award 1993, N.Y. Drama Critics Circle award 1993), And the World Goes Round, 1991, Steel Pier, 1997, Over and Over, 1999, (films) Something for Everyone, 1969, Cabaret, 1972, Funny Lady, 1975, A Matter of Time, French Postcards, Lucky Lady, 1976, New York, New York, 1977, Kramer vs. Kramer, 1980, Still of the Night, 1982, Blue Skies Again, 1982, Places in the Heart, 1984; composer for Liza Minnelli TV spl. Liza with a Z, 1974 (Emmy award), for Shirley MacLaine in Gypsy in My Soul, for Goldie Hawn and Liza Minnelli in Goldie and Liza Together, Baryshnikov on Broadway, An Early Frost, 1985, for Liza Minnelli in London, Steppin' Out, 1993 (Emmy award), Breathing Lessons, 1994, The Boys Next Door, 1995. Recipient Kennedy Ctr. Honoree, Disting. Achievement in Musical Theatre award Drama League Awards, 2007. Mem. Dramatists Guild., Nat. Inst. Music Theatre, Songwriters Hall of Fame.*

KANDERS, WARREN BEATTY, manufacturing executive, investment banker; b. NYC, Nov. 1, 1957; s. Ralph Franklin and Jeanne (Adler) K. Grad., Choate Sch., 1975; student, Inst. for Architecture and Urban Studies, 1978; AB, Brown U., 1979. Sr. analyst Morgan Stanley and Co., Inc., NYC, 1979-81; assoc. Oppenheimer and Co., Inc., NYC, 1981-83; exec. dir., head of mergers and acquisitions Orion Royal Bank Ltd., NYC, 1983-87; mng. dir. Great Pacific Capital Inc., NYC, 1987-89; pres. Kanders & Co., Inc., NYC, 1990—, Pembridge Holdings Inc., 1992—93; vice-chmn. Benson Eyecare Corp., 1992—96; chmn. Armor Holdings Inc., Jacksonville, Fla., 1996—2007, CEO, 2003—07; exec. chmn. Clarus Corp., 2002—, Net Perceptions Inc., 2004—; chmn. Langer Inc., Deer Park, NY, 2004—. Mem. Americas Soc., Choate Rosemary Hall Young Alumni Leadership Coun. Clubs: Can., City Athletic. Office: Langer Inc 450 Commack Rd Deer Park NY 11729*

KANDRAVY, JOHN, lawyer; b. Passaic, NJ, May 9, 1935; s. Frank and Anna (Chan) K.; m. Alice E. Sullivan, Feb. 17, 1962; children: Elizabeth Ann (Mrs. Joseph P. Cassidy), Katherine Ann. BA, Wesleyan U., Middletown, Conn., 1957; JD, Columbia U., 1960. Bar: N.J. 1960, D.C. 1969, U.S. Supreme Ct. 1973, N.Y. 1982. From assoc. to ptnr. Shanley & Fisher, Newark, 1961-80, ptnr. Morristown, NJ, 1980-99, mng. ptnr., 1983-85, 89-99; ptnr. Drinker Biddle & Reath LLP, Florham Park, NJ, 1999—. Bd. dirs. Tingue, Brown & Co., VHS Ins. Co., Ltd.; mem. adv. bd. Ridgewood Savs. Bank of N.J. (divsn. Boiling Springs Savs. Bank), 2001—04. Mem. Gov.'s Mgmt. Commn., State of N.J., 1970; chmn. Planning Bd., Ridgewood, N.J., 1981-85, Zoning Bd. Adjustment, 1979-81; mem. bd. advisors Coll. Bus. Adminstrn., Fairleigh Dickinson U., 1983-87, chmn. bd. advisors, 1985-86; mem. Soc. of Valley Hosp., Ridgewood, 1971—, chmn. bd. trustees Ctrl. Bergen Cmty. Mental Health Ctr., N.J., 1970-73; trustee Palisades Counseling Ctr., Rutherford, 1968-81, The Forum Sch., Waldwick, N.J., 1987—, The Forum Sch. Found., Waldwick, 1978—; trustee The Valley Hosp., Ridgewood, 1992-2004, chmn. 2001-04, hon. trusteee, 2004—; trustee Valley Hosp. Found., Ridgewood, 2001-04, Valley Home Care, 2004-, chmn., 2005—; trustee Peer Found. for Plastic Surgery and Rehab., Florham Park, 1996—, Valley Health Sys., Inc., Paramus, 1997—, Children's Aid and Family Svcs., Inc., Paramus, N.J., 1998—; lawyers' adv. coun. Rutgers Law Sch., Newark, 1994-98, vis. com., 1994-98. Edward John Noble Found. grant, 1957-60. Mem. ABA, N.J. Bar Assn., Essex County Bar Assn., D.C. Bar Assn., Morris County Bar Assn., Essex Club (gov. 1976-85), Wesleyan U. Alumni Assn. (chmn. 1981-83), Ridgewood Country Club, Park Ave. Club (gov. 1992-97). Republican. Presbyterian. Home: 56 Monte Vista Ave Ridgewood NJ 07450-2428 Office: Drinker Biddle & Reath LLP 500 Campus Dr Fl 4 Florham Park NJ 07932-1047 Home Phone: 201-652-4907; Office Phone: 973-360-1100. Business E-Mail: john.kandravy@dbr.com.

KANDT, RAYMOND S., neurologist; b. Rochester, NY, July 8, 1950; m. Irene Kandt; children: Melanie, Lauren. AB cum laude, U. Va., 1972; MD, U. Va. Sch. Medicine, 1976. Diplomate Am. Bd. Med. Examiners, Am. Bd. Pediatrics, Am. Bd. Psychiatry & Neurology with spl. competence in child neurology and with added qualifications in clin. neurophysiology; cert. neurovascular & pediat. neurosonologist; cert. MRI/CT. Intern, resident in pediatrics Johns Hopkins Hosp., Balt., 1976-78, resident in pediatric neurology, fellow in devel. pediatrics, 1978-81; instr. depts. neurology, pediatrics U. Mich., Ann Arbor, 1981-82, asst. prof. depts. neurology & pediatrics, 1982-84; asst. prof. pediatrics div. pediatric neurology Duke U. Med. Ctr., Durham, NC, 1984-89, assoc. prof. pediatrics div. pediatric neurology, 1989-92, asst. prof. medicine div. neurology, 1990-92; assoc. prof. neurology, pediatrics Bowman Gray Sch. Medicine, Winston-Salem, NC, 1992-97; clin. assoc. prof. pediatrics Wake Forest U./Bapt. Med. Ctr., Winston-Salem, 1997—. Chief sect. child neurology Bowman Gray Sch. Medicine, 1992-97, grad. med. edn. com. 1993-97, clin. faculty adv. coun., 1993-97; faculty advisor pediatric house staff U. Mich., 1981-84, faculty advisor med. students, 1983-84, com. on edn., 1982-84; pediatric rep. continuing med. edn. com. Duke U. Med. Ctr., 1985-92; mem. gen. clin. rsch. ctrs. com. nat. ctr. for rsch. resources NIH, 1991-95; cons. in field. Reviewer: Am. Jour. Human Genetics, 1995, Jour. Neurol. Scis., 1993—97, Nature Genetics, 1993, Annals of Neurology, 1998—2002; contbg. editor: Annals of Behavioral Medicine, 1991—93. Adv. bd. My Father's House Group Homes, 1993; med. adv. com. Children's Ctr. for the Physically Handicapped, Winston-Salem, N.C., 1993—. Grantee NIH, 1986-91, 89-92, Nat. Tuberous Sclerosis Assn., 1992-93, grantee Glaxo, 1995-96; recipient Merck award, 1976. Mem.: Profs. Child Neurology, Tuberous Sclerosis Alliance (mem. profl. adv. bd. 1990—, scientific adv. bd. 1995—, chmn. clin. care adv. bd. 1995—97, scientific grant rev. com. 1995—, chmn. med. adv. com. N.C. chpt. 1988—), Child Neurology Soc., N.C. Med. Soc., Am. Neurol. Assn., Phi Sigma, Alpha Omega Alpha. Home: 3428 Jameson Ln Winston Salem NC 27106-4771 Office: Johnson Neurologic Clinic 606 N Elm St High Point NC 27262-4336 Office Phone: 336-889-8877.

KANE, AGNES BREZAK, pathologist, educator; b. Danbury, Conn., Nov. 3, 1946; d. John Edward and Mary Elizabeth (Hatfield) Brezak; m. David E. Kane, June 22, 1970. BA, Swarthmore Coll., 1968; MD, Temple U., 1974, PhD, 1976. Diplomate Am. Bd. Pathology. Resident Temple U. Hosp., Phila., 1975-76, 77-78; postdoctoral fellow Karolinska Inst., Stockholm, 1976-77; asst. prof. Temple U. Sch. Medicine, Phila., 1977-82, Brown U., Providence, 1982-87, assoc. prof. pathology, 1987-95, prof. pathology, 1995-96, chair dept. pathology and lab. medicine, 1996—. Mem. merit rev. bd. for basic scis. VA, Washington, 1984-86; cons. R.I. Commn. for Safety and Occupational Health, Providence, 1986—; commr. Commn. to Identify Occupational Diseases, Providence, 1987-88; mem. rev. com. Nat. Inst. Environ. Health Scis., Research Triangle Park, N.C., 1988—. Assoc. editor Am. Jour. of Pathology, 1992—; contbr. articles on exptl. pathology to sci. publs. Lucretia Mott fellow Swarthmore Coll., 1969-71; recipient Rsch. Career Devel. award NIH, 1981-86. Mem. Am. Assn. Pathologists (women's com. 1987—, program com. 1990—), Assn. Women Med. Faculty Brown U. (founder, coord.), Women in Medicine (faculty advisor Brown U. chpt.; Mary Putnam Jacobi award 1986), Phi Kappa, Sigma Xi. Avocation: gardening. Office: Brown Univ Box G Providence RI 02912

KANE, ALAN HENRY, lawyer; b. Seattle, Nov. 7, 1940; s. Henry and Alice (Harbak) K.; m. Martha Dressler, June 25, 1966 (dec.); children: Karen, Graham, Amy. BA in Law, U. Wash., 1963, JD, 1965. Bar: Wash. 1965. Ptnr. Sax & Maciver, Seattle, 1966-84, Kirkpatrick Lockhart Preston Gales & Ellis, LLP, Seattle, 1985—. Fellow Am. Coll. Trusts and Estates Counsel (Wash. State chair 1985-88). Avocations: boating, water-skiing, fishing, skiing. Office: 925 Fourth Ave Ste 2900 Seattle WA 98104-1158 Office Phone: 206-623-7580. Business E-Mail: alan.kane@klgates.com.

KANE, CYNTHIA A., special education educator; b. Pitts., Sept. 11; d. Robert E. and Cleopha I. Kane. BS in English Edn., Ind. U., Bloomington, 1971; MS in Edn., Ind. U., Indpls., 1979. Lang. arts tchr. Indpls. Pub. Schs., 1974—84, spl. edn. tchr., 1984—93, spl. edn. resource tchr., 1993—2001, tchr. spl. assignment compliance monitor, 2001—07. Mem.: Coun. Exceptional Children, Ind. Coun. Tchrs. English (life), Ind. U. Alumni Assn. (life), Sierra Club (life).

KANE, JACQUELINE, human resources specialist; Various positions in fin. svcs. industry; sr. v.p. human resources capital raising and global capital markets group Bank of Am.; dir. exec. leadership devel., dir. strategic change Hewlett-Packard, 2000—03; v.p. human resources Clorox. Co., Oakland, Calif., 2004—05, sr. v.p., 2005—. Bd. trustees Oakland Mus. Calif. Office: Clorox Co 1221 Broadway Oakland CA 94612-1888 Office Phone: 510-271-7000. Office Fax: 510-832-1463.

KANE, JAY BRASSLER, banker; b. Bklyn., June 4, 1931; s. Arthur Ferris and Margaret (Brassler) K.; m. Marian Albertson, Oct. 15, 1960 (dec. 1993); children: Lisa Kane Brown, James Brassler. Grad., Poly. Prep. Sch., 1949; AB, Columbia, 1953; MBA, NYU, 1961. With Met. Life Ins. Co., NYC, 1954-55, Bankers Trust Co., NYC, 1955—, asst. v.p., 1965-68, v.p., 1968-88, BT Brokerage Corp., 1988-90; regional dir. Frank Russell Trust. Co., NYC, 1990-97; assoc. P.P.I. Internat., 1997—. Co-pres. Cotton Club, 1999—2000, mgr. corp. pension funds, mktg. dir. trust svcs.; spkr. Am. Bankers Assn.; lectr New Sch. Social Rsch.; Attach bd. dirs.; bd. dirs., pres. Pickwick Soc. Contbr. articles to profl. jours. Mem. N.Y. Soc. Security Analysts, Fin. Analysts Fedn., Am. Pension Conf., Riverside (Conn.) Yacht Club, N.Y. Yacht Club. Home and Office: Hilton Heath Cos Cob CT 06807 Office Phone: 203-661-9478. E-mail: jbkane1@aol.com.

KANE, JENNIFER LYNN, pharmacist, medical/surgical nurse; b. Quincy, Mass., Feb. 24, 1975; d. Stephen P. and Dolores K. Johnson; m. Daniel Edward Kane, June 9, 2002; 1 child, Benjamin Daniel. BS in Biology, Va. Tech., Blacksburg, 1997; BSN, Simmons Coll., Boston, 2001. Emergency svcs. asst. Brigham and Women's Hosp., Boston, 1999—2001; med. ICU staff RN Mass. Gen. Hosp., Boston, 2001—04; acute dialysis RN, CRRT educator Davita - Lahey Clinic, Burlington, Mass., 2004—07; pharmacovigilance specialist Cubist Pharmaceuticals, Lexington, Mass., 2007—. Bd. mem. Billerica Garden Club, Mass., 2007. Recipient Partners in Excellence award, Mass. Gen. Hosp., 2002. Mem.: AACN. Democrat. Avocations: travel, gardening. Home Phone: 978-667-7866. Personal E-mail: bstnhokie@aol.com.

KANE, JOHN LAWRENCE, JR., judge; b. Tucumcari, N.Mex., Feb. 14, 1937; s. John Lawrence and Dorothy Helen (Bottler) K.; m. Stephanie Jane Shafer, Oct. 5, 1993; children: Molly Francis, Meghan, Sally, John Pattison. BA, U. Colo., 1958; JD, U. Denver, 1961, LL.D. (hon), 1997. Bar: Colo. 1961. Dep. dist. atty., Adams County, Colo., 1961-62; assoc. firm Gaunt, Byrne & Dirrim, 1961-63; ptnr. firm Andrews and Kane, Denver, 1964; pub. defender Adams County, 1965-67; dep. dir. eastern region of India Peace Corps, 1967-69; with firm Holme Roberts & Owen, 1970-77, ptnr., 1972-77; judge U.S. Dist. Ct. Colo., Denver, 1978-88, U.S. sr. dist. judge, 1988—. Adj. prof. law U. Denver, U. Colo., 1996—; vis. lectr. Trinity Coll., Dublin, Ireland, winter 1989; adj. prof. U. Colo., 1996, philosophy, 2003. Contbr. articles to profl. jours. Recipient St. Thomas More award Cath. Lawyers Guild, 1983, U.S. Info. Agy. Outstanding Svc. award, 1985, Outstanding Alumnus award U. Denver, 1987, Lifetime Jud. Achievement award Nat. Assn. Criminal Def. Lawyers, 1987, Civil Rights award B'nai B'rith, 1988, Justice Gerald Le Dain award Drug Policy Found., 2000. Fellow Internat. Acad. Trial Lawyers, Am. Bd. Trial Advs. (hon.). Roman Catholic. Office: US Dist Ct US Courthouse 901 19th St Denver CO 80294-1929 Office Phone: 303-844-6118. Business E-Mail: John_L_Kane@cod.uscourts.gov. *There is a tendency to gild the past with uncritical generosity but an even more pronounced one to forget Santayana's dictum that one who forgets history is bound to repeat it. Law is that indispensable mechanism by which we may survive as a free people if we use it to apply a critical understanding of history to a confusing and dynamic present.*

KANE, KAREN MARIE, public affairs consultant; b. Colorado Springs, Colo., Mar. 7, 1947; d. Bernard Francis and Adeline Marie (Logan) K Student, Mills Coll., Oakland, Calif., 1965—66; BA, U. Wash., Seattle, 1970, MA, 1973, PhC, 1977, postgrad. Pub. affairs cons., housing subcom. Seattle Ret. Tchrs. Assn., 1981—84; pub. affairs cons. 1st US Women's Olympic Marathon Trials, 1982—83, Seattle, 1985—. Adminstr. sponsorships and grants Allied Arts Found., 2004—. Contbr. articles to newsletters and mags. Trustee Allied Arts of Seattle, 1987—96, past chmn. hist. preservation com., sec. bd. trustees, mem. exec. com., 1987—96; trustee Allied Arts Found., 1999—, sponsorship application approval com., 2002—04; active Mayor's Landmark Theatre Adv. Group, 1991—93, Pike Place Market Hist. Commn., Seattle, 1992—98, chmn., 1997—98; com. to rev. the Hildt agreement Pike Place Market, 1998—99; active Pike Market Constituency, 1999—; mem. Friends of Market, 1999—; vol. various polit. campaigns, Seattle; bd. dirs. Showboat Theatre Found./Bravo (formerly Showboat Theatre Found.), 1984—2002. Recipient Award of Honor Wash. Trust for Hist. Preservation, 1990, Recognition award Found. for Hist. Preservation and Adaptive Reuse, Seattle, 1991; Am. Found. grantee, 1989, 91 Mem.: LWV (chmn., hist. preservation Seattle chpt. 1989—, co-chmn. land use com. 2001—05, chmn. 2005—), AAUW, Hist. Seattle Preservation and Devel. Authority, Wash. Trust Hist. Preservation, San Francisco Archtl. Heritage, Hist. Hawai'i Found., Nat. Trust Hist. Preservation, U. Wash. Alumni Assn., Mills Coll. Alumnae Assn. Home Phone: 206-323-4721; Office Phone: 206-323-4721.

KANE, MARGARET BRASSLER, sculptor; b. East Orange, NJ, May 25, 1909; d. Hans and Mathilde (Trumpler) Brassler; m. Arthur Ferris Kane, June 11, 1930; children: Jay Brassler, Gregory Ferris. Student, Packer Collegiate Inst., 1920—26, Syracuse U., 1927, Art Students League, 1927—29, N.Y. Coll. Music, 1928—29, John Hovannes Studio, 1932—34; PhD (hon.), Colo. State Christian Coll., 1973. Head craftsman sculpture, arts and skills unit ARC, Halloran Gen. Hosp., NY, 1942—43; jury mem. Bklyn. Mus., 1948, Am. Machine & Foundry Co., 1957; com. mem. An Am. Group, Inc. Exhibitions include, Phila. Mus., Chgo. Art Inst., Am. Fedn. Arts, NY Bot. Garden, 1981, 60th Anniversary Exhbn. Lever House, 1987—98, Sculptors Guild 50th Anniversary Exhbn., Lever House, 1987—96, 1st Bi-Coastal exhibits San Francisco, Collection Donald Trump, 1988, Collection Rene Anselmo, 1991, Shidoni Galleries, Santa Fe, N.Mex., 1989, Am. Sculpture, Hofstra Mus., 1990, exhibitions include nat. tour Am. sculpture by EducArt Projects Inc., 1992, exhibitions include, Stamford Mus. and Nature Ctr., 1996, Zimmerli Art Mus. Historical Exhibit, 1999—2000, Treasures from the Smithsonian Am. Art Mus., 2000—02, numerous others, Represented in permanent collections, Zimmerli Art Mus., Rutgers U., NJ, 1992, Nat. Mus. Am. Art, Smithsonian Instn., Washington, 1993, 2000, Bruce Mus., Greenwich, Conn., 1996, Packer Collegiate Inst., Bklyn., 2003, one-woman shows include sculpture, Friends Greenwich (Conn.) Library, 1962, prin. works include 18 foot carving in limewood, 2002, prin. works include six foot carving Reaching the Galaxies, 2002—, prin. works include plaque Burro Monument, Fair Play, Colo., prin. works include bronze panels Earthbound, cast by Tallix Art Foundry Beacon, NY, 2005, Symbols, 2005, Micro-macrocosm, 2005, Five episodes in human history, bronze works placed against a cosmic background, 2006; reprodns. Contemporary Stone Sculpture, 1970, Contemporary Am. Sculptures, Am. References, Chgo.; CD-ROM, Smithsonian Nat. Mus. Am. Art, Washington, 1995; contbr. articles to mags. Recipient Hyatt Huntington award, 1942, Am. Artist Profl. League and Monclair Art Assn. awards, 1943, 1st Henry O. Avery prize, 1944, Sculpture prize, Bklyn. Soc. Artists, Bklyn. Mus., 1946, John Rogers award, 1951, Lawrence Hyder prize, 1952, 1954, David H. Zell Meml. award, 1954, 1963, Hon. Mention, U.S. Maritime Commn., 1941, A.C.A. Gallery Competition, 1944, medal of Honor for Sculpture, Nat. Acad. Galleries, N.Y., prize for carved sculpture, 1955, prize for animal sculpture, 1956, 1st award for sculpture, Ann. New Eng. Exhbns., Silvermine, Conn. Fellow: Internat. Inst. Arts and Letters (life); mem.: Nat. Trust Hist. Preservation, silvermine Guild Artists, Internat. Soc. Artists (charter), Internat. Sculpture Ctr., Greenwich Soc. Artists (mem. coun.), Bklyn. Soc. Artists, Artists Coun. U.S.A., Pen and Brush (emeritus 1992), Nat. League Am. Pen Women, Inc. (OWL award for the Arts 1991), Nat. Assn. Women Artists (2d v.p. 1943—44), Sculptors Guild, Inc. (life; sec. to exec. bd. 1942—45, chmn. exhbn. com. 1942, 1944). *It is not possible to overestimate the deep satisfaction experienced in having created countless direct carvings in marble, stone, wood and models for bronze. I strongly believe mankind needs to express itself in some meaningful way. My recent* *mahogany woodcarvings are dedicated to Peace, Love and an end to Violence. If these goals should inspire the many thousands of viewers of my art form, then I am content that my sculpture is a worthwhile contribution to American culture.*

KANE, MARY DEELY, former state official; b. Wilmington, Del., Mar. 10, 1962; d. Edward and Anna Teresa (Molloy) Deely; m. John Murray Kane, Apr. 12, 1986, 3 children BA in English, Mt. St. Mary's Coll., 1984, BS in Bus. & Fin., 1984; JD, Catholic U., 1999. Legis corr. to Senator J. R. Biden, Jr. US Senate, Washington, 1984-85; adminstr. spl. projects Am. Trucking Assn., Washington; of counsel Etheridge, Quinn, McAuliffe, Rowan & Hartinger, Rockville, Md., 2001—02; dep. sec. state State of Md., Annapolis, 2003—05, sec. state, 2005—07. Bd. dirs. Kane Co., Elkridge, Md., 1997—2003; alt. del. Rep. Party Nat. Conv., 2000; mem. Gov. Exec. Coun., Annapolis, Md., 2005—07; chair. Gov. Subcabinet for Internat. Affairs, 2005—07; mem. Gov. Commn. on Md. Mil. Monuments, 2005—07, Bd. State Canvasers, 2005—07, Gov. Interagency Coun. for Nonprofit Sector, 2005—07. Mem. Adv. Com.for the Jefferson Patterson Hist. Pk. & Mus., 2005—, Parish Coun., Our Lady of Mercy Cath. Church, 2000—03; bd. trustees Mater Dei Sch., Bethesda, Md. Mem.: Md. State Bar Assn., ABA. Roman Catholic.*

KANE, MARY KAY, academic administrator, law educator; b. Detroit, Nov. 14, 1946; d. John Francis and Frances (Roberts) K.; m. Ronan Eugene Degnan, Feb. 3, 1987 (dec. Oct. 1987). BA cum laude, U. Mich., 1968, JD cum laude, 1971. Bar: Mich. 1971. Rsch. assoc., co-dir. NSF project on privacy, confidentiality and social sci. rsch. data sch. law U. Mich., 1971-72, Harvard U., 1972-74; asst. prof. law SUNY, Buffalo, 1974-77; mem. faculty Hastings Coll. Law U. Calif., San Francisco, 1977—, prof. law, 1979—, assoc. acad. dean, 1981-83, acting acad. dean, 1987-88, acad. dean., 1990-93, dean, 1993—2006, chancellor, 2001—06, John D. Digardi Disting. Prof. Law. Vis. prof. law U. Mich., 1981, U. Utah, 1983, U. Calif., Berkeley, 1983-84, sch. law U. Tex., 1989; cons. Mead Data Control, Inc., 1971, 74, Inst. on Consumer Justice, U. Mich. Sch. Law, 1972, U.S. Privacy Protection Study Commn., 1975-76; lectr. pretrial mgmt. devices U.S. magistrates for 6th and 11th cirs. Fed. Jud. Ctr., 1983; Siebenthaler lectr. Samuel P. Chase Coll. Law, U. North Ky., 1987; reporter ad hoc com. on asbestos litigation U.S. Jud. Conf., 1990-91, mem. standing com. on practice and procedure, 2001—; mem. 9th Cir. Adv. Com. on Rules Practice and Internal Oper. Procedures, 1993-96; spkr. in field. Author: Civil Procedure in a Nutshell, 1979, 5th edit., 2003, Sum and Substance on Remedies, 1981; co-prodr.(with C. Wright and A. Miller): Pocket Supplements to Federal Practice and Procedure, 1975—; co-author (with C. Wright and A. Miller): Federal Practice and Procedure, vol. 7, 3d edit., 2001, 10, 10A and 10B, 3d edit., 1998, vols. 7-7C, 2d edit., 1986, vols. 6-6A, 2d edit., 1990, vols. 11-11A, 2d edit., 1995, vols. 7A-B, 3d edit., 2005; co-author: (with J. Friedenthal and A. Miller) Hornbook on Civil Procedure, 4th edit., 2005; co-author: (with C. Wright) Hornbook on the Law of Federal Courts, 2002, Federal Practice Deskbook, 2002; mem. law sch. divsn. West. Adv. Editl. Bd., 1986—; contbr. articles to profl. jours. Mem. standing com. on rules of practice and procedure U.S. Jud. Conf., 2000—. Mem. ABA (mem. bar admissions com. 1995-2000, mem. coun. sect. legal edn. and admission to bar 2004—), Assn. Am. Law Schs. (com. on prelegal edn. statement 1982, chair sect. remedies 1982, panelist sect. on prelegal edn. 1983, exec. com. sect. on civil procedure 1983, 86, panelist sect. on tchg. methods 1984, spkr. new tchrs. conf. 1986, 89, 90, chair sect. on civil procedure 1987, spkr. sects. civil procedure and conflicts 1987, 91, chair planning com. for 1988 Tchg. Conf. in Civil Procedure 1987-88, nominating com. 1988, profl. devel. com. 1988-91, planning com. for workshop in conflicts 1988, planning com. for 1990 Conf. on Clin. Legal Edn. 1989, chair profl. devel. com. 1989-91, exec. com. 1991-93, 2000-02, pres.-elect 2000, pres. 2001), Am. Law Inst. (co-reporter complex litigation project 1988-93, coun. 1998—), ABA/Assn. Am. Law Schs. Commn. on Financing Legal Edn., State Bar Mich. Home: 8 Admiral Dr Ste 421 Emeryville CA 94608-1567 Office: U Calif Hastings Coll Law 200 McAllister St San Francisco CA 94102-4707 Office Phone: 415-565-4777. E-mail: kanem@uchastings.edu.

KANE, MICHAEL ARTHUR CHRISTOPHER, plastic surgeon; b. Phila., Pa., Dec. 26, 1963; MD, Jefferson Med. Coll., 1984. Cert. Am. Bd. Surgery, Am. Bd. Plastic Surgery. Resident, gen. surgery NY Med. Coll., Valhalla, 1984—89; resident, plastic surgery Wright State Univ., Dayton, Ohio, 1989—91; fellow, anesthesia surgery Manhattan Eye, Ear & Throat Hosp., 1991—92, hosp. appointment; private practice NY, 1992—. Presenter in field. Contbr. articles to profl. publications; author: The Botox Book, 2002. Mem.: Internat. Soc. Hair Restoration Surgery, Med. Soc. State NY, NY County Med. Soc., Am. Soc. Plastic Surgeons, Hobart Hare Honor Soc. Achievements include Best known for work with Botulinum Toxin A-Botox; pioneered the use of Botox for cosmetic purposes. Office: 630 Park Ave New York NY 10021 Office Phone: 212-935-0030. Office Fax: 212-327-1045.*

KANE, MICHAEL BARRY, social science research executive; b. Taunton, Mass., July 2, 1944; s. Julius J. and Dorothy M. (Moscoff) K.; children: Jared E., Stacy E., Matthew D. BA in Polit. Sci., NYU, 1966; MA in Ednl. Adminstrn., Columbia U., 1968, MEd in Ednl. Adminstrn., 1970, EdD in Ednl. Adminstrn., 1974. Tchr. Roosevelt Sch., Stamford, Conn., 1966-67; asst. to dir. New Lincoln Sch., NYC, 1969; spl. asst. to dep. commr. for devel. U.S. Office of Edn., Washington, 1970-71; headmaster Downtown Community sch., NYC, 1971-73; coord. program for situational analysis and program for ednl. leadership Columbia U. Tchrs. Coll., NYC, 1970-73; group mgr., project dir. Abt Assocs., Inc., Cambridge, Mass., 1973-79; asst. dir., assoc. dir. Nat. Inst. Edn., U.S. Dept. Edn., Washington, 1979-82; pres. MCK Assocs., Inc., Tallahassee, Fla., and Annapolis, Md., 1982-87; prin. Pelavin Assocs., Inc., Washington, 1988-94; v.p. Am. Inst. for Rsch., Washington, 1995—98, sr. v.p., 1998—2006, exec. v.p., dir. adminstrn., 2007—. Chmn. Profl. Tchr. Career Devel. Coun., Fla.; vis. scholar Fla. State U.'s Ctr. for Needs Assessmtn and Planning; pres. Citizen's Coun. Edn., Fla.; chmn. Fla. Bus. and Edn. Coalition; lectr. numerous workshops. Author, co-author, editor: Minorities in Textbooks: A Study of Their Treatment in Social Studies Texts, Improving Schools: Using What We Know, Changing the Odds: Factors Increasing Access to College, Implementing Performance Assessments: Promises, Problems, and Challenges, Principles and Practices of Performance Assessment; contbr. articles to profl. jours. Avocations: boating, photography, scuba diving. Office Phone: 202-403-5144. Business E-Mail: mkane@air.org.

KANE, MICHAEL JOEL, physician; b. Erie, Pa., July 2, 1951; BS, U.S. Naval Acad., 1973; MD, N.J. Med. Sch., 1983. Diplomate Am. Bd. Internal Medicine. Med. intern Thomas Jefferson U. Hosp., Phila., 1983—84, resident medicine, 1984—86; fellow neoplastic diseases Mt. Sinai Med. Ctr., NYC, 1986—88; attending physician Jefferson Med. Coll., Phila., 1988—91, Med. Ctr. Princeton, NJ, 1991—96, Cancer Inst. N.J., Hamilton, 1996—2004, Cancer Ctr. Mountainside, Montclair, NJ, 2004—06, Cancer Ctr. Bayshore Hosp., Holmdel, NJ, 2007—. Served to lt. U.S. Navy, 1969-79. Decorated Navy Achievement medal. Fellow ACP, Am. Soc. Clin. Oncology, Am. Assn. Cancer Rsch., Am. Soc. Hematology, Oncology Soc. N.J. Office: Bayshore Hosp 668 N Beers St Holmdel NJ 07733

KANE, RICHARD JOSEPH, lawyer; b. NYC, Feb. 12, 1941; s. Joseph Thomas and Helen Elizabeth (Ward) K.; m. Lorraine Catherine Heckelmann, Nov. 21, 1964; children: Kevin Joseph, Robert Keith, Carol Aileen. BA, St. John's Coll., NYC, 1962; JD, St. John's U., NYC, 1965. Bar: NY 1965, Fla. 1967, US Dist. Ct. (So. Dist.) NY 1967, US Dist. Ct. (Ea. Dist.) NY 1967, US Ct. Appeals (2nd and 11th Cirs.) 1967, US Supreme Ct. 1969. Ptnr. Golenbock & Barell, NYC; ptnr., real estate dept. Thelen Reid & Priest LLP, NYC. Faculty mem. real estate financing and mortgage instruments NYU, Real Estate Inst. NYU., 1982; adv. bd., mem. First Am. Title Ins. Co., NY; lectr. in field. Contbr. articles to profl. jours. Jud. arbitrator Civil Ct. City of NY 1974—; active NYC Jud. Screening Com. 1982-84; chmn. law sch. homecoming program, 1983; vice-chmn. bldg. com. for the constrn. of Fromkes Hall; moderator TV series on real estate financing. Mem. ABA, Am. Judges Assn., Fla. Bar Assn. (real property law com.), NY State Bar Assn. (real property law sect., chmn. constrn. contracts 1980, lectr. real estate financing 1978), NY Assn. Arbitrators (pres. 1984, sec. 1982, v.p. 1982, bd. dirs. 1977—), St. John's U. Sch. Law Am. Alumni Assn. (bd. dirs. 1968—, pres. 1994-2000), Internat. Legal Frat., Phi Delta Phi Assn. of City of NY (pres. 1968-71, exec. com. 1971—, bd. govs. 1968). Office: Thelen Reid & Priest LLP 875 Third Ave New York NY 10022-6225 Office Phone: 212-603-2032. Office Fax: 212-603-2001. Business E-Mail: rkane@thelenreid.com.

KANE, ROBERT LEWIS, public health service officer, educator; b. NYC, Jan. 18, 1940; m. Rosalie Smolkin, June 17, 1962; children: Miranda, Ingrid, Kate AB, Columbia Coll., NYC, 1961; MD, Harvard U., 1965. Acting coordinator sr. clerkship program dept. community medicine U. Ky., Lexington, 1968-69; svc. unit dir. USPHS Indian Hosp., Shiprock, N.Mex., 1969-70; spl. asst. to regional health dir. USPHS HEW Region VIII, Denver, 1970-71; from asst. to assoc. prof. family and community medicine U. Utah Sch. Medicine, Salt Lake City, 1970-77; sr. researcher The Rand Corp., Santa Monica, Calif., 1977-85; from assoc. prof. to prof. medicine UCLA Sch. Medicine, 1978-85; prof. Sch. Pub. Health UCLA, 1980-85, U. Minn., 1985—, dean, 1985-90; intern U. Ky. Med. Ctr., Lexington, 1965-66, resident in community medicine, 1966-69. Adj. prof. Leonard Davis Sch. Gerontology, U. So. Calif., 1982-85; mem. expert com. on aging WHO, 1986-2002; Minn. endowed chair in long-term care and aging, 1989—; mem. adv. com. on Alzheimer's Disease, Washington, 1988-96; mem. com. on quality Inst. Medicine, 1988-90. Co-author: A Will and A Way, 1985, Long-term Care: Principles, Programs, and Policies, 1987, Essentials of Clinical Geriatrics, 5th edit., 2004, Understanding Health Care Outcomes Research, 2nd edit., 2005, The Heart of Long Term Care, 1998, Assessing Older Persons, 2000, It Shouldn't Be This Way, 2005, Meeting the Challenge of Chronic Illness, 2005. With USPHS, 1969-70. Home: 2715 E Lake Of The Isles Pky Minneapolis MN 55408-1053 Office Phone: 612-624-1185. Business E-Mail: kanex001@umn.edu.

KANE, ROBYN A., economist; b. New Britain, Conn., Aug. 2, 1959; d. Edwaed Isaac and Rosalie Rita Abraham; m. Gerard (Jerry) Francis Kane, Apr. 6, 1984; children: Michelle Marie, Abraham Joseph. BS in Math., Ctrl. Conn. State U., New Britain, Conn., 1982; MS in Math., U. ND, Grand Forks, 1987. Cert. Soc. Cost Estimating and Analysis, 2001. Instr. SD Sch. Mines & Tech., Rapid City, SD, 1988; adj. instr. iii Embry Riddle Aero. U., Ellsworth Air Force Base, SD, 1991—93; instr. Pikes Peak C.C., Colo. Springs, Colo., 1994—96; sr. cost analyst Analytic Svcs., Inc., Colo. Springs, 1996—2000; sys. analyst sencom divsn. Titan Sys. Corp., Colo. Springs, 2000—03; lead economist, bus. analyst The MITRE Corp, Colo. Springs, 2003—. Adj. instr. Embry Riddle Aero. U., 1994—98. Contbr. articles to profl. jours. Named Employee of Quarter, Analytic Svcs. Inc, Colo. Springs Divsn., 1997; recipient Dir.'s award, MITRE, 2006. Mem.: Inst. Ops. Rsch. and Mgmt. Scis., Mil. Ops. Rsch. Soc. (Cost Analysis Working Group Best Paper award 2005), Soc. Cost Estimating and Analysis (bd. dirs. 2004—06, co-founder Pike's Peak chpt., Best Paper in Risk Track award 2005, named Analyst of Yr. 2004). Roman Catholic. Avocation: weightlifting. Office: The MITRE Corp 1155 Acad Pk Loop Colorado Springs CO 80910 Home Phone: 719-535-0571; Office Phone: 719-572-8409. Office Fax: 719-572-8477. Business E-Mail: rkane@mitre.org.

KANE, SAM, meat company executive; b. Spisske Pohrdie, Czechoslovakia, June 23, 1919; came to U.S., 1948, naturalized, 1953. s. Leopold and Bertha (Narcisenfeld) Kannengiesser; m. Aranka Feldbrand, Jan. 15, 1946; children: Jerry, Harold Ira, Esther Barbara. Grad., Rabbinical Coll. Galanta, 1939. Pres. Sam Kane Wholesale Meat, Inc., Corpus Christi, 1956—, Sam Kane Meat, Inc., Corpus Christi, 1956—, Sam Kane Packing co., Corpus Christi, 1962—, Kane Enterprises, Inc., Corpus Christi, 1956—; pres., chmn. bd., CEO Sam Kane Beef Processors, Inc., 1956—. Pres., Jewish Welfare Appeal, 1962—; pres. Combined Jewish Appeal, 1962—, chmn. bd., 1962-65; mem. nat. cabinet United Jewish Appeal; bd. dirs. Tex. Coun. on Econ. Edn.; mem. Gov. Tex. 2000 Commn. Recipient award chmn. bd edn. B'nai Israel Synagogue, 1965, Israel Service award, 1966, Koach award State of Israel, 2976, Prime Minister of Israel Peace medal, 1980, Brotherhood award Corpus Christi chpt. NCCJ, 1984, Torch of Liberty award Anti Defamation League, 1984; named Outstanding Jewish Citizen of Corpus Christi, 1969. Mem. Tex. Coun. on Econ. Edn. (bd. dirs.), Tex. Taxpayers Assn., B'nai B'rith. Jewish (pres. synagogue 1964-65). Home: 27 Hewitt Dr Corpus Christi TX 78404-1662 Office: San Kane Beef Processors 9001 Leopard St Corpus Christi TX 78409-2502

KANE, SCOTT A., lawyer; b. Carson City, Mich., 1969; BS, Western Mich. U., 1994; JD, U. Cin., 1997. Bar: Ohio 1997, US Dist. Ct. Southern Dist. Ohio 1997, US Ct. of Appeals Sixth Cir. 1999. Ptnr. Squire, Sanders & Dempsey L.L.P., Cin. Mem., former chmn. Common Pleas Ct. Com.; mem., Electronic Data Discovery Task Force Squire, Sanders & Dempsey L.L.P, Cin.; mem., Adv. Bd. LexisNexis Applied Discovery. Served in USAR, vet., Operation Desert Storm. Named one of Ohio's Rising Stars, Super Lawyers, 2005, 2006. Mem.: Ohio State Bar Assn., Potter Stewart Inn of Ct. (barrister), Cin. Bar Assn. (mem., bd. of Professionalism Com.), FBA (exec. com., Cin./Northern Ky. chpt.). Office: Squire Sanders & Dempsey LLP 312 Walnut St Ste 3500 Cincinnati OH 45202-4036 Office Phone: 513-361-1240. Office Fax: 513-361-1201.

KANE, SIEGRUN DINKLAGE, lawyer; b. NYC, Sept. 21, 1938; d. Ralph Dieter and Lisbeth (Adam) Dinklage; m. David H.T. Kane, Jan. 24, 1964; children: David D., Brendon T. BA cum laude, Mt. Holyoke Coll., South Hadley, Mass., 1960; LLB, Harvard U., Cambridge, Mass., 1963. Bar: NY 1963, US Ct. Appeals (2d cir.) 1964, US Supreme Ct. 1967, US Ct. Appeals (7th cir.) 1984, US Ct Appeals (5th cir.) 1997. Ptnr. Kane, Dalsimer, Sullivan, Kurucz, Levy, Eisele & Richard, NYC, 1970—99, Morgan & Finnegan, NYC, 1999—. Lectr. trademarks Practicing Law Inst., NYC, 1980—, mem. adv. com. on copyright and trademarks, 1989—; mem. U.S. Patent and Trademark Office Pub. Adv. Com., Washington, 1985—95, 2000—04; bd. dirs. Bur. Nat. Affairs Adv. Com., Washington, 1988—; designated mem. INTA Panel Neutrals, 2000—; mem. adv. bd. McCarthy Ctr. Intellectual Property and Tech. Law, U. San Francisco, 2001—. Author: Trademark Law: A Practitioner's Guide, 1987, 5th edit., 2007, annual supplements, 1998—; contbr. articles to profl. jours. Mem. Briarcliff Zoning Bd. Appeals, Briarcliff Manor, NY, 1978-90, Briarcliff Hist. Soc. Bd., Briarcliff Manor, 1986-90. Named to The Best Lawyers in Am., 1997. Mem. ABA, Internat. Trademark Assn., NY Patent Law Assn. Avocations: tennis, aerobics, travel. Office: Morgan & Finnegan LLP 3 World Financial Ctr New York NY 10281-2101 Office Phone: 212-415-8778. Business E-Mail: skane@morganfinnegan.com.

KANE, STEVEN EDWARD, mediator, arbitrator; b. Milw., Sept. 7, 1949; s. Edward Thomas and Marion Jean (Regan) K.; m. Jacqueline Peacock; children: Clifford, Stacy. BS in Indsl. Relations, Cornell U., 1972, MBA, 1973; JD, U. Akron, 1977. Bar: Ohio 1977, Tex. 1977. Labor relations staff BF Goodrich, Akron, Ohio, 1973-77; cons. Modern Mgmt., Bannockburn, Ill., 1978; dir. employee relations Am. Hosp. Supply, Evanston, Ill., 1979-85; v.p. human resources adminstrn. Baxter Internat. (formerly Baxter Travenol Labs.), Deerfield, Ill., 1986-87, v.p. human resources, corp. groups, 1987-89, v.p. human resources hosp. and alternate site group, 1989-90, v.p. human resources alternate site group, chief labor counsel, 1990-91, v.p. employee rels., assoc. gen. counsel, 1992-94, v.p. compensation, 1995-96, v.p. govt. affairs, 1996-98; cons. StevenKane.com, Hillsborough, Calif., 1999; sr. v.p. human resources, legal, comm. Neoforma, Inc., 2000—03; mng. dir. Alternate Dispute Resolution, San Mateo, Calif., 2003—. Mem.: ABA, Tex. Bar Assn., Ohio Bar Assn. Home: PO Box 1421 San Mateo CA 94401 E-mail: sek17@cornell.edu.

KANE, THOMAS JAY, III, surgeon, educator; b. Merced, Calif., Sept. 2, 1951; s. Thomas J., Jr. and Kathryn (Hassler) Kane; m. Marle Rose Van Emmerik, Oct. 10, 1987; children: Thomas Keola, Travis Reid, Samantha Marie. BA in History, U. Santa Clara, 1973; MD, U. Calif., Davis, 1977. Diplomate Am. Bd. Orthopaedic Surgery. Intern U. Calif. Davis Sacramento Med. Ctr., 1977-78, resident in surgery, 1978-81; resident in orthopaedic surgery U. Hawaii, 1987-91; fellowship adult joint reconstruction Rancho Los Amigos Med. Ctr., 1991-92; ptnr. Orthop. Assocs. Hawaii, Inc., Honolulu, 1992—; asst. prof. surgery U. Hawaii, Honolulu, 1993—, chief divsn. implant surgery, 1993—, asst. chief orthopedics, 2003—04. Contbr. articles to profl. jours. Mem.: AMA, Am. Coll. Sports Medicine, Western Orthop. Assn., Am. Acad. Orthop. Surgery, Hawaii Orthop. Assn. (v.p. 2003—04, pres. 2004—), Hawaii Med. Assn., Am. Assn. Hip and Knee Surgeons, Phi Kappa Phi, Alpha Omega Alpha. Avocations: tennis, golf, skiing, music, surfing. Office: Orthopaedic Svcs Co LLP 1380 Lusitana St Ste 608 Honolulu HI 96813-2442 Office Phone: 808-521-8124. Personal E-mail: tkaneiii@yahoo.com.

KANE, THOMAS PATRICK, broadcast executive; b. NYC, Aug. 28, 1945; s. Thomas Patrick and Rosemary Ann (Tenanty) K.; m. Judith Ann Riccardo, m. Feb. 7, 1970; children: Thomas, Colby, F. Todd. Account exec. Edward Petry and Co., NYC, 1971-72, Peters Griffin and Woodward, NYC, 1972-74, Storer Broadcasting, NYC, 1974-75; account exec. nat. TV sales ABC, Detroit, 1977-78, NYC, 1978; ea. sales mgr. nat. TV sales ABC, NYC, 1978-82; account exec. Sta. WABC-TV, NYC, 1975-77, nat. sales mgr., 1982-86, gen. sales mgr., 1986-93, pres., gen. mgr., 1997—2004, WPVI-TV, Phila., 1993-97; pres. sales Viacom TV Stations Group, 2004—05; pres. & CEO CBS TV Stations Group, 2005—. Served to sgt. U.S. Army, 1966-68, Vietnam. Mem.: NY State Broadcasters Assn. Roman Catholic. Office: CBS Corp 51 W 52 St New York NY 10019-6188*

KANE, YVETTE, lawyer, judge; b. Donaldsonville, La., Oct. 11, 1953; d. Thomas R. Pregeant and Julia Tucker; children: Kathleen, Madeline. BA, Nicholls State U., Thibodeaux, La., 1973; JD, Tulane U., 1976. Bar: Pa. Trial atty. US Equal Employment Opportunity Commn., 1977-78; asst. atty. gen. Colo. Atty. Gen.'s Office, 1978-80; dep. dist. atty. Denver Dist. Atty.'s Office, 1980-86; dep. atty. gen. rev. and advice sect. Pa. Office Atty. Gen., 1986-91; chief counsel Pa. Ind. Regulatory Rev. Commn., 1991-92; sr. assoc. Wolf, Block, Schorr & Solis-Cohen, Harrisburg, Pa., 1993-95; sec. state Commonwealth of Pa., 1995-98; US dist. judge US Dist. Ct. (mid. dist.) Pa., Harrisburg, 1998—2006, chief judge, 2006—. Office: US Dist Ct Box 11817 228 Walnut St 8th Fl Harrisburg PA 17108 Office Phone: 717-221-3920.

KANEB, JOHN A., oil industry executive; m. Virginia Kaneb; 6 children. B., Harvard, 1956; LLD (hon.), St. Anslem Coll., 1984; PhD (hon.), U. Notre Dame, 1996. CEO Northeast Petroleum, 1959—83; pres. Catamount Cos.; co-founder, CEO Catamount Petroleum (acquired gen. partnership interest Gulf Oil L.P), 1986—94; chmn. Gulf Oil L.P., 1994—; CEO, pres., chmn. HP Hood, Chelsea, Mass., 1995—. Commr. Nat. Prison Rape Elimination Commn., 2004—; ptnr. Boston Red Sox. Trustee U. Notre Dame; trustee, fin. chmn. Partners Healthcare Sys.; trustee McLean Hosp. Jr. officer USN, 1957—59. Office: HP Hood 90 Everett Ave Chelsea MA 02150-2301

KANEHIRO, KENNETH KENJI, risk management consultant, educator; b. Honolulu, May 10, 1934; s. Charles Yutaka and Betty Misako (Hoshino) K.; m. Eiko Asari, June 23, 1962; 1 child, Everett Peter. BA in Counseling Psychology, U. Hawaii, 1956, grad. cert. in Counseling Psychology, 1957; grad. cert. in ins., The Am. Inst., RI, 1971; cert., Nat. Leadership Inst. CPCU; cert. continuing profl. devel. Claims adjustor Cooke Trust Co., Honolulu, 1959-62, underwriter, 1962-66; account supr. Alexander & Baldwin, Honolulu, 1966-68; spl. risk exec. Hawaiian Ins. & Guaranty, Honolulu, 1968-71, br. mgr. Hilo, Hawaii, 1971-72; chief of office Marsh & McLennan, Inc., Hilo, 1972-78; sr. mktg. rep. Occidental Underwriters, Honolulu, 1978-87; pvt. practice Honolulu, 1987—. Coord. Ins. Sch. of Pacific, Honolulu, 1978—; lectr. ins. Hawaii State Cts., 1986—; adv. bd. Ins. Commn., 2000—; mem. adv. bd. Real Estate Commn., 2003—; adv. Dai Tokyo Royal State Ins. Co., 1992—; mem. arbitration panel, ct. observer panel Hawaii State Cts., 1993-96, Hawaii Criminal Ct., 1994-98; proctor Hawaii State Bar Exam., 1994—; ins. expert witness, 1995—; instr. ins. agt.'s lic. course, 1995—; dir. edn. Profl. Ins. Agts. Hawaii, 2001—; bd. dirs. Royal Ins. Agy.; mem. bd. ethical inquiry Am. Inst. for Chartered Property Casualty Underwriters, 2002—. Adult leader Boy Scouts Am., Hilo and Honolulu, 1956—, risk mgr. Aloha coun., Honolulu, 1980—; edn. chmn. Gen. Ins. Assn., Hawaii, Hilo, 1971-77; ins. cons. Arcadia Retirement Residence, Honolulu, 1987—; cons. Waikiki Banyan Assn.; bd. govs. U. Hawaii Founders Alumni Assn., Honolulu, 1993—, scholarship chmn., 1993—. With U.S. Army, 1957-59. Recipient First Lady's Outstanding Vol. award, First Lady/State of Hawaii, 1990, Pres.'s award, Boy Scouts Aloha Coun., 1997. Mem.: Profl. Ins. Agts. Hawaii, Soc. Ins. Trainers and Educators Hawaii, Chartered Property and Casualty Underwriters Soc. (nat. gov. 2006—, pres. 1986—87, nat. publs. com. 1996—2000, nat. ethics com. 2000—06, nat. gov. 2006—, contbr. to jour., Excellence award 2000). Avocations: art, photography, music. Home: 1128 Ala Napunani St Apt 705 Honolulu HI 96818-1606

KANE HITTNER, MARCIA SUSAN, bank executive; b. NYC; d. Howard Eugene and Sydell (Friedman) Kane; m. Ellis Hittner. Cert. fin. planning, NYU, BA in Comm. Cert. Nat. Ret. Plans Tng. Ctr., software capability maturity model cert. interim profile adminstr. Carnegie Mellon U. Pension specialist Union Dime Savs. Bank, NYC, 1978—81; money market specialist Goldome (formerly Union Dime Savs. Bank), NYC, 1981—82; mgr. customer svc. Citibank, N.A., NYC, 1982—85, mgr. mktg. product, 1986—87, mgr. shareholder comm., 1988—89, asst. v.p., tax shelter conversions, 1990—93, asst. v.p. tech. client interface, 1993—95, asst. v.p. U.S., Europe consumer bank, 1995—99; with product design and devel. Software Engring. Process Group, 1995—99; v.p. mktg. strategy EAB subs. ABN-AMRO, 1999—2001, cons. bus. and mktg. strategy, 2001—04; exec. v.p. Howard Kane Assocs., Inc., 2001—; sr. v.p. Cambridge Home Capital, LLC, Great Neck, NY, 2004—06. Author: (with others) Critical Reading-Level G, 1980; pub.: Map of Destiny, 2004, Mommy, I Want To Kill Myself, 2007. Bd. dirs. Forest Hills Owners Corp., N.Y.C., 2000-05.

KANEKO, ISAO, air transportation executive; b. Mar. 1, 1938; married; 1 child. Grad. law dept., Tokyo U., 1960. Joined Japan Airlines, Tokyo, 1960, internat. cargo dept., indsl. rels. dept., with NYC, 1968—72, dep. v.p. indsl. rels. Tokyo, 1980, v.p. internat. rels., 1985, mng. dir., 1995—97, sr. v.p. human resources, 1995—98, sr. mng. dir., 1997—98, pres., 1998—2002; pres., CEO Japan Airlines System Co., Tokyo, 2002—04; chmn., group CEO Japan Airlines Corp. (formerly Japan Airlines System Co.), Tokyo, 2004—05; chmn. Japan Airlines Internat. Co. Ltd., 2004—05, Japan Airlines Domestic Co. Ltd., 2004—05. Co-chaired 28th ASEAN-

Japan Bus. Meeting; chmn. Internat. Air Transport Assn., 2002—04; vice-chmn. Japan Assn. Corp. Executives. Avocations: basketball, reading. Office: Japan Airlines Internat Co 4-11 Higashi Shinagawa Shinagawa-ku Tokyo 140 Japan

KANEKO, MASAO, radiology educator, researcher, specialist; b. Nagoya, Japan, May 6, 1933; s. Gensaku and Kaneko (Kitagawa) K.; m. Sachiko Yamazaki, May 11, 1961; children: Tomoo, Akio, Takeo. MD, Nagoya U., 1958, PhD, 1965. Intern St. Luke's Internat. Hosp., Tokyo, 1958-59; rsch. asst. Nagoya U., 1964, asst. prof., 1971-74; sect. chief Aichi Cancer Ctr., Nagoya, 1965-71; rsch. fellow UCLA, 1960-61; assoc. prof. radiology Hamamatsu U. Sch. Medicine, Japan, 1974-76, prof., 1976—99. Head radiology Hamamatsu U. Hosp., 1977-99; dir. Hamamatsu Red Cross Blood Ctr., 1999-2003, Tokoha Rehab. Hosp., 2003-. Author: Radiological Protection, 1982, Medical Optical Tomography, 1993. Recipient discovery promotion award Japan Discovery Assn., 1980. Mem. Japan Radiol. Soc. (emeritus; councilor), Radiol. Soc. N.Am. (corr.), Assn. Univ. Radiologists. Avocation: listening to classical music. Home: 347-5 Hatsuoi-cho Kita-ku Hamamatsu 433-8112 Japan Office: Tokoha Rehab Hosp 130 Nearai-Cho Kita-ku Hamamatsu 433-8108 Japan Home Phone: 81 53 436 7571. Home Fax: 81 53 436 7571. Personal E-mail: m.kaneko@oboe.ocn.ne.jp. Business E-Mail: d-tokoha-r-h@mail.wbs.ne.jp.

KANELLOS, NICOLÁS, language and liberal studies educator; b. NYC, Jan. 31, 1945; s. Constantino and Inés (de Choudens) K.; m. Cristelia Pérez, May 12, 1984; 1 child, Miguel José. BA in Spanish, Fairleigh Dickinson U., 1966; MA in Romance Langs., U. Tex., 1968, PhD in Spanish and Portuguese, 1974; postgrad. in Mexican Lit. and Culture, U. Autónoma Mex., Mexico City, 1964-65; postgrad. in Portuguese Lit. and Culture, U. Lisboa, Portugal, 1969-70; LHD (hon.), U. Ariz., 2001. From asst. to assoc. prof. Ind. U. N.W., Gary, 1970-79; assoc. prof. U. Houston, 1979-85, prof., 1985—, Brown Found. prof., endowed chair, 1996—. Founder, dir. Teatro Desengano del Pueblo, Gary, 1972-79; founder, pub. Arte Publico Press/U. Houston, 1979—; pub. The Americas Rev., 1973-99; apptd. Lit. Policy Panel NEA, 1987-90; apptd. to Arts Adv. Com., Ednl. Testing Svc./The Coll. Bd., 1987; apptd. Pres. Clinton Nat. Coun. on the Humanities, 1994; disting. vis. scholar Ctr. Humanities and Arts U. Ga., 2003; lectr., presenter in field Author: Mexican American Theatre: Legacy and Reality, 1987, Hispanic Bibliography, 1988, Biographical Dictionary of Hispanic Literature in the United States up to World War II, 1990, The History of Hispanic Theatre in the United States up to World War II, 1990 (SW Conf. Lat. Am. Studies Book award, 1991, Tex. Inst. Letters award, 1991, San Antonio Conservation Soc. Book award, 1990), A History of Hispanic Theatre in the United States: Origins to 1940, 1990, (chpts.) The Hispanic American Almanac: A Reference Work on Hispanics in the United States, 1993 (ALA award best reference work, 1990), 2004, Hispanic Almanac, 1994, Chronology of Hispanic American History, 1995; author: (edited with Bryan Ryan) Hispanic American Chronology, 1995; author: Hispanic Firsts: Three Hundred Years of Outstanding Achievement, 1997, Thirty Million Strong: Reclaiming the Hispanic Image in U.S. History, 1998, The Adventures of Don Chipote: When Parrots Breast Feed, 1999, Hispanic Periodicals in the United States: A Brief History and Comprehensive Bibliography, 2000, Los aventuras de Don Chipote, o Cuando los pericos mamen, 1985, 2000, Lucas Guevara, Spanish edit., 2001, English edit., 2003, Hispanic Literature of the United States: A Comprehensive Reference, 2004; author, prodr. Lalo Astol: El teatro en mi vida, 1982, author, rschr. The Bilingual Education Controversy: A Houston Perspective, 1982, author, cons. (brochure) Two Centuries of Hispanic Theater in the United States, 1984—85, Our Journeys/'Our Stories: Portraits of Latino Cambios/Nuestras Historias: Restratos del Logro Latino, 2004; editor (with Jorge Huerta): Nuevos Pasos: Chicano and Puerto Rican Drama, 1979, 2d edit., 1989; editor: (with Luis Dávila) Latino Short Fiction, 1980; editor: (with Robert E. Beck, Sharon L. Belshaw, others) (textbook series) Introduction to Literature, 1981, Exploring Literature, 1981, Understanding Literature, 1981, Types of Literature, 1981, American Literature, 1981, English Literature, 1981; editor: Mexican American Theater: Then and Now, 1983, Las aventuras de Don Chipote, 1984, English transl., 2000, Spanish transl., 2001, Hispanic Theater in the United States, 1985, Biographical Dictionary of Hispanic Literature in the United States, 1989, Short Fiction by U.S. Hispanic Authors, 1993, Hispanic American Almanac: A Reference Work on Hispanics in the United States, 1993, 2d edit., 2004; editor: (with Claudio Esteva Fabregat) Handbook of Hispanic Cultures in the United States, 1994; editor: Hispanic American Literature, 1995; co-editor: (textbooks for high sch. English) Ginn Literature Series, 2nd edit., 1989; mem. editl. bd. Latin Am. Theatre Rev., 1982—, Critica, 1983—, Confluencia, 1984—, SW Rev., 1990—, Latino Studies Jour., 1990—, MELUS, 1999—, Theater in the Ams. series; contbr. articles to profl. jours., chapters to books; editor, compiler The Hispanic Literary Companion, 1996, Noche Buena: Hispanic American Christmas Stories, 2000;: Noche Buena: Hispanic American Christmas Stories, 2000; gen. editor: Herencia: The Anthology of Hispanic Literature of the United States, 2002; dir. gen. En otra vez: antología de la literatura hispana de los Estados Unidos, 2002. Member Ind. Civil Rights Commn., Gary, 1974-75; mem. arts adv. com. NY Coll. Bd., 1989—; lit. cons. NEA, Washington, 1985-90; pres. Bishop's Com. Spanish Speaking, Gary, 1974-76; dir. nat. project. Named in honor of achievement as scholar, critic and educator, Soc. Study Multiethnic Lit. Modern Lang. Assn., 1980, 100 Most Influential Hispanic in US, Hispanic Bus. mag., 1989, 1993, 1997—98, Disting. Vis. Scholar, Ctr. Humanities and Arts, U. Ga., 2003; named to Tex. Inst. Letters, 1984, 1st Brown Found. Endowed Chair, U. Houston, 1996, Wall of Tolerance, Nat. Campaign Tolerance, 2003; recipient Outstanding Editor award, Coord. Coun. Lit. Mags., 1979, Hispanic Heritage award, Pres. Reagan, 1988, award, Tex. Assn. Chicanos Higher Edn., 1989, Commendation Gov. Tex. high stds. acad. excellence, 1989, Am. Book award pub., editor category, 1989, Best Reference Work of 1993 award, ALA, 1994, Denali Press award, 1996, PREMIO award, Hispanic Pub. Rels. Assn., 1995, Esther Farfel award, U. Houston, 1995, Hispanic Publ. award, Hispanic Caucus Am. Assn. Higher Edn., 1996, award for best article in MELUS, 1999, Estrella award, Assn. Hispanic Sch. Adminstrs., 2001, U. Houston award excellence in rsch. and scholarship, 2001, Cert. of Recognition, Tex. Inst. Letters, 2003, Houston Lit. Achievement award, Barnes and Noble and Bookstop, 2003, Golden Book award, Tex. Coun. for Reading and the Bilingual Child, 2005; fellow, NEH, 1979, Ford Found./NRC, 1986—87; Summer fellow, Ind. U., 1974, 1976, Eli Lilli Faculty Open fellow, 1976—77, Calouste Gulbenkian fellow rsch. in Portugal, 1976—90. Mem.: MLA (NYC chpt., lectr.), Tex. Com. Humanities, Coll. Bd. Task Force Arts in Edn., Nat. Coun. Humanities, Nat. Assn. Puerto Rican Studies, Nat. Assn. Chicano Studies, Hispanic Forum Houston, Inst. Hispanic Culture of Houston, Hispanic Soc. Am. (assoc.; hon., hon.), Am. Antiquarian Soc. Avocations: jogging, tennis, guitar, singing. Office: U Houston Arte Publico Press Houston TX 77204-0001 also: U Houston Dept Modern and Classical Langs 413 Agnes Arnold Hall Houston TX 77204-3006 Office Phone: 713-743-3128. Business E-Mail: artrec@mail.uh.edu.

KANET, ROGER EDWARD, political science professor; b. Cin., Sept. 1, 1936; s. Robert George and Edith Mary (Weaver) K.; m. Joan Alice Edwards, Feb. 16, 1963; children: Suzanne Elise Zelle, Laurie Alice Burhart. PhB, Berchmanskolleg, Pullach-bei-Muenchen, Ger., 1960; AB, Xavier U., Cin., 1961; MA, Lehigh U., 1963; AM, Princeton U., 1965, PhD, 1966. Asst. prof. polit. sci. U. Kans., Lawrence, 1966-69, assoc. prof., 1969-74; joint sr. fellow Russian Inst. and Rsch. Inst. Communist Affairs, Columbia U., NYC, 1972-73; from vis. assoc. prof. to assoc. prof. to prof. U. Ill., Champaign-Urbana, 1973—97, prof. emeritus, 1997—, head dept. polit. sci., 1984—87, assoc. vice chancellor for acad. affairs, dir. internat. programs and studies, 1989—97; prof. dept. internat. studies U. Miami, Fla., 1997—, dean Sch. Internat. Studies, 1997—2000, dir. undergrad. studies, 2002—04. Partipant exch. with Hungary and Poland, Internat. Rsch. and Exchs. Bd., 1976; cons. Inst. Pub. Policy Devel., Washington, 1977-79; assoc. Ctr. Advanced Study, U. Ill., 1981-82; mem. Coun. on Fgn. Rels., NY, 1991—; mem. Chgo. Coun. on Fgn. Rels., 1993-97; chair internat. edn. panel Com. Instl. Coop. Big 10 & Chgo., 1993-96; co-founder Ill. Consortium for Internat. Edn. Editor, co-editor: The Behavioral Revolution and Communist Studies, 1971, On the Road to Communism, 1972, The Soviet Union and the Developing Countries, 1974, Soviet and East European Policy, 1974, Soviet Economic and Political Relations with the Developing World, 1975, Background to Crisis: Policy and Politics in Gierek's Poland, 1981, Soviet Foreign Policy and East-West Relations, 1982, Soviet Foreign Policy in the 1980s, 1982, The Soviet Union, Eastern Europe and the Third World, 1987, Asia in Soviet Global Strategy, 1987, The Limits of Soviet Power in the Developing World: Thermidor in the Revolutionary Struggle, 1989, The Cold War as Cooperation: Superpower Cooperation in Regional Conflict Management, 1991, Soviet Foreign Policy in Transition, 1992, Regional Conflicts and Conflict Resolution, 1995, Coping with Conflict After the Cold War, 1996, Foreign Policy of the Russian Fed., 1997, Resolving Regional Conflicts, 1998, The New Security Environment. The Impact on Russian, Ctrl. and Ea. Europe, 2005, Russia: Re-emerging Great Power, 2007, From Superpower to Besieged Global Power: Restoring World Order After the Failure of the Bush Doctrine, 2008; guest editor spl. issue jours. including Nationalities Papers, 2007, Internat. Politics, 2008; contbr. more than 325 articles to scholarly jours. and books. Co-founder, pres. Kans. Parents Assn. Hearing-Handicapped Children, 1968-70. Recipient US Dept. State Rsch. award, 1976, Excellence in Undergrad. Teaching award U. Ill., 1981, 84, Faculty Achievement award Burlington No. Found., 1989, US Inst. Peace award, 1991; fellow NDEA, 1963-66, NATO, 1976, Internat. fellow Fed. Inst. for East European and Internat. Studies, Cologne, Fed. Republic of Germany, 1988; Am. Coun. Learned Socs. grantee, 1972-73, 78. Mem. Am. Assn. Advancement of Slavic Studies, Assn. Internat. Studies Assn. (chmn. Am.-Soviet rels. sect. 1990-92), Internat. Coun. for Ctrl. and Ea. European Studies (program chmn. 1st World Congress 1974, mem. program com. and gen. editor conf. publs. 7th World Congress 2005). Liberal. Roman Catholic. Home: 9225 SW 142d St Miami FL 33176 Office Phone: 305-284-3407. Business E-Mail: rkanet@miami.edu.

KANE-VANNI, PATRICIA RUTH, lawyer, paleontologist, educator; d. Joseph James and Ruth Marina (Ramirez); m. Francis William Vanni, Feb. 14, 1981; 1 child, Christian Michael. AB, Chestnut Hill Coll., 1975; JD, Temple U., 1985; postgrad., U. Pa. Bar: Pa. 1985, US Ct. Appeals (3d cir.) 1988. Freelance art illustrator, Phila., 1972—; secondary edn. instr. Archdiocese of Phila., Pa., 1980-83; contract analyst CIGNA Corp., Phila., 1983-84; jud. aide Phila. Ct. of Common Pleas, Pa., 1984; assoc. atty. Anderson and Dougherty, Wayne, Pa., 1985-86; atty. cons. Bell Tele. Co. of Pa., Pa., 1986-87; sr. assoc. corp. counsel Independence Blue Cross, Phila., 1987-96; pvt. practice law, 1996-97; dinosaur educator Acad. Natural Scis., Phila., 1997—; counsel Reliance Ins. Co., Phila., 1998—2000, contract atty., 2000—03; atty. Westmont Assoc., Haddonfield, NJ, 2002; legal counsel Housing Authority, Phila., 2003—05, atty. counsel, 2005—07; sr. corp. counsel Blue Cross of NE Pa., Wilkes-Barre, 2007—. Atty. cons., 1996-2003; counsel Reliance Ins. Co., Phila., 1998-2000, contract atty., 2000-2003; atty. Westmont Assoc., Haddonfield, NJ, 2002; legal counsel, Housing Authority, Phila., Pa., 2003-05, atty. counsel 2005—; cons. Coll. Consortium on Drug and Alcohol Abuse, Chester, Pa., 1986-89; paleo-sci. educator Pa. Acad. Natural Sci., 1997—; paleontology field expdns. include Mont., 1999. 2000, Isle of Wight, Eng., 1999, Bahariya Oasis, Egypt, 2000; spkr. in field. Contbr. articles and illustrations to profl. mag.; performer: Phila. Revels., 2001 03, 04. Judge Del. Valley Sci. Fairs, Phila., 1986, 87, 98, 99; Dem. committeewomen, Lower Merion, Pa., 1983-87; ch. cantor, soloist, mem. choir Roman Cath. Ch.; bd. dir. Phila. Assn. Ch. Musicians. Recipient Legion of Honor award Chapel of the Four Chaplins, 1983. Mem. ABA, Pa. Bar Assn., Phila. Bar Assn. (Theatre Wing), Phila. Assn. Def. Counsel, Phila. Vol. Lawyers for Arts (bd. dir.), Nat. Health Lawyers Assn. (spkr. 1994 ann. conv.), Hispanic Bar Assn., Soc. Vertebrate Paleontology, Pa. Acad. Nat. Sci. (vol.), Delaware Valley Paleontol. Soc. (v.p. 1998—); Guild of Natural Sci. Illustrators, DAR Independence Hall Chpt. Democrat. Avocations: choral and solo vocal music, portrait painting and illustrating, paleontology. Home: 119 Bryn Mawr Ave Bala Cynwyd PA 19004-3012 Personal E-mail: pkv1@erols.com, Paleopatti@hotmail.com.

KANFER, JULIAN NORMAN, biochemist, educator; b. Bklyn., May 23, 1930; s. Benjamin N. and Clara (Lichtenberger) K.; m. Beverly Kanfer; children— Brian, Rachel, Addison Slaeton Cressa. BSc, Bklyn. Coll., 1954; MSc, George Washington U., 1958, PhD, 1961. Biochemist Mass. Gen. Hosp., Boston, 1969-75; dir. biochem. research E.K. Shriver Center, Waltham, Mass.; also dir. research W.E. Fernald State Sch., Waltham, 1969-75; adj. asso. prof. biochemistry Brandeis U., Waltham, 1969-75; asso. prof. neuropathology Harvard, 1969-75, prin. research assoc., 1974-75; prof. U. Man., Winnipeg, Can., 1975—, head dept. biochemistry, 1975—. Cons. Health Scis. Centre, Winnipeg, 1976—; mem. med. adv. bd. Nat. Tay-Sachs Found., N.Y.C., 1970—; mem. study sect. on pathobiol. chemistry NIH, 1974—; postdoctoral fellowship com. NRC, 1983—; mem. Grant Commn. Nutrition and Metabolism Med. Rsch. Coun., Can., 1992—; vis. prof. dept. psychiatry U. Pitts. Med. Ctr., 1993-94; vis. prof. Stetson U., Deland, Fla., 1998—; adj. Daytona Beach C.C. Contbr. articles to profl. jours. Bd. dirs. Winnipeg chpt. Multiple Sclerosis Soc. Can., 1976. Named Hon. Citizen of New Orleans, 1997, Fellow Inst. de la Sante et de la Recherche Medicale (France); mem. Am. Soc. Biol. Chemistry, Am., Internat. neurochemistry socs., Am. Chem. Soc., AAAS, Soc. for Complex Carbohydrates, Fedn. Am. Socs. for Exptl. Biology, Can. Fedn. Biol. Socs., Canadian Biochem. Soc. Office: 1415 Ocean Shore Blvd Ormond Beach FL 32176-3673

KANG, ALVIN, bank executive; Field agent trainee IRS, LA; ptnr. KPMG LLP, Ernst & Young LLP; COO, CFO Broadway Fed. Bank; CFO Broadway Fin. Corp., Nara Bancorp, Inc., 2005—. Fin. officer, first lt. US Army, Fort Meade U.S. Army Base Md. Office: Nara Bancorp Inc 3731 Wilshire Blvd Ste 1000 Los Angeles CA 90010 Office Phone: 213-639-1700. Office Fax: 213-235-3033.*

KANG, BANN C., immunologist; b. Kyungnam, Korea, Mar. 4, 1939; d. Daeryong and Buni (Chung) K.; came to U.S., 1964, naturalized, 1976; A.B., Kyungpook Nat. U., 1959, M.D., 1963; m. U. Yun Ryo, Mar. 30, 1963. Intern, L.I. Jewish Hosp.-Queens Hosp. Center, Jamaica, N.Y., 1964-65, resident in medicine, 1965-67; teaching assoc. Kyungpook U. Hosp., Taegu, Korea, 1967-70; fellow in allergy and chest Creighton U., Omaha, 1970-71; fellow in allergy Henry Ford Hosp., Detroit, 1971-72; clin. instr. medicine U. Mich. Hosp., Ann Arbor, 1972-73; asst. prof. Chgo. Med. Sch., 1973-74; chief allergy-immunology Mt. Sinai Hosp., Chgo., 1975—; asst. prof. Rush Med. Sch., Chgo. 1975-84, assoc. prof., 1984-86; assoc. prof. U. Ky. Coll. Medicine, 1987-92, prof., 1992-2002, prof. emeritus, 2003—; cons., 1976—, Nat. Heart, Lung, Blood Inst., 1979—; mem. Exptl. Transplantation Adv. Bd., Ill., 1985-86, Diagnostic and Therapeutic Tech. Assessment (AMA), 1987—, Gen. Clin. Rsch. Com. (NIH), 1989-93; adv. com. Ctr. for Biologics and Rsch., FDA, 1993-96; counselor Chgo. Med. Soc., 1984-86, mem. policy com., adv. com. to health dept. Chgo. and Cook County, 1984-86. Recipient NIH award U. Mich., 1972-73. Diplomate Am. Bd. Internal Medicine, Am. Bd. Allergy-Immunology. Fellow ACP, Am. Acad. Allergy; mem. Am. Fedn. Clin. Research, AMA, Inter-Asthma Assn. Contbr. over 50 articles to profl. jours.

KANG, BENJAMIN TOYEONG, journalist, minister; b. Republic of Korea, Mar. 30, 1931; came to U.S., 1963, naturalized, 1979; s. Tae-Un and Kumjoo (Lee) K.; m. Katherine Chungcha Chung, Apr. 29, 1955; children: Jennifer, Mira, Gregory. BA, Yonsei U., Republic of Korea, 1954; MA, Kyungbuk U., Republic of Korea, 1959; BD, Temple U., 1967; ThD, Internat. Sem., 1981. Ordained to ministry Christian Ch., 1970. Instr. Yonsei U., 1956-58; exec. dir. Kyungju YMCA, Republic of Korea, 1958-59; asst. prof. Keimyoung U., Republic of Korea, 1959-61; pastor Korean Ch. of Lower Bucks, Levittown, Pa., 1974-84; pres. Korean Sch. of Lower Bucks, 1980-82; pastor Korean Gloria Ch., Phila., 1981-89; parish assoc. First Presbyn. Ch., Levittown, 1990—. Freelance writer, 1992—; columnist Dong-A Daily News, 1992-94, 99—, Christian Post, 2004-. Author: (hymn) In a Strange Land, 1992, The Wisdom to Live the American Life, 2005. Trustee Presbytery of Phila., Presbyn. Ch. USA, 1982-88, Met. Christian Coun. Phila., 1984-88, Coun. Korean Chs. in Phila., 1985-89; comdr. Vol. Student Army Kyungju, Republic of Korea, 1950-51. Home: 3128 Benjamin Rush Ct Bensalem PA 19020-1903

KANG, CHIL-YONG, virologist, immunology educator; b. Hadong, Kyung-Nahm, Republic of Korea, Nov. 28, 1940; arrived in Can., 1966, naturalized, 1971; s. Whashik and Ungee (Song) K.; m. Myung-Ja Oh (Kang), Dec. 17, 1966; children: Julie, Rosanne, Matthew. Diploma in Vet. Sci., Malling Agrl. Coll., Denmark, 1963; BSA, Kon-Kuk U., Korea, 1965; PhD, McMaster U., Hamilton, Ont., 1971; DSc, Carleton U., 1991. Postdoctoral fellow U. Wis., Madison, 1971—74; asst. prof. Southwestern Med. Sch. U. Tex., Dallas, 1974—78, assoc. prof. Southwestern Med. Sch., 1978—82; prof., chmn. dept. microbiology, immunology U. Ottawa, Ont., Canada, 1982—92; dir. U. Ottawa Biotech. Inst., Ont., 1987—92; dean sci., prof. medicine U. Western Ont., Canada, 1992—99, prof. virology, 1992—. Contbr. articles to profl. jours. Office: U Western Ont Siebens-Drake Inst Rm 129 1400 Western Rd London ON Canada N6G 2V4 Home Phone: 579-850-0718; Office Phone: 519-858-5125. Business E-Mail: cykang@uwo.ca.

KANG, HEESAM, investment analyst, educator; b. Taejon, Republic of Korea, Oct. 26, 1964; s. Doosik Kang and Bunok Jung; m. Myounghee Im, Jan. 11, 2003. BBA, Yonsei U., Seoul, 1990; MBA, Okla. City U., 1993; PhD, U. Tex., Arlington, 2002. Acting chief fin. sect. Kyungnam Chem. Inc., Taejon, Republic of Korea, 1989—91; grad. tchg. assoc. U. Tex., Arlington, 1997—2001; asst. prof. Bacone Coll., Muskogee, Okla., 2001—. Mem.: Fin. Mgmt. Assn. (assoc.). Avocations: fishing, travel. Address: 424 Burbank St Muskogee OK 74403 Office Phone: 918-781-7240. Business E-Mail: kangh@bacone.edu.

KANG, HONG TAE, engineering educator; PhD in Engring. Mechanics, U. Ala., Tuscaloosa. Asst. prof. U. Mich., Dearborn, 2003—. Mem.: ASME. Office: Univ Michigan 4901 Evergreen Rd Dearborn MI 48128

KANG, HYUN WOOK, research scientist; s. Dae Sung Kang and Myung Ae Kim; m. Min Ji Kim, Nov. 19, 2006. BS in Mech. Engring., Yonsei U., Seoul, 1994—2002; MME, U. Tex., Austin, 2002—04, PhD in Biomedical Engring., 2005—06. Rsch. asst. U. Tex., 2003—06; rsch. scientist Am. Med. Sys., Minnetonka, Minn., 2006—. Tchg. asst. U. Tex., 2005. Contbr. articles to profl. jours. Vol. St. Andrew Kim Ch., St. Paul. Pvt. 1st class Seung-Nam (K16), 1996—98, Kyung-ki, Rep. Korea. Grantee, Whitaker Found., 2004, Am. Soc. Laser Medicine and Surgery, 2004. Mem.: IEEE, Optical Soc. Am., Internat. Soc. Optical Engring. Achievements include patents pending for method for detection of atherosclerosis using the noninvasive photoacoustic technique assisted with biocompatible nanoparticles; research in laser ablation of tissue and materials; photoacoustic molecular imaging; thermal therapeutics on BPH treatment; laser therapeutics on BPH. Home Phone: 512-608-1602.

KANG, ISAMU YONG, retired nuclear medicine physician; b. Osaka, Japan, Aug. 27, 1939; came to U.S., 1966; s. Chi-Chieh and Ichi (Morita) K.; m. Midori Ishibashi, Mar. 15, 1971; children: Rika Florence, Hiroshi Frederick. MD, Kyushu U., Fukuoka, Japan, 1965. Diplomate Am. Bd. Pathology, Am. Bd. Nuc. Medicine. Intern Grad. Hosp. U. Pa., Phila., 1967-68; resident in pathology U. Calif., San Diego, 1972-74, Letterman Army Med. Ctr., San Francisco, 1974-76; resident in nuclear medicine Walter Reed Army Med Ctr., Washington, 1976-78; asst. chief nuclear medicine Walter Reed Army Med. Ctr., Washington, 1978-80; co-dir. clin. lab., nuclear med. staff physician Kaiser Permanente Med. Ctr., Oakland, Calif., 1980-86, chief nuclear medicine Walnut Creek, Calif., 1986—2000, radiation safety officer, 1986—2005; ret., 2005. Lt. col. U.S. Army, 1969-80, Vietnam; col. USAR, 1980-99, ret. Mem. Soc. Nuc. Medicine, Calif. Med. Assn. Buddhist. Avocations: jogging, golf, tennis, carpentry, reading. Home: 3554 Via Los Colorados Lafayette CA 94549-5332 Personal E-mail: i-kang@sbcglobal.net.

KANG, JING X., medical researcher, educator; PhD, MD. Assoc. prof. medicine Harvard Med. Sch.; prin. investigator Mass. General Hosp., Cardiovascular Rsch. Ctr. Contbr. articles to profl. jours. Studies the health effects of omega-3 polyunsaturated fatty acids, how they work and how genetic technologies can be used to further the benefits. Office: Cardiovascular Rsch Ctr Richard B Simches Rsch Ctr Ste 3209 185 Cambridge St Boston MA 02114 also: Cardiovascular Rsch Ctr Gate 5 Charleston Navy Yard 13th St Bldg 149 4th Fl Charlestown MA 02129 also: Cardiovascular Rsch Ctr 149 13th St Charlestown MA 02129 Home Phone: 978-682-0618; Office Phone: 617-726-8509. Office Fax: 617-726-6144. Business E-Mail: kang.jing@mgh.harvard.edu.

KANG, JUN-KOO, finance educator; 1 child, Clare J. BS in Bus. Adminstrn., Korea U., 1981; PhD, Ohio State U., Columbus, 1986—91. Asst. prof. U. R.I., Kingston, 1991—95, U. Calif., Riverside, 1995—96; assoc. prof. Korea U., Seoul, 1996—99; prof., fin. Mich. State U., East Lansing, 1999—, fed. credit union chair, fin., instns. and investments, 2001—. Assoc. editor Korean Jour. of Fin., Seoul, 1997—98, Internat. Rev. of Fin., Oxford, 1998—, Japan and the World Economy, Amsterdam, 2005—, Fin. Studies, Seoul, 2005—; editor Pacific-Basin Fin. Jour., Amsterdam, 2006—. Recipient Outstanding Paper award, U. R.I., 1994, Best Paper award, Korean Jour. of Fin., 2003, 2005, PACAP Best Paper award, Asian Fin. Assn., 2004, Excellence in Tchg. award, Mich. State U., 2004. Fellow: Asian Inst. Corp. Governance (assoc.); mem.: Korean Fin. Assn. (life), Korean and Am. Fin. Assn. (life), Pacific-Basin Fin. Mgmt. Soc. (life), Am. Economics Assn. (life), Am. Fin. Assn. (life), Western Fin. Assn. (life). Office: Mich State Univ Dept Finance Eppley 343 East Lansing MI 48824 Business E-Mail: kangju@msu.edu.

KANG, JU-SEOP, medical educator, consultant, medical researcher; b. Cheju, Republic of Korea, Feb. 2, 1961; s. Yong-Hee Lee; m. Tae-Eun Kim; children: Ji-Sook, Hyun-Sook, Ryun. PhD, Hanyang U., Seoul, 1993. Diplomate Korea Food and Drug Adminstrn., Korea Rsch. Found. Rsch. and tchg. asst. Hanyang U., Republic of Korea, 1988—92, asst. prof. Seoul, 1993—2002, assoc. prof., 2003—04; vis. scholar Hosp. U. Pa., Phila., 2000—06, assoc. prof., 2004—06, mem. edn. com., 2005—, chief sec. Inst. Biomed. Scis., 2005—, chief dept. pharmacology, head Hanyang Food and Drug Adminstrn. Ctr., 2005—. Dir. Mil. Gen. Lab., Republic of Korea, 1994—97; mem. drug rev. com. Korean Food and Drug Adminstrn., Seoul, 2000—02; mem. com. office rsch. integrity Hanyang U., Republic of Korea, 2007—. Author: Pharmacokinetic Books, Applied Pharmacokinetics, 2001; contbr. articles to profl. jours. Capt. Korean Mil., 1994—97. Mem.: Korean Soc. Food Sci. and Tech., Internat. Assn. Therapeutic Drug Monitoring and Clin. Toxicology, Korean Assn. Clin. Pharmacology and Therapeutics, Korean Assn. Pharmacology, Korean Assn. Applied Pharmacology. Avocation: golf. Office: Hosp Univ Pa Spruce St Philadelphia PA 19104 also: Hanyang Univ Pharmacology Coll Medicine 17 Haengdang Dong Sungdong Ku Seoul 133791 Republic of Korea Home: Hyundai Apt 106-301 Ungbong-dong Sungdong-ku Seoul 133-797 Republic of Korea Office Phone: 82-2-2220-0652. Business E-Mail: jskang@hanyang.ac.kr.

KANG, KYEONGPYO, transportation engineer, researcher; b. Seoul, July 17, 1970; s. Wansoon Kang and Kilsoon Kim; m. Misook Lee, Aug. 16, 1998; 1 child, Donghyo. Postgrad., U. Md., 2001—06; PhD in Transp. Engring. Cert. transp. engr., Korea. Rschr. Seoul Devel. Inst., 1998—2001; rsch. asst. U. Md., College Park, 2002—. Part-time rschr. Rsch. Assn. Rd. Traffic Safety, Seoul, 1997—98; presenter in field. Sgt. Republic of Korea Marine Corps, 1990—93. Mem.: Korean-Am. Scientists and Engrs. Assn. (scholar 2005). Home: 4335 Rowalt Dr # 303 College Park MD 20740 Office: U Md 1173 Glenn L Martin Hall College Park MD 20742 Home Phone: 301-927-5018; Office Phone: 301-405-6959. Office Fax: 301-405-2585. Personal E-mail: kkyeongpyo@hotmail.com. Business E-Mail: kpkang@wam.umd.edu.

KANG, QINJUN, mathematician; PhD in Mech. Engring., Johns Hopkins U., Balt., 1999—2003. Postdoctoral rschr. Los Alamos Nat. Lab., N.Mex., 2003—05, tech. staff mem., 2005—. Office: Los Alamos Nat Lab MS T003 Los Alamos NM 87545

KANG, SUNG-MO (STEVE KANG), electrical engineering educator; b. Seoul, Korea, Feb. 25, 1945; came to U.S., 1969; s. Chang-Shik and Kyung-Ja (Lee) K.; m. Myoung-A Cha, June 10, 1972; children: Jennifer, Jeffrey. BSEE, Fairleigh Dickinson U., 1970; MSEE, SUNY, Buffalo, 1972; PhD in Elec. Engring., U. Calif., Berkeley, 1975. Asst. prof. Rutgers U., Piscataway, NJ, 1975-77; mem. tech. staff AT&T Bell Labs., Murray Hill, NJ, 1977-82, supr., 1982-85; prof. U. Ill., Urbana, 1985-2000, head dept. electrical and computer engring., 1995-2000, assoc. Ctr. for Advanced Study, 1991-92, assoc. dir. microelectronics lab., 1988-95; univ. scholar U. Ill., Urbana, 1995-96. Dir. Ctr. for ASIC R&D, dean sch. engring. U. Calif., Santa Cruz, 2001—; pres. Silicon Valley Engring. Coun., 2002-03. Author 9 books; contbr. over 350 papers to internat. jours. and confs.; 12 patents. Recipient Meritorious Svc. award Cirs. and Sys. Soc., 1994, Humboldt Rsch. award for Sr. U.S. Scientists, 1996, Grad. Teaching award IEEE, 1996, IEEE CAS Soc. Tech. Achievement award, 1997, KBS award in Sci. and Tech., 1998, SRC Tech. Excellence award, 1999, Alumnus award U. Calif., Berkeley, 2001. Fellow AAAS, ACM, IEEE (various offices in Circuits and Systems Soc. including pres. 1991, founding editor-in-chief Trans. on VSLI systems, Disting. lectr. 1994-97, 2003-, Darlington award, SRC Inventor Recognition award 1993, 96, 99, 2001, 02, Meritorious Svc. award Computer Soc. 1990, CAS Soc. Golden Jubilee medal 1999, Millennium medal 2000, Mac Van Valkenburg award, 2005, Chang-Lin Tien Edn. Leadership award 2007), Nat. Acad. Engring. of Korea (fgn. mem.). Presbyterian. Avocations: tennis, travel. Office: U Calif Baskin Sch Engring Santa Cruz CA 95064 Home Phone: 831-421-9330; Office Phone: 831-459-2158. E-mail: kang@soe.ucsc.edu.

KANG, YOOGOO, anesthesiologist, educator; b. Seoul, Apr. 10, 1946; s. Kiduk and Samkum (Koh) K.; m. Young H. Kim, Nov. 9, 1972; children: Michael N., David H. BS, Seoul U., Republic of, 1967, MD, 1971. Diplomate Am. Bd. Anesthesiology. Intern St. Raphael Hosp., New Haven, Conn., 1974-75; resident in surgery Albert Einstein Med. Ctr., Phila., 1975-76; resident in anesthesiology Thomas Jefferson U. Hosp., Phila., 1976-78; fellow in obstetric anesthesia Magee Women's Hosp., Pitts., 1978-79; asst. prof. U. Pitts., 1979-88, dir. hepatic transplantation anesthesiology, 1984-98, assoc. prof., 1989-93, prof., 1994-98; prof., chmn. dept. anesthesiology Tulane U. Med. Ctr., New Orleans, 1998-2000; prof. vice chmn. dept. anesthesiology Thomas Jefferson U., Phila., 2000—. Head Internat. Symposium in Liver Transplantation, Pitts., 1984-88. Editor: Hepatic Transplantation: Anesthetic Management and Perioperative Care, 1985, Anesthesia and Intensive Care for Patients with Liver Diseasae, 1995; assoc. editor Liver Surgery and Transplantation, 1993—; mem. editl. bd. Current Opinions in Organ Transplantation, 1996—. Med. officer Korean Army, 1971-74. Mem. Am. Soc. Anesthesiologists, Internat. Soc. Rsch. in Anesthesiology, Internat. Liver Transplantation Soc. (pres. 1989-93, mem. exec. coun. 1993-95, adv. bd. 1995—), Liver Intensive Care Group Europe. Avocations: woodwork, photography. Office: Thomas Jefferson U Dept Anesthesiology 111 S 11th St Ste 5480 Gibb Philadelphia PA 19107-5092 Business E-Mail: yoogoo.kang@jefferson.edu.

KANGAS, EDWARD A., healthcare company and former diversified financial services company executive; b. 1942; m. Catherine Elizabeth Stephens, Sept. 17, 1994. BBA, U. Kansas, 1967, MBA. CPA NY, Conn. CPA, staff acct. Touche Ross & Co., Kansas City, 1967-74, ptnr., 1975-76, dir. mgmt. consulting ops., 1976-81, nat. dir. mgmt. consulting, 1981-85, mng. ptnr., CEO NYC, 1985-89; also CEO Touche Ross Internat.; mng. ptnr. Deloitte and Touche USA LLP, NYC, 1989-94; global chmn, chief exec. Deloitte Touche Tohmatsu Internat., 1989—2000; cons. Deloitte Touche, Wilton, Conn., 2000—; non-exec. chmn. Tenet Healthcare Corp., Dallas, 2003—. Bd. dirs. Electric Data Systems Corp., 2004—, Intuit Inc., 2007—, Eclipsys Corp., Hovnanian Enterprises, Inc., Com. for Econ. Develop.; chmn. Oncology Therapeutics Networks. Bd. dirs., mem. fin. com., mem. and chmn. fund raising com. Nat. Multiple Sclerosis Soc.; trustee Com. Econ. Devel., U. Kansas Endowment Assn.; bd. overseers The Wharton Sch.; mem. U. Kansas Bus. Sch. Advisors Office: Tenet Healthcare Corp 13737 Noel Rd Dallas TX 75240*

KANICK, VIRGINIA, retired radiologist; b. Coaldale, Pa., Nov. 10, 1925; d. Martin and Anna (Pisklak) K. BA, Barnard Coll., 1947; MD, Columbia U., 1951. Diplomate Am. Bd. Radiology. Intern Western Reserve U. Hosps., Cleve., 1951-52; resident in radiology St. Luke's Hosp., NYC, 1952-55, attending radiologist, 1955-74; acting dir. radiology St. Luke's Roosevelt Hosp., NYC, 1981-84, dep. dir. of radiology, 1984-89; ptnr. West Side Radiology, NYC, 1989—2003; ret., 2003. Clin. prof. radiology Coll. Physicians and Surgeons Columbia U., N.Y.C., 1975—; pres. Med. Bd. St. Luke's Roosevelt Hosp., 1980-82. Contbr. articles to profl. jours. Bd. dirs. Health System Agy. of N.Y.C., 1978-81. Fellow Am. Cancer Soc., 1955. Fellow Am. Coll. Radiology; mem. Am. Roentgen Ray Soc., Radiol. Soc. N.Am., N.Y. County Med. Soc. (sec., dir. 1978—), N.Y. State Radiol. Soc. (bd. dirs. 1975—). Independent. Avocations: skiing, travel, archaeology. Home: 560 Riverside Dr Apt 14B New York NY 10027-3240 Business E-Mail: vk3@columbia.edu.

KANIN, DENNIS ROY, lawyer; b. Boston, Feb. 22, 1946; s. Irving Lynwood and Doris May (Small) K.; m. Carol Ann Licht, July 9, 1978; children: Zachary Joshua, Jonah Louis, Franklin Jacob. AB, Harvard U., 1968, JD, 1971. Bar: Mass. 1971, DC 1978. Assoc. Mahoney Atwood & Goldings, Boston, 1971-73; legis. asst. to congressman Frank Evans U.S. Ho. Reps., Washington, 1973-74, adminstrn. asst. to congressman Paul Tsongas, 1975-78; adminstrv. asst. to senator Paul Tsongas U.S. Senate, Washington, 1979-84; ptnr. Foley, Hoag & Eliot, Boston, 1985—; prin. New Boston Ventures. Mgr. campaign Tsongas for US Senate, Boston, 1978; mem. Nat. Dem. Charter Commn., Washington, 1973-74, Nat. Commn. Dem. Platform Accountability, Washington, 1983-84; mem. exec. com. Mass. Ams. for Dem. Action, Boston, 1985-87; campaign mgr. Tsongas for pres.; vice chmn. Kerry Nat. Fin. Com., 2004, nat. adv. coun.; nat. exec. com., nat. commr., regional vice chair New Eng. bd. Anti-Defamation League, 1985—, chair- elect, 2003-04, regional chair, 2004—, nat. Washington affairs chair, 2006-; mem. bd. dirs. New Eng. Coun., 1993-98; bd. dirs. Concord Coalition Citizens Coun., 1995—; trustee, v.p. bd. dirs. Epiphany Sch., 1999—, Roxbury Latin Sch., 2000—, pres.; overseers cmty. health bd. com. Children's Hosp., Boston, 1996—, bd., 2006-. Jewish. Home: 65 Stuart Rd Newton MA 02459-1210 Office: 155 Seaport Blvd #1600 Boston MA 02210-2600 Office Phone: 617-542-3500. Personal E-mail: dkanin.nbv@verizon.net.

KANIN, JOSH DAVID, film studies educator; b. LA, May 19, 1950; s. Michael and Fay Kanin; children: Laurel Elizabeth, Jessica Naomi. MA, U. So. Calif., LA, 1973. Prof. Wright State U., Dayton, Ohio, 1973—74, Calif. State U., Fullerton, Calif., 1975—77; prodr., dir. Kanin Productions, Santa Monica, Calif., 1996—; prof. Santa Monica Coll., Calif., 1998—. Adj. prof. L.A. City Coll., 1974—75, Calif. State U., Long Beach, Calif., 1974—75, Northridge, Calif., 1997—2004, L.A. Valley Coll., Van Nuys, Calif., 1978—81, Art Ctr. Coll. Design, Pasadena, Calif., 1996—99, U. So. Calif., LA, 1996—97; lectr. cruise ships. Editor theatrical films, television, series. Mem.: Santa Monica Coll. Pres. Circle. Achievements include invention of video home tours for real estate firms; development of media literacy training course modules. Avocations: tennis, travel. Office: Santa Monica College 1900 Pico Boulevard Santa Monica CA 90405 Office Fax: 310-393-3683. Business E-Mail: kanin_josh@smc.edu.

KANJORSKI, PAUL EDMUND, congressman, lawyer; b. Nanticoke, Pa., Apr. 2, 1937; s. A. Peter and Wanda (Nedbalski) Kanjorski; m. Nancy Marie Hickerson, Nov. 22, 1962; 1 child, Nancy Marie Student, Temple U., 1957—62, Dickinson Sch. Law, 1962—65. Bar: Pa. Ptnr. Kanjorski & Kanjorski, Wilkes-Barre, Pa., 1966-84; mem. US Congress from 11th Pa. dist., 1985—, mem. oversight and govt. reform com., mem. fin. svcs. com., chmn. capital markets, ins. and govt. sponsored enterprises subcommittee. Acting solicitor City of Nanticoke, 1969-81; Pa. Workmen's Compensation referee, 1972-80; bd. dirs. Wyo. Valley Sanitary Authority, Wilkes-Barre, 1972-84 Served in USAR, 1960—61. Mem.: Wilkes-Barre Law Libr. Assn. Democrat. Roman Catholic. Avocation: fishing. Office: US House Reps 2188 Rayburn House Office Bldg Washington DC 20515-0001 Office Phone: 202-225-6511. Office Fax: 202-225-0764. E-mail: paul.kanjorski@mail.house.gov.*

KANJWAL, MOHAMMED Y., cardiologist; b. Sopore, Kashmir, India, June 14, 1955; s. Abdul Ahad and Sundari Kanjwal; m. Rubina H. Shah, Aug. 24, 1984; children: Hafsa Y., Shifa Y., Omar Y. MB, Govt. Med. Coll., Srinagar, Kashmir, 1979; MD, Govt. Med. Coll., Kashmir, 1983; DM, Post Grad. Inst. Med. Edn. and Rsch., Chandigarh, India, 1989; MD, SUNY, Buffalo, 1996. Cert. in clin. cardiac eledctrophysiology Tufts U., Boston, 1997, in cardiovascular medicine SUNY, Buffalo, 2000, registered Ohio, 2000, Mass., 2000. Sr. resident SK Inst. Med. Scis., Kashmir, India, 1984—86, cons. medicine, 1987—93; cardiology cons. King Fahad Hosp., Madina, Saudi Arabia, 1993—94; asst. prof. medicine Med. Coll. Ohio, Toledo, 2000—05; assoc. prof. medicine U. Toledo Med. Ctr., 2005—. Dir. cardiac electrophysiology lab U. Toledo Med. Ctr., 2003—. Adv. Islamic Ctr. Gt. Toledo. Fellow: Am. Coll. Cardiology (life); mem.: Heart Rhythm Soc. (assoc.). Home: 8853 Linden Lake Rd Sylvania OH 43560 Office: UToledo Med Ctr 3000 Arlington Ave Toledo OH 43614 Office Phone: 419-383-5066. Office Fax: 419-383-3041. Business E-Mail: yousuf.kanjwal@utoledo.edu.

KANN, PETER ROBERT, retired publishing executive, journalist; b. NYC, Dec. 13, 1942; s. Robert A. and Marie K. (Breuer); m. Francesca Mayer, Apr. 12, 1969 (dec. 1983); m. Karen Elliot House, 1984; children: Hillary Francesca, Petra Elliot, Jason Elliot, Jade Elliott. BA, Harvard U., 1964. Newspaper fund intern The Wall St. Jour., San Francisco, 1963, staff reporter Pittsburgh, Los Angeles, 1964, resident reporter Vietnam, 1967, roving reporter Hong Kong, 1969—75; pub. The Asian Wall Street Jour., Hong Kong, 1976-79; assoc. pub. The Wall St. Jour., NYC, 1979-88, pub., 1989—2002; v.p. Dow Jones & Co., NYC, 1979—85, exec. v.p., 1985—89, pres., COO, 1989-91; CEO Dow Jones Publications, 1991—2006; chmn. Dow Jones & Co., NYC, 1991—2007; editl. dir. Dow Jones Publications, NYC, 1989—2006; ret., 2007. Bd. dirs Dow Jones & Co., 1987—; chmn. bd. Far Ea. Econ. Rev., 1987—89; mem. Pulitzer Prize Bd., 1987—96, Coun. Fgn. Rels. Trustee Asia Soc., 1989—94, Aspen Inst., 1994—98, Spelman Coll., 1994—97, Inst. for Advanced Study, Princeton, N.J., 1990—. Recipient Pulitzer prize for internat. reporting, 1972. Mem.: Spee Club (Cambridge, Mass.). Office: Wall Street Journal Dow Jones & Co Inc 200 Liberty St New York NY 10281-1003*

KANNE, MICHAEL STEPHEN, federal judge; b. Rensselaer, Ind., Dec. 21, 1938; s. Allen Raymond and Jane (Robinson) Kanne; m. Judith Ann Stevens, June 22, 1963; children: Anne, Katherine. Student, St. Joseph's Coll., Rensselaer, 1957—58; BS, Ind. U., 1962, JD, 1968; postgrad., Boston U., 1963, U. Birmingham, Eng., 1975. Bar: Ind. 1968. Assoc. Nesbitt and Fisher, Rensselaer, 1968—71; sole practice Rensselaer, 1971—72; atty. City of Rensselaer, 1972; judge 30th Jud. Cir. of Ind., 1972—82, US Dist. Ct. (no. dist.) Ind., Hammond, 1982—87, US Ct. Appeals (7th cir.), Chgo., 1987—, Moot Ct. Competitions, 1998—; chmn. US Cts. Design Guide, 1988—95. Lectr. law St. Joseph's Coll., 1976—89, St. Frances Coll., 1990—91; faculty Nat. Inst. for Trial Advocacy, South Bend, Ind., 1978—88; mem. Ad Hoc Com. on Law Clerk Hiring, 2004. Bd. visitors Ind. U. Sch. Law, 1987—, Ind. U. Sch. Pub. and Environ. Affairs, 1991—; trustee St. Joseph's Coll., 1984—. 1st lt. USAF, 1962—65. Named Outstanding Alumnus, Today's Cath. Tchr., 1991; recipient Disting. Svc. award, St. Joseph's Coll., 1973, Disting. Grad. award, Nat. Cath. Ednl. Assn. Mem.: FBA, Tippecanoe County Bar Assn., Jasper County Bar Assn. (pres. 1972—76), Ind. State Bar Assn. (bd. dirs. 1977—79, Presdl. citation 1979), Law Alumni Assn. Ind. U. (pres. 1980). Roman Catholic. Avocations: horseback riding, weightlifting. Office: Charles A Halleck Federal Bldg 2447H 4th and Ferry St Lafayette IN 47902-1340 also: US Ct Appeals 219 S Dearborn St Chicago IL 60604*

KANNENBERG, LLOYD CHAMBERS, physicist, researcher; b. Sarasota, Fla., Mar. 23, 1939; s. Werner Frederick Ludwig Kannenberg and Nettie Louise Chambers; m. Susan Lippman, Aug. 10, 1963; 1 child, Susanna. SB, MIT, 1961; MS, U. Fla., 1963; PhD, Northeastern U., 1967. Elec. engr. Electro-Mech. Rsch., Inc., Sarasota, 1961-63; instr. physics Lowell (Mass.) Tech. Inst. (merged with Lowell State Coll.), 1966-67; from instr. to prof. physics U. Mass. (formerly U. Lowell), 1968—; instr. physics Northeastern U., Boston, 1967-68. Translator: (by H. Grassmann) A New Branch of Mathematics, 1994, Extension Theory, 2000; (by G. Peano) Geometric Calculus, 2000; contbr. articles to profl. jours. Mem. Am. Phys. Soc. (life), Am. Math. Soc., Am. Assn. Physics Tchrs., Math. Assn. Am, Sigma Xi, Sigma Pi Sigma, Phi Kappa Phi. Democrat. Office: U Mass-Lowell 1 University Ave Lowell MA 01854 Business E-Mail: lloyd_kannenberg@uml.edu.

KANNER, FREDERICK W., lawyer; b. NYC, Apr. 25, 1943; BA, U. Va., 1965; JD, Georgetown U., 1968. Bar: N.Y. 1969. Ptnr. Dewey Ballantine LLP, NYC, 1976—, chmn. corp. fin. group & mem. mgmt. com. Editor: Georgetown Law Jour., 1967-68. Dir. Lawyers Alliance for N.Y.; trustee Lawyers Com. for Civil Rights under Law. Mem. ABA, N.Y. State Bar Assn., Assn. Bar City N.Y. (former mem. securities regulation com.). Office: Dewey Ballantine LLP 1301 Avenue Of The Americas New York NY 10019-6092 Office Phone: 212-259-7300. Office Fax: 212-259-6333. Business E-Mail: fkanner@dbllp.com.

KANOF, NORMAN B., dermatologist; b. NYC, May 31, 1920; AB, MD, George Washington U., 1941; D in Med. Sci., Columbia U., 1949. Diplomate Am. Bd. Dermatology. Clin. prof. dermatology NYU Sch. of Medicine, NYC. Home: 737 Park Ave New York NY 10021-4256 Office: 10 E 70th St New York NY 10021-4913 Home Phone: 212-737-5514; Office Phone: 212-288-2600.

KANOFF, MARY ELLEN, lawyer; m. Chris Kanoff. BA in Econs., U. Calif., Berkeley, 1978, JD, 1984. Large systems mktg. rep. IBM, 1978—81; with Latham & Watkins, LA, 1984—, ptnr., 1991—. Bd. trustees St. Matthews Sch., Pacific Palisades, Calif., St. John's Hosp., Santa Monica, Calif.; bd. dirs. Chrysalis. Named one of Top 25 Lawyers in Calif. under 45, Calif. Law Bus., 1993, Up and Coming Bus. Persons in So. Calif., L.A. Bus. Jour., 1997; recipient Founders Spirit of Chrysalis award. Mem.: ABA (bus. law and entertainment law sects.), L.A. County Bar Assn., Calif. Bar Assn. Office: Latham and Watkins LLP 633 W Fifth St Ste 4000 Los Angeles CA 90071 Home Phone: 310-459-9082; Office Phone: 213-891-8728.

KANOJIA, CHET, communications executive; b. 1970; ME, Regional Engring. Coll. Bhopal, India; M in Computer Systems Engring., Northeastern U. Program mgr. Product Genesis, Inc.; CEO Navic Networks. Named one of 40 Executives Under 40, Multichannel News, 2006. Achievements include doctoral work on applications of artificial intelligence. Office: Navic Networks Bldg C-East 3rd Fl 140 Kendrick St Needham MA 02494 Office Phone: 781-433-3200. Office Fax: 781-453-2501.

KANOSKY, ALBERT LEO, history educator, small business owner; b. Kankakee, Ill., June 7, 1950; s. Leo George and Dorothy Eileen Kanosky; m. Rita Marie Regnier, Oct. 14, 1972; children: Michael, Caroline, Meghan. AA, Kankakee C.C., 1970; BS in History, Ill. State U., Normal, Ill., 1972; cert. in Elem. Edn., Olivet Nazarene U., Kankakee, Ill., 1974; student, Gov. State U., Park Forest, Ill., 1988. Tchr. Pestone Elem. Sch., Ill., 1972—73, Wilton Center Elem. Sch., Ill., 1974, Green Garden Elem. Sch., Manhattan, Ill., 1975—79, Peotone H.S., 1980—. Coach basketball Pastone H.S., Ill., 1980—95; offcl. Ill. H.S. Assn., 1977—2006; coach baseball, softball Kankakee Area, 1980—2000. Mem.: Nat. Coun. Social Studies. Independent. Roman Cath. Avocations: yardwork, bicycling, sports. Office: Peotone High Sch 605 W North St Peotone IL 60468-9182

KANOVITZ, HOWARD, artist, educator; b. Fall River, Mass., Feb. 9, 1929; s. Meyer Julius and Dora (Rems) K. BS, Providence Coll., 1949; postgrad., R.I. Sch. Design, 1949-51, NYU, 1959-61. Instr. Bklyn. Coll., 1962-64, Pratt Inst., 1964-66; prof. Southhampton Coll., 1977-78, Sch. Visual Arts, NYC, 1981-85. Artist, painter exhibited Tibor de Nagy Gallery, 1956, Stable Gallery, 1962, Jewish Mus., 1966, Waddell Gallery, 1969; one-man shows include U.S. and Europe, Stefanotty Gallery, N.Y.C., 1975, Galerie Jöllenbeck, Cologne, 1977, Benson Gallery, Bridgehampton, L.I., N.Y., 1977, Akademie der Kunste, Berlin, 1979, Kestner Gesellschaft, Hannover, 1979, Alex Rosenberg Gallery, 1982, Inge Baecker Gallery, 1987, 88, 91, Cologne, 1987, Marlborough Gallery, 1988, 90, Hokin-Kaufman Gallery, Chgo., 1989, Gana Art Gallery, Seoul, 1990, Ulrich Gering Gallery, Frankfurt, 1997, Nabi Gallery, Sag Harbor, L.I., 1998; group exhibits include Whitney Mus., N.Y.C., 1972, Dokumenta 5, Kassel, 1972, Berlin Nat. Gallery, 1976, Guild Hall, East Hampton, L.I., 1976, Dokumenta 6, Kassel, 1977, Alex Rosenberg Gallery, 1978, Louise Himmelfarb Gallery, Watermill, L.I., 1979, L.A. Mus. Contemporary Art, 1984, Indpls. Mus. Art, 1985, Ludwig Mus., Cologne, 1988, Parrish Art Mus., Southampton, L.I., 1988, Fla. Internat. U., Miami, 1989, Met. Mus., N.Y.C., 1991, Weatherspoon Art Gallery, Greensboro, N.C., 1991; represented in permanent collections Met. Mus., N.Y., Whitney Mus. Am. Art, N.Y., Hirshhorn Mus. and Sculpture Garden, Washington, L.A. County Mus. Modern Art, Guild Hall Mus., East Hampton, N.Y, Folkwang Mus., Essen, Germany. Studio: 361 N Sea Mecox Rd Southampton NY 11968-2829 Home Phone: 631-283-7179. Personal E-mail: nero@optonline.net.

KANSFIELD, NORMAN J., former seminary president; b. East Chicago, Ind., Mar. 24, 1940; s. Orval Russell and Margaret Jeannette (Norman) K.; m. Mary L. Klein, June 25, 1965; children: Ann Margaret, John Livingston. BA, Hope Coll., 1962; BD, Western Theol. Sem., 1965; M Sacred Theology, Union Theol. Sem., 1967; MA, U. Chgo., 1970, PhD, 1981. Pastor Second Reformed Ch., Astoria, Queens, 1965-68; interim pastor First Reformed Ch., Berwin, Ill., 1968-69; assoc. pastor Ivanhoe Reformed Ch., Riverdale, Ill., 1969-70; libr., prof. theology Western Theol. Seminary, Holland, Mich., 1970-83; dir. libr. svcs., assoc. prof. ch. history Colgate Rochester Divinty Sch., NY, 1983-92; dir. libr. svcs. St. Bernard's Inst., Rochester, 1983-92; pres. New Brunswick Theol. Seminary, NJ, 1993—2005; sr. resident scholar Drew U. Theol. Sch., Madison, NJ, 2006—. Commn. on history, mem. Reformed Ch. in Am., 1969-74; Rabbi Nathan Kellerman Meml. lectr. Temple Anshe Emmeth, New Brunswick, 1995; lectr. A.J. Muste Meml. lectr. Hope Coll., Holland, Mich., 2000; St. Columba lectr. Oxford U., 2002; 50th Anniversary lectr. Seoul Jang Sin U, 2004; sem. lectr. Near East Sch. Theology, Beirut, 2004; lectr. in field. Co-author: Evangelism: The Church's Proclamation, 1988; editor, contbr. (hymnbook) Rejoice in the Lord, 1985; editor: New Mercersburg Review, 2006-; mem. editl. bd. Perspectives, 1997-2004, Jour. Religion & Health, 2004-, Out in Scripture, 2007-; contbr. articles to profl. jours. Chair Hist. Adv. Com., Holland, 1970—83; dir. New Brunswick Tomorrow, 1994—2005; pres. Mercersburg Soc., 2002—; bd. trustee Blanton-Peale Inst., 2003—06; bd. dirs. Room for All, 2005—. Sealantic fellow Rockefeller Bros. Found., 1968-70, Conant fellow Episc. Ch. in USA, 1989-90, Pride Interfaith Coalition award, Boston, 2005, Human Rights Campaign Advocate award, 2005. Democrat. Avocations: book collecting, carpentry, fishing, gardening. Home: 28 3 Point Garden Rd East Stroudsburg PA 18301 Personal E-mail: nkansfield@verizon.net.

KANSTOROOM, DAVID ARNOLD, real estate developer, entrepreneur; b. Washington, Oct. 20, 1964; s. Allen Roy and Sara Eta Kanstoroom; m. Cynthia Marie Martinez, May 19, 1996; children: Summer, Jared. BSBA, U. Fla., Gainesville, 1987, MBA, 1991. V.p. network svcs. W2COM LLC, Dayton, Ohio, 1999-2000; CEO, pres., chmn. bd. dirs. Intelicom Holding Corp., Tampa, Fla., 1991—2002, chief devel. officer U.S. local holdings, 2001—02; pres., chmn. Oasis Custom Homes, Tampa, 2002—. Actor, stuntman live we. shows, 1978-84. Vol. Muscular Dystrophy Assn., Gainesville, Fla., 1984-89; pres. Bayport Colony Home Owners Assn., Tampa, 1999—; mem. Tampa Bay Performing Arts Ctr. Mem. Telecom Agent Assn., Ascent Assn. Comm. Enterprises, Tampa Bay C. of C., Sigma Chi (chmn. fundraising 1986-87, scholar 1987). Republican. Jewish. Avocations: football, basketball, boating, travel, skiing. Home: 155 45th Ave NE Saint Petersburg FL 33703 Office: David Kanstoroom Pa 155 45th Ave Ne Saint Petersburg FL 33703-4927 Office Phone: 813-855-0070. Fax: 813-854-4350. E-mail: dak1@tampabay.rr.com.

KANT, GLORIA JEAN, retired neuroscientist; b. Chgo., June 6, 1944; d. Hans Georg and Jo Sefa Kant; m. Philip Herbert Balcom, July 1, 1967 (div. 1976). BS in Chemistry, Mich. State U., 1965; PhD in Physiol. Chemistry, U. Wis., 1969. Chemist dept. psychiatry Walter Reed Army Inst. Rsch., Washington, 1970-71, neurochemist dept. microwave rsch., 1971-77, neurochemist dept. med. neuroscis., 1977-87, chief dept. med. neuroscis., 1987-95, dir. divsn. neuroscis., 1995—2001; ret. Mem. editl. bd. Pharmacology, Biochemistry and Behavior, 1991-2000; contbr. over 80 articles to sci. jours. Mem. AAAS, Soc. for Neurosci., Internat. Behavioral Neurosci. Soc., Women in Neurosci. Avocation: golf. Home: 1124 Dennis Ave Silver Spring MD 20901-2171

KANT, ROBERT S., lawyer; b. Little Rock, Sept. 25, 1944; BA, Univ. Pa., 1966; JD, Villanova Univ., 1970. Bar: Pa. 1970, Ariz. 1978. Shareholder, corporate and securities, bd. dir. Greenberg Traurig LLP, Phoenix. Named one of Best of the Bar in Corp. Law, Phoenix Bus. Jour., 2003, Best of Bar in Securities Law, 2004. Mem.: State Bar Ariz. (small bus. capital formation, chmn., securities sect. 1987—88). Office: Greenberg Traurig LLP Ste 700 2375 E Camelback Rd Phoenix AZ 85016 Office Phone: 602-445-8302. Office Fax: 602-445-8100. Business E-Mail: kantr@gtlaw.com.

KANTACK, CATHERINE MARGARET, retired music educator, retired international and bank broker; b. Cedar Rapids, Iowa, July 30, 1943; d. Roy William and Icel Margaret (Tiernan) Driscoll; m. Paul Wayne Kantack, Oct. 5, 1963; children: Keith C., Kelly A. Student, Creighton U., Omaha, 1961—62; attended, St. Joseph's Sch. Nursing, 1961—62; student, Jefferson Davis Coll., 1975—76. Tchr. piano Naval Bn. Constrn. Ctr., Gulfport, Miss., 1974—84; tchr. piano pvt. studio New Orleans, 1984—2003; ret., 1986—. Pres. C.M.II Fin. Svcs., Inc., New Orleans, 1986—2007; vol. pianist Vets. Hosp., 1980. ARC swimming instr. Keesler AFB, Biloxi, Miss., 1975—81. Recipient Ministry award, Keesler Med. Ctr., 1984, Spl. Recognition award, Nat. Security Studies Grad. Sch. Georgetown U., 1979, Wall of Tolerance, Montgomery, 2002, Internat. CPA Tax Box award, 2005. Mem.: Keesler Med. Wives Club, Keesler Officers' Wives Club. Roman Catholic. Avocations: reading, cooking, swimming. Home: 53 Dogwood Rd Columbus MS 39705-5348

KANTARCI, KEJAL, radiologist, researcher; b. Istanbul, Turkey, Dec. 1, 1969; arrived in U.S., 1998; d. Vehbi and Gülseren Aydin; m. Orhun H. Kantarci, Nov. 25, 1994. MS, Marmara U., Istanbul, 1993. Resident Istanbul U., 1993—97; radiologist pvt. practice, 1997—98; asst. prof., assoc. cons. Mayo Clinic, Rochester, Minn., 2004—. Contbr. chapters to books; mem. editl. bd.: Neurosci. Imaging, 2004—. Recipient Paul Beeson Career Devel. in Aging award, Nat. Inst. on Aging, 2007; fellow, Mayo Clinic, 1998—2004; scholar, NIH, 2005—, Beeson, 2007—. Mem.: Internat. Soc. Magnetic Resonance Medicine, Radiol. Soc. N.Am. Avocations: mountain climbing, scuba diving, bicycling. Office: Mayo Clinic 200 First St Rochester MN 55905 Office Phone: 507-284-9770. E-mail: kantarci.kejal@mayo.edu.

KANTARDZIC, MEHMED M., engineering educator; b. Sarajevo, Bosnia, Jan. 22, 1948; arrived in U.S., 1994; s. Muhamed and Rasema Kantardzic; m. Belma Numic Kantardzic, June 19, 1980; 1 child, Nermin. BS, U. Sarajevo, 1972, MS, 1976, PhD. Assoc. prof. U. Sarajevo, 1972—94, assoc. dean, 1987—94; from vis. prof. to prof. U. Louisville, 1995—2004, prof., 2004—, dir. Data Mining Lab., 2001—, dir. Online Data Mining Cert. Program, 2005—. Author: Data Mining: Concepts, Models, 2003; editor: Next Generation of Data Mining Appi, 2005; exec. prodr.: Next Generation of Data Mining Appi, 2004; editor: Next Generation of Data Mining Appi, 2004. Nominee Disting. Faculty award, U. Louisville, 2004. Mem.: IEEE (mem. data mining tech. com. 2005—), Internat. Conf. on Machine Learning and Applications (mem. steering com 2002—, Best Paper award 2003, 2005). Avocations: bridge, tennis. Home: 10616 Bracken Branch Rd Louisville KY 40223 Office: Univ Louisville Speed Sch Engring Louisville KY 40292

KANTER, ALAN MICHAEL, lawyer; b. Detroit, Apr. 24, 1954; s. Erwin Jack and Geraldine Ruth (Harvey) K.; m. Deborah Helen Avery, Dec. 11, 1983 (div. Oct. 2004); children: Amanda Danielle, Steven Joseph. BA with high distinction, Wayne State U., 1976, JD, 1979. Bar: Mich. 1979, U.S. Dist. Ct. (ea. dist.) Mich. 1979, U.S. Dist. Ct. (we. dist.) Mich. 1981, U.S. Ct. Appeals (6th cir.) 1982. Assoc. Robert F. Wick, P.C., Rochester, Mich., 1979-80, Shapack, Singer & McCullough, P.C., Bloomfield Hills, Mich., 1980-85; ptnr. Shapack, McCullough & Kanter, P.C. (formerly Shapack, McCullough & Frank, P.C.), Bloomfield Hills, 1986—; shareholder Strobl, Cunningham & Sharp PC, 2001. Adv. bd. Greater West Bloomfield Cable TV, 1987; alternative dispute resolution panel mem. Providers of Am. Health Lawyers Assn. Named one of Best Lawyers Am., Woodward/White, 2005, 2006, 2007. Mem. ABA, Oakland County Bar Assn. (chmn. pub. rels. com. 1985-86, chmn. case evaluation com. 1999-2000, alternative dispute resolution com., 1999—, cir. ct. com. 2001—, membership com. 2002—, computer tech. com. 2002—), Am. Arbitration Assn. (cert. and ct. approved arbitrator, mediator, case evaluator, nat. complex coml. panel, coml. law panel, employment law panel), Assn. Comml. Arbitrators (arbitration panel), Internat. Acad. Mediators (assoc.), State Bar Mich. (chmn. alternative dispute resolution sect. 2005-06), Phi Beta Kappa. Jewish. Avocations: music, photography, sports. Office: Ste 200 300 E Long Lake Rd Bloomfield MI 48304-2376 Home Phone: 248-738-9252; Office Phone: 248-540-2300. Business E-Mail: akanter@stroblpc.com.

KANTER, CARL IRWIN, retired lawyer; b. Jersey City, Feb. 17, 1932; s. Morris and Beatrice (Wilson) K.; m. Gail Herman, Nov. 27, 1963; children— Deborah, David, Andrew, Aaron AB, Harvard U., 1953, LL.B., 1956. Bar: Calif. 1956, N.Y. 1959. Assoc. Stroock & Stroock & Lavan, NYC, 1959-67, ptnr., 1967-92; sr. v.p., co-gen. counsel Merck-Medco Managed Care L.L.C., Montvale, NJ, 1992-97, spl. counsel, 1997-99; ret. Served with U.S. Army, 1957-58 Home: 993 Park Ave New York NY 10028 Personal E-mail: kanterart@yahoo.com.

KANTER, SANDRA MAY, lawyer; b. LA, Aug. 11, 1956; m. Michael Howard Kanter, May 15, 1983; children: Melanie Robin, Robert Joseph. BA magna cum laude, Brandeis U., 1978; JD cum laude, Harvard U., 1981. Bar: Calif. 1981. Assoc. Cox, Castle, & Nicholson, LA, 1981—86; prin. Law Offices of Sandra Kanter, Inglewood, Calif., 1986—88; assoc. Fine, Perzik & Singman, LA, 1989—90; contract ptnr. Nossaman, Guthner, Knox & Elliott, LA, 1991—. Mem.: ABA, Women's Transp. Seminar, LA County Bar Assn., Calif. Bar Assn. Office: Nossaman Guthner Knox & Elliott Ste 3100 445 S Figueroa St Los Angeles CA 90071 Office Phone: 213-612-7851. Office Fax: 213-612-7801. Business E-Mail: skanter@nossaman.com.

KANTER, STACY J., lawyer; b. NYC, 1958; d. Ronald I. and Elaine Kanter; m. Eric Martin Kornblau. BS magna cum laude, SUNY, Albany, 1979; JD cum laude, Bklyn. Law Sch., 1984. Bar: NY 1985. Law clk. to Hon. Raymond J. Dearie US Dist. Ct. Ea. Dist. NY, 1986—87; ptnr. Skadden, Arps, Slate, Meagher & Flom LLP, NYC, 1993—. Mng. editor Bklyn. Law Rev., 1983-84. Named one of NY's rising stars in bus. Crain's mag., 1997. Office: Skadden Arps Slate Meagher & Flom LLP 4 Times Sq New York NY 10036 Office Phone: 212-735-3497. Office Fax: 917-777-3497. E-mail: skanter@skadden.com.

KANTER, STEPHEN, lawyer, educator, dean; b. Cin., June 30, 1946; s. Aaron J. and Edythe (Kasfir) K.; m. Dory Jean Poduska, June 24, 1972; children: Jordan Alexander, Laura Elizabeth. BS in Math., MIT, 1968; JD, Yale U., 1971. Spl. asst. Portland (Oreg.) City Commr., 1971-72; from staff atty. to asst. dir. Met. Pub. Defender, Portland, 1972-77; prof. law Lewis and Clark Law Sch., Portland, 1977—, assoc. dean, 1980-81, acting dean, 1981-82, dean, 1986-94. Fulbright prof. law Nanjing (China) U., 1984-85, U. Athens (Greece) Faculty of Law, 1993; bd. dirs. Northwest Regional China Coun., 1996-00, pres.- elect, 1997-98, pres., 1998-99; exec. com. Owen M. Panner Am. Inns of Ct., pres., 1994-95; mem. judicial selection com. U.S. Dist. Ct. Oreg., 1993; cons. on drafting and implementation of Kazakhstan Constn., 1992, 94, cons. on Sch. Police funciton, Portland Sch. Dist. Author: The Bear and the Blackberry, 1999; contbr. articles to profl. jours. Mem. bd. overseers World Affairs Coun. Oreg., Portland, 1986-89; mem. Oreg. Criminal Justice Coun., Salem, 1987-92, Oreg. Bicentennial Commn., Portland, 1986-89; pres. Portland Baseball Group, 2000—. Named One of 10 Gt. Portlanders, Willamette Week newspaper, 1980; recipient E.B. MacNaughton Civil Liberties award, 1991. Fellow Am. Bar Found. (life); mem. ACLU (bd. dirs. Oreg. chpt. 1976-82, pres. 1979-81, lawyers com. 1976-2003), Oreg. State Bar Assn., Am. Law Inst. (ex-officio 1986-94), Fulbright Assn. (bd. dirs. 1987-93, exec. com. 1989-93). Home: 3142 SW Fairview Blvd Portland OR 97205-1831 Office: Lewis & Clark Law Sch 10015 SW Terwilliger Blvd Portland OR 97219-7768 Office Phone: 503-768-6757. Business E-Mail: kanter@lclark.edu.

KANTOFF, PHILIP W., oncologist; s. Sidney Michael and Liselotte Kantoff; m. Rochelle Gail Scheib, Nov. 1, 1981; children: Aaron Max, Emily Hannah, Sydney Sophia. MD, Brown U., Providence, RI, 1979. Dir. Lank Ctr. Genitourinary Oncology Dana Farber Cancer Inst., Boston, 1988, chief Divsn. Solid Tumor Oncology, 2002—, chief clin. rsch. officer, 2006—. Office: Dana Farber Cancer Institute 44 Binney Street Boston MA 02115 Office Phone: 617-632-1914.

KANTOR, DAVID, lawyer; b. Riverside, Calif., Aug. 10, 1952; BA, U. Mich., 1974, JD, 1980; MA, Stanford U., 1975. Bar: Minn. 1980, U.S. Dist. Ct. Minn. 1981. Assoc. O'Connor & Hannan, Mpls., 1980-85, ptnr., 1985-87; assoc. Leonard, Street and Deinard, Mpls., 1987-88, ptnr., 1989—. Vol. Peace Corps, 1975-77, Legal Advice Clinics, Mpls., 1980—. Mem. ABA, Minn. Bar Assn., Hennepin County Bar Assn. Office: Leonard Street & Deinard 150 S 5th St Ste 2300 Minneapolis MN 55402-4238 Office Phone: 612-335-1620. Business E-Mail: david.kantor@leonard.com.

KANTOR, GAIL, Internet company executive, concert producer; Background singer, mem. Bette Midler's Harlettes; founder Kantor Co., Kantor Prodns.; co-founder & CEO eJamming AUDiiO, San Francisco, 2001—. Background vocalist (with Bette Midler) Divine Miss M, 1972, Bette Midler, 1973, Songs for the New Depression, 1976, Experience the Divine: Greatest Hits, 1993, (with Leonard Cohen) New Skin for the Old Ceremony, 1974, (with Judy Collins) Bread and Roses, 1976, (with Ian Hunter) All American Alien Boy, 1976, Once Bitten Twice Shy, 2000, (with Barry Manilow) Complete Collection & Then Some., 1992, Another Life, 1995, (with Yoko Ono) Story, 1997, others; exec. prodr.: (TV films) Latin Nights, 1995. Office: eJamming AUDiiO 2nd Fl 77 Federal St San Francisco CA 94107-1414 Office Phone: 818-761-7268.*

KANTOR, HARVEY SHERWIN, medical educator; b. NYC, Apr. 30, 1938; s. Jack and Henrietta (Feingold) K.; m. Elvia Frostick, Nov. 8, 1992; stepchildren: Harold, Eric Frostick. Student, U. Miami, 1955-58; MD, Washington U., 1962; postgrad., MIT, 1967-69. Diplomate Am. Bd. Internal Medicine, Am. Bd. Pathology certification in Medical Microbiology, Am. Bd. Infectious Diseases. Instr. U. Miami Sch. Medicine, 1969-71; asst. prof. medicine and microbiology U. Ill. Sch. Medicine, Chgo., 1971-75; assoc. prof. medicine and pathology Chgo. Med. Sch., North Chgo., Ill., 1975—93; dir. divsn. infectious diseases VA Med. Ctr., North Chicago, 1975-85, chief med. microbiology, 1985-92; prof. internal medicine Tex. Tech. U. Health Sci. Ctr., Odessa, 1993—2002, dir. divsn. infectious diseases, 1993—2002, interim chmn. dept. internal medicine, 2000—02; clin. prof., dept. medicine Rosalind Franklin U. Medicine and Sci./Chgo. Med. Sch., 2005—. Contbr. chpts. to textbooks, articles to profl. jours. Capt. U.S. Army, 1964-66. Recipient NIH postdoctoral fellowship in infectious diseases New Eng. Med. Ctr. Hosp., Boston, 1966-69, U. Health Scis./Chgo. Med. Sch. Bd. Trustees Rsch. award, 1977. Fellow ACP, Infectious Diseases Soc. Am.; mem. Am. Soc. Microbiology, Soc. Hosp. Epidemiology in Am. Avocations: cooking, photography, computers. E-mail: hkantormd@yahoo.com.

KANTOR, ISAAC NORRIS, lawyer; b. Charleston, W.Va., Aug. 29, 1929; s. Israel and Rachel (Cohen) K.; m. Doris Sue Katz, June 17, 1956; children: Mark B., Cynthia Kantor Kraft, Beth Kantor Zachwieja. BA, Va. Mil. Inst., 1953; JD, W.Va. U., 1956. Bar: W.Va. 1956, US Dist. Ct. (so. dist.) W.Va. 1956, US Ct. Mil. Appeals 1957, US Ct. Appeals (4th cir.) 1978, US Dist. Ct. (no. dist.) W.Va. 1991, US Ct. Fed. Claims 1996. Judge adv. USAFR, 1956—58; ptnr. Katz Katz & Kantor, Bluefield, W.Va., 1958-70, Katz Kantor Katz Perkins & Cameron, Bluefield, W.Va., 1970-82, Katz Kantor & Perkins, Bluefield, 1982—. Town atty. Town of Bramwell, W.Va., 1970-75, Town of Petestown, W.Va., 1981-85; bd. dirs. First Cmty. Bank, First Cmty. Bancshares Inc., Bluefield, Va.; mem. vis. com. W.Va. U. Coll. Law, Morgantown, 1986-89; mem. dean's adv. coun. Appalachian Sch. of Law, Grundy, Va., 1998— Co-chmn. W.Va. Gov.'s Jud. Selection Com., 1988—97; chmn. W.Va. Ethics Commn., 1998—2000; chmn. W.Va. divsn. Am. Cancer Soc., 1990—92; pres. New River Pkwy. Authority, 1996—2006; adv. bd., chmn. Bluefield State Coll., 1997—2001, chmn. bd. govs., 2001—03, vice chmn. bd. govs., 2003—05, chmn. bd. govs., 2006, sec., bd. rsch. and devel. corp., 2004—; vice chair govt. affairs Bluefield C. of C., 1999—2001; chmn. bd. dirs. Greater Bluefield C. of C., 2002; dir. Bluefield Area Devel. Corp., 2005—; mem. Mercer County Equine com., 2006—; parliamentarian W.Va. Dem. Exec. Com., 1964—68; chmn. Mercer County W.Va. Dem. Exec. Com., 1966—70. Capt. USAR, 1953—61. Paul Harris fellow Rotary Internat., 1999; recipient Citizen of Yr. award Greater Bluefield Jaycees, 1980, Boss of Yr. award, 1992, St. George medal, Nat. Divsnl. award Am. Cancer Soc., 1993. Mem. W.Va. Trial Lawyers Assn. (pres. 1980-81), B'nai B'rith (pres. W.Va. coun. 1975-76), Rotary Internat. Jewish. Avocations: golf, reading, travel, civic activities. Home: 231 Oakdell Ave Bluefield WV 24701-4840 Office: PO Box 727 Bluefield WV 24701-0727 Office Phone: 304-327-0002. Personal E-mail: shale2@citlink.net. Business E-Mail: kantor@citlink.net.

KANTOR, MARK ALAN, lawyer, arbitrator; b. LA, Mar. 10, 1955; s. William Victor and Minerva (Wainess) K.; m. Lawranne Stewart. AB in Polit. Sci. and Internat. Relations, U. So. Calif., 1975; M in Pub. Policy, U. Mich., 1979, JD, 1979. Bar: N.Y. 1980, D.C. 1992. Assoc. Milbank, Tweed, Hadley & McCloy, NYC, 1979-81, 84-87, Hong Kong, 1981-84, ptnr. NYC and Washington, 1987-89, 90-99; gen. counsel Resolution Trust Corp. Oversight Bd., 1990. Adj. prof. Georgetown U. Law Ctr., 2000—; co-chair internat. dispute resolution com. D.C. Bar. Contbr. articles to profl. jours. Mem. ABA, Internat. Law Assn., Mid. East Inst. (sustaining mem.), Am. C. of C. Hong Kong (bd. govs. 1983-84, co-chair legal and fin. com. 1982-84), Phi Beta Kappa. Office Phone: 202-544-4953. Personal E-mail: mkantor@mark-kantor.com.

KANTOR, MICKEY (MICHAEL KANTOR), lawyer, former secretary of commerce; b. Nashville, Aug. 7, 1939; s. Henry Kantor; m. Valerie Woods (dec. 1978); children: Leslie, Douglas, Russell (dec.); m. Heidi Schulman, 1982; 1 child, Alix. BA, Vanderbilt U., 1961; JD, Georgetown U., 1968. Bar: Fla. 1968, D.C. 1972, Calif. 1974. Ptnr. Monatt, Phelps, Phillips & Kantor, LA, 1976—93; US Trade Rep. Exec. Office of the Pres., Washington, 1993-96; sec. US Dept. Commerce, Washington, 1996-97; ptnr., internat. trade practice Mayer Brown Rowe & Maw LLP, Washington, 1997—; sr. adv. Morgan Stanley & Co., 1997—. Mem. Mex.-Am. Legal Def. and Edn. Fund, 1977-87, spl. ind. commn. to review structure and operation of L.A. Police Dept.; bd. dirs. Nat. Legal Svcs. Corp., 1979-81, Ctr. Study Dem. Institutions, 1982—; chmn. L.A. Conservation Corp.; mem. Calif. Commn. on Campaign Fin., 1990-92; bd. dir. Pharmacia Corp., Monsanto Co., Korea First Bank. Participant various Dem. campaigns; mgr. Clinton for Pres. Campaign, 1992; mem. bd. vis. Georgetown Univ. Law Ctr.; trustee Internat. Comml. Diplomacy Proj.; bd. mem. Ctr. for Law in the Pub. Interest, 1989-92, Ctr. for Study of Democratic Inst., 1988-90. Order of the So. Cross, Govt. of Brazil, 2001; William O. Douglas award, Constitutional Rights Found.; Thomas Jefferson Disting. Pub. Svc. Medal, Ctr. for Study of Presidency; Albert Schweizer Leadership award, Hugh O'Brien Youth Found. Mem. ABA, Calif. Bar Assn., Fla. Bar Assn., D.C. Bar, Council Fgn. Rels. (Elihu Root Disting. Lectr.); dir. Nat. Assn. Pub. Interest Lawyers. Office: Mayer Brown Rowe & Maw 1909 K St NW Washington DC 20006-1101 Office Phone: 202-263-3295. Office Fax: 202-263-5295. Business E-Mail: mkantor@mayerbrownrowe.com.*

KANTOR, SIMON WILLIAM, chemistry professor; b. Brussels, Mar. 23, 1925; came to US, 1939, naturalized, 1946; s. Joseph Uszer and Josephine (Perez) K.; m. Karen Christine Duncan, 1989; children from previous marriage: Michael Bruce, Sharon Inez; stepchildren: Michael John Eisenbeiser, Jason James Eisenbeiser, Justin Ryan Eisenbeiser. BS, CCNY, 1945; PhD, Duke U., 1949. Postdoctoral fellow Duke U., Durham, NC, 1949—51; rsch. assoc. GE R & D Ctr., Schenectady, NY, 1951—60, sect. mgr., 1960—65, br. mgr., 1965—72; v.p. R & D. GAF Corp., Wayne, NJ, 1972—82; prof. chemistry U. Mass., Amherst, 1982—2000, prof. emeritus, 2000—. Contbr. articles to chem. jours.; patentee in field. Mem. Am. Chem. Soc., Phi Beta Kappa, Phi Lambda Upsilon. Avocation: bridge. Home: 153 Silver Lake Dr Agawam MA 01001-2351 Business E-Mail: swkantor@polysci.umass.edu.

KANTROVICH, ADAM J., education educator; b. Park Ridge, Ill., Sept. 2, 1971; s. Jerry M. and Fayette Kantrovich; m. Jennifer Eickhoff, June 10, 1995; 1 child, Elijah William; 1 child, Annika Evelyn. PhD, Va. Poly. Inst. and State U., Blacksburg, 2000. Instr., program leader Western Iowa Tech CC, Sioux City, Iowa, 2001—02; asst. prof. Morehead State U., Ky., 2002—. County dir., agrl. ext. educator U. Nebr. Coop. Ext., Hartington, 2000—01. V.p. Rowan County Ext. Coun., Morehead, Ky. Recipient Hon. Ky. State FFA degree, Ky. FFA, 2006, Hon. FFA Chpt. degree, Bath County FFA, 2005. Avocation: aerobics. Office: Morehead State U 325 Reed Hall Morehead KY 40351 Office Phone: 606-783-2662. Office Fax: 606-783-5067. Business E-Mail: a.kantrovich@moreheadstate.edu.

KANTROWITZ, ARTHUR, physicist, researcher, educator; b. NYC, Oct. 20, 1913; s. Bernard A. and Rose (Esserman) K.; m. Rosalind Joseph, Sept. 12, 1943 (div.); children: Barbara, Lore, Andrea; m. Lee Stuart, Dec. 25, 1980. BS, Columbia U., 1934, MA, 1936, PhD, 1947; DEng (hon.), Mont. Coll. Mineral Sci. and Tech., 1975; D.Sc. (hon.), N.J. Inst. Tech., 1981. Physicist NACA, 1935-46; prof. aero. engring. and engring. physics Cornell U., 1946-56; founder, dir., chmn., chief exec. officer Avco-Everett Research Lab., Everett, Mass., 1955-78; sr. v.p., dir. Avco Corp., 1956-79; prof. Thayer Sch. Engring., Dartmouth Coll., 1978—. Vis. lectr. Harvard U., 1952; Fulbright and Guggenheim fellow Cambridge and Manchester univs., 1954; fellow Sch. Advanced Study, MIT, 1957, vis. inst. prof., 1957—; Joseph Wunsch lectr. Technion, Haifa, Israel, 1968; mem., fellow lectr. Am. Inst. Chemists, 1977; Messenger lectr. Cornell U., 1978; 1st Hastings lectr. NIH, 1977; hon. prof. Huazhong Inst. Tech., Wuhan, China, 1980; mem. Presdl. Adv. Group on Anticipated Advances in Sci. and Tech., head task force on sci. ct., 1975-76; mem. tech. adv. bd. U.S. Dept. Commerce, 1974-77; mem. adv. panel NOVA, Sta. WGBH-TV, 1975—; bd. overseers Center for Naval Analyses, 1973-83; mem. adv. council Israel-U.S. Binational Indsl. Research and Devel. Found., 1978-81; bd. govs. The Technion (hon. life); mem. adv. council NASA, 1979, 80; life trustee U. Rochester; past mem. sci. and engring. adv. com. U. Rochester, Princeton U., Stanford U. and Rensselaer Poly Inst.; vis. prof. U. Calif., Berkeley, 1983. Contbr. articles to profl. jours.; patentee in field. Bd. dirs. Hertz Found., 1972—. Recipient award Am. Acad. Achievement, 1966, Theodore Roosevelt medal, 1967, Kayan medal Columbia U., 1973, MHD Faraday Meml. medal UNESCO, 1983, Beamed Energy Propulsion award First Internat. Symposium, 2002-. Fellow AAAS, AIAA (1st Von Kármán lectr. 1964, Fluid and Plasmadynamics medal 1981, Aerospace Contbn. to Soc. award 1990, hon. fellow 1998), Am. Acad. Arts and Scis., Am. Phys. Soc., Am. Astronautical Soc., Am. Inst. for Med. and Biol. Engring.; mem. NAS, NAE, Internat. Acad. Astronautics, Am. Inst. Physics, Sigma Xi. Achievements include lead developer of intra-aortic balloon pump and inventor of principle; scientific collaboration on MHD energy conversion US-USSR, 1968-78; high-energy lasers, interplanetary shock waves; solved missile nose cone heating problem during re-entry from space; early work in fusion, supersonic source for molecular beams and the total energy variometer noteable. Home: 4 Downing Rd Hanover NH 03755-1902 E-mail: arthur.kantrowitz@dartmouth.edu.

KANTROWITZ, JONATHAN DANIEL, publishing executive, educator, lawyer; b. Bridgeport, Conn., Apr. 14, 1945; s. Ralph Samson and Beatrice (Schine) K.; m. Monica Victoria Fractenberg, Dec. 26, 1970; children: Bethany Eve, Ralph Richard. BA, Brown U., 1966; JD, Harvard U., 1969. Bar: Conn. 1969, N.Y. 1980. Ptnr. Kantrowitz & Kantrowitz, Bridgeport, 1969-74; atty. So. New Eng. Tel. Co., New Haven, 1975-76; asst. gen. counsel Touche Ross & Co., NYC, 1977-81; founder, CEO Queue, Inc., Shelton, Conn., 1981. Adj. prof. Sch. Law Bridgeport, 1978-82. Author ednl. software Algebra Word Problems, 1984, How a Bill Becomes a Law, 1985. Vice chmn. Fairfield County Dem. Town Com., 1991-93, 96-2000; Dem. candidate for State Senate, 1972, 88, for U.S. Congress, 1994, 98; coach, mem. adv. bd. Fairfield Youth Soccer, 1985-90; coach Fairfield Little League, 1987, Joel Barlow H.S. Girls Varsity Soccer, 1991; mem. Fairfield Bd. Edn., 1991-93; chmn. bd. trustees Jewish Family Svcs., 1995-99; pres. bd. dirs. The Bridge Acad., 1997-99; mem. Fairfield Bd. Parks and Recreation, 1997-98; founder, pres. bd. Brooklawn Acad., 1998-99. Jewish. Avocations: soccer, tennis, biking, kayaking, books. Office: Queue Inc 1 Controls Dr Shelton CT 06484 Office Phone: 800-232-2224. E-mail: jdk@queueinc.com.

KANTROWITZ, SUSAN LEE, lawyer; b. Queens, NY, Jan. 15, 1955; d. Theodore and Dinah (Kotick) Kantrowitz; m. Mark R. Halperin; 1 child, Jacob Joseph Kantrowitz-Sirotkin. BS summa cum laude, Boston U., 1977; JD, Boston Coll., 1980. Bar: Mass. 1982. Assoc. producer Sta. KOCE-TV, Huntington Beach, Calif., 1980-81; acct. exec. Bozell & Jacobs, Newport Beach, Calif., 1981; atty. WGBH Ednl. Found., Boston, 1981-84, dir. legal affairs, 1984-86, gen. counsel, dir. legal affairs, 1986—, v.p., gen. counsel, 1993. Co-author: Legal and Business Aspects of the Entertainment, Publishing and Sports Industries, 1984. Mem. ABA, Mass. Bar Assn., Boston Bar Assn.

KANUK, LESLIE LAZAR, management consultant, educator; b. NYC; d. Charles and Sylvia Lazar; m. Jack Lawrence Kanuk; children: Randi Kanuk Dauler, Alan Robert. MBA, Baruch Coll., 1964; PhD, CUNY, 1974; PhD (hon.), Mass. Maritime Acad., 1981, Maine Maritime Acad., 1988. Pres. Leslie Kanuk Assocs., NYC, 1965—78, 1981—; Lippert Disting. chair Baruch Coll., NYC, 1981-84; prof. CUNY, 1974—99, prof. emeritus, 1999—. Mem. maritime transp. rsch. bd. NAS, 1975—78; commr., vice chmn., chmn. Fed. Maritime Commn., 1978—81; dir., pres., chmn. Containerization and Intermodal Inst., 1981—93; panelist NRC-NAS, 1975—78, 1991; vis. prof. grad. program Maine Maritime Acad., 1984—93; dir. Cleve. Cliffs Mining Co., 1991—2002. Author: Mail Questionnaire Response Behavior, 1974, Toward an Expanding U.S.M.M., 1976, Consumer Behavior, Prentice Hall, 1978, rev. edits., 1983, 87, 89, 94, 97, 2000, 04, 07, India, 1988, Australia, 1997, 2001, Brazil, 2000, Japan, 2001, China, 2002, Czech Republic, 2004, Croatia, 2004, Internat. Edit., 1997, 2004, Argentina, 2007; mem. editl. bd. Intermodal Forum, 1984-92. Bd. visitors Maine Maritime Acad., 1989—97; trustee United Seaman's Svc., 1988—. Recipient Connie award Containerization and Intermodal Inst., 1980, Diamond Superwoman award Harpers Bazaar mag., 1980, Person of Yr. award NY Fgn. Freight Forwarders and Brokers Assn., 1981, Person of Yr. award Baruch Fgn. Trade Soc., 1981, Disting. Alumnus award CCNY, 1984, Disting. PhD Alumni award CUNY, 1988, Townsend Harris medal, 1986. Mem. Beta Gamma Sigma. Office Fax: 212-717-8266.

KANUTH, JAMES GORDAN, chemical engineer; b. Lexington, Ohio, June 18, 1953; s. John Gordon and Helena Jane K.; m. Michelle Susan Cronk, Nov. 10, 2000; 1 child, Robert Gordon. BSChemE, U. Cin., 1976. Project engr. Joseph E. Seagram and Sons, Inc., Lawrenceburg, Ind., 1976-80; prodn. engr. Monsanto (name changed to Conoco), Alvin, Tex., 1980-81; sr. area engr. utilities Conoco (name changed to Oxy Chem), Alvin, 1981-89; regional mgr. Puckorius and Assocs., Inc. indsl. water treatment cons., League City, Tex., 1989-95; indsl. water treatment cons. Chemtreat, Inc., Nassau Bay, Tex., 1995—. Pres. Gulf Coast Energy Conservation Soc., Houston, 1988-89, Galveston County Mcpl. Utility Dist. 3, League City, 1983-88; city councilman City of League city, 1988-94; bd. dirs. Houston Galveston Area Coun., 1991; treas. Clear Lake Area Coun. of Cities, Webster, Tex., 1990-94. Mem. Nat. Assn. Corrosion Engrs. (com. mem. 1989—), Am. Inst. Chem. Engrs., Cooling Tech. Inst. (bd. dirs. 2005-), Cooling Tower Inst. (water treatment com. 1981—). Republican. Presbyterian. Avocations: boating, reading, sports cars. Home: 18124 Bal Harbour Dr Houston TX 77058 Office: Chemtreat Inc PO Box 412 League City TX 77574-0412 Office Phone: 800-521-2395. E-mail: jimk@chemtreat.com.

KANUTH, MICHELLE SUSAN, science educator; d. Robert Dale and Evelyn Lavonne Cronk; m. James Gordan Kanuth, Nov. 10, 2000; 1 child, Robert Gordon. BS, Ohio State U., Columbus, 1974; MS, U. Cin., Ohio, 1978; PhD, U. Ky., Lexington, 1992. Cert. med. technologist Am. Soc. Clin. Pathologists, 1974, specialist in blood banking Am. Soc. Clin. Pathologists, 1978, clin. lab. scientist Nat. Credentialing Agy. Lab. Pers., 1982. Blood bank specialist reference lab. Mass. Gen. Hosp., Boston, 1978—80; dir. med. tech. program Miriam Hosp., Providence, 1980—82; asst. prof. U. Ky., Lexington, 1983—86; assoc. prof. U. Louisville, 1987—2000, U. Tex. Med. Br., Galveston, Tex., 2000—. Chmn. immunology and immunohematology exam. com. Nat. Credentialing Agy. for Lab. Pers., 1993—97; pres. Ky. Soc. for Med. Tech., 1987—88. Named Med. Technologist of Yr., Ky. Soc. for Med. Tech., 1988. Mem.: Am. Soc. Clin. Pathologists, Am. Soc. Clin. Lab. Sci. (editor jour. 1995—, chmn. edn. and rsch. fund 1998—2002, Profl. Achievement Immunology award 1992, named Educator of Yr. Ky. chpt. 2001, Robin H. Mendelson award 2002, Joseph J. Kleiner award 2002), Omicron Sigma. Presbyterian. Avocations: reading, travel. Office: Univ Texas Med Br 301 Univ Blvd Galveston TX 77058 Home Phone: 281-335-0151; Office Phone: 409-772-9471.

KANY, JUDY C(ASPERSON), retired state senator; b. Ill., June 29, 1937; d. Helmer C. and Florence P. Casperson; m. Robert Kany, Aug. 16, 1958; children: Kristin, Geoffrey, Daniel. BBA, U. Mich., 1959; MPA, U. Maine, Orono, 1976. Mem. Maine Ho. of Reps., 1975-82, Maine Senate, 1982-92; project dir. for health professions regulation Med. Care Devel., Augusta, Maine, 1993—; mem. task force on health workforce regulation Pew Health Professions Commn., 1994-97; mayor Waterville, Maine, 1988-89; mem. issues and policy adv. com. Citizens Advocacy Ctr., Washington, 1994—2000; cmty. liaison Amity Circle Tree Ranch, Tucson, 2003—. Chmn. Maine's Adv. Commn. on Radioactive Waste, 1981-87, Joint Standing Com. Legal Affairs, 1987-88, Joint Standing Com. on State Govt., 1979-82, Joint Standing Com. Energy and Natural Resources, 1983-84, 89-90, Joint Standing Com. Banking and Ins., 1991-92, com. Maine Lakes, 1990-92, adv. com. on accountability to the Maine Health Care Reform Commn., 1994-95; mem. Commn. on Maine's Future, 1976, 87-89; project coord. Amity Found.'s Ariz Gov.'s Innovative Domestic Violence Prevention Grant, Amity, 2004-06. Democrat. Home: PO Box 508 81 Lakeshore Dr Belgrade Lakes ME 04918 also: 36832 S Stoney Flower Dr Tucson AZ 85739 Office Phone: 520-749-5980. Business E-Mail: jkany@amityfdn.org.

KANZER, ALAN, lawyer; b. NYC, June 28, 1944; BA magna cum laude, Columbia U., 1965; LLB, Yale U., 1968. Bar: NY 1969, US Tax Ct. 1971. Ptnr. Walter, Conston, Alexander & Green P.C. (now Alston Bird LLP), NYC; ptnr., mem. antitrust and investigations group Alston & Bird LLP, NYC, 2001—. Bd. editors Yale Law Jour., 1968. Mem. Assn. of Bar of City of NY, Phi Beta Kappa. Office: Alston & Bird LLP 90 Park Ave Fl 14 New York NY 10016-1301 Office Phone: 212-210-9480. Office Fax: 212-210-9444. Business E-Mail: alan.kanzer@alston.com.

KANZER, LYNN KAREN, medical record technician; b. Bronx, NY, Feb. 9, 1945; d. Carl Trost and Alma Cecile Zuckerman; m. Eli Fern, Oct. 6, 1965 (div. 1983); children: Dori Lisa Fern, Brian Allen Fern; m. Larry Kanzer, June 2, 1985; 1 stepchild, Glen Harris. LPN, Montefiore Hosp. Sch. Nursing, Bronx, 1962. Registered health info. technician 1988. LPN Montefiore Hosp., Bronx, 1962—66, Hebrew Hosp. Chronic Sick, Bronx, 1975—76, dir. med. records, 1976—87; dir. health info. Morningside House Nursing Home, Bronx, 1987—2003; admissions/hosp. rep. Orange County Residential, Goshen, NY, 2004—05; health info. coord. Elant at Fishkill, Beacon, NY, 2005—. Cons., NY, Pa., 1983—87; admissions/cmty. rels. rep., inservice educator Elant at Fishkill, Beacon, 2006—; negotiator contracts/rates various managed care cos.; presenter in field. Med. adv. bd. Drake Bus. Sch., Bronx, 1996. Mem.: NY Health Info. Mgmt. Assn., Am. Health Info. Mgmt. Assn. Avocations: knitting, travel. Home: 161 Marigold Ln Milford PA 18337 Office: 22 Robert R Kasin Way Beacon NY 12508

KANZLER, GEORGE, journalist, music critic; b. Elizabeth, NJ, Mar. 30, 1939; s. George and Helen K.; m. Margaret A. Dudas, Dec. 31, 1978; children: Sarah Ella Dudas-Kanzler. BA, Seton Hall U., 1960; postgrad. Bread Loaf Sch. of English, Middlebury Coll., 1960; MA, NYU, 1969; postgrad., U. Wis., 1972. Reporter, editor Linden (N.J.) Leader, 1961-63; instr., asst. prof. Ibadan (Nigeria) Polytech., 1966-68; writer, pop and jazz critic Star Ledger, Newark, 1968-90, writer, jazz critic, 1990—2002, Newhouse News Svc., Washington, 1975—2002; contbg. editor Hot House Jazz mag., 2002—; contbg. writer All About Jazz, NY, 2004—, JazzTimes mag., 2006—; arts critic The Beat, Greenville, SC, 2006—. Jazz disc jockey We. Nigeria Radio, Ibadan, 1966-68; instr. Essex C.C., Newark, 1970-73; elector Am. Jazz Hall of Fame, 1989—. Author: (TV show) One Way to Heaven, 1967; contbg. writer All About Jazz--New York, 2004—. Vice pres. bd. dirs. Newark Jazz Festival, 1991-93; vol. US Peace Corps., Nigeria, 1966-68. Specialist 4 US Army, 1963—65, Congo. Fellow Newspaper Fund, 1972, Music Critics Assn./Smithsonian Inst., 1974. Mem. Nat. Acad. Recording Arts and Scis., Friends of Nigeria, Mbari Artists and Writers Club (sec. pro-tem. 1966-68), Jazz Journalists Assn., N.Y. Jazz Critics Cir. Avocations: hiking, unicycling. Home: 406 Marseille Dr Simpsonville SC 29680 Office Phone: 201-306-6570. Business E-Mail: gkjazz@gmail.com.

KAO, CHARLES KUEN, electrical engineer, educator; b. Shanghai, Nov. 4, 1933; s. Chun-Hsien and Tsung Fong K.; m. May Wan Wong, Sept. 19, 1959; children: Simon M.T., Amanda M.C. B.Sc. in Elec. Engring., U. London, 1957, PhD in Elec. Engring., 1965. Devel. engr. Standard Telephones & Cables Ltd., London, 1957—60; prin. rsch. engr. Std. Telecomm. Lab. Ltd., Harlow, England, 1960—70; prof. electronics, chmn. dept., univ. pres. Chinese U. Hong Kong, 1970—74, prof. electronics, chmn. dept., vice chancellor, 1987—96; chief scientist Electro Optical Products div./ITT, Roanoke, Va., 1974—81, v.p., dir. engring., 1981—83; exec. scientist, dir. research ITT Advanced Tech. Ctr., Shelton, Conn., 1983—87; chmn., CEO ITX Svcs. Ltd., Hong Kong, 2000—. Author: Optical Fiber Technology II, 1981, Optical Fibers Systems: Technology, Design and Applications, 1982, Optical Fibre, 1988, A Choice Fulfilled--The Business of High Technology, 1991; contbr. articles to profl. jours.; patentee in field. Decorated comdr. Brit. Empire, 1993; recipient Morey award Am. Ceramic Soc., 1976, Stewart Ballantine medal Franklin Inst., 1977, Rank prize Rank Trust Funds, 1978, LM Ericsson Internat. prize, 1979, gold medal Armed Forces Comm. and Electronics Assn., 1980, Internat. C & C prize Found. for C & C Promotion, Japan, 1987, New Materials prize Am. Phys. Soc., 1989, Gold medal Internat. Soc. for Optical Engring., 1992, Japan prize The Sci. and Tech. Found. Japan, 1996, Morris Liebmann Meml. awrd, 1978, Alexander Graham Bell medal, 1985, Faraday medal, 1989, charles Stark Draper prize, 1999; Marconi Internat. fellow, 1985. Fellow: IEEE, Royal Acad. Engring. (U.K.), Royal Soc. (U.K.), Chinese Acad. Scis.; mem.: NAE, Academia Sinica (Taiwan), Royal Swedish Acad. Engring. Scis. Office: Unit 1708 Office Tower 1 Harbor Rd Wan Chai Hong Kong Hong Kong

KAO, JOHN STERLING, mathematician, educator; b. Salt Lake City, Aug. 30, 1967; s. Shih Kung and Yasuko Watanabe Kao. BS, U. Utah, 1985; MA, Princeton U., 1987, PhD, 1991. Asst. prof. U. San Francisco, 1991—97, assoc. prof., 1997—. Vis. assoc. prof. Princeton (N.J.) U., 1998—99. Assoc. editor: Advances and Applications in Statistics, 2002—; contbr. articles to profl. jours. Grad. fellow, NSF, 1985—91. Mem.: Math. Assn. Am., Inst. for Ops. Rsch. and the Mgmt. Scis., Soc. for Indsl. and Applied Math., Am. Math. Soc., Phi Beta Kappa, Golden Key. Office: Univ San Francisco 2130 Fulton St San Francisco CA 94117-1080 Office Phone: 415-422-6760.

KAO, MIN H., manufacturing executive; BS, Nat. Taiwan U.; MS in Elec. Engring., PhD in Elec. Engring., U. Tenn. With Magnavox Advanced Products; sys. analyst Teledyne Sys.; co-founder Garmin Corp., 1989, chmn., CEO; dir. Garmin Internat., Inc. Named one of Forbes' Richest Americans, 2006, 50 Who Matter Now, Business 2.0, 2007. Office: Garmin Internat Inc 1200 E 151st St Olathe KS 66062-3426*

KAO, PAI CHIH, clinical chemist; b. Nanking, China, June 20, 1934; came to U.S., 1965, naturalized, 1976; s. Gung and Chuu Hui (Chang) K.; m. Joyce Kao; 1 child, Wayne LeRoy. PhD in Biochemistry, U. Louisville, 1971. Diplomate Am. Bd. Clin. Chemistry, Am. Bd. Clin. Biochemistry. Instr. dept. social medicine Nat. Def. Med. Ctr., Taipei, Taiwan, 1958-65; postdoctoral investigator Oak Ridge (Tenn.) Nat. Lab., 1971-73; head dept. new methods devel. and radioimmunoassay CBL Lab., Columbus, Ohio, 1973-75; prof. emeritus clin. chemistry, dept. lab. medicine and pathology Mayo Clinic, Rochester, Minn., 1975—. Cons. clin. chemistry sect., clin. chemistry and hematology devices panel FDA. Contbr. articles to profl. jours. Fellow Nat. Acad. Clin. Biochemistry, N.Y. Acad. Scis.; mem. Am. Bd. Clin. Chemistry, Assn. Clin. Scientists. Home: 1432 Ridge Cliff Ln NE Rochester MN 55906-8705 Office: Mayo Clinic 1014 Plummer Rochester MN 55905-0001 Home Phone: 507-288-5946; Office Phone: 507-284-2691.

KAO, YASUKO WATANABE, retired library director; b. Tokyo, Mar. 30, 1930; arrived in US, 1957; d. Kichiji and Sato (Tanaka) Watanabe; m. Shih-Kung Kao, Apr. 1, 1959; children: John Sterling, Stephanie Margaret. BA, Tsuda Coll., 1950; BA in Lit., Waseda U., Japan, 1955; MSLS, U. So. Calif., 1960. Instr. Takinogawa H.S., Tokyo, 1950—57; catalog libr. U. Utah Libr., 1960—67, Marriott Libr., 1975—77, head catalog divsn., 1978—90; dir. libr. Teikyo Loretto Heights U., 1991—95. Contbr. articles to profl. jours. Vol. Utah Chinese Am. Cmty. Sch., 1974—80, Asian Assn. Utah, 1981—90; mem., vol. Asian Art Mus. San Francisco, 1996—. Waseda U. fellow, 1958—59. Mem.: Beta Phi Mu. Home: 2625 Yuba Ave El Cerrito CA 94530-1443 Personal E-mail: ykao@sbcglobal.net.

KAOUK, JIHAD, urologist; m. Rula Hajj-Ali; children: Sahar, Reem, Reda. BS, Am. U. Beirut, 1989, MD, 1993. Resident in urology Am. U. Beirut, 1993—99; fellow in advanced laparoscopic surgery Urol. Inst., Cleve. Clinic Found., 1999—2002, dir. robotic surgery, sect. minimally invasive surgery, 2002—. Contbr. articles to profl. jours. Mem.: So. Endourology, Am. Urol. Assn. (assoc.). Achievements include research in surgical techniques in urology such as Laparoscopic and minimally invasive surgery for bladder cancer, prostate cancer, and kidney diseases; development of new robotic urologic surgery techniques. Office: Cleve Clinic Found 9500 Euclid Ave Cleveland OH 44195 Home Phone: 440-498-8641; Office Phone: 216-444-2976.

KAPALA, FREDERICK J., federal judge; b. Rockford, Ill., Sept. 5, 1950; m. Jill Kapala; children: Katie, Candy. BA, Marquette U., 1972; JD, U. Ill. Coll. Law, 1976. Bar: Ill. 1976. Asst. state's atty. Winnebago County, 1976—77; atty. Pedderson, Menzimer, Conde Stoner & Killoren, 1977—82; assoc. judge 17th Jud. Cir., Ill., 1982—94, presiding judge juvenile ct., 1989—91, cir. judge, 1994—2001, presiding judge criminal ct., 1995—2001; judge 2nd Dist. Appelate Ct., Ill., 2001—07, US Dist. Ct. (no. dist.) Ill., 2007—. Served in USAR, 1970—80. Office: US Dist Ct 219 S Dearborn St Chicago IL 60604

KAPANY, NARINDER SINGH, physicist; b. India; m. Satinder Kapany; children: Rajinder, Kiren. Grad. with degree in physics, Agra U., India; advanced studies in optics, Imperial Coll. Sci. and Tech., London; PhD, U. London, 1955. Founder, chmn. bd., pres., dir. rsch. Optics Tech., Inc., Calif., 1960—72; founder, pres., CEO Kaptron, Inc.(sold to AMP Inc.), 1973—90; fellow, chief technologist for global comm. bus. AMP Inc., 1990—97; founder K2 Optronics, 2002—05. Regents prof. U. Calif., Berkeley, Santa Cruz, dir., Ctr. for Innovation and Entrepreneurial Develop.; vis. scholar, physics dept. and consulting prof., dept. electrical engring. Stanford U.; founding chmn., funder Sikh Found.; lectr. in field. Contbr. scientific papers to profl. jours.; artist of several dynoptic sculptures. Trustee U. Calif. Santa Cruz Found., Menlo Sch., Menlo Park, Calif. Named endowed chair of Sikh studies, U. Calif. Santa Barbara, 1998, endowed chair of opto-electronics, U. Calif. Santa Cruz, 1999; recipient Excellence 2000 award, USA Pan-Asian Am. C. of C. Fellow: AAAS, Optical Soc. Am., British Royal Acad. Engring.; mem.: Nat. Inventors Coun., World Presidents Orgn., Young Presidents Orgn. Achievements include being the father of fiber optics; patents in field. Avocations: philanthrophy, sculpting, art collecting. Office Phone: 650-496-2220. Personal E-mail: nkapany@hotmail.com.

KAPELMAN, BARBARA ANN, internist, hepatologist, gastroenterologist, educator; b. NYC, Apr. 30, 1949; d. Leonard A. and Helen (Hass) K.; m. Lawrence William Koblenz, Mar. 24, 1979; 1 child, Adam. BA, Barnard Coll., 1970; MS in Microbiology, Yale U., 1972; MD, Albert Einstein Coll. Medicine, 1975. Diplomate Am. Bd. Internal Medicine, Am. Bd. Gastroenterology. Clin. asst. prof. hepatology and gastroenterology Mt. Sinai Sch. Medicine Mt. Sinai Hosp., 1981—82; intern Roosevelt Hosp.-Columbia U., NYC, 1975-76, resident, 1976-78, fellow gastroenterology, 1978-80; fellow liver diseases Mt. Sinai Sch. Medicine-CUNY, NYC, 1980-81; attending physician liver diseases Mt. Sinai Hosp., NYC, 1981—82; asst. attending physician in gastroenterology Beth Israel Hosp., NYC, 1982-88, assoc. attending physician in medicine and gastroenterology, 1988-96, attending physician in medicine and gastroenterology, 1996—; clin. instr. in medicine Mt. Sinai Sch. of Medicine, NYC, 1981-87, asst. clin. prof. medicine, 1987-94; bd. dirs. Beth Israel Med. Ctr., NYC, 1984—, trustee, med. liaison, 1996-97; asst. clin. prof. medicine Albert Einstein Coll. Medicine, NYC, 1994—. Trustee Med. Bd. Liaison, 1996-97; attending physician Beth Israel North, Beth Israel Med. Ctr., N.Y.C., 1982—, Hosp. for Joint Diseases-Orthopedic Inst., N.Y.C., 1982—; vis. clin. fellow Columbia U. Coll. Physicians and Surgeons, N.Y.C., 1975-80; cons. gastroenterology and hepatology, 2004—. Co-author: Gastroenterology for the House Officer, 1989; contbr. articles to profl. jours. Fellow ACP, Am. Coll. Gastroenterology; mem. AMA, Am. Women's Med. Assn., Women's Med. Assn. NYC (officer), Am. Gastroent. Assn., Am. Assn. for Study of Liver Diseases, Am. Soc. for Gastrointestinal Endoscopy, Am. Med. Informatics Assn., NY Acad. Gastroenterology, NY Soc. for Gastrointestinal Endoscopy. Avocations: medical computer software, culinary arts, medical informatics, educational activities, Hebrew language studies. Home: 201 E 87th St Apt 20k New York NY 10128-3217 Home Phone: 212-860-9003. Business E-Mail: bkapelman@pol.net.

KAPIKIAN, ALBERT ZAVEN, physician, epidemiologist; b. NYC, May 9, 1930; s. Zareh Kaloust and Baizar (Bazikian) K.; m. Catherine Firth Andrews, Feb. 27, 1960; children: Albert Kaloust, Thomas Firth, Gregory Baird. BS cum laude, Queens Coll., 1952; MD, Cornell U., 1956; postgrad., Johns Hopkins U. Sch. Hygiene and Pub. Health, 1961-62, Royal Postgrad. Med. Sch. U. London, 1970; DSc (hon.), CUNY, Queens, 1999. Intern Meadowbrook Hosp., Hempstead, NY, 1956-57; commd. med. officer USPHS, 1957, advanced through grades to capt., ret., 1988; with USPHS Civil Svc., 1988-90, USPHS Sr. Exec. Svc., 1990-2000, Sr. Biomed. Rsch. Svc., 2000—01, sr. investigator, 2001—; with epidemiology sect. Lab. Infectious Diseases, Nat. Inst. Allergy and Infectious Diseases, NIH, Bethesda, Md., 1957—, asst. chief, head epidemiology sect., 1967—; rsch. prof. child health and devel. George Washington U. Sch. Medicine and Health Svcs., 1977—. Temporary advisor WHO, 1980-88, 91, 2006. Contbr. articles to profl. jours. Recipient Meritorious Svc. medal USPHS, 1970, 74, Disting. Svc. medal USPHS, 1983, Disting. Alumnus award Queens Coll., 1974, Stitt award Assn. Mil. Surgeons, 1974, Kabakjian award Armenian Students Assn. Am., 1974, Diagnostic Virology award (Murex) Pan Am. Soc. for Clin. Virology, 1993, joint recipient Pasteur award Children's Vaccine Initiative, 1998; invited to deliver Theobold Smith Lectr., 1995, Kinyoun Lectr., 1999, NIH Dirs. Lectr., 2000, Wyeth-Ayerst Rhesus Rotavirus Project Team award, 1995, Queens Coll Alumni Star award, 1998, Presdl. Disting. Exec. Rank award, 2000, award of distinction Cornell U. Weill Med. Coll. Alumni Assn., 2001, Butantan medal, Sao Paulo, Brazil, 2005, Albert B. Sabin Gold medal, Sabin Vaccine Inst., 2005, DHHS Secretary's Disting. Svc. award, 2006; named to Leon G. Smith Infectious Disease Hall of Fame, St. Michael's Med. Ctr., 2000. Fellow AAAS, Infectious Disease Soc.; mem. APHA, Am. Epidemiol. Soc. (pres. 1996-97), Am. Soc. Microbiology (Behring Diagnostics award 1987), Am. Soc. Virology, Phi Beta Kappa. Mem. Armenian Apostolic Ch. Home: 11201 Marcliff Rd Rockville MD 20852-3631 Office: NIH Lab Infectious Diseases Bethesda MD 20892-0001

KAPIKIAN, CATHERINE ANDREWS, artist; b. Cleve., Oct. 18, 1939; d. John Robert and Anne Alva (Cosgrove) Andrews; m. Albert Zaven Kapikian, Feb. 27, 1960; children: Albert, Thomas, Gregory. Student, Carnegie Mellon U., Pitts., 1957—59; BA, U. Md., Coll. Pk., 1963; MTS summa cum laude, Wesley Theol. Sem., Washington, 1979. Gen. illustrator NIH, Bethesda, Md., 1959—61; artist-in-residence Wesley Theol. Sem., 1979—, mem. faculty, 1980—, founder, dir. Ctr. Arts and Religion, 1984—2001, dir. Henry Luce III Ctr. for the Arts and Religion, 2001—. Designer, fabricator liturgical tapestries, banners, paraments and vestments; mem. commn. on worship and the arts Nat. Coun. Chs., 1991-97; mem. com. Washington Nat. Cathedral's Fabric and Fine Arts, 2006. Works exhibited in group shows including Interfaith Forum on Religion, Art and Architecture, Phoenix, 1979, Chgo., 1981, Phila., 1987, Houston, 1989, Boston, 1990, St. Thomas More Newman Ctr. Liturg. Arts Exhibit, Bowling Green U., Ohio1981, Archdiocese of Chgo., 1984, Biennial Exhbns. Liturgical Art Guild of Ohio, Columbus, 1985, 91, 93, 95, 97, 2001; author: Through the Christian Year: An Illustrated Guide, 1983, Art In Service of the Sacred, 2006; contbr. foreword to (book) Full Circle, 1988; contbr. articles and images to profl. jours. Mem. fabric and fine arts com. Washington Nat. Cathedral, 2006—; bd. dirs. Episcopal Ch. Visual Arts, 2002—06. Named to North Am. Acad. Liturgy, 2007; fellow, Coll. Preachers, Washington Nat. Cathedral, 1992. Mem. Arts and Religion Forum of Washington Theol. Consortium (founder, mem. steering com.), Interfaith Forum on Religion, Art and Architecture (bd. dir. 1983-85, 87-90), Schuyler Inst. Worship and the Arts (bd. dir. 1987-90). Democrat. Avocations: opera, remote control airplanes. Office: Wesley Theol Seminary Henry Luce III Ctr for Arts and Religion 4500 Massachusetts Ave NW Washington DC 20016-5632 Office Phone: 202-885-8617, 202-885-8608. Business E-Mail: ckapikian@wesleyseminary.edu.

KAPLAN, ALEXANDER EFIMOVICH, physics educator, engineering educator; b. Kiev, Ukraine, USSR, June 9, 1938; came to U.S., 1979; MS in Physics, Moscow Phys. Tech. Inst., 1961; postgrad., USSR Acad. Scis., Moscow, 1963-66; PhD in Physics and Math., Acad. Scis., Moscow, 1967. Rsch. scientist Radio R & D Lab., Moscow, 1961-63; rsch. staff mem. USSR Acad. Scis., 1963-79; rsch. staff mem., Francis Bitter Nat. Magnet Lab. MIT, Cambridge, 1979-82; prof. elec. engring. sch. Purdue U., West Lafayette, Ind., 1982—86; prof. elec. and computer engring. dept. Johns Hopkins U., Balt., 1987—. Cons. Bell Labs, Holmdel, N.J., 1980-81, Los Alamos (N.Mex.) Nat. Lab., 1981, Honeywell Rsch. Ctr., Mpls., 1982; guest scientist Max-Planck-Inst. for Quantum Optics, Garching, Munich, Fed. Republic Germany, 1981; Alexander-von-Humboldt prof. quantum physics dept. U. Ulm, Germany, 1996-97; invited lectr.; referee for several jours. and orgns.; invited fgn. prof., Kyoto U., Japan, 2006. Contbr. more than 370 rsch. publs., 120 jour. articles, 3 books, more than 40 Book Chpt., and conf. proceedings in the field; editl. bd. mem. Jour. Nonlinear Optical Physics & Materials, Internat. Jour. Optics Communications, 1997-99. Recipient Alexander von Humboldt award for sr. U.S. scientists Alexander von Humboldt Found. Germany, 1996, Max Born award, Optical Soc. Am., 2005. Fellow Optical Soc. Am. (Max Born award, 2005); mem. Am. Phys. Soc., IEEE Laser & Electro-Optic Soc. Achievements include patent in field. Office: Johns Hopkins U Elec and Comp Engring Dept 34th & Charles Sts Baltimore MD 21218 Home Phone: 410-366-3056; Office Phone: 410-516-7018, 410-516-5566. Business E-Mail: alexander.kaplan@jhu.edu.

KAPLAN, BARBARA JANE, retired city planner; b. NYC, Sept. 8, 1943; d. Richard S. and Fannie I. (Schutz) Benson; m. Jerry Martin Kaplan, May 29, 1966. BA, Barnard Coll., 1965; MS, U. Southern Calif., 1969. Asst. planner L.A. Regional Planning Commn., 1968-69; from asst. planner to assoc. planner San Diego Comprehensive Planning Orgn., 1969-71; asst. dir. of regional planning North Ctrl. Tex. Coun. of Govts., Arlington, 1971-73; dir. Pennsport Civic Assn., Phila., 1974; city planner III Phila. City Planning Commn., 1974-76, city planner V, 1976-80, dep. exec. dir., 1980-83, exec. dir., 1983-2000, ret., 2000. Trustee U. of the Arts, Phila., 1987—2001; pres. Ctr. for Literacy, Phila., 1991—96, bd. dirs., 1984—, Neighborhood Gardens Assn., Phila., 1987—. Mem.: Pa. Hort. Soc. (bd. dirs. 1993—, v.p. 2000—01, mem. coun.), Nat. Trust for Hist. Preservation, Am. Planning Assn. Avocations: reading, tennis.

KAPLAN, BARRY MARTIN, lawyer; b. NYC, Nov. 9, 1950; s. Stanley Seymour and Lillian (Schner) K.; m. Erica Green, July 26, 1981; children: Matthew Aaron, Elizabeth Rose, Andrew Nathan. BA, Colgate U., 1973; JD cum laude, U. Mich., 1976. Bar: Mich. 1976, Wash., 1978, U.S. Dist. (ea. dist.) Mich. 1976, U.S. Dist. Ct. (we. dist.) Wash. 1978, U.S. Dist. Ct. (ea. dist.) Wash. 1986, U.S. Tax Ct. 1983, U.S. Ct. Appeals (9th cir.) 1990. Law clk. to Hon. Charles W. Joiner U.S. Dist. Ct. (ea. dist.) Mich., Detroit, 1976-78; assoc. Perkins Coie, Seattle, 1978-85, ptnr., 1985—2005, Wilson Sonsini Goodrich & Rosati, Seattle, 2005—. Adj. prof. securities regulation U. Wash. Sch. Law; spkr. in field. Author: Washington Corporate Law, Corporations and LLCs, 2000; contbr. articles to legal jours. and procs. Mem. ABA (litigation sect., securities litigation com., bus. law sect., bus. and corp. litigation com., subcom. chmn. on control transactions 1993), Wash. State Bar Assn. (CLE spkr., bus. law sect., securities com., subcom. chair on dir.'s liability 1993), Wash. Athletic Club, Rainier Club. Home Phone: 206-324-0321; Office Phone: 206-883-2538. Business E-Mail: bkaplan@wsgr.com.

KAPLAN, BENJAMIN, judge; b. NYC, Apr. 9, 1911; s. Morris and Mary (Berman) K.; m. Felicia Lamport, Apr. 16, 1942; children: James L., Nancy L. Mansbach. AB, CCNY, 1929; LL.B., Columbia, 1933; LL.D., Suffolk U., 1974, Harvard U., 1981, Northeastern U., 1981. Bar: N.Y. 1934, Mass. 1950. Assoc., then mem. firm Greenbaum, Wolff & Ernst, NYC, 1933-42, 46; vis. prof. law Harvard, 1947, prof. law, 1948—, Royall prof. law, 1961-72, emeritus, 1972—; assoc. justice Supreme Jud. Ct. Mass., 1972-81; recalled to serve as judge Appeals Ct. Mass., 1983—2005. Reporter to adv. com. on civil rules Jud. Conf. U.S., 1960-66, mem., 1966-70; co-reporter restatement (2d) of judgments to Am. Law Inst., 1970-73 Served to lt. col. AUS, 1942-46. Mem. Am. Law Inst., Assn. Bar City of N.Y., Phi Beta Kappa. Achievements include assisting Justice Jackson on Nuremberg Trial, 1945. Home: 2 Bond St Cambridge MA 02138-2308 Office: Harvard Law Sch Cambridge MA 02138

KAPLAN, BETSY HESS, retired school board member; b. Bridgeton, NJ, Aug. 12, 1926; d. Alfred N. and Betsy (Bolton) Hess; m. Robert Leon Kaplan, June 11, 1953; children: Bruce Alfred, James Edward, Joan Ann. AB, Wesleyan Coll., 1947; BFA, Wesleyan Conservatory, 1948. Cert. tchr., Fla. Tchr. 4th grade Miami-Dade County Pub. Schs., Fla., 1950—53; edn. and cultural arts adv., 1961—88; instr. Miami Dade C.C., 1979—81; admintrv. asst. to Ethel K. Beckham Miami-Dade County Sch. Bd., 1980—82, mem. sch. bd., 1988—2004, chair, 1993—95; ret., 2004. Chair fed. rels. network Fla. Sch. Bds., Tallahassee, 1996-98; bd. dirs. New World Sch. Arts, Miami, 1996-2005, found. bd., 2004—; mem. Performing Arts Ctr. Trust, Miami, 1993-2004, student mentor 1997-2007; mem. Human Svcs. Coalition, 1995—. Mem. Emily's List, Washington, 1990—, Women's Emergency Network, Miami, 1990—; cultural amb. Heart of the City cultural series Miami-Dade Parks and Recreation Dept., 2002; bd. mem. Gay Lesbian and Straight Edn. Network, 1989—2001, co-chair, 2001—07; active Women's Polit. Caucus, 1988—. Named Woman Worth Knowing, Miami Beach Commn. on Status of Women, 1994, Woman of Yr., King of Clubs, 2000; named to Miami-Dade County Women's Park Wall of Honor, 2005; recipient Alumnae Disting. Achievement award, Wesleyan Coll., 1987, French Acad. Palms award, French Min. of Edn. of Youth and Sports, 1991, Ruth Wolkowsky Greenfield award, Am. Jewish Congress, 1993, Trailblazer award, Women's Com. of 100, 1993, Woman of Impact award, Cmty. Coalition for Women's History, 1995, Co. of Women, Pioneer award, Miami-Dade County Pks. Dept., 1997, Red Cross Spectrum award, Women in Edn., 1997, Lifetime Svc. to Music Edn. in Fla. and U.S., Fla. Music Educators Assn., 2000, Branches of Learning award, Women's Divsn. Greater Miami State of Israel Bonds Orgn., 2001, Heart of the Arts award, New World Sch. of the Arts, 2004, Pillar award, Black Heritage Planning Com., Miami-Dade County, 2004, Joseph R. Narot award, Temple Israel of Miami, 2004, Cervantes award, Nova U., 2004, Serving the Arts, Arts and Edn. award, Children's Cultural Coalition and Arts and Bus. Coun., 2004. Mem.: AAUW (Phoenix award 1999), LWV (Margery Rankin award 2004), M. Athalie Range Cultural Found. (bd. dirs. 1995—2002, exec. com. 2002—), Jewish Mus. Fla. (bd. dirs. 1999—2003, exec. bd. 2003—04, adv. bd. 2004—07), Alliance for Aging (mem. adv. bd. 1996—2004), Fla. Sch. Bds. Assn. (bd. dirs. 1990—99, Pres.'s award 2001), Phi Kappa Phi, Delta Kappa Gamma, Phi Delta Kappa. Democrat. Jewish. Avocations: studying art history, reading and interpreting poetry, studying and practicing French language, cooking. Home: 2 Grove Isle Dr # 1603 Miami FL 33133 Personal E-mail: bakaplan60@aol.com.

KAPLAN, CARL ELIOT, lawyer; b. NYC, Apr. 17, 1939; s. Lawrence S. and Pearl (Eisenberg) K.; m. Diane L. Garvin, Dec. 16, 1965; children: Lynn, Jonathan. BA, Columbia Coll., 1959; LLB, 1962. Bar: U.S. Dist. Ct. (so. and ea. dists.) N.Y. 1964, U.S. Ct. Appeals (2nd cir.) 1966, U.S. Supreme Ct. 1970. Assoc. Fulbright & Jaworski L.L.P., NYC, 1963—69, ptnr., 1969—2006. Bd. editors Columbia Law Rev., 1961-62. Mem. ABA, N.Y. Bar Assn., Assn. of Bar City of N.Y., Am. Soc. Corp. Secs., Univ. Club (N.Y.C.), Phi Beta Kappa. Avocations: biking, jogging. Office: 666 5th Ave Fl 31 New York NY 10103-3198 Office Phone: 212-318-3224. Business E-Mail: ckaplan@fulbright.com.

KAPLAN, CAROLYN SUE, elementary school educator; b. Childress, Tex., June 23, 1944; d. Irving and Juliette (Weiner) Kohn. Student, Hunter Coll. Cert. tchr., N.Y. Tchr. N.Y.C. Bd. Edn., 1966—79, 1991—; sec. Borough of Manhattan Community Coll., NYC, 1975—76, N.Y.C. Housing Authority, 1984—90; with Headstart program United People's Meth. Ch., 1993; peer specialist, intern, mental health worker Met. Hosp., NYC, 1998—99. Mem. legis. adv. com. N.Y. State Senate, Albany, 1991—; vol. Queens Woman's Ctr., 1994—; tutor adult literacy program Queens Librs., 1994—; bd. dirs. Venture House; mem. N.Y.C. Clubhouse Coalition; co-chmn. Queens Mental Health Coun., 1996-97; advocate The Bklyn. (N.Y.) Clubhouse, 1999—; co-chmn. Bklyn. (N.Y.) Mental Health Coun., 2003; tnr. Peer Specialist Ctr., 1999—; advocate Kingsbrook Jewish Med. Ctr., 2003— Mem. Assn. for Childhood Edn. Internat. Avocations: reading, cultural events, movies. Home: 19806 Pompeii Ave Jamaica NY 11423-1422 E-mail: carolyn.kaplan@worldnet.att.net.

KAPLAN, CATHY M., lawyer; b. NYC, Jan. 22, 1953; BA, Yale U., 1974; JD, Columbia U., 1977. Bar: N.Y. 1978. Ptnr. Brown & Wood, NYC; now ptnr. and co-head securitization practice Sidley Austin Brown & Wood LLP, NYC, and mem. exec. com. Contbr. articles to profl. journals. Mem.: ABA. Office: Sidley Austin Brown & Wood 787 Seventh Ave New York NY 10019 Office Phone: 212-839-5531. Office Fax: 212-839-5599. Business E-Mail: ckaplan@sidley.com.

KAPLAN, CHERYL L., theater educator; BA, Ind. U., Bloomington, 1994; MFA, U. Iowa, 2000. Dir. theater outreach edn. U. Tex. Med. Br., Galveston, 2002—. Dir.: (theatre prodn.) Picasso at the Lapin Agile, The Importance of Being Earnest, Driving Miss Daisy, The Devil and Ben Jones, The Firebugs, The Maids; author: (theatre prodn.) Till The Whistle Blows, Question of a Critical Illness: The Breast Cancer Journey, A Face to AIDS; dir.: (theatre prodn.) Wondergirl, (theatre production/utmb) Question of a Critical Illness:The Breast Cancer Journey, HIV/AIDS.it ain't over, Facing the Music, A Woman's heART, The Unspeakables, Unparalleled, Rumors. Mem.: Assn. Theatre Higher Edn., US Ctr. Internat. Assn. Theatre for Children and Young People, Soc. Am. Fight Dirs., Am. Alliance for Theatre Edn. (rep. Tex. state 2005—06). Office: Univ Tex Med Branch 301 University Blvd Galveston TX 77555-1311 Office Phone: 409-772-9395. Office Fax: 409-772-5640. Business E-Mail: clkaplan@utmb.edu.

KAPLAN, DAVID L., retired communications educator, actor, artist, sculptor; b. Chgo., Apr. 6, 1918; s. Maurice I and Emily (Seilin) Kaplan; m. Tea Stefancic, June 11, 1977. BS, Northwestern U., 1940, MA, 1941; postgrad., Stanford U., 1950—52. Actor, stage mgr. comml. Chicagoland theatre, Chgo. and Highland Park, 1953-76. Radio speech and theatre instr. Temple U., Phila., 1947—50; from instr. to prof. City Coll. Chgo., 1956—86; stage dir. Peninsula Players, Fish Creek, Wis., 1963—64; cmty. theatre dir., Wilmette, Lincolnwood, Wheaton, Winnetka, Ill., St. Joseph, Mich., 1965—70. Sculpture. Mem Equity Libr. Theatre, Chgo., 1953—99, pres., v.p., sec.-treas.; mem Skokie Art Guild, Ill., 1986—, Evanston Art Ctr, Ill. Recipient numerous artistic awards including Best Dir Award, Ill Community Theater Asn, 1970, Marge Dare Lifetime Achievment Award, Equity Library Theatre Chicago, 1999. Mem.: Actors Equity Assn., Chgo. Artists Coalition, Nat. Sculpture Soc. (assoc.).

KAPLAN, E. PAUL, urologist; b. Phila., Dec. 26, 1965; m. Lisa Greene Kaplan. BS, Emory U., Atlanta, 1987; MD, U. Pa., Phila., 1991. Bd. cet. urologist Am. Bd. Urology, 1999. Urologist Urology Assn. North Tex., Dallas, 2001—. Major, urologist USAF, 1997—2001. Mem.: Am. Soc. Urology. Office: Urology Assocs North Tex 7777 Forest Ln C-618 Dallas TX 75230

KAPLAN, EDWARD H., operations research specialist; BA, McGill U., Montreal, 1977; MSc in ops. rsch., MIT, 1979, MSc in stats., 1982, PhD, 1984. Instructor MIT, Cambridge, Mass., 1977—84; adj. lectr. & rsch. assoc. Harvard U. John F. Kennedy Sch. Govt., Cambridge, Mass., 1984—85, stats. instructor, Sloan Found. & Assn. Pub. Policy Analysis & Mgmt. (APPAM) Summer Sr. Inst., 1985—87; asst. prof. mgmt. sciences U. Mass., Boston, 1985—87; asst. prof. ops. rsch. & pub. mgmt. Yale Sch. Orgn. & Mgmt., New Haven, 1987—90, assoc. prof. policy modeling & pub. mgmt., 1989—93, prof. mgmt. sciences, 1993—2000, William N. & Marie A. Beach prof. mgmt. sciences, 2000—; assoc. prof. ops. rsch. Yale U., New Haven, 1989—93, affiliated faculty, Instn. Social & Policy Studies, 1989—; assoc. prof. medicine Yale Sch. Medicine, 1991—93, prof. medicine, 1993—98, prof. pub. health, 1998—; dir. Law, Policy & Ethics Core Ctr. Interdisciplinary Rsch. on AIDS, Yale U., 1999—2001, dir. Methodology & Biostatistics Core, 2001—. Vis. rsch. scholar U. Calif. Berkeley Survey Rsch. Ctr., 1991; Lady Davis vis. prof. medicine Hebrew U., Jerusalem, 1994, Lady Davis vis. prof. stats., 97; vis. prof., Davidson Sch. Mgmt. Technion Israel Inst. Tech., Haifa, Israel, 1998; vis. prof. ops. rsch. & stats. MIT Sloan Sch. Mgmt., 2000; scientific rev. bd. Am. Found. AIDS Rsch. (AmFAR), 1992—; exec. com. Yale Ctr. Interdisciplinary Rsch. on AIDS, 1997—. Recipient Alumni award for outstanding teaching, Yale Sch. Mgmt., 1991, AIDS Leadership award, Conn. Dept. Health Svcs., 1991, Franz Edelman award, Inst. Mgmt. Sciesnces, 1992, Hiscock award, Conn. Pub. Health Assn., 1997. Fellow: Inst. Ops. Rsch. & Mgmt. Sciences (INFORMS) (Lanchester award 1995, Pres.'s award 2002, Koopman prize 2003); mem.: Inst. Medicine, Conn. Acad. Sci. & Engring., Omega Rho (hon.). Office: Yale School of Mgmt Box 208200 52 Hillhouse Ave New Haven CT 06520-8200 Office Phone: 203-432-6031. Office Fax: 203-432-9995. E-mail: edward.kaplan@yale.edu.

KAPLAN, EDWARD L., retired electronics executive; b. Nov. 19, 1942; BSME, Ill. Inst. Tech., 1965; MBA, U. Chgo., 1971. Project engr. Seeburg Corp.; mech. engr. R&D Printer Divsn. Teletype Corp.; co-founder Zebra Technologies Corp. (formerly Data Specialties, Inc.), Vernon Hills, Ill., 1969—91; chmn., CEO Zebra Technologies Corp., 1991—2006, CFO, 1969—91, pres., 1969—95, 1997—98, 2001—02. Bd. trustees Ill. Inst. Tech., exec. com.; mem. coun. Grad. Sch. Bus. U. Chgo. Bd. dir. Anti-Defamation League. Named to Entrepreneurship Hall of Fame; recipient High Tech Entrepreneur award, Peat Marwick, 1988, Entrepreneur of Yr. award, Inc. Mag. and Ernst & Young, 1990, Disting. Entrepreneurial Alumnus award, U. Chgo., 1996. Fellow: NDEA; mem.: ASME, Chief Execs. Orgn., World Pres. Orgn., Soc. Advancement Mgmt., Tau Beta Pi.

KAPLAN, EUGENE ALKEN, psychiatry professor, department chairman; b. Syracuse, NY, Dec. 24, 1933; s. David S. and Florence F. Kaplan; m. Sandra Ecker Kaplan, May 14, 1961; children: Susan Beth Kaplan Lue, Karen Lynn. BA magna cum laude, Syracuse U., 1954; MD, SUNY, Syracuse, 1957. Diplomate Nat. Bd. Med. Examiners, cert. Am. Bd. Psychiatry and Neurology. Med. intern Albert Einstein Med. Ctr., NYC, 1957—58; psychiatry resident, chief resident SUNY Upstate Med. U., Syracuse, 1958—61, from instr. to prof., 1961—, prof., chair dept. psychiatry, 1987—99, prof., chair emeritus dept. psychiatry, 1999—. Cons. Peace Corps tng. programs Syracuse U., 1962—66; vis. prof. Sloan Sch. Cornell U., Ithaca, NY, 1967—82; lectr. Washington Sch. Psychiatry, 1967—69; vis. scientist The Tavistock Psychiat. Ctr., London, 1981; cons. psychiatrist Syracuse U. Health Svc., 1982—87. Co-editor: International Psychiatric Clinics, vol. 2 & 3, 1965; contbr. articles to profl. jours. Bd. dirs. Transitional Living Svc., Syracuse, 1975—82, Syracuse Opera, Syracuse, 1990—98, Syracuse Symphony, Syracuse, 1999—. Comdr. Med. Corps USN, 1967—69. Fellow: Am. Psychiat. Assn. (Disting. Life fellow); mem.: Am. Bd. Psychiatry and Neurology (sr. examiner 1974—98), Phi Kappa Alpha, Phi Beta Kappa. Avocations: sailing, piano. Home: 2804 West Lake Rd Cazenovia NY 13035 Office: SUNY Upstate Med Univ Dept Psychiatry 750 E Adams St Syracuse NY 13210 Home Phone: 315-655-8589; Office Phone: 315-464-3105. Business E-Mail: kaplane@upstate.edu.

KAPLAN, GABRIELA DIANA, radiologist; arrived in U.S., 1963; d. Isidor and Rosa Kaplan. MD, U. Autonoma Guadalajara, 1972; BA, Whittier Coll. Diplomate Am. Bd. Radiology. Fellow in body imaging Johns Hopkins U., Balt., 1980, fellow in neuroradiology, 1982; fellow in whole body magnetic resonance U. Mich., Ann Arbor, 1989, asst. prof. radiology Med. Ctr., 1988—89; asst. prof. Columbia U./Presbyn. Hosp., NYC, 1979; lectr. diagnostic radiology Johns Hopkins Hosp., Balt., 1980—82; pres. Lifewatch Group Ltd., Cleve., 1990—. Author: Wealth, Hunger and Peace, 1989—, Aquarelles, 2007, Reflections, 2007; contbr. articles to profl. jours. including Radiology Jour., Jour. Magentic Resonance Imaging. Named Amb. Poetry, Internat. Poetry, 2006; recipient Presdl. Rep. award of merit, Ptnrs. in Conservation award, World Wildlife Fund, 1999, Amb. Internat. award of Merit, Internat. Soc. Poetry, 2005. Mem.: Radiology Soc. N.A., P.I.B. Yacht Club (fleet surgeon). Republican. Roman Catholic. Achievements include invention of device to aid women in family planning. Avocations: environmental concerns, poetry, gardening. Personal E-mail: life_watch@msn.com.

KAPLAN, GARY, executive recruiter; b. Phila., Aug. 14, 1939; s. Morris and Minnie (Leve) K.; m. Linda Ann Wilson, May 30, 1968; children: Michael Warren, Marc Jonathan, Jeffrey Russell Wilson. BA in Polit. Sci., Pa. State U., 1961. Tchr. biology N.E. High Sch., Phila., 1962-63; coll. employment rep. Bell Telephone Labs., Murray Hill, NJ, 1966-67; supr. recruitment and placement Unisys, Blue Bell, Pa., 1967-69; pres. Electronic Systems Personnel, Phila., 1969-70; staff selection rep. Booz, Allen & Hamilton, NYC, 1970-72; mgr. exec. recruitment M&T Chems., Rahway, NJ, 1972-74; dir. exec. recruitment IU Internat. Mgmt. Corp., Phila., 1974-78; v.p. personnel Crocker Bank, Los Angeles, 1978-79; mng. v.p. ptnr. western region Korn-Ferry Internat., Los Angeles, 1979-85; pres. Gary Kaplan & Assocs., Pasadena, Calif., 1985—. Bd. dirs. Ptnrs. in Care, Greater L.A. Zoo Assn., Coll. Liberal Arts, Pa. State U. Alumni Assn. Mgmt. columnist, Radio and Records newspaper, 1984-85. Mem. alumni coun. Pa. State U.; former bd. dirs. The Wellness Cmty., Pa. State U. Indsl./Orgn. Psychology Adv. Bd., Vis. Nurs Assn. L.A., Hme Pharmacy of Calif., Calif. Exec. Recruiters Assn. Alumni fellow Pa. State U., 1998. Mem. World at Work, Soc. Human Resources Mgmt., Mount Nittany Soc. Pa. State U., Pa. State U. Alumni Soc., Big Ten Club So. Calif Office: Gary Kaplan & Assocs 201 S Lake Ave Ste 600 Pasadena CA 91101-3018 Office Phone: 626-796-8100.

KAPLAN, GEORGE WILLARD, urologist; b. Brownsville, Tex., Aug. 24, 1935; s. Hyman J. and Lillian (Bennett) Kaplan; m. Susan Gail Solof, Dec. 17, 1961; children: Paula, Elizabeth, Julie, Alan. BA, U. Tex., Austin, 1955; MD, Northwestern U., Evanston, Ill., 1959, MS, 1966. Diplomate Am. Bd. Urology. Intern Charity Hosp. of La. at New Orleans, 1959-60; resident Northwestern U., 1963-68, instr. Med. Sch. Chgo., 1968-69; clin. prof. U. Calif., San Diego, 1970—, chief pediatric urology, 1970—98. Trustee Children's Hosp. and Health Ctr., San Diego, 1978-90, Am. Bd. Urology, Bingham Farms, Mich., 1991-96; del. Am. Bd. Med. Specialties, Evanston, Ill., 1992-96. Author: Genitourinary Problems in Pediatrics; asst. editor Jour. Urology, Balt., 1982-89, 98-2002; assoc. editor Child Nephrology and Urology, Milan, Italy, 1988-94; contbr. articles to profl. publs. Pres. med. staff Children's Hosp., San Diego, 1980-82. Lt. USN, 1960-63. Recipient Joseph Capps prize Inst. of Medicine, 1967. Fellow ACS (pres. San Diego chpt. 1980-82), Am. Acad. Pediat. (chmn. sect. on urology 1986, Vadlogy medal 2007); mem. AMA, Soc. for Pediatric Urology (pres. 1993), Am. Urol. Assn., Soc. Internat. Urologie, Soc. Univ. Urologists, Am. Assn. Genito-Urin. Surgeons. Independent. Jewish. Avocation: rare books. Office: 7930 Frost St Ste 306 San Diego CA 92123-2740 Business E-Mail: gkaplan@chsd.org.

KAPLAN, GERSON NATHANIEL, retired radiologist; b. Feb. 18, 1939; s. Seymour Frayne and Rose Mandel Kaplan; m. Chaya Bernice Morman, June 14, 1959; children: Mara Leslie Hahn, Jana Lynn Fastow, Jason David. B in Chem. Engring., Cooper Union, NYC, 1960; MD, Georgetown U., Washington, 1966. Intern, resident Columbia Presbyn. Med. Ctr., NYC, 1966—68; surgeon NIH, Bethseda, Md., 1968—70; resident Johns Hopkins Hosp., Balt., 1970—73; radiologist Drs. Schultze and Assocs., Balt., 1973—97; ret. Instr. radiology Johns Hopkins Hosp., Balt., 1973—83. Mentor Big Bros. Big Sisters, Columbia, Md., 2000—04. Recipient Excellence Med. Studies, Hoffman La Roche, 1964. Mem.: Med. and Chirurgical Soc. Md., Radiol. Soc. N.Am. Avocations: golf, skiing. Personal E-mail: gersonk@verizon.net.

KAPLAN, GILBERT B., lawyer; b. Endicott, NY, July 9, 1951; s. Marek and Helene Christine (Freund) K.; m. Elizabeth Ann Piserchia, June 26, 1983; children: Katharine, Nicholas. Grad., Phillips Exeter Acad., 1969; AB, Harvard U., 1973, JD, 1977. Bar. Mass. 1977, D.C. 1989. Dir. office of investigations U.S. Dept. Commerce, Washington, 1983-85, dep. asst. sec. import adminstrn., 1985-87, acting asst. sec., 1987-88; sr. ptnr., head internat. trade practice Hale and Dorr, Washington, 1990—2004, chmn. govt. and regulatory affairs dept., 2001—04; ptnr., internat. trade King & Spalding, Washington, 2004—. Co-author (with Courtland Reichman): The ITC of the District Court? Where to Protect Your International Intellectual Property, 2006. Sec. Washington Exeter Alumni Assn., 1989-92; Rep. nominee and candidate State Rep. BackBay-Beacon Hill Sect., Boston, 1982; mem. Mass. Internat. Trade Adv. Bd., co-chmn. Export Promotion Task Force, 1992-97. Mem. ABA (co-chmn. com. on China, internat. law sect. 1989-91). Republican. Office: King & Spalding 1700 Pennsylvania Ave NW Washington DC 20006 Home Phone: 202-364-8159; Office Phone: 202-661-7981. Business E-Mail: gkaplan@kslaw.com.

KAPLAN, HARVEY L., lawyer; b. Kansas City, Mo., Nov. 11, 1942; BS in Pharmacy, U. Mich., 1965; JD, U. Mo., 1968. Bar: Mo. 1968, U.S. Tax Ct. 1971, U.S. Supreme Ct. 1971, U.S. Ct. Appeals (5th, 6th, 8th, 9th and 10th cirs.). Ptnr. Shook, Hardy & Bacon LLP, Kansas City, chair Pharm. and Med. Device Litig. Div. Mem. bd. editors Mo. Law Rev., 1967-68. Named Best of Bar, Kans. City Bus. Jour.; named one of 500 Leading Lawyers in Am., Lawdragon, 500 Leading Litigators in Am., Top 10 Super Lawyers Mo., Top 10 Super Lawyers Kans., Ams. Leading Lawyers for Bus., Chambers USA, Best Lawyers in Am. Fellow Internat. Acad. Trial Lawyers (bd. dirs. 1991-97, 98—, sec.-treas. 2001-02), Internat. Soc. Barristers, Am. Bar Found.; mem. Am. Soc. Pharmacy Law, Mo. Orgn. Def. Lawyers (bd. dirs. 1985-93), Internat. Assn. Def. Counsel (bd. dirs. 1991-94, def. counsel trial acad. 1989, dir.-elect 1992, dir. 1993, v.p., found. bd. dirs. 2001-03), Def. Rsch. Inst. (chmn. drug and med. device litigation com. 1991-94, bd. dirs. 1995-98), Phi Delta Phi. Office: Shook Hardy & Bacon LLP 2555 Grand Blvd 19th fl Kansas City MO 64108-2613 Office Phone: 816-474-6550. Business E-Mail: hkaplan@shb.com.

KAPLAN, HELENE LOIS, lawyer; b. NYC, June 19, 1933; d. Jack and Shirley (Jacobs) Finkelstein; m. Mark N. Kaplan, Sept. 7, 1952; children: Marjorie Ellen, Sue Anne. AB cum laude, Barnard Coll., 1953; JD, NYU, 1967; LLD (hon.), Columbia U., 1990. Bar: N.Y. 1967. Pvt. practice, NYC, 1967-78; ptnr. Webster & Sheffield, NYC, 1978-86, counsel, 1986-90; of counsel Skadden, Arps, Slate, Meagher & Flom, NYC, 1990—. Bd. dirs. The May Dept. Stores Co., Met. Life Inc. and Met. Life Ins. Co., JP Morgan Chase & Co., Exxon Mobil Corp. Trustee N.Y. Coun. for Humanities, 1976-82, chmn., 1978-82; trustee Barnard Coll., 1973-99, chair bd. trustees, 1984-94, trustee and chair emerita, 1999—; trustee Columbia U. Press, 1977-80, MITRE Corp., 1978-95, N.Y. Found., 1976-86, John Simon Guggenheim Meml. Found., 1981-98, NYU Law Ctr. Found., 1985-87, Neuroscis. Rsch. Found., 1986-92, Am. Mus. Natural History, 1989—, vice chair, 1993—; trustee Am. Trust for Brit. Libr., 1991-93, Com. for Econ. Devel., 1993-96, Commonwealth Fund, 1990-2003, vice chair, 1996-2003; trustee and chair emerita Inst. for Advanced Study, 1986-2002, trustee emerita, 2002—; trustee J. Paul Getty Trust, 1992—, vice chair 1997—; trustee Olive Free Libr.; trustee Carnegie Corp. N.Y., 1979—, vice-chair bd. trustees, 1981-84, 98-2002, chair, 1984-91, 2002-; chair, trustee Mt. Sinai Sch. Medicine, 1999-01, Mt. Sinai NYU Health, 1998-2001, vice-chair bd. trustees, 1993-99; trustee N.Y.C. Pub. Devel. Corp., 1978-83, vice-chair bd. trustees, 1978-82; mem. Adv. Com. on South Africa, U.S. Sec. of State, 1986-88; mem. N.Y. State Gov.'s Task Force on Life and the Law, 1985-90, Women's Forum, Inc., 1982—, Rockefeller U. Coun., 1984-94, Bretton Woods Com., 1985-96, Carnegie Coun. on Adolescent Devel., 1986-96; chair task force on sci. and tech. and jud. decision making Carnegie Commn. on Sci., Tech. and Govt., 1988-93; ptnr. N.Y.C. Partnership, 1987-92; bd. dirs. Am. Arbitration Assn., 1978-82. Mem.: N.Y.C. Bar Assn. (treas. 1991—93, mem. com. on philanthropic orgns. 1975—81, mem. com. on recruitment of lawyers 1978—82, mem. com. on profl. responsibility 1980—83), Am. Philos. Soc., Am. Acad. Arts and Scis., Century Assn., Cosmopolitan Club.

KAPLAN, HENRY JERROLD, ophthalmologist, educator; b. NYC, Dec. 29, 1942; s. Ralph and Henrietta (Davis) K.; m. Adele Lotner, June 26, 1966; children: Wendi Suzanne, Todd Daniel, Ariane Dev. AB, Columbia U., 1964; MD, Cornell U., 1968. Diplomate Am. Bd. Ophthalmology. Intern in medicine Lakeside Hosp., Univ. Hosps. Cleve., Case-Western Res. U., 1968-69; surg. resident Bellevue Hosp., NYU Med. Ctr., 1969-70; NIH rsch. fellow in immunology U. Tex. (Southwestern) Med. Sch., Dallas, 1972-74, asst. prof. dept. cell biology, 1974-75; resident in ophthalmology U. Iowa Hosps. and Clinics, Iowa City, 1975-78; retina-vitreous fellow dept. ophthalmology Med. Coll. Wis., Milw., 1978-79; assoc. prof. dept. ophthalmology Emory U. Sch. Medicine, Atlanta, 1979-84, prof., dir. rsch., 1984-88, assoc. prof. dept. microbiology, 1985-88; prof. dept. ophthalmology and visual scis. Washington U. Sch. Medicine, St. Louis, 1988-2000, chmn. dept. ophthalmology and visual scis., 1988-98; prof., chmn. dept. opthalmology and visual scis. U. Louisville (Ky.) Sch. Medicine, 2000—, William H. and Blondina F. Evans Prof. Ophthalmology, 2000—. Ophthalmologist in chief Barnes-Jewish Hosp., Washington U. Med. Ctr., 1988-98; affiliate scientist in pathology and immunology Yerkes Regional Primate Rsch. Ctr., Atlanta, 1981—; adj. prof. dept. small animal medicine U. Ga., Athens, 1985—; assoc. chief ophthalmology Emory U. Hosp., 1985-88; mem. visual scis. study sect. A-1 NIH, Bethesda, Md., 1985-89, chmn., 1987-89; pres. Barnes Eye Care Network, 1994-98; dir. Ky. Lions Eye Ctr., Louisville, 2000—; pres. Eye Specialists Louisville, Ky.,2000—; chmn. U. Physician Assocs., 2004—. Author, co-author or editor, co-editor more than 200 med. textbooks, chpts. and articles on uveitis and macular degeneration and retinal degeneration pub. in refereed sci. and med. jours., 1974—; mem. sci. jour. rev. bds. Archives Ophthalmology, 1978—, Retina, 1982—, Am. Jour. Ophthalmology, 1983—, Ophthalmology, 1983—, Current Eye Rsch., 1986—, Exptl. Eye Rsch., 1986—; mem. sci. rev. bd. Investigative Ophthalmology and Visual Sci., 1983—, mem. editorial bd., 1990-92; co-editor Ocular Immunology and Inflammation, 1994-98; editor: Ocular Immunology and Inflammation, 1999—. Maj. M.C., USAF, 1970-72. Recipient sci. award Alcon Rsch. Inst., 1987; Olga Keith Weiss rsch. scholar to Prevent

Blindness, Inc., N.Y.C., 1984. Fellow ACS, Am. Acad. Ophthalmology (Honor award 1984, Sr. Honor award 1994); mem. AMA, Assn. for Rsch. in Vision and Ophthalmology, Am. Assn. Immunologists, Macula Soc., Am. Uveitis Soc. (pres. 1997-99), Retina Soc., Louisville Ophthal. Soc., Ky. Acad. Eye Physicians and Surgeons. Jewish. Office: U Louisville Sch Medicine Dept Opthalmol & Visual Sci 301 E Muhammad Ali Blvd Louisville KY 40202-1511 Office Phone: 502-852-3716. Business E-Mail: hank.kaplan@louisville.edu. *Faith in pursuit of one's own ideas and persistence in the face of adversity will bring success, but more importantly - personal satisfaction.*

KAPLAN, HOWARD GORDON, lawyer; b. June 1, 1941; s. David I. and Beverly Kaplan. BS, U. Ill., 1962; JD, John Marshall Law Sch., Chgo., Ill., 1967. CPA Ill.; bar: Ill. 1967, D.C. 1980, N.Y. 1982, Wis. 1983, U.S. Supreme Ct. 1971. CPA Ill. Acct., Chgo., 1962—67; sr. ptnr. The Kaplan Group Ltd., Chgo., 1967—, The Kaplan Ptnrs. L.L.P., Chgo., 1975—. Asst. prof. Chgo. City Colls., 1967—78. Contbr. articles to profl. jours. Former treas. Ill. Devel. Fin. Authority. Mem.: ABA, AICPA, Ill. Soc. CPAs, Decalogue Soc., Bar Assn. 7th Cir., Chgo. Bar Assn., Ill. Bar Assn., B'nai B'rith, Friars Club (L.A.), Bryn Mawr Country Club (Chgo.), Standard Club. Office: 180 N La Salle St 25th Fl Chicago IL 60601-2501

KAPLAN, ISAAC RAYMOND, chemistry professor; b. Baranowicze, Poland, July 10, 1929; came to U.S., 1957; s. Morris and Anny (Chait) K.; m. Helen Fagot, Sept. 4, 1955; children: Debora, David Joel. BS, Canterbury U., Christchurch, New Zealand, 1951, MS, 1953; PhD, U. So. Calif., 1961. Rsch. scientist Commonwealth Sci. and Indsl. Rsch. Orgn., Sydney, Australia, 1953-57; postdoctoral fellow Calif. Inst. Tech., Pasadena, 1961-62; guest lectr. Hebrew U., Jerusalem, 1962-65; assoc. prof. UCLA, 1965-69, prof., 1969-93, prof. emeritus, 1993—. Contbr. over 300 articles to profl. jours. Guggenheim Found. fellow, Sydney, 1970-71. Fellow: AAAS, Geol. Soc. Am., Am. Inst. Chemists; mem.: Am. Assn. Petroleum Geologists (Pres. award 2002), Geochem. Soc. (Alfred Treibs medal 1993), Geophys. Union, Am. Chem. Soc., Russian Acad. Natural Sci. (fgn.) (Kapitsa medal 1998). Office: U Calif ESS Dept Plaza Circle Dr Los Angeles CA 90024

KAPLAN, JAMES I., lawyer; b. Chgo., Sept. 2, 1954; s. Jerome and Phyllis Enid (Rieber) K.; m. Elizabeth J. Taylor, May 7, 1989; children: William Taylor Kaplan, Caroline Taylor Kaplan. AB magna cum laude, Harvard U., 1977; JD, U. Chgo., 1981. Bar: Ill. 1982, U.S. Dist. Ct. (no. dist.) Ill. 1982, U.S. Ct. Appeals (7th cir.) 1984. Law clk. to Hon. Milton I. Shadur U.S. Dist. Ct. (no. dist.) Ill., Chgo., 1981-82; assoc. Mayer Brown & Platt, Chgo., 1983-88, Altheimer & Gray, Chgo., 1988, ptnr., 1988-91; gen. counsel, corp. sec. Cole Taylor Fin. Group, Inc., Wheeling, Ill., 1991-97; sr. v.p., gen. counsel, corp. sec. Reliance Acceptance Group, Inc., Chgo., 1997-98; assoc. gen. counsel No. Trust Co., Chgo., 1998—2004; mng. dir., gen. counsel Brown Bros. Harriman, NYC, 2004—. Mem. legal-legis. com. Chgo. Clearing House Assn., 1991—; adj. prof. Ill. Inst. Tech.-Chgo. Kent Coll. of Law, 1999. Bd. dirs., treas. Chgo. STRIVE, 1991—; trustee Latin Sch., Chgo., 1997-99. Mem. ABA, Chgo. Bar Assn., Am. Corp. Counsel Assn., Bank Counsel Group/Fin. Svcs. Roundtable, Phi Beta Kappa. Office: Brown Brothers Harriman 140 Broadway New York NY 10005

KAPLAN, JARED, lawyer; b. Chgo., Dec. 28, 1938; s. Jerome and Phyllis Enid (Rieber) K.; m. Rosellen Engstrom, Dec. 28, 1964 (div. 1978); children: Brian F., Philip B.; m. Maridee Quanbeck, June 2, 1990. AB, UCLA, 1960; LLB, Harvard, 1963. Bar: Ill. 1963, U.S. Dist. Ct. (no. dist.) Ill. 1969, U.S. Tax Ct. 1978. Assoc. Ross & Hardies, Chgo., 1963-69, ptnr., 1970, Roan & Grossman, Chgo., 1970-83, Keck, Mahin & Cate, Chgo., 1983-94, McDermott, Will & Emery, Chgo., 1994—. Bd. dirs. ESOP (Employee Stock Ownership Plan) Assn., Washington, 1987-90, Family Firm Inst., Boston, 1996-99, gen. counsel, 2003--; adv. coun. Ill. Employee-Owned Enterprise, Chgo., 1984-98; chmn. Ill. Adv. Task Force on Ownership Succession and Employee Ownership, 1994-95. Editor in chief: Callaghan's Fed. Tax Guide, 1988; author: Employee Stock Ownership Plans, 2005. Nat. pres. Ripon Soc., Washington, 1975-76; adv. coun. mem. Rep. Nat. Com., Washington, 1978-80; alt. delegate Rep. Nat. Conv., Detroit, 1980. Fellow Am. Coll. Employee Benefits Counsel, Am. Bar Found.; mem. ABA (chmn. sect. taxation, administrv. practice com. 1978-80), City Club, Chgo. (bd. govs. 1982-92), Univ. Club, Met. Club Republican. Jewish. Office: McDermott Will & Emery 227 W Monroe St 47th Fl Chicago IL 60606-5018 Home Phone: 313-943-2737; Office Phone: 312-984-6955. E-mail: jkaplan@mwe.com, jared.kaplan@att.net.

KAPLAN, JILL REBECCA, publishing executive; b. Feb. 27, 1966; d. Katherine and Arnold Kaplan; m. Wayne David Katz, Jan. 23, 1999; 2 children. With Economist group, NYC, Times Mirror mag. group, NYC; internat. sales mgr. Dow Jones & Co./Wall St. Jour. (WSJ), NYC, 1997—2000; dir. US sales Dow Jones internat. mag. group, 2000—06; gen. mgr. WSJ Jour. Report, WSJ Weekend Jour., 2000—06, WSJ Personal Jour., 2002—06, WSJ Weekend Edition, 2005—06; pub. Crain's NY Bus., NYC, 2006—. Office: Crains NY Bus 711 3rd Ave New York NY 10017 Office Phone: 212-210-0277. Office Fax: 212-210-0799. E-mail: jkaplan@crain.com.

KAPLAN, JOEL A., academic administrator; Sr. v.p. clin. affairs Mt. Sinai Med. Ctr., NY; dean, v.p. health affairs Sch. Medicine U. Louisville, 1998—2003, exec. v.p. and chancellor Health Scis. Ctr., 2003—04, dean emeritus, 2004—. Office: Abell Adminstrn Ctr U Louisville Louisville KY 40202

KAPLAN, JOEL DAVID, federal official; BA, JD, Harvard U. Law clk. for Hon. J. Michael Luttig US Ct. Appeals (4th cir.); law clk. for Justice Antonin Scalia US Supreme Ct.; policy advisor 2000 Presdl. Campaign, Austin, Tex.; spl. asst. to pres., Office of Chief of Staff The White House, Washington, 2001—03; dep. dir. Office Mgmt. & Budget Exec. Office of the Pres., Washington, 2003—06; asst. to Pres., dep. chief of staff for policy The White House, Washington, 2006—. Artillery officer USMC. Office: The White House 1600 Pennsylvania Ave Washington DC 20502

KAPLAN, JOEL H., lawyer; b. Bklyn., Jan. 10, 1946; BS, Cornell U., 1966; JD, U. Chgo., 1969. Bar: Ill. 1969, US Supreme Ct. 1978. Ptnr. Seyfarth Shaw LLP, Chgo., 1975—, chmn. Labor & Employment Practice Group, 1992—94, mem. exec. com. Bigelow teaching fellow, instr. criminal law & legal writing U. Chgo. Law Sch., 1969—70. Mem.: ABA (railway & airline labor law com.). Office: Seyfarth Shaw LLP 55 E Monroe St Ste 4200 Chicago IL 60603 Office Phone: 312-269-8821. Office Fax: 312-269-8869. Business E-Mail: jkaplan@seyfarth.com.

KAPLAN, JOEL STUART, lawyer; b. Bklyn., Feb. 1, 1937; s. Abraham Larry and Phayne (Moses) K.; m. Joan Ruth Katz, June 19, 1960; children: Andrea Beth, Pamela Jill. BA, Bklyn. Coll., 1958; LLB, NYU, 1961. Bar: NY 1962, US Dist. Cts. (ea. and so. dists.) NY 1964, US Ct. Appeals (2d cir.) 1966, US Supreme Ct. 1979, Fla. 1982, DC 1987. Asst. town atty. Town of Hempstead, Nassau County, NY, 1962-67; ptnr. Jaspan, Kaplan, Levin & Daniels and predecessors, Garden City, NY, 1970-83; sole practice Garden City, 1983-95; counsel Levin Belsky Ross and Daniels, Garden City, 1995—; ptnr. Kaplan Belsky Ross LLP, 2004—. Chmn. Hempstead Town Pub. Employment Rels. Bd., 1973-81; Rep. candidate for NY State Senate, 1974. Mem. ABA, NY State Bar Assn., Nassau County Bar Assn., B'nai B'rith Internat.(pres. 2002-06). Office: 666 Old Country Rd Ste 602 Garden City NY 11530-2006 Office Phone: 516-745-1100. Personal E-mail: joelskaplan@yahoo.com.

KAPLAN, JOHN, photojournalist, educator, consultant; b. Wilmington, Del., Aug. 21, 1959; s. Ralph Benjamin and Ruth Jillya (Denkin) Kaplan. BJ cum laude, Ohio U., Athens, 1982; MS in Journalism, Ohio U., 1998. Photojournalist, designer Spokesman Rev./Chronicle, Spokane, Wash., 1983—84; photojournalist, picture editor Pitts. Press, 1984—90; photojournalist Pitts. Post-Gazette, 1990—92; spl. corr. Block Newspapers, 1992—94. Tchr., lectr. numerous univs., seminars, profl. groups U.S., Can., 1984—; vis. lectr. Bradley U., Peoria, Ill., 1989; adj. prof. Syracuse U., London campus, 1993; assoc. prof. U. Fla., Gainesville, 1999—; dir. Media Alliance, cons., Pitts., 1990—2000; mem. Pulitzer Prize jury, 1994, 95; photojournalism mem. Ball State U., Muncie, 1998—99. Author: Mom and Me, 1996; contbr. to book series The Best of Photojournalism, Vols. 6, 7, 9, 10, 11, 14, 18, 1981-93; work in permanent collection Carnegie Mus. Art, Pitts.; author: Photo Portfolio Success, 2003. Named Pitts. Photographer of Yr., News Photographers Assn. Greater Pitts., 1986, 1989, 1992, Photographer of Yr., Pa. Photographers Assn., 1989, No. Photographer of Yr., 1992; named to, Ohio U. Coll. Comm. Hall of Fame, 1993; recipient Golden Quill Journalism award, Pitts. Press Club, 1986, 1989, Robert F. Kennedy Journalism award, Kennedy Found., 1989, 2003, Pulitzer prize for feature photography, 1992, 2003, Matrix Mag. award, Women in Comm., 1992, Ohio U. Disting. Grad. award, 1993, award for feature photography, Overseas Press Club, 2003, Harry Chapin award, 2003; Knight fellow, Ohio U., 1997—98. Mem.: Soc. Newspaper Design (Gold award 1989), Nat. Press Photographers Assn. (contest chmn. Region 3 1987—89, Regional Photographer of Yr. award 1985, 1986, 1987, 1989, Nat. Newspaper Photographer of Yr. award 1989, Nikon Documentary Sabbatical award 1990, Harry Chapin award 2023, others), Amnesty Internat. Avocations: racquet sports, furniture design, wines. Address: 3067 Weimer Hall Gainesville FL 32611-8400

KAPLAN, JOSEPH SOLTE, retired lawyer; b. Paterson, NJ, Mar. 14, 1935; s. Sidney C. and Estelle (Solte) K.; m. Lily Chariton, Dec. 28, 1958; children: Michele Kaplan Green, Andrew Ezra, David Baruch. BA, Yeshiva U., 1956; LLB, Harvard U., 1959. Bar: N.Y. 1966, U.S. Dist. Ct. N.J. 1960, U.S. Dist. Ct. (ea. and so. dists.) N.Y. 1967, U.S. Ct. Internat. Trade 1966, U.S. Ct. Appeals (fed. cir.) 1975, U.S. Supreme Ct., 1971. Assoc. Baker, Garber & Chazen, Hoboken, NJ, 1960—65; gen. atty. U.S. Dept. Treasury, NYC, 1965—66; assoc. Siegel Mandel & Davidson, NYC, 1966—70, Busby, Rivkin, Sherman, Levy & Rehm, NYC, 1970—71, ptnr., 1971—77, Rivkin, Sherman & Levy, NYC, 1977—81, Kaplan & Pellegrini, NYC, 1981—83, Baskin & Steingut, NYC, 1984—85, Ross & Hardies, NYC, 1985—2003, exec. com., 1992—95; of counsel McGuire Woods, LLP, NYC, 2003—06; ret., 2006. Mem. U.S. Ct. Internat. Trade Adv. Com., N.Y.C., 1989-97, chair 9th jud. conf. planning com. Articles editor Internat. Law Practicum, 1995-2003; contbr. articles to profl. jours. and pubs. Bd. dirs. Jewish Bd. Family and Children's Svcs., N.Y.C., 1985-93, v.p., 1996-97, pres.-elect, 1996-97, pres., 1998-2001, chmn. bd., 2002—, chmn. ct. and legal svc. com., 1976-84, chmn. cmty. edn. divsn. com., 1985-92, chmn. human resources com. 1989-97, chmn. exec. com., 1993-97; bd. dirs. The Shield Inst., N.Y.C., 2000—, chmn. bd., 2001—. With U.S. Army N.G., 1959-65. Mem. ABA (standing com. on customs law 1979-85), Am. Assn. Importers and Exporters (chmn. harmonized sys. com. 1980-90, bd. dirs. 1993-2003), Customs and Internat. Trade Bar Assn. (chmn. trial and appellate practice com. 1988-92, sec. 1992-94, bd. dirs. 1988-94), N.Y. State Bar Assn. (editor Internat. Trade Newsletter 1986-87) Office: McGuire Woods LLP 1345 Ave of Americas 7 New York NY 10105-0302 Office Phone: 212-548-7017. Business E-Mail: jskaplan@mcguirewoods.com.

KAPLAN, JUSTIN, author; b. NYC, Sept. 5, 1925; s. Tobias D. and Anna (Rudman) K.; m. Anne F. Bernays, July 29, 1954; children: Susanna Bernays, Hester Margaret, Polly Anne. BS, Harvard U., 1944, postgrad., 1944-46; LHD (hon.), Marlboro Coll., 1984. Free-lance editing, writing, NYC, 1946-54; sr. editor Simon & Schuster, Inc., NYC, 1954-59; lectr. English Harvard U., 1969, 73, 76, 78; prose writer in residence Emerson Coll., Boston, 1977-78. Vis. lectr. Griffith U., Brisbane, Australia, 1983; lectr. in field; judge Nat. Book Awards, 1968, 73, 78, 87, 93, Pulitzer prizes, 1989, 94, 97, 2003; resident Bellagio Study and Conf. Ctr., Italy, spring, 1990; Jenks prof. contemporary letters Coll. of Holy Cross, Worcester, Mass., 1992-95. Author: Mr. Clemens and Mark Twain, 1966, Lincoln Steffens, A Biography, 1974, Mark Twain and His World, 1974, Walt Whitman: A Life, 1980, (with Anne Bernays) The Language of Names, 1997, (with Bernays) Back Then, 2002, When the Astors Owned New York, 2006; editor: Dialogues of Plato, 1948, With Malice Toward Women, 1949, The Pocket Aristotle, 1956, The Gilded Age, 1964, Great Short Works of Mark Twain, 1967, Mark Twain, A Profile, 1967, Walt Whitman: Complete Poetry and Collected Prose, 1982, The Harper American Literature, 1987, 94, Best American Essays, 1990; gen. editor: Bartlett's Familiar Quotations, 17th edit., 2002; contbr. to NY Times, New Republic, Am. Scholar, Newsweek, Ploughshares, Yale Rev., others. Participant cultural programs USIA, Israel, Dominican Republic, Mex., 1985. Recipient Pulitzer prize for biography, 1967, Nat. Book award for arts and letters, 1967, Nat. Book award for biography, 1981, Guggenheim fellowship, 1975—76. Fellow: Mass. Hist. Soc., Soc. Am. Historians, Am. Acad. Arts and Scis.; mem.: Am. Acad. Arts and Letters, Harvard Club (NY), Phi Beta Kappa. Home: 16 Francis Ave Cambridge MA 02138-2010 Personal E-mail: jknames@aol.com.

KAPLAN, KEITH EUGENE, insurance company executive, lawyer; b. Rahway, NJ, Apr. 6, 1960; s. Eugene Aloysius and Barbara Ann (Dempski) Kaplan; m. Rita Marie Baker, Aug. 8, 1987; children: Matthew Joseph, William Alexander(dec.). BS, U. Pa., 1982; JD, Temple U., 1992. Bar: Pa. 1992. Underwriter Home Ins. Co., Phila., 1982—85, underwriting supr., 1985—86, product line mgr. NYC, 1987; underwriting dir. Reliance Ins. Co., Phila., 1987—88; asst. v.p. Reliance Nat., Phila., 1988—90, NYC, 1990—92, v.p., 1992—96, mng. v.p., 1996—2000, exec. v.p., 2000—. Bd. dirs. Assn. Ins. and Reins Runoff Cos., 2004—. Mem.: ABA, Assn. of Ins. and Reinsurance Run-off Cos. (bd. dirs.), Excess and Surplus Lines Claim Assn., Reinsurance and Ins. Arbitration Soc., Pa. Bar Assn. Home: 1240 Pickering Ln Chester Springs PA 19425-1423 Office: Reliance Ins Co Three Parkway Philadelphia PA 19102

KAPLAN, LAWRENCE JAY, retired economist, educator; b. Oct. 28, 1915; s. Harris and Estelle (Wilner) Kaplan; m. Jeanne Leon, June 9, 1946; children: Harriet Trackman, Sanford S., Marcia Pavone. BA, Bklyn. Coll., 1937; MA, Columbia U., 1938, PhD, 1958. Chief info. officer Bur. Labor Stats., Dept. of Labor, NYC, 1949—57; dir. planning and rsch. N.Y.C. Dept. City Planning, Dept. Relocation, 1957—65; prof. econs. John Jay Coll. Criminal Justice, NYC, 1965—86, prof. emeritus, 1986—; now lectr. and cons. Author: Elementary Statistics for Economics and Business, 1966, Ins and Outs of On-Track and Off-Track Betting, 1970, Retiring Right: Planning for A Successful Retirement, 2003; editor: An Economic Analysis of Crime, 1976. Vice-chmn., mem. profl. staff Congress-CUNY Welfare Fund, 1969—86, emeritus, 1986—; chmn. profl. staff Congress-CUNY Retirees chpt., 1991—2001, emeritus, 2001—; chmn. Coun. Mcpl. Retiree Organizations N.Y.C., 1995—2003, emeritus, 2003—. With mil. intelligence US Army, 1942—45, 6th Armored Divsn. Decorated NY State Conspcuous Svc. Cross, 5 Battle Stars; recipient citation, Republic of France. Mem.: Am. Statis. Assn., Am. Econ. Assn. Democrat. Jewish. Office: John Jay Coll Criminal Justice 899 10th Ave New York NY 10019-1104 Personal E-mail: ljkjj@aol.com.

KAPLAN, LEE LANDA, lawyer; b. Houston, Jan. 26, 1952; s. Charles Irving and Ara Celine (Seligman) K.; m. Diana Morton Hudson, Feb. 6, 1982. AB, Princeton U., 1973; JD, U. Tex., 1976. Bar: Tex., U.S. Dist. Ct. (no., we., ea. and so. dists.) Tex., U.S. Ct. Appeals (5th, 11th and Fed. cirs.), U.S Supreme Ct. Law clk. to sr. cir. judge U.S. Ct. Appeals (5th cir.), Houston, 1976-77; assoc. Baker & Botts, L.L.P., Houston, 1977-84, ptnr., 1985-94, Smyser Kaplan & Veselka, L.L.P., Houston, 1995—. Mem. Tex. Aerospace Commn., 1994-99. Mem. ABA, State Bar Tex., Houston Bar Assn., Am. Bd. Trial Advs. (assoc.), Am. Intellectual Property Law Assn., Houston Intellectual Property Law Assn. Democrat. Jewish. Avocation: history. Office: Smyser Kaplan & Veselka LLP 700 Louisiana St Ste 2300 Houston TX 77002-2728 Office Phone: 713-221-2323. Business E-Mail: lkaplan@skv.com.

KAPLAN, LEONARD EUGENE, accountant; b. Chgo., Mar. 3, 1940; s. David Solomon and Faye Gertrude (Grossman) K.; m. Myrna Dee Shellist, Dec. 20, 1959; children: Sheri Kaplan Mayes, Jodi Kaplan Hoffman, Jeffrey. Student, U. Ill., Chgo., 1958-59; BSc in Acctg., De Paul U., 1961. CPA, Tex., Ill.; cert. ins. counselor. Staff acct. Goldstein, Engerman & Shane, Chgo., 1960-63, BDO Seidman, Chgo., 1963-72, ptnr., 1972-79, Houston, 1979-95, regional tech. dir. region III, 1982-84, mng. ptnr., 1984-89, nat. dir. industry specialization, 1990-92; also bd. dirs.; exec. v.p., sec., CFO Delta Ins. Group Corp., Houston, 1995—. Mem. adv. coun. dept. acctg. U. Tex., 1989-95. Contbr. articles to various publs. Bd. dirs. Chocolate Bayou Theater Co.; mem. WYO Standards Com., FEMA, 2003—. Ill. State scholar, 1958-61, Jack Claitor Meml. scholar, 1988. Mem.: AICPA, Property Casualty Insurers Assn. Am., Tex. Surplus Lines Assn. (pres. 2006—07, Pres. award 2005), Bus. and Profl. Soc. of Jewish Fedn., Am. Assn. Mng. Gen. Agts., Soc. of Cert. Ins. Counselors, Ill. CPA Soc., Tex. Soc. CPAs (vice chmn. com. on rels. with attys. Houston chpt. 1984—85), B'nai B'rith (newsletter editor 1971—72), Royal Oaks Country Club (fin. com.). Jewish. Avocations: golf, tennis, crossword puzzles. Business E-Mail: lenk@deltains.com, lenk@houston.rr.com. *Concern for what might have been is never productive. Yesterday is what it is. Today and the rest of your life are what you make them. Focus on the future and never look back.*

KAPLAN, LEWIS A., federal judge; b. SI, NY, Dec. 23, 1944; s. Alfred H. and Dorothy A. Kaplan; widowed; 1 child, Merrill; m. Lesley Oelsner, Feb. 29, 2004. AB, U. Rochester, 1966; JD, Harvard U., 1969. Bar: N.Y. 1970, U.S. Ct. Appeals (1st and 2d cirs.) 1970, U.S. Dist. Ct. (so. and ea. dists.) N.Y. 1971, U.S. Ct. Appeals (3d cir.) 1973, U.S. Supreme Ct. 1973, U.S. Dist. Ct. (we. dist.) N.Y. 1975, U.S. Ct. Appeals (DC cir.) 1976, U.S. Dist. Ct. (no. dist.) Calif. 1980, U.S. Ct. Appeals (9th cir.) 1980, U.S. Dist. Ct. (ea. dist.) Mich. 1983, U.S. Ct. Appeals (6th cir.) 1983, DC 1985, U.S. Ct. Appeals (Fed. cir.) 1987, U.S. Dist. Ct. DC 1988. Law clk. to judge U.S. Ct. Appeals (1st cir.), 1969-70; assoc. Paul, Weiss, Rifkind, Wharton & Garrison, NYC, 1970-77, ptnr., 1977-94; judge U.S. Dist. Ct. (so. dist.) N.Y., NYC, 1994—, spl. master Westway litig., 1982. Trustee Lawyers Com. Civil Rights Under Law, 1992—94; mem. com. info. tech. Jud. Conf. U.S., 1997—2003; Brace Meml. lectr. Copyright Soc. U.S.A., 2001; mem., del. US-Finnish-Estonian Intellectual Property Workshop, 2007. Mem. US Del. US- Italian Intellectual Property Jud. Workshop (sponsored by US Embassy in Italy), 2003, 2005; mem. trustees' coun. U. Rochester, 1982—88, mem. trustees' vis. com. William E. Simon Grad. Sch. Bus. Adminstrn., 1986—88; village trustee NY, 1988—91. Fellow: Am. Coll. Trial Lawyers; mem.: ABA (jud. liaison to coun. antitrust sect. 2006—), Fed. Judges Assn. (dir. 1995—2001, exec. com. 1999—2001), Am. Law Inst., Fed. Bar Coun., N.Y. State Bar Assn. (Stanley H. Fuld award 2007). Office: US Courthouse 500 Pearl St New York NY 10007-1316

KAPLAN, MADELINE, legal administrator; b. NYC, June 20, 1944; d. Leo and Ethel (Finkelstein) Kahn; m. Theodore Norman Kaplan, Nov. 14, 1982. AS, Fashion Inst. Tech., NYC, 1964; BA in English Lit. summa cum laude, CUNY, 1982; MBA, Baruch Coll., 1990. Free-lance fashion illustrator, NYC, 1965-73; legal asst. Krause Hirsch & Gross, Esquires, NYC, 1973-80; mgr. communications Stroock & Stroock & Lavan Esquires, NYC, 1980-86; dir. adminstrn. Cooper Cohen Singer & Ecker Esquires, NYC, 1986-87, Donovan Leisure Newton & Irvine Esquires, NYC, 1987-93, Proskauer Rose Goetz & Mendelsohn, NYC, 1993-95, Kaye Scholer LLP, NYC, 1995—. Mem. adv. bd. Grad. Sch. Human Resources Mgmt. Mercy Coll., 1997—; bd. dirs. Suitability. Contbr. articles to profl. jours. Founder, pres. Knolls chpt. of Women's Am. Orgn. Rehab. Through Tng., Riverdale, N.Y., 1979-82, v.p. edn., Manhattan region, 1982-83; adv. bd. Suitability; vol. Starlight Found. Mem. ASTD, Assn. Legal Adminstrs. (program com.), MBA Alumni Assn. (bd. dirs.), Sigma Iota Epsilon (life). Office: 425 Park Ave New York NY 10022-3506

KAPLAN, MARJORIE, broadcast executive; married; 2 children. B in Semiotics, Brown U. Dir. advt. Kraft Gen. Foods; v.p. Ogilvy & Mather; exec. v.p. Lancit Media Entertainment; sr. v.p. children's programming and products Discovery Networks, US, 1997—, pres. Discovery Kids Media & Animal Planet Media, 2007—. Cons. Warner Amex Satellite Entertainment; developer Discovery Kids. Office: Discovery Comm 7700 Wisconsin Ave Bethesda MD 20814*

KAPLAN, MARK NORMAN, lawyer; b. NYC, Mar. 7, 1930; s. Louis and Ruth (Hertzberg) K.; m. Helene L. Finkelstein, Sept. 7, 1952; children: Marjorie Ellen, Sue Ann. AB, Columbia, 1951, JD, 1953. Bar: N.Y. 1953. Assoc. Garey & Garey, NYC, 1953; law clk. to Hon. William Bondy U.S. Dist. Ct. for So. Dist. N.Y., 1953-54; assoc. Columbia Law Sch., 1954-55, Wickes, Riddell, Bloomer, Jacobi & McGuire, NYC, 1955-59; from assoc. to sr. ptnr. Marshall, Bratter, Greene, Allison & Tucker, NYC, 1959-70; sr. ptnr. Burnham & Co., NYC, 1970-71; pres. Drexel Burnham Lambert Inc., NYC, 1972-77, also CEO, 1976-77; pres. Engelhard Minerals & Chem. Corp., NYC, 1977-79; mem. firm Skadden, Arps, Slate, Meager & Flom, NYC, 1979—. Bd. dirs. Am. Biltrite, Inc., Autobytel, Inc., REFAC Optical Group, DRS Techs. Inc., Volt Info. Sci., Inc., Jim Pattison, Ltd., Congoleum Corp., World Wide Spl. Fund N.V.; vice-chmn. Am. Stock Exch., N.Y.C., 1974, bd. govs., 1975, vice-chmn. bd. govs., 1975-76; trustee Bard Coll.; chmn. audit com. City of N.Y. Co-chmn. audit adv. com. Bd. Edn. of City of N.Y.; chmn. Early Edn. Leadership Group; bd. dirs. New Alternatives for Children. Mem.: Ednl. Broadcasting Corp., NY Acad. Sci., NY Acad. Medicine, Coun. Fgn. Rels., Century Assn. Home: 146 Central Park W New York NY 10023-2005 Office: Skadden Arps 4 Times Sq Fl 24 New York NY 10036-6595 Office Phone: 212-735-3800. Business E-Mail: mkaplan@skadden.com.

KAPLAN, MARK VINCENT, lawyer; b. Oct. 30, 1947; m. Cynthia Lang, Oct. 3, 1982 (div.); m. Carolyn Kozuch, Oct. 9, 1988. BA, U. Ill.; JD, Southwestern U., Calif. Ptnr. Kaplan & Simon, Los Angeles; div. atty. representing Paul Abdul, Chris Judd, Kevin Federline and others. Office: Kaplan & Simon 2049 Century Park E #2660 Los Angeles CA 90067 Office Phone: 310-227-9009. Fax: 310-552-1970. E-mail: mkaplan@kaplansimonlaw.com.

KAPLAN, MARSHALL MYLES, medical educator, researcher, gastroenterologist; b. Boston, Feb. 20, 1935; s. Harold and Ginda (Braverman) K.; m. Nancy Proger, June 5, 1960; children: Ginda, William, Thomas, Deborah. BS summa cum laude, Yale U., 1956; MD cum laude, Harvard U., 1960. Intern, resident Columbia-Presbyn., NYC, 1960-62; clin. assoc. NIH, Bethesda, Md., 1962-65; trainee liver disease Yale U., New Haven, 1965-66; asst. prof. medicine Tufts-New England Med. Ctr., Boston, 1966-69, assoc. prof. medicine, 1969-75, prof. medicine, 1975—, chief divsn. gastroenterology, 1972—2002. Chmn. merit rev. com. VA Hosps., Washington, 1975-77; mem. gastroenterology bd. Am. Bd. Internal Medicine, 1983-89, chmn., 1987-89, bd. govs., 1987-89, trustee, Tufts-New England Med. Ctr., 201-05; manuscript reviewer Annals Internal Medicine, Am. Jour. Medicine, Archives of Internal Medicine, Gastroenterology, Hepatology, Digestive Diseases and Sci., Am. Jour. Gastroenterology, Jour.

Hepatology Assoc. editor New Eng. Jour. Medicine, 1993-2001; editor Tufts Family Health Guides, 1979-82; mem. editl. bd. Hepatology, 1988-92; sect. editor Up to Date in Medicine, 2006—; contbr. over 300 articles to med. jours., chpts. to books. Lt. comdr. USPHS, 1962-65. Recipient Mentor Rsch. Scholar award, AGA Found., 2005. Master ACP (chair sci. program com. 1990-93, gastroenterology med. knowledge self-assessment program); mem. Assn. Am. Physicians, Am. Soc. Clin. Investigation, Am. Gastroenterology Assn., Am. Assn. for Study of Liver Disease (com. chair 1984-86), Am. Gastroenterology Assn. (Mentors award Am. Gastroenterology Assn. Found. 2005), Phi Beta Kappa, Alpha Omega Alpha (dir. 1983-89). Democrat. Jewish. Avocations: tennis, bridge, golf, gardening, music. Home: 30 Oakridge Rd Wellesley MA 02481-2504 Office: New England Med Ctr 750 Washington St Boston MA 02111-1526 Office Phone: 617-636-5877. Business E-Mail: mkaplan@tufts-nemc.org.

KAPLAN, MARTIN P., allergist, immunologist, pediatrician; b. Bklyn., Oct. 28, 1928; MD, SUNY Downstate Med. Ctr. Diplomate Am. Bd. Allergy & Immunology, Am. Bd. Pediat. Resident Jewish Hosp., Bklyn., 1954-55, SUNY Upstate Med. Ctr., Syracuse, 1957-58; fellow Children's Hosp., Washington, 1958-59; active staff mem. dept. medicine St. Joseph Hosp., Lexington, Ky., 1959—; clin. assoc. prof. pediatrics and medicine U. Ky. Coll. Medicine, 1982-97. Mem. Am. Acad. Allergy and Clin. Immunology, Am. Coll. Allergy, Asthma, and Immunology, AMA, Ky. Med. Assn. Office: 166 Pasadena Ste 150 Lexington KY 40503-3014 Personal E-mail: omkaplan@aol.com.

KAPLAN, MORTON A., political science professor; b. Phila., May 9, 1921; s. Lewis J. and Anthea (Ginsberg) K.; m. Azie Mortimer, 1967. BS, Temple U., 1943; PhD, Columbia, 1951. Instr. Ohio State U., 1951-52; asst. prof. polit. sci. Haverford Coll., 1953-54; mem. staff Brookings Instn., Washington, 1954-55; asst. prof. polit. sci. U. Chgo., 1956-61, asso. prof., 1961-65, chmn. com. internat. relations, 1959-85, prof. polit. sci., 1965-89, Disting. Svc. prof., 1989-91, Disting. Svc. prof. emeritus, 1991—; editor, pub. The World & I, 1985—2004. Dir. Ford. workshop program in internat. relations, 1961-76, dir. faculty arms control and fgn. policy seminar, 1970-75; dir. Ctr. for Strategic and Fgn. Policy Studies, 1976-85; cons. Japan War Coll. and Defense Agy., 1979; rsch. assoc. Ctr. of Internat. Studies, Princeton, 1958-62; vis. assoc. prof. polit. sci. Yale U., 1961-62; mem. staff Hudson Inst., 1961-78, cons., 1978-80; lectr. Command and Gen. Staff Sch., 1965-67, Fgn. Svc. Inst., 1967, Air War Coll., 1967-69, NAt. Def. Coll. Can., 1970-72; bd. assocs. Fgn. Policy Rsch. Inst., 1967-90; Gabrielson Disting. lectr. Bowdoin Coll., 1968; Nulton Disting. lectr. Goucher Coll., 1969; cons. NEH, 1972-74; pres. Cetra Music Corp., 1962—, Moraz Prodns., Inc., 1963—; cons. Com. Econ. Devel., 1965, Braddock, Dunn and McDonald, 1969, 72; cons. USIA, 1972; sect. chmn. Internat. Confs. in Unity Scis., 1975, 76, 78, 79, chmn., 1980-83; bd. dirs. Univ. Ctrs. for Rational Alternatives, 1969-96; bd. govs., rsch. com. Stratis, Israeli Inst. Strategic Studies and Policy Analysis, 1974-79; trustee U. Bridgeport, 1992-2004. Author: System and Process in International Politics, 1957, 2d edit., 2004, Some Problems in the Strategic Analysis of International Politics, 1959, The Communist Coup in Czechoslovakia, 1960, (with Nicholas de B. Katzenbach) The Political Foundations of International Law, 1961, (with Reitzel and Coblenz) United States Foreign Policy, 1945-55, 1956, Macropolitics: Essays on the Philosophy and Science of Politics, 1969, On Historical and Political Knowing: An Inquiry into Some Problems of Universal Law and Human Freedom, 1971, Dissent and the State in Peace and War: An Essai on the Grounds of Public Morality, 1970, On Freedom and Human Dignity: The Importance of the Sacred in Politics, 1973, The Rationale for NATO; Past and Future, 1973, (with others) Vietnam Settlement: Why 1973, Not 1969?, 1973, Alienation and Identification, 1976, The Life and Death of the Cold War: Selected Studies in Post-War Statecraft, 1976, Towards Professionalism in International Theory: Macrosystem Analysis, 1979, Science, Language and the Human Condition, 1984, rev. edit., 1989, Law in A Democratic Society, 1993; editor: The Revolution in World Politics, 1962, The New Approaches to International Relations, 1968, SALT: Problems and Prospects, 1973, Strategic Thinking and Its Moral Implications, 1973; editor, contbg. author: Great Issues of International Politics, 1970, 74, Isolation or Interdependence? - Today's Choices for Tomorrow's World, 1975, NATO and Dissuasion, 1974, Global Policy: Challenge of the 80s, 1983, Character and Identity vol. 1: Philosophical Foundations of Political and Sociological Perspectives, 1998, vol 2: Historical and Literary Perspectives, 2000; editor, co-author: Character and Identity: The Philosophical Foundations of Political and Sociological Perspectives, 1998, Character and Identity: The Sociological Foundation of Literary and Historical PErspectives, 2000; co-editor, contbg. author: Japan, America, and the Future World Order, 1976, Justice, Human Nature, and Political Obligation, 1976; co-editor: The Soviet Union and the Challenge of the Future, 4 vols., 1988-89; editor, pub. The World and I, 1986-2004; mem. editl. bd. Jour. Conflict Resolution, 1961-79; mem. editl. bd. World Politics, 1961-71, ORBIS, 1967-90; editor, contbr. The Many Faces of Communism, 1978; editor, Consolidating Piece in Europe, 1987; co-editor: Morality and Religion, 1992, The World of 2044: Technological Development and The Future of Society, 1994. Bd. trustees U. Bridgeport, 1994-2004; pres. Profs. World Peace Acad., 1983—. With AUS, 1943-46. Fellow Center Internat. Studies Princeton, 1952-53; Center Advanced Study in Behavioral Scis., 1955-56; Carnegie fellow, 1959-60 Mem. Am. Polit. Sci. Assn., Instituto Mexicano de Cultura (corr.), Internat. Cultural Soc. Korea (hon.), Profs. World Peace Acad. Internat. (pres. 1983—). Address: 5446 S Ridgewood Ct Chicago IL 60615-5315 *Constantly to seek new ideas, not for their newness, but for their ability to illuminate the condition of man.*

KAPLAN, MURIEL SHEERR, sculptor; b. Phila., Aug. 15, 1924; d. Maurice J. and Lillian J. (Jamison) Sheerr; BA, Cornell U., 1946; postgrad. Sarah Lawrence Coll., 1958-60, U. Calif. at Oxford (Eng.), summer 1971, U. Florence (Italy), summer 1973, Art Students League, N.Y.C., summers 1975-89. New Sch., N.Y.C., 1974-78, m. Murray S. Kaplan, June 3, 1946 (dec.); children: Janet Belsky, James S., S. Jerrold, Amy Sheerr Eckman. Exhbns. at Women's Clubs in Westchester, 1954-60, Allied Artists Am., 1958-73, Nat. Assn. Women Artists, 1966-05, Bklyn. Mus., 1968, Sculptors Guild, 1972, Bergen County (N.J.) Mus., 1974; 2-person shows: Camino Real Gallery, Boca Raton, Fla., 1980; represented in group shows at Norton Art Gallery, Palm Beach, Fla., 1980, Govt. Ctr., West Palm Beach, Fla., 1984, Northwood U. Gallery, 1993, 95, 96, 97; represented in permanent collections Columbia U., Brandeis U., U. Tex., Harvard Law Sch., 1990, Johnson Mus. at Cornell U., 1996, Weizman Inst., Israel, 1998, Portrait of Capt. David McCampbell aboard USS David McCampbell, 2002, Portrait of Itzahk Rabin in Internat. Exhibit Armory Art Ctr., 2002; executed twin 30 foot cor-ten steel sculptures, Tarrytown, N.Y., 1972, 2 large rotating steel sculptures Art Park, Trans-Lux Corp., 1978; art cons., interior designer, 1971-89; sec. commn. to establish art mus. in Westchester, 1956; chmn. Westchester Creative Arts Festival, 1956. Bd. dirs. Fedn. Jewish Philanthropies, 1956; chmn. 1st Sta. WNET, Channel 13 Art Auction; mem. com. art in pub. places, Palm Beach County, Fla., 1984; mem. art adv. com. Boca Raton Mus. Art, 1987-93; bd. dirs. Palm Beach County Cultural Coun. of Arts, 1992-94; tchr. sculpture Armory Arts Ctr., Palm Beach, 1987-92, bd. dirs., 1992—. Recipient prizes Nat. Assn. Women Artists, 1966, 96, 97, 2004, 06, Westchester Women's Club, 1955, 56, Allied Artists Am., 1969, Artists Guild, Palm Beach, 1987, 88, 90, 91, 92, 93, 94, 96, 97. Mem. NAD, Art Students League N.Y. Nat. Assn. Women Artists, Allied Artists Am., Nat. Sculpture Soc., Internat. Sculpture Ctr., Portraits Inc. N.Y. Address: 115 Lakeshore Dr North Palm Beach FL 33408 Personal E-mail: murielkaplan@aol.com.

KAPLAN, NADIA, writer; b. Chgo., Feb. 28, 1921; d. Peter and Aniela (Buchynska) Charydchak; m. Norman Kaplan, July 25, 1942 (dec. July 1989); children: Fawn Marie Stom, Norma Jean Martinez. BEd, Pestalozzi Froebel Tchrs. Coll, Chgo., 1948; postgrad., UCLA, 1947, LA City Coll., U. Hawaii, Honolulu, Pepperdine U., LA, 1970, Santa Monica Coll., 1981-87. Cert. tchr., Calif. Photographer, mgr. Great Lakes (Ill.) Naval Tng. Sta., 1942-45; primary/kindergarten tchr. L.A. Unified Sch. Dist., 1946-81. Contbr. articles to profl. jours.; creator puzzles various mags. Vol. recreational tchr. Found. for Jr. Blind, L.A., 1956-75, vol. camp counselor Camp Bloomfield, Calif., camp dir., 1956-61, leader cross-country study tour for blind teenagers, 1962; mem. dem. Nat. Com., 1985—. Pestalozzi Froebel Tchrs. Coll. scholar, 1938-41; recipient Norman Kaplan Life Achievement award, 2003. UK Blind, 2003. Mem. AAUW, Women Writers West (membership chair 1982-84), United Tchrs. L.A., Calif. Ret. Tchrs. Assn., Assn. Ret. Tchrs. Ukrainian Orthodox. Avocations: writing, bonsai cultivation, doll collecting, travel, golf. Home: 1827 Fanning St Los Angeles CA 90026-1439

KAPLAN, PAUL A., lawyer; b. Jersey City, Nov. 28, 1951; BA magna cum laude, Boston U., 1973; JD cum laude, U. Pa., 1976. Bar: DC 1976, Md. 1982, admitted to practice: US Ct. Appeals (4th Cir. and DC Cir.), US Dist. Ct, DC, US Dist. Ct., Md. Summer assoc. Wolf, Block, Schorr & Solis-Cohen, Phila., 1975; assoc. Arent, Fox, Kinter, Plotkin & Kahn, Washington, 1976—79, Shaw, Pittman, Potts & Trowbridge, Washington, 1979—82; prin., assoc. David, Hagner, Kuney & Davison, Washington, 1982—98; co-managing mem. Womble Carlyle Sandridge & Rice PLLC, Washington, mem. ethics com., mem. alternative dispute resolution com. Adj. faculty mem. Am. U. Washington Coll. Law. Mem. U. Pa. Law Review, 1974—76. Mem.: Bar Assn. Montgomery County, Md., ABA, Order of the Coif. Office: Womble Carlyle Sandridge & Rice PLLC 1401 Eye St NW 7th Fl Washington DC 20005 Office Phone: 202-857-4458. Office Fax: 202-261-0058. Business E-Mail: pkaplan@wscr.com.

KAPLAN, PAUL ELIAS, physiatrist, writer, educator; BA cum laude, Amherst Coll., 1962; MD, UCLA, 1966. Diplomate Am. Bd. Phys. Medicine and Rehab., Am. Bd. Electrodiagnostic Medicine. Intern in internal medicine Ohio State U. Hosp., Columbus, 1966-67; resident in internal medicine UCLA Med. Ctr. and Affiliate Programs, 1969-71; NIH fellow, resident in phys. medicine & rehab. U. So. Calif. Med. Ctr., LA, 1971-73; pvt. practice Beverly Hills, Calif., 1973-74; prof. rehabilitaion medicine and internal medicine Rehabilitation Inst. of Chgo./Northwestern U., 1974-86; prof., dept. chmn., med. dir. Rusk Rehab. Ctr. U. Mo., Columbia, 1986-89; Bert C. Wiley prof., chair phys. medicine and rehab. Ohio State U., Columbus, 1989-98; med. dir. PMR Northwest Orthopaedic Surgeons, Mt. Vernon, Wash., 1999—. Mem. acute and continuing care com. step 3 Nat. Bd. Med. Examiners, 1995-98. Author several textbooks on phys. medicine and rehab.; editor-in-chief jour. Yearbook of Rehab., 1984-89; alt. editor Archives of Phys. Medicine and Rehab., 1988-94; cons. editor Advance, 1995—; mem. editl. bd. Disability and Rehab., 1997—; contbr. more than 125 articles to profl. jours. Fellow ACP, Am. Acad. Phys. Medicine and Rehab., Am. Acad. PMR; mem. Assn. Acad. Psychiatrists (pres. 1987-89, pres. coun. of chairpersons), Am. Spinal Injury Assn. Avocation: bagpipes.

KAPLAN, PAUL MICHAEL, lawyer, educator; b. Lowell, Mass., Sept. 15, 1951; s. Samuel G. and Gladys G. Kaplan; 1 child, Karen D. AB with distinction, Boston U., 1973; JD, Northeastern U. Law Sch., 1974; LLM, London Sch. Econs., 1978. Bar: Mass. 1978, NY 1991, US Dist. Ct. (so. and ea. dist.) NY 1999, US Ct. Appeals (1st cir.) 1981, US Ct. Appeals (10th cir.) 2004, US Ct. Appeals (2nd cir.) 2005, US Supreme Ct. 2005. Law clk. to Judge R. Ammi Cutter Mass. Supreme Judicial Ct., 1980—81; v.p., sr. counsel Citbank (Citigroup), NYC, 1983—86; v.p., divsn. counsel Chem. Bank (JP Morgan Chase), 1986—90; ptnr. Shea and Gould, 1991—93, Baer Marks & Upham, 1993—98, Epstein Becker & Green, PC, 1998—2005, Sheppard, Mullin, Richter & Hampton LLP, 2005—06, Bryan Cave LLP, NYC, 2006—. Adj. prof. law Fordham Law Sch., NYC, 1991—. Contbr. articles to profl. jours. Legal counsel domestic and foreign corps. & fin. insts., NYC, 1998; bd. dirs. Am.-Israel Friendship League, 2006—. Scholar, Northeastern U. Law Sch., 1974—77; Trustee scholar, Boston U. Coll. Arts and Sci., 1969—73. Mem.: ABA, Clayton Act Com., Banking Law and Antitrust and Trade Regulation Coms., Assn. Bar City NY. Jewish. Avocation: marathon running. Office: Bryan Cave LLP 1290 Avenue of the Americas New York NY 10104 Home Phone: 212-280-0880; Office Phone: 212-541-1074. Office Fax: 212-541-1474; Home Fax: 212-878-8656. Business E-Mail: paul.kaplan@bryancave.com.

KAPLAN, PETER W., editor-in-chief; b. South Orange, NJ; s. Robert E. and Roberta Wennik Kaplan; m. Audrey Mary Walker, June 24, 1984; 3 children. BA in Am. Studies, Harvard Coll., 1976. Desk asst. ABC Radio; editor NY Times Mag., Esquire; Style sect. corr. Washington Post; cultural corr. NY Times, 1984; exec. editor & editl. dir. Manhattan, Inc.; with Conde Nast Traveler, 1992; editor-in-chief NY Observer, 1994—. Exec. prodr.: (TV series) The Charlie Rose Show, 1993. Office: NY Observer 9th Fl 915 Broadway New York NY 10010 Office Phone: 212-755-2400. Office Fax: 212-688-4889. E-mail: pkaplan@observer.com.

KAPLAN, RICHARD ALAN, government official; b. San Francisco; s. Murray M. and Beatrice (Ray) Kaplan. AA, Canada Coll., 1973; BA, San Francisco State U., 1975, BA, 1976, MA, 1981; postgrad., U. London, 1978—80, Nat. Def. U., 1984. Intelligence analyst US Govt., Washington, 1986—. Tech. advisor to arms control unit UN Hdqrs., Geneva, 1981—82; Army rep. numerous US Govt. Intra-Agy. Working Groups, 1986—. Author: An Interdisciplinary Study of the International Law of Armed Conflict, 1981; author 62 intelligence documents and studies for Army. With US Army, 1968. Recipient Commdrs. award for civilian svc., Dept. of the Army, 1991, Superior Civilian Svc. award, 1991, Civilian medal Humanitarian Svc., 1991, Superior Civilian Svc. award, 1995, Meritorious Civilian Svc. award, 1996, 2007, Commdrs. award for civilian svc., 1996, cert. of Commendation, FBI, 2001, others. Fellow Inter-Univ. Seminar on Armed Forces and Soc., Internat. Inst. Air and Space Law, Internat. Inst. Humanitarian Law; mem. Am. Fgn. Law Assn., Internat. Law Assn. (com. on internat. terrorism 1983—, com. on armed conflict 1983—), Am. Soc. Internat. Law, Royal Inst. Internat. Affairs, Internat. Inst. Strategic Studies. Home: Apt I 5701 Woodlawn Green Cir Alexandria VA 22309-4609 E-mail: richard.kaplan@mi.army.mil.

KAPLAN, RICHARD JAMES, film producer and director, educator, consultant, scriptwriter; b. NYC, Jan. 3, 1925; s. Benjamin David and Nathalie (Blaustein) K.; m. Blanche Beatrice Aanesen, Nov. 15, 1957 (div. 1981); children: Kjeld, Kirsti, Eve, Erica. BA in Polit. Sci., Antioch Coll., 1949; Diploma Cinema, U. So. Calif., 1951. Pres. Richard Kaplan Prodns., NYC, 1957—; dir., promotional films Am. Film Theater, NYC, 1973; media dir. Alternative Conf. on Environ., Stockholm, 1972; media cons. CUNY, 1974-75; dir. pub. programing Astoria Motion Picture and TV Studios, NYC, 1979-80; assoc. dean Pratt Inst. Sch Art and Design, NYC, 1984-85; producer ABC News, NYC, 1986; pres., exec. producer The Exiles Project, Inc., NYC, 1987-90. Cons. Harvard U., Cambridge, Mass., 1986-90; instr. NYU, CUNY, Parsons, Hunter Coll., U. Soc. Calif., U. Md., 1970-87; lectr., workshop dir. U.S. Info Svc., Arts Am., 1980, Israel, Egypt, India, Pakistan, Sri Lanka, Bangladesh, 1985; prof. Columbia U. Sch. of the Arts, 1991—; founder, dep. dir. Documentary Ctr. at Columbia U.; panelist NEH Pub. Media Program. Dir. documentary The Eleanor Roosevelt Story, 1965 (Oscar 1966); producer documentary King: Montgomery to Memphis, 1970 (numerous awards 1970-71); writer, dir., producer TV film A Look at Liv, 1976, others; dir., producer The Exiles, 1989 (Emmy award 1991), Assignment Rescue.The Story of Varian Fry and the Emergency Rescue Committee, 1997; exec. prodr., dir.: Varian and Putzi: A 20th Century Tale, 2001 Trustee Antioch Coll., Yellow Springs, Ohio, 1975-78; vice chmn. Rockland County Human Rights Commn., Rockland County, N.Y., 1968-71, Town of Ramapo (N.Y.) Housing Authority, 1972-76. Cpl. U.S. Army, 1943-46, ETO. Grantee NEH, Washington, 1987. Mem. Acad. Motion Picture Arts and Sci., Writers Guild of Am., Assn. Ind. Film and Video, N.Y. Film Video Council (bd. dirs.). Office Phone: 212-787-0258. E-mail: rkprods1@verizon.net.

KAPLAN, RICK (RICHARD N. KAPLAN), broadcast executive; b. Apr. 18, 1947; m. Priscilla A. Kaplan; 2 children. Grad., U. Ill., LittD (hon.), 1999. Assoc. prodr. The CBS Evening News with Walter Cronkite, NYC, 1974—79; sr. prodr. World News Tonight, ABC, 1979; exec. prodr. World News This Morning, Good Morning Am., Nightline, ABC, 1984-89, Viewpoint, The Koppel Report; creator, exec. prodr. Capitol to Capitol; coord. ABC News; exec. prodr. PrimeTime Live, 1989-94, World News Tonight with Peter Jennings, 1994-96; exec. prodr. spl. projects ABC Television Network, 1996-97; pres. Cable News Network-US, Atlanta, 1997—2000; teaching fellow Shorenstein Ctr. John F. Kennedy Sch. Govt. Harvard U.; sr. v.p. news ABC News, NYC, 2003—04; pres. MSNBC, Secaucus, NJ, 2004—06; exec. prodr. Evening News with Katie Couric, CBS, 2007—. Taught and lectured Duke U., Columbia U., Cornell U., Wellesley, U. Penn., Boston Coll., Columbia Coll., USC, Berkeley; adj. prof. U. Ill. Recipient 34 Emmy awards, 4 Overseas Press Club awards, 3 George Foster Peabody awards, 2 George Polk awards, 4 Alfred I. du Pont-Columbia U. awards, 2 Gold Batons, 12 Headliner awards; fellow, Harvard U. Office: CBS News 555 W 57th St New York NY 10019*

KAPLAN, ROBERT B., linguistics educator, consultant, researcher; b. NYC, Sept. 20, 1929; s. Emanuel B. and Natalie K.; m. Audrey A. Lien, Apr. 21, 1951; children— Robin Ann Kaplan Gibson, Lisa Kaplan Morris, Robert Allen. Student, Champlain Coll., 1947-48, Syracuse U., 1948-49; BA, Willamette U., 1952; MA, U. So. Calif., 1957, PhD, 1962. Teaching asst. U. So. Calif., Los Angeles, 1955-57, instr. coordinator, asst. prof. English communication program for fgn. students, 1965-72, assoc. prof., dir. English communication program for fgn. students, 1972-76, assoc. dean continuing edn., 1973-76, prof. applied linguistics, 1976-95, prof. emeritus, 1995—, dir. Am. Lang. Inst., 1986-91; instr. U. Oreg., 1957-60. Cons. field svc. program Nat. Assn. Fgn. Student Affairs, 1964-84; pres.-elect faculty senate U. So. Calif., 1988-89, pres., 1989-90; adv. bd. internat. comparability study of standardized lang. exams. U. Cambridge Local Exams. Syndicate; vis. sr. prof. grad. sch. applied lang. studies Meikai U., Urayasu City, Chiba, Japan, 1998-2000. Author: Reading and Rhetoric: A Reader, 1963; (with V. Tufte, P. Cook and J. Aurbach) Transformational Grammar: A Guide for Teachers, 1968; (with R.D. Schoesler) Learning English Through Typewriting, 1969; The Anatomy of Rhetoric: Prolegomena to a Functional Theory of Rhetoric, 1971; On the Scope of Applied Linguistics, 1980; The Language Needs of Migrant Workers, 1980; (with P. Shaw) Exploring Academic English, 1984; (with U. Connor) Writing Across Languages: Analysis of L2 Text, 1987; (with W. Grabe) Introduction To Applied Linguistics, 1991, Writing Around the Pacific Rim, 1995, Theory and Practice of Writing: An Applied Linguistics Perspective, 1996—; (with R.B. Baldauf) Language Policy from Practice to Theory, 1997, Language and Language-in-Education Planning in the Pacific Basin, 2003; co-editor: (with R.B. Baldauf) series The Language Situation in Malawi, Mozambique, The Philippines, 1998, Nepal, Taiwan, Sweden, 1999, Botswana, Côte d Ivoir, Hungary, Vanuatu, 2000, Paraguay, Tunisia, South Africa, European Union, 2001, Finland, 2002, Ecuador, 2002, No. Ireland, 2002, The Czech Republic, Fiji, 2004, Africa I: Botswana, Malawi, Mozambique and South Africa, 2004, Nigeria, Italy, 2005, Europe I: Finland, Hungary, Sweden, 2005, Europe 2: Czech Republic, European Union, Northern Ireland, 2005, Pacific I: Fiji, The Philippines and Vanuatu, 2006; mem. editl. bd.: Oxford Internat. Ency. of Linguistics, 1992, consulting editor 2d edit., 2003; editor: The Oxford Handbook of Applied Linguistics, 2002; mem. editl. bd. Jour. Asian Pacific Comm., Internat. Educator, BBC English Dictionary, Second Lang. Instruction/Acquisition Abstracts, Jour. Second Lang. Writing, Forensic Linguistics, Jour. Multilingual and Multicultural Devels., Asian Jour. English Lang. Tchg., Current Issues in Lang. Planning. Bd. dirs. Internat. Bilingual Sch. L.A., 1986-91, Internat. Edn. Rsch. Found., 1986-94. Served with inf. U.S. Army, Korea. Recipient U. So. Calif. Faculty Lifetime Achievement award, 2005; Fulbright sr. scholar, Australia, 1978, Hong Kong, 1986, New Zealand, 1992. Mem. AAAS, AAUP, Am. Anthrop. Assn., Am. Assn. Applied Linguistics (v.p., pres. 1992-94, award for disting. scholarship and svc. 1998), Assn. Internat. Linguistique Applique, Assn. Internat. Pour La Rsch. et La Diffusion Des Methodes Audio-Visuelles et Structuro-Globales, Assn. Tchrs. ESL (chmn. 1968-69), Calif. Assn. Tchrs. English to Spkrs. Other Langs. (pres. 1970-71), Can. Coun. Tchrs. English, Nat. Assn. Fgn. Student Affairs (nat. pres. 1983-84), Linguistics Soc. Am., Tchrs. English to Spkrs. Other Langs. (1st v.p., pres. 1989-91). E-mail: rkaplan@olypen.com.

KAPLAN, ROBERT DAVID, lawyer; b. Ossining, NY, July 9, 1939; s. Bernard I. and Helen Rosemarie (Gardner) K. AB, Brown U., 1961; LLM, JD, U. Wash., 1969. Bar: Wash. 1969, U.S. Dist. Ct. (we. dist.) Wash. 1969, U.S. Ct. Appeals (9th cir.) 1969. Ptnr. Bogle & Gates, Seattle, 1969—99; ptnr., chmn., Iraq practice Dorsey & Whitney LLP, Seattle, 1999—. Contbr. articles to law rev. Lt. USN, 1961-66. Named a Wash. Super Lawyer, Wash. Law & Politics Mag. Mem. ABA, Wash. State Bar Assn., U. Wash. Sch. Law Alumni Assn. (bd. dirs. 1975-85). Office: Dorsey & Whitney LLP Ste 3400 US Bank Ctr 1420 Fifth Ave Seattle WA 98101-4010 Office Phone: 206-903-8810. Office Fax: 206-903-8820. Business E-Mail: kaplan.robert@dorsey.com.

KAPLAN, ROBERT DAVID, journalist; b. NYC, June 23, 1952; s. Philip and Phylis (Quasha) K.; m. Maria Cabral, Aug. 26, 1983; 1 child, Michael. BA, U. Conn., 1973. Class of 1960 disting. vis. prof. in nat. security U.S. Naval Acad., Annapolis, Md. Author: Surrender or Starve, 1988, Soldiers of God, 1990, The Arabists, 1993 (Notable Book of Yr., NY Times Book Rev. 1993), Balkan Ghosts, 1993 (Best Book of Yr., NY Times Book Rev. 1993, Notable Book of Yr., ALA 1993), The Ends of the Earth, 1996 (Notable Book of Yr. ALA 1993), An Empire Wilderness, 1999, Eastward to Tartary, 2000, The Coming Anarchy: Shattering the Dreams of the Post Cold War, 2000, Warrior Politics: Why Leadership Demands a Pagan Ethos, 2001, Soldiers of God: With Islamic Warriors in Afghanistan and Pakistan, 2001, The Ends of the Earth: From Togo to Turkmenistan, from Iran to Cambodia, a Journey to the Frontiers of Anarchy, 2001, Surrender or Starve: Travels in Ethiopia, Sudan, Somalia, and Eritrea, 2003, Mediterranean Winter: The Pleasures of History and Landscape in Tunisia, Sicily, Dalmatia, and Greece, 2004, Imperial Grunts: The American Military on the Ground, 2005; nat. corr. Atlantic Monthly, Boston, 1993—; contbr. articles to profl. jours.

KAPLAN, ROBERT MALCOLM, health researcher, educator; b. San Diego, Oct. 26, 1947; s. Oscar Joel and Rose (Zankan) K.; children— Cameron Maxwell, Seth William AB in Psychology, San Diego State U., 1969; MA, U. Calif., Riverside, 1970, PhD, 1972. Lic. psychologist, Calif. Sr. rsch. assoc. Am. Inst. for Rsch., Palo Alto, Calif., 1972-73; from asst. prof. to prof. U. Calif., San Diego, 1973—2004, prof. dept. family and preventive medicine, 2004, chief health care svcs. divsn., 1989—96, chmn. health care svcs. divsn., 1997—2004; from asst. prof. to prof. psychology San Diego State U., 1974-88, dir. Ctr. for Behavioral Medicine; prof. medicine U. Calif., LA, 2004—. Mem. health svcs. rsch. study sect. Nat. Ctr. Health Svcs. Rsch., 1981-85, 88-92, VA Sci. Rev. and Evaluations Bd. for Health Svcs., 1989-91 (chair 1991-92); cons., lectr. in field. Faculty fellow San Diego State U., 1977; epidemiology fellow Am. Heart Assn.,

1983; recipient Career Rsch. Devel. award NIH, 1981-86, Alumni and Assocs. Disting. Faculty award San Diego State U., 1982, Exceptional Merit service award San Diego State U., 1984 Fellow APA (bd. dirs., Outstanding Sci. Achievement award health psychology divsn. 1987, 2001, pres. 1992-93); mem. AAAS (exec. com. Pacific divsn. 1978-82), Soc. Behavioral Medicine (bd. dirs., pres. 1996-97, pres. elect 2001—, editor-in-chief Annals of Behavioral Medicine, 2000-05, Health Psychology, 2005—), Inst. Medicine NAS. Office: UCLA Dept Health Svcs CH5-31-293-C PO Box 951772 Los Angeles CA 90095-1772 Home: 17748 Revello Dr Pacific Palisades CA 90272 Home Phone: 310-728-6667; Office Phone: 310-825-7652. Business E-Mail: rmkaplan@ucla.edu.

KAPLAN, ROBERT S., business educator, former investment banker; BS, U. Kans., 1979; MBA, Harvard U., 1983. Head Asia-Pacific investment banking The Goldman Sachs Group, NYC, 1990—93, head Ams. corp. fin. dept., 1994—98, co-chief oper. officer global investment banking, 1998—99, global co-head investment banking divsn., 1999—2001, vice chmn., 2002—06, sr. dir., 2006—; prof. Harvard Bus. Sch., Boston, 2005—. Bd. dirs. Bed Bath & Beyond, Inc. Co-chmn. bd. The TEAK Fellowship, Project A.L.S., The Harvard Ctr. Neurodegeneration and Repair; dir. The Jewish Theol. Sem. Office: Harvard U Soldiers Field Boston MA 02163

KAPLAN, SHELDON, lawyer, director; b. Mpls., Feb. 16, 1915; s. Max Julius and Harriet (Wolfson) K.; m. Helene Bamberger, Dec. 7, 1941; children— Jay Michael, Mary Jo, Jean Burton, Jeffrey Lee. BA summa cum laude, U. Minn., 1935; LLB, Columbia U., 1939. Bar: N.Y. 1940, Minn. 1946. Pvt. practice, NYC, 1940-42, Mpls., 1946—; mem. firm Lauterstein, Spiller, Bergerman & Dannett, NYC, 1939-42; ptnr. Maslon, Kaplan, Edelman, Borman, Brand & McNulty, Mpls., 1946-80. Chmn. Kaplan, Strangis and Kaplan, Mpls., 1980—; bd. dirs. Stewart Enterprises Inc., Creative Ventures Inc. Decisions editor Columbia Law Review, 1939. Served to capt. AUS, 1942-46. Mem. Minn. Bar Assn., Hazeltime Nat. Golf Club, Mpls. Club, Phi Beta Kappa. Home: 2950 Dean Pkwy Minneapolis MN 55416-4446 Office: Kaplan Strangis & Kaplan 5500 Wells Fargo Ctr Minneapolis MN 55402 Office Phone: 612-375-1138. Business E-Mail: sk@kskpa.com.

KAPLAN, STEVEN, lawyer; b. Washington, Sept. 20, 1953; s. Harry E. and Blanche G. (Friedman) K. BA, New Coll., 1975; JD magna cum laude, Georgetown U., 1978. Bar: D.C. 1978, U.S. Dist. Ct. D.C. 1979, U.S. Ct. Appeals (D.C. cir.) 1979. Assoc. Arnold & Porter, Washington, 1978-85, ptnr., Corp. Securities Practice Group, 1986—. Mem. faculty Bank Merger Tech. Conf., Washington, 1987, SEC Acctg. & Fin. Reporting, Washington, 1986, Bank Merger Seminar, Washington, 1985, Mcpl. Securities Rule-making Bd., 2004-07; speaker Va. Securities Assn., Virginia Beach, 1987. Editor, Georgetown Law Journal; contbr. articles to profl. jours. Mem bd. Washington Trustees Federal City Council; bd. dir. Washington Performing Arts Soc. Named one of Leading Lawyers Am., Lawdragon 3000, 2006, Ams. Leading Lawyers, Chambers USA, 2005, 2006, Best Lawyers in Am., 2007. Mem. ABA (sect. bus. law), Econ. Club of Washington, Japan Commerce Assn., Cosmos Club. Office: Arnold & Porter LLP Thurman Arnold Bldg 555 12th St NW Washington DC 20004-1206 Office Phone: 202-942-5998. Office Fax: 202-942-5999. Business E-Mail: steven.kaplan@aporter.com.

KAPLAN, SUSAN, lawyer; BA summa cum laude, Hofstra U., 1971; JD, Columbia U., 1974. Bar: N.Y. 1975, U.S. Dist. Ct. (so. and ea. dists.) N.Y. 1975. Assoc. Patterson Belknap & Webb, NYC, 1974-76; asst. dist. atty. Nassau County, NY, 1976-81; asst. chief prosecution Office Profl. Discipline State of N.Y., 1981—83, dep. dir. prosecution, 1983—85; pvt. practice NYC, 1985—2006. Mem. adv. bd. Employee Assistance Program Health Care Network, 1988-2002; lectr. in field. Contbr. articles to profl. jours. Mem. adminstrv. bd. Soc. Meml. Sloan-Kettering Cancer Ctr., 1975-78; mem. adv. coun. Nassau County Boy Scouts Am., 1977-87, v.p., 1981-84; sec., bd. dirs. Harkness Ballet Found., 1980-86. Assoc. fellow N.Y. Acad. Medicine 1990-91, fellow 1992-2004. Fellow N.Y. Bar Found.; mem. N.Y. State Bar Assn. (com. on pub. health 1975-78, com. on profl. discipline 1983-90, com. on health law 1985-88, 92-96, com. to confer with state med. soc. 1985-96, vice chair 1986-87, chair 1987-92, mem. health law sect. 1996—). Office: 165 W End Ave Ste 27P New York NY 10023-5515

KAPLAN, THEODORE NORMAN, insurance company executive; b. Newburgh, NY, July 23, 1935; s. Edward and Bella (Kesten) Kaplan; m. Madeline Kahn, Nov. 14, 1982; children: Garrett, Judith. BS in Acctg., Syracuse U., 1957. CLU. Ins. sales Aetna Life, NYC, 1959-67, Bankers Life, NYC, 1967-73, Conn. Mut., NYC, 1973-77; benefits cons. Theodore N. Kaplan Assocs., LLC, NYC, 1977—. Mem.: Life Underwriters Assn., Million Dollar Round Table (life; qualifying mem.). Office: Theodore N Kaplan Assoc LLC 515 Madison Ave New York NY 10022-5403 Office Phone: 212-826-3838. Business E-Mail: tkaplanins@aol.com.

KAPLAN, THOMAS ABRAHAM, physicist, educator; b. Phila., Feb. 24, 1926; s. Michael Jay and Nellie (Cohan) K.; m. Patricia Ruth Roe, Nov. 24, 1956; children: Melissa Ann, Andrea Jean, Laurie Michelle. BSME, U. Pa., 1948, PhD in Physics, 1954. Rsch. assoc. Engring. Rsch. Inst., U. Mich., Willow Run, 1954-56; rsch. assoc. Brookhaven Nat. Lab., Upton, NY, 1956-58; staff mem. Lincoln Lab., MIT, Lexington, Mass., 1959-70; prof. physics Mich. State U., East Lansing, 1970-95, prof. emeritus, 1995—. Cons. Naval Rsch. Lab., Washington, summer 1979-80; vis. scientist Max-Planck Inst. für Festkörperforschung, Stuttgart, Fed. Republic Germany, 1981-82, 88-89, summer 1983-84, Inst. für Festkörperforschung der Nuclear Physics Rsch. Inst. Jülich, Fed. Republic Germany, 1982; disting. vis. prof. U. Tsukuba, Ibaraki, Japan, 1989. Contbr. numerous articles on theoretical condensed matter physics to profl. jours. Petty officer 2nd class USN, 1944-46. Recipient Sr. Scientist award Alexander von Humboldt Stiftung, 1981. Fellow Am. Phys. Soc.; mem. Sigma Xi. Democrat. Jewish. Avocations: singing, playing piano and trumpet. Office: Mich State U Dept Physics Astronomy East Lansing MI 48824 Business E-Mail: kaplan@pa.msu.edu.

KAPLAN, TODD P., diversified financial services company executive; BA in Math. and Econs., Yale U., New Haven. With Merrill Lynch, 1986—, mng. dir., 1997, head corp. fin. grp. investment banking, COO global markets and investment banking, 2002—03, global head leveraged fin., sr. v.p., chmn. global leveraged fin., global markets and investment banking NYC, 2006—. Office: Merrill Lynch 4 World Fin Ctr 250 Vesey St New York NY 10080

KAPLAN, WAYNE S., lawyer; b. Chgo., July 13, 1946; BS magna cum laude, U. Pa. Wharton Sch. Finance and Commerce, 1968; JD cum laude, Harvard U., 1971. Bar: DC 1972, Ill. 1989, US Ct. Fed. Claims 1976, US Tax Ct. 1975, US Ct. of Appeals (11th cir.) 1991, US Supreme Ct. 1979, US Ct of Appeals (9th cir.). Clk. to hon. Arnold Raum US Tax Ct., 1971-73; ptnr. Covington & Burling, Wash., DC, 1973—79, Lee, Toomey & Kent, Wash., DC, 1980—87, Mayer, Brown , Rowe & Maw LLP, Chgo., 1987—2004; sr. councel Mayer, Brown, Rowe & Maw LLP, 2004—. Mem. ABA (sect. taxation, com. fgn. activities U.S. taxpayers, affiliated and rel. corps., adminstrv. practice, tax acctg. problems), D.C. Bar, Internat. Fiscal Assn., Internat. Tax and Fin. Forum, Beta Gamma Sigma. Office: Mayer Brown Rowe & Maw LLP 71 S Wacker Dr Chicago IL 60606 Office Phone: 312-701-7918. Office Fax: 312-706-9196. Business E-Mail: wkaplan@mayerbrownrowe.com.

KAPLITT, MICHAEL GORDON, neurosurgeon, medical educator; b. Bklyn., Sept. 1, 1965; m. Melissa Beth Rutkin. AB magna cum laude in Molecular Biology, Princeton U., 1987; MD, Cornell Med. Coll., 1995; PhD in Molecular Neurobiology, Rockefeller U., 1993. Bd. cert. neurological surgery. Resident neurosurgery, chief resident Cornell; fellow in stereotactic and functional neurosurgery U. Toronto; asst. prof. then assoc. prof. neurosurgery Weill Med. Coll., Cornell U., N.Y. Presbyn. Hosp., NYC, 2001—, assoc. attending neurosurgeon, dir. Ctr. for Stereostatic and Molecular Neurosurgery, 2001—. Clin. asst. attending divsn. neurosurgery dept. surgery Meml.-Sloan Kettering Cancer Ctr., NYC; adj. asst. prof. Lab. Neurobiology and Behavior The Rockefeller U., NYC; mem. admissions com. Weill Cornell Med. Sch., NYC. Editor: (web site) World Soc. for Stereotactic and Functional Neurosurgery; co-editor: Viral Vectors: Gene Therapy and Neuroscience Applications, 1995, Gene Therapy in the Brain: From Bench to Bedside, 2005; contbr. scientific papers. Named a Victor and Tara Menezes Clinical Scholar; named one of "Best Doctors in NY, NY Mag., 2004; named to, Crain's N.Y. Bus. "40 under 40", 2004; recipient Albert Cass Traveling Fellowship, 1992, Saul R. Korey award for exptl. neurology, Am. Acad. Neurology, 1994, Fellowship award, Med. Rsch. Coun. Can., 2000, Young Investigator Award, Am. Soc. for Gene Therapy, 2005, Disting. Housestaff Award, NY Hospital-Cornell Med. Ctr.; Charles Elsberg fellow in neurol. surgery, N.Y. Acad. Medicine, 2002, New Scholar award in aging rsch., Ellison Med. Found., 2002. Office: Weill-Cornell Med Coll Dept Neurosurgery 525 E 68th St New York NY 10021 Office Phone: 212-746-4966. Office Fax: 212-746-5592.*

KAPLOW, HERBERT ELIAS, journalist; b. NYC, Feb. 2, 1927; s. Solomon and Belle (Bernstein) K.; m. Betty Koplow, Aug. 10, 1952; children— Steven, Robert, Lawrence. BA, Queens Coll., NYC, 1948; MS, Northwestern U., 1951. News corr. NBC, Washington, 1951-72, ABC, Washington, 1972-94. Served with AUS, 1945-46. Recipient Alumni awards Queens Coll., 1963, Alumni awards Northwestern U., 1959 Mem. Sigma Delta Chi. Jewish. Home: 211 N Van Buren St Falls Church VA 22046-3654 Personal E-mail: herbkap@cox.net. *Curiosity and an open, receptive mind are essential characteristics of good journalism. So too is a certain humility growing from the realization that peoples' lives can be affected by a journalist's work. It is a sobering responsibility.*

KAPLOW, JULIE B., psychologist, educator; d. Lois S. and Robert D. Kaplow; m. Alan R. Prossin, June 25, 2005. BA, U. Mich., Ann Arbor, 1997; MA, Duke U., Durham, NC, 2000, PhD, 2002. Lic. psychologist NY State Edn. Dept., 2005, Mass. Bd. Registration Psychologists, 2003; registered nat. health svc. provider Nat. Register Health Svc. Providers. Asst. prof. Boston U., 2004, U. Medicine Dentistry NJ, Newark, 2004—06; assoc. prof. John Jay Coll. of Criminal Justice, CUNY, NYC, 2006—; asst. prof. Boston U. Med. Ctr., Boston, 2003—04. Dir. psychology tng. Boston U. Med. Ctr., Dept. Child and Adolescent Psychiatry, Boston, 2003—04; cons. Nat. Child Traumatic Stress Network, Traumatic Grief Task Force, Durham, NC, 2002—05. Author: (book) Samantha Jane's Missing Smile: A Story for Children Who Have Lost a Parent, Collaborative Treatment of Traumatized Children and Teens: A Trauma Systems Therapy Approach; contbr. articles to profl. and med. jours. Recipient J. P. Guilford Undergraduate Rsch. award, Psi Chi, 1997, Psychology award, Psi Chi Nat. Honor Soc., U. Mich., 1995—99; fellow, Terry Sanford Ctr. for Child and Family Policy, Duke U., 1999—2000; grantee Mentored Clin. Scientist Devel. award, NIMH, 2006—; Alcohol and Substance Abuse grant, NC Gov.'s Inst., 2000—02, Clin. Psychology fellow, Harvard Med. Sch., 2001—02, Carolina Consortium on Human Devel. Predoctoral fellow, NIMH, 2000—01, James B. Angell scholar, U. Mich., 1997. Mem.: APA, Soc. Prevention Rsch., Internat. Soc.Traumatic Stress Studies, Soc. for Rsch. in Child Devel., Am. Psychopathological Assn., Phi Beta Kappa. Achievements include research in Discovered link between different forms of anxiety and the initiation of adolescent alcohol use; Found link between children's coping strategies in immediate aftermath of sexual abuse and later post-traumatic stress symptoms; Identified various risk factors for the development of early-onset substance use in children. Office: John Jay College Criminal Justice 445 West 59th St New York NY 10019 Home Phone: 201-985-8048; Office Phone: 646-557-4405. Business E-Mail: jkaplow@jjay.cuny.edu.

KAPLOW, LOUIS, law educator; b. Chgo., June 17, 1956; s. Mortimer and Irene (Horwich) K.; m. Jody Ellen Forchheimer, July 11, 1982; children: Irene Miriam, Leah Rayna. BA, Northwestern U., 1977; AM, JD, Harvard U., 1981, PhD, 1987. Bar: Mass. 1983. Prof. law Harvard U., Cambridge, Mass., 1982—, assoc. dean for rsch. and spl. programs, 1989-91, Finn M.W. Caspersen and Household Internat. prof. law and econs., 2004—. Co-author: Antitrust Analysis, 1997, Fairness Versus Welfare, 2002; contbr. articles to profl. jours.; mem. editl. bd. Jour. of Law, Econs. and Orgn., 1989—, Nat. Tax Jour., 1995—, Legal Theory, 1995—, Jour. Pub. Econs., 2001—. Faculty rsch. assoc. Nat. Bur. Economic Rsch., Cambridge, Mass., 1985—. Mem. AAAS, Am. Acad. Arts and Scis., Am. Econ. Assn., Nat. Tax Assn., Am. Law and Econs. Assn. Jewish. Office: Harvard U 1575 Mass Ave Rm 322 Cambridge MA 02138-2801

KAPLOW, ROBERT DAVID, lawyer; b. Bklyn., Feb. 6, 1947; s. Herbert and Geraldine Rhoda Kaplow; m. Lois Susan Silverman, May 22, 1971; children: Julie, Jeffrey. BS, Cornell U., 1968; JD, U. Mich., 1971; LLM, Wayne State U., 1978. Bar: Mich. 1972, U.S. Dist. Ct. (ea. dist.) Mich. 1972, U.S. Tax Ct. 1976, U.S. Ct. Appeals (6th cir.) 1991. Assoc. Milton Y. Zussman, Birmingham, Mich., 1972-75, Rubenstein, Isaacs, Lax & Bordman, Southfield, Mich., 1975-89; ptnr. Maddin, Hauser, Wartell, Roth & Heller P.C., Southfield, 1989—. Mem. Fin. and Estate Planning Coun. Met. Detroit, Inc.; bd. dirs. Jewish Assn. Retarded Citizens. Mem.: ABA, Oakland County Bar Assn., Mich. Bar Assn., Cornell Club Mich. Office: Maddin Hauser Wartell Roth and Heller PC 28400 Northwestern Hwy Fl 3 Southfield MI 48034-1839 also: PO Box 215 Southfield MI 48037-0215 Office Phone: 248-354-4030. Business E-Mail: rdk@maddinhauser.com.

KAPLOWITZ, KAREN (JILL), lawyer, consultant; b. New Haven, Nov. 27, 1946; d. Charles Cohen and Estelle (Gerber) K.; m. Alan George Cohen, Aug. 17, 1980; children: Benjamin, Elizabeth. BA cum laude, Barnard Coll., 1968; JD, U. Chgo., 1971. Bar: Calif. 1971, U.S. Dist. Ct. (Cen. Dist.) Calif. 1971. Assoc. O'Melveny & Myers, LA, 1971-74; ptnr. Bardeen, Bersch & Kaplowitz, LA, 1974-80, Alschuler, Grossman & Pines, LA, 1980-96, of counsel, 1997—. Contbr. articles to profl. jours. Mem. vis. com. U. Chgo. Law Sch., 1990-93. Mem. ABA (chmn. employer-employee rels. com. of tors and ins. practice sect.), Assn. Bus. Trial Lawyers (pres.), Calif. Women Lawyers (Fay Stender award 1982), Women Lawyers Assn. L.A. Home: 1 Woodside Ln New Hope PA 18938-9281 Office: 100 Overlook Dr 2d Fl Princeton NJ 08540 Office Phone: 888-890-4240. Business E-Mail: kkaplowitz@newellis.com.

KAPLOWITZ, LISA GLAUSER, physician, educator; b. Phila., Apr. 18, 1951; d. Felix E. and Charlotte Glauser; m. Paul Bernard Kaplowitz, Dec. 28, 1970; children: Joshua Michael, Daniel Steven. BS, U. Mich., 1970; MD, U. Chgo., 1975; MS in Health Adminstrn., Va. Commonwealth U., 2002. Diplomate Am. Bd. Internal Medicine; Am. Bd. Infectious Diseases. Resident U. N.C., Chapel Hill, 1976—78, post grad. fellow, 1978—80, instr. dept. medicine, 1980—82; asst. prof., dept. medicine Med. Coll. Va., Richmond, 1982—89, assoc. prof., 1989—; dir. HIV/AIDS Ctr., Va. Commonwealth U., Richmond, 1993—2002, asst. v.p. fed. health policy; med. dir. ambulatory care Va. Commonwealth U. Health Sys., Richmond, 2000—02; dep. commr. for emergency preparedness and response Va. Dept. Health, Richmond, 2002—. Bd. dirs. AIDS Action Coun., Washington, 1995-96; mem., 1999-2000 class Exec. Leadership in Acad. Medicine Program for Women, MCP Hahnemann U. Contbg. (book chpt.) Conn's Current Therapy, 1985, 2d rev. edit., 1988, 3d edit., 1998; Principles of Critical Care Medicine, 1992. Mem. adv. bd. Va. League for Planned Parenthood, Richmond, 1993—, Richmond AIDS Ministry, 1988—92; mem. Leadership Metro Richmond, 1992—93; grad. Exec. Leadership in Acad. Med. for Women, MCP-Hahnemann U., 2000, Nat. Pub. Health Leadership Inst., U. N.C., 2003—04. Named Woman of Yr. Va. Commonwealth U., 1995; mem. Va. Women's Hall of Fame; fellow Inst. Medicine, 1996-97, Office of Senator Jay Rockefeller, 1997; recipient Local Legend award Nat. Libr. Medicine, 2004. Fellow ACP, Infectious Disease Soc. Am.; mem. APHA; Am. Soc. Microbiology. Avocation: piano. Office: Dept Commr Va Dept Health 109 Governor St 13th Fl Richmond VA 23219 Office Phone: 804-864-7025. Business E-Mail: Lisa.Kaplowitz@vdh.virginia.gov.

KAPLOWITZ, NEIL, gastroenterologist, educator; b. NYC, Mar. 16, 1943; s. Louis and Henrietta (Schall) K.; m. Fattaneh E. Enayat; children: Hillary C., Gregory D., Daria. BS, NYU, 1964, MD, 1967. Diplomate Nat. Bd. Med. Examiners; diplomate in internal medicine and gatroenterology Am. Bd. Internal Medicine. Intern, resident Bellevue Hosp., 1967-69; resident Albert Einstein Med. Ctr., 1969-70; asst. res. phys. Rockefeller Univ. Hosp., 1970-71; fellowship Cornell U. Coll. Medicine, 1970-72; guest investigator Rockefeller U., NYC, 1970-71; instr. in med. Cornell Univ. Med. Coll., 1971-72; asst. prof. Cornell U. Med. Coll., NYC, 1972-73, UCLA Sch. Medicine, 1975-77; chief hepatology Wadsworth VA Hosp., Los Angeles, 1975-79; dir. UCLA Wadsworth Gastroenterology/Hepatology Fellshp. Tng. Prog., 1980-84; chief gastroenterology/hepatology section Wadsworth VA Hosp., Los Angeles, 1980-89; assoc. prof. UCLA Sch. Medicine, 1977-82, prof., 1982-90, U. So. Calif. Sch. Medicine, LA, 1990—, chief div. gastrointestinal and liver diseases, 1990—; chief gastroenterology Wadsworth VA Hosp., LA, 1980-90; prof. molecular pharmacology & toxicology USC Sch. of Pharmacy, 1992—; prof. physiology USC Sch. Med., 1993—; dir. USC Liver Diseases Rsch. Ctr. (NIDDK Digestive Disease Core Ctr. Grant), 1994—. Affiliated investigator Ctr. for Ulcer Rsch., 1978-89, coord. for liver disease UCLA Affiliated Hosps., 1975-89, coord. gastroenterology/hepatology, UCLA Sch. Medicine, 1981-84; vice chair for rsch., bd. dirs., chmn. sci. adv. coun. Am. Liver Found., 1994-96. Editor: Liver and Biliary Diseases, 1992, Drug Induced Liver Dieseases, 2002; assoc. editor: Hepatology, 1985-90, Am. Jour. Physiology, 1991—; contbr. over 150 articles to profl. publs. Lt. comdr. USN, 1973-75. Recipient Western Gastroenterology Rsch. prize Western Gut Club, 1986, Tchr. of Yr., Wadsworth VA, 1977-78, NIH Merit awd. 1992, William S. Middleton awd., 1993, Solomon A. Berson Med. Alumni Achievement awd. in clin. sci., NYU Sch. Med., 1994. Fellow Am. Coll. Gastroenterology; mem. Assn. Am. Physicians, Am. Soc. Clin. Investigation, Western Soc. Clin. Investigation (pres. 1985-86), Am. Fedn. for Clin. Rsch., Am. Assn. for Study of Liver Disease, So. Calif. Gastroenterology Soc., So. Calif. Liver Rsch. Forum (founder), Am. Gastroenterology Soc., Am. Soc. for Pharmacology and Experimental Therapeutics, Internat. Biliary Assn., Internat. Assn. for Study of Liver Disease, Soc. for Exptl. Biology and Medicine, Am. Physiol. Soc., Western Assn. Physicians, Rsch. Soc. on Alcoholism, European Assn. for Study of Liver, Phi Beta Kappa, Alpha Omega Alpha. Achievements include research in regulation and role of hepatic glutathione in detoxification; transport of glutathione and organic anions; identification and characterization of cytosol proteins in liver which bind and transport bile acids, organic anions and tocopherol; mechanisms of cell death due to drugs and toxins; redox regulation of suceptibility to hepatotoxicity; role of endoplasmic stress in alcohol liver injury; role of the innate immune system in drug hepatotoxicity. Home Phone: 323-667-0371; Office Phone: 323-442-5576. E-mail: kaplowit@usc.edu.

KAPLUN, PAUL T., lawyer; b. Glen Cove, NY, Jan. 20, 1956; BSBA magna cum laude, Georgetown Univ., 1978, JD, 1984. CPA Va., 1980; bar: Md. 1985, DC 1986. Atty. Tucker Flyer (merged into Venable); ptnr.-in-charge, Greater Washington bus. practices group Venable LLP. Adj. faculty Georgetown Univ. Law Ctr., 1992—. Adv. bd. Entrepreneurship Inst.; bd. dir. Children's Chorus of Washington. Mem.: ABA, Am. Inst. CPAs, Md. State Bar Assn., DC Bar. Office: Venable LLP 575 7th St NW Washington DC 20004 Office Phone: 202-344-8535. Office Fax: 202-344-8300. Business E-Mail: ptkaplun@venable.com.

KAPNER, LEWIS, lawyer; b. West Palm Beach, Fla., May 21, 1937; s. Irving Michael and Mildred Leah (Pikelny) K.; m. Dawn Beth Grossman, Aug. 30, 1964; children: Steven, Kimberly, Michael, Allison. Student, Harvard U., 1956; BA, U. Fla., 1958; postgrad., George Washington U., 1961; JD, Stetson U., 1962; postgrad., Fla. Atlantic U., 1969-73. Bar: Fla. 1962, U.S. Dist. Ct. (so. dist.) Fla. 1963, U.S. Supreme Ct. 1968. Asst. county solicitor, West Palm Beach, 1962-65; ptnr. Kapner & Kapner, West Palm Beach, 1965-67; gen. counsel Palm Beach County Legis. Del., Tallahassee, 1967; judge Juvenile and Domestic Rels. Ct., West Palm Beach, 1967-73, Cir. Ct. West Palm Beach, 1973-81, chief judge, 1981-83; head marital and family law dept. Montgomery, Searcy & Denney and predecessor firm, West Palm Beach, 1984-88; pres. Lewis Kapner, P.A., West Palm Beach, 1988—. Faculty Nat. Jud. Coll., Reno, 1980-84, Fla. Jud. Coll., Gainesville, 1979-83, dean, 1982-83; adj. prof. law Nova U., 1982-84; mem. Supreme Ct. Commn. on Matrimonial Law, 1982-85. Contbr. articles to profl. jours. Pres. Internat. Found. Gifted Children, 1972-74; legal com. Am. Jewish Commn., 1998—. With USMC, 1959-60. Recipient Learned Hand award, 2005. Fellow Am. Acad. Matrimonial Lawyers (pres. Fla. chpt. 1983-84, bd. dir. 1999-2000), Outstanding Fla. Judge in matrimonial law 1982), Fla. Bar (past chmn. family law sect.), Actors Equity. Republican. Jewish. Office Phone: 561-655-3000.

KAPNICK, RICHARD BRADSHAW, lawyer; b. Chgo., Aug. 21, 1955; s. Harvey E. and Jean (Bradshaw) Kapnick; m. Claudia Norris, Dec. 30, 1978; children: Sarah Bancroft, John Norris. BA with distinction, Stanford U., 1977; MPhil in Internat. Rels., U. Oxford, 1980; JD with honors, U. Chgo., 1982. Bar: Ill. 1982, N.Y. 1993. Law clk. to justice Seymour Simon Ill. Supreme Ct., Chgo., 1982—84; law clk. to Justice John Paul Stevens U.S. Supreme Ct., Washington, 1984—85; assoc. Sidley Austin LLP, Chgo., 1985—89, ptnr., 1989—. Mng. editor: U. Chgo. Law Rev., 1981—82. Vestryman Christ Ch., Winnetka, Ill., 2000—03; trustee Chgo. Symphony Orch., 1995—, vice chmn., 2001—06; bd. dirs., chmn. Civic Orch. Chgo., 1999—2001; bd. dirs. Cabrini Green Legal Aid Clinic, 1990—94, chmn. bd., 1991—93, mem. adv. bd. dirs., 1995—2006, chmn., 2005—06; mem. bd. Stanford Inst. Econ. Policy Rsch., 1999—. Fellow, Leadership Greater Chgo., 1989—90; Marshall scholar, 1978—80. Mem.: Chgo. Club, Phi Beta Kappa, Order of the Coif. Republican. Episcopalian. fluency in Spanish.

KAPNICK, SAMUEL JASON, oncologist; b. Providence, Mar. 28, 1949; s. I.H. and Martha (Shaulson) K.; children: Senta Marie-Rose, Isrel Berndt-Stefan, Sesselja Edda, Finn MacComaill. BLS summa cum laude, boston U., 1974; MD, Harvard Med. Sch., 1981. Surg. rsch. assoc. Harvard Med. Sch., Boston, 1976-77, assoc. in ob/gyn., lectr., 1981-85; intern, resident in ob-gyn. Brigham & Women's Mass. Gen. Hosp., Boston, 1981—85; adminstrv. chief resident Mass. Gen. Hosp./Brigham Hosps., 1985; instr. in gynecology, fellow tumor surgery Harvard Med. Sch., Boston, 1985; cons. in gynecologic oncology Dana Farber Cancer Inst., Boston, 1985-87; clin. fellow Am. Cancer Soc., Boston, 1985-87; attending gynecologic oncologist West Palm Beach, Fla., 1989—; cert. gynecologic oncologist, 1991—. Asst. cons. prof. Duke U. Med. Ctr., Durham, NC, 1994—; reviewer rsch. submissions Cancer med. jour., Bethesda, Md., 1995—; invited lectr., 1995, Palm Beach County Hosps., 1990—, Am. Cancer Soc., Bethesda, 1995, also Switzerland, Germany, France and Eng., 1990-, bus. advisory bd. Admiralty Bank 1992-99. Contbr. articles to profl.

jours. Vol., contbr. Ctr. for Family Svcs., West Palm Beach, 1992—; mem., donor Mass. Gen. Hosp.; trustee, founder Helga Helgason BSRN Meml. Fund; dean's coun. and John Warren Fellow Med. Sch., Harvard U.; donor Covenant House Children's Shelter, 2004—; founder, dir. Kapnick Meml. Cancer Ctrl. Consortium, 2006; founder clinical care initiative Theresa Pratt RN Meml., 2006; active Cath. Diocese children's programs, 1998—; mem., donor First Unitarian Ch., North Palm Beach, Fla.; bd. dirs. Palm Beach Opera, 1992—. Henry Merritt Wriston scholarship Brown U. Mem. Bullfinch Soc., Harvard Club of Palm Beach. Achievements include research in colon, breast, and pelvic cancers. Avocations: philosophy, music. Address: PO Box 30053 Palm Beach Gardens FL 33420-0053 Office: 3345 Burns Rd Ste 203 Palm Beach Gardens FL 33410 Office Phone: 561-622-3810, 561-685-3183, 561-478-5190. Personal E-mail: jasonkapnick@yahoo.com.

KAPNICK, STEWART, investment banker; b. NYC, Mar. 10, 1956; s. Charles and Ruth Kapnick; m. Alison Sue Cherry, 1988; children: Jordan Leigh, Michael Taylor. BA with honors, George Washington U., 1978; MBA, Baruch Coll., 1986. Summer internship IBM Corp., White Plains, NY, 1977—78; acct. exec. L & C Pub. Inc., LA, 1979—82, 3M Corp., NYC, 1982—83; pres., fin. ops. prin. Ulysses Capital, NYC, 1983—87; lease fin. cons. SK Capital, NYC, 1987—; assoc. dir. product devel. and lease fin. Continental Info. Systems Corp., NYC, 1987-89; dir. equity fin. Info. Processing Systems Inc. subs. USF&G Fin. Svcs. Corp., Hackensack, NJ, 1989—92; v.p. lease acquisitions The CIT Group, Livingston, NJ, 1992—94; sr. v.p. corp. banking-lease fin. HSBC Bank USA (formerly Republic Nat. Bank of N.Y.), NYC, 1994—. Mem. Equipment Lessors Assn., Computer Dealers and Lessors Assn. Avocations: basketball, tennis, golf, playing options and foreign currency.

KAPOOR, ASHOK KUMAR, engineer; s. Ram Nath and Sarla Kapoor; m. Nisha Malhotra, May 9, 1984; 1 child, Shweta. BTech, Indian Inst. Tech., 1973; MS, U. Cin., 1979, PhD, 1981. Illumination engr. Philips India Ltd., Bombay, 1973-76; with Fairchild Rsch. Ctr., Palo Alto, Calif., 1981-87; mgr. tech. devel. ASIC div. Nat. Semicondr., Santa Clara, Calif., 1987-88; sr. mem. tech. staff HP Labs., Palo Alto, 1988-91; dir. device tech. LSI Logic, Santa Clara, 1991—96, dir. advanced modeling group, 1998—2000; dir. rsch. Nat. Semiconductor Corp., Santa Clara, 1997—98; founder, chief tech. officer Sensitron, Inc., San Mateo, Calif., 2000—04; founder, ptnr. SemiSolutions LLC, Palo Alto, 2004—; founder, CTO DSM Solutions Inc., Los Gatos, 2005—. Co-chair exec. tech. adv. bd. Semiconductor Rsch. Corp., 1995, mem. exec. tech. adv. bd., 1991-97; mem. tech. working group nat. tech. roadmap for Semiconductor Industry Assn., 1992, 94, mem. roadmap coord. group, 1996; spkr. at univs. Editor: Polysilicon Bipolar Transistors; contbr. tech. articles to profl. jours.; patentee in field. Named Inventor of Yr., LSI Logic, 1995. Mem. IEEE (sr., disting. lectr. 2006), IEEE Electron Devices Soc. (pres. Santa Clara Valley chpt. 1991-92), IEEE Bay Area Nanotech. Coun. Stearing Com. (treas. 2004-05), Material Rsch. Soc., Sigma Xi. Hindu. Avocations: bicycling, swimming, reading poetry and lit. Home: 1056 Amarillo Ave Palo Alto CA 94303-3705 Personal E-mail: akkapoor@comcast.net, akapoor@dcmsolutionsinc.com.

KAPOOR, NEERA, optometrist, research scientist; b. Melfort, Sask., Can., June 25, 1966; arrived in U.S., 1990; d. Ajit and Prem Kapoor. BSc, U. Toronto, 1989; MS, SUNY, NYC, 1993; OD, SUNY, 1994. Asst. clin. prof. optometry SUNY, NYC, 1995—2002, assoc. clin. prof., 2002—, dir. head trauma vision rehab. unit., 1996—2002, dir. Raymond J. Greenwald Rehab. Ctr., 2002—. Cons. neuro-optometry JFK Med. Ctr., NJ Neuro Sci. Inst., Edison, 2001—05. Co-author, co-editor: Visual & Vestibular Consequences of Acquired Brain Injury, 2001. Recipient Founder's award, Brain Injury Assn. NY State, 2002, Disting. Achievement award, NY State Optometric Assn., 2003, Chancellor's award, SUNY, 2005. Fellow: Am. Acad. Optometry; mem.: Assn. Rsch. in Vision and Ophthalmology, Coll. Optometrists in Vision Devel. (assoc.). Office: SUNY 5th Fl 33 W 42nd St New York NY 10036 Business E-Mail: nkapoor@sunyopt.edu.

KAPOOR, VISHAL, plastic surgeon; Grad. with honors, cum laude, U. Calif., San Diego; MD with honors, Alpha Omega Alpha, Tufts U. Sch. Med. Resident in gen. surgery, plastic & reconstructive surgery U. Wash., Seattle; fellow in cosmetic surgery Aesthetic Surgery Inst., San Francisco; pvt. practice LA. Affiliated Cedars Sinai Med. Ctr., LA, Olympia Midway Hosp., LA, Mercy Southwest Hosp., Bakersfield, Calif. Mem.: Am. Soc. Plastic Surgeons, Alpha Omega Alpha. Office: 1125 S Beverly Dr Ste 720 Los Angeles CA 90035 Office Phone: 310-277-4685. Office Fax: 310-277-4687. E-mail: drkapoor@drkapoormd.com.*

KAPOR, MITCHELL DAVID, application developer, foundation administrator; b. Bklyn., Nov. 1, 1950; s. Jesse and Phoebe L. (Wagner) K.; m. Judith M. Vecchione, June 4, 1972 (div. 1979); m. Ellen M. Poss, Aug. 7, 1983 (div. 1998); m. Freada Klein, June 19, 1999. BA, Yale U., 1971; MA, Campus-Free Coll. (now Beacon Coll.), Boston, 1978; postgrad., Sloan Sch. Mgmt., MIT, 1979; DHL (hon.), Boston U., 1985, Mass. Sch. Profl. Psychology, 1990; DSc (hon.), Suffolk U., 1988, U. Mass., 1996. Disc jockey WHCN-FM, Hartford, Conn.; tchr., transcendental mediation in Cambridge, Mass, and Fairfield, Iowa; entry-level computer designer Cambridge, Mass.; freelance cons., 1978-80; product mgr. Personal Software, Inc., Sunnyvale, Calif., 1980; founder Lotus Devel. Corp., Cambridge, Mass., 1982, dir., 1982—87, pres. Cambridge, Mass., 1982-84, CEO, chmn., 1984-86; chmn., CEO ON Tech. Inc., Cambridge, Mass., 1987-90; co-founder Electronic Frontier Found., Inc., Cambridge, Mass., 1990, chmn., 1990-94, chmn., pres., 1994-99; ptnr. ACCEL Ptnrs., Palo Alto, Calif., 1999—2001; pres. Kapor Enterprises Inc., 1985—; pres., chair Open Source Applications Found., San Francisco, 2001—; founding chair Mozilla Found., 2003—. Chmn. Mass. Commn. Computer Tech. and Law, 1992, 93, 2003—; mem., computer sci. and tech. bd. Nat. Rsch. Coun.; mem. adv. coun. Nat. Info. Infrastructure; adj. prof., Media Lab MIT, 1994—96; founding investor UUNET and Real Networks; chmn. bd. Linden Rsch.; bd. dir. Groove Networks; lectr. and co-taught, Open Source Development and Distribution of Information U. Calif. Berkeley, 2005—. Writer of articles, columns, & op-ed pieces on information infrastructure policy, intellectual property issues & antitrust to Scientific American, NY Times, Forbes, Tricycle: The Buddhist Review & Communications (Assn. Computing Machinery). Trustee Kapor Family Found., 1984—98, Level Playing Field Inst., San Francisco; founder, dir. Mitchell Kapor Found., 1997—. Recipient Fellow award, Computer History Mus., 1996. Jewish. Achievements include founder of Lotus Development Corporation and designer with other of Lotus 1-2-3 in 1983. Office: Mitchell Kapor Found 543 Howard St Ste 500 San Francisco CA 94105 Office Phone: 415-946-3016. Business E-Mail: mitch@kapor.com.

KAPP, C. TERRENCE, lawyer; b. Pine Bluff, Ark., Oct. 1, 1944; s. Robert Amos and Guenevere Patricia (DeVinne) Kapp; m. Betsy Langer, May 2, 1987. BA, Colgate U., 1966; JD, Cleve. State U., 1971; MA summa cum laude, Holy Apostles Coll., 1984. Bar: Ohio 1971, U.S. Dist. Ct. (no. dist.) Ohio 1973, U.S. Supreme Ct. 1980, U.S. Tax Ct. 1996. Ptnr. Kapp & Kapp, East Liverpool, Ohio, 1971-84; pvt. practice Cleve., 1984—; ptnr. Marshman, Snyder & Kapp, Cleve., 1991-93, Kapp Law Offices, Cleve., 1994—. Contbr. articles to profl. jours. Chair St. John's Cathedral Endowment Trust, Cleve., 1992—94; pres., bd. dirs. Lake Erie Nature and Sci. Ctr., Bay Village, Ohio, 1991—92. Mem.: ABA (judge finals nat. appellate adv. competition 1987, taxation com. exec. 1988—, nat. chmn. divorce laws and procedures com. family law sect. 1989—93, vice-chmn. step families com. 1991—93, task force client edn. 1991—, commr. presdl. commn. non-lawyer practice 1992—96, chmn. alternative funding com. 1992—, chair nat. symposium image family law atty-fact or myth 1993, domestic rels. taxatoin problems com. exec. tax sect., lit. sect., cert. Outstanding Svc. 1988, 1989, 1993, 1995), Cuyahoga County Bar Assn. (bar admissions com. exec. 1986—, cert. grievance com. 1990—, chair family law sect. 1991—92, jud. selection com. 1991—, unauthorized practice law com. 1992—, cert. Outstanding Leadership 1992), Ohio State Bar Assn. (family law com. exec. 1987—, family law curriculum com. Ohio CLE Inst. 1992—), Bay Men's Club, Cleve. Athletic Club (pres., bd.dirs.). Roman Catholic. Avocations: sailing, handball, racquet sports, dog training. Office: Kapp Law Offices PO Box 40447 Bay Village OH 44140-0447 Office Phone: 440-870-7500. Business E-Mail: kapplawoffices@ameritech.net.

KAPP, MICHAEL KEITH, lawyer; b. Winston-Salem, NC, Nov. 28, 1953; s. William Henry and Betty Jean (Minton) K.; m. Mary Jo Chancy McLean, Aug. 13, 1977; 1 child, Mary Katherine. AB with honors, U. N.C., 1976, JD with honors, 1979. Bar: N.C. 1979, U.S. Dist. Ct. (ea. dist.) N.C. 1980, U.S. Ct. Appeals (4th cir.) 1982, U.S. Dist. Ct. (mid. dist.) N.C. 1986, U.S. Supreme Ct. 1988. Law clk. to presiding justice N.C. Ct. Appeals, Raleigh, 1979—80, N.C. Supreme Ct., 1980—81; assoc. Maupin, Taylor & Ellis, Raleigh, 1981—85; ptnr. Williams, Mullin, Maupin, Taylor P.A. (formerly Maupin, Taylor & Ellis, P.A.), 1985—, mng. dir., 2002—07, v.p., 2007—. Research editor U. N.C. Jour. Internat. Law and Comml. Regulation, 1978-79; editor Survey of Significant Decisions of North Carolina Court of Appeals and North Carolina Supreme Court, 1979-81, 2d vol., 1981-82. N.C. teen Dem. advisor, 1983-85; mem. exec. coun. N.C. Dem. Party, 1983-85; founding dir. N.C. Vol. Lawyers for Arts, Raleigh, 1982-85; counsel Moravian Music Found., Winston-Salem, 1982-85, trustee, 1985-90, pres., 1990-92; counsel Raleigh Little Theatre, 1996-98, bd. dir., pres., 2003; bd. dir. Moravian Ch. Archives, Winston-Salem, 1984-89, Carolina Charter Corp., dir. 1995—; co-chair Raleigh First Night, 2000; bd. dirs. Soc. for Preservation of Historic Oakwood, Raleigh, 1981-83, Moravian Ministries Found., Inc., 2006-. Morehead scholar U. N.C., 1972. Mem. ABA, N.C. Bar Assn. (chmn. young lawyer div. continuing legal edn. 1980-82, membership 1984-86, bd. govs. 1983-86), N.C. State Bar (ethics com. 1981-91, chair com. on professionalism 2006—, jud. dist. councilor 2001-, chair ethics com. 2007), Wake County Bar Assn. (bd. dirs. 1988-90, pres.-elect 1995, pres. 1996), Raleigh Execs. Club (pres. 1998), Kiwanis (Raleigh Kiwanis Found. dir., 1996-98), Phi Beta Kappa, Phi Delta Phi, Pi Lambda Phi. Avocations: historic preservation, hiking, gardening. Home: 1615 Craig St Raleigh NC 27608-2201 Office: Williams Mullin Maupin Taylor PA Highwoods Tower One 3200 Beechleaf Ct Ste 500 Raleigh NC 27604-1670 Office Phone: 919-981-4000. Business E-Mail: kkapp@williamsmullin.com.

KAPP, ROBERT HARRIS, lawyer; b. Chgo., Mar. 9, 1934; s. Ben and Gladys (Harris) K.; m. Jean Schlusberg, June 22, 1958; children: Stephen, Lisa, Jonathan, Diana. BS in Econs., U. Pa., 1955; JD, U. Mich., 1958. Bar: Ill. 1958, D.C. 1961. Trial atty. U.S. Dept. Justice, Washington, 1958-61; ptnr. Hogan & Hartson, Washington, 1961—2003, of counsel, 2004—. Mem. adv. bd. Transnational Arbitration Assn., 1994-97. Bd. dirs. Global Rights (formerly Internat. Human Rights Law Group), 1978—, chmn., 1986-89, Lawyers' Com. for Civil Rights Under Law, 1976-06, chmn., 1983-85, Washington Lawyers' Com. for Civil Rights and Urban Affairs, 1974-96, chmn., 1980-82, ACLU of Nat. Capitol Area, 1983-95, chmn., 1992-94, Washington Sch. Psychiatry, 1980-86, Higher Achievement Program, 1991-94, Hope & Home, 2005-; mem. area I planning com. Montgomery County Pub. Schs., 1970; mem. adv. bd. Internat. Legal Studies Program, Am. U. Law Sch.; mem. bd. visitors U. Mich. Law Sch.; commr. Commn. on Independence for Nambia; co-founder, co-pres. Internat. Sr. Lawyers Project; sr. advisor REalizing Rights: The Ethical Globalization Initiative. Fellow Am. Bar Found. (Wiley A. Branton Sr. award Wash. Lawyers Com. for Civil Rights and Urban Affairs, Alan Barth Svc. award ACLU of Nat. Capitol Area, C. Anthony Friedrich Meml. award Internat. Human Rights Law Group). Office: Hogan & Hartson 555 13th St NW Ste 800E Washington DC 20004-1161 Office Phone: 202-637-8611. Office Fax: 202-637-5910. Business E-Mail: rhkapp@hhlaw.com.

KAPPAS, ATTALLAH, physician; b. Union City, NJ, Nov. 4, 1926; s. Attie and Sofia (Kozam) K.; m. Oct. 26, 1963; children: Peter, Michael, Nicholas. AB, Columbia U., 1947; MD with honors, U. Chgo., 1950; ScD, N.Y. Med. Coll., 1978. Diplomate: Am. Bd. Internal Medicine. Med. intern Univ. Service, Kings County Hosp., NYC, 1950-51; ACS rsch. fellow Sloan Kettering Inst., NYC, 1951-54; asst. resident physician and sr. asst. resident physician Peter Bent Brigham Hosp. Harvard Med. Sch., Boston, 1954-56; assoc. div. steroid biochemistry and metabolism Sloan Kettering Inst., NYC, 1956—57; from asst. prof. to assoc. prof. dept. medicine, head divsn. metabolism and arthritis U. Chgo. Med. Sch., 1957—67; Guggenheim fellow, guest investigator Rockefeller U., NYC, 1966—67, assoc. prof., physician, 1967—71, sr. physician, 1971—74, prof., 1971—91, physician-in-chief, 1974—91, physician-in-chief emeritus, 1991—, Sherman Fairchild prof., 1991—2004, prof. emeritus, 2004—; prof. medicine Cornell U., 1972—2002. Prof. medicine Cornell U., NYC, 1972—2002; Vincent Astor prof. clin. sci. Cornell U. Meml. Hosp. Sloan Kettering Inst., NYC, 1979—81; v.p. Rockefeller U., NYC, 1983—91; mem. coun. SUNY Health Scis. Ctr., Bklyn., 1998—2004; dir. Theresa and Eugene Lane Ctr. Rsch. and Edn. N.Y. Hosp. Queens Med. Ctr. Weill-Cornell Med. Coll., NYC, 1998—2002; emeritus Theresa and Eugene Lane Ctr. Rsch. and Edn. N.Y. Hosp. Queens Med. Ctr, Weill-Cornell Med. Coll., 2002; mem. dean's coun. U. Vt. Coll. Medicine, Burlington, 2000—04; prof. medicine emeritus Weill Cornell Med. Coll., NYC, 2002; mem. vis. com. divsn. biol. sci. and Pritzer Sch. Medicine U. Chgo., 2003—. Contbr. articles to profl. jours. Bd. dir. Vis. Nurse Service N.Y., 1982-86, 98—, Scenic Hudson, Inc., 2002-2007; mem. gov.'s com. on rev. sci. studies and devel. pub. policy on problems resulting from hazardous wastes N.Y. State, 1980; bd. dir. Beatrice Renfield Found., N.Y.C., 2003—. Served with U.S. Army, 1945-46. Named named Sr. Henry Hallet Dale Meml. lectr. and vis. prof., Johns Hopkins Hosp., 1975, Pfizer lectr. clin. pharmacology, Peter Bent Brigham Hosp., Harvard Med. Sch., 1977, Pfizer lectr., Pa. State U., 1980, first Rolf Blomstrand lectr., Karolinska Inst., 1988, first Glaxo lectr., Cornell U. Med. Sch., Gunner and Lillian Nicholson Found. exch. prof., Karolinska Inst., Stockholm, 1985—86, Barowsky Meml. lectr., N.Y. Med. Coll., 1986, First Annual Lang Rsch. lectr., N.Y. Hosp. Med. Ctr., Queens, 2000; recipient Spl. award in clin. pharmacology, Burroughs Wellcome Fund, 1973, Disting. Svc. award in med. scis., U. Chgo. Sch. Medicine, 1975, Citation for profl. achievement, U. Chgo. Alumni Assn., 1995, 1st Ann. award for excellence in clin. rsch., NIH, 1989; fellow Commonwealth Fund, 1961—62, Guggenheim fellow, 1966—67. Fellow ACP; mem. Assn. Am. Physicians, Am. Soc. Clin. Investigation, Am. Clin. and Climatol. Assn., Am. Soc. Pharmacology and Exptl. Therapeutics (pub. affairs com., award for exptl. therapeutics 1978), Practitioners Soc. N.Y., Harvey Soc., Endocrine Soc., Interurban Clin. Club, Cosmos Club (Washington), N.Y. Athletic Club, Lotos Club, Univ. Club (NY). Office: Rockefeller U Hosp 1230 York Ave New York NY 10021-6307 Office Phone: 212-327-8494. Office Fax: 212-327-8690.

KAPPAZ, MICHAEL H., engineering executive, energy executive; b. Cartagena, Colombia, May 14, 1942; came to the U.S., 1963; s. George and Elena (Hegel) K.; m. Chafica Maria Dau; children: George, Nur-Helene, Christine, Karen, William, Patricia. BS in Indsl. Engring. and Ops. Rsch., Poly. Inst. N.Y., 1970; MBA in Fin. Mgmt., Golden Gate U., 1976; cert. in Global Strategic Mgmt., U. Pa., 1984; cert. in exec. mgmt., Stanford U., 1986. Indsl. engr. for iron and steel Ramseyer and Miller, Inc., NYC, 1964-71; v.p., gen. mgr. internat. ops. Bechtel Power Corp., Bechtel Group, Gaithersburg, Md. and San Francisco, 1971-86; CEO K&M Engring. and Consulting Corp., Washington, 1987—; chmn. bd. dirs. KMR Power Corp., Arlington, Va., 1993-2000; chmn. K&M Global Constrn. LLC, 1995—, K&M Panam., LLC. Contbr. articles to various publs., papers to confs. and seminars. Mem. adv. bd. Rep. Nat. Com., 1993-2000; mem. Am. Rsch. Ctr. (Egyptology and Archeology), 1982-86; mem. engring. adv. com. Am. U., Cairo, 1982-86; co-chmn. coun. Latin Am. studies Johns Hopkins U., 1987-89, mem. adv. coun. 1987-97, mem. devel. com. 1993-98; bd. dirs. Washington Opera, Bus. Coun. for Internat. Understanding; chmn. emeritus U.S.-Colombia Bus. Partnership; trustee Latino Student Fund. Recipient Deal of Yr. award Project Fin. Internat. Yearbook, 1993, Infrastructure Fin. Mag., 1993, Blue Chip Enterprise award, 1995, Fast Track award, 1995, Inc 500 award, Nat. Tech. Fast 500 award, 1995, Fast 50 award 1996, Project Fin. Inter. 2000, Top 50 Hispanic High Tech Co. 2000. Mem. U.S. Energy Assn., Am. C. of C. (charter, Cairo), Am. Assn. Cost Engrs. (past v.p., dir. Capital chpt.), D.C. C. of C., Georgetown Club, Avenel Country Club, Damascus Lodge, Group of 50, Bretton Woods Com. Republican. Roman Catholic. Avocations: opera, baseball, golf, bridge. Home: PO Box 9865 Mc Lean VA 22102-0865 Office Phone: 703-442-3973. Business E-Mail: mkappaz@kmec.com.

KAPPES, PHILIP SPANGLER, lawyer; b. Detroit, Dec. 24, 1925; s. Philip Alexander and Wilma Fern (Spangler) K.; m. Glendora Galena Miles, Nov. 27, 1948; children: Susan Lea, Philip Miles, Mark William. BA cum laude, Butler U., 1945; JD, U. Mich., 1948. Bar: Ind. 1948. Assoc. Armstrong and Gause, 1948—49, C.B. Dutton, 1950—51; ptnr. Dutton, Kappes & Overman, 1952—85, of counsel, 1983—85; pres., dir. K&K Realty, Inc., Indpls., 1983—; ptnr. Lewis Kappes Fuller & Eads, Indpls., 1985—89; mgr. Labeco Properties, LLC, Indpls., 1985—; ptnr. Lewis & Kappes, Indpls., 1989—92, Creston Group, Indpls., 1989—98, Lewis & Kappes PC, Indpls., 1993—. Sec., Ind. Machine Works, Inc.(formerly named Laboratory Equipment Corp.), Mooresville, Ind., 1952-2000; instr. bus. law Butler U., 1948-49, chmn. bd. govs., 1965-66, bd. trustees, 1987-90; chmn. Ovid Butler Soc., 1982-83. Life bd. dirs. Crossroads Am. coun. Boy Scouts Am., 1965—, v.p. fin., mem. exec. com., pres., 1977-79, chmn. trustees endowment fund, 1987-92, trustee, 1987—, chmn. Gathering of Eagles dinner, 2000; bd. dirs. Fairbanks Hosp., Indpls., 1986-94, chmn. bd., 1988-91, exec. com., 1987-94, mem. audit and fin. com., 1992-94, life dir. emeritus, 1994—, chmn. nominating com., 1991; trustee Butler U., 1987-90, Children's Mus., Indpls., 1969-88, pres. bd. trustees, 1984-85, bd. disting. advisors, 1990-01, hon. trustee, 2001—; mem. First Meridian Heights Presbyn. Ch., 1933—, chmn. bd. trustees, 1958-61, 69-72, 1996— ruling elder 1982-85, 94-99, deacon, 1950-58; mem. planning com. and dir. Indpls. 32-Degree Masonic Learning Ctr. for Children, 1997-98, dir., 1998—, chmn. bd., 2002-2002, vice chmn., 2002—; chmn. Dyslexia Tutor Tng. Inst., 2000—; chmn. Lawyers Title Guaranty Fund Com., 1971-73; dir. Ind. Citizens for Modern Ct. Sys., 1970; vice chmn., mem. faculty Law in Am. Soc., 1971-73. Recipient Paul H. Buchanan award of excellence Indpls. Bar Found., Disting. Eagle award Boy Scouts Am., 2004, Disting. Alumnus award, Mortar award Butler U. Alumni Assn. Mem. ABA (ho. of dels. 1970-71), Ind. State Bar Assn. (ho. dels. 1959—, chmn. pub. rels. exec. com. 1966-69, sec. 1973-74, bd. mgrs. 1975-77, chmn. law practice mgmt. com. 1991-92, chmn. subcom. trial ct. judges, 2005-, chmn. jud. selection and retention subcom. improvement in jud. sys., standing com. 2005), Ind. Bar Found. of Ind. State Bar Assn. (Legendary Lawyers of Year, 2006), Indpls. Bar Assn. (treas., 1st v.p. 1965, pres. 1970, bd. mgrs. 1968-71, 75-77, chmn. law day com. 1991-92, settlement week com. 1989-95, co-chair Family Law Study Commn., co-chmn. ct. liaison com. 1992-93, family law implementation com. 1993-97, exec. com. bd. mgrs. 1994-96, counsel bd. mgrs. 1994, chmn. sr. lawyers divsn. 1999-2000, Bd. Mgrs. award for jud. sys. improvement 1995), Am. Judicature Soc., Indpls. Legal Aid Soc., Indpls. Jr. C. of C. (past 1st v.p., dir. ct. unification implementation com., chmn. 1995-98), Butler U. Alumni Assn. (past pres., Disting. Alumnus award, Mortar award), Mich. Alumni Assn., Meridian Hills Country Club, Lawyers Club, Gyro Club (pres. 1966), Masons (worshipful master 1975), Indpls. Valley Scottish Rite (33d degree, most wise master 1982-84, trustee 1996—, chmn. bd. trustees 1998-99, 2001—, pres. Indpls. Scottish Rite Cathedral Found., dir., chmn. 2001—, dir. Indpls. Scottish Rite Found.), Shriners, Phi Delta Theta (chpt. advisor 1950-82), Tau Kappa Alpha. Republican. Presbyterian. Office: 1 American Square Ste 2500 Indianapolis IN 46282-0003 Office Phone: 317-639-1210. Business E-Mail: pkappes@lewis-kappes.com.

KAPPES, STEPHEN R., federal agency administrator; b. Cin., Aug. 22, 1951; m. Kathleen Morgan; 2 children. BS in Anatomy & Chemistry, Ohio U., 1973; MS in Pathology, Ohio St. U. With CIA, 1981—2004, 2006—, chief counterintelligence ctr., 2000—02, assoc. dep. dir. ops. for counter-intelligence, 2000—02, asst. dep. dir. ops., 2002—04, dep. dir. ops., 2004, dep. dir., 2006—; exec. v.p. global strategy Armor Group Internat., 2005—06. Served in USMC, 1976—81. Office: CIA Office Dep Dir Washington DC 20505*

KAPPLER, ANN M., lawyer, finance company executive; b. New Brunswick, NJ, Dec. 24, 1957; AB magna cum laude, Darmouth Coll., 1979; JD, NYU, 1986. Bar: N.Y. 1988, DC 1989. Law clk. to Hon. Abner J. Mikva U.S. Ct. Appeals (DC cir.), Washington, 1986—87; law clk. to Hon. Harry Blackmun U.S. Supreme Ct., 1987—88; assoc. Jenner & Block, 1989—93, ptnr., 1994—98; sr. v.p., dep. gen. counsel Fannie Mae, Washington, 1999—2000, sr. v.p., gen. counsel, 2000—05; ptnr. Kelley Drye Collier Shannon, Washington, 2006—. Editor-in-chief: NYU Law Rev., 1985—86. Mem.: ABA, Order of Coif, DC Bar Assn., Internat. Human Rights Law Group (bd. dirs. 1999—2001), Coun. Ct. Excellence (bd. dirs. 1999—2001), Wash. Lawyers Com. Civil Rights and Urban Affairs (bd. dirs. 1999—2001). Office: Kelley Drye Washington Harbour, Ste 400 3050 K St, NW Washington DC 20007 Office Phone: 202-342-8441. Office Fax: 202-342-8451. E-mail: akappler@kelleydrye.com.*

KAPPLER, KAREN L., musician, educator; b. Maud, Okla., July 19, 1938; d. Raymond Maxwell and Verdena Mary (Caywood) Edwards; m. Samuel Houston Clifton, June 27, 1959 (div. Apr. 1, 1977); children: Mary Louise Clifton, Catherine Helen Sehorn; m. Karl Heinrich Kappler, Aug. 27, 1989. BA in Edn. and Music, U. Denver, 1965; postgrad., U. Colo., 1967, MMus in Piano performance, 1980; postgrad., U. No. Colo., 1970, U. Utah, 1971, Columbia U., 1976. Cert. tchr. Colo. Piano and remedial reading tchr. John Marshall H.S., Oklahoma City, 1954—56; tchr., piano, organ, voice, 1955—; tchr. Jefferson County Pub. Schs., Lakewood, Colo., 1965—73; tchr., tutor Colo. Dept. Social Svcs., Denver, 1973—75; instr. continuing edn. U. Colo., Boulder, 1977—78; tchr. Met. State Coll., Denver, 1978—80; paralegal specialist Solomon, Zimmerman, & Schwartz, P.C., 1978—85; paralegal John Dressler, Esq., Denver, 1982—84; prin., owner Paralegal Specialty Svcs., Denver, 1986—94; ch. music dir., 1980—. Pianist, organist, vocalist, primary tchr. Classen Blvd. Bapt. Ch., Oklahoma City, 1948—55; organist, choir soloist, dir. children's choirs Edgewater Meth. Ch., Denver, 1962—65; curriculum writer, nat. tchr. Jefferson County Pub. Schs., 1965—73, percussion ensemble coach, Colo., 2005; nat. coord., tchr. Robert Pace Piano Found., 1970—82; del. bd. edn. hearings on differentiated staffing Jefferson County Pub. Schs., 1971—73; dir. pilot program Colo. State Social Svcs., 1973—75; piano and voice coach dinner theaters, children's auditions, Denver, 1978—93; pvt. tchr. piano, organ, voice, theory, composition, improvisation Skinner Cmty. Sch., Denver Pub. Schs., 1980—93; weddings organist First Bapt. Ch., Denver, 1981—84; dir. music and choir, organist Highlands Christian Ch., Denver, 1983—87; prin. organist St. Thomas Moore Cath. Ch., Littleton, Colo., 1987—88; mem. Am. Guild Organists, 1988—2006, com. chair Young Artists' Competition, 1988, com. chair Denver study groups, 90; dir. music and choirs, organist First Ave. Presbyn. Ch., Denver, 1988—, festival of praise choral dir., 2004; pvt. tchr., coach to piano and voice students Denver Sch. Performing Arts, 1998—2004; piano tchr. grades 5-6 Britton Elem. Sch., Okla. Numerous recitals, concerts. Mem. exec. bd., officer, mem. com. Jefferson Symphony Orch., Golden, Colo., 1980—90; music stock advisor Jefferson County Libr., Lakewood, 1986; mem. Am. Guild Organists, 1988—2006; musician, spkr. Gideons Internat., Nashville and Denver, 1990—; cmty. capt. March of Dimes, Northglenn, Colo., 1992—, Am. Cancer Soc., 2004—06, Nat. Alzheimers Assn., 2004—06; performance music seminar leader Jefferson Symphony Orch., 1994, piano judge young artists competition, 2001; tchr. music, history Lewis and Clark Am. Indians Tour, Lewiston, Idaho, 2005; dir. music program, pianist Chaslou Acad., Denver, 1995—99. Grantee NDEA, 1963—65; NDEA Inst. fellow, 1968. Mem.: Thornton Arts, Sci. and Humanities Coun. (jr. artists festival piano divsn. judge 2000—07), Nat. Fedn. Music Clubs (judge coll. voice competition 1975, judge piano and organ 1998—99, 2003—04), Colo. Music Tchrs. Assn. (tchr. state conv. 1981, judge local panels, Denver chair State Theory JExam 1979—80, group class tchr. state conv. workshop 1979—80), Music Tchrs. Nat. Assn., Hist. Needlework Guild, Steinway Performance Club, Kappa Delta Pi, Sigma Alpha Iota (coll. chpt. pres. 1958—59, chair scholarship com. 1975, rec. sec. 1976—77, chair audit com. 1983, v.p. ritual 1996—97, v.p. music programs and ritual 1996—2001, del. Denver Alumnae chpt. to internat. conv. 1997, pres. state chpt. 1997—2000, chair scholarships com. 1998—2001, honors chair 2000, ex-officio treas. 2000—01, co-chair benefit concert 2000—02, chair bylaws com. 2000—06, Mozart 250th birthday concert co-dir., pianist, organist 2006, chair meml. svc., chair accompanists, Alumnae Chpt. Nat. Achievement award 1998, Rose of Honor 2000, chpt. cert. recognition 2001, 2003). Republican. Presbyterian. Avocations: reading, travel, needle-work design. Home and Office: 10449 Lafayette St Northglenn CO 80233-4249 Home Phone: 303-452-3863.

KAPPNER, AUGUSTA SOUZA, academic administrator; b. Bronx, NY, June 25, 1944; d. Augusto and Monica Thomasina (Fraser) Souza; m. Thomas Kappner, Aug. 14, 1965; children: Tania, Diana. AB, Barnard Coll., 1966; MSW, Hunter Coll., NYC, 1968; DSW, Columbia U., 1984. Cert. social worker, N.Y. Lectr., community affairs specialist Dept. Urban Affairs, Grad. Div., Hunter Coll., 1968-70; adj. instr., field supr. N.Y.C. C.C., 1970-71; instr., coord. urban leadership unit Columbia U. Sch. Social Wk., 1970-72; asst. prof., dir. admissions and student svcs. SUNY, Stony Brook, 1973-74; assoc. prof., chmn. human svcs. divsn. LaGuardia C.C., 1974-78, prof., dean continuing edn., 1978-84; dean acad. affairs Adult & Continuing Edn., CUNY, 1984, dean acad. affairs, instructional rsch., adult learning, 1984-86; pres. Borough of Manhattan C.C./CUNY, 1986-92; asst. sec. of vocat. and adult edn. Dept. of Edn., Washington, 1993-95; pres. Bank Street Coll., NYC, 1995—. Former chair Adult Literacy Media Alliance; bd. dirs. Nat. Writing Project; mem. panel Edn. Policy NYC Dept. Edn, Am. Coun. on Edn. Commn. for Advancement of Racial and Ethnic Equity; former mem. Commn. Nation Lifelong Learners; commr., Commn. Higher Edn., Middle States Assn.; former mem. adv. bd. Fund for the Improvement Post Secondary Edn., US Dept. Edn.; former mem. adv. panel Nat. Ctr. Innovation in Governing Am. Edn.; cons. and lectr. in field. Trustee Marymount Manhattan Coll.; mem. N.Y. State Edn. Commr.'s Task Force for the Edn. of Children and Youth at Risk, N.Y. State Gov.'s Coun. on Literacy, N.Y.C. Bd. Edn. Chancellor's U./Schs. Collaborative steering com.; appointed by Mayor of City of N.Y. to Joint Commn. on Integrity in Pub. Schs.; bd. dirs. N.Y. Urban Coalition; mem. N.Y.C. Coun. on Econ. Edn. Whitney M. Young Jr. fellow, 1982, USPHS awardee, 1981, Ford Found. fellow, 1973, Silverman Fund awardee, 1968, NIMH fellow, 1967, others; recipient Harlem Sch. Arts Humanitarian award, 1990, Am. Assn. Women in Community and Jr. Colls. Presdl. award, 1989, Asian Ams. for Equality Community Svc. award, 1989, Columbia U. Medal of Excellence, 1988, Barnard Coll. medal of distinction, 1988, Found. for Child Devel. Centennial award, 1999, Morris T. Keeton award Coun. for Adult and Exptl. Learning, others. Mem. Am. Coun. on Edn.

KAPPY, MICHAEL STEVEN, pediatrics educator; b. Bklyn., Feb. 8, 1940; s. Jack and Lilyan (Banchefsky) K.; m. Peggy Markson; children: Douglas Bruce, Gregory Louis. BA, Johns Hopkins U., 1961; MD, PhD, U. Wis., 1967. Asst. prof. U. Ariz. Med. Sch., Tucson, 1975-78; fellow pediatric endocrinology Johns Hopkins Hosp., Balt., 1978-80; assoc. prof. U. Fla. Med. Sch., Gainesville, 1980-85; clin. prof. U. Ariz. Med. Sch., Tucson, 1985-94; med. dir. Children's Health Ctr., Phoenix, 1985-94; prof. pediatrics U. Colo. Health Sci. Ctr., Denver, 1994—; chief pediatric endocrinology The Children's Hosp., Denver, 1994—. Editor: (jour.) Today's Child, 1985, Advances in Pediatrics, 2004, (book) Wilkins-The Diagnosis and Treatment of Endocrine Disorders in Childhood and Adolescence, 1994, Principles and Practice of Pediatric Endocrinology, 2005. Med. advisor Am. Diabetes Assn., Phoenix, 1985-94; bd. dirs. Ronald McDonald House, Phoenix, 1987-94. Named Tchr. of Yr., St. Joseph's Hosp., Phoenix, 1993, Disting. Alumni award, Johns Hopkins U., 1994, Med. Alumnus award, U. Wis., 2004. Mem. Assn. Pediatric Program Dirs. (pres. 1992-94), Soc. for Pediatric Rsch., Endocrine Soc., Am. Acad. Pediatrics, Physicians for Social Responsibility, Alpha Omega Alpha. Avocations: photography, cooking, four-wheel drive touring. Office: The Childrens Hosp 1056 E 19th Ave # B-265 Denver CO 80218-1088 Home: 460 S Marion Pkwy Apt 1706c Denver CO 80209-5547

KAPRAL, FRANK ALBERT, microbiologist and immunology educator; b. Phila., Mar. 12, 1928; s. John and Erna Louise (Melching) K.; m. Marina Garay, Nov. 22, 1951; children: Frederick, Gloria, Robert; m. Esther McKenzie, May 10, 2003. BS, U. of the Scis. in Phila., 1952; PhD, U. Pa., 1956. With U. Pa., Phila., 1952-66, assoc. in microbiology, 1958-66; assoc. microbiologist Phila Gen. Hosp., 1962-64, chief microbiology research, 1964-66, chief microbiology, 1965-66; asst. chief microbiol. research VA Hosp., Phila, 1962-66; assoc. prof. med. microbiology Ohio State U., Columbus, 1966-69, prof. med. virology, immunology and med. genetics, 1969—95, prof. emeritus dept. molecular virology, immunology and med. genetics, 1995—. Cons. Ctr. Disease Control, Atlanta, 1980, Proctor and Gamble Co., 1981-87. Contbr. articles to profl. jours. Active Ctrl. Ohio Diabetes Assn., 1992-93. With AUS, 1946-47. Grantee, Ctrl. Ohio Diabetes Assn., 1992—93; Rsch. grant, NIH, 1959—95. Fellow Am. Acad. Microbiology, Infectious Diseases Soc. Am.; mem. AAAS, Am. Soc. for Microbiology, Am. Assn. for Immunologists, Sigma Xi. Democrat. Roman Catholic. Achievements include patents for implant chamber. Home: 873 Clubview Blvd S Columbus OH 43235-1771 Personal E-mail: elaureo2@yahoo.com.

KAPRANOS, ALEXANDER (FRANZ FERDINAND), singer, musician; b. Almondsbury, Gloucestershire, England, Mar. 20; Studied English Lit., Glasgow. Singer, guitarist The Blisters (changed name to The Karelia); played bass The Yummy Fur; lead singer and guitarist Franz Ferdinand, 2001—. Performer: 9 Songs, 2004; notable guest appearences Musikprogrammet-programmet om musik, 2004, Friday Night with Jonathan Ross, 2004, Paskvil, 2004, lead singer, guitarist (albums) Darts of Pleasure, 2003, Franz Ferdinand, 2004 (Best Album, NME awards, 2005), You Could Have It So Much Better, 2005, (songs) Take Me Out, 2004 (Best Video, Q Awards, 2004, Best Track, NME awards, 2005, Ivor Novello award for Best Contemporary Song, 2005), Matinee, 2004, Michael, 2004, Do You Want To, 2005; performer: (DVD Single) Take Me Out, 2004, Matinee, 2004. Co-recipient Mercury Music prize, Britain, 2004, Award for GQ Internat. Band of Yr.; recipient Philip Hall Radar award, New Musical Express (NME) Awards, 2004, Best Live Band, 2006, Best Brit. Group & Best Brit. Rock Act, Brit Awards, 2005. Address: Domino Recording Co PO Box 47039 London SW18 1WD England

KAPRIELIAN, WALTER, advertising executive; b. NYC, June 2, 1934; s. Vartan and Shoushan (DerBargamian) K.; m. Julia Hachigian, July 7, 1957 (dec. Nov. 1983); children: Victoria Susan, Siran Marion, John Vartan; m. Dinaz Boga, May 20, 1988. AAS, SUNY, 1953. Licensed charterboat capt. Art dir. BBD&O, NYC, 1953-64; group head, art dir. Grey Advt., NYC, 1964-65; sr. art dir. Ketchum MacLeod & Grove, NYC, 1965-66; v.p., head art dir., 1966-67; v.p., assoc. creative dir., 1967-71; sr. v.p., creative dir., 1971-77; exec. v.p., asst. gen. mgr., 1977-80; gen. mgr., 1980-81; pres., chief exec. officer Ketchum New York, 1981-82; ptnr., co-creative dir., vice chmn. Fearon O'Leary Kaprielian, Inc., 1983-84; chmn., creative dir. Kaprielian O'Leary Advt., 1984-95; pres. Walter Kaprielian & Co., East Hampton, NY, 1995—. Instr. N.Y.C. Tech. Coll., 1971-79, Sch. Visual Arts, 1982-88; mem. adv. bd. N.Y.C. Tech. Coll., 1980—; lectr. Graphic Arts Tech. Found., 1970-81; v.p. ADC Pub. Co., N.Y.C., 1986-88. Author/illustrator: The Captain's Cookbook, 1976, rev. edit., 1979; designer: Bliss in Chrysalis, 1968; designer/editor: The Consecration of a Cathedral, 1968; contbr. articles to profl. jours. V.p. Visual Communicators Scholarship Fund, 1986-88, pres., 1988-90; chmn. parish coun. Holy Cross Ch. of Armenia, 1965-66, Armenian Ch. of Holy Martyrs, 1968-69; bd. dirs. N.Y.C. Tech. Coll. Found., 1985-99, Fish Unlimited, 1994-2000. Recipient awards Art Dirs. Club N.Y., awards Art Dirs. Club N.J., awards Soc. Illustrators, awards Am. Inst. Graphic Arts, awards Type Dirs. Club, awards Clio, awards Graphis, awards Advt. Club N.Y., awards Am. Advt. Fedn.; Theodore Rossevelt Meml. medal; St. Gauden's medal. Mem. Am. Inst. Graphic Arts, Art Dirs. Club (bd. dirs. 1974-76, 78-81, 91-93, pres. 1981-83, chmn. adv. bd. 1983-85, mem. adv. bd. 1984—, 1st v.p. 1993, pres. visual communicators scholarship fund 1988-90), U.S. Power Squadron, Nat. Party Boat Owners Alliance, Internat. Game Fish Assn., Maidstone Gun Club, Knights of Vartan. Republican. Avocations: seafood cooking, fishing. Personal E-mail: wkapriel@optonline.net.

KAPROV, SUSAN L., artist, photographer; BA, CUNY. Prin. works include Urban Helix at MetroTech Center, NYC, Precambrian Waltz, Port Authority NY and NJ, Swimmers, GSA, Time Travelers, Conn. State Commn. on the Arts, Nature Last Modified, NYC Health and Hosps. Corp., exhibitions include Bklyn. Mus. Art, Represented in permanent collections Mus. Modern Art, NYC. Recipient Stedman prize, Rutgers U., 1985; fellow, MacDowell Colony, 1977, 1994; Visual Artist fellow, NY Found. Arts, 1981. Mem.: AIA (assoc.). Home: 149 Willow St Brooklyn NY 11201 Home Phone: 718-624-2775. Personal E-mail: susan@kaprov.com.

KAPSCH, ROBERT JAMES, engineering and architectural historian; b. Elizabeth, NJ, July 25, 1942; s. Joseph Michael and Mary Elizabeth Kapsch; m. Elizabeth Perry Kephart, Nov. 11, 2000. BS in Engring., Rutgers U., 1964; MS in Mgmt., George Washington U., 1974, MA in Am. Studies, 1978; PhD in Engring. and Arch., Cath. U. Am., 1983; PhD in Am. Studies, U. Md., 1993. Chief HABS/HAER, 1980—95; spl. asst. to dir. Nat. Park Svc., Washington, 1996-2000, sr. scholar in hist. arch. and hist. engring., 2001—05. Author: Canals, 2004, Monocacy Aqueduct, 2005; mem. editl. bd. Bldgs. U.S. Publs. Series, 1991-94, The Potomac Canal: George Washington And The Waterway To The West, 2007 Participant various hist. preservation activities, Washington, 1975—. Capt. USAFR, 1964—68, Vietnam. Recipient DSM, U.S. Dept. Interior, 2002. Mem.: AIA, ASCE (history and heritage com. 2000—03), Constrn. History Soc., Nat. R.R. Hist. Assn., Hist. Medley Dist., Nat. Trust for Hist. Preservation, Nat. Preservation Inst. (bd. dirs. 2001—04), Am. Canal Soc., Soc. Archtl. Historians, Soc. for Indsl. Archeology (bd. dirs. 2001—04), Newcomen Soc., Cosmo Club. Avocations: antique toy trains, travel. Home: 15220 DuFief Dr North Potomac MD 20878-2411 Office Phone: 301-221-0244. E-mail: robertkapsch@aol.com.

KAPSNER, CAROL RONNING, state supreme court justice; b. Bismarck, ND, Nov. 25, 1947; m. John Kapsner; children: Mical, Caithlin. BA in English lit., Coll. of St. Catherine; postgrad., Oxford U.; MA in English lit., Ind. U.; JD, U. Colo., 1977. Atty. Kapsner and Kapsner, Bismarck, 1977-98; justice N.D. Supreme Ct., 1998—. Mem. N.D. Bar Assn. (past bd. govs.), N.D. Trial Lawyers Assn. (past bd. govs.), Burleigh County Bar Assn. (pres. 1980, mem. Jud. Conference 1988-96). Office: Supreme Ct State Capitol 600 E Boulevard Ave Dept 180 Bismarck ND 58505-0530 Fax: 701-328-4480. E-mail: ckapsner@ndcourts.com.*

KAPTEYN, HENRY CORNELIUS, physics professor, engineering educator; b. Oak Lawn, Ill., Jan. 21, 1963; m. Margaret Mary Murnane, 1988. BS, Harvey Mudd Coll., 1982; MA, Princeton U., 1984; PhD, U. Calif., Berkeley, 1989. Postdoctoral rschr. U. Calif., 1989-90; asst. prof. physics Wash. State U., Pullman, 1990-95, assoc. prof., 1995, U. Mich., Ann Arbor, 1996-99; prof. JILA, U. Colo., Boulder, 1999—. Contbr. articles to profl. jours. Regents fellow U. Calif., 1985, Sloan rsch. fellow, 1995. Fellow Optical Soc. Am. (Adolph Lomb medal 1993), Am. Phys. Soc.; mem. IEEE, Soc. Photo-Optical Instrumentation Engrs. (scholar 1988). Office: JILA Univ Colo Boulder CO 80309-0440 Home Phone: 303-449-5060. E-mail: kapteyn@jila.colorado.edu.

KAPTUR, MARCIA CAROLYN (MARCY KAPTUR), congresswoman; b. Toledo, June 17, 1946; BA in Hist., U. Wis., Madison, 1968; M in Urban Planning, U. Mich., Ann Arbor, 1974; postgraduate student, U. Manchester, Eng., 1974, MIT, 1981; LLD (hon.), U. Toledo, 1993. Urban planner Toledo-Lucas County Plan Commns., 1969—75; dir. planning Nat. Ctr. Urban Ethnic Affairs, 1975—77; asst. dir. urban affairs domestic policy staff Exec. Office of Pres., 1977-79; mem. US Congress from 9th Ohio dist., 1983—, mem. appropriations com., mem. budget com., co-chair Congl. Ukrainian Caucus. Author: Women in Congress. Adv. com. Gund Found.; exec. com. Lucas County Dem. Com.; mem. Dem. Women's Campaign Assn. Named Legislator of Yr., Nat. Mental Health Assn.; recipient Americanism award, VFW, 1999, Barbed Wire award, 1999, Director's award, Georgetown U. Edmund A. Walsh Sch. Fgn. Svc., Ellis Island Medal of Honor, 2002. Mem. Am. Planning Assn., Am. Inst. Cert. Planners, NAACP, Urban League, Polish Mus., U. Mich. Urban Planning Alumni Assn. (bd. dirs.), Polish Am. Hist. Assn., Lucas County Dem. Bus. and Profl. Women's Club, Fulton County Dem. Women's Club. Democrat. Roman Catholic. Office: DIst Office One Maritime Plz 6th Fl Toledo OH 43604 Office Phone: 202-225-4146, 419-259-7500. Office Fax: 419-255-9623.*

KAPUR, KAILASH CHANDER, industrial engineering educator; b. Rawalpindi, Pakistan, Aug. 17, 1941; s. Gobind Ram and Vidya Vanti (Khanna) K.; m. Geraldine Palmer, May 15, 1969; children: Anjali Joy, Jay Palmer. BS, Delhi U., India, 1963; M of Tech., Indian Inst. Tech., Kharagpur, 1965; MS, U. Calif., Berkeley, 1968, PhD, 1969. Registered profl. engr., Mich. Sr. rsch. engr. Gen. Motors Rsch. Labs., Mich., 1969-70; sr. reliability engr. TACOM, U.S. Army, Mich., 1978-79; mem. faculty Wayne State U., Detroit, 1970-89, assoc. prof. indsl. engring. and ops., 1973-79, prof., 1979-89; prof., dir. Sch. Indsl. Engring. U. Okla., Norman, 1989-92; dir., indsl. engring. U. Wash., Seattle, 1992—. Vis. prof. U. Waterloo, Can., 1977-78; vis. scholar Ford Motor Co., Mich., summer 1973. Author: Reliability in Engineering Design, 1977; contbr. articles to profl. jours. Grantee GM, 1974-77, U.S. Army, 1978-79, U.S. Dept. Transp., 1980-82. Fellow: Inst. Indsl. Engrs., Am. Soc. Quality; mem.: Ops. Rsch. Soc. Am. (sr.). Home: 4484 E Mercer Way Mercer Island WA 98040-3828 Office: U Wash PO Box 352650 Seattle WA 98195-2650 Office Phone: 206-543-4604. Personal E-mail: kalkapur@hotmail.com, kkapur@comcast.net. Business E-Mail: kkapur@u.washington.edu.

KAPUR, VISHESH, medical educator, epidemiologist; b. Rochester, NY; s. Kanwal and Kanta Kapur; m. Jennifer White; 1 child, Rohan. AB magna cum laude, Harvard Coll., Cambridge, Mass., 1984; MD, Yale Sch. Medicine, New Haven, Conn., 1989; MPH, U. Wash., Seattle, 1996. D.A.B.S.M. Am. Bd. Sleep Medicine, 1998, cert. Am. Bd. Internal Medicine, 1993, pulmonary medicine Am. Bd. Internal Medicine, 1996. Asst. prof. medicine U. Wash., Seattle, 1999—2005, assoc. prof. medicine, 2005—. Med. dir. UW Medicine Sleep Ctr., Seattle, 1999—; investigator Sleep Heart Health Study, Balt., 1999—. Mem. editl. bd.: Jour. Sleep, 2003—, Jour. Clin. Sleep Medicine, 2004—. Named one of Seattle's Top Physicians, Seattle Met. Mag., 2006—07, Seattle Mag., 2006; recipient John Harvard scholarship for Academic Achievement, Harvard Coll., 1980—83, Mentor award, UW Robert Wood Johnson Clin. Scholars Program, 2000. Mem.: Am. Acad. Sleep Medicine (mem. standards of practice com. 2005). Achievements include founding UW Medicine Sleep Center. Office Phone: 206-731-4999.

KAPUT, JIM L., lawyer; b. Toms River, NJ, May 28, 1960; BS, U Pa., 1982; JD, Cornell U., 1986. Bar: Ill. 1987. Assoc. Sidley & Austin (now Sidley Austin Brown & Wood), Chgo., ptnr., 1994—2000; sr. v.p., gen. counsel The ServiceMaster Co., Downers Grove, Ill., 2000—. Avocation: running. Office: The ServiceMaster Co 3250 Lacey Rd Ste 600 Downers Grove IL 60515-1700*

KARABEL, JEROME BERNARD, sociologist, educator; b. Phila., May 20, 1950; s. Henry Leon and Dorothy (Forstein) K.; m. Kristin Luker, Nov. 11, 1984; children: Alexander, Sonya. BA, Harvard U., 1972, PhD, 1977; postgrad., Nuffield Coll., Oxford, Eng., 1972-73, Ecole Pratique des Hautes Etudes, Paris, 1974-75. Sr. research assoc. Huron Inst., Cambridge, Mass., 1977-84; asst. prof. sociology U. Calif., Berkeley, 1984-86, assoc. prof., 1986-93, prof., 1993—, co-dir. Berkeley Project on Equal Opportunity. Author: The Chosen: The Hidden History of Admission and Exclusion at Harvard, Yale, and Princeton, 2005; co-author: (with Steven Brint) The Diverted Dream: Community Colleges and the Promise of Educational Opportunity in America, 1900-1985, 1989 Co-author and co-editor: (with A.H. Halsey) Power and Ideology in Education, 1977; sr. editor: Theory and Society, 1978-96; corr. editor: Theory and Soc., 1996-; assoc. editor: Sociology of Edn., 1982-85; contbr. articles to profl. jours., mags. and newspapers. Recipient Outstanding Book award Am. Ednl. Rsch. Assn., 1991, Sr. Scholar award for Rsch. and Publs., Am. Assn. Community & Jr. Colls., 1991, Nat. Jewish Book award Am. Jewish history, 2006, Max Weber award Am. Sociol. Assn., Disting. Scholarship award Pacific Sociol. Assn, 2007; grantee Nat. Inst. Edn., 1977-81, NSF, 1972-75, 81-87, Ford Found., 1981-83, 97-04; fellow Inst. Advanced Study, 1993-94. Mem. AAUP, Am. Sociol. Assn. (council mem. soc. edn. sect. 1984-87, Willard Waller award 2006, Disting. Book award 2007), Phi Beta Kappa. Home: 3015 Benvenue Ave Berkeley CA 94705-2509 Office: U Calif Dept Sociology 436 Barrows Hall Berkeley CA 94720 Business E-Mail: karabel@berkeley.edu.

KARÁDY, GEORGE GYÖRGY, electrical engineering educator, consultant; b. Budapest, Hungary, Aug. 17, 1930; arrived in U.S., 1976; s. Gyozo and Anna (Szamek) K.; 1 child, Gyuri. MSEE, Tech. U. Budapest, 1952, DEng, 1960, D (hon.), 1996. Registered profl. engr., NY, NJ, Que. From instr. to assoc. prof., docent Tech. U. Budapest, Hungary, 1952—66; lectr. U. Baghdad, Iraq, 1966—68, U. Salford, England, 1968—69; program mgr. Hydro Quebec Inst. of Rsch., Canada, 1969—76; chief elec. cons. engr. Ebasco Svcs., NYC, 1976—86; prof. Salt River Project Chair Ariz. State U., Tempe, 1986—. Adj. prof. McGill U., Montreal, 1972—76, Poly. Inst. NY, 1980—86; lectr. U. Montreal, 1970—76. Author: Operation of Electric Appliances and Network (in Hungarian), 1964; (with others) Advances in Electronics and Electron Physics, 1976; co-author: Electric Power Systems, Vol. V (in Hungarian), 1963, Electrical Power Systems and Networks (in Hungarian), 1964, Electrical Energy Conversion and Transport, 2005; contbr. articles to profl. jours. Fellow IEEE (paper award 1982, working group achievement award 1986); mem. U.S. Nat. Com. of Internat. Conf. of Large Elec. Network (sec.-treas. 1978-94), Princeton Ski Club (bd. dirs. 1977-86). Avocations: skiing, sailing, tennis, opera. Home: 11836 N 134th Way Scottsdale AZ 85259-3642 Office: Ariz State U Ira Fulton Sch Engring Dept Elec Engring Tempe AZ 85287-5706 Office Phone: 480-965-6569. Business E-Mail: karady@asu.edu.

KARAIM, BETTY JUNE, retired librarian; b. Devils Lake, ND, May 27, 1936; d. Erick Henry and Anna Caroline (Steen) Keck; m. William James Karaim, Dec. 7, 1955 (dec. 1983); children: Reed, Lisa, Ryan, Lynn, Rachel, Lee, Lara. BS in Edn., Mayville State U., ND, 1958; postgrad., U. N.D., summer 1961; MLS, U. Okla., 1972; postgrad., No. Mont. Coll., 1979-81. Libr. Cando (N.D.) High Sch., 1960-62; asst. libr., tchr. Mayville State Coll., 1962-79; libr. Havre (Mont.) Pub. Schs., 1979-82; libr. dir. Mayville State U., 1982-99, ret., prof. emerita, 1999. Bd. dirs. Mayville (N.D.) Pub. Libr., 1991-97, 2000—, pres., 1994-97, v.p., 2002-05, pres., 2005—; bd. dirs. Goose River Heritage Ctr., Mayville, 2000—, pres., 2002—; bd. dirs. M300 Assn. (arm of Mayville State U. Found.), 2000-06, sec., 2002—05. Recipient Orville Johnson Meritorious Svc. award, 1992, Disting. Alumni award Mayville State U. Alumni Found., 1997. Democrat. Avocations: reading, travel. Home: 320 1st St NW Mayville ND 58257-1107 Personal E-mail: bjkaraim@polarcomm.com.

KARAKEY, SHERRY JOANNE, real estate company executive, interior designer; b. Wendall, Idaho, Apr. 16, 1942; d. John Donald and Vera Ella (Frost) Kingery; children: Artist Roxanne, Buddy (George II), Kami JoAnne, Launi JoElla. Student, Ariz. State U., Tempe, 1960. Corp. sec., treas. Karbel Metals Co., Phoenix, 1963-67; sec. pub. Scottsdale (Ariz.) Daily Progress, 1969-72; with D-Velco Mfg. Ariz., Phoenix, 1959-62, dir., exec. v.p., sec., treas., 1972-87; mng. ptnr., financial real estate investment Karitage, Ltd., Scottsdale, 1987—. Personal E-mail: footnotes@cox.net.

KARAKLA, DANIEL W., otolaryngologist, surgeon; b. Springfield, Mass., Mar. 7, 1957; AA in Bus. Adminstrn., Holyoke C.C., 1978; BS in Zoology, U. Mass., 1981; MD, Uniformed Svcs. U. Health Scis., Bethesda, Md., 1986. Diplomate Am. Bd. Otolaryngology, Head and Neck Surgery, 1994. Intern Nat. Naval Med. Ctr., Bethesda, 1987, resident, 1993; clin. instr. surgery Uniformed Svcs. U. Health Scis., 1993—96; dir. residency edn. Naval Med. Ctr., Portsmouth, Va., 1995—99; asst. clin. prof. Ea. Va. Med. Sch., Norfolk, Va., 1996—2000, assoc. prof., 2000—, dir. med. edn., 2002—. Adj. asst. prof. surgery Uniformed Svcs. U. Health Scis., 1996—2002; dir. head and neck surgery Ea. Va. Med. Sch., Norfolk, 2002—; presenter in field. Contbr. articles to profl. jours., chapters to books. Advisor Head and Neck Cancer Patient Support Group, Norfolk, 2004—; mem. med. adv. coun. Am. Cancer Soc., Norfolk, 2000—. With USN, 1987—2000. Fellow, Meth. Hosp. Ind., Indpls., 1995. Fellow: Am. Head and Neck Soc., Am. Acad. Otolaryngology, Head & Neck Surgery, Am. Coll. Surgeons; mem.: Tidewater Otolaryngology and Ophthalmology Soc., Va. Soc. Otolaryngology, Head and Neck Surgery, Med. Soc.Va., Norfolk Acad. Medicine, Soc. U. Otolaryngologists, Assn. Mil. Surgeons US, Alpha Omega Alpha. Office: Ea Va Med Sch Dept Otolaryngology Head & Neck Surgery 825 Fairfax Ave Ste 510 Norfolk VA 23507

KARALEKAS, ANNE, media executive; b. Boston, Nov. 6, 1946; d. Christus and Helen (Vogiantzis) K. AB, Wheaton Coll., Norton, Mass., 1968; AM, Harvard U., 1969, PhD, 1974. Chief project mgr. def. and arms control project Commn. on Orgn. of Govt. for Conduct of Fgn. Policy, Washington, 1974-75; sr. staff mem. Senate Select Com. on Intelligence, Washington, 1975-78; sr. assoc. McKinsey & Co., Washington, 1978-85; mktg. mgr. The Washington Post, 1985-87, dir. mktg., 1987-89; pub. Washington Post Mag., 1989-96, dir. specialty products group, 1993-96; gen. mgr. Washington Sidewalk, Microsoft Corp., Washington, 1996-99; bd. dirs. Digital Globe, Longmont, 1999—. Author: History of the CIA, 1976; contbr. articles and book revs. to profl. jours. Advisor fgn. policy Mondale-Ferraro Presdl. Campaign, Washington, 1984; trustee Wheaton Coll., Norton, 1985-88. Mem. Council on Fgn. Relations, Phi Beta Kappa. Greek Orthodox. Avocation: twentieth century art and lit.

KARALEKAS, GEORGE STEVEN, advertising agency executive, political consultant; b. Boston, Nov. 26, 1939; s. Steven George and Sotiria (Sarris) K. BS, Boston U., 1962. Vice pres., assoc. media dir. Grey Advt., Inc., NYC, 1962-70; dir. advt. services Can. Dry Corp., NYC, 1970-72, dir. mktg. N.Y. ops., 1972-74; exec. v.p., dir. media and mktg., mgmt. account dir. deGarmo Advt., Inc., NYC, 1974-80; sr. v.p., exec. dir. media, mgmt. dir. D'Arcy-MacManus & Masius, NYC, 1980-85; pres. Karalekas & Co., NYC and Washington, 1985—. Sr. v.p., exec. dir. media November Group, Pres. Nixon, N.Y.C., Washington, 1971-72; sr. v.p., spl. advt. cons. Campaign 76, Pres. Ford, N.Y.C., Washington, 1975-76; sr. v.p., exec. dir. media Campaign 80, Pres. Reagan, N.Y.C., Washington, 1979-80; spl. advt. cons. Nov. Co., President Bush, N.Y.C., Washington, 1992. Mem. Republican Nat. Com., 1970—. Mem. Internat. Radio and TV Soc., Am. Mgmt. Assn. Republican. Greek Orthodox. Home: Holiday Point 8 Circle Dr Sherman CT 06784-1643 Office: Karalekas & Co 360 E 72nd St New York NY 10021-4753: 2433 Tracy Pl Washington DC 20008

KARALIS, JOHN PETER, computer company executive, lawyer; b. Mpls., July 6, 1938; s. Peter John and Vivian Karalis; m. Mary Curtis, Sept. 7, 1963; children: Amy Curtis, Theodore Curtis. BA, U. Minn., 1960, JD, 1963. Bar: Minn. 1963, Mass. 1972, Ariz. 1983, N.Y. 1986, Pa. 1986. Pvt. practice, Mpls., 1963-70; assoc. gen. counsel Honeywell Inc., Mpls., 1970-83, v.p., 1982-83; pvt. practice Phoenix, 1983-85; sr. v.p., gen. counsel Sperry Corp., NYC, 1985-87; v.p. gen. counsel Apple Computer Inc., Cupertino, Calif., 1987-89; of counsel Brown and Bain, Phoenix, 1989-92; sr. v.p. corp. devel. Tektronix, Inc., Portland, 1992-98; ret. Mem. bd. advisors Ctr. for Study of Law, Sci. and Tech., Ariz. State U. Coll. Law, Tempe, 1983-89, 2000—, adj. prof., 1990-91. Author: International Joint Ventures, A Practical Guide, 1992. Recipient Disting. Achievement award Ariz. State U., Tempe, 1985. Mem. Met. Club (N.Y.C.).

KARAN, DONNA (DONNA FASKE), fashion designer; b. Forest Hills, NY, Oct. 2, 1948; m. Mark Karan, 1971 (div.); 1 child, Gabrielle; m. Stephan Weiss, 1983 (dec. June 2001); 1 stepchild, Lisa. BFA, Parsons Sch. Design, 1987. Intern Liz Claiborne; With Addenda Co., to 1968; with Anne Klein & Co., NYC, 1968-84, assoc. designer, 1971-74, designer, 1974-84; owner, designer, ptnr. Donna Karan Co., NYC, 1984-96, created DKNY clothing line, 1988, chmn. bd., chief designer, 1996—2001; (Donna Karan merges with Louis Vuitton Moet Hennessy (LVMH), 2001); chief designer Donna Karan Co., NYC, 2001—. Launched fragrance Donna Karan for Women, 1992, Cashmere Mist, DKNY, 1994, Chaos, Donna Karan, 1996, Black Cashmere, 2002. Showed first complete collection for Anne Klein & Co. in 1974; collaborator on Anne Klein collections with Louis dell'Olio; author: DKNY: NYC, 1994. Bd. dirs. Design Industries Found. for AIDS; co-chair Kids for Kids, 1993, Ovarian Cancer Rsch. Super Saturday, East Hampton, NY, summers 1998, 1999. Recipient Coty award, 1977, Frontrunner award Sara Lee Corp., 1992, "Night of the Stars" Award The Fashion Group; co-recipient (with Louis dell'Olio) Coty Return award, 1981, Coty Hall of Fame citation, 1982, Coty award, 1984. Mem.: Coun. Fashion Designers Am. (bd. dirs., awards 1985, Menswear Designer of Yr. 1992, Womenswear Designer of Yr. 1996, Lifetime Achievement award 2004, awards 1986). Office: Donna Karan Internat West 40th St New York NY 10018 Office Phone: 212-789-1500.*

KARAN, PAUL RICHARD, lawyer; b. Providence, June 12, 1936; s. Aaron Arnold and Sadye (Persky) K.; m. Susan Clare Brody, Jan. 3, 1964 (dec. Apr. 1986); children: Jennifer Hilary, Steven Lee; m. Linda Doris Adler, July 2, 1987. BA, Brown U., 1957; JD, Columbia U., 1960. Bar: NY 1961, U.S. Dist. Ct. (so. dist.) N.Y. 1962, U.S. Supreme Ct. 1967, U.S. Tax Ct. 1975, U.S. Claims Ct. 1976. Assoc. Demov & Morris, NYC, 1960—65, ptnr., 1966—85, Gordon Altman Weitzen Shalov & Wein, NYC, 1985—2000, Tofel, Karan & Ptnrs., P.C., NYC, 2000—03, Todtman Nachamie Spizz & Johns P.C., NYC, 2003—. Contbr. articles to profl. jours. Chmn. Bd. Assessment Rev., Greenburgh, NY, 1978-86; mem. Planning Bd., Greenburgh, 1975-78, Bd. Edn., Greenburgh, 1980-83; mem. adv. bd. Am. Heart Assn., 2004—. Fellow Am. Bar Found., Am. Coll. Trust and Estate Counsel (chmn. downstate NY 1996-2001), NY Bar Found.; mem. ABA, NY State Bar Assn. (chmn. trusts and estates law sect. 1990-91), Assn. of Bar of City of NY. Avocation: golf. Office: Todtman Nachamie Spizz & Johns PC 425 Park Ave New York NY 10022 Office Phone: 212-754-9400. Business E-Mail: pkaran@tnsj-law.com.

KARANIKAS, ALEXANDER, language educator; b. Manchester, NH, Oct. 5, 1916; s. Stephen and Vaia (Kolias) K.; m. Helen J. Karagianes, Jan. 2, 1949; children: Marianthe Vaia, Diana Christine, Cynthia Maria. Student, U. N.H., 1934-36; AB cum laude, Harvard, 1939; MA, Northwestern U., 1950, PhD in English, 1953. With N.H. Writers Project, 1940-41; editor Allegheny-Kiski Valley Edit. The CIO News, 1941-42; radio news commentator Sta. WMUR, Manchester, 1946; grad. asst. Northwestern U., Evanston, Ill., 1950-52; instr. Kendall Coll., Evanston, Ill., 1952-53, Northwestern U., Evanston, 1953-54, 57-58; mem. faculty U. Ill. at Chgo., 1954—, prof. English, 1974-82, prof. emeritus, 1982—; owner Deerhaven Orchard, 1974-96. Cons. in field. Author: When a Youth Gets Poetic, 1934, In Praise of Heroes, 1945, Tillers of a Myth: The Southern Agrarians as Social and Literary Critics, 1966 (Friends of Lit. award 1967), (with Helen Karanikas) Elias Venezis, 1969, Hellenes and Hellions: Modern Greek Characters in American Literature, 1981; (musical) Nashville Dreams, 1991; (screenplay) Marika (Neptune award Moondance Film Festival 2003); (poetry) Stepping Stones, 1994. Mem. nat. cabinet Am. Youth Congress, 1937-39; exec. sec. Mass. Youth Coun., 1939-40; co-chmn. Nat. Bicentennial Symposium on the Greek Experience in Am., 1976; Publicity dir. N.H. Ind. Voters, 1946; sec. Manchester Vets. Council, 1946; Candidate for Congress, 1948; exec. com. United Hellenic Am. Congress, 1983—; exec. sec. Am. Coun. for Dem. Greece, 1947. With USAAF, 1942-45, Alaska corr. YANK, 1943-45. Named to Goffstown (NH) H.S. Hall of Fame, 2004. Mem. Hellenic Profl. Soc. Ill., Modern Greek Studies Assn., Screen Actors Guild, Friends of Lit., Harvard Club Chgo., Phi Eta Sigma, Order Ahepa (dist. sec. 1946). Mem. Greek Orthodox Ch. Home: 618 N Harvey Ave Oak Park IL 60302-1740 Office: Univ of Ill at Chicago English Dept Chicago IL 60680

KARAS, JAMES, public relations executive, engineering executive; b. New Brunswick, NJ, May 23, 1958; s. James Panayagelos and Angeliki (Karaviotis) Karas; m. Nancy Ann Davino, June 7, 1986; children: Jimmy Carl Panayagelos, Kristy Daniel, Nikki Ann. Attended, NY Inst. Tech., 1978, Rutgers U., 1979, Middlesex Coll., 1999. Cert. instr. NJ Defensive Driving, 2004. Promotor, sponsor Nat. Physique Com., NJ, 1986—91, Internat. Fedn. Body Builders, 1986—92; dir. devel. Internat. Ctr. for Ednl. Advancement, Newark, 1990—; CEO Savage Promotions, Somerset, NJ, 1990—; steward NJ Turnpike Authority, Newark, 2004—; exec. officer Internat. Peace Angles Project, NYC, 2002—. V.p. product devel. Xelat, East Brunswick, NJ, 1996—98; adv. Maxum Wireless, Ft. Lee, NJ, 1996—2000; cons. in field; bail enforcement agt./bounty hunter Tri-State area. Author: Sponsorship & Promotional Manual, 1985, 3d edit., 1987. Mem.: Am. Fedn. Labor and Congress of Indsl. Orgn. (steward), Internat. Fedn. Profl. and Tech. Engrs. (steward). Greek Orthodox. Avocations: weightlifting, football, baseball, reading. Office: Savage Promotions 36 S Dover Ave Somerset NJ 08873 Home Phone: 732-745-1898. Business E-Mail: savagepromotions@aol.com.

KARASEV, VLADIMIR, physicist, researcher; b. Samarkand, Russia, Nov. 6, 1951; s. Anatoly Karasev and Victoria Karaseva; m. Olga Smirnova, July 12, 1973; children: Maxim, Elena. PhD, Russia Acad. Sci., Shatura, 1999. Jr. staff scientist Phys.-Tech. Inst., Dushanbe, Tajikistan, 1974—86, staff scientist, 1986—87; head laser physics lab. Tadjikistan Acad. Sci., Dushanbe, 1987—89; sr. staff scientist Sci. Rsch. Ctr. for TL, Shatura, Russia, 1989—95; head optics and material processing lab. Rsch. Ctr. for TL, Shatura, 1995—2000; head laser processes and systems lab. Inst. on Laser and Info. Tech., Russia Acad. Sci., Shatura, Russia, 2000—. Contbr. articles to profl. jours. Avocations: tourism, photography, artistic laser cuttin. Office: Inst Laser and Info Techs 1 Svyatoozerskaya St Shatura 140700 Moscow Russia Office Phone: +7496 4522200/407. Fax: +7 4964522532. E-mail: vladkar@mail.ru.

KARASIK, MIRIYAM BETH, artist, writer; d. Warner Newton and Aleen Mildred (Hznkne) Oberly; m. Myron Solomon Karasik; stepchildren: Ruth Jacqueline, Jacob Edwin. BA in English, Grand Valley State Coll., Allendale, 1968; MA in Comms. Writing for Film and TV, Govs. State U., Park Forest South, Ill., 1978. Band dir. Kent City Cmty. Schs., Mich.; tchr. Grand Rapids Pub. Schs.; software tester Coldframe, Inc.; artist, musician, writer Miryem's Ink Studio, Cathedral City, Calif., 1985—. Author: (poetry) Word Windows, (film script) Return to Poland, 1978. Mem. Cmty. Action Tng. Svcs., Grand Rapids. Mem.: Writers Guild, Internat. Horn Soc. Democrat. Jewish.

KARASU, T(OKSOZ) BYRAM, psychiatrist, educator, writer; b. Feb. 11, 1935; MD, U. Istanbul, Turkey, 1959. Jr. intern St. Jeanne D'Arc Hosp., Montreal, Canada, 1963-64; resident in psychiatry Yale U., New Haven, 1969; prof. psychiatry Albert Einstein Coll. Medicine, Bronx, NY, 1981—, Silverman prof., chmn. psychiatry, 1993—, univ. chmn., 1998—. Chmn. Albert Einstein Coll. Medicine, 1993—; psychiatrist-in-chief Montefiore Med. Ctr., 1993—. Author: Wisdom in the Practice of Psychotherapy, 1992, Deconstruction of Psychotherapy, 1996, The Psychotherapists's Interventions, 1998, The Psychotherapist as Healer, 2001, The Art of Serenity, 2003, Of God and Madness, 2006; editor: Psychotherapy Research, 1982; The Spirit of Happiness, 2006; editor: The Psychiatric Therapies, 1984, Treatments of Psychiatric Disorders, 1989, others; editor-in-chief: Am. Jour. Psychotherapy, 1994—; contbr. articles to profl. jours. Recipient Sigmund Freud award, 1997. Mem.: Am. Psychiat. Assn. (chmn. commn. 1979—83, task force 1981—90, practice guidelines in major depression 1993, revised 2000, Disting. Svc. award 1983, Spl. Presdl. award 1988, Disting. Life fellow). Office: 2 E 88th St New York NY 10128-0555 Also: Albert Einstein Coll Medicine 1300 Morris Park Ave Bronx NY 10461-1975

KARATZ, WILLIAM WARREN, lawyer; b. Benton Harbor, Mich., Aug. 9, 1926; s. Harry E. and Grace M. (Campbell) K.; m. Barbara Lansburgh Low, May 25, 1989. Ph.B. (La Verne Noyes scholar), U. Chgo., 1948; postgrad., Sch. Pol. Sci., 1949; LL.B. (Harlan Fiske Stone scholar), Columbia U., 1952. Bar: N.Y. State 1953, U.S. Supreme Ct. 1960. Assoc. in law Columbia U. Sch. Law, NYC, 1952-53; assoc. firm Winthrop, Stimson, Putnam & Roberts, NYC, 1953-62, ptnr., 1963-86, sr. counsel, 1987-2000; retired ptnr. Pillsbury Winthrop, 2001—. Bd. editors: Columbia Law Rev, 1950-52. Served with USN, 1944-46. Fellow Am. Bar Found. (life); mem. ABA, Am. Law Inst. (life), Bar Assn. City of N.Y. (mem. exec. com. 1969-73, chmn. 1972-73, v.p. 1973-74), N.Y. State Bar Assn., (mem. ho. of dels. 1972-77), Am. Coll. Trial Lawyers, Am. Judicature Soc., Century Assn., Confrerie des Chevaliers du Tastevin (grand officer). Home: 100 E 50th St New York NY 10022-6805 Office: Pillsbury Winthrop 1540 Broadway New York NY 10036

KARAYAN, ANI A., psychologist, consultant; d. Armik Mike and Ida S. Karayan; m. Armen D. Avanessian, Aug. 31, 2003. BA, UCLA, 1996; MA, Calif. Sch. of Profl. Psychology, 1999, PhD, 2002. Cert. early childhood edn. Pacific Oaks Coll., Calif., 1996. Counselor Glendale Unified Sch. Dist./Healthy Start Program, Calif., 1998—2000; dir. mental health Merdinian Sch., Sherman Oaks, Calif., 1998—2001; coord. psychosocial programs in spina bifida Childrens Hosp., LA, 1999—2001; adj. faculty Antioch U., LA, 1999—; cons. Ctr. for Celebration for Diversity through Edn., LA, 2000—; child psychologist ENKI Health & Rsch. Sys., East L.A., 2002—. Cons. Transcultural Psychology Inst., Glendale, 2000—; lectr. UCLA Med. Residency Program, 2001; cons./lectr. Roosevelt Mid. Sch., Glendale, 2001—02; lectr. ENKI Health & Rsch. Sys., Commerce, Calif., 2004. Scholar, Calif. Sch. of Profl. Psychology, 1997—99. Mem.: Spina Bifida Assn. Am. (assoc.), APA (assoc.). Achievements include editing book on the topic of diversity education. Home Phone: 626-791-2674. E-mail: anikarayan@aol.com.

KARAYANIS, PLATO STEVEN, opera company executive; b. Pitts., Dec. 26, 1928; BFA, Carnegie Mellon U., 1952; artist's diploma in performance, Curtis Inst. Singer, stage dir., Luzern and Zürich, Switzerland, 1958-65, Met. Opera Nat. Co., 1965-67; exec. v.p., treas. Affiliate Artists Inc., 1967-77; mgr. rehearsal dept. San Francisco Opera, 1965; gen. dir. The Dallas Opera, 1977-2000; cons. Palm Beach Opera, 2002—. Chmn. Opera Am.; co-developer Affiliate Artists San Francisco Opera Program; dir. opera Fed. Republic of Germany and Switzerland. Vice chmn. alumni coun. Curtis Inst. Music, 2004—; bd. dirs. Santa Fe Opera. Recipient Excellence in the Creative Arts, Dallas Hist. Soc., 1993; grantee Martha Baird Rockefeller Fund Music. Mem.: Dallas Assembly, Opera Am. (chmn. bd. dirs. 1993—97), Sigma Alpha Iota.

KARBEN, SHELLEY VALERIE, elementary and special education school educator; b. Mt. Vernon, NY, Dec. 1, 1944; d. Sidney and Helen (Minskoff) Gross; children: Ryan Scott, Lori Jennifer. BS, 1966; MA, NYU, 1971. Cert. tchr. spl. edn., N.Y. Tchr. kindergarten and elem. East Ramapo Ctrl. Sch. Dist., Spring Valley, NY, 1966—, tchr. spl. edn. all areas/levels and early intervention, 2001—; adj. Tchr. Tng. Inst. Coll. New Rochelle, 2002—. Chairperson Child Study Team E. Ramapo Ctrl. Sch. Dist., 1995-; mem. pub. rels. panel, supt.'s adv. panel, 1992; cons. Jewish Day Schs, Yeshivas Schs., Hebrew Schs. Spl Edn., 1969—; dir. summer spl. edn. program Yeshiva; pvt. practice evaluation and remediation, 2001-; adj. tchr. Daemon Coll., 2003-. Mem. Profl. Cons. Staff, N.Y. State Sen. Commn. on Child Abuse, Albany, 1974; mem. Commn. of Ethnic Studies, Westchester County, 1975-76; exec. com. Dem. Party, Town of Ramapo, N.Y., 1985—, mem. task force affordable housing, 1991, mem. bd. assessment rev., 1988—; mem. Hebrew Programs for the Disabled, Nat. Commn. on Torah Edn., Yeshiva U., 1974-76, Fleetwood Synagogue Sisterhood, Mt. Vernon, N.Y., pres., 1976-77; pres. Hillcrest Civic Assn., 1990-98; dir. Club ARC Rockland County, 1994; facilitator site-based mgmt. team, 1998-2000; v.p. Kehillat, New Hempstead, 1997-2000; pres. Sisterhood Kehillat, New Hempstead, 1999-. Mem. ASCD, Assn. Children with Learning Disabilities, Coun. Exceptional Children, B'nai Brith (pres. Mt. Vernon 1975-77). Jewish. E-mail: skarben@yahoo.com.

KARBHARI, VISTASP M., engineering educator, researcher; b. Dec. 21, 1961; BCE, U. Poona, India, 1984, M in Structural Engring., 1985; PhD, U. Del., Newark, 1991. Rsch. asst. prof., scientist U. Del., Newark, 1991—95; asst. prof. U. Calif., San Diego, 1995—97, assoc. prof., 1997—2001, prof., 2001—. Editor: IIFC FRP Internat.; Am. editor: Internat. Jour. Materials and Product Tech., mem. editl. bd.: Composite Structures; mem. editl. bd. AGTM Jour. Testing and Evaluation; contbr. chapters to books, over 240 conf. proceedings, over 180 articles to profl. jours. Recipient Best Paper award Engring. Soc. Detroit, 1992, CIICE, 1999, ASC, 2000, Charles Pankow award for innovation in design Civil Engring. Rsch. Found., 1996, Career award NSF, 1997, Faculty award Am. Soc. Nondestructive Testing, 2003, International Institute for FRP in Construction (IIFC) Pres. award, 2006, Best Paper award European Workshop on Structrual Health Monitoring, 2006; Powell Faculty fellow, 1997-99, IIFC fellow, 2006. Mem.: ASCE (vice chair adv. materials resource com.), Soc. Materials and Process Engring., Internat. Inst. FRP in Contrn. (exec. com., editor-in-chief, Pres. award 2006), Internat. Soc. Structural Health Monitoring of Intelligent Structures, Am. Concrete Inst. (chair 44OL), Am. Soc. Metals (Best Paper award 1992). Office: U Calif San Diego Bldg 409 University Ctr 9500 Gilman Dr MC0085 La Jolla CA 92093-5004 Office Phone: 858-534-6470. Business E-Mail: vkarbhari@ucsd.edu.

KARCH, JACQUELINE, artist; b. Newark, Jan. 17, 1946; d. Samuel Arthur and Miriam Francis K.; m. William Clinton Keach, June 27, 1991. Student, Art Students League, 1962—66; BFA, Syracuse U., NYC, 1968; MAT, R.I. Sch. of Design, 1971. Art tchr. Providence Pub. Schs., 1972-2000; artist, ceramic tile Ceramic Tiles, Providence, 1983-2000, LeLand, NC, 2000—; tchr. art for trainable mentally disabled New Hanover H.S., Wilmington, NC, 2001—. Judge Spring Art Show Franklin Sq. Gallery, Southport, NC, 2005. One-woman shows include Gallery 401, Providence, RI, 1980, 1987, WHQR Gallery, Wilmington, NC, 2006, exhibited in group shows at San Regret Gallery, Boston, 1980, Am. Soc. on Aging, San Diego, 1988, Gallery 401, Providence, 1986, Bell St. Gallery, 1991—92, WHQR Gallery, Wilmington, NC, 2003, The Upstairs Gallery, Greensboro, NC, 2007, visual documentary, Trinity Square Repertory Theatre Productions, 1983—85, Jewish Home for the Aged, 1988; costume designer: (plays) The Charlatans, 1972; The Red Hat; author: Recipes Remembered, 1996. Mem. The Arts Students League (life). Avocations: calligraphy, costume design, cooking, gardening, animal rescue and training. Office: Ceramic Tiles-Jacqueline Karch 904 Woodridge Ct SE Leland NC 28451 Office Phone: 910-383-6108.

KARCHIN, LOUIS SAMUEL, composer, educator; b. Sept. 8, 1951; s. Isadore David and Ida (Kessler) K. MusB, U. Rochester, 1973; MA, Harvard U., 1975, PhD, 1978. Asst. prof. music NYU, NYC, 1979-85, assoc. prof. music, 1985-99, prof., 2000—. Pres. U.S. sect. Internat. Soc. for Contemporary Music, 1981-83, chmn., 1983-85; pub. C. F. Peters Corp. Composer: Capriccio for Violin and Seven Instruments, 1978, Duo for Violin and Cello, 1981, Viola Variations, 1982, Songs of John Keats, 1985, Songs of Distance and Light, 1988, Sonata for Cello and Piano, 1989, Romulus, an Opera in One Act, 1990, String Quartet, 1991, A Way Separate, 1992, Ricercare, 1992, Galactic Folds for chamber ensemble, 1993, Sonata da Camera, 1994, Summer Song, 1994, Rustic Dances, 1995, String Quartet No. 2, 1995, Rhapsody for Orchestra, 1996, Cascades, 1997, American Visions: Two Songs on Poems of Yevgeny Yevtushenko, 1998, Quartet for Percussion, 2000, Deux Poèmes de Mallarmé, 2001, Voyages for alto sax and piano, 2001, Carmen de Boheme, 2002, Orpheus, a Masque for baritone, instruments, and dance, 2003, Roethke Songs, 2004; commd. by Fromm Found., 1994, 2003, Koussevitzky Found., 1998, Barlow Found., 2001. Recipient Koussevitsky Composition prize Tanglewood, 1971, Joseph H. Bearns prize Columbia U., 1972, Composer award NEA, 1982, 83, Walter N. Hinrichsen award, AAAL, 1985, Heckscher Found. prize, 1999, Goddard Lieberson prize AAAL, 2001, Maurice Abravanel Disting. vis. composer U. Utah, 2002, Composition award Nat. Tchrs. Singing, 2004, Recording award Aaron Copland Fund, 2004. Office: NYU 24 Waverly Pl Rm 268 New York NY 10003-6757 Office Phone: 212-998-8303.

KARCZ, ANDRZEJ, literature educator; b. Radom, Poland, Oct. 17, 1961; arrived in U.S., 1988; s. Jan and Ewa Karcz; m. Anna Karcz, July 20, 1996; 1 child, Agatha. MA, Cath. U. of Lublin, Poland, 1986; PhD, U. Chgo., 1999. Instr./rschr. Cath. U. of Lublin, 1986—88; asst. prof. U. Kans., Lawrence, 1999—. Author: (book) The Polish Formalist School and Russian Formalism, 2002, Texts From Far and Near: Essays on Literature and Other Matters, 2003; contbr. articles and revs. to profl. jours., encys.; editor: Czeslaw Milosz "Moj Wilenski Opiekun" Listy Czeslawa Milosza Do Manfreda Kridla, 2005. Scholar, Stefan Batory Found., 1996. Mem.: Am. Assn. Advancement Slavic Studies, Am. Assn. Tchrs. Slavic and East European Langs., Polish Inst. Arts and Scis. of Am.

KARDIASMENOS, KATRINA SUZANNE, psychology professor; b. Lower Merion, Pa., Apr. 17, 1976; d. Pete Michael and Ronnie Joy Kardiasmenos. BS, St. Joseph's U., Phila., 1998, MS, 1999; PhD, Cath. U. Am., Washington, 2005. Postdoctoral fellow Washington Neuropsychological Inst., 2005—06; asst. prof. psychology Bowie State U., Md., 2006—. Mem.: APA, Am. Psychol. Soc., Internat. Neuropsychological Soc., Soc. for Neuroscience, Nat. Acad. Neuropsychology. Liberal. Greek Orthodox. Avocations: scuba diving, dog training. Office: Bowie State University Dept of Psych CLT 367 14000 Jericho Park Rd Bowie MD 20715 Office Phone: 301-860-3263. Office Fax: 301-860-3279. Business E-Mail: kkardiasmenos@bowiestate.edu.

KARDON, JANET, museum director; b. Phila. d. Robert and Shirley (Drasin) Stolker; m. Robert Kardon, Nov. 19, 1955; children: Ross, Nina, Roy. BS in Edn., Temple U.; MA in Art History, U. Pa. Lectr. Phila. Coll. Art, 1968-75, dir. exhbns., 1975-78; dir. Inst. Contemporary Art, Phila., 1978-89, Am. Craft Mus., NYC, 1989-95; ind. curator, 1996—. Adj. prof. Fashion Inst. of Tech., N.Y.C., Pratt Inst., Bklyn., Cooper Hewit; cons., panel mem. Nat. Endowment for Arts, 1975—; mus. panel mem. Pa. Coun. on Arts, Phila., 1988—; U.S. commr. Venice Biennale, Venice, 1980. Exhibitions include Labyrinths, Time, Artists SEts and Costumes, Laurie Anderson, Robert Mapplethorpe, David Salle, Gertrude and Otto Natzler; editor: Twentieth Century American Craft: A Centenary Project, The Ideal Home, 1900-1920, Revivals/Diverse Traditions, 1920-1945, Craft in the Machine Age, 1920-1945. Grantee Nat. Endowment for Arts, 1978. Home and Office: 150 E 69th St Apt 12G New York NY 10021-5704 Home Phone: 212-439-1803; Office Phone: 212-439-1803. Personal E-mail: jakardon@aol.com.

KARDUM, KARMEN ANA, lawyer; b. Rijeka, Croatia, Jan. 5, 1973; d. Vladimir Petar Kardum and Nella Lena Ahel; 1 child, Julian Manuel. BA, NYU, 1995; JD, SUNY, Buffalo, 1998. Bar: NY 1999. Legal advisor US Dept. Def., Sarajevo, Bosnia-Herzegovina, 1999—2004; sr. analyst Athena Innovative Solutions, Inc., Martinsville, Va., 2004—05; vice-pres., gen. counsel Loquitius, LLC, Greensboro, NC, 2005—. Govt. contractor US Dept. Def., Arlington, Va., 2005—. Recipient Medal of Svc. awrad, NATO, 1999—2004, Armed Forces Civilian Svc. medal, US Dept. Def., 2000, Plaque of Appreciation award, UN Spl. Rep. Sec. Gen., 2003. Mem.: ABA (licentiate), NY State Bar Assn. (licentiate). D-Conservative. Roman Catholic. Avocations: travel, reading, drawing. Office: Loquitius LLC 6060 W Elton Ave Ste A Las Vegas NV 89107 Office Fax: 866-530-2951. Business E-Mail: karmenak@loquitius.com.

KAREIVA, PETER MICHAEL, zoology educator, research ecologist; b. Utica, NY, Sept. 20, 1951; BS, Duke U., 1973; MS, U. Calif., Irvine, 1976; PhD in Ecology and Evolution, Cornell U., 1981. Lectr. environ. biology Calif. State U., LA, 1976; asst. prof. theoretical ecology and math. modelling Brown U., 1981—; prof. dept. zoology U. Wash., Seattle, 1981—2001; lead scientist Nature Conservancy, Seattle. Fellow Am. Acad. Arts & Scis.; mem. Ecol. Soc. Am., Entomol. Soc. Am. Office: Nature Conservancy 4722 Latona Ave NE Seattle WA 98105 Office Phone: 206-406-2249. Business E-Mail: pkareiva@tnc.org.*

KAREL, STEVEN, lawyer; b. 1950; BS, Stanford U.; JD, Harvard U. V.p., gen. counsel Robert Half Internat. Inc., Menlo Pk., Calif., 1989—, sec., 1993—. Office: Robert Half International Inc 2884 Sand Hill Rd Menlo Park CA 94025 Office Phone: 650-234-6000.*

KARELIS, KATHLEEN E., lawyer, communications systems company executive; b. 1960; BBA, Rollins Coll., Winter Park, Fla.; MBA, Fla. Inst. Tech., Melbourne, Fla.; JD cum laude, U. Miami, 1990. Ptnr. Miller & Chevalier; sr. ptnr. Jenner & Block, Washington, 2005—06; sr. v.p., gen.

counsel, corp. sec. L-3 Comm. Holdings, Inc., NYC, 2006—. Mng. editor: U. Miami Law Rev. Mem.: Order of the Coif. Office: L-3 Comm Holdings Inc 600 Third Ave New York NY 10016 Office Phone: 212-697-1111. Office Fax: 212-805-5477.*

KARELITZ, RICHARD ALAN, treasurer, lawyer; b. Elizabeth, NJ, Nov. 1, 1949; s. David Karelitz and Doris Frances (Tuck) Kahn; m. Virginia Lee Harris, Aug. 18, 1974; children: David Benjamin, Daniel Seth. AB, Coll. William and Mary, 1971; JD, Boston U., 1974, LLM, 1977. Bar: Mass. 1974, U.S. Supreme Ct. 1979; notary pub., Mass. Tax atty. Coopers & Lybrand, Boston, 1974-75; comptr. Internat. Forest Products Corp., Boston, 1975-79, treas., 1979-91, sr. v.p., 1991—. Treas. New Eng. TV Corp., 1987-91, Sta. WHDH-TV, Inc., 1987-91; gen. counsel New Eng. Patriots (NFL) Football Club, 1994—, Foxboro Stadium Assocs. L.P., Foxboro, Mass., 1989-2000, New Eng. Revolution Soccer Team, Foxboro, 1996—, NPS LLC, Foxboro, 2000—, Kraft Group LLC, 2000—; bd. dirs. Carmel Container System, Ltd., Tel Aviv, chmn. audit com., 1992—; treas. Chestnut Hill Mgmt. Corp., Boston, 1991—. Trustee Kraft Found., Boston, 1979-2002; bd. dirs. Temple Sinai, Sharon, Mass., 1995-99, Caritas Norwood Hosp., Mass., 2002—; exec. com. Boston U. Sch. Law, 2005—; hon. comdr. Hanscom AFB, 2006—. Mem.: ABA, Mass. Bar Assn., Boston U. Sch. Law Alumni Assn. (v.p. 2006—07, pres.-elect 2007—). Jewish. Avocation: travel. Home: 31 Sunset Dr Sharon MA 02067-1738 Office: Gillette Stadium One Patriot Pl Foxboro MA 02035

KARELITZ, ROBERT N(ELSON), lawyer; b. Elizabeth, NJ, May 20, 1948; s. David Karelitz and Doris Frances (Tuck) Kahn; m. Emily Louise Eisenberg, May 26, 1974; children: Jonathan, Andrew. BS in econs., U. Pa., 1970; JD, Harvard U., 1973. Bar: Mass. 1973, U.S. Dist. Ct. Mass. 1973. V.p. Fiduciary Trust Co., Boston, 1973—, bd. dirs., v.p., gen. counsel and corp. sec. Bd. dirs. Matanzas Creek Winery, Santa Rosa, Calif., dir. Royal St. Corp. With USAR, 1972-80. Mem. ABA, Mass. Bar Assn., Boston Bar Assn., Boston Estate Planning Coun. Clubs: Harvard, City, Am. Bankers Assn. (trust counsel com.), Nat. Conf. of Lawyers and Corp. Fiduciaries, fellow Am. Bar Found. Democrat. Jewish. Office: Fiduciary Trust Co 175 Federal St Boston MA 02110-2210 Office Phone: 617-574-3413.

KARELS, TIM J., ecology professor; arrived in US, 2003; BSc, U. Toronto, 1993, MSc, 1996, PhD, 2000. Postdoctoral fellow dept. biol. scis. U. Alta., Edmonton, Canada, 2000—01; postdoctoral fellow dept. zoology U. BC, Vancouver, Canada, 2001—03; postdoctoral fellow dept. biol. scis. Auburn U., Ala., 2003—05; asst. prof. dept. biology Calif. State U., Northridge, 2005—. Contbr. articles to profl. jours. Recipient Postdoctoral Fellowship (Hon.), Izaak Walton Killam Found., 2001-2003, award for Arctic Rsch. Excellence, Arctic Rsch. Consortium, 2001; fellow Postdoctoral Fellowship, Natural Sciences and Engring. Rsch. Coun. of Can., 2001-2003. Mem.: Ecol. Soc. Am., Brit. Ecol. Soc., Am. Soc. Mammalogists. Office: Dept Biol California State University 18111 Nordhoff St Northridge CA 91330 Home Phone: 818-267-7900; Office Phone: 818-677-2990. Office Fax: 818-677-2034. Business E-Mail: karels@csun.edu.

KARENTTE, BETTY, state legislator; b. Paducah, Ky., Sept. 13, 1931; m. Richard; 1 child, Mary. BA, MA, Calif. State U., Long Beach. Tchr. L.A. Unified Sch. Dist., 1961-92, cons., substitute tchr., 1994-96; mem. Calif. State Assembly, Sacramento, 1993—94, 2005—, Calif. State Senate, 1996—2004. Office: 3711 Long Beach Blvd Ste 801 Long Beach CA 90807 Office Fax: 562-997-0799. Business E-Mail: assemblymember.karnette@asm.ca.gov.

KARESH, WILLIAM B., science administrator, director, veterinarian; s. Karl and Anna (Bamberger) Karesh; m. Stacey Ann Beard, Dec. 29, 2000. DVM, U. Ga., Athens, 1982. Dir. field vet. program Wildlife Conservation Soc., Bronx, NY, 1989—; chief of party Global Avian Influenza Network for Surveillance, Bronx, NY, 2006—. Co-chair IUCN-SSC-Veterinary Specialist Group, Gland, Switzerland, 2000—. Author: Appointment at the Ends of the World. Recipient Emil Dolensek award, Am. Assn. of Zoo Veterinarians, 2001, Exceptional Svc. award, Wildlife Disease Assn., 2003, Svc. to Life award, Bio-Economics Rsch. Assoc., 2007. Office: Wildife Conservation Soc 2300 Southern Blvd Bronx NY 10460 Office Phone: 718-220-5892.

KARETZKY, JOANNE LOUISE, librarian; b. San Francisco, Apr. 20, 1952; d. Anthony Joseph and Augustina Clara (Armanino) Ballestrasse; m. Norman Martin Kunz, Dec. 28, 1975 (div. June 1984); m. Stephen Karetzky March 17, 1985. BA, U. San Francisco, 1972; MLS summa cum laude, San José State U., 1984; MA in Humanities summa cum laude, Calif. State U., Dominguez Hills, 1994. Cert. Calif. standard secondary tchr. Dir. libr. St. Paul H.S., San Francisco, 1977—85; spl. project libr., head tech. svc. Mercantile Libr., NYC, 1986—89; assoc. prof., head tech. svc., catalogue libr. Felician Coll., Lodi, NJ, 1989—. Author: The Mustering of Support for World War I by the Ladies Home Journal, 1998. Mem. Nat. Trust Hist. Preservation, Victorian Soc. Am., Found. for Study the Arts and Crafts Movement at Roycroft, Pursuing Our Italian Names Together (Pointers), Phi Alpha Theta. Avocations: music, needlecrafts, collecting books, vintage needlework/textiles, antiques. Office: Felician Coll Libr 262 S Main St Lodi NJ 07644-2117 Office Phone: 201-559-6133. Business E-Mail: karetzkyj@inet.felician.edu.

KARETZKY, STEPHEN, library director, educator, researcher; b. Bklyn., Aug. 29, 1946; s. Harry and Lillian Dorothy (Abrams) K.; m. Deborah Ann Shaw, Apr. 12, 1970 (div. July 1972); Joanne Louise Ballestrasse, Mar. 17, 1985. BA, CUNY, Flushing, 1967; MLS, Columbia U., 1969, DLS, 1978; MA, Calif. State U., Dominguez Hills, 1991. Libr. Bklyn. Pub. Libr., 1969-70; asst. prof. SUNY, Buffalo, 1974-76, Geneseo, 1977-78; assoc. prof. U. Haifa, Israel, 1978-81, San Jose (Calif.) State U., 1982-85; researcher, editor Shapolsky/Steimatzky Pub., NYC, 1981-82; sr. editor Shapolsky Pubs., NYC, 1985-86; libr. dir. Felician Coll., Lodi, NJ, 1986—. Author: Reading Research and Librarianship: A History and Analysis, 1982 (2d place award for Best Book of Yr. Am. Soc. Info. Sci 1983), The "Cannons" of Journalism, 1984; editor: The Media's War Against Israel, 1985, The Media's Coverage of the Arab-Israeli Conflict, 1989, Not Seeing Red: American Librarianship and the Soviet Union, 2002; bd. advisors Directory of American Scholars, 1999-2001; contbr. articles to profl. jours. Exec. dir. Ams. for a Safe Israel, N.Y.C., 1985-86. Mem.: Historians Am. Communism, Authors Guild, Am. Soc. Info. Sci. and Tech. Jewish. Avocation: book collecting. Office: Felician Coll Libr 262 S Main St Lodi NJ 07644-2117 Business E-Mail: karetzkys@felician.edu.

KARFF, SAMUEL EGAL, rabbi; b. Phila., Sept. 19, 1931; s. Louis and Reba (Margalit) K.; m. Joan Mag, June 29, 1959; children: Rachel Karff Weissenstein, Amy Karff Halevy, Elizabeth Karff Kampf. AB magna cum laude, Harvard U., 1953; MAHL, DHL, Hebrew Union Coll., 1956. Rabbi Congregation Beth Israel, Hartford, Conn., 1958-60, Temple Beth El, Flint, Mich., 1960-62, Chgo. Sinai Congregation, 1962-74; sr. rabbi Congregation Beth Israel, Houston, 1975-99, rabbi emeritus, 1999—; vis. prof. soc. and health U. Tex. Health Sci. Ctr., Houston, 1999—. Lectr. U. Chgo. Divinity Sch., 1968-75; vis. assoc. prof. U. Notre Dame, 1966-67; adj. prof. religious studies Rice U., Houston, 1976—; assoc. dir. McGovern Ctr. for Health, Humanities, and Human Spirit, U. Tex. Med. Sch., Houston, 2004-, vis. prof. family medicine, 2004-. Author: Agada: The Language of Jewish Faith, 1970, Permissions to Believe Finding Faith in Troubled Times, 2005; editor Centennial Vol. Hebrew Union Coll.-Jewish Inst. of Religion, 1981-84; contbr. chpts. Judaism Religions of the World, 1982. Bd. dirs. United Way, Houston, 1991—, Inst. Religion, Houston, 1990—. Recipient Homiletics award HUC-JIR, Cin., 1956; John Harvard scholar Harvard U., 1951-52. Mem. Cen. Conf. Am. Rabbis (pres. 1989-91), Houston Philos. Soc., Phi Beta Kappa, Kiwanis. Jewish. Avocations: tennis, walking, movies, reading. Office: Congregation Beth Israel 5600 N Braeswood Blvd Houston TX 77096-2901 E-mail: skarff@sph.uth.tmc.edu.

KARGLEDER, CHARLES LEONARD, language educator; b. Milbank, SD, July 19, 1939; s. George Leonard Kargleder and Ruby Teresa Gulck. BA, U. SD, 1960; MA, U. Ala., 1962, PhD, 1968; MS, U. South Ala., 1986. From instr. to prof. Spring Hill Coll., Mobile, Ala., 1963—83, prof., 1983—, chair dept. fgn. lang., 1971—, chair divsn. lang. and lit., 1992—99. Grad. asst. U. Ala., Tuscaloosa, 1965—67. Grantee Nat. Def. Edn. grant, US Govt., 1960—63. Mem.: South Ea. Coun. Latin Am. Studies, Am. Assn. Tchrs. Spanish and Portuguese, Kappa Delta Pi. Roman Catholic. Avocations: travel, reading, music, sports. Home: 1251 Henckley Ave # 207 Mobile AL 36609 Office: Spring Hill Coll 4000 Dauphin St Mobile AL 36608 Office Phone: 251-380-4646. Business E-Mail: kargleder@shc.edu.

KARGMAN, MARIE WITKIN, marriage and family therapist; b. Chgo., Aug. 28, 1914; d. Joseph and Clara (Zucker) Witkin; m. Max Kargman, 1935; children: Donna, William, Robert. JD, DePaul U., 1936; MA, Radcliffe Coll., 1951. Pub. defender Boys' Court, Chgo., 1936-37; ptnr. Kargman & Kargman, 1937-44, Boston, 1953-54, pvt. practice marriage counselor, family mediator, 1953—. Chmn. gov.'s council on home and family, Commonwealth of Mass., Boston, 1966-76. Author: How to Manage a Marriage, 1985; contbr. articles to profl. jours. Mem. Assn. of Practicing Sociologists (cited outstanding contbr.), Nat. Council on Family Relations, DePaul U. Law Sch. Alumni Assn. Avocations: tennis, tv appearances, golf. Home: 115 Rutledge Rd Belmont MA 02478-2631 E-mail: mariekargman@aol.com.

KARI, DAVEN MICHAEL, English and religious studies professor; b. Hot Springs, SD, Sept. 24, 1953; s. John Nelson and Corinna Nicolls (Morse) K.; m. Priya Perianayakam, Apr. 4, 1988; children: David Prem, Daniel Michael, Dante Gabriel. BA in English, Bibl. Studies, History, Fresno Pacific Coll., 1975, BA in Music, 1977; MA in English, Baylor U., 1983; MA, PhD in English, Purdue U., 1985-86; MDiv, PhD, So. Bapt. Theol. Sem., 1988-91. Lic. to ministry So. Bapt. Ch., 1971, ordained to ministry, 1996. Photography studio technician Johnson's Studio, Manteca, Calif., 1975-77; grad. teaching asst. Baylor U., Waco, Tex., 1978-79; minister of music Calvary Bapt. Ch., West Lafayette, Ind., 1984-85; grad. teaching asst. Purdue U., West Lafayette, Ind., 1979-85; lectr. in English Jefferson C.C., Louisville, 1987-90, Spalding U., Louisville, 1986-90, U. Louisville, 1986-90; asst. prof. English Mo. Bapt. Coll., St. Louis, 1991; assoc. prof. English Calif. Bapt. Coll., Riverside, 1991-93, assoc. prof. English, dir., Christian Ministry and Fine Arts, 1993-98; prof. Christian Studies and English Calif. Baptist U., 1998; acad. dean Washington Bible Coll., Lanham, Md., 1998-2000; adminstr., min. Bapt. Christian Sch., Hemet, Calif., 2000—01; freelance writer, 2001—02; assoc. prof. English Vanguard U. So. Calif., 2002—06, prof. English, 2006—. Author: T. S. Eliot's Dramatic Pilgrimage, 1990, Bibliography of Sources in Christianity and the Arts, 1995; co-editor: Baptist Reflections on Christianity and the Arts: Learning from Beauty, 1997, Contemporary Authors, 1997. Founder, co-dir. local Boys Brigade, Linden, Calif., 1969-71; asst. pastor Linden (Calif.) First Bapt. Ch., 1971; chair transp. com. Calvary Bapt. Ch., West Lafayette, 1982-83, dir. singles ministry, 1983-85; moderator Scholar's Bowl Quiz Contest, Riverside, 1993-94; min. First Bapt. Ch. Hemet, 2000-01. Recipient Lit. Criticism award Purdue U., 1983; named to Outstanding Young Men Am., 1985; named Faculty Mem. of Yr., Calif. Bapt. Coll., 1993; named to Contemporary Authors, 1997. Mem. Am. Acad. Religion, Conf. on Christianity and Lit., Evang. Theol. Soc. Democrat. Baptist. Avocations: poetry, stained glass windows, sculpture, photography, painting, music.

KARI, DONALD G., lawyer; b. Hood River, Oreg., Jan. 25, 1946; BS in Engring., with great distinction, Stanford U., 1967, MBA, JD, 1972. Bar: Wash. 1972, US Ct. Appeals (9th Cir.), US Dist. Ct. (We. Dist.) Wash. Ptnr., Energy & Utilities Practice Area Perkins Coie LLP, Bellevue, Wash. Mem.: Tau Beta Pi. Office: Perkins Coie LLP The PSE Bldg 10885 NE Fourth St Ste 700 Bellevue WA 98004-5579 Office Phone: 425-635-1406. Office Fax: 425-635-2400. Business E-Mail: dkari@perkinscoie.com.

KARI, ROSS, insurance company executive; BA in Math., U. Oreg., 1980, MBA in. Fin., 1983. Analyst in fin. Wells Fargo, 1983, v.p., 1987, sr. v.p. fin. and planning, gen. auditor, exec. v.p., 1995, head fin., mgr. controller's divsn./corp. tax., 1997, CFO, v.p., 1998—2001; CFO myCFO; exec. v.p., COO Fed. Home Loan Bank of San Francisco, 2002—07; exec. v.p., CFO Safeco Corp., Seattle, 2006—. Office: Safeco Corp Safeco Plz 4333 Brooklyn Ave Seattle WA 98185*

KARIM, JAWED, application developer; b. East Germany, 1979; s. Naimul and Christine Karim. BS in Computer Sci., Univ. Ill. at Urbana-Champaign, 2004; MS in Computer Sci., Stanford Univ., 2005—. Student rschr. Univ. Minn. Supercomputing Inst., 1997, Nat. Ctr. Supercomputing Applications, 1998—99; intern, advanced graphics divsn. Silicon Graphics Inc; intern, internet sys., tech. divsn. IBM, 1999; staff tech. architecture team PayPal (an eBay Co.), 2000—05; co-founder YouTube, Inc. (sold to Google in 2006), San Meteo, Calif., 2005, advisor, 2005. Contbr. articles to numerous profl. jours.

KARIM, KHURSHEED, engineering educator, researcher; s. Ghulam Mustafa and Anjuman Ara; m. Nazneen Ara, Feb. 12, 1998; children: Ahzam Mustafa, Madiha Anjum, Fatima Anjum. PhD, Indian Inst. Tech., Bombay, 2001. Asst. prof. U. Ark., Fayetteville, 2004—. Office: U Arkansas Dept Chem Engring 3202 Bell Engring Ctr Fayetteville AR 72701 Office Phone: 479-575-2484. Office Fax: 479-575-7926. Business E-Mail: kkarim@uark.edu.

KARIM, MOHAMMAD ATAUL, electrical engineering educator, researcher; b. Sylhet, Bangladesh, June 1, 1953; came to U.S., 1976; s. Muhammad Abdus and Anwara (Nuri) Shukur; m. Setara Karim, Dec. 20, 1977; children: Lutfi, Lamya, Aliya. BS in Physics with honors, U. Dacca, Bangladesh, 1976; MS in Physics, U. Ala., 1978, MS in Elec. Engring., 1979, PhD in Elec. Engring., 1981. Asst. prof. elec. engring. U. Ark., Little Rock, 1981-83, Wichita (Kans.) State U., 1983-86; dir. electro-optics program U. Dayton, Ohio, 1990-98, chair elect. and computer engring. dept. Ohio, 1994-98; head Elec. Engring. Dept. U. Tenn., Knoxville, 1998—2000; dean, engring. City Coll. of NY, NYC, 2000—04; v.p. rsch. Old Dominion U., Norfolk, Va., 2004—. Author: Digital Design, 1987, EO Devices and Systems, 1990, Optical Computing, 1992, Electro-Optical Displays, 1992; N.Am. editor Jour. Oprics and Laser Tech.; contbr. over 325 articles to profl. jours. and conf. procs.; editor 15 jour. spl. issues; holder 2 patents. Recipient Outstanding Scientist award Engring. and Sci. Found. (Dayton), 1994, Outstanding Engring. Scholarship award, 1998, Alumni award U. Dayton, 1991, NASA Tech Brief award 1990, Up-Comers award Muse-Machine, Dayton, 1990. Fellow Optical Soc. Am., Soc. Photo-Instrumentation Engrs., Bangladesh Acad. Scis.; mem. IEEE (sr. mem.), Inst. Physics, Instn. Engring. and Tech., Am. Soc. Engring. Edn. Muslim. Office: Old Dominion U Off Rsch 4807 Hampton Blvd Norfolk VA 23508 Home Phone: 757-463-0224; Office Phone: 757-683-3460. E-mail: mkarim@odu.edu.

KARIM, MUHAMMAD BAZLUL, political scientist, educator; b. Mymensingh, Bangladesh, Dec. 26, 1949; arrived in U.S., 1975; s. Abdul and Akika Khatoon Bari; m. Jean Ellickson, July 26, 1975. BA with honors, Dhaka U., Bangladesh, 1972, MA in Geography, 1973, Western Ill. U., 1978; cert. in computer programming, Strayer Coll., Washington, 1981; MA in Internat. Studies, U. Denver, 1984, cert. in devel. studies, 1985, PhD in Internat. Studies, 1991. Asst. dir. Integrated Rural Devel. Program, Dhaka, 1973-74; rsch. asst. Rajshahi (Bangladesh), 1974-75; rsch. assoc. Ethikos Rsch., Inc., Silver Spring, Md., 1980-81; rsch. asst. Internat. Food Policy Rsch. Inst., Washington, 1981; owner Asian Am. Net., 1996—; instr. Spoon River Coll., Macomb, 1991-95; asst. prof. Western Ill. U., Macomb, 1994—98; web content editor and rschr. Mayer, Brown, Rowe & Maw LLP, Chgo., 2000—. Cons. Ill. Dept. Human Rights, 1998-99; presenter in field. Author: A Farmer's Market in America, 1981, The Green Revolution: An International Bibliography, 1986, Structural Constraints to Participatory Development: An Examination of Social Stratification System in Rural Bangladesh, 1992, Participation, Development and Social Structure: An Empirical Study in a Developing Country, 1994; editor Who's Who of Asian Ams., 1998-; contbr. articles and rsch. reports to profl. jours. Vol. flood victims, Kampsville, Ill., 1993; election judge primary and gen. election Macomb City Precinct 7, McDonough County, Ill., 1990. Rsch. fellow Shell Cos. Found., 1987; grad. rsch. assistantship U. Denver, 1984-85, stipend and tuition scholar, 1983-84. Mem. Assn. Third World Studies (life, web master 1996—2000). Office Phone: 312-782-0600. Office Fax: 312-701-7711. Business E-Mail: info@asianamerican.net.

KARIN, MICHAEL, educator, molecular biologist, consultant; b. Tel Aviv, May 25, 1951; arrived in US, 1975; s. Emanuel and Elisheva (Gurevitz) K. BS in Biology, Tel Aviv U., 1975; PhD in Molecular Biology, UCLA, 1979. Postdoctoral fellow Inst. Cancer Research, Fox Chase, Pa., 1979-80; asst. research biochemist U. Calif., San Francisco, 1980-82; asst. prof. U. So. Calif. Med. Sch., Los Angeles, 1982-85; assoc. prof. U. Calif. San Diego Med. Sch., La Jolla, 1987, prof. pharmacology. Cons. and lectr. in field; mem. signal rsch. divsn. Celgene, 1992—; mem. Nat. Adv. Coun. for Environ. Health Sciences; rsch. prof. Am. Cancer Soc., 1999—. Contbr. articles to profl. jours. Searle scholar Chgo. Community Trust, 1984. Mem.: NAS, Endocrine Soc., Am. Soc. Microbiology, AAAS. Office: U Calif San Diego Sch Medicine 9500 Gilman Drive #0612 La Jolla CA 92093-0612 Office Phone: 858-534-1361. Office Fax: 858-534-8158. E-mail: karinoffice@ucsd.edu.

KARIYA, PAUL, professional hockey player; b. Vancouver, BC, Can., Oct. 16, 1974; Attended, U. Maine, 1992—93. Left wing Anaheim Mighty Ducks, 1994—2003, Colo. Avalanche, Denver, 2003—04, Nashville Predators, 2005—07, St. Louis Blues, 2007—. Mem. Team Can., Olympic Games, Lillehammer, Norway, 1994, Salt Lake City, 2002; player NHL All-Star Game, 1996, 97, 1999—2003. Named Rookie of Yr., Hockey East, 1993, Player of Yr., 1993; named to All-Rookie Team, NHL, 1995, NHL First All-Star Team, 1996, 1997, 1999, Second All-Star Team, 2000, 2003; recipient Hobey Baker Meml. Award, 1993, Lady Byng Meml. Trophy for Sportsmanship and Gentlemanly Conduct, 1996, 1997. Achievements include being a member of silver medal winning Canadian Hockey Team, Lillehammer Olympic Games, 1994, gold medal team, Salt Lake City Olympic Games, 2002. Office: St Louis Blues Scottrade Ctr 1401 Clark Ave Saint Louis MO 63103*

KARKHECK, JOHN PETER, physics professor, researcher; b. NYC, Apr. 26, 1945; s. John Henry and Dorothy Cecilia (Riebling) K.; m. Kathleen Mary Shiels, Nov. 8, 1969; children: Lorraine, Michelle, Eric. BS, LeMoyne Coll., 1966; MA, SUNY, Buffalo, 1972; PhD, SUNY, Stony Brook, 1978. Various positions Grumman Corp., Bethpage, NY, 1964-68; grad. asst. SUNY, Buffalo, 1968-70; tchr. secondary schs. Mattituck (N.Y.) Sch. Dist., 1970-71, Shelter Island (N.Y.) Sch. Dist., 1971-73; grad. asst. SUNY, Stony Brook, 1973-78, postdoctoral fellow, 1978-79, rsch. assoc., 1979-81; asst. prof. physics GMI Engring. and Mgmt. Inst., Flint, Mich., 1981-84, assoc. prof., 1984, prof., dir. physics, 1988-89, head. dept. sci. and math., 1989-93; prof., chmn. dept. physics Marquette U., Milw., 1993—2003, dir. physics for medicine program, 2003—, asst. vice provost for grad. studies, 2004—; dir. Marquette U., Bridging the Worlds: Physics Project for Lugazi Diocese, 2003—. Physics assoc. Brookhaven Nat. Lab., Upton, N.Y., 1975-79, cons., 1979-85, STS, Hauppauge, N.Y., 1983, BID Ctr., Flint, 1985-90; acad. assoc. Mich. State U., 1988, 90, vis. scholar, 1989, vis. scientist, 1991; reviewer Addison-Wesley Pub., 1990, 93; regional dir. Mich. Sci. Olympiad, 1991-92, 92-93; co-dir. NATO Advanced Study Inst., 1998, editor, 1999-2000. Contbr. numerous articles to profl. jours. Den leader Cub Scouts Am., Flint, 1987-91; leader Boy Scouts Am., 1991-98; bd. dirs. Flint Area Sci. Fair, 1991-93; mem. sci. curriculum adv. com. Milw. Acad. Sci., 2000-03; judge local sci. fairs. Dept. Energy rsch. grantee, 1977-79, NATO travel grantee, 1983-86, 89, NATO ASI grantee, 1998. Mem. Am. Phys. Soc., AAAS, AAPT, Sigma Xi (v.p. Marquette U. chpt. 1998-99, pres., 1999-2000). Roman Catholic. Avocations: swimming, reading, bicycling, travel, learning German. Home: 6592 N Bethmaur Ln Glendale WI 53209-3320 Office: Marquette Univ Dept Physics PO Box 1881 Milwaukee WI 53201-1881 Office Phone: 414-288-5321. Business E-Mail: john.karkheck@marquette.edu.

KARKOSCHKA, ERICH, planetary science researcher, writer; b. Stuttgart, Federal Republic of Germany, Nov. 6, 1955; came to U.S., 1983; s. Erhard Karkoschka and Rothraut Leiter. Diploma in math., U. Stuttgart, 1981; PhD, U. Ariz., 1990. Wissenschaftlicher Mitarbeiter U. Stuttgart, 1982; rsch. assoc. U. Ariz., Tucson, 1992—2003, sr. staff scientist, 2003—. Group leader Internat. Workshop Astronomy, Europe, 1981-89. Author: The Observer's Sky Atlas, 1990, German edit., 1988, Japanese edit., 1991, Czech edit., 1995, Drehbare Welt-Sternkarte, 1990; co-author: Das Himmelsjahr, 1982—. Recipient 2d European prize European Philips Contest for Young Scientists and Inventors, 1973. Avocations: playing violin in symphony orchestra, playing organ, amateur astronomy, worldwide travel. Office: Univ Ariz Lunar & Planetary Lab Tucson AZ 85721-0001 Business E-Mail: erich@lpl.arizona.edu.

KARL, DAVID MICHAEL, oceanographer, educator; b. May 9, 1950; BA magna cum laude, SUNY, Buffalo, 1971; MS, Fla. State U., 1974; PhD, U. Calif., San Diego, 1978. Rsch. asst. dept. oceanography Fla. State U., Tallahassee, 1972—73; rsch. asst. food chain rsch. group Scripps Instn. Oceanography, La Jolla, Calif., 1974—78; asst. prof. oceanography U. Hawaii, Honolulu, 1978—81, assoc. prof. oceanography, 1981—87, chmn. oceanic biology rsch. divsn., 1986—90, prof. oceanography Sch. Ocean and Earth Sci. and Tech., 1987—, chmn. biol. oceanography divsn. Sch. Ocean and Earth Sci. and Tech., 1990—91. Rsch. oceanographer Palmer Sta. Antarctica U.S. Antarctic Program, rsch. biologist Ross Ice Shelf Project; participant exptl. microbial ecology course Marine Biol. Lab., Woods Hole, Mass., 1974; participant Scandinavian summer sch. for microbial ecology U. Aarhus, Denmark, 1976; mem. grad. faculty oceanography U. Hawaii, Honolulu, 1978—, mem. grad. faculty marine biology, 1991—; mem. affiliate faculty Bermuda Biol. Sta. for Rsch., Ferry Reach, 1995—; mem. adv. com. for ocean scis. NSF, 1984—87, mem. global ocean flux subcom. on transformations in ocean interior, 1986—88; mem. subcom. on so. ocean process studies U.S.-Joint Global Ocean Flux Study, 1990—92; mem. adv. com. Office Polar Programs NSF, 1994—97; mem. search com. for dir. Hawaii Inst. Marine Biology, 1996—; co-chair NSF-Sponsored Workshop on Lake Vostok, Antarctica, 1998; mem. dir. search com. Inst. for Astronomy, 1999—2000. Mem. editl. bd.: Applied and Environ. Microbiology, 1980—82, 1983—85, 1985—88, 1989—94, Microbial Ecology, 1990—92, Ecosystems, 1999—2001, Biogeosciences, 2004—, guest editor: Deep-Sea Rsch., Rsch. on Antarctic Coastal Ecosystem Rates, 1991; editor: Microbiology of Deep-Sea Hydrothermal Vents, 1995; editl. advisor: Aquatic Microbial Ecology, 1995—96, guest editor: Deep-Sea Rsch., Oceanic Time-Series, 1996, subject editor: Aquatic Microbial Ecology, 1997—. Recipient Presdl. Young Investigator award,

NSF, 1984—89, A. G. Huntsman Medal, Bedford Inst. of Oceanography, 2001, Investigator in Marine Sci. award, Gordon and Betty Moore Found., 2004, Henry Bryant Bigelow Medal, Woods Hole Oceanog. Instn., 2004, David Packard Medal, Monterey Bay Aquarium Rsch. Inst., 2005. Fellow: Am. Geophys. Union (mem. exec. com. ocean scis. sect. 1996—98, mem. ad hoc com. on recognizing and encouraging the contbns. of biol. 1998—2000); mem.: NAS, Am. Soc. Limnology and Oceanography (mem. com. on edn. and human resources 1993—98, mem. selection com. Lifetime Achievement Award 1994, chairperson pub. policy com. 1998—, G. Evelyn Hutchinson Medal 1998), Am. Soc. for Microbiol. (v.p. Hawaii br. 1981—82, chmn.-elect divsn. aquatic and terrestrial microbiology 1984—85, mem. ann. meeting planning com. 1985—86, chmn. divsn. aquatic and terrestrial microbiology 1985—86), Oceanography Soc. (mem. membership com. 1996—99, coun. mem. 2000—), Hawaii Acad. Sci., Sigma Xi (councilor Hawaii br. 1991—92, mem. exec. com. Hawaii chpt. 1991—92). Office: U Hawaii Sch Ocean and Earth Sci and Tech 1000 Pope Rd MSB 629 Honolulu HI 96822 Home: 2499 Kapiolani Blvd Apt 503 Honolulu HI 96822

KARL, GEORGE, professional basketball coach; b. Penn Hills, Pa., May 12, 1951; children: Kelei Ryanne, Coby Joseph, Kaci Grace. Grad., U. NC, 1973. Draft pick NY Knicks, 1973; guard San Antonio Spurs, 1973-78, asst. coach, head scout, 1978-80; head coach Continental Basketball Assn. Mont. Golden Nuggets, 1980-83; dir. player acquisition Cleve. Cavaliers, 1983-84, head coach, 1984-86, Golden State Warriors, Oakland, Calif., 1986—88, Albany Patrons, NY, 1988—89, 1990—91, Real Madrid, Spain, 1991-92, Seattle SuperSonics, 1991—98, Milw. Bucks, 1998—2003, Denver Nuggets, 2005—; NBA analyst ESPN. Head coach USA Basketball Team Internat. Basketball Fedn. World Basketball Championships, Indpls., 2002. Named Coach of Yr., Continental Basketball Assn., 1981, 83, 91. Achievements include winning over 800 NBA games as head coach. Office: Denver Nuggets 1000 Chopper Cir Denver CO 80204*

KARLAN, PAMELA SUSAN, law educator; b. 1959; BA in History, magna cum laude, Yale U., 1980, MA in History, 1984, JD, 1984. Bar: US Supreme Ct., US Dist. Ct. So. Dist. NY, US Ct. Appeals 4th, 5th, 8th, 9th, and 11th Circuits. Law clk. to Judge Abraham D. Sofaer US Dist. Ct. So. Dist. NY, 1984—85; law clk. to Justice Harry A. Blackman US Supreme Ct., 1985—86; asst. counsel NAACP Legal Def. and Ednl. Fund, Inc., 1986—88; assoc. prof. law U. Va. Sch. Law, 1988—93, prof., 1993—98, Roy L. and Rosamond Woodruff Morgan rsch. prof., 1994—98; prof. law Stanford Law Sch., 1998—99, Kenneth and Harle Montgomery prof. pub. interest law, 1999—, academic assoc. dean, 1999—2000. Lectr. FBI Nat. Acad., 1990—2001; commr. Calif. Fair Polit. Practice Commn., 2003; vis. prof. Yale Law Sch., 1992, NYU Sch. Law, 1993, Harvard Law Sch., 1994—95, Stanford Law Sch., 1996, U. Va. Law Sch., 2002. Fellow: Am. Acad. Arts & Scis.; mem.: Am. Law Inst. Office: Stanford Law Sch Crown Quadrangle 559 Nathan Abbott Way Stanford CA 94305-8610 Office Phone: 650-725-4851. Office Fax: 650-725-0253. Business E-Mail: karlan@stanford.edu.*

KARLE, ISABELLA L., chemist; b. Detroit, Dec. 2, 1921; d. Zygmunt Apolonaris and Elizabeth (Graczyk) Lugoski; m. Jerome Karle, June 4, 1942; children: Louise Hanson, Jean Marianne, Madeleine Tawney. BS in Chemistry, U. Mich., 1941, MS in Chemistry, 1942, PhD, 1944, DSc (hon.), 1976, Wayne State U., 1979, U. Md., 1986, Athens U., Greece, 1997, U. Pa., 1999; LHD (hon.), Georgetown U., 1984; DSc (hon.), Harvard U., 2001; Doctor honoris causa, Jagiellonian U., Cracow, Poland, 2002. Assoc. chemist U. Chgo., 1944; instr. chemistry U. Mich., Ann Arbor, 1944—46; physicist Naval Rsch. Lab., Washington, 1946—. Paul Ehrlich lectr. NIH, 1991; exec. com. Am. Peptide Symposium, 1975—81; adv. bd. Chem. and Engring. News, 1986—89. Mem. editl. bd.: Biopolymers Jour., 1975—, Internat. Jour. Peptide Rsch., 1981—; contbr. articles to profl. jours. Named to Mich. Women's Hall of Fame, 1989; recipient Superior Civilian Svc. award, USN, 1965, Fed. Women's award, U.S. Govt., 1973, Annual Achievement award, Soc. Women Engrs., 1968, U. Mich., 1987, Dexter Conrad award, Office Naval Rsch., 1980, WISE Lifetime Achievement award, Women in Sci. and Engring., 1986, award for disting. achievement in sci., Sec. of Navy, 1987, Gregori Aminoff prize, Swedish Royal Acad. Scis., 1988, Adm. Parsons award, Navy League U.S., 1988, Ann. Achievement award, CCNY, 1989, Bijvoet medal, U. Utrecht, The Netherlands, 1990, Vincent du Vigneaud award, Gordon Conf. (Peptides), 1992, Bower Sci. award, Franklin Inst., 1993, Nat. medal of sci., Pres. of the U.S., 1995, Merrifield award, Am. Peptide Soc., 2007. Fellow: Am. Inst. Chemists (Chem. Pioneer award 1984), Am. Acad. Arts Scis.; mem.: NAS (Chem. Scis. award 1995), Biophys. Soc., Am. Philos. Soc., Am. Phys. Soc., Am. Chem. Soc. (Garvan award 1976, Hillebrand award 1970, Ralph Hirschmann award in peptide chemistry 1998), Am. Crystallographic Assn. (pres. 1976). Home: 6304 Lakeview Dr Falls Church VA 22041-1309 Office: Naval Rsch Lab Code 6030 Washington DC 20375-5341 Office Phone: 202-767-2624. Business E-Mail: isabella.karle@nrl.navy.mil.

KARLE, JEROME, physicist, researcher; b. NYC, June 18, 1918; married, 1942; 3 children. BS, CCNY, 1937; AM, Harvard U., 1938; MS, U. Mich., 1942, PhD in Phys. Chemistry, 1943. Rsch. assoc. Manhattan project, Chgo., 1943—44, U.S. Navy Project, Mich., 1944—46; head electron diffraction sect. Naval Rsch. Lab., Washington, 1946—58, head diffraction br., 1958—68, now head lab. for structure matter, 1968—. Mem. NRC, 1954—56, 1967—75, 1978—87; chmn. U.S. Nat. Com. for Crystallography, 1973—75. Recipient Nobel prize in Chemistry, 1985. Fellow: Am. Phys. Soc.; mem.: NAS (chair chemistry sect. 1988—91), Internat. Union Crystallography (mem. exec. com. 1978—87, pres. 1981—84), Am. Crystallograph Assn. (treas. 1950—52, pres. 1971—73), Am. Math. Soc., Am. Chem. Soc. Office: US Naval Rsch Lab Lab for Structure of Matter Code # 6030 Washington DC 20375-5341 *There is too much administration of everything creative. It distorts our society and its character. The solution is to select competent, well-qualified people and give them freedom and support to pursue their creative gifts.*

KARLEN, PETER HURD, lawyer, writer; b. NYC, Feb. 22, 1949; s. S. H. and Jean Karlen; m. Lynette Ann Thwaites, Dec. 22, 1978. BA in History, U. Calif., Berkeley, 1971; JD, U. Calif., Hastings, 1974; MS in Law and Soc., U. Denver, 1976. Bar: Calif. 1974, Hawaii 1989, Colo. 1991, U.S. Dist. Ct. (so. dist.) Calif. 1976, U.S. Dist. Ct. (no. dist.) Calif. 1983, U.S. Dist. Ct. (Hawaii) 1989, U.S. Supreme Ct. 1990. Assoc. Sankary & Sankary, San Diego, 1976; teaching fellow Coll. of Law U. Denver, 1974-75; lectr. Sch. of Law U. Warwick, United Kingdom, 1976-78; pvt. practice La Jolla, Calif., 1979-86; prin. Peter H. Karlen, P.C., La Jolla, 1986—. Adj. prof. U. San Diego Sch. of Law, 1979-84; mem. adj. faculty Western State U. Coll. of Law, San Diego, 1976, 79-80, 88, 92. Contbg. editor Artweek, 1979-95, Art Calendar, 1989-96, Art Cellar Exch. mag., 1989-92; mem. editl. bd. Copyright World, 1988—, IP World, 1997—; contbr. numerous articles to profl. jours. Mem. Am. Soc. for Aesthetics, Brit. Soc. Aesthetics. Office: 1205 Prospect St Ste 400 La Jolla CA 92037-3613

KARLGAARD, RICH, publishing executive; b. Bismarck, ND; married; 2 children. Co-founder Upside, 1989—92, editor, 1989—92; co-founder, editor Forbes ASAP, 1992—98; pub. Forbes Mag., NYC, 1998—. Co-founder, bd. dir. garage.com, 1977—; co-founder Churchill (public affairs) Club. Recipient Entrepreneur of Yr.-No. Calif. (for Churchill Club), Ernst & Young, 1997. Office: Forbes 60 5th Ave New York NY 10011-8882 also: Forbes 555 Airport Blvd 5th Fl Burlingame CA 94010 Office Phone: 650-558-4810. Office Fax: 212-620-2245. E-mail: publisher@forbes.com.*

KARLIN, EDWARD J., lawyer; b. Chgo., Mar. 10, 1952; BA with distinction, Ind. U., 1974; JD cum laude, Northwestern U., 1977. Bar: Ill. 1977, US Ct. Appeals (7th cir.), US Dist. Ct. (no. dist.) Ill. Mem. Seyfarth, Shaw, Fairweather & Geraldson, Chgo.; ptnr. Seyfarth LLP, Chgo., mem. exec. com., head, Corp. Practice Area. Bd. mem. Physician Insurers Assn. Am. Mem.: Chgo. Bar Assn. (banking law sect.), ABA (bus. law sect.), Phi Beta Kappa. Office: Seyfarth Shaw LLP 55 E Monroe St Ste 4200 Chicago IL 60603 Office Phone: 312-460-5875. Office Fax: 312-460-7875. Business E-Mail: ekarlin@seyfarth.com.

KARLIN, MICHAEL JONATHAN ABRAHAM, lawyer; b. London, Aug. 27, 1952; came to U.S., 1980; s. Eli Karlin and Miriam (Stahl) Henderson; m. Fiona Jane Wilson, July 20, 1973; children: Laura, Toby. BA with Hons., Cambridge U., Eng., 1973, MA, 1977. Bar: Calif. 1980, U.S. Dist. Ct. (cen. dist.) Calif. 1980, U.S. Tax. Ct. 1981; solicitor, Eng. and Wales 1977. Asst. solicitor D.J. Freeman & Co., London, 1975-80; assoc. Gelles, Singer & Johnson, LA, 1980-83, Morgan, Lewis & Bockius LLP, LA, 1983-88, ptnr., 1988—97, KPMG LLP, 1998—2000. Contbr. articles to profl jours., 1980—. Mem. ABA (tax sect. com. on U.S. Activities of Foreigners and Tax Treaties 2004, chmn. task force new and temporary immigrants 2004), Calif. State Bar Assn., L.A. County Bar Assn. (chmn. fgn. tax law com. taxation sect. 1989-90). Office: Karlin & Peebles LLP 8383 Wilshire Blvd #649 Beverly Hills CA 90211 Office Phone: 310-274-5275. Business E-Mail: mjkarlin@karlinpeebles.com.

KARLIN, SAMUEL, mathematics professor, researcher; b. Yonova, Poland, June 8, 1924; s. Morris Karlin; m. Elsie Karlin (div.); children: Kenneth, Manuel, Anna. BS in Math., Ill. Inst. Tech., 1944; PhD in Math., Princeton U., 1947; DSc (hon.), Technion-Israel Inst. Tech., Haifa, 1985. Instr. math. Calif. Inst. Tech., Pasadena, 1948—49, asst. prof., 1949—52, assoc. prof., 1952—55, prof., 1955—56; vis. asst. prof. Princeton U., 1950—51; prof. Stanford U., Calif., 1956—. Wald lectr., 1957; Andrew D. White prof.-at-large Cornell U., 1975—81; Wilks lectr. Princeton U., 1977; pres. Inst. Math. Stats., 1978—79; Commonwealth lectr. U. Mass., 1980; 1st Mahalanobis meml. lectr. Indian Statis. Inst., 1983; prin. invited spkr. XII Internat. Biometrics Meeting, Japan; prin. lectr. Que. Math. Soc., 1984; adv. dean math. dept. Weizmann Inst. Sci., Israel, 1970—77; Britton lectr. McMaster U., Hamilton, Ont., Canada, 1990; Cockerham lectr. N.C. State U., 1996; Elisha Netanyahu Meml. lectr. Technion-Israel Inst. Tech., 2005. Author: Mathematical Methods and Theory in Games, Programming, Economics, Vol. I: Matrix Games, Programming and Mathematical Economics, 1959, Mathematical Methods and Theory in Games, Programming, Economics, Vol. II: The Theory of Infinite Games, 1959, A First Course in Stochastic Processes, 1966, Total Positivity Vol. I, 1968; author: (with K. Arrow and H. Scarf) Studies in the Mathematical Theory of Inventory and Production, 1958; author: (with W.J. Sudden) Tchebycheff Systems: With Applications in Analysis and Statistics, 1966; author: (with H.Taylor) A First Course in Stochastic Processes, 2d edit., 1975; author: A Second Course in Stochastic Processes, 1980, An Introduction to Stochastic Modeling, 1984; author: (with C.a. Michelli, A. Pinkus, I.I. Schoenberg) Studies in Spline Functions and Approximation Theory, 1976. Recipient Lester R. Ford award, Am. Math. Monthly, 1973, Robert Grimmett Chair Math., Stanford U., 1978, The John Von Neumann Theory prize, 1987, award, U.S. Nat. Medal Sci., 1989, The Karlin prize in Math. Biology named in honor, Stanford U. Dept. Biol. Scis., 1992; fellow Proctor, 1945, Bateman Rsch., 1947—48, Guggenheim Found., 1959—60, NSF, 1960—61. Fellow: AAAS, Inst. Math. Statis., Internat. Statis. Inst.; mem.: NAS (award in applied math. 1973), Am. Philos. Soc., Human Genome Orgn., Am. Naturalist Soc., London Math. Soc. (hon.), Genetics Soc. Am., Am. Soc. Human Genetics, Am. Acad. Arts and Scis., Am. Math. Soc. Office: Stanford U Bldg 380 Stanford CA 94305-2125 E-mail: karlin@math.stanford.edu.

KARLINSKY, SIMON, language educator, writer; b. Harbin, Manchuria, Sept. 22, 1924; arrived in U.S., 1938, naturalized, 1944; s. Aron and Sophie (Levitin) Karlinsky. BA, U. Calif., Berkeley, 1960, PhD, 1964; MA, Harvard U., 1961. Conf. interpreter, music student Europe, 1947-57; tchg. fellow Harvard U., Cambridge, Mass., 1960-61; asst. prof. Slavic langs. and lits. U. Calif., Berkeley, 1963-65, prof., 1967-91, prof. emeritus, 1991—, chmn. dept., 1967-69. Vis. assoc. prof. Harvard U., 1966. Author: Marina Cvetaeva: Her Life and Her Art, 1966, The Sexual Labyrinth of Nikolai Gogol, 1976, 2d edit., 1992, Russian Drama from Its Beginnings to the Age of Pushkin, 1985, Marina Tsvetaeva: The Woman, Her World and Her Poetry, 1986, 2d edit., 1988, Italian edit., 1989, Spanish edit., 1990, Japanese edit., 1991; editor: The Bitter Air of Exile, 1977; editor, annotator: Anton Chekhov's Life and Thought, 1974, 2d edit., 1997, The Nabokov-Wilson Letters, 1979, 2d edit., 2001, French edit., 1988, German edit., 1995, Japanese edit., 2002; co-editor: Language, Literature, Linguistics, 1987, O RUS! Studia literaria slavica in honorem Hugh McLean, 1995; contbr. articles to profl. jours. Guggenheim fellow, 1969—70, 1977—78. Mem.: Phi Beta Kappa.

KARLL, JO ANN, retired judge, lawyer; b. St. Louis, Nov. 16, 1948; d. Joseph H. and Dorothy Olga (Pyle) K.; m. William Austin Hernlund, Sept. 9, 1990. BS magna cum laude, Maryville U.; JD, St. Louis U. Bar: Mo. 1993. Ins. claims adjuster, 1967-88; mem. Mo. Gen. Assembly dists. 104 and 105, 1991-93; dir. Mo. State Divsn. Workers' Compensation, Jefferson City, 1993-2000, adminstrv. law judge, 2000—03; pvt. practice High Ridge, Mo., 2003—. Founder, 1st pres. scholarship fund Mo. Kids' Chance, Inc., 1995-96, bd. dirs., 1995—2007, North Jefferson Ambulance Bd., 2004-06, pres. bd. dirs. 2005. Mem. Internat. Assn. Indsl. Accident Bds. and Commns. (past pres.). Office: Karll Law Ctr LLC 1682 Old Gravois Rd High Ridge MO 63049 Home Phone: 636-677-0757; Office Phone: 636-677-7000. E-mail: karll.law@sbcglobal.net.

KARLSEN, PAUL JOHAN, psychologist, researcher, writer; b. Bodø, Nordland, Norway, June 27, 1975; s. Hans and Else Regine Karlsen; life ptnr. Leo Andre Bull, Nov. 23, 1976. Student, Fribourg U., Switzerland, 1998; BA in Psychology and Philosophy, U. Oslo, 2000, PhD in Psychology, 2004; MA in Psychology, NYU, 2002. Freelance journalist Nordlandsposten, Bodø, Norway, 1991—97; postdoctoral fellow Dept Psychology U. Oslo, 2004—; vis. scholar Dept Psychology NYU, 2004—. Author: Daimler, 2002, Slik får du bedre hukommelse (How to improve your memory), 2004; contbr., articles to profl. jours. Recipient award, Thanks to Scandinavia Found., 2001, Andrew E. and G. Norman Wigeland award, The American-Scandinavian Found., 2001; fellow, Norwegian Rsch. Coun., 2004—; grantee, Lise and Arnfinn Heje's Fund, 2000—01, Norwegian Rsch. Coun., 2000—01; scholar, Fulbright Found., 2000—02. Mem.: Cognitive Neuroscience Soc., Norwegian Psychol. Assn., Norwegian Assn. Rsch. Workers, The Soc. North-Norwegian Authors, Norwegian Non-Fiction Writers and Translators Assn., The Norwegian Writers' Ctr., European Soc. Cognitive Psychology, Soho Ho Club, Psi Chi. Achievements include research in human memory. Home: 341 Lafayette St Ste 4006 New York NY 10012 Office: Dept Psychology U Oslo Postbox 1094 Blindern Oslo N 0317 Norway Office Phone: 4722352255. Office Fax: 4722845001. Business E-Mail: pjkarlse@psykologi.uio.no.

KARLTON, LAWRENCE K., federal judge; b. Bklyn., May 28, 1935; s. Aaron Katz and Sylvia (Meltzer) K.; m. Mychelle Stiebel, Sept. 7, 1958 (dec.); m. Sue Gouge, May 22, 1999. Student, Washington Sq. Coll., 1952-54; LL.B., Columbia U., 1958. Bar: Fla. 1958, Calif. 1962. Acting legal officer Sacramento Army Depot, Dept. Army, Sacramento, 1958-60, civilian legal officer, 1960-62; individual practice law Sacramento, 1962-64; mem. firm Abbott, Karlton & White, 1964, Karlton & Blease, 1964-71, Karlton, Blease & Vanderlaan, 1971-76; judge Calif. Superior Ct. for Sacramento County, 1976-79, U.S. Dist. Ct. (ea. dist.) Calif., Sacramento, 1979-83; formerly chief judge U.S. Dist. Ct., Sacramento, 1983-90, chief judge emeritus, 1990-2000, sr. judge, 2000—. Co-chmn. Central Calif. council B'nai B'rith Anti-Defamation League Commn., 1964-65; treas. Sacramento Jewish Community Relations Council, chmn., 1967-68; chmn. Vol. Lawyers Commn. Sacramento Valley ACLU, 1964-76. Mem. Am. Bar Assn., Sacramento County Bar Assn., Calif. Bar Assn., Fed. Bar Assn., Fed. Judges Assn., 9th Cir. Judges Assn. Clubs: B'nai B'rith (past pres.). Office: US Dist Ct 501 I St Sacramento CA 95814-7300

KARMALI, RASHIDA ALIMAHOMED, lawyer; b. Uganda, May 12, 1948; arrived in US, 1978; d. Alimahomed and Sakina (Govani) K. BSc, Makerere U., Kampala, Uganda, 1971; MSc, Aberdeen U., Scotland, 1973; PhD, U. Newcastle Upon Tyne, Eng., 1976; JD, Rutgers U., New Brunswick. NJ, 1993. Bar: NY 1994, US Patent Office. Fellow Clin. Rsch. Inst., Montreal, 1976-78; rsch. assoc. E. Carolina U., Greenville, NC, 1978-80, Meml. Sloan-Kettering Inst., NYC, 1980-84; adj. assoc. prof. Cook Coll., New Brunswick, NJ, 1984-90; practice in tech. law NYC, 1991—. Mem. ABA, Assn. Bar City NY, Am. Intellectual Property Law Assn., Licensing Execs. Soc. Office: 99 Wall St 10th Fl New York NY 10005 Office Phone: 212-651-9653. Personal E-mail: karmali@aol.com.

KARMAN, JAMES ANTHONY, manufacturing executive; b. Grand Rapids, Mich., May 26, 1937; s. Anthony and Katherine D. Karman; m. Carolyn L. Hoehn, Aug. 29, 1959; children: Robb Thomas, Janet Ellen, Edward John, Christopher James. BS cum laude, Miami U., Oxford, Ohio, 1959; MBA, U. Wis., 1960. Instr. corp. fin. U. Wis., Madison, 1960-61; asst. mgr. investment dept. Union Bank & Trust Co., Grand Rapids, 1961-63; treas. RPM, Inc., Medina, Ohio, 1963-69, v.p., treas., 1969-72, v.p., sec.-treas., 1972-73, exec. v.p., sec.-treas., 1973-78, pres., 1978—, also bd. dirs., CFO, 1982-93, vice chmn., 1999—. Instr. Am. Inst. Banking, 1962; bd. dirs. Metro. Fin. Corp., Shiloh Industries, Inc., A. Schulman, Inc. Trustee Trinity Cathedral, Cleve., Western Res. Hist. Soc., Boys & Girls Club, Cleve., The Leelanau Sch., Glen Arbor, Mich.; past bd. trustees Cleve. Orch., Boys Hope, Cleve., Cleve. Playhouse; mem. adv. coun. Miami U. Sch. Bus. Adminstrn.; mem. bd. visitors U. Wis.; mem. corp. coun., fin. com. Cleve. Mus. Art.; mem. Bluecoats, Inc., Cleve. Mem. U.S. Power Squadron, Gt. Lakes Hist. Soc., Mayfield Country Club, Cleve. Playhouse Club, Pine Lake Trout Club, Union Club (Cleve.), St. Louis Club, Order of Artus, Phi Beta Kappa. Home: 110 Seaspray Ave Palm Beach FL 33480-4227

KARMANOS, PETER, JR., computer company executive, professional sports team executive; m. Barbara Ann Karmanos (dec.); children: Peter III, Nick, Jason; m. Danialle Tynan. Grad., Wayne State U. Co-founder, corp. chmn., CEO Compuware, Detroit, 1973—; formed Gale Force Holdings, 1998. Gov., CEO Hartford Whalers, 1994—96; prin. owner, gov., CEO Carolina Hurricanes, 1996—. Sponsor youth hockey Detroit Jr. Whalers; Sponsor youth hockey programs New Eng. Jr. Whalers, Conn.; founder Barbara Ann Karmanos Cancer Inst., Detroit, 1995. Named Named Entrepreneur of Yr., Inst. Am. Entrepreneurs, 1989; recipient Lester Patrick Award, 1997. Achievements include being the owner of Stanley Cup Champion Carolina Hurricanes, 2006. Office: Carolina Hurricanes RBC Ctr 1400 Edwards Mill Rd Raleigh NC 27607-3624 also: Compuware Corp 1 Campus Martius Detroit MI 48226-5099

KARMAZIN, MEL, broadcast executive; b. NYC, Aug. 24, 1943; 2 children. BS, Pace U., 1967. Past sta. mgr. CBS radio, NYC, 1960—70; v.p., gen. mgr. Metromedia Inc., NYC, 1970—81; pres. Infinity Broadcasting Corp., NYC, 1981—2001, CEO, 1988—2001; chmn., CEO CBS Station Group, NYC, 1997; pres, COO CBS Corp., NYC, 1998—99; pres., COO Viacom Inc., NYC, 2000—04, ret., 2004, cons., 2004; CEO SIRIUS Satellite Radio Inc., NYC, 2004—. Bd. dir. Westwood One, Blockbuster, New York Stock Exchange. Named to Broadcasting Hall of Fame, Nat. Assn. Broadcasters, 2003; recipient Nat. Radio award, 1998, Gold Medal award, Internat. Radio & Television Soc., 2000. Office: SIRIUS Satellite Radio Inc 1221 Ave Americas 36th Fl New York NY 10020

KARMEIVER, DELBERT FRED, engineer, consultant, realtor; b. Okawville, Ill., Apr. 2, 1935; s. Wilbert and Ida (Harre) K.; m. Naomi Firnhaber, Oct. 18, 1958; children: Kenton Howard, Dianne Jill. BSCE, U. Ill., 1957, MS in Transp. Engring., 1959. Rsch. assoc. U. Ill., 1958-59; traffic engr. St. Louis County, Mo., 1959-65, traffic commr., 1965-69; dir. transp. City of Kansas City, Mo., 1969-74, dir. aviation and transp., 1974-90; dir. pub. works City of Hartford, Conn., 1990-92; assoc. exec. dir. Am. Pub. Works Assn., Chgo., 1992-94; cons. Torres Cons. Engrs., Kansas City, Mo., 1994-95; assoc. Reece & Nichols, Leawood, Kans., 1995—. Mem. Nat. Com. on Uniform Traffic Control Devices, 1971-85 Automotive Safety Found. fellow U. Ill., 1959. Mem. Inst. Transp. Engrs. (pres. Missouri Valley sect. 1965-66), Airport Operator's Coun. Internat., Am. Rd. and Transp. Builder's Assn. (dir. 1973-83, chmn. pub. transit adv. coun. 1980-83), Transp. Rsch. Bd., Am. Pub. Works Assn., U. Ill. Alumni Club Kansas City (pres. 1996—), Thrivent Fin. for Lutherans (v.p. West Jackson County chpt. 2003—06), Leawood Rotary Club, Beta Sigma Psi (nat. editor 1963-69, pres. Kansas City alumni 1981-82, Disting. Alumnus award 1971, nat pres. 1986-88, nat. treas. 1996-2004). Lutheran. Home: 12206 Avila Dr Kansas City MO 64145-1750 Office: Reece Nichols Realtor 12150 State Line Rd Leawood KS 66209-1255 Office Phone: 913-906-3722. Personal E-mail: delkarm@aol.com.

KARMEIER, LLOYD A., state supreme court justice; b. Washington County, Ill., Jan. 12, 1940; m. Mary Karmeier; 2 children. BS, JD, Univ. Ill. Bar: Ill. 1964, US Dist. Ct. (so. dist. Ill.), US Supreme Ct. Law clk. Justice Byron O. House, Ill. Supreme Ct., 1964—68; state's atty. Washington County, Ill., 1968—72; law clk. Judge James L. Foreman, US Dist Ct., Ill., 1972—73; atty. Hohlt, House, DeMoss & Johnson, 1964—86; resident cir. judge Washington County, Ill., 1986—2004; assoc. justice Ill. Supreme Ct., 2004—. Chmn. Com. on Pattern Jury Instructions Ill. Supreme Ct., 2003—04. Mem.: Ill. Judges Assn., Ill. State Bar Assn. (assembly mem. 1996—2002), Ea. St. Louis Bar Assn., St. Clair County Bar Assn., Washington County Bar Assn., So. Ill. Am. Inn of Ct. (pres. exec. com. 2003). Office: Illinois Supreme Court PO Box 266 Nashville IL 62263

KARMEL, ROBERTA SEGAL, lawyer, educator; b. Chgo., May 4, 1937; d. J. Herzl and Eva E. (Elin) Segal; m. Paul R. Karmel, June 9, 1957 (dec. Aug. 1994); children: Philip, Solomon, Jonathan, Miriam; m. S. David Harrison, Oct. 29, 1995. BA, Radcliffe Coll.; LLB, NYU, 1962; HHD (hon.), King's Coll., 1998. Bar: N.Y. 1962, U.S. Dist. Ct. (so. and ea. dists.) N.Y. 1964, U.S. Ct. Appeals (2d cir.) 1968, U.S. Supreme Ct. 1968, U.S. Ct. Appeals (3d cir.) 1987. Asst. regional adminstr. SEC, Washington, 1962-69, commr., 1977-80; assoc. Willkie Farr & Gallagher, NYC, 1969-72; ptnr. Rogers & Wells, NYC, 1972-77, of counsel, 1980-85; ptnr. Kelley Drye & Warren, NYC, 1987-94, of counsel, 1995—2002. Adj. prof. law Bklyn. Law Sch., 1973-77, 82-85, prof., 1985—, co-dir. Ctr. for Study of Internat. Bus. Law; trustee Practicing Law Inst. Author: Regulation by Prosecution, 1982; contbr. articles to profl. jours. Fellow Am. Bar Found.; mem. ABA, Assn. Bar City N.Y., Am. Law Inst., Fin. Women's Assn. Home: 66 Summit Dr Hastings On Hudson NY 10706-1215 Office: Bklyn Law Sch 250 Joralemon St Brooklyn NY 11201-3700 Office Phone: 718-780-7946. Business E-Mail: roberta.karmel@brooklaw.edu.

KARNAS, FRED G., JR., poverty and homeless specialist; b. Olean, NY, Sept. 9, 1948; BCP, U. Va., 1971; MSW, Va. Commonwealth U., 1980; PhD, Va. Tech. U., 1984. Gen. program dir. Cmty. Coun., Phoenix, 1983-87; exec. dir. Cmty. Housing Partnership, Phoenix, 1987-89, Ctrl. Fla. Coalition for the Homeless, Orlando, Fla., 1989-91, Nat. Coalition for the Homeless, Washington, 1991-95; with HUD, Washington, 1995-2000, dep. asst. sec., 1997-2000; cons. on homelessness, AIDS, housing policies, 2000—; pres. Ariz. Family Housing Fund, Phoenix, 2002—03; policy advisor Gov. of Ariz., 2003—06; sr. dir. Fannie Mae Found., Washington, 2006—07; adminstr. Ariz. Dept. Housing, 2007—. E-mail: fkarnas1@msn.com.

KARNAUGH, MAURICE, computer scientist, educator; b. NYC, Oct. 4, 1924; s. George Victor and Fannie (Weinstein) K.; m. Linn Blank; children: Robert Victor, Paul Joseph. BS, CCNY, 1948; MS, Yale U., 1950, PhD, 1952. Mem. tech. staff Bell Telephone Labs., Murray Hill, NJ, 1952—66, mgr. digital techs., 1956—66; chief scientist exploratory systems ctr., fed. system ctr. IBM, Gaithersberg, Md., 1966—70; mem. rsch. staff IBM Watson Rsch. Ctr., Yorktown Heights, NY, 1970—93. Disting. adj. prof. Poly. U., Bklyn., 1981-99. Contbr. articles on digital switching and artificial intelligence to profl. jours.; patentee in field. With U.S. Army, 1943-46, ETO. Fellow IEEE; mem. Internat. Coun. Computer Communications (gov. emeritus 1988—).

KARNAUSKAS, KRISTOPHER BENSON, research scientist; b. Edina, Minn., July 24, 1982; s. Frank and Vicki Karnauskas; m. Alexis Sarah Johnson, Aug. 20, 1981. BS, U. Wis., Madison, 2004; PhD, U. Md., College Park, 2007. Rsch. asst. NOAA Coop. Inst. Meteorol. Satellite Studies, U. Wis., Madison, 2003—04, Earth Sys. Sci. Interdisciplinary Ctr., U. Md., College Park, 2004—. Vis. scientist NOAA R/V Ka'imimoana, 2006—06. Mentor Adult Role Models Sci., Madison, 2004. Grantee, U. Md., 2004—07; Hilldale Undergraduate Rsch. fellow, 2003—04. Mem.: Am. Geophys. Union, Am. Meteorol. Soc. (mem. chpt. affairs com. 2006—, pres. U. Wis. chpt. 2003—04). Avocation: running.

KARNAZES, DEAN (CONSTANTINE KARNAZES), endurance athlete, writer; b. Aug. 1962; s. Nick and Fran Karnazes; m. Julie Karnazes; 2 children. Grad. in Food Sci. Tech., Calif. Polytechnic State U. Pharmaceutical sales representative; pres., co-founder EnergyWell Natural Foods, San Francisco; sponsored athlete The North Face. Author: Ultramarathon Man: Confessions of an All-Night Runner, 2005 (NY Times Bestseller List, Best of Amazon award, 2005); monthly columnist: Men's Health. Named one of Top 10 Ultimate Athletes, Outside mag. Achievements include ran 350 continuous miles in eighty hours 45 minutes, Oct. 12-15, 2005; ran across Death Valley in 126 degree temperatures; ran a marathon to the South Pole in negative 40 degrees, 2002; ran a 200-mile relay race solo, racing alongside teams of twelve on seven different occassions; swam across the San Francisco Bay; scaled Half Dome in Yosemite; mountain-biked for 24-hours straight; surfed the gigantic waves off the coast of Hawaii; accomplished windsurfer; Ten-time Western States 100-Mile Endurance Run Silver Buckle winner; Badwater Ultramarathon champion, 2004; The North Face Endurance 50 an expedition to run 50 marathons in all 50 states in 50 consecutive days, Sept. 17 to Nov. 5th ending with NYC Marathon followed by a run back across the contiguous US.*

KARNAZES, ELIZABETH MARIE BARNSON, lawyer, photojournalist; d. Paul Knudsen and Elizabeth Cardon Barnson; children: Shayne Peter Andrew, Alexander John Peter, Zachary Thomas Peter. BA, U. S.C., 1975; JD, Pace U., 1979. Bar: N.Y. 1981, Calif. Owner Law Offices of Elizabeth Karnazes, Foster City, Calif., 1985—, Insight Photography, Foster City, 1988—. Photographer Caught!; Sporting News (Best Sports Photos of the Yr., 1990), Yes! (Finalist Maj. League Baseball Photo of the Yr., 1989, Finalist UPI Sports Photo of the Yr., 1989), Karpov Wins! (Chess Journalists of Am. Photo of the Yr., 1998), Body Of Work (Chess Journalists of Am. Photographer of the Yr., 1998); contbr. photographs and articles to books. Calif. state del. U.S. Chess Fedn., Calif., 1998—2000; chmn. U.S. Chess Fedn. Women in Chess, 1998—2000; v.p. Foster City Little League, 1984—86; mem. internat. women's com. Fedn. Internationale des Echecs, Switzerland, 1997—99. Fellow: Redwings Horse Sanctuary (life); mem.: Omicron Delta Kappa (life), Delta Theta Phi (life). Avocations: sailboat racing, service dog training, travel, coaching, snowboarding. Office: Law Offices of Elizabeth Karnazes PO Box 4747 Foster City CA 94404 Office Phone: 650-345-9200.

KARNER, STEPHEN LESLIE, geophysicist; s. Garry David and Lois Gwenda Karner; m. Karen Ann Davies, Jan. 18, 1992. BS, Flinders U. of South Australia, 1986, BS with honors, 1987; MA, CUNY, Flushing, 1993; PhD, MIT, Cambridge, Mass., 1999. Intern Delhi Petroleum Inc., Adelaide, South Australia, Australia, 1986—87; geologist So. Australian Oil and Gas, Adelaide, Australia, 1987—88; geophysicist Wiltshire Geol. Svcs. Inc., Adelaide, South Australia, Australia, 1988—89; tchg. and rsch. asst. Queens Coll., CUNY, Flushing, NY, 1989—93; rsch. asst. Lamont-Doherty Earth Obs. of Columbia U., Palisades, NY, 1993; tchg. and rsch. asst. MIT, Cambridge, 1993—99, post-doctoral rsch. scientist, 1999—2000; post-doctoral rschr., rsch. scientist Tex. A&M U., Coll. Sta., 2000—04, adj. rsch. scientist, 2004—; post-doctoral rsch. scientist Wash. State U., Pullman, 2004—06; geomechanicist, geothermal energy Idaho Nat. Lab., Idaho Falls, 2004—06; geomechanicist Exxon Mobil Upstream Rsch. Co., Houston, 2006. Cons. Quantitative Basin Analysis Inc., Ramsey, NJ, 2004; steering com. Phys. Properties of Earth Materials, 2004—; attendee and spkr. UN Internat. Decade on Natural Disaster Reduction, Beijing, 1997—97. Author: (family history website) Blackadder - The Whole Damn Dynasty, (family history articles) 1804 First Settlers Association Newsletter; contbr. articles to profl. jours. County coord. FreeCen UK Census Project (freecen.rootsweb.com), 2001—04; dancer George Tomov Folkdance Ensemble, NYC, 1981—93; choreographer and dancer Adelaide Traditional Dancers, Adelaide, South Australia, Australia, 1984—89, Jedinstvo Folkdance Ensemble, Adelaide, 1986—89, KUD Biljana Folkdance Ensemble, Adelaide, 1984—86, Queanbeyan Folkdance Ensemble, Queanbeyan, New South Wales, Australia, 1983—83, Canberra Internat. Folkdance Assn., Canberra, Australian Capital Territory, Australia. Fellow David B. Harris Post-Doctoral fellow, Tex. A&M U., Coll. Sta., TX USA, 2003—04; grantee Keith Runcorn Travel award, European Geophys. Soc., 1997, Rsch. grantee, NSF, 2004—05. Mem.: Seismol. Soc. of Am, Am. Geophys. Union, Am. Assn. of Petroleum Geologists, 1804 First Settlers Assn., Borders Family History Soc., Herefordshire Family History Soc. Avocations: folklore, cultural heritage, dance, family history. Office: Exxon Mobil URC-URC N209 PO Box 2189 Houston TX 77252-2189 Home: 3118 Junegrass Ct Humble TX 77345 Office Phone: 713-431-4681. Business E-Mail: stephen.l.karner@exxonmobil.com.

KARNES, JOHN HERBERT, JR., corporate financial executive, lawyer; b. Glasgow, Mont., May 2, 1951; s. John Herbert and Sandra Marlene (Brickman) K. MBA, U. Tex., 1985; JD, So. Meth. U., 1988. Bar: Colo., Tex. Assoc. Kirkland & Ellis, Denver, 1988-91; dep. gen. counsel Appeche Corp., Houston, 1991-94; v.p., gen. counsel Hollywood Casino Corp., Dallas, 1994; various sr. exec. legal and fin. roles Pratt Hotel Corp., AMRE, Pillowtex Corp.; sr. v.p. FirstPlus Fin. Group; v.p., gen. counsel, corp. sec. Snyder Oil Corp, 1998—2000; v.p., gen. counsel CyberCash, 2000, exec. v.p., CFO, 2000; v.p., gen. counsel Encore Acquisition Co., 2002; sr. v.p., CFO Houston Exploration Co., 2002—06; exec. v.p., CFO Maxxam Inc., Houston, 2006—. Office: Maxxam Inc 1330 Post Oak Blvd Ste 2000 Houston TX 77056

KARNI, EDI, economics professor; b. Tel Aviv, Mar. 20, 1944; s. Eliezer and Sara (Vitis) K.; m. Barbara Shapiro, Mar. 16, 1980; children: Anat, Anna. BA in Econs., Hebrew U., 1965, MA in Econs., 1970, U. Chgo., 1970, PhD in Econs., 1971. Asst. prof. Ohio State U., Columbus, 1971-72; fellow Inst. for Advanced Studies/Hebrew U., Jerusalem, Israel, 1976-77; vis. prof. U. Chgo., 1977-79; assoc. prof. Tel Aviv U., 1972-81; prof. econs. Johns Hopkins U., Balt., 1981—. Disting. vis. prof. Vanderbilt U., 1987. Author: Decision Making Under Uncertainty, 1985; contbr. articles to profl. jours. Fellow: Econometric Soc.; mem.: Am. Econ. Assn. Jewish. Home: 6208 Sareva Dr Baltimore MD 21209-3530 Office: Johns Hopkins U Dept Econs Baltimore MD 21218

KARNOVSKY, MORRIS JOHN, pathologist, biologist; b. Johannesburg, June 28, 1926; arrived in U.S., 1955; s. Herman Louis and Florence (Rosenberg) Karnovsky; m. Shirley Esther Katz, Aug. 26, 1952; children: David Mark, Nina Jane. BS, U. Witwatersrand, Johannesburg, 1946, MB, BCh, 1950, DSc, 1984; diploma clin. pathology, U. London, 1954; MA (hon.), Harvard U., 1965. Prof. pathology Harvard U. Med. Sch., Boston, 1968—72, Shattuck prof., 1972—, chmn. program in cell and devel. biology, 1975—90, chmn. pathology dept., 1991—93. Recipient E.B. Wilson award, Am. Soc. Cell Biology. Fellow: Royal Microscopic Soc.; mem.: U.S. and Can. Acad. Pathology (Maude-Abbott award 1994), Am. Soc. for Investigative Pathology (Gold-Headed Cane award 1994), Am. Assn. Pathologists (co-pres. 1978—79, Rous-Whipple award), German Soc. for Cell Biology (hon.), Am. Soc. Cell Biology (pres. 1983—84), Inst. Medicine of NAS. Office: Harvard Med Sch 200 Longwood Ave Boston MA 02115-5701

KARNOW, STANLEY, journalist, writer; b. NYC, Feb. 4, 1925; s. Harry and Henriette (Koeppel) Karnow; m. Claude Sarraute, July 15, 1948 (div. 1955); m. Annette Kline, Apr. 21, 1959; children: Curtis Edward, Catherine Anne, Michael Franklin. BA, Harvard U., 1947; student, U. Paris, France, 1948—49; postgrad., Inst. d'Etudes Politiques, U. Paris, Paris, 1949—50. Corr. Time mag., Paris, 1950—57; bur. chief North Africa Time-Life, 1958—59, Hong Kong, 1959—62; spl. corr. London Observer, 1961—65, Time, Inc., 1962—63; Far East corr. Sat. Eve. Post, 1963—65, Washington Post, 1965—71, diplomatic corr., 1971—72; spl. corr. NBC News, 1973—75; assoc. editor The New Republic, 1973—75; columnist King Features, 1975—88, Le Point, Paris, 1976—83, Newsweek Internat., 1977—81; editor Internat. Writers Service, 1976—86; chief corr. PBS series Vietnam: A TV History, 1983; chief corr., narrator PBS Series The U.S. and the Philippines: In Our Image, 1989. Author: Southeast Asia, 1963, Mao and China: From Revolution to Revolution, 1972, Vietnam: A History, 1983 (Emmy award, 1984, DuPont award, 1984, Polk award, 1984, Peabody award, 1984), In Our Image: America's Empire in the Philippines, 1989 (Pulitzer Prize for history, 1990), Paris in the Fifties, 1997; co-author: Asian Americans in transition, 1992; contbg. author Passage to Vietnam, 1994, Mekong, 1995, Historical Atlas of the Vietnam War, 1995, Past Imperfect: History According to the Movies, 1995. Bd. advisors Vietnam Vets. Meml. Wall. With USAF, 1943—46. Recipient citation, Overseas Press Club, 1966, Ann. award for best newspaper interpretation of fgn. affairs, 1968, Lifetime Achievement award for coverage of Asia, Shorenstein Ctr. for Press and Politics, Harvard and Stanford Univs., 2002; fellow Neiman fellow, Harvard U., 1957—58; Inst. Politics John F. Kennedy Sch. Govt. fellow, East Asian Rsch. Ctr. fellow, 1970—71. Mem.: Soc. Am. Historians, Asia Soc., Coun. Fgn. Rels., PEN Am. Ctr., Signet Soc., Century Assn., Shek-O Club (Hong Kong). Home: 10850 Spring Knoll Dr Potomac MD 20854-1550

KARNS, ELIZABETH (LIBBY) A., retired daycare administrator; b. Lafayette, Ind., Aug. 26, 1946; d. Harris Lester III and Elizabeth Louise Karns. BA in Elem. Edn., Bethel Coll., Mishawaka, Ind., 1970; MS in Elem. Edn., Ind. U., South Bend, 1975, MLS, 1998. Cert. tchr. K-6 Ind. Tchr. day care Calvary Temple, South Bend, Ind., 1991—94, resource dir., 1994—95. Contbr. poetry to internat. libr. anthologies (Editor's Choice award Internat. Libr. Poetry, 1999, 2000, 2001, 2002, 2004, 2007). Pres. resident coun. Innwood Hills Estates, South Bend. Recipient Hon. Mention, Writer's Digest, 1998. Mem.: Uplifters, Calvary Temples Women's Ministries, Worship and Creative Arts Leaders (choir libr. 1994—2004). Republican. Avocations: reading, writing.

KARNSTEDT, DAVID, marketing executive; BA in Comms., U. Ill. V.p., gen. mgr. internet search group AltaVista; dir. western advt. Wired Digital Lycos; sr. v.p., gen. mgr. Yahoo! Search Mktg. (formerly Overture Services Inc.), 2001; head N.Am. sales Yahoo! Inc., 2007—. Co-founder search com. Interactive Advt. Bur., 2001; spkr. in field. Office: Yahoo! Inc 701 First Ave Sunnyvale CA 94089*

KAROL, FREDERICK JOHN, retired industrial chemist; b. Norton, Mass., Feb. 28, 1933; s. John and Valeria (Bzdula) K.; m. Ruth Helen Lindbom, May 31, 1958; children: Mark, Donald, Cynthia. BA, Boston U., 1954; PhD in Chemistry, MIT, 1962. With Union Carbide Corp., Bound Brook, NJ, 1956—, chemist, 1956-59, 62-65, project scientist, 1965-67, rsch. scientist, 1967-72, sr. rsch. scientist, 1972-76, rsch. assoc., 1976-80, corp. fellow, 1980-84, sr. corp. fellow, 1984-2000; ret., 2000. Contbr. numerous articles to profl. jours. With U.S. Army, 1954-56. Recipient Thomas Edison award R&D Coun. N.J., 1982, 99, Excellence in Catalysis award Met. N.Y. Catalysis Soc., 1987, Perkin Medal Soc. Chem. Industry, N.Y., 1989, ACS award for Creative Invention, 1991; named to Nat. Plastics Hall of Fame, 1997. Fellow: Soc. Plastic Engrs. (S.P.E. Conley award 1989, Internat. Gold medal 1990); mem.: Am. Chem. Soc., Nat. Assn. Engrs., Am. Inst. Chemists (Chem. Pioneer award 1988). Achievements include patents for 106 U.S. Home: 157 Skyline Dr Lakewood NJ 08701-5739 E-mail: fkarol@optonline.net.

KAROL, JOHN J., JR., producer, filmmaker; b. Mt. Kisco, NY, Apr. 1, 1935; s. John J. and Ann (Hale) Karol; m. Georgina P. Forbes, Oct. 1963 (div. 1977); children: Angelisse F., Christopher H.; m. Portia L. Fitzhugh, June 21, 1980; 1 child, Fitzhugh B. BA, Williams Coll., 1958; LLB, Yale U., 1962. Assoc. Lord, Day & Lord, NYC, 1962-64; parliamentary draftsman Atty. Gens. Chambers, Zomba, Malawi, 1964-67; dep. commr., gen. counsel State Vt. Dept. Taxes, Montpelier, Vt., 1967-69; prodr., filmmaker Apertura, Orford, NH, 1969—. Prodns. include (films) Brush Dance, 1985, Ben's Mill, 1982 (Acad. award nomination 1982, Golden Eagle award 1982), Main Street, 1979, A Place in Time, 1977 (Golden Eagle award 1977), Settling In, 1974, (video) Photographing with Fred Picker, 1991 (Telly award 1992), Printing with Fred Picker, 1990 (Golden Eagle award 1990, Telly award 1990), Ben's Water Tub, 1990. Dir. Inherit NH, Concord, 1984-90; trustee Upper Valley Land Trust, Norwich, Vt., 1987-90, mem. exec. bd. St. Martin's Ch., Fairlee, Vt., 1976-79, jr. warden, 1978. Mem. Soc. Motion Picture TV Engrs., Century Assn. (NYC), Tavern Club (Boston). Home and Office: Apertura Main St Orford NH 03777 Office Phone: 603-353-9067. Personal E-mail: karol@apertura.org.

KAROL, MICHAEL ALAN, editor; b. New Brunswick, NJ, Mar. 1, 1953; s. Reuben Hirsch and Sylvia (Gross) K. BA in Sociology and Comm., U. Pa., 1975; MS in Comm./TV Broadcasting, Boston U., 1977. Rhythm and blues editor Pop Top Mag. Little Face, Inc., Boston, 1976-78; staff photographer, prodn. editor Nat. Jewel Mag., NYC, 1978-79; assoc. editor Gift and Stationery Bus. Gralla Publs., NYC, 1979; mng. editor Modern Floor Coverings Charleson Pub. Co., NYC, 1979-82; editor-in-chief Floor Covering Bus. Thomson Retail Press, NYC, 1982-89; mng. editor Graphic Arts Monthly Cahners Pub. Co., NYC, 1990-96; copy chief Computer Shopper, Ziff-Davis, Inc., NYC, 1996-98; copy flow mgr. CMP, Inc., NYC, 1998-2000; spl. projects editor CNET Networks, 2001—04; editl. cons. Martha Stewart Living Omnimedia, 2002—03, 2004—; copy chief Soap Opera Weekly, Primedia Inc. Author: Lucy A to Z, 2001, Kiss Me, Kill Me, 2003, Lucy in Print, 2003, The Lucille Ball Quiz Book, 2004, The ABC Movie of the Week Companion, 2005, Sitcom Queens, 2006, Sleeps Well with Others, 2006; copy chief Soap Opera Weekly, 2003—. Recipient Silver awards for graphic excellence Modern Floor Coverings, MFC Mkt. Report, 1981, 84, Regional Design awards for Modern Floor Coverings covers Print Mag., 1985, 88, 65th Ann. Exhbn. Merit award Art Dirs. Club, 1986, Cert. of Distinction in editl. design for Elvis Lives!, Art Direction mag., 1992, Cert. of Merit, Cmty. Action Network, 1992, Bronze Editl. Medal of Excellence for How'd They Print That?, Cahners Pub. Co., 1995. Democrat. Avocations: travel, biking, reading, writing. E-mail: mkarol@nyc.rr.com.

KAROL, NATHANIEL H., lawyer, consultant; b. NYC, Feb. 16, 1929; s. Isidore and Lillian (Orlow) K.; m. Liliane Leser, July 20, 1967; children: David, Jordan. BS in Social Sci, CCNY, 1949; MA (fellow), Yale U., 1950; LL.B., N.Y. U., 1957, LL.M., 1959, JD, 1966. Bar: N.Y. 1957. Mgmt. trainee Curtiss Wright Corp., Wood-Ridge, NJ, 1956-57; practiced in NYC, 1957-58; contracting officer USAF, NYC, 1958-62; chief contract mgmt. survey and cost adminstrn. Office of Procurement, NASA, Washington, 1962-64; asst. dir. cost reduction, 1964-66; dep. asst. sec. Grants Adminstrn., HEW, Washington, 1966-69; univ. dean CUNY; exec. dir. Research Found., 1969-73; v.p. Hebrew Union Coll., Cin., 1973-75; partner, nat. chmn. cons. services for edn. Coopers & Lybrand (C.P.A.s), Chgo., 1975-81; pres. Nathaniel H. Karol & Assocs. Ltd., 1981—. Cons. to govt. agys. and ednl. instns. Author: Managing the Higher Education Enterprise. Served with U.S. Army, 1953-56. Recipient Outstanding Performance award HEW, 1968, Superior Performance award, 1969 Mem. N.Y. Bar, Nat. Assn. Coll. and Univ. Bus. Officers, Nat. Assn. Coll. and Univ. Attys. Home and Office: 1228 Cambridge Ct Highland Park IL 60035-1014 *What one is, is as important as what one does. I regard as successful the man who is able to establish a set of values and to observe them consistently. If there is a single thing for which I would wish to be remembered, it is that I was a man whose word was his bond.*

KARON, SHELDON, lawyer; b. Superior, Wis., Mar. 1, 1930; s. Bert and Betty Karon; m. Lee Goldwasser, Aug. 6, 1950; children: Maureen Byron, Laurie Feig, Peggy Pattis. BS, Northwestern U., 1952; JD, Harvard U., 1955. Bar: Ill. 1955. Assoc. Jenner & Block, Chgo., 1955-61; ptnr. Friedman & Koven, Chgo., 1962-75; ptnr., chmn. Karon, Morrison & Savikas, Chgo., 1975-88, Keck, Mahin & Cate, Chgo., 1988-97; of counsel Foley & Lardner, Chgo., 1997—. Arbitrator CPR Inst. Dispute Resolution, N.Y.C.; mem. Ill. Supreme Ct. Commn. for Jud. Reform, 1993-95. Bd. dirs. Kohl CHildren's Mus., Wilmette, Ill., 1988—, Highland Park (Ill.) Cmty. Edn., 1995—. Fellow Am. Coll. Trial Lawyers; mem. ABA, Ill. State Bar Assn., Chgo. Bar Assn., Fed. Cir. Bar Assn., Am. Arbitration Assn. (chair large complex case panel), Law Club, Legal Club. E-mail: skaron@foley.com.

KAROTKIN, ROSE A., marketing professional; d. Robert Edwin and Evelyn Rose (Carver) MacInnis; m. Mark Maynard Karotkin, Sr., Aug. 23, 2002; children: Mark Maynard Karotkin, Jr., Matthew Richard Lewis, Lisa Marie. BS in Bus. Mgmt. (hon.), Albertus Magnus Coll., New Haven, Conn., 2005. Mixology and bar mgmt. Boston Bartenders Sch., 2001. Mktg. Yankee Gas Services Co., Berlin, Conn., 2002—04; cons. Expressions by Rose, West Hartford, Conn., 2001—; mktg. coord. Phoenix Home Life, Hartford, 1997—2001; asst. to the dir. The Donaghue Found., Hartford, 1995—97; pres. M&R Auto Transport, 2004. Promotional assistance and hon. crew mem. for 2001 season Amistad Am., Mystic, Conn., 1999—2001; mktg. asst. Women's Am. Basketball League, Hartford, 1998—99. Co-author (environmental) R. Karotkin, K. Rook, S. Toelle (2002). Natural Gas Vehicle Marketing Plan 2002-2006. Yankee Gas Services Company, a Northeast Utilities System. Approved by the Connecticut Department of Utility Control August 8, 2002; contbr. criminology. Adv. Interval Ho., Hartford, 1998—2003; little league baseball coach Town of West Hartford, 1996—98; musician, singer, drama team Faith Living Ch., Plantsville, Conn.; co-chair representing Conn. Nat. Rep. Bus. Adv. Coun., Washington, 2003—04; sec., web designer Spl. Friends Charities, Inc., East Hartford, 2002—. Named Businesswoman of Yr., Nat. Rep. Congl. Committee's Bus. Adv. Coun., 2003; recipient Nat. Leadership award, Nat. Rep. Congl. Com., 2003. Mem.: Am. Assn. of Home-Based Bus. (assoc.), Nat. Assn. for the Self-Employed (assoc.), NAFE (assoc.), Am. Mktg. Assn. (assoc.), Kappa Gamma Pi. Independent. Avocations: riding, hiking, travel, volleyball. Office: Direct Energy 101 Barnes Rd Ste 301 Wallingford CT 06492 Office Phone: 203-284-3917. Personal E-mail: karotkin@comcast.net. Business E-Mail: rose.karotkin@directenergy.com.

KARP, BRAD S., lawyer; b. NYC, July 25, 1959; s. Marvin and Sondra (Fieldman) Karp; m. Roberta Schuhalter, Aug. 12, 1984; children: Meredith Dawn, David Matthew. BA summa cum laude, Union Coll., 1981; JD cum laude, Harvard U., 1984. Bar: NY 1986, U.S. Dist. Ct. (so. and ea. dist.), NY 1987, Fed. Cir. Ct. Appeals 1987, U.S. Claims Ct. 1988, U.S. Ct. Appeals (2d cir.) 1991. Law clk. to Hon. Irving R. Kaufman U.S. Ct. Appeals, 2d Cir., 1984—85; ptnr., chmn., litig. dept., co-chmn. securities litig., enforcement practice, mem. mgmt. com. Paul, Weiss, Rifkind, Wharton & Garrison LLP, 1985—. Bd. dir. Riverdale Country Sch., Practicing Attys. Law Students Program, Inc., Legal Action Ctr., NY Regional Am. Friends Hebrew U.; mem. program adv. bd. Brennan Ctr. Justice. Author: (monthly column) NY Law Jour., 1985—. Named one of 45 Under Forty-Five Leading Lawyers in U.S., Am. Lawyer Mag., 2003. Fellow: NY Bar Found.; mem.: ABA, Assn. Bar City of NY, Phi Beta Kappa. Office: Paul Weiss Rifkind Wharton & Garrison LLP 1285 Ave of the Americas New York NY 10019-6064 Office Phone: 212-373-3316. Office Fax: 212-492-0316. Business E-Mail: bkarp@paulweiss.com.

KARP, CAROL, ophthalmologist, educator; BA in Biol. Scis. magna cum laude, Brown U., Providence, RI, 1986, MD, 1989. Diplomate Am. Bd. Ophthalmology, 1995. Intern in transitional medicine St. Joseph Mercy Hosp., Ann Arbor, Mich., 1989—90; intern Kellogg Eye Ctr., U. Mich., Ann Arbor, Mich., 1990—93; resident Bascom Palmer Eye Inst., Miami, Fla., 1993—94, assoc. prof. clin. ophthalmology, 1994—. Mem.: Am. Acad. Ophthalmology (Achievement award 2004). Office: Bascom Palmer Eye Inst 900 NW 17th St Miami FL 33136 Office Phone: 305-326-6156.

KARP, DAVID BARRY, lawyer; b. Milw., Dec. 12, 1955; s. Joseph and Sally P. (Nashinsky) K.; m. Donna L. Boorse, Apr. 8, 1984. BA, U. Wis., Milw., 1977; postgrad., Am. U., 1978; JD, Marquette U., 1982. Bar: Wis. 1982, U.S. Dist. Ct. (we. and ea. dist.) Wis. 1982, U.S. Cir. Ct. (7th cir.) 1982. Assoc. Karp Law Offices, S.C., Milw., 1990—. Fellow Am. Acad. Matrimonial Lawyers; mem. ABA, ATLA, Wis. Assn. Trial Lawyers, Wis. State Bar, Inns of Ct., Soc. Family Lawyers. Avocations: golf, running, music. Office: 933 N Manfair Rd Ste 300 Milwaukee WI 53226 Office Phone: 414-453-0800. Business E-Mail: dbk@karplawfirm.com.

KARP, DAVID C., lawyer; b. Bklyn., July 12, 1968; AB magna cum laude, Harvard U., 1990; JD with honors, U. Chgo., 1993. Bar: NY 1994. Law clk. to Hon. J. Daniel Mahoney US Ct. Appeals (2nd cir.), 1993—94; corp. ptnr. Wachtell, Lipton, Rosen & Katz, NYC. Advisor Spl. Com. on Market Structure, Governance and Ownership NY Stock Exchange, spl. counsel Corp. Accountability and Listings Standards Com. Named a Dealmaker of the Yr., Am. Lawyer Mag., 2006. Mem.: ABA (vice chair Internat. Securities Transactions Com. 2002—03), NY State Bar Assn., Assn. of Bar of City of NY. Office: Wachtell, Lipton, Rosen & Katz 51 W 52nd St New York NY 10019-6150 Office Phone: 212-403-1327. Office Fax: 212-403-2327. E-mail: DCKarp@wlrk.com.

KARP, DIANE R., art educator; b. 1948; PhD in Art Hist., U. Pa. Prof. 20th century art hist. Temple U.; curator-Ars Medica Phil. Mus. Art; dir. New Observations Mag., Santa Fe Art Inst., 2001—. Exhibitions include with Dan Fox In Time of Plague, Am. Mus. Nat. Hist., N.Y., exhibitions include Art, Med. & the Human Condition, Phila. Mus. Art, 1985; author: (exhibition catalogue) Ars Medica, 1985. Office: Santa Fe Art Institute 1600 St Michaels Dr Santa Fe NM 87505 E-mail: dkarp@sfai.org.

KARP, DONALD MATHEW, lawyer, banker; b. Newark, Jan. 15, 1937; s. Michael N. and Beatrice (Laufer) K.; m. Margery Paula Lesnik, June 28, 1962; children: Jonathan David, Kathryn Jill. BA, U. Vt., 1958; JD, Cornell U., 1961. Bar: N.J. 1961, N.Y. 1981. With Broad Nat. Bank and Broad Nat. Bancorp., Newark, chmn. bd., 1985—, CEO, 1991; regional counsel SBA, N.J., 1966; atty., divisional bd. of N.Y., Sovereign Bank, Newark. Vice chmn., dir. Independence Cmty. Bank, 1999; mem. divisional bd. N.Y., Sovereign Bank. Mem. coun. trustees NJ Performing Arts Ctr.; mem. adv. com. Greater Newark Conservancy; bd. dirs. Ind. Cmty. Found., Newark Hist. Soc., Friends of Newark Pub Libr., Newark Preservation and Landmarks Commn., Local Initiatives Support Corp., Newark Mus.; mem. adv. bd. NJ Coll. Medicine and Dentistry; bd. dirs. Friends of Thirteen, Inc. Recipient CEO of the Yr. Bronze award Fin. World mag., 1994, Businessman of the Yr. award City of Newark, 1999; named City News 100 Most Influential, Newark, Rotary Club Person of the Yr., St. Philip's Acad. Role Model, 1998. Mem. ABA, N.J. Bar Assn., N.Y. State Bar Assn., Fed. Bar Assn., Assn. Bar City of N.Y., Essex County Bar Assn. Clubs: Mountain Ridge Country (West Caldwell). Office: Independence Community Bank 905 Broad St Ste 2 Newark NJ 07102-2695 Home Phone: 973-643-1800; Office Phone: 973-483-4500. Personal E-mail: dkarp95667@aol.com.

KARP, GERALD CHARLES, biologist, educator, writer; b. LA, Dec. 24, 1942; s. Harry and Sally Karp; m. Patrice Marie Patrick, Nov. 21, 1973; 1 child, Jennifer. BS, UCLA, 1964; PhD, U. Wash., 1970. Postdoctoral rschr. U. Colo. Med. Ctr., Denver, 1970—71; prof. biology U. Fla., Gainesville, 1971—84; vis. scientist U. Iowa, Iowa City, 1984, U. Calif., San Francisco, 1988—89; freelance writer Cin., 1990—. Ad hoc com. med. grants rsch. NIH, Bethesda, Md., 1976; cons. Morrison and Foerster, San Francicso, 1988, Wiley and Sons Publs., NYC, 1990— Author: Development, 1976, 2d edit., 1981, Cell Biology, 1979, 2d edit., 1984, Cell and Molecular Biology, 1996, 5th edit., 2007. Predoctoral fellow NSF, 1964-69, Postdoctoral fellow NIH, 1970-71. Mem. AAAS, Phi Beta Kappa. Personal E-mail: gkarpcell4@netscape.com.

KARP, HARVEY LAWRENCE, metal products executive; b. NYC, Nov. 26, 1927; s. Harry and Sadie (Zimmerman) K.; children: David, Nicholas. BA, Coll. City N.Y., 1949; LLB, Yale U., 1952. Bar: N.Y. 1952, Calif. 1954. Lawyer Chesapeake Industries, Inc., NYC, 1952-54; gen. counsel, v.p. Houston Fearless Corp., Los Angeles, 1955-60; founder, vice-chmn. bd. dirs., pres. Monogram Industries, NYC, 1960-83; chmn. bd. Mueller Industries, Inc., 1991—. With USNR, 1945. Mem.: Bel Air Country Club, Atlantic Golf Club. Home: PO Box 30 East Hampton NY 11937-0030 Home Phone: 631-324-2144; Office Phone: 631-324-2144. E-mail: harvey@karp.com.

KARP, HERBERT RUBIN, neurologist, educator; b. Atlanta, Apr. 13, 1921; s. Louis and Sadie (Fischer) K.; m. Hazel Berman, June 16, 1948; children: Eleanor Beth, Miriam Sarah, Benjamin Chaim. BA, Emory U., Atlanta, 1943, MD, 1951. Diplomate Am. Bd. Psychiatry and Neurology. Intern then resident in internal medicine Grady Meml. Hosp., 1951-54; resident in neurology Duke U. Med. Ctr., 1954-56; clin. and rsch. fellow in neurology and neuropathology Harvard U.-Mass. Gen. Hosp., 1956-58; asst. prof. neurology Emory U., Atlanta, 1958-63, prof., 1963-91, prof. emeritus, 1991—, disting. emeritus prof., 2006—, prof. medicine, 1983-91, chmn. dept. neurology, 1974-83, dir. geriat. program dept. medicine, 1983-90; dir. med. svcs. Wesley Woods Geriatric Ctr., 1983-91, med. dir. emeritus, 1991—. Med. dir. medicare svcs. Ga. Med. Care Found.; med. dir. for Medicare quality improvement, 2005—; trustee Atlanta Symphony Orch., 1975-95, bd. counselors 1996—, sec., 1979-80; pres. Ahavath Achim Synagogue, 1980-82; trustee Nat. Found. Jewish Culture, 1976-84, mem. bd. overseers, 1984-90. With USNR, 1943—46, with U.S. Public Health Svc. Reserve, 1946—. Recipient Thomas Jefferson award Emory U., 1984, Outstanding Med. Alumnus award, 1986, Disting. Med. Achievement award, 2001; Eternal Light award Jewish Theol. Sem. Am., 1985, Civic Endeavor award Med. Assn. Ga., 1989, Myrtle Wreath award Hadassah, 1990, Wakeman award Duke U., 1990; spl. fellow Nat. Inst. Neurol. Diseases, 1956-58; Herbert R. Karp Leadership award established in his name Dept. of Neurology, Emory U., 1999. Fellow Am. Acad. Neurology; mem. Am. Neurol. Assn. (mem. coun.), Assn. Univ. Profs. Neurology, Atlanta Interfaith Broadcasters (bd. dirs. 1991—, sec. 1997-2005, chair 2005—), Alpha Omega Alpha. Democrat. Jewish. Home: 880 Somerset Dr NW Atlanta GA 30327-3732 Office: Ga Med Care Found 1455 Lincoln Pkwy E Ste 800 Atlanta GA 30346 Office Phone: 678-527-3428. Personal E-mail: hkarp02@emory.edu. Business E-Mail: hkarp@gmcf.org.

KARP, JEFF, construction executive; BS in Civil Engring., Roosevelt U., Ill., 1979, MBA, 1984. Project engr. Del E. Webb Corp., Chgo., 1979—84, mgr. ops., 1984; project mgr. Power Constrn. Co., Schaumburg, Ill., 1986, sr. project mgr., v.p., exec. v.p., pres., COO, 2004—. Mem. adv. coun. Am. Subcontractors Assn.; mem. Fails Mgmt. Inst. Contracting Peer Group. Mem. bd. overseers Civil Engring. Dept. and Stuart Sch. Bus. Ill. Inst. Tech.; mem. coun. regents Loyola U. Chgo. Office: Power Constrn Co 2360 Palmer Dr Schaumburg IL 60173-3819 Office Phone: 847-925-1300.*

KARP, JONATHAN D., biology professor; s. Bernard and Charlotte Karp; m. Judy Karp, May 30, 1992. PhD, Vanderbilt U., Nashville, 1991. Biology prof. Rider U., Lawrenceville, NJ, 1997—. Co-author: The PhD Process: A Students Guide to Graduate School in the Sciences. Mem.: AAAS. Achievements include research in neural-immune interactions. Office: Rider University 2083 Lawrenceville Rd Lawrenceville NJ 08648 Home Phone: 609-466-3383; Office Phone: 609-895-5658. Business E-Mail: jkarp@rider.edu.

KARP, MARTIN EVERETT, management consultant; b. NYC, Apr. 30, 1922; s. Albert and Bessie (Ornstein) K.; m. Naomi Joslyn Kaplan, Mar. 14, 1948; children: Betsy, Leslie Karp Goldenberg, Jonathan. B.M.E., CCNY, 1942; student, Harvard U., 1944, MIT, 1945, Northeastern U., 1951-52. Lab. engr. Gen. Electric Co., Lynn, Mass., 1942-44; mgr. research and devel. Nat. Pneumatic Co., Boston, 1946-52; dir. product planning, engring. Remington Office Machine div. Sperry Rand Co., 1953-66, dir. mfg., 1966-68; staff asst. to office of pres. ITT, 1968-69, v.p., group gen. mgr., 1969-82, group exec., 1977-82, dir. product and mktg. strategy, 1980-82; mgmt. cons. Adj. prof. Stevens Inst. Grad. Sch. Mgmt., 1984—87. Contbr. articles to tech. jours.; patentee control systems. Dir. Coun. N.Y. Coops. Served as lt. (j.g.) USNR, 1944-46. Mem. ASME, Tau Beta Pi. Jewish (pres. congregation 1961-63). Home and Office: 250 E 87th St New York NY 10128-3115 Business E-Mail: nitram1@ix.netcom.com.

KARP, MARVIN LOUIS, lawyer; b. Milo, Maine, June 12, 1934; s. Harry and Rose Helen (Kiersh) K.; m. Lesley M. Ulevitch, Aug. 11, 1963; children: Harlan, Elissa, Douglas. BA, Yale Coll., 1955, JD, 1958. Bar: Ohio 1958, U.S. Dist. Ct. (no. dist.) Ohio 1960, U.S. Ct. Appeals (6th cir.) 1963, U.S. Supreme Ct. 1974. Ptnr. Ulmer & Berne, Cleve., 1958—, head litig. dept., 1968—. Pres. Park Synagogue. Fellow Internat. Acad. Trial Lawyers, Am. Coll. Trial Lawyers; mem. ABA (chmn. torts and ins. practice sects., chmn. standing com. on ethics), Cleve. Bar Assn. (trustee 1981-84, pres. 1988-89, Professionalism award 2001), Fedn. Ins. and Corp. Counsel (pres.), Am. Judicature Soc., Def. Rsch. Inst. Home: 3180 Lander Rd Cleveland OH 44124 also: 1660 W 2nd St Cleveland OH 44113-1454 Home Phone: 216-831-1244; Office Phone: 216-583-7014. Business E-Mail: mkarp@ulmer.com.

KARP, NOLAN S., plastic surgeon; b. NYC; BS, Northwestern U., Evanston, Ill., 1979; MD, Northwestern U., 1983. Lic. physician N.Y., diplomate Am. Bd. Surgery, Am. Bd. Plastic Surgery. Resident in gen. surgery NYU Med. Ctr., 1983—88; resident in plastic surgery Inst. Reconstructive Plastic Surgery, NYU Med. Ctr., 1989—91, exec. chief resident, 1990—91, fellow in microsurgery, 1991—92, craniofacial rsch. fellow, 1988—89; asst. prof. plastic surgery NYU Sch. Medicine, 1992—99, assoc. prof. clin. plastic surgery, 1999—; attending physician Tisch Hosp., 1992—, N.Y. VA Hosp., NYC, 1992—; asst. attending physician Bellevue Hosp. Ctr., NYC, 1992—; attending physician Manhattan Eye, Ear, Throat Hosp., NYC, 1992—. Contbr. articles to profl. jours. Recipient Award for best clin. paper, Am. Soc. Maxilofacial Surgery, 1990, 1st place for outstanding paper, N.Y. Acad. Medicine, 1990. Mem.: Am. Soc. Breast Disease, Tissue Engring. Soc., Am. Soc. for Laser Medicine and Surgery, Am. Soc. Plastic and Reconstructive Surgery, Plastic Surgery Rsch. Coun., N.Y. County Med. Soc., Med. Soc. State N.Y. Office: New York Univ Med Ctr 530 First Ave Ste 8Y New York NY 10016

KARP, PETER SIMON, marketing executive; b. New City, NY, Dec. 9, 1935; s. Joseph Bernard and Esther (Wexler) K.; m. Mona Leea Pecheux; children: Matthew Henry, Mark Andrew. BA, Hobart Coll., 1954; MFA, Columbia U., 1957. Rschr. Bur. Advt., Am. Newspaper Pubs. Assn., NYC, 1954-56; media dir. Smith, Hagl & Knudsen, Inc., NYC, 1957-59; media and rsch. dir. CAG Advt., Inc., NYC, 1960-62; exec. v.p. Bennett-Chaiken, Inc., NYC, 1963-66; founder, CEO BSI Global Rsch. Inc., NYC, 1967—; mng. dir. The Concept Testing Inst., NYC, 1972—; chairperson, CEO Pimi. Inc., NYC, 1986—. Dir. Office of the Future Panel, NYC, 1976—; co-dir. The Genesis Group, NYC, 1983—; Trendsetter Barometer and Global Mgmt. Barometer, Pricewaterhouse Cooper, 1991—. Co-author: Customer Satisfaction: How to Maximize, Measure and Market your Company's Ultimate Product, 1989, Competing on Value, 1991; creator BSI Tech. Value Assessments, 1989-90; editor BSI Newsletter, 1976—. Pollster Ken Keating Campaign, State of New York, 1964; vol. Grand Cen. YMCA, NYC, 1964-82. Fellow Inst. Dirs. (London); mem. Am. Mktg. Assn., Advt. Rsch. Found., Artificial Intelligence Assn., NY Acad. Scis., Palisades Tennis Club. Jewish. Avocations: art, sculpture, travel, music. Home: 159 Tweed Blvd Nyack NY 10960-4913 Office Phone: 845-359-8200. E-mail: psk@bsiglobal.com.

KARP, RICHARD M., advertising and communications executive; b. NYC, Aug. 17, 1929; s. Harry and Jo Golden (Bosk) K.; m. Jane Hausman, Nov. 26, 1978; 1 son, David. BS, BA, N.Y. U., 1950; postgrad., Boston U. Publicist 20th Century Fox Film Corp., 1954-56; sr. writer Donahue & Coe Advt., NYC, 1956-58; asso. creative dir., account supr. Reach, McClinton Advt., NYC, 1958-63; exec. v.p., creative dir. Grey Advt. Inc., NYC, 1963-93, ret., 1993—; v.p. Karp Devel. Co., 1993—; guest lectr. Baruch U., 1977-79; chmn. bd. L.A. Weekly, 1993-95. Author: monograph The Films of Buster Keaton, 1949. Mem. coun. of trustees Am. Friends of the Hebrew U., 1998; bd. dirs. Israel Cancer Assn. With AUS, 1950-51, USAF, 1951-54. Recipient Clio award, Internat. Advt. award, Screen Advt. award, Copywriters Club award. Mem. Brit. Inst. Practitioners in Advt. Office: 44 Cocoanut Row Ste 118B Palm Beach FL 33480-4069 Home Phone: 561-832-7525. Personal E-mail: Janekarp1@juno.com.

KARP, RICHARD MANNING, computer science educator; b. Boston, Jan. 3, 1935; s. Abraham Louis and Rose (Nanes) Karp; m. Diana Leigh Grand; 1 child, Jeremy Alexander. AB, Harvard U., 1955, SM, 1956, PhD in Applied Math., 1959; DSc (hon.), U. Pa., 1986, Technion, 1989, U. Mass., 1990, Georgetown U., 1992, U. Ctrl. Fla., 2000. Rsch. staff mem. IBM Watson Rsch. Ctr., Yorktown Heights, NY, 1959—68; visiting assoc. prof. elec. engring. U. Mich., Ann Arbor, 1964—65; prof. computer sci., indsl. engring., ops. rsch. U. Calif., Berkeley, 1968—96, assoc. chmn. elec. engring., computer sci., 1973—75, prof. math., 1980—95; co-chmn. program in computational complexity Math. Sci. Rsch. Inst., Berkeley, 1985—86; rsch. scientist Internat. Computer Sci. Inst., Berkeley, 1988—96; prof. computer sci. U. Wash., Seattle, 1995—99, adj. prof. molecular biotech., 1996—2000; univ. prof. U. Calif., Berkeley, 1999—; Hewlett-Packard vis. prof. Math Sci. Rsch. Inst., Berkeley, 1999—2000. Bd. govs. Weizmann Inst. Soc.; adv. bd. Computer Profns. for Social Responsibility; faculty rsch. lectr., Berkeley, 1981—82; Miller rsch. prof., Berkeley, 1980—81. Contbr. articles to profl. jours. Recipient Fulkerson prize in Discrete Math., Am. Math. Soc., 1979, Lanchester prize in Ops. Rsch., Inst. for Ops. Rsch. and the Mgmt. Sciences, 1977, ORSA/TIS von Neumann Theory prize, 1990, Babbage prize, 1995, Nat. medal of Sci. award, NSF, 1996, Harvey prize, 1998, Benjamin Franklin medal in Computer and Cognitive Sci., Franklin Inst., 2004; fellow Einstein, Technion, 1983, Lady Davis, 1983. Fellow: Assn. Computing Machinery (Turing award 1985), AAAS, Am. Acad. Arts and Scis.; mem.: NAS, NAE, Am. Philos. Soc., Inst. Combinatorics and Applications. Office: U Calif Computer Sci Divsn 387 Soda Hall # 1776 Berkeley CA 94720 E-mail: karp@icsi.berkeley.edu.

KARP, ROBERTA SCHUHALTER, retail executive, lawyer; b. Livingston, NY, 1958; m. Brad Karp; children: Meredith, David. BA in environ. studies, SUNY, Binghamton; JD, Hofstra U., 1983. Bar: NY 1984. Atty. Kramer, Levin, Naftalis & Frankel, NYC, 1983—86; from legal counsel to v.p., gen. coun. Liz Claiborne Inc., NYC, 1986—96, v.p. corp affairs, gen. counsel, 1996—2000, sr. v.p. corp. affairs, gen. coun., 2000—. Co-chair White House Apparel Industry Partnership, 1996—99; bd. dirs. Bus. for Social Responsibility, Volunteers of Legal Svc., NY. David Rockefeller Fellow, 2000—01. Office: Liz Claiborne Inc 1441 Broadway New York NY 10018 Office Phone: 201-295-7830.*

KARP, ROSANNE, oncology and women's health nurse; b. Lynn, Mass., Oct. 8, 1946; d. Max and Dorothy (Cohen) Sidman; children: Stacy, Matthew. ADN, Northeastern U., 1967; postgrad., Lesley Coll., 1990—2002. RN, Mass. Staff nurse Holy Family Hosp., Methuen, Mass., 1969-90; staff nurse Mass. Gen. Hosp., Boston, 1990-96, case mgr. gynecology/oncology svc., 1996—. Chair, prof. edn. Greater Lawrence unit Am. Cancer Soc., bd. dirs. Mass. div., 1990-92. Recipient Excellence in Med./Surg. Nursing award Merrimack Valley Area Health Edn. Ctr., 1988, Award for Disting. Vol. Leadership Greater Lawrence unit ACS, 1995, nat. leadership award Hadassah, 1997, Ptnrs. award Ptnrs. Healthcare Sys., Inc., 1999, Jeanette Ives Erickson award for Invaluable Contbns. to Resident Life and Tchg. Vincent Meml. Ob-Gyn. Svc., 2005.

KARP, STEPHEN R., real estate developer; m. Jill Karp; children: Douglass, Jana. Student in Pre-Med, Johns Hopkins U.; BA in Polit. Sci., Boston U., 1963. With Thomas Diab & Co., 1963; dir. devel. State Properties; founder, chmn., CEO New Eng. Devel., Newton, Mass., 1978—. Bd. trustees Children's Hosp. Boston, 2004—, Belmont HS, Union Coll.; bd. overseers Newton-Wellesley Hosp. Named one of 400 Richest Ams., Forbes mag., 2006. Mem.: Internat. Coun. Shopping Ctrs. (past chmn., mem. bd. dirs.), Urban Land Inst., Greater Boston Real Estate Bd., Belmont Country Club. Achievements include development of the first enclosed mall in the Northeast, 1972. Avocations: golf, skiing. Office: New Eng Devel 1 Wells Ave Newton MA 02459-3226 Office Phone: 617-965-8700. Office Fax: 617-243-7085.

KARP, STEVE, agent; b. Mt. Vernon, NY, Apr. 5, 1943; s. Mortimer Lester and Pearl Marion (Radding) K. BA, Tufts U., 1965; postgrad., Boston U., 1965-66, Am. Acad. Dramatic Arts, 1968. Actor Light Opera Manhattan, NYC, 1969-70, Am. Shakespeare Festival, Stratford, Conn., 1972, Long Wharf Theatre, New Haven, Conn., 1972-74, N.Y. Shakespeare Festival, NYC, 1974-75; founder, pres. Perk Prodns. Ltd., NYC, 1974-88; artistic dir. Maxwell Anderson Playwrights Series, Stamford, Conn., 1986-87; founder, producing dir. Stamford Theatre Works, 1988—. Tchr. playwriting Westport (Conn.) Playhouse Theatre Sch., 1986-87; tchr. screenwriting Fairfield (Conn.) U., 1986-87; cons. Perk Prodns. Ltd., N.Y.C., 1988—. Appeared in Broadway plays The Changing Room, 1973, Hertzl, 1975-76; writer, dir., prodr. (dramatic short films) The Tennis Lesson, 1976 (Silver medallion V.I. Film Festival 1976-77, Achievement award Am. Film Festival 1976-77, Achievement award Chgo. Film Festival 1976-77), Inside The Jogger, 1977 (Nat. Film Collection Libr. Congress 1979, Gold medallion V.I. Film Festival 1977-78, Excellent Achievement award Melbourne Film Festival 1977-78), The Tennis Match, 1978 (Nat. Film Collection Libr. Congress 1979, Achievement award Am. Film Festival 1978); playwright, dir. The Warehouse, 1991, Fraternity, 2005. Recipient Best Dir. Theatre award Conn. Critics Cir., 1991-92, Outstanding Contribution to Conn. Theatre award, 1996-97; Film Prodn. grantee Am. Film Inst.-Nat. Endowment, 1976. Avocations: jogging, tennis. Office: Stamford Theatre Works 95 Atlantic St Stamford CT 06901-2403 Home Phone: 212-724-6645; Office Phone: 203-359-4414. Personal E-mail: stevekarp@aol.com.

KARPEL, CRAIG S., journalist, editor; b. Midland, Tex., 1944; married. AB, Columbia U., 1965. Contbg. editor Harper's mag., NYC, 1985-92. Author: The Rite of Exorcism, 1974, The Retirement Myth, 1995; contbr. numerous articles to mags. and newspapers, U.S., S.Am., Europe, Africa, Asia. Office: c/o Don Congdon Assocs 156 5th Ave Ste 625 New York NY 10010-7002 Personal E-mail: craig.s.karpel@gmail.com.

KARPELES, DAVID, museum director; b. Santa Barbara, Calif., Jan. 26, 1936; s. Leon and Betty (Friedman) Karpeles; m. Marsha Mirsky, June 29, 1958; children: Mark, Leslie, Cheryl, Jason. BS, U. Minn., 1956, postgrad., 1956-59; MA, San Diego State U., 1962; postgrad., U. Calif., Santa Barbara, 1965-69; PhD, Atlantic Internat. U., 2003. Founder Karpeles Manuscript Libr. Mus., Montecito, Calif., 1983—, dir., founder Santa Barbara, Calif., 1988—, NYC, 1990—, Tacoma, 1991—, Jacksonville, Fla., 1992—, Duluth, Minn., 1993—, Charleston, SC, 1995—, Buffalo, 1995—, Newburgh, NY, 1999—, Shreveport, 2004—. Dir. 202 mini-museums throughout U.S. and Can.; established the 1st cultural literacy program, presented to schs. by respective mus. staffs, 1993—; tchg. fellow Buffalo State U., 2001—. Creator program to provide ownership of homes to low-income families, 1981. Named commencement spkr. to graduating class, U. Minn., 1996, hon. inductee, Acad. Sci. and Engring., U. Minn., 2002; recipient Affordable Housing Competition award, Gov. Edmund G. Brown Jr., State of Calif. Dept. Housing and Cmty. Devel., 1981, Disting. Alumni award, U. Minn., 1996. Jewish. Home: 465 Hot Springs Rd Santa Barbara CA 93108-2029 E-mail: kmuseumsb@aol.com.

KARPINSKI, HUBERTA, library trustee; b. Cato, NY, Jan. 4, 1925; d. Alfred Raymond and Lena Margaret (Fuller) Tuxill; m. Edward Karpinski, Nov. 17, 1956; children: Susan Tanielian, Rebecca Hitch, Amy Jaward. Student, U. Mich., Ann Arbor, 1943—45, Wayne U., Detroit, 1949—50; grad., NY Art Acad. Design, Detroit, 1972. Operator to svc. observer supr. Mich. Bell Telephone Co., Detroit, 1946—57; tchr. art Birmingham (Mich.) Pub. Sch., 1977—87; libr. trustee Redford (Mich.) Twp. Dist. Libr., 1971—. Chmn. Lola Valley Civic Assn., Redford, 1960-70; vice chmn. Redford Twp. Coun. Civic Assn., 1967-71; bd. dirs. 17th Dist. Mich. Dem. Party, Redford, 1968-71. Mem. Nat. Mus. Women in arts (charter), Mich. Porcelain Artists, Internat. Porcelain Art Tchrs. Avocation: painting. Home: 17418 Macarthur Redford MI 48240-2241

KARPLUS, PAUL ANDREW, biochemistry educator; b. Oakland, Calif., Sept. 25, 1957; s. Robert and Elizabeth Jane (Frazier) K.; m. Karen Elisabeth Andersen, July 26, 1980; children: Elisabeth Marie, Christina Jane, Timothy Robert. Student, U. Calif., Berkeley, 1974-76; BS in Biochemistry with highest honors, U. Calif., Davis, 1978. Postdoctoral rsch. assoc. Inst. Organic Chemistry and Biochemistry, U. Freiburg, Federal Republic of Germany, 1984-88; asst. prof. biochemistry, molecular and cell biology Cornell U., Ithaca, NY, 1988-93; assoc. prof. biochemistry, molecular and cell biology, 1993-98. Assoc. prof. dept. biochemistry and biophysics Oreg. State U., Corvallis, 1998-99, prof., 1999—. Recipient Nat. Rsch. Svc. award NIH-NIGMS, 1979, Pfizer award in enzyme chemistry Am. Chem. Soc., 1996, Milton Harris award for basic rsch., 2001; Alexander von Humboldt fellow, 1984-85, 90, Guggenheim fellow, 1996-97. Mem. Phi Kappa Phi. Home Phone: 541-758-6567; Office Phone: 541-737-3200. E-mail: karplusp@science.oregonstate.edu.

KARPMAN, HAROLD LEW, cardiologist, educator, writer; b. Belvedere, Calif., Aug. 23, 1927; s. Samuel and Dora (Kastleman) K.; m. Molinda Karpman. Student, UCLA, 1945-46; BA, U. Calif., Berkeley, 1950; MD, U. Calif., San Francisco, 1954. Diplomate Am. Bd. Internal Medicine. Rotating intern L.A. County Gen. Hosp., LA, 1954-55; cardiovascular trainee Nat. Heart Inst., LA, 1957-58; asst. resident Beth Israel Hosp., Boston, 1955-57; fellow Wyley Winsor Rsch. Found., LA, 1958-59; pvt. practice Beverly Hills, Calif., 1958—; clin. instr. medicine U. So. Calif., LA, 1958-64, asst. clin. prof., 1964-71, assoc. clin. prof., 1971-72; assoc. clin. prof. medicine UCLA Sch. Medicine, 1972-92, clin. prof. medicine, 1992—. Attending physician, bd. govs. Cedars-Sinai Med. Ctr., L.A., 1958-, UCLA Med. Ctr., 1958-04, Brotman Med. Ctr., 1958-, Culver City, Calif.; examiner in cardiovascular diseases Calif. Indsl. Accident Commn., Calif. Dept. Vocat. Rehab.; founder, bd. dirs., chmn. bd. Cardio-Dynamics Labs., Inc., 1969-82; gen. ptnr. Camden Med. Bldg., L.A., 1970-86; bd. dirs. Mcht. Bank Calif.; bd. dirs. med. rsch. Faberge, Inc., N.Y.C., 1980-84; cardiovascular cons. Delta Air Lines, 1992-94; founder, bd. dirs., chmn. bd., chief med. officer CORDA Med. Care, Inc., 1995-2000; chmn., founder, dir. Integrated Diagnostic Ctrs., Inc., 2000-07. Author: Your Second Life, 1979, Preventing Silent Heart Disease, 1989; assoc. editor Internat. Medicine Alert, 1992—; contbr. numerous articles to med. jours. Fellow ACP, Am. Coll. Cardiology, Am. Coll. Chest Physicians, Internat. Cardiovascular Soc., Am. Coll. Angiology, Internat. Coll. Angiology, Am. Thermographic Soc. (charter, pres. 1971-72), Am. Acad. Thermology; mem. AMA, Calif. Med. Assn., L.A. Med. Assn., Nat. Cardiovascular Network (exec. com., bd. dirs. 1994-98), Western Cardiovascular Network (chmn., med. dir. 1993-96), Am. Soc. Internal Medicine, Am. Heart Assn., Calif. Heart Assn., L.A. County Heart Assn. Office: 414 N Camden Dr #1100 Beverly Hills CA 90210-4532 Office Phone: 310-278-3400. E-mail: karpman@cumg.com.

KARR, CHARLES, lawyer; b. Coal Hill, Ark., Aug. 3, 1941; s. William Joe and Doris Jane (Coats) K.; m. Suzanne Mary Stoner, Dec. 23, 1962; children: Stephanie, Jennifer, Jeffrey BA, U. Ark., 1965, LLB, 1967. Bar: Ark. 1968, U.S. Dist. Ct. (we. dist.) Ark. 1979, U.S. Ct. Appeals (8th cir.), 1982, U.S. Supreme Ct. 1985. Law clk. to assoc. justice Ark. Supreme Ct., Little Rock, 1968; dep. pros. atty. Sebastian County, Ft. Smith, Ark., 1969-72; pros. atty. 12th Jud. Cir., Ft. Smith, 1973-78; ptnr. Law Offices Charles Karr, PA, Ft. Smith, 1979—. Mem. staff Ark. Constl. Revision Study Commn. Mem. Criminal Detention Facilities Bd., Pine Bluff, Ark., 1976-78, Gov.'s Commn. on Prisons, Little Rock, 1977; bd. dirs. United Way Ft. Smith, Inc., 1977-79, Bost Human Devel. Svcs., Inc., Ft. Smith, 1983-88. Mem.: ATLA, ABA (speedy trial com. 1976—77, prosecution discretion com. 1983—84), Ark. Pros. Attys. Assn. (pres. 1977), Ark. Bar Assn. (chmn. criminal law sect. 1976—77), W.B. Putman Am. Inn of Ct.

(pres. 1999). Democrat. Mem. Ch. of Christ. Home: 7415 Westminister Pl Fort Smith AR 72903-4250 Office: Law Offices Charles Karr PA 1st Nat Bank Bldg 602 Garrison Ave Ste 650 Fort Smith AR 72901-2535 Office Phone: 479-782-4028. Business E-Mail: karrlawfirm@aol.com.

KARR, DAVID DEAN, lawyer; b. Denver, Sept. 3, 1953; s. Dean Speece and Jean (Ransbottom) K.; m. Laura A. Foster, Apr. 10, 1982; children: Emily Ann, Bradley Foster. BA, U. Puget Sound, 1975; JD, Loyola U., 1979. Bar: Colo. 1979, U.S. Dist. Ct. 1979, U.S. Ct. Appeals (10th cir.) 1981, U.S. Supreme Ct. 1983. Assoc. Pryor Carney & Johnson, P.C., Englewood, Colo., 1979-84, ptnr., 1984-95, Pryor, Johnson, Montoya, Carney and Karr, P.C., Englewood, Colo., 1995—2005, Pryor Johnson Carney Karr Nixon PC, Englewood, Colo., 2005—. Mem. ABA (lead atty. pro bono team death penalty project Tex. chpt. 1988—), Colo. Bar Assn. (interprofl. com. 1990—), Arapahoe County Bar Assn. Denver Bar Assn., Def. Rsch. Inst., Colo. Def. Lawyers Assn. Home: 5474 E Hinsdale Cir Littleton CO 80122-2538 Office: Pryor Johnson Carney Karr Nixon PC 5619 DTC Pkwy Ste 1200 Greenwood Village CO 80111 Office Phone: 303-773-3500. Business E-Mail: dkarr@pjckn.com.

KARR, JAMES RICHARD, ecologist, educator, research director; b. Shelby, Ohio, Dec. 26, 1943; s. Rodney Joll and Marjorie Ladonna (Copeland) K.; m. Kathleen Ann Reynolds, Mar. 23, 1963 (div. Nov. 1982); children: Elizabeth Ann, Eric Leigh; m. Helen Marie Herbst Serrano, Dec. 22, 1984. BS, Iowa State U., 1965; MS, U. Ill., 1967, PhD, 1970. Fellow in biology Princeton (NJ) U., 1970-71, Smithsonian Tropical Rsch. Inst., Balboa, Panama, 1971-72, dep. dir., 1984-87, acting dir., 1987-88; asst. prof. biology Purdue U., Lafayette, Ind., 1972-75; assoc. prof. U. Ill., Urbana, 1975-80, prof., 1980-84; Harold H. Bailey prof. biology Va. Poly. Inst. and State U., Blacksburg, 1988-91; prof. zoology, fisheries, environ. health, civil engring. and pub. affairs U. Wash., Seattle, 1991—2006, dir. Inst. Environ. Studies, 1991-95, prof. emeritus, 2006—. Cons. on water resources EPA, 1978—, OAS, Washington, 1980, South Fla. Water Mgmt. Dist., West Palm Beach, 1989-2002, 06—; cons., gen. counsel Fla. Dept. Environ. Protection, 2002-03, 04—06. Recipient Carl R. Sullivan Fishery Conservation award, Am. Fisheries Soc., 2004, Environ. Stewardship award, N.Am. Benthological Soc., 2005; grantee, EPA, 1972—85, 1993—2000, U.S. Forest Svc., 1980—81, 1990—91, U.S. Fish and Wildlife Svc., 1979—82, NSF, 1982—84, 1997—2000, TVA, 1990—93, Dept. Energy, 1995—2002. Fellow: AAAS, Am. Ornithologists Union; mem.: N.Am. Ornithological Soc. Achievements include development of Index of Biotic Integrity, now used in North and South America, Asia, Australia, and Europe to assess directly the quality of water resources. Home Phone: 360-681-3163. Business E-Mail: jrkarr@u.washington.edu.

KARR, JANE, editor; Editor Edn. Life NY Times. Office: NY Times 229 W 43rd St New York NY 10036 Office Phone: 212-556-1234. E-mail: jakarr@nytimes.com.

KARR, JOANNE FERN, theater educator; b. LA, Feb. 18, 1955; d. Irving and Sylvia Zelda Karr. BA, U. So. Calif., LA, 1975, MA, 1978. Cert. secondary tchr. Calif. Tchr. LA Unified Sch. Dist., 1976—2000, Walnut Valley Unified Sch. Dist., Walnut, Calif., 2000—. Author: (script) Readers Theatre Scripts of Greek Mythology. V.p. Chino Cmty. Theatre, Calif., 2005; sec. So. Calif. Overseas Tchrs., 1994—97, 2005—. Named Fulbright Exch. Tchr. Office: Walnut HS 400 N Pierre Rd Walnut CA 91789 Office Phone: 909-594-1333.

KARR, RONALD DALE, librarian, historian; b. Pitts., Apr. 19, 1948; s. Emil and Vera J. Karr; m. Diane M. Beaudoin, July 13, 1974; children: Emilie R., Matthew B., Jeannine M. AB, Bucknell U., 1970; MA, Boston U., 1972, PhD, 1981; MS, Simmons Coll., 1978. Lectr. history Northeastern U., Boston, 1974—79; tech. editor Transp. Systems Ctr., U.S. Dept. Transp., Cambridge, Mass., 1974—77, libr., 1977—79; pub. svcs. libr. Transp. Libr. Northwestern U., Evanston, Ill., 1979—85; reference libr. U. Mass., Lowell, 1985—. Adj. faculty history dept. U. Mass., Lowell, 1997—. Editor: Indian New England, 1524-1674, 1999; author: Lost Railroads of New England, 1996, The Rail Lines of Southern New England, 1995; contbr. Encyclopedia of New Eng., Encyclopedia of Chgo. Mem., chmn. Planning Bd., Pepperell, Mass., 1989—2001; commr. No. Middlesex Coun. Govts., Lowell, 1989—95. Mem.: Urban History Assn. (bd. dirs.), Orgn. Am. Historians, Am. Hist. Assn., Beta Phi Mu. Office: Univ Mass Lowell 61 Wilder St Lowell MA 01854 Home: 30 Elm St Pepperell MA 01463-1603 Office Phone: 978-934-4554. Business E-Mail: ronald_karr@uml.edu. E-mail: ronkarr@charter.net.

KARR, STEPHEN WILLIAM, retired judge; b. Samos, Greece, June 20, 1919; arrived in US, 1920; s. William and Angeline Karr; m. Bette Jane LaVine; children: Carol, Steven, Alan, Catherine. BA, U. Mich., 1941, JD, 1947. Atty., Grand Rapids, Mich., 1947—71; US magistrate judge, 1971—87. Col. US Army, 1941—46. Recipient Santimala medal, King of Thailand, 1949. Mem.: FBA (Svc. to Profession award 1987), ABA, State Bar Mich.

KARRAKER, LOUIS RENDLEMAN, retired corporate executive; b. Jonesboro, Ill., Aug. 2, 1927; s. Ira Oliver and Helen Elsie (Rendleman) K.; m. Patricia Grace Stahlheber, June 20, 1952; children: Alan Louis, Sharon Elaine Cohen. BA, So. Ill. U., Carbondale, 1949, MA, 1952; postgrad., U. Wis., Madison, 1951—52, Washington U., St. Louis, 1954—56. V.p. pers. Am. Appraisal Assocs., Inc., Milw., 1969-73, v.p. adminstrn., 1973-74, group v.p., dir., 1974-77, exec. v.p., dir., 1977-79, pres., dir., 1979-82; bus. mgr. Concordia Coll., Ann Arbor, Mich., 1986-91; ret., 1991. Asst. to chmn. Parker Pen Co., Janesville, Wis., 1967-69, personnel mgr., 1964-67; asst. to pres. Augustana Coll., Sioux Falls, SD, 1962-64, acting chmn., dept. social scis., 1960-61, asst. prof. history, 1956-60; cons., spkr. in field Columnist The Jour. Times, Racine, Wis., 1993-99 Trustee Better Bus. Bur., Milw., 1979-82, Citizens Govtl. Rsch. Bur., Milw., 1979-82; speaker, canvasser Rep. Party, S.D., 1956-60. With USNR, 1952-53, Korea. Mem.: Hoover Presdl. Libr. Assn., Heritage Found., Am. Legion. Lutheran. Avocations: church activities, travel, fishing. Home: 217 S 7th St Apt 11 Waterford WI 53185-4500 Personal E-mail: karr217@webtv.net.

KARRAS, ALEX, actor, retired professional football player; b. Gary, Ind., July 15, 1935; m. Susan Clark Player Detroit Lions, 1958-71; host NFL Monday Night Football Preview WLS-TV, Chgo. Former commentator Monday Night Football, ABC-TV; numerous TV appearances including Tonight Show, TV movies: Paper Lion, The 500 lb. Jerk, Mad Bull, Mighty Moose & The Quarterback Kid, Babe, 1975, Mulligan's Stew, 1977, Centennial, 1978, Jimmy B. and Andre, 1979, Alcatraz: The Whole Shocking Story, When Fame Ran Out, 1980, Maid in America, 1982, Fudge-A-Mania, 1994; star TV series Webster, ABC-TV, 1983-86; films include: Blazing Saddles, 1974, Win, Place or Steal, 1977, FM, 1978, Nobody's Perfect, 1981, Victor, Victoria, 1982, Porky's, 1982, Against All Odds, 1984; author: (with Herb Gluck) Even Big Guys Cry, 1977, Alex Karras: My Life in Football, 1979, Tuesday Night Football, 1991. Named All-Pro, 1960, 61, 63, 65; recipient Outland Trophy, 1957, 79. Office: Ste 308 13400 Riverside Dr Sherman Oaks CA 91423-2541

KARRAS, RUTH MAZO, history professor; b. Chgo., Feb. 23, 1957; d. Robert Marc and Joan (Spector) Mazo; m. Christopher George Karras, Dec. 31, 1984; children: Nicola, Elena. BA in History, Yale Coll., New Haven, Conn., 1979; MPhil in European Archeology, Oxford U., Eng., 1981; MPhil in History, Yale U., New Haven, Conn., 1983, PhD in History, 1985. Asst. prof. U. Pa., Phila., 1985—93; assoc. prof. Temple U., Phila., 1993—96, prof., 1996—2000, assoc. dean, 1999—2000; prof. U. Minn., Mpls., 2000—. Gen. editor U. Pa. Press, Phila., 1994—. Author: (book) Slavery and Society in Medieval Scandinavia, 1988, Common Women: Prostitution and Sexuality in Medieval Europe, 1996, From Boys to Men: Formations of Masculinity in Later Medieval Europe, 2003, Sexuality in Medieval Europe: Doing Unto Others, 2005. Pres. Berkshire Conf. Women Historians, 2005—. Fellow, NEH, 1993—94; Rhodes Scholar, Oxford U., 1979—81. Avocation: knitting. Office: Univ Minn Dept History - Social Sci Bldg 267 19th Ave S Minneapolis MN 55455

KARRIKER, DANNY ALLEN, small business owner, protective services official; b. Covington, Ky., Dec. 13, 1962; s. Jerry Wayne Karriker and Shirlee Ann Stephenson; m. Joy Ellen Harness, June 4, 2005; m. Maggie Jane Bolen (div.); children: Daniel Wayne, Emilee Michele. AS, U. Ky., 1982; U.S. Armor Specialist, U.S. Armor Sch., 1983; BS, Ea. Ky. U., 1992; AS in Fire Sci., Ky. Cmty. and Tech. Coll. Sys., 2005. Cert. EMT Ky., 1981, med. lab. technician Ky., 1982; specialist US Army, 1983. Med. lab technician Lake Cumberland Regional Hosp., Somerset, Ky., 1980—82; tchr. Lincoln Co. H.S., Stanford, Ky., 1992—93; foreman, contractor Rio Grande Constrn., Lexington, Ky., 1993—98; owner/operator Karriker Bro's Fence, Eubank, Ky., 1998—; asst. chief Somerset (Ky.) Pulaski Co. Rescue Squad, 2000—, Spl. Response Team-Hazmat 12/WMD, Somerset, 2000—. Owner, operator Karriker Contracting, Eubank, Ky., 1985—; advisor, asst. chief Region 12 Haz-mat/Dept. Homeland Security, Somerset, 2000—; hon. chmn. Bus. Adv. Coun., Washington, 2003. Fireman Waynesburg Fire Dept., 1980—2006; mem., med. technician Waynesburg (Ky.) Rescue Squad, 1980—2002; mem., advisor Lincoln Co. Fire Dept. Sta. 5, Waynesburg, 1980—2006, Lincoln Co. Dive Rescue Team, Stanford, Ky., 2002—06; col. Boone's Raiders/Ky. Army N.G., Ky., 1984. Specialist US Army, 1983—90. Decorated Ky. Accomadation with Oak Leaf Clusters Ky. Army N.G., Army Achievement US Army, Best Recon Scout, Meritorous Svc.; named Rescue Squad Mem. of Yr., Somerset Pulaski Co. Rescue Squad, 2004. Mem.: DAV (life), PA Diving Instrs. (life; master diver), Am. Legion (life). Republican. Baptist. Avocations: diving, fishing, rapelling, hunting, motorcycling. Home and Office: 100 N Shady Ln Eubank KY 42567 Home Phone: 606-305-5834; Office Phone: 606-379-6124. Personal E-mail: karriker_a15@yahoo.com.

KARSEN, SONJA PETRA, retired literature educator; b. Berlin, Apr. 11, 1919; arrived in U.S., 1938, naturalized, 1945; d. Fritz and Erna (Heidermann) K. Titulo de Bachiller, Ministerio de Educación Nacional, Bogotá, 1937; BA, Carleton Coll., 1939; MA, Bryn Mawr Coll., 1941; PhD, Columbia U., 1950. Instr. Spanish Lake Erie Coll., Painesville, Ohio, 1943-45; instr. modern langs. U. PR, 1945-46; instr. Spanish Syracuse (NY) U., 1947-50, Bklyn. Coll., 1950-51; asst. to dep. dir. gen. UNESCO, 1951-52, L.Am. Desk, tech. assistance dept., 1952-53, mem. tech. assistance mission Costa Rica, 1954; asst. prof. Spanish Sweet Briar Coll., Va., 1955-57; assoc. prof., chmn. dept. Romance langs. Skidmore Coll., Saratoga Springs, NY, 1957-61, chmn. dept. modern langs. and lits., 1961-79, prof. Spanish, 1961-87, prof. emerita, 1987; cons. Hudson-Mohawk Assn. Colls. and Univs., 1990. Faculty rsch. lectr. Skidmore Coll., 1963; adv. and nominating com. Books Abroad, 1965-67; Fulbright lectr. Free U. Berlin, 1968; lectr. U. Gesamthochschule, Paderborn, Germany, 1995, 99. Author: Guillermo Valencia, Colombian Poet, 1951, Educational Development in Costa Rica with UNESCO's Technical Assistance, 1951-54, 1954, Jaime Torres Bodet: A Poet in a Changing World, 1963, Selected Poems of Jaime Torres Bodet, 1964, Versos y prosas de Jaime Torres Bodet, 1966, Jaime Torres Bodet, 1971, Ensayos de Literatura E Historia Iberoamericana/Essays on Iberoamerican Literature and History, 1988, Papers on Foreign Languages, Literature and Culture, 1982-87, 88, Bericht Über Den Vater: Fritz Karsen 1885-1951, 1993; translator: The Role of the Americas in History (Leopoldo Zea), 1992; editor Lang. Assn. Bull., 1980-83; mem. editl. adv. bd. Modern Lang. Studies, 1977-93; contbr. articles to profl. jours. Decorated Chevalier dans l'Ordre des Palmes Académiques, 1964; recipient Leadership award NY State Assn. Fgn. Lang. Tchrs., 1973, 76, 78, Nat. Disting. Leadership award, 1979, Disting. Svc. award, 1983, 86, Capital Dist. Fgn. Lang. Disting. Svc. award, 1987; recipient Spanish Heritage award, 1981, Alumni Achievement award Carleton Coll., 1982; exch. student auspices Inst. Internat. Ednl. at Carleton Coll., 1938-39; Buenos Aires Conv. grantee for rsch. in Colombia, 1946-47; faculty rsch. grantee Skidmore Coll., summer 1959, 61, 63, 64, 67, 69, 70, 73, ad hoc faculty grantee, 71, 78, 85; scholar in French, Bryn Mawr Coll., 1939-41 Mem.: Am. Soc. French Acad. Palms, MLA (life; del. assembly 1976—78, Mildenberger medal selection com. 1984—86), AAUW (life), AAUP (life), Nat. Assn. Self-Instrnl. Lang. Programs (v.p. 1981—82, pres. 1982—83), Am. Assn. Tchrs. Spanish and Portuguese (life; emeritus), El Ateneo Doctor Jaime Torres Bodet (founding mem.), Fulbright Alumni, UN Assn. U.S.A., Asociación Internacional de Hispanistas, Nat. Geog. Soc., Sigma Delta Pi, Phi Sigma Iota. Home: 1755 York Ave Apt 37A New York NY 10128-6875 *Perseverance, hard work and high ethical standards coupled with the opportunities for fulfilling one's potential, available in the United States to a greater extent than anywhere else in the world, have made my life what it is today.*

KARSH, PHILIP HOWARD, retired advertising executive; b. Salt Lake City, Sept. 19, 1935; s. Sol and Ruth (Marks) K.; m. Carol Hyman, July 3, 1962 (div. Sept. 1973); children: Michael David, Jill Ann; m. Linda Love, Sept. 7, 1984. BA, U. Colo., 1957. Account exec. Ted Levy/Richard Lane & Co., Denver, 1957-59; v.p. Jerome/Philip Advt., Denver, 1959—62, pres., 1962-65; v.p. Frye Sills Advt., Denver, 1965—77; pres. Karsh & Hagan Advt. Inc., Denver, 1977-85, chmn., 1985-97; ret., 1998. Trustee Nat. Jewish Med. and Rsch. Ctr., Denver, 1963—, chmn. 1991-95, Kern Rsch. Found., Denver, 1984—, Mile High United Way, Denver, 1986-92; mem. Denver Metro Conv. and Visitors Bur., 1994—, chmn., 1997. Named to Colo. Tourism Hall of Fame, 2004. Mem. Worldwide Ptnrs. (internat. chmn. 1986-87), Denver Advt. Fedn. (bd. dirs. 1968-69, 87-88), Colo. Hist. Soc. (trustee 1998—, chair 2003-06). Democrat. Jewish. Avocations: skiing, travel, golf. Home: 11704 W Auburn Dr Denver CO 80228-4758 Personal E-mail: philkarsh@comcast.net.

KARSKY, TIMOTHY J., state agency administrator; b. ND; m. Sharon Karsky; 2 children. BS in Mgmt./Mktg., No. State Coll., Aberdeen, SD, 1981. With FDIC, 1982—86; chief examiner ND Dept. Fin. Instns., 1986—89, asst. commr., 1989—97, 1999—2001, commr., 2001—; loan officer local bank, Bismarck, ND, 1997—99. Chmn. ND State Banking Bd., ND State Credit Union Bd. Mem.: Conf. State Bank Suprs. (treas. 2003, vice chmn. 2006—07). Office: ND Dept Fin Instns 2000 Schafer St Ste G Bismarck ND 58501-1204 Office Phone: 701-328-9933. Office Fax: 701-328-9955.

KARSNER, ANDY (ALEXANDER ARMAND KARSNER), federal agency administrator; BA with honors, Rice U.; MA, Hong Kong U. Internat. project dir. Tondu Energy Sys.; chief of staff for Hon. Moses Cheng Mo-Chi Legis. Coun. Hong Kong; dir. devel., sr. devel. mgr. Wartsila Power Devel., Wartsila Diesel Devel. Ltd.; mng. dir. Enercorp, LLC; asst. sec. for energy efficiency & renewable energy US Dept. Energy, Washington, 2006—. Office: US Dept Energy 1000 Independence Ave SW Washington DC 20585

KARSON, EMILE, lawyer; b. Berlin, Sept. 10, 1921; came to U.S., 1948, naturalized, 1955; s. Bogdan and Zorka (Natowa) Karastoyanoff; m. Lilia Usunowa, Dec. 31, 1944 (dec. June 27, 2005); 1 child, Danielle. LLB, U. Sofia, 1946, U. Paris, 1946, Docteur-en-Droit, 1948; LLM, Yale U., 1951, JSD, 1953; postgrad., U. So. Calif., 1953-54, U. Pa., 1978, Harvard U., 1978, Cornell U., 1991. Internat. atty. World Bank, Washington, 1951—53; gen. counsel Coast Fed. Savs., Great We. Savs., LA, 1954—58; F-104 exec. Lockheed Aircraft Internat., LA, 1959—63; treas. Europe, Zurich, Switzerland, Litton Industries, Inc., 1964-69; corp. treas. Continental Grain Co., NYC, 1969-72; v.p. fin. & adminstrn. Loctite Corp., Newington, Conn., 1972-81; founder, CEO, INTECH (internat. high tech. venture capital), Washington, 1981-85; internat. atty., 1998—. Vis. prof. law U. P.R., 1957; organizer 1st symposium on atomic energy and law for L.Am.; lectr. Naval War Coll., Fgn. Svc. Inst., U. So. Calif., Ind. U., U. Pitts.; mem. Rep. Assocs., 1954-56; Bus. Internat. Round Table, 1960-65; cons. Dept. State, 1983, U.S. Dept. Labor internat. programs, 1991, 92. Dir.: (documentaries, 2 films) shown at Cannes and Venice Film Festivals, 1947; (documentaries) Peace Treaty in Paris, 1947. Mem. adv. bd. Genetics Unique Fund, 1985-87; broadcaster Voice of Am., 1949-51; pres. Ea. European Orphans, Washington, 1990-92; steering com. Am. U. in Bulgaria, 1992-96; chmn., pres. Bulgarian-Am. Charitable and Ednl. Ctr., 1989-98. Fellow French Govt., 1946-48; recipient EE prize Lockheed Aircraft Internat., 1962. Mem. State Bar Calif., Bar U.S. Supreme Ct., World Affairs Coun. (founding mem. World Peace through Law sect.), Yale Club, Yale Law Sch. Club. Home and Office: 6020 California Cir #211 Rockville MD 20852 Home Phone: 301-230-3792; Office Phone: 301-230-3792. Personal E-mail: miltcho1921@yahoo.com.

KARSON, LILLIAN P., risk management consultant; b. Dec. 13, 1941; Diploma, Quincy City Hosp. Sch. Nursing; postgrad., U. Balt., Harvard U., Temple U. RN, Calif.; lic. property and casualty broker, Calif. Nurse Quincy (Mass.) City Hosp., 1962-63, Suburban Hosp., Bethesda, Md., 1963, Mercy Hosp., San Diego, 1963-64; head nurse oper. rm. Charleston (S.C.) Gen. Hosp., 1966-67; oper. rm. supr. North Arundel Hosp., Glen Burnie, Md., 1967-69; asst. dir. nurses, evening supr., house supr. Anne Arundel Hosp., Annapolis, Md., 1972-77; hosp. risk mgmt. cons. St. Paul Fire and Marine Ins. Co., Portland, Oreg., 1978-82, Brea, Calif., 1982-84; with Hosp. Ins. Svcs.,Inc., 1984-85; pres., ind. cons. QA/RM Cons., 1985—; prin., broker L&J Ins. Svcs., 1990—, LPK Enterprises, Inc., 1990—. Presenter in field. Contbr. Risk Management Handbook, 2d and 3d edits. Fellow: Am. Soc. Health Care Risk Mgmt. (disting. diplomate, cert., nat. legis. com. 1987—88, nat. pub. rels. and mktg. com. 1995, chmn. cpt. affairs com. 1996—97); mem.: Am. Soc. Outpatient Surgeons (nat. adv. bd. 1992—93), So. Calif. Assn. Healthcare Risk Mgrs. (bd. dirs. 1991—96, Most Contbg. Mem. to Field 1992), Soc. Healthcare Risk Mgrs., Am. Hosp. Assn. Home and Office: 76665 Chrysanthemum Way Palm Desert CA 92211-7460

KARSON, SAMUEL, psychologist, educator; b. Balt., Jan. 3, 1924; s. Norman Jacobson and Annie (Raskin) K.; m. Dorothy Faye Libert, Sept. 6, 1946; children: Linda Catherine, Michael Craig. BS, L.I. U., 1948; PhD, Washington U., St. Louis, 1952. Diplomate Clin. Psychology Am. Bd. Profl. Psychology. With psychiatric unit U.S. Naval Tng. Ctr., San Diego, 1952-55; asst. prof. dept. psychology U. N.H., 1957-58; chief psychologist, dir. rsch. Dade County Child Guidance Clinic, Miami, Fla., 1958-62; rsch. asst. prof. dept. nursing U. Miami, Fla., 1959-62; chief clin. psychologist, office aviation medicine FAA, Washington, 1962-66; prof., head dept. psychology Ea. Mich. U., Ypsilanti, 1966-77; chief psychologist, adminstr. overseas mental health program Dept. State, Washington, 1977-81; regional psychologist Southeast Asia Am. Embassy, Bangkok, Thailand, 1981-83; prof. clin. psychology Sch. Psychology Fla. Inst. Tech., Melbourne, 1983-85, prof., dir. grad. clin. tng., 1985-89; prin. investigator Second Genesis, Inc., Bethesda, Md., 1990-95. Cons. clin. psychology to office aviation medicine FAA, Washington, 1966-75. Author: (with J. O'Dell and M. Karson) 16PF Interpretation in Clinical Practice, 1997, The Karson Clinical Report, A Psychologist's Odyssey (Have PhD Will Travel), 1992, Pioneers in Personality Science: Autobiographical Perspectives, 2005. Served with USAAF, 1942-45, with USAF, 1955-57. Recipient Appreciation certificate Sec. State Alexander Haig, 1981, Personality Assessment award Thai Psychol. Assn., 1983, Disting. Profl. Contbns. award Md. Psychol. Assn., 1987. Fellow APA (life), Soc. Personality Assessment (life); mem. Assn. Aviation Psychologists (pres. 1973-74).

KARST, GARY GENE, retired architect; b. Barton County, Kans., Sept. 2, 1936; s. Emil and Clara (Nuss) K.; m. Loretta Marie Staub, Nov. 30, 1957; children: Kevin Gene, Sheri Lynn, Stacey Marie. BArch, Kans. State U., 1960. Registered profl. arch., Kans., Nat. Coun. Archl. Registration Bds., cert. NCARB. Staff architect Horst & Terrill Architects, Topeka, 1960—64; ptnr. Horst, Terrill & Karst Architects, Topeka, 1965—2001, dir. design, 1965—2001, sec., 1973—78, v.p., treas., 1978—92, v.p., 1992—99; pres., 1999—2001; ret., 2001; design architect Ruhnau, Evans, Brown & Steinman Architects, Riverside, Calif., 1964—65. Mem. Capital City Redevel. Agy., Topeka, 1978-86; mem. adv. bd. dept. architecture Kans. State U., Manhattan, 1986-87. Prin. works include Emporia (Kans.) H.S., 1972, (Kans. Soc. Architects award 1975), S.W. Bell Telephone Co. Equipment Bldg., 1974 (Bell Sys. award 1976), Durland Hall-Univ. Engring. Bldg., 1981 (Kans. Soc. Architects award 1983), Kans. State Prison Medium Security Facility, 1983 (Kans. Soc. Architects award 1985), Lansing H.S., 1988 (William W. Caudill citation Am. Sch. and Univ. Mag.), Leavenworth H.S., 1990 (citation Am. Sch. and Univ. Mag.), Plant Scis. Bldg., Kans. State U., 1994, Tomanek Hall, Ft. Hays State U., 1995; featured in publs. including Archtl. Record. Mem. Future Heritage Topeka, Capitol City Redevelopment Agy., Topeka, 1978—86. Recipient citation Am. Sch. and Univ. Mag.; Bales Organ Recital Hall, U. Kans., 1995, Weigel scholar Kans. State U., 1958-60; over 80 recognitions for design excellence. Mem. AIA (Henry W, Schirmer Disting. Svc. award 2001), Kans. Soc. Architects (pres. 1981-82), Optimists Internat. (pres. Topeka breakfast club 1970-71, lt. gov. Kans. dist. 1981-82). Republican. Lutheran. Avocations: woodworking, photography, sculpting. Home: 3535 SW Macvicar Ave Topeka KS 66611-1841 Personal E-mail: gkarst@cox.net.

KARST, KENNETH LESLIE, law educator; b. LA, June 26, 1929; s. Harry Everett and Sydnie Pauline (Bush) K.; m. Smiley Cook, Aug. 12, 1950; children— Kenneth Robert, Richard Eugene, Leslie Jeanne, Laura Smiley AB, UCLA, 1950; LL.B., Harvard U., 1953. Bar: Calif. 1954, U.S. Dist. Ct. (cen. dist.) Calif. 1954, U.S. Ct. Appeals (9th cir.) 1954, U.S. Supreme Ct. 1970. Assoc. Latham & Watkins, Los Angeles, 1954, 56-57; teaching fellow law Harvard U. Law Sch., 1957-58; asst. prof. Ohio State U. Coll. Law, Columbus, 1958-60, assoc. prof., 1960-62, prof., 1962-65; prof. law UCLA, 1965-90, David G. Price and Dallas P. Price prof. law, 1990—. Author: (with Harold W. Horowitz) Law, Lawyers and Social Change, 1969, (with Keith S. Rosenn) Law and Development in Latin America, 1975, Belonging to America: Equal Citizenship and the Constitution, 1989, Law's Promise, Law's Expression: Visions of Power in the Politics of Gender, Race, and Religion, 1993; assoc. editor Ency. of Am. Constn., 1986, co-editor-in-chief, 2d edit., 2000; contbr. articles to profl. jours. Served to 1st lt. JAGC, USAF, 1954-56. Law faculty fellow Ford Found., 1962-63. Fellow Am. Acad. Arts and Scis.; mem. State Bar Calif. Office: UCLA Law Sch PO Box 951476 Los Angeles CA 90095-1476 Business E-Mail: karst@law.ucla.edu.

KARTAGENER, CAROL A., lawyer; b. NYC, Feb. 26, 1955; d. Eugene and Helen Schneider; m. Martin H. Kartagener, Aug. 22, 1976. BA magna cum laude, SUNY, Binghamton, 1976; JD, U. Miami, Coral Gables, Fla., 1984. Bar: Fla. 1984, US Dist. Ct. (so. dist.) Fla. 1986. Law clk. hon. Norman C. Roettger, Jr. US Dist. Ct., Ft. Lauderdale, Fla., 1984—86; atty. Fleming O'Bryan & Fleming, Ft. Lauderdale, 1986—87, Weiss, Handler, Angelos & Cornwell, PA, Boca Raton, Fla., 1987—. Spl. master, guardian 17th Jud. Cir. Broward County, Ft. Lauderdale, 1996—98; lectr. Children First Classes, Palm Beach County, Fla. Mem.: South Palm Beach County Bar Assn. (family law sect.), Broward County Bar Assn. (family law sect.), Fla. Bar (family law sect., bd. cert. specialist in marital and family law 2000). Office: Weiss Handler Angelos & Cornwell PA 2255 Glades Rd Ste 218A Boca Raton FL 33431

KARTCHNER, GAYLA L., elementary school educator; d. Gaylan Clarence Roy and Dora Patterson; m. George H. Kartchner, Apr. 16, 1977. BS, No. Ariz. U., 1975; M In Edn., Ariz. State U., 2002. Post Degree Cert. No. Ariz. U., 1991. Tchrs. ast. Bloomfield Mcpl. Schs., N.Mex., 1988—90; substitute tchr. Farmington Mcpl. Schs., Farmington, N.Mex., 1990—91, tchr., 1992—. Pres. San Juan Basin Coun. of Reading, Farmington, 2004—, membership treas., 1994—2004; mem. Internat. Reading Assn., Newark, 1995—. Mem.: N.Mex Internat. Reading Assn. (assoc.), Internat. Reading Assn. (assoc.). Lds Ch. Home Phone: 505-327-2579; Office Phone: 505-599-8606.

KARTIGANER, JOSEPH, retired lawyer; b. Berlin, June 5, 1935; came to US, 1939; s. Harold and Lilly (Wolkowitz) K.; m. Audrey Gertsman Amdursky; children: Deborah Lynn, Alison Beth. AB, CCNY, 1955; LL.B., Columbia U., 1958. Bar: NY 1960, Fla. 1978, DC 1979. Assoc. White & Case, NYC, 1960-69, ptnr., 1969-88, Simpson Thacher & Bartlett, NYC, 1988-99; ret., 1999. Lectr. law Columbia Law Sch., NYC, 1973-80; vis. lectr. Sch. Law Yale U., 1997-2000; mem adv. com. NY Estates, Powers and Trust Law-Surrogate's Ct. Procedure Act, 1997-. Mem.: Columbia Law Rev. Fellow Am. Bar Found., Am. Coll. Trust and Estate Counsel (regent 1978-84), Am. Coll. Tax Counsel, NY State Bar Found.; mem. ABA (chmn. real property, probate and trust law sect. 1986-87, co-chair sect. standing com. on govt. submissions 1995—, Sect. Real Property and Trust advisor to conf. com., mem. editl. bds. for confs.), NY State Bar Assn., Am. Law Inst., Internat. Acad. Estate and Trust Law (exec. coun. 1980-94, 98-2002), Scarsdale Golf Club (Hartsdale, NY). Home: 812 5th Ave # 5B New York NY 10021-7253 Office: Simpson Thacher & Bartlett 425 Lexington Ave Fl 15 New York NY 10017-3954 Personal E-mail: joekart@yahoo.com.

KARWAN, MARK HENRY, engineering educator; b. Cleve., Nov. 16, 1951; B in Engring. Scis. with full honors, MS in Engring., Johns Hopkins U., 1974; PhD, Ga. Inst. Tech., 1976. From asst. prof. to assoc. prof. dept. indsl. engring. Univ. at Buffalo, SUNY, 1976-86, prof. dept. indsl. engring., 1986—, prof., chair dept. indsl. engring., 1987-92, prof., assoc. dean grad. edn. Sch. Engring. & Applied Scis., 1992-94, prof., acting dean Sch. Engring. & Applied Scis., 1994-95, dean Sch. Engring. & Applied Scis., 1996—2006. Chair U. at Buffalo Bus. Alliance, 1998-2001; cons. Mgmt. Adv. Svcs., Inc., Columbia, Md., 1974, Health Care Plan, Inc., Buffalo, 1984-87, Praxair, Inc., Tonawanda, N.Y., 1987—; faculty advisor student chpt. Inst. Indsl. Engrs. 849, 1977-83; proposal reviewer NSF-Sys. Theory and Ops. Rsch., NSF-Applied Math.; cluster chmn. ORSA/TIMS joint nat. meeting, 1986, session chmn., 1977—; dir. Ctr. for Indsl. Effectiveness, 1993-98, dir. grad. studies, 1982-87 Assoc. editor: Naval Research Logistics, 1987—2003, IIE Transactions, 1991-93; co-editor spl. issue Naval Rsch. Logistics, 1988; mem. editl. adv. bd. Computers & Ops. Rsch., 1984-2004; contbr. more than 70 refereed papers to profl. jours. including Annals of Discrete Math., European Jour. Operational Rsch., IEEE Transactions on Automatic Control, Jour. Mechanics Design, Mgmt. Sci., Math. Programming, Networks, Ops. Rsch., Water Resources Rsch.; patentee two-phase method for real time process control. Pres.'s fellow Ga. Tech. U., 1974-75. Mem. Alpha Pi Mu, Omega Rho (regional dir. N.E. U.S. chpt. 1982-84). Office: Univ at Buffalo Sch Engring And Applied Scis Buffalo NY 14260-1900 Office Phone: 716-645-2357 ext. 2131. Business E-Mail: mkarwan@buffalo.edu.

KARWOWSKI, WALDEMAR, adult education educator; b. Brzeg, Poland, Sept. 4, 1953; came to U.S., 1979; s. Ryszard and Maria (Kostur) K.; m. Bernarda Wanda Kaczmarek, June 23, 1979; children: Matteusz Piotr, Jessica Samantha. MS in Prodn. Engring., Tech. U., Wroclaw, Poland, 1978; PhD in Indsl. Engring., Tex. Tech. U., 1982; DSc in Mgmt. Sci., Inst. for Orgn. and Mgmt. in Intustry, Warsaw, Poland, 2004; DHC (hon.), South Ukrainian State Odessa Pedagogical U. Registered profl. engr.; cert. prof. ergonomist. Asst. prof. U. Louisville, 1983-87, assoc. prof., 1987-93, prof., 1993—, dir. Ctr. Indsl. Ervonomics, 1987—. Vis. asst. prof. Iowa State U., Ames, 1982-83. Contbr. articles to profl. jours. Fulbright scholar, 1990-91. Fellow Human Factors Ergonomics Soc.; mem. Ergonomics Soc., Internat. Found. Indls. Ergonomics & Safety (pres. 1992-93). Roman Catholic. Avocations: tennis, windsurfing, soccer, films. Office: U Louisville Lutz Hall Rm 445 Louisville KY 40292-0001 Home: 12405 Mistletoe Rd Louisville KY 40223-1515 Office Phone: 502-852-7173. E-mail: karwowski@louisville.edu.

KASAMA, HIDETO PETER, international business and investment advisor; b. Tokyo, Nov. 21, 1946; came to U.S., 1969; s. Toshiyoshi and Hamako (Yoshioka) K.; m. Evelyn P. Cruz (div. Apr. 1990); children: Jennifer, Nicole, Leona; m. Heidi W. Snare, June 29, 1991; 1 child, Serena. BABA, Seattle U., 1971, MBA, 1973. CPA. Mgmt. trainee Bank of Am., Seattle, 1972-74; audit supr. Ernst & Young, Seattle, 1974-79; pres. KASPAC Corp., Seattle, 1979-89; mng. ptnr. Kasama & Co., Seattle, 1980-98; shareholder AZ & Co., Seattle, 2000; pres. Kasama Internat., Las Vegas, 2000—. Contbr. articles to newspapers and mags. Mem. AICPA, Wash. Soc. CPA's, Wash. Assn. Realtors, Columbia Tower Club (founder). Avocations: golf, classical guitar, gardening. Office: 11620 Evergreen Creek Ln Las Vegas NV 89135 Office Phone: 702-531-3333. Business E-Mail: pkasama@windermere.com.

KASBAR, MICHAEL J., energy executive; Co-founder, officer, dir. TransTec New York, 1985—94; bd. dir. World Fuel Services Corp., Miami, Fla., 1995—, CEO marine fuel svc., 1995—2002, pres., COO, 2002—. Office: World Fuel Services Corp Ste 400 9800 NW 41st St Miami FL 33178*

KASBEER, STEPHEN FREDERICK, retired university official, investor; b. Princeton, Ill., Feb. 28, 1925; s. Virgil Sumner and Dorothy Marie (Uthoff) K.; m. Elizabeth Branning Royce, June 15, 1947 (div. 1978); children: Deborah Ann, William Royce.; m. Pamela Christine Rehm, Aug. 10, 1978. BS, Northwestern U., 1946, MA, 1951; JD, John Marshall Law Sch., 1966. Bar: Ill. 1967, U.S. Ct. Appeals (7th cir.) 1967. Supply and disbursing officer Naval Ammunition Depot, Guam, 1946; plant mgr. Boss Mfg. Co., Tiffin, Ohio, 1946-48; pres. Kasbeer Concrete Products, Princeton, Ill., 1948-49; dir. pers. Harper-Wyman Co., Hinsdale, Ill., 1951-69, sec., 1956-69, gen. counsel, 1967-69; v.p. indsl. rels. Bell & Howell Co., Chgo., 1969-71, group v.p., 1969-73; chmn. fin. com., trustee Evang. Hosp. Assn., Oak Brook, Ill., 1968-72, exec. v.p., COO, 1973-81; health care cons. Equitable Life Assurance Soc. U.S., NYC, 1980-81; v.p., asst. to pres. S & C Electric Co., Chgo., 1981; sr. v.p. Loyola U., Chgo., 1981-94, sr. v.p. adminstrn., treas., chief investment officer, 1985-94, ret., 1994; pres., dir. Loyola Mgmt. Co., Chgo., 1992-94, also bd. dirs. Lt. USNR, 1943—46. Mem. Econ. Club Chgo., Coronado Hist. Assn. (trustee, pres.), Rotary Club Coronado, Coronado Tennis Club. Republican. Presbyterian. Home: Unit 204 1710 Avenida Del Mundo Coronado CA 92118-3000

KASCH, MARY COURTEOL, occupational therapist; b. Chgo., Feb. 15, 1947; d. Paul and Bernice Zimmerman Courteol; children: Elizabeth Kasch Peter, David Michael. BS, Tufts U., 1970. Registered occupl. therapist, lic., cert. hand therapist. Pres. Hand Therapy Certification Commn., Sacramento, 2000—, exec. dir.; hand therapist Campus Commons Phys. Therapy, Sacramento, 1997—2001. Author: Rehabilitation of the Hand, 1979, 1985, 1991, 1996, 2001, Occupational Therapy: Practice Skills for Physical Dysfunction; mem. editl. rev. bd.: Jour. Hand Therapy, 1998—2005. Sec. Sacramento Choral Soc. Orch., Sacramento, 1998—2006. Recipient Award of Excellence, Occupl. Therapy Assn. Calif., 1986, Lillian Terris award, Profl. Exam. Svc., 1997, Nat. Svc. award, Arthritis Found., 1985, Pres.'s Gold award, Am. Soc. Hand Therapists, 1992. Fellow: Am. Occupl. Therapy Assn. Achievements include development of Certified Hand Therapist Credential. Avocations: singing, sewing. Office: Hand Therapy Certification Commission 1337 Howe Ave Ste 230 Sacramento CA 95825 Office Phone: 800-860-7097. Business E-Mail: mkasch@htcc.org.

KASDAN, LAWRENCE EDWARD, film director, screenwriter; b. Miami Beach, Fla., Jan. 14, 1949; s. Clarence Norman and Sylvia Sarah (Landau) K.; m. Meg Goldman, Nov. 28, 1971; children: Jacob, Jonathan. BA, U. Mich., 1970, MA in Edn., 1972. Copywriter W.B. Doner & Co. (Advt.), Detroit, 1972-75, Doyle, Dane Bernbach, Los Angeles, 1975-77; freelance screenwriter, 1977-80; motion picture dir., screenwriter Los Angeles, 1980—. Co-screenwriter: The Empire Strikes Back, 1980, Return of the Jedi, 1982; screenwriter: Continental Divide, 1981, Raiders of the Lost Ark, 1981; writer, dir.: Body Heat, 1981, Grand Canyon, 1992; co-screenwriter, dir., exec. prodr.: The Big Chill, 1983, Immediate Family, 1989, Jumpin' at the Boneyard, 1992, In the Land of Women, 2007; co-screenwriter, dir., prodr.: Silverado, 1985, The Accidental Tourist, 1988, Dreamcatcher, 2003; prodr. Cross My Heart, 1987; dir. I Love You to Death, 1989; co-screenwriter, dir. Wyatt Earp, 1994; screenwriter, co-prodr. The Bodyguard, 1992; dir. French Kiss, 1995, Mumford, 1999. Recipient Clio awards for advt., Writers Guild Am. award for the Big Chill, 1983, New York Film Critics Circle award for The Accidental Tourist, 1988; nominated 4 Acad. Awards. Mem. Writers Guild Am. West, Dirs. Guild Am. West.*

KASE, NATHAN GINDEN, dean; b. NYC, Apr. 6, 1930; s. Joseph and Flora (Ginden) Kosovsky; m. Judith Caryl Glass, July 8, 1956; children: Deborah Lillian, James, Nancy Kase O'Brasky. AB, Columbia U., 1951, MD, 1955; MA (hon.), Yale U., 1969; LHD honoris causa, Mt. Sinai Sch. Medicine, 2004. Instr. dept. ob-gyn. Yale U. Med. Sch., New Haven, 1962-63, asst. prof., 1963-66, assoc. prof., 1966-69, prof., chmn., 1969-78, prof., 1978-81; prof. ob-gyn. Mt. Sinai Sch. Medicine, 1981—, dean, 1984-98, acting chief exec. officer, 1986-88, emeritus dean, 1998—, interim dean, 2001—03, interim pres., CEO, 2001—02, prof. dept. medicine, 2005—. Chmn. adv. bd. Gateway Inst. Pre-Coll. Edn., NYC, 2002—05; pres., chair NY State Dept. Edn. Bd. for Medicine, 2007—. Co-author: Clinical Gynecologic Endocrinology and Infertility, Advances in Obstetrics/Gynecology, Principles and Practice of Gynecology, Medical Surgical and Obstetrical Complications of Pregnancy, Diagnosis and Management of Ovarian Disorders. Served to capt. USAF, 1957-59. Recipient Francis Gilman Blake award Yale U. Sch. Medicine, 1967. Fellow Am. Coll. Obstetricians and Gynecologists; mem. Am. Fertility Soc., Endocrine Soc., Associated Med. Schs. N.Y. (pres. 1989-91). Office: Mt Sinai Med Ctr Box 1025 One Gustave Levy Pl New York NY 10029 Home Phone: 914-232-8769; Office Phone: 212-659-9760. Business E-Mail: nathan.kase@mssm.edu.

KASER, DAVID, retired librarian, educator, consultant; b. Mishawaka, Ind., Mar. 12, 1924; s. Arthur Leroy and Loah (Steele) K.; m. Jane Jewell, Sept. 1, 1950; children: John Andrew, Kathleen Jewell. AB, Houghton Coll., 1949; MA, U. Notre Dame, 1950; A.M. in L.S, U. Mich., 1952, PhD, 1956. Serials librarian, instr. library sci. Ball State U., 1952-54; asst. in exchanges U. Mich. Library, 1954-56; chief acquisitions Washington U. Libraries, St. Louis, 1956-59, asst. dir., 1959-60; prof. library sci. Peabody Coll. and dir. libraries Vanderbilt U., 1960-68; dir. libraries Cornell U., 1968-73; prof. library sci. Ind. U., Bloomington, 1973-86, Disting. prof., 1986-91, Disting. prof. emeritus, 1991—; pres. Kaser Assocs., Inc., libr. bldg. cons., Bloomington, 1988-95. Fgn. assignments in Ireland, 1960, Korea, 1965, 81, 93, Laos, 1966, Taiwan, 1967, 79, 81, 88, 89, 93, S.E. Asia, 1969, Eng., 1971, France, 1972, Saudi Arabia, 1975-76, 83, Nigeria, 1978, Indonesia, 1978, Malaysia, 1992. Author: Messrs. Carey & Lea of Philadelphia, 1957, Cost Book of Carey & Lea, 1825-1838, 1963, Joseph Charless, Printer in the Western Country, 1963, Books in America's Past, 1966, Book Pirating in Taiwan, 1969, Library Development in Eight Asian Countries, 1969, Book for a Sixpence, 1980, Books and Libraries in Camp and Battle, 1984, The Evolution of the American Academic Library Building, 1997, Just Lucky I Guess, 2000; editor Mo. Libr. Assn. Quar., 1958-60, Coll. and Rsch. Librs., 1963-69. Guggenheim fellow, 1967 Mem. ALA (councilor 1965-69, 75-79), Assn. Coll. and Research Libraries (pres. 1968-69), Assn. Southeastern Research Libraries (chmn. 1966-68), Tenn. Library Assn. (pres. 1968-69), Am. Antiquarian Soc., Phi Beta Kappa, Beta Phi Mu (internat. pres. 1975) E-mail: kaserd@indiana.edu.

KASEY, ARTHUR R., III, secondary school educator; b. Louisville, Ky., Jan. 22, 1940; s. Arthur R. Kasey, Jr. and Ruth Prinz. BA, Vanderbilt U., 1962; MS in Geology, U. Tenn., 1965. Life cert. in teaching, Mo. Asst. instr. U. Mo., Columbia, 1965-71; tchr. Fox C-6 Sch. Dist., Arnold, Mo., 1971—. Tchr. Meth. Ch., Arnold, 1972—. Recipient Excellence in Teaching award Emerson Electric St. Louis, V.P. Fair, 1989; named Educator of Yr., Arnold, Mo., 1992, Arnold Walmart Tchr. of Yr., 2004 Mem. NEA, NSTA, Nat. Assn. Geology Tchrs.(Outstanding Earth Sci. Tchr., ctrl. states sect.), Nat. Speleological. Soc., Geol. Soc. Am. (Outstanding Tchr. Earth Sci. 1991), Sigma X. Avocations: travel, videography, photography. Home: 2631 Georgia Arnold MO 63010-1615 Office: Fox Sr High Sch 751 Jeffco Blvd Arnold MO 63010-1432 Personal E-mail: artkasey@webtv.net.

KASH, DON ELDON, political science professor; b. Macedonia, Iowa, May 29, 1934; s. Albert W. and Blanche Opal (Smith) K.; m. Elizabeth Gunn; children: Kelli Denise, Jeffrey Paul. BA, U. Iowa, Iowa City, 1959, MA, 1960, PhD, 1963. Instr. Tex. Tech. U., 1960-61; asst. prof. Ariz. State U., 1963-65, U. Mo., Kansas City, 1965-66; assoc. prof. Purdue U., West Lafayette, Ind., 1966-70; prof. polit. sci. U. Okla., Norman, 1970-91, George Lynn Cross rsch. prof. polit. sci., 1975-91, dir. Sci. and Pub. Policy Program, 1970-78; John T. Hazel Sr. and Ruth D. Hazel chair in pub. policy George Mason U., Fairfax, Va., 1991—. Vis. assoc. prof. Ind. U., 1969-70; chief conservation div. U.S. Geol. Survey, 1978-81; mem. Assembly Engring., Marine Bd. NRC; prof. Tsinghua U., Beijing. Author: The Politics of Space Cooperation, 1967, Energy Under the Oceans: A Technology Assessment of Outer Continental Shelf Oil and Gas Operations, 1973, North Sea Oil and Gas: Implication for Future U.S. Development, 1973, Energy Alternatives: A Comparative Analysis, 1975, Our Energy Future, 1976, U.S. Energy Policy: Crisis and Complacency, 1983, Perpetual Innovation: The New World of Competition, 1989, The Complexity Challenge: Technological Innovation in the 21st Century, 1999; contbr. articles to profl. jours. With AUS, 1952-54. Recipient Disting. Alumni award, U. Iowa, 1988. Fellow AAAS. Office: George Mason U Sch Public Policy 4400 University Dr Fairfax VA 22030-4444 Business E-Mail: dkash@gmu.edu.

KASHA, KENNETH JOHN, agriculturist, educator; b. Lacombe, Alta., Can., May 6, 1933; s. John Clarence and Mary Jennette (Proudfoot) K.; m. Marion Eileen Lenz, Aug. 14, 1958; children: Lorelei Marion, David John. BSc in Agr., U. Alta., Edmonton, 1957, MSc, 1958; PhD, U. Minn., 1962; LLD (hon.), U. Calgary, Alta., 1986. Rsch. asst. U. Minn., Mpls., 1958-61, fellow rsch. agronomy and plant genetics, 1961-62; rsch. scientist forages Agr. Can. Rsch. Sta., Ottawa, Ont., 1962-66; asst. prof. crop sci. dept. U. Guelph, Ont., 1966-69, assoc. prof. crop sci. dept. Ont., 1969-74, prof. crop sci. dept. Ont., 1974-98—, Univ. prof. emeritus Ont., 1998—. Cons. Ciba Geigy Seeds Ltd., Ailsa Craig, Ont., 1974-81, Monsanto Co., St. Louis, 1997-2002; organizing chair and editor 1st Internat. Symposium on Haploids in Plants, Guelph, 1974; dir. Plant Biotech Centre, Guelph Waterloo Biotech, 1984-87; program chmn. XVI Internat. Congress Genetics, Toronto, 1988; fgn. corr. Acad. d'Agriculture de France, 2003. Editor: Haploids in Higher Plants, 1974, Plant Cell Culture in Agriculture and Forestry, 1980, Mutation, In Vitro and Molecular Techniques for Environmentally Sustainable Crop Improvement, 2002, Doubled Haploid Production in Crop Plants, A Manual, 2003, Haploids in Crop Production II, 2005; contbr. articles to profl. jours.; mem. numerous jour. editl. bds. Decorated officer Order of Can., 1994; recipient Agrl. Inst. Can. Grindley medal, 1970; Can. Award of Excellence EC Manning Found., 1983, Disting. Rsch. award Ont. Agr. Coll. Alumni, 1984, Outstanding Achievement award U. Minn., 1999, Queen Elizabeth Golden Jubilee medal, 2002, named to Alumni Wall of Honor U. Minn., 2005. Fellow Royal Soc. Can. (fellow selection com., life scis. 2000-02); mem. Sigma Xi (Disting. Researcher award Guelph chpt. 1974), Genetics Soc. Can. (pres. 1976-77, sec. 1966-69, award of Excellence 1994), Internat. Assn. Plant Tissue Culture (nat. corr. 1990-94), Can. Soc. Plant Molecular Biology (founding mem.), Genetics Soc. Am., Am. Soc. Agronomy, Sigma Xi. Home: 28 Halesmanor Ct Guelph ON Canada N1G 4E2 Office: U Guelph Dept Plant Agr Guelph ON Canada N1G 2W1 E-mail: kkasha@uoguelph.ca.

KASHGARIAN, MICHAEL, pathologist, educator; b. NYC, Sept. 20, 1933; s. Toros and Arax K.; m. Jean Gaylor Caldwell, July 2, 1960; children: Michaele, Thea. AB, N.Y. U., 1954; MD, Yale U., 1958. Diplomate: Am. Bd. Pathology. Intern Barnes Hosp., St. Louis, 1958-59; asst. in medicine Washington U., St. Louis, 1958-59; asst. resident in pathology Yale New Haven Med. Center, 1959-61, resident in pathology, 1962-63; rsch. fellow in renal physiology U. Goettingen, Germany, 1961-62; practice medicine specializing in pathology New Haven, 1962—. Instr. Yale U., 1962-64, asst. prof., 1964-67, asso. prof., 1967-74, prof., 1974—, vice chmn. dept., 1976-89, chmn., 1990— assoc. pathologist Yale New Haven Hosp., 1964-66, asst. attending pathologist, 1966-69, attending pathologist, 1969—, pres. med. staff, 1983-84; cons. in pathology, 1962—. Author: (with J.P. Hayslett, B.H. Spargo) Renal Disease, 1974, (with G.N. Burrow) The Endocrine Glands; co-author (with A. Fogo) Diagnostic Atlas of Renal Pathology, 2005; editor: Yearbook of Nephrology, Yale Medicine, Current Opinion in Nephrology; mem. editorial bd. Nephron, 1970—, Am. Jour. Pathology, 1975—, Am. Jour. Kidney Diseases; contbr. articles to med. jours. Chmn. ednl. adv. council North Haven Bd. Edn., 1971; chmn. Christian edn. com. Ch. of Christ, Yale, 1970; bd. dirs. New Haven Symphony Orch.; v.p. Conn. Fund for Environ. 1st lt., M.C. USAR, 1954-65. USPHS fellow, 1963-65; research career devel. awardee, 1965-75. Fellow AAAS, Am. Soc. Clin. Pathologists, Coll. Am. Pathologists, Am. Soc. Nephrology, Am. Heart Assn.; mem. AMA, Internat. Acad. Pathology, Conn. State Med. Soc. (chmn. com. on organ and tissue transfer), New Haven County Med. Assn. (pres. bd. govs.), Am. Soc. Investigative Pathologists, Conn. Soc. Pathologists (pres. 1975), Am. Physiol. Soc., Gesellshaft Nephrologie (hon.), Renal Pathology Soc. (Jacob Churg award), Nat. Kidney Found. (Disting. Achievement award), Sigma Xi, Alpha Omega Alpha, Alpha Kappa Kappa. Home: 22 Old Orchard Rd North Haven CT 06473-3022 Office: 310 Cedar St PO Box 208023 New Haven CT 06520-8023 Home Phone: 203-248-9208; Office Phone: 203-785-2750. Business E-Mail: michael.kashgarian@yale.edu.

KASHIDA, JEFFREY SHINJI, diversified financial services company executive; b. Kyoto, Dec. 2, 1947; s. Kiyoshi and Yukiko (Noguchi) K.; m. Emily F. takagi, Apr. 15, 1972; children: Eugene, Leilani, Richard. BA, Kansai U., Japan, 1970; AA, Southwest Coll., LA, 1974; MIA, Columbia U., 1976. Pres. T.L.I. Inc., NYC, 1989-92; pres., CEO ACE USA, Inc., Bellevue, Wash., 1996—; treas. Systemland U.S.A., Inc., Honolulu, 1996—; mng. dir. ACE Co., Ltd., Tokyo, 1996—; pres., CEO Landmark Corp., Honolulu, 1998—, Ace Shoji Co. Ltd., Tokyo, 1999—, Pacific Angel Capital Corp., Honolulu, 2000—; CEO Pacific Asset Mgmt., LLC, Honolulu, 2003—. Com. mem. UNLV Internat. Gaming Inst., 1997—. Co-author: Challenge of Las Vegas. Mem. Am. Mgmt. Assn. Democrat. Buddhist. Avocations: movies, walking, golf, fishing, reading. Home: 107 Higuchi-Cho Nishino-kyo, Nakagyo-ku Kyoto 604 Japan Office Phone: 01181-3-5320-0733. E-mail: jkashida@tka.att.ne.jp.

KASICH, JOHN R., former congressman; b. McKees Rocks, Pa., May 13, 1952; BA, Ohio State U., 1974. Administrv. asst. Ohio State Senate, 1975-77; mem. Ohio Legislature, 1979-82, 98th-106th Congressses from 12th Ohio dist., Washington, 1983-2001; mem. nat. security com., armed svc. com.; mem. house budget com., chmn.; chmn. New Century Project, Columbus, 2001—. Author: Stand for Something, 2006.

KASINATH, BALAKUNTALAM S., medical researcher; b. Nov. 9, 1951; m. Uma Kasinath; children: Manasa, Vivek. MBBS in Medicine, Bangalore Med. Coll., India, 1975. With internal medicine Ill. Masonic Med. Ctr., Chgo., 1977-80; with nephrology U. Chgo. Hosps. and Clinics, 1980-83; asst prof. Rush-Presbyn.-St. Luke's Med. Ctr., Chgo., 1983-90; assoc. prof. dept. medicine divsn. nephrology U. Tex. Health Sci. Ctr., San Antonio, 1990-98; chief renal sect. Audie Murphy Meml. VA Hosp., San Antonio, 1991—2005, staff physician, 1991—. Prof. dept. medicine U. Tex. Health Sci. Ctr., San Antonio, 1998—. Contbr. articles to profl. jours., chpts in books; lectr. in field. Recipient Henry Christian award for excellence in rsch. Am. Fedn. for Clin. Rsch., 1994, Rsch. award Am. Diabetes Assn., 1995, 99, 2002, 05, Rsch. award VA, 1993, 97, 2002, 07, Rsch. award NIH, 1986, 90, 2003, 07. Mem. AAAS, Am. Soc. Nephrology, Internat. Soc. Nephrology, Indian Soc. Nephrology. Achievements include research in metabolic regulation of extracellular matrix molecules in diabetic renal disease. Office: U Tex Health Sci Ctr Dept Medicine-Nephrology Mail Code 7882 7703 Floyd Curl Dr San Antonio TX 78229-3900 Office Phone: 210-567-4707. Business E-Mail: kasinath@uthscsa.edu.

KASIRER, SURI, lobbyist; b. 1958; d. Moshe and Gloria Kasirer; m. Bruce Jay Teitelbaum, Apr. 3, 1997. Grad., Yeshiva U. Spl. asst. for Jewish affairs to Gov. Mario M. Cuomo State of NY, Albany, 1992—94; founder Kasirer Consulting, NYC, 1995—. V.p. leadership devel. EDAH; mem. Women's Leadership Forum; bd. dirs. Nat. Jewish Dem. Coun. Mem.: Ansonia Dem. Club. Office: Kasirer Consulting 321 Broadway Ste 201 New York NY 10007 Office Phone: 212-285-1800.

KASISCHKE, LOUIS WALTER, lawyer; b. Bay City, Mich., July 18, 1942; s. Emil Ernst and Gladys Ann (Stuady) K.; m. Sandra Ann Colosimo, Sept. 30, 1967; children: Douglas, Gregg. BA, Mich. State U., 1964, JD, 1967; LLM, Wayne State U., 1971. Bar: Mich. 1968, U.S. Dist. Ct. (southeastern dist.) Mich. 1968; CPA. Acct. Touche Ross & Co., Detroit, 1967-71; atty. Dykema Gossett, Detroit, 1971—; pres. Pella Window and Door Co., West Bloomfield, Mich., 1990-98. Bd. dirs. Barton Malow Co., Southfield. Author: Michigan Closely Held Corporations, 1986; contbr. articles to profl. jours. Mem. ABA, AICPA, State Bar Mich. (editor column Mich. Bar Jour. 1971-83), Mich. Assn. CPAs, Am. Coll. Tax Counsel Republican. Lutheran. Avocations: mountain climbing, skiing, running, squash, golf. Home: 3491 N Lakeshore Harbor Springs MI 49740 Office: Dykema Gossett 39577 Woodward Ave Ste 300 Bloomfield Hills MI 48304-5086

KASKELL, PETER HOWARD, professional society administrator, lawyer; b. Berlin, Mar. 29, 1924; s. Joseph and Lilo (Schaeffer) K.; m. Joan Folsom Macy, Nov. 30, 1968; stepchildren: Bryn, Alison. Grad., Horace Mann Sch., NYC, 1940; BA, Columbia U., 1943, LLB, 1948. Bar: N.Y. 1948. Assoc. White & Case, NYC, 1948-51; atty. Nat. Prodn. Authority, Washington, 1951-52, W.R. Grace & Co., NYC, 1952-54; div. counsel Curtiss-Wright Corp., Buffalo, 1954-56; with Olin Corp., Stamford, Conn., 1956-83, v.p. legal affairs, 1971-83; sr. v.p. CPR Inst. for Dispute Resolution, NYC, 1983-99, sr. fellow, 2000—. Former dir. CARE; former mem. adv. com. U.S. Dist. Ct. (ea. dist.) N.Y. Former trustee Aldrich Mus. Contemporary Art, Ridgefield, Conn., Boys' Athletic League, N.Y.C.; vice chmn. Conn. Humanities Coun.; organizer, chmn. lawyers com. conv. on contracts internat. sale goods, UN, Wilton ind. ethics com. With Intelligence Svc., AUS, 1943-45, ETO. Decorated Bronze Star. Mem. Assn. of Bar of City of N.Y., Wilton Riding Club (past gov.), Century Assn. Home: 226 Nod Hill Rd Wilton CT 06897-1717

KASKEY, RAYMOND JOHN, sculptor; b. Pitts., Feb. 22, 1943; s. Raymond John and Katherine (Stupak) K.; m. Sherrell Lewis. BArch, Carnegie-Mellon U., 1967; M Environ. Design, Yale U., 1969. Registered architect, Md., Va., D.C. Asst. prof. design Sch. Architecture, U. Md., College Park, 1969-76; architect Robert Bell Assoc., Washington, 1976-81; owner, sculptor Raymond Kaskey Studios, Brentwood, Md., 1981—. Vis. critic Sch. Architecture, Yale U., New Haven, 1977, Kans. State U., Manhattan, 1978; mem. adv. bd. James Wilbur Johnston Sculpture Competition, Washington, 1981—. Prin. works include civic sculpture Portland, Oreg., 1985, Nat. Law Enforcement Memorial, 1993, Nat. World War II Memorial, 2004. Fellow Nat. Sculpture Soc. (Mrs. Louis Bennett award 1981, Henry Hering Meml. medal 1986, 93); mem. AIA (Excellence award 1985). Office: Raymond Kaskey Studios 3804 38th St Brentwood MD 20722-1707 E-mail: kaskeystudio@earthlink.net.

KASKOWITZ, EDWIN, social services executive; b. St. Louis, May 15, 1936; s. Nathan and Fannie K.; children: Joy, Sara, Naomi. BA, Washington U., St. Louis, 1958, MSW. (grad. scholar), 1961. Lic. clin. social worker. Sr. social worker St. Louis County Health Dept., 1965-67; exec. dir. Gerontol. Soc. Am., 1967-80; pres. Business Radio Corp., Atlanta, 1981-82; pres., chief exec. officer The Association Mgmt. Group, Chevy Chase, Md., 1982-86; dir. JCCA Sr. Adult Services, Creve Coeur, Mo., 1986-89, The Forum on Aging Consumers and Employees, St. Louis U., 1989-90; pres. Gerontology Svcs. of Mo., 1991—; CEO, pres. People Sculptures Inc., 2002—. Pres. B'nai-Brith-Habirah, Washington, 1974-75; adv. bd. Over Easy program Sta. KQED-TV, 1977-81. With USAR, 1954-62. Fellow Royal Soc. Health; mem. Gerontol. Soc. Am., Am. Soc. Assn. Execs. (cert. assn. exec.), Nat. Assn. Social Workers, Acad. Cert. Social Workers.

KASLICK, RALPH SIDNEY, dentist, educator; b. Bklyn., Oct. 17, 1935; s. John J. and Dorothy K.; m. Jessica Hellinger, Oct. 24, 1976; 1 child, Andrew AB, Columbia U., 1956, D.D.S., 1959, cert. in periodontology, 1962. Instr. Fairleigh Dickinson U., Coll. Dental Medicine, Hackensack, NJ, 1965-67, asst. prof., 1967-70, assoc. prof., 1970-74, prof., 1974-88, asst. dean for acad. affairs, 1973-75, acting dean, 1975-76, dean, 1976-88, acting provost, Teaneck-Hackensack campus, 1983-85, sr. dean Teaneck-Hackensack campus, 1985-88; chief dentistry Coler-Goldwater Splty. Hosp., Roosevelt Island, NY, 1988—2003, pres. med. staff, 1992-94, 97-99, dir. consultative svcs., 1995—2003. Clin. prof. periodontics Coll. Dentistry, NYU, 1988—; cons. in field. Contbr. chpts. to textbooks, articles to profl. jours. Served to capt. U.S. Army, 1962-64. Recipient Journalism award of the Internat. Coll. of Dentists, 1972, medal of Japan Stomatological Soc., 1977, Stanley S. Bergen award for contbn. to dental edn. Seton Hall U., 1982, Disting. Alumnus award Columbia U. Periodontal Alumni Assn., 1984, Achievement award Fairleigh Dickinson U. Periodontal Alumni Assn., 1984, Hirschfeld Meml. medal and cert. Northeastern Soc. Periodontists, 1987, Disting. Practitioner medallion Nat. Acad. Practice, 1999, Disting. Alumni award Columbia U. Coll. Dental Medicine, 2007. Fellow Am. Coll. Dentists, N.Y. Acad. Dentistry; mem. ADA, AMA, Am. Dental Edn. Assn., Internat. Assn. Dental Rsch. (past pres. N.J. sect.), Am. Acad. Periodontology, Fedn. Spl. Care Orgns. in Dentistry, NY Acad. Scis., Sigma Xi, Omicron Kappa Upsilon.

KASLOW, FLORENCE WHITEMAN, psychologist, educator, family business consultant; b. Phila., Jan. 06; d. Irving and Rose (Tarin) Whiteman; m. Solis Kaslow; children: Nadine Joy, Howard Ian. AB in Sociology with distinction, Temple U., 1952; MA, Ohio State U., 1954; PhD, Bryn Mawr Coll., 1969. Lic. psychologist, marriage and family therapist, Fla.; bd. cert. psychologist Am. Bd. Clin. Psychology, Am. Bd. Forensic Psychology, Am. Bd. Family Psychology. Pvt. practice, Palm Beach Gardens, Fla., 1964—; dir. Fla. Couples and Family Inst., Palm Beach Gardens, 1982—; pres. Kaslow Assoc., Palm Beach Gardens, 1985—. Cons. USN Dept. Psychiatry Residency Tng. Programs, San Diego, Portsmouth, Va., Phila., 1976-88, Palm Beach Inst., 1983-90; adj. prof. med. psychology Duke U. Med. Ctr., Durham, N.C., 1982-2002; vis. prof. psychology Fla. Inst. Tech., Melbourne, 1985-; disting. vis. prof. Calif. Grad. Sch. Family Psychology, 1989-92; weekly radio guest Voice of Am., Focus on Families, 1993-2003; pres. Am. Bd. Forensic Psychology, 1977-80, Am. Bd. Family Psychology, 1996-2000; vis. prof. dept. psychiatry and behavior scis. med. ctr. Mercer U., Macon, Ga., 2006—. Editor: Voices in Family Psychology, 1990, The Military Family in Peace and War, 1993, Handbook of Relational Diagnoses and Dysfunctional Family Patterns, 1996, Handbook of Family Business and Family Business Consultation: A Global Perspective, 2006; editor: (with F. Shapiro and L. Makfield) EMDR & Family Therapy Processes, 2007; author (with L.L. Schwartz): Dynamics of Divorce: A Life Cycle Perspective, 1987; author: Painful Partings: Divorce and Its Aftermath, 1997, Handbook of Couple and Family Forensics, 2000, Comprehensive Handbook of Psychotherapy, 4 vols., 2002; author: (with L.L. Schwartz) Welcome Home: an International and Non Traditional Adoption Reader, 2004; mem. editl. bd. Jour. Marital and Family Therapy, 1976—, Jour. Family Psychology, 1987—, Jour. Sex and Marital Therapy, 1984—2002, Jour. Clin. Child Psychology, 1986—, Jour. Psychotherapy, 1988—2004, Profl. Psychology, 2002—, assoc. editor Jour. Family Psychotherapy, 1990—; contbr. chapters to books, articles to profl. jours. Recipient Outstanding Family Therapy Contbn. award, Am. Assn. Marriage and Family Therapy, 1991, NIMH trainee, 1969. Mem. APA (divsn. family psychology pres. 1987, sec. 1983-85, com. mem. 1987—, pres. divsn. media psychology 1993, coun. rep. 2002—, Disting. Lifetime Contbn. to Media Psychology award, 2000, Outstanding Conbtn. Internat. Advancement Psychology, 2002), Internat. Acad. Family Psychology (pres. 1998-2002), Am. Assn. Marital and Family Therapy, Am. Bd. Profl. Psychologists (trustee 2002-06, Disting. Psychology Contbn. award 1994), Am. Family Therapy Acad., Coalition Family Diagnosis (chmn. 1989-93), Am. Assn. Sex Educators, Counselors and Therapists, Internat. Family Therapy Assn. (founding pres. 1987-90), Acad. Family Mediators (bd. dir. 1982-88, treas. 1985-87). Office Phone: 561-625-0288. Personal E-mail: drfkaslow@bellsouth.net.

KASNOWSKI, CHESTER NELSON, artist, educator; b. Perth Amboy, NJ, Jan. 23, 1944; BFA, Dayton Art Inst., 1971; MFA, Tulane U., New Orleans, 1973. Curator New Orleans Mus. Art, 1971-74; tchr. So. Vt. Art Ctr., Manchester, 1981—2002. One-man show includes Bertha Undang Gallery, NYC, 1984, 85, 87, 91, 93, Carmen Llewellyn Gallery, New Orleans, 1996; group exhbns. at Dartmouth Coll., 1978, Robert Hall Fleming Mus., 1981, Franklin Furnace, 1982, 84, Bertha Undang Gallery, 1983, Hand Gallery, 1985; permanent collections include Cleve. Mus. Art, Bklyn. Mus., Franklin Furnace, Solomon R. Guggenheim Mus., Stedelijk Mus., Mus. Modern Art, Grantee Nat. Endowment Arts, 1974, 78. Home: PO Box 1 Weston VT 05161-0001 Personal E-mail: chesterk@sover.net.

KASOLD, BRUCE EDWARD, federal judge, lawyer; b. NYC, Apr. 26, 1951; s. Edward Frederick and Louise Catherine (Gebler) K.; m. Patricia Ann Gatz, June 16, 1973. BS, US Mil. Acad., 1973; JD, U. Fla., 1979; LLM, Georgetown U., 1982. Bar: Fla. 1979, US Ct. Mil. Appeals 1979, DC 1988. Commd. 2d lt. US Army, 1973, advanced through grades to lt. col., 1991, ret., 1994; commd. JAGC, 1979; legal counsel, Ft. Belvoir, 1979-81; legal counsel for affirmative claims litigation Sec. Army, Washington, 1981-83; chief legal counsel VII Corps Arty. Comdr., Augsburg, W.Ger., 1983-87; counsel to Sec. Army, 1987-89; legis. fellow US Senate Jud. Com., 1989-90, Senator Warner, 1990; legis. counsel Sec. Army, 1990-94; litigation atty. Holland & Knight, 1994-95; chief counsel US Senate Com. Rules & Adminstrn., 1995-98, Sec. US Senate & Senate Sgt. at Arms, 1998-2003; judge US Ct. Appeals Vets. Claims, Washington, 2003-. Spl. asst. US atty., 1980-81; spl. instr. Army Claims Svc., 1981-83, Judge Adv. Gen.'s Sch., 1982-83. Editor, pub.: Med. Care Recovery Newsletter, 1981-83; contbr. Army Lawyer, 1982—, articles to legal jours. Decorated Meritorious Svc. medal, Army Commendation with 2 oak leaf clusters. Mem. ABA, Fla. Bar Assn., DC Bar, Order of Coif. Roman Catholic. Office: US Ct Appeals Vets Claims 625 Indiana Ave NW Ste 900 Washington DC 20004*

KASOWITZ, MARC ELLIOT, lawyer; b. New Haven, June 28, 1952; s. Robert and Felice Beverly (Molaver) K. BA, Yale U., 1974; JD, Cornell U., 1977. Bar: N.Y. 1978, U.S. Dist. Ct. (so. and ea. dists.) N.Y. 1978; U.S. Ct. Appeals (2d cir.), 1989, U.S. Ct. Appeals (3rd cir.), 1993, U.S. Dist. Ct. Colo., 2001. Assoc. Rosenman & Colin, NYC, 1977-86, ptnr., 1986-88, Mayer, Brown & Platt, NYC, 1988-93, Kasowitz, Benson, Torres & Friedman LLP, NYC, 1993—. Editor: Cornell Law Review, 1975—77. Home: 1160 Park Ave Apt 4B New York NY 10128-1212 Office: Kasowitz Benson Torres & Friedman LLP 1633 Broadway New York NY 10019-6022 Office Phone: 212-506-1710. Office Fax: 212-506-1800. E-mail: mkasowitz@kasowitz.com.

KASPARAITIS, DARIUS, professional hockey player; b. Elektrenai, Russia, Oct. 16, 1972; m. Ingela Kasparaitis; 1 child, Elizabeth. Defenseman NY Islanders, 1992-97, Pitts. Penguins, 1996—2002, Colo. Avalanche, 2002, NY Rangers, 2002—07. Mem. Unified Team, Olympic Games, Albertville, France, 1992, Team Russia, Olympic Games, Nagano, Japan, 1998, Salt Lake City, 2002, Torino, Italy, 06. Achievements include being a member of gold medal Unified Hockey Team, Albertville Olympic Games, 1992. Avocations: fishing, tennis. Office: c/o NY Rangers 2 Pennsylvania Plaza New York NY 10121*

KASPERBAUER, MICHAEL JOHN, plant physiology educator, researcher; b. Manning, Iowa, Oct. 8, 1929; s. John Sixtus and Clara Mary (Balk) K.; m. Isabel Maria Giles, June 3, 1962; children: Maria, John, Paul, Sandra. BS, Iowa State Coll., 1954; PhD, Iowa State U., 1961. NSF postdoctoral fellow botany dept. U. Md., College Park, 1961-62; NRC/NAS rsch. assoc, rsch. plant physiologist USDA Pioneering Rsch. Lab., Beltsville, Md., 1962-63; rsch. plant physiologist USDA-Agrl. Rsch. Svc., Lexington, Ky., 1963-83, Florence, SC, 1983—. Mem. grad. faculty U. Ky., Lexington, 1965-83, adj. prof., 1965-83, Clemson (S.C.) U., 1983-2003. Editor, author: Biotechnology in Fescue Improvement, 1990; assoc. editor Agronomy Jour., 1975-83; contbr. over 200 articles to profl. jours. Bd. dirs. Gardenside Little League Baseball, Lexington, 1975-78; v.p. Turfland Babe Ruth Baseball League, Lexington, 1979-82. 1st lt. U.S. Army, 1954-56. Recipient L.M. Ware Rsch. award Am. Soc. Hort. Sci., 1990, Tech. Tranfer award Fed. Lab. Consortium , 1998, Superior Svc. award US Sec. Agrl., 2000. Fellow Am. Soc. Agronomy (Agronomic Rsch. award 1994, So. Branch Career Rsch award, 2002), Crop Sci. Soc. Am. (Crop Sci. Rsch. award 1990, Seed Sci. award 1999); mem. Am. Soc. Plant Physiologists, Am. Soc. Photobiology, Scandinavian Soc. Plant Physiology, Sigma Xi, Phi Delta Kappa, Gamma Sigma Delta, Phi Kappa Phi. Achievements include research in botany, crop science, photobiology, plant biochemistry, forage grasses, tissue and cell culture and molecular biology. Home: 1717 Williamsburg Ct Lexington KY 40504-2010 Personal E-mail: michaeljkasper@aol.com. *Awards and professional recognitions are nice, but family is the only thing that is really important to me.*

KASPRZAK, LUCIAN ALEXANDER, physicist, researcher, materials scientist; b. Scranton, Pa., July 22, 1943; s. Alexander Lucian and Helen Frances (Skubic) Kasprzak; m. Carole Anne Nowakowski, July 22, 1967; children: Brian, Dawn. BS in Physics, Stevens Inst. Tech., 1965, PhD in Materials, 1972; MS in Physics, Syracuse U., 1970. Engr. failure analysis IBM East Fishkill, Hopewell Junction, NY, 1965—69, engr. reliability Large Scale Integration, 1972—77, mgr. Very Large Scale Integration devel., 1977—81; mgr. vendor memory IBM Gen. Tech. Divsn. Assurance, Poughkeepsie, NY, 1981—82; tech. asst. to corp. v.p. IBM Corp. Hdqrs., White Plains, NY, 1982—83, mgr. memory tech., Gen. Tech. Divsn., 1983—84; program mgr., tech. support IBM Data Systems Divsn. Assurance, Poughkeepsie, 1984—85; program mgr. tech. profl. rels. IBM Corp. Hdqrs., Thornwood, NY, 1985—92; assoc. prof. physics and engrng. sci. Franciscan U. Steubenville, Ohio, 1992—96; reliability mgr. direct radiography Sterling Diagnostic Imaging, Newark, Del., 1996—97; dir. reliability Direct Radiography Corp., Newark, 1997—2001; reliability cons., 2001—03; staff reliability group Dade Behring Inc., 2004—. Bd. dirs. Internat. Reliability Physics Symposium, 1985—, chmn., 1986—87. Contbr. articles to profl. jours.; co-discoverer hot electron effect in Metal Oxide Semiconductor Field Effect Transistor; patentee in field. Mem. Environ. Bd., Wappingers Falls, NY, 1973; coach East Fishkill Youth Soccer League, 1974-82; coun. mem. St. Columba Parish, Hopewell Junction, 1985-91. Recipient Benefactors award Franciscan U. Steubenville, 1989; IBM resident fellow, Yorktown and Hoboken, NJ, 1969-72. Fellow IEEE (chmn. adv. bd. transactions on device and materials reliability, Third Millennium medal 2000); mem. Electron Devices Soc. of IEEE (adminstrv. com. 1986—, treas. 1988-99, adv. bd. Circuits and Devices mag. 1987-98, treas. trans. semiconductor mfg. 1992—, chmn. device reliability com. 1983-97, treas. Device Rsch. Conf. 1989-92, chmn. device reliability physics com. 1997-2005, Disting. Svc. award 2002), Am. Phys. Soc. Roman Catholic. Avocations: music, astronomy, philosophy, theology, art. Business E-Mail: l.kasprzak@ieee.org.

KASPUTYS, JOSEPH EDWARD, corporate executive, economist; b. Jamaica, NY, Aug. 12, 1936; s. Joseph John and Henrietta Viola (Derenthall) K.; m. Marilyn Patricia Kennedy, Oct. 29, 1953; children: Clare Victoria, Patricia Jeanne, Jacqueline Ann, Veronica Joy. BA magna cum laude, Bklyn. Coll., 1959; MBA with high distinction, Harvard U., Cambridge, Mass., 1967, DBA, 1972. With US Dept. Def., Washington, 1967-70; asst. adminstr. US Maritime Adminstrn., Washington, 1972-75; asst. sec. US Dept. Commerce, Washington, 1975-77; exec. v.p., COO Data Resources, Inc., Lexington, Mass., 1977-81, pres., CEO, 1981-84; exec. v.p. McGraw-Hill, Inc., NYC, 1984-87; pres., COO Primark Corp. Inc., Waltham, Mass., 1987-88, chmn., CEO, 1988-2000; chmn. Thomson Fin., 2000-01; chmn., CEO, pres. Global Insight, Inc., Waltham, 2001—. Lectr. Am. U., Washington, 1967-68, Bentley Coll., Boston, 1971-72; assoc. prof., lectr. George Washington U., Washington, 1967-77; bd. dirs. Logistics Mgmt. Inst., Washington. Chmn. adv. bd. Hitachi Found., Washington, Coun. for Excellence in Govt., Washington; mem. Com. for Econ. Devel., Washington. Comdr. USN, 1956-76. Decorated Legion of Merit; Warren G. Harding Aerospace fellow, 1971 Mem. Phi Beta Kappa. Clubs: Harvard Bus. Sch. (Boston); Capitol Hill (Washington). Republican. Roman Catholic. Home: 148 Sandy Pond Rd Lincoln MA 01773-2605 Office: Global Insight Inc 1000 Winter St Waltham MA 02451 Business E-Mail: joseph.kasputys@globalinsight.com.

KASS, BENNY LEE, lawyer; b. Chgo., Aug. 20, 1936; s. Herman and Ethel (Lome) Kass; m. Salme Lundstrom, Aug. 30, 1963; children: Gale, Brian. BS, Northwestern U., 1957; LLB, U. Mich., 1960; LLM, George Washington U., 1967. Bar: DC 1960. Atty. Maritime Adminstrn., 1960-61; counsel House Info. Subcom., 1962-65; asst. counsel Senate Adminstrv. Practice Subcom., Washington, 1965-69; pvt. practice law Washington, 1969—; mem. Kass, Mitek & Kass, PLLC, 2001; prof. communication law Am. U.; pub. mem. Nat. Advt. Rev. Bd., 1971-74. Life mem. Conf. Uniform State Laws. Columnist: Washington Post, L.A. Times; contbr. articles to profl. jours. Chmn. Ad Hoc Com. Consumer Protection, 1965—; chmn. consumer affairs subcom. Mayor's Econ. Devel. Com., 1968—70. With USAF, 1961—62. Mem.: FBA, ABA, Am. Polit. Sci. Assn. (Congl. fellow 1966), Sigma Delta Chi. Office: Kass Mitek & Kass PLLC 1050 17th St NW Ste 1100 Washington DC 20036-5596 Home Phone: 202-966-5703. Business E-Mail: blkass@kmklawyers.com.

KASS, DAVID NORMAN, accountant, lawyer; b. NYC, Mar. 8, 1951; s. Joseph Zane and Rosalind (Sperber) K.; m. Esta Gail Millman, Nov. 26, 1977; children: Sean N., Joshua A. BS in Acctg., SUNY, Albany, 1973; JD, St. John's U., Jamaica, NY, 1982. Bar: NY 1983. Staff acct. Touche Ross & Co., NYC, 1972-74; sr. acct. Reich Weiner & Co., NYC, 1974-76; ptnr. Brandt, Pollack, Kass & Wilkins, NYC, 1976-79, Kass & Kass CPAs PC, Roslyn, NY, 1979—; pvt. practice Roslyn, 1983—. Seminar leader Nassau Acad. Law, Mineola, NY, 1993, seminar leader/lectr., 1995. Contbr. articles to The Nassau Lawyer. Baseball coach Roslyn Little League, 1990-95; active in alumni fund campaign SUNY, Albany, 1994. Mem. Am. Arbitration Assn. (comml. law arbitrator), NY State Bar Assn., Nassau County Bar Assn. (mentor), Nat. Assn. CPA Practitioners, NY State Soc. CPAs, Nat. Arbitration Forum. Office Phone: 516-627-3136. Personal E-mail: dnkass@gmail.com.

KASS, JEROME ALLAN, writer; b. Chgo., Apr. 21, 1937; s. Sidney J. and Celia (Gorman) K.; children from previous marriage: Julie, Adam; m. Delia Ephron, May 21, 1982. BA, NYU, 1958, MA, 1959. Adj. prof. Film Sch. Colulmbia U. Playwright: Monopoly, 1965, Saturday Night, 1968, (mus.) Ballroom, 1978 (Tony nomination), (mus.) Norman's Ark, Montclair U., 2002, (TV) A Brand New Life, 1973, Queen of the Stardust Ballroom, 1975 (Writers Guild Am. award, Emmy nomination), My Old Man, 1979, The Fighter, 1982, Scorned and Swindled, 1984, Crossing to Freedom (aka Pied Piper), 1989, Last Wish, 1991, The Only Way Out, 1993, Secrets, 1995; screenwriter: The Black Stallion Returns, 1981, (miniseries) Evergreen, 1985; author: Four Short Plays by Jerome Kass, 1966, Saturday Night, 1969; adapted to concert form Finian's Rainbow, L.A., 1997, Pajama Game, L.A., 1998, Fiorello, L.A., 1999; musical version Queen of the Stardust Ballroom, Chgo., 1998. Mem. Dramatists Guild, Writers Guild Am., Actors Studio, Phi Beta Kappa. Personal E-mail: kasscade@aol.com.

KASS, LAWRENCE, hematologist, oncologist, educator; b. Toledo, Ohio, Sept. 30, 1938; AB magna cum laude, U. Mich., 1960; MD with hons., U. Chgo., 1964, MS Anatomy, 1964. Diplomate Nat. Bd. Med. Examiners, Am. Bd. Internal Medicine/Internal Medicine and Hematology, Med. Oncology, Am. Bd. Pathology/Hematology. Intern Peter Bent Brigham Hosp., Boston, 1964-65, asst. resident internal medicine, 1965-66; sr. asst. resident internal medicine U. Hosps. of Cleve., 1966-68; Elliott Hoyt fellow in hematology Univ. Hosps. of Cleve., 1967-68; various to rsch. assoc. U. Chgo., 1968-70; asst. prof. internal medicine U. Mich. Med. Sch., Ann Arbor, 1970-73, assoc. prof. internal medicine, 1973-78; prof. path., medicine Case Western Res. U. Sch. Medicine, Cleve., 1978—; head hematopathology MetroHealth Med. Ctr., Cleve., 1978—. Cons. in medicine, VA Hosp., Ann Arbor; editorial cons. Williams and Wilkins Pubs., Balt., 1974—, Archives of Pathology and Lab. Medicine Blood, The Jour. of Hematology, The Jour. of Histochemistry and Cytochemistry, Western Jour. of Medicine, Am. Jour. of Hematology, Biotechnic & Histochemistry, 1975—, Rsch. Career Selection Rev. Com., VA, Washington, 1976—; active numerous coms. in field. Contbr. articles to profl. jours. Maj. med corps. U.S. Army, 1968-70. Recipient Internat. Giovanni DiGuglielmo prize, Giovanni DiGuglielmo Found., Accademia Nazionale Die Lincei, Rome, 1976, Diamond Cover award Nat. Soc. Histotechnologists and Jour. of Histotechnology, 1988, C.V. Mosby award, 1964, Merck award 1964. Fellow Am. Coll. Phys., Coll. Am. Pathologists; mem. AAAS, Am. Soc. Hematology, Am. Fedn. Clin. Rsch., Am. Soc. Clin. Oncology, Soc. Exptl. Biology and Medicine, Cen. Soc. Clin. Rsch., Histochem. Soc., Biol. Stain Commn., Am. Soc. Clin. Path., Phi Eta Sigma, Phi Beta Kappa, Alpha Omega Alpha. Office: MetroHealth Med Ctr 2500 Metrohealth Dr Cleveland OH 44109-1900 Office Phone: 216-778-4945. Office Fax: 216-778-5701. Business E-Mail: lkass@metrohealth.org.

KASS, LEON RICHARD, humanities educator; b. Chgo., Feb. 12, 1939; s. Samuel and Anna (Shoichet) K.; m. Amy Judith Apfel, June 22, 1961; children: Sarah, Miriam. BS, U. Chgo., 1958, MD, 1962; PhD in Biochemistry, Harvard U., 1967. Intern Beth Israel Hosp., Boston, 1962-63; staff assoc. Lab. Molecular Biology, Nat. Inst. Arthritis and Metabolic Diseases, NIH, Bethesda, Md., 1967-69, staff fellow, 1969-70, sr. staff fellow, 1970; exec. sec. com. on life scis. and social policy NRC-NAS, Washington, 1970-72; tutor St. John's Coll., Annapolis, Md., 1972-76; Joseph P. Kennedy Sr. rsch. prof. in bioethics Kennedy Inst., Georgetown U., 1974-76; Henry R. Luce prof. liberal arts of human biology in coll. U. Chgo., 1976-84, prof. com. on social thought, 1984-90, Addie Clark Harding prof. in coll. and com. on social thought, 1990—; Hertog fellow Am. Enterprise Inst., Washington, 2002—. Founding fellow, bd. dirs. Hastings Ctr., 1969-96; bd. govs. U.S.-Israel Binat. Sci. Found., 1982-88; mem. coun. Nat. Humanities Coun., 1984-91, vice chmn. 1987-89; mem. Pres.'s Coun. Bioethics, 2001-, chmn. 2001-05. Author: Toward a More Natural Science: Biology and Human Affairs, 1985, The Hungry Soul: Eating and the Perfecting of Our Nature, 1994, (James Q. Wilson) The Ethics of Human Cloning, 1998, (Amy A. Kass) Wing to Wing, Oar to Oar: Readings on Courting and Marrying, 2000, Life, Liberty, and The Defense of Dignity: The Challenge for Bioethics, 2002, The Beginning of Wisdom: Reading Genesis, 2003; contbr. articles to profl. jours. Served with USPHS, 1967-69. NIH postdoctoral fellow, 1963-67, John Simon Guggenheim Meml. Found. fellow, 1972-73, Nat. Humanities Ctr. fellow, 1984-85, W.H. Brady, Jr. Disting. fellow Am. Enterprise Inst., 1991-92, 98-99; NEH grantee, 1973-74; recipient Bradley prize The Lynde and Harry Bradley Found., 2003. Mem. Phi Beta Kappa, Alpha Omega Alpha. Jewish. Office: American Enterprise Inst 1150 17th St NW Washington DC 20036-4603

KASS, PHILIP HOWARD, epidemiology educator; b. LA, Aug. 19, 1958; s. Leonard and Zita (Dunn) K.; children: Lauren, Alexander. DVM, U. Calif., Davis, 1983, M Preventive Vet. Medicine, 1984, MS in Stats., 1988, PhD in Epidemiology, 1990. Asst. prof. epidemiology U. Calif., Davis, 1990-95, assoc. prof. epidemiology, 1995—2004, prof. epidemiology, 2004—, dept. chair, 2006—. Mem. Am. Coll. Vet. Preventive Medicine (sec. epidemiology specialty 1993-95), Calif. Med. Assn., Am. Vet. Med. Assn., Soc. Epidemiologic Rsch. Home: 39330 Granite Bay Pl Davis CA 95616-7000 Office: U Calif Sch Vet Medicine Sect Biometrics/Prev Med Dept Population Health Davis CA 95616 Office Phone: 530-752-8631. Business E-Mail: phkass@ucdavis.edu.

KASSABOV, MARTIN, mathematics professor; PhD, Yale Univ., 2003. Postdoctoral fellow Univ. Alberta, 2003—04; H.C. Wang asst. prof., dept. math. Cornell U., Ithaca, NY, 2004—06, asst. prof. math, 2006—. Spkr. in field. Contbr. articles to profl. jours. Centennial Fellowship, Am. Math. Soc., 2007—08. Office: Cornell U Dept Math 590 Malott Hall Ithaca NY 14853-4201 Office Phone: 607-255-6868. Office Fax: 607-255-7149. Business E-Mail: kassabov@math.cornell.edu.

KASSAM, AMIN B., neurosurgeon, educator; m. Greta Kassam; children: Armand, Mikaeel. MD, U. Toronto, Can., 1991. Vis. instr. neurol. surgery U. Pitts., Sch. Medicine, 1997—98, asst. prof. neurol. surgery, 1998—2004, assoc. prof. neurol. surgery, 2004—. Dir. minimally invasive endoneurosurgery U. Pitts., Sch. Medicine, 1998—, interim chair dept. neurol. surgery, 2006—07, co-dir., skull base surgery ctr., 1998—, chair dept. neurol. surgery, 2007—. Mem. editl. bd. Neurol. Rsch., 2007—, ad hoc reviewer Jour. Neuroimaging, 1999—, Neurology, 2000, Jour. Neurology, Neurosurgery and Psychiatry, 2005—. Named one of Top Doctors, Pitts. Mag., 2006; recipient Frederick Urghart Acad. scholarship, 1985, Aga Khan Acad. scholarship, 1985, George Brown Meml. award for rsch., U.

Toronto, 1990, Track scholarship in surgery, 1991, Best Paper in eHealth award, Internat. Conf. on Telemedicine and Multi-media Comm., 2005, Endoscopics award, Beijing Neurosurg. Inst., 2006. Fellow: Royal Coll. Physicians and Surgeons Can. (life); mem.: Soc. Neuro-Oncology (life), Trigeminal Neuralgia Assn. (life), European Skull Base Soc. (life), North Am. Skull Base Soc. (life; mem. exec. bd. 2005), Congress Neurol. Surgeons (life), Am. Assn. Neurol. Surgeons (life). Achievements include development of the Expanded Endonasal Transplanum Approach (EEA) for minimally invasive brain surgery. Office: Univ Pitts Med Ctr 200 Lothrop St PUH B-400 Pittsburgh PA 15213 Home Phone: 412-967-9122; Office Phone: 412-647-6358. Office Fax: 412-647-1778. Business E-Mail: kassamab@upmc.edu.

KASSAN, STUART S., rheumatologist; b. White Plains, NY, Nov. 19, 1946; s. Robert Jacob and Rosalind (Suchin) K.; m. Gail Karesh, Apr. 4, 1971; children: Michael Andrew, Merrill Alissa. BA, Case Western Res., 1968; MD, George Washington U., 1972. Diplomate Am. Bd. Internal Medicine, Am. Bd. Rheumatology, Am. Bd. Geriatrics. Intern and resident Grady Meml. Hosp., Altanta, 1972-74; clin. fellow NIH, Bethesda, Md., 1974-76; fellow Hosp. for Spl. Surgery, Cornell Med. Ctr., NYC, 1976-78; head rheumatology clinic VA Med. Ctr., Denver, 1978-80; pvt. practice rheumatology, 1978—; asst. clin. prof. medicine U. Colo. Health Scis. Ctr., Denver, 1978-84, assoc. clin. prof. medicine, 1984-94, clin. prof. medicine, 1994—; med. dir. rehab unit. Luth. Med. Ctr., Wheatridge, Colo., 1983-87; med. dir. rehab. unit St. Anthony Hosp., Denver, 1987-93; chief med. officer Aspire Behavioral Health Inc., 2006—. Cons. Annals Internal Medicine, Phila., 1986—, Arthritis and Rheumatism, Atlanta, 1995—, Jour. of Rheumatology, 1996—; vis. alumni scholar George Washington U. Sch. Medicine, 1986; chmn. med. adv. bd. Sjögren's Syndrome Found., Bethesda, 1997-03, bd. dirs., 1996-03, Lupus Found. Colo., 2005-. Co-editor: Sjögren's Syndrome, 1987; contbr. over 40 articles to profl. jours. Bd. dirs. Rocky Mountain chpt. Arthritis Found., Denver, 1978-80, 03—, pres.-elect 2007Polachek fellow, 1976-77; bd. dirs. Lupus Found. Colo., v.p., 1995-96, pres., 1996-05; bd. dirs. Lupus Rsch. Inst., NYC, 2002-, Nat. Arthritis Found., 2006—. public policy coun., 2007-; pres. Metrowest IPA, Lakewood, Colo., 1997-03. With USPHS, 1974-76. Named Physician Honoree, Arthritis Found., Rocky Mt. Chpt., 2004, Annual Honoree, Lupus Found. Colo., 2005; recipient Disting. Alumni Svc. award, George Washington U., 2006. Fellow ACP, Am. Coll. Rheumatology (regional adv. com. 2005-, corp. affairs com. 2007-), Colo. Rheumatology Assn. (pres. 2004—), George Washington U. Sch. Medicine Alumni Assn.(pres. 2004—, mem. bd. dirs. 2004—); mem. Harvey Soc., Rocky Mountain Rheumatism Soc. (pres. 1997—), George Washington U. Alumni Assn. (bd. dirs.), Cosmos Club, Cactus Club. Jewish. Achievements include namesake for Lupus Found. of Colo. Stuart S. Kassan Humanitarian award. Office: Colo Arthritis Assoc 4200 W Conejos Pl Ste 314 Denver CO 80204-1311 Office Phone: 303-892-6033. Personal E-mail: skassan@earthlink.net.

KASSEL, ARTHUR DAVID, retired orthopaedic surgeon; b. NYC, June 13, 1925; s. Morris Bernard and Theresa Kassel; children: Laurie Ann, Daniel Robert, Hazel Susan. MB, MD, Chgo. Med. Sch. Resident in orthop. surgery VA Hosp., Bklyn.; orthop. surgeon Bklyn. and Oakland VA Hosps., 1954—59, Fremont Orthop. Med. Group, Calif., 1959—98, ret., 1998. Capt. US Army, 1952—54. Fellow: AOFAS, ACS, AAOS. Home: 1071 Belmarin Keys Blvd Novato CA 94949

KASSEL, CATHERINE M., community, maternal, and women's health nurse, consultant; b. Bklyn., Dec. 18, 1953; d. Christopher Frank and Ana Rosa (Sousa) Pannone; m. David L. Kassel, Dec. 27, 1979. Diploma in nursing, Kings County Hosp., Bklyn., 1974; BA in Cmty. Health, CUNY, 1979; BSN with honors, Columbia U., 1989. RN, N.Y. V.p. Kassel Mgmt. Co., NYC, 1985—; pres. Kassel & Co., LLC, NYC. Bd. dirs., co-chair legis. com. N.Y. Counties of RNs, Dist. 13, trustee, treas. polit. action com.; past bd. dirs. Nat. Abortion Rights Action League; bd. dirs., treas., chmn. fundraising, nominating com., adv. coun., Global Kids Inc.; mem. Women's Leadership Forum of Dem. Nat. Com. Mem. ANA (polit. action com.), ANA Found. (founding mem.), N.Y. State Nurses Assn., PAC. Home: 145 W 67th St Apt 7H New York NY 10023 Office Phone: 212-875-9945.

KASSEL, TERRY, human resources specialist; BA, NYU; JD, Seton Hall U. Pvt. practice, NY and NJ; various leadership positions including asst. gen. counsel and v.p. Office of Gen. Counsel; v.p. human resources U.S. private client group Merrill Lynch, NYC, 1985—2000, sr. v.p. human resources, 2001—05, sr v.p. exec. leadership develop., 2005—. Mem. bd. mgrs. Merrill Lynch Cmty. Devel. Co.; trustee Winthrop H. Smith Meml. Found., Merrill Lynch & Co. Found. Mem. adv. bd. NOW Legal Def. and Edn. Fund. Office: Merrill Lynch 4 World Financial Ctr New York NY 10080*

KASSEL, VIRGINIA WELTMER, television producer, scriptwriter; b. Omaha; d. Tyler and Inez (Willard) Weltmer. BA, Bryn Mawr Coll. Producer Sta. WGBH-TV, Boston; producer NET, NYC, coordinator nat. programs; mgr. spl. projects, exec. prodr. humanities programs WNET, NYC; sr. producer CBS Cable, NYC, 1981-83; dir. devel. and prodn. East Coast Primetime Entertainment, Inc., 1983-87; v.p. East Coast Primetime Entertainment, Inc., 1987-89; assoc. dir. performance programs, prodn. exec. Great Performances Sta. WNET-TV, NYC, 1989-91; producer, dir., writer Potter Prodns., 1991-92; dir. devel. Internat. Cultural Programming, 1992-94. Creator, prodr.: The Adams Chronicles; prodr.: The Soong Connection, 1995; founding prodr. Ch. of Heavenly Rest Players; contbr. articles to profl. jours. Recipient George Foster Peabody award, 1977, 2 Ohio State awards, 1977, Spl. Achievement award Nat. Assn. Ednl. Broadcasters, 1977, Triangle award, 1986; grantee NEH, Mellon Found Mem.: NATAS, NY Women in Film and TV, Brit. Acad. Film and TV Arts (NY and London), Am. Acad. TV Arts and Scis., Writers Guild Am. East, Nat. Com. on U.S. China Rels., Bryn Mawr Club NY (bd. dirs.), Women's City Club NY (bd. dirs., exec. com., co-chair commn. com.), Princeton Club (NY). Home: 4 E 89th St New York NY 10128-0636 Personal E-mail: virkassel@aol.com.

KASSELL, NEAL FREDERIC, neurosurgery educator; b. Phila., Mar. 17, 1946; s. Martin Buddy and Evelyn Abigail (Block) K.; m. Nancy Coffin, Dec. 14, 1967 (div.); children: Natasha Lynn, Lauren Tamara, Nicole Tristan; m. Denise Etheridge, Aug. 30, 1986 (div. 1987); m. Lynn Haire, Mar. 12, 1994 (div. 2000). MD, U. Pa., 1972. Diplomate Am. Bd. Neurol. Surgery. Intern Pa. Hosp., Phila., 1972-73, resident in neurology, 1973-74, resident in neurosurgery, 1974-75, U. Western Ont., London, 1975-77; asst. prof. neurosurgery U. Iowa, Iowa City, 1977-81, assoc. prof. neurosurgery, 1981-82, prof. neurosurgery, 1982-84; prof. and vice chmn. neurosurgery U. Va. Sch. Medicine, Charlottesville, 1984-97, prof., co-chmn. neurosurgery, 1993—; mem. staff U. Va. Hosp., Charlottesville. Chmn. bd., founder Multimedia Med. Sys., Inc., 1995-2000—; chmn., founder Med. Specialists, 1999; bd. dir. Va. Nat. Bank, LaGesse Found.; dir. NIH-Nat. Inst. Neurol. Disorders and Stroke study sects., 1984—; founder Focused Neurosound Surgery Found., bd. dir. Reviewer Neurosurgery, Jour. Cerebral Blood Flow and Metabolism, 1977—; mem. editl. bd. Stroke, Surg. Neurology, Neurosurgery; contbr. over 450 papers to profl. jours. Bd. dirs. Lagesse Found. Recipient numerous rsch. grants and contracts; recipient McKenzie Meml. award, 1977, Grass award. Republican. Avocations: classical music, hiking. Home: Wingate 2154 Garth Rd Charlottesville VA 22901-5412 Office: U Va Health Sys PO Box 800212 Charlottesville VA 22908-0212 Office Phone: 434-924-2735. Business E-Mail: neal@virginia.edu.

KASSELL, PAULA SALLY, editor, publisher; b. NYC, Dec. 5, 1917; d. Daniel Herman and Bertha Blanche (Jaret) K.; m. Gerson Gustav Friedman, Aug. 16, 1941 (dec.); children: Daniel Kassell, Claire Florence Friedman. BA, Barnard Coll., 1939. Tech. editor Bell Labs., Whippany, NJ, 1955-65, methods analyst Murray Hill, NJ, 1965-70; founder, editor, pub. New Directions for Women, Dover, NJ, 1971-77, assoc. editor Englewood, NJ, 1977-87, sr. editor, 1987-93, index editor Dover, 1993-98. V.p., UN rep. Women's Inst. for Freedom of Press, Washington, 1990—; convenor, mem. media task force Com. on Status of Women, UN, 1990-98. Contbr. chapters to books. Co-convenor Lakeland chpt. NOW, Dover, 1970; v.p. Dover (N.J.) Child Care Ctr., 1979-91; bd. dirs. Nat. Woman's Party, Washington, 1991-98; mem. media com. Forum 95, UN, N.Y.C., 1994-95; mem. adv. bd. Vet. Feminists Am., Lafayette, La., 1995—; mem. TV task force Morris County NOW, Morristown, N.J., 1995—; trustee Women's Media Initiative, 1997. Recipient First Feminist Action award NOW NJ, 1985, Women Making Herstory award, 1995, Elizabeth Cady Stanton award Women's Rights Info. Ctr., 1993, Woman of Achievement award Douglass Coll., 1994, Medal of Honor Vet. Feminists Am., 1998, Millicent Carey McIntosh Feminism Award Barnard Coll., 2004, Women Making History award NOW N.J. Found., 2006. Featured in exhibit on NJ feminists by Morris County (NJ) Hist. Soc., September 17, 2000 to March 18, 2001, Journalist of Month, on women's e-news, www.womensenews.org, 2002. Mem. Am. Journalism Historians Assn., Internat. Women's Media Found., Journalism & Women Symposium. Avocations: attending opera, concerts, ballet performances, visiting museums, travel. Home: 25 W Fairview Ave Dover NJ 07801-3417

KASSEWITZ, RUTH EILEEN BLOWER, retired public relations executive; b. Columbus, Ohio, May 15, 1928; d. E. Wallett and Helen (Daub) Blower; m. Jack Kassewitz, July 28, 1962 (dec.). BS in Journalism-Mgmt., Ohio State U., Columbus, 1951. Copywriter Ohio Fuel Gas Co., Columbus, 1951-55, Merritt Owens Advt. Agy., Kansas City, 1955-56; account exec. Grant Advt., Inc., Miami, 1956-59; account supr. Venn/Cole & Assocs., Miami, 1959-67; dir. comms. Ferendino/Grafton/Candela/Spillis Archs. & Engrs., Miami, 1967-69, Dade County dept. Housing and Urban Devel., Miami, 1969-72, Met. Dade County Govt., County Mgrs. Office, 1972-78; adminstr. pub. rels. U. Miami/Jackson Meml. Med. Ctr., 1978-90, ret., 1990. Bd. dirs. Girl Scouts USA, Tropical, Fla., 1974—76, 1981—83, Lung Assn. Dade-Monroe Counties, 1976—87, Met. YMCA, 1996—2003; exec. com. Miami-Dade C.C. Found., 1984—99; pres. Mental Health Assn. Dade County, 1982; mem. City of Miami Ecol. and Beautification Com. (now TREEmendous Miami, Inc.), 1978—2000; 1st vice-chmn., 1996—98; bd. govs. Barry U., Miami, 1981—83; trustee Nat. Humanities Faculty, 1981—83; treas., past chmn. Health, Edn., Promotion Coun., Inc.; adv. bd. Miami's For Me, 1987—88; mem. Coral Gables Cable TV Bd., 1983—86; cmty. adv. bd. Jr. League Greater Miami, Inc., 1989—92; founding mem. Nat. Honor Roll, Women in Pub. Rels., No. Ill. U., 1993; trustee emeritus United Protestant Appeal, 1992—99; ch. moderator Plymouth Congl. Ch., 1986—88, trustee, 1995—99, co-pres. Women's Fellowship, 2001—02. Recipient Disting. Svc. award Plymouth Congl. Ch., Miami, 1979; Ann Stover award, 1983; Golden Image award Fla. Pub. Rels. Assn., 1987; named Woman of Yr. Plymouth Congl. Ch., U. Miami Med. Sch., 1991, Humanitarian of Yr. YMCA of Gtr. Miami, 1998; honoree Fla. Women of Achievement. Fellow Pub. Rels. Soc. Am. (pres. South Fla. chpt. 1969-70, nat. chmn. govt. sect. 1973-74, nat. dir. 1974-76; cont. edn. coun. 1981-83; Silver anvil award 1973, del Assembly 1970-73, 86-89, Paul M. Lund Pub. Svc. award 1993, Miami chpt. Lifetime Achievement award 1995); mem. Women in Comms. (pres. Gtr. Miami chpt. 1962-63; Clarion awards 1973, 75, Cmty. Headliner 1985, Lifetime Achievement award Atlantic chpt. 2007), Miami Internat. Press Club (bd. dirs. 1986-87, treas. 1992), 200 Club Greater Miami (v.p. 1999-2000), Rotary Club of Miami (bd. dirs. 1988-97, pres. 1993-94, Disting. Rotarian of Yr. 1996, Rotarian of Yr. internat. dist. # 6990 1999), Delta Delta Delta (pres. Miami alumnae chpt. 1997-99), U. Miami Heritage Soc. E-mail: ruthbk@bellsouth.net.

KASSIN, SAUL, psychology professor; b. NYC, Apr. 25, 1953; s. Mordy and Betty K.; m. Carol Beth Goldner, Sept. 19, 1952; children: Briana Rachel, Marc Joseph. BS, Bklyn. Coll., 1974; MA, U. Conn., 1976, PhD, 1978. NIH postdoctoral fellow U. Kans., Lawrence, 1978-79, Stanford U., Calif., 1985-86; asst. prof. Purdue U., West Lafayette, Ind., 1979-81, Williams Coll., Williamstown, Mass., 1981-84; rsch. assoc. Fed. Jud. Ctr., Washington, 1984-85; from assoc. to full prof. Williams Coll., Williamstown, 1986—2006; disting. prof. John Jay Coll. Criminal Justice, 2006—. Jury, media cons., expert witness. Author: Psychology, 1995, 4th edit., 2004, Essentials of Psychology, 2004, Psychology in Modules, 2006; co-author: The American Jury on Trial, 1988, Confessions in the Courtroom, 1993, Social Psychology, 1990, 6th edit., 2005; co-editor: Developmental Social Psychology: Theory and Research, 1981, The Psychology of Evidence and Trial Procedure, 1985, On The Witness Stand: Controversies in the Courtroom, 1987, In the Jury Box: Controversies in the Courtroom, 1987, Readings in Social Psychology, 2002, Current Directions in Psychology, 2005, Psychology in Modules, 2006; cons. editor Jour. Exptl. Social Psychology, 1982-87, Jour. Personality and Social Psychology: Attitudes and Social Cognition, 1992-94; editl. cons. Law and Human Behavior, 1986—; ad hoc reviewer in field; contbr. articles to profl. jours. Rsch. grantee, Found. Child Devel., 1984—85, Jud. fellow, US Supreme Ct., 1984—85. Fellow APA, Am. Psychol. Soc., Am. Psychology-Law Soc.; mem. Soc. for Exptl. Social Psychology, Phi Beta Kappa. Office: Williams Coll Bronfman Sci Ctr Williamstown MA 01267 Business E-Mail: skassin@williams.edu.

KASSINGER, THEODORE WILLIAM (TED R. KASSINGER), lawyer, former federal agency administrator; b. Atlanta, Jan. 26, 1953; s. Edward Theodore and Sarah Mell (Laurent) K.; m. Ruth Lynn Good, Oct. 13, 1984; children: Anna Laurent, Austen Elizabeth, Alice Caroline. BLA, U. Ga., 1975, JD, 1978. Bar: Ga. 1978, D.C. 1986. Atty.-advisor U.S. Internat. Trade Commn., Washington, 1978-80; atty., advisor U.S. Dept. State, Washington, 1980-81; internat. trade counsel com. on fin. U.S. Senate, Washington, 1981-85, assoc., 1985-89; ptnr. Vinson & Elkins L.L.P., Washington, 1990—2001; gen. counsel U.S. Dept. Commerce, Washington, 2001—04, dep. sec., 2004—05; ptnr., co-chair global trade practice O'Melveny & Myers LLP, Washington, 2005—. Co-author: U.S. Regulation of International Trade, 1987, Basic Documents in International Economic Law, 1989. Republican. Roman Catholic. Office: O'Melveny & Myers LLP 1625 Eye St NW Washington DC 20006 Office Phone: 202-383-5170. Business E-Mail: tkassinger@omm.com.

KASSIRER, JEROME PAUL, medical educator; b. Buffalo, Dec. 19, 1932; Grad., U. Buffalo, 1953, MD magna cum laude, 1957; DS (hon.), U. Mass., 1992; D honoris causa, L'Universite Rene Descartes, Paris, 1992; DS (hon.), Thomas Jefferson U., 1994, SUNY, 1995. Diplomate Am. Bd. Internal Medicine (mem. certifying examination com. 1987-89, bd. dirs. 1989-96, mem. exec. com. 1993-96, chmn. 1995-96). Intern, asst. resident in medicine Buffalo Gen. Hosp., Buffalo, 1957—59; fellow in nephrology New Eng. Med. Ctr., Boston, 1959—61, sr. resident in medicine, 1961—62, asst. physician, 1961—65, physician renal svc., 1969-74, assoc. physician-in-chief, 1971—91, acting physician-in-chief, 1976—77; instr. medicine Sch. Medicine, Tufts U., Medford, Mass., 1961-65, asst. prof. medicine, 1965—69, assoc. prof., 1969—74, vice chmn. dept. medicine, 1971—91, acting chmn. dept. medicine, 1974—75, prof. medicine, 1974—, Sara Murray Jordan Prof. Medicine, 1987—91; editor-in-chief New Eng. Jour. Medicine, Boston, 1991—99. Lectr. in medicine Harvard U., 1991—; bd. dirs. Postgrad. Med. Inst. Mass. Med. Soc., 1988—91; vis. prof. Stanford U., 2007—. Editor in chief: Current Therapy in Internal Medicine, 1990; co-editor: Clin. Problem Solving, Hosp. Practice, 1985—91; cons. editor: Am. Jour. Medicine, 1976—86, mem. editl. bd.: New Eng. Jour. Medicine, 1972—75; co-editor: Nephrology Forum, Kidney Internat, 1978—91, ed. Decision Making, 1987—89; author: On the Take: How Medicine's Complicity with Big Business Can Endanger Your Health, 2004; editl. advisor: Outline of Knowledge, Part 4: Human Life, The New Encyclopaedia Britannica, 1989. Recipient Ednl. Rsch. Found. award, AMA, 1993. Master: ACP (gov. Mass. 1985—89, mem. exec. com. bd. govs. 1988—89, mem. health and pub. policy com. 1989—91, bd. regents 1990—91, chmn. sci.); mem.: Am. Acad. Arts & Scis., Soc. Clin. Decision Making (charter mem.), Buffalo Acad. Medicine, Nat. Libr. Medicine (chmn. bd. sci. counselors 1989—90, mem. biomed. journalism award com. 1992—), Assn of Am. Physicians, Inst. Medicine NAS. Jewish. Avocation: photography. Office: Tufts U Sch Med 136 Harrison Ave Boston MA 02111 Office Phone: 617-636-6523. Personal E-mail: jpkassirer@aol.com.

KASSNER, ANDREW CHARLES, lawyer; b. NYC, Dec. 12, 1959; s. Herbert Seymour Kassner and Sheilah Helen (Goodwin) Keat; m. Maureen Cummins, Mar. 25, 1984; children: Ethan, Gillian, Adam, Joshua, Claudia. BA in History, U. Pa., 1980; JD cum laude, N.Y. Law Sch., 1983. Bar: N.Y. 1984, U.S. Dist. Ct. (so. and ea. dists.) N.Y. 1984, Pa. 1985, Del. 2004, U.S. Dist. Ct. (ea. dist.) Pa. 1985, U.S. Dist. Ct. (no. dist.) Pa. 1990, U.S. Dist. Ct. (ctrl. dist.) Pa. 1995, U.S. Ct. Appeals (4th cir.) 2002. Bankruptcy atty., NYC; assoc. Arott, Nachamie, Benjamin et al, NYC, 1983-85, Fox, Rothschild, O'Brien & Frankel, Phila., 1985-86; from assoc. to mng. ptnr. Drinker, Biddle & Reath, Phila., 1986—2002, asst. to chmn., 1996—2005, ptnr.-in-charge, Wilmington and mem., mgmt. com., 2004—05, exec. ptnr., 2005—. Adj. prof. Rutgers U. Sch. of Law, Camden, N.J., 1989-2000; bd. trustees Consumer Bankruptcy Assistance Project, Phila., 1994—; bd. dirs. Farmers Mkt. Trust, Phila., 1994—. Mem. ABA, N.Y. Bar Assn., Pa. Bar Assn., Phila. Bar Assn., Am. Bankruptcy Inst., Ea. Dist. of Pa. Bankruptcy Conf., Mask and Whig Club (bd. dirs.), fellow, Am. Coll. Bankruptcy. Avocations: photography, travel, golf. Office: Drinker Biddle & Reath One Logan Sq 18th and Cherry Sts Philadelphia PA 19103 also: Drinker Biddle & Reath Ste 1000 1100 N Market St Wilmington DE 19801-1243 Office Phone: 215-988-2700, 302-467-4212. Office Fax: 215-988-2757, 302-467-4201. E-mail: andrew.kassner@dbr.com.

KASSNER, HERBERT SEYMORE, lawyer; b. NYC, Dec. 3, 1931; s. Abraham and Rose (Rosenblatt) K.; m. Sheilah Goodwin, 1957 (div. 1965); children: Andrew, Kenneth; m. Marjorie Fern Golding, 1974 (div. 1992); children: Robin, Jeffrey; m. Linda Rubinstein Finder, 1993. BA (hon.), Franklin and Marshall U., 1952; cert., Hague (Netherlands) Acad. of Internat. Law, 1953; MA, NYU, 1955; LLB (hon.), Harvard U., 1955. Bar: N.Y. 1955, Conn. 1986. Atty. Gallap, Climenko & Gould, NYC, 1955, Otterbourg, Steindler, Huston & Rosen, NYC, 1956; pvt. practice law NYC, 1957-65, 1969; atty. Dryer & Traub, NYC, 1966-68, Kassner & Detsky, NYC, 1970-80, Kassner & Haigney, NYC, 1981-90. Instr. Ohio State U., Columbus, 1956-57; asst. prof. Ark. State U., Pine Bluff, 1965. Contbr. articles to profl. jours. on 1st amendment law. Mem. Phi Beta Kappa. Home: 7221 Montrico Dr Boca Raton FL 33433-6931 Personal E-mail: Sonnykas123@aol.com.

KASSNER, MICHAEL ERNEST, materials science educator, researcher; b. Osaka, Japan, Nov. 22, 1950; (parents Am. citizens); s. Ernest and Clara (Christa) K.; m. Kelley M. Nichols, Nov. 23, 2005. BS, Northwestern U., 1972; MS, Stanford U., 1979, PhD, 1981. Metallurgist Sargent and Lundy Engrs., Chgo., 1977, Lawrence Livermore Nat. Lab., Calif., 1981—90, head phys. metallurgy and joining sect., 1988—90; lectr. San Francisco State U., 1983; prof. Naval Postgrad. Sch., Monterey, Calif., 1984—86; prof., dir. grad. program in materials sci. Oreg. State U., Corvallis, 1990—2003, Chevron endowed prof., 1996, Northwest Aluminium prof., 1997—2003; prof., chmn. dept. aero. and mech. engring. U. So. Calif., LA, 2003—. Temporary assignment as project mgr. Office Basic Energy Scis., U.S. Dept. Energy, 1991-96, 2000-03; vis. scholar dept. physics U. Groningen, Netherlands, 1985-87; vis. scholar dept. materials, sci. and engring. Stanford U., 1981-83; adj. prof. dept. mech. and aerospace engring. U. Calif., San Diego, 1999-2003. Author over 180 articles, book on binary phase diagrams, book on creep fundamentals, editor various sci. jours. Lt. USN, 1972-76; lt. comdr. USNR, 1976-81. Fulbright scholar, Netherlands; fellow ASM Internat., 1998. Mem. ASME, Am. Soc. Metals, Metall. Soc., Sigma Xi. Home: 321 S Irving Blvd Los Angeles CA 90020 Home Phone: 310-923-5576; Office Phone: 213-740-7212.

KASSOF, ALLEN H., foundation administrator; b. NYC, Dec. 17, 1930; s. Morris and Sophia B. Kassof; m. Arianne Scholz, 1953; children: Andrea, Arlen, Anita. BA, Rutgers U., 1952; AM, Harvard U., 1954, PhD, 1960. Asst. prof. Smith Coll., Northampton, Mass., 1957-60, Princeton (N.J.) U., 1961-65, assoc. prof., asst. dean coll., 1965-68; founder, exec. dir. Internat. Rsch. and Exchs. Bd., NYC and Princeton, 1968-92; pres. Project on Ethnic Rels. in Ea. Europe, Carnegie Corp. N.Y., Princeton, 1991—2005, pres. emeritus and sr. advisor, 2005—. Cons. conf. security and cooperation Europe, Hamburg, Germany, Budapest, Hungary, 1980, 85, Warsaw, Poland, 1993; mem. pres. com. fgn. lang., Washington, 1978-79; mem. U.S. task force Romania, Bucharest, 1990-92; prin. mediator between Govt. of Romania and Dem. Union Hungarians in Romania, 1993—; mem. Coun. for Ethnic Accord, 1992—; chair roundtable talks between Slovak and Ethnic Hungarian parliamentary parties of Slovakia, 1995—2001, Serb-Albanian Roundtable on Future of Kosovo, NYC, 1997; chmn. Regional Roundtable of Polit. Leaders from Southeast Europe on Rels. between Albanians and their Neighbors, Budapest and Athens, 2000, Lucerne, 2002, 04; co-chmn. Euro-Atlantic group on interethnic conflicts NATO, Brussels, 1998; chmn. Roundtable for Macedonian Parliamentary Parties on Fulfillment of the Ohrid Agreement, Mavroro, Macedonia, 2003-07. Decorated Grand Officer Nat. Order of Faithful Svc., Pres. of Romania. Mem.: Coun. Fgn. Rels., Am. Assn. Advancement Slavic Studies. Avocation: photography. Home: 949 Mercer Rd Princeton NJ 08540-4823 Office: Project on Ethnic Rels 15 Chambers St Princeton NJ 08542-3707 Personal E-mail: aakassof@cs.com. Business E-Mail: allen.kassof@per-usa.org. E-mail: allenkassof@patmedia.net.

KASSON, JAMES MATTHEWS, electronics executive; b. Muncie, Ind., Mar. 19, 1943; s. Robert Edwin and Mary Louise K.; m. Betty Roseman, Aug. 14, 1976. BSE.E., Stanford U., 1964; MSE.E., U. Ill., 1965. Engring. mgr. Santa Rita Tech., Santa Clara, Calif., 1963-69; engring. sect. mgr. Hewlett-Packard, Palo Alto, Calif., 1969-73; v.p. research and devel. ROLM Corp., Santa Clara, 1973-88; fellow IBM Corp., San Jose, Calif., 1988-95; v.p. engring. Echelon Corp., Palo Alto, Calif., 1995-98, CIO, 1998-2000. Patentee in field. Trustee Choate Rosemary Hall, Wallingford, Conn., 1990-96, Ctr. Photog. Art, Carmel, Calif., 2001-03, Monterey (Calif.) Mus. Art, 2005— Mem. IEEE (citation for contbn. 1981). Home: 33732 E Carmel Valley Rd Carmel Valley CA 93924 Personal E-mail: jim@kasson.com.

KASSOY, HORTENSE (HONEY KASSOY), artist, sculptor, painter; b. NYC, Feb. 14, 1917; d. Adolph and Mary (Apfel) Blumenkranz; m. Bernard Kassoy, June 30, 1946; children: Meredith, Sheila. Diploma, Pratt Inst., 1936; BS, Columbia U., 1938, MA, 1939; student, Parsons Sch. Design, Paris, U. Colo., 1966, NYU, 1966-67; studied sculpture with Sahl Swarz, Chaim Gross & Oronzio Maldarelli. One-woman shows include Caravan House Gallery, 1974, Women in the Arts Gallery, 1978, Ward-Nasse Gallery, 1986, Pioneer Gallery, Cooperstown, NY, 1987, 1991, 1997, 80th Birthday Retrospective Solo of Wood Sculpture Prints and Watercolors, Vladeck Hall Gallery, NY, 1997, 2002, Pioneer Gallery, Cooperstown, 1997, 2002, 90th Birthday Exhbn., Lehman Coll., Bronx, 2007, exhibited in group shows at Bronx Mus., NY, 1971, 1975, 1985—86, Toledo Mus. Art, Toronto Mus. Art, Hudson River Mus., Bklyn. Mus., New Age Gallery, Lever House, Bklyn. Coll., Fordham U., Lehman Coll., Cork Gallery, Nat.

Acad. Design, Represented in permanent collections Slater Meml. Mus. Co-chair visual arts Bronx Coun. Arts, 1973—76. Recipient 1st prize in watercolor, Painters Day NY World's Fair, 1940, Walker prize for Sculpture, Oneonta, NY, 2002; fellow, Va. Ctr. Creative Arts, 1986, 1988, 1989, 1992, 1995, 1997. Mem.: Fedn. Modern Painters and Sculptors, Contemporary Arts Guild (rec. sec. 1981—89), Internation Assn. Art (corr. sec. 1979—83, del. to 10th Congress 1983), NY Artists Equity Assn. (v.p. bd. dirs. 1971—83), Am. Soc. Contemporary Artists (v.p. 1989—94, 1999—2003, award in Sculpture 1979, 1980, 1983, 1990, 1992, 1996, 2000, 2002). Home: 130 Gale Pl Apt 6B Bronx NY 10463-2853 Home (Summer): Butternut Hill Studio 1577 County Route 16 Burlington Flats NY 13315-3211

KASTAN, DAVID SCOTT, literature educator, writer; b. NYC, Jan. 4, 1946; s. Peter Lewis and Audrey Brown (Kastan); 1 child, Marina Claire; m. Jane Ezersky, Nov. 26, 2004. AB, Princeton U., 1967; MA, U. Chgo., 1968, PhD, 1974. Asst. prof. Dartmouth Coll., 1973-79, 1973-79, assoc. prof., 1979-86; prof. Columbia U., 1987—. Disting. vis. prof. Am. U., Cairo, 1995, Copenhagen U., 1998; vis. prof., hon. rsch. prof. Univ. Coll. London, 1999—. Author: Shakespeare and the Shapes of Time, 1982, Shakespeare after Theory, 1999, Shakespeare and the Book, 2001; editor (with Marina Kastan): Poetry for Young People: William Shakespeare, 2000; editor: (with Peter Stallybrass) Staging the Renaissance, 1991; editor: Critical Essays on Shakespeare's Hamlet, 1995; editor: (with John Cox) New History of Early English Drama, 1997; editor: A Companion to Shakespeare, 1999, 1 Henry IV (Arden Shakespeare), 2002, Norton Critical Doctor Faustus, 2005, Paradise Lost, 2005, Oxford Encyclopedia of British Literature, 2006; editor: (series) Barnes and Noble Shakespeare, 2006—; co-editor: Bantam Shakespeare, 2004; gen. editor (with Richard Proudfoot and Ann Thompson): Arden Shakespeare, 1995. Woodrow Wilson fellow, 1968, Folger Libr. fellow, 1994, Huntington Libr. Mellon fellow, 1995, Burke Libr. fellow, 2003, Guggenheim fellow, 2004. Mem. MLA (divisional exec. com.), Renaissance English Text Soc. (coun. mem.), Shakespeare Assn. Am., Renaissance Soc. Am., Phi Beta Kappa. Office: Columbia U Dept English 116th St & Broadway New York NY 10027 Office Phone: 212-854-6257. Business E-Mail: dsk1@columbia.edu.

KASTELIC, DAVID ALLEN, lawyer, energy and food products executive; b. Ely, Minn., Apr. 19, 1955; m. Janice E Kastelic. BS cum laude, St. John's U., Collegeville, Minn., 1977; JD magna cum laude, U. Minn., Mpls., 1980. Bar: Minn. 1980, US Fed. Ct. 1980, US Ct. Appeals (8th cir.) 1985, US Supreme Ct. 1985, US Tax Ct. 1985. Sr. v.p. CHS Inc., Inver Grove Heights, Minn., gen. counsel, 2003—. Office: CHS Inc PO Box 64089 Saint Paul MN 55164-0089 Office Phone: 651-355-3712. Office Fax: 651-355-4554. E-mail: david.kastelic@chsinc.com.*

KASTELIC, ROBERT FRANK, aerospace transportation executive; b. Granite City, Ill., July 17, 1934; s. Joseph and Anna Marie (Kries) K.; m. Patricia Ann Dalton, Apr. 8, 1961; children: Michael J., Constance A., Robert J., Kirsten S. BS in Acctg., U. Ill., 1956. Sr. acct. Price Waterhouse & Co., St. Louis, 1956-63; v.p., CFO, comptroller Merc. Bancorp., St. Louis, 1963-72; exec. v.p., CFO Equimark Corp. and Equibank, Pitts., 1972-83, vice-chmn. bd., 1983-84; pres., COO Astrotech Internat. Corp., Pitts., 1986—; chmn., CEO X-Mark Industries, Washington, Pa., 1988—. Bd. dirs. Glenshaw (Pa.) Glass Co., Quasitronics, Inc., X-Mark Industries, Astrotech Internat., Pitts., Fidelity Savs. Bank; chmn. St. Francis Fin. Corp. Rev. com. United Way, Pitts., 1977-78; bd. dirs. St. Francis Hosp., Civic Light Opera. With U.S. Army, 1956-58. Mem. AICPA, Am. Mgmt. Assn., Am. Soc. Corp. Secs., Mo., Pa. insts. CPAs, Bank Adminstrn. Inst., Fin. Execs. Inst., Nat. Investor Relations Inst. Clubs: Duquesne. Home: 313 Fox Hunt Rd Pittsburgh PA 15238 Office: X-Mark Industries 2001 N Main St Washington PA 15301-6180 Personal E-mail: robertfkastelic@inbox.com.

KASTEN, ROBERT W., JR., former senator; b. Milw., June 19, 1942; s. Robert W. and Mary (Ogden) K. BA, U. Ariz., 1964; MBA, Columbia U., 1966. With Genesco, Inc., Nashville, 1966-68; dir., v.p. Gilbert Shoe Co., Thiensville, Wis., 1968-75; mem. Wis. Senate, Madison, 1972-75; mem. joint fin. com., 1973-75; chmn. joint survey com. on tax exemptions, 1973-75; mem. 94th-95th congresses from 9th Wis. Dist.; U.S. Senator from Wis., 1980-93; founder Kasten & Co., Thiensville, Wis., 1993—; sr. assoc. Strategic and Internat. Studies Ctr., Washington, 1993—. Mem. 100th Congress Com., appropriations com., budget com., commerce, sci. and transp. com., small bus. com. Regional dir. Milw. Coalition for Clean Water; active Milw. Soc. for Prevention of Blindness; founder Legis. Studies Inst. 1st lt. Wis. Air N.G., 1967-72. Named Jaycee of Yr., 1972; named Legis. Conservationist of Yr. Wis. Wildlife Fedn., 1973, 86; One of Best Legislators Senate Rep. Class of 1980 Nat. Jour., 1985. Mem. Nat. Audubon Soc., Ducks Unltd., Sigma Nu, Alpha Kappa Psi Office: Kasten & Co 1629 K St NW # 800 Washington DC 20006-4107

KASTEN, STANLEY HARVEY, professional sports team executive; b. Lakewood, NJ, Feb. 1, 1952; s. Nathan and Sylvia (Saltztreger) K.; m. Helen Weisz, Aug. 14, 1977; children: Alana Marie, Corey Richard, Sherry Leigh, Jay Bradley. AB, NYU, 1973; JD, Columbia U., 1976. Exec. asst. Turner Broadcasting Co., Atlanta, 1976-77; v.p. for sports TBS, Atlanta, 1986—; in-house counsel Atlanta Braves, 1976-77, pres., 1986—2003; v.p., asst. gen. mgr. Atlanta Hawks, 1978-79, v.p., gen. mgr., 1980-86, pres., 1986—2003, dir., 1986-90, pres., 1990—2003, also bd. dirs.; pres., gen. mgr. Atlanta Thrashers, 1999—2003; pres. Washington Nationals (MLB), 2006—. Bd. govs. NBA, NYC, 1978—, mem. Mktg., Player Pension, and Expansion Coms. Former trustee Naismith Basketball Hall of Fame; chmn. Player Personal Develop. Com. Named NBA Exec. of Yr., 1985-86, 86-87. Mem. ABA, N.J. Bar Assn., Sports Lawyers Assn. (bd. dirs., Award of Excellence, 2000) Office Phone: 703-437-4377.

KASTENBERG, WILLIAM EDWARD, engineering professor, former academic administrator; b. NYC, June 25, 1939; s. Murray and Lillian Kastenberg; m. Berna R. Miller, Aug. 18, 1963; children: Andrew, Joshua, Lillian; m. Gloria Hauser, May 3, 1992. BS, UCLA, 1962, MS, 1963; PhD, U. Calif., Berkeley, 1966. Asst. prof. Sch. Engring. and Applied Sci. UCLA, 1966-71, assoc. prof., 1971-75, assoc. dean Sch. Engring. and Applied Sci., 1981-85, chmn. mech. aerospace and nuc. engring., 1985-88, prof. mech., aerospace and nuc. engring. dept., 1975-94; sr. fellow U.S. NRC, Washington, 1979-80; prof. nuc. engring. dept. U. Calif., Berkeley, 1995—, chmn. nuc. engring. dept., 1995-2000, Chancellor's prof., 1996—99, Daniel Tellep disting. prof. engring., 1999—. Guest scientist Karlsruhe Nuc. Rsch., Germany, 1972—73; mem. Nat. Rsch. Com. Reactor Safety, 1985—86; chmn. peer rev. com. U.S. NRC, Washington, 1987—88; mem. adv. com. nuc. facility safety Dept. of Energy, 1988—92; mem. adv. com. Diablo Canyon Nuc. Power Plant, 1999—2000; dir. risk and sys. analysis control toxics program UCLA, 1989—95, chmn. Ctr. Clean Tech., 1992—94; project dir. Ctr. Nuc. and Toxic Waste Mgmt. U. Calif., Berkley, 1995—2000; facilitator Emotional Body Enlightenment, 2006—. Contbr. articles to profl. jours. Recipient Disting. Tchg. award, Am. Soc. Engring. Edn., 1973. Fellow: AAAS, Am. Nuc. Soc. (chmn. nuc. safety 1984—85, Arthur Holly Compton award); mem.: NAE. Office: Univ Calif Nuc Engring Dept 4155 Etcheverry Hall Berkeley CA 94720-1731 Home Phone: 510-527-9124; Office Phone: 510-643-0574. Business E-Mail: kastenbe@nuc.berkeley.edu.

KASTENMEIER, ROBERT WILLIAM, congressman; b. Beaver Dam, Wis., Jan. 24, 1924; s. Leo Henry and Lucille (Powers) K.; m. Dorothy Chambers, June 27, 1952; children: William, Andrew, Edward. LL.B., U. Wis., 1952. Bar: Wis. 1952. Dir. br. office claims service War Dept., Philippines, 1946-48; practiced in Watertown, 1952-58; justice of the peace, 1955-58; mem. 86th-101st Congresses from 2d Dist. Wis., 1959-91; mem. com. on judiciary, chmn. subcom. house jud. com.; mem. select com. on intelligence, 1989—. Served from pvt. to 1st lt., inf. AUS, 1943-46. Mem. Wis. Bar Assn. Office: 121 S Pinckney St Ste 300 Madison WI 53703-3338 also: 2328 Rayburn House Bldg Washington DC 20515-0001

KASTENSCHMIDT, BETTY M., elementary school educator, director; d. Edwin Riebe and Ruth S. Yohn-Riebe; m. David E. Kastenschmidt; children: Ruth, Karl, Edith. BS in Edn., Dr. Martin Luther Coll., 1990; MS in Edn., U. Wis., 1994. Tchr. grades 1-4 Palos Luth. Sch., Palos Heights, Ill., 1963—64; tchr. 1st grade Zion Luth. Sch., Columbus, Wis., 1964—67, North Trinity Sch., Milw., 1967—68; tchr. nursery, homebound Clinton Nursery Sch., Clinton, Minn., 1968—70; sales staff Knowledge Emporium, Greenlake, Wis., 1985—88; title I tchr., coord. Markesan Elem. Sch., Wis., 1988—. Chair English lang. arts Markesan Dist. Schs., 2000—04, fed. programs dir./Title I coord. No Child Left Behind team. Contbr. chapters to books. Sunday sch. tchr. Zion Luth. Ch., Kingston, 1990—, powerpoint coord., 2003—; bd. dirs. Kingston Libr., Wis., 1985—95. Grantee, Nat. Endowment for Humanities. Mem.: Delta Kappa Gamma (pres. 1999—2005). Avocations: reading, writing, history, gardening. Office: Markesan Elem Sch 200 S Margaret St Markesan WI 53946 Office Phone: 920-398-2373 ext. 281. Personal E-mail: bettykas@yahoo.com.

KASTER, LAURA A., lawyer; b. NYC, May 24, 1948; BA, Tufts U., 1970; JD magna cum laude, Boston U., 1973. Bar: Mass. 1973, Ill. 1975. Law clk. to Hon. Frank M. Coffin, U.S. Ct. Appeals for 1st circuit, Boston, 1973-75; assoc. Jenner & Block, Chgo., 1975-81, ptnr., 1981-97; gen. atty. law and govt. affairs AT&T Corp., Bedminster, NJ, 1997—2006, arbitrator, mediator, 2006—. Bd. trustees Lawyers Com. for Civil Rights. Co-author: Sanctions in Federal Litigation, 1991; co-editor: The Attorneys' Guide to the Seventh Circuit Court of Appeals, 3rd edit., 2005; note editor Law Rev. Boston U., 1973-72; contbr. chpt. to book and articles to profl. jours. Trustee Lawyers Com. for Civil Rights, 2005—. Master Granbaldi Inn Ct.; fellow Am. Bar Found. (life); mem. ABA, 7th Circuit Bar Assn., Fed. Cir. Bar Assn Personal E-mail: laura.kaster@gmail.com.

KASTIN, ABBA JEREMIAH, endocrinologist, researcher; b. Cleve., Dec. 24, 1934; s. Isadore I. and Ruth (Urdang) K. AB, Harvard U., 1956, MD, 1960; doctorate (hon.), U. Nacional Federico Villerarreal, Lima, Peru, 1980; DSc (hon.), U. New Orleans, 1984. Intern Vanderbilt U. Hosp., Nashville, 1960-61, resident in internal medicine, 1961-62; clin. assoc. USPHS, NIH, 1962-64; clin. investigator VA Hosp., New Orleans, 1965-68; chief endocrinology sect. VA Med. Ctr., 1968—2004; prof. dept. medicine Tulane U. Sch. Medicine, New Orleans, 1974—2004; grad. faculty U. New Orleans, 1976—; prof. and endowed chair Pennington Biomed. Rsch. Ctr., Baton Rouge, 2004—. Cons. prof. dept. psychology U. New Orleans, 1986—, FDA, 1979; mem. visual arts vis. com. Loyola U., New Orleans, 2004—; mem. med. adv. bd. Nat. Pituitary Agy., 1974-77; Wellcome vis. prof., 1990; pre-reviewer in endocrinology, mem. residency com. for internal medicine Accreditation Coun. for Grad. Med. Edn., 1984-95; vis. sr. scientist Japan Soc. Promotion Sci., 1997; spkr., lectr. in field. Editor-in-chief: Peptides, an Internat. Jour., 1980—; editor: Handbook of Biologically Active Peptides, 2006; mem. editl. bd. Jour. Clin. Endocrinology and Metabolism, 1976-80, Brain Rsch. Bull., 1986-95, Neurosci. and Biobehaviorial Rev., 1977-95, New Trends Exptl. Clin. Psychiatry, 1985-2001, Progress in Neuroendocrinimmunology, 1988-90, Pharmacology, Biochemistry and Behavior, 1989-1995, Molecular and Cellular Neuroscis., 1990-95, Physiology and Behavior, 1993-95, Endocrine Practice, 1994-2004, Neuroimmunomodulation, 1995-2000, Current pharm. Design, 2003—, Medicinal Chemistry, 2004—; contbr. more than 800 articles to profl. jours. Advisory bd. La. Philharmonic Orch., 1997—. Recipient Edward T. Tyler Fertility award Internat. Fertility Soc., 1975, Eagle award Fed. Bus. Assn., 1975, Copernicus medal Med. Faculty Krakow, Poland, 1979, William S. Middletown award VA, 1982, Strand award 2001; named in top 100 Most Cited Scientist List, Inst. for Scientific Info. Fellow Am. Coll. Endocrinology; mem. Am. Physiol. Soc., Am. Peptide Soc., Endocrine Soc., Soc. Exptl. Biol. Medicine, Soc. Neurosci., Internat. Soc. Psychoneuroendocrinology (introductory hon. scientific lectr. XVth Congress), Internat. Soc. Neuroendocrinology, Internat. Behavioral Neuroscience Soc. (keynote speaker first meeting, mem. adv. coun.), Internat. Neuropeptide Soc. (pres. 1993—) Brazilian Soc. Toxicology; hon. mem. La Soc. de Dermo-Chimie, Chilean Soc. Endocrinology, Phillippine Soc. Endocrinology and Metabolism, Peruvian Ob-Gyn Soc., Peruvian Endocrine Soc., Polish Endocrine Soc., Hungarian Endocrine Soc., Harvard Club La. (pres. 1991-95), Green Wave Masters Swim Club (pres. 1978-84). Jewish. Office: Pennington Biomed Rsch Ctr 6400 Perkins Rd Baton Rouge LA 70808-4124 Office Phone: 225-763-0266. Business E-Mail: peptides@pbrc.edu.

KASTNER, MARC AARON, physics professor; b. Toronto, Ont., Can., Nov. 20, 1945; came to U.S., 1952; s. Jacob and Ida Pearl (Shidlowsky) K.; m. Marcia Jill Paul, Aug. 27, 1967; 2 children. BS in Chemistry, U. Chgo., 1967, MS, 1969, PhD in Physics, 1972. Rsch. fellow Harvard U., Cambridge, Mass., 1972-73; asst. prof. physics MIT, Cambridge, 1973-77, assoc. prof., 1977-83, prof., 1983-89, Donner prof. of physics, 1989—. Dir. Consortium for Superconducting Electronics, 1989-91, Ctr. for Materials Sci. and Engring, 1993-98; head MIT Dept. Physics, 1998—. Recipient David Adler Lectureship award Am. Physical Society, 1995 Fellow AAAS, Am. Phys. Soc. (councillor at large 1991-94, Oliver E. Buckley prize 2000). Achievements include discovery of single electron effects in nanostructures and research in electronic, optical and magnetic properties of condensed matter, including semiconductors and high temperature superconductors.

KASTNER, MICHAEL JAMES, dentist; b. Huntington, Ind., Oct. 20, 1954; s. James H. and Barbara A. (Bartrom) K.; m. Kimberly A. Ricke, June 18, 1983; children: Kevin Michael, Ryan James, Derek Edward. BS in Biology and Chemistry, Manchester Coll., 1977; DDS, Ind. U., Indpls., 1981; postgrad., Armed Forces Inst. Pathology, 1989. Gen. practice dentistry, Toledo, 1981—. Asst. dentist Toledo Zoo, 1991—; mem. Ohio Mass Disaster Team, 1995—, team capt., 2001—; asst. Lucas County Coroner's Office, 1987—; asst. to N.Y. Med. Examiners Office in dental forensic identification of World Trade Ctr. victims, 2001. Bd. trustees Dental Ctr. Northwest Ohio, 1994-2000, nominating com., 1995-2001, long range planning com., 1999-2001, dental com., 1995-98, 2000; mem. Lucas County Oral Health Coalition. Recipient Alumni Honor award Manchester Coll., 1997, Recognition for Honor award Ohio State Senate Resolution, 1997, Honoring Am. Spirit award Gov. Ohio, 2002, cert. of recognition City of NY Office of Chief Med. Examiner, 2003, Congressman Vito Fosella, 13th Dist. NY, 2003. Fellow Pierre Fauchard Acad., Am. Coll. Dentists; mem. ADA (chmn. local chpt., chmn. area grassroots membership initiative, Recognition for Vol. Svc. Fgn. Country award Dominican Republic 1984, 87, Costa Rica 1990, Nepal 1994, Nicaragua 2000, 01), Ohio Dental Assn. (state del. 2002—, alt. del. 1999-01, statewide subcom. on peer rev. 2000—, chmn. 2004, dental OPTIONS program, 1999—, Humanitarian of Yr. 1995, 02), Toledo Dental Soc. (bd. dirs. 1996-99, peer rev. com. 1998—, nominating com. 1999-03, chmn. 2003, program and continuing edn. com. 1999—, relief fund subcom. 1999, fin. com. 2000, long range planning com. 2000, exec. office com. 2000-03, exec. bd. sec./treas. 2000, v.p. 2001, pres. 2002, constitution by-laws com., 2002—), Am. Acad. Cosmetic Dentistry, Am. Soc. Forensic Odontology, Am. Coll. Oral Implantology, Am. Soc. Osseointegration Internat. Congress Oral Implantologists, MENSA. Roman Catholic. Avocations: photography, basketball, travel, outdoor activities, oenology. Home: 6944 Hickory Ridge Rd Sylvania OH 43560

KASTOR, FRANK SULLIVAN, language educator; b. Evanston, Ill., Aug. 19, 1933; s. Herman Walker and Rebecca (Sullivan) K.; m. Tina Bennett, Oct. 28, 1979; children: Dacaeber, Mark, Harlan, Kristina, Patrick, Liam, Mary Elisabeth, Caroline. BA, U. Ill., 1955, MA, 1956; PhD, U. Calif., Berkeley, 1963. Teaching asst. U. Ill., 1955-56, U. Calif., Berkeley, 1960-63; asst. prof. English U. So. Calif., 1963—66, 1967—68; assoc. prof. English No. Ill. U., 1968-69; prof. English Wichita State U., 1969—, chmn. dept., 1969-75, prof. emeritus, 1998. Contbr. to: The Milton Ency., The Dictionary of Literary Biography; author books, articles, revs., TV documentaries, C.S. Lewis study guides. Served with USAF, 1956-59. Rsch. grantee U. Calif., Berkeley, 1962, U. So. Calif., 1964, No. Ill. U., 1969, Wichita State U., 1970, 72, 73, 74, 84, 86, 92; Fulbright lectr., Spain, 1966-67; Kans. Com. for Humanities grantee, 1973, 74, 94; recipient NEH award, 1971, 84. Mem. MLA, AAUP, Milton Soc. Am., N.Y. C.S. Lewis Soc., C.S. Lewis Soc. of Kans. (a founder), Phi Kappa Phi. Christian Ch. E-mail: fskdr3@cox.net.

KASTOR, JOHN ALFRED, cardiologist, educator; b. NYC, Sept. 15, 1931; s. Alfred Bernard and Ellen Voigt Bentley; m. Mae Belle Eisenberg, July 4, 1954; children: Elizabeth Mae, Anne Sarah, Peter John. BA, U. Pa., 1953; MD, NYU, 1962. Diplomate Am. Bd. Cardiology. With NBC, NYC, 1956-58; intern, asst. resident in medicine Bellevue Hosp., NYC, 1962-64; chief resident physician N.Y. U. Hosp., NYC, 1964-65; clin. and research fellow in medicine Mass. Gen. Hosp., Boston, 1965-68, clin. asst. and asst. in medicine, 1968-69; instr. in medicine Harvard Med. Sch., 1968-69; dir. med. intensive care unit Hosp. U. Pa., Phila., 1969-72, assoc. chief cardiovascular sect., 1972-77, chief, 1977-81; physician-in-chief U. Md. Hosp., 1984-97; prof. medicine U. Pa. Sch. Medicine, Phila., 1976-83; Theodore E. Woodward prof. medicine U. Md. Sch. Medicine, 1984-97, chmn. dept. medicine, 1984-97, prof. medicine, 1997—. Vis. prin. fellow Nat. Heart and Lung Inst., London, 1995. Author: Arrhythmias, 1994, 2d edit., 2000, Mergers of Teaching Hospitals in Boston, New York and Northern California, 2001, Governance of Teaching Hospitals: Turmoil at Penn and Hopkins, 2003, Specialty Care in the Era of Managed Care: Cleveland Clinic versus University Hospitals of Cleveland, 2005; founding editor Internat. Jour. Cardiology, 1981—84; contbr. articles to profl. jours. With US Army, 1953—55. Fellow: ACP, Coun. Clin. Cardiology of Am. Heart Assn., Am. Coll. Cardiology; mem.: Paul Dudley White Soc. (dir. 1977—86), Venezuelan Soc. Internal Medicine, Assn. Univ. Cardiologists, Assn. Am. Physicians, Am. Heart Assn. (bd. govs. southeaster Pa. chpt. 1975—81, bd. govs. Md. affiliate 1990—93), Am. Fedn. Clin. Rsch., Alpha Omega Alpha. Home: 2415 Boston St Baltimore MD 21224-4733 Office: U Md Hosp 22 S Greene St Baltimore MD 21201-1544

KASULIS, THOMAS PATRICK, humanities educator; b. Bridgeport, Conn., Mar. 5, 1948; s. Joseph John and Albina Anna (Checkanouskas) K.; m. Ellen Elizabeth Sponheimer, June 5, 1970; children: Telemachus, Matthias, Benedict. BA, Yale U., 1970, MPh, 1972, PhD, 1975; MA, U. Hawaii, 1973. Asst. prof. philosophy U. Hawaii, Honolulu, 1975-80; from asst. prof. to prof. philosophy and religion Northland Coll., Ashland, Wis., 1981-91; prof. comparative studies The Ohio State U., Columbus, 1991—, chair East Asian langs. and lit., 1993-95, chair comparative studies, 1995-98. Mellon faculty fellow in humanities Harvard U., Cambridge, Mass., 1979-80; vis. facility rschr. Osaka (Japan) U., 1982-83; Numata vis. prof. U. Chgo., Ill., 1988. Author: Zen Action/Zen Person, 1981, Intimacy or Integrity: Philosophy and Cultural Difference, 2002, Shinto: The Way Home, 2004; editor, co-translator: The Body: Toward an Eastern Mind-Body Theory, 1987; co-editor: Self as Body in Asian Theory and Practice, 1993, Self as Person in Asian Theory and Practice, 1994; contbr. chpts. to books and articles to profl. jours. Fellow Japan Found., 1982-83, 2004; NEH fellow, 1986-87, 2000; Sr. Rsch. fellow East West Ctr., Honolulu, 1988. Mem. Soc. for Asian and Comparative Philosophy (pres. 1988-91), Am. Soc. for the Study of Religion (pres. 1999-2002). Home: 1465 Montcalm Rd Upper Arlington OH 43221-3450 Office: Ohio State Univ Comparative Studies 451 Hagerty Hall 1775 College Rd Columbus OH 43210-1340 Home Phone: 614-487-9756; Office Phone: 614-292-7892. Business E-Mail: kasulis.1@osu.edu.

KATAI, ANDREW ANDRAS, chemical company executive; b. Gyor, Hungary, Sept. 17, 1937; came to U.S., 1956; s. Ivan and Clara (Szel) K.; m. Debbie Judwin, May 12, 1963 (div. 1970); children: Alisa, Gregory; m. Joan Eleanor Klein, July 30, 1972; children: Peter, Daniel. BS, Juniata Coll., 1960; MS, PhD, Syracuse U., 1965; MS, PhD in Chemistry, SUNY, Syracuse, 1965. Internat. mktg. asst. Esso chem. Co., NYC, 1965-66; asst. prof. Hunter-Lehman Coll. N.Y.C., 1965-70; research chemist Union Carbide Corp., Tarrytown, NY, 1966-67, internat. assoc. prodn. mgr. NYC, 1967-69, internat. product mgr., 1969-71; new bus. devel. mgr. W.R. Grace Constrn. Co., Cambridge, Mass., 1971-73; bus. mgr. internat. div. Inolex Corp., Chgo., 1973-77; Far East devel mgr. Eschem (Swift) Inc., Chgo., 1977, gen. mgr. internat. div., 1977-81, dir. internat. div., 1981-82, v.p. internat. div., 1982-83; pres. Swift Adhesives subs. Reichhold Chem. Co., Downers Grove, Ill., 1983-93; sr. Corridor fellow, assoc. prof. internat. bus. North Ctrl. Coll., Naperville, Ill., 1994-2000; adj. prof. Stuart Sch. Bus., Ill. Inst. Tech., 1997—2007; adj. prof. U. St. Francis, 2006—07. Contbr. articles to profl. jours. Chmn. coll. fundraising dr., Westchester County, N.Y., 1969; co-chmn. Homeowners' Assn., Flossmoor, Ill., 1981-82. Mem. Adhesive Mfrs. Assn. (treas. 1986-88, pres.-elect 1988, pres. 1990), East West Corp. Corridor Assn. (v.p. 1992-94), Am. Chem. Soc., Sigma Xi, Phi Lambda Upsilon. Avocations: bridge, classical music, kayaking, photography, travel. Home and Office: 1105 E Johnson Dr Naperville IL 60540-8245 Office Phone: 630-983-7591. Personal E-mail: aakatai@sbcglobal.net.

KATAKKAR, SURESH BALAJI, hematologist, oncologist; b. Poona, India, Feb. 9, 1944; arrived in USA, 1978, naturalized, 1985; s. Balaji Vasudeo Katakkar and Padmavati (Gangadhar) Varavandkar; m. Sunila Moghe; children: Smita, Sucheta, Swati. MB, BS, Poona U., India, 1969; grad., Ednl. Coun. Fgn. Med., 1970. Lic. Med. Coun. Can., diplomate in internal medicine and oncology Am. Bd. Internal Medicine, Am. Bd. Quality Assurance and Utilization Rev., Am. Bd. Forensic Medicine, Am. Bd. Thrombosis and Vascular Medicine, bd. cert. European Soc. Med. Oncology. Intern, then resident St. Paul's Hosp., Saskatoon, 1969-71; resident U. Hosp., Saskatoon, 1971-72; resident clin. hematology Gen. Hosp., Ottawa, 1973-74; fellow in med. oncology W.W. Cross Cancer Inst., Edmonton, Can., 1974-75; sr. cancer clin. assoc. Sasketchewan Cancer Commn., 1975-78; clin. investigator NCI, USA, 1975—; med. oncologist Madigan Army Med. Ctr., 1978-80; pvt. practice Tucson, Ariz., 1980—; med. dir., chmn. cancer com. N.W. Cancer Ctr., 1991—, Chmn. tumor bd. St. Mary's Hosp., Tucson, 1981-83, chmn. transfusion com., 1982-97; chmn. dept. med. Northwest Hosp., 1983-84, chief of staff, 1984-86, trustee, 1984-96, clin. lectr. Univ. Med. Ctr., Ariz. Cancer Ctr., 1989—. Contbr. articles to profl. jours.; spkr, presenter, abstracts in field. W.W. Cross Cancer Inst. fellow, 1974-75. Fellow ACP, Royal Coll. Physicians Can., Internat. Acad. Thrombosis/Hemostasis; mem. AMA, Am. Soc. Clin. Oncology, Internat. Soc. Preventive Oncology, Am. Geriatrics Soc., Am. Hosp. Assn., Am. Assn. Blood Banks, Am. Bd. Med. Dirs., Am. Coll. Med. Quality, N.Y. Acad. Scis., European Soc. Med. Oncology, European Assn. Cancer Rsch., European Hematology Assn., Am. Soc. Hematology Hindu. Avocations: swimming, stamp collecting/philately, coin collecting/numismatics, bicycling. Home: 1391 E Placita Mapache Tucson AZ 85718-3929 also: 1891 W Orange Grove Rd Tucson AZ 85704-1116 Home Phone: 520-742-4183; Office Phone: 520-742-4183. Personal E-mail: azhemonc@aol.com.

KATARIYA, KUSHAGRA, cardiothoracic surgeon, educator; MB BS, U. Delhi, 1989. Cert. Am. Bd. Surgery, Am. Bd. Thoracic Surgery. Resident in gen. surgery Beth Israel Med. Ctr., Albert Einsten Coll. Medicine, NYC, 1990—95, chief resident dept. surgery, 1995—96; resident divsn. cardiothoracic surgery Jackson Meml. Med. Ctr., U. Miami Sch. Medicine, 1996—98, attending physician, 1998—; asst. prof. dept. surgery U. Miami Sch. Medicine, 1998—2004, assoc. prof., 2004—; chief sect. cardiothoracic surgery Miami VA Hosp., 2001—; attending physician cardiothoracic surgery Cedars Med. Ctr., Miami, 2001—; chief exec. officer Artemis Health Scis., Gurgaon, India, 2006—. Spkr. in field. Contbr. chapters to books, articles to profl. jours.; guest reviewer Annals Thoracic Surgery, 2000—, Asian Annals Thoracic and Cardiovasc. Surgery, 2000—. Recipient Leon Ginzburg award, Albert Einstein Coll. Medicine, 1996, Resident Achievement award, Soc. Laparoendoscopic Surgeons, 1996, Best Tchr. award, Divsn. Cardiothoracic Surgery, U. Miami Sch. Medicine, 2001—02; grantee, U. Miami, Jackson Meml. Med. Ctr., 2001—, Aventis Pharm., 2001—02, St. Jude Med., Mpls., 2002—, Dept. Vet. Affairs, 2002—, Ethicon, Inc., 2003—. Mem.: ACS, Am. Assn. Physicians from India, Internat. Soc. Minimally Invasive Cardiac Surgery, Am. Coll. Cardiology (affiliate mem.), Assn. VA Surgeons, Soc. Thoracic Surgeons, So. Thoracic Surg. Assn. Office: Artemis Health Scis Apollo House 7 Institutional Area SEctor 32 Gurgaon Haryana 122001 India E-mail: kkatariya@artemishealthsciences.com.

KATAYAMA, ROBERT NOBUICHI, retired lawyer; b. Honolulu, Oct. 11, 1924; s. Sanji Katayama; married; children: Alice A. Katayama Jenkins, Robert Nobuichi Jenkins, Kent J. Jenkins, Susan H. Ono, Carole Y. Kaneshiro, Wendy L. Lee. BA, U. Hawaii, 1950; LLB, Yale U., New Haven, Conn., 1955; grad., Command and Gen. Staff Coll., 1964; LLM, George Washington U., Washington, DC, 1967; grad., Indsl. Coll. Armed Forces, 1971. Commd. 1st lt. JAGC U.S. Army, 1958, advanced through grades to col., 1973, ret., 1973; gen. counsel Overseas Mdse. Inspection Co., San Francisco, 1956-58, Army Contract Adjustment Bd., Washington, 1964-68; prof. law JAG Sch. U. Va., 1968—70; from assoc. to ptnr. Baker & McKenzie, Chgo., Tokyo and San Francisco, 1973-85; ptnr. Seki & Jarvis, San Francisco and San Jose, 1985-86, Nutter, McClennen & Fish, San Francisco, 1986-88; spl. counsel, sr. advisor Crosby, Heafey, Roach & May, Oakland, Calif., 1988; ptnr. Carlsmith Ball, Honolulu, 1988-95, counsel, 1994—2004, ret., 2004. Chmn., CEO Kapolei People's Inc. dba Kapolei Golf Course, Honolulu, 1996—99; pres. Kapolei Holding Corp., 1998—. Trustee Nat. Japanese Am. Meml. Found., 1995—97, gov., 1997—; mem. Hawaii Adv. Coun. to Japanese Am. Nat. Mus., 2001—03; bd. dirs. Japanese Cultural Ctr. Hawaii, 1997—98, bd. govs., 1998—. Named Real Dean, U. Hawaii, Honolulu, 1950; recipient Disting. Alumni award, 2001. Mem.: ABA, Ill. Bar Assn., 442d Regimental Combat Team Found. (trustee 1993—2004, pres. 1999—2002), Hawaii Army Mus. Soc. (trustee 2001—), Military Officers Assn. Am., Japanese Am. Soc. Legal Studies, Nat. Japanese Am. Hist. Soc. (legal officer 1984—89), Japan Am. Soc. Hawaii, Hawaii Bar Assn., Calif. Bar Assn., Oahu AJA Vets. Coun. (pres. 1997), Japanese C. of C. of No. Calif. (bd. dirs. 1987—89), 442d Vets. Club (legal advisor 1994—95, pres.-elect 1996, pres. 1997—98, legal advisor 2000—05, 1st v.p. 2006—). Democrat. Buddhist. Home: 4389 Malia St Apt 553 Honolulu HI 96821 Personal E-mail: bobkata@earthlink.net.

KATCHANOVSKI, IVAN G., political scientist, researcher; b. Lutsk, Ukraine, Sept. 11, 1967; arrived in Can., 2005; s. Sophia Katchanovska. Diploma in Econ. and Social Planning, Nat. U. Econs., Kyiv, Ukraine, 1990; diploma with hons. in Sociology and Politics, Ctrl. European U., Prague, Czech Republic, 1993; MA in Econs., George Mason U., Fairfax-Arlington, Va., 1996, PhD in Pub. Policy, 2001. Economist Lutsk Dist. Fin. Dept., Lutsk, Volyn Region, Ukraine, 1990—92; instr. Volyn State U., Lutsk, Volyn Region, Ukraine, 1993—94; rsch. asst. US Inst. of Peace, Washington, 1996—96, George Mason U., Fairfax, Va., 1997—2002; rsch. assoc. Smith Coll., Northampton, Mass., 2001—; post-doctoral fellow U. Toronto, Ont., Canada, 2005—. Cons. George Mason U., Fairfax, Va., 2000—04, adj. prof., 2004. Author: Cleft Countries: Regional Political Divisions and Cultures in Post-Soviet Ukraine and Moldova, 2006; co-author: Paradox of American Unionism: Why Americans Like Unions More Than Canadians Do, but Join Much Less, 2004; co-editor: Development of the Mathematical Ideas of Mykhailo Kravchuk, 2004; contbr. articles to profl. jours. Recipient Young Scholars award, Cosmos Club Found., 2001, Krawtchouk medal, XI Internat. Sci. Krawtchouk Conf., 2006; fellow, Inst. Humane Studies, 1997—98; grantee, Shevchenko Sci. Soc., 2004; scholar, Ctrl. European U., 1992—93, George Mason U., 1994—97; John Olin Jr. Faculty fellowship, Inst. Humane Studies, 1994, Russian and Eurasian fellow, NAFSA, 1994—96, Kluge fellow, Libr. Congress, 2002—03, Lubin-Winant Rsch. fellowship, Franklin and Eleanor Roosevelt Inst., 2005. Mem.: Am. Polit. Sci. Assn. Office: Department of Political Science University of Toronto Ontario Toronto Canada M5S 3G3 Office Phone: (416) 946-7008. Personal E-mail: ikatcha1@gmualumni.org. Business E-Mail: ivan.katchanovski@utoronto.ca.

KATCHER, JONATHON A., lawyer; b. Detroit, Oct. 2, 1954; BGS with distinction, Univ. Mich., 1976; JD, Lewis & Clark Coll., Portland, 1981. Asst. public defender State of Alaska, Anchorage, 1981—84; Supervising atty. Protection and Advocacy for Developmentally Disabled (PADD), Anchorage, 1984—85; Barrister I Alaska Inns of Court, Anchorage, 1993—2003; spec. edn. hearing officer State of Alaska, Dept. of Edn., 1990—. Mem.: ABA, Alaska Bar Assn. (pres. 2005—06). Office: Pope & Katcher Ste 220 421 W First Ave Anchorage AK 99501 Office Phone: 907-272-8577.

KATCHER, RICHARD, lawyer; b. NYC, Dec. 17, 1918; s. Samuel and Gussie (Appelbaum) K.; m. Shirley Ruth Rifkin, Sept. 24, 1944; children: Douglas P., Robert A., Patti L. BA, U. Mich., 1941, JD, 1943. Bar: Mich. 1943, N.Y. 1944, Ohio 1946. Assoc. Noonan, Kaufman & Eagan, NYC, 1943-46; from assoc. to ptnr. Ulmer, Berne & Laronge, Cleve., 1946-72; ptnr. Baker & Hostetler, Cleve., 1972-95. Lectr. in fed. income taxation Case Western Res. U. Sch. Law, Cleve., 1953-69, 71-72; mem. adv. bd. on intercollegiate athletics, U. Mich., 2001-2004; chmn. Nat. Conf. Lawyers and CPAs, 1982-. Contbr. articles on fed. tax to profl. jours. Recipient Disting. Alumni Service award U. Mich., 1987, Leadership medal Pres.' Soc. of U. Mich., 1991. Fellow ABA (coun. sect. taxation 1973-76), Am. Coll. Tax Counsel (regent); mem. Am. Bar Retirement Assn. (bd. dirs., v.p. 1986-87, pres. 1987-88), U. Mich. Pres. Soc. (chmn. exec. com. 1987-90), Nat. Conf. Lawyers and CPAs (chmn. 1982-83), U. Mich. Cleve. Club (pres. 1959, Outstanding Alumnus award 1987), U. Mich. Alumni Assn. (dir. 1994-98, sec. 1997-98). Avocation: tennis. Home: 26150 Village Ln Apt 104 Beachwood OH 44122-7527 Office: Baker & Hostetler 3200 National City Ctr 1900 E 9th St Ste 3200 Cleveland OH 44114-3475 Office Phone: 216-861-7476. E-mail: RKatcher@bakerlaw.com.

KATCHER, RICHARD DAVID, lawyer; b. Newark, May 26, 1941; s. Henry Edward and Eve M. (Kreiger) K.; m. Susan M. Scherer, June 28, 1964; children: Daniel, Andrew. AB, Lafayette Coll., 1963; LLB, N.Y. Univ., 1966. Assoc. Simpson Thacher & Bartlett, NYC, 1966-68, Wachtell, Lipton, Rosent Katz, NYC, 1968-71, pntr., 1971—. Office: Wachtell Lipton Rosen & Katz 51 W 52nd St Fl 29 New York NY 10019-6150 Office Phone: 212-403-1222. Business E-Mail: rdkatcher@wlrk.com.

KATEB, GEORGE ANTHONY, political science professor; b. Bklyn., Feb. 27, 1931; s. Anthony Francis and Victoria Anna (Mesnooh) K. AB, Columbia U., 1952, A.M., 1953, PhD, 1960; D.H.L. (hon.), Amherst, 1989. Mem. faculty Amherst Coll., 1957, prof., 1967-87, Kenan prof. polit. sci., 1974-78, Joseph B. Eastman prof. polit. sci., 1980-87; prof. politics Princeton U., 1987—, William Nelson Cromwell prof. politics, 1999—2002, William Nelson Cromwell prof. politics emeritus, 2002—. Vis. lectr. Mt. Holyoke Coll., 1958, Yale U., 1973, Harvard U., 1986. Author: Utopia and Its Enemies, 2d edit., 1972, Political Theory: Its Nature and Uses, 1968, Utopia, 1971, Hannah Arendt: Politics, Conscience, Evil, 1984, The Inner Ocean: Individualism and Democratic Culture, 1992 (Spitz prize Conf. for Study Polit. Thought 1994), Emerson and Self-Reliance, 1994; co-editor: (with David Bromwich) John Stuart Mill, On Liberty, Patriotism and Other Mistakes, 2006; mem. editl. bd. Mass. Rev., 1961-70, Polit. Theory, 1972—, Am. Polit. Sci. Rev., 1976-81, Jour. History Ideas, 1976—, Jour. Utopian Studies, 1977-80, Raritan, 1980-02; cons. editor: Polit. Theory, 1983-00. Univ. fellow Columbia U., 1953-54; fellow Soc. Fellows, Harvard U., 1954-57; Guggenheim fellow, 1971-72 Mem. AAUP, Am. Acad. Arts and Scis., New Eng. Polit. Sci. Assn. (exec. com. 1965-66, pres. 1978-79), Am. Soc. Polit. and Legal Philosophy (v.p. 1972-74), Conf. for Study of Polit. Thought, ACLU, Phi Beta Kappa. Office: Princeton U Dept Politics Princeton NJ 08544-0001 Business E-Mail: kateb@princeton.edu.

KATEHI, LINDA P.B., engineering educator; b. Athens, Greece, Jan. 30, 1954; arrived in US, 1979; d. Vasilios and Georgia (Begni) K.; m. Spyros Tseregounis, July 10, 1980; children: Erik Tseregounis, Helena Tseregounis. BSEE, Nat. Tech. U., Athens, 1977; MSEE, UCLA, 1981, PhD in Elec. Engring., 1984. Teaching asst. Nat. Tech. U. Athens, 1977—78; rsch. engr. Dept. Def. Naval Rsch. Lab, GETEN, Athens, 1978—79; rsch. asst. UCLA, 1979-84; asst. prof. elec. engring. U. Mich., Ann Arbor, 1984—89, assoc. prof. elec. engring. and computer sci., 1989—94, prof. electrical engring. and computer sci., 1994—2001, coll. engring. assoc. dir. grad. program, 1994—95, mem. exec. com. Coll. Engring., 1995—98, assoc. dean grad. edn., 1998—99, sr. assoc. dean academic affairs, 1999—2001; John A. Edwardson dean engring. Purdue U., West Lafayette, Ind., 2001—; prof. computer and elec. engring., provost and vice chancellor academic affairs The U. Ill., Urbana-Champaign, 2002—. Reviewer Army Rsch. Office, 1984—, NSF, 1984—, chair. adv. com. to Engring. Directorate, 2005—, mem. adv. com. to Directorate for Computer and Info. Sci. and Engring., 2002—; strategic directions com. U. Mich., 1999—, assoc. dean and assoc. provosts academic programs group, 1999—, chair, provost com. on faculty mentoring, 1999—; mem. adv. com. on electron devices Dept. Defense, 1999—; chair Pioneer Revolutionary Technologies Subcom., Aerospace Enterprise NASA, 2002—, mem. Aerospace Tech. Adv. Com., 2002—, mem. aeronautics technical adv. com.; mem. Army Rsch. Lab. adv com. on Sensors and Electrons Divsn. AUS, 2003—; mem. engring. adv. com. Iowa State U., 2003—; mem. nominating com. Nat. Medal Tech.; mem. Kauffman Nat. Panel for Entrepreneurship; mem. telecomm. bd. NRC, mem. Army Rsch. Lab adv. com. divsn. sensors and electonics; mem. DoD Adv. Group on Electron Devices. Contbr. articles to profl. jours. Recipient Rsch. Excellence Award, Elec. Engring. and Computer Sci. Dept., U. Mich. Ann Arbor, 1993, Humboldt Rsch. Award, 1994, Faculty Recognition Award, U. Mich. Ann Arbor, 1994. Fellow: AAAS (mem. bd.), IEEE (Antennas and Propagation Soc., Microwave Theory and Techniques Soc., Microwave Theory and Techniques Soc. 3d Millenium Medal 2000); mem.: NAE, Advanced Computational Electromagnetics Soc., Internat. Soc. Hybrid Microelectronics, Internat. Union Radio Sci. (Booker Young Scientist Award 1987), Union Radio Sci. Internat., Sigma Xi. Achievements include patents in field. Avocations: skiing, tennis, gardening. Office: U Ill Urbana Office Provost and Vice Chancellor Acad Affairs Swanland Adminstrn Bldg MC 304 601 E John St Champaign IL 61820

KATEN, KAREN L., retired pharmaceutical company executive; b. 1948; BA in Polit. Sci. and Econ., U. Chgo., 1970, MBA in Mktg. and Fin., 1974. Mktg. assoc. pharms. Pfizer Inc., 1974, various positions Roerig divsn. product mgmt. group, 1975—78, group product mgr. Pfizer Labs., 1980, dir. product mgr. Pfizer Labs., v.p. mktg. Roerig divsn., 1983—86, v.p., dir. ops. Roerig divsn., 1986—91, v.p., gen. mgr. Roerig divsn., 1991—93, v.p., 1992—99, exec. v.p. Pfizer US Pharms. Group, 1993—95, pres. Pfizer US Pharms. Group NYC, 1995—2002, sr. v.p., 1999—2001; exec. v.p. Pfizer, Inc., 2001—05, vice chmn., 2005—06; exec. v.p. Pfizer Global Pharmaceuticals (formerly Pfizer Pharmaceuticals Group), 1997—2001, pres., 2001—05, Pfizer Human Health, 2005—06; adv. health policy Pfizer Inc., 2006. Bd. dirs. GM, Harris Corp., Catalyst, Nat. Alliance Hispanic Health, Am. Bur. for Med. Advancement in China; mem. internat. coun. J.P. Morgan Chase & Co.; mem. coun. U.S. and Italy, U. Chgo. Grad. Sch. Bus.; trustee U. Chgo.; nat. bd. trustees Am. Cancer Soc. Rsch. Found., NCAA Found.; health bd. advisors RAND Corp.; bd. corp. advisors Am. Diabetes Assn.; appointee US-Japan Private Sector/Govt. Commn., 2003, Nat. Infrastructure Adv. Com., 2003; bd. trustees Healthcare Leadership Coun. Named one of Most Powerful Women in Bus., Fortune mag., 1998—2005, Top 50 Women to Watch, Wall St. Jour., 2005, Next 20 Female CEOs, Pink Mag. & Forté Found., 2006; recipient Salute to Women Achievers award, YMCA, Women Yr. award, Boy Scout Am. Greater N.Y. Coun., NY Women's Agenda Star award, Bus. Leadership award, Burden Ctr. Aging, Iphigene Ochs Sulzburger award, Barnard Coll., Am. Fedn. Aging Rsch. Distinction award, Woman of Yr. award, NYC Police Athletic League, 2001, Woman With Heart award, Am. Heart Assn., 2004. Mem.: Nat. Pharm. Coun. (mem. bd. dirs.), Am. Diabetes Assn. (mem. bd. corp. advisors, Women of Valor award), Am. Cancer Soc. Rsch. Found. (mem. nat. bd. trustees), Nat. Alliance Hispanic Health, European Fedn. Pharm. Industry Assns. (bd. mem.), Health Leadership Coun., Pharm. Rsch. and Mfrs. Assn. Am.*

KATEN-BAHENSKY, DONNA, health facility administrator; BA in Anthropology, U. Mo., Columbia, 1980, MS in Pub. Health Adminstrn., 1982. COO, assoc. hosp. dir., acting hosp. dir. U. Nebr. Hosp., Omaha, 1991—98; vice chancellor bus. and fin. U. Nebr. Med. Ctr., Omaha, 1996—97; v.p. ambulatory care Nebr. Health Sys., Omaha, 1997—98; COO Med. Coll. Va. Hosps., Richmond, 1998—2000, exec. v.p., COO, 2000—02, Clinics of Va. Commonwealth U. Health Sys., Richmond, 2000—02; dir., CEO U. Iowa Hosps. and Cilinics, Iowa City, 2002—. Adj. faculty, preceptor grad. program in health adminstrn. Med. Coll. Va. Hosps.; mem. U. Health Sys. Consortium, Am. Coll. Healthcare Execs.; mem. adv. bd. Pfizer Health Solutions. Office: Univ Iowa Hosps and Clinics 200 Hawkins Dr Iowa City IA 52242

KATES, CAROLYN LOUISE, physical therapist; b. Ann Arbor, Mich., Dec. 11, 1949; d. Phillip Brown and Sara Louise Kates; m. Gregory Van Dreps, Sept. 23, 1986. BS, U. Fla., 1982; MSc, U. Wash., Seattle, 2000. Phys. therapist Sunland Ctr., Gainseville, Fla., 1982—84, Metcalf Elem. Sch., Gainseville, 1983—85, Shand's Hosp. U. Fla., 1985—86, Swedish Med. Ctr., Seattle, 1994—99, Boyer Children's Clin., Seattle, 1987—. Asst. instr. Manual Therapy for the Pediatric Patient, Seattle, 1990—2002; clin. instr. phys. therapy U. Wash., 1994—; presenter in field. Contbg. author: Clinical GMT Measurement with Pedographs, 2005; med. illustrator Management of Common Neuromuscular Disorders, 2005. Mem. Assn. Comprehensive Early Intervention Practice, Seattle, 1999—2001. Mem.: Wash. State Phys. Therapy Assn., Am. Phys. Therapy Assn., Golden Key Nat. Honor Soc., Phi Kappa Phi. Democrat. Home: 2760 SW 116th St Seattle WA 98146 Office: Boyer Children's Clin 1850 Boyer Ave E Seattle WA 98112 Office Phone: 206-325-8477.

KATES, MORRIS, biochemist, educator; b. Galati, Romania, Sept. 30, 1923; arrived in Can., 1924, naturalized, 1944; s. Samuel and Toby (Cohen) K.; m. Pirkko Helena Sofia Makinen, June 14, 1957; children: Anna-Lisa, Marja Helena, Ilona Sylvia. Student, Parkdale Coll., 1936-41; BA, U. Toronto, Ont., Can., 1945, MA, 1946, PhD, 1948. Research asst. Banting Inst., U. Toronto, 1948-49; postdoctoral fellow Nat. Research Council Can., Ottawa, Ont., 1949-51, research officer bioscis. div., 1951-68; prof. chemistry U. Ottawa, 1968-69, prof. biochemistry, 1969-89, prof. emeritus, 1989—, vice-dean research Faculty Sci. and Engring., 1978-82, staff research lectr., 1981, chmn. dept. biochemistry, 1982-85. Author: Techniques of Lipidology, 1972, 2d edit., 1986; co-editor: Metabolic Inhibitors vols. II and IV, 1972, 73, Biomembranes vol. 12, 1984, Handbook of Lipid Rsch., vol. 6, 1990, Biochemistry of Archaea (Archaebacteria), 1993; co-editor: Can. Jour. Biochemistry, 1974-84; contbr. numerous articles on lipid rsch. to profl. jours. Fellow Chem. Inst. Can., Royal Soc. Can.; mem. Can. Biochem. Soc. (pres. 1987-88), Am. Chem. Soc., Am. Soc. Biol. Chemists, Biochem. Soc. (London, Morton lectr. 1995), Am. Oil Chemists Soc. (Supelco rsch. award 1984), Ottawa Biol. and Biochem. Soc. (Sci. prize 1977, pres. 1974-75). Achievements include rsch. on lipid biochemistry. Home: 1723 Rhodes Crescent Ottawa ON Canada K1H 5T1 Office: U Ottawa Dept Biochemistry adn Mibrobiology and Immunology MacDonald Hall 323 150 Louis Pasteur St Ottawa ON Canada KIN 6N5 Business E-Mail: mkates@science.uottawa.ca.

KATHERINE, ROBERT ANDREW, chemicals executive; b. Phila., May 26, 1941; s. John and Winifred Irene (Smith) K.; m. Lynda Ann Ketchell, Dec. 27, 1988. BSCh.E., Drexel Inst. Tech., 1964, MBA, 1968; P.MD, Harvard U. Grad. Sch. Bus., 1977. Plant mgr. synthetic phenol plastics div. Allied Chem. Corp., 1964-66; asst. to dir. Far East sales Air Products & Chems., Phila., 1966-70; product group mgr. corp. devel. P.Q. Corp., 1970-72, div. sales mgr. splty. chems., 1972-74; bus. dir. polymers Hooker Chem. & Plastics div. Occidental Petroleum Corp., Burlington, NJ, 1974-78, v.p., gen. mgr. Ruco div., 1978-80, v.p., gen. mgr. fabricated products div., 1980-81; pres. The McCloskey Corp., 1981-83, chmn. bd., pres., CEO, 1983—89. Chmn. bd. McCloskey Corp. (Calif.), 1981-89, McCloskey Corp. (Oreg.), 1981-89; instr. Villanova U., 1973-75; asst. prof. Phila. Coll. Textiles and Sci., 1969-75 Mem. adv. bd. Modern Paint & Coatings Mag.; contbr. numerous articles to profl. jours. and newspapers. Bd. dirs. Inter-Sci. Found., UCLA Med. Sch., 1983-86; bd. dirs., chmn. fin. com., exec. compensation com., mem. exec. com. Hahnemann U.; corp. adv. bd. Huntington's Disease of Am. Mem. Soc. Plastics Industry (chmn. vinyl film group, exec. com. plastic bottle inst.), Nat. Paint and Coatings Assn. (bd. dirs., indsl. coatings steering com.), Young Pres. Orgn., Am. Chem. Soc., Am. Mgmt. Assn. (pres.' assn.), Pa. Soc. Clubs: Harvard Bus. Sch. (Phila., N.Y.C.); Union League (Phila.); Aronimink. Republican. Baptist. Home: 4102 Battles Ln Newtown Square PA 19073-1602 Office: 7600 State Rd Philadelphia PA 19136-3404 Personal E-mail: bobkat41@hotmail.com, rakkat@comcast.net.

KATHREN, RONALD LAURENCE, health physicist; b. Windsor, Ont., Can., June 6, 1937; s. Ben and Sally (Forman) K.; m. Susan Ruth Krafft, Dec. 24, 1964; children: SallyBeth, Daniel, Elana (dec.). BS, UCLA, 1957; MSc, U. Pitts., 1962. Diplomate Am. Bd. Health Physics (bd. dirs. 1982-84, sec.-treas. 1984); Am. Acad. Environ. Engrs.; registered profl. engr., Calif. Health physicist Lawrence Radiation Lab. U. Calif., Livermore, 1962-67; mgr. external dose evaluation, Battelle Pacific N.W. Labs., Richland, Wash., 1967-70, sr. rsch. scientist, 1970-72, staff scientist, program mgr., 1978-89; dir. US Transuranium and Uranium Registries Hanford Environ. Health Found., 1989-92, prof., dir. US Transuranium and Uranium Registries, Wash. State U., 1992-99, prof. emeritus, 1999-; US expert Internat. Atomic Energy Agy., Caracas, Venezuela, 1977; affiliate assoc. prof. U. Wash., 1978-94, prof., 1994, program coordinator in radiol. scis., 1980-82, 86-88; cons. Adv. Com. Reactor Safeguards, Washington, 1979-89; cons. adv. com. Nuc. Waste, 1988-94; mem. adv. com. Richland City Schs., 1985-87; bd. dirs. Mid-Columbia Symphony, 1987-92; chmn. Nat. Coun. Radiation Protection and Measurements Sci. Com. on Collective Dose, 1991-95; cons. Com. Environ. Radioactivity, 2005-; mem. Nat. Coun. of Examiners for Engring. and Surveying Com. on Examinations for Profl. Engrs., 1993—; trustee, Richland Public Libr. Found, 2002-, pres., 2004, Herbert M. Parker Found, 1987-, Master Gardner Found, 2004-06, Richland Players, 2007—. Author: Ionizing Radiation: Tumorigenic and Tumoricidal Effects, 1983; Radioactivity in the Environment, 1984; Radiation Protection, 1985, The Plutonium Story, 1994. Editor: (with others) Health Physics: A Backward Glance, 1980; Computer Applications in Health Physics, 1984, Environmental Health Physics, 1993, Radiation Protection Dosimetry, 1990—, Internat. Jour. Low Level Radiation, 2002—. Contbr. numerous articles to profl. jours., tech. reports, and chpts. in books. USPHS fellow, 1961-62; recipient Arthur Humm award Nat. Registry Radiation Protection Technologists, 1988, Hartman medallist and Orator Radiology Centennial, 1995. Mem. NAS (com. on film badge dosimetry in atmospheric nuclear tests 1989, subcom. health effect depleted uranium 2005—), Health Physics Soc. (life fellow, pres. 1989-90, pres. Columbia chpt. 1971, dir. 1973-76, Elda E. Anderson award 1977, founders award 1985, Disting. Sci. Achievement award 2003, G. William Morgan Lectr. award, 2006), Am. Assn. Physicists in Medicine, Am. Acad. Health Physics (bd. dirs. 1984-86, pres. 93-96), Soc. Radiol. Protection (fellow cert. in applied health physics). Home: 137 Spring St Richland WA 99354-1651 Office: Wash State Univ 137 Spring Richland WA 99354-1641 Office Phone: 509-375-5643. Personal E-mail: kathren@bmi.net. Business E-Mail: rkathren@tricity.wsu.edu.

KATHURIA, RAJEEV S., cardiovascular surgeon, thoracic surgeon; b. New Delhi; MD, George Wash. U., DC, 1981—85. Lic. gen. surgery Am. Bd. Surgery, 1992, thoracic surgery Am Bd. Thoracic Surgery, 1994. Cardiovasc. surgeon Ariz. Heart Inst., Phoenix, 1993—2004. Fellow: ACS; mem.: Soc. Thoracic Surgeons. Office: AZ Cardiovascular & Thoracic Surgeons 8402 E Shea Blvd Scottsdale AZ 85253

KATIN, PETER ROY, pianist; b. Nov. 14, 1930; m. Eva Zweig, 1954;2 children. Student, Royal Acad. Music.; DMus (hon.), De Montfort U., 1994. Prof. Royal Acad. Music, 1956-60; prof. piano U. Western Ont., Can., 1978-84; prof. Royal Coll. Music, 1992—2001, Thames Valley Univ., 2001—04. Made 1st London appearance Wigmore Hall, 1948; leading interpreter of Chopin; concerts include Europe, Africa, Japan, Can., U.S., Hong Kong, India, New Zealand, Singapore, Malaysia; rec. artist for Athene, Decca, Everest, Unicorn, HMV, Philips, Lyrita, MFP, Carlton, Simax, Claudio, Olympia; formed The Katin Piano Trio, 1997. Pres. Camerata of London; v.p. Bridgwater Arts Centre. Recipient Chopin Arts award, NYC, 1977. Fellow Royal Acad. Music; assoc. Royal Coll. Music; mem. Inc. Soc. Musicians, Royal Soc. Musicians. Avocations: reading, writing, theater, tape recording, photography. Office: 41 First Ave Bexhill-on-Sea East Sussex TN40 2PL England Office Phone: +44 (0)1424 211167. Business E-Mail: peter.katin@btinternet.com.

KATINA, ELENA SERGEJEVNA, singer; b. Moscow; Attended, Moscow State U., Faculty of Psychology. Singer t.A.T.u., 1999—. Rep. for Russia Eurovision Song Contest, 2003. Singer: (albums) 200 km/h in the Wrong Lane, 2002, Dangerous and Moving, 2005. Recipient 3rd Place for song "Ne ver', ne bojsia", Eurovision Song Contest, 2003. Mailing: tATu Interscope Records 2220 Colorado Ave Santa Monica CA 90404

KATINSKY, STEVEN B., communications company executive; b. Phila., Feb. 6, 1959; BS in Comms., Rutgers U., 1981. Founder Hollywood Media, Inc. (formerly Hollywood.com), Santa Monica, Calif., 1993; founder, CEO, pres. Supertuner.com, Santa Monica, Calif.; founder AdEngage; founder, mng. dir. Fruition Ventures LLC. Office: Fruition Ventures LLC 6121 Avenida Cresta La Jolla CA 92037 Office Phone: 858-459-8999. Office Fax: 858-459-1673.*

KATLIC, JOHN EDWARD, management consultant; b. Washington, Pa., Nov. 3, 1928; s. Frederick John and Dorothy Ann (Gideon) K.; m. Nancy Jean Nicely, Aug. 26, 1950; children: Mark Richard, Kerry Leigh, Kevin

Edward, Kathleen Diane, Nancy Ellen. BS in Engring. of Mines, W.Va. U., 1955, MS in Engring. of Mines, 1961. Mine surveyor Rochester & Pittsburgh Coal Co., Indiana, Pa., 1948-49; mine supt. Consolidation Coal Co., Morgantown, W.Va., 1959-62, gen. supt., 1962-66, v.p. Pitts., 1973-75; sr. mining engr. Ea. Assn. Coal, Pitts., 1967-68, divsn. mgr., 1969, v.p. pers. safety and indsl. rels., 1970, v.p., gen. mgr. Semet-Solvay divsn. Allied Chem., 1970-73; exec.v.p. adminstrn. engring. and govt. rels. Island Creek Coal Co., Lexington, Ky., 1975-83; sr. v.p. fuel supply Am. Electric Power Svc. Corp., 1983-93; pres. So. Ohio Coal, Cen. Ohio Coal, Windsor Coal, Conesville Coal (all subs.), 1983-93. Mem. negotiating team Nat. Bituminous Coal Wage Agreement, Joint Industry Devel. Com., 1978; cons. projects in Russia, Siberia, Kazakhstan, S. Africa. Author: Miner Jack And His Unforgettable People In The Coal Fields, 2006. Mem. Morgantown City Coun., 1964-66, Marshall U. Found., 1979; bd. dirs. W.Va. Edn. Found., 1983-90, Inland Waterways Users Bd., 1992-93, Decorative Arts Ctr. Ohio, 1998-2001, Fairfield County Found.; mem. Steering com. W.Va. U.; chmn. bd. trustees Lancaster Fairfield Community Hosp., 1990-91; bd. dirs. Ohio Glass Mus. With inf. U.S. Army, 1946-47, C.E., 1950-52. Named Man of Yr., Coal Age Mag., 1987, Ohio Mining and Reclamation Assn., 1988; recipient Erskine Ramsay medal AIME, 1995, Kingery Safety award Pa. Coal Mining Inst. Am., 1995; named to W.Va. Coal Hall of Fame, 2000. Mem. AIME, VFW, Soc. Mining Engrs., Nat. Mine Rescue Assn., Nat. Mining Assn. (chmn. 1990-92), Mine Rescue Vets. of Pitts. Dist., Lancaster Fairfield C. of C. (pres. 1989), Symposiarchs, Ky. Cols., Cherry River Navy Club, Masons, Shriners. Republican. Presbyterian. Achievements include patents for mining machine indicator, dust control in longwall mining. Home: 1233 Ridgewood Way Lancaster OH 43130-1154 Office Phone: 740-654-2191. Personal E-mail: minerjack@aol.com.

KATO, RYOZO, ambassador; b. Saitama Prefecture, Japan, Sept. 13, 1941; m. Hanayo Kato; 3 children. Law degree, Tokyo U., 1965. Employee Ministry Fgn. Affairs, Japan, 1965—81, dir. security affairs divsn. N.Am. Affairs Bur., 1981—84, dir. treaties divsn. Treaties Bur., 1984—87, dir. gen. affairs divsn. Min.'s Secretariat, 1990—92, dep. dir.-gen. N.Am. Affairs Bur., 1992—94, dir.-gen. Asian Affairs Bur., 1995—97, dep. min. fgn. affairs, 1999—2001; min. Embassy of Japan, 1987—90; consul-gen. of Japan San Francisco, 1994—95; amb. Extraordinary and Plenipotentiary of Japan to US Washington, 2001—. Office: Embassy of Japan 2520 Mass Ave NW Washington DC 20008-2869 Office Phone: 202-238-6700.

KATO, SHUICHI, information scientist, educator; b. Agematsu, Nagano, Japan, Sept. 4, 1943; BSEE, Nagoya Inst. Tech., Japan, 1969; MS, Chiba U., Japan, 1976; DMS, Tokyo U., 1981. Cert. in biomed. engring., neurophysiology. Staff Devel. Ctr. of Abilities, Seiko Co. Ltd., Tokyo, 1971-73; vis. rschr. Physiol. Lab., Cambridge (Eng.) U., 1981-82; vis. rschr. dept. electronics and computer sci. U. Calif., Berkeley, 1982-83; prof. faculty informatics Teikyo Heisei U. (formerly Teikyo U. Tech.), 1988—. prof. Grad. Sch. Informatics, 1999—. Lectr. dept. materials sci. Chiba U., 1989—2005; pre-reviewer New Energy and Indsl. Tech. Develop. Orgn. Japan, 2001—; chmn. bd. dirs. NPO Inst. Intelligent Comm., 2003—. Author: Physiological Base of Creativity, 1988, Application of Microprocessor to Monitor and Conditioning during Sleep, 1979, Design of a Life Support Computer Network System for Aged People, 1998, Nonlinearity of the ABR frequency characteristic, 1998; cons. editor Contemporary WHO's WHO, 2002—. Mem. IEEE, N.Y. Acad. Sci., Physiol. Soc. Japan (nominated Internat. Educator of Yr., Internat. Biographical Centre Cambridge, 2003, Japan Soc. Med. Electronics and Biol. Engring., Japan Soc. EEG and EMG, Inst. Electronics, Info. and Comm. Engrs., Welfare and Med. Soc. Chiba (vice-chmn. 2002—). Home: 3-12-11-206 Yamadabashi Ichihara 290-0021 Japan Office: Tokyo Met Ctrl Libr 5-7-13 Minami-Azabu Minato-ku Tokyo 106 Japan Home Phone: 0436-42-1496; Office Phone: 0436-74-5783. E-mail: kato@grape.plala.or.jp, kato@ieee.org.

KATO, WALTER YONEO, physicist; b. Chgo., Aug. 19, 1924; s. Naotaro and Hideko (Kondo) K.; m. Anna Chieko Kurata, June 26, 1953; children: Norman, Cathryn, Barbara. BS, Haverford Coll., Pa., 1946; MS, U. Ill., 1949; PhD, Pa. State U., University Park, 1954. Rsch. assoc. Ordnance Research Lab., Pa. State U., 1949-52, Brookhaven Nat. Lab., Upton, NY, 1952-53, sr. nuclear engr., asso. chmn. dept. applied sci., 1975-77, assoc. chmn. dept. nuclear energy, 1977-80, dep. chmn., 1980-88, chmn., 1988-91, sr. nuclear engr., 1991-97, cons., 1997—; rsch. affiliate dept. nuclear engring. MIT, Cambridge, 1999—2005, rsch. affiliate dept. nuclear sci. & engring., 2005—. Sr. physicist Argonne Nat. Lab., Ill., 1953-75; vis. prof. dept. nuclear engring. U. Mich., Ann Arbor, 1974-75; cons. Office Nuc. Regulatory Rsch., US NRC, 1974-76. Contbr. articles to profl. jours. Bd. dirs. Naperville YMCA, Ill., 1966-74; mem. Order of Sacred Treasure 3d class Japanese Govt., 1992. Served with Ordnance Corps AUS, 1946-47. Fulbright rsch. fellow, 1958-59, Sci. and Tech. Agy. Japan fellow, 1998. Fellow AAAS, Am. Nuclear Soc. (dir.), Argonne Univ. Assn. (Disting. Appt. award 1974); mem. Am. Phys. Soc., Sigma Xi. Methodist. Home: 65 Grove St Unit 342 Wellesley MA 02482 E-mail: wykato@mit.edu, wykatov@verizon.net.

KATOH, YUTAI, materials scientist; s. Mitsuhiko and Ikuko Kato; m. Michiko Sakakibara, Oct. 3, 1994; children: Yuri Kato, Tatsuhiro Kato, Masahiro Kato. PhD, U. Tokyo, 1994. Rsch. assoc. Nat. Inst. Fusion Sci., Toki, Gifu, Japan, 1995—96; assoc. prof. Kyoto U., 1996—2003; staff scientist Oak Ridge Nat. Lab., Tenn., 2003—. Recipient Bd. Dirs.' Excellence in Fusion Engring. award, Fusion Power Assocs., 2006. Office: Oak Ridge National Laboratory 1 Bethel Valley Road Oak Ridge TN 37831 Office Phone: 865-576-5996.

KATOK, ANATOLE, mathematics professor; b. Washington, Aug. 9, 1944; married; 3 children. MA, Moscow State U., 1965, PhD, 1968. Junior scientific rsch. worker central economics USSR Acad. of Sci. Mathematics Inst., 1968—73, sr. scientific rsch. worker central economics, 1973—78; prof., chair in analysis U. Maryland, 1978—84; prof. Calif. Inst. Tech., 1984—90, Penn State U., 1990—, Raymond N. Shibley prof., 1996—. Vis. lectr. Federal U., Mexico City, 1986, Stanford U., 1979, Federal U., Mexico City, 1988; vis. prof. U. Rome, 1978, U. Paris, 1993, U. Rome, 1997, Tsin Hua U., Taiwan, 1999, Cambridge U., 2000, Independent U. Moscow, 2001—03, U. Paris, 2002; vis. fellow Japan Soc. for Promotion of Sci., 2003; mem. editorial bd. Mathematical Rsch. Letters Jour., 1994—, Discrete & Continuous Dynamical Systems, 1995—, Moscow Mathematical Jour., 2000—. Editor: (books) Cambridge Tracts in Mathematics, Cambridge Studies in Advanced Mathematics, Proceedings, Progress in Mathematics. Fellow: Am. Acad. Arts & Sciences; mem.: Inst. Math. and Applications (bd. govs. 1993—96). Office: Penn State U Mathematics Dept U Park State College PA 16802

KATON, WAYNE J., psychiatrist, researcher; BA cum laude, U. Vermont, 1971; MD, U. Oreg., Portland, 1976. Lic. physician Wash., 1977, diplomate Natiional Bd. Med. Examiners, 1977, Am. Bd. Psychiatry and Neurology, 1981. Resident psychiatry U. Wash., Seattle, 1976—79, asst. prof. psychiatry, 1979—90, prof. psychiatry, 1990—. Vice-chmn., dir. health svcs. rsch. and psychiat. epidemiology U. Wash. Editor: Gen. Hosp. Psychiatry, 2005—; contbr. articles to profl. jours. Named one of Best Doctors in Am., 2001—06; recipient Gerald L. Klerman Sr. Investigator award, Depression and Bipolar Support Alliance, 2003, Thomas Hackett Meml. award, Acad. Psychosomatic Medicine, 2003. Mem.: Acad. Psychosomatic Medicine, Am. Psychiat. Assn., Am. Psychosomatic Soc., Anxiety Disorders Assn. Am. Achievements include research in collaborative care in primary care. Office: U Washington Dept Psychiatry Box 356560 1959 NE Pacific St Seattle WA 98195-6560 Office Phone: 206-543-7177. Office Fax: 206-221-5414. Business E-Mail: wkaton@u.washington.edu.

KATONA, MICHAEL GEORGE, civil engineer, educator; b. Bridgeport, Conn., Apr. 28, 1940; s. George and Ruth Elanor (Schenk) K.; m. Patty Lou Sullivan, Aug. 22, 1959 (div. Sept. 1997); children: Michele Joy Katona Lankford, Teresa Noelle Katona Wickstrom. BA in Math., U. Mich., 1967, BSCE, 1967, MS in Structures, 1968; PhD in Structural Mechanics, U. Calif., Berkeley, 1976. Sr. rsch. engr. Naval Civil Engring. Lab., Port Hueneme, Calif., 1968-77; prof. civil engring. U. Notre Dame, South Bend, Ind., 1977-86; sr. sect. head TRW, Ballistic Missiles Divsn., San Bernardino, Calif., 1986-89; chief scientist Air Force Civil Engring. Lab., Panama City, Fla., 1989-97; prof., chair civil engring. Wash. State U., Pullman, Wash., 1997—. Group II chmn. Transp. Rsch. Bd., 1994-97; U.S. rep. NATO Com. Protective Structures, 1990-93; sci. advisor EPA Mid-Atlantic Ctr., Ann Arbor, Mich., 1994—; Air Force prin. mem. Joint Engrs. Mgmt., Dept. Def., 1992-97; chmn. Nat. Coop. Hwy Rsch. Program panel Transp. Rsch. Bd., Washington, 1995-98; v.p. Acad. Rsch. Coun. of Civil Engring.-Rsch. Found., 1998—. Mem. editl. bd. Internat. Jour. Numerical Methods, 1985—; contbr. more than 60 articles to profl. jours. With USN, 1959-62. Recipient Presdl. Young Investigator award NSF, 1984, Naval Civil Engring. award USN, 1970, Outstanding Civilan Career award USAF, 1998. Fellow ASCE; mem. Marina Club Home Owners Assn. (pres. 1995-97). Achievements include CANDE computer software program used for the design and analysis of buried structures such as culverts, pressure pipes, conduits, and soil bridges. Office: Wash State U Dept Civil Engring Pullman WA 99164-0001 Home Phone: 253-851-5242; Office Phone: 509-335-2692. Business E-Mail: mgk@wsu.edu.

KATONA, PETER GEZA, biomedical engineer, educator; b. Budapest, Hungary, June 25, 1937; came to U.S., 1956, naturalized, 1962; s. Stephan and Irene (Renner) K.; m. Jaroslava Blanar, Aug. 27, 1966; children—Catherine Iris, Andrew George. BS in Elec. Engring, U. Mich., 1960; S.M. in Elec. Engring. (Sloan fellow, 1960-62), M.I.T., 1962, Sc.D. in Elec. Engring, 1965. Asst. prof. elec. engring. M.I.T., 1965-69; assoc. prof. biomed. engring. Case Western Res. U., Cleve., 1969-78, prof., 1978-92, chmn. dept., 1980-87. Program dir. biomed. engring. and aiding the disabled NSF, 1989—91; v.p. biomed. engring. The Whitaker Found., 1991—95, exec. v.p. biomed engring., 1995—98, pres. biomed. engring., 1998—2000, pres., CEO, 2000—06; prof. elec. and computer engring. George Mason U., 2006—. Mem. editl. bd. Am. Jour. Physiology, 1975-81; contbr. articles on cardio-respiratory control and automated drug delivery to profl. jours. Recipient Alexander von Humboldt award, 1987-88, Disting. Achievement award, BMES, 2005, Pierre Galletti award, AIMBE, 2006. Fellow AAAS, Am. Inst. Med. & Biol. Engring. (founding); sr. mem. IEEE, Am. Physiol. Soc., Biomed. Engring. Soc. (bd. dirs. 1977-80, pres. 1984-85), Am. Soc. Engring. Edn. Office Phone: 703-993-9347. Business E-Mail: pkatona@gmu.edu. E-mail: peter@katonaconsulting.org.

KATOPODIS, LOUIS, supermarket chain executive; Grad., U. Houston, 1971. Joined Fiesta Mart, Houston, 1975—, various positions including non foods buyer, gen. mgr., pres., CEO. Bd. mem. Food Marketing Inst. Treas. bd. dirs. Chronic Lymphocytic Leukemia Global Rsch. Found. Office: Fiesta Mart 5235 Katy Fwy Houston TX 77007-2210

KATRANA, DAVID JOHN, plastic and reconstructive surgeon; b. Moline, Ill., Oct. 16, 1945; s. Nicholas John and Marilyn Ann Katrana; m. Carol; children: Nicole Elaine, Kimberly Ann. BA in Biology, Northwestern U., Evanston, Ill., 1967; DDS, Northwestern U., Chgo., 1971, MD, 1974. Diplomate Am. Bd. Plastic and Reconstructive Surgery. Resident oral surgery Northwestern U. Dental Sch., Chgo., 1971-72; intern surgery Northwestern U. McGraw Med. Ctr., Chgo., 1974-75, resident gen. surgery, 1975-77, resident plastic and reconstructive surgery, 1977-79; assoc. Houston Plastic Surgery Assocs., 1979-91; pvt. practice plastic surgery, 1991—; asst. clin. prof. plastic surgery Baylor Coll. Medicine, Houston, 1980—. Pres. Hyperbaric Mgmt. Assocs. Inc., 1997-2000; dental cons. The Chgo. Bulls, 1977-79; instr. surgery, dental cons. Northwestern U. Med. Sch., Chgo., 1978-79; dir. burn unit Humana Hosp. Southmore, Pasadena, Tex., 1982-88; div. chief surgery Rosewood Hosp., Houston, 1984-86, pres. med. staff, 1988-89; plastic surg. cons. Houston Gamblers Profl. Football Team, 1984; mem. courtesy staff St. Luke's Episcopal Hosp., West Houston Med. Ctr., Meml. Hosp. at Memorial City, also others; lectr. various univs. and hosps. Contbr. articles to profl. jours. Trustee Rosewood Med. Ctr., Houston, 1989—96, chmn. bd., 1995—2000; dir. Ctr. Wound Care and Hyperbaric Medicine, Spring Br. Med. Ctr., 2000—01. Fellow ACS; mem. Undersea and Hyperbaric Med. Soc., Internat. Soc. Burn Injuries, Am. Burn Assn., Am. Soc. Plastic and Reconstructive Surgeons, Tex. Soc. Plastic Surgeons, Tex. Med. Assn., Harris County Med. Soc., Houston Soc. Plastic Surgeons, Wound Healing Soc. Office: 909 Frostwood # 260 Houston TX 77024 Home: 5001 Woodway #1204 Houston TX 77056 Personal E-mail: dj2870@aol.com.

KATRITZKY, ALAN ROY, chemistry professor; b. London, Eng., Aug. 18, 1928; s. Frederick Charles and Emily Gertrude (Lane) K.; m. Agnes Juliane Dietlinde Kilian, Aug. 5, 1952; children: Margaret, Erika, Rupert, Freda. BA, Oxford U., 1951, BSc, 1952, MA, DPhil, Oxford U., 1954; PhD, Cambridge U., 1958, DSc, 1963; DSc (hon.), U. Nac. Madrid, 1986, U. Poznan, Poland, 1990, U. Gdansk, 1994, U. East Anglia, UK, 1995, U. Toulouse, France, 1996; Prof. (hon.), Xian Modern U., 1995, Beijing Inst. Tech., 1995; DSc (hon.), U. St. Petersburg, Russia, 1997, U. Bucharest, Romania, 1998, U. Rostov, Russia, 2000, U. Ghent, Belgium, 2001, Bundelkhand U., India, 2001, U. Timisoara, Romania, 2003, U. Wroclaw, Poland, 2005, U. Jena, Germany, 2007. ICI fellow U. Oxford, 1956-58; lectr. chemistry U. Cambridge, 1958-63; fellow Churchill Coll.; prof. chemistry U. East Anglia, 1963-80; dean U. East Anglia (Sch. Chem. Scis.), 1963-70, 76-80; Kenan prof. organic chemistry U. Fla., Gainesville, 1980—. Dir. Fla. Inst. Het. Cpds., 1986—. Editor: Advances in Heterocyclic Chemistry, vols. 1-85, 1963—; regional editor: Tetrahedron, 1980-98; chmn. editl. bd. Comprehensive Heterocyclic Chemistry, 1st edit., 9 vols., 1985, 2d edit., 10 vols., 1996, 3d edit. 12 vols., 2006, Comprehensive Organic Functional Group Transformations, 7 vols., 1995, 2d edit., 2004. Decorated Cavaliere Ufficiale. Fellow Royal Soc., St Catherine Coll. (hon.); mem. Am., Brit., Italian (hon. mem.), Polish (hon. mem.) Chem. Socs., Internat. Soc. Het. Chem., Polish Acad. Sci. (fgn. mem.), Real Catalan Acad., Slovenian Acad., Russian Acad. Sci. (fgn. mem. Siberian br.), Indian Nat. Acad. Sci. (fgn. mem.). Home: 1221 SW 21st Ave Gainesville FL 32601-8417 Office: U Fla Dept Chemistry Gainesville FL 32611 Business E-Mail: katritzky@chem.ufl.edu.

KATSAKIORES, GEORGE NICHOLAS, state legislator, retired food service executive; b. Derry, NH, Dec. 11, 1924; s. Nicholas G. and Agorista (Siatravinos) K.; m. Lucille Brunelle, Nov. 11, 1963 (div. July 1980); children: Sheila, Glen, Greg, Karen, Gary; m. Phyllis M. Harrie, Oct. 9, 1983 Student, U. N.H., 1946—48. Owner White's Restaurant, Derry, 1948—88, ret., 1988; mem. N.H. Ho. of Reps., 1982—, chair transp. com., 1982—91, chmn. emeritus, 1991—. Dir. Derry Devel. and Preservation Corp.; vice chmn. Airport Access Hwy. Task Force, Manchester, N.H.; mem. transp. task force Am. Legis. Exch. Coun., Washington, 1984—; apptd. to N.H. Integrated Trans. and R.R. Coun., 1985—, Internat. Hellenic Union, 2004- Dir. Derry Devel. and Preservation Corp.; vice chmn. Airport Access Hwy. Task Force, Manchester, NH; mem. transp. task force Am. Legis. Exch. Coun., Washington, 1984—; apptd. to NH Integrated Transp. and RR Coun., 1985—, Internat. Hellenic Union, 2004—; dir. NE Corridor Initiative, Boston, Greater Derry/Saleit Transp. Coun., Nutfield Sr. Devel. Corp., Cmty. Alliance Regional Transp.; mem. Rockingham County Com., Brentwood, NH, 1998—; chmn. Rock City Del., 1999—2004, Rep. Nat. Party, NH Rep. Com., 1982—; bd. dirs. Cmty. Alliance for Regional Transp. Cpl. med. corps US Army, 1943—45, ETO. Inducted into Pinkerton Acad. Hall of Fame, 1999 Mem. VFW (Post 1617), AARP, Nat. Coun. State Legislators (trans-com.), N.H. Transp. and Hwy. Users Coalition, N.H. R.R. Revitalization Assn., Internat. Hellenic Union, Am. Legion, Hoodkroft County Club (Derry) Greek Orthodox. Avocations: golf, politics. Home: 1 Bradford St Derry NH 03038-4258 Office Phone: 603-217-6689. E-mail: p.katsakiores@comcast.net.

KATSH, SALEM MICHAEL, lawyer; s. Abraham Isaac and Estelle (Wachtell) K.; m. Jennette Williams, Sept. 4, 1983; children: Halley Rachel, Emmet Walker. BA, NYU, 1970, JD cum laude, 1972. Bar: N.Y. 1973, U.S. Dist. Ct. (so., ea., no. dists. N.Y.) 1975, U.S. Ct. of Appeals (2d cir.) 1975, U.S. Ct. of Appeals (9th cir.) 1977, U.S. Supreme Ct. 1983, U.S. Ct. Appeals (fed. cir.) 1990, U.S. Dist. Ct. (no. dist.) Calif. 1993. Assoc. Weil, Gotshal & Manges, NYC, 1972-80, ptnr., 1980-97, Shearman & Sterling, NYC, 1997—2005, Kasowitz, Benson, Torres & Friedman, NYC, 2005—06. Adj. prof. New York Law Sch., 1980-84. Author: Industrial Power and the Law, 1980, (with others) The Limits of Corporate Power, 1981; founder Jour. Proprietary Rights; contbr. articles to profl. jours. Mem.: ABA, Bar Assn. City of NY, NY State Bar Assn., Order of Coif. Mailing: 44 W 62nd St Ste 16B New York NY 10023 Office Phone: 212-678-9214. Business E-Mail: yodeyah@yahoo.com.

KATSIFF, BRUCE, artist; b. Phila., Dec. 10, 1945; s. Myer and Rose (August) K.; m. Joane Mitnick, Dec. 30, 1965; 1 child, Timothy. BFA, Rochester Inst. Tech., 1968; MFA, Pratt Inst., 1973; postgrad., Oxford U., Eng., 1987. Film producer Eastman Kodak Co., Rochester, NY, 1968; adj. prof. Thomas Edison Coll., Trenton, NJ, 1970-74; chmn. fine art Bucks County Coll., Newtown, Pa., 1973-84, prof., 1984-88; chmn. art and music Bucks Coll., Newtown, 1988-89; dir. James A. Michener Art Mus., 1990—. Mng. bd. dirs. Photography Sesquicentennial, Phila., 1988-90. Exhibited at Mus. Modern Art, N.Y.C., 1968, Internat. Mus. Photography, Rochester, N.Y., 1969, Phila. Art Mus., 1970, Am. Arts Ctr., Exeter, Eng., 1970, Tainjan Inst., China, 1987, Pa. Acad. Fine Arts, 1990, Washington Photography Ctr., 1993. Grantee NEA, 1973; fellowship Pa. Arts Coun., 1990. Fellow Soc. Photographic Educators; mem. Pa. Coun. on Arts (mus. panel 1982-85, visual arts panel 1987-90). Mailing: PO Box 28 Lumberville PA 18933-0028 Home: 182 Short Rd Doylestown PA 18901 E-mail: bkatsiff@comcast.net.

KATSOULOMITIS, GEORGIA, foundation administrator, lawyer; Graduate, Tufts Univ.; JD, Catholic Univ., Washington. Spl. asst. US Labor Secy., Robert Reich, Washington; spl. asst. and counsel, oversight and investigations Dept. Labor, Washington; v.p. Robinson Lerer & Montgomery, NYC; now asst. exec. dir. Boston Bar Found. Class of 2004 LeadBoston leadership devel. program; past. exec. dir. Mass. Women's Polit. Caucus. Mem.: Women's Bar Assn. (legis. policy com.), Hellenic Bar Assn. (vice pres. 2005), Mass. Bar. Office: Boston Bar Found 16 Beacon St Boston MA 02108 Office Phone: 617-778-1948. Office Fax: 617-523-0127. Business E-Mail: gkatsoulomitis@bostonbar.org.

KATTA, RAJANI, dermatologist; b. Montreal; d. Satyanarayana and Swarajyalaxmi Katta; m. Samir P. Desai. MD, Baylor Coll. Medicine, Houston. Lic. Am. Bd. Dermatology, 1998. Assoc. prof. Baylor Coll. Medicine, Houston, 1998—. Fellow: Am. Contact Dermatitis Soc. Office: Baylor Dermatology 6620 Main St Ste 1425 Houston TX 77030 Office Phone: 713-798-6131.

KATTOUF, THEODORE E., former ambassador; b. Altoona, Pa., 1946; m. Jeannie Ajay; children: Jennifer, Jonathan, Paul, Michael. Grad., Pa. State U. With U.S. Fgn. Svc., 1972—2003, econ. and comml. officer Kuwait, 1973-75, polit. officer Damascus, Middle East analyst Bur. of Intelligence and Rsch. Washington, internat. relations officer Near East Bur., dep. chief of mission Baghdad, 1983, Sanaa, dep. dir. Office of Arab North Affairs Washington, 1988, dir. Office of Arab North Affairs, dep. chief of mission Damascus, Riyadh, Saudi Arabia; US amb. to United Arab Emirates US Dept. State, 1998—2001, US amb. to Syria Damascus, 2001—03; pres., CEO Am-Mideast Edn. & Training Services, Inc. (AMID-EAST), Washington, 2003—. Served in US Army, 1968—72. Recipient Cobb award, Meritorious Honor award (2), US Dept. State, Sr. Performance award (4), Presdl. Honor award. Office: AMIDEAST 1730 M St NW Ste 1100 Washington DC 20036*

KATTWINKEL, JOHN, pediatrician, educator; b. Newton, Mass., June 24, 1941; s. Egon Emil and Dorothy Lucile (Fish) K.; m. Phyllis Ann Denton, Sept. 14, 1963; children: Susan, Linda. BS, Rensselaer Poly. Inst., 1964; B in Med. Sci., Dartmouth Coll., 1966; MD, Harvard U., 1968. Diplomate Am. Bd. Pediatrics, Am. Bd. Neonatology (bd. dirs. 1981-86). Resident in pediatrics Duke Med. Ctr., Durham, NC, 1968-70; clin. assoc. NIH, Bethesda, Md., 1970-72; neonatology fellow Case Western Res. U., Cleve., 1972-74; asst. prof. pediatrics U. Va., Charlottesville, 1974-78, assoc. prof., 1978-84, prof., 1984—, dir. neonatology, 1974—, Charles Fuller chair in neonatology, 1998—. Founder Perinatal Edn. Ctr., Charlottesville, 1976—; Poland and China cons. Project HOPE, Milwood, Va., 1979-92; hon. prof. Zhejiang Med. U., Hangzhou, People's Republic of China, 1985. Mem. editl. bd. Pediatrics, 1999—2005; contbr. articles on newborn respiration and med. edn. to profl. jours.; inventor device for nasal ventilation of infants. Lt. comdr. USPHS, 1970-72. Named Disting. prof., U. Va. Alumni Assn., 2007; recipient Discovery Health Channel Med. Honor, 2004. Fellow: Am. Acad. Pediat. (fetus and newborn com. 1983—89, neonatal resuscitation program steering com. 1989—98, chair 1994—98, editor 1999—, Ross Profl. Edn. award 1989); mem.: Soc. Pediat. Rsch., Am. Pediat. Soc. Avocation: tennis. Home: 500 Rocks Farm Dr Charlottesville VA 22901 Office: U Va Dept Pediatrics Charlottesville VA 22908-0001 Office Phone: 434-924-5428. Business E-Mail: jk3f@virginia.edu.

KATYAL, NEAL KUMAR, law educator; b. 1970; married; 3 children. AB, Dartmouth U., 1991; JD, Yale U., 1995. Law clk. to Justice Stephen G. Breyer U.S. Supreme Ct.; law clk. to Hon. Guido Calabresi US Ct. Appeals (2nd Cir.); nat. security adv. to dep. atty. gen. US Dept. Justice, Washington, 1998—99; assoc. prof. law Georgetown U., 1997—2004, John Carroll rsch. prof. law, 2004—. Vis. prof. Yale U., 2001—02, Harvard U., 2002. Contbr. articles to profl. jours.; guest appearance (TV series) The Colbert Report, 2006. Named one of Top 40 Lawyers Under 40, The Nat. Law Jour., 2005, Litigation's Rising Stars, The Am. Lawyer, 2007; recipient Pro Bono award, The Nat. Law Jour., 2004. Office: Georgetown U Law Ctr 600 New Jersey Ave NW Washington DC 20001 Office Phone: 202-262-9000.*

KATZ, ABRAHAM, retired foreign service officer; b. Bklyn., Dec. 4, 1926; s. Alexander and Zina (Rabinowitz) K.; children: Tamar, Jonathan, Naomi; m. Marion Scheinberger, July 29, 1996. BA cum laude, Bklyn. Coll., 1948; M.I.A., Columbia U., 1950; PhD, Harvard U., 1968. Commd. fgn. service officer Dept. State , 1951; vice-consul, prin. officer Am. Consulate, Merida, Mexico, 1951—53; 2d sec. Am. Embassy, Mexico, 1953—56; chief Soviet fgn. econ. Bur. Intelligence Rsch., Washington, 1957—59; 1st sec. U.S. missions to NATO, OECD, Paris, 1959-64; counselor Am. Embassy, Moscow, 1964-66; dir. office of OECD European Communities and Atlantic Polit. Econ. Affairs, Washington, 1967-74; dep. chief of mission OECD, Paris, 1974-78; dep. asst. sec. for internat. econ. policy and research Dept. Commerce, Washington, 1978-80, asst. sec.

internat. econ. policy, 1980-81; U.S. rep., ambassador OECD, Paris, 1981-84; pres. U.S. Coun. Internat. Bus., 1984-99, pres. emeritus, 1999—. Employer mem. gov. body Internat. Labor Orgn., 1984-99; v.p. Internat. Orgn. Employers, 1984-99. Author: The Politics of Economic Reform in the Soviet Union, 1972. Pres. Internat. Orgn. Employers, 2006—. Decorated grand officier Ordre National du Merite (France); recipient U.S. Coun. Internat. Bus. Internat. Leadership award. Mem. Am. Polit. Sci. Assn., Assn. Advancement Slavic Studies, Am. Fgn. Svc. Assn., Am. Assn. Comparative Econ. Studies, Coun. Fgn. Rels., Internat. Orgn. Employers (pres. 2006), Cosmos Club, Harvard Club, B'nai Brith, Century Assn. Office: US Coun Internat Bus 1212 Avenue Of The Americas New York NY 10036-1602 Business E-Mail: akatz@uscib.org.

KATZ, ADRIAN IZHACK, medical educator; b. Bucharest, Romania, Aug. 3, 1932; came to U.S., 1965, naturalized, 1976; s. Ferdinand and Helen (Lustig) K.; m. Miriam Lesser, Mar. 31, 1965; children— Ron, Iris. MD, Hebrew U., 1961. Research fellow Yale U., 1965-67, Harvard U., 1967-68; intern Belinson Med. Center, Israel, 1961, resident, 1962-65; practice medicine specializing in internal medicine and nephrology New Haven, 1966-67, Boston, 1967-68, Chgo., 1968—; attending physician U. Chgo. Hosps., 1968—2002, head nephrology sect., 1973-82; asst. prof. medicine U. Chgo., 1968-71, assoc. prof., 1971-74, prof., 1975—2002, prof. emeritus, 2002—. Fogarty sr. internat. fellow, vis. scientist Lab Cell Physiology, Coll. de France, Paris, 1977-78; vis. prof. cellular and molecular physiology Yale U., 1988; vis. scientist dept. molecular medicine Karolinska Inst., Stockholm, 1994—. Co-author: Kidney Function and Disease in Pregnancy; contbr. chpts. to books, articles to profl. jours. Fellow A.C.P.; mem. Am. Physiol. Soc., Am. Soc. Clin. Investigation, Assn. Am. Physicians, Am. Soc. Nephrology, Internat. Soc. Nephrology, Central Soc. Clin. Research, N.Y. Acad. Scis. Home: 1125 E 53rd St Chicago IL 60615-4410 Office: U Chgo 5841 S Maryland Ave Chicago IL 60637-1463 Business E-Mail: akatz@medicine.bsd.uchicago.edu.

KATZ, ALAN CHARLES, toxicologist; b. Kearny, NJ, Nov. 10, 1946; s. Edward Myron and Margaret Ellen Katz; m. Marcia Anne Ellenwood, July 26, 1974; children: Bryan Jeffrey, Jeffrey Alan. BS in Biology, Fairleigh Dickinson U., 1970, MS in Human Physiology, 1977; Cert. in Mgmt., Ctrl. Conn. State U., 1981. Diplomate Am. Bd. Toxicology, Am. Bd. Forensic Examiners. Chemist Union Carbide Corp., Bound Brook, N.J., 1965-70; toxicologist Ortho Pharm. Corp., Raritan, N.J., 1971-74; sr. ophthalmic pharmacologist Cooper Labs., Cedar Knolls, N.J., 1974-76; sr. assoc. toxicologist J&J Rsch. Found., North Brunswick, N.J., 1976-79; study dir. Stauffer Chem. Co., Farmington, Conn., 1979-84; sr. toxicologist EPA, Washington, 1984-87; exec. dir. TAS, Inc., Washington, 1987-97; mgr. tech. affairs Sanachem USA, Inc., 1997-98; prin. Katz Assocs., 1985—, TOXCEL, LLC, 1999—; dir. TOXCEL Internat., Ltd., 2000—. Contbg. editor Acute Toxicity, 1991-97; editl. bd. Jour. Applied Toxicology. Fellow Am. Coll. Forensic Examiners; mem. N.Y. Acad. Scis., Soc. Comparative Ophthalmology (past pres.), Soc. Toxicology, Am. Coll. Toxicology, Am. Chem. Soc., Soc. Toxicologie du Can., Roundtable Toxicology Cons., Food & Drug Law Inst. Home: 16090 Simon Kenton Rd Haymarket VA 20169-2109

KATZ, ANDRES U., surgeon; b. Caracas, Venezuela, July 4, 1948; arrived in U.S., 1965; s. Alexander Katz and Isabel Ungar; m. Patricia Moreno; 1 child, Santiago. MD, U. Navarra, Pampcona, 1972. Resident St. Paul Hosp., Dallas, 1972—76; fellow in vascular U. Manitoba, 1976—77; clin. instr. surgery Southwestern Med. Sch., Dallas, 1977—. Mem.: Royal Coll. Surgery, Tex. Surg. Soc.

KATZ, ARNOLD MARTIN, medical educator; b. Chgo., July 30, 1932; s. Louis Nelson and Aline (Grossner) K.; m. Phyllis Beck, Apr. 18, 1959; children: Paul, Sarah, Amy, Laura. BA with honors, U. Chgo., 1952; MD cum laude, Harvard U., 1956; D.Med. (hon.), Carol Davila U., 1994. Diplomate Nat. Bd. Med. Examiners. Intern Mass. Gen. Hosp., Boston, 1956-57, asst. resident, 1959-60; rsch. assoc. NIH, Bethesda, Md., 1957-59; asst. registrar Inst. Cardiology, London, 1960-61; rsch. fellow dept. medicine UCLA, 1961-64; asst. prof. physiology Columbia U., NYC, 1963-67; assoc. prof. medicine and physiology U. Chgo., 1967-69; Philip J. and Harriet L. Goodhart prof. cardiology Mt. Sinai Sch. Medicine, NYC, 1969-77; prof. medicine U. Conn., Farmington, 1977—2000, prof. medicine emeritus, 2000—, head cardiology divsn., 1977—95; vis. prof. medicine Dartmouth Med. Sch., 1990—2001, vis. prof. medicine and physiology, 2001—. Cons. VA, 1970; coord. Problem Area #3, US-USSR Collaboration in Cardiovasc. Rsch., 1983—86; mem. adv. com. Chinese Acad. Med. Sci., 1982—89; R.T. Hall lectr. Cardiac Soc., Australia, 1991, New Zealand, 91; chair sci. bd. Stanley J. Sarnoff Endowment Cardiovasc. Sci. Inc., 1992—93; chair, sci. adv. bd. Patrick, Catherine, Weldon, Donaghue Med. Rsch. Found., 1994—97; mem. bd. sci. counsellors Nat. Heart Lung Inst., 1989—92. Author: Physiology of the Heart, 1977, Physiology of the Heart, 4th edit., 2006, Heart Failure: Pathophysiology, Molecular Biology and Clinical Management, 2000; editor: The Heart and Cardiovascular System, 1986, 1991; Am. Jour. Physiology, 1966—72, mem. editl. bd.: Jour. Molecular and Cellular Cardiology, 1970—92, editor-in-chief:, 1986—92, mem. editl. bd.: Am. Jour. Cardiology, 1970—75, Jour. Mechanochemistry and Cell Motility, 1970—72, Am. Jour. Medicine, 1971—77, Jour. Clin. Investigation, 1971—76, Circulation Rsch., 1974—80, Physiol. Rev., 1976—80, Cardiovasc. Pharmacol., 1979—88, Life Scis., 1979—88, Cardiology, 1980—85, Jour. Am. Coll. Cardiology, 1983—87, Can. Jour. Cardiology, 1988—91, Cardioscience, 1988—95, Circulation, 1992—, reviewer: several profl. jours.; contbr. articles to profl. jours. Served with USPHS, 1957-59. Humboldt fellow Alexander von Humboldt Found., 1975-76, Moseley traveling fellow Harvard U., 1960-61. Fellow ACP, Am. Coll. Cardiology (gov. Conn. 1984-87), Coun. on Basic Cardvasc. Sci. (charter); mem. Am. Heart assn. (advanced rsch. fellow 1961-63, established investigator 1963-68, v.p. couns. 1992-94, bd. dirs. 1992-94, chmn. coun. affairs com. 1992-94, chmn. exec. com. basic sci. coun. 1990-92, Conn. affiliate bd. dirs. 1986-94, Greater Hartford chpt. bd. dirs. 1977-84, sec. 1982-84, v.p. 1984-86, pres. 1986-88, Rsch. Achievement award 1989, Disting. Achievement award Basic Sci. Coun. 1991, award of Meritorious Achievement 1995, Honoree Louis N. and Arnold M. Katz prize Basic Sci. Coun. 1995), N.Y. Heart Assn. (bd. dirs. 1971-74, 75-77), Am. Physiol. Soc., Cardiac Muscle Soc. (pres. 1969-71), Assn. Am. Physicians, Internat. Soc. Heart Rsch. (pres. Am. sect. 1985, founding fellow 2000, Peter Harris Disting. Scientist award 2004), Assn. Univ. Cardiologists, Alpha Omega Alpha. Home: PO Box 1048 1592 New Boston Rd Norwich VT 05055-1048 E-mail: arnold.m.katz@dartmouth.edu.

KATZ, ARNOLD MARTIN, insurance brokerage firm executive; b. Schenectady, NY, Mar. 22, 1940; s. David and Minna Katz; 1 child, Sharon. BS in Pub. Rels., Boston U., 1962. Cert. life underwriter, Pa. Sales rep. Mass. Gen. Life Ins. Co., Hartford, Conn., 1964-66, sr. sales rep., 1966-67, asst. mgr., 1967; mgr. Phila., 1967-72; v.p. Boston, 1972-76; pres. Brokerage Concepts, Inc., Phila., 1977—. Pres. BCI Holdings Inc., Atlantic Adminstrs., Waltham, Mass., Group Source, Phila. Contbr. articles to profl. jours. Bd. dirs. Moss Rehab. Hosp., Phila., 1985-93, Police Athletic League, Phila., 1986—; vice chmn. Einstein Health Care Found., Phila., 1987—; chmn., mem. bd. Belmont Hosp. 1987—2002. Served to maj. U.S. Army, 1962-73. Mem. Life Underwriter Assn., CLU (bd. dirs. Phila. chpt.), Assn. Health Ins. Agts. (pres.). Jewish. Office: Brokerage Concepts Inc 1021 8th Ave King Of Prussia PA 19406 Office Phone: 610-491-4802. Business E-Mail: arnold.katz@bcitpa.com.

KATZ, AVI, lawyer; b. Boston, Jan. 15, 1959; s. I. Norman and Judith (Batt) K.; m. Rivi Kanarek, Aug. 25, 1982; children: Dena, Tamar, Yehoshua. BA, Yeshiva U., 1981; MA, Columbia U., 1984, JD, 1986. Bar: N.Y. 1987. Law clk. to Hon. Lawrence W. Pierce, U.S. Ct. Appeals for 2d Cir., NYC, 1986-87; assoc. Willkie Farr & Gallagher, NYC, 1987-96; assoc. gen. counsel Loral Space & Comm. Ltd., NYC, 1996-97, dep. gen. counsel, 1997-98, v.p., dep. gen. counsel, 1998-99, v.p., gen. counsel, sec., 1999—. Mem. ABA, N.Y. State Bar Assn., New York County Lawyers Assn., Assn. Bar City N.Y. Home: 1460 Hudson Rd Teaneck NJ 07666-2914 Office: Loral Space & Comm Inc 600 3rd Ave New York NY 10016-1901 Office Phone: 212-338-5340. Business E-Mail: avi.katz@hq.loral.com.

KATZ, AVRUM SIDNEY, lawyer; b. Melrose Park, Ill., Oct. 10, 1939; s. Joseph George and Bessie Goldie (Ancel) K.; m. Sheela Cara Cooperman, Sept. 1, 1963; children: Julie Anne, Aaron Richard, Michele Sharon. BSEE, Ill. Inst. Tech., 1962; JD, George Washington U., 1966. Bar: Ill. 1966, U.S. Dist. Ct. (no. dist.) Ill. 1967, U.S. Patent Office 1967, U.S. Supreme Ct. 1977, U.S. Ct. Appeals (7th cir.) 1978, D.C. 1991, cert.: U.S. Patent Office (examiner). Assoc. Leonard G. Nierman, Chgo., 1966—67, Fitch, Even, Tabin, Flannery & Welsh and predecessor firms, Chgo., 1967—70, ptnr., 1971—82, Welsh & Katz Ltd., Chgo., 1983—. Mem. intellectual property adv. bd. George Washington U. Law Sch., Washington, 2000—. Author (with others): Effective Litigation Against Knockoffs, 1984; author: Chip, Mask and Program Protection, 1985, Electronics and Computer Patent and Copyright Practice, 1988, 2d edit., 1990; mem. editl. bd. Mealey's Litig. Report on Intellectual Property, 1992—, mem. adv. bd. Licensing Jour., 1987—, The IP Litigator, 2000—. Mem. ad hoc com. Lake Forest City Coun., Ill., 1970; bd. govs. Hebrew U. Jerusalem, 2007; bd. dirs. Am. Friends of Hebrew U., 1999—, mem. exec. com. Midwest region, 1999—; panelist on trade secret law and alternative dispute resolution George Washington U. Law Sch. India Project, Mumbai, Bangalore and Goa, 2007. Recipient Distinction award for contbns. to area of intellectual propery law for protection video games, Patent Resources Group, 1983, Torch of Learning award, Am. Friends Hebrew U., 2006. Mem.: ABA, IEEE, Am. Intellectual Property Law Assn., Assn. Patent Law Firms (pres. 1998—99), Licensing Exec. Soc., Internat. Trademark Assn., Intellectual Property Law Assn. Chgo., Chgo. Bar Assn., Ill. Bar Assn., Std. Club Chgo., Union League Club Chgo., Sigma Iota Epsilon, Eta Kappa Nu, Tau Beta Pi, Delta Theta Phi. Home: 475 Turicum Rd Lake Forest IL 60045-3363 Office: Welsh & Katz Ltd 120 S Riverside Plz Fl 22 Chicago IL 60606-3913 Office Phone: 312-655-1500. Business E-Mail: askatz@welshkatz.com.

KATZ, BARBARA STEIN, special education educator; b. Springfield, Mass., July 22, 1933; d. Harry and Pearl (Black) Stein; m. Charles Murry Katz, July 14, 1957; children: Helen Lee, Robert Alan. BS, Am. Internat. Coll., Springfield, 1956, MA in Ednl. Psychology in Learning Disabilities, 1979. Cert. in elem. edn., moderate spl. needs, Mass. Elem. tchr. Springfield Pub. Schs., 1956-60; Jr. Great Books discussion leader, 1968-69; Gillingham remedial tchr. Pub. Schs., Longmeadow, Mass., 1975-78, spl. edn. tchr. Chicopee, Mass., 1978-98, reader, 1998—2002, Pioneer Valley Collaborative, East Longmeadow, Mass., 1998—2002; ret., 2002. Pres. Kodimoh Synagogue Women's Group, Springfield, 1972-74; troop leader Girl Scouts U.S., Longmeadow, 1967-70. Horace Mann grantee, 1988. Mem. NEA, Mass. Tchrs. Assn. Avocations: painting, reading, walking, swimming. Home: 407 Bliss Rd Longmeadow MA 01106-1538 Personal E-mail: lyncam5@aol.com.

KATZ, BARRY JAY, geologist, researcher; s. Manny and Sheila Beth Katz; m. Terry Gail Kormendy, Mar. 6, 1977; children: Rebecca Gayle, Michelle Patricia Gale. BS in Geology, Bklyn Coll., 1970—74; PhD in Marine Geology and Geophysics, U. Miami, Coral Gables, FL, 1974—79. Lic. geologist Bd. Profl. Geoscientists, Tex., 2003. Sr. geologist Texaco Inc., Bellaire Rsch. Labs., Bellaire, Tex., 1979—84; rsch. geologist Texaco Inc., Houston Rsch. Ctr., 1984—86; supr. geochemical applications Texaco Inc., Exploration & Prodn. Tech. Dept., 1985—90, sr. rsch. geologist, 1987—90, rsch. assoc., 1990—93, sr. rsch. assoc., 1993—97; rsch. cons. Upstream Tech. Dept., Houston, 1997—2001, ChevronTexaco, Bellaire, 2001—03, sr. rsch. cons., 2003—05, Chevron Energy Tech. Co., Houston, 2005—, team leader hydrocarbon charge, 2005—. Chmn. environ. protection & safety panel Integrated Ocean Drilling Program, Houston, 2002—. Editor: (monographs) Lacustrine Basin Exploration - Case Studies and Modern Analogs, 1990, Source Rocks in a Sequence Stratigraphic Framework, 1993, Petroleum Source Rocks, 1995, Petroleum Systems of South Atlantic Margins, 2000; contbr. articles to profl. jours. Recipient Best Paper award, Nigerian Petroleum Exploration Assn., 2001; fellow Chevron fellow, Chevron, 2001; grantee Texaco fellow, Texaco Inc., 1998. Fellow: Geol. Soc. London; mem.: Paleontol. Soc., Internat. Assn. Geochemistry & Cosmochemistry, Houston Geol. Soc., Geol. Soc. of Am., Geochemical Soc., European Assn. Organic Geochemistry, Am. Geophys. Union, Soc. Sedimentary Geology, Am. Assn. Petroleum Geologists (Steve Champlin Meml. award 1989, Robert H. Dott Sr. Meml. prize 2000). Achievements include research in hydrocarbon potential of lacustrine basins. Office: Chevron Energy Tech Co 1500 Louisiana St Houston TX 77002 Home Phone: 281-370-9912. Office Fax: 832-854-7070. Business E-Mail: barrykatz@chevron.com.

KATZ, BRIAN JEFFREY, dermatologist; b. Detroit, Jan. 28, 1975; s. Gerald Alan Katz and Dianne Faye Politzer; m. Tara Lynn Harrison, Dec. 23, 2000. BS with high distinction, U. Mich., Ann Arbor, 1997; MD, Sackler Sch. Medicine Tel Aviv U., 2002. Cert. M.D. Ednl. Commn. Fgn. Med. Grads., 2002. Rsch. fellow Skin and Cancer Assoc., Plantation, Fla., 1997—98; dermatology resident Robert Wood Johnson Med. Sch., New Brunswick, NJ, 2003—06; chief resident dept. dermatology Robert Wood Johnson Med Sch., 2005—06. Consensus bd. mem. 1st World Congress Dermoscopy, Rome. Contbr. chapters to books, articles to profl. jours.; co-author: American Academy of Dermatology CD on Dermoscopy, 2000. Med. asst. Salvation Army Free Med. Clinic, Fort Lauderdale, Fla., 1997—98; co-founder cafe 88 Orchard, Manhattan, NY, 2003—05. Mem.: AMA, Internat. Soc. Dermoscopy (bd. dirs. 2003—), Am. Acad. Dermatology (maintenence of cert. com. 2004—07, bd. dirs.). Achievements include development of 3 step diagnostic algorithm used in diagnosing pigmented lesions with dermoscopy. Office: Mt Sinai Med Ctr 4302 Alton Rd Ste 960 Miami Beach FL 33140 Office Phone: 305-674-7414. Office Fax: 305-674-1459. Personal E-mail: briankatz88@yahoo.com.

KATZ, BRUCE ELLIOT, dermatologist; b. NYC, Apr. 12, 1951; s. Solomon and Rita (Holtz) K.; m. Carol Katz. BS, McGill U., 1973, MD, 1977. Diplomate Am. Bd. Dermatology, 1983. Intern Royal Victoria Hosp., Montreal, Canada, 1977-78; resident in internal medicine Columbia-Presbyn. Med. Ctr., NYC, 1978-79, chief resident dermatology, resident dermatology, 1979-82, dir. Dermatologic Cosmetic Surgery Clinic, assoc. attending dermatologist, Dermatology Svc.; assoc. clin. prof. Coll. of Physicians and Surgeons Columbia U.; courtesy staff St. Luke's Roosevelt Hosp. Ctr. Current dir. Juva Skin-Laser Ctr., NY; state vice chmn. Dermatology Found., NYC, 1991; presenter in field. Editl. bd. Cosmetic Dermatology Jour.; contbr. numerous articles to profl. jours. Fellow Am. Acad. of Dermatology (public comms. com. 1994—, co-chmn. skin cancer screening NY State 1991-96), Am. Soc. for Dermatologic Surgery (minimum benefits package task force 1995—), Am. Acad. of Cosmetic Surgery, Am. Soc. for Laser Medicine and Surgery; mem. Assn. of Acad. Dermatol. Surgeons, NY State Soc. of Dermatology, Dermatol. Soc. of Greater NY (pres. 1993-94, v.p. 1992-93, scientific program chmn. 1990-93), NY Facial Plastic Surgery Soc., Dermatology Found., Skin Cancer Found., NY State Med. Soc., NY County Med. Soc. Office: Juva Skin-Laser Ctr NY 60 E 56th St New York NY 10022

KATZ, COLLEEN, publisher; b. Newark; BA in Math., Montclair State U., NJ; cert., Ctr. Linguistique Etrangers, Tours, France. Assoc. editor Fawcett Publs., NYC, 1972-73, editor, 1973-76; editorial dir. Butterick Fashion Mktg. Co., NYC, 1976-77; editor Ency. of Textiles, NYC, 1979; editor in chief N.J. Monthly, Morristown, 1982-85; dir. publs. Ins. Info. Inst., NYC, 1985-88; pub., editor-in-chief Jour. of Accountancy, NYC, 1988—2007. Adj. prof. Audrey Cohen Coll., 2000. Editor Ins. Rev., 1985-88; pub. mags. and newsletters AICPA, 1997—; editor Huguenot Heritage, 1999. Vol. tchr. Elizabeth (N.J.) Sch. System; vol. editor Nat. Council Jewish Women, NJ, 1967—71; vol. pub. relations worker Essex County Mental Health Assn., NJ, 1980—81. Named Woman of Yr., Cen. N.J. March of Dimes, 1984, Outstanding Alumnus, Montclair Coll., 1984; recipient Gold Cir. award Am. Soc. Assn. Execs., 1989, award for pub. excellence Comm. Concepts, 1990, Pub. Excellence award Mag. Week, 1990, Gen. Excellence award Soc. Nat. Assn. Publs., 1991, Golden Page award, 2000-01, 0102. Mem.: Conf. des Vins du Cahors, Soc. Nat. Assn. Publs. (Silver medal for gen. excellence 1997), Am. Soc. Mag. Editors, Soc. Profl. Journalists, Nat. Arts Club. Avocation: foreign languages. Office: Jour of Accountancy Harborside III Jersey City NJ 07311 E-mail: ckatz@aicpa.org.

KATZ, DAVID A., lawyer; b. Freeport, NY, Oct. 1, 1963; BA magna cum laude, Brandeis U., 1985; JD cum laude, NYU Sch. Law, 1988. Bar: NY 1988. Ptnr. corp. dept. Wachtell, Lipton, Rosen, & Katz. Sr. profl. fellow NYU Ctr. Law and Bus.; prof. mgmt. Owen Grad. Sch. Mgmt., Vanderbilt U.; adj. asst. prof. NYU Sch. Law, 1992—96, adj. prof., 1996—. Mem. editl. staff: NYU Law Rev., 1986—87, note and comment editor:, 1987—88. Named Dealmaker of Yr., Am. Lawyer Mag., 2005; named one of 45 Under Forty-Five, 2003; recipient Am. Jurisprudence awards. Mem.: ABA (chmn. dictionary task force com. on negotiated acquisitions, mem. Fed. securities laws com.), Nat. Assn. Corp. Dirs., Am. Soc. Corp. Secretaries, NY State Bar Assn., Assn. Bar City of New York, Order of the Coif, Phi Alpha Delta. Office: Wachtell Lipton Rosen & Katz 51 W 52nd St New York NY 10019-6150 Office Phone: 212-403-1309. Office Fax: 212-403-2309. Business E-Mail: dakatz@wlrk.com.

KATZ, DAVID LAWRENCE, preventive medicine physician, researcher; b. LA, Feb. 20, 1963; s. Donald I. and Susan Gail Katz; m. Catherine Sananes; children: Rebecca Wortman, Corinda, Valerie, Natalia, Gabriel. MD, Albert Einstein Coll. Medicine, 1988; MPH, Yale U., 1993; BA in French, Dartmouth Coll., 1984. Diplomate Am. Bd. Internal Medicine, Am. Bd. Preventive Medicine. Assoc. prof. pub., adj. public health Yale U. Sch. of Medicine, New Haven, 1998—; founder, dir. Integrative Medicine Ctr., Griffin Hosp., Derby, Conn.; dir. Prevention Rsch. Ctr. Yale U. Sch. Pub. Health, Derby, Conn., 1998—; nutrition columnist O, The Oprah Magazine, 2002—; med. contbr. ABC News, 2005—07; health columnist NY Times Syndicate, 2005—; founder, pres. Turn the Tide Found. Inc., 2007. Mem. editl. bd. Am. Jour. Preventive Medicine; mem. editl. adv. bd. Prevention Mag., Men's Health Mag., Health Mag. Author: Preventive Medicine, Epidemiology and Biostatistics, 1996 (Rising Star, American College of Preventive Medicine, 2001), Nutrition in Clinical Practice, 2000, Clinical Epidemiology and Evidence-based Medicine, 2001, The Way to Eat, 2002. Recipient numerous clin. rsch. grants, CDC, NIH, DHHS, USDA, AHA, 1996—. Fellow: Am. Coll. Preventive Medicine (bd. dirs. 2002, chmn. ann. meeting 2002, chmn. prevention practice com., N.W. regent); mem.: ACP, American College of Nutrition. Avocations: skiing, hiking, creative writing. Office: Yale Prevention Rsch Ctr 130 Division St Derby CT 06518 Office Phone: 203-732-1265. Office Fax: 203-732-1264.

KATZ, EDWARD MORRIS, banker; b. Passaic, NJ, Apr. 18, 1921; s. David and Badane (Gubersky) K.; m. Phyllis Kushner, June 20, 1948; children— David, Alan, Michael. BA, Bklyn. Coll., 1947; MA, NYU, 1948. Auditor Amalgamated Bank N.Y., NYC, 1951-55, cashier, 1955-73, v.p., 1957-61, sr. v.p., 1961-71, exec. v.p., 1971-78, pres., chief exec. officer, 1978-89, dir., 1966-89, ret., 1989. Home: 48 Windsor Rd Great Neck NY 11021-2740 E-mail: phyllisedkat@aol.com.

KATZ, ESTHER, historian, educator; b. Aug. 14, 1948; came to US, 1951; d. Harry and Rose AB, Hunter Coll., 1969; MA, NYU, 1973, PhD, 1980. Instr. SUNY, Brockport, 1976, NYU, 1976, Coll. New Rochelle, NYC, 1981; adj. asst. prof. NYU, 1983-90, rsch. scientist, 1989—, adj. assoc. prof., 1991—. Dir., editor Margaret Sanger Papers Project, 1987—; dep. dir. Inst. for Rsch. History, NYC, 1983-87; chair bd. dirs. Ctr. Lesbian and Gay Studies CUNY, 1991-94; mem. exec. bd., Nat. History Coalition, 2003—; cons., Ford Found., 1997-98; acting dir. program in archival mgmt. and hist. editing, 1993-94. Editor: The Selected Papers of Margaret Sanger, Vol. I: The Women Rebel, 1900-1928, vol. 2, 2003, Birth Control Comes of Age, 1828-1939, 2007, The Margaret Sanger Microfilm Edition, 1996, 97; co-editor: Woman's Experience in American, 1980, Procs. of Conf. on Women Surviving Holocaust, 1983; contbr. articles on history of edn., birth control, and Margaret Sanger to profl. jours. Moses Coit Taylor fellow NYU, 1976; ACLS grant-in-aid, 1989. Mem.: Am. Hist. Assn., Orgn. Am. Historians (com. on rsch. and access to hist. documents 2003—05), Assn. for Documentary Editors (exec. coun. 2001—03, pres. 2003—04, exec. coun. 2005). Office: NYU Dept History 53 Washington Sq S New York NY 10012-1098 E-mail: esther.katz@nyu.edu.

KATZ, FRIEDRICH, history educator; b. Vienna, June 13, 1927; came to U.S., 1970; s. Leo and Bronia (Rein) K.; m. Jana Badian, Feb. 8, 1956; children: Leo, Jacqueline. BA, Wagner Coll., NYC, 1948; PhD, U. Vienna, 1954; Dr Habilitatus, Humboldt U., Berlin, 1962; degree (hon.), U. Michoacan, Mexico, 2004; Golden Doctorate, U. Vienna, 2004; degree (hon.), U. Puebla, Mexico, 2005. Instr., then prof. Latin Am. history Humboldt U., Berlin, 1962-70; vis. prof. polit. sci. Nat. U. Mex., 1968; vis. prof. history U. Tex., Austin, 1970-71; vis. prof. history and anthropology U. Vienna, 1985; Morton D. Hull disting. svc. prof. history U. Chgo., 1983—. Mem. joint commn. on Latin Am. studies, Social Sci. Rsch. Coun., N.Y.C., 1977-80; mem. ednl. adv. bd., John Simon Guggenheim Meml. Found., N.Y.C., 1988—; mem. joint adv. com. to Pres. Social Sci. Rsch. Coun./Am. Coun. Learned Socs., 1988—. Author: Ancient American Civilizations, 1970, Secret War in Mexico, 1982 (Bolton prize 1982); author, editor: Riot, Rebellion and Revolution, 1988, The Life and Times of Pancho Villa, 1998 (Bolton prize, 1998, Beveridge prize, 1998, Bry6ce Wood award, 1998). Decorated, Order del Aguila Azteca Pres. Republic of Mex., 1988, Order of Academic Merit Gov. State of Jalisco, Mex., 1988. Named Honorary Citizen of Chihuahua, Congress of Chihuahua, 1995; recipient Doctor Honoris Causa, U. Colima, 1994, Free U. Berlin, 2002, Bundesverdienstkreuz Erster Klasse fur Wissenschaft und Kunst der Republik Österreich, Pres. Austria, 2003, Medalla Isidro Fabela, Facultad de Leyes, 2004, Designation of Ctr. for Mexican Studies, U. Chgo., Pres. Don Michael Randel, 2005. Mem.: AAAS, Mexican Acad. Scis. Office: U Chgo Dept History 1126 E 59th St Chicago IL 60637-1580 Business E-Mail: fkatz@uchicago.edu.

KATZ, GEORGE GERSHON, psychologist, lawyer; b. Aug. 3, 1927; s. Abraham Michael and Dora K.; 1 child, Esti Goodman. BA, Brooklyn Coll., 1950; JD with honors, Calif. Coll. Law, 1978; PhD with honors, N.Y. U., 1956. Diplomate Am. Bd. Clinical Psychology, Am. Bd. Forensic Psychology, Am. Bd. Profl. Psychology. Clin. assoc. U. So. Calif., Los Angeles, 1971-89; instr. Northwestern U., Evanston, Ill., 1960-64; assoc. prof. Calif. State U., Los Angeles, 1969-72; adj. prof. Fuller Inst., Pasadena, Calif., 1982-86; clin. prof. U. Calif., Los Angeles, 1974-94; dir. clin. tng. VAMC, Los Angeles, 1984-93, asst. chief psychology, 1984-94. Mem. pres. com. public health edn., White House, Washington, 1972; cons. senate com. on Vets. Affairs, Washington, 1972-74, Hathaway Sch.

for Children:, Calif., 1969-74; co-dir./cons. Project NOVA, L.A., 1971-72; author/presenter papers in field. Co-initiator of the unit system within VA; introduced the first ombudsman program in the VA. Oral commr. Bd. of Psychology, State of Calif., 1992—. With USCG, 1944-46. Grantee NIMH, Va., 1971-75; patient advocate VISTA program, 1973. Fellow: APA, Am. Acad. Forensic Psychology, Am. OrthoPsychiatric Assn., Am. Psychol. Soc.; mem.: State Bar Calif. (chair, legal profl. com. 1998—), Am. Bd. Profl. Psychology (treas. 1992—2001, v.p. 2001—), Acad. Clin. Psychology. Office: Forensic Psych Assocs 17337 Tramonto Dr Pacific Palisades CA 90272-3121 Home Phone: 310-454-6693. E-mail: psychlaw1@verizon.net.

KATZ, HADRIAN RONALD, lawyer; b. Cambridge, Mass., Aug. 12, 1949; s. Samuel and Alice (Greenstein) K.; m. Candace Kay Kaufman, Apr. 1, 1977; children: Gwendlyn Rebecca, Jonathan Harold. AB, Harvard U., 1969; MA, U. Calif., Berkeley, 1972; JD, Harvard U., 1976. Bar: DC 1977, Mass. 1977, US Dist. Ct. DC 1977, US Ct. Appeals (DC cir.) 1979, US Supreme Ct. 1983, US Ct. Appeals (6th cir.) 1985, US Ct. Appeals (4th cir.) 1989. Ptnr. Arnold & Porter, Wash., DC, 1976—. Lead trial counsel UMG Recs., Inc. Mem. ABA, IEEE, Am. Phys. Soc., Assn. for Computing Machinery, Math. Assn. Am. Democrat. Avocation: computer. Office: Arnold & Porter 555 12th St NW Washington DC 20004-1206 Office Phone: 202-942-5707. Office Fax: 202-942-5999. Business E-Mail: hadrian.katz@aporter.com.

KATZ, IRV, not-for-profit executive; BA, Ind. U., Bloomington; MSW, Ind. U., Indpls. V.p. planning, planning coun. dir. United Way of Ctrl. Ind., acting v.p. fund distribution, acting v.p. resource devel., pres., CEO; group v.p. cmty. impact svc. area United Way of Am.; joined Nat. Human Svcs Assembly, Washington, 2001, now pres., CEO. Bd. mem. Generations United, BBB Wise Giving Alliance, Joint Agencies Trust; steering com. mem. Coalition for Cmty. Schs. Office: Nat Human Svcs Assembly Ste 402 1319 F St, NW Washington DC 20004 Office Phone: 202-347-2080. Office Fax: 202-393-4517. E-mail: irv@nassembly.org.

KATZ, JASON LAWRENCE, lawyer, insurance executive; b. Chgo., Sept. 28, 1947; s. Irving and Goldie (Medress) K.; 2 children. B.A., Northeastern Ill. U., 1969; J.D., DePaul U., 1973. Bar: Calif. 1976, Ariz. 1973, U.S. Ct. Appeals (9th cir.) 1976. pvt. practice, Scottsdale, Ariz., 1973-76; v.p., corp. counsel Mission Ins. Group, Inc., Los Angeles, 1976-84; exec. v.p., gen. counsel Farmers Group, Inc., Los Angeles, 1984—, bd. dirs., 1986—; v.p., bd. dirs. Calif. Def. Counsel, 1986-88. Mem. Calif. Bar Assn. (exec. bd. ins. law subcom. 1991-94), Los Angeles County Bar Assn. (mem. exec. bd. corp. law sect. 1993-94), Conf. Ins. Counsel (v.p., pres. L.A. chpt. 1981-82), Assn. Calif. Tort Reform (bd. dirs. 1990-94), The Ins. Coun. So. Calif. (City of Hope chpt. 1991-94). Office: Farmers Group Inc 4680 Wilshire Blvd Los Angeles CA 90010-3807

KATZ, JEFF, television personality; s. Harold and Doris Katz; m. Heidi Jaillet, Aug. 15, 1999; children: Harrison Tabor Jaillet, Julia Jaillet, Joseph Jaillet. Cert., Labour Coll. Can., 1993; grad., Delawn County Police Acad. Cert. mcpls. police officer Commonwealth of Pa. Talk show host WRKO-AM, Boston, 1996—2000, KXNT-AM, Las Vegas, 2000—01, WPHT-AM, Phila., 2001—03, Liberty Broadcasting Network, Washington, 2004, KNEW-AM, San Francisco, 2004—06, WBT AM and WBFFM, San Francisco, 2006—. Spkr. in field. TV host (nat. TV show) Mass Madness (Best TV Host, Nat. Wrestling Alliance, 1999). Hon. mem. bd. dirs. Media Partners for Pets, Las Vegas, 2000—01; apptd. State Coun. Devel. Disabilities Napa County Bd. Suprs., 2005; vice-chmn. Calif. State Coun. Devel. Disabilities, 2006—, chmn. legis. com., 2006—; apptd. gen. plan adv. com. City Am. Canyon Calif., 2006—; bd. dirs. Am. Jewish Com. No. Calif.; media rels. dir. Rep. Liberty Caucus, LA, 2004; chmn. radio & tv com. Conn. State Rep. Party, Hartford, Conn., 1993—94; rep. town committeeman South Windsor Rep. Town Com., Conn., 1993—94; bd. dirs. Rep. Jewish Coalition No. Calif.; nat. bd. advisors Jews Against Anti-Christian Defamation, 2005; mem. bd. chpt. leaders Rep. Jewish Coalition, Phila., 2004—05. Named Man of the Yr., Shomrim Soc. Phila. and the Del. Valley, 2004, Best Talk Show Host In Phila., Achievement In Radio, 2003, Talk Show Host of Yr., Eagle Forum Calif., 2006; recipient Minuteman award, Conn. Taxpayers' Com., 1992, Rainbow medal, USMC League, 1995, Jack Anderson award Excellence Journalism, Calif. CCPOA, 1996, Quill and Badge award, Internat. Union of Police Associations, AFL-CIO, 1998, Best Radio Program award, Electronic Media Awards, 2001, Lights of Liberty award, Advocates for Self-Govt., 2005, James Madison award, Second Amendment Found., 2006; Abraham Lincoln fellow, The Claremont Inst., 2005. Mem.: Nat. Spkrs. Assn., Masons (Master 2004), Internat. Brotherhood Knights of Vine (Knight of Vine 2002), Ancient and Accepted Scottish Rite (32d Degree Mason 2004). Jewish. Avocations: wine appreciation, sailing, travel. Home Phone: 707-553-1242. Personal E-mail: radiokatz@aol.com.

KATZ, JEFFREY G., electronic games executive; m. Karen Katz; 2 children. BSME, U. of Calif., Davis; MS, Stanford U., 1978, MIT. Various positions including v.p. American Airlines, 1980—97; pres. SABRE, 1993—97; COO Swissair, 1997, pres., CEO, 1998—2000; chmn., CEO Orbitz, Inc., 2000—04; CEO, pres. LeapFrog Enterprises, 2006—. Bd. dirs. Northwest Airlines Corp., 2005—, friendster.com. Office: LeapFrog Enterprises 6401 Hollis St Ste 100 Emeryville CA 94608-1071

KATZ, JEROME CHARLES, lawyer; b. Boston, Sept. 25, 1950; s. Ralph and Thelma M. (Clark) K.; m. Nancy M. Green, Aug. 29, 1976; children: Jonathan Green, Elizabeth Rachel. AB magna cum laude, Duke U., 1972; JD, Columbia U., 1975. Bar: N.Y. 1976, U.S. Dist. Ct. (so. and ea. dists.) N.Y. 1976, U.S. Supreme Ct. 1979, U.S. Ct. Appeals (2d cir.) 1981, U.S. Dist. Ct. (we. dist.) N.Y. 1990. Assoc. Chadbourne & Parke LLP, NYC, 1975—83, ptnr., 1983—2007, Ropes & Gray LLP, NYC, 2007—. Ct.-apptd. neutral mediator U.S. Dist. Ct. (so. dist.) N.Y., 2001—; bd. dirs. The Legal Aid Soc., 2002-07. Assoc. editor Columbia Jour. Transnat. Law, 1974-75. Trustee Citizens Budget Commn., 2003—, Lawyers' Com. Civil Rights Under Law, 2005—. Harlan Fiske Stone scholar Columbia U., 1974. Mem. ABA (litigation sect.), Assn. Bar of City of N.Y., Phi Beta Kappa Home: 77 E 12th St New York NY 10003-5002 Office: Ropes & Gray LLP 1211 Ave Americas New York NY 10036 Office Phone: 212-596-9000. Business E-Mail: jerome.katz@ropesgray.com.

KATZ, JOEL ABRAHAM, lawyer; b. Bronx, NY, May 27, 1944; s. Harry and Hilda (Wiesenthal) K.; Kane Swims, 1994; children from previous marriage: Leslie Helaine, Jeni Michelle. BA in Econs., Hunter Coll., 1966; JD, U. Tenn., 1969. Bar: Tenn. 1969, Ga. 1971, U.S. Dist. Ct. (ea. dist.) Tenn. 1970, U.S. Dist. Ct. Appeals (11th cir.) 1971. Co-mng. shareholder emeritus, chair internat. entertainment practice Greenberg Traurig LLP, Atlanta. Gen. counsel, bd. dirs. Farm Aid Inc.; spl. counsel Country Music Assn.; former vice chmn. Gibson Found., Gibson Guitar Corp., Baldwin Piano Corp.; state music industry rep. State of Ga. Mem. bd. T.J. Martell Found. for Leukemia Rsch., NYC, Internat. Tennis Hall of Fame; bd. dirs. Very Spl. Arts, White Fence, Natrol, Inc., Yellowstone Club; Bd. govs. Buckhead Club; spl. council Rock and Roll Hall Fame. Named to Ga. Music Hall of Fame, 1995. Fellow Royal Soc. for Encouragement Arts, Manufactures, and Commerce; mem. NARAS (gen. counsel, past v.p., past nat. trustee, dir. found. bd., nat. chmn. bd. trustees, trustee Atlanta chpt., chmn. emeritus), ABA, Fed. Bar Assn., Ga. Bar Assn., Tenn. Bar Assn., Atlanta C. of C. (bd. advisors). Office: Greenberg Traurig LLP The Forum 3290 Northside Pkwy Ste 400 Atlanta GA 30327 Office Phone: 678-553-2100. Office Fax: 678-553-2212. Business E-Mail: katzj@gtlaw.com.

KATZ, JOETTE, state supreme court justice; b. Bklyn., Feb. 3, 1953; BA, Brandeis U., 1974; JD, U. Conn., 1977; LLD (hon.). Bar: Conn. 1977. Pvt. practice, 1977-78; asst. pub. defender Office Chief Pub. Defender, 1978-83; chief legal svcs. Pub. Defender Svcs., 1983-89; judge Superior Ct., 1989-92; assoc. justice Conn. Supreme Ct., Hartford, 1992—; adminstrv. judge Appellate Sys., Hartford, 1994-2000, 2006—. Instr. U. Conn. Sch. Law, 1981-84, Yale U. Sch. Law, 2006-; instr. ethics and criminal law Quinnipiac Coll. Sch. Law, 1999—; chair Evidence Code Drafting Com., chair Adv. Com. Appellate Rules, Client Security Fund; Am. Inns Ct. (past pres. Fairfield County br.), Assn. Reproductive Tech. (mem. com.). Co-author: (book) Connecticut Criminal Caselaw Handbook: A Practitioner's Guide, 1989. Mem. Justice Edn. Ctr. Recipient Maria Miller Stewart award, Conn. Women's Education & Legal Fund, 1993, Harriet Tubman award, Nat. Orgn. for Women, 1993, Women of Distinction award; Nat. Council of Jewish Women, 2001. Mem. Am. Law Inst., Conn. Bar Assn. (Henry J. Naruk Judiciary award 2004). Office: Conn Supreme Ct 231 Capital Ave Hartford CT 06106

KATZ, JOHN, investment banker; b. Washington, Aug. 2, 1938; s. Milton and Vivian (Greenberg) K.; divorced; children: Ellen, Allison; m. Laura Cherkis, May 29, 1988; stepchildren: Ann Cherkis, Nancy Gernstetter. AB, Harvard U., 1960, JD, 1963. Bar: N.Y. 1964. With Hall, Casey, Dickler & Howley, 1963-67; asst. corp. counsel City of N.Y., 1967-69; spl. asst. to Congressman Richard L. Ottinger, 1969; with Poletti, Freidin, Prashker, Feldman & Gartner, 1969-75; atty. Equitable Life Assurance Soc. of U.S., 1975-79, v.p., counsel, 1979-82, v.p. Office of Chief Investment Officer, 1982-86; sr. v.p. Equitable Investment Corp., 1986-88, exec. v.p., 1989-91; chmn., CEO Sam's Restaurant Group, Inc., NYC, 1991-92, investment banker, 1992-2000; mng. ptnr. Associated Mezzanine Investors, LLC, 2000—05, Boo Ventures, LLC, 2005—. Mem. Greater N.Y.C. Com. of Harvard Law Sch. Fund; chmn. admissions com. Harvard Club N.Y.C., 1988-89; bd. dirs. Resources for Children with Spl. Needs, Inc., 1985-98; bd. dirs. My Sisters' Place, 1995-2004, co-chmn., 1996-99, chmn., 1999-2000. Home and Office: 10 Hemlock Rd Hartsdale NY 10530-2951 E-mail: johnkatz@cloud9.net.

KATZ, JOHN W., lawyer, state official; b. Balt., June 3, 1943; s. Leonard Wallach and Jean W. (Kane) Katz; m. Joan Katz, June 11, 1969 (div. 1982); 1 child, Kimberly Erin. BA, Johns Hopkins U., 1965; JD, U. Calif., Berkeley, 1969; DDL (hon.), U. Alaska, 1994. Bar: Alaska 1971, Pa. 1971, U.S. Dist. Ct. D.C. 1971, U.S. Ct. Appeals (D.C. cir.), U.S. Tax Ct., U.S. Ct. Claims, U.S. Ct. Mil. Justice, U.S. Supreme Ct. Legis. and adminstrv. asst. to Congressman Howard W. Pollock of AK, Wash., 1969—70; legis. asst. US Sen. Ted Stevens of Alaska, Washington, 1971; assoc. McGrath and Flint, Anchorage, 1972; gen. counsel Joint Fed. State Land Use Planning Commn. for AK, Anchorage, 1972—79; spl. counsel Gov. Jay S. Hammond of Alaska, Anchorage and Washington, 1979—81; commr. Alaska Dept. Natural Resources, Juneau, 1981—83; dir. state fed. rels. and spl. counsel Gov. Bill Sheffield of Alaska, Washington and Juneau, 1983—86; dir. state-fed. rels., spl. counsel to Gov. Steve Cowper of Alaska, Washington, 1986—90, Gov. Walter J. Hickel of Alaska, Washington, 1990—94, Gov. Tony Knowles, 1994—2002, Gov. Frank Murkowski, 2002—. Mem. Alaska Power Survey Exec. Adv. Com. of FPC, Anchorage, 1972—74; com. hard rock minerals Gov.'s Coun. of Sci. and Tech., Anchorage, 1979—80; guest lectr. on natural resources U. Alaska, U. Denver. Contbr. articles to profl. jours.; columnist (Anchorage Times), 1991. Acad. supr. Alaska Externship Program, U. Denver Coll. Law, 1976—79; mil. history charity mem. Johns Hopkins U.; mem. Reagan-Bush transition team, U.S. Dept. Justice, 1980. Recipient Superior Sustained Performance award, Joint Fed. State Land Use Planning Commn. for Alaska, 1978, Resolution of Commendation award, Alaska Legis., 1988, Citation for svc. to people of Alaska, 2003, Cert. of Appreciation, Gov. of Alaska, 2004. Republican. Office: State of Alaska Office of Gov 444 N Capitol St NW Ste 336 Washington DC 20001-1529 Home Phone: 202-471-4468.

KATZ, JOSE, cardiologist, theoretical physicist, educator; b. Havana, Cuba, June 6, 1944; s. Lipa and Victoria (Masson) K.; m. Anke Ebsen; children: Susan, David, Rachel, Hannah. BS, U. Ill., 1963, MS, 1964, PhD, 1967; MD, Free U. Berlin, 1980. Rsch. assoc. physicist U. Hamburg, Germany, 1967—69; instr. physics Purdue U., West Lafayette, Ind., 1969—71; asst. prof. physics Free U., West Berlin, Germany, 1971—74, prof. physics, 1974—82; resident in internal medicine Cleve. Met. Gen. Hosp., Mt. Sinai Med. Ctr., 1982—85; cardiology fellow Southwestern Med. Sch., Dallas, 1985—88; asst. prof. medicine and radiology Columbia U. Coll. Physicians and Surgeons, NYC, 1988—94, assoc. prof. medicine and radiology, 1994—2004; dir. cardiovasc. MRI and spectroscopy Columbia-Presbyn. Med. Ctr., NYC, 1988—2004, co-dir. EKG lab., 1999—2004; pres., CEO, med. dir. Cardio-Med. Svcs., LLC, NJ, 2004—, Comprehensive Healthcare and Med. Svc. PLLC, NYC, 2004—. Staff attending Columbia-Presbyn. Med. Ctr., NYC, 1988-2004. Contbr. articles to profl. jours., chpts. to books. Fellow ACP, Am. Coll. Cardiology, Am. Coll. Chest Physicians, Am. Coll. Angiology, Am. Heart Assn. (coun. clin. cardiology, coun. on cardiovasc. radiology, coun. on basic scis.), Internat. Soc. Magnetic Resonance in Medicine; mem. AMA, Radiol. Soc. N.Am., Soc. Nuc. Medicine, N.Am. Soc. Cardiac Imaging, Sigma Xi, Phi Kappa Phi, Sigma Tau, Pi Mu Epsilon, Tau Beta Pi. Office: 595 Madison Ave 27th Fl New York NY 10022 Business E-Mail: jkatz@mdadvice.com. E-mail: jkatz@cardio-med.net.

KATZ, JOSEPH LOUIS, chemical engineer, educator; b. Colon, Panama, Aug. 4, 1938; naturalized, 1970; s. Adolfo and Margarita (Eisen) K.; m. Liliane Capelluto, Apr. 10, 1965; children: Daniel P., Alan R. BS, U. Chgo., 1960, PhD, 1963. Amanuensis U. Copenhagen Chem. Lab. III, 1963-64; mem. tech. staff N.Am. Aviation Sci. Ctr., Thousand Oaks, Calif., 1964-70; assoc. prof. chem. engring. Clarkson Coll. Tech., Potsdam, NY, 1970-75, prof., 1975-79, Johns Hopkins U., Balt., 1979—, chmn. dept. chem. engring., 1981-84, 2005—06. Prof. U. Aix-Marseille, France, 1976; vis. prof. MIT, Cambridge, 1977. Recipient John W. Graham Rsch. prize, Clarkson U., 1975; John Simon Guggenheim Meml. Found. fellow, 1976-77. Fellow AAAS, Am. Phys. Soc.; mem. AIChE, Am. Chem. Soc. (Md. sect. Chemist of Yr. 1982), Sigma Xi. Home: 5600 Greenspring Ave Baltimore MD 21209-4308 Office: Johns Hopkins U Dept Chem & Biomolecular Engring Baltimore MD 21218 Office Phone: 410-516-8484. Business E-Mail: jlk@sigmaxi.org.

KATZ, JULIAN, gastroenterologist, educator; b. NYC, Apr. 3, 1937; s. Abraham M. and Fay (Sher) K.; m. Sheila Moriber, Aug. 18, 1963; children: Jonathan Peter, Sara Katherine. AB, Columbia U., 1958; MD, U. Chgo., 1962. Diplomate Am. Bd. Internal Medicine. Intern U. Chgo. Hosps., 1962-63; resident in medicine Duke U., 1963-65; fellow in gastroenterology Yale U., 1965—67; practice medicine specializing in gastroenterology, internal medicine and geriatrics Phila., 1969—; prof. medicine and lectr. physiology and biochemistry Med. Coll. Pa., 1970—. Prof. medicine Jefferson Med. Coll., Phila., 1988—2001; chief clin. gastroenterology Med. Coll. Pa.; lectr. in field. Editor profl. jours. and books; contbr. articles to profl. jours. and books. Mem. Bd. Health, City of Phila. With USN, 1967-69. Fellow ACP, Am. Coll. Gastroenterology; mem. Am. Soc. Gastrointestinal Endoscopy, Am. Soc. Study Liver Disease, Am. Gastroent. Assn., Phila. County Med. Soc. (pres. 1997-98), Pa. Soc. Gastroent. (pres. 1999-2001), Del. Valley Geeriatrics Soc. (pres. 2004), Digestive Disease Nat. Coalition (exec. com.) Home and Office: 701 Dodds Ln Gladwyne PA 19035-1516 Office Phone: 610-645-6000. Business E-Mail: jkatz@icdc.com.

KATZ, KAREN W., retail executive; m. Alan Katz; 1 child. BA, Univ. Tex.; MBA, Univ. Houston, 1982. Asst. buyer, dept. mgr., buyer Foley's Dept. Stores; merchandise mgr. Neiman Marcus Town & Country, Houston, 1985—87; v.p., divsnl. merchandise mgr., handbags, designer accessories Neiman Marcus, 1987—91, v.p., gen. mgr., NorthPark Dallas, 1991—96, sr. v.p., dir. of stores, 1996—98, exec. v.p. of stores, 1998—2000, pres., CEO, Neiman Marcus Direct catalog, e-commerce bus., 2000—02, pres., CEO of stores, 2002—. Bd. dir. Pier 1 Imports, 2001—. Bd. dir. Dallas Theater Ctr., Charter 100. Named one of Next 20 Female CEOs, Pink Mag. & Forté Found., 2006. Mem.: Dallas Jewish Comty. Ctr. (bd. dir.). Mailing: Neiman Marcus Stores One Marcus Sq 1618 Main St Dallas TX 75201*

KATZ, KENNETH ARTHUR, lawyer, accountant; b. NYC, Apr. 4, 1955; s. Bernard and Shirley Anne (Schachter) K.; m. Gillian Lynn Bagg, Nov. 29, 1986; children: Melissa Lee, Ashley Dawn. AB in Econs. cum laude, Harvard U., 1976; JD, Yeshiva U., 1980; MBA in Pub. Acctg., Pace U., 1987. Bar: N.Y. 1994, U.S. Tax Ct. 1994, D.C. 1995; CPA, N.Y. Legal asst. Law Offices of Jerome A. Wisselman, Manhasset, N.Y., 1980-81, Law Offices of S. Mac Gutman, Forest Hills, N.Y., 1981-82; asst. contr. Tauck Tours, Inc., Westport, Conn., 1982-84; pvt. practice acct. Eastchester, N.Y., 1984-87; tax specialist KPMG Peat Marwick, White Plains, N.Y., 1987-88; atty., acct., ptnr. Bernard Katz & Co, P.C., Eastchester, 1988—. Mem. bus. coun., Westchester County, NY. Mem. ABA (taxation and internat. law sects.), N.Y. State Bar Assn. (tax sect.), D.C. Bar Assn. (taxation and sect. on corps., fin. and securities law), Westchester County Bar Assn. (tax and trusts and estates coms.), N.Y. State Soc. CPAs, Nat. Tax Assn.-Tax Inst. Am. (com. on internat. pub. fin.), Harvard-Radcliffe Club of Westchester. Avocations: sports, music, personal investing. Office: Bernard Katz & Co PC 1 Mayfair Rd Eastchester NY 10709-2701 Office Phone: 914-779-7555. Personal E-mail: bkatzcpc@aol.com. Business E-Mail: kkatz@bkatzcopc.com.

KATZ, LAWRENCE SHELDON, lawyer; b. Newark, Jan. 30, 1943; s. Edward and Pearl (Weiss) K.; divorced; 1 child, Scott. BBA in Govt., U. Miami, 1965, JD, 1968. Cert.: Fla. Supreme Ct. (mediator). Assoc. Hoffman & St. Jean, Miami Beach, Fla., 1968-70, Jack R. Nageley Law Office, Miami Beach, Fla., 1970-72, Swickle, Katz & Brotman, Miami Beach, Fla., 1972-77; pvt. practice Miami Beach, Fla., 1977—90, Coconut Grove, Fla., 1990—2001, Miami, 2001—. Gen. counsel Fraternal Order of Police, Hialeah, Fla., 1972-89; gen. counsel U.S. Shooting Team Found., Colorado Springs, 1978-95, chmn., 1978-83; mem. U.S. Olympic Com. Ho. Dels., 1978-83. 2d lt. U.S. Army, 1965-69. Recipient Pres.'s award Nat. Assn. Criminal Def. Attys., 1977, 11th Cir. Pro Bono award. Mem. ABA (com. on internat. criminal law 1971-94, criminal def. function com. 1989-98, family law sect. com. on internat. law and procedure, 1996-, vice-chmn. 2006-07, chmn. 2007—, internat. child abduction atty. network 1997-, mem. internat. law sect. com. on family law 2004—, mem. steering group 2006—, mentor), NRA (bd. dirs. 1977-83), First Family Law Inn of Ct., Internat. Soc. Family Law, Fla. Sportshooting Assn. (pres. 1985), The Fla. Bar (narcotics practice com. 1988-92, mental health profl. in litigation com. 1994-96, domestic violence com. 1994-98, legislation com. 1998-2004, com. on children's issues, 2005, 2006, com. continuing edn. 2006-), Acad. Fla. Trial Lawyers (vice chmn. criminal law sect.), Fla. Assn. Criminal Def. Attys. (sec. 1978-79, v.p. 1979-80), Fla. Smallbore Rifle Assn. (pres. 1968-70), Safari Club Internat. (v.p. 1992-98, sec. 1997-98, pres.-elect 1998-99, pres. 1999-2000, pres. Miami chpt. 2001-03, pres. So. Fla. chpt. 1988-90, Mem. of Yr. award 1999-2000, Presdl. award 1996, 98), Nat. Rifle Assn. (benefactor, mem. bd. dirs. 1977-83), Blackhawk Rifle Club, Nat. Sporting Clays Assn. (life), Ruffed Grouse Soc. (life sponsor), Phi Epsilon Pi (pres. 1964), Phi Alpha Delta, World Forum for Future of Sportshooting (v.p. 2000-01). Jewish. Avocations: flying, photography, scuba, skiing, hunting. Office Phone: 305-670-8656. Business E-Mail: katzlaw@bellsouth.net.

KATZ, LEONARD, psychology professor, researcher; b. Boston, Mar. 6, 1938; s. William and Ruth K.; m. Barbara A. Mahoney, May 28, 1962; children: Nicholas, Stephen, Alexis. BS, U. Mass., 1959, PhD, 1963. Postdoctoral fellow Stanford (Calif.) U., 1963-65; prof. psychology U. Conn., Storrs, 1965—2006; researcher Haskins Labs., New Haven, 1974—. Contbr. articles to profl. jours. Fulbright fellow, Yugoslavia, 1986. Fellow Am. Psychol. Soc., Am. Assn. Advancement of Sci. Office: U Conn Dept Psychology Wab U 20 Storrs Mansfield CT 06269-1020 Business E-Mail: leonard.katz@uconn.edu.

KATZ, LEWIS ROBERT, law educator; b. NYC, Nov. 15, 1938; s. Samuel and Rose (Turoff) K.; m. Jan Karen Daugherty, Jan. 14, 1964; children: Brett Elizabeth, Adam Kenneth, Tyler Jessica. AB, Queens Coll., 1959; JD, Ind. U., 1963. Bar: Ind 1963, Ohio 1971. Assoc. Snyder, Bunger, Cotner & Harrell, Bloomington, Ind., 1963-65; instr. U. Mich. Law Sch., Ann Arbor, 1965-66; asst. prof. Case Western Res. U. Law Sch., Cleve., 1966-68, assoc. prof., 1968-71, prof., 1971—, John C. Hutchins prof. law, 1973—. Dir. Ctr. for Criminal Justice, Case Western Res. U., 1973-91, dir. fgn. grad. studies, 1992—; cons. criminal justice agys. Author: Justice is the Crime, 1972, The Justice Imperative: Introduction to Criminal Justice, 1979, Ohio Arrest Search and Seizure, 2007; (with J. Shapiro) New York Suppression Manual, 1991, Know Your Rights, 1994; (with P.C. Giannelli, B. Blair, J. Lipton) Ohio Criminal Law, 2d edit., 2003; (with P.C. Giannelli) Ohio Criminal Justice, 2007; (with B.W. Griffin) Ohio Felony Sentencing Law, 2006, (with N.P. Cohen) Questions and Answers: Criminal Procedure, 2003. Mem. regional bd. Anti-Defamation League; trustee Women's Law Fund. Recipient Disting. Tchr. award Case West Res. U. Law Alumni Assn., Tchr. of Yr. award Case Western Res. U., 1999; Nat. Defender Project of Nat. Legal Aid and Defender Assn. fellow, 1968. Mem. ABA. Home: 29550 S Woodland Rd Pepper Pike OH 44124-5743 Office: Case Western Res U Law Sch Law Sch Cleveland OH 44106 Home Phone: 216-514-4744; Office Phone: 216-368-3287. Business E-Mail: lewis.katz@case.edu.

KATZ, LOIS ANNE, internist, nephrologist; b. Rockville Centre, NY, Dec. 1, 1941; d. Irvin Martin and Frances (Berenstein) Fradkin; m. Arthur A. Katz, Aug. 18, 1962; children: David, Brian. BA, Wellesley Coll., 1962; MD, NYU, 1966. Diplomate Am. Bd. Internal Medicine, Am. Bd. Nephrology. Intern medicine Bellevue Hosp., NYU, NYC, 1966-67, resident medicine, 1967-68; sr. resident medicine N.Y. Hosp., NYC, 1968-69; from chief resident medicine to assoc. chief staff N.Y. VA Med. Ctr., NYC, 1969—2000, assoc. chief of staff spl. emphasis programs and quality mgmt., 2000—; asst. prof. clin. medicine NYU Sch. Medicine, NYC, 1974-79, assoc. prof., 1979-94, prof. clin. medicine, 1994—2002, prof. medicine, 2002—. Fellow: ACP; mem.: Am. Soc. Hypertension, Women in Nephrology (treas. 1985—89), Soc. Gen. Internal Medicine, Am. Med. Women's Assn., Am. Soc. Nephrology, Wellesley Coll. Alumnae Assn. (region 2 admission rep. 1997—2001), Sigma Xi, Alpha Omega Alpha. Jewish. Avocations: reading, swimming, cooking, music. Office: Dept Vets Affairs NY Harbor Healthcare System 423 E 23rd St New York NY 10010-5013 Office Phone: 212-951-6875. Business E-Mail: lois.katz@med.va.gov.

KATZ, MICHAEL, pediatrician, educator; b. Lwow, Poland, Feb. 13, 1928; arrived in U.S., 1946, naturalized, 1951; s. Edward and Rita (Gluzman) Katz; m. Robin J. Roy, July 19, 1986; 1 child, Edward Alexander. AB, U. Pa., 1949, postgrad. (Harrison fellow), 1950—51; MD, SUNY, Bklyn., 1956; MS, Columbia U. Sch. Public Health, 1968. Intern UCLA Med. Ctr., 1956—57; resident Presbyn. Hosp. (Babies Hosp.), NYC, 1960—62, dir. pediatric svc., 1977—92, cons., 1992—; hon. lectr. pediat. Makerere U. Coll., Kampala, Uganda, 1963—64; instr. in pediat.

Columbia U., 1964—65, prof. tropical medicine Sch. Pub. Health, 1971—92, prof. pub. health emeritus, 1992—, prof. pediat. Coll. Physicians and Surgeons, 1972—77, prof. pub. health, 1977—92, Reuben S. Carpentier prof., 1977—92, Reuben S. Carpentier prof. emeritus, 1992—; sr. v.p. for rsch. and global programs March of Dimes Found., White Plains, NY, 1992—. Assoc. mem. Wistar Inst., Phila., 1965—71; asst. prof. pediat. U. Pa., 1966—77; cons. WHO, Guatemala, Venezuela, Egypt, Yemen; mem. U.S. del. 32d World Health Assembly, Geneva, 1979; cons. UNICEF, NYC, Tokyo, USAID, Egypt, 1982, Poland, 87; mem. bd. sci. councillors Nat. Inst. Dental Rsch., 1986—90, chmn., 1990—92; vis. prof. U. Würzburg, Germany, 1988; vis. prof. pediat. U. Negev, Beer Sheva, Israel, 1996. Author (with others): Parasitic Diseases, 1982, 2d edit., 1989; editor (with Volker ter Meulen): Slow Virus Infections of the Central Nervous System, 1977; mem. editl. bd.: Med. Microbiology and Immunology, 1975—90, Pediatric Infectious Diseases Jour., 1981—92, Vaccines, 1983—94; co-editor: Manuals in Pediatrics; contbr. articles to profl. jours. Pres. World Alliance Orgns. Prevention Birth Defects, Inc., 1995—2005. Lt. M.C. USNR, 1957—59. Recipient Jurzykowski Found. award in Medicine, 1983, Alexander von Humboldt Sr. U.S. Scientist award, 1988; grantee, NIH, 1968—76, WHO, 1972—76. Fellow: AAAS, Am. Acad. Pediat., Infectious Diseases Soc. Am.; mem.: Eastern Soc. for Pediatric Rsch., Inst. Medicine of NAS, World Alliance of Orgns. for the Prevention of Birth Defects (pres. 1995—2005), Pediatric Infectious Disease Soc., Royal Soc. Tropical Medicine and Hygiene (London), Deutsche Gesellschaft für Neuropathologie und Neuroanatomie E.V. (corr.), N.Y. Soc. Tropical Medicine (pres. 1976—77), Am. Soc. Tropical Medicine and Hygiene, Am. Soc. Microbiology, Harvey Soc., Am. Pediatric Soc., Soc. Pediatric Rsch., Sigma Xi. Home: 1 Griggs Ln Chappaqua NY 10514-1404 Office: March of Dimes Found 1275 Mamaroneck Ave White Plains NY 10605-5298 Office Phone: 914-997-4555. Personal E-mail: katzfamily@optonline.net. Business E-Mail: mkatz@marchofdimes.com.

KATZ, MICHAEL ALBERT, lawyer; b. Bklyn., May 8, 1942; s. Emanuel and Miriam (Fassler) K.; 1 child, Nathaniel P. BS, Bklyn. Coll., 1963; LLB, NYU, 1966; LLM, George Washington U., 1973. Bar: N.Y. 1966, D.C. 1970, Ill. 1976, N.J. 1995, U.S. Supreme Ct. 1975. Asst. U.S. atty., D.C., 1971-75; trial atty. United Airlines, Chgo., 1975-78; div. counsel ea. divsn. NYC, 1978-81; counsel indsl. rels. Trans World Airlines, Inc., NYC, 1981-86, asst. gen. counsel, 1986-91, assoc. gen., counsel, 1991-94; assoc. gen. counsel GAF/ISP Corp., Wayne, N.J., 1994-96; of counsel Pfaltz & Woller PA, Summit, N.J., 1996—. Capt. JAGC US Army, 1967—71, ret. col. res. Decorated Bronze Star. Home: 94 Canterbury Rd Chatham NJ 07928-1771 Office: 382 Springfield Ave Ste 217 Summit NJ 07901-2707 E-mail: makatz@att.net.

KATZ, MICHAEL JEFFERY, lawyer; b. Detroit, May 11, 1950; s. Wilfred Lester and Bernice (Ackerman) K. BE with honors, U. Mich., 1972; JD, U. Colo., 1976; cert. mgmt., U. Denver, 1985, cert. fin. mgmt., 1990. Bar: Colo. 1978; cert. franchise exec. Internat. Franchise Assn., 2007. Rsch. atty., immigration specialist Colo. Rural Legal Svcs., Denver, 1976-77, supervising atty. migrant farm lab., 1977-78; ind. contractor Colo. Sch. Fin., Denver, 1978-79; sole practice Denver, 1978-86; assoc. Levine and Pitler, P.C., Denver, 1986-88; gen. counsel, sec. Grease Monkey Internat., Inc., Denver, 1988-92; prin. Katz & Co., Denver, 1992—; ptnr. Corprom, Eyler & Katz LLC, Denver, 1999—. Lectr. on incorporating small bus. and real estate purchase agreements Front Range Coll., 1986—, condr. seminars on real estate and landlord/tenant law, 1980—; lectr. real estate Lorman Ednl. Svcs., Inc., 2001—; of counsel Levine and Pitler, PC, Englewood, Colo., 1985—. Contbr. Action Line column Rocky Mountain News; contbr. articles to profl. jours. Mem. ATLA, Am. Arbitration Assn. (panel of arbitrators 1989), Denver Bar Assn. (law day com. 1985—, real estate com. 1980—, pro bono svcs. com. 1984—), Colo. Assn. Bus. Intermediaries, US Yacht Racing Assn., Dillon Yacht Club. Avocations: sailing, bicycling, swimming, art collecting, reading. Office: 13710 E Rice Pl Aurora CO 80015-1058 Office Phone: 303-790-4103. Business E-Mail: michael@businesslawyer.com.

KATZ, MICHAEL RAY, Slavic languages educator; b. NYC, Dec. 9, 1944; s. Louis M. and Alice (Gordon) K.; m. Mary K. Dodge, Nov. 19, 1978; 1 child, Rebecca Marie Dodge-Katz BA, Williams Coll., Williamstown, Mass., 1966; MA, Oxford U., 1968, PhD, 1972. From asst. to assoc. prof. Williams Coll., Williamstown, Mass., 1972-83; prof., chmn. dept. Slavic langs. U. Tex., Austin, 1984-97, dir. Russian, East European and Eurasian studies; dean lang. schs. and schs. abroad Middlebury Coll., Vt., 1998—2004, C.V. Starr prof. Russian studies, 2005—. Author: The Literary Ballad in Early 19th Century Russian Literature, 1976, Dreams and the Unconscious in Russian Literature, 1984; translator: Who Is To Blame? (A. Herzen), 1984, Notes from Underground (Dostoevsky), 1989, What Is To Be Done: (Chernyshevsky), 1989, Tolstoy's Short Fiction, 1991, Devils (Dostoevsky), 1992, Polina Saks (Druzhinin), 1992, Fathers and Sons (Turgenev), 1994, Antonina (Turgenev), 1997, Prologue (Chernyshevsky), 1995, Antonina (Tur), 1997, Sanin (Artsybashev), 2001, The Five (Jabotinsky), 2005. Grantee NEH, 1981-82, 2007; recipient Max Haywood Translation prize, 1982, ADFL/MLA award for Disting. Svc. to Profession, 2005. Mem. Am. Assn. Advancement Slavic Studies, Am. Assn. Tchrs. Slavic and East European Langs. (v.p. 1989-92, pres.-elect 1995-96, pres. 1997-98, past pres. 1999-2000), Am. Coun. Tchrs. of Russian (bd. dirs. 1984-2001), Assn. Dept. of Fgn. Langs. (exec. com. 2000-02). Avocations: flute, jogging. Home: 1712 Sperry Rd Middlebury VT 05753-9442 Office: Middlebury Coll FIC 6 Middlebury VT 05753 Home Phone: 802-462-2899; Office Phone: 802-443-5122. Business E-Mail: mkatz@middlebury.edu.

KATZ, MITCHELL H., city health department administrator; b. 1959; BS, Yale U., New Haven, Conn.; MD, Harvard U. Med. Sch., Cambridge, Mass., 1986. Attending physician San Francisco Gen. Hosp., AIDS Clinic; chief, rsch., AIDS office San Francisco Dept. Pub. Health, dir., AIDS Office, 1992—97, interim dir., health, 1997—98, dir., health, 1998—. Author: Multivariable Statistics: A Practical Guide for Clinical Researchers. Office: San Francisco Dept Health 101 Grove St Rm 308 San Francisco CA 94102

KATZ, NATASHA, lighting designer; m. Dan Moses Schreier. Lighting design (Broadway plays) Pack of Lies, 1985, Aren't We All?, 1985, Honky Tonk Nights, 1986, Breaking the Code, 1987, Gypsy, 1989, The Cemetery Club, 1990, Shogun, The Musical, 1990, Peter Pan, 1990, Hamlet, 1992, Someone Who'll Watch Over Me, 1992, Company, 1993, A Grand Night for Singing, 1993, My Fair Lady, 1993, Beauty and the Beast, 1994, State Fair, 1996, Barrymore, 1997, The Scarlet Pimpernel, 1997, The Capeman, 1998, Twelfth Night, 1998, Ring Round the Moon, 1999, Aida, 2000 (Tony award best lighting design, 2000), Seussical, 2000, Dance of Death, 2001, Sweet Smell of Success, 2002, Flower Drum Song, 2002, Urban Cowboy, 2003, Taboo, 2003, The Glass Menagerie, 2005, The 25th Annual Putnam County Spelling Bee, 2005, Lennon, 2005, Tarzan, 2006, A Chorus Line, 2006, The Coast of Utopia, 2007 (Outer Critics Cir. award outstanding lighting design, 2007, Drama Desk award outstanding lighting design, 2007, Tony award best lighting design of a play, 2007), The Little Mermaid, 2007.*

KATZ, NICHOLAS M., mathematician; b. Balt., Dec. 7, 1943; BA, John Hopkins U., 1964; MA, Princeton U., 1965, PhD, 1966. Instr. Math. Dept., Princeton U., 1966—67, lectr., 1967—68, asst. prof., 1968—71, assoc. prof., 1971—74, prof., 1974—, dept. chair, 2002—. Author: Exponential Sums and Differential Equations, 1990, numerous other math. works. Co-recipient Levi L. Conant prize, Am. Math. Soc., 2003; fellow, Sloan, 1971, JSPS, 1983, Guggenheim, 1975, 1987; postdoctoral fellowship, NATO, 1968. Mem.: Am. Acad. Arts and Scis., NAS. Office: Princeton U Math Dept Fine Hall Washington Rd Princeton NJ 08544-1000

KATZ, PETER, lawyer; b. Boston, Nov. 18, 1947; s. Milton and Vivian (Greenberg) K.; m. Linda Weiss; children: Laura, Pamela, Joseph. AB, Harvard U., 1969, JD cum laude, 1972. Bar: Mass. 1972, Commonwealth Mass., US Dist. Ct. Mass. Law clk. to hon. Benjamin H. Kaplan Supreme Jud. Ct., Mass., 1972-73; dir. grant mgmt. Mayor's Office Criminal Justice, Boston, 1973-74, counsel, 1974-75; assoc. Hill & Barlow, Boston, 1975-81, ptnr., 1981—, Day Pitney LLP. Mem. editorial bd. Man's Impact on the Global Environment, 1970. Mem. staff MIT Conf. on Global Environ. Problems, 1970, Conf. on Taxes and Effluent Charges as Means of Pollution Control, Washington, 1971. Mem.: New Eng. Coun. Tech. Com. Office: Day Pitney LLP 1 Internat Place Boston MA 02110 Office Phone: 617-345-4808. Office Fax: 617-345-4745. Business E-Mail: pkatz@daypitney.com.

KATZ, REUVEN J., lawyer; b. Cin., 1924; m. Catherine S. Katz; children: Stewart, Sharon. BA, U. Cin., 1988, LHD (hon.), 2001; JD, Harvard Law Sch., 1950. Bar: Ohio 1950. Assoc. and ptnr. Paxton & Seasongood; pvt. practice Reuven J. Katz Co., L.P.A.; ptnr. Katz, Teller, Brant & Hild, 1980—. Pres. Big Brothers Assn. Cin., Coun. Aging Cmty. Chest; bd. mem. Johnny Bench Scholarship Fund, Greater Cin. Found., Jewish Vocat. Svc., Shetlering Oaks Hosp., U. Cinn. Coll. Medicine Cmty. Advisory Bd.; past chmn. bd. U. Cin. Found. Officer USAAF, World War II. Named one of Top 50 Lawyers Cin., Law and Politics Media, Inc., Top 100 Lawyers Ohio; recipient Lifetime Achievement award in Law, Cin. Bar Found., 1999, Chairman's award, U. Cin. Found., 1999. Mem.: Sports Lawyers Assn. (bd. mem.), Tournament Players Club Rivers Bend (bd. gov.), Palm Beach Polo and Country Club, Cin. Country Club, U. Club Cin. Avocations: golf, tennis, theater. Office: Katz Teller Brant & Hild 255 E Fifth St Ste 2400 Cincinnati OH 45202-4787 Office Phone: 513-721-4532. Business E-Mail: rkatz@katzteller.com.

KATZ, ROBERT JAMES, lawyer; b. NYC, Nov. 24, 1947; s. Seymour Milton and Naomi Bernice (Norek) K.; m. Jane Nan Lisman, Aug. 12, 1970; children: James Nicholas, Emily Austen. BA, Cornell U., 1969; JD magna cum laude, Harvard U., 1972; postdoctoral, London Sch. Econs., 1972-73. Bar: N.Y. 1973, U.S. Dist. Ct. (ea. and so. dists.) N.Y. 1973, U.S. Ct. Appeals (2d cir.) 1973, U.S. Supreme Ct. 1981. Law clk. to chief judge U.S. Ct. Appeals (2d cir.), NYC, 1973; assoc. Sullivan & Cromwell, NYC, 1974-80, ptnr., 1980-88; ptnr., gen. counsel Goldman, Sachs and Co., NYC, 1988—2000, sr. counsel, 2000—01, spl. counsel, adv. dir., 2001—04, sr. dir., 2004—. Trustee Cornell U., Ithaca, N.Y.; bd. councilors USC Shoah Found. Inst.; mem. exec. com. Dean's Advisory Bd., Harvard Law Sch., Cambridge, Mass.; chair emeritus Horace Mann Sch.; trustee emeritus Allen-Stevenson Sch.; bd. dirs. Achilles Track Club. Knox fellow Harvard U., 1972. Mem. ABA, N.Y. State Bar Assn., Assn. Bar City N.Y., Fed. Bar Coun., Cornell Club, Harvard Club (N.Y.C.). Office: Goldman Sachs & Co One NY Plaza New York NY 10004-2456

KATZ, ROBERT L., lawyer; BCL magna cum laude, McGill U., Montreal, Can., LLB; student, NYU Sch. Law. Assoc. Milbank, Tweed, Hadley & McCloy, NYC and London, 1986—95; asst. gen. counsel GM AG, Zurich, Switzerland, 1996—98; gen. counsel, regional compliance officer Europe, Mid. East and Africa ops. Delphi Corp., Paris, 1999—2006; sr. v.p., gen. counsel, mem. strategy bd. Fed.-Mogul Corp., Southfield, Mich., 2007—. Office: Federal-Mogul Corp 26555 Northwestern Hwy Southfield MI 48033-2146*

KATZ, ROBERT NATHAN, ceramics engineer, educator; b. Williamsport, Pa., Sept. 2, 1939; s. Louis and Rose Bernice (Golbitz) K.; m. Barbara Kurn Rubin, June 15, 1986; children: Pamela Lynn, Jonathan Adam. SB, MIT, 1961; MS, U. Mich., 1963; PhD, MIT, 1969. Rsch. asst. U. Mich., 1961-62; metallurgist Army Materials Rsch. Agy., Watertown, Mass., 1962-65; ceramic engr. Army Materials Tech. Lab., Watertown, 1965-70, chief ceramics rsch. divsn., 1970-87, chief materials technologist, 1987-95; prin. R. Nathan Katz Assocs., 1995—. Norton assoc. prof. mech. engrng. Worcester (Mass.) Poly. Inst., 1990—91, Norton rsch. prof., 1991—2003, rsch. prof., 2004—; apptd. spl. mem. grad. faculty U. Md., 2000—02; liaison mem. various coms. Nat. Materials Adv. Bd.; participant Nat. Rsch. Coun., Bd. of Army Sci. and Tech., Star-21, Strategic Techs. for the Army of the 21st Century study, 1988—92, Nat. Acad. Sci. Naval Studies Bd., Future Carrier Tech. Study, 1990—91, Nat. Acad. Sci., Nat. Materials Adv. Bd., Materials Rsch. for Def.-After-Next study, 2001—02; external examiner Bd. Grad. Studies, U. Cambridge, England, 1979; cons. Dept. Def., Dept. Energy, Congl. Office of Tech. Assessment; mem. U.S. del. NATO Com. on Challenges of Modern Soc., 1974; mem. organizing com., lectr. NATO Advanced Study Inst. Nitrogen Ceramics, 1976, 81. Editor: Ceramics for High Performance Applications, 1974, Vol. II, 1978, Vol. III, 1983; mem. editl. bd. Internat. Jour. High Tech. Ceramics, 1984-89, Jour. European Ceramic Soc., 1989-2005; columnist Ceramic Industry Mag., 1999-2001; contbr. articles to tech. publs. Trustee Temple Israel of Natick, 1979-80, Temple Beth Zion, Brookline, 1998-2006, chmn., 1999-2003; Eagle Scout, BSA, Troop 65, Scranton, Pa., 1956. Recipient Tech. Writing award, Dept. Army, 1981, Mass. Rep. of Yr. award, Nat. Rep. Congl. Com., 2002. Fellow Am. Ceramic Soc.; mem. Nat. Inst. Ceramic Engrs., New Eng. Ceramic Soc. (F.H. Norton award 1978), Am. Soc. Metals, Sigma Xi. Home: 1731 Beacon St Apt 1403 Brookline MA 02445-5329 Office: Dept Mech Engring Worcester Polytechnic Inst Worcester MA 01609 Office Phone: 617-738-4723. Business E-Mail: katz@wpi.edu.

KATZ, ROGER, pediatrician, allergist, immunologist, educator; b. Menominee, Mich., Feb. 23, 1938; s. Peter W. and Mae C. (Chudacoff) Katz; children: Carl, Gary, Robyn. BS, U. Wis., 1960; MD, U. Louisville, 1965. Diplomate Am. Bd. Allergy and Immunology, Am. Bd. Pediatric Allergy, Am. Bd. Pediat. Clin. prof. pediat. UCLA, 1978—. Spkr. in field; expert legal evaluator. Author and editor sci. books and manuscripts. Maj. U.S. Army, 1970-72. Named One of Best Drs. in Am., 1996, 97, 2001, 02, 05. Fellow Am. Acad. Allergy, Asthma and Immunology, Am. Coll. Allergy, Asthma and Immunology (bd. regents 1990-93), Am. Acad. Pediat., Am. Coll. Chest Physicians, Joint Coun. Allergy, Asthma and Immunology (pres. 1986-90). Office: UCLA Med Ctr 1304 15th St # 102 Santa Monica CA 90404-1810 Office Phone: 310-393-1550.

KATZ, RONALD ALAN, dermatologist; b. St. Joseph, Mo., July 13, 1942; s. Walter and Mildred (Talman) K.; m. Jane Ellen Markin, Dec. 26, 1968; children: Jennifer Lynn, Hilary Beth. BS, U. Cin., 1964; MD, U. Md., 1969. Diplomate Am. Bd. Dermatology. Intern Childrens Nat. Med. Ctr., Washington, 1969-70; resident Yale U., New Haven, Conn., 1972-75, chief resident in dermatology, 1974-75; pvt. practice College Park, Md., 1975—. Clin. prof. dermatology and pediats. George Washington U., 1975—. Contbr. articles to profl. jours. Founding vol. U.S. Meml. Holocaust Mus., Washington, 1993-96. Lt. comdr. USPHS, 1970-72. Named Outstanding Physician Specialist, Consumer Checkbook, 1998, 2002; named one of Top Doctors, Washingtonian, 1993, 1995, 1999, 2002, 2005, Best Doctors in Am., 2001, 2002, 2005. Mem. AMA, Md. State Med. Soc., Prince George's County Med. Soc., Washington Dermatol. Soc. pres. 1990-91), Am. Acad. Dermatology, Soc. for Pediatric Dermatology, Soc. for Investigative Dermatology, Alpha Omega Alpha. Democrat. Jewish. Avocations: photography, running marathons. Home: 9304 Sprinklewood Ln Potomac MD 20854-2257 Office: 6201 Greenbelt Rd College Park MD 20740-2354 E-mail: ronaldk204@aol.com.

KATZ, RONALD LEWIS, physician, educator; b. Bklyn., Apr. 22, 1932; s. Joseph and Belle (Charnis) K.; children: Richard Ian, Laura Susan, Margaret Karen. BA, U. Wis.-Madison, 1952; MD, Boston U., 1956; postgrad. in Pharmacology (NIH fellow), Coll. Physicians and Surgeons, Columbia U., 1959-60; postgrad. (John Simon Guggenheim fellow), Royal Postgrad. Med. Sch., U. London, 1968-69. Intern USPHS Hosp., SI, 1956-57; resident Columbia-Presbyn. Med. Center, 1957-60; asst. prof. anesthesiology Coll. Physicians and Surgeons, Columbia U., 1960-66, assoc. prof., 1966-70, prof., 1970-73; prof., chmn. dept. anesthesiology UCLA, 1973-90, prof. anesthesiology, 1990-94, chief staff Med. Ctr., 1984-86; prof., chmn. dept. anesthesiology U. So. Calif., LA, 1995—2000, prof., 1995—. Cons. NIH, FDA, numerous state agys. Author, editor: Muscle Relaxants, 1975; Contbr. numerous articles to profl. jours.; Mem. editorial bd.: Handbook of Anesthesiology, 1972—, Progress in Anesthesiology, 1973—; editor in chief Seminars in Anesthesia, 1982—. Mem. Am. Soc. Anesthesiologists, Am. Physiol. Soc., Am. Soc. Pharmacology and Exptl. Therapeutics, N.Y. Acad. Medicine; Faculty Anaesthetists of Royal Coll. Surgeons of Eng. Achievements include inventor peripheral nerve stimulator. Home: 2910 Neilson Way Apt 407 Santa Monica CA 90405-5323 Office: Harbor UCLA 1000 W Carson St Anesthesiology Box 10 Torrance CA 90509

KATZ, RONALD SCOTT, lawyer; b. Norwich, Conn., Dec. 14, 1946; s. Irving David and Joan (Lebovitz) K.; m. Ann Lisa Mark, Dec. 27, 1969; children: Benjamin, Cynthia. BA, Johns Hopkins U., 1968; JD, Columbia U., 1972. Bar: NY 1972, US Ct. Appeals (2d cir.) 1974, US Ct. Appeals (4th cir.) 1993. Assoc. Golenbock & Barell, NYC, 1972—80, ptnr., 1981—89, Whitman & Ransom, NYC, 1990—93; shareholder, dir. Shack Siegel Katz & Flaherty PC, NYC, 1993—2005; ptnr. Blank Rome LLP, NYC, 2005—. Mem. ABA, NY State Bar Assn. Home: 16 Paxford Ln Scarsdale NY 10583-3318 Office: Blank Rome LLP 405 Lexington Ave New York NY 10174 Office Phone: 212-885-5170. Business E-Mail: rkatz@blankrome.com.

KATZ, RONALD STANLEY, lawyer; b. St. Louis, May 1, 1945; s. Isadore and Lillian (Goldman) K.; m. June Schlesinger (dec. 1985); m. Libby Roth, Mar. 22, 1987; children: Hart Eddy, Jason, Elliot. BA summa cum laude, NYU, 1967; MA, Oxford U., Eng., 1969; JD, Harvard U., 1972. Bar: D.C. 1973, Calif. 1979. Fellow Internat. Legal Ctr., NYC, 1972-75; atty. antitrust div. U.S. Dept. Justice, Washington, 1975-77; dep. dir. office of Law of the Sea negotiations Dept. State, Washington, 1977-78; assoc. McCutchen Doyle Brown & Enersen, San Francisco, 1978-82; ptnr. Gaston Snow & Ely Bartlett, Palo Alto, Calif., 1982-86, Kadison & Pfaelzer, Palo Alto, 1986-87, Coudert Bros, San Francisco, 1987, Manatt Phelps & Phillips LLP, Palo Alto, Calif. Co-author: Survey of Indonesian Economic Law: Labor Law, 1974; contbr. articles to profl. publs. Rhodes scholar, 1967; Woodrow Wilson Found. fellow, 1967, recipient Atty. Gens. outstanding performance award. Mem. ABA, Bar Assn. San Francisco, coun. fgn. Rels., San Francisco com. fgn. Rels., Am. Law Inst., State Bar Calif., overseer NY U. coll. of arts & sci., overseas fellow Internat. legal ctr. Bandung, Indonesia. Office: Manatt Phelps & Phillips LLP 1001 Page Mill Rd bldg 2 Palo Alto CA 94304 Office Phone: 650-812-1346. Office Fax: 650-213-0260. Business E-Mail: rkatz@manatt.com.

KATZ, SAMUEL, retired geophysics educator; b. Berlin, Feb. 13, 1923; came to U.S., 1934, naturalized, 1940; s. Herman and Bertha (Low) K.; m. Jean Barbara Parker, July 10, 1953; children— David R., Daniel M., Miriam E. BS, U. Mich., 1943; A.M., Columbia, 1947, PhD, 1955. With radiation lab. Mass. Inst. Tech., 1943-46; mem. sci. staff Lamont Geol. Obs., Columbia, 1948-53; sr. physicist Stanford Research Inst., 1953-57; mem. faculty Rensselaer Poly Inst., 1957—, prof. geophysics, 1962-86, prof. emeritus, 1986—, chmn. dept. geology, 1964-69; ret., 1986. Contbr. articles in field to profl. jours. Mem. Am. Geophys. Union, AAAS, Sigma Xi. Home: 908 Karenwald Ln Schenectady NY 12309-6416

KATZ, SAMUEL LAWRENCE, pediatrician, researcher; b. Manchester, NH, May 29, 1927; s. Morris and Ethel (Lawrence) Katz; m. Betsy Jane Cohan, June 27, 1950; children: Samuel Lawrence Jr.(dec.) , John S.L., David L., Deborah Susan, William L., Susan Johanna, Penelope Jennifer; m. Catherine Minock Wilfert, July 23, 1971; stepchildren: Rachel Ann, Katie Claiborne. AB magna cum laude, Dartmouth Coll., 1948; MD cum laude, Harvard U., 1952; DSc (hon.), Georgetown U., 1996, Dartmouth Coll., 1998. Intern Beth Israel Hosp., Boston, 1952—53; resident Children's Hosp., Boston, 1953—54, 1955—56, Mass. Gen. Hosp., 1954—55; from rsch. fellow to asst. prof. Harvard Med. Sch., 1956—68; prof., chmn. dept. pediat. Duke Med. Sch., 1968—90, Wilburt C. Davison prof., 1972—97. Mem. sci. adv. bd. Hasbro Children's Found., St. Jude Children's Rsch. Hosp.; rschr. on virology, virus vaccines and immunization NIH couns. and study sects. WHO; chmn. India-US Vaccine Action Program, 1999—2004; chmn. adv. com. immunization practice Ctrs. for Disease Control, Atlanta, 1985—93. Developer (with John F. Enders) attenuated live measles-virus vaccine; contbr. chapters to books, articles to profl. jours. Chmn. bd. trustees Internat. Vaccine Inst., Seoul, Republic of Korea, 2003—07. With USNR, 1945—46. Recipient Rsch. Career Devel. award, NIH, 1965—68, Presdl. medal of achievement, Dartmouth Coll., 1991, Sabin Gold medal, Albert Sabin Vaccine Inst., 2003, Duke U. Founder's medal, 2004, Alfred duPont award Pediat. Rsch., Nemours Found., 2006, Pollin prize Pediat. Rsch., 2007; fellow, Nat. Found., 1956—58. Mem.: APHA (Needleman medal and award 1997), Inst. Medicine NAS, Pediat. Infectious Diseases Soc. (Disting. Physician award 1991), Assn. Med. Sch. Pediat. Dept. Chmn. (pres. 1977—79), Am. Acad. Pediat. (Grulee award 1975, Jacobi award 1986), Am. Assn. Immunologists, Infectious Diseases Soc. Am. (co-chmn. vaccine initiative 1998—99, co-chmn. nat. network for immunization info. 1999—2003, Bristol award 1988, Soc. citation 1993), New Eng. Pediat. Soc., Am. Pediat. Soc. (pres. 1986—87, St. Geme award 1988, Howland award 2000), Soc. Pediat. Rsch., Am. Soc. Clin. Investigation, Am. Fedn. Clin. Rsch. Home: 1917 Wildcat Creek Rd Chapel Hill NC 27516-9786 Office: Duke U Med Ctr PO Box 2925 Durham NC 27710-0001 Office Phone: 919-668-4852, 919-684-3734. Office Fax: 919-681-8934. Business E-Mail: katz0004@mc.duke.edu.

KATZ, SANDRA, educational consultant, psychologist, education educator; d. Victor Benaim and Anita de Benaim; m. Gabriel Katz, Aug. 14, 1977; children: Valerie Katz-Seibald, Alan, Denise. BA in Psychology, U. Tenn., 1978, MS in Ednl. and Counseling Psychology, 1980; lic. in psychology, U. Catolica Andres Bello, Caracas, 1983. Sch. intervention specialist Invedin: Venezuelan Inst. Child Devel., Caracas, 1980—81; pvt. practice child psychology Unit Psychoednl. Intervention, Caracas, 1981—95; head sch. psychologist Eutimio Rivas Pub. Sch. Sys., Miranda, Venezuela, 1984—89; mem. faculty dept. sch. psychology U. Catolica Andres Bello, Caracas, 1984—; mem. grad. faculty Andres Bello Cath. U., Caracas, 1991—2001, interim head grad. program on child devel., 1998; CEO, co-funder, sr. cons. Proyecto Armonia, Caracas, 1994—. V.p. bd. dirs. Ctr. Rsch. and Edn., Caracas, 1995—2000; mem. adv. bd. Retorno: Addiction Prevention Ctr., Caracas, 2001—02; mem. jury Tchr. Excellence Award, Caracas, 2002; presenter, leader workshops in field. Author: Armonia por la Paz, 2003, 100 Icebreakers for Harmony (in Spanish), 2005, Armonia in Preschool, 2006; contbr. numerous articles to profl. publs. Staff trainer Atenea's Found. for Abandoned Children and Youth, Caracas, 1996—98, Fundana Found. for Abandoned Children, Caracas, 2004—05, UCAB Cmty. Outreach Program, 2004—05; advisor, cons. Venezuelan Camping Assn., 2000—05; advisor, cons., staff trainer Crecer con Valores program, 1997—2001; bd. dirs. Cmty. Edn. Sys.-Fundasec, Caracas, 2005. Recipient award, Enhancing Jewish Cmty.'s Edn., Caracas, 2003, 2004, Teaching Excellence award, Herzl-Bialik Cmty. Edn. Sys.,

2003, Recognition award, Ctr. Rsch. and Edn., Venezuela, 2000, Contbn. award, Venezuelan Camping Assn., 2000. Mem.: Miranda Assn. Psychologists, Venezuelan Psychol. Assn. (honor award), Nat. Assn. Sch. Psychologists, Venezuelan Fedn. Psychologists (hon.), U. Tenn. Alumni Assn., Women Internat. Zonist Orgn. Achievements include development of ednl. programs in field. Avocations: dance, reading, travel. Office: Proyecto Armonia POBA Internat 158P-025255 Miami FL 33102-5255 Business E-Mail: sandra@proyectoarmonia.com.

KATZ, SANFORD NOAH, lawyer, educator; b. Holyoke, Mass., Dec. 23, 1933; m. Joan Raphael; children: Daniel, Andrew. BA in History with distinction, Boston U., 1955; JD, U. Chgo., 1958; postgrad., Yale U., 1963-64. Bar: D.C. 1959, U.S. Supreme Ct. 1963, Mass. 1970. Law clk. to chief judge U.S Ct. Claims, Washington, 1958-59; from instr. to assoc. prof. Cath. U. Sch. Law, 1959—64; assoc. prof. U. Fla., 1964-66, prof., 1966-68, Boston Coll., 1968-2000, Libby prof. law, 2000—. Vis. prof. U. Mich., summer 1967; lectr. in law and social work Smith Coll., summers 1965-69; assoc. Clare Hall Cambridge U., England, 1973; mem. Faculty of Laws, 1973; vis. fellow Hampstead Child Therapy Clinic, London, 1973; vis. fellow All Souls Coll. Oxford U., 1997, vis. fellow Pembroke Coll., 2000, 06; del. White House Conf. on Children, 1970; mem. Spl. Adv. Com. Atty. Gen. Mass., 1974, Joint Mass. House and Senate Commn. on Family, 1977, Mass. Jud. Nominating Commn., 1977—79; chief drafter HEW model acts; rsch. on child abuse and neglect, marriage, child custody in divorce, model legislation, contract law. Author: When Parents Fail, 1971, Adoptions Without Agencies: A Study of Independent Adoptions, 1978, Child Snatching-The Legal Response to the Abduction of Children, 1981; (with Weyrauch) American Family Law in Transition, 1983; (with Weyrauch and Olsen) Cases and Materials on Family Law-Legal Concepts and Changing Human Relationships, 1994; (with Eekelaar and Maclean) Cross Currents, 2000, Family Law in America, 2003, others; also book introductions; editor: The Youngest Minority: Lawyers in Defense of Children, vols. I and II, 1974; (with John Eekelaar) Family Violence: An International and Interdisciplinary Study, 1978, Marriage and Cohabitation in Contemporary Societies, 1980; editor-in-chief Family Law Quar., 1970-83; contbr. articles to profl. jours. Chmn. Lydia Rapoport Endowment Fund Smith Coll. Grantee Field Found., 1968-69, Grant Found., 1971-75, HEW, 1973-78. Mem. ABA (chmn. family law sect. 1980-81), Internat. Soc. Family Law (pres. 1981-84, exec. coun. 1985—).

KATZ, SHERMAN E., lawyer; b. Pitts., July 13, 1943; s. Saul H. Katz and Ann (Sklov) Cohen; m. Maureen Murphy, Jan. 26, 1980; 1 child, Barnaby Simon. Student, U. Stockholm, 1963-64; BA cum laude, Amherst Coll., 1965; JD, Columbia U., 1969, MA in Internat. Affairs, 1969; diploma in European Law, Oxford U., 1992. Bar: N.Y. 1969, D.C. 1969, U.S. Ct. Appeals D.C. 1970, U.S. Supreme Ct. 1973, U.S. Ct. Internat. Trade 1984. Ptnr. Coudert Bros., Washington, 1977-94, Squire, Sanders & Dempsey, Washington, 1994-98, Kelley, Drye & Warren, Washington, 1998—, of counsel; sr. assoc. Carnegie Endowment for Internat. Peace, Washington, 2006—. Prof. internat. trade Johns Hopkins Sch. Advanced Internat. Studies, 2001—; William Scholl chmn. internat. bus. Ctr. Strategic and Internat. Studies, Washington, 2000—06. Contbr. articles to profl. jours. Commr. D.C. Commn. on Arts & Humanities, Washington, 1987—; chmn. exec. com., hon. dir. Washington Performing Arts Soc., 1981—; bd. dirs. The Washington Opera, 1988—, The Source Theatre, Folger Poetry Series. Decorated Knight of the Royal Polar Star by King of Sweden. Mem. ABA (chmn. svcs. trade com. 1987-89, vice-chair internat. bus. transactions com. 1999), N.Y. State Bar Assn., Assn. of Bar of City of N.Y., D.C. Bar Assn., Am. Soc. Internat. Law (chmn. publs. com. 1984-87), Nat. Fgn. Trade Coun. (chmn. internat. trade com. 1986), Coun. Fgn. Rels., Washington Fgn. Law Soc., Cosmos Club. Office: Carnegie Endowment for Internat Peace 1779 Massachusetts Ave NW Washington DC 20036-2103 Office Phone: 202-939-2370. Business E-Mail: skatz@ceip.org.

KATZ, STANLEY NIDER, law educator; b. Chgo., Apr. 23, 1934; s. William Stephen and Florence (Nider) K.; m. Adria Holmes, Jan. 16, 1960; children: Derek Holmes, Marion Holmes. AB, Harvard U., Cambridge, Mass., 1955, MA, 1959, PhD, 1961; LLD (hon.), Stockton State Coll., 1981, U. Hartford, Conn., 1998, Ohio State U., 1998; DHL (hon.), U. Puget Sound, Tacoma, Wash., 1994, C.W. Post/LI U., 1997, Sacred Heart U., Fairfield, Conn., 1997, Roosevelt U., Chgo., 2003, Ursinus Coll., Collegeville, Pa., 2003; DLA (hon.), Dickinson Coll., Carlisle, Pa., 2003. Asst. prof. history Harvard U., 1961-65, U. Wis., Madison, 1965-71; prof. legal history Law Sch. U. Chgo., 1971-78; Class of 1921 Bicentennial prof. history Am. law and liberty Princeton U., 1978-86, sr. fellow Woodrow Wilson Sch., 1986-97, lectr. with rank of prof. Woodrow Wilson Sch., 1997—, dir. Ctr. for Arts and Cultural Policy Rsch., Woodrow Wilson Sch., 1998—, acting dir. law and pub. affairs Woodrow Wilson Sch., 2004—05; pres. Am. Council Learned Socs., NYC, 1986-97. Vis. prof. law U. Pa., 1978-86, 2003; mem. Oliver Wendell Holmes Devise, Washington, 1976-84; bd. govs. Inst. European Studies, Chgo., 1976—2002; chmn. Coun. on Internat. Exchange Scholars, Washington, 1981-85; adj. prof. Cardozo Law Sch., 1999-2000. Author: Newcastle's New York, 1968; editor: The Case and Tryal of John Peter Zenger, 1963, rev. edit., 1972, Oliver Wendell Holmes Devise History of U.S. Supreme Court, 1984—, Colonial America, 1971, 76, 83, 92, 2000, American History: Promise and Progress, 1983, Constitutionalism and Democracy, 1993, The Life of Learning, 1994, Philanthropy in the World's Traditions, 1998, Mobilizing for Peace, 2002. Active NJ Com. for Humanities, 1978—84, 1996—; trustee Nat. History Ctr., 2003—, So. Meth. U., 1988—2000, Nat. Cultural Alliance, 1990—97, chmn., 1997—98; trustee Rsch. Librs. Group, 1991—93, 1997—99, Brit.-Am. Arts Assn. CCC, 1991—, Newberry Libr., Chgo., ind. sector, 1989—92, Toynbee Prize Found., 1994—97, pres., 1995—97, Nat. Faculty, 1995—2001, Fulbright Internat. Ctr., 1995—, Copyright Clearance Ctr., 1997—, civic edn. project, 1997—; bd. dirs. Social Sci. Rsch. Coun., NYC, 2002—06; v.p. Friends of the Law Libr., Libr. of Congress, 1991—2003; v.p. disciplinary oversight com. Surpeme Ct. NJ, 1994—2000; v.p. NJ Ethics Commn., 1991—94, com. model rules of profl. conduct, 1982—83, com. sale of law practices, 1983—84, 1989. Fellow Am. Soc. Legal History (pres. 1978-81); mem. AAAS, Papers of the Founding Fathers, Inc. (chair 1985—), Internat. Soc. Cultural Property (treas. 2005—), Inst. Early Am. History and Culture (coun. 1974-76, 90-93, 97-98), Am. Hist. Assn. (v.p. rsch. 1997-2000, Troyer Steele Anderson prize, 2005), Orgn. Am. Historians (exec. com. 1976-79, pres. elect 1986-87, pres. 1987-88), Am. Antiquarian Soc., Mass. Hist. Soc., Am. Philos. Soc., Soc. Am. Historians, Cuban Acad. Sci., Coun. Fgn. Rels., Phi Beta Kappa. Clubs: Princeton (NYC). Democrat. Jewish. Office: Princeton U Woodrow Wilson Sch Princeton NJ 08544-0001 Office Phone: 609-258-5637. Business E-Mail: snkatz@princeton.edu.

KATZ, STEPHEN IRA, federal agency administrator; b. Bklyn., Jan. 26, 1941; BA with honors, U. Md., 1962; MD with honors, Tulane U., 1966; PhD in Immunology, U. London, 1974. Diplomate Am. Bd. Dermatology. Asst. dermatology Walter Reed Gen. Hosp., Washington, 1970-72; rsch. fellow dept. pathology Royal Coll. Surgeons Eng., London, 1972-74; sr. investigator dermatology Nat. Cancer Inst./NIH, Bethesda, Md., 1974-77, acting chief dermatology br., 1977-80, chief dermatology br., 1980—2001; dir. Nat. Inst. Arthritis and Musculoskeletal and Skin Diseases, Bethesda, 1995—. Marion B. Sulzberger prof. dermatology Uniformed Svcs. U. Health Scis., Bethesda, 1989-95, acting chmn. dermatology dept., 1993-95; cons. Georgetown U., 1970-72, Walter Reed Army Hosp., 1975-79, Nat. Naval Med. Ctr., 1976-95, Washington Dermatol. Soc., 1980-81. Editl. bd. Internat. Jour. Dermatology, 1977-81, Jour. Investigative Dermatology, 1979-82, Jour. Am. Acad. Dermatology, 1979-83, Jour. Immunology, 1981-85, Am. Jour. Dermatopathology, Epithelia, 1986-88, Regional Immunology, 1988-95, Medicine, 1992—, Am. Jour. Contact Dermatitis, 1992—, Dermatology Internat., 1992—, Proceedings Assn. Am. Physicians, 1995—, others; contbr. over 180 sci. articles and 50 book chpts. Goldberger Summer fellow AMA, 1965, Advanced Tng. fellow Dermatology Found., 1972-74; recipient Presdl. Exec. Meritorious Rank award, PHS Superior Svc. award, Sulzberger Lecture award Am. Acad. Dermatology, D. Martin Carer Mentor award Am. Skin Assn., Stephen Rothman Meml. award Soc. Investigative Dermatology, Messenger of Hope award Scleroderma Found., Inflamatory Skin Disorders Rsch. award. Mem. Inst. Med.-Nat. Acad. Sci. Achievements include research in Langerhans cells and epidermally derived cytokines, demonstrating that skin is a critical component of the immune system; the field of inherited and acquired blistering skin diseases. Office: Nat Inst Arthritis and Musculoskeletal and Skin Diseases Bldg 31 Rm 4C32D 31 Center Dr Bethesda MD 20892-2350 Office Phone: 301-496-4353.

KATZ, STEVEN MARTIN, lawyer, accountant; b. Washington, Feb. 8, 1941; s. Joseph and Pauline (Weinberg) K.; m. Lauri Gail Berman, Aug. 23, 1964; children: Benjamin, Aaron, Rebecca, Joshua. BS, U. Md., College Park, 1962; JD, George Washington U., 1965. Bar: D.C. 1966, Md. 1971; CPA, Md. Ptnr. Euzent, Katz & Katz, Washington, 1969-72; sr. ptnr. Katz, Frome & Bleecker, P.A., and predecessors, Rockville, Md., 1972-95; pvt. practice Rockville, 1995—. Mem. Md. State Grievance Commn., 1991—. Mem. Md. Bar Assn., Md. Assn. CPAs, D.C. Bar, Montgomery County Bar Assn., Md. State Bar Found. Jewish. Office: 401 E Jefferson St Ste 208 Rockville MD 20850-2613 Office Phone: 301-738-8441. Office Fax: 301-294-9484. Personal E-mail: smkatz7@verizon.net.

KATZ, STUART CHARLES, lawyer, musician; b. Chgo., June 9, 1937; s. Jerome H. and Sylvia L. (Singer) K.; m. Penny Schatz, Jan. 23, 1959; children: Steven, Lauren. BA, Roosevelt U., Chgo., 1959; JD with distinction, John Marshall Law Sch., 1964. Bar: Ill. 1964, U.S. Dist. Ct. (no. dist.) Ill. 1965, U.S. Supreme Ct. 1967. Exec. v.p., gen. counsel Heitman LLC, Chgo., 1972—. Jazz pianist and vibraphonist, appeared in concerts with Benny Goodman, Gene Krupa, Bud Freeman. Mem.: ABA, Chgo. Bar Assn., Ill. Bar Assn. Office: 191 N Wacker Dr Ste 2500 Chicago IL 60606-1885 E-mail: skatz@heitman.com.

KATZ, STUART Z., lawyer; b. NYC, July 14, 1942; BA, CCNY, 1964; JD, NYU, 1968. Bar: N.Y. 1968. Ptnr. Fried, Frank, Harris, Shriver & Jacobson, NYC, 1968—. Lectr. Practicing Law Inst., Prentice Hall, N.Y.C. and Mile, Minn. Mem.: ABA. Office: Fried Frank Harris Shriver & Jacobson 1 New York Plz Fl 27 New York NY 10004-1980

KATZ, THOMAS OWEN, lawyer; b. Killeen, Tex., Jan. 15, 1958; s. Herbert D. and Eleanor (Meyerhoff) K.; m. Elissa Ellant, Nov. 6, 1983; children: Joseph, Peyton, Jacob. BS in Econs., U. Pa., 1979; JD, Georgetown U., 1982. Bar: Fla. 1982, US Tax Ct. 1983. Shareholder, chair income tax dept. Ruden, McClosky, Smith, Schuster & Russell, P.A., Ft. Lauderdale, Fla., 1982—. Bd. dirs. CLAL-Ctr. for Jewish Learning and Leadership, NY, 1993—, chmn., 2002—05, Cmty. Found. of Broward, 2000-06, chmn. 2005-06; bd. overseers Ctr. Advanced Judaic Studies U. Pa., 2001—. Office: Ruden McClosky Smith Sch PO Box 1900 Fort Lauderdale FL 33302-1900 Office Phone: 954-527-2419. Business E-Mail: thomas.katz@ruden.com.

KATZ, TONNIE, newspaper editor; BA, Barnard Coll., 1966; MSc, Columbia U., 1967. Editor, reporter newspapers including The Quincy Patriot Ledger, Boston Herald Am., Boston Globe; Sunday/projects editor Newsday; mng. editor Balt. News Am., 1983-86, The Sun, San Bernardino, Calif., 1986-88; asst. mng. editor for news The Orange County Register, Santa Ana, Calif., 1988-89, mng. editor, 1989-92, editor, v.p., 1992-98, editor, sr. v.p., 1998—2003. Office: Orange County Register 625 N Grand Ave Santa Ana CA 92701-4347

KATZ, TREUMAN P., health facility administrator; b. 1942; m. Sue Ellen Katz. Pres., CEO Children's Hosp. and Regional Med. Ctr., Seattle, 1979—2005, pres. emeritus, 2005—. Office: Children's Hosp and Regional Med Ctr 4800 Sand Point Way NE Seattle WA 98106

KATZ, VERA, former mayor, college administrator, state legislator; b. Dusseldorf, Germany, Aug. 3, 1933; came to U.S., 1940; d. Lazar Pistrak and Raissa Goodman; m. Mel Katz (div. 1985); 1 child, Jesse. BA, Bklyn. Coll., 1955, postgrad., 1955-57; PhD (hon.), Lewis & Clark Coll., Portland State U., Oreg. Market research analyst TIMEX, B.T. Babbitt, NYC, 1957-62; mem. Oreg. Ho. of Reps., Salem, 1985—91; former dir. devel. Portland Community Coll.; mayor City of Portland, Oreg., 1992—2004. Mem. Gov.'s Council on Alcohol and Drug Abuse Programs, Oreg. Legis., Salem, 1985—; mem. adv. com. Gov.'s Council on Health, Fitness and Sports, Oreg. Legis., 1985—; mem. Gov.'s Commn. on Sch. Funding Reform; mem. Carnegie task Force on Teaching as Profession, Washington, 1985-87; vice-chair assembly Nat. Conf. State Legis., Denver, 1986—2003. Recipient Abigail Scott Duniway award Women in Communications, Inc., Portland, 1985, Jeanette Rankin First Woman award Oreg. Women's Polit. Caucus, Portland, 1985, Leadership award The Neighborhood newspaper Portland, 1985, Woman of Achievement award Commn. for Women, 1985, Outstanding Legis. Advocacy award Oreg. Primary Care Assn., 1985, Service to Portland Pub. Sch. Children award Portland Pub. Schs., 1985, Visionary Leadership award, 1998, Legal Citizen of Yr. award, 2002. Fellow Am. Leadership Forum (founder Oreg. chpt.); mem. Dem. Legis. Leaders Assn., Nat. Bd. for Profl. Teaching Standards. Democrat. Jewish. Avocations: camping, jogging, dance. Office: Office of the Mayor City Hall 1221 SW 4th Ave Rm 340 Portland OR 97204-1995

KATZ, WILLIAM EMANUEL, retired chemical engineer; b. Honesdale, Pa., June 12, 1924; s. Edward David and Aimee Helen (Rosenfelder) K.; m. Martha Elizabeth Legg, Feb. 13, 1960; children: Susan Katz Miller, Martha Katz Laserson, E. David II, James A.L. BSChE, MIT, 1948, MSChE, 1949. Chem. engr. Ionics Inc., Watertown, Mass., 1949-51, asst. treas., 1951-53, treas., 1953-58, v.p. and dir., 1958-81, exec. v.p. and dir., 1981—2003; ret., 2003. Author chapter in AWWA Manual of Water Quality and Treatment, 1964, and 30 articles on water and waste treatment; patentee in field. Mem. wastewater adv. com. Mass. Water Resources Authority, 2003-. With U.S. Army, 1942-46, PTO. Recipient Life Achievement award Internat. Desalination Assn., 1999. Mem. AIChE, Am. Water Works Assn., Am. Desalting Assn. (Water Quality Person of Yr. 1992). Avocations: piano, composing. Home: 11 Sunset Rd Weston MA 02493-1623

KATZ, WILLIAM LOREN, author; b. Bklyn., June 2, 1927; s. Bernard and Madeline (Simon) K.; m. Laurie Lehman, Sept. 10, 1994. BA, Syracuse U., 1950; MA, NYU, 1952. Tchr. Am. history, NYC, 1954—60, Hartsdale, NY, 1960—67; freelance author, 1967—. Cons. N.Y. State Edn. Dept., 1967-68, 83-84, USAF Sch. in Eng., Belgium and Holland, 1974-75; scholar in residence Tchrs. Coll. Columbia, 1971-73, NYU, 1987-91; tchr. Black history Tombs Prison, N.Y.C., 1973, N.Y. U. Afro-Am. Inst., 1973; faculty Inst. Urban and Minority Edn., Gen. Assistance Ctr., Tchrs. Coll. Columbia U., 1976; tchr. Am. history New Sch. for Social Rsch., N.Y.C., 1977-83; pres. Ethrac Publs., 1971—. Author: Eyewitness: The Negro in American History, 1967 (Gold medal for nonfition NCCJ), 1995, Teachers' Guide to American Negro History, 1968; author: (with Warren J. Halliburton) American Majorities and Minorities: A Syllabus of United States History for Secondary Schools, 1970, A History of Black Americans, 1973; author: The Black West: A Documentary and Pictorial History, 1971 (Mark Twain award for non-fiction), 2005, Teaching Approaches to Black History in the Classroom, 1973, The Constitutional Amendments, 1974, An Album of Reconstruction, 1974, An Album of the Civil War, 1974, Minorities in American History, Vols. I-VI, 1974—75, Making Our Way, 1975, Black People Who Made the Old West, 1977, 2d edit., 1994, An Album of the Great Depression, 1978, An Album of Nazism, 1979, Black Indians: A Hidden Heritage, 1986, 2d edit., 1997, The Invisible Empire: The Ku Klux Klan Impact on History, 1986, A History of Multicultural America, Vols I-VIII, 1993—94; author: (with Marc Crawford) The Lincoln Brigade: A Picture History, 1989, 2d edit., 2002, Proudly Red and Black, 1993, Black Women of the Old West, 1995, Flight From the Devil: Six Slave Narratives, 1996, Black Legacy: A History of New York's African Americans, 1997, Black Pioneers: An Untold Story, 1999, The Cruel Years: American Voices at the Dawn of the 20th Century, 2002; author: (with Laurie R. Lehman) 2d edit., 2003; editor: The American Negro: History and Literature., 1968—71; editor: (with James M. McPherson) The Anti-Slavery Crusade in America, 1969; editor: (with Henry Steele Commager and Arthur Schlesinger Jr.) Vital Sources in American History for High School Students, 1980; columnist: NY Daily Challenge, 1986—; contbr. articles to profl. jours. Exec. bd. Art Against Apartheid, 1984; nat. coun. Nat. Emergency Civil Liberties Com., 1983-85; curator Black West Exhibit, Schomburg Ctr. for Rsch. in Black Culture, NYC, 1985-86. With USNR, 1945-46. Recipient Imani White Dove Peace award, 2000. Office Phone: 212-533-6875. Personal E-mail: wlkatz@aol.com. *If you believe that people have no history worth mentioning, it's easy to assume they have no humanity worth defending.*

KATZBERG, ROBERT F., lawyer; b. Bklyn., Mar. 12, 1946; BA with honors, CUNY Brooklyn Coll., 1967; JD cum laude, George Washington U., 1971. Bar: NY 1972, US Dist. Ct., NY (Ea. Dist.) 1974, US Ct. of Appeals, Second Circuit 1974, US Supreme Ct. 1975, US Dist. Ct., NY (So. Dist.) 1976, US Ct. of Appeals, Eleventh Circuit 1981, US Tax Ct. 1985, US Ct. of Appeals, Third Circuit 1991. Law clerk to Judge Oliver Gasch US Dist. Ct., Washington, 1971—72; asst. US atty. Ea. Dist. of NY, 1972—77; now ptnr. Kaplan & Katzberg, NYC. Prof. Nat. Inst. of Trial Advocacy, Benjamin N. Cardozo Law Sch., 1983—; mem. bd. dirs. NY Council of Defense Lawyers, 1989—91, Ea. Dist. Assn., 1989—; prof. Legal Aid Soc. Trial Advocacy Program, 1990—93. Mem.: ABA (co-chmn, white collar crime com. 1993—97), NY County Lawyers Assn., NY State Bar Assn. Office: Kaplan & Katzberg 767 Third Ave New York NY 10017 Office Phone: 212-750-3100. Office Fax: 212-750-8628.

KATZEN, JAY KENNETH, retired diplomat, state legislator, government agency administrator; b. NYC, Aug. 23, 1936; s. Perry and Minerva (Rich) K.; m. Patricia Anne Morse, May 30, 1963; children: John Timothy Rich, David Mark Nicholas, James Alexander Scott. BA magna cum laude, Princeton U., 1958; MA, Yale U., 1959. Joined U.S. Fgn. Svc., 1959; fgn. svc. officer Dept. State, Washington, 1959-60, 62-63, 66-69; consular-comml. officer Am. consulate gen. Sydney, Australia, 1960-62; econ. officer Am. embassy Bujumbura, Burundi, 1963-64; labor attaché Am. Embassy, Kinshasa, Zaire, 1964-66, polit. officer Bucharest, Rumania, 1969-71, counselor of embassy Bamako, Mali, 1971—73; adviser U.S. Mission to UN, NYC, 1973-77; with Office of Vice Pres., Washington, 1977, Nat. War Coll., 1977; chargé d'affaires Am. Embassy, Brazzaville, Congo, 1977-78; polit. adv. to U.S. del. World Adminstrv. Radio Conf., 1979; pres., CEO Victims of Communism Meml. Found., Washington, 2003—04; regional dir., acting chief of staff Peace Corps., 2004—. Vis. prof. Boston Coll. Grad. Sch. Mgmt., 1978-79; vice-chmn. bd. dirs. African Devel. Found., 1988-90; bd. advisers Patterson Sch. Diplomacy and Internat. Commerce, U. Ky., 1989—, Duke U. Primate Ctr., 1986—. Chmn. Fauquier County (Va.) Rep. Com., 1992-94; elected to Ho. of Dels. of Va. Gen. Assembly, 1993, 95, 97, 99; Republican candidate lt. gov., Va., 2001; Republican candidate U.S. Congress, 2002. Mem. Princeton Quadrangle Club, Army and Navy Club, Dacor House Club, Lions Internat. Home: PO Box 9917 Arlington VA 22219

KATZEN, MOLLIE, writer; b. Rochester, NY, Oct. 13, 1950; d. Leon and Betty (Heller) K.; m. Jeffrey David Black, June 26, 1983 (div. Oct. 1985); 1 child, Samuel Katzen Black; m. Carl Shames, Dec. 12, 1986. BFA, San Francisco Art Inst., 1972. Author, illustrator: Mossewood Cookbook, 1977, Enchanted Broccoli Forest, 1982, Still Life with Menu, 1988, Molly Katzen's Still Life Sampler, 1993, Pretend Soup & Other Real Recipes: A Cookbook for Preschoolers & Up, 1994, Enchanted Broccoli Forest, 1995, Moosewood Cookbook Classics: Miniature Edition, 1996. Recipient Graphic Arts award Arnot Art Gallery, 1976, Cert. of Commendation, Calif. State Assembly, 1989. Jewish. Avocations: classical pianist, painter. Office: care Ten Speed Press PO Box 7123 Berkeley CA 94707-0123

KATZEN, RAPHAEL, consulting chemical engineer; b. Balt., July 28, 1915; s. Isidor and Esther (Stein) K.; m. Selma M. Siegel, June 19, 1938; 1 child, Nancy Katzen Riedel. B.Chem. Engring., Poly. U. Bklyn., 1936, M.Chem. Engring., 1938, D.Chem. Engring., 1942. Registered profl. engr. in 16 states. Tech. dir. Northwood Chem. Co., Phelps, Wis., 1938-42; project mgr. Diamond Alkali Co., Painesville, Ohio, 1942-44; mgr. engring. divsn. Vulcan, Cin., 1944-53; mng. partner Raphael Katzen Assos., Cin., 1953-80; chmn. Raphael Katzen Assos. Internat., Inc., 1956—97. Contbr. articles to profl. jours; patentee in field. Mem. Cin. Air Pollution Bd., 1972-75. Recipient Disting. Alumnus award Poly. Inst. Bklyn., 1970, Dedicated Alumnus award, 1977; Disting. cons. award Ohio Assn. Cons. Engrs., 1978; Profl. Accomplishment, Disting. Engr. award Tech. and Sci. Socs. Coun., 1978, 79, Personal Achievement in Chem. Engring. award Chem. Engring., McGraw Hill, 1988, Renewable Fuels Assn. Lifetime Achievement award, 1999, 16th Ann. Fuel Ethanol Workshop award of excellence, 2000, others; Poly. U. fellow, 1981. Fellow AIChE (Chem. Engring. Practice award 1986, Robert L. Jacks Meml. award 1990, Founders award 2001), Am. Inst. Chemists; mem. NAE (elected), TAPPI, PAPTAC, Am. Chem. Soc. (Spl. Lifetime Achievement award 2000), Am. Arbitration Assn., Am. Club Miami, Fla., Sigma Xi, Tau Beta Pi, Phi Lambda Upsilon. Home: 27901 Riverwalk Way Bonita Springs FL 34134-8692 Office: 9220 Bonita Beach Rd Ste 200 Bonita Springs FL 34135-4231 Office Phone: 239-498-2552. E-mail: rkatzenpe@aol.com. *We are put on this earth to produce to the best of our ability to improve the lot of mankind, and our talents should not be wasted through lack of effort or misguided direction.*

KATZEN, SALLY, lawyer, educator; b. Pitts., Nov. 22, 1942; d. Nathan and Hilda (Schwartz) K.; m. Timothy B. Dyk, Oct. 31, 1981; 1 child, Abraham Benjamin. BA magna cum laude, Smith Coll., Northampton, Mass., 1964; JD magna cum laude, U. Mich., Ann Arbor, 1967. Bar: DC 1968, US Supreme Ct. 1971. Congl. intern Senate Subcom. on Constl. Rights, Washington, 1963; legal rsch. asst. civil rights divsn. Dept. Justice, Washington, 1965; law clk. to Judge J. Skelly Wright US Ct. Appeals (DC cir.), 1967-68; assoc. Wilmer, Cutler & Pickering, Washington, 1968-75, ptnr., 1975-79, 81-93; gen. counsel Coun. on Wage and Price Stability, 1979-80, dep. dir. for policy, 1980-81; adminstr. Office of Info. and Regulatory Affairs Office of Mgmt. and Budget, Washington, 1993-98, counselor to the dir., 1999-2000, dep. dir. mgmt., 2000-2001; dep. dir. Nat. Econ. Coun. The White House, Washington, 1998-99; sr. policy advisor Joe Lieberman for Pres., 2003—04. Pub. mem. Adminstrv. Conf. US, 1988—93, govt. mem. and vice chmn., 1993—95; adj. prof. Georgetown U. Law Ctr., 1988, 1990—92; resident scholar and lectr. Smith Coll., 2001—04; vis. lectr., fellow Johns Hopkins U., 2002—04, 2006; adj. prof. U. Pa. Law Sch., 2003; vis. prof. U. Mich. Law Sch., 2004—05, 2007; lectr. U. Mich., 2005—07; vis. prof. George Mason U. Law Sch., 2006, 07. Editor-in-chief U. Mich. Law Rev., 1966-67. Mem. com. visitors U. Mich. Law Sch., 1972-2006, mem. dean's adv. coun., 2006-; mem. nat. rsch. couns. sci. review panel Nat. Acads. Sci., 2006. Fellow ABA (house of dels. 1978-80, 89-91, coun. adminstrv. law sect. 1979-82, chmn. adminstrv. law and regulatory practice sect. 1988-89, governing com. forum com.

comm. law 1979-82, chmn. standing com. Nat. Conf. Groups 1989-92, chmn. e-rule making com. 2007-); mem. DC Bar Assn., Prettyman-Leventhal Inn of Ct. (exec. com. 1988-90, counselor 1990-91), Women's Bar Assn., FCC Bar Assn. (exec. com. 1984-87, pres. 1990-91), Women's Legal Def. Fund (pres. 1977, v.p. 1978), Order of Coif. Home: 4638 30th St NW Washington DC 20008-2127 Personal E-mail: dykatzen@earthlink.net.

KATZENBACH, NICHOLAS DEBELLEVILLE, former United States attorney general; b. Phila., Jan. 17, 1922; s. Edward Lawrence and Marie Louise (Hilson) K.; m. Lydia King Phelps Stokes, June 8, 1946; children—Christopher Wolcott, John Strong Minor, Maria Louise Hiltson, Anne deBelleville. BA, Princeton U., 1945; LL.B., Yale U., 1947; Rhodes scholar, Balliol Coll., Oxford U., Eng., 1947-49. Bar: NJ 1950, Conn. 1955, NY 1972. With firm Katzenbach, Gildea & Rudner, Trenton, NJ, 1950; atty.-adviser Office Gen. Counsel Air Force, 1950-52, part-time cons., 1952-56; assoc. prof. law Yale Law Sch., 1952-56; prof. law U. Chgo. Law Sch., 1956-60; asst. atty. gen. US Dept. Justice, 1961-62, dep. atty. gen., 1962-64, acting atty. gen., 1964, atty. gen., 1965-66, under sec. state, 1966-69; sr. v.p., gen. counsel IBM Corp., 1969-84, sr. v.p. law and external relations, 1984-86, also bd. dirs.; ptnr. Riker, Danzig, Scherer, Hyland & Perretti, Morristown, NJ, 1986-91; non-exec. chmn. MCI, 2004—06. Author: (with Morton A. Kaplan) The Political Foundations of International Law, 1961; editor-in-chief: Yale Law Jour, 1947; contbr. articles to profl. jours. Served to 1st lt. USAAF, 1941-45. Decorated Air medal with three clusters; Ford Found. fellow, 1960-61 Mem. AAAS, ABA, Am. Law Inst. (mem. coun.), Am. Judicature Soc., Am. Philos. Soc. Democrat. Episcopalian.

KATZENBERG, JEFFREY, film company executive; b. NYC, Dec. 21, 1950; m. Marilyn Siegel, 1975; children: Laura, David. Asst. to chmn., chief exec. officer Paramount Pictures, NYC, 1975-77, exec. dir. mktg., 1977; v.p. programming Paramount TV, 1977-78; v.p., feature prodn. Paramount Pictures, 1978-80, sr. v.p., prodn. motion picture divsn., 1980—82, pres. prodn., motion pictures & TV, 1982—84; chmn. Walt Disney Studios, Burbank, Calif., 1984—94; co-founder (with Steven Spielberg & David Geffen), ptnr. DreamWorks SKG, Universal City, Calif., 1994—; CEO DreamWorks Animation, Inc., Glendale, Calif., 1994—. Chmn. Motion Picture and TV Fund; bd. dirs. Found. Motion Picture Pioneers; co-chmn. creative rights com. Directors Guild Am.; co-chmn. com. on profl. status of writers Writers Guild Am. Co-prodr.: Nightmare Before Christmas, 1993, exec. prodr.: Prince of Egypt, 1998, Road to El Dorado, 2000, Chicken Run, 2000, Joseph: King of Dreams, 2000, Shrek 2, 2004, Shark Take, 2004; prodr.: (films) Shrek, 2001, Spirit: Stallion of the Cimarron, 2002, Sinbad: Legend of the Seven Seas, 2003; exec. prodr.: (TV series) Father of the Pride, 2003, The Contender, 2005—. Bd. dirs. AIDS Project LA, Michael J. Fox Found. Parkinson's Rsch., Simon Wiesenthal Ctr., Calif. Inst. Arts, Cedars-Sinai Med. Ctr., Geffen Playhouse, Am. Mus. of Moving Image. Named one of 50 Most Powerful People in Hollywood, Premiere mag., 2005—06. Office: Dreamworks SKG 1000 Flower St Glendale CA 91201-7500

KATZEN-GUTHRIE, JOY, performance artist, engineering executive; b. Memphis, Nov. 11, 1958; d. Eli and Bess (Bloomfield) Katzen; m. Mark C. Guthrie, Aug. 7, 1983. BFA in Music cum laude, Stephens Coll., Columbia, Mo., 1980, BA in Comms. magna cum laude, 1980. Traffic dir. WPLP News/Talk Radio, Pinellas Park, Fla., 1981-83, ops. mgr., 1982-83; traffic reporter WUSA-FM and WDAE-AM, Tampa, Fla., 1985-86; announcer, programmer, pub. rels. mgr. WXCR-FM Classics 92, Safety Harbor, Fla., 1983-87; v.p., dir. Katzen and Guthrie Assocs., Inc., Palm Harbor, Fla., 1987—; pres. Tune-of-the-Century Music, 1989—. Creator, designer, owner website www.JoyfulNoise.net, 1998—. Co-author, composer musical comedy Once Around Manhattan, 1985; author: (one-act play) A Murder in Pine County, 1987; composer, lyricist some 750 songs; performance artist CD/Cassette albums Seasons of Joy, 1989, Heart of Ancient Promise, 1993, New State of Mind, 1993, How Good and Pleasant, 1996, Passages, 1998, SoulStream, 1998, Favorite Melody, 2005, A Steadfast Bridge, ltd. edit., 2005, Favorite Melody vol. 2, 2006; studio vocalist Jeff Arthur Prodns., St. Petersburg, Fla., 1985, 86, Studio C. Prodns., Tampa, 1991-92; studio vocalist, jingle writer West End Rec., Tampa, 1989, 90; session musician Hurricane Pass Studios, Clearwater, Fla., 1993—. Music dir. religious sch. Temple B'nai Israel, Clearwater, 1988-89; music dir. Perry-Mansfield Performing Arts Camp, Steamboat Springs, Colo., 1987; cantorial soloist B'nai B'rith Hillel Found., Tampa, 1990-93, Temple Shir Shalom, Gainesville, 1994-99, Congregation B'nai Emmunah, Tarpon Springs, 1996-99, Congregation Aliyah, Clearwater, 1999-2000, Temple B'nai Israel, Clearwater, 2000-2002, 2005, Temple Beth El, Sarasota, 2002-2004. Recipient 1st and 3d place awards Memphis Songwriters Assn. Competition, 1988, others; Pinellas County Arts Coun. grantee, 1997, 2004. Mem. AAUW (dir. pub. rels. 1985-97), ASCAP, Songwriters Guild Am., Dramatists Guild, Nat. Acad. Songwriters, Nashville Songwriters Assn. Internat., Guild of Temple Musicians, Fla. Music Assn., Women's Musicians' Alliance (bd. dirs. 1998—), Hadassah (life). Democrat. Jewish. Avocations: photography, travel, music, theater, films, books. Home and Office: 2487 Indian Trl E Palm Harbor FL 34683-2806 Home Phone: 727-785-4568; Office Phone: 727-785-4568, 800-354-1302. Personal E-mail: joyfulnoise@earthlink.net.

KATZENSTEIN, ANDREW M., lawyer; b. Pa., Oct. 13, 1957; BA magna cum laude, U. Mich., 1979, JD cum laude, 1982; LLM in Taxation, U. San Diego, 1985. Bar: Calif. 1982, NY 1990, US Tax Ct. Ptnr. Katten, Muchin & Rosenman, LLP, LA. Tchr. estate tax UCLA Law Sch.; tchr. estate planning Golden Gate U. Grad. Tax Prog. Contbr. articles to profl. publs. Named a So. Calif. Super Lawyer, LA Mag. and So. Calif. Super Lawyers mag., 2004, 2005, 2006; named one of Top 100 Wealth Advs. in N.Am., Citywealth, 2006, Top 100 Attys., Worth mag., 2006. Mem.: Am. Coll. Trust and Estate Counsel, Am. Com. for Weizmann Inst. of Sci., LA County Bar Assn., Beverly Hills Bar Assn., Cure Diabetes Now. Office: Katten Muchin Rosenman Ste 2600 2029 Century Park E Los Angeles CA 90067-3012 also: Ste 450 260 Sheridan Ave Palo Alto CA 94306-2047 Office Phone: 310-788-4540. Office Fax: 310-712-8420. E-mail: andrew.katzenstein@kattenlaw.com.*

KATZMAN, DAVID, investment company and professional sports team executive; BA in Acctg. and Fin., Mich. State U.; student, Detroit Coll. Law. Founder DeeKay Enterprises, Inc., 1987; pres. Home Depot S.O.C., 1997—2000; mng. ptnr. Camelot Ventures, 1999—; vice chmn. Cleve. Cavaliers, 2005—, Quicken Loans. Bd. dirs. 1-800-Contacts, 2003, RealAge.com, ePrize. Office: Camelot Ventures 20555 Victor Pky Ste 100 Livonia MI 48152 E-mail: dkatzman@camelotventures.com.*

KATZMAN, IRWIN, lawyer; b. Windsor, Ont., Can., June 29, 1931; s. Aaron and Rose (Tarnow) K.; m. Helen Frances Blecher, Dec. 20, 1952 (dec. Feb. 1998); children: Barry, Harriet, Kenneth, Rhonda, Aaron; m. Toby Lyman, Aug. 15, 1999. BS, Wayne State U., 1953, MBA, 1963; JD cum laude, Loyola U., LA, 1974. Bar: Calif. 1974, U.S. Dist. Ct. (cen. dist.) Calif. 1974, U.S. Ct. Appeals (9th cir.) 1980, U.S. Supreme Ct. 1980, U.S. Tax Ct. 1988. Chemist E.I. Dupont de Nemours, Phila., 1953-54; asst. quality mgr. Chrysler Corp., Detroit, 1956-63; mfg. plans mgr. Ford Motor Co., Newport Beach, Calif., 1963-70; prodn. control mgr. Dresser Industries, Huntington Park, Calif., 1970-73; purchasing mgr. Hughes Aircraft Co., Inglewood, Calif., 1973-74; v.p. First Alliance Mortgage Co., Santa Ana, Calif., 1976-77; pvt. practice Anaheim, Calif., 1975-94, San Jose, Calif., 1995—. Pres. Temple Beth Emet, Anaheim, 1988-90. With U.S. Army, 1953-56. Mem. State Bar of Calif., Orange County Bar Assn., Santa Clara County Bar Assn., Alpha Epsilon Pi (life). Avocations: sailing, golf, amateur radio. Office: 8346 Riesling Way San Jose CA 95135-1435 Office Phone: 408-223-9372.

KATZMAN, JOHN S., educational organization executive; b. Oct. 10, 1959; s. Lawrence and Shirley Katzman; m. Alicia Ernst, Aug. 7, 1993; 2 children. BA in Architecture, Princeton U., 1981. Founder The Princeton Review, NYC, 1981, CEO, 1981—2007, pres., 1981—2000, exec. chmn., 2007—; dir. Student Advantage. Adv. bd. Inst. Internat. Rsch., NYC; bd. advisors Silver Shield Found., NYC. Co-author: Class Action, 1995. Office: The Princeton Review 2315 Broadway New York NY 10024*

KATZMAN, LAUREN I., special education educator, consultant; b. Stuttgart, Germany, Mar. 17, 1961; EdD, Harvard U., Cambridge, Mass., 2004. Spl. edn. tchr. various sch., 1983—98; prof. spl. edn. Boston U., 2005—. Office: Boston Univ 2 Sherborn St Boston MA 02215 Office Phone: 617-353-3253. Business E-Mail: lkatzman@bu.edu.

KATZMAN, ROBERT, neurologist, educator; b. Denver, Nov. 29, 1925; s. Maurice and Leah K. (Schnitt) K.; m. Nancy Bernstein, Sept. 2, 1947; children: David Jonathan, Daniel Mark. BS, U. Chgo., 1949, MS, 1951; MD cum laude, Harvard U., 1953. Diplomate Am. Bd. Psychiatry and Neurology. Intern Boston City Hosp., 1953-54; chief resident Neurol. Inst. Columbia Presbyn. Hosp., NYC, 1956-57; faculty mem. Albert Einstein Coll. Medicine, NYC, 1957-84, prof., chmn. neurology dept., 1964-84, dir. Resnick Gerontology Ctr., 1979-84; chmn. dept. neuroscis. U. Calif., San Diego, 1984-90, Florence Riford prof. neuroscis. and rsch. in Alzheimer's disease, 1984-94, rsch. prof. neuroscis., 1994—2002, prof. emeritus neurosci., 2003—. Mem. clin. rsch. adv. com. Nat. Found. March of Dimes, 1975-76; mem. adv. coun. Nat. Inst. on Aging, 1982-85; chmn. med. and sci. bd. Alzheimer Disease and Related Disorders Assn., Chgo., 1979-85; mem. adv. panel on Alzheimer's disease HHS, 1987-93. Co-author: Brain Electrolytes and Fluid Metabolism, 1973, Neurology of Aging, 1983, Alzheimer Disease: The Changing View, 2000; co-editor: Basic Neurochemistry, 1972-81, Principles of Geriatric Neurology, 1992, Alzheimer Disease, 1994, Alzheimers Disease, 2d edit., 1999; mem. editl. bd. Clin. Neuroscience Rsch. Jour., ARNMD, 2001—. With USN, 1944-46, PTO. Recipient Humanitarian award Alzheimer's Disease and Related Disorders Assn., 1985, Disting. Svc. award, 1989, Allied Achievement in Aging award Allied Signal Corp., 1985, Henderson Meml. award Am. Geriatric Soc., 1986, 7th Ann. Chgo. Rita Hayworth Gala award Alzheimer's Assn., 1994, Crystal Tower award Alzheimer's Assn., 1998, IPA Luigi Amaducci Meml. award Internat. Psychogeriatric Assn., 2003, Genesis award Alzheimer's Assn., 2005; Robert Katzman Clin. Rsch. Tng. fellowship, Am. Acad. Neurology Found., 2006. Fellow Am. Acad. Neurology (S. Weir Mitchell award 1960, George W. Jacoby award 1989, co-recipient Potamkin prize Alzheimer's disease rsch. 1992); mem. Assn. Rsch. in Nervous and Mental Disorders (pres. 1977), Am. Physiol. Soc., Inst. Medicine NAS, Am. Neurol. Assn. (pres. 1985-86), Internat. Soc. Alzheimer's Disease Rsch., Alpha Omega Alpha. Office: U Calif San Diego Sch Medicine 9500 Gilman Dr Dept 0949 La Jolla CA 92093-0949 Office Phone: 858-622-5850. Business E-Mail: rkatzman@ucsd.edu.

KATZMANN, GARY STEPHEN, judge; b. NYC, 1953; AB summa cum laude, Columbia U., 1973; MLitt, Oxford U., 1976; MPPM, JD, Yale U., 1979. Bar: Mass. 1982, U.S. Dist. Ct. Mass. 1983, U.S. Ct. Appeals (1st cir.) 1983, D.C. 1984, U.S. Ct. Appeals (2d cir.) 1987, N.Y. 1990, U.S. Ct. Appeals (fed. cir.) 1991. Law clk. to judge U.S. Dist. Ct. (so. dist.) N.Y., NYC, 1979-80; law clk. to Hon. Stephen Breyer U.S. Ct. Appeals (1st cir.), Boston, 1980-81; rsch. assoc. ctr. criminal justice Law Sch. Harvard U., Cambridge, Mass., 1981-83; asst. U.S. atty., chief appellate atty., dep. chief criminal div., chief legal counsel U.S. Atty.'s Office, Mass., 1983—2004; assoc. dep. atty. gen. U.S. Dept. Justice, Washington, 1993-94; assoc. justice Mass. Appeals Ct., 2004—. Lectr. Harvard U. Law Sch., 1989-97; project dir. J.F. Kennedy Sch. Govt., Harvard U., 1997-2000; participant Yale Law Sch. Sentencing Seminar, 1999; mem. bd. visitors Discovering Justice. Author: Inside the Criminal Process, 1991, Securing Our Children's Future: New Approaches to Juvenile Justice and Youth Violence, 2002. Recipient Dir's. Superior Performance awards U.S. Dept. Justice, 1993, 2003; fellow Harvard U., 1997-2003, Governance Inst. Mem. ABA, Gov.'s Juvenile Justice Adv. Com., Phi Beta Kappa. Office: Mass Appeals Ct John Adams Courtho One Pemberton Sq Ste 3500 Boston MA 02108-1767

KATZMANN, ROBERT ALLEN, federal judge; b. NYC, 1953; AB summa cum laude, Columbia U., 1973; MA in Govt., Harvard U., 1975, PhD in Govt., 1978; JD, Yale U., 1980. Bar: Mass. 1982, NY, US Ct. Appeals (1st cir.) 1983, DC 1984, US Dist. Ct. Mass. 1984. Law clk. to judge US Ct. Appeals (1st cir.), Concord, NH, 1980-81; rsch. assoc. Brookings Instn., Washington, 1981-85, fellow, 1985-99, acting dir. govt. studies, 1998; adj. prof. law, pub. policy Georgetown U., Washington, 1984-92, William J. Walsh prof. govt., prof. law, 1992-99; pres. Governance Inst., Washington, 1986-99; judge US Ct. Appeals (2nd cir.), 1999—; adjunct prof. of Law New York University, New York, 2001—. Vis. prof. polit. sci. UCLA, Washington program, 1990-92; vis. chair, Wayne Morse prof. law and politics U. Oreg., 1992; cons. Fed. Cts. Study Com., 1990; adj. prof. law NYU, 2001— Author: Regulatory Bureaucracy: The Federal Trade Commission and Antitrust Policy, 1980, Institutional Disability: The Saga of Transportation Policy for the Disabled, 1986, Courts and Congress, 1997; co-editor: Managing Appeals in Federal Courts, 1988; editor: Judges and Legislators, 1988, The Law Firm and the Public Good, 1995; editor, co-author, Daniel Patrick Moynihan: The Intellectual in Public Life, 1998, 2d edit, 2004; article and book editor Yale U. Law Jour., 1979-80. Recipient Chas. E. Merriam award, Am. Political Sci. Assn., 2001. Fellow: Am. Acad. Arts and Scis.; mem.: ABA (vice chair com. on govt. ops. and separation of powers 1991—94, pub. mem. adminstrn. conf. 1992—95, adminstrv. law sect.), Am. Assn. Law Schs. (chmn. legis. sect. 1999—2000), Am. Polit. Sci. Assn. (Charles E. Merriam award 2001), Am. Judicature Soc. (bd. dirs. 1992—98), Phi Beta Kappa. Office: US Ct Appeals 2d Cir 40 Foley Sq New York NY 10007-1502*

KATZOWITZ SHENFIELD, LAUREN, philanthropy consultant; m. Marc Shenfield. BS in Comparative Lit. with honors, Brandeis U., 1970; MS with honors, Columbia U., 1971. With Newsweek mag.; then with Phila. Bull.; freelance writer, editor, cons., until 1975; cons. Ford Found., 1972-75; mgr. PBS programs Exxon Corp., 1978-81; mgr. Exxon Rsch. and Engrng. Co., 1981-84; regional liaison for Europe and Africa, Exxon Corp., 1984-86; exec. dir. Philanthropy Advisors - A Svc. of UJA-Fedn. of N.Y., 1986—; pres. Lauren Katzowitz Cons., Croton on Hudson, NY, 1986—. Mem. profl. adv. coun. Met. Mus. of Art, 2000-06, Central Park Conservancy, 2001—; bd. dirs. N.Y. Regional Assn. of Grantmakers, 2000-06, Women and Philanthropy, 2003-06. Named one of 12 Women to Watch in the Eighties, Ladies' Home Jour., 1979. Office: Philanthropy Advisors 130 E 59th St New York NY 10022 Home Phone: 914-271-3141; Office Phone: 212-836-1358. Business E-Mail: katzowitzl@philanthropyadvisorsny.org.

KATZUNG, BERTRAM GEORGE, pharmacologist; b. Mineola, NY, June 11, 1932; m. Alice V. Camp; children: Katharine Blanche, Brian Lee. BA, Syracuse U., 1953; MD, SUNY, Syracuse, 1957; PhD, U. Calif., San Francisco, 1962. Prof. U. Calif., San Francisco, 1958—. Author: Pharmacology, Examination and Board Review, 2007, Basic and Clinical Pharmacology, 2006; contbr. to profl. jours. Markle scholar. Mem. AAAS, AAUP, Am. Soc. Pharmacology and Exptl. Therapeutics, Biophys. Soc., Fed. Am. Scientists, Internat. Soc. Heart Rsch., Soc. Gen. Physiologists, Western Pharmacology Soc., N.Y. Acad. Sci., Astron. Soc. of Pacific, Internat. Dark-Sky Assn., Nat. Deep Sky Observers Soc., Planetary Soc., Royal Astron. Soc. Canada, San Francisco Amateur Astronomers Soc., Sonoma County Astron. Soc., Profl. Photographers Am., Golden Gate Computer Soc., Phi Beta Kappa, Alpha Omega Alpha. Office: U Calif San Francisco Dept Cellular/Molec Pharm PO Box 450 San Francisco CA 94143-0450

KAUDERER, BERNARD MARVIN, retired naval officer, consultant; b. Phila., July 21, 1931; s. Harry Thau and Anne Mae (Mandell) K.; m. Myra Frances Weissman, Mar. 21, 1954; children: Howard Todd, Heidi Susanne, Robin Beth. BS, U.S. Naval Acad., 1953. Commd. ensign U.S. Navy, 1953, advanced through grades to vice adm., 1983; comdr. Submarine Group Five, 1977-79; dep. dir. research, devel., test and evaluation Office Chief Naval Ops., Navy Dept., Washington, 1979-81; comdr. submarine forces U.S. Pacific Fleet, 1981-83; comdr. submarine force U.S. Atlantic Fleet, 1983-86; ret. U.S. Navy, 1986. Cons. to industry and govt. Decorated D.S.M., Legion of Merit, Meritorious Service medal, Navy Commendation medal, Navy Expeditionary medal. Mem. Naval Submarine League (dir.), Masons, Shriners. Home: 7025 Ibis Pl Carlsbad CA 92011-5011

KAUFFMAN, B. SUZANNE, historian, genealogist; b. Macomb, Ill., June 14, 1930; d. Kenneth Dill and Louise (Zimmerli) Murrell; m. Thomas Lindenfelser (div. 1953); children: Charles Thomas II, Donald Mark. BA, U. Fla., 1982. Field archaeologist Yorktown (Va.) Hist. Ctr., 1985-86; sr. assoc. First Investors Corp., NYC, 1986—2001; ret., 2001. Rschr. in field. Oral historian Ky. History Ctr.; historian, genealogist Anderson Pub. Libr. Mem. Nature Conservancy, Nat. Wildlife Assn., Whale Adoption/Friends of the Forest, Ky. Hist. Soc. (Rsch. fellowship 2005), Ky. Geneol. Soc., McDonough County Geneal. Soc. Avocations: herb gardening, yoga, painting.

KAUFFMAN, CARL HERBERT, retired music educator; b. Neptune, NJ, Nov. 15, 1944; s. Herbert Percival and Florence Ryan Kauffman; m. Lura Gretelle Nail, Aug. 12, 1966; children: Rebecca Ruth, Matthew Monroe. MusEdB, Loyola U., New Orleans, 1966; MusEdM, George Peabody Coll., Nashville, 1967; PhD, Peabody Coll. Vanderbilt U., Nashville, 1982. Cert. tchr., highly qualified tchr. State of Ala. Band dir. Metro Nashville Pub. Schs., 1969—96, Elberta Mid. Sch. Baldwin County Pub. Schs., Bay Minette, Ala., 1996—2006. Sec.-treas. Mid. Tenn. Sch. Band and Orch. Assn., Nashville, 1984—96; editor Tenn. Musician, 1990—94. Bd. dir. Lake Forest Property Owners Assn., Daphne, Ala., 2004—05. Named Tchr. of Yr., Elberta Mid. Sch., 2003—04. Mem.: NEA, Am. Fedn. Musicians, Music Educators Nat. Conf. Avocations: golf, travel, cooking. Home: 106 Betty Cir Daphne AL 36526

KAUFFMAN, DAVID LIN, lawyer; b. Mohrsville, Pa., June 13, 1930; s. James L. and A. Catherine (Mengel) Kauffman; m. Nancy Ruth Loose, July 18, 1953; children: Randolf, Eric, Scott. BA in Polit. Sci., Albright Coll., 1958; LLB, U. Md., 1964. CPA Md. Acct. Met. Edison Co., Reading, Pa., 1952—55, Easco Corp., Balt., 1958—71, sec., corp. counsel, 1971—2004; ret. With US Army, 1949. Mem.: Am. Assn. Attys.-C.P.A., Md. Soc. C.P.A.s, Md. Bar Assn., ABA. Republican. Meth.

KAUFFMAN, ERLE GALEN, geologist, paleontologist; b. Washington, Feb. 9, 1933; s. Erle Benton and Paula Virginia (Graff) K.; children: Donald Erle, Robin Lyn, Erica Jean; m. Claudia C. Johnson, Sept. 1989. BS, U. Mich., 1955, MS, 1956, PhD, 1961; MSc (hon.), Oxford U., 1970; DHC, U. Göttingen, Germany, 1987. Teaching fellow, instr. U. Mich., Ann Arbor, 1956-60; from asst. to full curator dept. paleobiology Nat. Mus. Natural History Smithsonian Instn., Washington, 1960-80; prof. geology U. Colo., Boulder, 1980-96, chmn. dept. geol. scis., 1980-84, interim dir. Energy, Minerals Applied Rsch. Ctr., 1989-91; prof. geology Ind. U., 1996—2003, prof. emeritus, 2004—. Adj. prof. geology George Washington U., Washington, 1962-80; cons. geologist, Boulder, 1980-96. Author, editor: Cretaceous Facies, Faunas and Paleoenvironments Across the Cretaceous Western Interior Basin, 1977; contbg. editor: Concepts and Methods of Biostratigraphy, 1977, Fine-grained Deposits and Biofacies of The Cretaceous Western Interior Seaway, 1985, High Resolution Event Stratigraphy, 1988, Paleontology and Evolution: Extinction Events, 1988, Extinction Events in Earth History, 1990, Evolution of the Western Interior Basin, 1993; contbr. articles. to profl. jours. Recipient U.S. Govt. Spl. Svc. award, 1969, NSF Best Tchr. award U. Colo., 1985 named Disting. Lectr. Am. Geol. Inst., 1963-64, Am. Assn. Petroleum Geologists, 1984, 85, 91, 92; Fulbright fellow Australia, 1986. Fellow Geol. Soc. Am., AAAS; mem. Paleontol. Soc. (councilor under 40, pres. elect 1981, pres. 1982, past pres. 1983, chmn. 5 coms.); mem. NRC (rep.), Palaeontol. Assn., Internat. Paleontol. Assn. (v.p. 1982-88), Paleontol. Research Instn., Soc. Sedimentary Geology (com. mem., Spl. Svc. award 1985, Best Paper award 1985, Raymond C. Moore Paleontology medal 1991, William H. Twenhofel medal 1998), Rocky Mountain Assn. Geologists (project chief) (Scientist of Yr. 1977), Paleontol. Soc. Wash. (pres., sec., treas.), Geol. Soc. Wash. (councilor), Md. Acad. Scis. (hon. Paleontology sect.), Sigma Xi, Phi Kappa Phi, Sigma Gamma Epsilon. Democrat. Avocations: music, fishing, climbing, photography. Office: Dept Geol Sci Ind Univ 1001 E 10th St Bloomington IN 47405-1405 Business E-Mail: claudia@indiana.edu.

KAUFFMAN, GEORGE BERNARD, chemistry professor; b. Phila., Sept. 4, 1930; s. Philip Joseph and Laura (Fisher) K.; m. Ingeborg Salomon, June 5, 1952 (div. Dec. 1969); children: Ruth Deborah (Mrs. Martin H. Bryskier), Judith Miriam (Mrs. Mario L. Reposo); m. Laurie Marks Papazian, Dec. 21, 1969; stepchildren: Stanley Robert Papazian, Teresa Lynn Papazian Baron, Mary Ellen Papazian. BA with honors, U. Pa., 1951; PhD, U. Fla., 1956. Grad. asst. U. Fla., 1951-55; rsch. participant Oak Ridge Nat. Lab., 1955; instr. U. Tex., Austin, 1955-56; rsch. chemist Humble Oil & Refining Co., Baytown, Tex., 1956, GE, Cin., 1957, 59; asst. prof. chemistry Calif. State U., Fresno, 1956-61, assoc. prof., 1961-66, prof., 1966—. Guest lectr. coop. lecture tours Am. Chem. Soc., 1971; vis. scholar U. Calif., Berkeley, 1976, U. Puget Sound, 1978; dir. undergrad. rsch. participation program NSF, 1972. Author: Alfred Werner-Founder of Coordination Chemistry, 1966, Classics in Coordination Chemistry, Part I, 1968, Part II, 1976, Part III, 1978, Werner Centennial, 1967, Teaching the History of Chemistry, 1971, Coordination Chemistry: Its History through the Time of Werner, 1977, Inorganic Coordination Compounds, 1981, The Central Science: Essays on the Uses of Chemistry, 1984, Frederick Soddy (1877-1956): Early Pioneer in Radiochemistry, 1986, Aleksandr Porfirevich Borodin: A Chemist's Biography, 1988, Coordination Chemistry: A Century of Progress, 1994, Classics in Coordination Chemistry, 1995, Metal and Nonmetal Biguanide Complexes, 1999; contbr. articles to profl. jours.; contbg. editor: Jour. Coll. Sci. Tchg., 1973—, The Hexagon, 1980—, Polyhedron, 1983—85, Industrial Chemist, 1985—88, Jour. Chem. Edn., 1987—, Today's Chemist, 1989—91, The Chemical Intelligencer, 1994—2000, Today's Chemist at Work, 1995—, Chemical Heritage, 1996—, The Chemical Educator, 1998—, Chem. 13 News, 1998—, Pathways of Science, 2007—; guest editor: Coordination Chemistry Centennial Symposium (C3S) issue, Polyhedron, 1994; editor tape lecture series: Am. Chem. Soc., 1975—81. Named Outstanding Prof., Calif. State U. and Colls. Sys., 1973; recipient Exceptional Merit Svc. award, 1984, Meritorious Performance and Profl. Promise award, 1986-87, 88-89, Coll. Chemistry Tchr. Excellence award Mfg. Chemists Assn., 1976, Chugaev medal, 1976, Kurnakov medal, 1990, Chernyaev medal, 1991, USSR Acad. Sci., George C. Pimentel award in chem. edn. Am. Chem. Soc., 1993, Dexter award in history of chemistry, 1978, Marc-Auguste Pictet medal Soc. Physique et d'Histoire Naturelle de Genève, 1992, Pres.'s medal of Distinction, Calif. State U., Fresno, 1994, Rsch. award at an Undergraduate Instn., Am. Chem. Soc., 2000, Laudatory Decree Inst. History of Sci. and Tech. Russian Acad. Sci., 2000; Rsch. Corp. grantee, 1956-57, 57-59,

59-61, Am. Chem. Soc. Petroleum Rsch. Fund grantee, 1963-64, 69-70, NSF grantee, 1960-61, 63-64, 67-69, 76-77, NEH grantee, 1982-83; John Simon Guggenheim Meml. Found. fellow, 1972-73, grantee, 1975; Strindberg fellow Swedish Inst., Stockholm, 1983. Fellow: AAAS; mem.: Mensa, Am. Chem. Soc. (chmn. divsn. history of chemistry 1969, mem. exec. com. 1970, councilor 1976—78, George C. Pimentel award in chem. edn. 1993, Helen M. Free Pub. Outreach award 2002), Soc. History Alchemy and Chemistry, History of Sci. Soc., Assn. Univ. Pa. Chemists, AAUP, Gamma Sigma Epsilon, Alpha Chi Sigma, Phi Kappa Phi, Phi Lambda Upsilon, Sigma Xi. Home: 1609 E Quincy Ave Fresno CA 93720-2309 Office: Calif State U Dept Chemistry Fresno CA 93740-8034 Home Phone: 559-323-9123; Office Phone: 559-323-9123. Business E-Mail: georgek@csufresno.edu.

KAUFFMAN, GORDON LEE, JR., surgeon, educator; b. Grand Rapids, Mich., Mar. 30, 1946; s. Gordon Lee Sr. and Jeanne (Klunder) K.; m. Christie Lyn VanSweden, June 28, 1969; children: Gordon Lee III, Christian Anthony. BS, Wheaton Coll., 1968; MD, U. Mich., 1972. Diplomate Nat. Bd. Med. Examiners, Am. Bd. Surgery. Resident in surgery U. Mich., Ann Arbor, 1972-77; rsch. assoc. VA Wadsworth, LA, 1977-80, staff surgeon, 1977-85; asst. prof. surgery UCLA Sch. Medicine, 1979-83, assoc. prof., 1983-85; prof. surgery and physiology, chief div. gen. surgery Pa. State U., Hershey, 1985—, vice chmn. dept. surgery, 1994—. Investigator Ctr. for Ulcer Rsch. and Edn., L.A., 1979-81, key investigator, 1981-85; cons. City of Hope Nat. Med. Ctr., Duarte, Calif., 1982-85, Harbor Gen. Hosp., Torrance, Calif., 1983-85; mem. surgery and bioengring. study sect. NIH, 1990-94, mem. consensus devel. panel on helicobacterpylori, 1994. Mem. editl. bd. Surgery, 1988—, Jour. Gastrointestinal Surg., 1997—, Jour. Surg. Rsch., 1990-97, Am. Jour. Surgery, 1994-97; contbr. chpts. to books, numerous articles to profl. jours. Grantee Coun. Tobacco Rsch., 1969, VA, 1980-85; Galens Fgn. fellow, 1971, Med. Assistance Program Fgn. fellow, 1971, Frederick Coller resident fellow, 1976, James IV fellow, 1991. Mem. ACS (sec.-treas. cen. Pa. chpt. 1990-96), Assn. Acad. Surgery (chmn. edn. com. 1985-87), Am. Fedn. for Clin. Rsch., Soc. for Exptl. Biology and Medicine, Am. Gastroenterol. Assn. (chmn. abstract rev. com. 1986-87, 95-96), Soc. Univ. Surgeons (chmn. com. on publs.), Soc. Surgery of Alimentary Tract (nominating com. 1990, publ. com. 1991-93, chmn. 1994, recorder 1994-97), Frederick A. Coller Surg. Soc., Collegium Internat. Chirurgiae Digestivae, Surg. Biology Club I, Soc. Clin. Surgery (membership com. 1992-95, chmn. 1995-96), Cent. Surg. Soc. (councilman at large 1995-96), Am. Surg. Assn. (membership adv. com. 1993-97). Office: Milton S Hershey Med Ctr H149 500 University Dr Hershey PA 17033-2391 Office Fax: 717-531-4335. Business E-Mail: gkauffman@psu.edu.

KAUFFMAN, MATTHEW, journalist; b. Princeton, NJ, Oct. 5, 1961; m. Wendy Nelson-Kauffman; 2 children. BA, Vassar Coll. Reporter Hartford (Conn.) Courant, 1986—. Co-recipient Worth Bingham prize, Nat. Press Found., 2007, George Polk award for Mil. Reporting, 2007; named Reporter of Yr., Hartford Courant. Office: Hartford Courant 285 Broad St Hartford CT 06155 Office Phone: 860-241-6200.*

KAUFFMAN, ROBERT A., lawyer; b. Atlantic City, Aug. 5, 1963; BA, U. Pa., 1985, JD, 1988. Bar: Pa. 1989, Fla. 1989. With Reed Smith, LLP, Phila., 1988—92; asst. U.S. atty. criminal and asset forfeiture divsn. Phila., 1992—96; ptnr. Reed Smith, LLP, Phila., 1997—2003; shareholder Berger & Montague, Phila., 2003—04; sr. v.p., gen. counsel Harleysville Group, Inc., Harleysville, Pa., 2004—, chief governace officer, 2004—. Office: Harleysville Group Inc 355 Maple Ave Harleysville PA 19438-2297 Office Phone: 215-256-5173. Office Fax: 215-256-5631.

KAUFFMAN, STEPHEN BLAIR, law librarian, educator; b. St. Louis, Sept. 25, 1948; s. William Porter and Patricia Mary (Cain) Kauffman; m. Susan Heffernan, Jan. 24, 1971 (dec. Aug. 1972); m. Mary Ann Royle, Aug. 24, 1979 (div. 1997); children: Ashley, Stephanie, Cameron. BS, U. Mo., St. Louis, 1971; JD, U. Mo., Kansas City, 1975, LLM, 1976; MLL, U. Wash., 1977. Bar: Mo. 1975. Law libr. Reiderer Eisberg, Kansas City, Mo., 1973—75; law libr. asst. U. Wash., Seattle, 1976—77; law libr. Nat. Jud. Coll., Reno, 1977—81; asst. prof. of law No. Ill. U., DeKalb, 1981—84, law libr. dir. and assoc. prof., 1984—88; prof. law., law libr. dir. U. Wis., Madison, 1988—94; affiliate faculty Sch. of Library and Info. Studies, 1992—94; prof. law., law libr. Yale U., New Haven, 1994—. Mem. adv. bd. Conn. State Law Libr. Sys., 1994—; bd. dirs. LLMC, 2000—04; bd. academic adv. Oceana Publ., 1999—2000; bd. adv. Assn. of Bar City NY, 1996—98. Contbr. articles to profl. jours.; co-author (with Bonnie Collier): Law in America: An Illustrated Celebration, 2001. Mem.: ABA, New England Consortium of Law Libraries (pres. 2000—02), Mo. Bar Assn., Spl. Librs. Assn., Am. Assn. Law Librs. Democrat. Office: Yale Law Sch PO Box 208215 New Haven CT 06520 Home: 41 Old Smugglers Rd Branford CT 06405 Business E-Mail: blair.kauffman@yale.edu.

KAUFFMAN, WILLIAM JOSEPH, editor, writer; b. Batavia, NY, Nov. 15, 1959; s. Edward Joseph and Sandra Jean (Baker) K.; m. Lucine Margaret Andonian, May 22, 1987; 1 child, Gretel. BA, U. Rochester, 1981. Rsch. asst. Senator D.P. Moynihan, Washington, 1981-82, legis. asst., 1982-83; asst. editor Reason, Santa Barbara, Calif., 1985-86, Washington, 1986-87; assoc. editor The Am. Enterprise, 1994—2006. Author: Every Man a King, 1989, Country Towns of New York, 1994, America First! Its History, Culture and Politics, 1995, With Good Intentions? Reflections on the Myth of Progress in America, 1998, Dispatches from the Muckdog Gazette, 2003, Look Homeward, America, 2006. Bd. dirs. Genesee Landmark Soc., 1993—, Holland Purchase Hist. Soc., 1993—, Genesee County Baseball Club, 2002-. Roman Catholic. Avocations: astronomy, music, collecting coins and political campaign items. Home: 28 Chapel St PO Box 266 Elba NY 14058-0266 Office Phone: 585-757-2455.

KAUFFMANN, STANLEY JULES, author; b. NYC, Apr. 24, 1916; s. Joseph H. and Jeannette (Steiner) K.; m. Laura Cohen, Feb. 5, 1943. B.F.A., NYU, 1935. Mem. Washington Sq. Players, 1931-41; asso. editor Bantam Books, 1949-52; editor-in-chief Ballantine Books, 1952-56, consulting editor, 1957-59; editor Alfred A. Knopf, 1959-60; film critic New Republic, NYC, 1958-65, 67—, assoc. lit. editor, 1966-67; theater critic NY Times, NYC, 1966, New Republic, NYC, 1969-79, Saturday Rev., 1979-85. Condr. program The Art of Film, Channel 13, N.Y.C., 1963-67; vis. prof. Sch. of Drama, Yale U., 1967-86, 95, 97; vis. prof. CUNY, 1973-76, 77-92, Hunter Coll, 1993-05; Disting. vis. prof. Adelphi U., 1992-94, profl. performing arts, 1994-96. Author: The Hidden Hero, 1949, The Tightrope, 1952, A Change of Climate, 1954, Man of the World, 1956, A World on Film, 1966, Figures of Light, 1971; editor: (with Bruce Henstell) American Film Criticism: from the Beginnings to Citizen Kane, 1973, Living Images, 1975, Persons of The Drama, 1976, Before My Eyes, 1980, Albums of Early Life, 1980, Theater Criticisms, 1983, Field of View, 1986, Distinguishing Features, 1994, Regarding Film, 2001, Albums of a Life, 2007. Recipient George Jean Nathan award for dramatic criticism, 1972-73, George Polk award for criticism, 1982, Outstanding Tchr. award Assn. for Theater in Higher Edn., 1995, Telluride Film Festival medal, 1998; Ford Found. fellow for study abroad, 1964, 71, hon. fellow Morse Coll., Yale U., 1964, Guggenheim fellow, 1979-80. Address: 10 W 15th St New York NY 10011-6838

KAUFFOLD, RUTH ELIZABETH, psychologist; b. Decatur, Ill., Sept. 5, 1946; d. James Henry and Elizabeth Opal Kauffold; m. Paul Dwight Entner, Aug. 23, 1968; 1 child, James Paul. BA, Cedarville Coll., Ohio, 1968; MEd, Wright State U., 1972; MS, U. Dayton, 1986; PhD, The Union Inst., 1997. Tchr. Springfield Pub. Schs., Ohio, 1968—72, Pomona Unified Sch. Dist., Calif., 1973—76, Bethel Sch. Dist., New Carlisle, Ohio, 1977—81; practicum Sycamore Hosp., Miamisburg, Ohio, 1994; intern, resident clin. psychology Agape Counseling Ctr., Centerville, 1995—2000. Co-hostess talk show Radio Sta. WHIO, Dayton, 1998; guest speaker Think TV, 2005—; lectr., spkr. in field. Active Missionary Project Ptnr., Lima, Peru, 1986; tchr. Far Hills Bapt. Ch., Dayton, Ohio, 1997, Fair Haven Ch., 2000-04 Jennings scholar Martha Holden Jennings Found., 1972. Mem. APA, AACC, Dayton Area Psychol. Assn. Avocations: interior design, architecture, gardening, reading, walking.

KAUFMAN, ANDREW LEE, law educator; b. Newark, Feb. 1, 1931; s. Samuel and Sylvia (Meltzer) K.; m. Linda P. Sonnenschein, June 14, 1959; children: Anne, David, Elizabeth, Daniel. AB, Harvard U., 1951, LL.B., 1954. Bar: DC 1954, Mass. 1979, US Supreme Ct. 1961. Assoc. Bilder, Bilder & Kaufman, Newark, 1954-55; law clk. to Justice Felix Frankfurter U.S Supreme Ct., 1955-57; ptnr. Kaufman, Kaufman & Kaufman, Newark, 1957-65; lectr. in law Harvard U., Cambridge, Mass., 1965-66, prof., 1966-81, Charles Stebbins Fairchild prof. law, 1981—, assoc. dean, 1986-89, vice dean acad. programming, 2005—. Author: (with others) Commercial Law, 1971, 82, Problems in Professional Responsibility, 1976, 84, 89, 2002, Cardozo, 1998. Treas. Shady Hill Sch., 1969-76; treas. Hillel Found. Cambridge, Inc., 1977-86. Mem. Mass. Bar Assn. (chmn. com. profl. ethics 1982—). Office: Harvard U Law Sch Cambridge MA 02138

KAUFMAN, ANDREW MICHAEL, lawyer; b. Boston, Feb. 19, 1949; s. Earle Bertram and Miriam (Halpern) K.; m. Michele Moselle, Aug. 24, 1975; children: Peter Moselle, Melissa Lanes, Caroline Raney. BA cum laude, Yale U., 1971; JD, Vanderbilt U., 1974. Bar: Tex. 1974, Ga. 1976, Ill. 1993, U.S. Ct. Appeals (5th and 11th cirs.) 1981. Assoc. Vinson & Elkins, Houston, 1974-76, ptnr., 1982-83, Austin, 1983-92, Dallas, 1992; assoc. Sutherland, Asbill & Brennan, Atlanta, 1976-80, ptnr., 1980-81, Kirkland & Ellis LLP, Chgo., 1993—. Adj. prof. Vanderbilt Law Sch., 2005—. Editor in chief Vanderbilt U. Law Rev., 1973-74. Mem. nat. alumni bd. Vanderbilt U.Law Sch., 1994—2000; Alumi fund raiser Yale U., 1971—, mem. alumni schs. com., 1986—92, 2003—; mem. med. ethics coun. Seton Hosp., 1988—92; participant Leadership Austin, 1987—88; bd. dirs. KLRU-TV, 1989—93; mem. Austin (Tex.) Entrepreneurs Coun., 1991—92; mem. adv. bd. Dallas Bus. Com. Arts Leadership Inst., 1992—93; governing bd. mem. Chgo. Symphony Orch.; bd. dirs. United Way, Austin, Tex.; pub. TV Ballet Austin, Tex., 1986—92; mem. adv. bd. Austin Tech. Incubator, 1989—93. Mem. ABA (bus. law sect. 1978—, chmn. lease financing and secured transactions subcom. of com. devels. in bus. financing 1993-99, UCC com., legal opinions com., comml. fin. svcs. com.), Tex. Bar Assn., Yale U. Alumni Assn., Order of Coif, Headliners Club, Yale Club, N.Y.C. and Chgo., Knights of the Symphony Austin. Avocation: sailing. Office: Kirkland & Ellis LLP 200 E Randolph St Fl 54 Chicago IL 60601-6636 Office Phone: 312-861-2313. Business E-Mail: Andrew.Kaufman@chicago.kirkland.com.

KAUFMAN, ANTOINETTE DOLORES, information technology manager; b. Phila., Mar. 10, 1939; d. Joseph and Maria Falcone; m. John R. Kaufman, Apr. 30, 1988. Student, St. Joseph's U., 1968. With N.W. Ayer & Son, Inc., NYC, 1956-81; adminstrv. asst. N.W. Ayer ABH Internat., 1960, asst. corp. sec., 1977, corp. sec., 1978-79, stock transfer agt., 1969-79, info. specialist, 1979-81; exec. v.p., sec., creative dir., COO Help Bus. Svcs., Inc., Glen Mills, Pa., 1981—. Mem.: Pa. State U. Alumni Assn. (life), Navy League US (life), Union League of Phila. Avocations: ballroom dancing, cooking, violin, piano, gardening. Home and Office: Help Bus Svcs Inc 519 Newlin Pointe Glen Mills PA 19342 Personal E-mail: hbsswarthmore@hotmail.com.

KAUFMAN, BARTON LOWELL, financial services company executive; b. Shelbyville, Ind., Mar. 28, 1941; s. Nathan and Hortense (Schwartz) K.; m. Judy Dorman, June 17, 1962; children: Grant, Wendy Kaufman Siegel, Emily Kaufman Frank, Hannah Kaufman Joseph. BS, Ind. U., 1962, JD, 1965. Bar: Ind. 1965. Agt. Kaufman Multi-Million Dollar Agy., Indpls., 1965-70; pres., CEO Kaufman Fin. Corp., Indpls., 1970—. Pres. Twenty-Five Million Dollar Internat. Forum, Chgo., 1989. Republican. Jewish. Office: Kaufman Fin Corp 600 East 96th Street, Suite 595 Indianapolis IN 46240 Home: 414 Springwood Dr Carmel IN 46032-7935 Office Phone: 317-581-7000. E-mail: bartk@kaufin.com.

KAUFMAN, BEL, author, educator; b. Berlin; d. Michael J. and Lala (Rabinowitz) K.; divorced; children: Jonathan Goldstine, Thea Goldstine. BA magna cum laude, Hunter Coll., 1934; DHL, Hunter Coll, 2001; MA with highest honors, Columbia U., 1936; LLD honors, Nasson Coll., Maine, 1965. Adj. prof. English CUNY; lectr. throughout country, also appearances on TV and radio. Mem. Commn. Performing Arts. Editorial bd., Phi Delta Kappan.; Author: Up the Down Staircase, 1965, Love, etc, 1979; also short stories, articles, TV play, translations from Russian, lyrics for musicals. Bd. dirs. Shalom Aleichem Found.; adv. council Town Hall Found. Recipient plaque Anti-Defamation League, and plaque United Jewish Appeal, Paperback of Year award, Ky. Col. award, Bell Movie award, Nat. Treasure awrd Seasoned Citizens Theatre, 2001, Flame Keepers award Perpetuity; also ednl. journalism awards; named to Hall of Fame Hunter Coll., winner short story contest sponsored by NEA and PEN, 1983. Mem. Author's Guild, Dramatists Guild, P.E.N., English Grad. Union, Phi Beta Kappa. Address: 1020 Park Ave New York NY 10028-0913 Personal E-mail: belkau@verizon.net.

KAUFMAN, BILLIE JO, law librarian, educator; BS, Ind. U., Bloomington, 1971, MS, 1974; JD, Nova Southeastern U., 1990. Asst. prof. law Shepard Broad Law Ctr., Nova Southeastern U., Fort Lauderdale, Fla., 1996—2003, assoc. prof., 2002, dir. Law Libr. & Tech. Ctr., 1996—2003; dir. Law Libr., prof. law Washington Coll. Law, Am. U., Washington, 2003—04, assoc. dean for libr. info. resources, prof. law, 2003—. Mem.: AALS, AALL, ABA, S.E. Fla. Info. Network, South Fla. Assn. Law Librs., Consortium of S.E. Law Librs., Law Librs. Soc. of Washington, DC, S.E. Assn. Law Librs. Office: Am U Washington Coll Law 4801 Massachusetts Ave, NW Washington DC 20016 Office Phone: 202-274-4374. E-mail: bkaufman@wcl.american.edu.*

KAUFMAN, CHRISTOPHER LEE, lawyer; b. Chgo., Mar. 17, 1945; s. Charles R. and Violet-Page (Koteen) K.; m. Carlyn A. Clement, Jan. 25, 1986; children: Charles Alexander, Caroline Clement. BA, Amherst Coll., 1967; JD, Harvard U., 1970. Bar: Ill. 1970, Calif. 1972. Law clk. to judge U.S. Ct. Appeals (2d cir.), NYC, 1970-71; from assoc. to ptnr. Heller, Ehrman, White and McAuliffe, San Francisco, Palo Alto, Calif., 1974-90; ptnr. Latham & Watkins, Menlo Park, Calif., 1990—. Editor: Harvard Law Review., 1968-70. Mem. ABA (com. on negotiated acquisitions, com. on fed. regulation of securities). Office: Latham & Watkins LLP 140 Scott Dr Menlo Park CA 94025-1008 Business E-Mail: christopher.kaufman@lw.com.

KAUFMAN, DAVID GRAHAM, construction executive; b. North Canton, Ohio, Mar. 20, 1937; s. DeVere and Josephine Grace (Graham) Kaufman; m. Carol Jean Monzione, Oct. 5, 1957 (div. Aug. 1980); children: Gregory Allan, Christopher Patrick. Student, Kent State U., Ohio, 1956; grad., Internat. Corr. Schs., Scranton, Pa., 1965, NY Inst. Photography, NYC, 1983, Calif. Coast U., 1983—86. Cert. constrn. insp., constrn. project mgr., asbestos insp., lead insp., lead risk assessor, asbestos project designer, lock-out/tag-out, environ. insp., environ. specialist, environ. mgr., EPA cert. lead insp. and risk assessor, cert. concrete constrn. spl. inspector Am. Concrete Inst., cert. field testing technician Am. Concrete Inst., constrn. cons., environ. cons., concrete testing technician Am. Concrete Inst. Machinist apprentice Hoover Co., North Canton, Ohio, 1955-57; draftsman-designer Goodyear Aircraft Corp., Akron, Ohio, 1957-60, Boeing Co., Seattle, 1960-61; designer Berger Industries, Seattle, 1961-62, Puget Sound Bridge & Drydock, Seattle, 1963, C.M. Lovsted, Seattle, 1963-64, Tracy, Brunstrom & Dudley, Seattle, 1964, Rubens & Pratt Engrs., Seattle, 1965-66; founder, owner Profl. Drafting Svcs., Seattle, 1965, Profl. Take-Off Svcs., Seattle, 1966, Profl. Representation Svcs., Seattle, 1967; pres. Kaufman Inc., Seattle, 1967-83, Kaufman-Alaska Inc., Juneau, 1975-83, Kaufman-Alaska Constructors, Inc., Juneau, 1975-83; constrn. mgr. U. Alaska, 1979-84; constrn. cons. Alaskan Native and Eskimo Village Corps., 1984—; prin. Kaufman S.W. Assocs., N.Mex., 1984—, Graham Internat., 1992—, Parsons-Brinckernoff, Los Alamos, 2000—. Trustee advisor Kaufman Internat., Kaufman Group, Kaufman Enterprises. Mem.: Internat. Code Coun., Am. Welding Inst., Am. Concrete Inst., Am. Contractors Inst., Prodrs. Coun. Alaska, Prodrs. Coun. Hawaii, Prodrs. Coun. Idaho, Prodrs. Coun. Wash., Prodrs. Coun. Oreg., Associated Gen. Contractors Seattle Constrn. Coun., Internat. Conf. Bldgs. Ofcls., Assn. Constrn. Insps., Constrn. Specifications Inst., Environ. Assessment Assn., Portland C. of C., Toastmasters (past gov.), Nat. Eagle Scout Assn., Elks, Lions. Republican. Roman Catholic. Office: PO Box 458 Haines AK 99827-0458 also: PO Box 1781 Santa Fe NM 87504 Home: 505 Oppenheimer # 409 Los Alamos NM 87544

KAUFMAN, DAVID MARC, pediatric neurologist; b. Bronx, NY, July 10, 1945; s. Harold M. and Edna M. (Markowtiz) K.; m. Harriet B. Kaufman, June 30, 1968; 1 child, Jill R. BS, Union Coll., 1967; MD, Boston U. Sch. of Medicine, 1975. Diplomate Am. Bd. Pediatrics. Intern-resident N.Y. Hosp., NYC, 1975-77; resident-fellow Mt. Sinai Med. Ctr., NYC, 1977-80; pvt. practice in pediatric neurology NYC, 1980—; med. dir. Premier Health Care / YAI Nat. Inst. for People with Disabilities, 1997—. Mem. admissions com. Mt. Sinai Sch. of Medicine, N.Y.C., 1992—, ethics com. Child Neurology Soc., Mpls., 1995—; adv. bd. Winston Prep Sch. Spl. Edn. Sch., N.Y.C., 1990, Young Adult Inst., N.Y.C., 1995—. Author: (with others) The Founders of Child Neurology, 1990. Fellow Am. Acad. Pediatrics; mem. Am. Acad. Neurology, Child Neurology Soc. Office: 3 E 83d St New York NY 10028 Office Phone: 212-737-4911. Personal E-mail: davidneuro@aol.com.

KAUFMAN, DONALD LEROY, building products executive; b. Erie, Pa., May 9, 1931; s. Isadore H. and Lena (Sandler) K.; m. Estelle Friedman, Aug. 15, 1954; children: Craig Ivan, Susan Beth, Carrie Ellen. BS in Bus. Adminstrn, Ohio State U., 1953, LL.B., 1955. Bar: Ohio 1955. Pres. Alside, Inc., Akron, Ohio, 1974—, chief exec. officer, 1982—. V.p., bd. dirs. Assoc. Materials Inc. Mem. adv. com. U. Akron; trustee Jewish Welfare Fund, Akron, 1958-65, young leaders div., 1961-65; trustee Akron City Hosp. Found., 1984-91, Menorah Park Home for Aged, Akron Children's Hosp. Found. Mem. Akron Bar Assn., Sigma Alpha Mu, Tau Epsilon Rho. Home: 2825 Roundhill Rd Akron OH 44333-2273 Office: PO Box 2010 Akron OH 44309-2010

KAUFMAN, DONALD WAYNE, research ecologist; b. Abilene, Tex., June 7, 1943; s. Leo Fred and Marcella Genevieve (Hobbie) Kaufman; m. Glennis Ann Schroeder, Aug. 5, 1967; 1 child, Dawn. BS, Ft. Hays Kans. State Coll., 1965, MS, 1967; PhD, U. Ga., Athens, 1972. Postdoctoral fellow U. Tex., Austin, 1971-73; asst. prof. U. Ark., Fayetteville, 1974-75, SUNY, Binghamton, 1975-77; assoc. program dir. Population Biology, NSF, Washington, 1977-80; asst. prof. biology Kans. State U., Manhattan, 1980-84, assoc. prof. biology, 1984-91, prof. biology, 1991—; adj. curator mammals Sternberg Mus. Nat. History Ft. Hays State U., Hays, Kans., 2000—. Adj. prof. biology U. N.Mex., 1998; vis. scientist Savannah River Ecology Lab., Aiken, SC, 1973-74; acting dir. Konza Prairie Rsch. Natural Area, 1986-87, coord., 1990-91; dir. Konza Prairie Long-Term Ecol. Rsch. Program, 1985-90; grant rev. panelist EPA, 1981-85, USDA, 1995-96; cons. NSF, 1984, Nat. Pk. Svc., 2000. Contbr. articles to profl. jours. Recipient Alumni Achievement award, Fort Hays State U., 2005; fellow NDEA, 1967—69. Mem. AAAS, Am. Soc. Mammalogists (award 1972, bd. dirs. 1989-92), Ecol. Soc. Am., Am. Inst. Biol. Scis., The Wildlife Soc. (pres. Kans. chpt. 2005-07), Soc. Conservation Biology, Ctrl. Plains Soc. Mammalogists (bd. govs. 2000-06), Sigma Xi. Office: Kans State U Div Biology Ackert Hall Manhattan KS 66506 Business E-Mail: dwkaufma@ksu.edu.

KAUFMAN, DONNA SOBLE, lawyer, director; m. Fred Kaufman; 2 children. BCL, McGill U.; LLM, U. Montreal. Bar: Que., Ont. Former broadcast exec. Sta. CHCH-TV, Hamilton, Toronto, Canada; former chmn., CEO Selkirk Comm. Ltd.; former ptnr. Stikeman Ellliott. Bd. dirs. BCE Inc., Bell Can., Hudson's Bay Co., Telesat Can., TransAlta Corp., 1989—, chmn. bd. dirs.; gov. Baycrest Centre for Geriatric Care. Author: Broadcasting Law in Canada: Fairness in the Administrative Process; contbr. articles to profl. jours. Recipient Award of Distinction, Faculty of Commerce, Concordia U., Montreal, 1995, Fellowship award, Inst. Corp. Dirs., 2001. Office: 2 Saint Clair Ave E Ste 800 Toronto ON Canada M4T 2T5 Business E-Mail: donna@dkaufman.com.

KAUFMAN, FRANCINE R., pediatric endocrinologist; m. Neal Kaufman; children: Adam, Jonah. B., Northwestern U., 1972; MD, Chgo. Med. Sch., 1976. Cert. pediatric endocrinology & metabolism. Intern Childrens Hosp. Los Angeles, 1976—77, resident, 1977—78, fellow, 1978—80, attending physician, head of Ctr. for Endocrinology, Diabetes & Metabolism; dir. Comprehensive Childhood Diabetes Ctr., Los Angeles; prof. pediatrics Univ. So. Calif. Keck Sch. Medicine. Diplomat Am. Bd. Pediatrics; co-principal investigator Keck Diabetes Prevention Initiative, Los Angeles; med. adv. bd. Mini-Med Technologies, 1993—2001, 2003—, Eli Lilly Corp., 1998—, Novo Nordisk, 1999—, Life Scan, Inc., 2000—01, 2003—; editorial bd. Internat. Diabetes Monitor, 1994—95, 1998—, Diabetes Forecast, 1998—, Diabetes Reviews, 1998—, Current Diabetes Reports, 2001—, Pediatric Diabetes, 2002—, DOC News, 2004—. Author: Diabesity, 2005; contbr. scientific papers, chapters to books. Del. WHO Assembly, Geneva, 2002, Calif. Task Force on Childhood Obesity; chair Los Angeles County Task Force on Children & Youth Physical Fitness, 2002; Calif. del. to Healthy Sch. Summit in Washington DC, 2003; chair Studies to Treat or Prevent Type 2 Diabetes in Youth (STOPP-T2); sci. adv. group Am. Diabetes Assn., 1997—, programs com., 1997—, bd. dirs., 1993—96, 2000, chair, Task Force on Health Care Reform, 1993—95, chair, Task Force on Signature Advocacy, 1993—94, chair, Pub. Policy Leadership Forum, 1995—96, Profl. Ed. Project Team, 1999—, Task Force on Schools, 2002—03, nominating com., 2003—04, pres., 2002—03; active Juvenile Diabetes Assn., Nat. Diabetes Ed. Program, Internat. Diabetes Fedn., Ctr. Disease Control & Prevention, UNESCO, NIH; profl. & patient ed. com. Am. Diabetes Assn. Los Angeles Chpt., 1985—, bd. dirs., 1986—, pres, 1988—90, caper com., 1986—, fundraising com., 1990—; pub. seminar com. Am. Diabetes Assn. Calif. Affiliate, 1985—, bd. dirs., 1988—, exec. com., 1991—, pres., 1996—97. Recipient Woman of Valor award, Am. Diabetes Assn., 2003, Banting Medal, 2003, Albert Renold award, European Assn. for the Study of Diabetes, 2003. Mem.: AAP (Endocrine exec. com. 1998—, Task Force on Obesity), Inst. Medicine. Achievements include invention of Extend Bar. Office: Childrens Hospital Los Angeles MS #1 4650 Sunset Blvd Los Angeles CA 90027 E-mail: fkaufman@chla.usc.edu.

KAUFMAN, GEORGE S., real estate company executive; BS, Ohio State U.; MS, NYU. Chmn. Kaufman Astoria Studios; pres., COO Kaufman Realty Corp. Trustee Whitney Mus. Am. Art, NYC, Hall of Sci. Mus., Fashion Inst. Tech., NYC, NY Coun. Motion Pictures & TV, Am. Mus. Moving Image. Mem.: Real Estate Bd. NY, Midtown Real Estate Owners Assn. (pres.). Office: Kaufman Astoria Studios 34-12 36th St Astoria NY 11106

KAUFMAN, GLEN FRANK, art educator; b. Fort Atkinson, Wis., Oct. 28, 1932; s. Eli J. and Elynor B. (Jensik) K. BS with honors, U. Wis., 1954; MFA, Cranbrook Acad. Art, 1959; cert., State Sch. Arts and Crafts, Copenhagen, 1960. Head fibers dept. Cranbrook Acad. Art, Bloomfield Hills, Mich., 1961-67; assoc. prof. art U. Ga., Athens, 1967-72, prof. art, 1972—, prof. in charge, fabric design, 1967—, grad. faculty, 1969—. Staff designer Dorothy Liebes Design Studio, N.Y.C., 1960-61; designer Regal Rugs, Inc., North Vernon, Ind., 1966-82; vis. artist Sch. Textiles, Royal Coll. Art, London, 1976; juror The Albuquerque (N.Mex.) Mus., 1981, Midland (Mich.) Art Coun., 1985, Itami Craft Ctr., Osaka, Japan, 1991, others; panelist Visual Artists Fellowship/Crafts, Nat. Endowment for the Arts, Washington, 1992—; cons. in field; lectr. and workshop presenter in field. One-man shows include Gallery Maronie, Kyoto, Japan, 1984, Sembikiya Gallery, Tokyo, 1985, Arrowmont Sch. Arts and Crafts, Gatlinburg, Tenn., 1986, Fiberworks, Berkeley, Calif., 1987, Madison (Ga.)-Morgan Cultural Ctr., 1988, Fuji Gallery, Osaka, Japan, 1988, Wacoal Ginza Art Space, Tokyo, 1989, Allrich Gallery, San Francisco, 1990, Azabu Mus. of Arts and Crafts, Tokyo, 1991, Lamar Dodd Art Ctr., LaGrange (Ga.) Coll., 1992, Gallery Gallery, Japan, 1992, Wacoal Ginza Art Space, Tokyo, 1994, Gallery Nouveau, Pusan, Korea, 1994, Ba Tang Gol Arts Ctr., Seoul, Korea, 1994, Wacoal Ginza Art Space, Tokyo, 1996, Gallery Gallery, Kyoto, Japan, 1996, others; exhibited in group shows at Columbia Mus. Art, SC, 1980, No. Ill. U., DeKalb, 1981, Visual Arts Ctr. Alaska, Anchorage, 1982, Robert L. Kidd Gallery, Birmingham, 1983, Am. Craft Mus., NY, 1986, Denki Kaikan Gallery, Nagoya, Japan, 1987, Gayle Wilson Gallery, Southampton, NY, 1988, Sch. Visual Arts, NY, 1989, Itami Craft Ctr., Osaka, 1989 (Silver prize), Farrell Collection, Washington, 1991, Allrich Gallery, San Francisco, 1991, Nagoya Trade and Industry Ctr., 1991; New Visions Gallery Contemporary Art, Atlanta, 1992, Mus. Kyoto, 1992, Smithsonian Instn., Washington, 1992-93, Atlanta (Ga.) Fin. Ctr., 1993, Nat. Mus. Modern Art, Kyoto, Japan, 1993, Art Inst. Chgo., 1993, Brenau U. Gallery, Gainesville, Ga., 1993, Mus. Kyoto, 1994, Asian Arts Ctr. Towson (Md.) State U., 1994, Am. Craft Mus., NY, 1995, Nogaya and Trade Industry Ctr., Japan, 1995, Gallery, Gallery, Kyota, Japan, 1995, Harbourfront Ctr., Toronto Can., 1995, Museé Marsil, Montreal, Can., 1995, Brown/Grotta Gallery, Wilton, Conn., 1995, NJ Ctr. for Visual Arts, Summit, 1997, Georgia State U. Gallery, Atlanta, 1997, Brown/Grotta Gallery, Wilton, Conn. 12997, Vanderbilt U. Sarratt Gallery, Nashville, 1997, Georgia Mus. Art, Athens, 1997, others; represented in permanent collections Am. Craft Mus., NYC, Juraku Mus, Kyoto, Cleve. Mus. Art, Art Inst. Chgo., U. Wis., Madison, Itami City Craft Ctr., Hyogo Prefecture, Japan, Ithaca (NY) Coll. Mus. Art, Long House Found., L.I., NY, Nat. Mus. Modern Art, Kyoto, Smithsonian Instn., Rockford Art Assn., Ill., S.C. Johnson Collection, U.S.A. Collection Contemporary Crafts, SUNY, Oneonta, Wichita Art Assn., Kans., pvt. collections; works illustrated in many books; contbr. articles to jours. Recipient Fulbright grant to Denmark, 1959-60, Grant for rsch. and travel to Europe, U. Ga., Dept. Art, 1973, Nat. Endowment for the Arts Craftsmen's Fellowship grant, 1976, Nat. Endowment for the Arts Svcs. to the Field grant, 1980-81, 81-82, Faculty Rsch. grant U. Ga. Athens Office of V.P. for Rsch., 1983-96, Nat. Endowment for the Arts Visual Artist's Fellowship grant, 1990, Ga. Coun. for the Arts Individual Artist grant, 1991, Sr. Faculty Rsch. grant U. Ga. Athens Rsch. Found., 1992, others. Fellow Am. Craft Coun.; mem. World Craft Coun., Surface Design Assn. (S.E. regional rep. 1977-80, pres. 1980-82, named hon. life mem. 1983), Phi Beta Delta. Office: Sch of Art Univ Ga Athens GA 30602

KAUFMAN, GORDON DESTER, theology studies educator; b. Newton, Kans., June 22, 1925; s. Edmund George and Hazel (Dester) K.; m. Dorothy Wedel, June 11, 1947; children: David W., Gretchen E., Anne Louisa, Edmund G. II. AB with highest distinction, Bethel Coll., Kans., 1947, LHD (hon.), 1973; MA in Sociology, Northwestern U., 1948; BD magna cum laude, Yale U., 1951, PhD in Philos. Theology, 1955; LHD (hon.), 2007. Ordained to ministry Mennonite Ch., 1953. Asst. prof. religion Pomona Coll., 1953-58; asso. prof. theology Vanderbilt U., 1958-63; prof. theology Harvard U. Div. Sch., Cambridge, Mass., 1963-95, Edward MallincKrodt Jr. prof. div., 1969-95, prof. emeritus, 1995—. Vis. prof. United Theol. Coll., Bangalore, India, 1976-77, Doshisha U., Kyoto, Japan, 1983, U. South Africa, Pretoria, 1984; vis. lectr. Oxford U., 1986, Chinese U. Hong Kong, 1991. Author: Relativism, Knowledge and Faith, 1960, The Context of Decision, 1961, Systematic Theology: a Historicist Perspective, 1968, God the Problem, 1972, An Essay on Theological Method, 1975, 3d edit., 1995, Nonresistance and Responsibility and other Mennonite Essays, 1979, The Theological Imagination: Constructing the Concept of God, 1981, Theology for a Nuclear Age, 1985, In Face of Mystery: A Constructive Theology, 1993, God—Mystery—Diversity: Christian Theology in a Pluralistic World, 1996, In the beginning.Creativity, 2004, Jesus and Creativity, 2006. Mem. Am. Acad. Religion (pres. 1981-82), Am. Theol. Soc. (pres. 1979-80) Democrat. Home: 6 Longfellow Rd Cambridge MA 02138-4736 Office: 45 Francis Ave Cambridge MA 02138-1911

KAUFMAN, HAROLD RICHARD, mechanical engineer and physics educator; b. Audubon, Iowa, Nov. 24, 1926; s. Walter Richard and Hazel (Steere) K.; m. Elinor Mae Wheat, June 25, 1948; children: Brian, Karin, Bruce, Cynthia. Student, Evanston C.C., 1947-49; BSM.E., Northwestern U., 1951; PhD, Colo. State U., 1971. Researcher in aerospace propulsion NACA, Cleve., 1951-58; mgr. space propulsion research NASA, Cleve., 1958-74; prof. physics and mech. engring. Colo. State U., Ft. Collins, 1974-84, prof. emeritus, 1984—, chmn. dept. physics, 1979-84; pres. Kaufman & Robinson, Inc., Ft. Collins, 1984—; v.p. R&D Commonwealth Sci. Corp., Alexandria, Va., 1984-96. Pioneer in field of electron bombardment ion thruster, 1960; cons. ion source design and applications. Contbr. over 150 publs. and 35 patents in field. Served with USNR, 1944-46. Recipient NASA medal for exceptional sci. achievement, 1971. Fellow Am. Vacuum Soc. (Albert Nerken award 1991), AIAA (assoc. fellow, James H. Wyld Propulsion award 1969), Electric Rocket Propulsion Soc. (Outstanding Achievement in Electric Propulsion medal 2005); mem. Tau Beta Pi, Pi Tau Sigma. Office: Kaufman & Robinson Inc 1306 Blue Spruce Dr Ste A Fort Collins CO 80524-2067

KAUFMAN, HENRY, diversified financial services company executive; b. Wenings, Germany, Oct. 20, 1927; came to US, 1937; s. Gustav and Hilda (Rosenthal) K.; m. Elaine Reinheimer, Sept. 15, 1957; children: Glenn, Craig, Daniel. BA, NYU, 1948; MS, Columbia U., 1949; PhD, NYU, 1958, LLD (hon.), 1982; LHD, Yeshiva U., 1986. Asst. chief economist research dept. Fed. Res. Bank NY, 1957-61; with Salomon Bros., Inc., NYC, 1962-88, gen. partner, 1967-88, mem. exec. com., 1972-88, mng. dir., 1981-88, chief economist, charge bond market research, industry and stock research and bond portfolio analysis research and corp. bond research depts., also vice-chmn.; founder Henry Kaufman & Co., NYC, 1988—. Pres. Money Marketeers, NYU, 1964-65; bd. dirs. Lehman Brothers Holdings Inc., 1995-. Bd. dirs. Fed. Home Loan Mortgage Corp. Trustee Whitney Mus. of Am. Art, Cambridge Ctr. for Behavioral Studies, Inst. Internat. Studies; pres. Animal Med. Ctr.; bd. govs. Tel-Aviv U.; chmn. bd. overseers Stern Sch. of Bus. NYU; chmn. Inst. Internat. Edn.; bd. dirs. Statue of Liberty - Ellis Island Found., Mem. Am. Econ. Assn., Am. Fin. Assn., Conf. Bus. Economists, Econ. Club NYC (dir.), UN Assn. (bd. dirs., co-chmn. econ. policy council), Council Fgn. Relations. Mailing: c/o Whitney Mus Am Art 945 Madison Ave New York NY 10021

KAUFMAN, HERBERT MARK, finance educator; b. Bronx, NY, Nov. 1, 1946; s. Henry and Betty (Fried) K.; m. Helen Laurie Fox, July 23, 1967; 1 child, Jonathan Hart. BA, SUNY, Binghamton, 1967; PhD, Pa. State U., 1972. Economist Fed. Nat. Mortgage Assn., Washington, 1972-73; asst. prof. Ariz. State U., Tempe, 1973-76, econs. prof., 1980-88, fin. prof. Tempe, 1988—, chair dept. fin., 1991—2004. Exec. dir. Ctr. for Fin. System, 1988-, cons. World Bank, Washington, 1985-86, Gen. Acctg. Office, Washington, 1985, Congl. Budget Office, Washington, 1980, N.Y. Stock Exch., 1995—. Author: Financial Markets, Financial Institutions and Money, 1983, (with others) The Political Economy of Policy Making, 1979, Money and Banking, 1991; contbr. articles to profl. jours. Mem. Am. Econ. Assn., Am. Fin. Assn., Nat. Assn. of Bus. Economists. Avocations: golf, piano. Home: 1847 E Calle De Caballos Tempe AZ 85284-2505 Office: Ariz State U Bin 3906 Dept Fin Tempe AZ 85287 Business E-Mail: herbert.kaufman@asu.edu.

KAUFMAN, JAMES JAY, lawyer; b. Newark, NY, Jan. 23, 1939; s. Joseph Julius and Ann Gertrude (Quick) K.; m. Patricia Ann Patterson, Sept. 3, 1966; children: Kristine, Jeffrey. BA, Bucknell U., 1960; LLB, JD, Union Coll., Albany, 1964. Bar: N.Y. 1965, U.S. Ct. Appeals (2nd cir.) 1966, U.S. Dist. Ct. (we. and no. dists.) N.Y. 1968, N.C. 1985, Pa. 1985, U.S. Supreme Ct. 1985, U.S. Dist. Ct. (ea. dist.) N.C. 1991, U.S. Ct. Appeals (4th cir.) 1991, U.S. Ct. Appeals (7th cir.) 1992, U.S. Dist. Ct. (mid. dist.) N.C. 1993; certified mediator, Wilmington, Conn. Legal counsel, legis. and adminstrv. asst. Rep. Theodore R. Kupferman, U.S. Congress, Washington, 1965-67; assoc. Houghton, Pappas & Fink, Rochester, NY, 1967-70; ptnr. Culley, Marks, Rochester, 1970-75; sr. ptnr. James J. Kaufman, P.C., Newark, 1975-84, Kaufman & Forsyth, Rochester, 1984-91, Barefoot & Kaufman, Wilmington, NC, 1991-93, Kaufman, Barefoot & Green, Wilmington, 1993-94; of counsel Hancock & Estabrook, Syracuse, NY, 1994-96; sr. ptnr. Kaufman & Green, L.L.P., Wilmington, 1994-2001, Maupin, Taylor & Ellis, PA, 2001—02. V.p. Fed. Bar Coun., 1968; mem. 7th Jud. Dist. Grievance Com., 1983-89; del. U.S./China Joint Session on Trade, Investment and Econ. Law, Beijing, 1987; strategic planning cons., Rochester, 1994-95; panel mem. Commerce Tech. Adv. Bd. on Noise Abatement, Washington, 1968; chmn. noise task force Genesee Region Health Planning, Rochester, 1970-71, mem./counsel noise task force, mem./counsel environ. health planning com., 1972-73; chmn. bd. dirs. Riviera Yachts of Americas. Author: What to Do Before the Money Runs Out—A Road Map for America's Automobile Dealers, 1993; contbr. articles to profl. publs. Justice Town of Arcadia, Newark, 1976-89. Mem. N.Y. State Bar Assn. (mem. spl. com. on environ. law 1974-77, mem. com. on profl. discipline, mem. com. on ct. in cmty. banking com. 1986—), Wayne County Bar Assn. (pres. 1986-87, v.p. 1985-86, chmn. family law sect. 1975-80, chmn. com. on profl. discipline 1975-89), N.C. Bar Assn., Pa. Bar Assn., New Hanover County Bar Assn., Monroe County Bar Assn., Wilmington Inns of Ct. (pres. 1994-97). Republican. Presbyterian. Avocations: boating, scuba diving, fishing, writing. Personal E-mail: jamesj.kaufman@gmail.com.

KAUFMAN, JEROME BENZION, retired neurosurgeon; b. Waterloo, Iowa, July 22, 1934; s. Louis and Dorothy (Rosenbloom) K.; m. Judith Ellen Lasker, June 29, 1967; children: David, Jonathan, Jefferey. BA, Wayne State U., 1955, MD, 1961; postgrad., U. Madrid. Diplomate Am. Bd. Neurol. Surgery 1975. Rotating intern Michael Reese Hosp. and Med. Ctr., Chgo., 1961-62; resident in internal med. Michael Reesee Hosp. and Med. Ctr., Chgo., 1962-63; resident in gen. surgery VA Hosp., Bronx, 1965-66, resident in neurology, 1966, resident in neurosurgery, 1967, from sr. to chief resident neurosurgery, 1969-70; resident neurosurgery Neurol. Inst. N.Y., Columbia Presbyn. Hosp., 1968; resident neuropathology Mt. Sinai Hosp. and Med. Sch., NYC, 1968; chief resident neurosurgery City Hosp., Elmhurst, N.Y., 1969; chmn. dept. neurosurgery Carle Clinic Assn. and Found. Hosp., Urbana, Ill., 1972—96, prof. emeritus, 1997—, U. Ill. Coll. medicine, Champaign-Urbana. Cons. neurosurgery McKinley Hosp., Urbana, Covenant Hosp., Urbana; asst. instr. internal medicine Chgo. Med. Sch., 1963; clin. assoc. prof. neurosurgery U. Ill. Coll. Medicine, Urbana, 1982-96, clin. prof., chmn. neurosurgery. Contbr. chapters to books to profl. jours. Capt. USAF, 1963—65. Named One of Best Drs. in Am.- Midwest, Ill. Fellow ACS, Am. Assn. Neurol. Surgeons (Continuing Edn. award in neurosurgery 1980, 83, 85, 87, 89, 93, 96), Internat. Coll. Surgeons (vice regent) N.Y. Acad. Scis.; mem. AMA (Physicians Recognition award 1980, 82, 85, 89, 93), Ill. Med. Soc., Champaign County Med. Soc., Congress Neurol. Surgeons, Ctrl. Neurosurg. Soc., Assn. Mil. Surgeons U.S., Chgo. Neurol. Soc. (Best Doctors in Am. Midwest). Home: 2104 Zuppke Dr Urbana IL 61801-6706 Personal E-mail: j-kauf@uiuc.edu.

KAUFMAN, JOEL DANIEL, medical educator, medical researcher; m. Anna Wald. MD, U. Mich., Ann Arbor, 1986; MPH, U. Wash., Seattle, 1990. Diplomate Am. Bd. Preventive Medicine, 1991. Assoc. med. dir. rsch. Wash. State Dept. Labor & Industries, Olympia, 1990—97; assoc. prof. U. Wash., Seattle, 1997—2006, prof., 2006—. Dir. U. Wash. Occupl. and Environ. Medicine Proram, 2002—. Grantee, US EPA, 2004—. Office: University of Washington DEOHS Box 354695 Seattle WA 98195 Office Phone: 206-897-1723.

KAUFMAN, JOSHUA JACOB, lawyer, editor; b. NYC., Oct. 31, 1950; s. Jay Herbert Kaufman and Aviva (Goodman) Kaufman-Penn; m. Nan Ellin, July 12, 1980; children: Jay Laurence, Aaron Michael. BA U. Md., 1972; JD George Washington U., 1975. Bar: Md. 1977, D.C. 1978, Fed. Dist. Ct. 1978, U.S. Tax Ct. 1981, US Ct. Claims 1981, NY 1983, US Supreme Ct. 1989. Ptnr. Lowe, Bressler & Kaufman, Washington, 1978-83; ptnr. Kaufman & Biel, P.C., Washington, 1984-86, Goldfarb, Kaufman & O'Toole, Washington, 1986-90, Kaufman & Silverberg, Washington, 1990-95, Tucker Flye, 1998-2000; ptnr., head copyright and licensing practice group Venable LLP, Washington; adj. prof. entertainment law Am. U. Law Sch., Washington, 1989—; exec. dir. Vol. Lawyers for Arts, Washington, 1977—82; exec. dir. Soc. To Prevent Trade in Stolen Art, Washington, 1995—2000. Author: Art of Investing in Art, 1980; columnist Artist Mag., Art Bus. News, Sculpture mag., Outdoors Unltd., Washington Lawyer mag., 1986—; contbr. articles to profl. jours.; segment producer, corr. (TV show) Washington's Business. Co-dir. City Coun. Task Force on Cable Regulation, 1974-75. Mem. ABA (forum on entertainment and sports industries, subcom. on copyright, various other sects.), Computer Law Forum, Computer Law Assn., Copyright Soc. USA (steering com. mem.). Democrat. Jewish. Avocations: sculpture, scuba diving, computers, computer art. Office: Venable LLP 575 7th St NW Washington DC 20004 Office Phone: 202-344-8538. Office Fax: 202-344-8300. Business E-Mail: jjkaufman@venable.com.

KAUFMAN, JULIAN MORTIMER, broadcasting company executive, consultant; b. Detroit, Apr. 3, 1918; s. Anton and Fannie (Newman) K.; m. Katherine LaVerne Likins, May 6, 1942; children: Nikki, Keith Anthony. Grad., H.S., Newark. Pub. Elizabeth (N.J.) Sunday Sun, Inc., 1937-39; account exec. Tolle Advt. Agy., San Diego, 1947-49; pub. Tucson Shopper, 1948-50; account exec. ABC, San Francisco, 1949-50; mgr. Sta. KPHO-TV, Phoenix, 1950-52; gen. mgr., v.p. Bay City TV Corp., San Diego, 1952-95; v.p. Jai Alai Films, Inc., San Diego, 1961—; TV cons. Julian Kaufman, Inc., San Diego, 1985—. Dir. Spanish Internat. Broadcasting, Inc., L.A.; chmn. bd. dirs. Bay City TV Inc. Contbr. articles to profl. jours.; prodr. (TV show) Pick a Winner. Mem. Gov.'s adv. bd. Mental Health Assn., 1958—; bd. dirs. Francis Parker Sch., San Diego BBB, 1979-84, San Diego Conv. and Visitors Bur., World Affairs Coun., Pala Indian Mission. Served with USAAF, 1942-46. Recipient Peabody award, 1975, Emmy award, 1980. Mem. San Diego C. of C., Advt. and Sales Club, San Diego Press Club, Univ. Club (San Diego), Sigma Delta Chi. Republican. Home: 3125 Montesano Rd Escondido CA 92029-7302 Office: 7677 Ronsen Rd Ste 210 San Diego CA 92111-1538 Home Phone: 760-745-0258. E-mail: consultingjmk@aol.com, janoskj66@aol.com.

KAUFMAN, KENNETH ROLAND, psychiatrist, educator; s. Jerome and Rebecca Kaufman; m. Christine Hanson Adams; children: Sarah Jennifer, Deborah Anne, Eliot Michael, Noah Shimon, Nathaniel David. BA summa cum laude, Columbia U., 1968; MA in Chemistry, Harvard U., 1970; MD, Washington U., St. Louis, 1974. Cert. Bd. Med. Examiners Mo., 1977, Pa., 1977, NY, 1978, Calif., 1978, NJ, 1995; Psychiatry Bd. Am. Bd. of Psychiatry and Neurology, 1981. Rsch. asst. dept. chem. pathology St. George's Hosp. U. London, 1966; tchg. fellow dept. chemistry Harvard U., Cambridge, 1968—70; tutor in chemistry Quincy House, Harvard U., Cambridge, 1969—70; asst. instr. psychiatry, NIMH trainee in psychiatry Washington U. Med. Ctr. (Barnes and Renard Hosp.), St Louis, 1974—77; psychiatry resident Washington U. Sch. Medicine, St. Louis, 1974—77; hon. clin. neurophysiologist Maudsley Hosp., London, 1976; rsch. fellow Inst. Psychiatry, U. London, 1976; advanced rsch. fellow Western Psychiat. Inst. and Clinic, U. Pitts., 1977; asst. prof. clin. psychiatry Western Psychiat. Inst. and Clinic, U. of Pitts., 1977—79; rsch. fellow Dept. Child and Adolescent Psychiatry Inst. Psychiatry U. London, 1976; asst. prof. psychiatry U. So. Calif. Sch. Medicine, LA, 1979—82, asst. prof. neurology, 1980—82, clin. asst. prof. psychiatry, 1982—84, clin. asst. prof. neurology, 1982—99; asst. clin. prof. of psychiatry and biobehavioral scis. UCLA, LA, 1984—96; pvt. practitioner Kenneth R Kaufman, MD Inc., LA, 1982—96; vis. asst. prof. psychiatry Columbia U. Coll. Physicians and Surgeons, NYC, 1986—86; assoc. prof. clin. psychiatry U. Medicine and Dentistry of NJ, Robert Wood Johnson Med. Sch., New Brunswick, 1995—98, assoc. prof. clin. neurology, 1996—98, assoc. prof. psychiatry, 1998—2002, prof. neurology, 2003—, assoc. prof. neurology, 1998—2003, prof. psychiatry, 2002—; attending psychiatrist U. Behavioral Health Care U. Medicine and Dentistry of NJ, Robert Wood Johnson Med. Sch., New Brunswick, 1997—98, Cmty. Mental Health Ctr. at Piscataway U. Medicine and Dentistry of NJ, Robert Wood Johnson Med. Sch., New Brunswick, 1996—97, Consultation Liaison Svc., Robert Wood Johnson U. Hosp., New Brunswick, NJ, 1997—, Splty. Psychopharmacology Clinics, New Brunswick, NJ, 1998—. Editl. bd. Annals of Clin. Psychiatry, 1988—2007, contr. editor editl. bd. Mt. Sinai Jour. Medicine, 1986—89, reviewer (19 profl. jours.); author: numerous articles, chpts., abstracts and internat. presentations in field. Team psychiatrist Mem. U.S. Med. Team, 16th Maccabiah Games, Tel Aviv, 2001. Recipient Gold medal in Cricket, 13th Maccabiah Games, 1989, Humanitarian award, Women's Am. O.R.T., 1993; fellow The Harvard Fellowship, Harvard U., 1968—69. Fellow: Am. Psychiat. Assn.; mem.: The Am. Epilepsy Soc., Am. Chem. Soc., Am. Psychopathological Assn., Assn. European Psychiatrists, Am. Acad. Clin. Psychiatrists (treas. 1997—99, program chair 1999—2001, v.p. 2001—02), Royal Coll. Psychiatry, AMA. Jewish. Avocations: travel, cricket, golf, theater, reading. Home: 8 Villa Dr Princeton Junction NJ 08550 Office: UMDNJ-Robert Wood Johnson Medical School 125 Paterson St Ste #2200 New Brunswick NJ 08901 Personal E-mail: adamskaufman@comcast.net. E-mail: kaufmakr@umdnj.edu.

KAUFMAN, LUNA AMALIA, musicologist; b. Nov. 28, 1926; came to U.S., 1952; Musicologist, Jagellonain U., Cracow, Poland, 1949. Pres. Temple Sholom, Plainfield, NJ, 1980-82; chmn. Liberty State Park (N.J.) Monument, 1982-85; pres., mgr. N.J. State Opera, Newark, 1987-94; chair Sister Rose Thering endowment for Judeo-Christian edn. Seton Hall U., West Orange, NJ, 1984—. Pub. spkr. on the Holocaust, 1976—; exec. bd. Anti-Defamation League of N.Y. Charter mem. Gov.'s Coun. on Holocaust Edn., 1982-92, Trenton, N.J.

KAUFMAN, MARK DAVID, lawyer; b. St. Louis, Feb. 24, 1949; s. Rudolf Ernst and Edith (Greiderer) K.; m. Margaret Taylor James, June 1, 2002; children: Mark, Thomas McLain. BA, Northwestern U., 1971; JD, Duke U., 1974. Bar: Ga. 1974, U.S. Ct. Appeals (11th cir.) 1974, U.S. Dist. Ct. (no. dist.) Ga. 1974. Assoc. Sutherland Asbill & Brennan LLP, Atlanta, 1974-81, ptnr., 1981—, exec. com., 1996-2000. Contbr. articles to profl. jours. Named to Best Lawyers in Am., 2005, Am. Leading Lawyers Bus., Chamber US, 2004. Mem. ABA, Ga. Bar Assn., Atlanta Bar Assn. (legal counsel 1979-2000, Exceptional Svc. award 1987, Pres.'s Disting. Svc. award 1979-80, Charles E. Watkins Jr. award 1989), Atlanta Bar Found. (legal counsel 1985-2000), Order of Coif. Lutheran. Home: 3181 Habersham Rd NW Atlanta GA 30305 Office Phone: 404-853-8107. Business E-Mail: mark.kaufman@sablaw.com.

KAUFMAN, MARK STUART, lawyer; b. Binghamton, NY, June 16, 1947; s. Leonard and Edith (Levinson) K.; m. Chris Kestle, Feb. 13, 1981; children: Olivia, Dylan. BS with high distinction, Cornell U., 1969; JD cum laude, Harvard U., 1973. Bar: Ga. 1973, US Dist. Ct. (no. dist.) Ga. 1973, US Ct. Appeals (5th cir.) 1973, US Ct. Appeals (11th cir.) 1981, US Ct. Appeals (6th cir.). Assoc. Troutman, Sanders, Lockerman, Ashmore, Atlanta, 1973-79, ptnr., 1979-87, Long, Aldridge & Norman, Atlanta, 1987—, McKenna Long & Aldridge, Atlanta. Chmn. Chpt. 11 bankruptcy Bench and Bar Conf., Ga. and Atlanta Bars, 1991. Chmn. Atlanta Mcpl. Ct. Task Force, 1985; organizing com. Citizens Conf. on Judiciary, 1982; participant Leadership Ga., 1977. Recipient Legal Elite, Ga. Trend Mag., 2003—06, Ga. Super Lawyer, Atlanta Mag., 2003—06, Am.'s Leading Lawyers for Bus., 2003—, Who's Who Legal USA-Insolvency & Restructuring, 2006, Best Lawyers in Am., 2006—07. Mem. Am. Bankruptcy Inst., Southeastern Bankruptcy Law Inst. (bd. dirs. 1994—), Atlanta Bar Assn. (bd. dirs. bankruptcy sect. 1990—, sec. 1993, pres. 1996), Lawyers Club Atlanta, Commerce Club, Ga. Citizens Conf. Office: McKenna Long & Aldridge 303 Peachtree St NE Ste 5300 Atlanta GA 30308 Office Phone: 404-527-4120. Office Fax: 404-527-4198. Business E-Mail: mkaufman@mckennalong.com.

KAUFMAN, MARTIN KEPLINGER, landscape artist; s. Thomas Richard and Karen Lynnette Kaufman; 1 child, Margaret Helen. AAS, Ohio State U., Wooster, 1995. Lic. pesticide applicators class 3 Tenn., 2006. Groundskeeper Pleasant Hill Golf Course, Perrysville, Ohio, 1993; intern Westchase Golf Club, Tampa, Fla., 1994; groundskeeper Kepperra Golf Club, Brisbane, Queensland, Australia, 1995; asst. superintendant The Jewel Golf Course/The Grand Hotel, Mackinac Island, Mich., 1995; groundskeeper Royal Melbourne Golf Club, Victoria, Australia, 1996, Capitol Golf Club, Melbourne, 1996; installer, office mgr. Oakland Irrigation, Columbus, Ohio, 1996—97; asst. field groundskeeper Charlotte Knights, Rock Hill, SC, 1997—98; asst. groundskeeper Greensboro Bats, NC, 1997—97; asst. landscape supr. Carolina Panthers, Charlotte, NC, 1998—99; asst. field mgr. Tenn. Titans, Nashville, 1999—2004; supt. grounds Tenn. State U., Nashville, 2004—05; head groundsman Ensworth Schs., Nashville, 2005—. Cons. Global LLC, Nashville, 2003. Coun. mem. First Evang. Luth. Ch., Nashville, Tenn., 2006—07. Mem.: Sports Field Mgrs. Assn. (cert.), Sports Turf Mgrs. Assn. Republican. Avocations: water sports, sports, travel. Office: Ensworth Schs 7401 Hwy 100 Nashville TN 37221 Home Phone: 615-604-8196; Office Phone: 615-301-5382. Office Fax: 615-304-5381. Personal E-mail: mkaufman7@comcast.net. Business E-Mail: kaufmanm@ensworth.com.

KAUFMAN, MATTHEW, otolaryngologist, plastic surgeon; b. Oct. 29, 1972; Grad. with honors, SUNY, Binghamton; MD, SUNY, Syracuse, 1998. Cert. Plastic Surgeon and Otolaryngologist-Head and Neck Surgeon. Surgical tng., otolaryngology-Head and Neck Surgery Mt. Sinai Hosp., Manhattan; tng., plastic and reconstructive surgery UCLA Med. Ctr. Cancer reconstruction and microsurgery cons., Head and Neck Oncology Group of Ctrl. NJ St. Peter's Univ. Hosp., New Brunswick, NJ; lectr. in field both nationally and internationally. Contbr. articles to publications on plastic surgery, chapters to books; featured in Cosmetic Surgery Times, med. cons. Untold Stories in the ER. Mem. adv. bd. FM World Charities.

Mem.: Alpha Omega Alpha, Phi Beta Kappa Soc. Office: Plastic Surgery Ctr 561 Cranbury Rd East Brunswick NJ 08816 Address: Plastic Surgery Ctr 308 E 79th St New York NY 10021-0906*

KAUFMAN, NATHAN, retired pathologist, educator; b. Lachine, Que., Can., Aug. 3, 1915; s. Solomon and Anna (Sabesinsky) K.; m. Rita Friendly, Sept. 10, 1946; children: Naomi, Michael, Miriam, Hannah, Judith. B.Sc., McGill U., Montreal, 1937, MD, C.M., 1941. Mem. faculty Western Res. U. Med. Sch., 1948-60, asst. prof., 1952-54, asso. prof., 1954-60; pathologist-in-charge Cleve. Met. Gen. Hosp., 1952-60; prof. pathology Duke Sch. Medicine, 1960-67; prof. dept. pathology Queen's U. Med. Sch., Kingston, Ont., Canada, 1967-81, prof. emeritus, 1981—, head dept., 1967-79; clin. prof. office of humanities Med. Coll. Ga., Augusta, 1980-85. Pathologist-in-chief Kingston Gen. Hosp., 1967-79; past cons. Hotel Dieu Hosp., St. Mary's of the Lake Hosp., Kingston Clinic, Ont. Cancer Treatment and Rsch. Found.; asso. editor Lab. Investigation Jour., 1952-66, editor, 1972-75, mem. editorial bd., 1975—; assoc. editor Am. Jour. Pathology, 1967, mem. editl. bd., 1967-71; Mem. grants panel Med. Rsch. Coun. Can., 1970-74, mem. coun., 1971-77, exec. com., 1971-74; active coms. Ont. Coun. Health, 1968-79, chmn. provincial lev. edl. subcom., 1972-75 Editor: Modern Pathology, 1988; mem. editl. bd. Modern Pathology, 1989—95. Served to capt. M.C., Royal Can. Army, 1942-4., Decorated mem. Order Brit. Empire; recipient Disting. Alumni award Duke U., 1975, Internat. Acad. Pathology Gold medal, 1996. Mem. Internat. Acad. Pathology (v.p. 1972-74, pres. elect 1974, pres. 1976-78, pres. U.S.-Can. div. 1973-75, sec.-treas. 1979-91, F.K. Mostofi Disting. Svc. award U.S.-Can. div. 1990), U.S. and Can. Acad. Pathology, Royal Coll. Physicians and Surgeons Can. (com. on exams. 1972), Cleve. Soc. Pathologists (past pres.), Am. Assn. Pathologists (editor Symposium series 1970-71), Am. Soc. for Investigative Pathology, Am. Soc. Clin. Pathologists, Am. Assn. Cancer Research, Am. Soc. Cytology, Coll. Am. Pathologists, Canadian Med. Assn., Can., Ont. assns. pathologists, Ont. Med. Assn., Can. Soc. Cytology. Home: 185 Ontario St # 704 Kingston ON Canada K7L 2Y7

KAUFMAN, PAULA T., university librarian; b. Perth Amboy, NJ, July 26, 1946; d. Harry and Clara (Katz) K.; m. L. Ratner, 1989. AB in Economics, Smith Coll., 1968; MLS, Columbia U., 1969; MBA, U. New Haven, 1979. Reference libr. Columbia U., NYC, 1969-70, bus. libr., 1979-82, dir. libr. svcs., 1982-86, dir. acad. info. svcs., 1986-87, acting v.p., univ. libr., 1987-88; dean of librs. U. Tenn., Knoxville, 1988-99; univ. libr. U. Ill., Urbana Champaign, 1999—, interim chief info. officer, 2006—. Reference coord. McKinsey & Co., NYC, 1970—73; founder, ptnr. Info. for Bus., NYC, 1973—76; prin. reference libr. Yale U., New Haven, 1976—79; bd. dir. Ctr. Rsch. Libr., 1994—2000, chmn., 1996—97; bd. dirs. CAUSE, 1996—98; bd. dir. Assn. Rsch. Libr., 1997—2003, v.p., pres.-elect, 2000—01, pres., 2001—02; bd. dir. ILCSO, 2000—04, chair, 2001—02; bd. dirs. Coun. on Libr. and Info. Resources, 2001—, vice chair, 2001—06, bd. dirs., 2005—, chair, 2006—. Contbr. articles to mags.; mem. editl. bd. Directory of Industry Data Sources, HARFAX, 1980-82, Jour. Academic Librarianship, 1987-92, Jour. Libr. Adminstrn., 1995-2001. Bd. dirs. Cmty. Shares, Knoxville, 1993—97, Lincoln Trails Libr. Sys., Champaign, Ill., 2001—; bd. trustees Champaign (Ill.) Pub. Libr., 2004—. Recipient Robert B. Downs Intellectual Freedom award, 1989. Mem. ALA, Soc. for Scholarly Pub., Solinet (bd. dirs., chmn. 1992-93). Office: Univ of Illinois 230 Main Library MC 522 1408 W Gregory Dr Urbana IL 61801-3607

KAUFMAN, PETER BISHOP, biological sciences educator; b. San Francisco, Feb. 25, 1928; s. Earle Francis and Gwendolyn Bishop (Morris) K.; m. Hazel Elizabeth Snyder, Apr. 5, 1958; children— Linda Myrl, Laura Irene BS, Cornell U., 1949; PhD in Botany, U. Calif.-Davis, 1954. Instr. botany U. Mich., Ann Arbor, 1956-58, asst. prof., 1958-62, assoc. prof., 1962-72, prof. botany, cellular and molecular biology and bioengring. program, 1972-97, emeritus prof. dept. biology, 1998—, 1st yr. seminar Residential Coll., 1997—2002, sr. rsch. scientist integrative medicine program. Cons. NASA Space Biology Program; vis. prof. U. Lund, Sweden, 1964-65, U. Colo., Boulder, 1973-74; mem. faculty agr. Nagoya U., Japan, 1981 Author: Laboratory Experiments in Plant Physiology, 1975, Plants, People and Environment, 1979, Botany Illustrated, 1983, 2d edit., 2005, Practical Botany, 1983, Plants: Their Biology and Importance, 1989; co-author: Handbook of Molecular and Cellular Methods in Biology and Medicine, 1995, 3d edit., 2007, Methods in Gene Biotechnology, 1997, 2d edit., 2006, Natural Products from Plants, 1998, 2d edit., 2006, Creating a Sustainable Future Living in Harmony with the Earth, 2002, Botany Illustrated, 2nd edit., 2006. Mem. Mich. Natural Areas Coun.; mem. exec. com. U. Mich. Program in Scholarly Rsch. for Urban Minority Students. Grantee NIH, NSF, NASA, Cherry Mktg. Inst. Mich. Fellow AAAS; mem. Am. Inst. Biol. Scis., Am. Soc. Plant Biologists, Am. Soc. Gravitational and Space Biology (sec.-treas., 1985-1993), Internat. Soc. Plant Molecular Biologists, Bot. Soc. Am., Mich. Bot. Club (pres. 1985-89), Sigma Xi. Democrat. Presbyterian. Office: U Mich B570E MSRB II West Medical Dr Ann Arbor MI 48109 Home: 7261 Hashley Rd Manchester MI 48158 Office Phone: 734-615-4675. Business E-Mail: pbk@umich.edu.

KAUFMAN, RAYMOND HENRY, retired physician, retired educator; b. Bklyn., Nov. 24, 1925; s. Morris and Anne (Markewich) K.; m. Patricia Ann Judson, June 23, 1946; children: Susan Jo (Mrs. Edward B. Kahn), Wendy Beth (Mrs. Seth Katzman), Murri Ellen (Mrs. Raymond Simonetti), Elisabeth Ann. Student, Coll. William and Mary, 1942-43, U. N.C., 1943-44; MD, U. Md., 1948. Diplomate: Am. Bd. Obstetrics and Gynecology. Intern Beth Israel Hosp., NYC, 1948-49, resident obstetrics and gynecology, 1949-53; fellow pathology Meth. Hosp., Houston, 1955-58; asst. prof. obstetrics, gynecology, pathology Baylor Coll. Medicine, Houston, 1959-65, assoc. prof., 1965-72, acting chmn. dept., 1968-72, prof., chmn. dept. ob-gyn, 1973-93, prof. pathology, 1973—2005, prof. dept. ob-gyn., 1973—2005, prof. emeritus, 2005—; prof. ob-gyn. Weill-Cornell Med. Sch., 2005—. Author: (with H.L. Gardner) Benign Diseases of Vulva and Vagina, 1969, 5th edit. (with S. Faro, D. Brown), 2005; contbr. articles to profl. jours. Served with USNR, 1943-45; to capt. USAF, 1953-55. Mem. Am. Coll. Obstetrics and Gynecology, ACS, Cen. Assn. Obstetrics and Gynecology (chmn. com. for cons. gynecol. pathology 1968-87, pres. 1976), Tex. Assn. Obstetrics and Gynecology (v.p. 1971, 81, pres. 1983), Am. Gynecol. and Obstet. Soc. (v.p. 1985-86), Houston Obstet. and Gynecol. Soc. (pres. 1971-72), Soc. Gynecol. Oncology (v.p. 1983-84), Am. Cytology Soc., Am. Fertility Soc., Am. Soc. Colposcopy, Internat. Soc. Vulvar Disease (pres. 1978-79), Phi Delta Epsilon (nat. sec. 1970-75). Office: Meth Hosp 6550 Fannin #900 Houston TX 77030-3411 Office Phone: 713-481-3199. Business E-Mail: rkaufman@tmh.tmc.edu.

KAUFMAN, RICHARD STUART, conductor; b. LA, Nov. 20, 1947; s. Walter S. and Margye L. (Whisler) Kaufman; m. Gayle Kaufman; 1 child, Whitney Claire. BA in Music, Calif. State U., Northridge, 1970. Music dir., condr. Sweet Charity, Two Gentlemen of Verona, Company, nat. tours, 1970-74, LA Civic Light Opera, 1975—80; condr. for various performers including Burt Bacharach, Juliet Prowse, Andy Williams, John Denver, nationwide, 1976—; music assoc. 20th Century Fox Studios, LA, 1982—84; music coordinator Metro Goldwyn Mayer/United Artists Communications, Culver City, Calif., 1984-87; dir. music for TV Metro Goldwyn Mayer/United Artists Comm., Culver City, Calif., 1988—; condr. Pacific Symphony, 1990—; prin. pops condr. Dallas Symphony Orch., 1997—. Mem. music adv. bd. Young Musicians Found., Henry Mancini Inst. Composer: Alma Mater for Calif. State U., 1969. Recipient Best Pop Instrumental Performance, Grammy Awards, 1993; fellow, Berkshire Music Festival, 1969, Tanglewood, 1969. Mem.: Phi Mu Alpha. Avocations: baseball, racquetball. Office: MGM/UA Communications Inc 10000 Washington Blvd Suite 2091 Culver City CA 90232 also: Dallas Symphony 2301 Flora St Dallas TX 75201 also: Pacific Symphony Ste 100 3631 S Harbor Blvd Santa Ana CA 92704*

KAUFMAN, ROBERT, lawyer; b. NYC, July 15, 1937; BA, UCLA, 1959; JD, Southwestern Univ., 1963. Bar: Calif. 1964, US Ct. Appeals, Ninth Circuit 1975. Referee State Bar Cts. Calif., 1969—84; family law mediator LA Superior Ct., 1981—2000; family law atty. Kaufman, Young, Spiegel, Robinson & Kenerson, LLP, LA. Asst. prof. law Pepperdine U., Malibu, Calif., 1988—96; spkr. in field. Contbr. articles to numerous profl. jours. Mem.: ABA (Professionalism Committee of the Family Law Section 1993), Assn. Trial Lawyers in Am., Orange Co. Bar Assn., California State Bar Assn. (family law and litig. svcs. 1975—), LA Co. Bar Assn. (exec. com., Family Law Section 1992—93, judicial liaison com. 1992—93), Beverly Hills Bar Assn. Office: Kaufman, Young, Spiegel Robinson and Kenerson Ste 300 301 North Canon Dr Beverly Hills CA 90210-4724*

KAUFMAN, ROBERT JULES, communications consultant, lawyer; b. NYC, Jan. 21, 1921; s. Ernst B. and Gertrude S. (Popper) K.; m. Susan H. Sanger, Feb. 22, 1951; children— Peter S., James H. Student, Columbia Coll., 1942, Yale U. Law Sch., 1948. Bar: N.Y. bar 1949. Assoc. Gale, Bernays, Falk & Eisner, NYC, 1948-53; ptnr. Gale & Falk, 1953-55; asst. gen. counsel DuMont TV Network, 1953-55; with ABC, NYC, 1955-86, v.p., gen. atty. network govtl. regulation, 1968-86; comm. cons. Scarsdale, NY, 1986—. Mem. internat. copyright panel Dept. State; guest speaker on radio and television matters at Practicing Law Inst. and N.Y. U. Law Sch. Served to lt. USN, 1942-46. Mem. Bar Assn. City N.Y. (communications com.), Copyright Soc. U.S.A., Nat. Acad. TV Arts and Scis. (mem. U.S. Olympic job opportunity program com.), Phi Beta Kappa. Home and Office: 33 Clarendon Rd Scarsdale NY 10583-2452

KAUFMAN, ROBERT MAX, lawyer, director; b. Vienna, Nov. 17, 1929; came to US, 1939, naturalized, 1945; s. Paul M. and Bertha (Hirsch) K.; m. Sheila Seymour Kelley. BA with honors, Bklyn. Coll., 1951; MA, NYU, 1954; JD magna cum laude, Bklyn. Law Sch., 1957. Bar: NY 1957, US Supreme Ct. 1961. Jr. economist, economist, sr. economist NY State Divsn. Housing, 1953—57; atty. antitrust divsn. US Dept. Justice, 1957—58; legis. asst. US Senator Jacob K. Javits, 1958—61; assoc. Proskauer Rose LLP, NYC, 1961—69, ptnr., 1969—. Past chmn. bd. Pirelli Cables & Systems, LLC, Pirelli Tires LLC; chmn. bd. Old Westbury Funds, Inc.; bd. dirs. Roytex Inc.; mem. NY State Legis. Adv. Com. on Election Law, 1973-74; chmn. adv. com. NY State Bd. Elections, 1974-78; chmn. NY State Bd. Pub. Disclosure, 1981-82, US Army Chief of Staff's Spl. Commn. on Honor System, 1988-89, NY Chief Judge's Com. on Availability of Legal Svcs., 1988-90; referee Commn. on Jud. Conduct; spl. master NY Supreme Ct. Appellate Divsn., 1999—; mem. Adminstrv. Conf. US (chair com. regulations), 1988-95; chmn. Fund for Modern Cts., 1990-95; mem. Def. Adv. Com. on Women in the Svcs., 1997-99, vice chair com. on equality mgmt., mem. exec. com. 1998. Co-author: Congress and the Public Trust, 1970, Disorder in the Court, 1973; co-gen. editor: Matthew Bender Treatise on Health Care Law, 4 vols., 1992-2002 Bd. dirs. NOW Legal Def. and Edn. Momentum; bd. dirs., mem. exec. com. Lawrence M. Gelb Found., Inc., Lawyers in Pub. Interest, 1986—95, emeritus bd. dirs., 1995—; bd. dirs., mem. exec. com. Am. Judicature Soc., pres., 1995—97; bd. dirs., chmn. exec. com. Cmty. Action Legal Svcs., Inc., 1976—78; dir., mem. exec. com. Legal Aid Soc., 1985—90; mem. exec. com. Vols. of Legal Svc., 1986—94; mem. platform com. N.Y. Rep. State Com.; mem. jud. selection adv. coms. Senator Javits, 1972—80, Senator Moynahan, 1977—2000; bd. dirs. Citizen's Union Found., 1986—, v.p., 1993—; bd. dirs. Women's Rsch. and Edn. Inst.; bd. visitors U. S. Mil. Acad., 1976—79; bd. dirs., vice chmn. N.Y. Cmty. Funds.; bd. dirs. Citizens Union NYC, 1986—, James Found., Vis. Nurse Svc. of N.Y.C., Med. and Health Rsch. Assn. N.Y.C., Sept. 11 Fund; mem. jud. selection adv. coms. of Senators Javitz and Moynihan, N.Y.C. Quadrennial Comm. on compensation of elected officials, 1995, 1999, mem. distbn. com., vice chair, 2001—, N.Y. Cmty. Trust; dir., mem. exec. com., past chmn. bd. Times Sq. Bus. Improvement Dist.; trustee Bklyn. Law Sch. With US Army, 1957—58. Fellow Am. Bar Found., NY State Bar Found.; mem. ABA, Assn. of Bar of City NY (pres. 1986-88, chmn. house com., co-chmn. com. on campaign fin. reform 1997-2001, past chmn. com. on 2d Century; past chmn. exec. com., past chmn. com. profl. responsibility, past chmn. spl. com. on campaign expenditures, past chmn. com. civil rights, past vice chmn. com. grievances, past chmn. delegation to state bar ho. dels.), NY State Bar Assn. (ho. of dels. 1978, 86-90), NY County Lawyers Assn. (past chmn. com. on civil rights), Am. Law Inst. Office: Proskauer Rose LLP 1585 Broadway New York NY 10036-8299 Office Phone: 212-969-3285. Business E-Mail: rkaufman@proskauer.com.

KAUFMAN, RUSSEL EUGENE, hematologist, oncologist; b. Kenton, Ohio, Mar. 7, 1946; s. George W. and Eileen M. (Risner) K.; m. Jane Ann Steinman; children: Jonathon R., Emily J. BS, Ohio State U., 1969, MD cum laude, 1973. Diplomate Am. Bd. Internal Medicine. Resident in medicine Duke U. Med. Ctr., Durham, NC, 1973-77, chief resident in medicine, 1977; rsch. hematologist NIH, Bethesda, Md., 1978-80; asst. prof. medicine Duke U. Med. Ctr., Durham, 1980-86, from asst. prof. to assoc. prof. biochemistry, 1985—2001, from assoc. prof. to prof. medicine, 1986—, prof. dept. biochemistry, 2000—02, prof. emeritus, 2002—, chief divsn. hematology and oncology, 1989-96, chief divsn. med. oncology & transplantation, 1996-98, vice chair dept. medicine, 1995-99, assoc. dean Sch. of Medicine, 1998-99, vice dean for edn. and acad. affairs, 1999—2002, assoc. vice chancellor acad. affairs, 2000—02; dir., CEO Wistar Inst., 2002—03, pres., CEO, 2004—; dir. Wistar NCI Cancer Ctr. Mem. sci. adv. com. Am. Cancer Soc., Atlanta, NYC, 1987—; mem. com. NAS, Washington, 1983-86; mem. sci. rev. coms. NIH, Bethesda, Md., 1985—; assoc. chief of staff edn. Durham VA Med. Ctr., 1998-99; Wistar prof. medicine Sch. Medicine U. Pa. Health Sys., 2003-; bd. dirs. U. City Sci. Ctr., 2002-, BioAdvance, 2004-06, chmn. 2006-, U. of Arts, 2005-, bd. advisors Osage Venture Ptnrs., 2005—, founding bd. mem. Pharm. Safety Inst. 2006—. Contbr. articles to profl. jours., chpts. to books. Mem. Pa. Cancer Ctr. Alliance, 2002—; bd. dirs., CEO Coun. for Growth Greater Phila. C. of C., 2003—; bd. mem. CEO Coun. for Growth, 2003—; mem. coun. for extramural grants Am. Cancer Soc., 2004—07, chair, 2007—. Searle Found. scholar, 1983-86, Leukemia Soc. scholar, NYC, 1986-90. Fellow ACP; mem. AAAS, Am. Soc. Biochemistry, Am. Soc. Hematology (head subcom. on red cell 1985-88, chmn. com. on tng. programs 1995-98), Assn. Subsplty. Profs. (exec. coun. 1994, treas. 1997-98, pres.-elect 1998-99, pres. 1999-2000, past pres. 2000-01), Assn. Hematology/Oncology Program Dirs. (chair 1997-98), U. the Arts (bd. mem. 2004-2007), Neuland Labs. (bd. mem. 2007—), Pa. Cancer Ctr. Alliance. Presbyn. Avocations: golf, tennis. Office: The Wistar Inst 3601 Spruce St Philadelphia PA 19104-4265 Office Phone: 215-898-3926. Business E-Mail: kaufman@wistar.org.

KAUFMAN, SHIRONA, cantor, educator; b. Bklyn., Apr. 25, 1953; d. Uriel and Annette (Berger) Levy; m. Berl H. Kaufman (div.); children: Lianne, Leora. BFA, SUNY, Purchase, 1980. Music tchr. Temple Israel Ctr., White Plains, NY, 1999—2001, Westchester Reform, Scarsdale, 2001—04; Cantor Congregation KTI, Port Chester, 2004—. Cantor Ahavat Achim, Colchester, Conn., 2001—04. Composer, prodr.: songs Shirona: Judaic Love Songs, 2000 (Best Jewish Album, Jewish Week, 2001), Songs of the Heart and Spirit, 2002; composer: Shabbat Anthology; contbr. articles to profl. jours. Mem.: Hanashir Music Network, Women Cantor's Network. Home: Apt 9 20 Chestnut St Rye NY 10580-2853 Office Phone: 914-967-4338. Personal E-mail: shirona@bellatlantic.net.

KAUFMAN, STEPHEN EDWARD, lawyer; b. NYC, Feb. 16, 1932; s. Herbert and Gertrude Kaufman; m. Marina Pinto, June 22, 1967; children: Andrew H. and Douglas P. BA, Williams Coll., 1953; LLB, Columbia U., 1957. Bar: N.Y. 1958, U.S. Ct. Appeals (2d cir.) 1958, U.S. Dist. Ct. (so. and ea. dists.) N.Y. 1960, U.S. Supreme Ct. 1963. Asst. U.S. atty. (So. dist.) NY US Dept. Justice, 1958, chief criminal divsn., 1964-69; pres. Stephen E. Kaufman, P.C., NYC, 1976—. Bd. dirs. Citigroup Mut. Funds. Trustee Mus. Jewish Heritage; dir. Police Athletic League. Fellow Am. Coll. Trial Lawyers; mem. ABA, N.Y. State Bar Assn., Assn. of Bar of City of N.Y. Office: 277 Park Ave New York NY 10172-0003 Office Phone: 212-826-0820. Business E-Mail: skaufman@sekpc.com.

KAUFMAN, STEPHEN LAWRENCE, radiologist, educator; b. Phila., Nov. 7, 1942; s. Abraham S. and Genevieve (Finestone) Kaufman. BA, U. Pa., 1963, MD, 1967. Resident in radiology, then fellow cardiovasc. radiology Johns Hopkins Med. Ctr., Balt., 1970-75, asst. prof. radiology, 1975-79, assoc. prof., 1980-88; prof. radiology, dir. cardiovasc. and interventional radiology Emory U., Atlanta, 1988—2003, prof. emeritus radiology, 2003—; attending radiologist Asheville VA Med. Ctr., 2003—, 2003—. Author: Techniques in Interventional Radiology, 1982; editor: Billiary Radiology, 1992; contbr. articles to profl. jours. Lt. comdr. USPHS, 1968—70. Fellow: Am. Heart Assn., Soc. Interventional Radiology; mem.: Am. Coll. Radiology, Radiol. Soc. N.Am. Avocations: hiking, white-water rafting, golf, computers. Personal E-mail: kauf8727@bellsouth.net.

KAUFMAN, SUSAN SHIFFMAN, psychologist; b. Bklyn., Mar. 26, 1954; d. Harvey Benjamin and Shirley Shiffman; m. Steven Robert Kaufman, Sept. 24, 1978; 1 child, Samantha Eve. BS cum laude, Bklyn Coll., 1975; MS, St. John's U., 1976, PD, 1977; MPhil, CUNY, 1979, PhD, 1990. Cert. sch. psychologist N.Y., 1977. Rsch. asst. dept. psychology Bklyn Coll., 1974—75; sch. psychology intern Coney Island Hosp., Bklyn., 1976—77; psychodiagnostic screener and evaluator Glen Cove Pub. Schs., NY, 1977; cons. in sch. psychology N.Y.C. Bd. of Edn., Bklyn., Queens, 1977—83; ind. profl. reviewer N.Y. State Dept. of Mental Hygiene, 1977; learning disability tutor Kingsborough C.C., Bklyn., 1978; sch. psychologist Mid. Country Ctrl. Sch. Dist. #11, Centereach, NY, 1978, Lindenhurst Pub. Schs., NY, 1980—. Workshop presenter Lindenhurst Pub. Schs., NY, 1981—, psychology budget coord., 1984—, psychologist interview com. for new hires, 1985—, mentor to new psychologists, 1990—, inclusion com. mem., 1993—, supr. psychology interns and sch. psychology PhD students, 1995—2003, co-author psychologist policy and procedure manual, 1999—, universal presch. com., 2002—03, com. on spl. edn. chairperson, 2002—. Contbr. conf. workshop. Mem. Syosset Pk. Civic Assn., NY, 1995—, sec., bd. dirs., 1997—2004; corresponding sec., exec. bd. Village Elem. Sch. PTA, NY, 1996—98; mem. Residents for a More Beautiful Syosset, NY, 1999—. Mem.: NASP. Home: 1 Pine Rd Syosset NY 11791 Office: Lindenhurst Pub Schs 350 Daniel St Lindenhurst NY 11757 Home Phone: 516-364-0953; Office Phone: 631-226-6894. Office Fax: 631-226-6428. Personal E-mail: sskaufman@aol.com. Business E-Mail: skaufm@lindenhurstschools.org.

KAUFMAN, THOMAS FREDERICK, lawyer, educator; b. Buffalo, Sept. 10, 1949; s. Frederick J. and Edna M. (Kilian) K.; children: Alycia, Thomas, Jonathan. BSEE, SUNY, Buffalo, 1971; JD, Georgetown U., 1976; MBA, Wharton Sch., U. Pa., 2001. Bar: Va. 1976, U.S. Ct. Appeals (6th cir.) 1976, DC 1977, U.S. Dist. Ct. DC 1981, Md. 1996, NY 2007. Law clk. to chief judge U.S. Ct. Appeals (6th cir.), 1976-77; assoc. Melrod, Redman & Gartlan, Washington, 1977-81, Willkie Farr & Gallagher, Washington, 1981-84, ptnr., 1985-95, Hunton & Williams LLP, Washington, 1995—. Adj. prof. law Georgetown U., Washington, 1986—; fed. city coun., Washington. Recipient Silver Vicennial medal, Georgetown U. Law Ctr. Mem. ABA, Am. Coll. Real Estate Lawyers (chmn. Capital Markets Com.). Avocations: skiing, bicycling, hiking, history. Office: Hunton and Williams LLP 1900 K St NW Washington DC 20006-1110 Office Phone: 202-955-1604. Business E-Mail: tkaufman@hunton.com.

KAUFMAN, VICTOR A., broadcast and retired film company executive; b. 1943; Various sr. positions Columbia, 1974—87; founding chmn., CEO Tri-Star Pictures, 1987—89; pres. CEO Columbia Pictures Entertainment, Inc., 1987—89; chmn. Savoy Pictures Entertainment, NYC, 1990—96; CFO, vice chmn. HSN, Inc., 1996—98; CFO, chmn. USA Networks, Inc., NYC, 1998—, vice chmn. and office chmn., 1999—2003; vice chmn. Interactive Corp., 2003—. Office: USA Networks Inc 42d Fl 152 W 57th St New York NY 10019-3310*

KAUFMAN, WILLIAM MORRIS, electrical engineer, consultant; b. Pitts., Dec. 31, 1931; s. Nathan and Sarah M. (Paper) K.; m. Iris F. Picovsky, June 21, 1953; children: Nathan E., Marjorie L., Emily M. BSEE, Carnegie Inst. Tech., 1953, MSEE, PhD in EE. Registered profl. engr. Supr. Westinghouse Electric Corp., Pitts., 1955-62; dir. rsch. Gen. Instrument Corp., Newark, 1962-65; cons. engr. GE, Valley Forge, Pa., 1965-66; mgr. med. engr. dept. Hittman Assocs. Inc., Columbia, Md., 1966-71; v.p. engring. ENSCO, Springfield, Va., 1971-83; v.p. Ocean Data Systems Inc., Rockville, Md., 1984-85; v.p. applied rsch., dir. Carnegie Mellon Rsch. Inst. Carnegie Mellon U., Pitts., 1985-97, mem. tech. transfer bd., 1989-94, mem. employee retirement and welfare benefit plan com., 1988-97. Chmn. tech. adv. group Fostin Capital, Pitts., 1986-95; mem. adv. bd. Pitts. Seed Fund, 1986-97; bd. dirs. Mellon Pitt Carnegie Corp., Maglev, Inc., Tech. Devel. and Edn. Corp. Patentee in field. Mem. adv coun. on regional devel. U. Pitts., 1986; bd. dirs. Ben Franklin Tech. Ctr. of Western Pa., 1988-97, treas., 1997; cons. tech. acquisition. Fellow IEEE (life); mem. Sigma Xi, Tau Beta Pi, Eta Kappa Nu. Home and Office: 38 Sheridan Rd Swampscott MA 01907-2045 Office Phone: 781-595-1434. Business E-Mail: billkaufman@cmu.edu.

KAUFMANN, HENRY MARK, mortgage banker; b. Basel, Switzerland, May 23, 1929; arrived in US, 1940; s. Ferdinand and Carola (Levy) K.; m. Barbara Lurie, Dec. 23, 1961; children: Frederic, Nancy. Student, Univ. Geneva, Switzerland, 1948; BA in Economics, Oberlin Coll., 1951; JD, Harvard U., 1954. Bar: NY 1957, US Ct. Appeals 1960, US Supreme Ct. 1960, US Tax Ct. 1974. V.p. Pearce Mayer & Greer, NYC, 1958—70, I.F.C. Capital Resources, NYC, 1970—75, Smith Barney Real Estate Corp., NYC, 1975—80; pres., chmn. Henry Kaufmann Assocs., Larchmont, NY, 1980—. With Mil. Intelligence Europe 1955-57. Mem. New Rochelle Bar Assn., NY Bar Assn., New York County Lawyers Assn., Harvard Club. Avocations: coin collecting/numismatics, travel. Home: 64 Greentree Dr Scarsdale NY 10583-7029 Office: Henry Kaufmann Assocs 2 East Ave Larchmont NY 10538-2462

KAUFMANN, JEFFREY BAER, finance educator; b. St. Louis Park, Minn., Aug. 27, 1959; s. Harold Ralph and Nora Jane (Baer) K.; m. Peggy Alicia Rouleau, May 9, 1994. BBA cum laude, James Madison U., 1987; JD, Coll. William and Mary, 1990; PhD, U. N.C., 1999. Bar: Va. 1990, U.S. Ct. Appeals (4th cir.) 1990. Summer assoc. Jeremiah Denton and Assoc., Virginia Beach, Va., 1989; rsch. asst. Coll. of William and Mary, Williamsburg, Va., 1988-90; instr. U. N.C., Chapel Hill, 1990-94; instr. corp. strategy and internat. bus. St. Mary's U., Winona, Minn., 1995—97; vis. asst. prof. mgmt. U. Ill., Urbana-Champaign, 1997—2001; asst. prof. mgmt. Iowa St. U., Ames, 2001—. Mem. Nat. Moot Ct. Team, Coll. William and Mary, Williamsburg, 1989; adj. assoc. prof. Ctrl. Mich. U., Mt. Pleasant, 1995, 1997. Mng. editor Adminstrv. Law Rev., 1989-90; contbr. chpt. to book and articles to profl. jours.; reviewer profl. jours. and assns. With USN, 1978-82. Decorated Expeditionary Forces medals (2); Richard D. Irwin Doctoral Dissertation fellow Richard D. Irwin Co., 1993-94, Nat. Doctoral Bus. Fellow Am. Assn. Colls. and Schs. of Bus, finalist Free Press Doctoral Dissertation award, Acad. Mgmt. Mem. ABA (vice chmn.

internat. law com. sect. adminstrv. law and regulatory practice), Va. Bar Assn., Acad. Mgmt. (5 Outstanding Reviewer awards), VFW, Phi Kappa Phi, Beta Gamma Sigma. Avocations: hiking, exercise, reading, history. Office: Iowa St U Coll of Business 3121 Gerdin Bus Bldg Ames IA 50011-1350 Office Phone: 515-294-1201. Business E-Mail: jkaufmnn@iastate.edu.

KAUFMANN, MARK STEINER, banker, director; b. NYC, Dec. 3, 1932; s. Milton L. and Elsa S. (Steiner) K.; m. Carole Richard, June 16, 1957; children: Jon Richard, Susan Helen. BS cum laude in Bus. Adminstrn., Lehigh U., 1953. V.p., dir. mktg. Standard Fin. Corp., NYC, 1958-64; sr. v.p., dir. Milberg Factors, Inc., NYC, 1964-73; dir. corp. devel. Chase Manhattan Bank, NYC, 1973-87, sr. v.p., 1987-96; chmn. Kaufmann & Ptnrs., LLC, NYC, 1996—. Past chmn. banking divsn. UJA/Fedn.; former chmn. bd. dirs. Industry Leaders Fund; adv. bd. Radar Logic, Inc. Hon. trustee Calhoun Sch., N.Y.C.; hon. dir. Lower Manhattan Cultural Coun.; chmn. emeritus Temple Israel, N.Y.C.; bd. mem. Matindale Inst., Lehigh U. 1st lt. USAF, 1953—55. Recipient human rels. award Anti-Defamation League, 1973, Am. Jewish Com., 1987. Mem. Harmonie Club (bd. mem.), Old Oaks Country Club (bd. mem.), Beta Gamma Sigma, Lambda Mu Sigma, Pi Gamma Mu, Omicron Delta Kappa. Home: 124 W 79th St New York NY 10024-6446 Office: Kaufmann and Ptnrs LLC 124 W 79th St New York NY 10024-6446 Office Phone: 212-496-3800. E-mail: mskaufmann@aol.com.

KAUFMANN, PATRICK J., business educator; b. Flint, Mich., Oct. 29, 1946; s. Joseph P. and Rose Ione Kaufmann; m. Joan Barry, May 10, 1979; 1 child, Christine. BA, Georgetown U., DC, 1964—68; JD, Boston Coll. Law Sch., 1971—74; MBA, U. Pa., Phila., 1978—80; PhD, Northwestern U., Evanston, Ill., 1980—84. Atty. Cohn, Riemer and Pollack, Boston, 1974—77; asst. prof. bus. adminstrn. Harvard Bus. Sch., Boston, 1984—91; prof. mktg. Ga. State U., Atlanta, 1991—98; prof., chair mktg. dept. Boston U. Sch. Mgmt., 1998—. Lt. USN, 1968—71. Recipient Outstanding Faculty Achievement award, Ga. State U., 1996. Mem.: Mass. Bar Assn., Am. Mktg. Assn., Internat. Soc. Franchising (chmn., exec. com. 1986), Beta Gamma Sigma. Office: Boston Univ Sch Mgmt 595 Commonwealth Ave Boston MA 02215 Office Phone: 617-353-4278.

KAUFMANN, URLIN MILO, English literature educator; b. Cleve., Aug. 27, 1934; s. Albert Walter and Alda Winona (Aiken) K.; m. Helen Elizabeth Olson, Sept. 1, 1956; children: Felice, Laurie, Andrew. BA, Greenville Coll., Ill., 1956; MA, U. Ill., 1957; PhD, Yale U., 1960. Instr. North Park Coll., Chgo., 1961-62, U. Ill., Urbana, 1962-63, asst. prof., 1963-67, assoc. prof. English, 1967-94, retired, 1994—. Author: The Pilgrim's Progress and Traditions in Puritan Meditation, 1967, Paradise in the Age of Milton, 1978, Heaven: A Future Finer Than Dreams, 1981, Measures of Breath, 2004; co-author: At Ease: Discussing Money and Values in Small Groups, 1998; contbg. author, editor: Households Under God, 1996, I May Be Different, But I'm Part of The Family, 1999. Pres. Light and Life men's aux. Free Meth. Ch. N.Am., Indpls., 1985-95; bd. dirs. Empty Tomb, Inc., Urbana-Champaign, 1980—. Democrat. Home: 1807 N Concord Ln Urbana IL 61802-7725 E-mail: ukaufman@uiuc.edu.

KAUFMANN, VICKI MARIE, social services administrator; b. Lansing, Mich., Nov. 7, 1946; d. Frank Richard and Sophia Mary (Scieszka) Marczynski; m. Felix Kaufmann May 28, 1988. BA, Carlow Coll., Pitts., 1970; MS in Pastoral Studies, St. Paul U., Ottawa, ON., Can., 1976, MA, 1977. Cert. family life educator, fund raising exec. Tchr. Mt. Nazareth Acad., Pitts., 1969—71; family svc. dir. Mt. Nazareth Ctr., Pitts., 1971—75, 1977—78; parish outreach worker St. Casimir Ch., Lansing, 1978—81; parish outreach cons. Diocese of Lansing, 1980—83; family life educator Cath. Social Svcs., Lansing, 1981—84; agy. dir. Cath. Social Svc., Brighton, Mich., 1984—93, Cath. Charities of Archdiocese Miami, Wilton Manors, Fla., 1994—2002, COO, 2002—04, dir. capital devel., 2004—07, cert. fund raising exec., 2005—; dir. spkrs. bur. Food for the Poor, Coconut Creek, Fla., 2007—. Chmn. Consortium on Aging, Howell, Mich., 1988-89; cons. (Lansing chpt.) Nat. Stepfamily Assn., 1982-84; facilitator Cath. Coun. on Aging, Livingston County, Mich., 1986-89. Co-author: Welcoming the Seasons, 1977, Parish Social Ministry, 1985. Co-chmn. Livingston County Emergency Shelter, Howell, Mich., 1988—, vice chmn., 1990; bd. dir. Livingston County United Way, Howell, 1988-89, Mich. Coun. of Family Rels., 1990-93; exec. sec. Coun. of Ch. Bd., Lansing, 1982-84; agy. rep. Energy Bank Coalition, Lansing, 1982-84. Mem. NAFE, Nat. Coun. Family Rels., Cath. Charities U.S.A., Mich. Coun. Family Rels. (bd. dir. 1990-93), Assn. Fundraising Profl. (cert.) Roman Catholic. Avocations: classical music, opera, the arts, travel. Office: Food for the Poor 6401 Lyons Rd Coconut Creek FL 33073

KAUGER, YVONNE, state supreme court justice; b. Cordell, Okla., Aug. 3, 1937; d. John and Alice (Bottom) K.; 1 child, Jonna Kauger Kirschner. BS magna cum laude, Southwestern State U., Weatherford, Okla., 1958; cert. med. technologist, St. Anthony's Hosp., 1959; JD, Oklahoma City U., 1969, LLD (hon.), 1992. Med. technologist Med. Arts Lab., 1959-68; assoc. Rogers, Travis & Jordan, 1970-72; jud. asst. Okla. Supreme Ct., Oklahoma City, 1972-84, justice, 1984-94, 1998—, vice chief justice, 1994-96, chief justice, 1997-98. Mem. appellate div. Ct. on Judiciary; mem. State Capitol Preservation Commn., 1983-84; mem. dean's adv. com. Oklahoma City U. Sch. Law; lectr. William O. Douglas Lecture Series Gonzaga U., 1990. Founder Gallery of Plains Indian, Colony, Okla., Red Earth (Down Towner award 1990), 1987; active Jud. Day, Girl's State, 1976-80; keynote speaker Girl's State Hall of Fame Banquet, 1984; bd. dirs. Lyric Theatre, Inc., 1966— , pres. bd. dirs., 1981; past mem. bd. dirs. Civic Music Soc., Okla. Theatre Ctr., Canterbury Choral Soc.; mem. First Lady of Okla.'s Artisans' Alliance Com. Recipient Herbert Harley award, 1999, Gov.'s Arts award, 2005; named Panhellenic Woman of Yr., 1990, Woman of Yr. Red Lands Coun. Girl Scouts, 1990; named one of 10 Most Notable Women in Okla. OKC Orch. League, 2005; named to Washita County Hall of Fame, 1992, Okla. Women's Hall of Fame, 2001. Mem. ABA (law sch. accreditation com.), Okla. Bar Assn. (law schs. com. 1977—, Jud. Excellence award 1999), Washita County Bar Assn., Washita County Hist. Soc. (life), St. Paul's Music Soc., Iota Tau Tau, Delta Zeta (Disting. Alumna award 1988, State Delta Zeta of Yr. 1987, Nat. Woman of Yr. 1988). Episcopalian. Office: Okla Supreme Ct State Capitol Building Rm 242 Oklahoma City OK 73105 Office Phone: 405-521-3841. E-mail: yvonne.kauger@oscn.net.

KAUK, JANET LEA, not-for-profit developer; b. Omaha, Nebr., Oct. 6, 1955; d. Walter Allen and Betty Galloway Bennett; m. Bruce Allen Kauk, Aug. 7, 1976; children: Justin Ryan, Blaine William. AA, Springfield Coll., Ill., 1978; degree in Nursing, U. Kans., Kans. City, 1981; MBA, U. Mo., Kans. City, 2006. Registered nurse, Bd. Healing Arts., Mo., 1979. Exec. dir. SafeHaven Kans. City, 1991—98, Synergy Svcs., Parkville, Mo., 1998—2000, Northland Cmty. Found., Kans. City, 2006—. Mem.charter com. Clay County, Liberty, Mo., 2000; founder Friends Shoal Creek, Kans. City, 1986—89; bd. dirs., pres., treas. North Kans. City Schs. Bd. Edn., Kans. City, 2002. Recipient Anne Robb Townsend award, Townsend Family, 2002. Mem.: Assistance League Kans. City (assoc.; founder 1983). Republican. Methodist. Avocations: travel, interior decorating, gardening, reading. Home: 4325 N Mulberry Kansas City MO 64116 Home Phone: 816-453-6885; Office Phone: 816-627-3402.

KAUL, MOHAN LAL, retired social worker, educator, writer; arrived in U.S., 1969, naturalized, 1976; s. Mahanand and Tarawati Kaul; m. Jaya Nagari, Aug. 8, 1950; children: Rajiv M., Sanjiv M., Prerna J. BSc, Panjab U., India, 1947; diploma in Social Work, Delhi Sch. Social Work, India, 1958; MSW, U. Pitts., 1967; PhD, Case Western Reserve U., Cleve., 1977. Warden Social Edn. Ctr., Delhi, 1950—59; cmty. organizer Dept. Urban Cmty. Devel., Delhi, 1959, chief cmty. organizer, 1959—63, dir., 1963—65; asst. dir. Dept. Cmty. Svcs., Delhi, 1967—69, East Akron (Ohio) Cmty. House, 1969—71; asst. prof. Kent (Ohio) State U., 1971—77, assoc. prof., 1977—94; ret., 1994. Mem. editl. bd. Pediatric Social Work, 1984—88. Author: My Account, Family Edition, 2004, Sheila, 2004; contbr. articles to profl. jours. Pres. Portage County Housing Advs., 1985—86; coord. Citizens Effort to Close Lucky Shoe Cafe, Akron, 1972. Fellow, Ford Found., 1965—67; grantee, Govt. India, 1957—58, NIMH, 1974—75. Mem.: NASW (Gold Card mem., cert.), Assn. Advancement Social Work Groups, Ohio Ret. Tchrs. Assn. (life), Coun. East Akron Block Club Pres. (founder 1972). Hindu. Avocations: gardening, exercise, writing, travel. Home: 1158 Morningview Dr Tallmadge OH 44278

KAUL, PRADMAN, communications executive; BSEE, George Washington U.; MSEE, U. Calif., Berkeley. Pres. Hughes Network Sys., LLC, Germantown, Md., 1990—2000, chmn., CEO, 2000—; pres., CEO Hughes Comms., Inc. Bd. dirs. PRIMUS Telecommunications, McLean, Va., 2002—, Optimos Inc., Tata Teleservices Maharashtra, Ltd. Contbr. articles to profl. jours. Chmn. Md. India Bus. Round Table; mem. Nat. Adv. Coun. George Washington U. Mem.: NAE, IEEE (sr.). Office: Hughes Network Sys, LLC 11717 Exploration Lane Germantown MD 20876

KAULAKIS, ARNOLD FRANCIS, management consultant; b. Lewiston, Maine, Oct. 6, 1916; s. Frank Kaulakis and Amelia (Vilaniskis) K.; m. Marguerite Marie Adams, Oct. 18, 1940; children: Bernadette, Robert, Michael, Marguerite. BS in Chem. Engring., MIT, 1938. V.p., dir. Exxon Research & Engring. co., Linden, N.J., 1961-66; dep. refining coordinator Exxon Corp., NYC, 1966-68; exec. chmn., chief exec. officer BOC-Airco Cryogenic Plant Ltd., London, 1968-71; mng. dir. Cryoplants Ltd., London, 1971-72; v.p. energy devel. The Pittston Co., Greenwich, Conn., 1972-81; chmn. bd., chief exec. officer Pittston Petroleum Inc., Montvale, N.J., 1977-83; mng. ptnr. Kensyntar Project Co., Greenwich, Conn., 1981-83; pres. Afkay Assocs., Rye, N.Y., 1983—. Patentee in field; contbr. articles to profl. jours. Mem. Welding Research Council (vice chmn. exec. com. 1964-68), Jr. Engring. Tech. Soc. (dir. 1962-68), Am. Petroleum Inst., Am. Mining Congress (synthetic fuels com.) Address: 5005 Theall Rd Rye NY 10580-1445 Office Phone: 914-925-0714.

KAUNITZ, JONATHAN DAVIDSON, physician; b. NYC, Nov. 6, 1950; s. Paul Ehrlich and Rita (Davidson) K.; m. Christine Lee, July 31, 1983; children: Justin Lee, Genevieve Jung. BA in Molecular Biology, Columbia Coll., 1972, MD, 1976. Diplomate Am. Bd. Internal Medicine, Am. Bd. Gastroenterology. Intern medicine Presbyn. Hosp., NYC, 1976—77, resident medicine, 1977—79; gastroenterology fellow U. Calif., San Francisco, 1979—80, gastrointestinal rsch. fellow, 1980—81, UCLA, 1981—82; asst. prof. medicine UCLA Sch. Medicine, 1983—91; assoc. investigator VA Career Devel. Series, 1984—85, rsch. assoc., 1985—88, clin. investigator, 1990—95; assoc. dir. UCLA Integrated Tng. Program in Digestive Diseases, 1986—90, co-dir., 1996—98, dir., 1998—2001; assoc. prof. dept. medicine Sch. Medicine UCLA, 1991—97, prof. dept. medicine Sch. Medicine, 1997—. Assoc. chief med. svc. gastrointestinal sect. Wadsworth VA Med. Ctr., 1993—; mem. legis. assembly UCLA, 1991-94, com. on appts. and promotions, 1991-2005; mem. gastrointestinal bd. Med. Rsch. Svc., Dept. VA, 1993-96, chair, 1995, mem. coun., 1996; mem. NIH study sects., chmn., 2006—; vis. lectr. Keio U. Med. Soc., Tokyo, 1994, 97, 2000, 05; vis. prof. Asahi (Japan) Gen. Hosp., 2003—, Hamamatsu Seirei Med. Ctr., 2003—. Mem. editl. bd. Am. Jour. Physiology. Bd. dirs. Cure Found., 2002—. Recipient numerous rsch. grants. Fellow Am. Coll. Gastroenterology; mem. Am. Gastroenterol. Assn., Am. Physiol. Soc., Columbia Coll. Physicians and Surgeons (alumni dir. 1976-86, dir. emeritus 1986—), Cure Autism Now (bd. dirs., sci. adv. group 1995-2004, chair 1996, sci. rsch. coun. 2000-06), Brentwood Biomed. Rsch. Inst. (bd. dirs., chair, 2003-06), Gastrointestinal Rsch. Group (pres.-elect 2006—), West Coast Salt and Water Club (program chmn. 1989, treas. 1989-98, pres. 1998—), Western Assn. Physicians, Alpha Omega Alpha. Avocations: soccer, bicycling, travel, collecting books. Office: CURE Wadsworth VA Med Ctr Los Angeles CA 90073 Home Phone: 310-450-4564. E-mail: jake@ucla.edu.

KAUPA, MIKE, musician, educator; s. Albert and Ruth Kaupa; m. Diana Loberant, Aug. 7, 2001; children: Simona Loberant, Raphael Loberant. BA, SUNY, Fredonia, 1986; MusM, U. of Miami, 1988. Cert. pub. sch. tchr. U. of the State of N.Y. Edn. Dept. Jazz educator Hot Clube de Portugal, Lisbon, 1980; prof. Taller de Musics, Barcelona, 1983—84; music tchr. Harley Sch., Rochester, NY, 1997—, Eastman Sch. of Music Cmty. Music Sch., Rochester, NY, 1997—; tchr. Tritone Jazz Fantasy Camp, Rochester, 1998—; interim prof. of jazz trumpet Eastman Sch. of Music, Rochester, 1999—2000; prof. of jazz trumpet, dir. of big band Zarauzko Nazioarteko Jazz Mintegia, Zarautz, Spain, 2001—02, Seminari Internacional de Jazz, Begues, Spain, 2004—05. Condr. Finger Lakes Music Educators Assn. Jr. Sr. High Festival, Geneva. Composer, prodr.: jazz CD This Is Spring; musician: Close Your Eyes, (jazz rec.) Orquestra Taller de Musics de Barcelona amb Tete Monoliu; prodr.: (jazz rec.) ONIX. Mem.: Music Educators Nat. Conf., Internat. Trumpet Guild. Avocations: golf, travel. Home: 707 Edgewood Ave Rochester NY 14618-4443 Office: Harley Sch 1981 Clover St Rochester NY 14618 Home Phone: 585-461-1177; Office Phone: 585-442-1770. Personal E-mail: mikekaupa@yahoo.com.

KAUR, MANDEEP, dermatologist, educator; b. Chandigarh, India, Feb. 25, 1978; d. Er. Kuldip Singh and Maj Balwinder Kaur Sahota; m. Lovinder Singh Gill, Sept. 29, 2001; 1 child, Smeena Kaur Gill. MBBS, Govt. Med. Coll., Amritsar, Punjab, India, 2001; MS in Clin. Epidemiology and Health Svcs. Rsch., Wake Forest U., 2006. Fellow in dermatology Sch. Medicine, Wake Forest U., Winston-Salem, NC, 2002—05, instr., 2005—06, asst. prof., 2006—. Assoc. faculty Women's Health Ctr. Excellence, Winston-Salem, 2006—. Recipient Friedrich E. Mohs Meml. award, 2006. Mem.: Soc. Photomedicine, Women's Dermatologic Soc., Soc. Investigative Dermatology, Nat. Psoriasis Found. (grantee 2005—06), Am. Acad. Dermatology (assoc.). Avocations: soccer, dance choreographing, music. Office: Wake Forest Univ Sch Medicine Medical Ctr Blvd Winston Salem NC 27157 Home Phone: 336-716-3273; Office Phone: 336-716-3273. Personal E-mail: docmandy78@yahoo.com. Business E-Mail: mkaur@wfubmc.edu.

KAUSHANSKY, KENNETH, medical educator; b. 1953; m. Lauren Kaushansky; 2 children. BS, UCLA, MD, 1979. Diplomate Am. Bd. Internal Medicine. Fellow in hematology U. Washington; prof. medicine U. Calif., San Diego, 1995—, chair dept. medicine, 2002—, Helen M. Ranney prof.; chief hematology sect. U. Washington Med. Ctr. Adj. prof. biochemistry U. Washington. Recipient Dameshek award, Am. Soc. Hematology, Outstanding Investigator award, Am. Soc. Med. Rsch. Fellow: Am. Acad. Arts & Sciences; mem.: Inst. Medicine, Assn. Am. Physicians, Am. Soc. Clin. Investigation (v.p.). Office: U Calif San Diego Dept Medicine 402 W Dickinson Ste 380 San Diego CA 92103-8811 Mailing: UCSD Med Ctr 8811 200 W Arbor Dr San Diego CA 92103-8811 Office Fax: 619-543-3931. E-mail: kkaushansky@ucsd.edu.

KAUSHIK, PRASHANT, rheumatologist, educator; b. Meerut, India, Aug. 25, 1970; s. Om Prakash and Kuntal Kaushik; m. Richa Pachaury, Feb. 21, 1996; children: Aadya, Aarya Aparna. MBBChir, All India Inst. Med. Scis., New Delhi, 1992, D, 1996; diploma in acupuncture and moxibustion, Indian Rsch. Inst. Integrated Medicine, 1992. Diplomate Am. Bd. Internal Medicine, Am. Bd. Rheumatology, Nat. Bd. Med. Examiners, India. Asst. clin. prof. medicine La. State U. Health Scis. Ctr., Baton Rouge, 2003—06, U. ND Sch. Medicine and Health Scis., Grand Forks, 2006—; rheumatologist St. Alexius Med. Ctr. Specialty Clinics, Bismark, 2006—. Author: Medical Principles and Practice; contbr. articles to profl. jours. Recipient Sir Dorabji Data award in Biochemistry, All India Inst. Med. Scis., 1988, Dr. Satyanand Gold medal, 1993, New Zealand High Commr.'s award, 1993. Fellow: Am. Coll. Rheumatology (licentiate); mem.: ACP (licentiate), Nat. Acad. Med. Scis. Office Phone: 701-530-6505. Personal E-mail: kaushikprashant@gmail.com.

KAUSLER, DONALD HARVEY, retired psychology professor; b. St. Louis, July 16, 1927; s Charles Richard and Pauline Ann (Svejkovsky) K.; m. Martha Blanche Roeper, Oct. 25, 1952; children— Rene, Donald Harvey, Jill, Barry. AB, Washington U., St. Louis, 1947, PhD, 1951. Rsch. psychologist USAF, Mather AFB, Calif., 1951—55; asst. prof., assoc. prof. U. Ark., 1955—60; assoc. prof., prof. St. Louis U., 1960—71, chmn. dept. psychology, 1963—71; prof. psychology U. Mo.-Columbia, 1971—89, Curator's prof., 1989—92; Curator's prof. emeritus, 1992—. Author: Psychology of Verbal Learning and Memory, 1974, Experimental Psychology and Human Aging, 1982, Experimental Psychology, Cognition and Human Aging, 1991, Learning and Memory in Normal Aging, 1994, The Graying of America: An Encyclopedia of Aging, Health, Mind, and Behavior, 1996, 2001, The Essential Guide to Aging in the 21st Century, 2007; editor: Readings in Verbal Learning, Contemporary Theory and Research, 1966—; columnist Scripps Howard News Svc., 2001-05; contbr. articles to profl. jours. Mem. APA, AAUP, Phi Beta Kappa, Sigma Xi. Home: 3905 Faurot Dr Columbia MO 65203-0309 Personal E-mail: dkausler2@aol.com.

KAUTT, GLENN GREGORY, financial planner, consultant; b. Arlington, Va., Jan. 25, 1948; s. Elmer Curtis and Phyllis Ruth (Schmalz) K.; m. Elisabeth B. Emerson, Aug. 19, 1971 (div. 1975); 1 child, Christopher Curtis; m. Elizabeth M. Dansereau, Dec. 22, 1989. BS, Purdue U., 1973; MBA, Harvard U., 1979. Cert. fin. planner; enrolled agt., admitted to practice before IRS. Commd. lt. USN, 1969, resigned, 1977; sr. assoc. ICF, Inc., Washington, 1979-81; mng. dir. The Challenger Group, Silver Spring, Md., 1981-85; sr. planner Fin. Svc. Group, Vienna, Va., 1985-87; prin., dir. Capitol Fin. Cons., Inc., Vienna, 1987-91; pres. Kautt Fin. Svcs., Inc., Vienna, 1991-99, The Monitor Group, Inc., Fairfax, Va., 1999—, chmn. bd., 2003—. Lectr. ADA, FPA, Am. Mgmt. Assn., US SBA, also maj. corps. Author: Stochastic Modeling: A New Way to Predict Your Financial Future, 2001; co-author: The Invincibility Shield for Investors, 2003; co-author, editor Inside the Real Estate Business, 1981; mem. editl. adv. bd. Jour. Fin. Planning, 1999-2002; contbr. articles to profl. mags. Mem. Registry Fin. Planning Practitioners, Fin. Planning Assn. Nat. Capitol Area (bd. dirs., pres. 1999, co-chair 2000, nat. chpt. leadership resource coun. 2000-02), Found. Fin. Planning (bd. trustees 2006-). Republican. Avocations: flying, skiing, scuba diving, singing. Office: 1430 Spring Hill Rd Ste 400 Mc Lean VA 22102 Home Phone: 703-893-1019; Office Phone: 703-288-0500. Business E-Mail: kautt@themonitorgroup.com.*

KAUTTER, DAVID JOHN, lawyer; b. Wilkes-Barre, Pa., Mar. 20, 1948; s. William George and Mary (Flanagan) K.; m. Kathy Jane Price, May 22, 1976; children: Hilary, David Jr. BBA, Notre Dame U., 1971; JD, Georgetown U., 1974. Bar: DC 1975, US Dist. Ct. DC 1981, US Tax Ct. 1981, US Supreme Ct. 1981. Staff acct. Coopers & Lybrand, Washington, 1971-74; mgr. Arthur Young and Co., Washington, 1974-78; legis. asst. Senator John Danforth, Washington, 1979-82; ptnr. Arthur Young and Co., Washington, 1982-89, dir. Wash. Nat. Tax Group, 1986-89; nat. dir. compensation and benefits tax svcs. Ernst & Young, Washington, 1989-98, mem. ptnrs. adv. coun., 1993-96, nat. dir. human resource svcs., 1998-2001, dir. nat. tax, 2001—. Contbr. articles to profl. jours. Mem. ABA, Fed. Bar Assn., AICPA. Republican. Roman Catholic. Avocation: cabinet making. Home: 8312 Summerwood Dr Mc Lean VA 22102-2212 Office: Ernst & Young 1225 Connecticut Ave NW Ste 700 Washington DC 20036-2621 Personal E-mail: david.kautter@ny.com.

KAUTZMAN, JOHN FREDRICK, lawyer; b. Indpls., Aug. 23, 1959; s. Fred L. and Barbara J. (Seeger) K. BA, Ind. U., 1981; JD, Ind. U., Indpls., 1984. Bar: Ind. 1985, U.S. Dist. Ct. (no. and so. dists.) Ind. 1985, U.S. Ct. Appeals (7th cir.) 1992. Law clk. Marion County Pros. Office, Indpls., 1981; bailiff Marion County Cir. Ct., Indpls., 1981-84, commr., judge pro tempore, 1985-89; assoc. Ruckelshaus, Roland, Hasbrook & O'Connor, Indpls., 1985-89, ptnr., 1990-98, Ruckelshaus, Roland, Kautzman, Blackwell & Hasbrook, Indpls., 1998—. Mem. faculty Ind. Trial Advocacy Coll., 1998—. Contbg. author The Indiana Lawyer newspaper, 1991—. Mem. bd. assocs. Ind. U. Found., Bloomington, 1993—, v.p. 1997-99, pres., 2000-05; precinct commiteeman Marion County Rep. Party, Indpls., 1994-96. Named Super Lawyer, 2004, 2005. Mem.: ABA, Indpls. Bar Assn. (chmn. young lawyers divsn. 1988—89, bd. mgrs. 1994—2002, v.p. 1998, first v.p. 2003, pres.-elect 2004, pres. 2005, Disting. fellow 1993), Ind. State Bar Assn., Phi Delta Phi. Methodist. Avocations: professional piano, golf. Office: Ruckelshaus Roland Kautzman Blackwell & Hasbrook Ste 900 107 N Pennsylvania St Indianapolis IN 46204-2424 Fax: (317) 634-8635.

KAUZLARICH, RICHARD DALE, retired ambassador, political scientist, consultant; b. Moline, Ill., Aug. 18, 1944; s. Victor and Eva Marie (Kronfeld) Kauzlarich; m. Anne Elizabeth Bregstone, Aug. 26, 1967; children: Richard Dale, Jr., Terri Lynne. AA, Black Hawk Coll., Moline, Ill., 1964; BA, Valparaiso U., 1966; MA, Ind. U., 1967, U. Mich., 1976. 2d sec. Am. Embassy, Addis Ababa, Ethiopia, 1973-75; fin. economist Office Devel. Fin., Dept. State, Washington, 1976-77, dep. office dir. Office Investment Affairs, 1977-80; counselor for econ. affairs Am. Embassy, Tel Aviv, 1980-83; office dir. ops. ctr. Dept. State, Washington, 1983-84, dep. asst. sec. internat. orgn. affairs, 1984-86, dep. dir. policy planning staff, 1986-89, office dir. regional polit.-econ. affairs, 1989-91, dep. asst. sec. Bur. European Affairs, 1991-93; prin. dep. to the amb.-at-large and spl. adviser S/NIS Dept State, Washington; U.S. amb. to Republic of Azerbaijan, 1994-97, Bosnia and Herzegovina, 1997-99; sr. advisor to undersec. state econ., bus. and agrl. affairs Dept. State, Washington, 1999-2001; pres. Kauzlarich Cons. Inc., Falls Church, Va., 2001—02; dir. spl. initiative on Muslim World U.S. Inst. Peace, Washington, 2002—03; nat. intelligence officer for Europe Nat. Intelligence Coun., Washington, 2003—. Mem. Am. Internat. Sch. Bd., Tel Aviv, 1981—83. Named Internat. Person of the Yr., Dnevi Avaz, 1997; recipient Presdl. Meritorious Svc. award, 1993, Hall of Fame award, Black Hawk Coll. Alumni Assn., 1993, Disting. Alumnus award, Valparaiso U., 1999. Lutheran. Home: 7019 Ted Dr Falls Church VA 22042-3943 Office: Nat Intelligence Coun Washington DC 20505 Personal E-mail: rdkauzlarich@yahoo.com. Business E-Mail: richadk0@dnl.gov.

KAUZMANN, WALTER JOSEPH, chemistry professor; b. Mt. Vernon, NY, Aug. 18, 1916; s. Albert and Julia Maria (Kahle) K.; m. Elizabeth Alice Flagler, Apr. 1, 1951; children: Charles Peter, Eric Flagler, Katherine Elizabeth Julia Kauzmann Pacala. BA, Cornell U., 1937; PhD, Princeton U., 1940; PhD (hon.), U. Stockholm, 1992. Westinghouse research fellow Westinghouse Mfg. Co., E. Pittsburgh, Pa., 1940-42; mem. staff Explosives Research Lab., Bruceton, Pa., 1942-44, Los Alamos Lab., 1944-46; asst. prof. Princeton U., 1946-51, asso. prof., 1951-60, prof. chemistry, 1960-82, chmn. dept., 1964-68, David B. Jones prof. chemistry, 1963-82, chmn. biochem. sci. dept., 1980-81; vis. scientist Atlantic Research Lab., NRC Can., 1983. Vis. lectr. Kyoto U., 1974; vis. prof. U. Ibadan, 1975 Author: Quantum Chemistry, 1957, Kinetic Theory of Gases, 1966, Thermal Properties of Matter, 1967, (with D. Eisenberg) Structure and Properties of Water, 1969. Recipient Linderstrom-Lang medal, 1966, Stein and Moore award, 1993; Jr. fellow Soc. Fellows, Harvard U., 1942. Fellow: AAAS, Am. Phys. Soc., Am. Acad. Arts and Scis.; mem.: NAS, Royal Astron. Soc.

Can., Fedn. Am. Scientists, Am. Chem. Soc., Am. Geophys. Union, Protein Soc., Am. Soc. Biochemistry and Molecular Biology, Sigma Xi. Home and Office: 301 N Harrison St PMB 152 Princeton NJ 08540-3512

KAVALEK, LUBOMIR, chess expert; b. Prague, Czechoslovakia, Aug. 9, 1943; came to U.S., 1970; s. Lubomir and Stepanka (Kavalkova) K.; m. Irena Koritsanska, Nov. 24, 1971; 1 child, Steven. Student, Faculty of Transp., U. Zilina, 1960-65, Faculty of Journalism, Charles U., Prague, 1967-68, George Washington U., 1970-71. Journalist Voice of Am., USIA, 1971-72; chief editor RHM Chess Pub., Great Neck, NY, 1973-89; mem. German chess team, Solingen, 1969-89, U.S. chess team in chess Olympiad, 1972, 74, 76, 78, 82, 84, 86; reporter world chess championship, chess columnist Washington Post, 1986—; exec. dir. Grandmaster Assn., Brussels, 1987-91, key organizer world cup, 1988-89; coach world championship Challenger, N. Short, 1990-93. Author: Wijk aan Zee 1975 - Grandmaster Chess Tournament, 1976, World Cup Chess, 1990, Tilburg, 1977; author: (with Efim Geller, Svetozar Gligoric and Boris Spassky) The Najdorf Variation - Sicilian Defense, 1976. Recipient Cramer award, 1999, Best Newspaper Chess Column award Chess Journalists Am., 2003, 06; inductee World and U.S. Chess Hall of Fame, 2001. Mem. Internat. Assn. Chess Journalists, U.S. Chess Fedn. Achievements include being the German chess team champion, 1969, 71, 72, 73, 74, 75, 80, 81, 86, SS Dutch Open champion, 1969, Czechoslovakian champion, 1962, 68, Internat. Grandmaster, 1965-, U.S. co-champion, 1972, 73; U.S. champion, 1978, European Cup team champion, 1976, Olympic champion, 1976, German Internat. champion, 1981; winner 30 internat. all-play-all tournaments; most Olympiad medals of any U.S. player (1 gold and 5 bronze medals) since 1924. E-mail: lkavalek@att.net.

KAVALER, THOMAS J., lawyer; b. NYC, Dec. 10, 1948; BA, CCNY, 1969; JD, Fordham U., 1972; LLM, NYU, 1975. Bar: N.Y., US Dist. Ct. (So., Ea., We. and No. Dists.) NY, US Ct. Appeals (2nd, 3rd, 4th, 5th, 6th, 7th, 8th, 10th, 11th and Fed. Cirs.), US Supreme Ct., US Tax Ct. Law clk. US Dist. Ct. NY, NYC, 1972-74; assoc. Cravath, Swaine & Moore, NYC, 1974-75, Cahill Gordon & Reindel LLP, NYC, 1975-80, ptnr., 1980—, mem. exec. com. Served to capt. USAR, 1969-77. Fellow Am. Bar Found., Internat. Acad. Trial Lawyers, NY Bar Found.; mem. Fordham Law Alumni Assn. (pres. 2000-02), Fed. Bar. Coun. (v.p. 2002-). Office: Cahill Gordon & Reindel LLP 80 Pine St Fl 17 New York NY 10005-1790 Office Phone: 212-701-3406. Office Fax: 212-269-5420. Business E-Mail: tkavaler@cahill.com.

KAVALERCHIK, BORIS YAKOVLEVICH, application developer, researcher; b. Luban, Minsk, Belarus, May 26, 1948; came to US, 1992; s. Yakov I. Kavalerchik and Liliya S. Rosengaus; m. Bella K. Kavalerchik, Dec. 27, 1979; 1 child, Inna. MS in Applied Mechanics with honors, Moscow Inst. Physics & Tech., 1969, PhD in Applied Math., 1972; DSc in Computer Sci., Glushkov Inst. Cybernetics, Kiev, Ukraine, 1990. Cert. specialist IBM, 2002, database adminstrn. solution expert 2002, application developer 2003. Project leader Belorussian Rsch. Inst. for Mgmt. Info. Systems, Minsk, USSR (Belarus), 1972-77, head system software dept., 1977-79, head systems devel. dept., 1979-90, prin. rschr., 1990-92; tech. specialist, cons., project leader info. tech. Guardian Life Ins. Co. of Am., NYC, 1992—. Assoc. prof. Belorussian Polytech. Inst., Minsk, 1975-78; leader of many nat. computer projects. Contbr. over 60 articles to Russian, Am. and German profl. jours. Recipient Outstanding Sci. and Engring. Rsch. prize USSR Coun. Ministers, Moscow, 1984. Mem. IEEE, Assn. for Computing Machinery. Jewish. Achievements include research in the fields of data and image compression; reliability and performance of data processing; operations research and its business and engineering applications. Home: 1 Grover Ter Fair Lawn NJ 07410-4506 Office: Guardian Life Ins Co 7 Hanover Sq New York NY 10004-2616

KAVANAGH, EILEEN J., librarian; BA, Ladycliff Coll.; MS in Libr. Sci., Columbia U., 1969; MA in Liberal Studies, SUNY, Stonybrook, 1980. Reference libr. Farmingdale (N.Y.) Pub. Libr., 1969-70; from reference libr. to libr. dir. Bay Shore-Brightwaters (N.Y.) Pub. Libr., 1970—. Recipient Disting. Citizen of Yr. award, Bay Shore-Brightwaters, 2005. Office: Bay Shore-Brightwaters Pub Libr 1 S Country Rd Brightwaters NY 11718-1513 Home Phone: 631-665-0133; Office Phone: 631-665-4350. Business E-Mail: ekavanag@suffolk.lib.ny.us.

KAVANAGH, RALPH WILLIAM, physics professor; b. Seattle, July 15, 1924; s. Ralph W. and Esther (Weken) K.; m. Joyce Eberhart, July 31, 1948; children: Kathleen, Janet, Stephanie, Linda, William Leonard. BA, Reed Coll., 1950; MA, U. Oreg., 1952; PhD, Calif. Inst. Tech., 1956. Mem. faculty Calif. Inst. Tech., Pasadena, 1956—, assoc. prof. physics, 1965-70, prof., 1970—2000, prof. emeritus, 2000—; rsch. assoc. Centre de Recherches Nucleaires, U. Strasbourg, France, 1967-68; rsch. assoc. Sch. Physics U. Melbourne, Australia, 1983. Contbr. articles to profl. jours. Served with USNR, 1942-46. Fellow Am. Phys. Soc. Home: 450 Bonita Ave Pasadena CA 91107-5064 Business E-Mail: kav@caltech.edu.

KAVANAUGH, BRETT MICHAEL, federal judge; b. Washington, Feb. 12, 1965; s. Edward and Martha Kavanaugh; m. Ashley Estes; 1 child. BA cum laude, Yale Coll., 1987; JD (hon.), Yale Law Sch., 1990. Bar: Md. 1990, DC 1992. Law clk. to Hon. Walter K. Stapleton US Ct. Appeals (3rd cir.), 1990—91; law clk. to Hon. Alex Kozinski US Ct. Appeals (9th cir.), 1991—92; atty., Office Solicitor Gen. US Dept. Justice, Washington, 1992—93; law clk. to Justice Anthony M. Kennedy US Supreme Ct., Washington, 1993—94; assoc. counsel Office Ind. Counsel Kenneth W. Starr, US Dept. Justice, 1994—98; ptnr. Kirkland & Ellis LLP, 1997—98, 1999—2001; assoc. counsel to Pres. The White House, Washington, 2001—03, sr. assoc. counsel to Pres., 2003, asst. to Pres., staff sec., 2003—06; judge US Ct. Appeals (DC cir.), 2006—. Roman Catholic. Office: US Ct Appeals E Barrett Prettyman US Courthouse 333 Constitution Ave NW Rm 3004 Washington DC 20001 Office Phone: 202-216-7180.*

KAVANAUGH, EVERETT EDWARD, JR., trade association executive; b. New Haven, June 9, 1941; s. Everett Edward and Marion (Gallagher) K.; m. Martha Gamble Murphy, Feb. 23, 1963; 1 son, Brett Michael. AB, Georgetown U., 1963; MBA, George Washington U., 1970; JD, Am. U., 1978. Bar: Md. 1979, D.C. 1990. Sales rep. Northwestern Mut. Ins. Co., Washington, 1963-68; asst. to exec. offices U.S. C. of C., Washington, 1970-72; pres. Cosmetic, Toiletry and Fragrance Assn., Washington, 1972—2005; ret. Mem.: Congressional Country, Burning Tree (Bethesda, Md.). Roman Catholic. Home: # 12 8500 River Rd Bethesda MD 20817

KAVANAUGH, FRANK JAMES, film producer, educator; b. Chgo., Sept. 12, 1934; s. Kenneth James and Carol Mae (Wilkey) K.; m. Barbara Ann Barrett, Nov. 16, 1957; children: Franklin James Jr., Christopher Barrett, Kenneth Wilkey. BA, Lake Forest Coll., Ill., 1956; PhD, Union Inst., Cin., 1982. Prodr., dir., exec. ABC-TV, Chgo., NYC, 1956-67; pres. Ravens Hollow Ltd., Warrenton, Va., 1967-69; exec. prodr. Airlie Prodns., Warrenton, 1979-89; prof. comm., prof. med. and pub. affairs, comm. chair George Washington U., Washington, 1983-89. V.p. Airlie Found., 1979-2006; adj. prof. Union Inst. Grad. Sch., 1987—; pres. Kavanaugh Assocs., Inc., 1989—; mentor Capella U.; pres. Internat. Acad. for Preventive Medicine. Asst. dir. TV Kukla, Fran & Ollie, 1958; prodr. (film) The Saving of the President, 1982 (Emmy award 1982); prodr. dir. films A Moveable Scene, 1968 (Emmy award nominee 1969), Flowers of Darkness, 1969 (Emmy award 1969), Bridge From No Place, 1970 (Emmy award 1970), The Possible Dream, 1970 (Emmy award 1970), More Than a Paycheck, 1978 (Emmy award nominee 1978), others; prodr., dir., writer film Each Child Loved, 1972 (Emmy award 1972), others. Bd. dirs. Performing Arts Trust. Recipient Cup of Italy Italian Film Festival, Salerno, 1982, highest award Edinburgh Film Festival, Scotland, 1982, Blue Ribbon Am. Film Festival, NYC, 1983, Gold medal Houston Internat. Film Festival, 1983. Mem. Nat. Acad. TV Arts and Scis. (life), C.I.N.E., Inc. (life), Dirs. Guild Am., Radio and TV Dirs. Guild, Mensa, Nat. Assn. TV Program Execs. (Iris award 1983), Broadcast Pioneers. Avocations: photography, scuba, boating, motorcycling.

KAVANDI, JANET LYNN, aerospace power engineer, chemist; b. Springfield, Mo., July 17, 1959; d. William Winfred and Wanda Ruth (Garner) Sellers; m. Farhad John Kavandi, June 5, 1982. BS magna cum laude, Mo. So. State Coll., 1980; MS, U. Mo., Rolla, 1982; PhD, U. Wash., 1990. Project engr. Eagle-Picher Industries, Joplin, Mo., 1982-84; prin. engr. power systems tech. Boeing Def., Seattle, 1984—95; Astronaut NASA, Houston, 1995—. Mem. AIAA, Am. Chem. Soc. Avocations: skiing, horseback riding, windsurfing, sailing, camping. Office: Astronaut Office MIC CB Lyndon B Johnson Space Center Houston TX 77058

KAVASCH, ELIZABETH BARRIE, writer, educator, illustrator; divorced; children: Christopher, Kimberlee. Author, illustrator: Pebbles & Cobbles, 1976, Native Harvests, 1977, Botanical Tapestry, 1979, Guide to Northeastern Wild Edibles, 1981, Herbal Traditions, 1982, Guide To Eastern Mushrooms, 1982, Introducing Eastern Wildflowers, 1982, Haiku, 1985, American Indian Cooking, 1989, Earthmaker's Lodge, 1994, Enduring Harvests, 1995, Earth Sense, 1996, A Student's Guide to Native American Genealogy, 1996, American Indian Healing Arts, 1999, Hands of Time, 1999, Zuni Children & Elders Talk Together, 1999, Crow Children & Elders Talk Together, 1999, Apache Children & Elders Talk Together, 1999, Seminole Children & Elders Talk Together, 1999, Blackfoot Children & Elders Talk Together, 1999, Lakota Sioux Children & Elders Talk Together, 1999, Earth Wise, 2000, The Seminole: Indian Nations, 2000, The Medicine Wheat Garden, 2002, Ancestral Threads, 2003, Dream Catcher, 2003, The Mound Builders of Ancient North America, 2004, Earth Lodge Horse Herbal, 2005, Sacred Cave, 2005. Home: 22 S Commons #9 Kent CT 06757 Office: Escape To The Arts 293 Main St Danbury CT 06810 Personal E-mail: ebarrie@msn.com.

KAVEESHWAR, ASHOK G., former federal agency administrator; b. Indore, India, 1942; arrived in US, 1961; m. Tuti Kaveeshwar; 1 child, Jaya. BS, Ujjian Univ., India; PhD in physics, SUNY, Buffalo, 1969. Pres., CEO Hughes STX Corp.; sr. v.p. Raytheon Tech. Svcs. Co., 1998—2002; pres. Orange Technologies, 2002—05; adminstr., rsch. & innovative tech. adminstrn. US Dept. Transp., Washington, 2005—06. Bd. dirs. SteelCloud, Inc., 2007—. Mem. dean's adv. council SUNY, Buffalo.*

KAVESH, ROBERT A., economist, educator; b. NYC, Sept. 12, 1927; s. Samuel and Pearl (Berlin) K.; m. Ruth Freidson, 1951 (div. 1980); children: Richard, Laura, Andrew, Joseph; m. Danielle Nisivoccia, July 11, 1990. BS, NYU, 1949; MA, Harvard U., 1950, PhD, 1954. Asst. prof. econs. Dartmouth Coll., 1953-56; bus. economist Chase Manhattan Bank, NYC, 1956-58; prof. econs. and fin. NYU Grad. Sch. Bus. Adminstrn., 1958-74, Marcus Nadler prof. fin. and econs., 1974—, chmn. dept. econs., 1968-83. Bd. dirs. Neuberger Berman Mut. Funds; econ. adv. bd. U.S. Dept. Commerce, 1968-70; investment adv. com. N.Y. State Comptroller, 1976-86; pres. The Money Marketeers, 1983-84. Author: Businessmen in Fiction, 1955, How Business Economists Forecast, 1966, Methods and Techniques of Business Forecasting, 1974; contbr. articles to profl. jours.; mem. editl. bd. Bus. Economics, 1965-99. Bd. dirs. Thomas A. Edison Coll. N.J., 1973-78. With U.S. Navy, WWII. Recipient Danforth Found. prize disting. teaching, 1968, Madden Meml. award for profl. achievement NYU, 1979, Gt. Tchr. award NYU, 1983, Lifetime Achievement award for mutual fund trustees Institutional Investor, 2004. Fellow Nat. Assn. Bus. Economists (council 1973-76); mem. Am. Fin. Assn. (exec. sec.-treas. 1961-79), Regional Sci. Assn. (past sec.), Am. Econ. Assn. Home: 60 E 8th St Apt 32B New York NY 10003-6501

KAVIS, GEORGE, engineer, photographer; b. Chgo., Feb. 2, 1935; s. Theodore and Margaret Marie Kavis; m. Patricia Marie Hewison, Dec. 17, 1978 (div. 1989); 1 child, Sherri Lynn. Design draftsman Pullman R.R. Car Mfg. Co., Chgo., 1953—55; design engr. adminstr. Fennell Corp., Harvey, Ill., 1957—66, F.H. Ayer Mfg. Co., Chicago Heights, Ill., 1966—. Cons. for design of machinery for mass prodn. Furniture design and mfg. With US Army, 1955—57. Achievements include patents for furniture, automotive, toys. Avocations: invention, art, photography, writing, collecting. Office: FH Ayer Mfg Co Box 247 Chicago Heights IL 60411 Office Phone: 708-755-0550.

KAVLI, FRED, retired manufacturing and engineering executive; b. Norway, Aug. 20, 1927; came to U.S., 1956; Grad. in physics, Norwegian Inst. Tech., 1955. Founder, CEO, sole shareholder automotive and aerospace sensor engring.-mfg. Kavlico Corp., Moorpark, Calif., 1958—2000; ret. Bd. dirs. The Found. for Santa Barbara City Coll.; trustee Found. for U. Calif., Santa Barbara; founder, chmn. The Kavli Found./The Kavli Operating Inst.; benefactor The Kavli Insts. (in neuroscience) at Columbia U., Yale U., U. Calif. at San Diego, (in nanoscience) at Caltech, Cornell U., Delft U. of Tech., (in astrophysics and cosmology) , Harvard U. (in nano), Stanford U., U. Chgo., MIT, (in theoretical physics), Peking U. (in astrophysics), U. Calif., Santa Barbara, Chinese Acad. Sci. (in theoretical); mem. pres. bd. on sci. and innovation U. Calif.; endowed several chairs, one in engring. at the U. Calif., Santa Barbara, another chair in Optoelectronics and Sensors, U. Calif., Irvine, in Nano-systems Sciences at UCLA, and Cosmology, Calif. Inst. Tech. Named Disting. Grand Patron, Alliance of the Arts, 1998, in honor of the Fred Kavli Theatre for Performing Arts at the Thousand Oak Civic Arts Plaza, Scientific American 50: Policy Leader Yr., Scientific American mag., 2005. Mem.: PCAST, Am. Acad. Arts & Sciences. Office Phone: 805-560-6500, 805-983-6000. Office Fax: 805-988-4800.

KAVNER, JULIE, actress; b. LA, Sept. 7, 1951; Grad., San Diego U., 1971. Actress: (TV series) Rhoda, 1974-78 (Emmy award 1978), Petrocelli, 1975, Lou Grant, 1977, Taxi, 1980, The Tracey Ullman Show, 1987-90, The Simpsons, (voice of Marge Simpson and others) 1990— (Emmy award, 1992), Sibs, 1991, Birdland, 1994, Tracey Takes On, 1996, (TV movies) Katherine, 1975, The Girl Who Couldn't Lose, 1975, No Other Love, 1979, Revenge of the Stepford Wives, 1980, Don't Drink the Water, 1994, Jake's Women, 1996, (feature films) National Lampoon Goes to the Movies, 1981, Bad Medicine, 1985, Hannah and her Sisters, 1985, Radio Days, 1987, Surrender, 1987, New York Stories, 1989, Awakenings, 1990, Alice, 1990, This Is My Life, 1992, Shadows and Fog, 1992, I'll Do Anything, 1994, Forget Paris, 1995, Deconstructing Harry, 1997, Doctor Dolittle (voice), 1998, A Walk on the Moon, 1999, Judy Berlin, 1999, Story of a Bad Boy, 1999, Someone Like You (voice), Barn Red, 2004, Click, 2006, The Simpsons Movie (voice), 2007. Office: The Simpsons c/o Twentieth Television PO Box 900 Beverly Hills CA 90213*

KAVOUKJIAN, MICHAEL EDWARD, lawyer; b. Mpls., Apr. 19, 1958; s. Antranik M. and Leikny Dorthea (Oines) K. AB with distinction, Stanford U., 1980; JD cum laude, Harvard U., 1984. Bar: Minn. 1984, NY 1986, US Dist. Ct. (dist. Minn.) 1985, US Dist. Ct. (so. dist. NY) 1988, Fla. 1999. Assoc. to ptnr. White & Case, NYC and Miami, Fla., 1985—. Spl. adv. to US Mission, Bosnia-Herzegovina, 1994—98. Bd. dir. Fla. Zool. Soc. Named one of Top 100 Attys., Worth mag., 2005. Mem.: ABA (chmn. com. estate planning and drafting 1992—94), Coun. Fgn. Rels., Assn. of the Bar of the City of NY, Soc. Trust and Estate Practitioners, UK, Fla. Bar, Minn. State Bar Assn., Fla. Zool. Soc. (bd. dirs. 2007—), Lincoln's Inn Soc. of Harvard Law Sch. (bd. govs. 1982—84), Nat. Press Club, Washington, Harvard Club, NYC, Washington, Boston. Republican. Presbyterian. Office: White & Case Wachovia Fin Ctr 200 S Biscayne Blvd Ste 4900 Miami FL 33131-2352 Office Phone: 305-995-5227. Office Fax: 305-358-5744.

KAVOUSSI, LOUIS RAPHAEL, urologist; b. NYC, Oct. 24, 1957; s. James P. and Margaret Kavoussi; m. Julie Kavoussi; children: Nicholas, Rebecca, Andrianna. BS, Columbia U., 1979; MD, SUNY, Buffalo, 1983. Resident in surgery and urology Washington U., St. Louis, 1991-93, asst. prof.; chief urology Jewish Hosp., St. Louis, 1989-91; asst. prof. Harvard Med. Sch., Boston, 1991-93; chief urology, assoc. prof. urology Johns Hopkins Bayview Med. Ctr., Balt., 1993—2006; prof. of urology NYU Sch. of Medicine, 2006—. Mem. med. bd. Johns Hopkins Bayview Med. Ctr., 1993—2006; dir. Stone Ctr. Johns Hopkins U., 1991—2006, Patrick C. Walsh Disting. prof. urologic surgery; cons., dept. of urology, Johns Hopkins U.; chmn. of urology, the N. Shore—LI Jewish Health System, Manhasset, NY Fellow Am. Urologic Assn., Endourology Soc. Achievements include first to perform laparoscopic nephrectomy, laparoscopic donor nephrectytor transplant; development of first clinical telesurgical system. Office: Johns Hopkins Bayview Med 4940 Eastern Ave Baltimore MD 21224-2735*

KAVRAKI, LYDIA, computer scientist, educator; BS, U. Crete, Greece, 1989; MS, Stanford U., 1992, PhD, 1995. Postdoctoral fellow Stanford U., research assoc.; assoc. prof. computer sci. Rice U., 1996—99, prof. bioengineering, 1999—; assoc. prof. structural & computational biology, molecular biophysics Baylor Coll. of Med., 1999—. Prog. com. mem. IJCAI, 1997—99; co-chair Internat. Workshop on Algorithmic Foundations of Robotics, 1998; prog. com. mem. IEEE Internat. Conference on Robotics Automation, 1999, ACM Annual Symposium on Computational Geometry, 1999; assoc. editor IEEE Transactions on Robotics and Automation, 1999—. Named one of Top 100 Young Innovators, MIT Tech. Review mag., 2002, Brilliant 10, Popular Sci. mag., 2003; recipient Career award, Nat. Sci. Found., Grace Murray Hopper award, Assn. for Computing Machinery, Early Career award, IEEE Robotics and Automation Soc.; grantee Alfred P. Sloan Rsch. Fellowship. Office: Rice U MS132 PO Box 1892 Houston TX 77251-1892

KAWACHIKA, JAMES AKIO, lawyer; b. Honolulu, Dec. 5, 1947; s. Shinichi and Tsuyuko (Murashige) K.; m. Karen Keiko Takahashi, Sept. 1, 1973; 1 child, Robyn Mari. BA, U. Hawaii, Honolulu, 1969; JD, U. Calif., Berkeley, 1973. Bar: Hawaii 1973, U.S. Dist. Ct. Hawaii 1973, U.S. Ct. Appeals (9th cir.) 1974, U.S. Supreme Ct. 1992. Dep. atty. gen. Office of Atty. Gen. State of Hawaii, Honolulu, 1973-74; assoc. Padgett, Greeley & Marumoto, Honolulu, 1974-75, Law Office of Frank D. Padgett, Honolulu, 1975-77, Kobayashi, Watanabe, Sugita & Kawashima, Honolulu, 1977-82; ptnr. Carlsmith, Wichman, Case, Mukai & Ichiki, Honolulu, 1982-86, Bays, Deaver, Hiatt, Kawachika & Lezak, Honolulu, 1986-95; propr. Law Offices of James A. Kawachika, Honolulu, 1996—2002; ptnr. Reinwald, O'Connor & Playdon LLP, Honolulu, 2002—. Mem. Hawaii Bd. of Bar Examiners, Honolulu; arbitrator Cir. Ct. Arbitration Program State of Hawaii, Honolulu, 1986— Chmn. disciplinary bd. Hawaii Supreme Ct., 1991-97; adv. com. civil justice reform act 1990 US Dist. Ct., 1991—; bd. dir. Hawaii Justice Found., 2004—, pres., 2007—. Mem. ABA (ho. of dels., standing com. ethics and profl. responsibility), Am. Judicature Soc. (bd. dirs. Hawaii chpt. 2003-), Hawaii State Bar Assn. (bd. dirs. 1975-76, young lawyers sect. 1983-84, 92-93, treas. 1987-88, v.p./pres.-elect 1997-98, pres. 1998-99), 9th Cir. Jud. Conf. (lawyer rep. Honolulu chpt. 1988-90), Legal Aid Soc. Hawaii (bd. dirs. 2005—). Avocations: running, tennis, skiing. Office: Pacific Guardian Ctr Makai Tower 733 Bishop St 24th Flr Honolulu HI 96813-4070 Home Phone: 808-373-1608; Office Phone: 808-524-8350. Business E-Mail: jak@roplaw.com.

KAWADA, JANET HANSEN, artist, educator; b. Newton, Mass., June 20, 1953; m. Charles Y. Kawada; children: Taylor Hansen, Russell Hansen. AS, Lasell Jr. Coll., Newton, Mass., 1973; BFA, Mass. Coll. Art, 1992; MFA, Vermont Coll., 1998. Studio mgr. Mass. Coll. Art., Boston, 1992-2001. Mem. adj. faculty Mass. Coll. Art, 1996—, New Eng. Sch. Art and Design, Boston, 1997—; dir. Kingston Gallery, Boston, 1999-2003; tech. dir. Devotion Pub. Sch., Brookline, Mass., 1985-92; workshop coord. World Batik Conf., Boston, 2005. Martin Godine fellow Mass. Coll. Art, 1992. Home: 197 Fuller St Brookline MA 02446-5774 Personal E-mail: jkawada@usa.net.

KAWAMOTO, HENRY K., plastic surgeon; b. Long Beach, Calif., 1937; Intern U. Calif. Hosp., LA, 1965; resident gen. surgery Columbia Presbyn. Med. Ctr., NYC, 1969-71; resident plastic surgery NYU, 1971-73; fellow crano-facial surgery Dr. Paul Tessier, Paris, 1973-74; clin. prof. plastic surgery U. Calif., LA. Mem. Am. Assn. Plastic Surgeons, Am. Soc. Plastic Surgeons, ASMS, AOA. Office: 1301 20th St Ste 460 Santa Monica CA 90404-2054 Office Phone: 310-829-0391.

KAWAMOTO, KEITH HITOSHI, protective services official; b. Granada Hills, Calif., Mar. 26, 1979; s. Bryce and Joanne Kawamoto. BA in History, U. Notre Dame, Ind., 2001. Lic. EMT County of LA, 2000. Firefighter LA City Fire Dept., 2002—04; fire insp. Glendale Fire Dept., Calif., 2006—. Scholar, LA Police Dept., 1997. Mem.: Mensa (assoc.). Home Phone: 818-335-4299.

KAWAMURA, GEORGINA K., finance company executive, state official; b. Lanai City, Hawaii, Sept. 19, 1952; m. Gary Kawamura, 1973; children: Bryan, Jon. AA in Acctg., Maui CC. Clk. to office mgr., budget dir. Maui (Hawaii) County Mayor's Office, 1987—88; planner Castle and Cooke Resorts, Lanai, Hawaii, 1998—2002; dir. fin. Dept. Budget and Fin., Hawaii, 2002—. Avocations: hula, reading. Office: Dept Budget and Fin PO Box 150 Honolulu HI 96810-0150*

KAWAMURA, KENJI, aerospace scientist; b. Tokyo, July 15, 1970; s. Hiroshi and Mine Kawamura; m. Makiko Watanabe, Mar. 21, 1999; 1 child, Ryuta. PhD of Sci. in Geophysics, Tohoku U., Sendai, Japan, 2001; MS in Geophysics, Tohoku U., 1996, BS in Geophysics, 1994. Rschr. Tohoku U., Sendai, 2001—02; fellow U. Bern, Switzerland, 2002—. Contbr. articles to profl. jours. Mem.: European Geosciences Union. Avocations: travel, sailing.

KAWAOKA, YOSHIHIRO, virologist, educator; m. Yuko Kawaoka. BS in Vet. Medicine, Hokkaido U., Japan, 1978; DVM, Ministry of Agriculture and Fishery, Japan, 1978; MS, Hokkaido U., Japan, 1980, PhD, 1983. Postdoctoral rschr. St. Jude Children's Rsch. Hosp., Memphis; prof. virology dept. pathobiological scis. U. Wis., Madison; prof. U. Tokyo Inst. Med. Sci. Contbr. articles to sci. jours. Office: Dept Pathobiological Scis U Wis Sch Vet Medicine 2015 Linden Dr W Madison WI 53706-1102 Office Phone: 608-265-4925. Office Fax: 608-265-5622. E-mail: kawaokay@svm.vetmed.wisc.edu.*

KAWASAKI, GUY, venture capitalist, investment banker, evangelist, entrepreneur, blog writer, writer; b. Honolulu, Hawaii, 1954; m. Beth Kawasaki; 4 children. BA in Psychology, Stanford U., 1976; MBA, UCLA, 1979; attended, U Calif. Davis Sch. Law, 1977, Billy Graham Sch. Envangelism, 1990; PhD (hon.), Babson Coll., 2003. V.p. mktg. Nova Stylings, Inc., LA, 1977—83; dir. mktg. Eduware Services (acquired by Peachtree Software), Agoura Hills, Calif., 1983; software evangelist, dir. software product mgmt. Apple Computer, Inc., Cupertino, Calif.,

1983—87, chief envangelist, 1995—97; CEO ACIUS, Cupertino, Calif., 1987—89, Fog City Software, 1993—95; ind. author, spkr., Forbes columnist, 1989—93; mng. dir. Garage Tech. Ventures, Palo Alto, Calif., 1997—. Bd. dir. Razz, FilmLoop, BitPass; advisor Kaboodle, Coghead, Simply Hired, TripWire. Frequent appearances on TV and radio including CNBC Power Lunch, CNN and Bloomberg; author: Hindsights: The Wisdom and Breakthroughs of Remarkable People, The Macintosh Way, How To Drive Your Competition Crazy, Selling the Dream, Rules for Revolutionaries: The Capitalist Manifesto for Creating and Marketing New Products and Services, The Art of the Start: The Time-Tested, Battle-Hardened Guide for Anyone Starting Anything; maintains blog website blog.guykawasaki.com, columnist Entrepreneur mag. Former bd. dir. Stanford Alumni Assn.; bd. dir. Hawaiian Island Ministry; bd. trustee Bowman Internat. Sch. Named to Technorati 100. Office: Garage Tech Ventures Ste 150 3300 Hillview Palo Alto CA 94304 Office Phone: 650-354-1854. E-mail: kawasaki@garage.com.*

KAWASHIMA, HOPE NOZOMI, musician; b. Auburn, Calif., Apr. 2, 1937; d. Peter Shinichi and Mary Etsuko Omachi; m. Mas Kawashima, June 14, 1964; children: Mariya Yoshiko Yamamoto, Rebekah Kawashima Wong. BA in Rec. and Music Therapy, Calif. State U., Sacramento, 1959; MA in Sacred Music, San Francisco Theol. Sem., 1964; postgrad., Juilliard Sch. Music, NYC, 1980—81. Ordained as deacon United Meth. Ch., consecrated to ministry United Meth. Ch., 1982; registered music therapist Calif., cert. dir. music. Music therapist State of Calif., Stockton, Napa, 1959—64; dir., organist 1st Presbyn. Ch., Altadena, Calif., 1964—71, Ontario (Oreg.) Cmty. Ch., 1972—80, J A United Ch., NYC, 1980—88, LaTijera United Meth. Ch., LA, 1988—93, Lake Park United Meth. Ch., Oakland, Calif., 1993—2002; min. music St. Paul's United Meth. Ch., Fresno, Calif., 2002—05, United Japanese Christian Ch., Clovis, Calif., 2005—. Dir. Music Mart Acad., Santa Monica, Calif., 1988—91. Musician: (CD's) Songs of Faith, Hope & Love, 1967; composer, musician: CD's Love Wider than an Ocean, 1977, prodr., composer, musician: CD's Reflections of Faith, Hope & Love, 2002 (CLPEP grantee); author: Learning to Play Piano is as Easy as ABC. Gen. conf. del. United Meth. Ch., St. Louis, 1988, mem. hymnal com. Nashville, 1985—88; chairperson Theol. Forum, Berkeley, Calif., 1994—2002. Recipient Famous Diamond Poet award, Famous Poets Soc., 1995; Sears Roebuck & Co. scholar, 1955, Calif. Civil. Liberties grantee, 2002. Mem.: Nat. Guild Piano Tchrs. (local chair 1979—89), Clergywoman Calif., Calif. Scholarship Fedn. (life), Native Daughters Calif. Office: United Japanese Christian Ch 136 N Villa Clovis CA 93612

KAWAZOE, ROBIN INADA, federal official; b. Wilkinsburg, Pa., Jan. 13, 1959; d. George and Hanako (Nishio) Inada; children: Amy, Steven. BA, U. Md., 1982. Program analyst Alcohol, Drug Abuse & Mental Health Adminstrn., Rockville, Md., 1981-85, 85-87, com. mgmt. officer, 1985—86, extramural programs officer, 1987-88; spl. asst. Nat. Inst. on Drug Abuse, Rockville, 1988-90, dep. dir. Office Sci. Policy and Comm., 1990-96; dir. Office of Sci. Policy and Planning, 1997—2005; sr. advisor to dir. Nat. Inst. Alcohol Abuse and Alcoholism, Bethesda, Md., 2005—, acting dep. dir., 2006—, assoc. dir. adminstr., 2007—. Recipient Recognition award, Pub. Health Svc., 1992, Dir.'s award, NIH, 1994, 2004, Dir.'s Group award, 2000, 2004, 2005, Group award for Disting. Svc., HHS Sec., 2004. Office: Nat Inst Alcohol Abuse and Alcoholism 5635 Fishers Ln Rm 2000 Bethesda MD 20892

KAWEWE, SALIWE MOYO, social work educator, researcher; children: Neo, Rujeko, Godfrey, Kudakwashe. BSW, U. Zambia, Lusaka, 1974; MSW, Washington U., St. Louis, 1979; PhD, St. Louis U., 1985. Cert. edn. accreditation reaffirmation Coun. on Social Work, 2001. Adminstrv. asst. U. Zambia, Lusaka, 1974—77; social svcs. officer, probation officer Dept. Social Svcs., Bulawayo, Zimbabwe, 1979—81; instr. St. Louis Pub. Schs., 1981—83; social svc. worker II Mo. Divsn. Family Svcs., St. Louis, 1984—85; asst. prof. Southea. La. U., Hammond, 1985—88, Ctrl. State U., Wilberforce, Ohio, 1989, James Madison U., Harrisonburg, Va., 1989—91, Wichita State U., 1991—96; assoc. prof. So. Ill. U., Carbondale, 1996—2001, dir. grad. program, 1996—98, prof., 2002—. Contbr. chapters to books; mem. editl. bd.: Social Devel. Issues, Jour. Social Work Edn., Jour. African Policy Studies, Jour. Immigrant and Refugee Svcs., Jour. Women and Lang., 1998—, mem. guest editl. bd.: Nat. Women Studies Jour., 1997—98; contbr. articles to profl. jours. and publs. Mem. Nat. Assn. Social Workers, Bulawayo, Matabeleland, Zimbabwe, 1980—82; Africa regional rep. Inter-Univ. Consortium for Internat. Social Devel., Wichita, 1992—94; mem. Tangipohoa Parish Mayor's commn. on Needs of Women, Hammond, 1985—88, Inter-Univ. Consortium for Internat. Social Devel., Carbondale, 1995—, Ill. Hunger Coalition, Chgo., 1998—; sec. Kans. Coun. on Social Work Edn., Topeka, 1992—93; mem. Com. to Enhance Minority, Human and Civil Rights, Springfield, 2000—; pres. Delmo Housing Corp., 2006—. Recipient Outstanding Scholastic Achievement award, George Warren Brown Sch. of Social Work, Wash. U., 1979, Superior Acad. Achievement award, St. Louis U. Internat. Student Assn., 1984, Appreciation for Continuing Svc. as a Faculty Advisor, Nat. Assn. Black Social Workers, 2001, Appreciation as Faculty Advisor, 2000, certificate of Dedication, African Student Coun. So. Ill. U. at Carbondale, 2001, Internat. Student Coun So. Ill. U. at Carbondale, 2001, Award of Appreciation of Svc., Nat. Assn. Black Social Workers, 2000, Recognition of Dedicated Svc., African Student Coun. So. Ill. U. at Carbondale, 1998, Dedication of Svc., African Student Coun., So. Ill. U. at Carbondale, 1997, Outstanding Leadership and Guidance, Student Orgn. of Social Work, Wichita State U., 1996, Outstanding Multilateral Study Del. award, World Congress on the Family, 1992; grantee Summer Rsch. Travel Grant, Wichita State U., 1994. Mem.: NASW (asst. dist. chair 1997—99), Internat. Coun. Social Welfare, Internat. Assn. for Schs. of Social Work, Soc. for Study of Social Problems, Peace and Social Justice Ctr. of So. Ctrl. Kans., Coun. on Social Work Edn., Internat. Assn. Feminist Econs., So. Ill. U. Women's Caucus, Nat. Women Studies Assn., So. Ill. HIV Care Consortium (bd. mem. 1997—2001), Internat. Fedn. Social Workers (life), Phi Alpha (hon.). Office: So Ill U Sch Of Social Work Mailcode 4329 Carbondale IL 62901 Office Phone: 618-453-3359. Business E-Mail: smkawewe@siu.edu.

KAWITT, ALAN, lawyer, arbitrator; JD, Chgo.-Kent Coll. Law, 1965; postgrad. Lawyers Inst., John Marshall Law Sch., 1966-68. Bar: Ill. 1966, U.S. Dist. Ct. (no. dist.) Ill. 1967, U.S. Ct. Appeals (7th cir.) 1971, U.S. Supreme Ct. 1971. Sole practice, 1970—; CEO Drexel Coy Pub., 1998—, Small Ships Cruises Group, 2001—. Mem. Am. Arbitration Assn. (arbitration panel). Office: PO Box 1514 Chicago IL 60690-1514 Office Phone: 312-786-2007.

KAY, ALAN C., computer scientist, nonprofit organization executive; b. Springfield, Mass., May 17, 1940; m. Bonnie MacBird. BS in Math., Molecular Biology, U. Colo., 1966; MSEE with distinction, U. Utah, 1968, PhD in Computer Sci. with distinction, 1969; PhD (hon.), Kungl Tekniska Hoegskolan, Stockholm, Ga. Inst. Tech., 2005; LHD (hon.), Columbia Coll., Chgo., 2005. Researcher Stanford Artificial Intelligence Lab., 1969—71, instr., 1970; group leader, principal scientist, Xerox Fellow Xerox Palo Alto Rsch. Ctr., Calif., 1971—81; chief scientist Atari, 1981—84; fellow Apple Computer, Brentwood, Calif., 1984-96; computer tchr. Open School, West Hollywood; fellow Walt Disney Imagineering, 1997—2001, v.p., rsch. & devel., 1996—2001; sr. fellow Hewlett-Packard Labs., 2002—05; adj. prof. computer sci. UCLA Henry Samueli Sch. Engring. and Applied Sci., 2002—; vis. prof. Kyoto U., Japan; pres., founder Viewpoints Rsch. Inst., Glendale, Calif., 2001—. Co-recipient Kyoto prize for Advanced Tech., Inamori Found., 2004; recipient Turing award, Assn. for Computing Machinery, 2003, Systems Software award, Edn. award, Assn. for Computing Machinery SIGCSE, Outstanding Contributions to Computer Sci. Edn., J-D Warnier Prix d'Informatique, NEC Computers & Communications Found. prize, Funai prize, Lewis Branscomb Tech. award, Fellow award, Computer History Mus., 1999. Fellow AAAS, NAE (co-recipient, Charles Stark Draper prize, 2004), Royal Soc. Arts; named to Computer History Mus. Achievements include invention of Dynabook; creator of Smalltalk, the first complete dynamic object-oriented programming (OOP) language; created an early model of the laptop computer and contributed. to the development of graphical user interfaces, Ethernet, laser printing, and the "client-server" and peer-peer networking model. Avocations: keyboards, guitar, pipe organist. Office: Viewpoints Rsch Inst 1209 Grand Central Ave Glendale CA 91201 Office Phone: 818-332-3000. Office Fax: 818-244-9761.

KAY, CHRISTOPHER K., retail executive, lawyer; b. Cin., Jan. 5, 1953; s. Robert and Joan Kay; m. Kristine Kenney, 1977; 1 child, Lauren. BA with honors in polit. sci. and history, U. Mo., 1975; JD, Duke U., 1978. Bar: 1978. Atty. Shughart, Thomson and Kilroy, Kans. City, Mo., 1978—84; chmn. litigation dept. Swann & Haddock, Orlando, Fla., 1984—90; ptnr. Foley & Lardner, Orlando, 1990—96; founding ptnr. Kay, Panzl & Latham, Orlando, Fla., 1996—98, Kay, Gronek & Latham, Orlando, Fla., 1998—2000; exec. v.p., gen. counsel, corp. sec. Toys "R" Us, Inc., Wayne, NJ, 2000—02, exec. v.p. ops., gen. counsel, corp. sec., 2002—03, exec. v.p. ops, corp. sec., 2003—. Mem. US-Japan Pvt. Sector/Govt. Commn., 2002. Presbyn. Fellow: Am. Bar Found.; mem.: ABA (vice chmn. antitrust sect. bus. torts and unfair competition com. 2000—), Am. Bd. Trial Advocates, Fla. State Bar. Office: Toys R Us Inc 1 Geoffrey Way Wayne NJ 07470-2030

KAY, CYRIL MAX, biochemist, educator; b. Calgary, Alta., Can., Oct. 3, 1931; s. Louis and Fanny (Pearlmutter) K.; m. Faye Bloomenthal, Dec. 30, 1953; children: Lewis Edward, Lisa Franci. B.Sc. in Biochemistry with honors (J.W. McConnell Meml. scholar), McGill U., 1952; PhD in Biochemistry (Life Ins. Med. Research Fund fellow), Harvard U., 1956; postgrad., Cambridge U., Eng., 1956-57. Phys. biochemist Eli Lilly & Co., Indpls., 1957-58; asst. prof. biochemistry U. Alta., Edmonton, 1958-61, assoc. prof., 1961-67, prof., 1967—, co-dir. Med. Rsch. Coun. Group on Protein Structure and Function, 1974-95, mem. protein engring. network Centre of Excellence, 1990—, chmn. internat. rsch. adv. com. to protein engring. network Centre of Excellence, 2000—; v.p. rsch. Alta. Cancer Bd., 1999—. Med. Rsch. Coun. vis. scientist in biophysics Weizmann Inst., Israel, 1969-70, summer vis. prof. biophysics, 1975, summer vis. prof. chem. physics, 1977, 80; mem. biochemistry grants com. Med. Research Council, 1970-73; mem. Med. Rsch. Coun. Can., 1982-88; Can. rep. Pan Am. Assn. Biochem. Socs., 1971-76; mem. exec. planning com. XI Internat. Congress Biochemistry, Toronto, Ont., Can., 1979; mem. med. adv. bd. Gairdner Found. for Internat. awards in Med. Sci., 1980-89; chmn. Internat. Scientific adv. com. on protein engring., 2000—. Contbr. numerous articles to profl. publs.; asso. editor Can. Jour. Biochemistry, 1968-82; editor-in-chief Pan Am. Assn. Biochem. Socs. Revista, 1971-76. Recipient Ayerst award in biochemistry Can. Biochem. Soc., 1970, Disting. Scientist award U. Alta. Med. Sch., 1988, Outstanding Contbn. to Alta. Sci. and Tech. Cmty. award, 2006. Fellow NY Acad. Scis., Royal Soc. Can.; mem. Order of Can. (decorated mem. 1995, officer 2006), Can. Biochem. Soc. (coun. 1971—, v.p. 1976-77, pres. 1978-79). Home: 9408-143d St Edmonton AB Canada T5R 0P7 Office: U Alta Dept Biochemistry Med Scis Bldg Edmonton AB Canada T6G 2H7 Office Phone: 780-492-4549. Business E-Mail: ckay@ualberta.ca.

KAY, DENNIS MATTHEW, retired publishing company official; b. Chgo., Sept. 20, 1936; s. Edward Francis and Rose Anne (Koziel) Kolodzinski; m. Judy R. Kalinsky, Jan. 9, 1965; 1 child, Alan Edward. BBA, Loyola U., 1976. Customer svc. agt. Am. Airlines, Chgo., 1959-69; expeditor Time Inc., Chgo., 1969-73, traffic mgr. People mag., 1973-75, Time mag. traffic mgr., 1975-78, ops. mgr., 1978-81, electronic data mgr., 1981-83, plant mgr. Waterloo, Wis., 1983-88, field ops. mgr., 1988-95, nat. prodn. analyst, 1995-96, field ops. mgr., 1996-99; ret., 2000. With U.S. Army, 1959-61. Recipient MM&D Excellence award Time Inc., 1989, Prodn. Excellence awards, 1993, 94, Pres. award, 1993. Mem. Moose Lodge River Grove 378 (gov. 1982-83). Roman Catholic. Avocations: stamp collecting/philately, piano, model building. Home: 604 Long Cove Dr Lake In The Hills IL 60156 Personal E-mail: denky1@aol.com.

KAY, GEORGE PAUL, environmental engineer; b. McKeesport, Pa., Sept. 25, 1954; s. George and Darlene Ann (Snyder) K.; m. Rosemary Ann Lynam, July 19, 1986; children: Brittany Elaine, Hope Elise, George Prescott. BS in Biology, U. Pitts., 1975, MS in Environ. Health, 1976, MSCE, 1982. Registered profl. engr., Pa., Ohio; cert. class A wastewater and water sys. operator Pa. Rsch. asst. U. Pitts., 1976-79; from asst. aquatic ecologist to sr. environ. engr. Michael Baker Corp., Beaver, Pa., 1979-87, sect. mgr. water and wastewater Coraopolis, Pa., 1987-89; mgr. water quality engring. Michael Baker Jr. Inc., Coraopolis, Pa., 2000—02, mgr. environ. engring., 2002—; sr. engr. water and wastewater AK Steel Corp. (formerly Armco, Inc.), Butler, Pa., 1989-2000. Contbr. articles to profl. jours. Avocations: archery, bonsai, guitar, aquariums. Home: 4596 Bucktail Dr Allison Park PA 15101-2120 Office: Michael Baker Jr Inc 100 Airside Dr Coraopolis PA 15108 Home Phone: 412-492-2065; Office Phone: 412-269-6028. Business E-Mail: gkay@mbakercorp.com.

KAY, HERBERT, retired energy executive; b. Johnsonburg, Pa., Mar. 19, 1924; s. Alexander S. and Carla Z. Racusin; m. Rita Inge Schmidt, May 4, 1956; children: Peter, Darcy, Philip. BS in Chem. Engring., Pa. State U., 1944; S.M., MIT, 1947; postgrad., Sloan Sch., 1968. Process engr. Stanolind Oil & Gas Co., Tulsa, 1947-49; group supr. Consolidation Coal Co., Library, Pa., 1949-55; sr. v.p. Climax Molybdenum Co., 1955-77; v.p. Amax Inc., 1977-85; also dir. U.K., Holland, Italy, France, Japan. Served with USNR, 1944-45. Mem. AIChE, Univ. Club (N.Y.), Madison Beach and Country Clubs (Conn.), Audubon Country Club (Fla.). Achievements include patents in field. Home: 111 E Wharf Rd PO Box 687 Madison CT 06443-0687 Business E-Mail: herbkay@alum.mit.edu.

KAY, HERMA HILL, law educator; b. Orangeburg, SC, Aug. 18, 1934; d. Charles Esdorn and Herma Lee (Crawford) Hill. BA, So. Meth. U., 1956; JD, U. Chgo., 1959. Bar: Calif. 1960, U.S. Supreme Ct. 1978. Law clk. to Hon. Roger Traynor Calif. Supreme Ct., 1959-60; from asst. prof. to assoc. prof. law U. Calif., Berkeley, 1960-62, prof., 1963, dir. family law project, 1964-67, Jennings prof., 1987-96, dean, 1992-2000, Armstrong prof., 1996—; co-reporter uniform marriage and div. act Nat. Conf. Commrs. on Uniform State Laws, 1968-70. Vis. prof. U. Manchester, England, 1972, Harvard U., 1976; mem. Gov.'s Commn. Family, 1966. Author (with D. Currie, L. Kramer and K. Roosevelt): Conflict of Laws: Cases, Comments, Questions, 7th edit., 2006; author: (with Martha S. West) Sex-Based Discrimination: Text, Cases and Materials, 6th edit., 2005; contbr. articles to profl. jours. Trustee Russell Sage Found., NY, 1972—87, chmn. bd. trustees NY, 1980—84; trustee, bd. dirs. Equal Rights Advs., Calif., 1987—88, chmn. Calif., 1976—83; pres. bd. dirs. Rosenberg Found., Calif., 1987—88, bd. dirs. Calif., 1978—. Recipient Rsch. award, Am. Bar Found., 1990, Margaret Brent award, ABA Commn. Women in Profession, 1992, Marshall-Wythe medal, 1995; fellow, Ctr. Advanced Study Behavioral Sci., Palo Alto, Calif., 1963. Mem.: ABA (sect. legal edn. and admissions to bar coun. 1992—99, sec. 1999—2001), Order of Coif (nat. pres. 1983—85), Am. Philos. Soc., Am. Acad. Arts and Scis., Assn. Am. Law Schs. (exec. com. 1986—87, pres.-elect 1988, pres. 1989, past pres. 1990), Am. Law Inst. (mem. coun. 1985—), Calif. Women Lawyers (bd. govs. 1975—77), Bar U.S. Supreme Ct., Calif. Bar Assn. Democrat. Office: U Calif Law Sch Boalt Hall Berkeley CA 94720-7200 Home Phone: 415-391-5158; Office Phone: 510-643-2671. Business E-Mail: hkay@law.berkeley.edu.

KAY, JOEL PHILLIP, lawyer; m. Marilyn Soltz, July 9, 1961; children: Arthur Hyman, Sarah Anne, Leslie Anette. BS in Econs., Wharton Sch., U. Pa., 1958; LLB, U. Tex., 1961; LL.M., Georgetown U., Washington, 1967. Bar: Tex. 1961, U.S. Dist. Ct. (so. and we. dists.) Tex., U.S. Dist. Ct (so. dist.) Ala., U.S. Ct. Appeals (5th cir.), U.S. Supreme Ct. Trial atty. tax div. Dept. Justice, 1963-67; U.S. atty. So. Dist. Tex., 1967-69; ptnr. Sheinfeld, Maley & Kay, P.C., Houston, 1969—2001; of counsel Hughes, Watters & Askanase, LLP , Houston, 2001—. Mem. Tex. Bd. Pub. Accountancy, 1984-85, quality rev. oversight bd., 1992-93; speaker at numerous institutes on comml. and bankruptcy law. Trustee, Am. Coll. Bankrupcy Found., 2002-. Capt. AUS, 1961—63. Recipient Banco Rotto award, Bankruptcy Law Sect., State Bar Texas. Fellow Am. Bar Found., Am. Coll. Bankruptcy (5th cir. regent 1998-2003); mem. ABA, Tex. Bar Assn. (dir. 1979-81, chmn. bd. 1981-82), Houston Bar Assn., Tex. Bar Found. (trustee 1983-86), Houston Bar Found. (dir. 1995-98), Tex. Supreme Ct. (grievance oversight com. 1987-94). Office: Three Allen Center 333 Clay 29th Fl Houston TX 77002 Office Phone: 713-759-0818.

KAY, KENNETH JEFFREY, real estate company executive; b. LA, Apr. 2, 1955; s. Morton M. and Beverly J. Kay. BS in Acctg., U. So. Calif., 1978, MBA in Fin., 1980. CPA, Calif. Staff acct. in charge Price Waterhouse and Co. (now PriceWaterhouse Coopers LLC), Century City, Calif., 1980-82; mgr. acctg. TRW-Fujitsu Co., LA, 1982-83; corp. controller Ameron Internat., Pasadena, Calif., 1983-88, sr. v.p. fin. and adminstrn., CFO, 1990-92, group v.p., 1992-94; pres., CEO, dir. Bishop, Inc., Westlake Village, Calif., 1988-90; sr. v.p. fin. and adminstrn., CFO Systemed, Inc., Torrance, Calif., 1994-96; sr. v.p., CFO Playmates Inc., Costa Mesa, Calif., 1997; exec. v.p., CFO Universal Studios Consumer Products Group, Universal City, Calif., 1998-99; v.p., CFO, Dole Food Co., Inc., Westlake Village, Calif., 1999—2002; sr. exec. v.p., CFO CB Richard Ellis Group, Inc., LA, 2002—. Chmn. supervisory com. Ameron Fed. Credit Union, South Gate, Calif., 1986. Bd. govs. Cedars-Sinai Med. Ctr.; mem. exec. com. Friends for Life, LA; mem. bd. dirs. Paralysis Project Am.; mem. bd. advisors U. So. Calif. Leven Sch. Acctg. Mem. AICPA, Am. Mgmt. Assn., Calif. Soc. CPAs, Assn. for Strategic Planning, Fin. Execs. Inst. Office: CB Richard Ellis Group Inc Ste 1600 11150 Santa Monica Blvd Los Angeles CA 90025 Office Phone: 310-405-8905. Business E-Mail: kenneth.kay@cbre.com.

KAY, MARCIA CHELLIS, writer; b. Boston, Mar. 13, 1940; d. Andrew Christopher and Dina Meland Quale; m. William G. Kay Jr. (dec.); m. Robert Dana Chellis (div.); children: Dana Chellis Keel, Bradford Adams Chellis. BS in Speech, Northwestern U., 1961, BS in Edn., 1961; EdM, Harvard U., 1979. With Boston Ednl. Rsch., Inc., Boston, 1970—71, Ednl. Recs. Am., Westport, Conn., Ednl. Writer's Collaborative, Cambridge, 1977—78; writer WGBH-TV (PBS), Boston, 1966—68; adminstrv. asst. to Joan Kennedy, 1979—82. Lectr. in field. Author: Living with the Kennedy's: The Joan Kennedy Story, 1985, The Joan Kennedy Story: One Woman's Victory Over Alcohol, Infidelity, Politics and Privilege, 1985, Ordinary Women, Extraordinary Lives, 1992. Bd. trustees Cantata Singers, Cambridge, 1968—96; 1st v.p., bd. mem. Jr. League Boston; chmn. program com. Harvard Club, New Bedford; storyteller Four Arts Children's Libr; active Am. Heart Assn.; bd. dirs. Harvard Club of Palm Beaches. Mem.: Nat. League Am. Pen Women, Author's Guild, Nat. Writers Union. Avocations: golf, tennis. Home: 200 N Ocean Blvd Palm Beach FL 33480

KAY, PAUL DE YOUNG, linguist; b. NYC, Nov. 7, 1934; s. William de Young and Alice Sarah Kay; m. Patricia Boehm, Feb. 13, 1934; children: Yvette, Suzanne de Young. BA in Econs., Tulane U., 1955; PhD in Anthropology, Harvard U., 1963. Asst. prof. MIT, Cambridge, 1964-65; assoc. prof., prof. Dept. Anthropology U. Calif., Berkeley, 1966-83, prof. Dept. Linguistics, 1983—, chmn. dept., 1986-91. Author: Words and the Grammar of Context, 1997; editor: Explorations in Mathematical Anthropology, 1971; co-author: Basic Color Terms, 1969; contbr. articles to Lang., Linguistic Inquiry, Foundations of Language, Linguistics and Philosophy, Lang. and Soc., Am. Anthropologist, Current Anthropology, Jour. of Linguistic Anthropology Grammars, Psychol. Scis., Cognition, others. Fellow Ctr. Advanced Study in Behavioral Scis., Stanford, Calif., 1965-66, Guggenheim Found., U. Hawaii, Oahu, 1972-73. Mem.: NAS, Am. Psychol. Soc., Soc. for Linguistic Anthropology (pres. 1988—89), Am. Anthrop. Assn., Linguistic Soc. Am. Office: Internat Computer Sci Inst 1947 Center St Ste 600 Berkeley CA 94704-1198 Office Phone: 510-666-2885. Business E-Mail: paulkay@berkeley.edu.

KAY, STEPHEN R., surgeon; b. Washington; MD, Cornell Med. Coll., NYC, 1978. Diplomate Am. Bd. Plastic Surgery, 1991. Plastic surgeon Chevy Chase Plastic Surgery, Md., 1986—. Pres. Nat. Capital Soc. Plastic Surgeons, Washington, 1995—96. Fellow: ACS; mem.: Am. Soc. Maxillofacial Surgeons, Am. Soc. Plastic Surgeons. Office: Stephen R Kay 5530 Wisconsin Ave #1510 Chevy Chase MD 20815 Office Phone: 301-951-5120.

KAY, THOMAS OLIVER, agricultural consultant; b. Anderson, SC, Sept. 29, 1929; s. Thomas Crayton and Gertrude (Whitworth) K.; m. Rebecca Moore, Aug. 29, 1954 (div. 1965); children— Michael (dec.), Mitchell; m. Bette Hutto, Oct. 1, 1966 (dec. Nov. 1991); stepchildren— Dallon Weathers, Bruce Weathers BA, Furman U., 1950; LL.D. (hon.), John Marshall Law Sch., Atlanta, 1960. Adminstrv. asst. U.S. Congress, Washington, 1966-73; legis. officer USDA, Washington, 1973-77; exec. asst. U.S. Senate, Washington, 1977-79; lobbyist Nat. Assn. Realtors, Washington, 1979-80; asst. to adminstr. Fgn. Agrl. Service USDA, Washington, 1981-82, dir. congl. relations, 1982-83, dep. asst. sec. govtl. and pub. affairs, 1983-85, dep. undersec. internat. affairs and commodity programs, 1985-86, adminstr. fgn. agrl. svc., 1986-90; pres. Kay Assoc., 1990—94. Mem. Litchfield Country Club (Pawleys Island, S.C.). Avocations: golf, swimming. Home: 17 Goodson Loop Pawleys Island SC 29585-8037

KAYAFAS, STEPHANIE ANN, special education educator, consultant, supervisor, actress; b. Pitts., Oct. 18, 1957; d. Nicholas and Helen Kayafas. BS, Rutgers U., 1979; MA, Georgian Ct. Coll., Lakewood, NJ, 1996. Cert. tchr. handicapped, elem. tchr., supr., prin., sch. bus. adminstr. N.J. N.J. spl. edn. tchr. Old Farmers Rd. Elem. Sch., Long Valley, NJ, 1979—82; spl. edn. tchr. Tinton Falls (N.J.) Mid. Sch., 1982-83, Rugby Sch., Wall, NJ, 1982—83; owner, operator Charlie's Auto Body Facility, Asbury Park, NJ, 1983—86; computer trainer Dendrite Internat. Inc., Morristown, NJ, 1998-99; actress Actor's Reps, NYC, 1998—; real estate referral cons. Ind. Referral Cons., Woodstown, NJ, 1999—; spl. edn. tchr. Marlboro (NJ) HS, 1987—2001, supr. spl. edn., 2002—. Mem. People to People Internat., 2001—; del. People's Republic of China Amb. Program, 2001. Mem.: ASCD, Am. Coun. Exercise, Rutgers Alumni Assn. Avocations: reading, poetry, weight training, guitar. Home: Riverview Twrs 28 Riverside Ave Unit 10G Red Bank NJ 07701 Office: Marlboro HS 95 N Main St Marlboro NJ 07746 Personal E-mail: stephanieknj@aol.com.

KAYATTA, WILLIAM J., JR., lawyer; b. Pawtucket, RI, Oct. 27, 1953; BA magna cum laude, Amherst Coll., 1976; JD magna cum laude, Harvard U., 1979. Bar: Maine 1980, US Dist. Ct. Dist. of Maine, US Ct of Appeals (1st & 9th cir.), US Supreme Ct. Law clerk to Chief Judge Frank M. Coffin

(1st cir.) U.S. Ct. Appeals, 1979-80; with Pierce, Atwood, Scribner, Allen, Smith & Lancaster, Portland, Maine; ptnr. Pierce Atwood, Portland, Maine. Mem. Maine Bd. Bar Examiners, 1986-90, chmn., 1988-89; mem. Maine Profl. Ethics Commn., 1995—. Contbr. articles to profl. jours. Named Best Lawyers Am., by Chambers USA, 2007, Am. Leading Bus. Lawyers. Mem. ABA (litigation sect., corp. coun. com.), Maine State Bar Assn., Maine Trial Lawyers Assn., Cumberland County Bar Assn., Am. Law Inst., pres. Maine Bar Found. 2004., fellow Am. Coll. Trial Lawyers. Editor & officer Harvard Law Review, 1977-79. Address: Pierce Atwood One Monument Sq Portland ME 04101 Office Phone: 207-791-1238. Office Fax: 207-791-1350. Business E-Mail: wkayatta@pierceatwood.com.

KAYDEN, JEROLD S., lawyer, urban planner; b. NYC, Sept. 12, 1953; AB, Harvard U., Cambridge, Mass., 1975, JD, MCRP, Harvard U., Cambridge, Mass., 1979. Bar: Mass. 1985, D.C. 1991, N.Y. 1992. Law clk. to judge U.S. Ct. Appeals for 2d Cir., 1979—80; law clk. to Justice William J. Brennan, Jr. U.S. Supreme Ct., Washington, 1980—81; lectr. Harvard Grad. Sch. Design, Cambridge, Mass., 1981—84, assoc. prof. urban planning, 1995—2003, dir. M in Urban Planning program, 1998—2000, dir. M in Urban Planning Program, 2004—, Frank Backus Williams prof. urban planning and design, 2004—, co-chair dept. urban planning and design, 2005—; of counsel Warner & Stackpole, Boston, 1987—99. Gerald D. Hines lectr. Harvard Grad. Sch. Design, 1986-87; sr. fellow Lincoln Inst. Land Policy, Cambridge, 1988-92; sr. advisor on land reform PADCO/U.S. Agy. for Internat. Devel., 1992-94; pres. Masterclass, Inc., L.A., 1976—; bd. dirs. PADCO, Inc., 1992-2004 Co-author: Landmark Justice, 1989, Privately Owned Public Space, 2000; co-editor: Zoning and the American Dream, 1989; contbr. articles to profl. jours. Bd. dirs. Kathmandu Valley Pres. Trust. Guggenheim fellow, 1989-90; grantee Nat. Endowment for Arts, 1979, 88, 20th Century Fund, 1989-92. Home: 11 Clement Cir Cambridge MA 02138-2205 Office: Harvard U Grad Sch Design 48 Quincy St Cambridge MA 02138 Business E-Mail: jkayden@gsd.harvard.edu.

KAYE, BARRY, insurance company executive; b. NYC, May 20, 1928; s. Herbert and Blanche (Sabin) K.; m. Carole Golison, Mar. 16, 1962; children: Fern L., Alan L., Howard S. CLU, Am. Coll. Life Underwriters. Pres. Barry Kaye, Inc., 1960—; owner Barry Kaye Assocs., Century City, Calif., 1970—; founder, chmn. Wealth Creation Ctrs., LA, 1980; mem. faculty Practicing Law Inst., 1969—; lectr. UCLA, 1970—. Co-owner, Carole & Barry Kaye Museum of Miniatures. Author: How to Save a Fortune on Your Life Insurance, 1980, rev. edit., 1991, Save a Fortune on Your Estate Taxes, 1990, (tape and audio book) Save a Fortune on Your Estate Taxes, (tape) Wealth Creation and Preservation, Die Rich and Tax Free!, 1995, Live Rich, 1996, The Investment Alternative, 1997, Die Rich 2, 2000, All New Investment Alternative, Give Your Estate Away Twice, 2003, You Buy, You Die, It Pays, 2006. Mem. bd. govs. Diamond Cir. of Hope; trustee City of Hope; fellow Ben Gurion Soc., Ben Gurion Soc. of the Negev; chmn. Love and Hope Ball Inst. Diabetic Rsch., U. Miami, 2002. Recipient Founders award Diamond Cir. City of Hope, 1972, Lifetime Achievement award Ben Gurion U. of the Negev, 1987, Man of Yr. award Gen. Agts. and Mgrs. Conf., 1965, 66, 67, Fin. Advisor of Yr. award Fin. Svcs. Advisor Mag., 1999; named Man of Yr. Anti-Defamation League, 2002, named Man or Yr. Jewish Fedn. Palm Beach County, 2002. Mem. NCCJ (trustee, bd. dirs.), Am. Soc. CLUs, B'nai B-rith (Pres. Club), Uncles of Vista del Mar, Internat. Forum. Office: Barry Kaye Assoc 5100 Town Center Tower II #550 Boca Raton FL 33486 Personal E-mail: barrykaye@barrykaye.com.

KAYE, DEBRA, composer, music educator; d. Fred R. and Barbara Seyburn Kaye. MusB, Mannes Coll. of Music, NYC, 1980; MA, NYU, 1995. Cert. in Dalcroze Eurhythmics Longy Sch. Staff composer Oliveri-oMusic, Atlanta, 1986—87; piano accompanist Coll. of the Siskiyous, Weed, Calif., 1988—91; mem. faculty Mannes Coll. of Music Prep. Divsn., NYC, 1991—; exec. dir. N.Y. Composers Cir., NYC, 2003—06; tchg. artist Alaria in residence at Mannes Coll. of Music, NYC, 2005—. Pianist 92nd St. Y, NYC, 1992—. Seven Stages Theatre, Atlanta, 1986; dir. music Cirque Gregoire, NYC, 1991, Genesius Guild, NYC, 2001, Lucy Moses Sch. for Music and Dance, NYC, 1993—94, Literally Alive Children's Theatre, NYC, 1999—2001. Composer: (performance (choral music) The North Wind and the Sun (commn., Ft. Wayne Children's Choir, 1991); composer, prodr.: performance Birds in the Night Ensemble; composer: (performance (children's theatre) The Ugly Duckling, 1999—2001, (performance) Rant (for viola da gamba or cello) (commn., 2003), (performance (piano trio) Three Voices (commn., 2004), (performance) Buscando (for harpsichord) (commn., 2005), My American Shtetl, text by Sholem Aleichem (commn., 2005), Selected, Emily Dickinson for baritone, 1999. Recipient travel and expenses grant, Meet the Composer, 1992, dean's scholarship, NYU, 1993, 1994, faculty devel. grant, The New Sch. U., 1992, 1995, 2004; grantee, Atlanta Music Tchrs. Assn., 1987, Millay Colony Arts, 2006, Edward T. Cone Fellowship, 2007. Mem.: N.Y. Composers Cir. (exec. dir. 2003—06), Am. Music Ctr., Dalcroze Soc. of Am. Avocations: dance, swimming, being in nature. Office Phone: 212-932-1376. Personal E-mail: dkaye1000@aol.com.

KAYE, DONALD, internist, educator; b. NYC, Aug. 12, 1931; s. Morris and Rose (Hirschtritt) K.; m. Janet Miriam Sovitsky, June 26, 1955; children: Kenneth Marc, Karen Lynne, Kendra Beth, Keith Steven. AB, Yale, 1953; MD, NYU, 1957. Diplomate Am. Bd. Internal Medicine, Am. Bd. Infectious Disease. Intern N.Y. Hosp., 1957-58, resident, 1958-60, fellow infectious diseases, 1960—63, asso. attending physician, 1961-69; physician-in-chief Hosp. Med. Coll. Pa., 1969-95; instr. medicine Cornell U. Med. Coll., 1961-63, asst. prof., 1963-66, asso. prof., 1966-69; prof., chmn. dept. medicine Med. Coll. Pa., Phila., 1969-94, Med. Coll. Pa. and Hahnemann U. Sch. Medicine, 1994-95, prof., 1995-96, Allegheny U. of Health Scis., 1996-98, MCP Hahnemann Sch. Medicine, 1998—2002, Drexel U., Coll. Medicine, 2002—. Cons. Phila. VA Hosp., 1969-95; CEO, pres. Med. Coll. Hosp., 1991-94, Med. Coll. Pa. and Hahnemann U. Hosp. Sys., 1994-96, Allegheny U. Hosps., 1996-98, Allegheny Integrated Health Group, 1996-97, Allegheny U. Health Scis., 1998; revision com. U.S. Pharmacopeia, 1975-95; mem. VA Merit Rev. Bd. in Infectious Diseases, 1976-78; com. on infectious diseases Am. Bd. Internal Medicine, 1976-84, cons., 1984-86. Author: Urinary Tract Infection and Its Management, 1972, Infective Endocarditis, 1976, Fundamentals of Internal Medicine, 1983, Internal Medicine for Dentists, 1983, 2d edit., 1990, Endocarditis, 1984, Infective Endocarditis, 1992; mem. editorial bd. Aging: Immunology and Infectious Diseases, Gerontology: Med. Sci., 1987-98, Antimicrobial Agts. Chemotherapy, 1972-98, Clinical Infectious Diseases, 2001-; contbr. articles to med. jours. Recipient Disting. Tchg. award Lindback Found., 1972; NIH grantee, 1967-76, 82-96; Pharm. Industry grantee, 1965-96, Emilio Ribas medal for disting svc. Brazilian Soc. of Infectious Diseases, 1994, Disting. Achievement award N.Y. Hosp.-Cornell Med. Ctr. Alumni Coun., 1994, Solomon A. Berson Alumni Achievement award NYU Sch. Medicine, 1996, Strittmatter award Philadelphia County Med. Soc., 1997. Master ACP (gov. Ea. Pa. region 1983-88, pres. Pa. chpt. 1987); fellow Gerontol. Soc. Am., Infectious Disease Soc. Am. (Mentor award 2005); mem. AMA, Pa. Med. Soc. (alt. del to AMA 1991-92), Phila. County Med. Soc. (pres. 1991-92), Am. Soc. for Microbiology, Am. Fedn. for Clin. Rsch., Am. Soc. for Clin. Investigation, Assn. Am. Physicians, Am. Clin. and Climatol. Assn., Phi Beta Kappa, Alpha Omega Alpha, Sigma Xi. Home: 1535 Sweet Briar Rd Gladwyne PA 19035-1216 Personal E-mail: donjank@aol.com.

KAYE, EDWARD MICHAEL, biotechnologist, physician, neurogeneticist; b. Chgo., Apr. 10, 1949; s. Peter Paul and Adeline Gertrude (Jacklin) K.; m. Alyssa Ann LeBel, Sept. 11, 1993; children: Michael Edward, Amy Jennifer, Dimitri Peter. BS, Loyola U., 1971, MD, 1975. Pediatric resident Loyola Medical Ctr., Maywood, Ill., 1975-78; child neurology fellow Boston City Hosp., Boston, 1978-81; rsch. fellow Boston U., Bedford, Mass., 1981-83; staff neurologist U. Tex., Houston, 1983-86, Floating Hosp. for Child, Boston, 1986-96; rsch. fellow Mass. Gen. Hosp., Charlestown, Mass., 1990-96; chief sect. neurology St. Christopher's Hosp. Children, 1996-98; dir. lab. for neurogenetics Allegheny U. Health Scis., 1997-98; chief sect. biochem. genetics Children's Hosp. Phila., Phila., 1998—2001; group v.p. clin. rsch. Genzyme Corp., 2001—. Mem. editl. bd.: Jour. Child Neurology, 1994, Jour. Pediat. Neurology, Annals Neurology. Sci. and med. adv. bd. United Lenckodystrophy Soc., Spinal Muscular Atrophy Found. Recipient Clinical Investigator Devel. award Nat. Inst. Health, Bethesda, 1990—. Mem. Child Neurology Soc., Soc. for Inborn Errors of Metabolism, Am. Acad. Neurology, AMS. Episcopalian. Avocations: sailing, running, biking, skiing, tennis. Office Phone: 617-638-6129. Business E-Mail: edward.kaye@genzyme.com.

KAYE, GORDON ISRAEL, pathologist, anatomist, educator; b. NYC, Aug. 13, 1935; s. Oscar Swarz and Rebecca (Schachman) K.; m. Nancy Elizabeth Weber, June 4, 1956; children: Jacqueline Elizabeth, Vivienne Rebecca. AB, Columbia U., 1955, AM, 1957, PhD, 1961. From rsch. asst. cytology to dir. Columbia U., NYC, 1953—63, dir. F. Higginson Cabot Lab. Electron Microscopy, 1963—76; rsch. and tchg. asst. cytology Rockefeller Inst., NYC, 1957-58; from Alden March prof. to prof. emeritus Albany (N.Y.) Med. Coll., 1976—99, prof. emeritus pathology, 1999—; prof. biomed. sci. SUNY Sch. Pub. Health, 1986-99; pres., CEO Waste Reduction by Waste Reduction, Inc., Troy, NY, 1993-98, chmn., 1998—, exec. v.p., 2002—06, acting CEO, 2006—. Mem. seminar on creative process Wenner-Gren Found., 1964-65; cons. electron microscopy dept. pathology N.Y. VA Hosp., 1965—99; Raymond C. Truex Disting. lectr. Hahnemann U., 1987. Co-author: Key Facts in Histology, 1985, Histology: A Text and Atlas, 1995, 4th edit., 2003; co-author: (in German) Atlas der Histologie, 1995; co-author: Histology, nat. med. series rev. series, 1997; editor: Current Topics in Cellular Anatomy, 1981; assoc. editor The Anat. Reocrd, 1972—98, editl. reviewer Exptl. Eye Rsch., 1964, Cancer, 1972—, Investigative Ophthalmology, 1973—, Gastroenterology, 1969—, Jour. Morphology, 1999—. Trustee Palisades free Libr., 1965-71; mem. Citizens Adv. Com., Sparkill Palisades Fire Dist., 1968-69; pres. Palisades Free Libr., 1969-71; trustee Orangetown Pub. Libr., 1971-73, Friends of Chamber Music, Troy, N.Y., 1988—; mem. citizens adv. com. Title III Program, S. Orangetown Ctrl. Sch. Dist., 1972-75; chmn. N.Y. State Low Level Waste Group, 1986-95; trustee Rockland Country Day Sch., 1974-78. Recipient Charles Huebschman prize in zoology Columbia U., 1954, Career Scientist award Health Rsch. Coun. N.Y.C., 1963-72, Rsch. Career Devel. award Nat. Inst. Arthritis and Metabolic Diseases, NIH, USPHS, 1972-76, Tousimis prize in biology, 1984; Ford Found. scholar, 1951-55; NSF predoctoral fellow, 1955-56, Nat. Inst. Neurol. Diseases and Blindness predoctoral fellow, 1959-61 Mem.: Lab. Animal Mgmt. Assn., Am. Assn. Lab. Animal Scis., Am. Assn. Vet. Lab. Diagnosticians, N.Y. Soc. Electron Microscopists (dir. 1964—67), Internat. Soc. Eye Rsch., Assn. Career Scientists Health Rsch. Coun., Harvey Soc., Am. Soc. Cell Biology, Am. Assn. Anatomists, Assn. Am. Med. Colls. (rep. con. acad. socs. 1979—2002, mem. adminstrn. bd. CAS 1985—86), Assn. Anatomy Chmn. (pres. 1980—81), Arthur Purdy Stout Soc. Surg. Pathologists (hon.), Waquoit Bay Yacht Club, Sigma Xi. Achievements include research in disposal of radioactively labeled animal carcasses; patents for methods for treatment and disposal of regulated medical waste; patents in field. Home Phone: 518-273-0292; Office Phone: 518-369-6399. Personal E-mail: wr2kaye@aol.com.

KAYE, JHANI, radio station executive, television producer and director; b. Maywood, Calif., June 18, 1949; s. Jimmie Eccak and Betty Jo (Holland) Kazaroff. BA, UCLA, 1971. Music dir. Sta. KFXM, San Bernardino, Calif., 1969-73; announcer Stas. KUTE-FM/KKDJ-FM, LA, 1972-74; asst. program dir. Sta. KROQ, LA, 1973-74, Sta. WCFL, Chgo., 1980-82, Sta. KFI, LA, 1982; program dir. Sta. KINT-FM, El Paso, Tex., 1975-80; sta. mgr., program dir. Sta. KOST-FM, LA, 1982-99; program dir. Sta. KBIG-FM, Glendale, Calif., 1999—2003, sta. mgr., 1999—2003. Dir. adult contemporary programming Clear Channel Radio, 1999—; owner Los Feliz Post Prodn. Video Svcs.; on-air host Radio Medium, radio program. Appeared in TV series Falcon Crest, 1985, Drew Carey Show, 1998; dir. TV commls., 1986—; voice-over motion picture The Couch Trip, 1987; dir., video editor Dick Clark TV Commls. Recipient Marconi Radio awards Nat. Assn. Broadcasters, 1990, 91. Office: Sta KBIG-FM 3400 West Olive Ave Ste 550 Burbank CA 91505 Office Phone: 818-566-4722. E-mail: jhanikaye@clearchannel.com.

KAYE, JUDITH SMITH, state appeals court judge; b. Monticello, NY, Aug. 4, 1938; d. Benjamin and Lena (Cohen) Smith; m. Stephen Rackow Kaye, Feb. 11, 1964; children: Luisa Marian, Jonathan Mackey, Gordon Bernard BA, Barnard Coll., 1958; LLB cum laude, NYU, 1962; LLD (hon.), St. Lawrence U., 1985, Union U., 1985, Pace U., 1985, Syracuse U., 1988, L.I. U., 1989. Bar: NY State 1963. Assoc. Sullivan & Cromwell, NYC, 1962-64; staff atty. IBM, Armonk, NY, 1964-65; asst. to dean Sch. Law NYU, 1965-68; ptnr. Connelly Chase O'Donnell & Weyher, NYC, 1969-83; assoc. judge NY State Ct. Appeals, NYC, 1983-93, chief judge Albany, NY, 1993—. Pres., Conf. of Chief Justices; chair bd. dir., Nat. Ctr. for State Cts., 2002-03; bd. dir. Sterling Nat. Bank. Bd. editor, NY State Bar Journal; contbr. articles to profl. jours. Former bd. dirs. Legal Aid Soc.; chair, Permanent Jud. Commn. on Justice for Children; founding mem., hon. chair, Judges and Lawyers Breast Cancer Alert (JALBCA); trustee, William Nelson Cromwell Found. Recipient Vanderbilt medal NYU Sch. of Law, 1983, Medal of Distinction, Barnard Coll, 1987, John Marshall award, ABA, 2005. Fellow Am. Bar Found.; mem. Am. Law Inst., Am. Coll. Trial Lawyers, Am. Judicature Soc. (bd. dirs. 1980-83), ABA (co-chair, Commn. on the Am. Jury, 2004-05). Democrat. Achievements include being the first women to serve on the New York state's Court of Appeals; being the first women to occupy the state judiciary's highest office, Chief Judge. Office: NY Court of Appeals Court of Appeals Hall 20 Eagle St Albany NY 12207-1009 also: NY Court of Appeals 230 Park Ave Ste 826 New York NY 10169-0007*

KAYE, MARC MENDELL, lawyer; b. Irvington, NJ, Nov. 25, 1959; s. Aaron Morton and Sandra (Hoch) K. AA, BA, Rutgers U., 1980; JD, U. Toledo, 1983. Bar: N.J. 1984, Fla. 1987, D.C. 1991, N.Y. 1998, U.S. Dist. Ct. N.J. 1984, U.S. Supreme Ct. 1992; cert. civil trial atty. 1991. Trial atty. Shevick, Ravich, Koster et al, Rahway, N.J., 1984-85, Greenberg, Margolis et al, Roseland, N.J., 1985-86, Brian Granstrand, Fairfield, N.J., 1986-90; pvt. practice Livingston, N.J., 1986-94, Short Hills, 1994—. Counsel CNA Ins. Co., Fairfield, 1986-90; apptd. arbitrator Union County Arbitrator Program, 1993, Essex County Arbitrator and Mediator Programs, 1995, Millburn Citizen Budget Com., 1998—; adv. coun. mem. Chmn.'s Club Summit Bank, 1989-91. Mem. exec. com. Young Leadership div. United Jewish Appeal, Metrowest, N.J. 1988-91; bd. dirs. Jewish Cmty. Ctr. of MetroWest, 1998—, Opera Music Theatre Internat., 1999—, Re'uth, 2004—. Mem. N.J. Bar Assn., Essex County Bar Assn. (subcom. chmn. legal med. com. 1992-94), Union County Bar Assn., Fla. Bar Assn., D.C. Bar Assn., Assn. Trial Lawyers Am., N.J. Trial Lawyers Assn., Lions Club (v.p. 1993-95), Prime Ministers Club, Israel Bonds. Avocations: golf, swimming, scuba diving, travel. Office: One N Brook Dr at S Orange Ave Short Hills NJ 07078-3126 Home Phone: 973-379-1870; Office Phone: 973-379-1870. Personal E-mail: Kayemarc@hotmail.com.

KAYE, MICHAEL S., corporate executive; b. Hackensack, NJ, Apr. 30, 1954; s. Alvin and Miriam Kaye; children: Philip, Aurora. BA, Stanford U., 1976; JD, Harvard U., 1980; studied Japanese law, U. Tokyo, Japan. Lawyer Gibson, Dunn & Crutcher, LA, 1980-83; pres., CEO Lark, Inc., Hong Kong, 1984-85, Westec Security (Secom Co.), Irvine, Calif., 1985-88, Secomerica, Inc. (Secom Co.), Newport Beach, Calif., 1987—; founder, mng. ptnr. ClearLight Ptnrs. LLC., 2000—. Office: ClearLight Ptnrs LLC 100 Bayview Cir Ste 5000 Newport Beach CA 92660 Office Phone: 949-725-6614. Office Fax: 949-725-6611.

KAYE, PETER FREDERIC, columnist; b. Chgo., Mar. 8, 1928; s. Ralph A. and Sara Corson (Philipson) K.; m. Martha Louise Wood, Mar. 20, 1955; children: Loren, Terry, Adam. BA in Govt., Pomona Coll., 1949. Reporter Alhambra (Calif.) Post-Advocate, 1950-53; reporter, editorial writer, polit. writer The San Diego Union, 1953-68; news and pub. affairs dir. KPBS-TV, San Diego State Coll., 1968-72; corr., producer Nat. Pub. Affairs Ctr. for TV, Washington, 1972-74; comm. dir. So. Calif. First Nat. Bank, San Diego, 1974-75; press sec. The Pres. Ford Com., Washington, 1975-76; mgr. Copley Videotex, San Diego, 1982-84; assoc. editor The San Diego Union, 1976-94; editl. dir. KNSD, San Diego, 1996-99. Freelance TV producer programs KPBS, PBS, BBC; San Diego corr. Newsweek, 1968-71, McGraw-Hill, 1959-67; lectr. comm. U. Calif., San Diego, 1971; copywriter Washburn-Justice Advt., San Diego, 1959-70. Producer 10 TV programs including including Jacob Bronowski: Life and Legacy, Twenty-Five Years of Presidency, The Presidency, The Press and the People. Press asst. Eisenhower-Nixon Campaign, L.A., 1952; asst. press sec. Richard Nixon Presdl. Campaign, Washington, 1960; dir. Pete Wilson for Mayor Campaign, San Diego, 1971; comm. dir. Flournoy for Gov. Campaign, Beverly Hills, Calif., 1974. With U.S. Mcht. Marines, 1945, U.S. Army, 1950-52. Jefferson fellow East-West Ctr., Honolulu, 1987; recipient Golden Mike awards So. Calif. TV News Dirs. Assn., 1969, 70, 71, Best Pub. Affairs Program award Nat. Ednl. TV, 1970, Best Local TV Series award Radio-TV Mirror, 1971, Nat. Emmy award Spl. Events Reporter, Watergate Coverage, 1973-74, Best Editorial awards Copley Newspapers Ring of Truth, 1979, Sigma Delta Chi, 1985, Calif. Newspaper Pubs. Assn., 1985; San Diego Emmy awards, 1985, 87, 91. Mem. NATAS, State Bar Calif. (bd. govs. 1991-97, v.p. 1993-94, 96-97), Sigma Delta Chi. Independent. Home: 240 Ocean View Ave Del Mar CA 92014-3322

KAYE, SAMUEL HARVEY, architect, educator; b. Columbia, SC, Sept. 27, 1940; s. James B. and Mary Louise (Harvey) K.; m. Patsy Cummings, June 27, 1964; children: Kimbelee Cummings, Elizabeth Harvey, Mary Catherine. BArch, Auburn U., 1963. Mem. staff Yeates & Gaskill, Architects, Memphis, 1965-68, Walk Jones & Francis Mah, Inc., Memphis, 1968-70, prin., 1970-74, Samuel H. Kaye, Architect, Columbus, Miss., 1974-91, Luke & Kaye, P.A., Columbus, 1991—. Instr. architecture Miss. State U., Starkville, 1983-84; instr. interior design Miss. U. for Women, Columbus, 1979-84, asst. prof., 1984-91; mem. Miss. Hist. Preservation Rev. Bd. Contbr. articles on urban design, usage study and historic archeol. research. Mem. St. Paul's Episcopal Ch. Vestry, Columbus, 1975-79, 83-85, bd. mgrs. Gray Ctr., Diocese of Miss., Canton, 1981-86, Salvation Army Adv. Bd., Columbus, 1983—; bd. trustees Miss. Heritage Trust, 1991—, pres. 1991-92, 2002-03. Lt. U.S. Army, 1963-65. Recipient preservation honor award Hist. Columbus, 1976, 81, 82, award of merit Miss. Hist. Soc., 1986, 91, 93, 94. Mem. AIA (bd. dirs. Miss. chpt. 1977, v.p. 1978, pres. 1979, state preservation coord. hist. resources com., urban design and planning com., honor award 1976), Nat. Trust Hist. Preservation (bd. advisors 1989-98, emeritus 1998—), Rotary (v.p. Columbus 1985-86, pres. 1986). Avocations: reading, photography. Home: 424 7th St S Columbus MS 39701-5752 Office: Luke & Kaye PA PO Box 48 114 5th St S Columbus MS 39703-0048 Home Phone: 662-327-5071. Business E-Mail: samkaye@ebicom.net.

KAYE, STUART MARTIN, lawyer; b. Bronx, NY, Dec. 2, 1946; s. Jules Krupnikoff and Gussie (Lipchinsky) Kaye; m. Nancy Elaine Carter, Oct. 19, 1967 (div. 1970); m. Christine Marie Heitkam, Sept. 25, 1970 (div. 1983); children: Joshua Brandon, Jeremy Jason; m. Eve C. Farkas, Apr. 2, 1988 (div. 1991); 1 child, Kimberly I. Morlan; m. Patricia S. Cruise, Mar. 9, 1996; 1 child, Trina S. Cruise. AA, Glendale Community Coll., 1971; BS in Polit. Sci., Ariz. State U., 1974; JD, Western State U., 1978. Bar: Calif. 1980, U.S. Dist. Ct. (no. dist.) Calif. 1980, (so. dist.) Calif. 1985, (cen. dist.) Calif. 1987. Assoc. mgmt. analyst State of Calif., Sacramento, 1978-84; pvt. practice Shingle Springs, 1981-84; legal counsel State of Calif., Sacramento, 1984-85, indsl. relations counsel San Diego, 1985-92; legal asst. Ariz. Atty. Gen., Phoenix, 1992-93; indsl. rels. coun. State of Calif., Santa Ana, 1993-95; atty. Don D. Sessions, APLC, Mission Viejo, 1995-98; pvt. practice La Mesa, 1998-2001; indsl. rels. coun. State of Calif., San Diego, 2001—04; judge U.S. Social Security Adminstrn., LA, 2004—. With U.S. Army, 1964-68. Democrat. Jewish. Avocation: camping. Office Phone: 213-894-3264. Personal E-mail: stuart7@msn.com.

KAYLAN, HOWARD LAWRENCE, musical entertainer, screenwriter, composer; b. NYC, June 22, 1947; s. Sidney and Sally Joyce (Berlin) Kaylan; m. Mary Melita Pepper, June 10, 1967 (div. Sept. 1971); 1 child, Emily Anne; m. Susan Karen Olsen, Apr. 18, 1982 (div. June 1996); 1 child, Alexandra Leigh. Student, UCLA; PhD in Philosophy, Am. Coll. Metaphys. Theology, St. Paul, Minn., 2000. Lead singer and founder rock group The Turtles, Los Angeles, 1965—; lead singer rock group Mothers of Invention, Los Angeles, 1970-72, Flo and Eddie, 1972-83; radio, TV, recording entertainer various broadcast organizations, Los Angeles, 1972—; screenwriter Larry Gelbart, Carl Gotleib prodns., Los Angeles, 1979-85; prodr. children's records Kidstuff Records, Hollywood, Fla., 1980-83; singer, prodr. rock band Flo and Eddie, Los Angeles, 1976-83; singer, prodr. The Turtles (reunion of original band), Los Angeles, 1980—; actor, TV and film Screen Actors Guild, Los Angeles, 1983—. Background vocalist various albums for numerous performers; syndicated talk show host Unistar Radio Network, 1989—; radio personality Sta. WXRK-FM, NYC, 1990—91, KLOU, St. Louis, 1993, WGRR, Cin., 1995—97. Author: Hi Bob, 1995, The Energy Pals, 1995; contbr. articles to profl. jours.; screenwriter (films) Death Masque, 1985, My Dinner With Jimi, 2003; actor: (films) 200 Motels, 1971, Get Crazy, 1985, General Hospital, Suddenly Susan, 1999, Riding the Bullet, 2004; performer: at White House, 1970; exec. prodr.(radio): Down Eerie Street, 1998; singer: numerous top ten hit songs with Turtles, Bruce Springsteen, The Ramones, Duran Duran, T. Rex, John Lennon and others; singer: (commls.) Chevrolet, Pepsi, Bruger King and NFL, 1970— (awards); singer: (albums) Dust Bunnies, 2005. Recipient 10 Gold and Platinum LP album awards while lead singer, 1995—, Fine Arts award, Bank of Am., 1965, Spl. award, Billboard Mag., 1992, Best Script award, Slam Dunk Film Festival, 2003, Bubblegum award, 2003. Mem.: AGVA, AFRTA, Am. Fedn. Musicians, Screen Actors Guild. Personal E-mail: kaylan@howardkaylan.com. E-mail: hkaylan@theturtles.com.

KAYLE, BRUCE E., lawyer; b. Bklyn., 1958; BA, BSE summa cum laude, Univ. Pa., 1979; JD cum laude, Harvard Univ., 1982. Bar: N.Y. 1983. Staff atty. Joint Com. on Taxation, U.S. Congress, Washington; ptnr. & chmn. Tax Dept. Milbank Tweed Hadley & McCloy, NYC. Contbr. articles to profl. jours. Bd. dir. Low-Income Taxpayer Clinic, Legal Aid Soc. Recipient Pro Bono award, Legal Aid Soc. Mem.: N.Y. State Bar Assn. (co-chmn. Com. Fin. Instruments, mem. exec. com. Tax sect.), Tax Club (pres.), Tax Forum. Office: Milbank Tweed Hadley & McCloy 1 Chase Manhattan Plz New York NY 10005-1413 Office Phone: 212-530-5956. Office Fax: 212-530-5219. Business E-Mail: bkayle@milbank.com.

KAYNE, JON BARRY, industrial psychologist; b. Sioux City, Iowa, Oct. 20, 1943; s. Harry Aaron and Barbara Valentine (Daniel) K.; m. Bunee Ellen Price, July 25, 1965; children: Nika Jenine, Abraham; m. Sandra Kay Fossbender, Jan. 5, 1985; 1 child, Shay-Marie Kathryn. BA, U. Colo., 1973; MSW, U. Denver, 1975; PhD, U. No. Colo., 1978. With spl. svcs. Weld County Sch. Dist. 6, Greeley, Colo., 1975-77; forensic diagnostician

Jefferson County (Colo.) Diagnostic Unit, 1977-78; assoc., dir. mktg. 1 Dow Ctr., assoc. prof. psychology Hillsdale (Mich.) Coll., 1978-87; pres. Jon B. Kayne, P.C., Hillsdale, 1980-87; pres. bd. dirs. Lang. Learners in Partnership of Omaha, 1989-93; chmn. bd. dirs., CEO Am. Internat. Mgmt. Assocs., Ltd., Denver, 1984-87; prof. bus. adminstrn. and psychology Bellevue (Neb.) U., 1987—, v.p. profl. and continuing edn. studies, 1987-93, v.p. acad. affairs, 1993—. Chmn. bd. dirs. Domestic Harmony, 1979-82; bd. dir. religious sch., Greeley, 1975-77; candidate for sheriff of Boulder County, 1974. With USAR, 1962. Mem. Am. Psychol. Assn., Am. Soc. Clin. Hypnosis, Am. Statis. Assn., Internat. Neuropsychol. Soc., Mich. Soc. Investigative and Forensic Hypnosis (chmn. bd., pres. 1982), N.Y. Acad. Scis., Phi Delta Kappa, Psi Chi, Alpha Gamma Sigma. Office: Bellevue U 1000 Galvin Rd S Bellevue NE 68005-3098

KAYS, WILLIAM MORROW, academic administrator, mechanical engineer; b. Norfolk, Va., July 29, 1920; s. Herbert Emery and Margaret (Fechteler) K.; m. Alma Campbell, Sept. 14, 1947 (dec. June 1982); children: Nancy, Leslie, Margaret, Elizabeth.; m. Judith Scholtz, July 17, 1983. AB, Stanford U., 1942, MS, 1947, PhD in Mech. Engring., 1951. Asst. prof. mech. engring. Stanford U., 1951-54, assoc. prof., 1954-57, prof., 1957-90, prof. emeritus, 1990—, chmn. dept. mech. engring, 1961-72, dean engring., 1972-84. Dir. Acurex Corp., Alcohol Energy Systems; cons. to numerous firms. Author: Compact Heat Exchangers, 1964, 93, Convective Heat and Mass Transfer, 1966, 80. Hon. editorial adv. bd.: Internat. Jour. Heat and Mass Transfer. Served with U.S. Army, 1942-46. Fulbright fellow, 1959-60; NSF sr. postdoctoral fellow, 1966-67 Fellow ASME (Heat Transfer Divsn. Meml. award 1965, Max Jacob award 1992); mem. Am. Soc. Engring. Edn., Nat. Acad. Engring. Office: Stanford U Dept Mech Engring Stanford CA 94305

KAYSE, KATHLEEN, publishing executive; b. Chgo., 1959; Grad., Univ. of Ill. Media planning Wells, Rich, Greene and J. Walter Thompson, Chgo., 1980—83; sales trainee Time, 1983; midwest advt. mgr. Time Mag., Chgo.; nat. advt. dir. Time for Kids; pub. Fortune Small Bus. (FSB), Time Mag., NYC, 1998—2001, Money mag., 2001—02, People mag., 2002—. Named Most powerful women in the US, Fortune. Mem.: Fin. Comm. Soc., Advertising Women of NY.

KAYSEN, CARL, economics professor; b. Phila., Mar. 5, 1920; s. Samuel and Elizabeth (Resnick) K.; m. Annette Neutra, Sept. 13, 1940 (dec. 1990); children: Susanna, Laura; m. Ruth Butler, 1994. AB, U. Pa., 1940; PhD, Harvard U., 1954. Rschr. Nat. Bur. Econ. Rsch., 1940-42; economist OSS, 1942; mem. faculty Harvard U., 1950—66; jr. fellow Harvard U. (Soc. Fellows), 1947-50, asst. prof. econs., 1950-55, asso. prof., 1955-57, prof., 1957-66, Lucius N. Littauer prof. polit. economy, 1964-66; assoc. dean Harvard U. (Grad. Sch. Public Adminstrn.), 1960-66; dir. Inst. Advanced Study, Princeton, NJ, 1966-76, prof., 1966-77; David W. Skinner prof. polit. economy MIT, 1977-90, dir. program in sci., tech. and soc., 1981-87, prof. emeritus, 1990—. Clk. to Judge C. E. Wyzanski, US Dist. C., 1950-52; dep. spl. asst. to Pres. Kennedy for nat. security affairs, 1961-63; mem. Carnegie Commn. on Higher Edn.; vice chmn., dir. rsch. Sloan Commn. on Govt. and Higher Edn.; faculty lectr. London Sch. Econs., 1956; Haynes lectr. Calif. Inst. Tech., 1966; Stafford Little lectr. Princeton U., 1968; Oliver W. Holmes lectr. Harvard Law Sch., 1969; Paley lectr. Hebrew U., Jerusalem, 1970; Godkin lectr. Harvard U., 1976; Bernard Brodie lectr., UCLA, 1994. Hon. Life trustee U. Pa. Served to capt. air intelligence AUS, 1942-45. Fulbright scholar London Sch. Econs., 1955-56; Guggenheim fellow, 1955-56; Ford Found. fellow Greece, 1959-60 Mem. Am. Philos. Soc., Am. Acad. Arts and Scis., Phi Beta Kappa. Clubs: Century (NYC). Office: MIT Security Studies Program E 38-614 292 Main St Cambridge MA 02139 Office Phone: 617-253-4054.

KAYSEN, GAVIN N., chef; b. Thousand Oaks, Calif., 1979; m. Linda Kaysen. Grad., New Eng. Culinary Acad., Montpelier, Vt., 2001. Chef Domaine Chandon, Napa Valley, Calif., 1996, Auberge de Lavaux, Lausanne, Switzerland, L'Escargot, London; sous chef Rancho Bernardo Inn, San Diego, 2002—04; chef de cuisine El Bizcocho, Rancho Bernardo Inn, San Diego, 2004—. Guest chef James Beard House, NYC, 2005; US rep. Bocuse d'Or World Cuisine Contest, Lyons, France, 2007. Named Best Chef in San Diego, San Diego Mag., 2004, Rising Star Chef, Restaurant Hospitality mag., 2006; named one of Best New Chefs, Food & Wine Mag., 2007; recipient Nat. Trophy of Cuisine and Pastry, 2003, third place, Internat. Trophy of Cuisine and Pastry, Paris, 2003. Avocations: travel, reading. Office: Rancho Bernardo Inn 1755o Bernardo Oaks Dr San Diego CA 92128*

KAYSER, BRIAN D., retired psychologist, writer; b. Heron Lake, Minn., Jan. 2, 1947; s. Lowell Norris Kayser and Margy Lucille Bassett; m. Ruth Ann Blanka, Mar. 27, 2002. BA, U. Ill., 1969; MA, U. Minn., 1970, PhD, 1972; PsyD, Forest Inst. Profl. Psychology, Springfield, Mo., 1995. Cert. in psychology Assn. State and Provincial Psychology Bds., 2001. Mktg. rschr. various orgns., 1976—83; asst. prof. sociology U. Akron, Ohio, 1972—75; pres. Kayser Mktg. Rsch. & Cons., Inc., 1983—92; clin. psychologist/neuropsychologist in pvt. practice, 1995—99; clin. psychologist/neuorpsychologist Panhandle Mental Health Ctr., Scottsbluff, Nebr., 1999—2001. Author: Secrets of Winning Baccarat; contbr. articles to profl. jours. Mem.: APA (life). Avocation: genealogy. Home Phone: 303-523-8557.

KAYSER, LEO, III, lawyer; b. Birmingham, Ala., Apr. 28, 1944; s. Leo and Simmie (Goldberg) K. BA in Polit. Sci. and Econs., Yale U., 1966; LLB, U. Va., 1969. Asst. counsel to pres. U. Va., Charlottesville, 1970; assoc. Shearman & Sterling, NYC, 1970-73, Baker & McKenzie, NYC, 1973—75; ptnr. Kayser & Redfern, NYC, 1975—. Bd. dirs. An Extraordinary Event, Inc. Trustee UN Devel. Corp., 1995-2003; bd.dirs. N.Y. League Conservation Voters, 2002-06. Mem. Fed. Bar Coun. (asst. sec. 1975-76), Assn. of Bar of City of N.Y. (mem. com. on drugs and the law 1994—). English Speaking Union, N.Y. Athletic Club, Yale Club of N.Y., Power Ten Inc., Union Club, The Econ. Club N.Y. Republican. Avocation: crew. Office: Kayser & Redfern 515 Madison Ave New York NY 10022-5403 Office Phone: 212-935-5057. Business E-Mail: lkayser@515law.com.

KAYTON, MYRON, engineering company executive; b. NYC, Apr. 26, 1934; s. Albert Louis and Rae K.; m. Paula Erde, Sept. 5, 1954; children: Elizabeth Kayton Kerns, Susan Kayton Barclay. BS, The Cooper Union, 1955; MS, Harvard U., 1956; PhD, MIT, 1960. Registered engr., Calif. Sect. head Litton Industries, Woodland Hills, Calif., 1960-65; dep. mgr. NASA, Houston, 1965-69; mem. sr. staff TRW, Inc., Redondo Beach, Calif., 1969-81; pres. Kayton Engring. Co., Inc., Santa Monica, Calif., 1981—. Chmn. bd. dir. WINCON Conf., L.A., 1985-92; founding dir. Caltech-MIT Enterprise Forum, Pasadena, Calif., 1984—; dir. Electronic Convs., Inc., 2000-01; tchr. tech. courses UCLA Extension, 1969-88. Author: Avionic Navigation Systems, 1966, 2d edit., 1997, Navigation: Land, Sea, Air and Space, 1990; contbr. articles to profl. jours Founding dir. UCLA Friends of Humanities, 1971-75; West coast chmn. Cooper Union Fund Campaign, 1989-93. Fellow NSF, Washington, 1956-57, 58-60; recipient Gano Dunn medal The Cooper Union, N.Y.C., 1975. Fellow IEEE (life; nominating com. 1999-2001, corp. bd. dirs. 1996-97, pres. aerospace 1993-94, exec. v.p. aerospace 1991-92, v.p. tech. ops. 1988-90, nat. bd. govs. 1983—2000, vice-chmn. L.A. coun. 1983-84, avionics editor Aerospace Transactions 2002—. M.B. Carlton award 1988, Disting. lectr., Millennium medal 2000); mem. ASME, Harvard Grad. Soc. (coun. mem. chmn. nominating com. 1988-91, Inst. Navigation (Kerschner award 2006), Soc. Automotive Engr., Harvard Club So. Calif. (pres. 1979-80), MIT Club (L.A.). Avocations: tennis, history, languages, flying. Office: Kayton Engring Co PO Box 802 Santa Monica CA 90406-0802 Office Phone: 310-393-1819.

KAYWOOD, SAM K., JR., lawyer; b. New Haven, June 14, 1957; BS with distinction, Babson Coll., 1979; JD with distinction, Emory Univ., 1986. CPA; bar: Ga. 1987. With Arthur Andersen; ptnr., chmn. fed. income tax group Alston & Bird LLP, Atlanta, 1993. Mem.: ABA (mem. tax sect.), IFA. Office: Alston & Bird LLP One Atlantic Ctr 1201 W Peachtree St NW Atlanta GA 30309-3424 Office Phone: 404-881-7481. Office Fax: 404-881-7777. Business E-Mail: skaywood@alston.com.

KAZ, NATHANIEL, sculptor; b. NYC, Mar. 9, 1917; s. I. Rudolph and Ida (Elkan) K.; m. Delfina Nahrgang, 1986; children: Naomi Della, Eric Justin. Student, Geo. B. Bridgeman, Samuel Cashwan, 1927, William Zorach; attended, Cooper Union. Tchr. Art Students League, NYC. One-man shows include Downtown Gallery, 1939, Assn. Am. Artists, 1946, Grand Central Moderns, 1954, Joan Avnet Gallery, 1965, Art Students League N.Y., 1991; traveling group exhbn. Bethlehem, Pa., Oshkosh, Wis., Annapolis, Md.; exhbns. include Whitney Mus., Met. Mus. Art, Bklyn. Mus., Art Inst. Chgo., U. Nebr., Phila. Mus. Fine Arts, Chgo. World's Fair; represented in permanent collections, Bklyn. Mus., Whitney Mus., Met. Mus., Jewish Mus., Nat. Acad. Mus., Ulrich Mus. at Wichita State U., N.Y.U., pvt. collections; designed and executed 10 ft. carving in limestone for Vine St. Temple, Nashville, 6 ft. bronze for Pub. Sch. 59, Bklyn., Realis Gallery, Winston-Salem, N.C., 2003, Alamance County Arts Coun., Graham, N.C., 2003, Circoscrizione Viareggio Nuova, Viareggio, Italy, 2004; exhibited 4 ritual works, Grand Central Moderns, 1957, Temple of Beth Emeth, Albany, N.Y., 1965; designed and executed two 7 ft. colored aluminum reliefs of Thespians-Tragedy and Comedy for Jr. High Sch. 164, Queens, NY, 1958. Grantee Nat. Inst. Arts and Letters, 1959; recipient Mich. Sculpture award, 1929, Sect. Fine Arts award, 1940, Artists for Victory award, 1942, Bklyn. Soc. Artists 32d ann. award, 1952, Sculpture prize Bklyn. Mus., 1952, Alfred G. B. Steel prize 148th ann. exhibit Pa. Acad. Fine Arts, 1953; winner nat. competition UN monument design, Nat. Council U.S. Art, 1955; Award for Sculpture Maury Leibovitz Competition, 1986; Nancy Dryfoos Meml. award Allied Artists Ann. Exhbn., N.Y.C., 1991, C. Percival Dietsch Sculpture prize Nat. Sculpture Soc., N.Y.C., 1992, Disting. Svc. award County of Westchester, 2006. Mem. Sculptors Guild, Nat. Sculpture Soc. (Exhbn. Gold medal, Maurice B Hexter prize, 2006), NAD (academician, Merit award 1976, Agop Agopoff award 1988, Saltus Gold medal 1989), Audubon Artists (Medals of Honor 1960, 1981, 83, 87, 88), Sculpture Soc. Office Phone: 212-724-3365.

KAZA, GREG JOHN, economist, educator; b. Wyandotte, Mich., Nov. 11, 1960; s. John J. and Mary A. Kaza. BA in Econs., U. Detroit, 1989; MSF in Internat. Fin., Walsh Coll., Troy, Mich., 1998. V.p. policy rsch. The Mackinac Ctr., Midland, Mich., 1989-91; adj. prof. Northwood Inst. and Walsh Coll., Troy, Mich., 1998—2000; state rep. State of Mich., 1993-98; exec. dir. Citizen Legislators' Caucus Found., Washington, 1999-2000, Ark. Policy Found., Little Rock, 2001—. Author 9 state laws. Contbr. articles to profl. jours. Mem.: Highpointers Club. Republican. Roman Catholic. Office: Ark Policy Found Stephens Bldg 111 Center St Ste 1200 Little Rock AR 72201 Office Phone: 501-537-0825.

KAZAKOV, ALEKSEY V., product designer; b. Moscow, Jan. 26, 1968; s. Victor A. Kazakov and Natalia A. Teplitskaya; 1 child, Kazimir A. AA in Art and Handicraft, Moscow Tchr.'s U., 1996; diploma in Design, Acad. Internat. Cooperation, Moscow, 2000. Designer Geoinformmark, Moscow, 1996—2000; artist designer Mir Parketa, Moscow, 2000—03; archl. designer FB Internat., Inc, Wood Ridge, NJ, 2004—05; lead designer Top Drawer Custom Cabinetry, New Rochelle, NY, 2005—06; artist designer Dfergos, Bronx, NY, 2006—. Freelance artist, 1988—. Video, Moscow Festival of Chamber Music Homecoming. Fax: 347-964-7153. E-mail: aleksey@dfergos.com.

KAZAMA, TOSHIO, retired humanities educator; b. Tokyo, Jan. 2, 1924; s. Kiichi and Mume (Yamana) K.; m. Kazuyo (Shimomura), May 10, 1955; children: Keiichi, Shinjiro, Naoto. Attended, Tokyo U., 1947—52. Instr., asst. prof. liberal arts Hosei U., Tokyo, 1969-74, prof. liberal arts, 1974-94. Bd. dir. Japanese Assn. Indian and Buddhist Studies. Author: A New Interpretation of Bi Yan Ji, 1978. Cadet, Japanese Shipping Engr., 1945. Avocation: seal engraving. Home: Shimorenjaku 6-4-23 Mitaka 181-0013 Japan Home Phone: 0422-43-1225. Personal E-mail: tkazm215@parkcity.ne.jp.

KAZAN, STEVEN, lawyer; b. NYC, Sept. 1, 1942; AB, Brandeis U., Waltham, Mass., 1963; LLB, Harvard U., Cambridge, Mass., 1966. Bar: NY 1967, Calif. 1970. Sr. and mng. ptnr. Kazan McClain, PLC, Oakland, Calif., 1974—. Office: Kazan McClain Abrams Lyons Farrise and Greenwood PLC 171 12 St # 300 Oakland CA 94607 Home Phone: 1 510 547 7817; Office Phone: 510-302-1000. Business E-Mail: skazan@kazanlaw.com.

KAZANCHYAN, GEVORK, public health educator; b. Yerevan, Armenia, Aug. 31, 1977; s. Hakop and Mary Kazanchyan. BS in Environ. and Occupl. Health, Calif. State U., Northridge, 1999, MS in Environ. and Occupl. Health, 2002; postgrad., Clayton Coll. Natural Health, 2003—. Cert. hazardous materials mgmt. Calif. State U., Northridge, 1999, registered environ. health specialist Calif., 1999, cert. lead prevention inspecto, assessor Calif., 2005, food safety profl. Nat. Environ. Health Assn., Colo., 2002, 40-hour hazardous waste worker Calif., 2001, profl. food mgr. Experior Assessments, Minn., 2005. Corp. health and safety assoc. Avery Dennison Corp. Health and Safety, Pasadena, Calif., 1999—2000; environ. health specialist III County LA Dept. Pub. Health, Baldwin Park, Calif., 2000—; adj. prof. dept. hotel and restaurant mgmt. Coll. of Canyons, Santa Clarita, Calif., 2002—, contracted instr. cmty. ext. and non-credit edn., 2006—. Mem. ask a food safety expert project panel Iowa State U. Ext., Iowa; project reviewer food safe schools com. Nat. Environ. Health Assn., Colo.; cons., spkr. in field. Prodr., co-writer: (documentary film) The Foundation Project; founder, ptnr. (food pairing-beer tasting dining events) Those Beer Guys; contbr. articles to profl. jours. Mem. Armenian Nat. Ice Hockey Team; advisor LEAF Certifications, LA, 2006; contbr. Pacoima Beautiful indoor air quality project, Pacoima, Calif., 1998—98; cons. GK Insights, LA, 2004—; youth athletic coach USA Hockey team West Valley Wolves, LA. Mem.: Calif. Environ. Health Assn., Nat. Environ. Health Assn. (corr.), Inst. Noetic Scis. (life), Calif. State U. Northridge Ice Hockey (corr.; gen. mgr. 1997—98, pres. 1998—99).

KAZANCI, DENIZ, mathematician; b. Aydin, Turkey, Aug. 2, 1982; d. Gürkan and Mürvet Kazanci. BS, U. Fla., Gainesville, 2005; PhD, Mich. State U., East Lansing, 2006. Tchg. asst. U. Fla., Gainesville, 2002—04, rsch. scholar, 2003—04; math. tchr. Okaloosa County, Ft. Walton Beach, Fla., 2005—06; fellow Am. Inst. Econ. Rsch., Gt. Barrington, Mass., 2006; with Mich. State U., East Lansing. Sec. Actuarial Student Soc. UF Chpt., Gainesville, Fla., 2002—03. Contbr. articles to profl. jours. Coord. team mem., internat. performance tent stage decoration 23rd Pfingst Festival, Germany, 2004. Recipient Hon. Scholars award, Broward C.C., 2000—01, Internat. Student Tuition award, U. Fla., 2002—04; fellow, Woods Hole Oceanog. Instn., 2003, Am. Inst. for Econ. Rsch., 2006—07; scholar, Jeanne Braddock Whiteworth Found., 2001—04, Booster Club, Blanche Ely H.S., 2001—02, Diversified Investment and Innovations Group, 2001—02, So. Scholar Found., 2002—05, U. Fla., 2003—04, Altrusa Internat. Club,f Gainesville, 2003—04; Internat. Student scholar, Broward C.C., 2000—01. Fellow: Phi Theta Kappa, Golden Key, Omicron Delta Epsilon; mem.: Actuarial Student Soc., Pi Mu Epsilon (pres. 2003—05, treas. 2002—03), Nat. Scholars. Achievements include research in incentives for IMF and World Bank reform of the structural policy change in developing debtor countries; curvature technique in diagnostic differentiation of low ejection fraction from healthy patients; Juan De Fuca Ridge. Avocations: travel, chess, music, painting, dance. Home Phone: 902122712138. Business E-Mail: kazancid@msu.edu.

KAZANJIAN, JOHN HAROLD, lawyer; b. Newport, RI, Jan. 25, 1949; s. Powel Harold and Louise T. (Alexander) K.; m. Jane Mitchell Kohlmeyer, Sept. 26, 1981; 1 child, Sara Jane. BA, Providence Coll., 1971; JD, Notre Dame U., 1975. Bar: N.Y. 1976, U.S. Dist. Ct. (so. dist.) N.Y. 1976, U.S. Dist. Ct. (ea. dist.) N.Y. 1977, U.S. Supreme Ct. 1980, U.S. Ct. Appeals (2d crct.) 1986, U.S. Ct. Appeals (fed. crct.) 1991. Assoc. Cadwalader, Wickersham & Taft, NYC, 1975-86; ptnr. Anderson, Kill & Olick, NYC, 1986-98, Beveridge & Diamond, NYC, 1999—. Mem. U.S. Naval War Coll. Found., Newport, 1985—. Mem. ABA (sects. on litigation, tort and ins. practice and internat. law), Assn. Bar City N.Y. (chair com. on product liability), N.Y. County Lawyers Assn. (chair com. on ins. law, tort law sect.), Metro. Club. Episcopalian. Avocations: caricatures, cartoons, long distance running. Office: Beveridge & Diamond 15th Fl 477 Madison Ave New York NY 10022-5802 E-mail: jkazanjian@bd.law.com.

KAZANJIAN, PHILLIP CARL, lawyer, educator; b. Visalia, Calif., May 15, 1945; s. John Casey and Sat-ten Arlene K.; m. Wendy Coffelt, Feb. 5, 1972; 1 child, John. BA with honors, U. So. Calif., 1967; JD with honors, Lincoln U., 1973. Bar: Calif. 1979, US Dist. Ct. (ctrl. dist.) Calif. 1980, US Tax Ct. 1980, US Ct. Appeals (9th cir.) 1980, US Mil. Ct. Appeals 1980, US Supreme ct. 1983. Ptnr. Brakefield & Kazanjian, Glendale, Calif., 1981-87; sr. ptnr. Kazanjian & Martinetti, Glendale, Calif., 1987—2005, of counsel, 2005—. Judge pro tem LA County Superior Ct., 1993—; instr. US Naval Acad., Annapolis, Md., 1981; adj. instr. Glendale CC, 1997-2005, instr., 2005—. Author: The Circuit Governor, 1972; editor-in-chief Lincoln Law Rev., 1973. Mem. Calif. Atty. Gen.'s Adv. Commn. on Cmty.-Police Rels., 1973; bd. dirs. LA County Naval Meml. Found., Inc., 1981-85, ARC, 1998-2003, Glendale CC Found., 1997—; pres., bd. trustees Glendale CC Dist., 1981-97, LA World Affairs Coun., Town Hall Calif.; vice chmn. bd. govs. Calif. Maritime Acad., 1986-94. Capt. USNR, 1969-99. Decorated Navy Commendation medal, Navy Achievement medal, knight Order of Knights Templar, 1990; recipient Patrick Henry medal Am. Legion, 1963, Congl. Record tribute U.S. Ho. of Reps., 1974, Centurion award Chief of Naval Ops., 1978; commendatory resolutions Mayor of L.A., L.A. City Coun., L.A. County Bd. Suprs., Calif. State Assembly and Senate, and Govt. of Calif., 1982, 2003, Justice award Calif. Law Student Assn., 1973. Mem. ABA (Gold Key 1972), Calif. Bar Assn., LA County Bar Assn., Am. Judicature Soc., ATLA, Glendale C. of C. (bd. dirs., Patriot Yr. 1986), Res. Officers Assn. (nat. judge adv., award 1981), Naval Res. Assn. (nat. adv. com.), US Naval Inst., Interallied Confedn. Res. Officers (internat. chmn. 1987-94), Explorers Club, Commonwealth of Calif. Club. Republican. Episcopalian. Office: Kazanjian & Martinetti 520 E Wilson Ave Ste 250 Glendale CA 91206-4346 Office Phone: 818-241-1011.

KAZANTSEV, ALEKSEY GREGORY, medical educator; b. Moscow, Dec. 25, 1958; s. Gregory Abramovich Shirman and Valentina Andreevna Kazantseva; m. Natalia Victor Mitlina; children: Yakov Alex, Masha Alex. BA, Pedagogical U., 1986; PhD, U. NC, Chapel Hill, 1997. Postdoctoral fellow MIT, Cambridge, Mass., 1997—2002; asst. prof. Med. Sch. Harvard U., Charlestown, Mass., 2002—. Dir. high throughput drug screening lab. Mass. Gen. Hosp., Charlestown, 2002—07. Contbr. articles to profl. jours. Grantee for eveloping potent and selective SIRT2 inhibitors, Cure Huntington's Disease Inc., 2006. Mem.: European Huntington's Disease Network (assoc.). Achievements include patents for discovery novel SIRT2 inhibitors. Home: 453 Washington St Apt 6 Brookline MA 02446 Office: Harvard Univ Medical School MGH Bldg 114-3300 16th St Charlestown MA 02129 Office Phone: 617-726-1274. Office Fax: 617-724-1480. Business E-Mail: akazantsev@partners.org.

KAZARIAN, POGHOS F., physicist, researcher, educator; b. Yerevan, Armenia, Sept. 2, 1973; arrived in USA, 1998; s. Frunzik H. and Tamara G. (Movsesyan) Kazarian. MS in Physics, Yerevan State U., Armenia, 1994, PhD in Physics, 1997. Post grad. rsch. asst. Dept. of Theory Physics, Yerevan State U., 1994—97, rsch. assoc., 1997—2000; instr. physics dept., math. dept. Glendale C.C., Calif., 2000—. Author: (Theory) Astrophysics, 1994—99, 8th Internat. Symposium on Light Sources, 1998, (book) Concepts in Physics: Classical Mechanics, 2003. Recipient Diploma with Honors, Faculty of Physics, Yerevan State Univ./Yerevan Armenia, 1994, Scholarship for Excellence, Yerevan State Univ./Yerevan Armenia, 1989—94, Diploma with Honors & Medal, AS Pushkin, Secondary Sch./Yerevan, Armenia, 1989. Mem.: AAAS, Internat. Soc. Gen. Relativity and Gravitation, Am. Chem. Soc., NY Acad. Sci. Bimetric scalar-tensor theory of gravitation-construction of pre-stellar objects of V. Ambartsumian's cosmogony concept, and full agreement with gen. relativity (GR included as partial case), 1993-1999; Abnormally intense radiation from dielectric, 1998. Office: Glendale Cmty Coll 1500 N Verdugo Rd Glendale CA 91208 Home: 342 N Belmont St Glendale CA 91206 Office Phone: 818-240-1000 5825. Business E-Mail: pkazarian@glendale.edu.

KAZAZIAN, HAIG HAGOP, JR., pediatrician, researcher, educator; b. Toledo, July 30, 1937; s. Haig Hagop and Hermine Adriene (Papelian) K.; m. Lillian Agnes Cleaver, Oct. 13, 1962; children: Haig Hagop III, Sonya Elizabeth. AB, Dartmouth Coll., 1959; MD, Johns Hopkins U., 1962. Diplomate Am. Bd. Pediatrics, Am. Bd. Medical Genetics (pres. 2000). Asst. prof. pediatrics Johns Hopkins U., Balt., 1969-74, assoc. prof. pediatrics, 1974-77, prof. pediats., 1977-94, prof. biology, 1979-94, prof. ob-gyn., 1985-94, prof. medicine, 1989-94, dir. Ctr. Med. Genetics, 1989-94, Sutland prof. pediat. genetics, 1991-94; prof., chmn. dept. genetics U. Pa. Sch. Medicine, Phila., 1994—. Mem. mammalian genetics study sect. NIH, Bethesda, Md., 1981-85; pres. bd. dirs. Citizens for Good Govt., Balt., 1973-75; bd. dirs. Am. Bd. Med. Genetics. Author more than 250 sci. papers; editor jour. Human Mutation, 1992. Sr. surgeon USPHS, 1966-68. Grantee NIH, 1968—; recipient Mead Johnson award Am. Acad. Pediatrics, 1976. Fellow Am. Acad. Arts & Scis.; mem. Inst. of Medicine, Am. Pediat. Soc., Am. Soc. Human Genetics (bd. dirs. 1982-85), Am. Soc. Clin. Investigation, Assn. Am. Physicians, Alpha Omega Alpha. Democrat. Episcopalian. Avocations: jogging, tennis, classical music. Office: U Pa Sch Medicine 475 Clinical Research Bldg 415 Curie Blvd Philadelphia PA 19104-4218*

KAZEMI, FARHAD, political scientist, educator; b. Tehran, Iran, Jan. 7, 1943; came to U.S., 1960; s. Parviz and Irandokht (Ehteshami) K.; m. Tina A. Garber, July 9, 1966 (div. 1975); children: Shirin, Sara; m. Jane Opper, Apr. 28, 1977; stepchildren: Lygeia, Maude. BA, Colgate U., 1964; MA, George Washington U., 1966, Harvard U., 1968; PhD, U. Mich., 1973. Teaching fellow U. Mich., Ann Arbor, 1968-70; from instr., asst. prof., assoc. prof. to prof. pol. sci. NYU, 1971-88, acting dean Grad. Sch. Arts and Sci., 1989-91, vice provost, 1999—2003. Vis. lectr. U. Pa., 1979; cons. U.S. Govt., 1980—; dir. Kevorkian Ctr. N.Y. U., NYC, 1982—85, 2004—06, chmn. dept. polit. sci., 1985—89, 1992—93, 1996—97; vis. prof. Princeton U., 1996; vis. sr. fellow Oxford (Eng.) U., 1997; apptd. mem. U.S. Adv. Group on Pub. Diplomacy for Arab and Muslim World, 2003. Author: Poverty and Revolution in Iran, 1980, Politics and Culture in Iran, 1988; author, editor: Iranian Revolution, 1980, Civil Society in Iran, 1995-96; co-editor: A Way Prepared: Studies on Islamic Culture, 1987, Peasants and Politics in the Modern Middle East, 1991 , other books and articles. Grantee NSF, 1973, Social Sci. Rsch. Coun., 1974-75, 84-85, Kervorkian Fund, 1985, Ford Found., 1992-93, 94-95, Rockefeller Found., 1993, 94. Fellow Middle East Studies Assn. (bd. dirs. 1985-88, pres. 1995-96); mem. Am. Polit. Sci. Assn., Internat. Polit. Sci. Assn., Internat. Studies Assn., Middle East Inst., Soc. Iranian Studies (coun., editor 1982-86, pres. 1998-99), Internat. Soc. Polit. Psychology, Coun. Fgn. Rels., Atlantic Coun. Washington (acad. assoc. 1985-98). Democrat. Avocations: tennis, bicycling, sailing. Office: NYU Dept Politics 19 W 4th St New York NY 10012-1119 Office Phone: 212-998-8506.

KAZEMI, HOMAYOUN, internist, educator; b. Teheran, Iran, Sept. 28, 1934; came to U.S., 1953, naturalized, 1970; s. Parviz and Irandokht K.; m. Katheryne McNulty, June 7, 1958; children: Paul, Laili. BA, Lafayette Coll., 1954; MD, Columbia U., 1958; MSc (hon.), Harvard U., 1990. Diplomate: Am. Bd. Internal Medicine. Intern M.I. Bassett Hosp., Cooperstown, NY, 1958-59; resident in medicine Mass. Gen. Hosp., Boston, 1963, chief pulmonary unit, 1967-89, chief pulmonary and critical care unit, 1989-98, chief emeritus, 1998—, sr. physician, 2005; assoc. prof. medicine Harvard U., 1971-78, prof., 1979—, prof. medicine Harvard/MIT program in health sci. and tech., 1980—. Hon. cons. in intrenal medicine Shanghai 1st People's Hosp., 1992—; vis. scholar dept. medicine, U. Calif., San Diego, 1998-99; bd. dirs. Boston Tb Assn.; vis. prof. U. Ghent, 1975-76, Peking Union Med. Coll., China, 1992; dir. U.S. Beryllium Case Registry, 1968-78; vis. fellow Hammersmith Hosp., London, 1965; cons. Fed. Aviation Agy., 1987. Author: (book) Poon C-S and Kazemi, H Editors, Frontiers in Modeling and Control of Breathing, 2001, Disorder of the Respiratory System, 1976, (with L.G. Miller) Manual of Pulmonary Medicine, 1982—, Acute Lung Injury, 1986; mem. editl. bd. New Eng. Jour. Medicine, 1981-90, Respiratory Mgmt., 1989-93, Current Opinion in Pulmonary Medicine, 1993-99, Current Opinion in Critical Care, 1993-2000; guest editor Respiration Physiology, 2000. Dir. Am. Lung Assn. Boston; mem. rsch. evaluation subcom. Am. Heart Assn., mem. cardiopulmonary coun., 1979—, v.p. 1985-87, pres. 1987-89, mem. rsch. rev. com.; bd. trustees Dublin (N.H.) Sch., 1987-97. Fellow Am. Heart Assn., 1961-63, Am. Heart Assn. (inaugural 2003); named Dickinson Richards lectr., 1996; recipient Chadwick medal Mass. Thoracic Soc., 1988, Lifetime achievement award AMA, 2000. Fellow ACP; mem. Am. Fedn. Clin. Rsch., Am. Thoracic Soc. (pres. Ea. sect. 1974-75), Mass. Med. Soc., Am. Physiol. Soc, Am. Soc. Clin. Investigation, Soc. Occupl. and Environ. Health, Sigma Xi. Office: Mass Gen Hosp Boston MA 02114 Home Phone: 978-371-9795. Business E-Mail: Hkazemi@partners.org.

KAZEMITABAR AMIRKOLAIE, SEYED JAVAD, engineer, researcher; b. Babol, Mazandaran, Iran, Mar. 31, 1981; s. Seyed Jamal Kazemitabar Amirkolaie and Razieh Tabari. BSc in Elec. Engring., Sharif U. Tech., Tehran, Iran, 1999; MSc in Engring., U. Calif., Irvine, 2005. Rsch. asst. Sharif U. Tech., Tehran, Iran, 2001—02, U. Calif., Irvine, 2003—. Cons. in field. Connexant-Broadcom fellow. Mem.: IEEE. Achievements include research in code design for multiple antenna channels. Personal E-mail: skazemit@uci.edu.

KAZEN, GEORGE PHILIP, federal judge; b. Laredo, Tex., Feb. 29, 1940; s. Emil James and Drusilla M. (Perkins) K.; m. Barbara Ann Sanders, Oct. 27, 1962; children: George Douglas, John Andrew, Elizabeth Ann, Gregory Stephen. BBA, U. Tex., 1960, JD with honors, 1961. Bar: Tex. 1961, US Supreme Ct., US Ct. Claims, US Ct. Appeals (5th cir.), US Dist. Ct. (so. dist.) Tex. Briefing atty. Tex. Sup. Ct., 1961-62; founder, first pres. Laredo Legal Aid Soc., 1966-69; assoc. Mann, Freed, Kazen & Hansen, 1965-79; judge US Dist. Ct. (so. dist.) Tex., Laredo, 1979-96, chief judge, 1996—; founder, first pres. Laredo Legal Aid Soc., 1966-69; judge Fgn. Intelligence Surveillance Ct., 2003—. Mem. Jud. Conf. Com. Criminal Law, 1990-96, chair com., 1996-99; mem. 5th Cir. Jud. Coun., 1991-94, 96-2003; adj. prof. law St. Mary's U. Sch. Law, 1990-2004. Pres. Laredo Civic Music Assn.; chmn. St. Augustine-Ursuline Consol. Sch. Bd.; bd. dirs. Boys' Clubs Laredo; trustee Laredo Jr. Coll., 1972-79; bd. dirs., v.p., pres. Econ. Opportunities Devel. Corp., 1968-70; past bd. dirs. D.D. Hachar Found. With USAF, 1962-65. Decorated Air Force Commendation medal; named Outstanding Young Lawyer, Larado Jaycees, 1970. Mem. ABA, Tex. Bar Found., Tex. Bar Assn., Tex. Criminal Def. Lawyers Assn., Tex. Assn. Bank Counsel, Tex. Assn. Def. Counsel, Laredo C. of C. (bd. dirs. 1975-76), 5th Cir. Dist. Judges Assn. (v.p. 1984-85, pres. 1986-88), U. Tex. Law Sch. Alumni Assn. (bd. dirs. 1976-77). Roman Catholic. Office: US Dist Ct PO Box 1060 Laredo TX 78042-1060

KAZI, SUMAYA, entrepreneur; b. 1982; B in Mktg. & Strategic Planning, U. Calif. Berkeley. Co-founder & exec. dir. The CulturalConnect, San Francisco; mktg. mgr. Sun Microsystems Global Comm. Group. Young Entrepreneur mentor BUILD, Oakland, Calif. Named one of Best Entrepreneurs Under 25, BusinessWeek, 2006. Mem.: Young Professionals Internat. Network (World Affairs Coun.). E-mail: sumaya@TheCulturalConnect.com.

KAZIMI, MUJID SULIMAN, nuclear engineer, educator; b. Jerusalem, Nov. 20, 1947; came to U.S., 1969; s. Suliman Ishak Kazimi and Fikrat Nuseibeh; m. Nazik D. Denny, Sept. 1, 1973. B. Engring., Alexandria U., Arab Republic of Egypt, 1969; MS, MIT, 1971, PhD, 1973. Sr. engr. Westinghouse Electric Corp., Madison, Pa., 1973-74; assoc. scientist Brookhaven Nat. Lab., Upton, NY, 1974-76; asst. prof. MIT, Cambridge, 1976-79, assoc. prof., 1979-86, prof., 1986—, head dept. nuclear engring., 1989-97. Tokyo Elec. Power Co. (TEPCO) chair for nuc. engring. at MIT, 2000—; dir. Ctr. Advanced Nuc. Energy Systems, 2000—; chmn. high-level waste task force adv. panel U.S. Dept. Energy, Washington, 1990-95, chmn. new prodn. reactor severe accident group, 1990-91. Co-author: (with Neil Todreas) Nuclear Systems: Volume I: Thermal Hydraulic Fundamentals, 1990, Nuclear Systems: Volume II: Elements of Thermal Hydraulic Design, 1990; editor: Perspectives on Technological Development in the Arab World, 1978. Pres. Assn. Arab-Am. Univ. Grads., Belmont, Mass., 1980, 87. Fellow Am. Nuclear Soc. (bd. dirs. N.E. chpt. 1978, 80, exec. com. thermal hydraulics divsn. 1988-90), AAAS; mem. ASME, AIChE (chmn. nuclear heat transfer com. 1980-83), Am. Soc. for Engring. Edn. (exec. com. nuclear engring. divsn. 1995-97). Office: MIT Dept Nuc Engring 77 Massachusetts Ave Rm 24-215 Cambridge MA 02139-4307 Home Phone: 617-965-2626; Office Phone: 617-253-4206. Business E-Mail: kazimi@mit.edu.

KAZIMIERCZUK, MARIAN KAZIMIERCZUK, electrical engineer, educator; b. Smolugi, Poland, Mar. 3, 1948; came to U.S., 1984; s. Stanislaw and Stanislawa (Tomaszewska) K.; m. Alicja Nowowiejska, July 5, 1973; children: Andrzej, Anna. MS, Tech. U. of Warsaw, Poland, 1971, PhD, 1978, DSc, 1984. Instr. elec. engring. Tech. U. of Warsaw, Poland, 1972-78, assoc. prof., 1978-84; project engr. Design Automation, Inc., Lexington, Mass., 1984; vis. prof. Va. Poly. Inst., Blacksburg, 1984-85, Wright State U., Dayton, Ohio, 1985—. Author: Resonant Power Converters, 1995, Electronic Devices: A Design Approach, 2003; contbr. articles to profl. jours. Recipient Univ. Edn. and Tech. award Polish Ministry of Sci. award, 1981, 84, 85, Polish Acad. Sci. award, 1983. Fellow IEEE (Harrel V. Noble award 1990); mem. Assn. Polish Engrs., Polish Soc. Theoretical and Applied Elec. Scis. Roman Catholic. Home: 3620 Cypress Ct Dayton OH 45440-4515 Office: Wright State U Dept Elec Engring Dayton OH 45435 Home Phone: 937-427-2834; Office Phone: 937-775-5059. Business E-Mail: mkazim@cs.wright.edu, marian.kazimierczuk@wright.edu.

KAZIN, MICHAEL, historian, writer; b. NYC, June 6, 1948; s. Alfred and Carol Bookman (Salvadori) K.; m. Beth Horowitz, Aug. 24, 1980; children: Daniel, Maia. BA, Harvard U., 1972; PhD, Stanford U., 1983. Instr. history San Francisco State U., 1978-82; asst. prof. history Stanford (Calif.) U., 1983-85; prof. history Am. U., Washington, 1986-99, Georgetown U., 1999—. Author: The Populist Persuasion, 1995, 2d edit., 1996, rev. edit., 1998, Barons of Labor, 1987, 2d edit., 89 (Gutman award 1988), America Divided, 1999, rev. edit. 2003, A Godly Hero: The Life of William Jennings Bryan, 2006; co-editor: Americanism New Perspectives on the History of an Ideal, 2006; contbr. articles to profl. jours., popular mags. and newspapers; book editor Tikkun, San Francisco/N.Y.C., 1987-96; assoc. editor Socialist Rev., San Francisco, 1978-84; hist. advisor several documentaries, 1982— Steering com. Com. for a Teach-In with Labor, NYC, 1996-97; spkr., local leader Nuc. Freeze Campaign, San Francisco, 1982-84. John Adams chair Am. Studies, Fulbright program, Utrecht, The Netherlands, 1996; Fulbright lectr. Ritsumeikan U., Tokyo/Kyoto, 1997; Sr. fellow William and Mary Coll. Commonwealth Ctr., Williamsburg, Va., 1990-91, postdoctoral fellow Smithsonian Instn., Washington, 1988-89, NEH fellow, 1998-99, Woodrow Wilson Ctr. fellow, 1998-99, Guggenheim fellow, 2004 Mem. Am. Hist. Assn., Orgn. Am. Historians (chair com. for Ellis Hawley award). Democrat. Jewish. Avocations: baseball, fiction. Office: Georgetown U Dept History Washington DC 20057-0001 Home Phone: 301-656-4863; Office Phone: 202-687-0007. Business E-Mail: mk8@georgetown.edu.

KAZMERSKI, LAWRENCE LEE, scientist, research facility executive; b. Chgo., June 9, 1945; s. Leonard Paul and Natalie Elizabeth (Turus) K.; m. Kathleen Ellen Scanlan, June 29, 1968; children: Keira Elisabeth, Timothy Lawrence. BSEE, U. Notre Dame, 1967, MSEE, 1968, PhD, 1970. Postdoctoral thin film specialist Radiation Rsch. Lab., AEC, Notre Dame, 1970-71; from asst. to assoc. prof. elec. engring. U. Maine, Orono, 1971-77; sr. scientist Solar Energy Rsch. Inst., Golden, Colo., 1977-79, prin. scientist, br. mgr., 1980—; dir. Nat. Ctr. for Photovoltaics, Nat. Renewable Energy Lab., Golden, Colo. Adj. prof. U. Colo., Colo. Sch. Mines, U. Denver; bd. dirs. Internat. Energy Found. Author: Polycrystalline and Amorphous Thin Films and Devices, 1980; editor: (with T.J. Coutts and S. Wagner) Copper Indium Diselenide for Photovoltaic Applications, 1986; editor in chief Solar Cells, 1979-91; mem. editorial bd. Jour. Vacuum Sci. and Tech., 1987—; contbr. over 240 articles to profl. jours. and tech. proc.; patentee in field. Instr. Jefferson County Outdoor Lab. Program for Elem. Edn., Colo., 1980— Recipient R & D IR-100 award R & D Mag., 1985, R & D 100 award, 1989, Dept. of Energy/Solar Energy Rsch. Inst. Pub. Servant award, 1989, AVS Peter Meml. award, 1981, Scientist of Yr. award World Renewable Energy Conf., 1994. Fellow IEEE (R&D 100 award 1992, William R. Cherry award photovoltaics, 1993), NAE, Am. Phys. Soc.; mem. NAE, Am. Vacuum Soc. (pres. 1991, trustee 1983-86, bd. dirs. 1988—, program chmn. nat. symposium 1982, chmn. thin films div., electronic materials and processing div. 1988, mem. short course exec. com. 1986—), Am. Radio Relay League. Roman Catholic. Avocations: amateur radio, running, computers. Home: 12799 W Atlantic Ave Lakewood CO 80228-4308 Office: Nat Renewable Energy Lab 1617 Cole Blvd Golden CO 80401-3305

KAZMIR, SCOTT, professional baseball player; b. Houston, Jan. 24, 1984; s. Eddie and Deborah Kazmir. Pitcher Tampa Bay Devil Rays, 2004—. Named to Am. League All-Star Game, 2006. Achievements include being the youngest pitcher in the major leagues in 2004; being one of three pitchers with more strikeouts than hits allowed in 2005; establishing a Devil Rays' franchise record in 2005 with 174 strikeouts; becoming the youngest Devil Rays All-Star in franchise history, 2006. Mailing: Tropicana Field One Tropicana Dr Saint Petersburg FL 33705 Office Phone: 727-825-3137.*

KEACH, MICHAEL ANDREW, library and information scientist; b. Inglewood, Calif., Sept. 8, 1949; s. Glenn Weseley Keach and Dorothy Louise Tovey; life ptnr. Douglas W.J. Ninow, Oct. 15, 1982. Student in theology and music, Park Coll., Parkville, Mo., 1968—73. Music dir. Theatre Under Stars, Houston, 1975—77; laser graphics specialist Automatic Data Processing, Balt., 1988—96; libr. sci. specialist Tampa-Hillsborough County Pub. Libr., Tampa, 2000—. Fibre arts educator Uncommon Threads, Palm Harbor, Fla., 1998—. Writer, dir.: (children's programming) Nat. Pub. Radio. Mem. adv. bd. Am. Assn. Museums, Tampa, 2000; developer, audio describer, dir. Md. Arts Access Task Force, Balt., 1993—96; pres. bd. dirs. York Rd. Devel. Assn., Balt., 1990—96, Cmty. Assn., Tampa, 1997—; mem. Rep. Ctrl. Com., Balt., 1994. Recipient Md.'s Most Beautiful People award, City of Balt., 1994, Gov.'s citation, State of Md., 1994, Citizen citation, City of Balt., 1994. Mem.: Intertel Soc., Mensa (Poetry award 1996). Hindu. Avocations: fiber arts, languages, spirituality, music, horticulture. Home: 17709 Nathan's Dr Tampa FL 33647 Office: Tampa-Hillsborough County Pub Libr 900 N Ashley Tampa FL 33602

KEACH, STACY, JR., actor, theater director and producer, musician, composer; b. Savannah, Ga., June 2, 1941; s. Stacy and Mary Cain (Peckham) K.; m. Malgosia Tomassi, 1986; children: Shannon and Karolina. AB in English and Drama, U. Calif., Berkeley, 1963; student, Yale Drama Sch., 1963-64, London Acad. Dramatic Art, 1964-65. Assoc. prof. drama Yale, 1967-68. Pres. Positron Prodns. Ltd. Contbr. articles to newspapers and mags.; mem. Lincoln Ctr. Repertory Co., Long Wharf Theatre, Washington Shakespeare Theatre, Williamstown Summer Theatre, Oreg. Shakespeare Festival, Tufts Arena Theatre; charter mem. The Yale Theatre Circle, 1986; Broadway debut in Indians, 1969; appeared in Broadway prodn. Deathtrap, 1979, Solitary Confinement, 1992, The Kentucky Circle, 1993 (Helen Hayes award for Best Actor 1993, Outstanding Performance award Drama League); off-Broadway appearances in Macbird, 1966-67, The Niggerlovers, 1967, Peer Gynt, 1969, Henry IV, 1 and 2, 1968, Hamlet, 1972, King Lear, 1968, Long Day's Journey Into Night, 1971, Cyrano de Bergerac, 1978, Hughie, London, 1980; Nat. Touring Co., Barnum, 1981; Kennedy Ctr. Prodn. of Idiot's Delight, 1986, Nat. Touring Co., Sleuth, 1988, The King & I, 1989, Love Letters, 1990-93, Richard III, 1991, Stieglitz Loves O'Keefe, 1995, MacBeth, 1995, The Ten Unknowns, 2003, King Lear, Chgo., 2006; (film) The Heart is a Lonely Hunter, 1968, End of the Road, 1969, Doc, 1970, The Traveling Executioner, 1970, The New Centurions, 1971, Fat City, 1971, Brewster McCloud, 1970, Luther, 1972, The Dion Brothers, 1973, Conduct Unbecoming, 1974, Jesus of Nazareth, 1967, The Killer Inside Me, 1974, The Squeeze, 1976, Gray Lady Down, 1976, The Greatest Battle, 1977, Two Solitudes, 1977, Cheech & Chong's Up in Smoke, 1977, The Ninth Configuration, 1978, The Long Riders, 1979, Road Games, 1980, Butterfly, 1980, Cheech & Chong's Nice Dreams, 1981, That Championship Season, 1982, Butterfly, 1982, The Class of 1999, 1990, The Forgotten, Milena, 1989, Escape from L.A., 1996, The Sea Wolf, 1996, Die Gang, 1996, American History X, 1998, Honeydripper, 2007, Come Early Morning, 2007; (TV) Orville and Wilbur, 1971, Particular Men, 1972, Classics For Today, 1972, Man of Destiny, 1973, all PBS, All the Kind Strangers, 1974, Caribe, 1974-75, both ABC, The Michener Dynasty, NBC, 1975, A Rumor of War, CBS, 1979, The Blue and the Gray, 1981, Wait Until Dark, 1982, Murder Me, Murder You, 1983, Princess Daisy, 1983, Mistral's Daughter, 1984, Intimate Strangers, 1986, More Than Murder, 1983, Mickey Spillane's Mike Hammer series, 1983, 86-87, Return of Mickey Spillane's Mike Hammer, 1986, starring role 6 hour mini-series on life of Ernest Hemingway, 1988 (Best Actor award Golden Globes 1988), Murder Takes All, 1989 (Emmy nominee Best Actor in Special or Miniseries), Body Bags, 1992 (Cable Ace Award nominee Best Actor), Against Their Will, 1994, Texas, 1995, Titus, 2000, The Santa Trap, 2002, The Simpsons, 2002-03 Frozen Impact, 2003, Prison Break, 2005-07, E/R, 2007; host TV programs Missing/Reward, 1988, Arts and Entertainment Stage Series, 1988-89, Circus of Stars, 1991, Case-Closed, 1993-94; dir.: Pullman Car Hiawatha, 1964-65, The Stronger, 1964-65, The Maids, 1964-65, The Repeater, 1971 (Cine Golden Eagle award, London Film Festival outstanding film), Incident at Vichy, 1974, Six Characters in Search of an Author, 1976, A Blinding Fear (episode of The New Mike Hammer), 1987; host PBS July 4th Festivities, 1995; narrator (TV documentary) Nova, Nat. Geographic, Am. Experience, Discover Channel Flight Over the Equator, 1995, Planet of Life, 1995, Stupid Behavior Caught on Tape, 2003; (books on tape) Hardboiled, 1994, Mickey Spillane's Works, 1990, CD-ROM, 1994, Ten Lost Tribes of Israel, Shakespeare's Sonnets; screen writer, producer The Long Riders, 1979. Sponsor Nat. Repertory Theatre Found. (Nat. Play Award Com.), 1986; hon. chair Cleft Palate Assn., 1995; spokesman United Indian Devel. Assn.; mem. Nat. Citizens Comm. Lobby, Entertainment Industries Coun. before House Select Com. on Drug Abuse, 1985; panelist Am. TV, Arts and Scis. Substance Abuse Conf., 1986, Artists Com. Kennedy Ctr. Honors, 1986—; mem. Players Club; charter mem. L.A. Classic Theatre Works, Artists Rights Found.; mem. artistic adv. bd. Nat. Found. for Advancement in Arts; mem. Helen Hayes Honorary Com. Fulbright award, 1964-65; recipient Best Actor award U. Calif., 1963, Best Actor award Oreg. Shakespeare award, 1963, Obie award, 1967, 71, 73, Vernon Rice Drama Desk award, 1967, 71, 72, Saturday Rev. award, 1967, Helen Hayes Best Actor award, 1994, Hon. chmn. Am. Cleft Palate Found., 1995—, Celebrity Outreach honoree, 1995, Master of Ceremonies, Capitol Mall, 1995. Address: 118 S Beverly Dr #201 Beverly Hills CA 90212 *The fundamental virtue of success is making your dreams come true. But without loved ones to share it with it means little or nothing.*

KEADY, GEORGE CREGAN, JR., judge; b. Bklyn., June 16, 1924; s. George Cregan and Marie (Lussier) K.; m. Patricia Drake, Sept. 2, 1950; children: Margaret Keady Goldberg, Marie E., George Cregan, Catherine A. Keady Sharp, Kathleen V. Student, U. Kans., 1943—44; BS, Fordham U., 1949; JD, Columbia U., 1950; LLD, We. New Eng. Coll., 1973. Bar: Mass. 1950. Assoc. Ganley & Crook, 1950—53, Peter D. Wilson, 1953—57; ptnr. Wilson, Keady & Ratner, 1958—79; justice Dist. Ct., Springfield, Mass., 1979—82; assoc. justice Superior Ct., Springfield, 1982—93; ret., 1993; freelance mediator and arbitrator, 1993—. Dean We. New Eng. Coll. Law Sch., 1970-73; dir. We. Mass. Bar Rev., 1956-63, We. New Eng. Coll. Bar Rev., 1965-72; chmn. Mass. Continuing Legal Edn., Inc., 1977-80; mem. Mass. Commn. on Jud. Conduct, 1988, chmn., 1990-93 Active United Fund, Springfield, 1950-72, Joint Civic Agys.; chmn. fund drive Am. Cancer Soc., 1962, selectman, Longmeadow, Mass., 1958-68, chmn. selectmen, 1960-61, 63-64, 66-68, moderator, 1968-73; vice chmn. Rep. Town Com., Longmeadow, 1956-60; alt. del. Rep. Nat. Conv., 1960, del., 1964; pres. Hampden Dist. Mental Health Clinic, Inc., 1968-71, Child Guidance Clinic, Springfield, 1962-64; corporator, trustee, chmn. bd. Baystate Med. Center, 1985-87, trustee, 1984-92, 94-99; chmn. bd. Baystate Health Sys., 1987-90; trustee We. New Eng. Coll., 1978-84, Baypath Jr. Coll., 1972-87, Baystate Health Sys., 1993-98; dir. BHIC, 1993-2007. Served with AUS, 1943-46 Decorated Bronze star. Mem. Am. Law Inst., Mass. Bar Assn., Hampden County Bar Assn. (exec. com. 1960-79, pres. 1965-67), Supreme Ct. Hist. Soc., Longmeadow Country Club, Phi Delta Phi. Roman Catholic. Home: 16 Meadowbrook Rd Longmeadow MA 01106-1341 Office Phone: 413-567-7412.

KEALA, FRANCIS AHLOY, security executive; b. Honolulu, June 1, 1930; s. Samuel Louis and Rose (Ahloy) Keala; m. Betty Ann Lyman, Nov. 28, 1952; children: Frances Ann, John Richard, Robert Mark. BA in Sociology, U. Hawaii, 1953. Patrolman Honolulu Police Dept., 1956-62, detective, 1962-65, lt., 1965-68, capt., 1968-69, chief of police, 1969-83; dir. security Hawaiian Telephone Co., 1983-93. Bd. dirs. Liliuokalani Trust; trustee St. Louis Sch., 1980—87, Keala Trust, 1989—, Kamehameha Schs. Bishop Estate, 1999—2001. Bd. dirs. Aloha coun. Boy Scouts Am., Sex Abuse Treatment Ctr., Hawaii Meml. Pk. Assn., St. Louis Found., ARC-Hawaii chpt., St. Francis Med. Ctr.-W.; bd. govs. Boys and Girls Clubs Honolulu; mem. civilian adv. group US Army; mem. Commn. Jud. Discipline; v.p., dir. Hawaiian Music Hall of Fame and Mus.; mem. Honolulu City and County Ethics Commn.; bd. dirs. 200 Club, Am. Automobile Assn. Hawaii. With US Army, 1953—55. Mem.: FBI Nat. Acad. Assocs., Hawaii State Law Enforcement Ofcls. Assn., Internat. Assn. Chiefs Police, Pacific Club, Oahu Country Club.

KEAN, HAMILTON FISH, lawyer; b. NYC, Mar. 1, 1925; s. Robert Winthrop and Elizabeth Stuyvesant (Howard) K.; m. Ellen Shaw Garrison, Mar. 25, 1950 (div. 1976); children: Leslie, Elizabeth K. Douglas, Lloyd Garrison, Lewis Morris; m. Alice Newcomer Baker, July 6, 1981 (dec. 1986); m. Edith Williamson Bacon, Sept. 23, 1989. AB cum laude, Princeton U., 1949; JD, Columbia U., 1954. Bar: NY 1954, NJ 1955. Asst. counsel Waterfront Commn. NY Harbor, 1954; law sec. NJ Supreme Ct., 1954-55; asst. U.S. atty. NJ Dist., 1955-57; ptnr. Clapp and Eisenberg and predecessors, Newark, 1957-62; trustee various funds, 1963—; lectr. law Rutgers U. Sch. Law, 1960; lectr. environ. law SUNY at Purchase, Westchester Cmty. Coll., 1974-76. Supervising atty. clin. program environ. law NYU Sch. Law, 1972-76; chmn. Livingston Nat. Bank, 1984. Assoc. editor: NJ Law Jour., 1957—62. Bd. dirs. Morris County Urban League, 1956-51; mem. Urban Crisis Task Force, 1976; bd. dirs. Youth Counseling League, 1969-93, pres., 1979-83, hon. dir.; bd. dirs. Citizens Com. for Children NY, 1971-2002, now hon. dir., pres., 1972-77, Eleanor Roosevelt award, 2001; chmn. Joint Action for Children, 1976; trustee Natural Resources Def. Coun., 1973-2002, hon. trustee, 2002—, treas., 1973-76; bd. dirs., sec. Environ. Advocates, 1972-78, hon. bd. dirs., 1999—; bd. dirs. Fountain House, 1966—, pres., 1975-78; mem. Adv. Coun. to NY State Office Mental Health, 1979-83; mem. Mental Health Svc. Coun., 1983-90; trustee Coro Found., 1979-85; mem. NY State Mental Hygiene Planning Coun., 1981-85; trustee Alice Desmond and Hamilton Fish Libr., 1981-98; trustee Schuyler Ctr. for Analysis and Avocacy, 1982-2007, pres., 1985-92, hon. trustee, 2007-; mem. adminstrv. bd. Lab. Ornithology Cornell U., 1982-87; trustee Hancock Shaker Village, 1986-92; mem. adv. bd. Panel of Ams., 1986—; bd. dirs., sec. Episc. Charities, 1995-2002, Citizens for Global Solutions Edn. Fund, 2004—; trustee World Federalist Assn. Endowment Fund, 1998—, chmn., 2001—; trustee Ctr. for UN Reform Edn., 2006—; chmn. Ctr. for War/Peace Studies, 2006—. Served to 2d lt. US Army, 1943-46. Decorated Purple Heart. Mem.: ABA, Assn. Bar City N.Y., NY State Bar Assn. (chmn. conf. on pub. interest law 1975), Columbia Law Sch. Alumni Assn. (treas. 1958—62), New Bedford Yacht Club, Millbrook Golf and Tennis Club, Princeton Club, Knickerbocker Club, Century Assn. Home: 130 East End Ave New York NY 10028-7553 Office: 120 E 56th St New York NY 10022

KEAN, JOHN VAUGHAN, retired lawyer; b. Providence, Mar. 12, 1917; s. Otho Vaughan and Mary (Duell) Kean. AB cum laude, Harvard U., 1938, JD, 1941; grad., U.S. Army War Coll., 1970. Bar: R.I. 1942, U.S. Dist. Ct. R.I. 1946, U.S. Ct. Appeals (1st cir.) 1950, U.S. Ct. Appeals (4th cir.) 1955, U.S. Ct. Claims 1963, U.S. Supreme Ct. 1982. With Edwards & Angell, Providence, 1941—, ptnr., 1954-87, ret. ptnr., 1987—. Bd. dirs. Greater Providence YMCA, 1964—76; chmn. Downtown Providence YMCA, 1964—67, Providence Com. on Fgn. Rels., 1994—2000. Capt. AUS US Army, 1943—46, capt. AUS US Army, 1950—52, brig. gen. R.I. Nat. Guard US Army, 1964—72. Decorated Legion of Merit. Mem.: ABA, R.I. Bar Assn., Res. Officers Assn., N.G. Assn., Soc. Cin. (hon.; R.I.), Assn. U.S. Army, Urban League R.I., Nature Conservancy (hon.), Alexis de Tocqueville Soc. R.I., Soc. Colonial Wars in R.I., Providence Art Club, Harvard Club R.I. (pres. 1964—66), Sakonnet Golf Club (Little Compton, R.I.), Army and Navy Club (Washington), Hope Club (bd. govs. 1996—2000, v.p.), Agawam Hunt. Office: c/o Edwards Angell Palmer & Dodge LLP 2800 Financial Plz Providence RI 02903-2499 Home: 355 Blackstone Blvd Apt 334 Providence RI 02906-4957

KEAN, STEVEN J., energy executive; B, Iowa State U., Ames; law degree, U. Iowa, Iowa City. With El Paso Natural Gas, Utilicorp, Enron; v.p. strategic planning Natural Gas Pipeline group Kinder Morgan, 2002, pres. Intrastate Pipeline Group Kinder Morgan Energy Ptnrs., L.P., exec. v.p. ops., exec. v.p., COO. Office: Kinder Morgan 500 Dallas St Ste 1000 Houston TX 77002 Office Phone: 713-369-9000.*

KEAN, THOMAS HOWARD, former academic administrator, governor; b. NYC, Apr. 21, 1935; s. Robert W. and Elizabeth Stuyvesant Kean; m. Deborah Bye; children: Thomas Jr., Reed, Alexandra. AB, Princeton; MA, Columbia; LLD (hon.), Dartmouth Coll., 2005. Mem. NJ Assembly, 1967-77, asst. majority leader, 1970—71, majority leader, 1971—72, speaker, 1972, minority leader, 1974; acting gov. State of NJ, Trenton, 1973, gov., 1981-89; pres. Drew U., Madison, NJ, 1990—2005. Chmn., The Nat. Commn. on Terrorist Attacks Upon the U.S. (The 9-11 Commn.), 2002-04; bd. dirs. Beneficial Corp., Carnegie Corp. of NY, Robert Wood Johnson Found. 1990- (chmn. 2005-). Co-author (with Lee H. Hamilton): Without Precedent: The Inside Story of the 9/11 Commission, 2006. Bd. dirs. World Wildlife Fund/Conservation Found. Recipient Rutgers Pub. Svc. award, 2006. Fellow: Am. Acad. Arts & Sciences.

KEAN, TOM, JR., (THOMAS HOWARD KEAN JR.), state senator; b. Livingston, NJ, Sept. 5, 1968; s. Thomas Howard Kean Sr. and Deborah (Bye) Kean; m. Rhonda Kean; 2 children. BA in Hist., Dartmouth Coll., Hanover, NH, 1990; MA in Law and Diplomacy, Tufts U., 1997. Aide former US Rep. Bob Franks; cons. Brit. Petroleum; special asst. US EPA; mem. NJ Assembly, 2001—03, NJ State Senate, Trenton, 2003—, dep. whip, 2003, minority whip, 2004—. Mem. Budget and Appropriations Com., Judiciary Com., Health, Human Services and Sr. Citizens com., Joint Com. on Pub. Schools, 2004—; vice chmn. State Govt. Com. Named a Legis. Leader, NJ Conf. Mayors, 2005; named Legis. of the Yr., Firemen's Benevolent Assn. Republican. Episcopalian. Office: 203 Elm St 1st Fl Westfield NJ 07090 Office Phone: 908-232-3673, 908-918-0414. Office Fax: 908-232-3345.*

KEANE, BIL, cartoonist; b. Phila., Oct. 5, 1922; s. Aloysius William and Florence Rita (Bunn) K.; m. Thelma Carne, Oct. 23, 1948; children: Gayle, Neal, Glen, Christopher, Jeff. Student pvt. schs., Phila. Staff artist, Phila. Bull., 1945-58, syndicated cartoonist, Register & Tribune Syndicate, Des Moines, 1954—; creator, cartoonist: Channel Chuckles, 1954-77, Family Circus, 1960—; author numerous books of cartoon collections; cartoonist: Stars and Stripes, 1945. Served with US Army, 1942-45, PTO. Named Cartoonist of the Yr. Nat. Cartoonist Soc., 1982, Reuben award. Mem. Nat. Cartoonists Soc. (Best Syndicated Panel award 1967, 71, 74, Cartoonist of yr. 1982), Newspaper Features Coun., Cartoonists Guild. Office: King Features 888 7th Ave Ph2 New York NY 10106-0003

KEANE, DOUGLAS, chef; b. Mich., May 5, 1971; s. Noel Patrick Keane, Kathryn Keane. BS in Hotel Adminstrn., Cornell U., Ithica, NY, 1993. Chef, sous chef Four Seasons, NYC; chef Lespinasse, NYC; chef, exec. chef Jardiniere, San Francisco; sous chef Restaurant Gary Danko, San Francisco; co-owner, exec. chef Market, St. Helena, Calif., 2003—, Cyrus, Healdsburg, Calif., 2005—. Asst. chef (TV series) Cooking with Claudine. Named Rising Star Chef, San Francisco Chronicle, 2002; recipient America's Best New Chef award, Food and Wine Mag., 2006. Office: Cyrus 29 North St Healdsburg CA 95448 Office Phone: 707-433-3311.

KEANE, JEFF, cartoonist; b. Mar. 8, 1958; s. Bil Keane and Thelma Carne; m. Melinda Keane, 1988; children: Spencer, Matilda, Olivia. BFA, U. So. Calif. Cartoonist, 1981—; asst. to Bil Keane. Co-author, inker & colorist (comic strips) Family Circus. Mem.: Nat. Cartoonists Soc. (pres. 2007—09). Office: c/o King Features 15th Fl 300 W 57th St New York NY 10019-5238 also: Nat Cartoonists Soc Ste 201 1133 W Morse Blvd Winter Park FL 32789*

KEANE, JEFFRY ROBERT, secondary school educator; s. Robert and Linda Keane. BA in Tchg. Social Studies, U. Ill., 1995; MA in Edn., Lewis U., 2003. Career services aide Victor J. Andrew HS, Tinley Park, Ill., 1997—2000, social studies tchr., 2000—. Office Phone: 708-342-5947.

KEANE, JOHN B., lawyer, electric power industry executive; b. Beverly, Mass., Aug. 25, 1946; m. Katherine Keane; 2 children. BA in Econs., Brown U., 1968; JD, Harvard U., 1972. Bar: Mass. 1972, Ohio (corp.) 2004. With Hill & Barlow, Boston, 1972—80, N.E. Utilities, Berlin, Conn., 1980—2002, v.p., sec., gen. counsel corp., 1992—93, v.p., treas., 1993—98, v.p. adminstrn., 1998—2002; pres. Bainbridge Crossing Advs., West Hartford, Conn., 2003—04; sr. v.p., gen. counsel, sec. Am. Electric Power Co. Inc., Columbus, Ohio, 2004—. Bd. dirs. Columbus Mus. Art. Office: Am Electric Power Co Inc 1 Riverside Plz Columbus OH 43215-2372 Office Phone: 614-716-2929. Business E-Mail: jbkeane@aep.com.*

KEANE, JOHN PATRICK, retired secondary school educator; b. NYC, Nov. 28, 1931; s. John and Mary (Walsh) K.; m. Lucille Ann Dunn, Apr. 3, 1976. BA in English, Iona Coll., 1954; JD, Fordham U., 1963, MS in Edn., 1965; EdM, Columbia U., 1973; MA in English, CUNY, 1984. Cert. secondary tchr. (English), adminstr., N.Y.C., N.Y. State. Tchr. area jr. h.s., NYC, 1962-65; tchr. h.s. English N.Y.C. Bd. Edn., Bklyn., 1965-93; dean of boys W.H. Taft H.S., Bronx, 1969-72; reading, writing coord. John F. Kennedy H.S., Bronx, 1985-91; tchr. English advanced placement John F. Kennedy H.S., Manhattan Coll., Bronx, 1991-93, retired, 1993. Editor, compiler: (manual) Handbook for Teachers of Reading and Writing, 1987, Writing Sampler (student's work), 1989-91 biannual. Founder Hamilton Heights Dems., 1965-69; candidate NY State Assembly, 1965; Dem. candidate 1st Selectman, North Stonington, Conn., 1997; active North Stonington Bd. Edn; justice of peace North Stonington; past chmn. North Stonington Dem. Town Com.; music min. St. Mary's Ch., Groton. MA thesis placed on permanent display as model, Lehman Coll., CUNY, Bronx, 1984. Mem. NEA (del. local 2), Am. Fedn. Tchrs. (del. local 2), United Fedn. Tchrs. (del N.Y. State, chpt. leader, unity com.), N.Y. State United Tchrs., Delta Kappa Pi, Phi Delta Kappa. Roman Catholic. Avocations: poetry, drama. Home: 6 Wyassup Lake Rd North Stonington CT 06359-1124

KEANE, MICHAEL E., computer services company executive; B in Acctg., Ill. State U., Normal; MBA, UCLA. CPA. CPA Price Waterhouse, Chgo.; with Litton, 1981, asst. treas., 1988—91, dir. pensions and ins., 1991; v.p., treas. Western Atlas, Inc., sr. v.p., CFO, 1996, UNOVA, Inc.; v.p. fin. Computer Scis. Corp., El Segundo, Calif., 2005—06, v.p., CFO, 2006—. Chmn. audit com. of bd. dirs. Zixcorp, 1998—2006. Mem.: AICPA, Ill. CPA Soc., Fin. Execs. Inst. Office: Computer Scis Corp 2100 E Grand Ave El Segundo CA 90245 Office Phone: 310-615-0311.*

KEANE, PATRICK, marketing executive; b. 1971; V.p., sr. analyst Jupiter Rsch.; head advt. sales strategy Google, Inc., 2003—07; exec. v.p., chief mktg. officer CBS Interactive, 2007—. Named one of 40 under 40, Advt. Age, 2007. Office: CBS Interactive 489 Fifth Ave 31st Fl New York NY 10017 Office Phone: 646-487-1000. Office Fax: 646-487-2597.

KEANE, PETER J., construction executive; With Pulte Homes Inc., 1993—, pres. Ill. divsn., pres. Gt. Lakes area, sr. v.p. homebuilding ops., 2006—. Office: Pulte Homes Inc 100 Bloomfield Hills Pky Ste 300 Bloomfield Hills MI 48304-2946 Office Phone: 248-647-2750.*

KEANE, WILLIAM FRANCIS, nephrology educator, research foundation executive; b. NYC, Sept. 21, 1942; s. William F. and Theresa (Crotty) K.; m. Stephanie M. Gaherin, June 10, 1967; children: Alicia Anne, Elizabeth Gaherin. BS, Fordham U., 1964; MD, Yale U., 1968. Diplomate Am. Bd. Internal Medicine, Am. Bd. Nephrology. Intern Cornell N.Y. Hosp. Med. Ctr., 1968-69, resident, internal medicine, 1969-70, 72-73; fellow nephrology U. Minn. Hosps., Mpls., 1973-75; chmn. dept. Hennepin County Med. Ctr., Mpls., 1991—; asst. prof. medicine U. Minn., Mpls., 1976-82, assoc. prof., 1982-87, prof., 1987-89; pres. Minn. Med. Rsch. Found., Mpls., 1989-95; nephrologist Hennepin County Med. Ctr., Mpls., 1995. Chmn. dept. medicine Hennepin County Med. Ctr., 1992—. Mem. Am. Coll. Physicians, Am. Fedn. Clin. Rsch., Am. Soc. Clin. Pharmacology and Therapeutics, Am. Soc. Nephrology. Office: Hennepin County Med Ctr 701 Park Ave Minneapolis MN 55415-1623 Home: PO Box 665 Spring House PA 19477-0665

KEANEY, THOMAS ADDIS, academic administrator, management consultant, educator, military officer; b. Boston, June 14, 1940; s. James Francis and Anna Catherine (Keefe) K.; m. Mary Beth Martin, June 22, 1963; children: Thomas M., Kathleen P., Maura E., Anna C. BS, USAF Acad., Colo., 1962; MA, U. Mich., 1971, PhD, 1975. Commd. 2d lt. USAF, 1962, advanced through grades to col., 1982; assoc. prof. history USAF Acad., Colo., 1973-77; flight comdr., ops. officer 7th Bomb Wing USAF, Fort Worth, 1977-79, squadron comdr. B-52, 43rd Strategic Wing Andersen AFB, Guam, 1980-81, dep. base comdr., 1981-82, mil. planner air staff Washington, 1983-85, base comdr. Wurtsmith AFB, Mich., 1985-86; chmn. dept. mil. strategy Nat. War Coll., Washington, 1986-91; rschr., author Dept. Air Force, Washington, 1991-92; prof. mil. strategy Nat. War Coll., Washington, 1993-98; exec. dir. Fgn. Policy Inst. Nitze Sch. Advanced Internat. Studies, Johns Hopkins U., Washington, 1998—, exec. dir. Merrill Ctr. Strategic Studies, 2004—. Author: Strategic Bombers and Conventional Weapons, 1984, Gulf War Air Power Survey, 2 vols., 1993, Revolution in Warfare?, 1995, U.S. Allies in a Changing World, 2000, Armed Forces in the Middle East: Politics and Strategy, 2001. Roman Catholic. Home: 3047 Holly St Falls Church VA 22044-2617 Office: Nitze Sch Advanced Intl Studies Fgn Policy Inst 1619 Massachusetts Ave NW Washington DC 20036-2213 E-mail: tkeaney@jhu.edu.

KEANY, SUTTON, lawyer; b. Limon, Costa Rica, Feb. 19, 1943; s. Francis Xavier and Winsome (Scoltock) K.; m. Susanne Elvera Andover, June 12, 1965; children: Damian Winsome, Alison Arwen, Courtney Vanessa, Sutton Andover. AB, Yale U., 1963; JD, Harvard U., 1966. Bar: P.R. 1967, N.Y. 1971, U.S. Supreme Ct. 1977. Assoc. McConnell, Valdes, Kelly & Sifre, San Juan, 1966-70, Winthrop, Stimson, Putnam & Roberts, NYC, 1970-75, ptnr., 1976—2001, Pillsbury Winthrop LLP, NYC, 2001—06; of counsel Bergery & Webb LLP, NYC, 2006—. Mediator, early neutral evaluator U.S. Dist. Ct. (ea. dist.) N.Y., 1992—. Author: (with Jay M. Vogelson) Complying with International Antitrust Regulations; contbr. articles to Bklyn. Law Rev. Trustee Aperture Found., N.Y.C., 1988-92; dir. The Fund for Modern Ctrs., 1992-99, The Legal Aid Soc., 1995-2001. Mem. ABA, Assn. Bar City N.Y., Am. Arbitration Assn. (arbitrator 1990-2000), Yale Club of N.Y. Avocation: squash. Office: Berger & Webb LLP 1633 Broadway New York NY 10019 Office Phone: 212-319-1900. Office Fax: 212-319-2017. Business E-Mail: skeany@bergerwebb.com.

KEAR, BERNARD HENRY, materials scientist, consultant; b. Port Talbot, South Wales, July 5, 1931; came to U.S., 1959, naturalized, 1965; s. Herbert and Catherine Ann (Rees) K.; m. Jacqueline Margaret Smith, Aug. 22, 1959; children: Andrew, Gareth, Edward, Gwyneth. B.Sc., U. Birmingham, 1954, PhD, 1957, D.Sc., 1970. With Tube Investments Ltd., Eng., 1957-59; staff scientist Franklin Inst., Phila., 1959-63; with United Technologies Corp., East Hartford, Conn., 1963-81, sr. cons. scientist, 1977-81; sci. adv. Exxon Research and Engring. Co., 1981-86; prof., chmn. dept mechs. and materials sci., dir. ctr. for materials synthesis Rutgers U., N.J., 1986—; dir. Ctr. for Nanomaterials Rsch., 1986—. John Dorn Meml. lectr., 1980, Henry Krumb lectr., 1983; mem. assessment panel Nat. Inst. Stds. & Tech.-Materials Sci. & Engring. Lab. Program, chmn., 1990; bd. dirs. Acta Metallurgica, Inc., chmn., 1989. Co-editor: (jour.) Nanostructured Materials, 1992-98; editor 10 books in field; contbr. 270 articles to profl. jours.; holder 45 patents. Bd. dirs., pres. Interfaith Housing for Elderly Project, Madison, Conn., 1974-79. Recipient Mathewson gold medal Am. Inst. Metall. Engrs., 1971 Fellow Am. Soc. Metals (Howe medal 1970); mem. Nat. Acad. Engring., Nat. Materials Adv. Bd. (chmn. 1986), Metall. Soc., Am. Soc. Metals. Office: Rutgers U Dept Materials Sci and Engring 607 Taylor Rd Piscataway NJ 08854-8065 Office Phone: 732-445-2245. Business E-Mail: bkear@rci.rutgers.edu.

KEAR, REBECCA JOANN, retired librarian; b. Everett, Wash., Apr. 28, 1941; d. Arvid John and Esther Freda Backlund; m. Ronald Eldred Kear, Aug. 23, 1964; children: Lee, Janice Lynn. BA, U. Calif., Santa Barbara, 1963; MLS, U. Calif., Berkeley, 1964. Libr. San Jose State U., Calif., 1964—67, Humboldt State U., Arcata, Calif., 1969—70; libr. local office, coord. firm libr. Dames & Moore, Atlanta, 1974—89, libr. govt. star wars program Washington, 1990—94; ret., 1994. Vol. March of Dimes, Westlake, Ohio, 2001—, Habitat for Humanity, Cleve., 1999—. Mem.: Assoc. New Westsiders, Prince of Peace Choir. Avocations: reading, bridge.

KEARFOTT, JOSEPH CONRAD, lawyer; b. Martinsville, Va., Sept. 24, 1947; s. Clarence P. and Elizabeth (Kelly) K.; m. Mary Jo Veatch, Feb.10, 1969; children: Kelly, David. BA, Davidson Coll., 1969; JD, U. Va., 1972. Bar: Va. 1972, U.S. Dist. Ct. (ea. and we. dists.) Va. 1973, U.S. Ct. Appeals (4th cir.) 1973, U.S. Tax Ct. 1979, U.S. Ct. Appeals (1st cir.) 1981, U.S. Ct. Appeals (5th cir.) 1982. Law clk. to presiding judge U.S. Dist. Ct. (ea. dist.) Va., Richmond, 1972-73; assoc. Hunton & Williams, Richmond, 1973-80, ptnr., 1980—. Lectr. NITA program, Washington and Lee U., 1982-83, Va. Com. on Continuing Legal Edn., 1984-2005; mem. 4th Cir. Jud. conf. Co-author: Virginia Evidentiary Foundations, 1998. Mem. Richmond Bd. Housing, 1977-85, Richmond Dem. Com., 1978-82; trustee Libr. Va. Found., 1994-, chmn., 2004-06, William Byrd Cmty. House, 1978-84, chmn., 1982-84; trustee United Way Svcs., Richmond, 1989-95, treas., 1993-95; trustee Libr. Va., 1989-94, vice chmn., 1990-91, chmn., 1991-92; trustee Trinity Episcopal Sch., 1986-94, treas., 1989-92, chmn., 1993-94; mem. Richmond Regional Bd., Thomas C. Sorensen Inst. Polit. Leadership, chmn., 2004-06; treas. St. Paul's Episcopal Ch., 2003—. Fellow: Va. Law Found.; mem.: ABA, Richmond Bar Assn., Va. Bar Assn. (Boyd Graves conf. chmn. 1999—2001), Order of Coif, Country Club Va. Avocations: golf, skiing. Home: 4436 Custis Rd Richmond VA 23225-1012 Office: Hunton & Williams East Tower Riverfront Pla 951 E Byrd St Richmond VA 23219-4074 Office Phone: 804-788-8446.

KEARNEY, CHRISTOPHER J., manufacturing executive, lawyer; b. Mount Pleasant, Pa., 1955; BA, U. Notre Dame, 1977; JD, DePaul U. Law Sch., 1981. Sr. atty. Borg-Warner Chems.; sr. counsel, global materials bus. GE; sr. v.p., gen. counsel Grimes Aerospace Co., 1995—97; v.p., sec., gen. counsel SPX Corp., Charlotte, NC, 1997—2004, pres., CEO, dir., 2004—07, chmn., pres., CEO, 2007—. Office: SPX Corp 13515 Ballantyne Corp Pl Charlotte NC 28277*

KEARNEY, DOUGLAS CHARLES, lawyer, journalist; b. Gloucester, Mass., June 24, 1945; s. Charles Matthew Kearney and Jean (Tarr) Thomas. Student, Brown U., Providence, 1963-64; BA, Fla. State U., Tallahassee, 1971, JD with high honors, 1973. Bar: Fla. 1974, Calif. 1976, US Ct. Appeals (5th cir.) 1977, US Dist. Ct. (mid. and so. dists.) Fla. 1978, US Ct. Appeals (11th cir.) 1981, US Supreme Ct. 1982, US Dist. Ct. (no. dist.) Tex. 1985, Tex. 1986. Asst. pub. defender Office of Pub. Defender 2d Jud. Cir., Tallahassee, 1973-76; asst. atty. gen. Atty. Gen.'s Office State of Fla., Tallahassee, 1977-78, chief antitrust enforcement unit Atty. Gen.'s Office, 1978-79; prin. Law Offices of Douglas C. Kearney, Tallahassee, 1979-85, Kearney & Assocs., Dallas, 1992—2006; assoc. Brice & Mankoff, PC, Dallas, 1985-87, mem., 1987-89, Choate & Lilly, PC, Dallas, 1989-92. Pres. Legal Aid Found. of Tallahassee, Inc., 1984. With US Army, 1965-68, Vietnam. Mem. Fla. Bar Assn., Tex. Bar Assn. Episcopalian. Avocations: sailing, tennis, swimming, gardening.

KEARNEY, JOHN WALTER, sculptor, painter; b. Omaha, Aug. 31, 1924; m. Lynn Haigh, June 2, 1951; children: Daniel Raymond, Jill Ann. Student, Cranbrook Acad. Art, 1946—48. Tchr., 1948—; co-founder, 1949; since pres. Contemporary Art Workshop Chgo. Mem. adv. bd. Art Inst. Chgo., A.R.S.G., Fine Arts Work Ctr., Provincetown, Mass., Chgo. Coun. on Fine Arts; vis. artist Am. Acad. in Rome, 1985, 92, 98, 03—; mem. summer faculty Fine Arts Work Ctr., Provincetown, 1996. Numerous one-man shows including A.C.A. Gallery, NYC, (5 shows) 1964-79, 03-04, Ft. Wayne (Ind.) Mus., 1966, Galleria Schneider, Rome, 1969, Ill. Inst. Tech., 1976, 91, Ulrich Mus. Art, Wichita State U., 1976, Dirksen Fed. Bldg., Chgo., 1979, Cherrystone Gallery, Wellfleet, Mass., 1980, 92, Contemporary Art Workshop, 1981, 84, Goldman-Kraft Gallery, Chgo., 1985, others in NYC, 1964-79, Venice, 1964, Rome, 1964, 68, Chgo., 1966-85, Berta Walker Gallery, Provincetown, Mass., 1992, 93, 95, 97, 2005, Mitchell Mus., Mt. Vernon, Ill., 1994, Chgo. Cultural Ctr., 2006, Art in Pub. Pls., Stamford, Conn., 2006; sculpture show 1998, Thomas McCormick Fine Art, Chicago, 1998. 2-person show, Art Inst. Chgo., A.R.S.G., 1977; represented in permanent collections, Mus. Contemporary Art, Chgo., Standard Oil Bldg., Chgo., Lawrence U., Appleton, Wis., Interfirst Plaza, Dallas, Mundelein Coll., Chgo., Norfolk Art Mus., Va., Ulrich Mus. Art of Wichita State U., Canton Art Inst., Capitol Bldg. Complex State Ill., Springfield, 1993, Detroit Children's Mus., Ft. Wayne Art Mus., Minn. Mus., St. Paul, New Sch. Social Rsch., NYC, City of Chgo. Park Dist., Northwestern U., Roosevelt U., Chgo., U. Wyo. Art Mus., St. Lawrence U., Canton, NY, Wichita Art Mus., Youth Art Ctr., Fayetteville, Ark., Peace Mus., Chgo., Kans. Coliseum, Wichita, Fourth Fin. Ctr., Wichita, Kresge Collection, Troy, Mich., Ill. State Mus., Ill. Capitol Bldg. Mitchell Mus., Mt. Vernon, Ill., Cranbrook Acad. Art, Bloomfield Hills., Mich., Oakton Coll., Des Plaines, Ill., Oz Park, Chgo., Tin Man, Screcrow, Cowardly Lion, Dorothy and Toto, Goudy Sch., Chgo.; also pvt. collections including, John D. Rockefeller IV collection, Robert Mayer collection, spl. sculpture in bronze and silver, Sculpture Park (4 works) Munster Ind., 2000, steel bumpers sculpture, others. Trustee Ill. Com. for Handgun Control. Served with USN, World War II, PTO. Named Man of Year in Arts in Chgo., 1963; Fulbright grantee, 1963-64; Italian Govt. grantee, 1963-64; grantee Nat. Endowment Arts, 1968 Mem. Provincetown Art Assn. (former v.p. and trustee) Home: 830 W Castlewood Ter Chicago IL 60640-4217 Studio: (summer) 638 Commercial St Provincetown MA 02657 also: (winter) Contemporary Art Workshop 542 W Grant Pl Chicago IL 60614 Office Phone: 773-472-4004, 508-487-0591. Personal E-mail: jaklynk830@aol.com.

KEARNEY, JOSEPH D., dean, law educator; b. Dec. 28, 1964; BA summa cum laude, Yale U., 1986; JD cum laude, Harvard U., 1989. Bar: Ill., Wis. Law clerk to Judge Diarmuid F. O'Scannlain U.S. Ct. Appeals, Ninth Cir., Portland, Oreg., 1989—90; to Justice Antonin Scalia U.S. Supreme Ct., Washington, DC, 1995—96; assoc. Sidley & Austin, Chgo., 1990—95, 1996—97; asst. prof. Marquette U. Law Sch., 1997—2001, assoc. prof., 2001—03, dean, prof. law, 2003—. Contbr. articles to law jours. Mem.: Am. Inns Ct. (mem. Thomas Fairchild Chap. 1999—), Federalist Soc., Milwaukee Lawyers' Chap. (mem. bd. dirs. 2000—), Wis. Bd. Bar Examiners, Wis. Bar Assn. (mem. bd. dirs. Ea. Dist. 2002—). Office: Marquette U Law Sch 1103 W Wisconsin Ave PO Box 1881 Milwaukee WI 53201 Office Phone: 414-288-1955. E-mail: joseph.kearney@marquette.edu.

KEARNEY, JOSEPH LAURENCE, retired athletic conference administrator; b. Pitts., Apr. 28, 1927; s. Joseph L. and Iva M. (Nikirk) K.; m. Dorothea Hurst, May 13, 1950; children: Jan Marie, Kevin Robert, Erin Lynn, Shawn Alane, Robin James. BA, Seattle Pacific U., 1952, LLD, 1979; MA, San Jose State U., 1964; EdD, U. Wash., 1970. Tchr., coach Paradise (Calif.) H.S., 1952-53; asst. basketball coach U. Wash., 1953-54, athletic dir., assoc. dir., 1964-76; coach, tchr. Sunnyside (Wash.) H.S., 1954-57; prin., coach Onalaska (Wash.) H.S., 1957-61; prin. Tumwater (Wash.) H.S., 1961-63; asst. dir. Wash. H.S. Activities Assn., 1963-64; athletic dir. intercollegiate athletics Mich. State U., East Lansing, 1976-80, Ariz. State U., Tempe, 1980; commr. Western Athletic Conf., Denver, 1980-95; ret., 1995. Hon. chmn. Holiday Bowl, 1994, commr. emeritus, 1994. Pres. Cmty. Devel. Assn., 1957-61; bd. dirs. U.S. Olympic Com., 1985-94, chmn. games preparation com., 1985-2001. With USN, 1945—47. Recipient Disting. Svc. award Mich. Assn. Professions, 1979, Citation for Disting. Svc. Colo. Sports Hall of Fame, U.S. Olympic Com. Order of Olympic Shield, 1996. Mem. Nat. Football Found. (ct. of honors com., Western Regional Leadership award 1999), NCAA, Nat. Assn. Collegiate Dirs. Athletics (Corbett award 1991, Adminstr. Excellence award), Collegiate Commrs. Assn. (pres., award of Merit 1998), Am. Football Assn. (Commrs. award 1996, Athletic Dir.'s award 1998). Home: 2810 W Magee Rd Tucson AZ 85742-1500 Personal E-mail: josephlkea@earthlink.net.

KEARNEY, MICHAEL JOHN, banker; b. Clinton, Iowa, Jan. 2, 1940; s. Vincent Joseph and Evelyn Lorraine (Lynch) K.; m. Lisa von Kaenel, Sept. 8, 1973 (divorced); children: Bridget, Andrew, Patrick. BSEE, Washington U., St. Louis, 1962; MBA, U. Pa., 1964. Tech. draftsman Alfred E. Teves K.G., Frankfurt, Fed. Republic of Germany, 1966-67, Hussmann Refrigerator Co., Mexico City, Mex., 1967-68, gen. mgr. Guatamala City, Guatamala, 1968-71, internat. sales mgr. Buenos Ares, Argentina, 1971-72; loan officer 1st Nat. Bank Chgo., Mexico City, 1972-76, asst. v.p. Chgo., 1976-79, v.p., 1979-86, Phila. Nat. Bank, Chgo., 1986-88; regional mgr. Valuation Rsch. Corp., Milw., 1988-90, v.p. internat. ops., 1990-94; v.p., group head credit Deutsche Genossenschaftsbank, NYC, 1995-97; v.p. Bank Hapoalim, Chgo., 1997—; pres. Pan Am. Bank, Chgo., 2001. Author: Midwest Families, 1979. Pres. St. Stephen's Green Property Owners, Northbrook, Ill., 1982-90, treas., 1980-82; mem. Northbrook Caucus, 1986-87, pres., 1987-89, chmn., Sesquicentennial Com., Clinton, Iowa, 2003-05, bd. dirs. Clinton County Hist. Soc., 2004-, chmn., Historic Preservation Commn., Clinton, 2004-05; bd. dirs. Clinton YMCA, solid waste commn. bd. Clinton County, 2006-, bd. Curtis Mansion Found., 2007-; councilman Clinton City Coun., 2005—. 1st lt. US Army, 1964—66. Recipient Jack Dermody Meml. Vol. of Yr. award, 2006—07. Mem. Beta Theta Pi (dist. chief 1982-90, Dist. Chief of Yr. 1987, asst. gen. treas. 1995—), Omicron Delta Kappa (pres. 1961-62). Republican. Roman Catholic. Avocations: genealogy, running, swimming. Home: 200 Fifth Ave S #304 Clinton IA 52732 Office: 419 S 2d St Clinton IA 52732 Office Phone: 847-877-0730, 563-242-0414. Business E-Mail: Michael.Kearney.WG64@Wharton.UPenn.edu.

KEARNEY, STEPHEN MICHAEL, federal agency administrator; b. Washington, Apr. 8, 1956; s. John James and Helen Joan (Gaffney) K.; m. Julie Elizabeth Mosio, June 30, 1984; children: Justin Samuel, Caitlin Elizabeth. BA, McGill U., 1978; MBA, George Washington U., 1985; AMP, Harvard Bus. Sch., 2000. CFA. Fin. economist US Treasury Dept., Washington, 1978-80; investment officer US Postal Svc., Washington, 1980-81, investment mgr., 1981-90, treas., 1990-99, v.p., treas., 1999—2000, sr. v.p. corp./bus. devel., 2000—01, v.p. pricing and classification, 2001—. First class honors, Univ. scholar McGill U., 1978; recipient Alexander Hamilton award for Excellence in Treasury Mgmt.,

1996, 98, 99, Postmaster Gen. award, 1997, 99. Mem.: Assn. for Fin. Profl., Washington Assn. Money Mgr. (pres. 1985—86), Fin. Execs. Internat., Beta Gamma Sigma. Democrat. Roman Catholic. Office: US Postal Svc 475 L Enfant Plaza SW Washington DC 20260-5014 Business E-Mail: skearney@usps.com.

KEARNS, DAVID RICHARD, chemistry professor; b. Urbana, Ill., Mar. 20, 1935; s. Clyde W. and Camille V. (French) K.; m. Alice Chen, July 5, 1958; children: Jennifer, Michael. BS in Chem. Engring., U. Ill., 1956; PhD., U. Calif., Berkeley, 1960. USAF doctoral fellow U. Chgo., 1960-61, MIT, Cambridge, 1961-62; asst. prof. chemistry U. Calif., Riverside, 1962-63, assoc. prof., 1964-67, prof., 1968-75, San Diego, 1975—. Assoc. editor Molecular Photochemistry, 1969-75, Photochemistry and Photobiology, 1971-75, Chem. Revs., 1974; assoc. editor Biopolymers, 1975-78, editorial bd., 1978-95. Sloan Found. fellow, 1965-67; Guggenheim fellow, 1969-70. Mem. Am. Chem. Soc. (Calif. sect. award 1973), Am. Phys. Soc., Am. Soc. Photobiology. Home: 8422 Sugarman Dr La Jolla CA 92037-2225 Office: U Calif San Diego Dept Chemistry La Jolla CA 92093 Office Phone: 858-534-2760. Business E-Mail: drk@chem.ucsd.edu.

KEARNS, ELLEN CECELIA, lawyer; b. Washington, Apr. 15, 1945; d. Lawrence Mark and Mary (Moran) K. AB, Regis Coll., 1967; JD, Boston Coll., 1976. Bar: Mass. 1977, U.S. Supreme Ct. 1989, U.S. Ct. Appeals (1st cir.) 1979, U.S. Dist. Ct. (Mass.) 1980. Ptnr. Kearns & Rubin, Boston, 1992—99, Epstein Becker & Green, Boston, 1999—2004; of counsel Foley & Lardner, Boston, 2005—. Mem. Gov.'s Commn. on Status of Women, 1983-86; del. Mass. Dem. Conv., 1988-90; trustee, Regis Coll.; mem. Reading Mcpl. Light Bd.; founder, bd. dirs. Sister Spirit, Inc., 1990-91; lector St. Agnes Ch. Recipient Cushing-Gavin award for Excellence in Labor-Mgmt. Rels., 1993, Regis Coll. Alumni Achievement award 1993, Boston Coll. Law Sch. Alumnae of Yr., 1992. Mem. ABA (chmn. fed. labor stds. legis. com. 1991-94), Mass. Bar Assn. (labor and employment sect. coun. 1990-93), Nat. Conf. Women's Bar Assns. (pres. 2004-), Women's Bar Assn. (bd. dirs. 1990-92, treas. 1993-95, v.p. 1995-96), Boston Bar Assn. (chmn. labor law sect. 1988-90), Boston Coll. Alumni Assn. (pres.), Reading Jaycees (treas.). Democrat. Roman Catholic. Home: 2 Beaver Rd Reading MA 01867-1103 Office: Foley & Lardner 111 Huntington Ave Boston MA 02199

KEARNS, JAMES JOSEPH, artist; b. Scranton, Pa., Aug. 7, 1924; s. David Joseph and Ann Mary (Keller) K.; m. Betty Ione Hough, June 19, 1948; children: David, Diane, Mark, Aaron, Lisa. B.F.A., Sch. Art Inst. Chgo., 1950. Instr. Sch. Visual Arts, NYC, 1960-90, Skowhegan (Maine) Sch. Painting, summers 1961-64. Illustrator: Can These Bones Live (E. Dahlberg), 1962, The Heart of Beethoven (S. Rodman), 1969; One-man shows include, Grippi Gallery, N.Y.C., 1956, 57, 60, 62, 68, Bloomfield (N.J.) Coll., 1967, 72, Sculpture Ctr., N.Y.C., 1973, Caldwell (N.J.) Coll., 1976, Trenton (N.J.) State Mus., 1984, Rider U., 2006; group shows include, Whitney Mus. Am. Art, 1959, 60, 61, 80, Am. Fedn. Art, Art Inst. Chgo., 1979, traveling exhbns., Pa. Acad. Fine Arts, Phila., 1964, 65, Butler Inst. Am. Art, Youngstown, Ohio, 1964, Monmouth (N.J.) Mus., 1969, Squibb Gallery, Princeton, N.J., 1974, sculpture, Schenectady Mus., 1976, 35th Audubon Artists, N.Y.C., 1977, Whitney Mus. Am. Art, N.Y.C., 1980; represented in permanent collections, Mus. Modern Art, N.Y.C., Whitney Mus. Am. Art, Newark Mus. Art, Montclair (N.J.) Mus., Topeka Pub. Library, Smithsonian Nat. Collection Fine Arts, Washington, Hirshhorn Mus., Washington, also numerous pvt. collections. Served with U.S. Army, 1943-46. Recipient Ann. Disting. Artist-Tchr. award Sch. Visual Arts, 1990; Nat. Inst. Arts and Letters grantee, 1959 Personal E-mail: jbkearns@verizon.net.

KEARNS, MARY HOYT, psychologist; m. Thomas Kearns. MS in Rsch. Methods & Statis. Analysis in Behavioral Scis., So. Conn. State U., New Haven, 1992—94; PhD in Devel. Psychology, Fordham U., Bronx, NY, 1994—2002. Owner, wellness cons. StellarSelf, Washington, 2003—. Chpt. founder, mem. Co. Friends, Norwalk, Conn., 2000—04; reviewer Contemporary Psychology, St. Louis, 2004—. Author: It's Your Time Now: What Will You Do With It? An 8-Week Plan for Figuring Out the What's Next in Your Life, Growing Toward Balance: Achieving Ideas for Bringing Harmony to Your Mind, Body and Spirit. Devel. co-chair, bd. trustees The Montessori Sch., Wilton, Conn., 1996—2002. Recipient Leadership Spotlight award, Women Pres. Ednl. Orgn., 2006. Mem.: APA, Women Pres. Ednl. Orgn., Women's Bus. Enterprise Nat. Coun., Assn. Psychol. Sci., Sigma Xi. Achievements include research in a multidimensional approach to the assessment of social support and its relationship to adults use of biomedical and alternative health care Services; the relationship of parental health beliefs, attributions and support to the health outcome of children with asthma. Office: StellarSelf Ste 400 1700 Pennsylvania Ave NW Washington DC 20006

KEARNS, MERLE GRACE, state agency administrator; b. Bellefonte, Pa., May 19, 1938; d. Robert John and Mary Katharine (Fitzgerald) Grace; m. Thomas Raymond Kearns, June 27, 1959; children: Thomas, Michael, Timothy, Matthew. BS, Ohio State U., 1960. Tchr. St. Raphael Elem. Sch., Springfield, Ohio, 1960-62; substitute tchr. Mad River Green Dist., Springfield, 1972-78; instr. Clark Tech. Coll., Springfield, 1978-80; commr. Clark County, Ohio, 1981-91; mem. Ohio Senate, Columbus, 1991-2000, majority whip, 1998—2000; mem. Ohio Ho. of Reps., Columbus, 2001—05, majority floor leader, 2005; dir. Ohio Dept. Aging, 2005—07; ret., 2007. Pres. Bd. County Commrs., 1982—83, 1987, 90. Sec. County Commrs. Assn. Ohio, 1988, 2d v.p., 1989—90, 1st v.p., 1990; mem. exec. com. Springfield Reps., 1984—2001; chair Ohio Children's Trust Fund, 1995—2000; past chair Legis. Office of Edn. Oversight; active NCSL Welfare Reform Task Force, 2001—05; vice-chair Policy Consensus Initiative Bd., 2002—; chair Head Start Plus Study Coun.; hon. chair Srs. 4 Kids, Ohio, 2007; bd. dirs. Springfield Symphony, 1980—86, Arts Coun., 1980—85; bd. dirs., mem. exec. bd. Nat. Conf. State Legislatures, 2000—03. Named Woman of the Yr., Springfield Pilot Club, 1981, Wittenburg Woman of Accomplishment, 1991, Watchdog of Treasury, 1991, 1996, 2000, Legislator of the Yr., Assn. Mental Health and Drug Addition Svcs. Bds., 1996, Pub. Childrens Svcs. Agys. Ohio, 1999, Ohio Cmty. Colls., 1997, Ohio Disting. Nurses, 2000, Advance Practice Nurse Assn., 2002, Legis. Co-Person of the Yr., Assn. Joint Vocat. Sch. Supts., 1996, Mental Health Adv. of the Yr., 2002, Outstanding Head Start Legislator of the Yr., Miami Valley, 2002, Legislator of Yr., Ohio Fedn. Tchrs., 2003, Advocate of Yr., Ohio County Alzheimer Assn., 2004, Alzheimer Legis. Advocate of Yr., 2004; recipient Pub. Policy Leadership award, 1997, Disting. Svc. Pub. Ofcls. award, Assn. Ohio Philanthropic Homes, 1999, 1st Ann. Jane Swart Disting. Svcs. to Nursing, 2000, Citizenship award, Ohio State U. Coll. Human Ecology, 2000, Legislator of Yr., Behavioral Health Authorities Assn., 2003, Ohio Better World award, Ohio Mediation Assn., 2004;, Ohio State U. scholar, 1957—59. Mem.: LWV (bd. dirs. 1964—78, pres. 1975—78), Ohio Nurses Assn. (Legislator of the Yr. 1995, 1999), Rotary, Omicron Nu. Roman Catholic. Avocation: reading.

KEARNS, RONALD EDWIN, music educator, performance artist; b. Raleigh, NC, May 16, 1952; s. Laura Henderson Kearns; m. Lillie Broughton, Feb. 5, 1950; 1 child, Tiffany. MusM, Cath. U. Of Am., 1980; MusB in Edn., Knoxville Coll., 1974. Tchr. Balt. City Pub. Schools, Baltimore, 1975—84, Montgomery County (Md.) Pub. Schools, 1985—2005, P. Mauriat performing artist, Vandoren performing artist. Record prodr. Ron Kearns Prodns., Columbia, Md., 1980—. Prodr.: (record) Time To Let Go, Terell Stafford, Candid Records, Ltd, 1990, (record sound recording) Centripetal Force, Terell Stafford, Candid Records, Ltd, 1992, (sound recording) Introducing Kenny Reed, 1990, Paul Carr - Pc 10, 1987, Buck Hill-up Hill, 1991, Ronnie Wells Live At Montpelier, 1998, (musician) The Ron Kearns Quintet Live At Blues Alley, 1999; musician: (sound recording) Hand Prints, 1997, Looking Back, Stepping forward, 2002, Live at Montpelier, 2005, Cheryl Jones Like Someone in Love. Regional pres. Md. Music Educators, Silver Spring, 1990—93; elder Presbyn. Ch., Washington, 1985—2002; hon. bd. mem. Fish Middleton Jazz Scholarship Fund, Silver Spring, Md., 1991—2002. Named one of 50 Outstanding Music Directors, SBO Magazine; recipient Jazz Achievement in Edn., Down Beat Magazine. Mem.: Nat. Acad. Recording Arts and Scis., Md. Music Educators, Internat. Assn. Of Jazz Educators, Music Educators Nat. Conf., Alpha Phi Alpha Frat., Inc. Presbyterian. Office: Ron Kearns Prodns Po Box 514 Columbia MD 21045-0514 Personal E-mail: ron@ronkearns.com.

KEARNS, WILLIAM MICHAEL, JR., investment banker; b. Orange, NJ, June 26, 1935; s. William Michael and Doris Mae (Hodgkinson) K.; m. Patricia Anne Wright, Aug. 17, 1957 (dec. 2006); children: William Michael III, Susan Elizabeth (Mrs. Eric R. Hubbard), Kathleen Anne, Michael Patrick, Elizabeth Anne (Mrs. James P. Leonard). AB, U. Maine, 1957; AM, NYU, 1960; postgrad., Boston Coll. Law, 1957-58, NYU, 1960-64; LLD (hon.), Gonzaga U., 1988. With Chase Manhattan Bank, 1958-59; security analyst Hayden, Stone & Co., Inc., NYC, 1960-62; assoc. instl. sales and syndicate dept. Kuhn, Loeb & Co., NYC, 1962-64, asst. v.p., 1964-66, v.p., 1966-68, sales mgr., 1968-69, gen. ptnr., 1970-75; mng. dir. Kuhn, Loeb & Co., Inc., 1976-77, Lehman Bros. Kuhn Loeb Inc., 1977-84, Shearson Lehman Bros. Inc., NYC, 1984—93; pres. W. M. Kearns & Co. Inc., Morristown, NJ, 1994—; vice chmn. Keefe Mgrs., LLC, NYC, 1998—2002, chmn., co-CEO, 2002—. Bd. dirs. Selective Ins. Group, Inc., Branchville, N.J., Transistor Devices, Inc., Cedar Knolls, N.J.; trustee EQ Advisors Trust, AXA Equitable Life Ins. Co., N.Y.C., AXA Enterprise Funds, AXA Fin., N.Y.C.; dir. U.S. Shipping Ptnrs. LP, Edison, N.J.; sr. adv. Proudfoot Cons., Plc, London, 1997—; adv. dir. Gridley and Co. LLC, N.Y.C., 2001—, Pvt. Client Resources LLC, 2005; investment adv. Young Nichols Gilstrap, Inc., Phoenix, 1982-1992; sr. cons. Ing Baring Furman Selz LLC, N.Y.C., 1994-98; mem. faculty Fairleigh Dickinson U. Coll. Bus. Adminstrn., 1959-68; instr. security analysis N.Y. Inst. Fin. 1961-67; adj. prof. Grad. Sch. Bus. Adminstrn., NYU, 1971-72, chmn. NYU Forum Fin., 1971; lectr. Columbia U., Fairleigh Dickinson U., U. Rochester, NYU. Trustee Drumthwacket Found., Inc., 1985-95, Morristown-Beard Sch., 1982-88, Rider Univ., 1982-88, Morristown Meml. Health Found., 1999-05, CBR Inst. for Biomed. Rsch., Boston, 2006—, New Vernon Cemetary Assn., 2006; trustee Morris Mus., 1968-86, mem. adv. bd., 1987—; trustee Tri-County Scholarship Fund, 1982—, v.p., 1985-86, pres., 1987-89, pres. emeritus, 1990—; bd. dirs. Greater N.Y. coun. Boy Scouts Am., 1986—, v.p., 1990—; bd. dirs. The Am. Friends of Covent Garden and the Royal Ballet, London, 1989—; mem. N.J. Rep. Fin. Com., 1978-84; adv. bd. Intrnat. Tennis Hall of Fame, 1984-86, bd. dirs., 1986-95, internat. coun., 1995-97; mem. adv. bd. Templeton Prize, Lyford Cay, Nassau, Bahammas, 1990—; exec. com. William E. Simon Grad. Sch., Bus. Adminstrn., U. Rochester, 1986-2006; devel. com. U. Maine, 1990-96, diocesan investment com., Diocese of Paterson N.J., 1986-03; mem. Cardinal's Com. of Laity, N.Y.C.; mem. 1910 Soc., Boy Scouts Am., 2000; dir. Malta Human Resources Found., 2004—. Decorated Am. Assn. Master Knights Sovereign Mil. Order Malta; Pontifical Order of St. Gregory The Great; recipient Silver Beaver award Boy Scouts Am., 1989, Leadership award Tri-County Scholarship Fund, 1990, Leadership award Morristown Meml. Hosp., 1998, Augusta Stone award Morristown Meml. Health Found., 1999. Mem. Nat. Assn. Security Dealers (corp. fin. com. 1976-80), Securities Industry Assn. (minority capital com. 1978-86, exec. com. N.Y. dist. 1970, vice chmn. 1973, chmn. 1974), New Eng. Soc., Soc. Friendly Sons St. Patrick City of N.Y., Univ.-Club (N.Y., trustee 1978-81), Bond Club N.Y., Econ. Club (N.Y.), Morris County Golf Club (Convent, N.J. gov. 1976-82), Green Jacket Club (Homestead, Va., founder 1991—), Morristown (N.J.) Club, Log Cabin Gun Club (Sterling, N.J.), Rolling Rock Club (Ligonier, Pa.), Mid-Ocean Club (Bermuda), Palm Beach (Fla.) Polo and Country Club, Skytop Lodge (Pa.), Beta Theta Pi, Kappa Phi Kappa. Roman Catholic. Office: W M Kearns & Co Inc 310 South St Morristown NJ 07960-7301 Business E-Mail: wkearnes@wesandsons.com.

KEARSE, AMALYA LYLE, federal judge; b. Vauxhall, NJ, June 11, 1937; d. Robert Freeman and Myra Lyle (Smith) K. BA, Wellesley Coll., 1959; JD cum laude, U. Mich., 1962. Bar: NY 1963, US Supreme Ct. 1967. Assoc. Hughes, Hubbard & Reed, NYC, 1962—69, ptnr., 1969—79; judge US Ct. Appeals (2nd cir.), 1979—. Lectr. evidence NYU Law Sch., 1968—69. Author: Bridge Conventions Complete, 1975, Bridge Conventions Complete, 3d edit., 1990, Bridge at Your Fingertips, 1980; transl., editor: Bridge Analysis, 1979; editor: Ofcl. Ency. of Bridge, 3d edit., 1976; mem. editl. bd.: Charles Goren, 1974—. Trustee NYC YWCA, 1976—79, Am. Contract Bridge League Nat. Laws Commn., 1975—; mem. Pres.'s Com. on Selection of Fed. Jud. Officers, 1977—78; Bd. dirs. NAACP Legal Def. and Endl. Fund, 1977—79, Nat. Urban League, 1978—79. Named Women's Pairs Bridge Champion Nat. div., 1971, 1972, World div., 1986, Nat. Women's Teams Bridge Champion, 1987, 1990, 1991; named to, Bridge Hall of Fame, 2004. Mem.: ABA, Lawyers Com. for Civil Rights Under Law (mem. exec. com. 1970—79), Am. Law Inst., Assn. of Bar of City of N.Y. Office: US Ct Appeals US Courthouse 40 Foley Sq Rm 2001 New York NY 10007*

KEASLER, MICHAEL EDWARD, judge; b. Dallas, Aug. 16, 1942; s. Lonnie Edward and Jane Cymbeline Keasler; m. Nancy Ann Lawson, June 21; 1 child, Christina Elizabeth. BA, U. Tex., Austin, 1964, LLB, 1967. Atty. Dallas County Dist., Grand Prairie, 1967—69, asst. dist. atty., 1969—81; judge 292d Dist. Ct., Dallas, 1981—99, Tex. Ct. Criminal Appeals, Austin, 1999—. Faculty mem. Nat. Judicial Coll., Reno, 1992—, Robert H. Jackson lectr., 2002, faculty council, 2004—05. Chair Dallas Ct. Juvenile Bd., 1985—86; presiding local adminstrv. judge Dallas County, 1987—88; dean Tex. State Jud. Edn., 1990—97; chair jud. sect. State Bar Tex., 1996—97; chair Tex. Ctr. for Judiciary, Inc., 1996—97. Fellow: Am. Bar Found., Tex. Bar Found.; mem.: ABA (chair state trial judges ethics com. 1997—98), Am. Law Inst. Republican. Episcopal. Avocations: reading, jogging, travel. Office: Tex Ct Criminal Appeals Supreme Ct Bldg 201 W 14th St Austin TX 78701

KEASLING, JAY D., chemistry professor, research scientist; b. 1961; BSc in Chemistry and Biology, U. Nebraska, 1986; MSc in Chemical Engring., U. Michigan, 1988, PhD in Chemical Engring., 1991; post-doctorate in Biochemistry, Stanford U., 1992. Rsch. asst. Dept. Chemical Engring., U. Mich., 1986—91; post-doctoral rsch. assoc. Dept. Biochemistry, Stanford U., 1991—92; asst. prof. chemical engring. U. Calif.-Berkeley, 1992—98, assoc. prof. chemical engring., 1998—2001, vice-chmn. Dept. Chemical Engring., 1999—2000; dir. U. Calif. BioSTAR Program, 2000—; exec. com. mem. UC BioSTAR Program, 2000—; prof. chemical engring. U. Calif.-Berkeley, 2001—. Contbr. scientific papers to profl. jours. Recipient CAREER award, Nat. Sci. Found., 1995, AIChE award for Chemical Engring. Excellence in Academic Teaching, 1999; fellow Chevron Young Faculty Fellowship, 1995, American Inst. of Med. and Biological Engring., 2000. Mem.: American Inst. of Med. and Biological Engring., American Soc. for Microbiology, American Inst. of Chemical Engrs., American Chemical Soc. Achievements include patents in field of "Reductive dehalogenation of organic halides in contaminated groundwater." US Patent No. 6,150,157 (1995). Office: Dept of Chemical Engring U California Berkeley CA 94720 Office Phone: 510-642-4862. Office Fax: 510-643-1228. E-mail: keasling@socrates.berkeley.edu.

KEATING, EUGENE KNEELAND, animal scientist, educator; b. Liberal, Kans., Feb. 15, 1928; s. Arthur Hitch and Nilie Charlotte (Kneeland) K.; m. Iris Louise Myers, Aug. 12, 1951; children— Denise Keating Schnagl, Kimberly Alan. BS, Kans. State U., 1953, MS, 1954; PhD, U. Ariz., 1964. Owner, mgr. ranch, Kans., 1954—; instr., farm mgr. Midwestern U., Wichita Falls, Tex., 1957-60; rsch. asst. U. Ariz., Tucson, 1960-64; prof. animal sci. Calif. State Poly. U., Pomona, 1964-98, prof. emeritus, 1998—, chmn. dept., 1971-78. Contbr. articles to profl. jours. Bd. dirs. Los Angeles County Jr. Livestock Fair, 1971-79, chmn., 1975. With USAAF, 1946-49. Recipient Farm Bur. Century award, 2000. Fellow: Am. Inst. Chemists; mem.: NRA Whittington Ctr. Founders Club, NRA (benefactor), Brit. Soc. Animal Prodn., Am. Soc. Lab. Animal Sci., Coun. for Agrl. Sci. and Tech. (life), Am. Soc. Animal Sci. (life), Nat. Intercollegiate Rodeo Assn. (West Coast regional faculty dir. 1972—76), Western Heritage Ctr., Rep. Nat. Com. (life), Calif Rifle and Pistol Assn. (Gold Eagle), Am. Legion, Block and Bridle Club, Santa Fe Trail and Gun Club (life), Ind. Order Foresters, Sigma Xi, Alpha Zeta, Gamma Sigma Delta, Phi Lambda Upsilon. Presbyterian. Mailing: PO Box 1920 Veradale WA 99037 Office Phone: 509-893-3804.

KEATING, FRANCIS ANTHONY, II, retired governor, lawyer; b. St. Louis, Feb. 10, 1944; s. Anthony Francis and Anne (Martin) K.; m. Catherine Dunn Heller, 1972; children: Carissa Herndon, Kelly Martin, Anthony Francis III. AB, Georgetown U., 1966; JD, U. Okla., 1969. Bar: Okla. 1969. Spl. agt. FBI, 1969-71; asst. dist. atty. Tulsa County, 1971-72; mem. Okla. Ho. of Reps., 1972-74, Okla. Senate, 1974-81; U.S. atty. No. Dist. Okla., 1981-84; asst. sec. U.S. Treasury Dept., Washington, 1985-88; assoc. atty. gen. Dept. Justice, 1988-89; gen. counsel, acting dep. sec. Dept. Housing and Urban Devel., Washington, 1989-93; gov. State of Okla., 1995—2003; pres. Am. Coun. Life Insurers, Washington, 2003—. Mem. Okla. Bar Assn. Republican. Office: Am Coun Life Insurers 101 Constitution Ave NW Washington DC 20001

KEATING, ISABEL, actress; b. Savannah, Ga. Actor: (Broadway plays) Enchanted April, 2003, The Boy From Oz, 2003 (nominee Outer Critics Cir. best actress, 2004, nominee Tony award best featured actress in a musical, 2004, Drama Desk award best featured actress in a musical, 2004, Theatre World award for outstanding musical debut, 2004), (off Broadway shows) Bonnie, Once in a Lifetime, Waiting at the Waters Edge, (regional stage shows) The Rise and Fall of Little Voice, Three Sisters, Chilean Holiday, One Foot on the Floor, Indian Ink, 2000 (Helen Hayes award best actress, 2000), On the March to the Sea, 2005, Lady Windermere's Fan, 2005; (films) The Nanny Diaries, 2006; (TV films) Judy Garland: By Myself, 2004. Office: c/o Blue Ridge Entertainment 41 Union Sq W New York NY 10003

KEATING, KEVIN, academic administrator, chef; AAS in Hotel Tech., Sullivan County Cmty. Coll. Cert. Exec. Chef Am. Culinary Fedn., Culinary Educator Am. Culinary Fedn., Vocat. Instr. in Quality Foods State of Fla. Chef Marriott Key Bridge Hotel, Washington, Stouffer's Nat. Ctr. Hotel, Washington, Hilton Hotel, Rye Town, NY; exec. chef SBR's Restaurant, Katonah, NY, Waccabuc Country Club; co-creator Am. Culinary Fedn. Culinary Apprenticeship Walt Disney World Co., Orlando; assoc. dean culinary arts Capital Culinary Inst., Keiser U., Tallahassee. Recipient regional award of Excellence, Kraft Foodservice, 1991, nat. award of Excellence, 1993. Mem.: Tallahassee Area Chefs Assn. (pres.), Am. Chef Fedn. (edn. chmn. 1992—99, Chef. of Yr. 1994, Pres. award for Outstanding Svc. 1995). Office: Capital Culinary Institute Keiser University 1700 Halstead Blvd Tallahassee FL 32309 Office Phone: 850-906-9494. Office Fax: 850-906-9497.*

KEATING, MARK TAYLOR, physician, medical educator; BS, Princeton U.; MD, Johns Hopkins U. Postdoctoral fellow Lewis Williams Labs. U. Calif., San Francisco; assoc. prof. medicine and human genetics U. Utah, Salt Lake City, L. George Veasy prof. pediat. cardiology; prof. cell biology Harvard Med. Sch.; prof. cardiology Children's Hosp., Boston; investigator Howard Hughes Med. Inst. Co-founder, co-chair sci. adv. bd. Hydra Biosciences, Inc., 2001. Contbr. articles to profl. jour. Recipient Basic Sci. prize, Am. Heart Assn., Cardiovascular Rsch. award, Pasarow Found. Fellow: Am. Acad. Arts & Sciences; mem.: NAS.

KEATING, MICHAEL BURNS, lawyer, educator; b. Cambridge, Mass., May 17, 1940; s. John Stuart and Anne Veronica (Burns) K.; m. Martha Harrison McGuire, OCt. 12, 1974; children: Michael Burns, Andrew Wade, Lucy Harrison. BA, Williams Coll., Williamstown, Mass., 1962; LLB, Harvard U., Cambridge, Mass., 1965. Bar: Mass. 1965, US District Ct. Mass. 1966. Law clk. to presiding justice Superior Ct. Mass., Boston, 1965-66, US Dist. Ct. Mass., Boston, 1966-67; assoc. Foley Hoag, Boston, 1967-74, ptnr., 1974—. Adj. prof. trial practice Northeastern Law Sch., Boston, 1985—. Trustee emeritus Brooks Sch., North Andover, Mas., 1978—, Foley & Hoag Found., Boston, 1981-89, Williams Coll., Williamstown, Mass., 1996—; pres. Crime & Justice Found., Boston, 1985-94; trustee Children's Mus. Boston, 2006-, Boston Found., 2004-. Lt. (j.g.) USNR, 1967—72. Fellow Am. Coll. Trial Lawyers, Harvard Club; mem. Boston Bar Assn. (pres. 2001-02). Democrat. Roman Catholic. Avocations: tennis, squash, skiing, sailing. Home: 3 W Cedar St Boston MA 02108-3535 Office: Foley Hoag 155 Seaport Blvd Boston MA 02210-2600 Home Phone: 617-723-7344; Office Phone: 617-832-1136. Business E-Mail: mkeating@foleyhoag.com.

KEATING, TEDD MICHAEL, adult education educator; b. S.I., NY, Apr. 26, 1971; s. Theodore F. and Annemarie Keating. BS, Manhattan Coll., Bronx, NY, 1993; MS, Slippery Rock U., Pa., 1995; PhD, U. Pitts., Pa., 2001. Cert. exercise specialist Am. Coll. of Sports Medicine, 1998; specialist Nat. Strength and Conditioning Assn., 1999, weightlifting coach USA Weightlifting, 2000. Instr., rschr., pers. supr. U. Pitts., 1996—98; assoc. prof. Manhattan Coll., Bronx, NY, 1998—; cons. Fitness Mag., NYC, 2003—04; lectr./cons. Nat. Fitness Trainers Assn., NYC, 2003—04; reviewer Strength and Conditioning Jour., Colorado Springs, Colo., 2003—; instr. anatomy, physiology Swedish Inst., NYC, 2006—. Dir. exercise physiology lab. Manhattan Coll., Bronx, NY, 1998—, coord. Jasperfit program, 2004—, faculty advisor to Phi Epsilon Kappa honor frat., 2004, personal trainer Jasperfit program, 2004—, editor Jasperfit newsletter, 2004—. Author: (research manuscript) Re-evaluation of a possible proximity effect, (column feature) Is the valsalva maneuver a proper breathig technique?, (research manuscript) Evaluation of a possible proximity effect of aspartame and vitamin C on muscular strength. Fundraiser Am. Cancer Soc., NYC, 2006—06, Manhattan Coll. Lasallian Action Com., Bronx, NY, 2005—06. Mem.: AAHPERD, Nat. Assn. for Kinesiology and Phys. Edn. in Higher Edn., Nat. Strength and Conditioning Assn. (Recertified with Distinction 2006), Am. Coll. of Sports Medicine, Phi Epsilon Kappa (chpt. advisor 2000—06). Achievements include first to Implemented First Campus-wide Wellness Program at Manhattan College; Expanded curriculum and facilities to meet the standards of major professional organization. Office: Manhattan Coll Manhattan College Pky Bronx NY 10471 Office Phone: 718-862-7495. E-mail: tedd.keating@manhattan.edu.

KEATING, TIMOTHY J., career military officer; b. Dayton, Ohio, Nov. 5, 1949; m. Wanda Lee Doerkson; children Daniel, Julie. Grad., U.S. Naval Acad., 1971; completed flight tng., 1973. Commd. ensign USN, 1971; advanced through grades to adm., 2004; duty USS Mason (DD-852) We. Pacific; ordered to VA-82 deploying USS Nimitz (CVN-68); reported to VA-122 NAS Lemoore, Calif., 1978; staff LSO with comdr. carrier air wing fifteen USS Kitty Hawk, We. Pacific, Indian Ocean; adminstrv. officer, ops. officer, maint. officer VA-94 USS Enterprise, We. pacific, 1982-84; aide, flat lt. to Comdr. in Chief U.S. Pacific Cmd., 1984-87; comdr. VFA-87, deployed with CVW-8 USS Theodore Roosevelt North Atlantic and Mediterranean, 1987; head aviation LCDR/jr. officer assignments br. naval mil. personnel cmd., Washington; dep.comdr. carrier air wing seventeen combat. ops. Desert Storm USS Saratoga, 1991; CNO fellow strategic studies group Newport, R.I.; temp. duty with joint task force S.W. Asia Riyadh, Saudi Arabia; comdr. Naval Strike Warfare Ctr., 1994—95; dep. comdr. carrier air wing nine USS Nimitz Arabian Gulf; dir. aviation officer distbn. divsn. naval mil. personnel cmd., 1995—96; comdr. Battle Force 7th Fleet (carrier group 5, carrier strike force) USN, 1998—2000, dep. chief naval ops., (plans policy & ops.), 2000—02; comdr. US Naval Forces Ctrl. Command, US Fifth Fleet, 2002—03; dir. The Joint Staff, The Pentagon, Washington, 2003—04; comdr. N.Am. Aerospace Def. Command (NORAD), Peterson AFB, Colo., 2004—07, US No. Command, 2004—07, US Pacific Command, Honolulu, 2007—. Decorated Def. Disting. Svc. Medal with Oak Leaf Cluster, Disting. Svc. Medal with Gold Star, Legion of Merit with three Gold Stars, Def. Meritorious Svc. Medal, Meritorious Svc. Medal with Gold Star, Air Medals (3), Navy Commendation Medal with two Gold Stars Office: US Pacific Command/JO1PA PO Box 64031 Camp H M Smith HI 96861*

KEATINGE, ROBERT REED, lawyer; b. Berkeley, Calif., Apr. 22, 1948; s. Gerald Robert and Elizabeth Jean (Benedict) Keatinge; m. Katherine Lou Carr, Feb. 1, 1969 (div. Dec. 1981); 1 child, Michael Towne; m. Cornelia Elizabeth Wyma, Aug. 21, 1982 (div. Jan. 2007); 1 child, Courteney Elizabeth. BA, U. Colo., 1970; JD, U. Denver, 1973, LLM, 1982. Bar: Colo. 1974, US Dist. Ct. Colo. 1974, US Ct. Appeals (10th cir.) 1977, US Tax Ct. 1980. Ptnr. Kubie & Keatinge, Denver, 1974-76; pvt. practice Denver, 1976; assoc. Richard Young, Denver, 1977-86; counsel Durham & Assoc. PC, Denver, 1986-89, Durham & Baron, Denver, 1989-90; project editor taxation Shepard's/McGraw-Hill, Colorado Springs, Colo., 1990-96; of counsel Holland & Hart, LLP, Denver, 1992—. Lectr. law U. Denver, 1982—92, adj. prof., 1983—94, 2005—; vis. assoc. prof. law Suffolk U. Law Sch., Boston, 2007—; spkr. in field. Author, cons. (CD-ROM) Entity Expert, 1996; co-author: Ribstein and Keatinge on Limited Liability Companies, 1992, 2d edit., 2004, Keatinge and Conaway on Choice of Business Entity, with ann. revisions, 2006—; contbr. articles to profl. jours. and treatises. Recipient Law Week award, U. Denver Bur. Nat. Affairs, 1974. Fellow: Am. Coll. Tax Counsel; mem.: ABA (chmn. subcom. ltd. liability cos. of com. on partnerships 1990—95, ABA adviser to Uniform Ltd. Liability Co. Act 1995, chmn. com. on taxation 1995—99, mem. ho. of dels. 1996—2002, ABA/Nat. Conf. Commrs. on Uniform State Laws joint editl. bd. on uninc 1996—, editl. bd. ABA/BNA Lawyer's Manual on Professional Conduct 1998—2002, chmn. com. on partnerships 2000—04, ABA adviser to Revision of Uniform Ltd. Partnership Act 2001), Am. Law Inst., Denver Bar Assn., Colo. Bar Assn. (taxation sect. exec. coun. 1988—94, sec.-treas. 1991—92, chmn. 1993—94, bd. govs. 1996—2004, bus. law sect. sec.-treas. 2001—03, vice chair 2003—05, chmn. 2005—, ethics com., corp. code revision com., co-chmn. ltd. liability co. revision com.). Home Phone: 303-668-7532; Office Phone: 303-295-8595. Business E-Mail: rkeatinge@hollandhart.com.

KEATING HEINEMANN, LORRIE T., state agency administrator; b. Thorp, Wis., July 12, 1961; d. Joseph M. and Mary Louise (Zander) Keating; m. Jack A. Heinemann, Aug. 27, 1988; 4 children: Katherine, Sarah, Margaret, Alexandra. BBA, U. Wis., Eau Claire, 1983; MBA, U. Wis., Oshkosh, 1992. Lic. securities profl. Pres., owner Wis. Investment Cons., Inc., Oshkosh, 1985—89; cash desk mgr. Valley Trust Co., Appleton, Wis., 1989; dir. corp. svcs. Valley Bancorporation, Appleton, 1989—94; with Associated Trust Co. Neenah, Wis.; investment adv. Virchow Krause Wealth Mgmt., LLC; sec. Wis. Dept. Fin. Instns., 2003—. Bd. dirs. Oshkosh Symphony, 1990; bd. chair Oshkosh Area Cmty. Found.; bd. mem. Oshkosh Cmty. YMCA, Oshkosh Pub. Mus. Mem. Internat. Assn. Fin. Planners (bd. dirs. 1986-90), Oshkosh C. of C. (mem. Leadership prog., fin. com. 1990), Oshkosh Country Club. Republican. Lutheran. Avocations: jogging, sailing, skiing, golf. Office: Office of Sec Wis Dept Fin Instns PO Box 8861 Madison WI 53703 Office Phone: 608-261-9555. Office Fax: 608-261-4334. E-mail: lorrie.keatingheinemann@dfi.state.wi.us.

KEATON, DIANE, actress; b. Santa Ana, Calif., Jan. 5, 1946; Student, Neighborhood Playhouse, NYC, 1968. Appeared on N.Y. stage in Hair, 1968, Play It Again Sam, 1969, The Primary English Class, 1976; appeared in numerous films including Lovers and Other Strangers, 1970, Play It Again Sam, 1972, The Godfather, 1972, Sleeper, 1973, The Godfather Part II, 1974, Love and Death, 1975, I Will, I Will.For Now, 1975, Harry and Walter Go To New York, 1976, Annie Hall, 1977 (Best Actress Acad. award 1978, Brit. Acad. Best Actress award 1978, N.Y. Film Critics Circle award 1978, Nat. Soc. Film Critics award 1978), Looking for Mr. Goodbar, 1977, Interiors, 1978, Manhattan, 1979, Reds, 1981 (Acad. award nominee), Shoot the Moon, 1982, Little Drummer Girl, 1984, Mrs. Soffel, 1984, Crimes of the Heart, 1986, Radio Days, 1987, Baby Boom, 1987, The Good Mother, 1988, The Lemon Sisters, 1990, The Godfather Part III, 1990, Father of the Bride, 1991, Manhattan Murder Mystery, 1993, Look Who's Talking Now, 1993 (voice), Father of the Bride 2, 1995, Marvin's Room, 1996, First Wives Club, 1996, The Only Thrill, 1997, The Other Sister, 1999, Hanging Up, 2000, Town and Country, 2001, Plan B, 2001, Something's Gotta Give, 2003 (Golden Globe for best actress in a musical or comedy, 2004, Acad. Award nomination for best actress, 2004, Screen Actors Guild Award nomination for best actress, 2004), The Family Stone, 2005, Because I Said So, 2007; (TV films) Running Mates, 1992, Amelia Earhart, 1994, Sister Mary Explains It All, 2001; actor, prodr: (TV films) Crossed Over, 2002, On Thin Ice, 2003, Surrender, Dorothy, 2005; dir. film: Heaven, 1987, Wildflower, 1991, Unstrung Heroes, 1995; exec. prodr.: (TV series) Pasadena, 2001; accomplished artist and singer; author book of photographs: Reservations, 1980; editor: (with Marvin Heiferman) Still Life, 1983, Mr. Salesman, 1994; prodr.: The Lemon Sisters, 1990; exec. prodr.: Northern Lights (TV), 1997. Recipient Golden Globe award, 1978*

KEATON, MARGARET-ANN COLEMAN, education educator; d. Raymond Thomas and Virginia Elizabeth Coleman; m. Christopher Bruce Keaton, May 31, 1986; 1 child, Christopher Ray James. B in Psychology with honors, Purdue U., 1998; M in Psychology, U. Ind., 2003; post grad., U. Indpls., 2005—. Pres. Key-Frame Corp., Indpls., 1986—2000; team leader Ind. U., Indpls., 1997—2001; adj. faculty Ivy Tech. State Coll., Indpls., 2004—, U. Ind., Indpls., 2004—. Cons., dir. Key-Frame Corp., 1986—2000. Prodr. (creator): (video) Main Frame Aerobics, 1986; choreographer creator (video) Indiana Pacemates NBA video, 1992; author (interviewer): (video) Sports Psychology, 1997. Co-dir. Ruthann Popcheff Meml. Fund, Indpls., 1986—. Mem.: Am. Coll. Sports Medicine, APA. Avocations: exercise, reading, writing, crafts. Home: 4930 N Kessler Blvd Indianapolis IN 46228 Business E-Mail: keatonma@uindy.edu.

KEATON, MICHAEL, actor, comedian; b. Coraopolis, Pa., Sept. 5, 1951; m. Caroline MacWilliams, 1982 (div. 1990); 1 child, Sean. Student, Kent State U. With comedy group Second City, LA. Appeared in movies Night Shift, 1982, Mr. Mom, 1983, Johnny Dangerously, 1984, Gung Ho, 1985, The Squeeze, 1987, Touch and Go, 1987, Beetlejuice, 1988 (Nat. Soc. Film Critics Best Actor award 1988), Clean and Sober, 1988 (Nat. Soc. Film Critics Best Actor award), The Dream Team, 1989, Batman, 1989, Pacific Heights, 1990, One Good Cop, 1991, Batman Returns, 1992, Much Ado About Nothing, 1993, My Life, 1993, The Paper, 1994, Speechless, 1994, Multiplicity, 1996, Jackie Brown, 1997, Inventing the Abbotts, 1997, Desperate Measures, 1998, Out of Sight, 1998, Jack Frost, 1998, A Shot at Glory, 2000, Quicksand, 2001, First Daughter, 2004, White Noise, 2005, Game Six, 2005, Herbie: Fully Loaded, 2005, (voice) Cars, 2006; TV series include All's Fair, 1976-77, The Mary Tyler Moore Hour, 1979, Working Stiffs, 1979, Report to Murphy, 1982; Studs Lonigan (mini-series), 1979; TV movies: Live From Baghdad, 2002; TV guest appearances include Mister Roger's Neighborhood, 1968, Maude, 1975, (voice) The Simpsons, 1989, Frasier, 1993, (voice) King of the Hill, 1997, (voice) Gary the Rat, 2003; exec. prodr. Body Shots, 1999.

KEATS, DONALD HOWARD, composer, educator; b. NYC, May 27, 1929; s. Bernard and Lillian K.; m. Eleanor Steinholz, Dec. 13, 1953; children: Jeremy, Jennifer, Jefery, Jocelyn. MusB, Yale U., 1949; MA, Columbia U., 1951; PhD, U. Minn., 1962; student, Staatliche Hochschule fur Musik, Hamburg, Germany, 1954-56. Teaching fellow Yale U. Sch. Music, New Haven, 1948-49; instr. music theory U.S. Naval Sch. Music, Washington, 1953-54; post music dir. Ft. Dix, NJ, 1956-57; faculty Antioch Coll., Yellow Springs, Ohio, 1957-76, prof., 1967-76, chmn. music dept., 1967-71; vis. prof. music U. Wash. Sch. Music, 1969-70, Lamont Sch. Music, U. Denver, 1975-76; composer-in-residence Colo. Music Festival, 1980, Arcosanti, 1986; vis. composer Aspen Music Festival, 1987; prof. music, composer-in-residence Lamont Sch. Music, U. Denver, 1975-99, Phipps Prof. in the humanities, 1982-85, prof. emeritus, 1999—. Concerts devoted solely to his music often with his participation as pianist, London, 1973, Tel Aviv, 1973, Jerusalem, 1973, N.Y.C., 1975, Denver, 1984, 91; Composer: Sonata for Clarinet and Piano, 1948, String Trio, 1948, Divertimento for Winds and Strings, 1949, The Naming of Cats, 1951, The Hollow Men, 1951, String Quartet 1, 1952, Concert Piece for Orchestra, 1952, Variations for Piano, 1955, First Symphony, 1957, Piano Sonata, 1960, An Elegiac Symphony, 1962, Anyone Lived in a Pretty How Town, 1965, String Quartet 2, 1965; ballet New Work, 1966; Polarities for Violin and Piano, 1968-70, A Love Triptych, 1970, Dialogue for Piano, and Winds, 1973, Diptych for Cello and Piano, 1975, Upon the Intimation of Love's Mortality, 1975, Branchings for Orch., 1976, Four Puerto Rican Love Songs: Tierras del Alma for soprano, flute and guitar, 1978, Musica Instrumentalis for chamber group, 1980, Concerto for Piano and Orch., 1990, Revisitations for Violin, Cello and Piano, 1992, Elegy for chamber orch., 1995, Fanfare for Brass, 1996, String Quartet No. 3, 2001. Served with U.S. Army, 1952-54. Recipient ASCAP awards, 1964—; awards from Ford, Danforth and Lilly founds., Nat. Endowment for Arts; winner Rockefeller Found. Symphonic Competitions, 1965, 66; Guggenheim fellow Europe, 1964-65, 72-73; Nat. Endowment for Arts grantee, fellow, 1975; Fulbright Scholar, 1954-56. Mem. ASCAP, Am. Music Ctr., Phi Beta Kappa. Home: 12854 Buckhorn Rd Littleton CO 80127 Business E-Mail: dkeats@du.edu.

KEATS, GLENN ARTHUR, manufacturing executive; b. Chgo., July 1, 1920; s. Herbert J. and Agnes H. (Streich) K.; m. Olga Maria Loor Hurtado, Feb. 13, 1946; children; Maria Susana Keats Eggemeyer, Allwyn Dolores Keats Nagel. BS in Commerce, Northwestern U., 1941. Sales exec. Keats-Lorenz Spring Co., Chgo., 1947-56; contr., auditor Plantaciones Ecuatorianas, S.A., Guayaquil, Ecuador, 1956-58; co-founder Keats Mfg. Co., Wheeling, Ill., 1958—. Lt. comdr. USN, 1941—47. Mem. Spring Mfrs. Inst., Northwestern U. Alumni Assn., Sigma Nu. Clubs: Evanston Golf, Amelia Island (Fla.). Republican. Lutheran. Home: 368 Woodland Rd Highland Park IL 60035-5055 Office: 350 Holbrook Dr Wheeling IL 60090-5812 Home Phone: 847-432-6540; Office Phone: 847-520-1133. Business E-Mail: gkeats@keatsmfg.com.

KEATS, THEODORE ELIOT, radiologist, educator; b. New Brunswick, NJ, June 26, 1924; m. Margaret E. McNamara, Aug. 27, 1949 (dec.); children: Matthew Mason, Ian Stuart B.; m. Patricia L. Hart, Mar. 30, 1974. BS, Rutgers U., 1945; MD, U. Pa., 1947. Diplomate Am. Bd. Radiology (trustee). Intern U. Pa. Hosp., Phila., 1947-48; resident U. Mich. Hosp., Ann Arbor, 1948-51; instr. U. Calif. Sch. Medicine, San Francisco, 1953-54, asst. prof., 1954-56; assoc. prof. U. Mo. Sch. Medicine, Columbia, 1956-59, prof. radiology, 1959-63, U. Va. Sch. Medicine, Charlottesville, 1963—, chmn. dept. radiology, 1963-92, alumni prof. radiology, 1992—. Vis. prof. Karolinska Hosp., Stockholm, 1963-64. Author: Atlas of Roentgenographic Measurement, 7th edit., 2001 (with Christopher Sistrom), An Atlas of Normal Roentgen Variants That May Simulate Disease, 8th edit., 2006, Self-Assessment of Current Knowledge in Diagnostic Radiology, 2d edit., 1980, An Atlas of Normal Developmental Roentgen Anatomy, 1978, 2d edit., 1988, (with Thomas H. Smith) Radiology of Musculoskeletal Injury, 1990; editor Emergency Radiology, 1984, 2d edit., 1989, editor-in-chief Current Problems in Diagnostic Radiology, 1981, 2001; Am. editor Skeletal Radiology, 1987-97; editor Applied Radiology, 1989-2001, Emergency Radiology, 1993-2001. Served with AUS, 1943-47; to capt., M.C. AUS, 1951-53. Fellow Am. Coll. Radiology (Gold medal 1995); mem. AMA, Am. Roentgen Ray Soc., Radiol. Soc. N.Am., Soc. Pediatric Radiology (hon.), So. Med. Assn., Internat. Skeletal Soc. (medal 1995), Soc. Emergency Radiology (gold medal 1999), Phi Beta Kappa, Sigma Xi, Alpha Omega Alpha. Home: 421 Key West Dr Charlottesville VA 22911-8423 Office: U Va Hosps Lee St Rm 1831 Charlottesville VA 22911 also: U Va Sch Medicine Dept Radiology Charlottesville VA 22908-0001 Home Phone: 434-296-2361; Office Phone: 434-924-9377. Business E-Mail: tek@virginia.edu.

KEATY, ROBERT BURKE, lawyer, business consultant; b. Baton Rouge, July 7, 1949; s. Thomas St. Paul and Alicia (Armshaw) K.; m. Erin Kenny, July 6, 1973; children: Kellen Elizabeth, Kathryn Ellen, Robert Burke II, Kaneil Erin, Rory Bridgette-Anne. BS, U. La., 1971; JD, Tulane U., 1974. Law clk. to judge U.S. Dist. Ct. for Ea. Dist. La., New Orleans, 1974-76. Mem. pres.'s com. Offshore Tng. and Survival Ctr., U. Lafayette, 1988-89; co-chmn. United Giver Fund Jud. Legal, 1994, Bishops Charity Ball Legal Com., 1995. Member dean's adv. com. Tulane U. Law Sch., New Orleans, 1987; mem. dean's exec. adv. com. Coll. Bus. Adminstrn., U. La., Lafayette, 1991. Sears scholar, 1971, Teagle scholar, 1973; recipient Most Outstanding Alumnus award U. La. Coll. Bus., Lafayette, 1991. Fellow La. Bar Found. (lifetime charter mem.). Avocations: reading, woodworking, tennis, fishing, carpentry.

KEBERT, KENT LERDY, ophthalmologist; b. Jackson, Miss., Oct. 3, 1957; s. F. Dean and LaVerne Jennings Kebert; m. Lynn Dianne Stone, Feb. 19, 1983; children: Alan, Karen, Laura. BS, Millsaps Coll., Jackson, 1979; MD, U. Miss., Jackson, 1983. Lic. Am. Bd. Ophthalmology, 1989. Intern Bapt. Meml. Hosp., Memphis, 1983—84; resident U. Tenn. Hosp., Memphis, 1984—87; ophthalmologist Kerbert Eye Clinic, McComb, Kans., 1987—. Chief surgery Southwest Miss. Regional Med. Ctr., McComb, 1993—94; chief staff SW Miss. Regional Med. Ctr., McComb, 1994—95. Vice chmn., mem. McComb City Sch. Bd., 1999—; med. missionary United Meth. Vol. in Mission, St. Ann's Bay, Jamaica, 2003, 2004, 2006. Mem.: Am. Acad. Ophthalmology. United Methodist. Avocations: tennis, skiing, music.

KECECIOGLU, DIMITRI BASIL, reliability engineering educator, consultant; b. Istanbul, Turkey, Dec. 26, 1922; arrived in US, 1946, naturalized, 1956; s. Basil C. and Mary (Melayios) Kececioglu; m. Lorene June Legan, Dec. 22, 1951; children: Zoe Diana, Draelos, John Dimitri. BS, Robert Coll., Istanbul, 1942; MS, Purdue U., 1949, PhD, 1953. Asst. instr. Purdue U., West Lafayette, Ind., 1943—47, instr., 1947—52; engring. scientist in charge mech. rsch. labs. Allis-Chalmers Mfg. Co., Milw., 1952—57, asst. to dir. mech. engring. industries group, 1957—60, cons. engr. industries group, 1960—63, dir. corp. reliability engring. program, 1960—63; prof. aerospace and mech. engring. U. Ariz., Tucson, 1963—, prof.-in-charge reliability engring. program, 1963—. Reliability and maintainability engring. cons., Tucson, 1963—; dir. Reliability Engring. and Mgmt. Inst., 1963—, Reliability Testing Inst., 1975—; applied reliability engring. and product assurance cons. Northrop Space Labs., GE, Ctr. Mgmt. and Indsl. Devel., Rotterdam, Netherlands, Delco Radio divsn. GM, Aerojet-Gen. Corp., Westinghouse Elec. Co., US Army Mgmt. Engring. Tng. Agy., Allied Signal, Data Gen., Polaroid, Storage Tek, Motorola, Digital Equipment, ITT, B. F. Goodrich, Gen. Dynamics, Xerox, Ford, JPL, Bendix, Cummins Engine, MOOG, Copeland, Eatman Kodak, Allied Chem., Honeywell, IBM, Ventara Med., Hamilton Sundstrand, Northrop-Grumman, numerous others; sr. ext. tchr. UCLA, 1983, vis. prof. reliability engring.; hon. prof. Shanghai U. Tech., 1984; assoc. prof. Tech. U., Bordeaux, France. Author: Bibliography on Plasticity, 1950, Introduction to Probabilistic Design for Reliability, 1975, Manual of Product Assurance Films and Videotapes, 1980, Reliability Engineering Handbook, Vols. 1-2, 1983, Maintainability Availability and Operational Readiness Engineering Handbook Vol. 1, 1995;: rev. edit., 2002, Robust Engineering Design by Reliability, Vol. 1, 2003; contbr. articles to profl. jours. Founder, fund raiser Dr. Dimitri Basil Kececioglu Reliability Engring. Rsch. Fellowships Endowment Fund, 1987. Recipient Presidency award, Milw. Tech. Coun., 1962, Automotive Industries Author award, 1963, Anderson prize, U. Ariz., 1983, Scholarship Devel. Office award, 1991; Fulbright scholar, Nat. Tech. U., Athens, 1971—72. Fellow: Am. Soc. Quality Control, Soc. Reliability Engrs., Soc. Automotive Engrs. (Ralph E. Teetor Outstanding Engring. Educator award 1977, Disting. Probabilistic Methods Educator award 1997), Am. Soc. Quality; mem.: IEEE, ASME, Hellenic Ops. Rsch. Soc. Greece, Am. Soc. Engring. Edn., Am. Hellenic Ednl. Progressive Assn. (Acad. Achievement award in Edn. 1991—92), Soc. Exptl. Stress Analysis, Nat. Golden Key Soc., Sigma Xi (pres. univ. chpt. 1990—91), Phi Beta Kappa (hon.), Phi Kappa Phi (pres. U. Ariz. chpt. 1988—89), Tau Beta Pi. Achievements include patents in field. Home: 7340 N La Oesta Ave Tucson AZ 85704-3119 Office Phone: 520-621-6120. Business E-Mail: dimitri@u.arizona.edu.

KECHIJIAN, PAUL, dermatologist, educator; b. Providence, Mar. 17, 1940; s. Harry Maderos and Annette (Rhia) Paré; m. Janice Ann Kechijian, July 31, 1976; children: Douglas Paul, Lisa Ann. AB in Psychology, Brown U., 1961, ScM in Biology, 1964; MD, Albany Med. Coll., 1968. Lic. Nat. Bd. Med. Examiners, N.Y. State Med. Lic.; diplomate Am. Bd. Dermatology, diplomate Dermatopathology Am. Bds. of Dermatology and Pathology. Med. intern, med. resident Barnes Hosp., St. Louis, 1968-69, 69-70; dermatology resident Mass. Gen. Hosp., Boston, 1970, U. Miami (Fla.) Sch. of Medicine, 1973-75; dermatopathology fellow NYU Med. Ctr., NYC, 1975-76; instr. clin. dermatology NYU Sch. of Medicine, NYC, 1975-78, clin. asst. prof. dermatology, 1978-84, clin. assoc. prof., 1984—2002; asst. attending physician to assoc. attending physician Bellevue Hosp., 1976—2002, NYU Med. Ctr., 1976-84, 84—; asst. attending dermatologist to sr. asst. North Shore Univ. Hosp., 1978—2002. Chief inpatient dermatology svc. Bellevue Hosp., 1976—86; cons. Holy Martyrs Armenian Day Sch., 1976—; hon. surgeon (dermatology) N.Y.C. Police Dept., 1981—; chief nail sect. NYU Med. Ctr., 1983—2002; presenter and lectr. in field. Contbg. editor: Jour. Dermatologic Surgery and Oncology, 1983-85; contbr. reports and articles to profl. jours. and chpt. to books. Fellow ACP, Am. Acad. Dermatology (com. on evaluation 1980-84, coun. on govtl. liaison key contact program 1986—96), Am. Soc. Dermatopathology; mem. AMA, N.Y. Acad. Scis., Dermatology Found., Soc. for Investigative Dermatology, Nassau County Med. Soc., L.I. Dermatol. Soc., Soc. for Dermatol. Surgery, Internat. Soc. Dermatol. Surgery, others. Office: 935 Northern Blvd Great Neck NY 11021-5309 Home Phone: 516-365-7312; Office Phone: 516-482-0650. Personal E-mail: kech1@optonline.net.

KECK, DONALD BRUCE, physicist; b. Lansing, Mich., Jan. 2, 1941; s. William G. and Zelda Divine Keck; m. Ruth A. Moilanen, July 10, 1965; children: Lynne Ann Vaia, Brian William. BS, Mich. State U., East Lansing, 1962, MS, 1964, PhD, 1967; DSc (hon.), Rensselaer Poly. Inst., Troy, NY, 2004. With Corning Glass Works, NY, 1968-76, mgr. applied physics NY, 1976-86; dir. optics and photonics Corning, Inc., 1986-91, v.p., dir. optics and photonics, 1997—2000, v.p., exec. dir. rsch., 2000—02; chief tech. officer Infotonic Tech. Ctr., 2002—04; cons. Big Flats, NY, 2004—. Bd. dirs. PCO, Inc., LA, 1985-90; bd. chmn. Opto-Electronics Inds. Develop. Assn., 1999-2002; mem. Nat. Inst. Standards and Tech. vis. com. advanced tech., 2003-06; lectr. in field. Editor: Jour. Lightwave Tech., 1989—94, co-author (5 books on optical fibers); contbr. more than 150 to profl. jours. Chmn. planning bd. Town of Corning, 1990—; mem. adv. bd. Corning Salvation Army; moderator 1st Congl. Ch., Corning, 1986—87, 1991—92; bd. dirs. ARC-Corning chpt., 1995—2007, Cmty. Found., 2000—06; chmn. troop com. Boy Scouts Am., Corning, 1968—71; pres. Civic Music Assn., Corning, 1971—75; bd. dirs. Nat. Inventors Hall of Fame Found., 1994—, pres., 2001—02; bd. dirs. Nat. Inventors Hall of Fame, 2000—06, sec., 2002—04, vice chair, 2003—. Recipient Tech. Achievement award Internat. Soc. Optical Engring., 1981, IR-100 award Indsl. Rsch., 1981, Engring. Achievement award Am. Soc. Metals, 1983, Am. Innovator award, 1995, John Tyndall award IEEE/Optical Soc. Am., 1992, Disting. Alumni award Mich. State U., 1996, Lauren Publishing, "Distinction in Photonics" award, 2002, Nat. medal of Tech., U.S. Pres., 2000, Macbeth award Greater Steuben Chpt. Am. Red Cross, 2007; inductee Nat. Innovators Hall of Fame, 1993; Paul Harris fellow Rotary Internat., 1998. Fellow IEEE, OSA, Optical Soc. Am. (bd. dirs. 1994-96), Nat. Acad. Engring., World Innovation Found.(hon.). Achievements include 36 patents in field. Avocations: skiing, music, woodworking, piano, photography. Home: 2877 Chequers Cir Big Flats NY 14814-9610 Home Phone: 607-562-3695. Personal E-mail: dkeck@stny.rr.com.

KECK, LEONHARD, retired small business owner; b. Leidrungen, Germany, Aug. 23, 1924; s. John George and Anna Keck; m. Florence M. Bartch, Apr. 6, 1947; children: Leonhard Jr., Kathleen, Gerald, Christeen. Butcher Keck Meat Market, Columbia, 1939—42, Keck-Swhippey, Mountville, Pa., 1946—51; butcher, owner, ptnr. Greenwalt and Keck Meat Market, Lancaster, Pa., 1951—66; salesman Dantro Assocs. Inc., Lancaster, 1966—85, owner, 1985—98; ret. Staff sgt. US Army, 1942—46. Decorated Purple Heart US Army, Good Conduct medal. Mem.: VFW (comdr. 1950—51). Avocations: hunting, fishing, archery.

KECK, PAUL E., JR., psychiatrist; b. Pitts., July 22, 1957; s. Paul Edgar and Shirley (Painter) K.; m. Susan Lynn McElroy; children: Timothy Daniel, Jason Samuel. AB, Dartmouth Coll., 1979; MD, Mt. Sinai Sch. Medicine, 1983. Intern internal medicine Beth Israel Med. Ctr., NYC, 1983-84; psychiat. resident McLean Hosp., Belmont, Mass., 1984-87, asst. psychiatrist, 1987-89; instr. in psychiatry Harvard Med. Sch., Boston, 1987-89, asst. prof. of psychiatry, 1989-91; assoc. prof. U. Cin. Coll. Medicine, 1991—2006, Lindner prof., 2006—, vice-chmn. rsch., 1997—2006, co-dir. biol. psyc. program, 1991—; dir. GCRC, Cin. VA Med. Ctr., 2004—06; pres., CEO, Lindner Ctr. of Hope, Mason, Ohio, 2006—. Asst. dir. Sleep Research Lab., McLean Hosp., Belmont, 1989-90. Contbr. 350 articles to profl. publs. Research grantee Nat. Inst. Arthritis Metabolism, 1982, Mass. Charitable Soc.; fellowship Tucker Found., 1983, Scottish Rite Schizophrenia Program, 1987, Stanley Found., 1994—, NIDA, 1995—, NIMH, 1994—, Am. Diabetes Assn. Fellow Soc. Biol. Psychiatry (disting.); mem. AAAS, Am. Psychiat. Assn., Collegium Internat. Psychopharmacologicum, MY Acad. Sci., Am. Coll. Physician Execs., Internat. Copernicus Scientists. Office: 1 Cin Coll Medicine Dept Psychiatry 231 Albert Sabin Way ML 559 Cincinnati OH 45267-0559 Office Phone: 513-558-8626. E-mail: paul.keck@uc.edu.

KEDES, LAURENCE HERBERT, biochemistry professor, physician, researcher; b. Hartford, Conn., July 19, 1937; s. Sammuel Ely and Rosalyn (Epstein) K.; m. Shirley Beck, June 15, 1958; children: Dean Hamilton, Maureen Jennifer, Todd Russell. Student, Wesleyan U., 1955-58; BS with distinction, Stanford U., 1961, MD, 1962. Intern Presbyn. U. Hosp., Pitts., 1962-63, asst. resident, 1963-64; rsch. assoc. lab. biochemistry Nat. Cancer Inst. Peterson, 1964-66; sr. asst. med. resident Peter Bent Brigham Hosp., Boston, 1966-67; surgeon USPHS, 1964-66; postdoctoral fellow dept. biology MIT, 1967-68; jr. assoc. in medicine and hematology assoc. Peter Bent Brigham Hosp., Boston, 1967-69; rsch. trainee in embryology Marine Biol. Lab., Woods Hole, Mass., 1969; instr. biology MIT, Boston, 1969-70; asst., assoc. then prof. medicine Stanford U., 1970-89, dir. admissions med. sch., 1978-81; William M. Keck prof. biochemistry and medicine U. So. Calif. Keck Sch. Medicine, LA, 1989—, dir. Inst. Genetic Medicine, 1989—, chair biochemistry, 1989—2002. Staff physician VA, 1970-92; vis. scientist Lab. Molecular Embryology, Naples, Italy, 1969-70, Dept. Animal Genetics, U. Edinburgh, 1970, Imperial Cancer Rsch. Fund, London, 1976-77; instr. embryology Marine Biol. Lab., Woods Hole, 1976; investigator Howard Hughes Med. Inst., 1974-82; founder, dir. IntelliCorp., Mountain View, Calif., 1980-90, chmn., 1982-86. Mem. editorial bd. Jour. Biol. Chemistry, 1982-88, Molecular and Cellular Biology, 1982-89, Jour. Applied Molecular Biology, 1982-85, Oxford Surveys on Eukaryotic Genes, 1983-94, Trends in Genetics, 1984-88; assoc. editor Jour. Molecular Evolution, 1982-90; cons. editor Circulation Rsch., 1994-99. Mem. fellowship award com. Am. Cancer Soc., 1978-81; co-principle investigator BIONET, 1984-89; mem. rsch. com. Am. Heart Assn., 1987; mem. sci. adv. bd. Muscular Dystrophy Assn., 1988-93. Fellow Med. Found. Boston, 1967-69, John Simon Guggenheim Found. fellow, 1976-77; Leukemia Soc. Am. scholar, 1969-74. Mem. Western Soc. for Clin. Rsch., Am. Soc. Clin. Investigation, Assn. Am. Psysicians, Am. Soc. Microbiology, Am. Soc. Biochemistry and Molecular Biology, Internat. Soc. Devel. Biology, Alpha Omega Alpha.

KEE, CHEA-SU, optometrist, educator; b. Johor Bahru, Malaysia, Nov. 26, 1970; s. Yien-siet Kee and Ah-mooi Ooi; m. Yuk-fung Yan, Dec. 27, 1997; children: Jocelin Qing, Alex Yin Ze. BS in Optometry (hon.), Hong Kong Poly. U., 1995; MA, CUNY, NYC, 1998; PhD, U. Houston, 2003. Rsch. asst. Hong Kong Poly. U., Hong Kong, 1995—96, CUNY, 1996—98; rsch. & tchg. asst. U. Houston, 1998—2003, rsch. assoc., 2003—05; rsch. asst. prof. New Eng. Coll. Optometry, Boston, 2005—06, asst. prof., 2006—. Recipient Outstanding Grad. Tchg. Asst. award, U. Houston, 2002; scholar, Ciba Vision, Hong Kong, 1995; William C. Ezell fellow, Am. Optometric Found., 1999—2002. Mem.: Am. Acad. Optometry (Vistakon Student Travel fellow 1999—2001), Assn. Rsch. Vision and Ophthalmology. Achievements include research in animal model for astigmatic development. Office: New England Coll Optometry 424 Beacon St Boston MA 02115 Office Phone: 617-236-6294. E-mail: cheasukee@gmail.com.

KEE, HOWARD CLARK, religion educator; b. Beverly, NJ, July 28, 1920; s. Walter Leslie and Regina (Corcoran) K.; m. Janet Burrell, Dec. 15, 1951; children: Howard Clark III, Christopher Andrew, Sarah Leslie. AB, Bryan Coll., Tenn., 1940; Th.M., Dallas Theol. Sem., 1944; postgrad., Am. Sch. Oriental Research, Jerusalem, 1949-50; PhD (Two Bros. fellow), Yale, 1951. Instr. religion and classics U. Pa., 1951-53; from asst. prof. to prof. N.T. Drew U., 1953-68; Rufus Jones prof. history of religion, chmn. dept. history of religion Bryn Mawr Coll., Pa., 1968-77; William Goodwin Aurelio prof. Biblical studies Boston U., 1977-89, chmn. grad. div. religious studies, 1977-86; sr. rsch. fellow U. Pa., 1987—. Vis. prof. religion Princeton U., 1954-55, Brown U., 1985; vis. lectr. U. of Durham, 1987, Claremont Sch. of Theology, 1991; Rsch. scholar, Miss. state U., 1992, vis. scholar, Princeton Theological Seminary, 1993; mem. archaeol. teams at Roman Jericho, 1950, Shechem, 1957, Mt. Gerizim, 1966, Pella, Jordan, 1967, Ashdod, Israel, 1968; chmn. Coun. on Grad. Studies in Religion; cons. for transls. Am. Bible Soc., 1989—. Author: Understanding the New Testament, 1957, 4th edit., 1983, 5th edit., 1992, Making Ethical Decisions, 1958, The Renewal of Hope, 1959, Jesus and God's New People, 1959, Jesus in History, 1970, 3d edit., 1995, The Origins of Christianity: Sources and Documents, 1973, The Community of the New Age, 1977, Christianity: An Historical Approach, 1979, Christian Origins in Sociological Perspective, 1980, Miracle in the Early Christian World, 1983, The New Testament in Context: Sources and Documents, 1984, Medicine, Miracle and Magic in New Testament Times, 1986, Knowing the Truth: A Sociological Approach to New Testament Interpretation, 1989, What Can We Know About Jesus?, 1990, Good News to the Ends of the Earth: The Theology of Acts, 1990, Christianity: A Social and Cultural History, 1991, 2d edit., 1998, Who Are the People of God? Early Christian Models of Community, 1995, To Every Nation Under Heaven: The Acts of the Apostles, 1997, The Beginings of Christianity: An Introduction to the New Testament, 2005; editor: Biblical Perspectives on Current Issues, 1976-83, Understanding Jesus Today, 1985—; editor Cambridge UP Annotated Study Bible, 1993, Cambridge Annotated Study Apocrypha, 1994, Cambridge Companion to the Bible, 1997, Removing Anti-Judaism From the New Testament, 1996, Removing Anti-Judaism From the Pulpit, 1998, The Evolution of the Synagogue, 1999The Beginnings of Christianity, 2005; librettist: New Land, New Covenant (Howard Hanson), 1976; contbr.: Interpreter's Dictionary of the Bible, 1962, supplement, 1976, Harper's Bible Dictionary, Dictionary of Bible and Religion, The Books of the Bible, Anchor Bible Dictionary. Bd. mgrs. Am. Bible Soc., 1956-89, chmn. transls. com., 1985-89; chmn. transls. com. United Bible Socs., 1985-89; bd. dirs. Mohawk Trail Concerts, Inc., Charlemont, Mass.; mem. adv. bd. Yale U. Inst. Sacred Music; exec. bd. Liberty Mus. Am. Assn. Theol. Schs. fellow Germany, 1960; Guggenheim fellow Israel, 1966-67; Nat. Endowment Humanities grantee Eng., 1984 Mem. Soc. Values in Higher Edn., Phila. Seminar on Christian Origins, Am. Acad. Religion, Soc. Bibl. Lit., Bibl. Theologians, Studiorum Novi Testamenti Societas, New Haven Theol. Discussion Group, Assn. for Sociology of Religion, Am. Interfaith Inst. (pres.). Presbyterian. Home: 3300 Darby Rd Haverford PA 19041-1061 *Life is a gift from the Creator. It is mediated to us through parents, family, friends, teachers. It is conveyed through love and learning, through challenge and conflict, through accomplishment and disappointment. The gift must be shared, not jealously guarded or proudly prized. By sharing life, we can approach others with candor and honesty, with joy and sympathy, with wonder and understanding. The shared gift brings gratitude and fulfillment.*

KEE, TERRY MICHAEL, lawyer; b. Kansas City, Mar. 12, 1953; s. James Jefferson and Ruth Anne (Brunton) K.; m. Jeanine Jackson, Aug. 17, 1976; children: Lucy Alice, Ruth Mildred, Johanna Grace. BA, U. Tex., Austin, 1975; JD, U. Tex., 1979. Bar: Calif. 1979, U.S. Dist. Ct. (no. dist.) Calif. 1979. Assoc. Pillsbury, Madison & Sutro, San Francisco, 1979-86, ptnr., 1987—; (Pillsbury, Madison & Sutro merged with Winthrop, Stimson, Putnam, 2001); ptnr., corp. & securities dept. Pillsbury Winthrop LLP, San Francisco, 2001—, former chair mergers & acquisitions, former chair, legal opinions com.; (Pillsbury Winthrop LLP merged with Shaw Pittman LLP, 2005); ptnr., corp. & securities dept. Pillsbury Winthrop Shaw Pittman LLP, San Francisco, 2005—. Mem.: ABA, San Francisco Bar Assn. Office: Pillsbury Winthrop Shaw Pittman LLP 50 Fremont St San Francisco CA 94105-2228 Office Phone: 415-983-1724. Office Fax: 415-983-1200. Business E-Mail: terry.kee@pillsburylaw.com.

KEEBAUGH, AARON CHRISTOPHER, music educator, historian; b. Wingfield, Ill., Aug. 23, 1978; s. Alfred Charles Jr. and Diane Louise Keebaugh; m. Cari Jo Crumrine, May 5, 2006. BA, Bridgewater Coll., Va., 2000; postgrad., U. Fla., Gainesville, 2002—. Music instr., band dir. Bishop Guilfoyle HS, Altoona, Pa., 2000—02; grad. tchg. asst. U. Fla., Gainesville, 2003—07, doctoral fellow in musicology, 2004—. Adj. instr. music Santa Fe CC, Gainesville, 2007—. Contbr. articles to profl. jours. Mem.: Coll. Music Soc., Am. Musicol. Soc. (student rep. 2005—07). Home: 1100 SW 8th Ave Apt 302 Gainesville FL 32601 Business E-Mail: ack78@ufl.edu.

KEECH, ELOWYN ANN, interior designer; b. Berrien County, Mich., Oct. 5, 1937; d. Earl Docker and Elizabeth Hall (Paullin) Stephenson; 1 child, Robert Earl Stephenson. Print designer, 1957-75; freelance interior designer, photoset and video set designer St. Joseph, Mich., 1975—; owner Fog Horn Records & Tapes; contract & resdential interior design cons., project coord., adminstr. pvt. practice, 1978—. 1st Fed. Savs. & Loan Assn., Three Oaks, Mich., 1975; interior designer Holland Ctrl. Trade Credit Union, Mich., 1978; 1st Fed. Savs. & Loan, Holland, 1978, Yonker Realty Co., 1979, People's Bank of Holland, 1979, Whirlpool Corp. Exec. Offices, 1980—, St. Joe Human Resources divsn., 1985—, Claeys Residence, 1984—, Calley Dental Office, 1985—, Sarett Nature Ctr., 1985—, Imperial Printing, 1986—, Schraders Super Market, 1986—, Dave's Garage, 1987—, Miller Residence, 1986—, Merritt Residence, Kalamazoo, 1987—88, Smith Residence, 1988, Emergency Shelter Svcs., 1991, Butzbach Residence, 1992, Merritt Residence, Del Mar, Calif., 1993—94, Fister Better Homes & Gardens Conf. Rm., 1994, Vanderboegh Residence, 1994—96; interior designer Vanderboegh Residence, 2006—07; S.W. Mich. regional Airport, 1994—, Berrien Hills Country Club, 1995—96, Butzbach Offices, 1995, Merritt Residence, Houston, 1996, Mich. Maritime Mus., 1996, St. Paul Episcopal Ch., 1996, Bacchiocchi Residence, 1996, Internat. Trade Assn. Greater Chgo., 1997, DeVries Residence, 1997, Kitchen Aid Small Appliance Display Whirlpool Tech. Ctr., 1998—99, Paullin Residence, Chgo., 1998—99, Pott, Laetz, Thomas & Hamilton Residences, 2000—01, Ft. Miami Heritage Soc. Exec. Offices, 2000, Benton Harbor-St. Joseph Herald-Palladium. Trustee Mich. Maritime Mus., 1994—97; bd. dirs., mem. steering and long-range planning coms. United Way Mich., 1980—87; bd. dirs. Blossomland United Way, 1981—86. Mem.: Internat. Interior Design Assn., Nat. Audubon Soc., Am. Rottweiler Club, Econ. Club S.W. Mich., Rotary Club (vol. chair, Ann. Rotary Track Meet S.W. Mich.). Office Phone: 269-369-4350.

KEEDY, CHRISTIAN DAVID, lawyer; b. Worcester, Mass., Jan. 9, 1945; BBA, Tulane U., 1967, JD, 1972. Bar: Fla. 1972; bd. cert. in admiralty and maritime law, Fla. Pvt. practice Christian D. Keedy, P.A., Miami, Fla., 1981—. Mem. Maritime Law Assn. US, Southeastern Admiralty Law Inst. (dir. 1982-83), The Fla. Bar (chmn. 1981-82, 03-04, admiralty law com.). Office: Christian D Keedy PA 7931 SW 59th Ave South Miami FL 33143-5513 Office Phone: 305-669-4478. E-mail: ckeedy@bellsouth.net.

KEEFE, ARTHUR THOMAS, III, non-profit fund raising executive; b. NYC, Mar. 1, 1953; s. Arthur Thomas and Marie Lorraine (Bernard) K.; m. Lorene Ann Lion, Aug. 7, 1981; children: Ryan Arthur, Garrett Thomas. BA in Econs., Yale U., 1975. Assoc. dir. The Campaign for Yale U., New Haven, 1976-79; dir. devel. Georgetown Prep., Rockville, Md., 1980-84; dir. resource devel. Greater S.E. Community Hosp., Washington, 1984-86, United Svcs. Orgn., Washington, 1987; dir. devel. Franklin Square Hosp., Balt., 1988-89, The Humane Soc. U.S., Washington, 1990-95; v.p. devel. AOPA Air Safety Found., Frederick, Md., 1995—2004. Bd. dirs., corp. sec. Nat. Catholic Cmty. Found. Named NCAA All-Am., Inter Collegiate Yacht Racing Assn. N. Am., 1973; recipient Gold Maxi, Direct Mktg. Assn. D.C., 1989. Mem. Nat. Soc. Fund Raising Execs. (cert.), The Planned Giving Study Group Washington, D.C. (pres. 1990-94), Nat. Com. on Planned Giving (bd. com. mem.). Republican. Roman Catholic. Avocations: duplicate bridge, numismatics, art collecting. Home: 9017 Willow Valley Dr Potomac MD 20854 E-mail: arthurkeefe3@aol.com.

KEEFE, CAROLYN JOAN, retired tax accountant; b. Huntington Park, Calif., Oct. 11, 1926; d. Paul Dewey and Mary Jane (Parmater) Keefe. AA, Pasadena City Coll., Calif., 1947; BA, U. So. Calif., 1950. Tax acct. Shell Oil Co., LA, 1950-71, Houston, 1971-91, ret., 1991. Advisor Midwest Mus. Am. Art, 1993—; vol. Houston Mus. Fine Arts, 1991—; vol. docent Houston Mus. Natural Sci., 1991—, Theatre Under the Stars, 1991—, Houston Pub. TV Channel 8, Houston, 1989—; donor Paul Dewey and Mary Jane Keefe scholarships. Mem. LWV, Inst. Mgmt. Accts. (emeritus life mem.), Desk and Derrick Club (bd. dir. 1994-95), Houston Alumni Club of Alpha Gamma Delta, USC Houston Alumni Club. Christian Scientist. Avocation: travel. Home: 1814 Auburn Trl Sugar Land TX 77479-6333

KEEFE, JAMES WASHBURN, educational writer, researcher, consultant; b. LA, Oct. 23, 1931; s. James E. and Leah M. (Washburn) K.; m. Jean Showalter, Dec. 6, 1980. BA maxima cum laude, St. Ambrose Coll., 1953; MusB, Mt. St. Mary's Coll., 1965, MA in Edn., 1966; EdD, U. So. Calif., LA, 1973. Cert. tchr., adminstr., Calif. Dean of studies Pius X H.S., Downey, Calif., 1962-67, prin., 1967-75; instr. U. So. Calif., 1972-75; lectr. Loyola Marymount U., LA, 1975-77, adj. prof. edn., 1977-78; coord. rsch. Nat. Assn. Secondary Sch. Prins., Reston, Va., 1978-80, dir. rsch., 1980-95. Mem. various nat. adv. bds. including Dept. of Edn. Ctr. on Orgn. and Restructuring of Schs., Nat. Study Sch. Evaluation-Evaluative Criteria Com., Sizer Coalition of Essential Schs. Author: Take Five: A Methodolgy for the Humane School, 1979, Student Learning Styles: Diagnosing and Prescribing Programs, 1979, Middle Level Principalship, 1981, 83, Student Learning Styles and Brain Behavior, 1982, High School Leaders and their Schools, 1988, 90, Instructional Leadership Handbook, 1984, 91, Learning Style Profile Handbook, 1989, The CASE-IMS School Improvement Process, 1991, Teaching for Thinking, 1992, Leadership in Middle Level Education, 1993, Instruction and the Learning Environment, 1996, Redesigning Schools for the New Century, 1997, Personalized Instruction: Changing Classroom Practice, 2000, Changing the School Learning Environment, 2004; PDK Fastback: Personalized Instruction, 2005; contbr. articles to profl. jours.; contbr. chpts. to books. Recipient Disting. Achievement award City of Downey, 1975, Award for Outstanding Ednl. Rsch. Calif. State U., Fullerton, 1992-93, Disting. Svc. award Nat. Cath. Edn. Assn., 1981. Mem. ASCD, Learning Environs. Consortium (pres., forum coord.), Nat. Assn. Secondary Sch. Prins., Nat. Cath. Honor Soc., Phi Delta Kappa. Office: JK Cons Ltd 1419 Belcastle Ct Reston VA 20194-1245 Personal E-mail: jimkeefe_j@hotmail.com.

KEEFE, MAUREEN RUTH, dean; b. Madison, Wis., Oct. 30, 1947; m. Michael Gaviglio; children: Erin, Ryan. BSN, U. Mich., 1970; MS, U. Colo., 1974, PhD, 1984, postgrad., 1985. Cert. PNP. Pub. health nurse Washtenaw County Health Dept., Ann Arbor, 1971-73; PNP Denver (Colo.) Health and Hosps., 1974-75, Univ. Hosp., Denver, 1978-85; instr. dept. psychology Univ. Colo., Denver, 1985-86; v.p. nursing The Children's Hosp., Denver, 1985—; assoc. dir. Kempe Rsch. Ctr., Denver, 1985—; asst. prof. Univ. Colo., Sch. Nursing, Denver, 1985-90, assoc. prof., 1990—; dean Coll. Nursing Med. U. S.C., Charleston, U. Utah, Salt Lake City. Cons. Emergent Tech. Corp., Boca Raton, Fla., 1985; vis. prof. Children's Hosp., Columbus, Ohio, 1990; mem. Nat. Adv. Bd. for Clin. Trials of the Preterm; mem. adv. bd. Johnson & Johnson Pediat. Inst. Co-author: A Primary Care Process Measure: The Nurse Practitioner Rating Form, 1981. Troop leader Brownies, Denver, 1983-84; bd. mem. Step Families Assn. Denver, 1984-85, pres., 1985. Recipient Book of Yr. award Am. Jour. Nursing, 1981, First award NIH/NCNR, 1987; named People to Watch, Denver Mag., 1988. Mem.: Western Inst. Nursing (exec. com. 1992—), Nat. Assn. Pediatric Nurse Assocs. and Practitioners (co-chair Internat. Yr. of the Child 1979), Sigma Theta Tau (perinatal grant selection com./Mead Johnson 1991, internat. rsch. com. 1992—, Alpha Kappa chpt. rsch. com. 1984—85, 1991—92, v.p. 1985—87, pres. 1988—90, bd. dirs. 2000—, Rsch. Excellence award 1988). Office: U Utah Coll Nursing Deans Office 10 S 2800 E Front Salt Lake City UT 84112-5880

KEEFE, RONALD D., lawyer; BA, Mich. State U., 1967; JD, Wayne State U., 1972. Bar: Mich. 1973. Ptnr. Kendricks Bordeau Adamini Chilman & Greenlee PC, Mich. Fellow: Am. Bar Found., Mich. State Bar Found.; mem.: State Bar Mich. (pres.-elect 2006—07). Office: Kendricks Bordeau Adamini Chilman & Greenlee PC 128 West Spring St Marquette MI 49855 Office Phone: 906-226-2543. Office Fax: 906-226-2819. E-mail: keefer@kendrickslaw.com.

KEEFER, JEFFREY L., chemicals executive; b. Fremont, Ohio, 1952; B in Econs., Wooster Coll., Ohio; MBA in Fin., Northwestern U. Fin. analyst titanium dioxide bus. DuPont, 1976, field sales position, 1982—85, customer svc. mgr., 1985—87, TiO2 market mgr. paper industry, 1987—89, sales mgr. Titanium Techs., 1989—93, mng. dir. Asia Pacific region for TiO2 Kuan Yin, Taiwan, 1993, dir. new ventures, 1997—99, v.p., gen. mgr. Titanium Techs., 1999—2004, group v.p. Performance Materials, 2004—06, exec. v.p., CFO, 2006—. Bd. dirs. Jr. Achievement Del. Office: DuPont 1007 Market St Wilmington DE 19898 Office Phone: 302-774-1000.*

KEEFER, LARRY KAY, medical researcher; b. Akron, Ohio, Oct. 28, 1939; s. Wesley Orville and Harriet Jane (Earhart) K.; m. Julie Ann Klestadt, June 24, 1962; children: Steven Howard, Simona Nicole. AB in Chemistry cum laude, Oberlin Coll., 1961; PhD in Organic Chemistry, U. NH, 1965. Asst. prof. oncology Chgo. Med. Sch., 1965-68; asst. prof. biochemistry U. Nebr. Med. Sch., Omaha, 1968-71; NIH spl. postdoctoral fellow Nat. Cancer Inst., Bethesda, 1971-72, sr. staff fellow, 1972-74, head analytical chemistry sect., 1974-83, chief chemistry sect. Frederick, Md., 1983—, chief lab. of comparative carcinogenesis, 1997—. Editl. adv. bd. Nitric Oxide Biology and Chemistry, 1997—. Mem. AAAS, Am. Chem. Soc., Am. Assn. Cancer Rsch. Achievements include discovery of and patents on compositions incorporating the nitric oxide-releasing diazeniumdiolate functional group, compositions useful for studying the physiological and pathophysiological effects of nitric oxide's critical bioregulatory actions; research the unique chemical properties of these compositions for a variety of possible clinical advances. Office: Nat Cancer Inst at Frederick Lab Comparative Carcinogenesis PO Box B Bldg 538 Rm 205F Frederick MD 21702-1201 Office Phone: 301-846-1467. Office Fax: 301-846-5946. E-mail: keefer@ncifcrf.gov.

KEEFFE, EMMET BRITTON, medical educator; b. San Francisco, Apr. 12, 1942; s. Emmet Britton and Corinne M. (Walsh) K.; m. Melenie M. Laskey, June 18, 1966; children: Emmet III, Brian, Meghan. BS, U. San Francisco, 1964, secondary teaching credential, 1965; MD, Creighton U., 1969. Intern Oreg. Health Sci. U., Portland, 1969-70, resident, 1970-73, fellow gastroenterology, 1973-74, asst. prof. medicine, 1979-83, assoc. prof. medicine, 1983-89, prof. med., 1989-92; fellow gastroenterology U. Calif., San Francisco, 1977-79, clin. prof. medicine, 1992—95; chief divsn. gastroenterology, hepatology Calif. Pacific Med. Ctr., San Francisco, 1992—95, med. dir. liver transplant program, 1992—95; prof. medicine, chief of hepatology, co-dir. liver transplant program Stanford Univ. Med. Ctr., 1995—. Author: Flexible Sigmoidoscopy, 1985, Handbook of Liver Disease, 1998, 2004, Atlas of Gastrointestinal Endoscopy, 1998; editor: Liver Update, 1991—94; mem. editl. bd. Hepatology, 1993—2006; mem. editl. bd.: Jour. Hepatology, 2000—07, Am. Jour. Gastroenterology, 2002—06, Ailimentary Pharmcology Therapeutics, 2003—, Liver Transplantation, 2006—; assoc. editor Liver Transplantation and Surgery, 1995—2000, Digestive and Nutrition, 1999—2004, Reviews in Gastroenterological Disorders, 2000—, sec. editor Current Opinion in Organ Transplantation, 2000—; exec. editor: GastroHep.com, 2000—; contbr. chapters to books, articles to profl. jours. Lt. comdr. USN, 1974-77. Master: ACP; fellow: Am. Gastroent. Assn., Am. Coll. Gastroenterology, Royal Coll. Physicians Ireland (hon.); mem.: AMA, Am. Bd. Internal Medicine (chair subspecialty bd. gastroenterology 2007—), Internat. Liver Cancer Assn., Found. Digestive Health and Nutrition (bd. dirs. 2004—), Am. Digestive Health Found. (bd. dirs. 1994—2001, vice chair pub. health programs 1997—2001), Am. Clin. and Climatology Assn., European Assn. Study of Liver, Western Gut Club (pres. 1991), Internat. Assn. for Study of Liver, Internat. Liver Transplantation Soc., North Pacific Soc. of Internal Medicine, Am. Fedn. Clin. Rsch., Am. Soc. Transplantation, Am. Soc. Gastrointestinal Endoscopy (sec. 1991—94, pres.-elect 1994—95, pres. 1995—96), Am. Assn. Study Liver Diseases, Am. Gastroenterologic Assn. (v.p. 2002—03, pres.-elect 2003—04, pres. 2004—05), Am. Liver Found. (bd. dirs. 1991—95). Home: 22 Weatherly Dr Mill Valley CA 94941-3272 Office: Stanford University Med Ctr 750 Welch Rd Ste 210 Palo Alto CA 94304-1509 Home Phone: 415-383-7192; Office Phone: 650-498-5691.

KEEFFE, JOHN ARTHUR, lawyer, director; b. Bklyn., Apr. 5, 1930; s. Arthur John and Mary Catherine (Daly) K.; m. Frances Elizabeth Rippetoe, July 24, 1952; children: Virginia Frances, Cynthia Louise, Amy Marie. AB, Cornell U., 1950; JD, U. Va., 1953. Bar: Va. 1953, NY 1956. Asst. US atty. so. dist. State of NY, 1955-57; assoc. Rogers, Hoge & Hills, NY, 1957-63; of counsel Havens, Wandless, Stitt & Tighe, NY, 1963-65; ptnr. Keeffe & Costikyan, NYC and Washington, 1965-74, Keeffe Bros., NYC and Washington, 1974-77; sec., mng. dir. Saud Al-Farhan Inc., NYC, 1979-80; pres., dir. J.A. Keeffe, PC, Eastchester, NY, 1981—2000. Bd. dirs., sec. The Street Theater, White Plains, NY, 1973-2002, trustee emeritus, 2002-, 1st lt. USAF, 1953-55. Mem. ABA, ATLA, NY State Bar Assn., Va. Bar Assn., Westchester County Bar Assn. (dir. 1989-90, chmn. com. on fed. courthouse plans and procedures 1994-2000), NY State Trial Lawyers Assn., Eastchester Bar Assn. (v.p. 1988-89, pres. 1989-90, bd. dirs. 1990-2000), Rotary (bd. dirs. 1991-2000, sec. 1991-92, pres.-elect 1992-93, pres. 1993-94, co-chair Eastchester Rotary Gift of Life 1993-94, co-chair dist. 7230 Gift of Life 1995-97). Republican. Congregationalist. Avocations: golf, reading. Home: 315A Heritage Hls Somers NY 10589-1716 Personal E-mail: fkeeffe@comcast.net.

KEEGAN, JAMES JOSEPH, entrepreneur; b. Phila., Sept. 6, 1947; s. George Washington and Kathryn Margaret (Eckels) K BBA in Acctg. cum laude, Tex. Christian U., 1969; MBA in Internat. Fin., U. Mich., 1970. CPA, Colo. Supervising sr. acct. KPMG, Denver, 1974-79; pvt. practice acctg. Englewood, Colo., 1979-81; pres. Trinity Securities, Englewood, 1981-83, Keegan Capital Devel., Englewood, 1983-89, Fairway Sys., Inc., Englewood, 1989—2005, Golf Converncе, Castle Rock, Colo., 2005—. CPA Small Bus. Adv. Coun., 1984-85; mem. rules and course rating coms. Colo. Golf Assn., committeeman, 1986-2002; rules ofcl. World Club Championship; mem. sectional affairs com. USGA, 1996-97, Golf Mag. panelist, 2002—; mem. Fellowship Christian Athletes. Capt. USAF, 1971-74. Mem. AICPA, Beta Gamma Sigma, Beta Alpha Psi, Delta Sigma Pi. Achievements include playing top 100 golf courses in U.S. Office Phone: 203-233-8880. Business E-Mail: jkeegan@golfconvernce.com.

KEEGAN, JANE ANN, insurance executive, consultant; b. Watertown, NY, Sept. 1, 1950; d. Richard Isidor and Kathleen (McKinley) K. BA cum laude, SUNY, Potsdam, 1972; MBA in Risk Mgmt., Golden State U., 1986. CPCU. Comml. lines mgr. Lithgow & Rayhill, San Francisco, 1977-80; risk mgmt. account coord. Dinner Levison Co., San Francisco, 1980-83; ins. cons. San Francisco, 1983-84; account mgr. Rollins Burdick Hunter, San Francisco, 1984-85; account exec. Jardine Ins. Brokers, San Francisco, 1985-86; ins. cons. San Francisco, 1986-87; ins. adminstr. Port of Oakland, 1987—, risk mgr., 1989—, mgr. accts. payable, 1996—. Vol. San Francisco Ballet vol. orgn., 1981-96, Bay Area Bus., Govt. ARC disaster conf.

steering com., 1987-88, 89, 90, 91-92; mem. Nob Hill Neighbors Assn., 1982—, City of Oakland Emergency Mgmt. Bd., 1990—. Mem. Safety Mgmt. Soc., CPCU Soc. (spl. events chairperson 1982-84, continuing profl. devel. program award 1985, 88, chair loss prevention), Calif. Assn. of Port Authorities (ins. chair 1998—), Risk and Ins. Mgr. Soc. (dep., sec. 1990—, dir. legis. 1993, dir. conf.). Democrat. Roman Catholic. Home: 17 Calafia Ct San Rafael CA 94903-2464 Office Phone: 510-627-1535. Business E-Mail: jkeegan@portoakland.com.

KEEGAN, JOHN CHARLES, former mayor, retired military officer, former state legislator; b. Tempe, Ariz., Feb. 21, 1952; s. William Edward and Lucille (Reay) K.; m. Lisa Graham, Dec. 18, 1995; children: Katherine, Mark, John II, Annie, Justin BS in Engring., Ariz. State U., 1975; MS in Geography and Urban Planning, Western Pacific U., 1990. Registered profl. engr., Az., Tex., Utah, Nev.; registered land surveyor, Ariz. Pres. Accels/Keegan Consulting Engrs., Peoria, Ariz., 1987—; mem. Ariz. Ho. Reps., Phoenix, 1991-95; mayor City of Peoria, Ariz., 1997—2007. Commr. Planning and Zoning Commn., Peoria, 1989-91; mem. criminal justice task force Am. Legis. Exch. Coun., 1991-96. Mem. selection com. Valley Leadership, Phoenix, 1988; chmn. Vision 2020 Com., Peoria, 1990-91. 1st lt. U.S. Army, 1975-79, comdr. USNR, 1988-2000. Recipient Silver Beaver award, Nat. Coun. Boy Scouts of Am., 2005. Mem. Ariz. Soc. Profl. Engrs. (pres. 1990-91, Young Engr. of Yr. award 1980, Disting. Svc. award 1991). Republican. Episcopalian. Avocations: sailing, scuba diving, flying.

KEEGAN, JOHN E., lawyer; b. Spokane, Wash., Apr. 29, 1943; BA, Gonzaga U., 1965; LLB, Harvard U., 1968. Bar: Wash. 1968, U.S. Ct. Appeals (9th cir.) 1976, U.S. Supreme Ct. Gen. counsel Dept. Housing and Urban Devel., Washington, 1968-70; instr. in bus. sch. and inst. environ. studies U. Wash., 1973-76, instr. land use and environ. law, 1976-78; now ptnr. Davis, Wright & Tremaine, Seattle. Author: (novels) Clearwater Summer, 1994, Piper, 2001, A Good Divorce, 2003. Office: Davis Wright Tremaine 2600 Century Sq 1501 4th Ave Seattle WA 98101-1688 Office Phone: 206-628-7688. Business E-Mail: johnkeegan@dwt.com.

KEEGAN, PETER W., diversified holding company executive; b. Providence, Sept. 11, 1944; s. James Francis and Lucile (Bowers) Keegan; m. Jane Louise Carpenter. AB, Brown U., 1966; MBA, Columbia U., 1970. With CBS Inc., NYC, 1970—96, dir. fin. analyst Broadcast Group divsn., 1972—74, asst. contr., records divsn., 1974—76, v.p., contr. radio divsn., 1976—83, v.p., contr., 1983—88, sr. v.p. fin., 1988—96; sr. v.p., CFO Loews Corp., NYC, 1996—. Served in US Army, 1966—68. Office: Loews Corp 667 Madison Ave Fl 7 New York NY 10021-8087 Office Phone: 212-521-2950.*

KEEGAN, ROBERT J., manufacturing executive; b. NY, July 27, 1947; m. Lynn Keegan; 2 children. BS in Math., LeMoyne Coll.; MBA in Fin., U. Rochester, 1972. With Kodak, Rochester, NY, 1972—95; gen. mgr. Kodak New Zealand, 1986—87; dir. fin. photographic products group Kodak, Rochester, NY, 1987—90; gen. mgr. Kodak Spain, 1990—91; gen. mgr. consumer imaging Kodak European Middle Ea. African Region, 1991—93; exec. v.p., global strategy officer Avery Dennison Corp., Pasadena, Calif., 1995—97; pres. Kodak Profl., 1997; corp. v.p. Kodak, Rochester, 1997—2000, pres. consumer imaging, sr. v.p., 1997—2000, exec. v.p., 2000; pres., COO Goodyear Tire & Rubber Co., 2000—03, chmn., pres., CEO, 2003—. Office: Goodyear Tire & Rubber Co 1144 E Market St Akron OH 44316*

KEEHN, ROBIN, community program specialist; b. Nov. 8, 1950; Attended, U. Calif., Santa Barbara, 1968—70; BA in Anthropology and Spl. Edn., Sonoma State U., 1972. Spl. edn. credential 1973. Learning disabilities tchr., developer K-8 grade So. Butte County Schs., Ashland, Mo., 1973—75; resource tchr., developer learning disabilities program Manila, Philippines, 1975—77; tchr. Sonoma Devel. Ctr., 1978; developer, tchr. citizenship and polit. process Santa Rosa Jr. Coll., Glen Ellen, Calif., 1978—82; county program specialist Area 2 Devel. Disabilities Bd., Chico, Calif., 1984—. Advisor non-profit orgn. People First of Eldridge, 1978—82, People First of Calif., 1990—95; organizer various People First confs., 1988—96; organizer first statewide conf. The Dream is Golden, 1996. Bd. mem. Hill Country Cmty. Health Clinic, Montgomery Creek; organizer Citizens Against Pesticide Application; vol tchr. sign lang. K-8th grade classes; bd. mem. KZFR Cmty. Radio Sta., Chico, chair. Recipient Tchr. of Yr. award, So. Boone Co. Mo., 1975—77, Lanterman People Who Make a Difference Lifetime Svc. award, Butte County Coordinating Coun.

KEEHN, SILAS, retired bank executive; b. New Rochelle, NY, June 30, 1930; s. Grant and Marjorie (Burchard) K.; m. Marcia June Lindquist, Mar. 26, 1955; children: Elisabeth Keehn Lewis, Britta Keehn Scott, Peter. AB in Econs, Hamilton Coll., Clinton, NY, 1952; MBA in Fin, Harvard U., 1957. With Mellon Bank N.A., Pitts., 1957-80, v.p., then sr. v.p., 1967-78, exec. v.p., 1978-79, vice-chmn., 1980; v.p. Mellon Nat. Corp., 1979-80, vice-chmn., 1980; chmn. bd. Pullman, Inc., Chgo., 1980; pres. Fed. Res. Bank Chgo., 1981-94; ret., 1994. Bd. dirs. Kewaunee Sci. Corp., Nat. Futures Assn. Trustee Rush U. Med. Ctr., Hamilton Coll., Clinton, N.Y. With USNR, 1953-56. Mem. Chgo. Club, Comml. Club Chgo., Econ. Club Chgo., Univ. Club, Links Club (N.Y.C.), Rolling Rock Club (Ligonier, Pa.), Indian Hill Club. Office: 707 Skokie Blvd Ste 600 Northbrook IL 60062-2841 Office Phone: 847-509-2757.

KEEHNER, MICHAEL ARTHUR MILLER, investment banking executive; b. Cedar Rapids, Iowa, Nov. 15, 1943; BS in Nuclear Physics, MIT, 1965; MBA in Fin. with high distinction, Harvard U., 1971. Registered securities rep. Engring. mgr. Gen. Dynamics Corp., Quincy, Mass., 1965-69; investment banking mgr. Kidder Peabody & Co., 1971-89, exec. mng. dir. individual investor svcs. NYC, 1991-94; chmn., dir. Kidder Peabody Internat. Corp., NYC, 1989-91; pres., chief exec. officer K P Exploration, Inc., NYC, 1982-88; mng. dir., mem. exec. com., bd. mem. Kidder Peabody Group, Inc., NYC, 1987-94; mng. ptnr. The Keehner Group, NYC, 1994—. Bd. dirs. Cross Border LLC, LDMI Telecom. Inc.; adj. prof. fin. Columbia U. Trustee Bklyn. Mus. Baker scholar Harvard U.; Loeb Rhodes fellow Harvard U. Mem. India House (N.Y.C.), Rembrandt Club (Bklyn.), Long Island Wyandanch Club (N.Y.). Address: PO Box 99 South Kent CT 06785-0099

KEEHNER, REBACCA LYNN, interior designer; b. Sacramento, Oct. 10, 1973; d. Kenneth Harvey Keehner Sr. and Carol Joy (Swan) Keehner. Student, Mills Coll., Oakland, Calif., 1991; BA, Calif. State U., Sacramento, 1999. Designer Eekistics Design Studio, Sacramento, 1999—2007, Chong Ptnrs., Sacramento, 2007. One-woman shows include Alley Cuts Gallery, 2003, exhibited in group shows at Brick Ho. Gallery, 2003. Mem. Sacramento Natural Foods Coop., PBS Pub. Broadcasting Sys. Scholar, Calif. Scholarship Assn., 1991. Mem.: Mensa. Avocations: art, guitar, violin.

KEEL, ALTON GOLD, JR., ambassador; b. Newport News, Va., Sept. 8, 1943; s. Alton Gold and Ella Clare (Kennedy) K.; 1 child, Kristen Ann; m. Lynn (Matti) K. BS in Aerospace Engring., U. Va., 1966, PhD in Engring. Physics, 1970; postdoctoral scholar, U. Calif., Berkeley, 1971. Staff Naval Surface Weapons Ctr., Silver Springs, Md., 1971-77; congl. sci. fellow Senate Armed Services Com., Washington, 1977-79, staff mem., 1977-81; asst. sec. for research, devel. and logistics USAF, Washington, 1981-82; assoc. dir., nat. sec. internat. affairs Office Mgmt. and Budget, Washington, 1982-86; exec. dir. Pres.' Commn. on Challenger Accident, Washington, 1986; acting asst. to pres. for nat. security affairs The White House, Washington, 1986; U.S. permanent rep. NATO, Brussels, 1987-89; dep. chmn. The Riggs Nat. Bank, Washington, 1989-92; pres., mng. dir. Carlyle Internat. The Carlyle Group, Washington, 1992-94; chmn. Carlyle SEAG, 1994-95; chmn., mng. dir. Atlantic Ptnrs., L.L.C., Washington, 1992—; chmn., CEO Land-5 Corp., 1999—2002; CEO, InoStor Corp., 2002—05. Chmn. F-16 fighter aircraft multinat. steering com.; nat. del., bd. dirs. Adv. Group for Aerospace R&D, 1982. Bd. dirs. Fondation pour la Promotion de la Recherche Fundamentale en Cancerologie, Belgium, 1988; mem. dean's adv. bd. U. Va., 1996-2005; trustee Engring. Sch. U. Va., 2005—. Recipient research award NRC, 1970; Nat. Congl. Sci. fellow AIAA, 1976; recipient Young Engr.-Scientist award AIAA, 1978, Air Force Exceptional Civilian Service award, 1982, NASA Group Achievement award, 1986, Disting. Alumni award U. Va., 1988. Fellow AIAA, Sigma Xi; mem. French Am. C. of C. (mem. sr. adv. group 1990-95), Belgian Am. Assn. (bd. dirs. 1990-94), Phi Eta Sigma, Tau Beta Pi. Office: Atlantic Ptnrs 2891 S River Rd Stanardsville VA 22973-2416 Office Phone: 434-990-9501. Business E-Mail: altonkeel@hughes.net.

KEELER, JAMES LEONARD, food products executive; b. Richmond, Va., Jan. 31, 1935; s. Joseph McCauley and Nora Elizabeth (Thomas) Keeler; m. Joan Sandra Barnhart, Aug. 14, 1954; children: Mark Leonard, Tracy Ann, Steven James, Gregory Wayne. BS, Bridgewater Coll., 1957; JD, U. Va., 1983. CPA Va.; bar: Va. 1983. Ptnr., acct. Hueston & Keeler, CPAs, Harrisonburg, Va., 1958-63; mng. ptnr., acct. Keeler, Phibbs & Co., CPAs, Harrisonburg, 1963-80; ptnr., atty. Wharton, Aldhizer & Weaver, Harrisonburg, 1983-88; CEO WLR Foods, Inc., Broadway, Va., 1988—2001, pres., 1990—2001, Wampler Foods, Inc., Broadway, 1997—2001. Mem. Va. Bus. Coun., 1995—2001, vice-chmn., 1999—2001; mem. Gov.'s Adv. Com. Va.'s Strategy, 1998; bd. dir. Massanutten Regional Libr., 2001—02; mem. exec. com. and trustee Bridgewater (Va.) Coll., 1974—, vice chmn. bd. trustees, 1974—91, chmn. com. bd. affairs, 1999—2003, mem. investment com., 2001—, chmn. bd. trustees, 2003—; exec. adv. coun. Coll. Bus. James Madison U., Harrisonburg, 1989—95; bd. dir. Rockingham Meml. Hosp., 1994—98, Va. Econ. Devel. Partnership, 1995—2001, Valley Va. Partnership Edn., 2000—04. Recipient Disting. Alumnus award, Bridgewater Coll., 1990, Outstanding Bus. Person award, Harrisonburg-Rockingham C. of C., 1995. Fellow: Va. Soc. CPAs (pres. 1970—71, Outstanding Mem. award); mem.: AICPA (mem. governing coun. 1969—70, 1974—75, 1976—77), ABA, Va. Bar Assn., Va. C. of C. (vice chmn. 1994—96, chmn. 1997—98, mem. exec. com., bd. dirs. 1994—98). Republican. Presbyn. Avocation: boating.

KEELER, THEODORE EDWIN, retired economics professor; b. Enid, Okla., Mar. 25, 1945; s. Clinton Clarence and Lorene Adda Keeler; m. Marjorie Ann Nathanson, Aug. 29, 1982; 1 child, Daniel C. BA, Reed Coll., 1967; S.M., MIT, 1969, PhD, 1971. Asst. prof. econs. U. Calif.-Berkeley, 1971-77, assoc. prof., 1977-83, prof., 1983—2006; prof. emeritus econs., 2006—. Key faculty Robert Wood Johnson Postdoctoral Fellows Program, 1993-01. Author: Railroads, Freight, and Public Policy, 1983; co-author: Regulating The Automobile, 1986; also articles; editor: Research in Transportation Economics, vol. I, 1983, vol. II, 1985. Grantee NSF, 1973-75, 80-82, dept. transp. program, 1988-90, 93-94, NIH, 1990-91, Nat. Inst. on Aging, 1995-96; prin. investigator Sloan Found., 1975-80, Robert Wood Johnson Found., 1996-99; sr. fellow, vis. scholar Brookings Instn., Washington, 1980-82; co-prin. investigator Tobacco Tax Project Calif. Tobacco-Related Disease Fund, 1990-94, 99-2000 Democrat. Office: U Calif Dept Econs Berkeley CA 94720-3880

KEELER, WILLIAM CONRAD, III, curator, librarian, archivist; b. Rochester, NY; s. William Conrad Jr. and Alice Prosonic Keeler; m. Caroline Van Brunt Beck, June 26, 1976; children: James William, Anna Jane. BA in Sociology, Fredonia State U., NY, 1974; MA in Libr. sci., U. Buffalo, 2000. Archivist, libr., curator Perinton Hist. Soc., Fairport, NY, 1989—; curator, libr. Landmark Soc. of Western N.Y., Rochester, 1999—; libr., archivist Rochester Hist. Soc., 2002—. Mem. Ecumenical and Interfaith Archives Mgmt. Team, Rochester, 2003—. Author, editor: Perinton, Fairport and the Erie Canal, 2001, Perinton and Fairport in the 20th Century, 2004; editor: (newsletter) Perinton Historigram, 2001—. Mem.: Assn. State and Local History, Soc. Am. Archivists, Rochester Regional Libr. Coun. (local history com. 1999—, coll. archives com. 2003—). Democrat. Roman Catholic. Avocations: woodworking, growing antique apples. Office: Landmark Soc Western NY 133 S Fitzhugh St Rochester NY 14608

KEELER, WILLIAM HENRY CARDINAL, retired cardinal; b. San Antonio, Mar. 4, 1931; s. Thomas. Love and Margaret T. (Conway) Keeler. BA, St. Charles Borromeo Sem., 1952; STL, Pontifical Gregorian U., Rome, 1956, JCD, 1961; DD (hon.), Lebanon Valley Coll., 1984, Gettysburg Coll., 1986, Susquehanna U., 1989; LHD (hon.), Mt. St. Mary's Coll., 1985; LLD (hon.), Gannon U., 1993; LHD (hon.), Loyola Coll., 1995, Shippensburg State U., 1995; DD (hon.), St. Mary's U., Winona, Minn., 1995, Elizabeth Coll., 1996, Western Md. Coll., 1996, St. Vincent Sem., 1996, Coll. of Notre Dame of Md., 1997, U. Notre Dame, 1998, Ateneo de Manila U., 1998, Sacred Heart U., 2000, Cath. U., Lublin, Poland, 2000. Ordained priest Roman Catholic Ch., 1955, consecrated bishop, 1979. Asst. pastor Our Lady of Good Counsel Ch., Marysville, Pa., 1956—58; sec. diocesan tribunal Diocese of Harrisburg, Pa., 1956—58, defender of the bond, 1961—66, vice-chancellor, 1965—69, chancellor, 1969—79, aux. bishop and vicar gen., 1979—83, bishop of Harrisburg, 1984—89; archbishop of Balt., 1989—2007; elevated to Cardinal Roman Cath. Church, 1994—; chmn. Md. Cath. Conf., 1989—. Newspaper publ. The Cath. Rev.; co-chmn. Pa. Conf. Inter-Ch. Coop., 1981—89; pres. Pa. Cath. Conf., 1983—89; chmn. com. on ecumenical and inter-religious affairs Nat. Conf. Cath. Bishops, 1984—87, mem., 1984—, sec., 1988—89, Episcopal moderator Cath.-Jewish rels., 1988—92, 1995—, v.p., 1989—92, pres., 1992—95; chmn. World Youth Day Celebration, Denver, 1993; cons. Com. Comm., 1995—; past pastor Marysville Parish; chmn. Com. Pro-Life Activities, 1998—2001; past titular bishop Ulcinium (Dulcigno); mem. Internat. Joint Com. for Cath.-Orthodox Theol. Dialogue, 1986—, Internat. Liaison Com. Caths. and Jews, 1987—, Synod of Bishops for Africa, 1994, World Synod of Bishops for the Consecrated Life, 1994, Synod of Bishops for Am., 1996; sec., spl. advisor 2d Vatican Coun., 1962—65; staff Coun. Digest, 1963—65; apptd. mem. Coun. for Assembly of Synod Bishops, 1997—. Active Black and Native Am. Missions Bd.; exec. bd. Keystone Area coun. Boy Scouts Am., 1979—89; trustee Cath. U. Am.; chancellor, chmn. bd. trustees St. Mary's Sem. and Univ., 1989—; chancellor Mt. St. Mary's Sem., 1989—; vice-chair North Am. Coll. Bd. Govs., 1998—; trustee Basilica of Nat. Shrine of Immaculate Conception, Washington, 1989—; active Interreligious Forum Greater Harrisburg, 1968—89; Pontifical coun. Promoting Christian Unity, 1994—; active Congregation for the Oriental Chs., 1994—; chmn. bd. trustees Associated Cath. Charities, 1989—, Basilica of Nat. Shrine of Assumption of the Blessed Virgin Mary, 1989—; v.p. Cath. Near East Welfare Assn. Named papal chamberlain, Pope Paul VI, 1965, prelate of honor, 1970, Marylander of Yr., Md. Colonial Soc., 1986, The Balt. Sun, 1994, Media Person of Yr., Md. Press Assn., 1994; recipient Gold medal, Pope John XXIII, 1961, John Baum Humanitarian award, Dauphin County unit Am. Cancer Soc., 1984, Americanism award, Anti-Defamation League, 1985, De Tocqueville Soc. award, 1988, Nat. award, Boy Scouts of Am., 1990, Disting. Citizen award, 1998, Weil medal, Jewish Chataqua Soc., 1993, Salvation Army award, 1995, Shaw award, Rotary Internat., 1995, Mahmoud Abu Sand Excellence award, Am. Muslim Coun., 1995, Nostra Aetate award, Inst. Christian Jewish Understanding, 1997, Silver St. George medal, Nat. Cath. Com. Scouting, 1998, Lifetime Achievement award, Shaare Zedek Med. Ctr., Jerusalem, 1999, Disting. Citizens award, Balt. coun. Boy Scouts Am., 1999. Mem.: Cath. Extension Soc. Govs., Am. Cath. Hist. Soc., Canon Law Soc. Am. Roman Catholic.

KEELEY, EDMUND LEROY, literature educator, writer, translator; b. Damascus, Syria, Feb. 5, 1928; came to U.S., 1931; s. James Hugh and Mathilde (Vossler) K.; m. Mary Stathatos-Kyris, Mar. 18, 1951. BA, Princeton U., 1949; DPhil, Oxford U., Eng., 1952; PhD (hon.), Athens U., 1994; LHD (hon.), Richard Stockton Coll., NJ, 2006. Fulbright tchr. English Am. Farm Sch., Salonika, Greece, 1949-50; Woodrow Wilson fellow, 1950-51; instr. English Brown U., 1952-53; Fulbright lectr. Salonika U., 1953-54; instr. English Princeton (N.J.) U., 1954-57, asst. prof., 1957-63, assoc. prof., 1963-70, prof. English and creative writing, 1970-92, Charles Barnwell Straut Class of 1923 prof. English, 1992-94; Straut prof. emeritus, 1994—; prof. creative writing and English emeritus Princeton (N.J.) U., 1994—, co-chmn. program in comparative lit., 1964-65, dir. creative arts program, 1966-71, dir. program creative writing and theatre, 1971-73, dir. creative writing program, 1974-81, mem. Hellenic studies com., 1979-94, chmn., 1985-94, dir. Hellenic studies program, 1985-94. Lectr. dept. Byzantine and Modern Greek Oxford (Eng.) U., 1960; vis. lectr. Writers Workshop, U. Iowa, 1962-63, U. of the Aegean, 1988; vis. prof. New Sch. Social Rsch., 1980, Sch. Arts Columbia U., 1981; writer-in-residence Knox Coll., spring 1963; Fulbright lectr. Athens U., 1985, U. Thessaloniki, 1986; vis. rsch. fellow U. Crete, Rethymnon, 1986; Fulbright rsch. fellow Athens U., 1987; sr. assoc. mem. St. Antony's Coll., Oxford, 1996; vis. prof., King's Coll., London U., 1996. Author: The Libation, 1958, (with Philip Sherrard) Six Poets of Modern Greece, 1960, George Seferis: Collected Poems, 1924-1955, 1967, C.P. Cavafy: Collected Poems, 1975, 92, Angelos Sikelianos: Selected Poems, 1979, 96, George Seferis: Collected Poems, 1979, 81, 95, The Dark Crystal, Voices of Modern Greece, 1981, Odysseus Elytis: Selected Poems, 1981, A Greek Quintet, 1992, The Gold-Hatted Lover, 1961, (with Mary Keeley) The Plant, The Well, The Angel (V. Vassilikos), 1964, The Impostor, 1970, (with George Savidis) C.P. Cavafy: Passions and Ancient Days, 1972, Odysseus Elytis: The Axion Esti, 1974, Voyage to a Dark Island, 1972, Cavafy's Alexandria, 1976, 1995, Ritsos in Parentheses, 1979, A Conversation with Seferis, 1982, Modern Greek Poetry: Voice and Myth, 1982, A Wilderness Called Peace, 1985, Yannis Ritsos, Exile and Return: Selected Poems, 1967-74, 1985, The Salonika Bay Murder: Cold War Politics and The Polk Affair, 1989, Yannis Ritsos: Repetitions, Testimonies, Parentheses, 1991, School for Pagan Lovers, 1993, George Seferis and Edmund Keeley: Correspondence, 1951-1971, 1997, Albanian Journal: The Road to Elbasan, 1997, Inventing Paradise: the Greek Journey, 1937-47, 1999, 2d edit., 2002, On Translation: Reflections and Conversations, 2000, Some Wine for Remembrance, 2001, Borderlines: A Memoir, 2005; editor: (with Peter Bien) Modern Greek Writers, 1972, (with Cone and Frank) The Legacy of R.P. Blackmur: Essays, Memoirs, Texts, 1987, The Essential Cavafy, 1995, (with Bien, Constantine, and Van Dyck) A Century of Greek Poetry: 1900-2000, 2004; bd. editl. direction: Princeton Alumni Weekly, 1964-77; adv. bd. Princeton Essays in the Arts, 1974-78; editl. bd. Byzantine and Modern Greek Studies, 1974-83, Translation Rev., 1978—, Jour. Modern Greek Studies, 1983-91; adv. editor Delos, 1988—; mem. Gennadius Libr. Bd. Trustees, 1995—. Scholarship fund com. Am. Farm Sch., Salonika, Greece, 1955-60, trustee, 1978—; chmn. McCarter Theatre Com., 1969, trustee, 1983-86; nat. bd. Translation Ctr., Columbia, 1975-77, governing bd., 1977-94; translation jury Nat. Book Awards, 1977; bd. dirs. internat. program Aegean U., 1989-90; trustee Internat. PEN Found., 2000-06, Coll. Yr. in Athens 2001—. With USNR, 1945-46; with USAF, 1953-56. Jr. fellow Coun. Humanities, 1956-57, Rome prize fellow Am. Acad. Arts and Letters, 1959-60, Guggenheim fellow, 1959-60, 73, McCosh faculty fellow, 1969-70, Ingram Merrill Found. fellow, 1977-78, resident fellow Va. Ctr. for Creative Arts, 1983, 84, 86, 90, NEA fellow, 1981, 88-89; Rockefeller Found. scholar Bellagio Study Ctr., Italy, 1982, 89; vis. fellow Inst. for the Humanities, U. Mich., 1994; NEH grantee, 1977-78, 83; recipient Columbia Transl. Ctr.-PEN award, 1975, Harold Morton Landon Transl. award Acad. Am. Poets, 1980, judge, 92, Howard T. Behrman award for Disting. Achievement in the Humanities, 1982, PEN/NEA fiction syndicate award, 1983, Pushcart Prize Anthology award, 1984, first European Prize for Transl. of Poetry, 1987, Acad. award in lit. Am. Acad. Arts and Letters, 1999, Ralph Manheim medal for translation PEN, 2000, Criticos prize London Hellenic Soc., 2000, Trustees' Annual award Gennadius Libr., 2003, Phiddipides award Hellenic Pub. Radio, 2004; comdr. Order of the Phoenix, Greece, 2002. Fellow Am. Acad. Arts and Scis.; mem. Authors Guild, Soc. Fellows Am. Acad. Rome (exec. com. 1975-77, 83-87), Am. Lit. Translators Assn. (exec. bd. 1983—), PEN (Am. Ctr. membership com. 1978-83, program com. 1979-82, exec. bd. 1980-96, del. internat. congress 1987, 91-93, 95-2000, v.p. 1989-91, pres. 1991-93, bd. trustees 1996-2001), Modern Greek Studies Assn. (pres. 1969-73, 80-82, exec. bd. 1995-98), Poetry Soc. Am. (v.p. 1977-78, 81-83), Acad. Athens (corr.), Hellenic Authors' Soc. (hon.), Phi Beta Kappa. Home: 140 Littlebrook Rd Princeton NJ 08540-4041 Also: 17 Loukianou St 10675 Athens Greece Business E-Mail: keeley@princeton.edu.

KEELEY, IRENE PATRICIA MURPHY, federal judge; b. 1944; BA, Coll. Notre Dame, 1965; MA, W.Va. U., 1977, JD, 1980. Bar: W. Va., 1980. Atty. Steptoe & Johnson, Clarksburg, W.Va., 1980-92; dist. judge U.S. Dist. Ct. (no. dist.), W. Va., 1992—. Adj. prof. law W.Va. U., 1990-91; bd. dirs. W.Va. U. Alumni Assn., 1995—, 1st v.p., 1997-98; mem. bd. advisors W.Va. U. Vis. com. W.Va. U. Coll. Law, 1987-91, 94-98; chmn. adv. bd. W.Va. U., 1997-98. Mem. ABA, Nat. Conf. Fed. Trial Judges (exec. com. 1996—,), W.Va. State Bar, W.Va. Bar Assn., Harrison County Bar Assn., Clarksburg Country Club, Oral Lake Fishing Club, Immaculate Conception Roman Cath. Ch. Office: US Courthouse PO Box 2808 500 W Pike St Rm 202 Clarksburg WV 26302-2808 Office Phone: 304-624-5850. Office Fax: 304-622-1928.

KEELEY, ROBERT VOSSLER, retired academic administrator, ambassador; b. Beirut, Sept. 4, 1929; s. James Hugh and Mathilde Julia (Vossler) K.; m. Louise Schoonmaker, June 23, 1951; children: Michal M., Christopher J. AB, Princeton U., 1951, postgrad., 1951-53; postgrad. (Princeton fellow in pub. affairs), 1970-71; postgrad. (Nat. Inst. Pub. Affairs fellow), Stanford U., 1965-66. With Fgn. Service, Dept. State, Washington, 1956-89; officer in charge Congo (Leopoldville) external affairs Washington, 1963-64; officer-in-charge Congo (Brazzaville), Rwanda and Burundi affairs, 1964-65; polit. officer Athens Greece, 1966-70; detailed Woodrow Wilson fellow Princeton U., 1970; dep. chief mission Kampala, Uganda, 1971-73; alt. dir. E. African affairs Washington, 1974; dep. chief mission Phnom Penh, Khmer Republic, 1974-75; dep. dir. Interagency Task Force for Indochina Refugees, 1975-76; ambassador Mauritius, 1976-78; dep. asst. sec. for African Affairs Dept. State, Washington, 1978-80; ambassador to Zimbabwe, 1980-84; sr. fellow Ctr. for Study Fgn. Affairs, Fgn. Service Inst., Washington, 1984-85; ambassador to Greece, 1985-89. Pres. Middle East Inst., Washington, 1990-95; writer, lectr., cons. Pub. Five and Ten Press, 1995—. Lt. (j.g.) USCGR, 1953-55. Mem. Am. Fgn. Svc. Assn., Washington Inst. Fgn. Affairs, Am. Acad. Diplomacy, Cosmos Club. Home: 3814 Livingston St NW Washington DC 20015-2803

KEELING, JOE KEITH, religious studies educator, retired dean; b. Muskogee, Okla., Apr. 21, 1936; s. William Lytle and Anna Madge (Watts) Keeling; m. Marjorie Ann Brotherton, 1957; children: Kara Kay, William Kent. BA in History, Northeastern State U., 1958; BD in Theology, So. Meth. U., 1962; MA in Theology, U. Chgo., 1967, PhD, 1974. Ordained to ministry United Meth. Ch., 1962. Dir. orientation, acad. advisor U. Chgo., 1964-68; asst. prof. religion Augustana Coll., Sioux Falls, SD, 1968-72; from asst. to assoc. prof. philosophy and religion Rockford (Ill.) Coll.,

1972-86, dean of spl. acad. programming, assoc. dean of coll., 1981-86; adj. assoc. prof. dept. medicine U. Ill. Coll of Medicine at Rockford, 1984-86; provost, dean, prof. religion and philosophy Baker U., Baldwin City, Kans., 1986-96; v.p., dean Ctrl. Meth. U., Fayette, Mo., 1996—2002, prof. emeritus philosophy and religion, 2002—. Mem. bd. ordained ministry Kans. Eastern Conf. United Meth. Ch., 1987—96; cons., evaluator, mem. accreditation rev. coun. Higher Learning Commn., North Ctrl. Assn. Colls. and Schs.; cons., evaluator, mem. accreditation rev. coun. Am. Conf. Acad. Deans, Midwest Bioethics Ctr.; author, lectr. in field. Mem. Kansas City Regional Coun. Higher Edn., 1986—94; mem. instl. rev. com. Swedish-Am. Hosp., Rockford, 1981—86. Mem.: AAUP (Ill. state coun. mem. 1979—81), Archeol. Inst. Am. (bd. dirs. Rockford chpt. 1984—86), Am. Acad. Religions (v.p. Midwest region 1981—82, pres. 1982—83), Rockford C. of C. (bd. dirs. 1983—86), Fayette Round Table Club (pres. 2005—06), Rotary (pres. 2006—07). Democrat. Avocations: fishing, camping, canoeing. Home: PO Box 429 878 Highway 5 And 240 Fayette MO 65248-9509 Office: Ctrl Meth U Stedman 313 411 Central Methodist Sq Fayette MO 65248-1129 Home Phone: 660-248-2692; Office Phone: 660-248-6276. Business E-Mail: kkeeling@centralmethodist.edu.

KEELING, J(OHN) MICHAEL, lawyer, trade association executive; b. Kilgore, Tex., Feb. 24, 1947; s. Frank Marion and Eva Mae (Buse) K.; m. Michaela Eleanora Halik, Aug. 2, 1969; children: Alexandra Halik, J. Michael Jr. BA, Yale U., 1969; JD, U. Tex., 1971. Bar: Tex. 1972, DC 1982. Rsch. dir. Tex. Legislature Interim Com. on Ad Valorem Taxation, Austin, 1971; rsch. dir. gubernatorial gov. campaign Frances T. Farenthold, Austin, 1972; legis. dir. office congressman J.J. Pickle 10th Dist. Tex., Wash., 1972-73; chief staff office Congressman J.J. Pickle, Washington, 1973—81; prin. David P. Stang, P.C., Washington, 1981-88; counsel Zuckert, Scoutt & Rasenberger, Washington, 1988-91; gen. counsel Employee Stock Ownership Plan Assn., Washington, 1984-91, pres., 1991—. Pub. (mag.) The ESOP Report, 1991—, (newsletter), 1991—. Recipient Disting. Svc. award Small Bus. Coun. Am., 1993. Mem. ABA, Nat. Assn. Royalty Owners (life), Am. Soc. Assn. Execs. (cert. Assn. Exec.). Democrat. Baptist. Avocation: civil war history. Business E-Mail: michael@esopassociation.org.

KEELING, LARRY DALE, journalist; b. Anderson County, Ky., May 5, 1947; s. Elmer Pascal and Ida Elizabeth (Gregory) K.; m. Cynthia Maria Taylor, Nov. 28, 1987 (div. Feb. 2001); m. Dorothy Elizabeth Cayce Wilson, Sept. 18, 2002. BA, U. Ky., 1969. Reporter Henry County Jour., Bassett, Va., 1972, Martinsville (Va.) Bull., 1972-74, Bradenton (Fla.) Herald, 1974-75, Lexington (Ky.) Herald, 1975-79; editl. writer Lexington Herald-Leader, 1979—. Columnist: Lexington Herald Leader, 2005—; contbr. articles to local newspapers. 1st lt. USAF, 1969-72, Taiwan. Recipient Sigma Delta Chi award for editl. writing, 1993, Nat. Headliner award for editl. writing, 1994, Green Eyeshade award for editl. writing, 1995, 97, spl. citation for opinion Nat. Awards for Edn. Reporting, 1997; fellow Knight Ctr. for Specialized Journalism, 1997. Mem. Soc. Profl. Journalists (Bluegrass chpt.), Nat. Conf. Editorial Writers. Office: Lexington Herald-Leader 100 Midland Ave Lexington KY 40508-1999

KEEN, CONSTANTINE, retired manufacturing executive; b. NYC, Jan. 1, 1925; s. Andrew and Sophie (Findani) K.; m. Kally Carajikis, Sept. 23, 1951; children: Katherine, Andrew. BA, NYU, 1952. Asst. treas. Sandz Indsl. Corp., NYC, 1951-55; with Fedders Corp., Edison, NJ, 1955—, asst. credit mgr., 1955-57, credit mgr., 1957-60, dir. credit, 1960-68, v.p., dir. credit, 1968-75, v.p., dir. distbr. relations, 1975-77, v.p., treas., 1980-87, v.p. internat., 1984-86; pres. Fedders Internat. Corp., 1987-93, dir., 1996—2004. With USAAF, 1942-45. Decorated D.F.C., Air medal. Mem.: Ahepa, Masons. Greek Orthodox.

KEEN, RACHEL, psychology professor; b. Burkesville, Ky., Oct. 5, 1937; d. James Em and Regina Elizabeth (Simpson) Keen; m. Charles E. Clifton, Aug. 20, 1965 (div. 2002); children: Ramona Clifton, Catherine Clifton. BA, Berea Coll., Ky., 1959; MA, U. Minn., 1960, PhD, 1963. Fellow U. Wis., Madison, 1963-65; rsch. assoc. U. Iowa, Iowa City, 1966-68; from asst. prof. to assoc. prof. U. Mass., Amherst, 1968-76, prof., 1976—2007, U. Va., Charlottesville, 2007—. Vis. prof. Stanford U., Palo Alto, Calif., 1975—76, U. Sussex, Brighton, England, 1981—82, U. Cambridge, England, 1989—90, Harvard U., 2002—04; mem. rsch. rev. com. NIMH, 1983—87; mem. human devel. study sect. NIH, 1990—94. Named Disting. Alumna, Berea Coll., 1994; recipient Rsch. Scientist award, NIMH, 1981—2001, Disting. Faculty award, U. Mass., 1988, Merit award, NICHD, 1999—, Disting. Sci. Contbn. award, Soc. Rsch. Child Devel., 2005; grantee, NIMH, NIH, NSF, 1968—; NIMH fellow, U. Minn., 1961—63. Fellow: AAAS, APA, Am. Acad. Arts and Scis., Acoustical Soc. Am.; mem.: Internat. Soc. Infant Studies (pres. 1998—2000), Soc. Psychophysiol. Rsch. (assoc. editor jour. 1972—75, bd. dirs. 1975—78), Fedn. Behavioral, Psychol. and Cognitive Scis. (sec. 1987—90), Soc. Rsch. Child Devel. (assoc. editor jour. 1977—79, sec. 1979—85, editor Monographs 1993—99). Democrat. Congregationalist. Avocations: playing piano, reading. Office: U Va Dept Psychology PO Box 400400 Charlottesville VA 22904 Office Phone: 413-243-4008.

KEENAN, ANTHONY LEE, trucking executive; b. Greenwood, SC, Mar. 18, 1949; s. Arthur Lee and Betty (Hart) K.; m. Cheryl Toney, Dec. 31, 1985; children: Andrew Lee, Anthony LeBrett, Aric Lane. BA, W.Ga. Coll., 1973; postgrad., Woodrow Wilson Coll. Law, 1975-79. Pres. Keenan, Inc., Decatur, Ga., 1975—; v.p. All Day Leasing Co., Decatur, 1977—; pres. United Trucker's Svcs., Conyers, Ga., 1978—; exec. dir. Ind. Trucker's United Co., Conley, Ga., 1979-80; pres. Southeastern Gen. Agy., Inc., 1983—; CEO Getaway Travel, 1996—. Pres. Am. Risk Reduction, Inc.; CEO, Am. Commerce and Shipping Assn., 1991-; mem. adv. bd. Rockdale Nat. Bank. Mem. White House Task Force To Develop Motor Carrier Act of 1980, 1979-80; com. chmn. Am. Mem. Profl. Truck Svcs. Assn., pres. 1987-89, chmn. bd. 1990; com. chmn. 354 Cub Scouts Am. Mem.: Ga. Surplus Lines Assn. (com. chmn. 1982—), Assn. Transp. Practitioners (com. chmn. 1992—), Aircraft Owners and Pilots Assn. (com. chmn.). Office Phone: 770-922-6200. E-mail: acsa@utsinfo.com.

KEENAN, BARBARA BYRD, professional society administrator; b. Martinsburg, W.Va., Aug. 31, 1952; d. James Leonard and Elizabeth (Somerfield) Byrd; m. Terrence James; 1 child, Marjorie Lynn. BS, Old Dominion U., 1973, MS, 1975; postgrad., U. Maryland, 1976. Cert. assn. exec. Instr. Old Dominion U., Norfolk, Va., 1972-75; asst. prof. U. Maryland, Balt., 1975-76; assoc. dir. Am. Dental Hygienists Assn., Chgo., 1976-79; dir. edn. Am. Coll. Preventive Medicine, Washington, 1979-81; dir. profl. affairs Tex. Pharm. Assn., Austin, 1981-83; dir. edn. and research Tex. Med. Assn., Austin, 1983-86; exec. v.p. Internat. Assn. Hospitality Accts., Austin, 1986-90; pres. Community Assn. Inst., Alexandria, Va., 1990—2002; exec. v.p. Inst. Food Technologists, Chgo., 2003—. Chair Assns. Advance Am. Com., 1994—; chair Internat. Food Info. Svc., 2003—; bd. mem. Partnership for Food Safety Edn., 2006—. Mem. editl. bd.: Jour. Assn. Leadership, 2003—, vice chmn.:, 2005—. Bd. dirs. Nat. Bd. Cardiopulmonary Credentialing, Gaitersburg, N.D., 1981-82, mem. exec. com. 1982; bd. dirs. South Tex. Arthritis Found., San Antonio, 1987-89, Capital Area Arthritis Found., Austin, 1986-89; founding chmn. Travis County Adult Literacy Coun., Austin, 1984-90, chmn. emeritus 1990—; bd. dirs. Am. Hotel and Motel Assn. Research Found., 1988-90. Recipient award Internat. Assn. Bus. Communicators, 1988; named one of Outstanding Young Women Am., 1981, Top 10 Bus. Women of Yr., Am. Bus. Women's Assn., 1986, Disting. Alumni award Old Dominion U., 1999; inaugural recipient Barbara Bird Keenan award Nat. Bd. for Cert. of Comty. Assn. Mgrs. Fellow Am. Soc. Assn. Execs. (charter, vice chmn. 1991-92, planning com. 1985-88, 91-92, chair Assn. Advance Am. com. 1994, bd. dirs. 1985-86, 88—, chmn. ednl. sect. 1985-86, chmn. task force on social responsibility 1989—, chair fellows 1989-90, chair univ. com. 2002-, Excellence award 1985, 88, 94, CAE commr. 1991-93, sec.-treas. 1993-94, gov. task force 1992-93, chair rsch. com. 1996-97, Mgmt. Achievement award 1983, Key award 1996, award of excellence in edn. 1997); mem. Town Lake Bus. Women's Assn. (Woman of Yr. 1986), Tex. Soc. Assn. Execs. (com. chair 1981—), Greater Washington Soc. Assn. Execs. (CAE cert. com., instr. and tutor 1991-92, cmty. svc. com. 1996-97, bd. dirs. 1997—, chair 2001-2002, Monument award in edn. 1992), Leadership Austin, Leadership Tex. (bd. dirs., tng. group 1987—), Internat. Assn. Hosp. Accts. (hon. 1990), William Smith Assn. (mem. rsch. coun. 2003—), U.S. C. of C. (mem. Com. of 100). Home and Office: 1322 Isabella St Evanston IL 60201-1623 Office: Inst Food Technologists 525 W Van Buren St Chicago IL 60607 Office Phone: 312-782-8424. E-mail: bbkeenan@ift.org.

KEENAN, BARBARA MILANO, state supreme court justice; b. Vienna, 1950; BA, Cornell U., 1971; JD, George Wash. U., 1974; LLM, U. Va., 1992. Asst. commonwealth atty., Fairfax County, Va., 1974—76; pvt. law practice, 1976—80; judge Gen. Dist. Ct., Fairfax County, 1980-82, Circuit Ct., Fairfax County, 1982-85, Ct. Appeals, Va., 1985-91; assoc. justice Va. Supreme Court, Richmond, 1991—. Recipient Am. Jurisprudence award, Fairfax Bar Assn., 1995. Office: Va Supreme Ct PO Box 1315 Richmond VA 23218-1315*

KEENAN, JAMES GEORGE, classics educator; b. NYC, Jan. 19, 1944; s. George F. and Cecilia Anna (Schmidt) K.; m. Laurie Haight; children: James, Kathleen, Kenneth, Mary, Lisa, Brian, Laura. AB, Holy Cross Coll., 1965; MA, Yale U., 1966, PhD, 1968. Asst. prof. Classics U. Calif., Berkeley, 1968-73; assoc. to full prof. Classics Loyola U. of Chgo., 1973—, chmn. classics, 1978-84, acting chmn., 1987-88. Cons. Petra Scrolls Conservation Project, 1995. Co-editor: Greek Papyri: The Tebtunis Papyri, vol. IV, 1976. Fellow Nat. Endowment for Humanities, 1973-74; travel grantee Am. Council Learned Socs., 1974, 83, 86; grant-in-aid Am. Philos. Soc., 1987. Mem. Am. Philol. Assn., Am. Soc. Papyrologists (pres. 1989-93), Chgo. Classical Club (pres. 1999-2001), Classical Assn. Midwest and South, Assn. Internat. des Papyrologues (mem. com. 1995-2004), Egypt Exploration Soc., Internat. Soc. Arabic Papyrology. Roman Catholic. Office: Loyola U Chgo Dept Classical Studies 6525 N Sheridan Rd Chicago IL 60626-5344 Home Phone: 773-761-9440; Office Phone: 773-508-3665. Business E-Mail: jkeenan@luc.edu.

KEENAN, JOHN FONTAINE, federal judge; b. NYC, Nov. 23, 1929; s. John Joseph and Veronica (Fontaine) K.; m. Diane R. Nicholson, Oct. 6, 1956; 1 child, Marie Patricia BBA, Manhattan Coll., NYC, 1951; LLD (hon.), Manhattan Coll., 1989; LLB, Fordham U., 1954; LLD (hon.), Mt. St. Vincent Coll., 1989. Bar: N.Y. 1954, U.S. Dist. Ct. (so. dist.) N.Y. 1983. From asst. dist. atty. to chief asst. dist. atty. N.Y. County Dist. Atty.'s Office, 1956-76; spl. prosecutor, dep. atty. gen. City of N.Y., 1976-79; chmn. bd., pres. N.Y.C. Off-Track Betting Corp., 1979-82; criminal justice coord. City of N.Y., 1982-83; judge U.S. Dist. Ct. So. Dist. N.Y., NYC, 1983—; chief asst. dist. atty. Queens County Dist. Atty.'s Office, NY, 1973. Adj. prof. John Jay Coll. Criminal Justice, N.Y.C., 1979-83, Fordham U. Sch. Law, N.Y.C., 1992, 93; mem. Fgn. Intelligence Svc. Ct., 1994-2001, Judicial Panel on Multi-Dist. Litigation, 1998-2006. Contbr. articles to law jours. Chmn. Daytop Village, Inc., NYC, 1981-83. With security agy. and mil. intelligence US Army, 1954—56. Recipient Frank S. Hogan award Citizens Com. Control of Crime in NY, 1975, Emory R. Buckner award Federal Bar Coun., 1993, cert. recognition Patrolmen's Benevolent Assn., 1976, 1st Ann. Hogan-Morgenthau Assocs. award NY County Dist. Atty.'s Office, 1976, Medal of Achievement NY County Lawyers Assn., 1992, Excellence award NY State Bar Assn., 1978, Outstanding Prosecution Svcs. award, 1978, award NY Criminal Bar Assn., 1979, Disting. Faculty award Nat. Coll. Dist. Attys., 1978, Louis J. Lefkowitz award Fordham U. Law Sch. Urban Law Jour., 1983, Charles Carroll award Guild Cath. Lawyers, 1994, Ellis Island medal of honor, Nat. Ethnic Coalition of Orgns. Found., Inc., 1998, Louis J. Lefkowitz Pub. Svc. award Fordham U. Law Sch., 2006. Mem.: Brehon Soc. (award 2002), Skytop Club, Amackassin Club. Republican. Roman Catholic. Office: US Dist Ct Daniel Patrick Moynihan US Courthouse 500 Pearl St Rm 1930 New York NY 10007-1312

KEENAN, JOHN PAUL, leadership and management educator, consultant, director, psychologist; b. Boston, Mar. 18, 1944; s. John W. and Claire (Gallagher) K.; m. Kathleen Lennon, Aug. 7, 1976; children: Christopher, Sean Patrick. BA, U. Santa Clara, 1967; MA, San Jose State U., 1969; PhD, U.S. Internat. U., San Diego, 1978. Instr. Chapman Coll., Orange, Calif., 1971-79; asst. prof. mgmt. Coll. of St. Rose, Albany, N.Y., 1979-83; dean C.C. Low County, Beaufort, S.C., 1983-86; pvt. practice, 1986—; assoc. prof. mgmt., dir. leadership devel. programs Mgmt. Inst., U. Wis. Sch. Bus., Madison, 1986-98; pres. Assn. Employment Practices and Prins., Norfolk, Va., 1992—; founder, pres., prof. leadership studies Inst. Leadership Global Edn., 2003—. Acting dean Sch. of Leadership and Human Devel. St. Bonoventure U., Amherst, NY, 1999—2001; exec. dir. leadership programs ACCEL-Medaille Coll., Amherst, NY, 2002; pres., CEO John P. Keenan & Assocs., Internat.; keynote spkr. and presenter in field. Co-author: Whistleblowing: Managing Dissent in the Work Place, 1985, Whistleblowing Research, 1985, Foundations of Leadership: New Manager Leadership Guide, 1997, Foundations of Leadership: Facilitator's Guide, 1997, Fastart: An Indepth Seminar for New Managers, 1998, Managing Human Resources, 2000, Organizational Leadership, 2000, Strategic Planning, Leadership Development, Problem Solving and Decision Making and Conflict Resolution, 2003; editor-in-chief Employee Responsibilities & Rights Jour., 1999—; contbr. over 120 articles to profl. jours. Mem. APA, ASTD, Acad. Mgmt., Decision Scis. Inst., Inst. Mgmt. Scis., Soc. for Indsl. and Orgnl. Psychology, Assn. on Employment Practices and Principles (program chmn. 1993, 97, 2000), Assn. Employment Practices and Prins. Avocations: swimming, hiking, all sports. Home: 2 Hillsboro Dr Orchard Park NY 14127-3411 Home Phone: 716-667-2516; Office Phone: 716-390-9657.

KEENAN, KATHLEEN, state legislator; b. Burlington, Vt., May 7, 1940; d. Roland and Madelyn M. (Cahill) K.; 8 children. Diploma, Jeanne Mance Sch. Nursing, 1961; diploma in nurse practitioner program, U. Vt., 1976. Nurse; mem. Vt. Ho. of Reps., Montpelier, 1989—, chair commerce com., appropriations com., 2007—. Mem. Hinesburg Dem. Com., 1954-68, chair, 1965-68; mem. St. Albans Dem. Com., 1968—; mem. Vt. Econ. Progress Coun., 1994-98; bd. dirs. Efficiency Vt., Vt. Electric Power Prodrs., State Human Resources Investment Coun., Vt. Interactive TV; hon. bd. mem. Vt. Capital Insurance Assn. Mem. St. Albans Skating Assn. (charter), Emergency Nurses Assn., Nat. Conf. Ins. Legislators (mem. exec. com., former pres.), Bus. and Profl. Women. Address: 8 Thorpe Ave Saint Albans VT 05478-1834 Office Fax: 802-828-2228. E-mail: kkeenan@leg.state.vt.us.

KEENAN, MICHAEL EDGAR, marketing professional; b. Columbus, Ohio, Mar. 15, 1934; s. Edgar Charles and Kathryn Ellen (Dowden) K.; divorced; children: Margaret, Matthew, Emily, Jennifer, Andrew, Martha. AB, Duke U., 1955. Media buyer Compton Advt., NYC, 1957-59; assoc. media dir. Foote, Cone & Belding, NYC, 1959-61; media dir. Lennen & Newell, NYC, 1961-63; sr. v.p., dir., cons. products div. Fuller & Smith & Ross, NYC, 1963-70; chmn. Keenan & McLaughlin Inc., NYC, 1970-82, cons., 1982-85; mng. dir. Western International Media Corp., NYC, 1985-98; CEO TELA Interactive, Inc., NYC, 1998—2003; pres. Keenan & Co., Inc., NYC, 1998—; sr. v.p. US Internat. Media, NYC, 2004—. Lectr. mktg. NYU, 1960-64; cons. FTC, Washington. Served with CIC, AUS, 1955-57. Mem. Am. Assn. Advt. Agys. (chmn. N.Y. coun. 1978), Nat. Agri-Mktg. Assn. (past pres. 1979), Rear Guard (treas., pres.), Thursday Club (chmn. 1960-2004). Independent. Roman Catholic. Avocation: sailing. Home: 63 Avenue A New York NY 10009-6539 Office: US Internat Media 572 Lexington Ave New York NY 10022 Home Phone: 212-673-5647; Office Phone: 212-572-0793. Personal E-mail: mikekeenan@nyc.rr.com. Business E-Mail: mkeenan@usintlmedia.com.

KEENAN, MIKE (MICHEAL EDWARD KEENAN), professional hockey coach, former professional sports team executive; b. Bowmanville, Ont., Can., Oct. 21, 1949; m. Nola Keenan; 1 child, Gayla. Student, St. Lawrence U., NYC. Hockey player St. Lawrence U. Skating Saints, 1969—72, U. Toronto, 1972—73, Roanoke Valley Rebels, Va., 1973-74, Whitby Warriors, 1976—77; coach Peterborough Petes, Ont. Hockey League, 1979-80; head coach Can. Nat. Jr. Team, 1980, Rochester Ams., Am. Hockey League, NY, 1980-83, Toronto Hockey Team, Can. Collegiate League, Ont., 1983-84, Phila. Flyers, 1984-88, Chgo. Blackhawks, 1988-92, gen. mgr., 1990-92; head coach NY Rangers, 1993-94; head coach, gen. mgr. St. Louis Blues, 1994-96; head coach Vancouver Canucks, 1998-99, Boston Bruins, 2000—01, Fla. Panthers, 2001—03, gen. mgr., 2004—06; head coach Calgary Flames, 2007—. Named MVP, Roanoke Valley Rebels, So. Hockey League, 1974; winning coach World Amateur Hockey Championships, 1980, Calder Cup Championship, 1982-83, Can. Collegiate Championship, U. Toronto, 1983-84, Stanley Cup Championship, 1994, Can. Cup Championship, 1987, 91; recipient Jack Adams award as NHL Coach of Yr., 1985; Coach of Yr. award Sporting News, 1985, Hockey News, 1985; Coach, NHL All-Star team 1985-86, 1987-88, 1992-93; Coach, Canadian Nat. Team, 1993. Achievements include being the coach of Stanley Cup Champion NY Rangers, 1994. Office: Calgary Flames PO Box 1540 Stn M Calgary AB Canada T2P 3B9*

KEENAN, NANCY, pro-choice association executive; b. Anaconda, Mont., Feb. 14, 1952; d. Patrick John and Anne Keenan. BA in Elem. and Spl. Edn., Mont. State U., 1974; MA in Edn. Adminstrn., U. Mont. Tchr. Yellowstone Boys' Ranch, 1974-75; tchr. spl. edn. Anaconda, Mont., 1975-88; mem. Mont. Ho. Reps., 1982-88; supt. of pub. instrn. State of Mont., 1988—2000; pres. NARAL Pro-Choice Am., Washington, 2004—. Mem. taxation, edn., local govt. and revenue oversight coms., 1982-84; chmn. ho. human svcs. and aging com.; asst. Dem. whip 1989. Active Anaconda Local Devel. Corp.; past pres. A.W.A.R.E.; past nat. pres. & chair legis. com. Coun. Chief State Sch. Officers; bd. dirs. Deer Lodge County Hospice; mem. Mont. Coun. for Exceptional Children. Recipient Pub. Svc. award Mont. Coun. for Exceptional Children, 1981. Mem. AAUW. Office: NARAL Pro Choice Am Ste 700 1156 15th St NW Washington DC 20005*

KEENAN, RICHARD, lawyer; b. Balt., Oct. 19, 1952; s. Robert Richard and Nance Yvonne (Baughman) K.; m. Kathleen McNamara, May 15, 1982. BBA summa cum laude, U. Notre Dame, 1974; JD, Yale U., 1977. Bar: Calif. 1977, U.S. Dist. (no. dist.) Calif. 1977, U.S. Dist. Ct. (so. dist.) Calif. 1981, U.S. Dist. Ct. (ea. dist.) Calif. 1984, U.S. Dist. Ct. (cen. dist.) Calif. 1985, U.S. Dist. Ct. (no. dist.) Ill. 1985, U.S. Dist. Ct. Hawaii 1986, U.S. Ct. Appeals (9th cir.) 1987. Law clk. to presiding judge William W. Schwarzer U.S. Dist. Ct. (no. dist.) Calif., 1977-78; assoc. Morrison & Foerster, San Francisco, 1979-81, Folger & Levin, San Francisco, 1981-84, ptnr., 1984—. Chmn. bd. dirs. Point Bonita YMCA, 1982-86; mem. Guardsmen, San Francisco, 1982—. Mem. ABA, Calif. Bar Assn., Notre Dame Bay Area Alumni Club (pres. 1984-85). Democrat. Roman Catholic. Office: Folger & Levin 275 Battery St Embarcadero Center W 23rd fl San Francisco CA 94111-3305 Office Phone: 415-986-2800. Office Fax: 415-986-2827. Business E-Mail: rkeenan@flk.com.

KEENAN, TERRY, anchor, correspondent; Degree in Math., Johns Hopkins U. Anchor bus. news programs CNBC; from segment prodr. to on-air corr. CNN Fin. News, NYC, co-anchor Street Sweep, sr. corr. The Moneyline News Hour with Lou Dobbs; anchor, Cashin' In FOX News Channel, NYC. Writer, prodr. Wall St. Week with Louis Rukeyser; editor fin. newsletter Going Pub. Recipient Cable Ace award. Office: Fox News Channel 1211 Ave Of Am New York NY 10036 Office Phone: 212-301-3000.

KEENAN, THOMAS J., chemicals executive; V.p., gen. mgr. Olefins and Polyolefins Mobil Chem. Co.; with Huntsman Corp., Salt Lake City, 1994—, sr. v.p. Hunstman Chem. Co. LLC, 1998—2000, pres. North Am. Petrochemicals and Polymers, 2000—03, divsn. pres. pigments, 2003—. Office: Huntsman Corp 500 Huntsman Way Salt Lake City UT 84108 Office Phone: 801-584-5700.*

KEENAN, WILLIAM W. (KIP), III, public relations executive; b. Charlottesville, Va., Sept. 15, 1963; BA in English, BA in French, Hampden-Sydney Coll., 1986; MA in French, Middlebury Coll., 1987. Journalist Sta. KISS FM, Paris, 1988-90; editor Alexander Graham Bell Assn. for the Deaf, Washington, 1989-90; journalist Le Figaro, Paris and Washington, 1989-91; editor, pub. info. officer Med. U. S.C., Charleston, S.C., 1991-94; pres. Keenan Comms., Charleston, 1994-97; mgr. brand mktg. practice Burson-Marsteller, NYC, 1997-99; v.p. The Portico Group, Lexington, Mass., 1999-2000, Alexander Ogilvy Pub. Rels. Worldwide, Cambridge, Mass., 2001—. Bd. dirs. Charleston Speech and Hearing, 1993-97, Trident United Way, 1995-97. Mem. Pub. Rels. Soc. Am. (Silver Anvil award 1995), Mass. Internet Coun. Episcopalian. Avocations: travel, languages, brand building, running. Home: 105 Gleneagles Saint Simons Island GA 31522-2452 E-mail: kipk@mail.com.

KEENE, DEBORAH M., law librarian; b. Nashville, Sept. 29, 1952; BA, Vanderbilt U., 1974, MLS, 1975; JD, U. Tenn., 1980. Assoc. dean libr. and tech. George Mason U. Sch. Law, Arlington, Va. Contbr. articles to profl. jours. Office: George Mason U Sch Law Rm 243 3301 Fairfax Dr Arlington VA 22201 Office Phone: 703-993-8110. E-mail: dkeene@gmu.edu.*

KEENE, DONALD, writer, translator, language educator; b. 1922; BA, Columbia U., 1942, AM, 1947, PhD, 1949; DLitt, U. Cambridge, 1978. Lectr. Cambridge U., 1948-53; guest editor Asahi Shimbun, Tokyo, 1982-92; prof. Columbia U., NYC, 1955-92, prof. emeritus, 1992—. Author: The Battles of Coxinga, 1951, The Japanese Discovery of Europe, 1952, 69, Japanese Literature: An Introduction for Western Readers, 1953, Living Japan, 1957, Bunraku, The Puppet Theatre of Japan, 1965, No: The Classical Theatre of Japan, 1966, Landscapes and Portraits, 1971, Some Japanese Portraits, 1978, World Within Walls, 1978, Meeting with Japan, 1978, Travels in Japan, 1981, Dawn to the West, 1984, The Pleasures of Japanese Literature, 1988, Travelers of a Hundred Ages, 1989, Seeds in the Heart, 1993, On Familiar Terms, 1994, Modern Japanese Diaries, 1995, The Blue-Eyed Tarokaja, 1996, Emperor of Japan, 2002, Five Modern Japanese Novelists, 2003, Yoshimasa and the Silver Pavilion, 2003, Frog in the Well, 2006; editor: Anthology of Japanese Literature, 1955, Modern Japanese Literature, 1956, Twenty Plays of the No Theatre, 1970; translator: The Setting Sun, 1956, Five Modern No Plays, 1957, No Longer Human, 1958, Sources of Japanese Tradition, 1958, Major Plays of Chikamatsu, 1961, The Old Woman, the Wife and the Archer, 1961, After the Banquet, 1965, Essays in Idleness, 1967, Madame de Sade, 1967, Friends, 1969, Chushingura, 1971, The Man Who Turned into a Stick, 1972, Three Plays by Kobo Abe, 1993, The Narrow Road to Oku, 1996, The Tale of the Bamboo Cutter, 1998, The Breaking Jewel, 2003. Office: Columbia Univ 509 Kent Hall New York NY 10027

KEENE, JACK DONALD, molecular genetics and microbiology educator; b. Jacksonville, Fla., June 21, 1947; s. Jack Donald and Stella Collene (Ellis) Keene; m. Judy May Keene, Sept. 6, 1969; children: Mike, Lisa E. Dugan. AB, U. Calif., Riverside, 1969; PhD, U. Wash., 1974. Staff fellow NINDS/NIH, Bethesda, Md., 1974-78; asst. prof. microbiology and immunology Duke U. Med. Ctr., Durham, NC, 1979-84, assoc. prof., 1984—88, prof., 1988—92, chmn., 1992—2002, James B. Duke disting. prof., 1997—, founder Ctr. RNA Biology dept. molecular genetics and microbiology, 1999—. Exptl. virology study sect. NIH, 1984—88, mem. molecular biology study sect., 1991—95, chmn., 1993—95; mem. nat. sel. and adv. bd. PEW Scholars in the Biomed Scis., 1991—96; co-chmn. Diversity Biotech. Consortium, Santa Fe, 1994—; dir. basic sci. rsch. Duke U. Comprehensive Cancer Ctr., 1995—2003; with program in genetics and genomics and molecular and cellular biology Duke U.; dir. combinatorial scis. ctr. Duke U. Med. Ctr., 1994—2000; biotech. cons. LipoGen, Inc., BioWhittaker, Inc., Med. and Biol. Labs., Inc., Nagoya, Japan; co-founder SARCO, Inc., Combinatorial Sci. Systems, Inc., ChemCodes, LLC; founder Ribonomics, Inc., Research Triangle Park, NC; bd. dirs. Alpha Vax, Inc. Assoc. editor Virology, 1983-2007, RNA Biology, 2005-; mem. editl. bd. Jour. of Virology, 1985-95, Molecular and Cellular Biology, 1991—, Alliance Cellular Signaling; editor Microbiology and Molecular Biology Revs., 1992-2000, editor-in-chief, 2000-05; editor Molecular Diversity, 1995-2003, Jour. Biol. Chemistry, 2003—; primary reviewer Jour. Immunology, 1996—. Mem. fellowship com. Arthritis Found., 1990-92, mem. rsch. com., 1990-92. Recipient Faculty Rsch. award Am. Cancer Soc., 1981-86, Devil's Bag award Arthritis Found., 1985-91; Nanaline Duke Faculty Scholar, 1981-84, PEW Scholar in the Biomed. Scis., 1986-90. Fellow Am. Acad. Microbiology; mem. Am. Soc. Virology, Am. Soc. Biochemistry and Molecular Biology, Am. Soc. Microbiology (mem. pub. bd. 2000-05), Ribonucleic Acid Soc., The Henry Kunkel Soc., Ny Acad. Scis. Office: Duke Univ Med Ctr Box 3020 Mol Gen and Microbiol Dept Research Dr/414 Jones Bldg Durham NC 27710 Office Phone: 919-684-5138.

KEENE, JOHN CLARK, lawyer, educator; b. Phila., Aug. 17, 1931; s. Floyd Elwood and Marthe (Bussiere) K.; m. Ana Maria Delgado, July 21, 1973; children: Lisa Keene Kerns, John, Suzanna Tonra, Katharine Metell, Peter; stepchildren: Carlos, René, Mario, Raúl, Silvio Navarro, Carmen Peláez. BA, Yale U., 1953; JD, Harvard U., 1959; M in City Planning, U. Pa., 1966. Bar: Pa. 1960. Assoc. Pepper, Hamilton & Scheetz, Phila., 1959-64; prof. city and regional planning U. Pa., Phila., 1968—2006, prof. emeritus, 2006—, chmn., 1989-93, ombudsman, 1978-84, 2006—, chmn. faculty senate, 1998-99, chair doctoral program in city and regional planning, 2002—05; ptnr. Coughlin, Keene & Assocs., Phila., 1981—2000, Keene and Assoc., Phila., 2001—. Vis. prof. U. Paris X, 1991, Bryn Mawr Coll., 2006; vis. adj. prof. Temple U., 2007. Author: (with Robert E. Coughlin) The Protection of Farmland, 1981, Growth Without Chaos, 1987, (with others) Untaxing Open Space, 1976, (with Samuel Hamill) Growth Mgmt. in NJ, 1989, (with Robert Coughlin and Joanne Denworth) Guiding Growth: Managing Urban Growth in Pa., 1991, 93, (with Julia Freedgood) Saving Am. Farmland: What Works, 1997; contbr. articles to profl. jours. Trustee ex officio Phila. Mus. Art, 1978-80; mem. sci. and tech. adv. com. Chesapeake Bay Program. Lt. USN, 1953-56. Recipient Lindback award for disting. tchg., 2004, Perkins award for disting. tchg., 2005; Fulbright fellow Tunisia, 1985. Mem.: Am. Inst. Cert. Planners, Phila. Club, Merion Cricket Club, Mil. and Hospitaller Order of St. Lazarus of Jerusalem. Home: 1527 W Montgomery Ave Bryn Mawr PA 19010-1659 Office: U Pa 309 Duhring Wing Philadelphia PA 19104 Home Phone: 610-510-1313; Office Phone: 215-898-7880. Business E-Mail: keenej@design.upenn.edu.

KEENE, LONNIE, lawyer; BS, U.S. Mil. Acad., 1976; MPA, Harvard U., 1984; JD, NYU, 1998. Bar: N.Y. Asst. prof., instr. U.S. Mil. Acad., West Point, NY, 1984-87; asst. army attache U.S. Embassy, Beijing, 1988-90; mem. policy planning staff U.S. Dept. State, Washington, 1990-94; sr. policy analyst, office sci. & tech. policy The White House, Washington, 1994-95; assoc. Linklaters, London, 1998-99, Milbank, Tweed, Hadley & McCloy, London, Hong Kong, 1999—2001, Wollmuth Maher & Deutsch, NYC, 2002; v.p., asst. gen. counsel Goldman, Sachs & Co., NYC, 2002—. Lt. col. US Army, 1976—95, ret. US Army. Decorated Legion of Merit; Olmsted scholar George and Carol Olmsted Found., Beijing, 1981-83. Mem. Coun. Fgn. Rels. (Internat. Affairs fellow 1990-91), Harvard Club N.Y.C. Avocations: golf, art, travel, skiing. Office: 85 Broad St New York NY 10004 Business E-Mail: Lonnie.Keene@gs.com.

KEENE, MARY ELLEN, federal agency executive; b. Washington, July 30, 1955; d. William Charles and Doris Eva (Springer) Keene; m. Randy Duane Ferryman, Dec. 4, 1982. BS in Edn. with honors, George Mason U., 1977; MPA, Harvard U., 1992. With CIA, Washington, 1974—79, imagery analyst specializing mil. assessments, 1979—84, mgr., sr. departmental requirements officer, 1984—86, first-line mgr., later middle mgr. planning/programming unit, 1986—87, first-line mgr. imagery analytic unit, 1987—88, with Intelligence Cmty. Staff, Com. Imagery Requirements and Exploitation, 1988—90, mid. mgr. customer svcs., 1990—93, mid. mgr. imagery analytic element, 1993—95, mgr. comptr. function, 1995—98, mid. mgr. all-source analytic unit, 1998—2000, sr. mgr. resource mgmt. function, cmty. staff, 2000—03, dep. exec. secretariat, 2003—05, dir. exec. secretariat, 2005—06; dep. exec. sec., sr. dr. adminstr. Nat. Security Coun., The White House, Washington, 2006—, office of the dir., 2007—. Mem. Kappa Delta Pi. Avocations: reading, gardening, collecting hummel figurines.

KEENE, RICHARD BRIAN, school system administrator, educational consultant; b. Falls Church, Va., Sept. 11, 1962; BS, U. State NY, 1987; MEd, U. Utah, 1991; EdS, U. Idaho, 1993, PhD, 2003. Behavioral specialist, tchr. math, sci., & phys. edn. Western Inst. Neuropsychiatry, Salt Lake City, 1986—87; instr. algebra & calculus Utah Valley C.C., Orem, 1988—89; tchr. algebra & geometry Payson H.S., 1987—89; tchr. pre-algebra & algebra Lehi Jr. H.S., 1989—90; supr. test ctr. Am. Coll. Testing Svc., Iowa City, 1990—91; dir. counseling & testing, counselor, psychology Delta H.S., Utah, 1990—91; test scorer, reader, test ctr. supr. Ednl. Testing Svc., Princeton, NJ, 1990—2003; dir. counseling & testing dir., counselor Hansen Sch. Dist., Idaho, 1991—92; counselor, adminstr. dist. office level Filer Sch. Dist., 1992—94; h.s. counselor, tchr.careers, ESL, math Minidoka County Sch. Dist., Rupert, 1994—97; dir., asst. dean, counselor Kern H.S. Dist., Bakersfield, Calif., 1997—2001; vice prin. Delano Elem. Sch. Dist., 2001—03; counselor, adminstr. computer sys. Clark County Team Acad., Las Vegas, 2003—04; coord. region data Clark County Sch. Dist., 2004—. Adj. faculty Nev. State Coll., Henderson, Nev., 2003—. Author: (study guide) Advanced Mathematics I (Pre-Calculus). Dist. commr. Boy Scouts Am., Las Vegas, 2007—; elected voting mem. Nev. State Dem. Ctrl. Com., Carson City, 2004—, Clark County Dem. Ctrl. Com., Las Vegas, Nev., 2004—. With USN, 1982—84, with USAR, 1984—. Mem.: NEA, ASCD, Am. Assn. Phys. Edn. Health Recreation and Dance, Nat. Coun. Tchrs.Math., Nev. Assn. Sch. Administrators, Toastmasters Internat., Am. Legion, Lions Internat., Optimist Internat., Phi Delta Kappa. Democrat. Avocations: scuba diving, travel, swimming. Home: 340 Abbington St Henderson NV 89074 Office Phone: 702-799-1719 5323. Office Fax: 702-799-3841. Personal E-mail: rbkeene@cox.net. Business E-Mail: rbkeene@interact.ccsd.net.

KEENE-BURGESS, RUTH FRANCES, military official; b. South Bend, Ind., Oct. 7, 1948; d. Seymour and Sally (Morris) K.; m. Leslie U. Burgess, Jr., Oct. 1, 1983; children: Michael Leslie, David William, Elizabeth Sue, Rachael Lee. BS, Ariz. State U., 1970; MS, Fairleigh Dickinson U., 1978; grad., U.S. Army Command and Gen. Staff Coll., 1986. Inventory mgmt. specialist U.S. Army Electronics Command, Phila., 1970-74, U.S. Army Communications-Electronics Material Readiness Command, Fort Monmouth, N.J., 1974-79; chief inventory mgmt. div. Crane (Ind.) Army Ammunition Activity, 1979-80; supply systems analyst Hdqrs. 60th Ordnance Group, Zweibruecken, Fed. Republic Germany, 1980-83; chief inventory mgmt. div. Crane (Ind.) Army Ammunition Activity, 1983-85, chief control div., 1985; inventory mgmt. specialist 200th Theater Army Material Mgmt. Ctr., Zweibruecken, 1985-88; analyst supply systems U.S. Armament, Munitions and Chem. Command, Rock Island, Ill., 1988-89; specialist logistics mgt. U.S. Army Signal Command, Ft. Huachuca, Ariz., 1989—. Troop leader Girl Scouts Am. Mem. Federally Employed Women (chpt. pres. 1979-80), NAFE, Soc. Logistics Engrs., Assn. Computing Machinery, Am. Soc. Public Adminstrn., Soc. Profl. and Exec. Women, AAAS. Democrat.

KEENER, CATHERINE, actress; b. Miami, Fla., Mar. 16, 1960; m. Dermot Mulroney, Nov. 1990 (separated May 2005); 1 child, Clyde. Grad., Wheaton Coll., Norton, Mass., 1983. Actor: (films) The Education Allison Tate, 1986, About Last Night, 1986, Survival Quest, 1989, Catchfire, 1990, Switch, 1991, Johnny Suede, 1991, The Gun in Betty Lou's Handbag, 1992, Living in Oblivion, 1995, Walking and Talking, 1996, The Destiny of Marty Fines, 1996, Boys, 1996, Box of Moon Light, 1996, The Real Blonde, 1997, Out of Sight, 1998, Your Friends and Neighbors, 1998, 8MM, 1999, Being John Malkovich, 1999, Death to Smoochy, 2002, Full Frontal, 2002, Simone, 2002, The Ballad of Jack and Rose, 2005 (Best Supporting Actress, Boston Soc. Film Critics awards, 2005), The Interpreter, 2005, 40 Year Old Virgin, 2005 (Best Supporting Actress, Boston Soc. Film Critics awards, 2005), Capote, 2005 (Best Supporting Actress, Boston Soc. Film Critics awards, 2005), Friends with Money, 2006; (TV films) Journeys North, 1994, Heroine of Hell, 1996, If These Walls Could Talk, 1996; (TV series) Ohara, 1987, (TV appearances) LA Law, 1986, Seinfeld, 1992. Address: c/o The Gersh Agy 232 N Canon Dr Beverly Hills CA 90210

KEENER, GAITHER MCDONALD, JR., corporate lawyer; b. Newton, NC, June 15, 1949; BA, Western Carolina U., 1972; JD, Wake Forest U., 1977. Bar: N.C. 1977, U.S. Supreme Ct. 1982. Assoc. counsel McElwee, Hall, & McElwee, 1977-86; sr. corp. counsel Lowe's Companies, Inc., North Wilkesboro, NC, 1986—98; v.p., asst. gen. counsel, sec. Lowe's Companies, 1998—2004, sr. v.p., gen. counsel, sec., 2004—. Commr. Wilkes Regional Med. Ctr. With U.S. Marines, 1968-71. Named to N.C. Baseball Hall of Fame, 1995. Mem. N.C. Bar Assn. Office: Lowe's Cos Inc PO Box 111 North Wilkesboro NC 28659-0111*

KEENEY, JOHN CHRISTOPHER, lawyer; b. Wilkes-Barre, Pa., Feb. 19, 1922; s. James M. and Mae M. (Clark) Keeney; widower; children: John C. Jr., Terence, Jean Marie, Joan, Kathleen. BS, U. Scranton, 1947; LLB, Dickinson Sch. of Law, Carlisle, Pa., 1949; LLM, Geo. Washington Law Sch., Washington, 1953. Chief Smith Act Unit, internal security sect. Dept. Justice, Washington, 1957-60, dep. chief organized crime sect. criminal divsn., 1966-69, chief fraud sect. criminal divsn., 1969-73, dep. asst. atty. gen. criminal divsn., 1973—. 1st lt. U.S. Army Air Force, 1943-45 ETO. Recipient Disting. Career award Pres. Reagan, 1983, Pres. Bush, 2004, Disting. Alumnus in Govt. award U. Scranton, 1997, Atty. Gen.'s Disting. Svc. award, 1987, DC Bar award for disting. govt. svc., 1996, Life Time Achievement award Dickinson Sch. Law, 2002, Atty. Gen. Levi award, 2006. Roman Catholic. Home: 11101 Lund Pl Kensington MD 20895-1624 Office: US Dept Justice 10th And Pennsylvania NW Washington DC 20530-0001 Home Phone: 301-946-0782; Office Phone: 202-514-2621.

KEENEY, JOHN CHRISTOPHER, JR., lawyer; b. Washington, Aug. 29, 1951; s. John Christopher and Eugenia M. (Brislin) Keeney; m. Kathleen V. Gunning; children: Katherine, Jaclyn. AB summa cum laude, U. Notre Dame, 1973; JD cum laude, Harvard U., 1976. Bar: Md. 1976, DC 1977, US Dist. Ct. DC 1978, US Dist. Ct. Md. 1977, US Ct. Appeals (4th cir.) 1977, US Ct. Appeals (DC cir.) 1978, US Supreme Ct. 1980, US Ct. Appeals (7th cir.) 1984, US Ct. Appeals (10th cir.) 1989, US Ct. Appeals (11th cir.) 1990, US Ct. Appeals (9th cir.) 1997, US Ct. Appeals (6th cir.) 1999, US Ct. Appeals (3rd cir.) 2005, US Ct. Appeals (8th cir.) 2006. Law clk. presiding judge US Dist. Ct. Md., Balt., 1976-78; assoc. Hogan & Hartson LLP, Washington, 1978-84, ptnr., 1985—, ptnr. charge pro bono cmty. svcs. dept., 1989—93. Adj. instr. legal ethics Am. U. Law Sch., 2000—02; mem. adv. com. on procedures US Ct. Appeals (DC cir,), 2006—. Co-author: (book) Civil and Criminal Remedies for Racially and Religiously Motivated Violence, 1983, 2d edit., 1999. Dir. Pub. Justice Ctr., Balt., 1990—95, 1997—2000; co-chair Dem. Nat. Lawyers Coun., 1999—2003; counsel del. selection Babbitt US Pres. campaign, 1987—88; counsel Dem. credentials com., 1989—91; hearing officer Dem. Nat. Conv., 1992, 1996; chmn. Berlage County Coun. campaign, Montgomery County, Md., 1989—94; bd. dirs. Washington Lawyers Com. Civil Rights Urban Affairs, 1999—. Mem.: ABA (former co-chair adjudication com., ad. law regulatory practice sec. 1999—2002, House of Dels. 2003—05, chair standing com. on election law 2007—), DC Bar (bd. govs. 2000—06, pres. elect 2003—04, pres. 2004—05), Phi Beta Kappa. Roman Catholic. Office: Hogan & Hartson LLP 555 13th St NW Ste 10W-206 Washington DC 20004-1109 Office Phone: 202-637-5750. Business E-Mail: jckeeney@hhlaw.com.

KEENEY, REGINA MARKEY, lawyer; b. Sumter, SC, Aug. 20, 1955; d. John Patrick and Margaret Mary (Rogers) Markey; m. Terence J. Keeney, Aug. 16, 1980; children: Teresa Marie, Anne Mairead. BS magna cum laude, Georgetown U., 1977; JD, Harvard U., 1980. Bar: DC. Assoc. Hamel, Park, McCabe & Saunders, Washington, 1980-83; atty., advisor FCC, Washington, 1983-85, bur. chief Wireless Telecom. Bur., 1994-95; sr. counsel comm. Senate Commerce Com., Washington, 1985-94; chief Common Carrier Bur., 1995-97, Internat. Bur., Wash., 1997—99; chief policy counsel Dell Computer; atty. Lawler, Metzger, Milkman & Keeney. Recipient top 45 pub. sector attys., Am. Lawyer, 1997. Mem.: DC Bar. Roman Catholic. Office: Lawler Metzger Milkman & Keeney 2001 K St NW Ste 802 Washington DC 20006 Office Phone: 202-777-7720. Office Fax: 202-777-7763. Business E-Mail: gkeeney@lmmk.com.

KEENEY, SCOTT NEAL, molecular biologist; b. Balt., Dec. 3, 1965; s. Grafton E. and Catherine K. Keeney. BS, Va. Tech, Blacksburg, 1987; PhD, U. Calif., Berkeley, 1993. Mem., molecular biology program Meml. Sloan-Kettering Cancer Ctr., NYC, 1997—; prof. molecular biology Cornell U., Weill Grad. Sch. Med. Scis., NYC, 1998—. Contbr. articles to profl. jours. Recipient Louise and Allston Boyer Young Investigator award, Meml. Sloan-Kettering Cancer Ctr., 2004; Postdoctoral fellow, Damon Runyon Cancer Rsch. Fund, 1993—97. Mem.: Leukemia and Lymphoma Soc. (scholar 2005—), Am. Cancer Soc. (grant reviewer 2004—), Harvey Soc., Amercia Soc. Microbiology, Am. Soc. Biochemistry and Molecular Biology, Genetics Soc. Am. Office: Meml Sloan-Kettering Cancer Ctr 1275 York Ave New York NY 10036 Office Phone: 212-639-5182.

KEENEY, STEVEN HARRIS, lawyer; b. Phila., Oct. 1, 1949; s. Arthur Hail and Virginia (Tripp) K.; m. Jean Ashburn, May 10, 1974 (div. Oct. 1986); 1 child, Christian Jeffrey; m. Lorri Caram Carty, Sept. 2, 2003. BA with honors, Trinity Coll., Hartford, Conn., 1971; MA, Hartford Sem. Found., 1973; JD, U. Conn., 1980. Bar: Ky. 1980, U.S. Dist. Ct. (we. dist.) Ky. 1981, U.S. Dist. Ct. (ea. dist.) Ky. 1983, U.S. Ct. Appeals (6th cir.) 2001. Staff reporter, edn. editor The Hartford Courant, 1971-74; asst. to supt. Hartford Pub. Schs., 1974-77; assoc. Igor Sikorsky & Assocs., Hartford, 1979-80, Brown, Todd & Heyburn, Louisville, 1980-82; ptnr. Barnett & Alagia, 1982—88, KLO The Keeney Law Office, 1988—90; prin. Amerilaw, 1990—93; pres. LawTech Svcs. Co., 1988—2002; mng. mem. Trautwein & Keeney PLLC, 1993—2002, Keeney Law Office, LLC, 2002—; city atty. City of Pineville, Ky., 2002—05; dean Profl. Learning Inst., 2005—. Chmn., CEO Write2U; co-founder InspectHomes4U; lectr. in field. Co-author/editor: Death Benefit: A Lawyer Uncovers A 20 Year Pattern of Seduction, 1993, 94, Reader's Digest Today's Best Non-Fiction Vol. 24, 1994; featured in Ct. TV's Forensic Files, 2004-2005, Cable TV's Inside Edition, Discovery Channel, others; contbr. articles to profl. jours. Bd. dirs. Hospice of Louisville, Inc., 1984-86; exec. dir. Juvenile Justice Pub. Edn. Project, West Hartford, Conn., 1978-80; pres. bd. dirs. Stage One: Louisville Children's Theatre, 1982-83; founding bd. dirs. Ky. Citizens for Arts, Frankfort, 1983; mem. Lebanon (Conn.) Bd. Edn., 1975-80; campaign mgr. Mazzoli 3d C.D. Ky., Jefferson County, 1982, 84; ruling elder 2d Presbyn. Ch., Louisville, 1984-86, Presbytery, 1990-, commr. counsel Recipient Disting. Contbn. award Nat. Com. for Prevention of Child Abuse, Ky. chpt., 1982, Disting. Svc. award Conn. Assn. Bds. of Edn., 1976, Profl. Achievement for Gen. Reporting Series award Soc. Profl. Journalists, Ch. History prize. Mem. ABA (editl. com. The Tax Lawyer 1984-89), ATLA, Nat. Assn. Criminal Def. Lawyers, Ky. Acad. Trial Attys., Ky. Bar Assn., Louisville Bar Assn., Million Dollar Advocates Forum, Order of Ky. Cols., Sigma Phi Epsilon, Sigma Delta Chi (Conn. chpt.). Democrat. Presbyterian. Avocations: bibliophile, marksman, golf. Office: Keeney Law Office PO Box 263 Harrods Creek KY 40027 Office Phone: 502-599-1154.

KEENEY, SUSAN E., pediatrician, educator; b. Texarkana, Tex., Jan. 7, 1956; BA, U. Tex., 1977; MD, U. Tex. Med. Br., 1987. Cert. pediats. Tex., neonatal/perinatal medicine Tex. Fellow in neonatology U. Tex., Houston, 1985—88; resident in pediats. U. Tex. Med. Br., Galveston, 1982—85, assoc. prof., 1988—. Office: U Tex Med Br Dept Pediats Galveston TX 77550 E-mail: skeeney@utmb.edu.

KEENEY, VIRGINIA T., retired child psychiatrist; b. Albany, NY, Mar. 23, 1920; d. Leon Lyle and Mabel Alice Tripp; m. Arthur Hail Keeney, 1942 (dec.); children: Steven Harris, Lee Douglas, Martha Heyburn; m. George Harrison Houston, 2003 (dec.). BS, Coll. of William and Mary, Williamsburg, Va., 1942; MD, U. Louisville, 1954. Dir. and creator program in ethics and humanities U. Louisville Sch. Medicine, 1974—2004, resident child psychiatry, 1979—84; assoc. prof. dept. comty. and family medicine U. Louisville, 1974—2004, asst. prof. dept. psychiatry, 1984—2004; ret., 2004. Bd. dirs. Buckhorn Presbyn. Child Welfare Agency. Co-author (with Arthur Keeney): (book) Dyslexia, 1966. Mem. adv. bd. Salvation Army, Louisville; program dir. Sabin Oral Polio Campaign, 1961—63; elder Presbyterian Ch.; chmn. bd. YWCA, Louisville, 1963—65; life bd. dir. Am. Printing House for the Blind, Louisville, 1998, Louisville Orch., 2003; chmn. bd. ARC, Louisville, 1994—96, life bd. dir., 1999; bd. dir. Louisville Hospice, 2000—06. Named Citizen Laureate of Louisville, Younger Women's Club, 1964, Woman of Distinction, Ctr. for Women and Families, 1992, Alumna fellow, U. Louisville, 2007; recipient Clara Barton award, ARC, 1980, 1996. Mem.: Jefferson County Med. Soc. Found. (trustee), Ky. Physicians Health Found. (trustee 1998—), River Valley Club, Alpha Omega Alpha. Presbyterian. Avocations: tennis, reading, walking, swimming.

KEENUM, MARK EVERETT, federal agency administrator, former legislative staff member; b. Starkville, Miss., Jan. 28, 1961; AA in Bus. Adminstrn., N.E. Miss. C.C., 1981; BS in Agrl. Econs., Miss. State U., 1983, MAgr in Agrl. Econs., 1984, PhD in Agrl. Econs., 1988. Grad. rsch. asst. Agr. and Forestry Exptl. Sta. Miss. State U., Starkville, 1983-84, ext. mktg. specialist Miss. Co-op Ext. Svc., 1984-86, rsch. assoc. Agr. and Forestry Exptl. Sta., 1986-88, asst. economist, prof. dept. agrl. econs., 1988-89; legis. asst. Office of Senator Thad Cochran, US Senate, Washington, 1989-96, staff dir., 1995-96, chief of staff, 1997—2006; under sec. for farm & fgn. agrl. services USDA, Washington, 2006—. Bd. dirs. Commodity Credit Corp., 2006—. Recipient Kiwanian of the Yr. award Starkville Kiwanis Breakfast Club, 1986, Outstanding Pub. Svc. award Coll. Agr. and Life Scis. Alumni Assn., Miss. State U., 1992, Outstanding Contbn. to Delta Agr. award Miss. Delta Coun., 1993, Farm Policy Commendation award Miss. Delta Coun., 1996; Varsity Football scholar N.E. Miss. C.C., 1979-81, Pres. scholar Miss. State U., 1982-83. Mem. Gamma Sigma Delta. Office: USDA Jamie L Whitten Fed Bldg 1400 Independence Ave SW Rm 205-E Washington DC 20250

KEENY, SPURGEON MILTON, JR., professional society administrator; b. NYC, Oct. 24, 1924; s. Spurgeon Milton and Amelia (Smith) K.; m. Sheila Spear, May 3, 1952; children: Christopher Spear, Christy Virginia, Spurgeon Milton III. BA, Columbia U., 1944, MA in Physics, 1946; postgrad., Sch. Internat. Affairs and Russian Inst., 1946—47; LLD (hon.), U. Notre Dame, 1991. With Directorate of Intelligence, Hdqrs. USAF, 1950—55; mem. staff Panel on Peaceful Uses Atomic Energy, Joint Congl. Com. Atomic Energy, Washington, 1955—56; chief atomic energy divsn. Office of Asst. Sec. Def. for Rsch. and Engring., Washington, 1956—57; mem. Gaither security resources panel Exec. Office of Pres., 1957; tech. asst. Pres.'s Sci. Adviser, Washington, 1958—69; sr. staff mem. Nat. Security Coun., 1963—69; asst. dir. for sci. and tech. U.S. Arms Control and Disarmament Agy., Washington, 1969—73, dep. dir., 1977—81; scholar-in-residence NAS, Washington, 1981—85; pres., exec. dir. Arms Control Assn., Washington, 1985—2001; sr. fellow NAS, Washington, 2002—. Dir. policy and program devel. Mitre Corp., McLean, Va., 1973-77; mem. U.S. del. to Geneva Conf. Experts on Nuc. Test Detection, 1958; to Geneva Conf. on Discontinuance Nuc. Weapons Tests, 1958-60; chief U.S. del. U.S./Soviet Talks on Theater Nuc. Forces, 1980; adv. com. Program Sci. and Internat. Affairs, Harvard, 1973-77; dep. chmn. com. environ. decision making NAS, 1974-77; chmn. Nuc. Energy Policy Study Ford Found., 1975-77; com. on internat. security and arms control NAS, 1981-; mem. com. on Tech. Issues Relating to Ratification of Comprehensive Test Ban Treaty, NAS, 2000-03. Co-author: Nuclear Power Issues and Choices, 1977; Nuclear Arms Control Background and Issues, 1985; Management and Disposition of Excess Weapons Plutonium, 1994, The Future of U.S. Nuclear Weapons Policy, 1997, Comprehensive Nuclear Test Ban Treaty, 2002, Monitoring Nuclear Weapons and Nuclear Explosive Materials, 2005. Served to 1st lt. USAF, 1948-50. Recipient Rockefeller Pub. Svc. award, 1970; Disting. Honor award U.S. Arms Control and Disarmament Agy., 1981. Fellow Am. Acad. Arts Scis., Am. Phys. Soc. (study group on light-water reactor safety 1974-75, forum award 1986); mem. Coun. on Fgn. Rels., Phi Beta Kappa. Home: 3600 Albemarle St NW Washington DC 20008-4216 Office: Nat Acad Scis CISAC 500 5th St NW Washington DC 20001 Home Phone: 202-966-1692. Personal E-mail: sskeeny@aol.com.

KEEP, CHARLES RUSSELL, JR., foundation administrator; b. NYC, Feb. 9, 1929; s. Charles Russell and Ada Keep; m. Nancy Garland (dec.); children: Charles Russell III, Christopher, Marcus, Courtney, Alison, Jonathan, Stephanie; m. Claudia Abigail, Dec. 30, 2005. BA, Dartmouth Coll., Hanover, NH, 1951; student, Harvard U., Cambridge, Mass., 1951—53. Acct. exec. Benton & Bowles Inc., NYC, 1955—59; mng. dir. Golden Acres Farm, Inc., Newtown, PR, 1959—65; dir. edn. Avco, Inc., Polahnospr, Maine, 1966—68, YWCA, Inc., Jersey City, 1968—72; dir. residential treatment Children's Aid and Adoption Soc. NJ, 1973—93; pres. Rosenstock-Huessy Fund, Norwich, Vt., 1994—2003. Founder, owner C.R. Keep Books, Huntington, NY, 1953—69; bd. dirs. 47 Main St., Inc., Castleton, Vt., 1999—2007. Editor: E. Rosenstock-Huessy, 1958. Mem.: St. Nicholas Soc. NY, Harvard Club NY. Democrat. Episcopalian. Home: PO Box 27 Solebury PA 18963

KEEP, MARCUS FLOYD, neurosurgeon; b. NYC, Mar. 15, 1959; s. Charles Russell Keep Jr. and Nancy Garland Stotz; m. Jenny Karlsson, Nov. 25, 2005; 1 child, Hannah Freyja. AB in Religion, Dartmouth Coll., Hanover, NH, 1980; BS in Chemistry, U. SC, 1981; MD, Med. U. SC, 1988; postgrad., Shanxi U., Taiyuan, China, 1981—82, St. George's U., 1984—85. Surgery intern Med. U. S.C., Charleston, 1988—89; neurosurgery resident Montreal Neurol. Inst., McGill U., Que., Canada, 1989—94; rsch. fellow Restorative Neurology Unit, Lund U., Sweden, 1994—96; pres. Restorative Neurosurgery Found., Honolulu, 1996—; CEO, founder Maas BioLab, LLC, Honolulu, 1997—; asst. prof. dept. neurosurgery U. N.Mex., Albuquerque, 2002—07; med. dir. Swedish Gamma Knife Ctr., Swedish Med. Ctr., Englewood, Colo., 2007—. Rsch. fellow INSERM-Neuromorphology Lab.-Salpetriere Hosp., Paris, 1989—90; asst. prof. dept. surgery John A. Burns Sch. Medicine, U. Hawaii, Honolulu, 1997—2002; rschr. Ctr. for Study of Neurol. Disease, Honolulu, 1997—98, Lab. Matrix Pathology, Honolulu, 1999—2002; asst. prof. dept. anatomy John A. Burns Sch. Medicine, U. Hawaii, Honolulu, 2000—02. Patentee in field; contbr. chapters to books, sci. articles to profl. jours. V.p. Nova Arts Found., Honolulu, 1997—2002; mem. instnl. rev. bd. St. Francis Med. Ctr., Honolulu, 1999—2001; mem. sci. adv. com. Clin. Rsch. Ctr., Honolulu, 2000—01; union rep. Montreal Neurol. Inst., Assn. Residents of McGill, Montreal, Que., 1992—94; pres. Fellows' Soc. of Montreal Neurol. Inst., 1993—94. Rsch. grantee Omina-Freundeshilfe Found., 1994, Bradley & Victoria Geist Found., 1998-2000, Ingeborg V.F. McKee Fund, 2001, RCMI-NIH, 2001-02, U. N.Mex. Dept. Surgery, 2004; fellow Phadhar Hosp., India, 1988, Burn Unit, Cali, Colombia, Ptnrs. of the Ams., 1987; recipient Innovative Albuquerque Entrepreneur/Small Bus. award Albuquerque C. of C., 2006. Fellow: ACS, Royal Coll. Surgeons of Can.-Neurosurgery; mem.: Rocky Mountain Neurosurg. Soc., Soc. Stereotactic and Functional Neurosurgery, Congress Neurol. Surgeons, Cell Transplant Soc., Hawaii Assn. Neurol. Surgeons (treas. 1997—2000, v.p. 2000—02), Soc. for Neurosci., Am. Soc. for Neural Therapy and Repair, Am. Epilepsy Soc., Am. Assn. Neurol. Surgeons., Internat. Brain Rsch. Orgn., NY Soc. Mayflower Descs., Mass. Soc. Mayflower Descs., Outrigger Canoe Club. Home: 1201 S Gaylord St Denver CO 80210 Business E-Mail: mkeep@maasbiolab.com.

KEEPHART, LYDIA FABBRO, lawyer, mediator; b. Trenton, NJ, Apr. 19, 1952; d. Leo Fabbro and Elide Agnes Romano; m. William Joseph Keephart; 1 child, Jonathan Fabbro. BA, Coll. N.J., 1973; MA, Rider U., 1978; JD, Seton Hall U., 1991; diploma in mediation, Rutgers U., Newark, 1998, Harvard U., 2000. Bar: N.J., Pa., Colo. Tchr. East Windsor Bd. Edn., Hightstown, NJ, 1973—81; test developer, program adminstr. Ednl. Testing Svc., Princeton, 1981—87; ptnr. Pellettieri, Rabstein & Altman, Princeton, 1991—. Mem. adv. bd. Fleet Bank Boston, NJ, 1995—2004, St. Lawrence & Morris Hall, NJ, 1999—, Bank Am., 2004—. Mem.: ABA, N.J. Bar Assn., Pa. Bar Assn., Colo. Bar Assn., Green Acres Country Club. Office: Pellettieri Rabstein and Altman 100 Nassau Park Blvd Ste 111 Princeton NJ 08540 Office Phone: 609-520-0900. Business E-Mail: lkeephart@pralaw.com.

KEEPIN, GEORGE ROBERT, JR., physicist; b. Oak Park, Ill., Dec. 5, 1923; s. George Robert and Erlene Marie (Bennett) K.; m. Madge Mary Twomey, June 13, 1948; children: Robert, William, Ardis, Mavis, Denice. PhB, U. Chgo., 1943; BS, MIT, 1946, MS, 1947; PhD in Physics, Northwestern U., 1949. Tchg. fellow dept. physics MIT, Cambridge, 1947; postdoctoral fellow U. Calif., Berkeley, 1950-52; rsch. physicist Los Alamos (N.Mex.) Sci. Lab., 1952-63, group leader nuclear safeguards rsch., 1966-76, dir. nuclear safeguards program, 1976-80; head physics divsn. IAEA, Vienna, Austria, 1963-65, spl. adviser to dep. dir. gen. nuclear safeguards, 1982-85; fellow Los Alamos Nat. Lab., 1985—. Mem. U.S. del. UN Atoms-for-Peace Conf., Geneva, 1955, 71, IAEA tech. adviser, 1964 Author: Progress in Nuclear Energy-Delayed Neutrons, 1956, Physics of Nuclear Kinetics, 1965; Arms Control Verification: The Technologies That Make It Possible, 1986; editor: Nuclear Analysis R and D; patentee in field. Fellow Los Alamos Nat. Lab, Am. Phys. Soc., Am. Nuclear Soc. (exec. com. 1967-69); mem. Inst. Nuclear Materials Mgmt. (nat. chmn. 1978-80, Disting. Service award 1984), N.Y. Acad. Scis., Sigma Xi. Home: 600 La Bajada Los Alamos NM 87544-3805

KEER, LEON MORRIS, engineering educator; b. LA, Sept. 13, 1934; s. William and Sophia (Bookman) Keer; m. Barbara Sara Davis, Aug. 18, 1956; children: Patricia Renee, Jacqueline Saundra, Harold Neal, Michael Derek. BS, Calif. Inst. Tech., 1956, MS, 1958; PhD, U. Minn., 1962. Registered profl. engr., Calif. Mem. tech. staff Hughes Aircraft Co., Culver City, Calif., 1956-59; research fellow, instr. U. Minn., Mpls., 1959-62; asst. prof. Northwestern U., Evanston, Ill., 1964-66, assoc. prof., 1966-70, prof. engring., 1970—, Walter P. Murphy prof. mech. and civil engring., 1994—, assoc. dean research and grad. studies, 1985-92, chmn. dept. civil engring., 1992-97. Preceptor Columbia U., NYC, 1963—64; dir. Ctr. for Surface Engring. and Tribology, 1997—; dept. acad. advisor civil and structural engring. Hong Kong U., 1998—2002; Chau Wei-Yin meml. lectr. Hong Kong Poly. U., 2000; S.W. Mechanics lecture tour, 2003—04. Co-editor: (monograph) Solid Contact and Lubrication, 1980; mem. editl. bd.: Jour. Mechanics of Materials; contbr. articles to profl. jours. Fellow, NATO, 1962, Guggenheim Found., 1972, Japanese Soc. for the Promotion of Sci., 1986. Fellow: NAE (elected 1997), ASME (life; tech. editor Jour. Applied Mechanics 1988—92, Innovative Rsch. award tribology divsn. 2001, Daniel C. Drucker medal 2003), ASCE (life; chmn. engring. mech. divsn. 1992—93), Acoustical Soc. Am., Am. Acad. Mechanics (sec. 1981—88, pres.-elect 1987—88, pres. 1988—89); mem.: Tau Beta Pi, Sigma Xi. Home: 2601 Marian Ln Wilmette IL 60091-2207 Office: Northwestern U Dept Civil Engring 2145 Sheridan Rd Evanston IL 60208-0834 Business E-Mail: l-keer@northwestern.edu.

KEESE, JAN, elementary school educator; Tchr. Crocker Elem. Sch., Ankeny, Iowa. Instr. Grad. Sch. Edn., Viterbo U. Named Ankeny Educator of Yr., 2005, Iowa Tchr. of Yr., Iowa Dept. Edn., 2007. Mem.: Iowa Literacy Coun. Office: Crocker Elem Sch 2910 SW Applewood Ankeny IA 50023 Business E-Mail: jkeese@ankeny.k12.ia.us.*

KEESHAN, LAWRENCE W., lawyer; b. Aug. 23, 1945; married; 3 children. AB cum laude, Georgetown U., 1967; MBA, JD, Stanford U., 1971. Bar: Calif. 1972. Assoc. Heller Ehrman White & McAuliffe, San Francisco, 1975—80, ptnr., 1980—87; sr. litig. ptnr. Gibson, Dunn & Crutcher, San Francisco, 1987—95; ptnr., global gen. counsel Pricewaterhouse Coopers, San Francisco & NYC, 1995—2006; shareholder Heller Ehrman LLP, San Francisco, 2007—, mng. dir. Internat. Practices, group leader, Securities & Litig. Practice. Articles editor Stanford Law Review, 1968-71. Served JAG Corps USN, 1972—75. Mem. Phi Beta Kappa. Office: Heller Ehrman LLP 333 Bush St San Francisco CA 94104-2878 Office Phone: 646-471-1101, 415-772-6113. Office Fax: 646-471-1117, 415-772-6268. E-mail: larry.keeshan@hellerehrman.com.

KEESING, FELICIA, biology professor; b. Santa Cruz, Calif., Jan. 24, 1966; d. Roger M Keesing and Zina Rose Vitcov; m. Richard S. Ostfeld, Nov. 2, 1996; children: Jacob Keesing Ostfeld, Benjamin Keesing Ostfeld. PhD, U. Calif., Berkeley, 1997. Asst. prof. Siena Coll., 1997—2000; assoc. prof. biology Bard Coll., Annandale, NY, 2000—. Vis. scientist Inst. Ecosys. Studies, Millbrook, NY, 2000—. Editor: Ecology of Infectious Diseases, 2007. Recipient Presdl. Early Career award, Pres. of U.S., 2000; grantee, NIH, Nat. Geog. Soc., 1997, NSF, 1998—2006; Patricia Robert Harris fellow, US Dept. Edn., 1991—96. Office: Bard Coll PO Box 5000 Annandale On Hudson NY 12504

KEESLING, KAREN RUTH, lawyer; b. Wichita, Kans., July 9, 1946; d. Paul W. and Ruth (Sharp) Keesling. BA, Ariz. State U., 1968, MA, 1970; JD, Georgetown U., 1981. Bar: Va. 1981, Fla. 1981, Ariz. 2000. Asst. dean of women U. Kans., Lawrence, 1970-72; exec. sec. , sec.'s adv. com. on rights and responsibilities of women HEW, Washington, 1972-74; dir. White House Office of Women's Programs, Washington, 1974-77; head civil rights and equal opportunity sect., Gov. Div., Congl. Rsch. Svc. Libr. Congress, Washington, 1977-80; legis. aide Sen. Nancy Kassebaum, Washington, 1979-81; mem. pers. office staff Office of Pres.-elect, Washington, Jan. 1981; pvt. practice Falls Church, Va. and Peoria, Sun City, Ariz., 1981-88, 90—; dept. for equal opportunity dept. Dept. Air Force, Washington, 1981-82, dep. asst. sec. manpower res. affairs and installations, 1982-83, prin. dep. asst. sec. manpower res. affairs, 1983-87, prin. dep. asst. sec. readiness support dept. Washington, 1987-88, prin. dep. asst. sec. manpower and res. affairs, 1988, asst. sec. manpower and res. affairs, 1988-89; acting wage and hour adminstr. U.S. Dept. Labor, Washington, 1992-93; pvt. practice Falls Church, Va., Peoria, Sun City, Ariz. Bd. advisers Outstanding Young Women Am., 1983—90. Mem. Nat. Women's Polit. Caucus, Washington, 1980, Nat. Fedn. Rep. Women's Club, Washington, 1975; pers. com. chair Faith Presbyn. Ch., 2000—04, elder, 2000—05, mission com. chair, 2005—07. Named One of Ten Outstanding Young Women of Am., 1975, Kans. Women's Golf Champion, 1966, Wichita Women's Champion, 1968, 1970, Outstanding Woman Golfer in Kans., 1966; recipient Alumni Achievement award, Ariz. State U., 1976, Elizabeth Boyer award, Women's Equity Action League, 1986, Meritorious Civilian award, USAF, 1987, Woman of Distinction award, Nat. Conf. Coll. Women, Student Leaders and Women of Distinction, 1988, Exceptional Civilian Svc. award, USAF, 1988. Mem.: Va. Bus. and Profl. Women's Found. (trustee 1985—93), The Women's Inst. Inc. (adv. coun. 1985—96), No. Va. Women atty.'s Assn. (steering com. 1990—95), Va. Fedn. Bus. and Profl. Women's Clubs (2d v.p. 1987—88, 1st v.p. 1988—89, pres.-elect 1989—90, pres. 1990—91), Fla. Bar Assn., Va. Bar Assn., Ariz. Bar Assn., PEO (treas. 2001—02, v.p. 2002—03, pres. chptr. 2003—05), U.S. Com. for UNIFEM (gen. counsel 1983—2002), Pi Beta Phi. Avocation: golf. Home: 9606 W Lindgren Ave Sun City AZ 85373 E-mail: Keeslingkr@aol.com.

KEESLING, RUTH MORRIS, foundation administrator; b. New Brunswick, NJ, Apr. 4, 1930; d. Mark Loren and Louise Weber Morris; m. Thomas Marion Keesling, June 30, 1956; children: Thomas Mark, James H., Frank M. BS in Journalism, U. Colo., 1953. Advt. dept. Burlingame Advance, Calif., 1953—54; news dept. Oakland Tribune, Calif., 1954; pub. rels. Mark Morris Assoc., Inc., Topeka, 1955; co-owner Pub. Rels., Inc., Denver, 1955—64; pres. Digit Fund, Denver, 1986—88; founder, sponsor Mountain Gorilla Vet. Project, Denver, 1986—2001; founder, pres. Mountain Gorilla Conservation Fund, Denver, 2001—. Founder Morris Animal Found., Denver, 1955—; pres. Dian Fossey Gorilla Fund, Denver, 1988—91, pres. internat., 1991—93; trustee Denver Zool. Found., Denver, 1969—; lectr. mountain gorillas; sponsor, founder Mt. Gorillas in Africa, 1987—; founder Wildlife Animal Medicine Dept. Makerene U., Uganda, 1994; head task force Rwandan Govt., 2000. Author: (brochures) Small Animal Clinical Nutrition, 1959; designer (exhibitions) Mus. Display Dian Fossey items, 1992—94. Named Woman of Distinction, Girl Scouts Am.; recipient Outstanding Alumni award, U. Colo., 1976, award for animal welfare, Collier County Humane Soc., 2002, Lifetime Achievement award, Brit. Airways, 2002, award, Collier County Humane Soc., 2002. Mem.: Port Royal Club, Naples Yacht Club, Denver Country Club, Pi Beta Phi (chmn. adv. bd. 1957—60, mem. house bd. 1958—61, Carolyn Lichtenberg Crest award 2000). Home: 3220 Cherryridge Rd Englewood CO 80113 Office: Mountain Gorilla Conservation Fund PO Box 2211 Englewood CO 80150-2211 Office Phone: 303-781-8484, 239-434-9447. E-mail: RuthKee@aol.com.

KEETON, J. E., retired psychiatrist; b. Brilliant, Ala., Oct. 8, 1925; s. James Willie and Mary Etta (Dodd) K.; m. Mary Ann Trantham, May 31, 1953 (dec. Dec. 1989); children: Jonathan Eric, David Wright, Adam Blake. BS, Birmingham So. U., 1951; MD, U. Ala., 1955. Intern U. Chgo. Clinics, 1955-56; resident psychiatry Inst. Living, Hartford, Conn., 1956-59; dir. day hosp. Vets. Hosp., Washington, 1960-61, asst. chief psychiatry, 1961-64; pvt. practice psychiatry Bethesda, Md., 1964-78; staff psychiatrist Vets. Med. Ctr., Tuscaloosa, Ala., 1978-97; ret., 1997. Dir. clozapine rsch. Vets. Hosp., Tuscaloosa, 1991-97. Pharmacist mate USN, 1944-46. Mem. Am. Psychiat. Assn. (life). Home: Capstone Village 601 5th Ave E Apt 223 Tuscaloosa AL 35407

KEETON, WILLIAM SCOTT, ecologist, educator; b. Ithaca, NY, Jan. 31, 1967; s. William Tinsley and Barbara Orcutt Keeton; m. Karen Lee Tyler, Mar. 10, 1968; children: William Tyler, Julia Tyler. BS, Cornell U., Ithaca, NY, 1990; M of Environ. Studies, Yale U., New Haven, Conn., 1994; PhD, U. Wash., Seattle, 2000. Polit. intern The Sierra Club, Legislative Office, Washington, 1989; regulatory analyst Sci. Applications Internat. Corp., 1990—92; cons. World Conservation Union, Gland, Switzerland, 1993—94; cons. conservation biologist Wilderness Soc., Seattle, 1994—96; field rsch. tech. U. Wash., 1996—2000, rsch. asst., 1997—2000; asst. prof. U. Vt., Burlington, 2000—07, assoc. prof., 2007—. Dir., Vt. forest ecosystem mgmt. demonstration project Vt. Monitoring Coop., Burlington, 2002—. Contbr. articles to profl. jours. Grantee, Fed. and state agencies and non-govl. orgns., 2000—06. Mem.: Soc. Conservation Biology, Am. Inst. Biol. Scis., Soc. Am. Foresters, Ecol. Soc. Am. Achievements include research in forest ecosystem structure and function, sustainable forestry climate change in parts, and ecosystem management and conservation. Avocations: hiking, backpacking, running, cross country skiing, guitar. Office: U Vt 343 Aiken Center Burlington VT 05405 Office Phone: 802-656-2518. Office Fax: 802-656-2623. Business E-Mail: william.keeton@uvm.edu.

KEETS, JOHN DAVID, JR., insurance company executive; b. Atlantic City, Apr. 1, 1948; s. John D. and Doris F. (Fleiss) Keets; m. Julianne Zellers, Nov. 3, 1973; children: J. David, Brian. BA, High Point Coll., 1970. CLU., cert. fin. planner, chartered fin. cons. Account exec. Mgmt. Recruiters, Phila., 1972-75; sales mgr. Cigna Fin. Svc., Miami (Fla.), Balt., 1975-82; agy. mgr. Fidelty Mut., Balt., 1983-85, Provident Mut. Ins. Co., Phila., 1985-88; regional v.p. Equitable Ins. Co., Mpls., 1988-90; prin. Keets & Assocs., Mpls., 1991—; mgr. Prudential Ins. Co., Mpls., 1993-94; v.p. bus. devel. Carlson Mktg. Group, Mpls., 1994-96; gen. mgr. Mut. of Omaha Cos., Mpls., 1998-2000; regional dir. 10F Foresters, 2000—03; treas., regional v.p. TransAm. Capital, Inc., 2004—. With U.S. Army, 1970-72, Germany. Mem. Mpls. Assn. Life Underwriters, Gen. Agts. and Mgrs. Assn, Internat. Assn. Fin. Planners, Am. Soc. CLU, Chartered Fin. Cons. Avocations: golf, boating. Home: 2420 Comstock Ln N Minneapolis MN 55447-2303 Office Phone: 612-801-1933. Personal E-mail: jkeets@msn.com.

KEEVER, MARY MOORE, elementary school educator; m. Wes Keever; children: Dory, Abby. BA, Wofford Coll., Spartanburg, SC, 1997; MEd, U. NC, Greensboro, 2005. Asst. dir. Camp Illahee, Brevard, NC, 1997—99; tchr., dean faculty mid. sch. Westchester Country Day Sch., High Point, NC, 1999—. Editor: Tchr. Edn. Quar. Action Rsch. Tchr. Empowerment, 2006; contbr. articles to newsletter. Mem. com. Family Svc. High Ponit, Oyster Roast, 2004—06, chmn., 2006—; mem. Jr. League High Point, 1999—2003. Presbyterian. Avocations: cooking, writing, reading. Office: Westchester Country Day Sch 2045 Old Greensboro Rd High Point NC 27265

KEEVEY, RICHARD FRANCIS, federal official, state official, educator; b. Phila., June 20, 1942; s. Richard Patrick and Eileen (Wright) K.; m. Elizabeth Regina Dwyer, Aug. 5, 1967; children: Richard, Michael, John. BA, La Salle Coll., Phila., 1964; M of Govt. Adminstrn., U. Pa., 1967. Various positions Commonwealth of Pa., City of Phila., State of N.J., 1967-70; dir. adminstrn., fiscal officer dept. community affairs N.J. Dept., Trenton, 1971-75, asst. to dir. div. budget and acctg. Treasury Dept., 1975-81, supr. Bur. Budget, Office Mgmt. and Budget, 1981-83, dep. budget dir., dep. comptr., 1983-89, dir. Office Mgmt. and Budget, 1989-94; dep. under sec. for fin. mgmt. Dept. Def., Washington, 1994-95, dir. defense fin. and acctg. agy., 1995-97; CFO U.S. Dept. Housing and Urban Renewal, 1997-99; dir. budget and fin. practice Arthur Andersen, Washington, 1999—2002; dir. adminstrv. and fin. programs Unisys corp., McLean, Va., 2002—03; dir. performance consortium Nat. Acad. Pub. Adminstrn., Washington, 2004—07; dir. policy rsch. Inst. Region Princeton U., NJ, 2007—. Instr. Rutgers U., New Brunswick, NJ, 1971-75; adj. prof. fin. Rider Coll., Lawrenceville, NJ, 1979-82, adv. com. grad. program in pub. mgmt., 1983-87; adj. prof. Seton Hall U., South Orange, NJ, 1990-93; adj. prof. budgeting sys. George Mason U., Fairfax, Va., 1999-2001; vis. prof. Princeton U., 2002-07, Am. U., 2005-07. Contbr. articles to profl. jours.; mem. bd. editors Pub. Adminstrn. Rev., 1979-84. Coach Little League Baseball and Soccer, 1975-82; trustee Police Athletic League Sports, Cinnaminson, N.J., 1978-81; mem. counsle president's adv. bd. La Salle U., 1984-87; bd. dirs. Zurbrugg Meml. Hosp., Willingboro, N.J., 1985-88; mem. Leadership N.J. Class of 1990, 1989—; pres. Cinnaminson Twp. Bd. Edn., 1980-90; mem. N.J. Commn. on Capital Budgeting and Planning, N.J. Bldg. Authority, N.J. Commn. on Health Benefits and Pensions, N.J. Transit Corp., N.J. Capital Joint Mgmt. Commn., N.J. Lease Mgmt.-Planning Bd. Recipient: Ken Howard award Career Achievement in Budget and Finance Am. Soc. Pub. Adminstrn., 2000; decorated DSM, medal for outstanding svc. U.S. Dept. Def., 1996. Mem. Nat. Assn. State Budget Officers, Nat. Assn. Comptrs., Am. Soc. for Pub. Adminstrn. (N.J. Pub. Adminstr. of Yr. award 1992), Assn. Govtl. Accts. (Disting. Leadership award N.J. chpt. 1991), Govt. Fin. Officers Assn. (tech. group to rev. budgets for nat. award certs.). Home: 1307 Wessex Pl Princeton NJ 08540 Office: Princeton U Princeton NJ 08540 Business E-Mail: rkeevey@princeton.edu.

KEEVIL, NORMAN B., mining executive; b. Cambridge, Mass., Feb. 28, 1938; s. Norman Bell and Verna Ruth (Bond) Keevil; m. Joan E. MacDonald, Dec. 1990; children: Scott, Laura, Jill, Norman Bell III. BA in Sci., U. Toronto, Ont., Can., 1959; PhD, U. Calif., Berkeley, 1964; LLD (hon.), U. BC, 1993. V.p. exploration Teck Corp., Vancouver, B.C., Canada, 1962-68, exec. v.p., 1968-81, pres., CEO, 1981-89, chmn., pres., CEO, 1989-94, pres., CEO, 1994-2000, CEO, 2000—; chmn. Teck Cominco Ltd., Vancouver, 2001—. Named Mining Man of Yr., No. Miner, 1979; named to Can. Mining Hall of Fame, 2004. Mem.: Soc. Exploration Geophysicists, Prospectors and Developers Assn. (Disting. Svc. award 1990, Viola R. MacMillan Developer's award 1997), Can. Inst. Mining and Metallurgy (Selwyn G. Blaylock medal 1990, Inco medal 1999), Royal & Ancient Golf Club (St. Andrews, Scotland), Shaughnessy Golf and Country Club, Vancouver Club. Office: Teck Cominco Ltd 200 Burrard St # 700 Vancouver BC Canada V6C 3L9 Office Phone: 604-687-1117.

KEEVIL, PHILIP CLEMENT, investment banker; b. London, Oct. 19, 1946; s. Ambrose Clement Arthur and Olwen Marjorie Enid (Gibbins) K.; m. Augusta Day McGrail, June 10, 1972; children: Adrian Ambrose Clement, Augusta Hall, Peter Larimer. BA, Oxford U., Eng., 1968, MA, 1972; MBA, Harvard U., 1975. Mgr. Unilever plc, Eng., 1968-73; assoc. Morgan Stanley & Co., NYC, 1975-78, Lazard Freres & Co., NYC, 1979-80, v.p., 1981-82, gen. ptnr., 1983-87; mng. dir., head mergers and acquisitions S.G. Warburg and Co. Inc., NYC, 1987-91, head investment banking, 1991-95; mng. dir. Salomon Brothers Inc. (now Citigroup Global Markets), 1995—2005, head internat. mergers and acquisitions NYC, 1995—97; head European mergers and acquisitions Salomon Smith Barney, London, 1997-2000; head mergers and acquisitions Schroder Salomon Smith Barney, London, 2000—02; sr. ptnr. Compass Advisers LLP, 2005—. Bd. dirs. S.G. Warburg & Co., Ltd., London, 1987-95, The Risk Adv. Group, 2006-, chmn., 2007-; adv. bd. NBD Sana Capital, Dubai, 2007-. Freeman City of London, 1968; liveryman Worshipful Co. of Poulters, London, 1968-, Worshipful Co. Internat. Bankers, London, 2006-; mem. of Ct., Poulters' Co., 1992-, renter warden, 1998-99, upper warden, 1999-2000, master, 2000-01; vestryman St. John's Ch., Locust Valley, NY, 1986-89; trustee St. Bernard's Sch., NY, 1991-97, St. Andrew's Sch., Del., 1993-2001; bd. dirs. Am. for Oxford Inc., 1995-02; bus. adv. forum. Said Bus. Sch., Oxford U., 1999-; bd. govs. City of London Sch. for Girls, 2002-; mem. adv. coun. London Symphony Orch., 2004-. Baker scholar Harvard Bus. Sch., Boston, 1975. Fellow: Royal Soc. Arts; mem.: Pilgrims Soc. UK, Brit.-Am. Bus. Inc. (dir. 1993—2000, dep. chmn. 1999—2001, dir. 2004—), Knickerbocker Club, London Rowing Club, Queenwood (Ottershaw, Eng.), Cavalry and Guards (London), Leander Club (Henley, Eng.), Brook Club, Piping Rock Club (Locust Valley) (gov. 1986—96). Episcopalian. Avocations: choral music, field sports, racquet sports. Business E-Mail: philip.keevil@ca-llp.com.

KEFALIDES, NICHOLAS ALEXANDER, physician, educator; b. Alexandroupolis, Greece, Jan. 17, 1927; came to U.S., 1947, naturalized; s. Athanasios and Alexandra (Aematidou) K.; m. Eugenia Georgia Kutsunis, Nov. 24, 1949; children: Alexandra Jane (dec.), Patricia Ann, Paul Thomas. BA, Augustana Coll., Rock Island, Ill., 1951; BS, U. Ill., Chgo., 1953, MS in Biochemistry, 1956, MD, 1956, PhD in Biochemistry, 1965; MS (hon.), U. Pa., 1971; doctorate (hon.), U. Reims, France, 1987. Resident in internal medicine U. Ill. Coll. Medicine, Chgo., 1960-62, NIH fellow in infectious disease, 1962-64, asst. prof. medicine, 1964-65, U. Chgo., 1965-69, assoc. prof. medicine, 1969-70; assoc. prof. medicine and biochemistry U. Pa., Phila., 1970-74, prof. medicine, 1974—96, prof. medicine emeritus, 1996—, prof. biochemistry and biophysics, 1975—; assoc. dean rsch. U. Pa. Sch. Medicine, 1994-95. Vis. prof. Oxford (England) U., 1977—78, 1984—85; mem., chmn. pathobiochemistry study sect. NIH, 1982—86, dir. project on burns, Peru, 1957—60; dir. Connective Tissue Rsch. Inst., Phila., 1977—2002; chmn. Instn. Rev. Bd. U. Pa., 1995—98, exec. chmn., 1998—2003; initiator, chair Gordon Rsch. Confs. on Basement Membranes, 1982; sci. mentor biotech. cos. Sci. Ctr., Phila., 2002—. Author: (with J. P. Borel) Basement Membranes: Cell and Molecular Biology, 2005; creator lecture series Lunch for Hungry Minds, Phila., 1998—; contbr. chpts. to books, articles to profl. jours. Lt. comdr., surgeon US Public Health Svc., 1957—60. Recipient Borden Rsch. Found. award, 1956, award for pioneering rsch. on connective tissue Collagen Gordon Confs. and Collagen Corp., 1997; Guggenheim fellow, 1977. Fellow AAAS; mem. Am. Assn. Pathologists, Am. Soc. Clin. Investigation, Am. Soc. Biochemistry and Molecular Biology, Am. Soc. Cell Biology. Achievements include discovery of Collagen type IV in basement membranes and its role in suppressing tumor cell growth and angiogenesis. Office: U Pa Univ City Sci Ctr 3701 Market St Rm 467 Philadelphia PA 19104-5502

KEFAUVER, WELDON ADDISON, publishing executive; b. Canal Winchester, Ohio, Apr. 3, 1927; s. Ross Baker and Virginia Marie (Burtner) K. BA, Ohio State U., Columbus, 1950. Mem. faculty Columbus Acad., 1956-58; mng. editor Ohio State U. Press, 1958-64, dir., 1964-84, dir. emeritus, 1984—. Dir. Am. Univ. Press Svcs., Inc., 1971-72, 76-79; mem. US del. 2d Asian Pacific Conf. Publs., Taiwan, 1978 Author: Scholars and their Publishers, 1977; editl. adv. bd. Scholarly Publishing. Served with AUS, 1945-46. Recipient Centennial Svc. award Ohio State U., 1970; citation Ohioana Libr. Assn., 1974; Disting. Svc. award Ohio State U., 1986; recognized for svc. to Ohio State U. by Ohio Senate and Ohio Ho.

of Reps., 1986. Mem. Assn. Am. Univ. Presses (v.p. 1971-72, dir. 1971-72, 76-79, pres. 1977-78), Soc. Scholarly Pub., Nathaniel Hawthorne Soc., AAUP, Phi Eta Sigma, Phi Kappa Phi Clubs: Torch (Columbus), Crichton (Columbus), Ohio State U. Faculty (Columbus). Home: 675 Eastmoor Blvd Columbus OH 43209-2252 Office: 1050 Carmack Rd Columbus OH 43210-1002

KEFFER, CHARLES JOSEPH, retired physics professor, academic administrator; b. Phila., Aug. 7, 1941; s. Raphael Joseph and Clara Emelia (Fefolt) K.; m. Barbara Franke, Aug. 27, 1966; children— Susan Marie, David Charles, Peter John, Dennis Paul BS, U. Scranton, 1963; AM, Harvard U., 1964, PhD, 1969. From instr. to assoc. prof. physics U. Scranton, Pa., 1967-73; dean coll. U. St. Thomas, St. Paul, 1973-77, v.p. acad. affairs, 1973-84, provost, 1977-98. Cons.-evaluator N. Central Assn., Chgo., 1980-98. Chmn. Midway Tng. Services, St. Paul, 1977-87. Grad. fellow NSF, Harvard U., 1963-65; summer leadership fellow Bush Found., 1977 Mem. Democratic Farm Labor Party. Roman Catholic Avocation: soccer.

KEFFLER, KARL JOSEPH, investment company executive, lawyer; b. St. Louis, July 1, 1943; s. Karl Leopold and Dorothea Agnes (Lucas) K. Student, U.Notre Dame, 1961-62; BA cum laude, Regis U., 1965; JD, St. Louis U., 1968; postgrad., Northwestern U., Chgo., 1972, Oxford U., Eng., 1995. Bar: Mo. 1969, U.S. Dist. Ct. D.C. 1970, Ill. 1987. Spl. agt. FBI, Washington, Mpls., San Francisco, 1968-71; asst. pros. atty. Office Pros. Atty. St. Louis County, Clayton, Mo., 1971-74; pvt. practice, St. Louis, 1974-81; trust officer Merc. Trust Co., NA, St. Louis, 1981-85; trust exec., head trust dept. People's Bank & Trust Co., Waterloo Iowa, 1985-86, Ill. Nat. Bank, Springfield, 1987-88, 1st Comml. Bank, Little Rock, 1988-89; pvt. investor St. Louis, 1989-97; exec. v.p., chief investments officer St. Louis Capital Mgmt., LLC, 1997—. Author investment newsletter Capital Idea, 1998. Bd. dirs. Springfield Symphony, 1987. Mem. Mo. Bar, Soc. Former Spl. Agts. FBI, Am. Mensa, Phi Delta Phi. Avocations: sports, art collecting, music. Home: 155 N Hanley Rd Apt 105 Saint Louis MO 63105-4106 Office: St Louis Capital Mgmt LLC 9845 Northbridge Rd Saint Louis MO 63124-1025 Home Phone: 314-863-2727; Office Phone: 314-863-2727. E-mail: karljkeffler@prodigy.net.

KEGEL, WILLIAM GEORGE, mining company executive; b. Pitts., Mar. 15, 1922; s. William G. and Gertrude (Holl) K.; m. Jacqueline Treacy, Feb. 17, 1942; children: Kathy, Danyele, Janice, Jacqueline, William, Madeline, Colleen, Lisa, Brian. Student elec. engring, U. Pitts., 1940-43; LLD (hon.), Ind. U. of Pa., 1986. Mgr. mech. and elec. depts. Lee Norse Co., 1941-50; with Jones & Laughlin Steel Corp., Pitts., 1950-76, gen. mgr. raw materials and traffic, 1975-76; pres. Cerro Marmon Coal Group, 1976-79; pres., chief exec. officer Rochester & Pitt. Coal Co., Indiana, Pa., 1979-88, chmn. bd., 1988-98. Dir. emeritus Savs. and Trust Co. Pa., Indiana. Mem. Indiana (Pa.) Airport Authority, 1980-2001; bd. dirs. Brownsville Gen. Hosp., 1964-71; mem. Centerville Borough Council, 1952-60. Mem. AIME, Coal Mining Inst. Am., Am. Mining Congress (dir.), Pitts. Coal Mining Inst., Duquesne Club, Ind. Country Club, Laurel Valley Country Club. Republican. Roman Catholic. Home: 61 Duck Woods Dr Southern Shores NC 27949 E-mail: wgkegel@charter.net.

KEGELES, SUSAN M., medical educator, researcher; b. Boston, Sept. 5, 1953; d. S. Stephen and Jane (Ainsworth) Kegeles; m. Jeffrey L. Lazarus, Aug. 23, 1982; children: Paul Thomas Kegeles Lazarus, Rebecca Ann Ainsworth Lazarus. PhD summa cum laude, U. Calif., Berkeley, 1984. Prof. medicine U. Calif., San Francisco, 1984—. Cons. in field. Recipient Karl Muenzinger award, 1984. Mem.: Phi Beta Kappa. Achievements include research in in social/behavioral HIV/AIDS prevention. Home: 2957 Shasta Rd Berkeley CA 94708 Office: Univ Calif Ctr for AIDS Prev Studies 50 Beale St San Francisco CA 94105

KEGERREIS, ROBERT JAMES, management consultant, marketing professional, educator; b. Detroit, Apr. 2, 1921; s. I. G. and A. M. (Merry) K.; m. Katherine L. Falknor, Oct. 30, 1943; children: Merry, Duncan, Melissa. BA, BS, Ohio State U., 1943, MBA, 1946, PhD, 1968, U. Dayton, 1982, EdD (hon.), EdD (hon.), U. Dayton; LLD (hon.), U. Akron, Wilberforce U.; ScD (hon.), Cen. State U., Japan, 1992; EconD (hon.), Okayama U., Japan, 1992. Economist Fed. Res. Bank, Cleve., 1946-49; pres. KV Stores, Inc., Woodsfield, Ohio, 1949-69; v.p., sec. KBK Devel. Co., Inc., 1955-62; assoc. prof. Ohio U., Athens, 1967-69; dean Coll. Bus. and Adminstrn. Wright State U., Dayton, Ohio, 1969-71, v.p. adminstrn., 1971-73, pres., 1973-85; cons. RJK Co., Dayton, 1985—. Lt. (j.g.) USN, 1943—46. Mem. Moraine Country Club, Bicycle Club, Pelican Bay Country Club. Methodist. Avocations: flying, golf.

KEGLEY, CHARLES WILLIAM, JR., political science professor; b. Evanston, Ill., Mar. 5, 1944; s. Charles William Kegley and Elizabeth Euphemia Meck; m. Ann Curry Taylor, Apr. 1, 1966 (div.); 1 child, Mrs. Suzanne, Mitchell Douglas; m. Pamela Ann Holcomb, July 2, 1975 (div.); m. Debra Annette Jump, July 6, 2002. BA, Am. U., 1966; PhD, Syracuse U., 1971. Asst. prof. Sch. Fgn. Svc., Georgetown U., 1971-72, prof., chmn. dept. polit. sci., 1981—85; dir. Byrnes Internat. Ctr. U. SC, Columbia, 1986—88, holder Pearce endowed chair in internat. rels., 1985—2005, disting. Pearce prof. internat. rels. emeritus, 2006—; founding ptnr. Kegly Internat., Inc., 2006—. Vis. prof. U. Tex., 1976; Moses Back Peace prof., Rutgers U., New Brunswick, N.J., 1989, People's U. China, Beijing, 1996, Grad. Inst. Internat. Studies, Geneva, 2004; corp. sec. Carnegie Coun. Ethics Internat. Affairs, NY, 2006; faculty fellow Moynihan Global Affairs Inst., Maxwell Sch., Syracuse U., 2006—. Author: A General Empirical Typology of Foreign Policy Behavior, 1973; co-author, co-editor (with William Coplin): A Multi-Method Introduction to International Politics: Observation, Explanation and Prescription, 1971, Analyzing International Relations: A Multi-Method Introduction, 1975, World Politics: Trent at Tronsfanatic, 11th edit., 2007; co-author: (with Eugene R. Wittkopf) American Foreign Policy: Pattern and Process, 1979, (with Eugene R. Wittkopf and Christopher Jones) 7th edit., 2007, World Politics: Trend and Transformation, 1981, 10th edit., 2005, Svetska Politika, 2005; (with Gregory A. Raymond) When Trust Breaks Down: Alliance Norms and World Politics, 1990, A Multipolar Peace? Great-Power Politics in the 21st Century, 1994, How Nations Make Peace, 1999, From War to Peace: Fateful Decisions in International Politics, 2002, Exorcising the Ghost of Westphalia: Building World Order in the New Millennium, 2002, The Global Future, 2006, 2d edit. 2007, After Iraq: The Imperiled American Imperium, 2007; co-editor: (with Robert W. Gregg) After Vietnam: The Future of American Foreign Policy, 1971; (with Gregory A. Raymond, Robert M. Rood, Richard A. Skinner) International Events and the Comparative Analysis of Foreign Policy, 1975; (with Patrick J. McGowan) Challenges to America: U.S. Foreign Policy in the 1980's, 1979, Threats, Weapons, and Foreign Policy, 1980, The Political Economy of Foreign Policy, 1981, Foreign Policy: USA/USSR, 1983; (with Eugene R. Wittkopf) Perspectives on American Foreign Policy, 1983, The Global Agenda: Issues and Perspectives, 1984, 6th edit., 2001 (with Patrick McGowan) Foreign Policy and the Modern World System, 1983; (with Eugene R. Wittkopf) The Nuclear Reader: Strategy, Weapons, War, 1985, 2d edit., 1989; (with Charles F. Hermann and James N. Rosenau) New Directions in the Study of Foreign Policy, 1987, (with Eugene R. Wittkopf) The Domestic Sources of American Foreign Policy, 1988, (with Kenneth Schwab) After the Cold War: Questioning the Morality of Nuclear Deterrence, 1991, (with Eugene R. Wittkopf) The Future of American Foreign Policy, 1992; editor: The Long Postwar Peace: Contending Explanations and Projections, 1990, International Terrorism: Characteristics, Causes, Controls, 1990, Controversies in International Relations Theory: Realism and the Neoliberal Challenge, 1995, The New Global Terrorism, 2003; contbr. chpts. to books, articles to profl. jours. Trustee Carnegie Coun. for Ethics in Internat. Affairs, 1992-98, 2000-06, vice chair 2007—. Recipient Disting. Alumni award Am. U., 1984; R.M. Davis scholar, 1962-66; Maxwell fellow, 1968-69, 70-71; NY State Regents fellow, 1969-70, Moynihon Faculty Rsch. fellow Syracuse U., 2006-; Fulbright sr. scholar, 1978, Russell rsch. awardee in humanities and social scis., 1982. Mem. Am. Polit. Sci. Assn., Am. Soc. Internat. Law, Am. Soc. Advancement Sci., Internat. Polit. Sci. Assn., Internat. Studies Assn. (assoc. dir. 1980-84, pres. 1993-94), Peace Sci. Soc., Peace Rsch. Soc., So. Polit. Sci. Assn., Pi Sigma Alpha, Omicron Delta Kappa, Delta Tau Kappa, Alpha Tau Omega. Home: 35 Veranda Ln Blythewood SC 29016-7602 Office: U SC Dept Polit Sci Columbia SC 29208-0001 Office Phone: 803-714-6049. Personal E-mail: jumpkegs@aol.com.

KEGLEY, JACQUELYN ANN, philosophy educator; b. Conneaut, Ohio, July 18, 1938; d. Steven Paul and Gertrude Evelyn (Frank) Kovacevic; m. Charles William Kegley, June 12, 1964; children: Jacquelyn Ann, Stephen Lincoln Luther. BA cum laude, Allegheny Coll., 1960; MA summa cum laude, Rice U., 1964; PhD, Columbia U., 1971. Asst. prof. philosophy Calif. State U., Bakersfield, 1973-77, assoc. prof., 1977-81, prof., 1981—, chair dept. philosophy and religious studies. Vis. prof. U. Philippines, Quezon City, 1966-68; grant project dir. Calif. Coun. Humanities, 1977, project dir. 1980, 82; mem. work group on ethics Am. Colls. of Nursing, Washington, 1984-86; mem. Am. Bd. Forensic Examiners; chair acad. senate Calif. State U., 2000-03, exec. com., 2003-04, chair fiscal and gov. affairs com. Author: Introduction to Logic, 1978, Genuine Individuals and Genuine Communities, 1997; editor: Humanistic Delivery of Services to Families, 1982, Education for the Handicapped, 1982, Genetic Knowledge, 1998; mem. editl. bd. Jour. Philosophy in Lit., 1979-84; contbr. articles to profl. jours. Active CSU Acad. Senate, 1999—; Bd. dirs. Bakersfield Mental Health Assn., 1982—84, Citizens for Betterment of Community. Recipinet Golden Roadrunner award Bakersfield Cmty., 1991, Wang Family Excellence award, 2000, Soc. Advancement Am. Philosophy Herbert Schneider award, 2006. Mem. Philosophy of Sci. Assn., Soc. Advancement Am. Philos. Soc. (chmn. Pacific divsn. 1979-83, 2005—, nat. exec. com. 1974-79, 2003-), Philosophy Soc., Soc. Interdisciplinary Study of Mind, Am. Philos. Assn. (bd. mem. 1999-2003, chair com. on tchg.), Dorian Soc., Phi Beta Kappa. Democrat. Lutheran. Avocations: music, tennis. Home: 7312 Kroll Way Bakersfield CA 93309-2336 Office: Calif State U Dept Philosophy Bakersfield CA 93311 Office Phone: 661-664-2249. Business E-Mail: jkegley@csub.edu.

KEHEW, GEORGE MANSIR, artist; b. Harvey, Ill., Aug. 17, 1923; s. George Henry and Blanche Willard (Holt) K.; m. Dolores Smith, Mar. 21, 1947; children: Eric Wayne, Roger Mark, Jai Lynne. Student, Chouinard Art Sch., LA, Art Ctr. Coll. of Design. Cert. indsl. edn. tchr. Calif., Calif. C.C. tchr. in art, design and photography. Various positions in field to illustrator Northrop Aircraft Corp., Hawthorne, Calif., 1957-59; lead man, tech. illustrators Cannon & Sullivan, San Diego, 1959-61; art dir. Applied Oceanog. Group, Scripps Inst. Oceanography U. Calif., San Diego, 1961-66, illustrator, photographer Office Learning Resources, 1966-67; artist Complete Art Svc., San Diego, Calif., 1966-68; illustrator, tng. visuals Grumman Aerospace, NAS Miramar, Calif., 1972-73; visual info. specialist Naval Edn. and Tng. Support Ctr., San Diego, 1973-85. Alt. mem. Equal Employment Opportunity Com., San Diego, 1983. Artist/author: Mac Goes to the Hospital, Best Friends Animal Coloring and Activity Book; creator ofcl. Squadron patch (Red Wolf) for VF-1 Mira Mar Naval Air Sta., logo for Scripps Applied Oceanographic Group, Point Loma, Calif., (game) Bushwacker; syndicated cartoon strip Hamalot; exhibiting cartoonist 1968 Terre Des Hommes, Man and His World, Pavilion de L'Humor, Montreal; designer, dir. TV show packaging for Art Around Us, San Diego Area Instrnl. TV Authority, 1965, others; represented in Vincent Price Sears travel show, 1965-67, others; contbr. articles to Desert Mag. Sgt. U.S. Army, PTO, 1942-46. Recipient art awards including Bicentennial First Ann. Best of Show award, 1976, Merit award in publs. San Diego C.C., 1972, award for best painting St. George Art Mus., 1999, Sweepstake award Washington County Fair Juried Show, 1999-2000, 04, Reserve Sweepstake award, 2004, 3d pl. award Springville Juried Art Show, 2000, 3d pl. award 17th Annual Dixie Invitational, 2004; grantee in field. Mem.: Am. Soc. Bot. Artists. Democrat. Avocations: mountain biking, cross country skiing, sailing, classic guitar.

KEHLER, ANDREW S., computer scientist, educator; b. Norristown, Pa., Jan. 14, 1966; s. Frank H. and Ruby A. Kehler; m. Jill E. Jarecki, June 28, 1997; 1 child, Jeremy R. BS in Computer Sci. and Engring., U. Pa., Phila, 1988; PhD in Computer Sci., Harvard U., Boston, 1995. Sr. computer scientist SRI Internat., Menlo Park, Calif., 1995—2000; assoc. prof. linguistics U. Calif. San Diego, La Jolla, 2000—. Author: Coherence, Reference, and the Theory of Grammar, 2002; contbr. scientific papers, articles to books and profl. jours. Mem.: Assn. Computational Linguistics (exec. bd. mem. N.Am. chpt. 2005—06). Office: U Calif San Diego 9500 Gilman Dr #0108 La Jolla CA 92093-0108 Business E-Mail: kehler@ling.ucsd.edu.

KEHLMANN, ROBERT, artist, critic; b. Bklyn., Mar. 9, 1942; BA, Antioch Coll., 1963; MA, U. Calif., Berkeley, 1966. Instr. glass design Calif. Coll. Arts and Crafts, Oakland, 1978-80, 91, Pilchuck Glass Ctr., Stanwood, Wash., 1978-80; guest curator Mus. Glass, Tacoma, Wash., 2001. One-man shows include Richmond Art Ctr., Calif., 1976, William Sawyer Gallery, San Francisco, 1978, 82, 86, Gallerie M. Kassel, Fed. Republic Germany, 1985, Anne O'Brien Gallery, Washington, 1988, 90, Dorothy Weiss Gallery, San Francisco, 1993, Hearst Art Gallery, Moraga, 1996; group shows include Am. Craft Mus., NYC, 1978, 86, Corning (NY) Mus. Glass, 1979, Tucson Mus. Art, 1983, Kulturhuset, Stockholm, 1985; represented in permanent collections at Corning Mus. Glass, Leigh Yawkey Woodson Art Mus., Hessesches Landes Mus., Germany, Bank of Am. World Hdqrs., San Francisco, Toledo Mus. Art, Hokkaido Mus. Modern Art, Sapporo, Japan, Huntington Mus. Art, W.Va., mus. Arts and Design, NYC, Mus. des Arts décoratifs, Lausanne, Switzerland, Oakland Mus.; rep. Heller Gallery, N.Y.C.; Author: Twentieth Century Stained Glass: A New Definition, 1992, The Inner Light: Sculpture By Stanislau Libensky and Jaroslava Brychtova, 2002; contbg. editor: New Glass Work mag., 1988-89; editor: Glass Art Soc. Jour., 1981-84. Chmn. Landmarks Preservation Commn., Berkeley, 1995-98. NEA grantee, 1977, 78. Mem. Glass Art Soc. (bd. dirs. 1980-84, 89-92, hon. life). Office Phone: 212-414-4014. Personal E-mail: robertkehlmann@yahoo.com.

KEHOE, JOHN KIMBALL, finance educator, consultant; b. Chgo., Ill., June 20, 1936; s. John J. and Eleanor M. Kehoe; m. Mary Corleen, Aug. 3, 1974; children: Megan Rose, Nancy Kimball. BA, Northwestern U., Evanston, Ill., 1958; MA, St. Louis U., 1964; D of Bus. Admin., Harvard U., Cambridge, Mass., 1975. Pers. rep. Eli Lilly and Co., Indpls., 1974—75, comp. analyst, 1976, sr. sales recruiter, 1977—78, internat. pers. adv., 1979—80, HR mgr. for rsch., 1981; dir. mgmt. devel. Eli Lilly & Co., Indpls., 1982—84; dir. exec. devel. SCH Healthcare Sys., Houston, 1985—89; dir. Exec. ed. Rice U, Houston, 1989—92; assoc. dean Fuqua Sch., Duke U, Durham, NC, 1992—93; dir. custom prog. Ctr. for Creative Leadership, Greensboro, NC, 1993—95; sr. cons. Pers. Decisions Internat., Mpls., 1995—97, Profit Link, Naperville, Ill., 1997—2002; lectr. in mgmt. Rice U, Houston, 2002—, dir. action learning projects, 2004—. Tchg. asst. Harvard U., Boston, 1970—72; instr. Harvard Bus. Sch., 1973—74; lectr. Ind. U., Indpls., 1977—83; assoc. dean exec. ed. Duke U, Durham, NC, 1992—93; adj. faculty Rice U, Houston, 1987—92, dir. exec. ed., 1989—92, lectr. in mgmt., 2001—. Bd. dirs. Northwest Assistance Ministries, Houston, 2003—. Mem.: Harvard Bus. Sch. Club of Houston (assoc.). Avocation: community svc. Home: 6010 Pin Oak Place Spring TX 77379-8825 Office Phone: 713-348-6267. Personal E-mail: kehoemck@rice.edu.

KEHOE, JOHN P., investor relations executive; b. NYC, Aug. 5, 1938; s. John M. and Mary K. (Denning) Kehoe; m. Veronica Lally, Dec. 1, 1984 (dec. 2007); children: John Michael, Maura Kehoe Collins, Kevin Dening, Brendan, Allise Dickson. Cert. in investment analysis, N.Y. Inst. Fin., 1960; MS in Bus. Policy, Columbia U., 1979; BA in English Lit., Fordham U., 1985. Sr. assoc. Baker Weeks & Co., Inc., NYC, 1957-61; v.p., asst. to pres. McDonnell & Co., Inc., NYC, 1961-65, sr. v.p., chmn. investment policy com., 1965-67; pres. McDonnell Fund, NYC, 1965-67; exec. v.p. Crosby M. Kelly Assocs. Ltd., NYC, 1967-69; pres., founder, chmn. Kehoe, White, Savage & Co. (Kehoe Ptnrs., Inc.), NYC, 1969—; chmn. Kehoe Ptnrs., Inc., NYC, 1998—; sr. counselor Abernathy MacGregor Group, NYC, 2000—. Trustee Fordham U. Served as sgt. USMCR, 1958-64. Mem.: Nat. Investor Rels. Inst. (charter), Ea. Yacht Club (Marblehead, Mass.), Princeton Club (N.Y.C.), Racquet and Tennis Club, Phi Kappa Phi, Beta Gamma Sigma. Home: 55 E 72nd St New York NY 10021-4149 Office: Kehoe Ptnrs Inc 501 Madison Ave Fl 13 New York NY 10022 Home Phone: 212-570-9861; Office Phone: 917-328-4872. Business E-Mail: jpk@abmac.com.

KEHOE, L. PAUL, state judge; b. West Carthage, NY, May 21, 1938; s. Leo A. and Mildred (Piddock) K.; m. Elizabeth M. Weber, 1963; children: L. Paul, John Michael, Patrick Lewis. BA, Syracuse U., 1959, JD, 1962. Bar: N.Y. 1962. Dist. atty., Wayne County, NY, 1967-71; mem. N.Y. Assembly, 1979-80, N.Y. State Senate, 1981-92; justice N.Y. Supreme Ct., 1993—; adminstrv. judge 7th Jud. Dist., 1996-2000; assoc. Justice Appellate Divsn., 4th Dept., 2000—. With AUS, 1962-63. Mem. ABA, N.Y. State Bar Assn., Wayne County Bar Assn., Monroe County Bar Assn., Elks. Republican. Office Phone: 585-368-8821. Personal E-mail: judgelpaulkehoe@yahoo.com.

KEHOE, THOMAS J., food products executive; b. NYC, Apr. 9, 1949; s. Thomas J. and Aileen F. Kehoe; m. Carole M. Cassidy, Oct. 1, 1994; m. Doreen A. Hydell, Sept. 1, 1975 (div. June 1, 1990); children: Yvonne, Thomas, Matthew, Veronica, Rebecca, Marrielle. BA, U. Dayton, 1971. Sales and mktg. exec. Xerox Corp., NYC, 1971—75; owner Bayville (N.Y.) Fish, 1976—78; polit. cons. Kehoe Assocs., Strafford, NH, 1978—80; dir. mktg. PG Assco Inc., Syosset, NY, 1980—82; pres., ptnr. Galilee Seafood, NYC, 1982—87; pres. Thomas J. Kehoe Inc., Northport, NY, 1982—90; pres., ptnr. K&B Seafood Inc., East Northport, NY, 1990—. Bd. dirs. Mid Atlantic Fishery Devel. Coun., 1985—88, Fish Polit. Action Com., Washington, 2006—; co-chmn. Molluscan Shellfish Inst. of Nat. Fisheries Inst., 2006—. Trustee Village of Northport, NY, 2006—, commr. of sanitation and commerce NY, 2006—; commr. LI North Shore Heritage Area Commn., 2006; exec. bd. Suffolk County coun. Boy Scouts Am., 2007—; coach Eaton's Neck Basketball, 1987—92; coach, v.p. Northport Little League, 1987—94. Named Bus. Man of Yr., Times Beacon Newspapers, 2006. Mem.: East End Marine Farmers Assn., Long Island Farm Bur., Pacific Coast Shellfish Growers Assn., East Coast Shellfish Growers Assn. (bd. dirs. 2003—), East Northport C. of C. (bd. dirs. 2005—07), Suffolk County Village Ofcls. Assn., Friends of Sagamore Hill, U.S. Fencing Assn., Nat. Eagle Scout Assn., Friends of Raynham Hall, AAU-Karate, Theodore Roosevelt Assn. (trustee 2006—), Nat. Fisheries Inst. (bd. dirs. 2006—), Aki Bokken Jutsu, Chowa Ryu Kobudo, Chowa-Ryu Karate, Juko Kai Internat., N.Y. Athletic Club. Achievements include becoming an Eagle Scout. Avocations: martial arts, history. Home: 51 Mariners Ln Northport NY 11768 Office: K&B Seafood Inc 176 Laurel Rd East Northport NY 11731 Office Phone: 631-261-8161. Personal E-mail: tjkehoe@verizon.net.

KEHOE, VINCENT JEFFRÉ-ROUX, photographer, cosmetics executive; b. Bklyn., Sept. 12, 1921; s. John James and Bertha Florence (Roux) K.; m. Gena Irene Marino, Nov. 2, 1966. Student, MIT, 1940-41, Lowell Technol. Inst., 1941-42, Boston U., 1942; BFA in Motion Picture and TV Prodn., Columbia U., 1957. Dir. make-up dept. CBS-TV, NYC, 1948-49, NBC Hallmark Hall of Fame series, 1951-53; make-up artist in charge of make-up numerous film, tv and stage prodns., 1942—; dir. make-up Turner Hall Corp., 1959-61, Internat. Beauty Show, 1962-66. Pres., dir. rsch., founder Rsch. Coun. Make-Up Artists, Inc., 1963-; chief press officer Spanish Pavilion N.Y. World's Fair, 1965; free-lance photographer, 1956-; founder 10th Rgt. of Foot, Am. Contingent, 1968, Nat. Assn. Taurino Clubs, 1961, Club Taurino N.Y., 1960. Author: The Technique of Film and Television Make-Up, 1958, For Color, 1970, The Make-Up Artist in the Beauty Salon, 1969, We Were There: April 19, 1775, 1974, A Military Guide, 1974, 2nd rev. edit., 1993, 3rd rev. edit., 1998-99, The Re-Created Officer's Guide, 5 vols., 1996-98, The Technique of the Professional Make-Up Artist, 1985, 2nd edit., 1995, Special Make-Up Effects, 1991, The British Story of the Battles of Lexington and Concord, 2000, The History of the 10th Regiment of Fort in Am., 3 vols., 2006; co-author The Professional Make-up Artist, 2006; author, photographer: (bullfighting book) Aficionado! (NY Art Dirs. Club award 1960), Wine Women and Toros! (NY Art Dirs. award 1962); prodr.: (documentary color film) Matador de Toros, 1959; contbr. photographs to numerous mags. including Time, Life, Sports Illustrated, Argosy, Popular Photography. Served with U.S. Army, WWII, ETO. Decorated Purple Heart, Bronze Star, CIB; recipient Torch award Coun. of 13 Original States, 1979. Fellow Co. Mil. Historians; mem. Tenth Foot Royal Lincolnshire Regimental Assn. (life; Hon. Col. 1968), Soc. Motion Picture and TV Engrs. (life), Acad. TV Arts and Scis., Soc. Army Hist. Rsch. (Eng., life), Brit. Officers Club New Eng. (life), Army Hist. Found. (life), 10th Mountain Divsn. Assn. (life), NRA (life), 70th Divsn. (life), Am. Chem. Soc., DAV (life), Eagle Scout Assn. (life), Naval Club (London). Home and Office: PO Box 850 Somis CA 93066-0850 Home Phone: 805-386-4744.

KEHOE, WILLIAM FRANCIS, lawyer; b. Stoneham, Mass., Dec. 3, 1933; s. William Andrew and Josephine Agnes (Crowley) K.; m. Dorothy Landry Kehoe; children by previous marriage: John William, Kathleen Emily. AB summa cum laude, Dartmouth Coll., 1955; MA, Yale U., 1956; LLB, Harvard U., 1963. Bar: Mass. 1963, U.S. Dist. Ct. Mass. 1964. Instr. English Middlebury (Vt.) Coll., 1956-57; ptnr. Gaston & Snow, Boston, 1970-91; counsel Hutchins, Wheeler & Dittmar, Boston, 1991-94, Taylor, Ganson & Perrin, Boston, 1995—. Mng. trustee Katharine L.W. and Winthrop Murray Crane, 3d Charitable Found.; mem. standing adv. com. on rules of civil procedure Supreme Jud. Ct.; lectr., panelist Mass. Continuing Legal Edn. Program and Mass. Jud. Inst. Author: Enjoying Ireland, 1966; contbr. articles and revs. to profl. jours. Served with U.S. Army, 1957-59. Fulbright scholar, Trinity Coll., Dublin, Ireland, 1959-60. Fellow Am. Coll. Trust and Estate Counsel; mem. Boston Bar Assn., Phi Beta Kappa. Office: Taylor Ganson & Perrin 160 Federal St Fl 20 Boston MA 02110-1722 Office Phone: 617-951-2777.

KEHRET, PEG, writer; b. LaCrosse, Wis., Nov. 11, 1936; d. Arthur Robert and Elizabeth (Showers) Schulze; m. Carl Edward Kehret, July 2, 1955 (dec. 2004); children: Bob. C., Anne M. Kehret Konen. Student, U. Minn., 1954—55. Trustee Pacific Northwest Writers Conf., Seattle, 1983-86. Author: Vows of Love and Marriage, 1979, Refinishing and Restoring Your Piano, 1985, Winning Monologs for Young Actors, 1986, Deadly Stranger, 1987 (Children's Choice award, 1988), The Winner, 1988, ENCORE!-More Winning Monologs for Young Actors, 1988, Nightmare Mountain, 1989 (Young Hoosier Book award, 1992, Golden Sower award Nebr. Libr. Assn., 1993, Iowa Children's Choice award, 1994, Maud Hart Lovelace award, 1995), Wedding Vows, 1989, Sisters, Long Ago, 1990,

Cages, 1991 (Maud Hart Lovelace award, 1996), Acting Natural, 1992, Terror at the Zoo, 1992 (Pacific N.W. Young Reader's Choice award, 1995, N.Mex. Land of Enchantment award, 1995, Iowa Children's Choice award, 1996), Horror at the Haunted House, 1992 (Sequoyah Children's Book award, 1995, Young Hoosier award, 1995), Night of Fear, 1994, Richest Kids in Town, 1994, Cat Burglar on the Prowl, 1995, Danger at the Fair, 1995, Bone Breath and the Vandals, 1995, Don't Go Near Mrs. Tallie, 1995, Desert Danger, 1995, The Ghost Followed Us Home, 1996, Earthquake Terror, 1996 (W.Va. Children's Book award, 1998, Children's Crown award Nat. Christian Sch. Assn., 1998, Utah Children's Book award, 1999, Va. Young Readers award, 1999), Race to Disaster, 1996, Screaming Eagles, 1996, Backstage Fright, 1996, Small Steps: The Year I Got Polio, 1996 (Soc. Children's Book Writers and Illustrators Golden Kite award nonfiction, 1997, PEN Ctr. USA West award, 1997, Dorothy Canfield Fisher award, 1998, Mark Twain award, 1999, Young Hoosier award, 2001), Searching for Candlestick Park, 1997, The Volcano Disaster, 1998 (Fla. Sunshine award, 2000), The Blizzard Disaster, 1998, The Flood Disaster, 1999, Shelter Dogs, 1999, I'm Not Who You Think I Am, 1999 (Lamplighter award), The Secret Journey, 1999, My Brother Made Me Do It, 2000, Don't Tell Anyone, 2000, The Hideout, 2001, Saving Lilly, 2001 (Henry Bergh award ASPCA, 2001), The Stranger Next Door, 2002 (Sequoyah award, 2005, Nev. Young Readers award, 2005), Five Pages a Day: A Writer's Journey, 2002, Spy Cat, 2003 (SD Prarie Pasque award, 2006), Escaping the Giant Wave, 2003 (Iowa Children's Choice award, 2006, Fla. Young Reader award, 2006, Nev. Young Reader award, 2006, Nebr. Golden Sower award, 2006, Minn. Maud Hart Lovelace award, 2007, Iowa Children's Choice award, 2007), Abduction!, 2004 (Edgar award nominee, 2005, Mark Twain award, 2007, S.Dak. Prairie Pasque award, 2007), The Ghost's Grave, 2005 (Pa. Keystone award, 2007, N.H. Gt. Stone Face award, 2007), Trapped, 2006, Tell It Like It Is, 2007, (plays) Cemeteries are a Grave Matter, 1977, Let Him Sleep 'Till It's Time for His Funeral, 1978, Spirit!, 1979 (Forest Roberts Playwriting award No. Mich. U., 1979, Best New Play award Pioneer Drama Svc., 1980), Dracula, Darling, 1980, Charming Billy, 1981, (musical) Bicycles Built for Two, 1985; contbr. articles to mags., short stories to mags. Vol. Humane Soc., SPCA, Bellevue, Wash., 1975—95, Pasado's Safe Haven, 1995-. Recipient Achievement award Pacific N.W. Writers, Celebrate Lit. award N.W. Reading Coun. of Internat. Reading Assn., 1993; named Artist of Yr., Redmond Arts Commn., 1998. Mem. Author's Guild, Soc. Children's Book Writers, Mystery Writers Am. Office: Curtis Brown Ltd Ten Astor Pl New York NY 10003

KEHRT, BETTIE F., medical transcriptionist; b. Phila., Aug. 20, 1948; d. Reed and Bettie Francis (MacKnight) Knox; m. Randy Mark Kehrt, Mar. 22, 1986; m. Fred Kaplan (div.). At in Paleontology, SD Sch. Mines and Tech., Rapid City, 1992—94. Sec., audit student U. Pa. Hosp., Phila., 1970—82; transcription sec. Salick Health Care, Phila., 1990—98; med. transcriptionist Temple U. Hosp., Phila., 1982—2000, Bapt. Hosp. East, Louisville, 2001—04, Norton Health Care, Louisville, 2004—. Docent Acad. Nat. Scis., Phila., 1982—2000; vol. editor, writer Mesozoic Times, 1987—93. Mem.: Soc. Vertebrate Paleontology. Libertarian. Avocations: paleontology, reading. Home: 7415 Crawfordsbire Ln Louisville KY 40220-2811 Office: Norton Health Care 224 E Broadway Louisville KY 40202

KEICHER, WILLIAM EUGENE, electrical engineer; b. Pitts., Dec. 28, 1947; s. William John and Gina Rina (Magrini) K.; m. Barbara Marie Gurgacz, Aug. 12, 1972 (dec. Mar. 2006); children: Lisa Anne, Kathy Marie, William Michael; m. Adrienne Lena Cordeau, June 10, 2007. BSEE, Carnegie-Mellon U., 1969, MSEE, 1970, PhD in Elec. Engring., 1974. Sr. elec. engr. CBS Labs., Stamford, Conn., 1974-75; mem. tech. staff Lincoln Lab., MIT, Lexington, Mass., 1975-83, asst. group leader, 1983-85, group leader, 1985—93, 2000—06, assoc. group leader, 1993—2000, 2006—07, sr. mem. tech. staff, 2007—. Cons. Sci. and Engring. Support Group for Strategic Def. Initiative, Arlington, Va., 1988; co-chair for numerous confs. in field. Editor: Millimeter Wave Technology, 1982, Applied Laser Radar Technology, 1993, Industrial Applications of Laser Radar, 1994; contbr. articles to profl. publs.; patentee spatial filter sys. Capt. US Army, 1974. Mil. Sensing Symposium fellow, 2003. Mem. IEEE (sr.), Optical Soc. Am., Nat. Rsch. Coun. (Air Force sci. and tech. com. on rev. of Air Force hypersonic tech. program 1997-98), Assn. Old Crows. Roman Catholic. Avocations: astrophotography, history, snorkeling, travel, microcomputers. Home: 6 Winn Valley Dr Burlington MA 01803-4727 Office: MIT Lincoln Lab 244 Wood St Lexington MA 02421-6426 Office Phone: 781-981-7483. Business E-Mail: keicher@ll.mit.edu.

KEIDERLING, TIMOTHY ALLEN, chemistry educator, researcher; b. Waterloo, Iowa, June 22, 1947; s. Glenn Allen and Ethel V. (Kalainoff) K.; m. Candace Ruth Crawford, Sept. 4, 1976; 1 son, Michael Crawford. B.S., Loras Coll., 1969; MA, Princeton U., 1971, PhD, 1974. NSF fellow Princeton U., 1969-72; rsch. assoc. U. So. Calif., LA, 1973-76; asst. prof. U. Ill., Chgo., 1976-81, assoc. prof. chemistry, 1981-85, prof., 1985—, acting head, 1997-2000, assoc. dean arts and scis., 2003-04; guest prof. Max Planck Inst., Garching, Germany, 1984, U. Freiburg, 2004, U. Padova, Italy, 2005; sr. vis. Oxford U., 1994. Contbr. chpts. to books, more than 230 articles to profl. jours. Fellow Fulbright Found. 1984, Guggenheim Found. 2004-05; grantee NSF, NIH, Petroleum Rsch. Found., various times; sr. rsch. scholar U. Ill., 1991-94. Mem. Am. Chem. Soc., Am. Phys. Soc., Biophys. Soc., Soc. Applied Spectroscopy (nat. sec. 2007—). Achievements include the development of technique of vibrational circular dichroism, making of first such measurements of polypeptides, proteins and nucleic acids, and first magnetic applications to small molecules; research in protein folding and theoretical modelling of peptide structure and spectra. Office: U Ill Dept Chemistry 845 W Taylor St M/C 111 Chicago IL 60607-7061

KEIL, JOHN MULLAN, advertising executive, artist; b. Rochester, NY, Dec. 30, 1922; s. Alvin Richard and Elizabeth (Mullan) K.; m. Barbara Louise Miller, Sept. 16, 1950; children: Peter Mullan, Nicholas John, Elizabeth Jane. BA, U. Rochester, 1946. Copywriter advt. dept. Armstrong Cork Co., Lancaster, Pa., 1946-48, Wendell P. Colton Advt., NYC, 1948-51, Needham & Grohmann, Inc., NYC, 1951-55, v.p., account exec., 1955-60; v.p., creative dir. Dancer, Fitzgerald, Sample, Inc., NYC, 1960-64, copy group head, 1964-67, v.p., 1967-70, sr. v.p., creative dir., 1970-75, dir., 1971-87, exec. v.p., 1975-87, chmn. creative planning con., 1973; exec. creative dir. Dancer, Fitzgerald, Sample, 1983-86; dir. creative devel. DFS-Dorland Worldwide, 1986-87; creative cons. Saatchi & Saatchi Adv. Worldwide, 1987—. Lectr. Amos Tuck Sch. Dartmouth Coll., Assn. Nat. Advertisers; Phillips Meml. lectr. U. Fla., 1987; painter acrylic on wood Frank J. Miele Gallery, N.Y.C., Toadhall Gallery, N.Y.C., Reed Gallery, Chester, Vt., So. Vt. Art Ctr., Manchester, Vt., Hartnett Gallery/U. Rochester, Hopper House Gallery, Nyack, NY, Minnebank Gallery, Mt. Vernon, Maine. Author: The Creative Mystique, How To Manage It, Nurture It, Make It Pay, 1985, How to Zig in a Zagging World, 1987; contbr. articles to Jour. Advt., Air and Space, Smithsonian, Time, N.Y. Times. Vice chmn. Zoning Bd. Appeals, Grandview-on-Hudson, N.Y., 1961-71; pres., trustee Rockland Country Day Sch., 1970-75; mem. trustees coun. U. Rochester, 1979-85, trustee, 1986-91 (life trustee, 1991—), U. Rochester Sports Hall of Fame, 2000, N.Y. State Coun. Governing Bds., 1989-94, Nat. Crime Prevention Coun., 1987—; trustee Tappan Zee Preservation Coalition, 1995—; mem. corp. Nyack Hosp., 2001-06. Served with USAAF, 1943-45. Decorated D.F.C., Air medal with two oak leaf clusters;, ETO ribbin with four battle starts, recipient Silver Bell award Advt. Coun., 1981, 84, Carl M. Loeb, Jr.-McGruff award Nat. Crime Prevention Coun., 1987. Mem.: So. Vt. Art Ctr., Alpha Delta Phi. Home: 7128 Westminster West Rd Putney VT 05346

KEIL, KLAUS, geology educator, consultant; b. Hamburg, Germany, Nov. 15, 1934; s. Walter and Elsbeth K.; m. Rosemarie, Mar. 30, 1961; children: Kathrin R., Mark K.; m. Linde, Jan. 28, 1984. MS, Schiller U., Jena, Germany, 1958; PhD, Gutenberg U., Mainz, Fed. Republic Germany, 1961; D (hon.), Friedrich-Schiller U., Jena, Germany, 2002; DSc (hon.), U. N.Mex., 2003. Rsch. assoc. Mineral. Inst., Jena, 1958-60, Max Planck-Inst. Chemistry, Mainz, 1961, U. Calif., San Diego, 1961-63; rsch. scientist Ames Rsch. Ctr. NASA, Moffett Field, Calif., 1963-68; prof. geology, dir. Inst. Meteoritics, U. N.Mex., Albuquerque, 1968-90; pres., prof. U. N.Mex., 1985-90, chmn. dept. geology Albuquerque, 1986-89; prof. geology U. Hawaii, Honolulu, 1990—, rsch. prof., head planetary geoscis. div., 1990-93, dir. Hawaii Inst. Geophysics and Planetology, 1994—2003, interim dean Sch. Ocean Earth Sci. and Tech., 2003—06, prof., 2006—; cons. Sandia Labs., others. Contbr. over 600 articles to sci. jours. Named new extraterrestrial mineral Keilite named after him; recipient Apollo Achievement award, NASA, 1970, Exceptional Sci. Achievement medal, 1983, George P. Merrill award, NAS, 1970, Leonard medal, Meteoritical Soc., 1988, Zimmerman award, U. N.Mex., 1988, J. Lawrence Smith medal, NAS, 2006, others. Fellow Meteoritical Soc., AAAS, Mineral. Soc. Am., Am. Geophys. Union, German Mineral. Soc., Microbeam Analysis Soc. (Pres.'s Sci. award 2002), others. Office: U Hawaii at Manoa Hawaii Inst Geophys & Planetology Honolulu HI 96822 Office Phone: 808-956-7755. Business E-Mail: keil@hawaii.edu.

KEIL, M. DAVID, retired international association executive; b. Hinsdale, Ill., Jan. 22, 1931; s. Milton Derby and Lydia Anne (Landwehr) K.; m. Marilyn Jean Martin, May 15, 1976 BSJ, Northwestern U., 1952. Brand mgr. Armour & Co., Chgo., 1953-60; sr. v.p. Young & Rubicam, Chgo., 1960-74, Sandy Corp., Detroit, 1974-75, D'Arcy-MacManus & Masius, Chgo., 1976-80; pres., mng. dir. Audit Bur. Circulations, Schaumburg, Ill., 1980-96; ret., 1996. Named to Medill Sch. Journalism Hall of Fame, 1997. Mem. Internat. Fedn. Audit Burs., Circulation (sec. gen. 1986-88), Hinsdale Golf Club, Univ. Club Chgo. Lutheran. Avocations: sports, reading, travel, music.

KEIL, STEPHEN LESLEY, astrophysicist; b. Billings, Mont., Feb. 21, 1947; s. Nolan F. and Billy Lou (Benjamin) K.; m. Alice Ann Orient, June 18, 1972; children: Pamela Lynn, Wesley Forrester. BS in Physics, Univ. Calif., Berkeley, 1969; PhD in Astronomy, Boston U., 1975. Teaching fellow Boston (Mass.) Univ., 1969-74; postdoctoral fellow Univ. Colo., Sunspot, N.Mex., 1975-76; rsch. fellow, applied math. dept. Univ. Sydney, Australia, 1976-78; NRC fellow Sacramento Peak Obs., Sunspot, 1978-80, rsch. scientist, 1980-83; chief, solar rsch. USAF Solar Rsch. Br., Sunspot, 1983-99; dir. Nat. Solar Observatory, Sunspot, 1999—. Mem. Nat. Solar Obs. adv. com., Tucson, 1983-89; prin. investigator USAF Solar Mass Ejection Imager, 1996-99; project dir. Advanced Tech. Solar Telescope, 2000—. Editor: (workshop proceedings) Small-Scale Dynamical Processes in Quiet Stellar Atmospheres, 1984; co-editor: (workshop proceedings) Solar Drivers of Interplanetary and Terrestial Disturbances, Innovative Telescopes and Instrumentation for Solar Astrophysics, SPIE 4853, 2003. Mayor Sacramento Peak Community, Sunspot, 1990-91, treas., 1981-87. Maj. USAF, 1980-85. Named Company Grade Officer of Yr., USAF, 1984, Officer of the Yr., Geophysics Lab., Boston, 1983. Mem. Internat. Astron. Union, Am. Astron. Soc., Am. Phys. Soc., Calif. Scholarship Fedn. (life). Achievements include first to make an accurate determination of the height variation of convective penetration in the solar atmosphere. Home: 3015 Corona Loop Sunspot NM 88349 Office: National Solar Observatory PO Box 62 Sunspot NM 88349-0062 Business E-Mail: skeil@nso.edu.

KEILL, STUART LANGDON, psychiatrist; b. Binghamton, NY, Oct. 5, 1927; s. Kenneth and Dorothy B. (Langdon) K.; m. Joanne Veness, Sept. 2, 1950; children: Elinor Anne Moran, Patricia J., Brian S., Victoria M. Keill Lo Russo. BA, Princeton U., 1947; MA, Cornell U., 1948; MD, Temple U., 1952. Intern Highland Hosp., Rochester, NY; resident in psychiatry N.Y. State Psychiat. Inst., Presbyn. Hosp., Columbia U., NYC, 1955-58; dir. edn., dir. West Side Community Mental Health Ctr., NYC, 1958-71, Roosevelt Hosp., NYC, 1958-71; regional dir. N.Y. State Dept. Mental Health, 1971-75; prof. clin. psychiatry SUNY, Stony Brook, 1975-80; chmn. dept. psychiatry Nassau County Med. Ctr., East Meadow, NY, 1975-80; clin. prof. psychiatry SUNY, Buffalo, 1980-86, emeritus prof. psychiatry, 1993—; chief psychiat. service VA Med. Ctr., Buffalo, 1981-86; prof. of psychiatry Sch. of Medicine U. Md., 1986-94, vice chmn. dept. psychiatry, 1986-93, prof. sch. social work, 1993-94, acting chmn., 1991-92; clin. prof. psychiatry Sch. Medicine NYU, 1994—; counselor Advocates Coalition for Psychiat. Patients, 1980-86; med. dir. Inst. for Psychiatry and Human Behavior, 1986-93. Mem. adv. com. mental health laws Md. Atty. Gen. Office, 1987-93; hon. rsch. fellow Dept. Psychol. Medicine U. Glasgow, 1994. Author: (with others) Textbook on Administrative Psychiatry, 1992; also 52 articles; mem. editl. bd. Social Work and Health Care, 1975—, Social Work in Mental Health Care, 2000—, Hosp. and Community Psychiatry; assoc. editor Gen. Hosp. Psychiatry Jour., 1981-94. Chmn. Nassau coun. Health Systems Agy., 1977-80; mem. adv. com. Dr. Glory's Children's Theatre, N.Y.C., 1980—; mental health laws adv. com. State's Atty. Gen., 1987; warden Christ Ch., Oyster Bay, 2002-07. Lt. USN, 1953—55. Recipient Julius T. Marcus award dept. psychiatry SUNY, Stony Brook, 1980, Jour. Social Work in Health Care editl. award, 1985; hon. sr. fellow U. Glasgow, Dept. Psychol. Medicine, Scotland, 1994. Fellow Am. Coll. Psychiatrists, Am. Psychiat. Assn. (Distinction in Adminstrn. award 1990); mem. MEDIPP Psychiatry Coun. (dist. chmn. 1981-86), Am. Assn. Psychiat. Adminstrs. (pres. 1981-82), Am. Hosp. Assn. (chmn. psychiat. svcs. sect. 1985), Am. Assn. Gen. Hosp. Psychiatrists (pres. 1985-87), N.Y. Soc. Clin. Psychiatry (pres. 1974-75, chmn. pub. psychiatry com.), Md. Psychiat. Soc. Business E-Mail: skeill@lords.com.

KEILLER, JAMES BRUCE, clergyman, dean; b. Racine, Wis., Nov. 21, 1938; s. James Allen and Grace (Modder) Keiller; m. Darsel Lee Bundy, Feb. 8, 1959; 1 child, Susanne Elizabeth. Diploma, Beulah Heights Bible Coll., 1957; BA, William Carter Coll., 1963, EdD (hon.), 1973; LLB, Blackstone Sch. Law, 1964; MA, Evang. Theol. Sem., 1965, BD, 1966, ThD, 1968; MA in Ednl. Adminstrn., Atlanta U., 1977; degree, Nat. Tax Tng. Sch., Monsey, NY, 1986; EdS, Ga. State U., 1987; DD, Heritage Bible Coll., 2001; postgrad., Atlanta Law Sch., Harvard U., 2001—03, North Ctrl. U., Ariz., 2005—. Ordained to ministry Internat. Pentecostal Assemblies, 1957. Pastor Maranatha Temple, Boston, 1957-58, Midland Full Gospel Ch., Mich., 1958-64; v.p. acad. dean Beulah Heights Bible U., Atlanta, 1964—, trustee, 1964—92; nat. dir. youth and Sunday sch. dept. Internat. Pentecostal Assemblies, 1958-64, dir. world missions Atlanta, 1964-76; missionary editor Bridegroom's Messenger, 1964—; dir. global missions Internat. Pentecostal Ch. of Christ, 1976—, mem. exec. com., 1976—; mem. exec. bd. Mt. Paran Christian Sch., 1980-91. Named Alumnus of Yr., William Carter Coll., 1965. Mem.: ASCD, Kappa Delta Pi, Assn. Coll. Adminstrv. Profls., Acad. Polit. Sci., Assn. Coll. Adminstrn. Profls., Nat. Assn. Alternative Cert., Soc. for Values in Higher Edn., Schomburg Soc., Am. Assn. Collegiate Registrars and Admin. Offices, Am. Assn. Higher Edn., Am. Conf. Acad. Deans, Nat. Assn. Scholars, Intercollegiate Studies Inst., Nat. Fedn. for Decency (bd. dirs.), Am. Bd. Master Educators (cert.), Am. Inst. Parliamentarians, Coll. of Tchrs., Soc. of Bibl. Lit., So. Accrediting Assn. Bible Colls. (exec. sec. 1970—93), Little Mountain Village Condo Assn. (bd. dirs. 1994—), Am. Acad. Religion, Evang. Theol. Soc., Ind. Order Foresters, Oxford Club, Kiwanis (lt. gov. Ga. dist. 1986—87, chmn. human values state com. Ga. dist. 1989—90). Republican. Home: 21A Little Mountain Vlg Ellenwood GA 30294-3150 Office: Beulah Heights Bible Coll 892 Berne St SE Atlanta GA 30316-1873 Office Phone: 404-627-2681. Business E-Mail: james.keiller@beulah.org.

KEILLOR, GARRISON EDWARD, writer, radio personality; b. Anoka, Minn., Aug. 7, 1942; s. John P. and Grace R. (Denham) K.; m. Jenny Lind Nilsson, 1995; children: Jason P., Maia Grace. BA, U. Minn., 1966. Former staff mem. The New Yorker. Author: Happy to be Here, 1982, Lake Wobegon Days, 1985, Leaving Home, 1987, We Are Still Married: Stories and Letters, 1989, WLT: A Radio Romance, 1991, The Book of Guys, 1993, Cat, You Better Come Home, 1995, The Old Man Who Loved Cheese, 1996, (with J. Nilsson) The Sandy Bottom Orchestra, 1996, Wobegon Boy, 1997, Me, by Jimmy (Big Boy) Valente, 1999, Lake Wobegon Summer 1956, 2001, Good Poems, 2002, Love Me, 2003, Homegrown Democrat, 2004, Daddy's Girl, 2005, Good Poems for Hard Times, 2005; creator, writer and host radio show A Prairie Home Companion; actor, writer: (films) A Prairie Home Companion, 2006; contbr. articles to mags. and newspapers (Harpers, The Atlantic Monthly, The N.Y. Times, others). Recipient Grammy award for best non-mus. recording Lake Wobegon Days, 1987, Ace award, 1988, Best Mus. and Entertainment Host awards, 1988, 89, medal for spoken lang. Am. Acad. and Inst. Arts and Letters, 1990, Nat. Humanities medal, 1999, Pres. Clinton; inducted into Radio Hall of Fame, 1994, Am. Acad. Arts and Scis., 1999. Democrat. Episcopalian. Office: A Prairie Home Companion 611 Frontenac Pl Saint Paul MN 55104-4947

KEIM, BETTY LOU, actress, literary consulant; b. Malden, Mass., Sept. 27, 1938; d. Buster and Dorothy Clair (Tracy) Keim; m. Warren Berlinger, Feb. 18, 1960; children: Lisa, David, Edward, Elizabeth. Grad., Lodge Acad., NYC, 1956. Appeared in films These Wilder Years, 1956, Teenage Rebel, 1956, Wayward Bus, 1957, Some Came Running, 1958; appeared on Broadway in Strange Fruit, Rip Van Winkle, Crime and Punishment, Texas Lil Darlin, The Remarkable Mr. Pennypacker, Roomful of Roses; appeared on TV in Omnibus, Playhouse 90, Alcoa Hour, Philco PlayHouse; appeared in TV series My Son Jeep, The Deputy. Assoc. Aid Project LA, 1984-97; life mem., vol. Actors Fund of Am. Recipinet Motion Picture award Calif. Women's Club, 1956, Filmdoms Famous Five award Film Daily Critics, 1956, Laurel award, 1956.

KEIM, DONALD BRUCE, finance educator; b. Bethlehem, Pa., Feb. 7, 1953; s. Elwood Benjamin and Doris Mae (Wanamaker) K.; m. Susan Langshaw, July 10, 1976; children: Sarah Elizabeth, Julia Diane BSBA, Bucknell U., 1975; MBA, U. Chgo., 1980, PhD, 1983; MS (hon.), U. Pa., 1988. Rsch. assoc. Fed. Deposit Ins. Corp., Washington, 1978; lectr. Loyola U. of Chgo., 1981—82; asst. prof., fin. U. Pa., Phila., 1982-88, assoc. prof. fin., 1988-94, prof. fin., 1994—98, John B. Neff prof. fin., 1998—. Vis. prof. INSEAD, Fontainebleau, France, 1994, 96-98, 2004; vis. scholar Dimensional Fund Advisors, Santa Monica, Calif., 1990, 1995-96; mem. acad. adv. bd. Brandywine Asset Mgmt., Wilmington, Del., 1993-2000. Assoc. editor Jour. of Fin. and Quant. Analysis, 1993-2001; co-editor European Fin. Rev., 1998-2003; contbr. articles to profl. jours. Rsch. grantee Inst. for Quantitative Rsch., 1984, 92, 99; recipient Graham and Dodd award Fin. Analysts Fedn., 1987, 99, N.Y. Stock Exch. award, 1996. Mem. Am. Fin. Assn., Western Fin. Assn. (program com. 1992-96, 2000-07), European Fin. Assn. (program com. 1996-2007). Avocations: music, photography, golf, gardening. Office: Univ Pa The Wharton Sch 2300 Steinberg Hall Philadelphia PA 19104 Business E-Mail: keim@wharton.upenn.edu.

KEIM, MICHAEL RAY, dentist; b. Sabetha, Kans., June 8, 1951; s. Milton Leroy and Dorothy Juanita (Stover) K.; m. Christine Anne Lorenzen, Nov. 20, 1971; children: Michael Scott, Dawn Marie, Erik Alan. Student, U. Utah, Salt Lake City, 1969-72; DDS, Creighton U., Omaha, 1976. Pvt. practice, Casper, Wyo., 1976—. Mem. vertical math. com. Natrona County Sch. Dist., 1997-2000; mem. Coll. Nat. Finals Rodeo Com., 2002—; equality of care advising mem. State or Wyo., 2007—. Mem. organizing bd. dirs. Ctrl. Wyo. Soccer Assn., 1976-77; mem. Casper Mountain Ski Patrol, Nat. Ski Patrol Sys., 1980-2000, 2005—, Big Horn Ski Patrol, 2001-05, avalanche and ski mountaineering advisor No. Divsn. Region III, 1992-96, outdoor emergency care instr. trainer, 1996-99, 1st asst. patrol dir., 1996-98, patrol dir., 1998-99; bd. dirs., dep. commr. for fast pitch Wyo. Amateur Softball Assn., 1980-84; bd. dirs. Ctrl. Wyo. Softball Assn., 1980-84; head coach Big Horn Mountain Ski Team, 2002-05; pres. Wyo. Spl. Smiles Found., 1995-96; mem. organizing com. Prevent Abuse & Neglect thru Dental Awareness Coalition, Wyo., 1996; mem. adv. com. Natrona County Headstart, 1985—; mem. City of Casper Leisure Svc. Adv. Com., 2002—, vice chair, 2007—. Recipient Purple Merit Star for Saving a Life, 1992, Hixon award, 2002. Master: Acad. Gen. Dentistry; mem.: ADA, Wyo. Donated Dental Svcs. (organizing bd. dirs. 1994, pres. 1995—96, Outstanding Vol. Dentist 2007), Wyo. Dental Hist. Assn. (bd. dirs. 1989—95), Ctrl. Wyo. Dental Assn. (sec.-treas. 1981—82, pres. 1982—83, sec.-treas. 2002—03, pres. 2003—04), Wyo. Dental Polit. Action Com. (sec.-treas. 1985—97), Wyo. Dental Assn. (chmn. conv. 1987—, bd. dirs. 1992—97, chmn. conv. 1993, v.p. 1993—94, ADA alt. del. 1994—95, pres.-elect 1994—95, pres. 1995—96, editor 1997—, chmn. conv. 1999), Wyo. Acad. Gen. Dentistry (sec.-treas. 1980—82, pres. 1982—87, del. 2007), Pierre Fauchard Acad., Fedn. Dentaire Internat., Am. Acad. Cosmetic Dentistry, Acad. Computerized Dentistry, Creighton Club (pres. 1982—84), Kiwanis (bd. dirs. 1986—96, v.p. Casper club 1988—89, pres.-elect 1989—90, internat. del. 1989—91, pres. 1990—91, chmn. internat. rels. com. 1992—99, Rocky Mountain dist. lt. gov.-elect divsn. 1 1997—98, lt. gov. divsn. 1 1998—99, Hixon award 2002). Methodist. Avocations: hunting, skiing, sports, woodworking, photography. Home: 58 Jonquil St Casper WY 82604-3863 Office: 1749 S Boxelder St Casper WY 82604-3538 Office Phone: 307-234-6358. Personal E-mail: mogul_mike@msn.com.

KEIM, WAYNE FRANKLIN, retired agronomist, geneticist; b. Ithaca, NY, May 14, 1923; s. Franklin David and Alice Mary (Voigt) K.; m. Ellen Joyce Neumann, Sept. 6, 1947; children: Kathryn Louise Keim Logsdon, David Wayne, Julie Anne Keim Hughes. BS with distinction, U. Nebr., 1947; MS, Cornell U., 1949, PhD, 1952. Instr., then asst. prof. Iowa State U., Ames, 1952-56; from asst. prof. to prof. Purdue U., West Lafayette, Ind., 1956-75; vis. prof., NSF sci. faculty fellow U. Lund, (Sweden), 1962-63; vis. prof. Colo. State U., Fort Collins, 1971-72, prof. dept. agronomy, 1975-92, chmn. dept., 1975-85. Recipient Best Tchr. award Sch. Agr., Purdue U., 1965, 68. Fellow AAAS, Am. Soc. Agronomy (Agronomic Edn. award 1971, Agronomic Svc. award 1991), Crop Sci. Soc. Am. (pres. 1983-84); mem. Am. Inst. Biol. Sci., Agronomic Sci. Found. (trustee). Home: 1441 Meeker Dr Fort Collins CO 80524-4311 Office: Colo State U Dept Soil Crop Scis Fort Collins CO 80523-0001

KEINER, CHRISTIAN MARK, lawyer; b. Omaha, Mar. 16, 1953; s. John Frederick Keiner and Geraldine Elizabeth (Smith) Eadie; m. Rosemary Monique White, Nov. 21, 1980; 1 child, Colin MacGregor. BA with high honors, U. Calif., Santa Barbara, 1977; JD with distinction, U. of Pacific, Sacramento, 1980. Bar: Calif. 1980, US Ct. Appeals (9th cir.) 1988, US Supreme Ct. 1991. Assoc. Biddle, Walters, Bukey, Sacramento, 1980-82, Biddle and Hamilton, Sacramento, 1982-92; pvt. practice Sacramento, 1992-98; ptnr. Girard and Vinson, Sacramento, 1998—2005; shareholder Kronick Moskovitz Tiedemann and Girard, Sacramento, 2005—. Contbr. articles to law jours. Bd. dirs. Calif. Found. for Improvement Employer-Employee Rels., Sacramento, 1994-99, Calif. Coun. Sch. Attys., Sacramento, 1996-98; instr., mem. labor-mgmt. adv. com. U. Calif. Davis Ext., Sacramento, 1986-99. Recipient award for adminstrv. law Am. Jurisprudence, 1979. Mem. ABA (pub. law sect.), Sacramento County Bar, Anthony M. Kennedy Inn of Ct., Harry S. Truman Club (pres. 1992), Order of Coif. Democrat. Office: Kronick Moskovitz Tiedemann and Girard 400 Capitol Mall 27th Fl Sacramento CA 95814 Office Phone: 916-321-4500. Business E-Mail: ckeiner@kmtg.com.

KEINER, R(OBERT) BRUCE, JR., lawyer; b. Washington, July 12, 1942; s. R. Bruce and Alice Miriam (Draeger) K.; m. Suellen Terrill, June 15, 1968; children: Scott, Grant, Terrill. BA, Dickinson Coll., Carlisle, Pa., 1964; LLB, U. Va., Charlottesville, 1967. Bar: DC 1968, US Supreme Ct. 1980. Assoc. to ptnr. Jones, Day, Reavis & Pogue, Washington, 1970-79; ptnr. Crowell & Moring LLP, Washington, 1979—; pres. Internat. Aviation Club of Washington, 1995. Pres., bd. trustees Maret Sch., 2000—04. Capt. US Army, 1968—69. Mem.: Columbia Country Club, Chevy Chase, Md., U. Club Washington, Internat. Aviation Club Washington (pres. 1995). Office: Crowell & Moring LLP 1001 Pennsylvania Ave NW Fl 10 Washington DC 20004-2595 Home: 46380 Greens Rest Way Great Mills MD 20634 Home Phone: 301-994-0339; Office Phone: 202-624-2615. Business E-Mail: rbkeiner@crowell.com.

KEIR, GERALD JANES, banker; b. Ludlow, Mass., Aug. 22, 1943; s. Alexander J. and Evelyn M. (Buckley) K.; m. Karen Mary Devine, July 22, 1972; children: Matthew J., Katherine B., Megan E. BA, Mich. State U., 1964, MA, 1966. Reporter Honolulu Advertiser, 1968-74, city editor, 1974-86, mng. editor, 1986-89, editor, 1989-95; exec. v.p. corp. comms. First Hawaiian Bank, Honolulu, 1995—. Co-author: Advanced Reporting: Beyond News Events, 1985, Advanced Reporting: Discovering Patterns in News Events, 1997. Bd. dirs. First Hawaiian Found., Salvation Army Bd. Hawaii, East-West Ctr. Found. Recipient Nat. Reporting award Am. Polit. Sci. Assn., 1971, Benjamin Fine Nat. award Am. Assn. Secondary Sch. Prins., 1981; John Ben Snow fellow, 1983, NEH fellow, 1973. Mem. Social Sci. Assn., Honolulu Cmty.-Media Coun. Office Phone: 808-525-7086. Business E-Mail: gerry.keir@fhwn.com.

KEISER, BERNHARD EDWARD, engineering executive, communications engineer, consultant; b. Richmond Heights, Mo., Nov. 14, 1928; s. Bernhard and Helen Barbara Julia (Buerkle) K.; m. Florence Evelyn Keiser, Jan. 22, 1955; children: Sandra, Carol, Nancy, Linda, Paul. BSEE, Washington U., St. Louis, 1950, MSEE, 1951, DScEE, 1953. Registered profl. engr., Va. Mgr. plans and programs RCA, Cape Canaveral, Fla., 1964-67, adminstr. advanced system planning Moorestown, NJ, 1967-69; v.p., tech. dir. Page Communication Engring., Washington, 1969-70; dir. advanced engring. Atlantic Rsch. Corp., Alexandria, Va., 1971-72; dir. anaylsis Fairchild Space & Electronics Co., Germantown, Md., 1972-75; pres. Keiser Engring., Inc., Vienna, Va., 1975—2003. Author: EMI Control in Aerospace Systems, 1979, Principles of Electromagnetic Compatibility, 1979, rev. edit. 1987, Broad band Coding, Modulation and Transmission Engineering, 1989, rev. edit. 1994; co-author: Digital Telephony and Network Integration, 1985, rev. edit. 1995. Fellow IEEE (chmn. No. Va. sect. 1980-81), Washington Acad. Scis., Radio Club Am. Republican. Lutheran. Home and Office: 2046 Carrhill Rd Vienna VA 22181-2917 *I am neither the master of my fate nor the captain of my soul. I owe everything to the Lord Jesus Christ, who is my Savior, my Redeemer.*

KEISER, DAVID WHARTON, pharmaceutical executive; b. East Orange, NJ, July 13, 1951; s. Robert Emil and Jean Gage (Van Buskirk) Keiser; m. Barbara Ann Biecher, Aug. 28, 1976; children: Stephanie, Amanda, Joseph. BA in Psychology, Gettysburg Coll., 1973; postgrad., Med. Sch. U. Basel, 1975-76. Area mgr. Hoffmann-La Roche, Basel, Switzerland, 1981-83; new bus. opportunities mgr. Mundipharma AG, Basel, 1984-85; mgr. licensing G.D. Searle and Co., Skokie, Ill., 1985-86, dir. licensing, Europe, 1987-89, sr. dir. licensing, 1989-90, sr. dir. Asia/Pacific ops., 1990-92; exec. v.p., COO Alexion Pharma, New Haven, 1992—2002, pres., COO, 2002—, also bd. dirs. Bd. dirs. Conn. United Rsch. Excellence. Bd. dirs. A Better Chance, Madison, Conn., 1997—99. With Swiss Army, 1978—85. Mem.: Licensing Execs. Soc. Avocations: travel, languages, golf, hiking, investing. Office: Alexion Pharma Inc 352 Knotter Dr Cheshire CT 06410 Personal E-mail: keiserd@aol.com.

KEISER, EDMUND DAVIS, JR., biologist, educator; b. Appalachia, Va., Feb. 18, 1934; s. Edmund Davis and Ora Elizabeth (Wade) K.; m. Alice Sue Tucker, Sept. 10, 1982; children: Mark Edmund, Julie Ann; stepchildren: Louis King III, Jenifer King. BA, So. Ill. U., Carbondale, 1956, MS, 1961; PhD in Zoology, La. State U., Baton Rouge, 1967. Tchr. sci. Kinmundy High Sch., Ill., 1956-57, Mt. Vernon Twp. Sch. Dist., Ill., 1957-58; dist. sci. coordinator Freeburg Sch. Dist. 70, Freeburg, Ill., 1958-62; instr. biology La Salle-Peru-Oglesby Jr. Coll., La Salle, Ill., 1962-64; teaching asst. La. State U., Baton Rouge, 1964-66; asst. prof. U. Southwestern La., Lafayette, 1966-70, assoc. prof., 1970-75, prof. biology, 1976, mem. coun. grad. coords., 1973-76; prof. biology U. Miss., Oxford, 1976—2005, 2007—, chmn. dept. University, 1976-87, prof. emeritus, chmn. emeritus, 2005—07. Rsch. assoc. Gulf South Rsch. Inst., 1972—74; mem. Atchafalaya River Basin Rsch. Coun., 1972—74; exec. coun., state dir. sci. tchg. La. Acad. Scis., 1972—74; exec. coun. Gopher Tortoise Soc., 1979—81; commr. Miss. Dept. Wildlife Conservation, 1978—79, 1980—84, chmn., 1983—84; cons. U.S. Fish and Wildlife Svc., 2001—, U.S. Army Corps of Engrs., 2001—; owner and cons. Ecol. Cons. Mem. Miss. Wildlife Heritage Com., 1980—84, Gov.'s Select Com. on Radioactivity and Radioactive Waste Depository, 1979—80; field assoc. Miss. Mus. Natural Sci., 2001—. Recipient numerous grants; Disting. Prof. award U. Southwestern La., 1973; Govs. Meritorious Service award State of Miss., 1979; citation for outstanding sci. teaching Nat. Sci. Tchrs. Assn.-Ill. Supt. Public Instrn., 1962 Fellow Explorers Club; mem. Soc. for Study Amphibians and Reptiles, Herpetologists League, Golden Key Honor Soc., Sigma Xi (chpt. pres. 1976, 79-80), Beta Beta Beta, Phi Eta Sigma, Phi Kappa Phi. Home and Office: Ecological Consulting 211 Saint Andrews Cir Oxford MS 38655-2518 Business E-Mail: bykeiser@olemiss.edu.

KEISER, PAUL HAROLD, retired hospital administrator; b. Dalton, Ohio, June 1, 1927; s. Austin R. and Elrena E. (Tschantz) K.; m. Nancy F. Homan, May 27, 1950; children— James William, Martha Ann Lee, Elizabeth Louise Green, Patricia Elrena Bell. BS, Mt. Union Coll., 1948; MS in Hosp. Adminstrn., Northwestern U., 1952. Adminstr. Community Hosp. Evanston, Ill., 1952-54, Burlington Hosp., Iowa, 1954-67; pres. York Hosp., Pa., 1967-88, ret. Pa., 1988. Lectr., seminar leader Northwestern U., Chgo., 1952-54, U. Iowa Hosp., Iowa City, 1955-59; lectr. George Washington U., 1969-86. Contbr. articles to profl. jours. Bd. dirs. United Way, York, Pa., 1970-78, York Habitat for Humanity, 1992-98, 99-2005, York County Parks Charitable Trust Bd., 1989-2007, vice chmn., 1990-2007; bd. dirs. York County Farm and Natural Land Trust, 1992-98, mem. adv. bd., 1998—2006; dir. adv. bd. Pa. State U., York, 1979—; sec. North Codorus Twp. Plan Commn., 1994-96; mem. North Codorus Twp. Bd. Suprs., 1995—2005, vice chmn., 1997-99, chmn. 2000-02, S.E. (York County) Regional Police Bd., chmn. 2002-05; mem. gov. bd. Byrnes Health Edn. Ctr., 1995—. Fellow Am. Coll. Hosp. Adminstrn. (life, regent 1964-67); mem. Iowa Interprofl. Assn. (pres. 1963-64), Iowa Hosp. Assn. (pres. 1961-62), Am. Hosp. Assn. (del. 1975-86), Hosp. Assn. Pa. (chmn. bd. dirs. 1983, bd. dirs. svcs. corp. 1986-89), Northwestern U. Hosp. Adminstrn. Alumni Assn. (pres. 1957-58), Rotary (bd. dirs. 1979-82), Sigma Alpha Epsilon. Republican. Presbyterian. Avocations: tennis, woodworking. Home: Apt J 404 950 Willow Valley Lakes Dr Willow Street PA 17584-9663

KEISLER, PETER DOUGLAS, federal agency administrator, lawyer; b. Hempstead, NY, Oct. 13, 1960; s. William and Sydelle (Prisand) K.; m. Susan Keisler; children: Sydelle, Alexander, Philip. BA, Yale U., 1981, JD, 1985. Bar: Pa. 1985, D.C. 1989. Law clk. to hon. judge Robert Bork US Ct. Appeals (D.C. cir.), Washington, 1985-86; assoc. counsel to Pres. of U.S. White House, Washington, 1986-88; law clk. to assoc. justice Anthony Kennedy US Supreme Ct., Washington, 1988-89; assoc. Sidley & Austin, Washington, 1989—93; ptnr. Sidley Austin Brown & Wood (formerly Sidley & Austin), 1993—2002; prin. dep. assoc. atty. gen. US Dept. Justice Civil Divsn., Washington, 2002, acting assoc. atty. gen., 2002—03, asst. atty. gen., 2003—. Mem. ABA, Pa. Bar Assn., D.C. Bar Assn. Republican. Jewish. Home: 4964 Allan Rd Bethesda MD 20816-2722 Office: US Dept Justice Civil Divsn 950 Pennsylvania Ave NW Washington DC 20530-0001

KEITEL, HARVEY, actor; b. Bklyn., May 13, 1939; m. Lorraine Bracco, 1982 (div. 1983); 1 child, Stella; m. Daphna Kastner, Oct. 7, 2001; 1 child. Studied with Lee Strasberg, Frank Corsaro, Actors Studio. Actor (films) Reflections in a Golden Eye, 1967, Who's That Knocking at My Door?, 1967, Mean Streets, 1973, Alice Doesn't Live Here Anymore, 1974, That's the Way of the World, 1975, Taxi Driver, 1976, Mother Jugs and Speed, 1976, Buffalo Bill and the Indians or Sitting Bull's History Lesson, 1976, Welcome to L.A, 1976, The Duellists, 1977, Blue Collar, 1978, Fingers, 1978, Eagle's Wing, 1979, La Mort en Direct, 1980, Saturn 3, 1980, Bad Timing: A Sensual Obsession, 1980, The Border, 1982, La Nuit de Varennes, 1982, Copkiller, 1983, Exposed, 1983, Une Pierre Dans la Bouche, 1983, Nemo, 1984, Falling in Love, 1984, Knight of the Dragon, 1985, A Complex Plot About Women, Alleys and Crimes, 1986, Off Beat, 1986, Wise Guys, 1986, The Men's Club, 1986, The American Bride, 1986, The Pick-Up Artist, 1987, The Inquiry, 1987, Down Where the Buffalo Go, 1988, The Last Temptation of Christ, 1988, Caro Gorbaciov, 1988, January Man, 1989, The Two Jakes, 1990, The Battle of the Three Kings, 1990, Two Evil Eyes, 1990, Bugsy, 1991 (Acad. award nominee), Mortal Thoughts, 1991, Thelma and Louise, 1991, Sister Act, 1992, Bad Lieutenant, 1992, The Piano, 1993, Point of No Return, 1993, Rising Sun, 1993, Dangerous Game, 1993, The Young Americans, 1993, Monkey Trouble, 1994, Pulp Fiction, 1994, Somebody to Love, 1994, Imaginary Crimes, 1994, Smoke, 1995, Clockers, 1995, Ulysses' Gaze, 1995, From Dusk Till Dawn, 1996, Head Above Water, 1996, City of Industry, 1997, Cop Land, 1997, Fairy Tale: A True Story, 1997, Shadrach, 1998, Lulu on the Bridge, 1998, Finding Graceland, 1998, Il Mio West, 1998, Holy Smoke, 1999, Presence of Minde, 1999, U-571, 2000, Prince of Central Park, 2000, Little Nicky, 2000, Nailed, 2001, Vipera, 2001, Taking Sides, 2001, Nowhere, 2002, Ginostra, 2002, Red Dragon, 2002, Beeper, 2002, Crime Spree, 2003, The Galindez File, 2003, Who Killed the Idea, 2003, Puerto Vallerta Squeeze, 2003, National Treasure, 2004, The Bridge of San Luis Ray, 2004, Be Cool, 2005, Shadows in the Sun, 2005; (TV films) A Memory of Two Mondays, 1974, The Virginia Hill Story, 1974, La Bella Otero, 1983, Baciami strega, 1985; actor, exec. prodr. (films) Blue in the Face, 1995, Three Seasons, 1999, The Grey Zone, 2001; actor, prodr. (films) Dreaming of Julia, 2003; actor, co-prodr. (films) Reservoir Dogs, 1992; TV appearances include Kojak, 1973, The FBI, 1974, Amazing Stories, 1985; stage appearances include A Lie in the Mind, Death of a Salesman, 1975, Hurlyburly, 1984. Recipient Lifetime Achievement award, Istanbul Film Festival, 2005. Office: c/o William Morris Agy 151 S El Camino Dr Beverly Hills CA 90212-2704 also: care Susan Culley Assoc 150 S Rodeo Dr Ste 220 Beverly Hills CA 90212-2409

KEITH, BRIAN THOMAS, automotive executive; b. Houston, Aug. 2, 1951; s. Thomas Ross and Elsie Ann (Carden) K.; m. Anna Lee Rogers, Nov. 17, 1973; children: Kevin Patrick, Lindsay Rogers. BSBA, Samford U., 1973. Educator installation IBM, Birmingham, Ala., 1971-73; salesman Albeco-Ala. Bus. Equipment Co., Birmingham, 1973-74; pres., owner Walter S. White Auto Parts, Inc., Birmingham, 1974—. Bd. dirs. Ala. Power Co. Vendor Rels. Bd., Birmingham, Automotive Wholesalers Worker Compensation Trust, 2001—; trustee Automotive Wholesalers Ins. Trust, Montgomery, 1985—, treas. investment com., 1992—, chmn. trust, 1996-99; industry spkr. Automotive Market Rsch. Coun., 1995, Automotive Aftermarket Assn. S.E., Automotive Aftermarket Industry Assn. Pub. mag. Auto Svc. and Repair, 1988-98; contbr. articles to publs. and mags. V.p. Park Bd. Patriot Baseball, Homewood, Ala., 1985-89; celebrity fundraiser Am. Cancer Soc., 1993; mem. canvass com. All Sts. Ch., Homewood, 1986-90, youth com., 1992-95; active St. Andrews Soc. of the Middle South. Named Outstanding Young Men in Am., U.S. Jaycees, 1983; recipient Tech. Tng. award Arvvin Industries, 1983-88. Mem. Automotive Aftermarket Assn. S.E. (bd. dirs. 1985—, chmn. 1986-91, treas. 1992-95, 98-2001, polit. action com. 1992-99, exec. com. 1991-2001, Leadership award 1991), Automotive Aftermarket Industry Assn. (bd. dirs. 1992-98, nat. polit. action com. 1993-99, co-chmn. automotive com. 1994-98), Birmingham C. of C., U.S. C. of C., Young Exec. Forum, Assn. Enterprises (pres. 1991-92), Jr. Achievement, Nat. Fedn. Ind. Bus. Episcopalian. Avocations: family, golf, travel.

KEITH, BRUCE EDWARD, sociologist; b. Decatur, Ill., Dec. 22, 1961; s. Donald and Elizabeth Keith; m. Kate Franklin, Dec. 17, 1988; children: Barbara, Mary. BA, Western Wash. U., Bellingham, Wash., 1984, MA, 1986; PhD, U. Nebr., Lincoln, Nebr., 1990. Asst. prof. sociology W.Va. U., Morgantown, W.Va., 1991—96; asst. dean acad. assessment US Mil. Acad., West Point, NY, 1996—2000, assoc. prof. sociology, 1996—2001, assoc. dean acad. affairs, 2000—, prof. sociology, 2001—; deployed to assist in devel. of nat. mil. acad. Kabul, Afghanistan, 2005—06. Pres. North Ctrl. Sociol. Assn., 2003—04; cons. Mid. States Commn. on Higher Edn., Phila., 1999—, Assn. Am. Colls. and Univs., 2005—, Am. Sociol. Assn., 2005—; deployed development nat. mil. acad. Govt. of Afghanistan, Kabul, 2005—06. Author: Inside West Virginia, 1999, Contexts for Learning, 2004; contbr. scientific papers, articles to profl. jour. Mem.: Am. Sociol. Assn., Assn. Am. Colls. and Univs. Office: US Mil Acad Office of the Dean Academic Affairs West Point NY 10996 Home Phone: 914-488-5093; Office Phone: 845-938-6321.

KEITH, COURTNEY S., lawyer; b. Waco, Tex., July 19, 1967; BS, Tex. Christian U., 1989; JD, Baylor U. Sch. Law, 1993. Bar: Tex. 1993. Asst. dist. atty. Tarrant County Criminal Dist. Atty.'s Office, 1993—95; ptnr. Keith Law Firm, P.C., Ft. Worth. Named a Rising Star, Tex. Super Lawyers mag., 2006. Mem.: Ft. Worth-Tarrant County Young Lawyers Assn., Assn. Trial Lawyers of Am., Texans for Civil Justice, Tex. Trial Lawyers Assn., Tarrant County Trial Lawyers Assn., ABA, Tarrant County Bar Assn. Office: Keith Law Firm PC Keith Bldg 1705 W 7th St Fort Worth TX 76102 Office Phone: 817-338-1400. E-mail: courtk@keithlaw.com.*

KEITH, DAMON JEROME, federal judge; b. Detroit, July 4, 1922; s. Perry A. and Annie L. (Williams) K.; m. Rachel Boone Keith, Oct. 18, 1953; children: Cecile Keith, Debbie, Gilda. BA, W.Va. State Coll., 1943; JD, Howard U., 1949; LLM, Wayne State U., 1956; PhD (hon.) (hon.), U. Mich., Howard U., Wayne State U., Mich. State U., NY Law Sch., Detroit Coll. Law, W.Va. State Coll., U. Detroit, Atlanta U., Lincoln U., Marygrove Coll., Detroit Inst. Tech., Shaw Coll., Ctrl. State U., Yale U., Loyola Law Sch., LA, Ea. Mich. U., Va. Union U., Ctrl. Mich. U., Morehouse Coll., Western Mich. U., Tuskegee U., Georgetown U., Hofstra U., DePaul U. Bar: Mich. 1949. Atty. Office Friend of Ct., Detroit, 1951—55; sr. ptnr. firm Keith, Conyers Anderson, Brown & Wahls, Detroit, 1964—67; mem. Wayne County Bd. Suprs., 1958—63; dist. judge US Dist. Ct. (ea. dist.) Mich., 1967—77, chief judge, 1975—77; judge US Ct. Appeals (6th cir.), Detroit, 1977—95, sr. judge, 1995—. Mem. Wayne County (Mich.) Bd. Suprs., 1958—63; chmn. Mich. Civil Rights Commn., 1964—67; pres. Detroit Housing Commn., 1958—67; commr. State Bar Mich., 1960—67; mem. Detroit Bar Assn., Mich. Com. Manpower Devel. and Vocat. Tng., 1964, Detroit Mayor's Health Adv. Com., 1969; rep. dist. judges 6th Cir. Jud. Conf., 1975—77; adv. com. on codes of conduct Jud. Conf. US, 1979—86; subcom. on supporting pers. Jud. Conf. Com. on Ct. Adminstrn., 1983—87; chmn. Com. on the Bicentennial of Constn. of Sixth Cir., 1985—; nat. chmn. Jud. Conf. Com. on the Bicentennial of Constn., 1987—; mem. Commn. on the Bicentennial of U.S. Constn., 1990; lectr. Howard U., 1972, Ohio State U. Law Sch., 1992, NY Law Sch., 1992; guest lectr. Howard U. Law Sch., 1981; Bicentennial of Constn. lectr. W.Va. State Coll., 1987; keynote speaker Black Law Students Assn., Harvard Law Sch., 1987. Contbr. articles to profl. jours. Trustee Med. Corp. Detroit, Interlochen Arts Acad., Cranbrook Sch., U. Detroit, Mich. chpt. Leukemia Soc. Am.; mem. Citizen's Adv. Com. Equal Ednl. Opportunity Detroit Bd. Edn.; gen. co-chmn. United Negro Coll. Fund Detroit; 1st v.p. emeritus Detroit chpt. NAACP; mem. com. mgmt. Detroit YMCA; mem. Detroit coun. Boy Scouts Am., Detroit Arts Commn.; vice chmn. Detroit Symphony Orch.; vis. com. Wayne State U. Law Sch.; adv. coun. U. Notre Dame Law Sch.; chmn. Citizen's Coun. for Mich. Pub. Univs.; deacon Tabernacle Missionary Bapt. Ch.; Deacon Bapt ch.; bd. dirs. Detroit Bd. Table, NCCJ. US Army, 1943—46. Named 1 of 100 Most Influential Black Ams., Ebony Mag., 1971—92, Damon J. Keith Elementary Sch. named in his honor, Detroit Bd. Edn., 1974, Damon J. Keith Ann. Civic and Humanitarian award established in his honor, Highland Park YMCA, 1984, 15th Mich. Legal Milestone The Uninvited Ear presented in honor of The Keith Decision, 1991; named one of The Century's Finest Michiganders, Mich. Chronicle, 1999; recipient Mich. Chronicle outstanding Citizen award, 1960, 1964, 1974, Alumni citation, Wayne State U., 1968, Ann. Jud. award, 1971, Citizen award, Mich. State U., Disting. Svc. award, Howard U., 1972, Jud. Independence award, 1973, Spingarn medal, NAACP, 1974, Fed. Judge of Yr. award, Black Law Students Assn., 1974, award for Outstanding Contbns. to Black Community, Nat. Assn. Black Social Workers, 1974, Judge of Yr. award, Nat. Conf. Black Lawyers, 1974, Bill of Rights award, Jewish Community Coun., 1977, A. Philip Randolph award, Detroit Coalition Black Trade Unionists, 1981, Human Rights Day award, B'nai B'rith Women's Coun. Met. Detroit, Robert L. Millender award, So. Christian Leadership Conf. Mich. chpt., 1982, Afro-Asian Inst. award, Histadrut in Israel, 1982, civil rights lectr. award, Creighton U. Ahmanson Law Ctr., 1983, Nat. Human Rels. award, Greater Detroit Roundtable of NCCJ, 1984, Knights of Charity award, Pontifical Inst. for Mission Extension, 1986, Disting. Pub. Svc. award, Mich. Anti-Defamation League of B'nai B'rith, 1987, Nat. Chpt. award, 1988, Black Achievement award, Equitable Fin. Cos., 1987, Menorah award, Afro-Asian Inst. Histadrut of Israel, 1988, Dr. George Derry award, Marygrove Coll. Detroit, One Nation award, The Patriots Found./GM, 1989, 1st Ann. Move Detroit Forward award, City of Detroit, 1990, Gov's. Minuteman award, Rotary Club Lansing, 1991, Disting. Warrior award, Detroit Urban League, 1998, Edward J. Devitt award for disting. svc. to justice, 1998, Pinnacle award, Turner Broadcasting Sys., 2000, Spirit of Excellence award, ABA, 2001. Mem.: ABA (coun. sect. legal edn. and admission to bar), Am. Judicature Soc., Nat. Lawyers Guild, Detroit Bar Assn. (pres'. award), Mich. Bar Assn. (champion of justice award), Nat. Bar Assn. (William H. Hastie award Jud. Coun., 8th Ann. equal Justice award), Detroit Cotillion Club, Alpha Phi Alpha. Office: US Ct Appeals US Courthouse 231 W Lafayette Blvd Rm 240 Detroit MI 48226-2779 also: Potter Stewart US Courthouse 100 E 5th St Cincinnati OH 45202-3988*

KEITH, DAVID, symphony orchestra conductor; b. Tacoma, Oct. 9, 1930; s. David and Barbara K.; m. Ginni Paynton, July 5, 1972. Student, San Francisco Conservatory of Music, 1948-50; studied choral conducting, Rodney Eichenberger, U. Wash., 1968; studied orchestral conducting, Dr. Stanley Chapple and Vilem Sokol, U. Wash., 1968-72; studied piano with, Ira Schwarz, Can., Louise van Ogle, U.S. Assoc. condr. Bellevue Philharm. Orch., Bellevue, Wash., 1968—70; condr., music dir. Seattle Concert Orch., 1970-73; founder, music dir. emeritus, condr. laureate L.A. Mozart Orch., 1974-91, also trustee, 1974-91. Avocations: breeding purebred, all-black German shepherds. Office: LA Mozart Orch 1771 Seaview Trl Los Angeles CA 90046 Office Phone: 360-468-3060.

KEITH, JENNIE, anthropology educator, academic administrator, writer; b. Carmel, Calif., Nov. 15, 1942; d. Paul K. and Romayne Louise (Fuller) Hill; m. Marc Howard Ross, Aug. 25, 1968 (div. 1978); 1 child, Aaron Elliot Keith Ross; m. Roy Gerald Fitzgerald, June 21, 1980; 1 child, Kate Romayne Keith-Fitzgerald. BA, Pomona Coll., 1964; MA, Northwestern U., 1966, PhD, 1968; Dr.Letters (hon.), Pomona Coll., 2002. NIMH fellow, Paris, 1968-70; asst. prof. anthropology Swarthmore Coll., 1970-76, assoc. prof., 1976-82, prof., 1982—, Centennial prof. anthropology, 1990—, chmn. sociology and anthropology, 1987-92, provost, 1992-2001; exec. dir. Eugene M. Lang Ctr. for Civic and Social Responsibility, 2002—07. Mem. rsch. edn. rev. com. NIMH, Washington, 1979-82; co-dir. workshop on age and anthropology Nat. Inst. Aging, Washington, 1980-81, task group leader nat. rsch. plan on aging, 1981; mem. human devel. rev. bd. NIH, 1985-89; mem. adv. coun. Brookdale Found., 1990-93. Author: Old People, New Lives, 1977, 2d paperback edit., 1982 (Am. Jour. Nursing Book of Yr. 1978), Old People as People, 1982; co-author: The Aging Experience, 1994 (Richard Kalish award Gerontol. Soc. Am. 1994); co-editor: New Methods for Old-Age Research, 1980, 2d edit., 1986, Age in Anthropological Theory, 1984; mem. editorial bd. Gerontologist, 1981-89, Jour. Gerontology, 1987-91, Jour. Aging Studies, 1989-98; assoc. editor Rsch. on Aging, 1981-88. Bd. dirs. Cmty. Svcs., Folsom, Pa., 1980-82, Inst. Outdoor Awareness, Swarthmore, 1980—; bd. dirs. Kendal-Crosslands, 1987-92, chmn., 1989-92, Kendal Corp., 1992-95; mem. gen. bd. Pendle Hill Quaker Study Ctr., 2005—. Conf. grantee Nat. Inst. Aging, 1980, rsch. grantee, 1982-90. Fellow Am. Anthrop. Assn., Gerontol. Soc. Am. (exec. bd. behavioral and social scis. sect. 1985-87, program chmn. 1989, chair 1989-90, publs. com. 1993-95); mem. Assn. Anthropology and Gerontology (founder, sec. 1980-81). Office: Swarthmore Coll Lang Ctr for Civic and Social Responsibi Swarthmore PA 19081 Office Phone: 610-690-5742. Business E-Mail: jkeith1@swarthmore.edu.

KEITH, JOHN A(UGUSTINE) C(HILTON), lawyer; b. Washington, Aug. 22, 1946; BA, U. Va., 1968, JD, 1974. Bar: Va. 1975, D.C. 1976. Law clk. Hon. Albert V. Bryan, Jr. U.S. Dist. Ct. (ea. dist.) Va., 1974-75; ptnr. Blankingship & Keith, Fairfax, Va. Fellow Am. Bar Found.; mem. ABA, Am. Counsel Assn., Va. State Bar (10th dist. com. 1983-86, chmn. 1985-86, chmn. standing com. on legal ethics 1996-97, bar coun. 1991—, exec. com. 1993—, pres.-elect 1997-98, pres. 1998—), Fairfax Bar Assn. Office: Blankingship Keith 4020 University Dr Ste 300 Fairfax VA 22030-6802 E-mail: JKeith@blankeith.com.

KEITH, KENT MARSTELLER, academic administrator, motivational speaker, lawyer, writer; b. NYC, May 22, 1948; s. Bruce Edgar and Evelyn E. (Johnston) K.; m. Elizabeth Misao Carlson, Aug. 22, 1976. BA in Govt., Harvard U., 1970; BA in Politics and Philosophy, Oxford U., Eng., 1972, MA, 1977; JD, U. Hawaii, 1977; EdD, U. So. Calif., 1996. Bar: Hawaii 1977, D.C. 1979. Assoc. Cades, Schutte, Fleming & Wright, Honolulu, 1977-79; coord. Hawaii Dept. Planning and Econ. Devel., Honolulu, 1979-81, dep. dir., 1981-83, dir., 1983-86; energy resources coord. State of Hawaii, Honolulu, 1983-86, chmn. State Policy Coun., 1983-86; chmn. Aloha Tower Devel. Corp., 1983-86; project mgr. Mililani Tech. Park Castle and Cooke Properties, Inc., 1986-89, v.p. pub. rels. and bus. devel., 1988-89; pres. Chaminade U., Honolulu, 1989-95; v.p. devel. and comm. YMCA Honolulu, 1998—2001, sr. v.p., 2001—04; pres. Carlson Keith Corp., 2004—. Author: The Paradoxical Commandments: Finding Personal Meaning in a Crazy World, 2001, Anyway: The Paradoxical Commandments, 2002, Do It Anyway, 2003, Jesus Did It Anyway, 2005; contbr. articles on ocean law to law jours. Trustee Hawaii Loa Coll., 1986—89, vice chmn., 1987—89; bd. dirs. St. Louis Sch., 1990—95, Hanahauoli Sch., 1990—98, Cath. Charities, 1997—2003; chmn. Manoa Neighborhood Bd., 1989—91; mem. platform com. Hawaii Dem. Conv., 1982, 1984, 1986; pres. Manoa Valley Ch., Honolulu, 1976—78; mem. Diocesan Bd. Edn., 1990—95, chmn., 1990—93; mem. Manoa Valley Ch. Rhodes scholar, 1970; named one of 10 Outstanding Young Men of Am., U.S. Jaycees, 1984; recipient Disting. Alumni award U. Hawaii, 1993. Mem. Am. Assn. Rhodes Scholars, Internat. House of Japan, Nature Conservancy, Soc. Sci. Assn., Family Promise Hawaii, Plz. Club, Pacific Club, Harvard Club Hawaii (Honolulu, bd. dirs. 1974-78, sec. 1974-76), Rotary (Honolulu Sunrise). Democrat. United Ch. Christ. Home: 2626 Hillside Ave Honolulu HI 96822-1716 Personal E-mail: kentkeith@hotmail.com.

KEITH, MICHAEL CURTIS, communication educator, writer; b. Albany, NY, Mar. 17, 1945; s. Frederick Curtis Keith and Margaret (McKenna) Harney; m. Susanne Riette, Jan. 1, 1986; 1 child, Marlo. MA, U. R.I., 1977, PhD, 1998. Broadcaster various radio stas., 1965-75; dir. radio and TV Dean Coll., Franklin, Mass., 1978-90; prof. George Washington U., Washington, 1990-92; chair edn. Mus. Broadcasting, Chgo., 1992-94; prof. Boston Coll., 1993—. Author: Signals in the Air, 1995, Voices in the Purple Haze, 1997, The Radio Station, 5th edit., 2004; co-author: (with R. Hilliard) The Broadcast Century: A Biography of American Broadcasting, 4th edit., 2004, The Next Better Place, 2003. With U.S. Army, 1962-65. Recipient Stanton fellow award, Boston Coll., 2005. Mem. Broadcast Edn. Assn., Popular Culture Assn., Mus. Broadcast Comm. Office: Boston Coll 3 Howard St South Easton MA 02375-1448 Office Phone: 617-552-8837. E-mail: keithm@bc.edu.

KEITH, PATRICIA, multi-media specialist; b. Houston, Sept. 21, 1946; m. Nicholas Keith, July 19, 1968; 1 child, Nicholas (deceased) Keith. BA, Tex. So. U., 1970, MA, 1971; MS, Towson U., Md., 2002. Cert. libr. media specialist 1985, English, journalism, speech tchr. Houston Ind. Sch. Dist., 1976—86; children's libr. Alexandria Pub. Libr., Alexandria, Va., 1986—89; libr. media specialist Kettering Elem. Sch., Upper Marlboro, Md., 1989—92; libr. media/tech. specialist Benjamin Stoddert Mid. Sch., Temple Hills, Md., 1992—2000; libr. media specialist Charles H. Flowers H.S., Springdale, Md., 2000—. Libr. media adv. com. Office of Libr. Media Svcs.-Prince George's County Pub. Schs., Landover, Md., 1996—; tech. asst. Sagebrush Automation Conversion-Prince George's County Pub. Sch., Landover, Md., 2004—07; sponsor Charles H. Flowers H.S. It's Acad. Team, Springdale, Md., 2000—; lectr. in field. Editor: (harmony chorus) Potomac Harmony Dispatch. Fellow Mentor Tchr. fellow, Md. Tech. Consortium and Md. Pub. TV, 2002, Md. Tech. Acad. fellow, Md. State Dept. of Edn., Johns Hopkins U. and Towson U., 1999—2000. Mem.: Md. Instrnl. Computer Coord. Assn. (workshop lectr. 1999—2002), Ednl. Media Assn. of Prince George's County (pres., v.p., historian 1993—2002), Consortium of Sch. Networks, Md. Ednl. Media Orgn. Avocations: reading, designing jewelry, theater, jazz. Office: Charles H Flowers High School 10001 Ardwick Ardmore Rd Springdale MD 20774 Home Phone: 301-577-5489; Office Phone: 301-636-8000 ext. 310. Office Fax: 301-636-8008. Personal E-mail: pkeith9214@comcast.net. Business E-Mail: pkeith@pgcps.org.

KEITH, PAULINE MARY, artist, illustrator, writer; b. Fairfield, Nebr., July 21, 1924; d. Siebelt Ralph and Pauline Alethia (Garrison) Goldenstein; m. Everett B. Keith, Feb. 14, 1957; 1 child, Nathan Ralph. Student, George Fox Coll., 1947—48, Oreg. State U., 1955. Illustrator Merlin Press, San Jose, Calif., 1980-81; artist, illustrator, watercolorist Corvallis, Oreg., 1980-94. Author 6 chapbooks including Christmas Thoughts, Retelling the Story, 1985, Poems, 1999; editor: Four Generations of Verse, 1979; author numerous poems; contbr. articles to profl. jour; one-woman shows include Roger's Meml. Libr., Forest Grove, Oreg., 1959, Corvallis Art Ctr., 1960, 98-99, Human Resources Bldg., Corvallis, 1959-61, Corvallis Pastoral Counseling Ctr., 1992-94, 96, Hall Gallery, Sr. Ctr., 1993-03, Consumer Power, Philomath, Oreg., 1994, 02, 03, 04, 05, 07, Art, Etc., Newburg, Oreg., 1995-2002; exhibited in group shows at Hewlett-Packard Co., 1984-85, Corvallis Art Ctr., 1992, Chintimini Sr. Ctr., 1992, 94, 01-04, Art Vine show, 2006. Co-elder First Christian Ch. (Disciples of Christ), Corvallis, 1988-89, co-deacon, 1980-83, elder, 1991-93; sec. Hostess Club of Chintimini Sr. Ctr., Corvallis, 1987, pres., 1988-89, v.p., 1992-94; active Luth. Ch. Coun., 1999-2000. Recipient Watercolor 1st price Benton County Fair, 1982-83, 88-89, 91, 2d prize, 1987, 91, 3d prize, 1984, 90, 92, 3d prize Newberg Festival, 2005. Mem. Oreg. Assn. Christian Writers, Internat. Assn. Women Mins., Am. Legion Aux. (post poet), ArtVine (Pres.'s Choice, 1999-2002, honorable mention, 2005, Newburg Annual Festival art show 3d prize 2006) Republican. Avocation: walking. Office: 304 S College St Newberg OR 97132-3114

KEITH, ROBERT WILLIAM, banker; b. Chgo., July 28, 1926; s. Nathan William Keith and Myrtle A. (Bull) Simons; m. Helen L. Weichel, Sept. 4, 1948; children— Melissa, Matthew, Andrew Student, Wentworth Military Acad., 1944; BS, U. Mo., 1947; MBA, Hofstra U., 1956. Employment mgr. Equitable Life Assurance Soc., NYC, 1947-56; asst. treas. Hanover Bank, NYC, 1956-59; asst. v.p. Mfrs. Hanover Trust Co., NYC, 1959-63, v.p., 1963-77, sr. v.p., 1977-83, exec. v.p., 1983-86. Regent Stonier Grad. Sch., Washington, 1981-84. Fellow Life Office Mgmt. Assn.; mem. CLU (chartered), Am. Inst. Banking (life), Am. Bankers Assn. (chmn. pers. divsn., dir. 1980-81), Beta Gamma Sigma, Beta Theta Pi, North Fork Country Club. Republican. Presbyterian.

KEITH, TOBY (TOBY KEITH COVEL), country singer, songwriter, producer; b. Clinton, Okla., July 8, 1961; s. H.K. and Joan Covel; m. Tricia Keith, Mar. 24, 1984; children: Shelly Reeve, Krystal, Stelen Keith Covel. Worked in oil industry; former band mem. The Easy Money Band; played defensive end Okla. City Drillers, minor league, semi-pro football team; football player Okla. Outlaws, US Football League (USFL) team; signed with Mercury Records, Nashville, 1984—99, DreamWorks, Nashville, 1999; founder Show Dog Nashville Records, 2005—. Singer: (albums) Toby Keith, 1993, Christmas to Christmas, 1995, Boomtown, 1995, Blue Moon, 1996, Dream Walkin', 1997, Greatest Hits, Vol. 1, 1998, How Do You Like Me Now?, 1999 (Album Yr., Acad. Country Music Awards, 2000), Pull My Chain, 2001, Unleased, 2002 (Favorite Country Album, Am. Music Awards, 2003), 20th Century Masters- The Millennium, 2003, Shock 'n Y'all, 2003 (Album Yr., Acad. Country Music Awards, 2003, Best Country Album, Am. Music Awards, 2004), Greatest Hits 2, 2004, Honkytonk University, 2005, White Trash with Money, 2006, Big Dog Daddy, 2007, (singles) Should've Been A Cowboy, 1993 (Named Most Played Song of Decade in th 90's, Billboard), He Ain't Worth Missing, 1993, Who's That Man, 1994, Upstairs Downtown, 1994, You Ain't Much Fun, 1995, Does That Blue Moon Ever Shine On You, 1995, Closin' Time at Home, 1996, We Were in Love, 1997, I'm So Happy I Can't Stop Crying, 1997, Getcha Some, 1998, How Do You Like Me Now?, 2000 (Named Most Played Song of 2000, Billboard); singer: (with Chris Le Doux) (songs) "Copenhagen", Rodeo Rock & Roll Collection, 1995; singer: (with Beach Boys) "Be True to Your School", Stars and Stripes, Vol. 1, 1996; singer: (with Lari White) "Only God Could Stop Me Loving You", Stepping Stones, 1998; singer: "I Can't Be A Slave", Prince of Egypt original soundtrack, 1998; prodr.: (song) "I Can't Be A Slave", Prince of Egypt original soundtrack, 1998; singer (guest appearance with Willie Nelson): (video) Beer for My Horses, Willie Nelson and Friends, Live and Kickin', 2003. Named Entertainer of Yr., Acad. Country Music Awards, 2002, 2003, Top Male Vocalist, 2000, 2003, Favorite Male Country Artist, Am. Music Awards, 2004, 2006, Country Artist of Yr., Billboard Music Awards, 2005; recipient Hottest Video of Yr. for song Whiskey Girl, Country Music Television Music Awards, 2005, Music Video of Yr. for As Good As I Once Was, Country Music Assn., 2005, Country Album Artist of Yr., 2005. Achievements include invited by George W. Bush to addresss at MacDill Air Force Base in Tampa Fla., site of US Cent. Command and headquarters of Gen. Tommy Franks; a super-patriotic response to Sept. 11th that became one of country's most highly charged political statements; songwriting, 12 of his 16 #1 hits have been self-penned; radio airplay, 8 Billboard country #1's and eight R&R country #1's from his DreamWorks Records alone; sales of more than $13.5 million. Avocations: hunting, fishing, golf, collecting baseball cards and memorabilia.*

KEITH, WILLIAM DOUGLAS, lawyer; b. Chgo., Apr. 11, 1950; s. William H. and Mary N. Keith; m. Jill Marie Keith, Nov. 27, 1977; children: William P., Robert D., Lauren M. BA, Rutgers U., 1972; JD, Stetson U., 1976. Bar: Fla. 1976; cert. civil trial lawyer, bus. litigation lawyer, civil trial advocate; cert. cir. mediator. Ptnr. Cardillo, Keith & Bonaquist, P.A., Naples, Fla., 1976—. Mem. judicial nominating commn. Twentieth Judicial Circuit, 2003—; mem. Fla. Bar Bus. Litigation Cert. Com., 2004—. Paul Harris fellow Rotary, 1988; bd. dirs. YMCA of Collier County, 1991-94. Mem. Am. Bd. of Trial Advocates (nat. bd. dirs. 2000-03), Am. Inns of Ct. (pres. 2000-01, master bencher), Assn. of Trial Lawyers of Am., Acad. Fla. Trial Lawyers (sustaining mem., bd. dirs. 1993-96), Collier County Bar Assn. (pres. 1983-84, pres. trial lawyers sect. 1986-87). Avocations: reading, golf, fly fishing. Office Phone: 941-774-2229.

KEITHLEY, BRADFORD GENE, lawyer; b. Nov. 23, 1951; s. Sanderson Irish and Joan G. (Kenneday) K.; m. Kathy Carrington, Nov. 6, 2004; children: Paul Michael, John N. Carrington III, Thomas Ryan Carrington. BS, U. Tulsa, 1973; JD, U. Va., 1976. Bar: Va. 1976, Okla. 1978, D.C. 1979. Atty. Office of Gen. Counsel to Sec. USAF, Washington, 1976-78; ptnr. Hall, Estill, Hardwick, Gable, Collingsworth and Nelson, Tulsa, 1978-84; sr. v.p. gen. counsel natural gas divsn. Arkla, Inc. (now Center-Point Energy, Inc.), Shreveport, La., 1984—90; ptnr. co-head global oil and gas practice team Jones Day, Dallas, 1990—. Mem. ABA, Fed. Energy Bar Assn., Va. State Bar, Okla. Bar Assn., D.C. Bar Assn., Am. Gas Assn. (mem. legal sect.), Dallas Petroleum Club. Office: Jones Day 2727 N Harwood Dallas TX 75201-1515

KEITHLEY, ROGER LEE, judge; b. Macomb, Ill., July 19, 1946; s. Gilbert Lee and Mary Jane (Torrance) K.; m. Karen Sue Metzger, Apr. 1, 1973; children: Roger Livingston, Terrance Christopher, Kathryn Suzanne. BS, U. Ill., 1968; JD, Harvard U., 1973. Bar: Colo. 1973, U.S. Dist. Ct. Colo. 1973, U.S. Ct. Appeals (10th cir.) 1976. Law clk. to justice Colo. Supreme Ct., Denver, 1973—74; trial atty. SEC, Denver, 1974—76; assoc. Morrato, Gueck & Colantuno, Denver, 1976—80; ptnr. Krys, Boyle, Golz & Keithley, Denver, 1980—86, Law, Knous & Keithley, Denver, 1986—90, Law, Keithley & Tuttle, Denver, 1990—93; pvt. practice Roger L. Keithley, P.C., Denver, 1993—98; presiding disciplinary judge Colo. Supreme Ct., 1998—2003. Prof. physics U. Asmara, Eritrea, Ethiopia, 1969-70. With U.S. Army, 1968-70. Mem.: ABA, Am. Law Inst., Denver Bar Asn., Colo. Bar Assn. Home: 5239 E 17th Ave Denver CO 80220-1313 Personal E-mail: rlkeithley@aol.com.

KEKER, JOHN WATKINS, lawyer; b. Winston-Salem, NC, Jan. 4, 1944; s. Samuel J. and Lucy Hearn (Spinks) K.; m. Christina Snowden Day, Sept. 11, 1965; children: Adam, Nathan. AB cum laude, Princeton U., 1965; LLB, Yale U., 1970. Bar: Calif. 1971, US Dist. Ct. (all dists. Calif.) 1971, US Ct. Appeals (9th cir.) 1971, US Supreme Ct. 1974. Law clk. to chief justice Earl Warren US Supreme Ct., Washington, 1970-71; staff atty. Natural Resources Def. Coun., Washington, 1971, Office Fed. Pub. Defender, San Francisco, 1971-73; ptnr. Keker & Van Nest and predecessor firms, San Francisco, 1973—. Assoc. counsel Iran/Contra Investigation, Washington, 1987—. Co-author: Effective Direct and Cross Examination, 1986; contbr. articles to profl. jours. Chmn. bd. Bay Area Water Quality Control, Oakland, Calif., 1980-82; v.p. San Francisco Fire Commn., 1988; pres. San Francisco Police Commn., 1990-91, 96-97. Served to 1st lt. USMC, 1965—67, Vietnam. Named Best Lawyer in Bay Area, San Francisco Chronicle, 2003; named one of 100 Most Influential Lawyers, Nat. Law Jour., 2006; named to Litig. Hall of Fame, Calif. State Bar, 2002; recipient Significant Contbn. to Criminal Justice award, Calif. Attys. for Criminal Justice, 1996. Fellow: Am. Bar Found., Am. Bd. Trial Advs., Internat. Acad. Trial Lawyers, Am. Coll. Trial Lawyers. Office: Keker & Van Nest 710 Sansome St San Francisco CA 94111 Office Phone: 415-391-5400.

KEKES, JOHN, philosopher, educator; b. Budapest, Hungary, Nov. 22, 1936; came to U.S., 1965, naturalized, 1977; s. Eugene and Anna (Borsodi) K.; m. Jean Justilliano, May 20, 1968. BA, Queen's U., Kingston, Ont., Can., 1961, MA, 1962; PhD, Australian Nat. U., 1967. Instr. to assoc. prof. philosophy Calif. State U., Northridge, 1965-71; prof. U. Sask., Regina, Canada, 1971-74, SUNY, Albany, 1974—, chmn. dept. philosophy, 1974-77, prof. philosophy and pub. policy, 1981—. Sr. rsch. fellow Ctr. for Philosophy of Sci., U. Pitts., 1984-85; vis. prof. U.S. Mil. Acad., West Point, N.Y., 1985-86, Nat. U. Singapore, 1989, Portuguese Cath. U., Lisbon, 2001. Author: A Justification of Rationality, 1976, The Nature of Philosophy, 1980, Dimensions of Ethical Thought, 1987, The Examined Life, 1988, Moral Tradition and Individuality, 1989, Facing Evil, 1990, The Morality of Pluralism, 1993, Moral Wisdom and Good Lives, 1995, Against Liberalism, 1997, A Case for Conservatism, 1998, Pluralism in Philosophy: Changing the Subject, 2000, The Art of Life, 2002, The Illusion of Egalitarianism, 2004, The Roots of Evil, 2005, The Enlargement of Life, 2006; gen. editor: Studies in Moral Philosophy, 1986—91; editor: Pub. Affairs Quar., 1999—2001. Recipient Comdrs. Pub. Svc. award U.S. Army, 1986; Rockefeller Found. humanities fellow, 1980-81, fellow Earhart Found., 1983, 88, 89, 98, 2002; resident scholar Rockefeller Found. Study Ctr., Bellagio, Italy, 1982, 89. Mem. Am. Philos. Assn., Royal Inst. Philosophy Home: 2041 Cook Rd Charlton NY 12019-2909

KELAHER, JAMES PEIRCE, lawyer; b. Orlando, Fla., Oct. 28, 1951; s. Philip James and Neva Cecelia (Peirce) K. BA, U. Cen. Fla., 1973; JD, Fla. State U., 1981. Bar: Fla. 1981, U.S. Dist. Ct. (mid. dist.) Fla. 1982, U.S. Ct. Appeals (11th cir.) 1983, U.S. Supreme Ct.; cert. civil trial law. Assoc. Law Office of Nolan Carter, P.A., Orlando, 1981-83, Law Office of James Kelaher, P.A., Orlando, 1983-87; ptnr. Kelaher & Wieland, P.A., Orlando, 1987—, Kelaher, Wieland and Hilado, P.A., Orlando, 1996-98, Kelaher Law Offices, P.A., Orlando, 1998—. Contbr. articles to profl. jours. Eagle benefactor Rep. Party. Mem. ABA, ATLA (sustaining), Orange County Bar Assn., Acad. Fla. Trial Lawyers (sec. 1994-95, treas. 1995-96, pres. 1997-98, bd. dirs. coll. diplomates, membership exec. com. bd. trustees Fla. lawyers action group), Ctrl. Fla. Trial Lawyers Assn. (pres. 1992-94). Roman Catholic. Avocations: tennis, golf, skiing, fishing. Office: Kelaher Law Offices 800 N Magnolia Ave Ste 1301 Orlando FL 32803-3255 E-mail: jim@kelaherlaw.com.

KELCH, ROBERT PAUL, former dean, pediatric endocrinologist; b. Detroit, Dec. 3, 1942; s. Paul and Iona Bertha (Schmitt) Kelch; m. Jeri Anne Parker, Aug. 17, 1963; children: Randall Paul, Julie Marie. PhB, Wayne State U., Detroit, 1964; MD, U. Mich., Ann Arbor, 1967. Intern then Wyeth pediatric residency fellow U. Mich. Med. Center, 1967—70, research fellow, 1969—70, mem. faculty, 1972—94, prof. pediatrics, 1977—94, acting chmn. dept., 1979—80, chmn. dept., 1981—94; physician-in-chief C.S. Mott Children's Hosp. U. Mich., 1983—94; chief clin. affairs U. Mich. Hosps., 1989—92; NIH trainee pediatric endocrinology U. Calif. Med. Center, San Francisco, 1970—72; prof. pediat., dean U. Iowa Coll. Medicine, Iowa City, 1994—2003, v.p. statewide health svcs., 2001—02; exec. v.p., med. affairs, prof. pediatrics U. Michigan, Ann Arbor, 2003—. Co-author: A Practical Approach to Pediatric Endocrinology, 1975; contbr. articles to med. jours. With USNR. Fellow: Am. Acad. Pediat.; mem.: Midwest Soc. Pediat. Rsch. (pres. 1983—84), Lawson Wilkins Pediat. Endocrine Soc., Ctrl. Soc. Clin. Rsch., Assn. Med. Sch. Pediat. Dept. Chmn. (pres. 1989), Am. Soc. Clin. Investigation, Am. Fedn. Clin. Rsch., Endocrine Soc., Am. Bd. Pediat. (sec.-treas. 1992, chmn. 1995), Soc. Pediat. Rsch. (pres. 1988), Inst. Medicine NAS. Methodist. Office: U Michigan Health Sys M7324 Med Sci Bldg Box 0626 1500 E Med Ctr Dr Ann Arbor MI 48109 Office Phone: 734-647-9351, 734-647-9351. E-mail: rkelch@med.umich.edu.

KELDER, DOROTHY MAE, science educator; b. Chgo., July 22; d. Peter Clarence and Dorothy (Vande Werken) Kelder. BA in Edn., Calvin Coll., Grand Rapids, Mich., 1964; MS in Edn., Bank St. Coll., NYC, 1985; postgrad., U. Mich., Ann Arbor, 1966. Music tchr. grade 3, 7-9 Hudsonville Christian Sch., Mich., 1964—70; 2st and 2d grade tchr. Ea. Christian Sch. Assn., North Haledon, NJ, 1971—77; elem. tchr. E.C.U.M.P. Dawn Treader, Paterson, NJ, 1977—83; 5th grade tchr. Paterson Bd. Edn., 1985—2001, 7th grade tchr. sci., 2001—. Mem. Sch. Leadership Com., Paterson, 2004—06; leader sci. activity Sci. Resource #8, Paterson, 2001—; mem. ACORN, Paterson, 2004. Recipient Tchr. of the Yr. Gov.'s award, Paterson Pub. Schs., 1996. Mem.: Paterson Edn. Assn., N.J. Edn. Assn. Democrat. Christian Reformed Ch. Avocations: tennis, reading, travel, knitting, singing.

KELEHER, DAVID, electronics executive; b. 1950; BA in Econ., U. NH; MBA, Cornell U. CPA, NH. Various sr. mgmt. positions in corp. fin. and ops. Digital Equipment Corp.; various exec. positions Raytheon Co., asst. corp. contr., group contr. comml. electronics div.; v.p., CFO Dynamics Rsch. Corp., Andover, Mass. Office: Dynamics Rsch Corp 60 Frontage Rd Andover MA 01810-5498

KELEHER, JAMES P., bishop; b. July 31, 1931; BA, St. Mary of the Lake Sem., Mundelein, Ill., 1954; DST, St. Mary of the Lake Sem., 1961, Licentiate in Sacred Theology, 1968; MA in Ednl. administrn., Loyola U., Chgo., 1967; PhD, Gregorian U., Rome. Ordained priest Roman Cath. Ch., 1958. Rector Quigley Sem. South, Chgo., 1976—78; pres., rector St. Mary of the Lake Sem., Mundelein, Ill., 1978—84; bishop Belleville, Ill., 1984—93; archbishop Archdiocese of Kansas City, 1993—2005, archbishop emeritus, 2005—. Mem. Papal Visitation Com. for Sems.; chmn. bishop's com. on priestly formation; mem. com. migration; mem. com. econ. concerns of the Holy See Nat. Conf. Cath. Bishops. Mem.: Midwest Assn. Theol. Schs., Nat. Cath. Edn. Assn. (sem. dept.). Office: Archdiocese of Kansas City Chancery Office 12615 Parallel Kansas City KS 66109

KELEHER, MICHAEL LAWRENCE, lawyer; b. Albuquerque, Sept. 21, 1934; s. William A. Keleher and Loretta Barrett; m. Margaret Anne Wills, June 10, 1961; children: Anne Barrett, Elizabeth Katherine, Margaret Mary, Mary Ann, Loretta Wills, Michael Wills. BA, U. N. Mex., 1956; MA, NYU, 1958; JD, U. Miss., 1962. Bar: N.Mex. 1962. Atty. Keleher & McLeod PA, Albuquerque, 1962—2001, of counsel, 2001—. Mem. N.Mex. Old Lincoln County Meml. Commn., 1969—76; chmn. N.Mex. Diamond Jubilee/U.S. constl. Bicentennial Commn., 1986—89; bd. dirs. Bernalillo County unit Am. Cancer Soc., 1966—74, pres., 1969—70; mem. Albuquerque Environ. Planning Commn., 1973—75, chair land controls bd., 1974—75; mem. Shared Vision, Inc., 1994—98; trustee U. Albuquerque, 1970—78, sec., 1974—78; chair N.Mex. State U. Rio Grande Hist. Collectors, 1978—79; chmn. Archdiocese Santa Fe Devel. Coun., 1990—93; trustee Archdiocese Santa Fe Cath. Found., 1991—2003, pres., 1997—99, Guadalupe Inst., 1987, chmn.; bd. dirs. Robert O. Anderson Schs. Mgmt. Found., 1995—99. Lt. (j.g.) USNR, 1956—58. Mem.: ABA, N.Mex. Bar Assn., U. N.Mex. Alumni Lettermen's Assn., Order Friars Minor (affiliate), Equestrian Order the Holy Sepulchre Jerusalem, Phi Theta Phi, Sigma Chi. Democrat. Roman Catholic. Office: Keleher & McLeod PA 201 3rd St NW Albuquerque NM 87102-3370 Business E-Mail: mlk@keleher-law.com.

KELEMEN, CHARLES F., computer science educator; b. Mt. Vernon, NY, Jan. 7, 1943; s. Frank K. and Eleanor E. K.; m. Sylvia J. Brown, July 26, 1975; children— Rebecca, Colin, Elizabeth. BA, Valparaiso U., 1964; MA, Pa. State U., 1966, PhD, 1969. Asst. then assoc. prof. Ithaca Coll., NY, 1969-80; prof. LeMoyne Coll., Syracuse, NY, 1980-84, Swarthmore Coll., Pa., 1984—, chmn. divsn. natural scis. and engring. Pa., 2000—03, Edward Hicks Magill prof. math. and natural scis., 2002—. Cons. in field; chair computer sci. dept. Swarthmore Coll., 1984-99, 2001—; vis. assoc. prof. Cornell U., Ithaca, N.Y., 1978, summers 1979-81. Co-author: (with others) Fundamentals of Computing II Abstraction Data Structures, and Large Software Systems, 1995, Fundamentals of Computing II C++ Laboratory Manual, 1995. Grantee NSF, 1977-81 Mem. Assn. Computing Machinery, IEEE, Computer Soc., Math. Assn. Am. Office: Swarthmore Coll Dept Computer Sci Swarthmore PA 19081 Business E-Mail: ckeleme1@swarthmore.edu.

KELEN, GABOR DAVID, emergency physician; b. Aug. 10, 1951; MD, U. Toronto, Can., 1979. Diplomate Am. Bd. Emergency Medicine. Intern St. Michael's Hosp., Toronto, Can., 1979-80, resident in internal medicine, 1981-82, Women's Coll. Hosp., Toronto, 1980-81; resident in emergency medicine Johns Hopkins Hosp., Balt., 1982-84, emergency physician-in-chief, 1993—; instr. Johns Hopkins U., Balt., 1984-85, asst. prof., 1985-89, assoc. prof., 1989-93, prof., 1993—, chair Emergency Medicine, 1993—, founder, Ctr. for Internat. Emergency Disaster Relief Studies, 1998—, dir. Johns Hopkins Office of Critical Event Preparedness & Response (CE-PAR), 2002—; dir. Nat. Ctr. for Study of Preparedness and Catastrophic Event Response. Vice chair, med. bd. Johns Hopkins Hosp., 2002—05, chair med. br., 2005—; editl. bd. Bioterrorism & Biosecurity, 2003—, Jour. Med. Disasters and Public Health Preparedness; pres. Assn. Academic Chairs of Emergency Medicine, 2004—06. Recipient Career Devel. award, Am. Coll. Emergency Physicians (ACEP)/Emergency Medicine Found., 1988, Clinician Scientist award, Johns Hopkins U., 1988—90, Academic Excellence award, Soc. Academic Emergency Medicine, 1992, Outstanding Contbn. to Rsch. award, ACEP, 1993. Fellow Soc. Acad. Emergency Medicine; mem. Am. Coll. Emergency Physicians, Am. Acad. Emergency Medicine, Royal Coll. Physicians Can., Inst. Medicine, Nat. Acad. Sci. Office: Johns Hopkins Hosp Ste 6-100 1830 E Monument St Baltimore MD 21287-0005 E-mail: gkelen@jhmi.edu.

KELL, JOSEPH WILLIAM, materials scientist; b. Bradenton, Fla., Jan. 6, 1980; s. William H. and Judie V. Kell. BS in Materials Sci. and Engring., Wright State U., Dayton, Ohio, 2003, MS in Materials Sci. and Engring., 2005. Materials scientist Air Force Rsch. Lab., Wright-Patterson AFB, Ohio, 2003—. Contbr. articles pub. to profl. jour. Scholar Outstanding Materials Sci. Undergraduate, Dean's Office, Coll. of Engring., Wright State U., 2002. Mem.: ASM Internat. (assoc.), Am. Ceramics Soc. (assoc.), Tau Beta Pi (rec. sec. of wsu chpt. 2002—03). Achievements include patents pending for Flux pinning of high temperature superconductors by minute additions; research in Minute doping of superconductors. Avocations: hiking, racing. Home: 4441 Glenheath Dr Kettering OH 45440 Home Phone: 937-545-9833; Office Phone: 937-255-6490.

KELL, LYLE NICHOLAS, retired minister, retired real estate broker; b. Sedro Woolley, Wash., May 8, 1924; s. Tate Maxville and Nancy Arzelia (Howard) Kell; m. Dorothy Jane Rasar; children: Nicholas Raymond, Brenda Jane. Student, U. Wash., Seattle U., 1960—62, Seattle Pacific Coll., 1960—62, Golden Gate Bapt. Theol. Sem., Federal Way, Wash., 60's—70's. Lic. ins. agt. Wash.; ordained minister Bapt. Ch., 1965; lic. real estate broker Wash. Log truck driver Lyman Timber Co., Sound View Pulp Co., Hamilton, Wash., 1947—51; switchman Gt. No. R.R., Seattle, 1953—59; broker, owner Spring Homes Realty/Kell Lynnwood Properties/Kell Realty Inc., Seattle/Lynnwood/Arlington, 1962—85; pastor Northgate Bapt. Ch., Seattle, 1965—72, First Bapt. Ch. of Martha Lake, Lynnwood, Wash., 1973—80. Author: Personal Biography of World War II, 1997. Mem. exec. bd., co-chmn. Snohomish County Vets. Assistance Fund Bd., Wash., 1995—; nat. chaplain WWII USN Armed Guard Hdqs., Rolesville, NC, 1995—; chaplain U.S. Senate, Washington, 1997; missionary to vets. Puget Sound Bapt. Assn. of Wash. State, 2002; chaplain Post 1561 VFW, Arlington, Wash., 1995. With USN, 1943—46. Decorated 2 Bronze Engagement Stars USN, China Svc. medal with clasp, Russian medal, World War II Combat Ribbon U.S. Govt.; recipient 2 Spl. Recognition awards, Downtown Seattle Kiwanis Club, 1963. Mem.: VFW (nat. chaplain 1995—96), DAV, SAR. Baptist. Achievements include research in for new major anesthetic. Home: 2821 180th St NE Marysville WA 98271 Personal E-mail: bkell@kell-co.com. Business E-Mail: lnk@wavecable.com.

KELL, MICHAEL JON, physician, researcher; b. Dhahran, Saudi Arabia, Nov. 1, 1949; arrived in U.S., 1951; s. Edgar Michael Kell and Elvira Therea Hannevig; children: Alexander Niels, Andrew Halvdan. BSChemE, U. Calif., Santa Barbara, 1971; MSChemE, MIT, 1972; MD cum laude, Emory U., 1985, PhD with highest honors, 1985. Diplomate Am. Bd. Anti-Aging Medicine, Am. Acad. Pain Mgmt., Am. Bd. Clin. Chem., Am. Bd. Froensic Medicine, Am. Bd. Clin. Hypnosis. Rschr. Dow Chem., Wayland, Mass., 1973—74; mgr. program Cordis-Dow, Concord, Calif., 1976—79; med. dir. Michael Jon Kell, PhD & Assoc., P.C., Atlanta, 1987—2000; dir. rsch. Urine Drug Testing, Inc., Marco Island, Fla., 1997—; med. dir. Pvt. Clinic Labs., Inc., Atlanta, 1991—2000; editor, author Harrison Publs., Suwanee, 2000—; founder Inst. Conscious Evolution and Human Devel., Atlanta, 2007—. Exec. dir. Expert Witness & Cons. Group; radio host Mind Brain Body. Author: (book) My Boyhood, 1965, Journey to Planet Earth, 1967, Electrostatic Fields and Surface Potentials from Individual, 1985, The Song of Solomon: A 3000 Year Postcript, 1985, The Journey of Self, 1987, Determining Disability and Personal Injury Damage, 4th edit., 2000, Medical Practice for Trial Lawyers, 5th edit., 2001; author: (with others) Noise, Impedance and Single Channels, 1983, Charged Membrane Proteins, Vault of Adepti, 1995; contbr. articles to profl. jours. Fellow, NSF, 1982; scholar, European Molecular Biology, 1982; Merit scholar, Brown U., 1967, Pres. Undgrad. Rsch. grantee, U. Calif., 1971, Grass Found. fellow, Marine Biol. Lab., 1982. Fellow: Am. Chem. Soc., Am. Soc. Clinic Hypnosis (approved cons.), Nat. Acad. Clin. Biochemistry, Am. Bd. Forensic Medicine, Am. Bd. Forensic Examiners, Am. Acad. Pain Mgmt. Achievements include invention of; patents for biotechnology; full foreign fillings. Avocations: writing, lecturing, meditating, philosophy, mathematics.

KELLAM, CARAMINE, volunteer; b. Painter, Va., Jan. 23, 1941; d. Emerson Polk and Amine (Cosby) Kellam; m. Isaac Somers White, Nov. 25, 1961 (div. 1975); children: Kellam White, Caramine White, Somers Farkas; m. Harry Sherman Holcomb, III, May 12, 1979 (div. Mar. 2001); m. Fred Greenway, Apr. 1, 2006. AA, St. Mary's Coll., Raleigh, 1960; cert., Richmond Bus. Coll., Va., 1961. Bd. dirs. Kellam Energy, Inc. Contbr. articles to profl. jours. Trustee Northampton-Accomack Meml. Hosp., Nassawadox, Va., 1986—98, v.p. aux., 1986—88, pres., 1988—90, sec. bd. trustees, 1989—91, vice chmn., 1991—94, chair, 1994—96; bd. dirs. Eastern Shore CC Found., 1998—, v.p. bd. dirs., 2001—03, pres., 2003—04; sec. E. Pol. Kellam Found., 1991—; mem. session Belle Haven Presbyn. Ch., 1999—2002; bd. dirs. Ea. Shore Hist. Soc., Onancock, Va., 1987—92, Shore Life Svcs., 1998—2007, pres., 2004—07; bd. dirs. Med. Soc. Va. Alliance, Richmond, Va., 1984—94, v.p., 1989—91, pres., 1992—93; trustee Shore Meml., 2003—, sec., 2004—07, vice chair, 2007—. Mem.: DAR (regent 2004—07), Med. Soc. Va. Trust, AMA Alliance Bd. (mem. ERF com. 1994, AMA-ERF com. chmn. 1994—95, field dir. 1995—98, bylaws chmn. 1999—2000), Garden Club Eastern Shore (pres. 1973—75, Garden Week chmn. 2001—02). Avocations: travel, reading, flower arranging. Home: PO Box 38 Franktown VA 23354-0038

KELLEHER, COLM, diversified financial services company executive; Grad., Oxford U. Chartered Accountant, 1983. Joined Arthur Andersen, London; various positions increasing responsibility Morgan Stanley, 1989—, co-head fixed income London, 2004—06, head global capital markets NYC, 2006—, apptd. CFO, 2007—. Office: Morgan Stanley 1585 Broadway New York NY 10036*

KELLEHER, HERBERT DAVID, air transportation executive, lawyer; b. Camden, NJ, Mar. 12, 1931; s. Harry and Ruth (Moore) K.; m. Joan Negley, Sept. 9, 1955; children: Julie, Michael, Ruth, David. BA cum laude, Wesleyan U., 1953; LLB cum laude, NYU, 1956. Bar: NJ 1957, Tex. 1962. Clk. NJ Supreme Ct., 1956—59; assoc. Lum, Biunno & Tompkins, Newark, 1959—61; ptnr. Mathews, Nowlin, Macfarlane & Barrett, San Antonio, 1961—69; sr. ptnr. Oppenheimer, Rosenberg, Kelleher & Wheatley, Inc., San Antonio, 1969—81, bd. dirs., 1971—; founder, gen. counsel, chmn. Southwest Airlines Co., Dallas, 1967—81, pres., CEO, chmn. bd. dir., 1981—2001, exec. chmn., bd. dir., 2001—. Recipient Bower award for Bus. Leadership, Franklin Inst., 2003. Home: 144 Thelma Dr San Antonio TX 78212-2516 Office: SW Airlines Co PO Box 36611 Dallas TX 75235-1611 Home Phone: 214-691-8558; Office Phone: 214-792-4110. Business E-Mail: vickie.shuler@wnco.com.

KELLEHER, KATHLEEN, marketing professional; b. Suffern, NY, May 3, 1951; d. John James and Carol (Re) K. BA, Fairleigh Dickinson U., 1973. CLU, chartered fin. cons., mut. fund counselor, advisor sr. living, advisor for sr. living. Ins. sales adminstr. Blyth Eastman Dillon & Co., 1977-79; product mktg. assoc. Dean Witter Reynolds, NYC, 1980-82; mgr. product mktg. annuities and ins. dept. Kidder, Peabody & Co., 1982-85; v.p. nat. sales mgr. ins. Paine Webber, 1985-88; v.p., dir. mktg. and sales support Landmark Fin. Corp., Oklahoma City, 1988-91; cons. fin. svcs., 1991—; dir. Mktg. Svcs. Protective Life investment product divsn., Cin., 1993-94, mktg. cons. fin. svcs., 1995—; dir. mktg. Prudential Annuity Svcs.; v.p. mut. funds and annuity tng. Prudential Investments, 1996, v.p. edn. strategy and integration, 2000; dir. annuity mktg. UBS Fin Svcs. Inc., Weehawken, NJ, 2002—07; pres., CEO Boomers & Beyond Cons. Svcs., LLC, Princeton, 2007—. Mem.: Soc. Fin. Svc. Profls. Republican. Office: 212 Carnegie Ctr Ste 206 Princeton NJ 08540 Office Phone: 609-919-6882. Business E-Mail: kathleen@kkboomerconsulting.com.

KELLEHER, KEVIN, music company executive; BA, Middlebury Coll.; MBA, Rutgers Grad. Sch. Mgmt. CPA. Ptnr. Price Waterhouse Media/Entertainment Group; controller Sony Music Entertainment, NYC, 1992—94, sr. v.p., 1992—99, exec. v.p. & CFO, 1999—2004, Sony BMG Music Entertainment, 2004—. Office: Sony BMG Music Entertainment 550 Madison Ave New York NY 10022 Office Phone: 212-833-8000.*

KELLEHER, KIMBERLY ANDERSON, magazine publishing executive; b. 1972; m. Dan Kelleher. BA History, U. of Wis. Spl. sect. mgr. ELLE Décor, 1993; several managerial sales positions ELLE, Mirabella and TEEN, 1993—98; beauty advt. dir. ELLE, 1998—2000; sr. v.p. of advt. and mktg. Cityspree Inc., 2000—01; advt. dir. Condé Nast's Mademoiselle, 2001, Golf For Women, 2001—02, pub., 2002—03, v.p., pub., 2003—04, SELF Mag., 2004—. Mem. bd. dirs. Fertile Hope Inc. Named an Industry Influencer, Folio Mag., 2005; named one of 40 under 40, Advt. Age, 2007; recipient Exec. Women's Golf Association's Leadership Award, Golf for Women, 2003. Office: Condé Nast Publications US HDQS 4 Times Sq New York NY 10001 Office Phone: 212-286-2860. Office Fax: 212-286-6763. E-mail: Kimberly_Kelleher@self.com.*

KELLEHER, NEIL L., chemist, educator; b. Clinton, Md., Apr. 28, 1970; s. William J. and Ann C. Kelleher; m. Jennifer Kelleher, Aug. 12, 1992; children: Emily, Lauren. BS in Chemistry, Pacific Luth. U., 1992, BA in German, 1992; postgraduate studies, U. Konstanz, Germany, 1992—93; MS in Bioanalytical Chemistry, Cornell U., 1995, PhD in Bioanalytical Chemistry, 1997. Fulbright scholar U. Konstanz, Germany, 1992—93; rsch. asst. Cornell U., Ithaca, NY, 1993—97; postdoctoral asst. Harvard Med. Sch., 1997—99; asst. prof. to assoc. prof. chemistry U. Ill., Urbana-Champaign, 1999—. Contbr. articles to profl. jours. Recipient Burroughs Wellcome award in pharm. scis., 2000—03, NIH, 2000—02, Rsch. Corp. Innovation award, 2001, Career award, NSF, 2002—; grantee, NIH, 1993—96; Searle scholar, 2000—03, Cotrell scholar, 2002, Packard fellow, 2002—. Mem.: AAAS, Am. Soc. Mass Spectrometry (Rsch. award 2001), Am. Chem. Soc. Office: Univ Ill Dept Chemistry 53 Roger Adams Lab 47-5 600 S Mathews Ave Urbana IL 61801 Office Phone: 217-244-3927. Office Fax: 217-244-8068. E-mail: kelleher@scs.uiuc.edu.

KELLEHER, PATRICK B., insurance company executive; B, Franklin & Marshall Coll. Fin. mgmt. positions Sun Life Assurance Canada, 1980—92; fin. mgmt. positions through CFO Manulife Fin., 1992—98; exec. v.p., CFO Transamerica Reinsurance, Charlotte, NC, 1998—2006; sr. v.p., CFO Genworth Fin. Inc., Richmond, Va., 2007—. Fellow: Canadian Soc. Actuaries, Soc. Actuaries; mem.: CGA Assn. Canada. Office: Genworth Fin Inc 6620 W Broad St Richmond VA 23230*

KELLEHER, ROBERT JOSEPH, judge; b. NYC, Mar. 5, 1913; s. Frank and Mary (Donovan) K.; m. Gracyn W. Wheeler, Aug. 14, 1940; children: R. Jeffrey, Karen Kathleen Kelleher King. AB, Williams Coll., 1935; LL.B., Harvard U., 1938. Bar: N.Y. 1939, Calif. 1942, U.S. Supreme Ct 1954. Atty. War Dept., 1941-42; asst. U.S. atty. So. Dist. Calif., 1948-50; pvt. practice Beverly Hills, 1951-71; U.S. dist. judge, 1971-83; sr. judge U.S. Dist. Ct. 9th Cir., 1983—. Mem. So. Calif. Com. Olympic Games, 1964; capt. U.S. Davis Cup Team, 1962-63; treas. Youth Tennis Found. So. Calif., 1961-64. Served to lt. USNR, 1942-45. Recipient Bicentennial Medal award Williams Coll., 2001; enshrined in Internat. Tennis Hall of Fame, 2000. Mem. So. Calif. Tennis Assn. (v.p. 1958-64, pres. 1983-85), U.S. Lawn Tennis Assn. (pres. 1967-68), Internat. Lawn Tennis Club U.S.A., Gt. Britain, France, Can., Mex., Australia, India, Israel, Japan, All Eng. Lawn Tennis and Croquet (Wimbledon), Harvard Club (N.Y./So. Calif.), Williams Club (N.Y.), L.A. Country Club, Delta Kappa Epsilon. Office: US Dist Ct 255 E Temple St Ste 1434 Los Angeles CA 90012-3334 Office Phone: 213-894-5255.

KELLEHER, TIMOTHY JOHN, retired publishing company executive; b. Massillon, Ohio, Jan. 4, 1940; s. John Joseph and Catherine Isabelle (Quinlan) K.; m. Mary Gray Thornton, Aug. 27, 1966; children— Catherine, Joseph, Sarah BS in Polit. Sci., Xavier U., Cin., 1962; postgrad., Xavier U., 1965, Morehead State U., Ky., 1975-76. Mgr. labor rels. GM, Norwood, Ohio, 1964-73; pers. mgr. Rockwell Internat., Winchester, Ky., 1973-77, dir. labor rels. Troy, Mich., 1977-82; v.p. human resources Detroit Free Press, 1982-89; sr. v.p. labor rels. Detroit Newspaper Agy., 1989—2004; ret. Dir. Detroit Macomb Hosp. Corp. Bd. dirs. Greater Detroit Alliance of Bus., annually 1983-89, Winchester/Clark Hist. Soc., Ky., 1975, pres., 1976-77; bd. dirs. New Detroit Inc., annually 1983-89. Served to sgt. U.S. Army, 1962-64 Mem. Coop. Edn. Assn. Ky. (bd. dirs. 1975-77, Employer of Yr. award 1976), Indsl. Rels. Rsch. Assn., Xavier U. Alumni Assn. (pres. Detroit chpt. 1991-93), Forest Lake Country Club (bd. dirs. 1991-94, 2000-02, pres. 2002). Republican. Roman Catholic. Avocations: golf, fishing. E-mail: TKelleher@cinci.rr.com.

KELLER, ARMOR, artist, arts advocate; b. Montgomery, Ala., June 16, 1937; d. Alton Mason and Margaret Elizabeth (Bell) ARmor; m. Ronald Thomas Keller, Nov. 28, 1958; 1 child, Kimberlin Marie. Student, Huntingdon Coll., 1955-56, U. Guam, 1972-74; BA, U. Ala., 1982. Planning bd. Nat. Book Makers Conf., Tuscaloosa, Ala., 1995; panelist grant rev. Ala. State Coun. on Arts, Montgomery, 1995-96, 98; judge HS art exhibn. 6th Congl. Dist. Arts Caucus, Birmingham, 1995-96; cons. Birmingham Mus. Art, 1996. Shows include Meridian (Miss.) Mus. Art, 1986, Vanderbilt U., Nashville, 1987, Birmingham Mus. Art, 1989, Birmingham So. Coll., 1990, Kennedy-Douglas Ctr. for the Arts, Florence, Ala., 1992, Wiregrass Mus. Art, Dothan, Ala., 1993, Ctr. Cultural Arts, Gadsden, Ala., 1994, Kentuck Mus., Northport, Ala., 1994, Ch. of the Nativity, Huntsville, Ala., 1996, Huntsville Mus. Art, 1999, Heritage Hall Mus., Talladega, Ala., 2000, Masur Mus. Art, Monroe, La., 2001, Mercedes-Benz Internat., Mus. and Visitor Ctr., Tuscaloosa, Ala., 2003, Space One Eleven ARt Ctr., 2007; spl. commns. for Ala. Symphony Orch. and Children's Aid Soc.; featured in Wild Wheels, 1992-93, Smithsonian, Japan Esquire, Spiegel; illustrator: Haiku: The Travelers of Eternity, 2001. Artist del. Sister City Commn., Japan, 1994, 2004; mem. Sister City Japan Com., Birmingham, 2002—06; project dir. Sister City Friendship, 2005; bd. dirs. Birmingham Sister City Commn., 2003—06. Fellow Escape to Create Seaside (Fla.) Inst., 1993, 94. Mem. Nat. League Am. Pen Women, Watercolor Soc. Ala. (pres. 1988-89), Birmingham Art Assn. (pres. 1982-83), Montgomery Art Guild (pres. 1976-78), Space One Eleven (pres. 1991-93), Bluff Park Art Assn. (project dir. 1997), Japan Am. Soc. Ala. (bd. dirs. 2002—). Avocations: tai chi, ikebana, travel, music. Home: 204 Vestavia Cir Birmingham AL 35216-1328

KELLER, BILL, executive editor; b. Jan. 18, 1949; m. Ann Cooper (div.); 1 adopted child, Tom; m. Emma Gilbey, Apr. 10, 1999; children: Molly, Alice. BA, Pomona Coll., 1970. Reporter The Portland Oregonian, 1970—79, The Congressional Quarterly Weekly Report, 1980—82, Dallas Times Herald, 1982—84; corr. NY Times, Washington, 1984—86, Moscow, 1986—91, bur. chief, 1989—91, Johannesburg, 1992—95, fgn. editor NYC, 1995—97, mng. editor, 1997—2001; op-ed columnist & sr. writer NY Times Mag., NYC, 2001—03; exec. editor NY Times, NYC, 2003—. Mem. bd. trustees Pomona Coll. Recipient Pulitzer Prize in Journalism for Internat. Reporting, 1989. Office: NY Times 229 W 43rd St New York NY 10036-3959*

KELLER, BRUCE P., lawyer; b. Nov. 28, 1954; BS, Cornell U., 1976; JD, Boston U., 1979. Bar: NY 1980, NJ 1981, Mass. 1981. Assoc. Debevoise & Plimpton LLP, NYC, 1982—88, ptnr., 1988—, head Intellectual Property Litig. practice. Mem.: ABA, Internat. Trademark Assn. Office: Debevoise & Plimpton LLP 919 Third Ave New York NY 10022 Office Phone: 212-909-6118. Office Fax: 212-909-6836. E-mail: bpkeller@debevoise.com.

KELLER, CASEY (KENNETH CHARLES KELLER JR.), communications executive; b. July 13, 1961; s. Kenneth Charles and Martha Keller; m. Donna Elizabeth Eplett, Mar. 23, 1992. BA in Econs., Cornell U.; MBA, Harvard U. Mktg. exec. Procter & Gamble Co.; global category leader sauces & condiments H.J. Heinz Co., mng. dir. US ketchup, condiments & sauces, chief growth officer; chmn., CEO Heinz Italy; exec. v.p., chief mktg. officer Motorola, Inc., Schaumburg, Ill., 2006—. Staff mem. of Dep. Chief Naval Ops for Surface Warfare, Washington. Officer USN. Named Grand Marketer of Yr., Brandweek mag., 2001. Office: Motorola Inc 1303 E Algonquin Rd Schaumburg IL 60196*

KELLER, DANIEL SYLVESTER, director; s. Richard Sylvester and Virginia Lynn Keller; m. Bernice Marie Worthington, Oct. 29, 1966; children: Jason Douglas, Cynthia Lynnette Hilyer. BS, U. Ga., Athens, 1975—79; ThD, Andersonville Theol. Sem., Camilla, Ga., 1996—97; MEd, U. Phoenix, 2002—05. Cert. K-8 tchr. Tenn., 2005. Sr. pastor Assemblies God, White Pine, Tenn., 1982—2002. Sgt. e6 US Army, 1968—86, Ft. Campbell, Ky. Mem.: Assn. Christian Schs. Internat., Assn. Supervison & Curriculum Devel. Office: Kodak Christian Acad 2941 Douglas Dam Rd Kodak TN 37764 Home Phone: 865-397-1726. Business E-Mail: drkeller@kodakchristian.com.

KELLER, DAVID PATRICK, real estate broker; s. Thomas Patrick Keller and Barbara Carol Graff; m. Stephanie Marie Rogers; children: Justin Patrick, Zachary Michael, Emma Marie. Lic. real estate broker Calif. Dept. Real Estate, 2001. Bus. operator Westley Fuel Svc. Inc., Calif., 1983—2000; real estate broker Keller Real Estate, Patterson, Calif., 1999—. Pres. Pattterson Rotary Club, 1999—2000; commr. Econ. Strategic Commn., Patterson, 1996—97, Planning Commn., Patterson, 1997—98; councilman City Coun., Patterson, 1998—2004, mayor, 2004—06; bd. mem. Stanislaus Workforce Alliance, 2003—05, Stanislaus Coun. Govts., Calif., 2004—06. Avocations: skiing, surfing. Home and Office: Keller Real Estate PO Box 1316 Patterson CA 95363 Home Phone: 209-613-6674; Office Phone: 209-892-5555. Office Fax: 209-892-8155. Business E-Mail: kellerre@inreach.com.

KELLER, DENNIS JAMES, management educator; b. July 6, 1941; s. Ralph and Dorothy (Barckman) K.; m. Constance Bassett Templeton, May 28, 1966; children: Jeffrey Breckenridge, David McDaniel, John Templeton. AB, Princeton U., 1963; MBA, U. Chgo., 1968. Account exec. Motorola Comm., Chgo., 1964-67; v.p. fin. Bell & Howell Comm., Waltham, Mass., 1968-70; v.p. mktg. Bell & Howell Schs., Chgo., 1970-73; pres. Keller Grad. Sch. Mgmt., Chgo., 1973-81, chmn., CEO, 1981—87. Chmn. bd., CEO DeVry Inc., 1987-04, chmn. bd. 2004-; cons., evaluator North Ctrl. Assn., Chgo., 1979-84; bd. dirs. Nicor Inc., 1994-, Ryerson Inc., Chgo., 2005-. Trustee Glenwood Sch. for Boys, Ill., 1980-02, Chgo. Zool. Soc., Brookfield, Ill., 1979-, Princeton U., NJ, 1994-98, 2000-, Lake Forest Acad.-Ferry Hall, Ill., 1980-87, George M. Pullman Found., Chgo., 1987-02, Mpala Wildlife Found., Nairobi, Kenya, 2001—, African Wildlife Found., Washington, chmn. 2005—; bd. trustees U. Chgo., 1998-; bd. dirs. Great Books Found., Chgo., 1986-98; chmn. U. Chgo. Grad. Sch. Bus. Coun., 1994-02, Princeton U. Sch. Engring. and Applied Scis. Leadership Coun., 1992-; commr. North Cen. Assn.-Commn. on Instns. of Higher Edn., 1985-88. Nat. Merit scholar, 1959-63; U. Chgo. Grad. Sch. Bus. fellow, 1967-68. Mem. Hinsdale Golf Club, Econ. Club, Comml. Club Chgo., Chgo. Club, Nantucket Golf Club, Sankaty Head Golf Club. Republican. Mem. United Ch. of Christ. Office: DeVry Inc 1 Tower Ln Ste 2350 Oakbrook Terrace IL 60181 Business E-Mail: dkeller@devry.com.

KELLER, ELIOT AARON, broadcast executive; b. Davenport, Iowa, June 11, 1947; s. Norman Edward and Millie (Morris) Keller; m. Sandra Kay McGrew, July 3, 1970; 1 child, Nicole. BA, U. Iowa, 1970; MS, San Diego State U., 1976. Corr. Sta. WHO-AM-FM-TV, Des Moines, 1969-70; newsman Sta. WSUI-AM, Iowa City, 1968-70; newsman, corr. Sta. WHBF-AM-FM-TV, Rock Island, Ill., 1969; newsman Sta. WOC-AM-FM-TV, Davenport, Iowa, 1970; freelance newsman and photographer Iowa City, 1969-77; pres., bd. dirs. mem. KZIA, Inc. (formerly KRNA, Inc. and Communicators, Inc.), Cedar Rapids, 1971—, treas., 2003—; gen. mgr. Sta. KRNA FM, Iowa City, 1974-98, Sta. KQCR FM, Cedar Rapids, 1994-95, Sta. KXMX FM, 1995—98, Sta. KZIA-FM, 1998—, Sta. KGYM-AM, 2006—. Dir. KZIA, Inc. (formerly KRNA, Inc. and Communicators, Inc.), Cedar Rapids, Iowa; adj. instr. dept. comm. studies U. Iowa, Iowa City, 1983, 84; mem. adv. bd. dept. comm. arts Wartburg Coll., Waverly, 2001—; mem. prof. adv. bd. Sch. Journalism and Mass Comm. U. Iowa, 2002—. Named Broadcaster of Yr., Iowa Broadcasters Assn., 2001; named to Hall of Fame, Advt. Fedn. Cedar Rapids, Iowa, 2004. Mem.: Iowa City Area C. of C. (chmn. local govt. task force 1981, chmn. transp. subcom. 2000—05, vice chmn. 2004—05, chmn. legis. coun. 2005—, named Vol. of Yr. 2004), Iowa Assn. R.R. Passengers (chmn. excursion 1988—), R.R. Passenger Car Alliance, Mid-Continent Rlwy. Hist. Soc. (bd. dir. 2000—03). Jewish. Home: 1244 Devon Dr NE Iowa City IA 52240-9628 Office: Sta KZIA FM and KGYM AM 1110 26th Ave SW Cedar Rapids IA 52404-3430 Office Phone: 319-363-2061. Business E-Mail: eliot@kzia.com. *The chance only comes once.*

KELLER, EVELYN FOX, philosophy of science professor; b. NYC, Mar. 20, 1936; divorced; children: Jeffrey, Sarah. BA, Brandeis U., 1957; MA, Radcliffe Coll., 1959; PhD, Harvard U., 1963; doctorate (hon.), Mt. Holyoke Coll., 1991, U. Amsterdam, 1993, Simmons Coll., 1995; LHD (hon.), Rensselaer Polytech. Inst., 1995; doctorate (hon.), Tech. U. Lulea, Sweden, 1996; LHD (hon.), New Sch. U., 2000, Alleghang Coll., 2000, Wesleyan U., 2001. Prof. math. and humanities Northeastern U., Boston, 1982-88; prof. U. Calif., Berkeley, 1988-92; prof. history and philosophy of sci. MIT, 1992—. Vis. fellow MIT Program in Sci., Tech. and Soc., 1979-80, vis. scholar, 1980-84, vis. prof., 1985-86; vis. prof. math. and humanities Northeastern U., 1981-82; Kregerb Wolf Disting. vis. prof. Northwestern U., 1985; sr. fellow Soc. for the Humanities, Cornell U., 1987; mem. Inst. for Advanced Study, Princeton, 1987-88; co-chair U. Calif. Systemwide Coun. on Women's Studies. Editor: A Feeling for the Organism: The Life and Work of Barbara McClintock, 1982, 2d edit., 1993, Reflections on Gender and Science, 1985, 10th edit., 1995, Refiguring Life: Metaphors of Twentieth Century Biology, 1995, Secrets of Life, Secrets of Death, 1992, The Century of the Gene, 2000, Making Sense of Life: Explaining Development with Medals, Metaphors and Machines, 2002; co-editor Body/Politics: Women and the Discourses of Science, 1990, Conflicts in Feminism, 1990, Keywords in Evolutionary Discourse, 1992, Feminism and Science, 1996; Am. editor Fundamenta Scientiae, Internat. Jour. for Critical Analysis of Sci. and the Responsibility of Scientists; edit. bd. Women's Review of Books, Hypatia, Biology and Philosophy, Literature and Sci. Series, Jour. of the History of Biology; contbr. articles to profl. jours. Numerous grants and fellowships. Fellow Am. Acad. Arts & Scis.; mem. History of Sci. Soc. Office: MIT E51-171 77 Mass Ave Cambridge MA 02139-4307 E-mail: efkeller@MIT.edu.*

KELLER, GLEN ELVEN, JR., lawyer; b. Longmont, Colo., Dec. 21, 1938; s. Glenn Elven and Elsie Mildred (Hogsett) K.; m. Elizabeth Ann Kauffman, Aug. 14, 1960; children: Patricia Carol, Michael Ashby. BS in Bus., U. Colo., 1960; JD, U. Denver, 1964. Bar: Colo. 1964, U.S. Dist. Ct. Colo. 1964, U.S. Ct. Appeals (10th cir.) 1982. Assoc. Phelps, Hall & Keller and predecessor, Denver, 1964-67, ptnr., 1967-73; asst. atty. gen. State of Colo., Denver, 1973-74; judge U.S. Bankruptcy Ct., Dist. Colo., 1974-82; ptnr. Davis, Graham & Stubbs LLP, Denver, 1982—2004, sr. counsel, 2004—. Lectr. law U. Denver, 1977-87; adj. prof., 1987-98, Frank E. Rickston Jr. adj. prof. law, 1998-2003; ct. adminstrn. com. Jud. Conf. US; fin. com. sch. constrn. Colo. Lawyers' Com., 1997-2000, exec. com., 1999-2000, chmn. task force on sch. discipline, 1999-2000; bd. dirs. Western Stock Show Assoc., 1985-; adj. instr. law U. Colo., 2003. Mem. Colo. Bd. Health, 1968-74, pres., 1970-74; pres., dir. The Westernaires, Golden, Colo., 1983-, Jefferson County R-1 Sch. Bd., 1984-89; dir. Jefferson County Sch. Fin. Corp., 1992—. Named Colo. Horse Person of Yr., Colo. Horse Coun., 1999, Best Lawyers in Am., 1995-. Fellow Am. Coll. Bankruptcy; mem ABA, Colo. Bar Assn., Denver Bar Assn., Nat. Conf. Bankruptcy Judges, Law Club. Republican. Office: Davis Graham & Stubbs LLP 1550 17th St Ste 500 Denver CO 80202-1202

KELLER, HERBERT BISHOP, mathematics professor; b. Paterson, NJ, June 19, 1925; BEE, Ga. Inst. Tech., 1945; MA, NYU, 1948, PhD in Math., 1954. Instr. physics & math. Ga. Inst. Tech., 1946-47; rsch. scientist divsn. electromagnetic rsch. Inst. Math Sci., NYU, 1948-53; head dept. math. Sarah Lawrence Coll., 1951-53; lectr. math. Washington Sq. Coll., 1957-59; assoc. prof. NYU, 1959-61; prof. applied math. Courant Inst., 1961-67; assoc. dir. AEC Computer & Appl. Math. Ctr., 1964-67; prof. applied math. Calif. Inst. Tech., 1967—2000, prof. emeritus, 2000—; rsch. scientist U. Calif., San Diego, 2000—. Vis. prof. Calif. Inst. Tech., 1965-66; mem. math. divsn. Nat. Rsch. Coun., 1969-72; mem. coun. Conf. Bd. Math. Sci., 1971-73; dist. vis. fellow Christ's Coll., Cambridge, 1993-94; cons. various industry & govt. concerns. Assoc. editor: (jour.) Jour. Appl. Math., Soc. Indsl. & Appl. Math., 1961-66, Jour. Computer & Systems Science, 1971-74; Japan Jour. Appl. Math., 1984—, Monogr. Ser. Assn. Computing Machinery, 1963-65, Jour. Numerical Analysis, 1964-71, Jour. Numerical Math., 1981—; ed. bd. ActaNumerica, 1992-. Recipient, Theodore von

Kármán Prize, Soc. of Industrial and Applied Mathematics, 1994; Guggenheim fellow, 1979-80. Fellow AAAS; mem. Am. Math. Soc., Math. Assn. Am., Soc. Indsl. & Applied Math. (pres. 1975-76), Assn. Computing Machinery. Office: Calif Inst Tech Dept Applied Math 1201 E California Blvd Pasadena CA 91125-0001 also: Univ Calif San Diego Math Dept La Jolla CA Office Phone: 626-395-4557. Business E-Mail: hbk@caltech.edu.

KELLER, JACK, agricultural engineering educator, consultant; b. Roanoke, Va., Jan. 5, 1928; s. Eugene and Clara (Lauber) Keller; m. Sara Altick, June 4, 1954; children: Andrew A., Jeffery S., Judith. BSCE, U. Colo., 1953; MS in Irrigation Engring., Colo. State U., 1955; PhD in Agrl. Engring., Utah State U., 1967. Registered profl. engr., Utah, Calif. Work unit engr. USDA Soil Conservation Svc., Victor, Colo., 1953; sales engr. So. Irrigation Co., Memphis, 1955-56; chief irrigation engr. W.R. Ames Co., San Jose, Calif., 1956-60; prof. Utah State U., Logan, 1960-88, dept. chmn., 1979-85, project mgr., 1978-88; pres., founder Keller-Bliesner Engring. Co., Logan, 1962—, CEO, 1989—. Co-dir. U.S. AID Water Mgmt. Synthesis Project, Logan, 1978—88, team leader tech. assistance teams, worldwide, 1980—98; chmn. Conservation Verification Cons. IID/MWD Conservation Agreement, Imperial, Calif., 1992—; sr. policy advisor to Egyptian Ministry Pub. Works and Water Resources U.S. AID WRSR Activity, 1995—98; sr. rsch. assoc. Internat. Water Mgmt. Inst., 1995—2000; sr. adv. agrl. water use efficiency program CALFED, 1999—2005; sr. irrigation policy advisor, bd. dirs. Internat. Devel. Enterprises, 2000—; team leader Project Advisor Cons. Navajo Indian Irrigation Project, 2001—03; chair water mgmt. sci. bd., mem. ind. sci. bd. Calif. Bay-Delta Authority, 2003—. Co-author: Trickle Irrigation Design, 1974, Sprinkle and Trickle Irrigation, 1990; contbr. NRC com. Soil and Water Rsch. Priorities for Devel. Countries, Washington, 1988; chmn. Red River Chloride Control Panel, Tulsa, 1988. With USN, 1945—47, PTO, sgt. USAF, 1951—53. Named Engr. of Yr., Utah Joint Engring. Coun., 1988. Fellow: ASCE (Royce J. Tipton award 2006), Am. Soc. Agrl. Engrs. (award for advancement of surface irrigation 2002); mem.: NAE, The Irrigation Assn. (Man of Yr. 1972), Internat. Commn. Irrigation and Drainage. Mem. Bahai Ch. Achievements include patents in field. Avocations: hiking, gardening, fishing. Home: 35 River Park Dr Logan UT 84321-4345 Office: Keller-Bliesner Engring 78 E Center St Logan UT 84321-4619 Office Phone: 435-752-9542. Business E-Mail: jkeller@kelbli.com.

KELLER, JAMES, retired state supreme court justice; b. Harlan, Ky., 1942; m. Elizabeth Keller; 2 children. Student, Ea. Ky. U.; JD, U. Ky. Pvt. practice, 1966—76; master commr. Fayette Cir. Ct., 1969-76, judge, 1976-99; justice Ky. Supreme Ct., 1999—2005; spl. counsel Gess Mattingly & Atchison, PSC, Lexington, Ky., 2005—. Former chair Lexington-Fayette Urban County Criminal Justice Commn.; mem. Judicial Advisory Com. to Governor's Office of Child Abuse & Domestice Violence Services; chair Child Support Guidelines Review Commn.; mem. Special Legislative Task Force on Parenting & Child Custody; chair Ky. Civil Filing Fees Com.; mem. Gubernatorial Task Force on Delivery, Funding Quality Public Defendant Services. Co-founder Kid's Time Clinic, Ky., Parents Education Clinic, Ky., Mediation Ctr. of Ky. Recipient 5th Annual Kentuckians Involved in Dependents' Support award, 1990, Mediation Ctr. award, Mediation Ctr. of Ky., 1992, Henry V. Pennington Outstanding Trial Judge award, Ky. Acad. Trial Attorneys, 1994, Bowling Green Bar Assn. award, 1995, Law Day award, 1998. Mem. Ky. Bar Assn., Fayette County Bar Assn. (Henry T. Duncan Memorial award 1987) Office: Gess Mattingly & Atchison 201 W Short St Lexington KY 40507*

KELLER, JENNIFER L., lawyer; b. Ft. Wayne, Ind., Feb. 26, 1953; AB, U. Calif., Berkeley, 1975; JD, U. Calif., Hastings Coll. Law, 1978. Bar: Calif. 1978, U.S. Dist. Ct., Ctrl. and So. Dists., Calif., U.S. Ct. Appeals, Ninth Cir. 1984, U.S Dist. Ct., No. and Ea. Dists., Calif. 1997, U.S. Dist. Ct., Ariz. 1998, U.S. Supreme Ct. 1999, cert.: Specialist in Criminal Law. Sr. rsch. atty. Ct. Appeals, 4th Dist., Div. 3, 1986—89; sr. dep. pub. defender Orange County Pub. Defender's Office; pvt. practice Law Offices of Jennifer L. Keller, 1992—. Bd. dir. Pub. Law Ctr. Orange County, 1995—2000; lawyer rep. 9th Cir. Jud. Conf., 1996—99; lectr. Calif. Pub. Defenders Assn., Continuing Edn. of the Bar, 1996. Mem. Hastings Constl. Law Quarterly, 1976—77. Bd. visitors Chapman U. Sch. Law, 1995—2003, Dean's Coun., 2004—. Named Atty. of Yr., Orange County Women Lawyers, 2003, Pub. Law Ctr. Orange County, 1996; named one of The One Hundred Most Influential Lawyers in Calif., Calif. Law Bus., 2001, California's 30 Top Women Litigators, 2002; recipient Wiley Manuel award for Pro Bono Svc., State Bar Calif., 1998, Lawyer of Yr., Constl. Rights Found. Orange County, 1983, Criminal Defense Trial Lawyer Yr., Orange County Trial Lawyers Assn., 2000, Jurisprudence Award, Anti-Defamation League of Orange County & Long Branch, 2001. Mem.: Orange County Trial Lawyers Assn. (named Criminal Def. Atty. of Yr. 2000), Calif. Attys. for Criminal Justice (bd. govs. 1992—93, lectr.), State Bar Calif. (commr., Bd. Legal Specializtion, Criminal Law Advisory Comn. 1990—92, vice-chair, Bd. Legal Specializtion, Criminal Law Advisory Comn. 1992—93, chair, Bd. Legal Specializtion, Criminal Law Advisory Comn. 1993—94, convention lectr., White Collar Crime 1994, commr. Bd. Legal Specialization 2002—05), Orange County Bar Assn. (bd. dir. 1991—93, officer 1993—97, pres. 1996, lectr., State Bar of Calif. President's Pro Bono Svc. award for Dist. 8), Orange County Women Lawyers (life; bd. dirs. 1984—86, Atty. of Yr. 2003). Office: 18500 Von Karman Ave Ste 560 Irvine CA 92612-1043 Office Phone: 949-476-8700. Office Fax: 949-476-0900. E-mail: jkeller@prodigy.net.

KELLER, JOHN FRANCIS, retired food products executive, mayor; b. Mt. Horeb, Wis., Feb. 5, 1925; s. Frank S. and Elizabeth K. (Meier) K.; m. Barbara D. Mabbott, Feb. 18, 1950; children: Thomas, Patricia, Daniel, David, John. BBA in Acctg., U. Wis., Madison, 1949; MBA, U. Chgo., 1963; grad., Stanford U. Sch. Bus., 1978. CPA, Wis., Ill. Acct. Bank of Am., 1949-51; mgr. statis. control and gen. accounting Miller Brewing Co., Milw., 1951—58; contr. Maremont Corp., 1958-68, Heublein, Inc., 1968-84; v.p. fin. Hamm's Brewing Co., 1968-70; v.p. fin., dir. United Vintners, Inc., San Francisco, 1970-80, chmn. bd., CEO, dir., 1980-84; group v.p. Heublein Wines Group, 1980-84; pres. ISC Wines of Calif., 1983-85; adminstrv. dir. Winegrowers of Calif. (a Calif. state mktg. order for wineries and grape growers), 1985-87; mgmt. cons. J.F. Keller & Assocs., 1985—2000. Lectr., assoc. prof. Calif. State U./Hayward Grad. Sch. Bus. and Econs., 1978-82; adj. prof. Golden Gate U. Grad. Sch. Bus., 1983-86, lectr., instr. Coll. San Mateo, 1990; bd. dirs. Servicor, Inc., Duckhorn Vineyards, Fife and Horn Vineyards. Active Boy Scouts Am., 1952—58; dir. Serra H.S. Bd., 1979—82; bd. dirs. U. Wis. Found., 1986—92, Seton Health Svcs. Found., 1988—2002, chmn., 1994—96; bd. dirs. Seton Med. Ctr., 1989—96; sec.-treas. St. Bartholomew Cath. Ch., 1992—94; bd. dirs. Cath. Health Care West, 1996—2001, fin. and investment com.; pres. bd. dirs. Alemany Scholarship Found., 1983—95; bd. dirs. Peace and Justice Task Force Commn., 1986—92; dir. St. Vincent de Paul-San Meteo County, 1997—; bd. dirs. Big Bros., San Francisco, 1971—75, Hill High St., St. Paul, 1969—70, Lesley Found., 1983—85; vol. Internat. Exec. Svc. Corp., 1995—2000; councilman City of Hillsborough, Calif., 1982—91, mayor, 1988—90; mem. parish coun. St. Lamberts Cath. Ch., 1966—68; pres. parish coun. St. Bartholomew Cath. Ch., 1980; mem. Pastoral Planning Commn., San Francisco, 1994—95; trustee St. Patrick's Sem., 1994—2006, investment advisor, 1990—. 2d lt. 82d Airborne divsn. AUS, 1944—46, ETO, with USAR, 1946—52. Decorated Knight of Magistral Grace in Obedience, Order of Malta, Knight of Grand Cross, Equestrian Order of the Holy Sepulchre of Jerusalem; recipient Disting. Bus. Alumnus award, U. Wis. Sch. Bus., 1990, St. Louise de Marillas award, Daughters of Charity. Mem.: VFW, AICPA, Nat. Assn. Accts., Calif. Soc. CPAs, Wis. Soc. CPAs, Fin. Execs. Inst., Junipero Serra Internat. (pres. San Mateo chpt. 1992—94, treas. Legatus chpt., San Francisco 1999—2005), Am. Legion, Peninsula Golf and Country Club, World Trade Club, Commonwealth Club, Phi Kappa Alpha (past treas., bd. dirs.). Republican. Roman Catholic. Home and Office: 785 Tournament Dr Hillsborough CA 94010-7423 Personal E-mail: jf.keller@comcast.net.

KELLER, JOHN WARREN, lawyer; b. Niagara Falls, Aug. 6, 1954; s. Joseph and Edith Lilian (Kilvington) K.; m. Sandra D. Hubbard, Dec. 18, 1981; children: Sean, Christopher. BA, Rider U., 1976; JD, Coll. William and Mary, 1979. Bar: Ky. 1980. Staff atty. Appalachian Rsch. & Def. Fund Ky., Inc., Barbourville, 1979-82; assoc. F. Preston Farmer Law Offices, London, Ky., 1982-88; ptnr. Farmer, Keller & Kelley, London, 1988-91, Taylor, Keller, Dunaway & Tooms, London, 1991—, Lexington, Ky., 1991—. Mem. Fla. Adv. Com. on Arson Prevention, 1990—; chmn. bd. dirs. Appalachian Rsch. & Def. Fund Ky., 1994-96; founder, chmn. bd. dirs. Ky. Lawyers for Legal Svcs. to the Poor. Contbg. editor: ABA Annotations to Homeowner's Policy, 3rd edit., 1995, ABA Bad Faith Annotations, 2d edit., 2001. Pres. Access to Justice Found., 1996—; bd. dirs. Christian Ch. in Ky., 1994—98; elder First Christian Ch., London, 1994—97, 2002—, chmn. bd. elders, 2002—03. Recipient Access to Justice award Ky. Legal Svcs. Programs, 1995, Outstanding Svc. award Ky. chpt. Nat. Soc. Profl. Ins. Investigators, 2000. Fellow: Ky. Bar Found. (bd. dirs. 2000—, pres. 2006—); mem.: ABA (vice chair property ins. law com. 1992—97), Nat. Soc. Profl. Ins. Investigators (bd. dirs. 2001—05, pres. 2004, F. Lee Breninger award 2004), Laurel County Bar Assn. (pres. 1992—93), Ky. Bar Assn. (bd. govs. 1996—2002, Donated Legal Svcs. award 2001), The Honorable Order of Ky. Cols. Office: Taylor Keller & Dunaway 1306 W 5th St London KY 40741-1615 also: Hamburg Place Office Park 1795 Alysheba Way Ste 2102 Lexington KY 40509 Home Phone: 859-264-1181. Business E-Mail: wkeller@tkdlaw.com.

KELLER, JOSEPH BISHOP, mathematician, educator; b. Paterson, NJ, July 31, 1923; s. Isaac and Sally (Bishop) Keller; m. Evelyn Fox, Aug. 29, 1963 (div. Nov. 17, 1976); children: Jeffrey M., Sarah N. BA, NYU, 1943, MS, 1946, PhD, 1948. Prof. math. Courant Inst. Math. Scis., NYU, 1948—79; chmn. dept. math. Univ. Coll. Arts and Scis. and Grad. Sch. Engring. and Sci., 1967—73; prof. math. and mech. engring. Stanford U., 1979—93, prof. emeritus, 1993—. Hon. prof. math. scis. Cambridge U., 1990—; rsch. assoc. Woods Hole Oceanographic Instn., 1965—; Gibbs lectr. Am. Math. Soc., 1977; von Neumann lectr. Soc. Indsl. and Applied Math., 1983; Rouse Ball lectr. U. Cambridge, Eng., 1993. Contbr. articles to profl. jours. Recipient von Karman prize, Soc. Indsl. and Applied Math., 1979, Eringen medal, Soc. Engring. Scis., 1981, Timoshenko medal, ASME, 1984, U.S. Nat. medal of Sci., 1988, NAS award in Applied Math. and Numerical Analysis, 1995, Frederic Esser Nemmers prize in math., Northwestern U., Evanston, Ill., 1996, Wolf prize in math., Wolf Found., Israel, 1997, Lagrange prize, Internat. Coun. for Indsl. and Applied Math., 2006. Mem.: NAS, Soc. Indsl. and Applied Math., Am. Phys. Soc., Am. Math. Soc., Am. Acad. Arts and Scis., Royal Soc. (fgn.), London Math. Soc. (hon.). Home: 820 Sonoma Ter Stanford CA 94305-1072 Office: Stanford U Dept Math Stanford CA 94305-2125

KELLER, JUAN DANE, retired lawyer; b. Cape Girardeau, Mo., Jan. 30, 1943; s. Irvin A. and Mercedes (Crippen) K.; m. Sandra Anne Solomon; children: Mary, John, Katharine, Robert, Michael, Cassandra. AB in History, U. Mo., 1965, JD, 1967; LLM, Georgetown U., 1971. Bar: Mo. Assoc. Bryan, Cave, St. Louis, 1971-78, ptnr., 1979—2004. Contbg. author: Missouri Bar Taxation Handbook, 1988-95. Capt. JAGC, U.S. Army, 1967-71. Mem. ABA, Mo. Bar (tax com. 1971—), Met. St. Louis Bar Assn., Order of Coif. Methodist. Home: 12512 Glencroft Dr Saint Louis MO 63128-2513 Personal E-mail: juandk@aol.com.

KELLER, KAREN A., library director; BA with honors, Mich. State U., East Lansing; MLS, U. Mich., Ann Arbor. Cert. libr.'s permanent profl. cert. Libr. Mich. Positions including head adult svcs. and asst. dir. Brighton Dist. Libr., Mich.; dep. dir. Anchorage Mcpl. Librs., 2006, acting mcpl. libr., 2006—07, dir., exec. sec./tech. advisor libr. adv. bd., 2007—. Mem.: ALA, Alaska Libr. Assn., Pacific NW Libr. Assn., Pub. Libr. Assn. Office: Anchorage Mcpl Librs ZJ Loussac Pub Libr 3600 Denali St Anchorage AK 99503 Office Phone: 907-343-2892. E-mail: KellerKA@muni.org.

KELLER, KASEY, professional soccer player; b. Olympia, Wash., Nov. 29, 1969; m. Kristin Keller; children: Cameron, Chloe. Student, U. Portland. Goalkeeper Millwall Football Club, England, 1990—96, Leicester City Football Club, England, 1996—99, Rayo Vallecano, Madrid, 1999—2001, Tottenham Hotspur FC, London, 2001—05, Southampton FC, 2004, Borussia Moenchengladbach, Germany, 2005—. 93 caps U.S. Nat. Soccer Team, 1990—; mem. U.S. World Cup Team, 1990, 94, 98, 2006. Named Male Athlete of the Yr., U.S. Soccer, 1997, 1999, 2005; named to All-Copa Am. Team, 1995, 1st Team All-American, 1990; recipient Silver Ball award, World Youth Championship, Saudi Arabia, 1989. Achievements include being the all-time leader in appearances, wins & shutouts (44) in goal for U.S. Nat. Soccer Team. Office: US Soccer Fedn 1801 S Prairie Ave # 1811 Chicago IL 60616-1319

KELLER, KENNETH HARRISON, engineering educator; b. NYC, Oct. 19, 1934; s. Benjamin and Pearl (Pastor) K.; m. Dorothy Robinson, June 2, 1957 (div.); children: Andrew Robinson, Paul Victor; m. Bonita F. Sindelir, June 19, 1981; children: Jesse Daniel, Alexandra Amelie. AB, Columbia U., 1956, BS, 1957; MS in Engring., Johns Hopkins U., 1963, PhD, 1964. Asst. prof. dept. chem. engring. U. Minn., Mpls., 1964-68, assoc. prof., 1968-71, prof., 1971—, assoc. dean Grad. Sch., 1973—74, acting dean Grad. Sch., 1974-75, head dept. chem. engring. and materials sci., 1978-80, v.p. acad. affairs, 1980-85, pres., 1985-88, prof. Hubert H. Humphrey Inst. Pub. Affairs, 1996—99, Charles M. Denny Jr. prof., 1999—2006, pres. emeritus, 2006—; Philip D. Reed sr. fellow for sci. and tech. Coun. on Fgn. Rels., 1990-96, sr. v.p., 1993-95; dir., prof. Bologna Ctr. Johns Hopkins U. Sch. Advanced Internat. Studies, Italy, 2006—. Cons. in field; cardiology adv. com. NIH, 1982-86; mem. sci. and tech. adv. panel to dir. CIA, 1995-99; commn. on phys. scis., math. and applications NRC, 1996-2000; bd. dirs. LASPAU: Acad. and Profl. Programs for the Ams., 1996-2003; trustee Sci. Mus. Minn., 1997-2003; chmn. Med. Technology Leadership Forum, 1998—2005. Adv. com. program for Soviet emigré scholars, 1974-82; bd. govs. Argonne Nat. Lab., 1982-85; bd. dirs. Walker Art Ctr., 1982-88, Charles Babbage Found., 1991-99. Lt. USNR, 1957-61. NIH Spl. fellow, 1972-73; vis. fellow Woodrow Wilson Sch. of Pub. and Internat. Affairs, Princeton U., 1988-90. Founding fellow Am. Inst. for Med. and Biol. Engring.; fellow AAAS; mem. Am. Soc. Artificial Internal Organs (pres. 1980-81), AIChE (Food and Bioengring. award 1980), Am. Coun. for Emigrés in the Professions (dir. 1972-80), Nat. Acad. Engring., Mpls. C. of C. (bd. dirs. 1985-88), Coun. Fgn. Rels., Phi Beta Kappa, Sigma Xi (nat. lectr. 1978-80). Office: Johns Hopkins Univ Sch Advanced Internat Studies via Belmeloro 11 40126 Bologna Italy

KELLER, MICHAEL ALAN, librarian, musicologist; b. Sterling, Colo., Apr. 5, 1945; s. Ephraim Richard and Mary Patricia (Warren) K.; m. Constance A. Kyle, Sept. 3, 1967 (div. Aug. 1979); children: Kristen J., Paul B.; m. Carol Lawrence, Oct. 6, 1979; children: Laura W., Martha M. BA, Hamilton Coll., 1967; MA, SUNY, Buffalo, 1970, postgrad., 1970-91; MLS, SUNY, Geneseo, 1972. Asst. libr. for reference and cataloging SUNY Music Libr., Buffalo, 1970-73; acting undergrad. libr. Cornell U., Ithaca, NY, 1976, music libr., sr. lectr., 1973-81; head music libr. U. Calif., Berkeley, 1981-86; assoc. univ. libr. for collection devel. Yale U., 1986-93; director Stanford U. Librs., Calif., 1993-94, univ. libr., dir. acad. info. resources Calif., 1994—; pub. HighWire Press, Stanford, 1995—, Stanford U. Press, 2000—. Mem. Nat. Digital Libr. Fedn., 1993—2005, chair exec. com., 2002—; mem. Bibliog Commn., Repertoire Internat. de la Presse Mus. de XIXve Siecle, 1981—84; chmn. music program com. Rsch. Librs. Group, 1982—86; reviewer NEH, 1982—88, panelist, 1979—95; chmn. Assoc. Music Librs. Group, Joint Com. Retrospective Conversion in Music, 1989—93; mem. collection mgmt. devel. com. Rsch. Librs. Group, 1986—91, chmn., 1989—91, mem. program adv. com., 1991—93; dir. Berkeley Italian Renaissance Project, 1985—95, Digital Libr. Fedn., 1994—; mem. bd. overseers Stanford U. Press, 1997—; mem. gov. com. Stanford-Japan Ctr. Rsch.; mem. adv. bd. Ebrary, Inc., 1999—; bd. dirs. Alibris Inc., 1999—; dir. Long Now Fedn., 1999—; trustee Hamilton Coll., 2001—05; mem. info. tech. adv. group New Libr. of Alexandria, Egypt, 2001—; mem. adv. bd. Groxis, Inc.; trustee Cisco Learning Inst., 2004—; chair adv. bd. rsch. libr. Los Alamos Nat. Lab., 2005—; vis. prof. Grad. Sch. Nat. Acad. Sci., China; cons. in field. Author: MSS on Microfilm in Music Libr. at SUNYAB, 1971, (with Duckles) Music Reference and Rsch. Materials; an annotated bibliography, 1988, 94; contbr. articles to profl. jours. Firefighter, rescue squad mem. Cuyuga Heights Vol. Fire Co., N.Y., 1980-81; bd. dirs. Long Now Found., 1998—; bd. trustees, Hamilton Coll., 2001-05; adv. bd. Digital Libr., Nat. Libr. China, 2005—, Global Edn. and Learning Cmty. Recipient spl. commendation Nat. Music Clubs, 1978, Berkeley Bronze medal U. Calif.-Berkeley, 1983, Deems Taylor award ASCAP, 1988; NDEA Title IV fellow SUNY-Buffalo, 1967-70, Pierson Coll., Yale U., Stanford U., 1994-95, World Econ. Forum, 2000, 01; Cornell Coll. Arts and Scis. rsch. grantee, 1973-81, U. Calif.-Berkeley humanities rsch. grantee, 1983-84, Coun. on Libr. Resources grantee, 1984, 93-99, Libr. Assn. U. Calif. grantee, 1985-86, NEH grantee, 1986; recipient various grants NSF, 1999—, State Libr. Calif., Mellon Found. Mem. ALA, AAUP, Music Libr. Assn. (bd. dirs. 1975-77, fin. com. 1982-83, editl. com. index and bibliography series 1981-85), Internat. Assn. Music Librs., Am. Musicol. Soc. (com. on automated bibliography 1982-83, coun. 1986-88), Conn. Acad. Arts and Scis. (bd. dirs.), Ctr. Rsch. Librs. (adv. com. 1988-90), Conn. Ctr. for Book (bd. dirs.), Book Club of Calif., Bohemian Club, San Francisco. Home: 809 San Francisco Ter Stanford CA 94305-1070 Office: Stanford U Cecil Green Libr Stanford CA 94305-6004 E-mail: michael.keller@stanford.edu.

KELLER, MICHELLE R., science educator; b. Rolla, ND, Aug. 15, 1951; d. Raymond Charles Halone and Yvonne M. (Klier) Edwards; m. Fred F. Keller, June 30, 1973; 1 child, Brent F. BS in Foods and Nutrition, N.D. State U., 1973; cert. sci. edn., Minot State U., 1977; MEd in Secondary Sci. Edn., N.Dak. State U., 2001. Instr. sci. Bisbee (N.D.)-Egeland H.S., 1975—. Judge Seiko Youth Challenge, 1993, 94; ND tchr. portfolio trainer, assessor. Access Excellence fellow Genentech/NSF, 1994; recipient Presdl. award for excellence in sci. tchg., 1993, Edn.'s Unsung Hero award 1998; named Hon. Mention Tchr., Radio Shack/Tandy scholars program, 1998, 99. Mem. Am. Assn. Physics Tchrs. (pres. N.D. sect. 2001—), Nat. Sci. Tchrs. Assn., N.D. Sci. Tchrs. Assn., N.D. Orienteering Alliance, Nat. Edn. Assn., N.D. Edn. Assn. Democrat. Roman Catholic. Avocations: walking, reading, gardening. Home: PO Box 265 201 3rd Ave W Bisbee ND 58317-0265 Office: Bisbee-Egeland H S P O Box 217 204 3rd Ave W Bisbee ND 58317 Home Phone: 701-656-3435; Office Phone: 701-656-3536. E-mail: mkeller@ndsualumni.net.

KELLER, PAUL, advertising executive, researcher; b. Mainz, Germany, Sept. 23, 1921; came to U.S., 1937, naturalized, 1942; s. Bernhard and Johanna (Metzger) K.; m. Ruth Ettinghouse, Dec. 25, 1948; children: Steven A., Richard M., Susan F. BA, NYU, 1948; MA, Columbia U., 1949. Research analyst N.W. Ayer, NYC, 1950-55; media research dir. Bryan Houston, NYC, 1955-57; v.p., dir. media and rsch., corp. sec., bd. dirs. Reach McClinton, NYC, 1957-69; v.p., assoc. rsch. dir. Ted Bates Advt., NYC, 1969-80, sr. v.p., rsch. dir., 1980-84; prin. Keller Cons. Co., 1985—89. Adj. prof. Hofstra U., 1970-75; vol. cons. Nat. Exec. Svc. Corps, 1985—2004; vol. tutor Archer St. Elem. Sch., Freeport. Soccer coach, 1971—75; village soccer commr., 1971—75. With US Army, 1942—45, PTO. Decorated Bronze Star, Purple Heart. Mem. Phi Beta Kappa, Pi Mu Epsilon. Personal E-mail: pkelrock@verizon.net.

KELLER, RACHAEL See ANDERSON, RACHAEL

KELLER, RANDAL JOSEPH, toxicology educator; b. Salem, Ind., Nov. 22, 1957; s. Frank Joseph and Virginia Francis (Barrett) K.; m. Pamela Marie Stroman, Sept. 17, 1994. BA, Eisenhower Coll., Seneca Falls, NY, 1979; MS, Utah State U., 1984, PhD, 1988. Cert. indsl. hygienist; cert. safety profl.; diplomate Am. Bd. Toxicology. Postdoctoral fellow Nat. Ctr. Toxicology Rsch., Jefferson, Ark., 1988-90; instr. U. Ark. for Med. Scis., Little Rock, 1990-91, coord. occupl. and environ. health program, 1991-96; assoc. prof. dept. occupl. safety and health Murray (Ky.) State U., 1996—. Peer reviewer Ctr. for Indoor Air Rsch., 1995—. Contbr. articles to profl. jours. Rsch. grantee U.S. EPA, Washington, 1993-96, NIOSH, Morgantown, W.Va., 1993-95. Fellow Am. Acad. Indsl. Hygiene; mem. Am. Indsl. Hygiene Assn. (pres. elect. Ark. sect. 1993-94, pres. 1994-95), Am. Conf. Govt. Indsl. Hygienists, Am. Soc. Safety Engrs., Am. Soc. Toxicology (1st pl. award metals splty. sect. 1986). Republican. Avocations: dog training, running, reading, microbrewing, triathlons. Home: 5317 Dunbar Rd New Concord KY 42076-9548 Office: Murray State U Dept Occupl Safety and Health 157 Industry and Tech Ctr Murray KY 42071-3347 Office Phone: 270-809-6655. Business E-Mail: randal.keller@murraystate.edu.

KELLER, RIC, congressman, lawyer; b. Orlando, Sept. 5, 1964; m. Cathy; children: Nick, Christy. BA, East Tenn. State U.; JD, Vanderbilt U. Former ptnr. Rumberger, Kirk and Caldwell; mem. U.S. Congress from 8th Fla. dist., 2001—; mem. edn. and workforce com., judiciary com., small bus. com. Mem. Congressional com. House Edn., Judiciary. Chmn. bd. Orlando/Orange County COMPACT program. Republican. Office: US House Reps 419 Cannon House Office Bldg Washington DC 20515-0908*

KELLER, ROBERTA LYNN, physician, researcher; d. William and Shirley Streifer; m. Bruce Adam Keller, May 18, 2000. MD, U. Calif., San Francisco, 1993. Cert. in neonatal-perinatal medicine Am. Bd. Pediat., 2003. Asst. prof. clin. pediat. U. Calif., San Francisco, 2005—.

KELLER, SHARI ANN, small business owner; d. Leslie Allen and Nancy Gail Hampton; m. Charles Arnold Keller, Dec. 23, 1986; 1 child, David J. Hampton; 1 child, Suzanne M. Restaurant mgr. Hardee's Food Sys., Tampa, 1994—2001; owner C & C Auton Salvage, Tampa, 2003—. Author: (book) World Peace Anthologies, 2003. Republican. Roman Catholic. Avocations: writing, mixing techno music, fishing, singing, fixing computers. Home: 12312 Pittsfield Ave Tampa FL 33624 Office Phone: 813-630-9201. E-mail: poetluver39@aol.com.

KELLER, STANLEY, lawyer; b. NYC, Aug. 16, 1938; s. Irving S. and Ceil (Silverstein) K.; m. Sandra Freshman, Dec. 25, 1960; children: Andrew J., Eric L., Matthew A. AB, Columbia U., 1959; LLB, Harvard U., 1962. Bar: Mass. 1962. Assoc. Palmer & Dodge LLP, Boston, 1962-68; ptnr. Palmer & Dodge LLP (now Edwards Angell Palmer & Dodge LLP), Boston, 1969—. Lectr. Boston U. Law Sch., 1969-79; treas., trustee Mass. Continuing Legal Edn., Inc., Boston, 1985-91; panelist continuing legal edn. programs for profl. orgns. Chmn. legal sect. United Way of Boston, 1982. Fellow Am. Bar Found., Mass. Bar Found.; mem. ABA (chair fed. regulation of securities com. 1999-2003), Mass. Bar Assn. (chmn. bus. law sect. 1983-85), Boston Bar Assn. (chmn. corp. law com. 1988-89, chmn. bus. law sect. 1989-91, co-chair legal opinions com. 1992-95, co-chair com. to revise Mass. Bus. Corp. Law 1992—), Tri Bar Opinion Com. Jewish. Office: Edwards Angell Palmer & Dodge LLP 111 Huntington Ave Boston MA 02199-7613 Office Phone: 617-239-0217. Business E-Mail: stanley.keller@eapdlaw.com.

KELLER, STEVEN RAY, security consultant; b. Williamsport, Pa., May 3, 1947; s. James N. and Betty J. K.; m. Kathy J. Billman, July 17, 1971; 1 child, Lindsey Allison. BA Govt., Pub. Adminstrn., Am. U., 1969. Cert. hypnotherapist, forensic hypnotist. Detective Met. Police Dept., Washington, 1969-74; spl. agt. Fed. Res. Bd., Washington, 1974-76, asst. dir. security, 1976-78; exec. dir. protection svcs. Art Inst. Chgo., 1979-86; pres. Steven R. Keller & Assocs., Inc., Ormond Beach, Fla., 1986—. Bd. dirs. Horizon Inst., Ormond Beach, 1986—, Internat. Assn. Profl. Security Cons. Author, books, film, numerous articles on security and mgmt. topics; exec. prodr. 24 video tng. programs for security industry. Bd. dirs. Am. Youth Soccer Orgn., Elmhurst, Ill., 1984-86. Recipient Exec. Achievement award, Security mag., 1986, Leadership award Smithsonian Inst. Mem. Am. Soc. Indsl. Security (chmn. profl. practice subcom., past chmn. mus. library archive com., mem. ethics com.; President's Award of Merit, Disting. Achievement award), Am. Assn. Mus. (security com., named to Centennial Honor Roll 2006), Internat. Assn. Profl. Securtiy Consultants (Outstanding Achievement award). Avocations: fishing, boating. Office: 555 Granada Blvd Ste G3 Ormond Beach FL 32174 Office Phone: 386-673-5043. Business E-Mail: steve@stevekeller.com.

KELLER, SUZANNE, sociologist, psychotherapist; arrived in U.S., 1942; d. Joseph and Martha Infield; m. Charles M. Haar, July 5, 1975. PhD, Columbia U., NYC, 1955; HHD (hon.), Hunter Coll., NYC, 1990. Rsch. assoc. ctr. internat. studies MIT, Cambridge, Mass., 1955—58; asst. prof. of sociology Brandeis U., Waltham, Mass., 1959—62, Vassar Coll., Poughkeepsie, NY, 1963—64; fulbright scholar Athens Ctr. of Ekistics, Greece, 1964—68; prof. of sociology Princeton U., NJ, 1967. Author: (books) Beyond the Ruling Class, 1963, Community: Pursuing the Dream, Living the Reality, 2003; editor: Bldg. for Women. Pres. Ea. Sociol. Soc., 1986, Queenston Common Homeowners Assn., 1992. Recipient Hon. Fellow, AIA, 1974, Malfi prize, 2005. Mem.: AIA (life hon.), Am. Sociol. Assn. (life; v.p. 1984), World Soc. for Ekistics (life; v.p. 1991, pres. 2005), Phi Beta Kappa. Achievements include first woman granted tenure in the 226 year history of Princeton University. Avocations: reading, opera, travel, philanthropy, writing. Office: Princeton U Dept of Sociology 107 Wallace Hall Princeton NJ 08544 Business E-Mail: skeller@princeton.edu.

KELLER, THEODORE G., JR., investment property owner and manager; b. Toledo, Ohio, July 22, 1933; s. Theodore George and Edna Louise (Christen) K.; m. Carolyn Mary Lord, Aug. 25, 1956 (dec. May 1985); children: Bradford W., Matthew C., Theodore G. III, Lathrop L.; m. Gayla Claire Rampel, Sept. 20, 1986. BS, Miami U., Oxford, Ohio, 1955; MBA, U. Pa., Phila., 1959. Advt. mgr. Procter & Gamble, Cin., 1959-73; v.p. Eastern Airlines, Miami, Fla., 1973-76, Sara Lee Corp., Chgo., 1976-78; corp. officer, exec. v.p. Pet Inc., St. Louis, 1978-92; v.p., gen. mgr. Right Assocs., St. Louis, 1992-96; owner, mgr. 22 Cottage St., LLC, South Orange, NJ, 1986—. Former pres., bd. govs. Naples Bath and Tennis Club, 2002-2004; dir. Naples Bath and Tennis Club Homeowners Assn. Lt. USNR, 1951-59. Conservative. Avocations: physical fitness, tennis, bridge. Home: 1031 Oriole Cir Naples FL 34105-7425 E-mail: gaylaandted@earthlink.net.

KELLER, THOMAS A., chef; Chef, owner The French Laundry, Yountville, Calif., 1994—, Bouchon, Yountville, Calif., 1998—, Bouchon Bakery, Yountville, Calif., Bouchon, Las Vegas, 2004—, Per Se, NYC, 2004—. Spokesperson Calif. Milk Adv. Bd., 1997—98. Author: The French Laundry Cookbook (Cookbook of the Year, Internat. Assn. Culinary Professionals, 1999, Versailles Cookbook award, 1999). Named Best Am. Chef: Calif., James Beard Found., 1996, Outstanding Chef Am., 1997, Outstanding Restaurateur, 2007, Best Chef, San Francisco Focus, 1997, Chef of Yr., Bon Appétit, 1998, Ams. Best Chef, Time Mag., 2001, Best Wine Dir., San Francisco Mag., 2002, Best Chef, Readers' Digest, 2004; recipient Ivy award, Restaurants & Instns., 1996, Robert Mondavi Culinary award of excellence, 1997, Wedgewood award, World Master Culinary Arts, 2001, Illy Best New Restaurant award, James Beard found., 2005, Outstanding Restaurant award, 2006. Mem.: Relais & Chateaux: Relais Gourmands, Traditions & Qualité. Office: 6640 Washington St Yountville CA 94599 also: Per Se Ten Columbus Cir at 60th St New York NY 10019 Office Phone: 707-944-2330.

KELLER, THOMAS FRANKLIN, business administration educator; b. Greenwood, SC, Sept. 22, 1931; s. Cleaveland Alonzo and Helen (Seago) K.; m. Margaret Neel Query, June 15, 1956; children: Thomas Crafton (dec.), Neel McKay, John Caldwell. AB, Duke U., 1953; MBA, U. Mich., 1957, PhD, 1960; HHD (hon.), Clemson U., 1987. CPA, N.C. Mem. faculty Fuqua Sch. Bus. Duke U., Durham, N.C., 1959—, assoc. prof., 1962-67, prof., 1967-74, R.J. Reynolds prof., 1974—2004, chmn. dept. mgmt. scis., 1974-96, vice provost, 1971-72, dean Fuqua Sch. Bus., 1974-96; dean Fuqua Sch. Bus. Europe, Frankfurt, 1999-2001; dean emeritus Fuqua Sch. of Bus., 2004—; prof. emeritus R.J. Reynolds, 2004—. Mem. editl. bd. Duke U. Press, 1970-87; vis. assoc. prof. Carnegie Mellon U., 1966-67, U. Wash., Seattle, 1963-64; cons. to govt. and industry; Fulbright-Hays lectr., Australia, 1975; bd. dirs. Wendy's Internat., Dublin, Ohio, Biogen Idec, Cambridge, Mass. Author: Accounting for Corporate Income Taxes, 1961, Intermediate Accounting, 1963, 68, 74, Advanced Accounting, 1966, Financial Accounting Theory vol. 1, 1964, 73, 84, vol. 2, 1969, Earnings or Cash Flows: An Experiment on Functional Fixation and the Valuation of the Firm, 1979; editor: monographs Financial Information Needs of Security Analysts, 1977, The Impact of Accounting Research on Practice and Disclosure, 1978; contbr. articles to profl. jours. Elder Presbyn. Ch.; trustee Stillman Coll., Tuscaloosa, Ala.; dir. N.C. Zool. Soc., Rsch. Triangle Regional Partnership, Research Triangle Park, N.C. With AUS, 1953-55. Recipient Outstanding Educator award, N.C. Assn. CPA's, 1997, Univ. medal, Duke Univ., 2001; fellow Haskins and Sells Found., U. Mich., 1959, Ford Found., Duke U., 1960, 1961. Mem. AICPA, Am. Acctg. Assn. (v.p. 1967-68, editor jour. 1972-75), N.C. Assn. CPAs, Fin. Execs. Inst., University Club, Phi Beta Kappa, Phi Kappa Sigma, Beta Gamma Sigma, Alpha Kappa Psi. Avocations: hiking, fishing, reading, sailing. Office: Duke U Fuqua Sch Bus Box 90120 Durham NC 27708-0120 Office Phone: 919-660-8045. Business E-Mail: tfk1@duke.edu.

KELLER, WILLIAM FRANCIS, publishing consultant; b. Meyersdale, Pa., May 22, 1922; s. Lloyd Francis and Dorothy Marie (Shultz) K.; m. Frances Jane Core, Mar. 31, 1944. AA, Potomac State Coll. of W.Va. U., 1941; BS, U. Md., 1943, MS, 1945. Ednl. rep. Blakiston Co., 1945-51, assoc. editor, 1951-54; editor coll. div. McGraw Hill Book Co., NYC, 1954-56; editor-in-chief Blakiston divsn. McGraw Hill Book Co., 1956-65, gen. mgr. div., 1965-68; pres. Year Book Med. Publs., Chgo., 1968-81, chmn. bd., 1968-82; pub. cons. Crystal Lake, Ill., 1982-95; adminstrv. sec. Am. Med. Pubs. Assn., 1985-91. Served with U.S. Army, 1945-46. Office: 7916 W Hillside Rd Crystal Lake IL 60012-2939

KELLERMAN, JONATHAN SETH, writer, pediatric psychologist, educator; b. NYC, Aug. 9, 1949; s. David Kellerman and Sylvia Fiacre; m. Faye Marilyn Marder, July 23, 1972; children: Jesse, Rachel, Ilana, Aliza. BA in Psychology, UCLA, 1972; MA in Psychology, U. So. Calif., 1973, PhD in Clin. Psychology, 1974. Lic. psychologist, Calif. Intern in psychology Children's Hosp. of Los Angeles, 1973-74, postdoctoral fellow, 1974-75, U. Southern Calif. Sch. Medicine, Los Angeles, 1974-75, staff psychologist, 1975-78, asst. clin. prof. pediatrics, 1978—79, clin. assoc. prof. pediatrics, 1979-98, clin. prof. pediats., psychology, 1998—. Founding dir. Psychosocial Program Children's Hosp., Los Angeles, 1977-81. Author: (non-fiction) Psychological Aspects of Childhood Cancer, 1980, Helping the Fearful Child, 1981, (fiction) When the Bough Breaks, 1985, Blood Test, 1986, Over the Edge, 1987, The Butcher's Theater, 1988, Silent Partner, 1989, Time Bomb, 1990, Private Eyes, 1991, Devil's Waltz, 1992, Bad Love, 1993, Daddy, Daddy Can You Touch the Sky?, 1994, Self-Defense, 1994, Jonathan Kellerman's ABC of Weird Creatures, 1995, The Web, 1995, The Clinic, 1996, Survival of the Fittest, 1997, Billy Straight, 1998, Savage Spawn, 1999, Monster, 2000, Dr. Death, 2000, Flesh And Blood, 2001, The Murder Book, 2002, A Cold Heart, 2003, Therapy, 2004, Twisted, 2004, Double Homicide, 2005, Gone, 2006 Recipient Samuel Goldwyn Creative Writing award UCLA, 1972, Edgar Allan Poe award, Mystery Writers of Amer., 1985, Anthony Boucher award, 1986, Disting. Alumnus award dept. psychology UCLA, 1997. Mem. Am. Psychol. Assn. (Media award 1994, Presdl. award 1998), Mystery Writers of Am. (Edgar Allan Poe award 1985, nominated Shamus award 2001). Jewish. Avocations: painting, guitar playing and collecting, book collecting, art collecting. Office: c/o Karpfinger Agcy 357 W 20th St New York NY 10011

KELLERMAN, SALLY CLAIRE, actress; b. Long Beach, Calif., June 2, 1937; d. John Helm and Edith Baine (Vaughn) K.; m. Richard Edelstein, Dec. 19, 1970; 4 step-daughters; m. Jonathan Krane, 1980. Student, Los Angeles City Coll., Actor's Studio, NYC. Stage appearances include Singular Man, N.Y.C., Breakfast at Tiffany's; films include Reform School Girl, 1959, The Third Day, 1965, The Boston Strangler, 1968, The April Fools, 1969, M*A*S*H, 1970 (Acad. award nominee 1970, Golden Globe award 1970), Brewster McCloud, 1970, Last of the Red-Hot Lovers, 1972, Slither, 1973, Reflection of Fear, 1973, Lost Horizon, 1973, Rafferty and the Gold Dust Twins, 1975, The Big Bus, 1976, Welcome to L.A., 1977, The Mouse and His Child, 1977 (voice), Magee and the Lady, 1978, It Rained All Night The Day I Left, 1978, A Little Romance, 1979, Foxes, 1980, Loving Couples, 1980, Serial, 1980, Head On, 1980, September Gun, 1983, Moving Violations, 1985, Lethal, 1985, Back to School, 1986, That's Life, 1986, Meatballs III, 1987, Three for the Road, 1987, Someone to Love, 1987, Paramedics (voice), 1988, You Can't Hurry Love, 1988, All's Fair, 1989, Limit Up, 1989, The Secret of the Ice Cave, 1990, Happily Ever After, 1990 (voice), The Player, 1992, Younger and Younger, 1993, Mirror, Mirror 2: Raven Dance, 1994, Ready to Wear (Prêt-à-Porter), 1994, It's my Party, 1995, She's So Lovely, 1997, The Maze, 1997, The Lay of the Land, 1997, Live Virgin, 1998, Bar Hopping, 1999; also TV roles Chrysler Theatre, Mannix, It Takes a Thief, Columbo: Ashes to Ashes; TV films Verna: USO Girl, 1978, For Lovers Only, 1982, Dempsey, 1983, Secret Weapons, 1985, Elena, 1985, Boris and Natasha, 1992; miniseries Centennial, 1978-79. Recipient nominations Acad. and Golden Globe awards for MASH. Mem. Actor's Equity, AFTRA. also: 7944 Woodrow Wilson Dr Los Angeles CA 90046

KELLEY, A. BENJAMIN, writer, educator, consultant; b. NYC, May 15, 1936; s. Hubert Williams and Anna Alberta (Davis) K.; children: Sumako Chongyol, Hubert Chongsu. Student, Def. Lang. Inst., 1955, Naganuma Inst., Tokyo, 1957-58, Sophia U., 1957, Harvard U. Bus. Sch., 1972. News editor Shipping and Trade News, Japan, 1957-60; Washington transp. corr. N.Y. Jour. Commerce, 1960-63; policy adviser ICC, 1963-65; mgr. transp. and communications dept. U.S. C. of C., 1966-67; dir. pub. affairs Fed. Hwy. Adminstrn., 1967-69; sr. v.p. Ins. Inst. Hwy. Safety, Washington, 1969-85; pres. A.B. Kelley Corp., Crofton, Md., 1985-96, Inst. for Injury Reduction, Crofton, 1988-95; pvt. auto safety cons., 1996—. Vis. faculty mem. Tufts U. Med. Sch., 2001-; exec. dir. Pub. Health Advocacy Inst., 2001-2003, dir. Hazards Archive project, 2003—; guest lectr. Johns Hopkins Sch. Pub. Hygiene and Pub. Health, 1974-95, U. So. Calif., 1974, U. Fla., 1972, UCLA, 1970, U. Calif., Davis, 1977; bd. dirs. Center Auto Safety, 1975—, Com. on Non-Theatrical Events, 1984—1992 Author: The Pavers and The Paved, 1971; author-narrator: Boobytrap!, 1971, Cars That Crash and Burn, 1973, Crashes That Need Not Kill, 1976, Faces in Crashes, 1984, Exhibit 44, 2006; also contbr. articles to profl jours. Served with AUS, 1954-57. Recipient Golden Eagle award Council Internat. Nontheatrical Events, 1971, 73, 76, 1st prize Zagreb (Yugoslavia) Film Festival, 1973, 75, Bronze Venus Medallion Virgin Islands Internat. Film Festival, 1976 Mem. Internat. Transp. Research Forum (past dir.), Nat. Safety Coun. (past dirs.), Am. Assn. Automotive Medicine, Soc. Automotive Engrs., Ctr. for Auto Safety (bd. dirs.). Business E-Mail: benjamin.kelley@tufts.edu.

KELLEY, ALLEN CHARLES, economist, educator; b. Everett, Wash., Sept. 5, 1937; s. Charles Edward and Velma L. (Allen) K.; m. Patty Ann Cochran, June 20, 1959; children: Brian Allen, Mark Andrew, Michael Charles. Student, Linfield Coll., 1955-57; AB, Stanford U., 1959, PhD, 1964. Vis. research fellow Australian Nat. U., 1962-63; cons. Rand Corp., 1962-67; acting asst. prof. Stanford U., 1963-64; faculty U. Wis., Madison, 1964-72, prof., 1970-72; prof. econs. Duke U., Durham, NC, 1972-81, James B. Duke prof., 1981—, chmn. dept., 1973-80; asso. dir. Center for Demographic Studies, 1973—. Vis. prof. Monash U., Melbourne, Australia, 1970-71; Esmee Fairbairn research prof. Herriot Watt U., Edinburgh, Scotland, 1978; research scholar Internat. Inst. Applied Systems Analysis, Laxenburg, Austria, 1979 Author: (with J.G. Williamson and R.J. Cheetham) Dualistic Economic Development, 1972, (with B.A. Weisbrod et al.) Disease and Economic Development, (with J.G. Williamson) Lessons from Japanese Development - An Analytical Economic History, 1974, The Professor's Guide to TIPS, 1975, (with R.M. Schmidt) The User's Guide to TIPS, 1975, TIPS Program Manual, 1976, (with J.G. Williamson) Modeling Urbanization and Economic Growth, 1980, (with A. Khalifa and M.E. El-Khorazaty) Population and Development in Rural Egypt, 1982; mem. editorial bd. Jour. Econ. Edn, 1973—; Contbr. articles, revs. to profl. jours. Scholar, fellow Weyerhaeuser Co., 1955-59; Scholar, fellow Ford Found., 1961-62; Scholar, fellow Earhart Found., 1959-61; Scholar, fellow Social Sci. Research Council, 1962-63; Richard I. Downing fellow econs. U. Melbourne, 1987-88; grantee Carnegie Found., 1964-65; grantee Exxon Edn. Found., 1965-67, 68-70, 71-74; grantee Ford Found., 1973-79; grantee Nat. Inst. Edn., 1974-75; grantee NSF, 1966-68; grantee Rockefeller Found., 1967-69; grantee Sloan Found., 1969-73, 79—; co-recipient Arthur Cole prize Econ. History Assn., 1972. Mem. Am. Econ. Assn. (chmn. com. econ. edn. 1978—), So. Econ. Assn. (v.p. 1981-82), Internat. Union for Sci. Study Population, Population Assn. Am., Joint Council on Econ. Edn. (trustee 1978— , exec. com. 1978—), Phi Beta Kappa. Home: 4607 Chicopee Trl Durham NC 27707-5208 Office: Duke U Econs Dept Durham NC 27708 Business E-Mail: kelley@econ.duke.edu.

KELLEY, ALOYSIUS PAUL, academic administrator, priest; b. Carlisle, Pa., Oct. 4, 1929; s. Aloysius Paul and Teresa (Barron) K. AB, St. Louis U., 1955, MA, PhL, St. Louis U., 1956; STL, U. Innsbruck, Austria, 1963; PhD, U. Pa., 1968; LLD (hon.), Sacred Heart U., 1985. Joined S.J., 1949; ordained priest Roman Catholic Ch., 1962; chmn. dept. classics Georgetown U., 1969-71, asst. acad. v.p., 1971-72, acting acad. v.p., 1972-74, exec. v.p. for acad. affairs and provost, 1974-79; pres. Fairfield U., Conn., 1979—2004; lectr. classical studies Fordham U., 2005—. Trustee Georgetown Prep. Sch., 1969-72, Loyola Coll., Balt., 1971-75, Scranton U., 1974-80, Bridgeport Area C. of C., 1979-82, St. Joseph's U., Phila., 1980-86, Georgetown U., 1982-88, 89-95, Conn. Grand Opera, 1980-82, John Carroll U., 1987-93, LeMoyne Coll., 1993-99, 2004—, Canisius Coll., 2006—, The Gesu Sch., 1993-97, St. Joseph's Prep. Sch., 1997—2002, St. Peter's Coll., 1998-2004, Nat. Assn. Ind. Colls. and Univs., 1997-2000; mem. D.C. Commn. Postsecondary Edn., 1974-79; vice chmn. Conn. Conf. Ind. Colls., 1980-81, chmn., 1981-83; pres. New Eng. Colls. Fund, 1993-95. Fulbright-Hayes fellow, 1971 Mem. Newcomen Soc. Democrat. Home and Office: Fordham Univ Spellman Hall 441 E Fordham Rd Bronx NY 10458

KELLEY, BARBARA BANNIN, retired physical education educator; b. Far Rockaway, NY, Feb. 29, 1952; d. Robert Joseph and Regina (Auspitzer) Bannin; m. Edward L. Kelley, Feb. 14, 1976; children: Ryan Patrick, Timothy Bannin. BS, Longwood Coll., 1974; MEd, U. Maine, 1976. Cert. tchr., Maine. Phys. edn. tchr. Mecklenburg County Schs., South Hill, Va., 1974-75, Bangor (Maine) Sch. Dept., 1975—2003. Mem. Nat. Bd. Profl. Teaching Standards, Washington, 1992; sr. cons. Asia Soc.; chair Coalition on Strengthening Teacher Knowledge, NC in the World. Bd. dirs. Hunt Inst., DonorsChooseNC; adv. bd. People to People Ambassador Programs. Named Coach of Yr., Maine High Sch. Coaches Assn., 1981, Tchr. of Yr., Maine Assn. Health, Phys. Edn., Recreation and Dance, one of ten people who shaped the decade in American edn. Teacher mag., 1999. Mem. NEA (bd. dirs. 1991—), Maine Tchrs. Assn. (bd. dirs. 1986—), Bangor Edn. Assn. (chief negotiator 1985-92), Nat. Bd. for Profl. Teaching Standards (chair, 1997-2003). Democrat. Avocation: tennis. Office: Vine St Sch Bangor ME 04401 Home: 1105 Ivy Ln Raleigh NC 27609-4733*

KELLEY, BRIAN P., beverage and former relocation services company executive; b. Cin. BA in Econs., Coll. Holy Cross, Springfield, Mass. With Procter & Gamble; sr. exec. appliance bus. GE, 1983; v.p. Global Consumer Services Ford Motor Co., 1999—2001, pres. Lincoln Mercury oper. unit, 2001—02; pres., CEO SIRVA, Inc., Westmont, Ill., 2002—07; pres., gen. mgr. Still Beverage Group Coca-Cola N. Am., Atlanta, 2007—. Office: Coca-Cola North America 1 Coca-Cola Plz Atlanta GA 30313*

KELLEY, BRUCE GUNN, insurance company executive, lawyer; b. Phila., Mar. 17, 1954; s. Robb Beardsley and Winifred Elizabeth Gray (Murray) K.; m. Susan Aldrich Barnes, Oct. 1, 1983; children: Dashle Gunn, Barnes Gunn, Onnalee Kinkaid. AB, Dartmouth Coll., 1976; JD, U. Iowa, 1979. Bar: Iowa 1979; CPCU; CLU. Assoc. Bradshaw, Fowler, Proctor & Fairgrave, Des Moines, 1979-84, ptnr., 1984-85; gen. counsel Employers Mut. Casualty Co., Des Moines, 1985-89, exec. v.p., 1989-91, pres., 1991—, also bd. dirs. Trustee Am. Inst. for Chartered Property Casualty Underwriters/Ins. Inst. Am.; bd. dirs. Property Casualty Insurers Assn. of Am. Bd. dirs. Property Loss Rsch. Bur. Recipient Disting. Eagle Scout award, Boy Scouts Am. Mem. Polk County Bar Assn., Beta Gamma Sigma, Des Moines Club, Rotary, Masons. Republican. Mem. United Church of Christ. Home: 14 Glenview Dr Des Moines IA 50312-2546 Office: EMC Ins Cos PO Box 712 Des Moines IA 50306-0712

KELLEY, CAROLYN, biotechnology educator; married. BS in Microbiology, U. NH, Durham, NH, 1996. Formerly in biotech pvt. industry; biotech. tchr. Seacoast Sch. Tech., Exeter, NH. Named NH Tchr. of Yr., 2007. Office: Seacoast Sch Tech 40 Linden St Exeter NH 03833 Business E-Mail: ckelley@sau16.org.*

KELLEY, COLLEEN M., labor union administrator; b. Pitts., 1944; B Acctg., Drexel U.; MBA, U. Pitts. CPA. Agt. revenue IRS; dir. membership and benefits programs Nat. Treasury Employees Union, pres., chief steward, v.p. chpt. 34 Pitts., nat. exec. v.p., exec. v.p., sr. leadership coun., nat. pres., 1999—, re-elected, 2003. Mem. labor mgmt. coun. IRS, Dept. Health & Human Svc.; mem. Comml. Activities Panel; mem., sr. rev. com. Dept. Homeland Security. Bd. dir. Fed. Employee Edn. and Assistance Fund; bd. gov. Partnership for Pub. Svc. Mem.: Fed. Retirement Thrift Investment Bd. (employee thrift adv. coun.), Fed. Salary Coun. Avocation: skiing. Office: National Treasury Employees Union 1750 H St NW Washington DC 20006-4600*

KELLEY, DARCY B., biology professor; AB, Barnard Coll.; PhD, Rockefeller U., 1975. Co-dir., neural sys., behavior Marine Biological Lab, Woods Hole, Mass.; prof., biological sciences Columbia Univ. Forbes lectr. Grass Found., and Marine Biological Lab.; spl. lectr. Soc. Neuroscience; plenary lectr. Soc. Neuroethology; rsch. prof. Howard Hughes Med. Inst., 2002—. Editor: Jour. Neurobiology; contbr. articles to profl. journals. Recipient Jacob Javits Neuroscience Investigator award (twice), Howard Hughes Med. Inst. grant, 2002. Office: Biological Sciences Columbia Univ MC 2432 911 Fairchild Ctr New York NY 10027 Office Phone: 212-854-5108. Business E-Mail: dbk3@columbia.edu.

KELLEY, DAVID CHRISTOPHER, philosopher; b. Lakewood, Ohio, June 23, 1949; s. Walter Carl and Patricia Kelley; m. Susan McCloskey, Mar 25, 1982. BA, MA, Brown U., 1971; PhD, Princeton U., 1975. Asst. prof. philosophy Vassar Coll., Poughkeepsie, NY, 1975-84; freelance writer, lectr., 1984-89; exec. dir. Objectivist Ctr., Poughkeepsie, 1990—2004, sr. fellow Washington, 2005—. Vis. lectr. in philosophy Brandeis U., Waltham, Mass., 1989-90 Author: The Evidence of the Senses, 1986, The Art of Reasoning, 1990, Unrugged Individualism, 1996, A Life of One's Own, 1998, Contested Legacy of Ayn Rand, 2000; co-author: Laissez Parler, 1985. Mem. Am. Philos. Assn. Office: Objectivist Ctr 1001 Connecticut Ave NW Ste 425 Washington DC 20036 Office Phone: 202-296-7263. Business E-Mail: dkelley@objectivistcenter.org.

KELLEY, DAVID E., producer, writer; b. Waterville, Maine, Apr. 4, 1956; m. Michelle Pfeiffer, Nov. 13, 1993; 1 adopted child, Claudia Rose 1 child, Jack Henry. BA, Princeton U., 1979; JD, Boston U., 1983. CEO David E. Kelley Prodns., Inc., LA. Writer, story editor, exec. story editor, supervising prodr., exec. prodr. L.A. Law (Emmy award for Outstanding Drama Series 1989, 90, Emmy award for outstanding writing in a drama series 1990); writer, exec. prodr. Picket Fences (Emmy award for outstanding drama series 1993, 94), Chicago Hope, 1994-2000, The Practice, 1997—2004 (Golden Globe award for best TV drama 1998, Emmy award for outstanding drama series, 1998, 99), Ally McBeal, 1997-2002 (Golden Globe winner, Emmy award for best TV series-musical or comedy 1997, 98, Emmy award for outstanding comedy series 1999), Snoops, 1999-2000, Boston Public, 2000—04, Girl's Club, 2002, The Brotherhood of Poland, New Hampshire, 2003, Boston Legal, 2004-, The Law Firm, 2005, The Wedding Bells, 2007. Office: David E Kelly Prodns care 20th Century Fox 10201 W Pico Blvd Bldg 80 Los Angeles CA 90064-2606 also: William Morris Agency One William Morris Pl Beverly Hills CA 90212*

KELLEY, DAVID N., lawyer, former United States attorney; b. Dec. 1, 1959; AB, Coll. William & Mary, 1981; JD, N.Y. Law Sch., 1986. Bar: 1986. Police officer East Hampton; co-chief organized crime and terror unit U.S. So. Dist. NY, 1993—2003, asst. U.S. atty. to deputy U.S. atty. (So. dist.) NY, 1988—2003, U.S. atty., 2003—05; sr. litig. ptnr. Cahill Gordon & Reindel LLP, NYC, 2005—. Adj. prof. N.Y. Law Sch. Office: Cahill Gordon & Reindel LLP 80 Pine St New York NY 10005

KELLEY, DELORES GOODWIN, state legislator; b. Norfolk, Va., May 1, 1936; d. Stephen Cornelius and Helen Elizabeth (Jefferson) Goodwin; m. Russell Victor Kelley, Jr., Dec. 26, 1956; children: Norma Kelley Johnson, Russell III, Brian. BA, Va. State Coll., 1956; MA, NYU, 1958, Purdue U., 1972; PhD, U. Md., 1977. Dir. religious edn. N.Y.C. Protestant Coun., Bronx, 1959-60; tchr. N.Y.C. Pub. Schs., Bklyn., 1962-64, Ctrl. Sch. Dist., Plainview, NY, 1965-66; asst. prof. Morgan State U., Balt., 1966-70; prof. speech comms. and English Coppin State Coll., Balt., 1973—2004; mem. Md. Ho. of Dels., Annapolis, 1991—94; former chmn. Joint Com. on Fed. Rels./Md. Senate, 1995—98; chmn. exec. nomination com. Md. Senate, 2007—. Joint com. legis. policy, joint com. legis. ethics, co-chair joint com. on fair practices Md. State Senate, 1999—, vice chair, joint com. on health care delivery and fin., 2000—, fin. com., 1998—; senate chair Joint Com. on Adminstrv., Exec. and Legis. Rev., 2001—02; vice-chair sen. com. exec. nomination; vice-chair Balt. County Senate Delegation, 2003—; panelist, reviewer NEH, Washington, 1978—82, Nat. Inst. Justice, 1998—; dean Coppin State Coll., Balt., 1979—82; fellow Am. Coun. on Edn., Washington, 1982—83; vice-chair bd. dirs. Harbor Bank Md., 1982—; mem. Gov.'s Commn. on Adoption, 1995, Atty. Gen.'s and Lt. Gov.'s. task force on family violence, 1996—, Md. Commn. on Criminal

Sentencing Policy, 1996—, Md. Commn. on Infant Mortality, 1999—2002; mem. strategic planning com. Balt. County Schs., 1999—2000; adv. com. Md. Medicaid, 1998—; commr. Edn. Commn. of States, 2004—. Editor (monograph) Concepts of Race, 1981; moderator (TV series) Teaching Writing: Process Approach, 1982. Sec. Md. Dem. Party, Annapolis, 1986-90; bd. dirs. Balt. Urban League, 1986-89; pres. Black Jewish Forum, Balt., 1990-92; commr. Md. Commn. on Values, Annapolis, 1980-85; bd. dirs. Balt. Mental Health Systems, 1991-95; host Internat. Visitors Ctr., 1976—; commn. mem. Md. Commn. Hereditary and Congenital Disorders, Balt., 1992-95; del. White House conf. on Aging, 1995; mem. Edn. Commn. States, 2004-; Presdl. elector, 2004; vice chair nat. conf. state legislatures fin. svcs. com., 2005-. Fellow Purdue U., 1970-72; grantee Md. Com. for Humanities, Balt., 1977-78, NEH, Washington, 1988-89; recipient Racial Justice award YWCA of Met. Balt., 1995; named to Md. Top 100 Women, Warfields Bus. Record, 1995, 97, 2004, Cir. of Excellence award The Daily Record, 2004. Mem. Nat. Inst. Justice (panelist, rev. 1997), Inst. Govtl. Svcs. (bd. dirs. 1993-94), Nat. Polit. Congress Black Women (bd. dirs., Balt. chair 1993-95), Women Legislators Md. (1st v.p. 1995-96, pres. 1998-99), 10th Dist. Dem. Club Md. (founder, pres. 1995—), Alpha Kappa Alpha (life). Baptist. Avocations: travel, public speaking, reading. Office: 302 James Senate Office Bldg Annapolis MD 21401-1991 Home Phone: 410-922-5085; Office Phone: 410-841-3606. Personal E-mail: dkelley428@earthlink.net. Business E-Mail: delores_kelley@senate.state.md.us.

KELLEY, ED, editor-in-chief; b. Perry, Okla., 1953; m. Carole Kelley; 3 children. BA Phi Beta Kappa, U. Okla., 1975. From roving reporter to editor Daily Oklahoman, Okla. City, 1975—99, editor editl. page, 1999—2003, editor, 2003—. Juror Puljtzer Prizes, 1998; mem. profl. adv. bd. Gaylord Coll. Journalism & Mass Communication, U. Okla. Named Editor of Yr., Nat. Press Found., 1996; named to Okla. Journalism Hall of Fame, 2003. Mem.: Am. Soc. Newspaper Editors, Phi Beta Kappa. Office: Oklahoman PO Box 25125 Oklahoma City OK 73125-0125 Office Phone: 405-475-3311. E-mail: ekelley@oklahoman.com.*

KELLEY, EDWARD ALLEN, publisher; b. Clinton, Mass., June 28, 1927; s. Edward Francis Kelley and Lillian Marion (Keigwin) French; m. Margaret Jordan Talbott, Feb. 24, 1962; children: Catherine, Edward, Michael. BA, Trinity Coll., Hartford, Conn., 1950; STM, Gen. Theol. Sem., NYC, 1953. Prodn. asst., customer svc. rep. Colonial Press, Clinton, 1953-57; mgr. bookstore Morehouse-Barlow Co. Inc., NYC, 1957-61, v.p., editorial dir., 1961-74; sr. v.p. Oxford U. Press, NYC, 1974-83; pres. Kelley Assocs., Ridgefield, Conn., 1983-87; pres., pub. Morehouse Pub. Co., Ridgefield, 1988-97; pvt. practice pub. cons. Ridgefield, 1997—. Editor The Episcopal Ch. Ann., 1967-74, 87-97. With USNR, 1945-47, World War II. Democrat. Episcopalian. Avocations: golf, reading.

KELLEY, FRANCES A., occupational therapist, consultant; b. Cheyenne, Wyo., July 26, 1925; BSin Occupl. Therapy, U. So. Calif., 1949; Occupl. Cert. in Supervision, Los Angeles Valley Coll., 1985. Asst. chief occupl. therapy, therapist San Fernando VA Hosp., Calif., 1948-53, rehab. medicine svc. coord., chief occupl. therapy, clin. edn. supr. Calif., 1963-71; dir., bd. dirs. IDEAS Assocs., Inc., 1989-93; chief. occupl. therapy, coord. GM&S occupl. therapy VA Med. Ctr., Sepulveda, Calif., 1971-89, cons., vol. Dept. Occupl. Therapy, 1989—. HHon. clin. faculty dept. occupl. therapy U. Soc. Calif., 1992-95, 95—; presenter in field. Contbr. articles to profl. jours., video. Mem. Am. Occupl. Therapy Found., Calif. Found. Occupl. Therapy. Recipient Lifetime Achievement award Occupl. Therapy Assn. Calif., 1990, Cert. Appreciation Govt. Affairs Commn., 1995. Mem. Am. Occupl. Therapy Assn. (Cert. Recognition commn. on edn. 1994), Am. Occupl. Therapy Polit. Action Com., Occupl. Therapy Assn. (Calif. We. area chpt.), World Fedn. Occupl. Therapy, Nat. Assn. Ret. Fed. Employees, V.A. Retirees, Disabled Am. Vets. Aux., Arleta C. of C., San Fernando Valley Japanese Am. Cultural Ctr., Gold Star Wives Am., Nat. History Assn. San Luis Obispo Coast, Inc., Tau Alpha Epsilon. Home: 9427 Obeck Ave Arleta CA 91331-5521 E-mail: fkelley725@aol.com.

KELLEY, FRANK JOSEPH, lawyer, former state attorney general; b. Detroit, Dec. 31, 1924; s. Frank Edward and Grace Margaret (Spears) Kelley; m. Nancy Courtier; children: Karen Ann, Frank Edward II, Jane Francis. Pre-law cert., U. Detroit, 1948, JD, 1951. Bar: Mich. 1952. Pvt. practice law, Detroit, 1952—54, Alpena, 1954—61; atty. gen. State of Mich., Lansing, 1962—98; pvt. practice Lansing, 1998—. Instr. econs. Alpena CC, 1955—56; instr. pub. adminstrn. Alpena County, 1956; atty. city real estate law U. Mich. Extension, 1957—61. Mem. Alpena County Bd. Suprs., 1958—61; pres. Alpena Cmty. Svcs. Coun., 1956; chmn. Gt. Lakes Commn., 1971; founding dir., 1st sec. Alpena United Fund, 1955; founding dir., 1st pres. Northeastern Mich. Child Guidance Clinic, 1958; pres. bd. dirs. Northeastern Mich. Cath. Family Svc., 1959. Mem.: ABA, Nat. Assn. Attys. Gen. (pres. 1967), State Bar Mich., 26th Jud. Cir. Bar Assn. (pres. 1956), Internat. Movement Atlantic Union, KC (4 deg., past legal adv.), Alpha Kappa Psi. Address: 101 S Washington Sq Fl 9 Lansing MI 48933-1731 Office Phone: 517-371-1400.

KELLEY, HENRY PAUL, academic administrator, psychology educator; b. Cleburne, Tex., July 4, 1928; s. Henry Rowell and Jane Frances (Wynn) K.; m. Lucerle DeCourcy Scott, Aug. 18, 1949; children: Roger Wynn, Scott Franklin, Gordon Henry. BA in Pure Math., U. Tex., 1949, MA in Ednl. Psychology, 1951; AM, PhD in Psychology, Princeton U., 1954. Cert. and lic. psychologist, Tex. Psychometric fellow Ednl. Testing Svc., Princeton, N.J., 1951-54; pers. mgmt. and evaluation psychologist pers. and tng. rsch. ctr. USAF, San Antonio, 1954; aviation exptl. psychologist U.S. Naval Sch. Aviation Medicine, Pensacola, Fla., 1955-57; coord. measurement svcs., testing and counseling ctr., from asst. to assoc. prof. ednl. psychology U. Tex. Austin, 1958-64, lectr., 1964-67, dir. measurement and evaluation ctr., prof. ednl. psychology, 1967—99, prof. emeritus ednl. psychology, 1999—; regional dir. southwestern office Coll. Entrance Exam. Bd., Austin, 1964-67. Regional coord. Project TALENT, Austin, 1959-61; mem. southwestern regional adv. com. Coll. Entrance Exam. Bd., Austin, 1968-73, vice-chmn. com. rsch. and devel., N.Y.C., 1970-73, chmn., 1973-76, mem. adv. panel econ. implications recognizing prior learning, 1979-80; vis. faculty mem. ann. inst. coll. entrance, acad. placement and student fin. assistance Coll. Entrance Exam. Bd. and U. N.C., Chapel Hill, 1975-94; tech. reviewer, panel mem. rsch. projects br., bur. edn. handicapped, office edn. HEW, Washington, 1977; asst. hearing officer minimum competency study Nat. Inst. Edn., 1980-81; mem. gen. faculty U. Tex. Austin, 1960-64, 67-99, sec., 1981-87, mem. faculty senate, 1972-74, 81-95, sec., 1975-79, adminstrv. adviser ednl. policy com., 1968-99; reviewer comprehensive program fund improvement secondary edn. U.S. Dept. Edn., 1983; mem. rsch. adv. panel, manpower and pers. divsn. Air Force Human Resources Lab., Brooks AFB, San Antonio, 1984-86; mem. com. testing, coordinating bd. Tex. Coll. and Univ. Sys., Austin, 1985-86, mem. adv. com. basic skills testing, coordinating bd., 1987; mem. basic skills test rev. panel Tex. Edn. Agy., Austin, 1987; mem. Tex. acad. skills coun. Tex. Higher Edn. Coord. Bd., 1987-93, chmn. adv. com. tests and measurements Tex. acad. skills coun., 1987-93; mem. planning com. Ann. Tex. Testing Conf., 1987-94; cons., spkr. in field. Author: (with Bruce Walker) Self-Audit of CLEP Policies and Procedures: A Guide to Policy Decisions for Colleges and Universities, 1981; contbr. articles to profl. jours. and publs. Lt. USNR. Recipient Edward S. Noyes award Coll. Bd., 1976, Advanced Placement Spl. Recognition award, 1985; recipient numerous grants in field. Fellow APA, Am. Psychol. Soc.; mem. Am. Assn. Applied and Preventive Psychology, Am. Ednl. Rsch. Assn., Nat. Coun. Measurement Edn., Nat. Soc. Study Edn., Am. Assn. Higher Edn., Am. Evaluation Assn., Measurement Svcs. Assn., Nat. Coll. Testing Assn., Psychometric Soc., Phi Beta Kappa, Phi Delta Kappa, Phi Eta Sigma, Phi Kappa Phi, Sigma Xi. Methodist. Avocations: reading, bridge. Office: U Tex Austin Ednl Psychology Dept 1 Univ Station D5800 Austin TX 78712-0383 Home: Apt 306 4100 Jackson Ave Austin TX 78731-6069 Home Phone: 512-419-9931; Office Phone: 512-471-0526. Business E-Mail: p.kelley@mail.utexas.edu.

KELLEY, IRENE W., retired librarian, musician, artist; b. Taunton, Mass., Mar. 24, 1932; d. Joseph John and Bronislawa Apalonia (Kowal) Gesiak; m. Thomas Francis Kelley, Aug. 11, 1956; children: Steven, Kenneth, Richard. AB magna cum laude, Boston U., 1954, MA, 1955, EdD, 1992; MLS, Simmons Sch. Libr. Sci., 1972. Physical sci. libr. Brown U., Providence, 1955—57; libr. Randolph Pub. Libr., Mass., 1957—64, Milton HS, Mass., 1964—87; ret., 1987. Musician: Brockton Symphony, Wellesley Symphony. Mem.: Quincy Art Assn., Braintree Art Assn., Norwood Art Assn., Canton Art Assn. Democrat. Roman Catholic. Home: 7 Surrey Ln Canton MA 02021 Personal E-mail: ikgesiak@aol.com.

KELLEY, JAMES EDWARD, actor, writer; b. Providence, Mar. 26, 1970; s. George Edward and Carlotta Marie Kelley; m. Lisa Marie Potter, Jan. 19, 2002. BA in Philosophy, RI Coll., Providence, 1994; postgrad., U. RI. Cameraman WSBE (Pub. Broadcasting), Providence, 1990; actor, 1981—; at & t relay operator AT&T, Providence, 1995—96; art therapist St. Joseph's Living Ctr., Providence, 1999—2001; artist, 1999; editor Poet Laureate Portugal- Jose Brites, Warwick, RI, 2002—02; cameraman Rites & Reason Theatre, Brown U., Providence, 2005; power-point image collater Rites & Reason Theatre, Providence, 2005, cameraman, 2006, props master, mgr., designer, 2006. Actor-in-residence Rites & Reason Theatre, Brown U., 2003—. Author: (play) A Venture into a Handicapped Person's Mind, Advection: A Transfer of Heat. Mem. Amnesty Internat., Providence, 1988, Sentinel Group, RI College's Sherlock Ctr., Providence, 2006; prayer line St. Philip's Ch., Smithfield, RI, 1996—99, coord. eucharistic adoration, 1997—99; actor Daydream Theatre, Providence, 2003—; actor-in-residence Brown University's Rites & Reason Theatre, 2003—. Recipient Henry Fonda Young Playwright's award, Conn., 1988. Mem.: SAG, AFTRA, Hearing Loss Assn., Mensa. Roman Catholic. Avocations: art, writing, travel, pool, poker. Home: 750 Church Ave Warwick RI 02889 Home Phone: 401-732-0759; Office Phone: 401-996-3958. Personal E-mail: mensanbeing@hotmail.com.

KELLEY, JAMES FRANCIS, lawyer; b. Dec. 30, 1941; s. James O'Connor and Marcella Cecilia (Salb) K.; m. Anne H. Morgan; children: Sarah, Leah; AB, Yale U.; JD, U. Chgo. Bar: N.Y. 1967, Tex. 1981. Assoc. Breed, Abbott & Morgan, NYC, 1967-75; dep. gen. counsel United Tech. Corp., Hartford, Conn., 1975-81; sr. v.p., gen. counsel Maxus Energy Corp (formerly Diamond Shamrock Corp.), Dallas, 1981-88; ptnr. Jones, Day, Reavis & Pogue, Dallas and Paris, 1988-93; sr. v.p., gen. counsel Georgia-Pacific Corp., 1993-00; exec. v.p. & gen. coun., 2000-05; Gov. Dallas Symphony Assn., 1985-89; bd. dir. North Tex. Pub. Broadcasting Found., Dallas, 1983-91, mem. exec. com., 1988-91; bd. dirs. Atlanta Symphony Orch., 1994-2007, mem. exec. com., 1996—, chair fin. com., 2002-07; bd. dirs. Piedmont Healthcare Inc., 2003-; mem. bd. visitors Emory U., 1999-01. Mem. ABA, Assn. Gen. Counsel.

KELLEY, JAN, publishing executive, musician; b. Stanford, Calif. BA, Carleton Coll., Northfield, Minn. Pres., editor, publ. Last Resort Music Pub., Inc., Studio City, Calif., 1997—; cellist, freelance musician LA, 1963—. Editor of music arrangements. Mem.: Am. Fedn. Musicians, Recording Musicians Assn. Avocation: gardening. Office: Last Resort Music Pub Inc 820 Thompson Ave Ste 14 Glendale CA 91201 Office Phone: 818-956-0088.

KELLEY, JANET GODSEY, lawyer; b. Ky., May 9, 1953; d. Paul and Christine Godsey; m. Peter Marcum (div.); m. Michael R. Kelley, Sept. 5, 1988; children: Megan Marcum, Christina Kelley. AB, Morehead State U., 1975; JD, U. Ky., 1978. Bar: Ky. 1978. Assoc. Wyatt, Tarrant & Combs, Louisville, 1978-83, ptnr., 1983-94; gen. counsel Sunbeam Corp., Ft. Lauderdale, Fla., 1994—99; v.p., sr. counsel The Limited Inc., 1999—2001; exec. v.p., gen. counsel Kmart, Troy, Mich., 2001—03; sr. v.p., sr. counsel Family Dollar Stores, Charlotte, NC, 2004—05, sr. v.p., gen. counsel, sec., 2005—. Notes editor Ky. Law Jour., 1990. Mem. Ky. Sch. Facilities Constrn. Com. Mem. ABA, Ky. Bar Assn. for Women, Women Laywers' Assn., Exec. Inst., Order of the Coif. Democrat. Office: Family Dollar Stores PO Box 1017 Charlotte NC 28201-1017 Office Phone: 704-849-7427. E-mail: jkelley@familydollar.com.*

KELLEY, JOHN JOSEPH, JR., lawyer; b. Cleve., June 17, 1936; s. John Joseph and Helen (Meier) K.; m. Gloria Hill, June 20, 1959; children: John Joseph III, Scott MacDonald, Christopher Taft, Megan Meredith. BS cum laude in Commerce, Ohio U., 1958; LL.B., Case Western Res. U., 1960. Bar: Ohio bar 1960. Clk. firm Walter & Haverfield, Cleve., 1957-60; assoc. Walter, Haverfield, Buescher & Chockley, Cleve., 1960-66, partner, 1967-72; chief exec. officer Fleischmann Enterprises, Cin., 1972-77; pvt. practice law Cin., 1977-87; ptnr. Kohnen & Patton, Cin., 1988—. Chmn. bd. Basic Packaging Systems, Inc., 1982-87; dir. Orgamac Leasing Ltd; pres. Naples Devel. Inc., 1974-87, Yankee Leasing Co. Mem. Lakewood (Ohio) City Council, 1965-72, pres., 1972; mem. exec. com. Cuyahoga County (Ohio) Republican Central Com., 1965-72; mem. Hamilton County (Ohio) Rep. Policy Com.; Ohio chmn. Robert Taft, Jr. Senate Campaign Com., 1970, 76; bd. govs. Case Western Res. U., 1961, 84-87. Mem. ABA, Assn. Ohio Commodores, Ohio State Bar Assn., Cin. Bar Assn., Cin. Country Club, Queen City Club (Cin.), Wendemer Country Club (Naples). Home: 5 Woodcreek Dr Cincinnati OH 45241-3255 Office: PNC Center 201 E Main St Ste 800 Cincinnati OH 45202 Office Phone: 513-381-0656. Business E-Mail: jkelley@kplaw.com.

KELLEY, JOHN PAUL, communications consultant; b. Columbus, Ohio, May 12, 1919; s. John Adrian and Josephine (Nash) K.; m. Dorothy Rose Peters, July 31, 1942 (dec. June 15, 2005); children: John M., Ann P., Daniel O., Peter D. BS in Journalism, Ohio State U., 1941; MBA, Harvard U., 1946. Mgr. sales promotion Seiberling Rubber Co., Akron, Ohio, 1946-48; account supr. Batten, Barton, Durstine & Osborn, Cleve., 1948-51; mgr. consumer advt. Monsanto Chem. Co., St. Louis, 1951-54; pres. Mumm, Mullay & Nichols, Advt. Agy., Columbus, 1954-59; v.p. Goodyear Tire and Rubber Co., Akron, 1959-84; communications consultant, 1984—. Lt. AUS, 1943-46. Mem. Assn. Nat. Advertisers (past chmn.), Advt. Coun. (past chmn. bd. dirs.). Republican. Roman Catholic. Home: 76240 Fairway Dr Indian Wells CA 92210-8822 E-mail: jpk340@verizon.net.

KELLEY, KITTY, writer; b. Spokane, Wash., Apr. 4, 1942; d. William V. Kelley; m. Michael Peter Edgley (div.); m. Johnathan Zucker. BA in English, Univ. Wash., Seattle, 1964. Employee Wash. Post, 1969—71. Author: The Glamour Spas, 1975, Jackie Oh!, 1978 (NY Times bestseller list), Elizabeth Taylor: The Last Star, 1981 (NY Times bestseller list), His Way: The Unauthorized Biography of Frank Sinatra, 1986 (#1 NY Times bestseller list, record sales made it best selling biography in publishing history), Nancy Reagan: The Unauthorized Biography, 1991 (NY Times bestseller list), The Royals, 1997 (#1 NY Times bestseller list, Publishers Weekly bestseller list), The Family: The Real Story of the Bush Dynasty, 2004 (Publishers Weekly bestseller list). Named one of The Most Famous, FAscinating and Influential Alumni of the Past 100 Years, Univ. Wash., 1999, the 20 Georgetowners of the Century, Georgetowner newspaper; named to Vanity Fair Hall of Fame; recipient Outstanding Author award, Am. Soc. Journalists and authors, Philip M. Stern award for outstanding svc. to writers and the writing profession, Medal of Merit, Lotos Club, NYC. Office: c/o Doubleday Author Mail Random House Inc 1745 Broadway New York NY 10019

KELLEY, LINDA ELAINE SPADAFORA, school psychologist, educator; b. Melrose, Mass., July 24, 1948; d. Guy Joseph Spadafora and Yolanda Elaine Maglio; children: Paul, Michael. BA in Sociology, Emmanuel Coll., Boston, Mass., 1970; MEd in Early Childhood & Spl. Edn., Ga. State U., 1980, EdS in Sch. Psychology, 1997. Learning disability specialist Atlanta Speech Sch., Atlanta, 1981—96; psychol. assoc. Child & Family Inst., Atlanta, 1997—99; sch. psychologist Holy Redeemer Cath. Sch., Alpharetta, Ga., 1999—. Bd. officer Kappa Delta Pi, Nat. Honor Soc. in Edn., Ga., 1982—88; ednl. cons. State Dept. Edn., Ga., 1988—90; bd. trustees Learning Disability Assn. Ga., 1998—2001; exec. bd. Ga. Assn. Sch. Psychologists, 2003—; sch. psychology del. to South Africa People to People Amb. Program, Spokane, Wash., 2005—. Grantee Rsch. in Reading Instrn., Ga. Assn. of Sch. Psychologists, 2000; scholar Dr. Kay Crouch Scholarship, Kappa Delta Pi, 1991; 1993. Mem.: NASP. Roman Catholic. Achievements include development of Prevention/detection and intervention: early reading failure. Avocations: tennis, hiking, dance, reading, calligraphy. Home: 1110 Morningside Pl NE Atlanta GA 30306 Home Phone: 404-876-6537. Personal E-mail: lekelley@bellsouth.net.

KELLEY, MALCOLM DAVID, actor; b. Bellflower, Calif., May 12, 1992; Actor: (films) Antwone Fisher, 2002, You Got Served, 2004; (TV films) Knights of the South Bronx, 2005; (TV series) Lost, 2004—05 (Outstanding Performance by an Ensemble in a Drama Series, Screen Actors Guild award, 2006), numerous TV series guest appearances. Avocations: basketball, politics. Mailing: ESI Network Inc #340 6310 San Vicente Blvd Los Angeles CA 90048

KELLEY, MARK ALBERT, physician, educator, health products executive; b. Boston, Oct. 31, 1947; s. Albert Joseph and Virginia Marie Kelley; m. Gail Riggs Kelley, Aug. 4, 1974; children: Christopher Riggs, Amy Morgan. AB, Harvard U., Cambridge, Mass., 1969; MD, Harvard U., Boston, 1973. Diplomate Am. Bd. Internal Medicine, Am. Bd. Pulmonary Disease, Am. Bd. Critical Care. Intern Hosp. U. Pa., Phila., 1973—74, resident, 1974—76, chief med. resident, 1977—78, fellow in pulmonary diseases, 1976—77; dir. pulmonary fellowship U. Pa., Phila., 1979—82, from asst. to assoc. prof. medicine, 1979—92, prof., 1992-2000; dir. pulmonary fellowship tng. program, 1979—82; vice chmn. med. U. Pa. Sch. Medicine, Phila., 1986—90; dir. pulmonary fellowship tng. program, 1979—82; assoc. chmn. clin. svcs., dir. med. residency tng. program, 1982—86; dir. faculty group practice, 1985—90; vice dean clin. affairs U. Pa. Sch. Medicine, Phila., 1990—99; chief of medicine Phla. VA Med. Ctr., 1999—2000; exec. v.p. Henry Ford Health Sys., Detroit, 2000—; CEO Henry Ford Med. Group, Detroit, 2000—; fellow in pulmonary disease Hosp. U. Pa., Phila., 1978—79. Spkr. in field. Mem. editl. bd. Annals Internal Medicine, 1990—93, Critical Care Medicine, 1992—98. Fellow: ACP, Am. Coll. Chest Physicians; mem.: Am. Bd. Med. Specialties, Soc. Critical Care Medicine, Am. Bd. Internal Medicine (critical care medicine test com. 1988—93, chmn. 1990—93, bd. govs. 1990—98, exec. com. 1993—98, sec.-treas. 1994—96, chmn. 1997—98, sec.-treas. found. bd. 1999—2003, chmn. 2003—06), Am. Thoracic Soc. (chmn. nat. manpower study 1996—2000, critical care work force project 2001—04), Alpha Omega Alpha. Office: 1 Ford Pl Detroit MI 48202-3450 Office Phone: 313-876-8701. Business E-Mail: mkelley1@hfhs.org.

KELLEY, MAURICE LESLIE, JR., gastroenterologist, educator; b. Indpls., June 29, 1924; s. Maurice Leslie and Martha (Daniel) K.; m. Carol J. Povec, Feb. 11, 1967; children: Elizabeth Ann, Mary Sarah. Student, U. Vt., Va. Poly. Inst., Princeton U., 1943-45; MD, U. Rochester, 1949. Intern, resident Strong Meml. Hosp., Rochester, NY, 1949-51, Bixby fellow in medicine, 1953-56; fellow in gastroenterology Mayo Clinic, Rochester, Minn., 1957-59; asst. prof. medicine U. Rochester, 1959-64, assoc. prof., 1964-67; practice medicine specializing in gastroenterology Rochester, NY, 1959-67; assoc. prof. clin. medicine Dartmouth Med. Sch., 1967-74, prof. clin. medicine, 1974-88; chmn. sect. internal medicine Hitchcock Clinic, 1972-74, chmn. sect. gastroenterology, 1974, 88; prof. medicine emeritus Dartmouth Med. Sch., 1988—; mem. staff Strong Meml. Hosp., Hitchcock Clinic, Mary Hitchcock Meml. Hosp. Cons. Canandaigua VA, Rochester Gen., Genesee hosps., VA. Med. Ctr., White River Junction. Contbr. articles to profl. jours., chpts. to books. Served with AUS, 1942-45; M.C. USAF, 1951-53. Fellow ACP (gov. for N.H. 1974-78, Laureate award 1993), Am. Gastroenterol. Assn.; mem. Am. Soc. Gastrointestinal Endoscopy, AMA (chmn. sect. gastroenterology 1970-71), Am. Physiol. Soc., Alpha Omega Alpha. Avocations: sports cars, cinema. Home: 15 Ledge Rd Hanover NH 03755-1612 Office: Dartmouth-Hitchcock Med Ctr 1 Medical Center Dr Lebanon NH 03756-0002 Office Phone: 603-650-5216.

KELLEY, MICHAEL A., state agency administrator; BA in Econs., Calif. State U., Sacramento, MPA. Dir. Dept. Consumer Affairs, Calif., 1987—91; divsn. chief Dept. Motor Vehicles, Calif., 1991—95; dep. commr. Dept. Ins., Calif., 1995—99, chief dep. commr. Calif., 1999—2000; prin. prog. budget analyst Dept. Fin., Calif., 2000—02, chief performance rev. Calif., 2002—04; chief fin. and adminstrv. officer for sec. Bus., Transp. and Housing Agy., Calif., 2004—06; acting commr. Calif. Dept. Fin. Instns., 2006, commr., 2006—. Office: Calif Dept Fin Instns 1810 13th St Sacramento CA 95814 Office Phone: 916-322-5967. Office Fax: 916-445-7643.

KELLEY, MICHAEL GARHART ROOSEVELT, historian, educator, writer; b. Cambridge, Mass., July 25, 1943; s. John Joseph Kelley and Elisabeth Ann Garhart. BA in History, Boston U., 1966, MA in History, 1967; PhD in Scottish History, U. Edinburgh, Scotland, 1973. Prof. history, chair history dept. Blackburn Coll., Carlinville, Ill., 1974—85; vis. prof. U. San Francisco, 1983—84, Calif. Poly. State U., San Luis Obispo, Calif., 1987—88; chmn. dept. history Utah State U., Roosevelt/Vernal, 1989—97. Accreditation team mem. North Ctrl. Coll. Assn., Ill., 1978—79; founding assoc. editor The Outlaw Trail Jour., 1991; apptd. nat. grader to grade SAT Am. history exam. Ednl. Testing Svc., 1996—98. Contbr. numerous articles to profl. jours. Charter mem. Outlaw Trail Assn., Utah, 1991; bd. dirs. Macoupin County Mental Health, Carlinville, 1980—85; bd. advisors Am. Biog. Inst., Raleigh, 1994—; dir. Am. Bicentennial, Carlinville, 1976; bd. dirs. 150th Hist. Anniversary, Macoupin County, 1979. Fellow Postgrad. fellow, U. Edinburgh, 1970—72, Midwest Faculty fellow, U. Chgo., 1979, Summer fellow, NEH, 1980. Fellow: Dutch Settlers Soc. of Albany (life), Internat. Biog. Assn. (life), The Augustan Soc. (life); mem.: We. Ill. Hist. Assn. (charter mem.), Scudder Family Assn. (life), Phi Alpha Theta, Phi Beta Kappa. Roman Catholic. Avocations: local and regional history, environmentalist, politics. Home: Apt 111 1008 Larkin St San Francisco CA 94109 Office Phone: 415-567-0579.

KELLEY, MICHAEL JOHN, newspaper editor; b. Kansas City, Mo., July 5, 1942; s. Robert Francis and Grace Lauretta (Schofield) Kelley; 1 child, Anne Schofield. BA, Rockhurst Coll., 1964. Reporter, polit. writer Kansas City Star & Times, 1960-69; asst. Sen. Thomas F. Eagleton, Washington, 1969-76; pres. Swensen's Midwest, Inc., Kansas City, 1976-80; exec. asst. Ctrl. States Pension Fund, Chgo., 1981-83, 85-87; asst. mng. editor Kansas City Times, 1984; editor The Daily Southtown, Chgo., 1987-97; mng. editor Las Vegas (Nev.) Sun, 1997—. Office: Las Vegas Sun 2275 Corporate Cir Henderson NV 89074

KELLEY, MIKE, artist; b. Detroit, 1954; BFA, U. Mich., Ann Arbor, 1976; MFA, Calif. Inst. Arts, 1978. Performances include L.A.C.E., L.A., 1978, 81, 83, La Jolla (Calif.) Mus. Contemporary Art, 1978, Found. Art Resources, L.A., 1979, 80, Calif. Inst. Arts, Valencia, 1980, Hallwalls, Buffalo, 1981, Mus. Contemporary Art, L.A., 1984, L.A. Mcpl. Art Gallery Theatre, 1985, Sta. KPFK, L.A., 1986, Artists Space, N.Y.C., 1986; one-person exhbns. include Mizuno Gallery, L.A., 1981, Felsen Gallery, L.A., 1983, Rosamund Felsen Gallery, L.A., 1984, 85, 87, 89, 90, Galerie Peter Pakesch, Vienna, 1989, 91, Galerie Ghislaine Hussenot, 1990, Hirshorn Mus., Washington, 1991, Galeria Juana de Aizpuru, Madrid, 1991, Jablonka Galerie, Colonge, Germany, 1991, Basel Kunsthalle, Basel, Swizerland, 1992, Inst. Contemporary Art, London, 1992, capcMusee, Bordeaux, France, 1992, Whitney Mus. Am. Art, N.Y.C., 1993, The Uncanny, Tate Liverpool, 2004, Day is Gone, Gagosian Gallery, N.Y.C., 2005; group exhbns. include Annina Nosei Gallery, N.Y., 1980, Mizuno Gallery, 1981, Rosamund Felson Gallery, 1983, 84, Newport Harbor Art Mus., Newport Beach, Calif., 1983, 84, 91, Mus. Contemporary Art, 1988, 89, 91, 92, Weatherspoon Art Gallery, Greensboro, N.C., 1983, Art Gallery New South Wales, Sydney, Australia, 1984, Whitney Mus. Am. Art, 1985, 87, 88, 89, 91, 92, 93, Milw. Art Mus., 1985, 90, 92, Concord Gallery, N.Y., 1985, L.A. Inst. Contemporary Art, 1985, Corcoran Gallery Art, Washington, 1986, L.A. County Mus. Art, 1987, 88, Mus. Modern Art, Tokyo, 1987, Mus. Fine Arts, Boston, 1988, 90, Inst. Contemporary Art, Boston, 1988, Kunsthalle Dusseldorf, 1988, Kunstsammlung Nordrheinn-Westfalen, 1988, Kunstverein fur die Rheinlande und Westfalen, 1988, La Biennale di Venezia, Venice, 1988, Stadmuseum Graz, Austria, 1988, Pat Hearn Gallery, N.Y., 1989, La Foret Art Mus. Tokyo, 1989, Rooseum Malmo, Sweden, 1989, Daniel Weinberg Gallery, L.A., 1989, 90, Suzanne Hilberry Gallery, Birmingham, Mich., 1989, Robbin Lockett Gallery, Chgo., 1989, Galerie Schurr, Stuttgart, 1989, Galerie Gisela Capitain, Koln, Germany, 1990, Interim Art, London, 1990, Jay Gorney Modern Art, N.Y., 1990, Loughelton Gallery, N.Y., 1990, Galerie Ghislaine Hussenot, Paris, 1990, 93, Villa Arson, Nice, France, 1990, Seibu Contemporary Art Gallery, Tokyo, 1990, Simon Watson Gallery, N.Y., 1990, John Good Gallery, N.Y., 1990, Fahey/Klein Gallery, L.A., 1990, Grazer Kunstverein, Graz, Austria, 1990, Stux Gallery, N.Y., 1990, Mincher/Wilcox Gallery, San Francisco, 1991, Fundacion Caja de Pensiones, Madrid, 1991, ALdrich Mus. Contemporary Art, Ridgefield, Conn., 1991, L.A. Mcpl. Art Gallery, 1991, Sezon Mus. Art, Tokyo, 1991, Tsukashin Hall, Osaka, Japan, 1991, Meyers/Bloom Gallery, L.A., 1991, Martin-Gropius-Bau, Berlin, 1991, 93, Carnegie Mus. Art, Pitts., 1991, Newport Harbor Art Mus., 1991, Galerie Max Hetzler, Cologne, 1992, 93, Anders Tornberg Gallery, Lund, Sweden, 1992, Hayward Gallery, London, 1992, Mus. Modern Art, N.Y.C., 1992, Musee d'Art Contemporarin, Pully/Lausanne, Swizerland, 1992, Castello di Rivoli, Turin, Italy, Deste Found., Athens, Greece, 1992, Deichtorhallen, Hamburg, Germany, 1992, Israel Mus., Jerusalem, 1992, Mus. Ludwig, Cologne, 1992, Museo d'Arte Sezione Contemporanea, Trent, Italy, 1992, Schurmann Sammlung, Ludwig Forum fur Internationale Kunst, Aachen, Germany, 1992, Galerie Nationale Du Jeu de Paume, Paris, 1992, Spazio Opos, Milan, 1992, Galerie Krinzinger, Vienna, 1992, Royal Acad. Art, London, 1993, Galerie Jennifer Flay, Paris, 1993, Kunstlerhaus Bethanien, Berlin, 1993; permanent collections include Whitney Mus. Am. Art, Mus. Modern Art, N.Y.C., Mus. Fine Arts, Boston, capc Musee, Bordeaux, L.A. County Mus. Art, Mus. Contemporary Art, L.A., Mus. Boymans van Beuningen, Rotterdam, Mus. van Hedendaadse Kunst, Ghent, Belgium, WOW (The Work of the Work), Henry Art Gallery, U. Washington, 2004. Recipient Skowhegan medal mixed media, 1997, U. Mich. Sch. Art and Design Disting. Alumnus award, 1998, Calif. Inst. Arts Disting. Alumnus award, 2000; Louis Comfort Tiffany Found grant, 1984, Nat. Endowment for Arts Visual Artists fellowship grant, 1985, Artists Space Interarts grant, 1986, Awards in the Visual Arts grant, 1987, Nat. Endowment the Arts Mus. Program Exhbn. grant, 1990, John Simon Guggenheim Meml. Found. fellowship, 2003. Office: Metro Pictures 519 W 24th St New York NY 10011-1104

KELLEY, PATRICIA HAGELIN, geology educator; b. Cleve., Dec. 8, 1953; d. Daniel Warn and Virginia Louise (Morgan) Hagelin; m. Jonathan Robert Kelley, June 18, 1977; children: Timothy Daniel, Katherine Louise. BA, Coll. of Wooster, 1975; AM, Harvard U., 1977, PhD, 1979. Instr. New Eng. Coll., Henniker, NH, 1979; asst. prof. U. Miss., University, 1979-85, assoc. prof., 1985-89, acting assoc. vice chancellor acad. affairs, 1988, prof., 1989-92, assoc. dean, 1989-90; program dir. NSF, Washington, 1990-92; prof., chmn. dept. geology U. N.D., Grand Forks, 1992-97; prof. U. NC, Wilmington, 1997—, chmn. dept. earth scis., 1997—2003. Editor several books; contbr. articles to profl. jours. Deacon Bethel Presbyn. Ch., Olive Branch, Miss., 1985-90. Rsch. grantee NSF, 1986-89, 90-99, 2000-03; NSF fellow, 1976-79. Fellow AAAS, Geol. Soc. Am., Paleontol. Soc. (coun. 1984-85, 95-96, 98-2004, chair S.E. sect. 1984-85, chair N.C. sect. 1995-96, pres.-elect 1998-2000, pres. 2000-02, past pres. 2002-04); mem. Assn. Women Geosci. (Outstanding Educator award 2003), Paleontol. Rsch. Inst. (trustee 2003-, pres. bd. trustees 2004-06), Soc. Econ. Paleontologists and Mineralogists, Nat. Assn. Geosci. Tchrs. (disting. spkr. 2007), Sigma Xi, Phi Beta Kappa. Presbyterian. Avocations: writing, music, travel. Office: Dept Geography and Geology Univ NC Wilmington NC 28403-5944 Office Phone: 910-962-7406. Business E-Mail: kelleyp@uncw.edu.

KELLEY, PATRICK ALAN, neurologist, educator; b. Hinsdale, Ill., Sept. 24, 1947; s. Joseph John and Carol (Obalil) K.; m. Anne Nancy Trifilo, Feb. 22, 1975 (div. Aug. 1979). BA, Knox Coll., 1969; MD, Loyola U., Maywood, Ill., 1973. Diplomate Am. Bd. Psychiatry and Neurology. Resident in neurology Tufts U., Boston, 1974-77; asst. clin. prof. U. Conn., Farmington, 1977-79, U. Tenn., Chattanooga, 1979-88; staff neurologist Group Health Assn., Washington, 1988-94; chmn. dept. neurology Humana Group Health Plan, Washington, 1994-97; asst. clin. prof. George Washington U., Washington, 1988—; staff neurologist Kaiser Permanent, Kensington, Md., 1997—2007. Neurol. cons., Washington Hosp. Ctr., 1988-2006, Meml. Hosp., Chattanooga, 1979-88; clin. instr. neurology, Northeastern U., Boston, 1976-77. Author: Clinical Medicine: Selected Problems with Pathophysiologic Correlations, 1988. Candidate for Ho. of Dels., Gen. Assembly of Commonwealth of Va., 1999; mem. Pres.'s club Rep. Nat. Com., Washington, 1996-2004. Fellow Am. Acad. Neurology; mem. AMA (Physician Recognition award 1998, 2006), Am. Epilepsy Soc., Am. Med. EEG Assn., Med. Soc. Va., Phi Beta Kappa. Republican. Roman Catholic. Avocations: art, collecting editions of thomas jefferson's work, horses. Personal E-mail: PAKIrishmD@aol.com.

KELLEY, PATRICK W., health science association administrator, preventive medicine physician; MD, U. Va.; PhD, Johns Hopkins Sch. of Hygiene and Public Health. Dir. Global Emerging Infections System US Dept. of Defense, Silver Spring, Md., 1990—2002; dir. Preventive Medicine Walter Reed Army Inst. of Research, Silver Spring, Md., 1990—2002; dir. bd. on Global Health Inst. Medicine, Washington, 2004—, dir. bd. on African Sci. Acad. Devel., 2005—. Fellow: Am. Coll. Preventative Medicine. Office: Inst Medicine 500 5th St NW Washington DC 20001 Office Phone: 202-334-1748. E-mail: africa@nas.edu.

KELLEY, RICHARD ROY, hotel executive; b. Honolulu, Dec. 28, 1933; s. Roy Cecil and Estelle Louise (Foote) K.; m. Jane Zieber, June 21, 1955 (dec. 1978); children: Elizabeth, Kathryn, Charles, Linda J., Mary Colleen; m. Linda Van Gilder, June 23, 1979; children: Christopher Van Gilder, Anne Marie. BA, Stanford U., 1955; MD, Harvard U., 1960. Pathologist Queen's Med. Ctr., Honolulu, 1962-70, Kapiolani Maternity Hosp., Honolulu, 1961-70; asst. prof. pathology John A. Burns Med. Sch., U. Hawaii, Honolulu, 1968-70; chmn. bd. Outrigger Enterprises, Honolulu. Bd. dirs. First Hawaiian Bank, Outrigger Internat. Travel, Inc. Former trustee, past chmn. Punahou Sch.; dean's adv. bd. Travel Industry Mgmt. Sch., U. Hawaii; former vice-dean Ednl. Inst. AH & MA Pres.'s Acad. Bd. Regents; former chmn. bd. councilors Hawaii Pacific divsn. Am. Cancer Soc., past chmn. commn. on performance stds. State of Hawaii; trustee Kent-Denver Sch., U. Denver, 2003, Colo. Neurol. Inst., 2005-. Named Marketer of Yr., Am. Mktg. Assn., 1985, Communicator of Yr., Internat. Bus. Communicators, 1987, Salesperson of Yr., Sales & Mktg. Execs. Honolulu, 1995; named to Hawaii Bus. Hall of Fame, 1993; recipient Hope award Multiple Sclerosis Soc., 1995, Ihe award Hawaii Army Mus. Soc., 2000, Lifetime Achievement award Nat. Assn. Indsl. and Office Properties, 2003, Legacy in Tourism award U. Hawaii Sch. Travel Industry Mgmt., 2004. Mem.: World Travel and Tourism Coun., World Pres.'s Orgn., Pacific Asia Travel Assn., Japan Hawaii Econ. Coun., Chief Execs. Orgn., Hawaii Visitors Bur. (bd. dirs., chmn. 1991—92). Office: Outrigger Hotels & Resorts 2375 Kuhio Ave Honolulu HI 96815-2992 Home Phone: 303-761-7465; Office Phone: 808-921-6610. E-mail: richard.kelley@outrigger.com.

KELLEY, ROBERT DARYL, retired biology professor, mathematics professor; b. Leadville, Colo., June 28, 1947; s. Daryl Dean and Beulah Kelley; 1 child, Sebrina. AS, Mesa State Coll., Colo., 1967; BA, Western State Coll., Colo., 1971, MA, 1972. Civil engr. tech. USDA White River NF, Glenwood Springs, Calif., 1965—91; prof. biology and math. Colo. Mt. Coll., Glenwood Springs, Calif., 1981—2007; ret. Bd. mem. Vet. Tech. Adv. Bd., Glenwood Springs, Colo., 1996—2002, Crystal River Caucus Wildlife Taskforce, Redstone, Colo., 2005—; adv. panel mem. USDA Forest Svc. Recipient Appreciation award, Colo. Divsn. Wildlife. Mem.: CDT Trl. Assn. Independent. Avocations: painting, writing. Office: Colo Mountain Coll 3000 Country Rd 114 Glenwood Springs CO 81601 Business E-Mail: rkelley@coloradomtn.edu.

KELLEY, ROBERT OTIS, anatomist, educator; b. Santa Monica, Calif., Apr. 30, 1944; s. David Otis and Onetia May (Nettles) K.; m. Marcia Jean Bell; children: Jennifer Leigh, Karin Michelle, Matthew Philip, Sarah Ann. BS, Abilene Christian U., 1965; MA, U. Calif., Berkeley, 1966, PhD, 1969. Asst. prof. U. N.Mex. Sch. of Medicine, Albuquerque, 1969-74, assoc. prof., 1974-79, prof., 1979—; chmn. dept. anatomy U. N.Mex. Sch. Medicine, Albuquerque, 1981-97; assoc. vice chancellor rsch., exec. dean grad. coll. U. Ill., Chgo., 1997-99; dean Coll. Health Scis., U. Wyo., Laramie, 1999—. Vis. scientist Okazaki (Japan) Nat. Labs., 1984-85; mem. study sect. NIH, Bethesda, Md., 1982-86, U.S. Med. Licensing Exam. Step 1, 1995—; anatomy com. Nat. Bd. Mex. Examiners, Phila., 1992—. Author: Basic Histology, 1989; editor Cell and Tissue Rsch., 1970—, Anat. Record, 1970-97; contbr. articles to profl. jours. Patroller Nat. Ski Patrol, 1970—. Recipient Rsch. Career Devel. award NIH, 1972-77, Kaiser award U. Calif., Irvine, 1976; Internat. Exch. Scholar NSF; NIH grantee, 1970—Mem. Fedn. Am. Socs. for Exptl. Biology (pub. affairs exec. com. 1993—), Am. Soc. Cell Biology, Soc. for Devel. Biology, Electron Microscopy Soc. Am. (bd. dirs. 1987—), Am. Assn. Anatomists (exec. com. 1988—), Assn. Am. Med. Colls. (exec. coun. 1995—, chair assembly 1997-99), Nat. Caucus of Basic Biomed. Sci. Chairs, Nat. Bd. Med. Examiners. Democrat. Avocations: sailing, skiing, hang-gliding, scuba diving, backpacking. Address: 1162 Granito Dr Laramie WY 82072-5027 Office: U Wyo PO Box 3432 Laramie WY 82071-3432

KELLEY, ROBIN DAVIS GIBRAN, history professor, writer; b. NYC, Mar. 14, 1962; BA, Calif. State Long Beach, 1983; MA African History, UCLA, PhD in US History. Assoc. prof. U. of Mich., 1991—95; prof. NYU, NYC, 1995—2003, chair History Dept.; prof. Anthropology Dept. Columbia U., 2003—06; prof. Dept. History U. So. Calif., LA, 2006—. Chair dept. history NYU, 2002—03. Author: (book) Freedom Dreams: The Black Radical Imagination, Yo' Mama's Disfunktional!: Fighting the Culture Wars in Urban America (best book of 1997 by Village Voice; outstanding book on human rights, Gustavus Myers Ctr. for the Study of human rights in the US, 1997-99, 1997), Race Rebels: Culture, Politics, and the Black Working Class (outstanding book, Nat. Conf. of Black Polit. Scientists, 1995), Hammer and Hoe: Alabama Communists During the Great Depression (Elliot Rudwick prize, orgn. of Am. Historians, 1991; co-winner, Francis Butler Simkins prize, So. Hist. Assn., 1991); editor: To Make Our World Anew: A History of African Americans (history book club; choice outstanding academic title; outstanding book on human rights, Gustavus Myers Ctr., 2001). Adv. bd. mem. North Star Fund, NYC, 1999—2002; bd. mem. Am. Social History Project, NYC, 1997—2002, Davis-Putter Scholarship Fund, Boston, 1995—2002, NY Workers Rights Bd., NYC, 1998—2003; exec. bd. mem. Soc. of Am. Historians, NYC, 2002—03. Recipient ABC Clio award, Orgn. of Am. Historians, 1995; Ctr. for Advanced Study in the Behavioral Sciences, Stanford U., 1997—98, Montgomery fellowship, Dartmouth Coll., 2000, 2002, Schomburg Scholars-in-Residence fellowship, NY Pub. Libr., 2000—01. Office: U So Calif Dept Hist SOS 277 Los Angeles CA 90089 Home: 8306 Wilshire Blvd # 2024 Beverly Hills CA 90211 Office Phone: 213-740-1679. Office Fax: 213-740-6999. E-mail: rdkelley@usc.edu.

KELLEY, SHANA O., biochemist; BS in Chemistry, Seton Hall U., 1992; PhD in Chemistry, Calif. Inst. Tech., 1999; postdoctoral rsch., Scripps Rsch. Inst., 1999—2000. Asst. prof. dept. chemistry Boston Coll., 2000—. Founding scientist and cons. GeneOhm Scis., La Jolla, Calif., 2001—. Contbr. articles to profl. jour. Named one of Top 100 Young Innovators, MIT Tech. Review, 2004; recipient NSF Career award, 2004; Alfred P. Sloan fellowship, 2004. Office: Merkert Chemistry Ctr 140 Commonwealth Ave Chestnut Hill MA 02467 Business E-Mail: shana.kelley@bc.edu.

KELLEY, STEPHEN MICHAEL, lawyer; s. Charles Francis and Dawn Priscilla Kelley; m. Susan Strong, Aug. 16, 1980; children: Harty Tilton, Benjamin James. BS, SUNY, Geneseo, 1978; MBA, St. John Fisher Coll., Rochester, NY, 1988; JD, SUNY, Buffalo, 1998. Bar: N.Y., D.C. Adj. instr. Monroe C.C., Rochester, NY, 1988—94; gen. counsel Rulison & Co., Rochester, NY, 1998—2001; v.p. Fleet Nat. Bank, Rochester, NY, 2001—04, Bank of Am., Rochester, NY, 2004—. With US Army, 1972—75. Recipient William E. McKnight Vol. Svc. award, Vol. Legal Svcs. Project, 2003. Mem.: ABA, D.C. Bar Assn., NY State Bar Assn. (assoc.), SUNY Geneseo Alumni Assn. (bd. dirs. 1989—2004, Meritorius Svc. award 2002), Hunt Hollow Ski Club (bd. dirs. 2000—04), Genesee Valley Club (bd. govs. 2003—04). Avocations: tennis, skiing, fox hunting, travel. Home: 371 Allens Creek Rd Rochester NY 14618 Office: Bank of Am One East Ave Rochester NY 14638 Home Phone: 585-461-4245; Office Phone: 585-546-9557. Office Fax: 585-546-9560. Business E-Mail: stephen.m.kelley@bankofamerica.com.

KELLEY, SYLVIA JOHNSON, financial services firm executive; b. Butte, Mont., Dec. 29, 1929; d. John O. and Hilja W. (Koski) J.; m. Dan H. Kelley, June 1, 1950 (div. Jan. 1973); children: David D., Bruce J., Sheila K. Miller, Mona K. Kelley; m. Richard T. Marshall, June 10, 1979. CLU; ChFC; cert. fin. planner; registered fin. cons.; cert. sr. advisor. Legal sec. various law firms, LA, 1959-69; registered rep. Met. Life, NYC, 1969-75, SMA Equities, Inc., Worcester, Mass., 1975-89, Multi-Fin. Securities Corp., Denver, 1989—2003; CEO Advance Funding, Inc., El Paso, Tex., 1981—; registered rep. Geneos Wealth Mgmt. Co., Denver, 2003—06, Nat. Planning Corp., 2007—. Contbr. articles to profl. jours. Bd. dirs., chmn. bus. adv. com. Marina Del Rey C. of C., 1974-75; bd. dirs., pub. rels. chmn. Am. Heart Assn., El Paso, 1972-74; charter pres. El Paso Exec. Women's Coun., 1972-73; mem. fin. adv. com. El Paso C.C., 1992-95; bd. dirs., past pres. El Paso Estate Planning Coun., 1993-2001. Mem. Am. Soc. CLUs and ChFC (past pres. El Paso chpt., bd. dirs. 1981-85), Soc. Sr. Adv. (cert.). Avocations: contract bridge, ballroom dancing, international travel, photography. Office: Advance Funding Inc 423 Executive Center Blvd El Paso TX 79902 Home Phone: 915-231-9575; Office Phone: 915-772-2277. Personal E-mail: syskelley@aol.com.

KELLEY, THOMAS JOSEPH, lawyer; b. L.A., Dec. 9, 1936; s. Thomas Joseph and Mary Pauline (O'Dea) K.; m. Kaye Saxon Baker, June 25, 1966; children: Sean, Thomas Joseph III, Scott. BS in History, U. Santa Clara, 1958; JD, Loyola U., Los Angeles, 1966. Bar: Calif. 1966, U.S. Dist. Ct. (so. dist.) Calif. 1966, U.S. Supreme Ct. 1970. Assoc. Schell and Delamer, Los Angeles, 1966-73; assoc. Musick, Peeler & Garrett, Los Angeles, 1973-76, ptnr., 1976-84; ptnr. Moneymaker & Kelley, 1984-91, Dear & Kelley, 1992—; hearing officer state bar cts., 1976-82. Served to maj. USMCR, 1958-78. Mem. ABA, Los Angeles County Bar Assn., Assn. Bus. Trial Lawyers, So. Calif. Def. Counsel, Lawyer-Pilots Bar Assn., Santa Clara Alumni Assn. (pres. 1981-82). Republican. Roman Catholic. Office: 35 Aloha Dr Pacific Palisades CA 90272-4639

KELLEY, TINA, journalist; b. Morristown, NJ; B, Yale Univ. Author: (Poetry Coll.) Gospel of Galore, 2003 (recipient Wash. State Book award, 2003). Recipient Bullis-Kizer Prize, Poetry Northwest, Theodore Roethke prize. Office: New York Times Newark Bur 111 Mulberry St Newark NJ 07102 Office Phone: 973-802-1877. Office Fax: 973-623-1368.

KELLEY, WILLIAM NIMMONS, physician, educator, science administrator, dean; b. Atlanta, June 23, 1939; s. Oscar Lee and Willa Nimmons (Allen) Kelley; m. Lois Faville, Aug. 1, 1959; children: Margaret Paige, Virginia Lynn, Lori Ann, William Mark. MD, Emory U., 1963; MA (hon.), U. Pa., 1989. Diplomate Am. Bd. Internal Medicine (chmn. 1985-1986). Intern in medicine Parkland Meml. Hosp., Dallas, 1963—64, resident, 1964—65; sr. resident medicine Mass. Gen. Hosp., Boston, 1967—68; clin. assoc., sect. on human biochem. genetics NIH, 1965—67; tchg. fellow medicine Harvard U. Med. Sch., 1967—68; asst. prof. to prof. medicine, asst. prof. to assoc. prof. biochemistry, chief divsn. rheumatic and genetic diseases Duke U. Sch. Medicine, 1968—75; Macy faculty scholar Oxford U., 1974—75; prof., chmn. dept. internal medicine, prof. dept. biol. chemistry U. Mich. Med. Sch., Ann Arbor, 1975—89; Robert G. Dunlop prof. medicine, biochemistry and biophysics U. Pa., Phila., 1989—2000, dean Sch. Medicine, 1989—2000; CEO U. Pa. Med. Ctr. and Health Sys., Phila., 1989—2000; prof., 2000—. Human gene therapy subcom. NIH, 1986—92, recombinant DNA com., 1988—92, dirs. adv. com., 1992—95; bd. dirs. Merck & Co., Beckman Coulter, Inc., Advanced Biosurfaces, Inc., GenVec, Inc., Polymedix, Inc. Author (with J.B. Wyngaarden): Gout and Hyperuricemia, 1976; author: (with I.M. Weiner) Uric Acid, 1979; author: (with Harris, Ruddy and Sledge) Textbook of Rheumatology, 1981, 5th edit., 1997, now Kelley's Textbook of Rheumatology, 7th edit., 2005, Arthritis Surgery, 1994; author: (with M. Osterweiss and E.R. Rubin) Emerging Policies for Bio-Medical Research (Health Policy Annual III), 1993; editor-in-chief: Textbook of Internal Medicine, 1989, Textbook of Internal Medicine, 3rd edit., 1997; editor-in-chief now Kelley's Textbook of Internal Medicine, 4th edit., 2000; editor-in-chief: Essentials of Internal Medicine, 1994; contbr. articles to profl. jours. Trustee Emory U., 1992—, Emory U., Woodruff Health Scis. Ctr. Recipient C.V. Mosby award, 1963, John D. Lane award, USPHS, 1969, Rsch. Career Devel. award, 1972—75, Geigy Internat. prize rheumatology, 1969, Heinz Karger Meml. Found. prize, 1973, Disting. Med. Achievement award, Emory U., 1985, John Phillips Meml. award and medal, ACP, 1990, Nat. Med. Rsch. award, Nat. Health Coun., 1993, Robert H. Williams award, Assn. Profs. of Medicine, 1995, David E. Rogers award, Assn. Am. Med. Coll., 1999, Emory medal, 2000; scholar, Mead Johnson, 1967, Josiah Macy Found., 1974—75; Clin. scholar, Am. Rheumatism Assn., 1969—72. Master: ACP, Am. Coll. Rheumatology; fellow: AAAS, Am. Philos. Soc., Am. Acad. Arts and Scis.; mem.: Assn. Profs. Medicine (sec.-treas. 1987—89), Am. Soc. Internal Medicine, Am. Soc. Human Genetics, Ctrl. Rheumatism Soc. (pres. 1978—79), Australian Rheumatism Assn. (hon.), Royal Coll. Physicians Ireland (hon.), Am. Coll. Rheumatology (editl. bd. 1972—77, pres. 1986—87, Gold Medal award 1997), Assn. Am. Physicians (Kober medal 2005), Am. Fedn. Med. Rsch. (pres. 1979—81), Am. Soc. Biochemistry and Molecular Biology (editl. bd. 1976—81), Am. Soc. Clin. Investigation (editl. bd. 1974—79, pres. 1983—84), Inst. Medicine of NAS (chmn. sect. 4 1988—90, chmn. membership com. 1990—94, coun. mem., exec. com. 1996—2001), Ctrl. Soc. for Clin. Rsch. (pres. 1986—87), Alpha Omega Alpha, Sigma Xi. Office: BRB II/III 421 Curie Blvd Ste 1403 Philadelphia PA 19104 Home: 203 Elgin Ct Wayne PA 19087 Office Phone: 215-573-9953. Personal E-mail: kelleywn@hotmail.com.

KELLEY-HALL, MARYON HOYLE, retired social worker; b. Anderson, Ind., Aug. 5, 1924; d. Arthur Dent and Mildred Madeline (Hall) Hoyle; m. Dean M. Kelley, June 8, 1946; 1 child, Lenore Wadsworth Hervey; m. Richard A. Hall, Oct. 14, 2000. AB, U. Denver, 1945; MSW, Columbia U., NYC, 1967. Psychiat. social worker Rockland State Hosp., Orangeburg, N.Y., 1963-67, psychiat. social work supr., 1967-70; dir. social svcs. Rockland Children's Psychiat. Ctr., Orangeburg, 1970—72, chief child care svc., 1972—73; chief children's habilitation svc. Suffolk Devel. Ctr., Melville, NY, 1974—79; med. social worker Suffolk County Health Svcs., Hauppauge, NY, 1983-89; med. social work supr. Brentwood (N.Y.) Family Health Ctr., 1990—93. Home: 800 S 15th St # I-869 Sebring OH 44672

KELLIHER, JOSEPH TIMOTHY, commissioner; b. Jan. 17, 1961; m. Karen Goff; 3 children. BSFS, Georgetown U., 1983; JD magna cum laude, Am. U., 1994. With Preston, Thorgrimson, Ellis & Holman; staff mem. of Rep. Joe Barton; with Am. Nuc. Energy Coun.; represented Pub. Svc. Electric and Gas Co., 1991—95; majority counsel House Com. on Commerce, 1995—2000; of counsel LeBoeuf, Lamb, Greene & MacRae; with Bush/Cheney Presdl. Transition Team; sr. policy advisor to sec. US Dept. Energy, Washington; commr. Fed. Energy Regulatory Commn, Washington, 2003—, chmn., 2005—. Office: Fed Regulatory Commn 888 First St NE Washington DC 20426

KELLIS, MICHAEL JOHN, osteopathic physician; b. Wheeling, W.Va., Dec. 2, 1958; s. John George and Mary (Moskos) K. BS magna cum laude, Bethany Coll., W.Va., 1981; DO, Ohio U., 1985. Resident Brentwood Hosp., Cleve., 1985-86, fellow, 1986-87; pvt. practice, Chardon, Ohio, 1987—; dir. sports medicine Geauga Hosp., 1987—; dir., pres. Dr. Mike's Vitamins, 1999—. Team physician Berkshire High Sch., Burton, Ohio, 1987—, Notre Dame-Cath. Latin High Sch., Chardon, 1989—. Basketball coach, speaker on drug abuse Sts. Constantine and Helen Green Orthodox Ch., Cleveland Heights, Ohio 1987—; mem. leadership com. Geauga County unit Am. Heart Assn., Chardon, 1990—; ch. bd. mem. Sts. Constantine and Helen Greek Orthodox Ch., 1996-98; founder, pres. Friends of St. Michael non-profit orgn., 1996—; dir. summer camp Monastery of St. Michael, Rhodes, Greece; active Hunger Task Force, Geauga County, 1998—, nat. rep. Joint Commn. Sports Medicine, 2004, 2005 Named one of Cleve.'s 50 Most Interesting People, Cleve. Mag., 1997. Fellow Am. Osteopathic Acad. Sports Medicine (bd. dirs. 1996—, dir. nat. conv. 1999); mem. Am. Coll. Osteo. Sports Medicine, Am. Coll. Gen. Practitioners, Am. Osteo. Assn. Republican. Avocations: biking, weightlifting, stamp collecting/philately. Office: 13207 Ravenna Rd Chardon OH 44024-7032

KELLISON, STEPHEN GEORGE, actuarial consultant; b. Ord, Nebr., Mar. 20, 1942; s. Orin Albian and Sarah Viola (Crouch) K.; m. Chery Le Wagner, June 14, 1963 (div. Jan. 1970); m. Erica Elizabeth Bowers, Jan. 27, 1978 (div. June 1985); m. Maureen Antoinette Gage, Nov. 15, 1986. AB, U. Nebr., Lincoln, 1963, MS, 1967. CFP. Actuarial supr. Occidental Life Ins. Co., LA, 1963-65; actuary Lincoln Liberty Life Ins. Co., Lincoln, Nebr., 1965-66; prof. U. Nebr., 1966-75; consulting actuary G.V. Stennes

& Assocs., Dallas, 1975-76; exec. dir. Am. Acad. Actuaries, Washington, 1976-88; chmn. Dept. Risk Mgmt. and Ins. Ga. State U., Atlanta, 1989-93; sr. v.p. instnl. svcs. Am. Gen. Retirement Svcs., Houston, 1994—2001. Chmn. tech. panel Social Security Adv. Coun., 1989—91; pub. trustee Social Security and Medicare, 1995—2000; mem. task force on interest methods Fin. Acctg. Stds. Bd., 1989—95; sec. Actuarial Edn. and Rsch. Fund, 1989—92; mem. tech. panel Social Security Adv. Bd., 2003—04; vis. prof. U. Ctrl. Fla., Orlando, 2005—. Author: The Theory of Interest, 1970, 2d edit., 1991, Fundamentals of Numerical Analysis, 1975. Fellow Soc. Actuaries (bd. dirs. 1973-75, 90-93, v.p. 1999-2001, pres. 2003-05); mem. Nat. Acad. Social Ins., Am. Acad. Actuaries (bd. dirs. 1975-76), Internat. Actuarial Assn., Phi Beta Kappa. Home and Office: 9301 Wickham Way Orlando FL 32836-5518 Office Phone: 407-909-0853. Personal E-mail: sgkellison@aol.com.

KELLMAN, SANDRA Y., lawyer; b. Mar. 21, 1952; BA with high honors, Univ. Ill., Urbana-Champaign, 1973; JD cum laude, Northwestern Univ., 1977. Bar: Ill. 1977. Ptnr. co-chmn. Lodging & Timeshare practice group DLA Piper Rudnick Gray Cary, Chgo. Editor (note & comment): Jour. of Criminal Law & Criminology; contbr. articles to profl. jours. Office: DLA Piper Rudnick Gray Cary Suite 1900 203 N LaSalle St Chicago IL 60601-1293 Office Phone: 312-368-4082. Office Fax: 312-236-7516. Business E-Mail: sandra.kellman@dlapiper.com.

KELLMAN, STEVEN G., literature educator, author; b. Bklyn., Nov. 15, 1947; s. Max and Pearl (Pomerantz) K BA, SUNY, Binghamton, 1967; MA, U. Calif., Berkeley, 1969, PhD, 1972. Asst. prof. Bemidji State U., Minn., 1972—73; lectr. Tel-Aviv U., 1973—75; vis. lectr. U. Calif., Irvine, 1975—76; asst. prof. U. Tex., San Antonio, 1976—80, assoc. prof., 1980—85, prof. comparative lit., 1995—, Ashbel Smith prof., 1995—2000. Vis. assoc. prof. U. Calif. Berkeley, 1982; columnist, critic The San Antonio Light, 1983-93; fiction critic Gettysburg Rev., 1991-93; editor lit. scene USA Today mag., Valley Stream, N.Y., 1985—; film critic San Antonio Current, 1986-89, 98—; NEH seminar, U. Natal, South Africa, 1996 Author: The Self-Begetting Novel, 1980, Loving Reading: Erotics of the Text, 1985, The Modern American Novel, 1991, The Plague: Fiction and Resistance, 1993, Perspectives on Raging Bull, 1994, The Translingual Imagination, 2000, Redemption: The Life of Henry Roth, 2005; editor: Approaches to Teaching Camus's The Plague, 1985, (lit. mag.) Occident, 1969-70, Switching Languages: Translingual Writers Reflect on their Craft, 2003; co-editor: Into the Tunnel, 1998, Leslie Fiedler and American Culture, 1999, Torpid Smoke: Vladimir Nabokov's Short Fiction, 2000, Magill's Literary Annual, 2000—, UnderWords: Perspectives on Don DeLillo's Underworld, 2002; contbg. writer The Tex. Observer, 1989—Pres. bd. dir. Gemini Ink, 1998-2002, bd. editors Jewish Jour. San Antonio, 1987—, chmn., 1991-95; adv. humanities Inter-Am. Book Fair, San Antonio, 1987-94; adv., judge Tex. Film Festival, San Antonio, 1986-87, Cine Festival, San Antonio, 1985-90; v.p., bd. dir. Tex. Humanities Resource Ctr., 1991-92; del. Dem. Nat. Conv., 1992 Named Fulbright lectr. Thilisi State U., Georgia, U.S. Govt., 1980, lectr. Peru, Ptnrs. of Ams., Washington, 1988, 1995, Fulbright Disting. prof. U. Sofia, Bulgaria, 2000; recipient H.L. Mencken award, Balt. Sun, 1986, Arts and Letters award, San Antonio Libr. Found., 2005, award, NY Soc. Libr. Bd., 2005, First Pl. in Arts Criticism, Assn. Alternative Newsweeklies, 2006, Nona Balakian Citation for Excellence in Reviewing, Nation Book Critics Cir., 2006; grantee People's Republic of China, Fulbright Found., 1995; Sawyer fellow, Harvard U., 1997. Mem. MLA, Nat. Book Critics Cir. (bd. dir. 1996-2002), PEN Am. Ctr., Tex. Inst. Letters Home: 302 Fawn Dr San Antonio TX 78231-1519 Office: U Tex Dept English Classics & Philosophy San Antonio TX 78249 Office Phone: 210-458-5216. E-mail: kellman@lonestar.utsa.edu.

KELLNER, IRWIN L., economist; b. NYC, Oct. 4, 1938; s. Phillip and Mildred (Isaacson) Kellner; m. Ann Heiman, Jan. 22, 1961; children: Lori, Shari. BA in Econs., Bklyn. Coll., 1960, MA in Econs., 1964; PhD in Econs., New Sch. for Social Rsch., 1973; LHD (hon.), Hofstra U.; LLD (hon.), St. Joseph's Coll. Asst. bus. outlook editor Bus. Week Mag., prior to 1960, 1966-70; rsch. analyst Philip Morris, Inc., 1960-63; sr. rsch. analyst William Esty Co., Inc., 1963-66; assoc. economist Mfrs. Hanover Trust Co., NYC, 1970-72, v.p., 1972-78, dep. chief economist, 1973-78, sr. v.p., 1978—; chief economist The Chase Regional Bank, NYC, 1980-97; Augustus B. Weller Disting. Chair of Econs. Hofstra U., Hempstead, NY, 1997—. Chief economist MarketWatch, 1997—, Northfork Bancorp.; adj. full prof. sch. bus. Adelphi U., 1983—91; adj. vis. lectr. colls.; spkr. bus. and cmty. groups. Author: Econ. Report/Hofstra U.; weekly guest News 12 L.I., Cablevision, Radio and TV; contbr. articles and commentaries to profl. publs. Mem. village planning bd. Port Washington, N.Y., 1972—; commr. Hist. Landmarks, Village of Port Washington North, 1971-74; former bd. dirs. Juv. Diabetes Found., 1986-92, N.Y. Inst. Tech., sch. bus. Adelphi U.; bd. dirs. Children's AIDS Network, 1986—, Don Monti Found., 1992—; assoc. trustee North Shore U. Hosp., 1992—; chmn. adv. bd. Barry Z. Levine Sch. of Health Scis., Touro Coll., 1991—; mem. L.I. Regional Transp. adv. com. N.Y. State Senate Com. on Transp., 1988—; mem. N.Y. Dist. Adv. Coun. of Sml. Bus. Adminstrn. Region II; mem. N.Y. State Comptroller's Econ. Adv. Com., 1995—; past mem. N.Y.C. Economist's Roundtable, 1991-93; mem. numerous pro bono bds. including North Shore Univ. Hosp., Don Monti Meml. Rsch. Found., Epilepsy Found. of L.I., Nassau County Coun. of Boy Scouts of Am.; mem. adv. bd. C.W. Post's Coll. of Mgmt., 1997; numerous other civic activities. Recipient award for tobacco econs. Tobacco Mchts. Assn., 1978; named Number One Prognosticator, Instl. Investor mag., Most Accurate Forecaster (twice), Bus. Week mag., one of Top 5 Interest Rate Forecasters, Wall St. Jour.; recipient Disting. Leadership award, Barry Z. Levine Sch., Human Rels. award Am. Jewish Com., Humanitarian award Juv. Diabetes Found., Gary Sherman Humanitarian award North Shore Health System; named Hon. Alumnus Hofstra U.; named one of 100 Most Influential Long Islanders, LI Bus. News. Mem. Conf. Bd. (mem. Econ. Forum), Forecasters Club N.Y. (past pres.), Money Marketeers (past gov.), N.Y. Assn. Bus. Economists (past pres.), Am. Econ. Assn., Am. Statis. Assn., Bus. Economists Council, Downtown Economists Luncheon Group, Nat. Assn. Bus. Economists, N.Y. Acad. Scis., Met. Econ. Assn., Am. Bankers Assn. (adv. com.). Achievements include the innovation of the Mfrs. Hanover (now Chase) Trade-Weighted Dollar and the Mfrs. Hanover (now Chase) Cost-of-Living Index.

KELLNER, LAWRENCE W. (LARRY KELLNER), air transportation executive; m. Susan Kellner; 4 children. BS Bus. Admin. magna cum laude, Univ. SC. CFO, exec. v.p. Am. Savings Bank; CFO, sr. v.p. Continental Airlines, Houston, 1995—96, CFO, exec. v.p., 1996—2001, pres., 2001—04, COO, 2003—04, chmn., CEO, 2004—. Bd. dir. Continental Airlines, Marriot Internat., Belden & Blake Corp., Air Tranp. Assn. Bd. dir. Spring Branch Edn. Found., YMCA Greater Houston Area, Houston Minority Bus. Council, Greater Houston Partnership. Recipient Disting. Alumni award, Univ. SC, 1998. Office: Continental Airlines PO Box 4607 Houston TX 77210*

KELLNER, LEON B., lawyer; b. 1945; BA cum laude, SUNY, Buffalo, 1967; JD, Harvard U., 1971. Bar: NY, Fla., DC. U.S. atty. so. dist. State of Fla., Miami, 1985—88; ptnr. Anderson Kill Olick & Oshinsky, L.L.P., 1988—96, Dickstein Shapiro, Wash., DC, 1996—. Recipient Am.'s Leading Lawyers for Bus., 2005—06. Mem.: ABA, DC Bar Assn., Fla. Bar Assn., Bisonhead Society, Phi Eta Sigma. Office: Dickstein Shapiro 1825 Eye St NW Washington DC 20006 Office Phone: 202-420-2283. Office Fax: 202-420-2201. Business E-Mail: kellnerl@dicksteinshapiro.com.

KELLNER, RICHARD GEORGE, mathematician, computer scientist; b. Cleve, July 10, 1943; s. George Ernst and Wanda Julia (Lapinski) K.; m. Charlene Ann Zajc, June 26, 1965; children: Michael Richard, David George. BS, Case Inst. Tech., 1965; MS, Stanford U., 1968, PhD, 1969. Staff mem. Los Alamos Sci. Lab., N.Mex., 1969—79, Los Alamos Nat. Lab., 1983—88; co-owner, dir. software devel. KMP Computer Systems, Inc., Los Alamos, 1979—84; mgr. spl. projects KMP Computer Systems divsn. 1st Data Resources, Inc., Los Alamos, 1986—87, with microcomputer divsn., 1988. Owner CompuSpeed, 1986—; co-owner Computer-Aided Communications, 1982-84; v.p., COO, bd. dir. Applied Computing Systems Inc., 1988-2003; cons., 1979—; owner Sys. Automation Tech., 2003-4; pres., Autonomous Innovations, Inc., 2004-; CTO Innovative Autonomous Sys., LLC, 2005—. Recipient Commendation award for outstanding support of operation Desert Storm. Mem. IEEE, Assn. Computing Machinery, Math. Assn. Am., Soc. Indsl. and Applied Math., Am. Math. Soc. Home: 8 Lookout Ln Santa Fe NM 87506-8258

KELLOGG, DAVID WAYNE, agricultural studies educator, researcher; b. Seymour, Mo., Aug. 19, 1941; s. Martin David and Lula May (Spurlock) K.; m. Mary Sue Powell, June 7, 1964; children: Kirk David, Susan Joann Franz, Kimberley Annelle Van Vacter, Gregory William. BS, U. Mo., 1963, MS, 1964; PhD, U. Nebr., 1968. Profl. animal scientist. Asst. prof. agriculture N.Mex. State U., Las Cruces, 1967-71, assoc. prof., 1971-78, prof., 1978-81; prof., dept. head U. Ark., Fayetteville, 1981-86, prof., 1986—. Cons. AID-N.Mex. State U. Mission, Asuncion, Paraguay, 1971; spkr. Ark. Farm Bur., Little Rock, 1981-90, ORFFA Seminar, Rennes, France, 1995, Breda, Holland, 1996, San Jose, Costa Rica, 1999; Brenen and Leipsig, Germany, 2002, Bergano and Piedmont, Italy, 2002, Santa Cruz, Bolivia, 2002, 04, Belo Horizonte, Brazil, 2004. mem. adv. com Ark. Livestock and Poultry Commn., 1989-94; reviewer rsch. proposals USDA, Small Bus. Innovation. Mem. editl. bd.: Jour. Dairy Sci., 1978—84, nutrition sect. editor:, 2000—06, editor-in-chief: Profl. Animal Scientist, 2006—; contbr. chapters to books, articles to profl. jour. Mem. Fellowship Bible Ch. Mem.: Ark. Nutrition Coun., Ark. Registry Profl. Animal Scientists (sec., treas. 1989—93, charter), So. Assn. Agrl. Sci. (bd. dir. 1993—94), Am. Grassland and Forage Coun., Am. Soc. Animal Sci. (awards com. 1990—92, spkr. symposium on chelated trace minerals 1996), Am. Dairy Sci. Assn. (sec. so. sect. 1991, v.p. 1992, pres. 1993, awards com. 1996—98, spkr. symposium on highest producing dairy herds 2000, Disting. Svc. award 2005), Am. Registry Profl. Animal Sci. (bd. dir. 1989—91, pres.-elect 1993—94, pres. 1994—95, nominating com. 1996—98), Gideons Internat. (trustee 1975—81). Office: U Ark Dept Animal Sci Fayetteville AR 72701 Business E-Mail: wkellogg@uark.edu.

KELLOGG, HERBERT HUMPHREY, metallurgist, educator; b. NYC, Feb. 24, 1920; s. Herbert H. and Gladys (Falding) K.; m. Jeanette Halstead, July 20, 1940; children— Thomas Bartlett, Jane Falding, David Humphrey, Elizabeth Ann. BS, Columbia U., NYC, 1941, MS, 1943. Asst. prof. mineral preparation Pa. State U., State Coll., 1942-46; faculty Columbia U., NYC, 1946—, Stanley-Thompson prof. chem. metallurgy, 1968-90, prof. emeritus, 1990—. Chmn. titanium adv. com. Office Def. Mblzn., 1954-58 Contbr. articles to profl. jours. Recipient Best Paper award extractive metals div. Am. Inst. Mining, Metall. and Petroleum Engrs.; James Douglas Gold medal Am. Inst. Mining, Metall. and Petroleum Engrs., 1973 Fellow AIME (chmn. extractive metallurgy div. 1958), Metall. Soc., Instn. Mining and Metallurgy (London); mem. NAE, Sigma Xi, Tau Beta Pi. Home: 95 Closter Rd Palisades NY 10964

KELLOGG, HUSTON GLENN, pediatrician, medical educator; b. LA, Apr. 6, 1924; s. William Pitt and Thelma Bernice Kellogg; m. Eleanor Katherine Duncan, June 16, 1990; 1 child, Brian McBride Hodge; m. Dorothy Zulick Kellogg (dec.); children: Jacob William, Paul Huston, Michael Sherman. BS, Yale U., New Haven, 1945; MD, Washington U., St. Louis, 1947. Diplomate Am. Bd. Pediat. Intern St. Luke's Hosp., St. Louis, 1947—48; resident pediat. St. Joseph's Infirmary, Lousiville, Ky., 1945—49, St. Louis U., 1949—50; pvt. practice pediat. San Diego, 1952—62, La Mesa, 1962—95; chief pediat. and infectious disease San Diego County Hosp., 1957—61; faculty U. Calif. San Diego, 1969—. Med. dir. Home of Guiding Hands, Lakside, Calif., 1967—79. Contbr. articles pub. to profl. jour., scientific papers. Bd., chair Grossmont Hosp. Found., La Mesa, 1996—2002; bd. dirs. Home of Guiding Hands, San Diego Regional Ctr. for Devel. Disabilities, 2000—06. Capt. M.C. USNR, 1943—84. Mem.: San Diego County Med. Soc. Found. Ret. Physicians Soc., Assn. Mil. Surgeons U.S., Naval Res. Assn., Res. Officers Assn., Rotary, Shriners. Republican. Presbyterian. Achievements include chief pediat. four times, Grossmont Hosp. Avocations: travel, real estate. Home: 3404 Cromwell Pl San Diego CA 92116-1927 Personal E-mail: hgkell@aol.com.

KELLOGG, PETER NEWMAN, pharmaceutical executive; b. Bryn Mawr, Pa., Mar. 20, 1956; s. Paul Vincent and Jean (Flynn) K.; m. Carol Anne Curley, Apr. 26, 1986; 1 child, Charlotte. BS in Engring., Princeton U., NJ, 1978; MBA in Mgmt., U. Pa., Phila., 1982. Sr. cons. Arthur Andersen and Co., Phila., 1978-80; job mgr. Booz Allen and Hamilton, NYC, 1981-87; dir. corp. planning PepsiCo, Inc., Purchase, NY, 1987-89, divsn. fin. dir. Pepsi Cola Internat. Somers, NY, 1989—91, v.p. fin., CFO, sr. v.p. Pepsi Cola South to sr. v.p. PepsiCo E-Commerce Dallas, 1991—2000; exec. v.p., CFO Biogen Inc., Cambridge, Mass., 2000—04, Biogen Idec Inc., Cambridge, 2004—07, Merck & Co., Inc., Whitehouse Station, NJ, 2007—. Mem. Planning Forum, Princeton Club, Merion Golf Club, Cap and Gown Club. Office: Merck & Co Inc PO Box 100 Whitehouse Station NJ 08889-0100 Office Phone: 908-423-1000.*

KELLOGG, PETER R., securities dealer; b. Sept. 1942; s. James C. Kellogg III; married; 3 children. Student, Babson Coll., 1963. With Stern Frank Meyer Fox, 1964-67; sr. ptnr. Spear Leeds & Kellogg, NYC, 1967—99; chmn., CEO Spear Leeds & Kellogg Securities Inc. (sold to Goldman Sachs for 6.5 billion in 2000), NYC, 1969—99. Bd. dirs. Nam Tai Electronics, Inc., Ziegler Companies; owner Hudson Farm, Andover, NJ, United States. Co-founder Cynthia K. & Peter R. Kellogg Found. Fund. Named one of Forbes' Richest Americans, 1999—, World's Richest People, Forbes mag., 2001—; recipient Julius Blegen Award, US Ski Assn., 2006. Mem.: bd. US Ski and Snowboard Assn.*

KELLOGG, WILLIAM WELCH, meteorologist, researcher; b. New York Mills, NY, Feb. 14, 1917; s. Frederick S. and Elizabeth (Walcott) K.; m. Elizabeth Thorson, Feb. 14, 1942; children: Karl S., Judith K. Liebert, Joseph W., Jane E., Thomas W. BA, Yale U., 1939; MA, UCLA, 1942, PhD, 1949. With Inst. Geophysics UCLA, LA, 1946-52, asst. prof., 1950-52; scientist Rand Corp., Santa Monica, Calif., 1947-59, head planetary scis. dept., 1959-64; assoc. dir. Nat. Ctr. Atmospheric Research, Boulder, Colo., also dir. lab. atmospheric scis., 1964-73, sr. scientist, 1973-87; sr. rsch. assoc. Nat. Ctr. Atmospheric Rsch., Boulder, Colo., 1994—. Mem. earth satellite panel IGY, 1956-59; space sci. bd. Nat. Acad. Scis., 1959-68, mem. com. meteorol. aspects of effects of atomic radiation, 1956-58, com. atmospheric scis., 1966-72, polar rsch. bd., 1972-77; mem. Rocket and Satellite Rsch. Panel, 1957-62; adv. group supporting tech. for operational meteorol. satellites NASA-NOAA, 1964-72; rapporteur meteorology of high atmosphere, commn. aerology World Meteorol. Orgn., 1965-71; chmn. internat. commn. meteorology upper atmosphere Internat. Union Geodesy and Geophysics, 1960-67, mem., 1967-75; internat. com. climate Internat. Assn. Meteorology and Atmospheric Physics, 1978-87; sci. adv. bd. USAF, 1956-65; chmn. meteorol. satellite com. Advanced Rsch. Projects Agy., 1958-59; panel on environment President's Sci. Adv. Com., 1968-72; space program adv. council NASA, 1976-77; chmn. meteorol. adv. com. EPA, 1970-74, nat. air quality criteria adv. com., 1975-76, air pollution transport and transformation adv. com., 1976-78; coun. on carbon dioxide environ. assessment Dept. Energy, 1976-78; adv. to sec. gen. on World Climate Program, World Meteorol. Orgn., 1978-79; dir. rsch. Naval Environ. Prediction Research Facility, Monterey, Calif., 1983-84; chmn. adv. com. Div. Polar Programs NSF, 1983-86; researcher on meteorology, dynamics and turbulence of upper atmosphere, prediction radioactive fallout and dispersal, applications of infrared techniques, atmospheres of Mars and Venus, theory of climate and causes of climate change Served as pilot-weather officer USAAF, 1941-46. Co-recipient spl. award pioneering work in planning meteorol. satellite Am. Meteorol. Soc., 1961; recipient Risseca award contbn. human relations in scis. Jewish War Vets. U.S.A., 1962-63, Exceptional Civilian Service award Dept. Air Force, 1966, Spl. award for pioneering meteorol. satellites Dept. Commerce, 1985, Spl. Citation award for atmospheric conservation Garden Club of Am., 1988. Fellow Am. Geophys. Union (pres. meteorol. sect. 1972-74), Am. Meteorol. Soc. (council 1960-63, pres. 1973-74), AAAS (chmn. atmospheric and hydrospheric sect. 1984); mem. Sigma Xi. Home: 445 College Ave Boulder CO 80302-7131 *If there is anything that generally characterizes a gratifying and successful career in science, it is the challenge of diversity. The really important problems of the universe, and especially of society, involve several disciplines, and we are compelled to work at these discipline interfaces. Pigeon holes are for pigeons, not scientists.*

KELLOGG FAIN, KAREN, retired history educator; b. Pueblo, Colo., Oct. 10, 1940; d. Howard Davis and Mary Lucille (Cole) Kellogg; m. Sept. 1, 1961; divorced; 1 child, Kristopher. Student, U. Ariz., 1958-61; BA, U. So. Colo., 1967; MA, U. No. Colo., 1977; postgrad., U. Denver, 1968, 72-93, Colo. State U., 1975-91, Chadron State Coll., 1975, U. No. Ill., 1977-83, Ft. Hayes State Coll., 1979, U. Colo., 1979, 86-87, 92, Ind. U., 1988. Cert. secondary tchr. Colo., 1967. Tchr. history and geography Denver Pub. Schs., 1967-96; tchr. West H.S., Denver, 1992-96. Area adminstr., tchr. coord. Close Up program, Washington, 1982-84; reviewer, cons. for book Geography, Our Changing World, 1990. Vol., chmn. young profls. Inst. Internat. Edn. and World Affairs Coun., Denver, 1980—; state selection com. U.S. Senate and Japan Scholarship Com., Denver, 1981-89, Youth for Understanding, Denver; active Denver Art Mus., 1970—; vol. Denver Mus. Natural History, 1989—, Am. Cancer Soc. Jail and Bail, 1996, Climb the Mountain, 1996, Denver Conv. Bur., 1997; bd. overseas Dept. Def. Dependents Sch., Guantanamo Bay, Cuba, 1990-91; screening panelist Tchr. to Japan Program Rocky Mtn. Regional Fulbright Meml. Fund, 1997; vol. tour guide Colo. State Capitol, 1997-2001; vol. aide Colo. State Rep. Nancy Todd Fulbright scholar Chadron State Coll., Pakistan, 1975; Geog. Soc. grantee U. Colo., 1986; recipient award for Project Prince, Colo. U./Denver Pub. Schs./Denver Police Dept., 1992. Mem.: AAUW, Colo. Coun. on Internat. Orgns. (mem. bd. 1999—), Colo. Geographic Alliance (steering com. 1986), Rocky Mountain Regional World History Assn. (steering com. 1984—87), Am. Forum for Global Edn., Fulbright Assn. (bd. dirs. and regional liaison Colo. chpt. 2001—), World History Assn., Nat. Coun. Social Studies (del. 1984), Colo. Coun. Social Studies (sec. 1984—86), Denver Bot. Gardens, Kappa Kappa Iota, Gamma Phi Beta. Episcopalian. Avocations: travel, hosting international visitors, swimming, reading. Home: 12643 E Bates Cir Aurora CO 80014-3315 Personal E-mail: karenfain@hotmail.com.

KELLS, MELVIN RICHARD See ROBERTS, MEL

KELLUM, DONALD ARTHUR, military officer; b. Schofield Barracks, Hawaii, Dec. 13, 1935; s. Harry Snow and Edna Lois (Pickels) Kellum; m. Martha Ann Myers, Mar. 10, 1957; children: Kathryn Ann Kellum Comer, Donald Wainright. B in Gen. Edn., U. Nebr., Omaha, 1962; MS in Pub. Adminstrn., George Washington U., 1966. Commd. officer USAF, 1953, advanced through grades to col., fighter, bomber navigator, 1956—75, numbered Air Force vice comdr., 1975—77, numbered Air Force dir., 1977—86, ret., 1986; def. cons. JAYCOR, 1986—88; co-founder, bd. dirs., sr. mil. scientist Simulation Techs., Inc., 1988—2004; sr. mil. analyst Anteon Corp., 2004—06; sr. analyst Gen. Dynamics Info. Tech., 2006—07; sr. mil. analyst Addx Corp., 2007—. Decorated Legion of Merit with two oak leaf clusters, DFC, Purple Heart, Air medal with eleven oak leaf clusters, Air Force Commendation medal.

KELLY, A. DAVID, lawyer; b. St. Paul, June 8, 1948; s. David and Katherine (Tappins) Kelly; m. Elizabeth Woehrle, Oct. 25, 1978; children: Charles, George. BA, Carleton Coll., 1970; JD, Harvard U., 1973. Bar: Minn. 1973. Ptnr. Faegre & Benson, Mpls., 1973-90, Oppenheimer, Wolff & Donnelly, Mpls., 1990-95, Kelly, Hannaford & Battles, Mpls., 1995—. Chmn. Voyageurs Nat. Pk. Assn., Mpls., 1984—90; pres. St. Paul Boys' and Girls' Club, 1992—95; trustee Union Gospel Mission, 1982—92, Carleton Coll., Northfield, Minn., 1972—76, Minn. Mus. Am. Art, 2003—. Office: 900 Baker Bldg 706 Second Ave S Minneapolis MN 55402

KELLY, ALEDA MAE, retired secondary education educator; b. Mayfield, Ky., June 18, 1926; d. William Aubrey and Nomye (Brandon) Farmer; m. Troy Wilbert Kelly, June 5, 1948 (dec., 2003); children: Gene Michael, Patricia Jane Hendren. BA, Murray State U., 1948. Cert. tchr., Ky., Mo., Ill. Tchr. Benton (Ky.) City Schs., 1948-49, East Prairie (Mo.) Sch., 1949-52, Colusa (Ill.) Sch. Sys., 1958-60, Nauvoo (Ill.) Sch. Sys., 1961-64; tutor doctoral students So. Ill. U., Carbondale, 1964-67. Author: 20th Anniversary Aldersgate United Methodist Church, 1975, 40th Anniversary Aldersgate United Methodist Church, 1995, The Flame Still Burns, History of Memphis Conference United Methodist Women, 1995, History of Alumni Association-Memphis State University, 1996, Love Made Visible, History of Memphis McKendree District United Methodist Women, 1997. Active YWCA, Memphis, 1997; mem., officer Aldersgate United Meth. Ch., Memphis, 1967-97; mem. nominating com. McKendree Dist. United Meth. Women. Mem. United Meth. Women (v.p., historian McKendree dist.), Alpha Sigma Alpha (editor 1946-48), Kappa Delta Pi. Democrat. Avocations: reading, writing, presenting programs and workshops. Home: 4482 E Dearing Rd Memphis TN 38117-6902

KELLY, ALFRED F., JR., diversified financial services company executive; married; 4 children. BA, Iona Coll; MBA, Iona Coll. Adj. asst. prof. Iona Coll., New Rochelle, NY, 1980—85; with Am. Express, 1987—, exec. v.p. gen. mgr. U.S. consumer card mktg., exec. v.p., gen. mgr. consumer mktg. TRS, 1997—98, pres. consumer card svcs. group TRS, 1998—2000, group pres. U.S. consumer and small bus. svc., 2000—07, pres., 2007—. Chmn. Wall St. Charity Golf Classic; trustee Iona Coll., New Rochelle, NY. Office: Am Express Co World Fin Ctr 200 Vesey St New York NY 10285

KELLY, ANASTASIA DONOVAN (STASIA KELLY), lawyer, insurance company executive; b. Boston, Oct. 9, 1949; d. Charles A. and Louise V. Donovan; m. Thomas C. Kelly, Aug. 23, 1980; children: Michael, Brian. BA cum laude, Trinity Coll, 1971; JD magna cum laude, George Washington U., 1981. Bar: DC 1982, Tex. 1982, Va. Analyst Air Line Pilots Assn., 1971-74; dir. employee benefits Martin-Marietta Corp., Bethesda, Md., 1974-81; assoc. Carrington, Coleman, Sloman & Blumenthal, Dallas, 1981-85, Wilmer, Cutler & Pickering, Washington, 1985-90, ptnr., 1990-95; sr. v.p., gen. counsel, sec. Fannie Mae, Washington, 1995-99, Sears, Roebuck & Co., 1999—2003; exec. v.p., gen. counsel MCI, Inc. (formerly WorldCom), Ashburn, Va., 2003—06, corp. sec., 2003—04; exec. v.p., gen. counsel, sr. regulatory & compliance officer Am. Internat. Group, Inc. (AIG), 2006—. Bd. dirs. Owens-Ill., Toledo, 1999—; chair Equal Justice Works; dir. Assn. Corp. Counsel. Trustee Trinity U., Washington, 2003—; bd. dirs. Equal Justice Works, 1999—. Named one of Outstanding Young Women of Am., 1980, The 50 Most Influential Women Lawyers in Am., Nat. Law Jour., 2007; recipient Aiing High award, Nat. League Def. Fund,

2002, Myra Blackwell award, Chgo. Women's Bar, 2002. Mem.: ABA, Am. Corp. Counsel Assn. (bd. dirs. 2001—), Am. Bar Found., Order of Coif. Republican. Roman Catholic. Office: Am Internat Group Inc (AIG) 70 Pine St New York NY 10270

KELLY, ANTHONY ODRIAN, textiles executive; b. Dublin, June 12, 1935; s. John Peter and Delia Mary (Finnegan) K.; m. Sheila Josephine Clancy, Sept. 4, 1963; children— Barbara Anne, Adrienne Elizabeth, Damian Anthony. Grad., Coll. Commerce, Dublin, 1958; MBA, Columbia U., 1965, doctoral degree, 1971. Adj. asst. prof. Columbia U., NYC, 1968-69; dir. econ. studies Sperry & Hutchinson Co., 1969-71, asst. to pres. furnishings divsn., 1975; dir. mktg. Irish Agrl. Devel. Co., 1971-74; sr. v.p. mktg. Bigelow-Sanford, Inc., Greenville, SC, 1976-79, exec. v.p., COO, 1979-85, pres., CEO, 1985-86; pres., chief ops. officer Mannington Mills Inc., 1992, pres., CEO, 1993-2000, ret., 2000. Ford Found. fellow; Samuel Bronfman fellow. Mem. Inst. Cost and Mgmt. Accts., Kiawah Island Club, Beta Gamma Sigma.

KELLY, ARTHUR LLOYD, investment company executive; b. Chgo., Nov. 15, 1937; s. Thomas Lloyd and Mildred (Wetten) Kelly; m. Diane Rex Cain, Nov. 25, 1978; children: Mary Lucinda, Thomas Lloyd, Alison Williams. BS with honors, Yale U., 1959; MBA, U. Chgo., 1964. With A.T. Kearney, Inc., 1959-75, mng. dir. Dusseldorf, Germany, 1964-70, v.p. for Europe Brussels, 1970-73, internat. v.p. London, 1974-75, ptnr., dir., 1969-75, mem. exec. com.; 1972-75; pres., COO, dir. LaSalle Steel Co., Chgo., 1975-81; pres., CEO, dir. Dalta Corp., Chgo., 1982—; mng. ptnr. KEL Enterprises L.P., Chgo., 1983—. Dir. BASF Aktiengesellschaft, Ludwigshafen, Germany, BMW A.G., Munich, DataCard Corp., Minnetonka, Minn., Deere & Co., Moline, Ill., No. Trust Corp., Chgo., Snap-On, Inc., Kenosha, Wis., Robert Bosch G.m.b.H., Stuttgart; trustee U. Chgo.; mem. adv. coun. Ditchley Found., Oxford, England; bd. dirs. Chgo. Coun. Fgn. Rels. Fellow: Royal Geog. Soc. London (life); mem.: Coun. Fgn. Rels. NYC, World Pres.' Orgn., Brook Club (NYC), Yale Club (NYC), Racquet Club, Econ. Club, Comml. Club, Casino Club, Everglades Club (Palm Beach), Chgo. Club, Beta Gamma Sigma. Office: 20 S Clark St Ste 2222 Chicago IL 60603-1805

KELLY, ARTHUR PAUL, physician; b. Asheville, NC, Nov. 23, 1938; s. Joseph Paul and Amanda Lee (Walker) Kelly; m. Beverly Gayle Baker, June 25, 1966; children: Traci Allyce, Kara Gisele. BA, Brown U., 1960; MD, Howard U., 1965. Intern Harper Hosp., Detroit, 1965-66; resident in dermatology Henry Ford Hosp., Detroit, 1968-71; instr. in dermatology Brown U., Providence, 1971-73; asst. prof. internal medicine Charles R. Drew U. Medicine and Sci., Los Angeles, 1973-77, prof. LA, 1983; chief div. dermatology King.-Drew Med. Ctr., LA, 1976—, interim chmn. dept. internal medicine, 1985-86, vice chmn., 1987-91, chmn., 1992-95; assoc. prof. medicine U. So. Calif., LA, 1977-80; prof. UCLA, 1995—. Contbr. articles to profl jours, chapters to books; editor-in-chief: Jour. Nat. Med. Assn., 1997—2004. Served to capt US Army, 1966—68, Vietnam. Recipient Act-So award, NAACP, 1983. Fellow: Am Acad Dermatology; mem.: Am Dermatology Asn (vpres 1997—98, pres 1998—99), Asn Profs Dermatology (pres-elect 1996—98, pres 1998—2000), Nat Med Asn (chmn sect dermatology 1978—80, Oustanding Minority Dermatology Fellow 1972), Metropolitan LA Dermatology Soc (vpres 1986—87, pres 1987—88). Democrat. Avocations: travel, tennis. Office: King/Harbor Med Ctr 12021 S Wilmington Ave Los Angeles CA 90059-3019 Office Phone: 310-668-4571. Business E-Mail: apkelly@cdrewu.edu.

KELLY, BEVERLY ANN, elementary school educator; b. LA, Nov. 28, 1952; d. Irene Andrews and Jerry Kelly. BA, Calif. State U., LA, 1977; MS, La Verne U., Calif., 1985. Cert. elem. multiple subjects State of Calif., 1978, children's ctr. permit State of Calif. Weekend day camp sec. Found. for Jr. Blind, View Park, Calif., 1975—77, multi-handicapped tchr., 1978—79; classroom vol. First St. Spl. Edn. Sch., East L.A., 1977; dormitory asst. Calif. State Disgnostic Sch. for Neurol. Handicapped Children, LA, 1977—78; spl. day class intern Marianne Frostig Ctr. Ednl. Therapy, West L.A., Calif., 1979—80; learning handicapped tchr. Queen Anne Elem. Sch., LA, 1980—85; resource specialist tchr. Century Pk. Elem. Sch., Inglewood, Calif., 1985—, d.a.t.e. coord., 2002—04. Asst. supr. Teen Post, LA, 1979—80; ESL tchr. Dorsey H.S., LA, 1999—2000; asst. dir. Youth Experience Summer Program, View Park, Calif., 1981; fellow Marianne Frostig, LA; npi UCLA, Brentwood, Calif.; work study aide Neurol. Sch., LA. Mem. Lambda Pi Zeta, South Bay, Calif.; sunday sch. tchr. West Angeles Ch. of God in Christ, LA, 1978—80; vol. Willie Jordan Mission, LA, 1998—99; mem. Voices In Praise Choir, LA, 1999—2004, West Angeles Prison Ministry, LA, 2004—05, Wildlife Fedn., 2005—06. Mem.: Sierra Club, Wildlife Fedn. (corr.), Four Seasons Ski Club (assoc.), West L.A. Sierra Club (assoc.), Zeta Phi Beta (assoc.; vice sec. 1998—2000). Democrat-Npl. Mem. Ch. Of God. Avocations: travel, photography, african dance, computer graphics, crocheting. Home Phone: 323-732-4828; Office Phone: 323-755-2800. Personal E-mail: bkellee@msn.com. E-mail: bkelly@lausd.k12.ca.us.

KELLY, BRIAN J., editor; b. Clifton, NJ, Sept. 13, 1954; s. John J. and Catherine M. Kelly; m. Patrice Winsect, May 27, 1983; children: Daniel, Laura. BA in Econs., Georgetown U., Washington, 1976. Reporter Daily Register, Shrewsbury, NJ, 1975-76, Chgo. Sun-Times, 1976-84; editor Regardie's Bus. Mag., Washington, 1985—92; dep. editor Outlook Washington Post, congl. editor; asst. mng. editor U.S. News & World Report, 1998, exec. editor, 2003—07, editor, 2007—. Lectr. journalism Northwestern U., 1984, George Washington U., 1986. Co-author: Amazon, 1985, The Four Little Dragons, 1999, The Last Forest, 2007; author: Adventures in Porkland: How Washington Wastes Your Money and Why They Won't Stop, 1993. Office: US News & World Report 1050 Thomas Jefferson St NW Washington DC 20007 Office Phone: 202-955-2000.*

KELLY, CHARLES ARTHUR, lawyer; b. Evanston, Ill., Mar. 2, 1932; s. Charles Scott and Bess (Loftis) K.; m. Frances Kates, Sept. 9, 1961 (div. 1979); children: Timothy, Elizabeth, Mary; m. Patricia Lynn Francis, June 28, 1979 (div. 1995); m. Jean E. Glazier, June 25, 2005. BA with honors, Amherst Coll., 1953; LLB, Harvard U., 1956. Bar: DC 1956, Ill. 1956. Assoc. Hubachek & Kelly, Chgo., 1956-64, ptnr., 1964-82, Chapman & Cutler, Chgo., 1982—2002, of counsel, 2002—. Sec. Speedfam Internat., Inc., 1992-99, gen. counsel, 1998-99. Bd. dirs. Gads Hill Ctr., Chgo., pres., 1977—82; bd. dirs. Quetico Superior Found., Mpls., v.p., 1964—; bd. dirs. Lakeland Found., Chgo., 1960—96, pres., 1970—85, Ernest C. Oberholtzer Found., Mpls., 1962—2002, v.p., treas., 1998—2002; bd. dirs. Chgo. Hearing Found., 1990—94, Wilderness Rsch. Found., Chgo. Recipient Legion of Merit, USAF, 1982. Fellow Am. Coll. Trust and Estate Counsel; Mem. ABA, Chgo. Bar Assn., Ill. Bar Assn., Fed. Bar Assn., Univ. Club, Mid-Am. Club, Mich. Shores Club (Wilmette, Ill.), Harvard Club (Boston). Republican. Presbyterian. Office: Chapman and Cutler 111 W Monroe St Ste 1800 Chicago IL 60603-4080 Office Phone: 312-845-3009. Business E-Mail: ckelly@chapman.com.

KELLY, CHARLES HAROLD, advertising executive; b. Omaha, Mar. 30, 1950; s. Kerwood Michael and Erma Lenore (Johnson) K.; m. Susan Marie Nielsen, Dec. 28, 1971; children: Matthew Michael, Laura Elizabeth. BA, Hastings Coll., 1972; MS, Iowa State U., 1973. Account exec. Kerker & Assocs., Mpls., 1977-80, v.p., dir. client services, 1983—99; account exec. Foote, Cone & Belding, Chgo., 1980-82; account supr. Bozell, Jacobs, Kenyon & Eckhardt, Mpls., 1982-83; chmn, CEO Kerker, Mpls. Bd. dirs. YMCA of Greater Mpls.; bd. of visitors Penn State U. , Coll. of Comm. Mem. Advt. Fedn. Mpls. (pres. 1987-88), Am. Assn. Advt. Agys. (past pres. Twin Cities). Republican. Lutheran. Avocations: jogging, golf, photography, music. Office: Kerker 7701 France Ave S Minneapolis MN 55435-5288 Office Phone: 952-897-9420.

KELLY, CHRISTOPHER M., lawyer; b. Buffalo, Apr. 27, 1961; BA summa cum laude, Canisius Coll., 1983; JD with honors, Duke Univ., 1986. Bar: New York 1988, Ohio 2001. Atty. Simpson Thacher & Bartlett, NYC; ptnr., chair capital markets practice Jones Day, NYC, Cleve., 2006—. Office: Jones Day 222 East 41st St New York NY 10017-6702 Office Phone: 212-326-3438. Business E-Mail: ckelly@jonesday.com.

KELLY, CRAIG JAMES, bank executive; b. Troy, NY, Oct. 21, 1945; BS in History, Springfield Coll., Mass., 1967. Dir. mktg. New Britain Bank & Trust Co., Conn., 1968-73; sr. v.p., dir. mktg. Signet Bank (formerly Bank of Va.), Richmond, 1973-87, Banc One Corp., Columbus, Ohio, 1987—97; group exec. v.p. strategic mktg. Crestar Fin. Corp., 1997; corp. exec. v.p., chief mktg. exec. SunTrust Banks, Inc. Bd. dirs. BAI, 2006—. Recipient Disting. Young Alumnus award Springfield Coll., 1974. Mem. Bank Mktg. Assn. (tchr., lectr. 1985-88), Consumer Bankers Assn. (coun. 1990), Ohio Bankers Assn. (tchr., lectr. 1990), Springfield Coll. Alumni Assn. (pres. 1973). Avocations: sailing, wine. Office: SunTrust Banks Inc PO Box 4418 Atlanta GA 30302-4418 Office Phone: 404-588-7711. Office Fax: 404-827-6173.*

KELLY, CURTIS HARTT, retired publishing executive; b. Ft. Atkinson, Wis., May 17, 1935; s. Curtis and Edna (Guenther) K. BA, Yankton Coll., 1957. With fin. divsn. Scott Foresman Co., Glenview, Ill., 1962-86, with info. sys. divsn., 1986-97. Home: 1363 W Estes Ave Apt 2-U Chicago IL 60626-5465

KELLY, DANIEL GRADY, JR., lawyer; b. Yonkers, NY, July 15, 1951; s. Daniel Grady and Helene (Coyne) K.; m. Annette Susan Wheeler, May 8, 1976; children— Elizabeth Anne, Brigid Claire, Cynthia Logan. Grad., Choate Sch., Wallingford, Conn., 1969; BA magna cum laude, Yale U., 1973; JD, Columbia U., 1976. Bar: N.Y. 1977, U.S. Dist. Ct. (so. and ea. dists.) N.Y. 1977, Calif. 1986, U.S. Dist. Ct. (cen. dist.) Calif. 1987. Law clk. to judge U.S. Ct. Appeals (2d cir.), NYC, 1976-77; assoc. Davis Polk & Wardwell, NYC, 1977-83; sr. v.p. Lehman Bros., NYC, 1983-85; sr. v.p., gen. counsel Kaufman & Broad, Inc., LA, 1985-87; ptnr. Manatt, Phelps, Rothenberg & Phillips, LA, 1987-90, Sidley & Austin, LA and NY, 1990-99, Davis Polk & Wardwell, NYC and Menlo Park, Calif., 1999—. Mem. editl. bd. Columbia Law Rev., 1975-76. Office: Davis Polk & Wardwell 1600 El Camino Real Menlo Park CA 94025-4119 Office Phone: 650-752-2001. E-mail: dankelly@dpw.com.

KELLY, DANIEL JOHN, physician; b. Binghamton, NY, June 23, 1940; s. William James and Mary Elizabeth (Schmitt) K.; m. Lois Ann Lanshe, Aug. 21, 1965; children: Britton James, Jeffrey Daniel, Reid William, Piper Ann. AB in History, Yale U., 1962; MD, Jefferson Med. Coll., 1966. Diplomate in Pathology, Nuclear Medicine, Dermatopathology. Intern Naval Hosp., Boston, 1966-67, resident Oakland, Calif., 1966-71, asst. chief lab. Great Lakes, Ill., 1971-73, chief lab. svcs., 1973-75; co-dir. lab. Highland Park (Ill.) Hosp., 1975-97, dir. lab., 1980-89, 96-97; co-dir. lab. Lake Forest (Ill.) Hosp., 1975-97, dir. lab., 1989-91; with Dean, Hoffman & Clark Pathologists S.C., Lake Forest, 1975-97, Associated Lab. Physician Svcs., Wauwatosa, Wis., 1997-99; chief of staff elect Highland Park (Ill.) Hosp., 1992-94, chief of staff, 1994-96, also bd. dirs.; with Consolidated Pathology Cons., S.C., Lake Bluff, Ill., 1999—. Med. exec. com. Highland Park Hosp., 1992-97, Lake Forest Hosp., 1989-91. Bd. dirs. Lake Forest Hist. Preservation Found., 1979-88; mem. bldg. rev. bd. City Govt., Lake Forest, 1989-93; mem. clin. lab. and blood bank adv. bd. Ill. Dept. Pub. Health, 1990-95; mem. Am. Pathology Found. Comdr. USNR, 1966-75. Fellow Coll. Am. Pathology, Am. Soc. Clin. Pathology, Internat. Acad. Pathologists; mem. AMA, Ill. Soc. Pathologists, Am. Soc. Dermatopathology, Internat. Soc. Dermatopathology, Am. Acad. Dermatology, Assn. Military Surgeons Roman Catholic. Avocations: reading, art, music, fishing. Home: 499 E Illinois Rd Lake Forest IL 60045-2364 Office: Dept Pathology Lake Forest Hosp 660 N Westmoreland Rd Lake Forest IL 60045-1659 Home Phone: 847-234-7942; Office Phone: 847-535-6218. Office Fax: 847-535-6237. Personal E-mail: danjkelly@pol.net.

KELLY, DAVID M., lawyer; b. Mt. Pleasant, Pa., Oct. 18, 1957; BCE, U. Pitts., 1979, MCE with highest honors, 1980; JD, Duquesne U., Pa., 1983. Bar: Pa. 1983, La. 1985, DC 1987, registered: US Patent & Trademark Office. Ptnr. Finnegan, Henderson, Farabow, Garrett & Dunner LLP, Washington, chmn., Trademark & Copyright Practice Group. Mem. Duquesne Law Rev., 1981—83. Co-author (with Monica Talley): The High Price of Popularity, 2004 (Burton award, 2005). Mem.: Internat. Trademark Assn., Am. Intellectual Property Law Assn., ABA, DC Bar. Office: Finnegan Henderson Farabow Garrett & Dunner LLP 901 New York Ave NW Washington DC 20001-3315 Office Phone: 202-408-4000. Office Fax: 202-408-4400. Business E-Mail: david.kelly@finnegan.com.

KELLY, DEE J., lawyer; b. Bonham, Tex., Mar. 7, 1929; s. Dee C. and Era L. (Jones) K.; m. Janice LeBlanc, Dec. 30, 1954; children: Cynthia Kelly Barnes, Dee J., Craig LeBlanc. BA, Tex. Christian U., 1950; LLB, George Washington U., 1954. Bar: Tex. 1954. Pvt. practice law, Ft. Worth, 1956-79; founding, sr. ptnr. Kelly Hart & Hallman LLP, Ft. Worth, 1979—. Bd. dirs. A.M.R. , 1983—2000, Justin Industries, Inc., 1986—2000, The SABRE Group Holdings, Inc., 1996—2000. Trustee Tex. Christian U., 1971—2007; bd. regents Tex. State U. Sys., 1969—75; trustee U. Tex. Law Sch. Found., 1983—2002, Scott and White Meml. Hosp. and Scott, Sherwood and Bridley Found., 1989—98, U. Tex. Southwestern Moncrief Radiation Ctr., 1985—; bd. visitors U. Tex. Cancer Ctr., 1980—87; mem. Joint Select Com. on Judiciary, 1988, Task Force on Jud. Selection, 1995—96, Fed. Jud. Evaluation Com., 1989—; dir. Southwestern Expn. and Livestock Show, 1986—; bd. advisors George Washington U. Law Sch., 2001—05; bd. dirs. Tex. Turnpike Authority, 1967—76, chmn., 1969—76; bd. dirs. Ctr. Am. and Internat. Law, 1986—2006. 1st lt. USAF, 1951—53. Named Disting. Alumni, Tex. Christian U., 1982, George Washington U., 2001, Ft. Worth's Outstanding Bus. Exec., 1993, Ft. Worth's Outstanding Citizen, 2000; recipient Horatio Alger award Horatio Alger Assn. Disting. Ams., 1995, Blackstone award, 1998, Disting. Citizen award Boy Scouts Am., 2003. Fellow Am. Bar Found.; mem. Tarrant County Bar Assn., Tarrant County Bar Found., Tex. Bar Found. (founding mem.). Avocation: golf. Home: 1315 Hillcrest St Fort Worth TX 76107-1577 Office Phone: 817-332-2500. E-mail: dee_kelly@khh.com.

KELLY, DENNIS MICHAEL, lawyer; b. Cleve., May 6, 1943; s. Thomas Francis and Margaret (Murphy) K.; m. Marilyn Ann Divoky, Dec. 28, 1967; children: Alison, Meredith. BA, John Carroll U., 1961-65; JD, U. Notre Dame, 1968. Bar: Ohio 1968. Law clk. U.S. Ct. Appeals (8th cir.), Cleve., 1968-69; assoc. Jones, Day, Reavis & Pogue, Cleve., 1969-75, ptnr., 1975—. Mem. Ohio Bar Assn., Bar Assn. Greater Cleve. Office: Jones Day Reavis & Pogue North Point 901 Lakeside Ave E Cleveland OH 44114-1190 Office Phone: 216-586-7180. E-mail: dmkelly@jonesday.com.

KELLY, DOROTHY HELEN, pediatrician, educator; b. Fitchburg, Mass., July 29, 1944; BS in Nursing magna cum laude, Fitchburg State Co., 1966; BS with distinction, Wayne State U., 1968, MD with distinction, 1972. Diplomate Am. Bd. Pediatrics, Pediatric Pulmonology. Intern Children's Svc. Mass. Gen. Hosp., Boston, 1972-73, resident in pediatrics, 1973-75, fellow in pediatrics pulmonary medicine, 1976-79, co-dir. pediat. pulmonary lab., 1976—83, assoc. dir. pediatric pulmonary unit, 1983—95; teaching fellow Harvard Med. Sch., Boston, 1973-75, clin. fellow, 1972-75, instr. in pediatrics, 1975-81, asst. prof. pediatrics, 1981-89, assoc. prof. pediatrics, 1989-95, U. Tex., Galveston, 1995-97, Houston, 1995—; assoc. dir. S.W. SIDS Rsch. Inst. Meml. Herman S.W. Hosp., Houston, 1995—. Cons. Bur. Community Health Svcs., NEW, 1979-80, FDA, 1986, 88-92, ECRI, 1987-88, also others; chmn. apnea adv. com. Nat. Sudden Infant Death Syndrome Found., 1979-81; mem. com. anesthesiology and respiratory devices panel Ctr. for Devices and Radiol. Health, FDA, 1990-94; chmn. physicians' com. Nat. Assn. Apnea Profls., 1990-91, also others; reviewer numerous jours. in field. Contbr. numerous articles to profl. jours. Recipient Woman of Vision award Nat. Soc. for Prevention of Blindness, Mass. Affiliate, 1981, First Disting. Alumni award Fitchburg State Coll., 1984, grants in field. Mem. Am. Med. Woman's Assn., Am. Acad. Pediatrics (task force on prolonged apnea 1978), Am. Thoracic Soc., Internat. Pediatric Soc., Assn. for Psychophysiol. Study Sleep, Soc. for Pediatric Rsch., Tex. Thoracic Soc., Tex. Med. Assn., Tex. Pediatric Soc., Am. Autonomic Soc., Am. Assn. SIDS Prevention Physicians (bd. dirs., pres.-elect), NH Pediatric Soc. Office: North Country Pediatrics Littleton Regional Hosp Littleton NH 03561 Office Phone: 603-484-2803. E-mail: dhkelly@aap.net.

KELLY, DOUGLAS LAIRD, lawyer, investment company executive; b. Pensacola, Fla., Mar. 4, 1949; s. John L. and Shirley (Perkins) K.; m. Cynthia Jane Benedict, Dec. 28, 1971; children: Laura Elizabeth, Michael Laird. BS in Fin., U. Colo., 1971; JD, Washington U., 1973. Bar: Mo. 1974. Assoc. Peper, Martin, Jensen, Maichel & Hetlage, St. Louis, 1974-78, ptnr., 1978—94; atty. A.G. Edwards, St. Louis, 1994—, exec. v.p., CFO, corp. sec., treas., dir. of law & compliance. Mem. NASD Nat. Adjudicatory Council. Mem. ABA, Mo. Bar Assn. Office: AG Edwards 1 N Jefferson Ave Saint Louis MO 63103

KELLY, EAMON MICHAEL, economic development professor, retired university president; b. NYC, Apr. 25, 1936; s. Michael Joseph and Kathleen Elizabeth (O'Farrell) K.; m. Margaret Whalen, June 22, 1963; children: Martin (dec.), Paul, Andrew, Peter. BS, Fordham U., 1958; MS, Columbia U., 1960, PhD, 1965. Officer in charge Office of Social Devel., Ford Found., NYC, 1969—74; officer in charge program related investments Ford Found., 1974—79; exec. v.p. Tulane U., New Orleans, 1979—81, pres., 1981—98; pres. emeritus; prof. Payson Ctr. Internat. Devel. and Tech. Transfer Tulane U., 1998—. Dir. policy formulation div. Econ. Devel. Adminstrn., Dept. Commerce, Washington, 1968; spl. asst. to adminstr. SBA, Washington, 1968-69; spl. cons. to sec. Dept. Labor, 1977; bd. dirs. So. Edn. Found., La. Land and Exploration Co., Nat. Captioning Inst., Assn. Gov. Bds. Colls. and Univ., Econ. Devel. Commn. State of La.; mem. Nat. Sci. Bd., 1996-2002 (chmn. 1998-2002), Nat. Security Edn. Bd., Humphrey Fellows Nat. Adv. Bd., Bus. Higher Edn. Forum, com. econ. devel. Gabelli Enterprises Inc., exec. com. Assn. Am. Univs.; pres. Commission NCAA, Found. for Biomed. Rsch., Nat. Sci. Bd., 1996; former chair Presidential Adv. Bd. Pres. city coun., councilman-at-large City of Englewood, N.J., 1974-77; bd. advocates Planned Parenthood of La. Mem. AAUP, La. Conf. Univs. and Colls., La. Assn. Ind. Colls. and Univs., Bus. Coun. New Orleans, City Club, Inc., Met. Area Com., New Orleans Ednl. Telecom. Consortium. Democrat. Roman Catholic. Office: Tulane University Tech Srvcs 1555 Poydras St Ste 1400 New Orleans LA 70112-5406

KELLY, EDMUND FRANCIS, insurance company executive; b. 1945; With Aetna Life & Casualty Co., 1974-92; pres., COO Liberty Mut. Ins. Co., Boston, 1992-98, pres., CEO, 1998—2001, chmn., 2000—01; chmn., pres., CEO Liberty Mutual Holding Co. Inc., Boston, 2001—. Office: Liberty Mutual Holding Company Inc 175 Berkeley St Boston MA 02116-5066

KELLY, EDMUND JOSEPH, lawyer, investment banking executive; b. Mount Vernon, NY, May 18, 1937; s. Hugh Joseph and Catherine (Rice) K.; m. Joan Anne Fee, Nov. 18, 1961; children: Kathleen Kelly Broomer, Edmund Murphy, Thomas More, Mary Kelly Mehr, Michael McNaboe. AB cum laude, Coll. of Holy Cross, 1959; JD (James Kent scholar), Columbia U., 1962. Bar: NY 1962. Sec. of Air Force Office of Gen.Counsel, Washington, 1962-65; assoc. White & Case, NYC, 1965-70, ptnr., 1971-84; vice chmn. Dominick & Dominick Co., NYC, 1984-91, Eighteen Seventy Corp., Purchase, NY, 1991—. Lectr. Practicing Law Inst., Am. Mgmt. Assn.; bd. dirs. Fed. Paper Bd. Co., Inc., Montvale, N.J., 1981-96; bd. dirs., mem. exec. com. Chgo. Pneumatic Tool Co., N.Y.C., 1980-86. Author: The Takeover Dialogues, A Discussion of Hostile Takeovers, 1987; editor Columbia Law Rev., 1961-62; contbr. articles to legal jours. Air Force mem. Armed Services Procurement Regulation Com., 1964-65. Office: Eighteen Seventy Corp Two Manhattanville Rd Purchase NY 10577-2118

KELLY, EDWARD J., III, diversified financial services company executive; AB, Princeton U., 1975; JD, U. Va., 1981. Mng. dir. J.P. Morgan & Co., 1997—2000; chmn., CEO Mercantile Safe Deposit & Trust Co., Balt., 2001—07; pres., CEO Mercantile Bankshares Corp., Balt., 2001—07, chmn., 2003—07; vice chmn. PNC Fin Services Group, Pitts., 2007—. Bd. dir. CSX Corp., Hartford Fin. Services Group Inc. Trustee Johns Hopkins Univ., Balt. Mus. Art. Office: PNC Fin Services Group One PNC Plz 249 Fifth Ave Pittsburgh PA 15222*

KELLY, ELLSWORTH, painter, sculptor; b. Newburgh, NY, May 31, 1923; Student, Pratt Inst., 1941—43, Boston Mus. Fine Arts Sch., Ecole des Beaux-Arts, Paris, 1946-48; DFA (hon.), Pratt Inst., 1993, Bard Coll., 1996; doctorate (hon.), Royal Coll. Art, London, 1997. Works exhibited: Salon de Realities Nouvelles, Paris, 1950, 51, Carnegie Inst., 1958, 61, 64, 67, 85, Sao Paulo Biennial, 1961, Tokyo Internat., 1963, Documenta III, Germany, 1964, Documenta IV, 1968, Documenta IX, 1992, Venice Biennale, 1966, Guggenheim Internat., 1967, Corcoran Ann., Washington, 1979, others; one-man shows include Galerie Arnaud, Paris, 1951, Galerie Maeght, Paris, 1958, 64, 65, Sidney Janis Gallery, N.Y.C., 1965, 67, 68, 71, Betty Parsons Gallery, N.Y.C., 1956, 57, 59, 61, 63, Tooth Gallery, London, 1962, Washington Gallery Modern Art, 1964, Inst. Contemporary Art, Boston, 1964, Dayton's Gallery 12, Mpls., 1971, Albright Art Gallery, 1972, Hans Mayer Gallery, Dusseldorf, Germany, 1972, Leo Castelli Gallery, N.Y.C., 1973, 77, 79, 81, 82, 84, 85, 86, 88, 89, 92, Irving Blum Gallery, Los Angeles, 1965-68, 73, Greenberg Gallery, St. Louis, 1973, 89, Whitney Mus. Am. Art, N.Y.C., 1982, St. Louis Mus. Art, 1983, N.Y. Mus. Modern Art, 1973, Pasadena (Calif.) Mus. Modern Art, 1974, Walker Art Mus., Mpls., 1974, 94, Detroit Inst. Fine Arts, 1974, Ace Gallery, Venice, Calif., 1975, Janie Lee Gallery, Houston, 1975, Blum/Helman Gallery, N.Y.C., 1975, 77, 79, 81, 82, 84, 85, 86, 88, 89, 92, Met. Mus., N.Y.C., 1979, Stedelijk Mus., Amsterdam, 1979, Hayward Gallery, London, 1980, Centre Georges Pompidou, Paris, 1980, Staatliche Kunsthalle, Baden Baden, 1980, Margo Leavin Gallery, L.A., 1984, 91, John Berggruen Gallery, 1991, Castelli Graphics, N.Y., 1988, BlumHelman Gallery, L.A., 1988, Daniel Templon, Paris, 1989, 92, Overholland Mus., Amsterdam, 1989, Susan Sheehan Gallery, N.Y.C., 1990, 92, 95, 96, Gallery Kasahara, Osaka, Japan, 1990, Portikus, Frankfurt, Fed. Rep. Germany, 1990, Matthew Marks Gallery, N.Y.C., 1992, 94, 96, 98, 99, 2001, Anthony D'Offay, London, 1992, 94, Paula Cooper Gallery, N.Y.C., 1992, 94, Modern Art Mus. Ft. Worth, 1987, Mus. Fine Arts, Boston, Art Gallery Ont., Toronto, Balt. Mus. Art, San Francisco Mus. Modern Art, Nelson-Atkins Mus. Art, Kansas City, Detroit Inst. Arts, 1987, Huntsville Mus. Art, Ala., Des Moines Art Ctr., Iowa, Neuberger Art Mus., Purchase, N.Y., Los Angeles County Mus. Art, U. Okla. Mus. Art, Berkshire Mus., Pittsfield, Mass., Univ. Art Mus., Berkeley, Calif., Hood Mus. Art, Hanover, N.H., Ellsworth Kelly, The French Years, 1948-54, Galerie Nationale du Jeu de Paume, Paris, 1992, Westfälisches Landesmus, Munster, Germany, 1992,

Nat. Gallery, Washington, 1993, Eli Broad Found., L.A., 1994, Milw. Art Mus., 1994, Gugghenheim Mus., 1996, Mus. Contemporary Art, L.A., 1997, Tate Gallery, 1998, Haus der Kunst, 1998, Met. Mus. Art, 1998, Fogg Art Mus., 1998, 99, Boston U., 1998, New Brit. Mus. Am. Art, 1998, Newcomb Gallery Art, 1998, High Mus. Art, 1999, Art Inst. Chgo., 1999, Kunstmuseum Winterthur, 1999, Stadtische Galerie, 1999, Kunstmuseum Bonn, 1999, Del. Art Mus., 1999, Smithsonian, 2000, Whitney Mus. Am. Art Philip Morris, 2000, San Francisco MOMA, 2002; represented in permanent collections Mus. Modern Art, Met. Mus., Whitney Mus., Carnegie Inst., Albright Art Gallery, Buffalo, Chgo., Art Inst., Worcester Mus., Toronto (Can.) Mus.,Tate Gallery, London, Walker Art Center, Mpls., Guggenheim Mus., N.Y.C., Los Angeles County Mus., Centre Georges Pompidou, Paris,Stedlijk Mus., Amsterdam, Kroller-Mueller Mus., Otterlo, Holland, Munster Mus., Germany, UNESCO, Paris, Centro Reina Sofia, Madrid, Lenbachhaus, Munster, Balt. Mus. Art, Nat. Gallery, Washington, San Francisco Mus. Modern Art. sculpture: lobby, Transp. Bldg., Phila., 1956, Barcelona, Spain, 1985, Balt. Mus. Garden, 1988, Walker Art Ctr. Garden, 1988, Mus. Fine Arts, Houston, 1986, Myerson Symphony Ctr., Dallas, 1989, Nestle S.A., Vevey, Switzerland, 1991, Carre d'Art, Museee d'Art Contemporain, Nimes, France, Holocaust Mus., Washington, 1993. Mem. USAAF, 1943—45. Decorated chevalier Ordre Arts et Lettres, Legion of Honor, comdr. Arts et Lettres (France); recipient Brandeis painting award, 1963, Edn. Min. award Tokyo Internat., 1963, 4th prize Carnegie Inst., 1962, painting prize, 1964; painting prize Art Inst. Chgo., 1964, 74, Showhegan, 1981, medal Pratt Inst., Bklyn., 1993, medal for outstanding achievement Sch. Mus. Fine Arts, Boston, 1996, ann. tribute award Friends Art and Preservation in Embassies, U.S. Dept. State, 1996, Govs. award N.Y. Sate Coun. on Arts, 1998; named Friend of Barcelona and recipient medal Mayor of Barcelona, 1993. Fellow Acad. Arts and Scis.; mem. Nat. Acad. Arts and Letters, NAD (academician, 1994-). Address: Matthew Marks Gallery 523 W 24th St New York NY 10011-1104

KELLY, ERIC DAMIAN, lawyer, educator; b. Pueblo, Colo., Mar. 16, 1947; s. William Bret and Patricia Ruth (Ducy) K.; children: Damian Charles, Eliza Jane, Valissitie Christina Heeren, Douglas Ray Heeren; m. Sandra Walker, 1996. BA, Williams Coll., 1969; JD, U. Pa., 1975, M of City Planning, 1975; PhD, Union Inst., 1992. Bar: Colo. 1975, U.S. Dist. Ct. 1976, U.S. Tax Ct. 1976, U.S. Ct. Appeals (10th cir.) 1986. Chief citizens' participation unit Region III EPA, Phila., 1971-72; project planner Beckett New Town, NJ, 1972-73; v.p., project mgr. Rahenkamp Sachs Wells & Assocs., Inc., Denver and Phila., 1973-76; sole practice Pueblo, 1976-83; pres. Kelly & Potter, P.C., Pueblo, Albuquerque and Santa Fe, 1983-90. Adj. prof. U. Colo. Coll. Architecture and Planning, 1976-90; chmn., prof. Dept. cmty. and regional planning Iowa State U., 1990-95; adj. asst. prof. grad. sch. bus. U. So. Colo., 1986-90; dean coll. architecture and planning Ball State U., 1995-98, prof. urban planning, 1999—; mem. city devel. bd. State of Iowa, 1991-95. Gen. editor Zoning and Land Use Controls, 1995—; author: Enforcing Zoning and Land Use Codes, 1988, Managing Community Growth: Policies, Techniques and Impacts, 1993, Selecting and Retaining Consultants, 1993, Planning, Growth and Public Facilities: A Primer for Public Officials, 1994; editor, prin. author: The Roadtripper, 1969; contbr. articles to profl. planning and legal jours. Mem. adv. bd. Mcpl. Legal Studies Ctr., S.W. Legal Found., 1989—; mem. nat. adv. bd. Rocky Mountain Land Use Inst. Coll. Law U. Denver, 1992—; bd. dirs. Broadway Theatre League, Pueblo, 1976-77, Pueblo Beautiful Assn., 1978-82, Better Bus. Bur., 1988-89; trustee Sangre de Cristo Arts and Conf. Ctr., 1981-87, chmn. 1986; trustee Christ Congl. Ch., 1982-83; mem. Ind. Land Resources Coun., 1999—; bd. dirs., mem. adv. bd. Nature Conservacy Ind. With U.S. Army, 1969-71. Named Outstanding Student, Am. Inst. Planners, 1976; recipient Outstanding Faculty award Order of Omega, 1992. Mem. ABA, Am. Inst. Cert. Planners (charter, elected Coll. of Fellows 1999), Am. Planning Assn. (nat. pres., 1997—, chair planning & law divsn. 1996-97, pres. Iowa chpt. 1994-95, amicus curiae com. 1988-94, 95-97, legis. & policy com. 1993-97, Colo. chpt. excellence award 1989), Williams Coll. Alumni Assn. (class sec. 1969-74, regional sec. 1980-82, class agt. 1985-89), Rotary (local dir. 1988-90, dir., pres. Pueblo Rotary Found. 1988-89, v.p. 1988-89, pres. 1989-90, area rep. for dist. gov. 1991-92), Phi Kappa Phi. Democrat. Home: 2312 W Audubon Dr Muncie IN 47304-2003 Office: Ball State U Coll Architecture Planning Muncie IN 47306-0001

KELLY, FRANCIS J., III, global marketing company executive; m. Heather Kelly; children: Whitney, Jay (twins). BA, Amherst Coll.; MBA, Harvard. With Young & Rubicam, NYC, 1978-81; from acct. exec. to sr. v.p., group acct. dir. Humphrey Browning MacDougall, 1983-88; prin., dir. client svcs., COO Leonard Monahan, Lubars & Kelly, Providence, 1989-94; chief mktg. officer, dir. planning and client svcs. Volkswagen, Am. Legacy Found., Talbots, Royal Caribbean, Titleist, FootJoy, The Hartford, Citizens Fin. Arnold Comm., 1994—; pres., COO Arnold Worldwide, Boston. Spkr. in field. Author (with Heather Kelly): What They Really Teach You at the Harvard Business School. Mem.: Essex County Club, Harvard Club Boston, Boston Ad Club (past pres.). Avocations: golf, paddle tennis, travel, reading, coaching youth sports. Office: Arnold Worldwide 101 Huntington Ave Boston MA 02199-7603

KELLY, GARY C., air transportation executive; m. Carol Kelly; children: Caroline, Elizabeth. BBA in Acctg., U. Tex., 1977. CPA, Tex. Audit mgr. Arthur Young & Co., Dallas; controller Sys. Ctr. Inc., Irving, Tex., Southwest Airlines Co., Dallas, 1986-89, CFO, 1989—2004, v.p. fin., 1989—2001, exec. v.p., 2001—04, vice chmn., CEO, 2004—. Office: Southwest Airlines Co 2702 Love Field Dr Dallas TX 75235*

KELLY, GEOFFREY J., lawyer, beverage company executive; JD, U. Sydney. Mem. legal dept. Coca-Cola Export Corp.; mgr. legal dept. Australasia area The Coca-Cola Co., Sydney, 1970, sr. counsel internat. ops., 2000, chief dep. gen. counsel Atlanta, 2003—05, sr. v.p., 2004—, gen. counsel, 2005—. Bd. mem., mem. Audit, Fin. and Compliance Com. Coca-Cola Amatil Ltd. Office: Coca-Cola Co PO Box 1734 Atlanta GA 30301*

KELLY, GERALD WAYNE, chemical coatings company executive; b. Charleston, W.Va., May 21, 1944; s. Wayne Woodside (dec.) and Sarrah (Myers) K.; m. (div.); children: Scott Wayne, Lauren Melissa (dec.); m. Elizabeth Long, Nov. 18, 1983. BS, W.Va. U., Morgantown, 1966. From sales corr. to regional mgr. duPont Corp., various locations, 1966-83; bus. mgr. Decatur (Ala.) divsn. Whittaker Corp., 1983-85; v.p. Decatur divsn. Morton Internat., 1985-86, pres. Decatur divsn., 1986-93; v.p. Morton Indsl. Coatings, Morton Internat., Chgo., 1993-99; pres./owner IRP Inc., Falkville, Ala., 1992-99; exec. v.p. D & K Group, Inc., Elk Grove Village, Ill., 2001—02; CEO D & K Laminex, Inc., Charlotte, NC, 2001—02; COO GW Resources, Murrells Inlet, SC; pres. TKO Resources, Murrells Inlet, SC; co-founder Mid Town Techs., Inc., Atlanta, 2006. Bd. dirs. Ind. Cystic Fibrosis Found., Indpls., 1971-73, Peninsula Polymers, Inc., 2002-05. Mem. Nat. Coil Coaters Assn., Nat. Paint and Coatings Assn., Beta Theta Pi. Republican. Methodist. Avocation: automobiles. Home: PO Box 2990 Murrells Inlet SC 29576 Office: GW Resources Inc PO Box 2540 Murrells Inlet SC 29576 Address: TKO Resources Inc PO Box 2990 Murrells Inlet SC 29576 Office: Mid Town Techs Inc Ste 1104 50 Biscayne Dr Atlanta GA 30309 Office Phone: 843-446-6457.

KELLY, GRACE DENTINO, secondary school educator; b. Peoria, Ill., Mar. 30, 1934; d. Michael and Arnita Balagna (Barto) Dentino; m. Robert N. Kelly, Aug. 31, 1957; children: Susan, James, Stephen, Patrick. Cert. med. tech., St. Francis Sch. Med. Tech., Peoria, Ill., 1955; BS, Bradley U., Peoria, Ill., 1971, MS, 1973. Tchr. sci. St. Mark Sch., Peoria, asst. prin., 1980-83, prin., 1992-98; prin., chmn. jr. HS curriculum com. for drug edn. St. Thomas Sch., Peoria Heights, Ill., 1983-89; tchr. biology and chemistry Woodruff HS, Peoria, 1989-90; prin. Blessed Sacrament Sch., Morton, Ill., 1991-92, Trewyn Mid. Sch., Peoria, 1998—2002, mem. math. curriculum com.; lead tchr. Glen Oak Primary Sch., Peoria, 2002—06; ret. Presenter Ill. Math Tchr. Conv., Peoria, 1992; tchr. Aurora U., Ill.; edn. cons. Two Rivers Profl. Devel. Ctr., 2002—; with Lakeview Mus. Mem. adv. bd. Peoria Jour. Star Newspaper, 1973-80. Bd. dirs. Spl. People Encounter Christ, 1997. Recipient Econs. Educator award Joint Coun. on Econ. Edn., NYC, 1982—, dedication to excellence in edn. and to justice and equality award NOW, 1998, Esmark Found. award Ill. Coun. Econ. Edn., 1984, Those Who Excell award Ill. State Bd., 1989, PARC award, 1989, Today's Cath. Tchr.'s Project: Sharing award, 1992, Adminstr. of Yr. award Today's Cath. Tchr. Mag., 1992, Jean Tucker award Ill. Valley Mental Health Assn., 1994, Positive Promotions 1st prize Midwest Exceptional Tchr. award, 2005; named Tchr. Who Makes a Difference, Positive Promotions, 2004, 06; grantee Nat. City Bank, 2003-06. Mem. AAUW (Outstanding Cmty. Svc. award, Justice Edn. award 1998), Nat. Sci. Tchrs. Assn., Am. Soc. Clin. Pathologists, Ill. Sci. Tchrs. Assn. (dir. region III, presenter papers), Ill. Jr. Acad. Sci. (dir. region I), Peoria Area Ret. Tchrs., Italian Am. Soc., Phi Delta Kappa. Roman Catholic. Home: 1815 W High St Peoria IL 61606-1635

KELLY, HENRY ANSGAR, language educator; b. Fonda, Iowa, June 6, 1934; s. Harry Francis and Inez Ingeborg (Anderson) K.; m. Marea Tancred, June 18, 1968; children— Sarah Marea, Dominic Tancred. AB, St. Louis U., 1959, A.M., Ph.L., St. Louis U., 1961; PhD, Harvard U., 1965. From asst. prof. English to prof. emeritus U. Calif., LA, 1967—2004, prof. emeritus, 2004—, dir. Ctr. for Medieval and Renaissance Studies, 1998—2003. Author: The Devil, Demonology and Witchcraft, 1968, 74, Divine Providence in the England of Shakespeare's Histories, 1970, Love and Marriage in the Age of Chaucer, 1975, The Matrimonial Trials of Henry VIII, 1976, Canon Law and the Archpriest of Hita, 1984, The Devil at Baptism, 1985, Chaucer and the Cult of St. Valentine, 1986, Tragedy and Comedy from Dante to Pseudo-Dante, 1989, Ideas and Forms of Tragedy from Aristotle to the Middle Ages, 1993, Chaucerian Tragedy, 1997, Inquisitions and Other Trial Procedures in the Medieval West, 2001, Satan: A Biography, 2006; co-editor Viator 1970-90, editor, 2003—. Jr. fellow Harvard Soc. of Fellows, 1964—67. Fellow Guggenheim fellow, 1971—72, Nat. Endowment Humanities, 1980—81, 1996—97. Fellow Medieval Acad. Am.; mem. Medieval Assn. of Pacific (pres. 1988-90). Roman Catholic. Home: 1123 Kagawa St Pacific Palisades CA 90272-3838 Office: UCLA Dept English 405 Hilgard Ave Los Angeles CA 90095-9000 Office Phone: 310-825-7486. E-mail: kelly@humnet.ucla.edu.

KELLY, HUGH RICE, lawyer, retired energy executive; b. Austin, Tex., Dec. 16, 1942; s. Thomas Philip and Cecilia Elizabeth (Rice) Kelly; m. Marguerite Susan McIntosh, Dec. 27, 1971; children: Susan McIntosh, Cecilia Rice. BA, Rice U., 1965; JD, U. Tex., 1972. Bar: Tex. 1972, U.S. Dist. Ct. (so. dist.) Tex. 1974, U.S. Ct. Appeals (5th cir.) 1975, U.S. Supreme Ct. 1975. Assoc. Baker Botts, Houston, 1972-78, ptnr., 1979-84; exec. v.p., gen. counsel Reliant Energy (formerly Houston Lighting & Power Co.), Houston, 1984—2003; gen. counsel Texans for Lawsuit Reform, 2003—. 1st lt. US Army, 1966—69. Fellow: ABA Found., Houston Bar Found., Tex. Bar Found.; mem.: ABA, Am. Law Inst., Houston Bar Assn., State Bar Tex., Coronado Club. Republican. Home and Office: 1936 Rice Blvd Houston TX 77005-1635 E-mail: hkelly00@gmail.com.

KELLY, J. MICHAEL, lawyer; b. Hattiesburg, Miss., Dec. 5, 1943; BA, Emory U., 1966; LLB, U. Va., 1969. Bar: Ga. 1969, U.S. Supreme Ct. 1978, D.C. 1980, Utah 1982, Calif. 1988. Law clerk to Judge Griffin B. Bell (5th cir.) US Ct. Appeals, Atlanta, 1969-70; ptnr. Alston & Bird (formerly Alston, Miller & Gaines), Atlanta, 1970-77, 81-82; counselor to atty. gen. US Dept. Justice, Washington, 1977-79; counselor to sec. US Dept. Energy, Washington, 1979-81; ptnr., shareholder, dir. Ray, Quinney & Nebeker, Salt Lake City, 1982-87; ptnr. Cooley Godward Kronish LLP, San Francisco, 1987—. Mem. Omicron Delta Kappa, Phi Alpha Delta. Democrat. Office: Cooley Godward Kronish LLP 101 California St 5th Fl San Francisco CA 94111-5800 Home Phone: 415-999-4446; Office Phone: 415-693-2076. Business E-Mail: kellyjm@cooley.com.

KELLY, JAMES, editor; b. Bklyn., Dec. 15, 1953; m. Lisa Henricksson; 1 child, Luke. Grad. in Pub. and Internat. Affairs, Princeton Univ., 1977. Worked on Bill Bradley senatorial campaign, NJ, 1977; joined Time Mag., NYC, 1978, dep. mng. editor, 1996—2001, mng. editor, 2001—06, Time Inc., 2006—. Bd. visitors Columbia U. Grad. Sch. Journalism. Office: Time Inc Time Life Bldg 1271 Avenue of the Americas New York NY 10020-1300*

KELLY, JAMES ANDREW, former federal agency administrator, policy research executive; b. Fond du Lac, Wis., Sept. 15, 1936; s. James Daniel and Clarice K.; m. Audrey Pool, July 30, 1960; children— James, Archer BS, U.S. Naval Acad., 1959; MBA, Harvard U., 1968; postgrad., Nat. War Coll., 1977. Commd. ensign US Navy, 1959, advanced through grades to capt.; comptroller US Pacific Fleet, Pearl Harbor, Hawaii, 1979-82, ret., 1982; dep. asst. sec. Dept. Def., Washington, 1983-86; spl. asst. to pres., sr. dir. Asian affairs NSC, 1986-89; pres. EAP Assocs. Inc., Honolulu, 1989-94, Pacific Forum/CSIS, Honolulu, 1994—2001; asst. sec. ea. Asian Pacific affairs US Dept. State, Washington, 2001—05.

KELLY, JAMES ANTHONY, priest; b. Worcester, Mass., Apr. 22, 1949; s. James and Elisabeth (Allen) K. BA in Philosophy and Govt., Harvard Coll., 1971; PhD in Philosophy, CUNY, 1979; postgrad., Pontifical U. of Holy Cross, Rome. ordained priest Roman Cath. Ch., 1982. Dir. Riverside Study Ctr., NYC, 1977-79; procurator Prelature of Opus Dei, Rome, 1984-88, vicar USA region New Rochelle, NY, 1988-98; work with vicar of Opus Dei, 1998—2002; work with Del. Vicar of Opus Dei in Calif., 2002—. Avocations: philosophy, jazz, literature. Home and Office: 765 14th Ave San Francisco CA 94118-3558 Office Phone: 415-386-0431. Business E-Mail: jakelly@prkvw.com.

KELLY, JAMES M., astronaut, military officer; b. Burlington, Iowa, May 14, 1964; s. William and Mary Ann Kelly; m. Dawn Renee Timmerman; 4 children. BS in Astronautical Engring. (with honors), USAF Acad., Colo. Springs, Colo., 1986; MS in Aerospace Engring., U. Ala., Moontgomery, 1996; Disting. grad., Undergraduate Pilot Tng. Euro-NATO Joint Jet Pilot Tng., Sheppard AFB, Wichita Falls, Tex.; Top-Gun at 426th F-15 replacement tng. unit for initial F-15 Eagle tng., Luke AFB, Phoenix, Ariz. Commd. 2d lt. USAF, Colo. Springs, 1986, advanced through grades to lt. col., fighter pilot F-15, 67th Fighter Squadron, 18th Fighter Wing Kadena Air Base, Okinawa, Japan, 1987—92, instr., mission commdr. Otis Air Nat. Guard Base, Cape Cod, Mass., 1992—93; student Test Pilot Sch., Edwards (Calif.) AFB, 1993—94; project test pilot, asst. ops. officer USAF Nellis AFB, Las Vegas, Nev., 1994—96; astronaut Johnson Space Ctr., Houston, 1996—, pilot space shuttle flight crew. Recipient Meritorious Svc. medal, Air Force Commendation medals (2), Outstanding Unit awards (2), Combat Readiness medals (2). Mem.: USAF Acad. Assn. Grads. 2,500 flight hours in 35 different aircrafts; over 370 hours in space; pilot on STS-102 (Discovery), March, 2001; pilot on STS-114(Discovery) Return to Flight mission in which the crew will test and evaluate new procedures for flight safety and shuttle inspection and repair techniques in July, 2005. Office: Astronauts Office Johnson Space Ctr Houston TX 77058

KELLY, JAMES MICHAEL, plant and soil scientist; b. Knoxville, Feb. 2, 1944; s. Woodrow Wilson and Thelma Lucille (Miller) K.; m. Susan Kay Morris, Aug. 9, 1969; children: John Kip, Christopher Kenneth. BS, E. Tenn. State U., 1966; MS, U. Tenn., 1968, PhD, 1973. Cert. profl. soil scientist. Assoc. ecologist NUS Corp., Pitts., 1973-74; rsch. assoc. Forestry Dept. Purdue U., West Lafayette, Ind., 1975-76; program mgr. Tenn. Valley Authority, Oak Ridge, 1977-88, sr. rschr., 1990-94; sr. tech. specialist, team leader, 1994-95; prof., chair dept. forestry Iowa State U., Ames, 1995—2001, chair dept. natural resource ecology and mgmt., 2002—04; dean Coll. Natural Resources Va. Tech. U., Blacksburg, 2004—. Vis. prof. agronomy Purdue U., 1988-89; adj. prof. U. Tenn., Knoxville, 1980-95, forestry dept. Purdue U., 1985-95. Author: Carbon Forms and Functions in Forest Soils, 1995; assoc. editor Soil Sci. Soc. Am. Jour., 1989-95, Forest Sci., 1998-01; editl. bd. Forest Ecology and Management, 2001-05; contbr. more than 100 articles to profl. jours. Head referee Ayso Youth Soccer, Oak Ridge, 1985-88; troop com. Boy Scouts Am., Oak Ridge, 1989-95. Oak Ridge Assoc. Univ. fellow, 1970-72; Elec. Power Rsch. Inst. grantee, 1978, 82, 89, 91, 95, NSF grantee, 1995; recipient Rsch. Champion award Elec. Power Rsch. Inst., 2002. Fellow Soil Sci. Soc. Am. (chmn. divsn. S7 1986-87, bd. dirs. 1988-89, awards com. 1992-93, fellows com. 1997-99, profl. svc. com. 2000-02); mem. AAAS, Ecol. Soc. Am., Soc. Am. Foresters, Exptl. Aircraft Assn. (chpt. pres. 1991-93), Trees Forever (bd. dirs. 1995-05), Sigma Xi, Gamma Sigma Delta, Xi Sigma Pi. Achievements include research and application of environmental science. Office: Va Tech Univ Coll Natural Resources Blacksburg VA 24061 Office Phone: 540-231-3479. Business E-Mail: jmkelly@vt.edu.

KELLY, JAMES PATRICK, lawyer; b. Twin Falls, Idaho, Mar. 25, 1946; s. James Patrick Sr. and Ynes Mary (Alastra) K.; m. Carol Louise White, June 6, 1968; children: Mary Louise, Christopher John. AB, Harvard U., 1968, JD, 1975. Bar: Ga. 1975, U.S. Dist. Ct. (no. and so. dists.) Ga. 1976, U.S. Ct. Appeals (5th cir. 1976, 6th cir. 1996, 1st cir. 1997, 11th cir.), U.S. Supreme Ct. 1999. Assoc. Kilpatrick & Cody, Atlanta, 1975-80; ptnr. Morris & Manning, Atlanta, 1980-83, Smith, Gambrell & Russell, Atlanta, 1983-85, Asbill, Porter & Churchill, Atlanta, 1985-86; sr. ptnr. Kelly Law Firm, P.C., Atlanta, 1986—. Bd. dirs. Sr. Citizen Services of Met. Atlanta, 1980-83. Served to capt. U.S. Army, 1968-72. Named Ga. Super Lawyer, 2005, 2006; named one of Best Lawyers in America, 2007. Mem. ABA (corp. and banking law sect., health law forum), Ga. Bar Assn., Atlanta Bar Assn., Ga. Acad. Healthcare Attys. (bd. dirs. 1987-89), Am. Health Lawyers Assn. (bd. dirs. 1993-99, arbitrator, mediator 2005-, fellow 2005-), Internat. Network Boutique Law Firms, Lawyers Club Atlanta, Harvard Alumni Assn. (bd. dirs. 1983-84), Harvard Law Sch. Assn. Ga. (v.p. 1988-89, pres. 1989-91), Cochise Club, Harvard Club (pres. 1982-83, bd. dirs. 1990—), Harvard Club Ga. (pres. 1980-81), Bar Register Pre-Eminent Lawyers, Georgian Club, Capital City Club, Kiwanis (pres.). Episcopalian. Avocations: public speaking, marathon running, travel, horseback riding. Office: 200 Galleria Pky NW Ste 1510 Atlanta GA 30339-5946

KELLY, JAMES PATRICK, JR., retired engineering executive; b. Bklyn., July 19, 1933; s. James Patrick and Marion Rita (Gleason) Kelly; children: Kathryn, Mark, Lisa Angelique, Trevor, Lisa, James(dec.). BSEngring., U.S. Naval Acad., 1955; postgrad., U. Houston, 1968-69. Registered profl. engr., Calif. Asst. site mgr. Pathfinder reactor Allis Chalmers Mfg. Co., Sioux Falls, SD, 1963-67; nuclear project mgr. Brown & Root, Houston, 1967-69; from constrn. project mgr. to asst. v.p. Gibbs & Hill, Omaha, NYC, 1969-75; pres. Dravo Lime Co., Pitts., 1975-77; group v.p. natural resources Dravo Corp., Pitts., 1976-81, sr. v.p. engring. and constrn., domestic and internat., 1982-84; pres., dir. C.F. Braun & Co., Alhambra, Calif., 1984-86; pres., CEO Hadson Power Sys., Inc., Irvine, Calif., 1986-91; ret., 1991. Bd. dirs. Hadson Corp., 1986—91. Mem. Sioux Falls Bd. Edn., 1965—66, Assn. Retarded Citizens Pitts., 1970—; pres. found. bd. dirs. Calif. State U., LA, 1985—95; pres. Santa Ana Com. Ednl. and Recreational Redevel. Plan, 1992—93; mem. Devel. Disabilities Area Bd., 1995—98; foreman Orange County Grand Jury, 1997—98; bd. dirs. S.D. Mental Health Assn., 1966—67, Western Pa. Sch. Blind Children, 1978—84. Mem.: NSPE, Sierra Club, Mensa. Home: 1413 Franzen Ave Santa Ana CA 92705-6926 Personal E-mail: JPK159@webtv.net.

KELLY, JANET, science educator; b. Shattuck, Okla., Aug. 15, 1949; d. Frank and Audrey Smith; children: Gregory Brant Halm, Ryan Jeffrey. BA, Houston Bapt. U., 1969; MAT, Tex. Christian U., Ft. Worth, 1975; PhD, U. North Tex., Denton, 1993. Asst. prof. U. Tex., Arlington, 1993—94; assoc. prof. sci. edn., dir. Inst. Math., Sci. and Tech. Edn. Tex. Christian U., Fort Worth, 2001—06. Contbr. articles to profl. publs. including Internat. Jour. Sci. Edn., Jour. Thought, Teaching Children Mathematics. Vol. Ft. Worth Clean City, 2002—05. Recipient Mortar Bd. Preferred Prof. award, Tex. Christian U., 1997, 1999, 2003, Dean's Tchg. award, 2004; grantee Inst. Math., Sci. and Tech. grantee, Sid Richardson Found., 2004, 2005—06, 2001—03, Lockheed Martin, 2004, Coppell Ind. Sch. Dist., 2004—05; Meadows Scholar, U. North Tex., 1991—93, Inst. Math., Sci. and Tech. grantee, Sid Richardson Found., 1999—2001. Office: Texas Christian U Box 297900 Fort Worth TX 76129 Office Phone: 817-257-6793. Business E-Mail: j.kelly2@tcu.edu.

KELLY, JANET LANGFORD, oil industry executive, lawyer; b. Kansas City, Mo., Nov. 27, 1957; BA, Grinnell Coll., 1979; JD, Yale U., 1983. Bar: NY 1985, Ill. 1989, Mich. 2004. Law clk. to Hon. James J. Hunter III US Ct. Appeals (3rd cir.), 1983-84; ptnr. Sidley & Austin LLP, Chgo., 1984-89; sr. v.p., sec., gen. counsel Sara Lee Corp., Chgo., 1995-99; exec. v.p. corp. devel., gen. counsel, sec. Kellogg Co., Battle Creek, Mich., 1999—2001, exec. v.p. corp. devel. & adminstrn., gen. counsel, sec., 2001—06; dep. gen. counsel ConocoPhillips Co., Houston, 2006—07, sr. v.p. legal, gen. counsel, sec., 2007—. Sr. editor Yale Law Jour., 1983. Bd. dirs. Am. Arbitration Assn., Constl. Rights Found.; mem. adv. bd. Chgo. Vol. Legal Svcs. Found. Mem.: ABA. Office: ConocoPhillips Co 600 N Dairy Ashford Rd Houston TX 77079 Office Phone: 281-293-1000. E-mail: janet.l.kelly@conocophillips.com.*

KELLY, JEFFREY D., bank executive; b. Aug. 13, 1953; BS in bus. adminstrn., Ohio State U., 1977; MS in econ., U. Akron, 1979. Mgmt. asst., bank investment divsn. Nat. City Corp., sr. v.p., 1990—94, exec. v.p., chief funds mgmt. officer, 1994—97, chmn. asset-liability com., 1997—2000; chmn. Nat. City Mortgage Co., 1997—2000, Nat. City Equity Ptnrs., 1998—2000; CFO, exec. v.p. Nat. City Corp., Cleve., 2000—04, vice-chmn., CFO, 2004—. Bd. dirs. Progressive Ins. Corp., 2000—; adv. bd. FTVentures. Sec., trustee Great Lakes Sci. Ctr.; bd. trustees Cuyahoga Cmty. Coll.; mem. Fin. Svcs. Roundtable. Office: Nat City Corp 1900 E 9th St Cleveland OH 44114-3484 Office Phone: 216-575-2000, 800-738-3888. Office Fax: 216-575-2353.*

KELLY, JEFFREY W., chemist, educator; BS in Chemistry, SUNY, Fredonia, 1982; PhD in Organic Chemistry, U. NC, Chapel Hill, 1986. Postdoctoral rschr. biochemistry Rockefeller U., 1987—89; asst. prof. chemistry Tex. A&M U., 1989—95, assoc. prof., 1995—97; Lita Annenberg Hazen prof. chemistry Scripps Rsch. Inst., 1997—. Vis. investigator Meml. Sloan-Kettering Inst., 1996; cons. Parke Davis, 1996—2001, Praecis Pharms., 1996—2000, Hoffman-LaRoche Allergy and Inflammation, 1996—97; dean grad. studies Scripps Rsch. Inst., 2001—, v.p. academic affairs, 2001—; mem. sci. adv. bd. Hereditary Disease Found., 2001—06, Celiac Sprue Rsch. Found., 2002—, Provid Pharms. Inc., 2002—; mem. external adv. com. Vanderbilt Inst. Chem. Biology, 2002—; co-founder FoldRx Pharms., Boston, 2003. Contbr. articles to sci. jours.; mem. editl. bd.: Jour. Amyloidosis, 1994—, mem. editl. adv. bd.: Protein Sci., 1999—, mem. editl. bd. and adv. bd.: Biopolymers, 2001—, bd.

mem.: Internat. Jour. Peptide Rsch. and Therapeutics, 2004—, mem. bd. consulting editors: Bioorganic and Medicinal Chemistry, 2004—. Recipient Searle Scholar award, 1991—94, Camille Dreyfus Tchr.-Scholar award, 1994, Nat. Lectr. award, Biophysical Soc., 1999, Young Investigator award, Protein Soc.-Dupont, 1999, Arthur C. Cope Scholar award, Am. Chem. Soc., 2001; grantee Rohm and Haas Organic Divsn. fellowship, 1985—86. Mem.: Protein Soc. (pres. 2005—). Office: Dept Chemistry Scripps Rsch Inst 10550 N Torrey Pines Rd La Jolla CA 92037 E-mail: jkelly@scripps.edu.

KELLY, JERRY BOB, social services administrator; b. Chgo., Feb. 6, 1942; s. Robert Lee and Mildred Florence (Griffin) Kelly; m. Diana Joyce Wilburn, Nov. 29, 1969; children: Jerold Robert, Joycelyn Reneé. BS in Acctg., Roosevelt U., Chgo., 1968. Lic. real estate salesman, Ill., life ins. prodr., Ill. Acct. Weather Bloc Mfg. Co., Chgo., 1967—68; programmer Morton Salt Co., Chgo., 1968—69; br. mgr. Chgo. Econ. Devel. Corp., 1970—77; ptnr. Smith Distbrs., 1977—79; mgr. fin. and adminstrn. Suburban Cook County Area Agy. on Aging, Chgo., 1979—85; exec. dir. Lawndale Bus. and Local Devel. Corp., Chgo., 1985—88; dir. No. Cook County Pvt. Industry Coun., Chgo., 1988—89; contr. Howard Area Cmty. Ctr., Chgo., 1989—99. Bd. dirs. Northside Cmty. Fed. Credit Union; treas. Day Care Crisis Coun. Met. Chgo., 1973—76; 1st v.p. West Side Health Planning Orgn., 1974—76; treas. Met. Chgo. chpt. Nat. Caucus and Ctr. on Black Aged, 1992—94; treas. bd. dirs. St. Leonard's House; Cook County State's atty. African-Am. Adv. Coun., 1995—; vol. Ill. CPA Soc.; treas. North Lawndale Small Grants Human Devel. Corp.; mem. adv. coun. John Marshall Metro H.S. Acad. Fin. With AUS, 1964—67. Recipient Appreciation award, Day Care Crisis Coun. Met. Chgo., West Side Health Planning Orgn., Chgo. Black Caucus, Am. Fedn. Tchrs., Chgo. Bd. Election Commrs., Comprehensive Health Planning Orgn. Chgo. Mem.: Assn. Photographers Internat. (fin. officer Milton Lee Olive post), Am. Legion, John Marshall H.S. Alumni Assn. (pres.), Elks (2d v.p. Ill.-Wis., past grand exalted ruler). Baptist. Achievements include research in redevelopment plan East Garfield. Home: 1415 N Mayfield Ave Chicago IL 60651-1015 Office Phone: 773-622-1073. Personal E-mail: jbk59@aol.com. *Personal philosophy: The things that have helped me most in my life is believing in myself, trusting in God and the strength of the Griffin Family.*

KELLY, JIM (JAMES EDWARD KELLY), former professional football player; b. Pitts., Feb. 14, 1960; B in Bus. Mgmt., U. Miami, Fla., 1982. With Houston Gamblers USFL, 1984-85, Buffalo Bills, 1986—97; founder & pres. Kelly Enterprise, Inc. Named Sporting News U.S. Football League Rookie of Yr., 1984, mem. All-Star team, 1985, Pro-Bowl team, 1987, 88, 90, 91, 92; named to Quarterback of NFL All-Pro Team, Sporting News, 1991; played in Super Bowl XXV, 1990, XXVI, 1991, XXVII, 1992, XXVIII, 1993; named to Pro Football Hall of Fame, 2002 Office: Kelly Enterprise 1961 Whirle Dr Ste 5 Buffalo NY 14221

KELLY, JOHN E., III, information technology executive; BS in Physics, Union Coll., 1976; MS in Physics, Rensselaer Poly. Inst., 1978, PhD in Materials Engrng., 1980; DSc (hon.), Union Coll., 2004. Numerous mgmt. and tech. positions IBM, 1980—90, dir. semiconductor rsch. and devel. ctr., 1990—94, v.p. bus. process reengring. divsn. microelectronics, 1994—95, v.p. sys., tech. and sci., divsn. rsch., 1995—96, v.p. strategy, tech. and ops., divsn. microelectronics, 1996—97, v.p. server devel., 1997—99, gen. mgr. divsn. microelectronics, 1999—2000, sr. v.p., group exec. tech. group, 2000—04, sr. v.p. tech. & intellectual property, 2004—. Trustee Union Coll. Fellow: IEEE; mem.: Semiconductor Industry Assn. (bd. dirs., former chmn.). Office: IBM Corp New Orchard Rd Armonk NY 10504*

KELLY, JOHN FLEMING, lawyer; b. Denver, Mar. 13, 1926; s. Charles James and Marjorie (Fleming) Kelly; children: Maureen Kelly Barker, Johanna Elizabeth, Alinka Flaminia, John Fleming Jr. BA, Yale U., New Haven, Conn., 1947, LLB, 1950. Bar: Colo. 1950, US Supreme Ct. 1957. Assoc. Holland & Hart, Denver, 1950—54, ptnr., 1954—89; pvt. practice, 1989—2006; sr. cons. Internat. Inst. for Conflict Prevention and Resolution (CPR), 1995—. Legal counsel, dir., mem. exec. com. Colo. Assn. Commerce and Industry, 1965—97; gen. counsel U. Corp. Atmospheric Rsch., Boulder, Colo., 1974—84, spl. counsel, 1984—89; mem. Denver panel dispute resolution CPP Inst., 1988—95, 2005—. Bd. dirs. Boys' Clubs Denver, 1961—71, treas., 1961—66; bd. dirs. Regional Transp. Dist. Colo., 1969—81, chmn., 1969—74, mem. exec. com., 1969—79; chmn. Gov.'s Spl. Com. Schs., 1970—71; trustee Kent Sch., Denver, 1971—74; pres. Ctrl. City Opera House Assn., 1972—74, chmn. bd. dirs., 1974—76, hon. dir., 1976—; chmn. Found. Denver Performing Arts Complex, Denver, 1988—94. With USNR, 1943—46, with USNR, 1952—53. Named Colo. Bus. Leader, Colo. Assn. Commerce and Industry, 1984; recipient Yale medal for Oustanding Svc., 1985, cert. appreciation, Denver City Coun., 1991, dedication of lobby, Buell Theatre, 1991. Mem.: ABA, Denver Bar Assn., Colo. Bar Assn. (bd. govs. 1961—65, v.p. 1964—65), Assn. Yale Alumni (bd. govs. 1977—82, vice chmn. 1978—80, chmn. 1980—82), University Club. Republican. Roman Catholic. Home and Office: 1818 Marion St Apt 301 Denver CO 80218 Office Phone: 303-832-2085.

KELLY, JOHN HUBERT, diplomat; b. Fond du Lac, Wis., July 20, 1939; s. James Daniel and Clarice L. Kelly; m. Helena Marita Ajo; children: David Snowdon, Maria Louise. BA, Emory U., 1961; advanced studies cert., Georgetown U., 1982. Vice consul Am. Consulate, Adana, Turkey, 1965-66; 3rd sec. Am. Embassy, Ankara, Turkey, 1966-67, 2nd sec. Bangkok, 1968-69; consul Am. Consulate, Songkhla, Thailand, 1969-71; 1st sec. Am. Embassy, Paris, 1976-80; fgn. svc. U.S. Dept. of State, Washington, 1972-76, dep. exec. sec., 1980-81, dep. asst. sec. of state, 1982-85, asst. sec. state for Near East and South Asia, 1989-91; U.S. amb. Am. Embassy, Beirut, 1986-88, amb. Helsinki, Finland, 1991-94; pres. John Kelly Cons., Conyers, 1994—; mng. dir. Internat. Equity Ptnrs., Atlanta, 1995-98. Mem. adv. coun. Una Chapman Cox Found., 1982-86; trustee Lebanese Am. U., 1996-2005. Mem. Coun. on Fgn. Rels., Mid. East Inst. Office: John Kelly Cons 2440 Wall St Ste D Conyers GA 30013-6341

KELLY, JOHN JAMES, lawyer; b. Rockville Centre, NY, July 4, 1949; s. John James Sr. and Eleanor Grace (Vann) K.; m. Clara Sarah Gussin; 1 child, John James III. AB in Govt., Georgetown U., 1971, JD, 1975. Bar: Pa. 1976, D.C. 1979, U.S. Dist. Ct. D.C. 1980, U.S. Claims Ct. 1982, U.S. Ct. Appeals (D.C. cir.) 1980, U.S. Ct. Appeals (fed. cir.) 1982. Law clk. to judge U.S. Dist. Ct., Washington, 1975-77; assoc. Corcoran, Youngman & Rowe, Washington, 1977-80, Capell, Howard, Knabe & Cobbs, Washington, 1980-83, Loomis, Owen, Fellman & Howe, Washington, 1983-86, ptnr., 1986-90; v.p., sec., gen. coun. Electronic Industries Alliance, Arlington, Va., 1990-96, exec. v.p., gen. counsel, 1997—2005, mem. exec. bd., bd. govs., 2005—; pres. JEDEC Solid State Tech. Assn., 2000—; counsel Howe, Anderson & Steyer, Washington, 1990—. Mem. Jud. Conf., D.C. Cir., Washington, 1983, Jud. Conf. Fed. Cir., Washington, 1988—. Contbr. articles to legal and profl. publs. Mem. ABA, D.C. Bar, Pa. Bar Assn., Am. Soc. Assn. Execs. (bd. dirs. legal section 1989-94, chmn. 1992-93), Fed. Bar Assn., Met. Club. Democrat. Roman Catholic. Office: JEDEC Solid State Tech Assn 2500 Wilson Blvd Arlington VA 22201-3834 Business E-Mail: johnk@jedec.org.

KELLY, JOHN JOSEPH, JR., federal official; b. Paterson, NJ, Dec. 28, 1940; s. John Joseph Sr. and Helen C. (Ebersach) K.; m. Brenda Ruth Miller, July 1, 1966; children: Elizabeth Ann, Kathleen Anne, John J. BS in Chemistry, Seton Hall, 1963; MS, Pa. State U., 1969; MPA, Auburn U., 1976. Commd. 2d lt. USAF, 1963, advanced through grades to brig. gen., 1976—78, dir. spl. projects, HQ Scott AFB, Ill., 1978-80; comdr. 15 WEA Squadron USAF, McGuire AFB, NJ, 1980-81; dep. dir. programs/policy Air Force info. systems USAF, Washington, 1981-84; vice comdr. 7th Weather Wing Scott AFB, 1984-85; comdr. 5th Weather Wing Langley AFB, Va., 1985-88; comdr. Air Weather Svc. Scott AFB, 1988-91; dir. weather AF/XOW Washington, 1991-94; dir. Nat. Weather Svc., 1998—2003; dep. under sec. oceans and atmosphere Dept. Commerce/NOAA, 2003—. Cons. Dept. Commerce, 1991. Decorated DSM, Legion of Merit, Bronze Star. Fellow Am. Meteorol. Soc., Air Force Assn., Nat. Weather Assn. Roman Catholic. Avocations: golf, reading. Office: Dept of Commerce 14th and Constitution NW Rm 6811 Washington DC 20230 Office Phone: 202-482-3565. Business E-Mail: jack.kelly@noaa.gov.

KELLY, JOHN MARTIN, lawyer; b. Oshkosh, Wis., Dec. 13, 1948; s. Martin Paul and Ivy Cecile (James) Kelly; m. Teresa Jean Wendland, July 24, 1982. BA, U. Wis., Madison, 1971; JD, Georgetown U., 1974; postgrad. in bus., Harvard Bus. Sch., 1976-77. Bar: Wis. 1974, D.C. 1975. Atty. office chief counsel IRS, Washington, 1974—76; assoc. Dempsey, Magnusem, Williamson & Lampe, Oshkosh, 1977—82; ptnr. Dempsey, Williamson, Kelly & Hertel, LLP, Oshkosh, 1983—. Mem. ABA, Wis. Bar Assn., D.C. Bar Assn., Winnebago County Bar Assn. Office: Dempsey Williamson Kelly & Hertel LLP 1 Pearl Ave Oshkosh WI 54903-0886 Business E-Mail: jmkelly@dempseylaw.com.

KELLY, JOHN PATRICK, lawyer; b. Boston, May 9, 1952; s. Patrick and Elizabeth (Glennon) K.; m. Eileen Linda Obuchowski, May 28, 1983; children: John Patrick, Laura Beth, Kevin Sean. AB, Coll. Holy Cross, 1974; JD, Vanderbilt U., 1978. Bar: Mass. 1978, Fla. 1979, US Dist. Ct. (so. dist.) Fla. 1980, US Supreme Ct. 1981; cert. trial lawyer, Fla., bus. litig. specialist, Fla. Law clk. to presiding justice Tenn. Supreme Ct., Nashville, 1978—79; assoc. Fleming, O'Bryan & Fleming, Ft. Lauderdale, Fla., 1979—84, ptnr., 1984—96, Gunster, Yoakley, Valdes-Fauli & Stewart, Ft. Lauderdale, 1996—2000, Lorusso Loud & Kelly LLP, Ft. Lauderdale, 2000—05, The Kelly Law Firm, Ft. Lauderdale, 2005—. Lectr. Ctr. for Internat. Legal Studies, Kitzbuhel, Austria, 1999. Co-author Florida Business Litigation Manual, 1989-2000. Mem. Fla. Bar Assn. (civil rules com., lectr. Continuing Legal Edn. 1988-2000, prof. edn. seminars 1991-2000), Am. Arbitration Assn. (arbitrator), Nat. Futures Assn. (arbitrator), Tower Club, St. Thomas More Soc., Nat. Bd. Trial Advocacy, Phi Beta Kappa. Roman Catholic. Avocations: skiing, scuba diving, photography. Office: Kelly Law Firm 2400 E Commercial Blvd Ste 211 Fort Lauderdale FL 33308 Office Phone: 954-568-5555. Business E-Mail: jkelly@businesslitigation.com.

KELLY, JOHN WILLIAM, JR., academic administrator; b. Greenville, SC, Jan. 5, 1955; s. John William and Betty (Kelly) K.; children: Christopher, Kimberly. BS, Clemson U., 1977; MS, Ohio State U., 1979, PhD, 1982. Asst. prof. Tex. A&M U., 1982-85, Clemson (S.C.) U., 1985-89, assoc. prof., 1989-91, prof., dept. head, dir. bot. garden, 1991-96, sch. dir., interim v.p. pub. svc. and agr., 1996-97, v.p. pub. svc. and agr., dir. S.C. Bot. Garden, 1997—. Cons. in field. Contbr. more than 50 articles to profl. jours. Bd. govs. S.C. BIO; chmn. bd. dirs. Am. Distance Edn. Corp., Pate Found., Forestry Assn. Recipient Outstanding Contbr. award S.C. Nurseryman's Assn., 1991. Fellow Am. Soc. Hort. Sci. (v.p. 1995-99, pres. 1999, chmn. bd. dirs. 2000, Outstanding Rschr. 1994, Outstanding Adminstr. 1995, So. region Outstanding Educator 1989); mem. So. Assn. Agrl. Scientists (past pres.), S.C. Greenhouse Growers Assn. (life, exec. sec. 1991). Avocations: gardening, nature. Office: Clemson U Pub Svc and Agr 130 Lehotsky Hall Clemson SC 29634-0101

KELLY, KATHLEEN DENNIS, international government affairs consultant; b. Ann Arbor, Mich., Aug. 20, 1952; d. Edward Wimberly and Beatrice Forrest Dennis; children: Charlotte, John. BA in Polit. Sci., U. Tex., 1974. Pres. Interisk, Inc., Houston, 1981-85; cons. Russell Reynolds & Assoc., Houston, 1985-88; exec. dir., pres. Houston Internat. Protocol Alliance, Houston, 1988-94; pres. Internat. Protocol Advisors, Houston, 1994; hon. consul New Zealand, 1995—. Chair Houston Com. Fgn. Rels., 1997, mem. exec. com., 1997—. Author booklet: Consular Ball, 1993. Bd. dirs. Houston World Affairs Coun., 1996—, Bolivian Charity Found., Houston, 1997—; bd. dirs. world trade divsn. Greater Houston Partnership; mem. internat. rev. bd. Park Plz. Hosp., Houston, 1993-95; mem. exec. com. Consular Corps of Houston. Recipient Cert. of Appreciation, U.S. Dept. State, 1992, U.S. Secret Svc., 1992, Cert. Merit, Bolivian Govt., 1994. Mem. Bus. Coun. for Internat. Understanding. Republican. Presbyterian. E-mail: KathleenKell@sbcglobal.net.

KELLY, KEVIN, editor; b. Penn State, Pa., Apr. 27, 1952; s. Joseph John and Patricia Kelly; m. Gia-Miin Fuh, Jan. 2, 1987; children: Kaileen, Ting, Tywen. Freelance photographer, 1971-80; editor, pub. Walking! Jour., Athens, Ga., 1982-84, Whole Earth Rev., Sausalito, Calif., 1984-90; exec. editor Wired Mag., San Francisco, 1992-98; chmn. All Species Found., 2001—. Editor: Signal, 1988; author: Out of Control, 1994, New Rules for the New Economy, 1998, Asia Grace, 2002, Cool Tools, 2003, True Films, 2004; pub. Cool Tools website. Recipient Gen. Excellence Nat. Mag. Award, 1993, 96. Mem.: Long Bets Found. (pres. 2002—). Avocation: beekeeping. Home and Office: 149 Amapola Ave Pacifica CA 94044-3102 Office Phone: 650-355-7676. E-mail: kk@kk.org.

KELLY, LUCIE STIRM YOUNG, retired nursing educator; b. Stuttgart, Germany, May 2, 1925; came to U.S., 1929; d. Hugo Karl and Emilie Rosa (Engel) Stirm; m. J. Austin Young, Aug. 30, 1946 (div. Feb. 1971); m. Thomas Martin Kelly, 1972 (dec. Aug. 2003); 1 child by previous marriage, Gay Aleta (Mrs. Donald Meyer). BS, U. Pitts., 1947, MLitt, 1957, PhD, 1965; D in Nursing Edn. (hon.), U. RI, 1977; LHD (hon.), Georgetown U., 1983; DSc (hon.), Widener U., 1984; D of Pub. Svc. (hon.), Am. U., 1985; DSc (hon.), U. Mass., 1989; DHL (hon.), SUNY, 1996. Instr. nursing McKeesport (Pa.) Hosp., 1953-57, asst. adminstr. nursing, 1966-69; asst. prof. nursing U. Pitts., 1957-64, asst. dean, 1965; prof., chmn. nursing dept. Calif. State U., LA, 1969-72; co-project dir. curriculum rsch. Nat. League for Nursing, 1973-74; project dir. patient edn., office consumer health edn., also adj. assoc. prof. cmty. medicine Coll. Medicine and Dentistry N.J.-Rutgers Med. Sch., 1974-75; prof. pub. health and nursing Sch. Pub. Health and Sch. Nursing Columbia U., NYC, 1975-90, prof. emeritus Sch Pub. Health, Sch. Nursing, 1990—, assoc. dean acad. affairs Sch. Pub. Health, 1988-90, hon. prof. nursing edn. Tchrs. Coll., 1977-93, acting head divsn. health adminstrn. Sch. Pub. Health, 1980-81, 86-88; on leave as exec. dir. Mid-Atlantic Regional Nursing Assn., 1981-82. Cons. U. Nev., Las Vegas, 1970-72, Ball State U., Ind., 1971, Long Beach (Calif.) Naval Hosp., 1971-72, Travis AFB, Calif., 1972, Brentwood VA Hosp., LA, 1971-72, Ctrl. Nursing Office VA, Washington, 1971-94, NJ Dept. Higher Edn., 1974-78, John Wiley Pub., 1974-76, Sch. Nursing and Sch. Pub. Health Am. U. Beirut accreditation visit, 1978; spl. med. adv. group VA Dept. Medicine and Surgery, Washington, 1980-84; cons. nursing com. AMA, 1971-74, Citizen's Com. for Children, NYC; v.p. Pa. Health Coun., 1968-69; adv. com. physicians assts. Calif. Bd. Med. Examiners, adv. com. Cancer Soc. LA, 1970-72, com. nursing VA, Washington, 1971-74, chair 1975-90, regional med. programs, Pa., 1967-69, Calif. 1970-72; spl. adv. com. on med. licensure and profl. conduct N.Y. State Assembly, 1977-79, nat. adv. com. Encore (nat. YWCA post-mastectomy group rehab. project), 1977-83; assoc. mem. NY Acad. Medicine, 1988-90; ethics com. Palisades Med. Ctr., 1993-05, bd. govs., 1995-05, mem. profl. and quality rev. com., 1995-05, chair, 1998-05, exec. com., 1998-99; 2d vice chair N.Y. Presbyn. Healthcare Sys., Palisades Med. Ctr., 1999-03, 1st vice chair 2003-05; lectr., cons., guest Beijing Med. Coll., China, 1982, Aga Khan U., Pakistan, 1990; bd. visitors U. Pitts. Sch. Nursing, 1986-93; editl. adv. bd. Am. Jour. Pub. Health, 1992, chair, 1993-97; chair adv. com. grad. program in pub. health U. Medicine and Dentistry NJ, 1995-00; vol. cert. mediator for Hudson County mcpl. cts., 2004-05; lectr. in field Author: (textbooks) Dimensions of Profl. Nursing, 8th edit., 1999, The Nursing Experience: Trends, Challenges, Transitions, 4th edit., 2002; contbg. editor: Jour. Nursing Adminstrn., 1975—82; columnist: jour. Nursing Outlook, editor-in-chief, 1982—91; mem. bd. advisors (jour.) Nurses Almanac, 1978, Nurse Manager's Handbook, 1979, Nursing Administration Handbook, 1992; editor (editl. bd.): (jour.) Am. Health, 1981—91; mem. editl. bd. Nursing and Health Care, 1991—95, Internat. Nursing Index, 1997—2001. Bd. dirs. ARC, LA, 1971-72; bd. dirs. Vis. Nurse Svc. N.Y., 1980-01, mem. exec. com., chmn. human resources, 1989-01; bd. dirs. Concern for Dying, 1983-89; bd. trustees Calif. State Coll. LA Found., 1971-72, U. Pitts., 1984-90, mem. exec. com. 1988-90; chair bd. visitors U. Pitts. Sch. Pub. Health, 1988-90; bd. visitors U. Miami Sch. Nursing, 1986-05; mem. health svcs. com. Children's Aid Soc., N.Y., 1978-84; v.p. Am. Nurses Found., 1980-82; mem. nat. adv. coun. on nurse tng. HRA, 1981-85; mem. nurses leadership coun. Chlorine Chemistry Coun., 1999-03; hon. bd. dirs. NOVA Found., 1998—, Health Professions Panel, Am. Legacy Found., 2000—. Named Outstanding Alumna U. Pitts. Sch. Nursing, 1966, Pa. Nurse of Yr., 1967, Roll of Honor N.J. State Nurses Assn., 1990; named to Tchrs. Coll. Columbia U. Nursing Edn. Alumni Hall of Fame, 1999; recipient Disting. Alumna award U. Pitts. Sch. Edn., 1981, Shaw medal Boston Coll., 1985, Bicentennial Medallion of Distinction, U. Pitts., 1987, R. Louise McManus Medallion for Disting. Svc. to Nursing, Tchrs. Coll. Columbia U., 1987, Dean's Disting. Svc. award Columbia Sch. Pub. Health, 1995, Second Century award in health care, Columbia U. Sch. Nursing, 1996; fellow HEW, 1965. Fellow Am. Acad. Nursing (named Living Legend 2001); mem. ANA (dir. 1978-82, Hon. Recognition award 1992), APHA (Ruth Freeman Pub. Health Nursing award 1993), Pa. Nurses Assn. (pres. 1966-69), Nat. League Nursing (bd. govs. 1991-95), Nurses Ednl. Funds Bd., U. Pitts. Sch. Nursing Alumni (pres. 1959), Vis. Nurse Assn. Ctrl. Jersey (bd. dirs. 1999-2001, mem. bd. trustees), Am. Hosp. Assn. (com. chmn. 1967-68), Assn. Grad. Faculty Cmty. Health/Pub. Health Nursing (v.p. 1980-81), Sigma Theta Tau (sr. editor Image 1978-81, pres.-elect 1981-83, pres. 1983-85, nat. campaign chair Ctr. for Nursing Scholarship 1987-89, chair devel. com. 1989-95, spl. advisor 1995-97, planned giving task force 1998-2001, Mentor award 1985, 93, 97, Spirit of Philanthropy award 1997), Pi Lambda Theta, Alpha Tau Delta (Cert. of Merit 1968). Achievements include collection of papers in Mugar Library, Boston U.

KELLY, MARGARET M., real estate company executive; b. Detroit; 2 children. AA in Accounting, Oakland Coll., Mich., 1979; BBA in Fin. and Accounting, Walsh Coll., Mich., 1981. Financial analyst Met. Hosp. and Health Ctr., Detroit, Am. Med. Internat., Denver, mgr. budgeting and financial analysis, mgr. alternative services financial planning and analysis; mem. services rep. for Colo. RE/MAX, 1989, regional dir. for Colo., 1992, v.p. and regional dir. for Mountain States, 1992, v.p. and zone dir. co. operated regions, 1993, sr. v.p., 1997, sr. v.p. external ops., 1999, pres., 2002, co-CEO, 2004, CEO, 2005. Named one of 25 Yoplait Champions, 2003, Real Estate's 25 Most Influential Thought Leaders, Realtor Mag., 2006; recipient Outstanding Alumni award, Am. Assn. Cmty. Colleges, 2005. Avocations: scuba diving, golf, gardening. Office: RE/MAX International Inc 5075 S Syracuse St Denver CO 80237 Office Phone: 303-770-5531. Office Fax: 303-796-3599.*

KELLY, SISTER MARIE, school system administrator; b. Phila., Aug. 8, 1937; d. Edwin Michael and Anne Marie Kelly. BA, Trinity Coll., Washington, 1960; MS, Scranton U., Pa., 1968; EdD, Nova U., 1984. Tchr. Miraculous Medal Sch., Bklyn., 1960—62, Maryvale Prep Sch., Brocklandville, Md., 1962—64; tchr., prin. St. Anthony Sch., Florence, SC, 1964—70; prin. Our Lady of Victory Sch., Balt., 1970—72; asst. supt. Cath. Schs. Office, Washington, 1972—76, supt. Charlotte, NC, 1976—84, Wilmington, Del., 1984—91, Burlington, Vt., 2004—. Mem. Burlington C. of C., 2005—; elected to province leadership of religious cmty., 1991—96, gen. leadership, 1996—2002, supt. of sch., 2004. Mem.: ASCD, Nat. Cath. Ednl. Assn. (elem. com., Presdl. award 1987). Democrat. Avocations: reading, walking, music. Home: 100 Mansfield Ave Burlington VT 05401 Office: Cath Schs Office 351 North Ave Burlington VT 05401 Fax: 802-860-0451. Business E-Mail: mkelly@vermontcatholic.org.

KELLY, MARILYN, state supreme court justice; b. Apr. 15, 1938; m. Donald Newman. BA, Ea. Mich. U., 1960, JD (hon.); postgrad., U. Paris.; MA, Middlebury Coll., 1961; JD with honors, Wayne State U., 1971. Assoc. Dykema, Gossett, Spencer, Goodnow & Trigg, Detroit, 1973-78; ptnr. Dudley, Patterson, Maxwell, Smith & Kelly, Bloomfield Hills, Mich., 1978-80; owner Marilyn Kelly & Assocs., Bloomfield Hills, Birmingham, Mich., 1980-88; judge Mich. Ct. of Appeals, 1989-96; justice Mich. Supreme Ct., 1997—. Tchr. lang., lit. Grosse Pointe Pub. Schs., Albion Coll., Ea. Mich. U.; past mem. rep. assembly, comms. com., family law coun. Mich. State Bar; co-chair Open Justice Commn., 1999—; mem. governing bd. Nat. Consortium for Racial & Ethnic Fairness in Cts. Active Mich. Dem. Party, 1963—; former bd. dirs. Channel 56-Pub. TV, Detroit, Women's Survival Ctr., Pontiac; former mem. citizens advisory com. Detroit Public Schools, Wayne County Community Coll., Oakland County Community Coll. Recipient Disting Alumni award Ea. Mich. U., Disting. Svc. award Mich. Edn. Assn., Eleanor Roosevelt Humanities award State of Israel Bonds Atty. Div., 2003. Mem. Soc. Irish-Am. Lawyers, Women Lawyers Assn. (past pres.), Oakland County Bar Assn. (past chair family law com.), State Bar Mich. (Michael Franck award 2003); Fellow Mich. State Bar Found. Office: Mich Supreme Ct 3034 West Grand Blvd Detroit MI 48202*

KELLY, MARK E., astronaut; b. Orange, NJ, Feb. 21, 1964; s. Richard and Patricia Kelly; m. Amelia Victoria Babis; 2 children. BS in Marine Engrng. and Marine Transportation (with highest honors), U.S. Merchant Marine Acad., 1986; MS in Aeronautical Engrng., U.S. Naval Postgrad. Sch., 1994. Commd. ensign USN, 1986, advanced through grades to lt. comdr.; with Attack Squadron 128, Naval Air Sta., Whidbey Island, Wash., Attack Squadron 115, Atsugi, Japan; combat pilot Persian Gulf, Operation Desert Storm; project test pilot Carrier Suitability Dept., Strike Aircraft Test Squadron, Naval Air Warfe Ctr., Patuxent River, Md.; instr. pilot U.S. Naval Test Pilot Sch.; astronaut NASA, Houston, 1996—, with Astronaut Office Computer Support Br. Pilot STS-108 (Endeavor) mission, 2001; co-pilot STS-121 (Discovery), a return-to-flight test mission and assembly flight to the International Space Station, 2006. Decorated Def. Superior Svc. medal, 4 Air Medals (2 indivdual/2 strike flight) with Combat "V", 2 Navy Commendation medals (one with Combat "V"), Navy Commendation medal with "V", Navy Achievement medal, Navy Expeditionary medal, 2 Southwest Asia Svc. medals, 2 Sea Svc. Deployment Ribbons, Overseas Svc. Ribbon and various other unit awards. Mem.: U.S. Merchant Marine Acad. Alumni Assn. Achievements include logged over 3,000 flight hours in over 40 different aircraft; over 375 carrier landings; logged 12 days in space; crew STS-108 Endeavour (2001). Avocations: bicycling, weightlifting, golf. Office: Astronaut Office/CB NASA Johnson Space Ctr Houston TX 77058

KELLY, MICHAEL JOSEPH, academic administrator, consultant; b. NYC, July 2, 1931; s. Hugh and Mary Agnes (Harrison) K.; m. Helen Janet Nee, Oct. 4, 1969; children: Joan T., Jean M. BA, Marist Coll., 1955; BEE, Cath. U., 1960, MEE, 1961; DEng, U. Detroit, 1968. Tchr. U. Detroit, 3 yrs., dir. Computer Ctr.; tchr., adminstr. Marist Coll., 4 yrs.; assoc. prof. electrical and mech. engring., dir. engring. case program Stanford U.; mgr. CAD, litho sys. IBM, East Fishkill, NY, 1969-79, mgr. Mfg. Tech. Ctr. Boca Raton, Fla., 1979-84, dir. Quality Inst., 1984, mgr. quality improvement and profl. devel. programs systems tech. divsn., 1986-87; dir.

computer integrated mfg. and tech. transfer NJ Inst. Tech., NJ, 1987-89; dir. def. mfg. office Def. Advanced Rsch. Projects Agy., 1989-91; exec. dir. Nat. Adv. Com. on Semiconductors, 1989-91; dir. Mfg. Rsch. Ctr. Ga. Inst. Tech., Ga., 1991-96, prof. technology mgmt. Ga., 1995-96; Northrop-Grumman endowed chair mfg. and design Calif. State U., LA, 1996-99; ind. mgmt. and ednl. cons., 1999—. Adj. prof. Stony Book U., 2003—. Home: 42 Tillotson Ave Saint James NY 11780-1728 Home Phone: 631-862-2664. Personal E-mail: jkelly931@optonline.net.

KELLY, MOIRA, actress; b. Queens, NY, Mar. 6, 1968; Student, Marymount Coll. Appeared in films The Boy Who Cried Bitch, 1991, Billy Bathgate, 1991, The Cutting Edge, 1992, Mr. Saturday Night, 1992, Chaplin, 1992, Twin Peaks: Fire Walk With Me, 1992, With Honors, 1994, Little Odessa, 1994, The Tie That Binds, 1995, (voice) The Lion King, 1994, Unhook the Stars, 1996, Entertaining Angels: The Dorothy Day Story, 1996, Changing Habits, 1997, Drive, She Said, 1997, Love Walked In, 1998, Dangerous Beauty, 1998, Hi-Life, 1998, Henry Hill, 1999, The Safety of Objects, 2001, (voice) The Lion King 1 1/2, 2004; TV movies include Monday After the Miracle, 1998; television appearances include (movies) Love Lies and Murder, 1991, Daybreak, 1993, To Have and To Hold, 1998, (series) The West Wing, 1999-2000. Office: care Gersh Agy 232 N Canon Dr Beverly Hills CA 90210-5302

KELLY, NANCY FOLDEN, art association administrator; b. Fredericksburg, Va., Oct. 28, 1951; d. Virgil Alvis Jr. and Frances Virginia (DeShazo) Folden; m. Frank R. Kelly, Aug. 11, 1973; 1 child, Katherine Elizabeth Kelly. BA in Theatre Arts, Va. Poly. Inst. and State U., 1973; MFA in Theatre Directing, So. Meth. U., 1975. Coord. student programs Lincoln Ctr. Inst., NYC, 1976-79; dir. NYC Opera Nat. Co. and edn. dept. Lincoln Ctr., 1979-93, mem. coun. on ednl. programs, 1979-93; mng. dir. Broadway Arts Theatre Young Audiences, NYC, 1994-96; dir. family and cmty. programs Ctrl. Park Conservancy, NYC, 1996-98; fin. mgr., assoc. dir. devel. Film Soc. Lincoln Ctr., NYC, 1999—2005, dir ops., 2006—. Office Phone: 212-875-5208. E-mail: nkelly@filmlinc.com.

KELLY, NANCY FRIEDA WOLICKI, lawyer; b. Chgo., Sept. 8, 1953; d. Samuel and Ingrid (Rappel) W. BA in Journalism and Sociology, U. Ariz., 1974, JD, 1977. Bar: Ariz. 1977. Law clk. Ariz. Ct. Appeals, 1977-78; legis. asst. fgn. policy and armed svcs. health, staff atty. Billy Carter investigation to U.S. Sen. Dennis DeConcini, 1979-81; staff dir. Senate Subcom. on Alcoholism and Drug Abuse, Washington, 1981-84; mem. staff Senator Gordon J. Humphrey, Washington, 1984-87; coord. adv. com. Voluntary Fgn. U.S. Aid, 1987; sr. analyst legal and drug related issues president's Commn. on the HIV Epidemic, 1987-88; sr. policy analyst Commn. Exec. Legis. Jud. Salaries, 1988-89; counselor Sec. Energy, 1989-93; v.p. Kelly, Anderson & Assocs., Alexandria, Va., 1993—. Recipient William Spaid Meml. award U. Ariz. Coll. Law, 1977, Senate commendation for Billy Carter investigation, 1980. Mem. Ariz. Bar Assn., Phi Kappa Phi. Jewish. Office: 424 N Washington St Alexandria VA 22314-2312 Home: 1290 Beresford Ct Mc Lean VA 22101-2426 Office Phone: 703-518-8828. Business E-Mail: nkelly@kellyanderson.com.

KELLY, PATRICK J., lawyer; BA, Marquette U., 1971; ed., Nat. U. Ireland; JD, Creighton U., 1975. Bar: Minn., Wis., US Dist. Ct. (Dist. Minn.), US Dist. Ct. (Dist. Wis.), US Ct. Appeals (8th Cir.), US Supreme Ct. Asst. corp. counsel and prosecutor City of New Brighton; asst. prosecutor City of White Bear Lake; city atty. City of Maplewood; spl. counsel eminent domain matters City of Osseo; spl. counsel City of St. Croix Falls; sr. ptnr. Kelly & Fawcett PA, St. Paul. Recipient Chgo. Tribune award. Mem.: Minn. State Bar Assn. (pres. 2006—07), Ramsey County Bar Assn. (chmn. ethics com., pres. 2002—04). Office: Kelly & Fawcett PA 444 Cedar St Saint Paul MN 55101 Office Phone: 651-224-3781. Office Fax: 651-223-8019.

KELLY, PATRICK JOSEPH, neurosurgeon, educator; b. Lackawanna, NY, Sept. 19, 1941; s. Joseph P. and Mary D. (Conner) K.; m. Carol Huey; children: Patrick D., Michael, Caitlin. BS, U. Mich., 1962; MD, SUNY, Buffalo, 1966. Cert. Am. Bd. Neurol. Surgery 1978. Intern U.S. Naval Hosp., Phila., 1966-67; resident neurosurgery Northwestern U., Chgo., 1970-72; resident neurosurgery med. branch U. Tex., Galveston, 1972—74; from asst. prof. to assoc. prof. U. Tex. Med. Sch., Galveston, 1974—79; assoc. prof. SUNY, Buffalo, 1979-84; prof., cons. Mayo Med. Sch./Mayo Clinic, Rochester, Minn., 1984-93; prof., chmn. neurosurg. dept. NYU Med. Ctr., 1993—. Cons., adv. bd. mem. Jet Propulsion Lab NASA, Pasadena, Calif., 1994—. Author: Tumor Stereotaxis, 1991; co-editor: Computers in Stereotactic Neurosurgery, 1992; mem. editl. bd. Neurosurgery, 1991—, Surg. Neurology, 1990—, Jour. Stereotactic and Functional Neurosurgery, 1986—; contbr. chpts. in books and articles to profl. jours.; profiled Am.'s Top Drs. and Top Drs.: New York Metro Area 2000-2002 of Castle Connolly Guide. Lt. comdr. MC USN, 1968—70. Recipient Scoville award World Fedn. Neurol. Surgery, 1997; named Citizen of Yr. Buffalo Evening News, 1982, Best Doctors in Am. Good Housekeeping, 1993, Town & Country, 1992, Am. Health, 1996, Top 100, Irish Am. mag., 1996, 99, Best Drs. N.Y., New York Mag., 1999, 2000-05, Woodward/White, Inc., 1998, 2000, 01, 02, Obrador medal Spanish Neurol. Soc., 1996, Sir Peter Freyer medal, Irish Surgical Soc., 2001, Invitee d'Honneur French Neurosurg. Soc., 2000, Olivacrona medal Karolinska Inst., Stockholm, 2002, Schneider Lectr. Am. Assn. Neurolog. Surgeons, 1996, 2002; named to Boys and Girls Clubs Am. Hall of Fame, 2001. Fellow ACS; mem. Am. Soc. Stereotactic Neurosurgery (past pres., bd. dirs.), Am. Assn. Neurol. Surgeons (Van Wagenen fellow 1977, com. chmn.), Acad. Neurol. Surgery, Soc. Neurol. Surgeons (com.), Soc. Neurochurgie de Lange Francaise., Brain Tumor Found. (founder 1997). Roman Catholic. Achievements include development of a computer-assisted image guiding stereotactic neurosurgery for brain tumors. Avocations: sailing, watercolor painting. Home: 7 Gracie Sq New York NY 10028-8001 Office: NYU Med Ctr 530 1st Ave New York NY 10016-6402 Home Phone: 212-251-7751; Office Phone: 212-263-8002. Business E-Mail: kellyp01@med.nyu.edu. E-mail: kelly@brainscans.com.

KELLY, PAUL J., lab administrator, physician, researcher; b. Australia; MB, BChir, MD, U. New S. Wales. Sr. rsch. physician Garvan Inst. for Med. Rsch., Sydney; co-founder, CEO Gemini Genomics, 1995—2001; CEO Orchid BioScis., Inc., 2003—. Former CEO, exec. dir. OmniViz, Inc.; dir. Nanovis, MedCenter Solutions, AgaMatrix. Contbr. articles to profl. jours. Fellow: Australasian Coll. Physicians. Office: Orchid BioScis Inc 4390 US Rte 1 Princeton NJ 08540 Office Phone: 609-750-2200. Office Fax: 609-750-6400.

KELLY, PAUL JOSEPH, JR., federal judge; b. Freeport, NY, Dec. 6, 1940; s. Paul J. and Jacqueline M. (Nolan) Kelly; m. Ruth Ellen Dowling, June 27, 1964; children: Johanna, Paul Edwin, Thomas Martin, Christopher Mark, Heather Marie. BBA, U. Notre Dame, 1963; JD, Fordham U., 1967. Bar: N.Mex. 1967. Law clk. Cravath, Swaine & Moore, NYC, 1964—67; assoc. firm Hinkle, Cox, Eaton, Coffield & Hensley, Roswell, N.Mex., 1967—71, ptnr., 1971—92; judge US Ct. Appeals (10th cir.), Santa Fe, 1992—. Mem. N.Mex. Bd. Bar Examiners, 1982—85, N.Mex. Ho. of Reps., 1976—81, chmn. consumer and pub. affairs com., mem. judiciary com.; mem. N.Mex. Pub. Defender Bd., US Jud. Conf. Com. on the Jud. Br., 1994—99, US Jud. Conf. Civil Rules Adv. Com., 2002—; chair 10th Cir. Rules com., 10th Cir. Uniform Criminal Jury Instrn. Com. Bd. visitors Fordham U. Sch. Law, 1992—2006; pres. Oliver Seth Inn of Ct., 1993—, Roswell Drug Abuse Com, 1970—71; mem. Appellate Judges Nominating Commn., 1989—92, Eastern N.Mex. State Fair Bd., 1978—83; pres. Chaves County Young Reps., 1971—72; vice chmn. N.Mex. Young Reps., 1969—71, treas., 1968—69; pres. parish coun. Roman Cath. Ch., 1971—76; bd. dirs. Zia coun. Girl Scouts Am., Roswell Girls Club, Chaves County Mental Health Assn., 1974—77, Santa Fe Orch., 1992—93, Roswell Symphony Orch. Soc., 1969—82, treas., 1970—73, pres., 1973—75. Mem.: State Bar N.Mex. (v.p. young lawyers sect. 1969, mem. continuing legal edn. com. 1970—73, co-chmn. ins. sub-com. 1972—73, mem. Bench-Bar com. 1994—), Fed. Bar Assn. Office: US Court Appeals 10th Circuit Federal Courthouse PO Box 10113 Santa Fe NM 87504-6113 Office Phone: 505-988-6541.*

KELLY, PAUL KNOX, investment banker; b. Boston, Feb. 18, 1940; s. Thomas Joseph and Rita Patricia Kelly; m. Nancy Lee Belden, July 17, 1978; 1 child, 3 stepchildren. AB in English, U. Pa., 1962; MBA in Fin., Wharton Sch., 1964; LLD (hon.), U. Auckland, New Zealand, 2006. Investment analyst bond dept. Prudential Ins. Co. Am., 1964-65; asst. treas. Comml. Credit Co., 1965-68; v.p. First Boston Corp., NYC, 1968-75; ptnr., mem. mgmt. com., dir. Prescott, Ball & Turben, Cleve., 1975-77; sr. v.p., dir. Butcher & Singer, Inc., 1977-78; exec. v.p., mem. exec. com., dir. Blyth Eastman Dillon & Co., NYC, 1978-80; mng. dir. Merrill Lynch White Weld Capital Markets Group, NYC, 1980-82; exec. v.p., dir. Dean Witter Reynolds, Inc., 1982-84; pres., dir. Quadrex Securities Corp., 1984-85, Peers & Co., NYC, 1985-90, PH II, Inc., Westport, Conn., 1988—, Knox & Co., NYC, 1992—. Trustee U. Pa.; bd. dirs. Knox Enterprises, Inc. Mem. Union Club (Cleve.), Chagrin Valley Hunt Club, Penn Club N.Y., The LInks, Union League (Phila.), The No. Club (Auckland, New Zealand). Office: Knox & Co 33 Riverside Ave Westport CT 06880-4223

KELLY, PAUL VINCENT, retired military officer, former federal agency administrator; BA in Econ., Merimack Coll.; MS in Mgmt. Sci., U. Lowell; diploma in nat. security studies, Indsl. Coll. of Armed Forces. Commd. ensign USMC, 1979, advanced through ranks to Col., various inf. and fin. mgmt. positions, sr. officer Dept. of Navy liaison to House and Senate appropriations com., ret., 1999; sr. officer legis. asst. to chmn. of Jt. Chiefs of Staff U.S. Dept. of State, dir. Marine Corps War Coll., asst. sec. of state for legis. affairs Washington, 2001—05.

KELLY, PETER, energy executive; B in Mgmt. Sci., U. Manchester Inst. Sci. and tech., Eng. Various sr. fin. and oper. positions semiconductor divsn. UK, France and Portugal Tex. Instruments; head fin. Sonae, Portugal; CFO largest divsn. ICL; COO Fujitsu-ICL Systems Inc., CFO; v.p. ops. Integrated Circuits divsn. Agere Systems, Inc., 2000—01, exec. v.p. global ops., 2001—05, exec. v.p., CFO, 2005—07; v.p. fin., CFO UGI Corp., 2007—. Bd. dirs., mem. audit com. Plexus Corp. Fellow: Inst. Chartered Mgmt. Accts. Office: UGI Corp PO Box 965 Valley Forge PA 19482 Office Phone: 610-337-7000.*

KELLY, PETER MCCLOREY, II, lawyer; b. Chgo., Mar. 23, 1948; s. John Stephen and Helen (Patterson) K.; m. Susan Barrett, Aug. 17, 1995; children: Peter, Eli, Eamon, Liam. A.B., U. Notre Dame, 1970; J.D. cum laude, Ind. U., 1973. Bar: Ill. 1973. Assoc. McDermott, Will & Emery, Chgo., 1973-78, ptnr., 1979-81; ptnr. Kirkland & Ellis, Chgo., 1981-84, Bell, Boyd & Lloyd, Chgo., 1984-91, Murphy, Smith & Polk, Chgo., 1991-98, Ogletree Deakins (formerly Murphy Smith & Polk), 1999—; adj. prof. Sch. of Law, Loyola U., Chgo., 1976-84, Ind. U. Law Sch., Bloomington, 1985; speaker to various profl. groups and orgns. Mem. U.S. C. of C. (employee benfits council 1981—), ABA (life fellow), charter fellow, bd. govs., Am. Coll. Employee Benefits Counsel Chgo. Bar Assn. (sec. employee benefits com. 1982-83, vice chmn. employee benefits com. 1983-84, chmn. 1984-85), Midwest Pension Conf. (exec. bd. 1984—), Order of Coif. Home: 1316 Davis St Evanston IL 60201-4104 Office: Ogletree Deakins 2 1st Nat Plz Fl 25 Chicago IL 60603 E-mail: kellypm@odnss.com.

KELLY, QUENTIN THORN, water and power company executive, writer; b. New Orleans, La., July 14, 1934; s. Edgar Joseph and Leola (Pilcher) Kelly; m. Peggy R. Richey; children: Lisa Scott Curtis, Carolyn Kelly Colella, Quentin T. Jr. Student, Kenyon Coll., Gambier, Ohio. Asst. to pres. Westinghouse Electric Corp., New York City, NY, 1965—72; chmn. and CEO WorldWater & Power Corp., Pennington, NJ, 1984—. Writer MGM Studios, Hollywood (Culver City), Calif. Named to N.J. Inventors Hall of Fame, 1998. Mem.: Army and Navy Club (Wash., DC), Williams Club (N.Y.C.). Achievements include invention of Solar Water Pumps, 1992. Office: WorldWater & Power Corp 55 Route 31 South Pennington NJ 08534

KELLY, R. (ROBERT SYLVESTER KELLY), musician, recording industry executive; b. Chgo., Jan. 8, 1967; Musician (with MGM): (songs) (first single) Why You Wanna Play Me, 1990; musician: (with Public Announcement) (albums) Born Into the '90s, 1992; musician: (with Jay-Z) The Best of Both Worlds, 2002, Unfinished Business, 2004; musician: 12 Play, 1993, R. Kelly, 1995; songwriter: for Changing Faces, Janet Jackson, Michael Jackson, 1995; musician: (albums) R., 1998, TP-2.com, 2000, Chocolate Factory, 2003, Happy People/U Saved Me, 2004, TP-3: Reloaded, 2005, Double Up, 2007, (songs) I Believe I Can Fly, 1996 (Grammy, Best R&B Song, Best R&B Male Vocal Performance, Best Original Song from a Soundtrack, 1998), Rise Up, 2007. Recipient Favorite Male R&B Artist, Am. Music Awards, 2005. Achievements include 15 Billboard Top 40 hits during the 1990s (highest among male artists). Studio: Jive Records 137 W 25th St New York NY 10001 Office Phone: 212-727-0016.

KELLY, R. JAMES, retail executive; From nat. dir. mid. market and fast growing cos. divsn. to mng. ptnr. Carolinas ops. Price Waterhouse LLP, 1973—97; vice-chmn., CFO, adminstrv. officer, bd. dir. Family Dollar Stores, Charlotte, NC, 1997—2006, pres., COO, 2006—. Past chmn. bd. dirs. Charlotte Symphony Orch. Office: Family Dollar Store PO Box 1017 10401 Old Monroe Rd Charlotte NC 28201*

KELLY, RAYMOND ALOYSIUS, JR., lawyer, educator; b. Yuma, Ariz., July 6, 1944; s. Raymond A. and Josephine V. (Schulz) K.; m. Mary Jo Battaglia, Mar. 8, 1980; 1 child, Kyle Patrick. B.A., Providence Coll., 1966; J.D., Albany Law Sch., 1973. Bar: N.Y. 1974, U.S. Dist. Ct. (no. dist.) N.Y. 1974, U.S. Ct. Appeals (2d cir.) 1984. Asst. dist. atty. Albany County, Albany, N.Y., 1974-80; asst. pub. defender Albany County, Albany, 1980; sole practice, Albany, 1980—; mem. adj. faculty Albany Law Sch., 1975—; mem. continuing legal edn. faculty N.Y. State Lawyers and Advs., Albany, 1981—. Mem. editorial bd. Albany Law Rev., 1972-73. Contbr. articles to N.Y. State Defender, 1983-84. Active Big Bros.-Big Sisters, Providence, 1962-66. Served to capt. U.S. Army, 1966-70; Vietnam. Decorated D.S.C., Bronze Star, Purple Heart with 3 oak leaf clusters. Mem. Nat. Inst. Trial advocacy, Assn. Trial Lawyers Am., Nat. Coll. Criminal Def., N.Y. State Trial Lawyers Assn., N.Y. State Bar Assn. (Denison Ray award 1998, Outstanding Practitioner of Yr. 2000). Democrat. Roman Catholic. Clubs: Wolferts Roost Country, Steuben Athletic (Albany). Home: 293 Loudonville Rd Albany NY 12211-2015 Office: 112 State St Suite 1005 Albany NY 12207 Office Phone: 518-463-4569. E-mail: rakelly@albany.net.*

KELLY, RAYMOND BOONE, III, lawyer; b. Ft. Worth, Oct. 12, 1947; s. Raymond Boone Jr. and Martha (Morehead) K.; m. Ellen McCarthy; children: Alice Katherine, Anne Rowan. BA, Tulane U., 1970; JD, So. Meth. U., 1974. Bar: Tex. 1974. Ptnr. Decker, McMackin & McClane, Ft. Worth, 1974—. V.p., trustee William E. Scott Found., Ft. Worth, 1978—. Bd. dirs., past pres. Goodwill Industries Ft. Worth, 1975-94; bd. dirs. Arts Coun. Ft. Worth and Tarrant County, 1980-91, 95-97, Conf. of S.W. Founds., Dallas, 1986-89, 97-2000, Davey O'Brien Found., 2001—, Ft. Worth Mus. Sci. and History, 2003-, Big Bros./Bis Sisters, Ft. Worth, 1987-94, Intercultura, Inc., Ft. Worth, 1989-96, chmn., 1992-94, Funding Info. Ctr., 1993-97, Ft. Worth Dallas Ballet, 1996-97, Cmty. Found. North Tex., 1996-2002, Bishop Davies Ctr, 1999-2005, Baylor All Saints Med. Ctr., 1997—; trustee All Saints Health Found., 1987-, chmn. 1991-2002; trustee Modern Art Mus. Ft. Worth, 1981—, Fort Worth Country Day Sch., 1996-2002, Goodwill Industries Ft. Worth Found., 1997—2003, Ft. Worth Club, 1999-2002. Mem. ABA, State Bar Tex., Tarrant County Bar Assn., Tarrant County Young Lawyers Assn. (v.p., sec. 1976-77), Tex. Bar Found. (life fellow), Tarrant County Bar Found., Ft. Worth Club, Exchange Club, Rivercrest Country Club, Steeplechase Club, Ind. Petroleum Assn. Am., Tex. Oil and Gas Assn. Republican. Episcopalian. Home: 301 Virginia Pl Fort Worth TX 76107-1611 Office: Decker, McMackin & McClane 801 Cherry St Ste 2000 Fort Worth TX 76102-3812

KELLY, RAYMOND CASE, anthropology educator; b. Bridgeport, Conn., Feb. 16, 1942; s. Rowland Leigh and Helen Janet (Varkala) K.; m. Mary Pfender, Aug. 28, 1966 (div. 1979); 1 child, Kathryn Elizabeth; m. Sherry Beth Ortner, Oct. 4, 1979 (div. 1991); 1 child, Gwendolyn Ida. BA in Anthropology, U. Chgo., 1965; MA in Anthropology, U. Mich., 1966, PhD in Anthropology, 1974. Lectr. dept. anthropology U. Mich., Ann Arbor, 1971-73, asst. prof. dept. anthropology, 1974-77, assoc. prof. dept. anthropology, 1977-86, full prof. dept. anthropology, 1986—2004, prof. emeritus, 2004—. Rackham divisional bd. social sci. U. Mich. Horace H. Rackham Grad. Sch., Ann Arbor, 1983-84, assoc. chair, mem. exec. com. dept. anthropology, 1984-85, 89-93, acting chair 1993-94; exec. com. U. Mich. Press, 1987-90. Author: Etoro Social Structure, 1977, The Nuer Conquest, 1985, Constructing Inequality, 1993, Warless Societies and The Origin of War, 2000; contbr. numerous articles to profl. jours. NEH fellow, 1979-80, Guggenheim Found. fellow, 1982-83, Ctr. for Advanced Study in Behavioral Scis. fellow, 1982-83. Mem.: NAS. Avocation: landscape gardening. Office: U Mich Dept Anthropology 1054 LSA Bldg Ann Arbor MI 48109

KELLY, RAYMOND CRAIN, toxicologist; b. Portland, Oreg., Sept. 4, 1945; s. Joyce Raymond and Evelyn Francis (Eaman) K.; m. Connie Lee McDaniel, June 28, 1968 (div. Aug. 1993); children: Clinton Samuel, Joel Christopher. BS in Biochemistry, Wash. State U., 1967; PhD in Chemistry, U. Oreg., 1975. Diplomate Am. Bd. Toxicology.; lic. clin. lab. toxicologist, Calif. With forensic toxicology staff Case Western Res. U. and Cuyahoga County Coroner's Office, Cleve., 1975-77; toxicology supr. Lab Procedures, Inc., Woodland Hills, Calif., 1977-78; asst. dir. dept. clin. & indsl. toxicology Bio-Sci. Labs., Van Nuys, Calif., 1978-83; chief toxicology Splty. Labs., Inc., LA, 1983-84; pres., chief lab. ops. Willow Toxicology Group, Pasadena, Calif., 1984-85; pres. Stat Tox Ctr., Mission Hills, Calif., 1985-89; tech. dir. Stat Lab, Inc., Mission Hills, 1986-89; lab. dir. MEDTOX Bio-Analytical, Woodland Hills, 1989—. Cons. toxicologist Tox-Tech, Simi Valley, Calif., 1984—; mem. clin. lab. tech. adv. com. Calif. Dept. Health Svcs., 1989—. Mem. editorial rev. bd. Jour. Analytical Toxicology; contbr. articles to profl. jours. Recipient Rsch. Svc. award Nat. Inst. Drug Abuse. Fellow Am. Acad. Forensic Scis. (toxicology sect.); mem. Am. Assn. Clin. Chemistry, Coll. Am. Pathologists (insp. forensic urine drug testing program), Calif. Assn. Toxicologists (past pres.), Assn. Drug Detection Labs., Toxicology Mgmt. Group. Achievements include research on convenient thin-layer chromatographic screening methods for acetaminophen in serum, on radioreceptor assays, on improved recovery and stability of ethanol in automated headspace analysis, on urinary phenylacetate and response to methylphenidate, and on drug testing in the workplace.

KELLY, RAYMOND WALTER, police commissioner; b. NYC, Sept. 4, 1941; married; two children. BBA, Manhattan Coll., 1963; LLM (hon.), St. John's U., 1971, NYU, 1974; MPA, Harvard U., 1984; Ph.D (hon.), Marist Coll., 1995, Manhattan Coll., 1996, Coll. St. Rose, 1997, St. John's U., 1998. Acting commr. N.Y.C. Police Dept., 1992, commr., 1992—94, 2001—; under sec. for enforcement U.S. Treasury Dept., 1996-98; commr. U.S. Customs Svc., 1998—2001; sr. mng. dir. global corp. strategy Bear, Stearns, & Co. Inc., 2001. Dir. internat. police monitors, Port-au-Prince, Haiti, 1994-95, v.p. Ams., INTERPOL, 1996-2000. Col. USMC, served in USMC, 1963—93. Recipient Alexander Hamilton medal for Exceptional Svc., US Dept. Treasury. Office: NYC Police Dept One Police Plz New York NY 10038

KELLY, REID BROWNE, lawyer; b. Kingston, Ont., Can., June 19, 1960; came to U.S., 1965; s. William Browne and Betty Lou (Rowland) K.; m. Debra Lee Carpenter, July 11, 1987 (dec. April 2003). BA magna cum laude, Colo. Coll., 1982; JD, U. Colo., 1985; cert., U. San Diego Inst., Oxford (Eng.) U., 1985. Bar: Colo. 1986, U.S. Dist. Ct. Colo. 1987, U.S. Ct. Appeals (6th cir.) 1997. Assoc. LaFrance & Assoc., Durango, Colo., 1986-87, Warren, Mundt, Martin & O'Dowd, Colorado Springs, Colo., 1987-93; ptnr. Warren, Mundt & Martin, Colorado Springs, 1993-95; mem. The Kelly Law Firm, L.L.C, Pagosa Springs, Colo., 1996—. Co-chair employment law com. El Paso County Bar Assn., Colorado Springs., 1992-94. Named Outstanding Young Men of Am., 1987-96. Mem. Colo. Bar Assn., S.W. Colo. Bar Assn. (sec. local chpt. 1997-99), Pi Gamma Mu. Avocations: Tae Kwon Do, yoga, running, skiing, chess. Office: The Kelly Law Firm LLC 4440 N Pagosa Blvd Pagosa Springs CO 81147-8312 Office Phone: 970-731-3710.

KELLY, RICHARD C., energy executive; BS in Acctg., Regis U., MBA; postgrad., U. Colo., U. Mich. With auditing dept. Pub. Svc. Co. Colo., 1968-74, staff asst. to mgr. acctg., 1974-76, corp. reports mgr., 1976-83, mgr. acctg., asst. contr., 1983-86, treas., 1986-87, v.p. fin. svcs., 1987-90, sr. v.p. fin., 1990—97; exec. v.p., CFO New Century Energies, Denver, 1997—2000; pres. enterprises Xcel Energy Inc., Minneapolis, Minn., 2000—02, v.p., CFO, 2002—03, pres., 2003—, COO, 2003—03, CEO, chmn., 2005—. Past pres. Arvada Optimist Club; past dir. Ronald McDonald House, Denver Metro C. of Colo. Pub. Expenditures Coun., Mercy Housing; bd. dir. Minneapolis Downtown Coun.; mem. Regis Acctg. Adv. Com. Office: Xcel Energy Inc 414 Nicollet Mall Minneapolis MN 55401-1993*

KELLY, ROBERT DONALD, management consultant; b. Chgo., Sept. 14, 1929; s. Donald Francis and Irene Sarah (Gardner) K.; m. Kay R. Black, Apr. 25, 1959; children: Kim Robert, Kris Donald, Candis Elizabeth. BS in Indsl. Engring., Iowa State U., 1951; MS, Purdue U., 1955, PhD, 1957. Cert. mgmt. cons.; lic. inds. psychologist, Ill. Mem. faculty Purdue U., West Lafayette, Ind., 1953—57; from assoc. prin. to ptnr., dir. Kearney Mgmt. Cons., Chgo., 1957—79; mng. ptnr. pers., internat. pers. Arthur Andersen World Hqtrs., Chgo., 1979—90; sr. internat. cons. Watson Wyatt Co., Chgo., 1990—2003; freelance cons. Chgo., 2003—. Bd. dirs. Allied Farm Equip., Duff Truck Line, Smith, U.S. Contbr. articles to profl. jours. Chmn. bd. trustees Clarendon Hills Presbyn. Ch., 1969-72; chmn. bd. deacons, 1966-69; pres. Bd. Edn. Hinsdale Sch. Dist. 1975-83; trustee and chmn. bd. Coll. DuPage, 1985-91; trustee, bd. dirs. Village of Hinsdale, 1995-99; chmn. Hist. Preservation Commn., Village of Hinsdale, 2001-03; bd. dirs. Hideaway Beach Assn., 2006—. With USAF, 1951-53. Mem. Am. Inst. Mgmt. Cons., Am. Compenstion Assn., Am. Psychol. Assn., Univ. Club, Econs. Club Chgo., Sigma Xi. Home: 120 S Elm St Hinsdale IL 60521-4227 Office: Unit 837 5000 Royal Marco Way Marco Island FL 34145 Personal E-mail: kelly80369@aol.com.

KELLY, ROBERT EDWARD, JR., lawyer; b. Pitts., Nov. 28, 1950; s. Robert E. Sr. and Adelaide Cecelia (Harris) K.; m. Noreen Theresa Quinn, Oct. 23, 1976; children: Robert E. III, Christopher Patrick, Andrew Clifford. BA, Siena Coll., 1972; JD, Georgetown U., 1975. Bar: Pa. 1975,

U.S. Dist. Ct. (we. dist.) Pa. 1975, U.S. Dist. Ct. (ea. and mid. dist.) Pa. 1978, U.S. Ct. Appeals (3d cir.) 1979, U.S. Supreme Ct. 1980, U.S. Dist. Ct. (no. dist.) N.Y. 1992, U.S. Dist. Ct. (no. dist.) Calif. 1994. Assoc. Houston, Harbaugh, Cohen & Lippard, Pitts., 1975-77; assoc., dep. atty. gen. Commonwealth of Pa., Harrisburg, 1977-80; assoc. Duane, Morris & Heckscher, Harrisburg, 1980-86, ptnr., 1986—2002, Kelly, Hoffman & Goduto, LLP, Harrisburg, 2002—07, Kelly, Parker & Cohen LLP, Harrisburg, 2007—. Mem. ABA, FBA, Pa. Bar Assn., Pa. Def. Inst., Dauphin County Bar Assn., Pa. Soc., Am. Inns of Ct., St. Thomas More Soc., West Shore Country Club (Camp Hill, Pa.). Republican. Roman Catholic. Home: 3610 Horsham Dr Mechanicsburg PA 17050-2204 Office: Kelly Parker & Cohen LLP Commerce Towers 10th Fl 300 N 2d St Harrisburg PA 17101 Office Phone: 717-920-2220. Business E-Mail: rkelly@kpc-law.com.

KELLY, ROBERT FRANCIS, federal judge; b. 1935; BS, Villanova U., 1957; LLB, Temple U., 1960. Pvt. practice law, Media, Pa., 1961-62, 64-76, Chester, Pa., 1962-64; law clk. to Hon. Francis J. Catania Ct. Common Pleas, Delaware County, Pa., 1964-72; prothonotary Delaware County, 1972-76; former judge Ct. Common Pleas 32d Jud. Dist. Pa.; judge U.S. Dist. Ct. (ea. dist.) Pa., Phila., 1987—, sr. judge, 2001—. Lectr. law Villanova U. Law Sch. Voluntary defender Delaware County, 1962; chmn. Delaware County Rep. Exec. Com., 1972-76, Subcom. on Libr. Programs; mem. Judicial Coun. com. on Automation and Tech., 1989—. Mem. ABA, Am. Judicature Soc., Pa. Bar Assn., Pa. Trial Judges Assn., Delaware County Bar Assn. (judicial counsel's com. automation and tech., 1989—, chmn. subcom. libr. programs). Office: US Dist Ct 11613 US Courthouse 601 Market St Philadelphia PA 19106-1713 Office Phone: 215-597-0736.

KELLY, ROBERT LYNN, advertising executive; b. Chgo., Oct. 25, 1939; s. Carl Robert and Annabel Pauline (Lindsay) K.; m. Maria Graciela Gonzalez, Oct. 26, 1963; children: Albert E., Elizabeth A. BA, Gettysburg Coll., 1961. Dir. pub. info. Oxnard AFB, Calif., 1961-64; with Armstrong World Industries, Lancaster, Pa., 1964-67; owner Bob Kelly Advt., Quito, Ecuador, 1967-70; ptnr., writer, acct. exec., mgr. Ibold & Kelly Advt., Lancaster, 1970-72; founder, pres. Kelly Advt., Inc., Lancaster, 1972-84; pres. Kelly Michener, Inc., Lancaster, 1984—2004, chmn., 2005—06. Guest lectr. F & M Coll., and Millersville U., 1971—; lectr. Lancaster Community Gallery, 1977. Contbr. articles to profl. jours. Active various civic orgns.; bd. dirs. Lancaster Cmty. Gallery, 1978-89, v.p., 1983-89; mem. campaign coms. Lancaster County Rep. orgns., 1973-75; bd. dirs. Rockford Plantation, 1979-89, v.p., 1988-89; v.p. Let's Lifebelt Lancaster, 1984-85. With USAF, 1961-64. Mem. Nat. Advt. Agy. Network (nat. chmn. 1984), Am. Assn. Advt. Agys. (chmn. regional bd. govs. 1989-90, mem. regional bd. govs. 1998—), Lancaster Advt. Agy Coun. (sec. 1987-61, pres. 1992—2004), N.G. Assn. U.S., Sales and Mktg. Exec., Hamilton Club, Lancaster Tennis and Yacht Club (bd. dirs., v.p. 1986-87, commodore 1988-89), Elk River Yacht Club, Port Herman Beach Assn. (pres. bd. dirs. 1998-99). Episcopalian. Office: Kelly Michener Inc PO Box 959 Lancaster PA 17608-0959 Home Phone: 717-394-6684. E-mail: rkelly@kellyadv.com.

KELLY, ROBERT P., bank executive; b. Mar. 17, 1954; B of Commerce, St. Mary's U., Halifax, NS; MBA, City U., London, England. cert. CPA. Sr. mgmt. Toronto Dominion Bank, Canada; exec. v.p., CFO First Union Corp., Charolette, NC, 2000—01; CFO Wachovia Corp., Winston Salem, NC, 2001—06; chmn., pres., CEO Mellon Fin. Corp., Pitts., 2006—07; CEO Bank of NY Mellon Corp., NYC, 2007—. Bd. dirs. Art Gallery Ontario; former chmn. Metro. Toronto YMCA capital campaign. Office: Bank of NY Mellon Corp 1 Wall St New York NY 10286*

KELLY, ROBERT SYLVESTER See KELLY, R.

KELLY, ROBERT VINCENT, JR., metal products executive; b. Phila., Sept. 29, 1938; s. Robert Vincent and Catherine Mary (Hanley) K.; m. Margaret Cecilia Taylor, Feb. 11, 1961; children: Robert V. III, Christopher T., Michael J., Tasha Marie. BS in Indsl. Mgmt., St. Joseph's U., Phila., 1960; postgrad., Roosevelt U., 1965-66. Gen. foreman prodn. Republic Steel Corp., Chgo., 1963-68; supt. prodn. Phoenix Steel Corp., Phoenixville, Pa., 1969-73; gen. supt. ops. Continental Steel Corp., Kokomo, Ind., 1973-77; gen. mgr. MACSTEEL div. Quanex Corp., Jackson, Mich., 1977-81; corp. v.p. Quanex Corp., Houston, 1979—, pres. MACSTEEL group Jackson, 1982—. Pres. La Salle Steel Co., Hammond, Ind., 1985-87, Arbuckle Corp., Jackson, 1984-88. Leader, com. mem. Boy Scouts Am., Jackson. Lt. USN, 1960-63. Mem. Am. Mgmt. Assn. (pres.), Inst. Indsl. Engrs., Assn. Iron and Steel Engrs., Am. Soc. for Metals, USN Inst., Jackson C. of C. Clubs: Jackson Country. Avocations: hiking, camping, sailing, scouting. Home: 1734 Metzmont Dr Jackson MI 49203-5379 Office: Macsteel, Quanex Corp 1 Jackson Sq Ste 500 Jackson MI 49201-1446

KELLY, SCOTT J., astronaut, military officer; b. Orange, NJ, Feb. 21, 1964; s. Richard and Patricia Kelly; m. Leslie Yandell; 2 children. BSEE, SUNY Maritime Coll., 1987; MS in Aviation Sysems, U. Tenn., Knoxville, 1996. Commd. ensign SUNY Maritime USN, 1987; advanced through grades to lt. comdr.; student pilot USN, Naval Air Sta. Beeville, Tex., 1987—89; naval pilot USN Fighter Squadron 101, Oceana, Va., 1989—90; pilot USN, Fighter Squadron 143, USS Dwight D. Eisenhower, 1990—93; test pilot student USN Test Pilot Sch., 1993—94; test pilot USN, Patuxent River, Md., 1994—96; astronaut NASA Johnson Space Ctr., Houston, 1996—. Served as NASA's dir. ops., Star City, Russia; back-up crew mem. ISS Expedition-5; astronaut office space station branch chief NASA; pilot STS 103 Mission, 1999; comdr. STS-118 Mission (Endeavour) to Internat. Space Station, 2007. Decorated Def. Superior Svc. medal, Navy Commendation medal, Navy Achievement medal, (2) Navy Unit Commendations Nat. Def. Svc. medal, Southwest Asia Svc. medal, Kuwait Liberation medal, Sea Svc. Deployment Ribbon; recipient NASA Space Flight medal, NASA Exceptional Svc. medal, Korolev Diploma, Fedn. Aeronautique Internationale, 1999. Fellow: Soc. Exptl. Test Pilots (assoc.); mem.: Assn. Space Explorers. Achievements include being the first flight pilot to fly an F-14 with an experiment digital flight control system installed and performed subsequent high angle of attack and departure testing; Logged over 3,700 flight hours in more than 30 Different aircraft and has over 250 carrier landings. Avocations: running, weightlifting. Office: Astronaut Office Johnson Space Ctr Houston TX 77058*

KELLY, SEAN, entrepreneur; b. 1983; Attended, Johns Hopkins U.; grad., Columbia U. Personal trainer & fitness cons.; rsch. assoc. NYU Hosp. for Joint Disease; co-founder Fit Fuel, Gardena, Calif., 2004—. Co-author: HealthPundits.com. Named one of Best Entrepreneurs Under 25, BusinessWeek, 2006. Office: Fit Fuel West 2140 W 139th St Gardena CA 90249 E-mail: sean@fitfuel.com.

KELLY, SEAN DORRANCE, philosophy educator; m. Cheryl K. Chen; 1 child. BS with honors, Brown U., 1989, MS in Cognitive and Linguistic Scis., 1989; PhD in Philosophy, U. Calif., 1998. Tchg. asst. philosophy U. Calif., Berkeley, 1989—97, Ralph K. Church departmental fellow in philosophy, 1997—98, instr. philosophy, 1996; lectr. philosophy Stanford U., Calif., 1998—99; asst. prof. philosophy Princeton U., 1999—2006, Jonathan Edwards Bicentennial preceptor, 2002—06, Old Dominion faculty fellow, 2000—01, chair Old Dominion Faculty Fellows, 2001—02; prof. philosophy Harvard U., 2006—. Vis. scholar U. Calif., Berkeley, 2000; lectr. in field. Author: The Relevance of Phenomenology to the Philosophy of Language and Mind, 2000; contbr. articles. Campbell's Coll. Scholarship, Brown U., 1985—89, Fellowship in Complex Sys., Santa Fe Inst. and Los Alamos Labs., 1989, Howison fellowship in philosophy, U. Calif., 1995—96, fellow, NEH Summer Inst. on Consciousness and Intentionality, 2002, James S. McDonnell sr. fellowship in philosophy and neuroscis., 2000—, fellow, John Simon Guggenheim Meml. Found., 2003—, vice-chancellor's rsch. grant in the humanities, U. Calif., 1995, Humanities Grad. Rsch. grant (2), 1996. Mem.: Am. Philosoph. Assn. Office: Harvard U Emerson Hall 25 Quincy St Cambridge MA 02138 Office Phone: 617-495-3915. E-mail: sdkelly@fas.harvard.edu.

KELLY, STANHOPE A., bank executive; b. Nov. 25, 1957; BA in Bus., N.C. State U. Head consumer fin. svcs. Wachovia Corp., regional exec. Raleigh, NC, Forsyth county exec. Winston-Salem, NC, mgmt. assignments in dealer fin., retail banking and corp. banking, sr. exec. v.p. banking and wealth mgmt. divsn., 2000—01, sr. exec. v.p., head wealth mgmt. Charlotte, NC, 2001—. Co-chair capital campaign drive Children's Mus., Winston-Salem; active Forsyth County Heart Gala, Wachovia Arts and Sci.; trustee Forsyth County Day Sch.; mem. bd. visitors Wake Forest U., Bapt. Med. Ctr. Mem.: Fin. Svcs. Roundtable. Office: Wachovia Corp Ste 400 301 S College St Charlotte NC 28288*

KELLY, SUE (SUSAN WEISENBARGER KELLY), former congresswoman; b. Lima, Ohio, Sept. 26, 1936; m. Edward W. Kelly; 4 children. BA in Botany and Bacteriology, Denison U., Granville, Ohio, 1958; MA in Health Advocacy, Sarah Lawrence Coll., Bronxville, NY, 1985. Biomedical rschr. Boston City Hosp., New Eng. Inst. Med. Rsch., 1958; tchr. sci. and math. John Jay Jr. HS, 1962-63, Harvey Sch.; real estate rehabilitator, 1963; campaign coord. Staff of US Rep. Hamilton Fish US Congress, 1971-72; intern Ruth Taylor Home, 1973-74; florist, owner Somerstown Flower Shop, 1978-79; patient advocate emergency room St. Luke's Hosp., NY, 1984-87; adj. prof. grad. prog. health advocacy Sarah Lawrence Coll., 1987-92; mem. US Congress from 19th NY dist., 1995—2007. Vice chmn. com. fin. svcs.; mem. transp. & infrastructure com., small bus. com.; chair fin. svcs. oversight and investigations subcommittee; founder Congl. anti-terrorist financing task force. Recipient Guardian of Seniors' Rights award, Hero of the Taxpayer award, Guardian of Small Bus. award, Nat. Fed. Ind. Bus., Friend of the Farm award, Am. Farm Bur., Sgt. Charles Valenti Legislator of Yr. award, Enlisted Assn. of NY Nat. Guard, Nat. Health Care Humanitarian award, Patient Adv. Found., 1999, Friend of the Nat. Pks. award, Nat. Pks. Conservation Assn., 2005. Republican. Presbyterian.*

KELLY, SUEDEEN G., commissioner; b. 1951; BA, U. Rochester; JD, Cornell U. Bar: DC 1976, N.Mex. With Leubben, Hughes & Kelly, N.Mex.; atty. Office of Atty. Gen., N.Mex.; chair N.Mex. Pub. Svc. Commn.; legis. aide to U.S. Senator Jeff Bingaman, 1999; counsel to Calif. Independent Sys. Operator, 2000; with Modrall, Sperling, Roehl, Harris & Sisk, Albuquerque, 2000—03; commr. Fed. Energy Regulatory Commn., Washington, 2003—. Office: Fed Energy Regulatory Commn 888 First St NE Washington DC 20426

KELLY, T. MARK, lawyer; b. Houston, May 5, 1957; BA magna cum laude, Tex. A&M U., 1978; JD, So. Meth. U., 1981. Bar: Tex. 1981. Ptnr., co-chair Corp. Fin. and Securities Practice, mem. Mgmt. Com. Vinson & Elkins, LLP, Houston. Fellow: Houston Bar Found., Tex. Bar Found.; mem.: ABA, Houston Bar Assn., Tex. Bar Assn. Office: Vinson & Elkins LLP First City Tower 1001 Fannin St, Ste 2300 Houston TX 77002-6760 Office Phone: 713-758-4592. E-mail: mkelly@velaw.com.

KELLY, THADDEUS ELLIOTT, medical geneticist; b. NYC, 1937; MD, Med. Coll. S.C.; PhD, Johns Hopkins U. Diplomate Am. Bd. Genetics (pres. 1993-94), Am. Bd. Pediat. Prof. pediat. U. Va., Charlottesville, dir. med. genetics. Office: U Va Hosp Div Med Genetics PO Box 800386 Charlottesville VA 22908-0386

KELLY, THOMAS CAJETAN, archbishop; b. Rochester, NY, July 14, 1931; s. Thomas A. Kelly and Katherine Eleanor (Fisher) Conley. AB, Providence Coll., 1953; STL, Dominican House of Studies, Washington, 1959; D in Canon Law, U. St. Thomas, Rome, 1962; STD (hon.), Providence Coll, 1979; DHL (hon.), Spalding Coll., 1983. Ordained priest Roman Cath. Ch. 58, aux. bishop 77. Sec. Dominican Province, NYC, 1962—65; sec. Apostolic Del., Washington, 1965—71; assoc. gen. sec. Nat. Conf. Cath. Bishops-U.S. Cath. Conf., Washington, 1971—77; gen. sec. U.S. Cath. Bishops Conf., Washington, 1977—82; archbishop Archdiocese of Louisville, 1982—. Chmn. Cath. Conf. Ky., Louisville, 1982—. Chancellor Bellarmine Coll.; bd. dirs. St. Luke Inst. Recipient Veritas medal, St. Catharine Coll., 1984. Mem.: Nat. Cath. Edn. Assn. (chmn. bd. dirs. 1991—94), Canon Law Soc. Am. Roman Catholic. Home and Office: 212 E College St Louisville KY 40203-2334

KELLY, THOMAS J., JR., lawyer; b. Williamsport, Pa., July 18, 1953; BS, LaSalle Coll., 1976; JD, Cath. U. Am., 1980. Bar: DC 1981. Law clk. to chief judge H. Carl Moultrie Superior Ct. of D.C., 1980—82; asst. US atty. Washington, 1986—89; with Venable LLP, Washington, 1989—, ptnr., corp. def./white collar, environ., 1992—. Founder Zacchaeus Free Legal Clinic, NW Washington, DC. Named a Top Lawyer, Washingtonian Mag., 2004; named Young Lawyer of the Yr. award, DC Bar Assn., 1991. Mem.: ABA, Assn. Asst. US Attys, Nat. Assn. Criminal Def. Lawyers, Bar Assn. DC, DC Bar. Office: Venable LLP 575 Seventh St NW Washington DC 20004 Home Phone: 301-738-8756; Office Phone: 202-344-4887. Office Fax: 202-344-8300. Business E-Mail: tjkelly@venable.com.

KELLY, THOMAS JESSE, JR., molecular biologist; b. Birmingham, Ala., Nov. 21, 1941; s. Thomas Jesse and Agnes (Allen) K.; m. Mary Lucinda Schwartz, June 25, 1969; children: Mark Thomas, Andrew Samuel. BA with honors, Johns Hopkins U., 1962, PhD in Biophysics, 1968, MD, 1969. Served with USPHS, 1970-72. Postdoctoral fellow Harvard Med. Sch., Boston, 1968, Johns Hopkins U. Sch. Medicine, Balt., 1969-70; staff assoc. Nat. Inst. Health, Bethesda, Md., 1970-72; asst. prof. microbiology Johns Hopkins U. Sch. Medicine, Balt., 1972-75, assoc. prof., 1976-79, Boury Prof. molecular biology and genetics, 1980—2002, dir. dept., 1982—2002; dir. Sloan-Kettering Inst., NYC, 2002—. Chmn. study sect. virology NIH, 1988-90. Mem. editorial bd. Jour. Biol. Chemistry, 1982-94, Jour. Virology, 1980-90, Virus Rsch., 1983-93, Oncogene Rsch., 1989-94, Seminars in Virology, 1989-95, Am. Soc. Biochem. Molecular Biology, 1989-94. Awards assembly Gen. Motors Cancer Prize; bd. dirs. Passano Found. Recipient Career Devel. award NIH, 1972-77, Alfred P. Sloane, Jr. award, GM Cancer Rsch. Found., 2004. Fellow Am. Acad. Arts and Sci.; mem. NAS, Am. Soc. Biological Chemists, Am. Soc. Microbiology, Am. Soc. Virology, Phi Beta Kappa, Alpha Omega Alpha, Inst. Medicine. Office: Sloan-Kettering Inst 1275 York Ave New York NY 10021

KELLY, THOMAS M., headmaster; BA, Fairfield U.; MEd, Columbia's Teachers Coll.; PhD & MPhil, Columbia U. Former prin. Hendrick Hudson HS; supt. Valhalla Union Free Sch. Dist., Westchester, NY, 1999—2005; head of sch. Horace Mann Sch., Riverdale, NY, 2005—. Adjunct prof. Columbia's Teachers Coll., 1994—. Pres. & bd. dirs. Hawthorne Found.; founder Valhalla Schools Found. Mem.: Nat. Psychology Honor Soc., Nat. Education Honor Soc. Office: Horace Mann Sch 231 W 246th St Bronx NY 10471*

KELLY, THOMAS MICHAEL, lawyer; b. Atlanta, Oct. 5, 1958; s. Edward (dec.) and Marie K. AB cum laude, Columbia U., 1979; JD cum laude, Harvard U., 1983. Bar: N.Y. 1985. Law clk. to Hon. Eugene Nickerson U.S. Dist. Ct. (ea. dist.) N.Y., Bklyn., 1983-84; assoc. Debevoise & Plimpton, NYC, 1984-93, ptnr., 1993—. Bd. dirs. Symphony Space, Inc.; mem. investment com. Social Sci. Rsch. Coun. Mem. Assn. of Bar of City of N.Y. Democrat. Office: Debevoise & Plimpton 919 3rd Ave 43d Fl New York NY 10022-6225 Home Phone: 212-982-1383; Office Phone: 212-909-6907. Business E-Mail: tmkelly@debevoise.com.

KELLY, THOMAS N., JR., telecommunications industry executive; Degree, Wofford Coll. With Howard Bedford Nolan, 1981—93; v.p. mktg. AT&T Wireless, 1993—96; exec. v.p., , chief mktg. officer Nextel Commn., 1996—2003, exec. v.p., COO, 2003—05; exec. v.p., chief strategy officer Sprint Nextel Corp., 2005, exec. v.p. transition integration, 2005—06. Bd. dir. Radioframe Networks Inc., Bellevue, Wash., Scotts Miracle-Gro Co., Gracenote Co., Broadsoft. Vol. sch. and youth athletic orgn., Va. Mailing: Scotts Miracle-Gro Bd Directors 14111 Scottslawn Rd Marysville OH 43041

KELLY, THOMAS PAINE, JR., retired lawyer; b. Tampa, Fla., Aug. 29, 1912; s. Thomas Paine and Beatrice (Gent) K.; m. Jean Baughman, July 25, 1940; children: Carla, Thomas Paine III (dec.), Josie. AB, U. Fla., 1935, JD, 1936. Bar: Fla. 1936, U.S. Dist. Ct. (no. dist.) Fla. 1936, U.S. Ct. Appeals (5th cir.) 1936, U.S. Dist. Ct. (mid. dist.) Fla. 1940, U.S. Dist. Ct. (so. dist.) Fla. 1939, U.S. Ct. Appeals (11th cir.) 1983, U.S. Supreme Ct. 1990. Since practiced in, Tampa; assoc. McKay, Macfarlane, Jackson & Ferguson, 1939-40; ptnr. McKay, MacFarlane, Jackson & Ferguson, 1940-48, Macfarlane, Ferguson, Allison & Kelly, 1948-83, sr. ptnr., 1983-91; of counsel Shear, Newman, Hahn & Rosenkranz, 1992-95; shareholder MacFarlane Ferguson & McMullen, P.A., Tampa, Fla., 1996—, ret., 2005. Author: Fifty Years of Courting, 1996, The Fighting 589th, 2001. Chmn. Tampa Com. 100, 1960-61; pres. Tampa Citizens' Safety Coun., 1961-62; Bd. dirs. Tampa chpt. ARC, 1955-62, pres., 1958-59; bd. dirs. Boys Clubs Tampa, 1956-67, pres., 1966-67. Col. F.A. AUS, 1940-45. Decorated Silver Star. Fellow Am. Coll. Trial Lawyers, Internat. Acad. Trial Lawyers; mem. Am. Bar Assn., Fla. Bar Assn. Hillsborough County, Fla. Bar (chmn. com. profl. ethics 1953-58, chmn. com. ins. and negligence law 1962-63, chmn. fed. rules com. 1969-70) Republican. Home: 5426 Lykes Ln Tampa FL 33611-4747

KELLY, TIMOTHY E., communications executive; B in Mktg., U. Fla. Various pos., including acct. mgr. Procter & Gamble, Burger King, and Arm & Hammer, D'Arcy, Masium Benten & Bowles, Inc., and Lever Bros. Co., NYC; asst. v.p. corp. brand, media and sponsorship mktg. initiatives, to v.p.-consumer long distance mktg. Consumer Svcs. Group, 1994—99; pres. Tickets.com, 1999—2002; pres.-Sprint Bus., Global Markets Group Sprint Corp., Dallas, 2002—05; pres. customer mgmt. Sprint Nextel, Reston, Va., 2005—. Office: Sprint Nextel 2001 Edmund Halley Dr Reston VA 20191*

KELLY, TIMOTHY JOHNSTON, secondary school educator; b. Carlisle, Pa., Feb. 6, 1953; s. John Edward and Jane (Oseth) Kelly; m. Sharon Lynn Weber, Apr. 5, 1980; children: Brian, Eric. BBA, Ga. State U., Atlanta, 1981, MEd, 1995; EdS, U. Ala., Tuscaloosa, 2004. Cert. tchr. Ga. Tchr. Ga. studies and econ. Gwinnett County Pub. Schs., Ga., 1987—. Scorer Nat. Bd. Profl. Tchg. Stds., 2001—02. Bldg. campaign chmn. United Way, Dacula and Osborne Mid. Sch., 1997—2004. Mem.: Ga. Assn. Educators. Avocations: photography, collecting records, travel, collecting neckties, reading.

KELLY, TIMOTHY MICHAEL, newspaper publisher; b. Ashland, Ky., Nov. 28, 1947; s. Robert John and Pauline Elizabeth (Henneman) K.; m. Carol Ann Knight, Aug. 2, 1969; children: Kimberly, Kevin. BA, U. Miami, Fla., 1970. Sports copy editor, writer The Courier-Jour., Louisville, 1970-71; exec. sports editor The Phila. Inquirer, 1971-75; dep. mng. editor Dallas Times Herald, 1975-81; mng. editor The Denver Post, 1981-84; exec. editor Dallas Times Herald, 1984; editor Daily News, LA, 1984-87; mng. editor The Orange County Register, Santa Ana, Calif., 1987-89; editor, sr. v.p. Lexington (Ky.) Herald-Leader, 1989-96, pub., 1996—. Juror Pulitzer Prize, 1987-88. Bd. dirs. YMCA of U.S.A., 2004—, nat. sec., 2005—07. Recipient Excellence Cmty. Svc. award Knight Ridder, 1995, Ida B. Wells award, 1999, Ky. Journalism Hall of Fame award, 2000, Byron B. Harless award Knight Ridder, 2003. Roman Catholic. Office: Lexington Herald Leader 100 Midland Ave Lexington KY 40508-1999 Office Phone: 859-231-3257. Business E-Mail: tkelly@herald-leader.com.

KELLY, TIMOTHY WILLIAM, lawyer; b. Apr. 27, 1953; s. George Raymond and Mary Therese (Kelly) K.; m. Mary Teresa Harms, May 24, 1980; children: Ryan Timothy, Colin Patrick, Kaitlynn Elizabeth. BS in Bus. Adminstrn., U. Dayton, 1975, JD, 1978. Bar: Ill. 1978, U.S. Dist. Ct. (cen. and no. dists.) Ill. 1979. Staff counsel Praire State Legal Aid, Bloomington, Ill., 1978-81; felony asst. McLean County Pub. Defenders, Bloomington, 1981-83; assoc. Jerome Mirza & Assocs., Bloomington, 1983-88; asst. prof. polit. sci. Ill. State U., Normal, 1980-83; faculty mem. Ill. Inst. Continuing Legal Edn. Lectr. in field. Contbr. articles to profl. jours. Bd. dirs. Bloomington/Normal Day Care Assn., 1982-83; civil actions arbitrator and mediator McLean County, 1996—. Named one of Top Three Attys. in McLean, Bus. to Bus. Mag., 1997. Fellow Ill. Bar Found.; mem. ATLA, Ill. State Bar Assn. (mem. civil practice and procedure sect. coun. 1992—, chmn. 1998, Allerton house steering com. 1994, 96, 98, tort law sect. coun. 1995—, assembly mem. 1995—), Ill. Trial Lawyers Assn. (mem. bd. mgrs. 1992—, continuing legal edn. com. 1995-96, exec. com. 1996, chmn. ins. law com. 1996-98), Chgo. Bar Assn., McLean County Bar Assn. (sec. 1984-85), McLean County Inns of Ct., IICLE (bd. dirs. 2000—). Democrat. Roman Catholic. E-mail: twkelly271@aol.com.

KELLY, TOM (JAY THOMAS KELLY), retired professional sports team manager; b. Graceville, Minn., Aug. 15, 1950; s. Joseph Thomas and Anna Grace (Heisenbottle) K.; children: Sharon Clare, Thomas John. Student, Mesa Jr. Coll., Ariz., 1968-69. Profl. baseball player Minn. Twins, Mpls., 1968-77, coach, 1982-86, mgr., 1987—2001, mgr. minor league team Toledo, 1978-82. Managed Minn. Twins team to World Series Championship, 1987, 91; named Am. League Mgr. of Yr. Sporting News, 1991. Mem. Assn. Profl. Baseball Players, U.S. Trotting Assn., Nat. Greyhound Assn. Avocation: harness racing. Office: Minn Twins Hubert H Humphrey Metrodome 34 Kirby Puckett Pl Minneapolis MN 55415-1596

KELLY, VICKY LELOIE, music educator; b. Amarillo, Tex., Feb. 17, 1949; d. Robert Bruce and Elizabeth Ann Kelly (Stepmother), Lavelle Hughes Kelly; m. Steven Alan Graham, May 14, 1999. MusB, Oklahoma City U., 1971, MusM, 1972; Cert. Attendance, U. Stranieri, Perugia, Italy, 2002. Adj. prof. voice Okahoma City U., 1975—79, instr. voice, 1979—83, asst. prof. voice, 1983—85, assoc. prof. voice, 1985—2000, prof. voice, 2000—. Singer, actor Lyric Theater Oklahoma City, Inc., 1967—70; singer Kansas City Starlight Theater, Mo., 1970—72; mgr., singer, dancer USO, Europe, 1976, Asia, 81, Dept. Def. Overseas Tours, Europe, 1983, mgr./singer/dancer, Europe, 91, mgr., singer, dancer, Asia, 85, Europe, 1993—93, 1992. Named Lady in tNews, Okla. Hospitality Club, 1982; recipient Okla. Amb. Good Will, Okla. Heritage Assn., 1991. Mem.: Coll. Music Soc., Okla. Music Tchrs. Assn., Can. Voice Care Found., Music Teachers Nat. Assn., Voice Found., Actors Equity Assn., Nat. Assn. Tchrs. Singing, Cardinal Key, Sigma Alpha Iota, Pi Kappa Lambda, Gamma Phi Beta. Methodist. Office: Oklahoma City U 2501 N Blackwelder Oklahoma City OK 73106 Home Phone: 405-842-0427; Office Phone: 405-208-5342.

KELLY, WILLIAM CHARLES, JR., retired lawyer; b. Mpls., June 9, 1946; s. William Charles and Marian Eileen (Moritz) K.; m. Cynthia Ann Churchill, June 28, 1969; children: Patrick, Brian. AB, Harvard U., 1968;

JD, Yale U., 1971. Bar: Maine 1972, D.C. 1973, U.S. Supreme Ct. 1973. Law clk. to Judge Coffin U.S. Ct. Appeals (1st cir.), Portland, Maine, 1971-72; law clk. to Justice Powell U.S. Supreme Ct., Washington, 1972-73; exec. asst. to sec. HUD, Washington, 1975-77; ptnr. Latham & Watkins, Washington, 1978—2003, ret., 2003. Bd. dirs. Nat. Low Income Housing Coalition, Washington, 1983-94, The Governance Inst., 1986—, Washington Legal Clinic for the Homeless, 1999—; trustee Sheridan Sch., 1992-98; mem. Ashoka World Coun., 1997—; dir. Ashoka Innovators for the Public, 1999—; pres. Stewards Affordable Housing for Future, 2004—. Lt. USNR, 1973-75. Mem. ABA, D.C. Bar Assn. Office: Latham & Watkins Ste 1000 555 11th St NW Washington DC 20004-1304 Office Phone: 202-637-2233. Business E-Mail: bill.kelly@lw.com.

KELLY, WILLIAM FRANKLIN, JR., lawyer; b. Houston, Feb. 12, 1938; s. William Franklin and Sara (McAshan) K.; m. Ingrid Leach, Sept. 11, 1965; children: Kristin Adams, Sara McAshan. BA, Stanford U., 1960; LLB, U. Tex., 1963. Bar: Tex. 1965. Assoc. Vinson & Elkins, Houston, 1965-72, ptnr., 1972-97. Served to 1st lt. U.S. Army, 1963-65. Fellow Houston Bar Found; mem. ABA, Tex. Bar Assn., Houston Bar Assn. Clubs: Forest (Houston), The Houston. Episcopalian. Avocation: sport diving. Home: 600 E Friar Tuck Ln Houston TX 77024-5707 Office: Vinson & Elkins LLP First City Tower 1001 Fannin St Ste 2300 Houston TX 77002-6706

KELLY, WILLIAM MICHAEL, investment company executive; b. Pittsfield, Mass., Feb. 3, 1944; children: Alyssa A., Eileen J.; m. Christina E. Houlihan, 2003. BA in Polit. Sci., St. Anselm Coll., 1966; MA in Polit. Sci., Duquesne U., 1968; MBA in Fin., NYU, 1972. Portfolio mngr., v.p. Chase Manhattan Bank, NYC, 1968-77; v.p. Nat. Aviation and Tech., NYC, 1977-80; assoc. Lingold Assocs., NYC, 1980—, pres., 1992—. Trustee 1st Eagle Funds, N.Y.C., 1999—; ind. gen. ptnr. ML Venture Ptnrs. II, N.Y.C., 1991-2001; dir., treas., Black Forest Consortium, Inc., Black Forest Preserve, N.Y., 1989—; trustee N.Y. Found., 1985-2005, chmn., 1992-95; asst. treas. Neuroscis. Rsch. Found., Calif, 1982-99; v.p., treas. Sergei Zlinkoff Fund Med. Edn., 1992—; trustee St. Anselm Coll., N.H., 1998—, NH Inst. Politics, 2007. Bd. govs. Eugene Lang Coll, 1994-02; trustee Pathways for Youth, 1976-2005, pres. 1981-84. Mem. AAAS, (investment and fin. com. 1985-99), N.Y. Acad. Scis. (fin. affairs com. 1987-2002), Sleepy Hollow Country Club. Office: 500 5th Ave Fl 50 New York NY 10110-5099 Office Phone: 212-391-8960.

KELLY, WILLIAM WATKINS, educational association executive; b. Asheville, NC, Sept. 21, 1928; s. John Jackson and Trula (Watkins) K.; m. Lura Jane Kelly, Feb. 14, 1953 (div. Jan. 14, 1983); children: William Watkins, Robert Jackson, Blair Massey, Gregory Clark.; m. Catherine Messer Penney, Jan. 22, 1983. BA, Va. Mil. Inst., 1950; A.M., Duke U., 1955, PhD, 1957. Commandant cadets, tchr. English John Marshall High Sch., Richmond, Va., 1950-52; instr. English Va. Mil. Inst., 1952-53, English Air Force Acad., 1957-58, asst. prof., 1958-60, English Va. Mil. Inst., 1960-62; asst. prof. Am. thought and language Mich. State U., 1962-65, assoc. prof., 1965-69; assoc. dir. The Honors Coll., 1965-68, dir., 1968-69; pres. Mary Baldwin Coll., 1969-76, Transylvania U., Lexington, Ky., 1976-81; sr. assoc. Univ. Assos., 1981-82; exec. v.p. L.Q.C. Lamar Soc., 1981-82; pres. Ala. Assn. Ind. Colls. and Univs., 1982-88, Ga. Found. for Ind. Colls. Inc., Atlanta, 1988-96; pres. emeritus, 1996—; pres. Assn. Pvt. Colls. and Univs. in Ga., Atlanta, 1990-96; sr. v.p. Jon McRae & Assocs. Inc., Atlanta, 1996—2001; dir. coll. and unv. rels. Connexxia, 2001—05; sr. adv. higher edn. divsn. James Tower, 2005—; sr. assoc. Jon McRae and Assocs., 2007—. Mem. Va. Commn. on Status of Women, 1973-76, Ky. Commn. on Status of Women, 1977-81; chmn. Ky. Rhodes Scholar Selection Com., 1978-79; pres. Coun. Ind. Ky. Colls. and Univs., 1978-80; bd. dirs. Ala. Humanities Found., 1983-88, chmn. bd. dirs., 1985-87; bd. dirs., exec. com. Ga. Humanities Coun., 1989-96, vice chair, 1991-93, chair, 1994-96. Author: Ellen Glasow: A Bibliography, 1964. Bd. dirs. ODK Found., 2002—, Ky. State C. of C., 1980—82; trustee Greensboro Coll., 1993—2000, 2002—. Ellis L. Phillips Found. intern Rutgers U., 1964-65; Ala. recipient IBM Disting. Performance award Ind. Coll. Funds Am., 1986, Outstanding Ala. Fund Raising Exec. award Nat. Soc. Fund Raising Execs., 1986, Leadership award Brunswick Pub. Charitable Found., 1993; Danforth fellow, 1953-57; Duke scholar, 1954-55; William Watkins Kelly Endowed Scholarship in the Humanities established Ga. Found. Ind. Colls., 1996. Fellow Found. Ind. Higher Edn. (nat. presiding officer 1992-94, Disting. Performance award 1996); mem. MLA, Am. Studies Assn., Soc. Values in Higher Edn., Am. Assn. Higher Edn., Ellen Glasgow Soc. (pres. 1973-75), Newcomen Soc. N.Am., Rotary (Paul Harris fellow), Phi Beta Kappa, The Fellows of Phi Beta Kappa (bd. dirs. 2000—), Omicron Delta Kappa (Found. bd. dirs. 2002—), Rotary. Home and Office: 4015 Brockton Close Marietta GA 30068-4931 Home Phone: 770-953-0315; Office Phone: 770-272-9040. Personal E-mail: drkelly@bellsouth.net. Business E-Mail: wwk@jonmcrae.com.

KELM, BONNIE G., art museum director, educator, art appraiser, consultant; b. Bklyn., Mar. 29, 1947; d. Julius and Anita (Baron) Steiman; m. William G. Malis; 1 child, Michael Darren. BS in Art Edn., Buffalo State U., 1968; MA in Art History, Bowling Green State U., Ohio, 1975; PhD in Arts Adminstrn., Ohio State U., 1987. Cert. uniform standards of profl. appraisal practice NYU, 2004. Art tchr. Toledo Pub. Schs., 1968—71; ednl. cons. Columbus (Ohio) Mus. Art, 1976—81; prof. art Franklin U., Columbus, 1976—88; legis. coord. Ohio Ho. of Reps., Columbus, 1977; pres. bd. trustees Columbus Inst. for Contemporary Art, 1977—81; tech. asst. cons. Ohio Arts Coun., Columbus, 1984—88; dir. Bunte Gallery Franklin U., Columbus, 1978—88; dir. art mus. Miami U., Oxford, Ohio, 1988—96, assoc. prof., 1988—96; dir. Muscarelle Mus. of Art Coll. William and Mary, Williamsburg, Va., 1996—2002, assoc. prof. art and art history, 1996—2002; dir. Univ. Art Mus. U. Calif., Santa Barbara, 2002—06. Adj. prof. dept. art history U. Art Mus. U. Calif., Santa Barbara; grant panelist Ohio Arts Coun., Columbus, 1985—87, Columbus, 1991—95, 2006—; art book reviewer William C. Brown Pub., Madison, Wis., 1985—92; mem. acquisitions adv. bd. Martin Luther King Ctr., Columbus, 1987—88; field reviewer Inst. Mus. Svcs., Washington, 1990—; chair grant panel Art in Pub. Places, 1992—95; trustee Ohio Mus. Assn., 1993—96; adv. bd. Women Beyond Borders, 2004—; state apptd. mem. adv. com. Ohio Percent for Art, 1994—96; spkr., presenter in field. Author, editor (mus. catalogues) Connections, 1985, Into the Mainstream: Contemporary Folk Art, 1991, Testimony of Images: PreColumbian Art, 1992, Collecting by Design: The Allen Collection, 1994, Photographs by Barbara Hershey: A Retrospective, 1995, Georgia O'Keeffe in Williamsburg, 2001; contbr. chpt. to books, articles to profl. jours. Founding mem., mem. adv. coun. Columbus Cultural Arts Ctr., 1977-81; coord., curator Cultural Exch. Program, Honolulu-Columbus, 1980; mem. acad. women achievers YWCA, 1991—; mem. adv. bd. Women beyond Borders, 2004—, Exploring Solutions Past: The Maya Forest Alliance, 2006-. Recipient Marantz Disting. Scholar award Ohio State U., 1995, Gelpe award YWCA, 1987, Cultural Advancement of City of Columbus award, The Columbus Dispatch, 1984, Disting. Svc. award, Columbus Art League, 1984, Critic's Choice award Found. for Cmty. of Artists, N.Y., 1981; Fulbright scholar USIA, 1988 (The Netherlands); NEH fellow East-West Ctr., Honolulu, 1991. Mem. Am. Assn. Mus. (advocacy task force, surveyor mus. assessment program 1996—, nat. program com. 2001), Assn. Coll. and Univ. Mus. and Galleries (bd. dirs. 1998-2006), Western Mus. Assn., Fulbright Assn., Coll. Art Assn. (session chair, mus. com. 2004-07), Internat. Coun. Mus., Calif. Assn. Mus., Internat. Soc. Appraisers. Office Phone: 805-815-5198. Business E-Mail: bgkelm@wavecable.com. *Pay attention to all of the potentials and resources that others overlook in your every day environment. Never let any one convince you that something you're committed to is impossible. Make an art of putting people and possibilities together.*

KELMAN, ARI, history professor, educator; b. Phila., Dec. 5, 1968; s. Samuel M. and Anna D. Kelman; m. Lesley Sophia Rosen, June 21, 1998; 1 child, Jacob. BA, U. Wis., Madison, 1991; PhD, Brown U., Providence, RI, 1998. Prof. honors coll. U. Okla., Norman, 1998—2000; assoc. prof., chmn. dept. U. Denver, 2000—05; assoc. prof. history U. Calif., Davis, 2005—. Contbr. articles to mags., to profl. jours. Recipient Abbott Lowell Cummings award, Vernacular Architecture Forum, 2004. Home Phone: 530-297-1234.

KELMAN, EDWARD MICHAEL, lawyer; b. NYC, Aug. 29, 1943; s. Jack H. and Evelyn (Karp) K.; children: Matthews S., Joshua K. AB, Cornell U., 1965; JD, NYU, 1968. Bar: N.Y. 1969, Conn. 1972. Asst dist. atty. N.Y. County Dist. Atty.'s Office, 1968-71; assoc. Glazer & Wechsler, Stamford, Conn., 1971-72, Squadron, Gartenberg, Elenoff & Plesent, NYC, 1972-73; sr. atty. CBS Records, CBS, Inc., NYC, 1973-76; asst. gen. atty. CBS Pub., CBS, Inc., NYC, 1976-77; v.p. law Chappell Music Co., NYC, 1977-80; of counsel Law Offices of Michael Sukin, NYC, 1980-82; v.p. bus. affairs and acquisitions Thorn EMI Video & TV, NYC, 1982-83; pvt. practice entertainment and media law NYC, 1983—. Recipient Spl. award Rec. Ind. Assn. Am., 1975. Mem. NARAS, Assn. Bar City NY., Conn. Bar Assn., Nat. Acad. Popular Music, Cornell Club of NY, NYU. Sch. Law Alumni Assn. (bd. dirs.). Avocations: sports, movies, theater. Office: 100 Park Ave 20th Fl New York NY 10017 Office Phone: 212-371-9490. Fax: 212-750-1356. E-mail: Emknyc@aol.com.

KELMAN, GLENN, Internet company executive, entrepreneur; b. 1972; BA summa cum laude, U. Calif. Berkeley. Product mgr. Stanford Tech. Group; co-founder Plumtree Software, San Francisco, 1996—2005; pres. & CEO Redfin, Seattle, 2006—. Bd. dirs. Naviance. Office: Redfin Puget Sound Area Real Estate Ops 308 Occidental Ave #205 Seattle WA 98104 Office Phone: 877-973-3346.*

KELMAN, MARYBETH, retired health care consultant, health policy analyst; AS in Nursing, Rutgers U., 1964; BA, Douglas Coll., 1977; MA, Rutgers U., 1988. Program dir. health promotion N.J. Hosp. Assn., Princeton, NJ, 1983-87; policy analyst N.J. Dept. Human Svcs., Trenton, NJ, 1988-89; exec. dir. Eye Screening Coord. Coun. N.J., Inc., Monmouth Junction, NJ, 1989-91; health care cons. N.J. Divsn. Pensions and Benefits, Trenton, 1992—2004; ret., 2004. Trustee Forums Inst. for Pub. Policy, Princeton, 1998—, chmn., 1998—2005. Home: 1500 Sawyer Ave Manasquan NJ 08736 Personal E-mail: mbkelman@verizon.net.

KELMAN, STEVEN JAY, education educator; b. NYC, May 1, 1948; s. Kurt and Sylvia (Etman) K.; m. Shelley Metzenbaum, July 5, 1980; children: Jody, Leora. AB summa cum laude, Harvard Coll., 1970; PhD, Harvard U., 1978. Asst. prof. pub. policy Harvard U., 1978-80; with Federal Trade Comm., Washington, 1980-81; assoc. prof. and prof. pub. mgmt. Harvard U., 1982-93, 97—; adminstr. Office of Fed. Procurement Policy, Washington, 1993-97. Editor: Internat. Pub. Managements Jour., 2005—. Democrat. Jewish. Office: Harvard Univ JFK Sch of Government Cambridge MA 02138 Office Phone: 617-496-6302. E-mail: steve_kelman@harvard.edu.

KELMENSON, LEO-ARTHUR, advertising executive; b. NYC, Jan. 3, 1927; s. Joseph A. and Ruth (Rothberg) K.; m. Gayle Frances Abrams, Sept. 1989; children from previous marriage: Todd-Arthur, Joel Adam. BS, Columbia U., 1951; postgrad., Grad. Sch. Bus., 1952. From TV prodn. to sr. v.p., asst. to pres. Lennen & Newell, 1951-65; exec. v.p., mem. exec. com. Norman Craig & Kummel, 1965-66; sr. v.p., dir., mem. exec. com. Kenyon & Eckhardt, 1967-68, chmn., chief exec. officer, 1968-86; chmn. Bozell, Jacobs, Kenyon & Eckhardt, 1986-93, chmn. exec. com.; chmn. Bozell Worldwide; chmn. bd. advisors, chmn. devel. com. Tisch Sch of Arts NYU, 1988—; chmn. Bozell de Mexico, 1992-99, FCB Worldwide, NYC, 1999—. Pres. Kelmenson Funds Ltd.; dir. Lorimar, Locations Unltd., On-Line Software Internat.; bd. trustees Am. Cinematheque; lectr. New Sch. Social Rsch.; Adviser communications office U.S. Atty. Gen., 1960-63; spl. project officer Dept. State, 1952-64; co-founder, v.p., dir. African Med. and Rsch. Found., 1957—. Author: (poetry) Epilogue, 1964; also short stories. Mem. pub. rels. com. Nat. Cancer Found., 1958—; adv. com. Nat. Cultural Center, 1962; pres. Shoes for Little Souls, 1960, Remsenburg Assn., 1968; bd. dirs. ASPCA, Stop Cancer Found., 1990, 91; mem. pres.'s adv. coun. Am. Diabetes Assn., 1977-78. Served with USMCR, World War II. Recipient Theodore Roosevelt Man of Year award, 1955; Silver Quill Poetry award, 1955; Res. Officers Assn. award, 1965; Guggenheim World Peace award, 1951; Am. Jewish Com. Humanitarian award; Humanitarian award St. Frances Cabrini. Mem. U.S. Olympic Com., N.Y. Advt. Club, Soc. Am. Businessmen Club, Sigma Phi Epsilon. Clubs: Sands Point, Ocean Reef, Key Largo, Sands Point Yacht, L.I. Polo, U.S. Yacht Racing Assn. (N.Y.). Office: NYU Tisch Sch Arts New York NY 10003 also: FCB Worldwide 100 W 33rd St #5 New York NY 10001-2921 Fax: 212-885-3399. E-mail: lkelmenson@fcb.com.

KELSEY, ANN LEE, library administrator; b. Kokomo, Ind., June 20, 1946; d. Harry Willard and JoAnn Kelsey. BA in Anthropology and English cum laude, U. Calif., Riverside, 1968; MLS, UCLA, 1969. Adminstrv. libr. U.S. Army Spl. Svcs., Cam Ranh Bay, Vietnam, 1969-70; children's libr. Elmont (N.Y.) Meml. Libr., 1970-71; libr. Queensborough Pub. Libr., Jamaica, N.Y., 1971-73; children's libr. Upper Saddle River (N.J.) Pub. Libr., 1973-75; prin. libr. Morris County Libr., Whippany, N.J., 1975-83; assoc. dir. Learning Resource Ctr., County Coll. Morris, Randolph, N.J., 1983—. Networked assoc. fellow 60s workgroup Inst. for Advanced Tech. in Humanities, U. Va., 1994—; ptnr., cons. libr. automation and planning DocuMentors, Rockaway, N.J., 1985—; ind. cons. infosys., Whippany, 1978—. Co-author: Planning for Automation: A How-To-Do-It Manual for Librarians, 1993, 2d edit., 1997, Writing and Updating Technology Plans: A Guidebook with Sample plans in CD-ROM, 1999, Planning for Integrated Systems and Technologies, 2001, Staffing the Modern Library, 2005; contbr. chpt. to: Insider's Guide to Library Automation, 1993; editor: Resources for Teaching the Vietnam War: An Annotated Guide, rev. edit., 1996; also articles. V.p. Project: Hearts and Minds, Inc., Greenwich, Conn., 1995-2005; bd. dirs. NJ Vietnam Vets. Oral History Project, Kean U., 1998, NJ Vietnam Vets. Meml. Found., 2001; edn. adv. com. N.J. Vietnam Vets. Meml. Found., Vietnam Era Ednl. Ctr., 1998; active Morris County Dem. com., 1992. Named to honor roll Vietnam Women's Meml. Project, Washington, 1993; recipient award African Am. Cultural Coun. Virginia Beach, 1999. Mem. ALA (travel grantee 1988), Am. Soc. Info. Sci., Spl. Libr. Assn. (pres. N.J. chpt. 1989-90, chairperson cataloging com. 1992-93), N.J. Libr. Assn. (chairperson automated libr. svcs. sect. 1992-93, mem. pers. adminstrn. com. 1986-87, mem. pay equity task force 1985-86), Women's Overseas Svc. League (scholarship com. chair 2003-), UCLA Alumni Club (chmn. scholarship com. N.Y. chpt. 2003—), Phi Beta Kappa. Avocations: bicycling, Web surfing, gardening. Office: DocuMentors 7 Valley View Dr Rockaway NJ 07866-1506 Business E-Mail: akelsey@ccm.edu.

KELSEY, CLYDE EASTMAN, JR., philosophy educator, psychology professor; b. Wadena, Minn., Mar. 30, 1924; s. Clyde Eastman and Lorraine (Lamb) Bagley) K.; m. Betty Jean Williams, Apr. 1, 1949 (dec.); children: Becky Kelsey Marcin, Nancy Kelsey Eargle; m. Jamie Lee Reagan, 1987. BA, U. Tex., El Paso, 1948; MA, U. Tulsa, 1951; PhD, U. Denver, 1960; degree (hon.), U. de Oriente, Venezuela, 1969. Dir. counseling bur. U. Tex., El Paso, 1951-61, prof., head dept. philosophy, psychology, 1961-62, vice chmn. dept. philosophy and psychology, 1951-61; dean students, dir. Inter-Am. Inst., 1962-66; program adv. Venezuela, Ford Found., 1966-69; vice chancellor public affairs U. Denver, 1969-72; v.p. devel. and univ. relations Tex. Tech U., Lubbock, 1972-81, prof. edn., 1981-88, prof. emeritus, 1988—; sr. rsch. fellow Nat. Center Higher Edn. Mgmt., 1983-87. Lectr. 4th Army U.S., 1961-65; cons. U.S. Dept. State, Peace Corps, 1961-66; mem. adv. bd. Kans. Wesleyan Coll., 1970-71; vis. scientist NSF, 1962-66; v.p. Colo. Ptnrs. of Alliance, 1971-73; examiner, cons. Tex. State Bd. of Examiners of Psychologists, 1992-98; cons. Agy. for Internat. Devel., Coll. Bd., Civil Svc. Commn., World Bank to India, Saudi Arabia, Turkey, Republic of Mauritius, InterAm. Bank to Guyana, S.A. Contbr. articles to profl. jours. Bd. dirs. El Paso Mental Health Assn., 1951-58, pres. 1953-55; bd. dirs. El Paso Sch. Retarded Children, 1952-57, pres., 1953-55; bd. dirs. Lubbock Goodwill Industries, 1972-85, v.p., 1973-77, pres., 1978-80; bd. dirs. St. Mary's Hosp. Found., 1986-2000, chmn., 1994-96. With USNR, 1942-45. Decorated Order San Carlos Republic Colombia, 1964; recipient Disting. Alumni Svc. award U. Denver, 1972; Fulbright scholar Colombia, 1960-61 Fellow Tex. Acad. Sci.; mem. APA, Tex. Psychol. Assn., Phi Beta Delta. Home: 13413 North Shore Dr Montgomery TX 77356

KELSEY, DAVID, manufacturing executive; Grad. in Civil and Geol. Engring., Princeton U.; MBA, Harvard Bus. Sch. With GE Co.; CFO Oglebay Norton Co.; v.p., CFO Sealed Air Corp., Saddle Brook, NJ, 2001—. Office: Sealed Air Corp Park 80 E Saddle Brook NJ 07663

KELSEY, ROBIN E., art history educator; m. Sara St. Antoine; 1 child, Adelaide Rose. PhD, Harvard U., 2000. Assoc. prof. history of art and architecture Harvard U. Recipient Arthur Kingsley Porter Prize, Coll. Art Assn. for essay "Viewing the Archive: Timothy O' Sullivan's Photographs for the Wheeler Survey, 1871-74", 2004; fellow, Sterling & Francine Clark Art Inst., Williamstown, Mass., 2004. Office: Harvard U Dept History of Art and Architecture Sackler Mus 485 Broadway Cambridge MA 02138

KELSO, CHARLOTTE ELIZABETH, elementary school educator, health and physical education specialist; d. James Edward and Charlotte Anne Kelso. BS, Appalachian State U., Boone, NC, 1979; MA, Tenn. Tech U., Cookeville, 1980. Cert. tchr. Va., 1984, athletic trainer NATABOC, 1984. Head women's basketball/prof. So. Ark. Unversity, El Dorado, 1980—82; math instr./athletic trainer/coach Richmond County H.S., Rockingham, NC, 1982—84; elem. phys. edn. specialist Roanoke City Schs., Va., 1984—89; head athletic trainer/prof. Mt. Olive Coll., Mount Olive, NC, 1989—90; head atletic trainer/prof. Morgan State U., Balt., 1990—96; health/phys. edn. specialist Swanson Mid. Sch., Arlington, Va., 1996—. Fire instr. Prince William County Fire Programs, Nokesville, Va., 1997; adj. instr. Va. Dept. of Fire Programs, Richmond, 1986; coach Roanoke Stars, Roanoke, Va., 1985—90; basketball coach Swanson Mid. Sch., Arlington, Va., 1999. Vol. fire fighter Evergreen Fire Dept., Evergreen, Va., 1997, Clearbrook Fire Dept., Roanoke, Va., 1985—89. Named Fire Fighter of the Yr., Clearbrook Vol. Fire and Rescue, 1996; recipient Va. State Recreation Educator or Yr. award, 2006, So. Dist. Assn. Recreation Profl. of Yr., 2007. Mem.: NEA., NATA, Va. Assn. Health Phys. Edn. Recreation and Dance (bd. dirs. 1997, v.p. 2003—06, Recreation Profl. of Year 2006). Avocations: travel, golf, flying. Home Phone: 571-332-9630.

KELSO, JOHN HODGSON, retired federal agency administrator; b. Iowa City, June 16, 1925; s. Edward Lewis and Eliza (Hodgson) K.; m. Marian Louise Towers, Aug. 22, 1948; 1 child, John T. BA, State U. Iowa, 1949, MA, 1950. Occupational research analyst Bur. Naval Personnel, Dept. Navy, Washington, 1951-55; orgn. and methods examiner Agr. Research Services, Dept. Agr., Washington, 1955-57; mgmt. analyst mgmt. adv. br. Bur. State Services, USPHS, HEW, Washington, 1957-58, chief survey group, 1958-60, chief mgmt. adv. br., 1960-62, asst. exec. officer, 1962-66; exec. officer USPHS, Bethesda, Md., 1966-68; asso. adminstr. mgmt. Health Services and Mental Health Adminstrn., 1968-73; dir. office regional operations USPHS, Office Asst. Sec. for Health, HEW, 1973-76; dep. adminstr. Health Services Adminstrn., 1976-81, acting adminstr., 1981-82; dep. adminstr. Health Resources and Services Adminstrn., 1982-94, acting adminstr., 1985-86, 88-89. Cons. United Network for Organ Sharing, Richmond, Va., 1994—2006. Served with AUS, 1943-46. Recipient Superior Svc. award USPHS, 1969, Disting. Svc. award HEW, 1972, Presdl. Meritorious Rank award 1983, Disting. Presdl. Rank award 1989, Surgeon Gen.'s medallion, 1989. Mem. Sigma Alpha Epsilon. Methodist.

KELSO, LINDA YAYOI, lawyer; b. Boulder, Colo., 1946; d. Nobutaka and Tai Ike; m. William Alton Kelso, 1968. BA, Stanford U., 1968; MA, U. Wis., 1973; JD, U. Fla., 1979. Bar: Fla. 1980. Assoc. Mahoney, Hadlow & Adams, Jacksonville, Fla., 1979-82, Commander, Legler, Werber, Dawes, Sadler & Howell, Jacksonville, 1982-86, ptnr., 1986-91, Foley & Lardner, L.L.P., Jacksonville, 1992—. Mem. ABA (bus. law sect.), Jacksonville Bar Assn., Phi Beta Kappa, Order of Coif. Avocations: music, gardening, cooking. Office: Foley & Lardner LLP PO Box 240 Jacksonville FL 32201-0240 Office Phone: 904-359-2000. E-mail: lkelso@foley.com.

KELSO, WILLIAM M., archaeologist; b. Mar. 1941; m. Ellen Kelso. BA in Hist., Baldwin-Wallace Coll.; M in Am. Hist., Coll. William and Mary, 1964; PhD, Emory U., 1971. Tchr. HS hist., Williamsburg, Va.; commr. archaeology Va. Hist. Landmarks Commn.; resident archaeologist Monticello, 1979—85; dir. archaeology Colonial Williamsburg's Carter's Grove, Monticello and Popular Forest, 1986, Assn. for the Preservation of Va. Antiquities, Jamestown Rediscovery project, 1993—; historical and chief archaeologist Jamestown, Va., 1994—. Asst. field archaeologist on Colonial Va. excavations with Ivor Noel Hume; lectr. throughout the US and Europe; adj. prof. Coll. William and Mary, 1995—. Author of an annual summary of the discoveries at Jamestown, (books) Jamestown: The Buried Truth, 2006. Achievements include began excavation at Jamestown, Virginia, the first permanent settlement on America in 1994, and by 1996 uncovered the remains of James Fort, which was thought to have been lost to the James River. Avocations: Bluegrass, banjo player, running. Office: Assn Preservation Va Antiquites (APVA) Jamestown Rediscovery 1367 Colonial Pkwy Jamestown VA 23081 Office Phone: 757-229-4997 ext. 102. Office Fax: 757-564-3844. Business E-Mail: wkelso@apva.org.

KELSON, RICHARD B., metal products executive; b. Pitts., Nov. 20, 1946; B in Polit. Sci., U. Pa.; JD, U. Pitts. Atty. Alcoa, Pitts., 1974-77, gen. atty., 1977-83, mng. gen. atty., 1983-84, asst. sec., mng. gen. atty., 1984-89, asst. gen. counsel, 1989-91, sr. v.p. environ. health and safety, 1991-94, exec. v.p. environ., health and safety, gen. counsel, 1994-97, exec. v.p., CFO, 1997—2006, chmn.'s counsel, 2006—. Bd. dirs. Meadwestvaco. Bd. dirs. Alcoa Found., U. Pitts. Law Sch. Bd. Visitors, Pitts. Civic Light Opera; mem. Fin. Exec. Inst. the Officers Conf. Group, The Pvt. Sector Coun.'s CFPs; mem. bd. trustees Carnegie Mellon. Mem. ABA. Office: Alcoa 390 Park Ave New York NY 10022

KELTNER, THOMAS NETHERY, JR., lawyer; b. Oklahoma City, June 1, 1946; s. Thomas N. and Tully Jo (Rowntree) K.; m. Paula Schonwald, June 17, 1972; children: Katherine, Jane. AB cum laude, Harvard U., Cambridge, Mass., 1968; JD, Columbia U., NYC, 1974. Bar: NY 1975. Law clk. to Judge Alfred P. Murrah US Ct. Appeals (10th cir.), Oklahoma City, 1974-75; gen. counsel, exec. com. Wien & Malkin LLC, NYC, 1978—, exec. com., 1978—; mem. Empire State Bldg. Assocs., LLC, 1995—. Pres. Wien & Malkin Securities Corp., 1986—; mem. adv. bd. Stewart Title Ins. Co., 2001—. Editor: Columbia Jour. Transnat. Law. Pres.

parish coun. St. Thomas More, NYC, 1982-83; trustee Convent Sacred Heart, NYC, 1986-92, Citizens Budget Commn., 1991-2001, HealthCare Chaplaincy, 1993-2004, Birch Wathen Lenox Sch., 1994-2000, East Side Assn., 1996-2002, Interfaith Neighbors, 1997-2005. Lt. (j.g.) USNR, 1968-70. Named to, Best Lawyers in Am., 2001—. Mem. ABA (real estate syndication com. 1985-87), NY State Bar Assn. (com. on corp. and other bus. entities 1999—), NY County Lawyers Assn. (chmn. real estate devel. com. 1985-86, exec. com. real property law sect. 1985-86), Tuxedo Club (Tuxedo Park, NY) Harvard Club (NYC)(mem. schs. com. 1982-92), Union Club (NYC). Republican. Roman Catholic. Office: Wien & Malkin LLC 60 E 42nd St New York NY 10165-0006

KELTON, ARTHUR MARVIN, JR., real estate developer; b. Bennington, Vt., Sept. 12, 1939; s. Arthur Marvin and Lorraine (Millington) K.; m. Elaine White, Nov. 1, 1986; 1 child, Ashley. BA, Dartmouth Coll., 1961; postgrad., U. Vt., 1963. Ptnr. Kelton and Assocs., Vail, Colo., 1966—77; pres. Kelton, Garton and Assocs. Inc., Vail, 1977—84, Kelton, Garton, Kendall, Vail, 1984—93, Christopher, Denton, Kelton, Kendall, Vail, 1993—2001, Kelton & Kendall, Vail, 2001—. Head agt. Dartmouth Alumni Fund, Hanover, NH, 1985-90, class pres., 1990-96; active Dartmouth Alumni Coun., 1996—, Eagle Valley Land Trust, 2001-; pres. Vail Valley Med. Ctr. Found., 1991—; bd. overseers Hanover Inn, 2002—, Dartmouth Real Estate Coun., 2003—; gov. bd. Vail Valley Med. Ctr., 2006—. Republican. Congregationalist. Avocations: skiing, golf, wingshooting. Home: 1034 Homestake Cir Vail CO 81657-5111 Office: Kelton & Kendall 225 Wall St Ste 200 Vail CO 81657-3615 Home Phone: 970-476-5411; Office Phone: 970-476-7995. E-mail: akjr@vail.net.

KELTON, ELMER STEPHEN, novelist; b. Andrews County, Tex., Apr. 29, 1926; s. Robert William and Neta Beatrice (Parker) K.; m. Anna Lipp, July 3, 1947; children: Gary, Stephen Lee, Kathryn Ann. BA in Journalism, U. Tex., 1948. Agrl. editor San Angelo (Tex.) Standard-Times, 1948-63; editor Sheep and Goat Raiser Mag., San Angelo, 1963-68; assoc. editor Livestock Weekly, San Angelo, 1968-90; ret., 1990. Author: (novels) Hot Iron, 1955, Buffalo Wagons, 1956, Barbed Wire, 1957, Shadow of a Star, 1959, The Texas Rifles, 1960, Donovan, 1961, Bitter Trail, 1962, Horsehead Crossing, 1963, Massacre at Goliad, 1965, Llano River, 1966, After the Bugles, 1967, Captain's Rangers, 1968, Hanging Judge, 1969, Shotgun Settlement, 1969, Bowie's Mine, 1971, The Day the Cowboys Quit, 1971, Wagontongue, 1972, The Time it Never Rained, 1973, Manhunters, 1974, Joe Pepper, 1975, Long Way to Texas, 1976, The Good Old Boys, 1978, The Wolf and the Buffalo, 1980, Eyes of the Hawk, 1981, Stand Proud, 1984, Dark Thicket, 1985, The Man Who Rode Midnight, 1987, Sons of Texas, Book One, 1989, Sons of Texas, Book Two, 1989, Sons of Texas, Book Three, 1990, Honor at Daybreak, 1991, Slaughter, 1992, The Far Canyon, 1994, The Pumpkin Rollers, 1996, Cloudy in the West, 1997, Bitter Trail, 1999, Way of the Coyote, 2001, Ranger's Trail, 2002, Lone Star Rising, 2003, Jericho's Road, 2004 Texas Vendetta, 2004, Sons of Texas, 2005, Six Bits a Day, 2005, Brush Country: Two Texas Novels, 2006; (non-fiction) Looking Back West, 1972, Frank C. McCarthy: The Old West, 1981, Permian, A Continuing Saga, 1986, Living and Writing in West Texas, 1988, The Art of Howard Terpning, 1992, The Art of Frank McCarthy, 1992, The Art of James Bama, 1993, The Indian in Frontier News, 1993, My Kind of Heroes, 1995 (rev. ed. 2004), Christmas at the Ranch, 2003, Tom Lovell, Storyteller with a Brush, 2005, Six Bits a Day, 2005, (memoir) Sandhills Boy, 2007. Bd. dirs., exec. com. West Tex. Boys Ranch, San Angelo. With U.S. Army, 1944-46. Recipient Western Heritage awards (4); Spur award (7); Nat. Cowboy Hall of Fame, Career award Western Lit. Assn., 1990. Mem. Western Writers Am. (7 Spur awards, pres. 1963-64), Tex. Inst. Letters (Tinkle-McCombs award for excellence 1985), Tex. Folklore Soc., West Tex. Hist. Soc. (pres. 1990-91). Methodist. Avocations: reading, classic films.

KEM, RICHARD SAMUEL, retired army officer; b. Richmond, Ind., Aug. 9, 1934; s. Charles Edward and Janice Allene (Beard) K.; m. Ann Callahan, May 7, 1960 (dec. June 2003); children: Michelle, John Samuel, Steven Edward; m. Ann Brown, Apr. 17, 2004; children: Deborah Ann Brown, Suzanne Marie Brown. BS, U.S. Mil. Acad., 1956; MS in Civil Engring., U. Ill., 1962; MS in Internat. Affairs, George Washington U., 1972; postgrad., Naval War Coll., 1972, Northwestern U., 1979, Harvard U., 1983. Commd. 2d lt. U.S. Army, 1956, advanced through grades to maj. gen., 1984; comdg. officer 577th Engr. Bn. Vietnam, 1968-69; staff, faculty U.S. Mil. Acad., West Point, N.Y., 1969-71; staff officer Mil. Personnel Center, 1972-74, Office Army Chief Staff, 1974-75; chief public affairs Office Chief Engrs., 1975-76; comdg. officer 7th Engr. Brigade, Germany, 1976-78; chief installations and constrn. U.S. Army Europe, 1978-79; dep. asst. chief engrs., 1979-80; dep. dir. civil works Office Chief Engrs., 1980; comdr., div. engr. Ohio River div., 1981-84; bd. engrs. Rivers and Harbors, 1982-84, Mississippi River Commn., 1982-84; comdg. gen. U.S. Army Engr. Sch. and Fort Belvoir, Va., 1984-87; dep. chief of staff, engr. U.S. Army, Europe, 1987-88, chief of staff, 1988-89; dep. chief of engrs. Washington, Washington, 1989-90; ret., 1990; dir. pub. works Arlington (Va.) County, 1990—2004; ret., 2004. Decorated DSM with oak leaf cluster, Legion of Merit with oak leaf cluster, Bronze Star, Gold Order of de Fleury medal. Mem. ASCE, Soc. Am. Mil. Engrs., Am. Def. Preparedness Assn., Army Engr. Assn. (bd. dirs. 1992—), Am. Pub. Works Assn. (bd. dirs. 1989-90). Episcopalian. Office: Burdeshaw Assoc Ltd 4701 Sangamon Rd Bethesda MD 20816 Office Phone: 301-229-5800. E-mail: samkem@comcast.net.

KEMBLE, JOE DAVID, mathematics professor; b. Port Arthur, Tex., Feb. 19, 1960; s. Joe Edward and Jackie Ruth Kemble. BS in Secondary Edn., Lamar U., 1984, MEd in Supervision, 1986; EdD in Curriculum and Instrn., U. Houston, 1995. Cert. secondary sch. tchr. Tex., math. and computer info. systems. Substitute tchr. Bridge City (Tex.) Ind. Sch. Dist., 1983—87; substitute and tutorial tchr. Orangefield (Tex.) Jr. HS, 1984—85; adult edn. tchr. West Orange (Tex.)-Cove Ctrl. Ind. Sch. Dist., 1986—87; adj. instr. Lamar U., Port Arthur, Tex., 1987, Orange, Tex., 1987—89, lectr. Beaumont, Tex., 1989—99, asst. prof. devel. math., 1999—. Book and software reviewer McGraw-Hill, Boston, 1999—, mem. adv. bd., 2004—05; book reviewer Addison-Wesley, Boston, 2001; advisor, webmaster Ctr. Gen. Studies Lamar U., 1999; book reviewer John Wiley & Sons, 2006. Author: Student's Solution Manual for Intermediate Algebra: A Real World Approach, 2005; book reviewer: John Wiley and Sons, 2006. Mem. faculty senate Campus Crusade for Christ, 1996—2000, 2002—06, faculty advisor, 1993—2003. Mem.: Am. Ednl. Rsch. Assn., Tex. Coun. Tchrs. Math., Nat. Coun. Tchrs. Math., Tex. Assn. Coll. Tchrs. (treas. for Lamar U. 1997—2003, Ea. Region v.p. 2003—07, host Ea. region Conf. 2004). Democrat. Baptist. Avocations: reading, travel, music, computers, church work. Home: 3000 Merriman Port Neches TX 77651 Office: Lamar U PO Box 10047 Beaumont TX 77710 Office Phone: 409-880-8048. Office Fax: 409-880-8602. Business E-Mail: joe.kemble@lamar.edu.

KEMELHOR, ROBERT E(LIAS), mechanical engineer; b. NYC, May 19, 1919; m. Shirley P. Tennen; children: Judith Ellen Bielecki, Joel Martin, Barry Alan. Student Pre-Law, Bklyn. Coll., 1936-38; BSME, George Washington U., 1949. Registered profl. engr., Washington. Sr. draftsman Bur. Ships Navy Dept., Washington, 1940-43, design engr. Bur. Ordnance, 1943-46, mil. billet weapon launching sect. Bur. Aeros., 1946-53; chief engr. design, devel. prodn. McLean Devel. Labs., Copiague, N.Y., 1953-58; dir. rsch. and devel. Pesco Products div. Borg-Warner Corp., Bedford, Ohio, 1958; with applied physics lab. Johns Hopkins U., Laurel, Md., 1958-91, program mgr., 1982-85, chief engr. tech. svcs. dept., 1986-91; pvt. practice cons. Bethesda, Md., 1991—. Cons. Advanced Tech. and Mfg. Enterprise Programs, Nat. Inst. Stds. and Tech., U.S. Dept. Commerce, Aeronautics Indsl. Tech. Program, NASA/JPL. Contbr. articles to profl. jours. U.S. del. Internat. Standards Orgn. Subcom., Mfg. Automation; mem. western region and inter-county recreation adv. bd. Montgomery County, Md.; bd. dirs. Alumni Assn., George Washington U. Fellow AIAA (assoc.); mem. AAAS (sr. sci. and engr.'s), Soc. Mfg. Engrs. (sr. mem., chmn. Washington chpt. No. 48), Sigma Tau, Tau Beta Pi. Achievements include patents in field. Home: 6211 Redwing Ct Bethesda MD 20817-5914

KEMENT, ISABELLA VINICONIS, retired construction company executive; b. Sept. 9, 1923; d. Paul and Mary (Karsokas) Viniconis; married Stanley J. Kement, Feb. 6, 1943 (dec. Dec. 1998); children: Stanley J. Jr., Joan Kement Turbie. Owner, mgr. tobacco farm, 1943-45; bookkeeper, dispatcher, sec., owner Kement Constrn. Co. Inc., Broad Brook, Conn., 1945-70; owner, bookkeeper, mgr., builder E-Z Living Suites, Broad Brook, 1959-84; owner restaurant and hotel, 1959-65; ptnr. Kement Park Landfill and Gravel, Broad Brook, 1947—; sec. Kement Devel. Corp.; mgr., pres., bookkeeper Apt. Complex, Broad Brook, 1959-84; ptnr. Depot St. Gravel Pit; pres. Manor House, Inc., 1959-84, E-Z Living Suite, 1959-84; ptnr. Kement Ltd. Partnership, Inc., Kement Investment Corp. Owner Sanibel (Fla.) Arms West Condos, 1973—2005. Mem. bd. North Cen. Health Dist.; mem. ch. coun. and social coms., Broad Brook, 1985-87; Cath. Christian Doctrine tchr.; active St. Catherine's Ch. Recipient First Place trophy East Windsor Bicentennial Parade, 1968. Mem. Tobacco Valley Art Assn., Univ. of Third Age, East Windsor Garden Club. Roman Catholic. Avocations: line dancing, travel, art, craft design, gardening. Home: 307 North Rd Broad Brook CT 06016-9607 Personal E-mail: ivk1923@cox.net.

KEMENY, M. MARGARET, oncologist, surgeon, hospital administrator, educator; b. Elizabeth, NJ, May 7, 1946; d. George Kemeny and Ellen Sagi. BS, Harvard U., 1968; MD, Columbia U., 1972. Dir. cancer ctr. Queens Cancer Ctr., NYC, 2001—; divsn. chief surg. oncology SUNY Stony Brook. Prof. surgery Mt. Sinai Sch. Medicine, 2005—; mem. editl. bd. Am. Jour. Surgery, Annals of Surgery, Oncology. Fellow: ACS (bd. govs., vice chair bd. govs.); mem.: Assn. Women Surgeons (pres.). Home: 36 Perry St New York NY 10014 Office: Queens Cancer Ctr at Queens Hosp 82-68 164th St Jamaica NY 11432 Office Phone: 718-883-4031. Business E-Mail: kemenym@nychhc.org.

KEMMELMEIER, MARKUS, sociologist, psychologist, educator; b. Balingen, Germany, May 31, 1967; s. Ulrich and Margarete Kemmelmeier; m. Heather Dawn Gillespie, Aug. 12, 2005; children: Christoph, Lena Lydia, Liesel Maria. PhD, U. Mich., Ann Arbor, 2001. Asst. prof. sociology and social psychology U. Nev., Reno, 2001—07, assoc. prof. sociology and social psychology, 2007—. Mem.: APA, Am. Sociol. Assn., Soc. Psychol. Study Social Issues. Achievements include research in the influence of student political orientation on academic outcomes. Office: Univ Nevada Mail Stop 300 Reno NV 89557 Home Phone: 775-787-8717; Office Phone: 775-784-1287. Business E-Mail: markusk@unr.edu.

KEMMERER, PETER REAM, financial executive; b. NYC, Dec. 20, 1942; s. Mahlon Sistie and Colette Noel (Fitch) K.; m. Lillian Reilly, Sept. 15, 1990. BS, Georgetown U., 1966; MBA, Am. U., 1970; MA, New Sch., 1975. Analyst corp. planning Otis Elevator Co., NYC, 1971-74; mgr. fin. and adminstrn. bus. equipment div. SCM Corp., NYC, 1975-80; pres. Mesa Verde, Inc., Cranbury, N.J., 1980—, also bd. dirs. Mng. ptnr. Jezel-Bezel Ptnrs., Cranbury, 1980—. Trustee Monmouth Conservation Found., 2005—. With fin. corps. US Army, 1966—68. Roman Catholic. Avocations: sailing, reading, sports. Office: 37 N Main St Cranbury NJ 08512-3203 Personal E-mail: kem344@aol.com.

KEMMERLY, JACK DALE, retired state official; b. El Dorado, Kans., Sept. 17, 1936; s. Arthur Allen and Eythel Louise (Throckmorton) K.; m. Frances Cecile Gregorio, June 22, 1958; children: Jack Dale Jr., Kathleen Frances, Grant Lee. BA, San Jose State U., 1962; cert. in real estate, UCLA, 1970; MPA, Golden Gate U., 1973; cert. labor-mgmt. rels., U. Calif., Davis, 1978; cert. orgnl. change, Stanford U., 1985. Right of way agt. Calif. Div. Hwys., Marysville, 1962-71; adminstrv. officer Calif. Dept. Transp., Sacramento, 1971-82, dist. dir. Redding, 1982-83, chief aeros. Sacramento, 1984-94; mgmt. cons. U.S. Dept. Transp., Riyadh, Saudi Arabia, 1983-84. Chmn. tech. adv. com. on aeronautics Calif. Transp. Commn. Bd. dirs. Yuba-Sutter Campfire Girls, 1972-73. With USN, 1954-57. Recipient superior accomplishment award Calif. Dept. Transp., 1981. Mem. Nat. Assn. State Aviation Ofcls. (nat. pres. 1989—), Am. Assn. State Hwy. and Transp. Ofcls. (aviation com. 1985-94), Calif. Assn. Aerospace Educators (adv. bd. 1984—), Calif. Assn. Airport Execs., Calif. Aviation Coun., Aircraft Owners and Pilots Assn. (dir. regional reps.), Elks (exalted ruler Marysville, Calif. 1974-75). Republican. Roman Catholic. Avocations: non-partisan political activities, reading, flying. Office: 1285 Charlotte Ave Yuba City CA 95991-2803 Office Phone: 530-674-3694. Personal E-mail: jdkemmerly@sbcglobal.net.

KEMMERLY, JAMES ROBERT, obstetrician, gynecologist; b. Baton Rouge, La., Aug. 15, 1936; s. Carl Edward and Edith May (Wright) Kemmerly; m. Sue L. Martin, June 12, 1960 (div. Jan. 1992); children: David Lee, Kelly Renee, Celeste Danielle; m. Dana Clawson Bell, Sept. 12, 1992 (div. Jan. 1999); m. Brenda Risner, July 30, 2005. BS, La. State U., 1953-56, MD, 1956-60; summer student, Perkins Sch. Theology, So. Meth. U., 1957, 58, 59. Diplomate Am. Bd. Ob-Gyn. Intern So. Bapt. Hosp., New Orleans, 1960-61, resident, 1963-66; practice medicine specializing in ob-gyn. Minden, La., 1966—; founding pres. The Women's Clinic A Med. Corp. Clin. asst. prof. La. State U. Med. Ctr., Shreveport, 1972—82; pres. med. staff Minden Med. Ctr., 1972, 1976—77, 1988—89, med. dir., 2002—; bd. dirs. Peoples Bank & Trust Co., Minden. Lay leader 1st United Meth. Ch., Minden, also past chmn. adminstrv. bd., pastor com., del. to state and nat. confs. With USAF, 1962-63. Fellow Am. Coll. Ob-Gyn.; mem. AMA, La. State Med. Assn., So. Med. Assn., Webster Parish Med. Soc. (pres. 1986-). Office: The Womens Clinic A Med Corp 431 Homer Rd Minden LA 71055-2933

KEMNITZ, JOSEPH WILLIAM, physiologist, researcher; b. Balt., Mar. 15, 1947; s. Harold Clarence and Alice Mae (Ziebarth) K.; m. Amanda Marye Tuttle, Jan. 5, 1991; children: Julia Ellen, Joseph Andrew. BA, U. Wis., 1969, PhD, 1976. Rsch. assoc. Wis. Nat. Primate Rsch. Ctr., Madison, 1976-79, asst. scientist, 1979-84, assoc. scientist, 1984-94, sr. scientist and assoc. dir., 1995-96, dir., 1996—; assoc. scientist dept. medicine U. Wis., Madison, 1991-94, sr. scientist dept. medicine, 1995-97, prof. dept. physiology. Cons. NIH, Bethesda, Md., 1981—; mem. Children's Diabetes Ctr., Madison, Wis., 1990—; steering com. Inst. on Aging, Madison, 1989—. Assoc. editor Hormones and Behavior, 1986-96; contbr. articles to profl. jours. Grantee (various) NIH, 1977—. Mem. Am. Physiol. Soc., Am. Inst. Nutrition, Am. Diabetes Assn., Am. Soc. Primatologists, Gerontol. Soc. Am., N.Am. Assn. Study of Obesity, Internat. Primatol. Soc. Office: Primate Rsch Ctr UW 1220 Capitol Ct Madison WI 53715-1237

KEMNITZ, THOMAS MILTON, publisher; b. Washington; s. Milton Neumann and Esther L. K.; m. Myrna Kaye Glick, Dec. 10, 1982; 1 son, Thomas Milton Jr. BA, U. Mich., 1964; PhD, U. Sussex, Eng., 1969. Prof. U. N.H., Durham, 1969-75; pres. Kemnitz Audio Video, Boston, 1976-78, Trillium Press Inc., Unionville, NY, 1978—. Pres. KAV Books, Inc., 1980—, Royal Fireworks Pub., 1989—, Silk Label Books, 1998—; chmn. bd. Royal Fireworks Printing Co., 1989—. Author: Kids Working with Computers (12 vol. series), 1983-85, Brain Booster, 1985, Computer Ethics, 1985, Buck Fang's Logo Challenge, 1985, other books and pieces of software; pub. Our Gifted Children mag. Office: Royal Fireworks Publ Co #41 1st Ave Unionville NY 10988-0399 Business E-Mail: tmk@rfwp.com.

KEMP, ALSON REMINGTON, JR., lawyer, retired educator; b. Rossville, Ga., July 3, 1941; s. Alson R. Dorothy (Walters) K.; m. Martha Gudenrath, Aug. 7, 1967; children: Alson Remington, Colin T. BS, U. Tenn., 1962; JD, U. Cin., 1965. Bar: Tenn. 1965, Ohio 1965, Calif. 1970, US Dist. Ct. (no. and ctrl. dists.) Calif. 1971, US Ct. Appeals (9th cir.) 1971, US Ct. Appeals (DC cir.) 1982. Asst. prof. Hancock Coll., Santa Maria, Calif., 1966-68; asst. prof. U. Tenn., Chattanooga, 1969; mem. Morgan & Garner, Chattanooga, 1968-70, Pillsbury, Madison & Sutro, San Francisco, 1970-75, ptnr., 1975-99; pvt. practice Healdsburg, Calif., 1999—. Dir. Green Diamond Resource Co.; dir Smith Bros. Holding Co., 2001—, vice chair, 2001—03, chair, 2003—05; bd. dirs. No. Sonoma County Healthcare Found. Capt. USAF, 1965—68. Grantee Benwood Found., 1962-65. Fellow: Am. Coll. Trial Lawyers; mem.: Calif. Bar Assn. Republican. Home and Office: 22190 Puccioni Rd Healdsburg CA 95448 Office Phone: 707-433-1199. Personal E-mail: arkemp@gmail.com.

KEMP, ANN, retired librarian; b. Providence, Ky., Aug. 2, 1941; d. Charlie and Rubye (Sigler) Kemp Page. BA, Belmont U., 1964; MLS, Vanderbilt U., 1965, postgrad., 1968-79. Cert. tchr. Ky. Libr. Nashville (Tenn.) Pub. Libr., 1965, U. Louisville Libr., 1965-67, Dawson Springs (Ky.) Ind. Schs., 1967-93; instr. Murray (Ky.) State U., 1973-78. Author: Poem, The ABC's of Parthenon. Mem.: DAR, Ky. Libr. Assoc., Ky. Edn. Assoc., Nat. Edn. Assoc., The Parthenon Patrons. Baptist. Avocations: studying architecture and folklore, poetry. Home: 703 S Clinton St Athens AL 35611

KEMP, BARRETT GEORGE, lawyer; b. Dayton, Ohio, Feb. 22, 1932; s. Barrett M. and Gladys M. (Linkhart) K.; children: Becky A., Barrett George II; m. Shirley, 1997. BSc, Ohio U., 1954; JD, Ohio No. U., 1959. Bar: Ohio 1959. With FBI, 1959-61; mem. B.G. Kemp Law Firm, St. Marys, Ohio, 1961—. Law dir. City of St. Marys, 1964-80. Sec., treas. Cmty. Improvement Corp., 1967-79; founder St. Marys Sister City, Inc.; founder, organizer sister city with Ho Kudan-cho, Japan, 1985. With US Army, 1954—56. Recipient Outstanding Citizen award City of St. Marys, 1973, Builder of Bridges award St. Mary's C. of C., 1995. Mem. Ohio Bar Assn., Auglaize County Bar Assn., Rotary (v.p. 1968, pres. 1969, Lifetime achievement 1997, Four Aves. of Cvs. citation 1999), Masons, Shriners, Scottish Rite. Address: 216 E Spring Saint Marys OH 45885 Office Phone: 419-394-3341. Personal E-mail: kemplaw@bright.net.

KEMP, EUGENE THOMAS, retired veterinarian; b. McDonough, NY, Mar. 22, 1930; s. Oswald Milton and Almira Dorothy (Allen) K.; m. Ruth Emer Stoll, Sept. 29, 1951 (dec. Sept. 1977); 1 child, William Allen; m. Margaret Atenna Rowland, Dec. 27, 1980. BS, Cornell U., 1951, DVM, 1957. Sr. ptnr. Day Hollow Animal Clinic, Owego, NY, 1957—2000; ret., 2000. Author: Serfs on a Fief, 2002; contbr. articles to profl. jours. Bd. dirs. First Ch. of Nazarene, Owego, 1991-98; v.p. Tioga County Bd. Health, 1988-96, pres., 1996-2005; mem. Owego-Apalachin Bd. Edn., 1961-71; mem. Broome-Tioga Bd. Coop. Edn. Svcs., Binghamton, 1969-83, pres., 1971-76; founding pres. Broome-Tioga Coun. Sch. Bd. Pres., 1973. Mem. So. Tier Vet. Med. Assn. (pres. 1992). Republican. Avocations: piano, creative writing, jazz. Home: 478 Hiawatha Rd Owego NY 13827-5307

KEMP, GEOFFREY THOMAS HOWARD, political scientist, consultant; b. UK, May 20, 1939; came to U.S., 1967, naturalized, 1974; s. Thomas Howard and Gwendoline (Reeves) K.; m. Vivian Reubens, Sept. 1968 (div. 1979); m. Tamara Levin Weisberg, Nov., 1998. BA, Oxford U., 1963, MA, 1967; PhD, MIT, 1971. Research assoc. Internat. Inst. Strategic Studies, London, 1965-67; research assoc. Ctr. Internat. Studies, MIT, Cambridge, 1967-71; assoc. prof. internat. politics Fletcher Sch. Law and Diplomacy, Tufts U., 1971-80; spl. asst. to Pres. for nat. security affairs White House, Washington, 1981-85; sr. fellow Ctr. for Strategic and Internat. Studies, Georgetown U., Washington, 1985-86; sr. assoc. Carnegie Endowment for Internat. Peace, 1986-95; dir. regional strategic programs Nixon Ctr., Washington, 1995—. Author: The Control of the Middle East Arms Race, 1991, Forever Enemies? American Policy and the Islamic Republic of Iran, 1994; co-author: Strategic Geography and the Changing Middle East, 1997. Served to lt. Army U.K., 1958-60 Mem. Council on Fgn. Relations (internat. affairs fellow 1976), Internat. Inst. Strategic Studies, Oxford Union Soc. Avocations: evelyn waugh literature, movies, english watercolor paintings, golf. Office: Nixon Ctr 1615 L St NW Washington DC 20036-5610 Home Phone: 301-941-1347. Business E-Mail: gkemp@nixoncenter.org.

KEMP, JACK FRENCH, former congressman; b. LA, July 13, 1935; m. Joanne Main; children: Jeffrey, Jennifer, Judith, James. BA, Occidental Coll., 1957; postgrad., Long Beach State U., Calif. Western U. Quarterback Pitts. Steelers, 1957, San Diego Chargers (formerly LA Chargers), 1960—62, Buffalo Bills, 1963—69; spl. asst. to gov. State of Calif., 1967; spl. asst. to chmn. Republican Nat. Com., 1969; mem. 92d-100th congresses from 31st N.Y. Dist., 1971-89; former sec. Dept. of Housing and Urban Development, 1989-92; co-dir. Empower America, Washington, D.C., 1993—. Pub. relations officer Marine Midland Bank, Buffalo; candidate for Rep. Presdl. nomination, 1987-88; Rep. nominee for v.p., 1996; bd. dirs. Six Flags Inc., 2005- Mem. Pres.'s Council on Phys. Fitness and Sports; mem. exec. com. player pension bd. NFL Named to Pro Bowl, 1961-66, 1969; Recipient Disting. Service award N.Y. State Jaycees; Outstanding Citizen award Buffalo Evening News, 1965, 74, Warner award, 2004 Mem. Nat. Assn. Broadcasters, Engrs. and Technicians, Buffalo Area C. of C., Sierra Club, Am. Football League Players Assn. (co-founder, pres. 1965-70) Republican. Office: Empower America 1775 Pennsylvania Ave Nw Washington DC 20006-4605

KEMP, KARL THOMAS, insurance company executive; b. Petoskey, Mich., Dec. 16, 1940; s. Vernon L. and Dorothy Jean (Olson) K.; m. Mary Ormston Graham, July 21, 1973; children: Karl Thomas Jr., John Walter, James Edward. BA, Harvard U., 1964. V.p. corp. fin. GEICO Corp., Washington, 1966-81; sr. v.p., pres. Resolute Reins. Co., NYC, 1981-90; pres., CEO White Mountains Ins. Group, Ltd., Hanover, N.H., 1997—. Bd. dirs. Folksamerica Holdings, Inc., N.Y.C., chair Human Resources Com., 1996—; bd. dirs. FSA Holdings, N.Y.C., chair human resources com., 1994—; bd. dirs. Eldorado Bancshares, Inc., Calif., chair human resources com., 1996—; bd. dirs. Main St. Am. Holdings, Keane, N.Y., exec. com., 1994—; pres., CEO White Mountain Holdings, Inc., Hanover, 1994—; bd. dirs. Amlin, plc., London. Mem. Am. Bonanza Soc., Aircraft Owners and Pilots Assn., Harvard Club (N.Y.C., Vt., N.H.). Avocation: flying. Home: 6 Goodfellow Rd Hanover NH 03755-4800 Office: White Mountains Ins Group Ltd 80 S Main St Hanover NH 03755-2053

KEMP, MARK D., construction executive; BBA in Acctg., Tex. Tech U. CPA. Various positions up to ptnr. Arthur Andersen, LLP, Dallas, 1983—2002; v.p., contr. Centex Corp., Dallas, 2002—04, sr. v.p., contr., 2004—, interim CFO, 2006. Mem.: AICPA, Tex. Soc. CPAs. Office: Centex Corp PO Box 199000 Dallas TX 75219-9000 Office Phone: 214-981-5000.*

KEMP, PAMELA JEAN, marriage and family therapist; d. Loren Eugene and Betty May Goodwin; m. Thomas Edward Kemp, Oct. 19, 1969; children: Brian Thomas, Christina Marie. BS in Edn., Ill. State U., Normal, 1969; MS, Purdue U., West Lafayette, Ind., 1973, PhD, 1977. Lic. tchr.

elem. self-contained grades 1-8 Tex. Edn. Assn., 1989, tchr. spl. edn. grades pre-K-12 Tex. Edn. Assn., 1989, tchr. kindergarten Tex. Edn. Assn., 1989, profl. counselor Tex. State Bd. Examiners Profl. Counselors, 1997, counselor pre-K-12 Tex. Edn. Assn., 2000. Assoc. prof. U. Wis., Stevens Point, 1977—87, asst. dean grad. studies, 1986—87; adj. asst. prof. psychology Amberton U., Garland, Tex., 1988—94; specialist early intervention Denton State Sch. Outreach, Terrell, Tex., 1992—94; therapist child and family Dallas Metrocare Svcs., 1994—2000; counselor Montclair Elem. Sch., Garland, Tex., 2000—. Mem.: Tex. State Tchrs. Assn., Tex. Counseling Assn., Tex. Assn. Infant Mental Health, Dallas Assn.Psychoanalytic Social Workers, Pax Christi, Results, Freedoms Found. Valley Forge, Dallas Trekkers. Avocations: walking, reading, travel, yoga. Office: Montclair Elem Sch 5200 Marketplace Dr Garland TX 75043 Home Phone: 972-841-0810. Home Fax: none. Personal E-mail: kempfamily5@tx.rr.com.

KEMP, THOMAS JOSEPH, retired electronics executive; b. Holy Cross, Iowa, Aug. 17, 1943; s. Joseph Peter and Margaret Gertrude (Wilgenbusch) K.; m. Ruth Anne Pfohl, Aug. 22, 1964; children: Geoffrey Joseph, Jennifer Anne, Julie Marie, Jack Thomas. BA in Bus. Acctg., Loras Coll., 1964; MS in Sys. Mgmt., St. Mary's U., San Antonio, 1978. Commd. 2d lt. USAF, 1964, advanced through grades to lt. col., 1980, pilot, mgr., 1964-85; ret., 1985; Instructional systems design mgr., dep. program mgr. United Airlines Svcs. Corp., Irving, Tex., 1985-87; divsn. mgr., project mgr. Flight Safety Svcs. Corp., Irving, 1987-90; program mgr. ElectroCom Automation, Arlington, Tex., 1990—2002; mgr. Integrated Logistics Support Siemens Dematic, Arlington, 1997—2002. Congl. advisor Vets. and Budget Com., Ft. Worth, 1994-2004; pres. Tarrant County Vets. Coun., Ft. Worth, 1995-96. Mem. VFW (life), Mil. Officers Assn. Am. (life), Air Force Assn. (life, state pres. Tex. 1995-97, nat. v.p. 1998-99, Texoma region pres. 1999-2000, nat. dir. 2000-03, exec. com. 2000-06, nat. sec. 2003-06, nat. dir. emeritus 2006-, Exceptional Svc. award 1990, 91, 94, Presdl. citation 2000, Mem. of Yr. 2002), Am. Legion, KC (Grand Knight 2003-05, Knight of Month award, Family of Month award). Republican. Roman Catholic. Avocations: fishing, golf, gardening. Home: 173 Rieti Crowley TX 76036-2009 Office Phone: 817-313-9187. E-mail: tjkafatx@flash.net.

KEMPER, ALEX R., pediatrician, educator; b. Richmond, Va., Apr. 16, 1967; s. Bennett Kemper and Marlyn Littman; m. Julie Firestone, Sept. 20, 1993; children: Benjamin, Anna. MD, Duke U., Durham, NC, 1993—96; MPH, U. NC, Chapel Hill, 1996—98, MS, 1998—2000. Diplomate Am. Bd. Pediat., 1996. Asst. prof. U. Mich., Ann Arbor, Mich., 2000—06; assoc. prof. Duke U. Sch. Medicine, 2006—. Dir. pediatric health svcs. rsch. program Duke U. Mem.: Ambulatory Pediatric Assn., Am. Acad. Pediat., Soc. Pediatric Rsch. Achievements include research in screening policy. Office: Duke Clin Rsch Inst PO Box 17969 Durham NC 27715

KEMPER, DAVID WOODS, II, banker; b. Kansas City, Mo., Nov. 20, 1950; s. James Madison and Mildred (Lane) K.; m. Dorothy Ann Jannarone, Sept. 6, 1975; children: John W., Elizabeth C., Catherine B., William L. BA cum laude, Harvard U., 1972; MA in English Lit., Oxford, Worcester Coll., 1974; MBA, Stanford U., 1976. With Morgan Guaranty Trust Co., NYC, 1975-78; v.p. Commerce Bank of Kansas City, Mo., 1978-79, sr. v.p., 1980-81; pres. Commerce Bancshares, Inc., 1982-86, pres., ceo, 1986-91, chmn., pres., ceo, 1991—; also dir. Commerce Bancshares, Inc; chmn. Commerce Bank N.A., St. Louis, 1985—. Bd. dirs. Kansas City, Tower Properties, Kansas City, Ralcorp Holdings, Inc. Contbr. articles on banking to profl. jours. Trustee Mo. Bot. Garden, Washington U., Donald Danforth Plant Sci. Ctr. Mem. Acad. Arts and Scis., Fin. Svcs. Roundtable, Kansas City Country Club, River Club (Kansas City), St. Louis Club, St. Louis Country Club, Racquet Club, Old Warson Country Club (St. Louis). Office: Commerce Bancshares Inc 8000 Forsyth Blvd Clayton MO 63105

KEMPER, DORLA DEAN EATON (DORLA DEAN EATON), real estate broker; b. Calhoun, Mo., Sept. 10, 1929; d. Paul McVay and Jesse Lee (McCombs) Eaton; m. Charles K. Kemper, Mar. 1, 1951; children: Kevin Keil, Kara Lee. BS in Edn., Ctrl. Mo. State U., 1952. Tchr. pub. schs., Twin Falls, Idaho, 1950—51, Mission, Kans., 1952—53, Burbank, Calif., 1953—57; sales rep. real estate Minn., 1967—68, Calif., 1971—73, Deanie Kemper, Inc. Real Estate Brokerage, Loomis, Calif., 1974—76, pres., 1976—91; sr. cons. Capital Holding Corp., Louisville, 1991—93. Ptnr. Kemper Properties, 2006—. Pres. Battle Creek Park Elem. Sch. PTA, St. Paul, 1966-67; mem. Placer County (Calif.) Bicentennial Commn., 1976; mem. Sierra Coll. Adv. Com., 1981—; active Placer County Hist. Soc. Named to Million Dollar Club (lifetime) Sacramento and Placer County bds. Realtors, 1978-94; designated Grad. Realtors Inst., Cert. Residential Specialist. Mem. Nat. Assn. Realtor, Calif. Assn. Realtors, Nat. Assn. Real Estate Appraisers, Placer County Bd. Realtors (profl. stds. com.), DAR (chpt. regent 1971-73, organizing chpt. regent 1977—, dist. dir. 1978-80, state registrar Calif. 1980-82, state vice regent 1982-84, state regent 1984-86, nat. resolutions com., nat. rec. sec. gen. 1986-89, nat. chmn. units overseas 1983-86, nat. pres. gen. 1995-98, hon. nat. pres. gen. 1998—, nat. chmn. WWII Meml. Campaign 1998-2001, pres. Nat. Officers Club 2006-), Nat. Gavel Soc., Daus. Am. Colonists, Colonial Dames Am., Internat. Platform Assn., Hidden Valley Women's Club (pres. Loomis chpt. 1970-71), Auburn Travel Study (pres. 1979), Calif. State Officer's Club (pres., 2007—). Republican. Home: 8165 Morningside Dr Granite Bay CA 95746-8163

KEMPER, J. MARINER, bank executive; b. 1973; Grad., U. of Puget Sound, Tacoma, WA. Pres. UMB Bank, Colo., 1997—2000, pres, CEO, 2000—04; chmn. UMB Bank, Western Region, 2004—; chmn., CEO UMB Bank, Denver, 2004—. Bd. mem. Mayor's Commn. on Art, Culture & Film, Denver, Boys and Girls Club Metro Denver, Cheyenne Mountain Zoo, Colo. Springs, Air Quality Transp. Mgmt. Coun., Denver, Western States Art Fedn., Denver; chmn. City of Sculpture Campaign for Denver Art, Culture & Film Found., Denver, Denver Art, Culture & Film Found.; bd. mem. Cherokee Ranch & Castle Found., Denver. Recipient 40 Under 40, Denver Bus. Jour., 1999, 22 to Watch in 2002, 5280 mag. Office: UMB Bank 1670 Broadway Denver CO 80202 Office Phone: 816-860-5607.

KEMPER, JAMES DEE, lawyer; b. Olney, Ill., Feb. 23, 1947; s. Jack O. and Vivian L. Kemper; m. Diana J. Deig, June 1, 1968; children: Judd, Jason. BS, Ind. U., Bloomington, 1969, JD summa cum laude, 1971. Bar: Ind. 1971. Law clk. U.S. Ct. Appeals (7th cir.), Chgo., 1971-72; ptnr. Ice Miller LLP, Indpls., 1972—, mng. ptnr., 1993—98. Note editor: Ind. U. Law Rev., 1970—71; contbr. articles to profl. jours. Past officer, bd. dirs. Marion County Assn. Retarded Citizens, Inc., Indpls.; past bd. dirs. Ctrl. Ind. Easter Seal Soc., Indpls., Crossroads Rehab. Ctr., Inc., Indpls.; pres., bd. govs. Orchard Country Day Sch., Indpls.; bd. dirs. Eiteljorg Mus. Native Ams., Butler U. Fellow: Ind. Bar Found.; mem.: ABA (mem. employee benefit com.), Gt. Lakes TE/GE Coun., Ind. Bar Assn., Stanley K. Lacy Leadership Alumni, U.S. C. of C. (mem. employee benefit com.), The Group, Inc. Office: Ice Miller LLP Ste 3100 1 American Sq Indianapolis IN 46282-0200 Business E-Mail: kemper@icemiller.com.

KEMPER, JOHN DUSTIN, mechanical engineering educator; b. Portland, Oreg., May 29, 1924; s. Clay Wallace and Leona Bell K.; m. Barbara Jeanne Kemper, June 28, 1947; 1 child: Kathleen Lynne. BS, UCLA, 1949, MS, 1959; PhD, U. Colo., Boulder, 1969. Chief mech. engr. Telecomputing Corp., North Hollywood, Calif., 1949-55, H.A. Wagner Co., Van Nuys, Calif., 1955-56; v.p. engring. Marchant div. SCM Corp., Oakland, Calif., 1956-62; faculty U. Calif., Davis, 1962-91, prof. engring., 1967-91, dean coll. Engring., 1969-83, ret., 1991. Panel chmn. Engring. Grad. Edn. and Research, NRC, 1985. Author: Engineers and Their Profession, 1967, 5th edit., 2001, Introduction to the Engineering Profession, 1985, 2d edit., 1993, (with G.C. Andrews) Canadian Professional Engineering Practice and Ethics, 1992, Birding Northern California, 1999, Southern Oregon's Bird Life, 2002, Exploring Southern Oregon's Beautiful Places, 2003, Wildflowers of Southern Oregon, 2006, The Rogue Valley, 2006. Served with USAF, 1944-46. Named engineering building in his honor, U. Calif., Davis campus. Fellow ASME (chmn. San Francisco sect. 1962-63), AAAS; mem. Am. Soc. Engring. Edn.

KEMPER, RANDY, fashion designer; Student, Parsons Sch. Design; tenured with Albert Nipon, JG Hook, Hana Mori, Bill Blass. With House of Givenchy, Paris; prin. Randy Kemper, NYC. Avocations: polo, piano. Office: 530 7th Ave Fl 14 New York NY 10018-4878

KEMPER, ROBERT VAN, anthropologist, educator, minister; b. San Diego, Nov. 21, 1945; s. Ivan L. and Roberta (King) K.; m. Sandra L. Kraft, Sept. 9, 1967; 1 child, John Kraft. BA, U. Calif., Riverside, 1966; MA, U. Calif., Berkeley, 1969, PhD, 1971; MDiv, So. Meth. U., 1999. Ordained to ministry Presbyn. Ch., 1999. Postdoctoral fellow U. Calif., Berkeley, 1971-72; asst. prof. So. Meth. U., Dallas, 1972-77, assoc. prof., 1977-83, prof., 1983—, chmn., 1992-94, 2004—, pres. faculty senate, 2005—06, trustee, 2005—06. Vis. rsch. scholar U. Iberoamericana, Mexico City, 1970, 79-80, Ctr. U.S.-Mex. Studies, La Jolla, Calif., 1983, U. Nat. Autónoma Mex., Mexico City, 1990-91, El Colegio de Michoacán, Zamora, Mex., 1991; sec. Inst. Study of Earth and Man, Dallas, 1989-92; Coun. Preservation Anthrop. Records; founding chair Commn. Anthropology Tourism, Internat. Union Anthrop. and Ethnol. Scis., 1993-96. Author: Migration and Adaptation, 1977; co-author: History of Anthropology, 1977; co-editor: Anthropologists in Cities, 1974, Migration Across Frontiers, 1979, (series) Contemporary Urban Studies, 1990—, Chronicling Cultures, 2002; editor Socio Cultural Anthropology, Am. Anthropologist, 1985-90, Human Orgn., 1995-98; mem. editl. bd. Ency. World Cultures, 1990-96, Ency. Urban Cultures, 1999—2002. Elder North Pk. Presbyn. Ch., Dallas, 1987-89, 95-97; parish assoc. Trinity Presbyn. Ch., 1999—; mem. Mcpl. Libr. Adv. Bd., Dallas, 1975-79; bd. dir. Oasis Housing Corp., 2000-04, Presbyn. Assn. Cmty. Transformation, 2003-04. Fulbright fellow, 1979-80, 91-92, Wenner-Gren fellow, 1974-76, 79-83, Woodrow Wilson fellow, 1966-67. Fellow AAAS, Am. Anthrop. Assn. (bd. dir. 1990-92), Soc. Applied Anthropology (chmn. Malinowski award com. 1979-80, bd. dir. 1995-98); mem. Latin Am. Studies Assn. (co-chmn. XI Internat. Congress 1983), Soc. Urban Anthropology (pres. 1988-90), Soc. Latin Am. Anthropology (pres. 1981-82), Phi Beta Kappa (pres. chpt. 1987-88). Home: 10617 Cromwell Dr Dallas TX 75229-5110 Office: So Meth Univ Dept Anthropology 3225 Daniel Ave Dallas TX 75205-1437 Home Phone: 214-350-1449; Office Phone: 214-768-2928. Business E-Mail: rkemper@smu.edu.

KEMPER, RUFUS CROSBY, JR., retired bank executive; b. Kansas City, Mo., Feb. 22, 1927; s. Rufus Crosby and Enid (Jackson) Kemper; m. Mary Barton Stripp; children: Rufus Crosby III, Pamela Warrick Gabrovsky, Sheila Kemper Dietrich, John Mariner, Mary Barton Wolf, Alexander Charles, Heather Christian. Grad., Phillips Acad., Andover, Mass., 1942; student, U. Mo.; LL.D. (hon.), William Jewel Coll., 1976; DFA (hon.), Westminster Coll., 1983. Joined City Nat. Bank & Trust Co. (now UMB Fin. Corp.), Kansas City, 1950; exec v.p. UMB Fin. Corp., 1957—59, pres., 1959—71, chmn. & CEO, 1971—2000; sr. chmn. UMB Fin. Corp. & UMB Bank, 2000—04; ret., 2004. Hon. trustee Thomas Jefferson Found.; mem. nat. com. Whitney Mus. Am. Art, NYC.; commr. Nat. Mus. Am. Art., Washington; founder, chmn. bd. trustees The Kemper Mus. Contemporary Art, Kansas City, 1994-; trustee Kemper family foundations; founder, mem. bd. dirs. The Agriculture Future of Am., 1996-. Served USNR, WWII. Recipient Key Man Kansas City Jr. C. of C., 1952, Disting. Svc., 1964, Man of Yr. Award Kansas City Press Club, 1974, Outstanding Kansas Citian Award Native Sons Kansas City, 1975, 82, 1st Advocacy Award Mid-Continent Small Bus. Assn., 1980, Banker Adv. of Yr. Award Small Bus. Adminstrn., 1981, Lester Milgram Humanitarian Award, 1982, Man of Yr. Award Downtown, Inc., 1982, Pirouette Award Kansas City Ballet Guild and Kansas City Tomorrow Alumni Assn., 1983, Faculty Alumni Award U. Mo. Columbia Alumni Assn., 1982, Mo. Arts Coun. Award, 1984, Kansas City Chancellor's Medal U. Mo., 1984, Disting. Svc. Award St. Paul Sch. Theology, 1987, Advocacy Award Mo. Citizens for the Arts, 1987, Outstanding Patron of Excellence in the Arts and Architecture Am. Inst. Architects - Kansas City, 1994, VIP Leadership Award Centurions Leadership Program Greater Kansas City C. of C., 1995; named Man of Yr. Kansas City Press Club, 1974, Kansas Citian of Yr., 1997; named one of Top 200 Collectors ARTnews mag., 2004. Mem. Am. Royal Assn. (v.p., bd. dirs.), Man of the Month Fraternity, Beta Theta Pi (Man of Yr. 1974) Clubs: River, Carriage, Kansas City Country, Kansas City, 1021, Mo, Chathan, Mass., Garden of the Gods, Cheyenne Mountain Country (Colorado Springs, Colo.). Republican. Episcopalian. Avocations: Collector Old Masters, modern and contemporary art, farming, tennis, sailing, horseback riding, raising cattle. Office: Kemper Mus Contemporary Art 4220 Warwick Blvd Kansas City MO 64111

KEMPER, R(UFUS) CROSBY, III, library director; s. R. Crosby Kemper, Jr. Tchr. English U. Sichuan, China; chmn., CEO United Mo. Bank, 2000—04; interim exec. dir. Kans. City Pub. Libr., 2005, exec. dir. Mo., 2005—. Bd. mem. Truman Presdl. Libr. and Inst. Editor: Winston Churchill: Resolution, Defiance, Magnanimity, Good Will, 1995. Bd. mem. Jefferson Nat. Pk. Assn., Kans. City Symphony, Thomas Jefferson Found.; chmn. Mo. Bankers Assn. Office: Kans City Pub Libr 14 W 10th St Kansas City MO 64105 Office Phone: 816-701-3501. Office Fax: 816-701-3401. E-mail: crosbyk@kclibrary.org.

KEMPER, TOM A., secondary school educator; b. Van Nuys, Calif., Mar. 13, 1964; s. Alfred M. and Harriet L. Kemper; m. Alison P. Trope, July 1, 2001; 1 child, Jackson T. BA, U. Calif., Berkeley, 1987; PhD, U. So. Calif., LA, 2006. Tchr. Crossroads Sch., Santa Monica, Calif., 1998—. Recipient Outstanding Tchr. award, U. Chgo., 2001, Tchr. Recognition award, US Dept. Edn. Presdl. Scholars Program, 2001, Outstanding Am. Tchrs. award, Nat. Honors Roll, 2006, Tchr. Recognition award, Nat. Found. Advancement Arts, 2006; scholar, Mary Pickford Found., 2004; Skaaren fellow, Harry Ransom Ctr., 2007. Mem.: MLA. Home: 3630 Purdue Ave Los Angeles CA 90066 Office: Crossroads Sch Arts and Scis 1714 21st St Santa Monica CA 94140 Home Phone: 310-397-3903; Office Phone: 310-829-7391. Personal E-mail: tomaskemper@aol.com.

KEMPF, DONALD G., JR., retired lawyer; b. Chgo., July 4, 1937; s. Donald G. and Verginia (Jahnke) K.; m. Nancy Kempf, June 12, 1965; children: Donald G. III, Charles P., Stephen R. AB, Villanova U., 1959; LLB, Harvard U., 1965; MBA, U. Chgo., 1989. Bar: Ill. 1965, U.S. Supreme Ct. 1972, N.Y. 1986, Colo. 1992. Assoc. Kirkland & Ellis, Chgo., 1965-70, ptnr., 1971-2000; exec. v.p., chief legal officer, sec. Morgan Stanley, NYC, 2000—05; ret., 2005. Trustee Chgo. Symphony Orch., 1995—, Am. Inns of Ct., 1997-2006, v.p., 2002-06; bd. govs. Chgo. Zool. Soc., 1975—, Art Inst. Chgo., 1984—; bd. dirs. United Charities Chgo., 1985-2003, chmn. bd., 1991-93; trustee NYC Opera, 2002-05; commr. Antitrust Modernization Commn., 2004-07. Capt. USMC, 1959-62. Recipient Stephen E. Banner award, 2004. Fellow Am. Coll. Trial Lawyers; mem. Am. Econ. Assn., ABA, Chgo. Club, Econ. Club, U. Club, Mid-Am. Club, Saddle and Cycle Club (Chgo.), Snowmass (Colo.) Club, Roaring Fork Club, Country Club Fla., Quail Ridge (Fla.) Club, Westmoreland Club. Roman Catholic. Personal E-mail: dkempf@kempflaw.com.

KEMPISTY, MICHAEL, artist, writer, actor; b. Willoughby, Ohio, Mar. 25, 1973; s. Walter and Johanna Kempisty; m. Crista Kempisty, Aug. 31, 1996; children: Alanna, Devin. Diploma in fine arts, Columbus Coll. of Art & Design, Ohio, 1992; diploma in theatre, Ohio State U., 1996. Box office sales, mgr. Alex Theatre, Glendale, Calif., 1998—; artist, owner Michael Lightsey Fine Arts, Encino, Calif., 2002—. Artist apprentice Pharmaka Art, LA, 2005—. Author: (poetry book, art) Abstractions, 2005, (screenplays) Vexation of A Dream, 2006. Ptnr. of conscience Amnesty Internat., Columbus, 1992—93; patron Environ. Def. Fund, Columbus, 1993—95. Mem.: Am. MENSA. Office: Michael Lightsey Fine Arts PO Box 17641 Encino CA 91416

KEMPNER, MAXIMILIAN WALTER, dean, lawyer; b. Berlin, Feb. 27, 1929; came to US, 1939; s. Paul H. and Marga Marie (von Mendelssohn) K.; m. Barbara Paige Mooney, 1952; children: Paul, Daphne, Emily Mayne. BA, Harvard U., 1951, LLB, 1954; LLM, Columbia U., 1957; LLD, Vt. Law Sch., 1997. Bar: NY bar 1954. With Webster & Sheffield, NYC, 1957-91; dean Vt. Law Sch., South Royalton, 1991-96. Chmn. Vt. Legis. Apportionment Bd.; dir. Lawyers Com. for Civil Rights under Law. Trustee Marlboro Sch. Music, Inc., Conservation Law Found.; former dir. Legal Aid Soc., Am. Coun. on Germany, Albert Schweitzer Fellowship, Coun. on Libr. Resources; active Coun. Fgn. Rels., Inc. With U.S. Army, 1954-56. Fellow Am. Bar Found. (life); mem. ABA (past chmn. legal edn. and admissions to bar sect.), Am. Law Inst. (life), Assn. Bar City N.Y., N.Y. State Bar Assn., Harvard Law Sch. Assn. N.Y.C. (past pres.). Office Phone: 802-763-2222. Business E-Mail: mkempner@vermontlaw.edu.

KEMPNER, MICHAEL W., public relations executive; b. Chgo., Jan. 31, 1958; s. Lester T. and Lois Kempner; m. Jacqueline Steinberg, Oct. 24, 1987; children: Zachary, Melissa. BS, Am. U., 1981. Spl. asst. to Gov. of N.J., Trenton, 1977-79; state campaign dir. Pres. Jimmy Carter, Washington, 1979-80; dep. fin. chair Dem. Nat. Comm., 1980-82; legis. dir. to Robert Torricelli US Congress, Hackensack, NJ, 1983-84; pres. Winter's Chocolates, Emerson, NJ, 1984-86; founder, pres., CEO The MWW Group, East Rutherford, NJ, 1986—. Bd. dirs. N.J. Drug Abuse Resistance Edn. Contbr. articles to popular mags. Former fin. vice chair Dem. Nat. Com.; regional chmn. fin. Dem. senatorial campaign, Washington, 1990, chmn. fin. com. Congressman Torriceli, Hackensack, 1984—, committeeman Bergen County Dem. Com., 1991, bd. advisors Ctr. Food Action, Englewood, N.J., 1990-91. Named Entrepreneur of Yr. finalist, 1991, 92, 93, 94; recipient Best Communications Exec., Am. Bus. Awards, 2007. Mem. Pub. Rels. Soc. Am., Young Pres. Orgns., mem. 1992 U.S Olympic Com., regl fin. chmn., mem. Am. Bankruptcy Inst., and Turnaround mgmt. Assn. Office: The MWW Group 1 Meadowlands Plz Fl 6 East Rutherford NJ 07073-2100*

KEMPSTER, NORMAN ROY, journalist; b. Sacramento, Jan. 4, 1936; s. Roy Dixon and Viola Alice (Cox) K.; m. Jane Leon, June 30, 1957; children: Jill Suzanne Zemke, David Norman. BA, Calif. State U., 1957. Reporter U.P.I., 1957-73, Washington Star-News, 1973-76; reporter Washington bur. L.A. Times, 1976—80, reporter Jerusalem bur., 1981—84, reporter Washington bur., 1984—2001. Joe Alex Morris meml. lectr. Harvard U., 1983, adj. prof. Lenoir-Rhyne Coll., Hickory, NC, 2003. Served with AUS, 1959-61. Profl. Journalism fellow, 1967; recipient Gerald Loeb award, 1980 Mem. Fgn. Press Assn. in Israel (v.p. 1982-83), White House Corrs. Assn. (dir. 1974-75), State Dept. Corrs. Assn. (treas. 1986, v.p. 1987, pres. 1988), Overseas Writers of Washington (pres. 1989-91). Episcopalian. Home and Office: 7505 Democracy Blvd Bethesda MD 20817 Personal E-mail: nrkempster@aol.com.

KEMPTHORNE, DIRK ARTHUR, secretary of the interior, former governor; b. San Diego, Oct. 29, 1951; s. James Henry and Maxine Jesse (Gustason) K.; m. Patricia Jean Merrill, Sept. 18, 1977; children: Heather Patricia, Jeffrey Dirk. BS in Polit. Sci., U. Idaho, 1975. Exec. asst. to dir. Idaho Dept. Pub. Lands, Boise, 1975-78; exec. v.p. Idaho Home Builders Assn., Boise, 1978-81; campaign mgr. Batt for Gov., Boise, 1981-82; lic. securities rep. Swanson Investments, Boise, 1983; Idaho pub. affairs mgr. FMC Corp., Boise, 1983-86; mayor City of Boise, 1985—92; US Senator from Idaho, 1993-98; gov. State of Idaho, Boise, 1999—2006; sec. US Dept. Interior, Washington, 2006—. 1st v.p. Assn. of Idaho Cities, 1990-93; chmn. U.S. Conf. of Mayors Standing Com. on Energy and Environment, 1991-93, mem. adv. bd., 1991-93; sec. Nat. Conf. of Rep. Mayors and Mcpl. Elected Officials, 1991-93; mem. Senate Armed Svcs. Com., 1993-98, Senate Small Bus. Com., 1993-98, Senate Environ. and Pub. Works Com., 1993-98, Nat. Rep. Senatorial Com., 1993-98; chmn. Senate Drinking Water, Fisheries and Wildlife Subcommittee, 1995-98, mem. advisory commn. on Intergovernmental Rels., 1995-96; chmn. Armed Svcs Personnel Subcommittee, 1996-98. Pres. Associated Students U. Idaho, Moscow, 1975; chmn. bd. dirs. Wesleyan Presch., Boise, 1982-85; mem. magistrate commn. 4th Jud. Dist., Boise, 1986-93; mem. task force Nat. League of Cities Election, 1988; bd. dirs. Parents and Youth Against Drug Abuse, 1987—; mem. bd. vis. USAF Acad., 1994—; chmn. Idaho Working Ptnrs. Ltd., 1993—; hon. chmn. Idaho Congressional Award, 1994—. Named Idaho Citizen of Yr. The Idaho Statesman, 1988, Legislator of the Year Nat. Assn. Counties, 1995, State Legislator of the Year Nat. Assn. of Towns and Townships, 1995; recipient U.S. Conference of Mayor's Nat. Legis. Leadership award, 1994, Disting. Svc. award Nat. Conf. State Legislatures, 1995, Disting. Congressional award Nat. League of Cities, 1995, Guardian of Freedom award Council of State Governments, 1995. Republican. Methodist. Office: US Dept Interior 1849 C St NW Mail Stop 7229 Washington DC 20240*

KEN, SUSANTO SUWARNO, engineer; PhD, U. So. Calif., LA, 2006. Mech. design engr. Honeywell, Torrance, Calif., 1998—99; rsch. fellow U. So. Calif., LA, 2001—. Reviewer: Internat. Jour. Robotics and Automation. Named winner Bio-Tech Applications Contest, IEEE, 2002; recipient Design News award, ANSYS, Inc. and Design News Mag., 2003; scholar, NAFSA and US Info. Agy., 1998. Mem.: ASME (reviewer Jour. Med. Devices). Achievements include invention of Miniature Piezoelectric Forceps Actuator. Office: U So Calif 3650 McClintock Ave Rm 430 Los Angeles CA 90089-1453 Home Phone: 310-544-9375. Business E-Mail: ksusanto@usc.edu.

KENAGY, CHERI LYNN, nurse; b. Houston, Nov. 12, 1958; d. Kenneth Leigh and Mary Louise Kenagy; m. William J. Balan, July 30, 1982 (dec. Jan. 15, 1991). Student, San Jacinto Coll., 1980. Lic. vocat. nurse, cert. physician asst., pediat. advanced life support. Hosp. staff relief Ace Med. Staffing, Houston, 1998—, AHA, Houston, 1998—. Conservative. Presbyterian. Avocations: travel, scuba diving. Home: Box 5885 Pasadena TX 77508-5885 Personal E-mail: txauburn2002@yahoo.com.

KENAGY, ROBERT COFFMAN, planning consulting company executive; b. Hartford, Conn., July 10, 1931; s. Herbert Glenn and Mary Emily (Hardesty) K.; m. Karen Miriam Emanuelson, June 8, 1957; children: Neil S., Lynn S., Gretchen P. BA, Princeton U., 1953; postgrad., U. Pa., 1953—54. Various mktg. mgmt. positions IBM, NYC, White Plains, Armonk, NY, 1957—69; v.p. mktg. Data Dimensions, Inc., Greenwich, Conn., 1969—73; fin. prin. Sidney A. Staunton, Inc., New Canaan, Conn., 1973—78; pres. RCK Mgmt. Co., Ltd., New Canaan, Litchfield, Conn., 1978—. Bd. dirs. Keystone Engring. Co., Los Angeles, 1983—89. Mem. Larchmont-Mamroneck Bd. Edn., N.Y., 1968-72; bd. dir. YMCA, New Canaan, 1975-81, pres., 1980-81, trustee The Aloha Found., Fairlee, Vt., 1976-91, pres., 1983-84, trustee emeritus, 1991—; trustee First Congl. Ch., Litchfield, 2002—, vice chair, 2002-05, chair, 2005—; bd. dir. United Way, New Canaan, 1979-82, campaign chmn., 1979-80; bd. dir. Northwest Conn. Assn. for the Arts, 2005-. 1st lt. US Army, 1954—56. Mem.:

Litchfield Country Club, Princeton Club NY. Avocations: singing, travel. Home and Office: RCK Mgmt Co Ltd 24 Fox Crossing Ln Litchfield CT 06759-2305 Home Phone: 860-567-0790; Office Phone: 860-567-0260. E-mail: kenagy@optonline.net.

KENAN, THOMAS STEPHEN, III, philanthropist; b. Durham, NC, Apr. 19, 1937; s. Frank Hawkins Kenan and Harriet Gregg (DuBose) Gray. BA in Econ., U. N.C., 1959. Trustee Sarah G. Kenan Found., Durham, 1968-74, N.C. Mus. Art, Raleigh, 1972-91, Randleigh Found. Trust, 1981-95, N.C. Sch. the Arts, Winston-Salem, 1983-91, W.R. Kenan Charitable Trust, Chapel Hill, NC, 1986-97, U. N.C. Arts and Sci. Found., Chapel Hill, 1989-91, The Nat. Tropical Bot. Gardens, Hawaii, The Coun. of Nat. Trust for Hist. Preservation, Henry Morrison Flagler Mus.; dir. William R. Kenan Jr. Fund, 1995—. Exec. com. Flagler System, Inc., Palm Beach, Fla., 1968-97; chmn. Kenan Transport Co., Chapel Hill, 1968-97; pres. Westfield Co., Durham, 1971-91. Founder Liberty Hall Restoration Commn., 1966, Duplin Outdoor Drama Soc., 1976; trustee The Duke Endowment; trustee Mary Duke Biddle Found., Durham, 1984-85. Mem. Hope Valley Country Club, Treyburn Golf and Country Club, Breakers Beach and Golf Club, Univ. Club, Landfall Golf and Tennis Club. Episcopalian. Avocations: music, horseback riding, golf, reading, gardening. Address: PO Box 4150 Chapel Hill NC 27515-4150

KENDALL, CHARLES TERRY, librarian; b. Chambersburg, Pa., Aug. 13, 1949; s. Guy William and Virginia Mae (Naugle) K.; m. Alice Marie Bienz, Aug. 21, 1971; children: Terri, Anita, Kendra. BA, Huntington Coll., Ind., 1971; MLS, George Peabody Coll., 1972; postgrad., Asbury Theol. Sem., 1982-83; MA in Religion, Anderson U., Ind., 1990. Head libr. Plymouth Pub. Libr., Ind., 1972—73; cataloger Mohave County Libr., Kingman, Ariz., 1975—78; resources libr. Starved Rock Libr. Sys., Ottawa, Ill., 1978—81; dir. Mifflin County Libr., Lewistown, Pa., 1981—82; cataloger Asbury Coll., 1982—83; dir. Byrd Meml. Libr. Anderson Sch. Theology, Anderson U., 1983-89; theol. studies libr. Anderson U. Libr., 1989-98, archivist, 1992-98; dir. Mabee Libr. Sterling Coll., Kans., 1998—2002; head circulation and tech. svc. Alexandrian Public Library, Mt. Vernon, Ind., 2003—05, head collection svcs., 2005—. Mem. ALA, Public Library Assn.

KENDALL, DAVID E., lawyer; b. Camp Atterbury, Ind., May 2, 1944; BA, Wabash Coll., 1966; MA, Oxford U., England, 1968; JD, Yale U., 1971. Bar: N.Y. 1974, U.S. Ct. Appeals (5th cir.) 1976, D.C. 1978, U.S. Supreme Ct. 1978, Md. 1993. Law clerk to Justice Byron R. White U.S. Supreme Ct., 1971-72; assoc. counsel NAACP Legal Def. & Ednl. Fund, 1973—78; assoc. Williams & Connolly LLP, Washington, 1978—81, ptnr., 1981—. Adj. prof. Columbia U. Law Sch., 1977-78, Georgetown U. Law Ctr., 1985-95. Note and comment editor Yale Law Jour., 1970-71; author (with Leonard Ross) The Lottery and the Draft, 1970; auth Constitutional Vandalism, 30 U. New Mexico Law Review 155, 2000, Opinion Is Protected Expression Under the Constitution, 2 Communications Lawyer 5, 1984, How to Keep Your Client Alive, 3 Criminal Defense 9, 1976, The Affirmative Duty to Integrate in Higher Education, 79 Yale Law Journal 666, 1970. 2nd lt. US Army, 1972—73. Rhodes scholar; named one of 75 Best Lawyers in Washington, Washingtonian survey mag. Mem. N.Y. State Bar Assn., Md. State Bar Assn., Washington, DC Bar Assn., bd. dirs., NAACP Legal Def.& Ednl. Fund Inc. Office: Williams & Connolly 725 12th St NW Washington DC 20005-5901 E-mail: dkendall@wc.com.

KENDALL, DOROTHY IRENE, secondary school educator; d. Alger Hugh Kendall, Sr. and Adelia Irene (Rasor) Kendall. BBA, U. Tex. Austin, 1967; MEd, U. Houston, Victoria, Tex., 1980. Cert. Tchr. Tex., 1969. Tchr. Victoria Meml. H.S. (formally Victoria H.S.), 1967—2006; ret., 2006. Owner Open Door Boutique, Karnes City, Tex., 1970—74, Kendall's Boutique, Victoria, 1974—77; tchr., coach Victoria H.S., 1968—73. Sponsor Student Coun. Victoria Meml. H.S., 1989—92; sponsor Meml. Christian Club, Victoria, 1993—2006; tchr. Sun. sch. Northside Bapt. Ch., Victoria, 1968—77; sponsor Bapt. Young Women's Assn., Victoria, Tex., 1968—75. Recipient Outstanding Tchr., Nat. Honor Roll's Outstanding Am. Teachers, 2006, Leadership Cert., E. I. duPont deNemours and Co., 1992. Mem.: Nat. Edn. Assn. (life), Tex. State Tchrs. Assn. (life), Tex. Exes (life). Avocations: photography, travel, horseback riding, tennis.

KENDALL, HARRY WESLEY, playwright, writer; b. Tarentum, Pa., Aug. 10, 1931; s. Wesley Chappell Kendall and Emma Jane Lucas; children: Victor, Michael Susan(dec.) , Harry, Rochelle, Joel, Mitchell. BA, Rutgers U., 1977; MFA, Norwich U., 1988. Sr. writer/editor Boeing Helicopter Co., Ridley Township, Pa., 1980—95; writer/reporter Phila. Bulletin, 1972—80, Trenton Times, Trenton, NJ, 1969—72; elec. tech. Radio Corp. of Am., Camden, NJ, 1963—69; field svc. tech. Jacy Inc. Cons. Engr., Camden, NJ, 1960—63. Author: (historical fiction) Truth Crushed to Earth, 1999, (plays) Resistance in Christiana, 2001. Pres. Willingboro Pub. Libr., Willingboro, NJ, 1989—; co-chair Communciations Com., 1987—2004; v.p., bd. dirs. Theater of Seventh Sister, 2002—04; pres. Kinsmen of Willingboro, 1968—70; v.p. Greater Willingboro Assn., 2000—; with Mt. Carmel Baptist Ch., Wash.; judge Optimist Internat., 1987—93. Recipient Cmty. Svc. award, Alpha Kappa Alpha Sorority, 2004, Commitment Youth award, Zion Bapt. Ch., 2004, Cert. of Appreciation, Mt. Carmel Bapt. Ch., Boeing Vertol Toastmasters, Dist. 38. Mem.: South Jersey Regional Libr. Coop. Democrat. Avocations: yoga, jazz. Office Fax: 609-871-8683. E-mail: kentehuti@aol.com.

KENDALL, JASON DANIEL, professional baseball player; b. San Diego, June 26, 1974; s. Fred Kendall. Selected first-round free-agt. draft Pitts. Pirates, 1992; catcher Gulf Coast League Pirates, 1992, Augusta (South Atlantic League), 1993, Salem (Carolina), 1994, Carolina (So. League), 1994-96, Pitts. Pirates, 1996—2004, Oakland A's, 2004—. Named to Nat. League All-Star team, 1996, 1998, 2000. Office: c/o Oakland A's 7000 Coliseum way Oakland CA 94621

KENDALL, JOHN WALKER, JR., internist, researcher, dean; b. Bellingham, Wash., Mar. 19, 1929; s. John Walker and Mathilda (Hansen) K.; m. Elizabeth Helen Meece, Mar. 19, 1954; children: John, Katherine, Victoria. BA, Yale Coll., 1952; MD, U. Wash., 1956. Intern, resident in internal medicine Vanderbilt U. Hosp., Nashville, 1956-59, fellow in endocrinology, 1959-60, U. Oreg. Med. Sch., Portland, 1960-62; asst. prof. medicine Oreg. Health Scis. U., Portland, 1962-66, assoc. prof. medicine, 1966-71, prof. medicine, 1971—, head divsn. metabolism, 1971-80; dean Oreg. Health Scis. U. Sch. Medicine, Portland, 1983—92; assoc. chief staff-rsch. VA Med. Ctr., Portland, 1971-83, dep. chief of staff, 1993, VA disting. physician, 1993-96, acad. affiliates officer, 1997—, grad. med. edn. adv. com., 2001—04. Cons. Med. Rsch. Found. Oreg., Portland, 1975-83; sec. Oreg. Found. Med. Excellence, Portland, 1984-89, pres., 1989-91; grad. med. edn. adv. com. Dept. Vets. Affairs, 2001—05; commn. mem. VA Cares, 2003-04; mem. VA Blue Ribbon Com. on Grad. Med. Edn., 2006—. Lt. comdr. M.C., USN, 1962-64 Recipient Outstanding Physician award Found. Med. Excellence, 1995. Mem. AMA (governing coun. med. sch. sect. 1989-93, chair 1991-92, alt. del. 1992-93, Oreg. del. 1994-98, rep. Coun. Grad. Med. Edn. 1993-94), Assn. Am. Physicians, Am. Soc. Clin. Investigation, Am. Fedn. Clin. Rsch., We. Soc. Clin. Rsch. (councillor 1972-75), Endocrine Soc., Multnomah County Med. Soc. (treas. 1989, pres. 1991), Med. Rsch. Found. (Mentor award 1992), Royal Soc. Medicine (endocrinology sect. coun. 1999—2004). Presbyterian. Home: 3131 SW Evergreen Ln Portland OR 97205-5816 Office: Oreg Health Scis U Sch Medicine L-607 3181 SW Sam Jackson Park Rd Portland OR 97239

KENDALL, KATHERINE ANNE, social worker; b. Muir-of-Ord, Scotland, Sept. 8, 1910; came to U.S., 1920, naturalized, 1940; d. Roderick and Annie Scott (Walker) Tuach; m. Willmoore Kendall, June 22, 1935 (div. Apr. 1950). BA, U. Ill., 1933; MA, La. State U., 1939; PhD, U. Chgo., 1950; D Public Service (hon.), Syracuse U., 1981; DSW (hon.), U. Pa., 1985, La. State U., 1987, U. Ill., 1989. Asst. prof. Richmond Sch. Social Work, 1941-42; asst. dir. home service A.R.C., 1942-44; lectr. U. Chgo. Sch. Social Service Adminstrn., 1944-45; asst. dir., tng. supr. Inter-Am. and Internat. Tng. units U.S. Children's Bur., 1945- 47; social affairs officer UN Secretariat, 1947-50; exec. sec. Am. Assn. Schs. Social Work, 1950-52; ednl. sec. Council on Social Work Edn., 1952-58, assoc. dir., 1958-63, exec. dir., 1963-66, dir. internat. edn., 1966-71; Carnegie vis. prof. U. Hawaii, 1960-61; mem. exec. bd. Internat. Assn. Schs. Social Work, 1954-66, sec.-gen., 1966-78, hon. pres., 1978—. Ofcl. non-govtl. rep. UN, 1954-94; Moses prof. Hunter Coll. Social Work, 1983-84; dir. Internat. Conf. on Social Work Edn., Population and Family Planning, East-West Ctr., Hawaii, 1970; exec. sec. Coun. of Advisors to Hunter Coll., Hunter Coll. Sch. Social Work and Lois and Samuel Silberman Fund, 1985-87. Author: Reflections on Social Work Education, 1950-1978, Social Work Education: Its Origins in Europe, 2000, The Council on Social Work Education: Its Antecedents and the First Twenty Years, 2002; UN reports International Exchange of Social Welfare Personnel, 1949, Training for Social Work: First International Survey, 1950; editor: Social Work Values in an Age of Discontent, 1970, Population Dynamics and Family Planning: A New Responsibility for Social Work Education, 1971, World Guide to Social Work Edn., 1984, Eileen Blackey; Pathfinder for the Profession, 1986; co-editor: Gerontological Social Work: International Perspectives, 1988; compiler: Social Casework— Cumulative Index 1920-1979, 1981. Active UN Internat. meeting experts on social work tng., Munich, 1956; faculty UN Seminar, Keeru, Finland, 1952; assignment social work edn., Guatemala, 1949, Brazil, 1952, Paraguay, 1954; dir. 1st seminar Schs. Social Work in Central Am., 1963. Mem. NASW, Mortar Bd., Internat. Assn. Schs. Social Work, Council on Social Work Edn., Internat. Council on Social Welfare, Phi Beta Kappa, Chi Omega. Home: Collington # 2003 10450 Lottsford Rd Mitchellville MD 20721-2734 E-mail: k.kend@erols.com.

KENDALL, KAY LYNN, interior designer, consultant; b. Cadillac, Mich., Aug. 20, 1950; d. Robert Llewellyn and Betty Louise (Powers) Kendall; 1 child, Anna Renee Easter. BFA, U. Mich., 1973. Draftsman, interior designer store planning dept. Jacobson Stores, Inc., Jackson, Mich., 1974-79, sr. interior designer store planning dept., 1981—98; prin., pres. Kay Kendall Designs LLC dba K.I.D.D. LLC (Kendall Interior Design and Devel. LLC), 1979—; sr. interior designer Maddalena's Inc., 1998—2002; realtor Edward Surovell Realtors, Ann Arbor, Mich., 2000—05, Citadel Group, Jackson, Mich., 2005—. Cons. in field. Big sister Big Bros./Big Sisters Jackson County. Mem. Am. Soc. Interior Designers (profl. mem., assoc. Ctrl. Mich. chpt.). Avocations: tennis, golf, gardening, skiing. Home: 701 Church St Grass Lake MI 49240-9206 Office: KIDD LLC 107 S Main St Chelsea MI 48118 Office Phone: 734-433-0811. Business E-Mail: kkendall@kidd-llc.com.

KENDALL, LEIGH WAKEFIELD, surgeon, hospital administrator; b. Brattleboro, Vt., Mar. 8, 1937; s. Irwin Samuel and Laura Eliza (Walbridge) Kendall; m. Grace Eleanor Fullarton, July 1, 1961; children: William Leigh, Bradley Edward. AB, U. Pa., Phila., 1959; D of Medicine, U. Vt., 1963; MS, U. Ill., Chgo., 1965. Diplomate Nat. Bd. Med. Examiners, Am. Bd. Surgery, cert. ACLS. Intern then resident surgery U. Ill. Hosp., Chgo., 1963-69; rsch. fellow Am. Cancer Soc., Chgo., 1964-65, clin. fellow, 1968-69; staff surgeon USN Hosp., Great Lakes, Ill., 1969; surgeon USN Hosp. Ships, Vietnam, 1969-70; pvt. practice Lancaster, Pa., 1971-93; med. dir. Alliance Health Plan, Lancaster, 1995—2005; assoc. med. dir. St. Joseph Regional Health Network, Lancaster and Reading, 1999—2000; med. dir. St. Joseph Hosp., Lancaster, 2000—01, Lancaster Regional Med. Ctr., 2000—. Instr. surgery U. Ill. Hosp., Chgo., 1968—69; active staff St. Joseph Hosp., Lancaster, 1971—, sect. chief gen. surgery, 1981—88, chmn. dept. surgery, 1989—93; mem. courtesy staff Lancaster Gen. Hosp., 1971—; cons. surgery Franklin & Marshall Coll., Lancaster, Pa., Masonic Homes, Elizabethtown, Pa.; staff physician Millersville U., 1993—2004; staff physician cardiac rehab. Lancaster Gen. Hosp. Health Campus, 1995—98. Lt. comdr. M.C. USNR, 1959—71, Vietnam. Decorated 1st Class Mil. Honor medal Republic of Vietnam. Fellow: ACS; mem.: AMA, Am. Coll. Physicians Execs., Royal Soc. Medicine (Eng.), Pa. Med. Soc., Internat. Soc. Surgeons, Warren H. Cole Soc. (pres. 1994—95), Intrepids Club, Sigma Nu. Republican. Episcopalian. Avocations: photography, travel. Home: 1314 Quarry Ln Lancaster PA 17603-2424 Office: Med Affairs Office Lancaster Regional Med Ctr Lancaster PA 17604-3434 Office Phone: 717-299-3875.

KENDALL, PETER LANDIS, television news executive; b. Toledo, Oct. 8, 1936; s. Roy Cline and Edythe Mae (Kindy) K.; m. Beate Margit Fritz, June 11, 1966; children: Adrian Peter, Stefanie Karin. BA, U. Cin., 1959; BS cum laude, U. Ill., Urbana, 1960. News producer-writer Voice of Am., Washington, 1961-64; corr. Deutsche Welle, Bonn, Germany, 1964-66; morning news producer CBS News, Washington, 1971-74, producer London, 1974-77, bur. chief, 1977-82, sr. producer-asst. bur. mgr. Washington, 1982-86, bur. chief Bonn, 1986-88; pvt. practice internat. TV cons. Washington, 1988-90; exec. producer Washington bur. Cable News Network, 1990—2002, cons., 2002—; exec. producer CNN Washington Coverage of Gulf War, 1991. Producer: Econ. Summits, London, 1977, 84, Bonn, 1978, Versailles, 1982; Iranian Hostages Return, Frankfurt, West Germany, 1980, Moscow Olympics, 1980, London, The Royal Wedding, 1981; numerous presdl. visits to Europe. Recipient Emmy award for Senate and Watergate coverage Nat. Acad. TV Arts and Scis., 1974 Mem. Am. Corrs. Assn. (exec. bd. London 1977-80), Health Vols. Overseas (bd. dirs. 1996-2002), Sigma Delta Chi. Espiscopalian. Club: Tamesis Sailing (London). Home: 4955 Quebec St NW Washington DC 20016-3230 Personal E-mail: pandbkendall@verizon.net.

KENDALL, PHILLIP ALAN, retired lawyer; b. Lamar, Colo., July 20, 1942; s. Charles Stuart and Katherine (Wilson) K.; m. Margaret Roe Greenfield, May 2, 1970; children: Anne, Timothy. BS in Engring., Stanford U., 1964; JD, U. Colo., 1969; postgrad., U. Freiburg, 1965—66. Engr. Siemens Halske, Munich, 1965; assoc. Kraemer, Kendall & Benson LLC, Colorado Springs, Colo., 1969—2004; ret., 2004. Gen. counsel Peak Health Care, Inc., Colorado Springs, 1979-87; bd. dirs. Wells Fargo Banks Colorado Springs. Pres. bd. Colorado Springs Symphony Orch. Assn., 1977-80; bd. dirs. Penrose Hosps., Colorado Springs, 1982-88; pres. bd. Citizen's Goals, Colorado, 1984-86; bd. dirs. Legal Aid Found., Denver, 1988-94, chmn., 1991-93; bd. dirs. Colo. chpt. Nature Conservancy, chair 2001-03; pres., bd. trustees Bee Vradenburg Found., 2004—. Recipient Medal of Distinction-Fine Arts, Colorado Springs C. of C., 1983. Mem. ABA, Am. Bar Found., Colo. Bar Found., Colo. Bar Assn. (bd. govs. 1985-88, Outstanding Young Lawyer 1977), El Paso County Bar Assn. (bd. trustees 1983-85), Colorado Springs Estate Planning Coun.(lectr. charitable estate planning). Avocations: triathlons, helicopter skiing, marathon swimming, windsurfing, sailing. Home: 1915 Wood Ave Colorado Springs CO 80907-6714 E-mail: pkendall@k2blaw.com.

KENDALL, ROBERT LOUIS, JR., lawyer; b. Rochester, NH, Oct. 13, 1930; s. Robert Louis and Marguerite (Thomas) K.; m. Patricia Ann Palmer, Aug. 13, 1955; children: Linda J., Cynthia J., Janet L. AB cum laude, Harvard U., Cambridge, Mass., 1952; JD cum laude, U. Pa., Phila., 1955; Diploma in Law, Oxford U., Eng., 1956. Bar: Pa. 1957, Ga. 1993. Assoc. Schnader, Harrison, Segal & Lewis, Phila., 1956-65, ptnr., 1966-95. Lectr. Temple U. Law Sch., Phila., 1976-77; spl. instr. U. Pa. Law Sch., 1959-62. Contbr. to Antitrust Law Developments, 2d edit. 1984 Bd. dirs. Mann Music Ctr., Inc., Phila., 1971-98, Settlement Music Sch., Phila., Pa., 1984—, Jr. C. of C., Phila., 1962-65; mem. Phila. Orch. Assn., 1983—. Fellow Soc. Values in Higher Edn.; mem. ABA, Pa. Bar Assn., Ga. Bar Assn., Phila. Bar Assn., Atlanta Bar Assn., U. Pa. Law Alumni Assn. (bd. mgrs.), Rotary, Order of Coif (pres. 1979-80), Lawyers Club Atlanta, Harvard Club. Democrat. Episcopalian. Home: 3500 West Chester Pike Newtown Square PA 19073-4101

KENDALL, SUSAN GARDES, librarian; b. Hagerstown, Md., Aug. 24, 1948; d. George Austin and Jeanne Faust (Smith) Gardes; m. Steven Walter Kendall, May 25, 1974; children: Kimberly Ann, Kristen Jeanne. BA, William Woods Coll., Fulton, Mo., 1970; MA, Ohio State U., 1971; MLS, Simmons Coll., 1974. Reference libr. Simmons Coll., Boston, 1973-74, Harper Coll., Palatine, Ill., 1976-81, Marquette U., Milw., 1982; head adult svcs. Brookfield (Wis.) Pub. Libr., 1982-87, Batavia (Ill.) Pub. Libr., 1988-90; reference libr. Cobb County Pub. Libr., Marietta, Ga., 1990-93, br. mgr., 1993—. Treas. Mgmt. Recruiters, Lithia Springs, Ga., 1990—; bd. dirs. Gardes Investments Ltd., Columbus, Ohio, 1972—. Contbr. articles to profl. jours. Vol. Olympic Games, Atlanta, 1996; leader Girl Scouts, 1982-94. Mem. S.E. Librs. Assn. (award com. 1993-95, 98—), Ga. Libr. Assn. (pub. librs. 1993-95, award com. 1996-97, v.p. 1997-98, scholarship chair 2000—). Methodist. Office: Cobb County Libr Sys 266 Roswell St NE Marietta GA 30060-2005

KENDALL, WILLIAM MELVIN, lawyer; b. Sept. 8, 1946; BA, Stanford U., Calif., 1970; JD, U. Santa Clara, Calif., 1976; MA, George Mason U., Fairfax, Va., 2006. Bar: Calif., US Ct. Claims. 1978, Fed. Dist. Ct. 1976. Criminal prosecutor Dist. Atty.'s Office, Crescent City, Calif., 1976—80; fgn. svc. officer US Dept. State, Washington, 1981—99. Contbr. numerous articles to profl. publs. Mem.: SCV (quartermaster 2000—06), Masons (32d degree). Home: 13740 Cabells Mill Dr Centreville VA 20120

KENDALL HULL, MARGARIDA, art educator, painter; b. Lisbon, Portugal; Attended studied history & philosophy, U. Lisbon; BFA, Corcoran Sch. Art, 1973; MFA, Catholic U., 1982. Visiting prof. studio art Towson State U., 1986; asst. prof. studio art George Mason U., 1987, assoc. prof., 1994, 2000—. Represented in permanent collections, Art Inst. Chgo., Gulbenkian Mus. Contemporary Art, Lisbon, Portugal, one-woman shows include, Osuna Gallery, Washington D.C., 1983, Gulbenkian Found., 1984, exhibitions include, Baltimore, Chgo., N.Y., Phila., Gallery K, Dupont Cir. Office: Art Dept George Mason U 4400 University Dr Fairfax VA 22030-4444

KENDE, ANDREW STEVEN, chemist, educator; b. Budapest, Hungary, July 17, 1932; arrived in U.S., 1941, naturalized, 1951; s. George and Elizabeth Kende; m. Frances Boothe, Sept. 14, 1954; 1 child, Mark. AB, U. Chgo., 1951; MS, Harvard, 1954, PhD, 1957. Sr. rsch. scientist Lederle Labs., Am. Cyanamid Co., Pearl River, NY, 1957-63, rsch. assoc., 1963-66, rsch. fellow, 1966-68, cons., 1968-94; prof. chemistry U. Rochester, NY, 1968—2002, prof. emeritus, 2002—, Charles Frederick Houghton prof. chemistry, 1981-2000, prof. oncology, 1982-2000, chmn., 1979-83, assoc. chmn., 1989-90. Vis. prof. SUNY, Buffalo, 1967, Mich. State U., East Lansing, 1968, U. Genève, 1974, U. Amsterdam, 1989; cons. study sect. NIH, 1972—76, chmn., 1974—76; vis. scholar Stanford U., 1975; cons. Dow Chem. Co., 1975—2001, Bausch and Lomb Co., 1985—90, Eastman Kodak Co., 1987—94, Procter and Gamble Pharms., 1988—2004, Dow Agrosciences, 1994—2002; Bicentenary lectr. Royal Australian Chem. Inst., 1988; pres. Organic Syntheses Inc., 1992—2002. Mem. bd. editors Organic Reactions, 1968—83; editor-in-chief: Organic Reactions, 1983—88; mem. bd. editors Chem. Revs., 1973—76, Organic Syntheses, 1978—87, Synthetic Comm., 1981—96; assoc. editor: Jour. Organic Chemistry, 1997—2002. Am. Cancer Soc. fellow, Glasgow (Scotland) U., 1956—57, Guggenheim fellow, 1978—79. Fellow: Japan Soc. Promotion Sci.; mem.: Am. Chem. Soc. (mem. exec. bd. Rochester sect. 1970—72, chmn. organic chem. divsn. 1978—79, mem. editl. bd. Jour. Am. Chem. Soc. 1995—2000, Arthur C. Cope Sr. scholar 2003). Home: 19 Larchwood Dr Pittsford NY 14534-2432 Office: U Rochester River Campus Dept Chemistry Rochester NY 14627-0216 Office Phone: 585-275-4236. E-mail: kende@chem.rochester.edu.

KENDE, CHRISTOPHER BURGESS, lawyer, educator; b. NYC, Apr. 28, 1948; s. Herbert Alexander and Helga Henrietta (Wieselthier) K.; m. Barbara Gonzales, May 22, 1976. BA, MA, Brown U., 1970; JD, NYU, 1973. Bar: NY 1974, Mass. 1975, DC 1988, Calif. 1996, US Dist. Ct. (So. and Ea. dists.) NY 1974, US Ct. Appeals (2nd cir.) 1976, US Ct. Appeals (9th cir.) 1996, US Supreme Ct. 1978. Staff atty. Legal Aid Soc., NYC, 1973-76; assoc. Dewey, Ballantine et al., NYC, 1976-78, Hill Betts & Nash, NYC, 1978-82, ptnr., 1982-89, Holtzmann, Wise & Shepard, NYC, 1989-96, Cozen O'Connor, NYC, 1996—. Adj. prof. maritime and admiralty law Bklyn. Law Sch., 2003—. Bd. editors: Law and Politics; contbr. articles to profl. jours. Named a Manhattan Super Lawyer, Law & Politics, 2006—07; recipient Silver medal, French Nat. Depository Bank, 1984. Mem. ABA (mem. tips sect.), NY County Lawyers Assn. (past chmn. com. admiralty and maritime law 1998-99), Maritime Law Assn. (marine ecology com., com. internat. orgns. and stds.), French Maritime Law Assn., Union Internat. des Avocats (pres. ins. law commn. 2003-06), India House, Edgartown Yacht Club, Univ. Club NY, Travellers (Paris), Yacht Club de France, Order of Coif, Phi Beta Kappa. Democrat. Presbyterian. Avocations: sailing, motorcycling, tennis, animal-assisted therapy, gardening. Home: 545 W End Ave Apt 2B New York NY 10024-2723 Office: Cozen & O'Connor 45 Broadway New York NY 10006-3007 Office Phone: 212-908-1242. Business E-Mail: ckende@cozen.com.

KENDELL, KEN, music educator; b. Midwest, Wyo., Dec. 14, 1932; s. Arnold Elmer and Mildred Iantha Franks. Student, U. Wyo., 1952—54; studied voice with, Sandy Oliver, 1955—60, Ruth Miller and Mario Chamlee, 1969—90. Pvt. practice, LA, 1972—2003, Las Vegas, Nev., 2003—. Cons. U. Sci. and Philosophy, Waynesboro, Va., 1994—96; asst. prodn. dir. Altru Entertainment, Inc., Las Vegas, 2003—. Author: Mystery of Voice, Mystery of Life, 1995; composer: (musical) Candid Hams, 1987, Road of Life, 1994; asst. cruise dir. and entertainer: Orient Overseas Line, 1976—80. Tour guide Liberace Mus., Las Vegas, 2003—. Named one of actors in Academy Award Nominated film Prelude, 1996; recipient Hon. Music award, Phi Mu Alpha, 1953. Mem.: SAG, Nat. Assn. Tchrs. Singing (pres. 1987—88). Republican. Avocations: writing, ventriloquist, timpanist. Home: 8764 Timber Mesa St Las Vegas NV 89139 Office Phone: 702-228-9646. Personal E-mail: kenkendell@netzero.com.

KENDER, WALTER JOHN, horticulturist, educator; b. Camden, NJ, Dec. 20, 1935; s. Walter and Martha K.; m. Carole Holm, May 26, 1957; children: David, Lily BS, Del. Valley Coll., 1957, DSc (hon.), 1993; MS, Rutgers U., 1959, PhD, 1962. From asst. prof. to assoc. prof. horticulture U. Maine, Orono, 1962-69; mem. faculty Cornell U., N.Y. State Agrl. Expt. Sta., Geneva, 1969-82, prof. pomology, 1975-82, head dept. pomology and viticulture, 1972-82; chmn. dept. pomology Cornell U., Ithaca, 1975-82; dir. citrus rsch. and edn. ctr. U. Fla., Lake Alfred, 1982-96, prof., 1982-2001, prof. emeritus, 2001—. Co-chmn. task force fruit rsch. N.E. USDA State Exptl. Stas., 1973-75; sec. Internat. Working Group Juvenility Woody Plants, 1974-82; cons. Winrock Internat. (USAID) Pakistan, 1989, Indonesia, 1992, P.R. Dept. Agr., 1996; disting. scientist Agrl. U., Wageningen, Netherlands, 1974; mem. adv. bd. Archbold Biol. Sta., 1991-2001. Contbg. author: Blueberry Culture, 1966; contbr. articles to profl. jours. Bd. dirs. Green Horizon Land Trust, 2004. Fellow AAAS, Am. Soc. Hort. Sci. (dir. 1975-85, trustee endowment fund 1982-87); mem. N.Y. State Hort. Soc., Internat. Soc. Hort. Sci., Internat. Citriculture Soc. (corr.), Am.

Pomological Soc. (mem. adv. com.), Fla. Inst. Food Tech., Coun. Agrl. Sci. and Tech., Fla. State Hort. Soc. (hon. mem. 2000, pres. 1996, chmn. of bd. 1997), N.Y. State Fruit Testing Assn. (sec.-treas. 1972-82), Farm Bur. Adv. Com., Haines City Citrus Growers Assn. (bd. dirs. 1991-96), Fla. Citrus Showcase (bd. dirs. 1996-2000), Sigma Xi (past chpt. pres.). Office: Citrus Rsch & Edn Ctr 700 Experiment Station Rd Lake Alfred FL 33850-2243 Home Phone: 863-422-7807. Personal E-mail: kenderw@aol.com.

KENDERIAN, SHANT, engineer, consultant; s. Hagop Kenderian and Janet Janoian; m. Ani Manjikian, Sept. 6, 1997; children: Nairy, Talar. BS in Prodn. Engring. & Metallurgy, U. Tech., 1985; MS in Mfg. Engring. & Tech., Calif. State U., 1996; PhD in Materials Sci. & Engring., The Johns Hopkins U., 2002, MS in Materials Sci. and Engring., 2002. Lic. profl. engr., Md., 2000. Mfg. engr. A&H Jewelry Mfg. Co, Glendale, Calif., 1995—96, Weckerle, Santa Monica, 1996—97, Space Systems/Loral, Palo Alto, 1997—98; rsch. scientist The Johns Hopkins U., Balt., 2002—03; sr. engr. Jet Propulsion Lab., Pasadena, Calif., 2003—04; sr. staff mem. The Aerospace Corp., El Segundo, Calif., 2005—. Cons. engr. MM & NDE, West Hills, Calif., 2003—. Exhibitions, Oil Paintings; contbr. scientific papers to profl. jours. Fellow, Am. Soc. Nondestructive Testing, 2001. Mem.: NSPE, Soc. Mfg. Engrs., Acoustical Soc. Am., Am. Soc. Nondestructive Testing. Achievements include patents for Laser-Air Hybrid Ultrasonic Non-Contact And Remote Testing of Railroad Wheels; Laser-Air Hybrid Ultrasonic Non-Contact And Remote Testing of Railroad Tracks. Personal E-mail: kenderian@msn.com.

KENDIG, LYNNE E., physician; b. Phila., Dec. 6, 1949; d. Carl M. and Marion (Conkle) Shetzley; m. William Lampe, 1969 (div. 1978); 1 child, Megan Alpert; m. Dan Spicer, Aug. 21, 1983 (div. 1998); m. Robert Kendig, Sept. 13, 2003. BS in Edn., U. Pa., 1971; MS in Computer Edn., Lesley Coll., 1985; MD with honors, U. Colo., 1994. Tchr. elem. edn. Tredyeffrin-East town Sch. Dist., Berwyn, Pa., 1976—81, Cherry Creek Sch. Dist., Englewood, Colo., 1982—87; intern, residency St. Joseph's Hosp., Denver, 1994—97; family practice physician Exempla Healthcare Orchard Family Practice, Englewood, 1997—; pvt. practice family physician Oasis Family Medicine, Denver, 2000—. IBM edn. cons., Englewood, 1986-87; resident physician St. Joseph Hosp. Family Practice, Denver, 1994-97; mem. admissions com. U. Colo. Med. Sch., Denver, 1993-94. Vol. student physician Stout Street Homeless Clinic, Denver, 1990-94; physician lectr., educator Tar Wars, Denver, 1995-96; mem. Denver Pub. Libr. Friends Found., 1996—; mem. Med. Mission Team, Guatemala, 2005, 07. Mem. AMA, Am. Acad. Family Physicians, Colo. Med. Soc., Alpha Omega Alpha. Avocations: hiking, travel, gardening, fly fishing. Home: 635 Bellaire St Denver CO 80220-4934 E-mail: lynnekendig@earthlink.net.

KENDIG, WILLIAM LAMAR, retired federal official, accountant; b. York, Pa., Apr. 11, 1938; m. Esther Delores Mostoller, Oct. 14, 1961; 1 child, Marc Daniel. BS, Elizabethtown Coll., 1960; MBA, Am. U., 1965, PhD, 1969. Spl. agt. U.S. Treasury Dept., Washington, 1960—65; staff asst. Procter & Gamble Co., Cin., 1965-66; mgr., cons. Price Waterhouse & Co., Washington, 1968-71; asst. vice chancellor U. Md., College Park, 1971-74, acting vice chancellor, 1974-75; dir., mgmt. cons. U.S. Dept. Interior, Washington, 1975-76, dep. dir. audit and investigations, 1977-78, acting insp. gen., 1978-79, dep. asst. sec., 1979-81, dir. fin. mgmt. and dep. chief fin. officer, 1981-94, chair mgmt. control coordinating com., 1987—92, acting prin. dep. asst. sec., 1988. Mem. Fed. Acctg. Stds. Adv. Bd., 1991-94; ind. cons., 1996—. Contbr. articles to profl. jours. Chmn. ops. com., chmn., mem. steering com. 69 Corridor Concerned Citizens, 2001—02; mem. Mayor's Compensation Com., Prescott, Ariz., 1999; fundraiser Leukemia and Lymphoma Soc., Tri-City "Light the Night" Walk, 2004—05; bd. dirs. Yavapai Coll. Roghrider, 2005—06; v.p. Yavapai Coll. Roughrider, 2006—. Named Meritorious Exec., Pres. of U.S., 1986, Disting. Exec., 1988; recipient Donald Scantlebury award Joint Fin. Mgmt. Improvement Program, 1990. Mem. Fed. Fin. Mgrs. Coun. (chmn. 1982-85), Assn. Govt. Accts. (nat. exec. com. 1984-87, Chpt. Outstanding Achievement award 1983, 86, Frank Greathouse Disting. Leadership award 1992, Cornelius E. Tierney/Ernst & Young Lifetime Rsch. Achiever award 1996), Pub. Employees Roundtable (bd. dirs. 1987-89, Dir.'s award 1988), Sr. Execs. Assn. (bd. dirs. 1985-91, Ted Kern award 1984), Worldwide Assurance for Employees Pub. Agys. (bd. dirs. 1993-96), Nat. Assn. Ret. Fed. Employees (1st v.p. Prescott chpt. 2001-02, pres. 2003, chpt. exec. com. 2004-05, bd. 2005-06). Avocations: reading, exercising. Personal E-mail: kendig@cableone.net.

KENDLER, BERNHARD, retired editor; b. Cin., Jan. 28, 1934; s. Harry Harlan and Mildred (Black) K.; m. Jill Ferguson, Dec. 12, 1975. BA in English, NYU, 1955; MA in Comparative Lit, U. Mich., 1956. Research asst. Calif. Tchrs. Assn., 1958-60; editor A.S. Barnes & Co., Inc., NYC, 1960-62; copy editor J.B. Lippincott Co., Phila., 1962-63; mng. editor, editor, exec. editor Cornell U. Press, Ithaca, NY, 1963—2005; ret. Mem. Phi Beta Kappa. Home: 500 Harbison Blvd Apt 1009 Columbia SC 29212

KENDLER, HOWARD H(ARVARD), psychologist, educator; b. NYC, June 9, 1919; s. Harry H. and Sylvia (Rosenberg) K.; m. Tracy Seedman, Sept. 20, 1941 (dec. July 2001); children: Joel Harlan, Kenneth Seedman. AB, Bklyn. Coll., 1940; MA, U. Iowa, 1941, PhD, 1943. Instr. U. Iowa, 1943; rsch. psychologist OSRD, 1944; asst. prof. U. Colo., 1946-48; assoc. prof. NYU, 1948-51, prof., 1951-63; chmn. dept. Univ. Coll., 1951-61; prof. U. Calif., Santa Barbara, 1963-89, prof. emeritus, 1989—, chmn. dept. psychology, 1965-66. Project dir. Office Naval Rsch., 1950-68; prin. investigator NSF, 1953-65, USAAF, 1951-53; mem. adv. panel psychobiology NSF, 1960-62; tng. com. Nat. Inst. Child Health and Human Devel., 1963-66; cons. Dept. Def., Smithsonian Instn., 1959-60, Human Resources Rsch. Office, George Washington U., 1960; vis. prof. U. Calif., Berkeley, 1960-61, Hebrew U., Jerusalem, 1974-75, Tel Aviv U., 1990; chief clin. psychologist Walter Reed Gen. Hosp., 1945-46. Author: Basic Psychology, 1963, 3d edit., 1974, Basic Psychology: Brief Version, 1977, Psychology: A Science in Conflict, 1981, Historical Foundations of Modern Psychology, 1987, Amoral Thoughts About Morality: The Intersection of Science, Psychology, and Ethics, 2000; co-author: Basic Psychology: Brief Edition, 1970; co-editor: Essays in Neobehaviorism: A Memorial Volume to Kenneth W. Spence; assoc. editor: Jour. Exptl. Psychology, 1963-65; contbr. to profl. jours., chpts. to books. Served as 1st lt. AUS. Fellow Ctr. for Advanced Studies in Behaviorial Scis., Stanford, Calif., 1969-70; NSF grantee, 1954-76. Mem. Am. Psychol. Assn. (pres. divsn. exptl. psychology 1964-65, pres. divsn. gen. psychology 1967-68), Western Psychol. Assn. (pres. 1970-71), Soc. Exptl. Psychologists (exec. com. 1971-73), Psychonomic Soc. (governing bd. 1963-69, chmn. 1968-69), Sigma Xi. Home and Office: 300 Hot Springs Rd Santa Barbara CA 93108 E-mail: kendler@psych.ucsb.edu.

KENDLER, KENNETH S., medical educator; b. NYC, July 12, 1950; married; 3 children. BA with hons., U. Calif., Santa Cruz, 1972; MD, Stanford U., 1977; DSc (hon.), U. Birmingham, Eng., 1999. Diplomate Am. Bd. Psychiatry and Neurology. Intern Yale U., 1977-78, resident, 1977-80, fellow biological scientist tng., 1978-80; asst. prof. Mt. Sinai Sch. Medicine, NYC, 1980-83, rsch. assoc., 1981-83; assoc. prof. Med. Coll. Va./Va. Commonweatlh U., Richmond, 1983-86, prof., dept. psych., dept. human genetics, 1987—, Rachel Brown Banks Disting. Prof. Psych., 1991—; dir. Va. Inst. Psychiat. and Behavioral Genetics, 1996—. Thomas William Salmon lectr. N.Y. Acad. Medicine, 2001. Mem. editl. bd. Archives of General Psych., Bipolar Disorders, Current Psychiatry Reports, Neuropsychiat. Genetics, Schizophrenia Research, Social Psychiat. and Psychiat. Epidemiology, British Jour. of Psych.; internat. adv. panel Indian Jourl. of Psychiatry; contbr. articles to profl. jours., chpts. to books. Named 2d most frequently cited author of high-impact papers in psychiatry, 1990—98; recipient First prize, Anna-Monika-Found., 1997, Stanley R. Dean award, Am. Coll. Psychiatrists, 1998, Kurt Schneider Sci. award, 1998, Outstanding Paper award in humility theology, Templeton Found., 1999, Edward Strecker award, 2000, Fundacion Castillo del Pino award, 2001, Edward J. Sachar award for outstanding contbns. to psych. rsch., 2001, Rema Lapouse award, Am. Pub. Health Assn., 2002, Philip R.A. May Meml. award Leadership Disting. Svc. Psychiatry, UCLA, 2002, Erik Stromgren medal and Meml. Lectureship, Stromgren Found., Denmark, 2003. Fellow: Am. Psychiatric Assn.; mem.: Am. Assn. for Advancement of Sci., Behavior Genetics Assn., Genetic Epidemiology Soc., Neuroscience Rsch. Program (assoc.), Am. Soc. Human Genetics, Am. Psychiatric Assn. Office: Va Commonwealth U/Med Coll Va Dept Psychiatry PO Box 980126 Richmond VA 23298-0126 Office Phone: 804-828-8590.

KENDRICK, BUDD LEROY, psychologist; b. Pocatello, Idaho, Apr. 19, 1944; s. Oscar Fredrick Kendrick and Miriam Stuart (Thorn) Stewart; m. Sue Lorraine Allen, Nov. 11, 1966; children: Aaron Matthew and Edgar Seth; m. Beverly Ann Dockter, Dec. 26, 1978; children: Cassandra Rachelle, Angela Priscilla. BA, Idaho State U., Pocatello, 1967, MEd, 1969, EdD, 1974. Lic. psychologist, lic. counselor, Idaho; lic. clin. profl. counselor Mont., Idaho; cert. health svc. provider in psychology, nat. cert. counselor; cert. clin. mental health counselor; nat. bd. cert. fellow hypnotherapist; cert. profl. qualification in psychology, critical incident stress mgmt. provider, Red Cross disaster mental health svc. provider; cert. supr. Idaho Profl. Counselors and Marriage and Family Therapists. Tchr. psychology Pocatello H.S., 1967-69; dir. counseling svcs. Midwestern Coll., Denison, Iowa, 1969-70; rehab. counselor Idaho Divsn. of Vocat. Rehab., Pocatello, 1970-73; counselor (doctoral internship) Counseling Ctr., Idaho State U., Pocatello, 1973-74; rehab. counselor Idaho Divsn. of Vocat. Rehab., Pocatello, 1974-75; chief of psychology Mental Health and Devel. Disabilities Program, Boise, Idaho, 1975—; pvt. practice psychology Boise, 1977—. Vice-chmn. Idaho State Counselor Licensing Bd., 1982-84, chmn. 1984-85, sec. 1985-86; sec., treas. Nat. Bd. Cert. Counselors Inc., Alexandria, Va., 1986-93; mem. licensure com. Idaho Pers. and Guidance Assn., 1975-78, chmn. 1977-78, rep. Am. Pers. and Guidance Assn. Licensure Network, 1977-78; allied clin. staff Intermountain Hosp., Boise, 1983-93, Northwest Passages Adolescent Hosp., Boise, 1986-93, Saint Alphonsus Regional Med. Ctr., Boise, 1986-93; designated examiner and dispositioner involuntary commitments, conservatorships and guardianships State of Idaho, 1981—; cons. Idaho Pers. Commn., 1982—; grad. sch. lectr. Idaho State U., 1975; grad. sch. faculty affiliate, Coll. of Idaho, Caldwell, 1981-86; presenter concerning counselor credentialing issues, 1981-86; treas. Idaho Mental Health Assn., 1980-81; mem. Idaho Psychology, Social Work reclassification task force, 1990-91; mem. Idaho Assn. Counseling and Devel. Legis. Task Force for Third Party Benefits for Lic. Profl. Counselors, 1990. Editor: Directory of the Idaho Psychol. Assn., 1983; author numerous articles on hypnosis, counseling and profl. credentialing. Mem. adv. bd. Trio (Upward Bound, Talent Search, Head Start), Idaho State U., 1975-76; mem. Human Rights Com., Idaho State Sch. and Hosp., 1977; mem. adv. com. Nat. Bd. Cert. Counselors and WHO Internat. Global Counseling Survey, Surrey, Eng., 2005. Recipient Disting. Svc. award Idaho Pers. & Guidance Assn., 1978, Profl. Achievement award Idaho State U., 1987, Spl. Recognition award Idaho Assn. for Counseling and Devel., 1989, Lawrence Schumacher Meml. Employee of Yr. award State of Idaho, 1995, Disting. Grad. award Idaho State U., 2001, Friend of Rsch. and Assessment for Counseling, Inc. Fellow Am. Coll. Advanced Practice Psychologists (founding mem. Idaho chpt.), Idaho Psychol. Assn. (sec. 1982-84); mem. SCV, Idaho Mental Health Counselors Assn. (charter), Idaho Counseling Assn. (leadership coun. 1977-78), ACA (pub. policy and legis. com., mem.-at-large 1992-94, chair nat. licensure subcom. 1992-94), Am. Mental Health Counselors Assn., APA (divsn. 17 counseling psychology, divsn. 30 psychol. hypnosis), Chi Sigma Iota, Idaho Hist. Soc. (cert. Idaho pioneer desc.), Stuart-Mosby Hist. Soc., Kappa Delta Pi, Honor Soc. Edn., Ancora Impara Hon. Soc. (co-founder, v.p.). Avocations: sword collecting, genealogy, history, collecting autographed celebrity photographs. Office Phone: 208-334-0900. Personal E-mail: psy108@cableone.net.

KENDRICK, DAVID ANDREW, economist, educator; b. Gatesville, Tex., Nov. 14, 1937; s. Andrew Green and Nina Alice (Murray) K.; m. Gail Tidd, July 4, 1964; children— Ann, Colin. BA, U. Tex., 1960; PhD (Woodrow Willson fellow 1961-62), MIT, 1965. Asst. prof. Harvard U., Cambridge, Mass., 1966-70; vis. scholar Stanford U., Calif., 1969-70; vis. prof. MIT, Cambridge, 1978-79; prof. econs. U. Tex., Austin, 1970—. Author (with A. Stoutiesdijk): The Planning of Industrial Investment Programs, 1978; author: (with P. Dixon and S. Bowles) Notes and Problems in Microeconomic theory, 1980; author: Stochastic Control for Economic Models, 1981, Feedback: A New Framework for Macroeconomic Policy, 1988, Models for Analyzing Comparative Advantage, 1990; author: (with P.R. Mercado and H.M. Amman) Computational Economics. Served with U.S. Army, 1960-61. Ford faculty fellow, 1969-70 Fellow AAAS; mem. Econometric Soc., Am. Econs. Assn., Soc. Econ. Dynamics and Control. (pres. 1980), Soc. Computational Econs. (pres. 1998). Home: 7209 Lamplight Ln Austin TX 78731-2119 Office: U Tex Dept Econs ECB 3-134E Austin TX 78712

KENDRICK, JOHN WHITEFIELD, economist, educator, consultant; b. NYC, July 27, 1917; s. Benjamin Burks and Elizabeth W.W. (Shields) K.; m. Maxine Fillyaw; children: Bonnie Elizabeth, Karen Johanna, John Burks. AB, U. N.C., 1937, MA, 1939; PhD, George Washington U., 1955. Economist Nat. Resources Planning Bd., Washington, 1941-43, U.S. Dept. Commerce, Washington, 1946-53, chief economist, 1976-77; sr. staff mem. Nat. Bur. Econ. Rsch., NYC, 1953-56, part-time, 56-78; prof. econs. George Washington U., Washington, 1956-88, prof. emeritus, 1988—. Univ. prof. U. Conn., Storrs, 1964-66; vis. prof. Georgetown U., UCLA, Stanford U., U. Hawaii, Simon Fraser U., v.p. for econ. rsch. The Conf. Bd., N.Y.C., 1972-73, part-time, 1973-76; dir., trustee Pioneer Mut. Funds, Boston, 1961-2000; bd. dirs. Am. Productivity and Quality Ctr., Houston, 1977—; cons. AT&T, 1964-83, Office Mgmt. and Budget, NSF, GAO, other cos. and govt. agys.; mem. Conf. on Rsch. in Income and Wealth, chmn. 1963-64; adj. scholar Am. Enterprise Inst., 1980-86. Author: Productivity Trends in the United States, 1961 (Pres. Kennedy Libr. award 1962), (with Daniel Creamer) Measuring Company Productivity: Handbook with Case Studies, 1961, rev. edit., 1965, Economic Accounts and Their Uses, 1972, The Formation and Stocks of Total Capital, 1976 (also Russian trans.), Improving Company Productivity, 1977, (with E. Grossman) Productivity in the United States: Trends and Cycles, 1980, (with John B. Kendrick) Personal Productivity, 1988 (trans. in Korean and Japanese), other books; editor 6 conf. vols.; mem. editl. bds. Rev. of Income and Wealth, Bus. Econs.; contbr. over 150 articles to profl. jours. 1st lt. A.C., U.S. Army, 1943-45; served with U.S. Strategic Bombing Survey, 1945-46, ETO. Recipient Graham Dodd award for article Fin. Analysts Jour., 1962, Abramson award for article in Bus. Econs. jour., 1987. Fellow Am. Statis. Assn., Nat. Assn. Bus. Economists; mem. Am. Econ. Assn., So. Econ. Assn. (pres. 1982-83), Nat. Economists Club (pres. 1975-76, chmn. bd. 1976-77), World Acad. Productivity Sci., Atlantic Econ. Soc. (disting. assoc., pres. 1992-93), George Washington U. Club, Phi Beta Kappa. Unitarian-Universalist. Avocations: swimming, walking, reading, tv talk shows. Office: George Washington U Dept Econ Washington DC 20052-0001 Home: Apt 1228 3440 S Jefferson St Falls Church VA 22041-3131 Home Phone: 703-578-7685; Office Phone: 202-668-6686.

KENDRICK, KATHERINE, lawyer; b. SC; BA, U. Calif., Berkeley; JD, Columbia U., 1986. Assoc. Latham & Watkins, Los Angeles; with legal dept. Walt Disney Studios, 1989—96; v.p. European legal affairs Walt Disney Co.; gen. counsel DreamWorks Animation SKG, Inc., 1996—2004, bd. dirs., gen. counsel, 2004—. Bd. mem. Next Generation Coun., Motion Picture and Television Fund; adv. bd. LA Sports and Entertainment Commn., Kernochan Ctr. Law, Media and Arts, Columbia U. Sch. Law, Western Region Bd. US Ski and Snowboard Assn. Office: DreamWorks SKG 1000 Flower St Glendale CA 91201

KENDRICK, KIM, federal agency administrator; BA, Bowdoin Coll.; JD, U. Pitts. Asst. gen. counsel insured housing and cmty. devel. litigation US Dept. Housing & Urban Devel., Washington, 1990—95; legal counsel DC Housing Authority, 1995—98, regional adminstr., 1998—2002; gen. counsel Covenant House Washington; sr. counselor to sec. US Dept. Housing & Urban Devel., Washington, asst. sec. for fair housing and equal opportunity., 2005—. Office: HUD 451 Seventh St SW Rm 5100 Mail Code E Washington DC 20410 Office Phone: 202-708-4252. Office Fax: 202-708-4483.

KENDRICK, PETER MURRAY, communications executive, investor; b. Winchester, Mass., Oct. 8, 1936; s. Wallace Dolloff and Esther (Burke) Kendrick; m. Grace Terry, June 17, 1967; children: Caroline, Timothy. BSBA, Babson Coll., 1962. Office mgr. Am. Hosp. Supply Corp., Chgo. and Charlotte, NC, 1962-65; registered rep. Hayden, Stone & Co., 1966-69; gen. mgr. Continental Cablevision, Concord, NH, 1969—72, Jackson, Mich., 1972—74; pres. New Eng. Cablevision, Portland, Maine, 1974-79, chmn. bd., 1980; pres. Home Theater Network, Portland, 1977-87, NYC; chmn. bd. Envirologic Data Corp., Portland, 1984-86; sr. v.p. Watson Techs., Portland, 1994-96; pres., chmn. Internet Maine, Internet N.E., Inc. (merger Harvard Net, Inc.), Portland, 1997; interim CEO Compass Cablesys., Portland, 1998—99. Founder, pres. The Travel Channel, 1981-86; founder The Disney Channel, 1981; vice chmn. bd. dirs., pres., treas. Internat. Cablevision, Inc., Bronxville, NY, 1987-93; chmn. bd. Kendrick Corp., Portland, Maine, 1986—, Kendrick Tech. Corp., 1992—, Legal Document Systems, Inc., Washington, 1992-94, The Film Channel, Inc., Portland, 1987-90, Yankee Books, Camden, Maine, 1989-91. Trustee North Yarmouth Acad., Yarmouth, Maine, chmn. ann. giving campaign, 1986-87; treas. Foreside Cmty. Ch., Falmouth and Cumberland Foresides, Maine, 2005—. With USAF, 1956-59. Recipient Highest Programming award, Cable TV Nat. Assn., 1973, 1986. Mem. New Eng. Cable TV Assn. (v.p. 1972, pres. 1975), Mich. Cable TV Assn. (v.p. 1973), Portland Country Club, Portland Yacht Club, Cable TV Pioneers. Office Phone: 207-781-5883. Personal E-mail: kendrick@maine.rr.com.

KENDRICK, RHONDA LYNN, poet, small business owner; b. Shreveport, La., Dec. 28, 1964; d. Dewey Stovall Kendrick Jr. and Mary Laverne Kendrick; 1 child, Jasmyn Lynn Davenport. Student, La. Tech. U., Ruston, Bassar Parish CC, La., Hunds Jr. Coll., Jackson, Miss., Century Coll., Shreveport. Co-owner D.S.K. Ltd., Inc., Minden, La. Author: Twilight Musings, 2005. Mem.: Internat. Soc. Poets (founding laureate mem.). Democrat. Avocations: writing, reading, computers. Home: PO Box 53227 Shreveport LA 71135

KENDRICK, WILLIAM BRYCE, biologist, consultant, editor, writer; b. Liverpool, Lancashire, Eng., Dec. 3, 1933; arrived in Can., 1958; s. William and Lillian Maud (Latham) K.; m. Laureen Anne Carscadden, Dec. 14, 1978; children: Clinton, Kelly. BSc with honors, U. Liverpool, 1955, PhD, 1958, DSc, 1980. Postdoctoral fellow NRC, Ottawa, Ont., Canada, 1958-59; rsch. scientist Agr. Can., Ottawa, 1959-65; asst. prof. U. Waterloo, Ont., 1965-66, assoc. prof. Ont., 1966-71, prof. Ont., 1971-94, disting. prof. emeritus Ont., 1994—, assoc. dean Ont., 1985-93. Adj. prof. U. Victoria, B.C., 1994—; propr. Mycologue Pub. and Cons., Ltd.; tech. adv. Aerobiology Lab. Assocs., Dulles, Va.; cons. in field. Author: The Fifth Kingdom, 1985, 2d rev. and enlarged edit., 1991, 3rd edit., 2001, CD Rom version 4.6, 2007, A Young Person's Guide To The Fungi, 1986; co-author: Genera of Hyphomycetes, 1980, An Evolutionary Survey of Fungi, Algae and Plants, 1992; editor: Taxonomy of Fungi Imperfecti, The Whole Fungus, Biology of Conidial Fungi; contbr. articles to profl. jours. Guggenheim fellow, 1979-80. Fellow Royal Soc. Can.; mem. Acad. Sci. (hon. sec. 1984-91), Mycol. Soc. Am. (Disting. Mycologist award 1995), Brit. Mycol. Soc. (centenary fellow 1996), Can. Bot. Assn. (Lawson medal 2001). Mem. Green Party. Avocations: reading, music, walking, photography, rowing. Home and Office: 8727 Lochside Dr Sidney BC Canada V8L 1M8 Office Phone: 250-655-5051. E-mail: bryce@mycolog.com. *Curiosity is the key to a full life. Keep on asking questions-and keep on trying to answer them-until the day you die.*

KENDZIOR, ROBERT JOSEPH, marketing executive; b. Mar. 24, 1952; s. Joseph W. and Josephine R. Kendzior. BArch, Ill. Inst. Tech., 1975. Account supr. Burger King Corp. Rogers Merchandising, Inc., Chgo., 1975-77; account exec. Walgreen Corp. Eisaman, Johns & Laws Advt., Inc., Chgo., 1977-78; v.p. mktg. Dunkin Donuts Am., Inc., Randolph, Mass., 1978-95; v.p., chief mktg. officer Factory Card Outlet Am., Inc., Chgo., 1995-98; v.p. internat. mktg. Allied Domecq Retailing, 1999—2005; v.p. Internat. Mktg. and Retail Concepts, Randolph, 2003—; chief mktg. officer Captain D's Seafood Restaurants, Nashville, 2005—. Bd. dirs. Baskin-Robbins, Japan. Recipient Most Valuable Promotion award PepsiCo, 1984. Mem. Triangle Fraternity. Achievements include guest spkr., Boston U. (Internat. Mktg.), 2004. Home Phone: 847-946-7619. Personal E-mail: rkendzior@msn.com.

KENEALLY, KATHRYN MARIE, lawyer; b. Dayton, Ohio, Apr. 30, 1958; d. William Henry and Joanna Gertrude K.; m. Thomas Marshall, Oct. 16, 1992. BA, Cornell U., 1979; JD, Fordham U., 1982; LLM in Taxation, NYU, 1993. Bar: N.Y., 1983, U.S. Dist. Ct. (so., ea. dists.) N.Y., 1983, U.S. Ct. Appeal (2d, 3d, 11th cirs.), U.S. Tax Ct. Law clk. to Hon. E. R. Neaher U.S. Dist. Ct. (ea. dist.) N.Y., Bklyn., 1982-83; assoc. Skadden Arps Slate Meagher & Flom, NYC, 1983-85, Kostelanetz Ritholz Tigue & Fink, NYC, 1985-90, ptnr., 1990-93, Kostelanetz & Fink, LLP, NYC, 1993-99; mem. Owen & Davis, PC, NYC, 2000—02; ptnr. Fulbright & Jaworski, LLP, NYC, 2002—. Columnist The Champion, 1996—, Jour. Tax Practice and Prodecure, 1999-; co-author: Practice Under Federal Sentencing Guidelines, 1998; contbr. articles to profl. jours. Mem. practitioners adv. group U.S. Sentencing Commn., 1993—. Mem. ABA (chmn. taxation sect., civil and criminal tax penalties com. 2000-02, stds. tax practice com., 2005-07), Nat. Assn. Criminal Def. Lawyers (life). Home: 48 Charlotte Pl Hartsdale NY 10530-2602 Office: Fulbright & Jaworski LLP 660 Fifth Ave New York NY 10103 Office Phone: 212-318-3000. E-mail: kkeneally@fulbright.com.

KENEALLY, THOMAS MICHAEL, author; b. Australia, Oct. 7, 1935; s. Edmund Thomas and Elsie Margaret (Coyle) K.; m. Judith Mary Martin, Aug. 21, 1965; children: Margaret Ann, Jane Rebecca. Student, St. Patrick's Coll., Strathfield, N.S.W. Writings include (fiction) The Place at Whitton, 1965, The Fear, 1965, Bring Larks and Heroes, 1967, Three Cheers for the Paraclete, 1968, The Survivor, 1969, A Dutiful Daughter, 1971, The Chant of Jimmie Blacksmith, 1972 (Heinemann award for lit. Royal Soc. Lit. 1973), Blood Red, Sister Rose, 1974, Gossip From the Forest, 1975, Moses the Lawgiver, 1975, Season in Purgatory, 1977, A Victim of the Aurora, 1977, (children's book) Ned Kelly and the City of Bees, 1978, Passenger, 1979, Confederates, 1979, The Cut-Rate Kingdom, 1980, Schindler's List, 1982 (Booker McConnell prize for fiction 1982, Fiction prize L.A. Times 1983), Outback, 1983, (play) Bullie's House, 1985, A Family Madness, 1985, The Playmaker, 1987, To Asmara, 1989, Flying Hero Class, 1991, (non-fiction) The Place Where Souls Are Born, 1992, (non-fiction) Now and in Time to Be, 1992, Woman of the Inner Sea, 1992, Jacko: The Great Intruder, 1994, A River Town, 1995, Homebush Boy-A Memoir, 1995; (plays) Halloran's Little Boat, 1966, Childermass, 1968, An Awful Rose, 1972; (non-fiction) The Great Shame, 1999, (fiction)

Bettany's Book, 2000, (non-fiction) An American Scoundrel, The Life of the Notorious Civil War General Dan Sickles, 2002, An Angel in Australia, 2002, (non-fiction) Lincoln, 2003, The Tyrant's Novel, 2004. Inaugural mem. Australia-China Coun., 1978-83; mem. adv. panel Australian Constn. Commn., 1985-88; mem. Literary Arts Bd. Australia, 1985-88; chmn. Australian Rep. Movement, 1991-93, dir., 1994—. Decorated Officer Order of Australia; recipient Miles Franklin award, 1967, 68, Captain Cook Bi-Centerary prize, 1970. Fellow Royal Soc. Lit. (London), Am. Acad. Arts and Scis.; mem. PEN, Australian Soc. Authors (chmn. 1987-90), Nat. Book Coun. Australia (pres. 1985-90. Office: Curtis Brown (Australia) P/L PO Box 19 Paddington NSW 2021 Australia

KENEN, PETER BAIN, economist, educator; b. Cleve., Nov. 30, 1932; s. Isaiah Leo and Beatrice (Bain) K.; m. Regina Horowitz, Aug. 21, 1955; children: Joanne Lisa, Marc David, Stephanie Hope, Judith Rebecca. AB, Columbia U., 1954; MA, Harvard U., 1956, PhD, 1958. Mem. faculty Columbia U., 1957-71, prof. econs., 1964-71, chmn. dept., 1967-69, provost univ., 1969-70; prof. econs. and internat. fin. Princeton U., NJ, 1971—2004, dir. internat. fin. sect., 1971-99; Ford rsch. prof. U. Calif., Berkeley, 1979-80; adj. sr. fellow internat. econs. Coun. on Fgn. Rels., 2004—. Rschr. on internat. monetary theory and policy; cons. Coun. Econ. Advisors, 1961, U.S. Treasury, 1962-68, 77-80, 95-98, Bur. Budget, 1964-68, IMF, 1990, 92. Author: British Monetary Policy and the Balance of Payments (1951-1957), 1960, Giant Among Nations, 1960; author: (with A.G. Hart and A. Entine) Money, Debt and Economic Activity, 4th edit., 1969; author: (with R. Lubitz) International Economics, 3d edit., 1971; author: A Model of the U.S. Balance of Payments, 1978; author: (with P.R. Allen) Asset Markets, Exchange Rates and Economic Integration, 1980; author: Essays in International Economics, 1980, Managing Exchange Rates, 1988, Exchange Rates and Policy Coordination, 1989, Exchange Rates and the Monetary System, 1994, Economic and Monetary Union in Europe, 1995, International Economy, 4th edit., 2000, The International Financial Architecture: What's New? What's Missing?, 2001; editor: International Trade and Finance, Frontiers for Research, 1975; editor: (with others) The International Monetary System Under Flexible Exchange Rates, 1982; editor: (with R.W. Jones) Handbook of International Economics, 1984; editor: Managing the World Economy, 1994, Understanding Interdependence, 1995; editor: (with A.K. Swoboda) Reforming the International Monetary and Financial System, 2000; contbr. articles to profl. jours. Recipient David A. Wells prize Harvard U., 1958-59, Univ. medal Columbia U., 1977; Ctr. Advanced Study Behavioral Scis. fellow, 1971-72, John Simon Guggenheim Found. fellow, 1975-76, Res. Bank Australia fellow, 1983-84, Royal Inst. Internat. Affairs fellow, 1987-88, German Marshall Fund fellow, 1987-88, Houblon-Norman fellow Bank of Eng., 1991-92, fellow Res. Bank New Zealand, 2002. Mem.: Am. Econ. Assn., Coun. Fgn. Rels., Royal Econ. Soc, Group of Thirty. Home: 176 Western Way Princeton NJ 08540-7208 Office: Princeton U Dept of Econs Fisher Hall Princeton NJ 08544-1021 Office Phone: 609-258-4051. Business E-Mail: pbkenen@princeton.edu.

KENISON, RAYMOND ROBERT, fraternal organization administrator, director; b. Mo., Sept. 23, 1932; s. Raymond Roy and Emma Oleta (Holder) Kenison; m. Marjorie White, Feb. 1, 1955; children: Debra Kenison Brown, Peggy Kenison Crim, Raymond Roger, Robert B. AA, Hannibal LaGrange Coll., 1953; BA, U. Mo., 1961; postgrad., Cen. Bapt. Sem., Kansas City, 1957, Midwestern Bapt. Sem., 1965; DivD, Hannibal LaGrange Coll., 1994. CFP; cert. instr. Pastor 1st Bapt.Ch., Bates City, Mo., 1954-56, Friendship Bapt. Ch., Mexico, Mo., 1956-62, Immanuel Bapt. Ch., Hannibal, Mo., 1962-77; dir. devel. Mo. Bapt. Children's Home, Bridgeton, 1977-80, exec. dir., 1980—; pres., 1992—. Pres. bd. trustees Hannibal-Lagrance Coll.; co-founder, pres. Viability R & D Group; pres. MBCH Found., 2001—; chmn. contract com. Spl. Care Homes of Mo., 2002—; pres. MBCH Properties, 2002—; pres., chmn. bd. MBCH Profl. Devel. Inst., 2003. Mem. Child Welfare League Am., Inc.; pres. Hannibal Coun. Alcohol and Drug Abuse; bd. dirs. Hannibal Cmty. Chest, 1974—79, Alliance Children and Families, Mo. Alliance Children and Families; pres. Hannibal Ministerial Alliance. Named Kenison Complex in his honor. Mem.: Viability R & D Group (co-founder, pres.), Inst. CFPs, S.W. Assn. Child Care Execs., Mo. Child Care Assn. (bd. dirs., pres. 1994—), So. Bapt. Child Care Execs. (pres.), Nat. Soc. Fund Raising Execs. (sec.), Nat. Assn. Homes Children, Nat. Foster Parents Assn., Hannibal Investment Club (pres. 1976—78, 1982—83). Home: 4 River Hills Hannibal MO 63401-6218 Office: Mo Bapt Children's Home 11300 Saint Charles Rock Rd Bridgeton MO 63044-2793 Office Phone: 314-739-6811.

KENISTON, KENNETH, psychologist, educator; b. Chgo., Jan. 6, 1930; s. Hayward and Roberta (Cannell) K.; m. Ellen Uviller, June 20, 1960 (div. Aug. 1975); children: Ann Rogers, Sarah Hayward; m. Suzanne Berger, Jan. 10, 1976; 1 child, Daniel Eben. BA, Harvard Coll., Cambridge, Mass., 1951; DPhil, Oxford U., 1956; LLD (hon.), U. Notre Dame, Ind., 1971; DSc (hon.), Colgate U., Hamilton, NY, 1972. From rsch. asst. to rsch. assoc. dept. social rels. Harvard U., Cambridge, Mass., 1955-62; from asst. prof. to assoc. prof. psych. Yale Med. Sch., New Haven, 1962-68, prof. psych., 1968-75; Andrew W. Mellon prof. human devel. Mass. Inst. Tech., Cambridge, 1975—. Lectr. on clin. psychology Harvard U., 1958-62, resident fellow, asst. sr. tutor Eliot House, 1953-59; assoc. dir., acting dir., then dir. Behavior Scis. Study Ctr., Yale Med. Sch., 1965-72; fellow Davenport Coll., Yale U., 1962-75; chmn., exec. dir. Carnegie Coun. on Children, New Haven, 1972-78; dir. program in sci., tech. and soc. Mass. Inst. Tech., 1987-92, dir. grad. studies, 1993-96, dir. projects, 1996—; dir. MIT India Program, 1998-06; mem. Carnegie Commn. on Higher Edn., 1968-73, bd. dirs. Overseers Harvard Coll., 1969-75, MacArthur Prize Fellows selection com., 1979-85; com. on selection Guggenheim Found., 1992-94; vis. scholar Ecole de Mines, Paris, 1980-81; vis. prof. U. Paris Sorbonne, 1986-87, Centro de Estudios Avanzados de Ciencias Sociales, Madrid, 1990, Nat. Inst. Advanced Studies, Indian Inst. Sci., Bangalore, 1999-2000, 01-02. Author: The Uncommitted, 1966, Young Radicals, 1968, All Our Children, 1977, (with D. Guston) The Fragile Contract, 1994, Earth, Air, Fire, Water, 1999, (with J. Ker Conway and L. Marx) Earth, Air, Fire, Water: Humanistic Studies of the Environment, 2000, (with Deepak Kumar) IT Experience in India: Bridging the Digital Divide, 2004, (with Rohit Raj Mathur and R.K. Bagga) The State, IT, and Development, 2005; contbr. articles to profl. jours., chpts. to books. Rhodes scholar Balliol Coll., Oxford U., 1951-53; jr. fellow Harvard U., 1953-56; Guggenheim fellow, 1980-81. Fellow AAAS; mem. Coun. Fgn. Rels., Phi Beta Kappa, Sigma Xi. Office: Mass Inst Tech E51-296A 77 Massachusetts Ave Cambridge MA 02139 Business E-Mail: kken@mit.edu.

KENLEY, DAVID LYNN, history professor; b. Salt Lake City, Jan. 24, 1968; s. Lynn Garden and Jean Hansen Kenley; m. Wendi Michelle Carlson, Aug. 17, 1991; children: Spencer David, Meili Elise, Maya Anne. BA, Brigham Young U., Provo, Utah, 1986—91; MA, U. Utah, Salt Lake City, 1992—94; PhD, U. Hawaii, Honolulu, 1994—99. Assoc. prof. history Marshall U., Huntington, W.Va., 1999—2004, Elizabethtown Coll., Pa., 2004—. Regional leader Nat. Consortium Tchg. About Asia, 2001—; editl. bd. mem. Am. Jour. Chinese Studies, 2004—06. Author: The China-Taiwan Conflict and its Historical Basis, 2000, New Culture in a New World: The May Fourth Movement and the Chinese Diaspora in Singapore, 1919-1932, 2003; contbr. articles to profl. jours. Bishop Ch. Jesus Christ Latter-Day Saints, Huntington, 2001—04, Lancaster, Pa., 2006. Mem.: Am. Assn. Chinese Studies, Assn. Asian Studies, Phi Alpha Theta (life). Lds Ch. Office: Elizabethtown Col History Dept 1 Alpha Dr Elizabethtown PA 17022 Home Phone: 717-361-1238.

KENLEY, HOWARD, state legislator; b. Ft. Stockton, Tex., Mar. 28, 1945; s. Howard A. Jr. and Elvira (Hayten) K.; m. Sally Butler; children: John, Bill, Betsy. AB, Miami U., Oxford, Ohio, 1967; JD, Harvard U., 1972. Atty. Cadick, Burns, Duck & Neighbours, Indpls., 1972-73; pres., owner Kenley's Supermarkets, Noblesville, Ind., 1974-93; owner Cambridge Investment Inc., 1998; judge Noblesville City Ct., 1974-89; senator Dist. 20 Ind. State Senate, 1992—, mem. fin., judiciary, edn., planning and pub. policy coms., mem. fin. com., judiciary com., planning/pub. svc. com., senator Indpls. Bd. dirs. Society Bank of Ind. Bd. dirs. Boys and Girls Club of Noblesville 1975, adv. bd. 1st United Meth. Ch., Key Bank Noblesville Edn. Found., mem. Noblesville Econ. Devel. Bd. 2000-. 1st lt. US Army, 1969—71. Decorated Army Commendation medal; named Bd. Mem. of Yr. Noblesville Boys and Girls Club, 1984-85. Mem. Ind. State Bar Assn., Hamilton County Bar Assn., 50 Club of Hamilton County, Elks, Beta theta Pi, mem. ELKS Club, 1980-, mem. HAM County 50 Club 1976-, mem. Am. Legion, 2000-. Office: Indiana State Senate 200 W Washington St Indianapolis IN 46204-2785 Office Phone: 317-232-9400, 317-232-9453. Office Fax: 317-232-9660.

KENNA, GEORGE ANTHONY, pharmacist, researcher; s. Merrill Carlton and Esther Ann Kenna; m. Nancy Constantino Kenna, May 17, 1981; 1 child, John. BS in Pharmacy, U. RI, 1975, MA in Psychology, 2001, PhD in Psychology, 2003. Registered pharmacist Va. Pharmacist Potomac Hosp., Woodbridge, Va., 1977—80, Liggett Rexall, Middletown, RI, 1980—81, Douglas Drug, RI, 1981—96; grad. asst. U. R.I., 1997, rsch. asst., 1999; pharmacist Walmart Pharmacy, North Kingstown, RI, 1998—2001; clin. pharmacist Kent County Hosp., Warwick, RI, 1999—2007, Westery Hosp., RI, 2007—. Tchg. asst. stats. U. RI, Kingston, 2001—02, asst. adj. prof., 2006—; rsch. fellow dept. biomedicine Brown U., Providence, 2003—04; postdoctoral fellow Ctr. for Alcohol and Addiction Studies, Providence, 2004—07; cons. Brown U., Providence, 2003—04, asst. prof. psychiatry and human behavior, 2007—. Contbr. articles to profl. jours., chapters to books. Recipient Young Investigator award, Rsch. Soc. Alcoholism, 2004, Rsch. Award grant, Ctr. for Alcohol and Addiction Studies, 2004. Mem.: APA, Coll. Psychiat. and Neurol. Pharmacists, Rsch. Soc. Am., Am. Pharm. Assn. Episcopalian. Avocations: skiing, bicycling, golf, writing. Home: 59 Bedford Ln North Kingstown RI 02852 Office: Brown U Box G-BH Providence RI 02908

KENNARD, JOYCE L., state supreme court justice; b. Bandung, West Java, Indonesia, May 6, 1941; AA, Pasadena City Coll., 1970, U. So. Calif., 1970, BA in German magna cum laude, 1971, MPA, JD, U. So. Calif., 1974, LLD (hon.), 2007; JD (hon.), Pepperdine Sch. Law, 1989; LLD (hon.), Calif. Western Sch. Law, 1990, Southwestern U. Sch. Law, 1991, Whittier Law Sch., 1994, Northwestern Sch. Law, Lewis and Clark Coll., 1997, Lincoln Law Sch., 1997, San Joaquin Coll. Law, 2004. Dep. atty. gen., LA, 1975—79; sr. atty. State Ct. Appeals, LA, 1979—86; judge LA County Mcpl. Ct., 1986—87; assoc. justice pro tempore State Ct. Appeal (divsn. three), LA, 1987; judge LA County Superior Ct., 1987—88; assoc. justice State Ct. Appeals (divsn. five), LA, 1988—89, Calif. Supreme Ct., San Francisco, 1989—. Chair appellate adv. com. Calif. Jud. Coun., 1996—. Recipient Contbg. Progress of Dignity and Self-Esteem Among Amputees award, Sacramento Women Amputees Group, 1990, Lifetime Achievement award, Ind. Living Ctr. So. Calif., 1990, award, Gov.'s Hall of Fame for People with Disabilities, 1990, San Fernando Valley Bar, 1990, Asian/Pacific Women's Network, LA, 1991, YWCA, LA, 1991, Ernestine Stahlhut award, Women Lawyers' Assn. of LA, 1990, Justice of Yr. 1991 award, Calif. Trial Lawyers Assn., 1992 Chinese-Am. Pioneers So. Calif. Judiciary award, Chinese Hist. Soc. of So. Calif., First Ann. Women of 90's award, Robinson's Dep. Store, LA, 1992, First Ann. Netherlands-Am. Heritage award, Netherlands-Am. Arts and Cultural Found., 1992, Atty. Gen. award, Asian and Pacific Islander Employee Adv. Com., Atty. Gen.'s Office, 1992, award, ABA Task Force on Opportunities for Minorities in Jud. Adminstrn. Divsn. and Commn. on Opportunities for Minorities in Profession, 1992, Marin Women's Hall of Fame, 1997, San Francisco Women Lawyers Alliance, 1997, Asian Pacific Am. Legal Ctr. So. Calif., LA, 1997, Coun. Asian Pacific Islanders Together Active Leadership (C.A.P.I.T.A.L.), 1997, Margaret Brent Women Lawyers of Achievement award, ABA, 1993, Trailblazer award, Nat. Asian Pacific Am. Bar Assn. (NAPABA), 1994, Founders award, Nat. Asian Pacific Am. Law Students Assn. (NAPALSA), 1994, Access award, LA County Commn. Disabilities, 1994, St. Thomas More Medallion award, St. Thomas More Law Honor Soc. and Loyola Law Sch., 1995, Spirit Excellence award, ABA's Commn. on Opportunities for Minorities in the Profession, 1996, Accompanying award, Asian Bar Assn. Sacramento, Legal Impact award, Asian Law Alliance, San Jose, Calif., 2000, First Justice Rose Bird Meml. award, Calif. Women Lawyers San Francisco, 2001, Pub. Svc. award, Asian Pacific Am. Bar Assn., 2001, Jud. Coun.'s award, San Francisco, 2004, Achieve with Inspiration and Courage award, Orgn. Chinese Ams., San Mateo, Calif., 2005, Cert. Spl. Congl. Recognition, Congressman Tom Lantos, 2005, Cert. of Recognition, Spkr. pro Tempore Leland Y. Yee Calif. State Assembly, 2005, Cert. of Commendation, Bd. Suprs. San Mateo County, 2005, Lifetime Achievement award, Japanese Am. Bar. Assn. LA, 2006, Alumni Merit award, U. So. Calif. Sch. Policy, Planning and Devel., 2006. Mem.: Alpha Gamma Sigma Soc., Alpha Mu Gamma, Phi Kappa Phi, Phi Beta Kappa. Office: Calif Supreme Ct 350 McAllister St San Francisco CA 94102-4783

KENNARD, LYDIA H., former airport terminal executive; b. 1954; BA, Stanford U., 1975; MS, MIT, 1979; JD, Harvard U., 1979. Former pres./prin.-in-charge KDG Devel. Constrn. Consulting, LA; former mem. L.A. Planning Commn.; dep. exec. dir. design and constrn. L.A. World Airports, 1994-99, interim exec. dir., 1999-2000, exec. dir., 1999—2003, 2005—07; chmn. KDG Develop. & Constrn. Cons., LA, 2003—05. Mem. Calif. Air Resources Bd., 2004-; bd. dir. IndyMac Bank; bd. trustees, The RAND Corp., 2002-05, 2007- Active UniHealth Found. Bd.; past mem. Calif. Med. Ctr. Found. Bd., Equal Opportunity Adv. Coun. So. Calif. Edison. Named Woman of Yr. L.A. chpt. Women's Trans. Seminar, 1995, Civic Leader of Yr. Nat. Assn. Women Bus. Owners-L.A., 2000.*

KENNARD, MARY ELIZABETH, lawyer; d. Rodman Ramos and Mary Elizabeth Kennard. BAS, Boston U., 1976; JD, Temple U., 1980; LLM, George Washington U., 1982. Bar: Pa. 1980, R.I. 1988, D.C. 1988, U.S. Dist. Ct. (we. dist.) Pa. 1985, U.S. Ct. Appeals (3d cir.) 1985, U.S. Dist. Ct. R.I. 1988, U.S. Ct. Appeals (1st cir.) 1989, U.S. Dist. Ct. D.C. 1996, U.S. Supreme Ct. 1985. Asst. exec. dir. Nat. Assn. Coll. and Univ. Attys., Washington, 1981-83; asst. univ. counsel U. Pitts., 1984-85; asst. to v.p. for legal affairs Howard U., Washington, 1985-87; legal counsel U. R.I., R.I. Coll. and C.C. of R.I., Kingston, 1987-94; v.p., gen. counsel, sec. Am. U., Washington, 1995—. Bd. dirs. Washington Trust Bank, Washington metro area Am. Corp. Counsels Assn. Mem. Nat. Assns. Coll. and Univ. Attys., R.I. Black Lawyers Assn. Democrat. Avocation: golf. Office: American Univ 4400 Massachusetts Ave NW Washington DC 20016-8165

KENNARD, WILLIAM EARL, former lawyer; b. LA, Jan. 19, 1957; s. Robert A. and Helen Z. (King) K.; m. Deborah D. Kennedy, Apr. 9, 1984. BA, Stanford U., 1978; JD, Yale U., 1981; degree (hon.), Howard U., Gallaudet U., Long Island U. Bar: Calif. 1981, D.C. Ct. Appeals 1985, U.S. Ct. Appeals (D.C. cir.) 1994, U.S. Supreme Ct. 1994. Fellow Nat. Assn. Broadcasters, Washington, 1981-82, asst. gen. counsel, 1983-84; assoc. Verner, Liipfert, Bernhard, McPherson & Hand, Washington, 1984-89, ptnr., 1990-93; gen. counsel FCC, Washington, 1993-97, chmn., 1997—2001; sr. fellow Aspen Commn. and Soc. Program, Wash., 2001; mng. dir. Carlyle Grp., Wash., DC, 2001—. Mem. bd. dir. Sprint Nextel Corp., NY Times Co., Hawaiian Telcom and Insight Comm. Office: Carlyle Grp 1001 Pennsylvania Ave NW Washington DC 20004 Office Phone: 202-729-5626. Office Fax: 202-347-1818.

KENNEALLY, MICHAEL E., diversified financial services company executive; BS in Econs., U. Mo., MBA. Rsch. analyst Boatmen's Trust Co., 1983—87, instl. portfolio mgr., sr. v.p., dir. rsch., 1993—97; pres.,chief investment officer NationsBank Pvt. Investments, 1997—98; chmn., chief investment officer Bank of Am. Capital Mgmt.; pres., investment mgmt. Bank of Am.; chmn., global CEO Credit Suisse Asset Mgmt., 2003—. Office: Credit Suisse First Boston LLC 11 Madison Ave New York NY 10010-3629 Office Phone: 212-325-2000.

KENNEDY, ADRIENNE LITA, playwright; b. Pitts., Sept. 13, 1931; d. Cornell Wallace and Etta (Haugabook) Hawkins; m. Joseph C. Kennedy, May 15, 1953 (div. 1966); children: Joseph C., Adam. BS, Ohio State U., 1953; student creative writing, Columbia U., 1954-56; student playwrighting, New Sch. Social Research, Am. Theatre Wing, Circle in the Sq. Theatre Sch., 1957-58, 62; doctorate (hon.), Ohio State U., 2003. Mem. playwriting unit Actors Studio, NYC, 1962-65; lectr. Yale U., New Haven, 1972-74; CBS fellow Sch. Drama, NYC, 1973; lectr. Princeton (N.J.) U., 1977; vis. assoc. prof. Brown U., 1979-80. Rep. to conf. Internat. Theatre Inst., Budapest, 1978; vis. lectr. Harvard U., 1990, 91, vis. prof., 1997—. Author: (plays) Funnyhouse of a Negro, 1961, Cities in Bezique, 1965, A Rat's Mass, 1966, A Lesson in Dead Language, 1966, The Lennon Plays, 1968, Sun, Cities of Bezique, 1969; A Movie Star Has To Star in Black and White, 1976, Ohio State Murders, She Talks to Beethoven, 1990, (with Adam Kennedy) Sleep Deprivation Chamber, 1995; (play) People Who Led to My Plays, 1987 (Manhattan Borough Pres.'s award 1988), Letter to My Students, Lancashire Lad; commd. by Empire State Youth Inst., 1979, Onestes, Electra, Juilliard Sch. Music, 1980, Black Children's Day, Rites and Reason, Brown U., 1980The Vanishing Literary Club, 2005, (adaptation) Madame Bovery, 2003, (with Adam Kennedy) Mom How Did You Meet the Beatles, 2006; represented in numerous anthologies Norton Anthology of Am. Lit., Adrienne Kennedy Reader. Recipient Obie award, 1964, 96, Pierre Lecomte du Novy award Lincoln Ctr., 1994, award AAAL, 1994, Anisfield-Wolf Lifetime Achievement award, 2003, PEN/Laura Pels Found. award drama, 2006; fellow Guggenheim Found., 1968, Rockefeller Found., 1967-68, NEA, 1993, Lila Wallace Readers Digest, 1994, Yale U., 1974-75; grantee Nat. Endowment Arts, 1973, Rockefeller Found., 1974, Creative Artists Pub. Svc., 1974; Disting. lectr. U. Calif., Berkeley, 1980, 86. Fellow: MLA (hon.); mem.: PEN (bd. dirs. 1976—77). Address: 325 W 89th St New York NY 10024 *I believe in listening to one's inner voices.*

KENNEDY, ALFRED PARKER, JR., pediatrician, surgeon; b. Bryn Mawr, Pa., Oct. 24, 1963; s. Alfred and Elizabeth Kennedy; m. Lisa Marie Kramer; children: Parker, Alexis, Amber. BA, Lehigh U., Bethlehem, Pa., 1986; MD, Hahnemann U., Phila., 1990. Dir. pediatric surgery U. Tenn., Knoxville, 2006—. Office: E Tenn Pediat Surgery Group 2100 Clinch Ave Ste 430 Knoxville TN 37916 Home Phone: 865-692-6675; Office Phone: 865-546-2131. Office Fax: 865-637-2535; Home Fax: 865-637-2535. Personal E-mail: akennedy@etch.com.

KENNEDY, ANTHONY MCLEOD, United States supreme court justice; b. Sacramento, July 23, 1936; s. Arthur J. and Gladys McLeod Kennedy; m. Mary Davis, June 29, 1963; children: Justin Anthony, Gregory Davis, Kristin Marie. AB, Stanford U., 1958; student, London Sch. Econs., 1957—58; LLB, Harvard U., 1961; JD (hon.), U. Pacific, 1988, U. Santa Clara, 1988. Bar: Calif. 1962, U.S. Tax Ct. 1971. Assoc. Thelen, Martin, Johnson, and Bridges, San Francisco, 1961—63; pvt. practice Sacramento, 1963—67; ptnr. Evans, Jackson & Kennedy, 1967—75; adj. prof. constl. law McGeorge Sch. Law, U. of Pacific, 1965-88; judge U.S. Ct. Appeals (9th cir.), Sacramento, 1975—88; assoc. justice U.S. Supreme Ct., Washington, 1988—. Mem. bd. student advisors Harvard Faculty, 1960-61, Advisory Com. on Codes of Conduct, 1979-87, Com. on Pacific Territories, 1979-88 (chmn., 1982-88), Fed. Jud. Ctr., 1987-88. With Calif. Army Nat. Guard, 1961. Recipient Golden Plate award, Acad. Achievement, 2005. Fellow Am. Bar Found. (hon.), Am. Coll. Trial Lawyers (hon.); mem. ABA, Sacramento County Bar Assn., State Bar Calif., Phi Beta Kappa. Office: US Supreme Ct One First St NE Washington DC 20543-0001*

KENNEDY, BRIAN JAMES, marketing executive; b. NYC, Nov. 7, 1941; s. James and Una K.; m. Donna Lee Rugendorf, Dec. 7, 1968; children: Kerry, Kelly. BS in Fgn. Service, Georgetown U., 1963; grad. Japanese lang., Def. Lang. Inst., 1965; postgrad., NYU, Monterey Inst. Fgn. Studies. Various positions, then v.p. advt. and sales TWA, NYC, 1967-83; sr. v.p. mktg. The Hertz Corp., NYC, 1983-87, exec. v.p. mktg and sales, 1987—. Pres. Duneview Devel. (real estate) Corp., Wainscott, N.Y. Home: 163 Bay Ln Water Mill NY 11976-3103 Office: Hertz Co 225 Brae Blvd Park Ridge NJ 07656-1888

KENNEDY, CARY, state official; b. Norwalk, Conn., June 28, 1968; d. J. Wade and Joycee Portnoy Kennedy; m. Saurabh Mangalik; children: David Kadin, Kyra Kennedy. BA, St. Lawrence U., 1990; MPA, Columbia U., 1993; JD, U. Denver, 1995. Budget officer for Gov. Roy Romer Office State Planning and Budgeting, Colo., 1995—98; fiscal analyst Colo. Dept. Health Care Policy and Financing, Children's Basic Health Plan, 1998—99; with Educare Colo. (now Qualistar), 2000—02, Colo. Children's Campaign; policy dir. for House Speaker Andrew Romanoff, 2004—05; state treas. State of Colo., 2007—. Guest lectr. U. Denver Coll. Law, U. Colo. Grad. Sch. Pub. Affairs, Bighorn Ctr. Pub. Policy; treas. Coffman's Adv. Com. on Constl. Reform. Vol. guardian ad-litem atty. Children's Legal Clinic (now Rocky Mountain Children's Law Ctr.); bd. dirs. Paddington Station Preschool. Office: Office of Treas 140 State Capitol Denver CO 80203 Office Phone: 303-866-2441. Office Fax: 303-866-2123. E-mail: treasurer.kennedy@state.co.us.*

KENNEDY, CHARLES, retired neuroscientist, retired medical educator; b. Buffalo, Aug. 27, 1920; m. Eulsum Kennedy, Aug. 27, 1968; 3 children from previous marriage. BA in Chemistry cum laude, Princeton U., 1942; MD, U. Rochester, 1945. Diplomate Am. Bd. Pediats., Am. Bd. Psychiatry and Neurology, lic. N.Y., Pa., DC, Maine, Md. Intern pathology New Haven Hosp., 1945—46; instr. pathology Sch. Medicine Yale U., New Haven, 1945-46; fellow in child psychiatry Children's Hosp., Buffalo, 1948-49, resident pediatrician, 1949-51; fellow in physiology Grad. Sch. Medicine U. Pa., Phila., 1951-53, assoc. pediats. Sch. Medicine, 1952-55, assoc. in neurology, 1955-58, asst. prof. neurology in pediats., 1958-61, assoc. prof., 1961-67; chief divsn. neurology, dir. child neurology Children's Hosp., Phila., 1959-67; prof. pediats., neurology Sch. Medicine Georgetown U., Washington, 1971-90, prof. emeritus, 1990—. Vis. fellow in neurology Neurol. Inst. Columbia Presbyn. Med. Ctr., 1957—58; mem. Lab. Clin. Sci. Nat. Inst. Mental Health, 1967—68, Lab. Cerebral Metabolism, 1968—95; lectr. U.S. Naval Hosp., Phila., 1962—68; mem. adv. com. dyslexia State of Tex., 1965; guest lectr. Nat. Naval Med. Ctr. Uniformed Svcs. U. Health Scis., 1977—87. Mem. editl. bd. Pediat. Rsch., 1978—84, Brain Rsch., 1980—96, Jour. Cerebral Blood Flow and Metabolism, 1981—88. Lt. (j.g.) USNR, 1946—48. Fellow, Life Ins. Med. Rsch. Fund, 1951—53. Fellow: Coll. Physicians Phila.; mem.: Profs. Child Neurology, Child Neurology Soc., Soc. Neuroscience, Assn. Rsch. Nervous and Mental Disease, Phila. Neurol. Soc. (v.p. 1967), Phila. Pediat. Soc. (pres. 1964), Internat. Soc. Cerebral Blood Flow and Metabolism, Internat. Soc. Neurochemistry, Nat. Bd. Med. Examiners (mem. pediat. com. 1960—64), Am. Soc. Neurochemistry, Am. Acad. Neurology (chmn. sect. child neurology 1964—66), Am. Neurol. Assn., Am. Acad. Pediats., Am. Pediat. Soc.

KENNEDY, CHARLES ALLEN, lawyer; b. Maysville, Ky., Dec. 11, 1940; s. Elmer Earl and Mary Frances Kennedy; m. Patricia Ann Louderback, Dec. 9, 1961; 1 child, Mimi Mignon. AB, Morehead State Coll., 1965, MA in Edn., 1968; JD, U. Akron, 1969; LLM, George Washington U., 1974. Bar: Ohio 1969. Asst. cashier Citizens Bank, Felicity, Ohio, 1961-63; tchr Triway Local Sch. Dist., Wooster, Ohio, 1965-67; with office of gen. counsel Fgn. Agr. and Spl. Programs Divsn. USDA, Washington, 1969-71; ptnr. Kauffman, Eberhart, Cicconetti & Kennedy Co., Wooster, 1972-86, Kennedy, Cicconetti, Knowlton & Buy-Tendyk, LPA, Wooster, 1986—. Mem.: ABA, Wayne County Bar Assn., Ohio Assn. Justice, Ohio State Bar Assn., Am. Coll. Barristers, Am. Assn. Justice, Fed. Bar Assn., Lions, Exch. Club, Elks, Phi Delta Kappa, Phi Alpha Delta. Republican. Home: 275 W Henrietta Wooster OH 44691 Office: Kennedy Cicconetti & Know Ken 558 N Market St Wooster OH 44691-3406 Office Phone: 330-262-7555. Personal E-mail: knndy558@netscape.net.

KENNEDY, CHESTER RALPH, JR., retired state official, art director; b. Middleboro, Mass., Apr. 22, 1926; s. Chester Ralph and Mary Carmen (Mello) K.; m. Barbara Ann Partridge, June 27, 1953; children: Karen Brooke, Scott Douglas. BFA, Mass. Coll. Art, 1951; postgrad., New Eng. Adult Edn. Inst., 1959, Boston U., 1966, Brandies U., 1985. Supr. pub. health edn. Mass. Dept. Pub. Health, Boston, 1953-56, coordinator health edn., 1956-74, asst. dir. health edn., 1974-81, dir. health edn., 1981-84, dist. health officer, 1984-89; ret., 1989. Asst. art dir. Barchét Studios, Middleboro, 1949-59, art dir., co-owner, Sherborn, Mass., 1959—; cons. USPHS, Assn. State and Territorial Health Officers; lectr., instr. Harvard, Boston U., Mass. Coll.; mem. Acad. Master Plan Adv. Commn., Mass. State Coll. System; exhibit chmn. 22nd World Health Assembly. Editor: Commonwealth of Mass. Secretarial Reference Manual, 1969; designer blue ribbon exhibit New Eng. Hosp. Assembly, 1969; designer five pvt. homes. Pres. Pub. Health Museum in Mass., 1991-93, mem. exec. bd., 1993-, exec. dir., 2002-; pres. Reach Out, Inc., 1970-74, bd. dirs., 1974-; bd. dirs. Greater Framingham Mental Health Assn., 1974-76; elected to Sherborn Bd. Health, 1974-86; mem. Solid Waste Recovery Tech. Com., 1975-84; co-chair Coalition Organized for Health Edn. in Schs., 1982-89. Served with USN, 1944-46. Recipient Boy Scouts Am. Organizer award, 1941, Commonwealth Mass. Disting. Svc. citation, 1971, Health Edn. citation New Eng. Consortium Health Edn. Assn., 1975, Coalition Organized for Health Edn. in Schs. citation, 1989, hon. award, 2002, Reach Out award, 1977, Southeastern Assn. Health Bds. award, 1989, Michael Dukakis Gov.'s award, 1989, Mass. Dept. Pub. Health award, 1989, Pub. Health Museum Organizer award Mass. Ho. of Reps., 1993, Gov. William Weld Museum Founder award, 1993. Mem. New Eng. Health Edn. Assn. (pres. 1971-72), Mass. Health Coun., New Eng. Health Promotion Coun., Soc. Pub. Health Edn., Mass. Audubon Soc., Mass. Archeol. Soc., Mass. Coll. Art Alumni (pres. 1968-72), Assn. Mass. State Colls. Alumni (pres. 1973-75), Mass. Pub. Health Assn. (health edn. chmn. 1974-76, 25 yr. award 1986, Paul Revere award 1990), Mass. Health Officers Assn. (emeritus, Curtis M. Hillard award 1989, exec. sec. 1992-98), Mass. Assn. Health Bds. (hon., exec. bd. 1990-94), New Eng. Pub. Health Assn. (pres. 1984-85, Ira Hiscock award 1980, 25 yr. award 1989, pres.'s award, 2001). Office: Barchét Studios 178 Washington St Sherborn MA 01770-1022 E-mail: chet.kennedy@att.net.

KENNEDY, CHRISTOPHER ROBIN, ceramics engineer, director; b. Ottawa, Ont., Can., June 25, 1948; s. Robert Alvin and Ruth Christina (Downie) K.; m. Christine Willa Wayman, Jan. 28, 1978; children: Scott Wayman, Stuart James. BS, Rutgers U., 1969; MS, Pa. State U., 1971, PhD, 1974. Asst. ceramist Argonne Nat. Lab., Ill., 1974-79, ceramist Ill., 1979-82; staff engr. Exxon Rsch. and Engring. Co., Florham Park, NJ, 1982-83, group leader materials devel. group, 1984; mgr. materials rsch. sect. Lanxide Corp., Newark, 1984-87, mgr. def. products devel. sect., 1987-92; mgr. composite devel. and engring. sect., 1992-93; v.p. tech. Lanxide Corp., Newark, 1993-98; dir. R&D Ceramco, Burlington, NJ, 1998—2003; dir. R&D Prosthetics Divsn. Dentsply Internat., York, PR, 2003—. Contbr. numerous articles to profl. jours. Patentee in field. Mem. Am. Ceramic Soc., Nat. Inst. Ceramic Engrs., Keramos. Office: 550 W College Ave York PA 17405 Office Phone: 717-849-4573.

KENNEDY, COLLEEN M., medical educator; MD, Med. Coll. Pa., Phila., 1995; MS, U. Iowa, Iowa City, 2004. Diplomate Am. Bd. of Obstetricians and Gynecologists, 2001. Assoc. U. Iowa, 2002—05, asst. prof., 2005. Dir., colposcopy clinic U. Iowa, 2005—; dir., vulvar vaginal disease clinic U. Iwa, 2006—. Achievements include research in vulvar pain; lower genital tract disorders. Office: U Iowa 200 Hawkins Dr Iowa City IA 52242

KENNEDY, CORNELIA GROEFSEMA, federal judge; b. Detroit, Aug. 4, 1923; d. Elmer H. and Mary Blanche (Gibbons) Groefsema; m. Charles S. Kennedy, Jr. (dec.); 1 son, Charles S. III. BA, U. Mich., 1945, JD with distinction, 1947; LL.D. (hon.), No. Mich. U., 1971, Eastern Mich. U., 1971, Western Mich. U., 1973, Detroit Coll. Law, 1980, U. Detroit, 1987. Bar: Mich. bar 1947. Law clk. to Chief Judge Harold M. Stephens, U.S. Ct. of Appeals, Washington, 1947-48; assoc. Elmer H. Groefsema, Detroit, 1948-52; partner Markle & Markle, Detroit, 1952-66; judge 3d Judicial Circuit Mich., 1967-70; dist. judge US Dist. Ct., Eastern Dist. Mich., Detroit, 1970-79, chief judge, 1977-79; circuit judge US Ct. Appeals, (6th cir.), 1979-99, sr. judge, 1999—. Mem. Commn. on the Bicentennial of the U.S. Constitution (presdl. appointment). Recipient Sesquicentennial award U. Mich. Fellow Am. Bar Found.; mem. ABA, Mich. Bar Assn. (past chmn. negligence law sect.), Detroit Bar Assn. (past dir.), Fed. Bar Assn., Am. Judicature Soc., Nat. Assn. Women Lawyers, Am. Trial Lawyers Assn., Nat. Conf. Fed. Trial Judges (past chmn.), Fed. Jud. Fellows Commn. (bd. dirs.), Fed. Jud. Ctr. (bd. dirs.), Phi Beta Kappa. Address: 744 Fed Ct House 231 1st Detroit MI 48226*

KENNEDY, CORNELIUS BRYANT, retired lawyer; b. Evanston, Ill., Apr. 13, 1921; s. Millard Bryant and Myrna Estelle (Anderson) K.; m. Anne Martha Reynolds, June 20, 1959; children: Anne Talbot, Lauren K. Mayle. AB, Yale U., 1943; JD, Harvard U., 1948. Bar: Ill. 1949, D.C. 1965. Assoc. Mayer Meyer Austrian & Platt, Chgo., 1949-54, 55-59; asst. to U.S. atty. Dept. Justice, Chgo., 1954-55; counsel to minority leader U.S. Senate, 1959-65; sr. ptnr. Kennedy & Webster, Washington, 1965-82; of counsel Armstrong, Teasdale, Schlafly & Davis, Washington, 1983-88; public mem. Adminstrv. Conf. U.S., 1972-82, sr. conf. fellow, 1982-90, chmn. rulemaking com., 1973-82; ret., 1988. Contbr. articles to profl. jours. Fin. chmn. Lyric Opera Co., Chgo., 1954; chmn. young adults group Chgo. Coun. Fgn. Rels., 1958-59; pres. English Speaking Union Jrs., Chgo., 1957-59; trustee St. John's Child Devel. Ctr., Washington, 1965-67, 75-87, pres., 1983-85; exec. dir. Supreme Ct. Hist. Soc., 1984-87. 1st lt., AC U.S. Army, 1942-46. Fellow Am. Bar Found.; mem. Am. Law Inst., ABA (coun. sect. adminstrv. law 1967-70, chmn. sect. 1976-77), Fed. Bar Assn. (chmn. com. adminstrv. law 1963-64), Legal Club Chgo., Explorers Club, NYC Club, Capitol Hill Club, Chevy Chase Club, Sailing Club of Chesapeake, Adventurer's Club, Hillsboro Club, Sulgrave Club. Home: 500 Crestwood Dr 2403 Charlottesville VA 22903

KENNEDY, DAVID, musician; b. Calif., July 8, 1976; Co-founder & guitarist Box Car Racer, 2002—03, Hazen Street, 2004—, Angels & Airwaves, 2005—. Musician: (albums) (with Boxcar Racer) Boxcar Racer, 2002, There Is, 2002, (with Hazen Street) Hazen Street, 2004, (with Angels & Airwaves) We Don't Need to Whisper, 2006. Co-recipient Woodie of Yr., mtvU Woodie Awards, 2006.*

KENNEDY, DAVID BOYD, foundation executive, lawyer; b. Ann Arbor, Mich., Sept. 2, 1933; s. James Alexander and Elizabeth (Earhart) K.; m. Sally Martin Pyne, 1964; children: Jane Elizabeth Mack, Douglas Earhart. Student, McGill U., 1951-52, U. Mich., 1952-54; AB, Ind. U., 1958; LLB, U. Mich., 1963. Bar: Mich. 1964, Wyo. 1965. Pvt. practive law, Sheridan, Wyo., 1964-84; pres. Earhart Found., Ann Arbor, Mich., 1985—2003, trustee, 1979—. Trustee Citizens Rsch. Coun. of Mich.; chmn., bd. dirs. Inst. for Justice, Washington; mem. bd. overseers Hoover Instn./Stanford U. Mem. Wyo. Ho. Reps., 1967-72; chmn. Wyo. Rep. State Ctrl. Com., 1971-73; Rep. nat. committeeman, 1976-80, vice chmn., 1978-80; atty. gen. State of Wyo., 1974-75; mem. Mont Pelerin Soc.; apptd. mem. Pres.'s Com. on Arts and Humanities, Washington, 1990-93; bd. dirs. Philanthropy Roundtable, Washington, 1993-2000; bd. dirs. Univ. Music Soc., 1986-90, pres., 1990; trustee World of Learning, Inc., Brattleboro, Vt., 1993-98. With U.S. Army, 1954-57. Mem. Wyo. Bar Assn., Mich. Bar Assn. Republican. Office: Earhart Found 2200 Green Rd Ste H Ann Arbor MI 48105-1569 Home Phone: 734-994-9010; Office Phone: 734-761-8592.

KENNEDY, DAVID L., cosmetics company executive; m. Shirley Kennedy; 2 children. BS in Acctg., U. North Ala.; MBA, UCLA. CPA. Acct. Ernst & Young, 1972; joined Coca Cola Co., 1980; various key fin. positions Columbia Pictures while it was divsn. of Coca-Cola Co., v.p., corp. bus. devel., 1988—91, gen. mgr. Coca-Cola USA Fountain Divsn., 1992—98, mng. dir. Coca-Cola Amatil Ltd. Sydney, Australia, 1998—2001; exec. v.p., pres. Revlon Internat., 2002—06; CFO Revlon, Inc., 2006, pres., CEO, 2006—. Office: Revlon Inc 237 Park Ave New York NY 10017*

KENNEDY, DAVID MICHAEL, historian, educator; b. Seattle, July 22, 1941; s. Albert John and Mary Ellen Kennedy; m. Judith Ann Osborne, Mar. 14, 1970; children: Ben Caufield, Elizabeth Margaret, Thomas Osborne. BA, Stanford U., 1963; MA, Yale U., 1964, PhD, 1968; MA, Oxford U., 1995; D (hon.), LaTrobe U., 2001. From asst. prof. history to prof. Stanford U., Calif., 1967—80, prof., 1980—, chmn. program in internat. relations, 1977—80, assoc. dean Sch. Humanities and Scis., 1981—85, William Robertson Coe prof. history and Am. studies, 1987—93, Donald J. McLachlan prof. history, 1993—, chair, history dept., 1990—94. Vis. prof. U. Florence, Italy, 1976—77; lectr. Internat. Comms. Agy., 1976—77; vis. prof. Am. history Oxford U., 1995—96, Tanner lectr., 2003; co-dir. Bill Lane Ctr. Study of the North Am. West, 2005—. Author: Birth Control in America: The Career of Margaret Sanger, 1970 (Bancroft prize, John Gilmary Shea prize), Over Here: The First World War and American Society, 1980, Freedom from Fear: The American People in Depression and War, 1929-1945, 1999 (Pulitzer prize, 2000, Francis Parkman prize, 2000, Ambassador's prize, 2000, Calif. Gold medal for lit., 2000); author: (with Thomas A. Bailey and Lizabeth Cohen) The American Pageant: A History of the Republic, 13th edit., 2006; co-editor: Power and Responsibility: Case Studies in American Leadership, 1986; mem. adv. bd. (TV program) The American Experience, Sta. WGBH, 1986—92. Mem. planning group Am. Issues Forum, 1974—75; bd. dirs. CORO Found., 1981—87, Environ. Traveling Companions, 1986—, Stanford U. Bookstore, 1994—2003, The Pulitzer Prizes, 2002—. Recipient Richard W. Lyman award, Stanford U. Alumni Assn., 1989, Laurance and Naomi Carpenter Hoagland prize for Undergraduate Teaching, Stanford U., 2005; fellow, Am. Coun. Learned Socs., 1971—72, John Simon Guggenheim Meml. Found., 1975—76, Ctr. for Advanced Study in Behavioral Scis., 1986—87, Stanford Humanities Ctr., 1989—90. Fellow: Am. Philos. Soc., Am. Acad. Arts and Scis.; mem.: Soc. Am. Historians, Orgn. Am. Historians (Disting. Svc. award 2007), Am. Hist. Assn. Democrat. Roman Catholic. Office: Stanford U Dept History Stanford CA 94305 Office Phone: 650-723-0351. Business E-Mail: dmk@stanford.edu.

KENNEDY, DAVID WILLIAM, law educator; b. Phila., Apr. 5, 1954; AB in History & Internat. Rels., with honors, Brown U., 1976; MALD in Internat. Rels., Fletcher Sch. Law & Diplomacy, Tufts U., 1979, PhD in Internat. Rels., 1984; JD magna cum laude, Harvard U., 1980. Bar: DC 1980. John Harvey Gregory lectr. on world orgn. Harvard Law Sch., Cambridge, Mass., 1981—83, asst. prof. law, 1983—86, prof. law, 1986—, Henry L. Shattuck prof. law, 1994—2003, Manley O. Hudson prof. law, 2003—, dir. European Law Rsch. Ctr., 1991—, faculty dir. grad. & internat. legal studies, 1991—97; of counsel Cleary, Gottlieb, Steen & Hamilton, Brussels, 1989—90. Vis. prof. U. Paris X, Nanterre, 1995—96, 1996—97, 1998, 2001—02, U. Paris II, 1998, U. Toronto, 1998, 99, NYU Law Sch., 1999, Australian Nat. U., 2000, U. Turin, 2001, 02, Paris I Pantheon Sorbonne, 2005; vis. scholar Sch. Oriental and African Studies, U. London, 2000—01. Author: The Dark Sides of Virtue: Reassessing International Humanitarianism, 2004. Fellow, Inst. Internat. Law, Kiel U. & Inst. Internat. Affairs, Hamburg U., Germany, 1980—81; Fulbright Fellow, Belgium, 1984, Alexander von Humboldt Stiftung and Sheldon Fellow, Germany. Mem.: Coun. Fgn. Rels. Office: Harvard Law Sch 1563 Massachusetts Ave Cambridge MA 02138 Office Phone: 617-495-3132. Office Fax: 617-496-4947. Business E-Mail: dkennedy@law.harvard.edu.

KENNEDY, DAVID WILLIAM, otolaryngologist, medical administrator, educator; b. York, Eng., June 27, 1948; s. Michael Leo and Winifred Pearl (Shepherd) K.; m. Edna Mae Schirmer, Apr. 20, 1978; children: Garrett David, Kirin Suzanne. Student in Pre-Med. Program, Ampleforth Coll., York, 1962-66; MD, Royal Coll. Surgeons, Ireland, 1972. Diplomate Am. Bd. Otolaryngology, Am. Bd. Head and Neck Surgery; lic. physician Pa., Md. Intern St. Laurence's Hosp., Dublin, 1972-73; asst. resident in surgery Johns Hopkins U., Balt., 1973-74, asst. resident in otolaryngology, 1974-77, mem. staff, 1977-91, chief resident in otolaryngology, asst. prof. otolaryngology, 1977-78, asst. prof., 1978-86, assoc. prof. otolaryngology-head and neck surgery, 1986-91, assoc. prof. neurosurgery, 1987-91; mem. staff Loch Raven VA Hosp., Balt., 1980-87, cons. physician, 1987-91; mem. staff Sinai Hosp. Balt., 1981-88; chmn. U. Pa. Med. Ctr., Phila., 1991—2003; mem. staff VA Hosp., Phila., 1991—; vice dean profl. svcs. U. Pa. Sch. Medicine, 2002—; sr. v.p. U. Pa. Health Sys., 1991—2002. Dir. Penn Internat. Rhinology Course, Phila., 1991—; spkr. in field; lectr. in field. Contbg. author: Rhinitis, 2d edit., 1991, Diseases of the Nose, Throat, Ear, Head and Neck, 1991, Otolaryngology, 3d edit., 1991, Surgery for Skull Base Tumors, 1991, Sinus Disease: Guide to First Line Management, 1994, Diseases of the Sinuses: Diagnosis and Management, 2000, Living with Chronic Sinusitis, 2004, others; mem. editl. bd. Ear, Nose and Throat Jour., 1983—, Am. Jour. Rhinology, 1986—, Laryngoscope, 1988—, Auris Nasus Larynx, 1996—, ACTA Oto-Rhino-Laryngologica Belgica, 1995—; editor-in-chief Am. Jour. Rhinology, 1988-, Current Opinion in Otolaryngology and Head and Neck Surgery, 1992—, Jour. Otolaryngology, 1993—; editor Auris Nasus Larynx, 1996—, ACTA Oto-Rhino-Larynngologica Belgica, 1995—; contbr. numerous articles to profl. jours. Recipient Leonard Abrahamson Meml. Gold medal, 1971, Lyons Meml. medal, 1971, gold medal Coombe Lying-In Hosp., 1971, Reuben-Harvey prize, 1972, Coun.'s prize and gold medal, 1972, Sr. William Wilde medal, 1995, Predl. Citation Am. Acad. Otolaryngology - Head and Neck Surgery, 2002; rsch. grantee Schering Corp., 1981, HHS, 1983-88, Norwich-Eaton Corp., 1984-86, Minn. Mining and Mfg. Co., 1984, Healthtek, 1990-91. Fellow Am. Acad. Otolaryngology-Head and Neck Surgery (mem. hearing subcom. 1985-91, mem. rhinology-paranasal sinus com. 1986-93, 97—, mem. CPT com. 1992-97, legis. alt. bd. gvs. 1991—, mem. adv. coun. on continuing edn. with TV subcom. 1994, instr. endoscopic sinus surgery 1985, mem. internat. otolaryngology com. 2000, bd. dirs., coord. govtl. rels. 2004—), Royal Coll. Surgeons (anatomy demonstrator/lectr. 1972-73, vis. prof. 1980-81, Sir William Wheeler Meml. medal 1972, Fitzsimmons Gold medal for surgery 1972, Bronze medal), Royal Coll. Surgeons (Ireland); mem. ACS (com. on emerging surg. tech. and edn. 1999), AMA (hon.), NAS-Inst. Medicine, Am. Rhinologic Soc. (bd. dirs. 1988-96, v.p. 1989-90, pres. 1992-93, cons. to bd. dirs. 1987-88), Internat. Rhinologic Soc. (bd. dirs. 1995—, v.p. 2004-07, pres.-elect 2007—), Phila. Laryngol. Soc., Soc. Univ. Otolaryngologists (mem. nominating com. 1985-86), Nat. Acad. Scis., Inst. of Medicine, Pa. Acad. Otolaryngology, John Morgan Soc., Johns Hopkins Med. and Surg. Assn., Danish Otolaryngology Soc. (hon.), Johns Hopkins Soc. Scholars. Achievements include introduction of endoscopic sinus surgery to U.S.; development of extended applications of endoscopic surgical techniques; clinical development of surgical localizers. Office: Univ Pa Med Ctr 5 Ravdin 3400 Spruce St Philadelphia PA 19104-4206 Office Phone: 215-662-6971. Business E-Mail: kennedyd@uphs.upenn.edu.

KENNEDY, DONALD, environmental scientist, educator, editor; b. NYC, Aug. 18, 1931; s. William Dorsey and Barbara (Bean) Kennedy; children: Laura Page, Julia Hale stepchildren: Cameron Rachel, Jamie Christopher. AB, Harvard U., 1952, AM, 1954, PhD, 1956; DSc (hon.), Columbia U., Williams Coll., U. Mich., U. Ariz., U. Rochester, Reed Coll., Whitman Coll., Coll. William & Mary. Mem. faculty Stanford (Calif.) U., 1960-77, prof. biol. scis., 1965-77, chmn. dept., 1965-72, sr. cons. sci. and tech. policy Exec. Office of Pres., 1976, commr. FDA, 1977-79, provost, 1979-80, pres., 1980-92, prof. emeritus, Bing prof. environ. sci., 1992—. Bd. overseers Harvard U., 1970—76; bd. dirs. Health Effects Inst., Nat. Commn. Pub. Svc., Carnegie Commn. Sci., Tech. and Govt. Author: Academic Duty, 1997; mem. editl. bd. Jour. Neurophysiology, 1969—75, Sci., 1973—77; editor-in-chief: Sci., 2000—; contbr. articles to profl. jours. Bd. dirs. Carnegie Endowment Internat. Peace, David & Lucile Packard Found. Fellow: AAAS, Am. Acad. Arts and Scis.; mem.: NAS, Am. Philos. Soc. Office: Stanford Univ Inst Internat Studies Encina Hall 401 Stanford CA 94305-6055 Home Phone: 650-326-9009; Office Phone: 650-725-2745. Business E-Mail: kennedyd@stanford.edu.

KENNEDY, DOUGLAS AYERS, education educator, dean; b. Glen Ridge, NJ, June 19, 1961; s. Robert Freeman and Edith Bess Kennedy; m. Elizabeth Jane Smith, Aug. 12, 1989; children: Samuel Freeman, Maxwell McClelland. BS, U. Del., Newark, 1983; MS in Edn., So. Ill. U., Carbondale, 1985; EdD, Temple U., Phila., 1988. Cert. pk. and recreation profl. Nat. Certification Bd. for Pk. and Recreation Pers., 1989. Dir. fitness svcs. Sheraton Corp., Hasbrouck Heights, NJ, 1985; student activities coord. C.C. Phila., 1985—87; instr. Temple U., Phila., 1987—88; prof., dept. coord. Va. Wesleyan Coll., Norfolk, 1988—, assoc. dean for campus recreation, 2005—. Chair Va. Profl. Certification Bd., Mechanicsville, 1990—2001; visitor Coun. on Accreditation of Pk. and Recreation Curricula, Ashburn, Va., 1998—, chair, 1999—2002; chair bd. dirs. YMCA Camp Silver Beach, Jamesville, Va., 2006—; exec. bd. mem. YMCA South Hampton Roads, Norfolk, Va., 2007—; bd. dirs. Found. of the Va. Recreation and Pk. Soc., Mechanicsville. Contbr. chapters to books, articles to profl. jours. Asst. dir. nat. camping sch. aquatics sect. Boy Scouts Am., Jamesburg, NJ, 1985—2007; event dir. Spl. Olympics, Carbondale, Ill., 1984—85; contbr. master plan City of Norfolk Recreation Bur., 1997; mem. Virginia Beach Parks and Recreation Youth Unit Rev. Com., 1999; del. leader Internat. Rep. Inst., Washington, 1994. Recipient Samuel Nelson Gray Disting. Tchg. award, Va. Wesleyan Coll., 1991, 2000, Outstanding Alumni award, So. Ill. U., 2007; Rsch. grantee, US Dept. Rehab. Svcs., 1990, Ednl. Tech. grantee, Bell Atlantic, 2003. Mem.: Va. Recreation and Pk. Soc. (pres. 1995, Fellows Award 2005), Rho Phi Lambda (advisor 1998—2007). Democrat. Achievements include research in employment patterns in therapeutic recreation; employe wellness needs; factors related to college student attrition; efficacy of computerized mentorship in parks and recreation; recreation facility usage and the measurement of participant attitudes; comparison of the perceptions of health care administrators and physically disabled adults concerning the factors that contribute to the psychological well-being of adults who have a physical disabili; effect of a recreation activity on work productivity. Avocations: triathlete, coaching youth sports, antique auto restoration. Office: Virginia Wesleyan College 1584 Wesleyan Dr Norfolk VA 23502 Home Phone: 757-460-5037; Office Phone: 757-455-3305. Office Fax: 757-455-5739. Business E-Mail: kennedy@vwc.edu.

KENNEDY, DUNCAN MCLEAN, law educator; b. Washington, March 4, 1942. AB in Econs., Harvard U., Cambridge, Mass., 1964; LLB, Yale U., 1970. Law clk. to Justice Potter Stewart, US Supreme Ct., 1970-71; asst. prof. law Harvard U., 1971-76, prof., 1976-, Carter prof. gen. jurisprudence, 1996-. Vis. prof. law U. Paris I, 1998; disting. vis. prof. Suffolk U. Sch. Law, 2002. Author: Legal Education and the Reproduction of Hierarchy, 1983, Sexy Dressing, etc., 1993, A Critique of Adjudication, 1997, Libertad y restriccion en la decision judicial, 1999, Legal Education and the Reproduction of Hierarchy: A Polemic Against the System, A Critical Edition, 2004. Office: Harvard Law Sch 1563 Massachusetts Ave Cambridge MA 02138 Office Phone: 617-495-4619. Office Fax: 617-496-4863. Business E-Mail: kennedy@law.harvard.edu.

KENNEDY, ELIZABETH, health facility administrator; b. Binghamton, NY, Mar. 19, 1944; d. Robert D. and Doris Beverly (Bryde) Courtright; m. Leon C. Kennedy, Aug. 29, 1964; children: Andrew, Tracey, Brian, Kristie. AAS, Ind.-Purdue U., 1986; BSN, Ind. Wesleyan U., 1996. RN, Ind.; lifetime ARC nurse. DON Summit House, Ft. Wayne, Ind., 1986-87; staff nurse Mark Souder, M.D., Auburn, Ind., 1988; DON Kendallville (Ind.) Nursing Home, 1988-89, Lifecare Ctr., Lagrange, Ind., 1989-91; asst. DON Arbors at Ft. Wayne, Ind., 1991-92; nursing supr. Allen Home, Health Care & Hospice, 1993-95; DON Courtland Health and Rehab. Ctr., Ft. Wayne, 1996—; staff nurse Interim Health Care, Ft. Wayne, Ind., 1996-97; agy. nurse The Arc of N.E. Ind., 1997-98; DON The Cedars, Leo, Ind., 1998-99; RN cons. Prof. Nursing Svc., 1989—99; clin. educator Parkview Health Sys., Ft. Wayne, Ind., 1999-2000; case mgr. mr/dd In Case Mgmt., Indpls., 1999-2000; mgr. extended care unit Don Adams County Meml. Hosp, Decatur, Ind., 2000; dir. nursing Englewood Health and Rehab. Ctr., Ft. Wayne, Ind., 2001—02; nursing mgr. Wash. House Treatment Ctr., 2001—; dir. nursing Riverbend H.C., Ft. Wayne, 2001; RN coord. Ft. Wayne State Devel. Ctr., 2002—; asst. dir. nursing Univ. Park Nursing Ctr., Ft. Wayne, 2002—03; with Don Kendallville Manor, Kendallville, Ind. Instr. ARC., 1986, AHA CPR, 1998; assoc. faculty dept. nursing Purdue U., Ft. Wayne, 2000. Recipient Scottish Rite Nursing scholarship. Home: 2620 E State Blvd Apt 209 Fort Wayne IN 46805-4781 E-mail: tishrn@comcast.net.

KENNEDY, ELIZABETH MAE, musician; b. Medford, Mass., Oct. 16, 1949; d. Thomas Power and Anne Cecelia (Coyne) Sullivan; m. William David Kennedy, Oct. 12, 1970 (div. 1984); children: Mary Elizabeth, Jonathan Martin. AS, N.S. C.C., 1969; student, Aquinas Coll., 1991—92. Cert. liturgical musician music and liturgy. Retail sales mgmt. Jordan Marsh Co., Peabody, Mass., 1966—69; retail mgmt. Sears, Roebuck and Co., Lynn, Mass., 1969—70; asst. bookkeeper Henry Leather Co., Peabody, 1970—76; office mgr. Bartlett and Steadman Co. Inc., Marblehead, Mass., 1981—90; music dir. Contemporary Choir St. Mary's HS, Lynn, Mass., 2006—. Music dir., contract organist St. John The Evangelist Ch., Swampscott, Mass., 1985-98; co-founder New Sch. Music and Performing Arts, Marblehead, 1994; dir. music St. Charles Borromeo Ch., Waltham, Mass., 1998-99, Incarnation Parish, Melrose, Mass., 1999-2003, choir dir. St. Mary's HS, Lynn, Mass., 2006—. Organizer Devereux Neighborhood Assn.; active North Shore Piano Tchrs. Guild, 1988—, v.p., 1998-2000, co-pres., 2000-02; chair Marblehead Festival of the Arts, 1998-99. Democrat. Roman Catholic. Avocations: reading, swimming, midi, computers. Home: 46 Ocean Ave Marblehead MA 01945-3616 Fax: 781-631-1519. Personal E-mail: elizmkenn@aol.com.

KENNEDY, EVELYN SIEFERT, foundation executive, textiles executive; b. Pitts., Nov. 11, 1927; d. Carmine and Assunta (Iacobucci) Rocci; m. George J. Siefert, May 30, 1953 (dec. 2000); children: Paul Kenneth, Carl Joseph, Ann Marie; m. Lyle H. Kennedy II, Oct. 12, 1974 (dec. 1990); m. Frederick J. Commentucci, Feb. 24, 2001. BS magna cum laude, U. RI, 1969, MS in Textiles and Clothing, 1970. Accredited appraiser of personal property, Internat. Soc. Appraisers. With Pitts. Pub. Schs., 1945—50, Goodyear Aircraft Corp., Akron, Ohio, 1950—54; clothing instr. Groton Dept. Adult Edn., Conn., 1958—68; pres. Sewtique, Groton, 1970—, Sewtique II, New London, Conn., 1986; v.p. Kennedy Capital Advisors, Groton, 1973—85, Kennedy Mgmt. Corp., Groton, 1974—85, Kennedy Intervest, Inc., Groton, 1975—85; pres., exec. dir. PRIDE Found., Inc., Groton, 1978—. Clothing cons. Coop. Ext. Svc., Dept. Agr.; internat. lectr. on clothing for disabled and elderly; adj. faculty U. Conn., Ea. Conn. State Coll., St. Joseph Coll.; hon. prof. U. RI, assoc. prof., 1987-2000; fed. expert witness Care Label Law, FTC, 1976; mem. Major Appliance Consumer Action Panel, 1983-89. Author: Dressing With Pride, 1980, Clothing Accessibility: A Lesson Plan to Aid the Disabled and Elderly, 1983, Textiles Speak, 1996. Regional adv. coun. SBA Active Corps Execs., Hartford, 1985-2006; bd. dirs. Small Bus. Devel. Ctr., 1989-2006, Easter Seal Rehab. Ctr. Southeastern Conn., Southeastern Conn. Women's Ctr., Women's Ctr. New London County; bus. adv. coun. U. RI, 1979-89, trustee, 1985—; active LWV; mem. Groton Vocat. Edn. Adv. Coun. Recipient award of distinction U. RI, 1969, Adv. of Yr. SBA, 1984, Outstanding Svc. in Cmty., 1991; named Woman of Yr. Bus. and Profl. Women's Club, 1977, Conn. Home Economist of Yr., 1987; named to Wall of Fame U. RI, 2004. Mem. Internat. Sleep Coun. (consumer affairs rep., SBA award 1991), Internat. Soc. Appraisers (accredited appraiser personal property, panelist FMHA roster, farmer's credit mediator 1989-92), Nat. Assn. Bedding Mfrs., Conn. Home Economists in Bus. (founder 1977, Women of Yr. 1987), Nat. Home Economists in Bus. (chmn. internat. rels., nat. fin. chmn. 1986), Am. Home Econs. Assn., Coll. and Univ. Bus. Instrs. of Conn., Am. Occupl. Therapy Assn. (resource cons. 1986—), Web-Re-Stor Assn. (wedding restoration specialist 1993-2000), Southeastern Women's Network, Textile Soc. Am., Fashion Group, Costume Soc. Am., New London Zonta Club, Bus. and Profl. Women's Club (Outstanding Women of Yr. 1977), Omicron Nu. Office: 391 Long Hill Rd Groton CT 06340-3812 Office Phone: 860-445-7320, 800-332-9122. Personal E-mail: textileappraisal@aol.com.

KENNEDY, FAYE, retired social worker, author; b. Kansas City, Mo., Apr. 3, 1931; d. Wiley Choice and Zella Rae (Jackman) K.; m. Patrick Joseph Daly, Jan. 7, 1961. AA, Pasadena City Coll., 1951; BA, Hunter Coll., 1955; cert., Alliance Francaise, Paris, 1956. Vocat. counselor N.Y. State Divsn. Employment, NYC, 1957-65; social worker N.Y. State Div. Parole, NYC, 1965-77. Author: Good-bye, Diane, 1976; assoc. editor Afro-Hawaii News, 1990-92. Hawaii adv. com. U.S. Civil Rights Commn., Honolulu, 1990-2007; active Hawaii State Commn. on Status of Women, Honolulu, 1993-95, Hawaii Civil Rights Commn., Honolulu, 1995-2003, Honolulu County Com. Status of Women, 2004—, Martin Luther King Jr. Commn., Honolulu, 1989-93; del. Hawaii Dem. Party State Cen. Com., 1994—, Dem. Nat. Conv., 1996, 2000, 04; bd. dirs. Hawaii Literacy, Inc., 1987-97, Hawaii Youth at Risk, 1991-94, ACLU of Hawaii, 1999-2002; 1st v.p. NAACP-Hawaii, 2003-07; chmn. Hawaii Friends Civil Rights, 2007—. Recipient Gov.'s Cert. of Appreciation, State of Hawaii, 1989-93, Making of the King Holiday award Martin Luther King Jr. Commn., 1991, Outstanding Achievement award Hawaii Literacy, Inc., 1988, 92, Outstanding African Ams. citation Mahogany, 1996, Afro-Hawaii News, 1992, Hawaii Personalities Recognition citation RSVP mag., 1989, Lifetime Dedication to Pub. Svc. cert. Honolulu City Coun., 1996. Mem. Hawaii Women's Polit. Caucus (pres. 2003-), Hawaii Yacht Club. Democrat. Avocations: reading, writing, movies, gardening. Home: 3071 Felix St Honolulu HI 96816-1911

KENNEDY, GARY F., air transportation executive, lawyer; b. May 13, 1955; m. Michele Valdez; 4 children. BA magna cum laude, U. Utah, 1977, JD, 1980. Atty. Roe & Fowler, Salt Lake City, 1980—82, Suitter, Axland, Armstrong and Hanson, Salt Lake City, 1982—84; atty. legal dept. Am. Airlines, 1984—87, sr. atty. legal dept., 1987—91, mng. dir.-properties corp. real estate dept., 1991—96, v.p. corp. real estate, 1996—2003, sr. v.p., gen. counsel, 2003—. Mem.: Phi Beta Kappa. Office: AMR Corp 4333 Amon Carter Blvd Fort Worth TX 76155*

KENNEDY, HAROLD EDWARD, lawyer; b. Pottstown, Pa., Oct. 18, 1927; s. Freeman S. and Alice (Brehm) K.; m. Eleanor Henry, Jan. 9, 1960; children: Kathleen, Nancy, Harold, Robert, Ellen, Anne, Susan. Student, Colgate U., 1945-47; LLB, Syracuse U., 1952. Bar: N.Y. 1952, U.S. Dist. Ct. (no. dist.) N.Y. 1954, U.S. Supreme Ct. 1956, U.S. Dist. Ct. (so. dist.) N.Y. 1962. Ptnr. Taylor & Kennedy, Amsterdam, NY, 1952-59; sr. assoc. Kissam & Halpin, NYC, 1959-60; vice chmn., gen. counsel, dir. mergers and acquisitions Foster Wheeler Corp., Clinton, NJ, 1960-94, legal advisor, 1994-97, also bd. dirs. Bd. dirs. W.I. Refining Ltd. Trustee First Presbyn. Ch., Orange, N.J., 1973-76, St. Barnabas Corp., 1996-2003; sec., 1996-2003, St. Barnabas Med. Ctr., 1986-2003, Kessler Inst. for Rehab., 1987-97, vice chmn., 1992-97, Union Hosp., 1994-2003, Beth Israel Hosp., 1996-2003; bd. visitors Syracuse U. Coll. of Law, 1987-2003. With USAF, 1945-47. Mem. Order of Coif, Baltusrol Golf Club, Sea Pines Country Club. E-mail: kennedyhe@aol.com.

KENNEDY, HAROLD LEE, physician; b. Amarillo, Tex., Oct. 1, 1948; s. Hugh L. and Marilyn Ruth (Kelley) K.; m. Cynthia Louise Garst; children: Rachael, Nikki, Jason, Megan, Jeremy, James, Josh., La. State Univ., 1969; MD, La. State, 1973. Diplomate Am. Bd. Surgery, Am. Bd. Colon Rectal Surgery. Intern Naval Hosp., Oakland, Calif., 1973-74, gen. surgery residency, 1974-78, staff surgeon Bremerron, Wash., 1978-81; colon rectal surgical fellow Univ. Minn., Mpls., 1981-82; colon rectal surgeon Sacramento, Calif., 1982—. Founding ptnr. Sacramento Colon Rectal Surgery, set up anal physiology lab., Sacramento, 1987—; lectr. numerous nat. meetings, numerous nat. com. Contbr. articles to profl. jours. Fellow Am. Coll. Surgeons, Am. Soc. Colon Rectal Surgery, Soc. Gasto-intestinal Endoceapic Surgery; mem. Calif. Medical Assn., Sacramento/El Dorado Medical Soc., Sacremento Surgical Soc., Northern Calif. Soc. Colon & Rectal Surgeons, The Northwest Soc. Colon & Rectal Surgeons, Alpha Omega Alpha. Avocations: hunting, snow and water skiing, fishing. Office: Sacramento Colon Rectal Surgery 1020 29th St Ste 350 Sacramento CA 95816-5173

KENNEDY, JACK LELAND, lawyer; b. Portland, Oreg., Jan. 30, 1924; s. Ernest E. and Lera M. (Talley) K.; m. Clara C. Hagans, June 5, 1948; children: James M., John C. Student, U.S. Maritime Commn. Acad., Southwestern U., LA; JD, Lewis and Clark Coll., 1951. Bar: Oreg. 1951. Pvt. practice, Portland; ptnr. Kennedy & King, Portland, 1971-77, Kennedy, King & McClurg, Portland, 1977-82, Kennedy, King & Zimmer, Portland, 1982-98, Kennedy, Watts, Arellano & Ricks L.L.P., Portland, 1998—. Trustee Northwestern Coll. Law, Portland; dir. Profl. Liability Fund, 1979-82. Contbr. articles to legal jours. Mem. bd. visitors Lewis and Clark Coll. With USNR, 1942-46. Recipient Disting. Grad. award Lewis and Clark Coll., 1983. Fellow Am. Coll. Trial Lawyers, Am. Bar Found. (life), Oreg. Bar Found. (charter); mem. ABA (ho. of dels. 1984-88), Oreg. State Bar (bd. govs. 1976-79, pres. 1978-79), Multnomah Bar Assn., City Club, Columbia River Yacht Club. Republican. Office: Kennedy Watts Arellano & Ricks LLP Ste 2850 1211 SW Fifth Ave Portland OR 97204-3733 Home Phone: 503-224-7521; Office Phone: 503-228-6191. Business E-Mail: kennedy@kwar.com.

KENNEDY, JACK STANNERS, lawyer; b. Terre Haute, Ind., Apr. 14, 1945; BA magna cum laude, Harvard U., 1967; JD, U. Va., 1972. Bar: Conn. 1972. With Robinson & Cole LLP, Hartford, mng. ptnr., 1994-2000. Mem. editorial bd. Va. Law Review, 1970-72. Mem. ABA (sect. bus. law), Conn. Bar Assn. (past chair sect. bus. law), Order of Coif. Office: Robinson & Cole LLP 280 Trumbull St Hartford CT 06103-3597 Office Phone: 860-275-8265. E-mail: jkennedy@rc.com.

KENNEDY, JAMES ALOYSIUS CHARLES, investment company executive; Investment analyst T. Rowe Price Inc., Balt., 1978—81, v.p., 1981—87, v.p., dir. equity rsch., 1987—97, bd. dir., 1996—, v.p., dir. equity div., 1997—2006, pres., CEO, 2007—. Office: T Rowe Price Inc 100 E Pratt St Baltimore MD 21202*

KENNEDY, JAMES COX, publishing and media executive; b. Honolulu, Nov. 1947; two sons, one daughter. BBA, U. Denver, 1970; LHD (hon.), Kennesaw State Univ., 2003. With Atlanta Newspapers, 1972-79, prodn. asst., 1972-76, exec. v.p., gen. mgr., 1976-79; pres. Grand Junction Newspapers, 1979-80; pub. Grand Junction Daily Sentinel, 1980-85; v.p. Cox newspapers div. Cox Enterprises Inc., Atlanta, 1985-86, exec. v.p., 1986-87, pres., chief oper. officer, exec. v.p., 1986-87, chmn., CEO, 1988—. Hon. chmn. Tour de Cure cycling event, Am. Diabetes Assn., 1997, Ga. chapter Nat. Multiple Sclerosis Soc. Bike Tour, 1993—95; bd. mem. Ducks Unlimited, PATH Found.; pres. Wetlands Am. Trust. Named Philanthropists of the Yr. (with wife Sarah), Greater Atlanta chapter Assn. Fund-raising Professionals, 2003; named to J. Mack Robinson Coll. Bus. Hall of Fame, Ga. State Univ., 2004. Past Masters Nat., Pan-Am. & World champion, 3000 meter pursuit cycling race; capt. of four man cycling team, winning Race Across America in 1992, setting a world record, and finished 2d in 1994, setting an Am. record; named to U.S. Cycling Fedn. Master's All-American team. Mailing: Cox Enterprises Inc PO Box 105357 Atlanta GA 30348-5357 Office: Cox Enterprises 6205 Peachtree Dunwoody Rd Atlanta GA 30328*

KENNEDY, JAMES W., aerospace transportation executive; b. Riverdale, Md. m. Bernadette Kennedy; 2 children. B in Mech. Engring., Auburn Univ., Ala., 1972; MBA, Ga. So. Univ., Statesboro, 1977. With Aerospace Engring. Coop. Edn. Program NASA Kennedy Space Ctr., 1968; dep. dir. of sci. and engring. NASA George C. Marshall Space Flight Ctr., 1998—99, dir. engring. Huntsville, Ala., 1999, dep. dir., NASA Kennedy Space Ctr., Fla., 2002—03, dir. Fla., 2003—. With USAF. Recipient Astronautics Engr. of Yr. award, Nat. Space Club, 2003. Office: Dir NASA Kennedy Space Ctr Orlando FL 32899

KENNEDY, JERRIE ANN PRESTON, public relations executive; b. Quanah, Tex. Student, Sunset Sch. Preaching, Lubbock, Tex., 1975-78, Jo-Susan Modeling Sch., Nashville, 1984, Film Actors Lab., 1986. Co-prodr. Vincent Cirrincione & Assocs., NY, 1986; paralegal Arlington Career Inst., 1998—; freelance internat. mktg. and pub. rels. exec., Papua New Guinea. Military del. NATO Allies for The French Liaison, Ft. Hood, Tex., 1992, Vietnam War (Diplomatic immunity) 1972-1975. Author screenplay, fed. and cmty. pub. spl. events prodn. US Activist Women's Rights in the State of Tex., 2003. Recipient 1st and 3d pl. awards Modeling Assn. Am., NYC, 1985.

KENNEDY, JOAN PACE, school librarian, educator; b. Bogalusa, La., Dec. 1, 1945; d. Winfred Dutch and Betty Duncan Pace; m. Jay Gould Kennedy, Aug. 15, 1964; children: Juanette Ladell, Jacqueline Kennedy Williams, Justin Ben. Master's degree, Southeastern La. U., Hammond, La., 1980. Libr. sci. state cert. La., cert. prin. La. Dept. of Edn., supr. student tchg. La. Dept. of Edn., parish or city sch. supr. of instrn. La. Dept. of Edn. Tchr. grades 1-2 Wesley Ray Elem. Wash. Parish Sch. Bd., Franklinton, La., 1973—94, libr. Wesley Ray Elem., 1994—. Asst. prin. Wesley Ray Elem. Washington Parish Sch. Bd., 1999—2000. Contbr. creative writing/poetry anthology, articles to profl. jours. and newspapers (1st Pl. Poetry Divsn. award, 1992). Dir. vacation Bible sch. Stateline Bapt. Ch., Franklinton, La., 2003—05. Named Washington Parish Elem. Tchr. of the Yr., Wash. Parish Sch. Bd., 1984, Wesley Ray Elem. Tchr. of the Yr., Wesley Ray Elem., 1989, 1994; recipient WST Mini-Grant, Washington-St. Tammany Electric, 1999, 2002; grantee Bell South Mini-Grant, Bell South Tel. Co., 2001. Mem.: Internat. Reading Assn., La. Libr. Assn., Washington Parish Reading Coun. (pres. 2000—01), La. Reading Assn. (pres. 2004—05, mini-grant 2000—01, Libr. of Yr. 2001), Washington Parish Art Assn., Kappa Kappa Iota (pres. 1998—99), Delta Kappa Gamma (sec. 1999—2001). Baptist. Avocations: reading, writing, singing, camping, painting. Home: 57244 Hwy 438 Angie LA 70426 Office: Wesley Ray Elem 30523 Wesley Ray Rd Angie LA 70426 Home Phone: 985-986-2949; Office Phone: 985-986-3130.

KENNEDY, JOE DAVID, JR., (JOEY KENNEDY), editor; b. Dayton, Tex., Mar. 28, 1956; s. Joe David Sr. and Patricia Ann (Harper) K.; m. Veronica Elaine Pike, Feb. 2, 1980. BA, U. Ala., Birmingham, 1988, MA, 2003. Reporter gen. assignments Houma Daily Courier, La., 1974-76; dir. news, sports Sta. KJIN-AM/KCIL-FM, Houma, 1976-77; reporter gen. assignments Cullman Times, Ala., 1977-78; asst. sports editor Anniston Star, Ala., 1978-81; sports copy editor Birmingham News, 1981-83, asst. editor lifestyle, 1983-85, editor photography, 1985-86, Sunday editor, 1986-89, editor book revs., 1986-95, editl. writer, columnist, 1989—. Adj. prof. dept. English, U. Ala., Birmingham, 2001—. Contbr. Redbook mag., 1997, 98, Iron Horse Lit. Rev., 2004, Aura Lit. Rev., 2005. Mem. Houma-Terrebonne Bicentennial Commn., 1975-76; press sec. rep. gubernatorial candidate Guy Hunt, Ala., 1978; tutor literacy Birmingham Pub. Schs. Adult Learning Ctr., 1990-91; judge J.C. Penney Golden Rule Awards for Vols., 1992; lectr. Lee Coll. Springs Art Festival, Baytown, Tex., 1992; mem. adv. bd. Sch. Journalism, U. Miss., 1992-98, Dept. Comm. Studies U. Ala. Birmingham, 2005-; bd. dirs. So. Mus. Flight, 1992-93; mem. Leadership Birmingham Class, 1994-95, AIDS Care Team, 1994-00; bd. dirs. A Baby's Place, 1996-97, PATH Orgn. for Homeless, 1997-99, Childcare Resources, 2004-05, Bridges Found., 2006—; mem. Ct. Appointed Spl. Advocates for Children, 1996—; mem. bd. deacons Southside Bapt. Ch.; reading tutor 4th graders Birmingham Pub. Schs., 1999. Nominee Pulitzer prize, 1994, Pultizer prize, 2006; named Comm. Alumnus of Yr., U. Ala., Birmingham, 1991, One of the Top 20 Grads., 1994; recipient various awards, La. Press Assn., 1974—77, Ala. Press Assn., 1989—2001, Best Commentary award, 1992, 2000, 2004, Ala. Sportswriters Assn., 1978—81, Hector award, Troy State U., 1991, 1992, 1994, 1995, Pulitzer prize for edtl. writing, 1991, Nat. Edn. Writers Assn., 1994, Ed. Press Award, John S. Coley award as Outstanding Graduate Student, U. Ala.-Birmingham, 2003, Nat. Headliner award, 2006; scholar Howton Scholarship in Creative Writing, U. Ala.-Birmingham, 2002—03. Mem. U. Ala. Birmingham Nat. Alumni Soc. (life; bd. dirs. 1999-2004, v.p. 2002-04), Outstanding Grad. Student Sch. Arts and Humanities 2003. Avocations: civil war history, reading, writing. Home: 1635 11th Pl S Birmingham AL 35205-5907 Office: Birmingham News 2200 4th Ave N Birmingham AL 35203-3840 Office Phone: 205-325-2466. Business E-Mail: jkennedy@bhamnews.com. E-mail: joey@bham.rr.com.

KENNEDY, JOHN EDWARD, lawyer; b. Mpls., Feb. 18, 1947; s. John Edward and Margaret (Greathouse) K.; m. Linda Bagwell, June 22, 1968; children: John Harlan, Linda Elizabeth. AB cum laude, Harvard U., 1968, JD magna cum laude, 1971. Bar: Tex. 1971, US Dist. Ct. (so. dist.) Tex. 1972, US Ct. Appeals (5th cir.) 1972, US Supreme Ct. 1975, US Ct. Appeals (DC cir.) 1984. Assoc. Vinson & Elkins LLP, Houston, 1971-80, ptnr., 1980—. Served to 2d lt. USAR, 1972. Mem. ABA, Houston Bar Assn., Energy Bar Assn, Downtown Club. Presbyterian. Home: 2617 Pemberton Dr Houston TX 77005-3441 Office: Vinson & Elkins LLP 2500 First City Tower 1001 Fannin St Houston TX 77002-6760 Office Phone: 713-758-2550.

KENNEDY, JOHN HARVEY, chemistry professor; b. Oak Park, Ill., Apr. 24, 1933; s. John Harvey and Margaret Helen (Drenthe) K.; m. Joan Corinne Hipsky, June 9, 1956 (div. Mar. 1969); children: Bruce Laurence, Bryan Donald, Brent Peter, Jill Amy.; m. Victoria Jane Matthew, July 2, 1970; 1 child, Karen Anne. BS, UCLA, 1954; AM, Harvard U., 1956, PhD, 1957. Sr. research chemist E.I. du Pont de Nemours, Wilmington, Del., 1957-61; asst. prof. chemistry U. Calif., Santa Barbara, 1961-63, 67-69, assoc. prof., 1969-76, prof., 1976-93, prof. emeritus, 1993—, chmn. dept., 1982-85; assoc. prof. Boston Coll., Chestnut Hill, 1963-64; head inorganic chemistry Gen. Motors, Santa Barbara, 1964-67. Cons. Eveready Battery Co., Cleve., 1983-2000; vis. prof. U. N.C., Chapel Hill, 1980-81, Japan Soc. Promotion of Sci., Nagoya, 1974-75, Leningrad State U., 1989, China Acad. Scis., 1990. Author: Analytical Chemistry, Principles, 1990, Analytical Chemistry, Practice, 1990; contbr. articles to profl. jours.; patentee in field. Mus. dir. Christ the King Episcopal Ch., Santa Barbara, 1982-98. Mem. Am. Chem. Soc., Electrochem. Soc. Democrat. Avocation: music. Home: 5357 Agana Dr Santa Barbara CA 93111-1601 Office: U Calif Dept Chemistry Santa Barbara CA 93106 Office Phone: 805-893-2429. Personal E-mail: jvkennedy@aol.com.

KENNEDY, JOHN NEELY, state official; b. Centreville, Miss., Nov. 21, 1951; m. Becky Kennedy; 1 child. BA magna cum laude, Vanderbilt Univ., 1973; JD, Univ. Va., 1977; BCL first class honors, Oxford Univ., 1979. Spl. counsel to La. Gov., 1988—92; sec. Dept. Revenue, 1996—99; atty. to ptnr. Chaffe, McCall, Phillips, Toler and Sarpy, LLP, Baton Rouge, New Orleans; state treas. State of La., 1999—. Adj. prof. LSU Law Sch.; candidate US Senate, La., 2004; bd. dir. La. Workers' Compensation Corp. Vol. tchr.; bd. dir. Coun. for a Better La., Friends of the New Orleans Ctr. for Creative Arts. Mem.: Nat. Assn. State Treas. (so. regional v.p.), Phi Beta Kappa. Democrat. Meth. Office: State Treas 900 N Third St--Fl 3 PO Box 44154 Baton Rouge LA 70804*

KENNEDY, JOHN PATRICK, lawyer, corporate financial executive; b. Oct. 2, 1943; s. Arch R. and Kathryn R. (Delahunty) K.; children: Kathleen, Elizabeth, Christina, Patrick, Lindsay. BA in Econs., U. Kans., 1965, JD, 1967; MBA in Fin., U. Mo., 1972, LLM, 1973. Bar: Kans. 1967, Mo. 1968, Ohio 1973, Wis. 1985, U.S. Supreme Ct. 1972, U.S. Dist. Ct. (we. dist.) Mo. 1972, U.S. dist. Ct. Kans. 1967. Trial atty. Kodas, Gingerich & Stites, Kansas City, Mo., 1967-69; sr. atty. Mobay Chem. Co., Kansas City, Mo., 1969-73; gen. counsel Johnson Controls, Inc., Milw., 1984—2004, corp. sec., 1987—2004, sr. v.p., 2002—04, pres. Controls Group, 2004—. Small bus. advisor, venture capitalist. Contbr. articles to profl. jours. Served with USAR, 1967-73. Recipient Wall St. Jour. award, 1972, A. Jurisprudence awards, 1966-67. Mem. ABA, Ohio Bar Assn., Columbus Bar Assn., Wis. Bar Assn., Am. Corp. Counsel Assn. Democrat. Roman Catholic. Office: Johnson Controls Inc 5757 N Green Bay Ave PO Box 591 Milwaukee WI 53201 Office Phone: 414-228-1200.*

KENNEDY, JOHN WILLIAM, engineering company executive; b. Summit, NJ, May 20, 1956; s. William John and Jean Mary (Krutisia) Kennedy; m. Cecelia Marie Hamrock, Dec. 26, 1981; 1 child, Sean Michael. BS with honors, North Adams State Coll., 1978; MBA with honors, Columbia Pacific U., 1987, BS in Indsl. Engring., 1988; PhD in Bus. Mgmt., LaSalle U., 1996. Cert. tchr. NJ. Tchr. Mountainside Sch. Dist., NJ, 1979—82, Chatham Boro Sch. Dist., NJ, 1982—83; plant mgr. Chatham Club Recreation Ctr., 1982—85; ops. mgr. Coleman Equipment, Inc., Irvington, NJ, 1985—91; project mgr., acct. mgr. automated sorting systems div. Sandvik Process Sys., Totowa, NJ, 1991—95; gen. mgr. sales and engring. Barnett Industries, Irvington, NJ, 1995—96; pres., owner Multitech Group Inc., South Plainfield, NJ, 1996—2006; corp. v.p. TMG-Thinkpath, South Plainfield, 2006—. Plant mgr., ops. mgr., cons. Madison Cmty. Pool, NJ, 1971—87. Contbr. tech. articles to tech. publs. Active Denville area Boy Scouts Am., NJ, 1984—, chmn. dist. advancement com. NJ, 1990—95, exec. bd. NJ, 1995—, dist. oper. com. chmn. NJ, 1998—; area com. Spl. Olympics, Flanders, NJ, 1987—, event dir. Morris, Sussex and Warren counties, 1998—; exec. bd. Morris-Sussex Boy Scouts Am., 1996—; active Madison Environ. Commn., Madison Planning Bd.; trustee Park Ave. Club Found. Named Eagle Scout, Boy Scouts Am., 1970, Alumni of Yr., Mass. Coll. Liberal Arts (formerly North Adams State Coll.), 2005, Disting. Alumni Profl., Mass. Coll., 2005; named to Eagle Scout Hall of Fame, Boy Scouts Am., 1999; recipient Lifetime Achievement award, Boy Scouts Am. Patrios' Path Coun., 2001, named Disting. Eagle Scout, Boy Scouts Am., 2005. Mem.: Am. Soc. for Quality Control, Inst. Indsl. Engring., Am. Mgmt. Assn. Republican. Roman Catholic. Achievements include co-pantentee vacuum lifter, air logic weightless circuit. Avocations: camping, bicycling, racquetball, softball, coin collecting/numismatics. Home: 198 Kings Rd Madison NJ 07940-2238 Office: TMG-Thinkpath 165A Ryan St South Plainfield NJ 07080-4206 Home Phone: 973-377-0373; Office Phone: 908-753-0400. Business E-Mail: jkennedy@thinkpath.com.

KENNEDY, JOSEPH PATRICK, II, utilities executive, former congressman; b. Brighton, Mass., Sept. 24, 1952; s. Robert F. and Ethel (Skakel) K.; m. Sheila Brewster Rauch, Feb 12, 1979 (div. 1991); 2 children: Joseph Patrick III, Matthew; m. Anne Elizabeth Kelly, Oct. 23, 1993. BA, U. Mass., Boston, 1976. Founder, chmn., pres. Citizens' Energy Corp., 1979-87, 98—; mem. 100th-105th Congress from 8th Mass. dist., 1987—99; ranking minority mem. banking & fin. svcs. subcom. on housing & cmty. devel., mem. com. on vets.' affairs. Active Can. Robert F. Kennedy Meml. Democrat. Office: Citizens Enterprises Corp Ctr Lobby Ste 342 88 Black Falcon Ave Boston MA 02210-2431

KENNEDY, JOSEPH PAUL, chemist, researcher; b. Budapest, Hungary, May 18, 1928; arrived in U.S., 1956; s. Laszlo and Rosa (Farkas) Kennedy; m. Ingeborg G. Hausen, Feb. 10, 1956; children: Katherine, Cynthia, Julie. PhD, U. Vienna, Austria, 1954; MBA, Rutgers U., 1961; D (hon.), Kossuth U., Hungary, 1989. Rsch. fellow Sorbonne, U. Paris, 1955; rsch. assoc. McGill U., Montreal, Que., Canada, 1956; rsch. chemist Celanese Corp., Summit, NJ, 1957-59; sr. rsch. assoc. Esso Rsch. Engring. Co., Linden, NJ, 1959-70; prof. polymer sci. U. Akron, Ohio, 1970-80, disting. prof. polymer sci. and chemistry, 1980—. Cons. Akron Cationic Polymer Devel. Co., 1983—. Author: (book) Cationic Polymerization, 1975, Carbonca-tionic Polymerization, 1982, Designed Polymers by Carbocationic Macromolecular Engineering: Theory and Practice, 1992. Named Outstanding Rschr., Alumni Assn. U. Akron, 1979; recipient Morley award and medal, Cleve. Am. Chem. Soc., 1982, award Disting. Svc. in Sci., Soc. Polymer Sci., Japan, 2000. Mem.: Am. Chem. Soc. (Polymer Chemistry award 1985, 1995, Applied Polymer Sci. award 1995, George Stafford Whitby award 1996), Hungarian Acad. Scis. Avocation: Japanese art of the Meiji. Home: 510 Saint Andrews Dr Akron OH 44303-1228 Office: U Akron Inst Polymer Sci Akron OH 44325-0001 Home Phone: 330-972-7512; Office Phone: 330-972-7512. Business E-Mail: josep19@uakron.edu.

KENNEDY, KAMELA DENISE, director; b. Mobile, Ala., Dec. 28, 1968; d. Kamel William and Dorothy Johnson Kennedy. BA, U. Ala., Tuscaloosa, 1991; MEd, Ala. State U., Montgomery, 2004, EdS, 2006. Dist. recruiter Ala. State U., Montgomery, 1991—2002, asst. coord. student activities, 2002—. Mem.: Ala. Counseling Assn. (editor newsletter 2004—05, co-editor newsletter 2005—), Chi Sigma Iota, Am. Counseling Assn., Delta Sigma Theta (co-chair com. 2005—06, bd. mem. project fundraiser 2005—06). Office: Alabama State University 915 S Jackson

Street Montgomery AL 36195 Home Phone: 334-284-5725; Office Phone: 334-229-4888. Personal E-mail: kamelakennedy@aol.com. E-mail: kkennedy@alasu.edu.

KENNEDY, KAREN SYENCE, advertising agency executive; b. Bklyn., May 7, 1943; d. Bruno Weinschel and Pearl Heyman; first marriage: Michael Syence; children: Sherry, Scott; m. Peter Kennedy, Aug. 25, 1979. BS, Boston U., 1963. Advt. mgr. Weinschel Engring., Gaithersburg, Md., 1965-68; mktg. svcs. mgr. Rixon Electronics, Silver Spring, Md., 1968-70; pres. Comm. Unltd., Chevy Chase, Ltd., 1970-74; v.p. Ehrlich Manes & Assocs., Bethesda, Md., 1974-77; pres. Rainbow Tree, St. Croix, V.I., 1978-80; advt. programs dir. GE, McLean, Va., 1980-81; pres. Karen Syence Kennedy Assocs., Fairfax, Va., 1981-83; pres., CEO, KSK Comm., LLC, Vienna, Va., 1983—2002; ptnr. EPB Comms., NYC, 1999—2002; pres. Karen Syence Kennedy Assocs., Great Falls, Va., 2002—. Pres., chmn. Treasure Beach Found., 2000—. E-mail: ksk001@earthlink.net.

KENNEDY, KATHLEEN, film producer; b. Jan. 1, 1954; m. Frank Marshall, 1987; 2 children. BA in Telecommunications and Film, San Diego State U., 1975. Various posts including camera operator, video editor, floor dir. and news prodn. coord. KCST, San Diego; co founder (with Steven Spielberg & Frank Marshall) and pres. Amblin Entertainment, Universal City, Calif., 1984—92; co-founder (with Frank Marshall), pres., prodr. Kennedy-Marshall Co., 1994—. Pres. Producers Guild of Am., 2001—06. Assoc. prodr.: (films) Poltergeist, 1982, Twilight Zone-The Movie, 1983, Indiana Jones and the Temple of Doom, 1984, Reform School Girls, 1986; prodr.: (films) E.T. The Extra-Terrestrial, 1982 (Academy award nomination for best picture 1982); (with Quincy Jones, Frank Marshall, and Spielberg) The Color Purple, 1985 (Academy award nomination for best picture 1985); (with Marshall and Art Levinson) The Money Pit, 1986; (with Marshall and Spielberg) Empire of the Sun, 1987, Always, 1989; (with Richard Vane) Arachnophobia, 1990; (with Marshall and Gerald R. Molen) Hook, 1991; (with Robert Watts) Alive, 1993; (with Molen) Jurassic Park, 1993, (with Marshall) Milk Money, 1994; (with Clint Eastwood) The Bridges of Madison County, 1995, Twister, 1996; (with Steven Spielberg), The Six Sense, 1999, Snow Falling on Cedars, 1999, A Map of the World, 1999, Artifical Intelligence: AI, 2001, Jurassic Park III, 2001, Seabiscuit, 2003, The Young Black Stallion, 2003, War of the Worlds, 2005; exec. prodr.: (films)Roller Coaster Rabbit, 1990, A Dangerous Woman, 1993, Schindler's List, 1993 (Academy award for best picture 1993), Trail Mix-Up, 1993, A Far Off Place, 1993, Balto, 1995, Congo, 1995, The Indian in the Cupboard, 1995; (with Marshall and Spielberg) Gremlins, 1984, The Goonies, 1985, Back to the Future, 1985, Young Sherlock Holmes, 1985, *batteries not included, 1987, Jurassic Park: The Lost World, 1997, Dad, 1989, Back to the Future Part II, 1990, Gremlins 2: The New Batch, 1990, Back to the Future Part III, 1990, Joe Versus the Volcano, 1990, Cape Fear, 1991, We're Back! A Dinosaur's Story, 1993, (with Marshall) Fandango, 1985; (with Marshall, Spielberg, and David Kirschner) An American Tail, 1986; (with Marshall, Spielberg, Peter Guber, and Jon Peters) Innerspace, 1987; (with Spielberg) Who Framed Roger Rabbit, 1988; (with Marshall, Spielberg, and George Lucas) The Land Before Time, 1988; (with Marshall and Lucas) Indiana Jones and the Last Crusade, 1989; (with Marshall and Kirschner) An American Tail: Fievel Goes West, 1991; (with Peter Bogdanovich) Noises Off, 1992; (with Marshall and Molen); (with Molen, Kirschner, William Hanna, and Joseph Barbera) The Flintstones, 1994, Olympic Glory, 1999, Signs, 2002; exec. prodr. TV Tummy Trouble, 1989, The Sports Pages, 2001 Bd. dir. Michael J. Fox Found. for Parkinson's Rsch. Named one of 100 Most Powerful Women in Entertainment, Hollywood Reporter, 2006. Office: Kennedy-Marshall Co 619 Arizona Ave Santa Monica CA 90401-1358*

KENNEDY, KENNETH ADRIAN RAINE, biological and forensic anthropologist; b. Oakland, Calif., June 26, 1930; s. Walter Burkhart and Margaret Miriam (Madge) K.; m. Mary Caroline Marino, Aug. 5, 1961 (div.); m. Margaret Carrick Fairlie, Aug. 10, 1969. BA, U. Calif., Berkeley, 1953, MA, 1954, PhD, 1962. Diplomate Am. Bd. Forensic Anthropology; lic. lay reader. Instr. U. Calif., 1962-63; asst. prof. anthropology Cornell U., Ithaca, NY, 1964-68, assoc. prof., 1968—81, prof. ecology, evolutionary biology, anthropology and Asian studies, 1981—2005, prof. emeritus, 2005—. Sec. Am. Bd. Forensic Anthropology, 1999—2002; cons. forensic anthropology N.Y. State, 1964—; field rsch. in India, Pakistan, Sri Lanka, 1963—. Author 12 books; mem. editl. bd. Am. Jour. Phys. Anthropology, 1998-2001, acting editor-in-chief, 1985; field editor Am. Anthropologist, 1982-85; contbr. numerous articles to sci. jours. Guest White House state dinner reception for Pres. Sri Lanka, 1984. Sgt. U.S. Army, 1954-57. Grantee NSF, Smithsonian Instn., Howard Found., NEA, Am. Inst. Indian Studies, numerous others. Fellow AAAS (mem. electorate nominating com. in anthropology 2004—), Am. Acad. Forensic Scis. (sec.-treas. forensic anthropology sect. 1993-94, chmn. 1994-95, chmn. phys. anthropology sect. 1994-95, T. Dale Stewart award in forensic anthropology 1987); mem. Am. Anthrop. Assn. (chmn. biol. anthropology sect. 1986-88, mem. long-range planning com. 2002-2004, William W. Howells Book award 2002), Am. Assn. Phys. Anthropologists (exec. bd. 1990-96, v.p. 1994-96), Cornell Rsch. Club (pres. 1978-80, 89-90), Sigma Xi (pres. 1984-85). Episcopalian. Avocations: violin, playing in chamber music groups. Office: Cornell U Ecology & Evolutionary Bio Corson Hall Ithaca NY 14853-2701 Office Phone: 607-254-4214. Business E-Mail: kak10@cornell.edu.

KENNEDY, KEVIN W., finance company executive; BA, Hamilton Coll., 1970; MBA, Harvard Bus. Sch., 1974. Head corp. fin. Goldman Sachs Group Inc., NYC, 1988—94, head Americas Group, 1994—99, mem. exec. office, 1999—2001, exec. v.p. human capital mgmt., 2001—. Life trustee, former chmn. bd. Hamilton Coll.; mng. dir., v.p. bd. dirs. Met. Opera; trustee N.Y. Pub. Libr.; hon. trustee Chewonki Found.; bd. dirs. Wallace Found. Served Nat. Guard US Army. Office: Goldman Sachs Group Inc 85 Broad St New York NY 10004

KENNEDY, LAWRENCE ALLAN, mechanical engineering educator; b. Detroit, May 31, 1937; s. Clifford Earl and Emma Josephine (Muller) K.; m. Valaree J. Lockhart, Aug. 3, 1958; children: Joanne E., Julie A., Janet A., Raymond L., Jill M., Brian G. BS, U. Detroit, 1960; MS, Northwestern U., 1962, PhD, 1964. Registered profl. engr., N.Y. Chmn. dept., prof. mech. and aero. engring. SUNY-Buffalo, 1964-83; chmn. dept. mech. engring., prof. Ohio State U., Columbus, 1983—94, Ralph W. Kurtz disting. prof., 1992-95; prof. mech. engring. and chem. engring. U. Ill., Chgo., 2004—, prof. emeritus mech. engring., 2004—, dean coll. engring., 1994—2004, dean emeritus, 2004—, Stanley Kaplan scholar, 2002—; prof. mech. engring. Ohio State U., Columbus, 2006—. Vis. assoc. prof. mech. and aero. engring. U. Calif.-San Diego, 1968-69, VonKarman Inst., Rhode-St. Genese, Belgium, 1971-72; Goebel vis. prof. mech. and aero. engring. U. Mich., Ann Arbor, 1980-81; vis. prof. mech. & aerospace engring. Princeton U., 1993-94; cons. Cornell Aero. Lab., Buffalo, 1968-72, Tech. Adv. Service, Fort Washington, Pa., 1969— , Ashland Chem. Corp., Dublin, Ohio, 1983-90, Mech. Engring. Sci. and Application, Buffalo, 1972-83, Columbia Gas, 1987-92; vis. faculty fellow mech. and aerospace engring. Princeton U., 1994. Contbr. numerous articles on engring. to profl. jours.; editor: Progress in Astronautics and Aeros., Vol. 58, 1978, Exptl. Thermal and Fluid Scis., 1987-95; editor in chief Jour. Thermal & Fluid Scis., 1997—; assoc. editor Applied Mechanics Revs., 1985-88, Jour. Propulsion & Power, 1992-98. Recipient Ralph R. Teetor award 1984, AT&T Found. award, 1987, Ralph Coats Roe award, 1993; NATO fellow, 1971-72, NSF fellow, 1968-69, W.P. Murphy fellow, 1960-63; Agard lectr., 1971-72. Fellow AIAA, ASME, AAAS, Am. Phys. Soc.; mem. Combustion Inst., Am. Soc. Engring. Edn., Soc. Automotive Engrs. Roman Catholic. Avocations: skiing, squash, hiking, music. Office: Ohio State Univ 201 W 19th Ave Columbus OH 43210 Office Phone: 614-292-2926. Personal E-mail: lkennedy@uic.edu.

KENNEDY, LEO RAYMOND, engineering executive; b. Cleve., Dec. 29, 1942; s. Leo Raymond and Jane (Brady) K.; m. Doris Elaine Jurgens, Feb. 18, 1967; children: James Raymond, Brian Robert, Kristin Lee. BS, U.S. Mil. Acad., 1965; EdM, U. Ill., 1972; MBA, L.I. U., Greenvale, NY, 1975; grad., Army War Coll., Carlisle, Pa., 1986. Commd. 2d. lt. U.S. Army, 1965, advanced through grades to col., 1987, adc Korea, 1970; assoc. dir. admissions U.S. Mil. Acad., West Point, N.Y., 1972-75; dir. pers. mgmt. armored divsn. U.S. Army, Killeen, Tex., 1976-78, chief staff divsn. Clay Kaserne, Germany, 1980-82, comdr. battalion Colorado Springs, Colo., 1982-85, inspector gen. inf. divsn., 1985-86, dir. resource mgmt. Pentagon Washington, 1986-92; pres., CEO Kennedy & Assocs., Fairfax, Va., 1993-96; divsn. mgr. Sci. Applications Internat. Corp., McLean, Va., 1996-2000, v.p., 2000—. Acquisition budget com. Army program, Washington, 1987-92; guest spkr. fed. budgeting process, Washington, 1988-92. Decorated Legion of Merit, Bronze Star medal. Mem. AUSA, TROA (life), USAWC (life), Soc. Mil. Comptrs., Non-Commd. Officers Assn. (hon. life), NY Acad. Sci., Am. Chem. Soc., Kappa Delta Pi. Republican. Roman Catholic. Avocations: squash, racquetball, basketball, railroading.

KENNEDY, LEONARD JERVEY, telecommunications industry executive, lawyer; b. Bklyn., 1951; m. Ellen Mears Kennedy; children: Julia Anne, Emma McMath, Kimberli Kennedy. BA, Cornell U., 1974, JD, 1977. Bar: Md. 1978, DC 2000. With Venable, Batjer, & Howard, 1977—78; from mem. staff to sr. legal advisor FCC, 1980—88, 1990—91; counsel Dow, Lohnes & Albertson, P.L.L.C., Washington, 1989—90, 1991—93, ptnr., 1993—2001; sr. v.p., gen. counsel Nextel Comm. Inc., 2001—05; gen. counsel Sprint Nextel Corp., Reston, Va., 2005—. Bd. dirs. Appleseed Found., Washington, 2002—. Office: Sprint Nextel Corp 2001 Edmund Haley Dr Reston VA 20191 Business E-Mail: len.kennedy@sprint.com.

KENNEDY, LESLIE W., criminal justice educator, former dean; s. William W. and Jean Kennedy; m. Ilona Poznanski; children: Alexis, Andrea. BA, McGill U., Montreal, 1971; MA, Western Ont., 1972; PhD, Toronto U., 1975. Asst. to prof. U. Alta., Edmonton, Canada, 1975—98; prof., dean Rutgers Sch. Criminal Justice, Newark, 1998—2007; prof. Rutgers U. Sch. Criminal Justice, Newark, 2007—. Dir. Rutgers Ctr. for Study of Pub. Security, Newark. Co-author: (book) Deadly Deeds, 1993, Crime Victims in Context, 1998, When Push Comes to Shove, 1999, The Criminal Event, 4th edit., 2007, Risk Balance and Security, 2007. Grantee, Fund for NJ., 2004—06. Office: Sch Criminal Justice Rutgers Univ 123 Washington St Newark NJ 07102 Office Phone: 973-353-3331. Business E-Mail: kennedy@andromeda.rutgers.edu.

KENNEDY, LINDA MANN, neuroscience educator, researcher; b. Malden, Mass., July 29, 1939; d. Alfred William Mann and Etta May (Maglue) Stenquist; m. Richard Dearman Kennedy, Apr. 15, 1961; children: Pamela Lea, Ruth Alexander. Diploma in nursing, New England Deaconess Hosp., 1959; AB, Simmons Coll., 1975; PhD, Harvard U., 1980. RN, Mass. Staff nurse Lahey Clinic, Boston, 1959-61, various hosps., Mass., Ga., 1962-72; tchg. asst. Simmons Coll., Boston, 1972-75; vis. rsch. fellow Cornell U., Ithaca, NY, 1978-81; rsch. assoc. Worcester (Mass.) Found. Exptl. Biology, 1980-83; rsch. asst. prof. Clark U., Worcester, 1983-84, asst. prof., 1984-91, assoc. prof., 1991—, U. Mass. Med. Sch., 1995—2000. Co-founder, co-dir., dir. interdisciplinary neurosci. program Clark U., Worcester, 1984—97, chair instnl. rev. bd. for human rsch., 1997—2000, Worcester, 2002—; vis. scientist Weizmann Inst. Sci., Rehovot, Israel, 1991—92; mem. adv. panel various programs NSF, Washington, 1993—, vis. program dir. Sensory Sys. program, 2000—02; mem. study sections various programs NIH, 1988—. Mem. editl. com. Univ. Press New England, 1989-91; contbr. articles to profl. jour. Mem. conservation com. Town of Framingham, Mass., 1973-74. Recipient Grad. fellowship for women Danforth Found., 1975-79, Rsch. Svc. award NIH, 1980-83, multiple Rsch. grants NSF, NIH, 1978—. Mem. New Eng. Psychol. Assn. (hon.), Assn. Chemoreception Sci. (exec. bd. councilor 1986-88), Soc. for Neurosci., Soc. for Values in Higher Edn., European Chemoreception Orgn., Internat. Brain Rsch. Orgn. Unitarian Universalist. Avocations: swimming, classical and jazz concerts, travel, reading mysteries, opera. Home: 98 Waterford Dr Worcester MA 01602-3512 Office: Clark Univ Dept Biology Worcester MA 01610

KENNEDY, LYDIA, human resources specialist; b. 1971; BA in Psychology, U. Ariz.; M in Ednl. Leadership, No. Ariz. U., Tucson. Worked in Human Resources dept. Ariz. Daily Star, Tucson Citizen, Tucson Newspaper; tng. mgr. Casino, Sun/Casino Del Sol; dir., Human Resources dept. Buffalo Exch., Tucson, 2002—. Eller Assoc. U. Ariz. Eller Coll. of Bus. and Pub. Policy. Mem. League of United Latin Am. Citizens, 1993—; mentor Wakefield Mid. Sch.; mem., Women's Leadership Conf. Com. YWCA; mem. Ariz. Compensation survey adv. steering com., Newman Cath. Cmty. Ctr. Named one of 40 Under 40, Tucson Bus. Edge, 2006. Mem.: Am. Soc. Tng. and Devel., Soc. Human Resources Mgmt., Knights of Columbus. Office: Buffalo Exchange PO Box 40488 Tucson AZ 85717 Office Phone: 520-622-2711. Office Fax: 520-622-7015.

KENNEDY, MARC J., lawyer; b. Newburgh, NY, Mar. 2, 1945; s. Warren G. K. and Frances F. (Levinson) K.; m. Karen Karatsu; children: Kayla R., Shawna D. BA cum laude, Syracuse U., NY, 1967; JD, U. Mich., 1970. Bar: NY 1971. Assoc. Davies, Hardy, Ives & Lawther, NYC, 1971-72, London, Buttenweiser & Chalif, NYC, 1972-73, Silberfeld, Danziger & Bangser, NYC, 1973; counsel Occidental Crude Sales, Inc., NYC, 1974-75; v.p., gen. counsel Internat. Ore & Fertilizer Corp., NYC, 1975-82; asst. gen. counsel Occidental Chem. Corp., Houston, 1982; v.p., gen. counsel Occidental Chem. Agrl. Products Inc., Tampa, Fla., 1982-87; v.p., gen counsel agrl. products group Occidental Chem. Corp., Tampa, 1987-91, assoc. gen. counsel Dallas, 1991—. Faculty mentor Columbia Pacific U., Mill Valley, Calif., 1981—88. Contbr. articles to profl. jours. Mem. governing bd. Ctr. for Brain Health U. Tex. Dallas, 2001—2005; trustee Bar Harbor Festival Corp., NYC, 1974-87; bd. dirs. Am. Opera Repertory Co., 1982-85; mem. com. planned giving NY Foundling Hosp., 1977-88; Explorer post advisor Boy Scouts Am., 1976-78. Mem. ABA (vice-chmn. com. internat. law liaison young lawyers sect. 1974-75, chmn. sub-com. proposed trade barriers to the importation of products into US 1985-88, vice chmn. corp. counsel com. 1992-93, co-chmn. corp. counsel com. 1993-98), NY State Bar Assn., Assn. Corp. Counsel, Tex. Bar Assn. Office: Occidental Chem Corp PO Box 809050 Dallas TX 75380-9050

KENNEDY, MARGARET ALEXIS, law educator, researcher; d. Lynne and Gerry Kennedy. BA, U. Toronto, Can., 1986—90; LLB, U. Man., Winnipeg, Can., 1990—93; MA, U. B.C., Vancouver, Can., 1996—98, PhD, 1998—2004. Bar: B.C. 1995. Asst. prof., dept. criminal justice U. Nev., Las Vegas, 2005—. Recipient 41 Dissertation award, APA, 2003, 37 Dissertation award, 2004. Office: Univ Nevada 4505 Maryland Pky Box 5009 Las Vegas NV 89154-5009 Home Phone: 702-242-8829; Office Phone: 702-895-5122. Office Fax: 702-895-0252. Business E-Mail: alexis.kennedy@unlv.edu.

KENNEDY, MARJORIE ELLEN, librarian; b. Dauphin, Man., Can., Sept. 14, 1946; d. Stanley Harrison and Ivy Marietta (Stevens) May; m. Michael P.J. Kennedy, Apr. 3, 1980. BA, U. Sask., Regina, 1972; BLS, U. Alta., Edmonton, 1974; BEd, U. Regina, 1981. Profl. A cert. edn., Sask. Elem. sch. tchr. Indian Head (Sask) Pub. Sch., 1965-66, Elgin Sch., Weyburn, Sask., 1967-68; tchr., libr. Ctrl. Sch., Prince Albert, Sask., 1970-71; elem. sch. tchr. Vincent Massey Sch., Prince Albert, 1969-70, 72-73; children's libr. J.S. Wood br. Saskatoon (Sask.) Pub. Libr., 1974-77, asst. coord. children's svcs., 1977-79; programme head, instr. libr. tech. SIAST-Kelsey Campus, Saskatoon, 1979—. Presenter workshops on reference materials for elem. sch. librs., storytelling and libr. programming for children, 1980—; vol. dir. Children's Lit. Workshops, Sask. Libr. Assn., 1979-80; mem. organizing com. Sask. Libr. Week, Saskatoon, 1988. Mem. Vanscoy (Sask.) and Dist. Agr. Soc., 1983-95. Named to Libr. Edn. Honor Roll ALA, 1987. Mem. Can. Libr. Assn. (instl. rep. 1984—), Sask. Libr. Assn. (insl. rep. 1984—, mem. children's sect. 1982-83), Sask. Assn. Libr. Techs. (instl. rep. 1984—), Can. Club (bd. mem. 1981-84). Mem. United Ch. Can. Avocations: antique doll restoration, antiques, gardening. Office: SIAST Kelsey Campus Box 1520 Libr Info Tech Program Saskatoon SK Canada S7K 3R5 E-mail: Kennedy@siast.sk.ca.

KENNEDY, MARK ALAN, secondary school educator; b. Oklahoma City, 1951; s. Millford and Lyn (Cheaney) Kennedy. BA with honors, Calif. State U., 1978; postgrad., Western Sem., 1978-79, Fuller Sem., 1980-83; MEd, U. LaVerne, 1997. Cert. tchr., Calif. Sales mgr. Kennedy Investments, Ontario, Calif., 1980-83; regional v.p. A.L. Williams, Rancho Cucamonga, Calif., 1983-89; loan officer Funder's Mortgage Corp., Covina, Calif., 1989-90; math., social sci. tchr., lang. devel. specialist Ontario-Montclair Sch. Dist., 1990-96, San Bernardino County Cmty. Sch., 1996—, lead tchr., 1998—2000, acting prin., 1998-99. Tchg. asst. Western Sem., Portland, Oreg., 1978-79; instr. Cmty. Inst., 1979; adj. prof. tchr. edn. Chapman U., 2001-05; soccer coach DeAnza Mid. Sch., Ontario, 1990-93, core team leader, coop tchr., 1992-95, student coun. advisor, 1992-93, bilingual adv. coun., 1992-96, dist. lang. arts/social sci. trainer, 1993-94; advisor U. Calif. Riverside Honors Students' Inner City Literacy Program, 1993-95; mentor tchr. Ontario-Montclair Sch. Dist., 1994-95; cons. Inst. in Local Self Govt., Sacramento, 1994-96, Assn. Calif. Sh. Adminstrs., 1994-2002; learning styles cons., 1994—; mem. sch. attendance rev. bd., 1996-99. Author: Lessons from the Hawk, 2001, Classroom Management: The Dance of the Dolphin, 2004; contbr. articles to profl. jours. With USN, 1971-75. Named Tchr. of Yr., Inland Coun. for Social Studies, 2000, San Bernardino County Alternative Educators, 2003. Mem.: Am. Soc. Journalists and Authors, Calif. Tchrs. Assn., Phi Alpha Theta (mem. chair 1976—78). Episcopalian. Avocations: philosophy, languages, kickboxing, Kung Fu, literature. Office: Caffry N Cmty Sch 7201 N Archibald St #5 Rancho Cucamonga CA 91730 Office Phone: 909-989-5712.

KENNEDY, MARK RAYMOND, former congressman; b. Benson, Minn., Apr. 11, 1957; m. Debbie Kennedy; 4 children. BA in Acctg., St. John's U., Minn., 1979; MBA, U. Mich., 1983. CPA. Campaign worker for election of Rudy Boschwitz to US Senate, 1978; certified pub. acct. Arthur Andersen & Co., 1978—81; dir. corp. & internat. fin. The Pillsbury Co., 1983—87; sr. v.p., treas. Federated Dept. Stores Inc., Cin., 1987—92; CFO, sr. v.p. merchandising, ops. & advt. ShopKo Stores, Green Bay, Wis., 1992—94; CFO, v.p. adminstrn. Dept 56 Inc., Eden Prarie, Minn., 1995—2000; mem. US Congress from 6th Minn. dist. (formerly 2nd), 2001—07. Mem. agriculture com., transportation & infrastructure com.; subcom. gen. farm commodities, risk mngmt., conservation, credit, rural devel. and rsch., aviation, highways and transit (vice ch.), co-chmn., Minn. Rep. Party Platform Co., 1998 Founder Minn. Rough Riders Issues Forum. Recipient Friend of the Farm Bur. award, Minn. Farm Bur. Fedn., 2002. Mem.: Toastmasters, Lions. Republican. Roman Catholic.*

KENNEDY, MARY THERESA, mental health services professional; b. NYC, Dec. 4, 1940; d. Owen and Theresa B. Reilly; m. James Anthony Kennedy, Dec. 28, 1968; 1 child, James Austin. BA, St. John's U., NY, 1962; MA, St. Johns U., NY, 1964; PD, St. John's U., NY, 1968; PhD, Fordham U., NY, 1971. Asst. prof. St. John's U., Jamaica, NY, 1968—78, CUNY, NYC, 1975—87; chief psychologist Office Mental Retardation and Develop. Disabilities, NYC, 1980—; psychologist pvt. practice, 1989—; assoc. prof. CUNY, NYC, 1975—. Forensic coord. Office Mental Retardation and Develop. Disabilities, NYC, 1980—; pres. Assn. Downstate Dirs. Psychology, NYC, 1992—95. Contbr. articles to profl. jours. Recipient Outstanding Educators award, City Hall, NYC, 1972. Mem.: APA, N.Y. State Psychol. Assn., Kappa Delta Phi. Office: Dr Mary T Kennedy 217-04 Northern Blvd Bayside NY 11361 Home Phone: 718-217-2765; Office Phone: 718-631-8939.

KENNEDY, MARY VIRGINIA, retired diplomat; b. Pocatello, Idaho, Sept. 5, 1946; d. Charles Millard and Martha Lorissa (Evans) K. BA, U. Denver, 1968, MA, 1969; MAT, U. Idaho, 1971, JD, 2001. Tchr. cert. Idaho. Recreation aide ARC, South Vietnam, 1969-70; ops. officer State Dept. Ops. Ctr., Washington, 1977-78; spl. asst. amb. Philip Habib, Washington, 1979-80, Sec. State, Washington, 1980-81; econ. officer U.S. Embassy, Cairo, 1981-84; consul Am. Consulate, Adana, Turkey, 1985-88; Pearson fellow Office Cong. Bereuter Ho. Reps., 1988-89; exec. asst. Dept. Sec. State, Washington, 1989-91; dep. chief mission Dept. State U.S. Embassy, Kuwait, 1991-93; consul gen. Am. Consulate, Karachi, Pakistan, 1994-96; dean Sch. Profl. Area Studies, Fgn. Svc. Inst., 1996-98; ret., 1998. Bd. trustees Idaho State Hist. Soc., 1999—2002. Mem. Am. Fgn. Svc. Protective Assn. (bd. dirs. 1988-91), Phi Beta Kappa, Mortar Bd. Home: 5137 Admiral Way SW Seattle WA 98116 Address: PO Box 16634 Seattle WA 98116-0634 Personal E-mail: niact@aol.com.

KENNEDY, MEGAN CATHERINE, music educator; b. Johannesburg, July 16, 1963; arrived in U.S., 1997; d. Vivian Hector and Shirley Margaret Granger; m. David Mark Kennedy, Apr. 1, 1987; children: Diana, Jane, Kimberley. Student, Trinity Coll. Music, Johannesburg, 1975—80, U. South Africa, 1985—87, student, 1988; CIDESCO diploma, Stellenbosch Acad., 1984. Instr. St. Clair Coll., Windsor, Ont., Canada, 1988—89; piano tchr. Windsor, 1992—94, Maxwell Music, White Lake, Mich., 2002—05, Piano Power, West Bloomfield, Mich., 2002—; Piano pedagogue Mich. Music Ctr, Commerce, Mich., 2005—. Mem.: West Oakland Music Tchrs. Assn., Music Tchrs. Nat. Assn., Mich. Fedn. Music Clubs, Mich. Music Tchrs. Assn., Nat. Guild Piano Tchrs., Am. Coll. Musicians. Episcopalian. Avocations: gardening, walking, travel, history, log homes. Office Phone: 248-505-8684. Personal E-mail: meegieloo@yahoo.com.

KENNEDY, PARKER S., finance company executive; b. Orange, Calif. m. Sherry Kennedy; children: Donald, Katie. AB in Econs., U. So. Calif., LA, 1970; JD, U. Calif., Hastings, 1973. Assoc. Levinson & Lieberman, Beverly Hills, Calif.; sr. v.p. First Am. Title Co. of LA; various positions including v.p.-nat. sales dir. First Am., 1977—84; dir. First Am. Title, 1981—, exec. v.p., 1984-89, pres., 1989—99, chmn., 2003—; exec. v.p. First Am. Corp., 1986-93, dir., 1987—, pres., 1993—2003, chmn., CEO, 2003—. Bd. dir. Ellie Mae. Bd. dir. Fletcher Jones Found., Orange County Council, Boy Scouts of Am., Bowers Mus. Named one of Best Performing Bosses, Forbes Mag., 2003. Mem. Calif. Bar Assn., Am. Land Title Assn. (past pres.) Office: First Am Corp One First American Way Santa Ana CA 92707*

KENNEDY, PATRICIA BERRY, retired music educator; b. Alexandria, La., May 8, 1944; d. Gerald Adair and Zennia Juanita (Francis) Berry. B of Music Edn., Va. Commonwealth U., 1968, MEd, 1974. Cert. music tchr., gen., choral and instrumental, adminstrn. and supervision, Va. Tchr. choral music Colonial Hgts. (Va.) Pub. Schs., 1968-71; tchr. choral, instrumental and gen. music King William (Va.) Pub. Schs., 1972—2002; ret., 2002; bookeeper Dominion Uniserv Unit, 2002—. Coun. chair Dominion UniServ Unit, Richmond, Va., 1987-90, 91-93, 1st v.p., 1996-98; bd. dirs. Va. Edn. Assn., 1987-90, 91-93, 96-2000, 04—, ret. coun., 2002-, NEA, 2002-.

Va. Wing CAP, Civil Air Patrol, Chesterfield, Va., 1971—. Named Sr. Mem. of Yr., Civil Air Patrol Va. Wing, 1984, 2000, PTA Mem. of Yr., Hamilton-Holmes PTA, 1985, Tchr. of Yr., Acquinton Elem. Sch., 1990, 96, King William County Schs., 1990-91, Exceptional Mem. of Yr., Acquinton PTA, 1993-94, 99-2000. Mem. NEA, Va. Educators Assn. (bd. dirs.), Music Educators Nat. Conf., Va. Elem. Music Edn. Assn. (pres. 1994-96), Va. Music Educators Assn., King William Edn. Assn. (faculty rep., sec. 1992-93, pres. 1994-97), Lions Club (bd. dirs. 2020-05). Independent. Baptist. Avocation: search and rescue work. Office: Dominon UniServ Unit 8001 Franklin Farms Dr #243 Richmond VA 23229 Home: 3518 Chesdin Blvd Sutherland VA 23885-9569 E-mail: patkennedy@mindspring.com.

KENNEDY, PATRICK F., federal agency administrator, former ambassador; b. Chgo., June 22, 1949; m. Mary Elizabeth Swope. BA, Georgetown U.; diploma Sr. Seminar in Fgn. Policy. Mem. Fgn. Svc., 1973, regional adminstrv. officer Africa, 1973-74; pers. officer Bur. African Affairs US Dept. State, 1975-76, spl. asst. to under sec. for mgmt. Washington, 1977-81, supervisory gen. services. officer Paris, 1981—85, exec. dir., then dep. exec. sec., 1985-90, adminstrv. counselor Cairo, 1991-93, asst. sec. for adminstrn. Washington, 1993—2001, acting under sec. for mgmt., 1996—97, acting asst. sec. for diplomatic security, 1998, coord. reorganization of fgn. affairs agencies, 1997—2001; amb., U.S. rep. for mgmt. and reform UN, 2001—03; chief of staff Coalition Provisional Authority, Baghdad, Iraq, 2003, Transition Unit, Baghdad, Iraq, 2004; dep. dir. mgmt. Office Nat. Intelligence, Washington, 2005—. Office: Office Nat Intelligence NEOB 725 17th St Washington DC 20500

KENNEDY, PATRICK JOSEPH, congressman; b. Brighton, Mass., July 14, 1967; s. Edward M. and Joan (Bennett) Kennedy. BS in Social Sci., Providence Coll., 1991. Mem. RI State Ho. Reps., 1989—95, US Congress from 1st RI dist., 1995—, mem. appropriations com., mem. natural resources com., co-founder Native Am. Caucus. Chmn. Ho. Rules Com., 1992; del. 1988 Dem. Nat. Conv.; co-founder, co-chmn. Congl. Portuguese-Am. Caucus; mem. New Eng. Caucus, Congl. Caucus on Armenian Issues, Older Ams. Caucus, Dem. Task Force on Tax Policy, AIDS PAC Congl. adv. bd., Italian-Am. Congl. Del.; co-sponsor amendment in Older Ams. Act, Higher Edn. Accumulation Prog. Bd. dirs. RI Spl. Olympics, RI March of Dimes, Nat. Com. for Prevention of Child Abuse (RI chpt.), Big Brother RI Co-recipient Pub. Svc. award, Soc. Neuroscience, 2002; recipient Order of the Infante D. Nenrique medal, Govt. of Portugal, 1996, Human Rights award, Am. Jewish Congress, Paul E. Tsongas Meml. award, Lymphoma Rsch. Found., Congl. Honors award, Leukemia and Lymphoma Found., Helping Move Lives Forward Reintegration award, Eli Lilly & Co., 2003, Pres.'s award, Am. Psychoanalytic Assn., 2003, Alliance award, Am. Psychiat. Assn., 2003, Paul Wellstone Mental Health award, Depression and Bipolar Support Alliance, 2003. Mem. RI Lung Assn. (bd. dirs.), RI Mental Health Assn. (bd. dirs.), Friends of Ireland. Democrat. Roman Catholic. Office: US House Reps 407 Cannon House Office Bldg Washington DC 20515-3901 Office Phone: 202-225-4911. Office Fax: 202-225-3290. E-mail: patrick.kennedy@mail.house.gov.*

KENNEDY, RANDALL L., law educator; b. Columbia, SC, 1954; BA, Princeton U., 1977; grad. studies in History, Balliol Coll., Oxford U., 1977-79; JD, Yale U., 1982. Bar: DC 1983. Law clk. to Hon. J. Skelly Wright US Ct. Appeals, 1982-83; law clk. to Hon. Thurgood Marshall US Supreme Ct., 1983-84; asst. prof. law Harvard Law Sch., Cambridge, Mass., 1984—89, prof., 1989—. Author: Race, Crime, and the Law, 1997, Nigger: The Strange Career of a Troublesome Word, 2002, Interracial Intimacies: Sex, Marriage, Identity and Adoption, 2003. Named one of 100 Most Influential Lawyers, Nat. Law Jour., 2006. Office: Harvard Law Sch 1563 Massachusetts Ave Cambridge MA 02138 Office Phone: 617-495-0907. Office Fax: 617-496-4866. Business E-Mail: rkennedy@law.harvard.edu.

KENNEDY, RAOUL DION, lawyer; b. San Jose, Calif., Feb. 6, 1944; s. Ralph and Maxine (Schoemake) Kennedy; m. Patricia Ann Bilby, Feb. 11, 1967 (dec. 2005); m. Martha Shaw Nolte, Oct. 18, 2006. BA, U. Pacific, 1964; JD, U. Calif., Berkeley, 1967. Bar: Calif. 1967, U.S. Supreme Ct. 1970. Assoc. Hagar, Crosby Heafey, Roach & May, Oakland, Calif., 1969-96, Morrison & Foerster, San Francisco, 1996-99; ptnr. Skadden, Arps, Slate, Meagher & Flom LLP, San Francisco, Calif., 1999—. Co-author: California Expert Witness Guide, 1983, 2d edit., 1991. Fellow Am. Coll. Trial Lawyers, Internat. Soc. of Barristers; mem. Am. Bd. Trial Advocates, Internat. Acad. of Trial Lawyers, Am. Acad. Appellate Lawyers, Calif. Acad. Appellate Lawyers (pres. 1983-84). Home: 1701 Gough St San Francisco CA 94109-4419 Office: Skadden Arps Slate Meagher & Flom LLP Four Embarcadero Ctr San Francisco CA 94111 Office Phone: 415-984-6450. Business E-Mail: rkennedy@skadden.com.

KENNEDY, RICHARD JEROME, writer; b. Jefferson City, Mo., Dec. 23, 1932; s. Donald and Mary Louise (O'Keefe) K.; m. Lillian Elsie Nance, Aug. 3, 1960; children: Joseph Troy, Matthew Cook. BS, Portland State U., 1958. Author: (novel) Amy's Eye, 1985 (Internat. Rattenfanger Lit. prize, Fed. Republic Germany 1988), also 18 children's books including Richard Kennedy: Collected Stories, 1988 and 3 musicals, including adaptation of H.C. Andersen's The Snow Queen; inclusion of stories in: The Oxford Book of Modern Fairy Tales, 1993, The Oxford Book of Children's Stories, 1993. With USAF, 1951-54. Home and Office: 415 W Olive St Newport OR 97365-3716

KENNEDY, ROBERT, political science professor; b. Newark, Sept. 20, 1939; s. Cecil L. (Stepfather) and Maria E. (Rega) Smith; m. Vevonna M. Clark, Nov. 4, 1966; children: Shaun C., Teague C. BS, USAF Acad., Colorado Springs, Colo., 1963; MA, Georgetown U., 1964, PhD, 1978; doctorate (hon.), Bulgarian Nat. Def. Acad., 2002. With USAF, 1963-71; fgn. affairs officer U.S. Arms Control and Disarmament Agy., Washington, 1974; sr. rschr. strategic studies inst. U.S. Army War Coll., Carlisle, Pa., 1974-83, Dwight D. Eisenhower prof. nat. security studies, 1983-85; dep. comdt. NATO Def. Coll., Rome, 1985-88; prof. dept. nat. security studies U.S. Army War Coll., 1988-89; prof. sch. internat. affairs Ga. Inst. Tech., Atlanta, 1989-97, prof. Sam Nunn Sch. Internat. Affairs, 2002—. Cons. Inst. Pub. Policy Devel., Washington, 1977—78; dep. dir., co. dir. Ctr. Internat. Strategy, Tech. and Policy, Atlanta, 1990—97; dir. Marshall European Ctr. Security Studies, Garmisch, Germany, 1997—2002; mem., prof. Acad. Security, Def., and Law Enforcement, Russia. Author, editor: The Defense of the West: Strategic and European Security Issues, 1984, U.S. Policy Towards the Soviet Union: A Long Term Western Prospective 1987-2000, 1988, Alternative Conventional Defense Postures for the European Theater, Vol. I, 1990, Vol. 2, 1992, Vol. 3, 1993; mem. adv. bd. and editl. bd., U.S., Europe; contbr. articles to profl. jours.; founding gen. editor: The Atlanta Papers, 1996—2000. Acad. assoc. Atlantic Coun. U.S., 1989—97; mem. exec. com., chmn. joint chiefs staff Process Accreditation Joint Edn., Washington, 1991—97. With USAFR, 1971—86. Decorated comdr. Pres. of Romania; named Outstanding Young Men of Am., U.S. Jaycees, 1972; recipient Superior Civilian Svc. award, U.S. Army, 1989, Joint Disting. Civilian Svc. award, 2002; fellow, Georgetown U., 1974; Fulbright scholar, 1965—66, Non-Resident Sr. fellow, Atlantic Coun. U.S., 1983—84. Mem.: Atlanta Coun. Internat. Rels. So. Ctr., Internat. Studies Assn. (chmn. sect. mil. studies 1985—87), Internat. Inst. Strategic Studies. Avocations: skiing, woodworking, furniture making, water-skiing, hiking. Home: 6975 Hunters Knoll Atlanta GA 30028 Office Phone: 404-894-0682. Personal E-mail: vnbkennedy@comcast.net.

KENNEDY, ROBERT ALAN, educational administrator; b. Benson, Minn., Sept. 29, 1946; s. William Henry and Mary Rose (Pothen) K.; m. Mary Ellen Rumpho, June 9, 1984; children: Caleb, Alex, Bryce, Curran. BS, U. Minn., 1968; PhD, U. Calif., Berkeley, 1974. Asst. prof. U. Iowa, Iowa City, 1974-78; assoc. prof. to prof. Wash. State U., Pullman, 1979-85; prof., chmn. Ohio State U., Columbus, 1987; program dir. NSF, Washington, 1987-89; v.p. res. U. Md., College Park, 1989-92; v.p. rsch., assoc. provost grad. studies Tex. A&M U., College Station, 1992-2000; from exec. v.p. to pres. U. Maine, 2000—04, pres., 2004—. Contbr. articles to profl. jours. Home: Presidents House Orono ME 04469 Office: Office of the President Ste 200 5703 Alumni Hall Orono ME 04469*

KENNEDY, ROBERT EMMET, JR., historian, educator; b. NYC, Dec. 19, 1941; s. Robert Emmet and Jean (MacLeod) K.; m. Jane Marie McMahon, June 23, 1968; children: Mara, Gaëlle Marie, Daniel Patrick, Robert Emmet III. BA, Johns Hopkins U., 1963; MA, Boston Coll., 1965; PhD, Brandeis U., 1973. Instr. history Merrimack Coll., 1964-66; instr. history Kent State U., Ohio, 1968-69; asst.-associé U. Toulouse, France, 1969-73; asst. prof. European history George Washington U., Washington, 1973-77, assoc. prof., 1977-82, prof., 1982—. Co-editor: The Shaping of Modern France: Writings on French History since 1715, 1969; author: A Philosopher in the Age of Revolution: Destutt de Tracy and the Origins of Ideology, 1978, A Cultural History of the French Revolution, 1989; co-author: Theatre, Opera and Audiences in Revolutionary Paris: Analysis and Repertory, 1996, Secularism and Its Opponents from Augustine to Solszhenitsyn. Fellow Am. Council Learned Socs., 1977-78, Woodrow Wilson Internat. Ctr. for Scholars, 1983-84 Mem. Soc. French Hist. Studies, Hist. Soc. Roman Catholic. Office: George Washington Univ Dept History Washington DC 20052-0001 Office Phone: 202-994-6254. Business E-Mail: ekennedy@gwu.edu.

KENNEDY, R(OBERT) EVAN, engineering executive, consultant, retired structural engineer; b. Worland, Wyo., Mar. 31, 1916; s. Robert Eaker and Addie Miranda (Pritchard) K.; m. Betty Lou Kaser, Feb. 3, 1945; children: Anne Louise, Carter Evan, Robert Gordon. Student, Jamestown Coll., ND, 1934-35; BS in Civil Engring., U. Colo., 1938. Recorder U. S. Geol. Survey, Denver, 1938-39; jr. hydraulic engr. Colo. Water Consv. Bd., Denver, 1939-41; structural draftsman, jr. designer Am. Bridge Co., Trenton, N.J., 1941-42; stress analyst Goodyear Aircraft Corp., Akron, Ohio, 1942-44, liaison engr., group leader, sect. head Phoenix, 1944-46; sales rep. Luby-Sonnen Co., Madison, Wis., 1946; project engr. Rentenbach Engring. Co., Knoxville, Tenn., 1946-47; field mgr. Kaser Constrn. Co., West Des Moines, Iowa, 1947; design engr. Moffatt, Nichol & Taylor, Portland, Oreg., 1947-49, Cooper & Rose, Portland, 1949-51; chief structural engr. Barrett & Logan Architects, Portland, 1951-52, Edmundson, Kochendoerfer & Kennedy A/E, Portland, 1952-53, chief engr., 1954-55, ptnr., 1955-68; mng. ptnr. Edmundson, Kochendoerfer, Kennedy-Daniel, Mann, Johnson, Mendenhall, Portland, 1968-74; v.p. Daniel, Mann, Johnson and Mendenhall, Baltimore, 1974-79; assoc. Tibbets, Abbott, McCarthy and Stratton, Washington, 1980-84; pres. Kennedy Assocs., Inc., Portland, 1984—. Bd. dirs. Terwilliger Plaza, treas. 2003; chmn. Seismic Design Com., Portland, 1948-50, bd. dirs., treas. Portland Bldg. Code Revisions Com., 1950-53; observer, cons. Effects Nuclear Test U.S. Dept. Commerce, Yucca Flats, Nev., 1955; instr. Oreg. Bd. Higher Edn. Architects Registration Exams., Portland, 1954-58, Engrs. Registration Exams., 1960-63; lectr. Oreg. Dental Sch. Disaster Planning, Portland, 1960-64; mem. A/E Selection Bd. U.S. Gen. Svcs. Adminstrn. NW Divsn., Auburn, Wash., 1973, Nat. Def. Exec. res. U. S. Bur. Pub. Rds., Washington, 1964-71; bd. mem. Portland Chess & Success, 1998—; cons. Seismic Structural Design, 2005. Contbr. articles to profl. jours. Vice chmn. Fernwood Grade Sch. PTA, Portland, 1952-53, Portland Traffic Safety Commn., 1964-74; chmn. scholarship Grant H.S. Dad's Club, Portland, 1964-67; chmn. engrs. divsn. Portland United Good Neighbors, 1965, chmn. profl. divsn., 1967, 68; pres. Portland City Club, 1968; chmn. Interfaith Housing Com., Portland, 1969-73; pres. Dulaney Towers Condo Bd., Towson, Md., 1975-78, Dulaney Towers Maintenance Bd., 1976-78, Waterford Condo. Bd., Kensington, Md., 1985-88, Am. Plz. Condo. Bd., 1999, Portland Housing Devel. Corp., Portland, 1970-74, Metrohousing, Inc., Portland, 1971-74;pres. chmn. Balt. Energy Coun., 1978; mem. Portland Symphonic Choir, 1958-64, Multnomah County Bldg. Code Appeals Bd., Portland, 1964, Nat. Mcpl. League, 1968-79, nat. conv. sect. convenor, 1976, 77, Mayor's Adv. Com., Portland, 1968-69, Congressman Wendell Wyatt Re-election Com., Portland, 1968; treas. Am. Plaza Condo Assn. Bd., Portland, 1991-96; mem., elder Towson Presbyn. Ch., 1974-79. Recipient Meritorious Svc. award City Portland, 1952, Nat. Design Honor award HUD, Washington, 1976, Grand Design award Am. Consulting Engrs. Coun., Washington, 1996, Outstanding Vol. award Am. Plz. Condo, 2001; named Vol. of Yr., Terwilliger Plz., 1999. Mem. ASCE (bd. dirs. Oreg. sect. 1953-55, Capital sect. 1980-90, sec. 1983, mem. Md. sect. 1974-90, Oreg. sect. 1990—), ASTM (chmn. NW dist. 1970), Am. Concrete Inst., Soc. Am. Mil. Engrs. (Merit award Portland Post 1973), Structural Engrs. Assn. Oreg. (life; founder, pres. 1949), Profl. Engrs. Oreg. (bd. dirs. 1948-74, chmn. Conv. 100 Yrs. Engring., founder Engr. Yr. award 1952), Prestressed Concrete Inst., Engring. Coun. Rsch. Inst., Consulting Engrs. Coun. Oreg. (treas. Oreg. 1960, Engring. Excellence Project award 1996, nat. 1997; certificate life mem., founding mem. 2004), Structural Engrs. Assn. Oreg., Toastmasters. Republican. Home and Office: 2545 SW Terwilliger Blvd 1121 Portland OR 97201-6312 Office Phone: 503-299-1108. Business E-Mail: rekblkk@tplaza.org.

KENNEDY, ROBERT FRANCIS, JR., lawyer, environmentalist; b. Washington, Jan. 17, 1954; s. Robert Francis and Ethel (Skakel) Kennedy; m. Emily Ruth Black, 1982 (div. 1992); children: Robert III, Kathleen; m. Mary Richardson, Apr. 15, 1994; children: Conor, Kyra, William, Aiden Vieques. BA, Harvard U., 1977; JD, U. Va., 1982; LLM, Pace U., 1987; studied at, London Sch. Econs., 1978. Former asst. dist. atty. NYC; sr. atty. Nat. Resources Defense Coun., 1991—; chief prosecuting atty. Hudson Riverkeeper, 1993—; pres. Waterkeeper Alliance; clin. prof., supervising atty. Pace U. Sch. Law Environ. Litig. Clinic, White Plains, NY, 1999—; host Ring of Fire, Air Am. Radio, 2005—. Author: Judge Frank M. Johnson, Jr.: A Biography, 1977, Crimes Against Nature: How George Bush and His Corporate Pals Are Plundering the Country and Hijacking Our Democracy, 2004, (children's book) Saint Francis of Assisi: A Life of Joy, 2005; co-author (with David K. Gordon): The Legend of City Water: Recommendations for Rescuing the New York City Water Supply, 1991; (with John Cronin) The Riverkeepers: Two Activists Fight to Reclaim Our Environment as Basic Human Right, 1997. Avocation: white-water paddling. Office: Nat Resources Defense Coun 40 W 20th St New York NY 10011 also: Pace Law Sch 78 N Broadway White Plains NY 10603 Office Phone: 212-727-2700.

KENNEDY, ROGER GEORGE, museum program and parks director; b. St. Paul, Aug. 3, 1926; s. Walter J. and Elisabeth (Dean) K.; m. Frances Hefren, Aug. 23, 1958; 1 dau., Ruth. Grad., St. Paul Acad., 1944; BA, Yale, 1949; LL.B., U. Minn., 1952. Bar: Minn. 1952, D.C. 1953. Atty. Justice Dept., 1953; corr. NBC, 1954-57; dir. Dallas Council World Affairs, 1958; spl. asst. to sec. Dept. Labor, 1959; successively asst. v.p., v.p., chmn. exec. com., dir. Northwestern Nat. Bank St. Paul, 1959-69; v.p. finance, exec. dir. Univ. Found., Minn., 1969-70; v.p. financial affairs Ford Found., NYC, 1970-78, v.p. arts, 1978-79; dir. Nat. Mus. Am. History Smithsonian Instn., Washington, 1979-92, dir. emeritus, 1993—; dir. Nat. Park Svc., Washington, 1993-97. Spl. asst. to sec. HEW, 1957, cons. to sec., 1969 Author: Minnesota Houses, 1967, Men on a Moving Frontier, 1969, American Churches, 1982, Architecture, Men, Women and Money, 1985, Orders from France, 1989, Greek Revival America, 1989; editl. dir.: Smithsonian Guide to Historic America, 12 vols., 1989-90, Rediscovering America, 1990, Mission 1993, Hidden Cities, 1993, Burr, Jefferson, and Hamilton, 1999, Mr. Jefferson's Lost Cause, 2003, HIstoric Homes of Minnesota, 2005, Wildfire and Americans, 2006; appearances on NBC radio and TV Today, also others, 1954-57; contbr. articles to mags. and profl. jours. Served with USNR, 1944-46. Address: 3131 Connecticut Ave NW Apt 2201 Washington DC 20008

KENNEDY, RUSSELL EDWARD, academic administrator; s. Russell Eugene and Alice Louise Kennedy; m. Karen Sue Janowiak, Mar. 26, 1977 (div. Oct. 18, 1988); children: Colleen June Kennedy Frazer, Matthew David, Brian Daniel, Curtis Russell. BS in Edn., Ind. U., Bloomington, 1973; MS in Adminstrn., U. Notre Dame, Ind., 1986. Cert. Am. Soc. for Hosp. Pub. Rels. and Mktg., 1984. News anchor, prodr., reporter Marion (Ind.) Cable TV, Inc., 1973; news reporter, announcer WGOM-AM/WMRI-FM, Marion, 1973—74; news anchor, prodr., reporter WNDU AM-FM-TV, South Bend, Ind., 1974—77, asst. news dir., 1977—80; cmty. rels. mgr. St. Joseph's Med. Ctr., South Bend, 1980—84, dir. cmty. rels., 1984—85, dir. mktg., 1985—86; dir. market comm. St. Joseph's Care Group, South Bend, 1986—89; adj. faculty, pub. speaking and radio news Ind. U., South Bend, 1989—91; dir. edn. Oaklawn Cmty. Mental Health Ctr. and Hosp., Elkhart/Goshen, Ind., 1989—93; mktg. dir. CPC Valle Vista Hosp., Greenwood, Ind., 1993—94; pvt. practice mktg. cons. Indpls., 1994—95; dir. edn. and pub. affairs Mental Health Assn. in Marion County, Indpls., 1995—98; media specialist Media Wise, Indpls., 1998—2000; gen. edn. instr. ITT Tech. Inst., Indpls., 2000—01, assoc. dean, 2001—. Chair nat. membership com. Soc. Profl. Journalists, 1979—80; pres. Michiana Chpt., Soc. Profl. Journalists, South Bend, 1979—80, South Bend Press Club, 1982—83, Ind. Soc. for Healthcare Pub. Rels. and Mktg., 1988—89; mem. coun. on pub. rels. Ind. Hosp. Assn., 1988. Contbr. articles to profl. jours. Chair of one of six pilot sites nationally for anxiety disorders edn. program NIMH, Washington, 1996—98; mem., subcommittee on outreach, edn., and communication Ind. Governor's Adv. Panel on Children's Health Ins., 1998; mem., cmty. adv. com., Marion County cmty. health assessment project Marion County Dept. of Pub. Health, Indpls., 1996; selected by u. adminstrn. to serve on 14-mem. student bd. Ind. U. Meml. Union, Bloomington, Ind., 1971—72. Recipient CASPER Award for Campaign on Clin. Depression, United Way Ctrl. Ind., 1998; Hoosier Scholar, State Ind., 1969. Mem.: Alpha Epsilon Rho, Phi Delta Kappa Internat. Office: ITT Tech Inst 9511 Angola Ct Indianapolis IN 46268

KENNEDY, STEPHEN DANDRIDGE, economist, researcher; b. NYC, Feb. 25, 1942; s. Joseph Conrad and Frances (Midlam) K.; m. Joanna Court Bartlett, Nov. 27, 1965; children: Julia Paca, Benjamin Bartlett. AB, Harvard U., 1963; PhD, MIT, 1972. Mem. staff com. on banking and currency U.S. Ho. of Reps., Washington, 1964-66; adminstrv. asst. The Fed. Home Loan Bank Bd., Washington, 1966-67; analyst Abt Assocs., Inc., Cambridge, Mass., 1970, v.p., 1975, chief scientist, 1988—. Adj. lectr. John F. Kennedy Sch. Govt., Harvard U., 1995. Bd. trustees The Commonwealth Sch., 1997—2002. Episcopalian. Avocations: gardening, sailing. Office: ABT Assocs Inc 55 Wheeler St Cambridge MA 02138-1192

KENNEDY, SUSAN ORPHA, physical education educator, consultant, sports official; b. Torrington, Conn., June 1, 1951; d. Sidney Robinson Jr. and Dorothy Rose (Deering) K. BS in Phys. Edn., Ithaca Coll., 1973; MS in Phys. Edn., U. Oreg., 1978; PhD in Phys. Edn., Tex. Woman's U., 1991. Cert. K-2 tchr., N.Y. Tchr., coach Regional Dist. #1, Housatonic Valley Regional H.S., Falls Village, Conn., 1973-76; grad. teaching fellow U. Oreg., Eugene, 1976-78; substitute tchr., girls basketball coach Lake County Sch. Dist. #7, Lakeview, Oreg., 1978-80; instr., coach, athletic trainer Chadron (Nebr.) State Coll., 1980-84; rsch. asst. Tex. Woman's U., Denton, 1984-86, 88-89. Adj. faculty, U. North Tex., Denton, 1988-90. Author: (video) Prevention and Care of Athletic Injuries: Taping Techniques, 1984; coord.: (puppet show) Kids on the Block, Tex. Woman's U., 1985-86.; contbr. articles to profl. jours. Sectional ofcl., 1992—; basketball ofcl., 1970-78, 1991-2000; ofcl. U.S. Field Hockey Assn.; nat. ofcl. U.S. Women's Lacrosse Assn., 1992—; bd. dirs. Conn. Field Hockey Ofcls., 1995—, sec., 1995-2004, rules interpreter, 2003—; vol. Conn. Vols. Svcs. for Visually and Physically Handicapped, 1992-2002, rec. sec., 1999-2000; chair Inland Wetlands Commn., Litchfield, Conn. 1998-05 Named to New Agenda: N.E. Women's Hall of Fame, 2005; recipient Outstanding Official, Conn. Field Hockey Coaches Assn., 2001, Vol. of Yr., Nutmeg State Games, 2000, Ofcl. of Yr., 2000; scholar Acad. All-Am., 1987, All-Am., U.S. Achievement Acad., 1989, 1991. Mem. AAHPERD, Nat. Athlete Trainers Assn., Am. Coll. Sports Medicine, Nat. Assn. Sport Ofcls., Conn. Interscholastic Athletic Conf. Avocations: sea kayaking, weight training, officiating, environmental science issues, raising orchids. Home and Office: PO Box 1426 266 Norfolk Rd Litchfield CT 06759-2517

KENNEDY, TED (EDWARD MOORE KENNEDY), senator; b. Boston, Feb. 22, 1932; s. Joseph Patrick and Rose (Fitzgerald) K.; m. Joan Kennedy, Nov. 30, 1958 (div. Dec. 6, 1982); children: Kara Anne, Edward Moore Jr., Patrick Joseph; m. Victoria Anne Reggie, July 3, 1992. AB, Harvard U., Cambridge, Mass., 1956; postgrad., Internat. Law Sch., The Hague, Netherlands, 1958; LLB, U. Va., Charlottesville, 1959. Bar: Mass. 1959, US Supreme Ct. 1963. Asst. dist. atty., Suffolk County, Mass., 1961-62; US Senator from Mass., 1962—; chmn. Health, Edn., Labor and Pensions Com.; mem. Judiciary, Armed Svcs. and Joint Econ. Coms.; mem. Dem. Steering & Outreach Com., Nat. Security Working Group. Author: Decisions for a Decade, 1968, In Critical Condition: The Crisis in America's Health Care, 1972, Our Day and Generation, 1979, American Back on Track, 2006, My Senator and Me, 2006; co-author: (with Mark O. Hatfield) Freeze: How You Can Help Prevent Nuclear War, 1979. Trustee John F. Kennedy Ctr. for Performing Arts. Served with AUS, 1951-53. Named One of 10 Outstanding Young Men, US Jaycees, 1967. Fellow Am. Acad. Arts and Sci. Democrat. Office: US Senate 317 Russell Senate Bldg Washington DC 20510-0001 Office Phone: 202-224-4543. Business E-Mail: senator@kennedy.senate.gov.

KENNEDY, THOMAS J., lawyer; b. Milw., July 29, 1947; s. Frank Philip and June Marian (Smith) K.; m. Cathy Ann Cohen, Nov. 24, 1978; children: Abby, Sarah. BA, U. Wis., 1969, JD cum laude, 1972. Bar: Wis. 1972, U.S. Dist. Ct. (ea. and we. dists.) Wis. 1972, Ariz. 1981, U.S. Dist. Ct. Ariz. 1981, U.S. Ct. Appeals (7th cir.) 1980, U.S. Ct. Appeals (9th cir.) 1981, U.S. Ct. Appeals (D.C. cir.) 1983, U.S. Supreme Ct. 1984, U.S. Ct. Appeals (11th cir.) 1986. Assoc. Goldberg, Previant, Milw., 1972-79, Brynelson, Herrick, Madison, Wis., 1979-81; ptnr. Snell & Wilmer, Phoenix, 1981-93, Lewis and Roca, Phoenix, 1993-96, Ryley, Carlock and Applewhite, Phoenix, 1996-99, Gallagher & Kennedy, 1999—2000, Sherman & Howard, 2000—. Contbg. editor The Developing Labor Laws, 2d, 3d edits., The Fair Labor Standards Act. Mem. ABA, Ariz. State Bar, State Bar Wis., Maricopa County Bar Assn. Avocations: tennis, reading, hiking. Office Phone: 602-636-2015. Business E-Mail: tkennedy@sah.com.

KENNEDY, THOMAS PATRICK, financial executive; b. NYC, Oct. 13, 1932; s. Andrew Francis and Marie P. (Scullen) K.; m. Mary P. Drennan, Jan. 14, 1956 (dec.); children: Thomas Patrick, Kevin M. (dec.), Michael J., Mary P. Kennedy Handsman, Deborah A. Kennedy Carter. BS, St. Peter's Coll., 1958; postgrad., Seton Hall U., 1959. Acct. Haskins & Sells CPAs, NYC, 1953-54, 1955—57; staff Emerson Radio & TV, NYC, 1957-58; various exec. positions CBS, NYC, 1958-67; with Ford Found., NYC, 1967; dir. fin. Pub. Broadcasting Lab., NYC, 1967-69; with Children's TV Workshop (Sesame St.), NYC, 1969-80, CFO, v.p. fin. and adminstrn., 1969-78, treas., 1969-78, sr. v.p., 1978-80; exec. dir. Ctr. Non-Broadcast TV, 1980-85; pres. Tomken Mgmt., Ltd., 1980—, chmn. bd., 1983—; chmn. bd., CEO, Effie Techs., Inc., 1984—. V.p., corp. fin. Jersey Capital

Mkts Group, Inc., 1987-88; chief exec. officer, chmn. bd. Corp. Strategies Group, Inc., 1988-89; v.p. Vantage Securities, Inc. (co-venture with Whitehall Fin. Group), 1991-94; cons. in field; bd. advisers Franciscan Comm. Ctr.; bd. dirs., exec. dir. Ctr. for Non-Broadcast TV, 1980-85; ptnr. Hunter Village Estates Realty; officer, dir. Hunter Village Country Club Estates, Inc. With C.E., U.S. Army, 1954-55, Korea. Mem. Fin. Execs. Inst., Internat. Radio and TV Soc., Inst. Broadcast Fin. Mgmt., Nat. Assn. Accts., Internat. Broadcast Inst., Internat. Inst. Comm., Internat. Assn. Fin. Execs., Am. Assn. Individual Investors, Am. Legion, Korean War Vets., Brevard Vets. Council, Vets. Fgn. Wars, N.Y. Athletic Club, Knights of Columbus. Republican. Roman Catholic. Home and Office: 420 E 54th St Apt 16A New York NY 10022 Office Phone: 212-980-6845.

KENNEDY, WILBERT KEITH, SR., agronomy educator, retired university official; b. Vancouver, Wash., Jan. 4, 1919; s. Wilbert Parsons and Gracie Evelyn (Woolf) K.; m. Barbara Josephine Barber, Dec. 9, 1941 (dec. Nov. 1999); children: Wilbert Keith, James Clayton. BS, Wash. State U., 1940; MS in Agr., Cornell U., 1941, PhD, 1947. Asst. prof., asst. agronomist Wash. State Coll., 1947-48, assoc. prof., assoc. agronomist, 1948-49; prof. agronomy Cornell U., Ithaca, N.Y., 1949—; assoc. dir. research N.Y. State Coll. Agr., Cornell U.; also assoc. dir. Cornell U. Agr. Exptl. Sta., 1959, dir. research and dir. expt. sta., 1959-65; assoc. dean N.Y. State Coll. Agr., 1965-67, vice provost univ., 1967-72, dean, 1972-78, provost univ., 1978-84, provost emeritus, 1984—; with Atlantic Philantropic Svc. Co., Ithaca, 1988—. Cons. Rockefeller Found., Kasetsart U., Thailand, 1968, Ford Found., Malaysia, 1970 Contbr. articles to profl. jours. Mem. sch. bd., Dryden, N.Y., 1953-55; exec. com. Louis Agassiz council Boy Scouts Am., 1955-70; active local Community Chest; bd. dirs. Tompkins Community Hosp., 1984-94, pres., 1986-88. Served to maj. AUS, 1942-46. Guggenheim fellow; Fulbright scholar, 1956-57; recipient N.Y. Farmers award, 1958, Merit Cert. award Am. Grassland Council, 1964 Fellow AAAS, Am. Soc. Agronomy; mem. Sigma Xi, Phi Kappa Phi, Alpha Zeta. Home: 223 Savage Farm Dr Ithaca NY 14850-6506

KENNEDY, W(ILBERT) KEITH, JR., retired electronics executive, transportation executive; b. Phoenix, Sept. 19, 1943; BSEE, MS, Cornell U., 1966, PhD, 1968. Researcher microwave solid-state devices Cornell U. and RCA Rsch. Labs., Princeton, NJ, 1964-68; researcher, leader devel. team thin-film fabrication facility Watkins-Johnson Co., Palo Alto, Calif., 1968-71, head R & D devel. dept., 1971-74, solid state div. mgr., 1974-78, also v.p., 1977, devices group v.p., 1978-86, v.p. shareowner rels. and planning coord., 1986-88, co. pres., chief exec. officer, 1988—2000; vice chmn. CNF, San Mateo, Calif., 2002—04; chmn. Con-Way, Inc., San Mateo, Calif., 2004—. Contbr. articles to profl. jours. and procs. Patentee microwave power generator. Bd. dir. & past chmn. Joint Venture: Silicon Valley Network; bd. dir. Lytton Gardens. Mem. IEEE (sr.); mem. Group Electronic Devices of IEEE, Group Microwave Theory and Techs. of IEEE, Calif. C. of C. (bd. dirs.), Phi Eta Sigma, Eta Kappa Nu, Tau Beta Phi, Phi Kappa Phi, Sigma Xi. Office: Con-way Inc 2855 Campus Dr Ste 300 San Mateo CA 94403-2512*

KENNEDY, WILLIAM JOSEPH, novelist, educator; b. Albany, NY, Jan. 16, 1928; s. William Joseph and Mary Elizabeth (McDonald) K.; m. Dana Daisy Segarra, Jan. 31, 1957; children: Dana Elizabeth, Katherine Anne, Brendan Christopher. BA, Siena Coll., 1949; LHD (hon.), Russell Sage Coll., 1980; ArtsD (hon.), Rensselaer Poly. Inst., 1987, LHD (hon.), 1987, L.I. U., 1989, Fordham U., 1992, Trinity Coll., 1998; Notre Dame, 2001, DePaul U., 2002, St. Lawrence U., 2005; LittD (hon.), Siena Coll., 1984, Coll. St. Rose, 1985. Asst. sports editor, columnist Glens Falls Post Star, N.Y., 1949-50; reporter Albany Times-Union, N.Y., 1952-56, spl. writer N.Y., 1963-70; asst. mng. editor, columnist P.R. World Jour., San Juan, 1956; reporter Miami Herald, Fla., 1957; corr. Time-Life Publs. in P.R., 1957-59; founding mng. editor San Juan Star, 1959-61; lectr. SUNY, Albany, 1974-82, prof. English, 1983—. Vis. prof. Cornell U., Ithaca, N.Y., 1982-83; founder N.Y. State Writers Inst., 1983. Author: (book) The Ink Truck, 1969, Legs, 1975, Billy Phelan's Greatest Game, 1978, O Albany, 1983, Ironweed, 1983 (Pulitzer prize, 1984, Nat. Book Critics Circle award, 1984, film script, 1987), Quinn's Book, 1988, Very Old Bones, 1992, Riding the Yellow Trolley Car, 1993, The Flaming Corsage, 1996, Roscoe, 2002, (film script with Francis Ford Coppola) The Cotton Club, 1984, (children's books with Brendan Christopher Kennedy) Charlie Malarkey and the Belly Button Machine, 1986, Charlie Marlarkey and the Singing Moose, 1994, (play) Grand View, 1996. Served U.S. Army, 1950-52. Recipient Creative Arts award Brandeis U., 1986, Gov. N.Y. Arts award, 1984, Comdr. Order of Arts and Letters, France, 1993; MacArthur Found. fellow, 1983, Nat. Endowment of the Arts fellow, 1981. Mem.: Am. Acad. Arts and Scis., Acad. Motion Picture Arts and Scis., Am. Acad. Arts and Letters. Office: NYS Writers Inst U Albany 1400 Washington Ave Albany NY 12222-0100

KENNEDY, X.J. (JOSEPH KENNEDY), writer; b. Dover, NJ, Aug. 21, 1929; s. Joseph Francis and Agnes (Rauter) K.; m. Dorothy Mintzlaff, 1962; children: Kathleen, David, Matthew, Daniel, Joshua. BSc, Seton Hall U., 1950; MA, Columbia U., 1951; cert., U. Paris, France, 1956; LHD (hon.), Lawrence U., 1988; DFA (hon.), Adelphi U., 1998; DLitt (hon.), Westfield State Coll., 2002. Teaching fellow U. Mich., Ann Arbor, 1956—60, instr. English, 1960-62; lectr. English Woman's Coll., U. NC, Greensboro, 1962-63; asst. prof. English Tufts U., Medford, Mass., 1963-67, assoc. prof., 1967-73, prof., 1973-79. Vis. lectr. Wellesley Coll., 1964, U. Calif., Irvine, 1966—67. Author: Nude Descending a Staircase, 1961, 2d edit., 1994, Introduction To Poetry, 1966, 12th edit., (with Dana Gioia) 2007, Growing into Love, 1969, Breaking and Entering, 1971, Emily Dickinson in Southern California, 1974, Celebrations After the Death of John Brennan, 1974, (with J.E. Camp, Keith Waldrop) Three Tenors, One Vehicle, 1975, One Winter Night in August, 1975, Introduction to Fiction, 1976, (with Dana Gioia) 10th edit., 2007, Literature, 1976, (with Dana Gioia) 10th edit., 2007, The Phantom Ice Cream Man, 1979, (with Dorothy M. Kennedy) The Bedford Reader, 1982, (with Dorothy M. Kennedy and Jane Aaron) 9th edit., 2006, Did Adam Name the Vinegarroon?, 1982, French Leave: Translations, 1983, Hangover Mass, 1984, (with Dorothy M. Kennedy) Knock at a Star: a Child's Introduction to Poetry, 1982, revised edit., 1999, The Owlstone Crown, 1983, 2nd edit., 2005, The Forgetful Wishing-Well, 1985, Cross Ties: Selected Poems, 1985, Brats, 1986; (with Dorothy M. Kennedy) The Bedford Guide for College Writers, 1987, 7th edit., (with Dorothy M. Kennedy, Sylvia A. Holladay and Marcia F. Muth) 2005, Ghastlies, Goops and Pincushions, 1989, Fresh Brats, 1990, Winter Thunder, 1990, The Kite That Braved Old Orchard Beach., 1991, (with Dorothy M. Kennedy) Talking Like the Rain, 1992, The Beasts of Bethlehem, 1992, Dark Horses: New Poems, 1992, Drat These Brats!, 1993, The Minimus Poems, 1996, Uncle Switch, 1997, The Eagle as Wide as the World, 1997, Elympics, 1999, Elefantina's Dream, 2002, Exploding Gravy, 2002, The Lords of Misrule: Poems, 1992-2001, 2002, The Seven Deadly Virtues, 2005, (with Dana Gioia and Mark Bauerlein) Handbook of Literary Terms, 2005, In a Prominent Bar in Secaucus: New and Selected Poems, 1955-2007, Peeping Tom's Cabin: Comic Verse, 2007; translator: Lysistrata in Penn Greek Drama Series, 1999; poetry editor: Paris Rev., 1961-64; editor: (with J.E. Camp) Mark Twain's Frontier, 1963, (with J.E. Camp, Keith Waldrop) Pegasus Descending, 1971, 2nd edit. 2003, Messages, 1973, Tygers of Wrath: poems of hate, anger and invective, 1981, (with Dorothy M. Kennedy) Knee-Deep in Blazing Snow: Poems by James Hayford, 2005; editor, pub. (with Dorothy M. Kennedy) Counter/Measures mag, 1971-74. Judge Nat. Coun. on Arts poetry book selections, 1969, 70, T.S. Eliot prize Thomas Jefferson Univ. Press, 1998, X.J. Kennedy poetry award Tex. Rev., 1998, 90, 2000. With USN, 1951-55. Recipient Lamont Poetry award Acad. Am. Poets, Bess Hokin prize Poetry mag., 1961; Golden Rose award New Eng. Poetry Club, 1974; Los Angeles Times book award for poetry, 1985, Michael Braude award for light verse Am. Acad. and Inst. Arts and Letters, 1989, Aiken-Taylor award U. of the South, 1999, Excellence of Poetry for Children award, Nat. Coun. Tchrs. of English, 2000, The Poets' prize, 2004; grant Nat. Council Arts and Humanities, 1967-68; Shelley Meml. award, 1970; Bread Loaf fellow in poetry Middlebury Coll., 1960; Guggenheim fellow, 1973-74; Bruern fellow in Am. civilization U. Leeds, 1974-75. Mem. Assn. Lit. Scholars and Critics, John Barton Wolgamot Soc., PEN (mem. coun. New Eng. 1996—), MLA, Poetry Soc. Am., Nat. Coun. Tchrs. English, Authors Guild, Phi Beta Kappa, Sigma Tau Delta (hon.). Home: 22 Revere St Lexington MA 02420-4424

KENNEL, CHARLES FREDERICK, atmospheric physics professor, academic administrator, government official; b. Cambridge, Mass., Aug. 20, 1939; s. Archie Clarence and Elizabeth Ann (Fitzpatrick) K.; m. Ellen Lehman; children: Matthew Bochner, Sarah Alexandra. AB, Harvard U., 1959; PhD in Astrophys. Scis., Princeton U., 1964; DSc (hon.), U. Ala., Huntsville, 2003. Prin. rsch. scientist Avco-Everett Rsch. Lab., Mass., 1960-61, 64-67; vis. scientist Internat. Ctr. Theoretical Physics, Trieste, Italy, 1965; faculty UCLA, 1967-71, prof. physics, 1971-98, chmn. dept., 1983-86, exec. vice-chancellor, 1996-98; mem. Inst. Geophysics and Planetary Physics, 1972-98, acting assoc. dir. inst., 1976-77; space sci. bd. NRC, 1977-80, chmn. com. space physics, 1977-80; Fairchild prof. Calif. Inst. Tech., 1987; assoc. adminstr. NASA, Washington, 1994-96; vice-chancellor, dir. Scripps Inst. Oceanography U. Calif.-San Diego, La Jolla, 1998—2006, founding dir. environment and sustainablility initiative, 2005—, disting. prof. atmospheric scis., 2006—. Space and earth scis. adv. com. NASA, 1986—89, adv. coun., 1998—2006, chmn., 2001—05; bd. physics and astronomy NRC, 1987—94, chmn., 1992—94, chmn. fusion sci. adv. com., 1998—2001, chmn. com. on global change rsch., 1999—2002, chmn. plasma sci., 1990; chmn. Partnership for the Observation of the Global Oceans, 1999—2002; co-chair Beyond Einstein Program adv. com. NRC, 2006—; fusion policy adv. com. DOE, 1990; Fulbright lectr., Brazil; visitor U.S.-USSR Acads. Exch., 1988—90; disting. vis. prof. U. Alaska, 1988—93; mem. Pew Oceans Commn., 2000—03; vis. scholar U. Cambridge, England, 2007, Christ Coll., Cambridge, 2007; cons. in field. Co-author: Matter in Motion, The Spirit and Evolution of Physics, 1977; co-editor: Solar System Plasma Physics, 1978. Bd. dirs. L.A. Jr. Ballet Co., 1977-83, pres., 1979-80; bd. dirs. Inst. for Theoretical Physics, Santa Barbara, Calif., 1986-90, San Diego Nat. History Mus., 1998-2002, Calif. Climate Action Registry, 2002-05; bd. dirs. Calif. Ocean Sci. Trust, 2002-06. Nat. scholar Harvard U., 1959, W.C. Peyton Advanced fellow, 1962-63, NSF postdoctoral fellow, 1965-66, Sloan fellow, 1968-70, Fulbright scholar, 1985, Guggenheim fellow, 1987; recipient Aurelio Peccei prize Acad. Lincei, 1995, Hannes Alfven prize European Geophys. Soc., 1998, Disting. Svc. medal NASA, 1996, Disting. Pub. Svc. medal NASA, 2006; named CP Snow Lectr., U. Cambridge, 2007. Fellow: AAAS, Am. Phys. Soc. (pres. divsn. plasma physics 1989, James Clerk Maxwell prize 1997), Am. Geophys. Union; mem.: NAS, Am. Philos. Soc., Calif. Coun. on Sci. and Tech., Internat. Acad. Astronautics, Am. Acad. Arts and Scis. Office: U Calif San Diego SIO/DO 9500 Gilman Dr La Jolla CA 92093-0210 Business E-Mail: ckennel@ucsd.edu.

KENNEL, RICHARD WAYNE, recording industry executive, consultant, small business owner, treasurer, finance company executive; b. Ft. Wayne, Ind., Aug. 11, 1952; s. John Charles and Betty June (Miller) K.; m. Leah Marie Waybright, Aug. 1, 1976. Student, Ind. U., Ft. Wayne, 1970—71, James Madison U., 1974. Rec. artist (bassist) Arista Records/Happy the Man, Reston, Va., 1974-79; rec. studio owner, prodr., bus. mgr. The Inner Circle, White Plains, NY, 1984-96; bus. mgr. Inner Workings, Briarcliff Manor, NY, 1996—2006; CFO Great No. Arts, Briarcliff Manor, 1990—2005, Invasion Group Ltd., Briarcliff Manor, 1990—, July 4th Music, Inc., Briarcliff Manor, 1990—, Castle Hill Pub. Ltd., Briarcliff Manor, 1990—, United for Opportunity, Inc., Briarcliff Manor, 2004—; treas. Happy the Man Inc., 1999—; co-owner Innermost Music, 1999—, Innertainment, Briarcliff Manor, 2000—; founder, dir. Indie Fin. Network, Briarcliff Manor, 2006—. Albums include Happy the Man, 1977, reissued, 1999, Crafty Hands, 1978, reissued, 1999, Better Late, 1983, Retrospective, 1989, Beginnings, 1990, Past, Present, Future, 1991, Happy the Man Live, 1994, Death's Crown, 1999, Beauty Gone Wild, 2001, The Muse Awakens, 2004, After the Storm, 2006. Served with US Army, 1971-73, 94th Mil. Police Battalion Kaiserslautern, Germany. Mem. ASCAP, Audio Engring. Soc., Am. Fedn. Musicians, NARAS. Avocations: travel, computers, reading, football, basketball. Office: 522 N State Rd Ste 102 Briarcliff Manor NY 10510-1540 Office Phone: 914-762-2238. Business E-Mail: rick@indiefinancialnetwork.com.

KENNELLY, BARBARA B., retired congressman, federal agency administrator; b. Hartford, Conn., July 10, 1936; d. John Moran and Barbara (Leary) Bailey; m. James J. Kennelly, Sept. 26, 1959 (dec. 1995); children: Eleanor Bride, Barbara Leary, Louise Moran, John Bailey. BA in Econs, Trinity Coll., Washington, 1958; grad., Harvard-Radcliffe Sch. Bus. Adminstrn., 1959; MA in Govt, Trinity Coll., Hartford, 1971. Mem. Hartford Ct. of Common Council, 1975-79; sec. of state State of Conn., Hartford, 1979-83; mem. 98th-105th Congresses from 1st Dist. Conn., Hartford, 1982-98; mem. ways and means com.; counselor, assoc. commr. Social Security Adminstrn., 1999-2000; sr. adv. Baker & Hostetler, Washington; currently pres. & CEO Nat. Com. to Preserve Social Sec. & Medicare. Trustee Trinity Coll., Hartford, Conn.; active in numerous polit., civic, and goft. orgns. Greater Hartford, Conn.; co-chair Ctr. for Democracy, Washington. Democrat. Roman Catholic. Office: Natl Com Preserve Social Security & Medicare 10 G St NE Ste 600 Washington DC 20004

KENNELLY, DENNIS L., lawyer; b. Jersey City, July 23, 1948; s. Lawrence William and Florence (Taylor) Kennelly; m. Anne Marie Gilles, Jan. 14, 1978; children: Margaret Anne, Maureen Elizabeth. AB cum laude, Coll. of Holy Cross, 1970; JD, Duke U., 1973. Bar: Iowa 1973, Hawaii 1974, Calif. 1975, US Supreme Ct. 1997. Labor rels. mgr., counsel San Francisco Newspaper Agy. (Chronicle/Examiner), 1976—79; dir. employee rels., labor counsel Peninsula Times Tribune, Palo Alto, 1979—85; prin. Dennis L. Kennelly Law Office, Menlo Park, 1985—. Lt. JAGC USNR, 1973—76. Republican. Roman Catholic. Avocations: golf, sports, basketball. Office: 1030 Curtis St Ste 200 Menlo Park CA 94025-4501 Office Phone: 650-853-1291. E-mail: secretarymim@aol.com.

KENNELLY, SISTER KAREN MARGARET, church administrator, nun, retired academic administrator; b. Graceville, Minn., Aug. 4, 1933; d. Walter John Kennelly and Clara Stella Eastman. BA, Coll. St. Catherine, St. Paul, 1956; MA, Cath. U. Am., 1958; PhD, U. Calif., Berkeley, 1962. Joined Sisters of St. Joseph of Carondelet, Roman Cath. Ch., 1954. Prof. history Coll. St. Catherine, 1962-71, acad. dean, 1971-79; exec. dir. Nat. Fedn. Carondelet Colls., 1979-82; province dir. Sisters of St. Joseph of Carondelet, St. Paul, 1982-88; pres. Mt. St. Mary's Coll., LA, 1989-2000, pres. emerita, 2000—; congl. dir. Sisters of St. Joseph of Carondelet, St. Louis, 2002—. Cons. N. Ctrl. Accreditation Assn., Chgo., 1974—84, Ohio Bd. Regents, Columbus, 1983—89; trustee colls., hosps., Minn., Mo., Wis., Calif., 1972—; chmn. Sisters St. Joseph Coll. Consortium, 1979—82. Editor, co-author: Am. Cath. Women, 1989; author (with others): Women of Minnesota, 1977; author: Women Religious and the Intellectual Life: The North American Achievement, 1996; co-editor: Gender Identities in American Catholicism, 2001;: Cath. Coll. Women in Am., 2002. Bd. dirs. Am. Coun. on Edn., 1997—99, Nat. Assn. Ind. Colls. and Univs., 1997—2000, Assn. Cath. Colls. and Univs., 1996—2000, Western Region Nat. Holocaust Mus., 1997—2000; coord. History Homes Religious Nature, 1988—. Fellow Fulbright, 1964. Mem.: Western Assn. Schs. and Colls. (sr. commn. 1997—2000), Assn. Cath. Colls. and Univs. (exec. bd. 1996—2000), Am. Coun. Edn. (bd. dirs. 1997—99), Nat. Assn. Ind. Colls. and Univs. (bd. dirs. 1997—99), Am. Assn. Rsch. Historians Medieval Spain, Medieval Acad., Am. Cath. Hist. Assn. Avocations: skiing, cuisine. Office: Congl Ctr 2311 Lindbergh Blvd Saint Louis MO 63131 Home Phone: 314-961-6189; Office Phone: 314-966-4048. Personal E-mail: kkennelly33@hotmail.com.

KENNELLY, LAURA BALLARD, literature educator, writer; b. Denton, Tex., July 28, 1941; d. E. Garrett and Laura L. (Hutchins) Ballard; m. Kevin J. Kennelly, Aug. 26, 1961 (div. 1996); children: Kathryn, Kevin G., Patrick J., Daniel T., Brendan C.; m. Robert Mayerovitch, Sept. 6, 1996. BA, U. North Tex., 1961, MA, 1969, PhD, 1975. Vis. prof. English U. N. Tex., Denton, 1975—95, prodn. assoc. Studies in the Novel, 1987—92; bibliographic editor Restoration: Studies in English Literary Culture, 1980—2000. Assoc. editor Bach: Jour. Riemenschneider Bach Inst., Baldwin-Wallace Coll., 2000—. Editor: Grasslands Rev., 1987—2006, A Certain Attitude: Poems, 1995; author: The Passage of Mrs. Jung: Poems, 1990; contbr. scholarly articles to profl. jours., poetry, essays, and fiction to various publs.; fine arts columnist: Morning Jour., 2002—. Dir. Birth Right of Denton, 1983—85. Fellow, Antiquarian Soc., 1994—95; grantee, S. Ctrl. MLA, 1990; Michael Kraus Rsch. grantee, Am. Hist. Assn., 1992, Rsch. grantee, Antiquarian Soc., 1990, NEA fellow, 2005. Mem.: MLA, Music Critics Assn. N.Am., Tex. Assn. Creative Writing Tchrs. (pres. 1993—95), E. Ctrl. Soc. 18th Century Studies, S. Ctrl. Soc. 18th Century Studies, Am. Hist. Assn., Am. Soc. 18th Century Studies (affil. socs. coord. 1991—98). Roman Catholic. Avocations: running, bicycling. Office: Bach Inst Baldwin-Wallace Coll 275 Eastland Rd Berea OH 44017 Office Phone: 440-826-8071. Business E-Mail: lkennell@bw.edu.

KENNELLY, MICHAEL J., neurologist, surgeon; s. William J. and Nancy T. Kennelly; m. Deanna R. Turner, Feb. 4, 1989; children: Megan E., Amanda R., Molly T. Student, U. Notre Dame, South Bend, Ind., 1981—85; MD, U. Cin., 1989. Cert. urologist Am. Bd. Urology, Mass., 1997. Intern U. Mich. Med. Ctr., 1990, urol. resident, 1994; clin. instr. U. Tex., Houston, 1994—95; clin. asst. prof. U. NC, Chapel Hill, 1995—2005, clin. assoc. prof., 2005—; dir., dept. urology Carolinas Rehab. Hosp., Charlotte, NC, 1995—; med. dir. Charlotte Continence Ctr., NC, 1995—. Neurology, urodynamics, and pelvic reconstruction fellow U. Tex., Houston, 1995. Mem.: Am. Spinal Injury Assn. (bd. mem. 2002—). Office: McKay Urology 1023 Edgehill Rd S Charlotte NC 28207 Office Phone: 704-355-8686. Office Fax: 704-355-8687.

KENNERLY, DAVID HUME, photographer, writer, producer; b. Roseburg, Oreg., Mar. 9, 1947; s. Orlie Alden and Joanne (Hume) K.; m. Susan Allwardt, 1967 (div. 1969); m. Mel Harris, Oct. 30, 1983 (div. 1988); 1 child, Byron Hume; m. Carol Huston, Dec. 22, 1989. Student, Portland State Coll., 1965-66. Photographer Oreg. Jour., 1966, The Oregonian, 1967, UPI, LA, 1967-68, NYC, 1968-69, Washington, 1969-70, Saigon, Vietnam, 1971-72; contract photographer Life and Time mags., S.E. Asia, 1972-74; personal photographer Pres. of U.S., Washington, 1974-77; photographer Time Mag., Washington, 1977—90; contbr. photog. George Mag., 1996—99; contbr. corr., Good Morning Am. ABC, 1996—98; contbr. editor NBC News, 2006—. Dir. photography Philip Morris mag., NY, 1987; prodr. Warner Bros. TV, 1990-92; pres. Red Star Prodns., 1990. Author: Shooter, 1980; co-writer, exec. producer (teleplay), Shooter, 1987; co-writer, dir., producer (script for Am. Film Inst.) Bao Chi, 1987; exec. producer The Taking of Flight 847-The Uli Derickson Story, 1988 (Emmy award nomination 1988). Recipient Pulitzer Prize Columbia U., 1972; 2 1st place awards World Press Photo, 1976, spl. citation Nat. Press Photographers, 1976, Olivier Rebbot award Overseas Press Club, 1985, Front Page award N.Y. Newspaper Guild, 1985-86; directing fellow Am. Film Inst., 1984-86. Mem. White House Press Photographers Assn., Writers Guild Am. Business E-Mail: PIX@kennerly.com.

KENNERLY, NANCY N., lawyer; BA, Stanford U., Palo Alto, Calif., 1976; JD, U. San Diego, 1979. Ptnr. Paul, Hastings, Janofsky & Walker LLP, LA, 1988—2004; co-managing ptnr. Kennerly, Lamishaw & Rossi LLP, LA, 2004—. Named one of Super Lawyers, LA Mag., 2004—07. Office: Kennerly Lamishaw & Rossi LLP 707 Wilshire Blvd Ste 1400 Los Angeles CA 90017 Office Phone: 213-312-1250.

KENNETT, LEE BOONE, JR., historian, educator; b. Greensboro, NC, Aug. 11, 1931; s. Lee Boone and Dorothy Mary Kennett; m. Julianne Smythe Hudgens, June 24, 1961 (div. July 1977); children: Caroline Allison, John Calvin; m. Anne Marie Lucille Durand, Feb. 17, 1987. Student, Guilford Coll., NC, 1948—50; BA, U. N.C., 1952; MA, U. Miss., 1956; PhD, U. Va., 1958. Asst. prof. Converse Coll., Spartanburg, SC, 1958—60; lectr. So. Ill. U., Carbondale, 1960—61; asst. prof. U. Ga., Athens, 1962—66, assoc. prof., 1968—78, prof. history, 1978—87, rsch. prof., 1987—93, prof. emeritus, 1993—; assoc. prof. Guilford Coll., NC, 1967—68. Founder, dir. Consortium on Revolutionary Europe, 1969—74; mem. fellowship selection bd. Inst. of Internat. Edn., 1978, 80; organizer Internat. Conf. on Aviation, Nat. Air and Space Mus., Washington, 1990; directeur d'études associé Ecole Pratique des Hautes Etudes, 4th sect., U. Paris, 1978; Lindbergh prof. Nat. Air and Space Mus., Smithsonian Instn., 1989—90; guest lectr. aero. sect. Inst. Phys. Sci. and Tech., Russian Acad. Sci., 1991. Author: (book) The French Armies in the Seven Years' War, 1968, The French Forces in America, 1780-1783, 1977, A History of Strategic Bombing, 1982, G.I.: The American Soldier in WW II, 1987, The First Air War, 1914-1918, 1990, French edit., 2005, Marching Through Georgia, 1995, Gettysburg: le tournant de la guerre de Sécession, 1997, Sherman: A Soldier's Life, 2001; co-author: The Gun in America, 1975; co-editor: French Military Aviation: A Bibliographical Guide, 1989; translator (editor): The Russian Campaign, 1812, 1970, Clement Ader's Aviation Militaire, 2003; contbr. numerous articles to profl. jours., chpts. to anthologies. Decorated Chevalier, Ordre des Palmes Académiques France; recipient Claiborne History prize, U. Miss., 1956, Fulbright Lectureship to France, 1966—67, Bicentennial Lectureship to France, Fulbright Found., 1974—75, Gilbert Chinard prize, Soc. for French Hist. Studies, 1978, Nat. Book prize, Phi Alpha Theta, 1979, Excellence in Rsch. award, U. Ga., 1980, Disting. Svc. award, Inst. Internat. Edn., 1981; fellow James Wilford Garner fellow, U. Miss., 1955—56, Virginia Mason Davidge fellow, U. Va., 1956—57; grantee Advanced Rsch. grantee, U.S. Army Mil. History Inst., 1979, Rsch. grantee, USAF Hist. Rsch. Ctr., 1988; Fulbright fellow, France, 1960—61. Mem.: So. Hist. Assn., Soc. for Mil. History, Orgn. Am. Historians, N.C. Civil War Roundtable, Greensboro Hist. Mus., Centre d'etudes d'histoire de la Défense, Am. Hist. Assn., Phi Beta Kappa. Office Phone: 336-674-0179. Personal E-mail: amd2ba@aol.com.

KENNEY, ANNE, university librarian; BA, Duke U., 1972; MA in History, U. Mo., St. Louis, 1975; MLS, U. Mo., Columbus, 1979. Assoc. dir. Dept. of Preservation and Conservation Cornell U. Libr., Ithaca, 1987—2001, assoc. univ. libr. instruction, rsch. and info. svcs., 2002—06, sr. assoc. univ. libr. pub. svcs. and assessment, 2006—, interim univ. libr., 2007—. Former commr. Nat. Hist. Pubs. and Records Commn.; mem. Clinton/Gore Transition Team; mem. Com. on Librs. and Archives of Cuba Social Rsch. Coun.; mem. adv. com. Portico; spkr. in field. Contbr. articles to profl. jours. Fellow: Soc. Am. Archivists (past pres.). Office: Cornell U 201 Olin Libr Ithaca NY 14853-5301 Office Phone: 607-255-3393. E-mail: ark3@cornell.edu.*

KENNEY, BELINDA JILL FORSEMAN, information technology executive; b. Oak Ridge, Tenn., Dec. 18, 1955; d. Jack Woodrow and Betty Jean Forseman; m. Ronald Gene Kenney, Feb. 23, 1985; 1 child, Brandon. BS, U. Tenn., Chatanooga, 1977, postgrad., 1977—78; MBA, Emory U., Atlanta, 2000; postgrad., U. Colo. Law Sch., 2006—. Sales rep. Xerox

Corp., Nashville, 1978—82, maj. account sales mgr., 1982—83, region sales ops. mgr. St. Louis, 1984—86, dist. sales mgr. Overland Park, Kans., 1987—89, dist. mgr. San Antonio, 1989—95, v.p. Houston, 1995—97, v.p., region gen. mgr. Bus. Svcs. Atlanta, 1998—99, sr. v.p. region mgr. NASG, 2000—01; corp. officer, exec. v.p. sales and mktg. SpectraLink Corp., Boulder, Colo., 2004—07. Exec. in residence Leeds Sch. Bus. U. Colo. Patron M.D. Anderson Cancer Ctr.; vol. ARC, Disaster Assistance Call Ctr.; mem. Emergency Family Assistance Assn. Guild, live auction chairperson; vol. The Gathering Place; bd. dirs. Wise Women's Coun., Women's Vision Found., Foothills United Way Boulder, United Way Found. Mem.: Foothills Mensa. Lutheran. Avocations: jogging, reading, tennis, health and fitness. Office: 5755 Central Ave Boulder CO 80301

KENNEY, BRIAN, editor-in-chief; MS in Libr. Sci., Pratt Inst. Reference libr. NY Pub. Libr.; mgr. Bklyn. Pub. Libr. Ctrl. Libr.; exec. editor, technology and web Library Journal; joined Reed Bus. Information, divsn. Reed Elsevier Inc., 2001—; editor-in-chief School Library Journal, Reed Bus. Information, divsn. of Reed Elsevier Inc., 2005—. Creator Library By Design. Fed. fellowship, Inst. Mus. and Librs. Svcs., 2004. Office: School Library Journal 360 Park Ave S New York NY 10010 Office Phone: 646-746-6756. Business E-Mail: bkenney@reedbusiness.com.

KENNEY, BRIGID, media company executive; b. 1965; Audit mgr. Arthur Andersen & Co., 1986—92; mgr. of acctg. and external reporting Tribune Co., 1993—94, dir., acctg. and fin. reporting, 1994—97, dir., treasury ops., 1997—99; asst. treas. Tribune Interactive, Inc., 1999—2002, v.p., 2002—04, v.p., gen. mgr., 2004—06, sr. v.p., network ops., 2006—. Named one of 25 Women to Watch, Crain's Chgo. Bus., 2007. Office: Tribune Interactive Inc 365 Canal St Ste 3100 New Orleans LA 70130*

KENNEY, BRIGID E., lawyer; b. Balt., Feb. 9, 1951; BA, Goucher Coll., 1973; student, U. N.C.; JD with honors, U. Md., 1977. Bar: Md. 1977. Law clk. to Hon. Rita C. Davidson Ct. Spl. Appeals, Md., 1977-78; ptnr. Venable, Baetjer and Howard, Balt.; now ptnr. Venable LLP, Balt. and Washington. Chair Alliance for the Chesapeake Bay, Inc., 2005. Mem. ABA, Md. State Bar Assn., Bar Assn. Balt. City, Order of Coif. Office: Venable LLP 1800 Mercantile Bank 2 Hopkins Plz Baltimore MD 21201-2930 also: Venable LLP 575 Seventh St NW Washington DC 20004 Office Phone: 410-244-7487. Office Fax: 410-244-7742. Business E-Mail: bekenney@venable.com.

KENNEY, CRANE H., lawyer; b. Quincy, Mass., Dec. 31, 1962; BA cum laude, U. Notre Dame, 1985; JD cum laude, U. Mich., 1988. Bar: Ill. 1988. Assoc. Schiff, Hardin & Waite; counsel Tribune Co., Chgo., 1994—95, sr. counsel, 1995—96, v.p., chief legal officer, 1996, v.p., gen. counsel, sec., 1996—2000, sr. v.p., gen. counsel, sec., 2000—. Office: Tribune Co 435 N Michigan Ave Ste 600 Chicago IL 60611-4001 Office Phone: 312-222-9100, 312-222-2491. Office Fax: 312-222-4206. E-mail: ckenney@tribune.com.*

KENNEY, DION PATRICK, information technology executive, entrepreneur; b. Middletown, NY, Apr. 26, 1962; s. John Michel Kenney and Joan Elizabeth (Bennett) Klein. BS in Physics, Fla. State U., 1984; MS in Physics, Tex. A&M U., 1989; MBA, U. Pa., 1995. Engr. Navair-Dept. of Navy, Lakehurst, NJ, 1985-86, Stratford, Conn., 1986-87; software engr. Unisys, Houston, 1990-93; mktg. and bus. planning profl. Health Care Devel. Internat., Tarrytown, NY, 1993-95; founder, pres. Cybernet Info. Systems, Yorktown Heights, NY, 1994—. Dir. bus. planning AHSC Group, LLC, Tarrytown, N.Y., 1995-2002; prin. cons. Y2 Mktg., N.Y.C., 2002—. Office: 777 Old Sawmill River Rd Tarrytown NY 10591 Home: 10 Sarah Bishop Rd Ridgefield CT 06877-1215

KENNEY, ESTELLE KOVAL, artist, educator; b. Chgo., Feb. 15, 1928; d. Hyman English and Florence (Browman) Koval; m. Herbert Kenney, Feb. 6, 1948; children: Carla, Robert. BFA, Art Inst. Chgo., 1976, MFA, 1978; postgrad., Yale U., 1980. Art therapist Grove Sch., Lake Forest, Ill., 1973—78, New Trier H.S., Ctrl. H.S., Winnetka, Ill., 1978—79, Mosely Sch., Chgo., 1979, Cove Sch., Evanston, Ill., 1979—82; dir. art therapy concentration, instr. painting and drawing Loyola U., Chgo., 1981—; pres., art dir. Nuts on Clark, Chgo. Pres., art dir. Nuts on Clark Inc., Chgo. One-woman shows include Evanston Libr., 1971, Zaks Gallery, Chgo., 1977, 1979, 1982, Renaissance Soc.-Bergman Gallery, U. Chgo., 1980, exhibited in group shows at Ill. State Mus., 1975, Women Artists, Here and Now, 1976, Chgo. Connections traveling exhbn., 1976—77, Bat, /wineb's Caucus for Art, 1977, Nancy Lurie Gallery, 1978, Marycrest Coll. Gallery, Davenport, Iowa, 1982, Chgo. Internat. Art Expo, 1981, 1982, 1983, Notre Dame U. Gallery, South Bend, Ind., 1982, Represented in permanent collections Ill. State Mus., Springfield, Union League Club. Chgo. Mem.: Coll. Art Assn., Ill. Art Therapy Assn. (pres. 1979—), Am. Art Therapy Assn. Personal E-mail: estellekenney@nutsonclark.com.

KENNEY, FRANK DEMING, lawyer; b. Chgo., Feb. 20, 1921; s. Joseph Aloysius and Mary Edith (Deming) K.; m. Virginia Stuart Banning, Feb. 12, 1944; children: Claudia Kenney Carpenter, Pamela Kenney Voetberg, Sarah Kenney Swanson, Stuart Deming Kenney AB, U. Chgo., 1948, JD, 1949. Bar: Ill. 1948, U.S. Dist. Ct. (no. dist.) Ill. 1949. Assoc. J.O. Brown, Chgo., 1948-49; assoc., ptnr. Winston & Strawn, and predecessors, Chgo., 1949-92, ret., 1992. 1st lt. AUS, 1942-46, CBI, PTO. Mem. ABA, Ill. Bar Assn., Chgo. Bar Assn. (chmn. real property law com. 1982-83), Lawyers Club Chgo., Fox River Valley Hunt Club, Quadrangle Club, Nat. Beagle Club Am. (bd. dirs. 1981-92), Spring Creek Basset Hunt Club (master 1977-93, chmn. bd., 1993-98, hon. chmn. bd. 1998-2002, hon. master 2002-), Kappa Sigma (nat. housing fin. commr. for U.S. and Can., 1959-91). Republican. Roman Catholic. Office: Winston & Strawn 35 W Wacker Dr Ste 3800 Chicago IL 60601-1695

KENNEY, H. WESLEY, JR., (HARRY WESLEY KENNEY JR.), television producer, television director; b. Dayton, Ohio, Jan. 3, 1926; s. Harry Wesley and Minnie Ruth (Keeton) K.; m. Kay Ann Snure (div. 1964); children: Nina, Harry Wesley III, Kara; m. Heather North, May 22, 1971; 1 child, Kevin. BFA, Carnegie Inst. Tech., 1950. Dir. Fights at St. Nicks, Rocky King Detective, Night Beat Dumont Network, NYC, 1950-57; producer, dir. TV shows True Story, Modern Romances NBC, NYC, 1957-61; freelance dir. Omnibus, NYC, 1958; dir. theater prodn. My Three Angels Totem Pole Playhouse, 1955; dir. theater prodn. The King and I Melody Fair Summer Theatre, Niagra Falls, 1959; dir. theater prodn. Twelfth Night Antioch, Yellow Springs, Ohio, 1962; dir. TV series The Doctors NBC, NYC, 1964-66, exec. producer, dir. TV series Days of Our Lives Los Angeles, 1967-77; dir. TV series All in the Family CBS, Los Angeles, 1974, dir. pilots The Jeffersons, Filthy Rich, Ladies Man, Rosenthal & Jones, Side By Side, exec. producer, dir. TV series The Young and the Restless, 1981-86; producer, dir. (spl.) Miss Kline, We Love You ABC, 1974, exec. producer, dir. TV series General Hospital Los Angeles, 1987-90; freelance dir., 1990—. Cons. Televisa-Mexico City UCLA Ext. Sch., 1990, guest instr. TV directing, 1975, guest instr. multiple camera directing, 1991, 93; instr. profl. seminar in TV for Televisa, 1990; guest lectr. profl. seminar dor srs. and students in drama Carnegie Mellon U., Pitts., 1990; assoc. prof. TV prodn. UCLA Sch. Theatre, Film and TV, 1993-99, 2001-; assoc. prof. TV prodn. Sch. Cinema and TV U. So. Calif., 1998, 99—, guest prof. Frostburg Mo. State U. summer TV Festival, 2004. Dir. closed cir. med. shows including Dr. Salk Polio Vaccine Report from U. Mich., Ann Arbor, 1956; dir. (theater prodns.) Ten Little Indians, Advent Theatre, L.A., 1991, The Best Christmas Pageant Ever, 1993, Love Letters, W.Va. Pub. Theatre, Morgantown, 1994, Shadowlands, Tracy Roberts Theater, 1995 (Dramalogue award for Directing), Scrooge, W.Va. Pub. Theatre, 1995; dir. Sebiyophrenin: The Relapse, 3-part series; dir. (infomercials) Elements of Beauty-The Merle Norman Experience, 1993, Therapy Without Tears-The EMLA Study, 1993; dir. (series spls.) Soap Break, CBS, 1994-95 (Emmy nomination). Served with USN, 1943-46. Recipient 7 Emmy awards Acad. TV Arts and Scis. 1973, 78, 79, 82, 83, 84, 86, 13 Emmy award nominations Acad. TV Arts and Scis., 1972-88, 95 Mem. Dirs. Guild Am., Producers Guild Am., Actors Equity, Omega Delta Kappa. Avocations: athletics, tennis, travel, bungy jumping. Home: 12996 Galewood St Studio City CA 91604-4045 Personal E-mail: marle333@aol.com. *I recognize myself as an "average guy" with an average intelligence and talent and more than average patience and luck. An awareness of this fact has allowed me to accept the success I have had, always working for something better, but recognizing those shortcomings that have at times made me fail. Also because of this, thank God, I have had more than my share of happiness.*

KENNEY, JOHN ARTHUR, lawyer; b. Oklahoma City, Aug. 3, 1948; m. Sept. 4, 1971; children: John Graham, Lauren Elizabeth. BS in Indsl. Engring. with distinction, U. Okla., 1971, JD, 1975. Bar: Tex. 1975, US Dist. Ct. (so. dist.) Tex. 1976, U. Ct. Appeals (5th cir.) 1977, Okla. 1981, US Dist. Ct. Okla. 1981, US Ct. Appeals (10th cir.) 1983, US Supreme Ct. 2003. Assoc. Baker & Botts, Houston, 1975-81; shareholder McAfee & Taft, Oklahoma City, 1982—. Temp. judge Okla. Ct. of Appeals, atty. appointed panels, Leadership Oklahoma City; magistrate judge merit selection com. and civil justice reform act adv. com. U.S. Dist. Ct. (we. dist.) Okla. Bd. advisors dept. indsl. engring., bd. visitors Coll. Engring., Okla. U.; past trustee, deacon Westminster Presbyn. Ch.; dir., past pres. Rebuilding Together with Christmas in April, Oklahoma City. Mem. ABA, Okla. Bar Assn. (adminstrn. of justice com. 1990-2000), Fed. bar Assn. Okla. City (chpt. pres. 2001-03), Okla. County Bar Assn. (dir. 1997-98, pres. 1999-2000), Order of Coif, Tau Beta Pi. Office: McAfee & Taft Two Leadership Sq 10th Fl Oklahoma City OK 73102

KENNEY, JOHN JOSEPH, lawyer; b. NYC, July 13, 1943; s. Joseph Charles and Regina Elizabeth (Hulbert) K.; m. Charlotte O'Brien, May 23, 1971; 1 child, Alexander Hulbert. BA, St. Michael's Coll., 1966; JD, Fordham U., 1969. Bar: N.Y. 1970, U.S. Dist. Ct. (so. dist.) N.Y. 1973, U.S. Ct. Appeals (2d cir.) 1973, U.S. Dist. Ct. (ea. dist.) N.Y. 1980, U.S. Supreme Ct. 1991. Assoc. Dunnington, Bartholow & Miller, NYC, 1969-71; asst. US atty. US Dist. Ct. (so. dist.) NY, NYC, 1971-80; assoc. Simpson, Thacher & Bartlett, NYC, 1980-81, ptnr., 1981—2005, Engel McCarney & Kenney LLP, NYC, 2006—07, Hugnet, Newman, Regal & Kenney LLP, NYC, 2007—. Mem. deptl. disciplinary com. Appellate Divsn. 1st Dept., 2002—. Counsel, Village of Bronxville, 1983-86; mem. Planning Bd. of Bronxville, 1992-98, counsel, 1981-83; trustee Hist. Deerfield Inc., 1992-98, Bennington Coll., 1999—, Bronxville Pub. Libr., 2003-06; bd. dirs. Citizens Crime Commn., 1998—, Am. Assn. for Internat. Commn. Jurists, 2000—. Recipient John Marshall award U.S. Dept. Justice, 1980. Fellow Am. Coll. Trial Lawyers (chmn. com. on fed. rules of evidence 2003-05); mem. ABA, Fed. Bar Coun. (pres. 1994-96), Assn. Bar City NY (chmn. criminal law com. 1992-95), New York County Lawyers Assn. (pres. 1996-97), NY State Bar Assn. (exec. com. 1997-2000, chmn. spl. com. bar exam and lawyer competence 2005—), NY State Bar Found. (bd. dirs. 2004—), Wong Sun Soc. San Francisco. Republican. Roman Catholic. Home: 8 The Byway Bronxville NY 10708-4934 Office: Hoguet Newman Regal & Kenny LLP 10 East 40th St New York NY 10016-0301 Home Phone: 914-337-5640; Office Phone: 212-689-8808. Business E-Mail: jkenney@hnrklaw.com.

KENNEY, JOHN PATRICK, dentist; b. Joliet, Ill., July 8, 1946; s. John Edward and Nellie Kenney; div.; 1 child, David J BS Mktg., Christian Bros. Coll., 1968; DDS, Loyola U., Maywood, Ill., 1977; MS Oral Biology, Loyola U., Chgo., 1979. Diplomate Am. Bd. Forensic Odontology. Supr. passenger svcs. Am. Airlines, Chgo., 1969—72; pvt. practice in pediat. dentistry Park Ridge, Ill., 1980—; asst. prof. pediat. dentistry Northwestern U., Chgo., 1993—97, clin. assoc. prof. pediat. dentistry, 1997—2000; assoc. prof. clin. surgery Northwestern U. Med. Sch., 2000—. Forensic odontologist Cook County Med. Examiner, Chgo., 1984-97, chief, 1991-97; forensic odontologist Kane County Coroner, Geneva, Ill., 1984-97; cons. forensic odontologist Am. Airlines, Chgo., 1979, Midwest Express Airlines, Milw., 1985, Am. Eagle Airlines, Ind., 1995, United Express Airlines, Quincy, Ill., 1996, Comair Airlines, Mich., 1997, U.S. Army Ctrl. ID Lab., Honolulu, 1997—, Amtrak, Ill., 1999, NYCME, 2001; mem. Nat. Disaster Med. Sys. D-Mort team USPHS, forensic oversight com., 2001—; dir. Identification Svcs. Dupage County Ill. Coroners Office, 1997— Mem. editl. bd. Jour. Forensic Scis., 1997—, Jour. Forensic Identification, 2004—; contbr. articles to profl. jours Dep. coroner DuPage County, 2001— Fellow Am. Acad. Pediat. Dentistry, Am. Coll. Dentists, Am. Acad. Forensic Scis., Pierre Fauchard Soc., Royal Soc. Medicine; mem. ADA, Internat. Orgn. Forensic Odonto-stomatology (v.p. 1984-87), Internat. Assn. for Identification (cert. sr. crime scene analyst 1991—), Am. Acad. Pediat. Dentists, Am. Bd. Forensic Odontology (bd. dirs. 1990-96, 2000-03, treas. 1991-93, v.p. 1994, pres. 1995-96, sec. 2003-04, v.p. 2004-05, pres. 2006-07), Ill. State Dental Soc., Ill. Soc. Pediat. Dentists (bd. dirs. 1987-90), Chgo. Dental Soc., Kiwanis (pres. 1983-84, Disting. Pres. 1984), Forensics Sci. Found. (trustee 2006—). Office: 101 S Washington Ave Park Ridge IL 60068-4200

KENNEY, KIMBERLY, elementary school educator; BA, Plymouth State U. Tchr. Boscawen (NH) Elem. Sch., 1989—. Named NH Tchr. of Yr., 2006. Office: Boscawen Elem Sch 1 BEST Ave Concord NH 03303 Business E-Mail: kkenney@mv.k12.nh.us. E-mail: fhcoach8999@aim.com.*

KENNEY, KRISTIE ANNE, ambassador; b. Washington; m. William R. Brownfield. BA in Polit. Sci., Clemson U., 1977; MA in Latin Am. Studies, Tulane U.; student, Nat. War Coll. Econ. cons. US Mission, Geneva; econ. officer US Embassy, Argentina, consular officer Jamaica; dir. Ops. Ctr. US Dept. State, Washington; mem. NSC; sr. adv. to asst. sec. for internat. narcotics & law enforcement US Dept. State, 2001—02, polit. mil. officer Office NATO Affairs, exec. sec. Washington, 1999—2001, US amb. to Ecuador Quito, Ecuador, 2002—05, US amb. to the Philippines Manila, 2006—. Recipient Disting. Honor award, US Dept. State, Arnold Raphel Meml. award. Avocations: skiing, tennis. Office: DOS Amb 8600 Manila Pl Washington DC 20521-8600*

KENNEY, MELISSA A., environmental scientist, educator; BA, U. Va., Charlottesville, 2002. Rsch. asst. ctr. expertise superfund site recycling U. Va., Charlottesville, 2001—02; tchg. asst. Duke U., Durham, NC, 2002—, rschr. environ. sci., 2003—. Instr. environ. Va. Gov.'s Sch., 1999—2005; cons. in field. Contbr. articles to profl. jours. Recipient Soil and Water Mgmt. Proficiency award, Nat. FFA, 2000; fellow, Duke U. Ctr. Tchg., Learning, and Writing, 2003—04, Nat. Water Resources Inst., 2006—07; scholar, Morris K. Udall Found., 2001. Mem.: North Am. Lake Mgmt. Soc., Am. Water Resources Assn., Ecol. Soc. Am., Inst. Ops. Rsch. and Mgmt. Scis., Sigma Xi (pres. Duke U. chpt. 2005—07). Achievements include research in using science and decision analysis to set water quality standards. Avocations: ballroom dancing, singing, cooking, reading, travel. Office Phone: 919-613-8116.

KENNEY, PHILIP G., construction executive; With F.A. Wilhelm Constrn. Co., Inc., Indpls., 1982, mgr. facilities constrn. group, 1985—95, pres., 2001—, Freitag-Weinhardt, 1995—2000. Vice chmn. Metro Indpls. Coalition Constrn. Safety. Office: FA Wilhelm Constrn Co Inc 3914 Prospect St Indianapolis IN 46203 Office Phone: 317-359-5411. Office Fax: 317-359-8346. E-mail: philipkenney@fawilhelm.com.*

KENNEY, ROBERT JAMES, JR., lawyer; b. Boston, Jan. 16, 1948; BA, Harvard Coll., 1969, JD, 1972. Bar: Mass. 1972, D.C. 1976. Assoc. Hogan & Hartson LLP, Washington, 1976-81, ptnr., 1981—, dir. gov. contracts practice group. Lt. USNR, 1973-76. Recipient Federal 100 award Fed. Computer Week, 1992. Mem. Fed. Bar Assn. (chmn. govt. contracts sect. 1992-94, chmn. ADP procurement com. 1990-92, Disting. Svc. award 1990, 91, 94). Office: Hogan & Hartson LLP 555 13th St NW Washington DC 20004-1161 Office Phone: 202-637-5707. Office Fax: 202-637-5910. Business E-Mail: rjkenney@hhlaw.com.

KENNEY, THOMAS FREDERICK, broadcast executive; b. Dearborn, Mich., Sept. 25, 1941; s. Charles B. and Grace M. (Wilson) K.; m. Beth H. Rockwood, Aug. 22, 1964; children: Sean, Blair. BS, Mich. State U., 1964. Program mgr. Sta. WMBD-TV, Peoria, Ill., 1969-71; exec. producer Sta. WJZ-TV, Balt., 1971-73; program mgr. Sta. KFMB-TV, San Diego, 1973-75; program mgr., then dir. broadcasting ops. Sta. KHOU-TV, Houston, 1975-79; v.p., gen. mgr. KHOU-TV, 1979-84, Sta. WROC-TV, Rochester, NY, 1984-90; owner Santa Fe Wireless, Inc., Gainesville, Fla., 1990—99; regional mgr. Trader Pub. Co., Phoenix, 1999—. Freelance TV cons., Houston, 1984. Home: 1858 E Campbell Ave Gilbert AZ 85234-8228 Office: Employment Guide 2902 W Aqua Fria Freeway Ste 1090 Phoenix AZ 85027 Office Phone: 623-869-8888. Personal E-mail: thoskenney@gmail.com.

KENNEY, WILLIAM FITZGERALD, lawyer; b. San Francisco, Nov. 4, 1935; s. Lionel Fitzgerald and Ethel Constance (Brennan) K.; m. Susan Elizabeth Langfitt, May 5, 1962; children: Anne, Carol, James. BA, U. Calif.-Berkeley, 1957, JD, 1960. Bar: Calif. 1961. Assoc. Miller, Osborne Miller & Bartlett, San Mateo, Calif., 1962-64; ptnr. Tormey, Kenney & Cotchett, San Mateo, 1965-67; pres. William F. Kenney, Inc., San Mateo, 1968—; gen. ptnr. All Am. Self Storage, 1985—, Second St. Self Storage, 1990-96, Cochrane Rd. Self Storage, 1996—, Marina Bus. Ctr., 1998—; pres. The Positive Edge, 2000—. Trustee San Mateo City Sch. Dist., 1971-79, pres., 1972-74; pres. March of Dimes, 1972-73; bd. dirs. Boys Club San Mateo, 1972-90, Samaritan House, 1989-2006, Lesley Found., 1992-2004. With U.S. Army, 1960-62. Mem. State Bar of Calif. (taxation com. 1973-76), San Mateo County Bar Assn. (bd. dirs. 1973-75), Calif. Assn. Realtors (legal affairs com. 1978—), San Mateo C. of C. (bd. dirs. 1987-93), Self Storage Assn. (we. region, pres. 1989-90, nat. bd. dirs. 1990-97, nat. v.p 1994-95, pres. 1996), Rotary (pres. 1978-79), Elks (exalted ruler 1974-75). Republican. Roman Catholic. Home: 221 Clark Dr San Mateo CA 94402-1004 Office: 120 N El Camino Real San Mateo CA 94401-2705 Office Phone: 650-347-3603. E-mail: bill1135@rcn.com.

KENNEY, WILLIAM JOHN, JR., real estate developer; b. Huntington Park, Calif., Mar. 9, 1949; s. William John, Sr. and Dorothy Marie (Smith) Kenney; m. Susan Louise Wattson, Sept. 26, 1987. BS in Econs., Calif. State U., Fullerton, 1970, BBA, 1971. Lic. real estate broker Calif., Ariz., cert. leasing specialist. Leasing agt. John S. Griffith, Irvine, Calif., 1972-78, dir. leasing, 1978-84; v.p. leasing John S. Griffith (name now Donahue Schriber), Newport Beach, Calif., 1984-85, sr. v.p., 1986-91, sr. v.p. devel., 1991-95; founder Kenney Co., Newport Beach, 1995—. Spkr. in field. Bd. dirs. Riverside (Calif.) YMCA, 1989—92, Promontary Bay Cmty. Assn. Recipient Cert. Appreciation, Hemet C. of C., Riverside Bd. Realtors, Hemet Valley Kiwanis, Riverside Kiwanis. Mem.: Newport Harbor Bd. Realtors (cert. Appreciation), Calif. Bus. Properties Assn. (dir. 1976—96, chmn. 1988—89), Internat. Coun. Shopping Ctrs. (assoc.; chair govt. affairs com. 1994—98), Balboa Yacht Club (sec. 2003, bd. dirs. 2004—), Frank Miller Club (life). Avocations: surfing, fishing, skiing. Office: The Kenney Co 824 Harbor Island Dr Newport Beach CA 92660-7228 Office Phone: 949-675-7038.

KENNEY-BADEN, LINDA, lawyer; b. 1957; m. Michael M. Baden, 2000. grad. magna cum laude, law degree magna cum laude, Rutgers U., NJ. Jud. clk. to Judge John F. Lynch Appellate Divsn.; atty. Meyner & Landis, Newark; asst. prosecutor Monmouth County Prosecutor's Office, 1980; pvt. practice, 1984—. Mediator Fed. Dist. Ct. NJ. Co-author (with Michael Baden): Remains Silent, 2005. Bd. trustees Brookdale CC; mem. Brookdale CC Found. Mem.: Am. Acad. Forensic Scis. Office: 2 Bridge Ave Bldg 5 2nd Fl Red Bank NJ 07701-4604 Office Phone: 732-219-0099. Office Fax: 732-219-9653.*

KENNICUTT, ROBERT CHARLES, JR., astronomer; b. Balt., Sept. 4, 1951; s. Robert Charles and Joyce Ann K.; m. Norma Graceila Crosa Kennicutt, Feb. 17, 1976 (div. Jan. 18, 1996); 1 child, Laura. BS in Physics, Rensselaer Polytech. Inst., Troy, NY, 1973; MS in Astronomy, PhD in Astronomy, U. Wash., Seattle, 1978. Carnegie fellow Hale Observatories, Pasadena, Calif., 1978-80; asst. prof. astronomy U. Minn., Mpls., 1980-85, assoc. prof. astronomy, 1985-88; assoc. prof., astronomer U. Ariz., Tucson, 1988-92, prof., astronomy, 1992—; Beatrice Tinsley Centennial prof. U. Tex., Austin, 1994; Plumian prof. astronomy and exptl. philosophy U. Cambridge, England, 2005—. V.p. AAS, Washington, 1998-01; com. on Astronomy and Astrophysics Nat. Rsch. Coun., Washington, 1998-2001; Space Telescope Sci. Inst. coun., AURA, Washington, 2000-2004; next generation space telescope interim sci. working group, NASA, Washington, 2000-01, adv. com., chmn. 1996-99; vis. com. chmn. NOAO Observatories, AURA, Washington, 1996-2000; vis. com. European Southern Observatory, Garching bei Munich, Germany, 1997-2003, Gemini Obs., AURA, 2003—. Author: Galaxies: Interactions and Induced Star Formation, 1998; editor-in-chief The Astrophys. Jour., 1999-2006. Named Alfred P. Aloan fellowship 1983-87, Beatrice M. Tinsley Centennial professorship, U. Tex. at Austin, 1994, Carnegie fellowship Carnegie Instn. Washington, 1978-80, Blaauw Prof. U. Groningen, 2001. Fellow Am. Acad. Arts and Scis.; mem. NAS, Am. Astron. Soc. (v.p. 1998-01, Heinmen prize, 2007), Internat. Astron. Union, Astron. Soc. of the Pacific. Office: Steward Observatory U Arizona Tucson AZ 85721 Fax: 520-621-1532. E-mail: rkennicutt@as.arizona.edu.

KENNING, GREGORY GEORGE, physicist, educator; b. Winnipeg, Manitoba, Canada, May 9, 1960; s. George and Joyce Kenning; m. Katalin Komjati, Apr. 4, 2003; children: Gregory George Vajk, Gabriel Andrew. PhD, Mich. State U., 1988. Asst. rsch. physicist UCLA, 1988—94; adj. assoc. prof. U. Calif., Riverside, 1994—2004; asst. prof. Indian U., Indiana, Pa., 2004—. Dir. rsch. KenGen Tech., Crestline, Calif., 1995—2000. Contbr. articles to profl. jours and pubs. NSF Equipment grant, NSF, 2002. Achievements include patents for Automated Electrophoresis; patents pending for Squid Magnetometry For Cancer Screening. Avocations: hockey, hiking, travel. Home: 891 White Farm Rd Indiana PA 15701 Office: Indiana U of Pa Indiana PA 15704 Home Phone: 724-463-0559. Personal E-mail: gregory.kenning@iup.edu.

KENNY, DEBORAH, marketing professional, finance educator; b. NJ, Nov. 13, 1962; BA, U. Pa., 1983; MA, PhD, Columbia U., 1994. Publ. Dimension Mag., NYC, 1987-90; pres. N.Am. opers. The Jerusalem Report, NYC, 1994-97; v.p. mktg. Parenting group Time Warner, NYC, 1998-99; pres. publ. divsn. Sesame St., NYC, 1999—. Bd. dirs. Domestic Abuse Prevention Project. Fellow IWF-Harvard Leadership Found., 1997-98; recipient Clarion Advt. award, 1997, Echo Leader award Direct Mktg. Assn., 1989. E-mail: dkenny2222@aol.com.

KENNY, GEORGE EDWARD, pathobiology educator; b. Dickinson, ND, Sept. 23, 1930; s. Frank S. and Anna M. (Kelsch) K.; m. Mary Elisabeth Pearson, Aug. 23, 1958; children: Francis, Michael, Beth, Maureen, John, Edward. BS, Fordham U., 1952; MS, U. N.D., 1957; PhD, U. Minn., 1961. Rsch. instr. pathobiology U. Wash., Seattle, 1961-63, asst.

prof., 1963-67, assoc. prof., 1967-70, 1970-71, prof., 1971—2003, emeritus prof., 2003—, chair dept. pathobiology, 1970-91. Contbr. articles to Jour. Immunology, Annals N.Y. Acad. Sci., Jour. Clin. Microbiology, Infection Immunity; contbr. 185 papers and articles to profl. jours. Chair Archdiocescan Edn. Bd., Seattle, 1978-81; treas. Seattle Youth Symphony, 1996-2003; mem. bd. trustees Holy Names Acad., 1997-2006. With US Army, 1953-55. Recipient Kimble Methodology award APHA, 1971, Disting. Alumnus award U. N.D., 1983. Fellow Infectious Diseases Soc. Am., Am. Acad. Microbiology; mem. Am. Soc. Microbiology, Am. Assn. Immunologists, Internat. Orgn. for Mycoplasmology (treas.). Achievements include patent for antigen for Trachoma LGV and non-gonococcal urethritis. Home: 1504 37th Ave Seattle WA 98122-3470 Office: U Wash Dept Pathobiology Box 357238 Seattle WA 98195-7238 Business E-Mail: kennyg@u.washington.edu.

KENNY, GREGORY B., industrial equipment executive; BS, Georgetown Univ.; MBA, George Washington Univ.; MPA, Harvard Univ. Fgn. svc. officer US Dept. State, 1975—82; from v.p. corp. devel. to group exec. for tech. prod. and svcs. Penn Central Corp., 1982—94; exec. v.p. General Cable, 1994—97, bd. dir., 1997—, exec. v.p., COO, 1997—99, pres., COO, 1999—2001, pres., CEO, 2001—. Bd. dir. IDEX Corp., 2002—07, Corn Products Internat., Cardinal Health, 2007—. Office: c/o General Cable 4 Tesseneer Dr Highland Heights KY 41076*

KENNY, JAMES CASEY, former ambassador, construction company executive; b. Evanston, Ill., June 29, 1953; s. John Edward and Rosalie (Casey) K.; m. Margaret Mackin, Apr. 21, 1979; children: Colleen, Courtney, Casey. BS in Bus., Bradley U., 1976; DHL (hon.), Lynn U., 2005. Safety and field engr. Kenny Constrn. Co., Wheeling, Ill., 1976-79, project supt. Chgo., 1979-82, bus. devel. dir. Wheeling, 1982-89, v.p., 1989—; pres. Kenny Mgmt. Svcs.; U.S. amb. to Ireland US Dept. State, Dublin, 2003—06. Bd. dirs. Ill. Rd. Builders Assn., Chgo., Am. Underground Space Assn., St. Paul. Bd. dirs. Met. Pier and Expo Authority, Chgo., 1991-92, Ill. Ambs., Chgo., 1992, Nat. Corp. for Housing Partnerships, Washington, 1991-92; co-fin. chmn. Bush/Quayle 1992 Campaign, Chgo., 1992. Named Contractor of Yr., Am. Pub. Works Assn., 1990, Minorities in Constrn., 1992; recipient Flax Trust award, 2004 Mem. North Shore Country Club, Pinehurst Nat. Club. Tavern Club. Roman Catholic. Avocations: golf, skiing, platform tennis.*

KENNY, JANE M., government relations consulting executive; b. Jersey City; m. Greg Myer; 3 children. B, Trinity Coll., Washington, 1974; M in English and Am. Lit., Rutgers U., 1982. Cabinet sec. to Gov. Tom Kean State of NJ, 1986—90, chief policy and planning to Gov. Christie Whitman, 1994—96; v.p. corp. cmty. affairs Beneficial Mgmt. Corp., Peapack, NJ, 1990—94; commr. NJ Dept. Cmty. Affairs, 1996—2001; regional adminstr. region 2 US EPA, 2001—03; sr. v.p. The Whitman Strategy Group, LLC, 2004—. Bd. dirs. New Jersey Resources, 2006—. Recipient Nat. Pub. Svc. award, Women in Govt. award, Good Housekeeping. Fellow: Nat. Acad. Pub. Adminstrs. Office: Whitman Strategy Group LLC 116 Village Blvd Princeton NJ 08540

KENNY, JOHN EDWARD, computer analyst; b. Buffalo, Oct. 28, 1945; s. Thomas Edmund and Dorothy Elizabeth (Krull) K. AAS, Erie C.C., 1972. Systems analyst Nat. Fuel Gas, Buffalo, 1969-70; programmer Svc. Systems Corp., Clarence, N.Y., 1974-77, Carborundum, Niagra Falls, N.Y., 1973-74; analyst, programmer A. Marine Midland Bank N.A., Buffalo, 1977-83; sr. analyst, programmer, project leader Empire of Am., FSA, Buffalo, 1983-85, applications project supr., 1985-89, asst. v.p. software devel., 1989-91; pres. Can.-Am. Bus. Svcs., 1991—, GPS Sys., 1995—; sr. analyst, programmer Cardinal Health Corp., Amherst, N.Y., 1995—. Data processing cons. First Union Nat. Bank, NC, Elec. Data Sys., Plano, Tex., 1996—, Ernst & Young LLP-Med. Mut. of Ohio, 1997—2000; computer analyst Citicorp Student Loan Corp., Pittsford, NY, 1996—97; tchr. programming langs. Advanced Tng. Ctr., Buffalo; cons. M&T Bank Corp., Buffalo, 2000—01, Tyco Electronics, Harrisburg, Pa., 2001—02, Antares Mgmt. Solutions, Cleve., 2002—03, N.Y.C. Taxation and Fin. Dept., Albany, NY, 2004—; sr. IT cons. Bank of N.Y., Syracuse, 2004—05, Med. Mutual of Ohio, Cleve., 2005—; instr. computer tech. Acad. Med. Arts and Bus., Harrisburg, 2001—02. Mem. Rep. Presdl. Task Force; mem. Town of Tonawanda Conservative Com., 1980-2002, chmn., 1993-96; state committeeman 29th U.S. Congl. Dist., 1996-1999; mem. Erie County Conservative Com., 1980-2002, mem. exec. bd., 1994-97; 911 asst. Erie County Ctrl. Police Svcs., 1995-1997; mem. Erie County Rep. Com., 2004—. Mem. AARP, Am. Inst. Banking, Assn. Sys. Mgmt., Kenton C. of C., Greater Fort Erie C. of C. Can., US Golf Assn., Judges and Police Conf. Erie County (NY), Tonawanda Chmn. Men's Club, Champion Club, KC, Lions, Internat. Order Alhambra, World Future Soc. (profl.). Republican (nat. com.). Roman Catholic. Home and Office: 212 McKinley Ave Kenmore NY 14217-2438 Office Phone: 216-687-6403. Business E-Mail: cabussrv@aol.com.

KENNY, MARY ALICE, lawyer; b. Evergreen Park, Ill., July 5, 1961; d. Ronald Stanley and Kathleen Regina (Fawcett) Adams; m. James Michael Kenny, Sept. 3, 1988; children: Daniel Patrick, Eileen Anne BS, Ill. State U., Normal, 1984; JD, De Paul U., Chgo., 1988; M Libr. and Info. Sci., Rosary Coll., River Forest, Ill., 1997. Bar: Ill. 1988, U.S. Dist. Ct. (no. dist.) Ill. 1988, U.S. Ct. Appeals (7th cir.) 1988; cert. instr. grades 6-12, Ill. Dir. law libr. br. Cook County Law Libr., Bridgeview, Ill., 1989—97; paralegal educator Am. Inst. Paralegal Studies, Oakbrook Terrace, Ill., 1990—97; pvt. practice Tinley Park, Ill., 1992—; adj. prof. law, ref. libr. Sch. Law Libr. Loyola U., Chgo., 1998—2005. Mem. adv. bd. Am. Inst. Paralegal Studies, Oakbrook Terrace, 1994—96; mem. adv. bd. Inst. Paralegal Studies Loyola U., Chgo., 2002—. Contbg. author: Bar None: 125 Years of Women Lawyers in Illinois, (booklet) Union List of Holdings of the Branch Libraries of the Cook County Law Library, 1995, 96; contbr.: (book) Legal Research and Writing Exercises for Paralegals, 1992 Mem.: ABA. Democrat. Roman Catholic. Office: 16335 Harlem Ave Ste 400 Tinley Park IL 60477-2594 Office Phone: 708-429-1900. E-mail: mkennyltd@aol.com.

KENNY, ROBERT WADE, social sciences and humanities educator, writer; arrived in U.S., 1989; BA in Psychology, St. Mary's U., Halifax, 1975, BEd cum laude, 1976, MA in Ednl. Psychology, 1979; PhD in Rhetoric, U. Pitts., 1994, MA in Sociology, 1995. Prof. U. Dayton, Pa., 1996—2005, Mt. St. Vincent U., Nova Scotia, Canada, 2005—. Contbr. articles to profl. jours.; author: The Attic, 1985. Office Phone: 937-229-2376. Personal E-mail: doctorwadekenny@hotmail.com. E-mail: wade.kenny@notes.udayton.edu.

KENNY, SHIRLEY STRUM, academic administrator; b. Tyler, Tex., Aug. 28, 1934; d. Marcus Leon and Florence (Golenternek) Strum; m. Robert Wayne Kenny, July 22, 1956; children: David Jack, Joel Strum, Daniel Clark, Jonathan Matthew, Sarah Elizabeth. BA, BJ, U. Tex., Austin, 1955; MA, U. Minn., Mpls., 1957; PhD, U. Chgo., 1964; LHD (hon.), U. Rochester, NY, 1988, Chonnam U., 1996, Donguk U., 2000, Ajou U., 2004. Chair English dept. U. Md., College Park, 1973-79, provost Arts and Humanities, 1979-85; pres. CUNY Queens Coll., Flushing, 1985-94, SUNY, Stony Brook, 1994—; chair Brookhaven Sci. Assocs. Author: The Conscious Lovers, 1968, The Plays of Richard Steele, 1971, The Performers and Their Plays, 1982, The Works of George Farquhar, 2 vols., 1988, British Theatre and the Other Arts, 1984, Reinventing Undergraduate Education: A Blueprint for America's Research Universities, 1998; contbr. articles to profl. jours. Bd. dirs. Goodwill Greater N.Y., LI Assn. Named Outstanding Woman, U. Md., 1983, Outstanding Alumnus, U. Tex. Coll. Comm., 1989, Disting. Alumna, U. Tex., 1999; recipient Disting. Alumnus award, U. Chgo. Club Washington, 1980, Svc. and Leadership award, NY Urban League, 1988, Lifetime Achievement award, Fulbright Assn., 2007. Mem.: Woodrow Wilson Found. Bd., Boyer Comm. Educating Undergrads. (chair), Assn. Am. Colls. and Univs. (bd. dirs. 1988—91, 2005—). Office: SUNY 310 Adminstrn Bldg Stony Brook NY 11794-0701 Business E-Mail: shirley.kenny@sunyab.edu.

KENNY, TOM, actor; b. East Syracuse, NY, July 13, 1962; m. Jill Talley, 1995; 2 children. Actor: (films) How I got Into College, 1989, Shakes the Clown, 1992, Plughead Rewired: Circuitry Man II, 1994, Dead Weekend, 1995, Run Ronnie Run, 2002, My Life with Morrisey, 2003, Comic Book: The Movie, 2004, Creep Tales, 2004, The Paul Decca Story, 2004, Surviving Christmas, 2004, Great North Pole Elf Strike, 2005, Sky High, 2005; Voice: Spuro 2: Ripto's Rage!, 1999; Escape From Monkey Island, 2000; Sponge Bob Square Pants: Super Sponge, 2001; Dr. Dolittle 2, 2001; Orange County, 2002; The Powerpuff Girls, 2002; Eight Crazy Nights, 2002; The SpongeBob Square Pants Movie, 2004; Hoodwinked!, 2005; A.T.O.M.: Alpha Teens on Machines, 2005; The Ant Bully, 2006; Happily N'Ever After, 2007; Meet the Robinsons, 2007; TV Voice SpongeBob Square Pants, 1999—2007, Striperella, 2004, Foster's Home for Imaginary Friends, 2004—06, Super Robot Monkey Team Hyperforce Go!, 2004—06, Sunday Pants, 2005, IGPX: Immortal Grand Prix, 2005, (TV series) The Batman, 2004—07; actor: (TV films) Re-Animated, 2006, Plastic Man, 2006. Office: Nickelodeon Networks 1515 Broadway 42nd Fl New York NY 10036*

KENO, LEIGH R., antiques dealer, appraiser; b. Mohawk, NY, 1957; BA in Art History, Hamilton Coll., 1979. Dir. Am. furniture dept. William Doyle Galleries, 1979—84; v.p. appraisal dept. and specialist in Am. furniture dept. Christie's, 1984—86; owner Leigh Keno Am. Antiques, NYC, 1986—. Vis. scholar Winterthur Mus., Del.; regular featured appraiser PBS' Antiques Roadshow, 1996—; co-host with Leslie Keno Find! on PBS, 2003—. Co-author (with Leslie Keno and Joan Barzilay Freund): Hidden Treasures: Searching for Masterpieces of American Furniture, 2000; co-author: (with Leslie Keno) (column) This Old House mag., 2003—. Fellow, Hist. Deerfield Summer Fellowship Program, 1979. Mem.: Antiques Dealers Assn. Am., Nat. Antique and Art Dealers Assn. Am. Avocations: fly fishing, racing vintage sports cars. Office: Leigh Keno Am Antiques 127 E 69th St New York NY 10021

KENO, LESLIE B., antiques dealer, appraiser; b. Mohawk, NY, 1957; s. Ronald and Norma Keno; m. Emily Keno; 2 children. Grad. in Am. art, Williams Coll., 1979. Joined Sotheby's, NYC, 1980, sr. v.p., dir. Am. furniture and decorative arts, 1983—. Regular featured appraiser PBS' Antiques Roadshow, 1996—; co-host with Leigh Keno Find! on PBS, 2003—. Co-author (with Leigh Keno and Joan Barzilay Freund): Hidden Treasures: Searching for Masterpieces of American Furniture, 2000; co-author: (with Leigh Keno) (column) This Old House mag., 2003—. Fellow, Hist. Deerfield Summer Fellowship Program, 1979. Avocations: fly fishing, skiing, racing vintage sports cars. Office: Am Furniture and Decorative Arts Sothebys 1334 York Ave New York NY 10021

KENOURGIOS, DIMITRIS, finance educator; b. Athens, Attica, Greece, Sept. 25, 1973; s. Fotios and Emilia Kenourgios; m. Dimitra Rapti. B in Econs., U. Athens, 2000; MSc in Money, Banking and Fin., U. Birmingham, UK, 1996; PhD in Fin., U. Athens, 2000. Rschr. U. Athens, 1997—2000, mem. distance learning devel. team, 1998, e-learning tutor, 1999—2004, mem. rsch. programs office, 2003—06, lectr. fin., 2006—; vis. lectr. dept. econs. U. Thessaly, Volos, Greece, 2002—03. Vis. lectr. dept. fin. and acctg. Athens U. Econs. and Bus., 2002—06; tutor Greek Open U., 2004—. Mem.: Profl. Risk Managers' Internat. Assn. (corr.), Multinational Fin. Soc. (corr.), European Econs. and Fin. Soc. (corr.), Econ. Chamber of Greece (life). Avocations: sports, travel. Office: U Athens 5 Stadiou Athens 10562 Greece Office Fax: 30 210 3225542. Business E-Mail: dkenourg@econ.uoa.gr.

KENRICH, JOHN LEWIS, retired lawyer; b. Lima, Ohio, Oct. 17, 1929; s. Clarence E. and Rowena (Stroh) Katterheinrich; m. Betty Jane Roehll, May 26, 1951; children: John David, Mary Jane, Kathryn Ann, Thomas Roehll, Walter Clarence. BS, Miami U., Oxford, Ohio, 1951; LLB, U. Cin., 1953. Bar: Ohio 1953, Mass. 1969. Asst. counsel B.F. Goodrich Co., Akron, Ohio, 1956-65; asst. sec., counsel W.R. Grace & Co., Cin., 1965-68, v.p. Splty. Products Group divsn., 1970-71; corp. counsel, sec. Standex Internat. Corp., Andover, Mass., 1969-70; v.p., sec. Chemed Corp., Cin., 1971-82, sr. v.p., gen. counsel, 1982-86, exec. v.p., chief adminstrv. officer, 1986-91, ret., 1991. Trustee Better Bus. Bur., Cin., 1981-90; mem. bus. adv. coun. Miami U., 1986-88; mem. City Planning Commn., Akron, 1961-62; mem. bd. visitors Coll. Law U. Cin., 1988-92; mem. area coun. trustees Franciscan Sisters of Poor Found., Cin., 1989-93; bd. govs. Ohio River Valley chpt. Arthritis Found., 1992-95, 2000—04; mem. Com. on Reinvestment City of Cin., 1991-93. 1st lt. JAGC U.S. Army, 1954-56. Mem. Beta Theta Pi, Omicron Delta Kappa, Delta Sigma Pi, Phi Eta Sigma. Republican. Presbyterian.

KENRICK, CHARLES WILLIAM, lawyer; b. Chgo., June 16, 1946; s. Ralph Schwarting and Angela Augusta (Shostrom) K.; m. Patricia June Ogilvie, Dec. 27, 1969; children: Hugh, Alex, Graham, Charlotte, Blair. AB cum laude, Kenyon Coll., 1968; JD, Duquesne U., 1972. Bar: Pa. 1972, U.S. Dist. Ct. (we. dist.) Pa. 1972, U.S. Ct. Appeals (3rd cir.) 1977, U.S. Supreme Ct. 1984, U.S. Ct. Appeals (6th, 7th and 10th cirs.), 1988. From assoc. to ptnr. Dickie, McCamey & Chilcote, Pitts., 1972—98, mng. ptnr., 1993-97; ptnr. Gorr Moser Dell & Loughney, Pitts., 1999-2000, Grogan & Graffam, Pitts., 2000—04, Meyers, Kenrick Giuffre & Evans, LLC, Pitts., 2004—. Articles editor Duquesne U. Law Rev., 1971; editor Pitts. Legal Jour., 1980-84. Fellow: ABA, Allegheny Bar Found. (ho. of dels. 1980—2000), Pa. Bar Found.; mem.: Pa. Bar Assn., Allegheny County Bar Assn. (bd. govs. 1984—, adminstrv. v.p. 1986—, pres.-elect 1990, pres. 1991), Kenyon Coll. Nat. Alumni Coun., Kenyon Coll. Alumni Assn. Pitts. (pres. 1983—84), Duquesne U. Law Alumni Assn. (pres. 1985—86), Duquesne Club, Valley Brook Club, Rivers Club. Democrat. Office: Meyers Kenrick Giuffre & Evans LLC US Steel Tower 600 Grant St Ste 5745 Pittsburgh PA 15219-1000 Office Phone: 412-281-4100. Business E-Mail: ckenrick@meyersmedmal.com.

KENSETH, MATT, race car driver; b. Madison, Wis., Mar. 10, 1972; Career highlights include: first NASCAR Busch Series circuit season posted seven top 10's in 21 races; winner track championship at Madison Internat. Speedway, 1994, Wis. Internat. Raceway, 1994, 95; finished runner-up to Dale Earnhardt Jr. in points, 1998, posting 23 top 10s in 31 races with three wins and one Bud Pole, 1998; third place finisher behind Dale Earnhardt Jr. and Jeff Green, 1999, winner four races -- Darlington, Calif., Nazareth, and Bristol, and two Bud Poles at Dover and Charlotte, 1999; primary sponsor for 2000, Visine; Radioshak 500, 2002; Checker Autoparts 500, 2002; Subaway 400, 2004; UAW Daimler-Chrysler 400, 2003-2004; Sharpie 500, 2005; Diamond Hill Plywood 200, 2005; IROC Series Daytona, 2006; Auto Club 500, 2006.

KENSINGTON, ANDREW JUSTUS, litigation specialist; b. Elmhurst, Ill., Oct. 3, 1950; s. Walter Alan Kerr and Esther Elizabeth Blanton. Cert. litigation specialist, Roosevelt U., Chgo., 1981; BA in Psychology, Ill. State U., Normal, 1984, BA in Sociology, 1984; grad., Gabriel Richard Inst., 1984. Cert.: (Westlaw specialist). Pres. US Justice Party Americále, 1976—2005; owner Orion Inst., Buckingham, Va., 2001—05; litigation specialist Niro, Scavone, Haller & Niro, Chgo., 1983—85; with Johnson, Cusack & Bell, Chgo., 1989—90; legal asst. Trexler-Bushnell, et al, Chgo., 1990; patent cons. Legal Pers., Northbrook, Ill., 1990; sales rep. Radio Am./APAC Corp., Chgo., 1991—93; litigation cons., asst. Paul Armstrong, Atty. at Law, Chgo., 1993—94; resident property mgr. Joel Kaplan, Herbert G. Dorsey III, Sedona, Ariz., 1994—98; patent cons. Office Tech. Develop. Office Vice Chancellor U. Ill. Asst. project mgr. Amoco Corp. (Olsten Svcs.), Chgo., 1989—90; rschr. in field. Author free verse poetry; creator, producer, engr., arranger (personalized audio tapes);, author press releases. Participant anti-war movement Vietnam War, 1968—76; candidate U.S. Presidency US J.P.A., Va., 2003—04; founder N.A.C.G., Ill., 1993—2005. Capt. USAR. Named Excellence in Mil. Sci., US Army, Howe, Ind., 1965. Mem.: ABA, Vietnam Vets. Against the War. Episcopalian. Avocations: music, yachting, boating. Home and Office: 100 Ridge St Apt 118 Charlottesville VA 22902 Office Phone: 434-806-5554.

KENSLEA, TIMOTHY JOSEPH, historian, educator; b. Boston, Nov. 15, 1954; s. Daniel Leo and Clare Lindberg Kenslea; m. Mary Frances Sprogell, Aug. 17, 1985; 1 child, Charles Daniel. BA, Yale U., 1976; MAT, Boston Coll., 1990, PhD, 1999. Editor Little, Brown & Co., Boston, 1978—82; sr. editor Silver Burdett Ginn, Lexington, 1984—87, mng. editor Needham, 1987—88; history tchr. Norwell H.S., 1995—2006, Needham H.S., Mass., 2006—. Author: (book (nonfiction historical narrative) The Sedgwicks in Love: Courtship, Engagement, and Marriage in the Early Republic. Mem.: Catharine Maria Sedgwick Soc., Soc. Historians Early Am. Republic, New Eng. History Tchrs. Assn., New Eng. Hist. Assn., Nat. Coun. Social Studies. Office: Needham H S 609 Webster St Needham MA 02494 Home Phone: 781-444-2056. Personal E-mail: timkens@aya.yale.edu.

KENT, ALLEN, library and information sciences professor; b. NYC, Oct. 24, 1921; s. Samuel and Anna (Begun) K.; m. Rosalind Kossoff, Jan. 24, 1943; children: Merryl Frances Kent Samuels, Emily Beth Kent Yeager, Jacqueline Diane Kent Maryak, Carolyn May Kent Hall. BS in Chemistry, CCNY, 1942. Sci. editor Intersci. Pubs., 1946-51; research assoc. Ctr. Internat. Studies, MIT, 1951-53; prin. documentation engr. Battelle Meml. Inst., Columbus, Ohio, 1953-55; asso. dir. Ctr. for Documentation and Communication Research; prof. library sci. Western Res. U., Cleve., 1955-63; dir. office communications programs, chmn. interdisciplinary doctoral program info. sci., prof. info. sci., edn. and computer sci. U. Pitts., 1963-76; Univ. Disting. Service prof. library and info. sci. and assoc. dean U. Pitts. Sch. Library and Info. Sci., 1976-91, interim dean, 1985-86, prof. emeritus, 1992. Mem. mgmt. info. com. Health and Welfare Assn. Allegheny County, Pa., 1972-80; dir. Marcel Dekker, Inc., N.Y., 1978-93. Author (with others): Machine Literature Searching, 1956; author: (with J.W. Perry) Documentation and Information Retrieval, 1957; author: Tools for Machine Literature Searching, 1958, Centralized Information Services, 1958, Mechanized Information Retrieval, 1962, 2d edit., 1966, also fgn. transls. Specialized Information Centers, 1965, Information Analysis and Retrieval, 1971, Resource Sharing in Libraries, 1977, On-Line Revolution in Libraries, 1978, Structure and Governance of Library Networks, 1979, Use of Library Materials, 1979, Information Technology, 1982; editor, co-editor numerous books in field, exec. editor Ency. Libr. and Info. Sci., 1968—2003, Ency. Computer Sci. and Tech., 1972—2002, Ency. Microcomputers, 1984—2001, Ency. of Telecomm., 1988—98. Chmn. bd. Interuniv. Comms. Coun. Inc., 1971-74. Served with USAAF, 1942-46. Recipient Info. Tech. Merit award Eastman Kodak Co., 1968. Fellow AAAS; mem. ALA, Assn. Computing Machinery, Am. Soc. Info. Sci. (award of merit 1977, award for Best Info. Sci. Book of Yr. 1980, Pioneer in Info. Sci. 1987), Acad. Sr. Profls. Eckerd Coll. Home: 5108 Brittany Dr S Apt 601 Saint Petersburg FL 33715-1525 *My goal has been to be useful. This entails service, dedication to my profession and to the institution which supports my work, and absolute standards of honesty.*

KENT, AMY ELIZABETH, criminologist; b. Grand Rapids, Mich., May 6, 1978; d. Kenneth R. and Linda C. Kent. BS in Biology, Ctrl. Mich. U., Mt. Pleasant, 2000; MS in Molecular Biotechnology, Wayne State U., Detroit, 2003. Rsch. assoc. U. Mich., Ann Arbor, 2003—04; criminalist Miami-Dade Police Dept., 2004—. Contbr. articles to profl. jours. Mem.: Internat. Assn. Bloodstain Pattern Analysts (assoc.), Am. Acad. Forensic Scis. (assoc.), Miami Sport and Social Club, Phi Eta Sigma, Golden Key. Avocations: softball, flag football, running. Office: Miami-Dade Police Dept 9105 NW 25th St Miami FL 33172 Home Phone: 786-512-1829; Office Phone: 305-471-3155. Personal E-mail: musta36@hotmail.com. Business E-Mail: akent@mdpd.com.

KENT, BARTIS MILTON, retired physician; b. Terrell, Tex., June 23, 1925; s. Bartis William and Annie (Smalley) K.; m. Ann L. Kiel, July 6, 1954; children: Susan Ruth, Martha Lucille, Bartis Michael. Student, So. Meth. U., 1942-44; MD, Baylor U., 1948. Diplomate Am. Bd. Internal Medicine. Intern Jefferson Davis Hosp., Houston, 1948-49; resident pathology Mass. Meml. Hosps., Boston, 1951; resident in internal medicine Baylor U., 1953-56; indsl. physician Humble Oil Co., Houston, 1949-51; instr. dept. medicine U. Iowa, 1956-58; staff physician Iowa City VA Hosp., 1956-58; practice medicine specializing in internal medicine Muskogee, Okla., 1958—2002. Cons. Muskogee VA Hosp.; clin. asst. prof. medicine U. Okla. Sch. Medicine, 1975-98. Chmn. Muskogee County chpt. Am. Nat. Red Cross, 1963-65. With USAF, 1951—53. Decorated Air medal. Fellow A.C.P.; mem. Indsl. Med. Assn., Soc. Nuclear Medicine, Am. Fedn. Clin. Research, Am. Heart Assn., Aerospace Medicine Assn., Am., Okla. socs. internal medicine, Muskogee C. of C. Methodist. Mason (Shriner). Avocations: fishing, gardening. Home: 800 N 45th St Muskogee OK 74401-1505 Personal E-mail: bmkent@cox.net.

KENT, CALVIN ALBERT, academic administrator; b. Kansas City, Kans., Sept. 8, 1941; m. Nita Sue Davis, Aug. 23, 1963; children: Nita Christine, Anna Elaine. BA, Baylor U., 1963; MA, U. Mo., 1965, PhD, 1967; postgrad., U. Va., 1967, Wichita State U., 1972, U. Chgo., 1975, Rice U., 1987. Instr. econs. U. Mo., Columbia, 1963-64; instr. social scis. Stevens Coll., Columbia, 1964-67; faculty U. SD, Vermillion, 1967-78, prof. econs., 1973-78, dir. public fin. studies, 1971-78; Herman W. Lay prof. pvt. enterprise, dir. Center Pvt. Enterprise Baylor U., Waco, Tex., 1978-90; adminstr. Energy Info. Adminstrn., Washington, 1990-93; dean Lewis Disting. chair bus. Coll. Bus. Marshall U., Huntington, W.Va., 1993—2003, v.p. tech. commercialization, 2003—04, v.p. bus. and econ. rsch., 2004—. Exec. dir. S.D. Council on Econ. Edn., 1969-78; chief economist taxation coms. S.D. Legislature; cons. S.D. Dept. Rev. Alderman, Vermillion, 1969-78; mem. Pres.'s Adv. Com. Entrepreneurship Edn., 1983-85. Author: Indian Poverty, 1969, Taxation of Cooperative Enterprise, 1970, Death Taxes in the American States, 1974, Municipal Regulation and Franchising, 1975, Encyclopedia of Entrepreneurship, 1981, The Environment for Entrepreneurship, 1984, Entrepreneurship and the Privatization of Government, 1987, The Texas Economy, 1989, Entrepreneurship Education: Present Practices Future Direction, 1990, The Public Utilities Holding Company Act: 1935-92, 1993, Agenda for Fair Taxation, 1998; contbr. articles to profl. jours. Pres. City Coun., Vermillion, 1974-78; vice chmn. S.D. Mcpl. League, Dist. 2, 1972-74; councilman City of Huntington, W.Va., 1997—, City of Woodway, Tex., 1985-90, mayor, 1986-90, chmn. City Coun., 2002-03; co-chair Gov.'s Commn. on Tax Fairness, 1997-2000; mem. Tri-State Airport Authority, v.p., 2001—; mem. tax moderation task force, Gov., 2006—; v.p. Huntington Mcpl. Devel. Corp., 2000—. Outstanding Tchr., U. S.D., 1970-72, Outstanding Prof., Baylor U., 1983; Outstanding Young Religious Leader, 1976, Disting. Prof. Baylor Sch. Bus., 1981, Piper Prof. Piper Found., 1988; recipient Freedoms Found. at Valley Forge award for excellence in pvt. enterprise edn., 1980, Sargent Americanism award, 1986, John Schramm Leadership award Nat. Assn. Econ. Edn. and Joint Coun. on Econ. Edn., NSF award, 1974, Gov.'s citation for disting. achievement, 1996. Mem. Nat. Assn. Econ. Educators (pres. 1978-80), Assn. Pvt. Enterprise Edn. (sec.-treas. 1982-90, Disting. Svc. award 1988, Outstanding Scholar award 1992, bd. dirs. 1994), Soc. Econ. Educators (sec.-treas. 1987-90, v.p. 1993, pres. 1994), Rotary (pres. 1999-2000, Paul Harris fellow), Masons. Republican. Presbyterian. Home: 133 Woodland Dr Huntington WV 25705-1349

KENT, DAVID CHARLES, lawyer; b. Shreveport, La., July 23, 1953; s. Keith C. and Louise (Goode) Kent; m. Carol Elizabeth Hittson, July 3, 1976; children: John, Meredith, Robert. BA, Baylor U., 1975, JD, 1978. Bar: Tex. 1978, U.S. Dist. Ct. (no. dist.) Tex. 1980, U.S. Ct. Appeals (5th cir.) 1980, U.S. Dist. Ct. (so. and we. dists.) Tex. 1981, U.S. Ct. Appeals (11th cir.) 1981, U.S. Dist. Ct. (ea. dist.) Tex. 1981, bd. cert. civil trial law, personal injury trial law:. Briefing atty. Supreme Ct. Tex., Austin, 1978-79, Hughes & Luce L.L.P., Dallas, 1979-2000; ptnr. Diamond McCarthy Taylor Finley Bryant & Lee, LLP, 2000—03, Sedgwick Detert Moran & Arnold LLP, 2003—. Editor: Managing Scarce World Resources, 1975, Crime and Justice in America, 1976, Medical Care and Health in America, 1977, Meeting America's Energy Needs, 1978; contbr. articles to profl. jours. Mem. nat. exploring com. Boy Scouts Am., Irving, Tex., 1982—92; coord. employee campaign United Way, Dallas, 1981—90; teamwalk March of Dimes, Dallas, 1981—87; mem. HOBY Tex. N., bd. dirs., 1999—, sec., 2000—06, pres., 2006—; mem. Baylor Parents League, pres. North Dallas area chpt., 1999—2001; pres. Twin Bridge Homeowners Assn., 2000—02; bd. dirs. High Adventure Treks Dads and Daus., Inc., chmn., 2005—; bd. dirs. Law Focused Edn. Inc., 1997—2006, pres., 2004—06. Named Outstanding Young Lawyer Dallas, Dallas Assn. Young Lawyers, 1989; recipient Cert. Recognition, United Way, 1983. Fellow: Tex. Bar Found., Dallas Bar Found.; mem.: ABA (life fellow ABA Young Lawyer Divsn.), Coll. of State Bar of Tex., Dallas Bar Assn. (chair spkrs. com. 2002, dir. tort and ins. practice sect. 2005—, sec./treas. tort and ins. practice sect. 2006, co-chair Bench Bar conf. com. 2006, bd. dirs. 2007, vice chair tort and ins. practice sect. 2007, Outstanding Com. Chair award 1998), Baylor U. Alumni Assn. (scholarship com. 1980—81). Republican. Methodist. Office: Sedgwick Detert Moran & Arnold LLP 1717 Main St Ste 5400 Dallas TX 75201 Office Phone: 469-227-4658. Business E-Mail: david.kent@sdma.com.

KENT, DENNIS V., earth scientist, educator; b. Prague, Czech Republic, Nov. 4, 1946; came to US, 1953; s. Frank D. and Olga Kent; m. Carolyn Ann Cook, Dec. 18, 1971; 1 child, Amanda Grace. BS in Geology, CCNY, 1968; PhD in Marine Geology and Geophysics, Columbia U., 1974; D honoris causa, U. Paris, 2005. Rsch. assoc. Lamont-Doherty Earth Obs., Palisades, NY, 1974-79, sr. rsch. assoc., 1979-84, Doherty sr. rsch. scientist, 1984-98, assoc. dir., 1987-89, interim dir., 1989-90, dir. rsch., 1993-94, adj. sr. rsch. scientist, 1998—; prof. dept. geol. sci. Rutgers U., 1998—, bd. govs. prof. geol. scis., 2007—. Adj. prof. dept. geol. scis. Columbia U., N.Y.C., 1987-98; Gast prof. Inst. for Geophysik, Swiss Tech. Inst., Zurich, 1982, 97, 2003; vis. scholar Scripps Inst. of Oceanography, 2003; mem. ocean history panel Joint Oceanographic Instns. for Deep Earth Sampling, 1987-90, mem. exec. com., 1989-90, 93-94, 1998-2003; mem. bd. govs. Joint Oceanog. Inst., Washington, 1989-90, 93-94, 98—, vice chair, 2002-04, chmn., 2004-2006; mem. bd. govs. IODP Mgmt. Internat., Inc., Washington, D.C., 2003-07; mem. forum organizing com. U.S. Continental Sci. Drilling Program, 1993-95; rev. and adv. com. Inst. Rock Magnetism, U. Minn., 1994-99; mem. U.S. Sci. Adv. Com., Compost II, 1996-97; founding mem. ISI Highly Cited Rschrs. database, 2002. Assoc. editor Jour. Geophys. Rsch., 1981-83, Geophys. Rsch. Letters, 1984-87, Paleoceanography, 1989-96, Terra Nova, 1997-99, G-cubed, 1999-2005; contbr. more than 230 refereed articles to profl. jours. Recipient VMSG medal Vening Meinesz Sch. Geodynamics, Delft, Holland, 2003, Petrus Peregrinus medal European Geophys. Union, 2006; NSF grantee, 1974—; named Conoco Disting. lectr. Woods Hole (Mass.) Oceanog. Inst., 1983, Turner/Conoco Disting. lectr. U. Mich., Ann Arbor, 1985, Cox lectr. Am. Geophys. Union, 1998. Fellow AAAS, Am. Geophys. Union (pres.-elect geomagnetism and paleomagnetism sect. 1992-94, pres. 1994-96), Geol. Soc. Am. (Arthur L. Day medal 2003); mem. NAS. Office: Lamont-Doherty Earth Obs 61 Rt 9W Palisades NY 10964 also: Rutgers U Dept Geol Scis Piscataway NJ 08854 Office Phone: 845-365-8544. Business E-Mail: dvk@rci.rutgers.edu.

KENT, DOLORES, obstetrician, gynecologist, plastic surgeon; BA, Northeastern U., Boston; MD, Harvard U., Boston. Pvt. practice, LA. Fellow: ACOG; mem.: Am. Assn. Cosmetic Gynecologists, Assn. Black Women Physicians, Am. Assn. Cosmetic Surgeons, Ob-Gyn Soc. So. Calif., Am. Assn. Gynecologic Laparoscopists, Women Painters W., Pasadena Soc. Artists, Collage Artists Am. Office: 9201 Sunset Blvd Ste 406 Los Angeles CA 90069

KENT, EDGAR ROBERT, JR., investment banker; b. Balt., May 28, 1941; s. E. Robert and Marian (Mueller) K.; children: E. Robert, Josephine Townsend, Louise Daniel. BS, Princeton U., 1963; MBA, Columbia U., 1966; JD, U. Md., 1975. CFA. Mng. dir. DeutscheBancAlex.Brown, Balt., 1968-2001; dir. Alex.Brown Realty, Balt., 2001—. Trustee Calvert Sch., Balt., Ctr. Stage, Balt., Endowment Fund U. Md.; chmn. Balt. Cmty. Found. Home: 103 Castlewood Rd Baltimore MD 21210-1360 Office: Alex Brown Realty Inc Ste 1200 300 E Lombard St Baltimore MD 21202-6740 Business E-Mail: bob.kent@abrealty.com.

KENT, ERNIE, men's college basketball coach; b. Jan. 22, 1955; m. Dianna Kent; children: Marcus, Jordan, McKenzie. BA in Cmty. Svc. and Pub. Affairs, U. Oreg., 1977. Freshman coach U. Oreg., 1977, 1979; head coach O'Hara Cath. Sch., Eugene, Oreg., 1979, al-Khaleeg Club, Sayhat, Saudi Arabia, 1980—87, St. Mary's Coll., Moraga, Calif., 1991—97, U. Oreg., 1997—; asst. coach Colo. State U., 1988—89, Stanford U., 1990—91. Asst. coach USA Basketball 21-and-Under Nat. Team Summer Games, Japan, 2001; head coach USA Basketball Jr. Nat. Team Internat. Basketball Fedn. World Championships, 2003, Global Games (gold medal), 2003; bd. dirs. Nat. Assn. Basketball Coaches; bd. govs. Wooden Award. Named Pacific-10 Coach of Yr., 2002, Dist. Coach of Yr., Nat. Assn. Basketball Coaches, 2002, US Basketball Writers Assn., 2002, Basketball Times, 2002; recipient Hope award, Nat. Multiple Sclerosis Soc., Oreg. chpt., 2004. Office: Mens Basketball Casanova Athletic Ctr 8835 University of Oreg Eugene OR 97403-8835 Office Phone: 541-346-0490. E-mail: ekent@uoregon.edu.*

KENT, GEORGIA L., obstetrician, gynecologist, healthcare executive, educator; b. NYC, May 30, 1950; d. Harry J. and Eva R. K. BS in Biology with honors, U. Pitts., 1971; MD, U. Pa., 1975; MBA, George Washington U., 1991. Diplomate Am. Bd. Obstetricians-Gynecologists; MD, Colo., Calif., N.Y., N.J., Pa. Sr. instr. ob-gyn. Hahnemann U., Phila., 1979-82; obstetrician-gynecologist Kaiser Group Health Assn., Washington, 1982-90; med. dir. Pacificare, Fountain Valley, Calif., 1991-93, Denver, 1993-94; v.p. med. svcs. The Prudential Ins. Co. of Am., Prudential Healthcare, Roseland, N.J., 1994-96; potter, healthcare cons. self employed, West Orange, N.J., 1997-99, Pitts., 1999—; coll. chair undergrad. bus. and mgmt. degree programs U. Phoenix-Pitts. Campus, 2000—03; pvt. practice, 2006—. Guest lectr. U. Calif. Riverside, 1992-93, Denver U., 1993-94; adj. faculty Duquesne U., 1999—; dept. chair undergrad. bus. & mgmt. U. Phoenix, Pitts., 2000-03, Cmty. Coll. Allegheny County, 2001—; pvt. practice Georgia L. Kent, MD FACOG PC, 2006—. Contbg. author, featured in: (book) Women in Medicine and Management: A Mentoring Guide, 1995; exhibited in group shows at N.J. Ctr. for Visual Arts Mem. Show, 1997, 98, Sweetwater Art Ctr., 1999, North Hills Art Ctr., 2000 (hon. mention). Mem. AAUW, Am. Coll. Obstetricians and Gynecologists, Phi Beta Kappa, Beta Gamma Sigma. Avocations: greyhound rescue/adoption, potter, gardening, walking.

KENT, JEFFREY FRANKLIN, professional baseball player; b. Bellflower, Calif., Mar. 7, 1968; Grad., Edison H.S., Calif. 2d baseman Toronto Blue Jays, 1992, N.Y. Mets, 1992-96, San Francisco Giants, 1997—2002, Houston Astros, 2003—04, Los Angeles Dodgers, 2004—. Named Nat. League MVP, 2000; named to Nat. League All-Star Team, 1999—2001, 2004, Nat. league All-Star Team, 2005; recipient Silver Slugger, MLB, 2005. Office: LA Dodgers 1000 Elysian Park Ave Los Angeles CA 90012

KENT, JILL ELSPETH, entrepreneur, art appraiser, lawyer; b. Detroit, June 1, 1948; d. Seymour and Grace (Edelman) K.; m. Mark Elliott Solomons, Aug. 20, 1978. BA, U. Mich., 1970; JD, George Washington U., 1975, LLM, 1979. Bar: D.C. 1975. Mgmt. intern U.S. Dept. Transp., Washington, 1971-73; staff analyst Office Mgmt. and Budget, Exec. Office of Pres., Washington, 1974-76; legis. counsel U.S. Treasury Dept., Washington, 1976-78, dir. legis. reference divsn. Healthcare Financing Adminstrn., 1978-80; sr. budget examiner Office Mgmt. and Budget, Exec. Office of Pres., Washington, 1980-84; chief Treasury, Gen. Svcs. Office of Mgmt. and Budget, Washington, 1984-85; dep. asst. sec. for departmental fin. and planning U.S. Dept. Treasury, Washington, 1985-86, dep. asst. sec. for dept. fin. and mgmt., 1986-88, asst. sec. of treasury, 1988-89; CFO U.S. Dept. State, Washington, 1989-93, acting under sec. of state for mgmt., 1991; exec. devel. program Office of Mgmt. and Budget, Washington, 1984; CFO George Washington U. Med. Ctr., Washington, 1993-97; v.p. IPAC, 1997-98, The Columbus Group; chief assessor Educated Eye Appraisals. Pres. CEO Atlantic Threadworks Inc.; gen. mgr. The Frogeye Co., 1995—; adj. prof. pub. policy U. Md., 1993—. Bd. dirs. Mobile Med. Care Inc., 1987-91; Trustee Newport Sch., 1988-91, Washington Civic Symphony, 1994-95; bd. dirs. China Found., 1997—; sr. counselor Atlantic Coun. U.S., 1997—; bd. dirs., sec. Wash. Bach Consort. Recipient Adminstrs. award Healthcare Financing Adminstrn., 1980; named on of Top 40 Performers, Mgmt. mag., 1987, Disting. Svc. award Dept. Treasury, 1989, Am. Assn. Govt. Accts. award, 1992, Disting. Svc. award Dept. State, 1993. Mem. ABA, D.C. Bar Assn., Pres's. Coun. on Mgmt. Improvement, CFO Roundtable Healthcare Forum, Fin. Execs. Inst., Exec. Women in Govt. (treas. 1991-92, pres. 1992-93), Va. Assn. of Female Execs. (adv. coun. 1990), Coun. Excellence in Govt. (prin. 1993—). Republican. Home: 2419 California St NW Washington DC 20008-1615 Office Phone: 202-483-7209. Personal E-mail: jekent@verizon.net.

KENT, JOHN BRADFORD, lawyer; b. Jacksonville, Fla., Sept. 5, 1939; s. Frederick Heber and Norma Cleveland (Futch) Kent; m. Monett Powers, Dec. 18, 1969; children: Monett, Susan, Sally, Katherine. AB, Yale U., 1961; JD, U. Fla., 1964; LLM in Taxation, NYU, 1965. Bar: Fla. 1964, US Dist. Ct. (mid. dist.) Fla. 1965, US Tax Ct. 1965, US Ct. Appeals (11th cir.) 1973, US Supreme Ct. 1973, US Dist. Ct. (so. dist.) Fla. 1981, Nebr. US Dist. Ct. 1995. Assoc. Ulmer, Murchison, Kent, Ashby & Ball, Jacksonville, 1965-67; ptnr., shareholder Kent, Watts & Durden, P.A. and predecessor firms, Jacksonville, 1967-85; shareholder Carlton, Field, Ward, Emmanuel, Smith, Cutler & Kent, Jacksonville, 1985-88, Kent, Crawford, P.A., Jacksonville, 1988—2003, Marks Gray, P.A., Jacksonville, 2003—. Past pres., trustee Fla. CC Found.; past. pres., bd. dirs. N.E. divsn. Children's Home Soc. Fla.; past bd. dirs. Jacksonville Legal Aid Soc.; bd. dirs. Children's Home Soc. Fla. Mem.: Nat. Assn. Theatre Owners Fla. (bd. dirs., officer 1969—2000), Rotary (past officer, Paul Harris fellow). Office: Marks Gray PA 1200 Riverplace Blvd Ste 800 Jacksonville FL 32207

KENT, JULIE, dancer, actress, model; b. Bethesda, Md., July 11, 1969; d. Charles Lindbergh and Jennifer Elsie Cox; m. Victor Barbee, 1996. Grad. high sch., Potomac, Md. Apprentice Am. Ballet Theatre, NYC, 1985-86, mem. corps de ballet, 1986-1990, soloist, 1990-93, prin. dancer, 1993—. Starring role (films) Dancers, 1986, Center Stage, 2000; performed as a guest artist nationally and internationally. Recipient Prix de Lausanne Internat. Ballet competition, 1986, 1st prize at Erik Bruhn Competition in Toronto, 1993, Prix Benois de la Danse, Stuttgart, Germany, 2000; named one of 50 Most Beautiful People, People Mag., 1993. Office: Am Ballet Theatre 890 Broadway Fl 3 New York NY 10003

KENT, LAWRENCE, retired association executive, education and mental health director; s. Charles Ernest Hollopeter and Roma Flae Thomas-Hollopeter. Certs., Am. Inst. Banking, Dayton, Beverly Hills, Los Angeles, 1953—75; grad., US Army Q.M. Sch., Fort Lee, Va., 1956; cert., Am. Savs. and Loan Inst., Tucson, 1973; student, Pima C.C., Tucson, 1973; AA, LA City Coll., 1977; student, LA Valley Coll., Van Nuys, Calif., 1977—78; BA, Calif. State U., Northridge, 1979; postgrad., City Coll. San Francisco, 1980—82, Skyline Coll., San Bruno, Calif., 1981—82; MA, San Francisco State U., 1981; PhD, Miami U., Oxford, Ohio, 1985; postgrad., Sinclair C.C., Dayton, Ohio, 1988—92, U. Cin., 1991. Lic. social worker Ohio Counselor, Social Worker, and Marriage and Family Therapist Bd., 1993. Head teller and gen. ledger Merchants Nat. Bank and Trust Co., Dayton, Ohio, 1953—56; br. utility and head office teller Winters Nat. Bank & Trust Co., Dayton, 1958—61; dept. mgr., pro-cashier Union Bank, Beverly Hills, Sherman Oaks, Calif., 1961—67; dep. county auditor Montgomery County Auditor, Dayton, 1968—70; asst. to savings and br. ops. mgr., loan officer Tucson Fed. Savs. and Loan Assn., 1970—73; asst. v.p. Mechanics Nat. Bank, Bell, Calif., 1974—76; instrnl. materials lab. asst. Calif. State U., Northridge, 1977—79; asst. to dept. chair, program dir. San Francisco State U., 1979—82; program developer Native Am. Indian Srs. Ctr., San Francisco, 1980; tchg. fellow Miami U., Oxford, Hamilton, Ohio, 1982—85; dir. edn. and vocat. tng. Dayton Job Corps Ctr., 1987—88; dir. adminstrn. Mental Health Resources Corp., Xenia, Ohio, 1988; dir. program devel. Interdenominational Ministerial Alliance, Dayton, 1990—91; counselor Dayton Urban League, 1990—92; dir. devel. Germaine Lang. Ctr., Dayton, 1992—92; chmn. bd., CEO Kent/Universal Co., Inc., Orlando, Fla., 1993—97. Founder, pres. emeritus Presdl. Families Am., 1995—. Author, editor: newsletter Presdl. Families Gazette, author poetry; contbr. articles to publs. Mem. NY br. The English-Speaking Union, NYC, 1995—96; founding mem. Wall of Tolerance Nat. Campaign, Montgomery, Ala., 2001—06; donor, patron San Francisco Opera, 1980—81; patron San Francisco Symphony Assn., 1980—81; patron, mem. Dayton Ballet, 1984—85, Dayton Opera Assn., 1984—91, 2007—, Dayton Art Inst., 1984—88, SE Land Use Commn., Dayton, 1991, Montgomery County Police and Cmty. Rels. Com., Dayton, 1991—92, Leadership for Equality and Action in Dayton, 2004, Grassroots Greater Dayton, 2005—06, Dayton Internat. Peace Mus., 2006—, Dayton Coun. on World Affairs, 2006—, Dayton Visual Arts Ctr., 2006—; co. chair mental health resources corp. United Way Greater Dayton, Xenia, Ohio, 1988; mem. adv. com. Drug Action Coalition, Dayton, 1990—92; rep. two precincts SE Priority Bd., Dayton, 1991; vol., mem. WMFE-TV-24 Pub. Broadcasting Ctr., Orlando, Fla., 1994—96; subscriber Dayton Philharm. Orch., 2005—06; sponsor Union Concerned Scientists, Cambridge, Mass., 1990; founder Fla. and SE states br., editor The Monarchist League, London, 1994—99; invited attendee White House Briefing on Fgn. and Domestic Affairs, Washington, 1988; election candidate San Mateo County C.C. Dist. Bd. Trustees, Calif., 1981; mem. adv. group to Ohio gov. Cmty. Mental Health Fin. Mgmt. Group, Columbus, 1988. Specialist, 5th class US Army and USAR, 1956—62, Korea and US. Decorated Korea Def. Svc. medal US Army, Nat. Def. Svc. medal. Mem.: AMVETS (life), VFW (life), Intertel, Am. Assn. Univ. Profs., Poetic Genius Soc., Am. Mensa (Top One Percent Soc.), Korean War Vet. Assn. (life), Korea Def. Vets. Am., Navy League US, Army and Navy Union USA, Assn. US Army, 24th Inf. Divsn. Assn., Cold War Vets. Assn., First Families Miami County, Ohio, Huguenot Soc. Am., Mil. Order Fgn. Wars US, Gen. Soc. War 1812, Mil. Order Loyal Legion US, Sons Union Vets. Civil War, Mil. Order Stars and Bars, Descendants Mexican War Vets., Sons Spanish-Am. War Vets., Nat. Soc. Sons and Daughters of the Pilgrims, Winthrop Soc., Vets. Battle of the Bulge (assoc.), Nat. Assn. Established Families in Am., Soc. of Colonial Wars in the State of Fla., Mil. Order Fgn. Wars US, Mil. Order of the Loyal Legion of the US, Sons Sherman's Mar. to the Sea, Nat. Soc. Sons Colonial New Eng., Huguenot Soc. Am., St. George's Soc. NY, First Families Franklin, The Lost State Hist. Soc. (life), Hereditary Order Descendants of the Loyalists and Patriots Am. Revolution (life), SR in the State of Calif. (life), Nat. Soc. SAR (life; sgt.-at-arms Tucson chpt. 1970), Nat. Soc. Sons Am. Colonists (life; 2nd v.p., nat. corr. sec. gen 1977), Huguenot Soc. Founders Manakin in the Colony of Va. (life; pres. Fla. state br. 1994—98), St. David's Soc. State NY (life), First Families Ohio (life), 1st Cav. Divsn. Assn. (life), First Families Miami County, Ohio, Soc. Ind. Pioneers, First Families Tenn., Tex. First Families, Nat. Soc. Sons Utah Pioneers, Soc. Ky. Pioneers, Established Families in Am., Soc. Colonial Wars in the State Fla., St. George's Soc. NY, Am. Legion, 4th Armored Divsn. Assn., US Cav. Assn., Antioch Temple, Ancient Arabic Order, Nobles of the Mystic Shrine, Dayton (Ky. Cols. unit mem. 1989—92), Reed Commandery 6, York Rite, Dayton, Scottish Rite, Valley of Dayton (choir mem. 1988—89), KP, 37 Muncie IN & 9 Orlando FL, Knight Masons (Ireland), Buckeye Coun. 64, Dayton (life), The Royal Order of Scotland, Tall Cedars of Lebanon, Three Rivers Forest 174, Springfield OH, The Ormazd Grott, Orlando, Quatuor Coronati Corr. Cir. Ltd., London, Eng., Order of DeMolay, Dayton OH & Winter Pk. FL (publs. and fundraising advisor 1990—95), DeMolay Found. (preceptor donor, leadership fund), Solar Craft Club, Dayton Masonic Temple, Scottish Rite, Orlando (vol. computer data base mgr. 1994—95), Silver Trowel Coun. 141, York Rite, Dayton, Mt. Moriah Chaper 230, Royal Arch Masons, York Rite, Dayton, Pi Lambda Theta, Phi Delta Kappa, Phi Alpha Theta. Episcopalian. Office: Presidential Families of America Chateaux L'Aiglon Kettering OH 45429-1474 Home Phone: 937-299-9896; Office Phone: 937-299-9896. Personal E-mail: dr_lawrence_kent@hotmail.com.

KENT, LINDA GAIL, dancer; b. Buffalo, Sept. 21, 1946; d. Jerol Edward and Dorismae (Kohler) K.; m. Nicholas Wolff Lyndon, June 9, 1996. BS, Juilliard Sch., 1968. Dancer Alvin Ailey Am. Dance Theater, 1968-74, then prin. dancer, 1970-74; prin. dancer Paul Taylor Dance Co., NYC, 1975-89; dir. dance Perry-Mansfield Performing Arts Sch. and Camp, Steamboat Springs, Colo., 2001—. Faculty Juilliard Sch., 1984—; artist-in-residence Union Theological Seminary, N.Y. Mem. Am. Guild Mus. Artists, Actors Equity. Democrat. Unitarian Universalist. Home: 91 Payson Ave New York NY 10034-2722 Office: The Juilliard Sch Dance Divsn 60 Lincoln Center Plz New York NY 10023-6588 Home Phone: 212-569-1569; Office Phone: 212-799-5000 x 7057. E-mail: lgk921@aol.com.

KENT, M. ELIZABETH, lawyer; b. NYC, Nov. 17, 1943; d. Francis J. and Hannah (Bergman) K. AB, Vassar Coll. magna cum laude, 1964; AM, Harvard U., 1965, PhD, 1974; JD, Georgetown U., 1978. Bar: DC 1978, US Dist. Ct. DC 1978, US Ct. Appeals (DC cir.) 1978, US Supreme Ct. 1983, US Dist. Ct. Md. 1985. From lectr. to asst. prof. history U. Ala., Birmingham, 1972-74; assoc. Santarelli and Gimer, Washington, 1978; sole practice Washington, 1978—. Mem. Ripon Soc., Cambridge and Washington, 1968-93; rsch. dir. Howard M. Miller for Congress, Boston, 1972; vol. campaigns John V. Lindsay for Mayor, 1969, John V. Lindsay for Pres., 1972, John B. Anderson for Pres., 1980. Woodrow Wilson fellow 1964-65; Harvard U. fellow 1968-69. Mem.: ACLU, ABA, Superior Ct. Trial Lawyers Assn., DC Assn. Criminal Def. Lawyers (bd. dirs. 2001—), Women's Bar Assn., DC Bar Assn., Phi Beta Kappa. Republican. Avocations: history, politics. Home: 35 E St NW Apt 810 Washington DC 20001-1520 Office: 717 D St NW Ste 210 Washington DC 20004 Office Phone: 202-347-6952. E-mail: kentlaw@earthlink.net.

KENT, MATTHEW, law clerk; b. Huntsville, Ala., Dec. 4, 1968; BS in Consumer Journalism, U. Ga., Athens, 1993; MPA, Valdosta State U., Ga., 1994; PhD in Elem. and Secondary Ednl. Adminstrn., Capella U., Mpls., 2003; JD, U. La Verne, Ontario, Calif., 2007. Tchr. spl. edn. Burke County Pub. Schs., Waynesboro, Ga., 2000—01; law clk. Disability Rights Legal Ctr., San Bernardino, Calif., 2006—. Contbr. articles to profl. jours., chapters to books. Vol. City Animal Control and Adoption Ctr., Rancho Cucamonga, Calif., 2006—07; state cmty. rels. dir. Young Democrats Ga., Atlanta, 1985—86. 1st lt. USAF, 1995—99. Recipient President's Spl. Svc. award, Young Democrats of Ga., 1985, Excellence Future Torts award, Ctr. Computer-Assisted Legal Instrn., 2005; scholar, USAF ROTC, 1993—95. Mem.: Chi Sigma Iota, Gamma Beta Phi. Conservative. Baptist. Avocation: running. Home Phone: 909-477-9337.

KENT, MUHTAR, beverage company executive; b. 1952; BS in Economics, Hull U.; MS in Adminstrv. Sciences, London City U. Various mktg. and operations roles Coca-Cola Co., Atlanta, 1978—85, gen. mgr. Coca-Cola Turkey & Ctrl. Asia, 1985—89, pres. East Central Europe divsn., 1989—95; sr. v.p. Coca-Cola Internat., 1989—95; mng. dir. Coca-Cola Amatil-Europe Coca-Cola Co., 1995—97; pres., CEO Efes Beverage Group, Istantbul, Turkey, 1999—2005; pres, CEO North Asia, Eurasia and Middle East Group Coca-Cola Co., 2005—06; pres. Coca-Cola Internat., 2006; pres., COO Coca-Cola Co., 2006—. Mem. internat. bd. dirs. Special Olympics, 2007—. Office: Coca-Cola Co One Coca-Cola Plz Atlanta GA 30313 Office Phone: 404-676-2121. Office Fax: 404-676-6792.*

KENT, PATRICIA ANNE, music educator, singer; d. Robert Emmett and Clara Mae Kent; m. John Francis Menard; children: Nicole, Paul. BA, Coll. St. Benedict, St. Joseph, Minn., 1973; MA, CUNY, NYC, 1976; DMA, U. Minn., Mpls., 2006. Lectr. in music St. John's U., Collegeville, Minn., 1983—; voice tchr. Carleton Coll., Northfield, Minn., 2004—. Soprano soloist St. Agnes Ch., St. Paul, 1996—; profl. singer, rep. to bd. Minn. Chorale, Mpls.; soloist Minn. Orch., St. Paul Chamber Orch., Duluth-Superior Symphony, Rochester Symphony. Singer: (CD) All in the Family: Songs of Fanny and Felix Mendelssohn, 1999, La Vie Interieure, 2005. Vol. DFL, 2004, 2006. Mem.: Nat. Assn. Tchrs. Singing. Home: 897 Sherburne Ave Saint Paul MN 55104

KENT, PHILIP I., broadcast executive, communications executive; BA, Lehigh U. With sales team Blair Television, 1975; co-founder subs. Blair Entertainment John Blair & Co., 1981, v.p. program develop., 1984; packaging agent TV dept. Creative Artist's Agency, 1986—93; pres. Turner Home Entertainment Turner Broadcasting Sys., Atlanta, 1993—96; pres. Turner Broadcasting Systems Internat. Inc., Atlanta, 1996—2000, pres., COO CNN News Group, 2000—01; chmn., CEO Turner Broadcasting System, Inc. Time Warner Corp., 2003—. Bd. dirs. Ad Coun., Atlanta Braves; mem. dean's exec. bd. UCLA Sch. Theater, Film & TV. Bd. dirs. Woodruff Arts Ctr., Atlanta, Ctrl. Atlanta Progress. Mem.: Metro Atlanta C. of C. (bd. dirs.), Nat. Cable and Telecommunications Assn. (bd. dirs.).*

KENT, ROBERT BRYDON, law educator; b. Lowell, Mass., Dec. 2, 1921; s. Silas Stanley and Madeleine (Brydon) K.; m. Barbara Tuttle, Mar. 31, 1951; children: Robert Brydon, Dorothy Clarke, Elizabeth Montgomery, Hugh Clarke. AB, Harvard Coll., 1943; LLB, Boston U., 1949; LLD (hon.), Roger Williams U., 2001. Bar: Mass. 1948. Pvt. practice, Ware, Mass., 1948—50; instr. Boston U. Sch. Law, 1950-52, asst. prof., 1952-54, prof., 1954-81; prof. law, dean U. Zambia Sch. Law, 1970-72; dir. Law Practice Inst., Zambia, 1970-71; Ford fellow in law tchg. Harvard U. Law Sch., 1960-61, part-time vis. prof., 1973-74; vis. prof. Cornell Law Sch., 1980-81, prof., 1981-92, prof. emeritus, 1992—, assoc. dean, 1982-86. Hon. vis. fellow Trinity Coll., Oxford U., 1976; reporter com. on civil rules Supreme Ct. RI, Superior Ct. RI, Dist. Ct. RI; disting. vis. prof. Roger Williams U. Sch. Law, 1997-2006, bd. dirs., 2006-; vis. prof. Boston U. Sch. Law, 2000-01. Author: (with Austin W. Scott) Cases and Other Materials on Civil Procedure, 1967, Rhode Island Practice: Civil Rules with Commentaries, 1969, (with Wollin, Flanders and Simpson) Rhode

Island Civil and Appellate Procedure, 2006. Moderator Town of Lexington, Mass., 1965-70, selectman, 1977-81; vice chmn. Civil Liberties Union of Mass., 1966-69; exec. com. Law Assn. of Zambia, 1970-72; trustee Kimball Union Acad., pres., 1973-76. With U.S. Army, 1943-46. Fulbright prof. sch. law U. Zambia, 1988. Mem.: Am. Law Inst. Democrat. Unitarian Universalist. Home: 1 Doran Farm Ln Lexington MA 02420-2128 Office Phone: 781-861-1855. Personal E-mail: rkent@earthlink.net.

KENT, STEPHEN SMILEY, lawyer; b. Reno, July 6, 1952; s. Robert Roe and Muriel (Smiley) K.; m. H. Mayla Walcutt, Dec. 19, 1976; children: Kristopher, Kimberly, Alisa. BS (hons.), U. Nev., 1975; JD, U. of the Pacific, 1980. Bar: Nev. 1980. Law clk. to Hon. William N. Forman, Reno, 1980-81; assoc. Vargas & Bartlett, Reno, 1981-86, Beckley, Singleton, Jemison & List, Reno, 1986-89, shareholder, 1989-97, Woodburn & Wedge, Reno, 1997—. Mem. exec. coun. Nev. State Bar Young Lawyers Assn., Reno, 1987-89; mem. fee dispute com. Nev. State Bar, Reno, 1985-88, mem. ins. com., 1986-87. Co-author: (manuals/seminars) Nevada Uninsured Motorist Insurance, 1985, Controlling Damages, 1991, Enforcing Judgments, 1989, Pretrial Discovery, 1988, Default Judgements, 1994, Insurance Coverage Law in Nevada, 1998, Advanced Personal Injury Practice, 2001. Mem. NW Reno Neighborhood Adv. Coun., Reno, 1992-98. Mem. ABA (litigation sect.), Internat. Assn. Def. Counsel, Nat. Bd. Trial Advocacy (cert. civil trial advocate), Reno Rodeo Assn., Rotary Club Reno, Meeks Bay Yacht Club, Porsche Club. Office: Woodburn & Wedge 6100 Neil Rd PO Box 2311 Reno NV 89505-2311 Home: 7029 Heatherwood Dr Reno NV 89523-2094 Office Fax: 775-688-3088. Business E-Mail: skent@woodburnandwedge.com.

KENT, STEVEN, lawyer; b. Port Chester, NY, Feb. 9, 1949; BA, Georgetown U., 1970; JD, St. John's U., 1978; LLM, NYU, 1983. Bar: NY 1978, US Dist. Ct. So. Dist. NY, US Dist. Ct. Ea. Dist. NY, US Ct. Appeals 2nd Cir. Ptnr. Wilson, Elser, Moskowitz, Edelman & Dicker LLP, NYC. Mem.: ABA, NY State Trial Lawyers Assn., NY State Bar Assn. Office: Wilson Elser Moskowitz Edelman & Dicker LLP 23rd Fl 150 E 42nd St New York NY 10017-5639 Office Phone: 212-490-3000 ext. 2268. Office Fax: 212-490-3038. Business E-Mail: kents@wemed.com.

KENT, SUSAN, library director, consultant; b. NYC, Mar. 18, 1944; d. Elias and Minnie (Barnett) Solomon; m. Eric Goldberg, Mar. 27, 1966 (div. Mar. 1991); children: Evan Goldberg, Jessica Goldberg Lee, Joanna Goldberg; m. Rolly Kent, Dec. 20, 1991. BA in English Lit. with honors, SUNY, 1965; MS, Columbia U., 1966. Libr., sr. libr. N.Y. Pub. Libr., 1965-67, br. mgr. Donnell Art Libr., 1967-68; reference libr. Paedergaat br. Bklyn. Pub. Libr., 1971-72; reference libr. Finkelstein Meml. Libr., Spring Valley, N.Y., 1974-76; coord. adult and young adult svcs. Tucson Pub. Libr., 1977-80, acting libr. dir., 1982, dep. libr. dir., 1980-87; mng. dir. Ariz. Theatre Co., Tucson, Phoenix, 1987-89; dir. Mpls. Pub. Libr. and Info. Ctr., 1990-95; city libr. L.A. Pub. Libr., 1995—2004, N.Y. Pub. Libr., NYC, 2004—. Tchr. Pima CC, Tucson, 1978; grad. libr. sch. U. Ariz., Tucson, 1978—81; panelist Ariz. Commn. Arts., 1981—85; bd. devel. and fundraising Child's Play, Phoenix, 1983; reviewer pub. programs NEH, 1985, panelist challenge grants, 1986—89, panelist state programs, 1988; bd. dirs., mem. organizing devel. and fundraising com. Flagstaff (Ariz.) Symphony Orch., 1988; bd. advisors UCLA Grad. Sch. Edn. and Info. Scis., 1998—2001; cons., presenter in field. Contbr. articles to profl. jours. Chair arts and culture com. Tucson Tomorrow, 1981—85; commr. Ariz. Commn. Arts, 1983—87; bd. dirs., v.p. Ariz. Dance Theatre, 1984—86; bd. dirs. Arizonans Cultural Devel., Ariz., 1987—89, YWCA Mpls., 1991—92; bd. dirs. women's studies adv. coun. U. Ariz., 1985—90; participant Leadership Mpls., 1990—91. Recipient Libr. of the Yr., Libr. Jour., 2002, Info. Assocs. Exec. Leadership award, UCLA Anderson Sch., 2001, Interfaith Leadership award, Archdiocese of L.A., 2004; fellow, Sch. Libr. Sci., Columbia U., 1965—66. Mem.: ALA (mem. membership com. S.W. regional chair 1983—86, mem. com. appts. 1986—87, gov. coun. 1990—98, planning and budget assembly del. 1991—93, chair conf. com. 1996—97, Joseph Lippincott award 2003), Coun. Libr. and Info. Resources (bd. dirs. 2000—), Libr. Adminstrn. and Mgmt. Assn. (mem. John Cotton Dana Award com. 1994—95), Urban Librs. Coun. (mem. exec. bd. 1994—2001, treas. 1996—98, vice chair/chair elect 1998, 1999, chair 1999—2000), Calif. Libr. Assn., Pub. Libr. Assn. (mem. nominating com. 1980—82, v.p. 1986—87, pres. 1987—88, chair publs. assmebly 1988—89, chair nat. conf. 1994, chair legis. com. 1994—95). Office: NYPub Libr Fifth Ave and 42d St New York NY 10018 Home Phone: 212-717-0728; Office Phone: 212-642-0120. Business E-Mail: skent@nypl.org.

KENTON, EDGAR JACKSON, III, neurologist; b. Phila., Mar. 5, 1940; s. Edgar Jackson Kenton Jr. and Jessie Elizabeth Kenton; m. Geraldine Davis Kenton, Aug. 13, 1994; m. Sandra Payne Kenton, June 24, 1967 (div. Dec. 20, 1991); children: Adrienne Danielle, Brian Michael. BA, Rutgers U., 1961; MD, Cornell Med. Coll., 1965. Diplomate Am. Bd. Psychiatry and Neurology, Nat. Bd. Med. Examiners. Intern in internal medicine Jefferson Med. Coll., Phila., 1965—66, resident in internal medicine, 1966—67, resident in neurology, 1967—70; fellow in cerebral blood flow studies Strok Rsch. Ctr., Phila. Gen. Hosp., Phila., 1970; pvt. practice in neurology, 1972—. Acting cheif dept. neurology Lankenau Hosp., 1972—73, chief dept. neurology, 1973—98; examiner Am. Bd. Psychiatry and Neurology, 1982—92, sr. examiner, 1992—96, dir., 1996—; chief cerebrovascular diseases sect. Main Line Health Sys. Hosps., 1998—; instr. neurology Thomas Jefferson U. Med. Coll., 1972—78, asst. prof. neurology, 1974—78, clin. assoc. prof. neurology, 1978—, prof. clin. neurology, 1999; vis. prof. Morehouse Med. Coll., Atlanta, 1994, Meharry Med. Coll., Nashville, 1998; vis. faculty Marion Merrell Dow Minority Scholars Program, 1994—; cons. Bryn Mawr Child Study Inst., Bryn Mawr Coll., 1975—85; cons. Hill Top Prep. Sch. for the Learning Disabled, 1973—, Lupus Found., 1975—90; presenter in field; bd. dirs. Am. Acad. Neurology, Assn. Black Cardiologists, Am. Heart Assn., stroke task force, 1998—, v.p. Southeastern Pa. Region, 1998—2000, pres. Southeastern Pa. Region, 2000—01; mem. search com. Nat. Inst. Neurologic Diseases and Stroke, 2001; mem. Accreditation Coun. for Continuing Med. Edn., 2001—; mem. med. adv. bd. Lupus Found., Guillian-Barre Found., Inglis House of the Chronically Disabled. Rschr. in field.; musician: Stroke Connection, Am. Heart Assn., 1996—2000; mem. editl. bd. Stroke Jour.; contbr. articles to profl. jours. Mem. adv. com. on stroke prevention and treatment Gen. Assembly, Commonwealth of Pa., 2001; mem. Spkrs. Bur. Alzheimer's Assn. Greater Phila., Lankenau Hosp.; mem. Union League Phila.; bd. trustees Hill Top Prep. Sch., 1973—96, The Shipley Sch., 1984—88. Maj. USAF, 1970—72. Named one of Am.'s Leading Physicians, Black Enterprise Mag., 2001; recipient Recognition award, Nat. Sclerosis Soc., 1983, Humanitarian award, NAACP, 1983, Disting. Svc. award, Hill Top Prep. Sch. for Learning Disabled, 1985, Spl. Recognition award, Am. Heart Assn., 1999, Edn. award, 2000, Heart and Torch award, 2001. Fellow: Am. Stroke Assn. (stroke coun. 1978), Am. Acad. Neurology; mem.: AMA, Phila. Stroke Coun., Montgomery County Med. Soc., Med. Soc. Ea. Pa., Pa. State Med. Soc., Phila. Coll. Physicians, Alpers Soc. Clin. Neurology (sec.-treas. 1980—82, pres. 1982—90), Phila. Neurol. Soc., Sigma Pi Phi. Avocations: volunteering, travel.

KENTY, DAVID EARL, lawyer; b. Columbus, Ohio, Nov. 2, 1945; m. Janice B. Asher, Sept. 15, 1984; children: Joanna, Nora. BA, Coll. Wooster, 1967; JD, Harvard U., 1970. Bar: Mass. 1970, Ill. 1980, Pa. 1990. Ptnr. Winston & Strawn, Chgo., 1981-88, Schnader, Harrison, Segal and Lewis, Phila., 1988—. Spkr. in feilds. Author: Tax Management Portfolio #389-2d, 1990, Tax Management Portfolio #388-3d, 1988, contbr. articles to profl. journs. Mem. ABA 1970-, Phila. Bar Assn. 1988-, Phi Beta Kappa. Office: Schnader Harrison Segal & Lewis 1600 Market St Ste 3600 Philadelphia PA 19103-7287 Office Phone: 215-751-2000. Office Fax: 215-751-2205. Business E-Mail: dkenty@schnader.com.

KENWORTHY, SCOTT, humanities educator; s. Joseph H. and Nevenka P. Kenworthy; m. Oana Kenworthy, 1976. MA, U. Calif., Santa Barbara, 1991, St. Vladimir's Orthodox Theol. Sem., Crestwood, NY, 1993; PhD, Brandeis U., Waltham, Mass., 2001. Fulbright Sr. scholar U. Bucharest, Romania, 2003—05; asst. prof. Miami U., Oxford, Ohio, 2004—. Contbr. articles to profl. jours. Advisor Orthodox Christian Fellowship, Oxford, Ohio, 2001—07. Recipient Sr. Scholar Tchg. award, Fulbright, 2003—05; Grad. Tng. fellow, Social Sci. Rsch. Coun., 1995—96, Individual Advanced Rsch. Opportunities in Eurasia, Internat. Rsch. and Exchs. Bd., 1997—98, Postdoctoral fellow, Havighurst Ctr. Russian and Post-Soviet Studies, 2001—03, Title VIII Rsch. scholar, Kennan Inst., Woodrow Wilson Ctr., 2006—07. Mem.: Am. Soc. Ch. History, Am. Assn. Advancement Slavic Studies, Am. Acad. Religion. Office Phone: 513-529-4308. Home Fax: 513 529-4308.

KENWORTHY, WILLIAM EUGENE, judge; b. Las Animas, Colo., Apr. 27, 1933; s. William Sydner and Joyce Lovelle (Thedford) K.; m. Lucille Nicoletta Capozzola, July 20, 1963; children: William D., Kathryn J., Randal A. BS, U. Denver, 1955, LLB, 1956. Bar: Colo. 1957, U.S. Dist. Ct. Colo. 1957, U.S. Ct. Appeals (10th cir.) 1962, U.S. Supreme Ct. 1972. Assoc. Fugate & Mitchem, Denver, 1960-63, ptnr., 1964-67; counsel Navajo Freight Lines, Denver, 1967-69; gen. counsel Rocky Mountain Motor Tariff Bur., Denver, 1970-87; ptnr. Rea, Cross & Auchincloss, Washington, 1988-97; adminstrv. law judge Office of Disability Evaluation and Rev. Social Security Adminstrn., Pitts., 1997—. Instr. Coll. Law, U. Denver, 1965-66. Author: Transportation of Hazardous Materials, 2d edit., 1992, Corporate Counsel's Guide to Occupational Safety and Health Law, 1993, with supplements, Transportation Safety and Insurance Law, 2 vols., 1998, with ann. supplements, Killer Roads, 1999; columnist Electric Light and Power, 1966-84, Heavy Duty Trucking, 1993—; contbr. articles to profl. jours. Served with USNR, 1957-60; comdr. Res. ret. Mem. Assn. Transp. Practitioners (pres. 1985-86), Denver Bar Assn., Colo. Bar Assn., Transp. Lawyers Assn., Fed. Bar Assn., Mil. Officers Assn., Exch. Club, Kiwanis (pres. local club 1965-66). Republican. Roman Catholic. Office Phone: 412-644-2751.

KENYHERCZ, THOMAS MICHAEL, pharmaceutical company executive; b. Jan. 6, 1950; s. William Stephen and Goldie Elizabeth (Matica) K.; m. Linda Jane Kostyshak, Mar. 20, 1973; 1 child, Craig Thomas. BS, Youngstown State U., 1971; MS, U. Cin., 1973, PhD in Analytical Chemistry, 1975. Cert. regulatory affairs profl. Postdoctoral fellow in bioanalytical chemistry Purdue U.; 1975-77; scientist, sr. scientist, mgr. prodn. support labs. Ortho Pharm. Corp., Raritan, NJ, 1977-80; dir. product devel., quality assurance & regulatory affairs Janssen Pharmaceutica Inc., Piscataway, NJ, 1980-85; pres. KROSS, Inc., Hillsborough, NJ, 1985—. Founder KROSS Coatings, Inc., 1987—, Telluride Pharm. Corp., 1994—; founder, pres. Telluride Analytics, 1997—; founder KROSS Devel. Corp., 2001-; participant FDA-approved Orphan Drug Devel. program, IND Treatment of Cachexic AIDS Patients, 1996. Mem. editl. bd.: Jour. Automated Chemistry, 1975—. Coach basketball St. Mary's Sr. H.S., 1979—83; active Ctr. for Creative Living, Religious Sci. Ch. Princeton. Recipient SBIR Rsch. award EPA Phase I and II for studies of marine contamination, 1987, 88, FDA Orphan Drug designation, 1994; Lowenstein Schubert Twitchell fellow U. Cin., 1975, Kissinger fellow Purdue U., 1975-77. Mem. Am. Mgmt. Assn., Am. Assn. Clin. Chemists, Am. Assn. Anti Aging Med., Am. Chem. Soc., Am. Assn. Pharm. Scientists, Am. Soc. for Quality Control, U.S.-N.I.S. C. of C., Electrochem. Soc., Parenteral Drug Assn., Pharm. Mfrs. Assn., Drug Info. Assn., Regulatory Affairs Profl. Soc., Am. Soc. Pharmacognosy, Western Electroanalytical Theoretical Soc., Licensing Execs. Soc., Aquinas Inst., Controlled Release Soc., Soc. for Biomaterials. Byzantine Catholic. Office: Telluride Compound 300 Valley Rd Bldg 278 Hillsborough NJ 08844 Office Phone: 908-369-1900. Personal E-mail: knyhrcz@yahoo.com. Business E-Mail: knyhrcz@ix.netcom.com.

KENYON, CYNTHIA J., medical researcher; BS in Chemistry and Biochemistry, U. Ga., 1976; PhD, MIT, 1981. Post-doctoral fellow Med. Rsch. Coun. Lab. Molecular Biology, Cambridge, England; prof. U. Calif., San Francisco, 1986—, Herbert Boyer Disting. prof. biochemistry and biophysics. Co-founder Elixir Pharmaceuticals, Inc., Cambridge, Mass. Contbr. articles to profl. jours. Mem.: AAAS, NAS, Inst. Medicine, 2004. Achievements include suppressing a single gene in Caenorhabditis elegans worms-nematodes and doubling their normal life span; in recent research and a few more changes, their lifespan was expanded sixfold. Office: U Calif San Francisco, Genentech Hall 600 16th St Box 2200 San Francisco CA 94143-2200 Office Phone: 415-476-9250, 415-476-9864. Office Fax: 415-514-4147. E-mail: ckenyon@biochem.ucsf.edu.

KENYON, DAPHNE ANNE, economist; b. Augusta, Ga., Aug. 14, 1952; d. Lawrence Austin and Shirley (Knaus) Kenyon; m. Peter George Kachavos, Oct. 22, 1988. BA, Mich. State U., East Lansing, 1974; MA in Econs., U. Mich., Ann Arbor, 1976, PhD in Econs., 1980. Asst. prof. Dartmouth Coll., Hanover, NH, 1979—83; sr. analyst U.S. Adv. Commn. on Intergovt. Rels., Washington, 1983—85; fin. economist U.S. Treasury Dept., 1985—87; sr. rsch. assoc. Urban Inst., 1987—88; fellow Lincoln Inst. Land Policy, Cambridge, Mass., 1988—89, vis. fellow, 2005—; asst. prof. econs. Simmons Coll., Boston, 1989—90, assoc. prof. econs., 1991—98, chair dept. econs., 1996—99, prof. econs., 1998—2000; pres. Josiah Bartlett Ctr. Pub. Policy, Concord, NH, 1999—2002; prin. D.A. Kenyon & Assocs., Windham, 2002—. Cons. U.S. IRS Adv. Panel, Washington, 1987-99; appt. to Mass. Dept. Revenue Adv. Group, 1991; bd. dir. New Eng. Econ. Project, v.p., 1997-98, pres., 1999; mem. N.H. State Bd. Edn., 2006—; commr. Edn. Commn. of the States, 2007-. Assoc. editor Urban Studies, 1988-93, mem. U.S. editl. adv. com., 1993-2004; co-editor: Coping with Mandates, 1990, Competition Among States and Local Governments, 1991; N.H. corr. State Tax Notes, 1990-93; mem. editl. bd. Mass. Benchmarks, 1997-99; columnist: State Tax Notes, 2003—; contbr. articles to profl. jours. Mem. gov.'s revenue adv. com., State of N.H., Concord, 1982, 98, consensus revenue estimating panel, 2000-03; bd. dirs. Windham (N.H.) Sch. Bd., 2000-03, vice chmn. 2002-03. Fellow Grad. fellow, NSF, 1974. Mem. Am. Econ. Assn. (com. status women in econs. profession 1995-98), Nat. Tax Assn. (bd. dir. 1996-99, chair intergovernmental fiscal rels. com. 1996-98, program chair 1999), Nat. Tax Jour. (referee Ea. Econ. Jour.). Episcopalian.

KENYON, EDWARD TIPTON, lawyer; b. Summit, NJ, Jan. 27, 1929; s. Theodore S. and Martha (Tipton) K.; m. Dolores Cetrule, July 11, 1953; children: David S., James N., Jonathan W., Theodore H. AB, Harvard U., 1950; LL.B., Columbia U., 1953. Bar: NY 1956, NJ 1957. Assoc. Thacher, Proffitt, Prizer, Crawley & Wood, NYC, 1955-56; law clk. presiding judge US Dist. Ct. NJ, Newark, 1956-57; assoc. Jeffers, Mountain & Franklin, Morristown, NJ, 1957-59, Bourne, Noll and Kenyon and predecessor firm, Summit, 1959-62, ptnr., 1962-97, of counsel, 1997—. Bd. dirs. Atlantic Mgmt. Corp., 1990-98. Trustee Summit Art Ctr., 1960—72, Trinity-Pawling Sch., Pawling, NY, 1977—2003, Pingry Sch., Martinsville, NJ, 1970—97, Martha's Vineyard Preservation Trust, 1999—, Overlook Hosp., Summit, 1967—75, pres., 1973—75; trustee Overlook Hosp. Found., 1975—84, sec., 1977—80, v.p., 1980—81, pres., 1981—84; trustee Winston Sch., Summit, 1986—93, v.p., 1987—90, pres., 1990—92; mem. planning bd. Town Chilmark, 1998—, chmn., 2000—; trustee Martha's Vineyard Cmty. Hosp., 2006—; deacon Ctrl. Presbyn. Ch., Summit, 1960—65, trustee, 1965—72, 1987—93, pres., 1970—72, 1988—91; deacon First Congl. Ch., West Tisbury, Mass., 2000—05; bd. dirs. Overlook Mgmt. Corp., 1988—97. With M.C. US Army, 1953—55. Mem. ABA, NY State Bar Assn., NJ Bar Assn., Summit Bar Assn. (pres. 1983-84), Union County Bar Assn., Am. Coll. Trust Estate Counsel, Am. Law Inst. Clubs: Beacon Hill (trustee 1977-81, pres. 1979-81), Edgartown Yacht Club, Harvard NYC, Harvard NJ (trustee 1958-69, pres. 1968-69). Home: 49 N Abels Hill Rd Chilmark MA 02535-2026 Office: 382 Springfield Ave Summit NJ 07901-2707 E-mail: kittip@vineyard.net.

KENYON, GARY MICHAEL, gerontologist, educator; b. Montreal, Que., Can., June 12, 1949; s. Raymond George and Frances Evelyn (Duhault) K. B in Commerce cum laude, Loyola U., Montreal, 1970; BA, Concordia U., Montreal, 1977, MA, 1981; PhD, U. B.C., 1985. Postdoctoral fellow Andrew Norman Inst. U. So. Calif., LA, 1985-86; postdoctoral fellow Swedish Inst. Linkoping U., Sweden, 1986-87; prof., chmn. dept. gerontology St. Thomas U., Fredericton, N.B., Canada, 1987—. Adj. prof. McGill U. Ctr. for Studies in Aging, Montreal; hon. rsch. assoc. U. N.B., 1996—. Author: Emergent Theories of Aging, 1988, Metaphors of Aging, 1991, Aging and Biography, 1996, Restorying Our Lives, 1997, Ordinary Wisdom, 2001, Narrative Gerontology, 2001; editor: jour. Gnosis, 1979—81; rev. editor: Can. Jour. on Aging, 1989—90; contbr. articles to profl. jours. Social Scis. and Humanities fellow, Can. Govt., 1983—85. Mem. Gerontology Soc. Am., Can. Assn. Gerontology, N.B. Assn. Gerontology (bd. dirs.). Avocations: skiing, cooking, wine, Tai Chi instructor, language study. Office: St Thomas U Dept Gerontology Fredericton NB Canada E3B 5G3 Office Phone: 506-452-0527. E-mail: kenyon@stu.ca.

KENYON, REGAN CLAIR, educational association administrator; b. St. Louis, Jan. 31, 1949; s. Robert Clair and Nina Naoma (Giesler) K.; m. Mary Margaret Quinlan, June 2, 1979; children: Regan Clair Jr., Moriah Quinlan. BA, U. Mo., 1969, MEd, 1973; EdD, Harvard U., 1983. Tchr., Ferguson, Mo., 1971—74; prin. Manor Sch., St. Croix, Vanuatu, 1974—77, Country Day Sch., St. Croix, 1977—78; exec. asst. US Dept. Edn., Washington, 1978—80; adminstrv. asst. Harvard U., Cambridge, Mass., 1980—81; cons. to pres. MA Higher Edn. Assistance Corp., Boston, 1981—83; pres. Secondary Sch. Admission Test Bd., Princeton, NJ, 1983—. Contbr. articles to profl. jours.; inventor, editor in field. Mem. NJ State Bd. Edn., Trenton, NJ, 1987-91. Fellow Edn. Policy for George Washington U. Inst. Ednl. Leadership, Washington, 1978-79; Gustav Harris scholar Harvard U., 1980-83; recipient Horace Mann Prof. Contbr. citation US Dept. Edn., 1980; named Disting Alumni Mo. U., 1996. Mem. Inst. Ednl. Leadership, Harvard Club, Nassau Club, Phi Delta Kappa. Roman Catholic. Avocations: tennis, golf, skiing, fishing, hiking. Office: Secondary Sch Admission Test Bd CN 5339 Princeton NJ 08543 Office Phone: 609-683-4440. Office Fax: 609-683-4507.

KEOGH, HEIDI HELEN DAKE, advocate; b. Saratoga, NY, July 12, 1950; d. Charles Starks and Phyllis Sylvia (Edmunds) Dake; m. Randall Frank Keogh, Nov. 3, 1973; children: Tyler Cameron, Kelly Dake. Student, U. Colo., 1972. Reception, promotions Sta. KLAK, KJAE, Lakewood, Colo., 1972-73; acct. exec. Mixed Media Advt. Agy., Denver, 1973-75; writer, mktg. Jr. League Cookbook Devel., Denver, 1986-88; chmn., coord. Colorado Cache & Creme de Colorado Cookbooks, 1988-90. Speakers bur. Mile High Transplant Bank, Denver, 1983-84, Writer's Inst., U. Denver, 1988; bd. dir. Stewart's Shops Corp., Jr. League, Denver, The Gathering Pl., chmn. gov. bd., 2005-06, co-chair capital companion, 2005-. Contbr. articles to profl. jours. Fiscal officer, bd. dirs. Mile High Transplant Bank; blockworker Heart Fund and Am. Cancer Soc., Littleton, Colo., 1978—, Littleton Rep. Com., 1980-84; fundraising vol. Littleton Pub. Schs., 1980-98; vol. Gathering Place Assn., bd. dirs., 2003—, pres., 2003—, chmn. Brown Bag benefit, 1996; bd. dirs. Jr. League Found., 2006—; vol. Hearts for Life, 1991—, Oneday, 1992, Denver Ballet Guild, 1992—, Denver Ctr. Alliance, 1993—, Newborn Hope, 1980—, Girls, Inc., 1995—, Girls Hope, VOA Guild, 1996—, Le Bal de Ballet, 1998—, The Denver Social Register and Record, 1999—. Mem. Jr. League Denver (pub. rels. bd., v.p. ways and means 1989-90, planning coun./ad hoc 1990-92, sustainer spl. events 1993-94, found. bd. 2006—), Community Emergency Fund (chair 1991-92), Jon D. Williams Cotillion at Columbine (chmn. 1991-93), Columbine Country Club, Gamma Alpha Chi, Pi Beta Phi Alumnae Club (pres. Denver chpt. 1984-85, 93-94, nat. conv. chmn. Denver 2001, Woman of Yr., 2002), Pi Beta Phi Found. (grantee 2000-05). Episcopalian. Avocations: travel, skiing, golf. Home: 63 Fairway Ln Littleton CO 80123-6648 Personal E-mail: hiheidi2@yahoo.com.

KEOGH, KEVIN, lawyer; b. Omaha, Dec. 24, 1941; s. James Charles and Verna Marion (Pedersen) K.; m. Susan Elizabeth Mary Griffiths, Apr. 26, 1975; children: James, Caroline, Colin, Brendan. AB with honors, Holy Cross Coll., 1963; JD, Harvard U., 1966. Bar: N.Y. 1969, Conn. 1977, U.S. Ct. Appeals (2nd cir.) 1975. Assoc. Breed, Abbott & Morgan, NYC, 1969-75, ptnr., 1975-88, White & Case, NYC, 1988—, exec. ptnr., 1992—, head U.S. securities practice, 2005—. Dir. United Hosp. Fund of N.Y., 1984-88; vol. U.S. Peace Corps., Nicoya, Costa Rica, 1966-68. Mem. Am. Yacht Club (commodore 1985-86, Disting. Svc. award 1989), Assn. Bar City NY (com. on securities regulation 2002-2005), Yacht Racing Assn. L.I. Sound (Pres. 1983-84, Disting. Svc. award 1985), N.Y. Yacht Club (competitions com. 1990-92). Republican. Episcopalian. Home: 18 Sherwood Farm Ln Greenwich CT 06831-4410 Office: White & Case 1155 Avenue Of The Americas New York NY 10036-2787 E-mail: kkeogh@whitecase.com.

KEOGH, RICHARD JOHN, firearms and explosives consultant; b. Woonsocket, RI, Sept. 23, 1932; s. Michael Joseph and Dora Marie (Rumgay) Keogh. BBA, U. Mass., 1958; MA, Pepperdine U., 1974. Lic. explosive disposal technician Mass. Commd. 2d lt. U.S. Army, 1958, advanced through grades to maj., 1967; stationed at various locations including Korea and Vietnam, 1958-73; ret. USAR, 1979; disposal specialist USN, Lualualei, Hawaii, 1973-76; mgmt. analyst Marine Corps Air Sta., Kaneohe Bay, Hawaii, 1976-93; firearms and explosives cons., 1993—. Expert witness explosives and firearms, Hawaii, Mass. Contbr. articles to profl. jours. Pres. Assn. Owners Palms Condominium, Honolulu, 1978—80. Decorated 3 Bronze Stars, 2 Purple Hearts, 2 Air medals, Cross of Gallantry, Commendation medal; recipient Founders award, Order of Arrow Boy Scouts Am., 1989, cert. of Appreciation, FBI, 1991, Silver Beaver award, Boy Scouts Am., 1993. Mem.: Gun Owners Action League, DAV (life), VFW (life), Internat. Assn. Bomb Technicians and Investigators (life; dir. Hawaii chpt. 2000—), Mil. Order Purple Heart (life), Hawaii Rifle Assn. (pres. 1994—96, 2000—02), Bay Colony Weapons Collectors, Ohio Gun Collectors Assn., Nat. Auto Pistol Collectors Assn., Am. Legion (life). Avocations: rifle shooting, photography. Home: 431 Nahua St Apt 203 Honolulu HI 96815-2915 Home Phone: 808-923-2283.

KEOHANE, NANNERL OVERHOLSER, political scientist, academic administrator; b. Blytheville, Ark., Sept. 18, 1940; d. James Arthur and Grace (McSpadden) Overholser; m. Patrick Henry III, Sept. 16, 1962 (div. May 1969); 1 child, Stephan Henry; m. Robert Owen Keohane, Dec. 18, 1970; children: Sarah, Jonathan, Nathaniel. BA, Wellesley Coll., 1961, Oxford U., Eng., 1963; PhD, Yale U., 1967. Faculty Swarthmore Coll., Pa., 1967—73, Stanford U., Calif., 1973—81; pres., prof. polit. sci. Wellesley (Mass.) Coll., 1981—93, Duke U., Durham, NC, 1993—2004, pres. emerita, 2004—; Laurance Rockefeller disting. vis. prof. Woodrow Wilson Sch., Princeton U., 2005—. Author: Philosophy and the State in France: The Renaissance to the Enlightenment, 1980; co-editor: Feminist Theory: A Critique of Ideology, 1982. Trustee Colonial Williamsburg Found., 1988—2001, Doris Duke Charitable Found., 1996—; mem. Harvard Corp., 2005—. Named to National Women's Hall of Fame, 1995; recipient Marshall Medal, 2003; fellow, Ctr. for Advanced Study in the Behavioral

Scis., 1978—79, 1987—88, 2004—05; Marshall scholar, 1961—63, Dissertation fellow, AAUW. Fellow: Am. Philos. Soc., Am. Acad. Arts and Scis.; mem.: Am. Acad. Achievement, Coun. on Fgn. Rels., Phi Beta Kappa. Democrat. Episcopalian.

KEOHANE, ROBERT OWEN, political scientist, educator; b. Chgo., Oct. 3, 1941; s. Robert Emmet and Mary Irene (Pieters) K.; m. Nannerl Overholser, Dec. 18, 1970; children: Jonathan, Sarah, Stephan, Nathaniel BA, Shimer Coll., 1961; MA, Harvard U., 1964, PhD, 1966; D (hon.), U. Aarhus, Denmark, 1998. From instr. to assoc. prof. Swarthmore Coll., Pa., 1965-73; from assoc. prof. to prof. Stanford U., Calif., 1973-81, chmn. dept. polit. sci., 1980-81; prof. politics Brandeis U., Waltham, Mass., 1981-85; prof. govt. Harvard U., Cambridge, Mass., 1985-96, chmn., 1988-92, Stanfield prof. internat. peace, 1989-96; James B. Duke prof. polit. sci. Duke U., Durham, NC, 1996—2005; prof. internat. affairs Princeton U., 2005—. Author: After Hegemony, 1984, International Institutions and State Power, 1989, Power and Governance in a Partially Globalized World, 2002; co-author: Power and Interdependence, 1977, Designing Social Inquiry, 1994; co-editor: Transnational Relations and World Politics, 1972, The New European Community, 1991, Institutions for the Earth, 1993, After the Cold War, 1993, Ideas and Foreign Policy, 1993, Global Interdependence and Local Communities, 1994, Internationalization and Domestic Politics, 1996, International Environmental Aid, 1996, Imperfect Unions, 1999, Exploration and Contestation in World Politics, 1999, Legalization and World Politics, 2001, Humanitarian Intervention, 2003, Anti-Americanisms in World Politics, 2006; editor: Neorealism and Its Critics, 1986; editor Internat. Orgn., 1974-80; contbr. articles to profl. jours. Chmn. New Democratic Coalition Delaware County, Pa., 1969-71; pres. Triangle Land Conservancy, 2000-02. Recipient Sumner prize Harvard U., 1966, Grawemeyer award, 1989, Skytte prize, Johan Skytte Found., Uppsala, Sweden, 2005; fellow Ctr. Advanced Study in Behavior Scis., 1977-78 87-88, 2004-05; Guggenheim fellow, 1992, Frank Kenan fellow Nat. Humanities Ctr., 1995-96. Mem. Am. Acad. Arts and Scis., Am. Polit. Sci. Assn. (pres. 1999-2000), Am. Econ. Assn., Coun. Fgn. Rels. (Internat. Affairs fellow 1968-69), Internat. Studies Assn. (pres. 1988-89), Nat. Acad. Scis. Home: 179 Prospect Ave Princeton NJ 08540 Business E-Mail: rkeohane@princeton.edu.

KEOUGH, DANIEL EMMET, retired magazine editor; b. Bklyn., Jan. 31, 1932; s. Daniel E. and Florence (O'Brien) Keough. BA in Advanced Writing, NYU, 1956; postgrad., NYU and CUNY, 1963—64. Tech. writer Union Carbide Corp., NYC, 1956—58; copy writer BBD&O Batten, Barton, Durstin & Osborn, NYC, 1958—60; asst. to advt. v.p. Am. Std. Corp., NYC, 1960—61; writer, editor Via Port Mag. Port Authority of NY and NJ, 1962—91. Internat. trade advisor Dean of Middlesex Coll., Edison, NJ, 1988—91. Author: No Tombstones in the Sea, 2006; contbr. articles to mags. Lt. USNR, 1949—53, lt. USNR, 1961—62. Recipient Navy-Marine Corps Combat Action medal, USN, 1952, China Svc. medal, 1952, Presdl. Unit citation, Republic of Korea, 1953. Mem.: VFW, US Naval Inst., Korean War Vets. Roman Catholic. Home: 42 Saratoga Dr Oakland NJ 07436

KEOUGH, DONALD RAYMOND, investment and former beverage company executive; b. Maurice, Iowa, Sept. 4, 1926; s. Leo H. and Veronica (Henkels) K.; m. Marilyn Mulhall, Sept. 10, 1949; children: Kathleen Anne, Mary Shayla, Michael Leo, Patrick John, Eileen Tracey, Clarke Robert. BS, Creighton U., 1949, LLD (hon.), 1982, U. Notre Dame, 1985, Emory U., 1993, Trinity U., Dublin, Ireland, 1993, Clarke U., 1994. With Butter-Nut Foods Co., Omaha, 1950-61; with Duncan Foods Co., Houston, 1961-67; v.p., dir. mktg. foods div. Coca-Cola Co., Atlanta, 1967-71, pres. div., 1971-73; exec. v.p. Coca-Cola USA, Atlanta, 1973-74, pres., 1974-76; exec. v.p. Coca-Cola Co., Atlanta, 1976-79, sr. exec. v.p., 1980-81, pres., COO, dir., 1981-93, advisor to bd., 1993-98; chmn. Coca-Cola Enterprises Inc., Atlanta, 1986-93, Allen & Co. Inc., Atlanta, 1993—. Bd. dirs. The Coca Cola Co., 1981-93, 2004-, Convera Corp., McDonald's Corp., USA Networks, Inc., YankeeNets LLC., Interactive Corp., Berkshire Hathaway Inc. Mem. president's coun. Creighton U.; trustee emeritus U. Notre Dame and Lovett Sch. With USNR, 1944-46. Named to Advt. Hall of Fame, 2006. Mem. Capital City Club, Piedmont Driving Club, Commerce Club, Peachtree Golf Club. Office: 200 Galleria Pky NW Ste 970 Atlanta GA 30339-5945

KEOUGH, PHILIP J., IV, retail executive; married; 3 children. Dist. mgr., registered pharmacist, store mgr. Reliable Drug Stores, Inc., 1990—93; various positions Revco Drug Stores, Inc., Twinsburg, Ohio, 1993—97; regional sales mgr. CVS Corp., 1997—99, dir. pharmacy ops. Woonsocket, RI, 1999—2002; sr. v.p. pharmacy ops. Rite Aid Corp., Camp Hill, Pa., 2002—. Office: Rite Aid Corp 30 Hunter Lane Camp Hill PA 17011 Office Phone: 717-761-2633.*

KEOUGH, SHAWN, state legislator; m. Mike Keough; 2 children. Student, North Idaho Coll.; student in bus. mgmt., Lewis Clark State Coll. In pub. rels.; mem. Idaho Senate, Dist. 1, Boise, 1996—, mem. transp. com., mem. health and welfare com., vice chair fin. com. Mem. Idaho Women in Timber, Greater Sandpoint (Idaho) C. of C. Republican. Protestant. Office: State Capitol PO Box 83720 Boise ID 83720-0081 Office Phone: 208-332-1349.

KEOWN, LAURISTON LIVINGSTON, JR., consulting psychologist; b. Balt., Feb. 24, 1942; s. Lauriston Livingston and Gladys May (Dykes) K.; m. Patje Alexandra Susemihl, Aug. 7, 1962 (div. 1977); children: Christina, Cassandra, Lauriston, Clayton; m. Nancy Ann Hastie, Mar. 18, 1978 (div. 1990). BA cum laude, U. Balt., 1965; MS, U. Alta., 1970, PhD, 1977. Registered psychologist, Alta.; Can. Register Health Svc. Providers in Psychology. Lectr. Nippissing Coll., Laurentian U., North Bay, Ont., Can., 1968-69; chief sys. analyst Dept. Youth, Edmonton, Alta., Can., 1969-71, rsch. dir., 1971-72; dir. planning and rsch. Dept. Culture, Youth and Recreation, Alta., 1972-74; dir. planning and devel. Dept. Recreation, Pks. and Wildlife, Edmonton, Alta., 1974-75; asst. dir. Transp. Safety Alta. Transp. Dept., 1975-87; dir. Motor Transp. Planning and Bus. Analysis Alta. Transp. and Utilities, 1987-93; sr. psychologist Wainwright Cmty. Mental Health Svcs. Project, Alberta Hosp., Ponoka, 1993-95; regional mental health mgr. East Ctrl. Health Region, 1995-99; psychologist The Family Ctr., 1999—2005, Insight Psychol. Inc., 2002—. Cons. R. Dehaas Assocs., Edmonton, 1979-80, Draherin Group, Edmonton, 1980-82, Denlaur Assocs., 1988—. Author: (with others) Evaluation of Traffic Safety Programs, 1980, Strategic Management of The Motor Transport Industry, 1989, The Obsessive Compulsive Organization, 1993; contbr. more than 200 articles to profl. jours. Mem. Alta. Planning Bd., 1974-82; bd. dirs. Alta. Royal Can. Mounted Police Hist. Celebrations Commn., 1974-75; exec. bd. Traffic Records Commn., Nat. Safety Coun., 1978-93; Minister's Adv. Com. on Traffic Safety, 1992-93; mem. mental health adv. com. Capital Health Region, 2006—. Indsl. psychology scholar Lamond Dewhurst & Assocs., U. Alta., 1966. Fellow Am. Traffic Safety Info. Profls., Can. Soc. Clin. Hypnosis (Alta. divsn.); mem. Eye Movement Desentization and Reprogramming Internat. Assn. Can., Alta. Psychologists Assn. Episcopalian. Home: 26-51331 RR 224 Sherwood Park AB Canada T8C 1H3 Office: Insight Psychol Inc 309A Town Centre Prof Bldg 6203-28 Ave Edmonton AB Canada T6L 6K3 Office Phone: 780-461-1717. Business E-Mail: directors@insightpsychological.ca.

KEOWN, LINDA JANE, language educator; b. Phila. d. Kenneth K. and Helen J. Keown; m. Richard Wayne Crow, July 29, 2000. BA, Mt. Holyoke Coll., South Hadley, Mass., 1971; MA in Tchg., Emory U., Atlanta, 1976. Tchr. Spanish Fulton County Pub. Schs., Atlanta, 1971—77, Columbia Pub. Schs., Mo., 1979—2002, Ctrl. Meth. U., Fayette, Mo., 2002—06, U. Mo., Columbia, 2006—. Cons. Ednl. Testing Svc., Princeton, NJ, 1992—2004, Coll. Bd., Evanston, Ill., 1997—2006; yoga instr. Wilson's Total Fitness, Columbia, Mo., 2002—; chair Final II Spanish Exam Com., 1997—99; chair Advanced Placement section Nat. Am. Assn. Tchr. of Spanish & Portuguese, 1995. Pres. Mus. Art & Archaeology, Columbia, 2004—06; treas. King's Daus. Cir., Columbia, 1976—99, v.p., 2002—04; mem. adminstrv. bd. Mo. United Meth. Ch., Columbia, 2000—. Named Disting. Tchr. from Mo., U.S. Dept. Edn., 1994; recipient Nat. Endowment for the Humanities, Seminar Inst., Spain, 1994; grantee Fgn. Langs. fellow, Nat. Endowment for the Humanities, Spain, 1996. Mem.: Am. Coun. Tchrs. Fgn. Langs., Am. Assn. Tchrs. Spanish and Portuguese. Democrat. United Methodist. Avocations: yoga, reading, travel, swimming. Office: U Mo Dept Romance Langs and Lit Columbia MO 65211 Office Phone: 573-882-4263. Business E-Mail: keownl@missouri.edu.

KEOWN, MICHAEL H., food products executive; BA in Econs., Northwestern U. With E&J Gallo Winery and Proctor & Gamble, 1984—97; v.p., gen. mgr. Minute Maid Co., Coca-Cola Co., 1997—2002; pres. Dean Branded Pfoducts Group, Dallas, 2003—. Office: Dean Foods Co 2515 McKinney Ave Ste 1200 Dallas TX 75201-1945 Office Phone: 720-565-2302. E-mail: mkeown@whitewave.com.

KEPCHER, CAROLYN, real estate company executive; b. Westchester, NY, 1968; d. Raymond and Marie Cassidy; m. George Kepcher; children: Connor, Cassidy. Degree in bus. mktg., Mercy Coll., Dobbs Ferry, NY. Dir. sales and mktg. Beck Summit Hotel Mgmt. Group, Boca Raton, Fla.; with Trump Orgn., 1994—2006, former exec. v.p.; former gen. mgr., COO Trump Nat. Golf Club, Briarcliff, NY, Bedminster, NJ. Featured on (TV series) The Apprentice, 2004—06; author: Carolyn 101: Business Lessons from The Apprentice's Straight Shooter, 2004—. Mem.: Nat. Golf Course Owners Assn., Profl. Club Mktg. Assn., Met. Club Mgr.'s Assn., Club Mgr.'s Assn. Am. Office: Trump Nat Golf Club 339 Pine Rd Briarcliff Manor NY 10510

KEPETS, HUGH MICHAEL, artist; b. Cleve., Feb. 6, 1946; s. Nathan and Frances K. B.F.A., Carnegie Mellon U., 1968; M.F.A., Ohio U., 1972. One-man shows include, Fischbach Gallery, N.Y.C., 1974, 75, 78, Vick Gallery, Phila., 1974, 76, 77, Michael Berger Gallery, Pitts., 1975, 82, G.W. Einstein Co., Inc., N.Y.C., 1976, Graphics 1, Graphics 2, Boston, 1976, 79, Rubicon Gallery, Los Altos, Calif., 1977, New Gallery, Cleve., 1978, Women's City Club, Cleve., A.J. Wood Gallery, Phila., Carnegie-Mellon U., Pitts., 1979, Orion Editions, N.Y.C., 1980, Houghton (N.Y.) Coll., 1980, Galerie 99, Bay Harbor Islands, Fla., 1981, Cumberland Gallery, Nashville, 1983, Mattingly Baker, Dallas, 1983, Marcus/Gordon, Pitts., 1981, 85, 90, Roger Ramsay Gallery, 1984, 88, David Adamson Gallery, Washington, 1986, Randall Beck Gallery, Boston, 1986, 89, Ingrid Cusson Gallery, N.Y.C., 1989, Leo Kamen Gallery, Toronto, Can., 1990, Lyman Allyn Mus. Art, New London, Conn., 1992, David Adamson Gallery, Washington, 1992, Brenda Kroos Gallery, Cleve., 1993, 96; exhibited in group shows including, Cleve. Mus. Art, 1968, 71-79, 93—, Bklyn. Mus., 1972, 76, Asso. Am. Artists, N.Y.C., 1972, 74, Butler Inst. Am. Art, 1972, U. Pa., Phila., 1972, Espace Cardin, Paris, Michael Berger Gallery, Yale U. Art Gallery, Tyler Art Gallery, Phila., 1973, New Gallery, 1973, 74, 79, Akron (Ohio) Art Inst., 1974, Virginia Mus. Art, Richmond, Vick Gallery, 1974, Boston Mus. Fine Arts, 1975-77, 82, Phila. Print Club, Westmoreland County Art Mus., Skidmore Coll., 1975, Queens Mus., N.Y.C., Albion Coll., Lehigh U., Indpls. Mus. Art, Grand Palais-Paris, McNay Art Inst. of San Antonio, U. Mo., Kansas City, 1976, Glassboro (N.J.) State Coll., Library of Congress, 1977, Yale U. Art Gallery, 1978, Am. Acad. Arts and Letters, N.Y.C., 1978, 79, 80, Hunt Inst. for Bot. Documentation, Pitts., 1979, Md. Inst. Coll. Art, Balt., 1980, Hudson River Mus., Yonkers, N.Y., 1982, U. Pitts., 1983, Pratt Graphics Ctr., N.Y.C., 1983, Mattingly Baker Gallery, Dallas, 1984, Franklin & Marshall Coll., 1984, U. Calif.-Davis, 1985, Honolulu Acad. Art, 1985, Cleve. Mus. Art, 1985, 86, N.Y. Inst. Tech., 1985, Montgomery Coll., Rockville, Md., 1985, The Del. Art Mus., 1986; represented in permanent collections, Met. Mus. Art, N.Y.C., Cleve. Mus. Art, Phila. Mus. Fine Arts, Library of Congress, Del. Mus. Art, Indpls. Mus. Art, Harvard U. Fogg Mus., N.Y. Public Library, Worcester (Mass.) Art Mus., Yale U. Art Gallery, Minn. Mus. Art, St. Paul, R.I. Sch. Design Mus. Art, Art Inst. Chgo., U. N.C. at Chapel Hill Ackland Art Center, Utah State U., Brandeis U., Middlebury (Vt.) Coll., Kresge Art Gallery, others, also various banks and corps. including, Atlantic-Richfield Corp., N.Y.C., Johns Manville Corp., N.Y.C., FMC Corp., Chgo., AT&T, IBM, Xerox Corp., RCA, Princeton, N.J., Amarada Hess Corp., N.Y.C., Prudential Ins. Co. Am., N.Y.C., Commerce Banchares, Kansas City, Mo., Bank of Am., San Francisco, Gen. Mills Co., N.Y.C., Westinghouse Electric Corp., Pitts., Oliver Realty, Pitts., Gen. Electric Co., N.Y.C., Chase Manhattan Bank, N.Y.C., Citicorp, N.Y.C., Rockwell Internat., Pitts., Lehman Bros., N.Y.C. Nat. Endowment for Arts grantee, 1976; Creative Artists Public Service grantee, 1975, 79-80; recipient Purchase awards Davidson Nat. Print and Drawing Competition Fashion Inst. Tech., 1976, Purchase awards Davidson Nat. Print and Drawing Competition Phila. Print Club, 1975, Cleve. Arts prize Women's City Club, 1979 Studio: 134 W 26th St #401 New York NY 10001 Home Phone: 917-593-5036; Office Phone: 917-593-5036. Personal E-mail: hughkepets@aol.com.

KEPKE, MATTHEW AARON, lawyer; b. NYC, Jan. 25, 1976; s. Herb and Linda Kepke; m. Jaclyn Michelle Kunis, Aug. 18, 2002. BA in Psychology, U. Mich., 1998; JD, Case Western Res. U., 2001. Bar: NY 2002. Assoc. Jenkens & Gilchrist Parker Chapin LLP, NYC, 2000—04, Loeb & Loeb LLP, 2004—. Office: Loeb & Loeb LLP 345 Park Ave New York NY 10154 Home Phone: 212-996-9566, 917-575-8664; Office Phone: 212-407-4833. Office Fax: 212-202-5138. Business E-Mail: mkepke@loeb.com.

KEPLER, DAVID E., II, chemicals executive; BSChemE, U. Calif. With western divsn. computer and process systems grp. Dow Chem. Co., 1975, computer svcs. mgr. U.S.A. ea. divsn. Strongsville, Ohio, 1984—88, comml. dir. performance products Can., 1989—91, dir. info. systems pacific area, 1991—93, dir. chems. and plastics info. systems, 1993—94, dir. global info. systems applications, 1995, dir. global info. application, 1995—98, v.p., chief info. officer, 1998—2000, corp. v.p. eBusiness, 2000—04, corp. v.p. advanced electronic materials bus., global purchasing and supply chain, 2002—04, corp. v.p. shared services, 2004, chief info. officer, 2004—, sr. v.p. shared svcs., environment, health and safety, mem. Office of the Chief Exec., 2006—. Bd. dirs. Midland Cmty. Cancer Svcs., Alden B. Dow Mus. Sci. and Art; campaign chair United Way Midland County, 2004; bd. dirs. US C. of C. Mem.: AIChE, Am. Chem. Soc. Office: Dow Chem Co 2030 Dow Ctr Midland MI 48674*

KEPLINGER, BRUCE (DONALD KEPLINGER), lawyer; b. Kansas City, Kans., Feb. 4, 1952; s. Donald Lee and Janet Adelheit (Viets) K.; children: Mark William, Lisbeth Marie, Kristen Michelle, Kailyn Emily, Courtney Nicole; m. Carol Ann Heinz, Apr. 12, 1991. BA with highest distinction, U. Kans., 1974; JD cum laude, So. Meth. U., 1977. Bar: Kans. 1977, U.S. Dist. Ct. Kans. 1977, Mo. 1980, U.S. Dist. Ct. Mo. 1980, U.S. Ct. Appeals (10th cir.) 1985, U.S. Supreme Ct. 1989. Assoc. Clark, Mize & Linville, Salina, Kans., 1977-79, Blackwell, Sanders et al, Kansas City, Mo., 1979-82; ptnr. Payne & Jones, Overland Park, Kans., 1982-94, Norris & Keplinger LLC, Overland Park, 1994—. Master Kansas Inns of Ct.; chmn. Kans. Lawyer Svcs Corp., 1992—2001. Contbr. articles to profl. jours. V.p. Friends of Libr., Johnson County, Kans., 1980-85; deacon Village Presbyn. Ch., 1982-86; trustee United Meth. Ch. of Resurrection, 2002—. Mem.: Fedn. Def. and Corp. Counsel, Def. Rsch. Inst., Kans. Assn. Def. Counsel (pres.-elect 1992—93, pres. 1993—94), Mo. Bar Assn., Kans. Bar Assn. (chmn. Kans. lawyer svc. corp. 1992—2001), Assn. Def. Trial Attys. (state chmn. 1996—, exec. coun. 1999—2002), Internat. Assn. Def. Counsel, Hallbrook Country Club. Republican. Avocations: reading, golf. Office: Norris & Keplinger LLC 6800 College Blvd Ste 630 Overland Park KS 66211-1556 Office Phone: 913-663-2000. Business E-Mail: bk@nkfirm.com.

KEPNER, WILLIAM RAYMOND, JR., retired secondary school educator; b. Osceola, Nebr., July 13, 1940; s. William Raymond and Zella (Gillmor) Kepner; m. Diane Gambill, 1968. BA, U. Nebr., Lincoln, 1963; postgrad., U. Houston, 1978—79. Cert. secondary tchr. Calif. Tchr. Los Banos Unified Schs., Calif., 1963—67, Clayton Valley HS, Mt. Diablo Unified Sch. Dist., Concord, Calif., 1968—2003, chmn. English dept., 1995—2001. Mem.: Men's Sr. Golf Assn., AARP (tax counselor 2003—), Journalism Edn. Assn. No. Calif. (mem. bd. 1985—), Bay Area Photographers. Democrat. Avocations: travel, photography, volunteer work, golf, running. Home: 5523 McMillan St Oakland CA 94618 Personal E-mail: bkep@aol.com.

KEPPEL, WILLIAM JAMES, lawyer, educator, writer; b. Sheboygan, Wis., Sept. 25, 1941; s. William Frederick and Anne Elizabeth (Cinealis) K.; m. Polly Holmberg, June 26, 1965; children: Anne Rusert, Timothy, Matthew. BA, Marquette U., 1963; JD, U. Wis., Madison, 1970. Bar: Minn. 1970, U.S. Dist. Minn. 1970, U.s. Ct. Appeals (8th cir.) 1973, U.S. Dist. Ct. (we. dist.) Wis. 1979, U.S. Supreme Ct. 1979, U.S. Ct. Claims 1982. Assoc. Dorsey & Whitney, Mpls., 1970-76, ptnr., 1979-96; assoc. prof. Hamline U. Sch. Law, 1976-79, disting. practitioner in residence, 1996-2000. Instr. U. Minn. Law Sch.; adj. prof. William Mitchell Coll. Law, St. Paul; state adminstrv. law judge, 1977-79, 98-2004; chmn., dir. Legal Advice Clinics, Ltd.; dir. Legal Assistance of Minn., Inc.; head Hennepin County Pub. Defender's Office for Misdemeanors. Author: (with Mc Farland) Minnesota Civil Practice (4 vols.), 1979, 3d edit., 1999, Administrative Practice and Procedure, 1999; co-author, editor: Minnesota Environmental Law Handbook, 2nd edit., 1995; contbr. articles and monographs to legal jours. Lt. USN, 1963-67, Vietnam. Home: 10 Luverne Ave Minneapolis MN 55419-2612

KEPPELMAN, NANCY, lawyer; b. Abington, Pa., June 28, 1950; d. H. Thomas and Helene A. (Harrow) Keppelman; m. Michael E. Smerza, Sept. 9, 1978. Student, Oberlin Coll., Ohio, 1968-70; BA, U. Mich., 1972, JD, 1978; Cert., Inst. for Paralegal Tng., Phila., 1972. Bar: Mich. 1978, US Dist. Ct. (ea. dist.) Mich. 1978, US Tax Ct. 1986. Legal asst. Dykema, Gossett et al, Detroit, 1972-75; assoc. Butzel, Keidan et al, Detroit, 1978-80, Law Offices of Brook McCray Smith, Ann Arbor, Mich., 1980-82, Miller, Canfield et al, Detroit, 1982-89, Stevenson Assocs., Ann Arbor, 1989-90; shareholder, lawyer Stevenson Keppelman Assocs., Ann Arbor, 1991—. Condr. seminars in field. Co-author, editor QDROs, EDROs and Division of Employee Benefits in Divorce, A Guide for Michigan Practitioners, 2002; contbr. articles to profl. jours. James B. Angell scholar, U. Mich., 1972. Fellow Mich. State Bar Found., Am. Coll. Benefits Counsel; mem. ABA, State Bar Mich. (mem. taxation coun. 1991-94), Washtenaw County Bar Assn., Women Lawyers Assn. Mich. (bd. dirs., pres. Washtenaw region 1990-93). Avocations: birdwatching, music, hiking. Office: 444 S Main St Ann Arbor MI 48104-2304 Office Phone: 734-747-7050. E-mail: kep@skalaw.com.

KEPPLE, THOMAS RAY, JR., college administrator; b. Pitts., Mar. 19, 1948; s. Thomas Ray and Virginia Grace (Hudson) K.; m. Jane Donaldson, Aug. 22, 1971 (dec. 1977); m. Patricia Witcher, May 24, 1994. BA, Westminster Coll., 1970; MBA, Syracuse U., 1973, EdD, 1984. Dir. tech. tng. Morse divsn. Borg-Warner Corp., Ithaca, NY, 1970-73; dir. adminstrv. svcs. Rhodes Coll., Memphis, 1975-81, dean adminstrv. svcs., 1981-86, provost, 1986-89; v.p. Univ. South, Sewanee, Tenn., 1989-98; pres. Juniata Coll., Huntingdon, Pa., 1998—. Founding chair bd. dirs. Prepaid Tuition Consortium, The Ind. 529 Plan; bd. mem. abroad Brethren Coll., chmn. Assn. Ind. Colls. Univs. Pa. Author: Incentive Early Retirement Programs for Faculty. Bd. dirs. Sewanee Housing Inc., 1993-98; mem. exec. com. Vollintine Evergreen Cmty. Assn., Memphis, 1976-85, pres., 1981; mem. Biomed. Rsch. Zone Bd., 1986; sec.-treas. Health and Ednl. Facilities Bd. of Franklin County; bd. dirs. Liberty Bowl Classic; co-chair Gov. Rendell's higher edn. transition com. Mem.: Coun. Ind. Colls. (mem. adv. com. N.Y. Times), Am. Coun. Edn. (mem. internat. com., adv. bd. Princeton Rev.), Coll. and Univ. Personnel Assn., Memphis Acad. Forum (pres. 1985—86), Nat. Assn. Coll. and Univ. Bus. Officers, Assn. Ind. Colls. and Univs. Pa. (bd. dirs., treas.), Internat. Soc. Planning and Strategic Mgmt. (v.p. coms. 1984—85, pres. 1985—87), Univ. Club (N.Y.), Omicron Delta Kappa. Mem. Brethren Ch. Avocations: swimming, painting. Home: 2201 Washington St Huntingdon PA 16652-9762 Office: Juniata Coll Office of the Pres 1700 Moore St Huntingdon PA 16652-2119 Office Phone: 814-641-3101. Business E-Mail: kepplet@juniata.edu.

KEPPLER, HERBERT, publishing executive; b. NYC, Apr. 21, 1925; s. Victor and Josephine T. (Windmann) K.; m. Louise M. Lyman, July 7, 1956; children— Kathryn Louise, Thomas Victor. BA, Harvard, 1945. Reporter N.Y. Sun, 1948-49; with Modern Photography, NYC, 1950-87, editorial dir., pub., 1967-87; v.p. photog. pub. div. ABC Leisure Mags. Inc. div. ABC, NYC, 1974-78, sr. v.p. photog. pub. div., 1978-87; v.p., pub. dir. photography CBS Mags. Am. Photo and Popular Photography, 1987-88, Diamandis Communications Inc., 1988-90, Hachette Mags. Inc., 1990-93, Hachette Filipacchi Media U.S., Inc., 1993—2004, v.p. sr. counselor, 2004—. Author: Official 35mm Camera Rating Guide, 1957, Keppler on the Eye-Level Reflex, 1960, How to Make Better Pictures in Your Home, 1962, 124 Ways to Test Cameras, Lenses and Equipment, 1962, The Pentax Way, 1966, The Nikon-Nikkormat Way, 1976. Served to ensign USNR, 1945-46. Mem. Rolls-Royce Owners Club. Home: 119 N Highland Pl Croton On Hudson NY 10520-2113 Office: Hachette Filipacchi Media US Inc 1633 Broadway New York NY 10019-6708 Business E-Mail: hkeppler@hfmus.com.

KERBER, FRANK JOHN, retired diplomat; b. Indpls., June 13, 1947; s. Charles John and Romilda Ida (Molengraft) Kerber; m. Melanie Alice Niewoehner, July 29, 1989; 1 child, Brandon Eric. BA in Philosophy cum laude, Athenaeum of Ohio, 1969; MS, Georgetown U., 1976. Faculty coll. prep. sch., Cin., 1970-74; mgmt. cons. USAID, various locations, 1976-80; program officer USAID Mission, Tunis, Tunisia, 1980-84, Dept. of State, 1984; vice consul US Consulate Gen., Winnipeg, Canada, 1985-86; econ./comml. affairs officer Jordan, Lebanon, Syria, 1986—88; officer East-West Affairs European Bur. Office Regional Polit. and Econ. Affairs, 1988-90; A.I.D. liaison officer Bangui, Central African Republic, 1991-93; econ. officer Kingston, Jamaica, 1993-96; internat. economist Bur. Internat. Orgn. Affairs, Washington, 1996-98; spl. asst. to Amb. Schifter, 1998-2000; Ireland desk officer to Amb. Schifter, 2000—02; with US Mission to European Union, Brussels, 2002—06; ret., 2006; adj. prof. U. Pitts., 2007—; mem. faculty Sewickley Acad., 2007—. Mem.: Am. Fgn. Svc. Assn. Home: 1650 Pine Tree Dr Pittsburgh PA 15241 E-mail: melfrank52@msn.com.

KERBER, LINDA KAUFMAN, historian, educator; b. NYC, Jan. 23, 1940; d. Harry Hagman and Dorothy (Haber) Kaufman; m. Richard Kerber, June 5, 1960; children: Ross Jeremy, Justin Seth. AB cum laude, Barnard Coll., 1960; MA, NYU, 1961; PhD, Columbia U., 1968; DHL, Grinnell Coll., 1992; MA (hon.), Oxford U., 2006. Instr., asst. prof. history Stern Coll., Yeshiva U., NYC, 1963-68; asst. prof. history San Jose State Coll., Calif., 1969-70; vis. asst. prof. history Stanford U., Calif., 1970-71; asst. prof. history U. Iowa, Iowa City, 1971-75, prof., 1975-85, May Brodbeck prof., 1985—. Vis. prof. U. Chgo., 1991-92, Oxford U., England, 2006—. Author: Federalists in Dissent: Imagery and Ideology in Jeffersonian

America, 1970, paperback edit., 1980, 97, Women of the Republic: Intellect and Ideology in Revolutionary America, 1980, paperback edit., 1986, Toward an Intellectual History of Women, 1997, No Constitutional Right to Be Ladies: Women and the Obligations of Citizenship, 1998, paperback edit., 1999 (Littleton-Griswold prize in legal history Am. Hist. Assn., Joan Kelley prize in womens history Am. Hist. Assn.); co-editor: Women's America: Refocusing the Past, 1982, 6th edit., 2004, U.S. History As Women's History, 1995; mem. editl. bd. Signs: Jour. Women in Culture and Society, Jour. Women's History; contbr. articles and book revs. to profl. jours. Fellow Danforth Found., NEH, 1976, 83-84, 94, Am. Coun. Learned Socs., 1975, Nat. Humanities Ctr., 1990-91, Guggenheim Found., 1990-91, Radcliffe Inst. for Advanced Study, 2003. Mem. Orgn. Am. Historians (pres. 1996-97), Am. Hist. Assn. (pres. 2006), Am. Studies Assn. (pres. 1988), Am. Soc. for Legal History, Berkshire Conf. Women Historians, Soc. Am. Historians, Japan U.S. Friendship Commn., PEN Am. Ctr., Am. Acad. Arts and Scis., Am. Philos. Soc. Jewish. Office: U Iowa Dept History Iowa City IA 52242

KERBER, RICHARD E., cardiologist; b. NYC, May 10, 1939; s. Max and Pauline Kerber; m. Linda K. Kaufman; children: Ross, Justin. AB in Anthropology, Columbia U., 1960; MD, NYU, 1964. Diplomate Am. Bd. Internal Medicine, Am. Bd. Cardiology. Med. intern/resident Bellevue Hosp., NYC, 1964—66; med. resident Stanford (Calif.) U. Hosp., 1968—69, cardiology fellow, 1969—71; asst. prof. internal medicine U. Iowa, Iowa City, 1971—74, assoc. prof. internal medicine, 1974—78, prof. medicine, 1978—. Editor: Echocardiography in Coronary Artery Disease, 1988. Capt. US Army, 1966—68. Grantee RO1 grant, NHLBI, 1995—. Fellow: Am. Coll. Cardiology, Am. Heart Assn., Am. Heart Assn. (chmn. coun. on cardiopulmonary and critical care 1997—99, 1997—99, award of Meritorious Achievement 1996, Scientific Coun. Dist. Achievement award 2001), Am. Coll. Cardiology (gov. for Iowa 1976—79, 1976—79); mem.: Assn. Am. Physicians, Assn. Univ. Cardiologists, Am. Soc. for Clin. Investigation, Am. Soc. Echocardiology (sec. 1978—80, treas. 1993—95, v.p. 1995—97, pres. 1997—99, sec. 1978—80, treas. 1993—95, v.p. 1995—97, pres. 1997—99). Office: U Iowa Dept Medicine 200 Hawkins Dr Iowa City IA 52242-1009

KERBER, RONALD LEE, industrial corporation executive; b. Lafayette, Ind., July 2, 1943; s. John Andrew Kerber and Edith Helen (McMaster) Kerkhoff; children: John, Mark, Stephen, Jacqueline. BS, Purdue U., 1965; MS, Calif Inst. Tech., 1966, PhD, 1970. Registered profl. engr., Mich. Tech. staff Aerospace Corp., Los Angeles, 1971-72; prof. Mich. State U., E. Lansing, 1969-85, assoc. dean, 1984-85; program mgr. Defense Advanced Research Projects Agy., Arlington, Va., 1983-84; dep. undersec. U.S. Dept. Defense, Washington, 1985-88; v.p. advanced systems and tech. McDonnell Douglas Corp., St. Louis, 1988-89, v.p. tech. and bus. devel., 1989-91; exec. v.p., chief tech. officer Whirlpool Corp., Benton Harbor, 1991—2000; pres. SBDC Corp., Charlottesville, Va., 2000—. Contbr. articles to profl. jours. Mem. ASME, IEEE, Am. Phys. Soc.

KERBIS, GERTRUDE LEMPP, architect; m. Walter Peterhans (dec.); m. Donald Kerbis (div. 1972); children: Julian, Lisa, Kim. BS, U. Ill.; MA, Ill. Inst. Tech.; postgrad., Grad. Sch. Design, Harvard U., 1949-50. Archtl. designer Skidmore, Owings & Merrill, Chgo., 1954-59, C.F. Murphy Assocs., Chgo., 1959-62, 65-67; pvt. practice architecture Lempp Kerbis Assocs., Chgo., 1967—; lectr. U. Ill., 1969; prof. William Rainey Harper Coll., 1970—95, Washington U., St. Louis, 1977, 82, Ill. Inst. Tech., 1989-91. Archtl. cons. Dept. Urban Renewal, City of Chgo.; mem. Northeastern Ill. Planning Commn., Open Land Project, Mid-North Community Orgn., Chgo. Met. Housing and Planning Council, Chgo. Mayor's Commn. for Preservation Chgo.'s Hist. Architecture; bd. dirs. Chgo. Sch. Architecture Found., 1972-76; trustee Chgo. Archtl. Assistance Ctr., Glessner House Found., Inland Architect Mag.; lectr. Art Inst. Chgo., U. N.Mex., Ill. Inst. Tech., Washington U., St. Louis, Ball State U., Muncie, Ind., U. Utah, Salt Lake City. Prin. archtl. works include U.S. Air Force Acad. dining hall, Colo., 1957, Skokie (Ill.) Pub. Library, 1959, Meadows Club, Lake Meadows, Chgo., 1959, O'Hare Internat. Airport 7 Continents Bldg, 1963; prin. developer and architect: Tennis Club, Highland Park, Ill., 1968, Watervliet, Mich. Tennis Ranch, 1970, Greenhouse Condominium, Chgo., 1976, Webster-Clark Townhouses, Chgo., 1986, Chappell Sch., 1993; exhibited at Chgo. Hist. Soc., 1984, Chgo. Mus. Sci. and Industry, 1985, Paris Exhbn. Chgo. Architects, 1985, Spertus Mus.; represented in permanent archtl. drawings collection Art Inst. Chgo. Active Art Inst. Chgo. Recipient award for outstanding achievement in professions YWCA Met. Chgo., 1984 Fellow AIA (bd. dirs. Chgo. chpt. 1971-75, chpt. pres. 1980, nat. com. architecture, arts and recreation 1972-75, com. on design 1975-80, head subcom. inst. honors nomination); mem. Chgo. Women in Architecture (founder), Chgo. Network, Internat. Women's Forum, Arts Club Chgo., Cliff Dwellers (bd. dirs. 1987-88, pres. 1988, 89), Lambda Alpha. Office: Lempp Kerbis Assocs 172 W Burton Pl Chicago IL 60610-1310 Personal E-mail: lk172@aol.com.

KERCHER, DAVID MAX, retired mechanical engineer; b. Goshen, Ind., Nov. 18, 1931; s. Maxwell Mease and Rosemary (Harper) K.; m. Betty Noreen Raycroft, June 7, 1958; children: Kimberly S., Matthew R., Andrew D.R., Steven R., Elizabeth J., Jason R., Amy N. BSME, Purdue U., 1958; MS in Aerospace Engring., U. Cin., 1967. Engr. large jet engine divsn. GE, Cin., 1968—71, sr. engr., 1966—71, unit mgr., 1968, engr. missile and space divsn. Burlington, Vt., 1959—60, unit mgr. gas turbine dept. Schenectady, 1973—81, sr. engr., 1982, sub-sect. mgr. aircraft engine group Lynn, Mass., 1983—84; sr. engr. GE Aircraft Engines, Lynn, 1985—89, prin. engr., 1989—2001; ret., 2002. V.p. Sunrise Orchards, Inc., Goshen, Ind., 1996—2002, also bd. dirs. Contbr. articles to profl. jours.; 15 patents on gas turbine cooling. Sgt. USAF, 1950-54, USAFR, 1955-58. Fellow ASME (gas turbine heat transfer com. 1980—, vice chmn. com. 1992-94, chmn. 1994-96); mem. AIAA (sr.), ASME Internat. Gas Turbine Inst., Am. Legion (life), Air Force Assn. (life), Tau Beta Pi, Pi Tau Sigma. E-mail: dave@Kercher.org.

KERCHEVAL, ALEC NORTON, mathematician; s. Basyl Hurley Kercheval and Edwina Simi Norton; m. Lilian Garcia-Roig, May 7, 1995; children: Claire Elizabeth Kercheval-Roig, Olivia Anne Kercheval-Roig. BS, Harvey Mudd Coll., 1980; MA, Merton Coll., U. Oxford, 1982; PhD, U. Calif., Berkeley, 1987. Asst. prof. Math., Univ. Tex., Austin, 1989—98; sr. cons. Barra, Inc., Berkeley, 1999—2001; assoc. prof. Math., Fla. State Univ., Tallahassee, 2001—. Marshall scholarship, Marshall Aid Commn., Brit. Govt., 1980-1982, Postdoctoral fellowship math. scis., NSF, 1989-1992. Mem.: Am. Math. Soc. Office: Dept Math Florida State U Tallahassee FL 32306-4510 Business E-Mail: kercheva@math.fsu.edu.

KERCHEVAL, JOHN WILLIAM, III, finance professor, aerospace and defense executive, vulture capitalist, former investment banker; b. Arlington, Va., Aug. 21, 1965; s. John William Kercheval II and Carolyn Ann Booth Kercheval. BS in Chemistry, U. Calif., Berkeley, 1987, MBA in Fin. and Ops. Rsch., 1993. Rsch. assoc. Genentech, Inc., South San Francisco, Calif., 1986—88; assoc. tech. corp. fin. Hambrecht & Quist, LLP, San Francisco, 1988—91, assoc. v.p., corp. fin. dept., 1991—93; v.p. merchant banking Pierce Group, Arlington, 1993—95; dir. fin. planning and analysis Orbital Scis. Corp., Dulles, 1995—97; v.p., treas. Orbital Scis. Corp. / ORBCOMM, Dulles, Va., 1997—2001, European Aeronautic Def. and Space Co., N.V., Amsterdam, Netherlands, 2001—03; exec. v.p., CFO AeroAstro, Inc., Ashburn, Va., 2003—05; sr. mng. dir. Mid-Atlantic Vulture Capital Fund, Washington, 2004—; fin. prof. Georgetown U., Washington, 2004—. Dir. ORBCOMM Global, LP, Dulles, 1997—2000, ORBCOMM Internat., LP, London, 1997—2000. Mem. St. John's Episcopal Ch., McLean, Va. Alumni scholar, U. Calif., Berkeley, 1984—87. Mem.: Anubis Soc. (dir.), Calif. Alumni Soc., Skull and Keys Soc., The Tuckahoe Club, Order of Golden Bear, Phi Beta Kappa (sec. Washington chpt. 1999—2002). Conservative. Episcopalian. Avocations: swimming, weightlifting, stereo and sound reproduction. Home Phone: 703-790-8601. Personal E-mail: johnwkercheval@aol.com. Business E-Mail: jwk44@georgetown.edu.

KERCHEVAL, MICHAEL P., real estate company executive; m. Dana Kercheval; 2 children. BA in Economics and Internat. Affairs, U. Colo.; MA in Economics, Columbia U. Sr. economist Equitable Life Assurance Soc., 1982, sr. v.p., portfolio mgr.; sr. exec. Lend Lease Real Estate Investments; prin. and CEO Lend Lease Latin American Realty Advisors Ltd.; exec. v.p. Internat. Coun. Shopping Centers, 2000, COO, 2000, pres. and CEO. Bd. dirs. Travel Bus. Roundtable. Mem.: NY Soc. Assn. Executives, Nat. Assn. Bus. Economics. Office: Internat Council Shopping Centers 1221 Avenue of Americas 41st Floor New York NY 10020 Office Phone: 646-728-3800. Office Fax: 732-694-1755. E-mail: mkercheval@icsc.org.*

KEREIAKES, DEAN JAMES, cardiologist; b. Louisville, Jan. 8, 1953; s. James G. and Helen (Christy) K.; m. Anne Sugar, June 20, 1981; children: Jennifer, David, Andrew, Nicholas. BS, U. Cin., 1974, MD, 1978. Diplomate Am. Bd. Internal Medicine, Am. Bd. Cardiology. Intern, resident U. Calif., San Francisco, 1978-80; sr. resident Mass. Gen. Hosp., Boston, 1980-81; chief med. resident H.C. Moffitt Hosp., San Francisco, 1981-82; adult cardiology fellow U. Calif., San Francisco, 1982-84; coronary angioplasty fellow San Francisco Heart Inst., 1984, Sequoia Hosp., Redwood City, Calif., 1984; med. dir., The Heart Ctr. for Greater Cin. The Christ Hosp., Cin., 1985—; CEO, dir. rsch. Ohio Heart Health Ctr., 2000—05. Med. dir. Carl & Edythe Lindner Ctr. Clin. Cardiovasc. Rsch., Cin., 1995—; prof. clin. medicine Ohio State U., 1995—; mem. ACC/AHA task force com on angioplasty and unstable angina guidelines AHA/ACC, 1987-2002. Mem. editl. bd. Circulation, sect. editor, mem. editl. bd. Jour. Invasive Cardiology, Am. Heart Jour., Am. Jour. Cardiology, Jour. Am. Coll. Cardiology. Fellow Am. Coll. Cardiology; mem. AMA, Am. Heart Assn., Alpha Omega Alpha, Phi Beta Kappa. Republican. Avocation: wine collecting. Office: The Ohio Heart and Vascular Ctr 2123 Auburn Ave Ste 136 Cincinnati OH 45219-2906 Office Phone: 513-585-1777. E-mail: lindner@fuse.net.

KEREN, KINNERET, biophysicist; b. Jerusalem; PhD in Physics, Technion Israel Inst. Tech. Postdoctoral rschr. Theriot Lab., Dept. Biochemistry Stanford U. Contbr. articles to profl. jour. Named one of Top 100 Young Innovators, MIT Tech. Review, 2004. Office: Stanford U Dept Biochemistry Stanford CA 94305 Business E-Mail: kinneret@stanford.edu.

KERESTAN, KITTY WILDE, music educator; b. Louisville, Oct. 12, 1946; d. Maurice Edward and Kitty Thurman Wilde; m. Richard Michael Kerestan, June 15, 1968; children: Aaron Richard, Brian Cameron. BA, Morehead State U., 1968; MEd, Wright State U., 1996. Music tchr. Edgewood City Schs., Trenton, Ohio, 1968—70, New Miami Local Schs., Hamilton, Ohio, 1980—. Pres. New Miami Edn. Assn., Hamilton, Ohio. Musician: Hamilton Fairfield Symphony, 1970—83. Trustee Butler Co. Health Plan, Ohio, 1985—2004; dir. Holy Cross Lutheran Ch., Fairfield, Ohio, 2000—. Lutheran. Home: 2706 Moeller Dr Hamilton OH 45014 Office: New Miami Local Schs 600 Seven Mile Ave Hamilton OH 45011 Personal E-mail: nm_kerestan@swoca.net.

KERGER, PAULA ARNOLD, broadcast executive; b. Dec. 20, 1957; married. BS, U. Balt., 1979. Mgmt. positions U.S. Com. UNICEF, Washington, 1979—84; head develop. Internat. Ho., 1984—89; mgmt. positions Met. Opera, 1989—93; v.p. WNET-TV, NYC, 1993—2004, dir. govt. affairs, 1993—2002, sta. mgr., 2002—04, exec. v.p., COO, 2004—06; pres., CEO PBS, 2006—. Bd. dirs. PBS Found.; vice chair, bd. trustees Am. Pub. TV. Named one of 100 Most Powerful Women in Entertainment, Hollywood Reporter, 2006. Office: PBS 2100 Crystal Dr Ste 100 Arlington VA 22202-3784 Office Phone: 703-739-5000. Office Fax: 703-739-5777.*

KERIAN, JON ROBERT, retired judge; b. Grafton, ND, Oct. 23, 1927; s. Cyril Robert and Elizabeth Antoinette (Kadlec) K.; m. Sylvia Ann Larson, Dec. 28, 1959; children: John, Ann. PhB, U. N.D., 1955, LLB, 1957, JD, 1971. Bar: N.D. 1957, U.S. Dist. Ct. N.D. 1958, U.S. Ct. Appeals (8th cir.) 1971, U.S. Supreme Ct. 1963. Pvt. practice law, Grand Forks, N.D., 1958-61; asst. atty. gen. State of N.D., Bismarck, 1961-67; ptnr. Bosard, McCutcheon, Kerian, Schmidt, Minot, N.D., 1967-80; dist. judge State of N.D., Minot, 1980—92, surrogate judge, 1993—, ret., 1992. History instr. Bismarck State Coll., 1965-67; asst. city atty. City of Minot, 1968-76; atty. Zoning & Planning Commn., Minot, 1969-76; lectr. in field. Contbr. articles to profl. jours.; editor ABA newsletter, The Judges News, 1990—95. Mem. ABA (bd. editors Judges Jour. 1990-95), Western States Bar Conf. (pres. 1982-83), N.D. Bar Assn. (pres. 1979-80), Nat. Conf. State Trial Judges (exec. com. 1983-89). Home: 1800 8th St SW Minot ND 58701-6410 Office: PO Box 340 Minot ND 58702-0340 Personal E-mail: judex1@srt.com.

KERIK, BERNARD BAILEY, security firm executive, former police commissioner; b. Newark, Sept. 4, 1955; s. Donald and Patricia Kerik; m. Hala Matli, 1998; 4 children. BS in Pub. Adminstrn., Empire State Coll. (SUNY), 2002. Security guard King Faisal Specialist Hosp., Riyadh, Saudi Arabia, 1982—84; comdr. spl. weapons and ops., warden Passaic County Jail, NJ; with NYC Police Dept., 1985—2001; exec. asst. to commr. NYC Dept. Corrections, first dep. commr., 1995—97, commr., 1997—2000; police commr. NYC Police Dept., 2000—01; sr. v.p. Giuliani Ptnrs., NYC, 2001—03; CEO Giuliani-Kerik LLC (name changed to Giuliani Security & Safety), NYC, 2003—04; chmn., CEO The Kerik Group LLC, NYC, 2004—; interim min. interior, sr. policy adv. U.S. Presdl. Envoy to Iraq's Coalition Provisional Authority, Baghdad, 2003; state security adv. to Pres. Bharrat Jagdeo Govt. of Guyana, Georgetown, 2007—. Mem. criminal justice adv. coun. St. John's U., NYC; mem. academe policy rsch. sr. adv. com. U.S. Dept. Homeland Security; prin. mem. Mayor's cabinet overseeing the rescue, recovery, and investigation of the World Trade Center attack; mem. bd. dirs. Taser Internat., Inc., 2002—05. Author: The Lost Son: A Life in Pursuit of Justice, 2002. Served in 18th Airborne Corps US Army, 1975—78, South Korea, Middle East. Named a Comdr. of the Most Excellent Royal Order of the British Empire (CBE); recipient Medal of Valor, NYC Police Dept., Presdl. Commendation for Heroism. Office: The Kerik Group LLC 275 Madison Ave 35th Fl New York NY 10016*

KERINS, FRANCIS JOSEPH, college president; b. NYC, Mar. 23, 1927; s. John and Ellen (Mulrooney) K.; m. Mary Elizabeth Costigan, June 2, 1951; children: Mary Ellen Kerins Hayes, Donna (Mrs. Joseph Zelinski), John, Edward, Francis, Joseph, James. AB, St. Francis Coll., 1949; AM, St. Louis U., 1951; EdD, U. Denver, 1959; LHD, Coll. Idaho, 1983; LLD, City U., 1986. Prof., adminstr. Loretto Heights Coll., 1952-68; prof. higher edn. U. Denver, 1968-69; pres. Coll. St. Francis, Joliet, Ill., 1969-74, Carroll Coll., Helena, Mont., 1974-89, No. Mont. Coll., Havre, 1989-90, St. Mary of the Plains Coll., Dodge City, Kans., 1990-91. Commr. Western Interstate Commn. Higher Edn.; chmn. Western Ind. Colls. Fund, Commn. on Colls. Northwest Assn.; chmn. bd. Bank of Mont.; bd. dirs. Am. Council on Edn., Council Ind. Colls.; active Nat. Commn. on Higher Edn. Issues; cons. in field. Contbr. articles to profl. jours. Chmn. Lewis and Cark County Bicentennial Com., 1975—; trustee Loretto Heights Coll., 1961-67, Coll. St. Francis, 1969-74, Carroll Coll., 1974—; pres. Helena Symphony Soc., 1981—; bd. dirs. Helena YMCA, United Way, Lewis and Clark Libr. Found.; mem. Helena Airport Bd., Coun. on Naturopathic Med. Edn. With AUS, 1950-52. Fellow Am. Council Edn.; mem. Mont. Com. for Humanities (past chmn.), Assn. Cath. Colls. and Univs. (chmn.); mem. Helena C. of C. (bd. dir.), N.W. Assn. of Schs. and Colls. (pres.), Waterton-Glacier Internat. Peace Park Assn. (bd. dirs.), Rotary (past pres.). Roman Catholic.

KERKORIAN, KIRK, investor, former motion picture company executive, consultant; b. Fresno, Calif., June 6, 1917; s. Ahron and Lily K.; m. Hilda Schmidt, Jan. 24, 1942 (div. 1951); m. Jane Maree Hardy, Dec. 5, 1954 (div.); children: Tracy, Linda; m. Lisa Bonder, 1998 (div.) Student pub. schs., LA. Comml. airline pilot, from 1940; founder L.A. Air Svc. (later Trans Internat. Airlines Corp.), 1948, Internat. Leisure Corp., 1968; co-chmn., pres., CEO Tracinda Corp., 1969—; controlling stockholder Western Airlines, 1970; chief exec. officer Metro-Goldwyn-Mayer, Inc., Culver City, Calif., 1973-74, chmn. exec. com., vice-chmn. bd., 1974-79, dir., 1996—; controlling stockholder MGM/UA Communications Co.; cons., 1979—. Served as capt. Transport Command RAF, 1942-44. Named one of 50 Most Generous Philanthropists, Fortune Mag., 2005, Forbes Richest Americans, 2006, World's Richest People, Forbes Mag., 1999—, Forbes 400, 1999—. Office: Tracinda Corp 150 Rodeo Dr, Ste 250 Beverly Hills CA 90212*

KERLIKOWSKE, KARLA, research scientist; BS (magna cum laude) in Med. Tech., Mich. State U., East Lansing, 1978; MS in Nutrition, U. Calif., Berkeley, 1984; MD, U. Calif., San Francisco, 1988. Intern, medicine U. Calif., 1988—89, resident, primary care medicine, 1989—91, clin. instr., asst. physician, dept. medicine, 1991—93, asst. prof. in residence, dept. medicine, 1994—, asst. prof. in residence, dept. epidemiology & biostatistics, 1994—, assoc. prof. in residence, dept. medicine, 2000—, assoc. prof. in residence, dept. epidemiology & biostatistics, 2000—, prof. in residence, dept. epidemiology & biostatistics, 2000—; fellow, gen. internal medicine Veterans Affairs Med. Ctr., San Francisco, 1991—93, assoc. dir., women's clinic, 1993—99, dir., women's clinic, 1999—. Mem. U. Calif. Comprehensive Cancer Ctr., San Francisco; prin. investigator Nat. Cancer Inst.-funded San Francisco Mammography Registry, Outcomes Core; co-investigator NIH-funded, U. Calif. San Francisco Breast Cancer SPORE. Contbr. articles to profl. publications. Recipient Tower Guard award for Scholastic Achievement, 1975, Am. Cancer Soc. award for Primary Care Physicians, 1994—96. Mem.: Alpha Omega Alpha. Office: Veterans Affairs Medical Center VAMC 111A1 San Francisco CA 94143 Office Phone: 415-750-2093. Office Fax: 415-379-5573. Business E-Mail: kerliko@itsa.ucsf.edu. E-mail: karla.kerlikowske@ucsf.edu.*

KERMAN, ARTHUR KENT, physicist, researcher; b. Montreal, May 3, 1929; s. Samuel and Ida (Birn) K.; m. Enid Ehrlich, Dec. 21, 1952; children: Ben, Daniel, Elizabeth, Melissa, James. B.Sc., McGill U., 1950; PhD, MIT, 1953. Mem. faculty dept. physics MIT, Cambridge, 1956, dir. Ctr. Theoretical Physics, 1976-83, dir. lab. nuclear scis., 1983-92, prof., 1964—2002, prof. emeritus, 2002—. Vis. prof. SUNY-Stony Brook, 1970-71; adj. prof. Bklyn. Coll., 1971-75; rsch. prof. U. Tenn. and ORNL, 2004-; cons. Argonne Nat. Lab., 1961-83, mem. sci. and tech. adv. com., 1984-90; cons. Brookhaven Nat. Lab., 1965-81, mem. relativistic heavy ion collider policy com., 1985-95, vis. com. 1973-78, chmn. 1977; cons. Lawrence Berkeley Lab., 1975-80, mem. vis. com., 1980-83, chmn. 1981; cons. Lawrence Livermore Lab., 1964—, chmn. phys. sci. advi. com. 1992-96; cons. Nat. Ignition Facility, 1997-99; cons. Los Almos Sci. Lab, 1961—, mem. physics div. adv. com., 1984-96, mem. theol. div. adv. com. 1972, LANSCE divsn. adv. com., 1998-2003, chair LANSCE adv. bd., 2006-07; cons. Nat. Bur. Stds., 1980-81, Oak Ridge Nat. Lab., 1979-85, Sandia Nat. Lab., 1998-99; mem. U. Calif. Pres.'s Sci. and Academic Adv. Com. 1981-92; mem. White House Sci. Coun., 1982-85, panel on sci. and tech. in govt., 1985, fed. lab. rev. panel, 1982-83; mem. adv. com. Woods Hole Sub-panel of US Dept. Energy, 1982, com. on sci., engring. and pub. policy rsch. briefing panel on sci. frontiers and superconducting super collider NRC, 1985, nuclear sci. adv. com. Dept. Energy and NSF, 1982-85; mem. U.S. Dept. Energy Fusion Policy Adv. Com., 1990, mem. US Dept. Energy Inertial Confinement Fusion Adv. Com. 1992-96; mem. vis. com. Stanford U. Physics Dept., 1984, Yale U. Physics Dept., 1984, FONDS F.C.A.C. Comite des centres de Recherches pour le Laboratoire de Physique Nucleaire U. Montreal, 1982; mem. NIF Coun., 1997-99, NIF Programs Rev. Com., 2000-02; mem. Physics and Advanced Tech. Adv. Com., 1996—; Nat. Acad. Scis. panel on Inertial Confinement Fusion and Sci. Based Stockpile Stewardship, 1996-97, dirs. adv. com. Lawrence Livermore Nat. Lab., 1994-96; Ligo oversight bd. for MIT and Caltech, 1998-2002; cons. ORNL, 2002-04, U. Rochester Lab. for Laser Energetics, 2002-03; sci. advisor to asst. dep. adminstr. rsch., devel. and simulation DOE/NNSA, 2000—. Assoc. editor: Rev. Modern Physics, 1968-71. NRC fellow Calif. Inst. Tech., 1953-54, Niels Bohr Inst., Copenhagen, 1954-56; Guggenheim fellow U. Paris, 1961-62. Fellow Am. Phys. Soc. (program com. 1978-79, exec. com. div. nuclear physics 1970-72, pub. com. div. nuclear physics, Tom W. Bonner prize com. 1982-83), Am. Acad. Arts and Scis.; mem. N.Y. Acad. Scis. Office: MIT Dept Physics Rm 6-306 77 Massachusetts Ave Cambridge MA 02139-4307

KERMAN, PETER F., lawyer; BA, MS, Stanford Univ., 1977; JD, Harvard Univ., 1984. Bar: Calif. 1984. Joined Latham & Watkins, LA, 1984, office mng. ptnr., Silicon Valley Menlo Park, Calif., 1997—2004, now ptnr., and global chair, corp. dept., 2004—. Mem.: ABA. Office: Latham & Watkins Silicon Valley 135 Commonwealth Dr Menlo Park CA 94025

KERMES, CONSTANTINE JOHN, artist, industrial designer; b. Pitts., Dec. 6, 1923; s. John Demetrios and Katina (Katerinis) K.; m. Bessie Saratopoulos, Sept. 14, 1952; children: Harriet Kermes Shuman, Kathy Kermes Dixon. BFA, Carnegie Mellon U. Designer Am.-Std. Co., Pitts., 1952-55; indsl. design cons. New Holland N.A. subs. Fiat, Modena, Italy, 1955-82, indsl. designer, 1982—. One man shows include Grimaldis Gallery, Balt., 1979-80, Reading Mus., Pa., 1980, Jacques Seligmann Gallery, NYC, 1951-52, 54, 56, 59, 61, 64-65, 70, 75, 78-79, Hancock Shaker Mus., Pittsfield, Mass., 1989, Demuth Found., Lancaster, Pa., 1987, Millport Mus., Lancaster, 1989, William Pa. Mus., Harrisburg, 2000, Balt. Watercolor Soc., 2001, Ctrl. Market Art Gallery, 2001-03, Lancaster Mus. of Art, 2003-04; exhibited in group shows at Butler Inst. Am. Art, Youngstown, Ohio, 1964, Pa. Watercolor Soc., 1979-80, 91, Art 81, Washington, 1985, 91, Mus. Art, Lancaster, 1996, Ctrl. Mkt. Art Gallery, Lancaster, 2002, Westmoreland Mus. Art., Greensburg, Pa., 2003-04; exhibited in group shows at Okla. Watercolor Soc., 2001-02, Millersville (Pa.) U., Elizabethtown (Pa.) Coll., Lancaster Mus. Art; represented in permanent collections Storm King Art Ctr., Mountain View, NY, Pa. State U., Hershey (Pa.) Med. Ctr., Case New Holland, Pa., Pa. Hist. Mus., Hancock Shaker Mus., Mus. Art, Lancaster; illustrator Shaker Architecture, 1970; author, illustrator: American Icons, 1975. Recipient Am. Design Rev. award Indsl. Design mag., 1962, 64, 68, 72, Design award Am. Iron and Steel Inst., 1963, 69, 73, 75, awards Lancaster CountyArt Assn., award Berks Art Alliance, 2000, Hazleton Art League, 2000, York Art Alliance, 2000, Lancaster County Art Mus., Potomac Soc. award, 2001, prize Mid-Atlantic States Water Color, 2001, award Balt. Watercolor Soc., Art of State award William Penn Mus., Harrisburg, York, Pa. Art Assn. 2000, 01, 02, 03, 04, 05, award Phila. Water Color Soc., 2003, 04, Chester County (Pa.) Art Assn., 2003, 04, Okla. Watercolor Soc., 2005, others. Mem. AHEPA (Lancaster), Pa. Watercolor Soc., Hamilton Club (Lancaster). Greek Orthodox. Achievements include patents for farm equipment designs. Home and Office: 981 Landis Valley Rd Lancaster PA 17601-4816

KERMODE, FRANK (JOHN KERMODE), literary critic, educator; b. Douglas, Isle of Man, Nov. 29, 1919; s. John Pritchard and Doris (Kennedy) K. BA, Liverpool U., 1940, MA, 1947; DHL (hon.), U. Chgo., 1975; DLitt (hon.), Liverpool U., 1981; PhD (hon.), Amsterdam U., 1988, Newcastle U., 1993, Yale, 1995, U. Wesleyan, 1997, U. London, 1997, U. Sewanee, 1999, Columbia U., 2003, Harvard U., 2004. J.E. Taylor prof. English Manchester U., Eng., 1958-65; Winterstoke prof. English Bristol U., Eng., 1965-67; Lord Northcliffe prof. English U. Coll. London, 1967-74; King Edward VII prof. English Cambridge U., 1974-82; vis. prof. humanities Columbia U., NYC, 1983, 85. Charles E. Norton prof. Harvard U., 1977-78; Henry Luce prof. Yale Y., 1994. Author: Romantic Image, 1957, Wallace Stevens, 1960, The Sense of an Ending, 1967, D.H. Lawrence, 1973, The Classic, 1975, The Genesis of Secrecy, 1979, The Art of Telling, 1983, Forms of Attention, 1985, History and Value, 1988, An Appetite for Poetry, 1989, The Uses of Error, 1991, Not Entitled, 1995, others; (with Anita Kermode) The Oxford Book of Letters, 1995, Shakespeare's Language, 2000, Pleasing Myself, 2001, Pieces of My Mind, 2003, The Age of Shakespeare, 2004; co-editor Encounter, 1965-67; (with Robert Alter) The Literary Guide to the Bible, 1987; editor Modern Masters Series, 1969-91, Oxford Authors, 1984—. Served to lt. Royal Navy, 1940-46. Decorated officier Ordre des Arts et Sciences (France), 1973; named Knight Bachelor granted by the Queen of Eng., 1991; King's Coll. hon. fellow, 1987—. Fellow Brit. Acad., Royal Soc. Lit.; mem. Am. Acad. Arts and Scis. (hon.), Am. Acad. Arts and Letters (hon.), Accademia dei Lincei. Home: 9 The Oast House Pinehurst Grange Rd Cambridge CB3 9AP England Home Phone: 01223 357931; Office Phone: 01223 357931. Personal E-mail: frank_kermode@tiscali.net.

KERN, BERNARD DONALD, retired physicist; b. New Castle, Ind., Oct. 31, 1919; s. William Bernard and Cecile McDonald (Hudson) K.; m. Nedda Wisler Burdsall, Aug. 20, 1946; children: Richard B., Jonathan K., Arthur R. BS, Ind. U., 1942, MS, 1947, PhD, 1949. Physicist Signal Corps and Manhattan Project, Chgo., 1942-43; sr. physicist Oak Ridge Nat. Lab., 1949-50; faculty U. Ky., 1950-85, prof. physics, 1958-85, chmn. dept. physics and astronomy, 1967-69, prof. emeritus, 1985—. Physicist U.S. Naval Radiol. Def. Lab., San Francisco, 1957-58, cons., 1957-69; prof. Inst. Teknologi Bandung, Indonesia, U Ky., State Dept. Ednl. Assistance Program, 1961- 62 Author articles on nuc. physics. Served to lt.(jg) USNR, 1943-46. Fellow Am. Phys. Soc.; mem. Am. Inst. Physics, Am. Assn. Physics Tchrs. Home: 681 Providence Rd Lexington KY 40502-2264 Personal E-mail: slrcamera@aol.com.

KERN, BRAD D., lawyer; s. Frank B. Kern and Donna Jacard. BA, U. Calif., Berkeley, 1995; JD, UCLA, 1999. Extern to Chief Justice Ronald M. George Supreme Ct. Calif., San Francisco, 1997; assoc. Shearman & Sterling, San Francisco, 1999—. Contbr. articles to profl. jours. Mem.: ABA, Calif. Bar Assn. Office: Shearman & Sterling 525 Market St Ste 1500 San Francisco CA 94105 Office Phone: 415-616-1100.

KERN, CHARLES WILLIAM, retired academic administrator, chemist, educator; b. Middletown, Ohio, July 13, 1935; s. Charles Albert and Charme (Bowman) K.; m. Regine Bouchard. BS, Carnegie Inst. Tech., 1957; PhD, U. Minn., 1961; postgrad., Columbia U., 1961-63. Postdoctoral fellow in chem. physics Columbia U., NYC, 1961-63; asst. prof. chemistry SUNY, Stony Brook, 1964-66; adj. assoc. prof. chemistry Ohio State U., Columbus, 1966-71, adj. prof. chemistry, 1971-76, acad. vice chmn., dept. chemistry, 1972-73, prof. chemistry, 1976-80; rsch. scientist Battelle Meml. Inst., Columbus, Ohio, 1966-72, mgr. chem. physics sect., 1972-76, dir. phys. scis. program, 1973-74, inst. scientist, 1973-76, dir. Battelle Inst. program, 1976-84, cons., 1976-84; program dir. theoretical chem. physics, div. chemistry NSF, Washington, 1978-80, sr. staff assoc., computer sci. rsch. network project dir., div. math. and computer scis., 1980-83, program dir. structural chemistry and thermodynamics, acting sect. head phys. chemistry and chem. dynamics, div. chem., 1983-84, acting dir. div. chemistry, 1984-85, dep. dir. div. chemistry, 1985-86; asst. dir. gen. sci., Office of Sci. and Tech. Policy Office of the Pres., Washington, 1986; dean Ohio State U., Columbus, 1986-92; prof. chemistry Coll. Math. and Phys. Scis. Ohio State U., Columbus, 1986-92; v.p. rsch., dean Grad. Sch., Northwestern U., Evanston, Ill., 1992-93, v.p. rsch. and grad. studies, 1993-98, prof. chemistry, 1992-98, prof. emeritus, 1998—. Chmn,. Sch. Many-Body Techniques in Chemistry, Seattle, 1969, Carnegie-Mellon U. Admissions Coun., 1970-72, Summer Rsch. Conf. on Theoretical Chemistry, Boulder, Colo., 1975; co-chmn. Current Biol. Problems, Sch. for Phys. Scientists, 1977; exec. sec. NSF Dir.'s Task Force on Advanced Sci. Computing Resources, 1983-84. Assoc. editor Chem. Physics Letter, 1967-81; contbr. numerous articles to profl. jours. Mem. Am. Chem. Soc. E-mail: wkern04@comcast.net.

KERN, DAVID GRAHAM, lawyer; b. Cin., Aug. 28, 1973; BA, U. South, 1996; JD, Ohio State U., 2000. Bar: Ohio 2000, US Dist. Ct. Southern Dist. Ohio 2001. Asst. atty. gen. Ohio, 2000—02, asst. solicitor; assoc. Kohnen & Patton LLP, Cin. Named one of Ohio's Rising Stars, Super Lawyers, 2006. Mem.: Federalist Soc. for Law and Pub. Policy Studies, Cin. Bar Assn. Office: Kohnen & Patton PNC Ctr Ste 800 201 E Fifth St Cincinnati OH 45202 Office Phone: 513-381-0656. Office Fax: 513-381-5823.

KERN, DAVID JEFFERY, military officer; b. Binghamton, NY, Aug. 24, 1959; s. Arthur John and Maryellen Kern; m. Pamela A. Kelley, Sept. 17, 1984; children: Michael David, Margaret Kelley. BS in Physics, US Naval Acad., Annaplois, Md., 1981; MA in Nat. Security Affairs, Naval Postgraduate Sch., Monterey, Calif., 1988. Commd. ensign USN, 1981, advanced through grades to capt., 1981—2002, commdg. officer USS San Francisco Pearl Harbor, Hawaii, 1999—2002, commdg. officer USS Va. Groton, Conn., 2002—04, commodore Undersea Surveillance Virginia Beach, Va., 2005—. Decorated Legion of Merit USN; recipient Stephen Decatur award for Operational Excellence, USN League, 1990. Mem.: Mil. Officers Assn. Am., US Naval Inst., US Naval Acad. Alumni Assn. (life), US Submarine Vets. (life). Office: Dir Submarine Requirements and Warfare Devel Comdr Naval Submarine Forces 7958 Blake Rd Norfolk VA 23551-2492 Personal E-mail: kerndj@gmail.com. Business E-Mail: david.j.kern@navy.mil.

KERN, GEORGE CALVIN, JR., lawyer; b. Balt., Apr. 19, 1926; s. George Calvin and Alice (Gaskins) K.; m. Joan Shorell, Dec. 22, 1962; 1 child, Heath. BA, Princeton U., 1947; LLB, Yale U., 1952. Bar: N.Y. 1952. Chief U.S. Info. Ctr., Mannheim, W.Ger., 1947-48; dep. dir. pub. info. Office U.S. Mil. Govt. for Germany, Berlin and Nurnberg, 1948-49; assoc. Sullivan & Cromwell, NYC, 1952-60, ptnr., 1960—. Publ. Cub newspaper, Tehachapi, Calif., 1974—; bd. dirs. McJunkin Corp., Charleston, W.Va. Lt. USN, 1944-46. Home: 830 Park Ave New York NY 10021-2757 Office: Sullivan & Cromwell 125 Broad St Fl 28 New York NY 10004-2489

KERN, IRVING JOHN, retired food company executive; b. NYC, Feb. 10, 1914; s. John and Min (Weitzner) Kleinberger; m. Beatrice Rubenfeld, June 22, 1941; children John Alan, Arthur Harry, Robert Michael. BS, NYU, 1934, student Grad. Sch. Art and Sci., 1960-65; DHL, Mercy Coll., Dobbs Ferry, NY, 1980. Asst. buyer Bloomingdale's Dept. Store, NYC, 1934-40; with Dellwood Foods, Inc., Yonkers, NY, 1945-82, pres., 1966-77, chmn. and chief exec. officer, 1977-82. Dir. Scarsdale Nat. Bank; adj. prof. polit. sci., San Diego State U., 1989-95. Mem. County Mental Health Svcs. Bd. of Westchester County, 1954-59; mem. bd. dirs., sec. Westchester County Assn., 1950-57, 76-80; exec. bd. Westchester County Better Bus. Bur., 1970-73; bd. dirs. Westchester Coalition, 1972-80, Westchester Minority Bus. Assistance Orgn., 1973-75, Milk Industry Found., 1976-82, Nat. Dairy Coun., 1979-81; bd. dirs., vice chmn. Westchester Pvt. Industry Coun., 1979-82; mil. adv. coun. Ctr. for Def. Info., 1986-97. Lt. col. AUS, 1940-45. Decorated Bronze Star. Mem. N.Y. Milk Bottlers Fedn. (pres., dir.), Met. Dairy Inst. (exec. v.p., dir.), Phi Beta Kappa, Tau Epsilon Phi.

KERN, JEANNE RUSTEMEYER WOOD, retired secondary school educator; b. Washington, Dec. 8, 1939; d. Joseph Howard Rustemeyer and Jeannetta Greever Rustemeyer Jameson; m. Richard Alan Kern, Dec. 14, 2001; 1 child, Kristin C. BA, BS, U. Kans., Lawrence; MEd, U. Houston, 1965. Tchr. Bridge City (Tex.) HS, 1963—96, acad. team coach, 1990—96. Author: (novels) Trips and Whales and Puppy Dog Tales, 2005 (Golden Triangle Writers Guild romance award), (poems) Armchair Detective (Pushcart Prize nominee); proofreader: Ozarks Monthly; actor: (video) Hospice: The Caregiver (nat. award-winner). Bd. dirs. v.p. Orange (Tex.) Cmty. Players, 1988—2001; pres., sec. SE Tex. Arts Coun., Beaumont, 1995—2001; pres. Golden Triangle Writers Guild, Beaumont, Tex., 1998—2000; officer Osher Lifelong Learning Inst. Lincoln, 2002—06. Named Woman of the Yr., Bus. and Profl. Women, 1978, Tchr. of the Yr., Bridge City HS, 1980. Mem.: Am. Mensa (Chmns. award 2006), Alumni U. Kans. (life), Friends of the Lied, Welcome Wagon, Kappa Kappa Gamma (life; province dir. alumnae 2005—06). Home and Office: 2600 Cheshire North Ct Lincoln NE 68512 Home Phone: 402-423-0428; Office Phone: 402-423-0428. Personal E-mail: jeanne@richkern.com.

KERN, JOHN MCDOUGALL, lawyer; b. Omaha, Nov. 28, 1946; m. Susan McDougall Kern, Oct. 15, 1977. BA, Creighton U., 1970; JD cum laude, George Washington U., 1973. Bar: DC 1973, Calif. 1980, US Dist. Ct. DC 1974, US Dist Ct. ND Calif. 1980, US Dist. Ct. C.D. Calif. 1996, US Ct. Appeals (D.C. Cir.) 1974, US Ct. Appeals (9th Cir.) 1978. Asst. US atty. criminal divsn. Office of US Atty. DC, Washington, 1973-78; asst. US atty. civil divsn. Office US Atty. N. D. Calif., San Francisco, 1978-82; v.p., dir. Crosby, Heafey, Roach & May P.C., San Francisco, Oakland, LA, 1982—2002, Carlson, Calladine & Peterson, LLC, San Francisco, 2003—04. Faculty Nat. Inst. Trial Advocacy, 1987—; spkr., lectr. in field. Contbr. abstracts, book chpt., articles to profl. jours. Fellow: Am. Coll. Trial Lawyers; mem.: Am. Inn of Ct., Am. Bd. Trial Advs. (adv.). Address: 80 Maywood Dr San Francisco CA 94127 Office Phone: 415-682-7374. Personal E-mail: jmckern@gmail.com.

KERN, JOHN WORTH, III, judge; b. Indpls., May 25, 1928; s. John Worth and Bernice (Winn) K.; children: John, Stephen. BA, Princeton U., 1949; LLB, Harvard U., 1952. Bar: D.C. 1953, U.S. Ct. Appeals (D.C. cir.) 1955. With CIA, 1952-54; law clk. to chief judge U.S. Ct. Appeals D.C. Cir. Ct., 1954-55; asst. U.S. atty. D.C. Dist. Dept. Justice, Washington, 1955-59; assoc. Kilpatrick, Ballard & Beasley, Washington, 1959-65; with Dept. of Justice, Washington, 1965-68; judge D.C. Ct. Appeals, Washington, 1968-84, sr. judge, 1987—. Dean Nat. Jud. Coll., Reno, 1984-87; chair Annual Harold R. Medina Seminar for State and Fede. Judges on Humanities & Sci., Princeton U. Mem. D.C. Bar. Presbyterian. Office: DC Ct Appeals 500 Indiana Ave NW Washington DC 20001-2138

KERN, MICHAEL J., chemicals executive; Mgr. oxides and olefins Texaco Chem. Co., 1988—89, mgr. PO/MTBE project, 1989—92, plant mgr. Port Neches facility, 1992—93, area mgr. Jefferson County Ops., 1993—95; sr. v.p. mfg. Huntsman Corp., Salt Lake City, 1995—2001, sr. v.p. environ., health & safety, 2001—. Office: Hunstman Corp 500 Huntsman Way Salt Lake City UT 84108 Office Phone: 801-584-5700.*

KERN, MICHAEL L., III, corporate financial executive; b. 1973; BS in Fin. and Bus. Economics, Wayne State U. Cert. CFA. Founder The Lawn Masters; analyst Shanker & Stout P.C., 1996; mng. dir., Valuation and Lit. Adv. Services Grp. Stout Risius Poss, Mich., mng. dir., Real Estate Valuation Grp. Farmington Hills, Mich., CFO, COO. Named one of 40 Under 40, Crain's Detroit Bus., 2006. Mem.: Assn. Mgmt. Consulting Firms, Investment Analysts Soc. of Detroit, CFA Inst. Office: Stout Risius Ross 32255 Northwestern Hwy Ste 201 Farmington Hills MI 48334 Office Phone: 248-432-1239. Office Fax: 248-208-8822. Business E-Mail: mkern@srr.com.

KERN, PAUL JOHN, retired military officer; b. West Orange, NJ, June 16, 1945; s. Bruno Michael and Marjorie (Bolan) K.; m. Dolores I. Mercaldo, Aug. 28, 1971; children: Paul John Jr., Alexander Matthew. BS, US Mil. Acad., 1967; MS in Mech. and Civil Engring., U. Mich., 1973; fellow in Nat. Security, Harvard U., 1986-87. Registered profl. engr., Va. Advanced through grades from commdg. 2nd lt. to gen. US Army, 1967—2001, platoon leader, staff mem., 1967-69, troop comdr. 11th Armored Cavalry Regiment Vietnam, 1969-70, ret., 2004; asst. prof., course dir. dept. engring. US Mil. Acad., West Point, NY, 1973-76; ops. officer 2nd bn., 33rd Armor, 3rd Armor Divsn., Kirch Goens, Germany, 1976-78; br. chief Bradley Prog. Mgmt. Office, Warren, Mich., 1979-82; team chief rsch. and devel. US Army Staff, Pentagon, Washington, 1982-84; bn. comdr. 5th bn., 32nd Armor, 24th Inf. Divsn., Ft. Stewart, Ga., 1984-86; mil. asst. to under sec. US Dept. Def., Washington, 1987-89, mil. asst. to sec., 1993-96; comdr. 2nd brigade, 24th Inf. Divsn., Saudi Arabia and Iraq, 1989-91; dir. requirements Army staff, 1991-92; asst. divsn. comdr.-maneuver, 24th Inf. Divsn. Ft. Stewart, Ga., 1992-93; commdg. gen. 4th Inf. Divsn., Ft. Hood, Tex., 1996-97; mil. dep. to asst. sec. acquisition, logistics & tech. US Army, Washington, 1997—2001; commdg. gen. US Army Materials Command, Alexandria, Va., 2001—04; sr. counselor The Cohen Grp., Washington, 2005—. Head internal investigation into abuses at Abu Ghraib prison US Army, 2004; bd. dirs. EDO Corp., NYC, 2005—, iRobot Corp. Co-author: Acquisition Managers - Role and Reality, 1987. Decorated Bronze Star with 3 oak leaf clusters, Silver Star, Purple Heart with 2 oak leaf clusters, Def. Disting. Svc. medal, Army Disting. Svc. medal, Def. Superior Svc. medal, Legion of Merit, German Cross of Honor Fed. Armed Forces; recipient Alumni Soc. medal U. Mich. Mem. NAE, Soc. Automotive Engrs. (Teetor award 1975), Armor Assn., Assn. US Army, Coun. Fgn. Rels., US Naval Inst., Chi Epsilon. Roman Catholic. Avocations: sailing, woodworking, computers. Office: The Cohen Group 1200 19th St NW Ste 400 Washington DC 20036 E-mail: pkern@cohengroup.net.*

KERN, RONALD PAUL, dean, consultant; b. Chickasha, Okla., Sept. 2, 1947; s. John Edward Kern and Winona Briscoe Kern; m. Stephanie Perry, May 30, 1970; children: Stephanie Rachel Nelson, Jayson Paul. BS, U. Ctrl. Okla., 1970; MA, U. Tex., San Antonio, 1977; PhD, U. North Tex., 1990. Computer info. sys. Wideband Gigabit Network Engr. Dept. chair, tchr. Permian HS, Odessa, Tex., 1981-84; prof. Odessa Coll., Tex., 1984-85, dean, curriculum dir. Tex., 1990-97; curriculum dir. Maypearl Ind. Sch. Dist., Tex., 1985-88; coord. Collin County CC, Plano, Tex., 1988-90; v.p. acad. affairs We. Okla. State Coll., 1997-99; dir. Tex. Tech Univ.-Acad. 2000, Plano, 1999—2002; prin., owner Xstream Computers, 2002—06; tchr. AP computer sci. Highland Park HS, 2004—06; graduate dean higher edn. Kaplan U., 2005—. Cons. Tex. colls. and univs., 1988—; tech. field reader Tex. Higher Edn. Coord. Bd., chair, standing com. on univ. transfer and dispute resolutions. Contbr. articles to profl. jours. Finalist Educator of Yr., Tex. Computer Edn. Assn., 1987; named Tchr. of Yr., Samuel Clemens HS, 1976, Disting. Bandmaster of Am., State of Ariz., 1981, Disting. Prof. Bus. and Industry Divsn., Collin County CC, 1989; recipient Tchg. Excellence award, Nat. Inst. Staff and Orgnl. Devel., 1991. Mem. Tex. Assn. Instructional Adminstrs., Tex. Assn. Tech. Educators, Tex. Tech. Soc., Am. Indian Sci. and Engring. Soc., Odessa Optimist Club (bd. dirs. 1991-93), Phi Kappa Phi. Personal E-mail: kerndoc@yahoo.com. Business E-Mail: rkern@kaplan.edu.

KERN, RUSSELL MARC, marketing executive; b. Maywood, Calif., Oct. 2, 1956; s. Arthur and Beatric (Lomberg) K.; m. Deborah Louise, Mar. 11, 1984; 1 child, Hillary. BA in Econs., UCLA, 1979. Acct. exec. Needham Harper & Steers, Los Angeles, 1979-80, Doyle Dane Burnbach, Los Angeles, 1980-81; exec. v.p. Parsons & Kern, Santa Monica, Calif., 1981-84; founder, CEO, pres. Kern Orgn. (formerly Kern/Mathai Direct Mktg.), Woodland Hills, Calif., 1984—. Mem.: Dir. Mktg. Assn. (instr., Silver Echo Award 1988, Pioneer Awards 1988, 1989). Office: Kern Orgn 20955 Warner Ctr Lane Woodland Hills CA 91367 Office Phone: 818-703-8775. Office Fax: 818-703-8458.*

KERN, TERRY C., judge; b. Clinton, Okla., Sept. 25, 1944; s. Elgin L. and Lora Lee (Miller) Kern; m. Charlene Heinen, Dec. 26, 1970 (dec. Feb. 2002); children: Lauren, Suzanne, Justin Hunter; m. Jeanette Martin, Dec. 31, 2004. BS, Okla. State U., Stillwater, 1966; JD, U. Okla., Norman, 1969; LLM, U. Va., Charlottesville, 2004. Bar: Okla. 1969, US Dist. Ct. (ea. dist.) Okla. 1974, US Dist. Ct. (we. dist.) Okla. 1979, US Dist. Ct. (no. dist.) Okla. 1993, US Ct. Appeals (10th cir.) 1979. Gen. atty. FTC, Washington, 1969—70; ptnr. Fischl, Culp, McMillin, Kern and Chaffin, Ardmore, Okla., 1971—86; founding ptnr., pres. Kern, Mordy and Sperry, Ardmore, 1986—94; dist. judge US Dist. Ct. (no. dist.) Okla., Tulsa, 1994—, chief judge, 1996—2003. Mem. Jud. Conf. Com. on Security and Facilities, 10th Cir. Jud. coun. Chmn. bd. dirs. Southern Okla. Meml. Hosp., Ardmore, 1982—92, chmn., 1989—91. With USAR, 1970—75. Named to, Beta Theta Pi Hall of Fame, 2000; recipient Leadership Legacy award, Okla. State U., 2000, Disting. Alumnus award, 2001. Fellow: Okla. Bar Found. (pres. 1991, Disting. Svc. award 1992), Am. Bar Found.; mem.: ABA, Tulsa County Bar Assn. (bd. dirs.), Fed. Judges Assn., U. Okla. Coll. Law Assn., Okla. Bar Assn., Am. Bd. Trial Advocates (Okla. chpt.), Coun. Oak/Johnson-Sontag Inns of Ct. (master of bench). Democrat. Methodist. Office: US Dist Courthouse 333 W 4th St Tulsa OK 74103-3839

KERN, WILLIAM BLIEM, JR., minister; b. Phila., Nov. 24, 1943; s. William Bliem Sr. and Helen Elizabeth (Kennedy)K.; m. Ellen (Evjen), Dec. 13, 1968 (div. Dec. 1972). BA, Wilmington Coll., 1967; MSc and MST, The New Seminary, 1990. Ordained min. NY State Bd. Regents. Graphic design cons. to chief arch. Gibbs and Hill, NYC, 1976-77; art dir. spl. projects The N.Y. Times Mag. Group, NYC, 1979-80; design dir. Moving House and Home Mag., NYC, 1981; assoc. art dir. Weight Watchers Mag., NYC, 1982-83; market analyst The Comex Commodity Exch., NYC, 1987-89; tv host Satellite Psychic, Internat. Satellite Network, NYC, 1991-92; min., pvt. practice spiritual counseling NYC, 1990—. Author: (book of poems) Meditation Meditations Meditations, 1973 (chosen one of top ten books of the yr. by Library Jour., 1973, Distintive Merit in Book Design Award, Art Dir. Club of NY., 1974), (book) Nuc. Prayer, 1978, The Text of Amen, 1981, (CD) The Jewel in the Lotus with Allen Won Quintet, 2003. Mem. masonic edn. com. Mem. Am. Rsch. Ctr. in Egypt, Nat. Coun. for Geosomic Rsch., Soc. for Sci. Exploration, The Rosicsucian Soc. Am. (dir. astrology 1985-92), Chakrasambara Buddhist Ctr., George Washington Lodge # 285(treas. lodge, 1993-98); Lodge Coun. Chpt. Consistory Scottish Rite in the Valley Of N.Y.C. Avocations: watercolor landscape painting, vajrayana buddhist meditation, spiritual astrology. Home: 230 Riverside Dr Apt 15CC New York NY 10025-6172 E-mail: wbkjr3@verizon.net.

KERNAN, BARBARA DESIND, senior government executive; b. NYC, Jan. 11, 1939; d. Philip and Anne (Feuer) Desind; m. Joseph E. Kernan, Feb. 14, 1973. 1 stepson, Joseph E. Kernan, III. BA in English Lit., cum laude, Smith Coll., 1960; postgrad. Oxford U., 1963; MA in Lit. and Tchg., Harvard U., 1963; postgrad. in edn. policy George Washington U., 1980. Editor Harvard Law Sch., 1960-62; tchr. English, Newton (Mass.) High Sch., 1962-63; editor Allyn & Bacon Pubs., Boston, 1963-64; edn. assoc. Upward Bound, Edn. Assocs., Inc., Washington, 1965-68; edn. program specialist Title I, Elem. and Secondary Edn. Act, US Office Edn., 1969-73; fellow Am. Polit. Sci. Assn., Senator William Proxmire and Congressman Alphonzo Bell, 1973-74; spl. asst. to dep. commr. for elem. and secondary edn. and dir. dissemination, sch. fin. and analysis, US Office Edn., 1975-77, chief program analysis br. divsn. edn. for disadvantaged, 1977-79; chief grant program coordination staff Office Dep. Commr. for Ednl. Resources, 1979-80; chief priority concerns staff Office Asst. Sec. Mgmt., US Dept. Edn., Washington, 1980-81; dir. divsn. orgnl. devel. and analysis Office of Dep. Undersec. for Mgmt., 1981-86; Sr. Exec. Svc. candidate on spl. project to improve status of women Sec. Transp., Washington, 1983-84; inducted Sr. Exec. Svc., 1986; assoc. adminstr. for adminstrn. Nat. Hwy. Traffic Safety Adminstrn., US Dept. Transp., 1986-94, career devel. leader to presdl. mgmt. interns, 1989-91; trustee Capricorn Galleries, Rockville, Md., 1996-97, pres., 1997—; owner Philip Desind Collection, Am. Realism Fine Arts, 1997—. Recipient awards U.S. Office Edn., 1969, 71, 77, US Dept. Edn., 1981-86, U.S. Dept. Transp., 1991, 94, Small Agy. Coun., 1990; scholarships U. Mich., 1956-58, Smith Coll., 1958-60, Harvard U., 1962-63; Am. Polit. Sci. Assn. fellow, 1973-74; Sr. Exec. fellow John F. Kennedy Sch. Govt. Harvard U., 1983. Office Phone: 301-340-6900. Personal E-mail: bkernan@prodigy.net.

KERNAN, JEROME BERNARD, retired marketing educator, researcher; b. Cin., Nov. 22, 1932; s. E. B. and Alice (Gerver) Kernan; children: Kathleen Kernan Bedree, Brian Michael. BA, U. Cin., 1957; MS, U. Ill., 1959, PhD, 1962; post-doctoral studies in computer simulation, Carnegie Mellon U., Pitts., 1962; post-doctoral studies in math., U. Kans., 1963. Prof. emeritus George Mason U. Consumer rsch. cons., 1965—. Co-author: (book) Perspectives on Marketing Theory, 1968, Comparative Marketing Systems, 1968, Explorations in Consumer Behavior, 1968, Promotion: An Introductory Analysis, 1970, Managerial Analysis in Marketing, 1970, Perspectives in Marketing Management, 1971; contbr. over 120 articles to profl. jours. Pres. Sacred Heart Sch. Bd., Austin, Tex., 1964—67. With USAF, 1951—53. Co-recipient Ferber award, Jour. Consumer Rsch., 1992, Best Article award, Am. Acad. Advt., 1993. Mem.: Soc. for Consumer Psychology, Assn. for Consumer Rsch. (pres. 1978). Avocations: motorsport, golf. Home: 879 Pine Valley Ln Cincinnati OH 45245 Personal E-mail: jkernan@gmu.edu.

KERNAN, JOSEPH EUGENE, III, former governor; b. Chgo., Apr. 8, 1946; s. Joseph E. Kernan II and Marion Kernan; m. Maggie McCullough, 1974. BS, U. Notre Dame, 1968, PhD (hon.), 1998. Product mfg. mgr. Proctor & Gamble Co., 1975—76; sales exec. Schwarz Paper Co., 1976-80; city contr. City of South Bend, Ind., 1980-84, mayor Ind., 1988—96; v.p., treas. MacWilliams Corp., 1984-88; lt. gov. State of Ind., Indpls., 1996—2003, acting gov., 2003, gov., 2003—05. Bd. trustees St. Joseph Med. Ctr. Bd. dirs. St. Joseph County Spl. Olympics, Notre Dame Club, Jr. Baseball Assn., Northside L.L.; campaign cabinet United Way, 1979-82; treas. Studebaker Music Inc. USN, 1969—74. Recipient two Purple Heart medals, Navy Commendation medal, Combat Action Ribbon, Disting. Flying Cross, 2 Air medals, award for Individual Excellence. Democrat.

KERNER, GERALD, lawyer; b. NYC, Dec. 8, 1950; AB magna cum laude, Rutgers U., 1972; JD, Harvard U., 1975. Bar: N.Y. 1976. Law clk. to Hon. John R. Bartels U.S. Dist. Ct. (ea. dist.) N.Y., 1975-77; mem. Willkie, Farr & Gallagher, NYC; mng. dir. & gen. counsel Duquesne Capital Mgmt. LLC, NYC. Mem. ABA, Securities Industry Assn. (compliance and legal divsn.), N.Y. State Bar Assn., New York County Lawyers Assn. (com. on supreme ct.), Assn. of Bar of City of N.Y. (sec. com. on fed. cts. 1983-85, membership com. 1988—), Phi Beta Kappa, Omicron Delta Epsilon. Sr. editor Harvard Law Jour. on Legis., 1974-75. Office: Duquesne Capital Mgmt LLC 40 W 57th St Fl 25th New York NY 10019-4001 Office Phone: 212-830-6655.

KERNER, MICHAEL PHILIP, lawyer; b. NYC, July 21, 1953; s. Arthur and Rosalind (Mehr) K. BA, Antioch Coll., 1976; JD, Lewis & Clark U., 1979; LLM in Taxation with honors, Golden Gate U., 1995. Bar: Calif. 1980 (cert. specialist probate, trusts & estate planning), U.S. Dist. Ct. (no. and ea. dists.) Calif. 1983, U.S. Ct. Appeals (9th cir.) 1983, U.S. Tax Ct., 1996. Staff atty. U.S. EPA, Washington, 1979-80, asst. regional counsel region 9 San Francisco, 1980-83; ptnr. Kerner, Weppner & Rosenbaum, San Francisco, 1983-95; prin. Kerner & Assocs., San Francisco, 1996-2000; ptnr. Janin, Morgan & Brenner, San Francisco, 2000—. Bd. dirs. Solano County Legal Assistance, Vallejo, Calif., 1983-86; arbitrator San Francisco Superior Ct., 1991-94. Editor law rev. and law jours. Mem. ABA, Solano County Bar Assn., Bar Assn. of San Francisco, Nat. Assn. of Trust & Estate Profls. Democrat. Jewish. Avocations: windsurfing, snowboarding, road and mountain biking. Office Phone: 415-981-0670. Business E-Mail: mpk@jmblaw.com.

KERNOCHAN, JOHN MARSHALL, lawyer, educator; b. NYC, Aug. 3, 1919; s. Marshall Rutgers and Caroline (Hatch) K. BA, Harvard U., 1942; JD, Columbia U., 1948. Bar: N.Y. 1949. Asst. dir. Legis. Drafting Research Fund Columbia U., NYC, 1950-51, acting dir., 1951-52, dir., 1952-69, lectr. law, 1951-52, assoc. prof., 1952-55, prof., 1955-77, Nash prof. law, 1977-89, Nash prof. law emeritus, 1990—; spl. lectr., 1991—2000. Cons. Temporary State Commn. to Study Orgnl. Structure of Govt. N.Y.C., 1953; exec. dir. Coun. for Atomic Age Studies, 1956—59, co-chmn., 1960—62; chmn. bd. Galaxy Music Corp., 1956—89; bd. dirs. E.C. Schirmer Music Co., Inc.; pres. Gaudia Music & Arts, Inc., 1987—2004. Author: The Legislative Process, 1980; co-author: Legal Method Cases and Materials, 1980; contbr. articles to profl. jour. Mem. civil and polit. rights com. President's Commn. on Status of Women, 1962-63; dir. emeritus Vol. Lawyers for the Arts; mem. legal and legis. com. Internat. Confedn. Soc. Authors and Composers. Mem. Assn. Bar City of N.Y. Internat. Lit. and Artistic Assn. (mem. d'honneur, internat. exec. com., mem. U.S.A. group), Copyright Soc. U.S.A. (exec. com. 1986-89), Assn. Tchrs. and Rschrs. in Intellectual Property. Office: Columbia Univ Sch Law 435 W 116th St New York NY 10027-7297

KERNS, CHRISTIAN RANDOLPH, chemist; b. Fredicksburg, Va., Apr. 8, 1953; s. Terrill D. and Mary Barbe Kerns. BS in Chemistry, W.Va. U., 1978. Chemist Fla. Dept. Agr., Tallahassee, 1986—96, Harbor Br. Oceanographic Instn., Ft. Pierce, Fla., 1997, Aerotek Sci., Ft. Lauderdale, Fla., 1999—2000; engr. Spectro Analytical Instruments, Fitchburg, Mass., 2000—01; chemist Adecco, Leominster, Mass., 2002—. Capt. Colo. State Championship Basketball Team, 1971; chmn. mission com. St. Paul United Meth. Ch., Tallahassee, 1994—96; mem. membership and evangelism com. Wesley United Meth. Ch., Worcester, Mass., 2002—. Named 1st Team All State Colo. Men's Basketball Team, 1971. Mem.: Am. Chem. Soc., Lions Club (past pres.), Phi Theta Kappa (hon.). Methodist. Avocation: stained glass artist. Home: 192 Central St Apt 301 Gardner MA 01440 Office: Adecco 14 Monument Sq #101 Leominster MA 01453 Personal E-mail: crkerns1@juno.com.

KERNS, DAVID VINCENT, lawyer; b. Jan. 29, 1917; s. Clinton Bowen and Ella Mae (Young) K.; m. Dorothea Boyd, Sept. 5, 1942; children: David V., Clinton Boyd. BPh, Emory U., Atlanta, 1937; JD, U. Fla., Gainesville, 1939. Bar: Fla. 1939, US Dist. Ct. (mid. dist.) Fla. 1939, (so. dist.) Fla. 1978, (no. dist.) Fla. 1981, US Ct. Appeals (11th cir.) 1981, US Supreme Ct. 1988. Assoc. Sutton & Reeves, Tampa, Fla., 1939-41, Fowler & White, Tampa, 1945-47; ptnr. Moran & Kerns, Tampa, 1948-49; resident atty. Fla. Road Dept., 1949-53; rsch. asst. Supreme Ct. Fla., 1953-58; dir. Fla. Legis. Reference Bur., 1958-68, Fla. Legis. Svc. Bur., 1968-71, Fla. Legis. Libr. Svcs., 1971-73; gen. counsel Fla. Dept. Adminstrn., 1973-82; mem. Fla. Career Svc. Commn., 1983-86; spl. master Fla. Senate, 1987-96; legal cons. chief inspector gen. Fla. Gov. Office, 1995-98. Contbr. articles to profl. jours. With US Army, 1941—45. Mem. Fla. Govt. Bar Assn. (pres. 1966, J. Ernest Webb Meml. award 1982), Fla. Bar (bd. govs. 1978-84), Tallahassee Bar Assn. (spl. dir. 1993-95). Democrat. Methodist. Home: Apt 221 4425 Meandering Way Tallahassee FL 32308-5742 Personal E-mail: drkerns@embarqmail.com.

KERNS, JOANNA DE VARONA, actress, writer, director; b. San Francisco, Feb. 12, 1953; d. David Thomas and Martha Louise (Smith) de V.; m. Richard Martin Kerns, Dec. 11, 1976 (div. Dec. 1986); 1 child, Ashley Cooper. Student, NYU, 1970-71. TV series include The Four Seasons, 1984, Growing Pains; TV movies includes A Wedding On Waltons Mountain, 1982, V, 1983, Stormin' Home, 1985, The Return of Marcus Welby, M.D., 1984, The Rape of Richard Beck, 1985, Mother's Day On Waltons Mountain, 1982, A Bunny's Tale, 1985, Robin Cook's Mortal Fear, 1994, Whose Daughter is She?, 1995, No One Could Protect Her, 1995, See Jane Run, 1995, Terror In the Family, 1996; movies include Cross My Heart, 1986, Mother Knows Best, 1997, Sisters and Other Strangers, 1997, Emma's Wish, 1998, Girl Interrupted, 1999. Democrat. Office: Creative Artists Agy 9830 Wilshire Blvd Beverly Hills CA 90212-1804

KERNS, VIRGINIA B., anthropologist, writer; b. San Diego, 1948; d. James T. and Ruth B. Kerns; m. Ronald Adam Hallett. BA in Anthropology, Coll. William and Mary, 1970; PhD in Anthropology, U. Ill., 1977. Vis. asst. prof. Coll. William and Mary, Williamsburg, Va., 1977—78, from asst. prof. to prof., 1985—, chair dept. anthropology, 1988—93; asst. prof. Va. Tech, Blacksburg, Va., 1978—83; vis. asst. prof. U. Iowa, Iowa City, 1981; rsch. anthropologist UN Food and Agr. Orgn., Rome, 1984. Author: Women and the Ancestors: Black Carib Kinship and Ritual, 1983, 2d edit., 1997, Scenes from the High Desert, 2003 (William P. Clements prize for Best Nonfiction Book on Southwestern Am., 2004, Evans Biography award, 2004); editor: In Her Prime, 1985, 2d edit., 1992; mem. edit. bd.: Am. Ethnologist, 1979—84. Named Writer-in-residence, Mesa Refuge, 2005; recipient Faculty award for Advancement of Scholarship, Phi Beta Kappa, Alpha of Va., 1988, Thomas Jefferson Tchg. award, Coll. William and Mary, 1989, Outstanding Faculty award, State Coun. for Higher Edn. in Va., 1991; fellow, Fulbright-Hays Commn., 1974—75, Va. Found. for Humanities, 1989; grantee, Wenner-Gren Found. for Anthrop. Rsch., 1974—75, 1976; Hon. fellow, Woodrow Wilson Found., 1974. Fellow: Am. Anthrop. Assn.; mem.: Phi Beta Kappa. Office: Coll William and Mary Dept Anthropology PO Box 8795 Williamsburg VA 23187-8795 Office Phone: 757-221-1054. E-mail: vbkern@wm.edu.

KERNS, WILMER LEE, researcher; b. Dayton, Va., May 17, 1932; s. Lee Doil and Madeline A. (Grim) K.; m. Marian Iris May, Mar. 21, 1957 (div. 1963); children: Mark Wayne, Susan Kaye Kerns Mitchell; m. Shirley Mitchell Walton, June 19, 1965; children: Robert Todd, Lynelle Madeline, Jacob Scott Walton. AB, Trevecca Nazarene Coll., Nashville, Tenn., 1957; AM, U. Mich., Ann Arbor, 1960; PhD, Ohio State U., Columbus, 1971. Cert. tchr., counselor, Va. Math. tchr. Norfolk (Va.) Pub. Schs., 1957-59; counselor Washington-Lee High Sch., Arlington, Va., 1960-65; social worker Arlington (Va.) County Pub. Schs., 1965-67; civil rights specialist U.S. Office Edn., Washington, 1967-69; rsch. assoc. Ohio State U., Columbus, 1969-71; assoc. regional commr. Social and Rehab. Svc., Chgo., 1971-74, planning officer Washington, 1974-75, divsn. chief, 1975-77; sr. rsch. analyst Social Security Adminstrn., Washington, 1977-97; ret., 1997. Author: Shanholtzer History and Allied Family Roots, 1980, Historical Records of Old Frederick and Hampshire Counties, Va., 1992, Frederick County, Virginia: Settlement and First Families, 1730-1830, 1995; co-editor Hampshire County West Virginia, 1754-2004, 2004, Waltons of Old Virginia and Sketches of Families in Central Virginia, 2005; columnist The W.Va. Advocate, 1982-92 (Excellence in Journalism award 1992). Lay minister Truro Episcopal Ch., Fairfax, Va., 1988-91. With USN, 1950-53. Decorated Air medal; named Disting. West Virginian, Gov. of W.Va., 1989. Mem. Morgan County Hist. Soc., Winchester-Frederick County Hist. Assn. Republican. Avocations: music, genealogy. Home: 4715 38th Pl N Arlington VA 22207-2914 Personal E-mail: wkerns4@comcast.net.

KERPA, GARY J., computer science consultant; b. Derby, Conn., Apr. 20, 1958; s. George B. and Marcia J. (Tiano) K. Cert., Tech. Careers Inst., West Haven, Conn., 1978. Auto. tech. Racebrook Auto., Orange, Conn., 1974-77; computer system integration cons. Lawson & Assocs., Ansonia, Conn., 1980—. Regional coord. Ams. for Perot, Dallas, 1992. Mem.: Aircraft Owners and Pilots Assn. Republican. Roman Catholic. Avocation: flying. Home and Office: 18 Fairview St Ansonia CT 06401-2707

KERR, ALEXANDER DUNCAN, JR., lawyer; b. Pitts., May 6, 1943; s. Alexander Duncan Sr. and Nancy Greenleaf (Martin) K.; m. Judith Kathleen Mottl, May 25, 1969; children: Matthew Jonathan, Joshua Brandon. BS in Bus., Northwestern U., 1965, JD, 1968. Bar: Ill. 1968, Pa. 1969, US Dist. Ct. (ea. dist.) Pa. 1969, US Dist. Ct. (no. dist.) Ill. 1969, US Ct. Appeals (3rd cir.) 1969, US Ct. Appeals (7th cir.) 1975, US Supreme Ct. 1975. Assoc. Clark, Ladner, Fortenbaugh & Young, Phila., 1968-69, 73-74; asst. U.S. atty. U.S. Dept. Justice, Chgo., 1974-79; assoc., ptnr. Keck, Mahin & Cate, Chgo., Oak Brook, Ill., 1979-90; shareholder Tishler & Wald, Ltd., Chgo., 1990—. Staff atty. Park Dist. La Grange, Ill., 1985-2001; active Ill. St. Andrew Soc., North Riverside, 1982—, pres., 1995-97; vestryman, lay reader, chancellor, chalice bearer Emmanuel Episcopal Ch., 1980-99; mem. Pack 177, Troop 19, Order of the Arrow, Boy Scouts Am., La Grange, 1980-2000. With USN, 1969-75. Mem. Am. Legion, DuPage Club, Atlantis Divers. Home: 709 S Stone Ave La Grange IL 60525-2725 Office Phone: 312-876-3800. Office Fax: 312-876-3816. Business E-Mail: akerr@tishlerandwald.com.

KERR, BAINE PERKINS, oil industry executive; b. Rusk, Tex., Aug. 24, 1919; s. James Herman and Myrta Blake (Perkins) K.; m. Mildred Pickett Caldwell, June 13, 1942; children: Baine Perkins, John Caldwell, James Robinson, Mary Blake Kerr Winters. BA, LL.B., U. Tex. at Austin, 1942. Bar: Tex. 1942. Practiced in, Houston, 1945-77; partner firm Baker & Botts, 1955-77; dir. Pennzoil Co., Houston, 1964-94, chmn. exec. com., 1972-94, pres., 1977-85, dir. emeritus, 1994—. Served with USMCR, 1942-55. Mem. Chancellors, Order of Coif, Phi Beta Kappa. Office: Esperson Bldg 808 Travis St Ste 2200 Houston TX 77002-5704 Office Phone: 713-546-8978.

KERR, CRISTIE, professional golfer; b. Miami, Fla., Oct. 12, 1977; m. Erik Stevens, 2006. Winner Longs Drugs Challenge, 2002, LPGA Takefuji Classic, 2004, ShopRite LPGA Classic, 2004, State Farm Classic, 2004, Michelob Ultra Open, 2005, Franklin Am. Mortgage Championship, 2006, US Women's Open, 2007; tied for second U.S. Open, 2000. Winner Fla. State Jr. Girls Championship, 1993, 94, 95; mem. U.S. Curtis Cup Team, 1996, U.S. Solheim Cup Team, 2002, 03, 05. Achievements include low amateur at 1996 U.S. Women's Open; fifth place LPGA money list, 2004; nine top-ten finishes, 2004; winner, Wendy's Championship for Children, 2005, John Q. Hammons Hotel Classic, 2006. Avocations: fishing, baking. Office: c/o LPGA 100 International Golf Dr Daytona Beach FL 32124-1092*

KERR, DARLENE DIXON, electric power company executive; b. Syracuse, NY, Nov. 26, 1951; d. James and Mary Dixon; children: E. Kaye, J. Craig. BA, SUNY, Potsdam, 1973; MBA, Syracuse U., 1984. V.p. sys. electric ops. Niagara Mohawk Power Corp., Syracuse, 1988-91, v.p. gas mktg. and rates, 1991-93, v.p. electric customer svc., 1993-94, sr. v.p. electric customer svc., 1994-95, sr. v.p. energy distbn., 1995—98, past mem. steering com. and past chmn. polit. action com., exec. v.p. energy delivery, 1998—99, exec. v.p., chief oper. officer, 1999—2000, pres., chief operating officer, 2000—01; sr. v.p. Nat. Grid U.S.A., 2001—, pres., Nat. Grid U.S.A. Svc. Co., 2001—. Former mem. adv. bd. Rural Metro; former mem. policy coun. Success by 6. Former trustee Onondaga C.C.; former bd. dirs. Cmty.-Gen. Hosp.; mem. Syracuse U. Thursday Morning Roundtable and Corinthian Found.; mem. task force Bus. Alliance for a New N.Y.; past pres. and bd. dirs. Onondaga Citizens League; past v.p. bd. dirs. Regional Learning Svc., Inc.; past mem. policy and planning com. Leadership Grater Syracuse; former mem. Downtown Improvement Task Force; former committeewoman and vice chmn. Onondaga Rep. Com.; former mem. numerous campaign ad. coms. and Onondaga County Rep. task forces; mem. chmn.'s coun. and fin. com. Onondaga County Rep. Com.; bd. dirs. Farmers and Traders Life Ins. Co., Utilites Mutual Ins. Co., Greater Syracuse C.C., M&T Bank, N.Y. State Women in Comm. and Energy, former pres., LeMoyne Coll., Mktg. Execs. conf., Ctrl. N.Y. Regional Compact, Greater Syracuse Econ. Growth Coun., Syracuse 20/20. Named Mover and Shaker for bus. Syracuse Herald Am., 1990, Woman of Achievement for career Post-Std., 1991, Alumni of Distinction, SUNY, 1993, Citizen of Yr. Temple Adath Yeshurun, Syracuse, Woman of Achievement N.Y. State-Gov. Pataki, Extraordinary Woman Nat. Women's Hall of Fame, Seneca Falls, N.Y.; recipient Spirit Am. Women award Girls Inc. Ctrl. N.W., 1993, Multiple Sclerosis Soc. Crusaders for a Cure award, Zonta Crystal award. Office: National Grid USA 300 Erie Blvd W Syracuse NY 13202-4250

KERR, DAVE, state official, marketing professional; m. Patty Kerr; children: Ryan, Dan. Degree in Biol. Sci., Psychology, Kans. State U., 1968; MBA, U. Kans., 1970. Leader com. on Econ. Devel., Edn.; mem. Kans. State Senate, 1984—2004, pres., 2000—04. Bd. dirs. Hutchinson Hosp. Corp., Reno County Mental Health Adv. Com.; with Hutchinson Hosp. Bd. Dirs., Bds. Leadership Hutchinson, Hutchinson C.of C., Healthy Families, Nickerson and Hutchinson HS booster clubs. Mem.: Kans. Tech. Enterprise Corp. (mem. bd. dirs. 1987—98), Republican Ctrl. Com. (sec. 1981—84), Kans. C. of C. and Industry, Kans. Farm Bur., Legis. Post Audit, Joint Pensions, Investments and Benefits (vice chmn.), Legis. Coordinating Coun. (chmn.), Interstate Coop. (chmn.), Ways and Means Com., Commerce Com., Calendar and Rules Com. (chmn.). Republican. Office: State Capitol PO Box 2620 Hutchinson KS 67504

KERR, DAVID WYLIE, corporate financial executive, director; b. Montreal, Que., Can., Dec. 14, 1943; s. Dudley Holden and Cecilia (Maguire) K.; m. Sheryl Lee Drysdale, Nov. 1, 1969; children: Ross, Tamara. BSc, McGill U., Can., 1965, chartered acct., 1969. Chartered acct. Touche Ross & Co., Montreal, 1965—72; CFO Edper Investments Ltd., Toronto, Ont., Canada, 1972-78; COO Hees Internat. Corp., Toronto, 1978-85; exec. v.p. Brascan Ltd., Toronto, 1985-86; sr. v.p. strategic planning Noranda Inc., Toronto, 1986-87, pres., 1987-90, pres., CEO, 1990—2002, chmn., 2002—06. Bd. dir. Sun Life Fin. Inc., Shell Can. Ltd., Sustainable Devel. Tech. Can. Found., Can. Spl. Olympics Found., Toronto Rehab. Hosp., Brookfield Asset Mgmt., Inc.; mem. Nat. Roundtable on the Environment, Economy. Mem. Granite Club, Rosedale Golf Club. Mem. United Ch. Can. Avocations: bicycling, farming, golf. Office: BCE PL 181 Bay St Ste 300 Toronto ON Canada M5J 2T3

KERR, DEREK J., transportation executive; BS in Aero. Engring., U. Mich., MBA. Various fin. positions Northwest Airlines; sr. dir., fin. planning Am. West Holdings, 1996—98, v.p., fin. planning and analysis, 1998—2002, sr. v.p., fin. planning and analysis, 2002; sr. v.p., CFO Am. West Holdings (now US Airways Group), 2002—. Office: America West Holdings 111 Rio Salado Pkwy Tempe AZ 85281*

KERR, DONALD CRAIG, retired minister; b. Pitts., July 29, 1915; s. Hugh Thomson and Olive (Boggs) K.; m. Nora Minetta Lloyd, Sept. 12, 1942; children: Donald Jr., Elizabeth, Douglas. BA, Princeton U., 1937; MDiv, Princeton Theol. Sem., 1940; ThD, U. Toronto, Ont., Can., 1942. Ordained to ministry Presbyn. Ch. (U.S.A.), 1940. Min. East Kiskacoguillas Presbyn. Ch., Reedsville, Pa., 1942-47, 1st Presbyn. Ch., New Haven, 1947-48, Roland Pk. Presbyn. Ch., Balt., 1948-80, pastor emeritus, 1980; pastoral assoc. Presbyn. Ch., Sarasota, Fla., 1980-87; chaplain Plymouth Harbor, Sarasota, 1982-91. Moderator Presbytery of Balt., 1960-61, mem. bd. pensions, exec. com., 1963-66. Author: How the Church Began, 1953, What the Bible Means, 1954, History of Religion in America, 1975; editor: Design for Christian Living, 1952. Bd. advisors Presbyn. Home of Md.; pres. Residents' Assn. Roland Park Pl., Balt. Recipient 50-yrs. in ministry plague Lake Joseph Community Ch., 1989, 50-yr. Ordination Recognition, 1992; honored for being 50 yr. mem. Balt. Presbytery. Mem. St. Andrew's Soc. (trustee, chaplain 1980-91, cert. appreciation 1990), Ivy League Club (v.p. 1991, pres. 1992-93), Princeton Club (pres. 1988-90, class coun. 1937), Univ. Club Sarasota, Sarasota Yacht Club, Sara Bay Club, Gibson Island Club, The Johns Hopkins Club, Shriners, Masons (32 degrees). Home: 700 John Rugling Blvd E202 Sarasota FL 34236

KERR, DONALD MACLEAN, JR., federal agency administrator, physicist; b. Phila., Apr. 8, 1939; s. Donald MacLean and Harriet (Fell) K.; m. Alison Richards Kyle, June 10, 1961; 1 dau., Margot Kyle. B.E.E. (Nat. Merit scholar), Cornell U., 1963, MS, 1964, PhD (Ford Found. fellow, 1964-65, James Clerk Maxwell fellow 1965-66), 1966. Staff Los Alamos Nat. Lab., 1966-76, group leader, 1971-72, asst. div. leader, 1972-73, asst. dir., 1973-75, alt. energy divsn. leader, 1975-76; dep. mgr. Nev. ops. office Dept. Energy, Las Vegas, 1976-77; acting asst. sec. def. programs Dept. Energy, Washington, 1978, dep. asst. sec. def. programs, 1977-79, dep. asst. sec. energy tech., 1979; dir Los Alamos Nat. Lab., 1979-85; sr. v.p. EG&G, Inc., Wellesley, Mass., 1985-88, exec. v.p., 1988-89, pres., bd. dirs., 1989-92; exec. v.p., bd. dirs. Sci. Applications Internat. Corps., San Diego, 1993-96, Info. Sys. Labs., San Diego, 1996-97; asst. dir. FBI, Washington, 1997—2001; dep. dir. sci. & tech. CIA, Washington, 2001—05; dir. Nat. Reconnaissance Office, 2005—. Mem. Navajo Sci. Com., 1974-77, Def. Sci. Bd., 1993-98; mem. sci. adv. panel U.S. Army, 1975-78; mem. engring. adv. bd. U. Nev., Las Vegas, 1976-78, Cornell U., 1985—; chmn. com. R&D Internat. Energy Agy., 1979-85; mem. nat. security adv. coun. SRI Internat., 1980-89; mem. adv. bd. U. Alaska Geophys. Inst., 1980-85; mem. sci. adv. group Joint Strategic Planning Staff, 1981-91; mem. adv. bd. Georgetown U. Ctr. Strategic Internat. Studies, 1981-87; mem. adv. com. Naval Rsch., 1982-85; mem. corp. Draper Lab., 1982-97; mem. DCI Nonproliferation Adv. Panel, 1993-98; mem. bd. San Diego Tech. Coun., 1994-97; bd. dirs. Resources for the Future, Washington. Published research on plasma physics, microwave electronics, ionospheric physics, energy and nat. security. Trustee New Eng. Aquarium, 1989-93. Fellow AAAS, Am. Phys. Soc.; mem. Am. Geophys. Union, Nat. Assn. Mfrs. (bd. dirs. 1986-92), Southwestern Assn. Indian Affairs, World Affairs Coun. Boston (bd. dirs. 1988-92), Atlantic Coun. (bd. dirs. 1991-97), Cosmos Club (Washington), Sigma Xi, Tau Beta Pi, Eta Kappa Nu. Office: Nat Reconnaissance Office 14675 Lee Rd Chantilly VA 20151 Office Phone: 703-808-1010.

KERR, DOUGLAS ANTHONY, neurologist, researcher; b. Aug. 12, 1966; BA in Biology (magna cum laude), Princeton U., 1988; PhD in Biochemistry and Molecular Biology, Coll. Grad. Studies, Thomas Jefferson U., Phila., 1995; MD summa cum laude, Thomas Jefferson U., Jefferson Med. Coll., 1995. Am. Bd. Psychiatry & Neurology, 2000. Resident, dept. internal medicine The Graduate Hosp., Phila., 1995—96; resident, dept. neurology John Hopkins Hosp., Balt., 1996—98, chief resident, dept. neurology, 1998—99; asst. prof., neurology John Hopkins Sch. Medicine, Balt., 1999—; asst. prof., dept. molecular microbiology and immunology John Hopkins Sch. Pub. Health, Balt., 1999—; dir. John Hopkins Transverse Myelitis Ctr., 1999—. Platform presentation, Neural Stem Cells in Motor Neuron Disease Soc. for Neuroscience, 2000; invited spkr. in field; bd. dir. Ctr. for Amyotrophic Lateral Sclerosis Rsch., John Hopkins U.; affiliated faculty, Barker Firm, Osler Med. Tng. Program John Hopkins Hosp.; mem. Data Safety Monitoring bd. NIH sponsored hematopoietic stem cell transplantation trials network; dir. John Hopkins Project RESTORE; invited testimony, State Senate and House of Representatives for the MD Stem Cell Act 2005, Annapolis, Md. Contbr. articles to profl. jours.; peer reviewer Annals Neurology, Human Molecular Genetics, Jour. Neurovirology, Jour. Immunology, Exptl. Neurology, Jour. Clin. Investigation, Jour. Neurological Sciences, Jour. Neurology, Neurosurgery & Psychiatry, Jour. Rheumatology, Neurology, Spinal Cord, Jour. Cerebral Blood Flow & Metabolism. Named Hero for Hope for work on spinal cord regeneration, Keck Ctr. for Collaborative Neuroscience (The Spinal Cord Injury Project), 2004; recipient Howard Hughes Med. Inst. award for Clinician Scientist, 1999, Mentored Scientist award, NIH, 1999, Rsch. Develop. award, Muscular Dystrophy Assn., 1999—2001, Rsch. Grant, Parkinson's Disease Found., 1999—2000, Clinician Scientist award, John Hopkins Hosp., 1999, Agarni Found. award for best Scientific Talk, 2nd Internat. Congress in Neuroscience, Terni, Italy, 2000. Mem.: Transverse Myelitis Assn. (bd. dir.), Soc. for Neuroscience, Internat. Assn. for Neurovirology, Am. Soc. Microbiology, Am. Acad. Neurology, Alpha Omega Alpha. Office: John Hopkins Hosp 615 N Wolfe St Ste E5132 Baltimore MD 21205 Office Phone: 410-502-7099. Office Fax: 410-502-6736. E-mail: dker@jhml.edu.

KERR, FREDERICK HOHMANN, retired health facility and academic administrator; b. Pitts., July 11, 1936; s. Nathan Frederick and Laura Marie (Hohmann) K.; m. Ethyl Nylene Bashline, 1960 (div. 1969); m. Phyllis Jensen, Aug. 21, 1970, 1 child, Linda Jean. BA, Pa. State U., 1958; MPA, U. Pitts., 1961; LLD (hon.), Luth. Coll. Health Professions, Ft. Wayne, Ind., 1996. Exec. sec. Pa. Economy League Fayette County Br., Uniontown, Pa., 1959, Armstrong County Br., Kittanning, Pa., 1959—62; exec. sec. Woodbury Tax Rsch. Conf., Sioux City, Iowa, 1962—65; dir. pub. svc. City of Sioux City, 1965—66; from asst. administr. to assoc. administr. St. Luke's Regional Med. Ctr., Sioux City, 1966—71; administr., CEO Meml. Hosp. of Michigan City, Inc., 1971—75; pres., CEO St. Luke's Hosp., Maumee, Ohio, 1975—86, Luth. Hosp. Ind., Luth. Coll. Health Professions, Ft. Wayne, 1986—95; v.p. for devel. Quorum Health Resources, Inc., Brentwood, Tenn., 1995—2001. Dir. Ohio Hosp. Ins. Co., Columbus, treas. 1981-84. Trustee Ohio Hosp. Assn., Columbus, 1983—85; dir. Siouxland United Way, 1968—71, Ft. Wayne Pub. TV, 1990—94, United Way Allen County, Ft. Wayne, 1990—; trustee Northwest Med. Ctr., Oro Valley, 2004—05; mem. Iowa Intergovtl. Rels. Com., Des Moines, 1964—67; mem. Rancho Vistoso Adv. Bd. N.W. Med. Ctr., Tucson, 2002—05. Mem.: ASPA (life; nat. coun. 1966—69), Am. Protestant Health Assn. (vice chmn. 1988—90). Avocations: wine appreciation, writing. Personal E-mail: fhkerr@earthlink.net. *Being a servant is the most distinguished career of all.*

KERR, GARY ENRICO, lawyer, educator; b. Kewanee, Ill., Feb. 8, 1948; s. Roy Harrison and Marietta (Dani) K.; m. Eileen Elizabeth Straeter, Aug. 18, 1978; 1 child, Victoria Elizabeth. BA, No. Ill. U., 1970; JD, Northwestern U., Chgo., 1973. Bar: Ill. 1974, U.S. Dist. Ct. (cen. dist.) Ill. 1982, U.S. Ct. Appeals (7th cir.) 1983, U.S. Supreme Ct. 1983. Adminstrv. asst. Office Supt. Pub. Instrn. State Ill., Chgo., Springfield, 1971-74; asst. legal advisor Ill. State Bd. Edn., Springfield, 1974-78; spl. counsel Ill. State Comptroller, Springfield, 1978-79; pvt. practice Springfield, 1979—. Adj. faculty Sangamon State U. (now Ill. State U.), Springfield, Ill., 1994; pres., dir. counsel Kerr Products, Inc., Kewanee, Ill., 1980—; instr. paralegal program Robert Morris Coll., Springfield, 1992. Atty. South County Democrats, Sangamon County, Ill.; founder, mgr., Springfield (Ill.) Area

Youth Jazz Band; bd. mem. U. Ill., Springfield. Fellow Ednl. Policy program Inst. Ednl. Leadership, George Washington U., 1976-77. Mem. Ill. State Bar Assn. (chmn. sch. law sect. coun. 1983-84), Sangamon County Bar Assn. Avocations: skiing, tennis, fishing. Office: Gary Kerr Ltd 1020 S 7th St Springfield IL 62703-2417 Office Phone: 217-522-2244. E-mail: kerrltd@aol.com.

KERR, JAMES WILSON, engineer; b. Balt., May 21, 1921; s. James W. and Laura Virginia (Wright) Kerr; m. Mary Thomas Montgomery, Feb. 25, 1945 (div.); children: April Kerr Miller, Catherine Kerr Wood(dec.) , Wilson(dec.) , Andrew; m. June Walker, Dec. 27, 1977 (div.); m. Janice White Bain, Jan. 19, 1985. BS with honors, Davidson Coll., 1942; MS, NYU, 1948; postgrad., Freiburg U., 1957—60, Brookings Inst., 1970, postgrad., 1975; PhD, Kennedy Western U., 1989. Registered profl. engr., Calif. Commd. 2d lt. U.S. Army, 1942, advanced through grades to lt. col., 1964, with inf., World War II, Korea, electronics staff Ft. Bragg, NC, 1948-51, weapons rsch. N.Mex., 1953-57, adviser French Army, 1957-60, staff electronics Ft. Monroe, Va., 1960-62, rsch. mgr., divsn. dir. CD Pentagon, 1962-64, as civilian, 1964-81; asst. assoc. dir. Fed. Emergency Mgmt. Agy. for Rsch., 1981-85; sr. staff, cons. Michael Rogers, Inc., Winter Park, Fla., 1986—2005. V.p. Latherow & Co., Arlington, Va., 1965—86; dr. Mt. St. Helen's Tech. Office, 1980; radiol. officer Talbot County, Md., 1997—. Author: Korean-English Phrase Book, 1951, 19th Century Korea Postal Handbook, 1965, 2d edit., 1990; editor: Korean Philately mag., 1971—80, 1985—95; contbr. articles to profl. jours. Active Boy Scouts Am., 1933—; vol. fireman NY, 1946—48; chmn. libr. bd. Orangeburg, NY, 1946—48; advanced English instr. French Army, 1957—60; cons. Am. Nat. Red Cross Mus., 1968—85, Smithsonian Instn. Dept. Postal History, 1966—85, NSF, 1976—85; vol. fireman, fire commr. Fairfax County, 1975—81, chmn., 1977—81, Orange County, Fla., 1986—, pres., 1987—90, Pike County, Ala., 1994—98, Talbot County, Md., 1997—. Decorated Bronze Star with three oak leaf clusters, Purple Heart; recipient Silver Beaver award, Boy Scouts Am., 1956, James E. West award, 1994; Fulbright fellow, Japan, 1986. Fellow: AAAS (life), Explorers Club (emeritus); mem.: SAR (Fire Safety medal 1995), NAS (mem. various coms. 1962—87), NSPE, IEEE (sr.), Presdl. Nat. Def. Execs., Nat. Fire Protection Assn. (chmn. hosp. disaster com. 1973—86), Fed. Fire Coun., Internat. Assn. Fire Chiefs (chmn. rsch. com. 1969—88, chief sci. adviser 1982—86), Korean War Vets. Assn. (nat. bd. dirs. 1999), Black Forest Mardi Gras (Germany), Univ. Club Fla., Nat. Comm. Club, Pentagon Officers Athletic Club, Elks, Phi Beta Kappa, Delta Phi Alpha, Gamma Sigma Epsilon. Presbyterian. Home: PO Box 1537 Easton MD 21601-8929 Personal E-mail: jbkjow@goestton.net.

KERR, KIRKLYN M., academic administrator, veterinarian, pathologist; b. Green Bank, W.Va., May 1, 1936; married, 1957; 3 children. BS, U. W.Va., 1961, MS, 1966; DVM, Ohio State U., 1961; PhD in Vet. Pathology, Tex. A&M U., 1970. Diplomate Am. Coll. Vet. Pathology. Vet. practitioner North Side Vet. Clinic, Carlisle, Pa., 1961-62; rsch. assoc. vet. microbiology & pathology W.Va. U., Morgantown, 1962-65; form instr. to assoc. prof. vet. pathology Tex. A&M U. Coll. Vet. Medicine, 1965-72; assoc. prof. vet. pathobiology, dir. divsn. applied pathology Ohio State U. Coll. Vet. Medicine, 1972-78, dir. Ohio Agrl. Rsch. & Devel. Ctr., prof. poultry sci., 1987-91, prof. vet. preventive medicine, mem. faculty dept. preventive medicine, 1991-93; asst. dean rsch. and advanced studies, head vet. sci. La. State U. Sch. Vet. Medicine, La. State U. Agrl. Ctr., 1978-87; dean, dir. Coll. Agr. and Natural Resources U. Conn., Storrs Mansfield, 1993—. Mem. AVMA, Am. Assn. Avian Pathologists, Am. Coll. Vet. Pathologists, Farm Bur., Conn. Vet. Medicine Assn. Achievements include research in veterinary pathology, mycoplasmatacea, cancer research in animals. Office: U Conn Coll Agriculture & Natural Rsch 1376 Storrs Rd U-66 Storrs Mansfield CT 06269-4066 Office Phone: 860-486-2918. Business E-Mail: kirklyn.kerr@uconn.edu.

KERR, LOU C., foundation administrator; d. Lem C. and M. Mae (Beck) Coker; m. Robert S. Kerr, Jr., July, 1972; children: Steven S., Laura Kerr Ogle. BS in Edn. and Health, Oklahoma City U., DHL (hon.), 1991. V.p. The Kerr Found., Inc., Oklahoma City, 1985-99, pres., chair, 1999—. Founder, dir. Red Earth, Inc., Oklahoma City; adv. com. Breast Cancer Prevention and Treatment, 1994—; mem. Commn. on the Status of Women, 1994-99, 2000—; mem. Gov.'s State White House Conf. on Aging; mem. selection com. for Truman Found. Scholars, 1991-2000; mem. Social Security Disability Task Force; chair State Capitol Preservation Commn., 1990—; adv. coun. for gov. Okla. Environ. Concerns Coun., vice chair for gov., others; pres. Ind. Coll. Fund. V.p. fundraising campaign Allied Arts, 1985, v.p. exec. com., 1988—89, sec. exec. com., 1990—; mem. adv. coun. Women's Pres. Orgn.; mem., founder Atty. Gen.'s Consumer Adv. Com.; founder Bizzell Libr. Soc., U. Okla.; exec. com., v.p. Ctr. of the Am. Indian/Red Earth, 1983—; founder, chair Okla. Internat. Women's Forum, 1990—; nat. trustee Nat. Symphony Orch., Washington, 1999—; trustee NPR Found., Washington, 2001—; chair State Capitol Preservation Commn., Oklahoma City, 1990—; women's leadership bd., exec. com. Harvard U., Cambridge, 1999; 3d v.p. Red Lands coun. Girl Scouts U.S., 1993—97; v.p. Global Family Found.; mem. exec. com. Lyric Theatre of Okla., Inc., 1992—; adv. trustee Oklahoma City U.; v.p. Sister Cities, Inc, 1989—, exec. bd.; trustee Okla. Sch. Sci. and Math Found.; adv. dir. Tulsa Ballet Theatre; chair Okla. Centennial Commn., 2006—; bd. visitors U. Okla. Coll. Nursing, 2006—, Sam Noble Okla. Mus. Natural History, 2006—; trustee United Meth. Found. for Christian Higher Edn., 1996—2006, others; nat. bd. Fund for Am., 1989—; bd. govs. Okla. Ctr. of Sci. and Arts, Inc., 1987—97; mem. adv. bd. U. Okla. Coll. Fine Arts, 1994—2000, U. Okla. Polit. Com., ANSER-Ctr. for Internat. Aerospace Coop., 1995—98, Hazel K. Goddess Fund for Stroke Rsch. in Women, Internat. Gymnastics Hall of Fame, 1997—; adv. bd. dirs. Okla. Breast Inst., 1992—97; bd. dirs., exec. com. Ctrl. Okla. Coun. of World Affairs; bd. dirs. Am. Cancer Soc., Oklahoma County unit, 1995—97, Internat. Women's Forum, Washington, 1992—; exec. bd. Norick Art Mus.; chair, exec. bd. Dulaney-Browne Libr. Soc.; bd. dirs., co-chair Okla. Ind. Colls. Found., 1994—; bd. trustees Totts Gap, 2000—; bd. vis. Okla. U. Health Sci. Ctr. Named to Okla. Commerce and Industry Hall of Honor, Oklahoma City U., 2000, Okla. City Pub. Sch. Found. Wall of Fame, 2001, Philanthropy World Hall of Fame, 2006; knighted into The Byzantine Order of the Holy Sepulchre; recipient Vis A Tergo award Women's Bus. Ctr., 1997, Women Who Make a Difference award Internat. Women's Forum, 1994, Cert. of Merit Vol. Action Com. of Cmty. Coun., Okla. Tourism and Recreation Indsl. Gov.'s award, Nat. Others award Salvation Army, Kirkpatrick Petree award for outstanding cmty. svc. Oklahoma City U. Music Theatre Soc., 1988, Gov.'s Arts award Okla. State Arts Coun., 1988, Woman of Distinction award, Girl Scouts Red Lands Coun., 2002, Leading Lights award Internat. Women's Forum, 2003, Urban Pioneer award, 2006, Spl. Recognition award Assn. for Continuing Higher Ed., 2006; named March 2, 2005 as Lou C. Kerr Day, Okla. Gov. Henry. Fellow: Nat. Acad. Pub. Adminstrn. (hon.); mem.: NAPA (hon. fellow 2005), Okla. Med. Rsch. Fdn. (bd. mem. 2000—), League of Hist. Am. Theatres (bd.mem. 2004—06). Democrat. Methodist. Office: The Kerr Foundation Inc 12501 N May Ave Oklahoma City OK 73120 Fax: (405) 749-2877. E-mail: lkerr@thekerrfoundation.org.

KERR, MICHAEL H., stock exchange executive, lawyer; BA, Duke U., 1969; JD, Columbia U., 1972. Bar: Ill. 1972. Former ptnr. Kirkland & Ellis LLP, Chgo., of counsel, 2007—; bd. dirs. Chgo. Stock Exchange, Inc. (CHX), Chgo., 2001—, chmn., 2007—; bd. dirs. CHX Holdings, Inc., Chgo., 2005—, chmn., 2007—. Office: Chgo Stock Exchange, Inc One Financial Place 440 S LaSalle St Chicago IL 60605 also: Kirkland & Ellis LLP Aon Ctr 200 E Randolph Dr Chicago IL 60601 Office Phone: 312-861-2094. Office Fax: 312-861-2200. E-mail: mkerr@kirkland.com.*

KERR, ORIN SAMUEL, law educator; b. NYC, June 2, 1971; s. Arnold D. and Berta B. Kerr. BSME, Princeton U., 1993; MSME, Stanford U., 1994; JD cum laude, Harvard U., 1997. Law clk. to Hon. Leonard I. Garth U.S. Ct. Appeals (3rd cir.), Newark; atty., criminal divsn. U.S. Dept. Justice, Washington, 1998—2001, spl. asst. U.S. atty. (ea. dist.) Va.; assoc. prof. George Washington Univ., Washington, 2001—; law clk. to Anthony M. Kennedy U.S. Supreme Ct., Washington, 2003—04. Exec. editor Harvard Jour. Law and Pub. Policy; contbr. articles to profl. jours. Adv. Battered Women's Advocacy Project, Harvard Law Sch., Cambridge, Mass., 1994—. Mem. ABA (law students div.), The Federalist Soc., Phi Beta Kappa, Sigma Xi, Tau Beta Pi. Office: George Washington University Law School 2000 H St NW Washington DC 20052 Business E-Mail: okerr@law.gwu.edu.*

KERR, ROBERT B., astronomer, atmospheric scientist; BS in Physics, Ohio U., 1979; MS in Atmospheric Sci., U. Mich., 1981, PhD in Atmospheric Sci., 1986. Mem. tech. staff Aerospace Corp., El Segundo, 1987; prof. astronomy Boston U., 1988—97; dir. rsch. Sci. Solutions Inc., North Chelmsford, Mass., 1997, CEO, 2000—; with Dartmouth Coll., U. Mich.; prog. dir. aeronomy NSF; dir. Arecibo Obs., PR, 2007—. Mem. sci. adv. com. Arecibo Obs. Recipient Presdl. Young Investigator award. Office: Arecibo Obs HC03 Box 53995 Arecibo PR 00612 Office Phone: 787-878-2612. Office Fax: 787-878-1861.*

KERR, STEVE (STEPHEN DOUGLAS KERR), professional sports team executive, retired professional basketball player; b. Beirut, Sept. 27, 1965; m. Margot Kerr; children: Nicholas, Matthew, Madeleine. Grad., U. Ariz. Guard Cleve. Cavaliers, 1989—92, Chgo. Bulls, 1993—98, San Antonio Spurs, 1998—2001, 2002—03, Portland Trail Blazers, 2001—02; pres. basketball ops., gen. mgr. Phoenix Suns, 2007—; NBA analyst Tuner Network TV, 2003—07. Mem. NBA championship team Chicago Bulls, 1996-98; participant NBA All-Star Weekend,1994, 95, 96, 97. Named to NBA All-Interview Second Team, 1997-98, 98-99, Winner AT&T Shootout NBA All-Star Weekend, Cleve., 1997. Office: Phoenix Suns 201 E Jefferson St Phoenix AZ 85004*

KERR, THOMAS JEFFERSON, IV, academic administrator; b. Columbus, Ohio, Oct. 8, 1933; s. Thomas Jefferson and Ruth Glenora (Powell) K.; m. Donna Jean Lawton, June 11, 1955; children: Thomas Jefferson V, Cheryl Lee, Kathleen Anne. BS, Cornell U., 1956; MA, U. Buffalo, 1959; PhD (univ. fellow), Syracuse U., 1965; LHD (hon.), Otterbein Coll., 1984; LLD (hon.), Kendall Coll., 1996. Asst. prof., then prof. history Otterbein Coll., Westerville, Ohio, 1963-71, acting acad. dean, 1969-70, pres., 1971-84, Grant Med. Ctr. Found., Columbus, 1984-89, Kendall Coll., Evanston, Ill., 1990-96, pres. emeritus, 1996—. Chmn. Assn. Ind. Colls. and Univs., Ohio, 1976-78, Ohio Found. Ind. Colls., 1978-80 Mem. Greater Columbus Arts Coun., 1975-78; trustee Nationwide Funds, 1971-2005, Blue Cross Ctrl. Ohio, 1978-84, Grant Hosp., 1975-84, Ill. Restaurant Assn. Ednl. Found., 1991-96; mem. exec. com. Ill. Ind. Colls. and Univs., 1993-95; mem. Franklin County Draft Bd., 1969-71. Recipient Cokesbury Grad. Coll. Tchg. award, 1963. Mem. Masons, Rotary, Phi Kappa Phi, Kappa Phi Kappa, Omicron Chi Epsilon, Phi Eta Sigma. Republican. Methodist. Home: 4890 Smoketalk Ln Westerville OH 43081-4431

KERR, THOMAS ROBERT, lawyer; b. Covington, Ky., July 25, 1950; s. Thomas Hoover and Joann (Moffett) K.; m. Janice Duncan, May 26, 1973; children: Julie Ann, Jennifer Suzanne, Jill Mackenzie. BBA, U. Ky., 1972; JD, Chase Coll. Law, 1977. Bar: Ky. 1977, U.S. Dist. Ct. (ea. dist.) Ky. 1977. Sole practice, Covington, 1977—. Mem. pro-bono panel, Covington, 1980—; pub. defender Kenton County Pub. Defender's Office, Covington, 1977—. State rep. Ky. Gen. Assembly, Frankfort, 1985—; dir. Community Coun. on Religious Edn., Covington, 1985—; dir. Victims Assistance Network, Frankfort, 1985—, Calvary Christian Sch., Covington, 1981-87; deacon Calvary Bapt. Ch., Latonia, Ky., 1982; bd. dirs. No. Ky. Area Devel. Dist., 1988-93, Good Will, 1993—. With Air NG, 1971-77. Named One of Outstanding Young Men of Am., 1980, 83. Mem. Ky. Bar Assn., No. Ky. Bar Assn., Am. Trial Lawyers Assn., Ky. Acad. Trial Attys., Covington Christian Businessmans Assn. Clubs: Taylor Mill (Ky.) Swim (bd. dirs. 1983-87). Democrat. Baptist. Avocations: tennis, reading, various sports. Home: 5415 Old Taylor Mill Rd Covington KY 41015-2239 Office: 732 Scott St Covington KY 41011-2418 Home Phone: 859-356-1344; Office Phone: 606-431-2222. E-mail: thomasrkerr@yahoo.com.

KERR, WALTER BELNAP, retired electrical engineer, language researcher, consultant; b. Salt Lake City, Oct. 14, 1926; s. Walter Affleck and Marion Adeline (Belnap) K.; m. Raida Nebeker, May 2, 1952 (dec. Mar. 1992); children: Valerie Jean Kerr Merritt, Grant Mercer, Janice Arlene Kerr Hahn, Marilyn, m. Lillian Hamilton Nelson Ettinger, Oct. 1, 1992; children: Edgar Nelson Jr., James Nelson, Patricia Nelson Hardwick, Douglas Nelson. BA in French, U. Utah, 1951, BSEE, 1955; MBA in Internat. Bus., U. So. Calif., 1972. Electrical engr. Hughes Aircraft Co., LA, 1955-61, 67-69; missile instrumentation engr. Hercules Inc., Salt Lake City, 1961-66, 84-89, Rockwell Internat., Anaheim, Calif., 1969-70; investment broker Titan Capital Corp., L.A., Ogden, Utah, 1970-79; electrical engr. White Motor Corp., Ogden, 1979-84; tax examiner IRS, Ogden, 1990-91, ret., 1991. Cons. Soc. for the Advancement of Good English, Pittsford, N.Y., 1985-86. Author: Instrumentation Methods, 1963, Stewart Lives, 2003, (card) Pocket Guide to Good English, 1984; columnist Concord Corner, Cherokee Scout newspaper, 1996-99; inventor. Juggler St. Benedict's Hosp., and various nursing homes, grade schs., h.s., univs., shopping ctrs. and chs., 1947—. With USN, 1945-46, 1st lt. U.S. Army, 1951-53. Mem. IEEE, The Planetary Soc., World Wildlife Fund, Soc. for the Preservation of English Lang. and Lit., Soc. for Alphanumeric Improvement, Sierra Club. Republican. Mem. Lds Ch. Avocations: tennis, juggling, planetoid research, computing, astronomical model building. Home: 1257A Kelley Dr Blairsville GA 30512 Personal E-mail: mtntennispro99@yahoo.com.

KERR, WILLIAM ANDREW, lawyer, educator; b. Harding, W.Va., Nov. 17, 1934; s. William James and Tocie Nyle (Morris) K.; m. Elizabeth Ann McMillin, Aug. 3, 1968 AB, W.Va. U., 1955, JD, 1957; LLM, Harvard U., 1958; BD, Duke U., 1968. Bar: W.Va. 1957, Pa. 1962, Ind. 1980. Assoc. McClintic, James, Wise and Robinson, Charleston, W.Va., 1958; assoc. Schnader, Harrison, Segal and Lewis, Phila., 1961-64; asst. prof. law Cleve. State U., 1966-67, assoc. prof. law, 1967—68; assoc. prof. law Ind. U., Indpls., 1968—69, 1972—74, prof., 1974—98, prof. emeritus, 1998—; contract atty. Indpls. Pub. Defender Agy., 1998—. Asst. U.S. atty. So. Dist. Ind., Indpls., 1969-72; exec. dir. Ind. Jud. Ctr., 1974-86; dir. research Ind. Pros. Attys. Council, 1972-74; mem. Ind. Criminal Law Study Commn., 1973-89, sec., 1973-83; reporter speedy trial com. U.S. Dist. Ct. (so. dist.) Ind., 1975-84; trustee Ind. Criminal Justice Inst., 1983-86; bd. dirs. Indpls. Lawyers Commn., 1975-77, Ind. Lawyers Commn., 1980-83; mem. records mgmt. com. Ind. Supreme Ct., 1983-86. Author: Indiana Criminal Procedure: Pretrial, 1991, Indiana Criminal Procedure: Trial, 2 vols., 1998. Bd. dirs. Ch. Fedn. Greater Indpls., 1979-87. Served to capt. JAGC, USAF, 1958-61. Decorated Air Force Commendation medal; Ford Found. fellow Harvard Law Sch., 1957-58; recipient Outstanding Prof. award Students Ind. U. Sch. Law, 1974, Disting. Service award Ind. Council Juvenile Ct. Judges, 1979, Outstanding Jud. Edn. Program award Nat. Council Juvenile and Family Ct. Judges, 1985. Mem. Ind. State Bar Assn., Indpls. Bar Assn., Phila. Bar Assn., W.Va. Bar Assn., Nat. Dist. Attys. Assn., Am. Judicature Soc., Fed. Bar Assn. (Outstanding Service award Indpls. chpt. 1975), Order of Coif, Phi Beta Kappa. Office: 55 Monument Cir Ste 1017 Indianapolis IN 46204-5901 Office Phone: 317-917-0608.

KERR, WILLIAM C., physics professor; s. George H. and Agnes Dye Kerr; m. Sandria J. Neidus, June 9, 1963; children: Tamara J., Elizabeth L. Fish. BA, Coll. Wooster, Ohio, 1962; PhD, Cornell U., Ithaca, NY, 1967. Rsch. assoc. Chalmers U. Tech., Gothenburg, Sweden, 1967—68, Argonne Nat. Lab., Ill., 1968—70; prof. physics Wake Forest U., Winston-Salem, NC, 1970—. Recipient Excellence in Tchg. award, Wake Forest U., 1976; fellow, Woodrow Wilson Found., 1962—63. Mem.: Am. Phys. Soc. Office: Wake Forest Univ 1834 Wake Forest Rd Winston Salem NC 27109-7507 Home Phone: 336-759-2012; Office Phone: 336-758-5339. Business E-Mail: wck@wfu.edu.

KERR, WILLIAM T., publishing and broadcast executive; b. Seattle, Apr. 17, 1941; m. Mary Lang, Oct. 15, 1966; 1 child, Susannah Gaskill Kerr Adler. BA, U. Wash., 1963, Oxford U., Eng., 1965; MA, Harvard U., 1967, MBA, 1969. V.p. Dillon Read & Co., NYC, London, 1969—73; cons. McKinsey & Co., NYC, 1973-79; v.p. New York Times Co., NYC, 1979-91; pres. New York Times Mag. Group, NYC, 1985-91; exec. v.p., pres. mag. group Meredith Corp., Des Moines, 1991-94, pres., chief oper. officer, bd. dirs., exec. com., 1994-96, pres., CEO, 1997-98, chmn., CEO, 1998—2006, chmn., 2006—. Bd. dirs. Prin. Fin. Group, Whirlpool Corp., Interpublic Group Cos., Arbitron, Inc.; trustee Oxford U. Press, Harvard Bus. Sch. Publs., Internat. Fedn. Periodical Press. Bd. dirs. Bus. Com. for Arts. Mem.: Lost Tree Club, Reform Club, Des Moines Club, Wakonda Club, Quogue Field Club, The Brook Club, Union Club, Century Assn. Roman Catholic. Office: Meredith Corp 1716 Locust St Des Moines IA 50309-3023

KERREST, JACQUES DOMINIQUE, broadcasting company executive; b. Toulon, France, Oct. 17, 1946; s. Jacques Marie and Adrienne (Cuvru) K.; m. Sandra Werth, Dec. 27, 1973; children: Frederic, Marc-Olivier, Juliana. Baccalaureat, Coll. St. Gregoire, Tours, France, 1966; M of Econs., Faculte Scis. Econs., Paris, 1970; MBA, Inst. Etudes Politiques, Paris, 1971; M of Internat. Mgmt., Am. Grad. Sch. Internat. Mgmt., 1973. Analyst Messina Transvaal Devel. Co., Johannesburg, 1971-72; v.p. Chem. Bank, NYC, 1974-90; pres. Plenum Assocs. Inc., Wilmington, Del., 1990-93; CFO Positive Comms. Inc., Pleasanton, Calif., 1993-95, Chancellor Broadcasting Co., Dallas, 1995—97; sr. v.p., CFO Harte-Hanks Inc., 1997—2003; mng. dir., CFO Equant, 2003—04; CFO Virgin Media Inc., NYC, 2004—. Bd. dirs. ISA Instruments Inc., Edison, N.J. Roman Catholic. Avocations: sailing, soccer. Office: Virgin Media Inc Ste 2863 909 Third Ave New York NY 10022*

KERREY, BOB (J. ROBERT KERREY), academic administrator, former senator; b. Lincoln, Nebr., Aug. 27, 1943; s. James and Elinor Kerrey; m. Sarah Paley; children: Benjamin, Lindsey, Henry. BS in Pharmacy, U. Nebr., 1965; LLD (hon.), NY Law Sch. Owner, founder, developer Grandmother's Restaurants, Omaha, 1972—75; owner, founder Prairie Life Ctr., Lincoln and Omaha, Nebr.; gov. State of Nebr., Lincoln, 1983—87; ptnr. Printon, Kane & Co., Lincoln, Nebr., 1987—89; US Senator from Nebr., 1989—2001; pres. New Sch., NYC, 2001—. Mem. The Nat. Commn. on Terrorist Attacks Upon the U.S. (The 9-11 Commn.), 2002—04; co-chair (with Newt Gingrich) Nat. Com. for Quality Long-Term Care; mem. adv. bd. U.S. Govt. Accountability Office; mem. Nat. Security Higher Edn. Adv. Bd. bd. dirs. Lincoln Ctr. Assn., Nebr. Easter Seal Soc. With USN, 1966—69, Vietnam. Decorated medal of Honor, Bronze Star, Purple Heart; recipient Robert L. Haig award for Disting. Pub. Svc., NY State Bar Assn. Mem.: Lincoln C. of C., DAV, VFW, Am. Legion, Sertoma, Lions, Phi Gamma Delta. Congregationalist. Office: The New School 66 W 12th St Rm 800 New York NY 10011

KERRICH, ROBERT, geologist, educator; b. Dec. 15, 1948; BSc, U. Birmingham, 1971; MSc, Imperial Coll., London, 1972, PhD, 1975; DSc, U. Saskatchewan, 1996. NATO postdoctoral fellow U. Western Ontario, 1975—77, asst. prof., dept. geology, 1977—80, assoc. prof., dept. geology, 1980—86, prof., dept. geology, 1986—87; George J. McLeod chair, dept. geological sciences U. Saskatchewan, 1987—. Contbr. chapters to books;, author book; contbr. to peer-reviewed papers. Fellow: Royal Soc. Can.; mem.: Am. Geophysical Union (Willet G. Miller medal 1999), Geological Soc. London, Geological Soc. Am., Geological Soc. Can. (W.H. Gross medal 1988), Mineralogical Assn. Canada, Canadian Inst. Mining and Metallurgy. Office: Rm 246 Dept Geological Sciences U Saskatchewan 114 Science Pl Saskatoon SK S7N 5E2 Canada Office Phone: 306-966-5719. Office Fax: 306-966-8593. Business E-Mail: robert.kerrich@usask.ca.

KERRICK, DAVID ELLSWORTH, lawyer; b. Caldwell, Idaho, Jan. 15, 1951; s. Charles Ellsworth and Patria (Olesen) K.; m. Juneal Casper, May 24, 1980; children: Peter Ellsworth, Beth Anne, George Ellis, Katherine Leigh. Student, Coll. of Idaho, 1969—71; BA, U. Wash., 1972; JD, U. Idaho, 1980. Bar: Idaho 1980, U.S. Dist. Ct. Idaho 1980, U.S. Ct. Appeals (9th cir.) 1981. Mem. Idaho Senate, 1990-96, majority caucus chmn., 1992-94, majority leader, 1994-96. Mem. S.W. Idaho Estate Planning Coun. Mem. ABA, ATLA, Idaho Bar Assn. (3d dist. pres. 1985-86), Idaho Trial Lawyers Assn., Canyon County Lawyers Assn. (pres. 1985), Elks. Republican. Presbyterian. Avocations: skiing, photography. Office: PO Box 44 Caldwell ID 83606-0044 Home Phone: 208-454-3373; Office Phone: 208-459-4574.

KERRIGAN, NANCY, professional figure skater, retired Olympic athlete; b. Woburn, Mass., Oct. 13, 1969; d. Daniel and Brenda Kerrigan; m. Jerry Solomon, 1995; children: Matthew Eric Solomon, Brian Russell Solomon. Bronze medalist World Championships, 1991, 92; U.S. nat. bronze medalist, 1991; U.S. nat. silver medalist, 1992; bronze medalist Olympic Games, Albertville, France, 1992; U.S. nat. champion, 1993; silver medalist Olympic Games, Lillehammer, Norway, 1994. Numerous comls. and product endorsements including Walt Disney Co., Reebok, Northwest Airlines, Frosted Cheerios, Ray Ban, Revlon, Aetna U.S. Healthcare, Salvino Bammers, AquaTrend, Tostitos, Tropican; author: In My Own Words, 1996; author: (with Mary Spencer) Artistry on Ice, 2002; choreographer Halloween on Ice; performer: (video) Fairy Tales on Ice, Champions on Ice Tour, 1992—2004, (TV spls.) Dreams on Ice, Breaking the Ice, Nancy Kerrigan and Friends, Holiday Celebration on Ice, One Enchanted Evening, Divas on Ice, Nancy Kerrigan's Winter Wonderland, Colors of Winter, 2003, Grease on Ice, 1998—99, Broadway on Ice, 2000, Footloose on Ice, 2001, Skating with Celebrities, 2005; host (TV series) Lifetime TV, 2002—04, commentator Comcast, TV host Nancy Kerrigan's World of Figure Skating, 2002, 2005, Grand Prix of Figure Skating, ISU Grand Prix Lifetime TV, 2003—04; co-host: (TV series) The Insider, 2006; singer: (albums) Reflections Off the Ice, 1999, Simply the Best, 2004; actor: (TV series) Boy Meets World, 1995, The Journey of Allen Strange, 1998, Ice Angel, Hollywood Squares, 2003, Family Feud, 2003, Intimate Portrait, 2004, (voice): (TV films) The Easter Egg Adventure, Blades of Glory, 2007. Spokesperson Lions Club, 1994, Children's Trust Fund, 1997, Spalding Rehab. Hosp., MADD, Fight for Sight, Found. Fighting Blindness, 2007; founder, benefactor Nancy Kerrigan Found.; hon. chair Nancy Kerrigan Golf Classic, 2000—. Named to Bay State Games Hall of Fame, 2007; recipient Bronze medal, World Figure Skating Championships, 1991, Silver medal, 1992, Bronze medal, U.S. Pro Championships, 1997, Goodwill Games, 2000, Outstanding Mother award, Mother's Day Found., 2001, Henry Iba Outstanding Citizen Athlete award, 2002. Office: care of StarGames Bldg 1 40 Salem St Lynnfield MA 01940 Office Phone: 781-224-9655.

KERRY, CAMERON F., lawyer; b. Washington, Sept. 6, 1950; s. Richard John and Rosemary (Forbes) K.; m. Kathy B. Weinman, June 28, 1983; children: Jessica Weinman Kerry, Laura Weinman Kerry. BA cum laude, Harvard U., 1972; JD magna cum laude, Boston Coll., 1978. Bar: Mass.,

D.C. Polit. cons., writer, Cambridge, Mass., 1973-76; law clerk to Hon. Elbert P. Tuttle U.S. Ct. Appeals (5th cir.), Atlanta, 1978-79; assoc. Wilmer, Cutler & Pickering, Washington, 1979-82; mem. Mintz, Levin, Cohn, Ferris, Glovsky & Popeo, P.C., Boston, 1983—. Adj. prof. law Suffolk U. Law Sch. Editor book chpts.; mem. Boston Coll. Law Review, 1977-78; contbr. articles to profl. jours. Campaign mgr. Paul Guzzi for Sec. State, Newton, Mass., 1974; campaign mgr. John Kerry for Lt. Gov., Boston, 1982; advisor and nat. surrogate John Kerry for Pres., 2003-04; trustee Boston Police Found., 1993-98; coop. counsel Civil Liberties Union Mass., Boston, 1985; mem. Brookline (Mass.) Dem. Town Com., 1985—; dir. New Eng. Nordic Skiing Assn., 1999—, Nat. Jewish Dem. Coun., 2005—. Recipient Internat. Security Mgrs. Assn. award, 1993, citation Nat. Press Photographers Assn., 1990. Mem. ABA, Mass. State Bar Assn., Boston Bar Assn., Def. Rsch. Inst. Office: Mintz Levin Cohn Ferris Glovsky and Popeo PC 1 Financial Ctr Fl 38 Boston MA 02111-2621

KERRY, JOHN FORBES, senator; b. Denver, Dec. 11, 1943; s. Richard John and Rosemary (Forbes) K.; m. Julia Stimson Thorne, May 23, 1970 (div. July 25, 1988), children: Alexandra, Vanessa; m. Teresa Heinz, May 26, 1995, stepchildren: John, Andre, Christopher. BA in Polit. Sci., Yale U., 1966; MA, JD, Boston Coll., 1976; PhD (hon.), U. Ma., 1988. Bar: Mass. 1976. Nat. coord. Vietnam Vets. Against The War, 1969-71; asst. dist. atty. Middlesex County, 1976-79; ptnr. firm Kerry & Sragow, Boston, 1979-82; lt. gov. State of Mass., 1983—85; U.S. senator from Mass., 1985—; chmn. Dem. Senatorial campaign com., 1986-88; Democratic candidate for U.S. pres., 2004. Mem. Fgn. Rels. Com., Fgn. Rels. subcom. Internat. Ops., Sen. Dem. Steering & Coordination Com.; mem. Com. Banking, Housing & Urban Affairs, ranking minority mem. Com. Small Bus., Select Com. on Intelligence; ranking minority mem. Commerce, Sci. & Transp. subcom. on Oceans & Fisheries; Com. Fin.; Com. Small Bus. and Entrepreneurship, ranking minority mem. Author: The New Soldier, 1971, The New War: The Web of Crime That Threatens America's Security, 1997, A Call to Service: My Vision for a Better America , 2003; co-author (with Teresa Heinz Kerry) This Moment on Earth: Today's New Environmentalists and Their Vision for the Future, 2007 Dem. candidate for Congress from 5th Mass. Dist., 1972; bd. vistors Walsh Sch. Fgn. Service, Georgetown U. Served to lt. (j.g.) USNR, 1966-69. Decorated Silver Star, Bronze Star with oak leaf cluster, Purple Hearts (3). Mem. Vietnam Vets. Am. (founder). Democrat. Roman Catholic. Office: US Senate 304 Russell Senate Bldg Washington DC 20510-0001 also: District Office Ste 1000 One Bowdoin Sq Boston MA 02114-2928 Office Phone: 202-224-2742, 617-565-8519. Office Fax: 202-224-8525, 617-248-3870.*

KERSCHNER, EDWARD, brokerage house executive; BS, MBA, NYU. CFA. Securities analyst, investment strategist Cowen & Co., 1974—82; chmn. investment policy com. Paine Webber Inc., 1982—2000; chief global investment strategist UBS Investment Rsch., 2000—03; mng. dir., U.S. equity rsch. Citigroup Smith Barney, NYC, 2004—. Adj. prof. Stern Sch. Bus. NYU, 2001—. Named to All-American Rsch. Team, Institutional Investor mag. Office: Citi Smith Barney 388 Greenwich St New York NY 10013*

KERSCHNER, LEE R(ONALD), academic administrator, political scientist, educator; b. May 31, 1931; m. Helga Koller, June 22, 1958; children: David, Gabriel, Riza. BA in Polit. Sci. (Univ. fellow), Rutgers U., New Brunswick, 1953; MA in Internat. Relations (Univ. fellow), Johns Hopkins U., Paul H. Nitze Sch. Advanced Internat. Studies, 1958; PhD in Polit. Sci. (Univ. fellow), Georgetown U., 1964. From instr. to prof. polit. sci. Calif. State U., Fullerton, 1961-69, prof., 1988—; state univ. dean Calif. State Univs. and Colls. Hdqrs., Long Beach, 1969-71, asst. exec. vice chancellor, 1971-76, vice chancellor for adminstrv. affairs, 1976-77, vice chancellor acad. affairs, 1987-92; exec. dir. Colo. Commn. on Higher Edn., Denver, 1977-83, Nat. Assn. Trade and Tech. Schs., 1983-85, Calif. Commn. on Master Plan for Higher Edn., 1985-87; interim pres. Calif. State U., Stanislaus, 1992-94, spl. asst. to the chancellor, 1994-97; exec. vice chancellor Minn. State Colls. and Univs., St. Paul, 1996-97; vice chancellor emeritus Calif. State U., 1997—; presdl. advisor Calif. Maritime Acad. Mem. Calif. Student Aid Commn., 1993-96; cons. in field. Mem. exec. com. Am. Jewish Com., Denver, 1978-83; internat. bd. dirs. Amigos de las Americas, 1982-88 (chmn. 1985-87); chair Blue Ribbon Comm., Univ. Park and Rsch. Ctr., Chula Vista, Calif. Served with USAF, 1954-58; col. Res., ret. Home: PO Box 748 Weimar CA 95736-0748 Office Phone: 530-878-0312. Personal E-mail: lkconslt@pacbell.net.

KERSEY, SCOTT N., mathematician, educator; s. Alfred F. and Shirley N. Kersey. PhD in Math., U. Wis., Madison, 1990—99. Vis. asst. prof. Case Western Res. U., Cleve., 1999—2003; asst. prof. math. Ga. So. U., Statesboro, 2003—. Mem.: Am. Math. Soc. Office: Ga So Univ Dept Math Scis Statesboro GA 30460 Home Phone: 912-541-1300.

KERSEY, TALANA S., mental health counselor; b. Joliet, Ill., May 5, 1947; d. Elgin L. and Virgil D. McMahon; m. Joel Allen Kersey, Dec. 7, 1991; children: Michelle Talana, Eric Charles, Kelly Brooke. BA in Edn., Ariz. State U., 1970; MS in Mental Health Counseling, Nova Southeastern U., 1996. Lic. mental health counselor, real estate salesman, Fla.; cert. tchr., Fla. Secondry tchr. Orange County Schs., Orlando, Fla.; acad. instr. Brevard Start Ctr., Titusville, Fla.; eligibility specialist Ill. Aid to Families and Dependent Children, Apopka; tchr. C.H. Price Mid. Sch., Interlachen, Fla.; instr., job developer displaced homemaker program Santa Fe C.C., Gainesville, Fla.; therapist, mental health counselor Meridian Behavioral Healthcare, Inc., Gainesville, 1996—, Nick Ungson MD, P.A., Leesburg, Fla. Pvt. tutor, Gainesville, 1991-93. Vol. tchr. Head Start, Phoenix, 1970, Sparc, shelter for abused women, Gainesville, 1989; mem. planning bd. Gainesville Area Women's Network, 1990. Mem. ACA, NEA, Real Estate Edn. Assn. Avocations: piano, decorating, sewing. Office: Meridian Behavioral Healthcare 4300 SW 13th St Gainesville FL 32608

KERSTEN, CHRISTIAN GEORGE, university administrator; b. Paris, Jan. 11, 1949; s. Henry George and Elisabeth (Reiter) K.; m. Mary Menasche, May 29, 1970 (div. 1983); children: Michael Kenneth, James Alexander; m. Mary Louise Coleman, Jan. 5, 1985; 1 child, Hilary Coleman. BA, L.I. U., 1971; postgrad., NYU, 1974-76. Dir. ann. giving Manhattan Coll., Riverdale, NY, 1972-73; assoc. dir. alumni fedn. NYU, 1973-76; assoc. dir. devel. Clark U., Worcester, Mass., 1976-80; assoc. dir. univ. devel. Tufts U., Medford, Mass., 1980-83; asst. chancellor univ. devel. U. Calif., Santa Barbara, 1983-87; dir. devel. Norman Rockwell Mus., Stockbridge, Mass., 1987-88; v.p. for univ. advancement SUNY, Albany, 1988—97; exec. dir. U. Albany Found., 1988—97; sr. v.p. Albany Law Sch., 1997—2003, sec. bd. trustees, 1997—2003; pres. Berkshire Hudson Group Ltd., 2003—07; chief advancement officer Abraham Lincoln Presdl. Libr. and Mus., Springfield, Ill., 2007—. Dir. Mohawk Hudson Cmty. Found., Albany, 1988-91; trustee Hillsdale Pub. Libr., 1993—, Albany Symphony Orch., 1993—; town justice Hillsdale, NY, 2000-07. Recipient Grand Award for Improvement Coun. for Advancement and Support of Edn./U.S. Steel, 1981, Gold Medal for fundraising publs., 1986; named Outstanding Fundraising Exec., Nat. Soc. Fund Raising Exec. Mem. Coun. for Advancement and Support of Edn., Nat. Soc. Fundraising Execs. Democrat. Unitarian-Universalist. Office: 500 E Madison St STe 200 Springfield IL 62701 Office Phone: 217-558-8877. Business E-Mail: ckersten@alplm.org.

KERSTEN, FREDERICK IRVING, retired philosopher, educator; b. Niagara Falls, NY, Sept. 26, 1931; s. Irving Wilhelm and Margaret Edna Kersten; m. Karen Jean McKie, Mar. 24, 1994; m. Raquel Brik (dec.); children: Stephen, Andrew. BA, Lawrence Coll., 1951; MA, New Sch., NYC, 1959, PhD, 1964. Halle fellow Grad. Faculty, New Sch., NYC, 1961—62; assoc. prof. U. Mont., Missoula, 1962—69; prof. U. Wis., Green Bay, 1969—94, Frankenthal prof., 1984—94, philosopher in residence Madison, 1985—94. Author: Phenomenological Method, 1989, Galileo, 1998. Scholar, Brown U., 1955—56. Home: 2366 Old Plank Rd De Pere WI 54115

KERSTETTER, WAYNE ARTHUR, law educator; b. Chgo., Dec. 1, 1939; s. Arthur Edward and Lillian (Asplund) K. BA, U. Chgo., 1964, JD, 1967. Bar: Ill. 1968. Gen. counsel Ill. Drug Abuse Treatment Program, 1968—70; admin. and rsch. assoc. Ctr. Studies in Criminal Justice U. Chgo. Law Sch., 1970—72; asst. commr. N.Y. Police Dept., NYC, 1972—73; supt. Ill. Bur. Investigation, Chgo., 1973—76; assoc. dir. Ctr. Studies in Criminal Justice U. Chgo., 1976—78; assoc. prof. criminal justice dept. criminal justice U. Ill., Chgo., 1978—2000. Sr. rsch. fellow Am. Bar Found., Chgo., 1982-93, fellow, 1993—; cons. U.S. Civil Rights Commn., U. Chgo., ABT Assoc., Univ. Rsch. Assoc., Police Found. Mem. transition team Mayor Washington, Chgo., 1983, Criminal Justice Project of Cook County, 1987. Served with USNR, 1962-64. Rsch. grantee Nat. Inst. Justice, 1976, Chgo. Bar Found., 1979-80, Am. Bar Found., 1983; fellow Ctr. for Studies in Criminal Justice, U. Chgo. Law Sch., 1978-82. Home: 1070 S Collier Unit 702 Marco Island FL 34145 Personal E-mail: wkerstett@aol.com.

KERSTIENS, GENE J., mathemagenician, consultant; b. Phoenix, Nov. 7, 1926; s. Joseph Henry and Evangeline Kerstiens; m. Dorothy Louise Bishop, Jan. 27, 1951; children: Rita, Theresa, Mark, Frank, Helen, John, Christopher, Fredryc. BA, U. Portland, 1951; MA, U. Ariz., 1952; EdD, Nova U., Ft. Lauderdale, Fla., 1978. Prof. English El Camino Coll., Torrance, Calif., 1956—71; vis. prof. edn. Western Wash. State U., Bellingham, 1971—72; dean learning assistance El Camino Coll., Torrance, 1972—86; acting dir. Nat. Ctr. for Developmental Edn., Boone, NC, 1987—88; dir. learning assistance Scottsdale C.C., Ariz., 1988—92; dir. Andragogy Assocs., Torrance, 1992—. Cons. adult learning programs Pub. Broadcasting Svc., NYC, 1970—73; developer, pub. English Modular Minicourses, 1972, Academic Skills series, 1977; pub. Study Behavior Inventory, 1994. Author: Study-Reading for College Courses, 1968 (Merit award, 1970); compiler (monograph) Junior-Community College Reading/Study Skills: An Annotated Bibliography, 1970; editor: Educulture, 1971—85; mem. editl. bd. Jour. Developmental Edn., 1980—. Mem. ACLU. With US Army, 1945—47. Fellow: Am. Coun. of Developmental Edn. Assns.; mem.: Coll. Reading and Learning Assn. (pres. 1971, Lifetime Achievement award 1981). Avocations: sailing, travel, hiking, parachuting, motorcycling. Home and Office: Andragogy Associates 3434 W 227 Pl Torrance CA 90505-2632

KERSZBERG, ANNIK DOQUIRE, language educator; PhD, Pa. State U., University Park, 2005. Instr. French Lock Haven U. of Pa., 2000—05, asst. prof. French, 2005—. Office: Lock Haven U of Pa Fairview St Lock Haven PA 17745 Home Phone: 814-237-1537; Office Phone: 570-484-2180. Business E-Mail: akerszbe@lhup.edu.

KERTÉSZ, IMRE, writer; b. Budapest, Hungary, Nov. 9, 1929; With Világosság, Budapest, Romania, 1948—51. Author: Sorstalanság, 1975, A nyomkeresö: Két regény, 1977, A kudarc, 1988, Kaddis a meg nem született gyermekért, 1990, Az angol lobogó, 1991, Gályanapló, 1992, A holocaust mint kultúra: három eloadás, 1993, Jegyzökönyv, 1993, Valaki más: a változás krónikája, 1997, A gondolatnyi csend, amíg a kivégzöosztag újratölt, 1998, A számüzött nyelv, 2001; writer: (films) Fateless, 2005. Active Mil. Svc., 1951—53. Recipient Brandenburger Literaturpreis, 1995, Leipziger Buchpreis zur Europaischen Verstandigung, 1997, Herder-Preis, 2000, WELT-Literaturpreis, 2000, Ehrenpreis der Robert-Bosch-Stiftung, 2001, Hans Sahl-Preis, 2002, Nobel prize in Lit., 2002. Achievements include being first Hungarian to win Nobel Prize for Lit. Office: Northwestern U Press 625 Colfax St Evanston IL 60208-4210

KERTH, LEROY T., physics professor; b. Visalia, Calif., Nov. 23, 1928; s. Lewis John and Frances (Niccolls) K.; m. Ruth Lorraine Littlefield, Nov. 19, 1950; children: Norman Lewis, Randall Thomas, Christine Jane, Bradley Niccolls. AB in Physics, U. Calif., Berkeley, 1950, PhD, 1957. Mem. staff Lawrence Berkeley Lab, U. Calif., Berkeley, 1950-59, sr. scientist, 1959-61; assoc. prof. physics U. Calif., Berkeley, 1961-65, prof., 1965-93, prof. emeritus, 1993—, assoc. dean Coll. Letters and Scis., 1966-70, spl. asst. to chancellor, 1970-71, assoc. dir. for info. and computing scis. div., 1983-87, assoc. lab. dir. for gen. scis., Lawrence Berkeley Lab., 1987-89, assoc. lab. dir. sci. and tech. resources, Lawrence Berkeley Lab., 1990-92. Fellow Am. Phys. Soc. Home: 5 Los Conejos Orinda CA 94563-2214 Office: U Calif Lawrence Berkeley Lab Berkeley CA 94720-0001 Business E-Mail: ltkerth@lbl.gov.

KERTZER, DAVID ISRAEL, academic administrator, anthropology educator, writer; b. Feb. 20, 1948; m. Susan Dana, May 24, 1970; children: Molly, Seth. BA, Brown U., 1969; PhD, Brandeis U., 1974. From asst. prof. to prof. Bowdoin Coll., Brunswick, Maine, 1973-89, Kenan prof., 1989-92; Dupee prof. Brown U., Providence, 1992—, provost, 2006—. Author: Ritual, Politics, and Power, 1988, Sacrificed for Honor, 1993, Politics and Symbols, 1996, The Kidnapping of Edgardo Mortara, 1997 (Nat. Jewish Book award, Nat. Book award finalist), The Popes Against the Jews, 2001, Prisoner of the Vatican, 2004. Fellow: Am. Acad. Arts and Scis. Business E-Mail: David_Kertzer@brown.edu.

KERTZMAN, MITCHELL E., former software company executive, venture capitalist; LHD (hon.), U. Mass., Lowell. Founder Computer Solutions, 1974; founder, CEO Powersoft Corp. (merged with Sybase, Inc.), 1993—95; chmn. bd. dirs., CEO Sybase, Inc., Emeryville, Calif., 1995-98; pres., CEO Liberate Techs., Redwood Shores, Calif., 1998—2003; ptnr. Hummer Winblad Venture Partners, San Francisco, 2003—. Bd. dirs. Sybase, Inc., Shiva Corp., CNET, Interconnect Syss., Inc., Bridgestream, Sapias, Five9, ActiveGrid, Palamida, Akimbi Sys. Founder, former chmn. Mass. Inst. New Commonwealth; mem. N.Y. State Commn. Indsl. Competitiveness, chair task force indsl. policy. Recipient Inc. Mag. and Ernst & Young's New England Entrepreneur of Yr. award, 1993, Disting. Achievement award Tech. Unit New England B'nai B'rith, 1993. Mem.: Mass. Software Coun. (pres. 1994—96), Am. Electronics Assn. (chmn. 1990). Office: Hummer Winblad Venture Partners 1 Lombard St Ste 300 San Francisco CA 94111-1130 Office Phone: 415-979-9600. Office Fax: 415-979-9601. E-mail: mkertzman@humwin.com.

KERWICK, COLLEEN, lawyer, artist; b. Kilkenny, Ireland, Mar. 9, 1976; d. Sean Kerwick and Eileen Brennan-Kerwick. B Corp. Law, Nat. U. Ireland, Galway, 1998, LLB, 1999. Bar: N.Y. 2001. Litig. assoc. Williamson & Williamson, NYC, 2002—03; counsel Cullen and Dykman, NYC, 2003—. Founder Young Irish Film Makers, Kilkenny City, Ireland, 1991—. Actor: (ctrl. character in ind. feature) Dagober; creative embroidery, The Creation of Man (Cork Internat. Film Festival, 1993). Mentor Vol. Lawyers Project, NYC, 2004—06; sec. Emerald Assn. L.I., NYC, 2005—06. Mem.: N.Y. State Trial Lawyers Assn. (assoc.). Avocations: painting, piano, drama, music, irish culture and language. Office: Cullen and Dykman Brklyn Heights 177 Montague St Brooklyn NY 11201 Home Phone: 917-257-9822. Office Fax: 718-935-1509. Personal E-mail: colleen_kerwick@yahoo.com. E-mail: ckerwick@cullenanddykman.com.

KERWIN, CORNELIUS MARTIN, academic administrator, educator; b. Waterbury, Conn., Apr. 10, 1949; s. Daniel Vincent and Mary Catherine (Shea) K.; m. Ann D. Londe, Sept. 3, 1972; children: Michael Barnett, Alex Daniel. BA, Am. U., 1971; MA, U. R.I., 1972; PhD, Johns Hopkins U., 1978; postgrad., Am. U., Washington. Program asst. Johns Hopkins U., Balt., 1972-75; instr. Am. U. Washington Semester Program, Washington, 1975—78, Sch Govt. and Pub. Adminstrn. Am. U., Washington, 1978—80, asst. prof., 1980—84, assoc. prof., 1984—88; acting dean Sch. Pub. Affairs Am. U., Washington, 1988—89, dean, prof., 1989—97; acting provost Am. U., 1997—98, full provost, 1998—2005, co-founder Ctr. Study of Rulemaking, 2004, acting pres., 2005, interim pres., 2005—07, pres., 2007—. Cons. IBM Corp., Rockville, Md., 1984—, U.S. Fed. Energy Regulatory Commn., Washington, 1983—88, US EPA, Washington, 1988—; co-founder Ctr. Study of Rulemaking Am. u., Washington, 2004. Author: Rulemaking, 1994; contbr. book chpts., conf. papers, and articles to profl. jours. Regional finalist White House Fellowship Competition, 1980. Fellow Nat. Acad. Pub. Adminstrn.; Mem. Nat. Assn. Schs. Pub. Affairs and Adminstrn. (commn. on peer rev. and accreditation 1990-93, exec. coun., 1993—), Am. Soc. Pub. Adminstrn. (bd. dirs. Nat. Capital area chpt. 1990—, chmn. sect. on pub. law and adminstrn. 1991—), Am. Polit. Sci. Assn. Avocations: running, golf, tennis. Office: Office of Pres 4400 Massachusetts Ave NW Washington DC 20016 Office Phone: 202-885-2121. Office Fax: 212-885-3279. Business E-Mail: president@american.edu.

KERWIN, THOMAS P., architect; BArch, Ball State U., Muncie, Ind., 1986; MBA, Northwestern U., 2007. With Skidmore, Owings & Merrill LLP, Chgo., 1986—, mng. ptnr., 2001—. Prin. works include White Magnolia Plz., Shanghai, Suzhou Internat. Expo Ctr., China, 444 North Mich. Ave. - Storefront and Lobby Renovation, Chgo., GM Renaissance Ctr., Detroit, Rockwell Ctr., Manila. Named to Crain's Chgo. Bus. 40 Under 40 list, 2001; recipient Disting. Alumni award, Ball State U., 2005. Fellow: AIA (pres. Chgo. chpt. 2005); mem.: Landmarks Preservation Coun. Ill., Chgo. Architecture Found., Urban Land Inst., Exec. Club Chgo., Comml. Club Chgo., Lambda Alpha Internat. Office: Skidmore Owings & Merrill LLP 224 S Michigan Ave Ste 1000 Chicago IL 60604 Office Phone: 312-554-9090. Office Fax: 312-360-4545.*

KERWIN, WALTER THOMAS, JR., career officer, consultant; b. West Chester, Pa., June 14, 1917; s. Walter Thomas and Mary Joseph (Farra) K.; m. Barbara Walker Connell, July 10, 1940 (dec. 1980); children: Bruce Richard, Ann Walker; m. Marion Thompson McCutcheon, Oct. 27, 1984. BS, U.S. Mil. Acad., 1939; postgrad., Command and Gen. Staff Coll., 1948, M (hon.) in Mil. Art and Sci., 1978; postgrad., Armed Forces Staff Coll., 1953, U.S. Army War Coll., 1957, Nat. War Coll., 1960; LLD (hon.), U. Akron, 1976. Commd. 2d lt. US Army, 1939, advanced through grades to gen., 1973, chief nuc. activities SHAPE NATO Paris, 1963—65, commdg. gen. 3d armored divsn. artillery Frankfurt, 1965—66, asst. dep. chief staff ops. gen. staff Washington, 1966—67, chief staff mil. asst. command Saigon, Vietnam, 1967—68, commdg. gen. II field force Vietnam, 1968—69, dep. chief staff pers. gen. staff Washington, 1969—72, commdg. gen. continental army command Norfolk, Va., 1973, commdg. gen. forces command Atlanta, 1973—74, Army vice chief staff Washington, 1974—78. Cons. Martin Marietta Corp., Bethesda, Md., 1978-94, Lockheed-Martin, 1994-97; assoc. dir. ops. Los Alamos (N.Mex.) Sci. Lab., 1953-56; bd. dirs. Gen. Employment Enterprises, Oakbrook, Ill., 1984-2001; mem. bd. mgrs. Army Emergency Relief, 1982—; mem. sci. adv. group Def. Nuc. Agy., 1980-86; mem. tactical tech. adv. group Land Warfare Def. Advance Rsch. Projects, 1983-88; Dept. Def. proxy dir. DKI Electronics-Electro, Tec Corp., Precision Products, Inc., Martin Electronics Fri Corp., Triangle Microwave Inc., 1986-89. Chmn. Army Air Force Mut. Aid Assn., Arlington, Va., 1982-97, chmn. emeritus 1997—; bd. advisors Army Hist. Found., 1995-97, bd. dirs., 1997—; mem. coun. trustees Assn. U.S. Army, 1979-82; bd. visitors Nat. Def. U., 1982-90. Recipient Disting. Svc. medal Commonwealth of Pa., 1975, Outstanding Alumnus award U.S. Army War Coll., 1997, Disting Grad. award Assn. Grads. U.S. Mil. Acad., 2003, numerous mil. awards and decorations; named to Henderson Hall of Fame, West Chester, Pa., 1991, Res. Officers Assn. of U.S. Minute Man Hall of Fame, 1978; honored with Papal Benemerenti medal Pope Paul VI, 1977; named in honor of Walter Thomas Kerwin Forces Command Hdqs. Conf. Rm., Ft. McPherson, Ga., 2003. Fellow: Nat. Def. U. Capstone Program (emeritus); mem.: U.S. Field Arty. Assn. (pres. 1980—97), West Point Soc. (Castle-Duty Hon. Country award 1993, Artillery Ctr. Auditorium, Ft. Sill, Okla., dedicated Kerwin Hall 2001), Am. Def. Preparedness Assn. (comdr. Chief award 1984). Avocations: fishing, wilderness hiking.

KERWIN, WILLIAM JAMES, electrical engineering educator, consultant; b. Portage, Wis., Sept. 27, 1922; s. James William and Nina Elizabeth Kerwin; m. Madolyn Lee Lyons, Aug. 31, 1947; children: Dorothy E., Deborah K., David W. BS, U Redlands, 1948; MS, Stanford U., 1954, PhD, 1967. Aero. research scientist NACA, Moffett Field, Calif., 1948-59; chief measurements research br. NASA, Moffett Field, Calif., 1959-62, chief space tech. br., 1962-64, chief electronics research br., 1964-70; head electronics dept. Stanford Linear Accelerator Ctr., 1962; prof. elec. engring. U. Ariz., Tucson, 1969-85, prof. emeritus, 1986—. Cons. Power Electronics, 1980—. Author: (with others) Active Filters, 1970, Handbook Measurement Science, 1982, Instrumentation and Control, 1990, Handbook of Electrical Engineering, 1993, 97; contbr. articles to profl. jours.; patentee in field. Served to capt. USAAF, 1942-46. Recipient Invention NASA, 1969, 70; recipient fellow NASA, 1966-67 Fellow IEEE (Centennial medal 1984) Home: 1981 W Shalimar Way Tucson AZ 85704-1250 Office: U Ariz Dept Elec And Computer Engring Tucson AZ 85721-0001 Home Phone: 520-297-8529; Office Phone: 520-297-8529.

KERXTON, ALAN SMITH, lawyer; b. Balt., Mar. 19, 1938; s. Benjamin and Eva (Smith) Kerxton; m. Leslie Lurie, Aug. 2, 1961; children: Amy Lynn, Susan Deborah, Katherine Diane. BA, Ohio State U., 1960, JD, 1962. Bar: DC 1963, Md. 1965. Atty. corp. reorganization br. SEC, Washington, 1963-66; pvt. practice Washington, Potomac, Md., 1966—; prin. Ezrin, West and Kerxton, Chartered, 1976-84, Dunnells and Duval, Washington, 1990-93, Holland and Knight, Washington, 1994-97; of counsel Stein, Sperling, Rockville, Md., 1998—. Lectr. Cath. U. Am. Law Sch., 1973. With US Army, 1962—63. Mem.: Montgomery County Bar Assn., DC Bar Assn. Home: 11815 Beekman Pl Potomac MD 20854-2177 Office: 25 W Middle Ln Rockville MD 20850-2214 Office Phone: 301-838-3213. E-mail: akerxton@steinsperling.com.

KERZ, LOUISE (LOUISE HIRSCHFELD), historian; b. NYC, Sept. 16, 1936; d. Louis and Catharine Sohn; m. Leo Kerz, Apr., 1965 (dec. 1976); children: Jonathan, Antony; m. Al Hirschfeld, Oct. 1996 (dec. 2003). Student, Queens Coll., 1954-56, Marymount Coll., 1972-74. Theatre producer Leo Kerz Prodns., NYC, 1960-74; theatrical curator N.Y. Cultural Ctr., NYC, 1974, Theatre of Max Reinhardt, 1974, N.Y. Pub. Libr. Lincoln Ctr., NYC, 1984, Calif. Mus. Sci. and Industry, LA, 1985, The Demille Dynasty, 1984; rsch. cons. CBS: On the Air, 1978, Smith-Hemion TV Prodns., LA, 1987—96, The Phantom of the Opera, 1995. Dir. rsch. Greengage Prodns., Julie Andrews/Greengage Prodns., LA, 1988, Tony Awards Telecast 50th Anniversary Show, 1947—96; rsch. cons. TV Acad. Hall of Fame and Tony Awards telecasts, 1993—96; dir. rights and permissions The Line King (The Al Hirschfeld Story-nominated for Oscar 1996) NY Times, TV documentary; rsch. historian six-part TV series Broadway, 1997; spl. cons. The Demille Family-Documentary Am. Movie Channel, 1997; exec. cons., liaison Hirschfeld Exhbns., catalogs, books and events Mus. of City of NY, cons. Hirschfeld's NY exhibit, 2001; cons. Hirschfeld's Hollywood exhibit Acad. Motion Picture Arts & Scis., Beverly Hills, Calif., 2001; cons. catalogues to exhibits Pub. Harry N. Abrams, 2001; exhibit organizer V&A Theatre Mus., Nat. Theatre Southbank, London, 2005, Al Hirschfeld's Brits on Broadway; organizer London 2005 Hirschfeld Celebration, V&A Theatre Mus. and Royal Nat. Theatre at Southbank; curator book Hirschfeld's British Aisles, 2005. Assoc. prodr. on

Broadway: Rhinoceros, 1961; contbg. editor: N.Y.C. Access, 1983; picture editor The DeMilles: An American Family, 1988, Al Hirschfeld: On Line, 1998, curator, dir. Exhibit Broadway, 1995, curator, photographer (exhibitions) Hirschfeld Celebration at Leica Gallery, N.Y.C., 2002; exhibitions include Art Students League, 2007, one-woman shows include The Leica Gallery, N.Y.C., 2002; curator, writer Hirschfeld British Aisles, 2005; author (organizer): (exhibit) Art Students League, NYC, 2007. Vol. Persian Gulf War Am. Jewish Congress, Israel, 1991; elected mem. Tony Awards nominating com. Am. Theatre Wing, 2000-2003; co-chair Al Hirschfeld Centennial, assoc. prodr. Al Hirschfeld 100th Birthday Salute, 2003; pres. Al Hirschfeld Found., 2004-. Mem. Theatre Libr. Assn. Democrat. Address: c/o Al Hirschfeld Found 122 E 95th St New York NY 10128-1705

KES, VICKI, museum director; b. Bessemer, Ala., June 2, 1952; d. Gerald Vance and Marjorie Jean (Bush) George; m. Pieter A. Kes, Sr., Nov., 2002; children: Alissa Henson, Rebecca Hubbard. Office worker Mining Corp. of the South, Vance, Ala., 1978-79; artist, sign painter Bob's Sign Shop, Midfield, Ala., 1980—; dir. Iron & Steel Mus. of Ala., McCalla, 1980—. Program completion Office of Mus Programs, Smithsonian, Washington, 1987. Artist (book) Tannehill Crafts, 1982. Events Planner Ala. Reunion State of Ala., Montgomery, 1989. Recipient Top 20 Events in the South East award SE Tourism Soc., Atlanta, 1986-87, 88, 91, Head Start Vol. award, 1994. Mem. Ala. Preservation Alliance, Soc. Indsl. Archaeology, Nat. Trust for Hist. Preservation, Birmingham Area Mus. Assn., Am. Assn. State and Local History (program completion 1980), Am. Assn. Mus., Ala. Mus. Assn. (sec.-treas. 1983-85, chair com. Southeastern Museums Conf. 1999, co-chair com. 2000, Meritorious Svc. award 1983), Ala. State Employees Assn. (pres. Tannehill chpt. 1993-99). Democrat. Baptist. Avocations: pen, ink drawings, painting. Home: 258 Stipes Rd West Blocton AL 35184 Office: Tannehill Historical State Park 12632 Confederate Pkwy Mc Calla AL 35111-2620 Business E-Mail: tannehillmuseum@att.net.

KESARI, SANTOSH, neurologist, oncologist, neuroscientist; s. Sriramloo and Sarojini Kesari; m. Jyothsna Ashili, Dec. 7, 2000; 1 child, Sneha Lakshmi. BA, U. Pa., 1992, PhD, 1996, MD, 1999. Diplomate Am. Bd. Psychiatry and Neurology, 2005. Med. intern Beth Israel Deaconess Med. Ctr., Boston, 1999—2000; neurology resident Mass. Gen. Hosp., Brigham and Women's Hosp., Boston, 2000—03; neuro-oncologist Dana-Farber Cancer Inst., Boston, 2003—; neurologist Brigham and Women's Hosp., Boston, 2003—. Asst. prof. Harvard Med. Sch., 2007—. Recipient Disting. Scientist award, Sontag Found., 2006. Mem.: Am. Acad. Neurology (Aux. Founders award 2003). Office: Dana-Farber Cancer Inst 44 Binney St Boston MA 02115 Office Phone: 617-632-2166. Office Fax: 617-632-4773. Business E-Mail: skesari@partners.org.

KESARWALA, HEMANT, pediatrician, educator; MD, U. Bombay, India, 1971. Diplomate Am. Bd. Pediatrics, Am. Bd. Allergy/Immunology. Intern in pediat. L.T.M.G. Hosp., Bombay, 1970—71; resident in pediat. Lincoln Hosp., Bronx, NY; fellow in pediatric allergy, immunology Children's Hosp. Med. Ctr. U. Cin., 1978—79, physician dept. pediat., 1992—2004; clin. prof. pediat. Robert Wood Johnson U. Hosp., New Brunswick, NJ; clin. prof. Drexel U. Coll. Medicine, 2005—. Clin. prof. Pediatrics Robert Wood Johnson Univ. Hosp., New Brunswick, NJ, 1992—. Mailing: 3084 Rt 27 6 Kendall Park NJ 08824 Office Phone: 732-821-0595.

KESHAVARZIAN, ABTIN, electrical engineer, researcher; b. Tehran, Iran, Sept. 17, 1977; arrived in US, 2001; s. Manouchehr Keshavarzian and Delroba Parsi. BS, Sharif U. Tech., Tehran, Iran, 1999; MS, Shairf U. Tech., Tehran, Iran, 2001; PhD in Elec. Engring., Stanford U., Calif., 2005. Rsch. asst. Stanford U., 2002—04; sr. rsch. engr. Bosch Rsch. and Tech. Ctr., Palo Alto, Calif., 2005—. Scholar, Stanford U., 2003. Mem.: Persian Student Assn. (pres. 2003—04). Achievements include patents pending for wakeup scheduling methods for wireless sensor networks; energy-efficient algorithms for wireless sensor networks; research in synchronization in optical CDMA networks; neighbor discovery in wireless networks. Home: 2257 Yale St Palo Alto CA 94306 Office: Bosch Rsch and Tech Ctr 4009 Miranda Ave Palo Alto CA 94304 Home Phone: 650-387-5390; Office Phone: 650-320-2947.

KESHIAN, RICHARD, lawyer; b. Arlington, Mass., Aug. 11, 1934; s. Hamayak and Takuhe (Malkesian) K.; m. Jacqueline C. Cannilla, Sept. 11, 1965; children: Carolyn D., Richard M. (dec. 1999). BSBA, Boston U., 1956, JD, 1958. Bar: Mass. 1958. Pvt. practice law, Arlington, 1964-71; ptnr. Keshian & Reynolds, PC, Arlington, 1971—. Instr. bus. law George Washington U., 1961—63; adv. bd. Coop. Bank Concord, Arlington, 1984—91; gen. counsel Arlington Coop. Bank, 1978—83; mem. curriculum com. Mass. Continuing Legal Edn., Inc. Chmn. Arlington Zoning Bd. Appeals, 1972—76; pres. Arlington C. of C., 1976; v.p. Mass. Fedn. Planning Bds., 1978—85; mem. Arlington Contributory Retirement Bd., 1984—. Mem.: ABA (standing com. on lawyer guaranty funds), Mass. Assn. Bank Counsel (bd. dirs. 1985—2002, pres. 1992—95), Real Estate Bar Assn. Mass. (chmn. title stds. com. 1996—2000, bd. dirs. 1996—, clk. 1999—2001, pres. 2003, curriculum com. Mass. CLE 2001—), Am. Arbitration Assn. (arbitrator 1975—), Mass. Bar Assn. Democrat. Congregationalist. Home: 93 Falmouth Rd W Arlington MA 02474-1007 Office: 1040 Massachusetts Ave Arlington MA 02476 Office Phone: 781-646-0600. Personal E-mail: j-dkeshian@comcast.net. Business E-Mail: rkeshian@krtlaw.com.

KESHVALA, SEELPA H, secondary school educator; b. Milw., June 30, 1975; d. Hamir K and Mani M Keshvala. BS, U. Wis., Milw., 1998, MS, postgrad., U. Wis., Milw., 2000—. Principal and Superintendency Licensure Wis., 2004, Professional Educator Wis. Dept. of Edn., 1998. Tchr. Milw. Pub. Schools, 1998—2002, Milw. Area Tech. Coll., 2002—. Recipient Barbara L. Jackson Scholar, UCEA, 2004, Holmes Scholar, Holmes Partnership Acad., 2005, Lura M. Currithurs Scholarship, Pi Lambda Theta, Beta Epsilon Chpt., 2000, Advanced Opportunity Program (AOP) Fellowship, Grad. Sch., 2002—03, 2003—04, 2004—05. Mem.: Holmes Partnership Acad. (Holmes Scholar 2005), U. Coun. of Ednl. Adminstrn., Am. Edn. Rsch. Assn., Pi Lambda Theta. Hindu. Home: 1100 W Wells St Apt 811 Milwaukee WI 53233 Office: Dept of Administrative Leadership Enderis Hall Room 658 Milwaukee WI 53201 Home Phone: 414-291-8868; Office Phone: 414-229-2868. Office Fax: 414-229-5300. Personal E-mail: keshvala@uwm.edu.

KESLER, JAY LEWIS, retired academic administrator; b. Barnes, Wis., Sept. 15, 1935; m. H. Jane Smith; children: Laura, Bruce, Terri. Student, Ball State U., 1953-54; BA, Taylor U., 1958, LHD (hon.), 1982; Dr. Divinity (hon.), Barrington Coll., 1977; DD (hon.), Asbury Theol. Sem., 1984, Anderson U., 1999; HHD (hon.), Huntington Coll., 1983; LHD, John Brown U., 1987; LLD (honoris causa), Gordon Coll., 1992; DD (hon.), Union U., 2000, Trinity Internat. U., 2001; LHD (honoris causa), So. Wesleyan U., 2002. Dir. Marion (Ind.) Youth for Christ, 1955-58, crusade staff evangelist, 1959-60, dir. Ill.-Ind. region, 1960-62, dir. coll. recruitment, 1962-63, v.p. pers., 1963-68, v.p. field coordination, 1968-73, pres., 1973-85, also bd. dirs.; pres. Taylor U., Upland, Ind., 1985-2000, chancellor, 2000—03, pres. emeritus, 2003—; tchg. pastor Upland Cmty. Ch., 2002—. Bd. dirs. Star Fin. Group, Christianity Today, Brotherhood Mut. Ins. Co., Nat. Ass. Evangs., Youth for Christ Internat., Youth for Christ U.S.A.; mem. bd. reference Christian Camps Inc.; mem. Council for Christian Colls. and Univs., bd. mem., 2001; chmn. United Christian Coll. Fund; mem. adv. bd. Christian Bible Soc.; co-pastor 1st Bapt. Ch., Geneva, 1972—85; mem. faculty Billy Graham Schs. Evangelism; lectr. Staley Disting. Christian Sch. Lecture Program; past gov.'s appointee Ind. Commn. on Youth; tchr. Upland Cmty. Ch., 2002—. Spkr. on Family Forum (daily radio show and radio program), 1973-98; mem. adv. com. Campus Life mag.; author: Let's Succeed With Our Teenagers, 1973, I Never Promised You a Disneyland, 1975, The Strong Weak People, 1976, Outside Disneyland, 1977, I Want a Home with No Problems, 1977, Growing Places, 1978, Too Big to Spank, 1978, Breakthrough, 1981, Parents & Teenagers, 1984 (Gold Medallion award), Family Forum, 1984, Making Life Make Sense, 1986, Parents and Children, 1986, Being Holy, Being Human, 1988, Ten Mistakes Parents Make With Teenagers (And How to Avoid Them), 1988, Is Your Marriage Really Worth Fighting For?, 1989, Energizing Your Teenagers' Faith, 1990, Raising Responsible Kids, 1991, Grandparenting: The Agony and the Ecstasy, 1993, Challenges for the College Bound, 1994, Emotionally Healthy Teenagers, 1998; contbr. articles to profl. jours. Bd. advisors Prison Fellowship Internat., Christian Camps Inc., Christian Educators Assn. Internat., Evangelicals for Social Action, Love and Action, Venture Middle East, Internat. Com. of Reference for New Life 2000. Named sr. fellow, Coun. Christian Coll., 2000, Sagamore of the Wabash, 2000; recipient Angel award, Religion in Media, 1985, Outstanding Youth Leadership award, Religious Heritage Am., 1989. Office: Taylor U Office Pres 236 W Reade Ave Upland IN 46989-1002

KESLER, JOHN A., lawyer, real estate developer; b. Clark County, Ill., Apr. 25, 1923; s. Hal H. and Clara (Hurst) K.; m. Maxine Ruth Weaver, May 13, 1948; children: Nicki Kesler Herrington, Bradley Weaver, John A. II. AB, Ind. State U., 1948; JD, Ind. U., 1951. Bar: Ind. 1951, Ill. 1951. Chief dep. prosecutor County Vigo, Terre Haute, Ind., 1954-58; probate commr. Cir. Ct., 1971-74; mem. ho. reps. Ind. Legis., 1969-73; asst. state atty. County Madison, Edwardsville, Ill., 1985-88; pvt. practice law Terre Haute, 1951—. Pres. Wabash Valley Land Developers, Inc., Terre Haute, 1979—. Staff sgt. U.S. Army, 1943-46. Recipient Legion of Honor, Am Legion Medal of Honor, Good Govt. award West Vigo Jaycees, 1971, Civic Svc. award U.S. Jaycees, 1957; named Outstanding Pub. Offcl. Terre Haute Jaycees. Mem. ABA, Nat. Assn. Criminal Def. Lawyers, Terre Haute Bar Assn., Ind. Bar Assn., VFW (life), Am. Legion (life), United War Vets. Coun. Vigo County (past commdr.), SAR (state pres., nat. trustee), Exchange Club (pres.), Ind. U. Emeritus Club, Sagamore of the Wabash, Shriners, Grand Soc. Sycamores, Honorable Order of Ky. Cols., Grotto. Democrat. Methodist. Avocations: bowling, genealogy, reading. Home: 76 S Thorpe Pl West Terre Haute IN 47885 Office: 219 Ohio St Terre Haute IN 47807-3420 Office Phone: 812-235-1255.

KESLER, STEPHEN EDWARD, geology educator; BS with honors, U. N.C., 1962; PhD, Stanford U., 1966. Asst. prof. econ. geology La. State U., Baton Rouge, 1966-70; assoc. prof. U. Toronto, Ont., Canada, 1970-77; prof. U. Mich., Ann Arbor, 1977—, assoc. chair, 1998—2007. Vis. scientist Nat. Inst. Geography, Guatemala, 1966-69, Consejo Recursos Minerales, Mexico City, 1974-75; with Dirrección General Minas, Santo Domingo, 1983-84; cons. exploration for metallic and non-metallic mineral deposits. Author: Our Finite Mineral Resources, 1975; (with others) Economic Geology of Central Dominican Republic, 1984, Mineral Resources: Economics and the Environment, 1994; assoc. editor Econ. Geology, 1981-91, Ore Geology Revs., 1999-2005; mem. editl. bd. Jour. Geochem. Exploration, 1984-98. Pres. bd. trustees Lord of Light Luth. Ch., 1989-91. Fellow Geol. Soc. Am., Soc. Econ. Geologists (councillor 1983-86, internat. lectr. 1989-90, v.p. 1990-91, Thayer Lindsley lectr. 1994-95, pres. 1998-99, Penrose medal 2007); mem. Assn. Exploration Geochemists (councillor 1981-84), Soc. Mining Engrs. of AIME (program chmn. 1977). Lutheran. Office: U Mich Dept Geol Scis Ann Arbor MI 48109 Office Phone: 734-763-5057.

KESLER, THEODORE B., educational consultant; b. Sept. 9, 1961; BA, Columbia U., NY, 1983, MA, 1988, EdD, 2007. Tchr. PSTS, NYC, 1988—98, The Spl. Music Sch. Am., NYC, 1998—2001; ednl. cons. The Reading and Writing Project Tchrs. Coll., NYC, 2001—. Co-author: (book) Raising the Quality of Personal Narratives, 2006. Grant, NEH, 1994. Mem.: Academic Educators Rsch. Assn., Nat. Coun. Tchrs. English.

KESSEL, BRINA, ornithologist, educator, researcher; b. Ithaca, NY, Nov. 20, 1925; d. Marcel and Quinta (Cattell) K.; m. Raymond B. Roof, June 19, 1957 (dec. 1968). BS, Cornell U., 1947, PhD, 1951; MS, U. Wis., Madison, 1949. Student asst. Patuxent Rsch. Refuge, 1946; student tchg. asst. Cornell U., 1945-47, grad. asst., 1947-48, 49-51; asst. Wis. Alumni Rsch. Found., 1948—49; instr. biol. sci. U. Alaska, summer 1951, asst. prof. biol. sci., 1951-54, assoc. prof. zoology, 1954-59, prof. zoology, 1959-96, head dept. biol. scis., 1957-66, dean Coll. Biol. Scis. and Renewable Resources, 1961-72, curator terrestrial vertebrate mus. collections, 1972-90, curator ornithology collection, 1990-95, adminstrv. assoc. for acad. programs, grad. and undergrad., dir. acad. advising, office of chancellor, 1973-80, sr. scientist, 1996-99, prof. emeritus, dean emeritus, curator emeritus, 1999—. Project dir. U. Alaska ecol. investigations for AEC Project Chariot, 1959—63; ornithol. investigations N.W. Alaska pipeline, 1976—81, Susitna Hydroelectric Project, 1980—83. Author books; contbr. articles to profl. jours. Recipient Outstanding Contbn. award Alaska Bird Conf.; U. Alaska with ann. award Brina Kessel Medal for Excellence in Sci. named in her honor; swale pond at Creamer's Field Migratory Waterfowl Refuge in Fairbanks named in her honor. Fellow AAAS, Am. Ornithologists' Union (v.p. 1977, pres.-elect 1990-92, pres. 1992-94), Arctic Inst. N.Am.; mem. Wilson Ornithol. Soc., Cooper Ornithol. Soc., Soc. Northwestern Vertebrate Biology, Pacific Seabird Group, Arctic Audubon Soc. (hon.), Assn. Field Ornithologists, Sigma Xi (pres. U. Alaska 1957), Phi Kappa Phi, Sigma Delta Epsilon. Achievements include research in European Starling in North America; biogeography, seasonality, and biology of birds in Alaska. Office: U Alaska Mus of the North PO Box 80211 Fairbanks AK 99708-0211 Business E-Mail: ffbxk@uaf.edu.

KESSEL, JOHN HOWARD, political scientist, educator; b. Dayton, Ohio, Oct. 13, 1928; s. Arthur V. and Helen (Hopkins) K.; m. Margaret Sarah Wagner, Aug. 22, 1954; children— Robert Arthur, Thomas John. Student, Purdue U., 1946-48; BA, Ohio State U., 1950; PhD, Columbia U., 1958. Instr. Amherst and Mt. Holyoke colls., 1957-58; instr., asst. prof. Amherst Coll., 1958-61; asst. prof. U. Wash., 1961-65; Arthur E. Braun prof. polit. sci. Allegheny Coll., Meadville, Pa., 1965-70; prof. polit. sci. Ohio State U., Columbus, 1970-94, prof. emeritus, 1994—. Vis. prof. U. Calif., San Diego, 1977, U. Wash., 1980, Am. U., 1980. Author: The Goldwater Coalition: Republican Strategies in 1964, 1968, The Domestic Presidency, 1975, Presidential Campaign Politics: Coalition Strategies and Citizen Response, 1980, 4th edit., 1992, Presidential Parties, 1984, Presidents, the Presidency, and the Political Environment, 2001; co-editor: Micropolitics-Individual and Group Level Concepts, 1970, Theory Building and Data Analysis in the Social Sciences, 1984, Researching the Presidency: Vital Questions, New Approaches, 1993; editor Am. Jour. Polit. Sci, 1974-76; contbr. articles to profl. jours. Mem. exec. council Inter-Univ. Consortium for Polit. Research, 1964-65, 67-68; Exec. dir. Nixon-Lodge Vols. Mass., 1960; dir. arts, scis. div. Republican Nat. Com., 1963-64. Served with USN, 1950-53. Guest scholar, Brookings Inst., 1972, vis. scholar, Am. Enterprise Inst., 1980—82. Mem. Am. Polit. Sci. Assn. (exec. council 1969-71), Midwest Polit. Sci. Assn. (pres. 1978-79) Home: 516 E Schreyer Pl Columbus OH 43214-2273 Business E-Mail: kessel.1@osu.edu.

KESSEL, LLOYD R., nursing administrator, educator; b. Dickinson, ND, Oct. 24, 1952; s. Wendell Kasper and Tomasita (Martinez) Kessel; m. Kathleen Kessel, Nov. 24, 1988; children: Taylor Steven, Danielle Rose. BSN, Mary Coll., Bismarck, ND, 1975; MSN summa cum laude, U. of Mary, Bismarck, 1989. Dir. nursing svcs. Richardton (N.D.) Community Hosp.; sr. staff nurse oper. room Whittaker Life Scis., Khamis Mushayt, Saudi Arabia; health care officer S.W. Milti-County Correction Ctr., Dickinson; instr. nursing Dickinson State U.; supr. oper. room, anesthesia, day surgery St. Joseph's Hosp., Dickinson, dir. respiratory care svcs., dir. acute care nursing; coord. therapeutic svcs. Dakota Juvenile Corrections Facility, 2000—04; advanced psychiatric nurse pvt. practice, 2004—. Prodr.(poet):; contbr. Mem.: ANA, N.D. Nursing Assn. (ethics com., psychiat./mental health nursing com.), S.W. Mental Health Assn., N.D. Psychiat. Nursing Edn. Coun., Assn. Oper. Rm. Nurses, Sigma Theta Tau. Home: 821 3rd Ave W Dickinson ND 58601-3810

KESSEL, MARK, lawyer; b. Krasnik, Poland, June 14, 1941; arrived in U.S., 1948; s. Leo and Erna (Friedman) Kessel; m. Elaine Keit, Aug. 29, 1966; children: Greer Kessel Hendricks, Robert W. BA with honors in Econs., CUNY, 1963; JD magna cum laude, Syracuse U., 1966. Bar: N.Y. Assoc. Shearman & Sterling, NYC, 1971-77, ptnr., 1977—2001, mng. ptnr., 1990-94; mng. dir. Symphony Capital LLC, NYC, 2002—. Bd. dirs. Antigenics, Inc., Global Alliance for Tb Drug Devel. Bd. dirs. San Francisco Psychoanalytic Inst., 1988—90, Mus. City of N.Y., 1993—2003, W.M. Keck Found., LA, 1985—86; dir. Heller Fin., Inc., 1992—2001; bd. visitors Syracuse U. Coll. Law, 2002—. Capt. JAGC US Army, 1963—71. Avocations: reading, running. Office: Symphony Capital LLC 875 3d Ave New York NY 10022 Business E-Mail: mark@symphonycapital.com.

KESSEL, PHIL, professional hockey player; b. Madison, WI, Oct. 2, 1987; Center Boston Bruins, 2006—. Player NHL YoungStars Game, 2007. Recipient Bill Masterton Trophy, 2007. Office: c/o Boston Bruins TD Banknorth Garden 100 Legends Way Boston MA 02114*

KESSEL, RICHARD GLEN, zoology educator; b. Fairfield, Iowa, July 19, 1931; BS in Chemistry summa cum laude, Parsons Coll., 1953; MS in Zoology and Physiology, U. Iowa, 1956, PhD in Zoology and Cytology, 1959; postgrad., Marine Biol. Lab., 1957. Trainee dept. anatomy Wake Forest U. Sch. Medicine, Winston-Salem, NC, 1959-60, Nat. Inst. Gen. Med. Sci. postdoctoral rsch. fellow, 1960-61, instr. anatomy, 1959-61, asst. prof., 1961; asst. prof. biology U. Iowa, Iowa City, 1961—64, assoc. prof., 1964-68, prof., 1968—97, prof. emeritus, 1998—. Vis. investigator Hopkins Marine Sta., Pacific Grove, Calif., 1966; ind. investigator Marine Biol. Lab., Woods Hole, Mass., summers 1960, 62, 64. Author: (with C.Y. Shih) Scanning Electron Microscopy in Biology: A Students' Text-Atlas of Biological Organization, 1974, (with R.H. Kardon) Tissues and Organs: A Text-Atlas of Scanning Electron Microscopy, 1979, (with C.Y. Shih) Living Images, 1982, (with R. Roberts and H. Tung) Freeze Fracture Images of Cells and Tissues, 1991, Basic Medical Histology, 1998; assoc. editor Jour. Exptl. Zoology, 1978-82; mem. editorial bd. Jour. Submicroscopic Cytology, 1980—; mem. internat. bd. editors Scanning Electron Microscopy in Biology and Medicine; contbr. articles to profl. jours., chpts. to books Grantee USPHS, 1961-78, NSF, 1969-71, Whitehall Found., 1982-84; Bodine fellow; George Lincoln Seeley scholar; Nat Inst. Gen. Med. Sci.-USPHS, 1964-69; established endowed med. scholarship U. Iowa Coll. Medicine, established embryology course lecture Marine Biol. Lab., Woods Hole, Mass. Mem. AAAS, Am. Soc. Cell Biology, Am. Assn. Anatomists, Electron Micros. Soc. Am., Am. Physiol. Soc., Soc. Study of Reprodn., Am. Soc. Zoologists, Am. Inst. Biol. Sci., Soc. Devel. Biology, The 1847 Soc., Whitman Soc., Sigma Xi, Phi Kappa Phi, Beta Beta Beta. Office: Univ Iowa Dept Biol Scis Iowa City IA 52242

KESSELER, MATTHEW JOHN, librarian; b. Mt. Lebanon, Pa., Oct. 21, 1969; s. Robert Charles and Georgia Ellen Kesseler. AA in Univ. Parallel Tchr. Edn., C.C. Allegheny County, Pitts., 1990; BA in History, U. Pitts., 1993, MLS, 1994. Libr. grad. intern Hillman Libr. U. Pitts., 1994-95, libr. specialist III Chemistry/Computer Sci. Libr., 1998-99; part-time reference libr. Gumberg Libr. Duquesne U., Pitts., 1995-97; asst. libr. Pfeiffer Libr. Tiffin (Ohio) U., 1997-98; asst. libr. N. Libr. Cambria County Area C.C., Ebensburg, Pa., 1999—2000; film libr. U. Pitts. Med. Ctr.-Montefiore Film Libr., Pa., 2001; asst. ref. libr. Maag Libr., Youngstown (Ohio) State U., 2001—02; libr. State Correctional Instn., Cresson, 2003—. Democrat. Roman Catholic. Avocations: reading, computers, piano, travel.

KESSELMAN, DAVID W., lawyer; b. Van Nuys, Calif., Jan. 20, 1973; BA, Univ. Calif., Irvine, 1994; MA, London Sch. Econ., 1995; JD, Univ. Calif., Davis, 1999. Bar: Calif. 1999, US Dist. Ct. Ctrl. Calif. Assoc., comml. litigation Blecher & Collins, LA, 2000—. Named a Rising Star, So. Calif. Super Lawyers, 2005—06. Mem.: ABA, State Bar Calif., LA County Bar Assn., Assn. Bus. Trial Lawyers. Office: Blecher & Collins 17th Fl 515 S Figueroa St Los Angeles CA 90071 Office Phone: 213-622-4222. Office Fax: 213-622-1656. Business E-Mail: dkesselman@blechercollins.com.

KESSELMAN, JONATHAN RHYS, economics professor, public policy researcher; b. Columbus, Ohio, Mar. 17, 1946; s. Louis C. and Jennie K.; m. Sheila Kaplan, Mar. 12, 1973; 1 child, Maresa. BA with honors, Oberlin Coll., 1968; PhD in Econs., MIT, 1972. Asst. prof. econs. U. B.C., Vancouver, Canada, 1972-76, assoc. prof., 1976-81, prof., 1981—2003, dir. Ctr. for Rsch. on Econ. and Social Policy, 1992—2003; prof. pub. policy Simon Fraser U., Vancouver, 2004—, Can. rsch. chair in pub. fin., 2004—. Rsch. assoc. Inst. for Rsch. on Poverty, Madison, Wis., 1974-75; vis. scholar Delhi Sch. Econs., New Delhi, 1978-79; cons. econs., 1973—; prin. investigator Equality, Security and Cmty. Rsch. Project, 1998-2004. Author: Financing Canadian Unemployment Insurance, 1983, Rate Structure and Personal Taxation, 1990, General Payroll Taxes, 1997, Tax Design for a Northern Tiger, 2004; co-editor: Dimensions of Inequality in Canada, 2006; mem. editl. bd. Can. Pub. Policy, 1997—, Can. Tax Jour., 1999—; contbr. numerous articles on taxation, income security, employment policy to profl. jours. Bd. dirs. Tibetan Refugee Aid Soc., Vancouver, 1980-82; mem. adv. panel Can. Ministry Employment and Immigration, Ottawa, Ont., 1982-83; mem. B.C. Econ. Policy Inst., 1983-86; trustee pension plan U. B.C., 1988-90; chmn. Musqueam Indian Band Taxation Adv. Coun., 1992-96, mem., 1996-98; mem. B.C. Premier's Forum on New Opportunities for Working and Living, 1994-95; mem. compliance adv. com. Revenue Can. Taxation, 1997-99. Sr. scholar Oberlin Coll., 1967-68; NSF fellow, 1968-70; grantee U.S. Dept. Labor, 1971-72; leave fellow Can. Coun., (locat.) New Delhi, 1978-79; grantee Social Sci. and Humanities Rsch. Coun. Can., 1983-84, 90—; vis. fellow Australian Nat. U., Canberra, 1985; professorial fellow in econ. policy Res. Bank of Australia, 1985; recipient Doug Purvis award, Can. Econ. Assn., 1998, 2007. Mem. Am. Econ. Assn., Can. Econs. Assn., Can. Tax Found. (Douglas Sherbaniuk award 2002). Office: Simon Fraser U Pub Policy Program 515 W Hastings St Vancouver BC Canada V6B 5K3

KESSELMAN, MARC L., federal agency administrator; b. 1971; married; 2 children. BA, Cornell U.; JD, U. Pa. Bar: 1997. Law clk. to Hon. Julia S. Gibbons US Dist. Ct., Memphis, 1996—97; assoc. Ropes & Gray, LLP; trial atty. fed. programs br. US Dept. Justice, sr. counsel office legal policy Washington; assoc. gen. counsel office Office Mgmt. & Budget, Exec. Office of the Pres.; dep. gen. counsel Office Mgmt. & Budget, Exec. Office of the Pres.; gen. counsel USDA, 2006—. Office: Jamie L Whitten Fed Bldg 14th and Independence Ave SW Rm 107-W Washington DC 20250 Office Phone: 202-720-3351. Office Fax: 202-720-8666.

KESSELRING, DEBBIE ANNE, systems engineer; b. Durham, NC, July 21, 1965; d. Henry G. and Maria K.; m. Timothy J. Dacey; 1 child, Denise. BS in Aero. Engring., U. Md., 1987; MS in Systems Engring., Va. Tech. Inst., 1995. Engring. cons. VEDA Inc., 1988-89; structural engr. Naval Air Sys. Command, 1989-93, air-to-air missile program analyst, 1993-95; sys. engr. Ballistic Missile Def. Orgn., 1995—98; prin. engr. Computer Scis. Corp., 1998—2001, dep. dir., 2003—. Mem. AIAA (sr.).

KESSINGER, KEVIN M., diversified financial services company executive; BA, So. Ill. Univ.; MBA, Capital Univ., Ohio; post-grad. studies, Ohio St. Univ. Mng. dir. BancOne Fin. Card Svcs., Columbus, Ohio; exec. v.p. strategic bus. American AAdvantage Credit Card Program; chmn. CitiBank USA; COO CitiCards; exec. v.p. global consumer group, pres. consumer fin. No. Am. Citigroup, now Chief Ops., Tech. officer. Office: Citigroup 399 Park Ave New York NY 10043

KESSINGER, THOMAS ANTHONY, education educator, social studies educator, researcher, consultant; b. Portsmouth, Ohio; s. William Thomas and Hilma Kathryn (Wade) Kessinger; m. A. Jane Kessinger; children: Amy K. Chelman, Ann Marie. BS summa cum laude, Xavier U., Cin., 1969, MEd, 1971; MA, U. Cin., 1978, PhD, 1997. Cert. permanent comprehensive social studies Dept. Edn., Ohio, 1980, profl. supr. cert. Dept. Edn., Ohio, 2005, adminstr. lic. in ednl. rsch. Dept. Edn., Ohio, 2005, cert. adminstrv. lic. HS prin. Dept. Edn., Ohio, 2005, adminstrv. lic. elem. sch. prin. Dept. Edn., Ohio, 2005. Mid. sch. tchr. Wyo. Mid. Sch., Ohio, 1972—81; secondary tchr. Wyo. HS, 1979—2002; adj. prof. Xavier U., Cin., 1986—2002, prof., 2002—, cons., 2003—; grad. tchg. asst. U. Cin., 1990—92. Project coord., svc. learning cons. Wyo. City Schs., 2002—. Co-author: Teacher's Guide for Here's Ohio, 1989, Japan: Lesson Plans for Junior High Schools, 1994, Learning About Our World: Japan, 1997, Lessons About Japan for P-12 Educators, 2003; contbr. articles to profl. jours. Mem. content adv. and range finding com. graduation tests Ohio Dept. Edn., Columbus, 2004—. Lt. col. US Army, 1969—96, Columbus, with USAR. Named Tchr. of yr., Ohio Coun. for the Social Studies, 1985; recipient Disting. Achievement award in Geography, Nat. Coun. Geog. Edn., 1984, Learn and Serve Am. awards, Ohio Dept. Edn., 2002—07, Wheeler grant award, Xavier U., 2003, Info. Fluency award, 2005. Mem.: Res. Officers Assn., Ohio Confederation of Tchr. Edn. Orgns., Mid-Western Ednl. Rsch. Assn., Midwest History Edn. Soc., History Edn. Soc., Ohio Assn. Tchr. Educators, Ohio Coun. Social Studies, Nat. Social Studies Supr. Assn., Assn. Tchr. Educators, Profl. Tchrs. Econs. Assn., Global Assn. Tchrs. Econs., Soc. for Study of Curriculum History, Nat. Coun. Social Studies, Econs. Ctr. Edn. and Rsch. (assoc.), Assn. of US Army, Phi Delta Kappa Internat. Roman Catholic. Avocations: reading, travel, volunteering. Home: 10008 Clydesdale Dr Cincinnati OH 45231-2776 Office: Xavier U 3800 Victory Pkwy Cincinnati OH 45207-6521 Office Phone: 513-745-3725. Office Fax: 513-745-1052. Business E-Mail: kessinger@xavier.edu.

KESSLER, A. D., business, financial, investment and real estate advisor, consultant, educator, lecturer, author; b. N.Y.C., May 1, 1923; s. Morris William and Belle Miriam (Pastor) K.; m. Ruth Schwartz, Nov. 20, 1944 (div. 1974); children: Brian Lloyd, Judd Stuart, Earl Vaughn; m. Jaclyn Jeanne Sprague. Student U. Newark, 1940-41, Rutgers U., 1941-42, 46, Albright Coll., 1942, Newark Coll. Engring., 1946; PhD in Pub. Adminstrn. U. Fla., 1972; MBA, Kensington U., 1976, PhD in Mgmt. and Behavioral Psychology, 1977. Sr. cert. rev. appraiser; cert. bus. counselor; cert. exchanger; registered mortgage underwriter; registered investment advisor. Pvt. practice real estate, ins. and bus. brokerage, N.J., Pa., Fla., N.Y., Nev., Calif., Hong Kong, 1946—; pres. Armor Corp. , 1947-68; pres. Folding Carton Corp., Am., N.Y.C., 1958-68; exec. v.p. Henry Schindall Assocs., N.Y.C., 1966-67; tax rep. Calif. State Bd. Equalization, 1968-69; aviation cons. transp. div. Calif., Dept. Aeros., also pub. info. officer; 1969-71; FAA Gen. Aviation Safety Counselor; broker, mgr. La Costa (Calif.) Sales Corp., 1971-75; chmn. bd. Profl. Ednl. Found., 1975—, Timeshare Resorts Internat., 1975—, Interex, Leucadia, Calif., 1975-82, The Kessler Orgn., Rancho Santa Fe, Calif., 1975—, The Kessler Fin. Group, Fin. Ind. Inst., 1977—; pres. Ednl. Video Inst., 1978—, Fin. Planning Inst., 1975—, Rancho Santa Fe Real Estate & Land, Inc., 1975—; treas., exec. bd. dirs. Nat. Challenge Com. on Disability, 1983-90; dir. Practice Mgmt. Cons. Abacus Data Systems, 1984—; broker mgr. Rancho Sante Fe Acreage & Homes, Inc., 1987-89; mktg. dir. Commercial Real Estate Services, Rancho Santa Fe, 1987—; cons. broker Glenct. Properties Ptnrs., 1989-90; dir. U.S. Advisors, 1989—; founder Creative Real Estate Movement, 1946—; pub., editor in chief Creative Real Estate Mag., 1975—; pub. Creative Real Estate Mag. of Australia and New Zealand; founder, editor Moderator of Tape of the Month Club; founder, producer, chmn. Internat. Real Estate Expo; chmn. bd. The Brain Trust, Rancho Santa Fe, Calif., 1977—; fin. lectr. for Internat. Cruise Ships, Cunard Line, Norwegian Am. Cruises, P&O, Princess, others; lectr. life enrichment and stress mgmt. Internat. Cruise Ships; Calif. adj. faculty, prof. fin. Clayton U., St. Louis; developer, operator Barnegat Baywood Seaplane Base, Barnegat Bay, N.J.; owner, operator Skyline Airport, Hunterdon County, N.J. Scoutmaster Orange Mountain coun. Boy Scouts Am., 1955-62; harbor master N.J. Marine Patrol, 1958-67; dep. sheriff, Essex County, N.J., 1951-65; mem. pres.' adv. bd. Seton Hall U., 1961-64; chmn. Stop Smoking, 1990, Quick Study, 1990; feature broadcaster/producer Kalaidascope Radio Mag., Am. Radio Network, 1990—. Served with USAF, 1942-45. Decorated D.F.C., Air medal, Purple Heart; named to French Legion of Honor, Order of Lafayette; named a flying col, a.d.c., Gov. of Ga., 1957. Mem. Am. Soc. Editors and Pubs., Author's Guild, Internat. Platform Assn., Nat. Speakers Assn., Nat. Press Photographers Assn., Guild Assn. Airport Execs., Aviation and Space Writers Assn., Nat. Assn. of Real Estate Editors, Internat. Exchangors Assn. (founder), Air Force Assn. (dep. comdr. N.J. chpt. 1955-57). Clubs: Nat. Press, Overseas Press, La Costa Country, Cuyamaca, Rancho Santa Fe Country, Passport. Lodges: Masons, Shriners. Author: A Fortune At Your Feet, 1981, How You Can Get Rich, Stay Rich and Enjoy Being Rich, 1981, Financial Independence, 1987, The Profit, 1987, A Fortune at Your Feet in the '90s, 1994, The Midas Touch, Turning Paper Into Gold, 1994; author, instr. Your Key to Success seminar, 1988, Your Key to Creative Real Estate Success tng. program, 1996; The A to Z of Lease Purchase and 11 Other Options Training Prog.; editor: The Real Estate News Observer, 1975—; fin. editor API, 1978—; fin. columnist Money Matters, 1986—; syndicated columnist, radio and TV host of "Money Making Ideas," 1977—; songwriter: Only You, 1939, If I'm Not HomeFor Christmas, 1940, Franny, 1940, Flajaloppa, 1940, They've Nothing More Dear Only They've Got It Here, 1941, The Summer of Life, 1956; producer (movies) The Flight of the Cobra, Rena, We Have Your Daughters, Music Row; speaker for radio and TV as The Real Estate Answerman, 1975—; host (radio and TV show) Ask Mr. Money; conceptualist, exec. prodr. (TV show) The Trading Game, 1994; exec. prodr., moderator (TV show) A.D. Kessler's Real Estate Roundtable, 1993—. Inventor swivel seat, siptop, inflatumbrella. Home: PO Box 1144 Rancho Santa Fe CA 92067-1144

KESSLER, ALAN CRAIG, lawyer; b. Wash., Sept. 16, 1950; s. Alfred Milton and Josephine (Taub) K.; m. Gail Elaine Strauss, June 16, 1974; children: Stacy Ilana, Mark Jay, Daniel Jordan. BA with honors, U. Del., 1972; JD with honors, U. Md., 1975. Bar: Pa. 1975, US Dist. Ct. (ea. dist.) Pa. 1975, US Ct. Appeals (3d and 6th cirs.) 1975. Assoc. Dilworth, Paxson, Kalish, Levy & Kauffman, Phila., 1975-77, Berger & Montague, P.C., Phila., 1977-81; ptnr. Mesirov, Gelman, Jaffe, Cramer & Jamieson, Phila., 1981-91, Buchanan Ingersoll, P.C., Phila., 1991-99, Wolf, Block, Schorr & Solis-Cohen, 1999—. Instr. Inst. for Paralegal Tng., Phila., 1977-96. Mem. Presdl. Transition Team, 1992—93; vice-chmn. Pres.'s Commn. on Risk Assessment and Risk Mgmt., 1993—97; vice-chmn., bd. govs. U.S. Postal Svc., 2000—; chmn. bd. Bldg. Stds. City of Phila., 1983—84, bd. licenses and inspections rev., 1984—91; mem. City Planning Commn., Phila., 1992—97; commr. Lower Merion Twp., Pa., 1988—2000, Mayor's Commn. Homelessness, 1990—, Mayor's Com. on Spl. Svcs. Dist., 1989—; bd. dirs., pres. Randolph Ct. Assn., Phila., 1980—85; bd. dirs., v.p. South St. Neighbors Assn., Phila., 1983—87, Park Towne Pl. Tenants Assn., 1977—79; exec. com. Ctrl. Phila. Devel. Corp., 1989—, Jewish Employment Vocat. Svcs., 1989—, Phila. 2000; chair Supreme Ct. of Pa. Commn. on CLE, 1999—; fin. com. Dem. City Com. Phila., 1981—84, dep. counsel, 1980—84; mng. trustee Dem. Nat. Com., 1992—, fin. vice-chair, 2000—; chair Pa. Dem. Fin., 2003—; bd. dirs. Support Ctr. for Child Advocates, 1983—94, Phila. Indsl. Devel. Corp. Mem. ABA, Pa. Bar Assn., Phila. Bar Assn. (exec. bd. dirs. young lawyers sect., legis. liaison com., officer various coms.), Racquet Club, Radnor Valley Country Club. Democrat. Jewish. Home: 204 Daisy Ln Wynnewood PA 19096-1654 Office: Wolf Block Schorr & Solis-Cohen 1650 Arch St Fl 22 Philadelphia PA 19103-2097 Office Phone: 215-977-2588. Business E-Mail: akessler@wolfblock.com.

KESSLER, CAROL FARLEY, retired English language educator; b. Grove City, Pa., May 9, 1936; d. Louis Riley and Emily Josephine (Puder) Farley; divorced; children: Jonathan Farley, Melissa Beth. BA in English Lit., Swarthmore Coll., 1958; MAT, Radcliffe Coll., 1959; MA, PhD, U. Pa., 1977. Prof. English, Am., women's studies Delaware County campus Pa. State U., Media, 1981—2001, grad. faculty assoc., mem. women's studies core faculty, 1981—2001, coord. women's studies for Commonwealth Ednl. System, 1990, coord. campus English faculty, 1989-90; ret., 2001. Mem. Commonwealth Ednl. Sys., English grad. studies com. Pa. State U., 1991-93, mem. dissertation com. Coll. Edn., mem. numerous coms. Coll. Liberal Arts; vis. lectr. English, U. Pa., Phila., 1980, lectr. The Woman's Inst., 1979, lectr. NEH Conf., 1980, West Chester U., 1986, Pa. Humanities Coun., 1987-91, Hood Coll., Frederick, Md., 1990; colloquium evaluator Pub. Com. for Humanities in Pa., 1978; presenter Internat. Interdisciplinary Congress on Women, Hunter Coll., CUNY, 1990; women's studies discussion group Pa. Humanities Coun., 1986—; mem. Penn Mid-Atlantic Seminar for Study Women Culture and Soc., 1983—; convener, moderator, presenter panel Women's Studies Conf., Gettysburg Coll., 1991; mem. libr. com. Mont Alto Campus, Pa. State U., 1980-81, coord. women's studies faculty, 1980-81, rep. Liberal Arts Coun. Senators, 1980-81; mem. promotion and tenure com. Coll. Arts and Arch., Univ. Librs., Delaware County Campus, Pa. State U.; mem. adv. com. New Eng. Osteopathic Heritage Ctr., Maine Women Writers Collection, U. New Eng., 2001—. Author: Elizabeth Stuart Phelps, 1982, Daring to Dream: Utopian Stories by United States Women, 1836-1919, 1984, intro. excerpted and reprinted in Feminist Literary Theory: A Reader, 1986, Jour. Gen. Edn., 1985, The Story of Avis, 1877, 1987, 92, Charlotte Perkins Gilman, 1994, Daring to Dream: U.S. Women's Utopian Fiction Before 1950, 1995; mem. editl. bd. Utopian Studies, U. Mo., 1990-2001, mem. adv. bd., 1989-2001; mem. adv. bd. Utopianism and Commitarianism series Syracuse U., 1989-2001; contbr. chpts. to books, articles to profl. jours. Mus. docent Maine Hist. Soc. Wadsworth Longfellow House, 2001—. Grantee Am. Philos. Soc., 1977, Inst. for Arts and Humanistic Studies, 1981, 88, rsch. devel. grantee, 1988, faculty interchange grantee, 1981, 96, 90-91; Ford Found. fellow English Inst., U. Wis., 1962; NEH residential fellow U. Md., 1981-82; NEH stipend recipient, 1986, NEH rsch. fellow, 1988-89; Fulbright sr. lectr. Slovakia, 1995-96. Mem. MLA (mem. divsn. women's studies lang. and lit. 1985-90, coord. divsn. women's studies forum 1983, participant spl. sessions 1977, 78), Am. Culture Assn. (panelist politics and lit. 1992), Am. Literature Assn. (panelist Charlotte Perkins Gilman Soc. 1991), Am. Studies Assn. (invited panel summarizer 1979, mem. women's caucus, participant convs. 1985, 91), Nat. Coun. Tchrs. English (conf. on coll. composition and comm., participant 1984 conv.), Nat. Women's Studies Assn. (founding conv. fellowship awardee 1977, panel convener, chair 1982, 84, panel participant 1989), Northeast Modern Lang. Assn. (sect. sec., chair Am. Women Writers 1981, 82, panelist 1981, mem. women's caucus), Popular Culture Assn. (panel chair 1977, 78, 81, panel convener, chair 1984, panelist 1976-78, 81, 84, 88, 92, mem. women's caucus), Soc. Utopian Studies (adv. bd. 1988-90, edit. bd. 1991—, conf. coord. 1987, chair steering com. 1984-86, mem. 1983-88, panel chair 1983, 84, 85, 86, 87, 90, 92, presenter 1980-86, 90, 92, 1st internat. conv. 1983), Soc. Study Am. Women Writers. Democrat. Home: 112 Parsons Rd Portland ME 04103-4538 E-mail: cfk1@psu.edu.

KESSLER, CRISTY, education educator; b. Havre de Grace, Md., Feb. 13, 1971; d. James Kessler and Barbara Buchanan, Robert Buchanan (Stepfather) and Joy Kessler (Stepmother). AA, Essex C.C., Balt., 1991; BS, Towson U., Md., 1993, MEd, 1998; EdD, Wilmington Coll., Del., 2003. Cert. Nat. Bd. Profl. Tchg. Stds., 2005. Mid. sch., HS social studies tchr. Harford County Pub. Schs., Bel Air, Md., 1993—97; HS social studies tchr. Cecil County Pub. Schs., Perryville, Md., 1997—2003; dir. grad. studies dept. secondary edn. Towson U., Md., 2003—04; prof. edn. U. Hawaii, Honolulu, 2004—. Motivational spkr. Contbr. articles to profl. jours., chpt. to book. Recipient Best Paper award, Clute Inst. Acad. Rsch., 2006. Mem.: ASCD, Nat. Coun. Social Studies, Self Study of Tchr. Edn. Practices, Am. Ednl. Rsch. Assn. Office: U Hawaii 1776 University Ave Honolulu HI 96822 Home Phone: 808-782-6763; Office Phone: 808-956-4408.

KESSLER, DAVID AARON, dean, medical educator; b. NYC, May 31, 1951; m. Paulette Kessler; children: Elise, Benjamin. BA, Amherst Coll., 1973; JD, U. Chgo., 1978; MD, Harvard U., 1979. Cert. Advanced Profl. Cert. NYU Grad. Sch. Bus. Adminstrn., 1986. Intern in pediatrics Johns Hopkins Hosp., 1979—80, resident in pediatrics, 1980—82; spl. asst. to pres. Montefiore Med. Ctr., NYC, 1982—84; med. dir. Hosp. of Albert Einstein Coll. Medicine, NYC, 1984—90; tchg. appts. dept. pediatrics and dept. epidemiology and social medicine; instr. food and drug law Columbia U., NYC, 1986—90; commr. FDA Dept. Health and Human Svcs., Rockville, Md., 1990—97; dean, prof. pediatrics, internal medicine and pub. health Yale U. Med. Sch., 1997—2003; dean, vice chancellor med. affairs, prof. pediatrics U. Calif. San Francisco Sch. Medicine, 2003—; attending pediatrician Children's Hosp. Cons. US Senate Labor and Human Resources Com., 1981—84; bd. dirs. Doctors of the World; bd. dirs. Nat. Ctr. for Addiction and Substance Abuse Columbia U.; mem. White House Commn. on Presdl. Scholars. Author: A Question of Intent, 2001, numerous articles in med. jours. Chmn. bd. dirs. Elizabeth Glaser Pediatric AIDS Found.; bd. dirs. Henry J. Kaiser Family Found. Recipient Medal of Honor, Am. Cancer Soc., 1996, Pub. Welfare Medal, NAS, 2001, Nat. Pub. Affairs Spl. Recognition Award, Am. Heart Assn., Sheldon W. Andelson Pub. Policy Achievement Award, Am. Fedn. AIDS Rsch., Pub. Svc. Award, Am. Acad. Pediatrics, Franklin Delano Roosevelt Leadership Award, March of Dimes. Fellow: Am. Acad. Arts and Scis.; mem.: Inst. Medicine. Office: U Calif San Francisco Sch Medicine Dean's Office 513 Parnassus Ave San Francisco CA 94143-0410 Office Phone: 203-785-4672, 415-476-2342. Office Fax: 415-476-0689. Business E-Mail: kesslerd@medsch.ucsf.edu.

KESSLER, DIANE COOKSEY, religious organization administrator, minister; b. Jan. 8, 1947; BA in Religion, Oberlin Coll., 1969; MA in Religion and Soc., Andover Newton Theol. Sch., 1971, postgrad., 1979—; DD (hon.), Episcopal Divinity Sch., 2001. Ordained to ministry United Ch. of Christ, 1983. Assoc. dir. for strategy and action Mass. Coun. Chs., Boston, 1975-88, exec. dir., 1988—. Ind. preacher; speaker in field. Author: Parents and the Experts, 1974, God's Simple Gift: Meditations on Friendship and Spirituality, 1988; co-author: Councils of Churches and the Ecumenial Vision, 2000; editor: Together on the Way, 1999, Receive One Another.hospitality in ecumenical perspective, 2005; co-editor Encounters for Unity, 1995; also articles; mem. editl. adv. bd. Theology and Pub. Policy, 1989, 18, Mid-Stream, 1995-98. Former mem. adv. bd. Mass. Dept. Revenue; active Wellesley Congl. Ch.; mem. coun. for ecumenism United Ch. of Christ, 1984-94, chairperson coun. 1988-89, 90-91; mem. Atty Gen.'s Adv. Com. on Pub. Charities, 1988—, World Coun. of Churches, Joint Working Group, 1998-2005, 2006—; trustee Hancock Variable Series Trust I, 1999-2005; bd. dirs. Howard Benevolent Soc., 1989-96, New Eng. Holocaust Meml. Com., 1st Ch. Legacy Fund. Recipient Outstanding Woman award Coll. Club, 1990, Focolare award, 1994, Social Action Ministries award, 1995, Patron of Christian Unity award, 1998, Spirit of Hill award Candones Newton Theol. Sch., 2006. Mem. Valiant Woman award 1991), Boston Min.'s Club. Office: Mass Coun Chs 14 Beacon St Ste 416 Boston MA 02108-3704 Business E-Mail: council@masscouncilofchurches.org.

KESSLER, EDWIN, meteorology educator, consultant; b. Bklyn., Dec. 2, 1928; s. Edwin and Marie Rosa (Weil) K.; m. Lottie Catherine Menger; children: Austin Rainier, Thomas Russell. AB, Columbia Coll., 1950; MS in Meteorology, MIT, 1952, ScD in Meteorology, 1957. Chief synoptic meteorology sect. Weather Radar br. Air Force Cambridge Rsch. Lab., Bedford, Mass., 1954-61; sr. rsch. scientist Travelers Rsch. Ctr., Hartford, Conn., 1961-62, dir. atmospheric physics div., 1962-64; dir. Nat. Severe Storms Lab., Norman, Okla., 1964-86; adj. prof. U. Okla., 1964—. Vis. prof. MIT, 1975-76, McGill U., Can., 1980; bd. dirs. N.Am. Transp. Inst. Editor: Thunderstorms, A Social Scientific and Technological Documentary, 3 vols., 1982, 2d edits., 1983-88, paperback edits., vol. 1, 1988, vol. 2, 1992; contbr. articles to profl. jours. State chair Common Cause, Okla., 1993-99, vice chair, 1999-. With U.S. Army, 1946-47. Recipient award for outstanding authorship NOAA, 1971. Fellow AAAS, Am. Meteorol. Soc. (nat. councilor 1966-69, past mem. coms. on hurricanes, atmospheric electricity, agr. and forestry, cloud and precipitation physics, severe local storms, past chmn. com. on weather radar, cert. cons. meteorologist, Cleveland Abbe award for disting. svc. 1988); mem. AIAA (sr. mem.), LWV, Royal Meteorol. Soc. (fgn.), Am. Geophys. Union, Sigma Xi. Achievements include research in agriculture and energy; manager of 350 acres of pasture, streams and wilderness in central Oklahoma. Office: U Okla 100 E Boyd St Rm 684 Norman OK 73019-1028 Personal E-mail: kess3@swbell.net.

KESSLER, ERIC, broadcast executive; b. 1956; MBA, U. Pa. Wharton Sch. Brand mgr. Gillette Co., Boston, Lever Bros., NYC; mktg. mgr. HBO, NYC, 1986—89, pres. home video divsn., 1989—95, sr. v.p. mktg., 1995—99, exec. v.p., 1999—2003, pres. sales & mktg., 2003—07, co-pres., 2007—. Recipient Cable Marketer of Yr. award, Advt. Age. Office: HBO 1 Time Warner Ctr New York NY 10019-8016*

KESSLER, GALE SUZANNE, psychologist, educator; b. Chgo., Sept. 5, 1940; d. George I. Alpert and Celia Larman-Alpert-Shaps; m. Marvin Charles Facktor, June 4, 1960 (dec.); children: Greg Facktor, Charles Facktor, Laura Meehan; m. John W. Kessler, Feb. 20, 1986 (dec. Apr. 4, 2001). BA in Edn., Roosevelt U., Chgo., 1961; MS in Orgnl. Behavior, Adminstrn., George Williams Coll., Aurora, Ill., 1980. Tchr. Chgo. Pub. Schs., 1961; dir. constituency rels. George Williams Coll., 1982—85; dir. alumni rels. Grad. Sch. Bus. U. Chgo., 1986; dir. devel. Nat. MS Soc., Chgo., 1986—87; tchr. Chgo. Pub. Schs., 1987; instr. Columbia Coll., Lake Ozark, Mo., 1993—95; exec. dir. Women's Coun., Mo., 1998—2001. Internat. liaison to human svcs. George Williams Coll., Downers Grove, Ill., 1982—85; advisor Inst. for Women's Policy Rsch., Washington, 2000—01. Columnist: Consultations, 1995—98; author: Male "Mid-Life Crisis In Relation To Job Change", 1980. Chair Elmhurst Citizens for Flood Control, Ill., 1987—90; pres. Arts Coun., Lake Ozark, Mo., 1991—93; candidate state rep. State of Mo., Lake Ozark, 1997—98. Recipient Key to City, City of Elmhurst, Ill., 1990. Fellow: World Affairs Coun. (Seattle); mem.: Women's Univ. Club (co-chair com. 2003, Seattle). Avocations: reading, travel, writing, golf, tennis. Personal E-mail: gale.kessler@yahoo.com.

KESSLER, GLADYS, federal judge; b. 1938; BA, Cornell U., 1959; LLB, Harvard U., 1962. Staff atty. enforcement divsn. Nat. Labor Rels. Bd., 1962-64; legis. asst. to Senator Harrison A. Williams US Senate, 1964-66; legis. asst. to Rep. Jonathan B. Bingham US Ho. Reps., 1966-68; spl. asst. Office Staff Relations N.Y.C. Bd. Edn., 1968-69; ptnr. Berlin, Roisman and Kessler (and successor firms), 1969-77; assoc. judge D.C. Superior Ct., 1977-94; judge U.S. Dist. Ct. D.C., Washington, 1994—. Asst. lectr. law sch. George Washington U., 1971-73; del. to judicial adminstrn. divsn. D.C. Superior Ct., 1985-90; mem. adv. bd. Ctr. for Dispute Settlement Inst. for Judicial Adminstrn., State Justice Inst., mem. adv. com. nat. judicial edn. project on domestic violence; mem BNA adv. bd. Alternative Dispute Resolution Report, 1987-90; mem. family law cirriculum planning com. Georgetown U.; lead judge permanency planning project Nat. Coun. Juvenile and Family Ct. Judges; chair Nat. Conf. on Bioethics, Family and the Law, D.C., 1991; mem. faculty Nat. Inst. Trial Advocacy; exec. com. Nat. ABA Jud. Divsn./Conf. of Federal Trial Judges, 1997-2000; with U.S. Jud. Conf. Com. on Ct. Adminstrn. and Mgmt., 1999. Contbr. articles to legal jours. Recipient Women Lawyer of Yr. award Women's Bar Assn., 1983, Svc. award D.C. Coalition Against Domestic Violence, 1987, Judicial Excellence award Trial Lawyers Assn. Washington, 1987. Fellow Am. Bar Found.; mem. ABA (judicial adminstrn. divsn., com. on bioethics and AIDS, adv. com. on youth, alcohol and drug problems, nat. adv. bd. on child support and criminal justice, individual rights and responsibilities sect.), Am. Judicature Soc. (bd. dirs. 1985-89), Nat. Assn. Women Judges (v.p. 1979-81, pres. 1981-82), Nat. Ctr. for State Cts. (bd. dirs. 1984-87), Women's Legal Def. Fund (founding pres. 1971), Women Judges' Fund. for Justice (bd. dirs. 1980—), Found. for Women Judges (pres. 1980-82). Office: US Courthouse 333 Constitution Ave NW Washington DC 20001-2802

KESSLER, HERBERT LEON, art historian, educator, academic administrator; b. Chgo., July 20, 1941; s. Ben and Bertha K.; m. Johanna Zacharias, Apr. 24, 1976; 1 dau., Morisa. AB, U. Chgo., 1961; MFA, Princeton U., 1963, PhD, 1965. Asst. prof. U. Chgo., 1965-68; assoc. prof., 1968-73; prof., 1973-76; chmn. dept. art, univ. dir. fine arts, 1973-76; prof. Johns Hopkins U., Balt., 1976—, chair dept. art, 1976-89, 95-98. Guest prof. Bibliotheca Hertziana, Rome, 1996-97, dean Sch. Arts and Scis., 1998-99; vis. prof. Harvard U., 2000, Ecole des Hautes Etudes, 2000; Croghan Bicentennial vis. prof. Williams Coll., 2006. Author: French and Flemish Illuminated Manuscripts, 1969, The Illustrated Bibles from Tours, 1977, The Cotton Genesis, 1986, The Dura Synagogue Frescoes and Christian Art, 1990, Studies in Pictorial Narrative, 1994, The Poetry and Paintings in the First Bible of Charles the Bald, 1997, The Holy Face and the paradox of Representation, 1998, Rome 1300: On the Path of the Pilgrim, 2000, Spiritual Seeing: Picturing God's Invisibility in the Middle Ages, 2000, Old St. Peter's and Ch. Decoration in Medieval Italy, 2002, Seeing Medieval Art, 2004. Sr. fellow Dumbarton Oaks, Washington, 1980-86; Woodrow Wilson fellow; Inst. Advanced Study fellow; Am. Council Learned Socs. fellow; Am. Philos. Soc. fellow; Guggenheim fellow; fellow Am. Acad. in Rome Fellow Medieval Acad. Am., Am. Acad. Arts and Scis.; mem. Coll. Art Assn., Phi Beta Kappa. Home: 3601 Greenway Apt 809 Baltimore MD 21218 Office: Johns Hopkins U Baltimore MD 21218 E-mail: hlk@jhu.edu.

KESSLER, IRVING ISAR, epidemiologist, consultant; AB in Math., NYU, 1952; MA in Endocrinology, Harvard U., 1955, PhD in Epidemiology, 1969; MD, Stanford U., 1960; MPH, Columbia U., 1962. Diplomate Nat. Bd. Med. Examiners, Am. Bd. Preventive Medicine; lic. physician Md. Prof. epidemiology Johns Hopkins U., 1972-84; chmn. dept. epidemiology and preventive medicine U. Md. Sch. Medicine, Balt., 1978-88; prof. oncology U. Md. Sch. Medicine Cancer Ctr., Balt., 1984—; prof. medicine U. Md. Sch. Medicine, Balt., 1985—, prof. dermatology, 1995—. Prof. dept. epidemiology & preventive medicine U. Md. Sch. Medicine, 1988-2001; emeritus, 2002-, exec. com. U. Md. Med. Sys., 1984-88; bd. dirs. Md. Med. Rsch. Inst.; v.p. for health scis., bd. dirs. ECRI, Plymouth Meeting, Pa., 1992-93; sci. adv. bd. Ctr. for Indoor Air Rsch., 1988-2001; mem. hazardous and toxic substances study commn., State of Md., 1983-84; cons. and lectr. in field. Bd. dirs. Israel Cancer Rsch. Found.;

chmn. advisory panel on toxic shock syndrome AMA, 1984-85. Capt. USPHS res. Recipient Faculty Rsch. award Am. Cancer Soc. Fellow Am. Pub. Health Assn., Am. Coll. Preventive Medicine; mem. AAAS, Am. Epidemiol. Soc., Am. Assn. for Cancer Rsch., Am. Coll. Occupl. Medicine, N.Y. Acad. Sci., Md. Gerontological Assn. (founder, bd. dirs., chmn., program com., pres. 1984-85, Gerontology Recognition award 1989), D.A. Boyes Soc. Gynaecologic Oncology (hon.), Phi Beta Kappa, Soc. Sigma Xi. Office: 9-34 MSTF 10 S Pine St Baltimore MD 21201-1596 Office Phone: 410-706-7866. Personal E-mail: ikessler@verizon.net. E-mail: ikessler@epi.umaryland.edu. *Epidemiology is the scientific discipline underlying preventive medicine which bridges the interface between medical science and human health. In an era of escalating healthcare costs and diminishing faith in the medical care system, my professional career has been dedicated to the development of preventive medicine as an academic discipline and an instrument of public health policy. Of no less concern to me has been the further development of preventive medicine as a rewarding career for the finest of our nation's young physicians. Unfortunately, in recent years, epidemiologists have increasingly emphasized the statistical rather than the biomedical significance of research findings, thereby rendering the field much less attractive to well-trained physicians who are devoted to educating the aetiology and implementing the control of disease.*

KESSLER, JEFFREY L., lawyer; b. NYC, Feb. 19, 1954; s. Milton M. and Edith H. Kessler; m. Regina T. Dessoff, May 21, 1977; children: Andrew Zalman, Leora Miriam. BA, JD summa cum laude, Columbia U., 1977. Bar: N.Y. 1978, U.S. Dist. Ct. (so. dist.) N.Y. 1978, U.S. Ct. Appeals (1st, 2d, 3d, 8th, 11th & Fed. cir.), U.S. Supreme Ct. 1985. Assoc. Weil, Gotshal & Manges, NYC, 1977-85, ptnr., 1985—2003, Dewey Ballantine LLP, NYC, 2003—, co-chair Litigation Dept., 2003—. Adj. assoc. prof. Fordham Law Sch., 1988-98; adj. prof. Law Sch. Columbia U., 2005—; founder, bd. advisors study pvt. antitrust litig. Georgetown U., 1983-85; mem. exec. and mgmt. com. Dewey Ballantine LLP, N.Y.C., N.Y., 2003— Mem. editl. bd.: Columbia U. Law Rev., 1976—77, Competition Laws Outside the U.S., 2001—03, editor-in-chief: State Antitrust Practice Statutes, 1999; co-author: International Trade and U.S. Antitrust Law; contbr. articles to profl. jours. Kent scholar, 1975—76, Stone scholar, 1976—77. Mem. ABA (antitrust law sect., vice-chmn. Sherman Act Sect. 2 com. 1989-90, chmn. internat. law com. 1990-94, co-chmn. pub. com. 1994-96, coun. mem. 1996-99, internat. task force 2001-03), Columbia Coll. Alumni Assn. (bd. dirs. 1996-99), Phi Beta Kappa. Democrat. Jewish. Office: Dewey Ballantine LLP 1301 Ave of the Americas New York NY 10019-6092 Home Phone: 212-772-8247; Office Phone: 212-259-8050. Office Fax: 212-259-6333. Business E-Mail: JKessler@DeweyBallantine.com.

KESSLER, JOAN F., judge, lawyer; b. June 25, 1943; m. Frederick P. Kessler, Sept. 1966; 2 children. BA, U. Kans., 1961-65; postgrad., U. Wis., 1965-66; JD cum laude, Marquette U., 1968. Law clk. Hon. John W. Reynolds U.S. Dist. Ct. (ea. dist.) Wis., Milw., 1968—69; assoc. Warschafsky, Rotter & Tarnoff, Milw., 1969-71; pvt. practice Milw., 1971-74; assoc. Cook & Franke, S.C., Milw., 1974-78; U.S. atty. Eastern Dist. Wis., Milw., 1978-81; ptnr. Foley & Lardner, Milw., 1981—2004; judge Ct. Appeals Wisc., Milw., 2004—. Lectr. profl. responsibility U. Wis. Law Sch., Marquette U. Law Sch., Milw., 1994-96; bd. govs. State Bar of Wis., 1985-95, chair, 1993, bd. dirs. family law sect., 1991-94; mem. Jud. Coun. Wis., Madison, 1989-92; mem. Milw. Bd. Attys. Profl. Responsibility, 1979-85. Bd. dirs. Legal Aid Soc., 1974-78, v.p., 1978, Urban League, 1980-82, Women's Bus. Initiative Corp., 1989-91, Girl Scouts U.S., Milw., 1994-96; bd. dirs., pres. Voters for Choice in Wis., 1989-93. Fellow Am. Matrimonial Lawyers (bd. govs. 1990-96, v.p. 1996-99), Am. Law Inst., Am. Bar Found.; mem. ABA (chair sect. individual rights and responsibilities 2003-04, coun. mem. 1997-2004, editor Human Rights 1997-99), ACLU. Office: Judge Ct Appeals Wis 633 W Wisconsin Milwaukee WI 53203 Office Phone: 414-227-4684. E-mail: joan.kessler@wicourts.gov.

KESSLER, JOHN OTTO, physicist, researcher; b. Vienna, Nov. 26, 1928; arrived in U.S., 1940, naturalized, 1946; s. Jacques and Alice Blanca (Neuhut) K.; m. Eva M. Bondy, Sept. 9, 1950; children: Helen J., Steven J. AB, Columbia U., 1949, PhD, 1953. With RCA Corp., Princeton, NJ, 1952-66, sr. mem. tech. staff, 1964-66, mgr. grad. recruiting, 1964-66; prof. physics U. Ariz., Tucson, 1966-93, prof. emeritus, 1994—. Vis. rsch. assoc. Princeton U., 1962-64; sr. vis. fellow, vis. prof. physics U. Leeds, Eng., 1972-73, sr. vis. fellow, 1990-91; vis. prof. Technische Hogeschool Delft, Netherlands, spring 1979; Fulbright fellow dept. applied math. and theoretical physics Cambridge U., Eng., 1983-84. Contbr. articles to profl. jours. Fellow: AAAS; mem.: Am. Phys. Soc. Achievements include patentee in field; research in low Reynolds number fluid mechanics; mechanisms of bacterial propulsion, interaction and formation of coherent swarms, leading to microturbulence; bioconvection and consumption patterns of micro-organism populations; locomotion, transport of metabolites, and signalling; complementary aspects of mobility of microorganisms; measurement of probability densities for swimming velocity of algae and bacteria; relationship of interorganism signalling, quorum sensing, and exchange of metabolites to individual and collective motility in Bacillus subtilis and the Volvocales. Home: 2740 E Camino La Zorrela Tucson AZ 85718-3126 Office: U Ariz Physics Dept Bldg 81 Tucson AZ 85721-0001 Home Phone: 520-299-6522; Office Phone: 520-621-2797. Business E-Mail: kessler@physics.arizona.edu.

KESSLER, JOHN PAUL, JR., financial planner; b. Bronxville, NY, Sept. 4, 1946; s. John Paul and Helen Claire (Hopper) K. BBA in Fin., Tex. Tech. U., 1965-71. CFP; registered investment advisor. Agt. Met. Life Ins. Co., Lubbock, Tex., 1970-73; pension trust adminstr. Rep. Nat. Life, Dallas, 1973-78, Am. Founders Life, Austin, 1979-81; acct. for state appropriations Tex. State Comptr., Austin, 1981-84; fin. planner J. Paul Kessler & Assocs., Dallas, 1984-95, Kessler Fin. Assocs., Dallas, 1995—. Pension cons. Kessler Fin. Group, Dallas, 1984—. Mem. Am. Mgmt. Assn., Dallas Estate Planning Coun., Dallas Benefit Soc., Nat. Assn. Securities Dealers (registered rep.), Tex. Tech Alumni Assn., McKinney C. of C. Republican. Presbyterian. Avocations: golf, travel. Office: Kessler Fin Assocs PO Box 2382 Mc Kinney TX 75070-1860 Office Phone: 972-529-2827.

KESSLER, JUDD LEWIS, lawyer; b. Newark, Apr. 10, 1938; s. Samuel W. and Ethel S. (Shapiro) K.; m. Marian Osterweis, Jan. 7, 1979 (div. 1986); m. Carol Ann Farris, Oct. 19, 1987; 1 child, Samuel Farris. AB, Oberlin Coll., 1960; LLB, Harvard U., 1963. Bar: N.J. 1963, D.C. 1972, Md. 1989, U.S. Dist. Ct. N.J., U.S. Dist. Ct. D.C., U.S. Dist. Ct. Md., U.S. Ct. Appeals (4th cir.), U.S. Supreme Ct. 1968. Assoc. Toner, Crowley, Woelper and Vanderbilt, Newark, 1963-66; asst. gen. counsel U.S. Agy. for Internat. Devel., Washington, 1966-82; ptnr., chmn. internat. bus. practice group Porter, Wright, Morris & Arthur, Washington, 1982—. Author: (with others) Legal Aspects of Exporting, 1986; contbr. articles to profl. jours. Recipient Outstanding Career Achievement award, U.S. AID, 1982; Presdl. appointee to Sr. Fgn. Svc., 1982. Master: London Court Internat. Arbitration; mem.: ABA, Internat. Ctr. for the Settlement of Investment Disputes (panel of arbitrators 2003—), Fed. Bar Assn. (chmn. internat. sect. 1983—87, nat. coord. Export Legal Assistance Network 1985—, Pres.'s E Excellence Export Svc. award 1997), Am. Soc. Internat. Law, Internat. C. of C. (mem. U.S. arbitration com. 2000), Inter-Am. Bar Found. (pres. 1994—), Inter-Am. Bar Assn. (Internat. Lawyer of Yr. award 2002), Am. Arbitration Assn. (mem. internat. panel arbitrators 1997—), Cosmos Club. Office: Porter Wright Morris & Arthur 1919 Penn Ave NW Washington DC 20006-3434 Office Phone: 202-778-3080.

KESSLER, KEITH LEON, lawyer; b. Seattle, July 18, 1947; s. Robert Lawrence and Priscilla Ellen (Allbee) K.; m. Lynn Elizabeth Eisen, Dec. 24, 1980; children: William Moore, Christopher Moore, Bradley Moore, Jamie Kessler. BA in Philosophy, U. Wash., 1969, JD, 1972. Bar: Wash. 1972, U.S. Dist. Ct. (we. dist.) Wash. 1973, U.S. Dist. Ct. (ea. dist. 1992); U.S. Ct. Appeals (9th cir.) 1973, U.S. Supreme Ct. 1975. Law clk. to Hon. Robert Finley Wash. Supreme Ct., Olympia, Wash., 1972-73; ptnr. Kessler, Tegland & Urmston, Seattle, 1973-75, Kessler & Urmston, Seattle, 1975-76, Kessler, Urmston & Sever, Seattle, 1976-77, Kessler & Sever, Seattle, 1977-79; assoc. Stritmatter & Stritmatter, Hoquiam, Wash., 1980-83; ptnr. Stritmatter, Kessler & McCauley, Hoquiam, Wash., 1983-93, Stritmatter Kessler, Hoquiam, Wash., 1993-97, Stritmatter, Kessler, Whelan, Withey, Hoquiam, Wash., 1997—2006, Stritmatter, Kessler, Whelan, Colvccio, Hoquiam/Seattle, Wash., 2006—. Chmn. LAW PAC, Seattle, 1991-93; mem. pattern jury instrns. com. Wash. Supreme Ct., 2000—. Editor: Trial Evidence, 1996, author: (with others) Motor Vehicle Accident Litigation Desk Book, 1988, 1995, 97; contbr. chpt. to book. Pres. Kairos Ctr., Aberdeen, Wash., 1984-86; co-founder Grays Harbor Support Group; bd. dir. Wash. State Head Injury Found., Bellevue, Wash., 1993-96. Recipient Founders award Wash. State Head Injury Found., 1990, Silver award United Way, 1992 Fellow Am. Coll. Trial Lawyers; mem. Am. Bd. Trial Advocates, (pres. Wash. chpt. 1997), Wash. State Trial Lawyers Assn. (pres. 1990-91, named trial lawyer of yr., 1994), Damage Attys. Round Table (pres. 2002-03), Wash. Trial Attys. Political Forum (chmn. 1993-95), Wash. Def. Trial Lawyers (named Outstanding Plaintiff Trial Lawyer 2002), Trial Lawyers for Public Justice (state exec. com. 1994—). Office: Stritmatter Kessler Whelan Withey 413 8th St Hoquiam WA 98550-3607 Office Phone: 360-533-2710. Business E-Mail: keith@skwwc.com.

KESSLER, LEONARD, writer, illustrator; b. Akron, Ohio, Oct. 28, 1921; s. Louis Kessler and Lili Kessler-Hertzan; m. Ethel Gerson (dec.); children: Paul, Kim. BFA, Carnegie Tech. U., 1949. Freelance author, illustrator, NYC, 1949—57, New City, NY, 1957—97, Sarasota, Fla., 1996—. Author, illustrator: What's In a Line?, 1951, Heavy is a Hippo, 1954, Big Red Bus, 1957, Mr. Pine's Purple House, 2001, Mr. Pine's Mixed-Up Signs, 2001, Mrs. Pine Takes a Trip, 2005. Sgt. US Army, 1942—45, ETO. Decorated Purple Heart, Bronze Star. Home: 1624 Treehouse Cl TR-120 Sarasota FL 34231-6724 Personal E-mail: lenkessler@comcast.net.

KESSLER, MARCIA LYNN, school psychologist; b. Piqua, Ohio, July 5, 1950; d. Dale Elsworth and Harriet Elizabeth (Sumner) Hall; m. Douglas Weis Kessler, July 30, 1983; children: Elisabeth Virginia, Anna Morgan. BS, Ind. State U., 1972, MS, 1976, postgrad., 1980. Lic. sch. psychologist Ind., psychologist Ind. Tchr. spl. edn. Sidney Sch. Corp., Sidney, Ohio, 1972—74, Logansport Joint Spl. Svcs., Logansport, Ind., 1974—75; intern, grad. asst. Porter Sch. Psychology Ctr., Terre Haute, Ind., 1975—76; doctoral fellow Ind. State U., Terre Haute, 1977—79; sch. psychologist Johnson County Spl. Svcs., Franklin, Ind., 1976—77, 1979—81, McClelland Sch. Dist. Wayne Twp., Indpls., 1981—. Presenter in field various confs.; chmn. Assessment Com. for Writing Best Practices in the State of Ind. for Autism, 1997. Co-author: (test) Paired Hands Test, Secondary, 1976, (tape) The School Psychologist and Death, 1979. Founder Wayne Twp. Autism Info. Exch., Indpls., Autism Awards Ceremony, 1996. Mem.: Ind. Autism Acad., Ind. Assn. Sch. Psychologists, Nat. Assn. Sch. Psychologists. Office: McClelland Elementary School 6740 W Morris Indianapolis IN 46241

KESSLER, MURRAY S., consumer products company executive; BS, Villanova Univ.; MBA, NYU. Gen. mgr. Swanson div. Campbell Soup Co., 1997—98, v.p., exec. officer, Vlasic Internat. Foods, & pres., Swanson Frozen Foods div., 1998—99; sr. v.p. U.S. Smokeless Tobacco Co., 2000, pres., 2000—05; pres., COO UST Inc., Greenwich, Conn., 2005—07, pres., CEO, 2007—. Office: UST Inc 100 W Putnam Ave Greenwich CT 06830*

KESSLER, PHILIP JOEL, lawyer; b. Detroit, Nov. 15, 1947; s. Herbert Jerome and Mary Rita (Bloomgarden) K.; m. Ruth Ann Kessler, Dec. 22, 1968 (div. 1981); children: Herbert Jeffrey, Jennifer Ann; m. Mary Ray Brophy, Jan. 29, 1988. AB in English with distinction, U. Mich., 1969; JD, U. Calif., Berkeley, 1972. Bar: Mich. 1972, U.S. Dist. Ct. (ea. dist.) Mich. 1972, U.S. Ct. Appeals (6th cir.) 1976, U.S. Dist. Ct. (no. dist.) Tex. 1990, U.S. Tax Ct. 1990. Assoc. Butzel Long Gust Klein & Van Zile, Detroit, 1972-79, ptnr., 1979-82; shareholder Butzel Long (and predecessor firms), 1982—, chmn., 2006—. Legal rsch. tchg. fellow Detroit Coll. Law, 1975-77; asst. prof. law 1977-85; lectr. in field; local rules adv. com. U.S. Dist. Ct. for Ea. Dist. Mich., mem. 1991-95, chair 1994-95; life mem. Jud. Conf. U.S. Ct. Appeals for 6th Cir.; bd. dirs. The Beaumont Found., 1995-96, THAW Fund, 1995—. Mem. Founders Soc. Detroit Inst. Arts, 1988—. Fellow Am. Bar Found., Am. Coll. Trial Lawyers, Internat. Soc. BarristersMich. Bar Found.; mem. Detroit Athletic Club, Franklin (Mich.) Hills Country Club. Avocation: golf. Office: Butzel Long 150 W Jefferson Ave Ste 100 Detroit MI 48226 Office Phone: 313-225-7018. Business E-Mail: kessler@butzel.com.

KESSLER, RICHARD PAUL, JR., lawyer; b. Latrobe, Pa., July 11, 1945; s. Richard Paul Sr. and Dorothy Henrietta (Comp) K.; m. Kathleen Jane Parker, June 17, 1973 (dec. May 11, 1996); 1 child, Grace Elizabeth; m. Susan Kessler, Oct. 2000. BA, Fairfield U., Conn., 1968; JD, Emory U., 1971. Bar: Ga. 1971, U.S. Dist. Ct. (no. dist.) Ga. 1973, U.S. Ct. Appeals (5th cir.) 1974, U.S. Ct. Appeals (11th cir.) 1981, U.S. Supreme Ct. 1995. Law clk. to presiding justice U.S. Dist. Ct. (no. dist.) Ga., 1971-73; ptnr. Macey, Wilensky and Kessler LLP and predecessor firm, Atlanta, 1973—. Lectr. Practising Law Inst., 1981, 83, Fin. Svc. Corp. Career Conf., Atlanta, 1986, Ga. and Ala. Insts. of Continuing Legal Edn., 1993-95; panelist Credit Union Nat. Assn., Inc. League Attys. Conf., 1980-82, 87, 88-93, ABA, 1990-91; participant Nat. Conf. Commrs. on Uniform State Laws Drafting Com. on U.C.C. Articles, 3, 4, 4A, 1985-90; chair corp. and banking law sect. State Bar Ga., 1995-96. Author: What You Should Know About the New Bankruptcy Code, 1979, Guide to the Bankruptcy Laws: The Bankruptcy Reform Act of 1978, 79, Guide to the Bankruptcy Laws: The Bankruptcy Reform Act of 1978 (Bankruptcy Code) as Amended by the Bankruptcy Amendments and Federal Judgeship Act of 1984, The Bankruptcy Judges, U.S. Trustees and Family Farmer Bankruptcy Act of 1986; contbg. editor Banking and Lending Instn. Forms, 1996-2007; contbr. articles to profl. jours. Mem.: East Lake Golf Club. Office: Ste 600 285 Peachtree Center Ave NE Atlanta GA 30303-1229 Office Phone: 404-584-1200. Business E-Mail: rkessler@maceywilensky.com.

KESSLER, RONALD, author; b. NYC, Dec. 31, 1943; s. Ernest Borek and Minuetta K.; m. Pamela Johnson Whitehead; children: Greg, Rachel Kessler. Student, Clark U., Worcester, Mass., 1962—64. Reporter Worcester Telegram, 1964; reporter, editl. writer Boston Herald, 1964-68; N.Y. bur. reporter Wall Street Jour., 1968-70; investigative reporter Washington Post, 1970-85; journalist/author, 1985—. Author: The Life Insurance Game, 1985, The Richest Man in the World: The Story of Adnan Khashoggi, 1986, Spy vs. Spy: Stalking Soviet Spies in America, 1988, Moscow Station: How the KGB Penetrated the American Embassy, 1989, The Spy in the Russian Club: How Glenn Souther Stole America's Nuclear War Plans and Escaped to Moscow, 1990, Escape from the CIA: How the CIA Won and Lost the Most Important KGB Spy Ever to Defect to the U.S., 1991, Inside the CIA: Revealing the Secrets of the World's Most Powerful Spy Agency, 1992, The FBI: Inside the World's Most Powerful Law Enforcement Agency, 1993, Inside the White House: The Hidden Lives of the Presidents and the Secrets of the World's Most Powerful Institution, 1995, The Sins of the Father: Joseph P. Kennedy and the Dynasty He Founded, 1996, Inside Congress: The Shocking Scandals, Corruption, and Abuse of Power Behind the Scenes on Capitol Hill, 1997, The Season: Inside Palm Beach and America's Richest Society, 1999 (basis for A&E TV prodn.), The Bureau: The Secret History of the FBI, 2002, The CIA at War: Inside the Secret Campaign Against Terror, 2003, A Matter of Character: Inside the White House of George W. Bush, 2004, Laura Bush: An Intimate Portrait of the First Lady, 2006, The Terrorist Watch: Inside the Desperate Race to Stop the Heart Attack, 2007; chief Washington corr. NewsMax. Recipient pub. affairs reporting award Am. Polit. Sci. Assn., 1965; citation Freedoms Found., 1966; 1st prize in newswriting UPI, 1967; Sevellon Brown Meml. award AP, 1967; sci. writers award ADA, 1968; 1st place in pub. svc. award Md.-Del.-D.C. Press Assn., 1972; outstanding series award AAUW, 1972; Bill Pryor Meml. Reporting award, 1973; Front Page award Washington-Balt. Newspaper Guild, 1973; George H. Polk Meml. award for cmty. svc., 1973; for nat. reporting, 1979; Washington Dateline award for bus. reporting Sigma Delta Chi-Soc. Profl. Journalists, 1987; 1st pl. in investigative reporting Assn. Area Bus. Publs., 1987; named Washingtonian of Yr. Washington Mag., 1972; Dow Jones Inc. Newspaper Fund intern, 1964. Home and Office: 2516 Stratton Dr Potomac MD 20854-6231 Personal E-mail: KesslerRonald@cs.com.

KESSLER, RONALD N., plastics company executive; b. Youngstown, Ohio; s. Milton and Justine Kessler; m. Linda Ann Schloss, Aug. 21, 1976; children: Daniel, JamieAnn, Samantha, Seth. Student, Lowell Inst. Tech., Lowell, Mass., 1967—69; BS, Youngstown State Univ., Youngstown, Ohio, 1973. R & D tech. Kessler Products, Youngstown, Ohio, 1973—74; sales Space-Links Inc., Youngstown, Ohio, 1974—75, v.p. mktg., 1975—78; pres., owner Willow Molded Plastics/SLI, Youngstown, Ohio, 1978—84; v.p. fin. Thermal Energy Inc., Youngstown, Ohio, 1980—85; pres. Boardman Molded Products, Youngstown, Ohio, 1986—91, Mr. Charles Shampoo, W. Bloomfield, Mich., 1991—93, Kessler Products, Youngstown, Ohio, 1993—2004. Bd. dir. Thermal Energy, Youngstown, Ohio, 1980—85, AAMA Am. Archtl. Mfg. Assn., NYC, 1993, NYC, 97. Bd. mem. Jewish Cmty. Ctr., 1977—80, Jewish Cmty. Rels. Coun., Youngstown, Ohio, 2001—, Jewish/Arab Dialog, Youngstown, Ohio, 2003—. Mem.: Soc. Plastics Industries, Soc. Plastic Engr., Squaw Creek Country Club, Masonic Lodge (32nd degree 2002). Republican. Jewish. Achievements include over 20 domestic and international patents; on AAMA board for developing test procedures for weatherstripping. Avocations: golf, tennis, skiing, basketball. Home: 2000 Twin Oaks Girard OH 44420 Office: Boardman Molded Products Inc 1110 Thalia PO Box 1858 Youngstown OH 44501 Office Phone: 330-788-2401. Business E-Mail: rkessler@spacelinks1.com.

KESSLER, ROSLYN MARIE, financial analyst; b. Bloomington, Ind., Dec. 5, 1953; d. Ivan Gordon and Carmen Karina (Babbensingh) Samuels; m. Terrance Jude Kessler, Mar. 19, 1982 (div. Mar. 19, 1993); 1 child, Jude. BS in Acctg., SUNY, Albany, 1990; MBA in Fin., U. Rochester, 1994; MS in Mgmt. and Sys., NYU, 2007. CPA, NY; cert. mgmt. acct., internal auditor, fin. mgr.; accredited purchasing practitioner; Microsoft Office Specialist, 2003. Staff tax acct., auditor Arthur Andersen & Co., Rochester, NY, 1990-92; fin. analyst Xerox Corp., Rochester, NY, 1993-2000; tech. mgr. Am. Inst. Cert. Pub. Accts., NYC, 2000—03; sr. internet auditor Hubbell Corp., Orange, Conn., 2003—; spl. acctg. United Tech. Corp., 2003—. Grad. tchg. asst. acctg., 1992-94; William E. Simon Grad. Sch. Bus. Adminstrn. scholar, 1992-94, Glenbrook Neighborhood Assn., 2001-. Legis. chair PTA, Winslow Elem. Sch., 1991-92, PTA Brighton HS, 1996-2000; com. mem. Boy Scouts Am., Rochester, 1991-92; vol. Wesley-on-East Nursing Home, Rochester, 1992-95. Mem. AICPA, NY Assn. CPA Candidates (dir. 1991-92, pres. 1992-93). Avocations: bicycling, statistics, futures/options, yoga, light weightlifting. Office Phone: 203-386-7090.

KESSLER, STUART, accountant, financial planner; b. Bklyn., May 17, 1929; s. Morris M. and Anne (Blacker) K.; m. Isabel Lois Knecht, Aug. 19, 1956; children: Jeffrey, Glenn, Bradley. BA, Bklyn. Coll., 1950; MBA, CCNY, 1953; JD, Bklyn. Law Sch., 1957; LLM, NYU, 1962. CPA, N.Y.; bar: N.Y. 1957. Staff acct. Klein, Hinds, & Finke, NYC, 1952-60; ptnr. Rothstein, Kessler & Co., NYC, 1960-70; sr. tax ptnr. Goldstein, Golub, Kessler LLP, NYC, 1970—; mng. dir. Am. Express Tax and Bus. Svcs., 1998—2005, RSM McGladery, 2005—. Pres. Found. Acctg. Edn., NYC, 1985. Mem. editl. bd. Fin. Planning Jour., 1985-93; editor estate planning column CPA Jour., 1983; contbr. articles to profl. jours. Trustee Greenburgh Hebrew Ctr., 1974-83. Staff sgt. USAF, 1951-52. Recipient James Kelly Pub. Svc. award Westchester CPA Soc., 1990; named one of 100 Most Influential People in Acctg., Acctg. Today, 1994, 1996-2003, 05-06, One of Am.'s Top Fin. Advisors, Worth Mag., 1994; named to Bklyn. Tech. Hall of Fame, 1998. Mem. AICPA (governing coun. 1982-90, 91—, chmn. coun. 1997-98, bd. dirs. 1991-99, chmn. pers. fin. planning divsn. 1990-94, chmn. responsibilities in tax practice com. 1988-90, pers. fin. specialist, Gold medal 2003), N.Y. State Soc. CPAs (pres. 1984-85, bd. dirs. 1978-83, Outstanding Svc. award 1990, Hall of Fame 2002), Bklyn. Coll. Acct. Alumni Assn. (pres. 1964-65), Bklyn. Coll. Alumni Assn. (bd. dirs. 1962-85, Alumnus of Yr. 2005, Jerome Milgram Svc. award), Internat. Standardization Orgn. (chair com. personal fin. planning 2001-). Avocations: running, gardening, collecting headlines, travel, music. Office: Goldstein Golub Kessler LLP 1185 Ave Of The Americas New York NY 10036-2601 Home Phone: 914-693-3656; Office Phone: 212-372-1304. Personal E-mail: uskesslers@yahoo.com. Business E-Mail: stuart.kessler@rsmi.com.

KESSLER, WILLIAM EUGENE, healthcare executive; b. St. Louis, Dec. 15, 1944; s. Joseph John and Margaret Mary (Burns) K.; m. Patricia Christine Wilson, Nov. 9, 1968; children: Christina, William, John, Timothy, Jennifer, Catherine, Joseph, Daniel. BS in Commerce, St. Louis U., 1966, MHA, 1968. Various positions St. John's Hosp., St. Louis, 1963-67; adminstrv. resident St. Mary's Hosp., Grand Rapids, Mich., 1967-68; pres. St. Anthony's Health Ctr., Alton, Ill., 1971—. Chmn., prof. and tech. adv. com. Joint Commn. on Accreditation Healthcare Orgn., 1990-94; speaker profl. and community settings, 1972—; preceptor St. Louis U., 1980—, U. Mo., Columbia, 1991; bd. dir. Hosp. Assn. Met. St. Louis, 1975-85. Contbr. articles to profl. jour., 1972—. Admissions advisor US Mil. Acad., 1973-83; treas., bd. dir. Cath. Childrens' Home Alton, 1981-89; v.p. diocesan bd. edn. Diocese of Springfield, Ill., 1981-82, pres. 1982-84, mem. bd. edn. 1986-92; mem. diocesan fin. coun., 1987—; chmn. ARC, Alton, 1983-85; bd. dir. Am. Cancer Soc., Alton, 1984-90; pres. St. Louis Metropolitan Hosp. Coun., 1996. Served to capt. US Army, 1968-71. Decorated Army Commendation medal; recipient Alton Jaycees Disting. Svc. award, Alumni Merit award St. Louis U., 1994; named Knight of the Equestrian Order of the Holy Sepulchre, 1997; recipient Pro Ecclesia et Pontifice Cross Pope John Paul II, 2002, Mercy H.S., Alumni Merit award, 2002. Fellow: Am. Coll. Healthcare Execs. (regent's adv. coun. 1987—93, nominating com. 1991—94, regent 2002, chair ethics com., Regent's award, Sr. Healthcare Exec. of the Yr. award 1993); mem.: Southwestern Ill. Indsl. Assn. (exec. com. 1983—88, bd. dirs. 1989—, chmn. 1997), St. Louis U. Hosp. Adminstrn. Alumni Assn. (pres. 1978), Cath. Health Assn. U.S.A. (bd. dirs. 1987—, exec. com. 1989—92, chmn.-elect 1990—, chair 1991), Ill. Hosp. Assn. (exec. com. 1981—86, chmn. 1984—85), Am. Hosp. Assn. (Ho. of Dels. 1984—88), Stadium (St. Louis), Stadium Club (St. Louis), Rotary (pres. Alton chpt. 1981-82, Paul Harris fellow 1985), Rotary (pres. Alton chpt. 1981—82, Paul Harris fellow 1979, 1985). Avocations: photography, sports, family travel. Home: 1216 N Hanser Ln Godfrey IL 62035-1840 Office: St Anthony's Health Ctr St Anthony's Way PO Box 340 Alton IL 62002-0340 also: St Clare's Hosp 915 E 5th St Alton IL 62002-6434

KESSLER-HODGSON, LEE GWENDOLYN, actress, performing company executive; b. Wellsville, NY, Jan. 16, 1947; d. James Hewitt and Reba Gwendolyn (Adsit) Kessler; m. Bruce Gridley, June 22, 1969 (div. Dec. 1979); m. Jeffrey Craig Hodgson, Oct. 31, 1987. BA, Grove City Coll., 1968; MA, U. Wis., 1969. Prof. Sangamon State U., Springfield, Ill., 1969-70; pers. exec. Bullock's, LA, 1971-74; owner Brunnen Enterprises, LA, 1982—. Author: A Child of Arthur, 1981, White King and The Doctor, 2005; prodr., writer: Anais Nin: The Paris Years, 1986; appeared in TV movies, mini-series including Roots, 1978, Backstairs at The White House, 1979, Blind Ambition, 1980, Hill Street Blues, 1984-87, Murder By Reason of Insanity, 1985, Hoover, 1986, Creator, 1987, Our House, 1988, Favorite Son, 1988, Lou Grant 1983-84, Barney Miller, 1979, L.A. Law, 1990, Hunter, 1991, (screenplay) Settlers Way, 1988; (TV series) Matlock, L.A. Law others. Knapp Prize fellow U. Wis., 1969. Mem. AFTRA, SAG, DAR, Actors Equity Assn. Republican. Mem. Ch. Scientology. Avocations: singer, directing, motivational speaking. Mailing: PO Box 1808 Eureka MT 59917 Office Phone: 877-478-0835. Business E-Mail: lee@thekesslergroupintl.com.

KESTENBAUM, HAROLD L., lawyer; b. Bronx, NY, Sept. 27, 1949; s. Murray Louis and Yetta (Weiner) K.; m. Felice Gail Kravit, Aug. 11, 1973; children: Michelle, Benjamin. BA, Queens Coll., 1971; JD, U. Richmond, 1975. Bar: N.Y. 1976, N.J. 1977, U.S. Dist. Ct. (so. and ea. dist.) N.Y. Assoc. Wayne and Reiss, NYC, 1975-76, Natanson, Reich and Barrison, NYC, 1976-77, Goldstein and Axelrod, NYC, 1977-81; pvt. practice NYC and L.I., 1981—2002; counsel Farrell Fritz, P.C., 2002—07, Ruskin Moscou, 2007—; chmn. of the bd. Franchise It Corp., Bohemia, N.Y., 1984-89; pres., chief exec. officer Mr. Sign Franchising Corp., 1987-89. Bd. dirs. YTB Internat. Inc., GarageTek, Inc., Ultimate Francluse Sys., Inc.; cons. in field. Mem. ABA, N.Y. Bar Assn., N.J. Bar Assn., Nassau County Bar Assn. Republican. Jewish. Avocations: softball, weight training. Office Phone: 516-745-0099. Business E-Mail: hkestenbaum@rmfpc.com.

KESTER, CHARLES MELVIN, lawyer; b. Batesville, Ark., Jan. 19, 1968; s. Monty Charles and Phyllis Smith Kester; m. Cheryl Goodwin, June 1, 1991. BA in Philosophy summa cum laude, Liberty U., 1991; JD magna cum laude, Georgetown U., 1994. Bar: Ark. 1994, U.S. Dist. Ct. (ea. and we. dists.) Ark. 1995, U.S. Ct. Appeals (8th cir.) 1995, U.S. Ct. Fed. Claims, 2002, U.S. Supreme Ct. 1998. Law clk. U.S. Ct. Appeals 8th Cir., Fargo, ND, 1994-95; atty. Lingle Law Firm, Rogers, Ark., 1995—96; pvt. practice law Fayetteville, Ark., 1996—. Assoc. editor Georgetown Law Jour., 1993-94; contbr. articles to profl. jours. Mem. Ark. Bar Assn. (appellate practice com. 1997-00, young lawyers sect. adv. coun. 1998-99, sec. labor and employment law sect. 2002, chair 2004), Ark. Trial Lawyers Assn. (amicus curiae com. 1997-07), Phi Alpha Delta. Avocations: camping, rock climbing, spelunking. Home: 13602 White Oak Ln Fayetteville AR 72704-8312 Office: 1160 N College Ave Ste 1 Fayetteville AR 72703-1907 Office Phone: 479-582-4600.

KESTER, HELEN MARY, minister; b. Three Springs, Pa., Jan. 19, 1953; d. James R. and Phoebe C. (Dalzell) Daniels; m. Hal W. Kester, July 5, 1975; children: Mary Beth, Timothy, William Shondelmyer. BS, Slippery Rock U., 1974, MEd, 1978; MDiv, Pitts. Theol. Sem., 2006. Cert. elem. tchr., reading specialist, Pa. 8th grade reading tchr. New Kensington (Pa.)-Arnold Sch. Dist., 1974—2006, chair reading dept., 1974—2006; pastor Derry Presbyn. Ch., Pa., 2006—. Mem. NEA, Pa. State Edn. Assn., Internat. Reading Assn., Phi Delta Kappa, Kappa Delta Pi. Home Phone: 724-568-1123; Office Phone: 724-694-5710. E-mail: hkester@comcast.net.

KESTER, RANDALL BLAIR, lawyer; b. Vale, Oreg., Oct. 20, 1916; s. Bruce R. and Mabel M. (Judd) K.; m. Rachael L. Woodhouse, Oct. 20, 1940; children: Laura, Sylvia, Lynne. AB, Willamette U., 1937; JD, Columbia U., 1940. Bar: Oreg. 1940, U.S. Dist. Ct. Oreg. 1940, U.S. Ct. Appeals (9th cir.) 1941, U.S. Supreme Ct. 1960. Assoc., then partner firm Maguire, Shields, Morrison & Bailey, Portland, 1940-57; justice Oreg. Supreme Ct., Salem, 1957-58; partner Maguire, Shields, Morrison, Bailey & Kester, 1958-66, Maguire, Kester & Cosgrave, 1966-71, Cosgrave & Kester, Portland, 1972-78, Cosgrave, Kester, Crowe, Gidley & Lagesen, Portland, 1978-89, Cosgrave, Vergeer & Kester, Portland, 1989—. Instr. Northwestern Coll. Law, 1947-56; gen. solicitor northwestern dist. U.P. R.R., 1958-79; sr. counsel UPRR Co., 1979-81 Co-author: The First Duty: History of the U.S. District Court of Oregon, 1993; contbr. articles to profl. jours. Past v.p. Portland area coun. Boy Scouts Am.; past pres. Mountain Rescue and Safety Coun. Oreg.; past trustee Willamette U.; past bd. dirs. Oreg. Symphony Soc., Oreg. Mus. Sci. and Industry, Oreg. Ind. Colls. Found., United Way; mem. Portland Com. on Fgn. Rels. Recipient Silver Beaver award Boy Scouts Am., 1956, alumni citation Willamette U., 1987. Fellow Am. Acad. Appellate Lawyers; mem. ABA, Am. Bar Found. (life), Multnomah Bar Assn. (past pres. 1956, Professionalism award 1991), Oreg. State Bar (treas. 1965-66, Disting. Svc. award pub. utility sect. 1991), Am. Law Inst. (life), Nat. Ski Patrol, Mt. Hood Ski Patrol (past pres.), Mazamas (past pres., climbing chmn.), Wy'east Climbers, Portland C. of C. (pres. 1973, chmn. bd. 1974), U.S. Dist. Ct. Oreg. Hist. Soc. (past pres, bd. dirs., Lifetime Svc. award) Oreg. Ethics Commons (co-founder, sec.), Phi Delta Phi, Beta Theta Pi, Tau Kappa Alpha. Clubs: Arlington (Portland), City (Portland) (v.p. 1978-80, pres. 1986-87), University (Portland), Multnomah Athletic (Portland). Republican. Unitarian Universalist. Office: Cosgrave Vergeer & Kester LLP 805 SW Broadway 8th Fl Portland OR 97205 Home Phone: 503-292-2462; Office Phone: 503-323-9000. Business E-Mail: rkester@cvk-law.com.

KESTER, STEWART RANDOLPH, banker; b. Bronxville, NY, July 30, 1927; s. Robert Livingston, Jr. and Mae Anna (Jones) K.; m. Marion Fay Syrett, Sept. 23, 1950; children: Cheryl, Stewart Randolph, Valerie, Marcia. BA, Colgate U., 1949. Sales rep. Procter & Gamble Co., NYC, 1949-55; mng. ptnr. Kester Bros., Pompano Beach, Fla., 1955-86, R&S Properties, Pompano Beach, 1956-90, Fla. Coast Banks, Inc., Pompano Beach, 1973-75, vice chmn. bd., 1975-84, chmn. bd., 1984-85, chmn. exec. com., dir.; dir. Barnett Bank So. Fla. N.A., 1985-89, also bd. dirs.; with Kester Bros. Realty Inc., 1991—; pres. Crail Creek Assocs. LC, 1997—. Bd. dirs. Big Sky Western Bank, Mont., chmn. bd., 2000—; pres. Jefferson Valley Ranch, Whitehall, Mont.; sec.-treas. Westfork Devel. Co. Inc., Big Sky, 1991—2000; ptnr. Big Sky Ranch, Inc. LLC. Vice mayor, commr., Pompano Beach, 1964-66, mayor, 1966-67; mem. Broward County Charter Commn., 1974-75; pres. United Way of Broward County, 1978-79; chmn. bd. trustees Pompano Police Edn. Fund, Inc., 1975-86; mem. exec. com. Broward chpt. NCCJ, 1983-86; bd. dirs. Ft. Lauderdale Symphony; founding bd. dirs. Broward Workshop, Inc., 1981-85; founding dir., pres. Pompano Beach Bd. Trade, 1978-86; founding dir., v.p. Broward Cmty. Found., 1985-89; founding bd. dirs. Big Sky Assn. for Arts, 1989-95, Vigilante Theatre Corp., 1992-94. With AUS, 1946-47. Named Outstanding Young Man Pompano Beach Jaycees, 1962; recipient Service award Ft. Lauderdale C. of C., 1975, Silver Medallion award NCCJ, 1984, Community Svc. award Pompano Beach C. of C., 1983, 85. Mem. Pompano Beach Hist. Soc. (founding bd. dirs.), Greater Pompano Beach C. of C. (past dir.), Pompano Beach Exch. Club (past pres., charter mem., Book of Golden Deeds award 1976), Montana Hist. Soc., Custer Battlefield Mus. and Hist. Commn., Custer Battlefield Preservation Commn., Mus. of the Rockies, Buffalo Bill Hist. Ctr., Mus. of Art (Ft. Lauderdale), Sons of the Revolution (N.Y.). Republican. Presbyterian. Office: Kester Bros Realty Inc 619 E Atlantic Blvd PO Box 91 Pompano Beach FL 33061-0091 Home Phone: 954-942-7222; Office Phone: 954-943-0876. E-mail: srkfsk@aol.com.

KESTERSON, DAVID BERT, language educator, dean, academic administrator; b. Springfield, Mo., Feb. 19, 1938; s. Homer Russell and Dorothy (Mace) K.; m. Cheryl Renee Monk; children: A. Todd, Chad Russell. BSE, S.W. Mo. State U., 1959; MA, U. Ark., 1961, PhD, 1965. NDEA fellow, 1959-62; grad. teaching asst. U. Ark., Fayetteville, 1962-64; asst. prof. English N.C. State U., Raleigh, 1964-68; from asst. prof. to prof. English North Tex. State U. (name now U. North Tex.), Denton, 1968—, disting. Alumni prof., 1979, chmn. dept. English, 1981-86, assoc. dean Coll. Arts and Scis., 1986-92; sr. Fulbright lectr. U. Würzburg (Germany), 1985; interim dean Coll. Arts and Scis. U. North Tex., Denton, 1992-93, vice provost, 1993-98, v.p. for acad. affairs, 1998-2000, provost, v.p. acad. affairs, 2000—03, prof. English, 2003—, spl. asst. to pres. for humanities, 2003—06. Cons. presses on manuscripts in Am. lit Author: Josh Billings, 1973, Bill Nye, 1980; monograph Bill Nye: The Western Writings, 1976; editor: Studies in the Marble Faun, 1971, Critics on Poe, 1973, Critics on Mark Twain, 1973, Critical Essays on Hawthorne's The Scarlet Letter, 1988; founding editor: Hawthorne Soc. Newsletter (now Nathaniel Hawthorne Rev.), 1974-82; assoc. editor: Studies in the Novel, 1970— , Nathaniel Hawthorne Jour., 1980-82. With USAR, 1956-60. Recipient Mortar Bd. Outstanding Educator award, 1980; Outstanding Alumnus award S.W. Mo. State U., 1986, Disting. Grad. Alumnus award Dept. English U. Ark., 1988. Mem. Nathaniel Hawthorne Soc. (co-founder, 1st pres. 1974-76), Am. Humor Studies Assn. (pres. 1980-81), South Ctrl. MLA (exec. com. 1976-77), MLA (del. assembly 1977-80, 84-87), Melville Soc., Soc. Study So. Lit. (pres. 1999-01), Mark Twain Circle, Thoreau Soc., Thomas Wolfe Soc., Fulbright Assn., POE Studies Assn., Phi Kappa Phi, Phi Beta Delta, Golden Key. Office: U North Tex Office PO Box 311307 Denton TX 76203-1307 Business E-Mail: kesterson@unt.edu.

KESTLER, RICHARD MICHAEL, mathematics educator; b. Jamestown, NY, Feb. 8, 1952; s. John William and Crystal Frederica Kestler; m. Susan Linda Zappia, Apr. 11, 1987; children: Lisa, Matthew. AS, Jamestown CC, 1973; BS, SUNY, Fredonia, 1974, MS in Edn., 1977. Substitute tchr. Jamestown Pub. Schs., 1974—79; HS math. tchr. Sherman Ctrl. Sch., NY, 1979—81; jr./sr. HS math. tchr. Falconer Ctrl. Sch., NY, 1981—. Mem.: Am. Fedn. Tchrs. Home: 311 S Main St Jamestown NY 14701

KESTNER, ROBERT STEVEN, lawyer; b. St. Louis, Aug. 6, 1954; s. Robert Steven Sr. and Josephine Ann (LiPuma) K.; m. Denise Marie Dalhart, Apr. 25, 1981; children: Alexander, Jonathan, Joseph. BA in Mathematics & Economics, Ohio Wesleyan U., 1976; JD, Ohio State U., 1979. Bar: Ohio 1979, U.S. Dist. Ct. (no. dist.) Ohio 1979. Assoc. Baker & Hostetler, Cleve., 1979—88, ptnr., gen. bus. practice coord., 1988—2003, exec. ptnr., mem. policy com., 2003—. Mem. exec. campaign cabinet United Way; bd. dirs. Greater Cleve. Partnership. Mem. ABA, Ohio Bar Assn., Cleve. Bar Assn., Cleve. Mus. of Art (bd. regents), The Country Club, Pepper Pike. Office: Baker & Hostetler LLP 1900 E Ninth St Cleveland OH 44114-3485 Office Phone: 216-861-7558. Office Fax: 216-696-0740. Business E-Mail: skestner@bakerlaw.com.

KETCHAM, RICHARD SCOTT, lawyer; b. Columbus, Ohio, Jan. 8, 1948; s. Victor Alvin and Dorothy Eloise (Becher) K.; m. Kim Michelle Halliburton, Apr. 7, 1984 (div. 1989); 1 child, Kate Erin; m. Christy M. Canaday, Sept. 9, 1990 (div. 1994). BS, Bowling Green State U., Ohio, 1970; JD cum laude, Capital U., Columbus, 1974. Bar: Ohio 1974, U.S. Dist. Ct. (so. dist.) Ohio 1979. Asst. pros. atty. Franklin County (Ohio) Pros., Columbus, 1974-79, sr. asst. pros. atty., 1979-84; ptnr. Ketcham & Ketcham, Columbus, 1984—. Mem. task force Legal Aid Referral Project, Columbus Bar Assn. Homeless Project, 1989—. Mem. Gov.'s Task Force on Family Violence, 1984-86. Mem. Nat. Assn. Criminal Def. Lawyers, Ohio Assn. Criminal Def. Lawyers (bd. dirs. 1989—, v.p. CLE, sec., strike force chair 2005-07), Ctrl. Ohio Assn. Criminal Def. Lawyers (pres. 1994-95, bd. dirs. 2001—), Ohio State Bar Assn., Columbus Bar Assn. (chmn. criminal law com. 1994-95, 95-96), Franklin County Trial Lawyers. Avocations: fishing, basketball, model railroads, gardening. Home: 1937 Elmwood Ave Columbus OH 43212-1112 Office: Ketcham & Ketcham 755 S High St Columbus OH 43206-1908 Office Phone: 614-444-3900. Personal E-mail: rsketch2@aol.com.

KETCHAND, ROBERT LEE, lawyer; b. Shreveport, La., Jan. 30, 1948; s. Woodrow Wilson and Attie Harriet (Chandler) K.; m. Alice Sue Adams, May 31, 1969; children: Peter Leland, Marjory Attie. BA, Baylor U., 1970; JD, Harvard U., 1973. Bar: Tex. 1973, Mass. 1973, DC 1981. Assoc., ptnr. Butler & Binion, Houston, 1976-85, Washington, 1981-82; shareholder Brodsky & Ketchand, Houston, 1985-88; ptnr. Webster & Sheffield, Houston, 1988-90; atty. pvt. practice, Houston, 1990-92; ptnr. Short & Ketchand, Houston, 1992-2001; dir. Boyer & Ketchand, P.C., Houston, 2001—. Founder, chmn. bd. dirs. Rolling Waters, d/b/a Houston Legal Clinic. Pres. Prisoner Svcs. Com. Houston, 1986; deacon South Houston Bapt. Ch., 1976—; gen. counsel, dir. Houston Met. Ministries, 1986-88; dir. Interfaith Ministries Greater Houston, 1996-98; gen. counsel Houston Bus. Roundtable, 1988—. Lt. USNR, 1973-76. Mem. ABA, Tex. Bar Assn., Houston Bar Assn. (chmn. dispute com. 1989-90). Avocation: reading. Home: 2707 Carolina Way Houston TX 77005-3423 Office: Boyer & Ketchand PC 9 Greenway Plz Ste 3100 Houston TX 77046 Office Phone: 713-871-2053. Office Fax: 713-871-2024. Business E-Mail: rketchand@boyerketchand.com.

KETCHERSID, WILLIAM LESTER, history professor; b. Rockwood, Tenn., Feb. 22, 1943; s. Newell Woodrow and Hazel Wyatt Ketchersid; m. Lee Douglas Ketchersid, Sept. 3, 1966; children: William, Elizabeth Rodriguez, Deborah Heath, John W. BA in History, Tenn. Wesleyan Coll., 1965; MA in History, U. Tenn., 1966; PhD in History, U. Ga., 1977. Prof. Bryan Coll., Dayton, Tenn., 1966—69, 1973—79, 1984—. Faculty chair Bryan Coll., Dayton, Tenn., 1971, 88, 2006—07; sales rep. Am. Express, Chattanooga, 1974—84; summer tchr., Mongolia, 1993; reviewer Tenn. Hist. Assn., 1995—. Author: The Gilded Age Presidency Reconsidered, 2003. Leader mission trip Meth. Ch., Jamaica, 1986—2006, Cuba, 1998, Haiti, 1998, 2007. Recipient Tchr. Yr., Bryan Coll., 1968, 1979, Outstanding Prof. award, 1984—, 2002. Mem.: So. Hist. Assn., Dayton Lions Club (past pres. and bd. 1993—2006, Lion of the Decade Dist. 12-0 1990), Gideons Internat. Democrat. Methodist. Avocations: coin collecting/numismatics, hiking. Home: 361 13th Ave Dayton TN 37321 Office: Bryan Coll P O Box 7806 Dayton TN 37321 Office Phone: 423-775-7267. Personal E-mail: wketchersid@aol.com.

KETCHUM, JAMES ROE, curator; b. Rochester, NY, Mar. 15, 1939; s. George Roe and Mary Louise (Frantz) K.; m. Barbara M. Van Ness, Aug. 18, 1962; children: John Van Ness, Sarah Graham, Timothy Roe, Chester Arthur. AB, Colgate U., 1960; postgrad., Georgetown U., 1960-61, George Washington U., 1961-62. Staff historian Dept. Interior, Washington, 1960-62; registrar The White House, Washington, 1962-63, curator, 1963-70, U.S. Senate, Washington, 1970-95, curator emeritus, 1995—. Editor: The White House: An Historic Guide, 1962-70; contbr. numerous articles to profl. jours. and encys. Mem. Com. Preservation of White House, 1964-70; trustee U.S. Capitol Hist. Soc., 1971-79; alt. mem. Fed. Council Arts and Humanities, 1974-95; trustee Woodrow Wilson Birthplace Found., 1980—. Member Am. Assn. Museums, City Mus. Washington, Nat. Trust Historic Preservation, Theta Chi. Office: US Senate Commn Art Us Capital Bldg Rm S-411 Washington DC 20510-0001

KETCHUM, MARK D., consumer products company executive; BS, Cornell U., 1971. Joined Procter & Gamble Co., 1971, with paper div., 1971—84, brand mgmt., 1984—90, v.p., gen. mgr. Tissue/Towel, 1990—96, pres. N.Am. Paper Sector, 1996—99, pres. Global Baby and Family Care, 1999—2004; interim CEO Newell Rubbermaid Inc., 2005—06, pres., CEO, 2006—. Bd. dir. Newell Rubbermaid Inc., 2004—, Hillenbrand Industries, Inc, Kraft Foods, 2007—. Mem.: Am. Forest & Paper Assn. (bd. dirs. tissue div.). Office: Newell Rubbermaid Inc 10B Glenlake Pky, Ste 600 Atlanta GA 30328*

KETCHUM, RICHARD G., stock exchange executive, lawyer; BA, Tufts U., 1972; JD, NYU, 1975. Bar: NY, DC. Assoc. Milbank, Tweed, Hadley and McCloy, NYC, 1975—77; with SEC, 1977—83, dir. divsn. market regulation, 1983—91; exec. v.p. Nat. Assn. Securities Dealers, 1991—93, COO, 1993—98, pres., 1998—2000; pres., dep. chmn. Nasdaq Stock Market, Inc., 2000—03; gen. counsel global corp. and investment bank Citigroup, Inc., NYC, 2003—04; chief regulatory officer NY Stock Exch., NYC, 2004—06; CEO NYSE Regulation, Inc. NYSE Group, Inc., NYC, 2006—; non. exec. chmn. Fin. Industry Regulatory Authority, Inc., Washington, 2007—. Bd. dirs. NYSE Regulation, Inc., 2006—. Office: NYSE Regulation Inc c/o Ray Pellecchia 11 Wall St New York NY 10005*

KETCHUM, WILLIAM CLARENCE, author, educator; b. Columbia, Mo., Mar. 29, 1931; s. William C. and Mildred Ann (Roberts) K.; m. Erica Stoller; children: Aaron, Alison, Ian. BA, Union Coll., 1953; JD, Columbia U., 1956. Bar: N.Y. 1960. Atty. Kriendler & Kriendler, NYC, 1956, Martin, Clearwater & Bell, NYC, 1960-65, R.S. Lane, NYC, 1965-69; law sec. to Judge Lane of Civil Court, New York County NYC, 1969-76; instr. course on Am. antiques New Sch., NYC, 1970-87; instr. antiques course CUNY-Hunter Coll., 1978-79; mem. faculty NYU, 1984—, Folk Art Inst., 1987—, Marymount Coll., Tarrytown, N.Y., 1987-92. Guest curator Mus. Am. Folk Art, N.Y.C., 1974—, curator spl. projects, 1985-90, mem. nat. adv. com., 1992—; guest curator Nassau County Fine Arts Mus., 1980, Boscobel Restoration, 1995; curator Female Folk Artists U.S., Japan, 1988-89, Am. Bd. Games Katonah (N.Y.) Mus. Art, 1992, Scarsdale (N.Y.) Hist. Soc., 1993-94; guest spkr. Seminar on Early Am. Life, Pa. Farm Mus., Lancaster, 1974, Smithsonian Instn., 1976, Mercer Mus., Hancock Shaker Mus., 1977; guest lectr. Flemington Hist. Soc., 1975-76, antiques seminar NYU, 1973-75, 78-79, 81-84, New Haven Hist. Soc., 1975, Shelburne (Vt.) Mus., 1976, 78, St. Mary's of the Woods Coll., Terre Haute, Ind., 1976-78, Cooper-Hewitt Mus., 1978, Nassau County Fine Arts Mus., 1980, Mus. Am. Folk Art, 1978-84, Peale Mus., Balt., 1984, Del. Art Mus., 1985, N.Y. State Mus., 1985, 2000, Seattle Art Mus., 1986-87, Jacksonville (Fla.) Mus. Art, 1987, Marymount Coll., 1987-92, Hiram (Ohio) Coll., 1988, Triton Mus., Santa Clara, Calif., 1988, Chautauqua (N.Y.) Inst., 1989, Art and Culture Ctr. Hollywood, Fla., 1990, Philbrook Mus. Art, Tulsa, 1991, Katonah (N.Y.) Mus. Art, 1993, 99, Scarsdale (N.Y.) Hist. Soc., 1993, Claremont State (N.Y.) Hist. Site, 1994, Edinboro (Pa.) Coll., 1994-2000, Bruce Mus., 1995, 2002, Mus. of City of N.Y., 1995, Canterbury (N.H.) Shaker Village, 1997, N.Y. State Archaeol. Assn., 1997, 2000, N.Y. Hist. Assn., 1999-2001, Conn. Ceramic Cir., 1997, 2002, Am. Soc. Appraisers, 2000, 03; cons. antique series Time-Life, Inc., 1976-78; series cons. Knopf Collectors' Guides to Am. Antiques, 1982-84; spokesperson QVC, 1993; cons. material culture, archaeol. excavations Ft. Edward and Ft. William Henry, N.Y., 1994-2004, N.Y. State Hist. Assn., 1996—, NJ State Hist. Soc., 2004, Md. Auctioneers' Assn., 2004. Author: Early Potters and Potteries of New York, 1970, second ed. 1987; The Pottery and Porcelain Collectors Handbook, 1971; American Basketry and Woodenware, 1974; American Bottles, 1975; American Hooked Rugs, 1976; A Catalog of American Antiques, 1977, rev., 1990; The Family Treasury of Antiques, 1978; Catalog of American Collectibles, 1979, rev., 1990; Western Memorabilia, 1980; Auction, 1980; Collecting American Craft Antiques, 1980; Toys; Furniture 2, 1981; The Catalog of World Antiques, 1981; The Book of Boxes, 1982; Chests, Cupboards, Desks and Other Pieces, 1982, A Guide to Bottle Collecting, 1985; Am. Folk Art of the Twentieth Century, 1983; Pottery and Porcelain, 1983; Collecting Toys for Fun & Profit, 1985; Collecting 40's and 50's Collectibles for Fun and Profit, 1985; Sports Collectibles for Fun and Profit, 1985; All American, Folk Arts and Crafts, 1986; American Country Pottery, 1987, Making a Living in Antiques, 1990, Holiday Collectables, 1990, American Redware, 1990, Am. Stoneware, 1991, Country Wreaths and Baskets, 1991, Collecting the West, 1992, Western Memorabilia Identification and Price Guide, 1993, American Pottery & Porcelain, Identification and Price Guide, 1994, American Cabinetmakers, 1995, American Folk Art, 1995, The Art of Grandma Moses, 1996, Simple Beauty: The Shakers in America, 1996, The Art of the Golden West, 1996, Remington and Russell, 1997, Native American Art, 1997; contbg. author: The American Sporting Collectibles Handbook, 1982, Is It Genuine, 1986, The Dictionary of Art, 1994, The Encyclopedia of New York, 2000, American Folk Articles: Les Primitife Americains, 2001, The Encyclopedia of Folk Art, 2003, Paul Cushman: The Work and World of an Early 19th Century Potter, 2007; also articles to profl. jours. Lt., USNR, 1956-60. Recipient Amb. of Honor award English Speaking Union, 1984. Mem. Assn. of Bar of City of N.Y. (mem. com. uniform state laws 1972-76, mem. art com. 1976-78), N.Y. State Hist. Soc., N.E. Archeol. Assn., Westchester County Hist. Soc. (bd. trustees 2005—). Home: 241 Grace Church St Rye NY 10580-4217 Personal E-mail: w.ketchum@optonline.net.

KETEFIAN, SHAKÉ, nursing educator; b. Beirut, Dec. 29, 1939; d. Krikor and Zaghganoush (Soghomonian) K. BSN, Am. U. Beirut, 1963; MEd, Columbia U., 1968, EdD, 1972. From asst. prof. nursing to prof. NYU Sch. Edn., Health, Nursing and Arts Professions, NYC, 1972-84; dir. continuing edn. in nursing NYU, NYC; with U. Mich., 1984—; prof., assoc. dean for grad. studies, dir. doctoral and postdoctoral studies U. Mich. Sch. Nursing, Ann Arbor, 1984—91, dir. internat. affairs, 1996—, acting dean, 1991-92. Contbr. articles to profl. jours. Fellow AAUW, Am. Acad. Nursing (governing coun.); mem. ANA, Am. Orgn. Nurse Execs., Midwest Nursing Rsch. Soc. (chair sci. integrity task force 1994-96, 2001-03), Mich. Nurses Assn., Internat. Network for Doctoral Edn. in Nursing (co-founder, pres.), Sigma Theta Tau. Office: U Mich Sch Nursing 400 N Ingalls Ann Arbor MI 48109 Home Phone: 734-665-0094; Office Phone: 734-763-6669. Business E-Mail: ketefian@umich.edu.

KETEYIAN, ARMEN, news correspondent; b. Detroit, Mar. 6, 1953; m. Dede Keteyian; 2 children. BA cum laude, San Diego State Univ., 1976. Newspaper reporter, Calif.; writer, reporter Sports Illustrated, 1982—89; reporter, prodr. NBC Sports; network corr. ABC News, NYC, 1989—97; corr., Real Sports with Bryant Gumbel HBO, NYC, 1998—2006; reporter CBS Sports, NYC, 1997—2006; chief investigative corr. CBS News, NYC, 2006—. Co-author: Rod Carew's Art and Science of Hitting, 1986, Catfish: My Life in Baseball, 1988, Raw Recruits, 1990 (NY Times Bestseller list), Why You Crying? Autobiography of George Lopez, 2004 (NY Times Bestseller list); author: Big Red Confidential: Inside Nebraska Football, 1989, Ditka: Monster of the Midway, 1993, Money Players: Days and Nights Inside the New NBA, 1997. Recipient 8 Emmy awards. Office: CBS News 530 W 57th St New York NY 10019

KETNER, KENNETH LAINE, philosopher, educator; b. Mountain Home, Okla., Mar. 24, 1939; s. Louis Elaine and Johnnie Lucille (Hannah) K.; m. Berti Gabriella Zehetmeier, Aug. 24, 1964 (dec. Oct. 1996); 1 child, Kenneth Laine Jr. BA in Philosophy, Okla. State U., 1961, MA, 1967; MA in Folklore, UCLA, 1968; PhD in Philosophy, U. Calif., Santa Barbara, 1972. Part-time instr. Okla. State U., 1964-67; tchg. asst. U. Calif., Santa Barbara, 1969-70; mem. faculty Tex. Tech U., Lubbock, 1971—, prof. philosophy, 1977-98, chmn. dept., 1979-81; founder, dir. Inst. Studies in Pragmaticism, 1972—, Charles Sanders Peirce prof. philosophy, 1981-98, Charles Sanders Peirce interdisciplinary prof., 1998—, Paul Whitfield Horn prof., 1999—. Asst. prof. philosophy and folklore UCLA, summers, 1972, 74; co-organizer C.S. Peirce Bicentennial Internat. Congress, Amsterdam, Netherlands 1976; Peirce Sesquicentennial Internat. Congress, Harvard U., 1989. Author: A Critical Study of Stephen C. Pepper's Approach to Metaphysics, 1967, An Essay on the Nature of World Views, 1972, An Emendation of R.G. Collingwood's Doctrine of Absolute

Presuppositions, 1973; editor, compiler: Charles Sanders Peirce: Contributions to the Nation, 4 parts, 1975, 78, 79, 87, Comprehensive Bibliography of Works of C.S. Peirce, 1977, rev. edit., 1986, Reasoning and the Logic of Things, 1993, A Thief of Peirce, 1995, His Glassy Essence: an Autobiography of C.S. Peirce, 1998; founder, gen. editor Peirce Studies, 1979—, Philosophical Inquiries, 1989—, more. Capt. USAR, 1962-64. Grantee NSF, Nat. Endowment Humanities, Am. Coun. Learned Socs. Fellow Charles S. Peirce Soc. (pres. 1983); mem. Am. Philos. Assn., Freemason, Tau Kappa Epsilon. Democrat. Home: PO Box 65135 Lubbock TX 79464-5135 Office: Texas Tech Univ Library 305 Lubbock TX 79409-0002

KETTELKAMP, DONALD BENJAMIN, retired orthopedist; b. Anamosa, Iowa, Jan. 21, 1930; s. Enoch George and Elsie (Norden) K.; m. Alice June Mencke, Dec. 30, 1954; children: Karen June, Lisa Marie, Suzanne D., Jonathan B.; m. Clemencia Oliveros Brandon, Apr. 28, 1989. BA, Cornell U., Mt. Vernon, Iowa, 1952; MD, U. Iowa, 1955, MS, 1960. Diplomate Am. Bd. Orthop. Surgery. Intern Thomas D. Dee Meml. Hosp., Ogden, Utah, 1955—56; resident orthopedic surgery U. Iowa, Iowa City, 1958—61; practice medicine specializing in orthopedic surgery Anchorage, 1961—64; asst. prof. Albany (N.Y.) Med. Coll., 1964—66, assoc. prof., 1966—68, U. Iowa, Iowa City, 1968—71, prof., 1971; prof., chmn. dept. orthopaedic surgery U. Ark., Little Rock, 1971—74, Ind. U., Indpls., 1974—84; assoc. dean Tex. Tech. U., El Paso, 1984—87; exec. dir. Am. Bd. Orthop. Surgery, Chgo., 1986—94. Trustee: Jour. Bone and Joint Surgery, 1991—96. With USPHS, 1956—58. Mem.: ACS, Knee Soc., Assn. Orthopaedic Chairmen (pres. 1981), Am. Orthopaedic Assn. (pres. 1989—90), Am. Soc. Surgery of Hand, Am. Acad. Orthopaedic Surgeons.

KETTER, DAVID LEE, lawyer; b. Portsmouth, Ohio, Jan. 7, 1929; s. William Leslie and Dorothy Aileen (Weidner) K.; m. Beverly Jane Kinker, June 10, 1951; children— Michael David, Sandra Lee, Beth Ann, Richard Douglass AB, Ohio U., 1953; JD, U. Cin., 1955. Bar: Ohio 1955, Pa. 1964. Trial lawyer Dept. Justice, Washington, 1955-56; trial lawyer Chief Counsel's Office, IRS, Pitts., 1956-62; assoc. Kirkpatrick, Pomeroy, Lockhart & Johnson, Pitts., 1962-65; ptnr. Kirkpatrick & Lockhart, LLP, Pitts., 1965-94, of counsel, 1995—. Served as sgt. USMC, 1946-47, 50-52 Mem. ABA (tax sect.), Pa. Bar Assn. (tax sect.), Allegheny County Bar Assn. (chmn. tax sect. 1964-66), Pitts. Tax Club (pres. 1985-86), Order of Coif, Duquesne Club, Rivers Club, Valley Brook Country Club (sec. 1977-78). Clubs: Duquesne, Rivers, Valley Brook Country (McMurray, Pa., sec. 1977-78). Republican. Methodist. Avocations: golf, shooting. Home: 160 Canterbury Rd Mc Murray PA 15317-2802 Office: Kirkpatrick & Lockhart Preston Gates Ellis LLP Henry W Oliver Bldg 535 Smithfield St Pittsburgh PA 15222-2312 Home Phone: 724-941-5313; Office Phone: 412-355-6420. Business E-Mail: david.ketter@hlgates.com.

KETTERLE, WOLFGANG, physics professor; b. Heidelberg, Germany, Oct. 21, 1957; came to the U.S., 1990; divorced; three children. Physics pre-diploma, U. Heidelberg, 1978; physics diploma, Tech. U., Munich, 1982; PhD in Physics, Ludwig-Maximilians U. Munich, 1986; PhD in Sci. (hon.), Gustavus Adolphus Coll., 2005. Rsch. asst. Max-Planck Inst. for Quantum Optics, Garching, Germany, 1982-85, staff scientist, 1985-88; rsch. scientist dept. phys. chemistry U. Heidelberg, 1989-90; rsch. assoc. MIT, Cambridge, Mass., 1990-93, asst. prof. physics, 1993-97, prof., 1997—, John. D. MacArthur prof. physics, 1998—. Officer Order of Legion of Honor, 2002, France. Decorated Medal of Merit Baden-Wurtemberg, Knight Comdr.'s Cross (Badge and Star) Order of Merit Fed. Rep. Germany; recipient Technology Innovation award Discover Magazine, 1998, Fritz London prize in low temperature physics, 1999, Dannie-Heineman prize Acad. Scis., Göttingen, Germany, 1999, Benjamin Franklin medal in physics, 2000, NATO/DAAD Postdoctoral fellow, 1990—91, Michael and Philip Platzman award, 1994, David and Lucile Packard fellow, 1996, The Nobel Prize in Physics, 2001, Killian award, MIT, 2004. Fellow Am. Phys. Soc. (Disting. Traveling lectr. 1998, Rabi prize 1997), Am. Acad. Arts and Scis., Inst. of Physics; mem. NAS, German Phys. Soc. (Gustav-Hertz prize 1997), Am. Optical Soc., European Acad. Arts, Scis. and Humanities (titular mem.), Acad. Scis. Heidelberg, Bavarian Acad. Scis. Office: Dept Physics MIT 77 Massachusetts Ave Rm 26-243 Cambridge MA 02139-4307 E-mail: ketterle@mit.edu.

KETTIMUTHU, RAJKUMAR, computer scientist; s. Kettimuthu Chennimalai and Padmavathi Kettimuthu; m. Kavithaa Rajavenkateshwaran, Dec. 11, 2005. BS in Computer Sci. and Engring. (hon.), Anna U., Madras, India, 1999; MS in Computer Sci., Ohio State U., Columbus, 2002. Cert. network assoc. Cisco. Sys. adminstr. Anna U., 1995—97, tchg. assoc., 1997—99; network engr. Cisco's Offshore Devel. Ctr., Madras, Tamilnadu, India, 1999—2000; rsch. assoc. Ohio State U., Columbus, 2000—02; rsch. engr. Argonne Nat. Lab., U. Chgo., Ill., 2002—05, sr. rsch. engr., 2005—. Mem. program com. for several internat. confs.; prin. investigator for projects funded by US Dept. Energy and NSF; presenter and reviewer in field. Contbr. numerous articles and papers to profl. jours. Recipient Best Poster award, Internat. Conf. High Performance Computing, 1999, Pace Setter award, Cisco Systems, 2000, Best Paper award, Internat. Conf. Parallel Processing, 2002, Best Tool award, Assn. Computing Machinery and IEEE SuperComputing Conf., 2003, Excellence award, Distributed Systems Lab., Argonne Nat. Lab., 2004, Outstanding Rsch. Contbns. Computer Sci. and Engring. Acheivement award, World Acad. Sci., 2005, Outstanding Achievement award, Nat. Cancer Inst., 2007; scholar, Ohio State U., 2001. Mem.: IEEE, Open Grid Forum, Assn. Computing Machinery. Achievements include playing a key role in developing a data movement mechanism and framework for moving data efficiently across the wide area networks; playing a key role in developing an Input/Output (IO) system for distributed computers; development of innovative strategies for job scheduling in parallel and distributed computing systems. Avocations: travel, running, movies, racquetball. Office Phone: 630-252-0915. Home Fax: 320-386-0405. Personal E-mail: kettimut@gmail.com.

KETTLER, CARL FREDERICK, airline executive; b. NYC, Dec. 19, 1936; s. William Henry and Martha Maria (Allmendinger) K.; m. Marianne Louis Slagboom, Dec. 19, 1970; 1 child, Patricia Heidi. BS in Aeronautics, St. Louis U., 1965; MBA, U. Calif., Berkeley, 1966. Project mgr. corp. planning Trans World Airlines, 1968-69; dir. internat. market planning Flying Tiger Ln., 1969-71; spl. asst. to U.S. Senator Henry Bellmon, 1971-74; dir. fed. affairs Air Transport Assn. Am., Washington, 1974-78; co-organizer Midway Airlines, Inc., 1974-79; asst. to pres. Airbus Industries No.Am., NYC, 1978-80; vice chmn. bd. govs. Flight Safety Found., 1979-81; prtnr. Sunburst Energy Inc., Enid, Okla., 1980-82; co-founder, exec. v.p., COO Trans-Cen. Airlines, Oklahoma City, 1980—; founder T.H.E. Airline Inc., 1981; chmn., pres. Kettler Korp, Inc., 1981—; founder Kettler Komputer Svcs. Inc., 1987—, Kettler Employee Leasing Inc., 1981—; co-founder Kettler & Kettler Employment Svcs., Inc., Flemington, NJ, 1981; founder, pres. Kettler Airline Planning Svcs., Inc. Advisor to Reagan White House on Nat. Security, 1980-84; lectr. St. Louis U., 1968—; cons. aviation and internat. trade. Founder, pres. Oak Summit Sch. Hist. Soc., Citizens Against Ruining the Environ (CARE), 1985—; del. Rep. Nat. Conv., 1992. With USAF, 1955—61. Recipient Outstanding Svc. award Smithsonian Astrophys. Obs., 1959, Alumni Merit award St. Louis U., 1991. Mem. Nat. Def. Transp. Assn., Am. Inst. Aeronautics and Astronautics (air transport tech. com.), Okla. Heritage Assn., Okla. State Soc., Internat. House (Berkeley), Calif. Alumni Assn., U. Calif. at Berkeley, Ducks Unltd., Grand Nat. Quail Club (exec. com.), Capitol Hill Club, Nat. Aviation Club, Internat. Aviation Club, Wings Club, Aero Club, Alpha Eta Rho, Alpha Sigma Chi, Alpha Sigma Nu (Nat. Jesuit Scholastic Honors award, 1965), Gamma Phi Epsilon. Roman Catholic. Avocations: politics, piloting, boating, travel, writing. Home: 59 Everitts Hill Rd Flemington NJ 08822-4005 E-mail: kettler@blast.net.

KETTLEWELL, GAIL BIERY, academic administrator, research professor; b. Dresden, Ohio, Apr. 5, 1939; d. Graydon Adams and Mildred K. (Cox) Biery; m. Charles G. Kettlewell, Sept. 9, 1960; children: Christian, Abigail, Nathaniel. BA, Muskingum Coll., 1961; MA, Old Dominion U., 1973; EdD, Va. Poly. Inst. and State U., Blacksburg, Va., 1985. Libr. Knox County Libr., Mt. Vernon, Ohio, 1961-62; tchr. Fairfax County Pub. Schs., Alexandria, Va., 1968-70, Portsmouth Pub. Schs., Va., 1962-68, 70-72; assoc. prof. Tidewater CC, Portsmouth, 1974-83; vice chancellor So. Ark. U. Tech., Camden, 1984-90; provost No. Va. CC, Manassas, 1990—2002; dir. higher edn. program George Mason U., Fairfax, Va., 2002—06, rsch. prof. internat. post secondary devel., 2006—. Chmn. Internat. Applied Arts and Scis. Inst., 1999—2001. Author: Guide for Peer Tutors, 1981; co-author: (with Alice Hedrick) An Approach to Language, 1978, (with Betty J. Perkinson) Reading/Thinking/Writing, 1983, 2d edit., 1989, 3d edit., 1994; mem. editl. bd. Workforce, 1994. Bd. dirs. Ark. Literacy Coun., Little Rock, 1988, Prince William County chpt. ARC, 1991-94, 96-01, 05, Prince William Litter Control Coun., 1991, Manassas Mus. Assocs., 1991-94, Manassas Ctr. for Arts, 1994-99, Prince William/I66 Partnership, 1994-2002, Prince William/Manassas Conv. and Visitors Bur., 2001, Gray Ghost Theater, 2006—, vice-chmn., 2006—; pres. Prince William Habitat for Humanity, 2001-04; mem. Ark. Tech. Com., Little Rock, 1989-90, Am. Coun. Edn. Commn. on Women, 1994-97, Manassas Tourism Coun., 1994-96, Manassas Bus. Coun., 1994-96; coord., organizer Ouachita-Calhoun Literacy Coun., Camden, Ark., 1987-89; active Cmty. Theatre, 1983—. Fellow Western Carolina U., 1976, Old Dominion U., 1967; recipient Community Svc. award, Portsmouth, Va. Mem.: DAR, NAFE, AAUW, ASTD, Ark. Assn. Devel. Edn. (pres. 1988—89), North Ctrl. Assn. Schs. and Colls. (rev. com. 1987—90), Manassas Bus. Coun., Va. Assn. Female Execs, Am. Coun. Edn. (com. on women 1994—97), Prince William/Greater Manassas C. of C. (bd. dirs. 1994—2002), Children Am. Revolution (orgn. sr. pres. 1989—90), Fedn. Civic Clubs (v.p. 1980, pres. 1981—), Rotary (bd. dirs. 1992—94, v.p. 2006, pres. 2007—), Phi Delta Kappa, Delta Kappa Gamma (v.p. 1980—81, internat. fellowship 1982, pres. 1988—89, 1st v.p. 1992—93), Phi Theta Kappa (hon.). Episcopalian. Office: George Mason Univ MS 1C8 4260 Chainbridge Rd A102 Fairfax VA 22030-4444 Home: 13456 Victory Gallop Ln Gainesville VA 20155 Office Phone: 703-993-8935. Business E-Mail: gkettlew@gmu.edu.

KEULEGAN, EMMA PAULINE, special education educator; b. Washington, Jan. 21, 1930; d. Garbis H. and Nellie Virginia (Moore) K. BA, Dumbarton Coll. of Holy Cross, 1954. Cert. tchr. elem. and spl. edn. Tchr. St. Dominic's Elem. Sch., Washington, 1954-56, Sacred Heart Acad., Washington, 1956-59, Our Lady of Victory, Washington, 1959-63, St. Francis Acad., Vicksburg, Miss., 1963-78, Culkin Acad., Vicksburg, 1978-91, substitute tchr. spl. edn., 1991—. Treas. PTA, Vicksburg, 1980; pres. Vicksburg Geneal. Soc., 1999. Mem.: DAR (chpt. regent 1967—69, sec. 1994, chpt. chaplain 1996, chpt. libr. 2002, chpt. membership chmn.), Daus. of United Confederacy (chpt. chaplain), Soc. Descs. of Knights of Most Noble Order of the Garter, Sovereign Colonial Soc. Am. Royal Descent, Soc. Magna Charta Dames and Barons (state chaplain 2001), Daus. of the War of 1812 (state chaplain 1998, hon. state pres. 2002—03, state pres. 2002—), Daus. Am. Colonists (chaplain 1985—89, state pres. 1992—94, hon. state pres. 1994—), Colonial Dames 17th Century (state v.p. 1987—89, state pres. 1989, hon. state pres. 1991—), Internat. Reading Assn. (pres. Warren County chpt.), Vicksburg Geneal. Soc. (pres. 2003). Republican. Roman Catholic. Avocations: needlecrafts, reading, coin collecting/numismatics, stamp collecting/philately. Home: 215 Buena Vista Dr Vicksburg MS 39180-5612

KEUM, JONG-HAE, mathematician, educator; b. Kunsan, Korea, Apr. 5, 1957; s. Ki-Soo and Jeong-Gyo (Kwon) K.; m. Soonyiel Park, June 13, 1984; children: Yong-Yeon, Goo-Tag. BS, Seoul Nat. U., 1980, MS, 1982; PhD, U. Mich., 1988. Cert. in math. Asst. prof. U. Utah, Salt Lake City, 1988-90; assoc. prof. Konkuk U., Seoul, 1991-96, prof., 1997-2000, Korea Inst. Advanced Study, Seoul, 2000—. Vis. prof. U. Mich., Ann Arbor, 1996-97; vice chmn. Korea Nat. Com. for Univ. Entrance Exam., Seoul, 1997-99; dept. head Konkuk U., Seoul, 1998-2000; chief coord. The 41st Internat. Math. Olympiad, Taejon, Rep. of Korea, 2000; dean Sch. of Math. KIAS, Korea, 2005—, liaison com. mem. PRIMA, 2006. Contbr. articles to profl. jours. Lt. Korean Army, 1982. Recipient Best Paper award in sci. and tech. Korean Fedn. Sci. and Tech., 1998; rsch. fellow Math. Scis. Rsch. Inst., 1993, Japan Soc. for Promotion of Sci. fellow Nagoya U., 1998, fellow Korea Inst. for Advanced Study, 1998-2000; Royal Soc. fellow U. Warwick, 2000, Sprint fellow Nat. U. Singapore, 2000, COE fellow Hokkaido U., 2004. Mem. Korean Math. Soc., Am. Math. Soc., Math. Assn. Am. Avocation: golf. Office: Korea Inst Adv Study 207-43 Cheongryangri-dong Dongdaemun-gu 130-722 Seoul Republic of Korea Office Phone: +82-2-958-3788. Business E-Mail: jhkeum@kias.re.kr.

KEVAN, LARRY, chemistry professor; b. Kansas City, Mo., Dec. 12, 1938; s. Glenn Herman and Myrtle Helena (Johnson) K. BS, U. Kans., 1960; PhD, UCLA, 1963. Research assoc. U. Newcastle, England, 1963; instr. U. Chgo., 1963-65; asst. prof. chemistry U. Kans., Lawrence, 1965-67, assoc. prof., 1967-69; prof. Wayne State U., Detroit, 1969-80; Cullen prof. U. Houston, 1980—. Vis. prof. U. Utah, 1971, Nagoya U., Japan, 1976, U. of Paris, 1977, Armed Forces U., Munich, 1979, Hokkaido U., Japan, 1987, U. Florence, Italy, 1987, 90; chmn. Gordon Conf. Radiation Chemistry, 1975; mem. chemistry rev. com. Brookhaven Nat. Lab., 1974-78, chmn., 1978, chemistry rev. com. Argonne Nat. Lab., 1980-86, chmn., 1982; rev. com. Notre Dame Radiation Lab., 1993, 94, NIH Spl. Study sects., 1982—; users com. mem. Nat. High Field Magnet Lab., 1996-99. Author: Electron Spin Double Resonance Spectroscopy, 1976, Time Domain Electron Spin Resonance, 1979, Advances in Pulsed and Continuous Wave Electron Spin Resonance, 1990; also over 800 articles; editor: Radical Ions, 1968, Electron-Solvent and Anion-Solvent Interactions, 1976; mem. editl. bd. Jour. Chem. Physics, Jour. Phys. Chemistry, Radiation Physics and Chemistry, Concepts in Magnetic Resonance, Jour. Chem. Soc.-Faraday Trans., Applied Magnetic Resonance, Nucleonika, Magnetic Resonance Reviews. Guggenheim fellow, 1970-71; recipient Faculty Rsch. award Wayne State U., 1978, Rsch. award Polish Soc. Radiation Rsch., Warsaw, 1979, Rsch. award Golden Key Nat. Honor Soc., 1986, Rsch. Excellence award U. Houston, 1987, Rsch. award Sigma Xi, 1989, Marie Curie medal, 1995, Silver Medal, Internat. EPR Soc., 2000. Fellow AAAS, Am. Phys. Soc., Royal Soc. Chemistry (London); mem. Am. Chem. Soc. (S.E. Tex. award 1986), S.W. Catalysis Soc. (chmn. 1986-88), Internat. Zeolite Assn., Internat. ESR Soc., Internat. Soc. Magnetic Resonance. Avocations: scuba diving, sailboat racing, skiing, tennis, wine tasting. Office: Univ of Houston Dept Chemistry 136 Fleming Bldg Houston TX 77204-5003 E-mail: Kevan@uh.edu.

KEVILLE, TERRI DONNA, lawyer; b. Phila., Mar. 5, 1951; d. Bernard Louis and Dora Duchovnay Jacobs; m. Thomas Joseph Keville, Aug. 25, 1974; children: James Thomas, Jordan Brian, Warren Lowell, Owen Stuart. BA, U. Pa., 1972; JD, U. So. Calif., Gould Sch. Law, 1992. Bar: Calif. 1992, US Dist. Ct. (ctrl. dist.) Calif. 1992, US Ct. Appeals (9th cir.) 1992, US Supreme Ct. 2000. Summer assoc. Horvitz & Levy, Encino, Calif., 1990; assoc. Manatt, Phelps & Phillips, LLP, Los Angeles, 1992—97, ptnr., 1998—. Bd. dirs. Friends of LA County Law Libr., 2006—. Recipient Order of the Coif, USC Chpt., 1992, Articles Editor, So. Calif. Law Rev., 1991-1992. Mem.: Calif. Soc. Healthcare Attys. (pres. 2004—05), LA County Bar Assn. (co-chair, bioethics com. 2000—02, LA County Med. Assn./LACBA joint com. on biomedical ethics, co chair), ABA Health Law Sect., Am. Health Lawyers Assn. Jewish. Avocation: classical music. Office: Manatt Phelps & Phillips LLP 11355 W Olympic Blvd Los Angeles CA 90064-1614 Home Phone: 310-201-5080; Office Phone: 310-312-4183. Office Fax: 310-914-5735. Business E-Mail: tkeville@manatt.com.

KEVLES, BETTYANN HOLTZMANN, writer, historian, educator; b. NYC, Aug. 20, 1938; d. David Marshal Holtzmann and Sondra Sara Arlosoroff; m. Daniel Jerome Kevles, May 18, 1961; children: Beth Carolyn, Jonathan David. BA, Vassar Coll., Poughkeepsie, NY, 1959; MA in Pub. Law and Govt., Columbia U., NYC, 1961. Mem. faculty history Westridge Sch., Pasadena, Calif., 1970—80; columnist, book reviewer LA Times, 1982—94; mem. staff U. Calif. Press, Berkeley, 1982—86; lectr. history Art Ctr. Coll. Design, Pasadena, 1988—96, Yale U., New Haven, 2000—. Charles A. Lindbergh chair in space history Smithsonian Nat. Air and Space Mus., Washington, 2002; spkr. in field. Author: Watching the Wild Apes: The Primate Studies of Goodall, Fossey and Galdikas, 1976, Thinking Gorillas: Teaching and Testing the Greatest Ape, 1980, Females of the Species: Sex and Survival in the Animal Kingdom, 1986, Naked to the Bone: Medical Imaging in the Twentieth Century, 1996, paperback edit., 1998, Almost Heaven: The Story of Women in Space, 2003, paperback edit., 2006; contbr. articles to profl. publs. Recipient Best Book award, NY Acad. Scis., NYC, 1976, Best Non-fiction award, Horn Book-Boston Glove, 1977, Lit. Arts award, Pasadena Arts Coun., 2000, Edn. award, Women in Aerospace, Washington, 2005; grantee, Alfred P. Sloan Found., 1992, 1998. Mem.: NY PEN. Avocations: swimming, walking, travel, art.

KEVLES, DANIEL JEROME, historian, educator, writer; b. Phila., Mar. 2, 1939; s. David and Anne (Rothstein) Kevles; m. Bettyann Holtzmann, May 18, 1961; children: Beth Carolyn, Jonathan David. BA in Physics, Princeton U., 1960; postgrad., Oxford U., 1960-61; PhD in History, Princeton U., 1964. From asst. to prof. history Calif. Inst. Tech., Pasadena, 1964-86, Koepfli prof. humanities, 1986-2001, head program in sci., ethics, and pub. policy, 1987-2001; vis. prof. Yale U., New Haven, 2000-01, Stanley Woodward prof. history, 2001—, dir. grad. studies program in history of sci. and medicine, 2002—05, chair program in history of sci. and medicine, 2005—. Vis. rsch. fellow U. Sussex, Brighton, Eng., 1976; vis. prof. U. Pa., Phila., 1979, Princeton U., 1999; dir. studies Ecole des Hautes Etudes en Sciences Sociales, Paris, 1991; chmn. faculty Calif. Inst. Tech., 1995-97. Author: The Physicists, 1978 (Nat. Hist. Soc. prize 1979), In the Name of Eugenics, 1985; (mag. series) Annals of Eugenics (Page One award 1985), The Baltimore Case, 1998 (Watson Davis prize); co-author: Inventing America, 2002, 2d edit., 2006; co-editor: The Code of Codes, 1992; contbr. articles to NY Rev. Books, other mags. Charles Warren fellow Harvard U., 1981-82, Ctr. for Advanced Study Behavorial Scis. fellow, 1986-87, Nat. Endowment for Humanities sr. fellow, 1981-82, Guggenheim fellow, 1983. Fellow: AAAS (chmn. sect. L 1983—85), Am. Philos. Soc., Soc. Am. Historians; mem.: PEN, History Sci. Soc. (coun. 1980—82, com. publ. 1984—88, Sarton lectr. 1985, com. honors and prizes 2001—04, nominations com. 2007—, George Sarton medal 2001), Am. Hist. Assn., Internat. Acad. Hist. of Sci. (corr.), Orgn. Am. Historians, Am. Acad. Arts and Scis., Author's Guild, Century Assn., Yale Club (N.Y.C.), Phi Beta Kappa. Democrat. Office: Yale U Dept History PO Box 208324 New Haven CT 06520-8324 Office Phone: 203-432-1356. E-mail: daniel.kevles@yale.edu.

KEVOIAN, BOB, radio personality; b. 1950; Grad., Long Beach State U., 1973. Radio host WFBQ-FM, Indpls., 1983—; nat. syndicated host Premiere Radio Networks, 1995—. Co-host The Bob & Tom Show, 1983—. Co-recipient Radio Personality of Yr. award, Billboard, 1991—98, Marconi Radio award, Nat. Assn. Broadcasters, 1993, 1995, 1997, 1999, Marconi Radio award for Network Syndicated Personality of Yr., 2006, The Sagamore of the Wabash, 1994, Nat. Chmn.'s Citation award, Leukemia Soc. Am., 1996. Office: WFBQ 6161 Fall Creek Rd Indianapolis IN 46220*

KEVORKIAN, JIRAIR, aeronautics and astronautics engineering educator; b. Jerusalem, May 14, 1933; came to U.S., 1952; s. Leon and Araxie (Kalemkerian) K.; m. Seta Tabourian, Mar. 8, 1980. BS, Ga. Inst. Tech., 1955, MS, 1956; PhD, Calif. Inst. Tech., 1961. Aerodynamicist Convair, Ft. Worth, 1956-57; rsch. fellow Calif. Inst. Tech., Pasadena, 1961-64; asst. prof. U. Wash., Seattle, 1964-66, assoc. prof., 1966-71, prof. applied math., aeros. and astronautics, 1971—2002, prof. emeritus, 2002—, acting chmn. applied math., 1986-87, 88-90. Vis. prof. U. Paris, 1971-72; Fulbright-Hayes vis. lectr., 1975-76. Author: Partial Differential Equations, 1990; co-author: Perturbation Methods in Applied Mathematics, 1981, Multiple Scale and Singular Perturbation Methods, 1996. Home: 3730 W Commodore Way Seattle WA 98199-1104 Office: U Wash Dept Applied Math PO Box 352420 Seattle WA 98195-2420 Business E-Mail: kevork@amath.washington.edu.

KEVORKIAN, RICHARD, artist; b. Dearborn, Mich., Aug. 24, 1937; s. Kay and Stana (Bedeian) K.; m. Salpy Bouroujian; children: Anna, Raffi, Soseh and Ellina (twins), Salpi Serar. BFA, Richmond Profl. Inst., 1961; MFA in Painting, Calif. Coll. Arts and Crafts, 1962. Instr. drawing and painting Richard Bland Coll., Petersburg, Va., 1961-64; instr. dept. fine arts Va. Commonwealth U., Richmond, 1962-66, asst. prof. dept. painting and printmaking, 1967-69, assoc. prof., 1969-77, prof., 1967-93, prof. emeritus, 1993, chmn. dept., 1969-81. One-man exhbns. include Aaron Gallery, Washington, Marita Gilliam Gallery, Raleigh, N.C.; exhbns. include Birmingham Mus. Art, Ala., 1977, Greenville County Mus. Art, S.C., 1977, Southeastern Ctr. Contemporary Art, Winston-Salem, N.C., 1977, 78, Hunter Mus. Art, Chattanooga, 1978, Va. Mus. Fine Art, 1983, U. Tenn., Knoxville, 1983, Lee Hansley Gallery, Raleigh, N.C. Mem. selection bd. for visual arts Va. Ctr. for Creative Arts, Sweet Briar. Served with N.G., 1955-63; guest curator Retrospective Exhib. Maurice Bonds Anderson Gallery, 2003. NEA individual sr. artists grantee, 1972, Va. Commonwealth U. Sch. Arts faculty creative research grantee, 1974, Nat. Endowment for Arts, Southeastern Ctr. Contemporary Arts grantee, 1976; Guggenheim fellow, 1978 Home: 7909 Rock Creek Rd Richmond VA 23229-6643 Personal E-mail: rekev@comcast.net.

KEWALRAMANI, LAXMAN SUNDERDAS, surgeon, consultant; b. Jaipur, India, Mar. 10, 1943; came to U.S., 1970, U.S. citizen; s. Sunderdas K. and Sugnidevi Kewalramani; m. Dropadi Chellani, May 29, 1970; children: Anupama, Mukul. MB, BS, U. Rajasthn, Jaipur, 1965, M of Surgery, 1969. Diplomate Am. Acad. Pain Mgmt., Am. Bd. Disability Analysts, Am. Bd. Phys. Medicine & Rehab., Am. Bd. Electrodiagnostic Medicine. Fellow neurol. surgery U. Calif. Davis-Sacramento Med. Ctr., 1970-71, resident in phys. medicine and rehab., 1971-73; asst. prof. dept. phys. medicine and rehab. U. Calif., Davis, 1973-76; asst. prof. depts. phys. medicine and rehab. Baylor Coll. Medicine, Houston, 1976-79; assoc. prof. sect. rheumatology and rehab. dept. medicine sch. medicine La. State U., New Orleans, 1979-82; dir. rehab. rsch., coord. patient care La. Rehab. Inst. and Charity Hosp., New Orleans, 1979-82; pvt. practice in phys. medicine and rehab., orthopedic medicine, electrodiagnostic medicine and thermography, 1982—; med. dir. Health South Rehab. Ctr., Harahan, La., 1989-91; med. dir. rehab. unit Chalmette Med. Ctrs., La., 1991-92; med. dir. spine and orthopedic inst. Elmwood Med. Ctr., Jefferson, La., 1993-95. Sr. disability analyst Am. bd. Disability Analysts, 2001; cons. rehab. medicine svc. crippled children svcs. sect. VA Hosp., 1975-76; mem. quality assurance com. Charity Hosp. and La. Rehab. Inst., New Orleans, 1979-82; presenter in field. Reviewer manuscripts, cons. editorial bd. Archives Phys. Medicine and Rehab., 1977-80; contbr. 2 chpts. to books and 96 articles to profl. jours. Cons. Cluster Living and Shared Providers, 1978; trustee New Orleans Pharmacy Mus., 1993—. Fellow: Am. Acad. Pain Mgmt., Am. Acad. Phys. Medicine and Rehab. (subcom. med. practice 1985—86, assessment diagnostic and therapeutic modalities and devices); mem.: Am. Assn. Indian Profls. (pres. New Orleans chpt. 2003), Internat. Med. Soc. Paraplegia, Orleans Parish Med. Soc., La. Phys. Medicine and Rehab. Soc., La. State Med. Soc., Am. Assn. Electromyography and Electrodiagnosis (liaison rep. to profl. stds. com. 1984), Am. Assn. Electrodiagnostic Medicine, Am. Assn. Physicians India (ethics and grievance com. 1992), Am. Spinal Injury Assn. Republican. Hindu. Avocations: reading, music, collecting time pieces and writing instruments, abstract painting. Home: 738 English Turn Ln New Orleans LA 70131-3349 Office: 3301 Saint Charles Ave New Orleans LA 70115-4533 Home Phone: 504-394-7145; Office Phone: 504-899-3041. Personal E-mail: laxman_kewalramani@yahoo.com.

KEY, JACK DAYTON, librarian; b. Enid, Okla., Feb. 24, 1934; s. Ernest Dayton and Janie (Haldeman) K.; m. Virgie Ruth Richardson, Aug. 12, 1956; children— Toni, Scot, Todd. BA, Phillips U., Enid, Okla., 1958; MA, U. N.Mex., 1960; MS, U. Ill., 1962. Staff supr. Grad. Library U. Ill., 1960-62; pharmacy librarian U. Iowa, 1962-64; med. librarian Lovelace Found. for Med. Edn. and Research, Albuquerque, 1965-70; dir. Mayo Med. Ctr. Librs., Rochester, Minn., 1970-94, dir. emeritus, 1994—; prof. emeritus biomed. comm. Mayo Med. Sch. Cons. in field; participant Naval War Coll. Conf., 1979; Alberta A. Brown lectr. Western Mich. U., 1979 Author: The Origin of the Vaccine Inoculation by Edward Jenner, 1977, William Alexander Hammond (1828-1900), 1979; editor: Library Automation: The Orient and South Pacific, 1975, Automated Activities in Health Sciences Libraries, 1975-78, Classics and Other Selected Readings in Medical Librarianship, 1980, Journal of a Quest for the Elusive Doctor Arthur Conan Doyle, 1982, Medical Vanities, 1982, William A. Hammond, M.D., 1828-1900: The Publications of an American Neurologist, 1983, Classics in Cardiology, Vol. 3, 1983, Vol. 4, 1989, Medical Casebook of Dr. Arthur Conan Doyle from Practitioner to Sherlock Holmes and Beyond, 1984, Medicine, Literature and Eponyms: An Encyclopedia of Medical Eponyms Derived from Literary Characters, 1989, Conan Doyle's Tales of Medical Humanism and Values, 1992; contbr. articles to profl. jours. Served with USN, 1952-55. U. N.Mex. fellow, 1958-59, N.Mex. Library Assn. Marion Dorroh Meml. scholar, 1960, Rotary Paul Harris fellow, 1979; recipient Outstanding Hist. Writing award Minn. Medicine, 1980, Spl. Svc. award Am. Acad. Dermatology, 1992, Farthing award Baker St. Jour., 1993; decorated knight Icelandic Order of Falcon, 1980; named to Phillips U. Hall Fame, 1988. Mem. Med. Library Assn., Am. Inst. History Pharmacy, Am. Assn. History Medicine, Am. Med. Writers Assn., Am. Osler Soc. (pres. 1990-91), Mystery Writers of Am., Alcuin Soc., Baker St. Irregulars, Ampersand Club, Sigma Xi (cert. of recognition 1982) Mem. Christian Ch. (Disciples Of Christ). Home: PO Box 231 54 Skyline Dr Sandia Park NM 87047-0231 Office: Mayo Clinic Rochester MN 55905-0001 Office Phone: 507-284-2691.

KEY, JAMES EVERETT, ophthalmologist; b. Freeport, Tex., July 19, 1944; s. James Everett and Margaret Ann (Parker) K.; m. Betty Wilson, Dec. 22, 1967; children: Peter Wilson and Courtney Brooke (twins). BA, U. Tex., 1966; MD, Baylor U., 1970. Diplomate Am. Bd. Ophthalmology. Mem. staff Coll. Medicine Baylor U., Houston, 1976-89, clin. assoc. prof. ophthalmology, 1989-93, clin. prof. ophthalmology, 1994—. Chief ophthalmology St. Luke's Episcopal Hosp., Houston, 1987—. Contbr. articles to jours., chpts. to books, editor medical textbooks. Trustee U. of South, Sewanee, Tenn., 1991-96, 98-2000. Lt. USN, 1972-73. Recipient Honor award Am. Acad. of Ophthalmology, 1990; named Outstanding Alumnus, Baylor Coll. Medicine, 2006. Fellow Am. Acad. Ophthalmology (Hon. award); mem. AMA, Contact Lens Assn. Ophthalmologists (past pres.), Harris County Med. Assn., Tex. Ophthal. Assn. (past bd. dirs.), Houston Ophthal. Soc. (past pres.), Phi Beta Kappa. Episcopalian. Office: 6624 Fannin St Ste 2100 Houston TX 77030-2333 Home Phone: 713-529-9025; Office Phone: 713-796-0120. E-mail: eyemed1@swbell.net.

KEY, TED, cartoonist; b. Fresno, Calif., Aug. 25, 1912; s. Simon Leon and Fanny (Kahn) K.; m. Anne Elizabeth Wilkinson, Sept. 30, 1937 (dec. July 5, 1984); children: Stephen Lewis, David Edward, Peter Lawrence; m. Bonnie Williams-Cohen, Nov. 17, 1987. BA, U. Calif., Berkeley, 1933. Assoc. editor Judge mag., NYC, 1937-39; radio staff writer J. Walter Thompson Advt. Agy., NYC, 1939-43; cartoonist Hazel Saturday Evening Post, Phila., 1943-70, King Features Syndicate, 1969—. Cartoonist, writer The Econs. Press, Inc., Fairfield, N.J., 1957—; screenwriter Walt Disney Prodns., Burbank, Calif., 1970-77. Writer, cartoonist for CBS, NBC, mags., books, newspapers; playwright (NBC radio prodn.) The Clinic (pub. in anthology Best Broadcasts Of 1939-40); creator (cartoon features) Diz and Liz for Jack and Jill mag., 1961-71, (TV series) Hazel, Peabody and Sherman for Bullwinkle and Rocky Show (TV series), 1959; writer: Hazel, NBC-TV (4 yrs.), CBS-TV (1 yr.), 1946, Here's Hazel, 1949, Many Happy Returns, 1950, If You Like Hazel, 1952, So'm I, 1953, Hazel Rides Again, 1955, Fasten Your Seat Belts, 1956, Phyllis, 1957, All Hazel, 1958, The Hazel Jubilee, 1959, The Biggest Dog in the World, 1960, Hazel Time, 1962, Life With Hazel, 1965, Diz and Liz, 1965, Squirrels in the Feeding Station, 1967, Hazel Power, 1971, Right On Hazel, 1972, Ms. Hazel, 1972, Hazel's Feline Funnies, 1982; story/screenwriter: Million Dollar Duck, The Cat From Outer Space (also wrote novel), Gus; writer: Positive Attitude Posters, 1965-2003, Sales Bullets, 1960-2003; cartoons included in New Yorker, Esquire, Look, Life, Ladies Home Jour., McCall's, Good Housekeeping, Better Homes and Gardens, People, Mademoiselle. Master sgt. Signal Corps AUS, 1943-46. Mem. Nat. Cartoonists Soc. (Best Syndicated Panel award 1977), Writers Guild Am. West.

KEYES, DANIEL, author; BA in Psychology, Bklyn. Coll., 1950, MA in English, 1961. Assoc. fiction editor Magazine Mgmt. Co., NYC, 1950-52; v.p. Fenko and Keyes Photography, Inc., 1952-53; tchr. English N.Y.C. Bd. Edn., 1955-62; instr. English Wayne State U., Detroit, 1962-66; mem. faculty Ohio U., Athens, 1966—, prof. English and creative writing, 1972-97, prof. emeritus, 2000—; agt. William Morris Agy., NYC, Calif. Author: (novels) Flowers for Algernon (Hugo award 1959, Nebula award 1966, movie version: Charly, 1968 (Acad. award), The Touch, 1968, The Fifth Sally, 1980, (nonfiction) The Minds of Billy Milligan, 1981 (Spl. award Mystery Writers Am., Kurd Lasswitz award, 1st prize Best Fgn. Book award 1986), Unveiling Claudia, 1986, Daniel Keyes Collected Stories, 1993 (Japan), The Milligan Wars, 1994 (Japan), Daniel Keyes Reader, 1995 (Japan), Until Death Do Us Part: The Sleeping Princess, 1998 (Japan), (TV movie) Flowers for Algernon, 2000, (non-fiction) Algernon, Charlie and I: A Writer's Journey, 2000; (13 episode TV series) flowers for Algernon (Japan), 2002, The Touch, revised 2003; supervising prodr. (TV movie) The Mad Housers, 1990. With U.S. Maritime Svc., 1945—47. Ohio Arts Council Individual Artist fellow, 1986-87; recipient Baker Fund award 1986-87, Disting. Alumnus Honor award Bklyn. Coll. CUNY, 1988. Mem.: PEN, Sci. Fiction Writers Am. (Author Emeritus award 2000), Mystery Writers Am., Dramatists' Guild. Office: 7491 N Federal Hwy C5-110 Boca Raton FL 33487-1625 Personal E-mail: dankeyes@usa.net.

KEYES, JAMES HENRY, manufacturing executive; b. LaCrosse, Wis., Sept. 2, 1940; s. Donald M. and Mary M. (Nodolf) K.; m. Judith Ann Carney, Nov. 21, 1964; children: James Patrick, Kevin, Timothy. BS, Marquette U., 1962; MBA, Northwestern U., 1963. Instr. Marquette U., Milw., 1963-65; CPA Peat. Marwick & Mitchell, Milw., 1965-66; with Johnson Controls, Inc., Milw., 1967—, mgr. sys. dept., 1967-71, divsn. contr., 1971-73, corp. contr., treas., 1973-77, v.p., CFO, 1977-85, exec. v.p., 1985-86, pres., 1986-99, chief operating officer, 1986-88, chief exec. officer, 1988—2002, chmn. bd. dirs., 1993—. Bd. dirs. Baird Capital Devel. Fund. 1st Wis. Trust Co., LSI Logic, Inc., Universal Foods Corp. Active Milw. Symphony Orch., 1980—. Mem. Fin. Execs. Inst., Am. Inst. CPA's, Wis. Inst. CPA's., Machinery and Allied Products Inst. Office: Johnson Controls Inc 5757 N Green Bay Ave Milwaukee WI 53209-4408

KEYES, JAMES WILLARD, film rental company executive; b. Worcester, Mass., Mar. 17, 1955; s. Harold L. and Dorothy M. (Anderson) K.; m. Margo Bernadette Ramirez, Apr. 20, 1991. BA, Coll. Holy Cross, 1977; postgrad., U. London; MBA, Columbia U., 1980. Dir. corp. planning Gulf Oil Corp., Pitts., 1980-85; v.p. nat. gasoline The Southland Corp., Dallas, 1985-93; sr. fin. officer The Southland Corp. subs. 7-Eleven, Inc., CFO, 1996—98, exec. v.p., COO, 1998—2000, pres., CEO, 2000—05; chmn., CEO Blockbuster Inc., Dallas, 2007—. Founder Education is Freedom Found. Bd. govs. Dallas Symphony Assn., Inc., chmn.; bd. govs. ARC; trustee The Cooper Inst.; bd. mem. Edwin L. Cox Sch. Bus., So. Methodist U. Recipient Horatio Alger award, 2005. Mem. Phi Beta Kappa. Avocations: pilot, musician. Office: Blockbuster Inc 1201 Elm St Dallas TX 75270*

KEYES, JEFFREY J., lawyer; BA magna cum laude, U. Notre Dame, 1968; JD cum laude, U. Mich., 1972. Bar: Minn. 1972. Shareholder Briggs and Morgan, P.A., Mpls.; fellow Am. Coll. Trial Lawyers, Mpls. Mem. Gov.'s Task Force on Tort Reform, 1986; chmn. fed. practice com. U.S. Dist. Ct. Minn., 1990-93, 2002—, chmn. adv. group on civil justice reform act, 1991-93; trainer U.S. Magistrate Judges Tng. Conf. on Settlement, Mpls., 1992; lectr. in field. Contbr. articles to law jours. Chmn. bd. dirs. The Playwright's Ctr. Mem. ABA (chmn. antitrust sect. franchise com. 1989-90, contbg. editor Antitrust Monograph 1987, co-editor Antitrust Sect. State Antitrust Law Handbook, Minn. chpt. 1990), Minn. State Bar Assn. (co-chair Women in the Legal Profn. task force 1996-97, chmn. civil litigation sect. 1985-86), Hennepin County Bar Assn. Office: Briggs & Morgan 80 S 8th St 2200 Minneapolis MN 55402-2157

KEYES, JOAN ROSS RAFTER, education educator, writer; b. Bklyn., Aug. 12, 1924; d. Joseph W. and Hermia (Ross) Rafter; m. William Ambrose, Apr. 26, 1947 (dec.); children: William, Peter, Dion, Kenzie. BA, Adelphi U., Garden City, NY, 1945; MS, Long Island U., Greenvale, NY, 1973. Prodn. asst. CBS Radio, NYC, 1943-44; cub news reporter Bklyn. Daily Eagle, 1945-46; advt. copywriter Gimbel's Dept. Store, NYC, 1946-47; adj. prof. L.I. U., Greenvale, NY, 1984—; tchr. Port Wash. Pub. Schs., NY, 1970-94. Lectr., cons. pub. sch. dists. nationwide, 1978—; workshop leader Tchrs. English to Speakers Other Langs. convs., 1981—; cons. Kids' Readers, 2005. Author: Beats! Conversations in Rhythm, 1983, (video program) Now You're Talking, 1987, (computer program) Quick Talk, 1990, Oxford Picture Dictionary for Kids Program, 1998; contbr. articles to ednl. mags. Lectr., catechist Our Lady of Fatima Ch., Port Washington, 1987—; vol. Earthwatch, Mallorca, 1988. Australia/New Zealand ednl. grantee Port Washington Pub. Schs., 1992. Mem. Tchrs. of English to Speakers of Other Languages, Am. Fedn. of Tchrs., N.Y. State United Tchrs., Port Wash. Tchrs. Assn. Republican. Roman Catholic. Avocations: music, painting, travel, tennis, photography. Personal E-mail: joanrosskeyes@aol.com.

KEYES, MARION ALVAH, IV, manufacturing executive; b. Bellingham, Wash., May 11, 1938; s. Marion Alvah and Winnefred Agnes (Nolte) K.; m. Loretta Jean Mattson, Nov. 17, 1962; children: Marion A., Zachary Leigh (dec.), Richard. BS in Chem. Engring., Stanford U., 1960; MSEE, U. Ill., 1968; MBA, Baldwin Wallace Coll., 1981. Registered rofl. engr., Calif., Wis., N.Y., Ill., Ohio. Tchg. asst. dept. math. Stanford U., 1958-59; tech. Stanford Aerosol Labs., 1957-59; chem. engr. Ketchikan (Alaska) Pulp Co., 1960-63; dir engring. Control Sys. divsn. Beloit (Wis.) Corp., 1963-70; gen. mgr. digital sys. divsn. Taylor Instrument Co., Rochester, NY, 1970-75; v.p. engring. Bailey Controls Co., 1975-80; sr. v.p., group exec. Indsl. Products and Svcs. Group; pres. Bailey COntrols, Ohio, 1980-85; mem. exec. operating bd. McDermott Internat. Inc., 1985-89; pres., CEO Bailey Controls Co., Wickliffe, Ohio, 1989-90; chmn. Dcom Corp., Eastlake, Ohio, 1990-93; sr. v.p. tech. and bus. devel. process group, pres. Rosemount Analytical Inc. divsn. Emerson, St. Louis, 1993—. Bd. dirs. Fibermark Corp. Author: Offshore Platform Automation, 1990; editor: A Glossary of Automatic Control Terminology, 1970; contbr. articles to profl. jours.; holder 54 U.S. and more than 100 fgn. patents. Past bd. advisors Fenn Coll. Engring., Cleve. State U.; bd. dirs. Baldwin Coll., United Cerebral Palsy, Cleve.; past prs., mem. exec. bd. N.E. Ohio coun. Boy Scouts Am.; past pres. Area 5 Boy Scouts Am. Named to, Measurement and Control Hall of Fame. Fellow ISA (hon. life), TAPPI (Pioneer award), IEEE, Am. inst. Chemists, Instrument Soc. Am. (life hon.), Ohio acad. Scis. (life, bd. dirs., Centennial honoree 1991); mem. AIChE, Cleve. Engring. Soc. (bd. dirs.), Soc. Am. Mil. Engrs. (life), Am. Assn. Artificial Intelligence (charter), Am. Mgmt. Assn., U.S. Automation Rsch. Coun., Am. Automatic Control Coun. (past. sec. and bd. dirs., Am. Chem. Soc., Wis. Acad. Arts, Scis. and Letters, Cleve. World Trade Assn. (Man of Yr. 1984), Canterbury Golf Club, Mo. Athletic Club. Republican. Roman Catholic. Home: 8 Washington Terr Saint Louis MO 63112-1914 Office: 8100 W Florissant Ave K-Annex Saint Louis MO 63136 Business E-Mail: bud@keyes.org.

KEYES, ROBERT W., physicist, researcher; b. Chgo., Dec. 2, 1921; s. Lee P. and Katherine K.; m. Sophie Skadorwa, June 4, 1966; children— Andrew, Claire. BS, U. Chgo., 1942, MS, 1949, PhD, 1953. With Argonne Nat. Lab., 1946-50; staff mem. Westinghouse Research Lab., Pitts., 1953-60; mem. research staff IBM Research Lab., Yorktown Heights, NY, 1960—. Vis. physicist Am. Phys. Soc. Vis. Indsl. Physicists Program, 1974-75, 77; vice chmn. Gordon Conf. on High Pressure Physics, 1970; chmn. Gordon Conf. on Chemistry and Physics of Microstructure Fabrication, 1976, Nat. Materials Adv. Bd. (ad hoc com. on ion implantation as a new surface treatment tech.), 1978, Internat. Conf. Heavily Doped Semiconductors, 1984; mem. Nat. Acad. Scis.-NAE-NRC evaluation panel Nat. Bur. Standards, 1970-73; cons. physics survey com., mem. statis. data panel Nat. Acad. Sci.-NRC Council Physics Survey Com., 1972; mem. data and info. panel Nat. Acad. Sci.-NRC Com. on Survey of Materials Sci. and Engring., 1974; Girling Watson vis. prof. elec. engring. U. Sydney, Fall 1996. Author: Physics of VLSI Systems, 1987; assoc. editor Revs. Modern Physics, 1976-95; corr.: Comments on Solid State Physics, 1970-85. With USN, 1944—46. Recipient Outstanding Contbn. award IBM, 1963 Fellow Am. Phys. Soc. (chmn. com. applications of physics 1976-78), IEEE (life, chmn. subcom. cultural and sci. relations 1976, mem. del. to USSR 1975, W.R.G. Baker prize 1976, awards bd. 1984, Sigma Xi. Office: IBM PO Box 218 Yorktown Heights NY 10598-0218 Business E-Mail: rwk4@sigmaxi.org.

KEYES, SAUNDRA ELISE, newspaper editor; b. Salt Lake City, June 28, 1945; d. Vernon Harrison and Mildred K.; m. William J. Ivey, June 13, 1969 (div. 1976). BA, U. Utah, 1966; MA, Ind. U., 1969, PhD, 1976. Tchr. Salt Lake City Pub. Schs., 1966-67; asst. prof. Fisk U., Nashville, 1971-76; reporter, city editor The Tennessean, Nashville, 1976-83; staff writer The Courier-Jour., Louisville, 1983-84; dep. mng. editor Orlando (Fla.) Sentinel, 1985-88; mng. editor Phila. Daily News, 1988-90; exec. editor, sr. v.p. Press-Telegram, Long Beach, Calif., 1991-93; mng. editor The Miami Herald, 1993-96, Contra Costa Times, 1996—2000; editor Honolulu Advertiser, 2000—. Ford Found. fellow, 1978. Mem.: Am. Soc. Newspaper Editors (pres. accrediting coun. on edn. in journalism and mass comm. 2004—). Office: Honolulu Advertiser 605 Kapiolani Blvd PO Box 3110 Honolulu HI 96802

KEYFITZ, NATHAN, sociologist, educator, demographer; b. Montreal, Que., Can., June 29, 1913; s. Arthur and Anna (Gerstein) K.; m. Beatrice Orkin, Oct. 8, 1939; children: Barbara Lee, Robert Norman. BS, McGill U., Montreal, 1934; PhD, U. Chgo., 1952; MA (hon.), Harvard U., 1972; LLD (hon.), U. Western Ont., 1973, U. de Montréal, 1984, McGill U., 1984, U. Alta, 1985, U. Siena, Italy, 1991, Carleton U., 1993, U. de Québec, 1993. Census clk., statistician, sr. research statistician Dominion Bur. Statistics, Govt. Can., 1936-59; dir. Colombo Plan Bur., Sri Lanka, 1956-57; prof. sociology U. Toronto, Ont., Canada, 1959-63, U. Montreal, 1962-63; prof. U. Chgo., 1963-68, chmn. sociology dept., 1965-68; prof. demography U. Calif., Berkeley, 1968-72; Andelot prof. sociology and demography Harvard U., 1972-82, chmn. dept. sociology, 1978-80, emeritus, 1982—; Robert Lazarus prof. social demography Ohio State U., Columbus, 1980-84, prof. emeritus, 1984—; with Internat. Inst. Applied Systems Analysis, 1984-93; researcher Initiatives on Children, Am. Acad. Arts and Scis., Cambridge, Mass., 1994—. Tech. assistance assignments, Burma, 1951, Indonesia, 1952-53, 64, 79, 85-89, Argentina, 1960, Santiago, Chile, 1963, Moscow, 1977, 85, People's Republic China, 1981; vis. fellow Stanford U., 1986. Author: Introduction to the Mathematics of Population, 1968, 2d edit., 1977, Applied Mathematical Demography, 1977, (with Hal Caswell), 3d edit., 2005, Population Change and Social Policy, 1982, (with Wilhelm Flieger) World Population Growth and Aging, 1990; contbr. articles to profl. jours. Trustee Nat. Opinion Research Ctr., 1966—. Recipient Lazarsfeld award Am. Sociol. Assn., 1990, Common Wealth award, 1991; decorated Cross of Honor for Sci., Austria, 1993; named Laureate, Internat. Union Sci. Study Population, 1997, Norberg award Population Coun. of N.Y. Fellow Royal Soc. Can., Am. Statis. Assn. (chmn. social stats. sect. 1961), Royal Statis. Soc. (hon.), Statis. Soc. of Can. (hon.); mem. NAS, Am. Acad. Arts and Scis., Can. Polit. Sci. Assn. (chmn. sociology and anthropology sect. 1961), Inter-Am. Statis. Inst., Internat. Statis. Inst., Population Assn. Am. (pres. 1969-70), Phi Beta Kappa. Home and Office: 1580 Massachusetts Ave Apt 7C Cambridge MA 02138-2928 Office Phone: 617-491-2845. Personal E-mail: nathankeyfitz@yahoo.com.

KEYS, ALICIA (ALICIA AUGELLO COOK), vocalist, musician, songwriter; b. NYC, Jan. 25, 1981; d. Craig Cook and Terri Augello. Student, Columbia U. Singer: (albums) Songs in A Minor, 2001 (Video Music Award, two Billboard Awards, two Am. Music Awards, two NAACP Image Awards, three Soul Train awards, two World Music Awards, an ECCHO award, Grammy Award for Best New Artist, Song of Yr., Best R&B Vocal Performance, Best R&B Song and Best R&B Album), The Diary of Alicia Keys, 2003 (MTV Video Music award Best R&B Video for the song "If I Ain't Got You", 2004, R&B/Hip-Hop Singles of Yr.:"If I Ain't Got You", Billboard Music Awards, 2004, R&B/Hip-Hop Airplay Single of Yr.:"If I Ain't Got You", Billboard Music Awards, 2004, Grammy Award for Best R&B Album, 2005); composer: (films) Hollywood Homicide, Dr. Dolittle 2, Ali; actor: (films) Smokin' Aces, 2006, The Nanny Diaries, 2007, (TV guest appearances) The Cosby Show, 1985, Saturday Night Live, 2001, Charmed, 2001, Tonight Show with Jay Leno, 2001, American Dreams, 2003, Oprah Winfrey Show, 2004; author: Tears for Water: Songbook of Poems and Lyrics, 2004. Named Female Artist of Yr., Billboard Music Awards, 2004, Hot 100 Artist of Yr., 2004, Female Hot 100 Artist of Yr., 2004, Hot 100 Songwriter of Yr., 2004; named one of Time Mag. 100 Most Influential People, 2005, 50 Most Influential African-Americans, Ebony Mag., 2004; recipient Favorite Female Artist-Soul/Rhythm & Blues Music, Am. Music Awards, 2004, Female R&B/Hip-Hop Artist of Yr., Billboard Music Awards, 2004, R&B/Hip-Hop Singles Artist of Yr., 2004, Best R&B Video for Karma, MTV Video Music Awards, 2005, Outstanding Female Artist, NAACP Image awards, 2006, Outstanding Music Video and Outstanding Song for Unbreakable, NAACP Image award, 2006.*

KEYS, JERRY MALCOM, lawyer, educator; b. Childress, Tex., Dec. 5, 1947; s. Earl Milas and Mary Maud (Furr) Keys. BSEE with honors, U. Tex., 1970, JD with honors, 1975. Bar: Tex. 1975, US Dist. Ct. (so. and we. dists.) Tex. 1980, US Patent and Trademark Office. Assoc. Pravel & Wilson, Houston, 1975—76, Brown, Maroney, Rose, Baker & Barber, Austin, Tex., 1975—81; ptnr. Brown, Maroney, Rose, Barber & Dye, Austin, 1981—88; prin. Hagans/Keys PC, Austin, 1988—90; sr. shareholder Thompson & Knight, PC, 1990—94, Locke Purnell Rain Harrell, PC, 1994—98; ptnr. Locke Liddell & Sapp LLP, 1999; sr. v.p., gen. counsel FundsXpress, Inc., 1999—2001; shareholder Winstead Sechrest & Minick, PC, Austin, 2001—. Adj. asst. prof. U. Tex., 1979—85; mem. tech. adv. com. Supreme Ct. Tex., 1983—85. Exec. coun. Greater Austin-San Antonio Corridor Coun., 1993—, co-chmn., 2004—05, chmn., 2005—07. Mem.: Austin Intellectual Property Law Assn. (pres. 1989—90), Tex. Bar Assn. (profl. efficiency and econ. rsch. com., chmn. office automation subcom 1982—86). Office: Winstead PC 401 Congress Ave Ste 2100 Austin TX 78701

KEYS, JOHN W., III, former federal agency administrator; b. Sheffield, Ala., 1942; m. Dell Keys. BCE, Ga. Inst. Tech., 1964; MS in Civil Engring., Brigham Young U., 1971. Registered engr., Colo., Wyo., Mont., N.D. Civil and hydraulic engr. Bur. Reclamation, US Dept. Interior, 1964—79, chief Colo. River Water Quality Office, 1976—79, asst. to regional dir. Washington, 1979—80, pacific N.W. regional dir., 1986—98, commr. Washington, 2001—06. Comml. pilot for Angel Flight, Air LifeLine, County Search & Rescue, Moab, Utah. Coll. football referee, 1970—; H.S. football referee, 1962—. Recipient Disting. Svc. award, 1995.

KEYS, PAUL ROSS, academic administrator, educator; b. St. Louis, Mar. 21, 1940; s. Charles and Josie (Jones) K.; m. Donnielesky Harrington, May 23, 1998; children from a previous marriage, Pamela, Roderick. BS, St. Louis U., 1963, MSW, 1971; PhD, U. Wis., Milw., 1983. Exec. dir. Champaign (Ill.) Urban League, 1969; dep. dir. Concentrated Employment Program, St. Louis, 1971; asst. dir. legis. NASW, Washington, 1971-74; exec. dir. Cmty. Svcs. Coun., Columbia, Mo., 1974-76; dir. Broward County (Fla.) Dept. Human Svcs., 1976-78; dep. adminstr. Cmty. Svcs. divsn. State of Wis., 1978-81; prof. Hunter Coll., CUNY, 1983-94; faculty doctoral program CUNY, 1987-94; dean Coll. Health and Human Svcs., S.E. Mo. State U., Cape Girardeau, 1994-2000, also assoc. provost. Fellow Ctr. Social Adminstrn., Hunter Coll., 1985-94. Author: New Management in Human Services, 1988, 2d edit., 1995; founding editor Jour. Multicultural Social Work, 1989—; contbr. articles to profl. jours. Capt. USAF, 1963-69. Recipient Martin Luther King/Woodrow Wilson fellowship, 1970, Commendation Resolution, Mo. Gen. Assembly, 1976, GARIOA/Fulbright Rsch. fellowship, Tokyo, 1990-91, Disting. Alumni Svc. award St. Louis U. Sch. Social Svcs., 1996, Exemplar Mgmt. Excellence award Nat. Network for Social Work Mgrs., 1999; named to Sumner H.S. Hall of Fame, 2001. Mem. Am. Pub. Welfare Assn. (exec. com. 1988), Omega Psi Phi (Cmty. Svc. award 1977). Avocations: travel, computer software, jazz. Office: Provost's Office Governors State Univ 1 University Pkwy University Park IL 60466 Home Phone: 708-367-1253; Office Phone: 708-534-4980. Personal E-mail: pkeys@prodigy.net. Business E-Mail: p-keys@gaust.edu.

KEYS, SCOTT, bank executive; BS in Acctg., Loyola Marymount U. CPA. With Ernst & Young, Columbus, Ohio, 1986—2002, ptnr., 1999—2002, ptnr. in charge Ohio Valley Banking Practice; exec. v.p., CFO IndyMac Bank, Pasadena, Calif., 2002—. Office: IndyMac Bank 888 East Walnut St Pasadena CA 91101 Mailing: IndyMac Bank PO Box 7137 Pasadena CA 91101 Office Phone: 626-535-5901. Office Fax: 626-535-8203.

KEYSER, RICHARD LEE, distribution company executive; b. Harrisburg, Pa., Oct. 28, 1942; s. Harold L. and Mary J. K.; m. Mary Ellen Carter, June 20, 1964; children: Jeffrey, Jennifer. BS, U.S. Naval Acad., 1964; MBA, Harvard U., 1971. Commd. ensign USN, 1964, advanced through grades to lt., 1966; resigned, 1969; mktg.-analysis mgr. Fleetguard, Inc., Dallas, 1971-72, dir. logistics Cookeville, Tenn., 1973-77; gen. mgr. parts ops. Cummins Engine Co., Inc., Columbus, Ind., 1977-83, exec. dir. mktg.

ops., 1983-84; pres. NL-Hycalog, Houston, 1984-86; v.p. ops. W.W. Grainger, Inc., Chgo., 1986-87, exec. v.p., 1988-90, pres., COO, 1991—95; pres., CEO W.W. grainger, Inc., Chgo., 1995—97; chmn., CEO W.W. Grainger, Inc., Chgo., 1997—. Bd. dirs. Morton Internat. County chmn. blood program ARC, Cookeville, 1976-77; bd. dirs. Preserve To Enjoy, Inc., Columbus, 1983-84, Irene Josselyn Clinic, Northfield, Ill., 1989-92, Lake Forest Grad. Sch. Mgmt., 1992—, Evanston Hosp. Corp., 1996—. Former lt. comdr. USNR. Fellow Am. Prodn. and Inventory Control Soc. (cert.); mem. Chgo. Club, Harvard Bus. Sch. Club Chgo. (v.p. 1988-89, pres. 1989-90), Comml. Club Chgo. Office: WW Grainger Inc 100 Grainger Pkwy Lake Forest IL 60045-5201*

KEYSER, SAMUEL JAY, linguist, educator; b. July 7, 1935; s. Abraham L. and Sabina (Shaplen) K.; children: Rachel Suzanne, Beth Rebecca, Benjamin Jay Kendall; m. Nancy Kelly, 2001. BA, George Washington U., 1956; BA with honors, Oxford U., Eng., 1958, MA, 1962, Yale U., 1960, PhD, 1962. Mem. staff Rsch. Lab. Electronics MIT, Cambridge, 1961-62; mem. faculty Brandeis U., Waltham, Mass., 1965-71, Univ. Coll. London, 1971-72; head dept. linguistics U. Mass., Amherst, 1972-77; head dept. linguistics and philosophy MIT, Cambridge, 1977—84, assoc. provost for inst. life, 1985—94, spl. asst. to the provost, 1994-98, spl. asst. to Chancellor, 1998—, emeritus, 1998—, interim alcohol coord., 1999-2000. Co-author: English Stress: Its Form, Its Growth and Its Role in Verse, 1971, Beginning English Grammar, 1973, CV Phonology, 1983, Rule Generalization and Optionality in Language Change, 1985, Prolegomenon to a Theory of Lexical Argument Structure, 2002; author: (poems) Raising the Dead, 1993, (children's stories) The Pond God and other stories, 2003 (Lee Bennett Hopkins honor book award, 2004); editor (with K. Hale): The View From Building 20, 1993; editor: Linguistic Inquiry, 1970—, Current Studies in Linguistics, 1972—, Linguistic Inquiry Monograph Series, 1976—; occasional commentator All Things Considered, NPR, 2004—, The Reluctant Traveler, 2007—. Peter de Florez chair MIT, 1989. With USAF, 1962-65. Recipient Disting. Alumnus award, George Washington U., 1992; Fulbright scholar, 1956—58, sr. Fulbright scholar, 1971—72. Mem. Linguistic Soc. Am., MIT Alumni Assn. (hon. mem.), Phi Beta Kappa. Home: 7 Frost St Cambridge MA 02140-1502 Office: Dept Linguistics & Philosophy Rm E32-D770 MIT Cambridge MA 02139-4307 Office Phone: 617-253-1917. Business E-Mail: keyser@mit.edu. *People, like organizations, are very good at starting things and very bad at stopping them. This goes for projects, marriages, and careers. I have found that the best way to stop something is to start something. It makes the stopping much, much easier, at least until the last stop.*

KEYT, DAVID, philosophy and classics educator; b. Indpls., Feb. 22, 1930; s. Herbert Coe and Hazel Marguerite (Sissman) K.; m. Christine Harwood (Mullikin) June 25, 1975; children by previous marriage: Sarah, Aaron. AB, Kenyon Coll., 1951; MA, Cornell U., 1953, PhD, 1955. Instr. dept. philosophy U. Wash., Seattle, 1957—60, asst. prof., 1960—64, assoc. prof., 1964—69, prof., 1969—, chmn. dept. philosophy, 1971-78, acting chmn. dept. philosophy, 1967—68, 1970, 1986, 1994. Vis. asst. prof. dept. philosophy UCLA, 1962-63; vis. assoc. prof. Cornell U., 1968-69; mem. Inst. for Advanced Study, 1983-84; vis. prof. U. Hong Kong, autumn 1987, Princeton U., autumn 1988, U. Calif., Irvine, autumn 1990; vis. scholar Social Philosophy and Policy Ctr., Bowling Green State U., autumn, 2001. Co-editor: (with Fred D. Miller Jr.) A Companion to Aristotle's Politics, 1991; Author: Aristotle Politics, Books V, VI, 1999; contbr. articles in field to profl. jours. With US Army, 1955—57. Inst. for Rsch. in the Humanities fellow U. Wis., 1966-67; Ctr. for Hellenic Studies fellow, 1974-75. Mem. Am. Philos. Assn., Soc. Ancient Greek Philosophy. Home: 12032 36th Ave NE Seattle WA 98125-5637 Office: U Wash Box 353350 Dept Philosophy Seattle WA 98195-3350 Business E-Mail: keyt@u.washington.edu.

KEYVAN, SHAHLA, nuclear engineer, educator; arrived in U.S., 1971; d. Mahmood Keyvan and Forough Mortazavi. BS in Engring., U. Wash., 1974; MS in Nuc. Engring., Nuclear Engr. in Nuc. Engring., MIT, 1978; PhD in Nuc. Engring., U. Calif., Berkeley, 1983. Reactor operating license Nuc. Regulatory Commn., Wash., D.C., 1979, U.S. Nuc. Regulatory Commn., Wash., D.C., 1993. Cons. Argonne Nat. Lab., Idaho Falls, 1989; assoc. prof. nuc. engring. dept. U. Mo., Columbia, 1990—2001, rsch. prof., dir. ctr. artificial intelligence engring. and edn., 2001—. Panelist grad. fellowship program NSF, Arlington, Va., 1993—96. Author: (electronic books) Fundamentals Of Nuclear Technology, Introduction to Nuclear Reactor Physics, A Demo Module on Radiation Energy Deposition, A Demo Module on Fundamentals of Radiation Measurement, A Demo Module on Radiation Decay, A Demo Module on Binding Energy; contbr. articles to profl. jours. Grantee, Dept. of Energy Small Bus. Innovation Rsch. Program, 1984—87, Dept. of Energy, 1998—2003, NSF, 1991—93, 1994—97, 1998—2001, Mo. Inst. Instrnl. Devel., 1997—98, Mo. Dept. Econ., 1998—2001. Mem.: Am. Soc. Engring. Edn., Am. Nuc. Soc. (faculty advisor 1990—93, sec. Mo. sect. 1991—94), Phi Kappa Phi, Sigma Xi, Tau Beta Pi. Achievements include patents pending for automated inspection system for nuclear fuel pellet; automated nuclear fuel size measurement; flame image features and their analysis. Office: U Mo E2403D MAE Dept Columbia MO 65211 E-mail: keyvan@missouri.edu.

KEYWORTH, GEORGE ALBERT, physicist, consulting company executive; b. Boston, Mass., Nov. 30, 1939; s. Robert Allen and Leontine (Briggs) K.; m. Polly Lauterbach, July 28, 1962; children: Deirdre Anne, George Albert III. BS in Physics, Yale U., 1963; PhD in Nuclear Physics, Duke U., 1968; DSc (hon.), Rensselaer Poly. Inst., 1982; D in Engring. (hon.), Mich. Tech. U., 1984; D.Sc. (hon.), U. Ala., 1985. Staff physicist Los Alamos (N.Mex.) Nat. Lab., 1968-74, group leader neutron physics, 1974-78, div. leader, 1978-81; sci. advisor to Pres., dir. Office Sci. and Tech. Policy The White House, Washington, 1981-85; dir. rsch. Hudson Inst., Indpls., 1988-90, disting. fellow, 1990-95; chmn. The Keyworth Co., Washington, 1986—; chmn. & co-founder Progress and Freedom Found., Washington, 1993—. Hon. prof. Fudan U., Shanghai People's Rep. of China, 1984; mem. V.P.'s Task Force on Regulatory Relief, 1982-85, Presl. Commn. on Indsl. Competitiveness, 1984-85, Alcoa Sci. and Tech. Coun., 1986-; trustee, Santa Fe Inst., 1986-89, chmn. bd. dir. NovaWeb Tech. Inc, 1995-, Encanto Networks Inc., 1997-; bd. dir. Hewlett Packard Co., 1986-2006, Gen. Atomics, 1995-, Yourtel Telecom, 1998-. Recipient Chmn.'s award Am. Assn. Engring. Sci., 1982, SDI award Am. Def. Preparedness Assn, 1986, Hertz Found. award, 1987, First Internat Sci. and Tech. Cooperation prize People's Rep. of China, 1992. Fellow Am. Phys. Soc, AAAS, mem. Phi Beta Kappa, Sigma Xi. Clubs: Cosmos (Washington).

KEZLARIAN, NANCY KAY, marriage and family therapist; b. Royal Oak, Mich., Aug. 26, 1948; d. Barkev A. and Nancy (Israelian) K.; m. Robert S. Vinetz, M.D., Aug. 1995. Student, U. Vienna, Austria, 1969; BA, Albion Coll., 1970; MA in Theatre and TV, U. Mich., 1971; MA in Clin. Psychology, Pepperdine U., 1992. Cert. secondary tchr., Mich., Calif.; lic. marriage family therapist. Tchr. West Bloomfield Hills (Mich.) High Sch., 1971-76; tchr. ESL, L.A. Pub. Schs., 1976-80; personnel dir. Samuel Goldwyn Co., LA, 1985-86; dir. adminstrn. and human resources (Norman Lear) Act III Communications, LA, 1986-90; dir. programs Salvation Army Booth Meml. Ctr., LA, 1993-94; asst. exec. dir. Florence Crittenton Ctr., LA, 1994-96, exec. dir., 1996-2000; pvt. practice marriage and family therapy, 2000—. Owner, mgr. KAZ, hand painted clothing co., L.A., 1980-85; mem. Screen Actors Guild. Actress My Seventeenth Summer, The Big Blue Marble, l979 (Emmy award for children's TV programming). Bd. dirs. Calif. Assn. Children's Homes. Named Tchr. of Yr., West Bloomfield Hills High Sch., 1976. Mem. SAG, Pers. and Indsl. Rels. Assn. (legis. rep. dist. 5 1989, 90), Calif. Assn. of Marriage and Family Therapists, L.A. Group Psychotherapy Soc., Rotary Internat., People for the Am. Way, Psi Chi. Avocations: writing, world mythologies, theater, abstract artist, vegetarian chef. Personal E-mail: rsvinetz@pol.net.

KEZSBOM, ALLEN, lawyer; b. NYC, July 5, 1941; BA cum laude, Bklyn. Coll., 1962; LLB magna cum laude, Harvard U., 1965. Bar: N.Y. 1966, U.S. Dist. Ct. (so. dist.) N.Y. 1968, U.S. Dist. Ct. (ea. dist.) N.Y. 1972, U.S. Ct. Appeals (1st cir.) 1982, U.S. Ct. Appeals (2d cir.) 1971, U.S. Ct. Appeals (6th cir.) 1986, U.S. Ct. Appeals (8th cir.) 1981, U.S. Ct. Appeals (11th cir.) 1983, U.S. Supreme Ct. 1978. Assoc. Kaye, Scholor, Fierman, Hays & Handler, NYC, 1966-71, ptnr., 1972-86, Fried, Frank, Harris, Shriver & Jacobson, NYC, 1986—. Vis. lectr. Yale Law Sch., New Haven, Conn., 1992-93. Mem. Harvard Law Rev., 1963-65; contbr. articles to profl. jours. Knox fellow Harvard Law Sch., 1965-66. Mem. ABA (antitrust sect., litigation sect., nat. resources, energy & environ. law), N.Y. State Bar Assn. (antitrust sect., litigation, environ.), Assn. Bar City N.Y. Office: Fried Frank Harris Shriver & Jacobson 1 New York Plz Fl 22 New York NY 10004-1980 E-mail: kezsbal@friedfrank.com.

KHABIBULIN, NIKOLAI, professional hockey player; b. Sverdlovsk, Russia, Jan. 13, 1973; Goaltender Winnipeg Jets (now Phoenix Coyotes), 1994—96, Phoenix Coyotes, 1996—99, Long Beach Ice Dogs (IHL), 1999—2000, Tampa Bay Lightning, 2001—05, Chicago Blackhawks, 2005—. Goaltender Team Russia, World Cup of Hockey Tournament, 1996, Team Russia, Olympic Games, Salt Lake City, 2002. Co-recipient James Gatschene Memorial Trophy (MVP), IHL, 2000; named to NHL All-Star Game, 1998, 1999, 2002, 2003. Achievements include being a member of Stanley Cup Champion Tampa Bay Lightning, 2004. Office: c/o Chicago Blackhawks 1901 W Madison St Chicago IL 60612

KHACHADURIAN, AVEDIS, physician; b. Aleppo, Syria, Jan. 6, 1926; s. Khachadur and Aznive (Demirjian) K.; m. Laura Hadidian, July 27, 1961; children: Cynthia, Linda. BA, Am. U. of Beirut, 1949, MD, 1953. Resident in internal medicine Am. U. of Beirut, 1953—56, asst. prof. biochemistry and medicine, 1959—64, assoc. prof., 1964—71, prof., 1971; fellow Postgrad. Sch. Medicine, London, 1956—57, Harvard Med. Sch., 1957—59; prof. pediat., dir. Clin. Rsch. Ctr. Northwestern U. Med. Sch., 1971—73; prof. medicine, head divsn. endocrinology, metabolism and nutrition U. Medicine and Dentistry NJ-R.W. Johnson Med. Sch., Piscataway, 1973—; mem. staff pediat. Children's Meml. Hosp., Chgo. Cons. U. Chgo. Sch. Medicine. Mem. Am. Diabetes Assn., NY Acad. Sci., Am. Fedn. Cin. Rsch., Am. Heart Assn., Am. Inst. Nutrition, Endocrine Soc., NY Lipid Rsch. Club, Sigma Xi, Alpha Omega Alpha. Achievements include research in genetics; natural history, pathogenesis and treatment of hereditary hyperlipidemias; diabetes; studies on various inborn errors of metabolism, osteoporosis. Office: One RW Johnson Place New Brunswick NJ 08901 Office Phone: 732-235-7749. Personal E-mail: khachaav5@yahoo.com.

KHAIRALLA, ERIC WILLIAM, plastic surgeon; s. William C. Khairalla and Gaby Koudim; m. Ghislaine Geagea Khairalla, Dec. 30, 1988; children: Thea, William. BSc in Biology, Am. U. Beirut, Lebanon, 1983, MSc in Physiology, 1985, MD, 1988. Bd. cert. Am. Bd. Internal Medicine, 1991, Am. Bd. Plastic Surgery, 2002, diplomate Am. Bd. Plastic Surgery, 2002, cert. Royal Coll. Physicians Surgeons Can. Plastic Surgery, 1997. Resident in intenal medicine Md. Gen. Hosp., Balt., 1988—91; resident in plastic surgery U. Toronto, Ont., 1991—97; fellow in plastic suregry Georgetown U. Med. Ctr., Washington, 1998; assoc., pvt. practice Bethesda, Md., 1998—2000; pvt. practice Chevy Chase, Md., 2000—. Active staff Suburban Hosp., Bethesda, 1998, Sibley Meml. Hosp., Washington, 1999, Inova Fairfax Hosp., Falls Church, Va., 2000. Contbr. articles and papers in field. Vol. reconstructive surgeon Luz del Sol, Dominican Republic, 1998. Fellow: Royal Coll. Surgeons Physicians Can.; mem.: Am. Soc. Plastic Surgeons. Greek Orthodox. Avocations: photography, skiing, windsurfing. Office: Chevy Chase Plastic Surgery 5530 Wisconsin Ave 1235 Chevy Chase MD 20815 Office Phone: 301-657-4744.

KHALID, HUMAYUN, computer scientist, consultant; b. Karachi, Sind, Pakistan, July 9, 1968; s. Khalid Yousuf and Maimoona Khalid; m. Nuzhat Sultana, July 4, 1997; children: Nimra, Nabihah. BSEE magna cum laude, CCNY, 1992, MSEE, 1993; PhD, CUNY, 1996. Rsch. assoc. U.S. Dept. Def., NYC, 1996; staff electronic engr., scientist Motorola, Inc., Austin, 1996—98, sr. staff scientist, 1998—2000; sr. cons. Dell Computer Corp., Austin, 2000—. Mem. program com. Symposium Performance Evaluation Computer and Telecom. Sys., 2000. Contbr. articles to profl. jours. Contbr. N. Austin Muslim Cmty. Ctr., 1996—2000. Univ. fellow, CUNY, 1995, Univ. Tuition scholar, 1995. Mem.: IEEE (editor papers and proceedings), Soc. Computer Simulation Internat., Inst. Elec. and Electronics Engrs. Pakistan (life). Muslim. Home: 1000 Cassat Cove Austin TX 78753 Office: Dell Computer Corp One Dell Way Round Rock TX 78682 Personal E-mail: humayun_khalid@sbcglobal.net. Business E-Mail: humayunn_khalid@dell.com.

KHALIL, MOHAMMAD ASLAM KHAN, environmental science educator, engineering educator, physics professor; b. Jhansi, India, Jan. 7, 1950; came to U.S., 1963; s. M. Ahsan Khan and Aleem-Un-Nisa K.; m. Giti Ara Eshraghi, June 1973; children: Kathayoon Azra, Kaviyaan Aslam. BPhys, BA in Math. and Psychology, U. Minn., 1970; MS in Physics, Va. Polytechnic Inst., 1972; PhD in Physics, U. Tex., 1976; MS in Environ. Sci., Oreg. Grad. Ctr., Beaverton, 1979; PhD in Eviron. Sci., Oreg. Grad. Ctr., 1979. Tchg. asst. dept. physics Va. Polytechnic Inst. and State U., 1970-71; grad. asst. dept. math. and physics U. Tex., Austin, 1971-72, tchg. asst. dept. physics, 1972-73, 76, rsch. scientist asst. Ctr. for Particle Theory, 1972-76; instr. dept. physics Pacific U., Forest Grove, Oreg., 1978; rsch. asst. dept. environ. sci. Oreg. Grad. Ctr., Beaverton, 1977-79, asst. prof. dept. environ. sci., 1980-82, assoc. prof. dept. environ. sci., 1982-84, prof. dept. chem., biol. and environ. sci., 1984-86, prof. Inst. Atmospheric Sci., 1986-90, prof. dept. environ. sci. and engring., dir. Global Change Rsch. Ctr., 1990-95; prof. dept. physics Portland (Oreg.) State U., 1995—, chmn. dept., 2004—05, dir. environ. sci. and resources program, 2005—. Owner Andarz Co., Portland, 1981—. Editor: Chemosphere: Global Change Science, 1990-05; mem. editl. bd. Handbook of Environ. Chemistry, Environ. Sci. and Pollution Rsch. Internat., Atmospheric Environment; contbr. some 200 articles to profl. jours. Recipient Oustanding Scientist award, Oreg. Acad. Sci., 2004, World's Most Cited Authors award, ICI, Branford Prince Miller award, Portland State U., 2006; grantee, NSF, EPA, Dept. Energy, NASA. Mem. Am. Phys. Soc., Am. Chem. Soc., Am. Geophys. Union, Sigma Xi. Avocation: marathon runner. Office: Portland State U Dept Physics PO Box 751 Portland OR 97207-0751 also: Andarz Co 9961 NW Kaiser Rd Portland OR 97231-2701 Office Phone: 503-725-8396. E-mail: khalilm@pdx.edu.

KHALIL, MOHAMMED K., research scientist, medical educator; DVM, U. Khartoum, Sudan, 1985; MS, U. Khartoum, 1989, Tuskegee U., Ala., 1995, Purdue U., West Lafayette, Ind., 2001; PhD, Purdue U., 2002. Asst. prof. dept. biomed. scis. Coll. Vet. Medicine, Tuskegee U., Ala., 2007—; asst. prof. Tuskegee U., 2007—. Mem.: Am. Assn Clin. Anatomists, Assn. Ednl. Comm. and Tech., Am. Assn. Anatomists. Home: 1999 Sunny Dale Dr Tallahassee FL 32312

KHALIL, MOUNIR A., librarian, educator; b. Ashiwai, Fayuum, Egypt, Nov. 14, 1936; arrived in U.S., 1969; s. Amin Khalil and Mounirah A. Kerolos; m. Sawsan G. Aziz, May 31, 1951; 1 child, Richard. BA in Geography, Cairo U., 1958, BA in Libr. Sci., 1962; MLS in Libr. and Info. Scis., Pratt Inst., 1971, MS in Computer Sci., 1977; adv. cert. in Grad. Sch. Libr. and Info. Scis., U. Pitts., 1977. Cert. med. libr. Med. Libr. Assn. Head libr. Higher Inst. Petroleum, Suez, Egypt, 1962—66, Higher Inst. Social Work, Cairo, 1966—69; reference libr. Queensborough Pub. Libr., Jamaica, NY, 1969—73; br. libr. Bklyn. Pub. Libr., 1974—86; tech. libr. Health Ins. Plan, NYC, 1986—89; chief access svcs. City Coll. CUNY, NYC, 1989—92, reference libr., 1993—; dir. tech. svcs. N.J. Inst., Newark, 1993. Part-time instr. Katharine Gibbs Sch., NYC, 1986—92; adj. asst. prof. GSLIS Queens Coll., 1990; spkr. in field; presenter in field. Contbr. articles to profl. jours. Mem. faculty senate, mem. librs. and info. tech. com. CUNY; mem. Coptic Orthodox Ch. Bd., Bklyn., 1995. Bailey scholar, Queens Borough Pub. Libr., 1972, ALA Libr. Automation fellow, Al-Bayyt U., Jordon, 1997, Rsch. award, CUNY Rsch. Found., 2003—. Mem.: ALA, Internat. Fedn. Libr. Assn.s and Instns. (roundtable on bookmobiles 1999—), Spl. Librs. Assn. (moderator conf.). Achievements include development of electronic ILL and document delivery services. Avocations: chess, gardening, soccer, reading, travel. Office: City Coll CUNY West 138th St & Convent Ave New York NY 10031

KHALILZAD, ZALMAY MAMOZY, ambassador; b. Mazar-i-Sharif, Afghanistan, Mar. 22, 1951; m. Cheryl Benard; children: Alexander, Maximilian. BA, MA, American U., Beirut, Lebanon; PhD, U. Chgo., 1979. Asst. prof. polit. sci. Columbia U., NYC, 1979—89; spl. adv. to under sec. for polit. affairs US Dept. State, Washington, 1985—89; assoc. prof. U. Calif., San Diego, 1989—91; asst. dep. under sec. policy planning US Dept. Def., Washington, 1991—92; sr. polit. scientist RAND Corp., Washington, 1989—91, dir. strategy, doctrine & force structure prog. Project Air Force, 1993—99; head, Bush-Cheney Transition Team US Dept. Def., Washington, 2000—01; spl. asst. to Pres. & sr. dir. for Southwest Asia, N. E. & North African Affairs NSC, Washington, 2001—02, spl. asst. to Pres. & sr. dir. for Islamic Outreach & Southwest Asia Initiatives, 2002; spl. envoy to Afghanistan US Dept. State, Kabul, 2002—03, US amb. & presdl. envoy to Afghanistan, 2003—05, US amb. to Iraq Baghdad, 2005—07, permanent US rep. to UN NYC, 2007—. Muslim. Office: Permanent Mission of US to UN 140 E 45th St New York NY 10017*

KHALSA, PRABHJOT SINGH, neurologist; s. Kewal Singh and Harbans Kaur Khalsa; m. Amritpal Kaur Sagoo, Jan. 3, 1997; children: Uptej Kaur, Anoop Kaur, Prabhteg Singh. BA, U. Calif., Berkeley, 1983; MD, UMDNJ, Camden, NJ, 1988. Diplomate neurology Am. Bd. Psychiatry and Neurology, 1997, clin. neurophysiology Am. Bd. Psychiatry and Neurology, 1997, Nat. Bd. Med. Examiners, 1989, internal medicine Am. Bd. Internal Medicine, 1991. Intern internal medicine U. Calif., Davis, 1988—89, resident internal medicine, 1989—91, resident neurology Martinez, 1991—94, fellow clin. neurophysiology, 1994—95; neurologist Fremont Neurology Med. Associates, Inc., Fremont, Calif., 1995—. Cons. neurologist Wash. Twp. Hosp., Fremont, Calif., 1995—; asst. clin. prof. neurology U. Calif., Davis, 1995—. Mem.: ACP, Alameda Contra Costa Med. Assn., Calif. Med. Assn., Am. Assn. Electrodiagnostic Medicine, Am. Acad. Neurology. Office: Fremont Neurology Medical Associates Inc 722 Mowry Ave Fremont CA 94536 Home Phone: 510-713-3390; Office Phone: 510-713-3390.

KHALSA, SAT BIR SINGH, biomedical researcher; b. Toronto, Canada, Dec. 20, 1951; arrived in US, 1985, naturalized, 2001; s. Frank and Anna Rak; m. Siri Krishna Kaur Arnold, June 26, 1987; children: Hansmukh Kaur, Harimander Singh. BS in Physics, Chemistry, Math., and Astronomy, U. Toronto, Can., 1974, PhD in Physiology, 1985. Postdoctoral fellow U. Va., Charlottesville, Va., 1985—96; from rsch. fellow to asst. prof. medicine Harvard Med. Sch. Brigham and Women's Hosp., Boston, 1996—2006, asst. prof. medicine Harvard Med. Sch., 2006—. Contbr. articles to profl. jours. Min. Sikh Dharma Internat., Espanola, N.Mex., 1989—2006; bd. dirs. Sikh Dharma Mass., Millis, Mass., 2005—06. Grantee, NIH, 2000, 2004. Mem.: Soc. Sleep Rsch. (assoc.), Assn. Applied Psychophysiology and Biofeedback (assoc.). Democrat. Sikh. Office: Brigham and Women's Hospital 75 Francis Street Boston MA 02115 Office Phone: 617-732-7994. Office Fax: 617-701-1296. Business E-Mail: khalsa@hms.harvard.edu.

KHAN, AHMED MOHIUDDIN, insurance company executive; b. Hyderabad, Andhra Pradesh, India, Nov. 14, 1955; s. Mohammad Mominuddin and Mehar-Unnisa Begum Hyderabad; m. Marjorie L. Klein-Khan, Mar. 31, 1983; 1 child, Yosef F. MBA, U. Palm Beach, Fla., 1975; PhD in Bus. Adminstrn., Northwestern U., Evanston, Ill., 2000; PhD in Fin., Madison U., Harrisonburg, Va., 2001. Inventory auditor RGIS, Inc., Chgo., 1975-78; staff acct. Sommerset, Inc., Chgo., 1978-85; fin. cons. Provident Mutual Fin. Svc., Inc., Phoenix, 1985-92; pres. Khan and Assocs., Fin./Ins. Svcs., Phoenix, 1992—. Author: Financial-Insurance Services in the New Millenium, 2000. Named Hon. Mem. Exec. Hall of Fame, 2000, named one of Outstanding Scholars of 20th Century; recipient Nat. Sales Achievement award, 2000, Nat. Quality award, 2000. Mem. Assn. MBA Execs., Nat. Assn. Ins. Fin. Advisors, Millon Dollar Round Table. Democrat. Muslim. Avocations: golf, travel, classical music. Personal E-mail: amkhan_2001@yahoo.com.

KHAN, AMMAN A., lawyer; b. Hyderabad, India, May 11, 1968; married; 2 children. BA with distinction, McGill Univ., 1990; LLB cum laude, Univ. Ottawa, 1993; LLM, UCLA, 1994. Bar: Ontario 1997, Calif. 1998, US Dist. Ct. So. & Ctrl. Calif. Judicial clk. Fed. Ct. Canada, 1994—95; asst. prof. law Univ. Ottawa, 1995—96; sr. assoc., bus. litigation Christensen, Glaser, Fink, Jacobs, Weil & Shapiro, LA. Editor (assoc.): Ottawa Law Rev. Named a Rising Star, So. Calif. Super Lawyers, 2006; recipient J.S.D. Tory award for legal writing, 1992. Mem.: State Bar Calif., Law Soc. Upper Canada. Office: Christensen Glaser Fink Jacobs Weil & Shapiro 19th Fl 10250 Constellation Blvd Los Angeles CA 90067 Office Phone: 310-556-7865. Office Fax: 310-556-2920. Business E-Mail: akhan@chrisglase.com.

KHAN, ARFA, radiologist, educator; b. Srinagar, Kashmir, India, Dec. 4, 1943; came to U.S., 1966; d. Ghulam Rasool and Ruqia Hayat; m. Faroque A. Khan, Apr. 16, 1966; children: Arif O., Shireen. B of Medicine, B of Surgery, Govt. Med. Coll., Kashmir, 1964. Diplomate Am. Bd. Radiology. Intern Barberton (Ohio) Citizen Hosp., 1966-67; resident in radiology L.I. Jewish Med. Ctr., New Hyde Park, NY, 1967-70, from instr. to assoc. prof. radiology, 1970-93, chief thoracic radiology, 1983—, prof., 1993—, assoc. chmn. radiology, 1994-2000; program dir., 1995. Contbr. over 65 articles to radiology jours. Fellow Am. Coll. Radiology; mem. Am. Coll. Radiology, Am. Soc. Neuroradiology, Am. Soc. Head & Neck Radiology, Am. Soc. Thoracic Radiology, Radiol. Soc. N.Am. Democrat. Muslim. Avocations: cooking, tennis, aerobics, gardening, skiing. Office Phone: 718-470-7164. Office Fax: 718-343-7463. Business E-Mail: akhan@lij.edu.

KHAN, CHAKA (YVETTE MARIE STEVENS), singer; b. Great Lakes, IL, Mar. 23, 1953; m. Hassan Khan, 1970 (div. 1971); m. Richard Holland, 1974 (div. 1980); m. Doug Rasheed, 2001; children: Damien Holland, Milini. D (hon.), Berklee Coll. Music, 2004. Singer musical group Rufus, 1972-76; solo performer Warner Bros. Records, 1978—96. Founder, chmn. Chaka Khan Found., Beverly Hills, Calif., 1999—; founder EarthSong Entertainment, Beverly Hills, Calif. Singer (with Rufus) (albums) Rufus, 1973, Rags to Rufus, 1974, Rufusized, 1974, Rufus Featuring Chaka Khan, 1975, Ask Rufus, 1977, Masterjam, 1979, Camouflage, 1981, Stompin' At the Savoy, 1983, (solo albums) Chaka, 1979, Naughty, 1980, Whatcha' Gonna Do For Me, 1981, Echoes of an Era, 1982, Chaka Khan, 1983 (Grammy award for Best Female R&B Vocal Performance, 1983), I Feel For You, 1984 (Grammy award for Best Female Vocal R&B Performance, 1984), Destiny, 1986, CK, 1989, Life is a Dance,

1989, The Woman I Am, 1992 (Grammy award for Best Female R&B Vocal Performance, 1992), Vol. 1: Epiphany: The Best of Chaka Kahn, 1996, Come 2 My House, 1998, Chaka Khan Live, 2003, ClassiKhan, 2004; singer (songs) Tell Me Something Good (Grammy award for Best Group R&B Performance, 1974), I'm Every Woman, 1978, Be Bop Medley (Grammy award for Best Vocal Arrangement, 1983), Reading Rainbow TV theme song, 1983, Ain't Nobody (Grammy award for Best Group Vocal R&B Performance, 1983), I'll Be Good to You (Grammy award for Best Vocal Duo, 1990), What's Going On, 2001 (Grammy award for Best Traditional R&B Vocal Performance, 2002); appearances include (films) The Blues Brothers, 1980 (TV series) Hunter, 1984, New York Undercover, 1994, The Good News, 1997, Living Single, 1993, Malcolm & Eddie, 1996 (stage) Mama, I Want to Sing, 1995, Signed, Sealed, Delivered, 2002; author (autobiography) Chaka! Through the Fire, 2003. Named one of 200 Extraordinary Women Who've Changed the World, Essence mag., 1995, 100 Greatest Women of Rock 'N Roll, VH1, 1999; recipient 8 Grammy awards, Diamond Life award, Internat. Assn. African Am. Music, 1992, Lena Horne Career Achievement award, Soul Train Lady of Soul Awards, 1998, Lifetime Achievement award, Music of Black Origin (MOBO) Awards, 2002, Emerging Artist & Tech. in Music, 2002, World Music Awards, 2003, Black Entertainment TV (BET), 2006, Beverly Hills C.A.R.E.S. award, 2004, Woman of Yr. award, I'm Every Woman Conf., 2004, Humanitarian award, Chaka Khan Found., 2004. Office: Chaka Khan Found E Tower Ste 515 9100 Wilshire Blvd Beverly Hills CA 90212

KHAN, IMRAN, research scientist, educator; (parents Am. citizens); s. Abdus Sobhan Khan and Murshida Zohra; m. Masuda Khan, Sept. 9, 1965; children: Irfan Sobhan, Tahsin Murshed. PhD in Pharmacology, Med. U. SC, Charleston, 1991. Pharmacist Bangladesh, 1984. Asst. project scientist U. Calif. San Diego, La Jolla, 1986—2000, asst. prof., 2001—. Grant reviewer Am. Heart Assn., Sacramento, 2005—. Contbr. papers to profl. jours. and pubs. Vol. educator Standley Mid. Sch., San Diego, 2004. Mem.: Am. Soc. Pharmacology and Exptl. Therapeutics, Rho Chi, Phi Kappa Phi. Independent-Republican. Achievements include discovery of genetic linkage between nicotinic receptor responses and hypertension. Avocations: photography, travel. Office: Univ Calif San Diego 9500 Gilman Dr La Jolla CA 92093-0636 Home Phone: 858-458-0964; Office Phone: 858-822-0328. Personal E-mail: imranmurshedkhan@gmail.com. Business E-Mail: ikhan@ucsd.edu.

KHAN, JAMIL AKBER, chemical company executive; b. Karachi, Pakistan, Mar. 17, 1952; came to U.S., 1976; s. Mehboob and Shamim Akhter Khan; m. Susan Mandelin, Feb. 27, 1981; children: Farooq J., Omar J. PhD, U. London, 1976; MBA, U. New Haven, 1987. Rsch. fellow Uniroyal, Inc., Middlebury, Conn., 1978-84, mktg. specialist, 1984—85; mktg. dir., v.p. Tech. & Mktg. Internat., Middlebury, 1985-87; mktg. mgr. Montedison/Ausimont, NYC, 1987-88; sales and mktg. mgr. Ausimont, Morristown, N.J., 1988-90, Enimont/Enichem, NYC, 1990-94; dir. sales Enichem Americas, Houston, 1994—2006; v.p. sales, mktg. Lianda Corp., Hudson, Ohio, 2006—. Editor: Physical Chemistry, 1974; numerous patents in field. Mem. edn. com. UNICEF; mem. Mt. Arlington (N.J.) Bd. Edn., 1998. Fellow Royal Soc. Chemistry U.K., Am. Inst. Chemistry; mem. AMA (hon. lectr. 1990-98), Am. Chem. Soc., Soc. Automotive Engrs. Avocations: tennis, reading, lecturing, writing. Home Phone: 936-271-3841.

KHAN, JUNAID H., surgeon; BS in Biomedical Sci. cum laude, U. Calif., Riverside, 1986; MD, U. Calif., LA, 1989. Lic. Calif., 1991, Am. Bd. Surgery, 1996, Am. Bd. Thoracic Surgery, 1999. Resident dept. surgery U. Calif., San Francisco, 1989—95, resident divsn. cardiac surgery San Francisco Medical Ctr., 1995—98; with Doctors Medical Ctr., San Pablo, Calif., 1998—, Summit Medical Ctr., Oakland, Calif., 1998—. Presenter in field. Mem.: AMA, Calif. Soc. Thoracic Surgery (bd. dirs. 2004), Am. Heart Assn. (bd. dirs. 2006), Internat. Soc. Minimally Invasive Cardiothoracic Surgery, We. Thoracic Surgical Assn., San Francisco Surgical Soc., Soc. Thoracic Surgeons (patient safety task force 2005), Calif. Medical. Assn., Bay Area Soc. Thoracic Surgeons, Am. Coll. Surgeons (admission com. 2005), Alameda-Contra Costa Medical Assn.

KHAN, M. WASIULLAH, academic administrator; MA in Lit., Panjab U., Pakistan, MEd with honors; PhD in Edn. Adminstrn., Ind. U., Bloomington. Chancellor East-West U., Chgo., 1980—. Office: East-West U 816 S Michigan Ave Chicago IL 60605-2185 Home Phone: 312-616-8042; Office Phone: 312-939-0111. Business E-Mail: chancellor@eastwest.edu.

KHAN, MOHAMMAD ASAD, geophysics educator, retired minister, former senator of Pakistan; b. Aima, Lahore, Pakistan, Aug. 13, 1940; came to U.S., 1964; s. Ghulam Qadir and Hajira (Karim) K.; m. Tahera Pathan, Jan. 4, 1974; 1 dau., Shehzi Samira. BS, U. Punjab, Lahore, Pakistan, 1957, MS, 1963; postgrad., Harvard U., 1964-65; PhD (East West Center scholar), U. Hawaii, 1967. Lectr. in geophysics U. Punjab, India, 1963-64; asst. prof. geophysics and geodesy U. Hawaii, 1967-71, assoc. prof., 1971-74, prof., 1974-96, prof. emeritus, 1996—; chmn. internat. advisors, 1987—. NSF and NASA fellow Summer Inst. Dynamical Astronomy at MIT, Cambridge, Mass., 1968—69; leader Am. Asian Studies and Contemporary Social Problems Seminar Series, Honolulu, 1968—69; sr. vis. scientist geodynamics Goddard Space Flight Ctr. NASA, Greenbelt, Md., 1972—74; sr. resident assoc. NAS, 1972—74; diplomatic minister/adviser Resource Survey and Devel. Pakistan, 1974—76; sr. scientist Computer Scis. Corp., Silver Spring, Md., 1974—76, sr. cons., 1976—77; minister of petroleum and natural resources Govt. of Pakistan, 1983—86; cabinet mem. Econ. Coord. Com. Cabinet Govt. of Pakistan, 1983—86, Nat. Econ. Council Govt. of Pakistan, 1984—86; chmn. Hydrocarbon Devel. Inst., Pakistan, 1984—86, Attock Oil Refinery, 1984—86; senator Govt. of Pakistan, 1984—86. Contbr. articles to profl. publs. Chmn. East and West: A Perspective for the 80's; mem. Hawaii Environ. Council, 1979-83, chmn. exec. com., 1979-83, vice chmn., 1981-83; chmn. Pakistan Relief Fund, Honolulu, 1971. Recipient Gold medal Rawalpindi Union of Journalists, 1985, Pakistan Engrng. Coun., 1985, Pakistan Assn. of Minorities, 1984, 85, Disting. Alumnus award for pofl. excellence and leadership U. Hawaii, 1995. Fellow Explorers Club; mem. Geol. Soc. U. Punjab (pres. 1962-63), Am. Geophys. Union, Pakistan Assn. Advancement Sci., Am. Geol. Inst., Am. Geophys. Union, East West Ctr. Alumni Assn. (dir. 1976-80), Internat. Alumni of East West Ctr. (exec. com., chmn. 1977-80, Disting. Alumnus award for Outstanding Career Achievements and Leadership 1984). Achievements include research in geophysics, geodetic and oceanographic applications of satellites, geodynamics, planetary interiors, global tectonics, global correlations, core-mantle boundary problems, equilibrium figures, gravity, isostasy, satellite altimetry, geodesy, earth models, geophysical exploration, ocean dynamics. Office: U Hawaii-Hawaii Inst Geophysics Planetology Post 602 Honolulu HI 96822-2219 *Most men stand the test of adversity quite well, but if you really want to test the character of a man, give him power.*

KHAN, MOHAMMED YOUSUF, physician, consultant; b. Multan, Pakistan, May 1, 1936; arrived in U.S., 1960; s. M.K. and H.K. Durrani; m. Yasmin Yousef Jan, Oct. 31, 1971; children: Irfan, Zeshan. MBBS, Punjab U., Pakistan, 1958; PhD, U. Minn., Mpls., 1969. Diplomate Am. Bd. Internal Medicine, Am. Bd. Infectious Diseases. Resident internal medicine U. Minn., 1962-66, fellow infectious disease, 1966-69; cons. Pakistan Internat. Airlines, Karachi, Pakistan, 1970-72; head infectious diseases Hennepin County Med. Ctr., Mpls., 1972-83; co-dir. Sexually Transmitted Diseases Clinic, 1972-83; asst. prof. Dept. Med., U. Minn., 1972-83; head infectious diseases King Fahad Hosp., Riyadh, Saudi Arabia, 1983-98, King Khalid Hosp., Jeddah, Saudi Arabia, 1998-2000; chief infectious disease Maricopa Med. Ctr., Phoenix, 2000—; assoc. prof. medicine Mayo Med. Sch., Rochester, Minn., 2001—. Keynote speaker Riyadh Med. Forum, Suadi Arabia, 1992. Contbr. articles to jours., chpts. to books. Recipient Physician Recognition award AMA, 1996. Fellow ACP, Infectious Disease Soc. Am., Royal Coll. Physicians. Avocations: fishing, hiking, reading, coin collecting/numismatics. Office: Maricopa Med Ctr Dept Medicine 2601 E Roosevelt Phoenix AZ 85008 Personal E-mail: myousuf_khan@yahoo.com.

KHAN, MUSHFIQUDDIN, neuropharmacologist, researcher; s. Noor Mohammad Khan and Aqila Begum; m. Salma Ansar, June 15, 1966 (dec.); children: Tooba, Talha, Hamza. BSc with honors, Aligarh Muslim U., India, 1976, MSc, 1978, MPhil, 1980. Postdoctoral rschr. Ehime U., Matsuyama, Shikoku, Japan, 1984—86; rsch. scientist-pool officer Aligarh Muslim U., Uttar Pradesh, India, 1986—88; lectr. Shibli Nat. Postgraduate Coll., Azamgarh, Uttar Pradesh, India, 1988—90; postdoctoral rschr. Med. U. SC, Charleston, 1994—98, asst. prof., 2002—. Scientist Modern Foam Industries, Janupur, 1990—94; sr. scientist Ariz. Inst. for Biomedical Rsch., Scottsdale, 1999—2001; grant reviewer NIH, Washington. Mem. AMU Rsch. Student's Assn., Aligarh, 1980—82. Recipient Mitchell I. Rubin rsch. award, Children's Hosp., MUSC; grantee, NINDS, NIH, Bethesda, MD, 2000—05; Monbusho fellow, Govt. of Japan, jr. rsch. fellow, CSIR, Govt. of India, sr. rsch. fellow. Mem.: AAAS, Indian Soc. for Mass Spectrometry, Am. Soc. for Neurochemistry, Am. Assn. for Biochemistry and Molecular Biology. Avocations: travel, classical music, humor, handball. Home: 3529 Ashwycke St Mount Pleasant SC 29466 Office: Med Univ SC 173 Ashley Ave 508 CRI Charleston SC 29425 Home Phone: 843-856-2779; Office Phone: 843-792-7991. Business E-Mail: khanm@musc.edu.

KHAN, SAJID A., management consultant, entrepreneur; s. Mohammad Rafiq Khan and Bushra Nasim; m. Aisha Khan, Aug. 25, 1991; children: Dabir, Shanzay, Yasmine, Danial. MBA, Stern Sch. of Bus., NYC, 1997. V.p. Merrill Lynch, NYC, 1998—2002; pres. MicroAgility, Inc., Plainsboro, NJ, 2003—. Producer. Mem.: OPEN (assoc.), The Exec. Forum. Achievements include development of PMO Methodology. Office: Microagility Inc 666 Plainsboro Rd Ste 1116 Plainsboro NJ 08536-3045 Personal E-mail: sajid@microagility.com.

KHAN, TAPAN KUMAR, adult education educator; m. Saswati Nandi. PhD, IIT, Kanpur, India, 1997. Postdoctoral rsch. assoc. Temple U. Sch. Medicine, Phila., 1997—2000, U. NC, Chapel Hill, 2000—04; asst. prof. Blanchette Rockefeller Neurosciences Inst., Rockville, Md., 2004—. Achievements include research in peripheral biomarker development of Alzheimer's disease. Home: 19761 Crystal Rock Dr Apt 24 Germantown MD 20874 Home Phone: 240-683-8211; Office Phone: 301-294-7183.

KHANDEKAR, JANARDAN DINKAR, oncologist, educator; b. Indore, India, Feb. 1, 1944; came to U.S., 1971; s. Dinker and Sulaochan (Dawlae) K.; m. Amita Oomen, Aug. 28, 1971; children: Manoj, Melin. MD, MBBS, U. Indore, 1969; sabbatical, Northwestern U., Baylor U., 1992. Diplomate Am. Bd. Internal Medicine, Am. Bd. Med. Oncology. Intern M.Y. Hosp., Indore, 1967-70; resident in medicine Allegheny Gen. Hosp., Pitts., 1972-73; head divsn. med. oncology Evanston (Ill.) Hosp., 1975-98, from asst. attending physician to assoc. attending physician, 1975-79, sr. attending physician, 1979—; fellow Med. Rsch. Coun., Montréal, Que., Canada, 1970-71, Tufts U., Boston, 1973-75; asst. prof. medicine Northwestern U., Chgo., 1975-80, assoc. prof., 1980-86, prof. medicine, 1986—, Kellogg/Scanlon chair in oncology, 1991-98; dir. cancer control Northwestern U. Cancer Ctr., Chgo., 1991—; assoc. dir. Kellogg Cancer Care Ctr. Evanston Hosp., 1979-87, dir., 1987—; Louise Coon chmn. dept. medicine Evanston Northwestern Healthcare, 1998—. Active NIH Ad Hoc Com. on Nat. Prostate Cancer Program, NIH Team for Audit Clin. Trials at Yale U., Roswell Park Meml. Inst., Mayo Clinic, etc.; chmn. rsch. com. and adv. com. Searle Clin. Pharmacology Unit; sr. investigator Eastern Coop. Oncology Group, 1976-83, Community Clin. Oncology Program, 1983—; lectr. in field. Author (with others): (novels) Radiation-Associated Thyroid Carcinoma, 1977, Adjuvant Therapy of Cancer, 1977; editor: (Archives) of Internal Medicine, 2004; contbr. articles. Recipient cert. of merit Nat. Cancer Inst. Humanitarian award Cancer Wellness Ctr., 2003; grantee Ill. Cancer Coun., 1983-98, Duke U., 1983-90, Nat. Cancer Inst., 1983—, Women's Health Inst., 1993, Evanston Hosp., 1993—, NIH, 1988-91, 93—. Fellow ACP (laureate); mem. AAAS, Am. Soc. Clin. Oncology, Am. Fedn. Clin. Rsch., Am. Assn. Cancer Rsch., Inst. Medicine (Chgo.). Office: Evanston Hosp 2650 Ridge Ave Evanston IL 60201-1781

KHANG, CHULSOON, economics professor; b. Kaesong City, Republic of Korea, May 10, 1935; s. Woon-sung and Ji-chung (Lim) K.; m. Yee Yu Lau, Sept. 15, 1959; children: Kenneth, Maurice. BA in Econs., Mich. State U., 1959; MA in Econs., U. Minn., 1962, PhD in Econs., 1965. Asst. prof. econs. San Diego State U., 1963-66, U. Oreg., Eugene, 1966-69, assoc. prof., 1969-73, prof., 1973-97, prof. emeritus, 1997—. Vis. prof., rsch. grantee U. New South Wales, Australia, 1972-73; vis. prof., Fulbright fellow Hanguk U. Fgn. Studies, Seoul, Korea, 1979; vis. prof. U. Hawaii, Honolulu, 1989. Referee Am. Econ. Rev., Jour. Internat. Econs., Rev. Econ. Studies, Jour. Fin., Jour. Polit. Econs., Jour. Banking and Fin., Jour. Econs. and Bus., Internat. Econ. Rev.; contbr. articles to profl. jours. Mem. Eugene Area Korean Assn. (past pres.), Am. Econ. Assn. Republican. Home: 224 Edgewood Dr Port Ludlow WA 98365-9225 Office: U Oreg Dept Econs Eugene OR 97403 Personal E-mail: yeeyuchul@gmail.com.

KHANNA, KANWAL, rheumatologist; b. Larned, Kans., Aug. 25, 1958; s. Jaswant Lal and Prabha Khanna; m. Marcia Gabriel Nino, Dec. 17, 1988; children: Deven Neal, Jacqueline. BS in Biol. Scis. with honors, Stanford U., 1980; MD, U. Calif., San Francisco, 1984. Diplomate Am. Bd. Internal Medicine, Am. Bd. Rheumatology. Resident in internal medicine Cedars-Sinai Med. Ctr., LA, 1984-87; fellow in rheumatology Harbor-UCLA Med. Ctr., Torrance, Calif., 1987-90; pvt. practice rheumatology Modesto, Calif., 1991—. Contbr. articles to profl. jours.; author abstracts in field. Relevance reviewer Am. Bd. Internal Medicine, 1995; mem. expert witness panel Med. Bd. Calif., 1996. Fellow ACP, Am. Coll. Rheumatology; mem. Calif. Med. Assn., Stanislaus Med. Soc., Mensa Soc., Phi Beta Kappa. Avocations: tennis, exercise, cooking, travel. Office: 1429 College Ave # M Modesto CA 95350-4046 Office Phone: 209-524-2041.

KHANNA, NITIN, engineering executive; BS in Computer Engrng., Drexel U. With Cisco Sys.; network engr. Verizon Comm.; pres., COO OmPay, LLC, Phila.; chief tech. architect Phila. Parking Authority implementation. Mem. Rep. Nat. Convention Tech. Team, 2000. Named one of 40 Under 40, Phila. Bus. Jour., 2006. Mem.: US-India Inst. of Greater Phila. (co-founder 2004, pres.). Office: OmPay 3225 Arch St Philadelphia PA 19104 Office Phone: 888-383-9911. Office Fax: 215-243-8207.

KHANNA, YASH KUMAR, family practice physician, pediatrician; b. Lahore, India, Dec. 28, 1941; came to U.S., 1970; s. Sohan Lal and Savitri (Mehra) K.; m. Christine Anne Warren, Sept. 22, 1972; children: Rajan Yash, Nisha, Dev Yash. MBBS, King George Michael Coll., Lucknow, India, 1964. Diplomate Am. Bd. Pediat., Am. Bd. Forensic Examiners, Child Health Royal Coll. Physicians and Surgeons, London. Sr. house officer Monsall Hosp., Booth Hall Children's Hosp., Manchester, England, 1966-68, Joyce Green Hosp., Dastford, England, 1969-70; house officer, emergency physician St. Mary's Hosp., Orange, NJ, 1971-87, resident in pediat., 1971-73; pvt. practice physician Orange, NJ, 1973—; med. dir. Quick Med.-West Essex Med. Group, Caldwell, NJ, 1983—, pres.-elect, 1997-2000, pres. med. staff, 2001—06. Asst. surgeon Ctrl. Health Svcs., New Delhi, 1965-66; house physician and surgeon Irwin Hosp., New Delhi, 1964-65; mem. med. staff Hosp. Ctrs. at Orange, N.J., 1973—2004, pres. med. staff, 1986-87, 2001-04; bd. govs. Cathedral Healthcare Sys. N.J., 2001-04. Mem. adv. com. to the handicapped Twp. of Livingston, N.J.; trustee Hosp. Ctr. at Orange, 1986-96; bd. govs. Cath. Healthcare, 2001-04. Recipient Med. Outreach award Grace Reformed Bapt. Ch., Newark, 1997, Hind Ratann award NRI Soc. India, 2002. Mem. Am. Assn. Physicians from India, N.J. Med. Soc., Orange Mountain Med. Soc., Indian Physicians Assn. N.J. (v.p. 2002-03, pres. 2004—), Asian Music Acad. (founder, pres. 1999—). Democrat. Hindu. Avocations: music, antiques. Home: 112 Shrewsbury Dr Livingston NJ 07039-3404 Office: Family Medicine/Pediat 310 Central Ave East Orange NJ 07018 also: Quick Med-West Essex Med Group 825 Bloomfield Ave Verona NJ 07044 Office Phone: 973-678-2900. Personal E-mail: yashk@aol.com.

KHANZADIAN, VAHAN, tenor; b. Syracuse, NY, Jan. 23, 1939; s. Avedis Sarkis and Araxey (Youghian) K. BS, SUNY, Buffalo, 1962; post grad., Curtis Inst. Music, Phila., 1961-63. Debut as Ruggero in La Rondine, San Francisco Spring Opera, 1968; leading roles in Wozzeck, Fra Diavolo, Les Troyens, Madama Butterfly, Lucia Di Lammermoor, Tosca; appeared throughout U.S., Can.; appeared in title role in Don Carlo, Basel, Switzerland, 1992; debut as Calaf in Puccini's Turandot with Bavarian State Opera, Munich, Germany, 1995; appeared with all major opera cos., and opera festivals, including San Antonio, Ravinia, Tanglewood, Saratoga, Opera de Colombia; numerous solo recitals throughout N.Am.; appeared with symphony orchs., including Chgo., Boston, Phila., Cleve., Minn., Indpls., St. Louis, Milw., Pitts.; TV appearances include Gherman in Tchaikovsky's Queen of Spades; soloist in world premier of Menotti's Landscapes and Remembrances, PBS, 1976; leading tenor Met. Opera, 1991-99; debut as Gustavo in Un Ballo in Maschera, Met. Opera, 1993, Lyric Opera Chgo., 1993. Appeared in Sondheim's "Follies" at Paperhill Playhouse, 1998, which is recorded on a new CD. Served with U.S. Army, 1964-65. Sullivan Found. grantee, 1971-74; Rockefeller Found. grantee, 1971-73 Address: PO Box 741 Hunter NY 12442-0741 Personal E-mail: vahan@optonline.net. *My ethnic background, Armenian, with its strong Christian influence was instrumental in projecting the importance of family, religion, education, and culture. The strength and knowledge attained in this environment guided me in the arts, where I was fortunate to have had the discipline and the opportunity to pursue my goal of making a contribution in serving music.*

KHANZHINA, HELEN P., language and literature educator, translator; b. Perm, Russia, Aug. 28, 1954; came to U.S., 1995; d. Pavel L. and Dina B. Wexler; m. Yevgenii A. Khanzhin, Dec. 4, 1975 (div. Jan. 1984); 1 child, Dmitri. MA in English Lit., U. Perm, 1976; PhD in World Lit., U. St. Petersburg, 1985; Assoc. Prof. Diploma, USSR State Com. Nat. Edn., Moscow, 1991. Asst. then assoc. prof. dept. world lit. U. Perm, 1976-95; lectr. dept. English div. continuing edn. U. Va., Charlottesville, 1996-98. Interpreter Lang. Learning Enterprises, Washington, 1996—; rsch. analyst joint state govt. commn. gen. assembly Commonwealth Pa., Harrisburg, 1998—; lectr. divsn. comm., arts and social sciences Harrisburg C.C., 1998—; lectr. Sch. of Humanities Pa. State U., Harrisburg, 1999—. Author: The Making of the National Tradition in American Romantic Poetry and William Cullen Bryant's Creative Work, 1987, Genre, Mode and Style in American Romantic Poetry, 1998; editor: Problems of Method and Poetics in World Literature of the Nineteenth and Twentieth Centuries, 1995, 2d edit., 1997; contbr. articles to profl. jours. Vis. scholar grantee USIA, 1993-94, Brit. Coun. Beatrice Ward Found., 1990. Mem.: AAUW, Nat. Assn. Ethnic Studies. Avocations: classical music, jazz, ballet, art, travel. Office: Joint State Govt Commn 108 Fin Bldg Harrisburg PA 17120 Business E-Mail: ykhanzhina@legis.state.pa.us, ypk1@psu.edu.

KHARE, MOHAN, chemist, researcher; b. Varanasi, India, May 15, 1942; arrived in U.S., 1967, naturalized, 1971; s. Dwarka Nath and Rampyari Devi Khare Srivastava; m. Meena K., Nov. 20, 1973; 1 child, Rohit. BSc, Banaras Hindu U., India, 1961, MSc, 1963, PhD, 1967. Rsch. assoc. U. Md., College Park, 1967-69, Oreg. State U., Corvallis, 1969-70; sr. rsch. assoc. Cornell U., Ithaca, NY, 1970-78; analytical specialist Hydroscience Inc., (subsidiary of Dow Chem. Co.), Knoxville, Tenn., 1978-80; tech. specialist IT Enviroscience subs. IT Corp., Knoxville, 1980-82; rsch. prof. chemistry U. Nev., Las Vegas, 1982-84, mgr. organic divsn. quality assurance lab. under coop. agreement with EPA, 1982-84; mgr. organic analysis lab. Environ. Monitoring Svcs. Rockwell Internat., Thousand Oaks, Calif., 1984-85; dir. environ. analytical lab. EA Engrng., Sci., and Tech., Inc., Sparks, Md., 1985-87; sr. v.p. Recra Environ., Inc., Columbia, Md., 1987-89; pres., CEO Envirosystems, Inc., Columbia, 1989—. Cons. to toxic and hazardous waste analytical labs.; mem. panel peer rev. Toxic Organics Lab. Contbr. articles to profl. jours. including protocols and std. oper. procedures for hazardous waste analytical program. Mem. Am. Chem. Soc., Internat. Union Pure and Applied Chemistry, Internat. Assn. of Environ. Testing Lab. Home: 10189 Maxine St Ellicott City MD 21042-6351 Office: Envirosystems Inc 9200 Rumsey Rd Ste 102B Columbia MD 21045-1934 Office Phone: 410-964-0330. Personal E-mail: moham.khare@gmail.com. Business E-Mail: info@envsystems.com.

KHARGONEKAR, PRAMOD PRABHAKAR, engineering educator; b. Indore, India, Aug. 24, 1956; s. Prabhakar K. and Leela P. K.; m. Seema P. Pai, Apr. 7, 1983; children: Aditya, Shivangi. BTech. in elec. engrng., Indian Inst. Tech., Bombay, 1977; MS in math., U. Fla., 1980, PhD in elec. engrng., 1981. Asst. prof. elec. engrng. U. Fla., Gainesville, 1981-84; assoc. prof. elec. engrng. U. Minn., Mpls., 1984-88, prof. elec. engrng., 1988-89; prof. elec. engrng. and computer sci. U. Mich., Ann Arbor, 1989—2001, Arthur F. Thurnau Prof., 1995—98, assoc. chair elec. engrng. and computer sci., 1995-97, chair elec. engrng. and computer sci., 1997—2001, Claude E. Shannon Prof. Engrng. Sci., 2000—01; dean Coll. Engrng. U. Fla., Gainesville, 2001—, assoc. v.p. Engrng. and Indsl. Expt. Sta., 2001—, Eckis Prof. Elec. and Computer Engrng., 2001—. Assoc. editor Math. Problems in Engrng. Contbr. more than 250 articles to profl. jours. Recipient Sigma Xi award for Outstanding Rsch. on Math. Sys. Theory, U. Fla., 1982, Best Faculty Paper award, Dept. Elec. Engrng., 1983, Presdl. Young Investigator award, NSF, 1985, George Taylor award for Rsch., U. Minn. Inst. Tech., 1987, Donald Eckman award, Am. Automatic Control Coun., 1989, O. Hugo Schuck Best Paper award, 1993, Tchg. Excellence award, Elec. Engrng. and Computer Sci. Dept., U. Mich., 1992, Rsch. Excellence award, U. Mich. Coll. Engrng., 1994, Disting. Alumnus award, Indian Inst. Tech., 1997. Fellow: IEEE (Control Systems Soc. George S. Axelby Best Paper Award 1990, W.R.G. Baker Prize Paper Award 1991). Avocations: reading, music. Office: U Fla Coll Engrng 300 Weil Hall PO Box 116550 Gainesville FL 32611-6550 Office Phone: 325-392-6000. Business E-Mail: ppk@eng.ufl.edu.

KHARINA, NINA YURIEVNA, science educator; b. Taganrog, Russia, Mar. 28, 1958; arrived in U.S., 1996; d. Yuriy Nikolaevich Yefimov and Galina Vasilievna Yefimova; m. Nikolay Alekseyevich Kharin, Feb. 24, 1979; 1 child, Ilya Nikolaevich Kharin. MD, Rostov-on-Don State Med. U., Russia, 1981. Physician/pediatrician State City Hosp., Taganrog, 1981—86; sr. tchr. pathophysiology Med. Coll., Taganrog, 1984—96, head dept. biomed. disciplines, 1986—96; adj. therapist Univ. Hosp., Taganrog, 1993—96; adj. faculty Cuyahoga C.C., Highland Hills, Ohio, 2003—. Maj. lt. Navy, 1981—96, Russia. Recipient Tchr. of Highest Category, State Health Dept., Rostov-on-Don, Russia, 1995, Excellent Worker, Nat. Edn. of Russian Fedn., 1995, Outstanding Adj. Faculty, Cuyahoga C.C., 2005. Russian Orthodox Christian. Avocation: reading. Home: 892 Pinewood View Rd Sagamore Hills OH 44067 Office: Cuyahoga CC 4250 Richmond Rd Highland Hills OH 44122 Personal E-mail: nkharin@aol.com.

KHASAWNEH, MOHAMMAD TURKI, industrial engineer, educator; s. Turki M. Khasawneh and Enam M. Alwahshat; m. Manal T. Athamnah, June 26, 2002; children: Omar M., Farah M. BSc, Jordan U. Sci. & Tech., Irbid, 1993—98, MSc, 1998—2000; PhD, Clemson U., SC, 2000—03. Tchg. asst. Jordan U. Sci. & Tech., 1998—2000, Dept. Indsl. Engring., Clemson U., 2000—02, rsch. asst., 2000—03; tchr. record Clemson U., 2002—03; asst. prof. SUNY, Binghamton, 2003—. Author: (conference article) An Evaluation of Systematic Search Strategies on Inspection Performance Using a Job-Aiding Tool; contbr. articles to profl. jours. Recipient Best Paper award, Indsl. Engring. Rsch. Conf., 2004; grantee Summer Faculty fellow, U.S. Air Force, 2006; Rsch. grant for digitization of health records in healthcare setting, United Health Svcs. Hosp., 2005—06, Rsch. grant for virtual reality decision support sys. for surface mount tech. placement machines set-up, Integrated Electronics Engring. Ctr., Binghamton U., 2005—06, Rsch. grant for adaptive human-centered automation for control of advanced microelectronics mfg. sys., Ctr. Advanced Microelectronics Mfg., Binghamton U., 2006. Mem.: Jordan Engrs. Assn., Am. Soc. Quality (faculty advisor Binghamton U. student chpt. 2001—), Human Factors & Ergonomics Soc., Inst. Indsl. Engrs., Alpha Pi Mu, Alpha Epsilon Lambda. Office: SUNY Binghamton Vestal Pky E Binghamton NY 13902 Home Phone: 607-206-1099. Office Fax: 607-777-4094. Personal E-mail: mkhasawneh@gmail.com. Business E-Mail: mkhasawn@binghamton.edu.

KHASAWNEH, SHADI TURKI, computer scientist; b. Irbid, Jordan, July 24, 1979; arrived in US, 2004; s. Turki Khasawneh and Enam Alwahshat. BSc in Computer Engring., Al-balqa' Applied U., Amman, Jordan, 2002; MS in Computer Sci., SUNY, Binghamton, NY, 2006. Cert. Oracle, 2002, Sun Microsystems, 2003. Sr. cons. oracle Computer and Engring. Bur., Amman, Jordan, 2001—04; rsch. asst. Rsch. Found. SUNY, Binghamton, NY, 2004—06; engr. hardware design Intel Corp., Austin, Tex., 2006—. Contbr. articles to profl. jours. Mem.: IEEE (assoc.), Jordan Engrs. Assn. (assoc.), Assn. Computing Machinery (assoc.). Achievements include research in low-power high-performance regsiter file design in chip multiprocessors.

KHATAMEE, MASOOD AHMAD, obstetrician, gynecologist; b. Mashhad, Iran, Feb. 12, 1936; s. Ahmad and Cobra (Tadbir Kashani) K.; married, Mar. 11, 1966; children: Pira, Neda, Yalda. MD, Shiraz U., Iran, 1961. Diplomate Am. Bd. Ob-Gyn. Intern Nemazee Hosp., 1960-61; resident in ob-gyn. Bellevue Hosp. Ctr., NYC, 1962-66, fellow in infertility, 1966-67; exec. dir. Fertility Rsch. Found., NYC; mem. staff Lenox Hill Hosp., NYC, Beth Israel-North Divsn., NYC, NYU Med. Ctr., NYC. Clin. prof. NYU Sch. Medicine; pres. Iranian Am. Med. Assn., 1998-2000; founder Soc. Prevention Human Infertility; founder, pres. Shiraz U. Sch. Medicine Alumni Assn. USA, Inc., 1988-89. Pres. Iranian Am. Rep. Party, N.Y.C., 1994—. Fellow ACOG; mem. Am. Fertility Soc., Fertility Rsch. Found. Home: 23 Church St Alpine NJ 07620 Office: Fertility Rsch Found 877 Park Ave New York NY 10021-0341 Office Phone: 212-288-3737.

KHATIB, KATHY, school administrator, educator; b. Chgo., July 25, 1943; d. John and Mary Samsuris; m. Ahmed Khatib, Oct. 27, 1973; children: Kate, John. BA, U. Ill., Chgo., 1968; diploma, Am. Montessori Internat., Perugia, Italy, 1973. Tchr. spl. edn. Southwest Sch., Chgo., 1968—70, Arc Sch., Madison, Wis., 1970—72; asst. tchr. trainer Centro Internat. Montessori, Perugia, 1973—77; tchr. Alexander Montessori Sch., Miami, 1978—79; adminstr., head tchr. Johnstown Montessori Sch., Pa., 1979—82, Cmty. Montessori Sch., Glasgow, Ky., 1985—2004. Spkr., presenter in field. Mem.: Internat. Montessori Coun., Am. Montessori Soc., Assn. Montessori Internat. Avocation: boating.

KHATIB, RUSTOM ATFAT, gynecologist, researcher, endocrinologist, consultant, economist; b. Beirut, Sept. 3, 1962; s. Atfat Rustom and Samia Ibrahim (Jannoun) K.; m. Mona Adnan Tabbara, Feb. 11, 1993; children: Samia Karla, Ryan Atfat. BS with honors, Am. U. Beirut, 1984, MD, 1988; MBA, Hamilton U., Wyo., 1995, PhD in Bus. Adminstrn., 2001; postgrad diploma in econs., U. London, 2000, MSc in Fin. Mgmt., 2006. Resident in ob-gyn. Am. U. Beirut, 1992-94; fellow in reproductive endocrinology Mich. State U., Saginaw, 1994, clin. instr., 1992-94; clin. cons. Rizk Hosp., Beirut, 1994—2005. Clin. cons., dir. fertility unit European Heart Ctr., Saida, 1994—96; chmn. ob-gyn. United Med. Group, Beirut, 1996—2007, dir. fertility unit, 1997—2007; sci. cons. Beirut Fertility Ctr., 1994—99; dir. fertility svc. Jubeily Hosp., Saida, 1996—99; cons. fertility unit Kasab Hosp., Saida, 2000—; dir., sr. cons. IVF Systems, Beirut, 2007—; prof. and cons. Janeen Fertility Ctr., Manama, Bahrain, 2006—; mem. acad. coun. London Diplomatic Acad. Contbr. articles to profl. jours. including Gynecologic Oncology, Fertility and Sterility, European Jour. Obstets., Clin. Consultation in Ob-Gyn. Founding cabinet mem. World Peace and Diplomacy Forum, Cambridge; sec. gen. United Cultural Conv., Raleigh, NC, 2000—. Recipient Physician's Recognition award AMA, 1994, Ob-Gyn. Rsch. award Saginaw Coop. Hosps., 1994. Fellow Am. Coll. Surgeons; mem. Am. Soc. for Reproductive Medicine, NY Acad. Scis., European Soc. for Human Reproduction and Embryology, Am. Soc. for Reproductive Medicine, Greenpeace. Office: United Med Group Abdul Aziz St Al Mabani Ctr 14-5354 Beirut Lebanon Office Phone: 9611741900. Office Fax: 9611749695. Personal E-mail: 362812@cyberia.net.lb, rustom@cyberia.net.lb.

KHAVARI, KHALIL AKHTAR, psychology professor; b. Tehran, Iran, Nov. 10, 1932; s. Ardeshir Akhtar and Rouhanghiz Khalili K.; m. Sue Williston, June 6, 1959; children: Paul, Katherine. BS, Bradley U., 1960, MS, 1963; PhD, Ind. U., 1967. Asst., assoc. then prof. psychology U. Wis., Milw., 1967-95, founder, dir. Midwest Inst. on Drug Use, 1974-77, co-founder, coord. peace studies program, 1987-89. Referee, cons. in field. Author: Creating a Successful Family, 1989, Together Forever: A Practical Guide to Successful Marriage, 1993, Introduction to the Baha'i Faith, 1997, Spiritual Intelligence, 2000. Mem. aux. bd. Baha'i Faith, Milw., 1981-86, founding mem. Baha'i Internat. Health Assn., Ft. Lauderdale, Fla., 1984-90; life mem. Tlinget Indian Tribe, Alaska. Avocations: reading, travel, tennis, hiking, gardening.

KHAWLI, LESLIE ALBERT, research scientist, educator; s. Albert Antoine and Corinne Khawli; m. Carole Chammas, July 2, 1995; children: Michelle Leila, Joelle Corinne. PhD, U. So. Calif., LA, 1986. Postdoctoral fellow Harvard Med. Sch., Boston, 1986—88; asst. prof. U. So. Calif., LA, 1988—94, assoc. prof., 1994—2001, prof., 2001—06; prin. scientist Genentech Inc., 2006—. Tchg. grad. and med. students U. So. Calif., LA, 1988—; cons. Peregrine Pharms., Tustin, Calif., 1989—, Cancer Therapeutics, Inc., LA, 1995—, NeoTherapeutics, Inc., Irvine, Calif., 1997—2002. Scientist (cancer research) Interface between immunochemistry and nuclear medicine, primarily on the generation of new approaches for the successful immunodiagnosis and therapy of human cancer using genetically engineered monoclonal antibodies. Recipient Rsch. Travel award, NSF, 1983, Rsch. Svc. award, NIH, 1986-1988, Rsch. award, Nat. Cancer Inst., 1992-1995, Contbn. and Excellence in Cancer Rsch. award, Found. for Better Medicine, 2000; Rsch. fellowship, Harvard Med. Sch., 1986-1988, Pilot Rsch. Project grant, Am. Cancer Soc., 1992-1993, Rsch. grant, Nat. Cancer Inst., 1992-1995, Tobacco-Related Disease Rsch. Program, 1994-1996, Cancer Therapeutics, 1994-2003, Perigrine Pharms., 1995-2003, NIH, 2000-2003, Calif. Cancer Rsch. Program, 2000-2003. Mem.: Am. Assn. of Pharm. Scientists, Am. Chem. Soc., Am. Assn. for Cancer Rsch., Soc. of Nuc. Medicine. Achievements include patents for Use Of Promising Immunoregulatory Antibody/Cytokine Fusion Proteins For The Immunotherapy Of Solid Tumors; M-aminophenyltrialkylstannane; Radiohalogenated Half-Antibodies and Maleimide Intermediate Therefor; Modified Antibodies with Controlled Clearance Time; Antibodies Modified at Two Separate Sites; Antibodies with Reduced Net Positive Charge; Vasopermeability Enhancing Peptide of Human Interleukin-2 and; Published many articles and chapters in the fields of cancer research. Office: Genentech Inc One DNA Way M570 South San Francisco CA 94080 Business E-Mail: khawli.leslie@gene.com.

KHAYAT, CLARK, bank executive; B in Econs., Dartmouth Coll., Hanover, NH; JD, U. Pa., Phila. With Derivative Products Group NatCity Investments, v.p. Corp. Fin. Group; engagement mgr. McKinsey & Co.; with Nat. City Corp., Cleve., 2003—, sr. v.p., CFO Instnl. Asset Mgmt. team, head Best in Class program officer, sr. v.p. corp. planning. Dir. governance bd. Make a Wish Found. Greater Ohio and Ky. Office: Nat City Corp Nat City Ctr 1900 E Ninth St Cleveland OH 44114-3484 Office Phone: 216-222-2000.*

KHAYAT, ROBERT CONRAD, academic administrator; b. Moss Point, Miss., Apr. 18, 1938; m. Margaret Denton; children: Margaret D. Khayat Bratt, Robert C. Jr. BA in Edn., U. Miss., 1961, JD, 1966; LLM, Yale U., 1981. Bar: Miss. 1966. With Wash. Redskins, 1960—64; pvt. practice in law, mcpl. judge City of Moss Point, Pascagoula, Miss., 1967-69; mcpl. judge City of Oxford, Miss.; pvt. practice in law Oxford, 1975-77; mem. faculty Sch. Law U. Miss., University, 1969—, vice-chancellor for univ. affairs, 1984-89; pres. NCAA Found., 1989—92; prof. law, interim dir. athletics U. Miss., University, 1994, chancellor, 1995—. Contbr. articles to profl. jours. Pres. C. of C., Oxford Lafayette County, Fellowship of Christian Athletes. Recipient Disting. Am. award, Nat. Football Found., 1987, 1989, 2003, Outstanding Law Prof. of the Yr.; scholarship established in his name, 1995, Oxford Lafayette County Citizen of the Yr., 1989, Career Achievement award, NFL Alumni Assn., 1998; fellow, Yale U., 1981; scholar, Miss Law Jour., 1994. Mem.: ATLA, ABA, Miss. Bar Found. (trustee 1988—89), Miss. State Bar Assn., Phi Kappa Phi, Phi Delta Phi, Omicron Delta Kappa, Lamar Order. Office: U Miss Chancellor's Office 331 Martindale University MS 38677 Office Phone: 662-232-7111. Office Fax: 662-915-5935. E-mail: chancllr@olemiss.edu.*

KHAZINS, DAVID MIKHAILOVICH, research scientist; b. Budennovsk Stavropol Region, Russia, June 24, 1941; s. Mikhail Davidovich and Feiga Pavlovna Khazins; m. Ludmila Mikhajlovna Zagarskikh, Apr. 24, 1965; children: Irina Davidovna Rashevskaya, Gene Davidovich Hazins. MS, Moscow U., 1966, DSc, 1986. Leading scientist Joint Inst. Nuc. Rsch., Dubna, Russia, 1966—91; guest scientist Rockefeller U., NYC, 1991—96; rsch. scientist Duke U., Durham, NC, 1997—2000; sr. devel. scientist Bruker AXS, Inc., Madison, Wis., 2000—. Contbr. more than 120 articles to profl. jours. Recipient Advancing X-ray Diffraction, Vantec 2000 award, R&D 100 Mag., 2005. Home: 6966 Park Ridge Dr Madison WI 53719 Office: Bruker AXS Inc 5465 E Cheryl Pkwy Madison WI 53711 Home Phone: 608-276-8217; Office Phone: 608-276-3094. Office Fax: 608-276-3015. Personal E-mail: david.khazins@charter.net. Business E-Mail: david.khazins@bruker-axs.com.

KHEEL, ROBERT J., lawyer; b. New Rochelle, NY, May 1, 1943; s. Theodore W. Kheel; m. Elizabeth Ann Diamond, June 24, 1995. BA, Cornell U., 1965; MSc, London Sch. Econs., 1966; JD cum laude, U. Mich., 1969. Bar: NY 1969, Fla. 1970, DC 1983, US Dist. Ct. (So. Dist. NY) 1971, US Dist. Ct. (Ea. Dist. NY) 1971, US Ct. Appeals (2nd Cir.) 1975, US Ct. Appeals (DC Cir.) 1984, US Ct. Appeals (9th Cir.) 1990. Atty. Willkie, Farr & Gallagher, NYC, ptnr. litig. dept. Gen. counsel Nat. League Profl. Baseball Clubs; lectr. sports law Columbia Law Sch., 1991—. Contbr. articles to profl. jours. Trustee Howard and Georgeanna Jones Inst. Reproductive Medicine. Mem. ABA, NY State Bar Assn., Fla. Bar Assn., DC Bar, Assn. Bar City NY Office: Willkie Farr & Gallagher 787 Seventh Ave New York NY 10019-6099 Office Phone: 212-728-8234. Office Fax: 212-728-9234. E-mail: rkheel@willkie.com.

KHERADPIR, SHAYGAN, information technology executive; B in Elec. Engring., Cornell U., M, PhD, Cornell U. Joined GTE, 1987; v.p. GTE Labs, Waltham, Mass., 1994—96; asst. v.p., info. tech. GTE, 1996—98, v.p. info. tech., enterprise sys., 1998—2000; pres., e-bus. group Verizon Comm. (following GTE merger), 2000—02; exec. v.p., chief info. officer, info. tech. Verizon Comm., 2002—. Adj. prof., elec. engring. Northeastern Univ., Mass., 1992—94; adv. bd. mem. Cornell Univ. Engring. Sch.; mem. tech. adv. coun. Sun Microsystems. Author: more than 20 jour. papers. Named one of nation's 85 outstanding young engineers, NAE, 1996. Mem.: IEEE (sr.). Achievements include holding one patent. Office: CIO Verizon Comm 1095 Ave of Americas New York NY 10036*

KHERDIAN, DAVID, writer; b. Racine, Wis., Dec. 17, 1931; s. Melkon and Veron (Dumehjian) K.; m. Kato Rozeboom, 1968 (div. 1970); m. Nonny Hogrogian, Mar. 17, 1971. BS in Philosophy, U. Wis., 1960. Lit. cons. Northwestern U., 1965; founder/editor Giligia Press, 1966-72; rarebook cons. Fresno State Coll., Calif., 1968-69, lectr., 1969-70; ofcl. poet-in-the-schs. NH, 1971; editor Ararat mag., 1971-72; dir. Two Rivers Press, Aurora, Oreg., 1978-86. Poetry judge, lectr., reader of own poetry; founder, editor (with Nonny Hogrogian) The Press at Butternut Creek, 1987-88. Author: On The Death of My Father and Other Poems, 1970, Homage to Adana, 1970, Looking Over Hills, 1972, The Nonny Poems, 1974, Any Day of Your Life, 1975, Country, Cat: City, Cat, 1978, I Remember Root River, 1978, The Road From Home: The Story of an Armenian Girl (Lewis Carroll Shelf award, Boston Globe/Horn Book award, Newbery Honor Book award, Jane Addams Peace award, Banta award), 1979, The Farm, 1979, It Started With Old Man Bean, 1980, Finding Home, 1981, Taking the Soundings on Third Avenue, 1981, The Farm: Book Two, 1981, Beyond Two Rivers, 1981 (Friends of Am. Writers award), The Song in the Walnut Grove, 1982, Place of Birth, 1983, Right Now, 1983, The Mystery of the Diamond in the Wood, 1983, Root River Run, 1984, The Animal, 1984, Threads of Light: The Farm Poems Books III and IV, 1985, Bridger: The Story of a Mountain Man, 1987, Poems to an Essence Friend, 1987, A Song for Uncle Harry, 1989, the Cat's Midsummer Jamboree, 1990, The Dividing River/The Meeting Shore, 1990, On a Spaceship with Beelzebub: By a Grandson of Gurdjieff, 1990, The Great Fishing Contest, 1991, Friends: A Memoir, 1993, Juna's Journey, 1993, Asking the River, 1993, By Myself, 1993, My Racine, 1994, Lullaby for Emily, 1995, Seven Poems for Mikey, 1997, The Rose's Smile, 1997, I Called It Home, 1997, The Golden Bracelet, 1998, Chippecotton: Root River Tales of Racine, 1998, The Neighborhood Years, 2000, The Revelations of alvin Tolliver 2001, Seeds of Light: Poems From a Gurdjieff Community, 2002, The Song of the Stork and Other Early and Ancient Armenian Songs, 2004, Letters To My Father, 2004, The Buddha: The Story of an Awakened Life, 2004, Nearer the Heart, 2006; also bibliographies.; editor: Visions of America by the Poets of Our Time, 1973, Settling America: The Ethnic Expression of 14 Contemporary Poets, 1974, Poems Here and Now, 1976, Traveling America with Today's Poets, 1976, The Dog Writes on the Window with His Nose and Other Poems, 1977, If Dragon Flies Made Honey, 1977, I Sing the Song of Myself, 1978, Beat Voices: An Anthology of Beat Poetry, 1995; co-editor: Down at the Santa Fe Depot: 20 Fresno Poets, 1970; translator: The Pearl: Hymn of the Robe of Glory, 1979, Pigs Never See the Stars: Armenian Proverbs, 1982, Monkey: A Journey to the West, 1992, Feathers and Tails: Animal Fables From Around the World, 1992, Forgotten Bread: Armenian American Writers of the First Generation, 2007; editor: Forkroads: A Jour. of Ethnic-Am. Lit., 1995-97, Stopinder: A Gurdjieff Jour. For Our Time, 2000-2003. Served with AUS, 1952-54. Home and Office: 5082 County Rte 7 Chatham NY 12037-2604 Office Phone: 518-392-0970. Business E-Mail: tavnon@taconic.net. *The poet understands that everything is connected and all is one. This is all he really knows. But knowing this he is permitted to speak, quietly, disturbing nothing, removing nothing, revealing only the new-old relationships he has been given to see.*

KHIDIATOVA, ALIA, transportation executive; b. Beloretsk, Russia, May 30, 1972; d. Musliha Khidiatova; m. Yevgeniy Matkovskiy, Mar. 11, 2001. BA, Bashkir State U., Ufa, Russia, 1992; MD, Bashkir State U., Ufa, Russia, 1996. Cert. linguistics Faculty of Roman and German Lit., 1994. Nature preservation program leader European Youth Ecol. Fund, Moscow, 1991—95; tourism recruitment asst., interpreter Internat. Students Union, Moscow, 1991—95; interpreter InterModa, Ufa, Russia, 1993—94; interpreter, translator Youth Union, Ufa, Russia, 1994—95; post-graduate studies tchr. Bashkir State U., Ufa, Russia, 1995—96; v.p., treas. West Coast Limousine Inc., San Jose, Calif., 2000—. Vol. ARC, San Jose, Calif., 1996. Home Phone: 408-255-9601; Office Phone: 408-255-9601. Personal E-mail: alia@westcoastlimousine.com.

KHILNANI, VINOD M., manufacturing executive; b. 1952; m. Gita Khilnani; 2 children. MS, Delhi U.; MBA, SUNY, Albany. CPA, CMA. Various positions Cummins Engine Co., Inc., 1978-96; CFO Dayton (Ohio) Superior Corp., 1996-97; v.p., CFO Simpson Industries, Inc.; v.p., corp. contr. Metaldyne Corp., 2000—01; sr. v.p., CFO CTS Corp., Elkhart, Ind., 2001—07, pres., CEO, 2007—. Office: CTS Corp 905 W Blvd N Elkhart IN 46514 E-mail: vkhilnani@ctscorp.com.*

KHIM, JAY WOOK, information technology executive; b. Taegu, Korea, Oct. 22, 1940; came to U.S., 1965; s. Joon Mook and Soon E. (Lee) K. BS in Agrl. Econs., Kyung Pook U., Korea, 1963, MA in Agrl. Econs., 1966; postgrad. PhD program in Econs., U. Md., 1965-69; LLD (hon.), Randolph-Macon Coll., 1988; PhD (hon.), Kyungpook Nat. U., Republic of Korea, 1990. Mem. rsch. staff Brookings Instn., Washington, 1967-69; sr. economist NAB, Dept. of Labor, Washington, 1969-72; sr. assoc. Planning Rsch. Corp., Washington, 1972-74; chmn., CEO JWK Internat. Corp., Washington, 1974—, Internat. Trade and Investment Corp., Washington, 1977—. Bd. dirs. Millennium Bank. Author: The Third Eye, 1998; author, editor more than 100 research reports, articles for fed. govt. in fields of health, energy, def., transp., housing and internat. affairs Bd. dirs. Fulbright Found., 1999—, Asia Soc., Washington, 1999—, George Mason Inst., George Mason U., Fairfax, Va., 1983—, United Bank, 1997—, No. Va. Cmty. Found., 1998—, Worf Trap Found. for Performing Arts, 1998—; mem. World Presidents Orgn., 1992—, chmn. Washington Met. chpt., 1994-2000; bd. govs. U. Md. Alumni Assn.; bd. trustees Fairfax Hosp. Assn., 1986-2001; candidate for U.S. Congress from 11th Va. dist., 1992; chmn. fin. com. Rep. Party, Va.; commr. Small and Minority Bus. Commn., Fairfax County, 1992. Fulbright scholar, 1965, 66; recipient Sam Ill Found. award Korea, 1962, 63 Mem. Young Pres.'s Orgn., Pres. Club of Am. Mgmt. Assn., Nat. Security Assn., Am. Def. Preparedness Assn., Am. Econ. Assn., Fairfax C. of C. (bd. dirs. 1984-87), World Pres.'s Orgn. (chmn. Washington Met. chtp. 1994-95), City Club, Tower Club, Robert Trent Jones Club, Tournament of Players Club, Internat. Club (D.C.), River Bend Country Club, Fairbanks Golf and Country Club (San Diego). Office: JWK Internat Corp Ste 1040 7617 Little River Tpke Annandale VA 22003-2689 also: 10900 Tara Rd Potomac MD 20854-1342

KHO, EUSEBIO, surgeon; b. Philippines, Dec. 16, 1933; came to U.S., 1964; s. Joaquin and Francisca (Chua) K.; m. Grace Casas Lim, May 24, 1964; children: Michelle Mae, April Tiffany, Bradley Jude, Jaclyn Ashley, Matthew Ryan. AA, Silliman U., The Philippines, 1955; MD, State U. Philippines, 1960. Diplomate Am. Bd. Surgery. Rotating intern Philippine Gen. Hosp., U. Philippines, 1959-60; resident gen. practice Silliman U. Med. Ctr., 1960-63; virology rschr. Van Howelling Lab. Silliman U., 1963-64; intern in surgery Francis Scott Key Med. Ctr., 1964-65, resident in gen. surgery, 1965-67; fellow in surgery Johns Hopkins, 1965-67; rsch. assoc. pediat. surgery U. Chgo. Hosps., 1967-68; resident in gen. surgery then chief resident U. Tex. Hosp., San Antonio, 1968-70; hosp. surgeon St. Anthony Hosp., Louisville, 1970-72; practice medicine specializing in surgery Scottsburg, Ind., 1972—. Chmn. dept. surgery Scott County Meml. Hosp., 1973—; cons. surgeon Washington County Meml. Hosp., Salem, Ind., Clark County Meml. Hosp., Jeffersonville, Ind., 1973—; courtesy surgeon Suburban Hosp., Louisville, 1973—; gen. surgeon 5010 U.S. Army Hosp., Louisville, 1980—. Bd. dirs. Make-A-Wish Found., Ind., 1992—. Col. M.C., USAR, 1980—, Operation Desert Storm, 1990-91. Named to Chgo. Filipino Am. Hall of Fame, 1998; recipient Outstanding Svc. Overseas award U. Philippines Med. Alumni Soc., 2002. Fellow: ACS, Am. Coll. Emergency Physicians, Am. Soc. Abdominal Surgeons; mem.: APHA, AMA (Physician's Recognition award 1969, 1972), Philipine Med. Assn. of Ky. (Disting. Svc. award 2000), Am. Heart Assn., Am. Soc. Law and Medicine, Am. Cancer Soc., Am. Soc. Parenteral and Enteral Nutrition, Soc. Laparoscopic Surgeons, N.Y. Acad. Scis., Surgeons in Am. (life), Assn. Philippine Practicing Physicians in Am. (life), Assn. Mil. Surgeons U.S. (life), Res. Officers Assn. U.S. (life), Soc. Philippine Surgeons in Am. (life), Bradley Aust. Surg. Soc., Mark Ravitch Surg. Assn., Ind. Philippines Med. Assn., Ky. Med. Assn., Soc. of The Philippines, Ind. State Med. Assn., Am. Coll. Internat. Physicians (founding, trustee 1974—), U. Chgo. Med. Alumni Assn., Philippine Heritage Endowment Found., Philippine Ednl. and Cultural Endeavor (life), Silliman U. Alumni Assn. (life), U. Philippines Med. Alumni Soc. Am. (life), Assn. U.S. Army (life), Silliman Alumni Internat., Johns Hopkins Med. Alumni Assn., Optimists, Masons, Hon. Order Ky. Cols. Presbyterian. Home: 14 Carla Ln Scottsburg IN 47170-9707 Office: 137 E Mcclain Ave Scottsburg IN 47170-1846 Office Phone: 812-752-5659.

KHODAREV, NIKOLAI NIKOLAEVICH, biologist, researcher; b. Moscow, June 28, 1952; s. Nikolai Nikolaevich Khodarev and Rema Borisovna Khodareva; m. Irina Anatolievna Sokolova, Mar. 23, 1986; children: Anatoliy Nikolaevich Sokolov, Igor Nikolaevich, Artem Nikolaevich Sokolov, Alexander Nikolaevich. MD, 1st Moscow Med. Sch., 1976, PhD, 1981; DSc, USSR Acad. Med. Sci., Moscow, 1989. Staff scientist Inst. Biomed. Chemistry, Moscow, 1981—83, leading scientist, 1983—89; chief of lab. Ctr. Med. Biotech., Moscow, 1989—92; Fogerty fellow NIH, Bethesda, Md., 1992—95; rsch. asst. prof. Loyola U., Chgo., 1995—98, U. Chgo., 1998—2004, rsch. assoc. prof., 2004—. Mem. sci. bd. Ctr. Med. Genetics, Moscow, 1989—92, Ctr. Med. Biotech., Moscow, 1989—92. Contbr. articles to profl. jours.; patentee in field. Recipient Best Annual Presentation award, Inst. Biomed. Chemistry, 1980, Best Presentation of Yr. award, Dept. Health/Acad. Med. Sci.; fellow Fogerty Internat. Ctr., NIH, 1992—95; grantee travel grantee, USSR Acad. of Med. Sci., 1991; USSR Acad. Med. Sci., 1982, 1984. Mem.: Internat. Soc. Cellular Oncology, Radiation Rsch. Soc., Am. Assn. Cancer Rsch. Achievements include detection of supermethylated regions of DNA in chromatin; discovery of irradiation dose-dependent tumor genes; role of interferon signaling in tumor radioresistance; role of chromatin conformation and repetitive sequences in apoptosis. Avocations: science fiction, bicycling. Office: U Chgo 5841 S Maryland Ave Chicago IL 60637 Home Phone: 630-941-7325. E-mail: nikolai@rover.uchicago.edu.

KHOLODENKO, YURI V., scientist, educator; b. Kiev, Ukraine, May 23, 1959; s. Vsevolod Grinshteyn and Irina Kholodenko. MS in Physics and Math., Kiev State U., Ukraine, 1981; PhD in Phys. Chemistry, Ukrainian Acad. Scis., Kiev, 1991, U. Pa., Phila., 1999. Rsch. scientist Inst. Phys. Chemistry, Kiev, 1984—91; tchg. & rsch. asst. U. Pa., 1992—99; asst. prof. Widener U., Chester, Pa., 2000—02, Bowdoin Coll., Brunswick, Maine, 2002—04, Albany Coll. Pharmacy, NY, 2004—. Mem. curriculum com. Albany Coll. Pharmacy, 2005—, mem. math curriculum grp., 2006—. Mem. strategic devel. FDLC Consulting, Phila., 1999—2001. Mem.: Am. Assn. Colls. Pharmacy. Achievements include discovery of a new type of photocatalytic reaction at solution/semiconductor interface; an unusual distributed conformational protein dynamics originated in restrained self-regulating diffusion; research in long-range electron/energy transfer with possible application to polymerization; the connection between protein motion and function via exploration of ligand dynamics; dynamics of electronic and vibrational energy dissipation and energy flow through proteins. Avocations: tennis, swimming. Office: Albany Coll Pharmacy 106 New Scotland Ave Albany NY 12208 Home (Summer): 12021 Bustleton Ave Unit 13 Philadelphia PA 19116

KHONSARI, MICHAEL M., mechanical engineering educator; b. Aug. 17, 1957; m. Karen Sue Troy, Sept. 1, 1990. BS in Mech. Engring. with honors, U. Tex., Austin, 1978, MS in Mech. Engring., 1979, PhD in Mech. Engring., 1983. Rsch. and tchg. asst. U. Tex., Austin, 1978-83; asst. prof. Ohio State U., Columbus, 1984-87, U. Pitts., 1988-90, assoc. prof., 1990-96; prof. So. Ill. U., Carbondale, 1996-99, prof., chmn. dept. mech. engring. and energy processes, 1996-99; Dow Chem. endowed chair, prof. mech. engring. La. State U., Baton Rouge, 1999—, Dow Chem. endowed chair in rotating machinery, 1999—. Apptd. project dir. and assoc. commr. Sponsored R&D at La. Bd. Regents, Exptl. Program to Stimulate Competitive Rsch., 2003—; mem. mech. engring. grad. com. U. Pitts., 1988-90, design interest group, 1988-96; mem. faculty ctr. motion control U. Pitts.; reviewer NSF, NASA, Am. Chem. Soc. Books, McGraw Hill Books, Addison Wesley Books, Prentice-Hall Books, Holt Rinehart and Winston Books; lectr. in field. Assoc. editor ASME Jour. Tribology, 1997—, STLE Tribology Transactions, 1990—; assoc. editor, Jour. Engring. Tribology, editl. bd., Tribology Internat.; mem. editl. bd., reviewer Jour. Engring. Design Graphics, 1987—; contbr., reviewer, mem. editl. bd. adv. com. CRC Handbook of Lubrication, vol. III, 1991-93; reviewer Lubrication Engring. Jour., Wear Jour., Rheology Jour., Heat Transfer Jour., Tribology Jour., Applied Mechanics Jour.; co-author: Applied Triology, 2001; pub. abstracts and reports; referee various jours.; contbr. articles to profl. jours. Recipient Found. award ALCOA, 1990, 91. Fellow Soc. Tribology Lubrication Engrs. (bearings com. 1985—, chmn. 1988-91, assoc. editor, rev. Tribology Transactions 1990—, assoc. editor Jour. Tribology 1997—, Presdl. Rsch. Coun. award 1993), ASME (conf. planning com. 1989-96, reviewer Jour. Tribology and conf. papers, chmn. ASME/Soc. Tribology and Lubrication Engrs. Internat. Conf. in Tribology 1996, Burt L. Newkirk award 1990). Achievements include research in thermal effects in hydrodynamic bearings, thermal effects in wet clutches, hot spot prediction in mechanical components, Thermoclastic instability, powder lubrication, multi-phase flows in bearings, friction associated with instrument pointing mechanisms operating under ultra low speeds. Office: La State U Dept Mech Engring 2508 Ceba Baton Rouge LA 70803-0001 Office Phone: 225-578-9192. Business E-Mail: khonsari@me.lsu.edu.

KHORANA, ALOK ANAND, oncologist, medical researcher; arrived in US, 1996; s. Anand Bhushan and Suman Anand Khorana; m. Melissa Marie Khorana; children: Ethan Alok, Matthew, Michael Cultrara, Benjamin Cultrara. MBBS, Maharaja Sayajirao U., Baroda, Gujarat, India, 1995; MD, SUNY, Buffalo, NY, 1999. Diplomate Am. Bd. Internal Medicine, 1999, in med. oncology Am. Bd. Internal Medicine, 2002. Fellow in hematology and oncology U. Rochester, Rochester, NY, 1999—2002, sr. instr. James P. Wilmot Cancer Ctr., 2002—04, asst. prof. medicine James P. Wilmot Cancer Ctr., 2004—. Mem. oncology expert com. U.S. Pharmacopoeia, 2005—; mem. sci. program com. ASCO, 2005—; mem. rsch. implementation workgroup comprehensive cancer control plan N.Y. State, Albany, NY; mem. gastrointestinal cancers com. S.W. Oncology Group, 2003—. Contbr. (TV series) Second Opinion, Sta. PBS-TV, 2005; contbg. author: Narrative Matters, 2006, mem. editl. bd.: Cancer Investigation; contbr. chapters to books, articles to profl. jours. Med. adv. coun. Gilda's Club, Rochester, 2005—06. Recipient Dr. H. P. Shastry Academic Excellence Gold medal, South Gujarat U., 1991, Academic Excellence in Pharmacology Gold medal, Maharaja Sayajirao U., 1993, Creative Excellence Faculty award, U. Rochester, Med. Humanities Divsn., 2001—02; grantee, Cancer Action, Gilda's Club, Rochester, 2001, Dr. Robert Cooper Trust, 2003, Nat. Cancer Inst., 2006—; James P. Wilmot Cancer Rsch. fellow, U. Rochester, 2001—04, V Found. fellow, 2006. Fellow: ACP; mem.: Internat. Soc. Thrombosis and Haemostasis, Am. Soc. Clin. Oncology (mem. venous thromboembolism guidelines panel 2006—). Hindu. Achievements include research in elucidating risk factors related to cancer-associated thrombosis. Office: University of Rochester 601 Elmwood Ave Box 704 Rochester NY 14467 Office Phone: 585-275-5863.

KHORANA, HAR GOBIND, chemist, educator; b. Raipur, India, Jan. 9, 1922; s. Shri Ganpat Rai Khorana and Shrimati Krishna (Devi) Knorana; m. Esther Sibler, 1952; children: Julia Elizabeth, Emilie Anne; 1 child, Dave Roy. BS, Punjab U., 1943, MS, 1945; PhD, Liverpool U., Eng., 1948; DSc (hon.), U. Chgo., 1967, Simon Fraser U., Vancouver, Can., 1969, U. Liverpool, Eng., 1971, U. Punjab, India, 1971, U. Miami, 1994; degree (hon.), U. Bergen, Norway, 1996; others (hon.). Head organic chemistry group B.C. Rsch. Coun., 1952—60; vis. prof. Rockefeller Inst., NYC, 1958—; prof. , co-dir. Inst. Enzyme Rsch. U. Wis., Madison, 1960—70, prof. dept. biochemistry, 1962—70, Conrad A. Elvehjem prof. life scis., 1964—70; Alfred P. Sloan prof. biology and chemistry MIT, Cambridge, 1970—97, Alfred P. Sloan prof. emeritus, sr. lectr., dept. Biology, 1997—. Vis. prof. Stanford U., 1964; mem. adv. bd. Biopolymers; rschr. chem. methods for synthesis of nuccleotides, coenzymes and nucleic acids, elucidation on the genetic code, lab. synthesis of genes, biol. membrane and light-transducing pigments. Author: Some Recent Developments in the Chemistry of Phosphate Esters of Biological Interests, 1961; editl. bd. Jour. Am. Chem. Soc., 1963—, contbr. numerous articles to profl. jours., —. Recipient Merck award, Chem. Inst. Can., 1958, Gold medal, Profl. Inst. Pub. Svc. Can., 1960, Dannie-Heinneman Preiz, Göttingen, Germany, 1967, Remsen award, Johns Hopkins U., 1968, Am. Chem. Soc. award for creative work in synthetic organic chemistry, 1968, Louisa Gross Horwitz prize, 1968, Lasker Found. award for basic med. rsch., 1968, Nobel prize in physiology or medicine, 1968, elected to Deutsche Akademie der Naturforscher Leopoldina, HalleSaale, Germany, 1968; fellow Overseas, Churchill Coll., Cambridge, Eng., 1967. Fellow: AAAS, Am. Acad. Arts and Scis., Chem. Inst. Can.; mem.: NAS, others, Japanese Biochem. Soc. (fgn. hon.), Royal Soc. Edinburgh, Pharm. Soc. Japan (hon.), Royal Soc. (London), Pontifical Acad. Scis. (Rome), Indian Acad. Scis. (fgn. mem.), Am. Philos. Soc. Office: 68-680A Dept Biol MIT 77 Massachusetts Ave Cambridge MA 02139-4307

KHOSHNOOD, KAVEH, epidemiologist, educator; b. Tehran, Iran, Sept. 6, 1964; (parents Am. citizens); s. Manouchehr Khoshnood and Parvaneh Khallaghi; m. Salma Madatali Mody, June 11, 1989; children: Naveed, Parisa. BS, Loyola Coll.; MPH, Yale U.; PhD, Yale U., New Haven, Conn., 1990—95. Rsch. assoc. Yale Sch. Medicine, New Haven, 1995—99; asst. prof. Yale Sch. Pub. Health, 1999—. Achievements include research in HIV/AIDS prevention. Home: 784 Orange St Apt 2 New Haven CT 06511 Office: Yale Sch Pub Health 60 College St New Haven CT 06520 Home Phone: 203-624-8575. Office Fax: 203-785-3260; Home Fax: 203-785-3260. Business E-Mail: kaveh.khoshnood@yale.edu.

KHOSLA, ANIL, lawyer; b. Pakistan, Aug. 7, 1945; S. O. P. and Santosh (Puri) K.; m. Barbara Lynn Hayes, May 17, 1991; 1 child, Mark Dameron Khosla. AB magna cum laude, Harvard Coll., 1968; JD cum laude, Harvard Law Sch., 1971. Bar: Mass. 1973, N.Y. 1992, U.S. Dist. Ct. Mass. 1974. Assoc. Debevoise & Plimpton, NYC, 1971-73, Bingham, Dana & Gould, Boston, 1973-75; assoc., ptnr. Hale and Dorr, Boston, 1975-92; ptnr. Schramm & Raddue, Santa Barbara, Calif., 1992-93, Peabody & Arnold, Boston, 1993—; mem. Eckert Seamans Cherin & Mellott, LLC., Boston. Adj. prof. Suffolk U. Law Sch. Dir. Santa Barbara Civ. Light Opera, 1992; mem. major gifts com. Santa Barbara Mus. Art, 1992. Mem. ABA, Am. Coll. Investment Counsel, NY State Bar Assn., Boston Bar Assn., Nat. Assn. Bond Lawyers. Republican. Avocations: reading, music, travel. Home: 47 Raymond St Cambridge MA 02140-3638 Office: Eckert Seamans Cherin & Mellott LLC 1 International Place Boston MA 02110-2602 Office Phone: 617-342-6868, 617-342-6800. Office Fax: 617-342-6899. Business E-Mail: akhosla@eckertseamans.com.

KHOSLA, CHAITAN S., chemical engineer; BTech, Indian Inst. of Tech., Mumbai, 1985; PhD, Calif. Inst. Tech., 1990; postdoctoral work, John Innes Ctr., U.K., 1990—91. Prof. chem. engring, chemistry and biochemistry Stanford Univ., and Wells H. Rauser and Harold M. Petiprin prof., sch. of engring. Recipient Dreyfus new Investigator award, 1991, Young Investigator award, NSF, 1994—99, Allan P. Colburn award, 1997, ACS Lilly award in Biological Chemistry, 1999, Alan T. Waterman award, NSF, 1999, ACS Pure Chemistry award, 2000, Disting. Alumni award, Calif. Inst. Tech., 2000. Fellow: Am. Acad. Arts & Scis. Achievements include being credited with pathbreaking work on erythromycin biosynthesis and elucidating molecular mechanisms. Office: Stanford Dept Chemical Engring Keck Science Bldg Rm 389 381 North-South Mall Stanford CA 94305-5025 Business E-Mail: ck@chemeng.stanford.edu.*

KHOSLA, PRADEEP KUMAR, engineering educator; b. Amritsar, Punjab, India, Mar. 13, 1957; arrived in US, 1982; s. Brijnath and Sharda (Behal) Khosla; m. Thespine Kavoulakis, June 20, 1987; children: Nathan, Alexander. B in tech. with honors, Indian Inst. Tech., Kharagpur, India, 1980; MSEE, Carnegie Mellon U., 1984, PhD, 1986. Asst. engr. Tata Cons. Engineers, India, 1980-81; project engr. Siemens Co., India, 1981-82; asst. prof. elec. and computer engring. and robotics Carnegie Mellon U., Pitts., 1986—90, assoc. prof., 1990—94, prof., 1994—, founding dir. Inst. for Complex Engineered Systems, 1997—99, Philip and Marsha Dowd Professor Coll. Engring. and Sch. Computer Sci., 1998—, head elec. and computer engring. dept., 1999—2004, founding dir. Ctr. for Computer and Comm. Security, 2001—03, founding co-dir. CyLab, 2003—, dean Carnegie Inst. Tech., 2004—; Program Mgr. Software and Intelligent Systems Tech. Office (SISTO), Def. Sciences Office (DSO), and Tactical Tech. Office (TTO) Def. Advanced Rsch. Projects Agy. (DARPA), 1994—96. Mem. bd. on mfg. and enring. design NRC, 2003—; bd. dirs. MPC Corp., Quantapoint Inc., Pitts., co-founder; mem. strategy review bd. Ministry Sci. & Tech., Taiwan; mem. IT adv. com. Commonwealth Sci. & Indsl. Rsch. Orgn. (CSIRO), Australia; mem. coun. deans of aeronautics adv. com. NASA; mem. sr. adv. group Program on Joint Unmanned Combat Air Systems Def. Advanced Projects Rsch. Agy. (DARPA). Bd. dirs. The Children's Inst., Indian Inst. Tech. Found. Recipient Ladd award for excellence in rsch., Carnegie Inst. Tech., 1989, Tech Brief Award, NASA, 1992, 1993, Leadership Award for Excellence in Academics and Tech., siliconindia, 2000, W. Wallace McDowell Award, IEEE Computer Soc., 2001, Cyber Edn. Champion award, Bus. Software Alliance, 2007; Inlaks Found. Fellowship, 1982. Fellow: AAAS, Am. Assn. Artificial Intelligence, IEEE (disting. lectr. Robotics and Automation Soc. 1998—2003); mem.: NAE, Am. Soc. Engring. Edn. (George Westinghouse Award for Edn. 1999). Avocations: travel, tennis, volleyball. Office: Carnegie Inst Tech Carnegie Mellon U 110 Scaife Hall Pittsburgh PA 15213-3890

KHOSLA, VED MITTER, oral and maxillofacial surgeon, educator; b. Nairobi, Kenya, Jan. 13, 1926; s. Jagdish Rai and Tara V. K.; m. Santosh Ved Chabra, Oct. 11, 1952; children: Ashok M., Siddarth M. Student, U. Cambridge, 1945; L.D.S., Edinburgh Dental Hosp. and Sch., 1950, Coll. Dental Surgeons, Sask., Can., 1962. Prof. emeritus, dir. postdoctoral studies in oral surgery Sch. Dentistry U. Calif., San Francisco, 1968—; chief oral surgery San Francisco Gen. Hosp. Lectr. oral surgery U. of Pacific, VA Hosp.; vis. cons. Fresno County Hosp. Dental Clinic.; Mem. planning com., exec. med. com. San Francisco Gen. Hosp. Contbr. articles to profl. jours. Examiner in photography and gardening Boy Scouts Am., 1971-73, Guatemala Clinic, 1972. Granted personal coat of arms by H.M. Queen Elizabeth II, 1959 Fellow Royal Coll. Surgeons (Edinburgh), Internat. Assn. Oral Surgeons, Internat. Coll. Applied Nutrition, Internat. Coll. Dentists, Royal Soc. Health, AAAS, Am. Coll. Dentists; mem. Brit. Assn. Oral Surgeons, Am. Soc. Oral Surgeons, Am. Dental Soc. Anesthesiology, Am. Acad. Dental Radiology, Omicron Kappa Upsilon. Clubs: Masons. Office Phone: 650-348-7587. *It is part of the cure to wish to be cured. With God all things are possible.*

KHOSLA, VINOD, investment company executive; b. New Delhi, Jan. 28, 1955; married; 4 children. BSEE, Indian Inst. Tech., New Delhi, 1976; M in Biomed. Engring., Carnegie Mellon U., 1978; MBA, Stanford U., 1980. Co-founder Daisy Sys.; co-founding CEO Sun Microsystems, 1982—86; gen. ptnr. Kleiner, Perkins, Canfield and Byers, Menlo Park, Calif., 1986—; founder Khosla Ventures, 2004—. Bd. dirs. Asera, Centrata, Infinera, Juniper Networks, 1996—2004, QWEST Comms., 1998—2005, Nanotectonica, Redback, Zambeel, Zaplet, eASIC Corp., 2004—. Named one of 50 Who Matter Now, CNNMoney.com Bus. 2.0, 2006. Office: Khosla Ventures 2744 Sand Hill Rd Menlo Park CA 94025*

KHOSROWSHAHI, DARA, travel company executive; BA, Brown U., 1991. With Allen & Co. LLC, v.p., 1995—98; v.p. strategic planning IAC, 1998—99, pres. USA Networks Interactive, 1999—2000, exec. v.p., ops. and strategic planning, 2000—02, exec. v.p., CFO, 2002—04, CEO IAC Travel, 2004—05; pres., CEO Expedia Inc., Bellevue, Wash., 2005—. Office: Expedia, Inc 3150 139th Ave SE Bellevue WA 98005*

KHOURY, BERNARD V., educational administrator; Asst. dean Grad. Studies and Rsch. U. Md.; assoc. exec. sec. Assn. Am. U.; exec. dir. Grad. Record Examinations Program Ednl. Testing Svc.; assoc. v.p. Academic Affairs U. Md. Sys., assoc. vice chancellor Policy and Planning; exec. officer Am. Assn. Physics Tchrs., 1990—. Office: Am Assn Physics Tchrs One Physics Ellipse College Park MD 20740-3845

KHOURY, COLLEEN A., law educator, former dean; b. 1943; BA, Colby Coll., 1964; JD, Ill. Inst. Tech., 1975. Dir. info. and devel. pvt. child welfare agy., Chgo.; pub. info. dir. Cook County Dept. Pub. Aid; assoc. Bell, Boyd & Lloyd, 1975—83, ptnr., 1983; gen. counsel Ventrex Labs.; prof. U. Maine Sch. Law, Portland, 1985—, assoc. dean, 1991—93, dean, 1998—2005. Bd. dirs. Justice Action Group, Banknorth Group, Inc.; chair Commn. on Gender, Justice and Cts., Maine Supreme Jud. Ct., 1993—96. Corporator Boys and Girls Clubs Greater Portland, Maine; trustee Portland Symphony Orch.; vice chair bd. trustees Colby Coll. Recipient Caroline Duby Glassman award, Maine State Bar Assn., 1997, Deborah Morton award, U. New Eng., 2002, Margaret Brent Lawyers Achievement award, ABA, 2003. Mem.: Am. Law Inst., Maine Bar Found. (bd. dirs.). Office: Univ Maine Sch Law 246 Deering Ave Portland ME 04102

KHOURY, GEORGE GILBERT, printing company executive, sports association executive; b. St. Louis, July 30, 1923; s. George Michael and Dorothy (Smith) K.; m. Colleen E. Khoury Czerny, Apr. 3, 1948; children: Colleen Ann, George Gilbert. Grad., St. Louis U., 1946. V.p. Khoury Bros. Printing, St. Louis, 1946—; exec. dir. George Khoury Assn. Baseball Leagues, Inc., St. Louis, 1967—. Author: (novel) Brothers Baseball Bombshells, 2003. Served with U.S. Army, 1943-45, NATOUSA, MTO. Decorated Purple Heart with oak leaf cluster. Roman Catholic. Office: George Khoury Assn Baseball Leagues 5400 Meramec Bottom Rd Saint Louis MO 63128-4624 Personal E-mail: czernyce@msn.com.

KHOURY, KENNETH F., lawyer, air transportation executive; b. NY, July 17, 1951; BA with honors, Rutgers Coll., NJ, 1972; JD, Fordham U., 1977. Bar: NY 1978, NJ 1979, Ga. Assoc. White & Case, 1977—82; sr. counsel THE BOC Group Inc., 1982—83; asst. v.p., assoc. counsel The Continental Corp., 1983—88; sr. v.p., assoc. gen. counsel Shearson Lehman Hutton, Inc., 1988—90; assoc. gen. counsel to v.p., dep. gen. counsel, sec. Georgia-Pacific Corp., Atlanta, 1990—2005; sr. v.p., gen. counsel Weyerhaeuser Co., 2006; exec. v.p., gen. counsel Delta Air Lines, Inc., Atlanta, 2006—. Office: Delta Air Lines Inc PO Box 20706 Atlanta GA 30320-6001 Office Phone: 404-715-2600.*

KHOURY, NAJI, engineering educator; BS in Engring., Lebanese Am. U., Byblos, 1999; MS in Civil Engring., U. Okla., Norman, 2001, PhD in Civil Engring., 2005. Undergraduate rsch. asst. Lebanese Am. U., 1995—99; rsch. grad. asst. U. Okla., 1999, grad. tchg. asst., 2004—05, rsch. assoc., instr., 2006—; internship Okla. Dept. Transp., Okla. City, 2001—03. Cons. Profl. Svc. Industries, Inc., Okla. City, 2000—, Engring. Svc. & Testing, Inc., Norman, 2002—, Midwest Engring. & Testing, Inc., Okla. City, 2004—, King Engring. & Constrn., Inc., Tulsa, 2006—. Contbr. articles to profl. jours. Founder, pres. U. Okla. Lebanese Student Assn., 2002; grad. senator U. Okla., 2004—05. Recipient 3d Place Holderchem award, Holderchem Bldg. Chem. SAL, 1999; grantee scholarship, Kailas & Becky Rao Found., 2003—04, 2004—05; Rsch. grant. for effect of soil suction & moisture on resilient modulus of subgrade soils in Okla., 2003—06, Rsch. grant for permeability & resilient modulus of different aggregate bases commonly used in Okla., Okla. Dept. Transportation, 2005—06, Rsch. grant for engring. properties of stabilized subgrade soils for implementation of the AASHTO 2002 patent design guide, 2005—, Rsch. grant for stability & permeability of proposed aggregate bases in Okla., Okla. Transportation Ctr., 2006—. Mem.: ASCE, Transp. Rsch. Bd. Nat. Academies, Okla. Microscopy Soc., Chi Epsilon. Achievements include patents pending for new construction materials. Office: Univ Oklahoma 202 W Boyd St Rm 334 Norman OK 73019 Home: 1220 E Brooks Norman OK 73071 Business E-Mail: nkhoury@ou.edu.

KHOURY, PHILIP S., academic administrator; b. Washington, Oct. 15, 1949; BA with honors, Trinity Coll., 1971; PhD, Harvard U., 1980. Asst. prof. MIT, Cambridge, 1981-84, assoc. prof., 1984-90, prof., 1990—, assoc. dean Sch. Humanities, Arts, and Social Sci., 1987-90, acting dean, 1990-91, dean, 1991—, Kenan Sahin dean, 2002—06, assoc. provost, 2006—, Ford internat. prof. history, 2006—. Author: Urban Notables and Arab Nationalism, 1983, Syria and the French Mandate, 1987; co-editor Tribes and State Formation in the Middle East, 1990, The Modern Middle East: A Reader, 1993, 2d edit. 2004, Recovering Beirut: Urban Design and Post-war Reconstruction, 1993; mem. editl. bd. Jour. Interdisciplinary History, 1987-, Hist. Abstracts, 1990-, The Beirut Rev., 1991-93. Trustee Am. U. Beirut, 1997—, vice chmn., 2005; trustee Toynbee Prize Found., 1998—, Trinity Coll, 2000—, Mus. Fine Arts, Boston, 2006—, Nat. Humanities Ctr., 2007—; bd dirs. World Peace Found., 1999—, chmn., 2004—; bd. overseers Koc U., Istanbul; bd. dirs. Harvard Coop. Soc., 1998-2004. Thomas J. Watson fellow Watson Found., 1971-72; Fulbright scholar, 1976-77; Post-Doctoral Social Sci. Rsch. Coun., 1983-84; Mellon fellow Aspen Inst., 1984-85; Class of 1922 Career Devel. Professorship, MIT, 1984-86. Fellow Am. Acad. Arts and Scis.; mem. AAAS, Am. Hist. Assn. (George Louis Beer Prize 1987), Mid. East Studies Assn. (pres. 1998, dir. 1990-92, 97-2000), Brit. Soc. for Mid. East Studies, Pi Gamma Mu. Avocation: tennis. Office: MIT 77 Massachusetts Ave Bldg 10-280 Cambridge MA 02139-4307 Office Phone: 617-253-0887. Business E-Mail: khoury@mit.edu.

KHOYNEZHAD, ALI, cardiothoracic surgeon, researcher; b. Mashad, Khorasan, Iran, Feb. 11, 1970; arrived in U.S., 1998; s. Reza Khoynezhad and Zhaleh Yousefein; m. Ziba Jalali, Mar. 31, 1998. MD, U. Cologne Coll. Medicine, 1996, PhD, 1998. Diplomate Am. Bd. Surgery, 2004, Am. Bd. Thoracic Surgery, 2006. Instr., prosector anatomy U. Cologne Coll. Medicine, Koeln, Germany, 1992—93; instr. surgery Humboldt-University, Berlin, 1996—98, North Shore U.-L.I. Jewish Med. Ctr., New Hyde Park, 2002—03, adminstrv. chief resident gen. surgery, 2002—03; instr. surgery Montefiore Med. Ctr. Affiliated Hosp., Bronx, 2004—05, adminstrv. chief resident cardiothoracic surgery, 2004—05; staff surgeon vascular and endovascular surgery Harbor-UCLA Med. Ctr., 2005—; asst. prof. Cardiovasc. and Thoracic Surgery divsn. U. Nebr. Med. Ctr., Omaha, 2006—. Exec. com. mem. Oper. Rm. Quality Assurance Com., New Hyde Park, NY, 2001—02, Grad. Med. Edn. Com., New Hyde Park, 2002—03, Credentials Com., Bronx, 2004—05, Thoracic Surgery Resident Assn., NYC, 2004—; rschr. in field. Recipient First Prize, Murry Friedman Competition, Coll. Surgeons, 2002; E. Ferdinand Sauerbruch Grant in Aid, E. Ferdinand Sauerbruch Competition, 1996-1998. Mem.: ACS (licentiate), Am. Coll. Cardiology (licentiate), Am. Coll. Chest Physicians (licentiate Poster of Distinction award 2002), Iranian AMA (licentiate), Soc. Am. Gastrointestinal and Endoscopic Surgeons (licentiate), So. Med. Assn. (licentiate), Mecklenburg County Med. Soc. (licentiate), Internat. Soc. Heart and Lung Transplantation (licentiate), Cardiothoracic Surgery Network (licentiate), Soc. Thoracic Surgeons (licentiate), German Soc. Thoracic & Cardiovasc. Surgery (licentiate). Avocations: photography, travel. Office: Univ Nebr Med Ctr Cardiothoracic Surgery Divsn 982315 UNMC Omaha NE 68138-2315 Home: 19915 Farnam St Elkhorn NE 68022 Office Phone: 402-559-4424. Personal E-mail: akhoy@lycos.com. Business E-Mail: akhoynezhad@unmc.edu.

KHOZEIMEH, ISSA, electrical engineer, educator; b. Tehran, Iran, Dec. 25, 1939; came to US, 1959; s. Ismail and Zohreh (Akhun) Khozeimeh; m. Nahid Khozeimeh; children: Lili, Nini. BSEE, George Wash. U., Washington, DC, 1966; MSEE, 1973, D in Engring., 1984, DSc in Engring. Mgmt., 1993. Registered profl. engr. Engr. Potomac Electric Power Co., Washington, 1967-68; substation engr., 1968-73; design standrads engr., 1973-79; sr. engr. substation design, 1979-80; dept. head, chief elec. engr. David Volkert and Assocs., Bethesda, Md., 1980-88; mgr. utilities svcs. divsn. Metro Washington Airports Authority Dulles Internat. Airport, 1988—; prof. engring. and mgmt. U. Md., Balt., 1998—; prof. mgmt. U. Balt., 1999—. Pres. Internat. Mktg. and Consulting Corp., Washington, 1980-82; v.p. Horizon Internat., Washington, 1982-88; pres. Forum Internat. Glen Echo, Md., 1988—; prof. U. Md., Balt., 1998—, U. Balt., 1999—; bd. dirs. industry adv. bd. U. Md. Balt. County, 1998—. Author: An Automated Maintenance Management System for International Airports, 1993; contbr. articles to profl. jours. Recipient Sch. of Engring Svcs. award, 1976, Gen. Alumni Assn. Svc. award, 1971, George Wash. U., 1976, Engr. Coun. Cert. of Appreciation, 1984, 85, Disting. Svc. award 1986, Disting. Alumni Svc. award George Wash. U. Alumni Assn., 1998, Tech. Forum Leadership award, 1999, Outstanding Profl Efforts award Met. Washington Airport Authority, 2000. Mem.: NSPE, IEEE (sr.; life), DC Coun. Engring. and Archtl. Socs. (bd. mem. 1999—, v.p. 2004—05, pres. 2005—06, Meritorious Svc. award 2007), Washington Soc. Engrs. (bd. dirs. 1975—, pres. 1995), Md. Soc. Prof. Engrs. (pres. 1995—96, 2002—04, Disting. Sr. Engr. award 1997), Instrument Soc. Am. Republican. Muslim. Avocations: water-skiing, snow skiing, hiking, reading, publishing, lecturing, travel. Home: PO Box 557 Glen Echo MD 20812-0557 Office: Metro Washington Airports Authority Dulles Internat Airport PO Box 17045 Washington DC 20041-7045 Office Phone: 703-572-2830. Personal E-mail: khozeimeh@hotmail.com. Business E-Mail: issa.khozeimeh@mwaa.com.

KHUONG, LOC HUU, finance educator; arrived in U.S., 1975; s. Ba Huu and Le Ngoc Tran Khuong; m. Hanh-Phuoc Khuong. BBA, Loyola U., Chgo., 1984, MBA, 1994; D of Bus. Adminstrn., Nova Southeastern U., 2002, PhD in Acctg., 2006. Pub. acct. Ernest Frier & Assocs., CPA's,

Chgo., 1980—82; internal mgr. AB Dick Co., Chgo., 1983—84; audit mgr. Cenco, Inc., Oak Brook, Ill., 1984—86; v.p., fin., CFO Indsl. Wastes/ChemLime, Elizabeth, NJ, 1986—89; v.p. fin. Chemstar Lime Corp., Phoenix, 1990—94; dir. bus. analysis Chem. Lime, Ft. Worth, 1995—98; asst. to the CEO Chem. Lime Inc., Ft. Worth, 1998—. Mem.: Nat. Lime Assn., Acad. Mgmt., Am. Mgmt. Assn., Sigma Beta Delta Internat. Avocations: writing, golf, astronomy.

KHURANA, SANJAY KUMAR, spine surgeon, director; s. Sudarshan Kumar and Ishwar Khurana. BA, U. Calif., Berkeley, 1993; MD, Stanford U., Calif., 1997. Chief spine surgery Kaiser Permanente, San Diego, 2003—05, Diagnostic and Interventional Spine Care, Marina Del Rey, Calif., 2005—. Designer, spine surgery devices Sanjay K. Khurana, MD Inc. Recipient Volvo prize for Rsch. on Back Pain, North Am. Spine Soc., 2000. Fellow: Acad. Orthop. Surgeons, Coll. of Surgeons (life). Achievements include patents for post-operative pain control and thermal cooling device; research in utility of discography in low back pain; comparison of ACF versus ACD; antifungal penetration into intervertebral disc. Office: Sanjay K Khurana MD FACS Spine Surgery 13160 Mindanao Way # 300 Marina Del Rey CA 90292 Office Phone: 310-279-4351. Office Fax: 310-854-3800.

KHURGEL, TATIANA, music educator, director; b. Gudos, Tajikiston, Russia, Sept. 15, 1959; arrived in US, 1995; d. Vasilif Ivanoff and Ninov Egoroff; 1 child, Glen Shikunov. BA in Piano Performance, Dushanbe Coll. Music, 1974; diploma, Coll. Music, Russia, 1978; MBA in Choral Conducting, Moscow State Conservatory Music, 1983. Music dir. Luth. Ch. the Master, Corona del Mar, Calif., 1999—; accompanist Santa Ana Unified Sch. Dist., Calif., 1999—; music tchr. Yamaha Music Sch., Fountain Valley, Calif., 2000—. Singer: Belarus Philharmonic Soc., 1985—95. dir.: (chamber choir) Belarus Philharmonic Soc., 1985—95. Mem.: Am. Guild Organist, Music Tchrs. Assn. Home: 30902 Club House Dr 1I Laguna Niguel CA 92677 Office: Luth Ch Master 2900 Pacific View Dr Corona Del Mar CA 92625 Office Phone: 714-206-1767.

KHURI, FADLO RAJA, oncologist, educator; b. Boston, Sept. 13, 1963; s. Raja Najib and Soumaya Makdisi Khuri; m. Lamya Raja Tannous, June 15, 1991; children: Raja, Layla, Rayya. Student, Am. U. of Beirut, 1982; BS, Yale U., 1985; MD, Columbia U., 1989. Cert. bd. cert. diplomate. Intern in internal medicine Boston City Hosp., Boston U., 1989—90; resident Boston City Hosp., 1990—92; fellow in hematology and med. oncology Tufts-New Eng. Med. Ctr., Boston, 1992—95; instr. medicine U. Tex. M.D. Anderson Cancer Ctr., Houston, 1995—96, asst. prof., 1996—2001, assoc. prof., 2001—02; assoc. dir. clin. and tranlational rsch., prof. hematology, oncology, medicine, pharmacology and otolaryngology, Blomeyer chair translational rsch. Winship Cancer Inst., Emory U., Atlanta, 2002—. 1st author: clin. investigation Nature Medicine, 2000, Journal of the National Cancer Institute, 1997, Journal of Clinical Oncology, 2000. Recipient Career Devel. award, Am. Cancer Soc., 1996; scholar R.G. Haddad scholar, 1985—89; grantee, NIH, Dept. of Def., 1996—. Mem.: Eastern Coop. Oncology Group (chmn. cancer control and prevention com. 2004—), Radiation Therapy Oncology Group (chmn. chemoprevention com. 1998—2002), Am. Soc. Clin. Oncology, Am. Assn. Cancer Rsch. Office Phone: 404-778-1900. Business E-Mail: fkhuri@emory.edu.

KHURI, NICOLA NAJIB, physicist, researcher; b. Beirut, May 27, 1933; came to US, 1959, naturalized, 1970; s. Najib N. and Odette (Joujou) K.; m. Elizabeth Anne Tyson, Dec. 9, 1955; children: Suzanne Odette, Najib Nicholas. B.A with high distinction, Am. U. Beirut, 1952; PhD, Princeton U., 1957. Asst. prof. Am. U. Beirut, 1957-58, 60-61, assoc. prof., 1961-62; mem. Inst. Advanced Study, Princeton U., 1959-60, 62-63; vis. assoc. prof. Columbia, 1963-64; assoc. prof. Rockefeller U., 1964-68, prof., 1968—. Cons. Brookhaven Nat. Lab., 1963-73; mem. Carnegie Panel on U.S. Security and Arms Control, 1981-83; vis. scientist European Ctr. for Nuclear Research, Geneva, Centre d'Etudes Nucléaires, Saclay, France, Max Planck Inst. für Physik, Munich, Fed. Republic Germany. Contbr. articles to profl. jours. Trustee Am. U. Beirut. Fellow Am. Phys. Soc.; mem. Coun. on Fgn. Rels., Century Club (N.Y.C.). Office: Rockefeller U New York NY 10021 Home: # 6B 433 E 51st St New York NY 10022-6472

KHURI, SOUMAYA MAKDISSI, mathematics professor; arrived in U.S., 1960; d. Ilyas Khuri-Makdissi and Wadia Mary Hourani; m. Raja Najib Khuri, July 8, 1959 (div. Mar. 13, 1996); children: Fadlo, Ramzi, Jananne. BS, American U., Beirut, 1960; MA, Harvard U., Cambridge, Mass., 1961; PhD, Yale U., Conn., 1974. Asst. prof. math. American U. Beirut, 1979, assoc. prof. math., 1979—85, prof. math. dept., 1985—87; vis. fellow math. Yale U., New Haven, 1984—85, 1986—87; assoc. prof. math. dept. East Carolina U., Greenville, NC, 1987—91, prof. math. dept., 1991—. Author: (rsch. papers) Jour. Algebra, Proceedings Am. Math. Soc., 1977, 1978, 1979, Com. Jour. Math., Proceedings London Math. Soc., 1980, 1981, 1982. Avocations: travel, reading. Home: 122 Longmeadow Rd Greenville NC 27858 Office: East Carolina Univ Math Dept Greenville NC 27858 Personal E-mail: khuris@ecu.edu.

KHVOST-VOSTRIKOVA, NATALIA S., art educator, consultant; d. Serg I Khvostionkov and Maya Jacob Khvostionkova; children: Kuzma Nick Vostrikov, Gavrela Nick Vostrikov. BD Arts, Tech. Inst., Moscow, 1981. Cert. Fashion design Russian Ministry of Fashion Industry, 1981. Exhibitions, perfomances, Forbidden Art-the postwar Russian Avant-gard. Achievements include Participation Biennale Internationale Firenze(Italy). Personal E-mail: nkhvost@msn.com.

KIANG, ASSUMPTA (AMY KIANG), brokerage house executive; b. Beijing, Aug. 15, 1939; came to U.S., 1962; d. Pei-yu and Yu-Jean (Liu) Chao; m. Wan-lin Kiang, Aug. 14, 1965; 1 child, Eliot Y. BA, Nat. Taiwan U., 1960; MS, Marywood Coll., Scranton, Pa., 1964; MBA, Calif. State U., Long Beach, 1977. Cert. fin. mgr. Data programmer IBM World Trade, NYC, 1963; libr. East Cleve. Pub. Libr., 1964-68; lectr. Nat. Taiwan U., Taipei, 1971-73; reference libr. U.S. Info. Svc., Taipei, 1971-74; v.p., sr. fin. advisor Merrill Lynch, Santa Ana, Calif., 1977—, v.p., sr. fin. cons. Costa Mesa, Calif., 1996—. Author numerous rsch. reports in field. Founder Pan Pacific Performing Arts Inc., Orange County, Calif., 1987; pres. women league Calif. State. U., Long Beach, 1980-82. Mem. AAUW (treas. Newport-Costa Mesa br. 1996—), Chinese Bus. Assn. Soc. Calif. (chmn. 1987—, v.p. 1986-87), Chinese Am. Profl. Women's League (treas. 1993, pres. 1997—), Pacific Rim Investment and trade Assn. (vice-chair 1994-96), U.C.I. Chancellor's Club, Old Ranch Country Club, Ctr. Club (bd. dirs. exec. women's coun. Orange County 1998—). Democrat. Roman Catholic. Office: Merrill Lynch 650 Town Center Dr Ste 500 Costa Mesa CA 92626-1905 Office Phone: 714-429-2806. Personal E-mail: amylkiang@yahoo.com. Business E-Mail: AKiang@pclient.ml.com, assumpta_kiang@ml.com.

KIANG, NELSON YUAN-SHENG, medical educator; b. Wuxi, China, July 6, 1929; came to US, 1934; naturalized, 1961; m. 1957, 1976. PhB, U. Chgo., 1947, PhD in biopsychology, 1955; MD (hon.), U. Geneva, 1981; MS (hon.), Harvard U., 1984. Rsch. asst. Eaton-Peabody Lab. Mass. Eye and Ear Infirmary, Boston, 1957-62, dir., 1962—96; staff mem. rsch. lab. electronics MIT, Boston, 1955—96, Eaton-Peabody prof. dept. brain and cognitive scis., 1986—96, Eaton-Peabody prof. health scis. and tech., 1993—96; neurophysiologist, neurology svc. Mass. Gen. Hosp., Boston, 1977—96; prof. physiology, dept. otology and laryngology Harvard Med. Sch., Boston, 1984—96; emeritus on all appts., 1996—. Mem. communicative scis. study sect. NIH, 1968-72, behavior and neuroscis. study sect. NIH, 1985-89; mem. Com. Hearing Bioacoustics and Biomechanics NAS/NRC, Collegium Otorhinology-Laryngology Amiticiam Sacrum, Deafness Rsch. Found, Internat. Brain Rsch. Orgn.; hon. prof. Zhejiang U., Hangzhou, China, 1997, Peking Union Med. Coll. of Qinghua U., Beijing, 2001, Sun Yat-sen Med. U., Guangzhou, China, 2001; adv. prof. Fudan U., Shanghai, China, 1997; hon. advisor Chinese Med. Assn. Recipient Beltone award, 1968. Mem. AAAS, Soc. Neurosci., Am. Physiol. Soc., Acoustical Soc. Am., Am. Otology Soc., N.Y. Acad. Sci., Am. Acad. Arts and Scis., Assn. for Rsch. in Otolaryngology, Eastern Psychol. Assn., History of Sci. Soc., Philosophy of Sci. Assn., Royal Soc. Medicine, Psychonomic Soc., Union Internat. Univs. (advisor), Triglav Cir., Sigma Xi. Rsch. in physiology of auditory and other sensory systems; relation of brain to behavior. Office: Eaton Peabody Lab MA Eye & Ear Infirmary 243 Charles St Boston MA 02114 Business E-Mail: bnk@epl.meei.harvard.edu.

KIANI, REZA, endocrinology and internal medicine educator; b. Iran, Feb. 23, 1939; came to U.S., 1969; s. Farjollah and Salamah Kiani; m. Mahshid Zameni, June 24, 1981; children: Mandy, Mary, Cyrus, Soroosh. D in Medicine, Shiraz Univ., Shiraz, Iran, 1966; F.A.C.P., Am. Coll. Physicians, 1981. Instr. in medicine Univ. Ill., Chgo., 1972-73, assoc. in medicine, 1973-74, asst. prof. medicine, 1974-79, assoc. prof. medicine, 1979-91, prof. medicine, 1991—. Dir. medicine clinic, Univ. Ill., Chgo., 1983-88; cons. ophthalmology, urology, orthopeadics, surgery, 1989—, dir. diagnostic clinic, 1990—, dir. diabetes program, 1992—. Recipient Physician's Recognition award AMA, 1971, 73-76, Golden Apple award Univ. Ill., 1982-85, 90-93, C.G. Pilz award Univ. Ill., 1979. Fellow Am. Coll. Physicians; mem. Am. Fedn. Clinical Rsch., Am. Assn. Univ. Profs., Am. Soc. Internal Medicine, Am. Diabetes Assn. Avocations: gardening, fishing, boating, horseback-riding, reading. Home: 730 Bentwood Trce Alpharetta GA 30005-4144 Office: Univ Ill Dept Medicine 840 S Wood St Rm E123 Msa Chicago IL 60612-7317

KIBBEY, HAL STEPHEN, science writer; b. West Point, NY, Oct. 29, 1943; s. Donald Eugene and Mary Elizabeth (Lichliter) K.; m. Martha Ann Harsanyi, Dec. 12, 1970; children: Carolyn Ann, Laura Ann. BA, Cornell U., 1965; MA, Ind. U., 1969. Rsch. asst., rsch. assoc. Ind. U., Bloomington, 1970-75, publ. editor, 1975-79, sci. writer, 1979—. Free lance writer and editor, Bloomington, 1985—. Editor: Science Development: The Building of Science in Less Developed Countries, 1975. Pres. Rogers- Binford Elem. Sch. PTo, 1991—93; bd. dirs. Monroe County Civic Theater, 1995—96, Bloomington Playwrights' Project, 2004—. Mem. Nat. Assn. Sci. Writers, U.S. Chess Fedn. (life). Democrat. Methodist. Avocations: chess, singing, acting, writing and directing plays. Home: 1109 E Hunter Ave Bloomington IN 47401-5035 Office: Ind U Office Media Rels 530 E Kirkwood Ave Bloomington IN 47408-4062 Business E-Mail: hkibbey@indiana.edu.

KIBLER, JAMES EVERETT, English language educator, writer; b. Newberry, S.C., June 24, 1944; s. James Everett Kibler and Juanita Connelly. BA, U. S.C., Columbia, 1966, PhD, 1970. Prof. English U. of Ga., Athens, 1970—. Author: (social history) A Carolina Dutch Fork Calendar (Confederation of Local S.C. Hist. Socs. award, 1988), (poetry) Poems From Scorched Earth (So. Heritage Soc.'s Lit. Achievement award, 2000), (short story cycle) Child to the Waters, (novel) Walking Toward Home, Our Fathers' Fields (Fellowship of So. Writers award, 1999), Memory's Keep; editor: (poetry collection) Selected Poems of William Gilmore Simms, (biographical dictionary) American Novelists Since World War II, (short story collection) Fireside Tales. Mem.: William Gilmore Simms Soc. (life; sec. 1993—), Phi Beta Kappa (life). Independent. Lutheran. Avocations: farming, gardening, conservation. Home: 211 Peters Creek Rd Whitmire SC 29178 Office: U Ga Park Hall 254 Athens GA 30602 Home Phone: 803-276-4337; Office Phone: 706-542-1261. Business E-Mail: jkibler@uga.edu.

KIBLER, WILLIAM BENJAMIN, orthopedist, surgeon; b. Kingsport, Tenn., Sept. 29, 1946; s. Jacob B. and Della M. Kibler; m. Elizabeth Fay Mugler, June 20, 1970; children: B. Chase, David. BA, Vanderbilt U., 1968, MD, 1972. Cert. Am. Bd. Orthopedic Surgery, 1978. Intern, surgery Parkland Hosp., Dallas, 1972—73; resident, orthop. surgery Vanderbilt U., Nashville, 1973—77; staff physician Lexington Clinic, Ky., 1977—, head sect. orthop surgery, 1998—2007, med. dir. Sports Medicine Ctr., 1984—; med. dir. Shoulder Ctr. Ky., 2006—. Bd. dirs. Am. Coll. of Sports medicine, Indpls., 1990—96; pres. Soc. Tennis Medicine and Sci., NYC, 1990—99; lectr. various national and internat. orthop. soc. Author: The Athletic Preparticipation Exam, 1990, Functional Rehabilitation of Sports Injuries, 1998; contbr. articles various profl. jours. Named Best Dr. of Am., NYC, 2004—07; recipient Citation award, Am. Coll. of Sports Medicine, 1998, Plagenhof Sci. award, Profl. Tennis Registry, 1998. Fellow: Am. Acad. Orthop. Surgeons; mem.: Am. Orthopedic Assn., Am. Coll. Sports Medicine, Am. Shoulder and Elbow Surgeons, Am. Orthop. Soc. for Sports Medicine. Methodist. Avocations: sports, travel, hiking, bible study. Home: 240 Mkt St Lexington KY 40507 Office: Lexington Clinic 1221 S Broadway Lexington KY 40504 Office Phone: 859-258-8575. Office Fax: 859-258-8562. Personal E-mail: wkibler@aol.com. Business E-Mail: bkibl@lexclin.com.

KIBLER, WILLIAM WESTCOTT, French language and literature educator; b. Rochester, NY, Jan. 22, 1942; s. Charles J. and Ruth Isabel (Westcott) K.; m. Nancy Irene Schwan, June 29, 1968; children: Mary Alis, Charlotte. AB, Notre Dame U., 1963; MA, U. N.C., 1966, PhD, 1968. Asst. prof. French U. Ark., Fayetteville, 1967-69, U. Tex., Austin, 1969-73, assoc. prof., 1973-81, prof., 1981-83. Superior Oil-Linward Shivers Centennial prof. medieval studies, 1983—2004, prof. emeritus, 2004—. Author: An Introduction to Old French, 1984; author, editor: Chrétien de Troyes' Lancelot, 1981, Chrétien de Troyes' Yvain, 1985; co-author: Lion de Bourges, 1980, Guillaume de Machaut, Judgement du roy de Behaigne and Remede de Fortune, 1988; editor: Eleanor of Aquitaine: Patron and Politician, 1976, Medieval France: An Encyclopedia, 1995, Raoul de Cambra, 1996. Mem. South Cen. MLA (pres. 1986-87), Medieval Acad. Am. (councillor 1993-96), Société Rencesvals (pres. 1978-82, editor-in-chief Am.-Can. br. jour. Olifant 1986-91), Internat. Arthurian Soc. (pres. 2006—). Episcopalian. Avocations: squash, stamp collecting/philately, gardening.

KIBRICK, ANNE, retired nursing educator, dean; b. Palmer, Mass., June 1, 1919; d. Martin and Christine (Grigas) Karlon; m. Sidney Kibrick, June 16, 1949; children: Joan, John. RN, Worcester Hahnemann Hosp., Mass., 1941; BS, Boston U., 1945; MA, Columbia Tchrs. Coll., 1948; EdD, Harvard U., Cambridge, Mass., 1958; LHD (hon.), St. Joseph's Coll., Windham, Maine, 1973. Asst. edn. dir. Cushing VA Hosp., Framingham, Mass., 1948—49; asst. prof. nursing Simmons Coll., Boston, 1949—55; dir. grad. div. Boston U. Sch. Nursing, 1958—63, dean, 1963—68, prof., 1968—70; chmn. dept. nursing Boston Coll. Grad. Sch. Arts and Sci., 1970—74; founding chmn. Sch. Nursing Boston State Coll., 1974—82; founding dean Sch. Nursing U. Mass., Boston, 1974—88, prof., 1988—93, prof. emeritus, 1993—. Mem. adv. coun. Coll. Nursing and Health Scis. U. Mass., Boston, 2004—. Mem. editl. bd. Mass. Jour. Cmty. Health. Mem. Brookline Town Meeting, 1995—2000; mem. nat. adv. bd. Hadassah Nurses Coun., 1996—; bd. dirs. Brookline Mental Health Assn., Met. chpt. ARC, Children's Ctr. Brookline and Greater Boston, Inc., 1984—89, Boston Health Care for Homeless, 1988—90, Landy-Kaplan Nurses Coun., 1992—, treas., 1994—96. Named to, Nursing Edn. Alumni Assn. Tchr.'s Coll., Columbia U. Hall of Fame, 1999. Fellow: Am. Acad. Nursing; mem.: Mass. Assn. RNs (charter mem., Living Legend award 2006), Inst. of Medicine of NAS, Mass. Blueprint 2000, Mass. Orgn. Elder Ams. (bd. dirs. 1988—2000), Mass. Med. Soc. (postgrad. med. inst. 1983—96, bd. dirs. 1983—96, exec. com. 1989—96), Nat. Acads. of Practice, Mass. Nurses Found. (v.p. 1983—86), AIDS Internat. Info. Found. (founding mem. 1985), Mass. Nurses Assn. (dir. 1982—86, charter inductee Hall of Fame 2000), Nat. Mass. League Nursing (pres. 1971—73), ANA, Pi Lambda Theta, Sigma Theta Tau. Home: # 312 130 Seminary Ave Auburndale MA 02466 E-mail: akibrick@lasell.edu.

KICE, JOHN EDWARD, engineer, educator, consultant; b. Wichita, Kans., Sept. 11, 1949; s. Jack and Ruth (Jones) Kice; m. Susan Pappas; children: Adam, Jason. BS in Flour Milling Sci. and Bus. Adminstrn., Kans. State U., 1972; BS in Engring., Wichita State U., 1980; grad. diploma, Glasgow Caladonian U., 2000. Registered profl. engr., Kans. Design engr. Kice Industries, Wichita, 1973-84, v.p. engring., 1984—2003; lectr. Kans. State U., 2003—. Lectr. Wichita State U., 1980-86. Recipient Disting. Svc. award Assn. Operative Millers, 1988, 90, 92, 94, 96. Achievements include patents for Positive Displacement Air Pump, Reciprocating Airlock Valve, Rotary Mixing Damper, Blade Type Mixing Damper, Conveying Air Velocity Control, Pneumatic Conveying Injector, Machinery Access. Office Phone: 785-341-5880.

KICHLER, JACK, dermatologist; s. Morris and Freida (Greenberg) Kichler; m. Adriane Frank, June 13, 1954; children: Rise Lynn Cole(dec.) , Marcia Ann Kichler Schuffman. BS in Pharmacy, U. Fla., Gainesville; MD, U. Miami, Coral Gables, Fla. Registered pharmacist Fla. Mgr., pharmacist Martin Mgmt. Corp., Tampa, Fla., 1958—60; physician tropical medicine NIH, Cartagena, Colombia, 1964; commd. 2d lt. US Army, 1965, advanced through grades to col., 1980, intern Ft. Lewis, Wash., 1965—66, resident Ft. Sam Houston, Tex., 1966—69, chief dermatol. svc. Frankfurt, Germany, 1969—73, chief outpatient svcs. Ft. Devins, Mass., 1973—74; chief dermatol. svc. Med. Ctrl Clinic, Pensacola, Fla., 1974—85; dir. Seville Sq. Owners Assn., Pensacola, 1985—87, Cordova Sq. Owners Assn., Pensacola, 1987—89; docent, writer tchg. program Mus. Art, Pensacola, 1989—92; tchr. ESL Project Literacy, Pensacola, 1992—96; co-chmn. curriculum com. UWFI Sr. Program, Pensacola, 1996—2000. Dermatol. cons. various hosps., Ala.; dermatologist St. Joseph Free Dermatology Clinic, Pensacola, 1974—85; cons., lectr. in field. Bd. dirs. Sister Cities Internat., Pensacola, 2000—06, Japan Am. Soc., Pensacola, 2006—06, Sr. Citizens, West Fla. Hosp., Pensacola, 2001—, Med. Ctr. Health Care Plan, Pensacola, 1983—85. Decorated Meritorious Svc. medal (5), Army Commendation medal, Army Achievement medal, Nat. Def. Svc. medal (2), Good Conduct medal; recipient Order Mil. Med. Merit, Office US Army Surgeon Gen., 1983; tropical medicine grantee, NIH, 1964. Fellow: Royal Soc. Tropical Medicine London, Am. Soc. Laser Medicine and Surgery, Internat. Soc. Tropical Medicine; mem.: AMA (life), Am. Acad. Dermatology (life), Am. Acad. Dermatology (life), Anna Soc. (charter). Avocations: travel, cooking, computers, theology, Japanese gardening. Home: 4870 Manolete Pensacola FL 32504-9041

KICKLIGHTER, CLAUDE MILTON (MICK KICKLIGHTER), federal agency administrator; b. Glennville, Ga., Aug. 22, 1933; s. Claude Wilton and Ruby Dell (Drake) K.; m. Elizabeth Exley, Apr. 24, 1954; children: Elizabeth Jane, Claude M., Richard Van. AB, Mercer U., 1955; MA, George Washington U.; grad. Nat. and Internat. Security Program, Harvard U., 1981, grad. Sr. Mgrs. in Govt. Program, 1982. Commd. officer U.S. Army, 1955, advanced through grades to lt. gen.; staff Dept. Army, 1968-70; with 101st Airborne Div., Vietnam, 1970-71; comdr. 1st Bn. 21st Field Arty., Ft. Carson, Colo., 1972-73; staff Office Joint Chief of Staff, 1974-75, Office Def. Rep-Iran, Teheran, 1975-76; comdr. 24th Inf. Div. Arty., Ft. Stewart, Ga., 1977-78; asst. div. comdr., 1978-79; asst. chief staff logistics Allied Forces Central Europe, The Netherlands, 1979-81; comdg. gen. Security Assistance Center, Alexandria, Va., 1981-83; chief of staff U.S. Army Materiel Devel. and Readiness Command, Alexandria, 1983-84; comdg. gen. 25th Inf. Div., Schofield Barracks, Hawaii, 1984-86; asst. dep. chief of staff of logistics Washington, 1986-87; dir. of army staff Office of Chief of Staff, Washington, 1987-89; comdg. gen. U.S. Army Western Command, Ft. Shafter, Hawaii, 1989-90; comdr. U.S. Army Pacific, Hawaii, 1989—91; dep. under sec. of army internat. affairs, U.S. Army US Dept. Def., Washington, 1995—99; asst. sec. for policy & planning U.S Dept. Veterans Affairs, Washington, 2001—03; asst. sec. for policy, planning & preparedness US Dept. Veterans Affairs, Washington, 2003—05, chief of staff, 2005; spl. adv. for stabilization & security ops. in Iraq & Afghanistan US Dept. State, Washington, 2004; insp. gen. US Dept. Def., Washington, 2007—. Bd. dirs. Habitat for Humanity, Internat., 1996—2001, chmn., 1998—2001. Contbr. article to mil. jours. Decorated D.S.M. with two bronze oak leaf clusters, Def. Superior Svc. medal, Legion of Merit with three bronze oak leaf clusters, Bronze Star, Meritorious Svc. medal with bronze oak leaf cluster, Air Medal with bronze oak leaf cluster, Army Comendation medal with four bronze oak leaf clusters, Argentina Order of May, Disting. Pub. Svc., US Dept. Def., 2004 others. Episcopalian. Office: US Dept Defense 400 Army Navy Dr Ste 1000 Arlington VA 22202*

KIDD, A. PAUL, health facility and government agency administrator; b. Orange, NJ, Nov. 1, 1939; s. Arthur T. Kidd and Virginia V. McMullen; m. Penelope Kinsey, Mar. 11, 1961; children— Margaret, Lawrence, William, Anne BA, Rutgers U., 1961; MA, George Washington U., 1973. Personnel specialist VA Med. Ctr., Lyons, N.J., 1962-63, personnel specialist Pitts., 1963-66; employee relations specialist VA Central Office, Washington, 1966-71; assoc. hosp. dir. trainee VA Med. Ctr., Washington, 1971-73, assoc. dir. Beckley, W.Va., 1973-75, Temple, Tex., 1975-77, East Orange, N.J., 1977-80, med. ctr. dir. Huntington, W.Va., 1980-83, Lyons, N.J., 1983-96. Bd. dirs. W. Va. Health Systems Agy., Charleston, 1980-82, W. Va. State Health Coordinating Coun., Charleston, 1980-83, Ctrl. Jersey Health Systems Agy., Princeton, N.J., 1983-90. Bd. dirs. Mountaineer Family Health Plan, Beckley, 1973-75; med. edn. and rehab. coun. Marshall U., Huntington, 1980-83; mem., v.p. No. N.J. Fed. Exec. Bd., Newark, 19873-86, chmn., 1987-89, 92-95; coach mcpl. soccer league. Fellow Am. Coll. Health Care Execs.; mem. Sr. Exec. Service, Phi Beta Kappa Avocations: golf, painting, horticulture. Home: 1110 Veronica St Port Charlotte FL 33952-1147

KIDD, CHIP, book designer, writer; b. Shillington, Pa., 1964; Grad., Pa. State U. Mem. design team Knopf Pub. Group, NYC, 1986—, book cover designer. Contbr. op-ed page NY Times; design cons. Paris Review, 1995—. Author: Batman Collected, 1996, Batman Animated, 1998, The Cheese Monkeys: A Novel in Two Semesters, 2001, Mythology: The DC Comics Art of Alex Ross, 2003, Peanuts: The Art of Charles M. Schulz, 2004, Chip Kidd: Book One; Work: 1986-2006, 2006; one-man shows include DDD Gallery, Osaka, Japan, 2001, GGG Gallery, Tokyo, Japan, 2001, Cooper Union Lubalin Ctr., N.Y., 2006, Cooper-Hewitt Third Trienniel, N.Y.C., N.Y., 2006; designed more than 1,500 book covers. Finalist Nat. Design award for comm., 2006; recipient award for Use of Photography in Graphic Design, Internat. Ctr. Photography, 1997. Mem.: Alliance Graphique Internationalle. Achievements include invited to be part of third design triennial Cooper Hewitt Mus., NY, 2006. Office: Knopf Publishing 1745 Broadway 19th Fl New York NY 10019 Office Phone: 212-572-2363. Business E-Mail: ckidd@randomhouse.com.

KIDD, JAMES MARION, III, allergist, immunologist, educator; b. Baton Rouge, Dec. 15, 1950; s. James Marion, Jr. and Germaine Elizabeth (Hunt) Kidd; children: Mackenzie Elizabeth, Katherine Anne. MD, La. State U., 1976. Diplomate Am. Bd. Allergy and Immunology, lic. physician La., Fla., Wis. Resident physician La. State U. Sch. Medicine, New Orleans, 1977—79; rsch. fellow Med. Coll. Wis., Milw., 1980-82; pvt. practice in allergy and immunology Allergy, Asthma, and Immunology Clinic, Baton Rouge, 1982—; clin. asst., prof. community medicine La. Sch. Medicine, New Orleans, 1982—; clin. asst., prof. community medicine and pub.

health Tulane U. Sch. Medicine, New Orleans, 1992—2003. Dir. Baton Rouge Pollen Counting Sta., Nat. Allergy Bur. Paul Harris fellow, Rotary. Fellow: ACP, Baton Rouge Allergy Soc. (pres. 1990—95), La. Allergy Soc. (pres. 1989—90, exec. sec.-treas. 1992—96), Royal Soc. Medicine (U.K.), Am. Acad. Allergy and Immunology. Office: 8017 Picardy Ave Baton Rouge LA 70809-3538 Fax: 225-768-7642. E-mail: drjmkidd3@aol.com.

KIDD, JASON, professional basketball player; b. San Francisco, Mar. 23, 1973; m. Joumana Kidd, Feb. 21, 1997 (separated 2007); children: Trey Jason (T.J.), Miah, Jazelle. Student, U. Calif., 1992—94. Guard Dallas Mavericks, 1994—96, Phoenix Suns, 1996—2001; player NJ Nets, 2002—. Mem. US Men's Olympic Basketball Team (Gold medal), 2000. Founder Jason Kidd Found., Jason Kidd Basketball Scholarship Fund. Named Pac-10 Player of Yr., 1993—94, Nat. Freshman of Yr., The Sporting News and USA Today, 1993—94, Co-Rookie of Yr. (with Grant Hill), 1994—95; named to Ea. Conf. All-Star Team, NBA, 1996, 1998, 2000—04, 2007, All-NBA 1st team, 1999—2002, 1st team All-Defensive, 1999, 2001—02, 2nd team All-Defensive, 2000; recipient Gold medal, US Men's Olympic Basketball team, 2000. Achievements include leading NBA in Assists, 1999-2001, 2003. Avocations: R&B music, movies, baseball. Office: NJ Nets 390 Murray Hill Parkway East Rutherford NJ 07073*

KIDD, RUTH PRICE, retired secondary school educator; b. New Orleans, Nov. 28, 1927; d. Author James and Louise Francis Price; m. Edward Alvin Rhone (div.); m. Wesley McMillan Kidd, Jan. 25, 1958; 1 child, Wesliane Marie Kidd-Johnson. BS in Health, So. U., Baton Rouge, 1951, MS in Health, 1963. Tchr. Orleans Parish Sch. Bd., New Orleans, 1951—90. Dir. Bethany Sr. Ctr. and Exercise for Srs. Program, New Orleans, 1990—2005. Dir. youth choir Bethany United Meth. Ch., 1981—85. Named Coach of Yr. for girls basketball, John McDonogh Sr. H.S.; recipient Svc. to Band award. Mem.: AARP (past pres., rec. sec., Andrus award), Gilbert Acad. Alumni (pres. 1986—93, 1997—2005, fin. sec. 2005—), Orleans Parish Sch. Tchrs. (rec. sec. retirees chpt. 1990—99, v.p. retirees chpt. 1999—2006), Sigma Gamma Rho (parliamentarian rec. sec. 1993—2005, Christian Svc. award). Home: 2715 W Rothland St 9B Gonzales LA 70737

KIDDA, MICHAEL LAMONT, JR., psychologist, educator; b. Jackson, Miss., May 24, 1945; s. Michael Lamont and Annie Laurie (McKeithen) K.; m. Ellen Gordon, Aug. 23, 1977 (div. 2005); children: Patrick Gordon, John McKeithen. BA in English, Centenary Coll. La., Shreveport, 1969; MDiv, U. South, Sewanee, Tenn., 1972; MS in Social Psychology, U. Ga., Athens, 1984, PhD in Social Psychology, 1987. Youth cons. Cathedral St. Philip, Atlanta, 1974—76; counselor All Saints' Sch., Vicksburg, Miss., 1977—79; coord. assessment J.C. Smith U., Charlotte, NC, 1989—94, assoc. prof. psychology, 1985—, dept. head, 1987—89, 1999—2002. Coord. Grad. Student Conf./Personality and Social Psychology, Athens, 1981; bd. trustees NE Ga. Area Cmty. Resource Coun., Athens, 1980—83, v.p., 1982, tech. adminstrn., 84; data analysis cons., Athens, 1980—83; corp. sec. Kidda Enterprises, 1999—2004, pres., 2005; corp. sec. Carolina Cupboard, 2002—04; pres. Higher Edn. Evaluation and Devel., 2002—; rsch. advisor Experience for Undergraduates U. NC, Rsch. advisor, Experience for Undergraduates U. NC, Charlotte, 2006—; evaluation cons. NSF; presenter in field. Contbr. articles to profl. jours. and to On-line and CD-Rom data bases; author newsletter ETS Higher Edn. Assessment, 1993. Com. mem. cub scouts pack 19 Boy Scouts Am., Huntersville, NC, 1994—97; com. mem. Lions Club, Huntersville, 1996—99, Davidson, 1999—2001, membership com., 2000—01, dir. Hickory Grove, 2003—06, Tail Twister, 2006; bd. dirs. Metrolina Assn. for the Blind, 2006—07; mem. adv. bd. Washington Heights Project Nat. Children's Def. Fund, Charlotte, 1994; chair evaluation com. Fighting Back Against Drugs, Charlotte, 1992—94; bd. dirs. Lions Svcs. for the Blind, Charlotte, 1999—2005, pers. com. vice chair, 2002—05. Recipient Nat. Retention Excellence award Noel-Levitz Ctrs., Cross of Nails award St. Michael's Cathedral, Coventry, Eng., cert. of appreciation Washington Hts. Youth Svcs. Acad., 1997; Retention and Performance grantee Pew Charitable Trusts, 1994, Equipment grantee AT&T Found., 1991, grantee APA, 1996, United Negro Coll. Fund, 1996; fellow Inst. Non-Traditional Ministries, 1994-99. Mem. Am. Stats. Assn., Soc. Southeastern Social Psychologists, Lions, Sigma Xi (site coord. celebration of undergrad. rsch. 1999), Sigma Tau Delta, Psi Chi (chpt. adviser 2001—). Achievements include empirical demonstration of superiority of college-level inquiry curriculum over remediation in post-secondary education; research on effects of social control on prosocial behavior; research of causal attribution on evaluation of people with disabilities; research on effects of accepting non-reciprocal aid; devel. of relationship mapping as a curriculum assessment tool. Office: Johnson C Smith Univ 100 Beatties Ford Rd Charlotte NC 28216-5398 Office Phone: 704-378-3538. Business E-Mail: mkidda@jcsu.edu.

KIDDER, C. ROBERT, finance company executive; b. 1943; BSIE, U. Mich., 1966; MS, Iowa State U., 1968. With Ford Motor Co., Detroit, 1968-69, McKinsey & Co., NYC, 1972-78, Dart Industries, 1978-80, Duracell Europe, 1980-81, Duracell Internat. Inc., 1981-95, pres., CEO, 1988-95, past chmn., CEO; chmn., CEO Borden, Inc., Columbus, Ohio, 1995—2002, chmn., 2002—04; pres. Borden Capital Inc., 2001—03; prin. Stonehenge Partners Inc., 2004—06; chmn. CEO 3Stone Advisors LLC, Columbus, Ohio, 2006—. Dir. Morgan Stanley. Bd. trustees Ohio U., 2003—. With USN, 1969—72. Office: 3Stone Advisors LLC Ste 600 191 W Nationwide Blvd Columbus OH 43215*

KIDDER, FRED DOCKSTATER, retired lawyer; b. Cleve., May 22, 1922; s. Howard Lorin and Virgina (Milligan) K.; m. Eleanor (Hap) Kidder; children— Fred D. III, Barbara Anne Donelson, Jeanne Louise Haffeman. BS with distinction, U. Akron, 1948; JD, Case Western Res. U., 1950. Bar: Ohio 1950, Tex. 1985, U.S. Dist. Ct. (no. dist.) Ohio 1950, U.S. Dist. Ct. (no. dist.) Tex. 1985. Assoc. Arter & Hadden and predecessors, Cleve., 1950-79, ptnr., 1960-79, Jones Day and predecessors, Cleve., 1980-89, regional mng. ptnr. Tex., 1985-86; gen. counsel Lubrizol Corp., Cleve., 1989-92, spl. counsel, 1993—2003; gen. counsel Lubrizol Found., 2003—. Gen. counsel The Lubrizol Found., 2003—. Contbr. articles to profl. jours. Trustee Ohio Found. Ind. Colls., 2004—; gen. coun. Lubrizol Found., 2003—; past pres. Estate Planning Coun.; past co-chmn. bd. trustees Lake Erie Coll.; past trustee, v.p., Alzheimer's Assn., Cleve.; trustee, sec. Cleve. Sight Ctr.; trustee Bus. Advisors Cleve.; past alumni coun. U. Akron; past. corp. coun. Dallas Mus. Art; past pres. Case Western Reserve U. Law Sch. Alumni Assn.; past chmn. Shaker Heights Recreation Bd. Mem. ABA, Tex. Bar Assn., Ohio State Bar Assn., Cleve. Bar Assn., Ohio Fedn. Ind. Colls. (trustee), Estate Planning Coun. (past pres.), Blue Coats, Soc. Benchers (past chmn.), The Country Club, Cleve. Skating Club, Tax Club Cleve. (past pres.), Order of Coif, Ct. of Nisi Prius (former judge), Pepper Pike Club (past sec.), Phi Eta Sigma, Beta Delta Psi, Phi Sigma Alpha, Phi Delta Theta, Phi Delta Phi. Office: Lubrizol Foundation Wickliffe OH 44092-2298

KIDDER, GEORGE HOWELL, lawyer; b. Boston, June 14, 1925; son of Henry Purkitt and Julia Edwards (Howell) K.; m. Ellen Windom Warren, Aug. 17, 1946 (dec. May 1956); children: Susan Warren, George Howell, Stephen Wells; m. Priscilla Peele Hunnewell, Sept. 3, 1958 (dec. Nov. 1993); children: Priscilla Hunnewell, Timothy Hurd, Peter Arnold; m. Nancy Drohan, June 3, 1995. Grad., St. Mark's Sch., Southborough, Mass., 1943; student Navy V-12 program, Williams Coll., 1943-44; B in Naval Sci., Tufts Coll., 1945; LLB, Harvard, 1950; DD (hon.), Episcopal Div. Sch., 1987. Bar: Mass. 1951. With Office Gen. Counsel CIA, 1952-54; assoc. Hemenway & Barnes, 1950—52, 1954—55, ptnr., 1956-97, of counsel, 1997—. Mem. panel neutral mediators and arbitrators Jud. Arbitration and Mediation Svc./Endispute, 1997—. Chair exec. coun. divsn. sleep medicine Harvard Med. Sch., 1999—2006; mem. dean's adv bd. Harvard Law Sch., 2001—; corp. mem. Perkins Sch. for the Blind; trustee Episcopal Divinity Sch., Cambridge, Mass., 1967—86, 1998—, pres. bd. trustees, 1977—86, hon. trustee, 1986—98; chancellor Episcopal Diocese of Mass., 1988—, dir., Trustees of Donations; trustee Harvard Med. Ctr., 1989—97, St. Mark's Sch., 1959—84, pres. bd. trustees, 1974—84; trustee Fenn Sch., Concord, 1956—77, pres. bd. trustees, 1960—73; bd. dirs. Greater Boston Legal Svcs., 1961—87; trustee Wellesley Coll., 1962—80, trustee emeritus, 1980—; trustee Concord Acad., 1963—78; dir. State St. Boston Corp., 1971—94; pres. bd. trustees Concord Acad., 1971—78; trustee Boston Symphony Orch., 1977—94, pres. bd. trustees, 1987—94, life trustee, 1994—; trustee Children's Med. Ctr. and Children's Hosp. Corp., 1982—97, chmn. bd. dirs., 1992—97; dir. Controlled Risk Ins. Co., Ltd., 1988—99, chmn. bd. dirs., 1991—98; dir. Risk Mgmt. Found. Harvard Med. Instns., Inc., 1988—98, chmn. bd. dirs., 1991—98; trustee, mem. exec. com. WGBH Ednl. Found., 1987—2004, vice chmn., 1998—2003, trustee emeritus, 2004—; overseer Curtis Inst. of Music, 1997—2007; mem. adv. coun. UN Assn. of Greater Boston. Mem. Am. Law Inst.(life), Internat. Acad. Estate and Trust Law; Mem. Tau Beta Pi. Home: 110 Spencer Brook Rd Concord MA 01742-5206 Office: 60 State St Boston MA 02109-1800 Business E-Mail: gkidder@hembar.com.

KIDDER, RAY EDWARD, physicist, consultant; b. NYC, Nov. 12, 1923; s. Harry Alvin and Laura Augusta (Wagner) K.; m. Marcia Loring Sprague, June 12, 1947 (div. Aug. 1975); children: Sandra Laura, David Ray, Matthew Sprague. BS, Ohio State U., 1947, MS, 1948, PhD, 1950. Physicist Calif. Rsch. Corp., La Habra, 1950-56, Lawrence Livermore Nat. Lab., Livermore, Calif., 1956—. Mem. adv. bd. Inst. for Quantum Optics, Garching, Germany, 1976-90; bd. editors Nuc. Fusion IAEA, Vienna, 1979-84; cons. Sci. Applications Internat. Corp., San Diego, 1991-94; mem. hon. adv. bd. Inst. for Advanced Physics Studies, La Jolla, Calif., 1991—. Contbr. chpts. to books. With USN, 1944-46. Recipient Humboldt award Alexander von Humboldt Found., 1988. Fellow Am. Phys. Soc. (Szilard award 1993); mem. AAAS, Sigma Xi. Achievements include research in physics of nuclear weapons, inertial confinement fusion, megagauss magnetic fields, laser isotope enrichment, containment of low-yield nuclear explosions. Home: 637 E Angela St Pleasanton CA 94566-7413 Office: Lawrence Livermore Nat Lab PO Box 808 Livermore CA 94551-0808

KIDDER, TRACY (JOHN TRACY KIDDER), writer; b. NYC, Nov. 12, 1945; s. Henry Maynard and Reine Marie (Tracy) K.; m. Frances Toland, Jan. 1971. AB, Harvard U., Cambridge, Mass., 1967; MFA, U. Iowa, Iowa City, 1974. Contbg. editor Atlantic Monthly, Boston, 1982—. Author: The Road to Yuba City, 1974, The Soul of a New Machine, 1981 (Pulitzer prize 1982, Am. Book award 1982), House, 1985, Among Schoolchildren, 1989 (Robert F. Kennedy book award), Old Friends, 1993, Home Town, 1999, Mountains Beyond Mountains, 2003, (non-fiction) My Detachment: A Memoir, 2005; author numerous articles, short stories and book revs. Served to 1st lt. U.S. Army, 1967-69, Vietnam.

KIDDOO, ROBERT JAMES, engineering service company executive; b. Kansas City, Mo., July 8, 1936; s. Robert Leroy and Margaret Ella (Wolford) K.; m. Patricia Anne Wakefield, Apr. 17, 1957; children: Robert Michael, Stacey Margaret Kiddoo. BSBA, UCLA, 1960; MSBA, Calif. State U., Northridge, 1969; MBA, U. So. Calif., 1972, DBA, 1978. Cert. mgmt. acct. Asst. v.p., nat. divsn. loan officer Crocker-Citizen's Nat. Bank, LA, 1958—69; v.p., CFO, dir. corp. sec. Kirk-Mayer, Inc., LA, 1969—87; prof. emeritus acctg. and info. sys. Calif. State U., Northridge, 1970—2005; region adminstr. mgr. CDI Corp.-West, Chatsworth, Calif., 1990; exec. v.p. Kirk-Mayer, Inc., LA, 1990—92; pres. Creative Software Designs, Inc., Northridge, Calif., 1995—2002. Asst. v.p. financial affairs, univ. contr. Calif. State U., Northridge, 1997-2000. With U.S. Army, 1955-56. Mem. Mensa, Ltd., Beta Gamma Sigma, Beta Alpha Psi. Office: Calif State Univ Acctg And Is Northridge CA 91330-8372

KIDMAN, NICOLE, actress; b. Honolulu, June 20, 1967; d. Anthony and Janelle Kidman; m. Tom Cruise, Dec. 24, 1990 (div. Aug. 8, 2001); children: Isabella Jane Kidman, Connor Antony Kidman; m. Keith Urban, June 25, 2006. Goodwill amb. UN Devel. Fund for Women, 2006—. Actress (films) BMX Bandits, 1983, Bush Christmas, 1983, Wills & Burke, 1985, Archer's Adventure, 1985, Windrider, 1986, Watch the Shadows Dance (aka Nightmaster), 1986, Bit Part, 1987, Emerald City, 1989, Dead Calm, 1989, Days of Thunder, 1990, Flirting, 1991, Billy Bathgate, 1991 (Golden Globe Award nomination 1992), Far and Away, 1992, Malice, 1993, My Life, 1993, Batman Forever, 1995, Portrait of a Lady, 1996, To Die For, 1995 (Golden Globe award), The Peacemaker, 1997, Practical Magic, 1998, Eyes Wide Shut, 1999, The Others, 2001 (nominee Best Performance by Actress in Motion Picture-Drama Golden Globe award 2002, Best Actress KCFCC award 2001), Birthday Girl, 2001, Moulin Rouge, 2001 (Best Actress in Motion Picture Musical/Comedy Golden Globe award 2001, nominee Best Actress in Leading Role Acad. award 2002, Best Actress London Film Critics Cir. award 2001), The Hours, 2002 (Best Actress Academy award, 2003, Best Actress in Leading Role, British Acad. Film Award (BAFTA), 2003, Best Actress Golden Globe, 2003), Dogville, 2003, The Human Stain, 2003, Cold Mountain, 2003, The Stepford Wives, 2004, Birth, 2004, The Interpreter, 2005, Bewitched, 2005, Fur: An Imaginary Portrait of Diane Arbus, 2006, (voice) Happy Feet, 2006, The Invasion, 2007; prodr. (films) In the Cut, 2003; (TV appearances) Five Mile Creek, 1983, Chase Through the Night, 1983, Matthew and Son, 1984, Bangkok Hilton, 1989 (Australian Film Inst. Best Actress in Miniseries), Vietnam, 1985 (Australian Film Inst. Best Actress in Miniseries); theatrical prodns. include The Blue Room, London, 1997-98, Broadway, 1998-99. Goodwill amb. UN Develop. Fund for Women, UNIFEM, 2006—. Named Australian of Yr., NSW, 2004, Companion of the Order of Australia, 2006; named one of 50 Most Powerful People in Hollywood, Premiere mag., 2003—06, 100 Most Powerful Celebrities, Forbes.com, 2007; recipient ShoWest Dist. Decade Achievement award, 2002, Citizen award, UN, 2004, Companion of Order of Australia, 2007. Address: Creative Artists Agy 9830 Wilshire Blvd Beverly Hills CA 90212*

KIDNEY, WILLIAM LESLIE, retired secondary school educator; b. Toledo, Jan. 3, 1936; s. Henry Leslie and Gertrude Mae (Adams) Kidney. BS, Purdue U., West Lafayette, Ind., 1958; MEd, U. Toledo, 1968. Dist. exec. Boy Scouts Am., Toledo, 1958—61; tchr. Sylvania City Schs., Ohio, 1962—89; ret. Mem. Civil Air Patrol, Ohio, 1982—2002, Fla., 1982—2002; precinct committeeman Rep. Party, Sumter County, Fla., 1995—2002. Recipient Wing Historian Yr., Civil Air Patrol, 1991. Mem.: Am. Soc. Mil. Insignia Colletors.

KIDONAKIS, NIKOLAOS, physicist; b. Thessaloniki, Greece, Jan. 7, 1969; came to US, 1986; s. Ioannis and Dimitra (Tseliou) Kidonakis; m. Natalia Miasnikova, Dec. 20, 1995; children: Dorian Euphorion, Dimitrios Apollon. BS with honors, Calif. Inst. Tech., Pasadena, 1990; cert. advanced study in math., U. Cambridge, Eng., 1991; PhD, SUNY, Stony Brook, 1996. Rsch. fellow U. Edinburgh (Scotland), 1996-98; rsch. assoc. Fla. State U., Tallahassee, 1998—2001; vis. asst. prof. So. Meth. U., Dallas, 2001—02; vis. scientist U. Rochester, NY, 2002; Marie Curie rsch. fellow U. Cambridge, England, 2002—04; asst. prof. physics Kennesaw (Ga.) State U., 2004—. Vis. scientist Brookhaven Nat. Lab., Upton, NY, 1996, CERN, Geneva, 1997, Aristotle U., Thessaloniki, Greece, 1998, Fermilab., Batavia, Ill., 1999, U. Valencia, Spain, 2003; Stanford Linear Accelerator Ctr., Menlo Park, Calif., 2006. Ref. The Phys. Rev., 1997—; contbr. articles on theoretical particle physics to profl. jours. Mem.: Am. Physical Soc. Achievements include research in top quark and Higgs physics, Quantum Chromodynamics, and collider phenomenology. Office: Kennesaw State Univ Physics 1202 1000 Chastain Rd Kennesaw GA 30144 Office Phone: 770-423-6607. Business E-Mail: nkidonak@kennesaw.edu.

KID ROCK, (ROBERT JAMES RITCHIE), singer; b. Romeo, Mich., Jan. 17, 1971; m. Pamela Anderson, July 29, 2006 (separated Nov. 2006); 1 child from previous marriage, Robert James Ritchie Jr. Performer: (albums) Grits Sandwiches for Breakfast, 1990, The Polyfuze Method, 1993, Fire It Up, 1994, Early Mornin' Stoned Pimp, 1996, Devil Without a Cause, 1998, Star Profile, 2000, Audio Biography CD, 2000, The History of Rock, 2000, Cocky, 2001, Kid Rock, 2003, Live Trucker, 2006; actor: (films) Joe Dirt, 2001, (voice) Osmosis Jones, 2003, (voice): (TV series) Stripperella, 2003, (guest appearance) Stacked, 2005, CSI: New York, 2006. Office: c/o Nick Stern Atlantic Records 1290 Avenue of the Americas New York NY 10104

KIEBACK, DIRK GUENTER, gynecologist, researcher; b. Schleswig, Federal Republic of Germany, Sept. 5, 1955; came to US, 1987; s. Guenter Rudolf and Ingeborg Anne (Gottschalk) K.; m. Christina Charlotte Honkomp, Mar. 23, 1985; children: Jan-Dirk, Sabrina. BA, BS, Staatliche Domschule, Schleswig, 1974; MD, Christian Albrechts U., Kiel, 1981. Staff physician Fed.l Republic Germany Navy, Kiel, 1980-82; resident ob/gyn. U. Tuebingen, 1982-86; resident U. Muenster, Federal Republic of Germany, 1986-88; postdoctoral fellow, dept. cell biology Baylor Coll. Medicine, Houston, 1988-90, adj. asst. prof., 1991—; postdoc. fellow ob-gyn. U. Tex./M.D. Anderson Cancer Ctr., Houston, 1990-92; chief resident OBGYN U. Ulm, 1992-94; assoc. prof. ob-gyn. cell biology Baylor Coll. Medicine, Houston, 1994—; adj. assoc. prof ob-gyn. M.D. Anderson Cancer Ctr., 1997—; prof. chmn. U. Freiburg, 1998—2001; prof., chmn. dept. U. Maastricht, Netherlands, 2001—05; prof. dept. ob/gyn. Baylor Coll. Medicine, Houston, 2005—. Contbr. articles to profl. jours. Staff physician German Navy, 1980-82. Recipient Interdisciplinary Rsch. award, rsch. grant M.D. Anderson Cancer Ctr., 1991. Mem. Endocrine Soc., Internat. Gynelogic Cancer Soc., Felix Rutledge Soc., Am. Soc. Clin. Oncologists. Achievements include co-discovery of the first hereditary mutation in a human steroid receptor causing disease; research in gene therapy of gynecologic cancer, steroid receptor as cancer research modulator.

KIEBURTZ, KARL DAVID, physician, educator, researcher; b. Seattle, Oct. 11, 1958; s. R. Bruce and Alvena B. Kieburtz; m. Victoria Frances Korth, Dec. 27, 1984. BA, Amherst Coll., 1980; MD, MPH, U. Rochester, 1985. Intern in family medicine Highland Hospital, 1985—86; resident in neurology Strong Memorial Hospital, NYC, 1986—89; fellowship Experimental Therapeutics, 1989—92; asst. prof. Departments of Neurology and Community and Preventive Medicine, U. Rochester Sch. of Medicine and Dentistry, Rochester, 1992—95, assoc. prof., 1995—2000, prof., 2000—; dir. Clinical Trials Coordination Ctr. Dept. of Neurology, U. Rochester Sch. of Medicine and Dentistry, Rochester, NY, 1993—, chief Movmt. and Inherited Neurological Disorders Unit, 1999—2005. Grant reviewer, grant prin. investigator NIH, Bethesda, 1993—; mem. exec. com. Parkinson Study Group, Rochester, 1993—, chmn.; mem. sci. adv. bd. Alzheimer's Disease Coop. Study, San Diego, 1996—; mem. Am. Assn. for Advancement of Sci., 1992, World Fedn. of Neurology Rsch. Com. on Parkinson's Disease & Related Disorders, 2001, NINDS NSD-K Study Sect., 2000-2004; mem. adv. com. FDA Peripheral & Central Nervous System Drugs, 2003—. Assoc. editor Neurology, 1996—; contbr. articles to profl. jours. Bd. dirs. Cmty. Health Network, Rochester, 1992-95; mem. Brighton Planning Bd., 1997—. George W. Merck tchg. scholar; Logan Clendening fellow U. Kans., 1982. Fellow Am. Acad. Neurology; mem Am. Neurol. Assn.(adv. com., 2003—), Movement Disorder Soc. (Scientific Issues Com., 2003—, Internat. Exec. Com., 2004—), Ame. Soc. for Experimental NeuroTherapeutics (Program Com., 1999—, treas., 2003—), Phi Beta Kappa, Sigma Xi. Office: U Rochester Dept Neurology 1351 Mount Hope Ave Ste 220 Rochester NY 14620-3917 Office Phone: 585-275-0553, 585-341-7500. Fax: 716-473-9745.*

KIECHEL, WALTER, JR., lawyer; b. Johnson, Nebr., Aug. 3, 1920; s. Walter Henri and Ita Elizabeth (Casey) Kiechel; m. Mary Maxine Hurst, May 15, 1943; children: Walter III, Mary Victoria, Conrad Daniel. BA, U. Nebr., 1941; LLB, Yale U., 1949; LLM, George Washington U., 1950, JD, 1952. Bar: U.S. Supreme Ct., Dist. Columbia Supreme Ct. Office of judge advocate gen. U.S. Air Force, 1944—53; dept. asst. atty. gen. U.S. Dept. Justice, 1960—67; environmental counsel Internat. Paper Co., NYC, 1967—85. Lt. col. USAF, 1953—86. Home: 9120 Belvoir Woods Pkwy Apt 224 Fort Belvoir VA 22066

KIECOLT-GLASER, JANICE KAY, psychologist; b. Okla. City, Okla., June 30, 1951; d. Edward Harold and Vergie Mae (Lively) Kiecolt; m. Ronald Glaser, Jan. 18, 1980. BA in Psychology with honors, U. Okla., 1972; PhD in Clin. Psychology, U. Miami, 1976. Lic. psychologist, Ohio. Clin. psychology intern Baylor U. Coll. Medicine, Houston, 1974-75; postdoctoral fellow in adult clin. psychology U. Rochester, N.Y., 1976-78; asst. prof. psychiatry Ohio State U. Coll. Medicine, Columbus, 1978-84, assoc. prof. psychiatry and psychology, 1984-89, prof. psychiatry and psychology, 1989—, dir. divsn. health psychology, 1994—, active various coms. Mem. AIDS study sect. NIMH, 1988-91. Editl. bd. Brain, Behavior and Immunity jour., 1986—, Health Psychology jour., 1989—, Brit. Jour. Health Psychology, 1996—, Jour. Behavioral Medicine, 1994—, Psychosomatic Medicine, 1990—, Jour. Cons. and Clin. Psychology, 1992—, Jour. Gerontology, 1992—; reviewer Jour. Personality and Social Psychology, Psychiatry Rsch. jour.; author: Detecting Lies, 1997, Unconscious Truths, 1998, Handbook of Human Stress and Immunity, 1994; contbr. articles to profl. jours., chpts. to books. NIMH grantee, 1985—; recipient Merit award NIMH, 1993; Ohio State Disting. scholar, 1994, Devel. Health Psychology award, Divsn. Health Psychology and Adult Devel. and Aging, Norman Cousins award, Psychoneuroimmunology Rsch. Soc., 1998. Fellow Am. Psychol. Assn. (Outstanding Contbns. award 1988), Acad. Behavioral Medicine Rsch.; mem. Phi Beta Kappa, Inst. Medicine. Avocations: jogging, fiction writing. Office: Ohio State U Coll Medicine Dept Psychiatry 1670 Upham Dr Columbus OH 43210

KIEDIS, ANTHONY, vocalist, recording artist, actor; b. Grand Rapids, Mich., Nov. 1, 1962; Mem. band The Red Hot Chili Peppers, 1983—. Appears in films F.I.S.T, 1978, Jokes My Folks Never Told Me, 1978, Tough Guys, 1986, Less Than Zero, 1987, Point Break, 1991, The Chase, 1994; musician: (albums) Red Hot Chili Peppers, 1984, Freaky Styley, 1985, The Uplift Mofo Party Plan, 1987, Mother's Milk, 1989, Blood Sugar Sex Magik, 1991, One Hot Minute, 1995, Californication, 1999, By the Way, 2002, Stadium Arcadium, 2006 (Best Album award, MTV Europe Music Awards, 2006, Best Rock Album, Best Ltd. Edit. Package, Grammy awards, 2007), (songs) Dani California, 2006 (MTV Video Music award for best Art Direction, 2006, Best Rock Vocal Performance & Best Rock Song, Grammy awards, 2007); author: (autobiography) Scar Tissue, 2004. Co-recipient Favorite Band, Duo or Group, Am. Music Awards, 2006, Favorite Alternative Artist, 2006. Office: care Q Prime 131 S 11th St Nashville TN 37206 Office Phone: 615-258-1050. Office Fax: 615-258-1040. E-mail: info@qprime.com.*

KIEF, PAUL ALLAN, lawyer; b. Montevideo, Minn., Mar. 22, 1934; s. Paul G. and Minna S. K. BA, LLB, U. Minn., 1957. Bar: Minn. 1957, U.S. Dist. Ct. Minn. 1964, U.S. Ct Appeals (8th cir.) 2004, U.S. Tax Ct. 1968, U.S. Supreme Ct. 1981; cert. criminal trial law specialist Nat. Bd. Trial Advocacy. Gen. practice, Bemidji, Minn., 1959—; ptnr. Kief, Fuller, Baer & Wallner, Ltd., Bemidji, Minn., 1973-97; owner Paul A. Kief Law Firm,

Bemidji, Minn., 1998—; pub. defender 9th Jud. Dist. Minn., Bemidji, Minn., 1966-98; panel atty. Fed. Pub. Defender Dist. Minn., 1999—. Chief pub, defender, Bemidji, Minn., 1968—94; vol. atty. Minn. Civil Liberties Union; mem. adv. bd. Innocence Project of Minn.; panel atty Legal Svcs., Northwest, Minn. Vice chmn. Beltrami County Planning Commn., 1964-68; chmn. adv. com. Gov.'s Crime Commn., 1971-77; mem. Minn. Task Force on Standards and Goals in Criminal Justice, 1975-76, Crime Victims Task Force, 1985, Jud. Selection Com., 1987, Com. on Criminal Jury Instrn. Guides, 1988-90; bd. dirs. Legal Svcs. Northwest Minn., 1990-96; capt. CAP, 1969—. Served with USAR, USNG, 1958-64. Mem. ABA, ATLA, NACDL, MACDL, Nat. Bd. Trial Advocacy (cert. crim. law trial specialist 1998), Minn. Bar Assn., Minn. Trial Lawyers Assn., 15th Dist. Bar Assn. (past sec.), Beltrami County Bar Assn. (past pres.), Lawyer-Pilots Bar Assn., Minn. Criminal Def. Lawyers Assn., Toastmasters, Phi Beta Kappa. Democrat. Congregationalist. Home: PO Box 212 Bemidji MN 56619-0212 Office: 514 America Ave NW PO Box 212 Bemidji MN 56619-0212 Office Phone: 218-751-2222. Personal E-mail: paky@paulbunyan.net.

KIEFER, ANSELM KARL ALBERT, artist; b. Donaueschingen, Germany, Mar. 8, 1945; s. Albert and Cacilia (Forster) K.; m. Monika Bornebusch, Feb. 9, 1971 (div.); children: Daniel, Sarah, Julian. Student, State Acad. Arts, Karlsruhe, Fed. Republic Germany, State Acad. Arts, Dusseldorf, Fed. Republic Germany. One-man shows include Galerie am Kaiserplatz Karlsruhe, 1969, Galerie Michael Werner, Cologne, Fed. Republic Germany, 1973, 74, 75, 76, 77, Galerie im Goethe-Institut/Provisorium, Amsterdam, 1973, Galerie Felix Handschine, Basel, Switzerland, 1973, Galerie t'Venster/Rotterdam Arts Found., The Netherlands, 1974, Bonner Kunstverein, Bonn, Fed. Republic Germany, 1977, Galerie Helen van der Meij, Amsterdam, 1977, 80, Galerie Maier-Hahn, Dusseldorf, 1978, Stedelijk Van Abbemuseum, Eindhoven, The Netherlands, 1979, (with George Baselitz) XXXIX Biennale Venedig at German Pavilion, 1980, Mannheimer Kunstverein, Mannheim, Fed. Republic Germany, 1980, Wurttembergischer Kunstverein, Stuttgart, Fed. Republic Germany, 1980, Galerie Paul Maenz, Cologne, 1981, 84, Marian Goodman Gallery, N.Y.C., 1981, 82, 95, 96, Museum Folkwang, Essen, Fed. Republic Germany, 1981, Whitechapel Art Gallery, London, 1982, Mary Boone Gallery, N.Y.C., 1982, Sonja Henie-Niels Onstad Founds., Oslo, 1983, Anthony d'Offay Gallery, London, 1983, Hans-Thoma-Museum, Bernau/Schwarzwald, Fed. Republic Germany, 1983, Mus. Contemporary Art, Los Angeles, 1983-84, Stadtische Kunsthalle, Dusseldorf, and Musee d'Art Moderne de la Ville de Paris, 1983, Israel Mus., Jerusalem, 1983, Kunsthalle Basle, Switzerland, 1986, Edward Tyler Nahem Fine Art, 1996-97, Gagosian Gallery, N.Y.C., 1997-98, Met. Mus. Art, 1999; group shows include Musee d'Art Moderne, Paris, 1977, Teheran Mus. Contemporary Art, Iran, 1978, Badischer Kunstvereine, Karlsruhe, Fed. Republic Germany, 1979, Royal Acad., London, 1981, Palais des Beaux Arts, Brussels, 1981, Kunsthalle, Dusseldorf, 1981, Galeria Stein, Turin, Italy, 1982, Documenta 7, Kassel, Germany, 1982,St. Louis Art Mus., 1983, Inst. for Art and Urban Researches, Long Island City, N.Y., 1983, Inst. Contemporary Art at U. Phila., 1983, Mus. Contemporary Art, Chgo., 1983, New Port Harbour Mus., New Port Beach, Calif., 1983, Corooran Gallery Art, Washington, 1983, Fondacion S. Moragas, Barcelona, Spain, 1983, Biblioteca Nacional, Madrid, 1984, Stedelijk Mus., Amsterdam, 1984-85, Castello di Rivoli, Torino, 1985, La Grande Halle de la Vilette, Paris, 1985, Mus. Art, Carnegie Inst., Pitts., 1985, Nationalgalerie, Berlin, 1985, Royal Acad., London, 1985; represented in permanent collections Art Inst. Chgo., Los Angeles County Mus. Art, Mus. Contemporary Art, Los Angeles, Mus. Modern Art, N.Y.C., Solomon R. Guggenheim Mus., N.Y.C., Mus. Art, Carnegie Inst., Phila. Mus. Art, Va. Mus., Richmond, Hirshhorn Mus., Smithsonian Instn., Washington, Tamayo Mus., Mexico City, Stadtische Galerie mit Sammlung Ludgie, Aachen, Nationalgalerie, Berlin, Kunsthalle, Bielefeld, Folkwang Mus., Essen, Staatsgalerie moderner Kunst im Haus der Kunst, Munich, Staatsgalerie, Stuttgart (all Fed. Republic Germany), Stedelijk Mus., Stedelijk Van Abbemuseum, Eindhoven, Groninger Mus., Groningen, Mus. Boymans-van Beuningen, Rotterdam (all The Netherlands), Kunsthaus Zurich, Switzerland, Tate Gallery, London, Musée Nationale d'Art Moderne Centre Georges Pompidou, Paris; author: A Book by Anselm Kiefer, 1988. Recipient Wolf prize in the arts, 1990, retrospective Nat. Galerie Berlin, 1991. Mem.: Am. Acad. Arts and Sciences (hon. fgn.).

KIEFER, HELEN CHILTON, emergency and trauma physician, neurologist; b. Washington; d. Frank McGloin and Sue (Stanford) Chilton; m. John Harold Kiefer (div.); 1 child, Steven Chilton. AB in Chemistry magna cum laude, Cornell U.; PhD in Biochemistry, U. Chgo.; MD with honors, Northwestern U., 1981. Diplomate Am. Bd. Emergency Medicine, 1998. Resident neurology U. Ill. Med. Sch., Chgo., 1983-85; physicist, computer programmer physics div. Los Alamos (N.Mex.) Sci. Labs.; asst. prof. dept. biochemistry Northwestern U. Med. Sch., Chgo.; editor Marcus Acad. Media, Chgo., 1978-81; clin. assoc. prof. dept. biochemistry Loyola Med. and Dental Sch., Chgo.; pvt. practice emergency/trauma medicine, 1985—; dir. med. rsch. for biotech., assoc. med. dir. high tech. Abbott Labs., Abbott Park, Ill., 1986-89; assoc. ctr. for biotechnology Northwestern U., 1992. Adj. assoc. prof. dept. biomed. engring. and grad. multidisciplinary program in neurosci. Northwestern U., Evanston, Ill., 1989-90; vis. prof. dept. bioengring. U. Wash., Seattle, 1982-83; mem. presdl. adv. com. devel. non-invasive imaging-MRI, pet, rapid high resolution CT scanning, program project rev. bds. NIH; CEO, pres. Childstone Prodns. and Pub., 2000—; owner ONCall Urgent Care, Santa Fe, 2003—. Woodrow Wilson fellow, NSF fellow, Danforth Found. fellow, NIH postdoctoral fellow. Mem. Phi Beta Kappa, Alpha Omega Alpha. Office: 431 St Michaels Dr Santa Fe NM 87505 Office Phone: 505-954-9949.

KIEFF, ELLIOTT DAN, medical educator; b. Phila., Feb. 2, 1943; s. Irving N. and Florence (Prussel) K.; m. Jacqueline Louise Silverman, June 11, 1944; children: David, Scott, Elizabeth. AB, U. Pa., 1963; MD, Johns Hopkins U., 1966; PhD, U. Chgo., 1971. Intern medicine U. Chgo., 1966-67, resident medicine, 1967-70, asst. prof. medicine, 1971-77, assoc. prof. medicine and molecular genetics, 1977-80, prof. medicine and molecular genetics, 1980-85, L. Block prof. biol. scis., 1985-87, chief infectious disease, 1971-87; Harriet Ryan Albee prof. medicine, microbiology and molecular genetics Harvard U., Boston, 1987—, chief infectious disease Brigham Hosp., 1987, chair virology, 1991—; Meyer hon. vis. prof. U. Calif., San Francisco, 1991—. Assoc. editor Virology, 1980—, Jour. of Virology, 1982—, reviewing editor, Science, 1996—. Recipient Langer award Langer Cancer Rsch., 1983, Finland award, 1987, Ricketts award, 1996. Mem. Nat. Acad. Scis., Am. Acad. Arts and Scis., Am. Soc. Clin. Ivestigation, Assn. Am. Physicians, Inst. Medicine, Inter Urban Club, Quadrangle Club (Chgo.), Harvard Club (N.Y.C.). Avocation: tennis. Home: 269 Lee St Brookline MA 02445-5914 Office: Havard Univ Med Sch 181 Longwood Ave Boston MA 02115-5804

KIEFFER, GEORGE DAVID, lawyer; b. NYC, Nov. 17, 1947; m. Judith Kieffer; 2 children. BA in history, U. Calif., Santa Barbara, 1969; JD, UCLA, 1973. Bar: Calif. 1973. Extern to Hon. David L. Bazelon US Ct. Appeals DC Cir., 1972; joined Manatt, Phelps & Phillips, LA, 1973, ptnr., bd. dirs., co-chair govt. divsn. Mem. transition team Gov. Arnold Schwarzenegger; chair Mayor's Council of Econ. Advisors, Mayor's LA Econ. Impact Task Force, City of LA Charter Reform Commn. Author: (book) The Strategy of Meetings, 1988. Former bd. dirs. Constl. Rights Found.; former chmn. bd. dirs. Ctr. for the Study of Dem. Institutions; former mem., vice chair bd. dirs. LA Urban League, bd. dirs. Automotive Training Ctr.; active Citizens Adv. Coun. on Corporations, 1975—82, Commn. for the Rev. of the Master Plan for Higher Edn. in Calif., 1985—87; trustee, chmn. U. Calif. Santa Barbara Found., 1972—82; bd. regents U. Calif., 1979—80; bd. governors Calif. Cmty. Colleges, 1981—87, pres., 1984—85; mem. exec. com., chair bd. dirs. LA C. of C.; bd. dirs. Calif. C. of C., chair edn. com.; mem. mus. coun. Mus. Contemporary Art, LA; mem bd. dirs., exec. com. Ctrl. City Assn. LA. Named one of 100 Most Influential Lawyers in Calif., Calif. Law Bus., 2000; recipient Social Responsibility Award, LA Urban League, 1999. Mem.: LA County Bar Assn. Avocations: writing and performing music, tennis, golf, basketball. Office: Manatt Phelps & Phillips 11355 W Olympic Blvd Los Angeles CA 90064 Office Phone: 310-312-4146.

KIEFFER, JAROLD ALAN, publishing executive, writer; b. Mpls., May 5, 1923; s. Charles O. and Edith Ida (Feinberg) K.; m. Frances Clarfield, Aug. 13, 1949; children: Edith Charlotte, Charles Edward, Philip William. BA, U. Minn., 1947, PhD, 1950. Tchg. asst. polit. sci. dept. U. Minn., 1949, tchg. asst. social sci. program, 1950-51; rsch. asst., world affairs program Mpls. Star, 1949-50; exec. sec. def. moblzn. manpower coms., staff asst. to exec. sec. Office Def. Moblzn., Exec. Office of Pres., 1951-52, staff sec., 1952, asst. to exec. officer, exec. sec. borrowing authority review bd., 1953, spl. asst. to dir., 1955-56, acting dep. asst. dir. nat. security affairs, 1956-57, cons., 1958; exec. asst. to dir. orgn. and personnel, exec. sec. personnel adv. com. AEC, 1952-53; asst. to Arthur S. Flemming, mem. 2d Hoover Commn., 1953-55; chmn. Herbert Hoover's liaison to Task Force on Pers. and Civil Svc., 1953-55; asst. to Arthur S. Flemming, mem. and asst. to chmn. Pres.'s Adv. Com. on Govt. Orgn., 1953-61, cons., 1958; asst. to Meyer Kestnbaum, spl. asst. to Pres. for Hoover Commn. and intergovtl. rels. commn. matters, The White House, 1955—56; adviser to Meyer Kestnbaum, 1956-57; asst. to Nelson Rockefeller for policy and issues studies, N.Y. gubernatorial campaign, 1957—58. Cons. to sec. HEW, Washington, 1958, asst. to sec., 1958-59, asst. to sec. for program analysis, 1959-61; sec. bd. trustees Nat. Cultural Ctr., 1959-63, exec. dir., 1961-63; renamed John F. Kennedy Ctr. for Performing Arts; assoc. prof. polit. sci. U. Oreg., 1963-67, acting chmn. polit. sci. dept., 1964, asst. to pres., 1963-67; chmn. pub. affairs and adminstrn. programs, prof. pub. policy and adminstrn. Lila Acheson Wallace Sch. Cmty. Svc. and Pub. Affairs, 1967-69; U. Oreg. chmn. Interdisciplinary Masters Program on Pub. Affairs, 1965-69; dir. Macalester Found. for Higher Edn., 1969-70; exec. officer bd. trustees Macalester Coll., 1970-71, also adj. prof. polit. sci., 1969-71; dir. Office Internat. Tng., AID, State Dept., 1971-72, asst. adminstr. for population and humanitarian assistance, 1972-75; adj. prof. internat. rels. Am. U., Washington, 1975, staff dir. pres.' panel on biomed. rsch., 1975-76. Dep. commr. social security U.S. Dept. HHS, 1976-77; staff dir. Task Force on House Adminstrv. Sys., Commn. on Adminstrv. Rev., U.S. Ho. Reps., 1977; dir. Nat. Com. on Careers for Older Ams., Acad. Ednl. Devel., Inc., 1978-80, staff dir., 1981 White Ho. Conf. on Aging, 1980-82; vice chmn. Gov. Planning Coun. Arts and Humanities, State of Oreg., 1965-67; chmn. Project 70's Task Force on State Govt. Reorgn., Oreg. Gov.'s Office, 1968-69; chmn. task force on Strategic Perspectives on Aging, Fairfax, Va., 1986; cons. Office High Speed Ground Transp., U.S. Dept. Transp., 1971; cons. U.S. Office Edn., 1971; officer, mem. exec. com. Lane County Auditorium Assn., Oreg., 1963-69; exec. com. United Way, Fairfax, 1985-88; bd. dirs. World Population Soc., 1983-2002 pres., 1990-92; bd. dirs. Fairfax Vol. Action Ctr., 1967-91, hon. bd. mem., 1991-93; mem. Gov.'s Job Tng. Coordination Coun., Commonwealth Va., 1987-94, chmn. older worker and youth com., 1989-94, mem. exec. com., 1990-94; mem., chmn. transp. com. Fairfax Area Commn. on Aging, 1991-95, exec. com., 1993-95; bd. dirs., sec. No. Va. Coalition of Vol. Interfaith Caregivers, Inc., 1991-94; bd. dirs. Fairfax Alliance for Human Svcs., 1996—, chmn., 2001-04; bd. dirs. Fairfax Symphony Orch., 2005-. With AUS, 1942-46. Mem. ASPA (life), Am. Polit. Sci. Assn., Advanced Transit Assn. (dir. 1976—, chmn. 1983-84, sec.-treas. 1985-95, chmn. 1995-2000), Sr. Employment Resources Inc. (chmn. 1985—, editor SER Publs., 1989-97), Kieffer Publs. (pres., editor 1998—). Home: 9019 Hamilton Dr Fairfax VA 22031-3075 Office Phone: 703-591-8328.

KIEFFER, SUSAN WERNER, geologist, educator, media consultant; b. Warren, Pa., Nov. 17, 1942; BS in Physics and Math., Allegheny Coll., 1964; MS in Geol. Scis., Calif. Inst. Tech., 1967, PhD in Planetary Scis., 1971; DSc (hon.), Allegheny Coll., 1987. Rsch. physicist UCLA, 1971-73, asst. prof. geology, 1973-79; geologist U.S. Geol. Survey, Flagstaff, Ariz., 1979-90; prof. geology Ariz. State U., Tempe, 1988—, Regents prof., 1991-93; prof., head dept. geol. sci. U. B.C., Vancouver, Canada, 1993-95; co-founder Kieffer & Woo, Inc., Palgrave, Ont., Can., 1996-2000; founder Kieffer Inst. for Devel. of Sci. Based Edn., 1997-99; Walgreen chair, prof. geology U. Ill., Urbana, 2001—. W.H. Mendnhall lectr. U.S. Geol. Survey, 1980. Editor (with A. Navrotsky): Microscopic to Macroscopic: Atomic Environments to Mineral Thermodynamics, 1985. Recipient Disting. Alumnus award, Calif. Inst. Tech., 1982, Meritorious Svc. award, Dept. Interior, 1986, Spendiarov award, Soviet Acad. Scis., 1990; Alfred P. Sloan Found. fellow, 1977—79, MacArthur fellow, 1995—. Fellow: Mineral Soc. Am. (award 1980), Meteoritical Soc., Geol. Soc. Am. (Arthur L. Day medal 1992), Am. Geophys. Union, Am. Acad. Arts and Scis.; mem.: NAS. Avocations: athletics, music. Office: U Ill Dept Geology MC 102 1301 W Green St Urbana IL 61801 Business E-Mail: skieffer@uiuc.edu.

KIEFT, GERALD NELSON, mechanical engineer; b. Chgo., Dec. 29, 1946; s. Ralph and Alice (Nelson) K.; m. Linda Louise Fank, Oct. 28, 1967; children: Gerald Nelson II, Dawn Michelle. BSME, Midwest Coll. Engring., 1971. Sr. designer Clark Equipment Co., Aurora, Ill., 1971—73; project engr. Elgin Sweeper Co., Ill., 1974—86, GPI Industries, West Chicago, Ill., 1986—. Inventor in field. Company chmn. United Way Campaign, Elgin, 1977. Presbyterian. Home: 42w192 Silver Glen Rd Saint Charles IL 60175-8339 Office: GPI Industries Ste 700 800 E Northwest Hwy Palatine IL 60074-6513

KIEHL, E. ROBERT, manufacturing executive, consultant; b. Phila., Apr. 28, 1920; s. Eugene Phillip and Ida Jean Kiehl; m. Margaret Eleanor Swigart, Oct. 7, 1944; children: Robert Edward, John Marsh, Christine Margaret. BSChemE, Drexel U., 1943; postgrad., Princeton U., 1960—65. Chemist, engr. Allied Chem. Corp., Phila., 1940—43, project engr., 1943—44, plant mgr. Bethlahem, Pa., 1944—47, plant and works mgr. Edgewater, NJ, 1947—65; dir. oper. Allied Chem. Corp. Barrett Divsn., NYC, 1965—67; mgr. Gypsum Divsn. Celotex Corp., Tampa, Fla., 1967—84; cons. Internat. Exec. Svc. Corps, Stamford, Conn., 1987—. Chmn. materials handling com. Gypsum Assn., 1971—76; spkr. All Soviet Conf. on Gypsum, Moscow, 1979; chmn. mfg. and mining com. Gypsum Assn., 1979—83; spkr. Bur. of Standards, Washington, 1981; vol. exec. internat. projects Internat. Exec. Svc. Corps, Stamford, Conn., 1987—. Mem. bd. of edn. N. Highland Regional High Sch., Allendale - Saddle River, NJ, 1960—67; com. chmn. Boy Scouts of Am., New Milford, NJ, 1957—59; mem. adv. bd. Comprehensive Zoning Plan, Clearwater, Fla., 1995—96. With US Army, 1938—43. Mem.: Pi Kappa Phi. Republican. Episcopalian. Achievements include research in prodn. of coal for chemicals and distallation polyurethane foam, microwave cured fiberboard, pvc panels and gypsum products. Avocations: auto restoration, gardening, bridge, stamp collecting/philately. Home: 3241 San Mateo St Clearwater FL 33759 Home Phone: 727-726-1707; Office Phone: 727-726-1707.

KIEHL, KRAIG ROBERT, military officer, law educator; b. Erie, Pa., Apr. 29, 1967; s. Lynn Robert and Nancy Jane Kiehl; m. Renae Lynn Kluk, Mar. 9, 1977. BA in Polit. Sci., Edinboro U., Pa.; MA in Criminology, Ind. U. Pa., Indiana, 1995, PhD in Criminology, 2003. Investigator, police officer USAF, 1986—93; investigator Erie County Dist. Attys. Office, Pa., 1993; intelligence mgr. IRG, Inc., Charlotte, NC, 1996—99; officer in charge Northeast Cons. Tng. Ctr., Pa., 2001—; intelligence officer US Army, Iraq, 2005—06. Editor: Excuding Violent Youths, 2001. Coach, hugger Spl. Olympics, 1993—. Capt. Pa. NG, 1999—. Mem.: NG Assn., Mil. Officers Assn., Am. Legion, Alpha Phi Sigma. Avocations: running, hiking, fly fishing, reading. Office: Northeast Counterdrug Tng Ctr Bldg 8-64 Ft Indiantown Gap Annville PA 17003

KIEHNE, FRANK CHARLES, JR., foundation administrator; b. Burlington, Iowa, Feb. 2, 1925; s. Frank Charles and Grace May (Archer) Kiehne; m. Dolores Yulon Gutman, June 17, 1945; children: John Charles, James Wesley, Thomas Matt, Jeffrey Scott. AA, Bowling Green State U., 1944; BS, George Williams Coll., Chgo., 1947, MS, 1951. Community and student dir. southtown dept. YMCA of Chgo., 1947-50; exec. dir. country club br. YMCA, Kans. City, Mo., 1950-55; asst. gen. dir. YMCA of Met. St. Louis, 1955-61; CEO, YMCA of Reading and Berks County, Pa., 1961-70; cons. US peace Corps, 1961; CEO, YMCA of Met. Washington, 1970-73; exec. dir. internat. com. YMCA of USA, NYC, 1973-80; refugee dir. ch. world svc. Nat. Coun. Chs., NYC, 1981-82; CEO Pvt. Agys. in Internat. Devel. (now Am. Coun. Vol. Internat. Action), Washington, 1982-84; sec. for refugees World Alliance of YMCAs, Geneva, 1986-90; fgn. affairs advisor to Congressman Donald M. Payne, Washington, 1990—96. Coord. fgn. affairs task force Congl. Black Caucus, 1992—95, fellow, 1996—. Editor: Palestinian Situation, 1989; author: (with others) Fair Play in Sports, 1979; contbr. articles to profl. jours. Mem. Greater Reading Coun. of Chs., 1962—64; co-founder World Affairs Coun., Reading and Berks County, Pa., 1963—70; Human Rels. Coun., 1967; sec. Am. Coun. Vol. Agys. Fgn. Svc., 1973—80; mem. nat. adv. bd. Nat. Peace Acad., Washington, 1976—80; pres. Reading Libr. Co., 2003—06; mem. Internat. Coun. Vol. Agys., Geneva, 1986—90; Mem. subcom. Mayor's Commn. on Human Rels., Chgo. and Kansas City, Mo, 1951—55; co-founder Econ. Opportunity Coun. Reading and Berks County, 1964; mem. Planned Parenthood Coun. Bd., 1964—68; planning divsn. United Cmty. Svcs. of Reading and Berks County, 1969—79, v.p. coordination in devel.; mem. U.S. Western Sahara Found. Bd. Advisors, 1996—; trustee Reading Pub. Libr., 2000—02, YMCA of Reading and Berks Counties, 2000—; mem. vestry Christ Episc. Ch., Reading, Pa., 2005—; mem. YMCA Assn. Profl. Dirs., Nat. YMCA US Archives com. Officer USMC, 1943—45, officer USMC, 1951—52. Named Disting. Alumnus George Williams Coll. Aurora U., 1970, 06; recipient Cert. of Merit Am. Cancer Soc., F. William Stahl Journalism award, 2005; named to YMCA of the USA Hall of Fame, 2007. Mem.: Latin Am. Paper Money Soc., Hist. Soc. Berks County, Internat. Bank Note Soc., Africare (life). Avocations: collecting international bank notes, swimming. Home: 512 Elm St Reading PA 19601-3306 Office Phone: 610-376-3185. Personal E-mail: kiehnef@aol.com.

KIEKHOFER, WILLIAM HENRY, lawyer; b. Madison, Wis., June 19, 1952; s. William and Emily (Graham) K.; m. Leslie A. Cohen., Jan. 27, 1956; children: Allison Laura, Phoebe Leigh, Rachel Elizabeth. BA, U. Wis., 1976; JD, U. So. Calif., 1980. Assoc. Sidley & Austin, LA, 1980-82, Fried & King, LA, 1982-83, McKenna Conner & Cuneo, LA, 1983-90; ptnr. Kelley Drye & Warren LLP, LA, 1990—2001, Mayer, Brown, Rowe & Maw LLP, LA, 2001—. Office: Kelly Drye Warren 101 Park Ave New York NY 10178-0062

KIEL, FREDERICK ORIN, lawyer; b. Columbus, Ohio, Feb. 22, 1942; s. Fred and Helen Kiel; m. Vivian Lee Naff, June 2, 1963; 1 child, Aileen Vivian. AB magna cum laude, Wilmington Coll., 1963; JD, Harvard U., 1966. Bar: Ohio 1966, U.S. Supreme Ct. 1972. Assoc. Peck, Shaffer & Williams, Cin., 1966—71, ptnr., 1971—80, Taft, Stettinius & Hollister, Cin., 1980—89; pvt. practice law Cin., 1990—. Co-founder Bond Attys.' Workshop, 1976. Editor: Bond Lawyer, 1982, Nat. Assn. Bond Lawyers Quarterly Newsletter, 1982, Bond Lawyers and Bond Law: An Oral History, 1993, Bondletter, 1991—, Anderson Insights, 1992—; contbr. articles to profl. jours. Arbitrator Mcpl. Securities Rulemaking Bd., 1985-92; sec. Anderson Twp. Greenspace Adv. Com., 1990—; rep. precinct exec. Precinct H Anderson Twp., 1991-92, 94-2001, Precinct X Anderson Twp., 2001—; twp. atty. Anderson Twp., 1997-2003; twp. law dir., 2003—. Mem. Ohio State Bar Assn., Cin. Bar Assn., Nat. Assn. Bond Lawyers (life, co-founder 1979, dir. 1979-84, pres. 1982-83, hon. dir. 1984—, bond attys. workshop steering com. 1976, 83, 85, scrivener com. stds. practice 1987-89, Disting. Svc. award 2002, 04). Office: 1095 Nimitzview Dr Ste 103 Cincinnati OH 45230-4392 Office Phone: 513-232-4449.

KIEL, JEFF E., publishing executive; b. 1959; m. Gayle Kiel; children: Ryan, Alexa. BS, U. Fla., 1981. CPA. Acct. Ernst & Young, 1981—87, Kauffman, Rossin & Co., 1987; with Miami Herald, 1988—2002, v.p. fin., CFO, 1999—2002; v.p. advt. San Jose (Calif.) Mercury News, 2002—07, pub., 2007—. Office: San Jose Mercury News 750 Ridder Park Dr San Jose CA 95190 E-mail: jkiel@mercurynews.com.*

KIELAROWSKI, HENRY EDWARD, marketing executive; b. Pitts., Dec. 29, 1946; s. Henry Andrew Kielarowski and Evelyn Marie Kline Boileau; m. Lynda Blair Powell, Aug. 1971 (div. 1976); children: Amorette, Blair. BA, Duquesne U., 1969, MA, PhD, Duquesne U., 1974. Pres. Communicators, Inc., Pitts., 1974—76; mktg. specialist McGraw-Hill, Inc., NYC, 1976—81; dir. mktg. Fidelity S.A., Allison Park, Pa., 1981—86; exec. v.p. ARC Sys., Inc., Pitts., 1986—88; v.p. mktg. Providian Fin. Corp., San Francisco, 1988—98; pres. La Playa Cons., Inc., San Francisco, 1999—; founder Moksha Tribe EDM Collective. Author: Microcomputer Consulting in the CPA Environment, 1987; contbr. articles to profl. jours. Mem. Am. Mktg. Assn. (mktg. excellence award 1988), Direct Mktg. Assn. Democrat. Avocations: writing, mobile DJ, filmmaking. Home: 1496 La Playa St San Francisco CA 94122-2813 E-mail: apollo@edmscience.org.

KIELMEYER, WILLIAM HENRY, ceramics engineer, researcher; b. Columbus, Ohio, Jan. 6, 1943; s. Petr Henry and Dorothy Ruth (Potts) K.; m. Marjorie E. Kaufman, Oct. 5, 1968; children: Cheryl A., Thomas W. BS in Ceramic Engring., Ohio State U., 1966, MS, 1973. Project engr. Owens-Corning Fiberglas Corp., Granville, Ohio, 1968-72; rsch. engr. Johns-Manville Sales Corp., Littleton, Colo., 1973-78, sr. rsch. engr., 1978-86, rsch. assoc., 1987—. Mem. Am. Ceramic Soc. Republican. Lutheran. Achievements include 17 patents, including co-patentee process for making high-purity silica fiber for use in space shuttle reusable surface insulation; loose-fill residential insulation, commercial insulation materials and systems, manufacturing processes for dual glass and cladglass fibers. Home: 3374 W Chenango Ave Englewood CO 80110-6312 Office: 10100 W Ute Ave Littleton CO 80127-5002

KIELY, DAN RAY, fund manager, consultant, real estate company executive; b. Ft. Sill, Okla., Jan. 2, 1944; s. William Robert and Leona Maxine (Ross) K. BA in Psychology, U. Colo., 1966; JD, Stanford U., 1969. Bar: Colo. 1969, DC 1970, Va. 1973; cert. property mgr. Assoc. Holme, Roberts and Owen, Denver, 1969—70; pres. DeRand Equity Group, Arlington, Va., 1973-89; pres., chmn. bd. Bankwest Corp and related banks, Denver; pres., dir. United Gibralter Corp. Del., Inc., 1987—92; ptnr. Starlin & Kiely, P.C., 1989-94; trustee DeRand Real Estate Investment Trust, 1974—; pres. Strategy Corp. Internat., 2005—. Chmn. Pace Holdings, Inc., Washington, 1988—93, Washington Capital Corp., 1989—; pres. Catelyst Comm. Inc., Palm Beach, Fla., 2001—, Strategy Corp. Internat., 2005—; spkr., lectr. in field. Deacon, McLean Bapt. Ch., Va., 1977-80. Officer USAF, 1969-73. Decorated Legion of Merit. Mem. ABA, Nat. Bd. Realtors, Inst. Real Estate Mgmt., Nat. Assn. Rev. Appraisers, Internat. Coun. Shopping Ctrs., Nat. Assn. Real Estate Investment Trusts, Internat. Inst. (cert. valuer), Colo. Indsl. Bankers Assn. (bd. dirs. 1985-87). Home: PO Box 6621 West Palm Beach FL 33405-6621 Personal E-mail: dankiely@aol.com. Business E-Mail: dkiely@scifunds.com.

KIELY, PAULA, city librarian; Student, U. Wis., Stevens Point; BFA, U. Wis., Milw., MLS, 1992. Libr. Brookfield Pub. Libr.; libr. Zablocki and Martin Luther King librs. and Ctrl. Libr. Betty Brinn Children's Rm. Milw. Pub. Libr., 1995—98, coord. children's svcs., 1998, dep. dir. Librs. Dept., dep. city libr., ctrl. libr. svcs. mgr., 2000—06, interim city libr., 2006, city libr., 2006—. Mem.: Wis. Libr. Assn., Pub. Libr. Assn., ALA. Office: Milw Pub Libr 814 W Wisconsin Ave Milwaukee WI 53233 Office Phone: 414-286-3020. E-mail: pkiely@mpl.org.*

KIELY, W. LEO, III, brewery company executive; b. Jan. 16, 1947; AB in Econ. summa cum laude, Harvard U., 1969; MBA, U. Pa., 1971. Brand asst., asst. brand mgr. Procter & Gamble, Cin., 1971—73; from bus. mgr. to v.p. mktg. Wilson Sporting Goods Co., Chgo., 1973—79; pres. Ventura (Calif.) Coastal Corp., 1979—82; v.p. brand mgmt. Frito-Lay, Inc., 1982—83, v.p. mktg., 1983—84, v.p. sales & mktg., 1984—89, sr. v.p. field ops., 1989—90, v.p., gen. mgr. central div., 1990—91, pres., central div., 1991—93; pres., COO Coors Brewing Co., Golden, Colo., 1993—2000, pres., CEO, 2000—05, Adolph Coors Co., 2002—05, Molson Coors Brewing Co., Golden, Colo., 2005—. Bd. dirs. SEI Ctr. for Advanced Studies Bd. Wharton Sch. Fin., Phila., Adolph Coors Co and Coors Brewing Co., Golden, Colo., 1998—, Nat. Assn. of Manufacturers, Washington. Trustee Boys & Girls Clubs Am.; bd. dirs. Met. State Coll. Denver Found. Bd., Denver Ctr. for Performing Arts; chmn. Mile High United Way Denver. Mem.: Nat. Assn. Mfrs. (bd. dirs.). Office: Molson Coors Brewing Co PO Box 4030 Golden CO 80401*

KIENBAUM, JANICE MAE, reading specialist; d. Harold James and Marilyn Mae Kienbaum; children: Jeffrey James Pagel, Jennifer Mae Buhrow. B in Elem. Edn., U. Wis., Whitewater, 1971; M in Tchg. Reading, U. Wis., Eau Claire, 1990. Lic. profl. educator reading specialist k-8 Wis. Dept. Pub. Instrn., elem. sch. libr. Wis. Dept. Pub. Instrn. Elem. sch. libr. East Troy Schs., Wis., 1971—74; substitute tchr. Rice Lake Schs., 1986—87, Prairie Farm Schs., 1986—87, Barron Area Schs., 1980—87, handicap instrnl. aide, 1987—89, Title I reading tchr. and reading specialist, 1989—. Coach Odyssey of the Mind then Destination Imagination, Barron, Wis., 1993—2003. Contbr. poetry to anthologies. Sunday sch. tchr. First Luth. Ch., Barron, Wis., 1982—95, 2006, planning com. gift from the heart, 1993—. Mem.: Internat. Soc. Poets, Internat. Reading Assn., Wis. State Reading Assn. (chair publs. com. 1999—), Northwest Wis. Reading Coun. (mem. planning com. young authors conf. 1993—, v.p. 1990, 1997, pres. 1991, 1998). Lutheran. Avocations: writing, poetry, reading, fishing. Home: 40 S 2d St Barron WI 54812 Office: Barron Area Schs Woodland Sch 808 Woodland Ave Barron WI 54812 Office Phone: 715-537-5621. Business E-Mail: kienbaumj@barron.k12.wi.us.

KIENBAUM, THOMAS GERD, lawyer; b. Berlin, Nov. 16, 1942; came to U.S., 1957; s. Gerd Wilhelm Kienbaum and Albertine Brigitte (Kramm) Kettler; m. Karen Smith, June 24, 1966 (div.); 1 child, Ursula; m. Elizabeth Hardy, Jan. 22, 1992. AB, U. Mich., 1965; JD magna cum laude, Wayne State U., 1968. Bar: Mich. 1968, Ill. 1991, U.S. Supreme Ct. 1983. Assoc. Dickinson, Wright, Moon, Van Dusen & Freeman, Detroit, 1968-76, ptnr., 1976-97; ptnr., founder Kienbaum Opperwall Hardy & Pelton, Detroit and Birmingham, 1997—. Adv. bd. Nat. Employment Law Inst.; bd. vis. Wayne State U. Law Sch., 1996—; mem. Atty. Discipline Bd., 2007—. Contbr. articles to profl. jours. Bd. dirs. Wayne County Neighborhood Legal Svc., 1972-76, 87-88. Fellow ABA, State Bar of Mich. Found.; mem. Am. Judicature Soc., Coll. Labor and Employment Lawyers, State Bar Mich. (pres. 1995-96), Detroit Bar Assn. (pres. 1985-86), Barristers Assn. (pres. 1978-79), Oakland County Bar Assn., Order of the Coif. Avocations: reading, skiing, squash, sailing. Office: Kienbaum Opperwall Hardy & Pelton 280 North Old Woodward Ave Ste 400 Birmingham MI 48009-6202 Home Phone: 248-594-8560; Office Phone: 248-645-0000. Business E-Mail: tkienbaum@kohp.com.

KIENER, JOHN LESLIE, retired judge; b. Ft. Madison, Iowa, June 21, 1940; s. Cyril Joseph and Lucille Olive (Golden) K.; m. Carol Lynn Winston, June 4, 1966; children: Susan, Gretchen. BA cum laude, Loras Coll., 1962; JD, Drake U., 1965. Bar: Iowa 1965, Tenn. 1972, US Supreme Ct. 1974. Practice law, Decorah, Iowa, 1965-68; asst. atty. gen. State of Iowa, 1968-72; ptnr. Cantor & Kiener, 1972-80; city judge City of Johnson City, Tenn., 1975-80, gen. sessions judge, 1980—2006. Continuing edn. tchr., bus. law East Tenn. State U., 1975—. Assoc. editor in Jonesborough Herald and Tribune, 2006-; contbr. articles to profl. jours. and newspapers. Mem.: Elks, Rotary. Republican. Avocations: stamp collecting/philately, genealogy. Home: 2403 Camelot Cir Johnson City TN 37604-2938 Office: Herald and Tribune PO Box 277 Jonesborough TN 37659 Office Phone: 423-753-3136. Personal E-mail: jkiener@charter.net.

KIENITZ, LADONNA TRAPP, lawyer, librarian, municipal official; b. Bay City, Mich. d. Orlin D. and Mary (Stanford) Trapp; m. John Kienitz, Feb. 9, 1951 (div. Dec. 1974); children: John, Jim, Rebecca, Mary, Timothy, David. BA, Westmar Coll., 1951; MA in Libr. Sci., Dominican U., River Forest, Ill., 1970; M Mgmt., Northwestern U., 1984; JD, Western State U., Fullerton, Calif., 1995; LLM in Taxation, U. San Diego, 2004. Head libr. Woodlands Acad., Lake Forest, Ill., 1973-77; project officer North Suburban Libr. Sys., Wheeling, Ill., 1977-78; libr. dir. Lincolnwood Pub. Libr. Dist., Ill., 1978—86; city libr. City of Newport Beach, Calif., 1986—2002, dir. cmty. svcs. Calif., 1994—2002; tax atty. Chapman U. Sch. Law Tax Law Clinic, Orange, 2003—, Tustin Law Offices, 2005—. Mem.: ALA, ABA, US Tax Ct. Bar, US Supreme Ct. Bar, Pub. Libr. Assn. (pres. 1995—96), State Bar Calif., Orange County Bar Assn. Office Phone: 949-300-6951. Business E-Mail: ladonnakienitz@taxsolutionsite.com.

KIENSTRA, MATTHEW ALLEN, plastic surgeon; b. St. Louis, Feb. 20, 1969; m. Kristie S. Kienstra, Oct. 11, 1997; 1 child, Katherine Victoria. BS, U. Notre Dame, Ind., 1991; MD, So. Ill. U., Springfield, 1996. Diplomate Am. Bd. Otolaryngology/Head and Neck Surgery, 2002, Am. Bd. Facial Plastic and Reconstructive Surgery, 2004. Asst. prof. U. South Fla., Tampa, 2002—06; facial plastic and reconstructive surgery St. John's Hosp. and Clinics, Springfield, 2006—. Dir. facial trauma svc. St. John's Hosp., Springfield, 2006—. Contbr. articles to profl. jours. Mem.: ACS (assoc.), Am. Acad. Otolaryngology/Head and Neck Surgery (com. mem. 2004—07), Am. Acad. Facial Plastic and Reconstructive Surgery (com. mem. 2002—07). Office: St John's Hosp and Clinics 1229 E Seminole Ste 520 Springfield MO 65804 Office Phone: 417-820-5750. Office Fax: 417-820-5097. Business E-Mail: makienstra@sprg.mercy.net.

KIENZLE, JOHN FRED, retired history educator; b. Allentown, Pa., Apr. 1, 1945; s. Fred John and Florence Mary K.; m. Patricia Catherine Evertsen, Aug. 22, 1970. BA in history, Albany State U., 1967; MA in History, NYU, 1969; PhD in History, Princeton U., 1972. Libr. aide NYU, NYC, 1967-69, Firestone Libr. Princeton (N.J.) U., 1969-70; tchr. history Maple Hill H.S., Castleton, NY, 1970—2006; ret., 2006. Dir. media svcs. Maple Hill H.S., 1974—; adj. prof. Stena Coll., 2005—; lectr. photography, astronomy,travel and edn. Mem. Met. Mus. Art, 1987—, Lake Chaplain Maritime Mus., 1994—, N.C. Maritime Mus., 1999—, Schodack Faculty Assn., 1970—; trustee Maple Hill H.S. Amateur Radio Club, 1975—; radio officer Rensselaer County (N.Y.) Civil Emergency Svcs., 1980—. Recipient Tchr. of Yr., Schodack Schs., 1996—97, Capital Dist. Coun. Social Studies, 1998—99. Mem. Archaeol. Inst. Am. Republican. Roman Catholic. Avocations: sailing, flying, amateur radio, astronomy, photography. Office: Maple Hill H S 1216 Maple Hill Rd Castleton On Hudson NY 12033-1604 Home Phone: 518-477-5177. Personal E-mail: jkienzle@nycap.rr.com.

KIER, ANN B. BURNETTE, pathology educator; b. Littlefield, Tex., June 26, 1949; d. Robert Merlin and Martha (Bond) Yarbrough; m. Friedhelm Schroeder, Dec. 9, 1978; 1 child, Hilary. BA, U. Tex., 1971; BS, Tex. A&M U., 1973, DVM, 1974; PhD, U. Mo., 1979. Diplomate, Am. Coll. Lab. Animal Medicine. NIH fellow U. Mo., Columbia, 1976-79, asst. prof., 1979-84, assoc. prof., 1984-87; assoc. prof. dept. pathology U. Cin. Med. Sch., 1987-91, prof., dir. divsn. comparative pathology, dept. pathology, 1991-93; prof., head dept. pathobiology Tex. A&M U., College Station, 1994—2005. Cons. NIH, Washington, 1983—. Comparative Pathology, Frann Sci., Cin., 1987—. Contbr. articles to profl. jours. NIH grantee, 1980—. Mem. AAAS, Am. Assn. Pathologists. Avocations: scuba diving, piano, reading. Home: PO Box 500 Wellborn TX 77881-0500 Office: Tex A&M Univ Dept Pathobiology College Station TX 77843-0001 Office Phone: 979-862-1509. Business E-Mail: akier@cvm.tamu.edu.

KIEREN, THOMAS HENRY, management consultant; b. Milw., July 23, 1941; s. Henry Lawrence and Hildegard (Luketelle) K. BS, Holy Cross Coll., 1963; MBA, U. Chgo., 1968; postgrad., Harvard U., 1963. Mgr. Deloittee & Touche, 1968-69; asst. v.p. Sunbeam Corp., Chgo., 1969-75; dir. bus. strategy ACF Industries, Inc., NYC, 1975-78; dir. bus. and fin. planning GAF Corp., NYC, 1978-82; dir. bus. planning Engelhard Corp., Edison, NJ, 1982-83; founder, pres., mng. dir. Manhattan Cons. Group, Inc., NYC, 1983—. Bd. dirs. Mothers Stores, Inc.; chmn. mergers and acquisitions, seminar program Exec. Enterprises, Inc., N.Y.C., 1984-87; founder, chmn. Ducks Unltd., Inc., Passaic County; bd. dirs., chmn. Custom Corporate Photography, Inc., 2002—. Author, editor, lectr.: for AMA in corp. strategy, acquisitions and turnaround mgmt., 1980—; contbr. articles to profl. jours. Del. to White House conf. on small bus., Washington, 1986; pres. Bus. Execs. for Bush, 1998; area coord., mem. fin. com. Courter for Gov. of N.J., 1989; mem. fin. com. Whitman for Gov. of N.J. Campaign, 1993, 1997, mem. Inaugural Ball com., 1998; mem. Task Force on Tech. Policy Nat. Assn. Mfrs., Commn. Regulatory Reform and Govt. Waste; bd. dirs. Boy Scouts of Am.; mem. coun. N.Y. Philharm., 1980—; founder Chgo. Symphony Soc., Ctr. for Industry and Corp. Performance, Oak Ridge, NJ; founder, chmn. Greater Wayne Area Young Reps., Inc., 1992—2002; bd. dirs. N.J.-Straight and Narrow, Inc. Mem.: Nat. Assn. Photoshop Profls., Am. Inst. Architects, Am. Soc. Media Photographers, Product Devel. and Mgmt. Assn. (nat. v.p., bd. dirs., founder N.Y. chpt., Leadership award 1993), U. Chgo. Bus. Sch. Alumni Assn. (bd. dirs. 1983—85), Baruch Sch. of Bus. (adj. prof. of bus. strategy), Fordham Grad. Sch. of Bus., Amateur Comedy Club, U. Chgo. Bus. Sch. Club of N.Y. (founder, bd. dirs.), Trout Unltd., Inc. (bd. dirs. N.Y. chpt.). Republican. Roman Catholic. Avocations: fly fishing, sports car racing, skiing, environmental portrait and architectural photography. Office: Manhattan Cons Group Inc PO Box 765 Oak Ridge NJ 07438 E-mail: manconsgroup@earthlink.net.

KIERNAN, JOHN S., lawyer; b. Nov. 22, 1954; BA magna cum laude, Harvard U., 1976, JD magna cum laude, 1980. Law clerk to Hon. Walter R. Mansfield US Ct. Appeals (2d cir.), NYC, 1980—81; assoc. Debevoise & Plimpton LLP, NYC, 1981—88, ptnr., 1988—, co-chair, litig. dept. Village atty. Village of Pelham Manor, NY, 1990—93, village trustee, 1993—99, mayor, 1999—2001; dir. Legal Svcs. for NYC, 1989—, vice-chair, 1993—2003, chair, 2003—06; exec. com. Lawyer Com. of Civil Rights, 1997—; pres. Vols. of Legal Svc., 2000—07, chair, 2007—. Mem.: NYC Bar (exec. com. 2004—). Office: Debevoise & Plimpton LLP 919 Third Ave New York NY 10022 Office Phone: 212-909-6692. Office Fax: 212-621-7692. E-mail: jskiernan@debevoise.com.

KIERNAN, RICHARD FRANCIS, publisher; b. NYC, Apr. 17, 1935; s. James J. and Grace (Nolan) K.; m. Jane V. Eickmeyer, Dec. 29, 1962; children: Christopher R., Peter T., Kathy Lynn. BS, U. Conn., 1957. Salesman Med. Econs. Co., Oradell, NJ, 1963-65, sales mgr., 1965-67, gen. mgr. Chgo., 1967-68; pub. Med. Econs. mag., Oradell, 1970-72, sr. v.p., pub., 1990-95; sr. v.p., pub., Redbook, Annual, Med. Econs. mag., Bus. and Health mag., Drug Topics mag., Montvale, NJ, 1991—; pres. Medical Econs. Profl. Info. Svc. Group, 1995—; pub. RN Mag., Oradell, 1968-70; pres. Cliggott Pub. Co., Greenwich, Conn., 1972-75; exec. v.p. Biomed. Info. Inc., NYC, 1975-79; pres. Hosp. Pubs., Inc., Secaucus, NJ, 1979-89; chmn. R.F. Kiernan Assocs., Ridgewood, NJ, 1989-90; pres., COO PISG, Med. Econs., 1994—. Bd. dirs. Argus Press Holdings, USA; treas. Pharm. Adv. Council, 1979-81, pres., 1981; v.p. Devel. Med. Econs. Co. With U.S. Army, 1957-63. Mem. Pharm. Advt. Coun. (pres.), Assn. Clin. Pubs. (pres.), N.Y. Athletic Club, Ridgewood Country Club, Leland (Mich.) Country Club. Home and Office: 153 Hamilton Rd Ridgewood NJ 07450-1102

KIERSCHT, MARCIA SELLAND, academic administrator, psychologist; b. Rugby, ND; d. Osmund Harold and Cynthia (Thoresen) Selland; m. Charles M. Kierscht, Aug. 19, 1961 (div. 1972); children: Cynthia Ann, Matthew Mason. BA, U. Iowa, 1960, MA, 1962; PhD, Vanderbilt U., 1975. Lic. psychologist, Ill., Minn. Sch. psychologist South Suburban Cook County, Homewood, Ill., 1962-64, Dist. 108, Highland Park, Ill., 1964-65, Spl. Edn. Dist. Lake County Ill., Gurnee, 1966-72; psychol. examiner John F. Kennedy Ctr., George Peabody Coll., 1972-73; instr. in pediatrics Med. Sch. Vanderbilt U., Nashville, 1975-76; assoc. prof. Moorhead (Minn.) State U., 1976-80, asst. to pres., 1980-86; provost, chief exec. officer Tri-Coll. U., Fargo, ND, 1986-90; dean grad. and profl. sch. Hood Coll., Frederick, Md., 1990-93; v.p. Consortium of Univs. of the Washington Met. Area, 1993-94; pres. Stephens Coll., Columbia, Mo., 1994—2003, pres. emeritus, 2003—. Contbr. articles to profl. jours. V.p. Plains Art Mus., Moorhead, 1986-88; chmn. bd. govs. Fargo-Moorhead Area Found., Fargo, 1983-90; bd. dirs. United Way, Columbia, 1994-2001; mem. mgmt. coun. div. III, NAAA, 2001-03. Recipient Pembina Trail award, Minn. Hist. Soc., 1994. Mem. Am. Coun. on Edn., Coun. of Fellows, Fargo C. of C., Columbia C. of C. (bd. dirs.), Montgomery County High Tech. Coun., Rotary Club (Moorhead, Columbia, Fredericktowne), Cosmos Club, Washington.

KIERST, DEBRA B., theater educator, director, actor; b. Lubbock, Tex., July 20, 1955; d. James Howard and Ysleta Reed Buckner; m. Peter Shea Kierst, July 11, 1998; 1 child, Mary Kathleen. MFA, Tex. Tech U., Lubbock, 1983. Humanities/theatre tchr. Sandia HS, Albuquerque, 2000—03; drama dir. Sandia Prep. Sch., Albuquerque, 2003—. Theatrical dir. Albuquerque Little Theatre, 2002—, Vortex Theatre, Albuquerque, bd. dirs. Mem.: Am. Assn. Theatre and Edn., Ednl. Theatre Assn. Office: Sandia Preparatory School 532 Osuna Dr NE Albuquerque NM 87113 Office Phone: 505-338-3033. Office Fax: 505-338-3099. Business E-Mail: dkierst@sandiaprep.org.

KIES, DAVID M., lawyer; b. NYC, Jan. 25, 1944; s. Saul and Lillian (Schultz) K.; m. Emily Bardack, July 6, 1966 (div. 1985); children: Laura, Adam, Abigail; m. Anne Monteith, Oct. 7, 1990 (div. 1998); 1 child, Samuel; m. Kathryn L. Danes, Mar. 11, 2001. AB, Haverford Coll., 1965; JD, NYU, 1968. Bar: N.Y. 1968, U.S. Dist. Ct. (so. dist.) N.Y. 1969, U.S. Ct. Appeals (2d cir.) 1969. Assoc. Sullivan & Cromwell, NYC, 1968-76, ptnr., 1976—, dir. London office, 1992-95; chmn. ImClone Systems, Inc., 2001—06. Bd. dirs. ImClone Systems, Inc., 1996—2006. Former trustee Haverford Coll. Root Tilden fellow, NYU Law Sch., 1965. Mem. ABA, N.Y. State Bar Assn., Assn. Bar City of N.Y. Democrat. Jewish. Office: Sullivan & Cromwell 125 Broad St Fl 28 New York NY 10004-2489

KIES, KENNETH J., lawyer; b. Ft. Benning, Ga., Jan. 4, 1952; s. Robert Herman K.; m. Kathleen Barbara Clark, Oct. 11, 1986. BA, Ohio U., 1974; JD, Ohio State U., 1977; LLM in Taxation, Georgetown U., 1986. Bar: Ohio 1977, U.S. Tax Ct. 1978, D.C. 1987, U.S. Supreme Ct. 1992. Assoc. Baker & Hostetler, Cleve., 1977-81; asst. minority tax counsel Com. on Ways & Means U.S. Ho. of Reps., Washington, 1981-82, chief minority tax counsel, 1982-87; ptnr. Baker & Hostetler, Washington, 1987-95; chief of staff joint com. on taxation U.S. Congress, Washington, 1995-98; mng. ptnr. Price Waterhouse Coopers, Washington, 1998—2002; mng. dir. Fed. Policy Group, Clark Cons., Washington, 2002—. Contbr. articles to profl. jours. Mem. Capitol Hill Club, Washington Golf and Country Club, Robert Trent Jones Golf Club, Calusa Pines Club, Currituck Golf Club. Republican. Office: Fed Policy Group 101 Constitution Ave NW 701E Washington DC 20001-2133 Office Phone: 202-772-2480.

KIESGEN, PAUL, music educator; b. Chgo. s. Elmer and Alice Keller Kiesgen; m. Meredith Mills Kiesgen, May 15, 1993. BMus, Northwestern U., 1963, MusM, 1964. Voice instr. Ohio State U., Columbus, 1971—73, Wichita State U., Kans., 1973—78; singing tchr. Northwestern U., Evanston, Ill., 1981—83, DePaul U., Chgo., 1983—89; assoc. prof. music Oklahoma City U., 1986—93, No. Ariz. U., Flagstaff, 1993—97; prof. music Ind. U., Bloomington, 1997—. Guest tchr. Royal Acad. Music, London, Guildhall Sch. Music and Drama, London, Internat. Acad. Art, Rome, Shanghai Conservatory. Mem. editl. bd.: Jour. Singing, 2004—; contbr. articles to profl. jours. Mem.: Chgo. Singing Tchrs. Guild, Am. Acad. Tchrs. Singing, Nat. Assn. Tchrs. Singing (v.p. 2002—, master tchr. intern program 2000). Office: Ind Univ Sch Music 1201 E Third St Bloomington IN 47405 Office Phone: 812-855-7577.

KIESLER, CHARLES ADOLPHUS, psychologist, academic administrator; b. St. Louis, Aug. 14, 1934; m. Teru Morton, Feb. 28, 1987; 1 child, Hugo; children from previous marriage: Tina, Thomas, Eric, Kevin. BA, Mich. State U., 1958, MA, 1960; PhD (NIMH fellow), Stanford U., 1963; D (hon.), Lucian Blaga U., Romania, 1995. Asst. prof. psychology Ohio State U., Columbus, 1963-64, Yale U., New Haven, 1964-66, assoc. prof., 1966-70; prof., chmn. psychology U. Kans., Lawrence, 1970-75; exec. officer Am. Psychol. Assn., Washington, 1975-79; Walter Van Dyke Bingham prof. psychology Carnegie Mellon U., Pitts., 1979-85, head psychology, 1980-83, acting dean, 1981-82, dean Coll. Humanities and Social Scis., 1983-85; provost Vanderbilt U., 1985-92; chancellor U. Mo., Columbia, 1992-96, Weil Disting. prof. health svcs. mgmt., 1996-98; prof., sr. advisor San Diego State U., 1998-99. Pres., CEO, Virtual Univ. Internat., 1996-97. Author: (with B.E. Collins and N. Miller) Attitude Change: A Critical Analysis of Theoretical Approaches, 1969, (with S.B. Kiesler) Conformity, 1969, The Psychology of Commitment: Experiments Linking Behavior to Belief, 1971, (with N. Cummings and G. VandenBos) Psychology and National Health Insurance: A Sourcebook, 1979, (with A.E. Sibulkin) Mental Hospitalization: Myths and Facts About a National Crisis, 1987, (with C. Simpkins) The Unnoticed Majority: Psychiatric inpatient care in general hospitals, 1993. Served with Security Service USAF, 1952-56. Recipient Disting. Alumnus award Mich. State U., 1987, Gunnar Myrdal award for Evaluation Practice Am. Evaluation Assn., 1989. Fellow AAAS, APA (Distng. Contbr. to Rsch. in Pub. Policy award 1989), Am. Psychol. Soc. (founding past pres. 1988-90); mem. AAUP, Inst. of Medicine of Nat. Acad. Scis., Sigma Xi, Psi Chi, Phi Kappa Phi. E-mail: ckiesler@san.rr.com.

KIESLING, ERNST WILLIE, civil engineering educator, dean; b. Eola, Tex., Apr. 8, 1934; s. Alfred William and Louise (Kern) K.; m. Juanita Haseloff, Aug. 25, 1956; children: Carol, Chris, Max BSME, Tex. Tech. Coll., 1955; MS in Applied Mechanics, Mich. State U., 1959, PhD, 1966. Registered profl. engr. Asst. prof. Tex. Tech. Coll., 1959—63; sr. rsch. engr. S.W. Rsch. Inst., San Antonio, 1966—69; prof. civil engring. Tex. Tech U., Lubbock, 1969—, chmn. dept. civil engring., 1969—88, assoc. dean engring., 1988—93; prof. civil engring. Tex. Tech. U., Lubbock, 1993—2004, sr. assoc. dean, 2004—06. NSF faculty fellow, 1963-64 Fellow ASCE; mem. NSPE (life), Am. Soc. Engring. Edn., Nat. Storm Shelter Assn. (exec. dir. 2001—), Sigma Xi, Chi Epsilon, Tau Beta Pi Achievements include pioneering work in storm shelter research and utilization. Home: 5111 97th St Lubbock TX 79424-4867 Office: Tex Tech U Dept Civil Engring Lubbock TX 79409

KIESSLING, B. ROBBINS, lawyer; b. Atlanta, June 23, 1950; BA cum laude, Yale U., 1973; JD cum laude, NYU, 1976. Bar: N.Y. 1977. Mem. Cravath, Swaine & Moore LLP, NYC, ptnr., corp. Mem. TriBar Opinion Com. Named one of 500 Leading Lawyers in Am., 2005, Top 500 US Dealmakers, Lawdragon, 2007, Leading Lawyers in Banking, Chambers USA, 2005—07. Mem. N.Y. State Bar Assn., Assn. of Bar of City of N.Y. Office: Cravath Swaine & Moore LLP Worldwide Plz 825 8th Ave Fl 44 New York NY 10019-7475 Office Fax: 212-474-3700. Business E-Mail: bkiessling@cravath.com.

KIESSLING, LAURA LEE, chemist, researcher; b. Milw., Sept. 21, 1960; d. William E. and LaVonne V. (Korth) K. SB, MIT, 1983; PhD, Yale U., 1989. Teaching asst. MIT, Cambridge, Mass., 1982-83, Yale U., New Haven, 1983-84, rsch. asst., 1984-89; rsch. fellow Calif. Tech. U., Pasadena, Calif., 1989-91; asst. prof. chemistry U. Wis., Madison, Wis., 1991-97, assoc. prof., 1997-99, prof. chemistry, prof. biochemistry, 1999—, dir., Keck Ctr. for Chem. Genomics, 2001—. Cons. Ophidian, Inc., 1997-99, Alfred P. Sloan Found. Chemistry Fellowships, 1997-, mem. selection com., 2003-; mem. bioorganic and natural products study sect. NIH, 1997-2000, chair bioorganic and natural products chemistry study sect., 2000-02; sci. adv. bd. Promega, Inc., 1999—; Dowd Lectr., Dept. Chemistry, U. Pitts., Pa., 1999; chair, organizer, NSF Workshop on Frontiers in Glycoscience, 2000; chair, spkr., Symposium on Chemical Biology, Am. Soc. for Cell Biology, San Francisco, Calif., 2000, Med. Glycobiology, Annual Soc. for Glycobiology Mtg., 2001; mem. vis. com. Lawrence Berkeley Lab., 2000; mem. Chancellor search com., U. Wis. Madison, 2000; mem. Com. on Summer Meeting, Am. Soc. for Cell Biology, 2001; reviewer, Dreyfus Found. Rsch. Grants, 2002. Mem. editl. bd. Chemistry and Biology, 1997-, Organic Reactions, 2000-; mem. editl. bd. Organic & Biomolecular Chemistry, 2002, Annual Reviews of Biochemistry, 2005-; selection com. for editor Jour. Organic Chemistry, 1999; reviewer, NIH and NSF; contbr. articles to profl. jour. Recipient Bausch and Lomb Sci. award, 1978, Dow Chems. New Faculty award, 1992, Shaw Scientist award, 1992-97, Procter and Gamble U. Exploratory Rsch. award, 1992-95, Shaw Scientist award, 1992-97, Nat. Young Investigator award NSF, 1994-99, Beckman Young Investigator award, 1994-96, Am. Cancer Soc. Jr. Faculty award, 1995-97, Zeneca Excellence in Chemistry award, 1996, Dreyfus Tchr.-Scholar award Dreyfus Found., 1996-2001, Lake Mills, Wis. Disting. Alumni, 1999, Carbohydrate Rsch. award for Creativity in Carbohydrate Chemistry, 2001, Tetrahedron Young Investigator award in Bioorganic or Medicinal Chemistry, 2005; Postdoctoral fellow Am. Cancer Soc., 1989-91, Alfred P. Sloan Found. fellow, 1997-99, MacArthur fellow John D. and Catherine MacArthur Found., 1999-2004. Fellow AAAS (repr., Divsn. Chemistry, 2001-04); mem. Am. Acad. Arts & Sciences, Am. Chem. Soc. (Arthur C. Cope scholar 1999, Horace Isbell award, Carbohydrate Divsn., 2000, Francis P. Garvan-John M. Olin medal, 2007, editor-in-chief, Chemical Biology, 2005-), Soc. Glycobiology, Am. Soc. for Biochemistry and Molecular Biology, NAS, Sigma Xi, Phi Lambda Upsilon. Avocations: canoeing, rowing, running. Office: U Wis Dept Chemistry 1101 University Ave Madison WI 53706-1322 also: U Wis Dept Chemistry Rm 471C 433 Babcock Dr Madison WI 53706-1544 Fax: 608-265-0764.*

KIEU, QUYNH DINH, pediatrician, not-for-profit developer; b. Hanoi, Vietnam, Mar. 18, 1950; m. Chan Kieu. MD, U. Saigon, Vietnam, 1975. Intern U. Calif., Irvine, Orange, 1976—77, resident, 1977—78, fellow, 1978—79, asst. clin. prof. pediat., 1985—; pvt. practice, 1979—; founder, pres. Project Vietnam, 1996—. Recipient Woman of Yr. award, Calif.

Assembly's 69th Dist., 2004. Mem.: AMA Found. (Pride in Profession award 2004), Healthcare Found. Orange County (bd. dirs.), Vietnamese Med. Assn., Am. Acad. Pediat. Office: Project Vietnam 11100 Warner Ave Ste 116 Fountain Valley CA 92708-7500 Office Phone: 714-641-0850. Business E-Mail: qkieu@aap.org.

KIFFIN, LANE, professional football coach; b. May 9, 1975; s. Monte and Robin Kiffin; m. Layla Kiffin; children: Landry, Pressley. BA in Leisure Svc. Mgmt., Fresno State U., 1998. Grad. asst. Fresno State U., 1997—98; offensive line asst. Colo. State U., 1999; def. quality control coach Jacksonville Jaguars, 2000; tight ends coach U. So. Calif., 2000, wide receivers coach, 2002—05, passing game coord., 2004, offensive coord., 2005—06, recruiting coord., 2005—06; head coach Oakland Raiders, 2007—. Office: Oakland Raiders 1220 Harbor Bay Pkwy Alameda CA 94502*

KIFFMEYER, MARY, former state official; b. Balta, ND, Dec. 29, 1946; m. Ralph Kiffmeyer, 1968; children: Christina, Patrick, James, John. RN, St. Gabriel's Sch. Nursing, Little Falls, Minn. RN Minn. Sec. state State of Minn., St. Paul, 1999—2007. Mem. Minn. State Exec. Coun., Minn. State Bd. Investment. Mem. adv. bd. The Heartland Inst., Election Assistance Commn. Standards; bd. dirs. Hope for the City, Cradle of Hope, Close-up Found., Downtown Mpls. YMCA. Recipient Leadership award, Nat. Electronic Commerce Coordinating Coun., In the Arena award, Ctr. for Digital Govt., Commitment to Absentee Voting for the Military award, Fed. Voter Assistance, Outstanding Woman in Govt. award, Minn. Women of Today, 2003. Mem.: Nat. Assn. Secs. of State (past pres., chair com. bus. services, pres. 2003). Republican.*

KIGER, ROBERT WILLIAM, botanist, science historian, educator, researcher; b. Washington, Oct. 4, 1940; s. William Joseph and Marian (Calvert) K.; m. Suellen Montgomery, June 11, 1968; children: David M., James R. AA with honors, Montgomery Jr. Coll., 1964; BA in Spanish with Social Scis. minor, Tulane U., 1966; MA in History, U. Md., 1971, PhD in Botany, 1972. Tchr. Poolesville Elem. Sch., Md., 1966-67; grad. teaching asst. dept. history U. Md., College Park, 1968-69, grad. teaching asst. dept. botany, 1969-70, grad. rsch. asst. dept. botany, 1969-70; assoc. editor, rsch. botanist Flora N.Am. Program dept. botany Smithsonian Inst., Washington, 1972-73; asst. dir., sr. rsch. scientist Hunt Inst. Bot. Documentation, Carnegie Mellon U., 1974-77, dir., prin. rsch. scientist, 1977—; rsch. assoc. sect. botany Carnegie Mus. Natural History, Pitts., 1978—. Adj. scientist Pitts. Poison Ctr., Children's Hosp., 1990—; adj. prof. biol. scis. Carnegie Mellon U., 1984-99, adj. prof. history of sci. dept. history, 1979—, disting. svc. prof. botany dept. biol. scis., 1999—; mem. internat. com. Internat. Congress Systematic and Evolutionary Biology, 1980-90, asst. treas., 1980-90, sec.-gen., 1990-96; mem. adv. com., editorial com. Flora of N.Am. Project, 1983—; cons. Chgo. Botanic Garden, Glencoe, Ill., 1980-83, 87-88, 89, Carnegie Mus. Natural History, Pitts., 1984, European Sci. Found., Stasbourg, France, 1987, Commn. Preservation and Access, Wye, Md., 1991, FBI, Martinsburg, W.Va., 1997. Editor: Memoirs of the Torrey Botanical Club, 1975-88, Huntia, 1978-92, bibliographic editor (all vols.) and taxonomic editor (various families), Flora of North America, 1987—; exec. editor Hunt Inst. publs., 1977—; contbr. articles to profl. jours. Chmn. Lawrence Meml. Award Com., 1979—; steering group Com. Organize a Flora of N.Am. Project, 1982-83; sec. for N.Am. Commn. Taxonomic Database Plant Sci. IUBS, 1986-89, working parties for devel. various standards, 1986—, program com., 1987-90, global plant species info. group, 1990—; mem. adv. com. computer databasing Mo. Bot. Garden, St. Louis, 1988-89, Rocky Mountain Flora Project, 1993—; botanical info. adv. workshop BIOSIS, Washington, 1990; chmn. judges for botany Internat. Sci. and Engring. Fair, Pitts., 1989. With USMC, 1960-61, USMCR, 1960-66. Grantee NSF, 1971-73, 78-80, 90; recipient Full Merit scholarship Montgomery Jr. Coll., 1963-64, Partial Merit scholarship Tulane U., 1964-66, NSF Grad. traineeship U. Md., 1970, Carroll E. Cox award U. Md., 1972-73. Fellow Linnean Soc. London; mem. AAAS, Bot. Soc. Am. (sec./treas. hist. sect. 1979-92, chmn. archives and history com. 1985-86), Am. Assn. Bot. Gardens and Arboreta, Am. Inst. Biol. Scis., Am. Soc. Plant Taxonomists, Internat. Assn. Plant Taxonomy, Internat. Soc. for History and Philosophy Sci., Assn. Tropical Biology, Coun. Botanical and Horticultural Librs., History Sci. Soc., Soc. Econ. Botany, Soc. Study Evolution, Soc. Systematic Biology, Torrey Bot. Club (assoc. editor 1975—), New Eng. Bot. Club. Avocations: music, model aviation, cooking, motorcycling, photography. Home: 1183 Bucknell Dr Monroeville PA 15146-4319 Office: Carnegie Mellon U Hunt Inst Bot Documentation 5000 Forbes Ave Pittsburgh PA 15213-3890 Office Phone: 412-268-2434. Business E-Mail: rkiger@andrew.cmu.edu.

KIGGINS, MILDRED L., marketing professional; b. Hempstead, NY, Sept. 14, 1927; d. Wolfgang and Hannah Ingeborg (Olsson) Weissmann; m. Andrew Edward Kiggins, Jan. 8, 1962 (div. 1982); children: Daniel Mark, David Bruce. Diploma, Donovan Bus. Coll., Hackensack, NJ, 1945, Luther Coll. Acad., 1947. Exec. sec. Greenwich Engring. divsn. Am. Machine & Foundry Inc., Stamford, Conn., 1954-61. Mktg. Dr. Andrew Becker MD, Becker Pharm. Cons., Redwood City, Calif., 2000— Tchr. Sunday sch. St. John's Luth. Ch., Stamford, 1948-50. Republican. Avocations: gardening, music, sports, church activities. Home: 39 Wisteria Ln Tracy CA 95377-8765 Office Phone: 209-836-6064.

KIHLE, DONALD ARTHUR, lawyer; b. Noonan, ND, Apr. 4, 1934; s. J. Arthur and Linnie W. (Ljunngren) K.; m. Judith Anne, July 18, 1964; children: Kevin, Kirsten, Kathryn, Kurte. BS in Indsl. Engring., U. ND, Grand Forks, 1957; JD, U. Okla., Norman, 1967. Bar: Okla. 1967, US Dist. Cts. (we. and no. dists.) Okla. 1967, US Ct. Appeals (10th cir.) 1967, US Supreme Ct. 1971. Assoc. Huffman, Arrington, Scheurich & Kincaid, Tulsa, 1967-71, ptnr., 1971-78; shareholder, dir., officer Arrington Kihle Gaberino & Dunn, Tulsa, 1978-97, pres., 1994-97; shareholder, dir. Gable & Gotwals, Tulsa, 1997-99, advisor, dir., 1999-2001, of counsel, 2001—06; ret., 2006. Dist. chmn. Boy Scouts Am., 1983-85, cubmaster, 1986-88, coun. coms., 1988-96, campiree chmn., 1990; mem. Statewide Law Day Com., 1982-86, chmn., 1983-85; trustee Brandon Hall Sch., Atlanta, 1991-06, chmn., 1995-99. Lt. US Army, 1957-59. Recipient Silver Beaver award Boy Scouts Am. Mem.: Okla. Bar Assn. (chmn. constl. bicentennial com. 1986—89), Tulsa Club (bd. govs. 1987—94, pres. 1992), Q Club (scribe 1991—), So. Hills Country Club, Rotary, Order of Arrow (vigil), Order of Coif, Sigma Chi (Tulsa alumni pres. 1995—97), Phi Delta Phi, Sigma Tau. Republican. Home: 4717 S Lewis Ct Tulsa OK 74105-5135 Office: 1100 ONEOK Plz 100 W 5th St Tulsa OK 74103-4240 Business E-Mail: dkihle@gablelaw.com.

KIJOWSKI, ROSEMARY JOAN, small business owner, retired music educator; b. Perth Amboy, NJ, Feb. 13, 1948; d. John Raymond and Rosaria Rosica Kijowski; children: Robert John, Edward Raymond. BA, The Coll. of N.J., Ewing, 1970, MA, 1976. Cert. Fitness Nutritionist Calif., 2004, Tchr. of Music, K-12 N.J., 1970. Vocal and music dir. Edison Bd. of Edn., NJ, 1970—2005; talent show/ advisor Woodrow Wilson M.S., Edison, NJ, 1998—2005, peer leadership advisor, 2000—01; owner, gen.mgr. fitness ctr. The Body Shoppe for Women, Edison, NJ, 2003—. Asst. coach Odyssey of the Mind, Edison, NJ, 1984—90. Mem.: N.J. Assn. Women Bus. Owners, Edison Twp. Edn. Assn. (assoc. Tchr. of Yr. 1998, 2004—05), N.J. Edn. Assn. (assoc.), Music Educators Nat. Conf. (assoc.), N.J. Edn. Assn. (assoc.), N.J. Ret. Educators Assn. (assoc.), N.J. Music Educators Assn. (assoc.). Home: 52 Riverview Ave Edison NJ 08817 Office: The Body Shoppe Fitness Ctr 1897 Woodbridge Ave Edison NJ 08817 Home Phone: 732-317-4400; Office Phone: 732-572-3953. Personal E-mail: bodyshpro@msn.com.

KIKAREAS, PANAGIOTIS, foundation administrator, retired military officer; BSc with honors, Naval Acad, 1964; grad. with honors, Naval War Coll., 1981; MSc in Ops. Rsch., Cranfield Inst. Tech., Eng., 1977; PhD in Strategic Analysis and Internat. Affairs with honors, Wiltshire U., Eng., 1999; PhD in Bus. Mgmt., Wexford U., Switzerland, 2001. Commd. ensign Greek Navy, 1964, advanced through grades to admiral, 1991, ret., 1999; founder, chmn. Hellenic Aspis and Assocs. Inc. Found. Worldwide Peace and Security, 2005—. Presenter in field. Decorated knight supreme comdr. Cross of the Order of Phoenix, knight comdr. Cross of Phoenix, knight comdr. Cross of Order of Honor. Achievements include first to create war games and crisis mgmt. ctr.

KIKER, BILLY FRAZIER, economics professor; b. Elkin, NC, Apr. 21, 1936; s. William James and Ruby Lucille K.; m. Martha Jane Parker, Aug. 4, 1962; children: Todd, Jonathan, David. AB, Lenoir-Rhyne Coll., 1961; PhD, Tulane U., 1965. From asst. prof. to prof. dept. econs. U. S.C., Columbia, 1965—2006, disting. prof. emeritus, 2006—, chmn. dept., 1973-87, dir. Ctr. Studies in Human Capital, 1972-75. Vis. prof. U. Edinburgh, Scotland, 1973, U. Minho, Portugal, 1995-96, Wirtschafts U., Vienna, Austria, 1997; cons. in field. Author: Human Capital in Retrospect, 1968, Macroeconomic Analysis, 1974; editor: Investment in Human Capital, 1971; contbr. articles to profl. jours. Fulbright scholar U. Porto, Portugal, 1988. Mem. Am. Econ. Assn., Nat. Assn. Forensic Econs. Methodist. Avocations: sailing, tennis. Office: Univ SC Moore Sch Bus Columbia SC 29208

KIKO, COLLEEN DUFFY, lawyer; BS, ND State; JD, George Mason U. Bar: DC, Va. Supervisory labor rels. specialist Fed. Labor Rels. Authority, 1976—83; atty. adv. Civil Rights Div., Dept. of Justice, 1986—89; spl. asst. US atty. (Ea. dist.) Va US Dept. Justice, Alexandria, 1986—89; assoc. counsel Judiciary Subcommittee of Civil and Constl. Rights, House Judiciary Com., US Ho. of Reps., 1989; atty. Law Offices of Colleen Duffy Kiko, PC; assoc. Ronald M. Cohen & Assocs., PC, Arlington, Va.; judge Employees' Compensation Appeals Bd., Dept. of Labor, 2002—05; gen. counsel US Fed. Labor Relations Authority, 2005—. Office: US Fed Labor Relations Authority 1400 K St NW Washington DC 20424 Office Phone: 202-218-7910. Office Fax: 202-482-6608.

KIKO, PHILIP GEORGE, lawyer; b. Massillon, Ohio, July 16, 1951; s. Willard LeRoy and Stella Jane (Schroeder) K.; m. Colleen Duffy; children: Jamie Lynn, Sarah Elizabeth, Philip George Jr., Michael Ryan. BA, Mount Union Coll., 1973; JD, George Mason Sch. Law, 1977. Bar: Va. 1977, D.C 1978, U.S. Ct. Appeals (D.C. cir.) 1978. Assoc. legal counsel, broadcast asst. Nat. Rep. Congl. Com., Washington, 1973-79; exec. asst., legis. counsel Congressman Sensenbrenner, Washington, 1979-83; assoc. counsel judiciary com. U.S. Ho. Reps., Washington, 1983-86; acting dir. policy and enforcement Office for Civil Rights U.S. Dept. Edn., Washington, 1986-87; officer, bd. dirs. Kiko Heating & Air Conditioning, Canton, Ohio, 1973-89; legis. counsel Dept. Interior, Washington, 1987-89, dir. budget and program resource mgmt., 1989-92, dep. dir. office hearings and appeals, 1992-94; assoc. adminstr. procurement and purchasing U.S. Ho. of Reps., Washington, 1995-96, dep. chief of staff, counsel sci. com., 1997—98; chief of staff, counsel Congressman James Sensenbrenner, 1999-2000; chief of staff, gen. counsel House Com. on the Judiciary, 2001—07, Foley & Lardner LLP, 2007—. Active Arlington Rep. Com., 1978-86, 1995-2001, Fair Housing Bd., Arlington, 1980, St. Charles Parish Coun., 1997—; v.p. Arlington Hts. Citizen Assn., 1991-96, 2002-; pres. St. Charles Sch. PTO, 1994-99, 2001--; scoutmaster Boy Scouts Am., 2000—. Recipient Exceptional Svc. award Sec. Interior, 1988, Presidl. Meritorious Svc. award, 1992. Mem. Va. State Bar Assn., D.C. Bar Assn. Roman Catholic. Avocations: running, hunting, fishing. Office: Foley & Lardner LLP 3000 K St Ste 500 Washington DC 20007-5143

KIKOLER, STEPHEN PHILIP, lawyer; b. NYC, Apr. 24, 1945; s. Sigmund and Dorothy (Javna) K.; m. Ethel Lerner, June 18, 1967; children: Jeffrey Stuart, Shari Elaine. AB, U. Mich., 1966, JD cum laude, 1969. Bar: Ill. 1969, U.S. Dist. Ct. (no. dist.) Ill. 1969, U.S. Ct. Appeals (7th cir.) 1988, U.S. Ct. Appeals (11th cir.) 1994, U.S. Ct. Appeals for the Armed Forces 1970, U.S. Supreme Ct. 1994. Capt. Judge Advocate Gen.'s Corps U.S. Army, 1970-73; with Much, Shelist, Denenberg, Ament & Rubenstein PC, Chgo. Mem. ABA, Ill. State Bar Assn., Chgo. Bar. Assn. (real property law com., mechanics' liens subcom.), Soc. Ill. Constrn. Attys. Home: 2746 Norma Ct Glenview IL 60025-4661 Office: Much Shelist Denenberg Ament & Rubenstein PC 191 N Wacker Dr Chicago IL 60606-1615 Home Phone: 847-965-8323; Office Phone: 312-521-2495. Business E-Mail: skikoler@muchshelist.com.

KILANI, AHMED FATHY, lab administrator, director; s. Fathy Mohamad Kilani and Amal Ali Otrok; m. Souad Ahmad Benromdhane, Aug. 28, 2001. PhD, U. Calif., Berkeley, 1999. MT ASCP Calif., 1991. Study dir., lab. mgr. Small Pvt. Co., Rockville, Md., 2002—04; pres., lab. dir. Clongen Labs., LLC, Germantown, Md., 2004—. Achievements include development of close to 85 different molecular detection assays for infectious diseases. Office: Clongen Labs LLC 12321 Middlebrook Rd Ste 120 Germantown MD 20874 Home Phone: 301-916-0173; Office Phone: 301-916-0173. Business E-Mail: akil@clongen.com.

KILANKO, OYENIKE EUNICE, obstetrician, gynecologist; b. Bklyn., Mar. 5, 1972; d. Isaian Olayemi Oyedijo and Elizabeth Olayemi Tugbiyele Otedijo; m. Isaac Taiwo Kilanko, Sept. 20, 1998; children: Bolutiwi, Iyanu. BS, CUNY, 1995; MD, NYU, 1997. Diplomate Am. Bd. Ob-gyn. Assoc. attending Woodhill Med. Group, Bklyn., 2001—. Pres., co-owner Dermacare Bklyn. Hts., 2005—. Author poems. Fellow: Am. Coll. Ob-gyn. Office: Dermacare Bklyn Hts 122 Atlantic Ave Brooklyn NY 11201 Home Phone: 347-439-3551; Office Phone: 718-625-7546.

KILANOWSKI, DANA MARCOTTE, historian, writer, filmmaker, archaeologist; b. Grand Forks, ND, Aug. 30, 1946; d. Virgil Wallace and Lucille Hogan (Weidel) Marcotte; m. Samuel Joseph Kilanowski, Aug. 30, 1975; children: Kristen Marcotte, Samantha Marcotte. BA, U. N.D., 1975. Acting dir. non-acad. employment U. N.D., Grand Forks, 1968-71; historian, archaeologist Computer Scis. Corp., Edwards AFB, Calif., 1987-94; pres. Dana Marcotte Kilanowski Prodns., Palmdale, Calif., 1994—; mng. ptnr. Kerosene Flats Entertainment LLC, 2005—. Guest historian The History Channel, N.Y.C., 1997; oral historian Soc. of Exptl. Test Pilots, 2005-. Co-author: The Quest for Mach One, 1997 (Best Book award Am. Libr. Assn. 1998, 99); contbr.: Our American Century: A Century of Flight, 1999; exec. prodr. (TV documentary series) The Legends of Flight, 2004-; exec. co-prodr. (TV show and video) Mach One, 1997; prodr. (video documentary) The Happy Bottom Riding Club, 1994; prodr., historian (documentary series) The Legends of Flight, 2005; contbr. articles to profl. jours. Pres. Officers Wives Club, Edwards AFB, 1985-86, PTA, Edwards AFB, 1986; dir. Flight Test Hist. Found., Lancaster Calif., 1991—; guest lectr. Antelope Valley (Calif.) Schs., 1987—. Recipient Commendation, Air Force Flight Test Ctr., 1989, Commendation, Jet Pioneers of Am., 1991, Key Rsch. Historian award Dept. of Def. and Ctr. Environ. Excellence, 1997. Mem. AAUW, Nat. Coun. Pub. History, Nat. Trust Hist. Preservation, South West Oral History Assn., Oral History Assn., Am. Film Inst. Republican. Roman Catholic. Avocations: reading, hiking, swimming, water-skiing. Home and Office: Dana Marcotte Kilanowski Prodns 41445 Almond Ave Palmdale CA 93551-2843 E-mail: skilano@prodigy.net.

KILBANE, KATHLEEN ANN, stage manager; b. Cleve., Nov. 30, 1971; d. John Philip and Joan Marie Kilbane. BA in Polit. Sci., Coll. Wooster, 1994. Info. resource specialist Solid Waste Assn. N.Am., Silver Spring, Md., 1994—97; stage mgr. Horizons Theatre, Arlington, Va., 1998—2000, The Theatre Conspiracy, Washington, 1999—2000, Wash. Shakespeare Co., Arlington, Va., 2001; prodn. asst. The Shakespeare Theatre, Washington, 2002—04, asst. stage mgr., 2005—; stage mgr. African Continuum Theatre Co., Washington. Rsch. analyst Solid Waste Assn. N.Am., 1997—2002. Recipient Outstanding Vol. of Yr., Theatre J, 2004. Mem.: African Continuum Theatre Co., Actors' Equity Assn. Avocations: travel, cycling. Home Phone: 202-387-3305. Personal E-mail: kkilb@juno.com.

KILBANE, THOMAS STANTON, lawyer; b. Cleve., Mar. 7, 1941; s. Thomas Joseph and Helen (Stanton) K.; m. Sally Conway Kilbane, June 4, 1966; children: Sarah, Thomas, Eamon, James, Carlin. BA magna cum laude, John Carroll U., 1963; JD, Northwestern U., 1966. Bar: Ohio 1966, US Dist. Ct. (no. dist.) Ohio 1969, US Supreme Ct. 1975, US Ct. Claims 1981, US Ct. Appeals (6th cir.) 1982, US Ct. Appeals (3d cir.) 1990, US Ct. Appeals (5th cir.) 1998, US Ct. Appeals (2d, 7th and 9th cirs.) 2002, US Ct. Appeals (4th cir.) 2003, US Ct. Appeals (1st cir.) 2004, US Ct. Appeals (8th cir.) 2005, US Ct. Appeals (10th cir.) 2005, US Ct. Appeals (11th cir.) 2005, US Ct. Appeals (DC cir.). Assoc. Squire, Sanders & Dempsey, Cleve., 1966-76, ptnr., 1976—, adminstrv. com., 1979-80, mgmt. com., 1981-83, 87-90, mng. ptnr. litigation practice area, 1991—. Fed. ct. panelist US Dist. Ct. (no. dist.) Ohio; mem. adv. bd. Inst. Transnat. Arbitration. Mem. editl. bd. Northwestern U. Law Rev., 1965-66. Active Rep. Presdl. Task Force; bd. dirs. United Way Svcs.; chmn. Supreme Ct. Hist. Soc., No. Ohio, 2003-. 1st lt. US Army, 1967—68, capt. US Army, 1968—69, Vietnam. Decorated Bronze Star; named Greater Cleve. Cath. Man of Yr., 1996. Fellow ABA, Am. Coll. Trial Lawyers, Internat. Acad. Trial Lawyers, Master Bencher of John M. Manos Inn of Ct.; mem. Fed. Bar Assn., Am. Coll. Barristers, Ohio Bar Assn. (AAA corp. counsel com., ctr. for pub. resources constrn. com.), Greater Cleve. Bar Assn., Def. Rsch. Inst., Jud. Conf. 8th Jud. Dist. Ohio (life), Union Club, The 50 Club, The Club, Alpha Sigma Nu. Republican. Roman Catholic. Office: Squire Sanders & Dempsey 4900 Key Tower 127 Public Sq Cleveland OH 44114-1304 Office Phone: 216-479-8564. Office Fax: 216-479-8780. Business E-Mail: tkilbane@ssd.com.

KILBERG, WILLIAM JEFFREY, lawyer, director; b. Bklyn., June 12, 1946; s. Jack and Jeanette Constance (Beck) K.; m. Barbara D. Greene, Sept. 27, 1970. BS, Cornell U., 1966; JD, Harvard U., 1969. Bar: NY 1970, DC 1972. White House fellow, spl. asst. to sec. Labor, Washington, 1969-70; gen. counsel Fed. Mediation and Conciliation Service, 1970-71; assoc. solicitor U.S. Dept. Labor, 1971-73, solicitor, 1973-77; dep. team leader Dept. Labor, Reagan-Bush transition, 1980-81; ptnr. Breed, Abbott and Morgan, 1977-80, Gibson, Dunn & Crutcher, 1980—, ptnr.-in-charge Washington, 1990—95, now sr. ptnr., 1995—. Mem. exec. and mgmt. coms. Gibson Dunn & Crutcher; pub. mem. Adminstrv. Conf. of U.S., 1990-95. Co-author: Pitfalls for Japanese Employers, 1993; editor-in-chief Employee Relations Law Jour., 1986—2003; co-editor Employers' Rights and Responsibilities, 1988; contbr. articles to profl. jours. Class rep. Harvard Law Sch. Fund, 1973-74, 2005-06; bd. dirs. Friends of U.S. Dept. of Labor, 1989—. Named Top Employment Litigator in Washington, Washington Bus. Jour., 2005; named one of 12 Leading Labor and Employment Litigators in DC Area, Legal Times, 2004, Topy Employment Lawyer Chambers, 2004—05, 500 Best Leading Lawyers in US, Law-Dragon, 2005, 2006; recipient Man of Yr. award, Lafayette HS, 1970, League United Latin Am. Citizens award for outstanding svc. to Spanish-speaking, 1973, Arthur S. Flemming award, 1975, Judge Groat award, 1977; Father William J. Kelly scholar, 1964—66. Fellow: Am. Coll. Employee Benefits Counsel (charter); mem.: FBA, ABA, Nat. Legal Ctr. for Pub. Interest (legal adv. coun. 2004—), Coll. Labor and Employment Lawyers (charter, bd. dirs. 2003—), DC Bar Assn., NY Bar Assn., Rep. Jewish Coalition (bd. dirs. 1988—), White Ho. Fellows Assn. (1st v.p. 1981—82, pres. 1982—83), Harvard Alumni Assn., Cornell Alumni Assn. Jewish. Office: Gibson Dunn & Crutcher 1050 Connecticut Ave NW Ste 900 Washington DC 20036-5306 Office Phone: 202-955-8573. Business E-Mail: wkilberg@gibsondunn.com.

KILBORN, PETER THURSTON, journalist; b. Providence, Apr. 7, 1939; s. John Wiggins and Eleanor Artemesia (McIntire) K.; m. Susan Holly Woodward, Jan. 29, 1966; children: David Thompson, Elizabeth Artemesia Wilhelm. BA, Trinity Coll., 1961; MSJ, Columbia U., 1962. Reporter Providence Jour.-Bulletin, 1963-64; Paris corr. McGraw-Hill World News, NYC, 1966-68; reporter, writer Bus. Week Mag., NYC, 1969-71, L.A. bur. chief, 1971-73; cos. editor Bus. Week, NYC, 1973-74; reporter N.Y. Times, NYC, 1974-75, London corr., 1975-77, editor Sunday bus. sect. NYC, 1979-82, econs. editor Washington bur., 1982-83, sr. econs. corr. Washington bur., 1983-89, nat. corr. Washington bur., 1989—2005; bus. editor Newsweek Mag., NYC, 1977-78. Freelance writer, Wash., DC, 2005—. Trustee Trinity Coll., Hartford, Conn., 1990-96. Profl. journalism fellow Stanford U., 1968-69. Mem.: Sakonnet Yacht Club, Sakonnet Golf Club, R.I. Univ. Club N.Y.C. Home: 4007 Oliver St Chevy Chase MD 20815 Office Phone: 202-262-8019. Personal E-mail: pkborn@aol.com.

KILBOURN, JOSEPH A., lawyer; b. Providence, June 16, 1926; s. Jonathan Francis Kilbourn and Clara Vivell Kent; m. Elaine Mary Deran, Aug. 1, 1959; children: Mary, Pamela, Kent, Connor, Andrew. BA, Yale U., 1948; LLB, Columbia U., 1952. Bar: N.Y. 1953. Assoc. Bigham, Englar, Jones & Houston, NYC, 1953-63, ptnr., 1963-98, of counsel, 1998—2004; ptnr. Cone & Kilbourn, Mt. Kisco, 2004—. Chmn. excess, surplus lines, reins. com. tort and ins. practice sect. ABA, 1991-92. Pres. Rowayton (Conn.) Hose Co. vol. fire co., 1975-80, 83-84. Staff sgt. U.S. Army, 1944-46. Mem. Comml. Bar Assn. (London, hon.), Order of Founders and Patriots Am. (atty. gen. 1994-96, sec. gen. 1996-98, gov. gen. 1998-2000, Disting. Svc. award 2000), Soc. Colonial Wars in State of Conn. (mem. coun. 1977—), Norwalk Yacht Club. Avocation: sailing. Home: Apt 206 114 Strawberry Hill Ave Stamford CT 06902 Office: Cone & Kilbourn 83 S Bedford Rd Mount Kisco NY 10549 Home Phone: 203-323-7177; Office Phone: 914-481-6249. Business E-Mail: jkilbourn@conekilbourn.com.

KILBOURN, WILLIAM DOUGLAS, JR., law educator; b. Colorado Springs, Colo., Dec. 9, 1924; s. William Douglas and Clara Howe (Lee) K.; m. Barbara Ruth Neff, Sept. 16, 1950; children: Jonathan VI, Katharine Ann. BA, Yale U., 1949; postgrad., Columbia U., 1949-50, LLB, 1953. Bar: Mass. 1962, Oreg. 1953, Minn. 1974. Acct. Arthur Andersen & Co., 1949-50; assoc. Davies, Biggs, Strayer, Stoel & Boley, Portland, Oreg., 1953-56; asst. prof. law U. Mont., 1956-57; assoc. prof. law U. Mo., 1957-59; prof. law, founding dir. grad. tax program Boston U., 1959-71; prof. law U. Minn., 1971-98, prof. emeritus, 1998—. Dir. U. Mont. Tax Inst., 1956; of counsel Palmer & Dodge, Boston, 1964-75, Oppenheimer, Wolff & Donnelly, St. Paul and Mpls., 1980-94; mem. exec. com. Fed. Tax Inst. New Eng., 1966-72; mem. adv. com. Western New Eng. Coll. Tax Inst; vis. prof. law Duke U., 1974-75, U. Tex., 1977, Washington U., St. Louis, 1977; past ednl. advisor Tax Execs. Inst.; lectr. in 31 states, Mex., The Caribbean, D.C.; expert witness in field. Editor: Estate Planning and Income Taxation, 1957; contbr. articles to profl. jours. Dist. dir. United Fund, Belmont, Mass., chair fair practices com. Recipient numerous tchg. awards; Kent scholar, Stone scholar Columbia U. Law Sch. Mem. ABA (tax sect., corp. stockholder rels. com. 1962-76, chair subcom. inc. 1968-73), Boston Bar Assn. (chair tax sect. 1967-70), Boston Tax Forum, Boston Tax Coun. Avocations: tennis, botany, landscape gardening.

KILBOURNE, BARBARA JEAN, health and housing executive; b. Milw., Mar. 21, 1941; d. Burton Conwell and Marjorie Janet (Tufts) K.; m. Kenneth Keith Kauffman, Feb. 10, 1962 (div. 1983) BA, U. Minn., 1972;

MBA, Coll. St. Thomas, St. Paul, 1980. Adminstr. Ebenezer Soc., Mpls., 1974—85; v.p., dir. housing Walker Residence and Health Svcs., Inc., Mpls., 1985—88; exec. v.p. Oblate Ministries Health and Aging, West St. Paul, Minn., 1988—94; cons., 1995—; pres. Barbara J. Kilbourne, Ltd., 1996—; exec. dir. Cath. Health Assn. Minn., 1997—2002; v.p. mem. svcs. and internal ops. Minn. Health and Housing Alliance, 2001—06. Chair Minn. State Operated Svcs., 2000-02 Author: Family Councils in Nursing Homes, 1981. Chmn. bd. dirs. LifeWorks, Eagan, Minn., 1985-96, Minn. Assn. Homes for Aging, 1991-92, Sem. Plaza, Red Wing, 1995-97; project chair Dialog 2000, Dakota County, Minn., 1988-91; bd. dirs. ARC, Mpls., 1997-2002, Common Bond Cmtys., 1999-2002, Villa Guadalupe, Chgo., chair, 1999-2006. Mem. Minn. Rural Health Assn. (bd. dirs. 1998-2001) Episcopalian. Avocations: poetry, golf, hiking. Home and Office: 435 Shelard Pky Minneapolis MN 55426

KILBOURNE, EDWIN DENNIS, virologist, educator; b. Buffalo, July 10, 1920; s. Edwin I. and Elizabeth (Alward) K.; m. Joy Schmid, Dec. 20, 1952; children: Edwin Michael, Richard Schmid, Christopher Norton, Paul Alward. AB, Cornell U., 1942, MD, 1944; DSc honoris causa, Rockefeller U., 1986. Asst. Rockefeller Inst., 1948-51; mem. faculty Tulane U., 1951-55, Cornell U. Med. Coll., NYC, 1955-68, prof. pub. health, dir. div. virus research, 1961-68; prof., chmn. dept. microbiology Mt. Sinai Sch. Medicine, CUNY, 1968-86, disting. svc. prof., 1986—; rsch. prof. N.Y. Med. Coll., 1999—2002, emeritus prof., 2002—. Chmn., bd. dirs. Aaron Diamond AIDS Rsch. Ctr. for the City N.Y., 1989-94. Author: (with Wilson G. Smillie) Human Ecology and Public Health, 4th edit, 1968, Influenza, 1987, Strategies of Sex, 2005; Editor: The Influenza Viruses and Influenza, 1975. Mem. Health Rsch. Coun. N.Y.C., 1968-75. Recipient R.E. Dyer Lectureship award NIH, 1973, Borden award Assn. Am. Med. Colls., 1974, Dowling Lectureship award, 1976, Thomas Francis Lectureship award, 1976, Nat. Acad. Scis. 1977, Harvey Lectureship award, 1978, award of distinction Cornell U. Med. Alumni Assn., 1979, acad. medal N.Y. Acad. Medicine, 1982, Jacobi Medallion award Mt. Sinai Alumni Assn., 1991, Fogarty scholar award NIH, 1992. Fellow N.Y. Acad. Scis., Am. Philos. Soc.; mem. Harvey Soc., So. Soc. Clin. Rsch., Ctrl. Soc. Clin. Rsch. (emeritus), AAAS, APHA, Am. Assn. Immunologists, Am. Acad. Microbiology, Soc. Exptl. Biology and Medicine, Am. Soc. Clin. Investigation (emeritus), N.Y. Acad. Medicine, Assn. Am. Physicians, Am. Soc. Microbiology, Infectious Diseases Soc. Am., Conn. Acad. Sci. and Engring. Achievements include research in and publications on hormonal influences, genetic studies and exptl. transmission of viruses, and recombinant virus vaccines; development of influenza vaccines in use since 1971. Home: 23 Willard Ave Madison CT 06443-3202 Personal E-mail: ekilbourne@snet.net.

KILBOURNE, GEORGE WILLIAM, lawyer; b. Berea, Ky., Mar. 29, 1924; s. John Buchanan and Maud (Parsons) K.; m. Helen Spooner, Dec. 25, 1945 (div. 1968); m. Carole Marko, June 12, 1970 (div. 1984); children: Stuart (dec.), Charles; m. Anne F. Lavine, Aug. 19, 1996. Student, Berea Coll., 1941-42, Denison U., 1944; BS in Mech. Engring., U. Mich., 1946; JD, U. Calif., Berkeley, 1951. Bar: Calif. 1952, U.S. Dist. Ct. (no. dist.) Calif. 1952, Ind. 1957, U.S. Appeals (9th cir.). Sole practice, Berkeley, 1952-57; assoc. Hays & Hays, Sullivan, Ind., 1957-59, Boyle & Kilbourne, Sullivan, 1961-63, Bernal, Rigney & Kilbourne, Berkeley, 1963-68, Sherbourne & Kilbourne, Pleasant Hill, Calif., 1968-75; sole practice Pleasant Hill and Martinez, Calif., 1975—. Lectr. Lincoln Law Sch., San Francisco, 1956-57, John F. Kennedy Law Sch., Orinda, Calif., 1977-78. Served to 2d lt. USMC, 1942—46, PTO. Mem.: Elks. Episcopalian. Avocations: tennis, bowling, outdoors. Home and Office: 661 Augusta Dr Moraga CA 94556-1035 Personal E-mail: gwkilbourn@aol.com.

KILBRIDE, THOMAS L., state supreme court justice; b. LaSalle, Ill. married; 3 children. BA magna cum laude, St. Mary's Coll., 1978; JD, Antioch Sch. Law, 1981. Practicioner U.S. Dist. Ct., Ill., U.S. Seventh Cir. Ct. Appeals; justice Ill. Supreme Ct., 2000—. Former mem. bd. dirs., former v.p., former pres. Ill. Twp. Attys. Assn. Vol. legal adv. Cmty. Caring Conf., Quad City Harvest Inc.; charter chmn. Quad Cities Interfaith Sponsoring Com.; former mem. Rock Island Human Rels. Com.; former vol. lawyer, charter mem. Ill. Pro Bono Ctr. Mem.: Rock Island County Bar Assn., Ill. State Bar Assn. Office: Ill Supreme Ct State of Ill Bldg 160 N LaSalle St Chicago IL 60601

KILBURN, PENELOPE WHITE, retired data processing executive; b. Freeport, NY, June 25, 1940; d. William Prescott and Marian (Churchill) White; m. Edwin Allen Kilburn, Feb. 7, 1964; children: Penelope Allen, Nancy Kitchen. BA, Barnard Coll., 1962. Elem. sch. tchr. Holmdel (N.J.) Bd. Edn., 1975-78; tech. writer Continental Data Ctr., Neptune, NJ, 1983-86; with Johnson & Higgins, NYC, 1986-89, asst. v.p., 1989-91, v.p., 1991-95, ret., 1995. Sustaining mem. Jr. League, Phoenix, 1995; chmn. St. Georges refugee com., Rumson, NJ, 1981—83; mem. vestry St. Lukes, Branchport, NY, 1995—2000, warden, 2000—03; trustee Keuka Coll., Keuka Park, NY, 1997—2006, trustee emeritus, 2006—. Anglican. Avocation: gardening. Home: 10801 E Happy Valley Rd Lot 88 Scottsdale AZ 85255

KILBY, THEODORE MORGAN, JR., auditor, educator; b. Washington, Mar. 2, 1948; s. Theodore Morgan Sr. and Doris Marie Kilby; m. Valerie Stamps, Aug. 18, 1974 (div. 1989); children: Stephanie Michelle, Eric Hamilton. BS, Columbia Union Coll., 1975; MPA, Southeastern U., 1984, MBA, 1985. Cert. fraud examiner, cert. govt. fin. mgr. Dialysis technician VA Hosp., Washington, 1971-75, sickle cell counselor, 1975-78; staff acct. Dept. Vet. Affairs, Washington, 1978-79; auditor office of inspector gen. Dept. Transp., Washington, 1979-93, audit project mgr. office of inspector gen., 1993—. Chmn. supr. com. Transp. Fed. Credit Union, Washington. Chmn. adv. coun. Childrens Nat. Med. Ctr., 1996, mem., 1997. With U.S. Army, 1970-71. Mem. Nat. Soc. Accts., Assn. Govt. Accts. Avocations: golf, travel, music, arts. Home: 1108 Beatrice Ct Fort Washington MD 20744-3654 Office: Dept Transp OIG/JA-40 400 7th St NW Rm 9201 Washington DC 20590-0001

KILDEE, DALE EDWARD, congressman; b. Flint, Mich., Sept. 16, 1929; s. Timothy Leo and Norma Alicia (Ullmer) K.; m. Gayle Heyn, Feb. 27, 1965; children: David, Laura, Paul. BA, Sacred Heart Sem., 1952; tchr.'s cert., U. Detroit, 1954; MA, U. Mich., 1961; postgrad. (Rotary Found. fellow), U. Peshawar, Pakistan, 1958-59. Tchr. U. Detroit HS, 1954-56, Flint Central HS, 1956-64; mem. Mich. Ho. of Reps., 1964-74, Mich. Senate, 1975-76, US Congress from 7th Mich. dist., 1977-93, US Congress from 5th Mich. dist. (formerly 9th), 1993—; sr. mem. edn. and the workforce com., ranking minority mem. subcom. on early childhood, youth, & families; chair Congl. Auto Caucus, 1993—; co-chair Native Am. Caucus, 1997; mem. resources com.; mem. edn. and the workforce com. Recipient Excellence in Public Svc. awrad, Am. Acad. Pediatrics, 1988, Disting. Svc. award, Mich. Edn. Assn., 1993, Civitas award, 1999, Lifetime Achievement award, Ctr. Civic Edn., 2002, Friend of CACFP award, Child and Adult Care Food Program, 2002, NAICU award advocacy independent higher edn., Nat. Assn. Independent Colleges and Universities, 2003, Friend of Nat. Parks award, Nat. Parks Conservation Assn., 2005. Mem. NAACP (life), Am. Fedn. Tchrs., Urban League, Phi Delta Kappa. Lodges: K.C; Optimists. Democrat. Roman Catholic. Office: US Ho of Reps 2107 Rayburn House Bldg Washington DC 20515-2209 also: District Office 432 N Saginaw St Ste 410 Flint MI 48502-2018 Office Phone: 202-225-3611, 810-239-1437. Office Fax: 202-225-6393, 814-239-1439.*

KILE, ROBERT MERLIN, emergency physician; b. St. Louis, Oct. 12, 1948; s. J. Ray and Loretta C. Kile; m. Elizabeth Ann Ferguson, June 10, 2006; children: Larisa K., William Arthur. BA, Columbia U., NYC, 1970; MD, U. Minn., Mpls., 1974. Diplomate Am. Bd. Family Practice, Am. Bd. Emergency Medicine. Emergency physician Kaiser Health Plan, 1979—89, 1989—91; dir. emergency medicine CUPH Hosp., Plattsburg, NY, 1989; emergency physician Emergency Physicians, Southern Mankato, Minn., 1991—2000, Good Thunder Emergency Physician, Minn., 2000—02, Health East, St. Paul, 2002—. Mem.: Am. Coll. Emergency Physicians (Careeer Longevity award 1999, 2004). Avocations: skiing, poker, collecting Grateful Dead memorabilia.

KILEY, KEVIN CHRISTOPHER, retired military officer; b. Oct. 18, 1950; BS in biology, U. Scranton, 1972; MD, Georgetown U., 1976; grad., U.S. Army War Coll., 1994. Diplomate Am. Bd. Ob-gyn. Commd. 2d lt. US Army, 1972, advanced through grades to lt. gen., 2004; surg. intern, then resident in ob-gyn. William Beaumont Army Med. Ctr., El Paso, Tex., 1976-80; chief ob-gyn. svcs. 121st Evacuation Hosp., Seoul, South Korea, 1980-82; chief family planning/counseling svc., then asst. chief dept. ob-gyn., William Beaumont Army Med. Ctr., El Paso, 1982-85; divsn. surgeon 10th mountain divsn. Ft. Drum, NY, 1985-88; comdr. 10th med. bn., 10th mountain divsn., 1985-88; asst. chief, then chmn. dept. ob-gyn. William Beaumont Army Med. Ctr., El Paso, 1988-90; comdr. 15th evacuation hosp. Ft. Polk, La., 1990-91; dep. comdr. for clin. svcs. Womack Army Med. Ctr., Ft. Bragg, NC, 1991-93; comdr. Landstuhl (Germany) Regional Med. Ctr., 1994-98; command surgeon US Army Europe & 7th US Army, 1995-98; asst. surgeon gen. for force projection US Army Med. Command, Ft. Sam Houston, Tex., dep. chief of staff for ops., health policy & services, 1998-2000, comdr. Army Med. Dept. Ctr. & Sch. and Ft. Sam Houston, chief med. corps, 2000—02; comdr. Walter Reed Army Med. Ctr. & North Atlantic Reg. Med. Command & Lead Agent for Region 1, Washington, 2002—04, US Army Med. Command, Ft. Sam Houston, Tex., 2004—07; surgeon gen. US Army, Ft. Sam Houston, Tex., 2004—07; acting comdr. Walter Reed Army Med. Ctr., Washington, 2007. Decorated Disting. Svc. medal, Def. Superior Svc. medal, Legion of merit (with 3 oak leaf clusters), bronze star, Meritorious Svc. medal (with 2 oak leaf clusters), Army Commendation medal, Defense Svc. medal, "A" Profl. Designator, Order of Mil. Med. Merit, Expert Field Med. Badge. Fellow ACOG.*

KILEY, THOMAS, rehabilitation counselor; b. Mpls., Aug. 28, 1937; s. Gerald Sidney and Veronica (Roberts) K.; m. Jane Virginia Butler, Aug. 25, 1989; children: Martin, Truman, Tami, Brian. BA in English, UCLA, 1959; MS in Rehab. Counseling, San Francisco State U., 1989. Cert. rehab counselor. Former rsch. profl., businessman various S.E. Asian cos., U.S. Army; sr. social worker Episcopal Sanctuary, San Francisco, 1986-88; dir. social svcs. Hamilton Family Ctr., San Francisco, 1988-89; rehab. specialist Intracorp, Honolulu, 1989-91; pres. Heritage Counseling Svc., Honolulu, 1991—. Pres. Hunter Employment Svcs., Yuma, Ariz., 1995—, Algo Enterprises, Yuma, 1998—; chief fin. officer Heritage Am., Phoenix, 2004, Pro-Block, Yuma, 2006; pres. Hunter Leasing Svc., Yuma, 2006—. Mem. Am. Counseling Assn., Nat. Assn. Rehab. Profls. in Pvt. Sector, Am. Rehab. Counselors Assn. (profl.), Nat. Rehab. Assn., Rotary, Phi Delta Kappa. Office: Heritage Counselling Svcs PO Box 5945 Yuma AZ 85366-5945

KILGANNON, COREY, journalist; Metro. reporter New York Times. Author: (articles) The Search for the Family Tree Moves to the Web, Bklyn. Golfers Ignore Possibility of Not Playing, 2004, Back in the Saddle Preaching Drug Legalization, 2005. Office: NY Times Queens Bur Ste 1240 118-35 Queens Blvd Forest Hills NY 11375

KILGARIFF, KAREN, television producer; b. Petaluma, Calif., May 11, 1970; Performer Young Comedians, 1995, Make Me Laugh, 1997, Heroes of Comedy: Women on Top, 2003, Tenacious D: The Complete Master Works, 2003; writer Hype, 2001, The Girls Guitar Club, 2001; actress Mr. Show with Bob and David, 1997—98, Pulp Comics, 1998, Punch Drunk Love, 2002; writer Ellen Degeneres Show, 2003; also prodr., 2003—. Recipient Best Television Series or Special (Variety), The Producers Guild Am., 2006. Office: The Ellen Degeneres Show Warner Bros Studio 4000 Warner Blvd Burbank CA 91522

KILGORE, CADA T., III, lawyer; b. Griffin, Ga., Aug. 11, 1952; s. Cada T. Kilgore, Jr. and Margaret Heard Kilgore; children: Cada T. Kilgore, IV, Christopher T. BBA magna cum laude, Ga. Coll., 1975; JD magna cum laude, U. Ga., 1979, MBA, 1979. Bar: Ga. 1979. Assoc. Henkel & Lamon, P.C., Atlanta, 1979—81, Henkel, Hackett, Edge & Fleming, Atlanta, 1981—83; assoc./ptnr. Paul, Hastings, Janofsky & Walker, Atlanta, 1983—93; ptnr. Sutherland Asbill & Brennan LLP, Atlanta, 1993—. Com. mem. Trinity Sch. Ann. Fund, Atlanta, 1998—2000, Westminster Sch. Ann. Fund, Atlanta, 2001—04. Named Ga. Super Lawyer, Law and Politics, 2004—07. Mem.: Elec. Coop. Bar Assn. (bd. dirs.), Atlanta Bar Assn., G&T Lawyers' Assn., Ga. Electric Membership Corp. Counsel Assn., Nat. Assn. of Bond Lawyers, Capital City Club, Order of the Coif. Home: 3280 Northside Pkwy Atlanta GA 30327 Office: Sutherland Asbill & Brennan LLP 999 Peachtree St NE Ste 2700 Atlanta GA 30309-3996 Home Phone: 404-275-3948; Office Phone: 404-853-8196. Office Fax: 404-853-8806. Personal E-mail: cada.kilgore@sablaw.com.

KILGORE, DONALD GIBSON, JR., pathologist; b. Dallas, Nov. 21, 1927; s. Donald Gibson and Gladys (Watson) K.; m. Jean Upchurch Augur, Aug. 23, 1952; children: Michael Augur, Stephen Bassett, Phillip Arthur, Geoffrey Scott, Sharon Louise. Student, So. Meth. U., 1943-45; MD Southwestern Med. Coll., U. Tex., Dallas, 1949. Diplomate Am. Bd. Pathology, Am. Bd. Dermatopathology, Am. Bd. Blood Banking; notary pub. Intern Parkland Meml. Hosp., Dallas, 1949—50; resident in pathology Charity Hosp. La., New Orleans, 1950—54, asst. pathologist, 1952—54; pathologist Greenville (S.C.) Hosp. Sys., 1956—, dir. labs., 1985—96, Greenville Meml. Hosp., 1972—96. Cons. pathologist St. Francis Hosp., 1963—, Shriners Hosp., Greenville, 1963—, Easley Baptist Hosp.; vis. lectr. Clemson U., 1963—; asst. prof. pathology Med. U. S.C., 1968—; pres. Pathology Assocs. of Greenville, 1983—96. Deacon Westminster Presbyn. Ch., 1961, ruling elder, 1969, trustee, 2001—; mem. bd. govs. S.C. Patient Compensation Fund, 1977—2001; bd. govs. Roper Mountain Sci. Ctr., 2001—07. Capt. M.C. USAFR, 1954—56. Recipient Disting. Svc. award S.C. Hosp. Assn., 1976; awarded Order of The Palmetto by S.C. Gov. David M. Beasley, 1996. Fellow: Am. Soc. Dermatopathology, Am. Soc. Clin. Pathologists (councilor S.C. 1959—62), Coll. Am. Pathologists (life; assemblyman S.C. 1968—71); mem.: AMA (life; ho. of dels. 1978—94), Greater Greenville C. of C. (pres. ednl. task force 1965—70, elected trustee sch. dist. of Greenville County 1970—90), S.C. Soc. Pathologists (pres. 1969—72), S.C. Inst. Med. Edn. and Rsch. (pres. 1974—80), Nat. Assn. Med. Examiners, Greenville County Dental Soc. (life), Am. Assn. Blood Banks (life; adv. coun. 1962—67, insp. committeeman Southeast dist. 1965—2001), Am. Numismatic Assn. (life), Am. Coll. Nuc. Medicine, Am. Soc. Cytology, S.C. Med. Assn. (exec. coun. 1969—76, pres. 1974—75, exec. coun. 1978—94, A.H. Robins award for Outstanding Cmty. Svc. 1985), So. Med. Assn., Soc. Med. Friends of Wine, Epicurean Assn. of Am. (selection com.), Confrerie de la Chaine des Rotisseurs (bailli and echanson de l'ordre mondial, Greenville chpt.), Clan Douglas Soc. N.Am., Ltd. (life), Richard III Soc. (co-chmn. Am. 1966—75), Hist. Greenville Found. (exec. com. 1994—2001, pres. 1998—2000), S.W. R.R. Hist. Soc., S.C. Gov.'s Task Force on Hist. Preservation and Heritage Tourism, Roper Mountain Sci. Ctr. Assn. (bd. dirs. 2001—07), Brit. Museum Soc., U.S. Power Squadron, Confrerie des Chevaliers du Tastevin (chevalier Atlanta chpt.), S.C. Hist. Soc. (life), Tex. State Hist. Assn. (life), Thomas Wolfe Soc. (life), Medieval Acad. Am. (life), Archeol. Inst. Am. (life), Brookgreen Gardens Found. (life), Friends of Tewkesbury Abbey (life), Canterbury Cathedral Trust in Am. (life), Assn. Friends of Lincoln Cathedral (life), Am. Numis. Soc. (life), Soc. Ancient Numismatics (life), Royal Numis. Soc. (life), S.C. Numis. Assn. (life), Mensa (life), S.C. Congress Parents and Tchrs. (life), Greenville County Hist. Soc. (life), Preservation Soc. of Charleston (life), Wine Acad. Am. (life), Les Amis du Vin (life), Clan MacDuff Soc. Am. (life; exec. coun. 1980—2000), So. Meth. U. Alumni Assn. (life), Highland Park H.S. Alumni Assn. (life), Am. Wine Soc. (life), Blue Ridge Numis. Assn. (life), Am. Numis. Assn. (life), Confrerie de Les Grapilleurs du Beaujolais (chevalier), St. Andrews Soc. Upper S.C. (bd. govs. 1991—93), L'Academie de Gastronomie Brillat-Savarin des Etats-Unis (founding mem.), Soc. Wine Educators, Soc. Med. Friends of Wine, Piedmont Econ. Club, Poinsett Club (life), Commerce Club (life), Greenville Country Club (life), Chandon Club, Thirty-Nine Club (pres. 1981—82), Torch Club (pres. 1964—65), Rotary (Paul Harris fellow 1988), Phi Chi, Phi Eta Sigma. Democrat. Home: 105 Wren Way Greenville SC 29605-5321 Office: 8 Memorial Medical Ct Greenville SC 29605-4400

KILGORE, EDWIN CARROLL, retired federal agency administrator; b. Coeburn, Va., Jan. 24, 1923; s. Cecil Abram and Elizabeth Delle (Horne) K.; m. Ann Hitch, Dec. 30, 1944; children: Ashby Caroline, Elizabeth Cato. BSME, Va. Inst. Poly., 1944; grad., Fed. Exec. Inst., 1969. With NASA (and predecessor), 1944-81; dep. assoc. adminstr. ops. Langley (Va.) Rsch. Ctr., 1975-76, dir. mgmt. ops., 1976-79, assoc. adminstr. mgmt. ops., 1979-81; cons. to NASA Washington, 1981—. Pres. Old Dominion U. Rsch. Found., Va. Air and Space Ctr. Recipient Outstanding Leadership award NASA, Disting. Svc. medal, Apollo Spl. Achievement award, Solid Propellant Spl. Achievement award, Roger Jones award Am. U. Va., State Sr. Tennis Champion, 1993, 94, 99, Nat. Sr. Olympic Tennis Champion, 2003. Mem. AIAA, Pi Tau Sigma, Omicron Delta Kappa. Clubs: Hampton Kiwanis (pres. 1969). Methodist. Office: Acad Pub Admin Washington DC 20005

KILGORE, JENNY A., education educator; b. Cin., Dec. 27, 1952; d. Denton Chapman Shafer and Mary Lewis Green; m. Timothy Stuart Kilgore; children: Erin, Brian. BEd, Xavier U., Cin., 1984, MEd, 1991; PhD in Ednl. Leadership, Miami U., Oxford, Ohio, 2006. Cert. tchr. Ohio. Tchr. Landmark Christian Sch., Cin., 1984—98; instr. So. Ohio Coll., Cin., 1997, Miami U., Cin., 1999—, Ind. Wesleyan U., Cin., 2005—. Presenter in field. Admissions rep. US Mil. Acad., West Point, NY, 2000—; mem. coun. Village of Glendale, Ohio, 2003—; vice mayor Glendale, 2006; Sunday sch. tchr. Landmark Bapt. Temple, 1978—. Mem.: Am. Ednl. Rsch. Assn. Home: 10805 Chester Rd Cincinnati OH 45246

KILGORE, JERRY WALTER, lawyer, former state attorney general; b. Kingsport, Tenn., Aug. 23, 1961; m. Marty Kilgore; children: Klarke, Kelsey. BA, U. Va., 1983; JD, Coll. William & Mary, 1986. Prin. Richmond law firm Sands Anderson Marks & Miller; asst. Commonwealth atty. Scott County; asst. U.S. atty. (We. dist.) W. Va. US Dept. Justice, 1988—92; sec. pub. safety State of Va., Richmond, 1994—97, atty. gen., 2002—05; ptnr. Williams Mullen, Richmond, 2005—. Republican. Office: Williams Mullen Two James Ctr 1021 E Cary St PO Box 1320 Richmond VA 23218 E-mail: jkilgore@williamsmullen.com.

KILGOUR, DAVID, Canadian member parliament; b. Winnipeg, Man., Can., Feb. 18, 1941; s. David Eckford and Mary Sophia (Russell) K.; m. Laura Mae Scott, June 22, 1974; children: Margot, Eileen, David, Hilary. Bar: B.C., 1967, Man. 1970, Alta. 1972. Asst. city prosecutor, Vancouver, B.C., Canada, 1967-68; adv. counsel Dept. Justice, Ottawa, 1968-69; chief crown atty. Dauphin Judicial Dist., Man., 1971-72; a sr. agt. Alta. Gen. and Constl. Adv., 1972-79; mem. House of Commons, 1979—; apptd. parliament sec. to pres. of privy coun., 1979; opposition critic for crime prevention, 1981-83; dep. critic external affairs, 1983-84; parliament sec. to min. external rels., 1984—85; parliament sec. to min. Indian affairs and no. devel., 1985—86; parliament sec. to min. transport, 1986—87; dep. speaker, chmn. coms. whole house House of Commons, Ottawa, Ont., Can., 1994-97; sec. state Latin America & Africa, 1997—2002, Asia-Pacific, 2002—03. Author: Uneasy Patriots: Western Canadians in Confederation, 1988, Inside Outer Canada, 1990, Betrayal: The Spy Canada Abandoned, 1994. Chair Canadian chpt. Internat. Com. for a Free Vietnam, subcom. Human Rights and Devel., Canadian chpt. PGA. Mem. Can. Bar Assn. Office: Wellington St Ottawa ON K1A 0A6 Canada E-mail: kilgour@parl.gc.ca.

KILGUS, EDWARD CHIP, singer, actor, writer, poet; b. Flushing, NY, Jan. 18, 1947; s. Edward Henry and Dorothy Keefanora (Vita) Kilgus. Student, St. Bonaventure U., 1964—66; BA in English, Adelphi U., 1970. Chief judge Jesters Open Vocal Competition, Ft. Lauderdale, Fla., 2003, Hurricane Lounge, Dania Beach, Fla., 2005, singing contests, 2005; judge Sea Escape Escape to Stardom, Ft. Lauderdale, 2003; chief judge Porters Pl. Vocal Competition, Ft. Lauderdale, 2004—05; chief judge jesters judge, talent scout Real Rock Entertainment, 2006—; chief judge Funky Nutz, Boca Raton, Fla., 2007; mem. judges panel, talent scout Real Rock ENT; talent scout, vocal talent evaluator Starmakers Internat. Michael Hayles, 2005—06. Author: The School Bus of Our Dreams, 1987, It's a Long Walk to Hollywood, 1991, Cloth Moth: A Lifes Love, 2007, numerous poems, Run The Floor, 2007; actor: (made for TV movie) Black Magic, Miami Vice, 1987, Oklahoma, 1962, Flower Drum Song, 1963, South Pacific, 1964, Little Mary Sunshine, The Sound of Music, 1988, 2x5, 1989; (TV series) South Beach, 2006. Vol. hurricane emergency team, Dade County, 1987; vol. Hurricane Andrew shelter ARC, Broward County; headliner, emcee, host Tommy D's Am. Eatery Nat. Spinal Chord Found., 2005—; headliner, emcee, host Sinker benefit March of Dimes benefit, 2007; judge competitions Star Search, 2006; mem. Rep. Nat. Com., 1987—, Fla. Rep. Com., 2004; alt. precinct capt. Broward Rep. Exec. Com., Ft. Lauderdale, 1987—92; team leader Bush-Cheney campaign, Ft. Lauderdale, 2003—04, precinct capt., grass roots team leader, 2004; vol. presdl. visits Ft. Lauderdale and Coral Gables, Fla., 2004; precinct capt. Congressman E. Clay Shaw Re-election Campaign, 2006, Charlie Crist for Gov., Ft. Lauderdale, 2006. Sgt. USAR, 1969—75. Named Vol. of Week, E. Clay Shaw Re-Election Campaign, 2006; named one of Outstanding Poets, Nat. Libr. Poetry, 1994, Best New Poets, 1995; recipient medal, NY Music Festival Assn., 1959, 22 Hon. Mention awards, World of Poetry, 1985—93, Golden Poet award, 1986—92, Hon. Mention, Iliad Lit. Awards Program, 2001—03, Editor's Choice Outstanding Achievement in Poetry award (6), Internat. Libr. Poetry, 2004—06, Editor's Choice Outstanding Achievement in Poetry award, 2007. Mem.: KC (coun., 4th degree knight, 3 yr. trustee coun. 2007—, 3d degree 2005, 3d Degree award 2006, 4th degree Sir Knight 2006), ASCAP (assoc.), Am. Numis. Assn. Roman Catholic. Avocation: numismatics.

KILIBARDA, ZORAN, geologist, educator; b. Niksic, Serbia-Montenegro, July 24, 1957; s. Gojko and Natalija Kilibarda; m. Vesna Milovic, Jan. 31, 1982; children: Ivana, Nikola. PhD, U. Nebr., Lincoln, 1994. Asst. prof. Winona State U., Minn., 2001—02, Ctrl. Mich. U., Mount Pleasant, Mich., 2002—03, Ind. U. NW, Gary, Ind., 2003—. Mem.: US Chess Orgn., Geol. Soc. Am. Home: 2702 McCord Rd Valparaiso IN 46383 Office: Indiana Univ Northwest 3400 Broadway Gary IN 46408 Home Phone: 219-476-0412; Office Phone: 219-980-6753. Office Fax: 219-980-6673. Business E-Mail: zkilibar@iun.edu.

KILIK, JON, film producer; b. Milburn, NJ, Dec. 26, 1956; Prodr. films including: Do the Right Thing, 1989, Mo' Better Blues, 1990, Jungle Fever, 1991, Fathers and Sons, 1992, (with Monty Ross and Preston Holmes) Malcolm X, 1992, (with Robert De Niro and Jane Rosenthal) A Bronx Tale, 1993, Crooklyn, 1994, (with Scott Bushnell) Pret-A-Porter, 1994, (with Martin Scorsese and Spike Lee) Clockers, 1995, (with Tim

Robbins and Rudd Simmons) Dead Man Walking, 1995, Basquiat, 1996, Cradle Will Rock, 1999, Pollack, 2000, Bamboozled, 2000, 25th Hour, 2002, Alexander, 2004, Broken Flowers, 2005, Inside Man, 2006. Office: 230 Central Park W New York NY 10024-6029

KILINC-BALCI, FATMA SELCEN, textile engineer, researcher; d. Mehmet Kilinc; m. Hakan Balci. PhD, Auburn U., Ala., 2004. Grad. rsch. asst. Auburn U., 2000—04; post doctoral rsch. assoc. Aubrun U., 2004—. Reviewer profl. jours. Bd. dirs. adv. com. Office Multicultural Affairs, Auburn, 2006—07. Recipient Presentation award, Auburn U., 2002, Outstanding Grad. Student award, Auburn U. Polymer and Fiber Eng. Dept., 2003, 2004, Presentation award, Auburn U. Textile Engring. Dept., 2003, 2004, Nat. Textile Ctr., 2004; fellow, Auburn U., 2000—04; grantee, Am. Textile Chemists and Colorists, 2003. Mem.: SWE (assoc.). Achievements include patents pending for Elmogahzy-Kilinc fabric handle method; development of comfort model; research in protective clothing comfort; composite fiber development using green chemicals; fabric handle modeling.

KILKEARY, KEVIN P., hospitality executive; Hotel gen. mgr., resident mgr., dir. sales & marketing Interstate Hotels Corp., regional v.p. ops., Northeast region, corp. v.p. sales & marketing, North Am., pres., COO, Crossroads Hospitality Co., LLC Pitts., 1972—99, pres., COO, pres. Office: Prospera Hospitality Foster Plaza 9 750 Holiday Dr Pittsburgh PA 15220 Office Phone: 412-921-6200. Office Fax: 412-921-5158.

KILLDEER, JOHN See MAYHAR, ARDATH

KILLE, JOHN WILLIAM, JR., toxicology and biomedical product consultant; b. Tampa, Fla., June 17, 1943; s. John William and Myrtle Kille; m. Elaine Anderson; children: Amy, Lindsey, Thomas; m. Camille Ragazzo, Sept. 22, 1991; 1 stepchild, Richard. AB, Lafayette Coll., 1965; MS, Villanova U., 1968; PhD, U. Va., 1972. Diplomate Am. Bd. Toxicology. NIH rsch. trainee Worcester Found. for Exptl. Biology, 1970-72; Lalor rsch. fellow Cambridge (Eng.) U., 1972-73; lectr., rschr. Northwestern U., Evanston, Ill., 1974-78; group leader for drug safety Ortho Pharm. Co. divsn. Johnson & Johnson, Raritan, NJ, 1978-88; assoc. dir. product safety and regulatory affairs McNeil Splty. Products Co. divsn. Johnson & Johnson, New Brunswick, NJ, 1988-93; sr. toxicologist Cantox, Inc., Bridgewater, NJ, 1994-96; prin. J.W. Kille Assocs., Stanton, NJ, 1996—. Cons. to various pharm., food and biotech. cos. and legal firms, 1994—96; cons. Johnson & Johnson, Emisphere Techs., Valera Pharm., Helicon Therapeutics, Norgine Internat. Ltd. (U.K.), various other domestic and internat. projects, Canada, Mexico, Australia, England, 1996—; advisor Office Tech. Assessment, U.S. Congress, 1984. Contbr. articles to sci. jours. Chmn. Family Life Edn. Com., Bloomsbury, N.J., 1985-86. Rsch. fellow Lalor Found., 1972-73, WHO, 1972-73. Mem. Am. Coll. Toxicology, Genetic Toxicology Assn., Inst. Food Technologists, Regulatory Affairs Profls. Soc., Soc. Toxicology (program com. Mid-Atlantic chpt. 1996—, chmn. edn. and pub. comms. com. 1999-2003, v.p. 2006-07, pres. 2007—), Roundtable of Toxicology Cons. (pres., 2005-06, past pres. 2007), Teratology Soc., Mid-Atlantic Reprodn. and Teratology Assn. (pres. 1986-87). Avocations: music, singing, camping, hunting, fishing. Office: PO Box 69 Stanton NJ 08885-0069 Home Phone: 908-236-6833; Office Phone: 908-236-6182. Fax: 908-236-0921. E-mail: jwkille@earthlink.net.

KILLEA, MICHAEL F., lawyer; b. 1962; BA, Washington & Lee U.; JD, Georgetown U., 1987. Bar: NY, Fla. Assoc. O'Sullivan LLP (now O'Melveny & Myers LLP), NYC, 1987—96, ptnr., 1997—99, Holland & Knight LLP, NYC, Jacksonville, Fla., 1999—2001; exec. v.p., gen. counsel Pacer Internat., Inc., Jacksonville, Fla., 2001—. Office: Pacer Internat One Independent Dr Ste 1250 Jacksonville FL 32202*

KILLEBREW, ELLEN JANE (MRS. EDWARD S. GRAVES), cardiologist, educator; b. Tiffin, Ohio, Oct. 8, 1937; d. Joseph Arthur and Stephanie (Beriont) K.; m. Edward S. Graves, Sept. 12, 1970. BS in Biology, Bucknell U., Lewisburg, Pa., 1959; MD, NJ Coll. Medicine, 1965. Diplomate in cardiovasc. disease Am. Bd. Internal Medicine. Intern U. Colo., 1965-66, resident, 1966-68; cardiology fellow Pacific Med. Ctr., San Francisco, 1968-70; dir. coronary care Permanente Med. Group, Richmond, Calif., 1970-83; asst. prof. U. Calif. Med. Ctr., San Francisco, 1970-83, assoc. prof., 1983-93; clin. prof. medicine U. Calif., San Francisco, 1992—, mem. admissions panel, 1998—. Admissions panel joint med. program U. Calif. San Francisco/U. Calif. Berkeley, 1998—; expert med. reviewer Calif. Med. Br., 1999, Bd. of Med. Examiners Calif., 1999—. Contbr. chapters to books. Contbr. Resolution Firm Calif. State Assmebly, 2005. Recipient Physician's Recognition award continuing med. edn., Lowell Beal award Permante Med. Group/House Staff Assn., 1992, Commendation State Assembly of Calif. for Contbr to Women and Heart Disease, 2005; Robert C. Kirkwood Meml. scholar in cardiology, 1970. Fellow ACP, Am. Coll. Cardiology; mem. Fedn. Clin. Rsch., Am. Heart Assn. (rsch. chmn. Contra Costa chpt. 1975—, v.p. 1980, pres. chpt. 1981-82, chmn. CPR com. Alameda chpt. 1984, pres. Oakland Piedmont br. 1995—, bd. dirs. western affiliate). Home: 30 Redding Ct Belvedere Tiburon CA 94920-1318 Office: 280 W Macarthur Blvd Oakland CA 94611-5642 also: 901 Nevin Ave Richmond CA 94801-3143 Business E-Mail: ellen.killebrew@kp.org.

KILLEBREW, FLAVIUS CHARLES, academic administrator, biology professor; b. Canadian, Tex., Apr. 2, 1949; s. Wilbur N. and Nellie M. (Davidson) K.; m. Kathy C. Bartley, Dec. 23, 1981; 1 child, Arian. BS in Biology, West Tex. State Univ., 1971; MS in Biology, West Tex. State U., 1972; PhD in Zoology, U. Ark., 1976. Asst. prof. biology West Tex. A&M U., Canyon, 1976-81, assoc. prof., 1981-88, prof., 1988—, grad. dir., 1988-91, grad. dean, 1991-94, interim provost, v.p. for acad. affairs, 1994—95, provost, v.p. for acad. affairs, 1995—2004; pres. Texas A&M U., Corpus Christi, 2005—. Adj. prof. Tex. A&M U., College Station, 1990—. Sponsor T-Anchor 4-H, Canyon, 1985-90, WT Speakers Bur., Canyon, 1986—. Grantee U.S. Army Corps Engrs, 1978, Killgore Rsch. Ctr., 1989-91 Mem. Herpetologists League, Soc. for Study of Amphibians, Am. Soc. Ichthyologists, Assn. Tex. Grad. Schs. (pres. 1993), Coun. Pub. Univ. Chief Acad. Officers (pres. 1999), Masons, Tri Bet, Alpha Chi. Methodist. Office: Texas A&M U 6300 Ocean Dr Corpus Christi TX 78412-5503 Office Phone: 361-825-2621.

KILLEEN, MICHAEL JOHN, lawyer; b. Washington, Oct. 5, 1949; s. James Robert and Georgia Winston (Hartwell) K.; m. Therese Ann Goeden, Oct. 6, 1984; children: John Patrick, Katherine Therese, Mary Clare, James Philip. BA, Gonzaga U., 1971, JD magna cum laude, 1977. Bar: Wash. 1977, U.S. Dist. Ct. (we. dist.) Wash. 1979, U.S. Ct. Appeals (9th cir.) 1984, U.S. Supreme Ct. 1990. Jud. clk. Wash. State Ct. Appeals, Tacoma, 1977—79; assoc. Davis Wright Tremaine LLP, Seattle, 1979—85, ptnr., 1985—. Bd. dirs. Seattle Goodwill, 1987—, sec., 1998-2002. Author: Guide to Strike Planning, 1985, Newsroom Legal Guidebook, 1996, Employment in Washington, 1984—. Mem. bd. advisors Gonzaga Law Sch., Spokane, Wash., 1988—, pres., 1992-96. Recipient Freedom's Light award Wash. Newspaper Pub. Assn., 1999, Disting. Alumni award Gonzaga U., 2002. Mem. ABA, Wash. State Bar Assn., King County Bar Assn. (treas. 1987-89, Pres. award 1989). Republican. Roman Catholic. Office Phone: 206-622-3150. Business E-Mail: mikekilleen@dwt.com.

KILLEEN, TIMOTHY LAURENCE, aerospace scientist, science administrator; b. Cardiff, Wales, Jan. 21, 1952; came to US, 1978; married. BS with 1st class honors in Physics, Univ. Coll., London, 1972, PhD in Atomic and Molecular Physics, 1975. Rsch. asst. Univ. Coll., London, 1975—78; postdoctoral scholar U. Mich., Ann Arbor, 1978-79, asst. rsch. scientist, 1979-84, assoc. rsch. scientist, 1984-87, assoc. prof. atmospheric, oceanic and space scis., 1987-90, prof. atmospheric, oceanic and space scis., 1990-2000, dir. Space Physics Rsch. Lab., 1993—98, assoc. v.p. rsch., 1997—2000; dir. Nat. Ctr. Atmospheric Rsch., Boulder, Colo., 2000—, sr. scientist high altitude obs., 2000—. Vis. scientist Nat. Ctr. Atmospheric Rsch., 1983, 85, 86, 87 summers, affiliate scientist, 1988-92; adj. prof. U. Mich., 2000-; cons. Rockwell Internat., Westinghouse GE Corp, 1989-92, PRC, Inc., NASA Hdqs., NSF, Taiwanese Space Prog.; referee for: Jour. Geophys. Rsch., Geophys. Rsch. Letters, NASA proposals, Applied Optics, Space Sci. Instrumentation, Phys. Scripta, Annales Geophysicae, Planetary and Space Scis, Radio Sci., AFOSR proposals, NSCF proposals, Cambridge U. Press, Am. Meteorol. Soc., NRC Can.; co-dir. Rsch. Experiences for Undergraduates Site at U. Mich., 1986; mem. US Nat. Com. Solar Terrestrial Energy Prog., prog. rev. com. for NSF CFS and UAF programs, 1989, 90; chmn. prog. rev. com. for the NSF Aeronomy prog., 1986-88, 89; mem. COSPAR Commn. C task force on the CIRA-86 model atmosphere, vice chmn. COSPAR Commn. C.; chmn. NSF CEDAR prog. sci. steering com., 1988-91; prin. investigator on projects for NASA, NSF, Phillip's Lab.; presenter in field. Contbr. articles to profl. jours.; assoc. editor Jour. Geophys. Rsch. (Space Physics), 1987-92; editor-in-chief Jour. Atmospheric and Solar-Terrestrial Physics 1997; presenter papers at over 200 sci. meetings, confs., symposiums. Mem. U. Mich. Civil Liberties Bd., 1990-93, chmn. 1992-93; mem. U. Mich. faculty grievance bd. Mem. AAAS (sci. prog. com., 2003-), AAUP, NAE, Am. Geophys. Union (solar-planetary rels. exec. com., meetings com., fed. budget rev. com., pub. affairs com., chmn. solar-planetary rels. prog. com. fall 1987; convenor and presider for spl. sci. sessions at nat. meetings, convenor of Chapman conf. on the lower thermosphere and upper mesosphere 1992, nominations com. 2002-, pres-elect 2004, pres. 2006-), Inst. Physics, Eng., Am. Meteorol. Soc. Office: Nat Ctr Atmospheric Rsch PO Box 3000 Boulder CO 80307-3000 Office Phone: 303-497-1111. E-mail: kileen@ucar.edu.*

KILLEFER, CAMPBELL, lawyer; b. Hermosa Beach, Calif., Mar. 14, 1950; s. Peter and Helen (Campbell) K.; m. Madeline G. Killefer, May 28, 1978; children: Harrison, Dana. BA, Stanford U., Calif., 1972; JD, U. Calif., San Francisco, 1977. Bar: Calif. 1977, DC 1979. Adminstrv. asst. Office of Coastal Zone Mgmt., NOAA U.S. Dept. of Commerce, Washington, 1972-73; planner Calif. Coastal Zone Conservation Commn., San Francisco, 1973-74; assoc. Fulbright & Jaworski, Washington, 1977-82; ptnr. Shaw, Pittman, Potts & Trowbridge, Washington, 1982—2000, Venable LLP, Washington, 2000—. Editor-in-chief, Hastings Constl. Law Quarterly, 1976-77; contbr. numerous articles to profl. jours. Office: Venable LLP 575 Seventh St NW Washington DC 20004 Office Phone: 202-344-8196. Office Fax: 202-344-8300. Business E-Mail: ckillefer@venable.com.

KILLENBERG, GEORGE ANDREW, publishing executive, consultant, retired editor; b. St. Clair County, Ill., Mar. 30, 1917; s. George W. and Lavina (Ruhl) K.; m. Therese Murphy, June 3, 1943; children: George M., Mary K. Riley, John A., Terry M. Hatcher, Susan M. McGinn. BS, St. Louis U., 1954, MA, 1958. Engaged in pub. rels., 1935-41; mem. staff St. Louis Globe-Democrat, 1941—; city editor St. Louis Globe-Dem., 1956-66, mng. editor, 1966-79, exec. editor, 1979-84. Past chmn. Mid-Am. Press Inst. Bd. dirs. Boys Town Mo., 1960-88. With AUS, 1942-46. Mem. Press Club (St. Louis, pres. 1964), Sigma Delta Chi. Roman Catholic. Home: 3042 Hatherly Dr Saint Louis MO 63121-4534 Personal E-mail: gkillenber@aol.com.

KILLGORE, ANDREW IVY, former ambassador; b. Greensboro, Ala., Nov. 7, 1919; s. Robert Morris and Mary Elmae (Wimberly) K.; m. Marjorie Davis Nicholls; children: Elizabeth Nicholls Krieger, Andrew Nicholls, Jane G., Roberta K. McInerney. BS, Livingston U., 1943; JD, U. Ala., 1949. Bar: Ala. bar. Selector-analyst U.S. Displaced Persons Commn., 1949-50, displaced populations officer Frankfurt, Fed. Republic Germany, 1950-51; visa officer Am. Embassy, London, 1951-53; evaluator Dept. State, 1953-55, internat. relations officer, 1961-62; polit. officer Beirut, 1956-57; consul Jerusalem, 1957-59; polit. officer Amman, Jordan, 1959-61; officer-in-charge Iraq-Jordan affairs, 1962-65; pub. affairs officer USIS, Baghdad, Iraq, 1965-67; polit. officer Dacca, East Pakistan (now Bangladesh), 1967-70; polit.-econ. officer Arab Region North Directorate, 1970-72; counselor polit. affairs Tehran, Iran, 1972-74; charge d'affaires Manama, Bahrain, 1974; dep. chief mission Wellington, N.Z., 1974-77; amb. to Qatar Doha, 1977-80; ret., 1980. Pub. Washington Report on Middle East Affairs. Former pres. Am. sect. Musa Al-Alami of Jericho Found.; pres. Am. Ednl. Trust. Lt. (j.g.) USN, 1943-46. Recipient Cert. of Appreciation, Bd. Dirs. of Jerusalem Fund for Edn. and Cmty. Devel., 1995, Fgn. Svc. Cup, 1996. Mem.: Army and Navy, Cosmos. Office: 1904 18th St NW Washington DC 20009-7738 Office Phone: 202-939-6050.

KILLIAN, EDWARD JAMES, retired pediatrician; b. Bklyn., Nov. 14, 1927; s. Edward James and Helen Marie K.; m. Henriette Marian Killian, 1957; children: Christopher Edward, Bryan Alfred, Paul Matthew. BS, St. John's Coll., 1950; MD, SUNY, 1954. Diplomat Am. Bd. Pediatrics, Nat. Bd. Med. Examiners; lic. physician, N.Y. Intern Bklyn. Hosp., 1954-55, resident, 1955-57, attending pediatrician, 1959-61, Southside Hosp., Bayshore, NY, 1961-93, Good Samaritan Hosp., West Islip, NY, 1961-93, ret., 1994. Capt. USAF Med. Corps, 1957-59. Fellow Am. Acad. Pediatrics; mem. AMA, Med. Soc. State N.Y. (life), Suffolk County Med. Soc. (life), Suffolk Pediatric Soc. (emeritus). Avocations: swimming, hiking, gardening. Home: PO Box 432 English Mills Way Woodstock VT 05091

KILLIAN, GEORGE ERNEST, retired educational association administrator; b. Valley Stream, NY, Apr. 6, 1924; s. George and Reina (Moeller) K.; m. Janice E. Bachert, May 26, 1951 (dec.); children: Susan E., Sandra J.; m. Marilyn R. Killian, Sept. 1, 1984 BS in Edn., Ohio No. U., 1949; EdM, U. Buffalo, 1954; PhD in Phys. Scis., Ohio Northern U., 1989; PhD (hon.), U.S. Sports Acad., 1998, Yeungam U., Korea, 2003, Sch. Physical Edn., Wroclaw, Poland, 2006. Tchr.-coach Wharton (Ohio) High Sch., 1949-51; insp. USN, Buffalo, 1951-54; dir. athletics Erie County (N.Y.) Tech. Inst., Buffalo, 1954-69, asst. prof. health, phys. edn., recreation, 1954-60, asso. prof., 1960-62, prof., 1962-69; exec. dir. Nat. Jr. Coll. Athletic Assn., Colorado Springs, Colo., 1969—2005; ret., 2005. Editor: Juco Rev., 1960—. Served with AUS, 1943-45. Recipient Bd. Trustees award Hudson Valley C. of C., 1969, Erie County Tech. Inst., 1969, Service award Ohio No. U. Alumni, 1972, Service award Lysle Rishel Post, Am. Legion, 1982; named to Ohio No. U. Hall of Fame, 1979, Olympic Order, IOC, 1996, Women's Basketball Hall of Fame, 2000. Mem. Internat. Fedn. U. Students (pres.), U.S. Olympic Com. (dir.), Internat. Olympic Com., Am. Legion, Internat. Basketball Fedn. (pres. 1990-98), Internat. U. Sports Fedn. (1st v.p. 1995, pres. 2000), Masons, Rotary, Phi Delta Kappa, Delta Sigma Phi. Home: 325 Rangely Dr Colorado Springs CO 80921-2655 Personal E-mail: gkillian7@adelphia.net.

KILLIAN, JOHN F., telecommunications industry executive; married; 2 children. BS magna cum laude, Providence Coll., 1977; M, Bentley Coll. CPA Peat, Marwick, Mitchell & Co., Providence; dist. mgr. budgets New Eng. Tel.; dist. mgr. fin. assurance AT&T, 1981—83; gen. mgr. ops. Ea. Mass., 1983—85; divsn. mgr. market planning NYNEX, 1985—87; pres. of RI NYNEX New Eng., 1987—91, v.p. of Mass.; pres., CEO NYNEX CableComms Ltd., 1995; grp. pres. Internat. Telecom. Bell Atlantic, 1997, v.p. investor rels.; sr. v.p. customer ops. Nat. Ops. Grp. Verizon Comm., 2000, sr. v.p., CFO Domestic Telecom. Grp., pres. Verizon Bus. Trustee Coll. New Rochelle, Providence Coll., Nat. Urban League. Office: Verizon Comm 140 West St New York NY 10007

KILLIAN, LAWRENCE HARDING, II, (LARRY H. KILLIAN), sculptor; b. San Antonio, May 6, 1943; s. Lawrence Harding and Dorothy Louise (Wright) K.; m. Beverly Gayle Schlueder, Dec. 21, 1963 (div. 1979); children: Lawrence Harding III, Michael Ray; m. Janice Kay Nelson, June 18, 1981. Student, Tex. A&M, 1961; BS in Indsl. Arts, Southwest Tex. State, 1971, postgrad., 1971-72, RIT Coll., 1981. Instr., job corps. and trade schs., Tex., 1971-75; owner of metal fabrication and welding bus. Austin, Tex., 1975-81; salesperson Hart Graphics, Austin (Tex.) Times Printing, Random Lake, Wis., 1982-93; freelance metal sculptor Gainesville, Tex., 1991—2002, Lubbock area, 2002—. Exhibitions include World Trade Ctr., Dallas. With Leadership Gainesville, 1999. Southwest Tex. State U. scholar, 1970. Mem.: Rotary, Lions (pres. 1993). Avocations: antiques, real estate, travel, online trading. E-mail: killian@poka.com.

KILLIAN, LEWIS MARTIN, sociology educator; b. Darien, Ga., Feb. 15, 1919; s. Lewis Martin and Edith (Robinson) K.; m. Katharine Newbold Goold, Apr. 11, 1942; children: Katharine Newbold, Lewis Martin, John Calhoun. AB, U. Ga., 1940, MA, 1941; PhD, U. Chgo., 1949. Asst. prof. sociology U. Okla., 1949-52; asso. prof. sociology Fla. State U., 1952-57, prof., 1957-68, chmn. dept. sociology, 1966-68; prof., head dept. sociology U. Conn., 1968-69; prof. U. Mass., Amherst, 1969-84, prof. emeritus, 1984—. Vis. prof. UCLA, 1965-66, U. Hawaii, 1972; vis. lectr. Thames Poly., London, 1980-81; adj. prof. U. West Fla., 1986—2000; Disting. vis. prof. U. Del., 1986. Author: (with Ralph H. Turner) Collective Behavior, 1957, 3d rev. edit., 1987, (with Charles M. Grigg) Racial Crisis in America, 1963, The Impossible Revolution, 1968, White Southerners, 1970, rev. edit., 1985, The Impossible Revolution: Phase II, 1974, Black and White: Reflections of a White Southern Sociologist, 1994. Cons. com. disaster studies NRC, 1952-57, cons. to atty. gen. of Fla., 1954-55; chmn. human rights advocacy com., dist. 1, State of Fla., 1991-93, 2000-02; mem. Fla. Statewide Human Rights Advocacy Com., 1994-2000; mem. Fla. Local Advocy Coun., 2002-04. Col. USAR, ret. Decorated Legion of Merit; Guggenheim fellow, 1975—76. Mem. Am. Sociol. Assn., So. Sociol. Soc. (pres. 1989-90), Phi Beta Kappa, Omicron Delta Kappa, Kappa Alpha, Phi Kappa Phi. Home: 10100 Hillview Rd Apt 1108 Pensacola FL 32514-5446 E-mail: killiansr@bellsouth.net.

KILLIAN, RICHARD M., library director; b. Buffalo, Jan. 13, 1942; m. Nancy Killian; children from previous marriage: Tessa, Lee Ann. BA, SUNY, Buffalo, 1964; MA, Western Mich. U., 1965; grad. advanced mgmt. library adminstrn., Miami U., Oxford, Ohio, 1981; grad. library adminstrn. devel. program, U. Md., 1985. Various positions Buffalo and Erie County Pub. Libraries, 1963-74, asst. dep. dir., personnel officer, 1979-80; dir. Town of Tonawanda (N.Y.) Pub. Library, 1974-78; asst. city librarian, dir. pub. svcs. Denver Pub. Library, 1978-79; exec. dir. Nioga Library System, Buffalo, 1980-87; library dir. Sacramento (Calif.) Pub. Library, 1987—. Mem. ALA, Calif. Library Assn., Rotary. Office: Sacramento Pub Libr Adminstrn Ctr 828 I St Sacramento CA 95814-2589 Home: PO Box 342 The Sea Ranch CA 95497-0342

KILLIAN, ROBERT KENNETH, JR., judge, lawyer; b. Hartford, Conn., Jan. 29, 1947; s. Robert Kenneth Sr. and Evelyn (Farnan) K.; m. Candace Korper, Oct. 6, 1979; children: Virginia, Carolyn. BA, Union U., 1969; JD, Georgetown U., 1972. Bar: Conn. 1972, U.S. Ct. Appeals (2nd cir.) 1973, D.C. 1974, U.S. Ct. Appeals (D.C. cir.) 1974. Bur. chief Sta. WTIC-AM-FM-TV, Washington, 1969-72; spl. asst. Senator Abe Ribicoff, Washington, 1972-73; ptnr. Gould, Killian, Wynne et al, Hartford, Conn., 1972—84; judge Conn. Probate Ct., 1984—; ptnr. Killian & Donohue, 1985—98, Killian Donohue & Shipman LLC, 1998—2001, Killian Donohue & Jaff LLC, 2001—05, Killian & Donohue, LLC, 2005—. Spl. counsel Lt. Gov. Conn., Hartford, 1974-78; mem. exec. com. Conn. Probate Assembly, 1987—, pres.-judge, 1997-99; mem. investment adv. coun. State of Conn., 1995-99; mem. Jud. Commn. on Attys.' Ethics, 1990-2004. Author: Basic Probate in Connecticut, 1990, 11th edit., 2006. Regent, U. Hartford; trustee Hartt Sch. Music; dir. Conn. chpt. March of Dimes, 1986—; bd. dirs. Yeats Drama Found., 1989—; trustee Conn. Children's Trust Fund, 2004—, Child HEalth Devel. Inst., 2004—; incorporator St. Francis Hosp. and Med. Ctr. Recipient 1st Pl. award New England Conv. Magicians, 1965; named Conn.'s Outstanding Probate Judge, Conn. Probate Assembly, 1990. Mem. ABA, ATLA, Nat. Coll. Juvenile and Family Ct. Judges, Nat. Conf. Probate Judges, Conn. Bar Assn., Conn. Trial Lawyers Assn., Psychic Entertainer's Assn. (treas. 2006—), Internat. Brotherhood Magicians, Soc. Am. Magicians (chmn. nat. conv. 1977). Democrat. Roman Catholic. Home: 83 Bloomfield Ave Hartford CT 06105-1007 Office: Killian & Donohue LLC 363 Main St Hartford CT 06106-1885 Office Phone: 860-560-1977. Business E-Mail: bob@kdjlaw.com.

KILLIAN, WILLIAM PAUL, manufacturing executive; b. Sidney, Ohio, Apr. 26, 1935; s. Ray and Erie K.; m. Beverly Ann Buchanan, Sept. 7, 1957; children: William, Katherine, Michael B in Chem. Engring. with honors, Ga. Inst. Tech., 1957; M in Engring. Adminstrn. with honors, U. Utah, 1968. Chem. engr. Esso, Baton Rouge, 1957—58; mgr. research and devel. mfg. engring., then plant mgr. Thiokol Corp., Brigham City, Utah, 1958—68; mgr. corp. project mgmt. Masonite Corp., Chgo., 1968—70, mgr. new bus. ventures, 1970—73; mgr. strategic planning, chem. and metall. group Gen. Electric Co., Pittsfield, Mass. and Columbus, Ohio, 1973—77; v.p. corp. planning and devel. Hoover Universal Inc., Ann Arbor, Mich., 1977—85; v.p. corp. devel. Johnson Controls Inc., Milw., 1985—87, v.p. corp. devel. and strategy, 1987—2000. Bd. dirs., vice chmn. Cleaver-Brooks, Inc., Milw.; bd. dirs. RBC Bearing Corp. (NASDQ Roll), Oxford, Conn., Premix Inc., North Kingsville, Ohio; chmn., bd. advisors iNUX, Inc., Tampa. Bd. advisors Salvation Army, Sarasota; bd. dirs. All Faiths Food Bank, Sarasota, Fla. Mem.: Coun. Strategy Planning & Devel., Strategic Leadership Forum, Mfrs. Alliance (past chmn.), Coun. Strategic Planning Execs. of Conf. Bd. (past chmn.), Assn. for Corp. Growth Internat. (past nat. pres., past pres. Wis. chpt.), Mensa Soc, Koseme Soc., Tau Beta Pi, Phi Eta Sigma, Pi Delta Epsilon, Phi Kappa Phi, Omicron Delta Kappa. Personal E-mail: wkillian@comcast.net.

KILLINGER, CLAYTON, energy executive; B in Acctg., U. Tex., San Antonio. CPA. Ptnr. Arthur Andersen LLP, San Antonio; asst. contr. Valero Energy Corp., San Antonio, 2001—03, v.p., contr., 2003—. Office: Valero Energy Corpn PO Box 696000 San Antonio TX 78269-6000

KILLINGER, KERRY KENT, bank executive; b. Des Moines, June 6, 1949; m. Debbie Roush. BBA, U. Iowa, 1970, MBA, 1971. Exec. v.p. Murphey Favre, Inc., Spokane, 1976-82; exec. v.p. fin. mgmt., investor rels., corp. mktg. Wash. Mutual, Seattle, 1983-86; sr. exec. v.p., 1986-88; pres. Wash. Mutual Savs. Bank, Seattle, 1988—2005, CEO, 1990—2005, chmn. bd., 1991—2005; chmn., CEO Washington Mutual, Inc., Seattle, 2005—. Mem. Thrift Inst. Adv. Coun. to Fed. Res. bd., 1992—94, NY Stock Exch. Listed Co. Adv. Com.; bd. dirs. Wash. Savs. League, Wash. Fin. League, Green Diamond Resource Co., Safeco Corp., 2003—. Bd. dirs. Fed. Home Loan Bank of Seattle, 1995—, Seattle Repertory Theatre, 1990—, Washington Roundtable, 1990—, Downtown Seattle Assn., 1991, Leadership Tomorrow, Seattle Found., 1992—, Com. to Encourage Corp. Philanthropy; mem. Alliance for Edn., 1992—, chair, 1994-96, co-chmn. AIDS Walk-a-thon, Seattle, 1990; chair Partnership for Learning, 1997. Fellow Life Mgmt. Inst.; mem. Soc. Fin. Analysts, Greater Seattle C. of C. (bd. dirs. 1992—), Rotary. Office: Washington Mutual Inc Washington Mutual Tower 1201 Third Ave Seattle WA 98101*

KILLIP, THOMAS, cardiologist; AB, Swarthmore Coll., 1948; MD, Cornell U., 1952. Diplomate in internal medicine and cardiovasc. disease

Am. Bd. Internal Medicine. Med. intern Strong Meml. Hosp., 1952—53; resident in medicine N.Y. Hosp., NYC, 1953—58, resident in medicine and cardiology, 1954—55, chief divsn. cardiology, 1961—74; rsch. fellow Karolinska Inst., Stockholm, 1960—61; Harriman prof. medicine Cornell U., 1968—74; chmn. dept. medicine Evanston (Ill.) Hosp., 1974—79; prof. medicine, assoc. dean Northwestern Med. Sch., Chgo., 1974—79; chmn. dept. medicine Henry Ford Hosp., Detroit, 1979—84; prof. medicine U. Mich.; attending physician Beth Israel Med. Ctr., NYC, 1984—86, exec. v.p. med. affairs, 1984—98, interim pres. and CEO, 2002—05; dir. Heart Inst. Continuum Health Ptnrs., Inc., 1998—2002. Prof. medicine Albert Einstein Coll. Medicine. Office: Beth Israel Med Ctr First Ave at 16th St New York NY 10003 Office Phone: 212-420-4010. Fax: 212-420-4498. Business E-Mail: tkillip@chpnet.org.

KILLORAN, THOMAS M., mathematics professor, department chairman; b. Syracuse, NY, Dec. 27, 1966; s. Neil E. and Shirley A. Killoran; m. Doreen P. Killoran, Dec. 9, 1994; children: Shawn M. Fahey, Samantha M. BS, SUNY, Cortland, 1989; MS, Syracuse U., NY, 1993. Computer tchr. Bishop Grimes Jr./Sr. H.S., East Syracuse, NY, 1994—95; 8th grade math tchr. Waianae (Hawaii) Intermediate Sch., 1995—97; math tchr. South West H.S., Edgecombe, Pinetops, NC, 1997—2000; math instr. Edgecombe C.C., Tarboro, NC, 2000—. Office: Edgecombe Community College 225 Tarboro St Rocky Mount NC 27801 Home Phone: 252-446-9128; Office Phone: 252-446-0436. Office Fax: 252-985-2212. Business E-Mail: killorant@edgecombe.edu.

KILLORIN, ROBERT WARE, lawyer; b. Atlanta, Nov. 12, 1959; s. Edward W. and Virgina (Ware) K. AB cum laude, Duke U., 1980; JD, U. Ga., 1983. Bar: Ga. 1984, US Dist. Ct. (no. dist.) Ga. 1984, US Ct. Appeals (11th cir.) 1984. Ptnr. Killorin & Killorin, Atlanta, 1984—2006, Chitwood, Harley & Harnes, LLP, Atlanta, 2006—. Mem.: ATLA, State Bar Ga. (chair SCOPE com. 1986, young lawyers sect. legis. affairs com. 1989—91, instr. mock trial program 1989—), Atlanta Bar Assn., Ga. Trial Lawyers Assn., Fed. Bar Assn., 11th Cir. Hist. Soc., Mil. Order of Carabao, Nat. Speliological Soc., Nat. Assn. Underwater Instrs., Explorers Club, U. Ga. Pres.'s Club, Ga. C. of C. (govtl. affairs com.). Avocations: forestry, scuba diving. Office: Chitwood Harley & Harnes LLP 2300 Promenade II 1230 Peachtree St Atlanta GA 30309 Home Phone: 404-847-0617; Office Phone: 404-873-3900. Personal E-mail: rwk@bellsouth.net.

KILLOUGH, ALVIN LYNARD, psychology professor, consultant; b. Wash., Mar. 15, 1952; s. James Walls and Goldie Killough; m. Eryn Margaret Gee, June 12, 2005; children: Noni Michaela Gee, Alvin Lynard II. BA in Internat. Affairs, U. NC, Chapel Hill, 1974; MA in Psychology, U. NC, 1992, MA in Indsl. & Orgn. Psychology, 1992; PhD in Psychology, NC State U., Raleigh, 1999. Cert. human subjects rsch. tng. Ctr. Edn. & Rsch. Therapeutics, 2002. Sr. rschr. NC Ctrl. U., Durham, 2000—01, vis. asst. prof., 2002—04, vis. rsch. assoc. prof., 2004—05; social behavioral health scientist cons. Cultural Ecol. Sys., Durham, 2001—; asst. prof. psychology U. Minn., Crookston, 2006—. Cons. US HHS, Substance Abuse & Mental Health Svcs. Adminstrn., Rockville, Md., 2001—; cons., guest reviewer Soc. Behavioral Medicine, Milw., 2005—06, Nat. Med. Assn., DC, 2005—. Contbr. chapters to books, articles to profl. jours. Sepulcher knight Order Holy Sepulcher of Jerusalem, Greeley, Colo., 2001—07. Lt. USN, 1974—78, Norfolk, Va. Recipient Best in Tchg. award, NC Ctrl. U., 1996, 2000, Best Sci. award, Soc. Behavior Medicine, Milw., Wis., 2000, Best in Tchg. award, NC Ctrl. U., 2002—03, Best Paper award, Coll. Tchg. & Learning Conf., Orlando, Fla., 2004. Democrat. Mem. Christian Ch. Avocations: swimming, sailing, gardening. Office: Univ Minn Crookston 2900 University Ave Crookston MN 56716 Office Fax: 218-281-8250. Personal E-mail: akillough@worldnet.att.net. Business E-Mail: killo010@umn.edu.

KILLOUGH, DAVID E., lawyer; b. Camp Gordon, Ga., Jan. 30, 1955; BA, North Tex. State U., 1977; JD, Southwestern U., 1983. Bar: Calif. 1983, Tex. 2001. Ptnr., co-head Intellectual Property / Tech. Litig. Sect. Vinson & Elkins LLP, Austin, Tex. Mem.: ABA, Am. Intellectual Property Law Assn. Office: Vinson & Elkins LLP Ste 100 2801 Via Fortuna Austin TX 78746 Office Phone: 512-542-8428. E-mail: dkillough@velaw.com.

KILMAN, JAMES WILLIAM, surgeon, educator; b. Terre Haute, Ind., Jan. 22, 1931; s. Arthur and Irene (Piker) K.; m. Priscilla Margaret Jackson, June 20, 1968; children: James William, Julia Anne, Jennifer Irene. BS, Ind. State U., 1956; MD, Ind. U., 1960. Intern Ind. U. Med. Ctr., Indpls., 1960-61, resident surgery, 1961-66, asst. prof., 1966-69, assoc. prof., 1969-73; prof. surgery Ohio State U. Coll. Medicine, 1973-91, prof. surgery emeritus, 1991—; chmn. dept. thoracic surgery Children's Hosp., 1975-91; attending surgeon Univ. Hosp., Columbus, Ohio; attending staff Children's Hosp., Columbus, pres. staff, 1978; attending staff Grant Hosp., Riverside Hosp. Cons. surgeon VA Hosp., Dayton; pres. Columbus Acad. Medicine, 1977. Contbr. articles to profl. jours. Trustee Central Ohio Heart Assn., Acad. Medicine Edn. Found., Children's Hosp., 1978—. Served with USNR, 1951-55. USPHS Cardiovascular fellow, 1963-64; recipient Alumni Achievement award, Ind. State U., 1989. Fellow ACS, Am. Coll. Cardiology, Am. Acad. Pediats., Coll. Chest Physicians; mem. Columbus Surg. Soc. (hon., pres. 1974), Columbus Acad. Medicine (coun. 1971-73), Am. Surg. Assn., Soc. Univ. Surgeons, Am. Assn. Thoracic Surgery, Cen. Surg. Assn., Western Surg. Assn., Soc. Vascular Surgery, Internat. Cardiovasc. Soc., Internat. Soc. Surgeons, Chest Club, Cardiovasc. Surgery Club, City Club, Palm Aire Country Club, Faculty Club, Capital Club, Columbus Athletic Club, Pickaway County Country Club, Am. Boxer Club (bd. dirs. 2000-03, pres. 2001-03, AKC del. 2002-05), Pinnacle Club (Grove City, Ohio), Sigma Xi, Alpha Omega Alpha. Achievements include research in infant cardiopulmonary bypass and surgery for congenital heart lesions. Home: 4231 Jackson Pike Grove City OH 43123 Personal E-mail: leoline@aol.com.

KILMANN, RALPH HERMAN, business educator; b. NYC, Oct. 5, 1946; s. Martin Herbert and Lilli (Leob) Kilmann; children: Catherine Mary, Christopher Martin, Arlette Martin. BS, MS, Carnegie Mellon U., Pitts., 1970; PhD, UCLA, 1972. Instr. U. Pitts. Katz Grad. Sch. Bus., 1972, asst. prof., 1972-75, assoc. prof., 1975-79, prof., 1979—, George H. Love prof. orgn. and mgmt., 1991—2001, coord. orgnl. studies group, 1981-84, 86-89, dir. program in corp. culture, 1983—; pres. Organizational Design Cons., Pitts., 1975—; vis. scholar Calif. State U. Long Beach Coll. Bus. Adminstrn., 2002—03. Author: Social Systems Design: Normative Theory and the MAPS Design Technology, 1977, Beyond the Quick Fix: Managing Five Tracks to Organizational Success, 1984, 2d edit., 2004, Managing Beyond the Quick Fix: A Completely Integrated Program for Creating and Maintaining Organizational Success, 1989, Escaping the Quick Fix Trap: How to Make Organizational Improvements That Really Last, 1989, Workbook for Implementing the Tracks: Vols. I and II, 1991, Logistics Manual for Implementing the Tracks: Planning and Organizing Workshop Sessions, 1992, Workbook for Implementing the Tracks: Vol. III, 1993, Quantum Organizations: A New Paradigm for Achieving Organizational Success and Personal Meaning, 2001; co-author: Methodological Approaches to Social Science: Integrating Divergent Concepts and Theories, 1978, Corporate Tragedies: Product Tampering, Sabotage and Other Catastrophes, 1984, The Management of Organization Design: Vols. I and II, 1976, Producing Useful Knowledge for Organizations, 1983, Gaining Control of the Corporate Culture, 1985, Corporate Transformation: Revitalizing Organizations for a Competitive World, 1988, Making Organizations Competitive: Enhancing Networks and Relationships Across Traditional Boundaries, 1991, Managing Ego Energy: The Transformation of Personal Meaning into Organizational Success, 1994; mem. editorial bd. Jour. Mgmt., 1983-86, Acad. Mgmt. Exec., 1987-90, Jour. Organizational Change Mgmt., 1988—; developed Kilmann Insight Test, Learning Climate Questionnaire, Thomas-Kilmann Conflict-Mode Instrument, Organization Courage Assessment, MAPS Design Tech. for Social Systems Design, Kilmann-Saxton Culture-Gap Survey, Kilmann's Organizational Belief Survey; contbr. chpts. to books, articles to profl. jours. Mem. Eastern Acad. Mgmt. (treas. 1975-76, dir. 1983-86), Am. Psychol. Assn., Inst. Mgmt. Scis. (1st prize Nat. Coll. Planning competition 1976), Beta Gamma Sigma, Sigma Xi. *Some live only for themselves, some sacrifice their lives for others. The space between is enjoying one's life while contributing to society. No one should have the full responsibility for saving the world, nor the complete freedom to ignore the future.*

KILMARK, ROBERT MARTIN, retired lab administrator; b. Coloma, Mich., Aug. 16, 1921; s. Martin Carl and Ethyl Ruth Kilmark; m. Edna Rhoads Kilmark; children: D. Lee, Robert Jr., E.T., Candace. AA, St. Petersburg Jr. Coll., Fla., 1941; BS in Medicine, Mercer U., Macon, Ga., 1948; MD, Med. Coll. Ga., Augusta, 1950. Med. dir. Edmark Lab., St. Petersburg, 1964—88. Maj. USAF, 1941—45, col. USAR, 1973—85. Decorated Silver Star, Disting. Flying Cross, Purple Heart, Bronze Star, 8 Air medals, 2 Presdl. citations, ETO ribbon with 5 battle stars. Fellow: Acad. Family Practice; mem.: Am. Acad. Family Physicians (life), Fla. Med. Soc. (life), Mil. Officers Assn. Am. (life). Home: 3640 SE 22d Pl Ocala FL 34471

KILMARTIN, JOSEPH FRANCIS, JR., information technology executive; b. Mar. 11, 1924; s. Joseph Francis and Lauretta M. (Collins) Kilmartin; children: Joanne, Diane. Student, St. Thomas Sem., 1944; BA, Holy Cross Coll., 1947. Prodn. mgr. A.C. Gilbert Co., New Haven, 1947—49; prodr. NBC-TV, NYC, 1950—53; v.p. sales Cellomatic Corp., NYC, 1953—59; sr. v.p. Transfilm Inc., NYC, 1959—62, MPO Videotronics, NYC, 1962—66; pres. Bus. Programs Inc., Larchmont, NY, 1966—75, Greenwich, Conn., 1975—. Pres. Kilarnold Corp.; lectr. in field, cons. Mexican Dept. Agrarian Affairs and Colonization, 1974—. Profl. performer: (Broadway show) Small Wonder, (TV shows) Your Hit Parade, Philco Playhouse, Armstrong Circle Theatre, 1949-50. Active fund-raising Cmty. Chest, 1947-49, ARC, 1947-49, Boy Scouts Am., 1958-66, United Fund, 1970-73; mem. Congl. Adv. Bd., Presdl. Task Force, Atlantic Coun., Conn. Venture Group, Mil. Affairs Coun., Fayetteville, N.C., Harnett County Strategic Planning Commn.; bd. dirs. Lee County Arts Coun.; mem. exec. com., chmn. Lee County Rep. Party Coun.; chmn. Carolina Trace Cmty. Action Com.; mem. Southport Homeowners Bd., 2006; mem. chaplain's vol. corps Falmouth Hosp., Mass., 2006-07. Recipient medal of excellence Mex. Agrarian Affairs and Colonization Dept., 1976, Golden Medallion award in bus. comm. Miami Internat. Film Festival, 1978, Cmty. Developer of Yr. award Nat. Mfg. Housing Inst., 1998, Cmty. Betterment award N.C. House of Reps., 1998-99, Sovereign Mil. Order of the Temple of Jerusalem, 1998. Mem. Am. Mgmt. Assn., TV Execs. Soc., Pres.'s Assn., Equestrian Order of the Holy Sepulchur of Jerusalem, Larchmont Club (N.Y.), Yacht Club, Westchester Country Club, Univ. Club (N.Y.C.), Carolina Trace Country Club, Lambs Club, KC. Home: 4 Classic Circle Mashpee MA 02649 Personal E-mail: jkilma5437@aol.com.

KILMER, NEAL HAROLD, application developer; b. Orange, Tex., Apr. 24, 1943; s. Harold Norval and Luella Alice (Sharp) Kilmer; m. Jody Geary, Oct. 24, 1998. BS in Chemistry and Math., Northwestern Okla. State U., 1964; MS in Chemistry, Okla. State U., 1971; PhD in Chemistry, Mich. State U., 1979. Rsch. assoc. N.Mex. Petroleum Recovery Rsch. Ctr., N.Mex. Inst. Mining & Tech., Socorro, 1979-81, rsch. chemist, 1981-85, lectr. geol. engring., 1984, asst. prof. mining engring., 1985-86; phys. scientist Phys. Sci. Lab., N.Mex. State U., Las Cruces, N.Mex., 1986-96; software engr. Honeywell (formerly AlliedSignal), Las Cruces, 1996—. Contbr. articles to profl. jours. Mem.: Optical Soc. Am., Am. Inst. Physics, Am. Chem. Soc., Sigma Xi, Phi Lambda Upsilon, Pi Mu Epsilon. Presbyterian. Avocation: square and round dancing. Home: 398 No Problem Dr Las Cruces NM 88005-3951 Office: Software Maintenance & Tng Facility PO Box 9000 Las Cruces NM 88004-9000

KILMER, VAL, actor; b. Los Angeles, Dec. 31, 1959; m. Joanne Whalley, Mar. 1988 (div. Feb. 1996); children: Mercedes, Jack. Educ., Hollywood's Professional Sch., Juillard. Appeared in plays Electra and Orestes, Henry IV, Part One, 1981, As You Like It, 1982, Slab Boys (Broadway Debut), 1983, Hamlet, 1988, 'Tis Pity She's A Whore, 1992, The Postman Always Rings Twice, (Playhouse Theatre, London), 2005; motion pictures include Top Secret!, 1984, Real Genius, 1985, Top Gun, 1986, Willow, 1988, Kill Me Again, 1989, The Doors, 1991, Thunderheart, 1991, True Romance, 1993, The Real McCoy, 1993, Tombstone, 1993, Wings of Courage, 1995, Batman Forever, 1995, Heat, 1995, The Island of Dr. Moreau, 1996, The Ghost and the Darkness, 1996, Dead Girl, 1996, The Saint, 1997, The Prince of Egypt (voice) 1998, Joe the King, 1999, At First Sight, 1999, Pollock, 2000, Red Planet, 2000, Hard Cash (aka Run for the Money), 2002, The Salton Sea, 2002, Masked and Anonymous, 2003, Wonderland, 2003, Mindhunters, 2004, Alexander, 2004, Kiss Kiss, Bang Bang, 2005, Moscow Zero, 2006, 10th & Wolf, 2006, Played, 2006, Summer Love, 2006, The Ten Commandments: The Musical, 2006, Deja Vu, 2006; TV appearances include The Murders in the Rue Morgue, 1986, The Man Who Broke 1,000 Chains, 1987, Gore Vidal's Billy the Kid, 1989, Bounty Hunters, 2004.*

KILNER, URSULA BLANCHE, genealogist, educator, writer; b. Chgo., Feb. 2, 1925; d. Frederic Russell and Blanche (Miller) Gamble; m. Glen Kilner, May 12, 1950 (dec. Feb. 1998). BA cum laude, Mt. Holyoke Coll., 1946; MA, Columbia U., 1947, postgrad., 1951. Asst. to editor Grolier Pub., NYC, 1947; mgr. Magnamusic Inc., Garrison, NY, 1954-55; publicity and fundraising Little Guild of St. Francis Inc., Cornwall, Conn., 1957-68; lectr. U. Conn., Torrington, 1964-66; genealogist Bird Bottom Genealogy, Salisbury, Conn., 1979—. Owner, mgr. The Tenth Muse, phonograph and stereo co., 1958-60; reporter The Comml. Record, 1960-61. Author, editor: A Revolutionary Cook Book, 1985, A Cook Book for All Seasons, 1994; columnist The Voice, 1993—2003, Animal Life, 2004—06, book reviewer Heritage Books; contbr. articles to profl. jours. Mem. Planning and Zoning Commn., Salisbury, Conn., 1981-82, NY State Hist. Assn. Mem.: DAR (chpt. registrar Salisbury Arsenal 1982—2004), N.Y. State Hist. Assn., Ill. Geneal. Soc., N.Y. Hist. Assn., Essex (Mass.) Soc. Genealogists, Nat. Geneal. Soc., Soc. Genealogists, Conn. Gravestone Studies, Assn. Gravestone Studies, Vt. Genealogists Soc., Suffolk County Hist. Soc., Conn. Soc. Genealogists, Am. Coll. Genealogists (asst. nat. registrar 1990—91, cert. genealogist), N.H. Genealogy Soc. (life), Nat. Soc. Huguenots (life; adv. bd. 1993—2001, Conn. registrar 1998—2001), N.H. Soc. Genealogists (life), N.Y. Geneal./Biog. Soc. (life), New Eng. Hist./Geneal. Soc. (life), Salisbury Assn., Sons and Daus. First Settlers Newbury, Van Voorhees Family Soc., Greyhound Friends West, Inc., Nat. Soc. Colonial Dames XVII Century (organizing pres. Winthrop Fleet chpt. 1990, Conn. state registrar 1995—99, chpt. pres. 1999—2001, ret.), Sheffield Hist. Soc. (life), Morse Family Soc. (life), Piscataqua Pioneers N.H. (life), Kewanee (Ill.) Hist. Soc. (life), Andover (Mass.) Hist. Soc. (life), Nat. Soc. Daus. Am. Colonists (ret. Conn. registrar), Seeley Family Soc., Whitlock Family Soc., Ea. Star. Avocations: knitting, lecturing, saving greyhounds, greenhouse plants. Home and Office: Bird Bottom Farm RR 1 Salisbury CT 06068-9802

KILPATRICK, AUSTON MARM (A. MARM KILPATRICK), research scientist; PhD in Zoology, U. Wis., Madison. Sr. rsch. scientist Consortium for Conservation Medicine, NY. Contbr. articles to profl. publications. Achievements include determing the drivers of spatial and temporal variation in West nile virus transmission; developing models for the risk of transmission of Brucella abortus from bison and elk to cattle in Yellowstone National Park; risk assessment for the introduction of pathogens, including West Nile virus and Avian Influenza to new areas. Office: Consortium for Conservation Medicine 460 W 34th St 17th Fl New York NY 10001 Office Phone: 212-380-4471. Office Fax: 212-380-4475. Business E-Mail: kilpatrick@conservationmedicine.org.*

KILPATRICK, CAROLYN CHEEKS, congresswoman; b. Detroit, June 25, 1945; d. Marvell and Willa Mae (Henry) Cheeks; divorced; children: Kwame, Ayanna. AS, Ferris State Coll., Big Rapids, Mich., 1965; BS, Western Mich. U., 1972; MS in Edn., U. Mich., 1977. Tchr. Murray Wright High Sch., Detroit, 1972-78; mem. Mich. Ho. of Reps., Lansing, 1978-96, U.S. Congress from 13th Mich. dist. (formerly 15th), Washington, 1997—; mem. appropriations com. Del. Dem. Convs., 1980, 84, 88. Participant Mich. African Trade Mission, 1984, UN Internat. Women's Conf., 1986; del. participant Mich. Dept. Agr. to Nairobi (Kenya) Internat. Agr. Show, 1986. Recipient Anthony Wayne award Wayne State U., Disting. Legislator award U. Mich., Disting. Alumni award Ferris State U., Woman of Yr. award Gentlemen of Wall St., Inc., Burton-Abercrombie award 15th Dem. Congrl. dist.; named one of Most Influential Black Americans, Ebony mag., 2006. Mem. Nat. Orgn. 100 Black Women. Democrat. Office: House of Reps 1610 Longworth House Office Bldg Washington DC 20515-2215 also: Dist Office 1274 Library Ste 1B Detroit MI 48226 Office Phone: 202-225-2261, 313-965-9004. Office Fax: 202-225-5730, 313-965-9006.*

KILPATRICK, CLIFTON WAYNE, book dealer; b. Pontiac, Mich., Nov. 16, 1949; s. Martin Laverne and Shirley Irene (Powell) Ball (dec.). Grad. high sch., Ortonville, Mich. With Royal Castle (restaurant), Miami, Fla., 1969-71, Yankee Clipper (restaurant), Ft. Lauderdale, Fla., 1971-73, Creightons (restaurant), Ft. Lauderdale, Fla., 1973-75; book collector Trivia King, Ft. Lauderdale, Fla., 1975-93. Author: Trivia Professor, 1980. Democrat. Methodist. Home and Office: 2805 NW 30th Ct Oakland Park FL 33311-1331

KILPATRICK, DONALD G., lawyer; b. Orange, NJ, July 11, 1954; BA, Yale Univ., 1977; JD, Columbia Univ., 1981. Bar: NY 1982. Mng. dir. D. George Harris & Assoc., 1993—2001; ptnr., co-chmn. Mergers & Acquisitions practice Pillsbury Winthrop Shaw Pittman, NYC, 2001—. Mem.: Assn. Bar City of NY. Office: Pillsbury Winthrop Shaw Pittman 1540 Broadway New York NY 10036 Office Phone: 212-858-1235. Office Fax: 212-858-1500. Business E-Mail: donald.kilpatrick@pillsburylaw.com.

KILPATRICK, FRANK STANTON, marketing executive; b. San Jose, Calif., Dec. 2, 1950; s. Frank George and Marian (Polk) K. Student, U. Wis., 1968—71; AB in Polit. Sci., U. Calif., Berkeley, 1975, postgrad., 1976. Writer, advt. sales rep., Midwest regional mgr., mktg. mgr. 13-30 Corp. (Whittle Comm.), 1970—74; with Grey Advt., 1977; mktg. mgr. East/West Network, 1978—79; mktg. dir. Calif. Bus. mag., LA, 1979—81; v.p. mktg. Harlequin Mags., 1981; gen. mgr. new venture devel. Knapp Comm. Corp., 1981—84; gen. ptnr. Pacific Cellular, 1982—86, Calif. Coast Comm., 1981—84; dir., pres. Pasadena Media Inc., 1984—85; mgmt. cons. Kilpatrick & Assocs., LA, 1984—97. Lectr. entrepreneur program U. So. Calif. Sch. Bus. Adminstrn., 1984-85, UCLA Extension, 1989-94; pres. Capital Equity Group, 1986-87, Healthcare Comm. Group, 1998—. Vol. counselor 1736 Teen Crisis Ctr., Hermosa Beach, Calif., 1989-90. Mem. L.A. Advt. Club (Belding award 1980), Direct Mktg. Club So. Calif., World Affairs Coun., Town Hall Calif., U. Calif. Alumni Assn., Stanford Grad. Bus. Sch. Alumni Assn. (sec. 1985-86, v.p. events 1986-87, dir. 1987-90, pres. 1990-92), L.A. Venture Assn. (charter mem.). Office: 909 N Sepulveda Blvd 5th fl El Segundo CA 90245 Office Phone: 310-606-5700. E-mail: fkilpatrick@hcg.com.

KILPATRICK, JAMES JACKSON, JR., columnist, writer; b. Oklahoma City, Nov. 1, 1920; s. James Jackson and Alma Mia (Hawley) K.; m. Marie Louise Pietri, Sept. 21, 1942 (dec. May 1997); children: Michael Sean, Christopher Hawley, Kevin Pietri; m. Marianne Means, June 19, 1998. BJ, U. Mo., 1941. Reporter Richmond (Va.) News Leader, 1941-49, chief editorial writer, 1949-51, editor, 1951-67; writer nat. syndicated columns, TV commentator. Author: The Sovereign States, 1957, The Smut Peddlers, 1960, The Southern Case for School Segregation, 1962, The Foxes' Union, 1977, (with Eugene J. McCarthy) A Political Bestiary, 1978, (with William Bake) The American South: Four Seasons of the Land, 1980, The American South: Towns and Cities, 1982, The Writer's Art, 1984, The Ear is Human, 1985, A Bestiary of Bridge, 1986, Fine Print - Reflections on the Writing Art, 1993; editor: We the States, 1964; co-editor: The Lasting South, 1957. Vice chmn. Va. Com. on Constl. Govt., 1962-68; chmn. Va. Magna Carta Com., 1965; trustee Thomas Jefferson Ctr. for Protection of Free Expression, 1990—2004, Supreme Ct. Hist. Soc., 1987—. Recipient medal of honor for distinguished service in journalism U. Mo., 1953; ann. award for editorial writing Sigma Delta Chi, 1954; William Allen White award U. Kans., 1979; Carr Van Anda award Ohio U., 1987; named to Okla. Hall of Fame, 1978 Fellow Soc. Profl. Journalists; mem. Nat. Conf. Editorial Writers (chmn. 1955-56), Black-Eyed Pea Soc. Am. (No. 1 Pea pro tem 1965—), Gridiron Club. Whig. Episcopalian. Office Phone: 202-293-6301. E-mail: kilpatjj@aol.com.

KILPATRICK, JOHN AARON, construction and development company executive; b. Norfolk, Va., Jan. 7, 1954; s. Marion Calvin and Maude Elaine (Simms) K.; m. Lynnda Christina Peterson, Aug. 19, 1978; children: Lynnda Madonna, Jonathan Simms, Richard Marion, William Valien. B.S., U. S.C., 1976, M.B.A., 1981, PhD, 2002. Bus. mgr. J. Allen Shumaker Builders, Columbia, S.C., 1979-81; stockbroker Dean Witter Reynolds, Columbia, 1981-83; teaching assoc. U. S.C., Columbia, 1982-83; v.p., co-owner Carolina Microsystems, Columbia, 1983; controller Shumaker Bldrs., Columbia, 1985-87; v.p., gen. mgr. Sand Creek Properties, Columbia, 1987-88; pres. The Kilpatrick Co., 1987-90; adj. prof. Webster U., Columbia, 1986-90; asst. sr. v.p. rsch., U.S.C, 1990-94, lectr., Moore Sch. Bus., 1992-98; admin. S.C. Supercomputer Network, 1994-96; exec. dir., Acad. Coalition Intelligent Mfg., 1994-1995; pres., Greenfield Advisors 1998—. editor: Ctrl. Puget Sound Real Estate Rsch. Report; Author; Financing Development and Construction in the 90's, 1991, utstanding Home Construction, 1995, Subdivision Development, 1998. fellow Am. Real Estate Soc.; mem. Am. Real Estate Urban Econ. Assn., Am. Econ. Assn., Am. Fin. Assn., ABA (Assoc.), Appraisal Inst, Royal Inst. Chartered Surveyors (U.K.), Real Estate Counseling Group Am., Internat. Code Coun., Wash. Athletic Club, Ranier Club, Rotary Club, Omicron Delta Kappa, Phi Delta Theta. Episcopalian. Home: 5561 248th Pl Se Issaquah WA 98029-7619 Office: Greenfield Advt LLC Ste 650 2601 4th Ave Seattle WA 98121 Office Phone: 206-623-2935.

KILPATRICK, KWAME MALIK, mayor; b. Detroit, June 8, 1970; s. Bernard Kilpatrick and Carolyn (Cheeks) Kikpatrick; m. Carlita Poles; children: Jelani, Jalil, Jonas. BS in Polit. Sci., Fla. A&M Univ.; JD, Detroit Coll. Law, 1999. Cert. teacher Florida A&M U. Mem. Mich. Ho. Reps., 1996—2001; mayor City of Detroit, 2002—. Designer Clean Mich. Initiative, 1998; former leader Democratic Caucus. Named an Most Influential Black Americans, Ebony mag., 2006. Democrat. Achievements include youngest elected mayor of any major US city. Office: Coleman A Young Municipal Ctr 2 Woodward Ave Rm 1126 Detroit MI 48226 Office Phone: 313-224-3400.*

KILRAIN, SUSAN, astronaut; b. Augusta, Ga., Oct. 24, 1961; d. Joe and Sue Still; m. Colin James Kilrain. MS in Aerospace Engring., GA. Inst. Tech., 1985; grad., Test Pilot Sch. Wind tunnel project officer Lockheed Corp., Marietta, Ga.; commd. ensign USN, 1985, advanced through grades to lt. comdr., flight instr. TA-4J Skyhawk; naval aviator EA-6A Electric

Intruders for Tactical Electronic Warfare Sq. 33, Key West, Fla.; with NASA Johnson Space Ctr., Houston, 1995—, with Vehicle Sys. and Ops. Br. Astronaut Office, pilot STS-83, 1997, pilot STS-94, 1997, spacecraft communicator in mission control. Decorated Def. Superior Svc. medal, Navy Meritorious Svc. medal, Navy Commendation medal, Navy Achievement medal, (2) NASA Space Flight medals, Nat. Def. Svc. medal; recipient 10 Outstanding Young Ams. award U.S. Jr. C. of C., Good Scout award, 1997. Mem. Assn. Naval Aviation, Assn. Space Explorers, Ga. Tech. Found. Avocations: triathlons, martial arts, playing piano. Office: NASA Lyndon B Johnson Space Ctr Houston TX 77058

KILROY, JOHN MUIR, lawyer; b. Kansas City, Mo., Apr. 12, 1918; s. James L. and Jane Alice (Scurry) K.; m. Lorraine K. Butler, Jan. 26, 1946; children: John Muir, William Terence. Student, Kansas City Jr. Coll., 1935-37; AB, U. Kansas City, 1940; JD, U. Mo., 1942. Bar: Mo. 1942. Practice in, Kansas City, 1946—; ptnr. Shughart, Thomson & Kilroy, 1948—, pres., 1977-86, chmn. bd. dirs., 1980-88, chmn. emeritus, 1988—. Instr. med. jurisprudence U. Health Scis., 1973-93; panelist numerous med.-legal groups ACS, Mo. Med. Assn., Kans. U. Med. Sch., S.W. Clin. Soc. Contbr. articles to profl. jours. Chmn. bd. dirs. Kansas City Heart Assn.; mem. adv. bd. Midwest Christian Counseling Svc.; bd. dirs., pres. Della Lamb Cmty. Svc., 1991, chmn. bd. dirs., 1993; bd. dirs. Laubach Literacy Coun., 1998-2001, Kingswood Manor, 1992-94, Mo. Meth. Found., 1993-2002. Named Man of Yr., Sigma Chi, 1989. Fellow Am. Coll. Trial Lawyers; mem. ABA, Mo. Bar Assn. (chmn. med. legal com.), Kansas City Bar Assn. (Litigator Emeritus award 1990), Internat. Assn. Barristers, Internat. Assn. Def. Counsel, Am. Coll. Legal Medicine, Am. Bd. Profl. Liability Attys., Fedn. Ins. Counsel, Law Soc. U. Mo., Order Barristers U. Mo., Lawyers Assn., Kansas City (pres. 1968), Kansas City C. of C., Univ. Club (v.p. 1984, pres. 1985), Indian Hills Country Club, Kansas City Club. Office: Shughart Thomson & Kilroy 120 W 12th St Ste 1800 Kansas City MO 64105-1922 Home: 8101 Mission Rd Apt 411 Prairie Village KS 66208-5248

KILROY, WILLIAM TERRENCE, lawyer; b. Kansas City, Mo., May 24, 1950; s. John Muir and Katherine Lorraine (Butler) K.; m. Marianne Michelle Maurin, Sept. 8, 1984; children: Kyle E., Katherine A. BS, U. Kans., 1972, MA, 1974; JD, Washburn U., 1977. Bar: Mo. 1977. Assoc. Shughart, Thomson & Kilroy, Kansas City, Mo., 1977-81, mem., dir., 1981—. Contbr. articles to profl. publs. Mem. Kans. City Citizens Assn., 1980—; pres., bd. govs. Sch. Law Washburn, 1992-94; with Civic Coun. of Greater Kansas City, 1999—; legal coun. Heart of Am. Coun. Boy Scouts Am., 1988-92, mem. exec. com., 1988-95, Cmty. adv. Greater Kans. City Cmty. Found. and Affiliated Trusts, 1993-2000; bd. dirs. Kansas City Neighborhood Alliance, 1998-2004, Greater Kansas City Crime Commn., 1999—. Mem. Lawyers Assn. Kansas City, Kansas City Bar Assn. (chmn. civil rights com. 1984), Mo. Bar Assn., ABA (subcom. on arbitration, labor law sect. 1977—), Greater Kansas City C. of C., Kansas City Club, Kansas City Country Club. Office: Shughart Thomson & Kilroy 12 Wyandotte Plz 120 W 12th St Ste 1800 Kansas City MO 64105-1929 Office Phone: 816-374-0533. Business E-Mail: tkilroy@stklaw.com.

KILTS, JAMES M., investment banker, former consumer products company executive; b. Chgo., Feb. 10, 1948; m. Sandra Kilts; 2 children. BA, Knox Coll., 1970; MBA in Mktg., U. Chgo., 1974. Various operations and mgmt. positions General Foods, v.p., divsn. mgr. consumer products divsn. Oscar Mayer; joined Kraft Ltd., 1985, pres., gen. mgr. Canada, 1986; sr. v.p. strategy and develop. Kraft, Inc., 1987; pres. Kraft USA Philip Morris Companies Inc., 1989-94, exec. v.p. Kraft Foods Worldwide, 1994-97; pres., CEO Nabisco Inc., 1998—99, Nabisco Holdings Corp., Parsippany, NJ, 1999—2000; chmn., CEO The Gillette Co., Boston, 2001—05, pres., 2003—05; vice chmn. The Gillette Co. (divsn The Procter & Gamble Co.), 2005—06; founding ptnr. Centerview Partners LLC, NYC, 2006—. Bd. dirs., The Gillette Co., 2001-05, Whirlpool Corp., 1999-2005, Mays Dept. Stores, MetLife, Inc., 2005-, NY Times Co., 2005-, Procter & Gamble, 2005-; mem. internat. adv. bd. Citigroup. Trustee Knox Coll., 1992-; chmn. adv. bd., U. Chgo. Sch. Bus.

KILTS, LAURIE DAWN, elementary school educator; b. Casper, Wyo., Oct. 20, 1968; d. George Allen Taylor; m. Dustin Lee Kilts, June 15, 1991; children: Marie Rose, Lynn Kristen, Cole Lee. M in Early Childhood, Lesley U., Casper, 1998. 3rd grade tchr. Midwest Elem., Wyo., 1996—2001; instrnl. facilitator, math tutor Paradise Valley, Casper, 2001—. Home: 1200 W Ormsby Rd Casper WY 82601 Office: Paradise Valley Elementary 22 Magnolia Casper WY 82604 Home Phone: 307-472-3359; Office Phone: 307-577-4584. Personal E-mail: ldkilts@yahoo.com. Business E-Mail: laurie_kilts@ncsd.k12.wy.us.

KILTY, JEROME TIMOTHY, playwright, theater director, actor; b. Balt., June 24, 1922; s. Harold Joseph and Irene (Zellinger) K.; m. Cavada Humphrey, May 11, 1956. BA, Harvard U., 1949. Prof. drama U. Okla., Norman, 1971, U. Tex., Austin, 1972, U. Kans., Lawrence, 1973; appointed to O'Conner Chair of Lit., Colgate U., Hamilton, N.Y., 1974-75, 91-92; instr. in drama Harvard U., Cambridge, Mass., 1983-85, 89. Co-founder, dir., actor Brattle Theatre Co., Cambridge, Mass., 1948-52; actor N.Y.C. stage and TV, 1952-57, including Relapse, 1951, Quadrille, 1952, Misalliance, 1953; played: Falstaff, Iago, City Centre, 1954; writer, actor Dear Liar, Chgo. and London, 1957 (Berlin Festival Critics award 1961, Baton Du Brigadier 1962-63, Palma D'Oro 1962-63, Stanislavsky Centenary medal 1963), dir. revival, Paris, 1974, 80, Rome, 1975, 85, for TV, Hallmark Hall of Fame, 1981, dir. Australian Premiere, 1993, Melbourne; writer, dir. for TV Ides of March, London, 1963, Long Live Life, San Francisco, 1967; dir. Marie Bell, Elisabeth Bergner, Maria Casares, Pierre Brasseur in various French, German, Italian prodns., 1962-65; assoc. dir., Am. Conservatory Theatre, San Francisco, 1966-68, Am. Shakespeare Co., Stratford, Conn., 1965-68; dir. Possibilities, N.Y.C., 1968, Sarah Ferrati in Mrs. Warren's Profession (in Italian), Rome, 1976; writer, dir. Don't Shoot Mable, It's Your Husband, 1968; writer, actor Dear Love, Boston, 1969, London, 1973, The Laffing Man, 1975; dir., actor Androcles and the Lion, 1985, Love's Labor's Lost, 1985; writer: The Little Black Book, N.Y.C., 1972, Look Away, N.Y.C.; musicals What the Devil, 1977, Barnum, 1978; play Hey Marie!, 1979; dir. Julius Caesar, San Diego Nat. Shakespeare Festival, 1979, Love's Labor's Lost, 1980, Misalliance, Denver, 1980, I, James McNeill Whistler, Hartford Stage Co., Peter Pan, Kansas City, Mo., 1985; appeared in play A Month in the Country, N.Y.C., 1979-80, Enter a Free Man, N.Y.C., 1984, Foxfire, Kansas City, Mo., 1985; mem., Hartman Theatre Co., 1981-82, 86-87, played the Doctor in Three Sisters and Ernest in Bedroom Farce; dir. Tammy Grimes in The Millionairess; star The Magistrate; mem., Am. Repertory Theatre Co., Cambridge, Mass., 1983-2000, created role: The King in Big River, 1983, directed, played Armado in Love's Labor's Lost, 1985, played Abel Bishop in Right You Are (If You Think So), 1988, played Don Antonio in Saturday, Sunday, Monday, 1988; played title role in King Lear, Col. Treletsky in Platonov, played James Tyrone with Claire Bloom in Long Day's Journey into Night, 1996, played Old Ekdal in Wild Duck, 1997; created role Chairman Bowman in Mastergate by Larry Gelbart, 1989, repeated role on Broadway, Criterion Theater, 1989; co-star: A Moon for the Misbegotten, Cort Theatre, N.Y.C., 1984; repeated role of Phil Hogan, Am. Repertory Theatre (Best Actor award Boston Theatre Critics 1984); mem. Hartford Stage Co., 1985-86, played in The Tempest, Twelfth Night, directed and acted in Androcles and the Lion; played Boss Mangan in Heartbreak House, Yale Repertory Theatre, 1986; dir. The Seagull, Am. Conservatory Theatre, San Francisco, 1987, The Man Who Was Peter Pan, Am. Repertory Theater, Cambridge, 1990, Arms and the Man, Alley Theater, Houston, 1995; co-star The Doctor's Dilemma, N.Y.C., 1990, played Harry Hope in The Iceman Cometh, Chgo., 1990 (Joseph Jefferson award 1991); author plays About to Begin, 1988, Margaret Sanger/Unfinished Business, 1989, The Hermit of Yalta, 1993; starred with Opera Co. of Boston in world premiere of The Balcony, 1990, Bolshoi Theatre, Moscow, 1991, starred in Gigli Concert, Court Theatre, Chgo., Spoleto Festival U.S.A., 1992, The Substance of Fire, Asolo Theatre, Sarasota, Fla., 1992, Stages Repertory Theatre, Houston, 1994, Love Letters, Asolo Theatre, 1993, King Lear, Asolo Theatre, 1993; played Horace Vandergelder in The Matchmaker, McCarter Theater, Princeton, N.J., 1994, Gov. Danforth in The Crucible, Alley Theater, Houston, 1994, King Lear, Nebr. Shakespeare Festival, 1995, Tobias in A Delicate Balance, Stages Repertory Theater, Houston, 1996. Athol Fugard's Valley Song, Arizona Theatre Co., 1997, Michael James in Playboy of the Western World, Steppenwolf Theatre, Chicago, 1998, Long Wharf Theatre, New Haven; guest starred as King Lear, Arizona State Univ., 1998; played Leo Tolstoy in world premiere of The Last Station, Vt. State Co., Burlington, 1999, Scrooge, Va. Stage Co., Norfolk, 1999, 2000, Drummond in Inherit the Wind, Mo. Repertory Co., Kansas City, Ford's Theatre, Washington, 2000; played Sean O'Casey in I Knock at the Door, Westport, Conn., 2001; co-starred in world premiere The Astronaut, Westport, Conn., 2002. Served to capt. USAAF, 1942-46, ETO. Decorated D.F.C., Air Medal with seven clusters. Mem. Signet Soc. Clubs: Players (N.Y.C.). Home: PO Box 1074 Weston CT 06883-0074

KILWAY, KATHLEEN VICTORIA, chemist, educator, researcher; b. Hill AFB, Utah, Mar. 21, 1963; d. James Bernard and Neoma Inez Kilway. BS in Chemistry cum laude, St. Mary's Coll., Notre Dame, Ind., 1985; MS in Chemistry, U. Calif. San Diego, La Jolla, 1987, PhD in Chemistry, 1992. Grad. tchg. asst. U. Calif. San Diego, LaJolla, 1985—91, grad. rsch. asst., 1985—92; postdoctoral rsch. fellow Faculté des Sci. de St. Jerome, Marseilles, France, 1992—93, U. Calif., Berkeley, 1994—96; asst. prof. chemistry U. Mo., Kansas City, 1996—2002, assoc. prof. chemistry, 2002—, chair dept. chemistry, 2007—. Contbr. chapters to books, articles to profl. jours. Recipient Area Rsch. Enhancement award, NIH, 2000, Gov.'s Tchg. award, 2002; grantee Petroleum Rsch. Fund grant, Am. Chem. Soc., 2000; scholar Trustee's Faculty scholar, U. Mo. Kansas City, 2001. Mem.: Am. Chem. Soc., Sigma Xi, Iota Sigma Pi. Avocations: water-skiing, walking, reading. Office: U Mo Kansas City 510 H Flarsheim Hall Dept Chemistry 5100 Rockhill Rd Kansas City MO 64110-2999 Personal E-mail: Kilwayk@umkc.edu.

KIM, ANA H., otolaryngologist, educator; b. Seoul, Republic of Korea, Sept. 16, 1967; d. Ki Hak John and Yeong Ja Jemma Kim. BA, Cornell U., Ithaca, 1990—90; MD, Albert Einstein Coll. Medicine, Bronx, 1999. Diplomate bd. cert, otolaryngology Am. Bd. Otolaryngology, 2006, neurotology bd. elligible Am. Bd. Otolaryngology, 2007. Asst. prof. NY Eye & Ear Infirmary, N.Y.C., 2006—, dir. otologic rsch., 2006—; asst. prof. NY Med. Coll., Valhalla, NY, 2006—. Ednl. resources subcom. NY Med. Coll., 2006—. Contbr. articles various profl. jours., scientific papers. Recipient NY Eye & ear Infirmary Resident Tchg. Award, NY Eye & Ear Infirmary, 2004, J. Swift Henley Excellence in Resident Rsch. Award, 2004, Deafness Rsch. Found. Fellowship Award, Deafness Rsch. Found., 2006, Neurotology Fellow award, 2006, Travel award, AAO/HNS, 2005; ARO Travel grant. Fellow: Am. Acad. Otolaryngology/Head & Neck Surgery (implantable hearing device com. mem. 2006—); mem.: Equilibrium Com., Implantable Hearing Device Com., Assn. Rsch. Otolaryngology (equilibrium com. mem. 2006—), Am. Acad. Otolaryngology. Catholic. Achievements include patents pending for analysis of growth factor gene expression patterns during the healing of tympanic membrane after traumatic perforation. Avocations: travel, music, skiing. Home: 215 E 96th St Apt 18C New York NY 10128 Office: NY Eye and Ear Infirmary 310 E 14th St New York NY 10003 Home Phone: 917-826-2499; Office Phone: 212-614-8387. Office Fax: 212-979-4315. Business E-Mail: hkim@nyee.edu.

KIM, ATTA, photographer; b. South Korea, 1956; BS in Mechanical Engring., Changwon U. Exhibited in group shows at Alienation & Assimilation, Mus. Contemporary Photography, Chgo., 1998, Odense Foto Triennale, Odense, Denmark, 2000, FotoFest, Houston, 2000, Awakening, Australian Centre Photography, 2001, San Paolo 25th Bienal, 2002, Translated Acts: Body and Performance Art From East Asia, Queens Mus. Art, 2002, Absent Voices, Gallery Korea, 2004, one-man shows include Pyschopath, Yechong Gallery, Seoul, 1987, The Korean People, Nikon Salon Gallery, Tokyo, 1993, The Museum Project, NauvoGallery, Busan, Korea, 1995, Samsung Photo Gallery, Seoul, 1996, Society for Contemporary Photography, Kansas City, Mo., 2001, Atta Kim: On Air, Internat. Ctr. Photography, 2006, photography book, Atta Kim: The Museum Project, 2005, Atta Kim, 2006, Represented in permanent collections Mus. Fine Arts Houston, LA Country Mus. Art, Museet for Fotokunst, Odense, Denmark, Nat. Mus. Contemporary Art, Seoul, Art Museum of Kyongnam Province, China. Recipient Annual Artist's Prize, Sajin Yesul, 1997, Internat. Photo prize, The 1st Hanam Internat. Photo Festival, Korea, 2002, 4th Lee Myoungdong Photo prize, Seoul, Korea, 2003. Office: care of Yossi Milo Gallery 525 W 25th St New York NY 10001

KIM, BONG-JO, molecular biologist, researcher; b. Pusan, Republic of Korea, Aug. 30, 1966; s. Youn-Sik Kim; m. Sun-Ok Park, Sept. 2, 1970; children: Jin-Mu, Jin-Su, Johnny. BS in Biotechnology, Pukyong Nat. U., Pusan, Republic of Korea, 1993, MS in Molecular Biology, 1995, PhD in Biochemistry and Molecular Biology, 1998. Postdoctoral fellowship Korea Sci. and Engring. Found., 1998—99, Yosu Nat. U., Republic of Korea, 2000—01; rsch. scientist Japan STA Fellowship, Sci. Tech. Agy., 2001—03; vis. rschr. LMBB, NIAAA, NIH, 2003—. Lectr. YangSan U., Republic of Korea, 1999—2001, Pukyong Nat. U., Pusan, 1999—2001. Recipient Rsch. award, NIH, 2006; fellow, Korea Sci. and Engring. Found., Dajeon, 1998—99, Yosu Nat. U., 2000—01, Nat. Food Rsch. Inst., Tsukuba, Japan, 2001—03. Achievements include patents for construction of active enzymes by co-refolding the fragments; manufacturing method of oligosaccharides using insoluble polysaccharides; the marine bacterium Pseudomonas aeruginosa BYK-2 producing rhamnolipid and; method of making agar-oligosaccharide using edible acetic acid; research in a novel mechanism for apoptosis; construction of active enzymes by co-refolding the fragments. Avocations: travel, reading, tennis. Home: 257 Congressional Ln #710 Rockville MD 20852 Home Phone: 301-468-0723; Office Phone: 301-496-3984. Office Fax: 301-594-3113. Personal E-mail: kbj6182@yahoo.com. E-mail: bjkim@nih.mail.gov.

KIM, BUM-JIN, research scientist; b. Seoul, Republic Of Korea, Aug. 18, 1972; s. Jae Won Kim and Young Ja Jeung; m. Ha Young Choi, May 28, 2005. PhD, U. Pa., Phila., 2006. Rsch. fellow U. Pa., 2001—07; rschr. Cath. U. Pa., DC, 2007—. Rsch. fellowship, NSF, 2002. Home: 6100 City Ave Apt 1402 Philadelphia PA 19131 Personal E-mail: bjkim818@gamil.com.

KIM, CHARLES WESLEY, microbiology educator; b. Nashville, Mar. 20, 1926; s. Herbert Hyungsik and Kyung Sook Kim; m. Soo Johung, June 9, 1956; 1 child, Charles W. Jr. BA, U. Calif., Berkeley, 1949; MS in Pub. Health, U. NC, 1952, PhD in Parasitology and Microbiology, 1956. Instr., asst. prof. NY Med. Coll., NYC, 1956-59, 59-64; assoc. scientist, scientist Brookhaven Nat. Lab., Upton, NY, 1965-68, 68-70; assoc. dean basic health sci. SUNY, Stony Brook, 1972-74, assoc. vice provost, 1974-83, assoc. prof., 1970-87, prof. microbiology and medicine, 1987—, prof. emeritus, 1996—. Author: Microbiology Review, 1962, 11th edit., 1995; editor: Trichinellosis, 1974, 4th edit., 1985; editl. bd. Exptl. Parasitology, 1984—; reviewer Am. Jour. Tropical Medicine and Hygiene, 1990-93. Moderator N.E. Synod Presbyn. Ch., 1997—98; bd. dirs. Mountain Retreat Assn., 2000—03; mem. gen. assembly coun. Presbyn. Ch. (USA), 2000—04, mem. exec. com. gen. assembly coun., 2003—04, chair worldwide ministries com., 2003—04; bd. govs. Friends of Sunwood, Stony Brook, 1973—85, Suffolk Symphonnic Soc., Suffolk County, NY, 1975—77; mem. devel. com. Mus. Stony Brook, 1983—85; bd. govs. L.I. Coun. Chs., 1999—2003; mem. gov. bd. Three Village Hist. Soc., 2000—01; trustee Med. Benevolence Found., 2005—. Tropical medicine fellow La. State U. Sch. Medicine, 1958, USPHS fellow Argonne Nat. Lab., U. Chgo., 1964-65, Royal Soc. Tropical Medicine and Hygiene fellow, London, 1975. Mem. Internat. Commn. Trichinellosis (pres. 1988-93), Am. Soc. Parasitologists (chmn. nominating com. 1987), Am. Soc. Tropical Medicine and Hygiene, NY Soc. Tropical Medicine (pres. 1985-86), Sigma Xi (chpt. pres. 1993-94), Delta Omega. Fax: 631-751-3010.

KIM, CHIN-WOO, linguist, educator; b. Chungju, Korea, Mar. 22, 1936; came to U.S., 1961, naturalized, 1983; s. Hyong-gi and Kyong-ok K.; m. Beverly Jean Kircher, June 14, 1964 (div. June 1982); children: Joseph H., Daniel H; m. Kui-Soon Choe, Oct. 29, 1988. BA in English, Yonsei U., 1958, Wash. State U., 1962; MA, UCLA, 1964, PhD in Linguistics, 1966. Asst. prof. linguistics U. Ill., Urbana, 1967—69, assoc. prof. linguistics, East Asian langs., speech, and English as an internat. language, 1969—72, prof., 1972—, chmn. dept. linguistics, 1979—86, dir. Ill.-Tehran Rsch. Ctr., 1974—78, assoc. dir. Linguistic Inst., 1977, dir. Program in East Asian Studies, 1990—91; assoc. dir. Konan Internat. Exch. Ctr. Konan U., Kobe, Japan, 1993—94, 2004—05; head linguistics U. Ill., 1999—2004. Vis. prof. linguistics U. Hawaii, 1972-73, 86-87, adj. prof. U. Tehran, Iran, 1974-76, vis. prof. English Yonsei U., Korea, 1983-84, Konan U., Kobe, Japan, 1993-94, Korea U., Seoul, 1995-96, chair prof. in humanities Yonsei U., Seoul, 2007-. Author works in field. Bd. dirs. East Asian Language Inst. Ind. U., 1984-93; pres., bd. trustees Korean Language Sch., Urbana, Ill., 1988-92. Served with Korean Air Force, 1958-61. Am. Council Learned Socs. fellow, 1965-66; postdoctoral fellow MIT, 1966-67; Ctr. Advanced Study Fellow, U. Ill., 1984-85, Overseas Korean of the Year Award, Korean Broadcasting Soc., 2001. Mem. Linguistic Soc. Am., Linguistic Soc. Korea, Internat. Cir. Korean Linguistics (pres. 1978-80), Phonology-Morphology Cir. (adv. bd. 1995—), Internat. Soc. Korean Studies (pres. N.Am. br. 2005—), Internat. Assn. Humanistic Studies Lang. (pres. 2000—), Korean Assn. Speech Scis. (sr. advisor 1999—) Home: 1401 N Raintree Woods Urbana IL 61802-7749 Office: U Ill Dept Linguistics 707 S Mathews Ave Urbana IL 61801-3625 Office Phone: 217-244-2824. Business E-Mail: cwkim@illinois.edu, cwk1401@yonsei.ac.kr. *I grew up in an economically poor and politically oppressive and unstable environment (Japanese colonial rule, World War II, Korean War). The educational system mirrored such a society (books were scarce, pencils were used down to the one-inch length, and classes were often cancelled), but I was determined to learn, as I did not want to let the poor environment be an excuse for ignorance. Now in the States, it saddens me to see many people not realize and make use of excellent opportunities they have, for I believe that in the presence of excellence, mediocrity is a sin.*

KIM, CHONG LIM, political science professor; b. Seoul, July 17, 1937; arrived in US, 1962; s. Soo Myung and Chung Hwa (Moon) K.; m. Eun Hwa Park, Aug. 21, 1963; children: Bohm S., Lahn S., Lynn S. BA, Seoul Nat. U., 1960; MA, U. Oreg., 1964, PhD, 1968. Instr. U. Oreg., Eugene, 1965-67; asst. prof. U. Iowa, Iowa City, 1968-70, assoc. prof., 1970-75, prof., 1975—. Author: Legislative Connection, 1984, Legislative Process in Korea, 1981, Patterns of Recruitment, 1974; editor: Legislative Systems, 1975, Political Participation in Korea, 1980; contbr. numerous articles to profl. jours. Mem. Am. Polit. Sci. Assn., Midwest Polit. Sci. Assn. Avocations: reading, travel. Office: U Iowa Dept Polit Sci Iowa City IA 52242 Home Phone: 319-337-7871. Business E-Mail: chong-kim@uiowa.edu.

KIM, CHUL SUNG, physicist, educator; b. Seoul, Republic of Korea, July 5, 1950; s. Jong Sun Kim and La Pa Oh; m. Sung Hee Choi, Mar. 26, 1983; children: Eun A, Hyung Joon. BS, Yonsei U., Seoul, Korea, 1972, MS, 1974, PhD, 1982. Prof. Air Force Acad., Seoul, 1977—80, Kookmin U., Seoul, 1980—, dir. Natural Sci. Inst., 1991—93, dir. Ctr. Interuniv. Facility, 1993—2001, dean natural sci., 2004—. Vis. prof. Johns Hopkins U., Balt., 1987—88. Contbr. over 300 articles in the field of Mossbauer and Magnetic materials. Capt. Air Force Acad., 1976—80. Recipient Outstanding Rsch. Paper award, 2002, Acad. Rsch. award, 2005, Sci. and Tech. Outstanding Rsch. Paper award, Korean Fedn. Sci. and Tech. Soc., 2004. Mem.: IEEE, Am. Phys. Soc., Korean Magnetics Soc. (v.p. 2001—07, editor in chief 2001—, gen. affairs com. 2003—, pres. 2007—, Outstanding Rsch. Paper award 1999, Kangil Goo award 2004), Korean Phys. Soc. (treas. 1997—99, v.p. 2005—, editor in chief 2005—, Best Paper award 1991), Mossbauer Century Club. Home: 105-406 Woo Sung Apt Sur Cho Ku Jam Won Dong Seoul 137-790 Republic of Korea Office: Kookmin Univ Dept Physics Seoul 136-702 Republic of Korea Office Phone: 82-2-910-4752. Office Fax: 82-2-910-4728. E-mail: cskim@phys.kookmin.ac.kr.

KIM, CHUNG-HA, music educator; d. Tai-Won and Ai-Kyung Kim. MusB, Manhattan Sch. Music, 1999; MusM, U. Cin., 2001, D in Musical Arts, 2005. Tchg. asst. U. Cin., 1999—2004; adj. asst. prof. Millikin U., Decatur, Ill., 2004—06; asst. prof. piano Western Ill. U., Macomb, 2006—. Musician (pianist): (lecture-recital) E. T. A. Hoffmann's Influence on Robert Schumann's Kreisleriana; musician: (clinician) (workshop) Musical Technique With Czerny, Liszt, and Co. Recipient 2nd prize, Steinway-Competition, Hamburg (Germany), 1988, 1st prize, Jugend musiziert (Germany), 1986, 1987, President's award, Manhattan Sch. of Music, 1996, 1997, 1998; grantee Arts in the Cmty., Decatur Area Arts Coun., 2006. Mem.: Peoria Area Music Tchrs. Assn, Coll. Music Soc., Music Tchrs. Nat. Assn., Ill. State Music Tchrs. Assn. (east dist. chair 2005—06), Decatur Area Music Tchrs. Assn (sec. 2005—06). Office: Western Ill U Sch Music Browne 217 University Circle Macomb IL 61455 Office Phone: 309-298-2163. Business E-Mail: c-kim@wiu.edu.

KIM, DAE RYONG, management information systems educator; b. June 18, 1959; m. Jung Hwa Lee, Apr. 24, 1988; children: Jennifer, Harrison. MS, Iowa State U., 1992; PhD, U. Miss., 1996. Instr. U. Miss., Oxford, Miss., 1993—95; asst. prof. U. Ulsan, 1996—2001; assoc. prof. Del. State U., Dover, 2001—, chmn. dept., 2005—. Dept. chmn. U. of Ulsan, 1998—2001; cons. Electronic Commerce Resource Ctr., Ulsan, 2000—01; web mgr. U. of Ulsan, 1997—2001, computer lab supr., 1997—2001; lab supr. Del. State U., 2001—. Author: The Complete Success II: The Christians Who Succeed at Their Home, 2000, Unemployment, Setting Out a New Life, 2000; translator: Computers, Communications, and Information, 2001; sect. editor Yeungsang Acad. Jour., 2000—, editl. bd. The Internat. Jour. Applied Mgmt. and Tech., 2004—, Logos Mgmt. Rev., 2002—, reviewer Jour. of Electronic Commerce Rsch., 2002—; contbr. articles to profl. jours. Recipient Disting. Rsch. award, DSU, SOM, 2004, Acad. Strategic e-commerce, 2004, Acad. Ino. and Mgmt. Sci., 2006; grantee Munsu Rsch. grant, U. Ulsan, 1998, Distance Learning Rsch. grant, Korea Rsch. Found., 2000, Rsch. grant, Del. State U., 2002. Mem.: Korean Mgmt. Scientists in Am. (mng. dir. 2003—), INFORMS (Korean chpt. bd. dird. 2003—), Korean Internet and Electronic Commerce Assn. (dir. 2000—), Korean Assn. Indsl. Bus. Adminstrn. (mng. dir. 2000—01), Korea Soc. Mgmt., Korea Soc. MIS, Korea Assn. Info. Sys., Decision Sci. Inst., Inst. Operating Rsch. and Mgmt. Scis., Assn. for Info. Sys. Avocations: tennis, golf, running, travel, reading. Office: Del State U Sch Mgmt Dept Mgmt 1200 N DuPont Hwy Dover DE 19901 Office Phone: 302-857-6933. Personal E-mail: drkim23@hotmail.com. Business E-Mail: dkim@desu.edu.

KIM, DANIEL DAE, actor; b. Pusan, South Korea, Aug. 4, 1968; 2 children. BA in Theatre & Polit. Sci., Haverford Coll./Bryn Mawr Coll.; MFA, NYU. Actor: (films) American Shaolin, 1991, Addicted to Love, 1997, The Jackel, 1997, No Salida, 1998, Brave New World, 1998, Crusade, 1999, For Love of the Game, 1999, Looking for Bobby D, 2001, Cradle 2 the Grave, 2003, Wrath of Heaven, 2003, Hulk, 2003, Ride or Die, 2003, Spider-Man 2, 2004, Crash, 2004, The Cave, 2005; (TV films) Murder, She Wrote: A Story to Die For, 2000, Momentum, 2003, (video) Sin, 2003; (TV series) Lost, 2004— (Outstanding Male TV Performance, Asian Excellence Awards, 2006, Outstanding Performance by an Ensemble in a Drama Series, Screen Actors Guild award, 2006); video game Saints Row, 2005, guest appearances Law & Order, 1994, Beverly Hills, 90210, 1997, NYPD Blue, 1997, The Pretender, 1998, Seinfeld, 1998, The Practice, 1998, Ally McBeal, 1998, Party of Five, 1998, Fantasy Island, 1998, Walker, Texas Ranger, 1999, Star Trek:Voyager, 2000, Angel (12 episodes), 2001—03, Charmed, 2001, CSI: Crime Scene Investigation, 2001, 24 (11 Episodes), 2003—04, Enterprise, 2003, ER (4 episodes), 2003—04, Without A Trace, 2004, The Shield, 2004, and several others. Named one of Sexiest Man Alive, People mag., 2005.

KIM, DAVID EDWIN, plastic surgeon; b. Chgo. Grad., U. Ill., Champaign, 1989; MD, U. Ill., Chgo., 1993. Cert. Am. Bd. Plastic Surgery. Gen. surgery resident Mt. Sinai Hosp., 1993—97; plastic surgery resident Montefiore Med. Ctr., 1997—99; pvt. practice Beverly Hills, Calif., 1999—. Rsch. U. Ill., Chgo., 1995—96. Co-author: Skin Deep mag. Office: 436 N Bedford Dr Ste 300 Beverly Hills CA 90210 Office Phone: 310-271-6996. E-mail: davidekimmd@yahoo.com.*

KIM, DAVID HANWUK, surgeon, orthopedist, researcher; b. NY, Nov. 4, 1965; s. Sung Ho and Yang Hi Kim; m. Yoon Chun, Aug. 2, 2003; 1 child, Audrey. AB summa cum laude, Harvard U., Cambridge, Mass., 1988, MD, 1992. Diplomate Am. Bd. Orthop. Surgery, 2004. Intern gen. surgery Wash. U. Med. Ctr., St. Louis, 1992—93, resident gen. surgery, 1993—94; fellowship Nat. Insts. Health, Bethesda, Md., 1994—96; resident orthop. surgery combined program Harvard Coll., Boston, 1996—2001; fellowship spinal surgery Thomas Jefferson U., Phila., 2001—02; ptnr. The Boston Spine Group, 2002—07; asst. clin. prof. orthop. surgery med. sch. Tufts U., Boston, 2005—. Cons. in field. Contbr. articles to profl. jours. Fellow, NIH, 2001—02. Mem.: North Am. Spine Soc. (grantee 2004), Phi Beta Kappa. Achievements include design of spinal implant device; research in clinical outcomes following spinal surgery. Office: New England Baptist Hosp 125 Parker Hill Ave Boston MA 02120 Office Phone: 617-754-5595. Office Fax: 617-754-6482.

KIM, DAVID SANG CHUL, publishing executive, evangelist, retired academic administrator; b. Seoul, Nov. 9, 1915; arrived in U.S., 1959; m. Eui Hong Kang, Jan. 6, 1942; children: Sook Hee, Sung Soo, Hyun Soo, Young Soo, Joon Soo. BA in English Lit., Chosen Christian Coll., Seoul, 1939; postgrad., U. Wales, 1954—55, Western Conservative Bapt. Sem., 1959—61, U. Oreg., 1962—63, MA, 1965; postgrad., Pacific Sch. Religion, Berkeley, Calif., 1965—66; PhD, Pacific Columbia U., 1988. Staff Chosen Rubber Industry Assn., Seoul, 1939-45; fin asst. US Mil. Govt., Kunsan City, Republic of Korea, 1945-48; govt. ofcl. Ministry of Fin., Ministry of Social Affairs and Health, Ministry of Fgn. Affairs Govt. of Republic of Korea, Seoul, Republic of Korea, 1948-59; charter mem. Unification Ch., Seoul, Republic of Korea, 1954—, 1st missionary to Eng., 1954-55, missionary, evangelist, 1959-70; counseling supr. Clearfield Job Corps Ctr., Utah, 1966-70; founder, pres., owner The Cornerstone Press (now Rose of Sharon Press), 1978-85; charter mem., trustee World Relief Friendship Found., Inc. (now Internat. Relief Friendship Found., Inc.), 1974—; pres. Internat. One World Crusade Inc., 1975—. Founder, United Faith, Inc., Portland, Oreg., 1970—, Global Edn. R & D Fund, Inc., 1981-96; pres. Unification Theol. Sem., 1974-94; charter mem., trustee Nat. Coun. Ch. and Social Action, 1976-96; adv. fin. supporter Global Congress of World Religions, Inc., 1978-96; charter mem. Internat. Religious Found., Inc., 1982—; v.p. Unification Thought Inst., 1989-97; founder, pres. Marriage and Family Inst. Am., 1994—; chmn. inauguration The Family Fedn. for Unification and World Peace, Netherlands, 1996—; pres. emeritus Unification Theol. Sem., 2000—. Author: Individual Preparation for His Coming Kingdom: Interpretation of the Principle, 1964, Victory Over Communism and the Role of Religion, 1972; editor: (book series) Day of Hope in Review, Part 1-1972-1974, 1974, Part 2-1974-1975, 1975; exec. prodr.: (radio) The Unification Hour, 1975—2001; editor: (book series) Part 3-1976-1981, 1981; exec. prodr.: (radio) True Love Journey, 1993—2001; contbr. articles to profl. jour. Recipient Byzantine Golden medal Am. Inst. Patristic Byzantine Studies, Inc., 1992, Spl. award for Disting. Svc. Unification Ch., Internat., 1996, Cheon Il Guk Owner award Family Fedn. for World Peace and Unification, Seoul, 2003. Address: PO Box 1755 South Rd Sta Poughkeepsie NY 12601-0755

KIM, DEOK-HO, biomedical researcher; b. Youngju, Kyungsangbuk-Do, Republic of Korea, July 3, 1975; s. Yeon-Ho Myung; m. Eun Hyun Ahn, May 8, 2005. BS in Mech. Engring. with honors, Pohang U. Sci. Tech., 1994—98; MS, Seoul Nat. U., Republic of Korea, 1998—2000. Rsch. asst. Inst. Advanced Machinery and Design, Seoul Nat. U., Seoul, 1998—2000; rsch. scientist Korea Inst. Sci. and Tech., Seoul, 2000—05; vis. rsch. scientist Swiss Fed. Inst. Tech., Zurich, 2004; grad. rsch. asst. Johns Hopkins Univ., Baltimore, 2005—. Grad. rsch. advisor Korea Inst. Sci. and Tech., Seoul, 2000—05; session co-chair IEEE Symposium on Micromechatronics and Human Sci., Nagoya, Japan, 2001; mem. IEEE Engring. in Medicine and Biology Soc., 2003—06; ad-hoc reviewer IEEE Transactions/Conf. and ASME Conf., 2003—06; invited spkr. Umr Cnrs, Besanson, 2004. Contbr. numerous papers to profl. jours. and pubs. Mem. Korean-Am. Scientists and Engrs. Assn., Balt., 2006. Recipient Best Student Poster Paper award, Korean Soc. Precision Engrs., 1999, Best Student Paper award, Korean Soc. Mech. Engring., 1999, Excellent Rschr. of Yr. prize, Future Tech. Rsch. Divsn., Korea Inst. Sci. and Tech., 2004, Disting. Achievement award, Korea Inst. Sci. and Tech., 2005, Best Presentation award, Inst. Control, Automation, and Sys., 2005; grantee scholarship, POSTECH, Korea, 1996, Hogil-Kim Meml. fellowship, U. Birmingham, U.K., 1996, fellowship, Korea Sci. and Engring. Found., 2003. Mem.: IEEE. Achievements include patents pending for microrobot gripping apparatus; development of design, fabrication, and tests of a piezoelectric PVDF polymer-based sensorized microgripper; a flexible microassembly system using visual and force feedback for manufacturing opto-electromechanical components; design, measurements and mechanical analysis of a biomimetic tadpole robot using IPMC actuators; design, control, and experimental performance evaluation of 3-DOF PZT-driven mobile microrobot; a micromechanical force sensing system for measuring cellular force; patents for multi-degrees-of freedom dexterous telerobotic system for microassembly; autonomous bio-manipulation factory system for manipulating single cells; method and device for assembling MEMS components; apparatus and method for assembling MEMS components using image of multiple magnification; smart pipette system and method for manipulating individual bio cells; patents pending for cell separation system using ultrasound field and traveling wave dielectrophoresis; smart pipette for cell manipulation and manipulation method for using the smart pipette; autonomous bio-manipulation factory system for manipulating single cells. Avocations: travel, marathon. Home Phone: 410-908-2281. Business E-Mail: dhkim@jhu.edu.

KIM, DO GYOON, biomedical researcher; b. Gimcheon, Republic of Korea, Oct. 20, 1966; arrived in U.S., 1996; s. Sang Yong Kim and Sook Yong Shin; m. Eun Joo Song, Apr. 3, 1996; children: Simon Han Soo, John Yoon Soo. BS, Yonsei U., Seoul, 1989, MS, 1991; PhD, Rensselaer Poly. Inst., Troy, NY, 2001. Assoc. engr. Inst. Advanced Engring., DAEWOO Co., Yongin, Kyonggi-do, Republic of Korea; rsch. fellow Rensselaer Poly. Inst., 2001—02, SUNY Upstate Med. U., Syracuse, 2002—03, Henry Ford Hosp., Detroit, 2003—05, rsch. scientist, 2005—. Reviewer Assn. Bone and Joint Surgeons, Clin. Orthopaedics and Related Rsch., Phila., 2006—. Reviewer: ASME, Jour. Biomech. Engring., 2004—, BioMed. Engring. OnLine, 2005—, Jour. Biomechanics, 2006—; contbr. articles to profl. jours. Prin. korean lang. sch. St. Andrew Korean Cath. Ch., Northville, Mich., 2005—06. Fellow, Rensselaer Poly. Inst., 1998—2001; scholar, Yonsei U., 1985, 1989—91, Rensselaer Poly. Inst., 1987. Mem.: Korean Soc. Orthop. and Related Rsch. (rep. 2003—06), Biomed. Engring. Soc., Orthopaedic Rsch. Soc. (assoc.), Nat. Assn. Korean Sch. (sec. Mich. chpt. 2000—01), Korean-Am. Scientist and Engrs. Assn. (pres. N.E. N.Y. chpt.). Achievements include patents for conducting polymer and bacterial adhesion receptor. Home: 1195 Woodside Ct Troy MI 48085 Office: Bone Joint Ctr Henry Ford Hospital 2799 W Grand Blvd Detroit MI 48202 Home Phone: 248-635-0689; Office Phone: 313-916-8066. Office Fax: 313-916-8064. Business E-Mail: kimdg66@hotmail.com.

KIM, DO KYUNG, science educator; b. Seoul, Republic Of Korea, Mar. 22, 1970; s. Tae Yoon and Jung Sook (Choi) Kim; m. Mi Jung Kang; 1 child, Sue Jung. PhD, Royal Inst. Tech., Stockholm, 2002. Sr. rschr. Royal Inst. Tech., Stockholm, 2002—; vis. scientist Rutgers U., Newark, 2003—05; postdoctoral fellow MIT, Cambridge, 2004—05; asst. prof., lectr. in biomagnetics Keele U., Stoke-on-Trent, Staffordshire, United Kingdom, 2005—. Presenter in field. Author: Nanomaterials for Cancer Therapy and Diagnosis. With Korean mil., 1995—97. Achievements include patents for au coated superparamagnetic nanoparticles. Office: Keele Univ Thronburrow Dr Hartshill Staffordshire Stoke-on-Trent ST4 7QB England Office Phone: 44 1782 554 600. Business E-Mail: d.k.kim@pmed.keele.ac.uk.

KIM, DONG H., neurosurgeon, medical geneticist, educator; b. Seoul, Republic of Korea, Feb. 11, 1964; m. Grace Kim, Oct. 11, 1992; 1 child, Katherine William. BS with honors, Stanford U., Palo Alto, Calif., 1986; MD, U. Calif., San Francisco, 1990. Cert. neurosurgeon Neurosurgery Bds., 1991. Neurosurgeon, faculty mem. Brigham and Women's Hosp., Harvard Med. Sch., Boston, 2003—. Recipient Partners in Excellence award, Brigham and Women's Hosp., 2005. Mem.: San Francisco Neurol. Soc. (Henry Newman award 1993), Am. Assn. Neurol. Surgeons (Bayer Cerebrovascular Rsch. award 1999), Congress Neurol. Surgeons. Independent. Presbyterian. Achievements include one US patent in Genetic gains and losses in gliomas. Avocations: reading, basketball, swimming, travel. Office: BWH Neurosurgery Harvard Med Sch 75 Francis Street Boston MA 02115 Home Phone: 781-894-2214; Office Phone: 617-525-7779.

KIM, DONGSOO, clinical neuropsychologist, researcher; b. Seoul, Republic Of Korea, July 17, 1964; s. Jinsup Kim and Jeongsun Park; m. Eunjee Chung, June 1, 1991; 1 child, Teddy. BA, Baldwin-Wallace Coll., Berea, Ohio, 1986—89; MA, New Sch. Social Rsch., NYC, 1989—91; PhD, Yeshiva U., Bronx, NY, 1996—2001. Lic. psychologist NY State Bd. Psychology, 2003, NJ State Bd. Psychol. Examiners, 2004. Counselor Ohio Boys Town, Berea, Ohio, 1988—89; psychology extern Counseling Assocs. Rockland, New City, NY, 1998—99; neuropsychology extern/tester dept. neurology Montefiore Med. Ctr., Bronx, 1998—2000; neuropsychology extern dept. psychiatry NJ Med. Sch., Newark, 1999—2000; clincial psychology fellow dept. psychiatry Yale U. Med. Sch., New Haven, 2000—01; post-doctoral fellow in cognitive neurosci. Nathan Kline Inst. Psychiat. Rsch., Orangeburg, NY, 2001—03; pvt. practice in clin. neuropsychology and clin. psychology Englewood, NJ, 2003; nys rsch. scientist Nathan Kline Inst. Psychiat. Rsch./NYS Office Mental Health, Orangeburg, 2003—05; clin. & rsch. assoc. dept. psychiatry Soonchunhyang U. Hosp, Chunann, Republic of Korea, 2005—. Guest spkr. NY RadioKorea AM1660, Flushing, NY. Contbr. articles to profl. jours. Vol. dir. counseling svcs. NJ Korean-Am. Youth Ctr., Palisades Park, 2002—03; curriculum com. chair Korean Sch. NJ, Tenafly, 2003; bd. mem. Korean YMCA Flushing, NY, 2006. With Korean Army, 1991—93. Mem.: APA (life), Korean Psychol. Assn. (assoc.), Neuropsychology (assoc.), Assn. Rsch. Vision & Ophthalmology (assoc.), Soc. Neurosci. (assoc.), Internat. Congress Schizophrenia Rsch. (assoc.), Internat. Neuropsychology Soc. (assoc.). Office: Dongsoo Kim PhD 163 Engle St #1A Englewood NJ 07631 Office Fax: 201-391-1799. Business E-Mail: drdongsookim@hotmail.com.

KIM, DONGWOOK, research and development company executive; b. Seoul, Republic of Korea, Aug. 18, 1965; arrived in US, 2000; s. Hyung Young and Young Ja Kim; m. Sook K. Koh, June 26, 1967; children: Minjoo children: Jennifer H. MS, U. Mo., 1991; PhD in Biomed. Engring., Hanyang U., Korea, 2007. Project mgr. Samsung Electronics Co., Ltd, Suwon, 1992—2000; sr. profl. GE, Global Rsch. Ctr., Niskayuna, NY, 2001—04; chief tech. officer Bionet Co., Tustin, Calif., 2005—07; cons. engr. GE, Energy, Schenectady, NY, 2004—06; chief. exec. officer Neurolinx Ltd., Pine Brook, NJ, 2007—. Advisor and tech. bd. Hearing Aid Forum, Small and Medium Bus. Adminstrn., Korean Ministry Commerce, Industry and Energy, Seoul, 1998—99; tech. bd. Stds. Multimedia and Acoustics, Agy. Tech. and Stds., Korean Ministry Commerce, Industry and Energy, Seoul, 2000—; vis. scientist Johns Hopkins U., Balt., 2000—01. Mem. editl. bd. Korean Acad. Speech Lang. Pathology and Audiology, Seoul, 1998—2000; contbr. articles to more than 35 jours. Mem.: IEEE (tech. program reviewer tech. program com. 2003, contbr. jour.), Sigma Xi, Sci. Rsch. Soc. Achievements include 10 patents in field. Home and Office: Neurolinx Ltd 2000 Rachel Ter Apt #14 Pine Brook NJ 07058 Business E-Mail: neurolinx@hotmail.com.

KIM, DOW, investment company executive; b. Republic of Korea; BSE, Wharton Sch., 1984, MBA, 1990. Credit analyst, comml. banker, derivatives trader Mfrs. Hanover Bank, NY, 1985—91; v.p., head Yen options trading Chem. Bank, Tokyo, 1991—94; mgr. debt derivatives trading desk Merill Lynch & Co., Inc., 1994, mng. dir., head debt and equity derivatives, mgr. integrated fixed income bus., 2000, mng. dir. and head global enterprise risk mgmt., head global debt markets, 2001—03, exec. v.p., pres. global markets & investment banking, 2003—07, sr. exec. adv., 2007—. Office: Merrill Lynch & Co Inc 4 World Fin Ctr 250 Vesey St New York NY 10080*

KIM, DUCKSOO, radiologist, inventor, educator; b. Seoul, Korea, Aug. 16, 1948; came to U.S., 1977; s. Changkun and Sunchom (Cho) K.; m. Eunjoo Lee, May 22, 1978; children: LeeAnn, SueAnn, Andrew. BS, Cath. U., Seoul, 1969, MD, 1973; postgrad., Stanford U., Calif., 1981-83. Diplomate Am. Bd. Radiology; lic. physician, Mass., N.Y., Calif. Intern St. Mary's Hosp., Seoul, 1976-77, McKeesport Hosp., Pa., 1977-78; resident in diagnostic radiology Beth Israel Hosp., Newark, 1978-81; NIH fellow in cardiovascular and interventional radiology Stanford U. Med. Ctr., Calif., 1981-83; instr. radiology Harvard Med. Sch., Boston, 1983-86, asst. prof. radiology, 1986-92, assoc. prof. radiology, 1992-98; dir. divsn. cardiovascular and interventl. radiology Beth Israel Hosp., Boston, 1983-96; co-dir. divsn. cardiovascular and interventional radiology Beth Israel Deaconess Med. Ctr., Boston, 1996-98; prof. radiology and surgery U. Mass. Med. Sch., Worcester, 1999—2006; prof. radiology Boston U. Med. Sch., 2006—; dir. divsn. cardiovascular and interventional radiology U. Mass. Med. Ctr., Worcester, 1999—2006, Boston U. Med. Ctr., 2006—. Vis. prof. radiology U. Zurich, 1987, Nat. Rsch. Ctr. of Surgery, Ministry of Health, Russia, 1992; lectr. in field; rschr. in field. Author: Peripheral Vascular Imaging and Intervention, 1992; reviewer Catheterization and Cardiovascular Diagnosis, 1992-94, Hepatology, 1993; contbr. articles to profl. jours., chpts. in books. Sec. Korean Cath. Community, Boston, 1988-89, v.p., 1989-91, pres., 1991-92. Capt. Korean Army, 1973-76. Cath. U. Med. Coll. scholar, 1969-73; NIH grantee, 1981-83. Fellow Am. Coll. Angiology, Internat. Coll. Angiology, Am. Heart Assn., Soc. of Cardiovascular and Interventional Radiology; mem. AMA, Radiol. Soc. N.Am., Am. Coll. Radiology, New Eng. Soc. for Cardiovascular and Interventional Radiology (pres. 1992-93), New Eng. Korean Med. Soc., Norfolk Dist. Med. Soc., Mass. Med. Soc., Soc. of Magnetic Resonance in Medicine, Soc. of Magnetic Resonance Imaging, New Eng. Alumni Assn. of Cath. U. Med. Coll. (pres. 1991-92). Roman Catholic. Avocations: tennis, golf. Home: 9 Cedar Hill Rd Dover MA 02030-1631 Office: Boston Med Ctr 88 East Newton St Boston MA 02118 Home Phone: 508-395-3110. Personal E-mail: dicksookim@comcast.net.

KIM, E. HAN, financial economist, educator; b. Seoul, Republic of Korea, May 27, 1946; came to U.S., 1966; s. Chang Yoon and Young Ja (Chung) K.; m. Tack Han, June 14, 1969; children— Juliane H., Elaine H., Deborah H. BS, U. Rochester, 1969; MBA, Cornell U., 1971; PhD, SUNY-Buffalo, 1975. Asst. prof. Ohio State U., Columbus, 1975-77, assoc. prof., 1979-80; assoc. prof., then prof. fin. and bus. adminstrn. U. Mich., Ann Arbor, 1980-84, Fred M. Taylor Disting. prof., 1984—, chmn. dept. fin., 1988-91; dir. Mitsui Life Fin. Rsch. Ctr., 1990—. Vis. assoc. prof. U. Chgo., 1978-79; vis. rsch. fellow Korea Devel. Inst., 1986-87; econ. cons. Govt. of Korea, 1985-87, 98; Cycle and Carriage vis. prof. Nat. U. Singapore, 1989; Yamaichi prof. econs. U. Tokyo, 1990-91; cons. Bank of Korea, 1985, U.S. Dept. Treasury, IRS, 1988-94, World Bank, 1989-91, 93, Posco, 1995-98, Korea Stock Exch., 1997-98; co-chair Citizens for Econ. Freedom, 1997-99; bd. dirs. Posco, Hana Bank, Mut. Savs. Bank. Assoc. editor Jour. Fin., 1979-83, 88-92, Fin. Rev., 1982—2003, Internat. Jour. Fin., 1990—94, Internat. Rev. Fin. Analysis, 1990-92, Rev. No. Am. Jour. of Econs. and Fin., 1990—99, Rev. Quantitative Fin. and Acctg., 1990—, Pacific Basin Fin. Jour., 1991-96; editl. bd. Jour. Bus. Rsch., 1977—; adv. bd. Asia-Pacific Jour. Mgmt., 1990-96, Jour. Asian Bus., 1996—; contbr. articles to profl. jours. Mem. Korea-Am. Econ. Assn. (sec. gen. 1985, v.p. 1986, pres. 1996), Am. Econ. Assn., Am. Fin. Assn., Western Fin. Assn. Avocations: tennis, golf. Office: Univ Mich Ross Sch Bus Ann Arbor MI 48109

KIM, HAKYONG, lawyer, accountant; b. Seoul, Republic of Korea; m. Mihe Kim, July 29, 1983; children: Haemin, Phillip Sunghun, Grace H. BS, Seoul Nat. U., 1980; MBA, Pa. State U., 1988; JD, Touro Law Sch., 2002. Bar: NY 2003, DC 2004. Ptnr. Kim, You, & Assocs., NYC, Kim & Kim CPAs, Flushing, Jason Choi CPA, Hyundai Engring. & Constrn. Co., Seoul. Mem.: ABA, AILA. Office: Law Offices of Hakyong Kim PC 159-15 Northern Blvd Ste 111 Flushing NY 11358 Office Phone: 718-445-0123. Business E-Mail: hakyong@hkimlaw.com.

KIM, HAN PYONG, researcher; b. Seoul, May 2, 1945; s. Koe Jin and Jung Bok (Park) K.; m. Young Sook Yoon, Apr. 27, 1974; 1 child, Sung Mo. MA, DDS, Seoul Nat. U., 1975; PhD, Yonsei U., Seoul, 1982; MA, Monterey Inst. Internat. Study, 1996. Prof. Yonsei U., Seoul, 1977-84; vis. scholar UCLA, 1982; project rschr. health care sys. Korea Dental Assn., Seoul, 1988-92. Mem. bd. health ins. Nat. HIC, Seoul, 1990-92. Mem. Pres.'s Leadership Circle, Washington, 1995. Avocations: golf, fishing, photography. Home: 2800 Keller Dr 11 Tustin CA 92782 Home Phone: 714-734-5728; Office Phone: 714-724-2580. Personal E-mail: greenzone6@yahoo.com.

KIM, HANSOO, materials scientist, researcher; b. Seoul, Aug. 14, 1968; s. Wontae Kim and Chunja Lee; m. Hyungsook Park, July 1, 2000; 1 child, Christopher. BS, Korea U., Seoul, 1996, MS, 1998; PhD, U. Fla., Gainesville, 2003. Rsch. engr. Hynix Electronics, Icheon, Kyunggido, Republic of Korea, 1998—2000; rsch. assoc. U. Pa., Phila., 2004—06; rsch. scientist U. N. Tex., Denton, Tex., 2006—. Author: Encyclopedia of Nanoscience and Nanotechnolgy, Trends in Crystal Growth Research; contbr. articles various profl. jours. Sgt. 1st Bn., 501st Rgt., 17 Aviati, 1989—91, Seoul. Decorated Army Achievement medal U.S. Dept. of the Army; fellow Rsch. Assoc., U. Pa., 2004 - 2006; scholar Disting. Freshman, Korea U., 1992, Excellent Achievement In Study, 1992, Outstanding Undergraduate Student, Moam Fund, 1992 - 1993, Outstanding Grad. Student, Hynix Electronics, 1996. Mem.: Microscopy Soc. Am. Achievements include development of highly efficient blue - emitting oxide phosphor; discovery of high temperature phase of iron stable at room temperature in carbon nanotubes by transmission electron microscopy; development of hierachical zinc oxide nanotubes; method to transform the room temperature phase of iron to a high temperature phase in carbon nanotubes by electron beam; zinc oxide nanowires standing on carbon nanotube; research in nanoscale aggregates in ionomers by electron energy loss spectroscopy; controlled modifications in physical and chemical properties of nanometer scale areas in conventional polymers; systematic analysis of a titanium alloy by atom and electron probes; development of assessment of strain distribution in niobium superconductor; research in controlled modifications of conventional polymers by fast electrons; finding of abnormal behavior of a titanium alloy in vanadium segregation; characterization of strain distribution in niobium superconductor. Home: 521 E Windsor Dr 105 Denton TX 76209 Office: U N Tex 3940 N Elm St E137 Denton TX 76207 Office Phone: 940-891-6775. Office Fax: 940-565-4824. Personal E-mail: hsluminesc@hotmail.com.

KIM, HEATHER, director; d. Kim; m. Justin Kim, Aug. 1, 1960. BS, Ewha Women's U., Seoul, 1986; MS, NC State U., Raleigh, 1991, EdD, 1994. Dir. instl. rsch., adj. faculty Sacred Heart U., Fairfield, Conn., 1997—99; sr. rsch., planning assoc. Cornell U., Ithaca, NY, 1999—2000; sr. rschr. Yale U., New Haven, 2000—04; dir. instl. rsch. New Sch., NYC, 2004—06, Dartmouth Coll., Hanover, NH, 2006—. Cons. NC State U., 1994—96; asst. dir. NC C.C. Leadership Inst., Raleigh, 1993; spkr. in field. Contbr. articles to profl. jours. Postdoctoral fellow, Ednl. Testing Svc., Princeton, NJ, 1995—96. Mem.: Assn. for Study of Higher Edn., Am. Edn. Rsch. Assn., Ivy League Instl. Rsch. Group, Consortium on Financing Higher Edn., North East Assn. Instl. Rsch., Assn. Instl. Rsch., Phi Kappa Phi. Office Phone: 603-646-1247.

KIM, HO GILL, poet; b. Sachon, South Korea, June 22, 1943; s. Jong Soo and Ul Soon (Lee) K.; m. Sherrie Chul Ja Park, Mar. 19, 1970; children: Brian Ki-Man, Eugene Yoo-Jin. BA, Gyeng Sang Univ., Jin-Joo, Korea, 1970; MS in Econs., Kun Kook Univ., Seoul, 1975. Airline pilot Korean Airlines, Seoul, 1972-81; columnist Korean Central Daily News, LA, 1981-83; pres. Everglobe Enterprises Inc. dba Sunflower Farms, LA, 1984—. Editor: Literary realm, 1987-95, Korean American Literature, 1982-86, SiJo World, 1999—; author poetry. Capt. Korean Army, 1965-71, Vietnam. Decorated Military Merit Vietnam War Korean Army, 1971; recipient Anti-Communist Poetry award Korea Def. Ministry, 1969, Overseas Korean Literary award Chu Kang Literary Soc., 1997, Modern Si Jo Poetry award Modern SiJo Publ. Co., 1998. Mem. SiJo Soc. Am. (pres. 1995), Korean Literary Soc. Am. (pres. 1982—, adv.), Internat. Pen Club, Acad. Am. Poets, World Korean Writers Network (pres. 2000—). Office: 1937 E Vernon Ave Vernon CA 90058

KIM, HONG NACK, political science professor; b. Youngchun, Korea, Aug. 20, 1933; came to U.S., 1956, naturalized, 1973; s. Sang Do and Nam Jo (Sung) K.; m. Boohi Suh, Mar. 26, 1967; children: Michael, Jeffrey, Brian Kim. BA, Seoul Nat U., Korea, 1956; MA, Georgetown U., 1960, PhD, 1965. Lectr. Georgetown U., Washington, 1965-66; asst. prof. North Tex. State U., Denton, 1966-67, 1967-72, assoc. prof., 1972-77; prof. polit. sci. W.Va. U., Morgantown, 1977—. Author: Scholars Guide to Washington, D.C. for East Asian Studies, 1979; editor-in-chief: Internat. Jour. of Korean Studies, 2000—2005; editor: Asian Forum, 1972-74, Polit. Studies Rev., 1984-87; co-editor: Essays in Political Science, 1972, Korean Reunification: New Perspectives and Approaches, 1984, North Korea: The

Politics of Regime Survival, 2006; contbr. articles to various publs. Pres. Korean Assn. W.V., 1981-82, Assn. Korean Polit. Scientists N.Am.83-85, Internat. Coun. on Korean Studies, Washington. Fulbright-Hays Faculty Rsch. Abroad grantee U.S. Dept. Edn., 1979, 82; Fulbright Lecturing/Rsch. grantee U.S. Info. Agy., 1990; recipient Outstanding Rsch. award W.Va. U., 1985. Mem. Am. Polit. Sci. Assn., Assn. Asian Studies. Democrat. Presbyterian. Home: 1270 Braewick Dr Morgantown WV 26505-3339 Office: W Va U Dept Polit Sci Morgantown WV 26505 Business E-Mail: Hongkim@wvu.edu.

KIM, IKSUK, marketing educator; b. Busan, Republic of Korea, July 7, 1963; Degree in Law, Han Yang U., Seoul, 1982; MS in Telecomm., U. Pitts., 1995; M in Engring., Purdue U., West Lafayette, Ind., 1997, PhD, 2001. Prof. Calif. State U., Hayward, 2001—03, LA, 2003—. Cons. Korea Culture and Contents Agy., LA, 2006—. Program coord. Korea Cultural Ctr., LA, 2007—. Mem.: Am. Mktg. Assn. Achievements include research in online consumers' perceived risk; mall entertainment industry review and shopping behaviors; the state of e-CRM in retailing; operational determinants of caller satisfaction in the banking/financial services call center; operational determinants of caller satisfaction in the call center; online consumers' risk reduction strategies. Office: Calif State U LA 5151 State University Dr Los Angeles CA 90032 Office Phone: 310-343-2960. Office Fax: 323-343-5462. Business E-Mail: iksuk@hotmail.com.

KIM, JAEGWON, philosophy educator; b. Taegu, Korea, Sept. 12, 1934; came to U.S., 1955, naturalized, 1966; AB, Dartmouth Coll., 1958; PhD, Princeton U., 1962. Instr. philosophy Swarthmore Coll., 1961-63; asst. prof. philosophy Brown U., 1963-67, vis. prof., 1975, William Perry Faunce prof. philosophy, 1987—; chair dept. Borwn U., 1990-99; assoc. prof. philosophy U. Mich., 1967-70, prof., 1971-87, chmn. dept., 1979-87, Roy Wood Sellars prof. philosophy, 1986-87. Assoc. prof. Cornell U., 1970-71; prof. Johns Hopkins U., 1977-78; vis. prof. Stanford U., 1967; Fulbright lectr., Republic of Korea, 1984, Seoul Nat. U., 2000; vis. McMahon-Hank prof. U. Notre Dame, 1999, 2001—. Author: Supervenience and Mind, 1993, Philosophy of Mind, 1996, Mind in a Physical World, 1998, Physicalism or Something Near Enough, 2005; editor: (with Alvin I. Goldman) Values and Morals, 1978, (with A. Beckermann and H. Flohr) Emergence or Reduction?, 1992; (with E. Sosa) A Companion to Metaphysics, 1995, Metaphysics: An Anthology, 1999, Epistemology: An Anthology, 2000, Supervenience, 2002; co-editor: Nous, 2005; contbr. numerous articles to profl. publs. Fellow Am. Coun. Learned Soc., 1980-81, NEH, 1985; NSF grantee, 1977-79. Mem. Am. Philos. Assn. (chmn. com. on status and future of profession 1976-81, mem. bd. officers 1976-81, 88-90, v.p. ctrl. divsn. 1987-88, pres. 1988-89), Philosophy of Sci. Assn. (mem. governing bd. 1979-81), Am. Acad. Arts and Scis., Coun. Philos. Studies. Office: Brown U Dept Philosophy Providence RI 02912-0001

KIM, JAI SOO, retired physicist; b. Taegu, Korea, Nov. 1, 1925; came to U.S., 1958, naturalized, 1963; s. Wan Sup and Chanam (Whang) K.; m. Hai Kyou Kim, Nov. 2, 1952; children: Kami, Tomi, Kihyun, Himi. BSc in Physics, Seoul Nat. U., Korea, 1949; MS in Physics, U. Sask., Can., 1957, PhD, 1958. Asst. prof. physics Clarkson U., Potsdam, NY, 1958-59, U. Idaho, Moscow, 1959-62, assoc. prof., 1962-65, prof., 1965-67; prof. atmospheric sci. and physics SUNY, Albany, 1967-95, chmn. dept. atmospheric sci., 1969-76; emeritus prof., 1995—; rep. Univ. Corp. for Atmospheric Research SUNY, Albany, 1970-76, cons. Korean Studies Program Stony Brook, 1983-85. Vis. prof. Advanced Inst. Sci. and Tech., Seoul, Korea, 1983; cons. U.S. Army Research Office, 1978-79, Battelle Meml. Inst., 1978-81, Environ. One Corp., 1978-84, N.Y. State Environ. Conservation Dept., 1976-82, Norlite Corp., 1982-84, Korean Antarctic Program, 1988—. Contbr. articles to profl. jours. Mem. Am. Inst. Physics, Am. Geophys. Union, Sigma Xi. Home: 22 Westover Rd Slingerlands NY 12159-3646 Office: 1400 Washington Ave Albany NY 12222-0100 Personal E-mail: kim9664@msn.com.

KIM, JAMES JOO-JIN, electronics company executive; b. Seoul, Korea, Jan. 8, 1936; came to U.S., 1955, naturalized, 1971; s. Hyang-Soo and Seung-Ye (Oh) K.; m. Agnes Chungsook Kil, Dec. 30, 1961; children—Susan, David, John. Student, Seoul Nat. U. Coll. Law, 1954-55; BS, U. Pa., 1959, MA, 1961, postgrad., 1961-63; D in Comml. Sci. (hon.), Villanova U., 1990. Asst. prof. econs. Villanova (Pa.) U., 1964-70; founder, pres. AMKOR Electronics, Inc., West Chester, Pa., 1970-98; chmn., CEO AMKOR Tech. Inc., Chandler, Ariz., 1998—. Founder, dir. Electronics Boutique Holding Corp.; bd. dirs. Visalign, LLC, Semiconductor, Inc., CFM Techs. Inc.; dir., chmn. Anam Semiconductor, Inc. (Korea), 1992—. Trustee U. Pa. Named one of Forbes' Richest Americans, 2006; recipient Presdl. Commendation award Pres. Park/Chung Hee, Republic of Korea, 1979, Korean Presdl. Order of Indsl. Svc. Merits, 1983, Korean Presdl. Tin-Tower award Pres. Roh/Tae Woo, Republic of Korea, 1990, Grand-Prix, New Industry Mgmt. Acad., 1996, Global Korea award Mich. State U., 1996, Semiconductor award as pioneer in merchant packaging industry, 1998. Mem. Union League Club (Phila.), Beta Gamma Sigma. Office: Amkor Technology 1900 S Price Rd Chandler AZ 85248*

KIM, JEONG H., telecommunications industry executive, communications engineer; b. Seoul, Rep. of Korea; married; 2 children. BS, Johns Hopkins U., MS in Tech. Mgmt.; PhD in Reliability Engring., U. Md., 1991. Founder, chmn., CEO Yurie Sys., 1992—98; pres. broadband carrier networks, then COO & pres. Optical network Group Bell Labs, Lucent Technologies, 1998—2001; prof. of practice in reliability engring. Clark Sch. Engring., U. Md., College Park, 2002—05; pres. Bell Labs, Lucent Technologies (now Alcatel Lucent), Murray Hill, NJ, 2005—. Nuclear submarine officer USN. Recipient Ernst & Young's Emerging Entrepreneur of Yr Award. Mem.: NAE. Office: Alcatel Lucent Bell Labs 600 Mountain Ave New Providence NJ 07974-0636*

KIM, JEONGBIN JOHN, mechanical engineering educator; arrived in US, 1972, naturalized, 1982; s. Wanson Kim and Ilyun Wu; m. Mee-Joo Julie Kim, June 18, 1977; 1 child, June M.; m. Stacy E. Lee, Dec. 27, 2003. BSME, Seoul Nat. U., 1970; MSME, Brown U., 1974; PhD in Mech. Engring., Stanford U., Calif., 1978. Nat. rsch. coun. fellow NASA Ames Rsch. Ctr., Moffett Field, Calif., 1978-80, rsch. scientist, 1982-87, sect. head., 1987-93, branch chief, 1992-93; asst. prof. Stanford U., 1980-82; Rockwell Internat. prof. U. Calif., LA, 1993—. Editor: Physics of Fluid, 1998—. Recipient Engring. prize, Ho-Am Found., 2002. Fellow Am. Phys. Soc. (Otto Laporte award 2001) Democrat. Presbyterian. Office: U Calif Dept Mech/Aerospace Engring 420 Westwood Plz Los Angeles CA 90095-1597 Home Phone: 818-222-5435. Business E-Mail: jkim@seas.ucla.edu.

KIM, JIM YONG, public health service officer, preventive medicine physician; b. South Korea, Dec. 8, 1959; BA, Brown U., 1982; MD, Harvard U., 1991, PhD in anthropology, 1993. Assoc. prof. med. Harvard U.; co- dir. Harvard's Program in Infectious Disease and Soc. Change, 1996; founding mem. World Health Orgn.'s Working Group. on DOTS-Plus, 1999; attending physician Dept. of internal Med., Brigham and Women's Hosp., Boston; chief. Div. of Soc. Med. and Health Inequalities Harvard Med. Sch.; advisor to dir. gen. WHO, Geneva, dir. HIV/AIDS dept., 2004—. Co-founder, exec. dir. Partners in Health, 1987—. Author: (book) Dying for Growth: Global Inequality and the Health of the Poor; contbr. book. Named a MacArthur fellow, John D. & Catherine T. MacArthur Found., 2003; named one of 100 Most Influential People, Time Mag., 2006. Mem.: Inst. Medicine. Office: WHO Headquarters Avenue Appia 20 1211 Geneva 27 CH 121 Geneva Switzerland

KIM, JIN YONG, research scientist; b. Seoul, Republic Of Korea, Feb. 5, 1968; s. Ho-Chan Kim and Soon-Yon Bae; m. Sung-Hee Yoon, June 2, 1995; children: Bertha, Marcia. BS, Seoul Nat. U., 1986—90; MS, Pohang U. Sci. & Tech., S.Korea, 1990—92; PhD, Carnegie Mellon U., Pitts., 1993—98. Postdoctoral rsch. assoc. Carnegie Mellon U., 1998—99, rsch. fellow, 1999—2000; materials scientist AMTEK Rsch. Internat., LLC, Lebanon, Oreg., 2000—02; sr. rsch. scientist Pacific NW Nat. Lab., Richland, Wash., 2002—. Contbr. articles to profl. jours., chapters to books. Recipient Tech. Brief award, NASA, 2004. Mem.: Electrochem. Soc., Am. Ceramic Soc., Sigma Xi. Cath. Achievements include patents for method of joining ceramic and metal parts. Office: Pacific NW Nat Lab 902 Battelle Blvd Richland WA 99352 Home Phone: 509-628-0426. Office Fax: 509-376-2248; Home Fax: 509-376-2248. Personal E-mail: jyk8z@naver.com. Business E-Mail: jin.kim@pnl.gov.

KIM, JOOCHUL, urban planner, educator; b. Seoul, Korea, June 21, 1948; came to U.S., 1969; s. Kubong and Kumsoon (Song) K.; m. Shinja Rhee Kim, Sept. 16, 1969; 1 child, Matthew. BA in Sociology, U. Calif., Berkeley, 1973; MUP, U. Mich., Ann Arbor, 1977, PhD in Urban and Regional Planning, 1979. Lectr. Boston U., 1977-80; asst. prof. Ariz. State U., Tempe, 1980-85, rsch. assoc., 1980—, assoc. prof., sch. of planning, 1985—. Participant Leadership Acad., Tempe, 1989-90; mgmt. intern Ariz. State U., 1990, dir. spl. project, 1990-2001, acad. program coord., 2001—; vis. prof., Seoul Nat. U., 1987, Hanyang U., 1986-87, vis. chief rsch. assoc., Seoul Devel. Inst., 1995. Editor: Planning Perspectives, 1983—85; author: Seoul: The Making of Metropolis, 1997; contbr. articles to profl. jours. Mem. Ariz. Solar Energy Assn., Phoenix, 1983-84; mem. task force City of Tempe, 1990—; founding bd. dirs. Friends of Internat. Films, Tempe, 1982-86; co-chair City of Phoenix Planning Com., 1982-83. Fulbright scholar Republic of Korea, 1986-87; named one of Outstanding Young Men of Am., U.S. Jaycees, 1982. Mem. Internat. Div. Planners Network, Korean Urban and Regional Planning Assn. Avocations: movies, piano, music, travel, reading. Office: Ariz State U Sch Planning PO Box 872005 Tempe AZ 85287-2005 Office Phone: 480-965-2768.

KIM, KEEHOON, cybernetic scientist; s. Yong S. and Youngkum Kim; m. Gyeong Sook Kim; children: Somang, Hannah, Samuel. BS, Yonsei U., Korea, 1986; MS Iowa State U., 1992; PhD, Iowa State U., 1994. Postdoctoral rsch. assoc. Adaptive Computing Lab., Ames, Iowa, 1994—95; postdoctorate fellow Korea Atomic Energy Rsch. Inst., Taejon, Republic of Korea, 1995; sr. mem. tech staff Korea Electric Power Rsch. Inst., Taejon, 1996—2001; dir. Physical Optics Corp., Torrance, Calif., 2001—. Session chair Am. Nuclear Soc., 1994—95, Korean Nuclear Soc., Taejon, Republic of Korea, 1996—2001. Contbr. articles various profl. jours. Recipient Author Recognition award, Am. Nuclear Soc., 1993, CEO honor, Korean Electric Power Corp., 1998, Electric Power Tech. Grand award, 2000. Mem.: IEEE, Internat. Neurol Network Soc., Internat. Soc. of Optical Engring. Avocation: carpentry. Office: Physical Optics Corp 20600 Gramercy Pl 100 Torrance CA 90501 Office Fax: 310-320-4667. E-mail: keehoon7@gmail.com.

KIM, KEUNWOO, electrical engineer, researcher; b. Daegu, Republic of Korea, Sept. 29, 1968; s. Unyong Kim; m. Hyeyun Jang, June 12, 1999; children: Daniel S., Samuel S. BS in Physics, Sung-Kyun-Kwan U., Seoul, Republic of Korea, 1993; MS in Elec. and Computer Engring., U. Fla., 1998, PhD in Elec. and Computer Engring., 2001. Rsch. asst. U. Fla., Gainesville, 1996—2001; rsch. staff mem. IBM T. J. Watson Rsch. Ctr., Yorktown Heights, NY, 2001—. Achievements include research in double-gate device design and modeling. Home: 18 Redwood Dr Somers NY 10589 Office: IBM T J Watson Rsch Ctr Yorktown Heights NY 10598 Home Phone: 914-669-5320; Office Phone: 914-945-1336. Office Fax: 914-945-1358. Business E-Mail: kkim@us.ibm.com.

KIM, KI HANG, mathematician; b. Moon Duck, Pyongnam, Korea, Aug. 5, 1936; arrived in U.S., 1953; s. Jin Gyong Kim and Mee Lan Hong; m. Myong Ja Kim, Aug. 1, 1963; children: John Churl, Linda Youngmee. BS in Math., U. So. Miss., 1960, MS in Math., 1961; PhD in Math., George Washington U., 1971. Instr. math. U. Hartford, 1961—66; lectr. math. George Washington U., Washington, 1970—72; assoc. prof. math. St. Mary's Coll. Md., St. Mary's City, Md., 1970—72, U. N.C., Pembroke, 1972—74; prof. math. Ala. State U., Montgomery, 1974—, disting. prof. math., 1983—. Vis. prof. U. Lisbon, 1974, Stuttgart (Germany) U., 1978, Chinese Acad. Scis., Beijing, 1983. Editor-in-chief: Math. Social Scis., 1981—94; editor: Jour. Pure and Applied Math., 1987—, Future Generations Computer Sys., 1983—; contbr. articles to profl. jours. Specialist US Army, 1955—57. Grantee, NSF, 1971—2003. Fellow: Korean Acad. Sci. and Tech. Home: 416 Arrowhead Dr Montgomery AL 36117 Office: Ala State U 915 S Jackson St Montgomery AL 36101 Home Phone: 334-277-4084; Office Phone: 334-229-4484. Business E-Mail: khkim@alasu.edu.

KIM, KWANG SEOG, medical educator; s. Hee Choong Kim and Bok Kyoung Ju; m. Ji Young Park, Apr. 17, 1998; children: Min Seo, Jinwoo. B in med. sci., Grad. Sch., Chonnam Nat. U., Republic of Korea, 1988; M in med. sci., Grad. Sch., Chonnam Nat. U., 1994, PhD, 1997. Cert. med. practice 1988, specialy bd. plastic and reconstructive surgery 1997, subspecialty bd. in surgery of the hand 2005. Intern. Chonnam Nat. U. Hosp., Gwangiu, Republic of Korea, 1991—92, resident, 1993—97; lectr. Chonnam Nat. U. Hosp., Grad. Sch., 1997—99; fellowship Chonnam Nat. U. Hosp., 1999—2000, clin. prof., 2000—04; asst. prof. Chonnam Nat. U. Hosp., Grad. Sch., 2004—. Dir. Chonnam Nat. U. Hosp., Hand Surgery Ctr., 2000—02, Chonnam Nat. U. Hosp., Microsurgery Ctr., 2003—. Contbr. articles various profl. jours. Pub. health br. Nat. Pub. Health Care Ctr., Chonnam, Republic of Korea, 1988—91. Lt., med. officer Korean Army, 1988, Korea. Grantee, Chonnam Nat. U. Hosp., 1999—. Mem.: Korean Cleft Palate-Craniofacial Assn. (award 1997), Korean Soc. for Surgery of the Hand (award 1997), Korean Soc. Aesthetic Plastic Surgery (award 1997), Korean Soc. Plastic and Reconstructive Surgeons (award 1997), Internat. Conf. for Plastic, Reconstructive and Aesthetic Surgery (award 1997). Avocations: swimming, climbing, golf, asian checkers. Office: Chonnam Nat U Med Sch Dept Plastic and Reconstructive Surgery 8 Hak-dong Dong-gu Gwangju 501757 Republic of Korea Office Phone: 82-62-220-6363, ext. 6352. Office Fax: 82-62-227-1639. Business E-Mail: pskim@chonnam.ac.kr.

KIM, KWANG-JIN, medical educator; s. Sang-Shin Kim and Kyung-Soo Shin; m. Soon-Ja Lee, Dec. 16, 1972; children: Min-Soo, Shirley. BSEE, Seoul Nat. U., Republic of Korea, 1971, MSEE, 1973; PhD, U. of Pa., Phila., 1980. Post-doc. training in physiology UCLA, 1980—82, asst. prof., 1982—86, Cornell U. Med. Coll., NYC, 1986—90; assoc. prof. U. of So. Calif., LA, 1991—2005, prof., 2005—. Contbr. articles to profl. jours., chapters to books. Ad hoc reviewer/editl. bd. Pharm. Rsch. Jour. Recipient New Investigator award, NIH, 1985. Mem.: Am. Physiol. Soc. (life). Office: USC - Keck School of Medicine 2011 Zonal Ave- Rm HMR914 Los Angeles CA 90033 Office Phone: 323-442-1217. Office Fax: 323-442-2611. Business E-Mail: kjkim@usc.edu.

KIM, KYEHEE, environmental engineer, consultant; b. Seoul, Republic of Korea, Aug. 26, 1967; d. Kisoo Kim and Suntae Bae; m. Jaeyoon Kim, July 2, 1995; 1 child, Ha-eun Mary. PhD, U. Calif., San Diego, 2004. Registered profl. engr., Calif., 2006. Rschr. San Diego State U., 1998—2004, lectr., 2006—; project engr. PBS&J, Encinitas, Calif., 2004—. Lectr. in field. Editor: Ch. Mag. Scholar, San Diego Found., 1999—2004. Mem.: ASCE (assoc.). Presbyterian. Achievements include patents for chemical methods to remove perchlorate by metallic iron. Office: PBS&J 175 Calle Magdalena Encinitas CA 92024 Home: 12184 Libelle Ct San Diego CA 92131-3842 Home Phone: 858-578-8056; Office Phone: 760-753-1120. Personal E-mail: kyeheekim@hotmail.com. Business E-Mail: kkim@pbsj.com.

KIM, LEE ANN, reporter, newscaster; b. Seoul, South Korea; arrived in US, 1971; m. Louis Song. BA in Broadcast Journalism, U. Md., Coll. Park. Gen. assignment reporter & anchor, 10News Live KGTV, San Diego, 1996—. Founder, exec. dir. San Diego Asian Film Festival, 2000—. Recipient Emmy award for investigative reporting, Calif. Teacher's Assn. award for best edu. reporting, Calif. Chicano News Media Assn. award. Mem.: Asian Am. Journalists Assn. (former pres., local chapter, Best Reporting awards). Office: KGTV 10News 4600 Air Way San Diego CA 92102

KIM, MI HYUN, professional golfer; b. Inch'on, South Korea, Jan. 13, 1977; Student, Yongin U., Korea, Sun Gkyun Kwan U. Profl. golfer Korean LPGA, LPGA, 1999—. Named Rookie of Yr., LPGA, 1999. Achievements include winning LPGA Tour events including the State Farm Rail Classic, 1999, First Union Betsy King Classic, 1999, Safeway LPGA Golf Championship, 2000, Giant Eagle LPGA Classic, 2002, Wendy's Championship for Children, 2002, Ginn Clubs & Resorts Open; 2006, Jamie Farr Owens Corning Classic, 2006. Avocations: shopping, pool, piano. Office: LPGA 1000 International Golf Drive Daytona Beach FL 32124-1092*

KIM, MI JA, dean, academic administrator; b. Seoul, Republic of Korea, Jan. 23, 1940; came to U.S., 1966; d. Si Hyung and Jung Kwon (Ahn) Lee; m. Heung Soo Kim, Jan. 14, 1964; children: Yoon Hi and Joseph. BS in Nursing, Yon Sei U., Seoul, 1962; PhD in Physiology, U. Ill., Chgo., 1975; JD (hon.), North Park Coll., 1995. Staff nurse Severance Hosp., Seoul, 1962-63; health nurse Am. Embassy, Seoul, 1963-66; asst. prof. Coll. Nursing/Univ. Ill., Chgo., 1975-79, assoc. prof., 1979-84, prof., 1984—, assoc. dean for rsch. dir. of grad. studies and assoc. dean acad. affairs, 1984-88, acting dean, 1988-89, dean, 1989-95, vice chancellor for rsch. and dean of grad. coll., 1995-99, dir. Acad. of Internat. Leadership Devel., 2001—. Cons. Nat. Ctr. Nursing Rsch., Bethesda, Md., 1987-91, Bd. Regents Higher Edn., Boston, 1989, WHO, Geneva, 2000, Nat. Inst. Gen. Med. Scis., NIH, 2000; mem. nat. adv. coun. Nat. Ins.; sci. and tech. rev. Nat. Ctr. Rsch. Resources, NIH, 2004—; treas., bd. trustees Commn. Grads. Fgn. Nursing Schs. Internat., 2004-; rschr. assessment exercise Higher Edn. Funding Agy., UK, 2005—. Mem. adv. bd. Health of the Pub., PEW Charitable Trust, Robert Wood Johnson found., 1992-96; adv. coun. Ctr. Bioethics and Human Dignity, 1994—. Named 100 Most Influential Women in Chgo., Chgo. Tribune, 1991, Univ. Scholar, U. Ill., 1985-88, Outstanding Nurse Educator, Korean Nurses Assn., Seoul, 1983; recipient Disting. Health and Edn. award Midwest Cmty. Coun. Chgo., 1994, Book of Yr. award Am. Jour. Nursing, 1984, Golden Apple award, students of Coll. Nursing, U. Ill., 1976, 78; Fulbright scholar Yon Sei U., Seoul, 2001. Fellow Am. Acad. Nursing; mem. North Am. Nursing Diagnosis (bd. dirs. 1985-92), Am. Thoracic Soc., Chgo. Lung Assn. (bd. dirs. 1977-97, Leadership Recognition award 1996), Chgo. Heart Assn. (bd. govs. 1980-88), Am. Physiol. Soc., Internat. Leadership Inst. (adv. coun. 1998-99), Sigma Theta Tau (Disting. lectr. 1987, Mary Tolle Wright award for Excellence in Leadership, 1997). Avocation: golf. Office: U Ill Chgo Rm 1156 Coll of Nursing Chicago IL 60612-7350 Home Phone: 773-871-0902; Office Phone: 312-996-5275. Business E-Mail: mjkuic@uic.edu.

KIM, MICAELA, speech pathology/audiology services professional; b. Seoul, Korea; arrived in US, 1971; BA in Comm., Boston Coll., 1993; MS in Speech-Language Pathology, St. Xavier U., 2001. Documentary rschr. Seoul Broadcast System, Seoul; with ChicagoLand TV, 1994; field prodr. & rschr. WBBM-TV, 1995; gen. assignment reporter then medical anchor/reporter WBTW-TV, Myrtle Beach, 1996—97; freelance reporter WYCC-TV, Chicago, 1997—99; speech-language pathologist Lutheran Gen. Hosp., U. Chicago Hosp., Edward Hosp., Ill. Early Intervention System; now founder Smiling Star Speech & Language, Hinsdale, Ill. Recipient Mark Twain award. Mem.: Ill. Speech-Language-Hearing Assn., Am. Speech-Language-Hearing Assn., Asian Am. Journalists Assn. (treas. Chicago chapter 1995, v.p. Chicago chapter 1996). Office: Smiling Star Speech & Language 112 S Grant St Hinsdale IL 60521

KIM, MICHAEL CHARLES, lawyer; b. Honolulu, Mar. 9, 1950; s. Harold Dai You and Maria Adrienne K. Student, Gonzaga U., 1967—70; BA, U. Hawaii, 1971; JD, Northwestern U., 1976. Bar: Ill. 1977, U.S. Dist. Ct. (no. dist., gen. and trial law.) Ill. 1977, U.S. Ct. Appeals (7th cir.) 1981, U.S. Supreme Ct. 1986. Assoc. counsel Nat. Assn. Realtors, Chgo., 1977-78; assoc. Rudnick & Wolfe, Chgo., 1978-83, Rudd & Assocs., Hoffman Estates, Ill., 1983-85; ptnr. Rudd & Kim, Hoffman Estates and Chgo., 1985-87; prin. Michael C. Kim & Assocs., Chgo. and Schaumburg, Ill., 1987-88; ptnr. Martin, Craig, Chester & Sonnenschein, Chgo. and Schaumburg, 1988-91, Arnstein & Lehr LLP, Chgo., 1991—2004; prin. Michael C. Kim & Assocs., Chgo., 2004—. Gen. counsel Assn. Sheridan Condo-Coop Owners, Chgo., 1988—; adj. prof. John Marshall Law Sch., Chgo. Author column Apt. and Condo News, 1984-87; co-author Historical and Practice Notes; contbr. articles to profl. jours. Bd. dirs. Astor Villa Condo Assn., Chgo., 1987-91, 2002-05, treas., 1987-89, 2002-03, sec., 2002, pres., 2003-05. Mem. ABA (mem. real property and probate sect., mem. forum on constrn. industry), Chgo. Bar Assn. (chmn condominium law subcom. 1990-92, chmn. real property legis. subcom. 1995-97, vice chmn. real property law com., 1998-99, chmn. real proprty law com. 1999-2000), Ill. State Bar Assn. (real estate law sect. coun. 1990-94, corp. and securities law sect. coun. 1990-92), Asian Am. Bar Assn. Greater Chgo. Area (bd. dirs. 1987-88, 90-91), Cmty. Assns. Inst. Ill. (bd. dirs. 1990-92, pres. 1992), Coll. Cmty. Assn. Lawyers (bd. govs. 1994-98), Assn. Condominium, Townhouse and Homeowner Assns., Univ. Club (Chgo.). Avocations: squash, photography, travel. Office: Michael C Kim & Assocs 19 S LaSalle St Ste 303 Chicago IL 60603 Office Phone: 312-419-4000. Business E-Mail: mck@mkimlaw.com.

KIM, MICHAEL S., lawyer; b. Korea; arrived in US, 1983; BA, Harvard Coll.; JD, Harvard U. Bar: NY, Conn., US Dist. Ct. (so. and ea. dists.) NY, US Ct. Fed. Claims, US Ct. Appeals (2nd cir.). Assoc. Davis Polk & Wardwell; asst. US atty. criminal divsn. US Dist. Ct. (so. dist.) NY; ptnr. Kobre & Kim LLP, NYC, 2003—. Exec. editor: Harvard Law Rev.; contbr. articles to profl. jours. With USAR. Named one of Litigation's Rising Stars, The Am. Lawyer, 2007; named to, Crain's NY Bus. "40 under 40", 2004.*

KIM, MIKYONG MINSUN, education educator; b. Shinan, Republic of Korea, Jan. 21, 1961; d. Bok-Soo Kim and Young-Soon Choi; m. Jang Wan Ko. BA, Ewha Women's U., Seoul, Republic of Korea, 1984; MEd, U. Nebr., 1988; MA, UCLA, 1992, PhD, 1995. Adj. asst. prof. U. Ariz., Tucson, 1997—98; asst. prof. U. Mo., Columbia, 1998—2004; assoc. prof. George Washington U., Washington, 2004—, dir. doctoral program, 2004—. Cons. NSF, Arlington, Va., 2003—, grant rev. panelist, 2004; expert witness US Commn. on Civil Rights, 2006. Contbr. articles to profl. jours. Mem.: Assn. for Instnl. Rsch. (grantee post-master's cert. program 2001—04), Assn. for Study of Higher Edn., Am. Ednl. Rsch. Assn. Avocations: tennis, painting, travel. Office: George Washington U 2134 G St NW Ste 109 Washington DC 20052 Office Phone: 202-994-5876, 703-726-3771, 202-994-3205. Office Fax: 202-994-5870. Business E-Mail: kimmi@gwu.edu.

KIM, MIN JUNG, bank executive; BSBA, U. So. Calif. Br. mgr. to v.p., lending officer Hanmi Bank, 1985—95; sr. v.p., chief credit officer Nara Bancorp, LA, 1995—2003, exec. v.p., COO, 2006—06, acting pres., 2006, pres., CEO, 2006—. Office: Nara Bancorp 3701 Wilshire Blvd Ste 220 Los Angeles CA 90010*

KIM, PETER SUNGBAI, pharmaceutical and research and development company executive, educator; b. Atlanta, Apr. 27, 1958; s. Mi Heh (Ryu) K.; m. Kathryn H. Spitzer; children: Michael, Jeremy, Alexander. AB magna cum laude with distinction, Cornell U., 1979; PhD, Stanford U., 1985. Whitehead fellow Whitehead Inst., Cambridge, 1985—88, assoc. mem., 1988—92, mem., 1992—2001; asst. prof. biology MIT, Cambridge, 1988—92, assoc. prof., 1992—95, prof. biology, 1995—2001; asst investigator Howard Hughes Med. Inst., Cambridge, 1990—93, assoc. investigator, 1993—97, investigator, 1997—2001; exec. v.p. R&D Merck Rsch. Labs., West Point, Pa., 2001—02, pres., 2003—. Bd. dirs. Fox Chase Cancer Ctr., 2003—, Whitehead Inst. Biomed. Rsch., 2005—; mem. coun. Inst. Medicine NAS, 2006—; mem. oversight com., divsn. earth and life studies The Nat. Acads., 2006—. Recipient Excellence in Chemistry award ICI Pharms., 1989, Walter J. Johnson prize Jour. Molecular Biology, 1989, Nat. Acad. Sci. Molecular Biology award, 1993, Eli Lilly Biol. Chemistry award Am. Chem. Soc., 1994, DuPont Merck Young Investigator award Protein Soc., 1994, Ho-Am prize for basic sci. Samsung Found., 1998, Hans Neurath award The Protein Soc., 1999, Harvey lectr., The Harvey Soc., 2002. Fellow AAAS, Biophys. Soc., Am. Acad. Microbiology; mem. NAS. Office: Merck Rsch Labs UG4CD-01 351 N Sumneytown Pike North Wales PA 19454

KIM, PYUNG-SOO, martial arts educator; b. Seoul, Republic of Korea, Dec. 4, 1939; arrived in U.S., 1968; s. Chong Won and Duk In (Lee) Kim; m. Sonnya Park Kim; children: Sean Kim, Tasha Kim. BA in Russian Lang. and Lit., Han Kuk U. Fgn. Studies, Seoul, 1963. 10th degree Black Belt, 1994. Founder Kong Soo Do Club, Joong Ang H.S., Seoul, 1954, Kwon Bop Martial Arts Club, Han Kuk U. Fgn. Studies, Seoul, 1957-63; tchr. Spl. Police Detachment Korean Pres., 1958; tchr. hand-to-hand combat tng. Republic of Korea Army, 8th Divsn., 1961-63; founder Korean Tae Kwon/Karate Acad., Seoul, 1963; chief instr. Kang Duk Won Martial Arts Assn., Seoul, 1964, 8th U.S. Army and HQ I Corps, 1964-67; founder Kim Soo Coll. Tae Kwon-Karate, Houston, 1968, ChaYon-Ryu, Houston, 1970—; founding pres. Byung in Martial Arts Friendship Assn., Houston, 1994-97. Lectr. in field; faculty martial arts instr. U. Houston and Rice U., 1970—; Tae Kwon Do coord. U.S. Olympic Festival '86, Houston; fight choreographer Houston Grand Opera, 1986; presdl. appt. to Com. on Unification of Korea, 1986-93; advisor World Martial Arts Coun., 1990; mem. adv. bd. Asia Houston Network; guest appearances on Inside Edit., 1997, 99; subject of Martial Arts in Daily Life, Korean News Channel YTN, 2004. Editor, corr. Black Belt Mag., 1964-67; author: Palgue 1,2,3, 1973, Palgue 4,5,6, 1974, Palgue 7 & 8: Black Belt Requirements, 1976, History of ChaYon-Ryu, 1990, Chayon-Ryu, Taekwondo, 2000 (in Russian). Advisor Asia Houston Network. Recipient citation for contbn. to elevating Korean nat. image in world Korean Govt., 1970, Leadership commendation Mayor Kathy Whitmire, 1987, commendation U.S. Pres. Bill Clinton, 1993, 98, Ednl. Leadership citation Gov. Ann Richards, 1993, Gov. G.W. Bush, 1998, Leadership commendation Mayor Bob Lanier, 1993, Lifetime Achievement award of honor World karate Union Hall of Fame, 1997, Leadership Commendation, Mayor Lee Brown, 2003, Leadership citation, Gov. Rick Perry, 2003, Leadership citation Mayor Bill White, 2004; named Best Karate Instr. in Houston, Houston Press, 1990, Grandmaster of the Yr., Tex. Martial Arts Hall of Fame, Man of Yr. Am. All-Open Hall of Fame, 1991, World Karate Union Hall of Fame, Internat. Martial Arts Hall of Fame, 1997. Avocation: golf. Office: ChaYon-Ryu Internat Martial Arts Assn 1740 Jacquelyn Dr Houston TX 77055-3604 Home Phone: 713-462-8613; Office Phone: 713-681-9261.

KIM, ROBERT J., cardiologist; b. Seoul, Republic of Korea, Sept. 26, 1970; arrived in US, 1982; s. Yong K. and Kyu S. Kim; m. Kyung W. Cho, Nov. 20, 1999; children: Nathan R., Joshua D. BA in Biochemistry, U. Calif., Berkeley, 1993; MD, Tufts U., Boston, 1998. Lic. NH, 2006. Surg. resident St. Elizabeth's Med. Ctr., Boston, 1998—2001; resident internal medicine med. ctr. U. Mass., Worcester, Mass., 2001—04; cardiologist-in-training Dartmouth-Hitchcock Med. Ctr., Lebanon, NH, 2004—. Contbr. articles to profl. jours. Personal E-mail: bobjkim2@hotmail.com.

KIM, S. PETER, psychiatrist, educator, health facility administrator, researcher; b. Seoul, Oct. 8, 1939; s. Chong Soon Kim and Soon Bok Lim; m. Oksuk Mary Lee, Mar. 30, 1963; children: John, Katherine. CPM, Seoul Nat. U., 1957; MD, Seoul Nat. U. Coll. of Medicine, 1963; PhD, Toho U. Grad. Sch., Japan, 1984; MBA, U. Hawaii Sch. Bus. Adminstrn., 2002. Asst. prof. psychiatry N.Y. U. Sch. of Medicine, NYC, 1976—82, assoc. prof. psychiatry, 1982—88; prof. psychiatry and pediat. U. Ga. Med. Sch., Augusta, 1988—94; prof. psychiatry Sungkyoon Kwan Sch. of Medicine, Seoul, Republic of Korea, 1994—97, U. Hawaii Sch. of Medicine, Honolulu, 1997—. Program dir. child and adolescent psychiatry N.Y. U. and Bellevue Med. Ctrs., NYC, 1979—88, dir. divsn. child and adolscent psychiatry; program dir. child and adolescent psychiatry U. Ga. Med. Coll. of Ga., Augusta, 1988—94; dept. chmn. psychiatry Sungkyoon Kwan U. Sch. of Medicine, Seoul, Republic of Korea, 1994—97; dir. Samsung-Johns Hopkins Internat. Clinics, Seoul, 1994—97; program dir. child and adolescent forensic psychiatry U. Hawaii Sch. of Medicine, 1999—2006. Pres. Hawaii Psychiatric Med. Assn., Korean Am. Med. Assn. of Hawaii, Honolulu, 1999—2001. Fellow: Pacific Rim Coll. Psychiatrists, Am. Orthopsychiatric Assn., Am. Coll. Psychiatrists, Am. Acad. Child and Adolescent Psychiatry, Am. Psychiatric Assn.; mem.: Hibiscus Lions Club (pres. 2002—03). Office: Dept Psychiatry 4th Fl U Hawaii Sch Medicine 1356 Lusitania St Honolulu HI 96813 Business E-Mail: kimp@dop.hawaii.edu.

KIM, SABRINA S., lawyer; b. Seoul, South Korea, Oct. 9, 1969; BA magna cum laude, UCLA, 1992; JD, Univ. Calif., Hastings, 1996. Bar: Calif. 1996. Dep. atty. gen. Calif. Dept. Justice; assoc., securities litigation Milberg Weiss Bershad & Shapiro, LA. Ad. prof. Loyola Law Sch. Named a Rising Star, So. Calif. Super Lawyers, 2006, Mem.: Assn. Bus. Trial Lawyers (bd. mem.), Phi Beta Kappa. Office: Milberg Weiss Bershad & Schulman Ste 3900 300 S Grand Ave Los Angeles CA 90071 Office Phone: 213-617-1200. Office Fax: 213-617-1975. Business E-Mail: skim@milbergweiss.com.

KIM, SEONG CHAN, environmental scientist, researcher; b. Busan, Republic of Korea, Feb. 28, 1973; s. Jeom Yeol and Yun Soon Kim; m. Jung Hee Byun; children: Sean Jae-Woong, Brian Jin-Woong. PhD, Pusan Nat. U., Republic of Korea, 2002. Post-doctoral rschr. Inst. Environ. Tech. and Industry, Busan, Republic of Korea, 2000—03; rsch. assoc. U. Minn., Mpls., 2003—. Office: University of Minnesota 111 Church St SE Minneapolis MN 55455 Home Phone: 612-781-2145; Office Phone: 612-624-7016. Business E-Mail: schankim@me.umn.edu.

KIM, SEUNG-BUM (SAB), research scientist; b. Jangsung, Chunnam, Republic of Korea, Aug. 7, 1972; m. Jiong Qiu, July 18, 2000; 1 child, Bryce N. Doctorate, U. Coll. London, 1998. Postdoctorl scholar Jet Propulsion Lab., Pasadena; scientist Remote Sensing Sys., Santa Rosa, Calif., 2006—. Recipient Best Paper prize, IEEE Korea, 1992, Outstanding Paper prize, Korean Soc. Remote Sensing, 2005; fellow Vis. Scientist, US Office Naval Rsch., 2000, 2002; grantee Satellite Terrain Mapping, Korean Ocean Rsch. Devel. Inst., 2000, 2001, Satellite Laser Reflector Devel., Korean Govt., 2002, Satellite Communication Device, 2002, NASA Aqua Satellite Ground Processor, Korean Meteorol. Adminstrn., 2003. Mem.: Am. Geophys. Union (assoc.). Achievements include patents for image processing technique, intelligent interpolation; design of terrain mapping software, HanDEM. Office: Remote Sensing Sys 438 1st St Ste 200 Santa Rosa CA 95401 Office Phone: 707-545-2904 20. Business E-Mail: biocpu@yahoo.com.

KIM, SOOK CHA, artist; b. Choong-Joo, Korea, Mar. 30, 1940; arrived in U.S., 1973; d. Kyung Nam Chai and Choon Yi Lim; m. Myung Hak Kim, Dec. 5, 1967; 1 child, Young Kyoon. BFA, Hong-Ik U., 1965, MFA, 1967. Owner Morning Star Art Gallery, Washington, 1995—2003. Featured artist Art Addiction Internat. Gallery. Recipient Gold medal--Art Addiction Internat. prize Most Talented Artists Competition, Sweden, 1997, Cert. of Merit 6th Internat. Female Artist Art Exhbn. on Internet Art Mus., 1999. Home: 6540 Braddock Rd Alexandria VA 22312-2206

KIM, SOONGUN, educational consultant; 1 child, Edward C. Degree in engring., Poly. U., Bklyn., 1991. Registered profl. engr., Korea, 1982. Edn. cons. Steve Kim Edn. and Consulting, Bklyn., 1991—; tchr. John Adams HS, Ozone Park, NY, 1998—. Pres. Korean Parents' Assn. Bklyn, 1990—98. Recipient Svc. award, Bklyn. Korean Parents Assn., 1988, Cmty. Svc. award, Korean Engr. and Scientist Assn. NY, 2004. Mem.: Mensa (corr.). Prebyterian. Avocations: travel, writing, classical music, opera. Home Phone: 516-708-9657. Personal E-mail: skim209@gmail.com. Business E-Mail: skim209@yahoo.com.

KIM, SUCK-WON, psychiatrist, educator; b. Seoul, Korea, Mar. 5, 1940; came to U.S., 1966; s. Kyu-Ho Kim and Yong-Ja Cho; m. Young-Ja Moon, Mar. 27, 1968; children: Samuel C., Sandra I. MD, Cath. U., 1966. Staff psychiatrist Hennepin County Med. Ctr., Mpls., 1971-94; assoc. prof. psychiatry U. Minn. Sch. Medicine, Mpls., 1994—2004, prof., 2004—. Fellow Am. Psychiat. Assn. (disting. life); mem. AMA, AAAS, Soc. Biol. Psychiatry. Achievements include research in obsessive-compulsive disorder. Office: U Minn Sch Medicine 420 Delaware St SE Minneapolis MN 55454-0374 E-mail: kimxx003@umn.edu.

KIM, SUKHAN, lawyer; b. Seoul, Nov. 20, 1949; BA in Polit. sci., Guilford Coll., 1976; MA in Internat. Politics, Columbia Univ., 1978; JD, Georgetown Univ. Law Ctr., 1981. Bar: DC 1981, US Ct. Internat. Trade 1985, US Supreme Ct. Ptnr., mgr. Korean practice Arnold & Porter, Washington; ptnr., internat. trade and mem. mgmt. com. Akin Gump Strauss Hauer & Feld LLP, Washington. First vice chmn. US-Asia Fgn. Policy Coun.; hon. v.p. Korean War Mem. Mus.; counsel US-Korean Found.; dir. Korea Soc., NYC, Korea Econ. Inst., Washington; adj. prof. internat. trade law Georgetown Univ. Law Ctr., 1994; disting. vis. prof., Grad. Sch. of Internat. Studies Yonsei Univ., Korea, 2001—02. Contbr. numerous articles on US-Korea trade rels. to Korean publications. Recipient Columbia fellowship, 1978. Fellow: Inst. Trade and Investment; mem.: Washington Fgn. Law Soc., Am. Soc. Internat. Law, DC Bar Assn., World Affairs Coun., Coun. on Fgn. Rels., Asia Soc., Phi Beta Kappa. Achievements include being founding pres., Sukhan Kim Found.: Korean-Am.Youth Svc. Orgn. 2001. Office: Akin Gump Strauss Hauer & Feld LLP Robert S Strauss Bldg 1333 New Hampshire Ave NW Washington DC 20036-1564 Office Phone: 202-887-4131. Office Fax: 202-887-4288. Business E-Mail: shkim@akingump.com.

KIM, SUNG WAN, chemistry professor; b. Pusan, South Korea, Aug. 21, 1940; came to U.S., 1966; BS, Seoul Nat. U., 1963, MS, 1965; PhD in Physical Chemistry, U. Utah, 1969. Asst. rsch. prof. U. Utah, Salt Lake City, 1971-73, asst. prof., 1974-76, assoc. prof., 1977-79, prof., 1980—2001, dir. Ctr. Controlled Chemical Delivery, 1986—, disting. prof. pharmaceutica and pharm. chemistry, disting. prof. bioengineering, 2002—. Mem. study section SGYB, NIH, Bethesda, Md., 1985-89, 95-; founder, co-chmn., Internat. Symposium on Recent Advancd in Dryg Delivery, 1983-. Editor numerous books; editl. bd., Journal of Controlled Release (Outstanding paper award, 1989, 1991, 1998), Pharm. Rsch., Jour. Biomedical Materials Sci., Biomaterials Sci. jours.; patentee in field; contbr. articles to profl. jours. Recipient Founders award Controlled Release Soc., 1995, Clemson Basic Biomaterials award Soc. for Biomaterials , 1987, Gov.'s medal for sci., State of Utah, 1988, Inst. Soc. Blood Purification award, 1994, Japanese Biomaterials Rsch. award, 1996, Volwiler award, Am. Assn. Coll. Pharmacy, 2002, Ho-Am prize in Medicine, Ho-Am Found., 2003. Fellow Am. Assn. Pharm. Scientists (Rsch. Achievement award in Drug Delivery, 1995, Dale Wurster award, 1998), Am. Inst. Med. Bioengring, Biomaterials Soc.; mem. IOM, NAE Home: 1711 Devonshire Dr Salt Lake City UT 84108-2562 Office: U Utah Ctr Controlled Chem Delivery 30 S 2000 E BPRB Rm 201 Salt Lake City UT 84112 Office Phone: 801-581-6801.

KIM, SUN-HAE, retired medical/surgical nurse, writer, retired nurse midwife, retired physical therapist; b. Jinju, Republic of Korea, July 16, 1941; arrived in U.S., 1971; d. Sampil Kim and Bok-Sun Lee. BA in Eng. Lit., Youngnam U., 1966. Chief nurse Swedish Saved Children Fedn., Pusan, Republic of Korea, 1966—70; staff nurse Cook County Hosp., Chgo., 1971—72, Harper Hosp., Detroit, 1972—73, Queens Hosp. Ctr., Jamaica, NY, 1973—90, Elmhurst (N.Y.) Hosp., 1990—97, ret., 1997. Author: Among Hibiscus and Roses, 2004. Army nurse South Korean Army, 1960—66. Avocations: reading, walking, TV, cats. Home: 152-18 Union Turnpike Apt 12F Flushing NY 11367 Office Phone: 718-969-7135. Personal E-mail: kimsunhae@webtv.net.

KIM, TAE HOON, biology professor; s. Jay Cho Nam and Jenny Jung Ja Kim. BA, Reed Coll., Portland, Oreg., 1994; PhD, Harvard U., Cambridge, Mass., 2002. Postdoctoral fellow Ludwig Inst. Cancer Rsch., San Diego, 2002—06; asst. prof. sch. medicine Yale U., New Haven, 2006—. Ruth L. Kirschstein Nat. Rsch. Svc. grant, Nat. Cancer Inst., 2004—06. Office: Yale Univ PO Box 208005 New Haven CT 06520-8005

KIM, WAN HEE, engineering educator; b. Osan, Korea, May 24, 1926; came to U.S., 1953, naturalized, 1962; s. Sang Chul and Duck Hyung (Chong) K.; m. Chung Sook Noh, Jan. 23, 1960; children: Millie, Richard K. B.E., Seoul Nat. U., 1950; MS in Elec. Engring, U. Utah, 1954, PhD, 1956. Rsch. asst. U. Ill., Urbana, 1955—56; rsch. staff IBM Rsch. Ctr., Poughkeepsie, NY, 1956—57; asst. prof. Columbia U., NYC, 1957—59, assoc. prof., 1959—63, prof. elec. engring., 1963—78; chmn., CEO Tech. Assessment Corp. Internat., Palo Alto, Calif., 1991—. Chmn. Tech. Cons., Inc., N.Y.C., 1962-69; chmn. KOMKOR Am., Inc., N.Y.C., 1970-72; spl. advisor for the pres. and govt. Republic of Korea, 1967-79; advisor Korea Advanced Inst. Sci., Seoul, 1971-73; chmn. Korea Inst. Electronics Tech., 1977-81; mem. bd. Korea Telecommunication Electric Rsch. Inst., 1977-81; pres. WHK Engring. Corp. Am., 1982-84, WHK Electronics Inc., 1982-84; chmn., chief exec. officer Industries Assn. Electronic Korea, 1978-81; chmn. WHK Industries Inc., 1984-88, AEA Corp., WHK-FJF&M Assocs., 1988-89; pres. Asian Electronics Union, 1979-83; pub. Electronic Times of Korea, 1982-83, Dr. Kim Report on Korea, 1988-2001; cons. The World Bank, Washington, other indsl. orgns.; chmn., CEO Tech. Assessment Corp. Internat. (TACI), 1991—93. Author (with R.T. Chien): Topological Analysis and Synthesis of Communication Networks, 1962; author: (with H.E. Meadows) Modern Network Analysis, 1970; author: (Auto Biography) Embracing Two Suns, 1999, numerous articles, —. U.S. rep. on U.S.-Japan Scientists Coop. Program.; trustee U.S.-Asia Inst., Washington, 1984-88. Served with Korean Army, 1950-53. Decorated Bronze Star; recipient Achievement medal U.S.-Asia Inst., Industry medal Republic of Korea, 1989; Guggenheim grantee, 1964, NSF rsch. grantee, 1958-78. Fellow IEEE, Union Radio Scientifique Internat. (mem. U.S. nat. com. Commn. Band C 1963-78), Sigma Xi, Tau Beta Pi. Achievements include being honorarily named the father of Korean electronics industry for his contbrn. to the development of Korea. Home: PO Box 778 Palo Alto CA 94302-0778 Personal E-mail: whkim@msn.com. *Be prepared five minutes earlier than others.*

KIM, WAN J., former federal agency administrator, lawyer; b. Seoul, South Korea, June 1968; arrived in US, 1973, naturalized, 1978; m. Sarah Whitesell; children: Anna, Abigail. BA in economics, Johns Hopkins U., 1990; JD, U. Chgo., 1993. Law clk. to Hon. James L. Buckley US Ct. Appeals (DC Cir.), 1993—94; trial atty. criminal divsn. US Dept. Justice, 1994—96, asst. US atty. DC, 1999—2003; dep. asst. atty. gen. Civil Rights Divsn., US Dept. Justice, 2003—05, asst. atty. gen., 2005—07; atty. Kellogg, Huber, Hansen, Todd & Evans, 1997—98. Served USAR, 1985—90.*

KIM, WON, architect; b. Seoul, Republic of Korea, Mar. 10, 1943; s. Jong-soo and Yong Kim; m. Joung-ai Park, May 20, 1967; children: Ji-young, Tae-yoon. BS in Arch., Seoul Nat. U., 1965; diploma, Bowcentrum Postgrad. Internat., Rotterdam, The Netherlands, 1973. Architect Kim Swoo-geun Atelier, Seoul, Republic of Korea, 1965-70; prin. ptnr. Wondoshi Archs., Seoul, 1973-75; prin. Archs.' Group Forum, Seoul, 1976—; prof. Grad. Sch. Architecture Konkuk U., 1998—. Pres. Feng-shui/Geomancy Rsch. Ctr., Seoul, 1981-91; chmn. mng. com. Seoul Archtl. Sch., 1997-2003. Prin. works include Hangang Cath. Ch., 1980, Master Plan Independence Hall, 1983, Nat. Theater for Traditional Performing Arts, 1984 (Korean Inst. Arch. spl. award 1991), Nat. Reunification Edn. Ctr., 1987 (Korean Inst. Arch. award 1992), Cath. Martyr's Monument and Memorial Chapel (Korean Inst. Architects award 1986), Kwang-ju Cath. U. (Korean Inst. Arch. award 1998), Seoul Film Complex Korean Motion Picture Promotion Corp., 1991, Russian Embassy to Korea, 1995; author: Mirror of Our Age, 1975, (essays on architecture) Light and Shadow, 1982, (essays on environ.) Let the River Run Through I, 1999, Let the River Run Through II, 2002, Essay on People and the Hours With Them, 2003. Rep. Civilian Environ. Group Against Dong River Dam Constrn., 1999, Donggang Nat. Trust, 2000; mem. Korean Cath. Bishop's Coun. for Arts, Seoul, Republic of Korea, 1995—2002; bd. dirs. Samsung Cultural Found., 2003—; chmn. Kim Swoo-geun Cultural Found., Seoul, Republic of Korea, 2003—. Recipient Order Indsl. Svc. merit, 1988. Mem.: NGO Purunnara Orgn. (rep. 2002—), Korean Inst. Interior Designers (hon. bd. dirs. 1992—), Korean Soc. Interior Designers (pres. 1982—84, hon. bd. dirs. 1985—, hon. pres. 1999—), Korean Inst. Architects (hon. bd. dirs. 1996—), Nat. Mus. Soc. (bd. dirs. 1995—), Soc. Nat. Modern Art Mus. (bd. dirs. 1995—2000). Roman Catholic. Office: Archs' Group Forum 1-94 Dong Soong-dong Jongro-gu Seoul 110-809 Republic of Korea Home Phone: 82-2-731-3331; Office Phone: 82-2-744-8225. Office Fax: 82-2-742-5394. Business E-Mail: master@kimwonarch.com.

KIM, WON GYU, research scientist; b. Chun Cheon, South Korea, Dec. 2, 1962; s. Myung Hee Kim and Pil Rea Lee; m. Jee Sun Moon, Dec. 20, 1997; children: Gloria, Grace. Staff scientist NIH, Bethesda, Md., 1998—. Mem.: Am. Med. Informatics Assn. Achievements include development of spell correction in PUBMED. Personal E-mail: moonjeesun@hotmail.com.

KIM, WONSUK, mechanical engineer, researcher; m. Deokeun Choi; 1 child, Sieun. BS in Mech. Engring., Seoul Nat. U., Rep. of Korea, 1988; PhD in Mech. Engring., U. Mich., Ann Arbor, 1999. Rschr. Inst. Advanced Machinery and Design, Seoul, 1994—95; rsch. assoc. U. Mich., Dearborn, 1999—2000, rsch. scientist, 2002—, vis. scholar Ann Arbor, 1999—2000; rsch. prof. Hanyang U., Seoul, 2001—02. Contbr. articles to profl. jours. Deacon Korean Bible Ch. of Ann Arbor. Rsch. grantee, Ford Motor Co., 2004—. Mem.: ASME. Presbyterian.

KIM, YONG CHOON, philosopher, theologian, educator; came to U.S., 1958, naturalized, 1972; s. Chang Ho and Chung Ja (Choe) K.; m. Joyce Chungja Whang, Dec. 18, 1965; 1 dau., Grace. BA, Belhaven Coll., Jackson, Miss., 1960; Th.M., Westminster Theol. Sem., Phila., 1964; PhD, Temple U., 1969. Asst. prof. Asian studies York Coll., Pa., 1969-70; asst. prof. philosophy and religion Cleve. State U., 1970-71; asst. prof. philosophy U. R.I., Kingston, 1971-74, assoc. prof., 1974-79, prof., 1979—2006, prof. emeritus, 2006—. Founder, dir. Korean-Am. Christian Studies Inst., 1981— Author: Oriental Thought, 1973, The Ch'ondogyo Concept of Man: An Essence of Korean Thought, 1978; cons. editor Dictionary World Philosophy, 2001; author, cons. editor Ency. of Asian Philosophy, 2001. Preacher Christian Chs., various countries. Korean Culture and Arts Found. grantee, 1977; Korea Found. fellow, 1992. Mem. Assn. Asian Studies, Am. Acad. Religion, Soc. for Asian and Comparative Philosophy, AAUP, Korean-Am. Univ. Profs. Assn. (dir. Eastern region 1986-90, 97—, chair law and ethics com. 1990-96). Home: 134 Parkwood Dr Kingston RI 02881-1600 Office: Univ RI Dept Philosophy Kingston RI 02881 Office Phone: 401-874-2418. Business E-Mail: yongkim@uri.edu.

KIM, YONGBOK, physicist; s. Byungwha Kim and Kumja Hong; m. Eun Jung An. BS, Hanyang U., Seoul, South Korea, 1996; MS, Seoul Nat. U., South Korea, 1998; PhD, U. Calif., Berkeley, 2003. Post-doctoral rschr. U. Calif., San Francisco, 2004—06; sr. med. physicist Allegheny Gen. Hosp., Pitts., 2006—. Mem.: Am. Assn. Physicists in Medicine. Office: Allegheny Gen Hosp 320 E N Ave Pittsburgh PA 15212 Home Phone: 412-366-9849; Office Phone: 412-359-3697.

KIM, YONG-HAK, microbiologist; b. Buyou, Korea, June 28, 1966; s. Kwansoo Kim and Hoja Shin; m. Young Mee Lee; 1 child, Hwajung. B, Seoul Nat. U., Korea, 1989, MSc, 1992; PhD, U. Stuttgart, Germany, 1999. Postdoctoral fellow FDA, Nat. Ctr. Toxicol. Rsch., Jefferson, Ark., 1999—2002; rsch. scientist Seoul Nat. U. Sch. Medicine, 2003; vis. scientist Biotech. Rsch. Inst., NRC Can., Montreal, Que., 2003—04; rsch. scientist Sookmyung Women's U. Coll. Pharmacy, Seoul, 2004—05, Seoul Nat. U. Sch. Biol. Sci., 2005—. Fellow, German Acad. Exch. Program, 1994—99, Oak Ridge Inst. Sci. and Edn., 1999—2002. Mem.: Am. Soc. Microbiology. Avocations: car care, travel. Home: 926 Wolgye (Hanil Apt 101-905) Nowon Seoul 139-050 Republic of Korea Office: Seoul Nat U San 56-1 Shinrim Kwanak Seoul 151-740 Republic of Korea Home Phone: 82-2-6317-2967; Office Phone: 82-2-880-6704. E-mail: yhkim660628@hotmail.com.

KIM, YONGMIN, electrical engineer, educator, biomedical engineer; b. Jeju, Korea, May 19, 1953; came to the U.S., 1976; s. Ki-Whan and Yang-Whi (Kim) K.; m. Eunai Yoo, May 21, 1976; children: Janice, Christine, Daniel. BEE, Seoul Nat. U., Republic of Korea, 1975; MEE, U. Wis., 1979; PhD in Elec. and Computer Engring., U. Wis., Madison, 1982. Asst. prof., dept. elec. engring. U. Wash., Seattle, 1982-86, assoc. prof., dept. elec. engring. and adj. assoc. prof., bioengineering and computer sci., 1986-90, prof., dept. elec. engring., 1990—, adj. prof. bioengineering, radiology, and computer sci. and engring., 1990—, prof. and chair bioengineering, 1999—, W. Hunter and Dorothy L. Simpson Endowed chair bioengineering, 1999—. Bd. dirs. Optimedx, Precision Digital Images, Redmond, Wash.; cons. MITRE Corp., McLean, Va., 1990, Lotte-Canon, Seoul, 1991, Seattle Silicon, Bellevue, Wash., 1990-93, U.S. Army, 1989-96, Neopath, Inc., Bellevue, 1989-90, Trinius Ptnrs., Seattle, 1989-91, Samsung Advanced Inst. Tech., Suwon, Republic of Korea, 1989-92, Daewoo Telecom. Co., Seoul, 1989-91, Intel Corp., Santa Clara, 1992, Aptec Sys., Portland, Oreg., 1992-93, Optimedx, Seattle, 1992-96, Precision Digital Images, Redmond, Wash., 1994-96, Micro Vision, Seattle, 1994-96, Hitachi, Tokyo, 1995, Fujitsu, Tokyo, 1995; bd. dirs. Image Computing Sys. Lab., 1984—, Ctr. for Imaging Sys. Optimization, 1991, Optimedx, 1993-96, U. Wash. Image Computing Libr. Consortium,

1995—; program evaluator Accreditation Bd. for Engring. and Tech., 1992—. Editor Procs. of the Annual Internat. Conf. of the IEEE Engring. in Medicine and Biology Soc., vol. 11, 1989, Procs. of the SPIE Med. Imaging Confs., vol. 1232, 1990, vol. 1444, 1991, vol. 1653, 1992, vol. 1897, 1993, vol. 2164, 1994, vol. 2431, 1995, vol. 2707, 1996, vol. 3031, 1997, vol. 3335, 1998, vol. 3658, 1999; editor Handbook of Medical Imaging, 2000; mem. numerous editl. bds.; contbr. chpts. to books and numerous articles to profl. jours.; inventor in field. Mem. various nat. coms., chmn. steering com. IEEE Transactions on Med. Imaging; chmn. numerous confs. Recipient Career Devel. award Physio Control Corp., 1982; grantee NIH, 1984—, NSF, 1984—, U.S. Army, 1986—, USN, 1986—; Whitaker Found. biomed. engring. grantee, 1986, recipient Ho-Am prize in Engring., Ho-Am Found., 2003. Fellow IEEE (Early Career Achievement award 1988, Disting. Lectr. 1991-98, both of the IEEE Engring. in Medicine and Biology Soc.), Am. Inst. Med. and Biol. Engring.; mem. Assn. Computing Machinery, Soc. Photo-Optical Instrumentation Engrs., Tau Beta Pi, Eta Kappa Nu. Presbyterian. Achievements include subspecialties in computer engineering, multimedia, high-performance media processors, image processing, computer graphics, medical imaging, and virtual reality. Home: 4431 NE 189th Pl Seattle WA 98155-2814 Office Phone: 206-685-2271. Office Fax: 206-221-6837. E-mail: ykim@u.washington.edu.

KIM, YONG-WOO, engineer, educator, consultant; b. Seoul, Republic of Korea, Feb. 23, 1972; s. Jwasang Kim and Jeong-ok Lee; m. Eunsu Na, May 2, 2003; 1 child, Ashley Yeseul. BSCE, U. Calif., Berkeley, 1995, MSCE, 1999, PhD, 2002. Cert. fundamental engr., Calif., 2002. Sr. engr. Samwhan Corp., Seoul, 1995—98; rschr. Lean Constrn. Inst., Oakland, Calif., 2000—03; asst. prof. U. Houston, 2003—04, SUNY, Syracuse, NY, 2004—. Cons. Il-Yang Constrn., Seoul, 2005—; prin. investigator SUNY Rsch. Found., Albany, NY, 2005—. Contbr. articles to profl. jours. Fellow Grad. Rsch. fellowship, Lean Constrn. Inst., 2001; grantee U. Rsch. grant, Constrn. Industry Inst., 2005—, Il-Yang Constrn., 2005—. Mem.: Korean Inst. Constrn. Engring. & Mgmt. (assoc.), Lean Construction Inst. (assoc.). Achievements include development of profit-point analysis; process variance analysis. Avocations: travel, reading, writing. Home: 3283 Greenleafe Dr Phoenix NY 13135 Office: SUNY 1 Forestry Dr Syracuse NY 13210 Home Phone: 315-695-5821; Office Phone: 315-470-6839. Personal E-mail: ywkim@esf.edu.

KIM, YOON BERM, immunologist, educator; b. Pyongnam, Republic of Korea, Apr. 25, 1929; arrived in U.S., 1959, naturalized, 1975; s. Sang Sun and Yang Rang (Lee) K.; m. Soon Cha Kim, Feb. 23, 1959; children: John, Jean, Paul. *Son John H. Kim, BA 1982, Yale University; MD 1990, The Chicago Medical School; Internship and Residency in Obstetrics and Gynecology, Women's and Infants' Hospital, Brown University School of Medicine 1990-94; Clinical Instructor OBG, Brown University School of Medicine 1994-95. Fellow, Reproductive Endocrinology and Infertility, Reproductive Endocrinology Center, UCSF School of Medicine 1995-97. Practice OBG, DuKane Obstetrics and Gynecology Ltd., 1997-00; Physician, Reproductive Endocrinology, Kaiser Permanente Hospital, Walnut Creek, Santa Clara and private practice, Loas Altos, Cali, 2000-present. Daughter Jean M. Kim, BA 1984, Yale University; JD 1987, Boston College Law School; Corporate Attorney 1987— present, private practice, non-profit work and church ministry. Son Paul J. Kim, BS 1990, Brown University; MD 1995, University of Illinois (Chicago), College of Medicine; Residency in Family Practice, Diplomate Am. Bd. Family Practice, 1998; is practice with Family Med. Group, Turlock, Calif., 1998-presnet.* MD, Seoul Nat. U., 1958; PhD, U. Minn., 1965. Intern Univ. Hosp. Seoul Nat. U., 1958-59; asst. prof. microbiology U. Minn., Mpls., 1965-70, assoc. prof., 1970-73; mem., head lab. ontogeny of immune sys. Sloan Kettering Inst. Cancer Rsch., Rye, NY, 1973-83; prof. immunology Cornell U. Grad. Sch. Med. Scis., NYC, 1973-83, chmn. immunology unit, 1980-82; prof. microbiology, immunology and medicine Rosalind Franklin U. Medicine and Sci., Chgo. Med. Sch., 1983—, chmn. dept. microbiology and immunology, 1983—2004, acting dean Sch. Grad. and Postdoctoral Studies, 1994-95. Mem. Lobund adv. bd. U. Notre Dame, 1977-88. Contbr. numerous articles on immunology to profl. jours. Recipient Rsch. Career Devel. award USPHS, 1968-73, Morris Parker Meritorius Rsch. award U. Health Scis., Chgo. Med. Sch., 1984, Ham Choon Disinction in Med. Rsch. Grand prize Seoul Nat. U. Coll. Medicine Alumni Assn., 2003, Disting. Alumni award Seoul Nat. U., 2004. Fellow Am. Acad. Microbiology; mem. AAAS, Korean Acad. Sci. and Tech., Assn. Gnotobiotics (pres.), Internat. Assn. for Gnotobiology (founding), Am. Assn. Immunologists, Am. Soc. Microbiology, Am. Assn. Pathologists, Korean-Am. Med. Assn., NY Acad. Scis., Soc. for Leucocyte Biology, Internat. Soc. Devel. Comparative Immunology, Harvey Soc., Internat. Soc. Interferon and Cytokine Rsch., Korean Acad. Sci. and Tech., Chgo. Assn. Immunologists (pres.), Assn. Med. Sch. Microbiology and Immunology Chairs, Internat. Endotoxin Soc. (charter), Soc. Natural Immunity (charter), Sigma Xi, Alpha Omega Alpha. Achievements include discovery of the unique germfree dolostrum-deprived immunologically "virgin" piglet model used to investigate ontogenic development and regulation of the immune system including T/B lymphocytes, natural killer/killer cells, and macrophages; research on ontogeny and regulation of immune system, immunochemistry and biology of bacterial toxins, host-parasite relationships, gnotobiology and immunotherapy of cancer. Home: 313 Weatherford Ct Lake Bluff IL 60044-1905 Office: Rosalind Franklin U Medicine and Sci Chgo Med Sch 3333 Green Bay Rd North Chicago IL 60064-3037 Office Phone: 847-578-8847. Business E-Mail: yoon.kim@rosalindfranklin.edu.

KIM, YOUNG-HOON, systems engineer, researcher; b. Seoul, Republic of Korea, Nov. 12, 1969; s. Hojin and Jungnam (Yoo) Kim; m. Heeseon Lim, Oct. 31, 1996; children: Gnoo, Jeffrey Sunwoo. BS, Seoul Nat. U., 1992, MS, 1994, PhD, 1998. Rsch. staff mem. Samsung Advanced Inst. Tech., Kiheung, Kyunggi-Do, Republic of Korea, 1998—2002; sr. staff engr. Samsung Info. Systems Am., San Jose, Calif., 2002—06, Western Digital Corp., San Jose, 2006—. Lectr. Soong Sil U., Seoul, 1997. Recipient Human Tech Thesis Prize, Samsung Electronics, 1995. Mem.: IEEE. Achievements include development of steady-state oscillation-based iterative learning/identification control theory and technique; various advanced servo control techniques for hard disk drives; a disk-vibration suppression technique using low track misregistration suspensions in hard disk drives; patents for low torque ripple driving technique for brushless DC motors using iterative learning control method. Avocation: electric guitar. Home: 7928 Woodlark Way Cupertino CA 95014 Office: Western Digital Corp 5853 Rue Ferrarie San Jose CA 95104 Office Phone: 408-363-4297. Personal E-mail: jakeykim@sbcglobal.net. Business E-Mail: jake.kim@wdc.com.

KIM, YOUN-SUK ERNEST, economist, educator; b. Kwangju, Korea, Sept. 15, 1934; arrived in U.S., 1959, naturalized, 1977; m. Y. Hannar, Apr. 24, 1966; children: Y. Herb, Nancy Y., John Y. BA, Seoul Nat. U., 1958; MA, New Sch., 1967, PhD, 1973. Statistician Am. Photog. Corp., 1963—67; econometrician Candeub, Fleissig & Assocs., planning cons. Newark, 1968—70; adj. prof. Fairleigh Dickinson U., Teaneck, NJ, 1971—73; mem. faculty, asst. prof. Kean U., Union, NJ, 1974—78, assoc. prof. econs., 1979—84, prof., 1985—. Vis. prof. Seoul (Republic of Korea) Nat. U., 1987—88; vis. prof. grad. sch. Hankuk U., 1999; pres. Korean-Am. U. Profs. Assn., 1996—98. Author: Political Economics of U.S. Trade, 1988, Postwar Japan's Foreign Trade, 1991, Japanese Foreign Trade, 1992, U.S.-Korea Economic Partnership, 1995, Vision of Korea's Economy in the 21st Century, 1996, Economics of the Triad: Conflicts and Congruence of the U.S.A., Japan and Korea, 1997, New Economics, 1998, The IMF Program and Korean Economy, 2001, The Role of Government in Competitive Economies; mem. editl. bd. Human Sys. Mgmt.; editor: Internat. Jour. Korean Studies, 2001—; contbr. articles to profl. jours., also books; exec. editor: Jour. Asian Econs., 2005—07, assoc. editor: North Korea Rev., 2005—. Nat. screening com. mem. (E. Asia) Inst. Internat. Edn. Fellow, Gateway Inst. for Regional Devel., 2001—; grantee, N.E. Asia Coun., Kean U., Korea Econ. Rsch. Inst., 1987. Mem.: Assn. Asian Studies, Korea-Am. Econ. Assn. (pres. 1993—), Japan Econ. Seminar, Atlantic Econ. Soc., Eastern Econ. Assn., Western Econ. Assn., Am. Econ. Assn. Democrat. Office: Kean Univ Morris Ave Union NJ 07083-7117 E-mail: ykim@kean.edu, younkim@aol.com.

KIMBALL, BRUCE ARNOLD, soil scientist; b. Aitkin, Minn., Sept. 27, 1941; s. Robert Clinton and Rica (Barneveld) K.; m. Laurel Sue Hanway, Aug. 20, 1966; children: Britt, Rica, Megan. BS, U. Minn., 1963; MS, Iowa State U., 1965; PhD, Cornell U., 1970. Soil scientist USDA-Agrl. Rsch. Svc. U.S. Water Conservation Lab., Phoenix, 1969—2006, rsch. leader Environ. and Plant Dynamics Rsch. Group, 1990—2006. Editor: Impact of Carbon Dioxide, Trace Gases and Climate Change on Global Agriculture, 1990; co-editor: Carbon Dioxide Enrichment of Greenhouse Crops, 1986; assoc. editor Global Change Biology; contbr. articles to profl. jours. Named Highly Cited Rschr. in agr., Ins. for Sci. Info. Fellow: Am. Soc. Agronomy (chmn. program divsn. A3 1988, assoc. editor 1977—83, bd. dirs. 1994—97), Soil Sci. Soc. Am.; mem.: AAAS. Avocations: computers, biking. Office: Arid Land Agrl Rsch Ctr USDA-ARS 21881 N Cardon Ln Maricopa AZ 85238 Office Phone: 520-316-6369.

KIMBALL, CATHERINE D., state supreme court justice; b. Alexandria, La., Feb. 7, 1945; d. William H. and Jane C. (Kelley) Dick; m. Clyde W. Kimball; 3 children. JD, La. State U., 1970. Law clerk US Dist. Court, Western Dist. La., 1970; spec. coun. La. Attorney Gen. Office, 1971—73; gen coun. La. Commn. Law Enforcement & Admin. Crim. Just., 1973—81; priv. law prac., 1975—82; asst. dist. atty. 18th Jud. Dist., 1978—82; judge La. Dist. Ct. (18th dist.), 1982—92; assoc. justice La. Supreme Ct., 1992—. Adjunct prof. law Tulane Law Sch. Summer Abroad Program; chair La. Supreme Ct. Case Mgmt. Info. Sys. Task Force, La. Supreme Ct. Tech. Com., Alternative Dispute Resolution Com.; ex officio mem. Complex Litigation Com.; chair Jud. Budgetary Control Bd.; mem. La. Data Base Commn.; bd. mem. Juvenile Justice Reform Act Implementation Commn.; mem. US Dept. Justice Nat. Integration Resource Ctr. Task Force; chair Integrated Criminal Justice Info. Sys. Policy Bd., Justice Funding Commn. Named one of Top 25 Women of Achievement, Baton Rouge Bus. Report, 1997; recipient Outstanding Jud. award, Victims & Citizens Against Crime, Inc., President's award, La. CASA Assn., 2002, Amb. for Children award., 2003. Mem.: Order of the Coif, Wex Malone Am. Inn of Ct., State-Federal Jud. Council, Am. Judicature Soc., La. State Bar Assn. Office: La Supreme Ct 400 Royal St New Orleans LA 70130*

KIMBALL, CLYDE WILLIAM, physicist, researcher; b. Laurium, Mich., Apr. 20, 1928; s. Clyde D. and Gertrude M. K. BS in Engring. Physics, Mich. Coll. Mining and Tech., 1950, MS, 1952; PhD in Physics, St. Louis U., 1959. Staff scientist aeronutronic div. Ford Co., 1960-62; assoc. physicist Argonne Nat. Lab., Ill., 1962-64; prof. physics No. Ill. U., De Kalb, 1964—, Presdl. rsch. chair, 1982-86, rsch. prof., 1986-88, disting. prof., 1988—, advisor to pres. sci. and tech., 1982-88, dir. lab. for nanosci., engring. and tech., 2002—. Program dir. low temperature physics Materials Research Div., NSF, Washington, 1978-79; chair, bd. govs. Consortium for Advanced Radiation Sources, 1994—; exec. com. Basic Energy Sci. Synchrotron Rsch. Ctr., 1994—; exec. dir. Inst. for Nanosci., Engring. and Tech., No. Ill. U., 1992—; chair bd. No. Ill. Nanotech, 1994—. Contbr. articles to profl. jours. Served with U.S. Army, 1952-54 Fellow Am. Phys. Soc.; mem. AAAS, Am. Assn. Physics Tchrs., Sigma Xi. Home: PO Box 842 Dekalb IL 60115-0842 Office: No Ill U Dept Physics Faraday West 217 Dekalb IL 60115 Business E-Mail: ckimball@niu.edu.

KIMBALL, GEORGE EDWARD, III, sports columnist; b. Grass Valley, Calif., Dec. 20, 1943; s. George Edward and Rita Sue (Laslie) K.; m. Marge Marash; children: Darcy Maeve, George E. IV. Student, Mass. Bay C.C., U. Kans., U. Iowa. Sports editor Boston Phoenix, 1970-79; sports columnist Boston Herald, 1980—2005; columnist The Sweet Sci. website, 2005—. Columnist for Irish Times; featured sports columnist N.Y. Post, 1993; boxing commentator Fox SportsNet, 2002—. Author: Only Skin Deep, Sunday's Fools, Four Kings, numerous poems; co-host SportsCall, Sta. WRKO, 1986-87, Old Colony Sports Network, 1996-97; appeared numerous TV programs; contbr. articles to mags. Dem. candidate for sheriff, Douglas County, Kans., 1970. Recipient Best Sports Column award UPI, 1984, 86, Nat Fleischer award Boxing Writers Assn., 1985, First pl. Best Story, 2002-03, Best Golf Column award Golf Writers Assn., 1992; named Boston's Best Sports Columnist Boston Mag., 1987. Mem. European Club (senate) Brittas Bay, Ireland), St. Andrews Golf Club (Scotland).

KIMBALL, HARRY RAYMOND, medical association administrator, educator; b. LA; MD, U. Wash., 1962. Intern King County Hosp., Seattle, 1962—63; resident in internal medicine U. Wash. Hosps., Seattle, 1963—64, 1967—68; fellow infectious diseases NIH Hosps., Bethesda, Md., 1964—67; pres. Am. Bd. Internal Medicine, Phila., 1991—2004; prof. medicine, sr. advisor to dean Sch. Medicine U. Wash., Seattle, 2004—. Office: U Wash Sch Medicine 1325 4th Ave Ste 2000 Seattle WA 98101 Office Phone: 206-221-4743. Office Fax: 206-221-2999. Business E-Mail: hkimball@u.washington.edu.

KIMBALL, JOHN DEVEREUX, lawyer; b. Orange, NJ, Mar. 18, 1949; s. Robert Maxwell and Audrey Josephine (Kerr) K.; m. Astri Jean Baillie; children: Astri, Emily, Elizabeth, Andrew. BA, Duke U., 1971; JD, Georgetown U., 1975. Bar: NY 1976. Assoc. Healy & Baillie LLP, NYC, 1975-80, ptnr., maritime law, 1980—2006; ptnr. Blank Rome LLP, NYC, 2006—. Adj. prof. law NYU, 1986—. Co-author: Time Charters, 2003; The Law of Salvage, 3A Benedict on Admiralty,2006;Voyage Charters, 2007; mem. editl. bd. Jour. Maritime Law and Commerce. Mem. ABA, Maritime Law Assn., Assn. of Bar City of NY. Office: Blank Rome LLP The Chrysler Bldg 405 Lexington Ave New York NY 10174 Home Phone: 973-377-0553; Office Phone: 212-885-5259. Business E-Mail: jkimball@blankrome.com.

KIMBALL, JULIE ELLIS, small press publisher, humorist, writer; b. Providence, Sept. 30, 1952; d. James Robert and Arlene Barker McDonnell; m. Penn T. Kimball, July 27, 1985; 1 child, Laura J. BA, Brown U., 1974; MS, Columbia U. Grad. Sch. Journalism, 1975. Reporter, copy editor, asst. Sunday editor Daily Register, Red Bank, NJ, 1975—80; headline writer NY Daily News, NYC, 1989—90; pub. Westmeadow Press, Vineyard Haven, Mass., 2001—. Adj. prof. Columbia U. Grad. Sch. Journalism, NYC, 1986—88; media critic The Woman's Reporter, NJ, 1980—87. Author: 45 Minutes to America: Dispatches from Martha's Vineyard, 2001; editor: (poetry anthology) Vineyard Poets, 2003. D-Liberal. Congregationalist. Home: PO Box 4148 Vineyard Haven MA 02568 Office: Westmeadow Press PO Box 4338 Vineyard Haven MA 02568 Home Phone: 508-696-7497; Office Phone: 508-696-7497.

KIMBALL, LYNN JEROME, historian; b. La Junta, Colo., Sept. 21, 1943; s. Stanley Jerome and Ruth Estelle (Wilson) K.; m. Kathleen May Seker Mitchell, Nov. 13, 1965 (div. Mar. 1974); children: Scott, Lori, Todd; m. Dorothy Jean Bumar, Dec. 15, 1984; children: Donald, Wendy. BS, U.S. Naval Acad., Annapolis, Md., 1965; MS, U.S. Naval Postgrad. Sch., Monterey, Calif., 1971. Commd. USMC, 1965, advanced through grades to lt. col., dir. plans & policies Joint Spl. Ops. Command Ft. Bragg, NC, 1980-83, ops. officer 3d Marine Divsn. Okinawa, Japan, 1983-84, battalion comdr. Marine Corps Base Camp Lejeune, NC, 1984-87; def. attache Am. Embassy, Santo Domingo, Dominican Republic, 1988-90; dir. ops. and tng. Marine Corps Base USMC, Camp Lejeune, 1990-91, dir. environ. tng. Marine Corps Base, 1991-92, ret., 1991; mus. historian Mus. of the Marine Corps, 2006—; writer, historian Onslow County Hist. Soc., 1992—. Vis. lectr. Profl. Mil. Edn., Camp Lejeune, 1990-01. Columnist Jacksonville Daily News, 1996—, Tideland News, 1996—, Richlands Advertiser, 1996—; author: Battle of New River, 1996, Diary of J.Q.A. Morris, 1997, Camp Lejeune Oral History Project, 2002, Semper Fidelis: A Brief History of Onslow County and MCB Camp Lejeune, 2002; contbr. articles to profl. jours. Adv. bd. Onslow County Bd. Tourism, Jacksonville, N.C., 1995-02, Onslow County Mus., 1995-. Mem. Marine Corps Assn., US Naval Inst., Co. Mil. Historians, Marine Corps Historical Found., Onslow Hist. Soc., Soc. Civil War Historians, Civil War Roundtable Eastern NC. Republican. Baptist. Avocations: weightlifting, bicycling, walking, history. Home: 227 Creedmoor Rd Jacksonville NC 28546-6028 Office Phone: 910-455-9873. E-mail: ljkimbal@cc.rr.com.

KIMBALL, REID ROBERTS, psychiatrist; b. Draper, Utah, June 29, 1926; s. Crozier and Mary Lenore (Roberts) Kimball; m. Barbara Joy Radmore, Aug. 3, 1962; children: Valery, Michael, Pauline, Karen, Kay. BS, Brigham Young U., 1949; MD, U. Utah, 1951. Intern Thomas D. Dee Hosp., Ogden, Utah, 1951-52; resident Norristown (Pa.) State Hosp., 1952-53, Oreg. State Hosp., Salem, 1953-55, Palo Alto (Calif.) VA Hosp., 1956; practice medicine specializing in psychiatry Eugene, Oreg., 1957-60, Salem, 1960-72, Portland, Oreg., 1972-77; pvt. practice Eugene, 1957-60, Salem, 1960-72, Portland, 1972-77, Eugene, 1977-89; mem. staff Sacred Heart Hosp., Eugene; consultation/liaison psychiatry, 1977-90; locum teneas numerous locations, 1990—. Dir. Out-Patient Clinic Oreg. State Hosp., Salem, 1956—57, dir. med. edn., 1984; asst. prof. psychology U. Oreg., Eugene, 1957—65, prof., 1977—, asst. prof., Portland, 1965, adj. asst. prof., 1982—83, clin. prof., 1983—92. Mem. adv. bd. Lane County Cmty. Mental Health, 1980—81. With USN, 1943—45. Mem.: AMA, Lane County Psychiat. Assn. (pres. 1979—80), N. Pacific Psychiat. Assn. (pres. 1988—89), Am. Psychiat. Assn. (pres. Oreg. dist. br. 1973—74), Lane County Med. Soc., Oreg. Med. Assn. (chmn. psychiatry sect. 1973—74). Home and Office: 4055oyal Ave #99 Eugene OR 97402

KIMBALL, RICHARD ARTHUR, JR., retired lawyer; b. NYC, Feb. 3, 1930; s. Richard Arthur and Josephine (Dodge) K.; m. Hopeton Drake Kneeland, Dec. 22, 1956; children: George J., Samuel W., Sylvia K. Perry. BA, Yale U., 1952, LLB, 1958. Assoc. Debevoise, Plimpton & McLean, NYC, 1958-61; asst. treas. Morgan Guaranty Trust Co., NYC, 1961-63; assoc. Debevoise, Plimpton, Lyons & Gates, NYC, 1963-69; ptnr. Hughes Hubbard & Reed, NYC, 1970-92, counsel, 1993—2001; ret., 2001. Bd. dirs. English-Speaking Union of U.S., N.Y.C., 1985-97, N.Y. br. English-Speaking Union, 1965-89, chmn., 1993-94; pres. Yale Glee Club Assocs., New Haven, 1980-85, Dutchess Land Conservancy, Millbrook, N.Y., 1988—, chmn., 1997-2005, The Nature Conservancy, Lower Hudson chpt., 1991-94. 1st lt. U.S. Army, 1953-55. Fellow Am. Coll. Trust and Estate Counsel; mem. ABA, N.Y. State Bar Assn., Assn. Bar City N.Y., Century Assn. (N.Y.C., treas. 1983-89), Yale Club (N.Y.C.).

KIMBAROVSKY, ROSS EDWARD, lawyer; b. Kiev, Ukraine, Apr. 2, 1970; s. Edward M. and Alla S. Kimbarovsky; m. Caren Debra Herbin, Aug. 6, 1995; children: Arielle Faye, Mason Colin, Emma Claire. BA in Polit. Sci. and Philosophy, Northwestern U., Evanston, Ill., 1992; JD, U. Ill., Champaign, 1995. Bar: Ill. 1995, US Supreme Ct. 1995, US Dist. Ct. (No. dist.) Ill. 1995, US Dist. Ct. (No. dist.) Fla. 1997, US Dist. Ct. Ariz. 1997, US Ct. Appeals (DC and 2d cirs.) 1997, US Ct. Appeals (Fed. cir.) 2006; lic. real estate broker Ill., 2002. Atty. Hopkins & Sutter, Chgo., 1995—2001; ptnr. Ungaretti & Harris LLP, Chgo., 2001—. Named SuperLawyer, Key Profl. Media, Inc., 2006; named one of 40 Under Forty Attys., Law Bull. Pub. Co., 2006. Mem.: ABA. Office: Ungaretti & Harris LLP 3500 Three First National Plz Chicago IL 60602

KIMBELL, ABIGAIL R., federal agency administrator; b. Jan. 9, 1953; BS in Forest Mgmt., U. Vt.; MS in Forest Engring., Oreg. State U., 1982. Forester Bur. Land Mgmt., US Dept. Interior, Medford, Oreg., 1974; pre-sale forester US Forest Svc., USDA, Kodiak, Alaska, 1977, dist. ranger Kettle Falls, Wash., 1985—88, LaGrande, Oreg., 1988—91; forest supr. Tongass Nat. Forest, Petersburg, Alaska, 1991—97, Bighorn Nat. Forest, Sheridan, Wyo., 1997—99, Cimarron Nat. Grassland, Kans., 1999—2002, Pike and San Isabel Nat. Forests, Colo., 1999—2002, Comanche Nat. Grassland, Colo., 1999—2002; assoc. dep. chief, nat. forest system US Forest Svc., USDA, 2002—04, regional forester, no. region, 2004—07, chief Washington, 2007—. Office: US Forest Service 1400 Independence Ave NW Washington DC 20250-8333*

KIMBER, KAREN BEECHER, ESL educator; b. New Brunswick, NJ, June 3, 1945; d. Stanley and Emma Beecher Kimber. BA, The College of NJ, 1967; MA, Hunter Coll., 2005. Tv prodn. asst. Dancer Fitzgerald Sample, NYC, 1967—72; tv advt. coord. McCaffrey & McCall, NYC, 1973—76, AC & R Advertising, NYC, 1976—77; mng. ptnr. Kimber Bus. Machines Co., North Brunswick, NJ, 1977—83; instr. John Jay Coll. of Criminal Justice, NYC, 2005—. Advt. mgr. NY State TESOL, 2001—02. Contbr. articles to profl. jours. and mags. Hospitality coord. St. Thomas Ch., NYC, 1996—. Mem.: Ch. Club N.Y., St. George's Soc., Order of St. John of Jersusalem. Republican. Episcopalian. Avocation: travel. Home: 200 East 33d St Apt 29A New York NY 10016 Office: John Jay Coll of Criminal Justice 445 West 59th St Rn 1201N New York NY 10019

KIMBERLIN, SAM OWEN, JR., financial consultant; b. Wichita Falls, Tex., Feb. 4, 1928; s. Sam Owen and Mary Ruth (Crowell) K.; m. Alison Gray, Dec. 20, 1955; children: S. Scott, David Winston. BBA, U. Tex., Austin, 1951, LLB, 1953; grad. in banking, Rutgers U., 1972. Bar: Tex. 1953. First asst. Office Dist. Atty., Austin, 1953-54; asst. atty. gen. Office Atty. Gen. State Tex., Austin, 1955; gen. counsel Tex. Dept. Banking, Austin, 1956-62; exec. dir. Assn. State Chartered Banks in Tex., Austin, 1962-64; exec. v.p. Tex. Bankers Assn., Austin, 1964-88; mng. dir. TBA Svcs. Co., Inc., Austin, 1988-90; cons. Austin Trust Co., 1990—, Thornhill Securities, Inc., Austin, 1990—. Chmn. devel. bd. Austin Trust Co., 1991—; mem. Third Age Coun., U. Tex., Austin Author: Banking in Texas, 1972 (honors award 1972); co-author: Fight Your Texas Tax Appraisal and Win, 1997. Adv. coun. on property tax cons. Tex. Dept. Licensing and Regulation, 1996-2005; chmn. appraisal rev. bd. Travis Ctrl. Appraisal Dist., 1995-96; trustee S.F. Austin High Continuing Edn. Found. With USMC, 1946-48. Mem. Am. Soc. Assn. Execs., Tex. Assn. Bank Counsel, Adms. Club. Methodist. Avocation: tennis. Home: 3503 Scenic Hills Dr Austin TX 78703-1044 Office: PO Box 5930 Austin TX 78763-5930 Office Phone: 512-477-2255. Personal E-mail: samkim@austin.rr.com.

KIMBERLING, CLARK HERSHALL, mathematics professor, small business owner; b. Hinsdale, Ill., Nov. 7, 1942; s. Delmer Hershall and Jocelyn Leigh (Babel) K.; m. Margaret Penelope Mitchell, May 30, 1966; children: Amy, David, Brian. BA, North Tex. State U., 1964; MA, La. State U., 1966; PhD, Ill. Inst. Tech., 1970. Instr. N.W. Mo. State Coll., Maryville, 1967-69, Ill. Inst. Tech., Chgo., 1969-70; asst. prof. U. Evansville, Ind., 1970-75, assoc. prof., 1975-81, prof., 1982—; pres. Math. Software Co., Evansville, 1987—. Author: (with others) Emmy Noether: A Tribute to Her Life and Work, 1982; author: (book and software) Triangle Centers and Central Triangles, 1998, Geometry in Action, 2003; author computer software programs including The Geometric Constructor, 1985-90; editor divsn. music U. Evansville Press, 1976-88; editor computer corner Ind. Math. Tchr., Ball State U., 1986-91; contbr. articles to profl. jours.; composer for ch. choirs: This Easter Morn, 1997, The King of Love My Shepherd Is, 1997, Ring Out the Glad Tidings, 2000, O God, Beneath Your

Hand, 2002, O God, Who at the Dawn of Time, 2002, The Hills are Hushed This Night of Nights, 2002, Four Anthems for Mixed Voices and Handbells, 2003, others. Choir dir. St. Paul's Episcopal Ch., Henderson, Ky, 1978-84; bd. dirs. Fibonacci Assn., Santa Clara, Calif., 1999—; adv. bd. Forum Geometricorum, Boca Raton, Fla., 2000—. Mem. Nat. Coun. Tchrs. Math., Am. Math. Soc. (spl. session organizer 1999), Math. Assn. Am., Fibonacci Assn. (assoc. editor 1990—, bd. dirs. 2000-), U. Evansville Alumni Assn. (Outstanding Faculty Rsch. and Scholarly Activity award 1987). Achievements include research in points in the plane of a triangle: isoperimetric point, Exeter point, other points on the Euler line; fractal sequences interspersions, dispersions and generalized Wythoff arrays. Home: 2316 E Gum St Evansville IN 47714-2338 Office: U Evansville 1800 Lincoln Ave Evansville IN 47714-1506 Business E-Mail: ck6@evansville.edu.

KIMBERLING, JOHN FARRELL, retired lawyer; b. Shelbyville, Ind., Nov. 15, 1926; s. James Farrell and Phyllis (Casady) K. B of Naval Sci. and Tactics, Purdue U., 1946; AB, Ind. U., 1947, JD, 1950. Bar: Ind. 1950, Calif. 1954. Assoc. Bracken, Gray, DeFur & Voran, 1950-51, Lillick McHose & Charles, and predecessor firms, 1953-63, ptnr., 1963-86, Dewey Ballantine, LA, 1986-89; ret., 1989. Author: What This Country Needs, 2005, How to Try a Jury Case, 2007. Bd. visitors Ind. U. Sch. Law, 1987—; bd. dirs. Ind. U. Found., 1988—. Lt. (j.g.) USNR, 1951-53. Fellow Am. Coll. Trial Lawyers, Acad. Law Alumni Sch. Law Indiana U. (Disting. Alumni Svc. award, 2001); mem. ABA (charter, litigation sect.), State Bar Calif., LA Bar Assn., LA Jr. C. of C. (past pres.), Beta Theta Pi, Phi Delta Phi., Calif. Club, Chancery Club, Lincoln Club. Home: 1180 Los Robles Dr Palm Springs CA 92262-4124 E-mail: jkimberling@dc.rr.com. *My goal in life is and has been to do the very best of which I am capable in my professional life and in helping to make my community a better place in which to work and live.*

KIMBERLY, JOHN ROBERT, management educator, consultant; b. New Haven, Sept. 16, 1942; s. John T. and Beatrice (Branch) K.; m. Barbara Lenox Christy, June 27, 1970; children: Laura Lenox, John Fowler, Nina-Charlotte Marie. BA, Yale U., 1964; MS, Cornell U., 1967, PhD, 1970. Asst. prof. sociology U. Ill., Champaign/Urbana, 1970—74; vis. fellow Ecole Polytechnique, Paris, 1975-76; from asst. to assoc. prof. Sch. Mgmt. Yale U., New Haven, 1977-82; from assoc. to full prof. Wharton Sch., U. Pa., Phila., 1983—, Henry Bower prof., 1989—. Rsch. prof. Ecole Polytechnique, Paris, 1989-91; cons. OECD, 1975—, Office Tech. Assessment U.S. Congress, 1982-84, Robert Wood Johnson Found., Princeton, N.J., 1984-85; mem. health care tech. study sect. HHS, Washington, 1986-89; Novartis prof. in healthcare mgmt. INSEAD, 1999-2002. Author: The End of an Illusion, 1984, Cases in Health Policy and Management, 1985, The Migration of Managerial Innovation, 1993; editor: The Organization Life Cycle, 1980, Managing Organizational Transitions, 1984; contbr. articles to profl. jours. Bd. dirs. Wissahickon Hospice, Phila., 1985—, Chestnut Hill Hosp. Health Care, 1992—, Bach Festival Phila., 1992—, Community Fin. Bancorp, 1993—. Grantee HCA Found., Nashville, 1984-86, HHS, Washington, 1986—, Commonwealth Found., N.Y.C., 1986-87, Robert Wood Johnson Found., Princeton, 1986-87, Kaiser Family Found., 1994-96; Salmon and Rameau fellow INSEAD, Fountainbleau, France, 1996-99, 2002—. Mem. Am. Sociol. Assn., Acad. of Mgmt., Am. Pub. Health Assn. Avocations: restoration of antique cars and boats, tennis, skiing. Office: U Pa Wharton Sch Philadelphia PA 19104

KIMBERLY, ROBERT PARKER, medical educator; b. New Haven, July 29, 1946; s. John Taylor and Beatrice Eileen (Branch) K.; m. Susan Johnson Alesbury, June 17, 1972; children: Christopher, Taylor, Sarah, Michael, Thomas. AB, Princeton U., 1968; MA, New Coll., Oxford, Eng., 1970; MD, Harvard U., 1973. Diplomate Am. Bd. Internal Medicine. Intern Hosp. of U. Pa., Phila., 1973—74, resident in medicine, 1974—75; fellow in rheumatology Applied Rsch. Br., NIAMDDK, NIH, Bethesda, Md., 1975-77, Hosp. Spl. Surgery-Cornell Med. Ctr., NYC, 1977-79; asst. prof. medicine Cornell U. Med. Coll., NYC, 1979-84, assoc. prof. medicine, 1984-91, prof. medicine, 1991—96; dir. biomedical component and program dir. Cornell Arthritis Ctr., 1988—96; prof. immunology Cornell Grad. Sch. Med. Sciences, 1991—96; Howard L. Holley Prof. Medicine U. Ala. Sch. Medicine, Birmingham, 1996—; program dir. and sr. scientist U. Ala. Arthritis Ctr., 1996—; prof. microbiology and sr. scientist U. Ala. Comprehensive Cancer Ctr., 1996—. Andrew Mellon Found. tchr., scientist, 1980; sci. adv. bd. Alliance for Lupus Rsch.; trustee Arthritis Found. Contbr. numerous articles to profl. jours. Lt. comdr. USPHS, 1975-77. Rhodes Trust scholar, 1968. Fellow ACP, Am. Coll. Rheumatology (pres. N.E. chpt. 1990-91); mem. NY Rheumatism Assn. (pres. NYC chpt. 1992-93), Am. Assn. Immunologists, Am. Soc. Clin. Investigation. Office: U Ala Dept Rheumatology/Immunology 1900 Univ Ave Birmingham AL 35294

KIMBLER, LARRY BERNARD, real estate executive, accountant; b. Lucasville, Ohio, Sept. 6, 1938; s. Benjamin F. and Elizabeth L. (Kerr) K.; m. Susanna Hayes, June 20, 1964; children: Beth Ann, Carolyn Sue. BBA, U. Cin., 1964. CPA, Ohio; lic. real estate broker, Tex. Acct. Peat, Marwick, Mitchell & Co., Cin., 1964-68; mgr. acctg. and taxes Andrew Jergens & Co., Cin., 1968-70; exec. v.p. Am. Lakes & Land Co., Houston, 1970-74; from group controller real estate and minerals to gen. mgr. land utilization Internat. Paper Co., 1974-81; pres. Internat. Paper Realty Co., NYC, 1977-81; v.p. corp. real estate GTE, Stamford, Conn.; also pres. GTE Realty Corp., 1981-89; prin. Kimbler Assocs., Inc., Stamford, 1989-91; exec. v.p. The Staubach Co., Dallas, 1991—2002, also bd. dirs.; chmn. Washington Staubach Addison Airport Venture, 2002—. Bd. dirs. Stamford Econ. Assistance Corp.; past pres. Westchester So. Conn. chpt., NACORE; trustee, treas. Low-Heywood Thomas Sch., Stamford; lectr., speaker in field; mem. adv. bd. Homer Hoyt Inst.; officer, bd. dirs. Indsl. Devel. Rsch. Coun.; editl. adv. bd. Bldg. Econs. Contbr. articles to profl. jours. With AUS, 1956-59. Mem. Am. Inst. Corp. Asset Mgmt. (bd. govs.), Nat. Assn. Corp. Real Estate Execs. (master corp. real estate designation, chpt. pres.), Am. Inst. CPAs, Indsl. Devel. Research Council (bd. dirs., Officer Disting. Svc. award 1983, 87, Master Profl. designation), Am. Found. for Blind (chmn. bd. dirs. Ctr. on Vision Loss, nat. trustee), Bent Tree Country Club (bd. dirs., exec. com. 1999-2002). Presbyterian. Republican. Home: 5403 Bent Trail Dallas TX 75248-2034 Office: 15601 Dallas Pkwy Ste 400 Addison TX 75001-6055 Office Phone: 972-713-2618. Personal E-mail: lkimbler@sbcglobal.net.

KIMBRELL, DEBORAH ANN, geneticist, educator; b. San Angelo, Tex., July 22, 1950; d. Billy Lee and Dorothy (Babish) K.; m. S. Ingemar C. Olsson, June 15, 1991. BA in Biology and Psychology with honors, Mills Coll., 1972; PhD in Genetics, U. Calif., Berkeley, 1985. Rsch. tech. dept. respiration physiology Max Planck Inst. Exptl. Medicine, Göttingen, Germany, 1973-74; NIH predoctoral trainee dept. genetics U. Calif., Berkeley, 1979-85; Am. Cancer Soc. postdoctoral fellow dept. genetics U. Cambridge, England, 1985-88; Swedish MRC vis. scientist fellow dept. microbiology U. Stockholm, 1988-90; asst. prof. dept. biology and Inst. Molecular Biology, U. Houston, 1991—97; sr. faculty fellow dept. biochemistry and cell biology Rice U., Houston, 1997—99; assoc. rsch. geneticist molecular and cellular biology U. Calif., Davis, 1999—. Ad hoc grant reviewer various books and profl. jours., 1990—, NIH, Wash., DC, 2002—; founder immunity workshops Annual Drosophila Rsch. Conf., 1995—; contbr. Sci. Am. On-Line, Ask the Experts, 1996. Contbr. articles to profl. jours. Mem. US Coast Guard Aux., Calif., 2001—. Pres. Rsch. and Scholarship Fund grantee U. Houston, Rsch. grantees Am. Cancer Soc., 1992-99, NIH, 1999-03, Cancer Rsch. Coordinating Com. U. Calif., 2001, 04, NASA, 2004-, NASA Flight Investigator Rsch. grantee, 2005-. Mem.: Am. Soc. Gravitational and Space Biology, Genetics Soc. Am.

KIMBRELL, GRADY NED, writer, educator, retired school system administrator; b. Tallant, Okla., Apr. 6, 1933; s. Virgil Leroy Kimbrell and La Veria Dee Underwood; m. Marilyn Louise King, May 30, 1953 (div.); m. Mary Ellen Cunningham, Apr. 11, 1973; children: Mark Leroy, Lisa Christine, Joni Lynne. BA, Southwestern Coll., Winfield, Kans., 1956; MA, Colo. State Coll., 1958. Cert. tchr. (life), Calif., Colo.; cert. adminstr., Calif. Bus. tchr. Peabody (Kans.) High Sch., 1956-58, Santa Barbara (Calif.) High Sch., 1958-65, coordinator work edn., 1965-75, dir. research and evaluation, 1975-88. Author: Introduction to Business and Office Careers, 1974, The World of Work Career Interest Survey, 1986; co-author: Succeeding in the World of Work, 1970, 7th rev. edit., 2003, Entering the World of Work, 1974, 4th rev. edit., 2006, The Savvy Consumer, 1984, Personal and Family Economics, 1996, Marketing Essentials, 1991, 4th edit., 2006, Office Skills, 1998, 3d edit., 2003, Advancing in the World of Work, 1992, Exploring Business and Computer Careers, 1998, Employment Skills for Office Careers, 1998. With U.S. Army, 1953-55. Mem. NEA, Calif. Assn. Work Experience Educators, Nat. Work Experience Edn. Assn., Calif. Tchrs. Assn., Coop. Work Experience Assn. Avocations: breeding and racing quarter horses, photography, travel. Personal E-mail: gradykim@cox.net.

KIMBRELL, ODELL CULP, JR., internist; b. Spartanburg, SC, May 2, 1927; s. Odell Culp and Leona (Nicholas) K.; m. Etta Lou; children from former marriage: Odell Culp III, Cynthia Anne. AB, Duke U., 1947; MD, U. Pa., 1951. Diplomate: Am. Bd. Internal Medicine, Am. Bd. Life Ins. Medicine. Intern Med. Coll. Va., Richmond, 1951-52, resident in internal medicine, 1954-56; sr. resident in internal medicine VA Hosp., Phila., 1956-57; practice medicine specializing in internal medicine and endocrinology Gallipolis, Ohio, 1957-60, Raleigh, NC, 1960-93; practice ins. medicine, 1967—; mem. hon. staff Wake Med. Ctr.; clin. prof. medicine U.N.C. Med. Sch., 1970-90. Med. dir., cons. Pa. Life Ins. Co., 1998—. Contbr. articles to med. jours. Bd. dirs. Wake County Hosp. System Inc., Raleigh, 1971-81, sec., 1973-74, chmn., 1974-76; bd. dirs. Wake Health Facilities and Service Inc., 1975-81, pres., 1975-76; chmn. Wake County Heart Fund, 1961; deacon Hudson Meml. Presbyn. Ch., Raleigh, 1971-73. Served with USAF, 1952-54. Fellow ACP; mem. AMA, N.C. Med. Soc., Wake County Med Soc., Am. Soc. Internal Medicine, N.C. Soc. Internal Medicine, Am. Acad. Ins. Med., Mid-Atlantic Med. Dirs. Club (pres. 1979-80, 92). Home: 1905 Hunting Ridge Rd Raleigh NC 27615-5515 Office: 201 Shannon Oaks Ste 200 Cary NC 27511 *Serving through devoted application of mind, body and spirit.*

KIMBRELL, WILLARD DUKE, textiles executive; b. Gaston County, NC, Dec. 28, 1924; s. Curtis C. and Carolyn (Carter) Kimbrell; m. Dorothy Rhyne; 3 children. BS in Textiles, N.C. State Coll., 1949; PhD, U. N.C., Charlotte. Various positions Parkdale Mills, Inc., Gastonia, NC, 1938—, CEO, 1961—2001, chmn. bd. dirs., 2001—. Bd. dirs. Am. Textile Mfg., Inman Mills. Pres. Gaston Cmty. Found.; bd. dirs. YMCA, Gastonia; trustee Bowman Gray Sch. Medicine, U. N.C. With USAF. Mem.: N.C. Textile Mfrs. Assn. (pres.), Am. Yam Spinners Assn. (pres.). Republican. Office: 531 Cotton Blossom Cir Gastonia NC 28054 Home Phone: 704-865-8312. E-mail: dkimbrell@parkdalemills.com.

KIMBROUGH, NATALIE, history professor; b. Hamburg, Germany, Jan. 24, 1970; d. Christa Renate Scholl; BA in Am. Studies, U. Hamburg, 1994, PhD in History, 2003; MA in US History, George Mason U., Fairfax, Va., 1998. Adj. instr. online U. Md. U. Coll., Adelphi, Md., 2003—; asst. prof. history CC Balt. County, 2005—. Instr. German lang. US Dept. State Fgn. Svc. Inst., Arlington, Va., 1999—2005, lead curriculum developer, distance edn., 2004—06; adj. instr. online Strayer U., Newington, Va., 2002—05; adj. prof. history George Mason U., 2003—04; faculty advisor History Club, 2005—06; organizing mem. UMOJA Com., 2006; presenter in field. Vol. Friends of the Vietnam Vets. Meml., Arlington, 1994—99; bd. mem. Ea. CC Social Sci. Assn, Va., 2006—. Recipient Quadrille Ball award, Inst. Internat. Edn., NY, 1997—98, Franklin award, US Dept. State Fgn. Svc. Inst., 2001, 2002, 2003, Hon. Faculty Svc. award, Student Life and Activities, 2005—06; German Academic Exch. Program scholar, German Govt. and Johns Hopkins U., 1994—95. Mem.: N.E. Popular Culture Assn., Popular Culture Assn./Am. Culture Assn., Orgn. Am. Historians, Am. History Assn, Am. Studies Assn., CC Humanities Assn., Oral History Assn. Avocations: poetry, reading, music, dance, walking. Office: CC Balt County 800 S Rolling Rd Baltimore MD 21228 Home Phone: 202-889-2397; Office Phone: 410-455-6916. Business E-Mail: nkimbrough@ccbcmd.edu.

KIMBROUGH, ROBERT AVERYT, lawyer; b. Sarasota, Fla., Nov. 2, 1933; s. Verman T. and Edith (Averyt) K.; m. Emilie Hudson, Aug. 24, 1957; children: James E., Robert A. Jr. BS, Davidson Coll., 1955; LLB to JD, U. Fla., 1960. Bar: Fla. 1960, U.S. Dist. Ct. Fla. 1962. Pvt. practice, Sarasota, 1960—. Chmn., bd. trustees, Ringling Coll. Art & Design, Sarasota, 1983-85; chmn. Sarasota Welfare Home Inc., 1986-89; pres. Fla. West Coast Symphony, Sarasota, 1986-90. Recipient Champion Higher Edn. in Fla., Ind. Coll. and Univs. of Fla., 1984-85, Alumnus of Yr. award Phi Delta Theta, 1997. Mem. Fla. Bar, Sarasota County Bar Assn., Kiwanis. Republican. Presbyterian. Avocations: flying, fishing, boating. Home: 7100 S Gator Creek Blvd Sarasota FL 34241-9729 Office: 1530 Cross St Sarasota FL 34236-7015 Office Phone: 941-951-1234. Business E-Mail: rak@kimbroughkoach.com.

KIMES, DON MARK, artist, educator; b. Oil City, Pa., Nov. 18, 1953; s. Norman Lloyd and Lois Elaine (Toy) K.; m. Lois Ann Jubeck, July 22, 1978; children: Jesse Mark, Jonathan Todd, Elaina Rose. BA, Westminster Coll., 1975; postgrad., U. Pitts., 1975-77; cert., N.Y. Studio Sch., NYC, 1979; MFA, Bklyn. Coll. CUNY, 1980. Founder, dir. Inst. Internat. Art, Corciano, Italy, 1995—. Artistic dir. fisual arts Chautauqua (N.Y.) Inst. Sch. of Art, 1986—; full prof. Art Am. U., Washington, 1988—; mem. faculty N.Y. Studio Sch., N.Y.C., 1979-89, program dir., 1980-84; vis. prof. art The Am. U. Rome, 1999—; guest artist Acad. Fine Arts, Perugia, Italy, Dartmouth Coll., Georgetown U., Internat. Sch. Art, Umbria, America Haus, Munich, Harvard U., Parsons Sch. Design; artist in residence Monte Malbe, Italy, 1999. One-man shows include Prince St. Gallery, N.Y.C., 1979-80, 82, 84, 86, 88, 90, 92, Villahermosa Exhbn. Ctr., Mex., 1992, NAS, Washington, 1992, Gauman Cicchino Gallery, Fla., 1990, Michael Rockefeller Gallery, Fredonia, N.Y., 1988, Watkins Gallery, Washington, 1989, 97, Galleria ISA, Montecastello, Italy, 1999, Am. Haus, Munich, Germany, 1996, Galleria Rocca Paolina, Perugia, Italy, 1996, Claudia Carr Gallery, N.Y.C., 2000, Stephen Gang, 2001, Dartmouth Coll, 2001, Chautauqua Ctr. for the Visual Arts, 2006, Elizabeth Roberts Gallery, Washington, 2003, Constn. Hall, Washington, 2003, others; exhibited in group shows at Balt. Mus. Art, 1986, 99, Nat. Acad. of Design, N.Y.C., 1986, Corcoran Gallery of Am. Art, 1994, 95, Piazza Broletto, Perugia, Italy, 1995, Arte Vivre, Milan, 1995, Kouros Gallery, N.Y.C., 1997, Internat. Visions, Washington, 1999, Kennedy Mus. Art, Athens, Ohio, 1999, Agosto Corcianese, Umbria, 1998, Florence Internat. Bienale, 2001, 03, Katzen Mus. Art, 2006; represented in collections at Katzen Mus., Washington, MIT, Rockefeller U., Washington U., others; contbr. articles to profl. mags. Mem. N.Y. Studio Sch. Bd. Govs., N.Y.C., 1980-85. Named Visual Del. to Villahermosa Conferencia de Literatura y Artes, 1992, Soviet Cultural Exch. Eisenhower Found., Chautauqua Inst., 1986; fellow Edna St. Vincent Millay Colony, 1986; recipient artist-in-residence award U.S. Dept. Interior, 1993, Mellon Found. award to live in Italy, 1994-95. Mem. Coll. Art Assn. Am. Home: Chautauqua School of Art PO Box 1098 Chautauqua NY 14722-1098 Office: The Am U Dept Art Washington DC 20016 Home Phone: 716-753-2517; Office Phone: 202-885-1670. E-mail: dkimes@american.edu.

KIMES, SHERYL ELAINE, business educator; b. St. Louis, Apr. 14, 1954; d. John Alfred and Alpha Louise (Johnson) K. AB, U. Mo., 1975; MA in Pub. Adminstrn., U. Va., 1977; MBA, N.Mex. State U., 1983; PhD, U. Tex., 1987. Energy coord. St. Louis County, St. Louis, 1978-79; energy analyst Londe-Parker-Michels, St. Louis, 1979-82; teaching asst. N.Mex. State U., Las Cruces, 1982-83; project mgr. Technol. Innovation Ctr., Las Cruces, 1983-84; asst. instr. bus. U. Tex., Austin, 1984-85, rsch. asst., 1985-86; asst. prof. bus. N.Mex. State U., Las Cruces, 1986-88, Cornell U., Ithaca, N.Y., 1988-93, assoc. prof., 1993-2000, prof., 2000—. U. Tex. fellow, 1984-86. Mem. INFORMS. Avocations: swimming, bridge, wine, puzzles. Office: Cornell U 335 Statler Hall Ithaca NY 14853-6902

KIMETHU, SUSAN WANJA, computer specialist, database manager; b. Nairobi, Kenya, Mar. 13, 1956; d. Samuel Kimama Ngaii and Mary Nyambura Kimama; m. Daniel Mburu Kimethu; children: Hosea Kimethu Mburu, Samuel Kimama Mburu, Esther Njeri Mburu. Diploma, Kenya Tech. Coll., 1983; MBA, Baldwin Wallace Coll., 1992; PhD in Bus. Adminstrn., Kennedy Western U., 2002. Cert. Oracle database adminstr.; h.s. tchr. Sr. acct. Ameritrust Bank, Cleve., 1993—94; sr. fin. analyst Key Bank, Cleve., 1994—98; instr. Sawyer Bus. Coll., Cleve., 1994—98; database mgr. Telesis Of Ohio, Cleve., 1997—99; sr. bus. analyst Emerald Health, Cleve., 1998—99; database mgr. Orbital Computers, Cleve., 2000—01; computer specialist United Labor Agy., Cleve., 2001—03; tchr. Life Skills Ctr., Columbus, 2003—04. Tchr. English as second lang. Southwestern City Sch. Dist., Columbus, Ohio, 2004—. Author: Following & Obeying God in Your Youth, 2001, Kids, Let's Follow Christ, 2002, Kids, Let's Follow Christ Workbook, 2002. Mem.: Ohio Edn. Assn., Network Administrs., Oracle User Group. Office: Dansu Pubs LLC PO Box 955 Grove City OH 43123-0937 Office Phone: 216-513-6753. Personal E-mail: skimethu@hotmail.com.

KIM-FARLEY, ROBERT JAMES, epidemiologist, educator; b. Troy, NY, Jan. 24, 1948; s. Robert James and Glennie Jean Farley; m. Han Ju Kim-Farley, Sept. 18, 1976; 1 child, Jean. BSEE, U. Calif., Santa Barbara, 1970; MPH, UCLA, 1975; MD, U. Calif., San Francisco, 1980. Cert. preventive medicine and pub. health. Med. epidemiologist Ctrs. Disease Control and Prevention, Atlanta, 1981—2004; dir. communicable disease control and prevention Los Angeles County Dept. Pub. Health, LA, 2004—. Regional advisor WHO, New Delhi, 1984—88, dir. expanded programme on immunization, Geneva, 1989—93, rep., Jakarta, Indonesia, 1994—99, New Delhi, 1999—2002; prof. UCLA, 2003—. Recipient Surgeon Gen.'s Exemplary Svc. medal, USPHS, 1993. Mem.: APHA. Baha'I. Avocation: swimming. Office Phone: 213-989-7161. E-mail: rkimfarley@ladhs.org.

KIMM, MICHAEL S., lawyer; b. Seoul, July 12, 1963; came to U.S., 1974; s. Chun Teak and Chong Sim K. BA, Fordham U., 1987; JD, Boston U., 1991. Bar: N.J. 1991, N.Y. 1992, U.S. Dist. Ct. N.J. 1991, U.S. Dist. Ct. (so. and ea. dists.) N.Y. 1993, U.S. Ct. Appeals (2nd, 3rd and Fed cirs.) 1994, U.S. Supreme Ct. 1995. Pvt. practice, Hackensack, NJ. Mng. editor: Boston U. Internat. Law Jour., 1990-91; contbr. articles to profl. jours. Gen. counsel Korean-Am. Assn. for Rehab. of Disabled, Queens, N.Y., 1992-94. Mem. ABA, N.J. State Bar Assn., N.Y. State Bar Assn. Office: 185 Great Neck Rd Great Neck NY 11021 Address: 190 Moore St # 272 Hackensack NJ 07601

KIMMEL, CHUCK, academic administrator, director; b. Hopkinsville, Ky., Sept. 30, 1954; s. Charles William and Roberta Smith Kimmel; m. Patricia Carol Hodge, Aug. 11, 1978; children: Chad, Meredith, Adam. BA, U. Ky., Lexington, 1976; MA, E. Tenn. State U., Johnson City, 1978. Lic. athletic trainer State of Tenn. Bd. Med. Examiners, 00. Grad. asst. athletic trainer E. Tenn. State U., Johnson City, 1976—78, asst. athletic trainer, 1978—81; head athletic trainer Austin Peay State U., Clarksville, Tenn., 1981—2006, asst. athletic dir., 1990—2006; dir. injury clinic, instr. Appalachian State U., Boone, NC, 2007—. Presenter in field. Contbr. articles to profl. jours. Named to Athletics Hall of Fame, Austin Peay State U., 2006; recipient Merit award, SE Athletic Trainers' Assn., 2005. Mem.: Tenn. Athletic Trainers' Soc. (mem. parliamentarian 1982—85, 1995—2000, pres. 1989—93, v.p. 1985—89, Hall of Fame 2002, Pres.' award of merit 2005, Gene Smith/Mickey O'Brien Coll. Athletic Trainer of Yr. 1991), NC Athletic Trainers' Assn., Mid-Atlantic Trainers' Assn., Nat. Athletic Trainers' Assn. (dir. dist. IX 2000—04, sec./treas. 2001—04, chair fin. com. 2001—04, chair investment com. 2001—04, pres. elect 2003—04, pres. 2004—, liaison convention com. 2000—04, Most Dist. Athletic Trainer award 2002, cert., Athletic Trainer Svc. award 1997). Roman Catholic. Office: Appalachian State Univ 614 Howard St Box 32070 Boone NC 28608-2070

KIMMEL, ELLEN BISHOP, psychologist, educator; b. Knoxville, Tenn., Sept. 16, 1939; d. Archer W. and Mary Ellen (Baker) Bishop; divorced; children: Elinor, Ann, Jean, Tracy. BA summa cum laude, U. Tenn., 1961; MA, U. Fla., 1962, PhD, 1965. Asst. prof., rsch. assoc. Ohio U., 1965-68; asst. prof. U. South Fla., Tampa, 1968-72, assoc. prof., dean Univ. Studies Coll., 1972-73, prof. psychology and ednl. psychology, 1975-95, chair, 1992-94, disting. prof., 1996—2003, prof. emerita, 2003—. Disting. vis. prof. psychology Simon Fraser U., Vancouver, B.C., Can., 1980-81; cons. numerous sch. systems, bus. and govt. Author books; contbr. articles to profl. jours., chpts. to books. Mem. Fla. Blue Ribbon Task Force on Juvenile Delinquency, 1976-77; mem. Fla. Gov.'s Commn. on Women, 1979-83; mem. adv. bd. Stop Rape, Good Govt., Inc.; bd. dirs. NCCJ. Recipient Outstanding Svc. award State of Fla., 1975, Outstanding Tchg. award U. South Fla., 1978, Career Achievement award U. Tenn., 1983, Professorial Excellence award Fla. State U. Sys., 1997, Disting. Sr. Scholar Spl. Commendation of Honor, AAUW, 2001; 17 rsch. grants. Fellow: APA (governing coun. 1982—85, pres. divsn. 1986—88, Disting. Leadership award 1993), Am. Assn. Applied and Preventive Psychology (bd. dirs. 1994—97, charter fellow, program chair 1991, Disting. Edn. award 1994), Am. Psychol. Soc. (charter fellow, conf. chair 1990); mem.: Southeastern Psychol. Assn. (pres. 1977—79), Assn. Women in Psychology (Disting. Publ. award 2000), Athena Soc., Omicron Delta Kappa, Delta Kappa Gamma, Sigma Xi. Democrat. Office: U South Fla EDU 162 Tampa FL 33620 Business E-Mail: kimmel@tempest.coedu.usf.edu.

KIMMEL, MARK, author, venture capital company executive; b. Denver, Feb. 15, 1940; s. Earl Henry and Gerry Claire Kimmel; m. Gloria J. Danielewicz, Jan. 29, 1966 (div.); children: Kenton, Kristopher; m. Heidi J. Moller, Sept. 5, 1999. BSEE, U. Colo., Boulder, 1963, BS in Mktg., 1963; MBA in Fin., U. So. Calif., L.A., 1966; MA in Psychology, Regis U., Denver, 2000. Sales engr., market rsch. analyst 3M Co., Calif. and Minn., 1963—70; mgr. mktg. Am. Computer and Comm., Calif., 1970—71; mgr. new bus. devel. Motorola, Inc., Schaumburg, Ill., 1971—76; v.p. corp. devel. Nat. City Lines, Denver, 1976—77; pres. Enervest, Inc., Denver, 1977—84; gen. ptnr. Columbine Venture Fund Ltd., 1983—91, Columbine Venture Fund II, 1983—91, Columbine Venture Mgmt. I, 1983—91, Columbine Venture Mgmt. II, 1983—91; pres. Columbine Venture Mgmt. Inc., 1983—91, Paradigm Ptnrs., Inc., 1992—96; writer, lectr., 1996; v.p. Paradigm Books, Inc. Author: Trillion, 2002, Decimal, 2004, Creating the Cosmic Paradigm, 2005, Birthing A New Civilization, 2007. Chmn. Cosmic Paradign Network; v.p. Paradigm Book, Inc. E-mail: 77@zqyx.org.

KIMMEL, MARK E., lawyer; b. 1959; BS, Lehigh U.; JD, Pa. State U. Dickinson Sch. of Law, 1985. Bar: Pa. 1985. Various legal positions Hershey Foods Corp., 1987—99; v.p. administration, gen. counsel New World Pasta Co., 1999—2001; various legal positions Harsco Corp., 2001—03, asst. gen. counsel, sec., 2003—04, gen. counsel, corp. sec., 2004—. Office: Harsco Corp 350 Poplar Church Rd Camp Hill PA 17011

KIMMEL, SIDNEY, apparel company executive, film producer; b. 1928; Founder, pres. Jones Apparel Group (Divsn. W.R. Grace & Co.), Bristol, Pa., 1970-75, chmn., CEO, 1975—, pres., 1994-96; ptnr. Cipriani Internat.; owner, ptnr. Miami Heat; owner Sidney Kimmel Entertainment. Prodr. (films) 9 1/2 Weeks, 1986, The Clan of the Cave Bear, 1987, The Night We Never Met, 1993, Mother, 1996, Seperation Anxiety, 1997, Curtain Call, 1999, Famous, 2000, Town & Country, 2001, STRUT!, 2001, The Perfect You, 2001, The Emperor's Club, 2002, Neverwas, 2005, Trust the Man, 2005, Slow Burn, 2005, Alpha Dog, 2006, Copying Beethoven, 2006, Griffin & Phoenix, 2006, Death at a Funeral, 2007, Breach, 2007 Lead donor Kimmel Ctr. Performing Arts, Phila.; founder, chmn. Sidney Kimmel Found., Phila., 1993—; founder Sidney Kimmel Comprehensive Cancer Ctr. at Johns Hopkins U., Balt. Recipient Humanitarian award, Am. Cancer Soc., 1999. Office: Jones Apparel Group 250 Rittenhouse Cir Bristol PA 19007-1616 Fax: 215-785-1795.*

KIMMEL COHN, ROBERTA, art dealer, educator; b. Milw., Feb. 1, 1937; d. Maurice David and Helen Theresa Kimmel; m. Richard A. Cohn, May 28, 1971. BFA, Boston U., 1959. Prin. Roberta Kimmel Advertising, NYC, 1967—90; ptnr. Kimmel Cohn Arts, NYC, 1976—. Guest curator Goethe Inst., 1993, NYC, 2002; lectr. Georgia O'Keefe Mus., Santa Fe, 2002, Mus. Fine Arts, Boston, 2004. Author: (portfolio) George Grosz Erste Landing, 1977; author, illustrator (book) In Artists Homes, 1992. Jewish. Office: Kimmel Cohn Arts 1 W 64th St New York NY 10023

KIMMELMAN, MICHAEL SIMON, art critic; b. NYC, May 8, 1958; s. David Brown and Edythe Miriam (Weinstock) K.; m. Maria Kathleen Simson, Sept. 10, 1988. BA in History, Yale U., 1980; MA in Art History, Harvard U., 1982. Teaching fellow dept. fine arts, Arthur Kingsley Porter Fellow Harvard U., Cambridge, Mass., 1982-84; music critic Atlanta Journal-Constitution, 1984, Phila. Inquirer, 1985-87; culture editor U.S. News and World Report, Washington, 1987; art critic NY Times, 1988-90, chief art critic, 1990—. Lectr. in field; sr. fellow, Nat. Arts Journalism Program Columbia U., 2000. Author: Portraits: Talking With Artists at the Met, the Modern, the Louvre and Elsewhere, 1999 (named Notable Book of Yr., Washington Post and The Times, named Best Book of Yr., Publisher's Weekly), The Accidental Masterpiece: On the Art of Life and Vice Versa, 2005; contbr. to the New York Review of Books, articles to other magazines. Named a finalist in criticism for the Pulitzer Prize, 2000. Mem. Phi Beta Kappa. Office: NY Times 229 W 43rd St New York NY 10036-3959

KIMMES, NICOLE S., dentist, educator; BS, No. State U., Aberdeen, SD, 2001; DDS, Creighton U., Omaha, 2001. Dentist Summit Dental Assoc., PC, Omaha, 2001—. Adj. prof. Creighton U., Omaha, 2001—02, clin. educator, 2002—04, asst. prof. gen. dentistry, 2004—, dir., One World Clinic Screening, 2006—. Contbr. articles to profl. jours. Recipient Orgn. Tchrs. of Oral Diagnosis award, Creighton U., Dept. Gen. Dentistry, 2001; grantee, Health Future Found., 2005, 2006. Mem.: Am. Dental Edn. Assn., Am. Assn. Dental Rsch., Internat. Assn. Dental Rsch., Omicron Kappa Upsilon, Phi Eta Sigma Nat. Honor Soc. Office: Creighton Univ Sch Dentistry 2500 California Plaza Omaha NE 68178

KIMMEY, JAMES RICHARD, JR., foundation administrator; b. Boscobel, Wis., Jan. 26, 1935; s. James Richard and Frances Dale (Parnell) Kimmey; m. Sarah Webster Eastman, June 21, 1958; children: Elisabeth Webster, James Richard III. BS, U. Wis., 1957, MS, 1959, MD, 1961; MPH, U. Calif., Berkeley, 1967. Diplomate Am. Bd. Preventive Medicine. Intern Univ. Hosps., Cleve., 1961-62; med. resident Univ. Hosp., Madison, 1962-63; served from surgeon to med. dir. USPHS, 1963-68, chief kidney disease br., 1964-66, regional health dir. NY, 1967-68; exec. dir. Cmty. Health Inc., NYC, 1968-70, Am. Pub. Health Assn., 1970-73; sec. Health Policy Coun. Wis., 1973-75; pres. James R. Kimmey Assos., Inc., 1975-85; dir. Midwest Ctr. Health Planning, 1976-79; exec. dir. Inst. Health Planning, 1979-87; prof. pub. health, dir. Ctr. for Health Svcs. Edn. Rsch. St. Louis U. Med. Ctr., 1987-91; dean sch. pub. health St. Louis U., 1991-93, v.p. health scis., 1993-98, exec. v.p., 1998-2000; dir. Inst. Urban Health Policy, 2000-2001; pres. Mo. Found. for Health, 2001—. Adj. prof. NYU, NYC, 1968—70; lectr. Johns Hopkins, 1971—73; clin. instr. U. Wis., 1974—87; pres. Inst. Health Planning, 1979—86; chair Task Force Accreditation Health Professions, 1997—99, St. Louis ConnectCare, 1998—2001; dir. Ctr. Engring. Tech., 1998—2001; vice chair St. Louis Access Health, 1999—2001. Editor: (book) The Nation's Health, 1972—73; mng. editor: Am. Jour. Pub. Health, 1970—73, mem. editl. adv. bd.: Health Cost Mgmt., 1983—87; contbr. articles to profl. jours. Pres. World Fedn. Pub. Health Assns., 1972—73; mem. sci. adv. bd. Gorgas Inst., 1970—73; bd. dirs. Internat. Union Health Edn., 1970—73. Decorated USPHS Commendation medal. Fellow: APHA (governing coun. 1978—81, chmn. cmty. health planning sect. 1979—80, governing coun. 1983—87, 1989—92), Am. Coll. Preventive Medicine; mem.: Prospective Payment Assessment Commn. (commr. 1991—97), Mo. Pub. Health Assn. (Mo. Communicator of the Yr. award 1994), Am. Coll. Health Adminstrs., Am. Health Planning Assn. (dir. 1974—75, 1977—78, corp. sec. 1977—78, pres. 1980—81, Richard H. Schlesinger award 1978, James R. Kimmey award 1994), Alpha Sigma Nu, Delta Omega, Alpha Omega Alpha, Phi Eta Sigma. Democrat. Episcopalian. Office: Grand Ctrl Bldg Ste 400 1000 St Louis Union Sta Saint Louis MO 63103 Home: 1805 Park Ave #2D Saint Louis MO 63104 Home Phone: 314-621-3424; Office Phone: 314-345-5500. Business E-Mail: jkimmey@mffh.org.

KIMMICH, CHRISTOPH MARTIN, academic administrator, educator; b. Dresden, Jan. 16, 1939; s. Emil and Dora (Dreher) K.; m. Flora Graham Horne, July 10, 1965. BA, Haverford Coll., 1961; DPhil, U. Oxford, Eng., 1964. Asst. then assoc. prof. Columbia U., NYC, 1965-73; assoc. then full prof. Bklyn. Coll., CUNY, 1973—, assoc. provost, 1984-88, provost, v.p. acad. affairs, 1988-97; interim chancellor CUNY, NYC, 1997-99; pres. Bklyn. Coll., 2000—. V.p. bd. dirs. rsch. and devel. fedn. Bklyn. Coll., 1989—; chmn. bd. dirs. rsch. found. of CUNY, 1997-1999, mem., 2000-03. Author: The Free City, 1968, Germany and the League of Nations, 1976, German Foreign Policy: 1918-1945, 1981, 2d edit., 1991. Trustee St. Antony's Coll. Trust, N.Y.C., 1978-2000; bd. dirs. Northeastern Sci. Found., Troy, 1987-98, Coll. Cmty. Svcs., Inc., Bklyn., 1988-95, chmn., 2000—; bd. trustees Cranbury Pub. Libr., 1997-2000; bd. dirs. Bklyn. Philharm. Orch., 2003—; mem. adv. bd. Princeton Rev. Admissions Policy Divsn., 2004—. Recipient Yigal Allon Excellence in Edn. award, 2006; Fulbright scholar, 1961; Internat. Affairs fellow, 1974; Guggenheim fellow, 1983; decorated Order of Merit Comdr.'s Cross, Republic of Hungary, 2001. Mem. Phi Beta Kappa. Home: 183 Plainsboro Rd Cranbury NJ 08512-2603 Office: Bklyn Coll Office of the Pres 2900 Bedford Ave Brooklyn NY 11210-2889

KIMMITT, ROBERT MICHAEL, federal agency and former business executive; b. Logan, Utah, Dec. 19, 1947; s. Joseph Stanley and Eunice L. (Wegener) K.; m. Holly Sutherland, May 19, 1979; children: Kathleen, Robert, William, Thomas, Margaret. BS, U.S. Mil. Acad., 1969; JD, Georgetown U., 1977. Bar: D.C. 1977. Commd. 2d lt. U.S. Army, 1969, advanced through grades to maj., 1982, served in Vietnam, 1970-71; maj. gen. USAR, 1999—2004; law clk. U.S. Ct. Appeals, Washington, 1977-78; sr. staff mem. NSC, Washington, 1978-83, dep. asst. to Pres. for nat. security affairs and exec. sec. and gen. counsel, 1983-85; gen. counsel U.S. Dept. Treasury, Washington, 1985-87; ptnr. Sidley & Austin, Washington, 1987-89; undersec. for polit. affairs US Dept. State, Washington, 1989-91, US amb. to Germany Berlin, 1991-93; mng. dir. Lehman Bros., Washington, NYC, 1993-97; sr. ptnr. Wilmer, Cutler & Pickering, Washington, 1997-00; vice-chmn., pres. Commerce One, Pleasanton, Calif., 2000—01; exec. v.p., global pub. policy Time Warner Inc., Washington, 2001—05, chmn. internat. adv. coun., 2005; sr. internat. counsel Wilmer, Cutler, Pickering, Hale & Dorr, Washington, 2005; dep. sec. US Dept. Treasury, Washington, 2005—. U.S. mem. panel of arbitrators Ctr. Settlement of Investment Internat. Disputes, 1988—89. Decorated Bronze star (3), Purple Heart, Air medal, Vietnamese Cross of Gallantry, German Svc. Cross, German Army Cross in Gold; recipient Arthur Flemming award Downtown Jaycees, 1987, Alexander Hamilton award U.S. Dept. Treasury, 1987, Presdl. Citizens medal, 1991, Def. Disting. Civilian Svc. medal, 1993. Mem. Am. Acad. Diplomacy, Assn. Grads. U.S. Mil. Acad. (trustee 1976-82), Coun. Fgn. Rels. Roman Catholic. Office: US Dept Treasury 1500 Pennsylvania Ave NW Rm 3000 Washington DC 20220

KIMNACH, MYRON WILLIAM, botanist, horticulturist; b. LA, Dec. 26, 1922; s. Elmer Edward and Ida (Johnson) K.; m. Maria Jaeger, Nov. 17, 1961. Grad. h.s. Asst. mgr. U. Calif. Botanic Garden, Berkeley, 1951-62; dir. Huntington Bot. Gardens, San Marino, 1962—86, dir. emeritus, 1986; book-dealer Monrovia, Calif. Contbr. articles profl. jours. Pres., bd. dir. Palm Soc., 1976-78. With USCG, 1943-46. Fellow Cactus and Succulent Soc. Am. (pres. 1970-71, bd. dir. 1968-74, editor jour. 1993-2003). Home and Office: 509 Bradbury Rd Monrovia CA 91016-3704 Office Phone: 626-358-3043. Personal E-mail: mkimnach@aol.com.

KIMPTON, JEFFREY S., academic administrator; b. 1950; m. Julie Kimpton; children: Meghan, Adam. Attended polit. sci. & pre-law, Augustana Coll., Rock Island, Ill., 1968—70; BS in music edn., cum laude, U. Ill., 1973, MS in music edn. & sch. adminstr., 1975; cert. in corp. financial mgmt. & acctg., Am. Mgmt. Assn., 1995. Cert. teaching & adminstr. Ill., N.Y., Minn., Kans. Various teaching & adminstr. positions Pub. Sch. Sys., Wichita, Kans., Apple Valley, Minn., Corinth, NY, 1973—88; dir. instl. edn. Yamaha Corp. Am., 1988—96; dir. pub. engagement Annenberg Inst. Brown U., 1996—99; dir. sch. music U. Minn., 1999—2003, prof. music edn., 1999—2003; pres. Interlochen Ctr. for Arts, 2003—. Mem. Rotary Club Traverse City; corp. bd. Munson Healthcare; bd. dir. Traverse Area Arts Coun., ArtServe Mich. Office: Office of the Pres Interlochen Ctr for Arts PO Box 199 Interlochen MI 49643

KIMPTON, LAURA, artist; BA in Art Edn., U. Iowa, 1986; BFA in Photography, San Francisco Art Inst, 1990; MA in Counseling Psych., U. San Francisco, 1996. One-woman shows include Still Lights Gallery, San Francisco, 1988, Felix Kopala Gallery, Santa Cruz, Calif., 2005, Who's the Judge, supperclub, 2006, Mynd Too, Schomburg Gallery, LA, 2006, exhibitions include Eye Gallery Photography Auction, San Francisco, 1989, San Francisco Art Inst., 1989, South of Market Cultural Ctr., San Francisco, 1989, Artist Television Access, 1989, Diego Rivera Gallery, San Francisco Art Inst., 1989, Arts Guild of Sonoma, 2002, The Color of Woman, 2003, La Haye Art Ctr., Sonoma, 2003, Mus. Contemporary Art, Santa Rosa, Calif., 2004, di Rosa Preserve, Napa, 2005—06, Donna Seager Gallery, San Rafael, Calif., 2006, installations, Arts Guild of Sonoma, 2002, 2004, Pigman Gallery, San Francisco, 2005, NY Studio Gallery, 2007. Office: c/o FabryHess Fine Art Representation 4001 San Leandro St Ste 10 Oakland CA 94601

KIMREY, KAREN GOSS, secondary school educator; b. Oxford, NC, July 22, 1956; d. Mildred Currin Goss; m. Clay Hansen Kimrey, June 30, 2004; m. Michael McLendon, May 11, 1985 (div.); 1 child, Tracy Lynn McLendon. B cum laude, Meredith Coll., Raleigh, 1991. Tech. advisor Nortel Networks, Research Triangle Park, NC, 1995—2001; tchr. Granville County Sch., Creedmoor, 2001—04; tchr. 8th grade Heritage Mid. Sch., Wake Forest, 2004—. Chair dept. social studies Heritage Mid. Sch., 2005—, team leader aviators track 4, 8th grade, 2005—. Recipient Employee Excellence award, Granville County Schs., 2001—03. Mem.: DAR (life), United Daus. Confederacy (life), Phi Alpha Theta (life). Conservative. Baptist. Avocations: motorcycling, needlecrafts, reading. Home: 7605 Bud Morris Road Wake Forest NC 27587 Office: Heritage Middle School 3400 Rogers Road Wake Forest NC 27587 Home Phone: 919-556-0752; Office Phone: 919-562-6204. Personal E-mail: karenkimrey@nc.rr.com. Business E-Mail: kkimrey@wcpss.net.

KIM-RUPNOW, WEOL SOON, education educator; d. Dae-Soo Kim and Ye-Soon Yim; m. Robert James Rupnow; children: Kenneth Rupnow, Hana Rupnow. Degree, Seoul Nat. Tchrs. Coll., 1974; PhD, U. Hawaii, Manoa, 1991. Co-project dir., rschr. U. Hawaii-Manoa Ctr. on Disability Studies, Honolulu, 1997—2001, project dir., 2001—. Contbr. articles to profl. jours. Grantee Dept. Edn., 2001—03. Mem.: Am. Ednl. Rsch. Assn. (corr.). Office: Ctr on Disability Studies 1776 University Ave UA4-6 Honolulu HI 96826 Home Phone: 808-247-5708; Office Phone: 808-956-5712. Office Fax: 808-956-7878.

KIMURA, DOREEN, psychology professor, researcher; b. Winnipeg, Man., Can. 1 child, Charlotte Vanderwolf. BA, McGill U., Montreal, Que., Can., 1956, MA, 1957, PhD, 1961; LLD (hon.), Simon Fraser U., 1993, Queen's U., 1999. Lectr. Sir George Williams U. (now Concordia U.), Montreal, 1960-61; rsch. assoc. otol. rsch. lab. UCLA Med. Ctr., 1962-63; rsch. assoc. Coll. Medicine, McMaster U., Hamilton, Ont., 1964-67; assoc. prof. psychology U. Western Ont., London, 1967-74, prof., 1974-98, coord. clin. neuropsychology program, 1983-97. Supr. clin. neuropsychology Univ. Hosp., London, 1975-83; vis. prof. psychology Simon Fraser U., 1998—. Author: Neuromotor Mechanisms in Human Communication, 1993, Sex and Cognition, 1999, French, Japanese, Swedish, Spanish, Portuguese, and Polish edits.; contbr. numerous articles to profl. jours. Recipient Outstanding Sci. Achievement award Can. Assn. Women in Sci., 1986, John Dewan award Ont. Mental Health Found., 1992, Kistler prize for lifetime achievement in human rsch. Found. for the Future, 2006; fellow Montreal Neurol. Inst., 1960-61, Geigy fellow Kantonsspital, Zürich, Switzerland, 1963-64, D.O. Hebb Disting. Contbn. award, Can. Soc. Brain, Behav. & Cogn. Sciences, 2005. Fellow Royal Soc. Can., Can. Psychol. Assn. (Disting. Contbns. to Sci. award 1985); mem. Soc. Acad. Freedom and Scholarship (founding pres. 1992-93, 98-2000). Office: Simon Fraser U Dept Psychology Burnaby BC Canada V5A 1S6 Office Phone: 604-291-3356. Business E-Mail: dkimura@sfu.ca.

KIMYAI-ASADI, ARASH, surgeon; s. Taghi Kimyai-Asadi and Fatemeh Milani; m. Ming Hewy Jih, May 24, 2003; children: Leila, Zane Alabidin. BA, MD, Johns Hopkins U., Balt., 1999. Diplomate Am. Bd. Dermatology. Mohs surgeon DermSurgery Assocs., Houston, 2004—. Contbr. Mem.: Am. Acad. Dermatology, Am. Soc. for Dermatologic Surgery, Am. Coll. Mohs Micrographic Surgery and Cutaneous Oncology (assoc.), Phi Beta Kappa. Office: DermSurgery Assocs 7515 Main Ste 290 Houston TX 77030 Home Phone: 713-665-2780; Office Phone: 713-791-9966. Office Fax: 713-791-9927. Personal E-mail: akimyai@yahoo.com.

KINARD, CYNTHIA COCHRAN, artist, writer; b. Columbia, SC, Dec. 8, 1952; d. Thomas Louie and Eleanor (Bannister) Cochran; m. James Borden Kinard, Oct. 5, 1948. BA in Art with honors, BA in Modern Fgn. Langs. with honors, Western Carolina U., 1975; student, Angel Acad. Art, Florence, Italy, 2005. Exec. dir. Alleghany Arts Coun., Sparta, N.C., 1995—96. One-woman shows include Alleghany County Art Gallery, 1992, 1995, 1996, exhibitions include Pisgah Forest, Davidson River Gallery, 1997 (Merchants award, 1997, Honorable Mention, 1998), Macon County Fair (Watercolor Portrait, Grand Champion, 1999, 2004, Watercolor Floral, 2nd place, 2001), Spiritual III Internat. Juried Exhibit, Period Gallery (Spl. Recognition, 2000), Watercolor Mo. Nat. Annual Juried Exhibit, Mo. Watercolor Soc. Winston Churchill Meml. Gallery, Westminster Coll., 2001, 2002, 2003, Western Region Exhibit, YMI Cultural Ctr. (Watercolor Portrait, 3rd place, 2001), Bascon-Louise Annual Juried Exhibit, Highlands Visual Arts Ctr. (Watercolor Portrait, Merit award, 2001), 2002, Small Works Nat. All Media Invitational Exhibit, Period Gallery (Spl. Recognition, 2001), I Am Woman, Art 1 Gallery (Watercolor Portrait, Patron award, 2002), Watercolor Soc. North Carolina 57th Annual Juried Exhibit, 2002, Watercolor and Oil Portraits, Still Life's, Floral and Landscape, Swain County Ctr. Arts, 2003, 7th Annual All Media Internat. Juried Online Art Exhibit, Upstream People Gallery, 2004, Focus on Art 12th Annual Exhibit, TCarts Gallery, 2004, Graceworks 4th Annual Juried Fine Art Exhibit, Grace Ctr., 2004, Watercolor Soc. North Carolina 59th Annual Juried Exhibit, Appalachian Cultural Mus. Appalachian State U. (Strathmore Paper award, 2004), Watercolor Soc. North Carolina 60th Annual Juried Exhibit, Salem Fine Arts Ctr. Gallery, Salem Coll. (Watercolor Portrait Signature Mem., 2005). Pres. Friends of the Libr., Sparta, 1996—97; pastor's wife Burningtown Bapt. Ch., Franklin, NC, 2000—06; exec. dir. Alleghany Arts Coun., Sparta, 1996—97. Mem.: Art Renewal Ctr. (assoc.), Art League of the Smokies (assoc.), Am. Soc. Portrait Artists (assoc.), Watercolor Soc. N.C. (assoc.), Portrait Soc. Am. (assoc.), Nat. Watercolor Soc. (assoc.), Mo. Watercolor Soc. (assoc.), Am. Watercolor Soc. (assoc.), So. Watercolor Soc. (assoc.), Nat. Mus. Women in the Arts (assoc.). Conservative. Christian. Avocations: travel, hiking, raising dogs, photography, writing, languages. Home: 1480 Mica City Rd Franklin NC 28734 Home Phone: 828-421-1287; Office Phone: 828-421-1287. Personal E-mail: cckinard@earthlink.net.

KINBERG, JUDY, television producer and director; b. Freeport, NY, Sept. 15, 1948; d. Jack H. and Rose M. (Schwartz) K. BA, Hofstra U., 1970. Prodn. asst. various programs including Camera Three CBS TV, NYC, 1970-75; assoc. producer PBS-WNET/Dance in America, NYC, 1975-76, producer, 1977—. NBC co-producer: He Makes Me Feel Like Dancin', 1984 (Acad. award, Emmy award, Chgo. Internat. Film Festival Silver Hugo, CINE Golden Eagle award, Christopher awards); prodr., dir. Who's Dancin' Now? (AFI L.A. Internat. Film Fest. Audience award, Best Documentary, Cine Golden Eagle award, Parents' Choice award), 1999; producer: PBS Dance in America: The Feld Ballet, 1979, The Green Table (with Joffrey Ballet), 1982, The Magic Flute (with N.Y.C. Ballet), 1983, San Francisco Ballet: A Song for Dead Warriors, 1984, A Choreographer's Notebook: Stravinsky Piano Ballets by Peter Martins, 1984, Balanchine, Parts I and II, 1984 (27th Ann. Internat. Film and TV awards of N.Y., gold medal Chgo. Internat. Film Festival Silver Plaque Monitor award, Emmy nomination), San Francisco Ballet in Cinderella, 1985 (Internat. Film and TV Festival of N.Y. gold medal, CINE Golden Eagle award, Parent's Choice award), Mark Morris, 1986 (CINE Golden Eagle award, Am. Film & Video Festival Red Ribbon award), Choreography by Jerome Robbins, 1986 (Chgo. Internat. Film Festival Silver Hugo, CINE Golden Eagle award), Dance Theatre of Harlem in A Streetcar Named Desire, 1986 (Chgo. Internat. Film Festival Silver Hugo), In Memory of.A Ballet by Jerome Robbins, 1987 (Chgo. Internat. Film Festival Silver Hugo, CINE Golden Eagle award), Agnes, the Indomitable de Mille, 1987 (Emmy award, Chgo. Internat. Film Festival Silver Hugo, CINE Golden Eagle award), Paul Taylor: Roses and Last Look, 1988, Balanchine and Cunningham: An Evening at Am. Ballet Theatre, 1988, La Sylphide (with the Pa./Milw. Ballet), 1989, A Night at The Joffrey, 1989, (Emmy nomination, Gold medal Internat. Film and TV Festival of N.Y., Best Video Creation IMZ Video Danse Awards, Gold Hugo award Chgo. Internat. Film Festival), The Search for Nijinsky's Rite of Spring, 1989 (producer/dir., Best Documentary IMZ Video Danse Awards, Internat. Film & TV Festival N.Y. Bronze medal), Baryshnikov Dances Balanchine, 1989 (Emmy nomination, finalist Internat. Film and TV Festival of N.Y.), Paul Taylor's Speaking in Tongues (Gold medal Internat. Film and TV Festival N.Y. Gold Plaque award Chgo. Internat. Film Festival), 1991, The Hard Nut with Mark Morris Dance Group, 1992 (Gold medal Internat. Film and TV Festival of N.Y., Emmy nomination), Balanchine Celebration, 1993 (with N.Y.C. City Ballet, Emmy nomination), The Wrecker's Ball, Three Dances by Paul Taylor, 1996 (Rose d'or de Montreaux Festival finalist); producer, dir. Bob Fosse/Steam Heat, 1990 (Emmy award, Ohio State award, Chgo. Film Festival Silver Plaque, Festival Internat. du Film Sur L'Art, Festival Rose d'Or, Montreux), A Tudor Evening with Am. Ballet Theatre, 1990, Balanchine in Am. with the N.Y.C. Ballet, 1990, Ballerinas: Dances by Peter Martins, 1991, A Renaissance Revisited, 1996 (N.Y. Festivals finalist award), (documentary) Variety and Virtuosity/American Ballet Theatre Now, 1998 (Chris award Columbus Internat. Film & Video Festival), Am. Ballet Theatre in Le Corsaire, (Emmy award 2000)From Broadway: Fosse, 2001 (CINE Golden Eagle award); producer PBS Great Performances: Out of Our Fathers' House, 1978; co-producer PBS Dance in America: Pilobolus Dance Theatre, 1977, Trailblazers of Modern Dance, 1977 (1st pl. 9th Ann. Dance Film and Video Festival), San Francisco Ballet: Romeo and Juliet, 1978, Choreography by Balanchine, Part III, 1978 (Chgo. Internat. Film Festival Silver Plaque, Emmy nomination), Choreography by Balanchine, Part IV, 1979 (Emmy award), The Martha Graham Dance Company: Clytemnestra, 1979 (Chgo. Internat. Film Festival Golden Hugo), Two Duets with Choreography by Jerome Robbins and Peter Martins, 1980, Nureyev and the Joffrey Ballet: In Tribute to Nijinsky, 1981 (Peabody award 1981, Emmy nomination), The Tempest: Live with the San Francisco Ballet, 1981, L'Enfant et Les Sortileges, 1981, Paul Taylor: Three Modern Classics, 1982, Paul Taylor: Two Landmark Dances, 1982, Bournonville Dances (with mems. ofN.Y.C. Ballet), 1982; co-producer PBS Theater in America: When Hell Freezes Over I'll Skate, 1979; prodr., dir. PBS Great Performances: The World of Jim Henson, 1994 (Parents Choice honor, 1995, Emmy award), Born to Be Wild: The Leading Men of American Ballet Theatre, 2002 (Festival Rose d'Or Montreux, N.Y. Festivals Gold World medal, Parents' Choice Silver Honor, Berkeley Video and Film Grand Festival Winner, Chris Statuette 2003, Ojai Film Festival Jury award), 22nd Festival Internat. Du Film Sur L'Art, 4th Constellation Change Screen Dance Festival, London, (with Am. Ballet Theatre) The Dream, 2004, Swan Lake (with Am. Ballet Theatre); prodr. PBS Stage on Screen: The Man Who Came to Dinner, 2000, The Women, 2002. Mem. Dirs.' Guild Am., Acad. TV Arts and Scis. Office: Thirteen/WNET/Dance In America 450 W 33rd St Fl 6 New York NY 10001-2603

KINBERG, ROBERT, lawyer; b. St. Louis, Feb. 24, 1948; BSEE, Washington Univ., 1970; JD with honors, George Washington Univ., 1975. Bar: Va. 1975, DC 1982. Patent examiner, 1970—72; patent adv., office of JAG Dept. of Navy, 1972—73, Dept. of Air Force, 1973—75; mem., office gen. counsel NASA, 1975—82; ptnr. Spencer & Frank, 1982—87, 1989—98; ptnr., intellectual property litig. Venable LLP, Washington, 1998—; and co-chair, patent prosecution group Power Internat., Inc, Washington, v.p., 1987—89. Instr. Patent Resources Group, 1990—2000. Mem.: Internat. Assn. Protection of Industrial Property, Am. Intellectual Property Law Assn., Va. State Bar, DC Bar, Eta Kappa Nu, Tau Beta Pi. Office: Venable LLP 575 Seventh St NW Washington DC 20004 Office Phone: 202-344-4051. Office Fax: 202-344-8300. Business E-Mail: rkinberg@venable.com.

KINCAID, JAMAICA, writer; b. St. John's, Antigua and Barbuda, May 25, 1949; came to US, 1966; d. Annie Richardson; 2 children. Degree (hon.), Williams Coll., 1991, LI Coll., 1991, Amherst Coll., 1995, Bard Coll., 1997, Middlebury Coll., 1998. Author: At the Bottom of the River, 1983 (Morton Dauwen Zabel award Am. Acad. and Inst. of Arts and Letters 1984), Annie John, 1985, A Small Place, 1988, Lucy, 1990, Autobiography of My Mother, 1996, My Brother, 1997; editor: My Favorite Plant, 1998, My Garden, 1999.

KINCAID, JOHN, political science professor, editor; b. Phila., May 5, 1946; s. John and Louise M. (Berger) K.; children: Karen Louise, Sarah Jeanenne. BA, Temple U., 1967, PhD, 1981; MA, U. Wis., 1968. Instr. St. Peter's Coll., Jersey City, 1969-70; dir. Phoenix Peace Ctr., 1970-72; v.p., treas. Pentagon Papers Fund for Civil Liberties, LA, 1972-73; instr. Temple U., Phila., 1975-79; asst. prof. North Tex. State U., Denton, 1979-84; assoc. prof. U. North Tex., Denton, 1984-86; dir. rsch. U.S. Adv. Commn. on Intergovtl. Rels., Washington, 1986-87, exec. dir., 1987-94; Robert B. and Helen S. Meyner prof. govt. and pub. svcs. Lafayette Coll., Easton, Pa., 1994—, dir. Meyner Ctr. for Study State and Local Govt., 1994—. Rsch. fellow Ctr. for Study Federalism, Phila., 1982-85. Editor, contbr.: Political Culture, Public Policy and the American States, 1982, Covenant, Polity, and Constitutionalism, 1983, The Covenant Connection: Federal Theology and the Origins of Modern Politics, 2000, Competition among States and Local Governments, 1991, Constitutional Origins, Structure, and Change in Federal Countries, 2005; editor The Covenant Letter, 1979-92, Publius: Jour. Federalism, 1981-2006, (book series) State Government and Politics, 1983-2006; contbr. articles to profl. jours. Numerous grants NEH, Earhart Found., Ford Found., Fund for Improvement Postsecondary Edn., North Tex. State U., Nat. Inst. Edn., USIA. Mem. Am. Polit. Sci. Assn., Nat. Acad. Pub. Adminstrn., Acad. Polit. Sci., Southwestern Polit. Sci. Assn. (v.p., program chmn. 1984-86, pres. 1993-94). Episcopalian. Avocation: stamp collecting/philately. Office: Lafayette Coll Meyner Ctr Easton PA 18042-1785 Office Phone: 610-330-5597. Business E-Mail: meynerc@lafayette.edu.

KINCAID, JOHN BRUCE, lawyer; b. Chgo., Aug. 25, 1938; s. Cecil Eldred and Marguerite (Donahue) K.; m. Sharon Louise Middleton, Jan. 8, 1966; children: Stacy, Sarah, Tara. BS, No. Ill. U., 1960; JD, Chgo. Kent Coll. Law, 1963. Bar: Ill. 1963, US Dist. Ct. (no. dist. Ill.) 1964, US Ct. Appeals (7th cir.) 1978, US Supreme Ct. 1973. Ptnr. Hinshaw-Culbertson, Chgo., 1963-70, mng. ptnr. Mirabella & Kincaid, Wheaton, Ill., 1970—. Pres. United Way, Wheaton, 1982-84; trustee, elder First Presbyn. Ch., Wheaton, 1981-83. Mem. Assn. Trial Lawyers Am., Ill. Trial Lawyers Assn., Ill. Bar Found. (pres 1996-98), Ill. State Bar (Ill. tort coun. 1983-85), DuPage Bar Assn. (bd. dirs. 1972-75, chmn. profl. responsibility com. 1980-85, pres. 1991-92). Republican. Office: Mirabella & Kincaid Ste 100 1737 S Naperville Rd Wheaton IL 60187 Office Phone: 630-665-7300. Office Fax: 630-665-7609. E-mail: mkpclaw@aol.com.*

KINCAID, JOHN PETER, science educator; b. Pitts., Sept. 16, 1942; s. John Franklin and Nancy Ange Kincaid; m. Calliopi D Kincaid, Jan. 29, 1966; 1 child, John F. BA, Oberlin Coll., 1964; MS, Roosevelt U., 1966; PhD, Ohio State U., 1971. Modeling and Simulation Professional Cert. Nat. Indsl. Def. Assn., 2002. Rsch. psychologist Air Force Human Resources Lab, Dayton, Ohio, 1966—69; assoc. prof. Ga. So. U., Statesboro, 1970—77; rsch. engr. Martin-Marietta Aerospace, Orlando, Fla., 1977—78; rsch. psychologist USN, Orlando, 1978—85, US Army, Orlando, 1985—88; grad. rsch. prof., prin. scientist U. Ctrl. Fla., 1988—. Dir. Internat. Disaster Tng. Inc., Orlando, 1999—. Author (and editor): Computer Based Training School Safety Drills, 2004, (book series) Naval Junior Reserve Officer Training Curriculum, 1989. Chair, edn. com. Nat. Ctr. for Simulation, 2002—. Rsch. grant, State of Fla., 1989. Mem.: Am. Hellenic Ednl. Progressive Assn. Democrat. Greek Orthodox. Avocations: travel, woodworking. Home: 1345 Sawgrass Ct Winter Park FL 32792 Office: Inst for Simulation and Tng U Ctrl Fla 3100 Technology Pkwy Orlando FL 32826 Office Phone: 407-882-1330. Business E-Mail: pkincaid@ist.ucf.edu.

KINCAID, KAREN OWERS, nursing educator; d. Harold Wesley and Katherine Ophelia Owers; children: Angela Marie Fontenot, Phillip Todd. BSN, U. Tex., San Antonio, Tex., 1971, MSN, 1974; PhD in Health Scis., Tex. Woman's U., Denton, Tex., 2002. RN Tex., 1972, Alaska, 2004; cert. health edn. specialist The Nat. Commn. Health Ed Credentialing, Inc., 2002. Asst. prof. Auburn U., Montgomery, Ala., 2002—03; asst. prof. Sch. Nursing U. Alaska, Anchorage, 2004—. Vice chmn. adv. coun. Older Alaskans Program Salvation Army, Anchorage, 2004—06. Decorated Chief Nurse Officer award USPHS; named Outstanding Pub. Health Nurse, Tex. Nurse's Assn., 1986. Mem.: Commisssioned Officers Assn. (assoc.; chmn. by-laws com. 1992—94), Sigma Theta Tau (life; chmn. nominations com. 2004). Avocations: travel, reading. Office: Univ of Alaska Anchorage Sch of Nrsing 3211 Providence Drive Anchorage AK 99508 Home Phone: 907-786-4021; Office Phone: 907-786-4021. Business E-Mail: afkdk@uaa.alaska.edu.

KINCAID, RICHARD D., real estate company executive; B, Wichita State U.; MBA, U. Tex. With First Nat. Bank Chgo., Barclays Bank PLC; sr. v.p. finance Equity Group Investments, Inc., 1990—95; exec. v.p., CFO Equity Office Properties Trust, exec. v.p., COO, 1997—2001, pres., CEO, 2001—. Mem.: Real Estate Capitol Adv. Com. Office: Equity Office Properties Trust Two N Riverside Plaza Chicago IL 60606*

KINCAID, RODNEY LYLE, construction company executive; b. Orlando, Fla., Feb. 9, 1933; s. Marion Troy and Thelma (Sellers) K.; m. Sue Sims, Dec. 16, 1961; 1 child, James Clay. B of Bldg. Constrn., U. Fla., 1958. Estimator H.J. High Constrn. Co., Orlando, 1958—59; office mgr. Innanen Bros. Constrn. Co., Orlando, 1959—60; estimator R.C. Stevens Constrn. Co., Orlando, 1960—62, Sorensen-Fletcher Constrn. Co., Winter Park, Fla., 1962—63; pres. Kincaid Constrn. Co., Winter Park, 1963—. Pres. Cen. Fla. Builder's Exchange, Orlando, 1978-79. Pres. Assoc. Bd. of Fla. Symphony, 1968; chmn. City of Orlando Bldg. Code Bd., 1973-76, City of Winter Park Code Bd., 1987—; mem. hist. bldg. com. City of Orlando, 1976; mem. econ. devel. task force Greater Orlando Aviation Authority, 1981; 2d v.p. Ctrl. Fla. Fair, Orlando, 1987, pres., 1990-91; bd. dirs. Better Bus. Bur. Ctrl. Fla., Inc., 1989-92, chmn. bd., 1993; pres., founder Oldsmobile Club Fla., 1995-97. With U.S. Army, 1953-55. Mem. Greater Orlando C. of C. (v.p. 1981), Pi Kappa Alpha. Clubs: Country of Orlando (bd. dirs. 1983-86), Econs. of Orlando (pres. 1983-84). Republican. Presbyterian. Avocations: swimming, collecting classic automobiles. Office: Kincaid Constrn Co PO Box 80 861 W Morse Blvd Winter Park FL 32790 Office Phone: 407-647-6178. E-mail: kincaid@kincaidconstruction.com.

KINCAID, STEVEN RANDALL, marketing professional; b. Oklahoma City, July 19, 1953; s. William Calvin Hoover and Mary Elizabeth (Cochran) K. BA, Okla. State U., 1975; MA, U. Ill., 1977, PhD, 1980. Rsch. analyst Gen. Foods Corp., White Plains, N.Y., 1980-82; rsch. assoc. Opinion Rsch. Corp., Princeton, N.J., 1982-85, rsch. dir., 1985-86, rsch. exec., 1986-87, account exec., 1989-91; cons. John Hancock Life Ins. Co., Boston, 1987-88, dir. rsch., 1988-89, Prudential Ins. Co., Newark, 1991-93; sr. assoc. Abt Assocs., Cambridge, Mass., 1993-95; pres. Kincaid Assocs., Boxford, Mass., 1995-98; v.p. Fidelity Investments, Boston, 1998—2003, Bank of Am., 2003—04; pres. Kincaid Assocs., Topsfield, Mass., 2004—. Named Eagle Scout Boy Scouts Am., 1968. Mem. Am. Assn. Pub. Opinion Research, Am. Polit. Sci. Assn., Applied Polit. Sci. Study Group. (charter), Mktg. Sci. Inst. (trustee), Phi Kappa Phi. Republican. Methodist.

KINCANNON, CHARLES LOUIS (LOUIS KINCANNON), federal agency administrator; b. Waco, Tex., Dec. 1940; m. Lois Claire Green; 2 children. Grad., U. Tex., 1963; postgrad., George Washington U., 1963—65, U. Md., 1966, Georgetown U., 1967. Statistician US Census Bur., US Dept. Commerce, Washington, 1963—74; chief of program rev. staff Social and Econ. Statis. Adminstrn., US Dept. Commerce, Washington, 1974; mem. staff Office Mgmt. & Budget, Exec. Office of the Pres., Washington, 1975—77, br. chief, 1978—82; dep. dir., COO US Census Bur., US Dept. Commerce, 1982—92, acting dir., 1983—84, 1989, dir., 2002—; first chief statistician Orgn. for Econ. Cooperation and Devel., Paris, 1992—2000. Mem.: Washington Statis. Soc., Nat. Assn. for Bus. Econs., Am. Statis. Assn., Inter-Am. Statis. Inst., Internat. Statis. Inst. Office: US Dept Commerce US Census Bur Federal Center Bldg 3 Washington DC 20233*

KINCANNON, LOUIS See KINCANNON, CHARLES

KINCART, ROBERT OWEN, technological executive; b. Youngstown, Ohio, Feb. 8, 1949; s. Robert E. and Mary Louise (Briach) K.; children: Jeffrey, Jennifer, Michael. Student, Ohio U., 1967-70; BS in Chemistry, U. Fla., 1972. Registered environ. profl., environ. property assessor, environ. lending analyst, Nat. Registry of Environ. Profls.; lic. radon measurement specialist, 1988; cert. hazardous materials mgr.; lic. pollutant storage sys. contr., Fla. Rsch. chemist Roux Labs., Inc., Jacksonville, Fla., 1972-73; sr. control chemist Kerr-McGee Chem. Corp., Jacksonville, 1973-77; ops. mgr. The UpJohn Co./Asgrow, Plant City, 1977-82; pres., founder Resource Recovery Am., Mulberry, 1980-87, Am. Compliance Tech., Lakeland, 1987—. Bd. dirs. Fla. Spillage Com., Jacksonville, Fla. Author: Chemical Handling, 1986, Detection and Measurement of Radon Progeny, 1988, Radon Gas Information, 1988. Judge local sci. fair Little Miss Am. Beauty contest, Fla. State Sci. and Engrng. Fair; judge Lakeland Ledger Silver Garland, 1996—2001; bd. dir. Traviss Vo-Tech Inst., Lakeland, Fla., 1984, Goodwill Industries Fla., Lakeland, 1985, Polk County Disaster Com., 1988, Local Emergency Planning Coun., Polk County, Fla., 1989—, Habitat for Humanity. Named to Hon. Order of Ky. Cols., 1994. Mem. Am. Chem. Soc., U. Fla. Alumni Assn., Fla. Physics Soc., Fla. Assn. Water Quality (dir.), Polk County Transp. Soc., Tampa Com. of 100, Fla. Bar Assn., Fla. Petroleum Assn., Inst. Hazardous Material Mgmt., Am. Water Works Assn., Am. Soc. Safety Engrs., So. Environ. Bus. Coun., Fla. Environ. Assesors Assn (bd. dirs.), Propeller Club (bd. dirs.), Rotary (chartered; Paul Harris fellow), Bartow C. of C., Lakeland C. of C., Gator Boosters of U. Fla., U. Fla. Pres.'s Coun. Republican. Methodist. Avocations: golf, outdoor activities, community involvement, travel. Office: Am Compliance Techs Inc 1875 W Main St Bartow FL 33830-7718 Office Phone: 863-533-2000. E-mail: rokincart@act-environmental.com.

KINCHEN, THOMAS ALEXANDER, college president; b. Thomasville, Ga., Dec. 28, 1946; s. George H. and Annie L. (Castleberry) K.; m. Ruth Ann Hunter, Aug. 27, 1967; children: Alex, Lisa Ann. AB summa cum laude, Ga. So. Coll., 1969; MEd, U. Ga., 1975; MDiv, New Orleans Bapt. Theol. Sem., 1979, PhD, 1982. Pastor several chs., 1972-76; v.p. New Orleans Bapt. Theol. Sem., 1982-86; exec. dir., treas. W.Va. Conv. So. Bapt., Scott Depot, 1986-90; pres. The Bapt. Coll. of Fla., Graceville, 1990—. Editor Laos: All the People of God, 1984; contbr. articles to profl. jours. Bd. dirs. Area Devel. Coun., Graceville, 1991; mem. edn. commn. So. Bapt. Conv., 1992—; pres. bd. dirs. Jackson County Devel. Coun., 1996. Mem. So. Bapt. Adult Edn. Assn. (pres. 1996-98, v.p. 1994-96), Assn. Southern Bapt. Colls. and Schs.(bd. dir. 2000-03), Graceville C. of C. (pres. 1993), Kiwanis, Jackson County C. of C. (bd. dir. 2003-06, vice chmn. 2004, chmn. 2005), New Orleans Bapt. Theol. Sem. (Outstanding Alumnus 2000), Phi Kappa Phi, Alpha Psi Omega. Avocations: golf, fishing, woodworking. Office: Bapt Coll Fla 5400 Coll Dr Graceville FL 32440-1831 Office Phone: 850-263-3261. E-mail: takinchen@baptistcollege.edu.

KIND, RONALD JAMES, congressman, lawyer; b. La Crosse, Wis., Mar. 16, 1963; s. Elroy and Greta Kind; m. Tawni Zappa; 2 children. BA with honors, Harvard U., 1985; MA, London Sch. Econs., 1986; JD, U. Minn., 1990. Atty. Quarles and Brady, Milw., 1990—92; district atty. La Crosse County, 1992—96; mem. US Congress from 3rd Wis. dist., 1997—, mem. edn. and the workforce com., mem. resources com., mem. budget com. Active Freshman Bipartisan Campaign Fin. Reform Task Force; cofounder Upper Miss. River Congl. Caucus. Active Boys' and Girls' Club, La Crosse YMCA; bd. dirs. Coulee Coun. Alcohol or Other Drug Abuse. Mem. New Dem. Network, La Crosse Optimists Club. Democrat. Lutheran. Office: US Ho Reps 1406 Longworth Ho Office Bldg Washington DC 20515-4903 Office Phone: 202-225-5506.*

KINDBERG, SHIRLEY JANE, pediatrician; b. Newark, Feb. 4, 1936; d. John Bertil and Mabel Jacoba (deJonge) Kindberg; m. Charles Dale Coln, May 12, 1962; children: Sara Goldstein, Eric Coln, Lois Thompson, Ruth Skipper, Mary Mielenz. BS, Wheaton Coll., 1957; MD, Baylor U., 1961. Intern Tex. Children's Hosp., Houston, 1961-62; resident Children's Med. Ctr., Dallas, 1962-63; fellow in pediat. pulmonary disease U. Tex. S.W. Med. Sch., Dallas, 1963-64, fellow in pediat. infectious disease, 1965-67; pvt. practice gen. pediat. Dallas, 1969-81; pvt. practice newborns, 1981—2004. Active Park Cities Bapt. Ch.; mem. Dallas Symphony Assn. Republican. Avocations: cooking, travel, music, exercise. Personal E-mail: colnoma@sbcglobal.net.

KINDER, JOSEPH DONALD, principal; b. Wheeling, W.Va., Nov. 29, 1936; s. Joseph and Helen Agnes Kinder; married, June 8, 1963; children: Joseph F., Kathleen, Thomas E., Barbara; 1 child, Theodore. BA, West Liberty State Coll., W.Va., 1960; MA, Chapman U., Orange, Calif., 1971; EdD, No. Ariz. U., Flagstaff, 1983. Tchr. Imperial HS, Calif., 1970—72, 1989—99, prin., tchr., 1972—76; prin. summer sch. Imperial Unified Sch. Dist., 1978; prin. Westside Elem. Sch., Imperial, 1985—88, Frank Wright Intermediate Sch., Imperial, 1976—89; ret., 1999. Maj. USMC, 1954—70. Decorated Purple Heart. Democrat. Roman Catholic. Avocations: genealogy, coin collecting/numismatics, history. Home: 449 Allen St Brawley CA 92227-3001

KINDER, PETER D., lieutenant governor, former state senator; b. Cape Girardeau, Mo., May 12, 1954; s. James A. and Mary Frances (Hunter) K. Attended, U. Mo. Columbia, SE Mo. State U.; JD, St. Mary U., 1979. Spl. asst. to Rep. Bill Emerson US Congress, Washington, 1981-82; mem. Mo. State Senate from 27th dist., Jefferson City, 1992—2005, pres. pro. tempore, 2000—05; lt. gov. State of Mo., Jefferson City, 2005—. Staff counsel, real estate rep., 1983-87; assoc. publ., S.E. Missourian Newspaper, 1987-2002, asst. to the pres., 1987-94. Mem. Mo. Bar Assn., Am. Cancer Soc., Mo. Farm Bur., Area Wide United Way, Lions Club. Republican. Methodist. Office: Office Lt Governor State Capitol Bldg Rm 121 Jefferson City MO 65101 Office Phone: 573-751-4727. Office Fax: 573-751-9422. E-mail: ltgov@mail.mo.gov.

KINDER, RICHARD DAN, natural gas pipeline, oil and gas company executive; b. Cape Girardeau, Mo., Oct. 19, 1944; s. Luke Frazelle and Edna (Corbin) Kinder; m. Anne Lamkin; 1 child, Kara; m. Nancy McNeil, 1997. BA, U. Mo., 1966, JD, 1968. Sole practice, Cape Girardeau, Mo., 1972—80; sr. atty. Continental Resources/Fla. Gas Cos., Winter Pk., 1981—82, v.p., gen. counsel Winter Park, 1982—84; sr. v.p., gen. counsel Houston Natural Gas Corp., 1985, HNG/InterNorth Inc., Houston, 1985—86; exec. v.p. law and corp. devel. Enron Corp., Houston, 1986—87, exec. v.p., chief of staff, 1987—88, vice chmn. bd., 1988—89, pres., COO, 1989—96; chmn., CEO Kinder Morgan Inc., Houston, 1997—. Bd. dirs. Soc. Performing Arts, Houston, 1986—, Mus. Fine Arts, Houston, 1987—. Capt. US Army, 1968—72. Named one of Forbes' Richest Americans, 2006. Mem.: Houston Bar Assn., Mo. Bar Assn., ABA, Nat. Bd. of Smithsonian Instn., Petroleum Club, Houston Racquet. Methodist. Office: Kinder Morgan Inc 500 Dallas St, Ste 1000 Houston TX 77002*

KINDER, SUZANNE FONAY WEMPLE, retired historian, retired educator; b. Veszprem, Hungary, Aug. 1, 1927; arrived in U.S., 1948; d. Ernest and Magda (Mihalyfy) Fonay; m. George Barr Wemple, June 17, 1957 (dec. Apr. 1988); m. Gordon T. Kinder, May 26, 1990. B, English Sisters, Budapest, Hungary, 1945, U. Calif., Berkeley, 1953; MLS, Columbia U., 1955, PhD, 1967. Ref. asst. Columbia U., 1955—58; instr. Stern Coll. Women, NYC, 1962-63; asst. prof. Tchrs. Coll., Columbia U., NYC, 1964-66; from asst. prof. to prof. Barnard Coll., Columbia U., NYC, 1966-92, ret., 1992. Author: Atto of Vercelli: Church, State and Christian Society, 1979, Women in Frankish Society, 1981, 1983 (Berkshire prize, 1981); co-editor: Women in Medieval Society, 1985; contbr. chapters to books, articles to ency. and profl. jours. Recipient grant NEH, 1975, 80, 81-85, Spivack summer grant Barnard Coll., 1970, 81, Fulbright grant, 1982. Mem.: AAUP. Personal E-mail: gtkinder@aol.com.

KINDLER, JEFFREY B., pharmaceutical company executive, lawyer; b. Upper Montclair, NJ, May 13, 1955; m. Sharon Sullivan; children: Joshua, Samantha. BA summa cum laude, Tufts Univ., 1977; JD magna cum laude, Harvard Law Sch., 1980. Bar: DC 1980. Law clk. to Hon. David L. Bazelon U.S. Ct. Appeals (DC Cir.); law clk. to Justice William J. Brennan, Jr. US Supreme Ct.; ptnr. Williams and Connolly, Wash., DC; sr. counsel litig. and legal policy GE, Fairfield, Conn., 1990—94, v.p., sr. counsel litig. and legal policy, 1994—96; sr. v.p., gen. counsel McDonald's Corp., Oak Brook, Ill., 1996—97, exec. v.p. corp. rels., gen. counsel, 1997—2001, chmn. CEO Boston Market Corp., 2000—01, pres. Partner Brands, 2001—02; sr. v.p., gen. counsel Pfizer, Inc., NYC, 2002—04, vice-chmn., gen. counsel, chief compliance officer, 2004—06, CEO, 2006—, chmn., 2007—. Mem. Civil Justice Reform Group, Corp. Exec. Bd. Gen. Counsel Roundtable, Lex Mundi Client Adv. Council; mem bd. overseers RAND ICJ; mem. gen. counsel com. Nat Ctr. for State Courts. Editor: Harvard Law Rev. Bd. mem. Brennan Ctr. for Justice, Corporate ProBono.Org, Inst. for Legal Reform U.S. C. of C., Legal Aid Soc., Manhattan Theatre Club, NY Philharmonic, Partnership for NYC, Ronald McDonald House Charities, Bus. Council for NY State, Transparency Internat., UNited Way NYC. Recipient Stephen E. Banner award, UJA Fedn., Lawyers divsn., 2002, Stand Tall with NY award, Greater NY Chapter of the Am. Corp. Counsel Assn., 2002, Pro Bono Publico award, ABA, 2003, Northeast Region Employer of Choice award, Minority Corp. Counsel Assn., 2004, Exemplar award, The Nat. Legal Aid & Defender Assn., 2005, Expeditioner's award, NYC Outward Bound, 2005, Pro Bono Publico, The Legal Aid Soc., 2005, Pub. Svc. Corp. award, 2005, Exemplar award, Nat. Legal Aid & Defender Assn., 2005, Expeditioner's award, NYC Outward Bound, 2005, Laurie D. Zelon award, Pro Bono Inst. Georgetown Univ., 2006. Mem.: Assn. of Gen. Coun. Office: Pfizer Inc 235 E 42nd St New York NY 10017*

KINDLER, ROBERT ALAN, investment banker; b. Feb. 7, 1954; m. Pamela Kindler. BA, Colgate U., 1976; JD, NYU, 1980. Sr. ptnr. Cravath, Swaine & Moore, 1980—2000; global head mergers and acquisitions JP Morgan, 2000—06; vice chmn. investment banking Morgan Stanley, 2006—. Bd. trustees Colgate U. Bd. dirs. March of Dimes NY divisn.; bd. dirs. Knight-Bagehot fellowship program Columbia U. Office: Morgan Stanley 1585 Broadway New York NY 10036

KINDLUND, NEWTON CARLTON, retail executive; b. Detroit, Mich., June 25, 1940; s. Newton K. and Virginia M. Kindlund; children: Anne Kirsten, Erika Page; m. Joanne Weber Kindlund, May 29, 1974; 1 child, Darien F. BA, Mich. State U., 1963; postgrad., Boston Coll., 1969; student, U. Pa., 1977. Nat. sales mgr. Vesely Co., Inc., Lapeer, Mich., 1963-68; v.p. sales and mktg. Midas Internat. Corp., Chgo., 1968-70; pres. Recreation Enterprise Corp., Gainesville, Fla., 1970-73, N.C. Kindlund & Assoc., Glenville, N.C., 1974-75; regional v.p. Recreational Vehicle Industry Assn., Washington, 1976-77; founder, pres. Holiday of Orlando (Fla.), Inc., 1977-85, Holiday RV Rental/Leasing, Orlando, 1985-90; bd. chmn., founder, pres. Holiday RV Superstores, Inc., Orlando, 1987—. Pres. Holiday RV Superstores of N.Mex., Inc., Holiday RV Assurance Svcs., Inc. of Ariz., Holiday RV Superstores of S.C., Inc., Holiday RV Superstores West, Inc.; bd. dirs. Recreational Vehicle Industry Assn., Chgo., 1970-72, Cen. Fla. World Trade Coun., Orlando, 1985-87; adv. bd. Trailer Life Publs., 1985-90; co-founder Kindlund Investments, Inc., Winter Pk., Fla., Gryon, Switzerland. Contbr. articles to profl. jours. Bd. dirs. Fla. Recreational Vehicle Trade Assn., Tampa, 1978; bd. dirs. Ctrl. Fla. Better Bus.Bur., Winter Park, 1994-95, Orlando Festival of Orchestras, 1999, RV Industry Hall Fame; bd. edn. found. Recreational Vehicle Dealer Assn., founder Kindlund family industry scholarship; adv. bd. Crummer Sch. of Bus., Rollins Coll., Winter Park, Fla., 1998, 99; judge Students in Free Enterprise, Clearwater, Fla., 1998, 99; bd. dirs. Recreational Vehicle Found., 1999. Recipient Small Bus. Person of Yr. award Small Bus. Adminstrn., State of Fla., 1982, Entrepreneur of Yr. award Ernst & Young, Inc., Tampa, 1990, 100 award Miami Herald, 1992, 93, semi-finalist Jim Moran Entreprenurial Excellance award Fla. State U., 1996; named one of 500 fastest growing pvt. cos. Inc. Mag., 1983, one of top 150 Fla. pub. corps. Fla. Travel mag., 1993, one of Fla. top 100 cos. Orlando Metro 100, 1993, Industry Exec. of Yr., RV News Mag., 1995; named to RV Industry Hall Fame. Mem. Fla. RV Trade Assn. (founding mem., bd. dirs. 1987-90), Family Motor Coach Assn. (adv. bd. 1990—), Nat. RV Bus. Assn. (adv. bd. 1989-90), Recreational Vehicle Rental Assn. (nat. chmn. 1992, 93), Recreational Vehicle Dealers Assn. (exec. bd. 1992, 93), Orlando C. of C. (bd. dirs., exec. com. 1984-88, Silver 100 award 1992). Republican. Episcopalian. Avocations: skiing, golf, sailing, yachting. Address: 280 Stirling Ave Winter Park FL 32789 Home Phone: 407-628-4291; Office Phone: 407-628-4211. Personal E-mail: jmkindlund@cfl.rr.com.

KINDRED, LYNN HERBERT, cardiologist; b. Emporia, Kans., July 6, 1937; MD, U. Kans., 1963. Diplomate Am. Bd. Internal Medicine, Am. Bd. Cardiology. Intern U. Kans., Kansas City, 1963-64, resident, 1964-66, fellow in cardiology, 1966-67; mem. staff St. Luke's Hosp., Kansas City; clin. prof. U. Mo. Med. Sch., Kansas City; prnr. group practice Mid Am. Cardiology, Kansas City, Mo. Named a Kans. City Super Doctor, Kans. City mag., 2007. Fellow ACP, Am. Coll. Cardiology, Am. Coll. Chest Physicians; mem. CCC. Office: Mid Am Cardiology 4321 Washington St Kansas City MO 64111-5905 also: 3901 Rainbow Blvd. Mail Stop 4023 Kansas City KS 66160 Office Phone: 913-588-1227.*

KINDREGAN, CHARLES PETER, law educator; b. Phila., June 18, 1935; s. Charles Peter and Catherine (Delaney) K.; m. Patricia Ann. Patterson, Aug. 18, 1962 (dec. 1998); children: Chad, Helen, Tricia, Brian. BA, LaSalle U., 1957, MA, 1958; JD, Chgo.-Kent Coll. Law, 1966; LLM, Northwestrn U., 1967. Bar: Ill. 1966, Mass. 1968, U.S. Dist. Ct. Mass. 1970. Instr. Va. Mil. Inst., 1960-62, Loyola U., Chgo., 1964-67; prof. law Suffolk U., Boston, 1967—, assco. dean, 1990-94. Author: The Quality of Life, 1969, Malpractice and the Lawyer, 1981, Professional Responsibility of the Lawyer, 1995; co-author: Massachusetts Family Law and Practice, 3d edit., 2003; (with M. Inker) Mass. Domestic Relations Rules Annotated, 2005; contbr. articles to profl. jours. Mem. Hull Bd. Zoning Appeals, Mass., 1969; pres. Beacon Hill PTA, Boston, 1974-75. Mem. ABA (academic rep. to publications bd. family law sect.), Mass. Bar Assn. (task force on model rules of profl. conduct 1982-84, co-chair com. on crisis in private and family ct. 1994-97), Suffolk Ctr. for Advanced Legal Studies (dir. 1982-87). Democrat. Roman Catholic. Home: 150 Staniford St Apt 710 Boston MA 02114-2597 Office: Suffolk U Law Sch 120 Tremont St Boston MA 02108-4977 Office Phone: 617-573-8193.

KINDT, JOHN WARREN, lawyer, educator; b. Oak Park, Ill., May 24, 1950; s. Warren Frederick and Lois Jeannette (Woelffer) K.; m. Anne Marie Johnson, Apr. 17, 1982; children: John Warren Jr., James Roy Frederick. AB, Coll. William and Mary, 1972; JD, U. Ga., 1976, MBA, 1977; LLM, U. Va., 1978, SJD, 1981. Bar: D.C. 1976, Ga. 1976, Va. 1977. Advisor to gov. State of Va., Richmond, 1971-72; asst. to Congressman M. Caldwell Butler, U.S. Ho. of Reps., Washington, 1972-73; staff cons. White House,

Washington, 1976-77; asst. prof. U. Ill., Champaign, 1978-81, assoc. prof., 1981-85, prof., 1985—. Cons. 3d UN Conf. on Law of Sea; lectr. exec. MBA program U. Ill. Author: Marine Pollution and the Law of the Sea, 4 vols., 1981, 2 vols., 1988, 92, Economic Impacts of Legalized Gambling, 1994; contbr. articles to profl. jours. Caucus chmn., del. White House Conf. on Youth, 1970; co-chmn. Va. Gov.'s Adv. Coun. on Youth, 1971; mem. Athens (Ga.) Legal Aid Soc., 1975-76. Rotary fellow, 1979-80; Smithsonian ABA/ELI scholar, 1981; sr. fellow London Sch. Econs., 1985-86. Mem. Am. Soc. Internat. Law, D.C. Bar Assn., Va. Bar Assn., Ga. Bar Assn. Home: 801 Brookside Ln Mahomet IL 61853-9545 Office: U Ill 350 Wohlers Hall Champaign IL 61820 Office Phone: 217-333-6018.

KINDT, MONICA V., lawyer; b. San Juan, Nov. 21, 1974; BA, St. Olaf Coll., 1996; JD, Fla. Costal Sch. Law, 1999. Bar: Ohio 1999, US Dist. Ct. Southern Dist. Ohio 1999. Assoc. Cohen, Todd, Kite & Stanford, LLC, Cin. Named one of Ohio's Rising Stars, Super Lawyers, 2006. Mem.: Nat. Assn. Bankruptcy Trustees (trustee Cin. Chpt. 7 panel), Ohio State Bar Assn., Cin. Bar Assn. Achievements include fluency in French, Spanish, Portuguese. Office: Cohen Todd Kite & Stanford LLC 250 E Fifth St Ste 1200 Cincinnati OH 45202-4139 Office Phone: 513-421-4020. Office Fax: 513-241-4490.

KING, ALFRED MEEHAN, financial executive; b. Boston, Mass, Oct. 31, 1933; s. Lester S. and Marjorie C. (Meehan) K.; m. Mary Jane Oliver, Dec. 19, 1976; 1 child, Thomas A.; stepchildren: Tina Marie Oliver, Katherine Mary Lefebre. AB magna cum laude, Harvard Coll., 1954, MBA, 1959. Acctg. supr. Gen. Motors Co., LaGrange, Ill., 1959-64; asst. contr. J.I. Case Co., Racine, Wis., 1964-69; v.p. fin. Valuation Rsch. Corp., Milw., Minn., 1978—81, 1991—2005, chmn. bd. dirs., 1996—2005; vice chmn. Marshall and Stevens Inc., Spotsylvania, Va., 2005—. Mng. dir. Nat. Assn. Accts., Montvale, NJ, 1981-91; adj. asst. prof. U. Wis.-Parkside, Kenosha, 1978-81; adj. instr. Fordham U., NYC, 1989-96, U. Washington, 2006—; vis. com. Fordham Grad. Sch. Bus. Adminstrn. Author: Increasing the Productivity of Company Cash, 1969, Total Cash Management, 1994; Valuation, 2002, Fair Value, 2006; mem. editl. adv. bd. Jour. Cost Mgmt. and Strategic Fin. Treas. Village of North Bay, Wis., 1972-76, Racine Symphony Orch., 1979-81; mem. Saddle River (NJ) Sch. Bd., 1992-95. Mem. Inst. Mgmt. Acctg. (regent 1978-81, bd. dir. 1995-98), Fin. Exec. Inst., Valley Club (pres. 1983-84). Republican. Presbyn. Office Phone: 540-972-4704, 540-809-3497. Business E-Mail: alfredking@erols.com.

KING, ALGIN BRADDY, retired marketing educator; b. Latta, SC, Jan. 19, 1927; s. Dewey Algin and Elizabeth (Braddy) K.; m. Barbara I. Kelley, Nov. 29, 1997: children: Drucilla Ratcliff, Martha Louise. BA in Retailing and Polit Sci. cum laude, U. S.C., 1947; MS, NYU, 1953; PhD, Ohio State U., 1966. Exec. trainee Sears, Roebuck & Co., 1948; instr. retailing U. S.C., 1948—51; chief econ. analysis br. dist. OPS, 1951—53; exec. dir. Columbia (S.C.) Mchts. Assn., 1953—54; asst. prof. Tex. A&M U., 1954—55; mem. faculty Coll. William and Mary, 1955—72, prof. bus. adminstrn., 1959—72, dir. Bur. Bus. Research, 1959—63, assoc. dean Sch. Bus. Adminstrn., 1968—72; prof., dean Ctrl. Conn. State U. Sch. Bus., Avon, 1972—73; prof., head dept. bus. and econs. James Madison U., 1973—74; prof., dean Western Carolina U. Sch. Bus., Cullowhee, NC, 1974—76; prof. mktg. and mgmt. Christopher Newport U., Newport News, Va., 1976—87, dean Sch. Bus. Adminstrn. and Econs., 1977—87, head, dept. of mktg., 1987—96; prof. mgmt. and mktg. Towson (Md.) State U. Sch. Bus. and Econs., 1987—2003; ret., 2003—. Pres. Bus. and Adminstrv. Cons. Ltd. (mgmt. and mktg. cons.); teaching asst. Ohio State U., 1963-64; professorial lectr. George Washington U.; mgmt. cons. CSC, U.S. Army. Author: (with others) Hampton Waterfront Economic Study, 1967, The Source Book of Economics, 1973, Management Perceptions, 1976, International Marketing by Dabringer & Muellach Instrn. Manual, 1991; contbr. chpts. to books and articles to profl. jours. Mem. finance resource group Conn. Council Higher Edn., 1972-73; mem. U.S. Senatorial Bus. Adv. Bd. W.T. Grant Retailing scholar, 1947. Mem. Am. Mktg. Assn., Acad. Mgmt., Am. Inst. Decision Scis., Phi Beta Kappa. Episcopalian. E-mail: e-lecturer@comcast.net.

KING, ALLEN B., tobacco company executive; Dir. Universal Corp., Richmond, Va., 1989—, chmn. exec. com., mem. fin. com., pres., COO, 1996—2003, chmn., pres., CEO, 2003—06, chmn., CEO, 2006—. Office: Universal Leaf Tobacco Co Inc 1501 N Hamilton St Richmond VA 23230-6003*

KING, AMY CATHRYNE PATTERSON, retired mathematics educator, researcher; b. Douglas, Wyo., Dec. 30, 1928; d. John Francis and Mabel Eloise (Wear) Patterson; m. Don R. King, Aug. 8, 1949 (dec. 1985). BS, U. Mo., 1949; MA, U. Wichita, 1960; PhD, U. Ky., 1970. Tchr. Goddard (Kans.) Pub. Schs., 1956-58, U. Wichita, 1960-62; asst. instr. U. Kans., Lawrence, 1962-65; instr. Washburn U., Topeka, 1966-67; teaching asst. U. Ky., Lexington, 1967-70; prof. math. Ea. Ky. U., Richmond, 1970-98; Found. prof. emeritus, 1998—. Presenter in field. Author: instr.'s manual for College Algebra, 1981; (with Cecil B. Read) Pathways to Probability, 1963; contbr. (with others) articles to profl. jours. Departmental rep. for United Way, 1983; pres. Cokesbury Sunday Sch., Centenary United Meth. Ch., 1995-96, tchr. 3-yr.-olds. Recipient Award in Teaching, Ea. Ky. U., Richmond, 1982, Ea. Ky. U. Found. Professorship, 1993. Mem. Am. Math. Soc., Math. Assn. Am. (mem. various coms., 1st award for Disting. Coll. or Univ. Teaching 1992), Nat. Coun. Tchrs. Math., Assn. for Women of Math., Ky. Coun. Tchrs. Math. (Maths. Edn. Svc. and Achievement award 1998), Women in Math. Edn., Ky. Acad. Computer Users' Group, AAUP (treas. local chpt. 1984-86), Pi Mu. Epsilon, Kappa Mu Epsilon, Pi Lambda Theta, Sigma Delta Pi, Delta Kappa Gamma (pres. Omicron chpt., 1994-96), Sigma Xi. Phi Kappa Phi. Methodist. E-mail: amyking@infionline.net.

KING, ANDRE RICHARDSON, architectural graphic designer; b. Chgo., July 30, 1931; s. Earl James and Margie Verdetta (Doyle) K.; children: Jandra Maria, Andre Etienne; m. Sally M. Ryan, Sept. 19, 1980. Student, Chgo. Tech. Coll., 1956-57, U. Chgo., 1956-59; BAE., Art Inst. Chgo., 1959; grad., Gemological Inst. Am., 1992. ARK, Archtl. & Environ. Graphic Design Firm est., 1982—; With Skidmore, Owings & Merrill, Chgo., 1956-82; ind. designer, cons., 1982—. Mem. alumni bd. Chgo. Art Inst. Served with USAF, 1951-55. Recipient Design award Art Inst. Chgo., 1959, DESI award, 1982; Hon. consul of Barbados, W.I., 1971— Mem. AIA (assoc.), Am. Inst. Graphic Designers, Soc. Environ. Graphic Designers, Soc. Topographic Arts, Chgo. Soc. Communicating Arts, Art Dirs. Club of Chgo. (pres. 1979-80, 80-82), Art Inst. Chgo. Alumni (bd. dirs.), Arts Club of Chgo., Consular Corps of Chgo., Tavern Club of Chgo., Sigma Pi Phi, Beta Boule. Home: 6700 S Oglesby Ave Apt 1603 Chicago IL 60649-1301 Office Phone: 773-667-5963. Business E-Mail: arkdesign@sbcglobal.net. *To provide creative excellence for the future through my works.*

KING, ANGUS S., JR., former governor; b. Mar. 31, 1944; m. Mary J. Herman; children: Angus III, Duncan, James, Benjamin, Molly. BA, Dartmouth Coll., 1966; JD, U. Pa., 1969. Bar: Maine 1969. Staff atty. Pine Tree Legal Assistance, Showhegan, Maine, 1969-72; chief counsel Office Senator William D. Hathaway U.S. Senate Subcom. on Alcoholism and Narcotics, Washington, 1972-75; former ptnr. Smith, Lloyd & King, Brunswick, Maine, 1975—83; gov. State of Maine, Augusta, 1995—2003. TV host Maine Watch, Maine Pub. Broadcasting Network, 20 yrs.; v.p., gen. counsel Swift River/Hafslund Co., 1983; founder, pres. N.E. Energy Mgmt. Inc., Brunswick, Maine, 1989-94. Independent. Mailing: PO Box 457 Brunswick ME 04011-0457

KING, BARBARA SACKHEIM, travel company executive; b. Chgo., Apr. 9, 1948; d. Norman Robert and Pauline Huft Sackheim; m. Michael Raymond King, May 24, 1998; children: Lauren Marissa, David Elliott Weiner, Joshua Neal. BS, Northwestern U., 1970. Realtor Prudential Henry and Burrows, Overland Park, Kans., 1990—92; pres. Gt. Getaways, Leawood, 1992—. Life mem. Nat. Coun. Jewish Women, Kansas City, Mo.; v.p. Fine Arts Guild William Jewell, Liberty, Mo., 1986—87; mem. March Dimes, 1992—93. Mem.: Ctrl. Exch., Internat. Coun. Tourism Ptnrs., Airline Reporting Corp., Internat. Airline Travel Assn., Cruise Line Internat. Assn., Am. Soc. Travel Agts., Virtuoso, Pi Lambda Theta. Avocations: cooking, travel, knitting, crocheting. Office: Great Getaways 4600 College Blvd Ste 103 Leawood KS 66211 Home: 7853 W 157th Ter Overland Park KS 66223 Home Phone: 913-851-9719; Office Phone: 913-338-2244.

KING, B.B. (RILEY B. KING), singer, guitarist; b. Itta Bene, Miss., Sept. 16, 1925; LHD (hon.), Tougaloo Coll., Miss., 1973; MusD (hon.), Yale U., 1977, Berklee Coll. of Music, 1982; D of Fine Arts, Rhodes Coll. of Memphis, 1990; PhD (hon.), U. Miss., 2004. Began teaching self guitar, 1945, later studied Schillinger System, past disc jockey and singer Memphis radio stas., internat. appearances throughout world, recs. RPM, Crown, Bullet, Kent, ABC Records, ABC/Dunhill Records, toured Russia, 1979, albums Back in the Alley, B.B. King in London, Do the Boogie!, Completely Well, Electric B.B.-His Best, The Fabulous B.B. King, Guess Who, Heart and Soul, Live at Cook County Jail, Six Silver Strings, 1985, King of the Blues, Indianola Mississippi Seeds, 1989, Live at San Quentin, 1990 (Grammy award), Blues is King, 1990, Live at the Apollo, 1991 (Grammy award), Live at the Regal, 1991, Spotlight on Lucille, There is Always One More Time, 1992, Singin' the Blues, 1993, On the Road with B.B. King: An Interactive Autobiography, 1996, B.B. King & Friends, 2005 (Grammy for Best Traditional Blues Album, 2006); albums: 80, 2005; albums Blues d'Azur, 2006, Things Spiritual, 2006, Flyleaf, 2007, (guest appearance) Six Pack, 1993, Blues on the Bayou, Let the Good Time roll, 1998, guest artist with U2's Rattle and Hum, 1988, Deuces Wild, 1997, subject, collaborator B.B. King, B.B. King Blues Guitar, 1970, B.B. King Songbook, 1971, B.B. King, The World's Greatest Living Blues Artist, Blues Guitar, A Method by B.B. King, 1973, Riding with the King, 2000, Auld Lang Syne, 2002 (Grammy award, 2003), A Christmas Celebration of Hope, 2002 (Grammy award, 2003), Reflections, 2003, The Ultimate Collection, 2005; performer: at closing ceremonies Summer Olympics, 1996; author (with David Ritz): Blues All Around Me, 1996 (2d prize 8th Ann. Ralph J. Gleason Music Book awards); author: (with Dick Waterman) The B.B. King Treasures, 2005; appeared (films) When We Were Kings, 1996, Blues Brothers, 1998, 2000. Co-founder Found. Advancement Inmate Rehab. and Recreation, 1972—; founding mem. Kennedy Performing Arts Ctr., 1971. Co-recipient Grammy award for Best Rock Instrumental Performance, 1996; named Best Blues Instrumentalist, Ebony Mag., 1974—75, Best Male Blues Singer, 1974—75, Blues Guitarist of Yr., Guitar Player Mag., 1970—74, Best Blues Singer Nat. Assn. TV and Radio Announcers, 1974, Blues Act of Yr., Performance Award Polls, 1985, Most Outstanding Blues Singer, Living Blues Mag., 1993—94, 1996—97, Blues Act of Yr., Performance Award Polls, 1987, 1988, Blues Artist of Yr., 1994; named to Rock and Roll Hall of Fame, 1987, Hall of Fame and Best Blues Vocalist and Guitarist , Ebony mag., 1974, Blues Found. Hall of Fame, 1980, Rock Walk, 1989, Amsterdam Walk of Fame, 1989, Hollywood Walk of Fame, 1989; recipient Humanitarian award, Fed. Bur. Prisons, 1972, B'nai B'rith Music and Performance Lodge, N.Y.C., 1973, Gallery of Greats and Best Blues Guitarist, 1974, Artist of the Decade and Humanitarian award, Record World mag., 1974, Grammy award Best Rhythm & Blues Vocal Performance, Male, 1970, Grammy award Best Traditional Blues Album, 1981, 1983, 1986, 1985, 1991, 1993, 1999, 2000, 2002, 2005, Grammy Lifetime Achievement award, 1987, Grammy award Best Pop Collaboration with Vocals, 2000, Grammy award Best Pop Instrumental Performance, 2002, Hall of Fame award Nat. Assn. for Campus Activities, 1986, Presdl. medal of the Arts, 1990, Songwriter's Hall of Fame Lifetime Achievement award, 1991, Orville H. Gibson Lifetime Achievement award, Gibson Guitar Co., Nat. award of distinction, U. Miss., 1992, Kennedy Ctr. Honors, 1995, W.C. Handy award Blues Found., 1983, 1985, 1987, 1988, 1991, Lifetime Achievement award, 1997, MTV Video Music award for Best Video from a Film, 1988—89, Image awards, NAACP, 1975, 1981, 1993, Pioneer in Music award, Nat. Assn. Black Owned Broadcasters, 1997, Living Legend award Trumpet Awards, 1997, Golden Mike award, NATRA, 1969, 1974, Polar Music prize, Swedish Acad. Music, 2004, Presdl. Medal of Freedom, 2006, Golden Plate award, Acad. Achievement, 2004; Nat. Heritage fellow Nat. Endowment of the Arts, 1991. Office: care Sidney A Seidenberg Inc 1414 Ave Of The Americas New York NY 10019-2514 *I would say to all people, but maybe to young people especially— black and white or whatever color— follow your own feelings and trust them; find out what you want to do and do it, and then practice it and practice it every day of your life and keep becoming what you are, despite any hardships and obstacles you meet.**

KING, BILLIE JEAN MOFFITT, retired professional tennis player; b. Long Beach, Calif., Nov. 22, 1943; d. Willard J. and Betty Moffitt; m. Larry King (div. 1987), Sept. 17, 1965. Student, Calif. State U. at Los Angeles, 1961-64; PhD (hon.), Calif. State U., 1997; degree (hon.), Trinity Coll., 1998; PhD (hon.), U. Pa, 1999, U. Mass., 2000. Amateur tennis player, 1958-67; profl., 1968—84; mem. Tennis Challenge Series, 1977, 78; dir., ofcl. spokesperson World Team Tennis, Chgo., 1985—; commentator, analyst Wimbledon and other tennis events HBO, NYC. Winner, Singles champion tournaments include: Wimbledon, 1966-68, 72, 73,75, U.S. Open, 1967, 71, 72, 74, Australian Open, 1968, French Open, 1972; Doubles champion Wimbledon, 1961, 62, 65, 67, 68, 70-73, 79 U.S. Open, 1965, 67, 74, 80, French Open, 1972; mixed doubles champion Wimbledon, 1967, 71, 73, 74, U.S. Open, 1967, 71, 73, French, 1967, 70, Australian, 1968; winner 29 Virginia Slims singles titles, 1970-77, 4 Colgate titles, 1977, Fedn. Cup, 1963-67, 76-79, Wightman Cup, 1961-67, 70, 77, 78; World Tennis Team All-Star, 3 times; host Colgate women's sports TV spl. The Lady is a Champ, 1975; sports commentator ABC-TV, 1975-78;founder Women's Tennis Assn., 1973, pres., 1973-75, 80-81; founder, Women's Sports Found, 1974, Profl. World TeamTennis, 1974, World TeamTennis Profl. League, 1981, World TeamTennis Recreational League, 1985, World TeamTennis Charities, 1987; co-founder, pub. WomenSports mag., 1974, Kingdom, Inc., San Mateo, Calif.; founding mem., Women's Sports Legends; first woman commr. (Team Tennis League) profl. sports history, 1984; TV commentator HBO-Sports Wimbeldon coverage; capt. Fed. Cup for USA, 1995; cons. Virginia Slims World Championship Series;mem., Planned Parenthood, US Profl. Tennis Assn., US Profl. Tennis Registry, Chgo. Area Women's Sports Assn., advisory bd, Areta Sports award nomination com., Jim Thorpe Pro sports nomination com. award, sports advisory bd. for the Vic Braden Neurology Rsch. Inst., USTA Player Devel. Com.; bd. dirs. Challenger Ctr., Elton John AIDS Found., S.A.F.E., Nat. AIDS Fund, Altria Group, Inc., Women's Sports Found.; amb. Adventures in Movement Charity; coach Fed. Cup Women's Tennis Team, 1995-96, 98-2003, USA Olympic Women's Tennis Team, 1996, 2000; nat. spokesperson Literary Vols. Am.; tennis tchr. to profls. Author: Tennis to Win, 1970, (with Kim Chapin) Billie Jean, 1974, (with Greg Hoffman) Tennis Love: A Parent's Guide to the Sport, 1978, (with Frank Deford) The Autobiography of Billie Jean King, 1982 (with Cynthia Starr) We Have Come a Long Way, The Story of Women's Tennis, 1988. Named Sportsperson of Yr., 1972, Top 40 Athletes, 1994, Sports Illustrated; Woman Athlete of Yr., A.P., 1967, 73, Top Woman Athlete of Yr., 1972; Woman of Yr., Time mag., 1976, One of 10 Most Powerful Women in Am., Harper's Bazaar, 1977, One of 25 Most Influential Women in Am., World Almanac, 1977, One of 100 Most Important Ams. of 20th Century, Life mag., 1990, woman of the Year, Women in Sports & Events, 2002; named to Internat. Tennis Hall of Fame, 1987, Nat. Women's Hall of Fame, 1990, Chgo. Gay and Lesbian Hall of Fame, 1999, Court of Champions, USTA Nat. Tennis Ctr., 2003; WTA Hon. Membership award, 1986, Female Teaching Pro of the Decade, 1994, Lifetime Achievement award, March of Dimes, 1994, Flo Hymnal award, Women's Sports Found, 1997, "Player Who Makes a Difference award", 1997, US Olympic Com. Nat. Tennis Coach of the Year award, 1997, Nat. Women's Law Ctr. honoree, 1997, Elizabeth Blackwill award for Courage, William & Hobart Smith Colleges, 1998, Arthur Ashe award for Courage, ESPN, 1999, Community Role Model award, LA Gay & Lesbian Ctr., 1999, NFL Players Assn. Lifetime Achievement award, 1999, Sports Illustrated "Athletes Who Changed the Game award, 1999, Capitol award, GLAAD, 2000, Radcliffe medal, Radcliffe Coll., 2002, Internat Olympic Com. Women & Sport World Trophy, 2002, Nat. Assn. Collegiate Women Athletic Administrators award of Honor, 2002, Pillipe Chatrier award, Internat. Tennis Fedn., 2003. Won 71 singles titles, including 12 Grand Slam singles titles; won 20 Wimbledon titles;First woman to win more than $100,000 in a single season in any sport; Highest singles ranking 1(5 times between 1966-72); defeated Bobby Riggs in "The Battle of the Sexes" tennis match, Sept. 20, 1973, Houston, Tex. Office: Billie Jean King Ste 983 960 Harlem Ave Glenview IL 60025

KING, BILLY, professional sports team executive; b. Jan. 23, 1966; m. Melanie King; 1 child, Natane Alexandra. Grad. in Polit. Sci., Duke U., 1988. Color analyst Ohio Valley Conf. ESPN, 1988—89; asst. Ill. State U., 1989—93; asst. coach Ind. Pacers, 1993—97; v.p. basketball adminstrn. Phila. 76ers, 1997—98, gen. mgr., 1998—, pres., 2003—. Mem. US Men's Team World U. Games, 1987; athlete rep. on exec. com. USA Basketball, 1997—2000, mem. Men's Sr. Nat. Team com., 1997—2000, 2001—04, treas., 2001—04, mem. Men's Sr. Nat. Team Prog. Adv. Panel, 2005, bd. dirs., 2005—. Named Sports Exec. of Yr., Rainbow Sports Awards, 2000, NBA Exec. of Yr., African-Am. Ethnic Sports Hall of Fame, 2003; named one of Forty Under 40, St. and Smith's Bus. Jour., 2001, 101 Most Influential Minorities in Sports, Sports Illus., 2003; named to Duke U. Hall of Honor, 2001. Avocation: movies. Office: c/o Phila 76ers 1st Union Ctr Philadelphia PA 19148*

KING, BOOKER TERRY, JR., surgeon; b. Bklyn., Jan. 1, 1969; s. Booker T. King Sr. and Barbara Ann King; m. Dionne R. King, Sept. 13, 1994; children: Tyrique, Elijah, Booker III, Hezekiah, Genesis. BS cum laude, CUNY, NYC, 1992; MD, NYU, NYC, 1994. Diplomate Am. Bd. Surgery, Am. Bd. Surg. Critical Care. Resident in gen. surgery SUNY, Buffalo, 1994—99; commd. 2d sgt. US Army, 1999, advanced through grades to maj., 2001; chief gen. surgery Moncrief Army Hosp., Ft. Jackson, SC, 1999—2002, US Army Hosp., Heidelberg, Germany, 2002—05; staff surgeon 212th Mobile Army Hosp., Miesau, Germany, 2002—05; surg. critical care fellow U. Miami, Fla., 2005—06, trauma surgery fellow, 2006—07. Presenter in field. Contbr. articles to med. jours. Decorated Army Achievement medal, Army Commendation medal, Meritorious Svc. medal; Harry A. Kersner scholar in surgery, 1994. Fellow: ACS; mem.: Nat. Med. Assn., Assn. Mil. Surgeons US, Soc. Critical Care Medicine. Democrat. Office: U Miami Jackson Meml Hosp 1600 NW 10th Ave Miami FL 33126 Office Phone: 305-585-1293.

KING, CAROLE (CAROLE KLEIN), lyricist, singer; b. Bklyn., Feb. 9, 1942; m. Gerry Goffin; m. Charles Larkey; m. Rick Evers, 1977 (dec., 1978); m. Rick Sorensen, 1982; children: Louise, Sherry, Molly, Levi. Student, Queens Coll. Co-writer (with Gerry Goffin) Will You Love Me Tomorrow?, Go Away, Little Girl, Up on the Roof, (with Jerry Wexler) Natural Woman, The Locomotion, Take Good Care of My Baby, (with Toni Stern) It's Too Late, 1971; albums include Music, 1971, Tapestry, 1971 (4 Grammy awards), Simple Things, Pearls: Songs of Goffin and King, Rhymes & Reasons, 1972, Fantasy, 1973, Wrap Around Joy, 1974, Really Rosie, 1975, Thoroughbred, 1975, Her Greatest Hits: Songs of Long Ago, 1978, One To One, 1982, Speeding Time, 1983, City Streets, 1989, Colour Of Your Dreams, 1993, In Concert, 1994, A Natural Woman, 1994, The Carnegie Hall Concert, 1996, Pearls/Time Gone By, 1998, Super Hits, 2000, Love Makes the World, 2001, The Living Room Tour, 2005, Love Makes the World-Deluxe Edition, 2007; composer for films Head, 1968, Murphy's Romance, 1985, The Care Bears Movie, 1985; off-Broadway theater appearance in A Minor Incident, 1989; Broadway appearance in Blood Brothers, 1994; appeared in (films) Murphy's Romance, 1985, Russkies, 1987, (TV film) Hider in the House, 1989; (TV series) The Tracy Ullman Show, Gilmore Girls, 2002, 2005. Inducted in Rock & Roll Hall of Fame, 1990. Office: Carole King Prodns 11684 Ventura Blvd 273 Studio City CA 91604

KING, CAROLYN DINEEN, federal judge; b. Syracuse, NY, Jan. 30, 1938; d. Robert E. and Carolyn E. (Bareham) Dineen; m. Thomas M. Reavley; children: James Randall, Philip Randall, Stephen Randall. BA summa cum laude, Smith Coll., 1959; LLB, Yale U., 1962. Bar: D.C. 1962, Tex. 1963. Assoc. Fulbright & Jaworski, Houston, 1962—72; ptnr. Childs, Fortenbach, Beck & Guyton, 1972—78, Sullivan, Bailey, King, Randall & Sabom, 1978—79; judge US Ct. Appeals (5th Cir.), 1979—, chief judge, 1999—2006; mem. US Jud. Conf., 1999—2006, exec. com., 2000—05, chmn. exec. com., 2002—05. Trustee, exec. com., treas. Houston Ballet Found., 1967—70; Houston dist. adv. coun. SBA, 1972—76; Dallas regional panel Pres.'s Commn. White House Fellowships, 1972—76, mem. commn., 1977; bd. dirs. Houston chpt. Am. Heart Assn., 1978—79; nat. trustee Palmer Drug Abuse Program, 1978—79; trustee, sec., treas., chmn. audit com., fin. com., mgmt. com. United Way Tex. Gulf Coast, 1979—85; trustee, exec. com., chmn. bd. trustees U. St. Thomas, 1988—98. Recipient Smith Coll. medal, 1997, Outstanding Alumnus award, Phi Beta Kappa Alumni of Greater Houston, 1998, Margaret Brent Women Lawyers of Achievement award, ABA, 2005; rsch. fellow, Ctr. for Am. and Internat. Law, 1989—. Mem.: ABA, Philos. Soc. Tex., Houston Bar Assn., State Bar Tex., Am. Law Inst. (coun. 1991—, chmn. membership com. 1997—99), Fed. Bar Assn. Roman Catholic. Office: US Ct Appeals 11020 US Courthouse 515 Rusk Avenue Houston TX 77002-2694*

KING, CARRIE ANNE, publishing executive, advertising executive; b. Evansville, Ind., Mar. 20, 1971; d. Peggy Pauline Morgan and Gary Richard Noel Drazewski, Gary Richard Noel Drazewski and Peggy Pauline Morgan; m. Wayne V. King, Oct. 8, 2005; children: James Darrin Utley, Troy Jonathon Utley. CEO UDAC Advt., Price, Utah, 2002—, Mojocastle Press, Price, 2006—. Owner Nextime Wireless, Price, 2004—. Grantee SUESBIF, State of Utah, 2002. Mem.: EPPIC, Carbon County Employer Coun. Home: 753 N 400 E Price UT 84501 Office: Mojocastle Press 94 N 200 E Price UT 84501 Home Phone: 435-613-6398; Office Phone: 435-650-0009. Fax: 435-613-0320. Business E-Mail: carrie@mojocastle.com.

KING, CARY JUDSON, III, chemical engineer, educator, academic administrator; b. Ft. Monmouth, NJ, Sept. 27, 1934; s. Cary Judson and Mary Margaret (Forbes) K., Jr.; m. Jeanne Antoinette Yorke, June 22, 1957; children: Mary Elizabeth, Cary Judson IV, Catherine Jeanne. B in Engring., Yale U., 1956; MS, MIT, 1958, DSc, 1960. Asst. prof. chem. engring. MIT, Cambridge, 1959-63; dir. Bayway Sta. Sch. Chem. Engring. Practice, Linden, NJ, 1959-61; asst. prof. chem. engring. U. Calif., Berkeley, 1963-66, assoc. prof., 1966-69, prof., 1969—2003, prof. emeritus, 2003—, vice chmn. dept. chem. engring., 1967-72, chmn., 1972-81, dean Coll. Chemistry, 1981-87, provost profl. schs. and colls., 1987-94, dir. Ctr. for Studies in Higher Edn., 2004—; vice provost for rsch. U. Calif. Sys., Oakland, 1994—95, interim provost, sr. v.p. acad. affairs, 1995-96, provost, sr. v.p. acad. affairs, 1996—2004. Bd. assessment Nat. Bur. Stds.

Programs; dir. chem. engring. program divsn. Lawrence Berkeley Lab.; chair coun. chem. rsch. Gov.'s Task Force Toxics, Waste and Tech.; chair Calif. Coun. on Sci. and Tech., 2002—04; chmn. bd. dirs. Am. U. of Armenia Corp., 1995—2006. Author: Separation Processes, 1971, 80, Freeze Drying of Foods, 1971; contbr. numerous articles to profl. jours.; patentee in field. Active Boy Scouts Am., 1947-86; pres. Kensington Cmty. Coun., 1972-73, dir., 1970-73. Recipient Malcolm E. Pruitt award Coun. for Chem. Rsch., 1990. Mem. AIChE (Inst. lectr. 1973, Food, Pharm. and Bioengring. Divsn. award 1975, William H. Walker award 1976, Warren K. Lewis award 1990, bd. dirs. 1987-89, Clarence G. Gerhold award 1992); mem. AAAS, NAE, Am. Soc. Engring. Edn. (George Westinghouse award 1978), Am. Chem. Soc. (Separations Sci. and Tech. award 1997), Calif. Assn. for Rsch. in Astronomy (chmn.bd. 2003-06). Home: 7 Kensington Ct Kensington CA 94707-1009 Office: Ctr Studies Higher Edn Univ Calif MC 4650 Berkeley CA 94720-4650 Business E-Mail: cjking@berkeley.edu.

KING, CHARLES ROSS, physician; b. Nevada, Iowa, Aug. 22, 1925; s. Carl Russell and Dorothy Sarah (Mills) K.; m. Frances Pamela Carter, Jan. 8, 1949; children— Deborah Diane, Carter Ross, Charles Conrad, Corbin Kent Student, Butler U., 1943; BS in Bus., Ind. U., 1948, MD, 1964. Diplomate Am. Bd. Family Practice. Dep. dir. Ind. Pub. Works and Supply, 1949-52; salesman Knox Coal Corp., 1952-59; rotating intern Marion County Gen. Hosp., Indpls., 1964-65; family practice medicine Anderson, Ind., 1965—. Sec.-treas. staff Cmty. Hosp., 1969-72, pres.-elect, dir., chief medicine, 1973—, bd. dirs., 1973-75; sec.-treas. St. John's Hosp., 1968-69, chief medicine, 1972-73, chief pediatrics, 1977—; bd. dirs. Rolling Hills Convalescnet Ctr., 1968-73; pres. Profl. Ctr. Lab., 1965—; vice chmn. Madison County Bd. Health, 1966-69, chmn., 1986—; chmn. bd. dirs. Star Fin. Bank, Anderson. Bd. dirs. Family Svc. Madison County, 1968-69, Madison County Assn. Mentally Retarded, 1972-76, Anderson Fine Arts Ctr., 1996—; trustee St. Johns Health System., 1898—; chmn. bd. dirs. Anderson Downtown Devel. Corp., 1980—; mem. Paramont Restoration Steering Com., 1994—; trustee, sec.-tread. St. John's Med. Ctr., 1989—; mem. exec. com. Madison United Way Fund, vice-chmn., 1995, chmn., 1996; mem. exec. com. Stop Teen Pregnancy Program, 1995—; exec. commr. Health Search Madison County, 1995—. With U.S. Army, 1944-46. Recipient Dr. James Macholtz award, Spl. Olympics, 1986, Sagamore of Wabash award, State of Ind. Gov., 2002. Fellow Royal Soc. Health, Am. Acad. Family Practice (charter); mem. AMA (numerous Physicians Recognition awards), Ind. Med. Assn., Pan Am. Med. Assn., Am. Acad. Gen. Practice, Madison County Med. Soc. (pres. 1970), 9th Dist. Med. Soc. (sec.-treas. 1968), Anderson C. of C. (bd. dirs. 1979-82), Indpls. Mus. Art (corp. mem.), Anderson Country Club (bd. dirs. 1976-79), Phi Delta Theta (pres. Alumni Assn. 1952), Phi Chi. Clubs: Anderson Country (bd. dirs. 1976-79). Methodist. Office: 2015 Jackson St Anderson IN 46016-4337 Personal E-mail: chardrkm@aol.com.

KING, CHERYL BREA, elementary, secondary and music educator; b. McKeesport, Pa., Apr. 10, 1951; d. Edgar David and Eleanor Coates Brea; m. Richard Wayne King, PhD, June 22, 1974; children: Ashley, Adam, Allyson. B in Music Edn., Grove City Coll., 1973. Cert. instrnl. II grades K-12 music. Elem. music tchr. Grove City (Pa.) City Schs., 1973—74; elem. and middle sch. music tchr. Shaler Area Schs., Pitts., 1974—89; pvt. tchr. piano, dir. ch. choir, 1989—98; middle and sr. high vocal music tchr. East Allegheny Sch. Dist., North Versailles, Pa., 1998—, prodr., dir. H.S. musicals, 1998—. Mem., bd. dirs. McKeesport Little Theatre, 1998—2004; children's choir dir. First United Meth. Ch., East McKeesport, Pa., 1984—95. Mem.: Pa. State Edn. Assn., Pa. Music Edn. Assn., Music Edn. Nat. Coun. Democrat. Methodist. Avocations: reading, crafts, dance, Broadway musicals. Home: 412 Third St North Versailles PA 15137 Office: East Allegheny Sch Dist 1150 Jacks Run Rd North Versailles PA 15137 Office Phone: 412-824-9700. Business E-Mail: cking@eawildcats.net.

KING, CHI-YU, research scientist; b. Nanking, Jian-Su, China, Aug. 14, 1934; came to the U.S., 1958; s. Cheng-Wei and Chan-Ron (Chu) K.; m. Bi-Shia Wang, Sept. 8, 1962; children: Tsu-Jae, Hans Tsi-han, Henry Tsi-heng. BSEE, Nat. Taiwan U., Taipei, 1956; MS, Duke U., 1961; PhD, Cornell U., 1965. Rsch. fellow Calif. Inst. Tech., Pasadena, 1965-66; asst. rsch. geophysicist U. Calif., LA, 1966-68; geophysicist U.S. Geol. Survey, Menlo Park, Calif., 1968-70, 73-95, Nat. Oceanic and Atmospheric Adminstrn., San Francisco, 1970-73; PNC Internat. fellow, guest rschr. U. Tokyo, 1997-99. Vis. prof. Nat. Ctrl. U., Chung-Li, Taiwan, 1973-74; geophysicist, chmn. Earthquake Prediction Rsch. Inc., Los Altos, Calif., 1995—. Editor: Earthquake Hydrology and Chemistry, 1985, (with R. Scarpa) Modeling of Volcanic Processes, 1988; editor or co-editor spl. publs. Jour. Geophys. Rsch., 1980, 86, Geophys. Rsch. Letters, 1981, Pure and Applied Geophysics, 2006; mem. edit. bd. Jour. Geodesy and Geodynamics, 2003—; contbr. articles to profl. jours. Preacher, Bible tchr. various Christian chs. Calif., Taiwan, Hong Kong, China, Japan, Saipan, Persian Gulf, Europe, New Zealand, 1972—; chmn. bd. Ch. in Palo Alto, 1972-81, House of Christians, Los Altos, 1981-97. Mem. Am. Geophys. Union (assoc. editor Jour. Geophys. Rsch 1995-97). Home and Office: 381 Hawthorne Ave Los Altos CA 94022-3845 Office Phone: 650-948-4438. Personal E-mail: chiyuking@aol.com.

KING, CLIFFORD THOMAS, protective services official, martial arts instructor, educator; b. Austin, Tex., Sept. 29, 1980; s. Ira Thomas and Deborah Thomas King. BA in Criminal Justice summa cum laude, U. Tex., San Antonio, 2006. Supplemental instrn. leader U. Tex., 2006; police officer trainee Dallas Police Dept., 2007—. Martial arts instr. CTK Martial Arts, San Antonio, 1999—. Author: (books) Through Wolves Eyes: Dark Moon, In the Shadow of the Dragon. Vol. judo coach for children & young adults K-Bar Judo Club, Fredericksburg, Tex., 2002—04; vol. tchrs. asst. Ortega Elem. Sch., Austin, 2003; vol. swimming instr., Red Sross summer sports sch. aquatic program U. Tex., 2003—04. Sgt. USMC, 1998—2006, San Antonio, Texas. Decorated Armed Forces Res. Medal award USMC, Combat Action Ribbon, Navy Presdl. Unit Citation, Navy Meritorious Unit Commendation, Iraq Campaign medal, Global War Terrorism Expeditionary & Svc. medals, Nat. Def. Svc. medal, Selected Marine Corps Res. medal, Commdg. Gen. Cert. of Commendation award, Commdg. Officer Letter Appreciation award; recipient First Pl. Baylor/Tom Landry Triathlon, Baylor Med. Ctr., Dallas, 1998, Martial Artist of Yr. award, US Martial Arts Assn., 2004, Texas Judo Collegiate State Championship Silver Medal award, Tex. Judo, 2004, Texas Judo Sr. All Star Tournament Gold Medal award, 2004, Mil. Martial Artist of Yr. award, US Martial Arts Assn., 2005, Collegiate All-American Scholar award, US Achievement Acad., 2006, Cert. Appreciation award, U. Tex., 2006. Mem.: USMC Force Recon Assn., US Martial Arts Fedn. (life), Tex. Judo, Inc. (life), US Martial Arts Assn. (life), US Jiu-Jitsu Fedn. (life), US Judo Assn. (life), Omicron Delta Kappa, Alpha Phi Sigma, Alpha Chi, Sigma Iota Lambda, Golden Key. Methodist. Avocations: swimming, reading, creative writing. Home: 5349 Amesbury Apt 1404 Dallas TX 75206 Office: Dallas Police Dept 1400 S Lamar St Dallas TX 75215

KING, COLBERT ISAIAH, editor; b. Washington, Sept. 20, 1939; s. Isaiah and Amelia (Colbert) K.; m. Gwendolyn Ann Stewart, July 3, 1961; children: Robert, Stephen, Allison. BA, Howard U., 1961, postgrad., 1969. Attache Dept. State, Washington, 1964—70; dir. govt. rels. Potomac Elec. Power Co., Washington, 1976-77; legis. asst. to Md. Senator Charles McMathias Jr. Washington, 1972-76; dep. asst. sec. of treasury Dept. Treasury, Washington, 1977-79; U.S. exec. dir. World Bank, 1979-81; exec. v.p., bd. dirs. Riggs Nat. Bank, Washington, 1984—89; mem. editl. bd. Washington Post, 1990—, dep. editor editl. page, 2000—. Mem. Coun. for Excellence in Govt. With US Army, 1961-63. Named one of Outstanding Young Men of Am., US Jaycees, 1974; recipient spl. citation Nat. Rehab. Assn., 1975, Svc. award Ctr. for Sickle Cell Disease, Howard U., 1975, Disting. Svc. award US Treasury, 1979, Outstanding Alumnus award, Howard U., 1984, Pulitzer Prize, 2003. Mem. Kappa Alpha Psi. Democrat. Episcopalian. Office: The Washington Post 1150 15th St Washington DC 20071 Office Phone: 202-334-7475.

KING, CURTIS STEEBLE, history professor; b. Atlantic City, Oct. 1, 1959; s. George Allman and Cecelia Marie King. BS, U.S.Mil. Acad., West Point, NY, 1982; MA in History, U. of Pa., Phila., 1992; PhD in History, U. of Pa., 1999. Commissioned U.S. Army, 1982, advanced through grades to maj.; platoon leader, exec. officer, and asst. ops. officer Combat Support Bn., Berlin Brigade, Berlin, 1982—85; adj. and co. comdr. 4-37 Armor Bn., 1st Inf. Divsn., Fort Riley, Kans., 1986—89; asst. divsn. ops. officer 85th Divsn. (Exercise), Arlington Heights, Ill., 1995—98; asst. prof. of history U.S. Mil. Acad., West Point, NY, 1992—95; asst. prof. Combat Studies Inst., Fort Leavenworth, Kans., 1998—99, assoc. prof., 2000—; asisstant historian Stabilizaion Forces, Bosnia, Sarajevo, Bosnia-Herzegovina, 1999—2000. Adj. prof. Kans. State U., Manhattan, 2004—. Author: The Overland Campain Staff Ride Handbook; contbr. articles to profl. jours., chapters to books. Decorated Joint Svc. Commendation Medal US Dept. of Def., NATO medal, Army Commendation medals (4); recipient Omar N. Bradley Award for Excellence in Writing and Rsch., U.S. Mil. Acad., 1982. Mem.: Army Hist. Found., Nat. Trust for Hist. Preservation, US Armor Assn. (Order of St. George 1995), Soc. for Mil. History, Assn. for the Advancement of Slavic Studies, Am. Hist. Assn., The Soverign Mil. Order of the Temple of Jerusalem (assn. historian for the grand priory of the U.S. 2000—, Legion of Merit and St. Louis the Crusader Medal 2002 and 2002), Phi Alpha Theta, Phi Kappa Phi. Home: 51 Saint Mary's St Apt D Leavenworth KS 66048 Office: Combat Studies Institute US Army Command and Staff College Fort Leavenworth KS 66027 Home Phone: 913-680-1610; Office Phone: 913-684-2082. Personal E-mail: kingphillie@aol.com.

KING, CYNTHIA BREGMAN, writer; b. NYC, Aug. 27, 1925; d. Adolph and Elsie (Oschrin) Bregman; m. Jonathan King July 26, 1944 (dec 1997); children: Gordon Barkley, Austin Arthur (dec.), Nathaniel Bregman. Student, Bryn Mawr Coll., 1943-44, U. Chgo., 1944-46, N.Y.U., 1964-67. Assoc. editor Hillman Periodicals, NYC, 1946-50; mng. editor Fawcett Publs., NYC, 1950-55; creative writing tchr. The Awty Sch., Houston, 1974-75. Book reviewer, N.Y. Times Book Rev., 1976-83, Detroit News, 1980-88; dir. short story symposium Friends of Detroit Pub. Libr. and Detroit Women Writers, 1985; creative writing residencies Mich. Coun. of the Arts, Detroit, 1976-86. Author: In the Morning of Time, 1970, The Year of Mr. Nobody, 1978, Beggars and Choosers, 1980, Sailing Home, 1982; editor Fripp Island Audubon Club Natural History Publs., 1990-92 Mem. Pritchards Island adv. bd. U. SC, Beaufort, 1991—2006; pres. Fripp Island Audubon Club, 1991—92; asst. to chmn. Beaufort County Dem. Party, 1989—91. Recipient Spring Readings award, Detroit Working Writers, 2003; Creative Artist's grantee, Mich. Coun. for the Arts, 1985—86. Mem. The Authors Guild, Poets and Writers, Inc., Detroit Women Writers, Inc. (pres. 1979-81). Personal E-mail: tonibking@verizon.net.

KING, D. KENT, school system administrator; b. Preston, Mo., 1943; m. Sandy King; 3 children. BA, Ctrl. Mo. State U., 1964; MA, Drury Coll., Springfield, 1967; PhD in Ednl. Adminstrn., Okla. State U., 1972. From tchr. to prin. Houston Sch. Dist., Tex. County, Mo., 1964—70; supt. Licking Sch. Dist., Mo., 1971—77, Rolla Sch. Dist., Mo., 1977—96; dir. Mo. Sch. Improvement Program, 1996—99; dep. commr. Mo. Dept. Edn., Jefferson City, Mo., 1999—2000, commr., 2000—. Office: Mo Dept Edn PO Box 480 Jefferson City MO 65102-0480 Office Phone: 573-751-4446. Office Fax: 573-751-1179.*

KING, DAVID A., aerospace engineer; m. Lisa King; 2 children. BS in Mech. Engring., U. S.C., 1983; MS in Bus Adminstrn., Fla. Inst. Tech., 1991. Space shuttle main propulsion sys. engr. NASA, 1983—93, flow dir. Space Shuttle Discovery, 1993—95, dep. dir. shuttle processing, 1996—97, shuttle launch dir., 1997—99, dep. dir. Marshall Space Flight Ctr., 2002—03, dir. Marshall Space Flight Ctr., 2004—. Recipient Exceptional Svc. medal, NASA, 1996, Oustanding Leadership medal, 2000, 2004, Presdl. Rank award for Meritorious Execs., 2001, Presdl. Rank award for Disting. Execs., 2005. Fellow: Am. Inst. Aeronautics & Astronautics Found. (assoc.). Office: Marshall Space Flight Ctr DAO1 NASA Huntsville AL 35812 E-mail: david.a.king@nasa.gov.

KING, DAVID A., lawyer; b. LA, Feb. 26, 1960; married; 2 children. BS, Univ. Tenn., 1982, JD, 1985. Bar: Tenn. 1985. Mem., litigation & healthcare practices Bass Berry & Sims PLC, Nashville. Editor (student materials): Tenn. Law Rev. Named one of Best Lawyers in Nashville, Nashville Post, 2003. Fellow: Nashville Bar Found.; mem.: Am. Health Lawyers Assn., Def. Rsch. Inst., Tenn. Bar Assn., Nashville Bar Assn. Office: Bass Berry & Sims PLC Ste 2700 315 Deaderick St Nashville TN 37239-3001 Office Phone: 615-742-7890. Office Fax: 615-742-2815. Business E-Mail: dking@bassberry.com.

KING, DAVID ALAN, ecologist; b. River Falls, Wis., Dec. 6, 1949; s. Chauncy Byron and Rose Marie King. BS, U. Wis., River Falls, 1972; MS, Calif. Inst. Tech., Pasadena, 1974; PhD, U. Wis., Madison, 1979. Postdoctoral assoc. Stanford U., Stanford, 1979—81, U. Calif., Davis, 1981—83; rsch. assoc. prof. U. Portland, Oreg., 1983—87; sr. postdoctoral assoc. Smithsonian Tropical Rsch. Inst., Balboa, Panama, 1990—91; rsch. fellow U. NSW, Sydney, NSW, Australia, 1991—94, Australian Nat. U., Canberra, ACT, 1994—97, Harvard U., Cambridge, Mass., 2003—04. Contbr. articles to profl. jours. Achievements include the construction of ecological models for predicting effects of pollutants and high CO2 on crops and forests, research on tree architecture in Australia, Borneo, Central America, and North America and studies linking the growth of trees to their form and proportions.

KING, DAVID PAUL, health services executive, lawyer; b. Washington, June 20, 1956; s. Ivan Robert and Alice King. AB, Princeton U., 1977; JD, U. Pa., 1982. Bar: Ga. 1984. Law clk. to Hon. Alvin B. Rubin, US Ct. Appeals (5th cir.), Baton Rouge, 1982-83; assoc. Rogers & Hardin, Atlanta, 1983-85, Covington & Burling, Washington, 1985-87, Hogan & Hartson, L.L.P., Balt., 1990-92, ptnr., 1992—2001; asst. US atty. Dept. Justice, Balt., 1987-90; sr. v.p., gen. counsel, chief compliance officer Lab. Corp. Am. Holdings, 2001—04, exec. v.p. strategic planning and corp. devel., 2004—05, exec. v.p., COO, 2005—06, pres., CEO, 2007—. Adj. prof. U. Md. Law Sch., Balt. Mem. ABA, Md. Bar Assn., DC Bar Assn., Ga. Bar Assn. Office: Lab Corp Am Holdings 358 S Main St Burlington NC 27215

KING, DAVID ROY, lawyer; b. NYC, Jan. 5, 1950; s. Joseph S. and Doris (Kagan) K.; m. Eunice Searles, Aug. 22, 1971; children: Mark B., Anna M. BA, U. Pa., 1971; JD, Harvard U., 1974. Bar: Pa. 1974, US Dist Ct. (ea. dist.) Pa. 1974. Assoc. Morgan, Lewis & Bockius LLP, Phila., 1974-81, ptnr., 1981-2000; CEO Principia Pharms., Inc., 2000; pres. Delsys Pharms., Inc., 2001—; CEO BioRexis Pharm. Corp., 2002—.

KING, DON, boxing promoter; b. Cleve., Aug. 20, 1931; s. Clarence and Hattie K.; m. Henrietta King; children: Deborah, Carl, Eric. D (hon.), Shaw U. Boxing promoter, 1972—; owner Don King Prodns., Inc., Fla., 1974—. Promoter various fighters including Muhammad Ali, Sugar Ray Leonard, Mike Tyson, Ken Norton, Joe Frazier, Larry Holmes, Roberto Duran, George Foreman. Achievements include being featured on the covers of Time, Sports Illustrated, Ebony, Jet and other magazines; appearing in movies, TV shows and on numerous TV and radio talk shows; creating the phrase "Only in America"; establishing the Don King Foundation. Supporter NAACP, United Negro Coll. Fund, Martin Luther King Jr. Found., Simon Wiesenthal Ctr., Nat. Hispanic Scholarship Fund, Nat. Coalition of Title 1/Cptr. 1 Parents, Wheelchair Charities, Our Children's Found.; bd. trustee Shaw U. Named Man of Yr., Black United Fund and Brotherhood Crusade, in his honor "Don King Day", Newark, NJ, Greatest Promoter in History, Internat. Boxing Fedn., World Boxing Assn., World Boxing Coun.; named to Boxing Hall of Fame, 1997, the list of 40 Most Influential Sports Figures of the Past 40 Yrs., Sports Illustrated; recipient Black Achievement award, Martin Luther King Jr. Humanitaitan award, So. Christian Leadership, 1987, President's award, NAACP, Lifetime Achievement, Grambling State U. Office: care Don King Prodns Inc 501 Fairway Dr Deerfield Beach FL 33441-1865*

KING, DOUGLAS MICHAEL, lawyer, accountant; b. Ft. Worth, Dec. 31, 1962; s. King Raymond Earl and Barbara Ruth King (Stepmother). BBA, Baylor U., Waco, Tex., 1986; JD, Tex. Weslyan U., Dallas, 1994; M of Legal Letters in Tax, NYU, NYC, 1995. CPA Tex., 1989; bar: Tex. 1996. V.p., trust officer Lawyers Trust Co., Fort Worth, 1981—86; staff supr. litig. support PriceWaterHouseCoopers, L.L.P., Dallas, 1986—89; v.p. valuations Gordon Capital, inc., Toronto, Canada, 1989—92; assoc. Law, Snakard, Gambill & King, L.L.P., Fort Worth, 1992—96, Law, Snakard & Gambill, P.C., Fort Worth, 1997; pres. King & Assocs., P.C., Weatherford, Tex., 1997—. Lectr. database systems MBA program U. Tex., Austin, 1987—89. Author: (book) The New Copernican Revolution, 2004. Agnostic. Avocation: skiing. Home: Ste 117 711 Santa Fe Dr Weatherford TX 76086 Office: King & Associates PC 2110 Fort Worth Hwy Weatherford TX 76086 Home Phone: 817-598-1007; Office Phone: 214-642-3143. Office Fax: 208-693-3007; Home Fax: 208-693-3007. Personal E-mail: doug@dmkingpc.com. Business E-Mail: doug@reversemergershome.com.

KING, ED, musician; b. Glendale, Calif., Sept. 14, 1949; Band mem. Strawberry Alarm Clock, LA, 1966—72; guitarist with Lynyrd Skynyrd, 1972—75, 1987—96. Musician: (albums) (with Stawberry Alarm Clock) Incense & Peppermints, 1967, Psych Out, 1968, The World in a Seashell, 1968, Wake Up.It's Tomorrow, 1968, Good Morning Starshine, 1969, Beyond the Valley of the Dolls, 1970, Changes, 1971, (with Lynyrd Skynyrd) Pronounced Leh-Nerd Skin-Nerd, 1973, Smokes, 1973, Second Helping, 1974, Nuthin' Fancy, 1975, Southern By the Grace of God, 1988, Lynyrd Skynyrd 1991, 1991, The Last Rebel, 1993, Endangered Species, 1994. Named to Rock and Roll Hall of Fame, 2006. Office: c/o Vector Mgmt PO Box 120479 Nashville TN 37212

KING, EDWARD JOSEPH, clinical chemist, laboratory administrator; b. Bronx, NY, Nov. 17, 1955; s. Edward Paul and May Frances (Kern) K. BS, Manhattan Coll., Riverdale, NY, 1978; PhD in Analytical Chemistry, Pacific Western U., 1997. Cert. clin. chemist Nat. Registry Clin. Chemistry. Sr. technologist MetPath, Teterboro, N.J., 1979-91, MetLife Lab., Elmsford, NY, 1991—93; lab. mgr. East Side Physicians P.C., NYC, 1993—2003; clin. chemist ALX Lab c/o Animal Med. Ctr., NYC, 2004—. Contbg. author Procs. of Clinichem -96, Vol. 11, 1996, Procs. of Soc. Forensic Toxicology, 2000. Fellow Nat. Acad. Clin. Biochemists (assoc.); mem. Am. Assn. Clin. Chemistry (Clin. Chemist Recognition award 2000), Am. Soc. Clin. Pathologists (cert.), Am. Chem. Soc. Achievements include research and development of wet chemistry urinalysis methodology. Home: 1173 A Second Ave Box 246 New York NY 10021 Office: ALX Lab c/o Animal Med Ctr 510 E 62d St New York NY 10021 Business E-Mail: eking3@optonline.net.

KING, EDWARD LOUIS, retired chemistry professor; b. Grand Forks, ND, Mar. 15, 1920; s. Edward Louis and Beatrice (Nicholson) K.; m. Joy Kerler, Dec. 20, 1952; children: Paul, Marcia (dec.). Student, Long Beach Jr. Coll., Calif., 1938—41; BS, U. Calif., Berkeley, 1942, PhD, 1945. Rsch. chemist Manhattan Project U. Calif., Berkeley, 1942-46; mem. chemistry faculty Harvard U., 1946-48, U. Wis., 1948-62, U. Colo., Boulder, 1963-90, chmn. dept. chemistry, 1970-72; ret., 1990. Author: How Chemical Reactions Occur, 1963, Chemistry, 1979; Editor: Inorganic Chemistry, 1964-68. Guggenheim fellow, 1957-58. Mem. Am. Chem. Soc., Phi Beta Kappa, Sigma Xi. Office: U Colo Dept Chemistry PO Box 215 Boulder CO 80309-0215

KING, ELAINE A., curator, art historian, critic; b. Oak Park, Ill., Apr. 12, 1947; d. Casimir Stanley and Catherine Mary (Chmel) Czerwien. BS, No. Ill. U., 1968, MA, 1974; PhD, Northwestern U., 1986. Cert. Fine Arts Appraisal, 2002. Intern George Eastman House, Rochester, NY, 1977; lectr. history of photography Northwestern U., Evanston, Ill., 1977-81; curator Dittmar Meml. Gallery, Evanston, 1978-81; dir. Artemesia Gallery, Chgo., 1976-77; exec. dir., chief curator Carnegie-Mellon Art Gallery, Pitts., 1985—91; prof. critical theory and history of art Carnegie Mellon U., Pitts., 1981—. Ind. curator, 1991—; exhbn. rev. panel Pa. Coun. on Arts, 1991; exec. dir., chief curator Contemporary Art Ctr., Cin., 1993-95; guest curator Pitts. Cultural Trust, 1992, 93, 95, 96, Maria de Mater O'Neill mid-career survey, Mus. Arts, P.R., 2007; 10 year Retrospective of Diane Samuels, Mus. of Art, Györ, Hungary, Györ, 1999, bd. dirs. Mid-Am. Coll. Art Assn.; panel chair Midwest CAA Conf., 1997, 2003, Am. Assn. Culture Conf., 2007; co-coord. Wats:ON Festival, 1996-2003; adj. prof. U. Cin., 1994; art critic-in-residence U. Ariz., Tucson; guest curator Hungarian Bienale Exhbn. II, Györ, 1993, Master Graphic Arts Internat. Biennial, 1995, 97, 99, 2001, 03, 05, 07; pres. Internat. Jury, 2003, 07; panelist NEA Visual Arts, 1993; grant reviewer Inst. Mus. Sci., Washington, 1994, Ohio Arts Coun. fellowship and grant evaluator, 1994-95; Internat. Rev. panel AAUW internat. fellowships, Washington, 2000-03; mem. organizing com. Midwest Mus. Con., 1994-95; rep. Inter Arts Spring 1996 Budapest (Hungary) Crossroads; critic rep. Assn. Internat. Critics Art Conf. The Edge, Zagreb, Croatia; chmn. com. disting. exhbn. award Coll. Arts Assn., 1995-98, Assn. Internat. Critics Art XXXIV Congress Internat. Art Critics, Zagreb, Assn. Internat. Critics Art conf. ctrl. European cross-roads, 1996, 97, Assn. Internat. Critics Art Congress 2000, Barbados, 2003, Slovania, 2005, Assn. Internat. Critics Art Congress, Sao Paulo, 2007, Coll. Art Assn. Vanity and Desperation, 2007, London, Assn. Internat. Critics Art Congress, 2007; juror exhbn. 3rd Prague Internat.; nominator 4th Prague Internat., 2004; art-historian in residence internat. program Am. U., 2006, chair Sch. Visual Arts Plenary Session Conf., 2005, Internat. Popular Culture Assn. Conf., Wales, 2005, Chautauqua Inst., summer 2006, 2007; mem. panel censorship Ann Arbor Film Festival, 2007, Sch. Visual Arts, NYC; guest curator, spkr. in field. Curator, author: Crossing Borders: USA/Europe, Alleghany Coll. Art Galleries, 2000, Marking, 1999, The Figure As Fiction, 1993, Alfred DeCredico: Drawings, 1985-93, Emily Cheng: Monoprints, 1994, Passion Puzzles of Francisco Alvarado-Juárez, Secrets of Flora & Fauna, Institute of Culture, De Morales, 2006; (exhbn. catalogues) Barry LeVa: 1966-88, Mel Bochner: 1973-85, Elizabeth Murray: Drawings: 1980-86, Michael Gitlin: Sculpture & Drawings, 1990, New Generations: Chgo., 1990, New Generations: N.Y., 1991, Magdalena Jetalová, 1991, Martin Puryear: Sculpture & Drawings, 1987, Abstraction/Abstraction, Tishan Hsu, Paintings, Drawings & Sculpture, 1987, N.Y. Painting Today, Michel Gerand: Drawings and Site Works, 1989, Drawings and Sculpture, 1990, Art in the Age of Information, 1993, Five Artists at the Airport: Insights into Public Art, 1992, Martha Rosler: In Place of the Public, 1994, Shari Zolla, 1997, Lyzabeth Bayard: 2 Installations, Light Into Art: From Video to Virtual Reality (also booklet), David Humphrey: Paintings and Drawings 1987-95 (also catalogue), others; author: The Misunderstood Patron, The National Endowment for the Arts; co-editor: Ethics and the Visual Arts, 2006, Artist Observed, Signature of a Culture with Harvey Stein, 1988; critic-in-residence Sch. Art, San Juan, PR; free lance art critic, Washington Post, Grapheion, Tema Celeste, & Sculpture, Cin. Enquirer; Grapheion; Art on Paper, Pitt. Post-Gazette, art critic in residence Delaware Contemporary Ctr. for the Arts, 1992, Mid-Atlantic Arts Fellow, 1991, No. Ill. U., 1997; corr. critic, regional editor Diaglogue, Columbus, Ohio, 1984-89; corr. critic Sculpture; co-editor: (with Gail Levin) Ethics and the Visual Arts, 2006; contbr. articles, essays to various pubs. Active Dem. Party, Evanston, ward judge, 1977-78, precinct capt., 1977. Recipient Hunt Art award, 1977, Disting. Art Historian Residency award Am. U., 2006; scholar Pa. Humanities Coun., 1997, Nat. Mus. Am. Art, 2000; grantee Carnegie Mellon U., 1985, 87, 89-90, 96-99, 2002, Grant Trust for Mut. Understanding, Rockefeller Found., 1994, Thendora Found., 1995, Pa. Coun. on Arts, 2000, IREX, 2000; fellow Pa. Coun. on Arts, 1985, 89, 95, 99, 2000, Smithsonian Inst., 1998, 2000—, Nat. Portrait Gallery, 2001, Inst. for Art History, Acad. Scis., Budapest, Hungary, 2002, Ctrl. European Cultural Inst., 2002; named disting. art historian Am. U., Corcino, Italy, 2006. Mem. Coll. Art Assn., Am. Assn. Mus., Assn. Historians Am. Art, Assn. Internat. Critics Art (Am. sect.), Art Table, Midwest Coll. Art Assn. Avocations: cooking, gardening, tennis, swimming, sailing. Office: Carnegie Mellon U Coll Fine Arts Pittsburgh PA 15213 Office Phone: 412-268-1970. Personal E-mail: eaking13@yahoo.com. Business E-Mail: ek06@andrew.cmu.edu.

KING, SISTER ELEACE, special education services professional; b. Greenport, NY, Oct. 10, 1946; d. Gerald C. King and Alice Cecelia Ward. BA, Marywood Coll., 1969; MS, Yeshiva U., 1974; EdD, Johns Hopkins U., 1983. First grade tchr. St. John the Evangelist Sch., Scranton, Pa., 1969—70; spl. edn. tchr. Archdiocese of NY, New York, 1970—74; asst. prof. Marywood Coll., Scranton, 1974—86; sr. rsch. assoc. Ctr. Applied Rsch. Apostolate/Georgetown U., Washington, 1988—94; asst. supt. spl. edn. Diocese of Bridgeport, 1994—. Adv. bd. mem. St. Catherine Acad., Bridgeport, 1999—; bd. of trustees Nat. Cath. Partnership Disabilities, Washington, 2003—, treas. bd. trustees. Contbr. chapters to books. Adv. coun. mem. State Dept. Mental Retardation, Southwest Region, Conn., 1999—2000, mem., human rights com., 1998—2003. Scholar, The Inner-City Found. Charity and Edn., 1999—2004, Pitt Found., 2004. Mem.: Coun. Exceptional Children (assoc.), Nat. Cath. Edn. Assn. (assoc.). Roman Catholic. Achievements include Founder, St. Catherine Academy, a special education school for children with intellectual disabilities. Avocations: reading, knitting, walking. Office: Diocese of Bridgeport 238 Jewett Ave Bridgeport CT 06606 Home Phone: 203-333-2877; Office Phone: 203-372-4301 330. Office Fax: 203-372-1961. Personal E-mail: sreleace@aol.com. E-mail: srking@diobpt.org.

KING, ELIZABETH MAUREEN, business systems executive; b. Bellefonte, Pa., Nov. 13, 1957; d. Richard A. and Joanne Sellers King. BA, Pa. State U., University Park, 1979. Sys. analyst R.H. Macy, Newark, Fla., 1979-81; mgr. applications Eckerd Corp., Clearwater, Fla., 1981-93; dir. retail sys. Rite Aid Corp., Camp Hill, Pa., 1993; mgr. applications devel. IBM Global Svcs. Corp., Clearwater, Fla., 1993-96; sr. cons. McCready, Manigold, Ray and Co., Dunedin, Fla., 1996-97; v.p. bus. sys. Starbucks Coffee Co., Seattle, 1997—. Active Tribute to Women and Industry, 1989. Betty J. Lockington scholar, Martin Marietta scholar. Mem. NAFE, Pa. State U. Alumni Assn., Phi Beta Kappa, Phi Kappa Phi, Pi Sigma Alpha. Home: 4601 174th Pl SE Bellevue WA 98006-6549

KING, FREDERICK W., chemistry professor, researcher; s. Francis and Bernice King. BSc, U. Sydney, 1965—68; MSc, U. Calgary, 1969—71; PhD, Queens U., Kingston, 1972—75. Chemistry prof. U. Wis., Eau Claire, 1988—. Contbr. articles to profl. jours. Grantee Camille & Henry Dreyfus Tchr.-Scholar award, Dreyfus Found., 1983—88, Camille & Henry Dreyfus Scholar/Fellow award, 1991—93. Mem.: Am. Phys. Soc., Am. Chem. Soc. Achievements include contributions in theoretical chemistry/theoretical atomic physics. Avocation: Go. Office: Univ Wis Dept Chem Eau Claire WI 54702

KING, GARR MICHAEL, federal judge; b. Pocatello, Idaho, Jan. 28, 1936; s. Warren I. King and Geraldine E. (Hanlon) Appleby; m. Mary Jo Rieber, Feb. 2, 1957; children: Mary, Michael, Matthew, James, Margaret, John, David. Student, U. Utah, 1957-59; LLB, Lewis and Clark Coll., 1963. Bar: Oreg. 1963, U.S. Dist. Ct. Oreg. 1965, U.S. Ct. Appeals (9th cir.) 1975, U.S. Supreme Ct. 1971. Dep. dist. atty. Multnomah County Dist. Atty.'s Office, Portland, Oreg., 1963-66; assoc. Morrison, Bailey, Dunn, Carney & Miller, Portland, 1966-71; ptnr. Kennedy & King, Portland, 1971-77, Kennedy, King & McClurg, Portland, 1977-82, Kennedy, King & Zimmer, Portland, 1982-98; judge U.S. Dist. Ct. Oreg., Portland, 1998—. Active various pvt. sch. and ch. bds. Served as sgt. USMC, 1954-57. Fellow Am. Coll. Trial Lawyers (regent 1995-98), Am. Bar Found.; mem. ABA, Oreg. Bar Assn., Multnomah County Bar Assn. (pres. 1975), Jud. Conf. 9th Cir. (del.), Northwestern Coll. Law Alumni Assn. (pres.), Multnomah Athletic Club. Democrat. Roman Catholic. Avocations: tennis, reading, gardening. Office: 907 US Courthouse 1000 SW 3rd Ave Portland OR 97204-2930 E-mail: garr-king@ord.uscourts.gov.

KING, GARY K., state attorney general; b. Albuquerque, Sept. 29, 1954; s. Bruce King; m. Yolanda Jones, 1986. B in Chemistry, N.Mex. State U., 1976; PhD in Organic Chemistry, U. Colo., Boulder, 1980; JD, U. N.Mex., 1983. Founding ptnr. King & Stanley LLP, Moriarity, N.Mex., 1983—90; mem. N.Mex. State Ho. Reps., 1986—98, chair consumer and pub. affairs com.; corp. gen. counsel, sr. environ. scientist Advanced Sciences, Inc.; policy adv. to asst. sec. for environ. mgmt. US Dept. Energy, Washington, 1998; dir. Office of Worker and Cmty. Transition; atty. gen. State of N.Mex., Santa Fe, 2007—. Mem.: Sierra Club, NRA. Democrat. Office: Office of Atty Gen PO Drawer 1508 Santa Fe NM 87504-1508*

KING, GAYLE, editor, radio personality, television personality; b. Chevy Chase, Md., 1955; BS in Psych., U. Md., 1976. Reporter, weekend anchor WDAF-TV, Kansas City, 1977—80; reporter WFSB-TV, Hartford, Conn., 1981—99; co-host Cover to Cover, 1991; host The Gayle King Show, 1997; editor-at-large O, The Oprah Mag., 1999—, O at Home, 2003—; corr. The Oprah Winfrey Show; co-host XM Satellite Radio's Oprah & Friends, 2006—. Office: O, The Oprah Mag 300 W 57th St 36th Fl New York NY 10019*

KING, GEORGE RALEIGH, retired manufacturing executive; b. Benton Harbor, Mich., May 13, 1931; s. Maurice Peter and Opal Ruth (Hart) King; m. Phyllis Stratton, July 30, 1950; children: Paula King Zang, Angela King Young, Philip. Student, Adrian Coll., 1950-51. Cert. purchasing profl. exec. status. With Kirsch Co., Sturgis, Mich., 1951—, data processing trainee, 1951-53, data processing mgr., 1953-59, asst. purchasing agt., 1959-62, purchasing agt., 1962-68, dir. purchasing, 1968-91, ret., 1991; corp. cons., 1991—. Author: Rods & Rings, 1972. Elder 1st Presbyn. Ch., Sturgis, 1970; pres. Sturgis Civic Players, 1972. Recipient citation Boy Scouts Am., 1966, Jr. Achievement, 1967; nominated candidate for adminstrn. Fed. Procurement Policy, Reagan Adminstrn., Washington, 1980. Mem. Am. Purchasing Soc. (pres. 1979-81), Nat. Assn. Purchasing Mgmt., southwestern Purchasing Assn., Exchange (pres. Sturgis 1959, dis. gov. dist. and nat. clubs 1961), Berrien Hills Country Club, Rotary (Lakeshore), Masons, Elks. Home: 1804 Lakeshore Dr Apt 16 Saint Joseph MI 49085-1616 Office Phone: 269-369-9279. Personal E-mail: kinggeorgemi@aol.com.

KING, GLEN (LENARD GLEN KING), broadcasting educator, composer; b. NYC, Oct. 13, 1935; s. Lawrence Herbert and Marcia Helen (Berger) K.; m. Margaret Elizabeth Gabler, Aug. 26, 1989. BA, Calif. State U., LA, 1960, MFA, 1964. Prodn. asst. Sta. KABC-TV, LA, 1963-64; news asst. Sta. KTLA-TV, LA, 1964-65; disc jockey Sta. KUTE, LA, 1965-66, Sta. KFOX, LA, 1966; instr. theater arts Elizabeth Seton Coll., Yonkers, N.Y., 1966-67; assoc. prof. broadcasting West L.A. Coll., Culver City, Calif., 1977-84; prof. broadcasting Los Angeles Valley Coll., Van Nuys, Calif., 1985—95; founder Silver Kat Music BMI, 1985—. Supr. student cable internships West L.A. Coll., Culver City, Calif., 1980-85; designer broadcasting and TV aesthetics and documentary curriculums area colls.; owner, mgr. Silver Kat Music Pub. affiliate Broadcast Music Inc.; broadcast cons. CBS News, 1991, KMNY, 1992; prodr., dir. Pub. Access TV Adelphia Cable Co., Charlottesville, 1996-2000, dir. M.S. Telethon, 1996-98. Composer popular, country and gospel songs, 1976—. With USN, 1953-56, Republic of Korea. Winner internat. competition Song Writers Hall of Fame and N.Y. Music Pubs. Group, 1985; recipient 1st prize Am. Song Festival, L.A., 1976, Grand prize, 1979. Mem. BMI (affiliate), Nat. Music Pubs. Assn. Avocations: music, antiques, automobiles. E-mail: silverkatmusic@yahoo.com.

KING, GRAHAM, film producer; b. Eng., Dec. 19, 1961; Pres. & CEO Initial Entertainment Group, 1995—. Prodr.: (films) Dr. T and the Women, 2000, The Aviator, 2004, The Departed, 2006, Blood Diamond, 2006, Next, 2007, Time to Kill, 2007; exec. prodr.: Ping!, 2000, Traffic, 2000, Ali, 2001, The Dangerous Lives of Altar Boys, 2002, Desert Saints, 2002, Gangs of New York, 2002, The Ballad of Jack and Rose, 2005, An Unfinished Life, 2005, Gardener of Eden, 2006, First Born, 2007; (TV miniseries) Traffic, 2004. Mem.: Acad. Motion Picture Arts and Sciences.*

KING, GREGORY C., energy executive; b. NYC, July 1, 1960; m. Leigh Ann King; children: Gregory Jr., Allison, Andrew, Carolyn. BBA in Finance, U. Tex., Austin, 1982; JD, U. Houston, 1985. Ptnr. Bracewell & Patterson, LLP, Houston, 1985-93; assoc. gen. counsel Valero Energy Corp., Houston, 1993-97, v.p., gen. counsel, 1997-99, sr. v.p., COO, 1999—2003, pres., 2003—. Bd. dirs. Mission Rd. Devel. Ctr., San Antonio Zoo; mem. exec. com., trustee United Way of San Antonio and Bexar County. Mem. Tex. State Bar Assn.*

KING, GUNDAR JULIAN, retired dean; b. Riga, Latvia, Apr. 19, 1926; came to U.S., 1950, naturalized, 1954; s. Attis K. and Austra (Dale) Kenins; m. Valda K. Andersons, Sept. 18, 1954; children: John T., Marita A. Student, J.W. Goethe U., Frankfurt, Germany, 1946-48; BBA, U. Oreg., 1956; MBA, Stanford U., 1958, PhD, 1964; DSc (hon.), Riga Tech. U., 1991; D Habil. Oecon., Latvian Sci. Coun., 1992. Asst. field supr. Internat. Refugee Orgn., Frankfurt, 1948-50; br. office mfr. Williams Form Engring. Corp., Portland, Oreg., 1952-54; project mgr. Market Rsch. Assocs., Palo Alto, Calif., 1958-60; asst. prof., assoc. prof. Pacific Luth. U., 1960-66, prof., 1966—, dean Sch. Bus. Adminstrn., 1970-90. Vis. prof. mgmt. U.S. Naval Postgrad. Sch., 1971-72, San Francisco State U., 1980, 1987-88; internat. econ. mem. Latvian Acad. Scis., 1990—; regent Estonian Bus. Sch., 1991-99; vis. prof. Riga Tech. U., 1993-97 Author: Economic Policies in Occupied Latvia, 1965, additional books on business, last six in Latvian, 1999—2007; contbr. articles to profl. publs. Gov.'s com. Wash. State Govt., 1965-88; study group on pricing U.S. Commn. Govt. Procurement, 1971-72; pres. N.W. Univs. Bus. Adminstrn. Conf., 1965-66. With AUS, 1950-52. Decorated officer Order of Three Stars, Latvian, 2006; Fulbright-Hayes scholar, Thailand, 1988, Fulbright scholar, Latvia, 1993-94, 2007; recipient Spidola prize Latvian Culture Found., 1999, Recognition award, 2005 Mem. AAUP (past chpt. pres.), Am. Mktg. Assn. (past chpt. pres.), Assn. Advancement Baltic Studies (pres.), Alpha Kappa Psi, Beta Gamma Sigma. Office Phone: 253-535-7302. E-mail: Kingga@plu.edu.

KING, GWENDOLYN S., retired utility company executive, federal official; b. East Orange, NJ; d. Frank M. and Henryne (Walker) Stewart; m. Colbert I. King. BA cum laude, Howard U., 1962; postgrad., George Washington U.; doctorate (hon.), U. Md., 1990, U. New Haven, 1992. Legis. asst. to Sen. John Heinz, Washington, 1978-79; dir. Commonwealth of Pa. Office, Washington, 1979-86; dep. asst. to the pres. and dir. Office Intergovtl. Affairs, The White House, Washington, 1986-88; exec. v.p. Gogol & Assocs., 1988-89; commr. Social Security Adminstrn., Balt., 1989-92; sr. v.p. corp. and pub. affairs PECO Energy Corp., Phila., 1992-98; pres. Podium Prose, LLC, Washington. Bd. dirs. Lockheed Martin, Marsh & McLennan Cos., Monsanto Corp. Mem. Pres.'s Commn. to Strengthen Social Security, 2001. Recipient Drum Major for Justice award So. Christian Leadership Conf., 1990, Disting. Alumni award Howard U., 1991, Black Achievement Bus. and Fin. award Ebony Mag., 1992. Mem. Nat. Assn. Corp. Dirs. (bd. dirs.). Office: Podium Prose LLC Ste 1012 1025 Connecticut Ave NW Washington DC 20036

KING, HENRY LAWRENCE, lawyer; b. NYC, Apr. 29, 1928; s. H. Abraham and Henrietta (Prentky) King; m. Barbara Hope, 1949 (dec. May 1962); children: Elizabeth King Robertson(dec.) , Patricia King Cantlay-(dec.) , Matthew Harrison; m. Alice Mary Sturges, Aug. 1, 1963 (div. 1978); children: Katherine Masury King Baccile, Andrew Lawrence, Eleanor Sturges; m. Margaret Gram, Feb. 14, 1981. AB, Columbia U., 1948; LLB, Yale U., 1951. Bar: N.Y. 1952, U.S. Supreme Ct., other fed. cts. 1952. With Davis Polk & Wardwell, NYC, 1951—, ptnr., 1961—, mng. ptnr., chmn., 1982-96. Mng. editor Yale Law Jour., 1951. Trustee, chmn. bd. Columbia U., 1983-95, chmn. emeritus, 1995—; chmn. bd. Columbia Presbyn. adv. coun.; pres. Assn. Alumni Columbia Coll., 1966-68, Alumni Fedn. Columbia U., 1973-75; chmn. Coll. Fund, 1972-73; pres. Yale Law Sch. Assn., 1984-86, chmn., 1986-88; pres. Cathedral St. John the Divine, NYC; bd. dir. Population Coun., NY Acad. Medicine, Citizens Com. NYC, Inc., Am. Skin Assn., Fishers Island Devel. Co.; vestryman Trinity Ch., NYC, 1991-98; trustee Chapin Sch., 1977-89, Columbia U. Press, 1978-92. Recipient Columbia Alumni medal for conspicuous svc., 1968, John Jay award, 1992, Nicholas Murray Butler medal, 2005, Servant of Justice award Episcopal Diocese NY, 2007. Fellow Am. Coll. Trial Lawyers; mem. ABA, Coun. Fgn. Rels., Am. Law Inst., NY State Bar Assn. (pres. 1988-89), NYC Bar Assn., Am. Judicature Soc., Fishers Island Club, Century Assn., Union Club NYC, Blind Brook Club, Fishers Island Yacht Club, Pilgrims, Church Club NYC, Links Club. Home: 115 E 67th St New York NY 10021-5951 Office: Davis Polk & Wardwell 450 Lexington Ave 27th Fl New York NY 10017-3982 Office Phone: 212-450-4284. Business E-Mail: hking@dpw.com.

KING, HUESTON CLARK, retired otolaryngologist, educator; b. Bklyn., Feb. 3, 1929; s. William Clark and Alice Packard (Hueston) K.; m. Wilma Marguerite Grove, June 13, 1953; children: Brian G., Melinda K. AB in Biology, Princeton U., 1950; MD, Columbia U., 1954. Diplomate Am. Bd. Otolaryngology; lic. physician, Fla.; cert. Nat. Bd. Med. Examiners. Intern Jackson Meml. Hosp., U. Miami (Fla.) Sch. Medicine, 1954-55; resident in otolaryngology Walter Reed Army Med. Ctr., Washington, 1956-58; staff Coral Gables (Fla.) Hosp., 1962-82, Bapt. Hosp., 1962-82, Mercy Hosp., 1962-82, South Miami Hosp., Fla., 1962-82, Cedars of Lebanon Hosp., 1962-82, Jackson Meml. Hosp., 1962-82; with Venice (Fla.) Hosp., 1983-94. From clin. faculty to assoc. prof. dept. otolaryngology U. Miami Med. Sch., 1962-82; clin. prof. dept. otolaryngology U. Tex. Southwestern Med. Ctr., Dallas, 1998-2006, U. Fla.; lectr. in field. Author: (textbook) An Otolaryngologist's Guide to Allergy, 1991; sr. author: (textbook) A Practical Guide to Management of Nasal and Sinus Disorders, 1993, Allergy in ENT Practice: A Basic Guide, 1998, 2d edit. 2004; editor: Otolaryngologic Allergy, 1981; editor Allergy Digest, food allergy sect. Current Sci., allergy sect. Current Opinion, 1999-01; contbr. chpts. to books, articles to profl. jours. Bd. dirs. Woodmere at Jacaranda, Venice, 1997—99; committeeman Venice Found., 1995—97. Fellow ACS (emeritus), Am. Acad. Facial Plastic and Reconstructive Surgery (emeritus), Am. Acad. Otolaryngic Allergy (past pres. 1979-80, dir. med. edn. 1983-88), Am. Coll. Allergy, Asthma and Immunology; mem. Fla. Med. Assn., Sarasota Cmty. Med. Assn., Venice Yacht Club. Office Phone: 941-488-1739. Personal E-mail: huestoncking@verizon.net.

KING, IMOGENE M., retired nursing educator; b. West Point, Iowa, Jan. 30, 1923; Diploma, St. John's Hosp., 1945; BSN, St. Louis U., 1948, MSN, 1957; EdD, Columbia U., NYC, 1961; PhD (hon.), So. Ill. U., Edwardsville, 1990, Loyola U., Chgo., 1998. Instr. med.-surg. nursing, asst. DON St. John's Hosp., St. Louis, 1947-58; from asst. prof. nursing to assoc. prof. Loyola U., Chgo., 1961-66, prof., dir. grad. program in nursing, 1972-80; prof. U. South Fla., Tampa, 1980-90, dir. rsch., 1982-85, prof. emeritus, 1990—. Asst. chief rsch. grants br. divsn. nursing HEW, Washington, 1966—68; prof., dir. sch. nursing Ohio State U., Columbus, 1968—72; mem. def. adv. com. women svcs. Dept. Def., 1972—75; adj. prof. U. Miami Sch. Nursing, 1986—89; cons. VA Hosp., health care agys. Author: Toward a Theory for Nursing, 1971, transl. to Japanese, 1975, A Theory for Nursing Systems, Concepts, Process, 1981, transl. to Japanese, 1983, transl. to Spanish, 1985, Curriculum and Instruction in Nursing, 1986; mem. editl. bd. Theoria: Jour. Nursing Theorica, 2000—06; contbr. articles to profl. jours., chapters to books. Alderman, chmn. fin. com. Ward 2, Wood Dale, Ill., 1975—79; bd. dirs. operation PAR Inc., Pinellas County, Fla., 1990—92. Recipient Founders award, St. Louis U., 1969, Recognition of Contbns. to Nursing Edn. award, Columbia U. Tchrs. Coll., 1983, Disting. Scholar award, U. So. Fla., 1988—89, award for Outstanding Cmty. Svc., U. Tampa, 1997, Imogene King Rsch. award, 1997, Fla. Gov.'s medal for Contbn. to Nursing and Health Care, 1997, Dirs. award, Fla. League Nursing, 1997, award, Am. Acad. Nursing Living Legend, 2005. Fellow: Am. Acad. Nursing (hon. Living Legends 1994, hon. inducted 1996); mem.: ANA (conv. lectr. 1996, Jessie M. Scott award 1996), Fla. Nurses Found., Fla. Nurses Assn. (life; dir. region 2 1981—83, pres. dist. NC 1982—83, 2d v.p. 1983—85, bd. dirs. 1997—2001, Dist. IV bd. dirs. 2004—06, Nurse of the Yr. 1984, Nursing Rsch. award 1985, Hall of Fame award 2003, Advancing the Nursing Profl. award), Ill. Nurses Assn. (Highest Recognition award 1975, award 19th dist. 1975), Sigma Theta Tau Internat., Phi Kappa Phi (Scholar award 1988), Sigma Theta Tau (counselor Delta Beta chpt. 1983—85, pres-elect 1986—87, pres. 1987—89, disting. lectr. 1990—91, co-chmn. biennial conv. 1991, mem. nominating com. 1993—95, co-editor The Lang. of Nursing Theory and Metatheory 1997, Founders award for Excellence in Nursing Edn. 1989, Virginia Henderson fellow 1993). *Develop a healthy self-concept and know thyself. Practice the Golden Rule. Be honest and sincere in working with individuals and groups. Live each day to the best of your ability.*

KING, IVAN ROBERT, astronomy educator; b. Far Rockaway, NY, June 25, 1927; s. Myram and Anne King; m. Alice Greene, Nov. 21, 1952 (div. 1982); children: David, Lucy, Adam, Jane; m. Judith Schultz, Apr. 20, 2002. AB, Hamilton Coll., 1946; AM, Harvard U., 1947, PhD, 1952; Laurea Honoris Causa (hon.), U. Padua, Italy, 2002; ScD (hon.), Hamilton Coll., 2005. Instr. astronomy Harvard U., 1951—52; mathematician Perkin-Elmer Corp., Norwalk, Conn., 1951—52; methods analyst U.S. Dept. Def., Washington, 1954—56; with U. Ill., 1956—64; assoc. prof. astronomy U. Calif., Berkeley, 1964—66, prof., 1966—93, chmn. astronomy dept., 1967—70, prof. emeritus, 1993—; rsch. prof. U. Wash., Seattle, 2002—. Mem. faint object camera team Hubble Space Telescope. Contbr. numerous articles to sci. jours. Served with USNR, 1952-54. Fellow AAAS (chmn. astronomy sect. 1974), NAS, Am. Acad. Arts & Scis., Am. Astron. Soc. (councillor 1963-66, chmn. divsn. dynamical astronomy 1972-73, pres. 1978-80), Internat. Astron. Union. Achievements include research in structure of stellar systems. Office: U Wash Dept Astronomy Seattle WA 98195-1580

KING, JACK A., lawyer; b. Lafayette, Ind., July 29, 1936; s. Noah C. and Mabel E. (Pierce) K.; m. Mary S. King, Dec. 10, 1960; children: Jeffrey A., Janice D., Julie D. BS in Fin., Ind. U., 1958, JD, 1961. Bar: Ind. 1961. Ptnr. Ball, Eggleston, King & Bumbleburg, Lafayette, 1961-70; judge Superior Ct. 2 of Tippecanoe County, Ind., 1970—78; v.p., assoc. gen. counsel Dairyland Ins. Co., 1978—79, v.p., gen. counsel, asst. sec., 1980—85; asst. gen. counsel Sentry Corp., 1979—85; v.p., gen. counsel, asst. sec. Gt. S.W. Fire Ins. Co., 1980-85; v.p., gen. counsel Dairyland County Mut. Ins. Co. Tex., 1980-85; v.p., counsel Sentry Ctr. West, 1981-85; v.p., gen. counsel, asst. sec. Gt. S.W. Surplus Lines Ins. Co., 1981-85; v.p. legal, asst. sec. Scottsdale Ins. Co., 1985-95; asst. sec. Nat. Casualty Co., 1985-95; v.p. Ariz. Ins. Info. Assn., 1988-96; v.p. legal, asst. sec. Scottsdale Indemnity Co., 1992-95; sr. v.p., gen. coun. TIG Excess & Surplus Lines, Inc., 1995-96; exec. dir. Ariz. Ins. Guaranty Funds, 1998-2001. Cons., mediator and arbitrator, 1996-97, 2001—; exec. com. Ariz. Joint Underwriting Plan, 1980-81; mem. Ariz. Property & Casualty Ins. Commn., 1985-86, vice-chmn., 1986; mem. Ariz. Study Commn. on Ins., 1986-87, Ariz. Task Force on Ct. Orgn. and Adminstrn., 1988-89; adv. com. Ariz. Ho. Rep. Majority Leaders, 1989, Ariz. Dept. Ins. Fraud Unit, 1997-97; mem. Ariz. Dept. Ins. Comml. Lines Ins. Market Task Force, 2002. Contbr. to The Law of Competitive Business Practices, 2d edit. Bd. dirs. Scottsdale Art Ctr. Assn., 1981-84, Midwest Ins. Coalition, 2006-. Mem.: ABA, Ind. Bar Assn.

KING, JACK BURGE, academic librarian; b. Mpls., Sept. 9, 1931; s. Frederick Warren and Iva Burge King; m. Geraldine Elizabeth Beaty, Feb. 15, 1958. BA magna cum laude, U. Minn., 1953, MA in Econ. History, 1957, MLS, 1962. Spl. collections libr. U. Iowa, 1962—64; serials cataloger U. Minn., 1964—65; catalog libr. Hamline U., St. Paul, 1965—66, head tech. svcs., 1966—71, assoc. univ. libr., 1971—73, prof., 1973—96. Adj. prof. Coll. St. Catherine, St. Paul, 1993—2004; co-prin. investigator Nat. Sci. Found., St. Paul, 1968—71, prin. investigator, 1971—73. Contbr. articles to profl. and history jours. Donor U. Iowa Libr. Friends, 2000—, U. Minn. Libraries, 2001—, Hamline U. Libr., 1990—. First lt. US Army, 1954—56. Mem.: ALA, Econ. History Soc., Econ. History Assn. Avocation: writing. Home: 595 Cretin Ave South Saint Paul MN 55116

KING, JAMES C., retired military officer; b. Mar. 18, 1946; BS in Polit. Sci., Utah State U.; MS in Pub. Adminstrn., U. Mo., Kansas City; grad., Command and Gen. Staff Coll., Army War Coll. Commd. 2d lt. U.S. Army, 1968, advanced through grades to lt. gen., 1998, various assignments U.S. and overseas, 1968-88; chief mil. intelligence br. U.S. Total Army Personnel Command, Alexandria, Va., 1988-89; chief intelligence, electronic warfare and reconnaissance Office of Dep. Chief of Staff for Ops. and Plans, Washington, 1989-90; comdr. 66th Mil. Intelligence Brigrade, Europe and Germany, 1990-92; exec. officer to dep. chief of staff for intelligence U.S. Army, Washington, 1992; chief of ops. and targeting group Nat. Security Agy., Ft. Meade, Md., 1993-94; dir. intelligence U.S. Ctrl. Command, MacDill AFB, Fla., 1994-96; dir. for intelligence The Joint. Staff, Washington, 1996—98; dir. Nat. Geospatial-Intelligence Agy. (formerly Nat. Imagery and Mapping Agy.) US Dept. Def., Bethesda, Md., 1998—2001; sr. exec. v.p. for nat. security affairs MZM, Inc., Washington, 2001—05, pres., 2005; pres., CEO Athena Innovative Solutions, Inc. (formerly MZM, Inc.), Washington, 2005—. Office: Athena Innovation Solutions Inc 1523 New Hampshire Ave NW Washington DC 20036

KING, JAMES CALVIN, mathematics educator; s. James Allison King and Mabel Wilma Johnson; m. Marcella L. Duvall; children: Laura René Kendrick, James David. BS in Math., Mid. Tenn. State U., 1963, MST in Natural Sci., 1970; postgrad., U. Louisville, 1972. Cert. secondary tchr. math., biology, sci. Ala., Tenn., Ky. Math. tchr. Jefferson County Pub. Schs., Louisville, 1963—73, Huntsville (Ala.) City Pub. Schs., 1973—97; ret., 1997. Cpl. USMC, 1954—59. Mem.: SAR. Avocations: genealogy, writing. Personal E-mail: king11311@aol.com.

KING, JAMES CECIL, retired language and literature educator, medievalist; b. Uniontown, Pa., Sept. 14, 1924; s. Joseph Herbert and Eliza Ann (Kelley) K.; m. Diana Hanbury, Sept. 5, 1952 (div. Apr. 1958); children—Christopher Hanbury, Sheila Anne. BA, George Washington U., 1949, MA,

1950, PhD, 1954. Master for French, German and Latin St. Albans Sch. for Boys, Washington, 1952-55; asst. prof. German George Washington U., 1955-60, asso. prof., 1960-65, prof., 1965-90, prof. emeritus, 1990—. Rschr. Langs.-of-the-World Archives, 1960-61. Editor (with Petrus W. Tax) of series Die Werke Notkers des Deutschen, 1972—. With US Army, 1943—46. German Acad. Exch. Svc. grantee, 1963. Mem. Linguistic Soc. Am., Medieval Acad. Am., Am. Assn. Tchrs. German, MLA, Am. Goethe Soc., Soc. Germanic Linguistics, AAUP, Phi Beta Kappa. Home: 9296 Bailey Ln Fairfax VA 22031-1930

KING, JAMES EDWARD, retired museum director, consultant; b. Escanaba, Mich., July 23, 1940; s. G. Willard and Grace (Magee) K. BS, Alma Coll., 1962, DSc (hon.), 2002; MS, U. N.Mex., 1964; PhD, U. Ariz., 1972. Lab asst. in biology Alma Coll., Mich., 1960-62; rsch. asst. dept. biology U. N.Mex., Albuquerque, 1962-64; teaching asst. dept. botany and plant pathology Mich. State U., East Lansing, 1964-66; plant industry inspector Mich. Dept. Agriculture, Lansing, 1966-68; rsch. asst. dept. geochronology U. Ariz., Tucson, 1968-71, rsch. assoc. dept. geoscis., 1971-72; assoc. curator paleobotany Ill. State Mus., Springfield, 1972-78, head sci. sects. and full curator, 1978-85, asst. dir. for sci., 1985-87; adj. assoc. prof. dept. geology U. Ill., Urbana, 1979-88; dir. Carnegie Mus. Natural History, Pitts., 1987-96, Cleve. Mus. Natural History, 1996—2001; mus. cons., 2001—. Adj. prof. biology Sangamon State U., Springfield, Ill., 1983-87; adj. rsch. scientist Hunt Inst. Bot. Documentation, Carnegie Mellon U., Pitts., 1988—; adj. prof. dept. geology and planetary sci., U. Pitts., 1988-96; vis. scientist in residence Alma (Mich.) Coll., 1985; mem. adv. bd. dept. geosci. U. Ariz., 2005—. Author sci. papers on topics related to geology and paleobotany; mem. editorial bd. Jour. Archaeol. Sci., 1980-87. Bd. dirs. Western Pa. Conservancy, 1996-97, Allegheny Land Trust, 1995-96; trustee Chagrin River Watershed Ptnrs., 1997-2001; mem. exec. com. Univ. Cir., Inc., 1996-2001. Fellow Ill. State Acad. Sci. (pres. 1981-82); mem. Am. Assn. Mus. (bd. dirs. 1994-97), Am. Quaternary Assn., (treas., exec. com. 1976-84), Am. Assn. Stratigraphic Palynologists, Assn. Sci. Mus. Dirs. (v.p. 1992-93, pres. 1993-96), Assn. Systematics Collections (v.p. 1989-91, pres. 1991-93), Sigma Xi (pres. Springfield chpt. 1985-86). Home and Office: Ste 326 6336 N Oracle Rd Tucson AZ 85704

KING, JAMES LAWRENCE, federal judge; b. Miami, Fla., Dec. 20, 1927; s. James Lawrence and Viola (Clodfelter) K.; m. Mary Frances Kapa, June 1, 1961; children— Lawrence Daniel, Kathryn Ann, Karen Ann, Mary Virginia BA in Edn., U. Fla., Gainesville, 1949, JD, 1953; LHD (hon.), St. Thomas U., Miami, 1992. Bar: Fla. 1953. Assoc. Sibley & Davis, Miami, Fla., 1953-57; ptnr. Sibley Giblin King & Levenson, Miami, 1957-64; judge 11th Jud. Cir. Dade County, Miami, 1964-70; temp. assoc. justice Supreme Ct. Fla., 1965; temp. assoc. judge Fla. Ct. Appeals (2d, 3d and 4th dist.), 1965-68; judge US Dist. Ct. (so. dist.) Fla., Miami, 1970-84, chief judge, 1984-91, sr. judge, 1991—. Temp. judge US Ct. Appeals 5th cir., 1977-78; mem. Jud. Conf. US, 1984-87, mem. adv. commn. jud. activities, 1973-76, mem. joint commn. code jud. conduct, 1974-76, mem. commn. to consider stds. for admission to practice in fed. cts., 1976-79, chmn. implementation com. for admission attys. to fed. practice, 1979-85, mem. com. bankruptcy legis., 1977-78; mem. Jud. Conf. US, 1984-87; mem. Jud. Coun. 11th Cir., 1989-92; pres. 5th cir. U.S. Dist. Judges Assn., 1977-78; chief judge US Dist. Ct. C.Z., 1977-78; long range planning commn. Fed. Judiciary, 1991-95. Mem. state exec. council U. Fla., 1956-59; mem. Bd. Control Fla. Governing State Univs. and Colls., 1964. Served to 1st lt. USAF, 1953-55 Recipient Outstanding Alumnus award U. Fla. Law Rev., 1980, Lifetime Achievement award Greater Miami Jewish Fedn. Commerce and Professions Attys. Divsn., 1992, 18th Annual Edward J. Devitt Disting. Svc. to Justice award, 2000; The James Lawrence King Fed. Justice Bldg. named in his honor U.S. Congress, 1996. Mem. Fla. Bar Assn. (pres. jr. bar 1963-64, bd. govs. 1958-63, Merit award young lawyer sect. 1967), ABA, Am. Law Inst., Inst. Jud. Adminstrn., Fla. Blue Key, Pi Kappa Tau, Phi Delta Phi Democrat. Office: US Dist Ct James Lawrence King Fed Justice Bldg 99 NE 4th St Rm 1127 Miami FL 33132-2139 Office Phone: 305-523-5000.

KING, JAMES M., lawyer; b. Denver, July 17, 1948; BSEE with spl. honors, Univ. Colo., 1970, JD, 1976. Bar: Colo. 1976, U.S. Ct. Appeals tenth cir. 1979, U.S. Ct. Appeals ninth cir. 1984. Law clk. Colo. Ct. Appeals, 1976—77; ptnr. Baker & Hostetler, Denver, 1977—. Pres. Rocky Mountain Mineral Law Found., 2004—05. Mem.: ABA, Colo. Bar Assn., Tau Beta Pi, Order of the Coif. Office: Baker & Hostetler Suite 1100 303 E 17 Ave Denver CO 80203-1264 Office Phone: 303-861-0600. Business E-Mail: jking@bakerlaw.com.

KING, JANE CONNELL, mathematics professor; b. Shelbyville, Ky., May 3, 1939; d. Charles Edward Connell and Bobbye Jane Williams; m. Jerry Porter King, Sept. 5, 1962; children: Elizabeth Robinson, David Williams. BA, U. Ky., 1961, MS, 1962. Tchr. math. Moravian Prep. Sch., Bethlehem, Pa., 1967—69; asst. prof. math. Cedar Crest Coll., Allentown, Pa., 1969—80, dir. internship program, 1974—80; vis. lectr. math. Lehigh U., Bethlehem, 1981—86, supr. math. tutoring ctr., adj. prof., 1996—. Referee Two Yr. Coll. Math. Reader, 1978; vis. instr. math. Lafayette Coll., Easton, Pa., 1988—89; vis. asst. prof. Moravian Coll., Bethlehem, 1989—90. Bd. dirs., violinist Lehigh Valley Chamber Orch., Bethlehem, 1982—88, Pa. Sinfonia Orch., Allentown, 1993—97. Mem.: Am. Fedn. Musicians, Math. Assn. Am., Lehigh U. Women's Club (treas., v.p., pres. 1981—87). Conservative. Roman Catholic. Avocations: violin, jogging. Home: 1351 Gaspar Ave Bethlehem PA 18017 Office: Lehigh U 35 Sayre Dr Bethlehem PA 18015 Home Phone: 610-865-4937. Business E-Mail: janeking@lehigh.edu.

KING, JANE CUDLIP COBLENTZ, volunteer educator; b. Iron Mountain, Mich., May 4, 1922; d. William Stacey and Mary Elva (Martin) Cudlip; m. George Samuel Coblentz, June 8, 1942 (dec. June 1989); children: Bruce Harper, Keith George, Nancy Allison Coblentz Patch; m. James E. King, August 23, 1991 (dec. Jan. 1994). BA, Mills Coll., 1942. Mem. Sch. Resource and Career Guidance Vols., Inc., Atherton, Calif., 1965-69, pres., CEO, 1969—. Exec. asst. to dean of admissions Mills Coll., 1994-99. Proofreader, contbr. Mills Coll. Quarterly mag. Life gov. Royal Children's Hosp., Melbourne, Australia, 1963—; pres. United Menlo Park (Calif.) Homeowners Assn., 1994—; nat. pres. Mills Coll. Alumnae Assn., 1969-73, trustee, 1975-83; bd. govs. Mills Coll. Alumnae Assn., 1966-73, 75-83, 98-2006, life bd. govs., 2006—, v.p., 2001-06. Named Vol. of Yr., Sequoia Union H.S. Dist., 1988, Disting. Woman Mid-Peninsula (forerunner San Mateo County Women's Hall of Fame), 1975; recipient Golden Acorn award for Outstanding Cmty. Svc., Menlo Park C. of C., 1991. Mem. AAUW (Menlo-Atherton br. pres. 1994-96, v.p. programs 1996-97, editor Directory and Acorn, 1994—), Atherlons, Palo Alto (Calif.) Area Mills Coll. Club (pres. 1986), Phi Beta Kappa. Episcopalian. Avocations: reading, gardening.

KING, JEFF, dog musher; b. Calif., Feb. 6, 1956; m. Donna Gates King; children: Cali, Tessa, Ellen. Winner Yukon Quest, 1989, Kusko 300, 1991, 92, 93; plumber, contractor, kennel operator; 28th pl. finisher Iditarod, 1981, 12th pl. finisher, 1991, 6th pl. finisher, 1992, 1st pl. finisher, 1993, 1996, 1998, 2006. Oper., Goose Lake Kennel, Husky Homestead Tours Chief McKinley Vol. Fire Dept. Recipient 1st to Yukon award, 1991, 93, Halfway award, 1993, Fastest Time Safety to Nome, 1993, Golden Harness Lead Dogs Herbie & Kitty, 1993, Humanitarian award Alaska Airlines, Leonhard Seppala Humanitarian Award, 2003. Achievements include oldest musher to win the world's longest sled dog race at age 50, 2006.

KING, JEFFREY J., lawyer; Dir. taxation & legal services Expeditors Internat. of Wash., 1990—92, v.p., gen. counsel, 1992—94, v.p., gen. counsel, sec., 1994—98, sr. v.p., gen. counsel, sec., 1998—. Office: Expeditors Internat of Wash 1015 Third Ave Seattle WA 98104 Office Phone: 206-674-3400.

KING, JERRY WAYNE, chemist, researcher, engineer; b. Indpls., Feb. 19, 1942; s. Ernest E. and Miriam (Sanders) King; m. Bettie Maria Dunbar, Aug. 8, 1965; children: Ronald Sean, Valerie Raquel, Diana Lynn. BS, Butler U., Indpls., 1965; MS, Butler U., 1969; PhD, Northeastern U., Evanston, Ill., 1976. Rsch. chemist Union Carbide Corp., Bound Brook, NJ, 1968-70; postdoctoral fellow Georgetown U., 1973—74; asst. prof. dept. chemistry Va. Commonwealth U., Richmond, 1974-76; rsch. scientist Arthur D. Little, Inc., Cambridge, Mass., 1976-77; rsch. assoc. Am. Can Co., Barrington, Ill., 1977-79; rsch. scientist CPC Internat., Summit-Argo, Ill., 1979-86; lead scientist NCAUR-ARS divsn. USDA, Peoria, Ill., 1986—2002; program mgr. chem. divsn. Los Alamos Lab., 2002—05; Ansel and Virginia Condray prof. chem. engring. U. Ark., Fayetteville, 2005—. Guest lectr. in field; v.p. Supercritical Confs.; adj. prof. dept. food sci. U. Ark., 2004. Mem. editl. bd. Italian Jour. Food Sci., Jour. Supercritical Fluids, Supercritical Fluid Sci. and Tech. Series; contbr. articles to profl. jours. Recipient Scientist of Yr. award Nat. Ctr. Agrl. Utilization Rsch., Agrl. Rsch. Svc., USDA, 1993, Chgo. Chromatography Discussion Group Merit award, 1995, 8th Internat. Symposium on Supercritical Fluid Chromatography and Extraction excellence award, 1998, Merit award Midwest & Tri-State Supercritical Fluid Discussion Group, 1998, Rsch. award for supercritical fluids commercialization Thar Designs, 1998, Underwood Fund award Biotech. and Biol. Scis. Rsch. Coun., U.K., 1998, 1st Pl. award for consumer products Fed. Lab. Consortium for Tech. Transfer-Midwest Area, 2001, honorable mention award for health and medicine, 2001; named v.p. Supercritical Confs. Mem. AIChE, Assn. Ofcl. Analytical Chemists (Harvey W. Wiley award 1997, Keene P. Dimick award Pitts. conf. 2000), Inst. Food Technologists, Am. Oil Chemists Soc. (Herbert J. Dutton award 2003), Am. Chem. Soc., Assn. Advancement of Indsl. Crops, Acad. Georgofili (Italy, corr.), Internat. Soc. for Advancement of Supercritical Fluids. Office: U Ark Dept Chem Engring 3202 Bell Engineering Ctr Fayetteville AR 72701 Office Phone: 479-575-5979. Personal E-mail: kingjw100@hotmail.com. Business E-Mail: jwking1@uark.edu.

KING, JOAN CALUDA, medical educator, neuroscientist; b. New Orleans, Mar. 6, 1938; BS, St. Mary's Dominican Coll., 1961; MS, U. New Orleans, 1970; PhD, Tulane U., 1973. Rsch. assoc. in neuroanatomy U. Iowa Coll. Medicine, Iowa City, 1973-74; NIH postdoctoral fellow (neurosci.) Tulane U., New Orleans, 1974-76, rsch. assoc., vis. asst. prof. neurosci., 1976-79; asst. prof. anatomy Tufts U. Sch. Medicine, Boston, 1979-85, assoc. prof. anatomy and cellular biology, 1985-92, prof., chmn. anatomy and cellular biology, 1992-97, dir. reproductive ctr., 1992-97, prof. emeritus, 1997—. Mem. many nat. rev. coms., NSF, NIH, NICHD, 1979—. Co-author: Exploring the Basic Structures of the Brain, 1991, A Responsive Learning Environment for Medical Neurosciences: Sensory and Motor Pathways in the Spinal Cord, 1991; contbr. articles to profl. jours., chpts. to books; presenter in field; invited participant in numerous rsch. seminars and symposia; editl. bd. Biotechniques; ad hoc reviewer Science, Nature, Biology of Reproduction, Brain Rsch., Brain Rsch. Bull., Endocrinology, Jour. Histochemistry Cytochemistry, Jour. Neurosci., Neuroendocrinology, Neurosci., Peptides. Recipient Career Devel. award USPHS, 1979-84. Mem. Am. Assn. Anatomists, Internat. Soc. Psychoneuroendocrinology, Soc. Neurosci., Endocrine Soc. (animal welfare subcom. 1989), Kappa Delta Pi. Office: 14640 Swanson Ranch Rd Loveland CO 80538-9144

KING, JOHN CHARLES PETER, editor, writer; b. Vancouver, BC, Can., Dec. 13, 1949; s. Charles and Pauline K.; m. Jennifer; children: Sheila, James. BA, York U., 1973. Mem. staff The Globe and Mail Ltd., Toronto, 1970—2004, night city editor, 1973-75; bur. chief Ottawa, Can., 1975-78; nat. editor Toronto, 1978-81; bur. chief Washington, 1981-84; assoc. editor Report on Bus., Toronto, 1984-87, exec. editor, 1987-93; from dep. mng. editor to dir. editl. tech. Globe and Mail, Toronto, 1993—2004; asst. fin. editor Toronto Star, 2005—. Dir. Can. Mng. Editors Conf., 1997-98, v.p., 1998-99. Akela 65th Toronto Wolf Cub Pack, 2002—04; skipper 65th Toronto Sea Scouts, 2004—. Spanish lang. fellow Nat. Press Found., 1987; Thomson scholar, 1987. Mem. Can. Assn. Newspapers Editors (pres. 1999-2000), Toronto Press Club.

KING, JOHN ETHELBERT, JR., retired academic administrator; b. Oklahoma City, r, July 29, 1913; s. John Ethelbert and Iosa (Koontz) K.; m. Glennie Beanland, Dec. 25, 1936; children: Wynetka Ann King Reynolds, Rebecca Ferriss King Stevens. BA, N. Tex. U., 1932; MS, U. Ark., 1937; PhD, Cornell U., 1941; LLD (hon.), Coll. of Ozarks, 1965; LHD (hon.), No. Mich. U., 1966, U. SC, 1988. Latin tchr., coach Frisco Pub. HS, Tex., 1933-35; missionary to Native Ams. Presbyn. Ch. U.S.A., Okla., 1938-43, Ariz., 1938—43; asst. prof. NY State Coll. Agr., Cornell U., Ithaca, 1945-47; acad. dean, provost, prof. U. Minn., Duluth, 1947-53; pres., prof. Emporia U., Kans., 1953-66; prof., pres. U. Wyo., Laramie, 1966-67; prof., chmn. dept. So. Ill. U., Carbondale, 1967-83; Disting. vis. prof., interim dean U. SC, Columbia, 1984-90; ret., 1990. Ednl. adviser Civilian Conservation Corps, US Forest Svc., Ozone, Ark., 1935-37; mentor Assn. Governing Bds. Univs. and Coll., Washington, 1977-90. Editor: Work and the College Student, 1967, Money, Marbles and Chalk, 1978. Life trustee U. Ozarks, Clarksville, Ark., 1965—. Officer USN, 1943-45, PTO. Recipient Disting. Alumnus award N. Tex. U., Denton, 1965, U. Ark., Fayetteville, 1983. Mem. NEA (life), Am. Assn. Colls. Tchr. Edn. (pres. 1966-67), Rotary, Blue Key, Omicron Delta Kappa, Lambda Chi Alpha, Sphinx Club, Phi Delta Kappa. Avocations: history, Native American Studies. Personal E-mail: texasglennie@aol.com.

KING, JOHN JOSEPH, manufacturing company executive; b. Toledo, Jan. 12, 1924; s. Walter and Frances (Gwozd) Kawecka; m. Joy G. Mohler, Jan. 28, 1950; children: Catherine M., Carolyn S., David J., Michael R., Mark A.R. BSME magna cum laude, U. Toledo, 1957, MS in Indsl. Engring., 1961. Registered profl. engr., Ohio. Draftsman, Tecumseh Products Co., 1941-42; die designer Bingham Stamping Co., 1942-46; tool designer Spicer Mfg. Co., 1946-47; product designer Am. Floor Surfacing Co., 1947-50; founder, mgr. engr. Kent Industries, 1950-52; mech. engr. Owens Ill. Inc., Toledo, 1953-63; mgr. rsch. and devel. Permaglass Inc., Genoa, Ohio, 1963-69; founder, pres. Ashur Inc., Rossford, Ohio, 1969—, also chmn. bd. dirs. Patentee in field. Mem. Am. Ceramic Soc., Soc. Mfg. Engrs., Phi Kappa Phi, Tau Beta Pi. Republican. Roman Catholic. Clubs: Devils Lake Yacht. Lodges: KC, Eagles. Home: 1111 W Elm Tree Rd Rossford OH 43460-1338 Office: Ashur Inc 28663 Glenwood Rd Perrysburg OH 43551-3011

KING, JOSEPH, JR., federal agency administrator; b. Charleston, W.Va., June 8, 1950; s. Joseph and Jessie Ree (May) K.; m. Linda Streeter, Sept. 4, 1986. BA, Ohio State U., 1972; MS, Xavier U., 1975; EdD, U. Cin., 1982; diploma, U.S. Army War Coll., 1999. Investigator US EEOC, Cin., 1976-79, tng. officer Washington, 1979-82; EEO advisor US Army, Washington, 1982-84, EEO officer Giessen, Germany, 1984-86, Nurenburg, Germany, 1986-89, dir. EEO St. Louis, 1989-99. CEO King Group, St. Louis, 1989—, command exec. officer, 1999-2006, chief human capital officer, 2006-; prof. Boston U., 1984-89, Webster U., 1989—; expert witness US Fed. Dist. Ct., 1996; cons. in field. Author: Discretionary Equality, 1982, Strategic Leadership, 1999. Unit commr. Boy Scouts Am., St. Louis, 1990; congrl. intern. Congrl. Black Caucus, Washington, 1980. Sgt. USAF, 1979-82. Mem.: ASTD, Human Capital Inst., Soc. for Profls. in Dispute Resolution, Soc. Human Resource Mgmt., Am. Mgmt. Assn., World Future Soc. Independent. Avocations: jogging, exercise, martial arts. Home: 4520 Chouteau Ave Saint Louis MO 63110-1518 Office Phone: 973-724-9739. Business E-Mail: joseph.king@usarmy.mil.

KING, JOSEPH BERTRAM, architect; b. Greenville, SC, Sept. 14, 1924; s. Joseph A. and Bertram (Kerns) K.; m. Julia Nelson Hipps, Aug. 2, 1945; children: Allen, David, Thomas. Student, Memphis State Coll., 1943; B in Arch. Engring., N.C. State U., 1949. Prin. J. Bertram King, Asheville, N.C., 1952-94. Chmn. Planning and Zoning Commn., Asheville, 1966—; vice chmn. Met. Planning Bd., 1966-74 Prin. works include Humanities, Social Sci., Art and Mgmt. bldgs., residence hall, student center, U. N.C.-Asheville, occupational edn. bldg, Asheville High Sch., Bank of Asheville, Madison County High Sch, City-County Central Library Bldg, Reynolds High Sch, Sealtest Dairies. Bd. dirs. United Fund; Bd. dirs. N.C. Design Found., mem., 1983-87. Served as pilot USAAF, 1942-45, ETO. Decorated Air medal with 2 oak leaf clusters.; Recipient various archtl. honor awards. Fellow A.I.A. (pres. N.C. chpt. 1973); mem. N.C. Bd. Architecture (past pres.), Asheville C. of C. (past pres. 1972), Tau Beta Pi, Sigma Pi Alpha, Phi Kappa Phi. Home: 222 Country Club Rd Asheville NC 28804-2608

KING, JOSEPH WILLET, child psychiatrist; b. Springfield, Mo., Aug. 26, 1934; m. Doris Ann Toby; children: Pamela Renee, Timothy Wells, Michael Brian, Bradley Christopher. BA, So. Meth. U., Dallas, 1956; MD, U. Tex. Southwestern, Dallas, 1962. Diplomate Am. Bd. Psychiatry and Neurology; ordained vocat. deacon Episcopal Ch., 1996. Intern Baylor U. Med. Ctr., Dallas, 1962-63; clin. instr., asst. clin. prof. U. Tex. Southwestern Med. Sch., Dallas, 1962—78; fellow in child psychiatry Parkland Meml. Hosp. Programs, 1962—67; resident in gen. psychiatry Timberlawn Psychiat. Hosp., 1963-64, Lisbon VA Hosp., 1965; fellow in child psychiatry Hillside Hosp., Glen Oaks, NY, 1967; staff child psychiatrist, dir. child and adolescent svcs. Timberlawn Psychiat. Ctr., Inc., Dallas, 1967-78; assoc. attending child psychiatrist dept. psychiatry Baylor U. Med. Ctr., Dallas, 1967-78; active attending child psychiatrist Children's Med. Ctr., Dallas, 1967-78; attenting staff Dallas County Hosp. Dist./Parkland Meml. Hosp., 1967-78; cons. child psychiatry Girls Day Care Rehab. Ctr. Dallas County, Dallas, 1970-73; cons. child psychiatry and adminstrn. Meridell Achievement Ctr., Austin, Tex., 1971-73; dir. adolescent svcs. Portsmouth Psychiat. Ctr., Va., 1978-79; active attending child psychiatrist Maryview Hosp., Portsmouth, 1978-80; med. dir., chief exec. officer Psychiat. Inst. Richmond, Va., 1980-86; chief exec. officer, psychiatrist-in-chief Shadow Mountain Inst., Tulsa, 1987-90; v.p. Century Healthcare, Tulsa, 1987-90; med. dir. adolescent svcs. Commanche County Meml. Pavilion, Lawton, Okla., 1997-98; pres., CEO, med. dir. Desert Hills Ctr. for Youth and Families, Tucson, 1998-99; staff psychiatrist Sierra Tucson, Tucson, 1999—2004, Cottonwood de Tucson, Tucson, 2003—. Assoc. clin. prof. Med. Coll. Va., Va. Commonwealth U., 1980-90, Med. Sch. U. Okla., Tulsa, 1987-96; clin. prof. U. Okla., Oklahoma City, 1996-1998. Contbr. articles to profl. jours. Canonical resident Diocese of Ariz.; asst. chaplain Ret. Episcopal Clergy, Diocese of Ariz. Fellow: Am. Othropsychiat. Assn., Am. Psychiat. Assn. (disting. life, Ariz. dist. br.), Am. Coll. Psychiatrists (life; emeritus), Am. Soc. Adolescent Psychiatry (life; nat. pres. 1975—76); mem.: AMA, Tucson Psychiat. Soc. (treas.), Ariz. Psychiat. Assn., Tulsa Psychiat. Assn. (bd. dir.), Tulsa County Med. Soc., Okla. Med. Soc., Nat. Assn. Pvt. Psychiat. Hosps. (chmn. adolescent care com. 1971—81, pres. ind. for profit sect. 1991—92, trustee 1992—95, multiple com./task force functions), Am. Acad. Child and Adolescent Psychiatry (ins. com. 1981—86, pres. Okla. coun. 1991—92, state del. to nat. coun.), Dallas County Med. Soc. (various coms.), Alumni Assn. U. Tex. SW Med. Sch. (pres. 1982—85), Blue Key (elected mem.), Beta Theta Pi (pres. Gamma Omega chpt.). Office: Cottonwood de Tucson 4110 West Sweetwater Dr Tucson AZ 85745 Office Phone: 520-572-1343. Office Fax: 520-573-2186. Personal E-mail: jdking@aol.com.

KING, JOY RIEMER, art educator, linguist; d. Bjarne Viggo and Thora Yrsa Xenia (Riemer) Ferdinandsen; m. Charles Banks King, Jr. IV, July 4, 1992; stepchildren: Captain Charles Pat, Dorothy Marie 1 child, Nanette Joy Xenia Riemer. Diploma, Sorbonne, 1959; BA, Principia Coll., 1961; MA, Columbia U., 1968; art specialist diploma, Fla. Internat. U., 1999. Cert. tchr. Ill., 1961, Fla., 1972. Tchrs. aide Columbia U. Team, Kabul, Afghanistan, 1961—62; tchr., curriculum coord. Parents' Coop. Sch., Jeddah, Saudi Arabia, 1967—68; prin., tchr. Latin, French, civics, arts So. Acad., Miami, 1972—77; instr. art Internat. Fine Arts Coll., Miami, 1977—78; instr. French & English Internat. Sch. Langs., Miami Shores, 1978—79; mgr./artist Frances W. Cary Antiques, 1983—89; instr. French & Danish Inlingua, Coral Gables, 1989—90; tchr., art, French, U.S. history Dade County Pub. Schools, 1990—2002; art therapist St. Mary Cathedral Sch., 2002—. Dir. Paul Abrams Found., Miami, Fla., 1998—2001, So. Acad., 1972—77. Exhibitions include Jackie Hinckey Sipes Gallery, Dublin-Kitzen Fine Arts Gallery, Coral Gables, Fairchild Tropical Garden, Bok Tower Gardens, S.E. Pastel Soc., Salmagundi Club, N.Y.C., Hispanic C.C., Miami, Paula Insel Gallery, N.Y., Stern's Gallery, Roselyn Gallery, N.C., Art Works Gallery, Miami, Nat. Art Edn. Assn. Elec. Gallery, Washington; contbr. articles to profl. jours. Pub. rels. dir. Civitan, North Miami, 2000—01. Named in U.S. Congl. Record for art edn. program with at risk students, U.S. Congress, 1992; recipient Marge Pearlson award, Dade Coalition Cmty. Edn., 1997, award of Excellence, Goya Foods, Fla., 1996, cert. of Appreciation, Metro-Dade Police Dept, Northside Sta., 1996. Mem.: ASPCA, Southeastern Pastel Soc., Fla. Watercolor Soc., Nat. Art Edn. Assn., French Teachers Am., Alliance Francaise, Fla. Art Edn. Assn., Nat. Assn. Women Artists, Dade Art Educators Assn., The Nature Conservancy, Friends the Everglades, Nat. Wildlife Fedn., Smithsonian Instn., St. Joseph's Indian Sch., North Shore Animal League, Farm Sanctuary, World Vision, Friends Bok Tower, Internat. Fund for Animal Welfare, Navy League, Nat. Gardening Club (life). Avocations: reading, swimming, painting, sculpting, writing. Office Phone: 305-799-2610. Personal E-mail: joyscapes@bellsouth.net.

KING, KENTON J., lawyer; b. Aberdeen, Md., 1954; BA, Stanford Univ., 1977; JD, Univ. Calif., Berkeley, 1987. Bar: Calif. 1987. Law clerk to the Hon. Kenneth W. Starr, US Ct. of Appeals (DC cir.), 1987—88; ptnr. Skadden, Arps, Slate, Meagher & Flom LLP. Editor-in-chief Calif. Law Rev., 1986—87; contbr. articles to profl. journals. Named one of The World's Leading Lawyers, Chambers Global, 2002—03, America's Leading Business Lawyers, Chambers U.S.A., 2003—05. Mem.: Calif. Law Rev. Inc. (pres. 1996—98), Boalt Hall Alumni Assn. (bd. dir.), Order of Coif. Office: Skadden Arps Slate Ste 1100 525 University Ave Palo Alto CA 94301 Office Phone: 650-470-4530. Office Fax: 888-329-2950. Business E-Mail: kking@skadden.com.

KING, K(IMBERLY) N(ELSON), computer science educator; b. Apr. 28, 1953; s. Paul Ellsworth and Marcelia Jeannette King; m. Cynthia Ann Stormes, Sept. 5, 1981 (div. Nov. 1991); m. Susan Ann Cole, Aug. 9, 1996. BS with highest honors, Case Western Res. U., 1975; MS, Yale U., 1976; PhD, U. Calif., Berkeley, 1980. Asst. prof. info. and computer sci. Ga. Inst. Tech., Atlanta, 1980-86, rsch. scientist, 1986-87; assoc. prof. computer sci. Ga. State U., Atlanta, 1987—. Cons. Norfolk So. Rwy., 1991. Author: Modula-2: A Complete Guide, 1988, C Programming: A Modern Approach, 1996, Java Programming: From The Beginning, 2000; columnist Jour. Pascal, Ada, and Modula-2, 1989-90; contbr. articles to profl. jours. Vol. Ga. Radio Reading Svc., Atlanta, 1989—. Grad. fellow NSF, 1975-78; NSF grantee, 1981-84. Mem. AAUP, IEEE Computer Soc., Assn. for Computing Machinery (chmn. program com. 36th annual southeast conf. 1998), Tau Beta Pi. Office: Ga State U Computer Sci Atlanta GA 30303 Office Phone: 404-413-5727. Business E-Mail: knking@gsu.edu.

KING, LARRY (LARRY ZEIGER), broadcaster, radio personality; b. Bklyn., Nov. 19, 1933; s. Eddie and Jennie Zeiger; m. Alene Akins, 1961 (div. 1963), Mickey Sutphin, 1964 (div. 1966), remarried Alene Akins, 1967 (div. 1971); 1 child, Chaia; m. Sharon Lepore, 1976 (div. 1982); m. Julia Alexander, Oct. 7, 1989 (div. 1992); 1 child, Andy; m. Shawn Southwick, Sept. 5, 1997; 1 child, Chance Armstrong. Disc jockey various radio stas., Miami, Fla., 1957-71; freelance writer, broadcaster, 1972-75; radio personality Sta. WIOD, Miami, 1975-78; writer entertainment sects. Miami Herald, 7 yrs.; radio talk show host The Larry King Show, 1978—; host Larry King Live CNN, 1985—. Columnist USA Today, 1982—2001; host Goodwill Games, 1990. Appeared in films Ghostbusters, 1984, Lost in America, 1985; voice of Ugly Stepsister, Shreck 2, 2004; author: Larry King, Tell It To The King, (with B. D. Colen) Mr. King, You're Having a Heart Attack, 1989, Larry King: Tell Me More, When You're From Brooklyn, Everything Else Is Toyko, 1992, (with Mark Stencel) On the Line: The New Road to the White House, 1993. Chmn. Larry King Cardiac Found.; hon. trustee Am. Women in Radio and TV Com.; mem. Washington Ctr. for Politics and Journalism, The Read-Am. Adv. Bd., Hart Assist Found. Bd. Recipient Radio award Nat. Assn. Broadcasters, 1985, Jack Anderson Investigative Reporting award, 1985, Peabody award for Larry King Show U. Ga. Sch. Journalism, 1987, award for Larry King Live shows Awards for Cablecasting, 1987, 88, 89, also for excellence in cable TV, 1990, Marconi award Nat. Assn. Broadcasters, 1990, Allen H. Neuharth Award for Excellence in Journalism, Gracie Allen Award, Found. Am. Women in Radio and Television, 2003; named Best Radio Talk Show Host Washington Jour. Rev., 1986, Broadcaster of Yr. Internat. Radio and TV Soc., 1989; named to Emerson Hall of Fame, Broadcasters Hall of Fame, 1992, Man Of Yr. Am. Heart Assn., 1992. Mem. Friars Club. Office: CNN Larry King Live 820 1st St NE Washington DC 20002-4243

KING, LARRY L., playwright, actor; b. Putnam, Tex., Jan. 1, 1929; s. Clyde Clayton and Cora Lee (Clark) K.; m. Jeanne Casey, Nov. 25, 1950 (div. Nov. 1964); children: Alexandria, Kerri Lee, Bradley Clayton; m. Rosemarie Courmaris, Feb. 20, 1965 (dec.); m. Barbara Sue Blaine, May 6, 1978; children: Lindsay Allison, Blaine Carlton. Student, Tex. Tech U., 1949-50. Oil field worker El Paso Natural Gas Co., Jal, N.Mex. and Midland, Tex., 1943-45; reporter Hobbs (N.Mex.) Daily Flare, 1949, Midland Reporter-Telegram, 1950-52, Odessa (Tex.) Am., 1952-54; adminstrv. asst. U.S. Congress, Washington, 1954-64; freelance writer Washington, 1964—; pres. Texhouse Corp., Washington, 1979—. Ferris prof. journalism and polit. sci. Princeton (N.J.) U., 1973-75; Disting. Lyndon B. Johnson lectr. Southwest Tex. State University, 1991. Author: (books) The One-Eyed Man, 1966,. And Other Dirty Stories, 1968, Confessions of a White Racist, 1971, The Old Man and Lesser Mortals, 1974, Wheeling and Dealing, 1978, Of Outlaws, Con Men, Whores, Politicians and Other Artists, 1980, The Whorehouse Papers, 1981, That Terrible Night Santa Got Lost in the Woods, 1981, None But a Blockhead: On Being a Writer, 1986, Warning: Writer At Work, 1986, Because of Lozo Brown, 1988, True Facts, Tall Tales, and Pure Fiction, 1997, Reflections In A Bloodshot Eye: A Writer's Life in Letters, 1999, In Search of Willie Morris, 2006, (plays) The Best Little Whorehouse in Texas, 1978, The Kingfish, 1979, The Night Hank Williams Died, 1986, The Golden Shadows Old West Museum, 1987, Christmas: 1933, 1987, The Best Little Whorehouse Goes Public, 1994, The Dead Presidents' Club, 1995; also numerous articles; starred in: The Best Little Whorehouse in Texas (on Broadway), 1979, The Night Hank Williams Died (off-Broadway), 1989; contbg. editor Harper's, 1967-71, New Times, 1974-77, Tex. Monthly, 1973-78, Tex. Observer, 1964-74. Sgt. AUS, 1946-49. Recipient Stanley Walker Journalism award Tex. Inst. of Letters, 1972, Tony award League of N.Y. Theatres and Producers, 1978-79, Mary Goldwater award Theatre Lobby, 1988, Helen Hayes award, 1989; elected to Tex. Walk of Stars, 1988, Best Non-Fiction Article of Yr. award Tex. Inst. of Letters 2002, Bookends award Tex. Book Festival, 2004; Nieman fellow Harvard U., 1969-70, Duke U. fellow, 1975-76; Second Stage at Austin Playhouse Theatre named in his honor, 2006. Mem. Authors Guild, PEN, Writers Guild Am. East, Actors Equity Assn., Nat. Acad. TV Arts and Scis. (Emmy award 1981), Nat. Writers Union, Screenwriters Guild East, Dramatists Guild, Sandhills Club (Monahans, Tex.), Pelican Club (Odessa), Mystic Knights of the Sea. Democrat. Avocations: breeding show dogs, singing opera, ballet dancing. Personal E-mail: famousarthur@excite.com. *I have always avoided strong drink and evil companions.*

KING, LAURA JANE, librarian, genealogist; b. Pemberville, Ohio, Jan. 19, 1947; d. Richard D. and Jessie Florence (Brown) Zepernick; m. Bruce William King, June 17, 1972; 1 child, Christian Andrew. BA, Bowling Green State U., Ohio, 1969, MEd, 1976; MLS, Kent State U., 1995. Cert. pub. libr. Cert. geneal. lectr. County ext. agt. home econs. Ohio Coop. Ext. Svcs., Paulding County, 1970-77; asst. dir., historian Pemberville (Ohio) Pub. Libr.; asst. dir., br. coord. Pemberville Pub. Libr.; mem. PRIDE com., vocat. home econs. dept. Paulding Exempted Village, 1975—. Instr. genealogy Continuing Edn. Bowling Green State U., Eastwood Sch. Dist. Cmy. Edn. Mem. Paulding County Bicentennial Commn., 1975—77; state chmn. Friends of Libr., 1992—95; advisor 4-H; mem. Wood County Citizens Com. fo Bicentennial of U.S. Constn. and N.W. Ordinance; chmn. Pemberville com. Ohio Bicentennial; mem. Wood County Literacy Bd., Pemberville Sch. Adv. Com.; past pres. Eastwood Local Schs. Band Boosters; corr. docent DAR Mus., Washington; organist First Presbyn. Ch., Pemberville, ch. historian; trustee Pemberville-Freedom Area Hist. Soc. Recipient Tenure award, Coop. Ext. Svc., 1975, Oustanding Svc. award, 4-H, 1999. Mem.: SAR (medal of appreciation), DAR (vice regent chpt. 1975—77, state vice chmn. pages 1978—80, regent chpt. 1979—83, state and divsn. outstanding jr. mem. 1980, state chmn. lineage rsch. 1980—87, state chmn. membership commn. 1983—87, registrar chpt. 1985—, state rec. sec. 1987—89, state corr. sec. 1989—92, area spkr.'s staff, state chmn. Friends of the Libr. 1992—95, chpt. libr. 1998—), ALA, Coun. Ohio Genealogists (v.p. 1992), Ohio Libr. Assn., Berks County Geneal. Soc., Ohio Geneal. Soc. (pres. Wood County chpt. 1978—80, chmn. pub. rels. com. 1982—83, state program chmn. ann. conf. 1991, state chmn. History Writing Contest 1993, state program chmn. ann. conf. 1995, trustee 1995—, chmn. First Families of Wood County com.), Libr. Adminstrn. and Mgmt. Assn., Flag of the U.S. of Am. (sr. state registrar 1994—, sr. state chmn. govt. studies 1998—, sr. state organizing sec. 2000—, sr. state chmn.), Mary Sherman Hayes Soc. (past sr. v.p.), Bus. and Profl. Women's Club (v.p. 1974—75, pres. Paulding 1975—76), Order Ea. Star, Colonial Order Crown of Charlemagne, Daus. Am. Colonists (chpt. regent 1986—, state chmn. pub. rels. 1987, chmn. mideast region pub. rels.), Colonial Dames 17th Century (grave marker state chair 2006—07), Nat. Soc. Magna Charta Dames, Daus. Union Vets., First Families Ohio, U.S. Daus. of 1812 (chmn. state insignia), Palantines to Am., Children of Am. Revolution (past sr. state historian, sr. state rec. sec.). Home: 14553 N River Rd Pemberville OH 43450-9797 E-mail: lking@wcnet.org.

KING, LAWRENCE EDMUND, lawyer; b. Fairbanks, Ark., Sept. 16, 1965; s. Robert Wendell and Helen Jane (Lamar) K.; m. Tamara Kay Biby, July 21, 1988; c. three. BA in Polit. Sci., U. ND, 1989, JD, 1992. Bar: ND 1992, US Dist. Ct. (Dist. ND) 1992, Minn. 1995, Sisseton Wahpeton Sioux Tribal Ct., Turtle Mountain Band Chippewa Indians Tribal Ct., Three Affiliated Tribes Tribal Ct., Spirit Lake Sioux Nation Tribal Ct., Standing Rock Sioux Nation Tribal Ct. Assoc. Zuger Kirmis & Smith, Bismarck, ND, 1992, ptnr. Chmn. fin. com. McCabe United Meth. Ch., Bismarck, 1995. Recipient William Holland scholarship U. N.D., 1990, William Depuy scholarship, 1990. Mem. ABA (dist. rep. young lawyers divsn. 1994, pres ND young lawyers sect. 1993), ND Bar Assn. (pres. 2006-07), Big Muddy Bar Assn. (past pres.). Mailing: Zuger Kirmis & Smith PO Box 1695 Bismarck ND 58502 Office Phone: 701-223-2711. E-mail: lking@zkslaw.com.

KING, LEON, investment advisor; b. Phila., 1921; s. Abraham and Ethel (Walton) K.; m. Diane Averbach, Nov. 30, 1946; children: Cheryl, Elliot, Louis. BS in Econs, Wharton Sch., U. Pa., 1945; grad. with honors, Bank Adminstrn. Inst., 1970. CPA, Pa. Pub. acct., 1946-52; contr. hotel divsn. Bankers Securities Corp., 1952-57; contr. Sun-Ray Drug Co., 1957-60, Bellevue Stratford Hotel, 1960-64; with Indsl. Valley Bank and Trust Co., Phila., 1964-83, exec. v.p., 1973-83; with Indsl. Valley Title Ins. Co., Phila., 1964-86, chmn. bd., 1983-86; pres. Bancshares Inc., 1987-97; gen. ptnr. King Assocs. LP, 1996—; pvt. practice, 1987—. Mem. AICPA, Pa. Inst. CPAs, Beta Gamma Sigma. Home: 4030 Woodruff Rd Lafayette Hill PA 19444-1618 *Always be polite and courteous. Treat all people the same regardless of rank, station, or position. We are all human beings and each deserves civility and respect. From a small child to a chief of state, from a beggar to a captain of industry, all should be treated in the same friendly and courteous way.*

KING, LINDA ORR, museum director, consultant; b. Washington, June 21, 1948; d. William Baxter and Jayne (Reiser) Orr; m. James McClain King (dec. Aug. 1997); children: David, Adam, Lindsay. BA, La. State U., 1970, MA in Fine Arts, 1971; postgrad., Ga. State U., 2003—. Fine arts history asst. La. State U., Baton Rouge, 1967-70, grad. asst., 1970-71; assoc. curator La. State Mus., New Orleans, 1971-74; curator Coastal Ga. Hist. Soc./St. Simons Island Lighthouse Mus., St. Simons Island, 1984-87; dir. Coastal Ga. Hist. Soc., St. Simons Island, 1987-2000; dir. exhibitions and collections Atlanta Hist. Ctr., 2000-01; ind. mus. profl., 2001—. Romanian Mus. advisor U.S. State Dept., 2002. Co-editor: (photograph essay) George Francois Mugnier, 1975. Pres. Glynn County Soc. of St. Vincent de Paul, 1990-94; mem. Glynn County Courthouse Renovation Com., 1989-2000; Ga. state dir. S.E. Mus. Conf., 1990-94, also membership chair; mem. adv. coun. Brunswick Downtown Devel. Authority; mem. Leadership Glynn, 1992; mem. Commn. on Preservation of Ga. State Capitol; chmn. adv. coun. on hist. preservation Coastal Regional Devel. Ctr., 1987-98, chmn., 1996-98. Recipient Kellogg Career Enhancement award, Kellogg Found., 1989, Leadership award, Southeastern Mus. Conf., 1995, Nat. Mus. award, 1999, Ga. History Mus. Exhibit of 2002 award, 2002; fellow Internat. Partnership Among Mus. fellow to Sierra Leone, 1992. Mem. Ga. Assn. Mus. and Galleries (treas. 1987-89, Mus. Profl. of Yr. 1993), Coastal Mus. Assn. (treas. 1987-89), Am. Assn. Mus., Low Country Mus. Network (treas. 1993-99). Roman Catholic. Home: 3472 Paces Pl NW Atlanta GA 30327 E-mail: lindaorrking@bellsouth.net.

KING, LONNIE J., dean; m. Sylvia King; 2 children. BS, Ohio State U., 1966, DVM, 1970; MS in Epidemiology, U. Minn., 1980; MPA, Am. U., Washington, DC, 1991. Cert. Am. Coll. Vet. Preventive Medicine. Pvt. practice as vet., Dayton, Ohio, Atlanta; dir. govtl. rels. divsn. Am. Vet. Med. Assn., Washington; various staff assignments as chief vet. officer, sta. epidemiologist, dir. devel. Nat. Animal Health Monitoring Sys. USDA Animal and Plant Health Inspection Svc.; dep. adminstr. USDA Animal and Plant Health Inspection Svc. Vet. Svcs., 1988—91, dir. Nat. Animal Health Monitoring Sys.; adminstr. USDA Animal and Plant Health Inspection Svc., 1995—; dean Mich. State U. Coll. Vet. Medicine, 1996, dean and prof., large animal clin. sciences, initiated the CTr. for Emerging Diseases, campus leader in food safety. Sr. exec. fellowship program Harvard U.; oversees Nat. Food Safety and Toxicology Ctr.; designated leader for counter-bioterrism activities Michigan State U., leader in re0establishing public health programs; vice-chair Nat. Commn. on Vet. Econ.; contbr. to start of Nat. Alliance for Food Safety; served Governor's Task Force on Chronic Wasting Disease; mem. Inst. of Medicine's Com. on Microbial Threats to Health; cons. and bd. sci. advisors, Nat. Ctr. for Infectious Diseases CDC, dir. strategy & innovation. Editor: OIE Scientific Review on Emerging Zoonoses. Chmn. Nat. Academics Com. on Assessing the Nation's Framework for Addressing Animal Diseases; developer Science, Politics and Animal Health Policy Fellowship Program. Mem.: Inst. Medicine, Inst. Medicine, Am. Vet. Epidemiology Soc. (pres.), Assn. of Am. Vet. Med. Colleges (pres. 1999—2000). Office: Mich State U Coll Vet Medicine G100 Vet Med Center East Lansing MI 48824-1316

KING, LOWELL RESTELL, pediatric urologist; b. Salem, Ohio, Feb. 28, 1932; s. Lowell Waldo and Vesta Ethylwin (Snyder) K.; m. Mary Elizabeth Hill, July 9, 1960; children: Andrew Restell, Erika Lillie. BA, Johns Hopkins U., 1953, MD, 1956. Intern Johns Hopkins Hosp., Balt., 1956-57, resident in urology, 1957-62; asst. prof. urology Johns Hopkins U., 1962-63, Northwestern U., 1963-67, assoc. prof., 1967-70, prof., 1970-81, prof. urology and surgery, 1974-81; prof. urology and pediatrics Duke U., Durham, NC, 1981-97, prof. emeritus, 1997; prof. surgery/urology U. N.Mex., Albuquerque, 1997—. Prof., chmn. dept. urology Presbyn.-St. Luke's Hosp., 1968-70; surgeon-in-chief Children's Meml. Hosp., Chgo., 1974-80; examiner Am. Bd. Urology, 1968-94, trustee, 1975-81. Author: (with P.P. Kelalis) Clinical Pediatric Urology, 1976, (with A.B. Belman) 5th edit., 2007, Bladder Replacement and Continent Urology Diversion, 1986, 2d edit., 1991, Urologic Surgery in the Neonate and Young Infant, 1992, Reconstructive Urology, 1992, Urologic Surgery in Infants and Children, 1997, Office Guide to Pediatric Urology, 2002; cons. editor Urology; editor profl. jours.; contbr. articles to profl. jours. Vestryman, sr. warden Ch. of Our Savior, 1974-80; bd. dirs. Gads Hill Settlement House, 1969-73. Recipient Gold medal All India Urologic Congress, 1996, Gold medal Mex. Coll. Urology, 1991, Valentine medal N.Y. Acad. Medicine, 2002, Kretchmer medal Chgo. Urol. Soc. Mem. AMA, Am. Urol. Assn. (hon., career achievement award 1996, Merit award 2005), Am. Acad. Pediats. (chmn. sect. urology 1969-72, sec. 1975-76, pres. 1977-78, Urology medal 1992), Soc. Pediat. Urology (pres. 1983), Soc. Univ. Urologists, Am. Assn. Genitourinary Surgeons, Clin. Soc. Genitourinary Surgeons (pres. 1996). Episcopalian. Office: U NMex Health Scis Ctr Sch Medicine Dept Surgery Divsn Urology 2211 Lomas Blvd NE Albuquerque NM 87106-2745 Home: 2301 Via Granada NW Albuquerque NM 87107 Office Phone: 505-272-5504. Personal E-mail: octopus@cybermesa.com.

KING, LYNDEL IRENE SAUNDERS, museum director; b. Enid, Okla., June 10, 1943; d. Leslie Jay and Jennie Irene (Duggan) Saunders; m. Blaine Larman King, June 12, 1965. BA, U. Kans., Lawrence, 1965; MA, U. Minn.-Mpls., 1971, PhD, 1982. Dir. Frederick R. Weisman Art Mus., U. Minn., Mpls., 1979—; dir. exhbns. and mus. programs Control Data Corp., 1979, 80-81; exhbn. coord. Nat. Gallery of Art, Washington, 1980. Recipient Cultural Contbn. of Yr. award Mpls. C. of C., 1978; Honor award Minn. Soc. Architects, 1979. Mem. Assn. Art Mus. Dirs. (chair art issues com. 1998-2000, chair tech. comm. com. 2000, bd. trustees 1998—), Art Mus. Assn. Am. (v.p. bd. dirs. 1984-89), Assn. Coll. and Univ. Mus. and Galleries (v.p. 1989-92), Am. Assn. Mus., Internat. Coun. Mus., Upper Midwest Conservation Assn. (pres. bd. dirs. 1980—), Minn. Assn. Mus. (steering com. 1982), Am. Fedn. Arts Bd. Home: 326 W 50th St Minneapolis MN 55419-1247 Office: Weisman Art Mus 333 E River Rd Minneapolis MN 55455-0367 E-mail: wamdir@umn.edu.

KING, MARCIA GYGLI, artist; b. Cleve., June 4, 1931; d. Robert Prescott and Ruth (Farr) Gygli; m. Rollin White King, May 10, 1956 (div. 1974); children: Rollin White King Jr., Edward Prescott King. BA, Smith Coll., 1953; MFA, U. Tex., San Antonio, 1981. Docent Nat. Gallery Art, Washington, 1956-60; organizer, dir. docent program McNay Art Mus., San Antonio, 1964-76; art critic Express news, San Antonio, 1976-77; artist NYC, 1979—. Lectr. Nat. Gallery Art, Washington, 1956-60, div. continuing edn. U. Tex., 1976, So. Meth. U., Dallas, 1984, McNay Art Mus., San Antonio, 1984, Washington Project for the Arts, 1985, Monserrat Coll. Art, Beverly, Mass., 1987, Whitney Mus., Phillip Morris, N.Y.C., 1988, Lehman Coll. CUNY, 1988, MTA Pub. Art Commn. for Creative Stations, N.Y., 1995; panelist Panel on Women in the Arts, Alexandria, Va., 1978, Washington Project for the Arts, 1985, Corpus Christi (Tex.) State U., 1986, Dallas Mus., 1991, New Mus., N.Y., 1993, Mus. Mod. Art, N.Y., 1995. One woman shows include McNamara O'Connor Mus., Victoria, Tex., 1975, Charleton Gallery, San Antonio, 1980, Douglas Coll. Rutgers U., New Brunswick, NJ, 1981, McNay Art Mus., San Antonio, 1984, Mattingly Baker Gallery, Dallas, 1984, White Columns, NY, 1985, Parker Smalley Gallery, NY, Manhattan Marymount, NY, 1986, Ferver Gallery, NY, 1987, Katzen Brown Gallery, NYC, 1988, 90, Haines Gallery, San Francisco, 1988, Wallace Wentworth Gallery, Washington, 1988, U. NC, 1989, Valerie Miller Gallery, Palm Desert, Calif., 1989, Cleve. Ctr. for Contemporary Art, 1989-90, Hal Katzen, NY, 1992, 94, Guild Hall Mus., NY, 1995, Renee Fotouhi Fine Art, NY, 1995, Arts Acad., Md., 1996, Kouros Gallery, NY, 1999, Parchman Stremmel Gallery, San Antonio, 2000, San Antonio Art League Mus., 2000, Bklyn. Botanic Garden, 2001, Gallery Camino, Real, Fla., 2002, Gallery 668, NY, 2003, Blue Star Gallery, San Antonio; represented in permenant collections Bklyn. Mus., Cleve. Mus., Guggenheim Mus., Johnson Mus., Cornell U., Nat. Mus. Women in Arts, Newark Mus., Robert Coll., Istanbul, Ark. Art Ctr., Guild Hall, L.I., McNay Art Mus., San Antonio Art League, Best Products, Richmond, Va., British Petroleum, Cleve., Cadillac Fairview, Dallas., Laurel Sch., Cleve., Phillip Morris Co., NYC., Continental Life Ins. Corp., NYC, Goldman Sachs Co., NYC. Recipient Internat. Women's Yr. Panel award, Tex., 1977, Artist of Yr., San Antonio, 2000, James Kirkeby Nat. Meml. award Tex. Watercolor Soc., 1976, Brewer's Digest award Lone Star Brewery Day, 1963, Annual Z.T. Scott award & cir. Tex. Fine Arts Assn., 1970, Ethel T. Drought Meml. award San Antonio Art League Exhbn., 1971, Best of Show award Tex. Watercolor Show, 1971, First Purchase Prize, Tex. Watercolor Show, 1972, First Purchase Prize, 17th Delta Annual, Ark. Art. Ctr., 1974; named Outstanding Woman in San Antonio, Women's Polit. Caucus, 1979. Avocations: swimming, bicycling. Office: 477 Broome St Apt 63 New York NY 10013-5311

KING, MARGARET LEAH, history professor; b. NYC, Oct. 16, 1947; d. Reno C. and Marie (Ackerman) King; m. Robert E. Kessler, Nov. 12, 1976; children: David King Kessler, Jeremy King Kessler. BA, Sarah Lawrence Coll., 1967; MA, Stanford U., 1968, PhD, 1972. Asst. prof. dept. history Calif. State Coll., Fullerton, 1969-70; asst. prof. Bklyn. Coll., CUNY, 1972-76, assoc. prof., 1976-86, Broeklundian prof., 2006—; prof. Bklyn. Coll. and Grad. Ctr., CUNY, 1987—, Claire and Leonard Tow disting. prof., 2000—02, Broeklundian prof., 2006—. Disting. guest prof. Centre for Reformation and Renaissance Studies, U. Toronto, 1995. Author: Western Civilization: A Social and Cultural History, 3rd edit., 2004, The Renaissance in Europe, 2005; co-editor, translator: (with Diana Robin) Complete Works of Isotta Nogarola, 2004; co-editor: (with Albert Rabil Jr.) Teaching the Other Voice: Women and Religion in Early Modern Europe, 2007, (series) The Other Voice in Early Modern Europe; contbr. articles to profl. jours. Recipient Howard R. Marraro prize, Am. Cath. Hist. Assn., 1986, Tow award for distinction in scholarship, Bklyn. Coll., 1994—95, Scaglione prize, MLA, 2006; fellow, Danforth Found., 1967—72, Woodrow Wilson Found., 1967—68, Am. Coun. Learned Socs., 1977—78, NEH, 1986—87, Leonard and Claire Tow Disting. fellow, 2000—; grantee, Am. Coun. Learned Socs., 1976, Gladys Krieble Delmas Found., 1977—78, 1980—81, 1990, Am. Philos. Soc., 1979, 1990, NEH, 1984; Broklundian Professorship, Bklyn. Coll., 2006—. Mem. Am. Hist. Assn. (Howard and Helen Mararro prize 1996), Hist. Soc.(bd. govs. 2004-06), Renaissance Soc. Am. (exec. dir. 1988-95, editor Renaissance Quar. 1984-88, 97-2002). Home: 324 Beverly Rd Little Neck NY 11363-1125 Office: CUNY Bklyn Coll Dept History 2900 Bedford Ave Brooklyn NY 11210-2814 Home Phone: 718-224-5066; Office Phone: 718-951-5303. Personal E-mail: mking@nyc.rr.com.

KING, MARY-CLAIRE, geneticist, educator; b. Evanston, Ill., Feb. 27, 1946; m. 1973; 1 child, Emily King Colwell. BA in Math. (cum laude), Carleton Coll., Northfield, Minn., 1966; PhD in Genetics, U. Calif., Berkeley, 1973; PhD (hon.), Carleton Coll., Bard Coll., Smith Coll., Dartmouth Coll. Postdoctoral tng. U. Calif.-San Francisco; prof. genetics and epidemiology U. Calif. Berkeley, 1976—95; Am. Cancer Soc. rsch. prof. genome scis. and medicine U. Wash., Seattle, 1995—. Mem. bd. sci. counselors Nat. Cancer Inst., Meml. Sloan-Kettering Cancer Ctr., mem. NRC com. to advise Dept. Def. on the Breast Cancer Rsch. Program., NIH Genome Study Sect.; served on Nat. Commn. on Breast Cancer of the President's Cancer Panel; mem. adv. bd., NIH Office of Rsch. on Women's Health, Coun. of the NIH Fogarty Ctr., Nat. Action Plan for Breast Cancer, NIH Breast Cancer Program Review Group; affiliate mem. Fred Hutchinson Cancer Rsch. Ctr., Seattle; cons. Com. for Investigation of Disappearance of Persons, Govt. Argentina, Buenos Aires, 1984; carried out DNA Identifications for the UN War Crimes Tribunial; mem. UN Forensic Anthropology Team; mem. adv. bd. Robert Wood Johnson Found. Minority Med. Faculty Develop. program Contbr. articles to profl. jours. Named Woman of Yr., Glamour Mag.; recipient Clowes award, Basic Rsch., Am. Assn. Cancer Rsch., Jill Rose award, Am. Breast Cancer Found., Brinker award, Susan G. Komen Breast Cancer Found., 1999, Genetics prize, Peter Gruber Found., 2004, Weizmann Women & Sci. award, Am. Com. for Weizmann Inst. Sci., 2006. Fellow AAAS, Inst. Medicine, Acad. Arts and Sciences; mem. Am. Soc. Human Genetics, Soc. Epidemiologic Research, NAS, Phi Beta Kappa, Sigma Xi. Achievements include identifying the close similarity of the human and chimpanzee genomes; discovery of a gene (BRCA1) that predisposes to breast cancer; introduced direct sequencing of PCR-amplified segments of mitochondrial DNA for identifying people or their remains by comparing their DNA to that of relatives. Office: Dept Medicine and Genome Sciences Health Sciences RM K-160 U Washington Sch Medicine Box 357720 Health Sciences Room K-160 Seattle WA 98195-7720 Office Phone: 206-616-4294. Office Fax: 206-616-4295. E-mail: mcking@u.washington.edu.*

KING, MEGAN CHRISTINE, cell biologist; b. Middletown, NY, May 1975; d. F. Terence and Christine King; children: Forrest, Lorelei. BA, Brandeis U., Waltham, Mass., 1993—97; PhD, U. Pa., Phila., 1999—2004. Rsch. assoc. Cubist Pharms., Cambridge, Mass., 1997—99; postdoctoral fellow Rockefeller U., NYC. Grantee Predoctoral fellowship, Dept. Def. Breast Cancer Rsch. Program, 2003—05, Postdoctoral fellowship, NIH, 2006—. Mem.: Am. Soc. Cell Biology. Business E-Mail: mking@rockefeller.edu.

KING, MICHAEL HOWARD, lawyer; b. Chgo., Mar. 10, 1943; s. Warren and Betty (Fine) K.; m. Candice M. King, Aug. 18, 1968; children: Andrew, Julie. B.S. Washington U., St. Louis 1967, J.D. 1970. Bar: Ill. 1970, U.S. Dist. Ct. (no. dist.) Ill. 1970, U.S. Dist. Ct. (ea. dist.) Wis. 1972, U.S. Ct. Appeals (7th cir.) 1974, U.S. Ct. Appeals (5th cir.) 1979, U.S. Ct. Appeals (8th cir.) 2007, U.S. Supreme Ct. 1975, U.S. Ct. Appeals (3d cir.) 1983, U.S. Tax Ct. 1987, U.S. Ct. Appeals (10th cir.) 1987, U.S. Dist. Ct. (no. dist.) Calif. 1987, U.S. Dist. Ct. Nebr. 1988, U.S. Dist. Ct. (ctrl. dist.) Ill. 1992, U.S. Dist. Ct. (no. dist.) N.Y. 1992, U.S. Ct. Appeals (2nd cir.) 1994. Spl. atty. organized crime, racketeering sect. U.S. Dept. Justice, Washington, 1970-73; asst. U.S. atty. No. Dist. Ill., Chgo., 1973-75; assoc. Antonow & Fink, Chgo., 1976, ptnr., 1977-79; ptnr. Ross & Hardies, Chgo., 1979-2003, McGuire Woods LLP, 2003-05, LeBoeuf, Lamb, Greene and MacRae LLP, 2005—; chmn. Bd. Commr. Office of State Appellate Defender. Co-author Model Jury Instructions in Criminal Antitrust Cases, 1982, Handbook on Antitrust Grand Jury Investigations, 1988; contbr. articles to profl. jours. Bd. dirs. Chgo. Youth Ctrs., 1977-82; trustee Cove Sch., 1984-88, the Goodman Theatre, 1993. Mem. ABA (litigation sect., antitrust sect., criminal practice procedure com.), Ill. Bar Assn., Chgo. Bar Assn. (judiciary com., antitrust com.), Am. Judicature Soc., Fed. Bar Assn., Assn. Trial Lawyers Am., Mid-Am. Club (bd. govs.), Econ. Club, Chgo. Inn of Cts., Phi Delta Phi, Alpha Epsilon Pi.

KING, NICOLE, molecular biologist, educator; BA, Ind. U., Bloomington, 1992; AM, Harvard U., 1996, PhD, 1999. Postdoctoral fellow U. Wis., 2000—03; asst. prof., genetics and develop., dept. molecular and cell biology and integrative biology U. Calif., Berkeley, 2003—, faculty affiliate, Ctr. for Integrative Genomics. Contbr. articles to profl. jour. Named a MacArthur Fellow, John D. and Catherine T. MacArthur Found., 2005. Office: Univ Calif Berkeley Dept Molecular & Cell Biology 142 Life Sciences Addition #3200 Berkeley CA 94720-3200 Office Phone: 510-643-9395, 510-643-9417 (lab). Office Fax: 510-643-6791. E-mail: nking@berkeley.edu.

KING, ORDIE HERBERT, JR., oral pathologist; b. Memphis, Aug. 11, 1933; s. Ordie Herbert and Hazel (Eaton) King; m. Violette Papagianis, Mar. 21, 1974; children: Catherine Ann, Alexander Carlos;children from previous marriage: Anna LaVelle, Ordie Herbert III. BS, Memphis State U., 1957; DDS, U. Tenn., 1959, PhD, 1965. Diplomate Am. Bd. Oral and Maxillofacial Pathology. USPHS postdoctoral fellow U. Tenn., 1960-62, rsch. assoc. dept. pathology, 1963-65, asst. prof. pathology, 1965, resident oral pathology City of Memphis Hosps., 1962-63; asst. prof. pathology Northwestern U., 1966; assoc. prof. oral pathology St. Louis U., 1967-69, prof., 1969-70, chmn. dept., 1967-70, chmn. dept. dentistry univ. hosps., 1967-70; acting chmn., vis. assoc. prof. oral pathology Washington U., St. Louis, 1969-70, clin. prof. pathology Sch. Dental Medicine, 1979-80; prof. oral pathology, assoc. prof. pathology W.Va. U., Morgantown, 1970-74, prof. pathology, 1974, dir. Cytopathology Lab., Med. Ctr., 1971-74; prof. pathology Sch. Dental Medicine So. Ill. U., Alton, 1974-97, chmn. dept. diagnostic specialties Sch. Dental Medicine, 1979-92. Dir. So. Ill. Pathology Lab., Ltd., Godfrey, 1977—; dental cons. to chief med. examiner State of Tenn., 1963—65; mem. exec. com. St. Louis U. Hosps., 1967—70; mem. med. staff W. Tenn. Cancer Clinic, 1962—65, W.Va. U. Hosp., 1970—74; mem. med./dental staff dept. pathology Alton Meml. Hosp., 1986—; cons. VA Hosp., Clarksville, W.Va., 1973—74; dental cons. St. Louis County Med. Examiner, 1968—70; cons. cancer control program Nat. Ctr. Chronic Disease Control, USPHS, 1967—70; mem. Mo. Bd. Dental Splty. Examiners, 1982—84. Fellow: Am. Acad. Oral Pathology; mem.: ADA, Am. Cancer Soc. (bd. dirs. W.Va. divsn. 1972—74), Am. Soc. Cytopathology, Ill. Walking Horse Assn. (bd. dirs. 2000—), Spotted Saddle Horse Assn. Ill. (v.p. 2001, 2005—07, pres. 2002—04), Tenn. Walking Horse Breeders and Exhibitors Assn., Spotted Saddle Horse Breeders and Exhibitors Assn., Omicron Kappa Upsilon, Phi Rho Sigma, Kappa Alpha Order, Delta Sigma Delta. Home: 6111 Vollmer Ln Godfrey IL 62035-1062 Office: So Ill Path Lab Ltd Godfrey IL 62035

KING, PATRICIA ANN, law educator; b. Norfolk, Va., June 12, 1942; d. Addison A. and Grayce (Wood) K.; m. Roger W. Wilkins, Feb. 21, 1981; 1 child, Elizabeth. BA, Wheaton Coll., 1963; JD, Harvard U., 1969. Bar: D.C. 1969, U.S. Supreme Ct. 1980. Spl. asst. to chair EEOC, Washington, 1969-71; dep. dir. civil rights office HEW, Washington, 1971-73; prof. law Georgetown Law Ctr., Washington, 1973—, Carmack Waterhouse Prof. Law, Medicine, Ethics, and Public Policy. Adj. prof. Sch. Hygiene and Pub. Health Johns Hopkins U., 1990—; bd. dirs. Wheaton Coll., Womens Legal Defense Fund. Co-author: Law, Science and Medicine, 1984; contbr. articles to profl. jours. Chmn. Redevelopment Land Agy., Washington, 1976-80. Fellow Hastings Ctr.; mem. Am. Soc. Law and Medicine, Am. Law Inst., Inst. Medicine. Office: Georgetown Law Ctr 600 New Jersey Ave NW Washington DC 20001-2075

KING, PEGGY MARSHA, special education educator, researcher; b. Chgo., May 4, 1950; d. Thomas Edgar and Rhoda Newsom Hollingsworth; m. James Francis King, Mar. 21, 1972; children: James Ryan, Jessica Marie. BA, MS; postgrad., Aurora U., 2003—05. Cert. sch. adminstr. Ill., 2004. Inclusion specialist Glen Ellyn Sch. Dist. # 89, Ill., 1996—2004, spl. edn. dir., 2004—. Presenter in field. Mem. Wall of Tolerance, So. Poverty Law Ctr., Ala., 2004—05; life mem. PTA, Bensonville, Ill., 1990—; mem. HOPE Found. Mem.: ASCD, Ill. Alliance Adminstrs. of Spl. Edn. (assoc.). Office: Ccsd # 89 22W600 Butterfield Rd Glen Ellyn IL 60137 Home Phone: 630-790-9243; Office Phone: 630-469-8900. Business E-Mail: pking@ccsd89.org.

KING, PETER THOMAS, congressman, lawyer; b. NYC, Apr. 5, 1944; m. Rosemary Wiedel; children: Sean, Erin. BA in Hist., St. Francis Coll., Bklyn., 1965; JD, U. Notre Dame Law Sch., 1968. Bar: NY 1968. Lawyer pvt. practice; dep. atty. Nassau County, NY, 1972—74, exec. asst. to county exec. NY, 1974—76; gen. counsel NY Off-Track Betting Corp., 1977; mem. Town Coun., Hempstead, NY, 1977-81; comptr. Nassau County, NY, 1981-93; mem. US Congress from 3rd NY dist., 1993—, ranking mem. homeland security com., 2005—, mem. fin. svcs. com. Author: Terrible Beauty, 1999, Deliver Us From Evil, 2002, Vale of Tears, 2003. Chmn. Town Bd. Com. on Conservation and Waterways. With USNG, 1968—73. Named Patriot of Yr., Res. Officers Assn., Man of Yr., FBI Emerald Soc.; recipient Cert. of Achievement, Excellence in Fin. Reporting, Gov. Fin. Officers Assn., 1985—91, Cert. of Honor, LI Com. Soviet Jewry, Huey award, Vets. of Vietnam War, Frederick Olmstead award, Labor Enforcement Alliance, 2003, Disting. Svc. award, Inst. Pub. Affairs of the Orthodox Jewish Congregations of Am., Interfaith Understanding award, Jewish Chatauqua Soc. of the Wantagh Suburban Temple, Spirit of Enterprise award, US C. of C., Guardian of Small Bus. award, Nat. Fedn. Ind. Bus., Friend of Labor award, Civil Svc. Employees Assn. Mem.: Nassau County Fire Fighters Emerald Soc. (hon.), Cath. War Vets. (Cert. of Achievement), Sons of Italy, Vets. Corps of 69th Inf., AMVETS (life), Am. Legion, Ancient Order of Hibernians, KC (Citizen of Yr.). Republican. Roman Catholic. Office: 1003 Park Blvd Massapequa Park NY 11762 Office Phone: 202-225-7896, 516-541-4225.*

KING, QUINTIN L., trade association administrator, lobbyist; s. Harrison and Nora Lee King; m. Michelle White, June 16, 1986; 1 child, Samantha. BA Polit. Sci., DePaul U., Chgo., 1983; JD, U.Pa., Phila., 1986. Sr. ptnr. Lord & King Assocs., Chgo., 1992—. Bd. dirs. Kingdom Bus. Inst., South Holland, Ill.; chmn. bd. dirs. Consol. Bus. Group, Chgo., 2004—, Aron Comm. Pub. Rels. Firm; mem. ins. adv. bd. Rand Corps. Inst. for Civil Justice, Santa Monica, Calif., 1989—90; mem. policy and econs. coun. Gerson Lehrman Group, NYC, 2005—. Mem. Longfellow Adv. Coun., Oak Park, Ill., 2002—05; mem. adv. bd. liberal arts and scis. DePaul U., Chgo., 2002—; chmn. Coun. on Urban Rsch. and Edn., Chgo., 2002—; chmn. reunion com. DePaul U., Chgo., 1993; mem. advocacy adv. bd. midwest chpt. Am. Heart Assn., Chgo., 2004—. Named Man of Yr., Chgo. Coun. on Urban Rsch. and Edn., 2002—03. Mem.: Def. Rsch. Inst., Am. League Lobbyists, Pi Sigma Alpha, Pi Gamma Mu. Democrat. Avocations: collector old time radio shows, tennis, golf. Home Phone: 708-848-4012; Office Phone: 888-690-2048 ext. 84. Business E-Mail: qking@nailm.org. E-mail: nailminfo@aol.com.

KING, RAY JOHN, electrical engineering educator, engineering company executive; b. Montrose, Colo., Jan. 1, 1933; s. John Frank and Grace (Rankin) K.; m. Diane M. Henney, June 20, 1964; children: Karl V., Kristin J. BS in Electronic Engring., Ind. Inst. Tech., 1956, BS in Elec. Engring., 1957; MS, U. Colo., 1960, PhD, 1965. Instr. Ind. Inst. Tech., 1956-58, asst. prof., 1960-62, acting chmn. dept. electronics, 1960-62; research asso. U. Colo., 1962-65; research assoc. U. Ill., 1965; assoc. prof. elec. engring. U. Wis., Madison, 1965-69, prof., 1969-82, assoc. dept. chmn. for research and grad. affairs, 1977-79; staff rsch. engr. Lawrence Livermore Nat. Lab. (Calif.), 1982-90, sr. scientist high power microwaves program, 1989-90; co-founder KDC Tech. Corp., 1983, v.p., 1990—, cons. Vis. Erskine fellow U. Canterbury, N.Z., 1977; guest prof., Fulbright scholar Tech. U. Denmark, 1973-74 Author: Microwave Homodyne Systems, 1978; contbr. articles to profl. jours.; patentee in field; guest editor spl. issue Subsurface Sensing Techs. and Applications jour., 2000. NSF Faculty fellow, 1962-65. Fellow IEEE (life); mem. IEEE Soc. on Antennas and Propagation (adminstrv. com. 1989-91, chmn. wave propagation stds. com. 1986-89, gen. chmn. symposium 1989), IEEE Soc. Microwave Theory and Techniques, IEEE Soc. Instrumentation and Measurements, Forest Products Soc. (life), Electromagnetics Acad., Internat. Sci. Radio Union (commns. A, B, F), Sigma Xi, Iota Tau Kappa, Sigma Phi Delta. Home: 2595 Raven Rd Pleasanton CA 94566-4605 Office: KDC Tech Corp 2011 Research Dr Livermore CA 94550-3803 Home Phone: 925-462-8197; Office Phone: 925-449-4770. Personal E-mail: rayking@ieee.org.

KING, RAYMUND CAMILO, lawyer, physician; b. Manila, July 18, 1964; came to U.S., 1965; s. Constancio Yuzon and Rosalinda (De La Rosa) K.; m. Sandra Berninger, Aug. 2, 1997. BA in Biology, U. Dallas, 1986; MD, U. Tex., Houston, 1990; JD, Oklahoma City U., 1990. Diplomate Am. Bd. Forensic Examiners, Am. Bd. Forensic Medicine. Intern Health Scis. Ctr. U. Okla., 1990-92, resident dept. otolargngology Health Scis. Ctr., 1992-96; med. dir. Quality Med. Clinic, Oklahoma City, 1996—; pres. RKMD, Inc., Oklahoma City, 1996—. V.p. bd. govs. Sch. Law Oklahoma City U., 1997-98. Recipient Resident Rsch. award Am. Laryngol., Rhinol., and Otol. Soc., 1996. Fellow: Am. Coll. Legal Medicine, Internat. Coll. Surgeons; mem.: AMA, ABA (spl. com. on med. profl. liability), Tex. State Bar Assn., Dallas Bar. Assn., Am. Acad. Otolaryngology. Home: 8913 Greenwood Trl Rowlett TX 75088-6858 Office: 901 Main St Ste 4000 Dallas TX 75202

KING, REBECCA J., lawyer, consultant; b. Hazard, Ky., Aug. 7, 1951; d. Roger William and Fannie Jane (Starkey) Richmond; m. Colbert Sylvester King, Nov. 10, 1982; children: Justin, Allison. BA, Wright State U., 1977; MA, Miami U., Oxford, Ohio, 1978; JD, Tulane U., 1988. Bar: La. 1988, U.D. Dist. Ct. (ea. dist.) La. 1989, U.S. Dist. Ct. (we. dist.) La. 1992, U.S. Ct. Appeals (5th cir.) 1992, U.S. Dist. Ct. (ctrl. dist.) La. 1998. Law clk. Civil Dist. Ct., New Orleans, 1988—91; assoc. Carter & Cates, New Orleans, 1991—92; sr. law clk. La. Supreme Ct., New Orleans, 1992—94; ptnr. Middleberg Riddle & Gianna, New Orleans, 1994—2003. V.p. King Consulting, Inc., New Orleans, 1999—. Past corp. counsel Union Bethel Cmty. Devel. Corp., New Orleans; past chair pro tem, bd. trustees Union Bethel AME Ch., New Orleans. Recipient Black Achiever in Bus. and INdustry award, Dryades YMCA, New Orleans, 1992. Mem.: ABA (award, sect. urban, state and local govt. 1988), ATLA, New Orleans Bar Assn., La. State Bar Assn., Louis A. Martinet Legal Soc., Nat. Bar Assn. Democrat. African Methodist Episcopal. Personal E-mail: hazardkin@yahoo.com.

KING, RICHARD GENE, superintendent; b. Indpls., July 1, 1952; s. Ronald Gene and Rosemary King; m. Kathie Sue Duggan, Aug. 11, 1984; 1 child, Alexander Nicholas. BA, Purdue U., 1974; MS, Ind. U., 1980, EdS, 1990. Tchr. Decatur Twp. Schs., Indpls., 1974—91; asst. prin. Martinsville Schs., Ind., 1991—95; prin. Greencastle Cmty. Schs., Ind., 1995—97; asst. supt. North West Hendricks Schs., Lizton, Ind., 1997—. Mem. adv. bd. United Way of Hendricks County, 2002—, Purdue Sch. Edn., 2003—; elder Clermont Christian Ch., Ind., 1986—; bd. dirs., treas. Ind. Staff Devel. Coun., 2001—05; bd. dirs., pres. Hendricks Coll. Network, Danville, Ind., 2000—; bd. dirs. Hendricks Regional Health found., Danville, 2001—, v.p., 2005—; bd. dirs. At Your School, Indpls., 2004—. Recipient Cmty. Svc. award, Purdue U. Sch. Edn., 2005. Mem.: Am. Assn. Sch. Adminstrs., Ind. Assn. Pub. Sch. Supts., Nat. Staff Devel. Coun., John Purdue Club, Phi Delta Kappa. Avocations: growing roses, church activities, travel. Office: NW Hendricks Schs 104 N Church St PO Box 70 Lizton IN 46149 Office Phone: 317-994-4100. Office Fax: 317-994-5963. Business E-Mail: kingr@hendricks.k12.in.us.

KING, RICHARD HOOD, retired newspaper executive; b. Boston, Jan. 24, 1934; s. Gilbert and Frances (Hood) K.; m. Reta Schoonmaker, July 25, 1959; children: D. Whitney, Richard H. Jr., Nanci A. AB, Harvard U., 1955, MBA, 1961. Mgr. acctg. Hitchiner Mfg. Co., Inc., Milford, NH, 1963-68, div. contr. Wallingford, Conn., 1968-71; sec., treas. Smyth Mfg. Co., Inc., Bloomfield, Conn., 1971-72; v.p. fin. Progressive Trade Corp., Glastonbury, Conn., 1972-73; v.p., treas. Hartford Courant Co., Conn., 1973-85, v.p., asst. to gen. mgr. Conn., 1986-90, v.p. adminstrn. Conn., 1990-96, ret. Conn., 1996. Treas. Hartford Courant Found., 1974—96, trustee, 1993—98; v.p., sec., bd. dirs. Better Bus. Bur., Hartford, 1978; bd. dirs. Camp Courant, Inc., 1980—96, treas., 1980—96; bd. dirs. Conn. Prison Assn., 1984—91, treas., 1985, chmn. bd. dir., 1986—89; bd. dirs. Hartford Symphony Orch., 1990—98; bd. dirs., regional v.p. Conn. Audubon Soc., 1991—92, chmn., 1993—95, chmn. emeritus, 1995—98. bd. overseers, 1988—; bd. dir. Penikese Is. Sch., 1998—2006, treas., 2001—06; bd. dirs., treas. Falmouth Hist. Soc., 2007—. Lt. j.g. USNR, 1955—57. Mem.: Conn. Daily Newspapers Assn. (treas. 1992, 1st v.p. 1993—95, pres. 1995, exec. dir. 1996—2004), Fin. Exec. Inst. (treas. Hartford chpt. 1980—81, sec. 1981—82, v.p. 1982—83, pres. 1983—84), Glastonbury C. of C. (treas., exec. bd. dirs. 1991—94), Chapoquoit Yacht Club (West Falmouth, Mass., treas. 1973—74, vice commodore 2002, commodore 2003—04), Harvard-Radcliffe Club No. Conn. (v.p. 1989—90, pres. 1990—92). Home: 11 Snug Harbor Ln PO Box 456 West Falmouth MA 02574-0456

KING, RICHARD WAYNE, principal; b. Pitts., Mar. 27, 1952; s. Ralph Lewis and Pauline (Pyle) K.; m. Cheryl Louise Brea, June 22, 1974; children: Ashley, Adam, Allyson. BA in Psychology, Mt. Union Coll., 1974; MEd in Spl. Edn., U. Pitts., 1976, PhD in Ednl. Adminstrn., 1989. Cert. tchr., prin., Pa. Tchr. multiple-handicapped students Allegheny Intermediate Unit, Pitts., 1976-88, tchr. life skills support class, 1989-93; prin. Barrett Elem. Sch. Steel Valley Sch. Dist., Munhall, Pa., 1993—, chair Title I com., 1993—. Assoc. dir. summer program for exceptional children Camp Shining Arrow, Penn Hills, Pa., 1979-86, dir. adult program, 1980-84; chair Ea. Area Pub. Rels. Com., Pitts.,1 981-82, Ea. Area Vocat. Edn. Com., Pitts., 1987; insvc. trainer Allegheny Intermediate Unit, Pitts., 1988; sci. edn. amb. Carnegie Sci. Ctr., Pitts.; co-chair Steel Valley Strategic Planning Tech. Com., 1994; mem. site leadership com. Barrett Elem. Sch., 1993—. Dir. edn. 1st United Meth. Ch., East McKeesport, Pa., 1989—; cub den leader North Versailles area Boy Scouts Am., 1990—; bd. dirs. Family Ctr. for Child Devel.; mem. Steel Valley Elem. Adv. Coun., Steel Valley Adminstrv. Cabinet, 1993—, Steel Valley Communications Curriculum Com., 1994—. Mem. NEA, ASCD, Pa. State Edn. Assn. Avocation: home remodeling. Home: 412 3rd St North Versailles PA 15137-1220 Office: Barrett Elem Sch 221 E 12th Ave Homestead PA 15120-1690

KING, ROBERT ALAN, lawyer; b. Mt. Pleasant, Pa., July 15, 1947; s. Robert O. and D. Juanita (Buskey) King; m. Betsy Reynolds, Aug. 22, 1970; children: Brooke, Blythe, Brice. BA, Colgate U., 1969; JD magna cum laude, U. Pitts., 1972. Bar: Pa., 1972, US Dist. Ct. We. Dist. Pa., 1972, US Supreme Ct., 1979, US Ct. Appeals 3rd Cir., 1975, US Ct. Appeals 2nd Cir., 1988, US Ct. Appeals 11th Cir., 2002, Supreme Ct. Pa., US Dist. Ct. No. Dist. Calif. Assoc. Buchanan Ingersoll, Pitts., 1972-78, ptnr., shareholder, 1979-91, Babst, Calland, Clements & Zomnir, Pitts., 1991—2000; ptnr. Reed Smith LLP, Pitts., 2000—, also practice group leader constrn. group. Spl. master civil cases Ct. of Common Pleas of Allegheny County; arbitrator & mediator US Dist. Ct. We. Dist. Pa. Contbg. author Proving and Pricing Construction Claims, 2nd edit., 1996. Active Govt. Orgn. Com., Hampton Twp., Pa., 1974. Fellow Am. Bar Found; mem. ABA (mem. forum on constrn. industry), Pa. Bar Assn., Allegheny County Bar Assn. (inaugural chair constrn. sect.), Am. Coll. Trial Lawyers, Acad. Trial Lawyers Allegheny County , Am. Arbitration Assn., Master Builders Assn. Avocation: golf. Office: Reed Smith LLP 435 Sixth Ave Pittsburgh PA 15219 Office Phone: 412-288-4128. Office Fax: 412-288-3063. Business E-Mail: rking@reedsmith.com.

KING, ROBERT ALAN, psychiatrist, educator; b. Chgo., Jan. 29, 1943; m. Ruth G. King, 1983; children: Benjamin, Claire, Adam. BA, Oxford U., 1965; MD, Harvard U., 1968; BA, Cornell U., 1963. Cert. psychiatry, child psychiatry. Clin. assoc., staff psychiatrist NIMH, Rockville, Md., 1972—75; dir. for inpatient psychiatry Children's Hosp. Nat. Med. Ctr., Washington, 1976—81; dir. adolescent day svcs. Chestnut Lodge, Rockville, 1981—88; mem. faculty Yale Med. Sch., 1988—; prof. child psychiatry Yale Child Study Ctr., New Haven, 1998—. Mng. editor: Psychoanalytic Study of the Child. Lt. comdr. USPHS, 1972—75. Home: 165 Everit St New Haven CT 06511 Office: 230 S Frontage Rd New Haven CT 06520-7900 Home Phone: 203-772-0083; Office Phone: 203-785-5880. E-mail: robert.king@yale.edu.

KING, ROBERT BRUCE, federal judge; b. White Sulphur Springs, W.Va., Jan. 29, 1940; m. Julia Kay Doak, Apr. 16, 1965. BA, W.Va. U., 1961; JD, W.Va. Coll. of Law, 1968. Bar: W.Va. 1968, US Dist. Ct. (so. dist.) W.Va. 1968, US Ct. Appeals W.Va. 1968, US Ct. Appeals (4th cir.) 1970, US Dist. Ct. (no. dist.) W.Va. 1972, US Supreme Ct. 1974, US Dist. Ct. (ea. dist.) Ky. 1975, US Claims Ct. 1985, US Tax Ct. 1991. Asst. mgr. Sam Snead All-Am. Golf Course, Sharpes, Fla., 1965; rsch. asst. State and Cmty. Planning Office, Office of R&D, W.Va. U., Morgantown, W.Va., 1966—68; law clk. Chief Judge John A. Field, Jr. US Dist. Ct. (so. dist.) W.Va., Charleston, 1968—69; assoc. Haynes and Ford, Lewisburg, W.Va., 1969—70; asst. US atty. So. Dist. of W.Va., Charleston, 1970—74; assoc. Spilman, Thomas, Battle and Klostermeyer, Charleston, 1975, ptnr., 1976—77, 1981; US atty. So. Dist. of W.Va., Charleston, 1977—81; ptnr. King Allen Guthrie & McHugh, 1981—98; judge US Ct. Appeals (4th cir.), Richmond, Va., 1998—. Mem. Jud. Investigation Commn. of W.Va., 1990—94; vis. com. Coll. of Law of W.Va. U., 1997—; mem. 4th Cir. Jud. Coun. Mem., W.Va. N.G., 1957—59, mem. USAF, 1961—64. Scholar Patrick Duffy Koontz. Fellow: Am. Bar Found., Am. Coll. Trial Lawyers; mem.: ABA, Am. Bd. Trial Advocates (W.Va. chpt. pres. 1986—90), Jud. Conf. of 4th Cir. Ct. Appeals, W.Va. Law Sch. Assn., W.Va. U. Alumni Assn., Greenbrier County Bar Assn., Kanawha County Bar Assn., W.Va. Bar Assn., W.Va. Golf Assn., US Golf Assn., Order of the Coif, Phi Alpha Delta, Pi Sigma Alpha. Presbyterian. Office: Ste 7602 300 Virginia St Charleston WV 25301*

KING, ROBERT CHARLES, biologist, educator; b. NYC, June 3, 1928; s. Charles James and Amanda (McCutchen) King. BS, Yale U., 1948, PhD, 1952. Scientist biology dept. Brookhaven Nat. Lab., 1951-55; mem. faculty Northwestern U., 1956—, prof. biology, 1964-99, prof. emeritus, 2000—. Chmn. 8th Brookhaven Symposium in Biology, 1955; vis. investigator, fellow Rockefeller U., 1959; NSF sr. postdoctoral fellow U. Edinburgh, Scotland, 1958, Commonwealth Sci. and Indsl. Research Orgn. Div. Entomology, Canberra, Australia, 1963, Sericultural Expt. Sta., Tokyo, Japan, 1970 Author: Genetics, 2d edit., 1965, A Dictionary of Genetics, 7th edit., 2006, (with W.D. Stansfield and P.K. Mulligan) Ovarian Development in Drosophila melanogaster, 1970, also numerous papers; editor: Handbook of Genetics Series, 5 vols., (with H. Akai) Insect Ultrastructure, 2 vols., 1982. Fellow AAAS; mem. Am. Soc. Zoologists, Histochem. Soc., Am. Soc. Cell Biology (treas. 1972-75), Electron Microscopy Soc. Am., Genetics Soc. Am., Am. Soc. Naturalists, Soc. Devel. Biology, Entomol. Soc. Am., Genetics Soc. Can., Genetics Soc. Korea, Sigma Xi (pres. Northwestern U. chpt. 1966-67) Home: 2890 Fredric Ct Northbrook IL 60062-7504 Business E-Mail: r-king@northwestern.edu.

KING, ROBERT HOWARD, marketing professional; b. Excelsior Springs, Mo., June 28, 1921; s. Howard Churchill King and Nancy (Henry) King Eaton; m. Nancy Brown (dec.); children: John Mcfeeley (dec.), Mary Nan King Murphy, Sarah Ann King Robinson; m. Marjorie Kerr, Feb. 26, 1966 (dec.); m. Carol Flaumenhaft, 2005. Student, Kenyon Coll., 1938—40. V.p. sales Ency. Britannica, Inc., Chgo., 1946—61; pres. Spencer Internat., Inc., Chgo., 1961—66; v.p. Dill-Clitherow & Co., Chgo., 1966—68; pres. Time-Life Librs., Inc., Chgo., 1968—79; chmn., pres., CEO World Book, Inc., Chgo., 1979—83; pres. Consumer Mktg. Internat., Inc., Christiansted, St. Croix, U.S. Virgin Islands, 1983—. Bd. dirs. Good Will, Inc., Charlotte, N.C Capt. U.S. Army, 1942-46, WW II Mem. Direct Selling Assn. (chmn., Hall of Fame 1980), World Fedn. Direct Selling Assns. (founder, chmn. 1978-81), Direct Selling Edn. Found. (chmn. Cir. of Honor 1992), Direct Mkgt. Assn., Chgo. Club, Lighthouse Point Yacht & Racquet Club Home: 35445 Highland Dr Eustis FL 32736-7737 Office Phone: 352-483-0411.

KING, ROBERT L., foundation and former academic administrator; m. Karen King; 4 children. BA, Trinity Coll., 1968; JD, Vanderbilt U., 1971. Prosecutor Monroe County Dist. Atty.'s Office; N.Y. State Assemblyman Rochester, 1987—91; Monroe County exec.; dir. Gov.'s Office of Regulatory Reform, NY, 1995—98; budget dir. N.Y. State, 1998—99; chancellor SUNY, 1999—2005; CEO Ariz. Cmty. Found., Phoenix, 2006—. Prof. bus. law St. John Fisher Coll., Rochester; appointed mem. US Commn. on Presdl. Scholars, 2001, US Nat. Commn. for UN Ednl., Sci., and Cultural Orgn., 2004. Avocations: baseball, golf, sailing, reading. Office: Ariz Cmty Found 2201 E Camelback Rd, Ste 202 Phoenix AZ 85016

KING, ROBERT LEROY, business administration educator; b. Decatur, Ga., Jan. 22, 1931; s. John Todd and Charlotte (Stringer) K.; m. Helen Butler Leaptrott, Mar. 25, 1956; children: Robert Todd, Keith Alan, John Christopher. BBA, U. Ga., 1952; MA, Mich. State U., 1953, PhD, 1960; Dr honoris causa, Oskar Lange Acad. Econs., Wroclaw, Poland, 1992. Asst. prof. mktg. U. S.C., Columbia, 1957-61, assoc. prof., 1961-65; prof. mktg. Va. Poly. Inst. and State U., Blacksburg, 1965-82, head dept., 1969-76; prof. bus. adminstrn., head dept. The Citadel, Charleston, SC, 1982-85, Robert A. Jolley chair bus. adminstrn., 1985-90; dir. internat. bus. studies, prof. mktg. U. Richmond, 1990-96, prof. emeritus, 1996—. Cons. in field; vis. rsch. Warsaw Tech. U., Acad. Econs. in Wroclaw; overseas tchr. in field. Author: An Annotated Index to the Procs. of the Am. Mktg. Assn. Educators Confs., 1973, 90, Procs.: So. Mktg. Assn. 1973 Conf., 1974, Marketing and the New Science of Planning, 1969, Retailing: Theory and Practice for the 21st Century, 1985, Marketing in an Environment of change, 1986, Minority Marketing: Issues and Prospects, 1987, Retailing: Its Present and Future, 1988, Procs. of the 1988 Conf. of the Acad. of Internat. Bus. S.E. U.S. Region, Mktg.: Positioning for the 1990s, 1989, Marketing: Toward the 21st Century, 1991, Retailing: Reflections, Insights and Forecasts, 1991, Developments in Marketing Science, Vol. XIV, 1991, Marketing: Perspectives for the 1990s, 1992, Minority Marketing: Research Perspectives for the 1990s, 1993, Retailing: Theories and Practices for Today and Tomorrow, 1994, Retailing: End of a Century and a Look to the Future, 1997, Internat. Conf. Procs. of Am. Acad. Advt.: 2001 Asia-Pacific Conf., 2001, Internat. Conf. Procs. of Am. Acad. Advt., 2003, Asia-Pacific Conf., 2003; contbr. numerous articles to profl. jours. With AUS, 1953-55, maj. Res., 1955-76. Grantee Ford Found., 1964-65, Va. Poly. Inst. and State U., 1979-82, Citadel Devel. Foun., 1982-90. Mem. Am. Acad. Advt. (exec. sec. 1986-2002, dir. conf. svcs. 2002—, book rev. editor Jour. Advt. 1983-94), Am. Mktg. Assn., Acad. Mktg. Sci. (bd. govs. 1988-94, chmn. bd. govs. 1988-90, v.p. fin., treas. 1986-88), Assn. for Consumer Rsch., Acad. Internat. Bus., Am. Ass. for Advancement of Slavic Studies, Decision Scis. Inst., So. Conf. Slavic Studies, So. Mktg. Assn. (pres. 1972-73), Delta Sigma Pi, Omicron Delta Epsilon, Omicron Delta Kappa, Beta Gamma Sigma. Baptist. Avocations: classical music, history, travel, photography. Home: 2440 Edgeview Ln Midlothian VA 23113-9618 Office: U Richmond Sch Bus Am Acad Advertising Richmond VA 23173

KING, ROBERT LUCIEN, retired lawyer; b. Petaluma, Calif., Aug. 9, 1936; s. John Joseph and Ramona Margaret (Thorson) King; m. Suzanne Nanette Parre, May 18, 1956 (div. 1973); children: Renee Michelle,

Candyce Lynn, Danielle Louise, Benjamin Robert; m. Linda Diane Carey, Mar. 15, 1974 (div. 1981); 1 child, Debra; m. J'an See, Oct. 27, 1984 (div. 1989); 1 child, Jonathan F.; m. Marilyn Collins, June 15, 1991 (div. 2006). AB in Philosophy, Stanford U., 1958, JD, 1960. Bar: Calif., N.Y. 1961. Asst. U.S. atty. U.S. Atty's. Office (so. dist.), NYC, 1964-67; assoc. Debevoise & Plimpton, NYC, 1960-64, 67-70, ptnr., 1970—2003, mng. ptnr. LA, 1989—95. Lectr. Practicing Law Inst., N.Y.C., ABA, Asia/Pacific Ctr. for Resolution of Internat. Bus. Disputes, CPR Inst. for Dispute Resolution. Fellow: Am. Coll. Trial Lawyers; mem.: Calif. Bar Assn., Assn. Bar City NY. Democrat. Avocation: poetry. Business E-Mail: rlking@debevoise.com.

KING, ROBERT THOMAS, editor, writer; b. Hillside, NJ, Oct. 29, 1930; s. Philip Arthur and Lucy (Davis) K.; m. Fredericka Bredow, 1978 Student, Emmanuel Coll., Cambridge, Eng., 1948-50; BA, Birmingham U., Eng., 1955; postgrad., Shakespeare Inst., Stratford-Upon-Avon, Eng., 1955-56. Trainee Oxford U. Press, NYC, 1957-59; chief copy editor NYU Press, 1959-61, editor, 1961-63, mng. editor, 1963-66; dir. U. SC Press, Columbia, 1966-84. Contbr. articles to profl. jours., mags., newspapers. Recipient Lucy Hampton Bostick award, 1978. Mem. Am. Assn. Univ. Presses (bd. dirs. 1972-74, chmn. goals and long-range problems com.), Andiron Club, Grolier Club, Torch Club (Columbia). Episcopalian (dir. The Episcopalian, vestry, lic. lay reader).

KING, ROBERTA B., lawyer; b. Feb. 2, 1975; BA in Politics cum laude, Wake Forest U., Winston-Salem, NC, 1997, JD, 2002. Bar: NC 2003. Assoc. Bennett & Guthrie, Winston-Salem, NC, 2003—. Mem.: NC Assn. Def. Attys. (young lawyers exec. com. 2004—), Def. Rsch. Inst., Forsyth County Young Lawyers (treas, mem. exec. com.), NC Bar Assn. (chair, mem. exec. bd. young lawyers divsn. 2006—07, divsn. dir. 2007—08, com. mem. 2005—06). Office: Bennett & Guthrie 1560 Westbrook Plz Dr Winston Salem NC 27103

KING, RONALD LEE, retired accountant, government agency administrator; b. Scottsbluff, Nebr., Aug. 23, 1941; s. Fred and Dorothy Eldean (Lang) K.; m. Bouala Phannavong Oudomvilay Phasiboribounbane, Dec. 7, 1974; children: Donald, Naransra, Terry. Student, Oceanside-Carlsbad Coll., 1961-62; BS in Acctg., Golden Gate U., 1966. CPA, Calif. Office mgr. Nat. Auto Supply, San Francisco, 1963-66; acct. GAO, San Francisco, 1966-68, supervisory auditor Saigon, Vietnam, 1969-72, Bangkok, 1973-75, Washington, 1975-80, GAO evaluator, 1980-83, group dir., 1983-89, asst. dir. RTC issues, 1989-95, asst. dir. facility mgmt. issues, 1996—2004, retired, 2004. Agy. rep. constrn. sector Nat. Metric Council, Washington 1979-89, Fed. Constrn. Council, 1983-94; mem. conf. planning com. Adv. Bd. on Built Environment, Nat. Acad. Sci., Washington, 1981-83; vol. on assignment in Indonesia, Fin. Svc. Vol. Corps, N.Y., 2002. Cpl. USMC, 1959—63. A.P. Giannini Found. scholar, 1965. Democrat. Lutheran.

KING, ROSALYN MERCITA, social sciences educator, researcher, psychologist; b. Jacksonville, Fla., Aug. 16, 1948; d. Morris Charles and Marie (Coleman) K. BS, Howard U., 1970, MA, 1972; EdD, Harvard U., 1979. Dir. police youth project NCCJ, Washington, 1970-73; placement coord. U. North Fla., Jacksonville, 1973-74, instr., student support counselor, 1973-75; career edn. program coord. Roxbury/Harvard Sch. Program, Cambridge, Mass., 1976; rsch. analyst Spl. Commn. on Unequal Ednl. Opportunity Mass. Ho. of Reps., Boston, 1977; program coord. Freedom House, Inc., Roxbury, Mass., 1977-78; sr. program assoc. Expand Assocs., Inc., Silver Spring, Md., 1979; sr. assoc., dir. rsch. Mark Battle Assocs., Inc., Washington, 1980; dir. planning, program devel. and tech. assistance PUSH-Excel Inst. Research and Tng., Washington, 1981; rsch. assoc. So. Ctr. Studies in Pub. Policy Clark Coll., Atlanta, 1981-84; pres. Info. Rsch. Network Svc., Alexandria, Va., 1984—, Bathshua's Greetings, Alexandria, 1988—. Chief racial stats. U.S. Bur. Census, Washington, 1988; vis. prof. psychology Coppin State Coll., Balt., 1989-90; faculty rsch. assoc. U. Md., College Park, 1990-91; adj. lectr. dept. psychology George Mason U., Fairfax, Va., 1991—; adj. prof. psychology Prince George's C.C., Andrews AFB, 1991-94, Mary Washington Coll., Fredericksburg, Va., 1992-93, Catonsville (Md.) C.C., 1991-96, lectr., 1994-96; sr. pub. health analyst Agy. for HIV/AIDS Comm. Pub. Health, Washington, 1992-94; from assoc. prof. to prof. psychology and chair Ctr. for Tchg. Excellence No. Va. Region, No. Va. C.C., Loudoun campus, Sterling, Va., 1996—, planning com. Nat. Assessment Ednl. Progress, writing framework and specifications devel. ACT Inc., 2006, Nat. Assessment Governing Bd.; presenter papers in field; paticipant Oxford Roundtable on Psychology of the Child, 2006. Contbr. articles to profl. jours. Mem. APA, Assn. Psychol. Sci., Soc. for Tchg. of Psychology, Eastern C.C. Social Scis. Assn. (bd. trustees 2003—, chair bd. trustees 2005), Psi Chi, Phi Delta Kappa. Office Phone: 703-450-2629. E-mail: rosalynmercita.king@worldnet.att.net, roking@nvcc.edu.

KING, ROYCE ARTHUR, retired farm equipment executive; b. Lime Springs, Iowa, July 8, 1923; s. Harold Jackson and Ruth King; m. Frances Kwasnicka King, Sept. 16, 1944; children: James R., Susan K. Bilodeau. Student, Iowa State Coll., Ames, 1942—43, Mich. State U., East Lansing, 1943. Ptnr. Farm Equip. Dealership, Oelwein, Iowa, 1946—80; maintenance Oelwein Cmty. Pub. Schs., 1980—2004; ret., 2004. Lt. col. USAF, 1942—68. Named Eagle Scout, Boy Scouts Am., 1970; recipient Silver Beaver award, 1970. Methodist. Avocations: reading, history, antiques, camping.

KING, SHARON LOUISE, lawyer; b. Ft. Wayne, Ind., Jan. 12, 1932; AB, Mt. Holyoke Coll., 1954; JD with distinction, Valparaiso U., 1957; LLM in Taxation, Georgetown U., 1961. Bar: Ind. 1957, D.C. 1958, Ill. 1962. Trial atty. tax divsn. U.S. Dept. Justice, 1958—62; sr. counsel Sidley Austin LLP, Chgo. Bd. dirs., past pres. Lawyer's Com. for Better Housing, Inc.; mem. North Shore Sr. Ctr., 2006—, bd. dirs., 2006—. Fellow Am. Coll. Tax Counsel; mem. ABA (chmn. com. closely-held corps. taxation sect. 1979-81, regulated pub. utilities com. taxation sect. 1982-83, coun. dir. taxation sect. 1983-86), Chgo. Bar Assn. (bd. mgrs. 1973-75, chmn. fed. tax com. 1983-84), Ill. State Bar Assn. (counsel dir. sect. fed. taxation 1989-91), Women's Bar Found. (bd. dirs., past pres.). Office: Sidley Austin LLP One S Dearborn St Chicago IL 60603

KING, SHELDON SELIG, health facility administrator, educator; b. NYC, Aug. 28, 1931; s. Benjamin and Jeanne (Fritz) King; m. Ruth Arden Zeller, June 26, 1955 (div. 1987); children: Tracy Elizabeth, Meredith Ellen, Adam Bradley; m. Xenia Tonesk, 1988. AB, NYU, 1952; MS, Yale U., 1957. Adminstrv. intern Montefiore Hosp., NYC, 1952, 1955; adminstrv. asst. Mt. Sinai Hosp., NYC, 1957—60, asst. dir., 1960—66, dir. planning, 1966—68; exec. dir. Albert Einstein Coll. Medicine-Bronx Mcpl. Hosp. Ctr., Bronx, NY, 1968—72; asst. prof. Albert Einstein Coll. Medicine, NYC, 1968—72; dir. hosps. and clinics Univ. Hosp., assoc. clin. prof. U. Calif., San Diego, 1972—81; acting head div. health care scis., dept. cmty. medicine U. Calif. Sch. Medicine, 1978—81; assoc. v.p. Stanford U., Calif., 1981—85, clin. assoc. prof. cmty., family and preventive medicine; exec. v.p. Stanford U. Hosp., 1981—85, pres., 1986—89, Cedars-Sinai Med. Ctr., LA, 1989—94, CEO, 1989—94; exec. v.p. Salick Health Care, Inc., LA, 1994—99, pres. ea. region, 1996—98; interim dir. UCLA Med. Ctr., 1995; interim COO INFOHEALTH Mgmt. Corp., 1999—2000, bd. dirs., 2000—; prin. Creative Intellectual Commerce, 2001—. Mem. adminstrv. bd. Coun. of Tchg. Hosps., 1981—86, chmn. adminstrv. bd., 1985; preceptor George Washington U., Ithaca Coll., Yale U., U. Mo., CUNY; chmn. health care com. San Diego County Immigration Coun., 1974—77; adv. coun. Calif. Health Facilities Commn., 1977—82; chmn. ad hoc bd. advisors Am. Bd. Internal Medicine, 1985—91; mem. exec. com. St. Joseph Health Sys., 1990—94; acting chmn. Am. Health Properties, 1996—; nat. adv. com. Robert Wood Johnson Exec. Nurse Fellows Program, 1998—; trustee Carondelet Found., Carondelet Health Sys., Tucson, 2003—; mem. health care adv. coun. TLContact Inc., 2003—; mem. adv. coun. Precyse Solutions, Inc., 2004—; mem. exec. adv. coun. The Beryl Cos., 2006—. Mem. editl. adv. bd. (book) Who's Who in Health Care, 1977, mem. editl. bd. Jour. Med. Edn., 1979—84. Bd. dirs. hosp. coun. San Diego and Imperial Counties, 1974—77, treas., 1976, pres., 1977; bd. dirs. United Way San Diego, 1975—80, Vol. Hosps. Am., 1990—94; mem. Accreditation Coun. for Grad. Med. Edn., 1987—90, Prospective Payment Assessment Commn., 1987—90; bd. dirs. Hosp. Fund, 1987—2000, Tucson Zool. Soc., Reid Park Zoo, 2006—. With US Army, 1952—55. Fellow: APHA, Am. Hosp. Assn. (governing coun. Met. sect. 1983—86, coun. on fin. 1987, ho. of dels. 1987—89), Am. Coll. Health Care Execs.; mem.: Ariz. Arts, Sci. and Tech. Acad. (founder), Inst. of Medicine, Am. Podiatric Med. Assn. (project coun. 2000 1985—86), Calif. Hosp. Assn. (trustee 1978—81). Office Phone: 520-546-7890. Personal E-mail: xenshel@theriver.com.

KING, SHERYL JAYNE, retired secondary school educator, counselor; b. East Grand Rapids, Mich., Oct. 29, 1945; d. Thomas Benton III and Bettyann Louise (Mains) K. BS in Family Living, Sociology, Secondary Edn., Cen. Mich. U., 1968, M in Counseling, 1971. Educator Newaygo Pub. Schs., Mich., 1968-72; interior decorator Sue King Interiors, Grand Rapids, Mich., 1972-73; dir. girl's unit Dillon Family and Youth Svcs., Tulsa, 1973-74; mgr. Fellowship Press, Grand Rapids, Minn., 1974-76; educator, counselor Itasca CC, Grand Rapids, 1977-81, Dist. 318, Grand Rapids, 1977—2007, dept. head, 1977-81, 85-87; ret., 2007. Bd. dirs., chair program com. Marriage and Family Devel. Ctr., Grand Rapids, 1985-89. Treas. Cove Whole Foods Coop., 1978-80; chmn. bd. Christian Cmty. Sch., 1977-78; jr. high softball coach, 1983-86; issues com. No. Minn. Citizens League, Grand Rapids, 1984—, Blandin Found. Study, 1985-86; chair Itasca County Women's Consortium, Grand Rapids, 1983-87, Women's Day Conf., Grand Rapids, 1983-87; bd. dirs. audio tech. Fellowship of Believers, Grand Rapids, 1974-87, 90-98, deaconess, 1974—; bd. dir. audio tech Camp Dominion, Cass Lake, Minn., 1976-80; fitness com., chmn. aquatic com., YMCA, Grand Rapids, 1974-87; sec. Grand Rapids Libr. Bd., 2003—. Recipient 6 Outstanding Svc. awards Fellowship of Believers, 1974-79. Mem. Alpha Delta Kappa. Independent. Avocations: photography, tennis, sailing, travel, writing.

KING, SPENCER BIDWELL, III, cardiologist, educator, medical educator; b. Charleston, SC, May 12, 1937; s. Spencer B. and Caroline Paul King; m. Judith Gail Hayes; children: Spencer B., Susan Gail. AB, Mercer U., Macon, Ga., 1959; MD, Med. Coll. Ga., Augusta, 1963. Diplomate in internal medicine, cardiovasc. disease and interventional cardiology Am. Bd. Internal Medicine. Intern, internal medicine Walter Reed Army Med. Ctr., Washington, 1963—64; capt. M.C., U.S. Army, Honolulu and Vietnam, 1964—66; med. resident, cardiology Emory U. Sch. Medicine, Atlanta, 1966—68, cardiology fellow, 1968—70, dir. Cardiat Catheterization Labs., 1972—90, dir. interventional cardiology, 1985—2000, clin. prof. medicine; cardiologist St. Luke's Hosp. / U. Colo., Denver, 1970—72; dir. Andreas Cardiovasc. Ctr., Atlanta, 1986—2000; Fuqua chair interventional cardiology Fuqua Heart Ctr., Piedmont Hosp., Atlanta, 2000—; co-dir. Atlanta Cardiovasc. Rsch. Inst., Atlanta, 2000—. Bd. dirs. GMP Cos., Ft. Lauderdale, Fla., Surgivision, Inc., Columbia, Md.; chair interventional cardiology bd. Am. Bd. Internal Medicine, 1997—. Co-author: (book) Coronary Angiography and Angioplasty, Atlas of Interventional Cardiology, Hurst's the Heart; author and co-author of other books., mem. editl. boards for several publications, editl. cons. The New England Journal of Medicine; contbr. several articles to profl. jours. Trustee Mercer U., Macon, Ga., 1982—2002; bd. of visitors Mercer U. Sch. Medicine, Macon, Ga., 1982—84. Capt. US Army, 1963—66. Decorated Bronze Star; recipient Disting. Alumnus award, Med. Coll. Ga., 1992, RO1 Rsch. award, NHLBI, 1987-1997. Fellow: Am. Coll. Physicians, European Soc. Cardiology (Ethica Award 2000), Soc. Cardiac Angioplasty and Interventions (pres. 1990—91, First Founders Lecture 1990), Am. Coll. Cardiology (pres. 1998—99, Master). Achievements include invention of beta radiation catheter endovascular brachytherapy. Avocations: golf, travel. Office: Fuqua Ctr for Prevention Piedmont Hosp 1938 Peachtree Rd NW Suite 705 Atlanta GA 30309 Office Phone: 404-605-3567. Office Fax: 404-609-6759.*

KING, STEPHEN C., lawyer, commissioner, educator; b. Washington; s. Colbert and Gwendolyn (Stewart) King; m. Kathryn Dwight Siebert, Aug. 8, 1992; children: Willaim Isaiah, Robert Samuel, Henry Stephen, Audrey Elizabeth. BA, Wesleyan U., 1987; JD, Columbia U., 1990. Bar: NY, US Supreme Ct., US Ct. Appeals (2d cir.), US Dist. Ct. NY (ea. and so. dists.). Articles editor Columbia U. Human Rights Law Rev., 1989—90; assoc. Sidley & Austin, 1990—93; asst. US atty. criminal divsn. (ea. dist.) NY US Dept. Justice, 1994—2001, 2003—04; dir. law enforcement and investigations White House Homeland Security Coun., Washington, 2001—03; of counsel Hunton & Williams LLP, NYC, 2004—. Part-time commr. Fgn. Claims Settlement Commn., 2006, commr., 2006—; adj. asst. prof. Bklyn. Law Sch., 2006—. Bd. mgrs. Westbury Friends Sch. Named NY Super Lawyer, NY Super Lawyers Magazine, 2006. Mem.: ABA (litigation and bus. law sects.), Rep. Nat. Lawyers Assn. advisory coun., Federalist Soc., Fed. Bar Assn. (govt. contracts sect. com. homeland security, pres. eastern dist. NY chpt.), Fed. Bar Coun., FBI Citizens' Acad. NY (v.p. class of 2004), Met. Black Bar Assn., Nassau County Bar Assn., Nat. Def. Indsl. Assn., NY State Bar Assn. (comml., fed. litigation and trial law sects., food, drug and cosmetics law sect.). Office: Hunton & Williams LLP 200 Park Ave New York NY 10166-0136 Office Phone: 617-951-7000. Office Fax: 212-309-1100. Business E-Mail: sking@hunton.com.

KING, STEPHEN EDWIN, novelist, scriptwriter; b. Portland, Maine, Sept. 21, 1947; s. Donald and Nellie Ruth (Pillsbury) K.; m. Tabitha Jane Spruce, Jan. 2, 1971; children: Naomi Rachel, Joseph Hillstrom, Owen Phillip. BS, U. Maine, 1970. Tchr. English, Hampden (Maine) Acad., 1971-73; writer in residence U. Maine at Orono, 1978-79. Author: (novels) Carrie, 1974, 'Salem's Lot, 1975, The Shining, 1976, The Stand, 1978, The Dead Zone, 1979, Firestarter, 1980, Cujo, 1981, Different Seasons, 1982, The Dark Tower I: The Gunslinger, 1982, Christine, 1983, Pet Sematary, 1983, Cycle of the Werewolf, 1985, It, 1986, The Eyes of the Dragon, 1987, Misery, 1987, The Dark Tower II: The Drawing of the Three, 1987, The Tommyknockers, 1987, The Dark Half, 1989, The Stand, the Complete and Uncut Edition, 1990, The Dark Tower III: The Waste Lands, 1991, Needful Things, 1991, Gerald's Game, 1992, Dolores Claiborne, 1992, Insomnia, 1994, Rose Madder, 1995, Desperation, 1996, The Green Mile, 1996, The Dark Tower IV: Wizard & Glass, 1997, Bag of Bones, 1998, The Girl Who Loved Tom Gordon, 1999, Dreamcatcher, 2001, From A Buick 8, 2002, Dark Tower V: Wolves of the Calla, 2003, Dark Tower VI: Song of Susannah, 2004, The Dark Tower VII: The Dark Tower, 2004, The Colorado Kid, 2005, Cell, 2006, Lisey's Story, 2006, The Gingerbread Girl, 2007; (collections) Night Shift, 1978, Different Seasons, 1982, Skeleton Crew, 1985, Four Past Midnight, 1990, Nightmares and Dreamscapes, 1993, Hearts in Atlantis, 1999, Everything's Eventual: 14 Dark Tales, 2002; (non-fiction) Danse Macabre, 1981, On Writing: A Memoir of the Craft, 2000; (novels as Richard Bachman) Rage, 1977, The Long Walk, 1979, Roadwork, 1981, The Running Man, 1982, Thinner, 1984, The Bachman Books: Four Early Novels, 1986, The Regulators, 1996, Blaze: A Posthumous Novel, 2007; co-author (novels with Peter Straub) The Talisman, 1984, Black House, 2001; (non-fiction with Stewart O'Nan) Faithful: Two Diehard Boston Red Sox Fans Chronicle the Historic 2004 Season, 2004 (Quills award for sports book, 2005); author (original screenplays) Creepshow, 1982, Cat's Eye, 1984, Silver Bullet, 1985, Maximum Overdrive, 1986, Golden Years, 1991, Sleepwalkers, 1992; creator, writer (TV mini-series) The Stand, 1994, The Shining, 1997, Storm of the Century, 1999, Kingdom Hospital, 2004; actor (films): Knightriders, 1981, Creepshow, 1982, Maximum Overdrive, 1986, Creepshow II, 1988; actor, dir. (films) Maximum Overdrive, 1986. Recipient Medal for Disting. Contbn. to Am. Letters, The Nat. Book Found., 2003. Mem. Author's Guild Am., Screen Artists Guild, Screen Writers of Am., Writer's Guild. Democrat. Office: 49 Florida Ave Bangor ME 04401-3005*

KING, STEVE, congressman; b. Storm Lake, Iowa, May 28, 1949; m. Marilyn King; 3 children. Student, N.W. Mo. State U., 1967-70. Mem. Iowa State Senate from 6th dist., Des Moines, 1996—2002; vice chair natural resources and environ. com.; mem. appropriations com., mem. bus. and labor rels. com.; mem. commerce com., mem. state govt. com.; mem. US Congress from 5th Iowa dist., 2003—; mem. Ho. Judiciary com. Mem. St. Martin's Cath. Ch.; bd. dirs. Odebolt Cmty. Housing. Mem. Iowa Cattleman's Assn., Land Improvement Contractors Am., U.S. C. of C., Odebolt C. of C., SAC County Farm Bur. Republican. Office: US Ho Reps 1432 Longworth Ho Office Bldg Washington DC 20515-1505*

KING, STEVE MASON, judge, lawyer; b. Graham, Tex., Dec. 17, 1951; s. Beverly W. and Chloe (Stalcup) K.; m. Julia Ellen Milford, Mar. 30, 1974; children: Cassandra, Mason. BA cum laude, U. Tex., 1974; JD, Baylor U., 1976. Bar: Tex. 1977, US Dist. Ct. (no. dist.) Tex. 1978, US Ct. Appeals (5th cir.) 1981, US Supreme Ct. 1981, US Tax Ct. 1984, US Dist. Ct. (ea. dist.) Tex. 1989. Pvt. practice, Ft. Worth, 1977—94; judge Tarrant County Probate Ct. 1, Ft. Worth, 1994—; presiding judge, statutory probate Tex. Cts., 2002—05. Faculty Tex. Coll. Probate Judges; mem. Tex. Guardianship Manual Revision Com., Tex. Supreme Ct. Commn. Info. Tech., 1997-99, 2002-07, State Bar Tex. Trust Code Revision Commn., 2001, Probate Code Revision com., 2007. Mem. Capacity Assessment Handbook Adv. Panel, ABA Commn. Law & Aging APA; note contbr.: The Handbook of Tex., 3rd edit. Trustee Buckner Bapt. Benevolences, Dallas, 1981-2002, 2007—; vice chair Buckner Found., 2002-04, chair, 2004-07; parliamentarian Bapt. Gen. Conv. Tex., 1988-90; mem. Fort Worth Sesquicentennial Celebration History Commn.; pres. Archival Holdings, Inc.; dir. Fort Belknap Archives, Inc.; deacon Travis Ave. Baptist. Ch. Fellow Tex. Bar Found., Tarrant County Bar Found.; mem. State Bar Tex., Tarrant County Bar Assn., Tarrant County Probate Bar Assn. (bd. dirs., pres. 1993-94), Nat. Coll. Probate Judges (life, mem. nominating com. 1999, chair membership com. 2001-03, exec. com. 2002-07, pres. 2005-06), Magna Carta Barons (Somerset chpt.), Ft. Worth Club, Phi Delta Phi. Avocations: woodworking, history, genealogy. Office: Tarrant County Courthouse Rm 260A 100 W Weatherford St Fort Worth TX 76196-0241 Office Phone: 817-884-2028. Business E-Mail: probatecourt1@tarrantcounty.com.

KING, SUSAN BENNETT, retired glass company executive; b. Sioux City, Iowa, Apr. 29, 1940; d. Francis Moffatt Bennett and Marjorie (Rittenhouse) Sillin; m. Stephen P. Glantz. AB, Duke U., 1962. Legis. asst. U.S. Senate, Washington, 1963-66; dir. Nat. Com. for Effective Congress, Washington, 1967-71, Ctr. Pub. Financing of Elections, Washington, 1972-75; exec. asst. to chmn. Fed. Election Commn., Washington, 1975-77; chmn. U.S. Consumer Product Safety Commn., Washington, 1978-81; dir. consumer affairs Corning (N.Y.) Glass Works, 1982, v.p. corp. communications, 1983-86; pres. Steuben Glass, NYC, 1987-92; sr. v.p. corp. affairs Corning Inc., 1992-94. Trustee Duke U., Durham, NC, 1987—2001, Nat. Pub. Radio Found.; chmn. bd. Making a Difference in Cmtys., Inc., 1995—, Triangle Cmty. Found., 2002—, trustee; bd. dirs. MPC, Inc., 1995—. Fellow Inst. Politics, Harvard U., 1981.

KING, TALMADGE E., physician; b. Feb. 24, 1948; BA, Gustavus Adolphus Coll., 1970; MD, Harvard U., 1974. Vice chair dept. medicine U. Colo., Denver, 1992-97; exec. v.p. Nat. Jewish Med. and Rsch. Ctr., Denver, 1992-95; vice chmn. medicine U. Calif., San Francisco, 1997—; chief med. svc. San Francisco Gen. Hosp., 2003. Editor: Interstitial Lung Disease, 2003; co-editor: Medical Management of Vulnerable and Underserved Patients, 2006; sect. editor: Baum's Textbook of Pulmonary Diseases, 2004. Trustee Gustavus Adolphus Coll., St. Peter, Minn., 1993—2002. Mem.: Inst. Medicine, Am. Bd. Internal Medicine (bd. dir. 2006—), Am. Thoracic Soc. (pres. 1997—98). Office: San Francisco Gen Hosp Med Svcs 1001 Potrero Ave Rm 5h22 San Francisco CA 94110-3594 Office Phone: 415-206-3465. Business E-Mail: tking@medsfgh.ucsf.edu.

KING, THOMAS ROY, voice educator, music educator, director; b. St. Loui, Aug. 31, 1945; s. Roy Tilman and Kathleen Fowler King; m. Vicki Lynn Ball, June 12, 1970. MusB in Edn., U. Kans., Lawrence, 1968; MusM, Ind. U., Bloomington, 1970; MA in German, U. Miss., Oxford, 1989, ArtsD, 1992. Choral dir. North Springs HS, Atlanta, 1971—80; opera singer Pfalztheater, Kaiserslautern, Germany, 1980—81, Stadttheater, Oberhausen, Germany, 1981—82, Lueneburg, Germany, 1982—85; prof. voice Austin Peay St. U., Clarksville, Tenn., 1988—; co-artistic dir. Am. Inst. Musical Studies, Graz, Austria, 2004—. Lectr., 1985—. Mem.: SAR (pres. 2003—04), Coll. Music Soc. (pres. 2000—01), Phi Mu Alpha Sinfonia (deputy gov. 2003—). Episcopal. Avocations: genealogy, sailing, travel. Office: Austin Peay St U 601 College Ave Clarksville TN 37044 Office Phone: 931-221-7818. Business E-Mail: kingt@apsu.edu.

KING, TIM, charter school administrator; b. Chgo., 1967; BA, LLD, Georgetown U. Pres. Hales Franciscan HS, Chgo., 1994—2005; founder & CEO Urban Prep Charter Acad. for Young Men, Chgo., 2006—. Named one of 40 Under 40, Crain's Chgo. Bus., 2006. Office: Urban Prep Academies Ste 203 420 N Wabash Chicago IL 60611 also: Englewood Campus 6201 S Stewart Ave Chicago IL 60621 Office Phone: 312-276-0259. Office Fax: 312-755-1050.

KING, TRACY LYNN, science educator; b. Chgo., Jan. 15, 1966; d. Larry H. and Loretta Joyce (Yarbrough) Witherington; m. Junior Owen King, Aug. 26, 1989; children: Sara Lynn, Jefferson Allen. BS Biol. Sci., U. Tenn., Martin, 1991, History Endorsement, 1999. Tchr. sci. Starkville City Schs., Miss., 1993, Obion County HS, Troy, Tenn., 1994—95; spl. edn. asst. Weakley County Schs., Sharon, Tenn., 1997—2000; tchr. sci. and math. Carroll Acad., Huntingdon, Tenn., 2000—. Remediation tchr. Weakley County Schs., Martin, 1997—98, substitute tchr., Dresden, Tenn., 1995—96, Bradford Spl. Sch. Dist., Tenn., 1995—96. Leader Reel Foot Coun. Girl Scouts, Jackson, Tenn., 1997—99; asst. Horse Bowl and Hippology Team 4-H, Dresden, 2002—04; adv. Jr. Nat. Young Leaders Conf., Washington, 2004; parent vol. FFA chpt. Westview HS, Martin, 2003—. Mem.: Tenn. Sci. Tchrs. Assn., Order Ea. Star. Avocations: reading, horseback riding, needlecrafts, piano, gardening. Office: Carroll Academy 625 High St Ste 101 Huntingdon TN 38344-1731 Personal E-mail: double-K-ranch1@yahoo.com.

KING, TROY, state attorney general; b. Elba, Ala., Aug. 22, 1968; m. Paige Pinson; children: Briggs, Colden, Asher. BS in Hist. and Social Sci., Troy State U., 1990; JD, U. Ala., 1994. Bar: Ala. 1994. Asst. legal adv. to Gov. State of Ala., Montgomery, 1995, dep. legal adv. to Gov., 1995—97, acting exec. sec. to Gov., 1997, dep. exec. sec. to Gov., 1997—99, asst. atty. gen., 1999—2003, legal adv. to Gov., 2003—04, atty. gen., 2004—. Mem. Ala. Law Inst., 1994—, Alternative Dispute Resolution Task Force, 1998—99. Republican. Office: Office of Atty Gen 3rd Fl 11 S Union St Montgomery AL 36130 Office Phone: 334-242-7300.*

KING, VERNON DALE, art educator; b. Houston, Sept. 24, 1948; s. Walter Lee and Lois Louise King; m. Lillie Doris Jamerson (dec.); 1 child, Tahir Kamal. BA, North Tex. State U., 1973; MA, U. Houston, 1981;

postgrad., Art Inst. Houston, 1988—89. Tech. illustrator Lockheed Elecs. Corp., Houston, 1973—74; chem. oper. E.I. DuPont de Nemours Co., Inc., La Porte, 1974—99; educator art E.A. Olle Mid. Sch., Houston, 2000—01, R.W. Dowling Mid. Sch., Houston, 2001—02, M.B. Smiley HS, Houston, 2002—04, Crosby Mid. Sch., Crosby, 2004—. Adj. prof. art Cy-Fair Coll., Houston, 2003—06; presenter in field. Exhibitions include All Media, Omaha, Nebr., 2005, Upstream People Gallery, 2005, Nat. Juried Arts Competition and Exhbn., Winston-Salem, N.C., 2005, Sharjah Arts Mus., UAE, 2005, Face Value, Winston-Salem, 2005, others. Recipient award of Excellence, Manhattan Arts Internat. Coun., N.Y.C., 2003, Pres.'s Citation award, U. North Tex., 2007; J.O. Patterson Fine Arts scholar, Ch. of God In Christ, Memphis, 1977. Mem.: Houston Art Educators Assn., Tex. Art Edn. Assn., Nat. Art Edn. Assn. Democrat. Home: 7219 Seminole St Baytown TX 77521 Office: Crosby Mid Sch 14705 FM 2100 Crosby TX 77532 Mailing: PO Box 2503 Baytown TX 77522 Office Phone: 281-328-9265. Business E-Mail: vking@crosbyisd.org.

KING, VICKIE RUTH, minister; b. Birmingham, Ala., Aug. 19, 1951; d. Oliver Julian and Nellie Ruth Haynes; m. Donald C. King, Aug. 14, 1970; children: Paul C., Angie D. Chappell. Min. Ind. Pentecostal Holiness Ch., Birmingham, 1975—; oil painter Cullman Art Guild, Ala., 1994—97; pastor New Hope Ch., Springville, Ala., 1995—97; evangelist, mem. Gospel Revelation Inc., Ind., 1997—. Storyteller Cherokee Tribe of Northeast Ala., 2000—. Recipient Diamond Hope Trophy, Famous Poets Soc. Calif., 1999, First Prize for oil painting, Cullman Art Guild, 1997, Shakespeare Trophy of Excellence, Famous Poets Soc., 2003. Avocations: writing, porcelain faires. Home: 1091 Jim Thomas Road Hayden AL 35079

KING, VIRGINIA SHATTUCK, painter, retired school nurse, educator; b. Bklyn., Feb. 8, 1921; d. Harold James Shattuck and Lillian Elizabeth Shatluck; m. Stuart G. King, May 26, 1946 (dec. July 1988); children: Richard D.(dec.) , Stuart George, Harold James, Douglas Louis. BS in Nursing, Columbia U., NYC, 1944; postgrad., Adelphi U., Garden City, NY, SUNY, Stony Brook. RN NY, 1946; cert. sch. nurse tchr. NY, 1960. Head nurse, obstet. fl. Columbia - Presbyn. Hosp., NYC, 1945—46; pub. health nurse Suffolk County, NY, 1953, sch. nurse, tchr., 1959—79, tchr. health edn., 1970—79, ret., 1979. Author: From Then.To Who Knows When, 1996; one-woman shows include King Ctr. Performing Arts, 2000—01, Maxwell C. King Ctr. Performing Arts, 2001—02, exhibited in group shows at Strawbridge Art League, 2006—07, So. Watercolor Soc., 2007, Brevard County Govt. Ctr., Viera, Fla., 2007, exhibitions include King Ctr. Performing Arts, 1993, Fla. State Soc. Nat. Soc. DAR, 1993, Spacecoast Art League, 1996—97 (3d pl., 1996, 2d pl., 1997), Brevard Mus. Arts and Scis., 1997, 1999, Fla. Hist. Soc. Tebeau Libr., 1998, George Plimpton Zoo-to-Do, Cape Canaveral, 1998, Moffitt Cancer Rsch. Ctr., 1999, Fla. Watercolor Soc., 1999, 2001 (Strathmore award), Charlotte Country Art Guild, 2000, Ridge Art League, 2000, Bayard Ho. Exhibit, 2000, Strawbridge Art League, 2002, 2004—06 (Merit award, 2006), Orlando Mus. Art, 2001, So. Watercolor Soc., 2002, 2005, Melbourn Internat. Airport, 2004, Nat. Wildlife Ctr., Merrit Island, Fla., 2004—05, Ga. Water Color Soc., 2006, others, Represented in permanent collections Brevard County Libr., Brigantine Gallery, Cocoa Beach, 2007, Strawbridge Art League, pictures, Moffitt Cancer Ctr. mag., 1999. Second v.p. Friends of Eau Gallie Pub. Libr., 1999—. Named Artist of Mo., Brigantine Gallery, Cocoa Beach, 2007; recipient Strathmore Paper award, Fla. Water Color Soc., 2001. Mem.: DAR, Nat. League Am. Pen Women, NSDAR (chpt. regent 1990—92, vice regent 2005—06), Strawbridge Art League, Ga. Watercolor Soc. (ribbon and prize 2003, signature mem.), So. Watercolor Soc. (signature), P-2 Fla. Watercolor Soc., Brevard Watercolor Soc., N.Y. State Tchrs. Retired in Fla. (pres. Spuce coast chpt. 1992—94, Svc. award 2001). Republican. Achievements include the Virginia Shattuck Archives at Health Scis. Divsn. of Columbia U. Avocations: watercolor artist, writing, swimming, music. Home and Studio: 2419 Apache Dr Melbourne FL 32935 Office Phone: 321-259-1074. Personal E-mail: hglartiste@aol.com.

KING, WARREN R., judge; Grad., Rensselaer Polytech. Inst.; JD, Am. U.; LLM, Yale U. Atty. U.S. Dist. Ct. DC, Washington; chief grand jury/intake divsn., dep. and acting chief divsn. Superior Ct. Washington; with Office of Improvements in Adminstrn. of Justice U.S. Dept. Justice; assoc. judge Superior Ct. D.C., Washington, 1981—91, D.C. Ct. Appeals, Washington, 1991—98, sr. judge, 1998—; civil dispute atty. The McCammon Group. Mem. faculty Antioch Sch. Law, 1975—; mem. staff Atty. Gen.'s task force on violent crime; mem. hearing com. Bd. Profl. Responsibility. With USN. Office: Dist of Columbia Court of Appeals 500 Indiana Ave NW Rm 6000 Washington DC 20001-2131

KING, WAYNE EDGAR, journalist, educator; b. McDowell County, NC, Mar. 31, 1939; s. Weldon Edgar and Mary King; m. Nina Davis, (div. June 1978); m. Paula Theodore Carroll, July 16, 1984. BA in Journalism, U. N.C., 1964. Reporter, editor The Detroit Free Press, 1964-69; editor, bur. chief, corr. The N.Y. Times, NYC, 1969-93; dir. journalism program Wake Forest U., Winston-Salem, NC, 1993—. Working group on disability in U.S. Pres. The White House, 1996. Mem. editl. bd. Acad. Mag., Washington, 1996-2002. Recipient Pulitzer prize, 1968. Mem. AAUP Home: 1901 Waycross Dr Winston Salem NC 27106-3416 Office Phone: 336-758-4399. E-mail: kingwe@wfu.edu.

KING, WILLIAM, sculptor; b. Jacksonville, Fla., Feb. 25, 1925; Student, U. Fla., 1942-44, Cooper Union Art Sch., 1945-48, Bklyn. Mus. Art Sch., 1949, Acad. dei Belle Arti, Rome, 1949-50, Ctrl. Sch., London, 1952. Art instr. Bklyn. Mus. Art Sch., 1952-55, U. Calif., Berkeley, 1956-66, Art Students' League, 1968-69, U. Pa., Phila., 1972-73. Artist in residence, SUNY at Fredonia, New Paltz, Jamestown, Oswego, Plattsburgh. One person art exhibitions include: Alan Gallery, N.Y.C., 1954, 55, 61, San Francisco Mus. Art, 1970, Santa Barbara Mus. Art, 1970, Ringling Mus., Sarasota, Fla., 1971, Dag Hammerskjold Pla., N.Y.C., 1971, Jacksonville (Fla.) Art Mus., 1972, Worcester (Mass.) Art Mus., 1972, Elvehjom Art Ctr., U. Wis., Eau Claire, 1973, William Benton Mus., U. Conn., 1973, U. Ga., Athens, 1973, Traveling Exhbn. SUNY, 1974, Benson Gallery, Bridgehampton, N.Y., 1976, Louise Himmelfarb Gallery, Water Mill, N.Y., 1980, Wingspread Gallery, N.E. Harbor, Maine, 1981, Alpha Gallery, Boston, 1971, 82, Hunter Mus., Chattanooga, 1987, David Heath Gallery, Atlanta, 1987, Marilyn Pearl Gallery, N.Y.C., 1988, Internat. Sculpture Ctr., Sothebys, 1989, Simmons Visual Arts Ctr., Brenau Coll., Gainesville, Ga., 1992, U. Pitts., 1995, Seacon Sq., Bangkok, Thailand, 1996, Terry Dintenfass Gallery, N.Y.C., 1962, 64-71, 73, 76, 80-84, 86, 89-92, 94, 97. and others: group exhibitions include: Mus. Modern Art, N.Y.C., 1955, Ann. Exhbn. Whitney Mus. Am. Art., 1952, 54, 56, 58, 60, 62, 64, 66, 68, Fogg Art Mus., Dartmouth Coll., Vassar Cool, Bowdoine Coll. (traveling exhbn. 1972-73), Art Gallery Budapest, Hungary, 1973, Weatherspoon Art Gallery, U. N.C., 1974, Galeria Tonay Schubert, Marbella, Spain, 1976, Grand Palais, Paris, 1976, Inst. Contemporary Art, Boston, Dayton Art Inst., 1982, Chgo. Internat. Art Exhbn., 1982, Am. Acad. Arts and Letters, 1995, White House, 1995, many others; collection Met. Mus. Art, N.Y.C., Guggenheim Mus., Whitney Mus., Nelson and John Rockefeller Collections, others; also commissions. Recipient Sculpture prize, Cooper Union Art Sch., 1948, Fulbright grant, 1949-50. Margaret Tiffany Blake fresco award, 1951, Augustus St. Gaudens medal, Cooper Union, 1964, Creative Artist Pub. Svc. award and grant, 1974, Hakone Open-Air Mus., Japan, Distinction prize, 1980, Nat Acad. Design gold medal, 1986, Am. Acad. Arts and Letters, Louise Nevelson award, 1995. Mem.: NAD (academician 1991—, past pres.), Am. Acad. Arts and Letters.

KING, WILLIAM BRUCE, retired lawyer; b. Boston, June 3, 1932; s. Gilbert and Frances (Hood) K.; m. Sheila Malone, July 9, 1955; children: Stephen Bruce, Rachel Creath, Christopher Bruce. AB, Harvard U., 1954, LL.B., 1959. Bar: Mass. 1959. Assoc. firm Goodwin Procter, Boston, 1959-67, ptnr., 1968-99, of counsel, 2000—; prin. William B. King P.C., 1981-99. Mem. bd. investment Cambridge Savs. Bank, 1973-2007, trustee, 1969-2007, corporator, 1965-2007; sec. Bradley Real Estate, Inc., 1963-99; trustee Cambridge Heritage Trust, 1984—; dir. mem. exec. com. Cambridge Fin. Group, Inc., 1998-2007, hon. trustee, 2007—, Cambridge Appleton Trust, N.A., 1999-2006; corp. dir. Cambridge Homes, 2005-. Author: (with others) Real Estate Investment Trusts: Structures, Analysis, and Strategy, 1997. Trustee Buckingham Browne and Nichols Sch., 1970-76, sec., 1970-73, vice chmn., 1974-76; mem. Cambridge (Mass.) Hist. Commn., 1973—, vice chmn., 1973-86, chmn., 1986—; pres Cambridge Civic Assn., 1963-65; bd. govs. Nat. Assn. Real Estate Investment Trusts, 1982-88, chmn. state regulation subcom. of govt. rels. com., 1989-91. Served with USN, 1954-56. Recipient Industry Leadership award Nat. Assn. Real Estate Investment Trusts, 1995. Home: 25 Hurlbut St Cambridge MA 02138-1603 E-mail: basking@comcast.net.

KING, WILLIAM COLLINS, retired oil industry executive; b. Pitts., Aug. 11, 1921; s. William Raffington and Anne Blatchford (Collins) K.; m. Carolyn Ottilie Thorne, Sept. 1, 1951; children: William R., John Thorne, Louise R., Andrew C. BSChemE, Carnegie-Mellon U., 1943; MSChemE, MIT, 1948. With Gulf Rsch. & Devel. Co. div. Gulf Oil Corp., Pitts., 1948-55, with chems. dept., 1955-57, dir. market rsch. and econ. planning chems. dept., 1957-63, world wide coord. chem. ops., 1963-67, v.p. chem. ops. in Europe and Middle East, 1967-72, dir. corp. policy analysis, 1972-80, v.p. corp. planning, 1980—85, ret., 1985. Bd. dir. Fertiberia, S.A., Spain, Rio Gulf Petrolquimica, S.A., Spain, Kuwait Chem. Fertilizer Co., Kuwait; spkr., 1975—, participant nat. and local programs, participant local radio programs. Author: Building For Victory, WW-II and The CBI, and 1875 Engr. Av'n Bn., 2004, contbr. to Am. Heritage website, articles to profl. publs. Bd. dir. Hist. Soc. We. Pa., 1977-99, pres., 1986-90, chmn., 1990-98, vice-chmn., 1998-99, trustee emeritus, 1999 (honored with William Collins King Atrium of Senator John Heinz Pitts. Regional History Ctr., 1996); v.p., bd. dir. Civic Light Opera Co., Pitts., 1978-86 (Golden Hall of Fame, 1996); councillor of the Atlantic Coun. of the U.S., 1985-93. Served with C.E., U.S. Army, 1943-46, CBI. Recipient Alumni Merit award Carnegie Mellon U., 1998. Fellow Am. Chem. Soc.; mem. N.Am. Soc. Corp. Planning (bd. dir. chpt. 1982-85), Strategic Mgmt. Soc., Coun. Planning Execs. (conf. bd.), Am. Inst. Chem. Engrs. Clubs: Duquesne; Fox Chapel Golf (Pitts.). *Do all that you do in that way most likely to enhance the self esteem of others.*

KING, WILLIAM H., JR., lawyer; b. Richmond, Va., Nov. 4, 1940; AB, Dartmouth Coll., 1963; LLB, U. Va., 1967; MA (hon.), Dartmouth Coll., 1992. Bar: Va. 1967, Tex. 1993. Mem. McGuireWoods LLP, Richmond. Fellow Am. Bar Found., Am. Coll. Trial Lawyers; mem. ABA. Office: McGuireWoods One James Ctr Richmond VA 23219-4030 E-mail: wking@mcguirewoods.com.

KING, WILLIAM RICHARD, business educator, writer, consultant; b. McKeesport, Pa., Dec. 24, 1938; s. Dewey Clark and Cambria Edith (Jones) K.; m. Fay Eileen Bickerton, June 20, 1958; children: James David, Suzan Lorain, Cambria H.L. BS with honors, Pa. State U., 1960; MS Case Inst. Tech, 1962, PhD, 1964. Indsl. engr. Pitts. Steel Co., 1960; instr., research fellow, research asst. Case Inst. Tech., 1960-64; asst. prof. ops. research, 1964-65; asst. prof. stats. and ops. research Air Force Inst. Tech., 1965-67; assoc. prof. bus. adminstrn. U. Pitts., 1967-69, prof., 1969-85, univ. prof., 1986—, dir. doctoral program, 1971-74, dir. Strategic Mgmt. Inst., 1980-85. On leave as profl. staff mem. US Senate Budget Com., 1976-77; v.p., dir. Cleland-King, Inc., 1969-85; mgmt. cons., chmn. Internat. Conf. on Info. Systems Profl. Corp., 1987-88, 2006—07; vis. prof. U. Auckland, New Zealand, 1994, Nat. U. Singapore, 1997, City U. Hong Kong, 1997, 98; chair/co-chair Internat. Conf. on Info. Sys., 1987, 2005. Author: Quantitative Analysis for Marketing Management, 1967, Probability for Management Decisions, 1968, (with David Cleland) Systems Analysis and Project Management, 1968 (McKinsey Found. award 1969), 3d edit., 1983, Management: a Systems Approach, 1972, Marketing Management Information Systems, 1977, (with David Cleland) Strategic Planning and Policy, 1978, (with John Grant) The Logic of Strategic Planning, 1982; editor: (with David Cleland) Systems, Organizations, Analysis, Management, 1969, Project Management Handbook, 1983, 2d edit., 1989 (Inst. Indsl. Engrs. Book of Yr. award 1984), (with Gerald Zaltman) Marketing Scientific and Technical Information, 1979, (with D. I. Cleland) Strategic Planning and Management Handbook, 1987, (with P. Gray, E. McLean and H. Watson) Management of Information Systems, 1989, 2nd edit., 1994, (with V Sethi) Organizational Transformation Through Business Process Reengineering, 1998, OMEGA: Internat. Jour. Mgmt. Sci. Spl. Issue on Knowledge Mgmt. and Oranizational Learning, 2007, (with R. Torkdazeh) MIS Quarterly Spl. Issue on Offshoring, 2007, Planning for Info. Sys., 2007; assoc. editor: Strategic Mgmt. Jour., 1985-89, Mgmt. Sci., 1971-89, MIS Quar., 1980-82, editor-in-chief, 1983-85; area editor: Internat. Jour. Info. and Mgmt. Scis.; cons. editor: Prentice Hall Info. Mgmt. Series, 1989-99; mem. editl. adv. bd. Omega: Internat. Jour. of Mgmt. Sci., Info. Systems Rsch., Jour. Global Info. Mgmt., Jour. Mgmt. Info. Sys., Jour. Global Info. Tech. Mgmt., Jour. Market-Focused Mgmt., Info. Sys. Mgmt., Acad. Press, Ency. Info. Sys., Idea Group Press Ency. Knowledge Mgmt.; contbr. articles to profl. jours. Active YMCA; v.p., dir. Pitts. Commerce Inst., 1971-80; bd. dirs. Western Pa. Montessori Sch., 1968-71, pres., 1968-69. Served to 1st lt. USAF, 1965—67. Ford Found. Systems rsch. fellow, 1960-62; Travelers Ins. Co. rsch. fellow, 1963-64, External Examiner City U. Hong Kong, 1996-99. Fellow AAAS, Decision Sci. Inst., Assn. Info. Sys. (founding pres., Inaugural fellow 1999, Leo Lifetime Achievement award 2004), Inst. Mgmt. Sci. and Ops. Rsch. (pres. 1989-90, Inaugural fellow 2002); mem. Planning Forum, Ops. Rsch. Soc. Am., Acad. Mgmt., Strategic Mgmt. Soc., Inst. Mgmt. Scis. (v.p. 1986-89, pres. 1989-90), Assn. Computing Machinery, Am. Mktg. Assn., Soc. Info. Mgmt., World Future Soc., Tau Beta Pi, Beta Gamma Sigma, Alpha Pi Mu, Sigma Tau. Office: Katz Grad Sch Bus U Pitts Pittsburgh PA 15260 Business E-Mail: billking@katz.pitt.edu.

KINGDON, JOHN WELLS, political science professor; b. Wisconsin Rapids, Wis., Oct. 28, 1940; s. Robert Wells and Catherine (McCune) K.; m. Kirsten Berg, June 16, 1965; children: James, Tor. BA, Oberlin Coll., 1962; MA, U. Wis., 1963, PhD, 1965. Asst. prof. polit. sci. U. Mich., Ann Arbor, 1965-70, assoc. prof., 1970-75, prof., 1975-98, prof. emeritus, 1998—, chmn. dept. polit. sci., 1982-87. Author: Candidates for Office, 1968, Congressmen's Voting Decisions, 1973, 3d rev. edit., 1989, Agendas, Alternatives and Public Policies, 1984, 2d edit., 1995, America the Unusual, 1998. NSF grantee, 1978-82, Soc. Sci. Research Council grantee, 1969-70; Guggenheim fellow, 1979-80, Ctr. for Advanced Study in Behaviorial Scis. fellow, 1987-88. Fellow Am. Acad. Arts and Scis.; mem. Midwest Polit. Sci. Assn. (pres. 1987-88). Office: U Mich Dept Polit Sci Ann Arbor MI 48109

KINGDON, ROBERT MCCUNE, historian, educator; b. Chgo., Dec. 29, 1927; s. Robert W. and Anna Catherine (McCune) K. AB, Oberlin Coll., 1949; MA, Columbia U., 1950, PhD, 1955; postgrad, U. Geneva, 1951—52, PhD (hon.), 1986; HHD, Oberlin Coll., 1999. Instr., asst. prof. history U. Mass., 1952-57; asst. prof., assoc. prof., prof. history State U. Iowa, Iowa City, 1957-65; prof. history U. Wis., Madison, 1965-98, Hilldale prof. history, 1988-98; mem. Inst. Research Humanities, 1974-98, dir., 1975-87. Vis. instr. Amherst (Mass.) Coll., 1953-54; vis. prof. Stanford U., 1964, 80; bd. dirs. Ctr. Reformation Rsch., St. Louis, pres., 1967-2000. Author: Geneva and the Coming of the Wars of Religion in France, 1555-1563, 1956, Geneva and the Consolidation of the French Protestant Movement, 1564-1572, 1967, The Political Thought of Peter Martyr Vermigli, 1980, Church and Society in Reformation Europe, 1985, Myths About the St. Bartholomew's Day Massacres, 1572-1576, 1988, Adultery and Divorce in Calvin's Geneva, 1995, (with John Witte) Sex, Marriage, and Family in John Calvin's Geneva, vol. 1, 2005; editor: Sixteenth Century Jour., 1973-97; co-editor: Registres de la Compagnie des Pasteurs de Geneve au temps de Calvin, 1962-64, Registres du Consistoire de Geneve au temps de Calvin, t. 1-4, 1996-2007, Bibliography of the Works of Peter Martyr Vermigli, 1990; contbr. articles to profl. jours. Mem. Am. Soc. Reformation Rsch. (v.p. 1970, pres. 1971), Am. Soc. Ch. History (pres. 1980, Disting. Career award 2004), Cen. Renaissance Conf., Renaissance Soc. Am. (exec. bd. 1972-92), Internat. Fedn. Socs. and Insts. for Study of Renaissance (sec.-treas. 1967-89). Home: 4 Rosewood Cir Madison WI 53711-2723 Business E-Mail: rkingdon@wisc.edu.

KINGHAM, RICHARD FRANK, lawyer; b. Lafayette, Ind., Aug. 2, 1946; s. James R. and Loretta C. Kingham; m. Justine Frances McClung, July 6, 1968; 1 child, Richard Patterson. BA, George Washington U., 1968; JD, U. Va., 1973. Bar: DC 1973, US Dist. Ct. DC 1974, US Ct. Appeals (8th cir.) 1977, US Supreme Ct. 1977, US Ct. Appeals (5th cir.) 1980, registered: Law Soc. Eng. and Wales (fgn. lawyer) 1994. Editl. asst. Washington Star, 1964-68, 69-70; assoc. Covington & Burling, Washington, 1973-81, ptnr., 1981—, mng. ptnr. London office, 1996-2000, mem. mgmt. com., 2000—04, co-head Life Scis. Industry Group, 2000—. Lectr. law U. Va., Charlottesville, 1977—90; mem. com. issues and priorities new vaccine devel. Inst. Medicine, NAS, 1983—86, mem. com. on accelerating biowarfare countermeasures, 2002—04, 2003—04, Nat. Adv. Allergy and Infectious Diseases Coun. NIH, 1988—92; mem. adv. bd. World Pharms. Report, 1990—96; mem. WHO Coun. Internat. Orgns. Med. Scis. Working Party in Pharmacovigilance, 1997—99; lectr. grad. program in pharm. medicine Cardiff U., Wales, 1999—; adj. prof. Georgetown U., 2003—. Contbr. articles to profl. jours. Pres. Am. Friends of St. Peter's Eaton Sq., 2001—; treas., mem. parochial ch. coun. St. Peter's Ch. Eaton Sq., London, 1998—2001. With US Army, 1968—69. Mem.: ABA, European Forum for Good Clin. Practice, Soc. Vertebrate Paleontology, Food Law Group (U.K.), European Soc. Pharmacovigilance, Food and Drug Law Inst., Drug Info. Assn., Brussels Pharm. Law Group, Reform Club (London), Order of Coif. Republican. Episcopalian. Avocation: vertebrate paleontology. Home: 4821 Dexter St NW Washington DC 20007 Office Phone: 202-662-5268. Business E-Mail: rkingham@cov.com.

KING-NING, TU, materials science and engineering educator; b. Canton, China, Dec. 30, 1937; came to U.S., 1962; s. Ying-Chiang Tu and Sau-Yuk Chen; m. Ching Chiao, Sept. 25, 1964; children: Olivia, Stephen. BSc, Nat. Taiwan U., 1960; MSc, Brown U., 1964; PhD, Harvard U., 1968. Rsch. staff mem. IBM Watson Rsch. Ctr., Yorktown Heights, NY, 1968-93, sr. mgr. thin film sci. dept., 1978-85, sr. mgr. materials sci. dept., 1985-87; prof. dept. materials sci. & engring. UCLA, 1993—. Co-author: (textbook) Electronic Thin Film Science, 1992. Recipient Acta/Scripta Metallurgica Lecturer, 1990; grantee Alexander von Humboldt, 1996. Fellow Am. Phys. Soc., The Metall. Soc. (Applications to Practice award 1988), Churchill Coll. (U.K.), Academia Sinica Republic of China. Achievements include 8 patents on thin film technology for microelectronics. Office: UCLA Boelter Hall 6532 B Los Angeles CA 90095-0001 E-mail: kntu@ucla.edu.

KINGSBERY, WALTON WAITS, JR., retired accounting firm executive; m. Helen Elizabeth Clayton; children: Walton Waits, III, J. Clayton, Peter C. Student Washington and Lee U., 1945—47; BS with honors, U. Ala., 1950. CPA, N.J., N.Y., Calif., Ohio. With Price Waterhouse & Co., 1950, 1953—88, mng. pntr. Cleve., 1977—82, mng. ptnr. Western area LA, 1982—87; mgmt. commn. Price Waterhouse Bd., 1979—87; ret., 1988. Bus. adv. bd. Bateman Eichler, Hill Richards, LA, 1988-90, Employee Office of Atty. Gen. NJ, 1988-95; adv. bd. NJ Bur. Securities, 1993-98, NJ Supreme Ct. Com. on Unauthorized Practice of Law, 1990-2005; mem. NJ Commn. to Deter Criminal Activity, 1998-01; dir. NJ Citizens Against Crime, Inc., 1998-01. Contbr. articles to profl. jours. Mem. Shrewsbury (N.J.) Planning Bd., 1972—75; trustee Beech Brook, 1979, Cleve. Playhouse, 1980; clk. Village of Hunting Valley, Ohio; mem. Planning Bd., Spring Lake, NJ, 1997—; trustee Jersey Shore Med. Ctr. Found., 1999—; mem. audit com. Meridian Health Sys., 1999—2005; bd dirs. Greater Cleve. Growth Assn., 1978—82. With US Army, 1950—53. Mem. AICPA, SAR, Nat. Assn. Accts., Ohio Soc. CPAs, N.J. Soc. CPAs, N.Y. Soc. CPAs, Calif. Soc. CPAs, Bluecoats, Newcomen Soc. N.Am., Cleve. Country Club, Union Club, Cleve. Racquet Club, Duquesne Club (Pitts.), Fifty Club, Calif. Club, Jonathan Club, Lincoln Club (L.A.), Univ. Club (N.Y.C.), Spring Lake Golf Club (trustee, exec. com., chmn. fin. com., treas.), 200 Club, Beverly Hills Country Club (bd. govs.). *From a small town in Alabama to partner of Price Waterhouse in New York, then board member, management committee, head of the Cleveland office, then the West Coast practice was a long, interesting road made easier by professional mentors, a loving wife and an understanding family. Service to the government and charitable organizations has enriched career and retirement.*

KINGSBURY, ELLEN ANN DAGON, anesthesiologist, general practitioner; b. Balt., Feb. 3, 1936; d. Emmett Paul and Annie (Sollers) Dagon; m. Lyle Jordan Millan IV, Dec. 21, 1963; children: Lyle Jordan V, Elizabeth Lyle, Ann Sheridan Worthington.; m. T. Marshall Duer, Jr., Aug. 23, 1985; m. Milton D. Kingsbury, Oct. 13, 2006. AB, George Washington U., 1959; MD, U. Md., 1964; postgrad., Johns Hopkins U., 1965—68. Intern Union Meml. Hosp., Balt., 1964—65; resident in anesthesiology Johns Hopkins Hosp., Balt., 1965—68, fellow in surgery, 1965—68; practice medicine specializing in anesthesiology Balt., 1968—; faculty Ch. Home and Hosp., Balt., 1969—; attending staff Union Meml. Hosp., Ch. Home and Hosp., Franklin Sq. Hosp., Children's Hosp., James Lawrence Kernan Hosp., Balt., 1982—94; co-chief anesthesiology James Kernan Hosp., 1983—94, med. dir. out-patient surgery dept., 1987—94. Affiliate cons. emergency room Ch. Home and Hosp., Balt., 1969—, med. audit and utilizaions com., 1970-72, mem. emergency and ambulatory care com., 1973-74, chief emergency dept., 1973-74; cons. anesthesiologist Md. State Penitentiary, 1971; fellow in critical care medicine Md. Inst. Emergency Medicine, 1975-76; infection control com. U. Md. Hosp., 1975—; instr. anesthesiology U. Md. Sch. Medicine, 1975—; staff anesthesiologist Mercy Hosp., 1978—, audit com., 1979-80, 82; asst. prof. anesthegiology U. Md. Med. Sch., 1989-94; med. exec. com. Kernan Hosp., 1990-94, v.p. 1990, chief of staff, 1992—; active Tappahannock Family Practice, 1994-96, Rappahannock Gen. Hosp. Family Practice, 1996—, Rappahannock Gen. Hosp., 1996—, ethics com., 1997—; med. examiner No. Neck of Va., 1996—; active Commonwealth of Va. Med. Bd. Mem. AMA, Am. Coll. Emergency Physicians, Am. Acad. Gen. Practitioners, Met. Emergency Dept. Heads Am., Md. Soc. Anesthesiologists, Balt. County Med. Soc., Mid. Peninsula Med. Soc., No. Neck Med. Soc., Med. Soc. Va., Med. and Choir Faculty Med., Chirurg. Soc., Internat. Congress Anaesthesiologists, Internat. Anesthesia Rsch. Soc., Am. L'Hirondelle Club, Annapolis Yacht Club, Chesapeake Bay Yacht Racing Assn., Rappahannock River Yacht Club. Anglican. Address: PO Box 347 White Stone VA 22578-2021 Office Phone: 804-462-5155.

KINGSBURY, JOHN MERRIAM, botanist, educator; b. Boston, July 4, 1928; s. Willis Albert and Constance Elizabeth (Merriam) K.; m. Louise Arnold Gerken, June 6, 1956; 1 dau., Joanna Merriam. BS, U. Mass., 1950; A.M., Harvard U., 1952, PhD, 1954; Sc.D. (hon.), Dickinson Coll., 1985. Instr. Brandeis U., Waltham, Mass., 1953-54; mem. faculty N.Y. State Coll. Agr. and Life Scis., Cornell U., Ithaca, NY, 1954—83, prof. botany emeritus, 1983—; prof. clin. scis. Coll. Vet. Medicine, Cornell U., 1978-83, dir. arboretum and bot. garden, 1982-83. Instr. Marine Biol. Lab., Woods Hole, Mass., summers 1958-61; founding dir. Shoals Marine Lab., 1972-79; adj. prof. U. N.H., 1976-78; cons. Upstate Med. Ctr., Syracuse, N.Y.,

1977-86; instr. Aquavet course Cornell U.-U. Pa., 1978-2001; lectr. Cornell U. Adult U., 1978-2001; propr. Bullbrier Press, 1983—; lectr. Columbus project Sta. WGBH/Pub. Broadcasting Svc., Boston, 1990; mem. endowment com., chmn., 1992-94; vis. faculty U. Tasmania, Australia, 1980. Author: Poisonous Plants of the United States and Canada, 1964, Deadly Harvest-A Guide to Common Poisonous Plants, 1965, Seaweeds of Cape Cod and the Islands, 1969, rev. edit., 1997, The Rocky Shore, 1970, Oil and Water: The New Hampshire Story, 1975, 200 Conspicuous, Unusual, or Economically Important Tropical Plants of the Caribbean, 1988, Here's How We'll Do It-An Informal History of the Construction of the Shoals Marine Laboratory, 1991, Recollections and Reminiscences, 2000; mem. editl. bd. Cornell U. Press, 1985-86; compiler: Catalog of the Library at the Bullard Colonial Farm, 1999. NSF faculty fellow, 1958; Fulbright sr. scholar, 1980; recipient Profile Svc. award U. N.H., 1998; named in his honor: Rsch. Vessel John M. Kingsbury, 1984, John M. Kingsbury Dir., Shoals Marine Lab., Cornell U., 2001, John M. & Louise G. Kingsbury Scholarships, Cornell U., 2001, Kingsbury House, Appledore Island, 2001. Fellow Am. Acad. Vet. and Comparative Toxicology (hon.); mem. Bullard Meml. Farm Assn. (clk. 1978-2003, pres. 1990-94), Sea Edn. Assn. (trustee 1977-92, emeritus, 2002—, pres. 1982-87), Marine Biol. Lab. (life), Nature Conservancy (trustee N.Y. state bd. 1983-90), Audubon Soc. (lectr. Mass. chpt. 1987-89), Mass. Soc. Cin. Office: Cornell U 135A Guterman Lab Ithaca NY 14853-5903 Business E-Mail: jmk11@cornell.edu.

KINGSBURY, MICHAEL BRYANT, organist, retired elementary school educator, retired secondary school educator; b. Wilmington, NC, Dec. 25, 1933; s. Walter Russell and Olga Loretta (Lewis) K. BA, Emory U., 1957; MA, Atlanta U., 1978. Cert. mid. sch. sci. tchr., sci. tchr. K-12, social studies tchr., Ga. Tchr. Bouldercrest Elem. Sch., Atlanta, 1958-62; sci. tchr. Northcutt Elem. Sch., College Park, Ga., 1962-66, G.P. Babb Jr. H.S., Forest Park, Ga., 1966-84, Pointe South Mid. Sch., Jonesboro, Ga., 1984-94; organist, choir master Episcopal and Cath. Chs., Atlanta and Decatur, Ga., 1955—; organist, dir. Cath. music Ft. McPherson/U.S. Army, Atlanta, 1994—. Author, editor: Laboratory Manual for Earth Science, 1970. Bd. dirs. Camelot Homeowners Assn., Jonesboro, 1978-84; patron Atlanta Symphony Orch., 1992—; lector St. Luke's Episcopal Ch. Recipient Ritter Music award Atlanta Pub. Schs., 1951, Cmty. Svc. award Clayton County Ret. Tchrs., 1998, Service Playing cert. Am. Guild Organists, Cert. of Appreciation, Clayton County Educators Assn., 1999, others; NSF grant, 1970. Mem. Clayton County Ret. Tchrs. Assn. (pres. 1996—, dirs. dir. 2000-02, Cert. of Appreciation, Plaque 2002), Clayton County Ret. Educators Assn. (pres. 1996-98, dir. 10th dist.), Ga. Ret. Tchrs. Assn. (10th dist. dir. 2000-02), Am. Guild of Organists (membership com. 1958—), Atlanta Music Club (v.p. 2004—, pres. elect), Lake Jodeco Homeowners Assn. (bd. dirs.), Atlanta Music Club (v.p. programs, pres.-elect 2005, pres. 2006—). Democrat. Episcopalian. Avocations: walking, bicycle riding, collecting southern writings and gone with the wind memorabilia. Home: 2669 Lake Jodeco Dr Jonesboro GA 30236-5355 Office: Ft McPherson US Army Lee St Atlanta GA 30330 E-mail: kingsburymb@aol.com.

KINGSBURY, TOM (THOMAS A. KINGSBURY), retail executive; b. Wis. Student, U. Wis. Various mgmt. positions from exec. trainee Famous-Barr divsn. to sr. v.p. Filene's May Dept. Stores, 1976—2000, pres., CEO Filene's-Kaufmann's divsn., 2000—06; sr. exec. v.p. Kohl's Corp., Menomonee Falls, Wis., 2006—. Office: Kohls Corp N56 W17000 Ridgewood Dr Menomonee Falls WI 53051-5660 Office Phone: 262-703-7000.*

KINGSLEY, SIR BEN, actor; b. Scarborough, Eng., Dec. 31, 1943; s. Rahimtulla Harji and Anna Lyna (Goodman) Bhanji; m. Angela Morrant, 1966 (div. 1972), children: Thomas Alexis, Jasmine Anna; m. Alison Sutcliffe, July 1, 1978 (div. 1992), children: Edmund William Macaulay, Ferdinand James Macaulay; m. Alexandra Christmann, Oct. 3, 2003. MA (hon.), Salford U. Assoc. artist Royal Shakespeare Co., Eng., 1968—. Appeared in plays including Hamlet, 1975-76, Othello, 1985-86, Edmund Kean, 1981-83; actor (films) Fear Is the Key, 1972, Gandhi, 1981 (Acad. award for best actor, 1982), Betrayal, 1982, Turtle Diary, 1984, Sleeps Six, 1984, Harem, 1985, Maurice, 1987, Testimony, 1987, Pascali's Island, 1988, Without a Clue, 1988, Slipstream, 1989, (voice only) Romeo-Juliet, 1990, The Children, 1990, O, Quinto Macacao, 1990, Una Vita Scellerata, 1991, L'Amore Necessario, 1991, Bugsy, 1991, (voice only) Freddie as F.R.O.7, 1992, Sneakers, 1992, Dave, 1993, Innocent Moves, 1993, Searching for Bobby Fisher, 1993, Schindler's List, 1993, Death and the Maiden, 1994, Species, 1994, Twelfth Night: Or What You Will, 1996, The Assignment, 1997, Photographing Fairies, 1997, Parking Shots, 1998, Rules of Engagement, 1999, (voice only) A Force More Powerful, 1999, The Confession, 1999, Sexy Beast, 2000, Spooky House, 2000, What Planet Are You From, 2000, (voice only) Artificial Intelligence: A.I., 2001, The Triumph of Love, 2001, Tuck Everlasting, 2002, House of Sand and Fog, 2003 (Acad. Award nomination for best actor, 2004, Golden Globe nomination for best actor in a drama, 2004, Screen Actors Guild Award nomination for best actor, 2004), Thunderbirds, 2004, Suspect Zero, 2004, A Sound of Thunder, 2005, Mrs. Harris, 2005, Oliver Twist, 2005, BloodRayne, 2005, The Inquiry, 2006, Lucky Number Slevin, 2006, You Kill Me, 2007, The Last Legion, 2007; (TV movies) A Misfortune, 1973, Barbara of the House of Grebe, 1973, Antony and Cleopatra, 1974, The Brotherhood, 1975, An Impeccable Elopement, 1975, Remember Me, 1975, Beata Beatrix, 1975, The Artisan, 1975, Thank You Comrades, 1978, Kean, 1982, The Merry Wives of Windsor, 1982, Camille, 1984, Stanley's Visoipn, 1986, Murderers Among Us: The Simon Weisenthal Story, 1988 (Disting. Svc. award 1989), Leini: The Train, 1990, The War That Never Ends, 1991, Joseph, 1995, Moses, 1996, Weapons of Mass Distraction, 1997, Crime and Punishment, 1998, The Tale of Sweeny Todd, 1998, Alice in Wonderland, 1999, Anne Frank: The Whole Story, 2001; (TV mini-series) Dickens of London, 1976, The Seret of the Sahara, 1987; (TV series) Coronation Street, 1966-67, Oxbridge Blues, 1986, Crime and Punishment, 1998; (TV appearances) Orlamdo, 1966, Skin Deep, 1966, The Rhyme, But No Reason, 1966, The Adventurer, 1973, Wessex Tales, 1973, Play for Today, 1973, Silas Marner, 1987, The Sopranos, 2006. Recipient Padma Shri award Govt. of India, 1984, Grammy award, 1984, Oscar award, 1983; named Best Actor and Best Newcomer Brit. Acad. Film and TV Arts, 1982, Best Actor Standard Film Awards, London, 1983; knighted by Queen Elizabeth II, 2001 Mem. Brit. Acad. Film and TV Arts, Acad. Motion Picture Arts and Scis. (Golden Camera Berlin award, Evening Standard Film award for Best Actor for Schindler's List 1995). Office: Internat Creative Mgmt Inc 4-6 Soho Sq London W1D 3PZ England*

KINGSLEY, BOB, radio personality; Announcer Armed Forces Radio, Keflavik, Iceland, KFOX, KGBS, KFI, KLAC, LA; prodr. Am. County Countdown, 1974—78, host, 1978—2005, Bob Kingsley with America's Musicmakers, 1978—2005, Bob Kingsley's Country Top 40, 2006—, Bob Kingsley with Today's Hit Makers, 2006—. Bd. dirs. Acad. Country Music. Served in USAF. Named to County Music DJ Hall of Fame, 1998; recipient Nat. Broadcast Personality of Yr. award, Country Music Assn., 2001, 2003, Nat. On-Air Personality of Yr. award, Acad. Country Music, 2007. Office: Bob Kingsley's Country Top 40 PO Box 1575 Burbank CA 91507*

KINGSLEY, JEAN-PIERRE, federal official; b. Ottawa, Ont., Can., July 12, 1943; s. Oscar and Françoise (Charette-Bertrand) K.; m. Suzanne Potvin, Aug. 19, 1967; children: Marie-France, Justin, Michèle. B. Comm., U. Ottawa, 1965, MA in Hosp. Adminstrn., 1969. Programmer IBM, Ottawa-Hull, 1965-66; field supr. Travelers Ins., Ottawa-Hull, 1966-67; chief hosps. Dept. Vets.' Affairs Govt. Can., Ottawa-Hull, 1969-71, profl. officer Can. Mortgage & Housing Corp., 1971; assoc. exec. dir. and exec. dir. Charles Camsell Hosp., Edmonton, Alta., Canada, 1971-73; prin. exec. officer Office of Dep. Min. Health and Welfare, Dept. Nat. Health and Welfare Govt. of Can., Ottawa-Hull, 1973-74, group chief, Treasury Bd. Secretariat, 1974-76; dir. gen. audit br. Pub. Svc. Commn., Ottawa-Hull, 1976-77; pres., CEO Ottawa Gen. Hosp., 1977-81; dep. sec., Ministry of State for Social Devel. Govt. of Canada, Ottawa-Hull, 1981-84, dep. sec. pers. policy, Treasury Bd. Secretariat, 1984-87, asst. dep. registrar gen. Dept. Consumer and Corp. Affairs, 1987-90; chief electoral officer Parliament of Can., Ottawa, 1990—. Chmn. Monfort Hosp., 1981-90; bd. dirs. Internation Found. for Election Sys., Inst. for Democracy and Electoral Assistance. Avocations: music, community activities, windsurfing, carpentry, swimming. Office: Elections Canada 257 Slater St Ottawa ON Canada K1A OM6 E-mail: jean-pierre.kingsley@elections.ca.

KINGSLEY, JUDITH, artist; b. NYC; d. Fred and Minna Evelyn (Weisman) Gladstone; m. Theodore Kingsley, Oct. 26, 1950 (dec. May 1964); children: Ellen Kingsley Hirschfeld (dec. Mar. 2007), Melinda Kingsley Nester (dec.); m. John Fitting Jr., Apr. 9, 1976 (dec. Dec. 1997). Student, Syracuse U., 1948-49, Adelphi U., 1949-50, Pratt Inst., Art Students League, NYC, Nat. Acad. Fine Arts, Positano Art Inst., Italy, 1972, China Inst., NYC, 1977. One-woman shows include Galerie Internat., NYC, 1969, Weiner Gallery, NYC, 1970, Palm Beach Gallery, 1971, Lobster Pot Gallery, Nantucket, Mass., 1972, Crystal House Gallery, Miami Beach, Fla., 1973, Springfield Art Assn., Ill., 1975, East River Savs. Bank Gallery, Rockefeller Ctr., NY, 1976, Bergdorf Goodman Art Gallery, NYC, 1977, Adelphi U. Art Gallery, Garden City, NY, 1978, Multiple Images Gallery, Palm Beach, Fla., 1982, Valand Gallery, Naples, Fla., 1983, La Galeria De Santa Fe, 1984, Reece Gallery, NYC, 1979-80, Nelson Rockefeller Collection, NYC, 1981-82, L'Atelier Gallery, Piermont, NY, 1991-92, Jain Marunouchi Gallery, NYC, 1995-96, G.G. Rein Gallery, Houston, 1995-96, The Darvish Collection, Naples, 1995-98, Hofburg Palace Exhibit, Vienna, Austria, 1993, No. Trust Bank, Naples, 1998, Naples Art Gallery, Gallery Botero, Marco Island, Fla., 1998-99, Artsforum Gallery, NYC, 1998-2000, Gallery at the Registry Resort, Naples, 1999-2000, Alpers Fine Art, Andover, Mass., Charles Hecht Gallery, Palm Desert, Calif., 2001, Marco Polo Galleries, Carmel, Calif., 2001, Cofer Gallerie, Carmel, 2001, Julie Baker Fine Art, Grass Valley, Calif., 2002, Monkey Tree Gallery, Santa Fe, 2002, Vero Beach Art Guild Gallery, Fla., 2004, Tadu Gallery, Santa Fe, 2004-05 Sec. bd. dirs. NY Artists Equity, 1984-93. Recipient Morilla Oil award, New Rochelle Art Assn., 1973. Mem.: Nat. Mus. Women in the Arts, Sierra Club (Santa Fe), Quail Run Club (Santa Fe), Nat. Arts Club NY. Avocations: golf, tennis, swimming, yachting. Home and Office: Quail Run 3101 Old Pecos Trail Santa Fe NM 87505 Studio: The Lofts 3100 Cerrillos Rd Santa Fe NM 87505 Office Phone: 505-982-8292. Personal E-mail: princesskingsley@aol.com. E-mail: jkingsleyart@aol.com.

KINGSLEY, MARY LEE, writer, researcher, consultant, retired marketing executive; d. Thomas Drowne and Martha Bush (Clark); m. William Charles Johnson, Apr. 23, 1980 (div.); children: Lee Hart Johnson, William Kingsley Johnson. BA in English, Am. U., 1975; MS in Mktg., Johns Hopkins U., 2001, MA in Nonfiction Writing, 2005. Dir. mem. relations and mktg. Bank-Fund Staff Fed. Credit Union, 1992—2006. Editor-in-chief: World Bank Family Network, 2006—, columnist contbr. editor: WBFN Mosaic Mag., —; contbr. articles to profl. jours. Mem.: Wash. Independent Writers, Nat. Mil. Intelligence Assn., Nat. Defense Univ. Found., Nat. Cryptologic Mus. Found., Assn. Intelligence Officers, Car Club of Am., BMW Riders. Episcopalian. Avocations: writing, motorcycling, cars. Home and Office: 8204 Old Georgetown Rd Bethesda MD 20814-1452 Business E-Mail: mlkingsley@msn.com.

KINGSMORE, STEPHEN FRANCIS, physician, research scientist; b. Motherwell, Scotland, Sept. 3, 1960; came to U.S., 1988; s. Brian and Rona K. (Ritson) K.; m. Fiona J. McQuaid, Nov. 7, 1987; children: Daniel R., Rebekah F.P., Francesca S. BSc in Med. Microbiology, Queen's U., Belfast, Ireland, 1982; MB, ChB, BAO, Queen's U., Belfast, No. Ireland, 1985. Diplomate Am. Bd. Internal Medicine. Intern Craigavon Hosp., Portadown, No. Ireland, 1985-86; resident Queen's U., Belfast, 1986-88; fellow Duke U., Durham, NC, 1988-89, intern, 1989-90, resident, 1990-91, fellow, 1991-93, assoc. in medicine, 1993-94; asst. prof. U. Fla., Gainesville, 1994-97; COO Molecular Staging Inc., New Haven; v.p. rsch. CuraGen Corp., New Haven, 1997—2004; pres., CEO Nat. Ctr. for Genome Resources, Santa Fe, 2004—. Contbr. articles to profl. jours. Recipient Sr. Scholar awrd Am. Coll. Rheumatology, 1994, Arthritis Investigator award Arthritis Found., 1995, Jr. Faculty Rsch. award Am. Cancer Soc., 1996. Mem. Am. Fedn. Clin. Rsch. (Trainee Investigator award 1994, Jr. Faculty award 1996), Internat. Mammalian Genome Soc. Office: Pres Nat Ctr for Genome Resources 2935 Rodeo Pk Dr East Santa Fe NM 87505 Home Phone: 505-820-7852; Office Phone: 505-995-4466. Business E-Mail: sfk@ncgr.org.

KINGSOLVER, BARBARA ELLEN, writer; b. Annapolis, Md., Apr. 8, 1955; d. Wendell and Virginia (Henry) K.; m. Steven Hopp, 1993; 2 children. BA, DePauw U., 1977; MS, U. Ariz., 1981; LittD (hon.), DePauw U., 1994. Sci. writer U. Ariz., Tucson, 1981-85; free-lance journalist Tucson, 1985-87; novelist, 1987—. Book reviewer N.Y. Times, 1988—, L.A. Times, 1989—. Author: The Bean Trees, 1988 (ALA award 1988), Homeland and Other Stories, 1969 (ALA award 1990), Holding the Line: Women in the Great Arizona Mine Strike of 1983, 89, Animal Dreams, 1990 (PEN West Fiction award 1991, Edward Abbey Ecofiction award 1991), Another America, 1992, Pigs in Heaven, 1993 (L.A. Times Fiction prize 1993, Mountains and Plains Fiction award 1993, Western Heritage award 1993, ABBY Honor Book 1994), Essays, High Tide in Tucson, 1995, The Poisonwood Bible, 1998 (ABBY Honor Book 2000, PEN/Faulkner honoree 1999, Pulitzer runner-up 1999, Orange Prize short list 1999), Prodigal Summer, 2001, Small Wonder, 2002; co-author (with Annie Belt) Last Stand: America's Virgin Lands. Recipient Feature-writing award Ariz. Press Club, 1986; citation of accomplishment UN Nat. Coun. of Women, 1989; Woodrow Wilson Found./Lila Wallace fellow, 1992-93; Andrea Egan award Nat. Writers Union, 1998, Nat. Humanities Medal, 2000, Best Am. Sci. and Nature Writing, 2001, Gov.'s Nat. Award in the Arts, Ky., 2002, John P. McGovern award for Family, 2002, Nat. award Physicians for Social Responsibility, 2002. Mem. PEN Ctr. USA West, Nat. Writers Union, Phi Beta Kappa. Avocations: human rights, environmental conservation, gardening, history. Office: PO Box 160 Meadowview VA 24361

KINGSTON, ALEX (ALEXANDRA KINGSTON), actress; b. London, Mar. 11, 1963; m. Ralph Fiennes, 1993 (div. Oct. 28, 1997); m. Florian Haertel, Dec. 29, 1998; 1 child. Student, Royal Acad. Dramatic Arts. T.V. and movie actress. Appeared in TV films Foreign Affairs, 1993, Woman of the Wolf, 1994, The Infiltrator, 1995, Weapons of Mass Distraction, 1997, The Poseidon Adventure, 2005; films include The Cook, The Thief, His Wife & Her Lover, 1989, A Pin for the Butterfly, 1994, Carrington, 1995, Virtual Encounters 2, 1998, Croupier, 1998, This Space Between Us, 2000, Essex Boys, 2000, Warrior Queen, 2003, Sweet Land, 2005, Alpha Dog, 2006, Crashing, 2007; TV series include The Knock, 1996, ER, 1997-2004; TV miniseries include Crocodile Shoes, 1994, The Fortunes and Misfortunes of Moll Flanders, 1999; theatre appearances in Much Ado About Nothing, King Lear, Love's Labour's Lost, The Curse of the Starving Class, The Bright and Bold Design, Othello, The Alchemist, Traveling Players, Saved, Julius Caesar, See How They Run, One Flew Over the Cuckoo's Nest, 2006. Recipient SAG award for Outstanding Performance by Ensemble in a Drama Series, 1994. Office: c/o The Gersh Agy 232 N Canon Dr Beverly Hills CA 90210-5302*

KINGSTON, JACK, congressman; b. Bryan, Tex., Apr. 24, 1955; m. Libby Kingston; children: Betsy, John, Ann, Jim. BA in Economics, U. Ga.; attended, Mich. State U., 1973—74. Salesman, v.p. Palmer & Cay Carswell Ins. Co., 1979-92; mem. Ga. State Ho. Reps., 1985-93, US Congress from 1st Ga. dist., 1993—. Mem. Ways & Means Com., 1985-93, Appropriations Com., Congl. Rural Caucus Exec. Bd., 1993—, chmn. Theme Team (house Rep. comm. team). Vol. Hospice, United Way; mem. Atlantic Coast Conservation Assn., Isle of Hope Community Assn. Recipient Guardian Small Bus. award, Nat. Fed. Ind. Bus. 103, 104, 105, 106, 1992, Sound Dollar award Free Cong. Found., 1994, Golden Bulldog award mems. 103rd, 104th, 105th, 106th cong., 1994, 96, Golden Eagle award Nat. Security Caucus, 1994, cert. recognition inspector. gen. Criminal Investigator Acad., 1994, plaque of appreciation Camden county bd. realtors, 1995, disting. cit. award Armstrong state coll., 1996, merit award the Seniors Coalition, 1996, comm. police award city of Statesboro, 1997, numerous others. Mem. Am. Legislative Exchange Coun., Soc. Chartered Property & Casualty Underwriters, Solomon's Lodge F&AM, Rotary (Paul Harris fellow). Republican. Episcopalian. Office: US House Reps 2242 Rayburn House Office Bldg Washington DC 20515-1001*

KINGSTON, MAXINE HONG, writer, educator; b. Stockton, Calif., Oct. 27, 1940; d. Tom and Ying Lan (Chew) Hong; m. Earll Kingston, Nov. 23, 1962; 1 child, Joseph Lawrence. BA, U. Calif., Berkeley, 1962; D (hon.), Ea. Mich. U., 1988, Colby Coll., 1990, Brandeis U., 1991, U. Mass., 1991. Tchr. English, Sunset H.S., Hayward, Calif., 1965-66, Kahuku (Hawaii) H.S., 1967, Kahaluu (Hawaii) Drop-In Sch., 1968, Kailua (Hawaii) H.S., 1969, Honolulu Bus. Coll., 1969, Mid-Pacific Inst., Honolulu, 1970-77; prof. English, vis. writer U. Hawaii, Honolulu, 1977; Thelma McCandless Disting. Prof. Eastern Mich. U., Ypsilanti, 1986, sr. lectr. emerita U. Calif., Berkeley, 1990-2003. Author: The Woman Warrior: Memoirs of a Girlhood Among Ghosts, 1976 (Nat. Book Critics Cir. award for non-fiction; cited by Time mag., N.Y. Times Book Rev. and Asian Mail as one of best books of yr. and decade), China Men, 1981 (Nat. Book award; runner-up for Pulitzer prize, Nat. Book Critics Cir. award nominee 1988), Hawai' One Summer, 1987 (Western Books Exhbn. Book award, Book Builders West Book award), Tripmaster Monkey-His Fake Book, 1989 (PEN USA West award in Fiction), Through the Black Curtain, 1988, To Be The Poet, 2002, The Fifth Book of Peace, 2003 (Best Spiritual Book award, Spirituality and Health, 2003); editor: The Literature of California, 2001 (Commonwealth Club Book award 2001), Veterans of War, Veterans of Peace, 2006 (Spl. Recognition in Pub. award, No. Calif. Book Reviewers 2007, Pacific Justice and Reconciliation Ctr. Peace Book award, 2007); contbr. short stories, articles and poems to mags. and jours., including Iowa Rev., The New Yorker, Am. Heritage, Redbook, Mother Jones, Caliban, Mich. Quarterly, Ms., The Hungry Mind Rev., N.Y. Times, L.A. Times, Zyzzyva; prodr. The Woman Warrior, Berkeley Repertory Co., 1994, The Huntington Theater, Boston, 1994, The Mark Taper Forum, L.A., 1995; host: (TV series) Journey to the West, 1994; subject of documentaries Talking Story, Stories My Country Told Me, Writers and Places; interviews on Dick Cavett, Bill Moyers, Ken Burns' The West, The News Hour with Jim Lehrer; actor Truck Girl, 2004. Guggenheim fellow, 1981; recipient Nat. Endowment for the Arts Writers award, 1980, 82, Mademoiselle mag. award, 1977, Anisfield Wolf Book award, 1978, Calif. Arts Commn. award, 1981, Hawaii award for lit., 1982, Calif. Gov.'s award art, 1989, Major Book Collection award Brandeis U. Nat. Women's Com., 1990, award lit. Am. Acad. & Inst. Arts & Letters, 1990, Lila Wallace Reader's Digest Writing award, 1992, Spl. Achievement Oakland Bus. Arts award, 1994; named Living Treasure Hawaii, 1980, Woman of Yr. Asian Pacific Women's Network, 1981, Cyril Magnin award for Outstanding Achievement in the Arts, 1996, Disting. Artists award The Music Ctr. of L.A. County, 1996, Nat. Humanities medal NEH, 1997, Fred Cody Lifetime Achievement award, 1998, John Dos Passos prize for lit., 1998, Ka Palapola Po'okela award 1999, Profiles of Courage honor Swords to Plowshares, 1999, Alumna of Yr. award U. Calif.-Berkeley, 2000, Gold medal Calif. State Libr., 2002, Asian Am. Writers Workshop Lifetime Achievement award, 2006. Mem. Am. Acad. Arts and Scis. (KPFA Peace award 2005, Red Hen Press Lifetime Achievement award 2006).

KING-STURDIVANT, CONSTANCE MARIA, social services administrator; b. Nov. 3, 1951; d. Delloyd Ervin and Lucinda Amelia King-Davis; m. Jimmie Sturdivant (div.); children: Byron Vanquez, Ashley Monique, Jamal Kevin. AA, East St. Louis CC, Ill., 1973; BA, U. Ill., Springfield, 1975; MS in Edn., No. Ill. U., Dekalb, 1998. Juvenile parole officer Dept. Corrections, Rockford, Ill., 1975—83; child welfare specialist Dept. Children and Family Svcs., Rockford, 1983—98, adminstrv. case reviewer, 1998—. Recipient Worker Yr., Ill. Dept. Children and Family Svcs., 1997. Democrat. Baptist. Avocations: poetry, genealogy, reading. Office: Ill Dept Children and Family Svcs 200 So Main St Rockford IL 61104 Business E-Mail: cmsbigmama@insightbb.com.

KINGTON, BARRY CLARK, investor, consultant; b. Sept. 2, 1942; s. William Hayes and Margret Elisabeth (Clark) K.; children: Barry Clark, Paige Dawson. BS, Murray State U., 1969, MSAE, 1990. Owner coal and oil rights; investor stocks and commodities; bus. cons., pres. Point One Adv. Group, Inc., Am. Soc. Farm Mgrs. and Rural Appraisers. Fellow Internat. Soc. Philos. Enquiry (sr.); mem. AAAS, N.Y. Acad. Scis., Triple Nine Soc. (past regent), Appoloosa Horse Club, Archaeol. Inst. Am., Mensa (pres. Evansville area 1986-88), Am. Angus Assn., Prometheus Soc (past treas.)., Am. Soc. Agr. Cons., Internat. Soc. Agr. Cons., Aircraft Owners and Pilots Assn., Exptl. Aircraft Assn., Masons, Shriners, KT. Home: Kilmarnock Ln Madisonville KY 42431 Office: PO Box 1111 Madisonville KY 42431-0022

KINIGAKIS, PANAGIOTIS, research scientist, engineer, inventor, writer; b. Chanea, Greece, July 11, 1949; s. John and Evangelia (Vozinakis) K.; m. Kalliopi Paleologos, July 31, 1977 (div. Sept. 2000); children: Evangelia, Maria Anna; m. Tracey Dawn Quart, Jan. 3, 2003. BS, Superior Agrl. Sch., Athens, Greece, 1971, MS, 1973; MS in Food Sci., Rutgers U., 1979. Packaging devel. specialist Am. Cyanamid Co., Clifton, NJ, 1979-81; sr. packaging engr. Warner Lambert Co., Morris Plains, NJ, 1981-83; tech. svcs. supr. M&M Mars Inc., Hackettstown, NJ, 1983-87; sr. tech. prin. Kraft Foods Inc., Glenview, Ill., 1987—, Kraft Food fellow, 2001—. Agrl. engr. Food Agrl. Orgn. div. of UN, Chanea, 1975-77; lectr. in field. Patentee pkg. equipment and mfg. systems; contbr. articles to profl. jours. Advisor Greek Orthodox Youth Assn., Randolph, N.J., 1986, Hamilton, N.J., 1990. Mem. ASM, TAPPI, Internat. Materials Info. soc., Inst. Food Tech., Inst. Packaging Profls. (cert.), Soc. Plastics Engrs., N.Y. Acad. Scis. Greek Orthodox. Achievements include inventions in field. Avocations: golf, volleyball, soccer, tennis, scuba diving. Office: Kraft Foods Inc 801 Waukegan Rd Glenview IL 60025-4391 Home Phone: 815-979-7667; Office Phone: 847-646-5383. Business E-Mail: pkinigakis@kraft.com.

KINIRY, WILLIAM F., JR., lawyer; b. Phila., Dec. 5, 1950; AB, Villanova U., 1972; JD, U. Balt., 1976; student, U.S. Army JAG's Sch. Bar: Pa. 1976, U.S. Dist. Ct. (ea. dist.) Pa. 1978, U.S. Ct. Appeals (3rd cir.) 1978, U.S. Dist. Ct. (mid. dist.) Pa. 1991. Atty. Harvey, Pennington, Herting & Renneisen Ltd., Phila.; mng. ptnr. Phila. off. DLA Piper Rudnick Gray Cary, Phila. Served as co. comdr. US Army spl. ops. forces, USAR. Recipient Dean Joseph Curtis award, Univ. Pres. award. Mem. ABA, Pa. Bar Assn., NY State Bar Assn., Phila. Bar Assn., Product Liability Adv. Council, Def. Rsch. Inst., Soc. Automotive Engineers, Nat. Assn. Railroad Trial Counsel. Office: DLA Piper Rudnick Gray Cary One Liberty Pl Ste 4900 1650 Market St Philadelphia PA 19103-2762 Office Phone: 215-656-3340. Office Fax: 215-656-3301. Business E-Mail: william.kiniry@dlapiper.com.

KINLAW, DENNIS FRANKLIN, clergyman, religious organization administrator; b. Lumberton, NC, June 26, 1922; s. Wade Hampton and Sally (Burney) K.; m. Elsie Blake, Dec. 31, 1943; children: Elizabeth Kinlaw Coppedge, Dennis Franklin Jr., Katherine Kinlaw Key, Susan Kinlaw Masters, Sally Kinlaw Babcock. BA, Asbury Coll., 1943, LHD (hon.), 1980; MDiv, Asbury Theol. Sem., 1946; MA, Brandeis U., 1961, PhD, 1967; LLD (hon.), Houghton Coll., 1971; DD (hon.), Asbury Coll., 1990. Ordained deacon N.C. Conf. United Meth. Ch., 1949, ordained elder, 1951; transferred to Ky. Conf., 1969, ret., 1984. Pastor Meth. Ch., Faison, 1949-53, Loudenville (N.Y.) Community Ch., 1955-61; assoc. prof., prof. Old Testament langs. and lit. Asbury Theol. Sem., Wilmore, Ky., 1963-68, prof. bibl. theology, 1982-83; pres. Asbury Coll., Wilmore, 1968-81, 86-92; founder, pres. Francis Asbury soc., Wilmore, 1982—. Pres. Francis Asbury Soc., Wilmore, 1982—; vis. prof. Seoul (Republic of Korea) Theol. Coll. Author: This Day with the Master, Let's Start with Jesus, The Mind of Christ, We Live as Christ, Preaching in the Spirit, 1985; contbr. commentaries in bibl. publs. Recipient Alumnus award Asbury Theol. Sem., 1961. Mem. Soc. Bibl. Lit. and Exegesis, Wesley Theol. Soc., Evang. Theol. Soc. Home: 140 Lowry Ln Wilmore KY 40390-1219 Office: Francis Asbury Soc PO Box 7 Wilmore KY 40390-0007 Personal E-mail: fasdennis@aol.com.

KINMAN, GARY W., landscape company executive; Owner, CEO Kinman Assocs., Inc., Dublin, Ohio. Conducts seminars in field. Office: PO Box 1129 Dublin OH 43017 Office Phone: 614-764-8733. Office Fax: 614-793-0104. E-mail: gary@kinmaninstitute.com.

KINNAIRD, ELEANOR GATES, state legislator, lawyer; b. Rochester, Minn., Nov. 14, 1931; d. E. Vernon and E. Madge (Pollock) Gates; m. Richard W. Kinnaird, July 27, 1954 (div. June 1982); children: Robinson S., Michael G., Paul N. BA, Carleton Coll., 1953; MM, U. N.C., 1973; JD, N.C. Ctrl. U., 1992. Bar: N.C. 1992, U.S. Dist. Ct. (ea. and mid. dists.) N.C. 1992, U.S. Ct. Appeals (4th cir.) 1992. Staff atty. N.C. Prisoner Legal Svcs., Inc., Raleigh, 1993—2004; senator N.C. Gen. Assembly, 1997—; pvt. practice, 2004—. Mayor, Town of Carrboro, 1987-95. Mem.: Phi Alpha Delta. Episcopalian. Avocations: political and civic activities, movies, reading, gardening. Home: 207 W Poplar Ave Carrboro NC 27510-1613 Office: 211 N Columbia St Chapel Hill NC 27514 Office Phone: 919-942-4445. E-mail: elliek@ncleg.net.

KINNAMAN, THOMAS CHRISTOPHER, economics professor, researcher; b. Detriot, July 5, 1965; s. Fred Mershon Kinnaman and Marcia Ann Dickinson, Albert Lester Simmons (Stepfather); m. Catherine Mary O'Connor, Aug. 17, 1996; children: Peter Thomas, Bridget Claire. BA, George Mason U., 1987; PhD, U. Va., Charlottesville, 1994, MA, 1991. Asst. prof. Bucknell U., Lewisburg, Pa., 1994—99, assoc. prof., 1999—. Co-editor: The Economics of Household Garbage and Recycling Behavior, 2002; editor: The Economics of Residential Solid Waste Management, 2003; contbr. articles to profl. jours. Chmn. Lewisburg (Pa.) Planning Commn., 1998—2002, sec., 1999—2002. Mem.: Am. Econ. Assn. Home: 340 St Catherine Street Lewisburg PA 17837 Office: Bucknell University Department of Economics Lewisburg PA 17837 Home Phone: 570-523-0118; Office Phone: 570-577-3465. Office Fax: 570-577-3451; Home Fax: 570-577-3451. Business E-Mail: kinnaman@bucknell.edu.

KINNAN, SHARON JO, elementary school educator; b. Hays, Kans., Oct. 28, 1953; d. Vernon Leroy and Arlyne Carmen Hutton; m. Gene Ralph Kinnan, Nov. 30, 1975; children: David, Aaron. BA, Wayne State Coll., Nebr., 1974; MA, Doane Coll., Crete, Nebr., 1994. Elem. educator Neligh-Oakdale Pub. Schs., Nebr., 1975—. Republican. Home: Box 174 Oakdale NE 68761 Office: Neligh-Oakdale Pub Schs Box 149 Neligh NE 68756

KINNE, DAVID WEIR, retired surgeon; b. Amityville, NY, July 19, 1936; s. Charles Stanley and Angeline Marian (Simpson) K.; m. Frances Paytas (div. Dec. 1985); children: Lisa Ann, Jonathan Charles, James Andrew; m. Kathleen Liddy. AB, Columbia U., 1957; MD summa cum laude, SUNY Downstate Med. Ctr., NYC, 1964. Diplomate Am. Bd. Surgery. Chief breast svc. Meml. Sloan-Kettering Cancer Ctr., NYC, 1979—93, attending surgeon, 1982—93, dir. surg. edn., 1985—91, mem. Meml. Hosp. in cancer ctr., 1988—93; prof. surgery and chief breast svc. Columbia-Presbyn. Med. Ctr., 1993—2001; ret., 2001. Prof. surgery Cornell U. Med. Ctr., N.Y.C., 1978-1993; cons. Rockefeller Hosp. N.Y.C., 1978-1993; co-dir. Breast Exam. Ctr. of Harlem, N.Y.C., 1983-1993. Editor: Breast Diseases, 1987-91. Tour guide Met. Mus. Art, NYC, Carnegie Hall. Fellow ACS; mem. N.Y. Surg. Soc., Soc. Surg. Oncology, Ea. Surg. Soc., N.Y. Met. Breast Cancer Group (pres. 1987-89), N.Y. Athletic Club, St. Andrews Golf Club (Hasting-on-Hudson, N.Y.). Republican. Episcopalian. Avocations: golf, walking. Home: 340 E 64th St Apt 30B New York NY 10021-7507 E-mail: katnkin@aol.com.

KINNE, FRANCES BARTLETT, academic administrator; b. Story City, Iowa; d. Charles Morton and Bertha (Olson) Barlett; m. Harry L. Kinne, Jr. (dec.); m. M. Wothington Bordley, Jr. (dec.). Student, U. No. Iowa; B of Music Edn., M of Music Edn., Drake U., degree (hon.); PhD cum laude, U. Frankfurt, Fed. Republic of Germany, 1957; LHD (hon.), Wagner Coll., NY; LLD (hon.), Lenoir Rhyne Coll.; DHL (hon.), Jacksonville U., 1995; LLD (hon.), Flagler Coll.; DFA (hon.), Drake U., 1981. Tchr. music Kelley (Iowa) Consol. Sch.; supr. music Boxholm Consol. Sch., Des Moines, Des Moines pub. schs.; sr. army hostess Camp Crowder, Mo.; dir. recreation VA, Wadsworth, Kans.; lectr. music, English and Western culture Tsuda Coll., Tokyo; cons. music U.S. Army Gen. McArthur's Hdqrs., Tokyo; mem. faculty Jacksonville (Fla.) U., 1958—, Disting. Univ. prof., 1961-62, prof. music and humanities, 1963—, dean, founder Coll. Fine Arts, interim pres., 1979, pres., 1979-89, chancellor, 1989-94; chancellor emeritus, 1995—. Past chmn. Ind. Colls. and Univs. Fla.; mem. adv. coun. Nat. Soc. Arts and Letters; hon. mem. staff Mayo Clinic, Jacksonville; coporator Charles Schepens Eye Rsch. Inst. Havard U., Cambridge, Mass., mem. adv. bd. Women's Eye Task Force. Author: A Comparative Study of British Traditional and American Indegenous Ballads, 1958, Iowa Girl: The President Wears a Skirt, 2000, (CD) Memories (in memory of friend, Bob Hope), 2004; contbr. chapters to books, articles to profl. jours. Mem., chmn. adv. bd. Ronald McDonald House; bd. dirs., life mem. Jacksonville Symphony Assn., Bert Thomas Scholarschip Found., Doug Milne Found.; bd. dirs., mem. exec. com. Eye Rsch. Found.; trustee Drake U.; past mem. bd. govs. Jacksonville C. of C., past v.p.; mem. pres.'s adv. coun. Flagler Coll. Named Eve of Decade, hon. mem., 3d Armored Divsn., U.S. Army, Woman of Achievement, Ponte Vedra Woman's Club, 2005; recipient hon. awards, Bus. and Profl. Women's Clubs, 1962, Disting. Svc. award, Drake U., 1966, 1st Fla. Gov.'s award for achievement in arts, 1972, EVE award in edn., 1973, Arts Assembly Individual award, 1978—79, Roast award, Soc. for Prevention of Blindness, 1980, Brotherhood award, NCCJ, 1981, Top Mgmt. award, Jacksonville Sales and Mktg. Execs., 1981, Alumni Achievement award, U. No. Iowa, Ann. Burton C. Bryan award, Pub. Svc. award, Physicians Edn. Network, Freedom Found. Valley Forge, Disting. Svc. award, Fla. Soc. Ophthalmology, Women of Achievement award, 1st Coast Bus. and Profl. Women's Club Jacksonville, Disting. Educator award, Internat. Longshoremen's Assn., Hope award, Nat. Multiple Sclerosis Soc., Disting. Am. award, Nat. Football Fedn., Fla. State Mus. Tchrs. award, Outstanding Civic Leader award, Civic Roundtable of Jacksonville, Vol. Jacksonville 2d Ann. Bernard Gregory Servant Leader award, Elaine Gordon Lifetime Achievement award, Fla. Fedn. Bus. and Profl. Women, 1996, Order of the South award, So. Acad. Letters, Arts and Scis., Nat. Soc. Arts and Letters, Lifetime Achievement award, Arthritis Found., 2004, Davis award for Lifetime Achievement, Outstanding Philanthropist, 2005, Vision award, Schepen's Eye Rsch. Inst.; inducted into Fla. Women's Hall of Fame, Outstanding Svc. to Theatre Edn. Fla. Assn. for Theatre Edn., day named in her honor, Women's Club of Jacksonville and other orgns., one of six women featured on History Week posters apptd. by Mayor Jacksonville, bldgs. named in honor, Frances Bartlett Kinne Univ. Ctr. Jacksonville U., Frances Bartlett Kinne Alumni and Devel. Ctr. Drake U., Frances Bartlett Kinne Auditorium at Mayo Clinic, Jacksonville, north wing of Bertha Bartlett Pub. Libr., Kinne Garden (Wilma's Little People Sch.), Jacksonville. Mem.: AAUW, PEO, Nat. Soc. Arts and Letters (adv. coun.), Internat. Coun. Fine Arts Deans (past chmn.), So. Acad. Letters, Arts and Scis., Ind. Colls. and Univs. Fla. (past chmn.), Nat. Assn. Schs. Music (past chmn. region 7), Fla. Coll. Music Edn. Assn. (past pres., v.p.), Friday Musicale, Assn. Am. Colls. (past bd. govs., mem. exec. com.), Fla. Music Edn. Assn. (past bd. dirs.), Music Educators Nat. Conf., Fla. Music Tchr. Assn., Nat. Music Tchrs. Assn., Fine Art Forum (hon.), Jacksonville Women's Network Inner Wheel, Fla. Women's Hall of Fame (Gov.'s 1st award), Delius Assn. Fla. (life), Ret. Officers Assn. (hon.), River Club (first women mem.), Exch. Club (Golden Deeds award), St. John's Dinner Club (past pres., first women pres.), Rotary (pres. 2000, pres. Jacksonville 2000—, bd. dirs. Jacksonville chpt., first woman mem. and pres., Paul Harris fellow), Green Key (hon.), Alpha Xi Delta (Woman of Distinction award), Beta Gamma Sigma, Mu Phi Epsilon (Elizabeth Mathias award), Alpha Xi Delta, Omicron Delta Kappa (hon.), Alpha Kappa Psi (hon.), Alpha Kappa Pi (hon.), Alpha Psi Omega (hon.). Home: 4032 Mission Hills Cir W Jacksonville FL 32225-4635 *It has been a delightful challenge to amalgamate my career with happy experience as a U.S. Army wife - as a young bride assigned to China and evacuated to Occupied Japan - in pursuit of my Ph.D. at the University of Frankfurt in Occupied Germany (the lone American student) as a professor, dean, president, chancellor and now Chan. Emer. of Jacksonville University.*

KINNEAR, GREG, actor, film producer; b. Logansport, Ind., June 17, 1963; m. Helen Labdon, May 1, 1999; 1 child. Diploma in broadcast journalism, U. Ariz. With Armed Forces Radio, Athens, Greece. Appeared on TV series College Mad House, 1989, The Best of the Worst, 1991, Talk Soup, 1991-94, Later with Greg Kinnear, 1994-1996, TV movies What Price Victory, 1988, Murder in Mississippi, 1990, Dillinger, 1991, Based on an Untrue Story, 1993, Dinner with Friends, 2001, films, Blankman, 1994, Sabrina, 1995, Dear God, 1996, A Smile Like Yours, 1997, As Good As It Gets, 1997, You've Got Mail, 1998, Mystery Men, 1999, What Planet Are You From, 2000, Nurse Betty, 2000, Loser, 2000, The Gift, 2000, Someone Like You, 2001, We Were Soldiers, 2002, Auto Focus, 2002, Stuck On You, 2003, Godsend, 2004, The Matador, 2005, (voice) Robots, 2005, Bad News Bears, 2005, Fast Food Nation, 2006, Little Miss Sunshine, 2006 (Outstanding Performance by a Cast in a Motion Picture, SAG, 2007), Invincible, 2006; co-exec. prodr. TV series The Best of the Worst, 1991; exec. prodr. Talk Soup, 1991-94, Later with Greg Kinnear, 1994-1996,. Mem.: Alpha Tau Omega.*

KINNEAR, PETER D., energy executive; BSCE, Vanderbilt Univ., 1969; MBA, Univ. Chgo., 1971. Joined FMC Corp., 1971, mgr. bus. develop., 1972—75, mgr. Far East wellhead bus. Singapore, 1975—79, other mgmt. positions, 1979—82, global wellhead ops. mgr., 1982—85, div. mgr. fluid control & wellhead equip., 1982—94, gen. mgr. petroleum equip. & systems, 1994—2001, v.p., 2001, FMC Technologies Inc., Houston, 2001—04, exec. v.p. energy systems, 2004—06, pres., COO, 2006—07, pres., CEO, 2007—. Chmn. U.S. nat. com. World Petroleum Council; bd. dir. Tronox Inc.; bd. mem. Petroleum Equip. Suppliers Assn., Offshore Energy Ctr. Office: FMC Technologies Inc 1803 Gears Rd Houston TX 77067*

KINNEBREW, JACKSON METCALFE, lawyer; b. Oklahoma City, June 29, 1941; s. Jackson A. and Mary Lucille (Metcalfe) K.; m. Carole A. Vadner, Sept. 23, 1967; children: Scott, Sarah. BBA in Acctg., U. Okla., 1963; JD, So. Meth. U., 1967, LLM in Taxation, 1973. Bar: Tex. 1968, U.S. Dist. Ct. (no. dist.) Tex. 1968, U.S. Tax Ct. 1970, U.S. Ct. Appeals (5th cir.) 1971, U.S. Supreme Ct. 1971; CPA, Tex. Assoc. Strasburger & Price, Dallas, 1968-74, ptnr., 1975—98, of counsel, 1999—. Lectr. Wills and Probate Inst., 1980, 81, 83, 89, Practicing Law Inst., 1983; bd. trustees Ctr. Am. and Internat. Law (formerly Southwestern Legal Found.), 1987-; dir. exec. bd. So. Meth. U. Sch. Law, 2002-. Contbr. legal articles to profl. jours. Fund raising chmn. Boy Scouts Am., Dallas, 1984—86; chmn. legacy com. Am. Cancer Soc., Dallas, 1978—82; outside gen. counsel Cmtys. Found. of Tex., Dallas, 1987—2005; interim exec. dir. Cmtys. Found. Tex., Dallas, 2001—05; trustee Cmtys. Found. of Tex., Dallas, 2005—. Lt. US Army, 1963—65. Recipient Disting. Alumni award Pub. Interest, So. Meth. U. Sch Law, 2002. Fellow Am. Coll. Trust and Estate Counsel (state chmn. 1984-89, bd. regents 1988-94, membership selection com. 1993-99), Internat. Acad. Estate and Trust Law (academician 1990—); mem. ABA (subcom. chmn. 1979), State Tex. Bar Assn. (lectr. 1981, 82), Dallas Bar Assn. (chmn. probate sect. 1985), Tex. Soc. CPAs, Dallas Estate Planning Coun. (pres. 1985, program v.p. 1984, treas. 1982, sec. 1981), Tex. Bd. Legal Specialization (cert.). Avocations: golf, sports, bridge. Office: Strasburger & Price LLP Bank Am Plz 901 Main St Ste 4400 Dallas TX 75202-3724

KINNELL, GALWAY, poet, translator; b. Providence, Feb. 1, 1927; s. James Scott and Elizabeth (Mills) K.; children: Maud, Fergus. AB summa cum laude, Princeton U., 1948; MA, U. Rochester, 1949. Instr. English Alfred U., N.Y., 1949-51; dir. liberal arts program U. Chgo., 1951-55; Am. lectr. U. Grenoble, France, 1956-57; Fulbright lectr. U. Iran, Teheran, 1959-60; adj. assoc. prof. Columbia U., NYC, 1972, adj. prof., 1974, 76; Citizens' prof. U. Hawaii at Manoa, Honolulu, 1979-81; dir. writing program NYU, NYC, 1981-84, Samuel F.B. Morse prof. arts and scis., 1985-92, Erich Maria Remarque prof. creative writing, 1992—. Lectr. summer session U. Nice, France, 1957; vis. prof. Queens Coll. of CUNY, 1971, Pitts. Poetry Forum, 1971, Brandeis U., 1974, Skidmore Coll., 1975, U. Del., 1978; poet-in-residence Juniata Coll., 1964, Reed Coll., 1966-67, Colo. State U., 1968, U. Wash., 1968, U. Calif., Irvine, 1968-69, U. Iowa, 1978, Holy Cross Coll., 1977; vis. poet Sarah Lawrence Coll., 1972-78, Princeton U., 1976; resident writer Deya Inst., Mallorca, Spain, 1969-70; vis. writer Macquarie U., Sydney, Australia, 1979; poetry dir. Squaw Valley Cmty. of Writers, 1979—. Author: (poetry) What a Kingdom It Was, 1960, Flower Herding on Mount Monadnock, 1964, Body Rags, 1968, Poems of Night, 1968, The Hen Flower, 1969, First Poems: 1946-1954, 1970, The Shoes of Wandering, 1971, The Book of Nightmares, 1971, The Avenue Bearing the Initial of Christ into the New World: Poems 1946-1964, 1974, Mortal Acts, Mortal Words, 1980, Selected Poems, 1982 (Nat. Book award for poetry 1983, Pulitzer Prize for poetry 1983), The Fundamental Project of Technology, 1983, The Past, 1985, When One Has Lived a Long Time Alone, 1990, Imperfect Thirst, 1994, A New Selected Poems, 2000, Strong is Your Hold, 2006; (novels) Black Light, 1966; (children's) How the Alligator Missed Breakfast, 1982; (non-fiction) The Poetics of the Physical World, 1969, Walking Down the Stairs: Selections from Interviews, 1978, Thoughts Occasioned by the Most Insignificant of All Human Events, 1982, Remarks on Accepting the American Book Award, 1984; translator: Rene Hardy's Bitter Victory, 1956, Henri Lehmann's Pre-Columbian Ceramics, 1962, The Poems of Francois Villon, 1965, Yves Bonnefoy's On The Motion and Immobility of Douve, 1968 (Cecil Hemley Poetry prize Ohio U. Pr. 1968), Yvan Goll's The Lackawanna Elegy, 1970, Yves Bonnefoy's Early Poems, 1947-1959, 1990, The Essential Rilke, 1999; editor: The Essential Whitman, 1987. Fulbright scholar, 1955-56; Guggenheim fellow, 1961-62, 74-75; grantee Ford Found., 1955, Nat. Inst. Arts and Letters, 1962, Rockefeller Found., 1962-63, 68; Amy Lowell travelling fellow, 1969-70, MacArthur fellow, 1984; recipient Longview Found. award, 1962, Bess Hokin prize Poetry Mag., 1965, Eunice Tietjens prize Poetry Mag., 1966, Ingram Merrill Found. award, 1969, Brandeis U. Creative Arts award, 1969, Shelley prize Poetry Soc. Am., 1974, Medal of Merit Nat. Inst. Arts and Letters, 1975, Landon Translation prize, 1979, Hutchinson medal U. Rochester, 2001, Frost medal Poetry Soc. Am., 2002; named Vt. State Poet, 1989-93. Mem. Nat. Acad. and Inst. Arts and Letters, Am. Acad. Arts and Sci., Acad. Am. Poets (chancellor). Office: New York Univ Creative Writing program New York NY 10003-6607*

KINNEY, ARTHUR FREDERICK, humanities educator, writer; b. Cortland, NY, Sept. 5, 1933; s. Arthur F. and Gladys (Mudge) K. BA magna cum laude, Syracuse U., 1955; MS, Columbia U., 1956; PhD, U. Mich., 1963. Instr. Yale U., New Haven, Conn., 1963-66; asst. prof. U. Mass., Amherst, 1966-69, assoc. prof., 1969-73, prof., 1973-85, Copeland Prof., 1985—. Adj. prof. Clark U., 1973—, NYU, 1990—; dir. Mass. Ctr. for Renaissance Studies, Amherst; spkr. in field. Author: Faulkner's Narrative Poetics, 1978, Resources of Being: Flannery O'Connor's Library, 1984, Humanist Poetics, 1986, John Skelton: Priest as Poet, 1987, Continental Humanist Poetics, 1989, Dorothy Parker Revisited, 1997, Renaissance Drama, 1999, 2nd edit., 2005, Cambridge Companion to English Literature 1500-1600, 2000, Blackwell Companion to Renaissance Drama, 2001, Lies Like Truth: Shakespeare, Macbeth and the Cultural Moment, 2001, New Critical Essays on Hamlet, 2001, Shakespeare by Stages, 2003, Shakespeare's Webs: Networks of Meaning in Renaissance Drama, 2004, Shakespeare and Cognition, 2006; editor: Rogues, Vagabonds, and Sturdy Beggars, 1973, 2nd edit., 1990, Elizabethan Backgrounds, 1974, revised edit., 1990, Renaissance Historicism, 1987, Sidney in Retrospect, 1988, Tudor Encyclopedia, 2001, Challenging Humanism, 2005, English Literary Renaissance jour., (book series) Twayne English Authors Series-Renaissance, Massachusetts Studies in Early Modern Culture; mem. editl. bd. several jours.:, editl. cons. in field:. With AUS, 1956-58. Recipient Disting. Tchg. award U. Mass., 1990, Chancellor's medal, 1985, Univ. Rsch. fellowship, 1976; named Fulbright fellow, Christ Ch., Oxford U., 1977-78, Sr. Huntington Libr. fellow, 1973-74, 78, 83, Sr. NEH fellow, 1973-74, 87-88, 2003-06, Sr. Folger Shakespeare Libr. fellow, 1974, 90, 92. Mem. MLA (pres. coun. of editors of learned jours. 1971-73, 81-83), Shakespeare Assn. Am. (trustee 1995-1997), Renaissance Soc. Am. (coun. mem., Paul Oskar Kristeller Lifetime Achievement award 2006), Renaissance English Text Soc. (pres. 1985—), Sixteenth-Century Studies Conf. Assn, Internat. Sidney Soc. (pres.). Avocations: published photographer, jazz. Home: 25 Hunters Hill Cir Amherst MA 01002-3116 Office: English Dept U Mass Amherst Amherst MA 01003 also: Ctr Renaissance Studies PO Box 2300 Amherst MA 01004-2300 Office Phone: 413-577-3600. Office Fax: 413-577-3605.

KINNEY, CAROLYN, physician; b. Philipsburg, Pa., Feb. 18, 1957; MD, Boston U., 1981. Intern Thomas Jefferson U. Hosp., Phila., 1981, resident, 1982—84; staff Good Samaritan Regional Hosp. Med. Ctr., Phoenix, 1995—; phys. Health South Meridian Point Rehab., Scottsdale, Ariz., 1996—; sec. Am. Bd. Phys. Medicine & Rehab. Office: 9630 E Shea Blvd Scottsdale AZ 85260 also: Health South Meridian Point Rehab Hospital 11250 N 92nd St Scottsdale AZ 85260

KINNEY, CATHERINE R., stock exchange executive; married; 2 children. BS magna cum laude, Iona Coll.; cert. advanced mgmt., Harvard Sch. Bus.; DHL (hon.), Georgetown U., 2004; degree (hon.), Rosemont Coll. Various positions NY Stock Exch., 1974—86, mgr. trading-floor opers. and tech., 1986—95, group exec. v.p., 1995—2002, pres. & co-COO, 2002—06, NYSE Group, Inc., 2006—07; pres., co-COO NYSE Euronext, 2007—. Bd. mem. Met Life Ins. Co., 2002—04, Depository Trust & Clearing Corp., US India Bus. Coun. Trustee Iona Coll.; bd. dirs. Georgetown U.; mem. bd. Jr. Achievement NY, NY Stock Exch. Found., Catholic Charities. Office: NYSE Euronext 11 Wall St New York NY 10005*

KINNEY, EARL ROBERT, mutual funds company executive; b. Burnham, Maine, Apr. 12, 1917; s. Harry E. and Ethel (Vose) K.; m. Margaret Velie Thatcher, Apr. 23, 1977; children: Jeanie Elizabeth, Earl Robert, Isabella Alice. AB, Bates Coll., 1939; postgrad., Harvard U. Grad. Sch., 1940. Founder, North Atlantic Pack Co., Bar Harbor, Maine, 1941, pres., 1941-42, treas., dir., 1941-64; with Gorton Corp. (became subs. Gen. Mills, Inc. 1968), 1954-68, pres., 1958-68; v.p. Gen. Mills, Inc., 1968-69, exec. v.p., 1969-73, chief fin. officer, 1970-73, pres., chief operating officer, 1973-77, chmn. bd., 1977-81; pres., chief exec. officer IDS Mut. Fund Group, Mpls., 1982-87. Bd. dirs. Idexx Labs., Inc. Trustee Bates Coll., also chmn. alumni drives, 1960-64. Office: 4900 IDS Ctr Minneapolis MN 55402 Office Phone: 612-332-1369.

KINNEY, ELEANOR DE ARMAN, law educator; b. Boston, Jan. 17, 1947; d. Thomas DeArman and Eleanor Shepard (Roberts) K.; m. Charles Malcolm Clark Jr., June 25, 1983; children: Janet Marie, Brian Alexander, Margaret Louise. AB, Duke U., 1969, JD, 1973; MA, U. Chgo., 1970; MPH, U. N.C., 1979. Bar: Ohio 1973, N.C. 1977, U.S. Dist. Ct. (no. dist.) Ohio 1974. Assoc. Squire, Sanders & Dempsey, Cleve., 1973-77; estate planning officer Duke U. Med. Ctr., Durham, N.C., 1977-79; program analyst HHS, Washington, 1979-82; asst. gen. counsel Am. Hosp. Assn., Chgo., 1982-84; vis. prof. Ind. U. Sch. Law, Indpls., 1984-85, asst. prof., 1985-88, found. dir. William S. & Christine S. Hall Ctr. for Law and Health, 1987—, assoc. prof., 1988-90, Hall Render prof. law & exec. dir. Latin Am. Law Program, 1990—; adj prof. Ind. U. Sch. Public & Environ. Affairs & Sch. Medicine. Cons. Adminstrv. Conf. U.S., Washington, 1985—91; mem. exec. bd. Ind. State Bd. of Health, 1989—99; Fulbright fellow Nat. Univ. LaPlata, Argentina, 1999—2000. Author: Protecting American Health Care Consumers, 2002. Ed., Guide to Medicare Coverage Decision-Making and Appeals, 2002. Contbr. articles to legal jours., also monographs, chpts. to books. Mem.: ABA (coun. sect. on adminstrv. law and regulatory practice 1997—, vice-chair 2003—04, chair-elect 2004—05), Am. Law Inst., Am. Assn. Law Schs. (bd. mem. sect. on on adminstrv. law law 1998—, vice chair 2003—04, chair-elect 2004—05, chair 2005—), Am. Pub. Health Assn. Office: Indiana U School of Law Inlow Hall Room 136F 530 W New York St Indianapolis IN 46202-3225 Office Phone: 317-274-4091. Business E-Mail: ekinney@iupui.edu.

KINNEY, GILBERT HART, investor; b. NYC, May 11, 1931; s. Gilbert and Anna Dudley (Hart) Kinney; m. Ann Baker Rasmussen, Aug. 11, 1959; children: Sarah Kinney Contomichalos, Eleanor Hart. BA, Yale U., New Haven, Conn., 1953, MA, 1954; MPA, Harvard U., John F. Kennedy Sch., Cambridge, Mass., 1973. Fgn. svc. officer Dept. State, Washington, 1958—60, Security Office, Tokyo, 1960—62, Econ. Office, Saigon, Vietnam, 1962—64, Vietnam and Japan Desk, Washington, 1964—69, Prin. Office Consulate, Surabaya, Indonesia, 1969—72, JFK Kennedy Sch., Cambridge, 1972—73. Trustee Corcoran Gallery Art, Washington, 1974—94, CEO, 1977—78; trustee Archives Am. Art, Washington, 1974—91, pres., 1978—82; trustee Am. Fedn. Art, NYC, 1971—, pres., 2000—05, chmn., 2005—06; dir. Am. Arts Alliance, Washington, 1986—91; chmn. Yale Alumni Fund, 1986—88; trustee Yale U. Art Gallery, New Haven, 1991—; active Baseball Commn., DC Baseball Commn. Lt. j.g. USN, 1954—57. Recipient Yale medal, Yale U., 1997. Mem.: Union Club NYC, River Club NYC. Democrat. Roman Catholic. Avocations: art collecting, political fundraising. Home and Office: 19 E 72nd St New York NY 10021

KINNEY, GREGORY HOPPES, lawyer; b. Anderson, Ind., July 15, 1947; s. Dalton Roth and Effie Eleanor (Hoppes) Kinney. BA, Mich. State U., East Lansing, 1969, M in Labor Rels., 1971; JD, U. Detroit, 1974. Bar: Mich. 1975, US Dist. Ct. (ea. dist.) Mich. 1975, US Dist. Ct. (we. dist.) Mich. 2000, US Ct. Appeals (DC cir.) 1975, US Ct. Appeals (6th cir.) 1987. Labor law editor Bur. Nat. Affairs, Washington, 1974; pension cons. Edward H. Friend & Co., Washington, 1975, Wyatt Co., Detroit, 1976-84;

pvt. practice Detroit, 1984-86, Troy, Mich., 1986-99, Decatur, Mich., 1999—. Office: PO Box 243 Decatur MI 49045-0243

KINNEY, JAMES HOWARD, lawyer, real estate company executive; b. Oklahoma City, Mar. 2, 1937; s. William Edgar and Chrissie (Ballingall) Kinney; m. June Lassick, Mar. 26, 1961; children: Karen Jill, Scott James. BS cum laude in Bus. Mgmt., Calif. State U., Long Beach, 1963; JD, UCLA, 1966. Bar: Calif. 1966, US Dist. Ct. (so. dist.) Calif. 1966. Dep. dist. atty. Ventura County, Calif., 1966-68; ptnr. Collins, Gleason & Kinney, Torrance, Calif., 1968-85, O'Melveny & Myers, LA, 1985—2000; sr. v.p., chief real estate counsel The Macerich Co., Santa Monica, Calif., 2000—. Lectr. Harbor Coll., LA, 1971-72. Councilman City of Palos Verdes Estates, Calif., 1983-1990, Mayor, 1985-86, 88-89. With USMC, 1955-58. Mem. LA County Bar Assn., Internat. Coun. Shopping Ctrs., Sigma Alpha Epsilon. Republican. Office: Macerich Co Ste 700 401 Wilshire Blvd Santa Monica CA 90401-1452

KINNEY, JANIS MARIE, librarian, consultant; b. Cresson, Pa., Dec. 26, 1935; d. Cecil and Ruth Ellen (Moyer) Powell; m. James Leroy Kinney; 1 child, Janis Cecilia. BS in Libr. Sci., Clarion U., Pa., 1957; MEd in Curriculum and Instrn., Pa. State U., University Park, 1987. Librarian N. Huntingdon Sch. Dist., Irwin, Pa., 1957-58, Greater Gallitzin (Pa.) Schs., 1959-61, Hollidaysburg (Pa.) Area Sch. Dist., 1961-90; storyteller Altoona, Pa., 1990—. Chair Allegheny Storytellers of Pa., 1991—; rostered artist Pa. Coun. on the Arts in Edn. Program; cons. various sch. dists.; cons. Old Bedford Village Storytelling Festival, Bedford, Pa., West Overton Village Tellabration; cofounder interdisciplinary arts group Stories in Motion; spkr. Pa. Commonwealth Spkr. in Humanities, 2006-. Author/producer audio cassettes; featured teller Corn Island Storytelling Festivals, Louisville; contbr. articles to profl. jours. Active Blair County Arts Found., Altoona, 1991—, Blair County Tourist & Conv. Bur., 1992—, Blair County Hist. Soc., 1994—; Pa. Rural Arts Alliance, 1992—. Recipient Disting. Educator award Hollidaysburg Alumni, 1996. Mem. Internat. Order E.A.R.S. (Disting. Svc. award 2001), Nat. Storytelling Assn., Allegheny Storytellers Pa. (founder), Cen. Pa. Harp Soc. Avocations: reading, bicycling, hiking, music, travel. Home and Office: 1900 16th Ave Altoona PA 16601-2502 Office Phone: 814-943-1080. Personal E-mail: jan.kinney@verizon.net.

KINNEY, LISA FRANCES, lawyer; b. Laramie, Wyo., Mar. 13, 1951; d. Irvin Wayne and Phyllis (Poe) Kinney; m. Rodney Philip Lang, Feb. 5, 1971; children: Cambria Helen, Shelby Robert, Eli Wayne. BA, U. Wyo., 1973, JD, 1986; MLS, U. Oreg., 1975. Reference libr. U. Wyo. Sci. Libr., Laramie, 1975-76; outreach dir. Albany County Libr., Laramie, 1975-76, dir., 1977-83; mem. Wyo. State Senate, Laramie, 1984-94, minority leader, 1992-94; with documentation office Am. Heritage Ctr. U. Wyo., 1991-94; assoc. Corthell & King, 1994-96, shareholder, 1996-99; owner Summit Bar Rev., 1987—2004; fin. planner VALIC, 2001—. Author: (with Rodney Lang) Civil Rights of the Developmentally Disabled, 1986; (with Rodney Lang and Phyllis Kinney) Manual For Families with Emotionally Disturbed and Mentally Ill Relatives, 1988, rev. 1991, 99, Lobby For Your Library, Know What Works, 1992, Understanding Mental Illnesses: A Family Legal Guide, 2004; contbr. articles to profl. jours.; editor, compiler pub. rels. directory of ALA, 1982. Bd. dirs. Big Bros./Big Sisters, Laramie, 1980-83, Children's Mus., 1993-97; bd. dirs. Am. Heritage Ctr., 1993-97, Citizen of the Century, 1997-99, govt. chmn. 1997-99; pres. Friends Cmty. Recreation Project, 2001-06. Named Outstanding Wyo. Libr. Assn., 1977, Young Woman, State of Wyo., 1980; recipient Beginning Young Profl. award, Mt. Plains Libr. Assn., 1980, Arts and Scis. Disting. Alumni award, U. Wyo., 1997, Making Democracy Work award, Wyo. LWV, 2000, Cmty. Svc. award, Laramie and Lions Club, 2006. Mem.: ABA, Nat. Conf. State Legislatures (various coms. 1985—90), Laramie Area C. of C. (bd. dirs. 1996—2000, mem. 1999, Top Hand award 1997), Zonta, Kiwanis. Democrat. Avocations: photography, dance, reading, travel, languages. Home: 1415 E Baker St Laramie WY 82072 Office: PO Box 1710 Laramie WY 82073-1710 Office Phone: 307-742-6644. Personal E-mail: lfkl@aol.com.

KINNEY, STEPHEN HOYT, JR., lawyer; b. Albuquerque, Feb. 27, 1948; s. Stephen Hoyt and Harriet May (Gadsden) K.; m. Leslie vanLiew, June 10, 1972; 1 child, Erin. BS, MIT, 1970; JD, Harvard U., 1973. Bar: NY 1974, US Dist. Ct. (so. dist.) NY 1974, US Dist. Ct. (ea. dist.) NY 1974, US Dist. Ct. (no. dist.) NY 1978, US Ct. Appeals (2d cir.) 1975, US Supreme Ct. 1982. Programmer, analyst MIT, 1968-70; law clk. NJ Organized Crime Unit, Trenton, 1972; assoc. Reid & Priest, NYC, 1973-85, sr. atty., 1985-86, ptnr., 1986-98, Thelen Reid & Brown Raysman & Steiner, NYC, 1998—2006, ThelenReid Brown Raysman & Steiner, NYC, 2006—. Dir. The Friends of Thirteen, Inc., 2005—. Author, editor: Outline of Arbitration, 1984; contbr. articles to profl. jours.; creator software. Mem.: ABA. Office: Thelen Reid Brown Raysman & Steiner 875 Third Ave New York NY 10022-6225 Home Phone: 516-883-3112; Office Phone: 212-603-2168. Business E-Mail: skinney@thelen.com.

KINNEY, WILLIAM LIGHT, JR., editor, publishing executive; b. Bennettsville, SC, Oct. 26, 1933; s. William Light and Annie Laurie (Mayer) K.; m. Margaret Rene Pegues, Mar. 21, 1964; children: Elisabeth Mayer Kinney McNiel, William Light III (dec.). BS, Wofford Coll., 1954, DHL, 1999; BA in Journalism, U. S.C., 1977. Copy editor The State, Columbia, SC, 1955-58; reporter Marlboro Herald-Advocate, Bennettsville, 1958-59, advt. mgr., 1959-60, bus. mgr., 1960-65, mng. editor, 1965-70, editor, pub., 1970—; pres. Marlboro Pub. Co. Inc., 1970—. Sec. Marlboro Savs. & Loan Assn., Bennettsville, 1970-82, First Nat. Bank SC, Bennettsville, 1973-84; adv. bd. SC Nat. Bank, Bennettsville, 1984-94, Wachovia Bank, 1994-2000; sec., adv. bd. Security Fed. Savs. & Loan, 1982-90, bd. dirs., 1986-89; pres. Greater Pee Dee Press Inc., 1972-82, Bennettsville Parking and Devel. Co., 1964; v.p. Hamlet (NC) News Inc., 1973-82 Editor, pub.: Three Who Dared, 1960, Sherman's March—A Review, 1961, The Story of the Sculpture Light, 2001. Pres. United Fund, Bennettsville, 1963-64; chmn. Marlboro County com. S.C. Tricentennial, 1970, U.S. Bicentennial, 1974—81; councilman, mayor pro tem City of Bennettsville, 1967-69; mem. Marlboro County Devel. Bd., 1958-81; bd. dir. Kinney Found., 1971-99, chmn. bd. dir., 1975-99; bd. dir. Indian Mus. of Carolinas, 1972-2005; trustee Whipple Found., 1979—, chmn., 1981—; trustee S.C. Press Found., 1978-93, 2000—, vice-chmn., 1985-92, chmn., 1992-93; trustee Neil Monroe Trust Fund, 1965-91, chmn., 1977-91; adv. bd. SBA, 1962-64; chmn. fin. com. 1st Meth. Ch., 1985-87, staff parish com. chmn., 1990-92; active Chancel Choir, 1951—; trustee S.C. Meth. Adv., 1968-78, S.C. Hall of Fame, 1980-88, 2005—, v.p., 1980-82; dir. S.C. Confedn. Local Hist. Socs., 1974-75, treas., 1975-78, v.p., 1979, pres., 1980-82; warden St. David's Soc., 1978-80, pres., 1980-81; chmn. Jennings-Brown House Restoration, 1974-76, Bennettsville Downtown Commn., 1977-82; v.p. Bennettsville Downtown Devel. Assn., 1993—; trustee Am. Folklife Ctr., Libr. Congress, Washington, 1982—, chmn. 1987, 92-93, 98-2000, vice-chmn., 1990-92, 94—; mem. S.C. Archives and History Commn., 1987—, vice-chmn., 1988-90, 98—, chmn., 1990-93; SC rev. bd. Nat. Register of Hist. Places, 1988—, chmn., 1990—, S.C. State Devel. Bd., 1993; bd. dir. Friends Brookgreen Gardens, 1991-97, 2001-, pres., 1993-96, trustee, 1993-96; bd. visitors Coker Coll., 1986-89; bd. dirs. S.C. Com. for Humanities, 1981-85, Pawleys Island Civic Assn., 1979—, dir., 2004—; dir. Palmetto Trails, 1993-97; trustee Scotia Village Retirement Cmty., 1995—; v.p. Marlboro Civic Ctr. Found., 1994—; bd. mgrs. S.C. Hist. Soc., 2005—, v.p. 2007-. Named Bennettsville and S.C. Young Man of Yr., 1961, S.C. Amb. for Econ. Devel., 1990, Knight of Justice of the Order of St. John, Knights of Malta, Sovereign Order of St. John of Jerusalem, 1995—; recipient Govs. award Hist. Preservation 1996, Elizabeth O'Neill Verner Gov.'s award for the arts 2002, Jean Laney Harris Folk Heritage award S.C. Gen. Assembly, 2003. Mem. SAR, Nat. Trust for Historic Preservation (bd. advisors So. Region 1997-2006, chmn., 2000-02, nat. exec. com. 1999-2002), S.C. Press Assn. (pres. 1972-73), Palmetto Conservation Found. (dir. 1997-2001), Palmetto Trust Hist. Preservation (trustee 2002—), Marlboro County Hist. Preservation Com. (chmn. 1986-96), S.C. C. of C. (bd. dir. 1964-68, 75-78), Bennettsville C. of C. (bd. dir. 1964-67, 75-78), Bennettsville Jaycees (pres. 1962), S.C. Jaycees (v.p. 1963, nat. dir. 1964), Marlboro Hist. Soc. (bd. dir. 1967-79, 2000-, pres. 1975-79), U. S.C. Soc. (bd. dir. 1972-82, vice chmn. 1977-82), Wofford Coll. Alumni Assn. (bd. dir. 1968-72), Marlboro Country Club, Marlboro Cotillion Club (pres. 1984-86, 2004-06), Nat. Debutante Cotillion (sponsor 1987-95), Sans Souci Club (pres. 1980-82), Rotary (bd. dir. 1968-70, 99-2001, pres. 1970-72), McLeod Med. Ctr. Found. (trustee 1997-2007), SC Hist. Soc. (bd. mgrs. 2005—, v.p. 2007—), Phi Beta Kappa, Sigma Alpha Epsilon, Sigma Delta Chi. Home: Magnolia 508 E Main St Bennettsville SC 29512-0656 Office: Marlboro Herald-Adv Shiness PO Box 656 100 Fayetteville Ave Bennettsville SC 29512-0656 Business E-Mail: wlkinneyjr@mecsc.net. *"Service to humanity is the best work of life" is a tenet of the Jaycee Creed that still drives me to work through my avocations as well as my vocation to help make my community, state and nation better than I found. These efforts have broadened my horizons, enriched my life and heightened my spirit. I recommend active service to one's home community, state and nation to all.*

KINNISON, DANIEL E., manufacturing engineer; b. Weld County, Colo., Feb. 6, 1924; s. Daniel Calvin and Nellie Lillian Kinnison; m. Shirley Anne Wood, June 1, 1952; children: Patricia Anne, James Allen. Grad. HS, Keota, Colo. Farmer, rancher, Buckingham, Colo., 1946—49, Grover, Colo., 1949—54; farm equipment retailer Kimball, Nebr., 1954—85; owner, operator Prestige Mfg., Inc., Kimball, 1984—. Councilman City of Kimball, 1968—74, airport authority, 1975—78; exec. bd. Longs Peak coun. Boy Scouts Am., Greeley, Colo., 1975—89; bd. trustees Meth. Ch., Kimball, 1985—2000. With USAAF, 1944—45. Named Boss of Yr., Kimball C. of C., 1975; recipient Disting. Svc. award, 1970, Silver Beaver award, Boy Scouts Am., 1987. Mem.: Rotary (pres. 1960, 1986). Republican. Achievements include patents for post hole digger, air intake pre-cleaner. Avocations: furniture building, woodworking, flying. Home: 119 E 9th St Kimball NE 69145 Office: Prestige Mfg Inc 105 S Webster Kimball NE 69145

KINNISON, ROBERT WHEELOCK, retired accountant; b. Des Moines, Sept. 17, 1914; s. Virgil R. and Sopha J. (Jackson) K.; m. Randi Hjelle, Oct. 28, 1971; children: Paul F., Hazel Jo Lewis. BS in Acctg., U. Wyo., 1940. CPA, Wyo., Colo. Ptnr. 24 hour auto service, Laramie, Wyo., 1945-59; pvt. practice acctg. Laramie, Wyo., 1963-71, Las Vegas, Nev., 1972-74, Westminster, Colo., 1974-76, Ft. Collins, Colo., 1976-97; ret., 1997. Served with U.S. Army, 1941-45, PTO. Mem. Wyo. Soc. CPAs, Am. Legion (past comdr.), Laramie Soc. CPAs (pres. 1966), VFW, Laramie Optimist Club (pres. 1950), Sertoma Club. Home: 401 N Timberline Rd Lot 288 Fort Collins CO 80524-1431

KINNISON, WILLIAM ANDREW, retired university president; b. Springfield, Ohio, Feb. 10, 1932; s. Errett Lowell and Audrey Muriel (Smith) K.; m. Lenore Belle Morris, June 11, 1960; children— William Errett, Linda Elise, Amy Elisabeth. AB, Wittenberg U., 1954, BS in Edn., 1955; MA, U. Wis., 1963; PhD (1st Flesher fellow), Ohio State U., 1967; postgrad., Harvard U. Inst. Ednl. Mgmt., 1970; LL.D., Calif. Luth. Coll., 1983; Th.D., John Carroll U., 1983; LLD, Lenoir-Rhyne Coll., 1987; LHD, Capital U., 1995. Asst. dean admissions Wittenberg U., Springfield, 1958-65, asst. to pres., 1967-70, v.p. for univ. affairs, 1970-73, v.p. adminstrn., 1973, pres., 1974-95, pres. emeritus, 1995—; pres., CEO Heritage Ctr. of Clark County, 1997—2002. Author: Samuel Shellabarger: Lawyer, Jurist, Legislator, 1969, Building Sullivant's Pyramid: An Administrative History of the Ohio State University, 1970, Concise History of Wittenberg University, 1976, An American Seminary, 1980, Springfield and Clark County: an Illustrated History, 1985, also articles. Asst. to dir. Sch. Edn. Ohio State U., Columbus, 1965-67; past chmn. Assn. Ind. Colls. and Univs. Ohio; trustee Ohio Found. Ind. Colls., 1974-95, chair bd. trustees, 1995; chmn. standing com. Luth. World Ministries, 1976-82; mem. exec. coun. Luth. Ch. in Am., 1978-86; mem., chmn. Commn. for a New Luth. Ch., 1982-86; bd. dirs. Am. Assn. Colls., 1982-84. With U.S. Army, 1956-58. Mem. Clark County Hist. Soc. (trustee 1963—), Orgn. Am. Historians, Blue Key, Phi Beta Kappa, Phi Delta Kappa, Kappa Phi Kappa, Pi Sigma Alpha, Tau Kappa Alpha, Delta Sigma Phi, Omicron Delta Kappa. Clubs: Cosmos, Rotary. Home: 1820 Timberline Dr Springfield OH 45504-1236

KINNO, HITOSHI, mechanical engineer, educator; b. Tokushima, Japan, Mar. 10, 1917; s. Keihichi and Maki (Isoda) K.; m. Chikako Nii, Dec. 27, 1950 (dec. 1995); children: Hiroshi, Yukio. Grad., Tokushima Tech. Coll., 1939; DEng, Osaka U., Japan, 1959. Design engr. Sumitomo Machine Co., Niihama, Japan, 1939-45; asst. prof. Tokushima Tech. Coll., 1945-51; asst. U. Tokushima, 1951-54, lectr., 1954-56, asst. prof., 1956-61, prof., 1961-82, prof. emeritus, 1982—; pres. Earth Sci. Lab. Corp., Tokushima, 1996—2005. Dir. Yoko Civilization Rsch. Inst., Tokyo, 1986-90. Author: Waterhammer Control in Centrifugal Pump Systems, 1958, On the Mechanisms of the First Breakup of Pangaea in Early Mesozoic, 1991, The Origin of Earthquake Caused by Plate Motion, 1996, Land Protect Systems Against Sea Level Rise, 1998, Multiple Tidal Pumped Storage Power Generation Arrangement and the Method of Constructing the Same at a Tidal Power Site, 1999, System for Protecting Coastal Land from the Rise of Surface of the Sea, 2000, The Mechanism Discovery of the Glacial Age Cycle, 2003, Global Cooling Technology, 2004. Named to 3d Imperial Order of Rising Sun Emperor of Japan, 1990. Mem. N.Y. Acad. Scis. Shinto. Avocations: fishing, photography. Home: Tomidabashi 8-1-1-1105 Tokushima shi 770-0937 Japan Office Phone: (+81) 88-656-0552. E-mail: kinno_hitoshi@yahoo.co.jp.

KINO, GORDON STANLEY, electrical engineering educator; b. Melbourne, Australia, June 15, 1928; came to U.S., 1951, naturalized, 1967; s. William Hector and Sybil (Cohen) K.; m. Dorothy Beryl Lovelace, Oct. 30, 1955; 1 child, Carol Ann. BSc with 1st class honours in Math, London U., Eng., 1948; MSc in Math, London U., 1950; PhD in Elec. Engring, Stanford U., Calif., 1955. Jr. scientist Mullard Research Lab., Salford, Surrey, England, 1947-51; research asst., then research assoc. Stanford U., 1951-55, research assoc., 1957-61, mem. faculty, 1961—, prof. elec. engring., 1965—, assoc. dean facilities and planning Sch. Engring., 1986-92, assoc. chmn. elec. engring., 1984-88, W.M. Keck Found. chair engring., 1992-97, W.M. Keck Found. chair engring. emeritus, 1997—; dir. Ginzton Lab., 1994-96. Mem. tech. staff Bell Telephone Labs., 1955-57; cons. to industry, 1957— Author: (with Kirstein, Waters) Space Charge Flow, 1968, Acoustic Devices, 1987, (with Corle) Confocal Scanning Optical Microscopy and Related Imaging Systems, 1996; also numerous papers on microwave tubes; electron optics, plasma physics, bulk effects in semiconductors, acoustic surface waves, acoustic imaging, optical microscopy, fiber optics, non-destructive testing, optical storage. Guggenheim fellow, 1967-68; recipient Applied Research Achievement award Am. Soc. Non-destructive Testing, 1986. Fellow IEEE (Centennial medal, Sonics and Ultrasonics Group Achievement award 1984), Am. Phys. Soc., AAAS; mem. Nat. Acad. Engring. Inventor Kino electron gun, 1959; co-inventor real-time scanning optical microscope, 1987, solid immersion lens, 1989, microfabricated miniature microscope, 1995. Home: 867 Cedro Way Stanford CA 94305-1002 Business E-Mail: kino@stanford.edu.

KINOSHITA, TOICHIRO, physicist; b. Tokyo, Jan. 23, 1925; came to U.S., 1952; s. Tsutomu and Fumi (Ueda) K.; m. Masako Matsuoka, Oct. 14, 1951; children: Kay, June, Ray. BS, Tokyo U., 1947, PhD, 1952. Mem. Inst. for Advanced Study, Princeton, NJ, 1952-54; postdoctoral fellow Columbia U., NYC, 1954-55; rsch. assoc. Cornell U., Ithaca, NY, 1955-58, asst. prof., 1958-60, assoc. prof., 1960-63, prof., 1963-92, Goldwin Smith prof., 1992-95, Goldwin Smith prof. emeritus, 1995—. Mem. tech. adv. panel U.S. Dept. Energy, Washington, 1982-83; com. fundamental constants Nat. Rsch. Coun., Washington, 1984-86. Author: Quantum Electrodynamics, 1990; contbr. over 100 articles to profl. jours. Guggenheim fellow, 1973-74; recipient Sun-Amco medal Internat. Union Phys. & Applied Sci., 1998. Fellow NAS, AAAS, Am. Physical Soc. (Recipient J.J. Sakurai prize 1990). Democrat. Home: 5 Winthrop Pl Ithaca NY 14850-1740 Office: Cornell U Newman Lab Ithaca NY 14853 Home Phone: 607-257-0886. Business E-Mail: tk@hepth.cornell.edu.

KINSBRUNER BUSH, JENNIFER, lawyer; AB in History & Latin Am. Studies summa cum laude, Princeton U., 1996; Fulbright Scholar, Universidad Católica, Santiago, Chile, 1996—97; JD, Yale Law Sch., 2000. Bar: Calif., US Ct. of Appeals, Federal Circuit. Rsch. assoc. Wiggin & Dana; summer assoc. Kirkland & Ellis, 1998, Cleary Gottlieb, 1999; law clerk to Judge Stanley Marcus US Ct. of Appeals, 11th Circuit, 2000—01; assoc. Irell & Manella, 2001—02; assoc., intellectual property litigation Fish & Richardson, San Diego, 2002—. Office: Fish & Richardson 12390 El Camino Real San Diego CA 92130 Office Phone: 858-678-5070. Office Fax: 858-678-5099. Business E-Mail: bush@fr.com.

KINSELLA, THOMAS, poet; b. Dublin, May 4, 1928; s. John Paul and Agnes (Casserly) K.; m. Eleanor Walsh, 1955, 3 children. PhD (hon.), U. Iceland, 1984, U. Turin, 2005, Freedom of the City of Dublin, 2007. With Irish Civil Svc., 1946-65, asst. prin. officer Dept. Fin., 1960-65. Artist in residence So. Ill. U., 1965-67, prof. English, 1967-70; prof. English Temple U., Phila., 1970-90; dir. Dolmen Press Ltd., Cuala Press Ltd, Dublin; founder Peppercanister, Dublin, 1972. Author: Poems, 1956, Another September, 1958, Downstream, 1962, Nightwalker and Other Poems, 1968, Notes from the Land of the Dead, 1972, Butcher's Dozen, 1972, Finistere, 1972, New Poems, 1973, Selected Poems 1956-68, 1973, Song of the Night and Other Poems, 1978, The Messenger, 1978, Fifteen Dead, 1979, One and Other Poems, 1979; Songs of the Psyche, 1984; Her Vertical Smile, 1984; St. Catherine's Clock, 1987; Out of Ireland, 1987, Blood and Family, 1988, Poems From Center City, 1990, Personal Places, 1990, Madonna and Other Poems, 1991, Open Court, 1991, From Centre City, 1994, The Dual Tradition: an Essay on Poetry and Politics in Ireland, 1995, Collected Poems, 1996, The Pen Shop, 1997, The Familiar, 1999, Godhead, 1999, Citizen of the World, 2000, Littlebody, 2000, Collected Poems 1956-2001, 2001, Marginal Economy, 2006, Readings in Poetry, 2006; editor: Selected Poems of Austin Clarke, 1976; (with Sean O'Tuama) Poems of the Dispossessed 1600-1900 with translations, 1980; The New Oxford Book of Irish Verse (with translations), 1986; transl. (from Old Irish) The Tain, 1970. Recipient Guinness Poetry award, 1958, Triennial Book award, Irish Arts Coun., 1960, Denis Devlin Meml. award, 1966, 1969, 1988, 1994, Field Day/Keough-Notre Dame Centre/Commons Tundish award, 2001; Guggenheim fellow, 1968—69, 1971—72, hon. sr. fellow, Sch. of English, Univ. Coll., Dublin, 2003. Mem.: Irish Acad. Letters, Am. Acad. Arts and Scis. Home: 639 Addison St Philadelphia PA 19147

KINSELLA, TIMOTHY J., radiation oncologist; BS, St. John Fisher Coll., Rochester, NY, 1969; MS, MD, U. Rochester, 1974. Diplomate in radiation oncology Am. Bd. Radiology, in internal medicine and med. oncology Am. Bd. of Internal Medicine. Mem. radiation discipline working group NASA, Cleve., 2003—; mem. radiation sensitization working group divsn. of cancer treatment and diagnosis Nat. Cancer Inst., Bethesda, Md., 2002—, mem. integrative cancer biology program, 2004—. Recipient USPHS, NIH Spl. Achievement, 1983, NIH Award of Merit, 1984. Achievements include first to Photosensitizing Drug in 2003; Radiosensitizing Drug in 2005. Office: Univ Hospitals Case Medical Ctr 11100 Euclid Ave Cleveland OH 44106 Office Phone: 216-844-2530. Office Fax: 216-844-4799. Business E-Mail: timothy.kinsella@uhhospitals.org.

KINSER, CYNTHIA D., state supreme court justice; b. Pennington Gap, Dec. 20, 1951; d. Morris and Velda (Myers) Fannon; m. H. Allen Kinser, Jr., March 17, 1974; children: Charles Adam, Terah Diane. Student, Univ. of Ga., 1970-71; BA, Univ. of Tenn., 1974; JD, Univ. of Va., 1977. Bar: Va. 1977, U.S. Dist. Ct. (we. dist.) Va. 1977, U.S. Ct. Appeals (4th cir.) 1977, U.S. Supreme Ct. 1988. Law clk. to Judge Glen M. Williams U.S. Dist. Ct., 1977-78; pvt. law practice, 1978-90; commonwealth's atty. Lee County, Va., 1980-83; magistrate judge U.S. Dist. Ct. (we. dist.) Va., Abingdon, 1990-98; justice Va. Supreme Ct., Richmond, 1998—. Trustee Chapter 7 Panel, U.S. Bankruptcy Ct., 1979-90. Mem. Va. Bar Assn., Va. Trial Lawyers Assn., Am. Bar Assn. Methodist. Office: Va Supreme Ct PO Box 1315 Richmond VA 23218-1315*

KINSEY, ANGELA, actress; b. Lafayette, La., June 25, 1971; married. Grad., Baylor U. Intern for Max Weinberg Late Night with Conan O'Brien, 1994; operator 1-800-Dentist. Mem. Improv Olympic Theater. Actor: (TV series) King of the Hill, 1997—98, Step by Step, 1998, Run of the House, 2003, All of Us, 2003, Mad TV, Fire Me Please, Spy TV, The Blame Game, The Office, 2005— (Outstanding Performance by an Ensemble in a Comedy Series, SAG, 2007); (films) Career Suicide, 2004, Tripping Forward, 2006.*

KINSEY, CHARLES JOHN, industrial auctioneer, consultant, farmer, cattle breeder; b. Regina, Sask., Can., Aug. 4, 1922; came to U.S., 1929; s. Alfred Richardson and Lola Mae (Lagergren) K.; m. Shirley Elaine Grady, June 25, 1950; children: Rebecca Diane, David Allan, Jane Elizabeth, Thomas Charles. BS, U. Ill., 1951. Fieldman Am. Hampshire Swine Registry Am. Hampshire Herdsman, Peoria, Ill., 1946—48; exec. sec. Park Ridge C. of C., Ill., 1953; indsl. auctioneer S.L. Winternitz & Co., Inc., Chgo., 1954—57; ptnr. Kinsey-Koploy Co., Detroit, 1957—65; pres., prin. Charles Kinsey & Co., Inc., Detroit, 1965—. Cons. A-Line Mfg. Co., Centralia, Ill., 1982— Author: The Lives and The Times of The Kinsey Brothers, Ernest and Alfred, 1997. Mem. First Presbyn. Ch. Choir, Farmington Hills, Mich., 1959—. Served U.S. Army, 1944-46, Persian Gulf Command, ETO Recipient Am. Farmer Degree Future Farmers Am. Vocat. Agrl., Urbana, 1940, State Pres. Ill. Assn. Future Farmers Am., 1940-41, Thomas E. Wilson award Ill. 4-H Club, Chgo., 1943, State Ill. 4-H Livestock Champion, Nat. Hampshire Pig Club contest winner, 1939 Mem. U. Ill. Alumni Assn. (life), Sigma Phi Epsilon (life). Independent. Avocations: baritone soloist, creative writing, voice concerts. Home and Office: Charles Kinsey & Co Inc 40011 Jefferson Novi MI 48375-2026

KINSEY, JAMES LLOYD, chemist, educator; b. Paris, Tex., Oct. 15, 1934; s. Lloyd King and Elaine Mills K.; m. Berma McDowell, July 28, 1962; children: Victoria, Samuel, Adam. BA, Rice U., 1956, PhD, 1959; NSF fellow, U. Uppsala, Sweden, 1959-60; postdoctoral fellow, U. Calif., Berkeley, 1960-62. Asst. prof. dept. chemistry M.I.T., 1962-67, asso. prof., 1967-74, prof., 1974-88, chmn. dept., 1977-82; D.R. Bullard-Welch Found. prof. sci. Rice U., Houston, 1988—; dean natural scis., 1988-98; interim provost Rice U., Houston, 1993-94. Cons. Los Alamos Nat. Labs., external rev. com. chemistry and laser sci. divsn., 1983—89; Miller rsch. fellow, 1960—62; bd. chem. scis. NAS-NRC, 1980—83, 2004—, co-chmn. bd. chem. scis., 1981—83; steering com. U.S. Army Basic Sci. Rsch.-NRC, 1981—86; oversight rev. com. chemistry divsn. NSF, 1989; vis. com. divsn. chemistry and chem. engring. Calif. Inst. Tech., 1999—2004; com. of chemistry facilities and infrastructure U. Calif., Berkeley, 1992—93; corp. vis. com. dept. chemistry MIT, 1994—2004; vis. com. for chemistry Stanford U., 1993—96; external rev. com. chemistry U. Pa., 2000; adv. com. rsch. projects State of Tex. Higher Edn. Coordinating Bd., 2000—02; adv. bd. for engring. and scis. Internat. U. Bremen, Germany, 2000—04. Assoc. editor Jour. Chem. Physics, 1981-84; mem. editorial adv. bd. Jour.

Phys. Chemistry, 1984-88, Ann. Rev. Phys. Chemistry, 1985-89; mem. adv. editorial bd. Chem. Physics Letters, 1992-97; mem. Coun. of Am. Acad. of Arts and Scis., 1997-2001; contbr. articles to profl. jours. Chmn. sci. adv. bd. Robert A. Welch Found., 2006—. Recipient E.O. Lawrence award U.S. Dept. Energy, 1987; Alfred P. Sloan fellow, 1964-68, Guggenheim fellow, 1969-70. Fellow AAAS, Am. Phys. Soc. (exec. com. divsn. chem. physics 1985-88, Earle K. Plyler prize 1995), Am. Acad. Arts and Scis.; mem. NAS, Am. Chem. Soc. (chmn. divsn. phys. chemistry 1985, Nobel Laureate Signature award for grad. edn. 1990), Acad. Medicine, Engring. and Sci. Tex., Houston Philos. Soc. (pres. 2006-07), Sigma Xi. Office: Rice U MS-600 PO Box 1892 Houston TX 77251-1892 Business E-Mail: jlkinsey@rice.edu.

KINSEY, JOHN ALLEN, systems engineer, technical director; b. Salem, NJ, Jan. 24, 1933; s. Charles Allen Kinsey and Margaret Elizabeth Summerlin; m. Becky Lou Schergens, Jan. 1, 1994; children from previous marriage: Steven A., John D., Robert G. BSME, Rutgers U., 1954; postgrad., N.Mex. A&M U., 1955—56, U. Calif., Santa Barbara, 1972—73, U. Houston, Clear Lake, 1989—90, George Mason U., 1991. Test engr. Texaco, Inc., Beacon, NY, 1954—55; sr. design engr. Gen. Dynamics/Convair, Edwards Rocket Base, Calif., 1957—61; mgr. The Aerospace Corp., Vandenberg AFB, 1961—75, systems engring. dir. El Segundo, 1975—79, prin. dir. Johnson Space Ctr., Tex., 1979—91, prin. dir., program exec. office for space Arlington, Va., 1991—2004; tech. dir. Futron Corp., Bethesda, Md., 2004—. Rules com. Homeowners Assn., Arlington, Va., 1998—99, landscape com., 2002—03, cmty. rep., 2002—03. 1st lt., test engr. US Army, 1955—57, White Sands Proving Ground. Fellow: AIAA (assoc.); mem.: Women in Aerospace, Am. Rocket Soc. Avocations: bridge, boating, reading. Home: 1541 22d St N Arlington VA 22209 Office: Futron Corp 7315 Wisconsin Ave Ste 900Wl Bethesda MD 20814-3202 Home Phone: 703-525-7627; Office Phone: 301-280-2650. Business E-Mail: jkinsey@futron.com.

KINSINGER, JACK BURL, chemist, educator; b. Akron, Ohio, June 23, 1925; s. William Franklin and Idelle (Althaus) K.; m. Addie Jean Parker, Sept. 2, 1946 (div. 1987); children: Paul Craig, Amy Jo; m. Gladys Styles Johnston, 1997. BA, Hiram Coll., 1948; MS, Cornell U., 1951; PhD, U. Pa., 1958. Group leader rsch. Rohm & Haas Co., Phila., 1951-56; from asst. prof. to prof. chemistry Mich. State U., East Lansing, 1957-82, assoc. chmn. dept. chemistry, 1965-69, chmn. dept., 1969-75, asst. v.p. rsch. and devel., 1977, assoc. provost, 1977-82; prof. chemistry Ariz. State U., Tempe, 1982-87, v.p. acad. affairs, 1982-87; pres., CEO, Chgo. Osteo. Health Systems and Midwestern U., 1987—96, pres. emeritus, 1996—. Cons. Union Carbide Co., 1958-80, vice chmn. divsn. polymer chemistry, 1966-68, chmn., 1969; dir. chemistry divsn. NSF, 1975-77; trustee Kirksville Osteo. Med. Coll., 1984-87, Ariz. State U. Res. Park; exec. com. Fed. Independent Colls. and Univs., 1993-95. Editor computer symposium Jour. Polymer Sci., 1968. 2nd lt. USAAF, 1943-45. Recipient Disting. Alumnus award Hiram Coll., 1984. Fellow AAAS; mem. Am. Chem. Soc., Coun. Chem. Rsch. (vice chair exec. com. 1980-81). Home: 24548 N 121st Pl Scottsdale AZ 85255 Personal E-mail: jbkgsj623@msn.com.

KINSINGER, ROBERT EARL, property company executive, educational consultant; b. Chgo., Aug. 5, 1923; s. Elmer John and Frances Louise (Ballenger) K.; m. Sylvia Kading, May 20, 1950; children: William, Candace, Lisa. AB, Stanford U., 1948, MA, 1951; Ed.D., Columbia U., 1958; LL.D., Simpson Coll., 1977; L.H.D., Hahnemann U.; Litt.D., Thomas Jefferson U., 1986. Staff mem. U.S. del. 3d Gen. Assembly UN, Paris, France, 1948; regional field rep., mgr. chpt. and regional blood center ARC, Boise, Ida., 1949-56; lectr. Columbia U., 1956, Queens Coll., 1957; ednl. cons. Nat. League Nursing, 1957-60; dir. health careers project SUNY, 1960-66; program dir. W.K. Kellogg Found., Battle Creek, Mich., 1966-70, v.p., 1970-83; chmn. Ednl. Services for the Professions, Inc., 1983-87; pres. Kinland Properties. Cons. in field; vice-chmn., adv. coun. Mich. Comprehensive Health Planning Bd.; chmn. Commn. on Physicians Assts.; dir. Jossey-Bass Inc., Publs., 1982-89; dir., chmn., trustee, exec. com. Fielding Grad. Inst., 1985-92, 95-2002; adv. com. Corp. Cmty. Coll. TV; trustee Aviation Safety Inst. Author: Education for Health Technicians-An Overview, 1965; co-author: Clinical Nursing Instruction by Television, 1965; Editor: Career Opportunities for Health Technicians, 1971. Chmn. bd. overseers U. of State of N.Y. Regents Coll.; mem. exec. com. Commn. for a Nation of Lifelong Learners; dir. Sierra Repertory Theatre; trustee Excelsior Coll.; chmn., trustee Sierra Nonprofit Support Ctr.; counselor Svc. Corps of Ret. Exec. Lt. USNR, World War II. Recipient commn. of honor SUNY, Farmingdale, 1970; Man of Yr. award Nat. Council Community Services, 1971; Honors of Soc. award Am. Soc. Allied Health Professions. Fellow: Am. Soc. Allied Health Profls.; mem.: Village West Yacht Club. Avocation: hot-air balloons. Home and Office: 21901 Confidence Rd Twain Harte CA 95383-9688 Business E-Mail: bob@rkinsinger.com. *While the "Golden Rule" should always guide one's relationships, of equal importance is steadfast delivery of what you promise to yourself and to others, and a constant effort to exceed the original promise.*

KINSLEY, MICHAEL E., newspaper columnist; b. Detroit, Mar. 9, 1951; s. George and Lillian (Margolis) K.; m. Patty Stonesifer, 2002. AB, Harvard U., 1972, JD, 1977; postgrad., Magdalen Coll., Oxford U., Eng., 1972-74. Bar: D.C. Mng. editor The Washington Monthly, 1975, The New Republic, Washington, 1976-79, editor, 1979-81, 85-89, sr. editor, 1989-95; editor Harper's Mag., NYC, 1981-83; Am. Survey editor The Economist, London, 1988-89; contbg. writer Time mag., 1987—; Editor Slate Mag., 1996—2002, contbg. editor, 2002—04; editl. and opinion editor LA Times, 2004—05; columnist Washington Post, 2005—. Co-host CNN Crossfire, 1989-95.

KINSLEY, WILLIAM BENTON, literature educator; b. Montpelier, Vt., Sept. 11, 1934; emigrated to Can., 1965; s. Benton Rufus and Ann Magadline (Finnegan) K.; m. Therese Huang, Dec. 30, 1964 (dec. Mar. 1996); children: Anne-Marie, Claire, Eliane. Student, Wesleyan U., 1952—55; BA, U. Toronto, 1958; postgrad., U. Lyon, France, 1959; PhD, Yale U., 1965. Instr. St. Michael's Coll., Winooski, Vt., 1958-59, U. Rochester, NY, 1963-64; asst. prof. English lit. U. Montreal, Canada, 1965—71, assoc. prof., 1971—81, prof., 1981—2001, chmn. dept. etudes anglaises, 1970—71, 1975—79, 1990—91, 1998—99; ret., 2001. Editor: Contexts 2: The Rape of the Lock, 1979. Warden St. Pascal-Baylon Catholic Ch., Montreal, 1981-84, 2003. Can. council fellow, 1972-73 Mem. MLA, Am. Soc. Eighteenth Century Studies (pres. English 1974-75), Can. Soc. Eighteenth Century Studies, Assn. Can. Coll. and Univ. Tchrs. English, Can. Comparative Lit. Assn. Home: 3782 Kent Ave Montreal PQ Canada H3S 1N3 Office: U Montreal Etudes Anglaises Case Postale 6128 Sta A Montreal PQ Canada H3C 3J7 Office Phone: 514-343-5615. E-mail: wbkinsley@sympatico.ca.

KINSLOW, MARGIE ANN, volunteer; b. Salt Lake City, Dec. 7, 1931; d. Diamond and Sarah (Chipman) Wendelboe; m. James Ferol Kinslow, Apr. 6, 1954 (dec. July 1982). Student, U. Utah, 1949—53. Jr. vol. chmn. various hosps., Okla., Mont., Colo., 1967—87; pres. Ch. Woman's Orgn., Bartlesville, Okla., 1968; fin. advisor, jr. v.p., vol. chmn. Swedish Med. Ctr., Englewood, 1971—92; pres. Delta Gamma Alumnae, Denver, 1975—76; jr. vol. chair Colo. Assn. Hosp. Aux., Denver, 1977—82, 2d v.p., 1982—84; transp. chair, master class chmn. Rocky Mountain Regional Auditions, Met. Opera, Denver, 1986—. Office vol. Rep. Office, Billings, Mont., 1969-70, Colo. Senator, Denver, 1974-76; vol. various polit. candidates, Denver, 1974-90; various offices Newcomers, Okla., Mont. and Colo., 1967-75; bd. dirs. Anchor Ctr. for Blind Children, 2000—, Denver Lyric Opera, 2002—. Recipient Stellar award, 1979, Cable award, 1991. Mem. PEO, Gen. Fedn. of Women's Clubs (bd. dirs. 1994—, corr. sec. Western region), Colo. Gen. Fedn. of Women's Clubs (pres. 1994-96, various offices 1986-94), Denver Lyric Opera Guild (bd. dirs. 2002—), Cherry Creek Woman's Club (pres. 1985, Hoby corp. bd. 1997—), Littleton Rep. Women's Club. Episcopalian. Avocations: bridge, travel, people, the arts.

KINSMAN, ROBERT PRESTON, biomedical plastics engineer; b. Cambridge, Mass., July 25, 1949; s. Fred Nelson and Myra Roxane (Preston) Kinsman. BS in Plastics Engring., U. Mass. Lowell, 1971; post grad in bus. adminstrn., Air Force Inst. Tech., 1972—74; MBA, Pepperdine U., 1982. Cert. biomed. engr., Calif.; lic. real estate salesperson, Calif. Product devel. engr., plastics divsn. Gen. Tire Corp., Lawrence, Mass., 1976—77; mfg. engr. Am. Edwards Labs. divsn. Am. Hosp. Supply Corp., Irvine, Calif., 1978—80, sr. engr. Am. Edwards Labs. divsn., 1981—82, mgr. mfg. engring. Edwards Labs., Inc. subs. Añasco, PR, 1983; project mgr. Baxter Edwards Critical Care divsn. Baxter Healthcare Corp., Irvine, 1984—87, mgr. engring. and prodn. Baxter Edwards Critical Care divsn., 1987—93; pres. Kinsman & Assocs., Irvine, Calif., 1993—2001, Billerica, Mass., 2001—; expert/auditor Med. Device Certification GmbH, Memmingen, Germany, 1995—; dir. engring. CardioVasc. Dynamics, Inc., Irvine, 1997—2000, HemoDynamics, Inc., Irvine, 1999—2000; dir. biomaterials engring. Anchor Med. Tech., Inc., Irvine, 2000—01; dir. ops. Triage Med., Irvine, 2001. Mgmt. adv. panel Modern Plastics mag., N.Y.C., 1979-80; elected Nat. Hon. Soc., 1967. Vol. worker VA, Bedford, Mass., 1967-71; instr. first aid ARC, N.D., Mass., Calif., 1971-82; pres., bd. dirs. Lakes Homeowners Assn., Irvine, 1985-91; chmn., bd. dirs., newsletter editor Paradise Park Owners Assn., Las Vegas, Nev., 1988-99; bd. dirs. Orange County (Calif.) divsn. Am. Heart Assn., 1991-2001, chmn. devel. com., 1993-95, v.p. bd. dirs., 1993-94, chmn.-elect bd. dirs., 1994-95, chmn. bd. dirs., 1995-96, adv. coun. rep., 1994-96, immediate past chmn. bd. dirs., 1996-97, nominating com., 1995-98, chmn. nominating com., 2000-01, strategic planning com., 1998-2001, Golden Gavel emeritus mem. bd. dirs., 2001; steering com. Heart and Sole Classic fundraiser, 1988-2001, event chmn., 1991-92, 2001, devel. com. Calif. affiliate, 1993-95; bd. dirs. Billerica Hist. Soc., Mass., 2001- , treas., 2001-02, pres., 2002-05; Historical Museum Organizing Committee, Billerica, 2002- mem. Town of Billerica 350th Anniversary Celebration Com., 2003-06, co-treas., 2003-06; chmn. Beginnings of Billerica, 350th Anniversary Signature Event, 2005; mem. Town Meeting, Billerica, 2006-, Bennett Publ. Libr. Assn., Billerica, 2007-. Capt. USAF, 1971—75, capt. USAFR, 1975—81. Recipient Cert. of Appreciation, VA, 1971, Cert. of Merit for Outstanding Contbn. and Svc. to Mission, USAF Strategic Air Command, 1972-74, Baxter/Allegiance Found. Community Svc. grantee, Deerfield, Ill., 1992, 93, Cert. Appreciation Am. Heart Assn., 1991-95, Outstanding Svc. award, 1996, Cmty. Hero Torchbearer, 1996, Olympic Games, United Way Am. and Atlanta Com. for Olympic Games, Cert. of Recognition, U.S. Dept. Def., 2002. Mem. Soc. Plastics Engrs. (sr., Mem. of Month So. Calif. sect. 1989), Soc. for Biomaterials, Soc. Mfg. Engrs. (sr.), Am. Mgmt. Assn., Am. Soc. Quality (sr.), Arnold Air Soc. (comptr. 1969-70, pledge tng. officer 1970-71), Plastics Acad., Demolay, Profl. Ski Instrs. Am., Mensa (life), Am. Legion, Elks, DAV (Life), Lions, Phi Gamma Psi. Avocations: skiing, scuba diving, marathon running, golf, music. Office: Kinsman & Assocs PO Box 505 Billerica MA 01821-0505 Office Phone: 978-764-7587. Business E-Mail: kinsmanassociates@comcast.net.

KINSOLVING, CHARLES MCILVAINE, JR., marketing executive; b. NYC, Jan. 27, 1927; s. Charles McIlvaine and Florence Natalie (Hogg) K.; m. Coral May Eaton, July 13, 1963 (dec. Jan. 1988); m. Jolie Brockman Hammer, Apr. 26, 1993 (dec. Aug. 1995); m. Jacqueline Wolf Vogelstein, Aug. 22, 1998. Student, U. Paris, 1948; AB, U. Pa., 1949; postgrad., Harvard Med. Sch., 1949-50, Columbia U., 1951-53. Stockholder rels. AT&T, NYC, 1950-51; rsch. assoc. Young & Rubicam, Inc., NYC, 1951-53; asst. mgr. media rsch. McCann-Erickson, Inc., NYC, 1953-58; mgr. plans devel. Nat. Broadcasting Co., NYC, 1958-60; v.p., mktg. new tech. Newspaper Advt. Bur., NYC, 1960-87, sr. v.p. mktg. group, 1987-92; ind. comm. investor NYC, 1992—. Media cons. U.K., Belgium, South Africa; speaker Internat. Fedn. of Editors and Jours. Contbr. articles to profl. jours. Dem. candidate for State Assembly, Manhattan, 1954, 98; 1st vice chmn. N.Y. County Dem. Exec. Com., N.Y.C., 1963-71; mem., chmn. Planning Bd. #6 Manhattan, N.Y.C., 1969-84. Served with U.S. Army, 1945-46. Mem. Union Club, Century Assn., Dutch Treat Club (bd. govs. 1994-99), City Club (v.p. 1987-89), Coffee House Club (bd. dirs. 1984—), St. Anthony Club Phila., Travelers Century Club, St. Paul's Sch. Alumni Assn. (exec. com. 1994-99, v.p. 1995-99), Phi Beta Kappa, Delta Psi Episcopalian. Avocations: travel, photography, stamp collecting/philately. Mailing: 1107 5th Ave New York NY 10128-0145 Home: 27 Horseshoe Dr N East Hampton NY 11937 Personal E-mail: cjkinsolving@nyc.rr.com.

KINSTLER, EVERETT RAYMOND, artist; b. NYC, Aug. 5, 1926; s. Joseph E. and Essie K.; m. Lea C. Nation, June 23, 1958 (div. 1984); children: Katherine G., Dana C.; m. Peggy Chartier, 1996. Student, Art Students League, NYC, 1943—45; D (hon.), Rollins Coll., 1983, Lyme Acad. Art, 2002. Started career as illustrator, NYC, 1943; began specializing in portraiture, 1955; instr. Art Students League, NYC, 1969-74. Portraits include over 50 U.S. cabinet officers, ofcl. White House portrait former Pres. Gerald R. Ford, former Pres. Ronald Reagan, former Pres. Richard Nixon, J. Edgar Hoover, Richard K. Mellon, Mrs. Irenee duPont, Jr., Kurt Waldheim, sec.-gen. UN, Casper Weinberger, sec. of def., William Casey, dir. CIA, Cyrus Vance, sec. of state, Astronaut Alan B. Shepard, Jr., William Bowen, pres. Princeton U., James Cagney, John D. Rockefeller III, Byron Nelson, Frank Cary, pres. IBM, Charles Scribner, Jr., John Wayne, John Kemeny, pres. Dartmouth Coll., William Simon, sec. Treasury, Elliot Richardson, ambassador to Gt. Britain, Tennessee Williams, John Connally, gov. of Tex., Charles Brown, CH., ATT, Russel Long, U.S. Senator, Morris Udall, mem. U.S. Congress, Katharine Hepburn, Gregory Peck, former Pres. Richard M. Nixon; Bartlett Gramatti, pres. Yale U., George P. Shultz, former U.S. Sec. of State, Paul Newman, Thomas Kean, former Gov. N.J., former Pres. George Bush, Arthur Ashe, Tony Bennett, Carol Burnett, Elizabeth Dole, Betty Ford, Lady Bird Johnson, William Webster, Ruth Simmons Pres. Smith Coll., former dir. CIA, Harry Blackmun, U.S. Supreme Ct. Justice, former U.S. Sec. of State Warren Christopher, Placido Domingo, President Bill Clinton, Gene Hackman, Ruth Bader Ginsburg, U.S. Supreme Ct. Justice, Donald Rumsfeld U.S. Sec. Def., U.S. Senator Daniel Patrick Moynihan, NY Gov. George Pataki, Peter O'Toole, Sen. Robert Dole, Lawrence Summers, pres. Harvard U., John D. Ong, U.S. amb. to Norway, Dave Brubeck, Donald Trump, Charles Osgood, pres. U. Pa. Judith Rodin, Rudolph Giuliani, former mayor N.Y.C., also numerous others; one-man shows include Mus. City of N.Y., 2006, Gotleib Archival Rsch. Ctr. Boston U., 2006-07; represented in permanent collections, Butler Inst. Am. Art, Nat. Portrait Gallery, Washington, Nat. Acad. Design, Mus. City N.Y., Met. Mus. Art, N.Y.C., The Pentagon, Am. Embassy, Paris, Carnegie Mus., N.Y. Stock Exchange, Bklyn. Mus., White House, Smithsonian Instn., Retrospective Exhbn. Boston U., Butler Inst. Am. Art, Fairfield, Conn., 1999; numerous colls., univs., bus. firms; author: Painting Portraits, 1971, Painting Faces, Figures, Landscapes, 1981, My Brush with History, 2005; (documentary) An Artists Journey, PBS, 2001, PBS documentary, 2004—. Recipient Artists' Fellowship Medal, 1986, Nat. Arts Club medal, 1993, Allied Artists medal, 1997, Copley medal Nat. Portrait Gallery, 1999, Lifetime Achievement medal Salmagundi Club, 2002, medal honoree Nat. Acad. Design, 2002. Mem. Allied Artists Am. (dir. 1958-60), Artists Fellowships, Inc. (pres. 1967-70), Am. Watercolor Soc., Pastel Soc. Am., Audubon Artists, NAD, Actor's Fund Am. (life), Soc. Illustrators (hon.), Copley Soc. Boston (life), Lambs Club (N.Y.C.) (life),), Century Assn. Club (N.Y.C.), Lotos Club (N.Y.C.) (life), Nat. Arts Club (N.Y.C.), Dutch Treat Club (N.Y.C.), Players Club (life), Yale Club N.Y. (life). Office: care Nat Arts Club 15 Gramercy Park S New York NY 10003-1705

KINSTLINGER, JACK, engineering executive, consultant; arrived in US, 1939, naturalized, 1944; s. Joseph and Rose (Lichtblau) K.; m. Marilyn Wiseman, July 16, 1967; children: Michael, Jeremy. BSCE, Rensselaer Polytechnic Inst., 1952; MSCE, MIT, 1954. Registered profl. engr., NY, Pa., Wash., NH, Colo., Del., Md., Mass., Fla., NJ. Assoc. Tippetts, Abbett, McCarthy, Stratton, NYC, 1957-68; dep. sec. Pa. Dept. Transp., Harrisburg, 1968-75; state hwy. dir. State of Colo., Denver, 1975-82; v.p. Daniel-Mann-Johnson-Mendenhall, Denver, 1982-84; CEO KCI Techs., Inc., Balt., 1984-99, chmn. bd. dirs., chmn. emeritus, 2000—. Appt. chmn. Md. Coun. Mgmt. and Productivity, 1998—2002. Bd. dir. Am. Jewish Com., Balt.; mem. adv. bd. Rensselaer Poly. Inst., Troy, NY, Morgan State U., Balt. With civil engrs. corps USN, 1984—87. Named Transp. Adv. of Yr., Md. for Efficient and Safe Hwys., 2001; recipient Disting. State Svc. award, Fed. Exec. Bd., Denver, 1980, Leo Reithmeyer Outstanding Pub. Adminstrn. award, U. Colo., 1981, Cmty. Transp. award, Inst. Transp. Engrs., 1994, Fellows award, Rensselaer Polytechnic Inst. Alumni Assn., 1998, Chmns. award, High Speed Ground Transp. Assn., 2000, Sparky award. Fellow ASCE (Civil Engr. of Yr. award Md. sect. 1994), Am. Cons. Engrs. Coun. (Cmty. Svc. award 1998); mem. Am. Rds. and Transp. Builders Assn. (vice chair, bd. dir., Guy Kelcey award 1997), Civil Engring. Soc. Mem. (hon.), Sci. Rsch. Soc. (hon.), US Maglev Coalition (bd. dir.), Md. Assn. Non-Profit Orgns. (treas., bd. dir.), Chi Epsilon, Sigma Xi. Democrat. Jewish. Office: KCI Techs Inc 10 N Park Dr Hunt Valley MD 21030-1841 Home Phone: 410-484-5490; Office Phone: 410-316-7803. Business E-Mail: jkinstlinger@kci.com.

KINTER, KERRI ANNE, elementary school educator; b. Woodbury, NJ, Feb. 14, 1980; d. Thomas Lee and JoAnne Kinter. AA with honors, Burlington County Coll., Pemberton, NJ, 2002; BA with honors, Fairleigh Dickson U., Teaneck, NJ, 2005, cert. cum laude, 2005; MA in Art of Tchg., Fairleigh Dickinson U., Teaneck, NJ, 2006. Asst. tchr. preschool Goddard Sch., Burlington, NJ, 1998—2002, lead tchr. prekindergarten, 2002; ednl. asst. prekindergarten Burlington City Sch. Dist., NJ, 2002—05; lead tchr. preschool Just Children, Mount Laurel, NJ, 2005—06; substitute tchr. Pennsauken Sch. Dist., NJ, 2006—, Gibbsboro Sch. Dist., NJ, 2006—. Companion Lancaster Mennonite Home, Pa., 1999—2000; leader Awana Grace Fellowship Ch., Ephrata, Pa., 1998—99; tchr. Sunday sch. United Meth. Ch., Pennsauken, NJ, 2004—05, dir. music, 2004—, dir. youth group, 2006—. Mem.: Hist. Mil. Impressions. Avocations: piano, reading, crafts, scrapbooks, singing. Home Phone: 856-662-1838.

KINTNER, PHILIP L., history professor; b. Canton, Ohio, Jan. 23, 1926; s. William Wagner and Effie (Erwin) K.; m. Anne Genung, Dec. 27, 1951 (dec. June 2003); children: Karen, Judith, Jennifer. BA, Wooster Coll., 1950; MA, Yale U., 1952, PhD, 1958. Instr. Trinity Coll., Hartford, Conn., 1954-56, Reed Coll., Portland, Oreg., 1957-58, Trinity Coll., 1958-59, asst. prof., 1959-64; vis. assoc. prof. U. Iowa, Iowa City, 1964-65; assoc. prof. Grinnell (Iowa) Coll., 1964-69; coll. entrance bd. exam commissioner European History, Princeton, NJ, 1968-70; chief reader advanced placement European history, 1969-72; ACM prof. Florence (Italy) Program, 1989-90; prof. Grinnell Coll., 1970-96, Rosenthal prof. humanities, 1976-96; prof. emeritus, 1996—. With U.S. Army, 1944-46. Recipient numerous travel/study grants for rsch. and publ. in Germany. Mem. Sixteenth Century Studies Conf. Avocations: woodworking, cooking, mineral hunting. Home: 716 Broad St Grinnell IA 50112-2226 Office: Grinnell Coll PO Box 805 Grinnell IA 50112-0805 E-mail: kintner@grinnell.edu.

KINTSCH, WALTER, retired psychology professor; b. Temesvar, Romania, May 30, 1932; arrived in US, 1955; s. Christof and Irene (Hollerbach) Kintsch; m. Eileen Hoover, June 27, 1959; children: Anja, Julia. PhD, U. Kans., 1960. Prof. U. Colo., Boulder, 1968—2004; ret., 2004. Editor: Pyschol Rev, 1989—94; author: books. Office: U Colo Dept Psychology Institute Cognitive Scis Boulder CO 80309-0344 Office Phone: 303-492-8663. Business E-Mail: walter.kintsch@colorado.edu.

KINTZELE, JOHN ALFRED, lawyer; b. Denver, Aug. 16, 1936; s. Louis Richard and Adele H. Kintzele; children: John A., Marcia A., Elizabeth A.; m. Suzanne Hinsberger; stepchildren: William Karp III, Christopher Karp. BS in Bus., U. Colo., 1958, LLB, 1961. Bar: Colo. bar 1961. Assoc. James B. Radetsky, Denver, 1962-63; pvt. practice law Denver, 1963—; 2. Corp. officer, dir. Kintzele, Inc.; rep. 10th cir. U.S. Ct. of Claims Bar. Chmn. Colo. Lawyer Referral Service, 1978-83, Election commr., Denver, 1975-79, 83-86 Mem. AAJ, ABA, Colo. Bar Assn., Denver Bar Assn., Am. Judicature Soc., Roscoe Pound Found. Democrat. Roman Catholic. Home: 10604 E Powers Dr Englewood CO 80111-3957 Office: 1317 Delaware St Denver CO 80204-2704 Office Phone: 303-892-6494. Personal E-mail: jkintlaw@aol.com. Business E-Mail: jkintlaw@comcast.net.

KINZER, ALLEN SHAWN, lawyer; b. Euclid, Ohio, Feb. 22, 1963; s. Allen Odell and Wilma Kinzer; m. Brenda Burchfield, Dec. 21, 1991; children: Adah, Leah, Anna. BA in Econs. summa cum laude, Vanderbilt U., 1985; JD with honors, U. NC, 1988. Bar: Ohio 1988, U.S. Dist. Ct. (so. dist.) Ohio 1988, U.S. Ct. Appeals (6th and 10th cirs.) 1991. Assoc. Jones, Day, Reavis & Pogue, Columbus, Ohio, 1988-90; ptnr. Vorys, Sater, Seymour & Pease, LLP, Columbus, 1990—. Contbg. author: ABA's Labor and Employment Section Annual Equal Pay Act Reprt, 1995-2003, The Fair Labor Standards Act, 1999; co-author articles in profl. mags., 2001, 03; contbg. editor: The Fair Labor Standards Act, 2006; staff editor N.C. Law Rev, BNA Books; editl. adv. bd. Employer's Guide to the Fair Labor Standards Act, FLSA Employee Exemption Handbook; contbr. articles profl. jours. Elder, session mem., chair pers. com. capital campaign, Worthington Presbyn. Ch., 2003-; form father, Columbus Sch. girls, 2004-05. Mem. ABA (labor law sect., fair labor standards com. 1991—, chair Equal Pay Act subcom. 1995-03, Sarbanes Oxley subcom., 2003-), Ohio State Bar Assn. (labor law sect.), Columbus Bar Assn. (labor com., vol. lawyers for Justice Program, 1992—), AHA (Heartwalk company leader 1994, 95), Phi Beta Kappa. Republican. Avocations: reading, golf, jogging. Office: Vorys Sater Seymour & Pease 52 E Gay St Columbus OH 43215-3161 Office Phone: 614-464-6400. Business E-Mail: askinzer@vssp.com.

KINZER, DONALD MARSHALL, banker; b. Hillsville, Va., Aug. 28, 1943; s. Ellis Greene and Ida Belle (Marshall) K; m. Bonnie Theresa Hare, Apr. 7, 1969. Student, Coll. William and Mary, 1966-68; BBA, Roanoke Coll., 1974; MA, Hollins Coll., 1980. Computer programmer Coll. William and Mary, Williamsburg, Va., 1965-66, Celanese Corp., Narrows, Va., 1966-67; systems analyst Eaton Corp., Salem, Va., 1967-72, Dominion Bank, Roanoke, Va., 1972-73, investment officer, 1973-80, sr. v.p. investments, 1980-88, exec. v.p., chief fin. officer, 1988—91, responsible for investment mgmt., asset-liability and profitability analysis, 1991—94; second v.p. investments Shenandoah Life Ins. Co., Roanoke, Va. Tchr. Am. Bankers Assn., Washington, 1981—, Va. Bankers Assn., Richmond, 1982—, Hollins Coll., 1985—, Roanoke (Va.) Coll., Salem, 1986—. Contbr. articles on mgmt. to profl. jours. Sgt. USAF, 1962-66. Lutheran. Office: Shenandoah Life Ins Co 2301 Brambleton Ave SW Roanoke VA 24015

KINZIE, BRENDA ASBURRY, counselor; b. Roanoke, Va., Oct. 25, 1945; d. Omar Lee and Nadine Myrl (Sublett) Asburry; m. Samuel Joseph Kinzie, Mar. 30, 1973. BA, Hollins U., 1990; MS, Radford U., 1991. Case mgr./counselor Total Action Against Poverty, Roanoke, 1993—95; interagy. case coord. City of Roanoke, 1995—98. Vol. Am. Cancer Soc. Mem.: ACA, Hunting Hills Garden Club. Democrat. Divine Sci. Ch. Avocations: music, reading, walking, flower gardening. Home: 1051 Starmount Ave Roanoke VA 24019-3135

KINZIE, JACK L., lawyer; b. Ponca City, Okla., Sept. 3, 1948; BS, Okla. State Univ., 1971; JD, Univ. Okla., 1975. Bar: Okla. 1976, Tex. 1989, US Dist. Ct. (no., so., ea., we. dist. Tex., no., we. dist. Okla.), US Ct. Appeals 3d, 5th, 10th cir. Ptnr., mem. exec. com., chmn. bankruptcy & insolvency practice & ptnr. in charge Dallas office Baker Botts LLP, Dallas. Editor (assoc.): Okla. Law Rev. Dir. Greater Dallas C. of C., Dallas Ctr. for Contemporary Art; mem. Dallas Citizens Council. Named a Texas Super Lawyer, Texas Monthly mag. & Law & Politics mag., 2003—04. Mem.: Order of the Coif. Office: Baker Botts LLP 2001 Ross Ave Dallas TX 75201-2980 Office Fax: 214-953-6727, 214-661-4727. Business E-Mail: jack.kinzie@bakerbotts.com.

KINZIE, JEANNIE JONES, radiation oncologist, nuclear medicine physician; b. Great Falls, Mont., Mar. 14, 1940; d. James Wayne and Lillian Alice (Young) Jones; m. Joseph Lee Kinzie, Mar. 26, 1965 (div. Sept. 1982); 1 child, Daniel Joseph; m. Johnson Wachira, Oct. 7, 1991. Student, Oreg. State U., 1960; BS, Mont. State U., 1961; MD, Washington U., 1965; MBA, U. Phoenix, 1997. Diplomate Am. Bd. Radiology; diplomate Am. Bd. Nuclear Medicine; cert. advanced master gardener Colo. State U., 1997. Intern. in surgery U. N.C., Chapel Hill, 1965-66; resident in therapeutic radiology Washington U., St. Louis, 1968-71, instr. in radiology, 1971-73; asst. prof. in radiology Med. Coll. of Wis., Milw., 1973-75, U. Chgo., 1975-78, assoc. prof. in radiology, 1978-80; assoc. prof. of radiation oncology Wayne State U., Detroit, 1980-85; prof. radiology U. Colo., Denver, 1985-95; dir. radiation oncology U. Hosp., Denver, 1985-91; fellow in nuclear medicine U. Colo., 1996-98, asst. clin. prof. nuclear medicine, 1998—2005; staff radiologist Denver Vets. Hosp., Denver, 2003—. Cons. Denver Vets. Hosp., 1985-98, Denver Gen. Hosp., 1985-95, Rose Med. Ctr., 1986-95, FDA Ctr. for Devices and Radiologic Health, 1986-2003; mem. sci. adv. bd. Cancer League Colo., 1985-88; examiner Am. Bd. Radiology, 1985-88; adv. physician Colo. Med. Found., 1988-98; chmn. faculty promotion com. U. Colo. Health Scis. Ctr., 1988-89. Assoc. editor Internat. Jour. Radiation Oncology Biology and Physics, 1985-95; contbr. articles to profl. jours.; chpts. to books. Mem. Faith Bible Chapel Ch. NIH grantee, 1973-75. Fellow: Am. Coll. Radiology; mem.: AMA, Am. Cancer Soc. (bd. dirs. Denver unit 1986—87), Am. Soc. Therapeutic Radiologists, Rocky Mountain Oncology Soc. (bd. dirs. 1989—93, pres. 1991—93), Colo. Radiol. Soc., Denver Med. Soc., Colo. Med. Soc. (del./alt. del. ho. of dels. 1989—2006), Am. Coll. Nuclear Physicians. Republican. Avocations: gardening, rug latching, mountain climbing. Personal E-mail: jeannie.kinzie@att.net.

KINZLER, THOMAS BENJAMIN, lawyer; b. NYC, June 19, 1950; s. David and Rhoda Lenore (Wolgel) K.; m. Carol Ada Loebel, Aug. 24, 1975; children: Katherine Diane, David James. BA, Columbia Coll., 1971; JD, Boston U., 1975. Bar: N.Y. 1976, U.S. Dist. Ct. (no., so., ea. and we. dists.) N.Y. 1976, U.S. Ct. Appeals (2d cir.) 1976. Assoc. Kreindler, Relkin & Goldberg, NYC, 1975-77, Arthur, Dry & Kalish, NYC, 1977-80, Kelley Drye & Warren LLP, NYC, 1980-85; ptnr. Kelley Drye & Warren, NYC, 1985—. Mem. ABA, Assn. of the Bar City of N.Y.C. (products liability com. 1983-86, com. on state legis. 1978-80). Office: Kelley Drye & Warren 101 Park Ave Fl 30 New York NY 10178-0062

KIOVSKY, DOUGLAS GEORGE, land use planner; b. Montreal, Que., Can., Feb. 25, 1962; s. George and Alice Kiovsky. A in Recreational Land Mgmt., SUNY, Cobleskill, 1983; BS in Forestry Mgmt., Rutgers U., New Brunswick, 1986. Landscaper, Princeton, NJ, 1983—87; pk. ranger Monmouth County Pk. Sys., Lincroft, NJ, 1987—89, Hunterdon County Pks. Dept., Flemington, NJ, 1989—2001, asst. county pk. planner, 2001—. Hist. program coord. Hunterdon County Pks. Dept., 2002—; crew mem. NJ State Wildlands Fire Fighters, 2003—. Contbr. NJ Parks, Forests and Natural Areas, 2004, New Jersey Walk Book, 2004, Skiing in New Jersey, 2005. Exhibits co-chmn. Plainsboro Hist. Soc., NJ, 1997—2002; co-planner Franklin Twp. Rd. to Battle of Monmouth Planning Com., Kingston, 2003; garden designer City of Bordentown, 2003; co-planner Bass River State Forest Centennial Com., Tuckerton, NJ, 2004—05; treas. Kingston Hist. Soc., NJ, 2004—; vol. Rockingham State Hist. Site, 2006—; co-planner Princeton Treaty of Paris Region Planning Com., Kingston, 2007—. Recipient Vol. Recognition award, NJ Dept. Environ. Protection-State Pks. Svc., Bass River State Forest, Voorhees State Pk., Delaware and Raritan Canal State Pk., 2005—. Mem.: Nat. Trust Hist. Preservation. Avocations: photography, landscaping, writing, historical research. Home: 14 Fairfield Rd Princeton NJ 08540 Office: Hunterdon County Dept Pks and Recreation 1020 State Hwy 31 Flemington NJ 08822 Personal E-mail: georgesilverfox@aol.com.

KIPER, MEL, JR., sports commentator; b. July 25, 1960; married; 1 child. Student, Essex C.C., Balt. Expert analyst NFL draft ESPN, 1984—, coll. football, NFL analyst. Contbr. on NFL draft topics SportsCenter ESPN; pres. Mel Kiper Ent., Inc., Jarrettsville, 1981—. Office: PO Box 9711 Baldwin MD 21013-0711*

KIPKE, MICHELE DIANE, education and social services administrator, former hospital director; b. Glendale, Calif., Mar. 4, 1962; d. Arthur Harold and Anne Stuart (Mills) K. BA, NYU, 1984; PhD, Yeshiva U., 1989. Rsch. asst. Montefiore Med. Ctr., Bronx, N.Y., 1984-86; psychology intern Albert Einstein Coll. Medicine, Bronx, 1986-87; dir. AIDS prevention Montefiore Med. Ctr., Bronx, 1987-89; coord. substance abuse program Childrens Hosp. L.A., Calif., 1990-92, assoc. dir. rsch. and evaluation Calif., 1992-98; dir. bd. rsch. children, youth & families Nat. Res. Council, Washington, 1998—. Cons. HHS, SAMSA, HRSA, Washington, 1990—; coun. rep. elect Homeless Caucus, APHA, 1992-93; peer reviewer NIH, Washington, 1993—; cons. WHO/Mentor Found., Geneva, 1994—; spl. advisor Primary Health Care Initiative, Office of Treatment Improvement, Alcohol, Drug Abuse and Mental Health Adminstrn.; presenter in field. Reviewer AIDS Edn. and Prevention: An Interdisciplinary Jour., Jour. Adolescent Health Care; contbr. articles to profl. jours. Grantee Ctrs. for Disease Control (AIDS Evaluation of Street Outreach Project), 1992-95, Universitywide AIDS Rsch. Program (HIV Prevention Intervention Study with Seropositive Youth, 1993-95, Nat. Inst. on Drug Abuse (Investigation of Drug Use and HIV-Risk Sexual Behaviors Among Homeless Youth, 1993—, Substance Abuse and Mental Health Svc. Adminstrn./Ctr. for Substance Abuse Treatment, 1993—, Health Resources and Svcs. Adminstrn./Bur. Health Cre and Delivery and Assistance, 1993—, others. Mem. APA, Soc. Adolescent Medicine (ad hoc com. on health needs of homeless youth).

KIPLER, JAMES MICHAEL, musician, educator; b. Lackawanna, NY, Mar. 24, 1944; s. Michael James Kipler and Finkley; m. Deborah Anne Rutkowski, Apr. 6, 2007; m. Audrey Susan Miller, June 8, 1963 (div. Mar. 8, 1979); children: , David Wayne. CLU in fin. and ins. Gen. Motors Acceptance Corp., 1999. Commd. lt. US Army, 1984, advanced through grades to sgt. first class, 1989, recruiter Buffalo, 1984—93, resigned, 1993; musician Buffalo Musician's Assn., 1980—84; fin. mgr. Braun Cadillac-Buick, Buffalo, 1993—98; lease mgr. Culligan Pontiac-Volvo, Buffalo, 1998—2002; ind. musician Buffalo, 1998—. Guitarist Buffalo Philharm. Orch., 1990—92. Musician: (TV series) Dick Clark's Am. Bandstand, 1962. Decorated Meritorious Svc. medal US Army; recipient Recruiter ring, 1986. Mem.: Am. Fedn. Musicians (mem. exec. bd. local chpt. 1998—2002, v.p. local chpt. 1994—98), Amvets, Masons (most wise master 2004—05, grand sword bearer 2002—04). Reform. Avocations: travel, music, golf. Home and Office: 61 Elmleaf Dr Cheektowaga NY 14227 Office Phone: 716-668-3510. Personal E-mail: jkipler@adelphia.net, james.kipler@verizon.net.

KIPLINGER, KNIGHT AUSTIN, journalist, publishing executive; b. Washington, Feb. 24, 1948; s. Austin Huntington and Mary Louise (Cobb) K. BA, Cornell U., 1969; postgrad., Princeton U., 1969-70. Reporter Montgomery County Sentinel, Rockville, Md., 1970; Washington corr. Griffin-Larrabee News Bur., Washington, 1970-73, bur. mgr., 1976-78; Washington bur. chief, chief news svc. Ottaway Newspapers div. Dow Jones & Co., Washington, 1978-83; with Kiplinger Washington Editors, Washington, 1983—, v.p. for publs., 1983-89, exec. v.p., 1989-92, pres., 1992—; assoc. editor The Kiplinger Letter, Washington, 1983-99, editor-in-chief, 1999—; editor in chief Kiplinger's Personal Fin. Mag., Washington, 1985—. Author: World Boom Ahead, 1998; co-author: Washington Now, 1975, The New American Boom, 1986, America in the Global '90s, 1989. Bd. dir. The Washington Chorus, 1975—85, chmn., 1991—99; mem. adv. bd. Levine Sch. Music, Washington, 1975, Mount Vernon Ladies' Assn., 1986—92; bd. trustees White Ho. Hist. Assn., 2003—, Landon Sch., 1995—2000, chmn., 2003—. Mem. Soc. Profl. Journalists, Soc. Am. Bus. Editors and Writers, Nat. Press Club. Office: Kiplinger Washington Editors 1729 H St NW Washington DC 20006-3925

KIPNIS, DAVID MORRIS, physician, educator; b. Balt., May 23, 1927; s. Rubin and Anna (Mizen) Kipnis; m. Paula Jane Levin, Aug. 16, 1953; children: Lynne, Laura, Robert. AB, Johns Hopkins U., 1945, MA, 1949; MD, U. Md., 1951. Intern Johns Hopkins Hosp., 1951—52; resident Duke Hosp., Durham, NC, 1952—54, U. Md. Hosp., 1954—55; asst. prof. medicine Washington U. Sch. Medicine, St. Louis, 1958—63, assoc. prof., 1963—65, prof., 1965—, Busch prof., chmn. dept. medicine, 1972—92; disting. prof. medicine Washington U. Sch. of Medicine, St. Louis, 1992—; asst. physician Barnes Hosp., assoc. physician, 1963—72, physician-in-chief, 1972—93, disting. univ. prof., 1993—. Chmn. endocrine study sect. NIH, 1963—64, diabetes tng. program com., 1970—; chmn. Nat. Diabetes Adv. Bd. Editor: Diabetes, 1973; mem. editl. bd.: Am. Jour. Medicine, 1973, Am. Jour. Med. Scis.; contbr. articles to profl. jours. With US Army, 1945—46. Named Banting lectr., Brit. Diabetes Assn., 1972; scholar Markle scholar in med. scis., 1957—62. Mem.: NAS (coun. mem. 1997—2000), Nat. Acad. Scis., Inst. Medicine, Am. Acad. Arts and Scis., Am. Soc. Biol. Chemists, Endocrine Soc. (Oppenheimer award 1965), Am. Diabetes Assn. (Lilly award 1965, Banting medal 1977, Best medal 1981), Am. Fedn. Clin. Rsch., Assn. Am. Physicians (Kober medal 1994), Am. Soc. Clin. Investigation. Home: 7200 Wydown Blvd Saint Louis MO 63105-3023 Office: Barnes Hosp Dept Medicine PO Box 8212 660 S Euclid Ave Saint Louis MO 63110-1010

KIPNISS, ROBERT, artist; b. NYC, Feb. 1, 1931; s. Sam and Stella Anita K.; m. Jean Elizabeth Prutton, July 6, 1954 (div. 1982); children: Max, Ivan, Ruby, Benjamin; m. Laurie Lisle, 1994. Student, Wittenberg Coll., 1948-50; PhD (hon.), Wittenberg U., 1980; BA, U. Iowa, Iowa City, 1952, MFA, 1954; PhD (hon.), Ill. Coll., 1989. One man exhbns. include Museo de Arte Moderno, Cali, Columbia, 1977, Kalamazoo Art Inst., Canton Art Inst., Enatsu Galerie, Tokyo, Gallery New World, Dusseldorf, Germany, Redfern Gallery, London, Venable Neslage, Washington, Hexton Gallery, NYC, Tyler Mus., Tex., 1999, Butler Art Inst., Ohio, 1999, Bassenge Gallery, Berlin, 1999, Beadleston Gallery, NYC, 2001, 03, Weinstein Gallery, 1999, 2000, 01, 02, 04, New Orleans Mus. Art, 2006, Orlando Mus. Art, 2006, 07, Hartnett Mus., Richmond, Va., 2006, McNay Mus., San Antonio, 2007; represented in permanent collections Chgo. Art Inst., Whitney Mus. Am. Art, NYC, Nat. Collection Fine Arts, Victoria and Albert Mus., London, Libr. of Congress, LA County Mus., Detroit Inst. Art, Cleve. Mus., NY Pub. Libr., Butler Art Inst., De Young Mus., Fogg Mus., Cambridge, Mass., Boston Mus. Fine Arts, Indpls. Mus. Art, Portland Mus. Art, Yale Mus., New Haven, Conn., Brit. Mus., London, The Fitz William Mus., Cambridge, UK, New Orleans Mus. Art, Met. Mus. Art., Biblioteque Nat. France, Paris, Carnegie Mus., Pitts., Fine Arts Mus. San Francisco, Everson Mus., Syracuse, NY, Nelson-Atkins Mus., Kansas City, Mo., Pinakothech der Moderne, Munich. Served with U.S. Army, 1956-58. Recipient Ralph Fabri prize in lithography Nat. Acad. Design, 1976, James R. Marsh Meml. award in lithography Audubon Artists, 1978, Charles M. Lea prize Print Club Phila., 1978, prize for lithography Soc. Am. Graphic Artists, 1979, Medal of Honor in Graphics Audubon Artists, 1983, Childe Hassam purchase award Am. Acad. Arts and Letters, 1988, The Cannon prize Nat. Acad. Design, 1999, Graphics award Boston Printmakers, 1999, Daniel Serra-Badue Meml. award Audobon Artists, 1998, Medal of Honor, Audobon Artists, 1999, 2000, Purchase prize Delta Nat., 2001, Ark. State U., Prints U.S.A., 2001, Springield Mus. of Art, Mo., Leo Meissner award Nat. Acad., 2003. Mem. Nat. Acad. Design, The Century Assn., Soc. Am. Graphics Artists, Royal Soc. Painter Printmakers (London), The Boston Printmakers. Personal E-mail: rkipniss@msn.com.

KIPNISS MACDONALD, BETTY ANN, artist, educator; b. Bklyn., 1936; d. Samuel Simon and Stella Anita (Blackton) Kipniss; m. Gordon James MacDonald (div.); children: Gordon, Maureen, Michael, Bruce. BA, Adelphi U., 1958; MA, Columbia U., NYC, 1960. Instr. Montshire Mus., Hanover, NH, 1979—84, Lebanon Coll., NH, 1984, Smithsonian Instn., Washington, 1985—95. Instr. Corcoran Mus. Art, 1996-98; pres., bd. dirs. Washington Printmakers Gallery; bd. dirs. Washington Print Club Exhbns. include Nat. Mus. Women in Arts, Washington, 1994-95, Mesquite Fine Arts Gallery, Nev., 2006; permanent collections include Cmty. for Creative Nonviolence, Washington, Mus. Modern Art, Buenos Aires, Am. Cultural Ctr., New Delhi, India, Pa. State U., New Orleans Mus. Art, Montgomery Mus. Fine Arts, Ala., Miss. Mus. Art, NY Pub. Libr., Jane Voorhees Zimmerli Art Mus., Rutgers U., NJ, House of Humour and Satire, Gabrove, Bulgaria; featured in William and Mary Rev., 1992-96, Quarterly mag., 2006. Nominee Beaux & Eros II exhibit, Peninsula Mus. Art, Belmont, Calif., 2007 recipient 1st prize printmakers Washington Women's Art Ctr., 1986, Past Pres.'s award Mus. Fine Arts, Springfield, Mass., 1982, de Cordova Mus., Soc. Am. Graphic Artists N.Y., Merit award Currier Gallery Art, 1987, Purchase prize Print Club Albany, N.Y., 1998, Purchase award Permanent Collection Ark. State U., 2001, Mus. Graphics award Washington County Mus. Fine Arts, Md., 2003, First prize Miniature Painters, Sculptors and Gravers Soc., 2005; grantee Giorgio Cini Found., 1962, NEA, 1981 Mem. L.A. Printmaking Soc., Soc. Am. Graphic Artist, Boston Printmakers

KIPPER, BARBARA LEVY, wholesale distribution executive; b. Chgo., July 16, 1942; d. Charles and Ruth (Doctoroff) Levy; m. David A. Kipper, Sept. 9, 1974; children: Talia Rose, Tamar Judith. BA, U. Mich., 1964. Reporter Chgo. Sun-Times, 1964-67; photo editor Cosmopolitan Mag., NYC, 1969-71; vice chmn. Chas Levy Co., Chgo., 1984-86, chmn., 1986—. Trustee Spertus Inst. Jewish Studies, Chgo.(Ill.) Hist. Soc., Golden Apple Ind., Joffrey Ballet of Chgo. Recipient Deborah award Com. Women's Equality, Am. Jewish Congress, 1992, Shap Shapiro Human Rels. award The Anti-Defamation League of B'nai B'rith, Personal PAC's Leadership award, 1996, Disting. Cmty. Leadership award, ADL, Jewish Culture, 2004, Golden Sceptre award Nat. Found. Jewish Culture; named Nat. Soc. Fund Raising Execs. Disting. Philanthropist, 1995. Mem.: Chgo. Network, Com. of 200, Internat. Women's Forum, Econ. Club of Chgo., Chgo. Network, The Standard Club. Jewish. Office Phone: 708-356-3601. Business E-Mail: bkipper@chaslevy.com.

KIPRUSOFF, MIIKA, professional hockey player; b. Turku, Finland, Oct. 26, 1976; Goalie Ky. Thoroughblades (AHL), 1991—2001, San Jose Sharks, 2001—03, Clagary Flames, 2003—. Named to First All-Star Team, NHL, 2006; recipient William M. Jennings Trophy, 2006, Vezina Trophy, 2006. Office: Calgary Flames PO Box 1540 Stn M Calgary AB Canada

KIRAKOSYAN, ARMAN, physicist, researcher; b. Yerevan, Armenia, Mar. 8, 1969; s. Sasha S. Kirakosyan and Ida D. Hacobian; m. Satenik S. Vardanyan, Apr. 4, 2006; 1 child, Michael. PhD, Tashkent Phys. Tech. Inst., 2000; degree in physics and math., Nat. U. Uzbekistan, 2000. Postdoctoral rsch. assoc. Tex. A&M U., College Station, 2001—03; rsch. assoc. Jackson State U., Miss., 2004—. Mem.: Am. Phys. Soc. (assoc.). Home Phone: 601-979-1391; Office Phone: 601-979-1391. E-mail: arman.kirakosyan@jsums.edu.

KIRAWANICH, PHUMIN, electrical engineer; arrived in U.S., 1996; s. Wiwit and Arunee Kirawanich. BS, Prince of Songkhla U., 1995; PhD, U. Mo., 2002. Asst. rschr. Nat. Electronics and Computer Tech. Ctr., Ministry of Sci. and Tech., Bangkok, 1995—96; rsch. asst. Power Electronics Rsch. Ctr., Columbia, Mo., 1997—2002; fellow High Power Electromagnetic Radiation Lab., U. Mo., Columbia, 2002—. Contbr. articles to profl. jours., chapters to books. Grantee, Anechoic Electromagnetic Test Chamber, 2005. Mem.: IEEE (reviewer). Achievements include discovery of a process for the generation and use of transfer functions for electromagnetic topological simulations; charge collection improvement in metal-semiconductor-metal detectors by adding gratings in the active region. Home: 319 Nikki Way Columbia MO 65203 Office: Univ Mo 343 Engring Bldg West Columbia MO 65203 Office Phone: 573-884-4389. Office Fax: 573-884-0397. E-mail: kirawanichp@missouri.edu.

KIRAZ, BAHRI, plastics and mechanical engineer, consultant; b. Adana, Karatas, Turkey, Jan. 3, 1950; s. Rabia Kirnik and Kemal Kiraz; m. Gülden Kaya, Nov. 11, 1988; children: Talha, Yasin, Furkan, Kadir, Emine Nisanur. Degree in mech. engring., Cukurova U., Adana, 1975; degree in plastics engring., Fachhochschule Darmstadt, Germany, 1986. Process engring. WOCO, Steinau an der Strasse, Hessen, Germany, 1986—88, dir. assembling tech. dept., 1988—90; tchr. Tech. Sch. for Plastics Engring., Weissenburg, Germany; dir. tech. innovation and cons. Alfmeier Corp., Greenville, SC, 2004—. Cons. WOCO, Bad Soden-Salmünster, Hessen, 1990—93, dir. of process engring. dept., 1993—97; devel. engr. Alfmeier Präzision, Treuchtlingen, Germany, 1997—98, cons., 1998—99; dir. tech. innovation and cons. Alfmeier Präzion AG, Treuchtlingen, Mexico, 1999—. Composer: (song) Yok yok deme; prodr.: (devel.) template-ruler for kids; contbr. articles to profl. jours. Lt. Aircraft, 1975—77, Ankara. Mem.: VDI German Engring. Club. Muslim. Achievements include development of Control unite for Sitting comfort; research in Assistance diploma study cross linked polyethylen for joining technology; invention of Development Barb For Joining Technology; Assistance diploma study; Design of Experiment solve (finding the best set up for different processes); TolPro (tolerance program for thermoplastic parts); it is availible on the market; zero-defect Floats production made of NBR foam with my own DOE program; development of Testing method for Floats, hoses, resistor cards for tanks; Design standards for tank valves made of Polyethylen; Geometry for rotation welding (Tube-Fitting); research in Assistance Of Diploma Study For Rotation Welding Process; Assistance of diploma study about Orientation of extruded hoses; design of Design Of Barb For Rotation Welding; development of Finding The Best Process For Rotation Welding; research in Assistance diploma study process technology for rotation welding process; Assistance diploma study Orientation status in tubes for rotation weldig. Avocations: swimming, movie, music, playing guitar. Office Phone: 49914270342. Business E-Mail: bahri.kiraz@alfmeier.com.

KIRBY, ALLAN PRICE, JR., investment company executive; b. Wilkes-Barre, Pa., June 18, 1931; s. Allan Price and Marian (Sutherland) K.; children: Jessie Ann, Allan Price III, Slater Baran, Coray Sutherland, Milan Stanton. BA, Lafayette Coll., 1953. Pres. Liberty Sq., Inc., Mendham, NJ, 1960—; dir., chmn. exec. com. Alleghany Corp., 1987—. Chmn. bd. dirs. A.P. Kirby Jr. Found. Inc., 1989—. Lt. (j.g.) USNR, 1953-55. Mem. Mendham (N.J.) Golf and Tennis Club, Morris County Golf Club (Convent, N.J.), Yale Club (N.Y.C.), Black River Fish and Game Club (Pottersville, N.J.), Delta Kappa Epsilon. Office: 14 E Main St PO Box 90 Mendham NJ 07945-0090

KIRBY, C. EUGENE, JR., bank executive; Exec. v.p., head retail banking SunTrust Banks, Inc., exec. v.p., dir. internat and e-bus. svcs. Atlanta, 1999—2002, corp. exec. v.p. retail line of bus. and corp. mktg. Office: SunTrust Banks Inc PO Box 4418 Atlanta GA 30302-4418 Office Phone: 404-588-7711. Office Fax: 404-827-6173.*

KIRBY, CHARLES WILLIAM, JR., dancer, choreographer; b. Little Rock, Apr. 28, 1926; s. Charles William and Eva Rose (Horton) K. AA, Little Rock Jr. Coll., 1945. Adv. bd. George Brown Coll. Tech., Toronto; exec. com. Canadian Actors Equity Assn.; pres. Southeastern Regional Ballet Festival Assn., 1965; co-founder, co-owner (with Jacques Wensvoort) Abundance Restaurant, Inc., Toronto, 1980— Prin. soloist Ballet Soc. Ark., 1947, assoc. dir. Acad. Ballet Arts, Little Rock, 1948-50, prin. dancer Ark. State Musicals, 1949, Memphis Open Air Theatre, 1950, co-dir. Acad. Dance Arts, Memphis, 1950-65, prin. dancer, costume designer, choreographer Front St. Theatre, Memphis, 1954-64, choreographer Memphis Opera Theatre, 1954-64, performer Dallas Summer Musicals, 1964; co-organizer, choreographer ballets Memphis Civic Ballet, 1953-65; mem. Nat. Ballet Can., 1965-72, soloist, 1972-76, prin. dancer, 1976-85, prin. character artist, 1985-98; appeared: CBS-TV spls. Swan Lake, 1967, Cinderella, 1968 (Emmy award), Sleeping Beauty, 1972 (Emmy award), Giselle, 1975, La Fille Mal Gardee, 1979, Onegin, 1985, The Merry Widow, 1987, The Planets, 1994; choreographer: CBC-TV spls. CBC Opera prodn. La Rondine, 1971, Jacob's Pillow Dance Festival, 1971, Maurice Ravel Centennial Concert, 1975, summer opera festivals, Nat. Arts Centre, Ottawa, Can., Canadian Opera Co.; co. mgr. Dance Repertory Co., N.Y.C., 1972; author:, dir., choreographer, narrator: spl. ednl. program Spectrum: A Retrospective Look at Dance, 1973. With US Army, 1944. Recipient key to City of Little Rock, 1965 Mem.: Assn. Canadian TV and Radio Artists. Episcopalian. Home: 7518 Silver Trumpet Ln # 101 Naples FL 34109

KIRBY, D'LYLA, speech pathology/audiology services professional, educator; d. Harold Wright Kirby and Louise Veronica Engling. BS in Edn., Abilene Christian U., Tex., 1974; MS, Tex. Tech. U., Lubbock, 1978. Speech/lang. pathologist West Tex. Rehab. Ctr., Abilene, 1974—78, 1978—80; asst. prof. Abilene Christian U., 1980—. Author: Literature Lincs II, 2006; co-author: Camp Literacy, 2007. Bd. dirs. West Tex. Autism Ctr., Abilene, 2005—, King David's Kids, Abilene, 2006—. Mem.: Tex. Speech-Lang.-Hearing Found., Am. Speech-Lang.-Hearing Assn., Tex. Speech-Lang.-Hearing Assn. (v.p. pub. info. 1999—2001, Honor award 1996). Avocations: reading, cross stitch. Office: Abilene Christian U 1600 Campus Ct Abilene TX 79699 Business E-Mail: kirbyd@acu.edu.

KIRBY, DAVID V., prosecutor; b. 1950; BA, Pomona Coll.; JD, Northwestern U. Chief criminal divsn. US Dept. Justice, Burlington, Vt., asst. U.S. atty, 1996—2001, acting U.S. atty., 2001, 1st asst. U.S. atty., 2001—, U.S. atty., 2004—06. Office: US Atty 11 Elmwood Ave 3rd Fl PO Box 570 Burlington VT 05402-0570*

KIRBY, DOROTHY MANVILLE, social worker; b. Burke, SD, Oct. 23, 1917; d. Charles Vietz and Gail Lorena (Coonen) Manville; m. Sigmund Kirby, July 11, 1941 (div. 1969); children: Paul Howard, Robert Charles. BA, Wayne State U., 1970, MSW, 1972. Cert. social worker, Mich.; lic. marriage and family therapist, Mich. Pvt. practice social work, Allen Park, Mich., 1973—. Instr. stress, personal effectiveness and comm. Pres. Allen Park Symphony Orch., 1990-92. Mem.: LWV (pres. Allen Park 1965—66), NASW (clin.), AAUW, Mich. Assn. Marriage and Family Therapy (sec. 1982), Nat. Assn. Marriage and Family Therapy. Presbyterian. Avocation: playing violin. Home and Office: 15720 Wick Rd Allen Park MI 48101-1535 Office Phone: 313-382-0623. E-mail: dmkirby@ameritech.net.

KIRBY, FRED MORGAN, II, finance company executive; b. Wilkes Barre, Pa., Nov. 23, 1919; s. Allan P. and Marian G. (Sutherland) K.; m. A. Walker Dillard, Apr. 30, 1949; children: Alice Kirby Horton, Fred Morgan III, Dillard, Jefferson. Grad., Lawrenceville Sch., 1938; AB, Lafayette Coll., Easton, Pa., 1942; postgrad., Harvard Grad. Sch. Bus., 1947; LLD, St. Joseph's U., 1981, Lafayette Coll., 1984, Wake Forest U., 2002; LHD, Drew U., 1997. From v.p. to pres., bd. dirs. Allan Corp., 1953-75; pres., chmn. bd. dirs. Filtration Engrs., Inc., 1951-56; dir. Alleghany Corp., 1958—61, 1963—2007, v.p., 1961, exec. v.p., 1963-67, chmn. bd., 1967—2007, pres., 1968-77, mem. exec. com., 1968—2007. Pres., bd. dirs. F.M. Kirby Found., Inc.; bd. dirs. Nat. Football Found. and Coll. Hall of Fame, Inc. Served to lt. (s.g.) USNR, 1942-46. Recipient 25th Anniversary citation NCAA, 1966, Silver Anniversary All-Am. award Sports Illustrated, 1966, Gold medal Pa. Soc., 1982, Gold medallion Internat. Swimming Hall of Fame, 1989, Gold medal Nat. Football Found. and Coll. Hall Fame, Inc., 2000, Lawrenceville medal Lawrenceville Sch., 2001. Mem. Westmoreland Club, (Pa.), Spring Valley Hounds (N.J.), Treyburn Country Club (N.C.), Morris County Golf Club (N.J.), Zeta Psi. Office: PO Box 151 17 Dehart St Morristown NJ 07963-0151

KIRBY, HARMON ELWOOD, retired ambassador; b. Hamilton, Ohio, Jan. 27, 1934; s. Cecil and Julia Emma Catherine (Tucker) Kirby; m. Françoise Rolande Chatelain, Dec. 26, 1963; children: Caroline Patricia, Christopher Harmon. AB, Harvard U., 1952; MA, George Washington U., 1977. With pers. and labor rels. Diamond Nat. Corp., Middletown, Ohio, 1959-60; exec. asst. to exec. v.p. Hudson Pulp and Paper Co., NYC, 1960-61; joined Fgn. Svc., Dept. State, 1961; vice consul U.S. Mission, Geneva, 1961-63, U.S. Consulate Gen., Madras, India, 1964-66; internat. rels. officer Dept. State, 1966-69; polit. officer U.S. Embassy, New Delhi, 1969-72, Micronesia Status Negotiations, 1973; Turkish desk officer Dept. of State, 1974-76, dir. Pakistan/Afghanistan/Bangladesh affairs Washington, 1982-84, dir. UN polit. affairs, 1987-89, dir., performance evaluation, 1989-90; polit. counselor U.S. Mission European Cmtys., Brussels, 1976-79; counselor, dep. chief of mission U.S. Embassy, Khartoum, 1979-81, min.-counselor dep. chief of mission Rabat, Morocco, 1984-87; sr. seminar Nat. and Internat. Affairs, Washington, 1981-82; amb. to Togo, 1990-94; ret., 1995. With State Dept., Washington, 1996—. Bd. dirs. Internat. Eye Found. Fellow: Tangier Am. Legation Mus. Soc.; mem.: Am. Fgn. Svc. Assn., Diplomatic and Consular Officers Ret., Phi Beta Kappa. Avocations: travel, photography, tennis, swimming. Home: 6811 Barrett Ln Bethesda MD 20814-1205

KIRBY, J. SCOTT, air transportation executive; BS, USAF Acad.; MS, George Washington Univ. Economist, prog. acquisition & evaluation office U.S. Dept. of Defense; ops. rsch. cons. Sabre Decision Technologies; sr. dir. Am. West Airlines, 1995—97, v.p. planning, 1997—98, v.p. revenue mgmt., 1998—2000, sr. v.p. e-bus., 2000—01, exec. v.p. sales & mktg., 2001—05, US Airways Group, Tempe, Ariz., 2005—06, pres., 2006—. Office: US Airways Group 111 W Rio Salado Pkwy Tempe AZ 85281*

KIRBY, JEFFERSON W., investment company executive; b. Summit, NJ, Dec. 12, 1961; s. Fred Morgan II and Walker (Dillard) K.; m. Karen McCabe, Sept. 30, 1989; children: F. Morgan IV, J. Walker Jr., Jane J., Samuel S. BA, Lafayette Coll., Easton, Pa., 1984; MBA, Duke U., 1987. Analyst Morgan Stanley & Co., NYC, 1984-85; assoc. Bankers Trust Co., NYC, 1987-92; dir. corp. devel. Alleghany Corp., NYC, 1992-94, v.p., 1994—2003; mng. mem. Broadfield Capital Mgmt. LLC, Morristown, NJ, 2003—. Bd. dirs. Alleghany Corp. Bd. dir. F.M. Kirby Found., Inc., Morristown, N.J., 1984—; Nat. Football Found. and Coll. Hall of Fame, Morristown, NJ, 1998—; trustee The Peck Sch., Morristown, 1992-2000, Lafayette Coll., 1996—; mem. bd. visitors The Fuqua Sch. Bus., Duke U., 2002—; vol. Green Village Vol. Fire Dept., 1983-87. Mem.: Rolling Rock Club, Mendham Valley Gun Club, The U. Club, Morris County Golf Club (bd. dirs. 2002—), Zeta Psi. Republican. Episcopalian. Office: Broadfield Capital 86 Maple Ave Morristown NJ 07960

KIRBY, JOHN JOSEPH, JR., lawyer; b. Washington, Oct. 22, 1939; s. John Joseph and Rose Elizabeth (Mangan) Kirby; m. Susan Rita Cullman; children: John Pickens, Timothy James, Perrin Patricia Lucia. BA, Fordham Coll., 1961; BA (Rhodes scholar), Oxford U., 1964, MA, 1967; LLB, U. Va., 1966. Bar: Va 1966, NY 1969. Asst. prof. law U. Va., 1966-67; spl. asst. civil rights divsn. U.S. Dept. Justice, Washington, 1967-68; assoc. Mudge Rose Guthrie Alexander & Ferdon, NYC, 1968-70, ptnr., 1971-95, chmn., 1991-95; ptnr. Latham & Watkins, NYC, 1995—2007. Dep. dir. Pres's Commn. Campus Unrest, 1970. Bd. dirs. Georgetown U., 1976—92, Merton Coll. Charitable Corp., 1995—, pres., 2006—; bd. dirs. Fund Modern Cts., 1998—, Legal Aid Soc., 2006—; trustee fellow Fordham U., 1994—2000. Mem.: ABA, DC Bar, Va State Bar, Asn Bar City NY. Home: 812 Park Ave New York NY 10021 also: 88 Saddle Rock Rd Stamford CT 06902 Office: Latham & Watkins 885 3d Ave Ste 1000 New York NY 10022-4834 Office Phone: 212-906-1222. E-mail: john.kirby@lw.com.

KIRBY, LISA ANNE, literature educator; d. Dale Allen and Jo-Carole Cooper; m. Matthew Walker Kirby, Apr. 12, 2003. BA in English and Polit. Sci., Tex. Christian U., Ft. Worth, 1997; MA in English, U. Nebr., Lincoln, 1998; PhD in English, Tex. Christian U., Ft. Worth, 2003. Assoc. project editor Harcourt Coll. Pubs., Ft. Worth, 1998—2000; grad. instr. English Tex. Christian U., Ft. Worth, 2000—03; prof. English Collin County C.C., Plano, Tex., 2003—04; asst. prof. English NC Wesleyan Coll., Rocky Mount, NC, 2004—. Presenter in field. Contbr. chapters to books, articles to profl. jours. Recipient The Leslie H. and Evelyn G. Garner Faculty Leadership ward, NC Wesleyan Coll., 2006. Mem.: MLA, Bus. and Profl. Women (chmn. young careerist com. 2005—06, Young Careerist award 2005), Nat. Coun. Tchrs. English. Democrat. Avocations: reading, travel, films. Home Phone: 919-342-2804; Office Phone: 252-985-5337.

KIRBY, ODELL, retired small business owner, newswriter, writer; b. Vivan, Okla., 1921; s. Auda and Matilda (Brasfield) Kirby. Student, Inst. of Children's Lit., West Redding, Conn. Printer's devil Indian Jour., Eufaula, Okla., 1936; with various newspapers, 1936—72; owner vacuum cleaner sales and svc. bus., 1972—97.

KIRBY, RONALD EUGENE, fish and wildlife research administrator; b. Angola, Ind., Nov. 26, 1947; s. Robert Waye and Lorraine Alice (Hoag) Kirby; m. Dona J. Kirby; children: Cyrus Robert, William Emil, Peter Waye, Joshua M. Brosten, Emily A. Brosten, Andrew J. Brosten. BS, Duke U., 1969; MA, So. Ill. U., 1973; PhD, U. Minn., 1976. Staff biologist Coop. Wildlife Rsch. Lab., So. Ill. U., Carbondale, 1969-72; collaborating biologist U.S. Forest Svc., St. Paul and Cass Lake, Minn., 1970-72; rsch. biologist Antarctic Rsch. Program NSF, McMurdo Station, Antarctica, 1974; NIH rsch. trainee dept. ecology and behavioral biology U. Minn., Mpls., 1972-76; wildlife biologist, Patuxent Wildlife Rsch. Ctr. U.S. Fish and Wildlife Svc., Laurel, Md., 1976-80, population mgmt. specialist div. refuge mgmt. Washington, 1980-82, rsch. coord. Nat. Wildlife Refuge System, 1982-83, regional assessment biologist, office info. transfer Ft. Collins, Colo., 1983-88, leader info. transfer sect., 1988-90; asst. dir. No. Prairie Wildlife Rsch. Ctr., Jamestown, ND, 1991-92, dir., 1993; dir. U.S. Nat. Biol. Svc. No. Prairie Sci. Ctr., Jamestown, ND, 1993-96; dir. U.S. Geol. Survey No. Prairie Wildlife Rsch. Ctr., Jamestown, ND, 1997-2001; dir. U.S. Geol. Survey Forest and Rangeland Ecosys. Sci. Ctr., Corvallis, Oreg., 2001—03; sr. adv. biologist We. regional office U.S. Geol. Survey, Seattle, 2003—04, sci. quality coord., 2004—06, bur. approving ofcl., 2006—. Mem. waterfowl adv. com. Minn. Dept. Natural Resources, 1970—72; mem. black duck subcom. Atlantic Flyway Coun., 1976—80; mem. tech. sect. Central Flyway, 1991—. Editorial referee to sci. jours. and profl. reports; contbr. articles to profl. jours. Active Boy Scouts Am., 1984—. Grantee AEC, 1972—76. Mem.: The Wildlife Soc., Lambda Chi Alpha. Avocations: hiking, camping, birdwatching, motorcycling, hunting. Office: Western Regional Office US Geol Survey 909 1st Ave Ste 800 Seattle WA 98104 Home Phone: 253-833-7766; Office Phone: 206-220-4640. Business E-Mail: ronald_kirby@usgs.gov.

KIRBY, RUSSELL STEPHEN, epidemiologist, researcher, geographer; b. New Haven, June 8, 1954; s. Frank Eugene and Emily (Baruch) K.; m. Elizabeth Margaret Ivens, July 9, 1977; children: Rachel Anne, Amelia Jeanne, Jocelyn Eileen. BA, U. Wis., 1974, MS, 1977, PhD, 1981, MS, 1991. Lectr. U. Wis., Madison, 1980, 82-83; rsch. analyst 3 Wis. Ctr. for Health Stats., Madison, 1981-83, rsch. analyst 5, 1983-85, rsch. analyst 6 maternal and child health statistician, 1985-88; sr. rsch. analyst maternal and child health Ark. Ctr. Health Statistics, Little Rock, 1988-91; instr. dept. pediat. U. Ark. Med. Scis., Little Rock, 1989-93, asst. prof., 1993-96; assoc. prof. dept. ob.-gyn. Milw. Clin. Campus U. Wis. Med. Sch., 1996-01, prof., 2001—02; prof., vice chair dept. maternal and child health, sch. pub. health dept. of pediat. and ob-gyn U. Ala. at Birmingham, 2002—. Vis. asst. prof. Beloit Coll., 1987—88; adj. asst. prof. U. Ark., Little Rock, 1988—95; adj. assoc. prof. Coll. Bus. and Mgmt. Cardinal Stritch U., 2000—02; sci. dir. Ark. Reproductive Health Monitoring Sys., 1991—94, dir., 1994—96, cons., 1996—. Book rev. editor Jour. Perinatology, 1992-99; mem. bd. editors Jour. Childs Health, 2003-04, Birth, 2003—, Pediatric and Perinatal Epidemiology, Am. Jour. Perinatology, 2005; contbr. articles to profl. jours. Recipient Callon-Leonard award Wis. Assn. for Perinatal Care, 1994, Byron L. Hawks award Ark. Perinatal Assn., 1995, Fraternalist of Yr. award Ct. Razorback Ind. Order Foresters, 1996, Pres.'s award Nat. Birth Defects Prevention Network, 2005; named Vol. of Yr. SE chpt. Wis. March of Dimes Birth Defects Found., 1998, Outstanding Advocate for Maternal and Child Health Wis. Maternal and Child Health Coalition, 1999. Fellow Am. Coll. Epidemiology; mem. APHA, Assn. Am. Geographers (life), Agrl. History Soc. (life), So. Hist. Soc. (life), Wis. Assn. for Perinatal Care (bd. dirs. 1996-2002, pres.-elect 1998-99, pres. 1999-2000, past pres. 2000-01, Pres. award, 2003), Perinatal Found. (bd. dirs. 1996-2002, treas. 2000-02), Ark. Perinatal Assn. (pres. 1991-92), Soc. for Epidemiologic Rsch., Nat. Perinatal Assn. (bd. dirs. 1990-92, 95-98, ann. conf. chair 1999), Nat Birth Defects Prevention Network (pres. 1999, past pres. 2000, exec. com. 1997—, pres. award, 2005), Soc. for Pediatric and Perinatal Epidemiologic Rsch. (exec. com. 2000-04), Teratology Soc., Ala. chpt. Mar. of Dimes (bd. dirs. 2002—, chpt. chair 2005—), Assn. Tchrs. of Maternal and Child Health (treas. 2005-06, pres.-elect 2007). Avocations: camping, writing book reviews, computer cartography and graphics, used books. Home: 713 Kendall Dr Vestavia Hills AL 35226 Office: RPHB 320 1530 3rd Ave S Birmingham AL 35294-0022 Home Phone: 205-822-3388; Office Phone: 205-934-2985. Business E-Mail: rkirby@uab.edu.

KIRBY, WILLIAM C., history professor, former dean; b. Mt. Vernon, NY, July 31, 1950; s. Theodore Burnett and Jean Elizabeth (Tompkins) K.; m. Yvette Sheahan, May 14, 1977; children: Theodore, Elizabeth. AB summa cum laude, Dartmouth Coll., 1972; AM, Freie U., Berlin, 1973, Harvard U., 1974, PhD, 1981. Asst. prof. Washington U., St. Louis, 1980-86, dir. internat. affairs, 1983-88, assoc. prof., 1987-91, dir. Asian studies, 1988-91, dean, 1988-92, prof. history, 1991-92, Harvard U., Cambridge, Mass., 1992—, chmn. Coun. on East Asian Studies, 1993-97, chmn. dept. history, 1995—2000, Edith and Benjamin Geisinger prof. history, 1999—, dir. Fairbank Ctr. for East Asian Rsch., 1999—, dean Faculty of Arts and Scis., 2002—06. Vis. prof. Harvard U., Cambridge, 1989-90; gen. editor Modern China series Cambridge U. Press, N.Y.C., 1996—. Author: Germany and Republican China, 1984, State and Economy in Republican China, 2000; editor: Realms of Freedom in Modern China, 2003; co-editor: Normalization of U.S.-China Relations: An International History, 2006; mem. editl. bd. The China Quar., 1994—; contbr. articles to profl. jours. NEH Rsch. grant, 1994-97, ACLS Rsch. grant, 1984-85, 94, Chiang Ching-Kuo Found. grant, 1993-96, Fulbright grant, 1997-98. Mem. Assn. for Asian Studies, Am. Hist. Assn. Office: Harvard U, FAS Dept History CGIS S Bldg #S128 1730 Cambridge St Cambridge MA 02138 Office Phone: 617-495-5119. Office Fax: 617-495-9976. E-mail: william_kirby@harvard.edu.

KIRCH, DARRELL GENE, medical association and former academic administrator, dean; b. Denver, May 3, 1949; m. Deborah M. Kirch; children: Samantha M., Madeline A. BA in Philos., U. Colo., 1971, MD magna cum laude, 1977. Diplomate Am. Bd. Psychiatry and Neurology. Resident in psychiatry U. Colo. Health Scis. Ctr., Denver, 1977—82; med. staff fellow adult psychiatry br. NIMH, Washington, 1982—84, sr. staff fellow neuropsychiatry br., 1984—87, med. dir. Neuropsychiatric Rsch. Hosp., 1987—89, dep. sci. dir. Bethesda, Md., 1992—93; prof. Sch. Grad. Studies, prof. dept. psychiatry Med. Coll. Ga., Augusta, 1994—2000, dean Sch. Medicine, 1994—2000, dean Sch. Grad. Studies, 1995—99, sr. v.p. clin. activities, 1998—2000; prof. dept. psychiatry, sr. v.p. health affairs Pa. State U., Hershey, 2000—06, dean Coll. Medicine, 2000—06; CEO Milton S. Hershey Med. Ctr., 2000—06; pres. Assn. Am. Med. Colls., Washington, 2006—. Examiner Am. Bd. Psychiatry and Neurology, Deerfield, Ill., 1985—. Assoc. editor: Psychopharmacology Bull., 1990—98, Schizophrenia Bull., 1989—95. Capt. USPHS, 1986—94. Decorated Commendation medal. Mem.: AMA, Assn. Am. Med. Coll. (chair sec. on med. schs. 1998—99, chair 2003, mem. coun. deans adminstrv. bd. 2000—05), Soc. Exec. Leadership in Acad. Medicine, Am. Psychiat. Assn. Office: Assn Am Med Colls 2450 N St NW Washington DC 20037-1126 Home: 9409 Eagle Ridge Dr Bethesda MD 20817 Office Phone: 202-828-0460. E-mail: aamcpresident@aamc.org.*

KIRCH, DONALD ALLEN, writer, composer; b. Culver City, Calif., Jan. 24, 1967; s. Donald Raymond and Ruth Mae (White) K. Student, United Broadcast Sch., 1989. FCC permit. Author: Still Waters, 1997, KA-RE, 2000, A Stake in Murder, 2001, A Port By Any Other Name, 2002, A Funny Thing Happened on the Way to Roswell, 2003, The Christ Project, 2007; songwriter This Is America, 1991, The Working Man, 1991, Oh What A Gift is Christmas Day, 1991, The Miracle of Christmas, 1999. Mem. Titanic Hist. Soc. Roman Catholic. Avocations: history, films, naval ships and history of naval ships, sherlock holmes mysteries, study of strange phenomena. Home: 311 E 91st Ter Kansas City MO 64114-3738 Office Phone: 816-523-3945. Personal E-mail: dkirch@hotmail.com.

KIRCHER, CHRISTOPHER, neurologist, consultant; b. Niagara Falls, NY, May 30, 1942; s. Charles Edmund and Nancy Page Kircher; m. Amy Nichols Kircher, May 8, 1982; children: Caroline Anna, Madeline Catherine. BS, Xavier U., Cin., 1963; MD, Ind. U., 1973. Diplomate Am. Bd. Psychiatry and Neurology. Clin. clk. Nat. Hosp. Nervous and Mental Disorders, London, 1973; intern St. Joseph Infirmary, Louisville, 1973—74; resident neurology U. Minn., Mpls., 1974—75; sr. and chief resident U. Cin., 1975—77; vis. fellow Cleve. Clinic, 1977; neurologist Mayfield Clinic, Cin., 1977—97; neurology and clin. rsch. Riverhills Healthcare, Cin., 1997—2001. Dir. med. adv. bd. Alzheimer's Corp., Albuquerque, 1999—2005; dir. clin. adv. bd. Panacea Pharm., Gaithersburg, Md., 2001—06; cons. ProScan Imaging, Cin., 2002—05; co-developer nuclear scanning method Dual Tracer Emission Computer Tomography, 1998; moderator Challenging Views of Alzheimer Disease Conf., 2001—04; lectr. in field; reviewer rsch. grants Alzheimer's Assn., 2004—06. Editor: (book) Readings in Neurophysiology, 1968; contbr. articles to profl. jours. Fellow, NIH, 1965—68; scholar, Cmty. Inst. Cooperation, U. Mich., 1966—67. Mem.: Am. Acad. Neurology. Republican. Achievements include patents for Correlative Brain Regional Activity (COBRA) which is a dementia screening method; Omega 3 fat use to stimulate brain perfusion for diagnosis and possible therapy of dementia. Avocations: golf, travel, reading. Home and Office: Cincinnati Bio-Med and Fin Cons Ltd 3444 Arnold St Cincinnati OH 45208-4408 Office Phone: 513-871-1322. E-mail: ckircher@one.net.

KIRCHER, JOHN JOSEPH, law educator; b. Milw., July 26, 1938; s. Joseph John and Martha Marie (Jach) K.; m. Marcia Susan Adamkiewicz, Aug. 26, 1961; children: Joseph John, Mary Kathryn. BA, Marquette U., 1960, JD, 1963. Bar: Wis. 1963, U.S. Dist. Ct. (ea. dist.) Wis. 1963, U.S. Ct. Appeals (7th cir.) 1992. Sole practice, Port Washington, Wis., 1963-66; with Def. Research Inst., Milw., 1966-80, research dir., 1972-80; with Marquette U., 1970—, prof. law, 1980—, assoc. dean acad. affairs, 1992-93. Chmn. Wis. Jud. Council, 1981-83. Author: (with J.D. Ghiardi) Punitive Damages: Law and Practice, 1981, 2d edit (with C.M. Wiseman), 2000; editor Federation of Defense and Corporate Counsel Quarterly; mem. editorial bd. Def. Law Jour.; contbr. articles to profl. jours. Recipient Teaching Excellence award Marquette U., 1986, Disting. Service award Def. Research Inst., 1980, Marquette Law Rev. Editors' award, 1988. Mem. ABA (Robert B. McKay Professor award 1993), Am. Law Inst., Wis. Bar Assn., Wis. Supreme Ct. Bd. of Bar Examiners (vice chair 1989-91, chair 1992), Am. Judicature Soc., Nat. Sports Law Inst. (adv. com. 1989—), Assn. Internationale de Droit des Assurances, Scribes. Roman Catholic. Office: PO Box 1881 Milwaukee WI 53201-1881 Home Phone: 414-351-5242; Office Phone: 414-288-7095. Business E-Mail: john.kircher@marquette.edu.

KIRCHER, MORITZ FLORIAN, radiologist, researcher; b. Würzburg, Bavaria, Germany, Nov. 3, 1972; arrived in US, 2001; s. Stefan and Almut (Rauser) Kircher. MD with highest honors, Humboldt U., Berlin, 2000, PhD, 2001. Postdoctoral fellow Mass. Gen. Hosp., Harvard Med. Sch., Boston, 2001—04; surgery intern Cleve. Clinic Health Sys., 2004—05; resident in diagnostic radiology Beth Israel Deaconess Med. Ctr., Harvard Med. Sch., Boston, 2005—, advisor, resident rsch., 2005—. Reviewer Magnetic Resonance Medicine, 2006—. Recipient Eduard Ceraldi award, Cleve. Clinic Health Sys., 2005, Lawrie B. Morrison Rsch. award, Beth Israel Deaconess Hosp., 2007; grantee, German Rsch. Found., 2001—03; scholar, European Union, 1997—98; Postdoctoral fellowship, Am. Heart Assn., 2003—05. Mem.: German Soc. Immunology, Assn. U. Radiologists, Am. Roentgen Ray Soc., Radiol. Soc. N.Am. (Rsch. Trainee prize 2003, 2002). Achievements include development of highly derivatized tat-derivatized superparamagnetic nanoparticles for in vivo cell tracking by MRI; dual-wavelength optical reporters for in vivo protease sensing; magneto-optical nanoparticles for pre-operative and intra-operative brain-tumor delineation; magneto-optical nanoparticles for combined in vivo protease sensing and detection by MRI; discovery of three-dimensional recruitment pattern of CD8+ T cells into tumors. Avocations: photography, music. Office: Beth Israel Deaconess Medical Ctr One Deaconess Rd Boston MA 02215 Personal E-mail: mkircher@bidmc.harvard.edu.

KIRCHHEIMER, ARTHUR E(DWARD), lawyer, business executive; b. NYC, June 26, 1931; s. Arthur and Lena K.; m. Esther A. Jordan, Sept. 11, 1965. BA, Syracuse U., 1952, LL.B., 1954. Bar: N.Y. 1954, Calif. 1973. Ptnr. Block, Kirchheimer, Lemax & Failmezger, Syracuse, NY, 1954-70; corp. counsel Norwich Pharmacal Co., NY, 1970-72; sr. v.p., gen. counsel Wickes Cos., Inc., San Diego, 1972-84; prin. Arthur E. Kirchheimer, Inc., P.C., San Diego, 1984-90; writer, cons. in bus. matters La Jolla, Calif., 1990—. Sec., dir. Corp. Fin. Council San Diego, 1975 Pres. Mental Health Assn. Onondaga County, 1970; chmn. Manlius (N.Y.) Planning Commn., 1969-72; mem. Alternatives to Litigation Spl. Panel, 1984—; mem. San Diego County Grand Jury, 1991-92. Mem. ABA, Calif. Bar Assn. Home and Office: 2876 Palomino Cir La Jolla CA 92037-7066

KIRCHICK, WILLIAM DEAN, lawyer; b. Oceanside, NY, Nov. 20, 1950; s. Julian Gilbert and Jean (Kostinsky) K.; m. Carol Bonnie Rudnick, May 29, 1977; children: James Rory, Jeffrey Scott. BA in Polit. Sci. magna cum laude, U. Mich., 1973; JD cum laude, Boston Coll., 1976. Bar: Mass. 1978, Ill. 1976, US Dist. Ct. Mass. 1978, US Ct. Appeals (1st cir.) 1978, US Tax Ct. 1976, US Supreme Ct. 1982; accredited estate planner designation. Assoc. Arnstein, Gluck, Lehr & Milligan, Chgo., 1976-77; assoc., ptnr. Peabody & Brown, Boston, 1977-88; ptnr. Bingham Dana LLP, Boston, 1988—2002, Bingham McCutchen LLP, Boston, 2002—. Mem. Boston Probate and Estate Planning Forum, 1987—, program events coord., 1989-90, moderator, 1990-91; mem. Boston Estate Planning Coun., 1986—, exec. com., 1989-92, sec. 1995-96, treas., 1996-97, v.p. 1997-98, pres.-elect, 1998-99, pres. 1999-2000; mem. Norfolk and Plymouth Bus. and Estate Planning Coun., 1990—; mem. Planned Giving Group of New Eng., Inc., 1997-; curriculum adv. com. for Mass. Continuing Legal Edn., Inc. Contbg. author: Estate and Protective Planning Techniques in Massachusetts, 1990, A Practical Guide to Estate Planning in Massachusetts, 1996, Preparing Estate Tax Returns, 1997, Drafting Wills and Trusts in Massachusetts, 2002, Drafting Irrevocable Trusts in Massachusetts, 2005; contbr. articles to profl. jours. Chmn. young lawyers team spl. events com. Combined Jewish Philanthropies of Greater Boston, Inc., 1982-84, chmn. young lawyers team, 1984-85, mem. lawyers team cabinet, 1985-89, 91-94; trustee The CJP Disabilities Trust, 1998--, The Acorn Found., 2000-03. Recipient Campaign Leadership award Combined Jewish Philanthropies of Greater Boston, Inc., 1984, Estate Planner of Yr. award Boston Estate Planning Coun., 2004. Fellow Am. Coll. Trust and Estate Counsel; mem. ABA (mem. sect. probate, trusts and real property), Mass. Bar Assn. (mem. tax sect. exec. com. 1989-92, probate sect. exec. com. 1992-93), Boston Bar Assn. (mem. estate planning com. 1981—, chmn. 1984-88, chmn. subcom. to study income, gift and estate tax proposals of Tax Reform Act of 1986 1985-86, chmn. subcom. on proposed temporary regulations concerning Chpt. 13 Internal Revenue Code 1988-89, mem. probate sect. 1978—), U. Mich. Club Greater Boston, Boston Coll. Law Sch. Alumni Assn. Phi Beta Kappa, Phis Eta Sigma. Avocations: jogging, swimming, walking, skiing. Office: Bingham McCutchen LLP 150 Federal St Fl 15 Boston MA 02110-1726 Office Phone: 617-951-8590. Business E-Mail: william.kirchick@bingham.com.

KIRCHMAN, ERIC HANS, lawyer; b. Washington, May 2, 1962; s. Charles Vincent and Erika Ottilie (Knoeppel) K.; m. Hillary Bronkie Hutson, Apr. 19, 1991; children: Erika B., Thomas E., Kristen N. BA, Univ. Md., 1985; JD, Univ. Balt., 1990. Bar: Md. 1990, U.S. Dist. Ct. Md. 1991, U.S. Ct. Appeals (4th cir.) 2000, U.S. Dist. Ct. D.C. 2005. Assoc. Hillel Abrams, Rockville, Md., 1990-92; ptnr. Kirchman & Kirchman, Wheaton, Md., 1992—. Of counsel Md. Coun. for Gifted and Talented Children, Inc., Silver Spring, 1994. With U.S. Army Reserve, 1985-98. Mem.: Montgomery County Bar Assn., Md. State Bar Assn.

KIRCHNER, JAMES WILLIAM, retired electrical engineer; b. Cleve., Oct. 17, 1920; s. William Sebastian and Marcella Louise (Stuart) K.; m. Eda Christene Landfear, June 11, 1950 (dec. May 1977); children:

Kathleen Ann Kirchner Duda, Susan Lynn Kirchner Buonpane; m. Mary Jane Freebairn, Sept. 17, 2004; children: Lisa Ann Freebairn, Robert V. Freebairn III. BSEE, Ohio U., 1950, MS, 1951. Registered profl. engr., Ohio. Instr. elec. engring. Ohio U., Athens, 1950—52; mgr. liaison engring. Lear Siegler Inc., Maple Heights, Ohio, 1952—64; coord. engring. svcs. Case We. Res. U., Cleve., 1964—72, gen. mgr. Med. Ctr. Co., 1972—91; ret., 1991; sec. corp. Thermagon, Inc., Cleve., 1992. Mem. Portage County Republican Exec. Com., 1961-62; treas. PTA, Aurora, Ohio, 1963-65, v.p., 1965-66; mem. The Ch. in Aurora, 1956—. Served with USAAF, 1942-45, PTO Mem. NSPE (life), IEEE (life), VFW (life), Ohio Soc. Profl. Engrs. (life), Cleve. Engring. Soc. (chmn. environ. com. 1976), Am. Soc. Engring. Edn. (life). Home: Reserves of Aurora 535 Treetop Ct Aurora OH 44202-7317 Personal E-mail: jwkfph@aol.com.

KIRCHNER, JOHN SHIRK, orthopedic surgeon; BA in Chemistry cum laude, Washington and Lee U., Lexington, Va., 1988; MD, Hahnemann U., Phila., 1992. Bd. cert. Am. Bd. Orthopedic Surgery, diplomate Nat. Bd. Med. Examiners. Intern gen. surgery Hahnemann U. Hosp., Phila., 1992—93; resident orthopaedic surgery Allegheny U. Health Scis., Phila., 1993—97; fellow foot and ankle surgery Am. Sports Medicine Inst., Birmingham, 1997—98, asst. to staff, 1998; asst. prof. U. Pitts. Physicians, 1999—2002; orthop. surgeon Ala. Sports Medicine and Orthop. Ctr., Birmingham, 2002—05, Orthop. Specialists Ala., Birmingham, 2005—. Presenter in field. Contbr. articles to profl. jours. Fellow: Am. Acad. Orthopaedic Surgeons (foot and ankle evaluation subcom.); mem.: AMA, AOFAS, AAOFAS, Jefferson County Med. Soc., Pa. Orthopaedic Soc., Clin. Orthopaedic Soc. Achievements include research in neuropathic arthropathies; surgical treatment of adjacent simultaneous Morton's neuromas; results of the use of a trephine system for iliac crest bone graft harvest. Avocations: golf, scuba diving, mountain biking, tennis, swimming. Home: 979 Cobble Creek Dr Hoover AL 35226 Office: Orthopaedic Specialists Ala 720 Montclair Rd #200 Birmingham AL 35213

KIRCHNER, LISA BETH, actress, vocalist; b. LA; d. Leon and Gertrude (Schoenberg) K. BA, Sarah Lawrence Coll., NYC, 1975. Picture rschr. McGraw-Hill, 1985-87, John Wiley & Sons, 1988, Simon & Schuster/Globe Book Co., 1992—2000, Chelsea House Pubs., 1987-94, Oxford Univ. Press, 1997, Facts on File, 2001—02, Greenwood Pub. Co., 1997, Lazard Freres, 1998—, The Oryx Press, 1999—, Abbeville Press, 2001—02. Songwriter, BMI. Broadway appearances include The Threepenny Opera, 1975, The Human Comedy, 1985; off-Broadway appearances include the Radiant City, 1993, Hotel for Criminals, 1974, The American Imagination, others; TV shows include Songs From the Heart, Another World, The Guiding Light, As The World Turns, Out of Our Father's House; appearances at The White House and Gracie Mansion; performed as featured soloist and back-up singer with Judy Collins (numerous TV appearances); prodr., solo vocalist CD releases (Albany Records) entitled One More Rhyme, 1999, When Lights Are Low, 2002. Mem. AFTRA, SAG, BMI, Equity, Actor's Equity Assn. Avocations: painting, crafts, poetry. E-mail: kirchl@aol.com.

KIRCHNER, PETER THOMAS, nuclear medicine physician, educator, consultant; b. July 2, 1939; s. Elek and Julia (Kossy) K.; m. Mary Coleman Kirchner, Dec. 18, 1965 (div.); children: David, Annette, Julie. BA Physics, Yale U., 1960; MD, Columbia U., 1964. Diplomate Am. Bd. Internal Medicine, Am. Bd. Nuclear Medicine (sec. 1992-94, chmn. exam. com. 1991-94, vice chmn. 1994, 95). Intern, then resident, chief resident in internal medicine Nat. Naval Med. Ctr., Bethesda, Md., 1964-70; fellow in nuclear medicine Johns Hopkins U., Balt., 1970-72; head nuclear medicine Nat. Naval Med. Ctr., Bethesda, Md., 1972-77; asst. prof. radiology George Washington U., Washington, 1974-77; assoc. dir. nuclear medicine U. Chgo., 1978-81, assoc. prof. radiology, 1981—84, U. Iowa, Iowa City, 1981-84, prof. radiology, 1984—2002, prof. medicine, 1989—2002, emeritus prof. radiology, 2003—; dir. nuclear medicine U. Iowa Hosps. and Clinics, Iowa City, 1981-98; IPA contractee Dept. of Energy, Germantown, Md., 1998—2002; disting. R&D staff ORNL, 2002—; IPA staff Dept. of Energy, Germantown, Md., 2005—. Mem. radiology study sect. NIH, 1995-99; bd. dirs. Joint Rev. Com. Nuclear Medicine Tech., exec. com., 1996—; mem. nat. adv. com. Nat. Isotope Ctr., Dept. Energy, 1996-98; mem. Accreditation Coun. for Grad. Med. Edn. Editor Nuclear Medicine Review Syllabus, 1980; co-editor Nuclear Medicine Self Study I, 1988, Self Study II, 1996; author more than 80 sci. articles, 12 book chpts. Ea. Iowa alumni schs.com. chair Yale U., 1989-94. Capt. USNR, 1963-92. Out Svc. Tng. grantee USN, 1970; recipient Von Hevessy award Hungarian Soc. Nuclear Medicine, 1993. Fellow ACP (hon.), Am. Coll. Nuc. Physicians (hon., chmn. quality assurance and practice cert. com. 1993-95, bd. regents 1993—), Am. Coll. Radiology (hon.); mem. Radiol. Soc. N.Am. (sci. program com. 1992-98), Inst. Clin. Positron Emission Tomography (bd. dirs. 1992-97, pres. 1993-94), Soc. Nuc. Medicine (exec. com. 1988-93, bd. dirs. 1993-97, house of dels. 1993—, chair sci. program com. 1988-90, v.p. 1992-93, pres. 1995-96, gen. program chair 1999-2005, bd. dirs. 1999-2005), Joint Rev. Commn. on Edn. Programs in Nuc. Med. Tech. (sec.-treas. 1998-2001, chair 2001-04), Edn. Rsch. Found. Soc. Nuc. Medicine (bd. dir. 1994-, exec. com. 2004-), NIH-NIBIB (acting dir. intramural sci. program 2003-). Avocation: tennis.

KIRDAR, NEMIR AMIN, banker; b. Kirkuk, Iraq, Oct. 28, 1936; s. Amin and Nuzhet (Mohamad Ali) K.; m. Nada Adnan Shakir, Feb. 1, 1967; children: Rena, Serra. BA, Coll. of the Pacific, 1960; MBA, Fordham U., 1972; postgrad., Harvard U., 1979. Trainee, asst. treas., asst. v.p. Allied Bank Internat., NYC, 1969-73; v.p. Nat. Bank N.Am., NYC, 1973-74; v.p., head Gulf Div., Chase Manhattan Bank, NYC, 1974-81; pres., chief exec. officer INVESTCORP Bank E.C., Manama, Bahrain, 1982—; also bd. dirs. Chmn. Advisory Council Center for Contemporary Arab Studies, Georgetown U. Contbr. articles to profl. jours. Trustee London Philharmonic Trust, London. Mem. Overseers Committee on University Resources, Harvard U., Bd. Advs. World Economic Forum, Switzerland, Internat. Bd. Councillors Center for Strategic and Internat. Studies, Washington, D.C., Visiting Committee Fordham U., visiting committee JFK Sch. of Govt., Harvard U., bd. Trustees Heart Research Found. N.Y.C.; Friend of Somerville, Somerville Coll. Oxford U. Clubs: Metropolitan. Office: Investcorp 37th Fl W 280 Park Ave Rm 37W New York NY 10017-1216 also: Investcorp PO Box 5340 Manama Bahrain

KIRGIS, FREDERIC LEE, law educator; b. Washington, Dec. 29, 1934; s. Frederic Lee Sr. and Kathryn Alice (Burrows) K.; children: Julianne, Paul Frederic. BA, Yale U., 1957; JD, U. Calif.-Berkeley, 1960. Bar: Colo. 1961, Va. 1983. Atty. Covington & Burling, Washington, 1964-67; from asst. prof. to prof. law U. Colo., Boulder, 1967-73; prof. law UCLA, 1973-78; from prof. law to prof. emeritus Washington & Lee U., Lexington, Va., 1978—2005, prof. emeritus, 2005—, dir. Frances Lewis Law Ctr., 1978-83, dean law sch., 1983-88. Author: International Organizations in their Legal Setting, 1977, 2d edit. 1993, Prior Consultation in International Law, 1983, The American Society of International Law's First Century: 1906-2006, 2006; contbr. articles to profl. jours. Pres. Maury River Soccer Club, Lexington, 1978-85. Served to capt. USAF, 1961-64 Recipient Deak award 1974; research fellow NATO, Brussels, 1978 Mem. Am. Soc. Internat. Law (v.p. 1985-87, sec. 1994—), Am. Law Inst., Internat. Law Assn. (Am. br.), Am. Jour. Internat. Law (bd. editors 1984-96, 98-2003, hon. editor 2003—), State Bar Va., Order of Coif. Democrat. Presbyterian. Home: 15 Grey Dove Rd Lexington VA 24450-2269 Office: Washington and Lee U Sch of Law Lexington VA 24450 Office Phone: 540-458-8532. Business E-Mail: kirgisr@wlu.edu.

KIRICK, DANIEL JOHN, agronomist; b. Port Jervis, NY, Nov. 8, 1953; s. Daniel and Mary Theresa Kirick; m. Jean Marie Guse, Sept. 27, 1986; children: Nicholas, John, Kristina, Kimberly. BA in Biology, History, U. Minn., Duluth, 1976; BS in Agronomy, U. Minn., St. Paul, 1977. Cert. profl. agronomist. Agronomist Delft (Minn.) Farm Chems., 1978, Skelly Fertilizer, Trimont, Minn., 1978-80, Mower County Svc. Co., Sargeant, Minn., 1980-86, Cenex Supply, Ellis, SD, 1986-88, Rice (Minn.) Farm Supply, 1988-91, Kirick Agronomy Svcs., St. Cloud, Minn., 1992—. Mem. Comty. Edn. Devel. Adv. Coun., Sauk Rapids, Minn., 1990-94, Youth Devel. Bd., Sauk Rapids, 1990, Benton County Ext. Com., 1993-98, Ctrl. Minn. Forage Coun., 1994—. Mem. AAAS, Weed Sci. Soc. Am., Soil Sci. Soc. Am., Crop Sci. Soc. Am., Am. Soc. Agronomy. Roman Catholic. Home: PO Box 206 Rice MN 56367-0206 Office: Kirick Agronomy Svcs 9144 County Road 4 Saint Joseph MN 56374-9748

KIRILA, JILL S., lawyer; b. Sharon, Pa., 1972; BA, Ohio State U., 1994; JD, Georgetown U., 1997. Bar: Ohio 1997, US Ct. of Appeals Sixth Cir., US Dist. Ct. Northern Dist. Ohio, US Dist. Ct. Southern Dist. Ohio. Sr. assoc. Squire, Sanders & Dempsey L.L.P., Cin. Mem., Alumni Admissions Com. Georgetown U.; mem., Parenthesis and Human Resources Com. Ctr. Vocat. Alternatives. Named one of Ohio's Rising Stars, Super Lawyers, 2006. Office: Squire Sanders & Dempsey LLP 1300 Huntington Ctr 41 South High St Columbus OH 43215-6197 Office Phone: 614-365-2700. Office Fax: 614-365-2499.

KIRINCIC, PAUL E., health products executive; B in Hist. and Comm., St. Norbert Coll., De Pere, Wis.; MBA, Ind. U. V.p. human resources Whirlpool Europe Whirlpool Corp., Benton Harbor, Mich.; v.p. human resources consumer health divsn. Pfizer Corp.; sr. v.p. corp. human resources McKesson Corp., San Francisco, 2001, exec. v.p. corp. human resources. Office: McKesson Corpn One Post St San Francisco CA 94104*

KIRK, ARTEMIS G., university librarian; BA in Music, Vassar Coll.; M in Libr. and Info. Sci., Simmons Coll., Boston; MusM, Harvard U. Past asst. libr. Hellenic Coll., Brookline, Mass.; head libr. Pine Manor Coll., Chestnut Hill, Mass.; dir. libr. and co-dir. info. tech. Simmons Coll.; asst. dir. libr. for collections and budget U. Miami; dir. univ. libr. U. RI, 1998—2001; univ. libr. Georgetown U., 2001—. Bd. dir. RI Higher Edn. Libr. Info. Network; bd. mem. RI libr. bd. Fellow, U.S. Info. Agency, Am. Assoc. Libr. Mem.: Assn. Coll. and Rsch. Libr. Office: Lauinger Library Georgetown Univ 37th and N Streets NW Washington DC 20057-1174 Office Phone: 202-687-7425. Office Fax: 202-687-7501. E-mail: agk3@georgetown.edu.*

KIRK, BALLARD HARRY THURSTON, architect; b. Williamsport, Pa., Apr. 1, 1929; s. Ballard and Ada May (DeLaney) K.; m. Vera Elizabeth Kitchener, Mar. 13, 1951; children: Lisa Lee, Kira Alexandria, Dayna Allison, Courtlandt Blaine. BArch, Ohio State U., 1959. Pres. Kirk Assocs., Architects, Columbus, Ohio, 1963—. Mem. Ohio Bd. Bldg. Standards, Columbus, 1973-78, 92-99; pres. Nat. Coun. Archtl. Registration Bds., Washington, 1983-84, Ohio Bd. Examiners Architects, Columbus, 1973-93; bd. dirs. Nat. Archtl. Accrediting Bd., Washington, 1986-89. Mem. AIA (bd. dirs. Columbus chpt. 1988-92), Coll. of Fellows. Republican. Mem. Brethern Ch. Home: 2557 Charing Rd Columbus OH 43221-3673 Office Phone: 614-284-5706. Personal E-mail: kirkarch@sbcglobal.net.

KIRK, CARMEN ZETLER, data processing executive; b. Altoona, Pa., May 22, 1941; d. Paul Alan and Mary Evelyn (Pearce) Zetler. BA, Pa. State U., 1959-63; MBA, St. Mary's Coll. Calif., 1977. Cert. in data processing. Pub. sch. tchr. State Ga., 1965-66; systems analyst US Govt. Dept. Army, Oakland, Calif., 1967-70; programmer analyst Contra Costa County, Martinez, Calif., 1970-76; applications mgr. Stanford U., Calif., 1976-79; pres. Zetler Assocs., Inc., Palo Alto, Calif., 1979—. Cons. State Calif., Sacramento, 1985-88.

KIRK, CAROL, lawyer; b. Henry, Ill., Dec. 23, 1937; d. Howard P. and Mildred Root McQuilkin; m. Robert James Kirk, Aug. 20, 1961; children: Kathleen, Nancy, Sally. BS in Music Edn., U. Ill., 1960; JD, Ind. U., Indpls., 1989. Bar: Ind. 1989. Pvt. piano tchr., 1957-85; pub. sch. music tchr., 1960-62; dir. Ind. State Ethics Commn., Indpls., 1989-97; atty. and investigator Disciplinary Commn., Supreme Ct. Ind., Indpls., 1997—. Pres. Coun. on Govtl. Ethics Laws, (Internat.), 1993-94. Exec. editor Articles & Prodn. Ind. Law Rev., 1988-89. Mem. Met. Devel. Commn., Indpls., 1982-87; chairperson Pub. Radio Adv. Bd., Indpls., 1983-84, treas. Cmty. Svc. Coun., Indpls., 1988-91. Invitee to Nat. 4H Congress, Chgo., 1956; named 4H Family of Yr., Washington Twp., 4-H, Indpls., 1980, Vol. of Week, Voluntary Action Ctr., Indpls., 1980. Mem. LWV (pres. Indpls. 1979-83), Ind. Bar Assn., Indpls. Bar Assn., Phi Alpha Delta, Mu Phi Epsilon. Avocation: choir singing. Office: Discip Commn Supreme Ct Ind 1165 South Tower 115 W Washington St Indianapolis IN 46204-3420 E-mail: rkirk1937@aol.com.

KIRK, CASSIUS LAMB, JR., retired lawyer, investor; b. Bozeman, Mont., June 8, 1929; s. Cassius Lamb and Gertrude Violet (McCarthy) K. AB, Stanford U., Calif., 1951; JD, U. Calif., Berkeley, 1954. Bar: Calif. 1955. Assoc. Cooley, Godward, Castro, Huddleson & Tatum, San Francisco, 1956-60; staff counsel for bus. affairs Stanford U., 1960-78; chief bus. officer, staff counsel Menlo Sch. and Coll., Atherton, Calif., 1978-81; chmn. Eberli-Kirk Properties, Inc. (dba Just Closets), Menlo Park, 1981-94; ret. Faculty Coll. Bus. Adminstrn. U. Calif., Santa Barbara, summers 1967-73; past adv. bd. Allied Arts Guild, Menlo Park; past nat. vice-chmn. Stanford U. Annual Fund; past pres. Menlo Towers Assn.; endowed 2 professorships Stanford U., 2004 Past v.p. Palo Alto C. of C. With US Army, 1954-56. Mem. VFW, Stanford Faculty Club, Order of Coif, Phi Alpha Delta. Republican. Home: 1330 University Dr Apt 52 Menlo Park CA 94025-4241 Office Phone: 650-366-6285.

KIRK, CONNIE ANN, writer; b. Wellsville, NY, Feb. 14, 1957; d. Leonard A. and Mary Arlene Lewis; m. Kenneth Andrew Kirk, May 21, 1983; children: Benjamin Lewis, Johnathan Patrick. BA in English and Creative Writing, Binghamton U., 1986, MA in English and Creative Writing, 1988, PhD in English and Creative Writing, 2004. Adj. prof. English Mansfield (Pa.) U., 1988—2004. Designer, tchr. 1st online English course Mansfield U. Author: First Peoples: The Mohawks of North America, 2001, J. K. Rowling: A Biography, 2003, Emily Dickinson: A Biography, 2004, Sylvia Plath: A Biography, 2004, Sky Dancers, 2004, Mark Twain: A Biography, 2004, A Student's Guide to Robert Frost, 2006, (reference book) A Companion to American Children's Picture Books, 2005. Mem.: MLA, Author's Guild, Soc. of Children's Book Writers and Illustrators, Am. Lit. Assn., Emily Dickinson Internat. Soc. Personal E-mail: connieannkirk@hotmail.com.

KIRK, DARCY, law librarian, educator; BA, Vassar Coll., 1970; MLS, Simmons Coll., 1973, MBA, 1979; JD, Boston Coll., 1989. Libr. Widener Libr., Harvard U., 1971—80, Boston Coll. Libr., 1981—90; assoc. law libr. pub. svcs. Georgetown U., 1989—96; mem. law faculty U. Conn. Sch. Law, Hartford, 1996—, prof. advanced legal rsch., dir. Law Libr. Mem.: Law Librs. New England (v.p., pres.-elect), Rsch. Librs. Group, Am. Assn. Law Librs. Office: U Conn Sch Law 45 Elizabeth St Hartford CT 06105-2290*

KIRK, DAVID B., computer scientist; BS, MIT, MS in Mech. Engring.; MS in Computer Sci., PhD in Computer Sci., Calif. Inst. Tech. Engr. Apollo Sys. Div. Hewlett-Packard Co., 1989—91; chief scientist, head tech. Crystal Dynamics, 1993—96; chief scientist NVIDIA Corp., Santa Clara, 1997—. Recipient SIGGRAPH Computer Graphics Achievement Award, 2002. Mem.: NAE. Office: NVIDIA 2701 San Tomas Expressway Santa Clara CA 95050

KIRK, DENNIS DEAN, lawyer; b. Pittsburg, Kans., Dec. 13, 1950; s. Homer Standley and Maida Corena (Rouse) K.; 1 child, Dennis Dean II AA, Hutchinson Cmty. Jr. Coll., 1970; BS with distinction, No. Ariz. U., 1972; JD, Washburn U., 1975. Bar: Kans. 1975, U.S. Dist. Ct. Kans. 1975, D.C. 1977, U.S. Ct. Appeals (D.C. cir.) 1978, U.S. Supreme Ct. 1979, U.S. Ct. Appeals (5th cir.) 1981, U.S. Dist. Ct. Md. 1984, U.S. Tax Ct. 1984, U.S. Claims Ct. 1984, U.S. Ct. Appeals (fed. cir.) 1984, U.S. Ct. Mil. Appeals 1984, Va. 1990, U.S. Ct. Appeals (4th cir.) 1990; lic. pvt. investigator; lic. personal protection specialist; strategic integration and bus. transformation highly qualified expert US Army. Trial atty. ICC, Washington, 1975-77; assoc. Goff, Sims, Cloud & Stroud, Washington, 1977-82; pvt. practice Washington, 1982-90; ptnr. Slocum, Boddie, Murry & Kirk, Falls Church, Va., 1990-93; pvt. practice Falls Church, Va., 1993—2005; spl. asst. to gen. counsel Pentagon, U.S. Army, Washington, 2005—07, assoc. gen. counsel strategic integration and bus. transformation Pentagon, 2007—. Pres. Law Facilities, Inc., Washington, 1982-2005 Vol. parole and probation officer Shawnee County, Kans., 1973-74; citizens adv. task force group Md. Nat. Park and Planning Commn., 1978-80; citizens task force on gen. plan amendments study Fairfax County Coun., Va., 1981-82; active Seven Corners Task Force, Fairfax County, 1981-82, chmn. transp. and housing subcoms.; pres. Seven Springs Tenants Assn., College Park, Md., 1976-80, Ravenwood Park Citizens Assn., 1981-82; dir. Greenwood Homes, Inc., Fairfax County Dept. Housing and Cmty. Devel., 1983—2005; mem. gala com. Spotlight the Kennedy Ctr., Pres. Adv. Com. on the Arts, 1986-87, Mason Dist. Rep. Com., 1981-91, Fairfax County Young Reps., Fairfax County Rep. Com., 1982—; founding chmn., charter mem. Mason Dist. Jaycees, 1984-86; sec., gen. counsel, bd. dirs. U.S. Assocs. for the Cultural Triangle in Sri Lanka, 1983-90; commr. Consumer Protection Commn., Fairfax County, 1982—, chmn., 1996-97; vice chmn., 2004, towing adv. bd. Fairfax County, 1993-; Ravenwood precinct chmn. Rep. Orgn., Falls Church, 1982-90, 94—2005; bd. dirs. PTA Baileys Elem. Magnet Sch., 1995-99, v.p., 1996-97; spl. litigation coun. Pa. Bush-Cheny '04. Named to Honorable Order Ky. Cols. Mem. ABA, NRA (life), Am. Fedn. Musicians (life, emeritus), Assn. Former Intelligence Officers, Masons (Grand Sword Bearer 1992), The Federalist's Soc., The Heritage Found., Shriners, Tall Cedars, Scottish Rite, Moose, Royal Arch, Rep. Nat., Rep. Nat. Lawyers Assn. (adv. coun.), Rep. Nat. Com. (life), Phi Kappa Phi, Phi Alpha Delta (nat. capital area alumni chpt. justice 1984-86, 94-96) Methodist. Avocation: music. Home: 6315 Anneliese Dr Falls Church VA 22044-1620 Office: Office Gen Counsel US Army 104 Army Pentagon 3C546 Washington DC 20310-0104 Office Phone: 703-695-1277. Business E-Mail: dennis.kirk@hqda.army.mil.

KIRK, DONALD, journalist; b. New Brunswick, NJ, May 7, 1938; s. Rudolf and Clara (Marburg) K.; m. Susanne Smith, May 31, 1965 (div.); m. Emiko Hayashi, Dec. 12, 1985 (div.); children: James Paul, John Winston, Christian Daryl. AB, Princeton U., 1959; MA, U. Chgo., 1965; postgrad. (Ford Found. fellow), Columbia U., 1964—65; LittD (hon.), U. Md., 2004. Reporter Chgo. Sun-Times, 1960—61, N.Y. Post, 1961—64; free lance corr., writer, 1965—; Asia corr. Washington Star, 1967—70; Far East corr. Chgo. Tribune, 1971—74, N.Y. and UN corr., 1975—76; world editor, spl. corr. USA Today, 1982—90; Seoul corr. Internat. Herald Tribune, 1998—2003. Vis. fellow Cornell U., Ithaca, N.Y., 1986-88; Fulbright rschr., Philippines, 1995-96. Author: Wider War: The Struggle for Cambodia, Thailand and Laos, 1971, Tell It To The Dead: Memories of a War, 1975, Korean Dynasty: Hyundai and Chung Ju Yung, 1994, Tell It To The Dead: Stories of a War, 1996, Looted: The Philippines After the Bases, Business Guide to the Philippines, 1998, Korean Crisis: Unraveling of the Miracle in the IMF Era, 2000, Philippines in Crisis, 2005; co-editor: Korea Witness, 2006. Recipient Page One award Chgo. Newspaper Guild, 1960; citations Overseas Press Club, 1967, 72, 73, Best Asia article award 1974; George Polk Meml. award for fgn. reporting, 1975, Fulbright scholar, New Delhi, India, 1962-63; Edward R. Murrow fellow Coun. Fgn. Rels., N.Y.C., 1974-75. Mem. Am. Soc. Journalists and Authors, Soc. Profl. Journalists. Clubs: Nat. Press (Washington); Overseas Press (N.Y.C.); Fgn. Corrs. (Hong Kong); Internat. House of Japan. Home: 4343 Davenport St NW Washington DC 20016-4513

KIRK, DONALD EVAN, electrical engineering educator, dean; b. Balt., Apr. 4, 1937; m. Judith Ann Sand, Sept. 4, 1962; children: Kara Diane, Valerie Susan, Dana Elizabeth. BSEE, Worcester Poly. Inst., 1959; MSEE, Naval Postgrad. Sch., Monterey, Calif., 1961; PhD in Elec. Engring., U. Ill., 1965. From asst. to full prof. Naval Postgrad. Sch., Monterey, Calif., 1965-87; assoc. dean engring. San Jose (Calif.) State U., 1987-90, prof. elec. engring., 1990-93, dean engring., 1994—2002. Vis. scientist MIT Lincoln Lab., Lexington, Mass., 1981-82; program officer NSF, Arlington, Va., 1993-94. Author: Optimal Control Theory: An Introduction, 1970; co-author: First Principles of Discrete Systems and Digital Signal Processing, 1988, Contemporary Linear Systems, 1994. Bd. dirs. Carmel (Calif.) Sanitary Dist., 1973-77. Fellow IEEE, ASEE; mem. Sigma Xi, Tau Beta Pi, Eta Kappa Nu. Personal E-mail: kirkjd@sbcglobal.net.

KIRK, EDGAR LEE, retired musician, educator; b. Harrisburg, Pa., May 28, 1923; s. Arthur Lee and Bertha May (Berthel) K.; m. Ellen Calhoun Gray, June 18, 1947; children: Arthur Lee, Douglas Gray. MusB, Eastman Sch. Music, U. Rochester, 1947, MusM, 1948, PhD, 1957. Mem. faculty Mich. State U., East Lansing, 1948-89, now emeritus, prof. bassoon, chmn. applied music, 1973-89, chmn. grad. studies, 1978-87, dir. admissions dept. music, 1982, assoc. chmn., 1987-88; prof. bassoon Eastman Sch. Music, U. Rochester, summers, 1954-65; instr. bassoon Interlochen Arts Acad., 1975-79; ret., 1989. Bassoonist, Rochester Philharmonic Orch., NY, 1946-47, 54-55, staff bassoonist, radio sta. WHAM, Rochester, 1947-48, 1st bassoonist, Lansing Symphony Orch., Mich., 1960-73, 87-89, mem., Richards Woodwind Quintet, 1965-88; Rec. artist: Wind Quintets of Peter Muller, Crystal Records, Anton Reicha, Wind Quintets Opus 99, No. 2 and Opus 100, No. 6, Mus. Heritage Soc. With U.S. Army, 1943-46. Mem. Internat. Double Reed Soc. (pres. 1973-74) Home: 1281 Scott Dr East Lansing MI 48823-5213 Business E-Mail: kirk1@msu.edu.

KIRK, JILL, management consultant; BA, U. Oreg. Corp. dir. human resources/orgnl. devel. Tektonix, Inc., group human resources mgr.; dir. cmty. affairs Tektronix, Inc., 1994; exec. dir. Tektronix Found., 1991; founder The Kirk Group LLC, 1999—; ptnr. Lindberg/Kirk/Millar, 2000—; v.p. Oreg. Bus. Coun., 2005—. Mem. bd. dirs., exec. bd., govt. affairs com. Am. Electronics Assn.; bd. dirs. Associated Oreg. Industries; chair deputies com. Oreg. Bus. Coun., vice chair edn. com., mem. higher edn. task force, mem. pub. fin. com. Mem. Oreg. State Bd. Edn., 1996—, chairperson, 2001—, mem. exec. com., mem. joint bds. working group, mem. econ. devel. joint bds. working group; trustee Portland Art Mus., 1998—2001, 2001—; mem. adv. com. Portland Ctr. for the Performing Arts; bd. dirs. Portland Youth Philharm.; mem. strategic planning com. United Way Columbia-Willamette; active Oreg. Profl. Devel. Coun.; bd. chair Lintner Ctr. for Advanced Edn.; active Govs. Task Force on Higher Edn., Govs. Task Force on Quality Edn.; bd. dirs. Japanese Garden Soc., 2001, STARS, Portland Edn. Network, N.W. Bus. for Culture and the Arts, Nat. Alliance Bus. Western Region. Mem.: Portland C. of C. (bd. dirs.). Office: Oreg Bus Coun 1100 SW 6th Ave Ste 1608 Portland OR 97204-1090

KIRK, JOHN MACGREGOR, lawyer; b. Flint, Mich., Mar. 9, 1938; s. R. Dean and Berenice E. (Mac Gregor) K.; m. Carol Lasko, June 8, 1971; children: John M. Jr., Caroline Dwyer. BA, Washington & Lee U., 1960, LLB, 1962; LLM in Taxation, NYU, 1967. Bar: Mich. 1962, U.S. Ct. Mil. Appeals 1966, U.S. Supreme Ct. 1966, U.S. Tax Ct. 1969, U.S. Dist. Ct. (ea. dist.) Mich. 1982, U.S. Ct. Appeals (6th cir.) 1983. Trial atty. tax divsn. U.S. Dept. Justice, Washington, 1967-72; assoc. Boyer & Briggs, Bloomfield Hills, Mich., 1972-74; ptnr. Butzel, Long, Gust, Klein & Van Zile, Detroit, 1975-78; mem. Meyer, Kirk, Snyder & Lynch P.L.L.C., Bloomfield Hills, 1978—. Mem., past pres. Friends of Baldwin Pub. Libr., Birmingham, Mich., 1972—. Mem. ABA, State Bar Mich., Oakland County Bar Assn., Detroit Bar Assn., Birmingham Rotary, Walloon Yacht Club (treas., past commodore 1960-2004). Republican. Presbyterian. Home: 4350 Yale Ct Bloomfield Hills MI 48302-1669 Office: Meyer Kirk Snyder and Lynch PLLC 100 W Long Lake Rd Ste 100 Bloomfield Hills MI 48304-2773 E-mail: jkirk@meyerkirk.com.

KIRK, JOHN ROBERT, JR., retired lawyer, consultant; b. Stuart, Va., June 21, 1935; s. John Robert and Mary Elise (Mustaine) K.; m. Margarite Conover Kirk; children: Karen Louise, Laura Elise, Rebecca Elizabeth. Student, Rice Inst., 1953-56; BSChemE, U. Tex., 1959; JD, U. Houston, 1966. Bar: Tex. 1966, U.S. Patent and Trademark Office 1967, U.S. Supreme Ct. 1973, U.S. Dist. Ct. (so. dist.) Tex. 1974, U.S. Ct. Claims 1975, U.S. Dist. Ct. (no. dist.) Tex. 1977, U.S. Ct. Appeals (5th cir.) 1980, U.S. Ct. Appeals (11th cir.) 1981, U.S. Ct. Appeals (Fed. cir.) 1983. Patent atty. Jefferson Chem. Co., Houston, 1966-69, mgr. patent divsn., 1969-72; mem. Pravel, Gambrell, Hewitt, Kirk & Kimball, P.C., Houston, 1972-84, ptnr., 1973-84, Baker & Kirk, P.C., 1984-87, Baker, Kirk & Bissex, P.C., 1987-90, Baker, Kirk & Lindsay, P.C., 1990-93, Jenkens & Gilchrist, 1993—2006, ret., 2007. Cons. in field. Dir. Nat. Inventors Hall of Fame Found, Inc., 1979-82, 87-97, treas., 1983-84, v.p., 1984-86, pres., 1986-87; adv. bd. Intellectual Property Law Program U. Houston, 1991-2000, John Marshall Law Sch., 1999—, chair; adv. bd. Gulf Coast Regional Small Bus. Devel. Ctr., 1994-2004, Tex. Mfg. Assistance Ctr., Inc., 1995-2005. Lt. USMCR, 1958-60. Fellow: Coll. State Bar Tex., Houston Bar Found. (life), Tex. Bar Found. (life); mem.: ABA (com. chmn. 1982—90, intellectual property law sect. coun. 1990—94, vice chmn. 1994—95, chmn. 1996—97, com. chmn. sect. on specialization 2002—03, standing com. on specialization 2002—05), Am. Intellectual Property Law Assn., State Bar Tex. (chair intellectual property law sect. 1977—78), Nat. Inventive Thinking Assn. (adv. dir. 1990—2000), Licensing Exec. Soc., Houston Bar Assn., Houston Intellectual Property Law Assn. (bd. govs. 1986—92, pres. 1990—91), Commn. of Patents Edn. Roundtable (commr. 1987—95), Nat. Coun. Intellectual Property Law Assns. (vice chmn. 1986—87, chmn. 1987—88), Lakeside Country Club. Republican. Baptist. Personal E-mail: jkirk@msn.com.

KIRK, JUDD, real estate development executive; b. Salt Lake City, Apr. 29, 1945; s. George and Mary Kirk; m. Barbara Sharon Almvig, June 15, 1968; children: Lisa, Jon. BA in fin., U. Wash., 1967; JD, Harvard U., 1970. Bar: Wash. 1970. Ptnr. Davis, Wright & Jones, Seattle, 1970-86; pres. Skinner Devel. Co., Seattle, 1986-90, Port Blakely Communities, Seattle, 1990—. Vestryman, treas., St. Stephens Ch., Seattle, 1983-86; pres. bd. dirs., Epiphany Sch., Seattle, 1984-86. Mem. ABA, Wash. State Bar Assn. (chmn. real property, probate and trust sect. 1980-81), Urban Land Inst., Nat. Assn. Indsl. and Office Parks, Am. Coll. Real Estate Lawyers, Kirkland C. of C. (bd. dirs. 1987-90), U. Wash. Alumni Assn. (trustee 1989-97, pres., 1995-96), Issaquah C. of C. (bd. dirs. 1991—, pres. 1997-98), bd. Cascade Land Conservancy. Office: Port Blakely Communities 1325 4th Ave 10th Fl Seattle WA 98101 Office Phone: 206-624-5810. Office Fax: 206-624-9745.

KIRK, LINDA LOUISE, elementary school educator; b. Pitts., Mar. 29, 1958; d. Robert and Marion Di Agostino Kirk. BS in Elem. Edn., Ind. U. Pa., 1980; MEd in Curriculum and Instrn., Calif. U. Pa., 2005. Cert. prin. K-12. Tchr. adv. panel People's Gas Co., Pitts.; after sch. dir. Eastern Area YMCA, Wilmerding, Pa.; 2d and 3d grade math. specialist St. Bernadette Sch., Monroeville, Pa.; elem. tchr. Diocese Pitts., 1980—; lead tchr. trainer U. Pitts., 1994—98. Co-author video tapes. Mem.: Assn. Supervision and Curriculum Devel., Nat. Assn. Elem. and Secondary Prins., Pa. Assn. Elem. and Secondary Prins., Nat. Coun. Tchrs. Math., Renewed Inc. Avocations: golf, reading, music. Office: St Bernadette Sch 245 Azalea Dr Wilmerding PA 15148

KIRK, LYNDA POUNDS, biofeedback therapist, neurotherapist, counselor; b. Corpus Christi, Tex., Dec. 17, 1946; d. James Arthur and Elizabeth Pauline (Sanders) Pounds; children: Leslie Jennifer, Edward Christopher. BA, U. Tex., Austin, 1977; MA, St. Edwards U., 1996. Lic. profl. counselor. Therapist Austin (Tex.) State Hosp., 1977-80; dir. stress mgmt. The Hills Med./Sports Complex, Austin, 1980-82; founder, owner Austin Biofeedback Ctr., 1982—, Health Mastery Concepts, Austin, 1982—, Optimal Performance Inst., 2000—; CEO Healthy Life Options, Inc., Austin, 1998—. Cons. State of Tex., Austin, 1983—, City of Austin, 1985—, Lower Colo. River Authority, Austin, 1984—. Author: (book/cassette series) Regenerative Relaxation, 1981; Urological Applications of Biofeedback, Stress Mastery and Peak Performance, 1986. Bd. dirs. South Austin Civic Club, 1983—, pres., 1987; bd. dirs., treas. Texans for the Preservation of Hist. Structures, 1990—; bd. dirs. Austin Ctr. for Attitudinal Healing, 1992—. Fellow Biofeedback Cert. Inst. Am. (sr.), Internat. Soc. for Neuronal Regulation (pres. 1997-98); mem. Assn. Applied Psychophysiology and Biofeedback (pres. 2003-2004, found. bd. 2005), Internat. Soc. for Study of Subtle Energies and Energy Medicine, Biofeedback Soc. Tex. (pres. 1995-97, exec. bd., citation award 1989), Behavioral Medicine Soc. Am., Am. Holistic Med. Assn., Diplomate Cert. Quantitative Electroencephalography Technologists, Acad. Cert. Neurotherapists, Phi Beta Kappa Episcopalian. Avocations: jogging, snorkeling, mountain biking, designs for world peace. Home: 420 Brady Ln Austin TX 78746-5502 Office: Austin Biofeedback Ctr 3624 N Hills Dr Ste B205 Austin TX 78731-3061

KIRK, MARK STEVEN, congressman; b. Champaign, Ill., Sept. 15, 1959; s. Francis Gabriel and Judith Ann (Brady) Kirk; m. Kimberly Vertolli. BA, Cornell U., 1981; MS, London Sch. of Econs., 1982; JD, Georgetown U., 1992. Bar: Ill. 1992, D.C. 1993. Parliamentary aide Julian Critchley, London, 1982-83; chief of staff US Rep. John Porter, Washington, 1984-90; officer World Bank, Washington, 1990; spl. asst. to asst. sec. of state US Dept. State, Washington, 1991-93; atty. Baker & McKenzie, Washington, 1993-95; counsel Ho. Internat. Rels. Com., Washington, 1995-99; mem. US Congress from 10th Ill. dist., Washington, 2001—; mem. armed svcs. com., transp. and infrastructure com., budget com.; mem. Ho. appropriations com. Bd. dirs. Population Resource Ctr., Princeton, NJ. Contbr. articles to various newspapers. Organizer Bush/Quayle Campaign, No. Ill., 1988, Dole for Pres., 1988, various states; campaigner Porter for Congress, No. Ill., 1984-90. Lt. USNR, 1989—. Kellogg Fellow, Chgo., 1980, Radm James Fellow, Washington, 1984; recipient Coun. of Jewish Fedn. award Washington, 1988. Mem. Navy League, Naval Res. Assn., New Trier Rep. Orgn. Republican. Presbyterian. Avocations: backpacking, skydiving. Office: US House Reps 1531 Longworth House Office Bldg Washington DC 20515-1310 Home: 275 Whistler Rd Highland Park IL 60035-5947*

KIRK, NANCY A., state legislator, nursing home administrator; m. Henry Kirk. BS, Ill. State U., 1964; MSW, U. Kans., 1976. Nursing home adminstr.; mem. from dist. 56 Kans. State Ho. of Reps., Topeka. Address: 932 SW Frazier Ave Topeka KS 66606-1948

KIRK, PATRICK LAINE, lawyer; b. South Bend, Ind., May 12, 1948; s. Jerry W. and Vivian E. (Evans) K.; m. Cheryl A. Ensminger, Dec. 30, 1967; children: Kevin P., Travis S. BA, Valparaiso U., 1970, JD, 1973. Bar: N.Y. 1974, U.S. Dist. Ct. (no. dist.) N.Y. 1977, U.S. Supreme Ct. 1986. Ptnr. Grilli & Kirk, Herkimer, N.Y., 1974-89; asst. dist. atty. Herkimer County, Herkimer, N.Y., 1976-78, chief asst. dist. atty., 1978-86, 1978-86, dist. atty., 1986-91, county judge and county surrogate, 1992—; acting justice Supreme Ct. of N.Y., 1997—; judge Herkimer County Treatment Ct., 2003—. Counsel Herkimer Ctrl. Sch., 1974-76; asst. counsel Village of Herkimer, N.Y., 1981-89; lectr. Police Tng. Sch., Utica, N.Y., 1979-91, Arson Seminar, 1987, Rape Crisis Tng.; tchr. Herkimer County C.C., 1981; criminal justice com. Nat. Conf. State Trial Ct. Judges. Advisor Law Explorer Post, Herkimer, 1974-76; bd. dirs. Martin Luther Home, Clinton, N.Y., 1980, Herkimer County Drug Task Force; chmn. sect. Mohawk Valley United Fund, Ilion, N.Y., 1985; mem. Arson Task Force, 1986-91. Mem. ABA (N.Y. del. to nat. conf. of spl. court judges 1995), N.Y. State Bar Assn. (jud. adminstrn. com.), Internat. Narcotics Enforcement Officers Assn., Drug Enforcement Assn. N.Y. (v.p. 1990-91), N.Y. State County Judges Assn., N.Y. State Surrogate Judges Assn., Am. Judges Assn., Elks. Republican. Lutheran. Home: 840 W German St Herkimer NY 13350-2136 Office: Herkimer County Facility 301 N Washington St Herkimer NY 13350 Office Phone: 315-867-1171. Business E-Mail: pkirk@courts.state.ny.us.

KIRK, REA HELENE (REA HELENE GLAZER), special education educator; b. NYC, Nov. 17, 1944; d. Benjamin and Lillian (Kellis) Glazer; 3 stepchildren. BA, UCLA, 1966; MA, Ea. Mont. Coll., 1981; EdD, U. So. Calif., 1985. Cert. spl. edn. tchr. Calif., Mont. Tchr. spl. edn., LA, 1966—73; clin. sec. speech and lang. clinic Missoula, Mont., 1973—75; tchr. spl. edn. Missoula, Gt. Falls, Mont., 1975—82; br. mgr. YWCA LA, Beverly Hills, Calif., 1989—91; sch. adminstrn., ednl. coord. Adv. Schs. Calif., 1991—94; dir. Woman's Resource Ctr., Gt. Falls, 1981—82, Battered Woman's Shelter, Rock Springs, Wyo., 1982—84, Battered Woman's Program, Sweetwater County, Wyo., 1984—88, San Gabriel Valley, Calif., 1988; with Spl. Edn., Pasadena, 1994—96, prin., 1995; from asst. prof. to prof. U. Wis., Platteville, 1996—2007, prof., 2007—. Mem. Wyo. Commn. Aging, Rock Springs; vis. prof. U. Wuhan, China, 2003—04, Miss. Valley State U., Itta Bena, 2005; adv. bd. New Tchr. Advocate; sec. faculty senate U. Wis., Platteville, 2005—06. Pres., bd. dirs. Battered Women's Shelter, Gt. Falls; founder, advisor Rape Action Line, Gt. Falls; 4-H leader; hostess Friendship Force, amb. Wyo., Germany, Italy; v.p. Coun. Devel. Disabilities, Wis.; bd. dirs. Coun. Children with Behavior Disorders, Wis., Family Advs., Platteville, 1996—; organizer Women's Readers Theater, Platteville; active YWCA, Mont., Wyo., Cmty. Action Bd. City of LA; pres., bd. dirs. religious congregation, Rock Springs; founder Jewish religous svcs., Missoula. Named Advisor of the Yr., U. Wis., 2000, Woman of Yr., U. Wis., Platteville, 2006—07, Significant Wyo. Woman as Social Justice Reformer and Peace Activist, Sweetwater County, Wyo.; recipient honors, Missoula 4-H, Underkoffler Tchg. Excellence award, U. Wis., 2000, honor for Anti-Poverty work, LA Mayor Bradley, Support Staff award, U. Wis., Platteville, 2006; Gladys Byron scholar, U. So. Calif., 1993, Dept. Edn. scholar, 1994. Mem.: Assn. Children with Learning Disabilities (Named Outstanding Mem. 1982), Wis. Assn. Children with Behavior Disorders, Wis. Coun. Exceptional Children (bd. dirs., pres. S.W. region), Wis. Divsn. Mentally Retarded/Developmentally Disabled, Coun. Exceptional Children (v.p. Gt. Falls 1981—82, bd. dirs., Professionally Recognized Spl. Educator 1998), Pioneer Svc. Club (adv.), Pi Lambda Theta, Kappa Delta Pi (co-counselor 2000—, sec. 2002—), Phi Kappa Phi, Delta Kappa Gamma (sec. 2002—06). Office Phone: 608-342-1279. Business E-Mail: kirkr@uwplatt.edu.

KIRK, RICHARD DILLON, lawyer; b. Washington, Jan. 23, 1953; s. William Edward and Mary Elizabeth (Dillon) K.; m. Bridget Louise Stillwagon, June 27, 1981; children: Catherine Dillon, Suzanne Grace. AB, Georgetown U., 1975; JD, U. Va., 1978. Bar: Del. 1978, U.S. Dist. Ct. Del. 1980, U.S. Ct. Appeals (3rd cir.) 1984, U.S. Supreme Ct. 1984. Law clk. Del. Supreme Ct., Wilmington, 1978-79; assoc. Richards, Layton & Finger, Wilmington, 1979-82; dep. atty. gen. Del. Dept. Justice, Wilmington, 1982-84; assoc. Morris, James, Hitchens & Williams, Wilmington, 1984-86, ptnr., 1987—. Mem. Del. State Bar Assn. (pres. 1993-94, New Lawyers Disting. Svc. award 1988). Democrat. Roman Catholic. Office: Morris James Hitchens & Williams 222 Delaware Ave Wilmington DE 19801-1621 E-mail: rkirk@morrisjames.com.

KIRK, SHERWOOD, retired librarian; b. Kermit, W.Va., July 12, 1924; s. James Douglas and Magdalene (Elkins) Kirk; m. Ora Ward, Jan. 9, 1958; children: Diana, James Sherwood, Philip Lindsey. Student, Mich. State U., East Lansing, 1944; AB, U. Ky., Lexington, 1949; postgrad., U. Ill., Arbora, 1949—50. Student asst. U. Ky., 1946-49; circulation asst. U. Ill., 1949-51; head reference and circulation Marshall U., 1951-52; sr. asst., agrl. libr. U. Neb., 1952-54; spl. project asst. Nat. Agr. Libr., Washington, 1954-55; reference asst., liaison loan div. Libr. Congress, 1955-56, catalog asst., 1956-57; coord. pub. libr. svcs. Ky. Dept. Librs., Frankfort, 1957-63, asst. state libr., 1963-69; state libr. Fla., 1969-71; assoc. dir. libr. ops. Ill. State Libr., Springfield, 1971-82; exec. dir. Western Ill. Libr. System, Monmouth, 1982-94; delivery cons. Alliance Libr. Sys., 1994-95, Galesburg, Ill., 1994-95; ret., 1995. Mem. Ky. Gov.'s Planning Com. Librs., 1968; scholarship com. Ill. State Libr.; chmn. com. libr. svc. to state govt. Fla. Sec. of State, 1970; pres. Ill. Book Pac; vol. cataloger Bartow Fla. Pub. Libr.; adv. com. libr. svcs. and constrn. Fla. State Libr.; sec., adv. com. edn. Resource Sharing Alliance W. Ctrl. Ill.; bd. dirs. Friends of Lincoln Libr., Springfield, Ill., 1977—, Aledo-Mercer Carnegie Pub. Libr. Dist., 1997—. Recipient plaques for outstanding libr., Ky. Libr. Trustee Assn., 1968. Mem.: ALA (coun. 1967—69), Assn. State Libr. Agys. (administrv. bd.), Ill. Libr. Assn. (chmn. local arrangement 1974, mem. bicentennial com. 1974—, mem. legis.-libr. devel. com., chair pub. policy com. 1991, Robert R. McClarren Legis. award 1990), Fla. Libr. Assn., Ky. Libr. Assn. (pres. 1965—66), Springfield Lit. Club (pres. 1972), Optimist, Shriners, Masons. Home: 527 Eastlake Dr Haines City FL 33844-6339 Personal E-mail: kirk@ithink.net, sherd@copper.net.

KIRK, SUSANNE SMITH, editor; b. Washington; d. Harold Clair and Theodora Smith; m. Donald Kirk, 1965 (div. 1985); m. Samuel Alexander Tomlinson III, 1989. Student, Kaiserin-Theophanu Sch., Cologne, W.Ger., 1958; AB, Smith Coll., 1963; cert., Goethe Inst., Berlin, 1963; MS, Columbia U., 1965. Reporter South China Morning Post, Hong Kong, 1965-67; corr. German News Agy., Saigon, Vietnam, 1968-69; editor Charles Tuttle Pubs., Tokyo, 1972-74; freelance journalist, 1965-74; asst. editor Charles Scribner's Sons (now Scribner div. Simon & Schuster), NYC, 1975, editor, 1976-80, asst. v.p., 1977-98, fgn. rights dir., 1978-82, sr. editor, 1980-85, exec. editor, 1985—2004, v.p., exec. editor, 1998—2004, editl. cons., 2004—. Spkr. various writers' confs. Contbr. articles to newspapers. Mem. Mystery Writers Am. (Ellery Queen award 2000), Crime Writers Assn. (U.K.), Internat. Assn. Crime Writers, Snarks Ltd. (N.Y.C., v.p. 1983-84, pres. 1985-86), Columbia Club, Pilgrimage Garden Club (Natchez), Smith Coll. Club (N.Y.C.). Home: PO Box 2056 Natchez MS 39121-2056 Personal E-mail: suskirk@aol.com.

KIRK, TERRENCE, lawyer; b. Austin, Tex., Feb. 3, 1950; s. E.J. and Maryann Kirk. B in English, U. Tex., 1978, JD, 1982. Bar: Tex. 1992, bd. cert. criminal law:. Briefing atty. Tex. Ct. Criminal Appeals, Austin, 1982—83; assoc. Minton, Burton, Foster & Collins, Austin, 1983—83, Law Offices of Joseph A. Turner, P.C., Austin, 1985—99; pvt. practice Austin, 1999—. Mem. criminal jury charges com. State Bar Tex., spkr. advanced criminal law course, 1995—. Editor: (legal treatise) Meeker's Guide to Arrest, Search and Seizure. Sponsor Montopolis Little League, Austin, 2004—07. Named Tex. Superlawyer, Tex. Monthly, 2004, 2005; named to, Best Lawyers in Am., 2005, 2006; recipient Cora Crawford award-Best Undergraduate in English Dept., U. Tex. English Dept., 1978. Mem.: Tex. Assn. Criminal Def. Lawyers (Presdl. award for Contbns. to Amicus Com.). Socialist. Zen. Avocations: chess, movies & acting, travel, Yankees baseball, Notre Dame football. Office: Law Office of Terrence W Kirk 600 West 13th St Austin TX 78701 Office Phone: 512-236-8511. Office Fax: 512-476-5346. Personal E-mail: terry_kirk@sbcglobal.net. Business E-Mail: tkirk@defenselawyer.net.

KIRK, TERRI G., library media specialist; m. Dale Kirk; children: Chad, Dylan, Nora. B in Libr. Sci. and History, Western Ky. U.; M in History, Murray State U., Rank I in Sch. Adminstrn. Libr. media specialist Reidland High Sch., Paducah, Ky. Mem.: AASL (rep. to ALA coun. 2003—, mem. exec. bd., mem. conf. com.), Ky. Edn. Assn., NEA, Ky. Sch. Media Assn. (past pres., chair Eleanor Simmons grant com., Outstanding Sch. Libr. award 2001), ALA (mem. exec. bd. 2006—), Ky. Libr. Assn. (past pres., chair comm.). Avocations: reading, sailing, running, hiking. Office: Reidland High Sch 5349 Benton Rd Paducah KY 42003 Office Phone: 270-538-4225. Office Fax: 270-538-4211. Business E-Mail: terri.kirk@mccracken.kyschools.us.*

KIRK, THOMAS GARRETT, JR., librarian; b. Phila., Aug. 2, 1943; s. Thomas Garrett and Bertha (C.) K.; m. Elizabeth B. Walter, Aug. 29, 1964; children: Jennifer E., Cynthia M., Kristen A. BA, Earlham Coll., Richmond, Ind., 1965; MA, Ind. U., 1969; postgrad., Drexel U., 1987-88. Sci. libr. Earlham Coll., 1965-79; libr. cons. Richmond, Ind., 1972—; acting dir. librs. U. Wis., Parkside, Kenosha, 1979-80; dir. libr. Berea (Ky.) Coll., 1980-94, Earlham (Ind.) Coll., 1994-2000, dir. librs., coord. info. svcs., 2001—. Vis. instr. Ind. U. Libr. Sch., summers 1977, 78; bd. dirs SOLINET, 1981-84, 85-86, treas., 1982-84; bd. dirs. Ky. Libr. Network, 1985-87, 91-93, OCLC Mems. Coun., 1986-92, 1999-2005, exec. com. 2001-02, mem. standing joint com. on membership, 2003-05, mem. fin. com., 2003—05; v.p. Pvt. Acad. Libr. Network Ind., 1995-96, pres., 1996-97, 2005-06, OCLC Strategic Directions and Governance Adv. Com., 2000-01; adv. bd. OCLC Coll. and Univ. Librs., 1995-98. Author: Library Research Guide to Biology, 1978, College Libraries in Encyclopedia Library of Information Science, 2003; editor: Course-related Library and Literature Instruction, 1979, Increasing the Teaching Role of Academic Libraries, 1984; editl. bd. Coll. and Rsch. Librs., 1996-2002, Internet Reference Svcs. Quar., 1996-2002. Bd. dirs. Coll. Libr. Dirs. Mentor Program, 2002—; mem. midwest adv. com. NITLE, 2002—; mem. exec. com. Acad. Librs. Ind., 2003—05; sr. advisor Coun. Ind. Colls., 2003—. Mem. ALA (coun. 1986-90), Assn. Coll. Rsch. Librs. (v.p., pres.-elect 1992-93, pres. 1993-94, exec. com. 1984-85, 86-90, 92-95, rep. to Coalition for Networked Info. 1990-95, info. literacy adv. com. 2000-2002, Miriam Dudley Bibliog. Instrn. Libr. of Yr. award 1984, Acad./Rsch. Libr. of Yr. 2004), Inst. for Info. Literacy (adv. com. 1998-2003, chair 2001-03), Ind. Libr. Fedn., Ind. Coop. Libr. Svcs. Authority (exec. com. 1999-2001), Ky. Libr. Assn. (Acad. Libr. of Yr. award 1984), Phi Kappa Phi. Mem. Soc. Of Friends. Office: Earlham Coll Lilly Libr Richmond IN 47374 Office Phone: 765-983-1360. Business E-Mail: kirkto@earlham.edu.

KIRKBY, MAURICE ANTHONY, oil industry executive; b. Southwell, Notts, U.K., Apr. 12, 1929; emigrated to Can., 1983; s. George Sydney and Rose (Marson) K.; m. Muriel Beatrice Longmire, 1954; children: Peter Michael, Susan Margaret. BA with 1st class honors in Mech. Sci., King's Coll., Cambridge, Eng., 1952, MA, 1955. Chief petroleum engr. Brit. Petroleum Co. p.l.c., London, 1969-74, gen. mgr. exploration and prodn. dept., 1976-80, dirs.' support staff, 1982-83; gen. mgr. BP Petroleum Devel., Aberdeen, Scotland, 1974-76; sr. v.p. oil and gas Standard Oil Co., Cleve., 1980-82; pres., chief exec. officer, dir. BP Can. Inc., Calgary, Alta., Can., 1983-88; chmn., chief exec. officer Hope Brook Gold Inc., Calgary, Alta., Can., 1986-88; dep. chmn. N.Am. Gas Investment Trust, London, 1989-95. Contbr. articles to profl. jours. Mem. Bus. Council on Nat. Issues, Ottawa, Ont., Can., 1983-88. Served with RAF, 1947-49. Fellow Inst. Mining and Metallurgy (dir. 1980), Royal Acad. Engring.; mem. Inst. Mech. Engrs., Soc. Petroleum Engrs. (dir. 1980, 81-83).

KIRK-DUGGAN, MICHAEL ALLAN, retired law, economics and computer sciences educator; b. Stevens Point, Wis., Dec. 15, 1931; s. Frank E. and Dorothy Ada (Darrow) Duggan; m. Shirley M. Spencer, July 1956 (div. Jan. 1981); children: Michelle, Cheryl, Michael, Christopher, Robert, Siobhan, Mary; m. Cheryl Ann Kirk, Jan. 1, 1983. BS in Math., Coll. Holy Cross, 1953; postgrad., U. Minn., 1953—55; JD, LLB, Boston Coll., 1956; M in Patent Law, Georgetown U., 1959. Bar: Mass. 1956, U.S. Supreme Ct. 1961; qualified trial/def. counsel Gen. Cts. Martial, 1965; cert. cmty. based conflict resolution, 1994. Sr. engr. Sylvania Programming Lab., Needham, Mass., 1960—61; trial atty. antitrust divsn. U.S. Dept. Justice, 1961—67; asst. prof. econs. Whittemore Sch. U. N.H., Durham, 1967—69; comdr. U.S. Naval Intelligence Res., 1956—78; adminstrv. judge Atomic Safety and Licensing Bd. Panel, Washington, 1972—89; prof. bus. law and computer scis. U. Tex., Austin, 1969—93, prof. emeritus, 1993—. Apptd. adv. procurator Tribunal, Diocese of Raleigh, 1995-97, 2004—; editor-in-chief Computing Revs., N.Y.C., 1969-74. Author: Antitrust & U.S. Supreme Court, 1829-1984, 1984, Computer Utility, 1972, Law and the Computer, 1973, Paul Robeson Movies and Discography, 1998, Annulments & Divorce for Practicing Catholics, Bibliograph, 2006, Amazon Reviews, Bibliographies, 2006; editor: Legal Developments, Jour. Mktg., 1967-93, Legal Comments; contbr. articles to profl. jours. Head profs. Johnson, Durham, 1968; vol. IRS Vol. Income Tax Assistance, 1993—97; del. Tex. Dem. Com., Austin, Tex., 1972; eucharistic min., lector and lay pres. St. Columba Cath. Ch., Oakland, Calif., 1997—2004, Holy Cross Cath. Ch., Durham, NC, 1993—97, 2004—. Mem.: Mensa, Friend of Bill W. Democrat. Avocations: computers, photography, singing. Home: 5117 Spoolin Ct Raleigh NC 27604-6126 Office Phone: 919-250-9272. Personal E-mail: mkirkduggan@nc.rr.com.

KIRKGAARD, VALERIE ANNE, media group executive, radio host, writer, radio producer, consultant; b. Merced, Calif., Aug. 18, 1940; d. Basil Stuart and Audrey (Thompson) Coghlan; m. Alonzo Bryson Kirkgaard, Oct. 6, 1962 (div. Aug. 1983); children: Jennifer Alexandra, John Erik. AA, Santa Monica City Coll., 1961; BA, UCLA, 1968; M in Counseling, Goddard Coll., LA, 1982; M in Enlightenment, Sci. of Mind Ch., San Diego, 1992; PhD (hon.), Harrington U., 1999. Bd. and care organizer Norwalk State Hosp., LA, 1976-78; liaison to bd. dirs. Gay and Lesbian Cmty. Svcs. Ctr., 1976—79; therapist in pvt. practice Kirkgaard & Assocs, Pasadena, Pacific Palisades, Santa Monica, Calif., 1975—; pvt. practice relationship cons., 1976—; CEO Kirkgaard Media. Ear coning educator, mfr., 1992—; prodr., host radio and TV Waking Up In America, 1987—, Vital Issues, 2006—; radio prodr. Terry Cole Whittaker; radio prodr., host Open Forum, Waking Up In America, 2 programs for KFNX, Phoenix, KTBL, Albuquerque, WHLD, WMNY, Buffalo; spkr. in field. Author: Breakfast At Bob's, 1982, Take Two Breaths and Call Me in the Morning, 1988, environ. editor United Fitness Mag., 1992; columnist Hollywood Times, 1976, Century City News, 1990-92, Topanga Messenger, 1996—; contbr. articles to profl. jours.; inventor in field. Founder Golden Hearts Found. Olympic Torch bearer, 1984. Mem. Calif. Assn. Marriage Family and Child Counselors, Women's Mus. Art, LA County Mus. Art, World Vision, State of the World Forum, The Hunger Project, Mus. of Tolerance, Greater LA Press Club, Scriptwriters Network, Pacific Palisades C. of C., Roar Found., Global Security Inst. Avocations: horseback riding, hiking, reading, gardening. Home: 19733 Sunset Trl Topanga CA 90290 Office: Kirkgaard & Assocs 869 Via De La Paz Ste F

Pacific Palisades CA 90272-5202 Home Phone: 310-455-8623; Office Phone: 310-459-4824. Personal E-mail: valerieannekirkgaard@mac.com. Business E-Mail: val@wakingupinamerica.com.

KIRKHAM, D. COLLIER, lawyer; b. Ames, Iowa, May 29, 1947; AB magna cum laude, Harvard Coll., 1969; MS, Stanford Univ., 1971; JD with highest distinction, Univ. Iowa, 1975. Bar: NY 1976. Assoc. Cravath Swaine & Moore LLP, NYC, 1975—82, ptnr., corp., 1982—. Articles editor Iowa Law Rev. Mem.: ABA, NY State Bar Assn. Office: Cravath Swaine Moore LLP Worldwide Plz 825 Eighth Ave New York NY 10019-7475 Office Phone: 212-474-1204. Office Fax: 212-474-3700. Business E-Mail: ckirkham@cravath.com.

KIRKHAM, JAMES ALVIN, manufacturing executive; b. Sumner County, Tenn., June 18, 1935; s. Shirley Barnes and Ouida Redempta (Bursby) Kirkham; m. Shirley Ann Clouse, Sept. 3, 1954; children: Denise Anne, James Alvin II, Hughe Allan. Welder Ind. Wire Co., 1952-54; driver Arthur Lowe Cigar & Candy Co., 1954-56; time study Insley Mfg. Co., 1957; salesman Am. Chicle Co., 1958-59; mgr. Ace Battery, Inc., Indpls., 1967—; v.p. L. P. Industries, Inc., Indpls., 1977—; pres. Rubber Recycling Corp., 1989—; ptnr. TKT Leasing, Indpls., 1978—, LDJ Leasing, Indpls., 1979—, Vets. Interstate Plan, Inc. Chmn. fundraising equestrian events 10th Pan Am. Games; sec. Johnson County Pk. Bd.; bd. dirs. English Ave. Boys Club, State 4-H Horse and Pony Orgn.; pres. bd. dirs. Ind. Horse Coun. Found., Inc.; pres. PTO Clark Twp. Sch. Dist.; v.p. Johnson County 4-H Fairboard; active Boy Scouts Am.; treas. Ind. Horse Coun. Inc. Named Outstanding Show Mgr., Ind. State Fair, 1971; named to Ind. Horseman Hall of Fame, 1998; recipient Golden Boy award, Indpls. Boys Club Alumni Assn., 1970. Mem.: Indpls. Motor Truck Assn., Ind. Motor Truck Assn., Ind. Saddle Horse Assn., Am. Horse Show Assn., Indpls. C. of C., U.S. C. of C., Ind. Shetland Pony Breeders Club, Ind. Pony Am. Club, Am. Hackney Club, Ind. Pony Exhibitors Club, Moose, Shriners, Masons. Home: 1213 N Matthews Rd Greenwood IN 46143-8343 Office: 2166 Bluff Rd Indianapolis IN 46225-1983 Office Phone: 317-786-2717. Personal E-mail: jakirkham@sbcglobal.net.

KIRKHAM, JOHN SPENCER, lawyer, director; b. Salt Lake City, Aug. 29, 1944; s. Elbert C. and Emma Kirkham; m. Janet L. Eatough, Sept. 16, 1966; children: Darcy, Jeff, Kristie. BA with honors, U. Utah, 1968, JD, 1971. Bar: Utah 1971, U.S. Dist. Ct. Utah 1971, U.S. Ct. Appeals (10th cir.) 1990, U.S. Supreme Ct. 1991. Assoc. Senior & Senior, Salt Lake City, 1971-73; ptnr. VanCott, Bagley, Cornwall & McCarthy, Salt Lake City, 1973-92, Stoel Rives LLP, Salt Lake City, 1992—. Mem. exec. bd. Great Salt Lake coun. Boy Scouts Am., 1987—, exec. com. v.p. legal, 2003-06, pres., 2006—; mem. Utah Statewide Resource Adv. Coun., 1995-97; trustee Met. Water Dist. Salt Lake and Sandy, 2003; mem. bd. govs. Salt Lake Chamber, 2005-. Mem. Utah Bar Assn., Utah Mining Assn. (bd. dirs. Salt Lake City chpt. 1987—), Rocky Mountain Mineral Law Found. (trustee 1989-92). Republican. Mem. Lds Ch. Office: Stoel Rives LLP 201 S Main St Ste 1100 Salt Lake City UT 84111-4904 Office Phone: 801-328-3131. Business E-Mail: jskirkham@stoel.com.

KIRKHAM, M. B., plant physiologist, educator; b. Cedar Rapids, Iowa; d. Don and Mary Elizabeth (Erwin) K. BA with honors, Wellesley Coll.; MS, PhD, U. Wis. Cert. profl. agronomist. Plant physiologist U.S. EPA, Cin., 1973-74; asst. prof. U. Mass., Amherst, 1974-76, Okla. State U., Stillwater, 1976-80; from assoc. prof. to prof. Kans. State U., Manhattan, 1980—. Guest lectr. Inst. Water Conservancy and Hydroelectric Power Rsch., Inst. Farm Irrigation Rsch., China, 1985, Inst. Exptl. Agronomy, Italy, 1989, Agrl. U. Wageningen, Inst. for Soil Fertility, Haren, Netherlands, 1991, Massey U., New Zealand, 1991, Lincoln U., New Zealand, 1998, Environ. and Risk Mgmt. Group Hort. Rsch., 1998, Palmerston North, New Zealand, 1998, U. Hannover, Germany, 2003; William A. Albrecht seminar spkr. U. Mo., 1994; vis. scholar Biol. Labs., Harvard U., 1990; vis. scientist environ. physics sect. dept. sci. and indsl. rsch. Palmerston North, 1991, The Hort. and Food Rsch. Inst. New Zealand, Ltd., Crown Rsch. Inst., Palmerston North, 1998, 2005, Landcare Rsch., Lincoln, New Zealand, 1998; mem. peer rev. panel USDA/Nat. Rsch. Initiative, Washington, 1994; mem. rev. panel USDA Office Sci. Quality Rev. Water Quality Nat. Program, 2001; apptd. mem. US Nat. Com. for Soil Sci. of NAS, 2001—04; participant confs. and symposia; spkr., presenter in field. Author: Principles of Soil and Plant Water Relations, 2005; editor: Water Use in Crop Production, 1999; co-editor (with I.K. Iskander): Trace Elements in Soil, 2001; cons. editor Plant and Soil Jour., 1979—2005, mem. editl. bd. BioCycle, 1978—82, Field Crops Rsch. Jour., 1983—91, Soil Sci., 1997—, Jour. Crop Improvement, 1996—, Jour. Environ. Quality, 2002—, Crop Sci., 2004—, mem. editl. adv. bd. Internat. Agrophysics, 2000—, Australia Jour. Soil Rsch., 2004—; contbr. more than 220 articles and papers to sci. jours. Recipient Best Reviewer award, Water Resources Engring. divsn. Jour. Irrigation and Drainage Engring., ASCE, 1996, grad. faculty tchg. award, Coll. of Agr., Kansas State Univ., 2001; grantee, NSF, USDA, US Dept. Energy, Kans. Ctr. Agrl. Resources and the Environ., Manhattan; NSF postdoctoral fellow, U. Wis., 1971—73, NDEA fellow, E.I. du Pont de Nemours and Co. summer faculty fellow, 1976. Fellow: AAAS, Crop Sci. Soc. Am. (editl. bd. 1980—84, 2004—, chair crop physiology and metabolism divsn. 2007), Royal Meteorol. Soc., Soil Sci. Soc. Am. (travel grantee to internat. congress Japan 1990), Am. Soc. Agronomy (editl. bd. 1985—90); mem.: Am. Chem. Soc., Am. Math. Assn., Am. Phys. Soc., Internat. Assn. Hydrol. Sci., Royal Soc. New Zealand, Internat. Water Resources Assn., Am. Geophys. Union, Internat. Assn. Vegetation Sci., Am. Phytopathol. Soc., Water Environment Fedn., Growth Regulator Soc. Am., Soc. Exptl. Biology (London), NY Acad. Sci., Scandinavian Soc. Plant Physiology, Japanese Soc. Plant Physiology, Soc. Francaise de Physiologie Végétale, Am. Meteorol. Soc., Bot. Soc. Am., Internat. Union Soil Sci. (1st vice chmn. commn. soil physics 1994—98, sec. commn. on soils, food security and human health 2002—), Internat. Soil Tillage Rsch. Orgn., Am. Soc. Hort. Sci., Am. Soc. Plant Physiology (editl. bd. 1982—87), Sigma Xi (sec. chpt. 1997—99, Outstanding Sr. Scientist award 2002), Gamma Sigma Delta (Disting. Faculty award Kan. State U. chpt. 2001), Phi Kappa Phi (scholar award 2000). Home: 1420 McCain Ln Apt 244 Manhattan KS 66502-4680 Office: Kans State U Dept Agronomy Throckmorton Hall Manhattan KS 66505-5501 Office Phone: 785-532-0422. Business E-Mail: mbk@ksu.edu.

KIRKHART, MATTHEW WAYDE, psychology professor; b. Charleston, W.Va., June 26, 1965; s. Jerry Wilson and Mary Grace Kirkhart; m. Patricia Roberts, Feb. 14, 2003; m. Katherine Kaminsky, Oct. 11, 1992 (div. Apr. 6, 1997). BA, W.Va. U., Morgantown, 1987, MA, 1991; PhD, U. N.C., Greensboro, 1997. Lic. psychologist Bd. Examiners Psychologists, Md., 1999. Asst. prof. Loyola Coll., Balt., 1997—2003, assoc. prof., 2003—. Dir. masters edn. Loyola Coll., 2003—05, dir. undergraduate edn. dept. psychology, 2005—. Author: jour. articles in field of psychology. Recipient Presenter at The Dean's Symposium, Loyola Coll., 2001. Mem.: Md. Psychol. Assn. (assoc.). Methodist. Avocations: tennis, military history, painting. Office: Loyola Coll 4501 N Charles St Baltimore MD 21210-2699 Home Phone: 410-628-4804; Office Phone: 410-617-5498. Business E-Mail: mkirkhart@loyola.edu.

KIRKHORN, LEE-ELLEN CHARLOTTE, community health nurse, educator; b. Kennewick, Wash., Aug. 19, 1956; d. Ernest Arnold and Ellen Lillian Mathilda (Landstrom) Copstead. ADN, Columbia Basin Coll., 1976; BSN summa cum laude, Wash. State U., 1978; M Nursing, U. Wash., 1979; PhD, Gonzaga U., 1983. Rsch. asst. Wash. State U., Pullman, 1976-77; clinic nurse Profl. Mall, Pullman, 1976-77; charge nurse St. Brendan Nursing Home, Spokane, Wash., 1977-78; rsch. asst. U. Wash., Seattle, 1979; instr. Intercollegiate Ctr. for Nursing Edn., Spokane, 1979-81; pub. health nurse Spokane County Vis. Nurses Assn., 1980, 82, Zion Luth. Ch., Deer Park, Wash., 1993; asst. prof. Intercollegiate Coll. Nursing, Spokane, 1981-85, assoc. prof., 1985—2001; assoc. dean Western Campus U. Wis. Madison Sch. Nursing, 2001—05; assoc. prof. U. Wis., Eau Claire Coll. Nursing and Health Scis., 2005—. Cons., presenter in field; adj. clin. faculty mem. Hawaii Pacific U., Honolulu, 1994; assoc. prof. Intercollegiate Coll. Nursing U. Guam, 1991; external grant reveiwer Alta. Can. Found. for Nursing Rsch., 1991—. Editor: Perspectives on Pathophysiology, 1995, 2001, 05; contbr. articles to profl. publs., chpts. to books; mem. editl. bd. Geriatric Nursing, 1991—; rsch. cons. Spokane Planning Affiliates Network, 1989—; geriatric cons. Nehalem Valley Care Ctr., 1988, Hood River Care Ctr., 1989; expert witness Reed & Giesa, P.S., 1986. Mem. exec. bd., chair grantwriting subcom. Inland Empire br. Nat. Arthritis Found., 1991-2001; team capt. fundraising dr. Am. Heart Assn., 1988-2001; mem. task force on aging Sacred Heart Ctr., 1984-2000; co-leader fund dr. United Way, 1980. Postdoctoral fellow Gerontol. Soc. Am., 1986, 87. Mem. ANA (cert. gerontol. clin. nursing specialist), Am. Mental Health Counselors Assn. (cert. gerontol. counseling trainer), AAUP, Nat. League Nurses, Bus. and Profl. Women, Gerontol. Soc. Am., Internat. Coun. Nurses, Internat. Rehab. Inst., Wash. State Nurses Assn., Wash. State Pub. Health Assn., Inland Empire Nurses Assn. (nominating com. 1981-82), Western Gerontol. Soc., Intercollegiate Ctr. for Nursing Edn. Alumni Assn., Mensa, Sigma Theta Tau (2d v.p. Delta Chi chpt.-at-large). Lutheran. Avocations: photography, people watching, classical music. Home: 1412 Nixon Ave Eau Claire WI 54701-6575 Office: Univ Wisconsin Eau Claire Coll Nursing and Health Scis Eau Claire WI 54701 Office Phone: 715-836-5005. Personal E-mail: lecopstead@aol.com.

KIRKLAND, GEOFFREY ALAN, motion picture production designer; b. Derby, Eng., Oct. 7, 1939; came to U.S., 1980; s. Cyril George and Florence Kathleen Kirkland; m. Elspeth Mary Kennedy, Mar. 23, 1970. AA, Royal Coll. of Art, London, 1961. Designer BBC, London, 1961-66; freelance art dir. London, 1966-75; freelance prodn. designer LA, 1975—. Prodn. designer: (films) Bugsy Malone, 1975 (British Film Academy award, 1975); Midnight Express, 1978; Fame, 1980; Shoot the Moon, 1982; The Right Stuff, 1983 (Academy award nomination best art direction, 1983); Birdy, 1984; Leonard Part 6, 1987; Journey to the Center of the Earth, 1987; Mississippi Burning, 1988; Wildfire, 1989; Come See the Paradise, 1990; Renaissance Man, 1994; Space Jam, 1996; Desperate Measures, 1998; Angela's Ashes, 1998; The Life of David Gale, 2001; After the Sunset, 2001; Glory Road, 2004. E-mail: geoffreykirkland@netzero.com.

KIRKLAND, GEORGE L., oil industry executive; b. Aug. 1950; BS in civil engring., U. Fla., 1972, MS in civil engring., 1974. Constrn. engr. Chevron, New Orleans, 1974—78; with Caltex Pacific Indonesia, Sumatra, 1978—80, project engring. mgr. Duri Steam Flood project, 1980—85; sr. project mgr. Chevron U.S.A. Prodn. Co., Denver and Midland, Tex., 1985—88, San Francisco, 1988—90; group mgr. upstream tech. Chevron Rsch. and Tech. Co., 1990—92; gen. mgr. prodn. Chevron Nigeria Ltd., 1992—96, gen. mgr. asset mgmt., chmn., mng. dir., 1996—2000; pres. Chevron U.S.A. Prodn. Co., 2000; v.p. exploration and prodn. ops. Chevron Corp., 2000—; pres. N.Am. Upstream ChevronTexaco Corp., San Ramon, Calif., 2001—02; pres. ChevronTexaco Overseas Petroleum, San Ramon, Calif., 2002—05; v.p. Chevron Corp., San Ramon, Calif., 2002—05, exec. v.p., upstream & gas, 2005—. Trustee Africa Am. Inst.; bd. dirs. Corp. Coun. on Africa. Mem.: U.S.-Kazakhstan Bus. Assn. (bd. dirs.). Office: ChevronTexaco Corp 6001 Bollinger Canyon Rd San Ramon CA 94583-2324*

KIRKLAND, JOHN C., lawyer; b. Omaha, Nebr., Dec. 28, 1963; s. John and Marilou (Witt) K. AB, Columbia U., 1986; JD, UCLA, 1990. Bar: Calif. 1990. Assoc. Cadwalader Wickersham & Taft, LA, 1990-97; of counsel Weissmann Wolff Bergman Coleman & Silverman, LLP, Beverly Hills, Calif., 1997-2000; ptnr. Brown Raysman Millstein Felder & Steiner LLP, LA, 2000-01; shareholder Greenberg Traurig LLP, LA, 2001—. Bd. dirs. Oaktree Found., Inc. Mem. ABA, L.A. County Bar Assn., Beverly Hills Bar Assn. Home: 754 Swarthmore Ave Pacific Palisades CA 90272-4355 Office: 2450 Colorado Ave Ste 400E Santa Monica CA 90404 E-mail: kirklandj@gtlaw.com.

KIRKLAND, JOHN DAVID, oil and gas company executive; b. McAllen, Tex., June 6, 1933; s. O.D. and Daisy (Donohoe) K.; m. Ann Wales, June 15, 1957 (div. Feb. 1985); children: David, Solace, Robert; m. Kate Sayen, May 15, 1993. BA, Yale U., 1955, LLB, 1958. Bar: Tex. 1958. Atty. Baker, Botts, Shepherd & Coates, Houston, 1958-67; v.p. in charge fin. Pennzoil Co., Houston, 1967-73, exec. v.p., dir., 1973-78; dir. exec. edn. Jones Sch. Mgmt. and Adminstrn. Rice U., Houston, 1978-79; vice chmn., dir. Sandefer Oil & Gas, Inc., Houston, 1980; exec. v.p., dir. Roy M Huffington, Inc., Houston, 1980-86; chmn. Heritage Trust Co., Houston, 1986-89; chmn., CEO Antara Resources Inc., Houston, 1996-2000; chmn. Huntington Exploration, LLP, 2002—. Pres. Houston Ballet Found., 1972-74, trustee, 1979-, chmn., 1979-84; treas., chmn. fin. com. United Way of Houston, 1983-84; trustee Chinquapin Sch., 1991-94; bd. dirs. Houston chpt. Juvenile Diabetes Found., 1995-97; mem. adv. coun. Ctr. for Am. History, U. Tex. at Austin, 2002-. Mem. Tex. Bar Assn. Office: 989 S Post Oak Ln Houston TX 77056-2203 Office Phone: 713-888-0120. Business E-Mail: kirklandjohnd@sbcglobal.net.

KIRKLAND, JOSEPH, voice educator; b. Honey Island, Tex., Oct. 8, 1929; s. Earl Elmo and Frances Alice Kirkland; m. Jessie May Foster, Jan. 20, 1963; 1 child, Audrey. Associates, Lon Morris Coll., 1949; MusB, Centenary Coll., 1956; MusM, New England Conservatory of Music, 1958. Lead tenor Tangelwood Opera, Lenox, Mass., 1958; tenor Neopolitan Sextet, NYC, 1960—61, NBC Opera, NYC, 1961; singer, actor NYC; soloist tenor Grace Episc. Ch., NYC, 1968—72; voice instr. McLean (Va.) Arts Ctr., 2003—04, E. Valley Yamaha Music Sch., Chandler, Ariz., 2005—. Singer: Christian Children's Home, 1976; prodr.(musical dir.): Am. Lyric Theatre, 1988—90; conductor: Nat. Lyric Opera Co., 1987. Judge Mid-Atlantic Songwriters' Competition, 1991—92. Airman USAF, 1950—55, U.S. Recipient Dist. Alumni award, Lon Morris Coll., 1994. Mem.: Nat. Assn. Tchrs. Singing, Bohemians NY Musicians Club, Pi Kappa Lambda. Home: PO Box 67384 Phoenix AZ 85082-7384

KIRKLAND, REBECCA TRENT, endocrinologist; b. Durham, NC, Dec. 27, 1942; d. Josiah Charles Trent and Mary Duke (Biddle) Trent-Semans; m. John Lindsey Kirkland III, June 24, 1965. BA, Duke U., 1964, MD, 1968. Intern Baylor Coll. Medicine, 1968-69, resident in pediatrics, 1969-70, fellow in pediatric endocrinology, 1971-73, asst. prof. dept. pediatrics, 1975-81, assoc. prof., 1981-88, prof., 1988—, sr. assoc. dean med. edn. London, 2000; registrar Guy's Hosp., Hosp. for Sick Children, London, 1970; with U. Pa. Sch. Medicine, 1973-74, fellow, 1974-75. Asst. physician divsn. endocrinology Children's Hosp. Phila., 1973-75; mem. staff Tex. Children's Hosp., 1975—, Harris County Hosp. Dist., 1975—; head ambulatory svcs. Tex. Children's Hosp., 1984—, dir. jr. league outpatient dept., 1984—. Contbr. articles and revs. to profl. jours. Active Leadership Tex., Leadership Houston; pres. Greater Houston Women's Found., 1994—96; bd. dirs. AVANCE, Inc., 1992, YWCA, 1992; trustee Mus. Med. Sci., 1984—88; pres. Josiah C. Trent Meml. Found., Inc., 1983—, v.p., 1977—83; bd. dirs. Am. Leadership Forum, 1991, mem. selection com., 1989, 1990, sec. bd. dirs. Houston/Gulf Coast chpg., 1989, 1990, pres.-elect, 1991, pres., 1991—93; bd. dirs. Mus. Health and Med. Scis., 2001—. NIH fellow, 1971-73; recipient Alumnae award Baldwin Sch., 1983, Disting. Alumni award Durham Acad., 1984, Goodheart Humanitarian award B'nai B'rith, 1986, Disting. Svc. award Duke U. Med. Alumni Assn., 1992, Recognition award Ctr. for Interaction: Man, Sci. and Culture, 1993, One Voice for Children award Tex. Network for Medically Fragile and Chronically-Ill Children, 1993; named one of five Outstanding Women of Yr. Channel 13, Houston, 1984, Woman on the move Houston Post, 1989. Fellow Am. Acad. Pediatrics; mem. Endocrine Soc., Am. Fedn. For Clin. Rsch., So. Soc. for Pediatric Rsch., Lawson-Wilkins Pediatric Endocrine Soc., Houston Pediatric Soc., Tex. Pediatric Soc., Tex. Med. Assn., Soc. for Pediatric Rsch., Pediatric Endocrinology Soc. Tex., Ambulatory Pediatric Assn., Am. Pediatric Soc., Am. Acad. Pediatrics (pediatric endocrine sect.) 1990), Tex. Diabetes and Endocrine Assn. Business E-Mail: rebeccak@bcm.tmc.edu.

KIRKLAND, RICHARD IDE (RIK), JR., magazine editor; b. Ithaca, NY, May 11, 1951; s. Richard Ide and Alice Creel Kirkland; m. Jo ann Fulk, June 4, 1973 (div. 1978); m. Virginia Gonzalez, Jan. 30, 1982; children: Matthew, James, Allegra. BA, Birmingham-So. Coll., 1973; MA, Duke U., 1978. Instr. U. N.C., Greensboro, 1978; reporter Fortune Mag., NYC, 1978-81; writer Fortune, NYC, Washington, 1981-85, European editor London, 1985-89, sr. editor NYC, 1989-95, asst. mng. editor, 1995, dep. mng. editor, 1996-2001; dep. mng. editor Bus. Info. Group Time Inc., 1997—98; mng. editor Fortune, NYC, 2001—05, global editor, 2005—. Named Outstanding Student Ala., Birmingham News, 1969, Distinguished Alumnus, Birmingham-So. Coll., 1999. Mem. Am. Soc. Mag. Execs., Coun. Fgn. Rels. Avocations: rhythm & blues guitar (in band the Prowlers), reading, gardening, hiking.

KIRKLAND, RONALD E., insurance company executive; children: Michael S., Jonathan S. Sales assoc. AFLAC Inc., 1975, dist. sales coord. to regional sales coord. to state sales coord., state sales coord. Mo., v.p., West Territory dir., 2004—05, sr. v.p., dir. US sales, 2005—. Office: AFLAC Inc 1932 Wynnton Rd Columbus GA 31999 Office Phone: 706-323-3431. Office Fax: 706-324-6330.*

KIRKLAND, VIRGIL WAYNE, retired electrical engineer; b. Carthage, Tex., July 29, 1939; s. J.B. and Evelyn Virginia K.; 1 child, Olga Lynn. BSEE, Lamar State U., 1962. With Hughes Aircraft Co., Fullerton, Calif., 1962-94, mgr. tech. staff, 1979-94, asst. program mgr., 1995; with Butler Svc. Group Consulting, Orange, Calif., 1995; ret. Hughes Aircraft Co., Orange, 1995. Republican. Baptist.

KIRKLAND, WILLIAM MICHAEL, history professor; s. William Landon and Shirley Dianne Kirkland; m. Katina Elizabeth Brackin, July 18, 1998; children: Gracen Elizabeth, Landon Joel. Student, Bainbridge Coll., Ga., 1992—94; BA, U. Ga., Athens, 1996; MA, Valdosta State U., Ga., 1998. Instr. history Bainbridge Coll., 2003—06, asst. prof. history, 2006—. Coun. mem. Iron City Coun., Ga., 2001—05; deacon Iron City Bapt. Ch., 2000—. Mem.: CC Humanities Assn. (assoc.), Ga. Assn. Historians (assoc.), Lions Club (Lion Yr. 2001). Republican. Office: Bainbridge Coll 2500 E Shotwell St Bainbridge GA 39818 Home Phone: 229-774-2187; Office Phone: 229-248-2560. Business E-Mail: mkirkland@bainbridge.edu.

KIRKLIN-DARIF, DIANNA LYNN, small business owner; b. Moline, Ill., Oct. 9, 1957; d. Robert Edward and Bonita Pearl (Myers) Kirklin; m. Scott Martin Griffin, Dec. 1, 1982 (div. May 1995); 1 child, Robert Edward Griffin; m. William Brown Jr., 1978 (div. 1982); 1 child, Heidi Lynn Brown; m. Anouar Darif, Dec. 5, 2000. Student, Black Hawk Coll., 1977, student, 1996. Shipper, truck driver, mail expediter Desaulniers Printing Co., Moline, Ill., 1975—89; propr. Angelic Fashions, Moline, Ill., 1989—94; dir., propr. Angelic Pageants, Mystical Starr Pageants, Moline, Ill., 1988—; propr. Golden Birthday Co., 1995—. Inventor numerous bridal and party goods. Author: The Complete Guide to Children in Pageant, 1995, The Complete Guide to Children in Pageantry, 2002; creator: (party goods lines) Golden Birthday, 1995, (party goods line) Star Birthday, 1995. Tchr. Literacy is for Everyone, Moline, Ill., 2001, 2002; tchr. poise and charm Y and Cmty. Pk. Bd., Moline, Ill., 2002; electoral judge Voter Registration, Moline, Ill., 1998. Democrat. Avocations: dance, sewing, crafts, writing, reading. Home: 2627 - 51/2 Ave Rock Island IL 61201 Office Phone: 309-631-5141.

KIRKPATRICK, ANDREW BOOTH, JR., lawyer; b. Asheville, NC, Jan. 16, 1929; s. Andrew Booth and Gertrude Elizabeth (Ingle) K.; m. Frances Gordon Cone, Oct. 9, 1954; children: Christine, Melissa, Charles. BS cum laude, Davidson Coll., 1949; LLB magna cum laude, Harvard U., 1954. Bar: Del. 1954, Fla. 1955. Law clk. U.S. Ct. Appeals 3d Cir., 1954-55; assoc. Morris, Nichols, Arsht & Tunnell, Wilmington, Del., 1955-58, ptnr., 1958-95, of counsel, 1995—. Chmn. censor com. Supreme Ct. Del., 1970-78. Trustee U. Del., chmn., 1988-99; trustee Unidel Found., Inc.; pres. Young Republicans of New Castle County, 1957-58; chmn. Kennett Pike Assn., Wilmington, 1967-68; chmn. Gov.'s Commn. on Organized Crime, 1972-73; trustee Tatnall Sch., Inc., 1972-82. 1st lt. inf. U.S. Army, 1951-53. Fellow Am. Coll. Trial Lawyers; mem. Del. Bar Assn. (pres. 1978-79), Wilmington Club, Wilmington Country Club, Vicmead Hunt Club, Phi Beta Kappa. Presbyterian. Home: 9 Barley Mill Dr Wilmington DE 19807-2217 Office: Morris Nichols Arsht & Tunnell PO Box 1347 Wilmington DE 19899-1347

KIRKPATRICK, ANNE SAUNDERS, systems analyst; b. Birmingham, Mich., July 4, 1938; d. Stanley Rathburn and Esther (Casteel) Saunders; children: Elizabeth, Martha, Robert, Sarah. Student, Wellesley Coll., 1956-57, Laval U., Quebec City, Can., 1958, U. Ariz., 1958-59; BA in Philosophy, U. Mich., 1961. Sys. engr. IBM, Chgo., 1962-64; sr. analyst Commonwealth Edison Co., Chgo., 1981-97. Treas. Taproot Reps., DuPage County, Ill., 1977—80; pres. Hinsdale (Ill.) Women's Rep. Club, 1978—81. Mem.: Wellesley Chgo. (bd. dirs. 1972—73). Home: 22 E Chestnut St Unit 8B Chicago IL 60611-2376 Personal E-mail: a.kirkpatrick@sbcglobal.net.

KIRKPATRICK, CHARLES HARVEY, immunologist, researcher; b. Topeka, Nov. 5, 1931; s. Hazen Leon and Clarice Opal (Privott) K.; m. Janice Faye Fosha, July 11, 1959; children: Heather, Michael, Brian. BA, U. Kans., 1954; MD, U. Kans., Kansas City, 1958. Diplomate Am. Bd. Internal Medicine, Am. Bd. Allergy and Immunology. Asst. prof. U. Kans., Kansas City, 1965—67, assoc. prof., 1968; sr. investigator Nat. Inst. Allergy and Infectious Diseases, NIH, Bethesda, Md., 1968-79; dir. allergy and clin. immunology Nat. Jewish Ctr., Denver, 1979-93; prof. U. Colo., Denver, 1979—; dir. rsch. Innovative Therapeutics, Inc., 1993-96; pres. Cytokine Sci., Inc., Denver, 1996-99. Active NIH study sects., Bethesda. Editor: 4 books; contbr. numerous articles to profl. jours. NIH research grantee, 1981-86. Fellow ACP, Am. Acad. Allergy and Immunology, Molecular Med. Soc.; mem. Am. Soc. Clin. Investigation, Am. Assn. Immunologists. Episcopalian. Avocations: enology, antique corkscrews, antique automobiles. Office Phone: 303-315-6596. Business E-Mail: charles.kirkpatrick@uchsc.edu.

KIRKPATRICK, DAVID D., news correspondent; Media reporter New York Times, conservative beat reporter. Office: 1627 I St NW 7th Fl Washington DC 20006

KIRKPATRICK, DONALD ROBERT, secondary school educator; b. Ft. Belvoir, Va., Aug. 15, 1956; s. Robert Wilbur and Marsha Beatrice (Watson) K. BS, James Madison U., 1979; postgrad., U. Kans., 1979-81; MEd, U. S.C., 1994. Aid dept. paleobiology Nat. Mus. Natural History, Washington, 1979; rsch. asst. U. Kans., Lawrence, 1979-81; sci. tchr. 8th grade Johnakin Mid. Sch., Marion, SC, 1989—2003; sci. tchr. grades 9-12 Marion HS, 2003—. Rsch. assoc. Horry County Mus., Conway, 1990—;

fossil collector/donor Nat. Mus. Natural History, 1979—; presenter in field; instr. part-time Coastal Carolina U., Conway, S.C., 1992—, Francis Marion U., Florence, S.C., 1998—. Lt. USNR, 1981-89. Mem.: NEA, Planetary Soc., Nat. Ctr. Sci. Edn., Soc. Vertebrate Paleontology, S.C. Acad. Sci., S.C. Sci. Coun., Nat. Assn. Biology Tchrs., Nat. Sci. Tchrs. Assn. Avocations: collecting fossils, walking, reading. Home: 1321 Snider St Conway SC 29526-3120 Office: Marion High Sch 1205 S Main St Marion SC 29571 Home Phone: 843-248-3310; Office Phone: 843-423-2571. Personal E-mail: drki@verizon.net. Business E-Mail: dkirkpatrick@marion1.k12.sc.us.

KIRKPATRICK, EDWARD THOMSON, retired academic administrator, mechanical engineer; b. Cranbrook, BC, Can., Jan. 15, 1925; arrived in U.S., 1954, naturalized, 1981; s. John Thomson and Mary Pauline (Jones) Kirkpatrick; m. Barbara Jane Kelsberg, May 22, 1948; children: Allan, Karen, Ann, Keith. BA in Sci., U. BC, 1947; MS, Carnegie Inst. Tech., 1956, PhD, 1958. Registered profl. engr., N.Y., Ohio. Sales engr., mgr. F.D. Bolton, Ltd., Vancouver, B.C., Canada, 1948—54; asst. prof. Carnegie Inst. Tech., Pitts., 1954—58; dept. head U. Toledo, 1958—63; engring. dean Rochester Inst. Tech., NY, 1963—71; pres. Wentworth Inst. Tech., Boston, 1971—90, ret., 1990. Contbr. articles to profl. publs.; author: 1620 Fortran II-D Program, 1963. Recipient Outstanding Civilian Svc. award, U.S. Army, 1971. Fellow: Am. Soc. Engring. Edn. (bd. dirs. 1982—86); mem.: ASME, NSPE. Republican. Episcopalian. Avocations: homebuilt aircraft, flying, travel. Office: Wentworth Inst Tech Office of Pres 550 Huntington Ave Boston MA 02115-5998

KIRKPATRICK, GARLAND PENN, retired pediatrician; b. Chgo., Aug. 23, 1932; m. Dorothy Ann McCluster, Jan. 31, 1958; children: Garland Penn, Dawn Annette. AB, Talladega Coll., Ala., 1954; BS, U. Ill., Chgo., 1956, MD, 1958. Diplomate Am. Bd. Pediatrics. Fellow in devel. and behavioral pediatrics U. N.C., Chapel Hill; clin. instr. pediatrics U. Ill. Coll. Medicine, Chgo., 1959-64; pvt. practice pediatrics Kirkpatrick & Germain, Chgo., 1963-89; clin. asst. prof. pediatrics U. Chgo., 1983; clin. assoc. prof. pediatrics Northwestern Med. Sch., Chgo., 1985; clin. asst. prof. pediatrics U. Mich. Sch. Medicine, Ann Arbor, 1995, asst. clin. prof. pediatrics, 1996—2003, ret., 2003. Chmn. dept. pediatrics USAF Hosp., Richards Gebaur AFB, 1961-63; cons. Chgo. Bd. Edn., 1983-84; spkr. in field. Contbr. articles to profl. jours. Capt. USAF Med. Corps. Fellow Am. Acad. Pediatrics (exec. com. Ill. chpt. 1984); mem. AMA, Nat. Med. Assn., Soc. for Behavioral and Devel. Pediatrics. Baptist. Avocations: chess, gardening, reading, music: classical, jazz and gospel.

KIRKPATRICK, HAROLD (KIRK) WAYNE, telecommunications industry executive; b. Roanoke, Va., Dec. 30, 1960; s. David Albert Kirkpatrick, III and Hildred Lautrell Huffman; m. Zhe Feng, Apr. 20, 2004; 1 child, Ang Li. BA in English, Kans. State U., Manhattan, 1982. Faculty coord. City Colls. Chgo., Stuttgart, Germany, 1987—88; tech. dir. Amextra (Apple Computer IMC), Sulgen, Germany, 1988—89; microcomputer systems engr. Radio Free Europe/Radio Liberty, Munich, 1989—92, asst. dir. remote sites, 1992—94; dir. info. systems KEMS (Kuwait PDN), Kuwait City, 1994—95; gen. mgr. Apple Computer Distbr., Kuwait City, 1995—97; pres., CEO AdvanceNet, S.A.E., Cairo, 1997—98, Jerusalem, 1998—2000, MDS Am., Inc., Stuart, Fla., 2000—. Cons. Telcons, Stuart, 1989—2006. With US Army, 1984—87. Decorated Commendation medal US Army. Mem.: Mensa (corr.), Triple Nine Soc. (corr.). Independent. Unitarian Universalist. Achievements include lobbying for equitable assignment of RF spectrum. Avocations: stringed instruments, programming. Home: 3290 SW Island Way Palm City FL 34990 Office: MDS America Inc 800 Lincoln Ave Stuart FL 34990 Home Phone: 561-809-6372; Office Phone: 877-677-6372. Office Fax: 772-463-8220; Home Fax: 772-419-8335. Business E-Mail: kirk@mdsamerica.com.

KIRKPATRICK, JAMES JOSEPH, psychologist; b. Washington, Aug. 3, 1922; s. Luther James and Helen Jordan Kirkpatrick; m. Shirley Ann Mathews, Dec. 31, 1965; children: Martha M., Alan, Lori, James. AB in Psychology, U. Tenn., 1948, MA in Psychology, 1949; PhD in Psychology, Syracuse U., 1953. Diplomate Indsl. Psychology, Am. Bd. Examiners in Profl. Psychology. Project dir. Am. Inst. Rsch., Pitts., 1952—54; v.p. Harless & Kirkpatrick, Assocs., Tampa, Fla., 1954—65; assoc. prof. NYU, NYC, 1965—67; prof. Calif. State U., Long Beach, 1967—87, prof. emeritus, 1987—. Expert witness on equal employment opportunity issues, 1967—2001; cons. U. Chgo. IRC, 1975—81. Contbg. author: Readings Psych Tests and Measures, 1964, sr. author: Testing and Fair Employment, 1968, contbg. author: Comparative Studies of Blacks and Whites, 1973. Pilot USAF, WW II. Named Boss of Yr., Am. Bus. Women's Assn., 1962. Fellow: APA (chair ethics); mem.: Fla. Psychology Assn. (pres. elect 1965), Kiwanis. Democrat. Baptist. Avocations: photography, tennis. Home: 12331 Kensington Rd Los Alamitos CA 90720 Personal E-mail: volunteers1@mac.com.

KIRKPATRICK, JOHN PAXTON, oncologist, educator; b. NJ, Dec. 13, 1953; m. Rosemary Luthi, July 19, 1980; children: Sarah, John, Samuel. BS in Engring., Princeton U., NJ, 1975; PhD, Rice U., Houston, 1978; MD, U Tex. Health Sci. Ctr., San Antonio, 1999. Dir. polymer tech. Vista Chem. Co., Austin, Tex., 1990—93, mgr. corp. planning Houston, 1993—94, bus. mgr. plastic compounds, 1994—95; resident Duke U. Med. Ctr., Durham, NC, 2000—04, asst. prof., 2004—. Mem.: ASCO, Radiation Rsch. Soc. (Marie Curie award 2003), ASTRO. Avocations: cooking, gardening. Home: 104 New Parkside Dr Chapel Hill NC 27516 Office: Duke U Med Ctr Durham NC 27516 Home Phone: 919-960-2569; Office Phone: 919-668-5213. Office Fax: 919-668-7345. E-mail: jkirk@radonc.duke.edu.

KIRKPATRICK, ROBERT HUGH, communications executive; b. Kingston, NY, Mar. 3, 1954; s. Oscar Hugh and Ann (Page) K.; m. Debra Cook, Oct. 25, 1986; 1 child, Page. BA in Polit. Sci. with high honors, SUNY, Oneonta, 1977; M in Pub. and Pvt. Mgmt., Yale U., 1979. Cert. comml. pilot. Policy analyst edn. com. N.Y. State Assembly, 1977; mgr. mktg. Cummins Engine Co., Columbus, Ind., 1980-81, mgr. mktg. ops., 1982-83, dir. electronics mktg., 1984-86, dir. bus. devel. Svc. Products Co. subs., 1987-89; pres. Intelesis Inc., Columbus, 1989-97, CEO, 1996-97; pres. transp. and power divsn. AFFINA Corp., Columbus, 1998-2000; ptnr. Intelesis LLC, Columbus, 2001—03; COO, Servco LLC, Indpls., 2002—. Cons. in field. Contbr. articles to bus. jours. Trustee SUNY, Albany, 1975-76; pres. Student Assn. State Univ., Inc., 1975-76, v.p. 1974-75; vice-chmn. Nat. Student Lobby, 1976-77; pres. Columbus Arts Guild, 1981-82; treas. San Souci, Inc., Columbus, 1983-85; allocations com. United Way, 1990-92; mem. City Transp. Commn., Oneonta, N.Y., 1973-74; bd. dirs. Leadership Bartholomew County Alumni Assn., 1991-92, Young Mothers' Ednl. Devel., Inc., 1994-96; adminstrv. bd. First United Meth. Ch., 1994-96, trustee 1997-99; exec. com. ABC-Stewart Montessori Sch., 1996-99, sec. 1997; vol. pilot Angel Flight Am., 2001—, Ind. Wing Leader, 2003—05. Mem. Yale Club Ind. (treas. 1981-85), Rotary (bd. dirs. 1994-2000, pres. 1996-97, treas. 1997-99), Flying Rotarians Internat. Fellowship (bd. dirs. Americas 2004-05). Methodist. Home: 9727 Summerlakes Dr Carmel IN 46032 Office: Servco LLC 720 N High School Rd Indianapolis IN 46214 Office Phone: 317-814-0034.

KIRKPATRICK, R(OBERT) JAMES, geologist, educator; b. Schenectady, NY, Dec. 31, 1946; s. Robert James and Audrey (Rech) K.; m. Susan A. Wilson, Sept. 4, 1968 (div. 1984); children: Gregory Robert, Geoffrey Stephen; m. Carol A. Hanna, Sept. 3, 1985. AB, Cornell U., 1968; PhD, U. Ill., 1972. Asst. U.S. Geol. Survey, Denver, 1968; rsch. and teaching asst. U. Ill., Urbana, 1968-72; sr. rsch. geologist prodn. rsch. div. Exxon, Houston, 1972-73; rsch. fellow in geophysics Harvard U., Cambridge, 1973-75; asst. rsch. geologist Scripps Instn. Oceanography, La Jolla, Calif., 1976-78; asst. prof. dept. geology U. Ill., Urbana, 1978-80, assoc. prof., 1980-83, prof., 1983-88, prof., head dept., 1988-97, exec. assoc. dean Coll. Liberal Arts & Scis., 1997—2007; dean. Coll. Natural Sci. Mich. State U., 2007—. Mem. ocean crust panel Joint Oceanographic Instns. for Deep Earth Studies, 1977-78, active margin panel, 1978, downhole measurements panel, 1977-78; chair, Cements Divsn., Am. Ceramic Soc., 2004-05, trustee, 2006-; R.E. Grim prof. U. Ill., Urbana, 2005-07, emeritus, 2007-; cons. various corps. Editor: Initial Reports of the Deep Sea Drilling Project, Vols. 46 and 55, 1979, 80; co-editor: Kinetics of Geochemical Processes, 1981; assoc. editor American Mineralogist, 1987-90; contbr. over 200 articles to profl. jours. Overseas fellow Churchill Coll., Eng., 1985-86; grantee NSF, 1977—, Dept. Energy, 2000—, various other orgns., 1978—. Fellow Geol. Soc. Am., Mineral. Soc. Am. (councillor 1990-93, Dana medal 2004), Am. Ceramic Soc.; mem. Am. Geophys. Union (VGP award com. 1985-88, chmn. 1986-88), Internat. Mineral. Assn. (alt. U.S. del. 1982, coord. com. 1986 meeting, chmn. program com. 1986, U.S. rep. Commn. on Crystal Growth, v.p. 1986-90, sec. Commn. on Mineral Physics 1986-91). Office: Mich State U Coll Natural Sci 103 Natural Sci Bldg East Lansing MI 48824 Office Phone: 517-355-4470.

KIRKSEY, AVANELLE, nutrition educator; b. Mulberry, Ark., Mar. 23, 1926; BS, U. Ark., Fayetteville, 1947; MS, U. Tenn., Knoxville, 1950; PhD, Pa. State U., University Park, 1961; postdoctoral, U. Calif., Davis, 1976; DSc honoris causa, Purdue U., Ind., 1997. Assoc. prof. Ark. Polytechnic U., Russellville, 1950—55; rsch. asst. Pa. State U., University Park, 1956—58, fellow Gen. Foods, 1958—60; assoc. prof. Purdue U., West Lafayette, Ind., 1961—69, prof. nutrition, 1970—85, disting. prof., 1985—96, disting. prof. emeritus, 1997. Prin. investigator nutrition project in rural Egypt; coord. nutrition program Indonesian Univs., 1987—91. Contbr. articles to profl. jours. Named Meredith Disting. Prof. Nutrition, Purdue U.; named to Nutrition Hall of Fame, 2007; recipient endowment, Kirksey Annual Lecture Series, 1997, Borden award, Am. Home Econs. Assn., 1980. Fellow Am. Inst. Nutrition (Lederle award 1994); mem. N.Y. Acad. Scis., Phi Kappa Phi, Sigma Xi. Office: Purdue U Dept Food Nutrition West Lafayette IN 47907 Office Phone: 479-452-2340. Personal E-mail: akirksey01@cox.net.

KIRKWOOD, CAROL, literature and language educator; BA summa cum laude, Colo. State Univ., 1971; M with honors in French lang. and lit., Middlebury Coll. Sch. French, Paris, 1972. French tchr. Laramie (Wyo.) H.S., 1973—. Named Albany County Sch. Dist. One Tchr. of Yr., 2005, Wyo. Tchr. of Yr., 2006, Most Influential Pre-Coll. Tchr. (four times), Univ. Wyo. Honors Program. Office: Laramie High Sch 1275 North 11th St Laramie WY 82073*

KIRKWOOD, JOHN ROBERT, neuroradiologist; b. Albany, NY, Mar. 19, 1941; s. John Kinloch and Rita Arline (Schwick) K.; m. Norma Starr Miller, June 17, 1967 (dec. Mar. 1973); 1 child, Timothy; m. Gale Arcuni Duncan, Aug. 3, 1974; children: James Duncan, Christopher, Allison. BA in Psychology magna cum laude, Yale U., 1963, MD, 1967. Diplomate Am. Bd. Med. Examiners; diplomate in diagnostic radiology and neuroradiology Am. Bd. Radiology. Intern Children's Hosp. Med. Ctr., Boston, 1967-68; resident in diagnostic radiology U. Calif. Med. Ctr., San Francisco, 1968-71; fellow, instr. neuroradiology Brigham Hosp., Boston, 1971-72; chief neuroradiology Walter Reed Army Med. Ctr., Washington, 1972-73; asst. prof. radiology George Washington U. Hosp., Washington, 1973-74; from asst. prof. to assoc. prof. radiology Tufts U. Sch. Medicine, Boston, 1974—. Vice chmn. dept. radiology, Baystate Med. Ctr., Springfield, Mass., 1987-95, chmn. dept., 1997—, pres. Baystate Radiology and Imaging, Inc., 1997—; pres. Radiology and Imaging, Inc., Springfield, 1995-97, chmn., 2000—. Author: Essentials of Neuroimaging, 1990, 2d edit., 1995; contbr. rsch. articles to profl. jours. Major U.S. Army, 1972-73. Fellow Am. Coll. Radiology (councilor 2001—); mem. AMA, Am. Soc. Neuroradiology, Mass. Radiology Soc. (sec. 1995, v.p. 1998, pres.-elect 1999, pres. 2000—). Avocations: sailing, skiing, golf, art, music. Office: Dept Radiology Baystate Med Ctr 758 Chestnut St Springfield MA 01199-0001 E-mail: robert.kirkwood@bhs.org.

KIRKWOOD, ROBERT KEITH, applied physicist; b. Santa Monica, Calif., Mar. 10, 1961; s. Robert Lord and Patricia Cathrine (Keith) K.; m. Kimberly DeNeve Saunders, May 2, 1991; children: Rebekah Marie, Rachel Kathryn. BS, UCLA, 1982, MS, 1984; PhD, MIT, 1989. Rsch. asst. dept. elec. engring. UCLA, 1982-84; mem. tech. staff TRW Space and Tech. Group, Redondo Beach, Calif., 1984-85; rsch. asst. MIT, Cambridge, 1985-89, vis. scientist Plasma Fusion Ctr., 1992-94; postdoctoral fellow Calif. Inst. Tech., Pasadena, 1989-91; rsch. assoc. geophysics divsn. Air Force Phillips Lab., Hanscom AFB, Mass., 1991-92, physicist, 1992-94, Lawrence Livermore (Calif.) Lab., 1994—. Contbr. articles to Nuc. Fusion, Physics of Plasmas, Rev. Sci. Instruments, Physics Letters A, Phys. Rev. Letters. Recipient Rsch. Associateship award NRC, 1991; postdoctoral fellow Dept. Energy, 1989; doctoral fellow TRW Space and Tech. Group, 1985. Mem. Am. Phys. Soc. (Simon Ramo award in plasma physics 1991), Am. Geophys. Union. Achievements include development of wave transmission diagnostics for plasmas and demonstration of the interaction between multiple laser beams in plasmas. Office: Lawrence Livermore Lab L-479 PO Box 808 Livermore CA 94551-0808 Office Phone: 925-422-1007. E-mail: kirkwood1@llnl.gov.

KIRMAN, IGOR, lawyer; b. Kharkov, Ukraine, Nov. 28, 1970; came to the U.S., 1979; s. Vladimir and Ida Kirman; m. Galina Krasilovsky, Aug. 29, 1998. BA, Yale U., 1993; JD, Columbia U., 1996. Assoc. Sullivan & Cromwell, NYC, 1996-99, Wachtell, Lipton, Rosen & Katz, NYC, 1999—, ptnr. Adv. bd. mem. U.S. L.Am. Aid Found. NYC, adj. prof. Columbia Law Sch. Winner Nat. writing competition and awarded Scribes Law Rev. Writing award 1996, named a Dealmaker of Yr., Am. Lawyer mag., 2007. Mem. ABA, Assn. Bar City N.Y. (com. on symposium). Notes Editor Columbia Law Rev. Office: Wachtell Lipton Rosen & Katz 51 W 52d St New York NY 10019 Office Phone: 212-403-1393. Office Fax: 212-403-2393. Business E-Mail: ikirman@wlrk.com.*

KIRPALANI, SUSHEEL, lawyer; JD, Fordham U. Sch. Law. Assoc. Milbank, Tweed, Hadley & McCloy, NYC, ptnr. fin. restructuring grp., 2001—07; nat. chmn. bankruptcy litig. practice Quinn, Emanuel, Orquhart, Oliver & Hedges, NYC, 2007—. Assoc. editor: Fordham Law Rev. Office: Quinn Emanuel 22nd Fl 51 Madison Ave New York NY 10010 Office Phone: 212-849-7000. Office Fax: 212-849-7100.*

KIRPES, ANNE IRENE, elementary school educator; b. Dubuque, Iowa, Oct. 6, 1966; d. Raymond Louis and Norma Jean Margaret (Kern) K. BA, U. No. Iowa, 1989; EdM, Harvard U., 1997. Lic. elem. edn. Tchr. 1st grade Western Ave Sch., Sch. Dist. 161, Flossmoor, Ill., 1989-93, Serena Hills Sch., Sch. Dist. 161, Chicago Heights, Ill., 1993-96; tchr. 3d grade Wheelock Lab. Keene (N.H.) State Coll., 1997-98; reading/lang. arts test devel. specialist Riverside Pub. Co., Itasca, Ill., 1998—2002; reading test devel. dir. Data Recognition Corp., Maple Grove, Minn., 2002—. Exch. team mem. Rotary Group, Paris, 1995. Recipient Silver Congl. award U.S.A., 1988, Gold Congl. award, 1991; Young Alumni award U. No. Iowa Alumni Assn., Cedar Falls, 1994. Mem. ASCD, Nat. Coun. Tchrs. English, Whole Lang. Umbrella, Internat. Reading Assn., Kappa Delta Pi (internat. nominations com. 1988-90), Phi Delta Kappa (2007-08 Class of Emerging Leaders), Alpha Upsilon Alpha (internat. ad hoc com. mem., 2005-, internat. com. chair 2007-), Omicron Delta Kappa. Avocations: reading, travel, puzzles, butterfly memorabilia, board games. Home: 9461 Jewel Ln North Maple Grove MN 55311

KIRPILENKO, GRIGORY GRIGOR'EVICH, engineer, researcher; b. Irkutsk, Russia, Sept. 11, 1948; s. Grigory Karpovich and Emiliya Ivanovna Kirpilenko; m. Irina Vasil'evna Mamaeva; children: Andrey Grigor'evich, Michail Grigor'evich. Degree in Engring. and Physics, Moscow U. Electronics, 1972; PhD, Moscow Inst. Steel and Alloys, 1985. Rschr. Inst. Phys. Problems, Moscow, 1972—79; prin. rschr. Inst. Comm. Sys., Moscow, 1979—83; chief lab. Inst. Sci. Ctr., Moscow, 1983—90; dep. dir. Zelax Ctr., Moscow, 1990—96; mng. dir. Closed Joint Stock Co. Patinor Coatings Ltd., Moscow, 1996—. Mem. Freedom orgn., Moscow, 1996. Achievements include patents for technology and equipment of hard coating deposition; development of infrared emitter based on nanocomposite carbon coating. Avocations: tennis, travel. Home: ap 253 bld 162 Zelenograd Moscow 124305 Russia Office: Closed Joint Stock Co Patinor Coatings Ltd PO Box 10 Zelenograd Moscow 124460 Russia Home Phone: 7-495-536-32-59; Office Phone: 7-495-536-09-11.

KIRSANOW, PETER N., federal agency administrator; b. Oct. 30, 1953; BA, Cornell U., 1976; JD with honors, Cleve. State U. Atty. Calfee, Halter & Griswold, LLP; labor counsel City of Cleve.; sr. legal counsel Leaseway Transp. Corp., Cleve.; ptnr. Benesch, Friedlander, Coplan and Aronoff LLP; commr. U.S. Commn. on Civil Rights, 2001—06; mem. NLRB, 2006—. Chmn. bd. dirs. Ctr. New Black Leadership; mem. adv. bd. Nat. Ctr. Pub. Policy Rsch. Republican. Office: NLRB 1099 14th St NW Washington DC 20570-0001

KIRSCH, ABIGAIL, culinary productions executive; b. Bklyn., Jan. 22, 1930; d. Joseph and Mollie (Langbert) Greenberg; m. Robert B. Kirsch, June 19, 1951; children: Richard, James, Billy, Jo-Ellen. BA, Adelphi U., 1951; culinary cert., Cordon Bleu, Paris, 1967, Culinary Inst. Am., 1968. Founder, owner, chef, instr. Abigail Kirsch Sch. Cookery, Chappaqua, N.Y., 1964-75; founder Abigail Kirsch Culinary Prodns., Ltd., Tarrytown, N.Y., 1975—; chef, owner Abigail Kirsch's Husband's Pl., Chappaqua, 1975; owner, operator Abigail Kirsch at Tappan Hill, Tarrytown, N.Y., 1989—. Author cookbooks: Teen Cuisine, 1968, The Bride and Groom's First Cookbook, 1996, Invitation to Dinner, 1998, The Bride and Groom's Menu Cookbook, 2002; contbr. articles to profl. publs.; appeared on TV programs on CNN, Food Network, Discovery, Our Home, 1996. Bd. dirs. Westchester County Assn., White Plains, N.Y., 1997-99, March of Dimes West Divsn., White Plains, 1989-90; mem. exec. bd. Food Patch of Westchester, Millwood, N.Y., 1993-97; ann. gala advisor Westchester C.C., Valhalla, N.Y., 1990. Recipient Small Bus. award for Women U.S. C. of C., 1987, Vol. of Yr. award March of Dimes, 1992, Headliner award Women in Comms., 1995, Woman of Distinction award roundtable for Women in Food Svc., 1995, Pacesetter award Nat. Roundtable of Women in Food Svc., 1996, Restaurateur of Yr. award N.Y. State Restaurant Assn., 1996, Silver Plate award Internat. Food Svc. Mfrs. Assn., 1997, Family of Yr. award Family Svc. of Westchester, 1997; named to New York's 100 Most Influential Women in Bus., Crain's N.Y. Bus., 1999. Mem. Culinary Inst. Am. (chair ednl. policies com. 1988-95, sec. 1991-93, vice chair 1993-95, trustee emeritus 1995—), Les Dames d'Escoffier Internat. (sec. N.Y. chpt. 1995-96, pres. 1996-98, internat. pres. 1999—). Avocations: reading, travel, swimming. Home: 18 Robin Hood Rd Pound Ridge NY 10576-2306 Office: Abigail Kirsch at Tappan Hill 81 Highland Ave Tarrytown NY 10591-4206

KIRSCH, DARREN MATTHEW, music educator; b. Hollywood, Fla., Oct. 4, 1973; s. Donald Lee and Linda Ann Kirsch; m. Kathryn Maricena Thomas, Nov. 27, 1999; children: Jackson Lowell, Mary Eileen (Molly). BA in Music Edn., Music Performance, Va. Tech., 1995. Dir. bands 6-12 Glenvar H.S./Mid. Sch., Roanoke County, Va., 1995—96; dir. bands 9-12 Grafton H.S., York County, Va., 1996—. Mem.: Va. Band and Orch. Dirs. Assn., Va. Music Educators Assn., Delta Omicron. Office: Grafton HS 403 Grafton Dr Yorktown VA 23692-2173 Office Phone: 757-890-2468. Office Fax: 757-898-0533. E-mail: dkirsch@ycsd.york.va.us.

KIRSCH, DONALD, financial consultant; b. NYC, Oct. 9, 1931; s. William and Eva (Wasserman) Kirsch; m. Dorothy Ann Tejw, June 6, 1959; children: Mark Adam, Karen Rebecca Hoffman, Jonathan Bradford. BS, NYU, 1952. Editorial staffer Wall Street Jour., NYC, 1952-53; writer AP, NYC, 1954-55; pres. Wall Street Cons., NYC, 1955—; chmn. Wall St. Group, Calif., Inc., Los Angeles, 1963—; chmn., pres. The Wall Street Group, Inc., NYC, 1959—. Adj. assoc. prof. NYU Grad. Sch. Arts and Sci., 1974—79; founding chmn. Typesetting Products, Inc., Talleres Graficos de Interamericanos, San Juan, 1962—80; chmn. Eurofinancing Ltd., 1968; bd. dirs. Co-star Entertainment Inc.; bd. dirs., chmn. stategic planning com. MedNet Inc.; bd. dirs. Medi-Mail, Inc., Dialscan Sys., Audiofidelity Enterprises Inc., Interstate Nat. Dealers Svcs., Inc. Author: Financial and Economic Journalism: Analysis Interpretation and Reporting, 1978 (Librarian Assn. award, 1978), Investor Relations for the Over-the-Counter or Newly Public Company; author: (with others) The Handbook of Investor Relations; contbr. articles to profl. jours. Trustee Nat. Symphony Orch. John F. Kennedy Ctr. Performing Arts, treas. bd. trustees, 1996—98; trustee Big Bros.; mem. bd. mgrs. Episcopal Social Svcs., NY. Mem.: Am. Assocs. Royal Acad. Trust, Chief Execs. Orgn., Young Pres. Orgn., Met. Pres.' Orgn., NY Soc. Security Analysts, The Metropolitan (NYC), Firar's Club, Econs. Club NY, Masons. Office: The Wall St Group Inc 32 E 57th St New York NY 10022-2513 Home Phone: 212-348-7709; Office Phone: 212-888-4848. Personal E-mail: dkirsch1@aol.com.

KIRSCH, JAMES F., materials executive; B in Mktg., Ohio State U., Columbus. Various positions including Global Bus. Dir. Propylene Oxide and Derivatives and Global V.P. Electrochemicals Dow Chem. Co.; v.p. Ballard Power Systems, Burnaby, BC; pres., dir. Ballard Generation Systems; pres. Premix, Inc. and Quantum Composites; pres., COO Ferro Corp., Cleve., 2004—05, pres., CEO, 2005—, chmn., 2006—. Bd. dirs. United Way Greater Cleve., John Carroll U., University Heights, Ohio; bd. dirs. Greater Cleve. chpt. ARC. Office: Ferro Corp 1000 Lakeside Ave Cleveland OH 44114-1147 Office Phone: 216-641-8580.*

KIRSCH, LAURENCE STEPHEN, lawyer; b. Washington, July 20, 1957; s. Ben and Bertha (Gomberg) K.; m. Celia Goldman, Aug. 19, 1979; children: Rachel Miriam, Max David. BAS, MS, U. Pa., 1979; JD, Harvard U., 1982. Bar: DC 1982, US Ct. Appeals (3d cir.) 1983, (5th cir.) 1997, (9th cir.) 2001, US Dist. Ct. DC 1985, US Ct. Appeals (DC cir.) 1985, US Supreme Ct. 1987; registered environ. assessor, Calif. 1988. Law clk. to presiding judge Pa. Dist. Ct., Phila., 1982-83; vis. asst. prof. law U. Bridgeport (Conn.) Law Sch., 1983-84; assoc. Cadwalader, Wickersham & Taft, Washington, 1984-90, ptnr., 1991—2002; with Shea Gardner, Washington, 2002—04, Goodwin Procter LLP, 2004—. Chmn. steering coms. Superfund. Editor-in-chief Indoor Pollution Law Report, 1987-91; mng. editor Harvard Environ. Law Rev., 1981-82; contbr. articles to profl. jours. Mem. ABA, Fed. Bar Assn., AAAS, Air and Waste Mgmt. Assn. (indoor air quality com.), Environ. Law Inst., Am. Soc. Testing and Measurement (vapor intrusion com.), Phi Beta Kappa. Home: 7212 Longwood Dr Bethesda MD 20817-2122 Office: Goodwin Procter 901 New York Ave NW Washington DC 20001 Office Phone: 202-346-4440. Office Fax: 202-346-4444. E-mail: lkirsch@goodwinprocter.com.

KIRSCH, LLOYD, academic administrator; BS, Cornell U. Cert. Hotel Adminstr. Am. Hotel and Lodging Assn. Dir. food and beverage Americana Hotels, Albany, NYC; resident mgr. Shoreham Hotel, Washington; gen. mgr. Helmsley Hotel, Hartford, Conn., Springfield, Conn.; mng. dir. Loews Glenpointe Hotel, Loews Santa Monica Beach Hotel; regional v.p. ops. Hilton Hotels Corp.; v.p. ops. Meristar Hotels, West Coast Hotels; pres. The Cooking and Hospitality Inst. Chgo. Guest lectr. U. Mass., Farleigh Dickinson U., Santa Monica Cmty. Coll. Pres. Monterey Peninsula C. of

C., Conv. and Visitor's Bur. Recipient Top of Vanity award, Hospitality and Lodging Mag., Outstanding Food and Beverage Operation award, Loews Hotels. Mem.: Monterey County Hospitality Assn. (pres.), Internat. Assn. Culinary Professionals, Le Torque Blanche, Am. Inst. Wine and Food, Cornell Hotel Soc. Office: Cooking and Hospitality Inst Chgo 361 W Chestnut Chicago IL 60610*

KIRSCH, LYNN, lawyer; b. New Orleans, Oct. 31, 1964; d. Henry C. and Therese M. ((Guenther) K. BS in Bus. Mgmt., Fla. State U., Panama City, 1992; JD, U. Ariz., 1995. Bar: Nev. 1995, U.S. Dist. Ct. Nev. 1995, U.S. Ct. Fed. Claims 1997, U.S. Ct. Appeals (9th cir.) 1998, U.S. Supreme Ct. 1999. Law clk. U.S. Atty.'s Office, Phoenix, 1993, Slutes, Sakrison, Evan, Grant & Pelander, Tucson, 1993-94, Lionel, Sawyer & Collins, Las Vegas, 1994; judicial extern Fed. Dist. Ct., Tucson, 1994; rsch. asst. U. Ariz., Tucson, 1994-95; law clk. Jacob & Fishbein, Tucson, 1994-95; assoc. Goold, Patterson, DeVore & Rondau, Las Vegas, 1995-97, Curran & Parry, Las Vegas, 1997-99, Bernhard & Bradley, Las Vegas, 1999—2001; gen. counsel Unlt. Holdings, Inc., 2001—04; ptnr. Lynn Kirsch Chtd., 2004—. Mem. Justice of the Peace pro-tempore panel, Las Vegas Twp., County of Clark, 1998-2000; alt. mcpl. ct. judge City of Las Vegas, 1999-2004; vol. mediator clerk county social svs. Neighborhood Justice Ctr.; arbitrator BBB AutoLine; instr. The Nonprofit Corp., Nevada, UNLV Continuing Edn., 2002, 03, 05. Article editor U. Ariz. Law Rev., 1994-95. Mem. Jr. League of Las Vegas, 1998—, league atty., 2000—; mem. State of Nev. Commn. on Postsecondary Edn., 1998-01, Social Register of Las Vegas, House of Blues Found. Adv. Bd. Recipient Cert. Appreciation, U.S. Atty.'s Office, Phoenix, 1993, AmJur award Lawyers Coop. Publ., Tucson, 1993. Mem. ABA (litigation sect., assoc. editor The Affiliate 1999-2000), ATLA, State Bar Nev. (chair young lawyers sect. 1999-2000, so. Nev. disciplinary bd., fee dispute arbitration com.), Clark County Bar Assn. (trial by peers com., cmty. svc. com.), Nev. Trial Lawyers Assn., So. Nev. Assn. Women Attys. Avocations: horseback riding, hiking, skydiving. Office: 102 Gorcos Ave Ste 202 Las Vegas NV 89101 Home Phone: 702-737-3806. Personal E-mail: lynn@lynnkirsch.com.

KIRSCH, MARK A., lawyer; b. Washington, Sept. 25, 1958; BA cum laude, Univ. Rochester, 1980; JD, George Washington Univ., 1984. Bar: DC 1985, Md. 1985, Va. 2003, US Dist. Ct. (DC, Md. dist.) 1985. Ptnr., co-chmn. Consumer practice group DLA Piper Rudnick Gray Cary, Reston, Va. Contbr. articles to profl. jours. Mem.: ABA, Md. State Bar Assn. (chmn. com. on franchise & distribution law 1999—2001), DC Bar Assn., Va. Bar Assn. Office: DLA Piper Rudnick Gray Cary Suite 400 1775 Wiehle Ave Reston VA 20190-5159 Office Phone: 703-773-4241. Office Fax: 703-773-5052. Business E-Mail: mark.kirsch@dlapiper.com.

KIRSCH, ROBERT L., lawyer; b. Methuen, Mass., Aug. 23, 1957; s. Richard Alan and Gloria Maria (Russo) K.; m. Anne Elizabeth Renner, Nov. 18, 1989; children: Samuel, Jack. BS in Polit. Sci., Middlebury Coll., 1979; JD, Cornell Law Sch., Ithaca, NY, 1983. Bar: Mass. 1983, U.S. Dist. Ct. Mass. 1983, U.S. Ct. Appeals (1st cir.) 1983, N.H. 1985, U.S. Dist. Ct. N.H. 1985. Assoc. Hale and Dorr, Boston, 1983—92, ptnr., 1992—2004; ptnr., chmn. Environ. dept., mem. Litigation dept. & Energy Law group Wilmer Cutler Pickering Hale & Dorr, Boston, 2004—. Pres. exec. com. Mt. Washington Obs., North Conway, N.H., trustee, 1985—. Named a Mass. Super Lawyer, Boston Mag., 2004. Mem. ABA, NH Bar Assn., Boston Bar Assn., Phi Beta Kappa. Office: Wilmer Cutler Pickering Hale & Dorr 60 State St Boston MA 02109-1816 Office Phone: 617-526-6779. Office Fax: 617-526-5000. Business E-Mail: rob.kirsch@wilmerhale.com.

KIRSCH, ROSLYN RUTH, artist, educator, painter, printmaker; b. NYC, Dec. 30, 1928; d. Harry Morris and Lillian (Zemachson) Friedenberg; m. Louis Kirsch, Dec. 26, 1948; children: Libby Ann, Andrew Lawrence. Student, Queens Coll., 1946-48; BA, Hunter Coll., 1950. Art dir. Ladies' Ready-to-Wear Buying Office, NYC, 1948-50; art educator Armory Art Ctr., West Palm Beach, Fla., 1987—, Boca Raton Mus. Art Sch., Boca Raton, Fla., 1990—. Presenter in field; condr. painting workshops. One-person shows include J&W Gallery, New Hope, Pa., Capitol Gallery, Tallahassee, Fla., Peter Drew Gallery, Fla., Ken Elias Gallery, Habitat Gallery, West Palm Beach, Fla., Joel Kessler Gallery, Fla., Indigo Gallery, Fla., Palm Beach Internat. Airport, others; exhibited in group shows Ann. Hortt Exhbn., Mus. Art, Ft. Lauderdale, 1994, 98, Nat. Assn. Women Artists, West Palm Beach, 1995 (award), Boca Raton Mus. Art, Fla., 1999; represented in permanent collections including Mus. Art., Ft. Lauderdale, Boca Raton Mus. Art. Mem. Norton Mus. Art, Boca Raton Mus. Art, Ft. Lauderdale Mus. Art. Recipient various awards. Mem. Nat. Assn. Women Artists, Boca Raton Mus. Artists Guild, others. Avocations: golf, fundraising. E-mail: kirschfineart@yahoo.com.

KIRSCH, SCOTT DOUGLAS, family practice physician, director; b. Bronx, NY, Nov. 4, 1946; s. Max Milton Kirsch and Linda Paley Sokoloff; m. Bonnie E. Becker; children: Geoffrey Z., Laura G. BA, Queens Coll., 1967; MD, SUNY, Buffalo, 1971. Diplomate Am. Bd. Family Practice. Asst. dir. family practice residency program South Nassau Cmtys. Hosp., Oceanside, NY, 1980—82, dir., 1982—99, dir. dept. family practice, 1989—99, emeritus mem. dept. family practice, 2001—; assoc. dir. family practice residency program Southside Hosp., Bayshore, 1999—2006, Presbyn. Intercmty. Hosp., Whittier, Calif., 2006—. Recipient award for dedication to Hispanic Cmty., Nat. Hispanic Med. Assn., 2002, legis. resolution for disting. svc., N.Y. State Senate, 1999. Mem.: N.Y. State Acad. Family Physicians (pres. 2001—02, Family Practice Educator of Yr. 2005), Am. Acad. Family Physicians (del. to nat. conv. 1999—2006, mem. commn. on continuing med. edn. 2002—06, chair adv. bd. home study program 2004—06). Avocations: history, travel, baseball, martial arts. Home: 507 Valley Forge Dr Placentia CA 92870 Office: Presbyn Intercmty Hosp 12291 Whittier Blvd Whittier CA 90606 Home Phone: 714-524-0250; Office Phone: 562-698-0811 ext. 8578. Personal E-mail: scottkirsch@roadrunner.com.

KIRSCHBAUM, ALAN IRA, air force officer, systems integration specialist; b. Balt., Oct. 3, 1948; s. Marvin and Nadine (Gross) K.; m. Cheryl Louise Demming, Sept. 2, 1984. BME, U. Md., 1971; MBA, N.Mex. Highlands U., 1984; diploma, Def. Systems Mgmt. Coll., Alexandria, Va., 1981, Nat. Def. U., Washington, 1986. Registered profl. engr., Ohio. Commd. 2d lt. U.S. Air Force, 1971, advanced through grades to col., 1993, engine performance analyst aero. systems div. Dayton, Ohio, 1971-76, space def. project mgr., space div. LA, 1976-79, satellite integration mgr., space div., 1979-81, concept devel. br. chief, weapons lab. Albuquerque, 1981-84, advanced systems integration chief, rsch. office Washington, 1985-89; chief seismic systems acquisition div. USAF Tech. Applications Ctr., Melbourne, Fla., 1989-93; dep. dir. Acquisitions Tech. Applications Ctr., Melbourne, Fla., 1991-93; dep. dir. tech. Ballistic Missile Def. Orgn., Washington, 1993-95; dir. systems engring. Space and Missile Systems Ctr. USAF, LA, 1995—98; program mgr. space sys. and tech. AT&T Govt. Solutions, Santa Barbara, Calif., 1999—. Adviser Program Mgmt. Assistance Group, Dayton, 1981, Launch Readiness Rev., L.A., 1977. Contbr. articles to profl. jours. Big brother, Big Bros. Am., L.A., 1978; judge Internat. Sci./Engring. Fair, L.A., 1978; assoc. Kennedy Ctr. Performing Arts, Washington, 1985; grant evaluation panel United Way Santa Barbara County Cmty., 2001-05. Decorated Legion of Merit. Fellow AIAA (assoc., orgn. rep. 1977-79); mem. ASME, Air Force Assn., Mil. Ops. Rsch. Soc., Bard House Officers Club, Temple Beth Torah Brotherhood, Tau Beta Pi, Pi Tau Sigma, Omicron Delta Kappa. Home: 2210 Bermuda Dunes Pl Oxnard CA 93036-2778 E-mail: akirschbaum@att.com.

KIRSCHBAUM, MYRON, lawyer; b. NYC, Nov. 20, 1949; s. Jonas and Doris (Rose) K.; m. Esther Weiner, June 23, 1971; children: Rachel, Shoshana Stein, Yisrael. BA, Yeshiva U., 1971; JD, Harvard U., 1974. Bar: N.Y. 1975, U.S. Dist. Ct. (so. dist.) N.Y. 1975, U.S. Dist. Ct. (no. dist.) Calif. 1989, U.S. Ct. Appeals (2d cir.) 1975, U.S. Ct. Appeals (9th cir.) 1990, U.S. Ct. Appeals (fed. cir.) 1994, U.S. Ct. Appeals (3d cir.) 2001. Law clk. U.S. Ct. Appeals (2d cir.), NYC, 1974-75; assoc. Kaye, Scholer LLP, NYC, 1975-82, ptnr., 1983—. Mem. dept. disciplinary com. Appellate Divsn., Supreme Ct. NY. Editor Harvard Law Rev., 1972-73, case and comment editor, 1973-74. Fellow: NY State Bar Found.; mem.: ABA, NY State Bar Assn., Assn. Bar City NY. Office: Kaye Scholer LLP 425 Park Ave New York NY 10022-3506 Office Phone: 212-836-8159. Business E-Mail: mkirschbaum@kayescholer.com.

KIRSCHENBAUM, ALEXANDER, medical educator; b. Svalova, Ukraine, Jan. 17, 1952; arrived in US, 1974; s. Moisey and Etela Kirschenbaum; m. Alice Carla Levine, Jan. 17, 1988; 1 child, Benjamin. MD, Mt. Sinai Sch. Medicine, NYC, 1980. Diplomate Am. Bd. Urology, 1986. Assoc. prof. urology and oncology Mt. Sinai Sch. Medicine, 1976—. Contbr. articles to profl. jours. Mem.: Basic Rsch. Soc., Am. Urol. Assn., Alpha Omega Alpha. Office: 58A E 79th St New York NY 10021 Office Phone: 646-422-0926. Office Fax: 212-452-2605. Personal E-mail: akirschenb@aol.com.

KIRSCHENMANN, HENRY GEORGE, JR., management consultant, retired government official, accountant; b. Bklyn., June 11, 1930; s. Henry Godfrey and Eva Helen (Gellert) Kirschenmann; m. Pam Hirst; children: Victoria Mary, Henry George III, Ronald William. BS, Md. U.; MPA, Am. U. CPA; cert. gov. fin. mgr. Mem. auditor staff Price Waterhouse & Co., Washington; mem. auditor staff U.S. Army Audit Agy.; mem. internal auditor staff Martin-Marietta Co., Orlando, Fla.; various fin. and adminstrv. positions HEW, Washington; dep. asst. sec. HHS, Washington; assoc. cons. Bearing Point, Inc., Tyson's Corner, 1988—. Bd. dirs., assoc. dir. tng. Pub. Svc. Inst., Silver Spring, Md.; exec. dir. Nat. Edn. Inst., Rockville, Md. Pres. Support Groups, Inc.; dir. Soc. Not for Profit Orgns.and Cmtys., Inc. Recipient Superior Svc. award, HHS, Disting. Svc. award, Presdl. Rank award. Mem.: AICPA, Md. Assn. CPA, Inst. Cost Analysis, Assn. Govt. Accts., Nat. Grants Mgmt. Assn. (bus. officer 1997—2001, bd. dirs.), Soc. Rsch. Adminstrs. Home Phone: 301-460-9276.

KIRSCHNER, BARBARA STARRELS, gastroenterologist; b. Phila., Mar. 23, 1941; m. Robert H. Kirschner (dec.). MD, Women's Med. Coll. Pa., 1967. Diplomate Am. Bd. Pediatrics; cert. in pediatric gastroenterology and nutrition. Intern U. Chgo., 1967-68, resident, 1968-70; mem. staff U. Chgo. Children's Hosp., 1977-83, asst. prof. pediatrics, 1984-88, prof. pediatrics and medicine, 1988—, mem. com. on nutrition and nutritional biology. Contbr. articles to profl. jours. Pediatric Gastroenterology fellow U. Chgo., 1975-77; recipient Davidson award in Pediatric gastroenterology Acad. Pediatrics, 1993, Joseph Brenneman award Chgo. Pediat. Soc., 2001. Mem. Am. Gastroenterologic Assn., N.Am. Soc. Pediatric Gastroenterology, Soc. Pediatric Rsch., Alpha Omega Alpha. Office: U Chgo Med Ctr 5839 S Maryland Ave # MC 4065 Chicago IL 60637-5417 Home Phone: 773-288-2299; Office Phone: 773-702-6152.

KIRSCHNER, KENNETH HAROLD, lawyer; b. Bklyn., Dec. 1, 1953; s. Samuel and Stella K.; m. Andrea Chase, Feb. 8, 1997. BS, Cornell U., 1975; JD, NYU, 1978, LLM, 1981. Bar: N.Y. 1979, U.S. Ct. Appeals (2d, 5th and D.C. cirs.), 1979, U.S. Dist. Ct. (so. and ea. dists.) N.Y., 1979, U.S. Supreme Ct. 1982. Assoc. Kelley Drye & Warren, NYC, 1978-82, Breed Abbott & Morgan, NYC, 1982-86, ptnr., 1986-93, Kelley Drye & Warren LLP, NYC, 1993—2006. Adj. asst. prof. mgmt. NYU, 1988—. Contbr. articles to profl. jours. Office: Heller Ehrman LLP 7 Times Sq New York NY 10036 Office Phone: 212-847-8569. Business E-Mail: kenneth.kirschner@hellezarman.com.

KIRSCHNER, MARC ALAN, neuroscientist; b. Cin., July 3, 1956; s. Jack Robert and Lucretia (Einstein) K. BA, Middlebury Coll., 1978; MD, Case Western Res. U., 1982. Neurology resident McGill U., 1987; postdoctoral fellow Howard Hughes Med. Inst., New Haven, 1988-89; assoc. rsch. scientist Yale U., New Haven, 1989-91; instr. Oreg. Health Scis. U., Portland, 1991-92, asst. prof., 1992—; asst. clin. prof. neurology U. Wash., 1997—. Rsch. asst. prof. Vollum Inst. for Advanced Biomed. Rsch. Mem. Am. Acad. Neurology, Soc. for Neurosci. Achievements include research in isolation and characterization of mouse high-affinity excitatory amino acid transporters. Office: Univ Wash 1570 N 115th St Ste 14 Seattle WA 98133 Office Phone: 206-365-0111.

KIRSCHNER, WILLIAM STEVEN, lawyer; b. LA, Jan. 9, 1950; s. Robert and Ethel Ada (Bershad) K.; m. Sandy Bernstein, Aug. 31, 1976 (div. 1981); m. Laurie Kay Miller, Aug. 11, 1983; 1 child, Beryl Susan Elizabeth Miller. BA, Bklyn Coll., 1971; JD, Fordham U., 1976. Bar: N.D. 1980, Minn. 1981, Ga. 1977, N.Mex. 1995, U.S. Dist. Ct. N.D. 1981, U.S. Dist. Ct. Minn. 1985, U.S. Ct. Appeals (8th cir.) 1985. Assoc. Brian Nelson, Fargo, N.D., 1980-82; sole practice Fargo, 1982-84; ptnr. Kirschner & Baker Legal Clinic, Fargo, 1984-86; mng. atty. William Kirschner & Assocs., Fargo, 1986—2001; asst. county atty. Dona Ana County, N.Mex., 2001—02; city atty. City of Alamogordo, N.Mex., 2002—03; assoc. Holt & Babington, Las Cruces, N.Mex., 2003—04; exec. v.p., gen. counsel, sec. Conseco Inc., 2003—06. Bd. dirs. Alcohol Out Reach, Fargo, 1983-85, Youth Depot, Fargo, 1985, Temple Beth El, Fargo, 1986-88; sec. legal com. N.D. ACLU, 1986-95. Francis Kneller scholar Bklyn. Coll., 1969. Mem. Cass County Bar Assn., Nat. Lawyers Guild, N.D. Trial Lawyers Assn., Fargo Criminal Def. Lawyers Assn. (organizer), N.D. State Bar Assn. (ethics com. 1987-91). Office Phone: 317-817-6100. Office Fax: 317-817-2847.

KIRSCHSTEIN, RUTH LILLIAN, physician; b. Bklyn., Oct. 12, 1926; d. Julius and Elizabeth (Berm) Kirschstein; m. Alan S. Rabson, June 11, 1950; 1 child, Arnold. BA magna cum laude, L.I. U., 1947; MD, Tulane U., 1951, LLD, PhD, Tulane U., 1997; DSc (hon.), Mt. Sinai Sch. Medicine, 1984; LLD, Atlanta U., 1985; DSc (hon.), Med. Coll. Ohio, 1986; LHD (hon.), L.I. U., 1991; PhD (hon.), U. Rochester Sch. Medicine, 1998, Brown U., 1999; DSc (hon.), Spelman Coll., 2001, Georgetown U., 2001. Intern Kings County Hosp., Bklyn., 1951-52; resident pathology VA Hosp., Atlanta, Providence Hosp., Detroit, Clin. Ctr., NIH, Bethesda, Md., 1952-57; fellow Nat. Heart Inst. Tulane U., 1953-54; asst. dir. div. biologics standards NIH, 1971-72; dep. dir. Bur. Biologics, FDA, 1972-73, dep. assoc. commr. sci., 1973-74; acting assoc. dir. woman's health NIH, Bethesda, 1974-93, acting dir., 1993, dep. dir., 1993—99, acting dir., 2000—02, sr. advisor to dir., 2003—. Chmn. grants peer rev. study team NIH; mem. Inst. Medicine NAS, 1982—; co-chair, sec. Spl. Emphasis Oversight com. on Sci. and Tech., 1989—; mem. Office Tech. Assessment Adv. Com. on Basic Rsch., 1989—; co-chair PHS Coordinating Com. on Women's Health Issues, 1990—. Recipient Superior Svc. award, 1980, 1993, Presdl. Disting. Exec. Rank award, 1985, 1995, Pub. Svc. award, Fedn. Am. Soc.s Exptl. Biology, 1993, Nat. Pub. Svc. award, Am. Pub. Adminstrn./Nat. Acad. Pub. Adminstrn., 1994, Roger W. Jones award for exec. leadership, Am. U., 1994, Georgeanna Seegar Jones Women's Health Lifetime Achievement award, 1995, Albert Sabin Hero of Sci. award, 2000, Women Achievement award, Anti-Defamation League, 2001, J. Richard Nesson award, Harvard Med. Sch., 2002, Pub. Svc. award, Am. Soc. for Biochemistry and Molecular Biology, 2003. Mem.: NAS-IOM, AMA (Dr. Nathan Davis award 1990), Am. Acad. Arts and Scis., Am. Acad. Microbiology, Am. Assn. Pathologists, Am. Assn. Immunologists. Office: NIH 1 Center Dr Msc 0148 Rm 158 Bethesda MD 20892-0001 Business E-Mail: rk25n@nih.gov.

KIRSH, MICHAEL ALAN, financial estate planner; b. Bklyn., Aug. 3, 1952; s. Lawrence and Pauline (Goldberg) K.; m. Marcia Beth Fabrikant, Sept. 11, 1976; children: Jordana Erin, Ross Morgan. Grad. high sch., Bklyn. CFP; CLU; accredited estate planner. Prin. Kirsh Fin. Svcs., Inc., NYC, 1978—. Mem. Nat. Assn. Estate Planners, Nat. Assn. Ins. and Fin. Advisors, Fin. Planning Assn., Soc. Fin. Svc. Profls., Assn. Advanced Life Underwriting, Million Dollar Roundtable (Honor Roll, Top of the Table award), The Internat. Forum. Republican. Jewish. Avocations: tennis, skiing, reading. Office: 1776 Broadway New York NY 10019 Home Phone: 201-569-4429; Office Phone: 212-246-7030. Business E-Mail: mkirsh@kirshfinancial.com.

KIRSHBAUM, DANIEL JOSEPH, researcher; s. Ronald M. and Adrienne Kirshbaum. BS in Mech. Engring., U. Ill., Urbana-Champaign, 1996; MS in Elec. Engring., Johns Hopkins U., 1999; PhD, U. Wash., Seattle, 2004. Rsch. asst. U. Wash., Seattle, 1999—2004; postdoctoral fellow Nat. Ctr. Atmospheric Rsch., Boulder, Colo., 2004—06; postdoctoral assoc. dept. geology and geophysics Yale U., New Haven, 2006—. Recipient Bronze Tablet, U. Ill., 1996. Mem.: Am. Meteorol. Soc. Home: 508 Chapel St #2 New Haven CT 06511 Office: Dept Geology and Geophysics Yale Univ Box 208109 New Haven CT 06520 Office Fax: 203-432-3134. Personal E-mail: dkirshbaum@hotmail.com.

KIRSHBAUM, HOWARD M., retired judge; b. Oberlin, Ohio, Sept. 19, 1938; s. Joseph and Gertrude (Morris) K.; m. Priscilla Joy Parmakian, Aug. 15, 1964; children: Audra Lee, Andrew William. BA, Yale U., 1960; AB, Cambridge U., 1962, MA, 1966; LLB, Harvard U., 1965. Ptnr. Zarlengo and Kirshbaum, Denver, 1969-75; judge Denver Dist. Ct., 1975-80, Colo. Ct. Appeals, Denver, 1980-83; justice Colo. Supreme Ct., Denver, 1983-97; arbiter Jud. Arbiter Group, Inc., Denver, 1997—, sr. judge, 1997—2006. Adj. prof. law U. Denver, 1970-; dir. Am. Law Inst. Phila., 1982-2002, Am. Judicature Soc., Chgo., 1979-2002, Colo. Jud. Inst. Denver, 1979-89; pres. Colo. Legal Care Soc., Denver, 1974-75. Bd. dirs. Young Artists Orch., Denver, 1976-85; pres. Cmty. Arts Symphony, Englewood, Colo., 1972-74; dir. Denver Opportunity, Inc., Denver, 1972-74; vice-chmn. Denver Coun. on Arts and Humanities, 1969. Mem.: ABA (standing com. pub. edn. 1996—2001), Assn. for Conflict Resolution, Denver Bar Assn. (trustee 1981—83), Colo. Bar Assn. Avocation: music performance. Office: Jud Arbiter Group Inc 1601 Blake St Ste 400 Denver CO 80202-1328 Office Phone: 303-572-1919.

KIRSHBAUM, JON ALAN, systems analyst, consultant, retired systems administrator; b. LA, Nov. 5, 1942; s. George Alexander and Mary Elizabeth (Ball) K.; m. Anne Nofrey, Aug. 11, 1961 (div.); 1 child, Warren Ashley (dec.); m. Linda Louise Carl, Dec. 15, 1976; stepchildren: Gary Nicholas, Grant Adam. BS in Comprehensive Mktg., No. Ill. U., 1965, MBA in Fin., 1971, postgrad., 1988-93; MDiv, McCormick Theol. Seminary, Chgo., 1980. Cert. chief sch. bus. ofcl., data warehouse cons. IRD sales/DPD br. office adminstr. IBM Corp., Chgo., 1965-67, systems analyst/sr. assoc. planner Endicott, NY, 1967-71; seminary asst. Lincoln Park Presbyn. Ch., Chgo., 1972-73; team/project leader Chgo. Pub. Schs., 1974-89, data base adminstr., 1989-92, supr. desktop pub., 1992-94, core team mem., Time re-engring. project, 1994-95; project leader Info. Technologies, Chgo., 1995-96; prin. cons. Keane, Inc., Lisle, Ill., 1996-99; sr. analyst Mantiss a Dynegy Co., Chgo., 2000-2001. Freelance travel writer and editor, 1998—. Mng. editor: Today's Traveler Mag., Chgo., 1991-92, exec. editor/v.p. mktg., 1997-98. Mem. DuPage County (Ill.) Geneal. Soc. (bd. dirs. 1986-89, pres. 1989-90), DuPage County Hist. Soc., Glen Ellyn (Ill.) Hist. Soc., Salem (Ohio) Hist. Soc., Project Mgmt. Inst. (Olympia chpt.), Soc. Profl. Journalists (Western Washington pro chpt.), N.Am. Travel Journalists Assn. (regional v.p. 1993-94), US Lighthouse Soc., New Dungeness Light Sta. Assn., Dama Internat. (Puget Sound chpt.), River Ctr. Found., Near East Archaeol. Soc., Soc. Descs. of Colonial Clergy, Morse Soc., Soc. Descs. Henry Wolcott, Magna Charta Soc., Clallam County Geneal. Soc., Clallam County Hist. Soc. (bd. dirs. 2007—). Republican. Presbyterian. Avocations: fishing, genealogy, travel, weaving. Personal E-mail: jon_kirshbaum@usa.net.

KIRSHENBAUM, ARI P., engineering educator; m. Molly C. Millwood; 1 child, Noah. Applications engr. MED Assoc.; prof. St. Michael's Coll., Colchester, Vt., 2005—. Cons. Grantee, Vt. Genetics Network, NIH, NIDA. Home Phone: 802-453-2403; Office Phone: 802-654-2846.

KIRSHENBAUM, RICHARD IRVING, retired public health physician; b. Bklyn., Aug. 19, 1933; s. Joseph and Anne (Hantman) K.; m. Jean Shicher, Aug. 17, 1957; children: Miriam, Susan, Rachel. AB, Temple U., 1955; DO, Phila. Coll. Osteo. Medicine, 1959; MPH, Columbia U., 1971. Diplomate Am. Bd. Preventive Medicine. Resident intern Met. Hosp., Phila., 1959-60; pvt. practice medicine Bklyn., 1960-70; resident in pub. health N.Y.C. Dept. Health, 1970-73, pub. health physician, 1973-81, regional health dir. for Queens County, 1977-80, chief epidemiologist for Manhattan Borough, 1980-81; pub. health physician N.Y. State Dept. Health, NYC, 1981-98; retired, 1998. Contbr. articles to profl. jours. Lt. col. Med. Corps N.Y. Army NG, 1981-91, USAR, 1991-93. Recipient Physician's Recognition award AMA 1973, 76, 79, 82, 85, 88, 90, 93, 96, 98. Home: 313 Whitman Dr Brooklyn NY 11234-6935 Personal E-mail: bd67124@optonline.net.

KIRSHNER, ALAN I., insurance company executive; Grad., Vanderbilt U. Dir. Markel Corp., Glen Allen, Va., 1978—, pres., 1979—92, chmn., CEO, 1986—. Office: Markel Corporation 4521 Highwoods Pkwy Glen Allen VA 23060*

KIRSHNER, JACOB, physician; b. NYC, Jan. 9, 1927; s. Philip and Irene (Walzer) K.; m. Sylvia Ann Shyken, Aug. 19, 1956; children: Daniel, Miriam, Eli, Ruth. BS magna cum laude, CCNY, 1945; AM, Columbia U., 1947; MD, SUNY, 1951. Diplomate Am. Bd. Internal Medicine. Rotating inter Mt. Sinai Hosp., NYC, 1951-52, asst. resident internal medicine, 1953-54; jr. asst. resident Montefiore Hosp., Bronx, NY, 1952-53; sr. resident VA Hosp., Bronx, 1954-55, fellow cardiology, asst. chief cardiac sect. dept. medicine, 1955-57; cons. medicine dept. medicine South Amboy Meml. Hosp., NJ, 1957-94; sr. attending physician dept. medicine St. Peter's Med. Ctr., New Brunswick, NJ, 1957-94; clin. asst. prof. Coll. Medicine & Dentistry N.J. Robert Wood Johnson Med. Sch, New Brunswick, 1971-82, clin. assoc. prof., 1982-93, prof., 1993—2005; clin. prof. medicine Drexel U. Coll. Medicine, Phila., 2005—. Mem. exec. com. med. dental staff St. Peters Med. Ctr., New Brunswick, 1962-94, sec.-treas., 1985-86, v.p., 1987-88, pres., 1989-90. V.p. Congregation Anshe Emeth of South River, 1971-72, pres., 1972-75, 2003-04; v.p. Jewish Fedn. Raritan Valley, 1976-78, pres., 1978-80; life mem. bd. dirs. Jewish Fedn. Greater Middlesex County, 1985—; chmn. local com. State of Israel Bonds; mem. State Bd. Jewish Nat. Fund; co-chmn. Jewish Cmty. Rels. Coun. Middlesex County, 1985-87; mem. exec. com. Nat. Jewish Cmty. Rels. Adv. Coun., 1986-89, 90-97, co-chmn. strategy com. World Jewry and Internat. Human Rights, 1990-95, co-chmn. strategy com. on Israel and other world affairs, 1995-2000, vice chmn., 1993-97; vice chair NJ Bd. Anti-Defamation League, 1998-2002, area chair, 2002—; vice chair Jewish Coun. on Pub. Affairs, 1999-2003. With USN, 1945-46. Recipient David Ben Gurion award State of Israel Bonds, 1976, Samuel I. Hoddeson Humanitarian award Jewish Fedn. Raritan Valley, 1981, Presdl. award Jewish Fedn. Greater Middlesex County, 1988. Mem. Med. Soc. NJ, Middlesex County Med. Soc., Alpha Omega Alpha, Phi Beta Kappa. Home: 53 Ferris St South River NJ 08882-1829 Personal E-mail: efghijk@verizon.net.

KIRSNER, JOSEPH BARNETT, physician, educator; b. Boston, Sept. 21, 1909; s. Harris and Ida (Waiser) K.; m. Minnie Schneider, Jan. 6, 1934 (dec. Dec. 4, 1998); 1 son, Robert S. MD, Tufts U., 1933; PhD in Biol. Scis., U. Chgo., 1942; DSc (hon.), Tufts U., 1993. Intern Woodlawn Hosp., Chgo., 1933—34, resident in internal medicine, 1934—35; asst. in medicine U. Chgo., 1935—37, from asst. prof. to assoc. prof., 1937—51, prof., 1951—, Louis Block Disting. Service prof. medicine, 1968—, chief of staff, also dep. dean for med. affairs, 1971—76. Cons. NIH, 1956-69; hon. pres. Gastrointestinal Research Found., 1961-; Mem. drug efficacy adv. com. to NRC; chmn. adv. group Nat. Commn. on Digestive Diseases, 1978; chmn. emeritus sci. adv. com. Nat. Found. Ileitis and Colitis. Editor, author: Kirsner's Inflammatory Bowel Disease, 6th edit., 2004, The Growth of Gastroenterologic Knowledge During the 20th Century, 1994, Early Days of American Gastroenterology, 1996; contbr. more than 800 articles to profl. jours. Served with M.C. AUS, 1943-46, ETO, PTO. Recipient Julius Friedenwald medal disting. work gastroenterology, 1975, Horatio Alger award, 1979, hon. Gold Key for Disting. Service U. Chgo. Med. Alumni Assn., 1979, Alumni medal U. Chgo. Alumni Assn., 1989, Disting. Educator award Am. Gastroenterological Assn., 1999, Tufts U. Dean's medal, 2006; Joseph B. Kirsner award for excellence in rsch. in clin. gastroenterology established in his honor, Am. Gastroent. Assn., 1990; G. Brohée lectr. World Cong. Gastroenterology, 1994, Laureate award Lincoln Acad. Ill., Dean's medal Tufts U., 2006. Mem. Am. Assn. Physicians, ACP (master, John Phillips award), Am. Gastroent. Assn. (past pres., governing bd.), Am. Gastroscopic Soc. (past pres.), Am. Soc. Gastrointestinal Endoscopy (past pres., Rudolf Schindler award), Am. Soc. Clin. Investigation, Ctrl. Soc. Clin. Rsch., Chgo. Soc. Internal Medicine (past pres.), Inst. Medicine Chgo. (George H. Coleman medal, Lifetime Achievement award 2004) Achievements include research in gastrointestinal disorders, inflammatory disease of gastrointestinal tract. Home: 5805 S Dorchester Ave Top C Chicago IL 60637-1730 Office: U Chgo Med Ctr 5841 S Maryland Ave MC 2200 Chicago IL 60637-1470 Office Phone: 773-702-6101. Business E-Mail: jkirsner@medicine.bsd.uchicago.edu. *We need a return to higher standards, personally and professionally. Striving for personal excellence and achievement promotes universal excellence and peace.*

KIRSTEUER, ERNST KARL EBERHART, biologist, curator; b. Vienna, Sept. 28, 1933; came to U.S., 1965; s. Ernst and Barbara (Reichhalter) K.; m. Erika Stepnitz, Jan. 18, 1958. PhD (research fellow 1958-60), U. Vienna, 1961. Instr. U. Vienna, 1961-62; prof. marine biology U. Cumana, Venezuela, 1963-65; asst. curator Am. Mus. Natural History, NYC, 1965-70, assoc. curator, 1970-75, curator, 1975-87, chmn., 1977-84, ret., 1987. Contbr. articles to profl. jours. NSF grantee, 1968-71.

KIRTLEY, JAMES L., JR., electrical engineer, educator; BSEE, MSEE, MIT, PhD in Elec. Engring. Internship student employee to assoc. rsch. scientist to sr. rsch. scientist Raytheon Corp., Waltham, Mass., 1965—71; mem. faculty to prof. elec. engring. MIT, Cambridge, 1971—. Cons. SatCon Tech. Corp., Boston, 1985—, bd. dirs., 1992—, v.p., 1998—2005, gen. mgr., 1998—2000, v.p., chief scientist, 2000—05; vis. prof. Swiss Fed. Inst. Tech., Zurich, 1993—94. Contbr. articles to sci. jours.; co-author: Electric Motor Handbook, 1998. Fellow: IEEE (Third Millennium medal 2000, Nikola Tesla award 2002); mem.: AAAS, NAE, Sigma Xi. Achievements include patents in field. Office: Lab Electromagnetic and Electronic Systems MIT Rm 10-171 77 Massachusetts Ave Cambridge MA 02139 Office Phone: 617-253-2357. Office Fax: 617-258-6774. E-mail: kirtley@mit.edu.*

KIRTLEY, JANE ELIZABETH, law educator; b. Indpls., Nov. 7, 1953; d. William Raymond and Faye Marie (Price) Kirtley; m. Stephen Jon Cribari, May 8, 1985. BS in Journalism, Northwestern U., 1975, MS in Journalism, 1976; JD, Vanderbilt U., 1979. Bar: N.Y. 1980, U.S. Dist. Ct. (we. dist.) N.Y. 1980, DC 1982, U.S. Dist. Ct. DC 1982, U.S. Ct. Claims 1982, U.S. Ct. Appeals (4th cir.) 1982, U.S. Ct. Appeals (DC cir.) 1985, U.S. Supreme Ct. 1985, Va. 1995, U.S. Ct. Appeals (10th cir.) 1996, U.S. Ct. Appeals (5th cir.) 1997, U.S. Ct. Appeals (6th and 11th cirs.) 1998. Assoc. Nixon, Hargrave, Devans & Doyle, Rochester, NY, 1979-81, Washington, 1981-84; exec. dir. Reporters Com. for Freedom of Press, Arlington, Va., 1985-99; Silha prof. media ethics & law Sch. Journalism & Mass Comm. U. Minn., Mpls., 1999—, mem. affiliated faculty Law Sch., 2001—; dir. Silha Ctr. Study Media Ethics and Law, Mpls., 2000—. Mem. adj. faculty Am. U. Sch. Comm., 1988—98; mem. affiliated law faculty U. Minn., 2001—; disting. vis. prof. Suffolk U. Law Sch., 2004. Exec. articles editor: Vanderbilt U. Jour. Transnational Law, 1978—79; editor: The News Media and the Law, 1985—, The First Amendment Handbook, 1987, 4th edit., 1995, Agents of Discovery, 1991, 1993, 1995, Pressing Issues, 1998—99; columnist: NEPA Bull., 1988—89, Va.'s Press, 1991—99, Am. Journalism Rev., 1995—, W.Va.'s Press, 1997—99, Tenn. Press, 1997—99, mem. editl. bd.: Comm. Law and Policy. Bd. dirs. Sigma Delta Chi Found., Indpls. Mem.: ABA, Va. State Bar Assn., DC Bar Assn., N.Y. State Bar Assn., Sigma Delta Chi. Home: 3645 46th Ave S Minneapolis MN 55406-2937 Office: 111 Murphy Hall 206 Church St SE Minneapolis MN 55455-0488 Home Phone: 612-728-0651; Office Phone: 612-625-9038. Business E-Mail: kirtl001@tc.umn.edu.

KIRTON, JENNIFER MYERS, artist; b. Berwick, Pa., Sept. 16, 1949; d. Fred H. and Jean I. Myers; m. Timothy Kirton, Aug. 8, 1970; children: Timothy James, Andrea Jolene, Andrew Joseph. Diploma, Orange Meml. Sch. Nursing, Orlando, Fla., 1970. RN. Galleries in Paris; represented by Mt. Dora, Fla., art-exchang.com, IRRA Registry, NMWA Gallery Artisan Inn, Deland. Tchr. drawing Mt. Dora Ctr. for Arts; overseas prodn. exhibitor, Paris, 1992—; lectr. in field; chair, judge juried art shows. Exhibited in group shows at Nat. Red Cross Scholastic (Nat. award, 1961), Apopka Art & Foliage (1st Place, 1975, 1982, Purchase award, 1978, 3rd Place, 1983, Hon. Mention, 1980, 1986), Winter Park Mall (Best of Show, 1977), Longwood Artist League of Orange County / Cen. Fla. Artists (3rd Place, 1980), Colonial Plz. (Hon. Mention, 1982, 1st Place, 1988, 1989), Springs Plz. (Hon. Mention, 1983), Howell Branch Plz. (1st Place, 1984), Under the Trees (2nd Place, 1984, Special Judges award, 1985), Fashion Sq. (Hon. Mention, 1986), Artist League (Hon. Mention, 1986), Centrust (1st Place, 1988), Lake County Art Show (Hon. Mention, 1992), Working Area Artist, Altamonte Libr., Pine Hills, Fiesta in Pk., Art Addiction Sweeden, Mount Dora Ctr. Arts (hon. mention), Internat. Judeo Christian Upstream Gallery, 2005 (spl. recognition Merit award, 2005, 2006, 2007), Artists Fla., Vol. IV, 1994—95, one-woman shows include Meritor Bank, Seminole CC, 5th St., Overseas European Corp., Mayor's Show Apopka City Hall, Fruitland Park Libr., Winter Park Fine Art Gallery, 2005, Biennial Deland Mus. Art, Serious Studios, Miami, Fla., 2004, exhibited in group shows at Serious Studio, Galveston, 2005, Serious Studios, Berlin, mural, Apopka H.S. Stadium, Represented in permanent collections City of Apopka, Mt. Dora Ctr. Arts, exhibited in group shows at 1st Leesburg Art Assn. Spring Show, 2006 (Best of Show, 2007), others; featured in Indie Arts Digital mag., 2007, Lake mag., 2007, represented in (permanent collections) Art Exch., Chgo., Art Expo, NYC. Named Artist of Month, artexchange website, 2004, artisrepublik.com, 2005, Mount Dora Mus. Art, 2006, Co-artist of Month, Legacy Fine Art, 2005; named one of Best of Fla. Artists and Artisan, Gallery Direct Am. Art Collector Book One and Two, vol. 4; named to promote Art Exch. site, Art Expo, N.Y., Best of Fla. Artist Registry; recipient trophy, Fla. com. Nat. Mus. Art, 2005, spl. recognition awards, Upstream People Gallery. Mem.: Internat. Registry Artist and Artwork, Art Exch. (rep.), Leesburg Art Assn. (Best of Show), Ctrl. Fla. Artists, Orange County League Artists (past pres.), Nat. League Pen Women, Nat. Mus. Women Arts (mem. Fla. com., historian ecentfl.com, historian). Baptist. Avocation: collecting fine art. Home: 4700 Meadowland Dr Mount Dora FL 32757-9661 Office Phone: 407-353-8332. Personal E-mail: kirtonart@aol.com.

KIRVEN, TIMOTHY J., lawyer; b. Buffalo, Wyo., May 26, 1949; s. William J. and Ellen F. (Farrell) K.; m. Elizabeth J. Adams, Oct. 31, 1970; 1 child, Kristen B. BA in English, U. Notre Dame, 1971; JD, U. Wyo., 1974. Bar: Wyo. 1974. Ptnr. Kirven & Kirven, PC, Buffalo, 1974—. Author Rocky Mountain Mineral Law, 1982. Mem. Johnson County Libr. Br., Buffalo. Mem. ABA (ho. of dels. 2002—), Wyo. State Bar (pres. 1998-99), Johnson County Bar Assn., Western States Bar Conf. (pres. 1998-99), Rotary (pres. Buffalo club 1988-89, youth exch. program chmn. 1993-98). Home: PO Box C Buffalo WY 82834-0060 Office: Kirven & Kirven PC 104 Fort St PO Box 640 Buffalo WY 82834-0640

KIRWAN, BETTY-JANE, lawyer; b. Rockeville Center, NY, Feb. 4, 1947; d. Franklin Ira and Pearl Elias; m. Ralph D. Kirwan (div.); children: Katherine, Andrew, Kerrigan; m. John Terence Hanna, Sept. 15, 1985. AB, U. Calif., Berkeley, 1968, JD, 1971. Bar: Calif. 1972, U.S. Dist. Ct. (cen. dist.) Calif. Atty. McCutchen, Black, Verleger, Shea, LA, 1972-85; founding ptnr. McClintock, Kirwan, Benshoof, Rochefort, Weston, LA, 1985-89; environ. atty., chair dept. environment L.A. office Latham & Watkins, LA, 1989—, ptnr., 1989—. Pres. Boalt Hall Alumni Assn., Berkeley, 1983-84; vice chair Hathaway Children's Svcs., L.A., 1984-89. Bd. dirs. Hathaway Children's Svcs., 1985-90, PLI Environ. Law Adv. Com., 1992—. Mem. ABA (vice chair air quality com. Natural Resource sect. 1980-88, chair environ. quality com. Natural Resource sect., chair environ. controls com. Bus. Law sect. 1986-90, coun. Bus. Law sect. 1990-94), Boalt Hall Alumni Assn. (pres. 1984). Office: Latham & Watkins 633 W Fifth St Ste 4000 Los Angeles CA 90071 Home: 1300 Chelten Way South Pasadena CA 91030-3912 Office Phone: 213-485-1234. Business E-Mail: bj.kirwane@lw.com.

KIRWAN, R. DEWITT (KYLE), lawyer; b. Albany, Calif., Aug. 30, 1942; s. Patrick William and Lucille Anne (Vartanian) K.; m. Betty-Jane Elias, June 29, 1969 (div. 1982); children: Katherine DeWitt, Andrew Elias; m. Nancy Jane Evers, Oct. 27, 1984; 1 child, Fletcher Evers. BA, U. Calif., Berkeley, 1966; JD, U. San Francisco, 1969. Bar: Calif. 1971, U.S. Dist. Ct. (ctrl. dist.) Calif. 1971, U.S. Ct. Appeals (9th cir.) 1971. Assoc. Schell & Delamer, LA, 1971-73; ptnr. Lillick & McHose, LA, 1973-90, Pillsbury Madison & Sutro, LA, 1990-98, Akin, Gump, Strauss, Hauer & Feld, LA, 1998—. Chmn., exec. bd. U. Calif., Berkeley, 1988-97, trustee U. Calif. Berkeley Found., 1995-98; bd. dirs., trustee Pacific Crest Outward Bound Sch., 1993-99; bd. dirs. L.A. Philharm. Assn., 1985-89, pres., 1986-88, mem. bus. and profl. com.; bd. dirs. Pasadena (Calif.) Symphony Assn., 1978-82. Capt. USAR, 1966-71. Mem.: ABA, Am Bd. Trial Advs., Bohemian Club, Calif. Club. Democrat. Roman Catholic. Avocations: fly fishing, mountain climbing, hunting, skiing. Office: Akin Gump Strauss Hauer & Feld Ste 2400 2029 Century Park E Los Angeles CA 90067-3012 Office Phone: 310-229-1000. Business E-Mail: rkirwan@akingump.com.

KIRWAN, WILLIAM ENGLISH, II, academic administrator, mathematics professor; b. Louisville, Apr. 14, 1938; s. Albert Dennis Kirwan and Elizabeth (Heil) Kirwan; m. Patricia Ann Harper, Aug. 27, 1960; children: William English III, Ann Elizabeth. BA, U. Ky., 1960; MS (NDEA fellow 1960-63), Rutgers U., 1962, PhD, 1964. Instr. Rutgers U., 1963—64; mem. faculty U. Md., College Park, 1964, prof. math., 1972, chmn. dept., 1977—81, vice chancellor for acad. affairs, 1981—86, provost, 1986—88, acting pres., 1988—89, pres., 1989—98, Ohio State U., Columbus, 1998—2002; chancellor U. System Md., 2002—. Vis. lectr. London U., 1966—67; program dir. NSF, 1975—76. Contbr. articles to profl. jours. MS 2000 Com. for NRC; mem. adv. bd. Montgomery County (Md.), 1975—79; bd. dirs. Nat. Assn. State Univs. and Land Grant Colls., 1995—, Greater Washington YMCA, 1994—; World Trade Ctr. Inst., 1990—. Decorated officer Order King Leopold II (Belgium); named Disting. Alumnus, U. Ky., 1989, Rutgers U.; recipient First Citizen of Md. award, Md. State Senate, 1998, Nat. Innovators award, Minority Access, Inc., 2004, Career Achievement award, Rutgers U., Speaker's medallion, Md. Ho. Dels., 2007. Fellow: Am. Acad. of Arts & Sciences; mem.: NCAA (pres. commn. 1995—), Coun. for the Internat. Exch. of Scholars, Math. Assn. Am., Am. Assn. Colls. and Univs. (bd. dirs. 1993—), Am. Math. Soc. (editor Proc. 1977—82, coun. 1980—82), Phi Kappa Phi, Phi Beta Kappa. Office: University System of Maryland Chancellor's Office 3300 Metzerott Rd, Suite 2C Adelphi MD 20783 Office Phone: 301-445-1901. Office Fax: 301-445-1931. E-mail: bkirwan@usmd.edu.*

KIRWIN, BARBARA ROSA, forensic specialist; d. Ernest Joseph and Isolene Smith Rosa; m. Thomas Joseph Kirwin, Sept. 26, 1971; 1 child, Damon Thomas-Joseph. BA in Psychology, CUNY Queens Coll., 1970, MA in Psychology, 1972; PhD in Clin. Psychology, New Sch. U., 1980; postdoctoral cert., LI U., 1984. Cert. psychologist NY, 1981. Narcotics parole officer NY State Office Drug Abuse Svcs., Long Island City, 1974—76; drug abuse specialist Nat. Drug Rsch. Inst., NYC, 1976—78; psychology intern OMH Ctrl. Islip PC, Brentwood, NY, 1978—79; rsch. neuropsychologist NIMH, Creedmoor PC, Queens Village, NY, 1979—80; chief svc., svc. unit Creedmoor PC, Queens Village, 1980—82; asst. dir. adminstrn. NY State Office Mental Health Creedmoor PC, Queens Village, 1982—84, assoc. psychologist, 1984—87; dir. Harborview Psychol. Svcs., Huntington, NY, 1984—. Forensic cons. Def. Attys., 1980—; expert witness State and Fed. Cts., NYC, 1980—; forensic cons. Met. Area Dist. Attys., NY, 1981—; forensic cons., state atty. gen. Office of State Atty. Gen., Fla., 2001—. Author: The Mad, The Bad and The Innocent: The Criminal Mind on Trial; prodr.: (broadband prodn.) Madness, (documentary) The Chameleon Killer, The Queen of Cons. Bd. dirs. Ind. Living Assn., Bklyn., 1989, Acad. St. Joseph, Brentwood, NY. Fellow, Am. Coll. Forensic Examiners Internat., 2003. Mem.: APA, Nat. Register Svc. Providers in Psychology, Am. Coll. Forensic Psychology. Office: Harborview Psychol Svcs 75 Prospect St Ste 104 Huntington NY 11743 Home Phone: 631-423-4701; Office Phone: 631-367-4200. Personal E-mail: harborviewpsych@optonline.net, barbara.kirwin@gmail.com.

KIRWIN, KENNETH FRANCIS, law educator; b. Morris, Minn., May 10, 1941; s. Francis B. and Dorothy A. (McNally) K.; m. Phyllis J. Hills, June 2, 1962; children— David, Mark, Robert. BA, St. John's U., 1963; JD, U. Minn., 1966. Bar: Minn. 1966, U.S. Dist. Ct. Minn. 1968, U.S. Ct. Appeals (8th cir.) 1969. Law clk. to assoc. justice Supreme Ct., Minn., 1966-67; assoc. Lindquist & Vennum, Mpls., 1967-70; prof. law William Mitchell Coll. Law, St. Paul, 1970—2006, prof. emeritus, 2006—. Staff dir. Uniform Rules Criminal Procedure, 1971-74, reporter, 1982-87; reporter Uniform Victims of Crime Act, 1991-92; adj. prof. U. Minn. Law Sch., 1977, 80; active Minn. Lawyers Profl. Responsibility Bd., 1975-81, Minn. Bd. Continuing Legal Edn., 1975-83. Author: (with Maynard E. Pirsig) Cases and Materials on Professional Responsibility, 1984. Mem. Ramsey County Bar Assn., Minn. State Bar Assn. (chair rules of profl. conduct com., 2002-05, co-chair multi jurisdictional practice task force, 2005-06), ABA (mem. standing com. on discipline 1983-89), Am. Law Inst. Home: 1418 Brookshire Ct New Brighton MN 55112-6390 Office: William Mitchell Coll Law 875 Summit Ave Saint Paul MN 55105-3030 Home Phone: 651-633-7581; Office Phone: 651-290-6346. Business E-Mail: kenneth.kirwin@wmitchell.edu.

KIRZ, JANOS, physicist; b. Budapest, Hungary, Aug. 11, 1937; came to U.S., 1957; s. Andras and Emma (Teller) K.; m. Micheline Barthez, Dec. 19, 1964 (div. Aug. 1985); 1 child, Steven; m. Regina Moreno, Jan. 5, 1988. BA, U Calif., Berkeley, 1959; PhD, U Calif., 1963. Physicist Lawrence Berkeley Lab., Berkeley, Calif., 1964-67, acting divsn. dir., Advanced Light Source Divsn., 2004—06; lectr. U. Calif., Berkeley, 1967; assoc. prof. SUNY, Stony Brook, 1968-72, prof., 1973—, Disting. prof., 1995—, chmn. dept. physics and astronomy, 1988—2001. Acting divsn. dir. Advanced Light Source Divsn. Lawrence Berkeley Lab., 2004—06, sci. advisor, 2007—. Contbr. articles to profl. jours. Fellow Woodrow Wilson Found., 1959, A.P. Sloan Found., 1970, Guggenheim Found., 1985; recipient A.H. Compton Advanced Photon Source award, 2005 Fellow AAAS, Am. Physical Soc.; mem. Optical Soc. Am. Achievements include development of scanning X-ray microscope. Office: MS 80R0114 Lawrence Berkeley Lab Berkeley CA 94720

KISCHER, CLAYTON WARD, human embryologist, educator; b. Des Moines, Mar. 2, 1930; s. Frank August and Bessie Erma (Sawtell) K.; m.Linda Sese Espejo, Nov. 7. 1964; children: Cynthia Ann, Eric Armine, Frank Henry. BS in Biology, U. Omaha, 1953; MS, Iowa State U., 1960, PhD, 1962. Asst. prof. biology Ill. State U., 1962-63; rsch. assoc. Argonne (Ill.) Nat. Lab., 1963; asst. prof. zoology Iowa State U., 1963-64; NIH postdoctoral fellow in biochemistry M.D. Anderson Hosp, Houston, 1964-66; chief sect. electron microscopy S.W. Found. Rsch. and Edn., San Antonio, 1966-67; assoc. prof. anatomy U. Tex. Med. Br., Galveston, 1967-77, U. Ariz. Coll. Medicine, Tucson, 1977—95, prof. emeritus, 1995—. Dir. Scanning electron microscopy lab. Shrine Burns Inst., Galveston, 1969-73, cons. Am. Life League, Stafford, Va., other right to life groups; chmn. Am. Bioethics Adv. Commn.; lectr. in biomed. ethics Pima C.C., 2002-05. Co-author: The Human Development Hoax: Time to Tell the Truth; author sci. and pub. policy; contbr. articles to profl. jours. Cubmaster pack 107 Island Dist., Galveston, 1974-76; bd. dirs. YMCA. With USN, 1947-49. NIH Rsch. grantee, 1968-89; Morrison Trust grantee, 1975-76. Mem. SAR, Galveston Rsch. Soc. (pres. 1971-72), Am. Soc. Cell Biology, Electron Microscopy Soc. Am., Am. Assn. Anatomists, Tex. Soc. Electron Microscopy (hon.) (editor newsletter 1969-73, pres. 1975-76), Ariz. Soc. Electron Microscopy (pres. 1980-81), Gamma Pi Sigma. Home: 6249 N Camino Miraval Tucson AZ 85718-3024 Office: U Ariz Coll Medicine Dept Cell Biology and Anatomy Tucson AZ 85724-0001 Office Phone: 520-626-6084. Personal E-mail: wkisch@netzero.net.

KISCHUK, RICHARD KARL, insurance company executive; b. Detroit, Mar. 14, 1949; s. Russell and Aubrey Ann (Artt) K.; m. Sandra Jean Dierkes, June 26, 1971; children: Robert Charles, Kirsten Grace, Erin Michelle, Danielle Laraine, Russell Olan, Erika Anne. BS, U. Mich., 1969, M in Actuarial Sci., 1971; MS in Bus. Adminstrn., Ind. U., 1979. Enrolled actuary. Actuarial trainee Lincoln Nat. Life, Ft. Wayne, Ind., 1971-72, actuarial asst., 1972-1973, asst. actuary, 1973-77, asst. v.p., 1977-80, 2d v.p., 1980-82; v.p. Lincoln Nat. Corp., Ft. Wayne, Ind., 1982-86; v.p., dir. Lincoln Nat. Health and Casualty Ins. Co., 1985-87, Lincoln Nat. Life Reins. Co., 1985-87, Lincoln Nat. Adminstrv. Service; chief operating officer, dir. Lincoln Intermediaries, Inc., 1985-87, Spl. Pooled Risk Adminstrs., Inc., 1985-87, Underwriters and Mgmt. Services, Inc., 1985-87; pres. Crown Point Mgmt. Cons., Inc., 1987—, Benefficient Solutions, Inc., 1998—. Mem. editorial adv. bd. CLU Jour., 1983-91; contbr. articles to profl. jours. Fellow Soc Actuaries (chmn. fin. reporting sect. 1982-85, bd. govs. 1986-89), mem. Am. Acad. Actuaries. Avocations: camping, backpacking, canoing, photography. Office: Crown Point Mgmt Cons Inc PO Box 355 Pendleton IN 46064-0355 Office Phone: 765-778-4340. E-mail: rkischuk@umich.edu.

KISELIK, PAUL HOWARD, manufacturing executive; b. Newark, Nov. 29, 1937; s. Jerome W. and Rose Kiselik; m. Teri Nimaroff, Sept. 6, 1959; children: Daniel, Jonathan. BS in Indsl. Engring., Lehigh U., 1960; MS in Mgmt. Engring., N.J. Inst. Tech., 1965. Registered profl. engr., N.J., Pa. V.p. Nimrow Carton Co., Elizabeth, NJ, 1961-71; pres. Sebro Packaging Corp., Livingston, NJ, 1971—. Pres. Rayart Folding Box Co., Livingston, 1971—, Lane Graphics, Livingston, 1984—. Author: (book) Equity Financing of a Small Business, 1965. Lt. US Army, 1960—61. Mem.: TAPPI, Asa Packer Soc., Morristown-Beard Sch. Alumni Assn. (v.p. 1979—81), Newtonian Soc., Alpha Pi Mu, Tau Beta Pi. Avocation: raising dogs.

KISER, CHÉRIE R., lawyer; BA, Univ. Minn., 1983; JD specialization in Comm., Catholic Univ. Am., 1987. Bar: Pa. 1987, D.C. 1988. Ptnr. Mintz Levin Cohn Ferris Glovsky & Popeo PC, Washington, mng. ptnr. DC office. Chair comm. sect. Mintz Levin Cohn Ferris Glovsky & Popeo PC, chair diversity com., mem. policy com.; spkr. at numerous confs. in field. Contbr. articles to profl. jour. Mem.: ABA, Nat. Assn. Women Lawyers, Women in Cable and Telecom., Internat. Tech. Law Assn., Fed. Comm. Bar Assn. Office: Mintz Levin Cohn Ferris Glovsky & Popeo 701 Pennsylvania Av NW Washington DC 20004 Office Phone: 202-434-7325. Office Fax: 202-434-7400. Business E-Mail: crkiser@mintz.com.

KISER, COLIN LEE, military officer, government contractor; b. Houston, Apr. 17, 1960; s. John Overby Jr. and Mary Delle (Fitzgerald) Kiser. BS, US Naval Acad., Annapolis, Md., 1983; M in Strategic Studies, US Naval War Coll., Newport, RI, 1996, US Army War Coll., Carlisle, Pa., 2004. Analyst CACI Co./Combined Joint Task Force-76, Bagram, Afghanistan; collection mgr. MPRI Co./Iraq Survey Group, Baghdad; comdr. USN, Washington, officer; strategic planner MPRI Co./Combined Forces Command-Afghanistan, Kabul, Afghanistan, 2003—. Cons. Afghan Ministry Fin. Capt. USN, 1983—. Named Jr. Officer of Yr., Surface Group 6, 1993, Naval Res. Outstanding Jr. Officer of Yr., Res. Officers Assn., 1994. Mem.: Mensa, Army & Navy Club. Avocations: scuba diving, travel, visiting historical sites, jogging. Home: 292 Becky Ln Waxahachie TX 75165

KISER, JACKSON L., federal judge; b. Welch, W.Va., June 24, 1929; m. Carole Gorman; children: Jackson, William, John Michael, Elizabeth Carol. BA, Concord Coll., 1951; JD, Washington and Lee U., 1952. Bar: Va. Asst. U.S. atty. Western Dist. Va., 1958-61; assoc., then ptnr. R.R. Young, Young, Kiser, Haskins, Mann, Gregory & Young P.C., Martinsville, Va., 1961-82; judge U.S. Dist. Ct. (we. dist.) Va., 1982-93, chief judge, 1993-97, sr. judge, 1997—. Mem. Martinsville City Sch. Bd., 1971-77. With JAGC U.S. Army, 1952-55, capt. Res., 1955-61. Mem. Am. Coll. Trial Lawyers (state com.), Va. Bar Assn. (exec. com.), Va. State Bar, Va. Trial Lawyers Assn., 4th Cir. Jud. Conf. (permanent), Martinsville-Henry County Bar Assn., Order of Coif. Office: US Dist Ct PO Box 3326 700 Main St Danville VA 24543-3326

KISER, NAGIKO SATO, retired librarian; b. Taipei, Republic of China, Aug. 7, 1923; came to U.S., 1950; d. Takeichi and Kinue (Soma) Sato; m. Virgil Kiser, Dec. 4, 1979 (dec. Mar. 1981). Secondary teaching credential, Tsuda Juku U., Tokyo, 1945; BA in Journalism, Trinity U., 1953; BFA, Ohio State U., 1956, MA in Art History, 1959; MLS, cert. in Libr. Media, SUNY, Albany, 1974. Cert. community coll. librarian, Calif., cert. jr. coll. tchr., Calif., cert. secondary edn. tchr., Calif., cert. tchr. library media specialist and art, N.Y. Pub. rels. reporter The Mainichi Newspapers, Osaka, Japan, 1945-50; contract interpreter U.S. Dept. State, Washington, 1956-58, 66-67; resource specialist Richmond (Calif.) Unified Sch. Dist., 1968-69; editing supr. CTB/McGraw-Hill, Monterey, Calif., 1969-71; multi-media specialist Monterey Peninsula Unified Sch. Dist., 1975-77; librarian Nishimachi Internat. Sch., Tokyo, 1979-80, Sacramento City Unified Sch. Dist., 1977-79, 81-85; sr. librarian Camarillo (Calif.) State Hosp. and Devel. Ctr., 1985-93. Editor: Short Form Test of Academic Aptitude, 1970, Prescriptive Mathematics Inventory, 1970, Tests of Basic Experience, 1970. Mem. Calif. State Supt.'s Regional Coun. on Asian Pacific Affairs, Sacramento, 1984-91. Library Media Specialist Tng. Program scholar U.S. Office Edn., 1974. Fellow Internat. Biog. Assn. (life); mem. ALA, Am. Biog. Inst. (life, dep. gov. 1988—), Libr. Congress (nat.

mem.), Calif. Libr. Assn., Med. Libr. Assn., Asunaro Shogai Kyoiku Kondankai (Lifetime Edn. Promoting Assn., Japan), The Mus. Soc., Internat. House of Japan, Matsuyama Sacramento Sister City Corp., Japanese Am. Citizens League, Japanese Am. Nat. Mus., Japanese Am. Cultural and Cmty. Ctr., Ikenobo Ikebana Soc. Am., L.A. Hototogisu Haiku Assn., Ventura County Archeol. Soc., Internat. Soc. Poets, AAUW, Ventura County Chpt. Mem. Christian Science Ch. Avocations: flower arranging, ballroom dance, classical music.

KISHNANI, PRIYA SUNIL, medical geneticist; arrived in U.S., 1991; MB, BChir, Bombay U., 1985, MD, 1990; DCH, Coll. Physicians and Surgeons Bombay, 1989. Cert. Am. Bd. Pediat., Am. Bd. Med. Genetics, Am. Bd. Clin. Biochem. Genetics. Co-dir. Down Syndrome Clinic Duke U. Med. Ctr., Durham, NC, 1996—, dir. Lysosomal Storage Disease Program, 1997—, dir. biochem. genetics, 1997—, dir. Metabolic Clinic, 1998—, assoc. prof. pediat., dir. clin. trials, 2002—, interim chief, 2005—. Contbr. articles to profl. jours. Recipient Spl. Recognition Honors, Triangle Down Syndrome Network, 2001, Exceptional Parent Maxwell J. Schleffer Disting. Svc. award, Exceptional Parent, 2005. Mem.: Am. Glycogen Storage Disease Assn. (sci. adv. bd. for pompe disease 1997—), Itnernat. Collaborative Gaucher Group (adv. bd. 2005—), Assn. for Glycogen Storage Diseases (chairperson 2005—), Soc. for the Study Inborn Errors Metabolism, Am. Coll. Med. Genetics, Am. Soc. Human Genetics. Achievements include involvement in clinical trials for treatment of cognitive deficits in Down Syndrome and for enzyme replacement therapy of infantile and late onset Pompe disease. Avocations: singing, cooking, writing. Office: Duke Univ Med Ctr Pediat Med Genetics Bell Bldg Rm 237 Box 3528 Durham NC 27710

KISIEL, IDA MARIE, education educator, writer; d. Salvatore and Mary Rose Collura; m. Theodore Kisiel, Dec. 26, 1963; children: Caroline Marya, Cassandra Louisa. EdB, Duquesne U., 1949; MA, Pa. State U., 1951; PhD, U. Pitts., 1962—62. Myers-Briggs Type Indicator Ill., 1998. Drama coach/script writer Pitts. Radio Sch., 1952—54; asst. prof. Duquesne U., Pitts., 1953—62, dir. writers' workshop, 1955—60; program dir., children's lit. series WDUQ, Duquesne U., Pitts., 1955—58; program host, modern novel series Duquesne U., Pitts., 1958—61; biography reviewer Pitts. Press, 1959—60; assoc. prof. Canisius Coll., Buffalo, 1965—69; adj. prof. Mundelein Coll., Chgo., 1972—74; prof. humanities Roosevelt U., Chgo., 1974—2000, dir. discovery workshop for women, 1975—80; exec. dir. Carrus Ednl. Resources, Winfield, Ill., 1979—; freelance writer Winfield, Ill., 1980—; radio talk show host WFMT, Chgo., 1980; guest columnist for careers Chgo. Tribune, 1981; dir., job retraining programs for tchrs. DuPage Bd. Edn., Wheaton, Ill., 1982; radio program host, women in nontraditional roles WFMT, Chgo., 1988; consulting ptnr. Redirections, Inc., Chgo., 1988—91; academic dir., ptnrs. in corp. Roosevelt U., Chgo., 1990—95, prof. emeritus, 1992—2005, dir. tng. and devel. Chgo., 1995—2000, dir. in tng., 1995—2000. Writing cons. AC Davenport Co., Palatine, Ill., 1975; cons./expert vocat. witness various law firms, Chgo., 1979—; exec. dir. Carrus Ednl. Resources, Winfield, Ill., 1979—; dir. comprehensive employment tng. act job skills program U.S. Fed. Govt., Chgo., 1979—80; lectr. Women in Mgmt., North Shore Conf., Chgo., 1980—85; lectr., women's roles Women in Radio & TV, Chgo., 1982; lectr. on setting goals, linkages Coll. DuPage, Glen Ellyn, Ill., 1989; employment dir., paralegal program Roosevelt U., Chgo., 1992—98. Author: (columnist/articles) Chgo.Tribune, (memoir) Thank You, Miss Mackelroy; contbr. book/memoir; author: (book) Design for Change, Presentation Skills for Trainers; editor: Pittsburgh Festival: Special Bicentennial Issue; author: New Directions: Contemporary Issues in Career and Lifestyle Management, How to Get a Job as a Paralegal (3rd Edition), Career Strategies for Secretaries; contbr. book; author: (poems) Portraits & Promises, (nonfiction) Season of Grace; careers editor, columnist: Chgo. Tribune; author: numerous articles in newspapers, modules. Civic dir., cmty. resources program No. Ill. U. Lab Sch., DeKalb, 1972—73; mem. Citizens for a Better Environment, Winfield, 1980—89, Winfield United, 2004—05, Regional Commn. on Higher Edn. in Western Pa., Pitts., 1962; judge Sec. of Yr. Profl. Secretaries Internat., Chgo., 1981—82; dir., job skills retraining program North Shore Edn. Ctr., Evanston, 1974—75; mem. Friends of Winfield Libr., Winfield, Ill., 2004—05. Recipient Woman of Yr., Sigma Lambda Phi, 1955, Recognition award, GSA, 1985, Spl. Recognition award, Diversity Coun. of Lucent Tech., 1989, Recognition award, Women in Mgmt., 1990; fellow Project for the Study of Adult Learning, State of Ill., 1995; grantee, Am. Philos. Soc., 1962. Mem.: AAUW, Nat. Career Devel. Assn., Assn. Psychol. Type (licentiate), Wellsley Ctrs. for Women (assoc.), Am. Bd. Vocat. Experts (assoc.), Nat. Assn. Women in the Arts. Avocations: reading, travel, writing, counseling young adults. Home Phone: 630-665-3292. Personal E-mail: mkisiel1@comcast.net.

KISKA, TIMOTHY OLIN, communications educator, radio producer; b. Detroit, July 26, 1952; s. Edward Frederick and Mary Clare (Barnhart) K.; m. Patricia Irene Anstett, May 23, 1981; children: Caitlin, Amy, Eric. BA, Wayne State U., 1980, MA, 1995, PhD, 2003. Mem. staff Detroit Free Press, 1970-74, reporter, 1974-85, automotive writer, 1985-87; columnist Detroit News, 1987—2002. Asst. prof. comm. U. Mich., Dearborn, 2001-; mem. student newspaper publs. bd. Wayne State U., 1994-97, 99-2001; prodr. Sta. WWJ, 2004-. Author: Detroit's Powers and Personalities, 1989; From Soupy to Nuts! A History of Detroit TV, 2005. Mem.: Assn. Edn. in Journalism and Mass Communication. Home: 20050 Marford Ct Grosse Pointe Woods MI 48236-2324 Office: Univ Mich Dearborn 4901 Evergreen Rd Dearborn MI 48128 Home Phone: 313-886-2401; Office Phone: 313-583-6381. Business E-Mail: tkiska@umd.umich.edu.

KISKER, CARL THOMAS, pediatrician, educator; BA, Johns Hopkins U., 1958; MD, U. Cin. Coll. Medicine, 1962. Diplomate Am. Bd. Pediatrics, Am. Bd. Pediatric Hematology-Oncology. Lic. physician Ohio, Iowa. Intern U. Oreg. Coll. Medicine, 1962-63; sr. asst. surgeon NIH, 1963-65; jr. resident pediat. Children's Hosp., Cin., 1965-66, sr. resident pediat., 1966-67, fellow pediat. hematology, 1967-69, asst. attending pediatrician, 1968-69, attending pediatrician, 1969-73, dir. hemophilia project, 1971-73, dir. clin. hematology lab., 1972-73; asst. prof. pediat. U. Cin., 1969-72, assoc. prof. pediat., 1972-73, U. Iowa, Iowa City, 1973-79, dir. divsn. pediat. hematology-oncology, 1973-97, prof. pediat., 1979—. Med. lectr. various student and profl. groups; active mem. Pediat. Hematology-Oncology Group, Cin., Children's Cancer Study Group, L.A.; pres. Midwest Blood Club; mem. adv. coun. Nat. Hemophilia Ctrs., 1979—.$D Mem. editl bd. Pediat. Today; contbr. numerous sci. papers to profl. jours. and chpts. in books. Mem. Iowa Found. Fund Raising Com. Lederle Med. Student Rsch. fellow, 1959; recipient state and fed. grants, Alumni of Yr. award U. Cin. Coll. Medicine, 2002. Mem. Am. Soc. Hematology, Mid-west Soc. for Pediat. RSch., Am. Fedn. for Clin. RSch., Am. Heart Assn., Internat. Soc. Thrombosis and Haemostasis (sub-com. on neonatal hemostasis), Ctrl. Soc. for Pediat. Rsch., Soc. Pediat. Rsch., Johnson County Med. Soc., Prairie Region Affiliated Blood Svcs., Am. Pediat. Soc.

KISLAK, JEAN HART, art director; b. 1931; d. Frank Ernest and Isabelle Taylor (Ellis) Hart; m. William I. Herendeen, Aug. 23, 1952 (div. Feb. 1956); m. Louis G. Johnson, Jan. 31, 1959 (div. Feb. 1975); 1 child, Jennifer Taylor Johnson; m. Jay Kislak, Apr. 7, 1985. Student, Peace Jr. Coll., Raleigh, NC, Queens Coll., Charlotte, NC. With Storer Broadcasting Co., Miami, Fla., S.E. Banks, N.A., Miami, 1974-84, art dir., 1974-84; mem. Gov. Fla. Panel Visual Arts, 1979-81; art cons., 1974—. Internat. rep. Christies, Inc., 1998—2001; mem. art and archtecture com. Libr. of Congress, Washington, 2003. Bd. dirs. Viscaya Mus., Miami, 1963, Beaux Arts, U. Miami, 1968, Theatre Art Patrons, Miami, 1968, Theatre Art Patrons, Miami, 1965, Nat. Wildflower Assn., 1991, NEH, Fla., 1992, Miami (Fla.) Humane Soc., 2006, Farnsworth Mus., Rockland, Maine, 2006; trustee Dade County Zool. Soc., 1988—, Miami Art Mus., Barry Coll. Charter Sch.; mem. Bacardi Imports Art Bd., 1983-89, 98—, Fla. State Bd. Art Coun., 1987, Miami Art Mus. (formerly Dade County Ctr. for the Arts Bd.), 1989-99; mem. exec. bd. Zool. Soc. Fla., 1994; mem. Fla. Humanities Bd., 1994; mem. visual arts com. Libr. Congress, 2002. Recipient Gov. Fla. award art, 1976, 79, Miami Dade Pub. Libr. award, 1978, Bus. Com. for Arts award, 1975-79, WPBT Pub. TV award, 1976, 77, 80, Lowe Gallery, U. Miami cert. recognition, 1980, Dade County Art in Pub. Places cert. recognition, 1981, 82. Mem. 1805 Club (London) (hon. v.p. 1993—), Kislak Found. (bd. dirs. 1997—). Address: 720 NE 69th St Miami FL 33138-5738

KISLIK, RICHARD WILLIAM, publishing executive; b. NYC, Oct. 31, 1927; s. Louis K. and Isabelle (Deutelbaum) K.; m. Audrey Gerber, June 19, 1949; children: Nancy J., Andrew R., Laurie S., Wendy J AB, Harvard U., Cambridge, Mass., 1948, MBA, 1949. Rsch. asst. Bus. Sch. Harvard U., 1949-50; asst. contr. Maidenform Brassiere Co., 1950-54; contr. Doubleday & Co., Inc., 1954-60; treas., dir. Ziff-Davis Pub. Co., 1961—68; v.p. fin., dir. Random House, Inc., 1961-68; cons., 1968; v.p. Intext, Inc., 1968-69, pres., 1969—, exec. v.p., 1970-71, pres., 1971-77, chmn. bd., chief exec. officer, 1972-80, cons., 1980—85; pres., dir. W.H. Smith Pubs. Inc., 1986—95, ret., 1995; v.p. M. Evans & Co., 1987—96; pvt. practice, 1986—. Dir. Lin Broadcasting, 1969—95. Mem.: Harvard Bus. Sch. Club Greater NY, Pubs. Lunch Club, Harvard Club (NYC), Dutch Treat Club. Home: 176 E 71st St New York NY 10021-5159

KISLING, FANNY, counselor, educator; b. Preble County, Ohio, Jan. 14, 1931; d. William Benjamin and Anna Viola (Wing) Banis; m. Donald Robert Kisling, May 14, 1950 (dec. 1991); children: Emily Margaret, Rebecca Jane, Karen Lea, Suzanne Michele, Orval William, David Guy. BS with honors, Miami U., Oxford, Ohio, 1973, MEd, 1974, PhD, 1986. Lic. profl. counselor; cert. tchr. Commuter advisor Miami U., 1975-76, program cons., 1976-78; prof., counselor Sinclair C.C., 1978-96, retired, 1996. Lectr. Kent (Ohio) State U., 1990; presenter in field. One-woman shows include Preble County Art Ctr., Eaton, Ohio, 2006; author: An Eaton Chronicle, An Abbreviated History of Eaton, Ohio, 2006. Mayor Eaton, Ohio, 1995-97; mem. Eaton City Coun., 1993-97, Eaton Bicentennial Com.; bd. dirs. SCOPE Cmty. Action Agy., Ohio, 1993, Preble County Coun. on Aging, Preble County Art Assn., Preble County Retired Tchrs. Assn.; elder First Presbyn. Ch., Eaton, 1993. Mem.: AAUW, Ohio Coll. Pers. Assn., Am. Coll. Pers. Assn., Am. Counseling Assn., Alpha Garden Club (pres.), Phi Delta Kappa, Kappa Delta Pi, Phi Kappa Phi. Republican. Avocations: writing, bird watching, gardening, painting, hiking. Home: 305 East Ave Eaton OH 45320-2005 Personal E-mail: fkisling@woh.rr.com.

KISOR, HENRY DU BOIS, retired editor, columnist, critic, writer; b. Ridgewood, NJ, Aug. 17, 1940; s. Manown and Judith (Du Bois) K.; m. Deborah L. Abbott, June 24, 1967; children: Colin, Conan. BA, Trinity Coll., 1962, LittD (hon.), 1991; MS in Journalism, Northwestern U., 1964. Copy editor Wilmington News-Jour. (Del.), 1964-65, Chgo. Daily News, 1965-73, book editor, 1973-78, Chgo. Sun-Times, 1978—2006; ret., 2006. Adj. prof. Medill Sch. Journalism Northwestern U., Evanston, Ill., 1979-82 Author: What's That Pig Outdoors?: A Memoir of Deafness, 1990, Zephyr: Tracking a Dream Across America, 1994, Flight of the Gin Fizz: Midlife at 4,500 Feet, 1997, Season's Revenge, 2003, A Venture into Murder, 2005, A Cache of Corpses, 2007. Bd. dirs. Chgo. Hearing Soc., 1975-76. Recipient Stick-O-Type award Chgo. Newspaper Guild, 1981, 85, Outstanding Achievement award Ill. UPI, 1983, 85, 1st pl. award Ill. UPI columns divsn., 1985, James Friend Meml. Critic award Friends of Lit., 1988, Best Non-fiction award, 1991; finalist Pulitzer Prize nomination in criticism Columbia U., 1981; named to Chgo. Journalism Hall of Fame, 2001; NEH seminar fellow, 1978. Mem.: Deaf Pilots Assn. Avocations: photography, aviation. Personal E-mail: h.kisor@comcast.net.

KISS, ELIZABETH, academic administrator, philosophy educator; d. Sandor and Eva Ilona Kiss; m. Jeffrey Holzgrefe, Mar. 18, 1989. BA magna cum laude, Davidson Coll., NC, 1983; B of Philosophy, Oxford U., UK, 1985, D. Philosophy, 1990. Instr. in politics Princeton U., 1988—89, asst. prof., 1990—96; vis. prof. of humanities Deep Springs Coll., Deep Springs, Calif., 1990—91; fellow, ethics prog. Harvard U., Cambridge, Mass., 1992—93; fellow Nat. Humanities Ctr., NC, 1995—96; vis. prof. Deep Springs Coll., Deep Springs, Calif., 1999; assoc. prof. Duke U., Durham, NC, 1997—, Nannerl O. Keohane dir. Kenan Inst. for Ethics, 1997—2006; pres. Agnes Scott Coll., Decatur, Ga., 2006—. Bd. of directors Ctr. for Documentary Studies, Durham, NC, 1997—2003; dean's adv. com. on svc. learning Duke U., Durham, NC, 1997—; co-chair Academic Integrity Assessment Com., Durham, NC, 1999—. Author: (article) Moral Ambition within and beyond Political Constraints: Reflections on Restorative Justice, Democracy and the Politics of Recognition, In Praise of Eccentricity: Character, Moral Education, and Democracy, Alchemy or Fools Gold: Assessing Feminist Doubts and Rights. Represented Hungarian Human Rights Found. Conf. on Non-Governmental Organizations and Human Rights, UN, Geneva, 1987—87; Martin Luther King day planning com. Duke U., Durham, NC, 2000—01; interpreter at Hungarian elections Alliance of Free Democrats, Budapest, Hungary, 1990—90. Recipient Bowen Presdl. Preceptorship, Princeton U., 1994-1997; grantee Postdoctoral grant, Am. Coun. of Learned Societies, 2000-2001; scholar Rhodes Scholarship, Oxford U., 1983-1986. Mem.: N. Am. Soc. for Social Philosophy, NAS (treas.), Ctr. for Academic Integrity (bd. of directors 1997—2003), Davidson Coll. (bd. of trustees 1997—2003), NC Rhodes Scholarships (sec., selection com. 1998—2003). Office: Agnes Scott Coll 141 E College Ave Decatur GA 30030 Office Phone: 404-471-6280. Office Fax: 404-471-6067. E-mail: president@agnesscott.edu.*

KISSA, ERIK, retired chemist, consultant; b. Apr. 7, 1923; came to U.S., 1951, naturalized, 1956; s. Mats and Selma (Jakobson) K.; m. Selma Alide Tamm, Sept. 6, 1952; children: Erik Harold, Karl Martin. MS, Tech. U., Karlsruhe, Germany, 1951; PhD, U. Del., 1956. Rsch. chemist E. I. du Pont de Nemours & Co. Inc., Wilmington, Del., 1951-67, sr. rsch. chemist, 1967-74, rsch. assoc. Jackson Lab., 1974-86, sr. rsch. assoc., 1986-90, rsch. fellow, 1990-93; ret., 1994. Cons., 1994—; UN tech. expert, India, 1978, 79, China, 1982, Korea, 1986-88. Author: Fluorinated Surfactants, 1993, Dispersions, 1999, Fluorinated Surfactants and Repellents, 2001; editor: Detergency Theory and Technology, 1987; contbr. articles, chpts. on surface chemistry, textile chemistry, and analytical chemistry to profl. publs.; U.S. and internat. patentee in field. Recipient Soap and Detergent Assn. award, 1991. Mem.: Am. Chem. Soc., Del. Photographic Soc., Du Pont Country Club. Lutheran. Home and Office: 1436 Fresno Rd Wilmington DE 19803-5122 E-mail: ekissa@aol.com.

KISSA, KARL MARTIN, electrical engineer; b. Wilmington, Del., June 5, 1961; s. Erik and Selma (Tamm) Kissa; m. Wendy Sue Earle, Mar. 8, 2003; 1 child, Emily Elisabeth. BS, Duke U., 1982; MEE, U. Del., 1986, PhD, 1989. Tech. staff C.S. Draper Lab., Cambridge, Mass., 1989-94; photonic device engr. United Techs. Photonics, Bloomfield, Conn., 1994-95; sr. optical engr. JDSU, Bloomfield, 1995—. Vol. Harvard Sq. Meals Program, Cambridge, Mass., 1991-94. Mem. IEEE, Conn. Acad. Scis. & Engring., Phi Beta Kappa, Tau Beta Pi, Eta Kappa Nu. Congregationalist. Home: 1 Grant Estate Dr West Simsbury CT 06092-2101 Office: JDSU 45 Griffin Rd S Bloomfield CT 06002-1302

KISSAM, LUTHER C., IV, lawyer, chemicals executive; Assoc. gen. counsel Monsanto Co.; v.p., gen. counsel, sec. Merisant Co., Albemarle Corp., Richmond, Va., 2003—05, sr. v.p., gen. counsel, sec., 2005—. Office: Albemarle Corp 330 S Fourth St PO Box 1335 Richmond VA 23219 Office Phone: 804-788-6000.*

KISSANE, SHARON FLORENCE, writer, consultant, educator; b. Chgo., July 2, 1940; d. Bruno William and Agnes Evelyn (Payne) Mrotek; m. James Quin Kissane, July 2, 1966 (dec. June 1989); children: Laura Janine Ehrke, Elaine Marie Kissane Zachrel. BA, De Paul U., Chgo., 1962; MA, Northwestern U., Evanston, Ill., 1963; PhD, Loyola U., Chgo., 1970. Cert. tchr., Ill. Tchr. Notre Dame H.S., Chgo., 1959-61, Our Lady of Solace Sch., Chgo., 1961-62; tech. writer, editor Commerce Clearing House, Chgo., 1962-63; tchr. U. Ill., Chgo., 1963-66; mgr. Amalgamated Ins. Co., Chgo., 1966-68; writer Herald Newspapers, Des Plaines, Ill., 1968-69; assoc. dir. Montague Coll. Psycho-Ednl. Clinic, Chgo., 1970-72; dir. Learning Ctr., libr. Stevenson Elem. Sch., Des Plaines, 1972-73; dir. Park Ridge Reading Ctr., Ill., 1973-78; pres. Kissane Comms. Ltd., Barrington, Ill., 1979—. Learning disabilities specialist Montessori Sch., Lake Forest, Ill.; gifted coord. Winfield Pub. Schs.; spkr. in field. Author: What is Child Abuse?, 1993, 2001, Gang Awareness, 1995, 2001; co-author: Polish Biographical Dictionary, 1992, Career Success for People With Physical Disabilities, 1996, Autobiography of Mousie Garner, Vaudeville Stooge; contbr. articles to profl. jours. and encyclopedia of advt. Bd. dirs. Barrington (Ill.) Children's Choir, 1984-85, LA FEP Student Exch. Program, Barrington, 1983-84, Barrington Area United Way, Operation Smile Internat., Chgo.; mem. task force Dist. # 220, Barrington, 1983-86; founding mem. Barrington Area Arts Coun., 1980, Park Ridge Hist. Soc., 1972; mem. curriculum com. Barrington H.S., 1981-84; elections judge South Barrington Precinct, 1989—; mem. bus. adv. coun. Nat. Rep. Congl. com.; pres. small bus. advisory council. Recipient Dale Carnegie Speech scholarship Jr. Achievement, 1958, Ronald Regan Gold Medal Winner, Pres. Small Bus. Adv. Council, 2004, La Cittá del Sole, Italy, Disting. Bus. Leader award, 2001, Ill. Businessman of Yr. award, 2003, Poetry.com award; named Hon. Citizen of Korea, 1965, Women of the Yr. Am. Biog. Assn., 2004; honored as local author, Ill. Assn. Conv., 1999; Literacy grantee, 2000. Mem. Nat. Assn. Women Bus. Owners (bd. dirs. 1982-83), Ralph Metcalfe Found. (bd. dirs.), Internat. Platform Assn., MIT Forum, Ill. Libr. Assn. (Conn. chpt.), Barrington Profl. Women, Midwest Soc. Profl. Cons., Northwestern U. Entertainment Alliance, Authors Guild, Writers Guild Am., Loyola U. Grad. Alumni Soc. (bd. mem. exec. bd.), South Barrington Hist. Soc. (chmn.), Phi Delta Kappa, Kappa Gamma Pi. Republican. Avocations: painting, post-card art, music, sports. Office: Kissane Comms Ltd 15 Turning Shore Dr South Barrington IL 60010-9597 Office Phone: 847-381-7192. Personal E-mail: kissanecom@sbcglobal.net.

KISSEL, HOWARD WILLIAM, drama critic; b. Milw., Oct. 29, 1942; s. Leo and Ruth (Miletzky) K.; m. Christine Buck, May 5, 1974. BA, Columbia U., 1964; MS in Journalism, Northwestern U., 1966. Arts editor Women's Wear Daily, NYC, 1971-86; drama critic N.Y. Daily News, 1986—97, 2001—, columnist, 1997—2001. Juror Pulitzer Prize for Drama, 1994; bd. dirs. Theater Devel. Fund., 1982--; adj. prof. Marymount Manhattan, 1998-01. Author: David Merrick, The Abominable Showman; Dictionary of Literary Biography, 1982-97, Words with Music; editor: Stella Adler: The Art of Acting. Named to Hall of Achievement Northwestern U., 1997. Mem. N.Y. Drama Critics Circle (pres. 1984-86), N.Y. Film Critics Circle (chmn. 1975, 82), Players Club. Jewish. Home: 275 Central Park W New York NY 10024-3015 Office: NY Daily News Inc 450 W 33rd St Fl 3 New York NY 10001-2681 Office Phone: 212-210-1541.

KISSEL, PETER CHARLES, lawyer; b. Watertown, NY, Sept. 29, 1947; s. Laurence Haas and Catherine Cantwell (Weldon) Kissel; m. Sharon Darlene Murphy, June 14, 1970. AB, Syracuse U., 1969; JD, Am. U., 1972. Bar: DC 1973, US Court Claims 1976, US Court Appeals (3d cir) 1976, US Supreme Court 1978, US Dist Ct DC 1979, US Ct Appeals (9th cir) 1979, US Ct Appeals (DC cir) 1983, US Ct Appeals (5th cir) 1988. Atty.-advisor Fed. Power Commn., Washington, 1972-74; atty. pub. utilities, 1974-77; assoc. O'Connor & Hannan, Washington, 1977-79, ptnr., 1979-87, Baller Hammett, Washington, 1987-93; ptnr., CFO, Grammer, Kissel, Robbins, Skancke & Edwards (GKRSE), Washington, 1993—. Co-bus. mgr. Energy Law Jour., 1981, asst. editor, 1982—89, bus. mgr., 1989—92; contbr. articles to profl. jours. Mem Washington adv. bd. Syracuse U., 1995—, mem. chancellor's coun.; mem. adv. bd. Maxwell Sch. Citizenship and Pub. Affairs, 2002—; bd. dirs. Episcopal Caring Response to AIDS Inc., 1988—93, v.p., 1990—91, pres., 1992, mem. exec. com., 1990—93; mem vestry St Patrick's Episcopal Ch, Washington, 1975—78, chmn. ann. fundraising campaign, 1987—89; bd. dirs. PRISM, 1996—97, Waterpower XII Steering Com., 2000—01. Recipient Spl Award, Fed Power Comn, 1973. Mem.: Electric Coop. Bar Assn., Syracuse Univ. Chancellors Coun., Syracuse Univ. Soc. Fellows, Bar Assn. DC, John Sherman Myers Soc., Nat. Hydropower Assn., Energy Bar Assn. (vice chmn com on publs 1984—85, chmn com on hydroelectric regulation 1991—92), Phi Kappa Psi. Democrat. Episcopalian. Avocations: gardening, American history, Irish history, Irish music. Home: 5604 Utah Ave NW Washington DC 20015-1230 Office: GKRSE 1500 K St NW Ste 330 Washington DC 20005 Office Phone: 202-408-5400. Business E-Mail: pckissel@GKRSE-law.com.

KISSEL, RICHARD JOHN, lawyer; b. Chgo., Nov. 27, 1936; s. John and Anne T. (Unichowski) K.; m. Donna Lou Heidersbach, Feb. 11, 1961; children: Roy Warren, David Todd, Audrey Anne. BA, Northwestern U., 1958; JD, Northwestern U., Chgo., 1961. Assoc. Peterson, Lowrey, Rall, Barber & Ross, Chgo., 1961-65; divsn. counsel Abbott Labs., North Chicago, Ill., 1965-70; mem. Pollution Control Bd., Chgo., 1970-72; adminstrv. asst. Gov.'s Staff, Chgo., 1972; ptnr. Martin, Craig, Chester & Sonnenschein, Chgo., 1973-88, Gardner, Carton & Douglas, Chgo., 1988—2000, chmn. mgmt. com., 1996-98, of counsel, 2000—. Adj. prof. U. Ill. Sch. Pub. Health, Chgo., 1973-76; instr. Kent. Sch. Law, Ill. Inst. Tech., Chgo., 1974-78; vis. com. Northwestern U. Law Sch., 1996-99. Recipient Ill. award IAWA, 1996; bd. dirs. Harbour Ridge Realty, Co. Contbr. articles to profl. jours. Mem. Lake Forest (Ill.) Sewer Adv. Com.; pres. Lake Forest Lake Bluff Sr. Citizens Found. Fellow Internat. Soc. Barristers; mem. Ill. State Bar Assn., Chgo. Bar Assn., Ill. State C. of C. (chmn. environ. affairs 1973-76), Com. on Cts. for 21st Century, Knollwood Club (Lake Forest; gov. 1976-82), Lake Forest/Lake Bluff Sr. Citizens Found (bd. dirs., pres.), 100 Club Lake County (bd. dirs.), Harbour Ridge Yacht & Country Club, Harbor Ridge Realty (bd. dirs.). Roman Catholic. Office: Drinker Biddle Gardner Carton 191 N Wacker Dr Chicago IL 60606-1698 Home Phone: 847-295-4028; Office Phone: 312-569-1442. Business E-Mail: rkissel@gcd.com.

KISSELGOFF, ANNA, dance critic; Chief dance critic NY Times, NYC, 1972—2005, contbr. dance pieces, 2005—. Office: NY Times 229 W 43rd St New York NY 10036 Office Phone: 212-556-7238. Office Fax: 212-556-1516.

KISSINGER, HENRY ALFRED, international consulting company executive, former secretary of state; b. Fuerth, Germany, May 27, 1923; came to U.S., 1938, naturalized, 1943; s. Louis and Paula (Stern) K.; m. Ann Fleischer, Feb. 6, 1949 (div. 1964); children: Elizabeth, David; m. Nancy Maginnes, Mar. 30, 1974. AB summa cum laude, Harvard U., 1950, MA, 1952, PhD, 1954. Exec. dir. Harvard Internat. Seminar, 1951-69; mem. faculty dept. govt., Ctr. for Internat. Affairs Harvard U., 1954-69; dir. def. studies program Harvard Internat. Seminar, 1958-69, assoc. prof. govt., 1959-62, prof., 1962-69; faculty Ctr. Internat. Affairs, Harvard U., 1960-69; asst. to Pres. for nat. security affairs NSC, Washington, 1968—75; sec.

US Dept. State, Washington, 1973-77; founder, chmn. Kissinger Assocs., Inc., NYC. Chmn. Nat. Bipartisan Commn. on Ctrl. Am., 1983-84; study dir. nuclear weapons and fgn. policy Coun. Fgn. Rels, 1955-56; dir. spl. studies project Rockefeller Bros. Fund, Inc., 1956-58; cons. Ops. Rsch. Office, 1950-61; cons. to dir. Psychol. Strategy Bd., 1952; cons. Ops. Coordinating Bd., 1955, Weapons Systems Evaluation Group, 1959-60, US Dept. State, 1965-69; hon. chmn. World Cup USA, 1994; advisor to bd. Am. Express Co., Forstmann Little & Co.; internat. coun. J.P. Morgan Chase, Am. Internat. Group; trustee Ctr. Strategic and Internat. Studies; bd. mem. ContiGroup Companies; exec. com. Trilateral Commn.; bd dirs. Internat. Rescue com.; U.S. Olympic Com. Author: Nuclear Weapons and Foreign Policy, 1957, A World Restored: Castlereagh, Metternich and the Restoration of Peace, 1812-22, 1957, The Necessity for Choice: Prospects of American Foreign Policy, 1961, The Troubled Partnership: A Reappraisal of the Atlantic Alliance, 1965, White House Years, 1979, For the Record, 1981, Years of Upheaval, 1982, Observations: Selected Speeches and Essays, 1984, Diplomacy, 1994, Years of Renewal, 1999, Does America Need A Foreign Policy?, 2001, Ending the Vietnam War, 2003, Crisis, 2003; Editor: Problems of National Strategy: A Book of Readings, 1965, Confluence, An Internat. Forum, 1951-58; contbr. to profl. jours. Hon. mem. Internat. Olympic Com. Recipient citation Overseas Press Club, 1958, Woodrow Wilson prize for best book fields of govt., politics, internat. affairs, 1958, Disting. Pub. Svc. award Am. Inst. Pub. Svc., 1973, Nobel Peace Prize, 1973, Presdl. Medal of Freedom, 1977, Medal of Liberty, 1986; named Hon. Knight Comdr. of St. Michael and St. George, 1995; Guggenheim fellow, 1965-66. Mem. Am. Polit. Sci. Assn., Council Fgn. Relations, Am. Acad. Arts and Scis., Phi Beta Kappa. Clubs: Metropolitan (Washington); Century, River Club, Brook Club (N.Y.C.), Bohemian (San Francisco). Republican.

KISSINGER, WALTER BERNHARD, retired automotive executive; b. Furth, Germany, June 21, 1924; came to U.S., 1938, naturalized, 1939; s. Louis and Paula (Stern) K.; m. Eugenie Van Drooge, July 4, 1958; children: William, Thomas, Dana Marie, John. BA, Princeton U., 1951; MBA, Harvard U., 1953; PhD (hon.), Hofstra U., 2001. Asst. to v.p. fgn. operations Gen. Tire & Rubber Co., Akron, Ohio, 1953-56; pres. Advanced Vacuum Products Co., Stamford, Conn., 1957-62; exec. v.p., dir. Glass-tite Industries, Providence, 1960-62; asst. to pres. Jerrold Corp., 1963-64; exec. v.p., Chmn. exec. com., dir. Jervis Corp., Hicksville, NY, 1964-68; chmn., pres., chief exec. officer Allen Group Inc., Melville, NY, 1969-88; pres. WBK Assocs., Melville, NY, 1988—. Chmn. bd. of the Long Island Res. Inst., Melville, NY, 1992-98; vice chmn. bd. of trustees & chmn. of academic affairs comm., Hofstra U. Dir. Kissinger Family Found., mem. bd. Stony Brook Found.; served to capt. AUS, 1943-46, 50. Decorated Commendation medal. Mem.: The Lakes (Palm Desert, Calif.), Princeton Club of N.Y. Home: Lower Dr Huntington NY 11743 also: Lazy K Ranch Divide CO 80814 Office: WBK Assocs 200 Broadhollow Rd Melville NY 11747-4806 E-mail: ludwigwbk@aol.com.

KISSLING, FRED RALPH, JR., publishing and insurance agency executive; b. Nashville, Feb. 10, 1930; s. Fred Ralph and Sarah Elizabeth (FitzGerald) K.; m. Mary Jane Gallaher (dec. 1999); children: Sarah FitzGerald, Jayne Kirkpatrick. BA, Vanderbilt U., 1952, MA, 1958. Spl. agt. Northwestern Mut. Life Ins. Co., Nashville, 1953-58, gen. agt. Lexington, Ky., 1962-80, New Eng. Mut. Life Ins. Co., 1981-87; mgr. life dept. Bennett & Edwards, Kingsport, Tenn., 1958-62; pres. Employee Benefit Cons., Inc., Lexington, 1961—. Owner Lexington House, Inc., 1966—, Kennington Assocs., 1967—; prin. Kissling Orgn., 1980—, pub. Leader's mag., 1967—, editor, 1996—; owner, editor Fin. and Estate Planners Quar., 1993—; owner and pub. Fin. Svcs. Advisor, 1993—, Fraternal Monitor, 1999—; owner, pub., editor Probe Pub. Inc., 1997—; pub. Estate Rsch. Inst. Inc. Author: Sell and Grow Rich, 1966; editor: Questionnaire in Pension Planning, 1970, Questionnaire in Estate Planning, 1971. Adv. bd. Salvation Army, Lexington, 1971—, chmn., 1988-91; gen. chmn. United Way of Blue Grass, 1975, bd. dir., 1975-78, 80-83; trustee, chmn. bd. Lexington Children's Theatre, 1979-81, pres., 1981-83; mem. Ea. Ky. U. Friends Libr. Bd., 2007—. Mem. Am. Soc. CLU's (chpt. pres. 1969-70, 80-81, 2001-02, regional v.p. 1971-73), Ky. Gen. Agts. and Mgrs. Assn. (pres. 1965-66), Million Dollar Round Table (life mem., v.p., program chmn. 1976), Assn. for Advanced Underwriting (bd. dirs. 1976-84, pres. 1982-83), Am. Soc. Pension Actuaries (bd. dir. 1971-78, pres. 1974-90), U. Akron Sales Insts. (adv. dir. 1996-2004), Am. Philatelic Soc., Ea. Ky. Friends of Libr. (bd.), Sigma Chi, Lexington Club, Iroquois Hunt Club, Spindletop Hall, Masons, Shriners, Thoroughbred Club Am. Avocations: horse breeding, horse racing. Office: 98 Dennis Dr Lexington KY 40503-2915 Office Phone: 859-277-6135. Business E-Mail: fred@kisslingorganization.com.

KISTENBROKER, DAVID H., lawyer; BA magna cum laude, U. Wis., 1975; MA, Marquette U., 1977, JD, 1980. Bar: Ill. 1980, Wis. 1980, US Ct. Appeals, 2nd, 6th and 7th Cir., US Dist. Ct., No. Dist. Ill., US Dist. Ct., We. Dist. Mich., US Supreme Ct. Ptnr., chmn. Securities Litig. Practice, co-chair Corp. Governance Practice, mem. exec. com. and bd. dirs. Katten Muchin Zavis Rosenman, Chgo. Office: Katten Muchin Zavis Rosenman 525 W Monroe St Chicago IL 60661 Office Phone: 312-909-5452. Office Fax: 312-577-4481. E-mail: david.kistenbroker@kmzr.com.

KISTIAKOWSKY, VERA, physical researcher, educator; b. Princeton, NJ, Sept. 9, 1928; d. George Bogdan and Hildegard (Moebius) K.; m. Gerhard Emil Fischer, June 16, 1951 (div. 1970); children: Marc Laurenz Fischer, Karen Marie Fischer. AB, Mt. Holyoke Coll., 1948, ScD (hon.), 1978; PhD, U. Calif., Berkeley, 1952. Staff scientist U.S. Naval Rsch. Def. Lab., San Francisco, 1952-53; fellow U. Calif., Berkeley, 1953-54; rsch. assoc. Columbia U., NYC, 1954-57, instr., 1957-59; asst. prof. Brandeis U., Waltham, Mass., 1959-62, adj. assoc. prof., 1962-63; staff mem. MIT, Cambridge, 1963-69, sr. rsch. scientist, 1969-72, prof. physics, 1972-94, prof. emerita, 1994—. Author: Atomic Energy, 1959, One Way Is Down, 1967; contbr. articles to profl. jours Dir. Coun. for a Liveable World, 1983—2005, dir. Edn. Fund, 1983—2001, pres., 1997—2000. Recipient Centennial award, Mt. Holyoke Coll., 1972. Fellow AAAS, Am. Phys. Soc. (councilor 1974-77); mem. Assn. for Women in Sci. (pres. 1982-83), Phi Beta Kappa (vis. scholar 1983-84, senator 1988-96), Sigma Xi (lectr. 1990-92). Achievements include research in nuc. and elem. particle physics and astrophysics. E-mail: verak@mit.edu.

KISTLER, RIVES, state supreme court justice; BA, Williams Coll., 1971; MA, U. N.C., 1978; JD, Georgetown U. Law Sch., 1981. Law clerk Chief Judge Charles Clark U.S. Ct. of Appeals Fifth Circuit; law clerk Justice Lewis F. Powell, Jr. U.S. Supreme Ct.; litigation assoc. Stoel Rives, Portland, Oreg., 1983—87; asst. atty. gen. Oreg. Dept. Justice, 1987—99; judge Oreg. Ct. of Appeals, 1999—2003; justice Oreg. Supreme Ct., 2003—. Adjunct prof. constitutional law Lewis & Clark Law Sch., Portland, Oreg.; former mem., vice-chair Oreg. Bd. of Bar Examiners; former mem. Nat. Assn. of Attorneys Gen. Working Groups. Office: Oreg Supreme Ct 1163 State St Salem OR 97301 Office Phone: 503-986-5713. Business E-Mail: rives.kistler@state.or.us.

KISTNER, DAVID HAROLD, biology professor; b. Cin., July 30, 1931; s. Harold Adolf and Hilda (Gick) K.; m. Alzada A. Carlisle, Aug. 8, 1957; children— Alzada H., Kymry Marie Carlisle. AB, U. Chgo., 1952, BS, 1956, PhD, 1957. Instr. U. Rochester, 1957-59; instr., asst. prof. biology Calif. State U., Chico, 1959-64, assoc. prof., 1964-67, prof., 1967-92, prof. emeritus, 1992—; rsch. assoc. Atlantica Ecol. Rsch. Sta., Salisbury, Zimbabwe, 1970-95. Dir. Shinner Inst. Study Interrelated Insects, 1968-75; cons.-developer DowAgro Scis., Indpls., 1995—. Author: (with others) Social Insects, Vols. 1-3; editor Sociobiology, 1975—; contbr. articles to profl. jours. Patron Am. Mus. Natural History. Recipient Outstanding Prof. award Calif. State Univs. and Colls., L.A., 1976; John Simon Guggenheim Meml. Found. fellow, 1965-66; grantee NSF, 1960-92, Am. Philos. Soc., 1972, Nat. Geog. Soc., 1988. Fellow Explorers Club, Calif. Acad. Scis.; mem. AAUP, AAAS, Entomol. Soc. Am., Pacific Coast Entomol. Soc., Kans. Entomol. Soc., Am. Soc. Naturalists, Am. Soc. Zoologists, Soc. Study of Systematic Zoology, Internat. Soc. Study of Social Insects, Field Mus. Natural History (life, rsch. assoc.), Chico State Coll. Assocs. (charter). Home: 3 Canterbury Cir Chico CA 95926-2411

KIT, SAUL, retired biochemist, educator; b. Passaic, NJ, Nov. 25, 1920; s. Isadore and Minnie (Darvick) K.; m. Dorothy Anken, Sept. 28, 1945; children: Sally, Malon, Gordon. AB, U. Calif.-Berkeley, 1948, PhD, 1951. Post-doctoral fellow U. Chgo., 1951-52; rsch. assoc. biochemistry dept. U. Tex./M.D. Anderson Hosp. and Tumor Inst., Houston, 1953-55, asst. biochemist dept. biochemistry, 1956-57, assoc. biochemist, 1957-60, biochemist and chief sect. nucleoprotein metabolism, 1961-62; asst. clin. prof. biochemistry Baylor U. Coll. Medicine, Houston, 1956-57, assoc. clin. prof., 1957-58, vis. prof. virology and epidemiology dept., spring 1962, prof. biochemistry and head divsn. biochem. virology, 1962-92, prof. emeritus, 1993—; ret., 1993. Vis. prof. Inst. Venez Olano, Caracas, Venezuela, 1971, U. Buenos Aires, 1971, Calouste Gulbenkian Found., Lisbon, 1973; disting. vis. prof. La Trobe U., Victoria, Australia, 1982; mem. del. U.S.-Soviet Health Exch. in Virology, 1967; mem. del. on indsl. biochemistry Program to People's Republic of China, 1990; chmn. pathobiol. chemistry study sect., 1975-79; cons. NIH, 1970-92; sci. adv. bd. Am. Genetics Internat., Inc., 1981-84, Novagene Inc., 1983—. Assoc. editor: Cancer Research, 1960-79; mem. editorial bd. Intervirology, 1972-85, Internat. Jour. Cancer, 1964-90; contbr. 250 articles to profl. jours. With AUS, 1942—46. Recipient Rsch. Career award NIH, 1962-88, Disting. Inventor of 1987 award Intellectual Property Owners, Inc. Mem. Am. Soc. Cell Biology (treas. 1965-68, pres. 1970), Am. Assn. Cancer Rsch. (pres. S.W. sect. 1965-66), Am. Soc. Biol. Chemists, Am. Chem. Soc., Am. Soc. Microbiology, Am. Soc. Virology, Argentine Soc. Virology (corr.), Am. Assn. Vet. Lab. Diagnostics. Achievements include patents in field. Home: 11935 Wink Rd Houston TX 77024-7134 Personal E-mail: saulkit@aol.com.

KITADA, SHINICHI, biochemist; b. Osaka, Japan, Dec. 9, 1948; came to U.S., 1975; s. Koichi and Asako Kitada. MD, Kyoto U., 1973; MS in Biol. Chemistry, UCLA, 1977, PhD, 1979. Intern Kyoto U. Hosp., Japan, 1973-74; resident physician Chest Disease Research Inst., 1974-75; rsch. scholar lab. nuclear medicine and radiation biology UCLA, 1979-87, rsch. scholar Jules Stein Eye Inst., 1988-91; rsch. biochemist La Jolla (Calif.) Cancer Rsch. Found., 1992—. Author papers in field. Japan Soc. Promotion Sci. fellow 1975-76. Mem. Am. Oil Chemists Soc., N.Y. Acad. Scis., Sigma Xi. Office: The Burnham Inst 10901 N Torrey Pines Rd La Jolla CA 92037-1062 E-mail: skitada@ljcrf.edu.

KITASHIRAKAWA, MICHIHISA, head of religious order; b. Tokyo, Feb. 5, 1937; s. Nagahisa Kitashirakawa and Sachiko Tokugawa; m. Shimazu Kieko, 1967; children: Naoko, Nobuko, Akiko. Grad. in Politics and Econs., Gakusshuin U. Mng. dir. bd. trustees Toshiba Internat. Found.; 5th head Imperial Ho. Kitashirakawa, 1940—; chief priest Grand Ise Shrine (Shinto), 2001—. Office: Dept Gen Affairs Jingu Adminstrn Office (Jingo shicho) 1 Ujitachi-cho Ise Mie 516 0023 Japan

KITCH, EDMUND WELLS, law educator; b. Wichita, Kans., Nov. 3, 1939; s. Paul R. and Josephine (Pridmore) K.; m. Joanne Steiner, 1966 (div. 1976); 1 child, Sarah; m. Alison Lauter, Jan. 29, 1978 (div. 2000); children: Andrew, Whitney; m. Gail Lettwich Apr. 26, 2003. BA, Yale U., 1961; JD, U. Chgo., 1964. Bar: Kans. 1964, Ill. 1966, US Supreme Ct. 1973, Va. 1986. Asst. prof. law Ind. U., 1964-65; mem. faculty U. Chgo., 1965-82, prof., 1971-82, dir. law & economics program, 1980—82; mem. Ctr. Advanced Studies U. Va., Charlottesville, 1982-85; prof. U. Va. Sch. Law, 1982—85, Joseph M. Hartfield prof., 1985—2003, Sullivan and Cromwell rsch. prof., 1996-99, Mary and Daniel Loughran prof. law, 2003—, E. James Kelly, Jr. - Class of 1965 rsch. prof., 2003—. Vis. prof. Bklyn. Law Sch., 1995, Northwestern U., 1996, Georgetown U., 2002, U. Nebr., 2002; spl. asst. to solicitor gen. US Dept. Justice, 1973-74; exec. dir. Adv. Com. on Procedural Reform CAB, 1975-76; reporter Com. on Pattern Jury Instruction, Ill. Supreme Ct., 1966-69; mem. com. on pub.-pvt. sector rels. in vaccine innovation Inst. of Medicine, NAS, 1982-85, mem. com. on evaluation polio vaccine, 1987-88. Co-author: (with Harvey Perlman) Intellectual Property and Unfair Competition, 5th edit., 1997, (with Paul Goldstein) Selected Statutes and International Agreements on Unfair Competition, Trademarks, Copyrights and Patents, 2005. Mem. ABA, Va. Bar Assn., Am. Law Inst., Order of Coif, Phi Beta Kappa. Office: U Va Sch Law 580 Massie Rd Charlottesville VA 22903-1789 Office Phone: 434-924-7047. E-mail: ewk@virginia.edu.

KITCH, PAUL R., lawyer; b. Southfield, Mich., 1966; BSEE summa cum laude, U. Mich., 1989, MBA with high distinction, 1993, JD, 1993. Bar: Ill. 1993, US Ct. Appeals Fed. Cir., US Dist. Ct. No. Dist. Ill., registered: US Patent & Trademark Office. Shareholder Jenkens & Gilchrist, P.C., Chgo., 2001—, firm co-leader intellectual property practice group. Mem.: ABA, Intellectual Property Law Assn. Chgo., Am. Intellectual Property Law Assn., Chgo. Bar Assn. Office: Jenkens & Gilchrist PC Ste 2600 225 W Washington St Chicago IL 60606-3418 Office Phone: 312-425-3900. Office Fax: 312-425-3909. Business E-Mail: pkitch@jenkens.com.

KITCHEN, CHARLES WILLIAM, lawyer; b. July 17, 1926; s. Karl K. and Lucille W. (Keynes) K.; m. Mary Applegate, July 22, 1950; children: Kenneth K., Guy R., Anne Kitchen Campbell. BA, Western Res. U., 1948, JD, 1950. Bar: Ohio 1950, U.S. Dist. Ct. Ohio 1952, U.S. Ct. Appeals (6th cir.) 1972, U.S. Supreme Ct. 1981. Ptnr. Kitchen, Derry & Barnhouse Co., LPA, Cleve., 1950-97, sr. ptnr., 1972, ret., 1997; life mem., exec. com. 8th Jud. Dist. Conf., 1988-91. Mem. Regional Coun. on Alcoholism, 1981-86, chmn., 1985-86; bd. dirs. Scarbourgh Hall, 1992-94. With AC USAAF, 1944—45. Fellow Internat. Acad. Trial Lawyers, Am. Coll. Trial Lawyers (sr. mem.); mem. Ohio State Bar Assn. (coun. of dels. 1985-86), ABA (sect. tort and ins. practice, sec. litigation), Am. Arbitration Assn. (panelist 1961-91), Am. Bd. Trial Advocates (advocate), Cleve. Assn. Civil Trial Attys. (pres. 1971-72), Ohio Assn. Civil Trial Attys. (pres. 1975-76), Ohio State Bar Assn., Greater Cleve. Bar Assn. (chmn. med.-legal com. 1974-75, chmn. lawyers assistance program 1981-83, chmn. mentor com. 1988-95, jud. campaign com. chmn. 1993-95, trustee 1984-87), Am. Legion, Order of Coif, Beta Theta Pi, Phi Delta Phi. Presbyterian. Home: 3800 Rosemont Blvd Apt 109A Fairlawn OH 44333 Personal E-mail: ckitch26@aol.com.

KITCHEN, E.C. DEENO, lawyer; b. Tallahassee, May 1, 1942; s. Oscar Edward and Rose (Deeb) K.; m. Patricia Gautier, June 22, 1968; children: Anne-Elizabeth K. Williams, Kimberly Gautier K. Robson, William Gautier, Deeb-Paul II. JD cum laude, U. Fla., 1967. Bar: 1968, U.S. Dist. Ct. (no. and ctrl. dists.) Fla., U.S. Ct. Appeals (3d and 11th cirs.), U.S. Supreme Ct., 1975. Ptnr. Ervin, Varn, Jacobs, Odom & Kitchen, Tallahassee, 1971-88, Kitchen & High, Tallahassee, 1988-93, Kitchen, Judkins, Simpson & High, Tallahassee, 1993—2004; pntr. Dobson, Kitchen & Smith, Tallahassee, 2004—06, Ervin, Kitchen & Ervin, Tallahassee, 2006—. Past mem. editl. bd. U. Fla. Law Rev. Chmn. exec. com., Leon County (Fla.) Dem. Party, 1971-73, mem. state exec. com., 1971-75; trustee U. Fla. Law Ctr. Assn. Named one of Best Lawyers in Am., Fla. Legal Elite, Fla.'s Top Lawyers, Fla. Super Lawyers. Master Tallahassee Am. Inn of Ct. (charter); fellow Am. Coll. Trial Lawyers, Internat. Soc. Barristers, Am. Bar Found., Fla. Bar Found.; mem. ABA (bd. regents Nat. Coll. Criminal Def., 1981-84, litigation and criminal justice sects.), Am. Bd. Trial Advocates (charter, Tallahassee chpt., advocate, pres. 1996), Nat. Assn. Criminal Def. Lawyers, Acad. Fla. Trial Lawyers (bd. dirs. 1983-85, past Eagle sponsor), Florida Bar (bd. cert. trial lawyer 1983, exec. coun. trial lawyers sect. 1980-88, chmn. steering com. trial lawyers sect., chmn. trial advocacy program 1982, 88, faculty mem., lectr. 1979—, faculty advanced trial advocacy program, exec. coun. criminal law sect. 1976-85, chmn. legis. com., chmn. grievance com. 2d Jud. Cir. Fla. 1979-80, mem. 1977-80), chmn. Professionalism Com., 2nd Jud. Cir. Fla. (by appt. of Chief Judge), Leading Am. Attys. (adv. bd.), Order of Coif, Phi Kappa Phi, Phi Alpha Delta (past pres.). Avocations: karate (black belt cuong nhu oriental martial arts, black belt isshin-ryu karate). Office: Ervin Kitchen & Ervin PO Drawer 1170 Tallahassee FL 32302 Home Phone: 850-385-8204; Office Phone: 850-224-9135. Office Fax: 850-222-9164. Business E-Mail: dkitchen@ervinkitchenlaw.com.

KITCHEN, JOHN MARTIN, historian, educator; b. Nottingham, Eng., Dec. 21, 1936; s. John Sutherland and Margaret Helen (Pearson) K. BA with honors, U. London, 1963, PhD, 1966. Mem. Cambridge (Eng.) Group Population Studies, 1965-66; mem. faculty Simon Fraser U., Burnaby, B.C., Canada, 1966—. Author: The German Officer Corps 1890-1914, 1968, A Military History of Germany, 1975, Fascism, 1976, The Silent Dictatorship, 1976, The Political Economy of Germany 1815-1914, 1979, The Coming of Austrian Fascism, 1980, Germany in the Age of Total War, 1981, British Policy Towards the Soviet Union During the Second World War, 1986, The Origins of the Cold War in Comparative Perspective, 1988, Europe Between the Wars, 1988, 2d edit., 2006, A World in Flames, 1990, Empire and After: A Short History of the British Empire and Commonwealth, 1994, Nazi Germany at War, 1994, The Cambridge Illustrated History of Germany, 1996, Empire and Commonwealth, 1996, Kaspar Hauser, 2001, The German Offensives of 1918, 2001, Nazi Germany: A Critical Introduction, 2004, A History of Modern Germany 1800-2000, 2006. Fellow Royal Hist. Soc., Royal Soc. Can. Home: 24B-6128 Patterson Ave Burnaby BC Canada V5H 4P3 Office: Simon Fraser U Dept History Burnaby BC Canada V5A 1S6 Home Phone: 604-433-0119; Office Phone: 604-291-3521. Business E-Mail: kitchen@sfu.ca.

KITCHEN, MIKE, professional hockey coach, retired professional hockey player; b. Schomberg, Ont., Can., Feb. 1, 1956; m. Jill Kitchen; children: Amy, Megan. Defenseman Colo. Rockies, 1976—82, NJ Devils, 1982—84; asst. coach Toronto Maple Leafs, 1990—98, St. Louis Blues, 1998—2004, head coach, 2004—06; asst. coach Fla. Panthers, 2007—. Office: Fla Panters One Panther Parkway Sunrise FL 33323*

KITCHEN, PAUL HOWARD, hockey historian; b. Toronto, Ont., Can., Nov. 14, 1937; s. Percy Floyd and Mary Henrietta (Price) K.; m. Anne Margaret Heaney, Aug. 23, 1963; children: Kevin, Peter. BA, Carleton U., 1963; BLS, U. B.C., 1964. Librarian Nat. Library Can., Ottawa, 1964-66, chief bibliography div., 1966-70, spl. asst to nat. librarian, 1970-72, liaison officer govt. libraries, 1972-75; exec. dir. Can. Library Assn., Ottawa, 1975-85; pres. Paul Kitchen and Assocs., Ottawa, 1986-98. Dir. Book and Periodical Devel. Council, Toronto, 1975-85. Ann. contbr. Am. Library Assn. Yearbook, 1975-85. Recipient Brian McFarlane award for outstanding rsch. and writing (hockey), 2000. Mem. Soc. for Internat. Hockey History Rsch. (pres. 1996-2000). Personal E-mail: pkitchen@magma.ca.

KITCHEN, RICHARD, history professor, researcher; s. Darrell Rowley and Karen Garner Kitchen; m. Stephanie Mickelson, Aug. 26, 1983; children: Joshua Richard, Mickell, Kristen Camille, Jared Darrell. PhD in History, Ariz. State U., Tempe, 2002—02. Asst. prof. history N.Mex Mil. Inst., Roswell, 2002—. E-5 sgt. US Army, 1986—90. Office: New Mexico Military Institute 101 W College Blvd Roswell NM 88201 Office Phone: 505-624-8177. Business E-Mail: kitchenr@nmmi.edu.

KITCHENS, DEAN J., lawyer; b. Nov. 4, 1952; BA, Univ. Calif., Berkeley, 1974; JD, UCLA, 1978. Bar: Calif. 1978, Calif. Supreme Ct., Ct. of Appeals (ninth cir.). Assoc. Gibson Dunn & Crutcher LLP, LA, 1978—86, ptnr. litig. dept., 1986—, also gen. counsel to the firm, 2000—. Mem. exec. com. Gibson Dunn & Crutcher, LA, 1996—2000, LA, 2003—, mem. mgmt. com., 1998—. Articles editor UCLA Law Rev. Mem.: LA County Bar Assn. (past mem. Judicial appointments com.), Order of Coif. Office: Gibson Dunn & Crutcher 333 S Grand Ave Los Angeles CA 90071-3197 Office Phone: 213-229-7416. Office Fax: 213-229-6416. Business E-Mail: dkitchens@gibsondunn.com.

KITCHENS, FREDERICK LYNTON, III, education educator, researcher; s. Frederick Lynton Kitchens, Jr. and Carol Ann (Crane) Kitchens. BBA, Ga. So. U., 1984—88, MBA, 1991—92; PhD, U. of Miss., 1994—2000. PIA; Comml. Ins. Profl. Ins. Agents, 1988, Ins. Inst. of Am., 1988. Am. scholar Lloyd's of London, 1987—87; comml. underwriter Fireman's Fund Ins. Co., Atlanta, 1988—90; temp. instr. Ga. So. U., Statesboro, 1993—94; grad. instr. The U. of Miss., Oxford, 1996—2000; asst. prof. Ball State U., Muncie, Ind., 2000—05, assoc. prof., 2005—. Asst. underwriter Cherokee Ins. Co., Nashville, 1984—84; mgmt. trainee Hamilton-Lines Mfg., Bognor, England, 1985—85; asst. agt. Coastal Plains Ins. Assoc, Jacksonville, Fla., 1986; v.p. to pres. Doctoral Student Orgn., Oxford, Miss., 1998—99; dir. Cluster Computing Rsch. Project, Muncie, Ind., 2001—; advisor Assn. of Info. Tech. Professionals, Muncie, 2001—; adv. software development FSA Based Lang. Translator, 2002. Author: (book chpt.) Neural Networks in Bus.: Techniques and Applications, Encyclopedia of Information Science and Technology, 2005; contbr. articles to profl. jours. including Rev. of Bus. Rsch., Jour. Info. Tech. Edn., Asian Jour. Info. Sys., Jour. Enterprise Info. Mgmt., Electronic Jour. E-Learning, Jour. Computer Info. Sys., others. Recipient Eagle Scout, Boy Scouts of Am., 1982, First Pl. award, Ind. Cyberstar Awards, 2002, Innovation in Leadership of Bus. Edn. award, The Assn. Advance Collegiate Schs. Bus., 2003, Disting. Paper award, Decision Scis. Inst., 2004, Internat. Acad. Bus. and Pub. Adminstrn., 2005, 2006—07; grantee George A. and Frances Ball Rsch. Grant, Ball State U., 2001, Miller Coll. Bus., 2005, Ball State U., 2003, 2004—05, 2005—06. Mem.: Omicron Delta Kappa (assoc.), Mu Kappa Tau (assoc.), Beta Gamma Sigma (assoc.). Avocation: travel. Office: Ball State U WB 203 Muncie IN 47306

KITCHENS, WILLIAM CHARLIE, accountant; b. Jacksonville, Fla., Oct. 21, 1945; s. William Othar and Mazie Alice (Dugger) K. BBA, postgrad., Ga. Coll., Milledgeville, 1981. Cert. enrolled agt., accredited tax advisor. Income tax practitioner H&R Block, Macon, Ga., 1976-86; cost acct., dept. head West Point Pepperell, Milledgeville, 1981-82; asst. fin. examiner Ga. Dept. of Banking and Fin., Dublin, 1980; tax acct. Ga. Farm Bur. Fedn., Macon, 1982-97; pvt. practice income tax svc. Macon, 1997—. Served as staff sgt. USAF, 1965-68. Mem. Nat. Assn. Enrolled Agts., Ga. Assn. Enrolled Agts., Nat. Soc. Pub. Accts., Nat. Assn. Income Tax Practitioners. Republican. Baptist. Home and Office: Bill Kitchens Income Tax Svcs 544 Orange St Macon GA 31201-8622 Address: PO Box 7885 Macon GA 31209-7885 Personal E-mail: billkitc@bellsouth.net.

KITCHENS, WILLIAM H., lawyer; b. Newnan, Ga., Aug. 3, 1948; m. Ellen Parker Kitchens; children: William H. Jr., Nathan P., Madison H., Claire C. BA with high honors, Emory U., 1970; JD, U. Ga., 1973. Bar: Ga. 1973, US Dist. Ct. (no. dist.) Ga. 1974, US Ct. Appeals (1st. cir.) 1981, US Ct. Appeals (5th cir.) 1974, US Ct. Appeals (11th cir.) 1981, US Supreme Ct. 1977. Mng. ptnr. Arnall Golden Gregory, LLP, Atlanta. Adj. prof. food and drug law Emory U. Sch. Law, 1979—; bd. dirs. Ga. Biomed. Partnership; mem. Metro Atlanta Biosci. Coun.; mem. S.E. task force Med. Tech. Leadership Forum; Acad. Programs Com., Food and Drug Law Inst. Notes editor Ga. Law Review, 1972-73; mem. editl. adv bd. Food and Drug

Law Jour., 1981-87, 96-2001; author: Tactical Approaches to Common Problems FDA-Regulated Companies in Inside The Minds Food and drug Law Settlements and Negotiations, 2006,Georgia Jurisprudence Environmental Law, 1995, 96, The Georgia Environmental Law Handbook, 1996, FDA Regulation of Tissue Engineering in Synthetic Biodegradable Polymer Scaffolds, 1997; contbr. articles to profl. jours. Mem. Leadership Atlanta; trustee Profl. Assn. Ga. Educators Found.; bd. dir. Met. Atlanta C. of C. Named one of Best Lawyers in Am., Biotech., 2007; recipient Biomed. Cmty. award, Ga. Biomed. Partnership, 2006. Mem. ABA, Am Judicature Soc., State Bar Ga., Lawyers Club Atlanta, Atlanta Bar Assn, Food and Drug Law Inst., Lawyers Club Atlanta, Commerce Club, Omicron Delta Kappa Office: Arnall Golden & Gregory LLP 171 17th St NW Ste 2100 Atlanta GA 30363-1031 Office Phone: 404-873-8500.

KITCHER, PHILIP STUART, philosophy educator; b. London, Feb. 20, 1947; came to U.S., 1969; s. Ernest Lewis and Millicent Irene (Barrow) K.; m. Patricia Young Williams, Aug. 21, 1971; children— Andrew, Charles BA first class honors in Math./History & Philosophy Sci., Christ's Coll., Cambridge, 1969, MA, 1996; PhD Dept. Philosophy/Prog. in History and Philosophy Sci., Princeton U., 1974. Asst. prof. philosophy Vassar Coll., Poughkeepsie, NY, 1973-74, U. Vt., Burlington, 1974—78, assoc. prof. philosophy, 1979-83; prof. philosophy U. Minn.-Mpls., 1983-86; dir. Minn. Ctr. Philosophy of Sci., Mpls., 1984-86; prof. philosophy U. Calif., San Diego, 1986-93, faculty coord. for Sci. Studies, 1989—91, presdl. prof., 1993-99; prof. philosophy Columbia U., NYC, 1998—, John Dewey prof. philosophy, 2003—, James R. Barker prof. contemporary civilization, 2005—. Vis. asst. philosophy prof. U. Mich., Ann Arbor, 1979; prog. chair, Philosophy Sci. Biennial Mtg., 1984,; mem. Coun. for Philos. Studies, 1986-1991; mem.-at-large, US Com., Internat. Union of Logic, Methodology and Philosophy of Sci., 1988-93; mem., working group on the ethical responsibilities of scientists, 1994-1996, Internat. Coun. for Sci., com. on responsibility and ethics in sci., 1996-98; mem. NIH/Dept. Energy working group on the ethical, legal and social implications of the human genome project, 1995-97; mem. bd. electors for the chair in history & philosopht of sci., Cambridge U., 1996-97; mem. mgmt. com., Centre for the Philosophy of Sci., London Sch. Economics, 1996-; selector, Imre Lakatos award, 1988-99, steering com. mem., 1999-; philosophy referee for John Simon Guggenheim Found., 1994-; philosophy reader, Am. Coun. of Learned Societies, 1998-, Nat. Humanities Ctr., 1998-; com. mem. Mellon Fellowship, 2001-; invited lectr. in field. Author: Abusing Science" The Case Against Creationism, 1982, The Nature of Mathematical Knowledge, 1983, Vaulting Ambition: Sociobiology and the Quest for Human Nature, 1985, The Advancement of Science, 1993, The Lives to Come: The Genetic Revolution and Human Possibilities, 1996, Science, Truth & Democracy, 2001, In Mendel's Mirror: Philosophical Reflections on Biology, 2003; co-author (with Richard Schacht) Finding an Ending: Reflections on Wagner's Ring, 2004; mem. editl. bd., Philosophy Sci., 1985-1994, editor-in-chief, 1994-99; mem. editl. bd., Journal Philosophy, 2000-;philosophy editor (surrogate delegate), Oxford U. Press, NY, 1994-; contbr. articles to profl. jours. Recipient Schuman prize History of Sci. Soc., 1971; co-recipient Imre Lakatos award 1986; named Disting. scholar U. Vt., 1983, Phi Beta Kappa Romanell prof., 2003-2004; fellow Am. Coun. Learned Socs., 1982, NEH fellow, 1984, John Simon Guggenheim Found. Fellow, 1988-89, Libr. Congress Sr. Fellow: Bio-Ethics Issues in Molecular Genetics, 1993-94. Fellow Am. Acad. Arts and Sciences; mem. Philosophy of Sci. Assn.(governing bd., 1987-91), Am. Philos. Assn. (v.p. Pacific divsn. 1996-97, bd. officers 1996-99, pres, 1997-98, (also awarded by Prometheus Books) Prometheus prize, 2006), Soc. for Study of Evolution. Avocations: music, singing, golf, bridge, chess. Office: Dept Philosophy Columbia U 717 Philosophy Hall MC 4971 1150 Amsterdam Ave New York NY 10027 Office Phone: 212-854-4884. Business E-Mail: psk16@columbia.edu.*

KITE, MARILYN S., state supreme court justice, lawyer; b. Laramie, Wyo., Oct. 2, 1947; BA with honors, U. Wyo., 1970, JD with honors, 1974. Bar: Wyo. 1974. Sr. asst. atty. gen. State of Wyo., 1974—78; atty. Holland & Hart, Jackson, Wyo., 1979—2000; justice Wyo. Supreme Ct., 2000—. Contbr. articles to profl. jours. Mem. ABA (nat. resources sect., litigation sect.), Wyo. State Bar. Address: Wyo Supreme Ct 2301 Capitol Ave Cheyenne WY 82002*

KITE, STEVEN B., lawyer; b. Chgo., May 30, 1949; s. Ben and Dolores (Braver) K.; m. Catherine Lapinski, Jan. 13, 1980; children: David, Julia. BA, U. Ill., 1971; JD, Harvard U., 1974. Bar: Ga. 1974, U.S. Dist. Ct. Ga. 1974, U.S. Ct. Appeals (5th and 11th cirs.) 1981, Ill. 1985, Fla. 1986. Ptnr. Kutak Rock, Atlanta, 1974—84, Gardner Carton & Douglas LLP, Chgo., 1984—2005, Sonnenschein Nath & Rosenthal LLP, Chgo., 2005—. Author, editor: Law For Elderly, 1978; author: Tax-Exempt Financing for Health Care Organizations, 1996; co-author: Bond Financing, 1994. Bd. dirs. Atlanta Legal Aid Soc., 1979-84; trustee Sr. Citizens Met. Atlanta, 1980-83. Mem. ABA, Ill. Bar Assn., State Bar Ga., Chgo. Bar Assn., Fla. Bar Assn., Nat. Assn. Bond Lawyers. Avocations: travel, sports, reading. Office: Sonnenschein Nath & Rosenthal LLP 233 S Wacker Dr Ste 7800 Chicago IL 60606 Office Phone: 312-876-8195. Business E-Mail: skite@sonnenschein.com.

KITMAN, MARVIN, journalist; b. Pitts., Nov. 24, 1929; s. Myer and Rose (Kaufman) K.; m. Carol Sibushnick, Oct. 28, 1951; children: Jamie Lincoln, Suzy, Andrea Jordana. BA, CCNY, 1953. Columnist Armstrong Daily, NYC, 1956-63; media critic Newsday, Melville, NY, 1969—2005, Huffington Post.com, 2007—; pres., CEO The Kitman Group, Leonia, NJ, 1999—. Cons. Al Capp Enterprises, N.Y.C., 1961-63; staff writer Saturday Evening Post, N.Y.C., 1965-66; news mng. editor, founding mem. Monocle Mag., N.Y.C., 1963-69, TV critic New Leader mag., N.Y.C., 1967-89; TV critic 10 O'clock News WNEW-TV, N.Y.C., 1980-87. Author: The Number One Best Seller, 1966, The Marvin Kitman TV Show: Encyclopedia Televisiana, 1972, You Can't Judge a Book By Its Cover, 1970, The Coward's Almanac, or The Yellow Pages, 1975, I am a VCR, 1989, The Making of the Prefident 1789, 1989; co-author: George Washington's Expense Account, 1970; author: (under pseudonymn William Randolph Hirsch) The Red Chinese Air Force Diet, Exercise and Sex Manual, 1967, The Man Who Would Not Shut Up: The Rise of Bill O'Reilly, 2006; co-creator, writer (TV show) Ball Four, 1976. Avocations: riding trains, writing movie scripts, watching Steelers football games on TV. Office: 147 Crescent Ave Leonia NJ 07605

KITNA, JON, professional football player; b. Tacoma, Washington, Sept. 21, 1972; m. Jennifer Kitna; children: Jordan, Jada, Jalen. Postgrad in math edn., Ctrl. Wash. Quarterback Seattle Seahawks, 1997—2000, Cin. Bengals, 2001—06, Detroit Lions, 2006—. Office: Detroit Lions 222 Republic Dr Allen Park MI 48101

KITNER, DAVID N., lawyer; b. Brownwood, Tex., Aug. 25, 1948; BA, Rice U., 1970; JD with honors, U. Tex., 1973. Bar: Tex. 1973; bd. cert. labor and employment law, Tex. Bd. Specialization. Mem. Strasburger & Price L.L.P., Dallas. Instr. trial advocacy So. Meth. U., 1982-86. Named Tex. Super Lawyer, Tex. Monthly Mag. Fellow Am. Coll. Trial Lawyers, Tex. Bar Found. (life, named to Best Lawyers in Am.); mem. Tex. Assn. Def. Counsel, Dallas Bar Assn., Order Coif, Defense Rsch. Inst.; fellow Tex. Bar Found. Office: Strasburger & Price LLP 901 Main St Ste 4300 Dallas TX 75202-3724 E-mail: david.kitner@strasburger.com.

KITSOS, CONSTANTINE NICHOLAS, plastic surgeon; b. Athens, Greece, Aug. 10, 1938; came to U.S., 1946; s. Nicholas E. and Bessie N. Kitsos; children: Katie, Kristina, Nicholas. BA, U. Wash., 1960, MD, 1964. Diplomate Am. Bd. Surgery, Am. Bd. Plastic Surgery. Intern U. Miami, 1964-65, resident in gen. surgery; resident in plastic surgery Loyola U.; pvt. practice Miami, Fla., 1973—; chief of staff Highland Park Gen. Hosp., Miami, Fla.; staff S. Fla. Ctr. Costmetic Surgery, Miami. Capt. M.C., U.S. Army, 1965-67. Mem. Am. Soc. Plastic Surgeons. Greek Orthodox. Office: S Fla Ctr Cosmetic Surgery 9000 NE 2d Ave Miami FL 33138*

KITT, EARTHA MAE, actress, singer; b. St. Matthews, SC, Jan. 17, 1927; d. John and Anna K.; m. William McDonald, June 1960 (div.); 1 child, Kitt Shapiro. Grad. high sch. Soloist with Katherine Dunham Dance Group, 1948; night club singer, 1949—, appearing in France, Turkey, Greece, Egypt, N.Y.C., Hollywood, Las Vegas, London, Stockholm; actress: (plays) Dr. Faustus, Paris, 1951, New Faces of 1952, N.Y.C., Mrs. Patterson, N.Y.C., 1954, Shinbone Alley, N.Y.C., 1957, Timbuktu, 1978, Blues in the Night, 1985, Mimi Le Duck, 2006; (films) including New Faces, 1953, Accused, 1957, Anna Lucasta, 1958, Mark of the Hawk, 1958, St. Louis Blues, 1957, Saint of Devil's Island, 1961, Synanon, 1965, Up The Chastity Belt, 1971, Dragonard, Ernest Scared Stupid, 1991, Boomerang, 1992, Fatal Instinct, 1993, Harriet the Spy, 1996, Ill Gotten Gains (voice), 1997, (TV) The Wild Thornberrys (voice), 1998, The Emperor's New Grove (voice), 2000, Feast of All Saints, 2001, Santa Baby!, 2001, Standard Time, 2002, Holes, 2003, also 2 French films, also numerous TV appearances including Cat Woman role in Batman series, (broadway shows) The Wizard of Oz, 1998, The Wild Party, 2000 (Tony nominee), Rodgers & Hammerstein's Cinderella, 2001; star: (documentary film) All By Myself, 1982; albums include That Bad Eartha, 1953, Down to Eartha, 1955, Thursday's Child, 1956, St. Louis Blues, 1958, The Fabulous Eartha Kitt, Eartha Kitt Revisited, 1960, Bad But Beautiful, 1962, My Way: A Musical Tribute to Rev. Dr. Martin Luther King Jr., 1987, Best of Eartha Kitt, 1983, Thinking Jazz, 1991, Miss Kitt, To You, 1992, Back in Business, 1994, Sentimental Eartha, 1995, Standard/Live, 1998, The Best of Eartha Kitt: Where Is My Man, 1998, Lovin' Spree, 2005, She's So Good, 2006; author: Thursday's Child, 1956, A Tart Is Not a Sweet, Alone With Me, 1976, I'm Still Here, 1990, Confessions of a Sex Kitten, 1991; co-author: Down to Eartha, 2000, How to Rejuvenate: It's Not Too Late, 2000 Recipient Nightlife Legend award, 2006; named Woman of Yr. Nat. Assn. Negro Musicians, 1968; nominated 2 Grammys, 2 Tony awards, 1 Emmy.*

KITT, OLGA, artist; b. NYC, July 29, 1929; d. Elias and Mary (Opiela) K.; m. Nicholas Rawluk, Aug. 6, 1955 (div. 1960); 1 child, Wade. BA, Queens Coll., 1951; MA, State U. Iowa, 1952; studied with Meyer Schapiro, NYC, 1954; studied with Hans Hofmann, NYC, Provincetown, 1954-55; postgrad., Inst. Fine Arts, NYU, 1955, NYU, 1960-62; studied with Robert Beverly Hale, NYC, 1979. Gallery asst. Chappellier Gallery, NYC, 1952—53; asst. to Walter Pach NY, 1953—56; tchg. asst. CCNY, 1953—58; tchr. art NY, 1962—80. One-woman shows include CCNY, 1957, Manhattan Coll., Riverdale, N.Y., 1980, Blackout Gallery, N.Y.C., 1997, Coll. Mt. St. Vincent, 2001, 2002, 2003, The Corridor Gallery of Riverdale Temple, 2001, 2002, The Corridor Gallery of Interchurch Ctr., 2002, Starving Artists Gallery, 2005, Bronx Borough Pres. Carrion's Gallery, 2005, Hall of Fame Gallery, Bronx C.C., 2006, exhibited in group shows at Whitney Mus., N.Y.C., 1954, Bronx County Hist. Soc., 1978, Mus. Modern Art, N.Y.C., 1978, Art Students League, 1979, Bronx Mus. Arts, 1979, Coll. Mt. St. Vincent, 2000, Broome St. Gallery, N.Y.C., 2002, 2003, 2004, 2005, 2006, Longwood Gallery, NYC, 2007, Represented in permanent collections Bronx Council of the Arts, Bronx Arts Ensemble, Riverdale Press, Riverdale YM-YWHA, U. Iowa, Iowa City, Fordham U., Fordham Prep. Sch., Hostos Coll., N.Y.C., Harris Sch. of Art, Tenn., numerous pvt. collections. Home: Apt 4D 5610 Netherland Ave Bronx NY 10471-1703 Studio: 495 S Broadway Yonkers NY 10705-3221 E-mail: olgakitt@aol.com.

KITTA, JOHN NOAH, lawyer; b. San Francisco, Aug. 26, 1951; s. John E. and Norma Jean (Noah) K. BS, U. Santa Clara, 1973, JD, 1976. Bar: Calif. 1976. Asst. mgr. Transamerica Title Co., Dublin, Calif., 1977-78; assoc. Rhodes, McKeehan & Bernard, Fremont, Calif., 1978-79; sr. atty. Law Offices of John N. Kitta & Assoc., Fremont, 1979—. V.p. Californians Against Fraud, 1996—. Author: Wrongful Discharge.Look Before You Leap, 1990. Commr. Calif. Crime Resistance Task Force, Sacramento; trustee Alameda County Bd. Edn.; del. Dem. Cen. Com., Alameda County, 1980-81, 83-84. Democrat. Home: 2135 Ocaso Camino Fremont CA 94539-5645 Office: 39560 Stevenson Pl Ste 217 Fremont CA 94539-3074 Office Phone: 510-797-7990. Personal E-mail: jkitta@aol.com.

KITTEL, PETER, research scientist; b. Fairfax, Va., Mar. 23, 1945; s. Charles and Muriel K.; m. Mary Ellen, Aug. 12, 1972; 1 child, Katherine. BS, U. Calif., Berkeley, 1967; MS, U. Calif., La Jolla, 1969; PhD, Oxford U., 1974. Rsch. asst. U. Calif., La Jolla, 1967-69, Oxford (Eng.) U., 1969-74; rsch. assoc., adj. assoc. prof. U. Oreg., Eugene, 1974-78; rsch. assoc. Stanford (Calif.) U., 1978; rsch. assoc. Nat. Rsch. Coun. Ames Rsch. Ctr. NASA, Moffett Field, Calif., 1978-80, rsch. scientist, 1980—2004, Ames assoc., 2005—. Dir. Internat. Cryogenic Engring. Conf., 1998—, Cryogenic Engring. Conf., 1983-89, 92—, internat. CryoCooler conf., 1996-2004; co-chmn. Internat. CryoCooler conf., 1996-98. Adv. editor: Cryogenics, 1987—; editor: Advances in Cryogenic Engineering, 1992-98; contbr. articles to profl. jours. Fellow Oxford U., 1972-74, Nat. Rsch. Coun., 1978-80; recipient medal for Exceptional Engring. Achievement NASA, 1990, Space Act award NASA, 1989, 91. Fellow: Cryogenic Soc. Am.; mem.: AAAS, Am. Phys. Soc. Home: 3132 Morris Dr Palo Alto CA 94303-4037 Office: NASA 244-10 Ames Research Ctr Moffett Field CA 94035-1000 Home Phone: 650-493-2792; Office Phone: 650-604-4297. Business E-Mail: pkittel@mail.arc.nasa.gov.

KITTELBERGER, LARRY E., engineering executive; B in Computer Sci., Pa. State U., Univ. Park; MBA in Fin. and Quantitative Analysis, Old Dominion U., Norfolk, Va. Various leadership positions in engring. and info. systems Tenneco, Inc.; sr. v.p., chief info. officer AlliedSignal, Inc., 1994—99, Lucent Techs., Inc., 1999—2001; sr. v.p. adminstrn., chief info. officer Honeywell Internat., Inc., Morristown, NJ, 2001, sr. v.p. tech. and ops. Office: Honeywell Internat 101 Columbia Rd Morristown NJ 07962 Office Phone: 973-455-2000. Office Fax: 973-455-4807.*

KITTELSEN, RODNEY OLIN, lawyer; b. Albany, Wis., Mar. 11, 1917; s. Olen B. and Nellie Winifred (Atkinson) K.; m. Pearle M. Haldiman, Oct. 12, 1940; children: Gregory S., James E., Bradley J. PhB, U. Wis., 1939, LLB, 1940. Spl. agt. FBI, Washington, 1940-46; ptnr. Kittelsen, Barry, Ross, Wellington & Thompson, Monroe, Wis., 1946—. Dist. atty. Green County, Monroe, 1947-53; pres. State Bar Wis., Madison, 1976-77, 83-85; dir. Wis. Law Found., Madison, 1992—. Pres. Monroe Police and Fire Commn., 1947—; legal counsel X-FBI Inc., Quantico, Va., 1986—; mem. Am. Coll. Trust and Estate Coun., Chgo., 1983—. Recipient Outstanding Citizen award Monroe Jaycees, 1977, Outstanding Svc. award Albany FFA, 1991, Disting. Svc. award U. Wis. Law Sch., 1995, Disting. Svc. award U. Wis. Law Alumni Assn., 1995., Hon. Am. Famer award, 2003, award Wilaw Found., 2005. Fellow: Am. Bar Found.; mem.: Wis. Bar Found., Wis. Law Found. (life Truman McNulty award for Lifetime Achievement 2005), Wis. Bar Assn. Achievements include being chosen by We the People as the visiting delegate for a group of 20 lawyers from the US to China to improve inter-country relations. Home: 708 26th Ave Monroe WI 53566-1620 Office: 916 17th Ave Monroe WI 53566-2003 Office Phone: 608-325-2191.

KITTERMAN, LAURA ANN, occupational therapist; b. Hartford City, Ind., May 9, 1965; d. James Lee and Karen Sue (Stanley) K. BS in Biology, Ind. Cen. U., 1981; MS in Occpl. Therapy, U. Indpls., 1988. Registered occpl. therapist. Occpl. therapist Union Hosp., Terre Haute, Ind., 1989, St. Francis Hosp., Beech Grove, Ind., 1989—. Fieldwork coord./educator, St. Francis Hosp., crisis clin., CISD team mem. Mem. comm. events com. Homeowners Assn. of Neighborhood, 1997; notary pub. Avocations: geneology, music, writing, church involvement, swimming. Home: 4010 Cherry Blossom Blvd Indianapolis IN 46237-3808

KITTLE, CHARLES FREDERICK, surgeon; b. Athens, Ohio, Oct. 24, 1921; s. Frederick F. and Ida (Falls) K.; m. Jeane Mignon Groenier, 1945 (div. 1973); children: Candace Mignon, Bradley Dean, Leslie Jeane, Brian David; m. Ann Catherine Bates, 1981. AB with honors, Ohio U., Athens, 1942, LLD, 1967; MD with honors, U. Chgo., 1945; MS in Surgery, U. Kans., 1950. Diplomate Am. Bd. Surgery, Am. Bd. Thoracic Surgery (mem. bd. 1967-75, chmn. 1973-75). Intern U. Chgo. Clinics, 1945-46; resident gen. and thoracic surgery U. Kans. Med. Center, 1948-52; spl. tng. radio-isotopes for med. use Oak Ridge Inst. Nuclear Studies, 1950, cons. med. div., 1950-55; mem. faculty U. Kans. Sch. Medicine, 1950-66; assoc. prof. surgery, lectr. history medicine, 1959-66; cons. thoracic surgery VA Hosp., Wadsworth, Kans., 1954-57, cons. gen. surgery, 1957-60; attending gen. surgery VA Hosp. Kansas City, Mo., 1954-66, Wichita, Kans., 1955-62; prof. surgery, head sect. thoracic and cardiovascular surgery U. Chgo. Clinics, 1966-72; prof. surgery, dir. thoracic surgery sect. Rush Med. Coll. and Presbyn.-St. Luke's Hosp., 1973-92, prof. emeritus, 1992—; dir. Rush Cancer Ctr., 1978-86; mem. staff McNeal Hosp., Berwyn, Ill., 1986-92. Cons. Mcpl. TB Sanatorium, Chgo., 1968-74, Hines VA Hosp., Maywood, Ill., 1973-92; spl. rsch. cardiovascular surgery, control of blood flow. Life trustee Newberry Libr., Chgo. Served as lt. (j.g.) USNR, 1946-48. Recipient Konneker award Ohio U., 2004; clin. fellow Am. Cancer Soc., 1950-52; Markle scholar med. scis., 1952-58. Mem. AAAS, ACS (bd. dirs. Kans. 1965-68), Am. Assn. History Medicine, Am. Assn. Thoracic Surgery, Am. Coll. Cardiology (bd. dirs. Kans. 1963-66), Chgo. Surg. Soc. (pres. 1972-73), Am. Heart Assn. (chmn. program com. cardiovasc. surgery 1965-88, exec. com. cardiovasc. surgery coun. 1962-74, chmn. coun. 1972-74), Am. Physiol. Assn., Cen. Surg. Soc., Chgo. Med. Soc., Am. Surg. Assn., Internat. Cardiovasc. Soc. (sec. 1965-71), Internat. Soc. Surgery, Soc. Med. Hist. (pres. Chgo. 1983-85), N.J. Thoracic Surgery Soc., Ill. Thoracic Surgery Soc. (pres. 1983-84), Soc. Clin. Surgery, Soc. Surg. Oncology, Soc. Vascular Surgery, Soc. Univ. Surgeons (pres. 1966-67), Soc. Thoracic Surgery, Univ. Village Assn. (bd. dirs. 1986-89, pres. 1989), Arthur Conan Doyle Soc., Caxton Club (pres. 1999-2001), Chgo. Literary Club, Hounds of Baskerville, Baker Street Irregulars, Grolier Club, Phi Beta Kappa, Sigma Xi, Alpha Omega Alpha. Home: 856 S Laflin St Chicago IL 60607-4026 Office Phone: 312-243-4310. E-mail: kittle856@mindspring.com.

KITTLESON, HENRY MARSHALL, lawyer; b. Tampa, Fla., May 13, 1929; s. Edgar O. and Ardath (Ayers) K.; m. Barbara Clark, Mar. 20, 1954; 1 dau., Laura Helen. BS with high honors, U. Fla., 1951, JD with high honors, 1953. Bar: Fla. 1953. Ptnr. Holland & Knight, Lakeland and Bartow, Fla., 1955—. Mem. adv. bd. Fla. Fed. Savs. & Loan Assn., 1974-86; mem. Fla. Law Revision Commn., 1967-76, vice chmn., 1969-71; mem. Gov.'s Property Rights Study Commn., 1974-75, Nat. Conf. Commrs. Uniform State Laws, 1982—. Mem. coun. U. Fla. Law Ctr., 1974-77. Served to maj. USAF, 1953-55. Fellow Am. Bar Found.; mem. ABA (chmn. standing com. on ethic and profl. responsibility 1980-81), Am. Law Inst., Am. Coll. Real Estate Lawyers, Fla. Bar (chmn. standing com. profl. ethics 1965-66, tort litig. rev. commn. 1983-84), Blue Key, Sigma Phi Epsilon, Phi Delta Phi, Phi Kappa Phi, Beta Gamma Sigma. Presbyterian. Home: 1111 S Lakemont Ave Apt 511 Winter Park FL 32792

KITTLITZ, RUDOLF GOTTLIEB, JR., chemical engineer, researcher; b. Waco, Tex., Apr. 19, 1935; s. Rudolf Gottlieb and Lena Hulda (Landgraf) Kittlitz; children: Lenell, Theresa, Liesel, Rolf. BSChemE, U. Miss., 1957; MS in Engring., U. Ala., 2003. Registered profl. engr., Calif. Engr., polychems. rsch. E.I. du Pont de Nemours & Co., Wilmington, Del., 1957-60, engr., textile fibers dept. Seaford, Del., 1960-62, sr. engr., textile fibers dept., 1962-67, Chattanooga, 1967-68, sr. research engr., 1968-83, sr. research engr. textile fibers Seaford, 1983-87, research assoc. textile fibers, 1987-92, sr. rsch. assoc. fibers, 1992-94, Chattanooga, 1995—2000; statis. cons. Rudy Kittlitz & Assocs., Alpine, Tex., 2001—. Lectr. in field; adj. prof. U. Tenn.-Chattanooga, 1980—82, Sul Ross State U., 2001—; Citizen Am. Program del. to Russia, 1991. Co-author: Quality Assurance for the Chemical and Process Industries--A Manual of Good Practices, 1987, 2d edit., 1999, ANSI/ASQC Q90/ISO 9000: Guidelines for Use by the Chemical and Process Industries, 1992, Specifications for the Chemical and Process Industries--A Manual for Development and Use, 1996, Glossary and Tables for Statistical Quality Control, 4th edit., 2004. Vice chmn. Cmty. Action Com., Seaford, 1966; mem. Alpine Pks. and Recreation Bd., 2001—, chmn., 2005—; chmn. U.S. tech. adv. group to tech. com. Internat. Orgn. Standardization, 2001—. Fellow: Am. Soc. for Quality (chmn. Chattanooga sect. 1975—76, councilor region 11 chem. divsn. 1975—80, chmn. Del. sect. 1984—85, regional dir. 1986—87, exec. regional dir. 1987—91, dir.-at-large 1991—93, parliamentarian 1993—99, 2000—05, cert. quality and reliability engr., W.G. Hunter award 1989); mem.: Internat. Orgn. for Standardization, Am. Statis. Assn., Nat. Assn. Parliamentarians. Democrat. Baptist. Home: 2006 Ceredo Dr Alpine TX 79830 Office: 2006 Ceredo Dr Ste 3 Alpine TX 79830-8501 Office Phone: 432-837-9937.

KITTO, JOHN BUCK, JR., mechanical engineer; b. Evanston, Ill., Dec. 22, 1952; s. John Buck and Marie (Comstock) K.; children: Christopher Daniel, Andrew Comstock. BSME, Lehigh U., 1975; MBA, U. Akron, 1980. Registered profl. engr., Ohio, Pa. Sr. engr. McDermott Tech. Inc. subs. Babcock & Wilcox Co., Alliance, Ohio, 1975-80, research engr., 1980-81, program mgr., 1981-94, bus. devel. specialist, 1995-99; bus. devel. mgr. The Babcock and Wilcox Co., Barberton, Ohio, 1999—. Editor: Heat Exchangers for Two Phase Flow, 1983, Two-Phase Heat Exchanger, 1985, Maldistribution of Flow, 1987, Steam: Its Generation and Use, 2005; author and patentee in field. Fellow ASME (chmn. chpt. 1983-84, chmn. exec. com. of heat transfer divsn. 1992-93, v.p. region V 1992-95, officer bd. comms. 1991-95, sr. v.p. 1995-98, mem. bd. govs. 1998-2002, Prime Movers award 1992, Dedicated Svc. award 1992, George Westinghouse Silver medal 1991); mem. Tau Beta Pi, Pi Tau Sigma, Beta Gamma Sigma, Sigma Iota Epsilon. Republican. Avocations: reading, hiking, board games, coaching soccer. Home: 1225 Arrowhead Dr SW Dellroy OH 44620 Office: Babcock & Wilcox Co PO Box 351 20 S Van Buren Ave Barberton OH 44203-0351 Home Phone: 330-735-2473; Office Phone: 330-860-2303. Office Fax: 330-860-1409.

KITTREDGE, WILLIAM ALFRED, humanities educator; b. Portland, Oreg., Aug. 14, 1932; s. Franklin Oscar and Josephine (Miessner) K.; m. Janet O'Connor, Dec. 8, 1952 (div. 1968); children: Karen, Bradley. BS, Oreg. State U., 1953; MFA in Creative Writing, U. Iowa, 1969. Rancher Warner Valley Livestock, Adel, Oreg., 1957-67; prof. U. Mont., Missoula, 1969—, now Regents Prof. emeritus. Author: The Van Gogh Field, 1979, We Are Not In This Together, 1984, Owning It All, 1987, Hole in the Sky, 1992, Who Owns the West, 1996, The Portable Western Reader, 1997, Taking Care, 1999, Balancing Water, 2000, The Nature of Generosity, 2000, Southwestern Homelands, 2002, The Best Stores of William Kittredge, 2003, The Willow Field, 2006. With USAF, 1954-57. Named Mont. Humanist of Yr., 1989; recipient award for lit. Gov. of Mont., 1988, Charles Frankel prize in Humanities, NEH, 1994, Earl A. Chiles Lifetime Acheivement award, 2006, LA Times Kirsch Lifetime Acehivement award, 2007. Home: 143 S 5th St E Missoula MT 59801-2719 Office Phone: 406-549-6605. Personal E-mail: kittredgeb@aol.com.

KITTRELL, PAMELA R., lawyer; b. Athens, Ga., June 15, 1965; d. John Edison and Anne (Hagins) K. AB summa cum laude, U. Miami, 1987; JD, U. Mich., 1990. Bar: Fla. 1990, U.S. Dist. Ct. (so. dist.) Fla. 1991, D.C. 1992, Colo. 1994, U.S. Ct. Appeals (11th cir.) 1994, U.S. Dist. CT. (mid. dist.) Fla. 1995. Assoc. Stearns, Weaver, Miller, Weissler, Alhadeff & Sitterson, PA, Miami, 1990-93; sr. assoc. Cooney, Mattson, Lance, Blackburn, Richards & O'Connor, P.A., Ft. Lauderdale, Fla., 1994-98. Mem. Fla. Bar (appellate practice sec.). Democrat. Business E-Mail: kittrellaw@aol.com.

KITTRELL, STEVEN DAN, lawyer; b. Winfield, Kans., Aug. 4, 1953; s. William Dan and Jeanette E. (Miller) Kittrell; m. Susan K. Hattan, May 30, 1987. BA cum laude, Baylor U., 1974; JD cum laude, George Washington U., 1978; LLM in Taxation, Georgetown U., 1981. Bar: DC 1978, Md. 1991, US Ct. Fed. Claims 1979, US Tax Ct. 1979, US Supreme Ct. 1984. Legis. asst. to senator Bob Dole of Kans. US Senate, Washington, 1976-78; assoc. O'Connell & Associates, Washington, 1978-84; ptnr. O'Connell & Kittrell, Washington, 1984-88, Golden, Freda & Schraub, Washington, 1989-91, McGuire, Woods, Battle & Boothe LLP (now McGuireWoods LLP), Washington, 1991—, mng. ptnr. DC office. Mem. ABA (mem. tax sect. 1978- , chmn. com. on domestic rels. tax problems 1984-86), DC Bar Assn. (mem. sect. taxation), Delta Theta Phi. Republican. Baptist. Avocation: Tae Kwon Do. Office: McGuireWoods LLP Washington Sq 1050 Conn Ave NW, Ste 1200 Washington DC 20036-5317 Office Phone: 202-857-1701. Office Fax: 202-828-2975. Business E-Mail: skittrell@mcguirewoods.com.

KITTRIE, NICHOLAS, international lawyer, writer; b. nr. Bilgoraj, Silesia, Mar. 26, 1930; (parents Brit. citizens); s. S.K. Kronenbergh and Perla F. (Ver Standijk) K.; m. Sara Yudovic de Burak, June 1, 1962; children: Orde Felicien, Norda Nicole, Zachary McNair. Student, U. Cairo, 1946, U. London, 1947; LLB, U. Kans., 1950, MA, 1951; postgrad., U. Chgo., 1954-55; LLM, Georgetown U., 1963, SJD, 1968. Bar: Kans. 1953, D.C. 1958, U.S. Supreme Ct. Instr. Western civilization dept. U. Kans., 1948-50; legal analyst Kans. Govt. Rsch. Ctr., 1951-54; asst. to dir. legis. svc. ABA, 1955-56, project dir., 1956-58; rsch. assoc. Yale Law Sch., 1958; legal counsel to U.S. Senator Wiley, 1959; counsel to U.S. Senator Estes Kefauver, antitrust and monopoly subcom. U.S. Senate, 1959-62; ptnr. DeGrazia & Kittrie, Washington, 1962-67; prof. criminal and comparative law Washington Coll. Law, Am. U., 1963—, dir. Inst. Advanced Studies in Justice, 1970-78, dean, 1977-79, Mooers scholar and prof. law, 1983—; univ. prof. Am. U., Washington, 1994—. Lectr. U. Ottawa, summer 1966; vis. lectr. Salzburg Law Sch., summers 1999—; rsch. scholar Univs. Warsaw and Berlin, summers 1967, 68; rsch. assoc. Ctr. Studies Criminal Justice U. Chgo., 1967-68; dir. Law and Policy Inst., Jerusalem, summers 1970-76, Inst. Law and Mass Media, 1978—; chmn. Eleanor Roosevelt Inst. for Justice and Peace, 1989—; vis. fellow Inst. Advanced Legal Rsch. U. London, 1973-74, Nat. Inst. Justice U.S. Dept. Justice, 1979-80; vis. prof. London Sch. Econs., 1974; prof. internat. criminal law, Salzburg Law Sch., 2000-; cons. US Pres.'s Commn. Marijuana and Drug Abuse, 1972, US v.p.'s commn. to combat terrorism, 1985; permanent rep. AIDP to UN Social and Econs. Coun., 1975—; mem. task force on role of psychology in criminal justice Am. Psychol. Assn.; dir. Dulles Internat. Bank, 1998-, Bank of Chios, Athens, Greece; dir., gen. counsel Liberty House Investments; chmn. KVK Comm. Ltd.; chmn. finance com. U. Bridgeport, 1998—. Author: International Legal Responsibility for Colonial People, 1951, The Mentally Disabled and the Law, 1959, The Right to be Different: Deviance and Enforced Law, 1971, The Comparative Law of Israel and the Middle East, 1971, The Real Estate Settlement Process and Its Cost, 1972, Crescent and Star: Arab-Israeli Perspectives on the Middle East Conflict, 1972, Medicine, Law and Public Policy, 1975, The Tree of Liberty: Rebellion and Political Crime in America, 1986, 2d edit., 1998, The Uncertain Future: Gorbachev's Eastern Bloc, 1988, The War Against Authority: From the Crisis of Legitimacy to a New Social Contract, 1995, Rebels With a Cause: The Minds and Morality of Political Offenders, 2000, Sentencing, Sanctions and Corrections: Federal and State Law, Policy and Practice, 2002, The Future of Peace in the 21st Century, 2003, International Criminal Law and Procedure, 2003, International Crimes and Punishments: The Law of Peace and the Law of War, 2005; chmn. editl. bd. Jour. Criminology, 1973-75; mem. editl. bd. Law and Human Behavior, 1976-80; mem. editl. adv. bd. The Washington Times; mem. exec. bd. Paragon House Pubs.; sr. cons. U.S. News and World Report Books; contbr. articles to profl. jours. Chmn. UN Alliance of NGOs on Crime Prevention and Criminal Justice, 1998—, sci. com. U. Messina, Italy. Served with Brit. Middle East Command. Raymond fellow U. Chgo., 1954-55; rsch. fellow Yale Law Sch., 1955; sr. fellow NEH, 1973-74. Mem. ABA, AAAS (mem. coun. 1972—), Am. Soc. Criminology (pres. 1975), Internat. Assn. Penal Law (v.p. Am. sect., sec.-gen. 1975-80), Internat. Assn. Comparative Pub. Law (bd. dirs. 1976—), Am. Soc. Pub. Adminstrn., Am. Soc. Internat. Law (chair interest group on status of minorities), Internat. Inst. Space Law, Inter-Am. Bar Assn., Kans. Bar Assn., DC Bar Assn., Manorial Soc. Gt. Britain, Knight, Order of St. John, Rose Haven Yacht Club (bd. dirs.), Cosmos Club, Phi Delta Phi (Sam Green award). Home: 6908 Ayr Ln Bethesda MD 20817-4902 also: Ramsbridge Farm 42427 Cochran Mill Rd Leesburg VA 20175-4617 Office: Am U Sch Law 4801 Massachusetts Ave NW Ste 354 Washington DC 20016 Home Phone: 301-229-0446; Office Phone: 202-387-3624. Fax: 202-387-3629. Personal E-mail: genih@aol.com.

KITZ, RICHARD JOHN, anesthesiologist, educator; b. Oshkosh, Wis., Mar. 25, 1929; s. Edward G. and Lona M (Schneider) Kitz; m. Jeanne Hogan, Feb. 27, 1954; 1 child, Anne Marie. BS, Marquette U., Milw., 1951, MD, 1954, DSc (hon.), 2000; MA (hon.), Harvard U. Med. Sch., Cambridge, Mass., 1969. Diplomate Am. Bd. Anesthesiology (dir.). From intern in surgery to assoc. prof. Columbia U., 1954—66, assoc. prof., 1966—69; prof. rsch. and tchg. in anesthesia Harvard U.-MIT, co-dir. divsn. health scis. tech., 1985—91; anaesthetist-in-chief Mass. Gen. Hosp., Boston, 1969—94; from prof. to prof. Med. Sch. Harvard U., 1969—2004, prof. emeritus, 2004—. Cons. FDA; prin. investigator Harvard Anaesthesia Rsch. and Rsch. Tng. Ctr., 1969—93. Editor: This is No Humbug! Reminiscences of the Department of Anesthesia at the Massachusetts General Hospital, 2002; editor: (with E.M. Papper) Uptake and Distribution of Anesthetic Agents, 1963; editor: (with M.B. Laver) Sci. Basis of Anesthesia; editor-in-chief Jour. Clin. Anesthesia, 1987—95; contbr. articles to profl. jours. With M.C. USN, 1955—57. Fellow: Coll. Anesthesiologists; mem.: Harvard Club (Boston), Royal Coll. Surgeons Ireland (hon. mem. faculty anesthetists), Mass. Soc. Anesthesiologists, Am. Soc. Anesthesiologists, Royal Coll. Anesthetists Eng. (hon.), Japan Soc. Anesthesiologists (hon.), German Soc. Anesthesiologists and Intensive Care (hon.), Australian Soc. Anesthetists (hon.), Assn. Univ. Anesthetists, AMA, Inst. Medicine, NAS, Blue Water Sailing Club, Beverly Yacht Club. Roman Catholic. Home: 6 Pond St Dover MA 02030-2432 Office: Mass Gen Hosp Dept Anesthesia Boston MA 02114 Business E-Mail: richard_kitz@hms.harvard.edu, rkitz@partners.org.

KITZES, WILLIAM FREDRIC, lawyer, advocate, researcher; b. Bklyn., Nov. 24, 1950; s. David Louis and Rhoda Rachel (Feldman) K; m. Sandra Shimasaki, Apr. 7, 1979; children: Justin, Dana. BA, U. Wis., 1972; JD, Am. U., 1975. Bar: D.C. 1977. Legal advisor on product recalls U.S. Consumer Products Safety Commn., Washington, 1975-77, program mgr., 1977-80, regulatory counsel, 1980-81; v.p., gen. mgr. Inst. for Safety Analysis, Rockville, Md., 1981-83; prin. Consumer Safety Assocs., Potomac, Md., Boca Raton, Fla., 1983—. Cons. Toro Co., Bloomington, Minn., 1987, Vendo Co., Fresno, Calif., 1987, Nat. Assn. Attys. Gens., Washington, 1987, Arctic Cat, Inc., Thief River Falls, Minn., 1995—, Global Furniture, Toronto, Ont., 1997, Product Safety Online, Boca Raton, 1997—, Cisco Sys., Inc., San Jose, Calif., 2001-. Contbg. columnist CCH Product Safety Guide and Products Liability Reporter, 2000-01. Counsel Friends of Charlie Gilchrist, Montgomery County, Md., 1983; chmn. Fla. Consumers Coun., 1995—. Recipient silver medal for meritorious svc. U.S. Consumer Products Safety Commn., 1976. Mem. Am. Soc. Safety Engrs., Human Factors Soc., System Safety Soc., Nat. Safety Coun., Internat. Consumer Product Health and Safety Orgn. Home and Office: Consumer Safety Assocs 4501 NW 25th Way Boca Raton FL 33434-2506 Office Phone: 561-241-1900. Business E-Mail: kitzes@productsafety.com.

KITZKE, EUGENE DAVID, research and development company executive; b. Milw., Sept. 2, 1923; s. Leo R. and Regina R. (Tomczyk) Kitzke; m. Lorraine Grace Shummon, Sept. 2, 1946; children: Mary Victoria, Paul Simon, Patrice Lynn, Jerome Peter. BS, Marquette U., 1945, MS, 1947; diploma in basic clin. sci., Med. Coll. Wis., 2002. Instr. microbiology St. Mary's Sch. Nursing, Grand Rapids, Mich., 1946-47; assoc. prof. Aquinas Coll., 1947-51; lab researcher S.C. Johnson & Son, Inc., Racine, Wis., 1951-57, research mgr., 1957-76, v.p. corp. R&D, 1976-81; pres. Oak Crete Block Corp., South Milwaukee, Wis., 1980—; developer Wind Crest Subdiv., Wind Lake, Wis., 1993. Adj. prof. dept. environ. medicine Med. Coll. Wis., Milw., 1973—81; owner Danel Enterprise, South Milwaukee; judge Marquette U. Sci. Fair; bd. dirs. Songcards, inc. Author: (book) For the Next Generation, 1986; contbr. articles to tech. jours., fiction and poetry to mags.; author pubs. in field. Mem. pres.' coun. Alverno Coll., 1979—87. Recipient H. F. Johnson Cmty. Svc. award, 1996; Disting. scholar, Marquette U., 1995. Mem.: AAAS, Hist. Sci. Soc., Palm Soc. (exec. bd., past pres.), Sigma Xi, Sigma Tau Delta, Phi Sigma. Roman Catholic. Achievements include patents in field. Home: 616 Aspen St South Milwaukee WI 53172-1702 Office: PO Box 413 South Milwaukee WI 53172-0413 also: 7101 S Pennsylvania Ave Oak Creek WI 53154-2439 *Honor thyself. Be in control. Be paid.*

KITZMILLER, HOWARD LAWRENCE, retired lawyer; b. Shippensburg, Pa., May 6, 1930; s. Franklin Leroy and Emma Corrinna (Bedford) K.; m. Shirley Mae Pine, Apr. 4, 1953; children: David Lawrence, Diane May. BA summa cum laude, Dickinson Coll., 1951; JD, Dickinson Sch. of Law, 1954; LLM, George Washington U., 1958. Bar: Pa. 1955, D.C. 1984. Commr. U.S. Ct. Mil. Appeals, Washington, 1958-59; various positions to assoc. gen. counsel FCC, Washington, 1959-80; various positions to dir., sr. v.p. and sec. Washington Mgmt. Corp., 1983—2005; ret., 2005. Editor Dickinson Law Rev., 1954. Deacon, elder Westminster Presbyn. Ch., Alexandria, Va.; bd. dirs. S.E. Fairfax Devel. Corp., Fairfax County, Va., 1977-98, also past pres.; various positions including pres., parents adv. coun., bd. assocs., trustee, investment com. Randolph-Macon Coll., Ashland, Va., 1984-95. Capt. JAGC, U.S. Army, 1955-58. Mem. ABA, City Club Washington, Masons, Phi Beta Kappa. Republican.

KIVELSON, MARGARET GALLAND, physicist; b. NYC, Oct. 21, 1928; d. Walter Isaac and Madeleine (Wiener) Galland; m. Daniel Kivelson, Aug. 15, 1949; children: Steven Allan, Valerie Ann. AB, Radcliffe Coll., 1950, AM, 1951, PhD, 1957. Cons. Rand Corp., Santa Monica, Calif., 1956-69; asst. to geophysicist UCLA, 1967-83, prof., space physics, dept. earth and space scis., Inst. Geophysics & Planetary Physics, 1983—, also chmn. dept. earth and space scis., 1984-87, acting dir. Inst. Geophys. Planet Physics, 1999—2000; prin. investigator of magnetometer, Galileo Mission Jet Propulsion Lab., Pasadena, Calif., 1977—2004. Overseer Harvard Coll., 1977-83; adv. coun. NASA, 1987-93; chair atmospheric adv. com. NSF, 1986-89, Com. Solar and Space Physics, 1977-86, com. planetary exploration, 1986-87, com. solar terrestial physics, 1989-92; adv. com. geoscis. NSF, 1993-97; space studies bd. NRC, 2002-05. Editor: The Solar System: Observations and Interpretations, 1986; co-editor: Introduction to Space Physics, 1995; contbr. articles to profl. jours. Named Woman of Yr., LA Mus. Sci. and Industry, 1979, Woman of Sci., UCLA, 1984; recipient Grad. Soc. medal Radcliffe Coll., 1983, 350th Anniversary Alumni medal Harvard U., 1986, Alfvén medal European Geophys. Union, 2005. Fellow AAAS, NAS (councilor 2007-), Internat. Inst. Astronautics, Am. Geophys. Union (Fleming medal 2005), Am. Acad. Arts and Scis., Am. Phys. Soc., Am. Philisophical Soc., Royal Astron. Soc.; mem. Am. Astron. Soc. Office: UCLA Dept Earth & Space Scis 6843 Slichter Hall Los Angeles CA 90095-1567 Home Phone: 310-454-3581; Office Phone: 310-825-3435. Business E-Mail: mkivelson@igpp.ucla.edu.*

KIVIKOSKI, ASKO ILMARI, retired obstetrician, gynecologist; b. Helsinki, Finland, Aug. 3, 1932; came to U.S., 1984; MD, U. Turku, Finland, 1958, DSc, 1967. Diplomate Am. Bd. Ob-gyn. Intern U. Turku, 1962, resident in ob/gyn., 1962-65, asst. prof., 1966-76; resident in surgery City Hosp., Turku, 1965-66; researcher Washington U., St. Louis, 1971-72; fellow in perinatology Mt. Sinai Hosp., NYC, 1978-79; head dept. ob/gyn. Ctrl. hosp., Lahti, Finland, 1976-84; staff Barnes Hosp., St. Louis, 1984-87, 97—; chief gynecol. svcs. St. Louis Regional Med. Ctr., 1987-97; Connect Care, 1998-2001; asst. prof. Washington U., St. Louis, 1984-92, assoc. prof., 1992-2001, assoc. prof. emeritus, 2001—. Author articles on anatomy, obstetrics, perinatology and ultrasound.

KIZER, CAROLYN ASHLEY, poet, educator; b. Spokane, Wash., Dec. 10, 1925; d. Benjamin Hamilton and M. (Ashley) K.; m. Stimson Bullitt, Jan., 1948 (div.); children: Ashley Ann, Scott, Jill Hamilton; m. John Marshall Woodbridge, Apr. 11, 1975. BA, Sarah Lawrence Coll., 1945; postgrad. (Chinese govt. fellow in comparative lit.), Columbia U., 1946-47; studied poetry with Theodore Roethke, U. Wash., 1953-54; LittD (hon.), Whitman Coll., 1986, St. Andrew's Coll., 1989, Mills Coll., 1990, Wash. State U., 1991. Specialist in lit. U.S. Dept. State, Pakistan, 1964-65; first dir. lit. programs Nat. Endowment for Arts, 1966-70; poet-in-residence U. N.C. at Chapel Hill, 1970-74; Hurst Prof. Lit. Washington U., St. Louis, 1971; lectr. Spring Lecture Series Barnard Coll., 1972; acting dir. grad. writing program Columbia U., 1972; poet-in-residence Ohio U., 1974; vis. poet Iowa Writer's Workshop, 1975; prof. U. Md., 1976-77; poet-in-residence, disting. vis. lectr. Centre Coll., Ky., 1979; disting. vis. poet East Wash. U., 1980; Elliston prof. poetry U. Cin., 1981; Bingham disting. prof. U. Louisville, Ky., 1982; disting. vis. poet Bucknell U., Pa., 1982; vis. poet SUNY, Albany, 1982; prof. Columbia U. Sch. Arts, 1982; prof. poetry Stanford U., 1986; sr. fellow in humanities Princeton U., 1986; vis. prof. writing U. Ariz., 1989, 90, U. Calif., Davis, 1991; Coal Royalty chair U. Ala., 1995. Participant Internat. Poetry Festivals, London, 1960, 70, Yugoslavia, 1969, 70, Pakistan, 1969, Rotterdam, Netherlands, 1970, Knokke-le-Zut, Belgium, 1970, Bordeaux, 1992, Dublin, 1993, Glasgow, 1994; sr. fellow humanities council Princeton U., 1986. Author: Poems, 1959, The Ungrateful Garden, 1961, Knock Upon Silence, 1965, Midnight Was My Cry, 1971, Mermaids in the Basement: Poems for Women, 1984 (San Francisco Arts Commn. award 1986), Yin: New Poems, 1984 (Pulitzer prize in poetry 1985), The Nearness of You, 1987 (Theodore Roethke prize, 1988); Proses: On Poems & Poets, 1994, Picking & Choosing: Prose on Prose, 1995, Harping On: Poems 1985-1995, 1996, The Complete Pro Femina, 2000, Cool, Calm and Collected Poems, 1960-2000; editor: Woman Poet: The West, 1980, Leaving Taos, 1981, The Essential Clare, 1993, 100 Great Poems by Women, 1995; translator Carrying Over, 1988; founder, editor: Poetry N.W., 1959-65; contbr. poems, articles to Am. and Brit. jours. Recipient award Am. Acad. and Inst. Arts and Letters, 1985, Pres.'s medal Ea. Wash. U., 1988, 5 Gov.'s awards State of Wash., 1965, 85, 95, 98, 2001, Silver medal Commonwealth Club, 1997, 2002, Aiken Taylor prize Sewanee Rev., 1998, Patterson prize, 2002, Western State Lifetime Achievement award, 2002, 1st prize Ind. Pub. Book award, 2002, L.A. Times Top Ten Books award, 2002, Acad. prize, 2003, Poets' prize, 2003. Mem. PEN, Amnesty Internat., Poetry Soc. Am. (Masefield prize 1983, Frost medal 1988). Episcopalian. Address: 19772 8th St E Sonoma CA 95476-3849

KIZER, JORGE RUBEN, cardiologist, epidemiologist; arrived in U.S., 1979; s. Saul Kizer and Fanny Dejman; m. Carol A. Lillienstein, May 28, 2000; children: Jacqueline Elizabeth, Sabrina Gabriella. BS, SUNY, Stony Brook, 1990; MD, U. of Pa., 1994; MSc, Harvard U., 1999. Diplomate internal medicine Am. Bd. of Internal Medicine, cardiovasc. disease Am. Bd. of Internal Medicine. Medicine intern and resident Brigham and Women's Hosp./Harvard Med. Sch., Boston, 1994—97; fellow in cardiovasc. medicine U. of Pa. Med. Ctr., Phila., 1997—2001; asst. prof. medicine and pub. health Weill Med. Coll. of Cornell U., NYC, 2001—, Bruce B. Lerman clin. scholar, 2004—. Co-author over 20 peer reviewed pubs. and book chpts. Recipient Mentored Patient-Oriented Rsch. Career Devel. award, NIH, 2002—07; Clinically Applied Rsch. grant, Am. Heart Assn., 2004—05. Mem.: Phi Beta Kappa, Alpha Omega Alpha. Avocations: jogging, swimming, reading, languages, travel. Home: 430 E 63rd St Apt 6N New York NY 10021-7927

KIZER, KENNETH WAYNE, emergency physician, executive, educator; b. Decatur, Ind., May 28, 1951; s. Homer Martin Kizer and Ellen Hope Howland; m. Suzanne A. Stoddard, Aug. 26, 1972; children: Kelli Christina, Kimberly Casey. BS with honors, Stanford U., 1972; MD with honors, MPH in Epidemiology, UCLA, 1976. Rotating internship Naval Regional Med. Ctr., Portsmouth, Va., 1977; undersea medicine fellowship Naval Undersea Med. Inst., Groton, Conn., 1977; resident in diagnostic radiology U. Calif, San Francisco, 1980-81, resident in occupl. medicine, 1982-83; firefighter; emergency physician; dir. Emergency Med. Svcs. Authority State of Calif., 1983-84; chief dep. dir. and chief of pub. health Calif. Dept. Health Svcs., Sacramento, 1984-85, dir., 1985-91; prof., chmn. dept. cmty. and internat. health U. Calif., Davis, 1991-94; undersec. for health US Dept. Vets. Affairs, Washington, 1994-99; dir. Health Sys. Internat., Inc., 1994-97; pres., CEO Nat. Quality Forum, Washington, 1999—2005; chmn. Medsphere Sys. Corp., Aliso Viego, Calif., 2002—, pres., 2005—, CEO, 2005—. Contbr. numerous articles to profl. jours.; chpts. to books. Chair Radiation Emergency Screening Team, 1988-91, Hazardous Waste Appeal Bd., 1990; co-chair Calif. AIDS Leadership Com.; mem. Diving Control Bd. U. Calif., 1980-91, Gov.'s Emergency Ops. Exec. Coun., 1984-91, Governing Bd. Calif YMCA Model Legislature Program, 1986-90, Chem. Emergency Planning and Response Commn., 1988-90; chair S.W. Low Level Radioactive Waste Compact Commn., 1990-91, tobacco edn. oversight com. State Calif., 1990-91, bd. dirs. Calif. Wellness Found., 1992-2003, Matthews Found., 1991-94, Ctr. for AIDS Rsch., Edn. and Svcs., 1992-94, Infection Control Coun., 1991-94; mem. adv. bd. Preventive Sports Medicine Inst., 1991-94. Lt. USN, 1976-80. Recipient Humanitarian Svc. medal Dept. of Def., 1979, Spl. Recognition award No. Calif. Emergency Med. Care Coun., 1984, Golden State Med. Assn., 1986, Calif. Div. Am. Lung Assn., 1988, Calif. Health Fedn., 1988, cert. of Recognition Calif. Asian Pacific Health Coalition, 1989, Spl. Achievement award Calif. Emergency Physician Med. Group, 1989, Jean Spencer Felton award for Excellence in Sci. Writing, 1989, spl. awards from March of Dimes, Am. Cancer Soc., Calif. State Senate, Calif. Conf. Local Health Officers, others, 1991—, Healthcare Heroes award Calif. State Assembly, 1996, Cert. of Recognition award, 1996, Dr. Nathan Davis award AMA, 1998, Literacy Achievement award Am. Coll. Physician Execs., 1998, Founders award Wilderness Med. Soc., 1998, Justin Kimball Innovator's award Am. Hosp. Assn., 1998, Lifetime Achievement award Assn. Health Systems Pharmacists, 2002, Founders award Am. Coll. Med. Quality, 2004, Gustov O. Lienhand award, Inst. Medicine/Nat. Acad. Scis., 2004, Ernest S. Codman award Joint Commn. Accreditation Healthcare Orgs., 2005; named Toll fellow Coun. State Govts., 1987. Fellow Am. Coll. Physician Execs. (disting.), Am. Coll. Preventive Medicine, Am. Coll. Emergency Physicians, Am. Coll. Occupl. Environ. Medicine, Am. Acad. Clin. Toxicology, Royal Soc. Health, Royal Soc. Medicine, Am. Coll. Med. Toxicology, Am. Acad. Med. Adminstrs., Explorers Club; mem. APHA, Internat. Soc. Toxicology, Inst. Medicine NAS, Wilderness Med. Soc., Undersea and Hyperbaric Med. Soc., Nat. Soc. YMCA Youth Govs., Nat. Assn. Underwater Instrs. (Outstanding Contribution to Diving award 1984), Inst. Medicine, Delta Tau Delta (Beta Rho chpt. Hall of Fame 1987), Alpha Omega Alpha, Delta Omega. Independent. Avocations: scuba diving, hiking and backpacking, photography, racquet sports, book collecting. Office: Medsphere Systems Corp 120 Vantis Ste 405 Aliso Viejo CA 92656

KIZILISIK, AYDIN TARIK, surgeon, researcher; b. Istanbul, Turkey, July 20, 1959; s. Karani Ozer Akra and Gulen Kizilisik, Suat Kizilisik (Stepfather); m. Semiha Reha Duldur, Nov. 19, 1984; 1 child, Basak. MD, Ankara U. Med. Sch., 1984; M in Exptl. Surgery, U. Alta., Edmonton, Alta, Can., 1994. Intern Ankara U. Hosps., 1983—84; resident in surgery Gulhane Mil. Med. Acad. and Hosps., Ankara, 1986—91; sr. med. examiner, med. advisor to the gov. Tosya, Kastamonu, Turkey, 1984—86; fellow in liver transplantation U. Alta. Hosps., Edmonton, 1991—93; cons. liver transplant and hepatobiliary surgeon King Fahad N.G. Hosp., Riyadh, Saudi Arabia, 1994—98; fellow in multiorgan transplantation U. Tenn. Hosps., Memphis, 1999—2001, transplant surgeon, 2001—02; asst. prof. surgery Vanderbilt U. Med. Ctr., Nashville, 2002—06; attending transplant surgeon VA Med. Ctr., Nashville, 2002—06, St. Thomas Hosp., Nashville, 2002—06; dir. kidney transplant program Luth. Hosp. of Ind., Fort Wayne, 2007—. Instr. ACLS program King Fahad N.G. Hosp., Riyadh, 1994—98, instr. advanced trauma life support program, 1994—98; presenter in field. Contbr. articles more than 100 to profl. jours. Named to 2007 Guide to Am.'s Top Surgeons, Consumers' Rsch. Coun. Am.; Helen Boone scholar, Nora's Life Gift Found., 1999. Fellow: ACS, Internat. Coll. Surgeons, Am. Soc. Transplant Surgeons, Internat. Soc. Surgery, Am. Soc. Transplantation (Trainee Travel award 2000), Transplantation Soc.; mem.: European Soc. Organ Transplantation, Internat. Liver Transplantation Soc., Mid. Ea. Soc. Organ Transplantation, Turkish Nat. Soc. Surgery, NY Acad. Scis., Turkish Med. Assn. Achievements include research in graft versus host disease after small bowel transplantation; analysis of donor criteria and its implications on the outcome of liver transplants; development of microsurgery training for transplantation research purposes; research in impact of long term chronic immunosuppressive therapy on health and quality of life after orthotopic liver transplantation; development of pancreas transplantation with portal-enteric drainage. Home Phone: 260-271-1181. Business E-Mail: tkizilisik@ioheart.com.

KJELLMARK, ERIC WILLIAM, JR., management consultant, performing company executive; b. New Rochelle, NY, May 14, 1928; s. Eric William and Anna Sophia (Fogelstrom) K. BCE, Cornell U., 1950. Mgr. mktg. planning E. I. DuPont de Nemours, Wilmington, Del., 1980-87, dir. Far East task force, 1987-89; gen. dir. Opera Del., Inc., Wilmington, 1985-95; cons. Condux, Inc., Wilmington, 1985-94. Cons. Monkman-Rumsey, Inc., Wilmington, 1986-92. Treas., v.p. Grand Opera House, Inc., Wilmington, 1971-91, bd. trustees 1992-95; panelist Del. State Arts Coun., Wilmington, 1987-89, 96, 97; sec.-treas. Opera Del., 1994-96, bd. dirs., 1956-04, Wilmington Waterways, Inc., 1985-89; chmn. oversight com. Delaware Art Stabilization, 1993-96, chmn. level IV cos. Opera Am., 1989-91, bd. dirs., 1991-94; panelist Mid-Atlantic States Arts Consortium, 1990, NEA, 1991-94; pres. Opera for Youth, 1997-00; bd. dirs. Nat. Opera Assn., 1998, 99. Recipient W.W. Laird award DE, 1992, Partners in Excellence award Opera Guild Internat., 1994. Mem. Am. Chem. Soc., Am. Inst. Chem. Engrs., Alpha Chi Sigma. Republican. Episcopalian. Office: 3300 NE 36th St #821 Fort Lauderdale FL 33308

KLAAS, NICHOLAS PAUL, management consultant; b. Kieler, Wis., June 25, 1925; s. Paul Francis and Ida Klaas; m. Ruth Elizabeth Barry, Nov. 5, 1949; children: Paul, Patricia, Kathleen, James. BA, Loras Coll., 1945; PhD, U. Notre Dame, 1948. Registered to practice before U.S. Patent Office, 1970. Product mgr. Rohm & Haas Co., Phila., 1948-52; mgr. research and devel. 3M Co., St. Paul, 1952-65; exec. v.p., dir. Wyomissing Corp., West Reading, Pa., 1965-71, v.p. comml. develop., 1972—74; group v.p. chems. GAF Corp., NYC, 1974—77; gen. mgr. splty. chems. Ga. Pacific Corp., Portland, Oreg., 1977; pres. J.T. Baker Chem. Co., Phillipsburg, NJ, 1977-84; chmn. bd. J.T. Baker B.V., Deventer, Netherlands, 1978-84; pres. Klaas Assocs., 1984—. Adj. prof. chemistry San Diego State U., 1985-98; mem. bd. visitors chair, undergrad. rsch. com. U. N.C., Asheville, 1986-91, Council for Chem. Research, 1987-98. Patentee in field; contbr. articles to profl. jours. Trustee St. Joseph Hosp., Reading, Pa., 1968-71; bd. regents Loras Coll., Dubuque, Iowa, 1974-76. Mem.: AAAS, Am. Chem. Soc., Ocean Hills Country Club. Address: 4965 Alicante Way Oceanside CA 92056 Home Phone: 760-639-5404.

KLAAS, PAUL BARRY, lawyer; b. St. Paul, Aug. 9, 1952; s. N. Paul and Ruth Elizabeth (Barry) K.; m. Barbara Ann Bockhaus, July 30, 1977; children: James, Ann, Brian. AB magna cum laude, Dartmouth Coll., 1974; JD cum laude, Harvard U., 1977. Bar: Minn. 1977, US Dist. Ct. Minn. 1977, US Ct. Appeals (8th cir.) 1979, US Ct. Appeals (10th cir.) 1980, US Supreme Ct. 1982, US Ct. Appeals (9th cir.) 1989, US Ct. Appeals (fed. cir.) 1994; solicitor Eng. and Wales 2006. Assoc. Dorsey & Whitney, Mpls., 1977-82, ptnr. trial group, 1983—, ptnr.-in-charge London, 2005—, ptnr.-in-charge (internat.), 2007—. Co-chair Internat. Arbitration and Litigation Practice Group, 1996—, chair, Trial Group, 2000-06; adj. prof. William Mitchell Coll Law, St. Paul, 1980-85. Bd. dirs. St. Paul Chamber Orchestra. Fellow: Am. Coll. Trial Lawyers; mem.: Law Soc. Eng. and Wales, Phi Beta Kappa. Office: Dorsey & Whitney 50 S 6th St Ste 1500 Minneapolis MN 55402-1498 also: Dorsey & Whitney 21 Wilson St London EC2M 2TD England Office Phone: 612-340-2817, 44-020-7826-4567. Office Fax: 612-340-2868, 44-020-7588-0555. Business E-Mail: klaas.paul@dorsey.com.

KLAASSEN, PAUL J., personal care industry executive; m. Terry Klaassen. Founder, chmn., CEO Sunrise Sr. Living, 1981—. Founding chmn., dir Assisted Living Fed. Am.; bd. trustees Hudson Inst., Inst. Am. Values, Ethics Public Policy Ctr., Trinity Forum; adv. com. Dept. Health-care Policy Harvard Univ. Med. Sch. Office: Sunrise Sr Living 7902 Westpark Dr Mc Lean VA 22102 Office Phone: 703-273-7500. Office Fax: 703-744-1601.

KLABUNDE, KENNETH J., chemistry professor, researcher; BA in Chemistry, Augustana Coll., 1965; PhD in Chemistry, U. Iowa, 1969. Postdoctoral work Pa. State U., 1969—70; with Kans. State Univ., Manhattan, Kans., 1979—, head, dept. chemistry, 1979—88, univ. disting. prof., sch. chemistry, 1988—; founder, cons. NanoScale Corp., Manhattan, Kans. Contract cons. Catalytica, 3M, Amoco, and others; helped establish the Coun. for Chem. Rsch.; lectr. in field. Published several scientific papers, mem. editl. bd. Critical Reviews in Surface Chemistry, Chemistry of Material and Nanostructured Materials; author: Nanoscale Materials in Chemistry, 2001. Named Alumni Fellow, U. Iowa Coll. Liberal Arts & Sciences, 2003; recipient Conoco Disting. Grad. Faculty Mem., 1992, Olin Petefish award in Basic Sciences, 1995, Tech. of Yr. award, Silicon Prairie Tech. Assn., 1996, Popular Mechanics Breakthrough award, 2005. Mem.: Am. Chem. Soc. (Midwest award for Outstanding Achievements in Chemistry (St. Lewis sect.) 1998), Sigma Xi, Phi Lambda Upsilon, Alpha Chi Sigma. Achievements include being internationally recognized for work in catalysis, nanoparticles and destructive absorbants; designed the first metal atom reactor for general commercial use; developer of FAST-ACT (First Applied Sorbent Treatment-Against Chemical Threats), a formulation of non-toxic nanomaterials effective for neutralizing a wide range of toxic chemicals with the added potential to destroy chemical warfare agents; patents in field. Office: Dept Chemistry Kans State Univ 111 Willard Hall Office CB323 Manhattan KS 66506-3701 Office Phone: 785-532-6849, 785-532-6829 (lab). Office Fax: 785-532-6666. Business E-Mail: kenjk@ksu.edu.

KLAEHNE, EBERHARD O.W., pharmaceutical executive, chemist; b. Hamburg, Germany, Jan. 31, 1951; arrived in U.S., 1993; s. Walter and Hedwig (Jaster) Klaehne; m. Soumontha Phommachack, Dec. 21, 1987; m. Gabriele Jacobsen (div.); children: Maurice Nicolas, Somsay Phommachack. Diploma in chemistry, U. Hamburg, 1977, Dr. rerum naturalium, 1982. Dir. quality control Ichthyol Gesellschaft Cordes, Hermanni and Co., Hamburg, 1982—85; dir. quality control/quality assurance LTS Lohmann Therapie Systeme AG, Neuwied, Rheinland Pfalz, Germany, 1985—93; dir. quality assurance LTS Lohmann Therapy Systems Corp., West-Caldwell, NJ, 1993—96; dir. quality control, clin. supply LTS Lohmann Therapie Systeme AG, Andernach, Rheinland-Pfalz, Germany, 1996—2001, dir. quality assurance, 2001—02; exec. dir. quality Mylan Technologies Inc., St. Albans, Vt., 2002—. Rsch. assoc. DFG German Rsch. Soc., U. of Hamburg, Hamburg, Hamburg, Germany, 1977—77; sci. asst. lectr. U. of Hamburg, Hamburg, Hamburg, Germany, 1977—78; predoctoral rsch. assoc. Centre d'Etudes Nucléaires de Saclay, Saclay, 1979; rsch. assoc. DFG, German Rsch. Soc., Hamburg, Hamburg, Germany, 1980; sci. asst. U. of Hamburg, Hamburg, Hamburg, Germany, 1979—81; presenter in field. Contbr. articles to profl. jours. Leader table tennis sporting group Glashuetter Sporting Club, 1968—74. Scholar, DAAD German Academic Exch. Svc., 1978, DAAD German Academic Exch. Svc., Centre d' Etudes Nucléaires de Saclay, Paris, France, 1979. Achievements include research in synthesization and characterisization of novel class of neutral, anionic and cationic trigonal-bipyramidal coordinated Uranium(IV) organyls; photo reduction of Uranium(IV) to U(III) organyls with Trispentahaptocyclopentadienyl U(IV)alkyls; homolytic cleavage of U(IV)-C bonds with excess of Li-organyls. Personal E-mail: eklaehne@web.de.

KLAERNER, CURTIS MAURICE, gas industry executive; b. Fredericksburg, Tex., Sept. 7, 1920; s. Elgin and Irene (Wagner) K.; m. Aileen E. Eitt, Sept. 4, 1942 (dec. Oct. 1998); children: Sherilyn Kay, Curtis Elgin; m. Jean L. Patton, Aug. 26, 2000. BS in Chem. Engring, U. Tex., 1942; grad. program sr. execs., Mass. Inst. Tech., 1956. Process engr., then chief process engr. Magnolia Petroleum Co., 1942-53; refinery mgr., then mgr. Eastern region mfg. Socony Mobil Oil Co., 1953-59; regional exec., then regional v.p. Mobil Internat. Oil Co., 1959-61; pres. Mobil Inner Europe, Geneva, 1962-65; corp. v.p. charge marine transp. and internat. sales Socony Mobil Oil Co., 1965-69; exec. v.p. internat. div. Mobil Oil Corp., 1969-72, pres., 1972-79, also exec. v.p., dir., mem. exec. com. corp.; vice chmn., dir. Commonwealth Oil Refining Co., San Antonio, 1979, pres., chief operating officer, 1979-83; ret., 1983; pres. Klaerner Enterprises, 1984—; vice chmn. Weed Instrument Co. Mem. adv. coun. Engring. Found., U. Tex., Austin. Recipient Disting. Grad. award Coll. Engring., U. Tex., 1983 Mem. Phi Eta Sigma, Omega Chi Epsilon, Phi Kappa Sigma. Clubs: Circumnavigators (N.Y.C.); Oak Hills Country, Optimists, Exchange, Petroleum (San Antonio), Country Club San Antonio. Republican. Episcopalian. Home: 11 Chelsea Way San Antonio TX 78209-7400

KLAFTER, CARY IRA, lawyer; b. Chgo., Sept. 15, 1948; s. Herman Nicholas and Bernice Rose (Maremont) K.; m. Kathleen Ann Kerr, July 21, 1974; children: Anastasia, Benjamin, Eileen. BA, Mich. State U., 1968, MS, 1971; JD, U. Chgo., 1974. Bar: Calif. 1972. Assoc. Morrison & Foerster, San Francisco, 1972-79, ptnr., 1979-96; v.p. legal and corp. affairs, dir. corp. legal, corp. sec. Intel Corp., Santa Clara, Calif., 1996—. Lectr. law Stanford Law Sch., 1990-99. Capt. USAR, 1971-78. Mem.: Soc. Corp. Secs. and Governance Profls.

KLAGES, KAREN LOUISE, musician, educator; b. Pasadena, Calif., Nov. 10, 1964; d. Henry Eugene and Marjorie Bakker Klages. MusB in Edn., Ind. U., 1986, MusM, 1989. Profl. clear tchg. credential Calif., cert. gifted and talented edn. Pasadena Unified Sch. Dist., Calif. Tchr. instrumental music Pasadena (Calif.) Unified Sch. Dist., 1987—; French horn performer Fresno (Calif.) Philharm., 1999—; freelance musician various LA area orchs., 1987—; horn instr. Pasadena City Coll., 2000—04. Creator Eliot Mid. Sch. Jazz Band, 1991—. Musician (soloist): (with La Mirada Symphony) Schumann's Konzertstuck for Horns, (with Pasadena Orch.) Mozart's Horn Concerto #2. Vol. Lake Ave. Ch., Pasadena, 1983—2005; dir. performing groups Altadena (Calif.) Arts Coun., 2003—05; precinct worker nat. elections 2000 and 2004 Pasadena, 2000—04. Recipient Cert. of Recognition for Mus. Excellence in Pasadena Schs., City of Pasadena, 2003, Cert. of Recognition for Outstanding Dedication to Pasadena Schs., Bd. of Edn., Pasadena Unified Sch. Dist., 2003; grantee, Mr. Holland's Opus Found., 2002, Pasadena Ednl. Found., 2002, 2003, 2004. Mem.: NEA (assoc.; local site rep. 2003—05), Internat. Horn Soc. (assoc.), Am. Fedn. of Musicians (assoc.), Music Educators' Nat. Conf. (assoc.), So. Calif. Sch. Band and Orch. Assn. (assoc.). Avocations: backpacking, bicycling, dog shows, travel, reading. Home: 1915 Homewood Dr Altadena CA 91001 Home Phone: 626-794-6314; Office Phone: 626-795-6981. Personal E-mail: usermusic2264@aol.com.

KLAHR, GARY PETER, retired lawyer; b. NYC, July 9, 1942; s. Fred and Frieda (Garson) K Student, Ariz. State U., 1958—61; JD high honors, U. Ariz., 1964. Bar: Ariz. 1967, U.S. Dist. Ct. Ariz. 1967. Assoc. Brazlin & Greene, Phoenix, 1967—68; sr. ptnr. Gary Peter Klahr, P.C., Phoenix, 1968—2002; owner Klahr Paralegal Svc., Phoenix, 2002—. Judge adv. Camelback Civitan Club, 1970—73. Asst. editor Ariz. Law Rev., 1963-64; contbr. articles to profl. jours. Bd. dirs. CODAMA, 1975-89, pres., 1980-81; bd. dirs. Tumbleweed Runaway Ctr., 1972-76, Mrtro Youth Ctr., 1986-87, East McDowell Youth Assn., 1992-94, Svc., Employment, Redevel. Jobs for Progress, Phoenix, 1985-90, pres., 1986-87; bd. dirs. Internat. Found. Anti-Cancer Drug Discovery, 1998-2002, chair exec. com., 1999-2002; chmn. Citizens Criminal Justice Commn., 1977-78; elected Phoenix City Coun., 1974-76; co-chmn. delinquency subcom. Phoenix Forward Task Force; vol. referee Maricopa County Juvenile Ct., 1969, juvenile hearing officer, 1985-89; vol. adult probation officer; vol. counselor youth programs Dept. Econ. Security and Dept. Corrections, Phoenix; ex-officio mem., spl. cons. Phoenix Youth Commn.; mem. citizen adv. coun. Phoenix Union H.S. Dist., 1985-90, 95-99, co-chmn. 1998-99, elected Governing Bd., 1991-95, 2001-05, v.p., 1991-93; mem. rev. bd. Phoenix Police Dept., 1985-94; v.p. local chpt. City of Hope, 1985-86; Justice of Peace pro tem Maricopa County Cts., 1985-89; mem. City License Appeals Bd., 1987-97, vice chmn. 1988-93, chmn. 1993-97; v.p., co-founder Cmty. Leadership for Youth Devel.; del. Phoenix Together Town Hall on Youth Crime, 1982; bd. dirs. Murphy Trail Estates Neighborhood Assn., 2006—, v.p., 2006—; cmty. columnist Ariz. Rep., 2004—. Mem. ACLU (v.p. ctrl. chpt. Ariz. 1990-95, 2007—, pres. 1995-2001, state bd. 1990-2001, Disting. Citizen award 1976), Ariz. State Bar (past sec., bd. dirs. young lawyers sect., co-chmn. unauthorized practice com. 1988-89, other coms.), Maricopa County Bar Assn. (past sec., bd. dirs. young lawyers sect., vice-chmn. juvenile practice com. 1998-99), Am. Judicature Soc., Jewish Children's and Family Svc., Joint Jewish Task Force on Pub. Edn., Common Cause, NAACP, Ariz. Consumers Coun., Phoenix Jaycees (named 1 of 3 Outstanding Young Men Phoenix 1969), Temple Beth Israel, Order of Coif, Phi Alpha Delta. Democrat. Jewish. Office: 317 E Berridge Ln Phoenix AZ 85012 Home Phone: 602-265-3150; Office Phone: 602-265-3150. Personal E-mail: garyk57647@aol.com.

KLAHR, LEWIS, film director; Prof., dept. film Pratt Inst., NYC, Mass. Coll. Art, Cal. Arts; vis. artist several univ. Lectr. in field of film studies. Contbr. articles to numerous profl. jours.; dir.: (films) Her Fragrant Emulsion, 1987, Altair, 1994, Lulu, 1996, Calendar the Siamese, 1997, Pony Glass, 1998, Daylight Moon, 2002, The Aperture of Ghostings, 2002, Daylight Moon (A Quartet), 2004; Two Minutes to Zero, 2006, exhibited in group shows at Whitney Biennial, Whitney Mus. Art, NYC, 2004, 2006.

KLAIN, RONALD ALAN, lawyer; b. Indpls., Aug. 8, 1961; s. Stanley Hugh and Sarann (Horwitz) K.; m. Monica Medina, June 22, 1986; children: Hannah, Michael, Daniel. BA summa cum laude, Georgetown U., 1983; JD magna cum laude, Harvard U., 1987. Bar: Pa., 1992, D.C. 1999. Law clk. Hon. Byron R. White, Washington, 1987-89; spl. asst. Senate Judiciary Com., Washington, 1986-87, chief counsel, 1989-92; assoc. general counsel for Washington issues Clinton/Gore Campaign, 1992; assoc. counsel to the Pres. The White House, Washington, 1993-94; chief of staff and counselor for Atty. Gen., Janet Reno Dept. Justice, Washington, 1994-95; staff dir. Senate Dem. Leadership Com., Washington, 1995; chief of staff Vice President Gore, The White House, Washington, 1995-99; gen. counsel Gore-Lieberman Recount Com., Tallahassee, 2000; ptnr. O'Melveny & Myers LLP, Washington, 1999—2005; exec. v.p., gen. counsel Revolution LLC, Washington, 2005—, ptnr. Editor: Harvard Law Review, 1985—86. Commr. Pres.'s Commn. on Fed. Appointments Process, Washington, 1990; dir. debate preparation Kerry-Edwards for Pres., Washington, D.C., 2004. Named Lawyers of the Yr., Nat. Law Jour., 2000, Top Lawyer in Washington Under the Age of 40, Washingtonian; named one of 50 Most Promising Leaders in Am. Under the Age of 40, Time Mag., Top 20 Young Lawyers Nationwide. Mem.: ABA. Democrat. Jewish. Home: 3912 Rosemary St Chevy Chase MD 20815 Office: Revolution LLC 1717 Rhode Island Ave N 10th Fl Washington DC 20008 Office Phone: 202-776-1400. Office Fax: 202-383-5414. Business E-Mail: rklain@omm.com.

KLAINERMAN, SERGIU, mathematics professor; Diploma de Licenta, U. Bucharest, 1973; PhD, NYU, 1978. Miller fellow U. Calif., Berkeley, 1978—80; asst. prof. NYU Courant Inst. Math. Sciences, 1980—83, assoc. prof., 1983—86, prof., 1986—87, Princeton U., 1987—. Vis. prof. Stanford U., U. Miami, Hebrew U. of Jerusalem, Tel Aviv U., U. Bonn, Heidelberg U., Kyoto U., U. Canberra. Editor: Am. Jour. Mathematics, 1993—99; editl. bd. Jones and Barlett Publishers, Internat. Math. Rsch. Notices, Jour. Differential and Integral Equations, Advances in Differential Equations, Jour. of Am. Math. Soc., Nodea, Communications in Contemporary Mathematics, Selecta Mathematics, Jour. European Math. Soc. Guggenheim fellow, 1997—98, MacArthur fellow, 1991—96, Sloan fellow, 1983—85. Fellow: Am. Acad. Arts and Sciences; mem.: Am. Math. Soc. (Bocher prize 1999), French Acad. Sciences (fgn. mem. 2002—, Le Conte prize 1996), NAS. Office: Dept Mathematics Princeton Univ 1108 Fine Hall Washington Rd Princeton NJ 08544-1000 Office Phone: 609-258-4188. Office Fax: 609-258-1367. E-mail: seri@princeton.edu.

KLAMANN, JOHN MICHAEL, lawyer; b. Fresno, Calif., Aug. 23, 1952; s. Michael J. and Jacqueline C. K.; m. Brigid A. Cleary, Apr. 17, 1982; children: Conor, Seth, Zachary, Hannah, Kaitlin, Abbye. BS in Psychology, Kans. State U., 1974; JD, U. Kans., 1978. Bar: Mo. 1978, Kans. 1979. Atty. Popham Law Firm, Kansas City, Mo., 1978-88, Payne and Jones, Overland Park, Kans., 1989-96, Klamann and Hubbard, P.A., Overland Park, 1996—. Adj. prof. U. Mo., Kansas City Sch. of Law, 1998-2001. Author: (with others) Am Jur Trials, 1988, 90, 92. Mem. ABA, ATLA, Mo. Assn. Trial Attys., Kans. Trial Lawyers Assn., Mo. Bar Assn., Kans. Bar Assn. Home: 70 Dunfold Cir Kansas City KS 64112 Office: Klamann & Hubbard PA 929 Walnut St Ste 800 Kansas City MO 64106 Fax: 913-327-7800. E-mail: jklamann@kh-law.com.

KLAMMER, JOSEPH FRANCIS, retired management consultant; b. Omaha, Mar. 25, 1925; s. Aloys Arcadius and Sophie (Nadolny) K. Student, US Mil. Acad., West Point, 1947; BS, Creighton U., Omaha, 1948; MBA, Stanford U., Calif., 1950; cert. in polit. econs. Grad. Inst. Internat. Studies, U. Geneva, 1951. Cert. mgmt. cons. Adminstrv. analyst Chevron Corp., San Francisco, 1952-53; staff asst. No. Natural Gas Co., Omaha, 1953-57; mgmt. cons. Cresap, McCormick and Paget, Inc., NYC, 1957-75, v.p., mgr. San Francisco region, 1968-75, bd. dirs.; mgmt. cons., prin. J.F. Klammer Assocs., San Francisco, 1975-2000; semi-ret. practice mgmt. cons., San Francisco, 2000—03; ret., 2003. Bd. dirs. Conard House. Mem. adv. coun. Creighton U. Coll. Arts and Scis., 2000—03; CEO.pres. Broadway Towers Homeowners Assn., San Francisco, 1993—94, mem. maintenance com., 2000—, bd. dirs., 2002—, sec., 2005—, mem. rules com., 1995—96, bd. dirs., mem. fin. com., 1994—95. 1st lt. USAAF, 1943—46, lt. col. USAF, ret. Recipient Sovereign Mil. Hospitaller Order of St. John of Jerusalem of Rhodes and of Malta, Alumni Merit award Creighton U. Coll. Arts and Scis., 1998. Mem. Knights of Malta, Alpha Sigma Nu. Republican. Roman Catholic. Home: 1998 Broadway St #805 San Francisco CA 94109-2281

KLAMON, LAWRENCE PAINE, lawyer; b. St. Louis, Mar. 17, 1937; s. Joseph Martin and Rose (Schimel) K.; m. Jo Ann Karen Beatty, Nov. 1957 (div. Feb. 1974); children: Stephen Robert, Karen Jean, Lawrence Paine; m. Frances Ann Estes, Mar. 1980. AB, Washington U., St. Louis, 1958; JD, Yale U., 1961. Bar: N.Y. 1964, Ga. 1992. Confidential asst. Office Sec. Def., Washington, 1961-62, spl. asst. to gen. counsel, 1962-63; asso. Cravath, Swaine & Moore, NYC, 1963-67; v.p., gen. counsel Fuqua Industries, Inc., Atlanta, 1967-73, sr. v.p. fin. and adminstrn., 1971-81, pres., 1981-89, chief exec. officer, 1989-91; chmn., 1991; sr. counsel Alston & Bird, Atlanta, 1991-95; pres., CEO Fuqua Enterprises, Inc., Atlanta, 1995-97. Chmn. Gov.'s Internat. Adv. Coun., 1992-95. Mem. bd. editors Yale Law Jour., 1959-61. Mem. State Bar Ga., Order of Coif, Phi Beta Kappa, Omicron Delta Kappa.

KLANDERMAN, BRUCE HOLMES, retired chemist; b. Feb. 27, 1938; BA, Calvin Coll., Grand Rapids, Mich., 1959; MS in Chemistry, U. Ill., Urbana, 1961, PhD in Chemistry, 1963. Rsch. assoc. Eastman Kodak Co., Rochester, NY, 1963—78, environ. dir., 1978—92; prin. assoc. Radian Corp., Rochester, 1992—98; ret., 1998. Contbr. articles to profl. jours. Recipient Outstanding Svc. award, Calvin Coll. Alumni Assn., 1977. Mem.: Am. Chem. Soc., Am. Guild Organists. Achievements include patents in field.

KLAPER, MARTIN JAY, lawyer; b. Chgo., Jan. 12, 1947; s. Carl and Kate F. (Friedman) K.; m. Julia Warner, Nov. 14, 1973. BS in Bus. summa cum laude, Ind. U., 1969, JD summa cum laude, 1971. Bar: Ind. 1971, U.S. Dist. Ct. (no. and so. dists.) Ind. 1971, U.S. Ct. Appeals (7th cir.) 1972, U.S. Supreme Ct. 1979. Ptnr. Ice Miller, Indpls., 1972—. Mem. ABA, Ind. Bar Assn. Office: Ice Miller PO Box 82001 Indianapolis IN 46282-2001 Home Phone: 317-691-6594; Office Phone: 317-236-2322. Personal E-mail: Klaper@comcast.net. Business E-Mail: Klaper@Icemiller.com.

KLAPHOLZ, HENRY, obstetrician, gynecologist, educator; b. NYC, Oct. 13, 1941; s. Jakob and Frida (Nussbaum) Klapholz; m. Madelyn Hyman, June 6, 1971; children: Meredith, Judith, Lauren, Jacob. BEE, CCNY, NYC, 1963; MEE, NYU, NYC, 1964; MD, Albert Einstein U., NYC, 1971. Diplomate Am. Bd. Ob-Gyn. Intern Montefiore Hosp., NY, 1971—72; resident Beth Israel Hosp., Boston, 1972—76, vice chmn. ob-gyn., 1989—2001; assoc. prof. Harvard Med. Sch., Boston, 1989—; assoc. prof. HST divsn. MIT, Cambridge, Mass., 1998—; clin. prof. Tufts U. Sch. Medicine, Boston, 2001—; chmn. ob-gyn. Metrowest Med. Ctr., Framingham, Mass., 2001—. Host, prodr. (cable TV program) Dr.'s on Call, 2001—. Maj. US Army, 1976—78. Named one of Best of Boston, Boston Mag.; recipient S. Robert Stone Tchr. award, Harvard Med. Sch. Fellow: ACOG, Boston Obstet. Soc. Jewish. Avocations: photography, videography, TV production, piano, computers. Home: 25 Rockport Rd Weston MA 02493 Office: MetroWest Med Ctr 115 Lincoln St Framingham MA 01701 Office Phone: 508-383-8727.

KLAPHOLZ, MARC, cardiologist; b. July 16, 1960; MD, Albert Einstein Coll. Medicine, 1986; grad. summa cum laude, Yeshiva U., 1981. Diplomate Am. Bd. Internal Medicine. Dir. heart failure program U. Medicine and Dentistry N.J., Newark, 1997, dir. cardiac care unit, 1998, dir. cath. lab, 1999; chief heart failure program St. Vincent's Hosp., NYC, 1999—. Contbr. articles, abstracts. Named one of Best Drs. in N.Y., N.Y. Mag., 1999, 2000, 2001. Fellow: Am. Coll. Cardiology; mem.: Heart Failure Soc. Am., Am. Coll. Physicians, AHA. Office: 153 W 11th New York NY 10011 also: 140 Bergen St F Level Newark NJ 07103 Business E-Mail: klapholz@umdnj.edu.*

KLAPKA, JINDŘICH LUDVÍK, mathematician, physicist, educator, researcher; b. Zlín, Moravia, Czech Republic, Mar. 19, 1936; s. Ludvík Klapka and Frantiska (Cihalová) Klapková. M Physics, Masaryk U., 1959, D Natural Sci., 1967; PhD Phys. and Math. Sci., Charles U., 1968; postgrad., Czech Tech. U., 1961. Cert. mathematician, theoret. physicist, computer sci., automation, assoc. prof. Tech. U. Brno, 1987. Head rsch. group for math. methods Arms Factory Zbrojovka, Brno, Czech Republic, 1959—66; scientist Inst. Theory and Methods Engring. Prodn. Mgmt. Tech. U., Brno, 1966—68, sr. scientist, 1968—89, head sci. sector, 1989—91, assoc. prof. dept. computer sci., 1991—94, assoc. prof. Inst. Automation and Computer Sci., 1994—, coord. PhD studies faculty mech. engring., 1996—2005. Cons. Czech Com. Sci. Mgmt., Brno, 1970—91, head revision commn., 1970—91; referee Elsevier Sci. and World Sci. Publ., 2001—; head sci. grant projects Inst. Automation and Computer Sci. Tech. U., Brno, 1992—97, chmn. Pedagogical and Methodical Bd. Inst. Theory and Methods Industry Mgmt., 1976—90, mem. profl. bd. Inst. Automation and Computer Sci., 1999—; vis. prof. U. Pisa, Italy, 1975; head state rsch. project Tech. U. Brno, 1986—90; head sci. grant project Fund for Devel. Univ. Tech. U. Brno, 1995—97. Author: Dynamic Programming, 1970, Optimization of Multistage Production System, 1975 (Honor of the Merits, 1975), Decision Support System for Multicriterial R&D and Information Systems Projects Selection, 2002; contbr. articles to profl. jours. Mem. bd. reps. Brno-North, 1990—94. Recipient award for excellent grant results, Min. Edn. Czech Republic, 1997, Honor of Merit award, Tech. U. Brno, 1975, Legion Honor, United Cultural Conv., 2005, Internat. Peace prize, 2007; grantee, Tech. U. Brno, 1992—94, Coun. Econ. Rsch. Czech Republic, 1986—90. Fellow: Moravian and Silesian Acad. Edn., Sci., and Art (promoting fellow 1994—, vice-chmn. 1996—2005, head Natural, Tech. and Econ. Scis. sect. 1996—, chmn. 2005—), Czech Ops. Rsch. Soc. (promoting fellow 1995—); mem.: Unity Czech Mathematicians and Physicists, Project Mgmt. Soc. Roman Catholic. Achievements include research results in theory of transient processes in waveguides; methods for optimize of production processes; methods for multicriterial projects selection; methodology of operational research education; methods for projects scheduling. Avocations: philosophy, music history, railway transport history. Office: Tech U Brno Faculty Mech Engring Inst Automation Computer Science Technická 2 616 69 Brno Moravia Czech Republic Office Fax: 00420541142330. Business E-Mail: klapka@fme.vutbr.cz.

KLAPPA, GALE E., energy executive; BA in mass communications, U. Wis.-Milw., 1972. Pres., CEO, SWEB; pres. N.Am. Group, Mirant; with So. Co., Atlanta, 1974—2003, chief mktg. officer, chief strategic officer, exec. v.p., CFO, treas.; pres., CEO, Wis. Energy Corp., 2003—, chmn., 2004—. Dir. Edison Electric Inst.; vice chmn. Nuclear Electric Ins. Ltd. Adv. coun. U Wis.-Milw. Sch. Bus.; bd. dir. United Way Greater Milw., Met. Milw. Assn. Commerce. Office: Wis Energy Corp 231 W Michigan St Milwaukee WI 53203*

KLAPPER, ANDREW MARK, plastic surgeon; Grad., CUNY, Binghamton; MD, U. of Buffalo; grad., New York U. Inst. of Reconstructive Plastic Surgery (IRPS). Cert. American Bd. of Plastic Surgery, 2005. Tng., residency Gen. Surgery and Plastic Surgery at New York U. Med. Ctr.; dir. New York U. Downtown Plastic Surgery Clinic; on-staff doctor Manhattan Eye, Ear and Throat Hosp.; founder, doctor Outer Beauty. Author rsch. in peer reviewed journals. Achievements include first to a new procedure for Reduction Mammaplasty (Breast Reduction) that addressed the reconstructive efforts and symptomatic relief on an equal footing with Breast Aesthetics; a new Mastopexy (breast lift) technique that addresses the upper pole of the breast, increasing its projection; designing a new generation of Breast Scissors so that plastic surgeons could have better tools at their disposal; designing a Breast Marking Device for Vertical Breast Reduction and Breast Lift Surgery; designing an Abdominoplasty (tummy tuck) Marking Device. Office: Outer Beauty Plastic Surgery 308 East 79th St New York NY 10021 Office Phone: 212-717-5000.*

KLAPPER, RICHARD H., lawyer; b. White Plains, NY, 1954; AB, Hamilton Coll., 1975; MA, JD, Yale U., 1979. Bar: NY 1981. Assoc. Sullivan & Cromwell, NYC, 1980—87, ptnr., 1987—, mng. ptnr. litig. practice group, 1999—2004. Mem.: Fed. Bar Coun., Am. Law Inst. Office: Sullivan & Cromwell 125 Broad St Fl 28 New York NY 10004-2489 Office Phone: 212-558-3555. Office Fax: 212-558-3588. Business E-Mail: klapperr@sullcrom.com.

KLAPPERICH, FRANK LAWRENCE, JR., investment banker; b. Oak Park, Ill., Oct. 11, 1934; s. Frank Lawrence and Marjorie (Doan) K.; m. Margaret Monroe Touborg, Mar. 9, 1957; children: Margaret Friis, Susan Doane, Frank Lawrence III, Elizabeth Monroe. AB, Princeton U., 1956; MBA, Harvard U., 1961, postgrad., 1979. With Kidder, Peabody & Co., Inc., Chgo., 1961—, v.p., 1964—, dir., 1972-86, mng. dir., 1986-88, sr. v.p., 1988-90, ret., 1990; pres. Charter Capital Corp., 1991—. Governing mem. Orchestral Assn. Chgo. Symphony Orch., 1995—; vice chmn. governing mems., 1996-98; bd. dirs. Cmty. Found. Collier County, 2005— With USN, 1956—59, ret. LCDR USNR. Mem.: Inst. Chartered Fin. Analysts, Securities Industry Assn. (chmn. Ctrl. States dist. 1986—87), Investment Analysts Soc. Chgo., Harvard Bus. Sch. Alumni Assn. (bd. dirs. 2005—), Classic Chamber Concerts Inc. (bd. dirs. 2005—), Harvard Bus. Sch. Assn. Chgo., English Speaking Union (bd. dirs.Naples chpt. 2005—), Hole-in-the-Wall Golf Club (Naples), Indian Hill Club (Winnetka, Ill.), Princeton Club SW Fla. (bd. dirs. 2003—, pres. 2007—), Harvard Club of Naples (Fla., pres. 2001—03), Forum Club SW Fla. (bd. dirs. 2002—05), Econ. Club, Bond Club (pres. 1983—84), Mid-Day Club (trustee 1987—90), Chgo. Club, Charter Club (governing bd. 1987—97), Princeton Club (Chgo., pres. 1970—71). Home: 345 Woodley Rd Winnetka IL 60093-3740 Office Phone: 312-984-0984.

KLAPTHOR, JAMES, broadcast executive; BS in Commn. Arts & Sci., Broadcasting, Journalism, Western Mich. U., Kalamazoo, 1987. News dir. WGHN-AM/FE, Mich., 1987—90; sports dir. KBNN-FM/KCBQ-AM, San Diego, 1991—95, CBS TV, Calif., 1996; dir. media relations Albion Coll., Mich., 1997—99; chief exec. Rocket to Top Sports Enterprises, San Diego, 1994—2000, Prepare For Media, Chgo., 2000—; media rels. mgr. Inst. Food Technologists, Chgo., 2001—. Photographer MAC Report Online. Vol. US Postal Svc. Elf, Operation Santa; mem. Albion Coll. Presdl. Inauguration Com., Mich.; past bd. mem. San Diego Basketball Coaches Assn., San Diego HS Sports Assn. Recipient Spl. Teams Player of Yr., We. Mich. U., 1985—86. Mem.: Mid-Am. Conf. News Media Assn., Pub. Rels. Soc. Am. Avocations: photography, history, football, boating. Office: Prepare For Media PO Box 802206 Chicago IL 60680-2206 Home Phone: 312-371-9926. Business E-Mail: jim@prepareformedia.com.

KLARE, MICHAEL THOMAS, social sciences educator, director; b. NYC, Oct. 14, 1942; s. Charles and Mildred (Smith) K. BA cum laude, Columbia U., 1963, MA in Art History, Archaeology, 1968; postgrad. in Architecture, Yale U., 1963—65; PhD, Union Inst., 1976. Instr. Parsons Sch. Design, NYC, 1967-70; research dir. N.Am. Congress on Latin Am., Berkeley, Calif., 1970-76; vis. lectr. Tufts U., 1973; vis. fellow Center of Internat. Studies, Princeton U., 1976-77; program dir. Inst. Policy Studies, Washington, 1977-84; prof. peace & world security studies Hampshire Coll., Amherst, Mass., 1985—, dir. 5 colls. program in peace and world security studies, 1985—. Vis. assoc. prof. of peace studies Wellesley Coll., 1992-93; def. corr. The Nation, 1983—. Author: War Without End, 1973, Supplying Repression, 1978, Beyond the Vietnam Syndrome, 1981, American Arms Supermarket, 1985, Rogue States and Nuclear Outlaws, 1995, Resource Wars, 2001, Blood and Oil, 2004; co-author: A Scourge of Guns, 1996; editor: Peace and World Security Studies: A Curriculum Guide, 6th edit., 1994; co-editor: Low Intensity Warfare, 1988, Peace and World Security Studies: A Curriculum Guide, 5th edit., 1989, World Security: Challenges for a New Century, 1991, 3d edit., 1998, Lethal Commerce: The Global Trade in Small Arms and Light Weapons, 1995, Light Weapons and Civil Conflict, 1999; contbg. editor Current History, 1997-. Bd. dirs. Arms Control Assn., 1994—. Home: 17 Columbus Ave Northampton MA 01060-4252 Office: Hampshire Coll Sch Social Sci Amherst MA 01002 Home Phone: 413-584-5666; Office Phone: 413-559-5563. Business E-Mail: mklare@hampshire.edu.

KLARFELD, JONATHAN MICHAEL, journalism educator; b. Springfield, Mass., Dec. 11, 1937; m. Patricia Holland, Sept. 7, 1974; children: Victoria, Alexander. AB, Colgate U., 1960. Reporter, editor Holyoke (Mass.) Transcript-Telegram, 1962-65, UPI, Springfield, Boston, 1965-66, Boston Globe, 1966-68; press sec. Boston Parks/Redevel. Auth., 1968-70; reporter, writer Boston Record-Am., 1970-72; mgr. pub. info. Mass. Blue Cross, 1972-74; assoc. professor journalism Boston U., 1975—, dir. print journalism, 1979-96, dir. print and online journalism program, 1996—. Editl. cons. Lawyers Weekly Pubs., Boston, Lansing, Mich., Richmond, Va., Providence, 1983-92; press analyst Oxbow Corp., West Palm Beach, Fla., 1984-96; news media critic/columnist Boston Herald, 1994, 95; cons. in libel and invasion of privacy cases. Contbr. articles to numerous newspapers, periodicals. Mem. New Eng. Gilbert and Sullivan Soc., W.S. Gilbert Soc. UK, Sorcerers Rugby Club (pres. 1974-80), Newton Squash and Tennis Club (bd. govs. 1999-2003), Badminton and Tennis Club, Boston, Delta Kappa Epsilon. Avocations: squash, tennis, Gilbert and Sullivan. Office: Boston U Sch Journalism Boston MA 02215 Office Phone: 617-353-4978. E-mail: jklar@bu.edu.

KLARFELD, PETER JAMES, lawyer; b. Holyoke, Mass., Aug. 19, 1947; s. David Nathan and Gloria (Belsky) K.; m. Mary Myrtle, July 7, 1985; children: Peter Marcus (dec.), Mary Elizabeth, Louis Edward. BA, U. Va., 1969, JD, 1973; MA, U. Chgo., 1970. Bar: Va. 1973, DC 1975, US Dist. Ct. DC 1977, US Dist. Ct. (ea. dist.) Va. 1977, US Dist. Ct. (ea. dist.) Wis. 1987, US Dist. Ct. (no. dist.) Calif. 1990, US Ct. Appeals (4th cir.) 1978, US Ct. Appeals (3rd & 9th cirs.) 1986, US Ct. Appeals (2d cir.) 1998, US Ct. Appeals (7th cir.) 2003, US Supreme Ct. 1977. Law clk. to Hon. Robert R. Merhige, Jr. US Dist. Ct. (ea. dist.) Va., Richmond, 1973-74; atty., office of legal counsel US Dept. Justice, Washington, 1974-76; ptnr. Brownstein Zeidman & Lore, Washington, 1977-96, Wiley Rein LLP, Washington, 1996—. Editor: Covenants Against Competition in Franchise Agreements, 2002; contbr. articles to profl. jours. Trustee Dalkon Shield Other Claimants Trust, Richmond, 1990-96, chmn., 1991-96. Recipient Spl. Commendation for Outstanding Svc., Office of Legal Counsel US Dept. Justice, 1976. Mem. ABA (mem. forum on franchising governing com. 2007-). Home: 434 E Columbia St Falls Church VA 22046-3501 Office: Wiley Rein LLP 1776 K St NW Washington DC 20006-2304 Office Phone: 202-719-4464.

KLARICH, DAVID JOHN, lobbyist, lawyer; b. Hamilton, Ohio, July 17, 1963; s. Victor Martin and Janet Dawn (Carlson) K.; m. Cheryl Ruth O'Donnell, June 18, 1988. BA in Biology and Chemistry, U. Mo., 1985; MA in Pub. Policy, Regent U., 1990, JD, 1990. Bar: Mo. 1990. Mem. Mo. Ho. of Reps. from 92nd & 94th dists., Jefferson City, 1990-94, Mo. Senate from 26th dist., Jefferson City, 1994—2002, Riezman and Berger, P.C., Clayton, Mo., 1995—2002; apptd. commr. Mo. Indsl. Rels., 2002—03; mng. mem. Citizens for Policy Reform, LLC. Chmn. judiciary com. Mo. State Senate, 2001—02. Chmn. judiciary com. Mo. State Senate, 2001—02; chmn. West County Rep. Orgn. Recipient Adminstrn. of Justice award Jud. Conf. Mo., 1991, 99, Mo. Bar award, 1993, 97, 2000, 01, Mo. Hosp. Assn. award, 1995, Jud. Conf. award, 2000, 02, Legal Svcs. award, 2000, award Mo. Assn. Probate and Assoc. Cir. Judges, 2001; named Mo. Bar Outstanding Legis. of Yr., 1996, Voice of Bus. award Assoc. Industries, 1998. Mo. Lawyers weekly v.p. and coming Lawyer Mem. Bar Assn. Met. St. Louis, Young Lawyers Assn., Vol. Lawyers Assn., St. Louis Lawyers Assn., Mo. Assn. Trial Attys., St. Louis Eagle Scout Assn., Nat. Eagle Scout Assn., Jaycees, Lions, Mo. C. of C. (Spirit of Enterprise award 1997), Theta Xi. Mem. Assembly of God Ch. Personal E-mail: dklarich@sbcglobal.net.

KLARIK, BELA WILLIAM JAMES CLARK, retired school system administrator; b. Masontown, Pa., Aug. 7, 1931; s. Louis Klarik and Margaret Irma (Soltesz) Clark; children: Frank, Roxana, Steven, Louis M. AB in Edn. cum laude, Fairmont State Coll., W.Va., 1957; postgrad., W.Va. U., Morgantown, 1958, postgrad., 1959, Antioch Coll., Yellow Springs, Ohio, 1960, U. Md., Coll. Pk., 1965—75; MEd, U. Ga., Athens, 1961. Cert. ednl. supr. and adminstr., math. sci. and phys. edn. tchr. Ohio, Md. Profl. baseball player minor leagues Bklyn. Dodgers, 1953-55; tchr. math., coach Madison (Ohio) Meml. HS, 1957-60; tchr. math. and sci. Euclid (Ohio) City Schs., 1961-62; head dept. math. Richard Montgomery High Sch., Montgomery County Pub. Schs., Rockville, Md., 1962-65; Nat. Assn. Secondary Sch. Prins. adminstrv. intern John F. Kennedy HS, Silver Spring, Md., 1965-66; vice-prin. Col. E. Brooke Lee Jr. HS, Silver Spring, 1966-67; supr. math. Montgomery County Pub. Schs., Rockville, 1967-75, dir. dept. acad. skills, 1975-91; ret., 1991. Leader Md. delegation People to People Internat. Am.-Soviet Youth Exch., 1987; mem. edn. policy fellowship Inst. for Ednl. Leadership, Washington, 1988—89; mem. Md. Stds. for Schs. Com., 1989—91. Staff sgt. USAF, 1949—52. NSF Summer Inst. fellow, Antioch Coll., 1960, NSF Acad. Yr. Inst. fellow, U. Ga., 1960—61, NSF summer fellow, W.Va. U., 1963, U. Ga. summer fellow, 1961. Mem.: Inst. for Ednl. Leadership, Burnt Store Isles (Fla.) Assn., Montgomery County Ret. Pub. Sch. Employees Assn., Md. Ret. Pub. Sch. Employees Assn., Burnt Store Isles Boat Club, Am. Legion. Democrat. Roman Catholic. Avocations: travel, boating, sports, genealogy. Home: 5006 Ovideo St Punta Gorda FL 33950-8000 Personal E-mail: ldsleigh@comcast.net.

KLASKO, HERBERT RONALD, lawyer, educator, writer; b. Phila., Nov. 26, 1949; s. Leon Louis and Estelle Lorraine (Baratz) K.; m. Marjorie Ann Becker, Aug. 27, 1977; children: Brett Andrew, Kelli Lynn. BA, Lehigh U., 1971; JD, U. Pa., 1974. Bar: Pa. 1974, U.S. Dist. Ct. (ea. dist.) Pa. 1974, U.S. Ct. Appeals (3d cir.) 1981. Assoc. Fox, Rothschild, O'Brien & Frankel, Phila., 1974-75; ptnr., chmn. immigration dept. Abrahams & Loewenstein, Phila., 1975-88, Dechert, Price & Rhoads, Phila., 1988—2003; mng. ptnr. Klasko, Rulon, Stock & Seltzer, LLP, Phila., 2004—. Instr., mem. adv. bd. Inst. for Paralegal Tng., Phila., 1974-81; instr. Temple Law Sch. Grad. Legal Studies, Phila., 1984; adj. prof. Villanova U. Law Sch., Pa., 1985-90. Co-author: (with Matthew Bender and Hope Frye) Employer's Immigration Compliance Guide, 1985; bd. editors: Immigration Law and Procedure Reporter. Exec. committeeman, bd. dirs. Jewish Cmty. Rels. Coun., Phila., 1977—; chmn. exec. com., com. on unprosecuted Nazi war criminals Nat. Jewish Cmty. Rels. Adv. Coun., NYC, 1983-90; v.p. Hebrew Immigrant Aid Soc., Phila., 1977—; pres. Coun. of Tenants Assn., Southeastern Pa., 1980-81. Recipient Legion of Honor award, Chapel of Four Chaplains, 1977. Mem. ABA (coordinating com. on immigration), Phila. Bar Assn., Am. Immigration Lawyers Assn. (chmn. Phila. chpt. 1980-82, bd. govs. 1980—, nat. sec. 1984-85, 2d v.p. 1985-86, 1st v.p. 1986-87, pres.-elect 1987-88, pres. 1988-89, exec. com. 1984-90, 96-99, gen. counsel 1996-99, Founders award 1999), Am. Immigration Law Found. (bd. dirs. 1987-90). Avocations: politics, sports, travel, organizations. Office: Klasko Rulon Stock & Seltzer LLP 1800 JFK Blvd Ste 1700 Philadelphia PA 19103 Home Phone: 856-424-7721; Office Phone: 215-825-8608. Business E-Mail: rklasko@klaskolaw.com.

KLASS, PERRI ELIZABETH, pediatrician, writer; b. Tunapuna, Trinidad, Apr. 29, 1958; d. Morton and Sheila Solomon K.; children: Benjamin Orlando Klass, Josephine Charlotte Paulina Wolff. AB, Harvard U., 1979; postgrad., U. Calif., Berkeley, 1979-81; MD, Harvard U., 1986. Diplomate Am. Bd. Med. Examiners. Researcher Inst. Parasitology, Rome, 1981-82; instr. expository writing Harvard U., Cambridge, Mass., 1982-83; resident in pediatrics Children's Hosp., Boston, 1986-89, staff pediatrician, 1989-90; rsch. fellow Boston City Hosp., 1990; prof. journalism pediatrics NYU; pres. and med. dir. Reach Out and Read Nat. Ctr. Author: (novels) Recombinations, 1985, Other Women's Children, 1990, The Mystery of Breathing, 2004, (short stories) I Am Having an Adventure, 1986, Love and Modern Medicine, 2000, Two Sweaters For My Father, 2003, (essay collection) A Not Entirely Benign Procedure: Four Years as a Medical Student, 1987, Baby Doctor: A Pediatrician's Training, 1992; co-author (with Eileen Costello): Quirky Kids: Understanding and Helping Your Child Who Doesn't Fit In, 2003; co-author: (with Sheila Solomon Klass) Every Mother Is A Daughter, 2006. Recipient O. Henry award Doubleday, 1983, 84, 90, Women's Nat. Book Assn. award, 2006. Fellow Am. Acad. Pediatrics (media spokesperson 1989—); mem. Am. Med. Women's Assn., Mass. Med. Soc., Tilling Soc., PEN. Avocations: knitting, travel, spicy foods. Office: Reach Out and Read National Ctr 29 Mystic Ave Somerville MA 02145-1302 Office Phone: 617-629-8042, 617-629-8842.*

KLASS, RONI, literature and language professor; b. Paterson, NJ; d. Solomon Klass and Silvia Schwartz; divorced; 1 child, Jay; children: Seth, Rachel, Alexis. BA in English, Douglass Coll., New Brunswick, NJ, 1967; MS in TESL, Fla. Internat. U., Miami, 1992; PhD in Rhetoric, Linguistics, Ind. U. of Pa., 2004. Cert. TESOL. Prof. Fla. Internat. U., Miami, Fla., 1993—98; tutor Barry U., Miami Shores, 1995—, prof., 2005. Color cons. Beauty All Seasons. Mem.: TESOL, Nat. Coun. Tchrs English, Phi Kappa Phi. Avocations: yoga, weightlifting, reading, movies. Home: Apt 206 20850 San Simeon Way Miami FL 33179-1811 Office Phone: 305-899-4577.

KLASSEN, MARGRETA, clinical psychologist, educator; b. LA, May 4, 1928; d. David Charles and Jessie Irene (Asseltine) K.; m. Richard Caddell Calhoun, May 31, 1946 (div. 1962); children: Cathleen, Melissa, Nancy, Richard; m. Norman K. Dunn, July 25, 1963 (div. 1969); m. Donald Cole Wargin, Feb. 14, 1970 (dec. Jan 1984). BA, Pitzer Coll., Claremont, Calif., 1968; MS, Calif. State U., LA, 1972; PhD, Claremont Grad. U., Calif., 1982. Cert. practioner Biofeedback Inst. Am., 2002. Instr., counselor Chaffey C.C., Alta Loma, Calif., 1972-74; dir. bio-feedback program U. La Verne, Calif., 1974-76; owner Assocs. for Wellness, Claremont, Calif., 1979—; with Cert. Inst. of Am., Wheatridge, Colo., 1984-92; asst. prof. Calif. State Poly. U., Pomona, 1986-88; oral commr. Calif. Dept. Consumer Affairs, Sacramento, 1986-88; stress mgmt. program coord. Claremont Coll., 1988—97. Participant Golden Poet, World Congress of Poets, NYC, 1991; presenter joint meeting European Space Agy., German Rsch. Soc., Internat. Soc. for Bio-Behavioral Self-Regulation, Munich, 1991; program dir. Juvenile Connection, 1998-99; mem. adv. coun. Continuing Edn. in Mental Health, U. Calif. Irvine, 1998-2000; mem., presenter Soc. for Rsch. in Adult Devel., 2005. Editor: History of the Arabian Horse, 1968; reviewer: Jour. of the Assn. for Assessment in Counseling, Am. Counseling Assn., 1996-99. People to People del., USSR, 1989; mem. Claremont Hist. Soc., 1989-90, Internat. Soc. Police Surgeons, 2000-06; mem. steering com. Families First Collaborative of Orange County, 1998-99; mem. centennial heritage com. Newport Beach, 2005-06. Sr. fellow emeritus, Biofeedback Cert. Inst. of Am., 2002. Fellow Coll. for Advanced Practice in Psychology, Am. Coll. Advanced Practice Psychologists (founder); mem. APA, Calif. Psychol. Assn. (bd. dirs. 2006-07), NY Acad. Scis., Assn. for Applied Psychology and Bio-feedback, Orange County Psychol. Assn. (contbr. newsletter), Internat. Stress Mgmt. Assn. (sec., treas. 2003—), Inland Empire Bus. Women's Assn. (pres. Upland (Calif.) chpt. 1984), Internat. Soc. Police Surgeons, Laguna Poets Assn. (presenter), Pitzer Coll. Alumni Assn. (mem. leadership com. Orange County chpt. 2000-01). Avocations: swimming, writing. Home: 230 Lille Ln Apt 212 Newport Beach CA 92663-2665 Office: Newport Psychology Group 20371 Irvine Ave Ste A-160 Santa Ana CA 92707 Office Phone: 714-540-5010. Personal E-mail: drpsyreal8@aol.com.

KLATELL, ROBERT EDWARD, retired electronics executive, lawyer; b. Tampa, Fla., Dec. 11, 1945; s. Jack S. and Arla M. (Bragin) K.; m. Penelope E. Manegan, June 14, 1970; children: Christopher J., James M., Jeremy N. BA, Williams Coll., 1968; JD, NYU, 1971. Bar: N.Y. 1972. Assoc. Kramer, Lowenstein, Nessen, Kamin & Soll, NYC, 1970-76; gen. counsel, sec. Arrow Electronics, Inc., NYC, 1976—2002, v.p., 1979—93, sr. v.p., 1988-93, treas., 1990-96, CFO, 1992-96, exec. v.p., 1993—2003, cons., 2003—04; chmn. TTM Technologies, 2005—; CEO DICOM Group plc, London, 2006—. Bd. dirs. Datascape Corp., TTM (Time-to-market) Technologies, 2004—, Medoagrif Interactive Techs. Inc. Mem. ABA, Assn. Bar City N.Y., Fin. Execs. Inst. Office: TTM Technologies 4 Old Monson Rd Stafford CT 06075

KLATSKY, ARTHUR LOUIS, cardiologist, epidemiologist; b. NYC, Oct. 24, 1929; s. Martin Max and Rose M. (Hurwitz) Klatsky; m. Eileen Selma Rohrberg, June 21, 1953; children: Jennifer Ann, Benjamin Paul. BA, Yale U., 1950; MD, Harvard U., 1954. Diplomate Am. Bd. Internal Medicine, Am. Bd. Cardiovascular Disease. Intern in medicine Boston City Hosp., 1954-56; resident in internal medicine and cardiology Boston VA Hosp., 1958-60; trainee in cardiology U. Calif., San Francisco, 1960-61; clin. instr. in medicine U. Calif. Med. Ctr., San Francisco, 1961-68, asst. clin. prof. medicine, 1968-80; staff physician internal medicine and cardiology Kaiser Found. Hosp., Oakland, Calif., 1961-80, sub-chief dept. medicine, 1973, chief divsn. cardiology, 1978-94; assoc. divsn. rsch. Kaiser Permanente Med. Care Program, Oakland, 1975—; sr. cons. in Cardiology, 1995—. Mem. med. adv. coun. Wine Inst., San Francisco, 1978—. Contbr. articles to profl. jours., chpts. to books. Mem. profl. edn. com. Alameda County Heart Assn., 1969—. With Med. Corps, 1956-58. Recipient rsch. award, Med. Friends of Wine, 1984, 1st Thomas Turner award for Excellence in Alcohol Rsch., Alcoholic Beverage Med. Rsch. Found., 1992, Morris Collen Lifetime Rsch. Achievement award, 2004; fellow Am. Heart Assn. Coun. on Epidemiology, 1975—. Fellow ACP, Am. Coll. Cardiology; mem. Am. Wine Alliance for Rsch. and Edn. (bd. dirs. 1989—), Disting. Practioner in Medicine, Nat. Acad. of Practice (Disting. Practitioner award 1995). Avocations: long distance running, music, gardening, travel. Office: Kaiser Found Hosp 280 W Macarthur Blvd Oakland CA 94611-5642 Office Phone: 510-752-6538. Business E-Mail: arthur.klatsky@kp.org.

KLATT, WAYNE ROY, editor, writer; b. Chgo., Sept. 11, 1940; s. Waldemar George Klatt and Agnes Sophie Scannell; m. Marilyn Louise Koeppel, Aug. 7, 1965; children: Theresa Ann, Catherine Louise, Jennifer Marie. BA in Comm., U. Ill., 1962. Reporter City News Bureau of Chgo., 1963—64, editor, 1965—2005; freelance writer, 2005—. Co-author: Freed to Kill, 1990, I Am Cain, 1994, Homicide: 100 Years of Murder in America, 1998; contbr. articles to mags. Recipient Short Story Contest awards, U. Ill., 1958, 1st prize, Nit & Wit Mag., 1983. Mem.: Chgo. Press Vets. Assn. Avocations: reading, history, literature, films, psychology. Home: 4722 N Avers Ave Chicago IL 60625-6201 Home Phone: 773-267-1967.

KLATTEN, SUSANNE QUANDT, pharmaceutical executive; b. Bath Homburg, Germany, Apr. 28, 1962; d. Herbert Quandt and Johanna; m. Jan Klatten; 3 children. BA, BS; MBA, IMD Bus. Sch. Lausanne. Mgmt. bd. asst. Hubert Burda Media, 1989—90; mem. adv. bd., majority shareholder Altana Group, Bod Homburg, Germany, 1993—; mem. supervisory bd. BMW, 1997—. Chmn. bd. counsellors Herbert-Quandt-Stiftung Found. Named one of World's Richest People, Forbes Mag., 2003—07, Most Powerful Women in the World, Forbes mag., 2005. Office: Herbert-Quandt-Stiftung Herbert-Quandt-Haus Am Pilgerrain 15 Bad Homburg D-61352 Germany Office Phone: 49-06172-1712500. Office Fax: 49-06172-1712545. Business E-Mail: h-quandt-stiftung@altana.de.*

KLATZKY, ROBERTA LOU, psychologist, educator; b. Duluth, Minn., Jan. 6, 1947; d. Arnold and Rena (Brusin) Klatzky. BS, U. Mich., 1968; PhD, Stanford U., 1972. Asst. prof. U. Calif., Santa Barbara, 1972-77, assoc. prof., 1977-82, prof. psychology, 1982-93; prof. Carnegie Mellon U., Pitts., 1993—, head dept., 1993—2003. Author: Human Memory, 1980, Memory and Awareness, 1983. Ctr. Advanced Study fellow, Stanford, Calif., 1982. Fellow: AAAS (chair psychology sect. 2000—01), APA (chmn. bd. sci. affairs 2005), Am. Psychol. Sci. (treas. 1999—); mem.: Vision Scis. Soc., Soc. Exptl. Psychologists, Internat. Soc. Attention and Performance (mem. exec. com. 2001—07), Psychonomic Soc. (chmn. governing bd. 1998), Phi Beta Kappa. Avocation: piano. Office: Carnegie Mellon Univ Dept Psychology Pittsburgh PA 15213 Office Phone: 412-268-8026. Business E-Mail: klatzky@cmu.edu.

KLAUBERG, LAURA, marketing executive; 3 children. BS, Cornell U., 1976; MBA, NYU. With Clairol; v.p media Americas Cheseborough Pond's; sr. v.p. global mktg. Unilever Cosmetics Internat., Englewood Cliffs, NJ; v.p. mktg. shared svcs. Unilever, Englewood Cliffs, NJ, 2005—07, v.p media Americas, 2007—. Bd. dirs. Ad Coun. Bd. mem. Northern NJ Maternal Child Health Consortium; mem. Pres.'s Coun. Cornell Women; bd. mem. Schola Ministries, Starfish Children's Fund. Named a Woman to Watch, Advt. Age, 2007. Office: Unilever 800 Sylvan Ave Englewood Cliffs NJ 07632*

KLAUBERG, WILLIAM JOSEPH, information technology executive; b. NYC, June 30, 1926; s. Leo V. and Marian (Casey) K.; m. Kathleen Kelly, Feb. 18, 1950; children: Christine Anne, Kathleen Noel, Angela Ellen, William Jr. BS in Nautical Sci., Mcht. Marine Acad., 1947; BS in Fgn. Svc., Georgetown U., 1949. Mgr. US Lines, Inc., Japan, 1949-65, v.p. Tokyo, 1965-68, v.p. European Div. London, 1968-71, v.p. West Coast Div. San Francisco, 1971-73, v.p. East Coast Div. NYC, 1973-81; project mgr. Vinnell Corp., Balt., 1981-82, v.p. Fairfax, Va., 1982-83, exec. v.p., 1983-88, pres., CEO, 1988-93, chmn., chief exec. officer, 1993-94; chmn., 1994-97. Lt. (j.g.) USNR, 1947-52.

KLAUS, CHARLES, retired lawyer; b. Freiburg, Baden, Germany, Feb. 11, 1935; came to U.S., 1939; children: Charles, Kathryn, Richard; m. Elaine S. Jones, Jan. 6, 2002. BA, Cornell U., 1956, MBA, JD with distinction, 1961; postdoctoral, Case Western Res. U., 1964, Lakeland Cmty. Coll., 1976, 2004. Bar: Ohio 1961, U.S. Dist. Ct. (no. dist.) Ohio 1962. Assoc. Baker & Hostetler, Cleve., 1961-71, ptnr., 1972-94, formerly mng. ptnr. Cleve. office; ret., 1995. Past hon. trustee and pres. Cleve. Music Sch. Settlement; past trustee Cleve. Audubon Soc.; past trustee, sec. Cleve. Area Arts Coun., Lake Erie Opera Theatre, N.E. Ohio chpt. Arthritis Found.; former mem. Group Svc. Coun. Welfare Fedn. Cleve.; corp. mem. Holden Arboretum, 1993—, mem. coun., 2003-. Recipient Award of Merit, Cleve. Audubon Soc., 1979. Mem. Millard Fillmore Soc., Rowfant Club (past sec.), Kirtland Country Club (past dir., past sec., Willoughby, Ohio).

KLAUSE, ANNETTE CURTIS, librarian, writer; b. Bristol, Eng., June 20, 1953; came to US, 1968; d. Graham Trevor and Mary Frances (Kempe) C.; m. Mark Jeffrey Klause, Aug. 11, 1979. BA in English Lit., U. Md., 1976, MLS, 1978. Various positions libr. contracting cos., 1979-81, Montgomery County Dept. Pub. Librs., Md., substitute libr., 1981-82; children's libr. I Silver Spring Cmty. Libr., Md., 1981; children's part-time libr. I Kensington Park Cmty. Libr., Md., 1982-84, head children's svcs., 1991-92; children's full-time libr. I Bethesda Regional Libr., Md., 1984-89; head children's svcs. Olney Cmty. Libr., Md., 1989-91, Aspen Hill Cmty. Libr., Md., 1992—. Contbr. articles to profl. jours., short stories; author: The Silver Kiss, 1990 (Best Book of Yr. Honor Book, Mich. Libr. Assn., 1990, Booklist Best Books and Editor's Choice, 1990, named one of Sch. Library Journal's Best Books, 1990, named one of Best Books for Young Adults, ALA, 1991, named one of Best Books for Reluctant Readers, ALA, 1991, SC Young Adult Book award, 1993, Calif. Young Reader medal, 1993, Md. Black-eyed Susan award, 1993, Sequoyah Young Adult award, 1993, named one of 100 Best of the Best from Best Books for Young Adults lists, ALA, 1994), Alien Secrets, 1993 (Booklist Best Books, 1993, Sch. Libr. Jour. Best Books, 1993, Golden Duck Honor Book, 1994, named one of Notable Books for Children, ALA, 1994), Blood and Chocolate, 1997 (Booklist Editor's Choice, 1997, named one of Best Books of Yr., Sch. Libr. Jour., 1997, named one of Best Books for Young Adults, ALA, 1998, SC Young Adult Book award, 2000, Garden State Teen Book award, 2000, named one of Top Ten Challenged Books of Yr., ALA, 2001), Freaks: Alive, On the Inside!, 2006. Mem. ALA, Assn. Libr. Svc. to Children, Young Adult Libr. Svc. Assn., Children's Book Guild Washington, DC. Avocations: reading science fiction, fantasy and horror, attending science fiction conventions. Office: c/o Margaret K McElderry Books Simon & Schuster Childrens Pub Divsn 1230 Ave of the Americas New York NY 10020-1586 Personal E-mail: humanoddity@verizon.net.*

KLAUSEN, RAYMOND, theatre set and television production designer, sculptor; b. Jamaica, NY, May 29, 1949; s. Jens and Ane Kathrine (Jensen) K. BA, Hofstra U., 1961; MA in Art, NYU, 1963; MFA in Theatre Design, Yale U., 1967. Prodn. designer TV and theater. Hoffman eminent scholar prof. theatre, Fla. State U., 1993—. Theatrical set designer, 1967—, freelance TV art dir., 1970—; designer sets for Dreams, Soul Possessed, Brother's of the Knight, Pepito's Story, Kennedy Ctr., Waiting in the Wings, Comedy Tonight, Broadway, A Few Good Men.Dancin', New Victory Theatre, My Favorite Broadway, Ira Gershwin at 100, Carnegie Hall, Jubilee!, Bally's Grand, Las Vegas, Hello Hollywood, Hello!, MGM Grand, Reno, Jazz Legs, Berlin, Pete 'N' Keely, off Broadway, The Subject Was Roses, How to Succeed in Business Without Really Trying, You Can't Take it With You, Mary, Mary, Gypsy, John Drew Theatre, Scenes Formthe Life of Ggalileo, Johnny Johnson, Yale U., Summer and Smoke, Palmer Theatre, New Haven, Conn.; numerous TV series, individual spls. for Sammy Davis Jr., Elvis Presley, Neil Diamond, Bing Crosby, Perry Como, Jackie Gleason, Cher, Smothers Brothers, Pearl Bailey, The Muppets, Natalie Cole, Roberta Flack, Lynda Carter, plus the Kennedy Ctr. Honors, Omnibus, AFI Tributes to Bette Davis, John Huston, Fred Astaire, Jimmy Stewart, Henry Fonda, Alfred Hitchcock and Elizabeth Taylor, also Nat. Tours for Lionel Richie, Kenny Rogers, Julio Iglesias, Travis Tritt, Bally's Casino Prodns., The Kennedy Ctr. Homors, Gala for the Pres. at Ford's Theatre, Night of 100 Stars, The Tony Awards (2 times), The Am. Music Awards Show (28 times), The Academy Awards Show (9 times), Miss America (5 times), The 50th Anniversary of TV, Texaco Salutes Broadway, Happy Birthday Hollywood, (series) Vibe; solo exhbns. include LBJ Gallery, Newport Beach, Calif., 1990, Wade Gallery, L.A., 1991, Gallery Sanyo, Tokyo, 1991, 92, Ruth Bachofner Gallery, L.A., 1992, 95, Fla. State U. Mus., Tallahassee, 1993,; group exhbns. include Zantman Galleries, Carmel, Calif., 1991, Long Beach (Calif.) Mus. Art, 1992, Ward-Nasse Gallery, N.Y.C., 1992, Ettinger Gallery, Laguna Beach, Calif., Boise (Idaho) State U. Art Gallery, 1993, LACE, L.A., 1993, Alder Gallery, Eugene, Or., 1993, Clara Kott Von Storch Gallery, Mich.,1993, Michael Stone Collection, Va., 1993, San Diego Art Inst., Calif., 1993, Roy G. Biv Gallery, Palm Springs, Calif., 1994, Palm Springs Desert Mus., Calif., 1994, La Quinta Sculpture Park, La Quinta, Calif., 1994, Quietude Garden Gallery, East Brunswick, N.J., 1995, Hunter Mus. Am. Art, Chatanooga, Tenn., 1995, SUNY Plattsburg Art Mus., 1995, San Bernadino Coungy Mus., Calif., 1995, Paris Gibson Mus., Great Falls, Mont., 1995, Eva Cohen Gallery, Chgo., Ill., 1995, D.O.C.S. Gallery, New Orleans, 1997. With U.S. Army, 1962-63. Bates Travel fellow Europe, 1967; TDK Corp. grantee, 1991, 92; recipient 3 Nat. Acad. TV Arts and Sci. Emmy awards for Cher series, 1976, Acad. awards, 1982, 83, nominations for 1980, 91 Acad. Awards and Lynda Carter's Celebration, 1981, Kennedy Ctr. Honors, 1984, 86, Am. Music Awards, 1985, 90, Happy Birthday Hollywood, 1987, Acad. awards, 1991, 96. Home: 203 W 90th St Apt 7b New York NY 10024-1227

KLAUSMEYER, DAVID MICHAEL, scientific instruments manufacturing company executive; b. Indpls., Aug. 29, 1934; s. David M. and V. Jane (Donnellan) K.; m. Julie Ann Johnson, Oct. 29, 1955; children: Kathleen M., Kevin M., Gregory J. BS, Georgetown U., 1955. Asst. to pres. White Cons. Ind., Cleve., 1957; auditor Ernst & Ernst, Cleve., 1957—58; pres. Photopipe, Inc., Cleve., 1960—63; v.p. McGregor & Werner Internat., Inc., Washington, 1964—70; internat. cons. Stratford of Tex., Houston, 1971—72; pres. FLR Corp., Houston, 1972—74, Southwest Cons., Houston, 1981—86, Imaging Products, Houston, 1987—90; sec. Nanodyanmics-88, Inc., NYC, 1988—, also bd. dirs.; pres. Corp. Devel., Houston, 1974—81; ptnr. Klausmeyer & Assoc., Houston, 1970—2001; ret., 2001. Dir. U.S. investment banking Secured Electronic Global Order Execution Sys. Securities, Grand Cayman Island, 1995—2001; bd. dirs. S.ure Reification, Houston. Bd. dirs. Cath. Endowment Found. Galveston-Houston, 1999-02; mem. nat. fin. and ops. com. St. Vincent de Paul Soc., St. Louis, 2004—, chmn. audit com., 2006-; mem. Internat. Strategic Planning Com., Paris, 2006—. With USCG, 1955-57. Republican. Roman Catholic. Home: 10811 Brenner Creek Houston TX 77079-7300 Office Phone: 713-827-8947. E-mail: dklausmeyer@houston.rr.com.

KLAUSNER, JACK DANIEL, lawyer; b. NYC, July 31, 1945; s. Burt and Marjory (Brown) K.; m. Dale Arlene Kreis, July 1, 1968; children: Andrew Russell, Mark Raymond. BS in Bus., Miami U., Oxford, Ohio, 1967; JD, U. Fla., 1969. Bar: N.Y. 1971, Ariz. 1975, U.S. Dist. Ct. Ariz. 1975, U.S. Ct. Appeals (9th cir.) 1975, U.S. Supreme Ct. 1975. Assoc. counsel John P. McGuire & Co., Inc., NYC, 1970-71; assoc. atty. Hahn & Hessen, NYC, 1971-72; gen. counsel Equilease Corp., NYC, 1972-74; assoc. Burch & Cracchiolo, Phoenix, 1974-78, ptnr., 1978-98; judge pro tem Maricopa County Superior Ct., 1990—, Ariz. Ct. Appeals, 1992—; ptnr. Warner Angle, Phoenix, 1998—. Bd. dirs. Hunter Contracting Co. Bd. dirs. Santos Soccer Club, Phoenix, 1989-90; bd. dirs., pres. south Bank Soccer Club, Tempe, 1987-88. Office: Warner Angle Hallam Jackson & Formanek 3550 N Central Ave Ste 1500 Phoenix AZ 85012-2112 Home: 1702 E Becky Cir Payson AZ 85541-3363

KLAUSNER, MICHAEL DAVID, law educator; b. Phila., Dec. 12, 1954; s. Gilbert and Edith (Quitman) Klausner; m. Barbara Ann-Pei Sih, Sept. 2, 1984; children: Jill, Gregory. BA in Polit. Sci./Urban Studies, summa cum laude, U. Pa., 1976; MA in Economics, Yale U., 1981, JD, 1981. Bar: DC 1983. Law clk. to Judge David Bazelon US Ct. Appeals DC Cir., 1981-82; law clk. to Justice William Brennan US Supreme Ct., 1983-84; vis. scholar & lectr. dept. law Peking U., China, 1984-85; assoc. Paul, Weiss, Rifkind, Wharton & Garrison, Washington, 1982—83, Gibson, Dunn & Crutcher, Washington, Hong Kong, 1986-89; White House fellow, dep. assoc. dir. Office Policy Devel. White House, Washington, 1989-90; asst. prof. to prof. NYU Sch. Law, 1991—97; prof. law Stanford Law Sch., 1997—, Bernard D. Bergreen faculty scholar, 1997—2003, Nancy and Charles Munger prof. bus., 2003—, assoc. dean rsch. and academics, 2004—. Vis. prof. Stanford Law Sch., 1995—96. Avocation: scuba diving. Office: Stanford Law Sch Crown Quadrangle 559 Nathan Abbott Way Stanford CA 94305-8610 Office Phone: 650-723-6433. E-mail: klausner@stanford.edu.

KLAUSNER, RICHARD DANIEL, cell biologist, researcher; b. NYC, Dec. 22, 1951; BS, Yale U., 1973; MD, Duke U. Med. Sch., 1976. Rsch. assoc. Harvard Med. Sch., 1977-79; rscher., med. officer, mathematical biology program Nat. Insts. Health, Bethesda, Md., 1979-84; branch chief, cell biology, metabolism branch Nat. Inst. of Child Health & Human Devel., Bethesda, Md., 1984-95; dir. Nat. Cancer Inst., Bethesda, Md., 1995—2001; exec. dir. Global Health (Bill and Melinda Gates Found.), Seattle, 2002—05. Chmn., Scientific Advisory Bd., Ariad Pharmaceuticals, 1991, bd. dirs. Pathwork Diagnostics, 2006- Medicine, 1976; numerous articles in prof. journals. Recipient Meritorious Svc. Award, 1986, PHS, Damashek Prize, 1992, Am. Soc. for Hematology Mem. NAS, Am. Soc. for Clinical Investigation, Inst. Medicine.*

KLAUSNER, SAMUEL ZUNDEL, sociologist, educator; b. Bklyn., Dec. 19, 1923; s. Edward Solomon and Bertha (Adler) K.; m. Bracha Turgeman, Oct. 26, 1948 (div. 1960); children: Rina Ellen Klausner Spence, Jonathan David; m. Madeleine Suringar, Feb. 20, 1964 (div. 1982); children: Daphne Klausner Genyk, Tamar; m. Roberta Sands, Nov. 26, 1992. BS, NYU, 1947; MA, Columbia U., 1951, EdD, 1952, PhD, 1963. Cert. psychologist, N.Y., D.C. Lectr. edn. CCNY, 1951-52, 55-57; lectr. sociology Columbia U., 1957-63; instr. psychology Hebrew U., Jerusalem, 1952-53; lectr. religion and psychiatry Union Theol. Sem., 1961-63; assoc. prof. sociology U. Pa., Phila., 1967-70, prof., 1970-96; dir. Ctr. for Rsch. on the Acts of Man, 1971-88, chmn. grad. group in sociology, 1984-86; prof. emeritus U. Pa., Phila., 1996—. Clin. psychologist Govt. Mental Hosp., Jerusalem, 1954-55; program dir. Bur. Applied Social Rsch., Columbia U., 1956-61; sr. rsch. assoc. Bur. Social Sci. Rsch., Washington, 1964-67; exec. sec. Soc. for Study of Religion, 1964-70; cons. U.S. Dept. Commerce, 1968-69, U.S. Naval Chaplains Sch., 1973-81, Nat. Libr. Medicine, 1969, NRC, 1967-81, others; vis. prof. Al Mansoura U., Egypt, 1983, Muhammad V. Univ., Morocco, 1986. Author: Psychiatry and Religion, 1964, The Quest for Self-Control, 1965, The Study of Total Societies, 1967, Why Man Takes Chances, 1968, Society and Its Physical Environment, 1970, On Man in His Environment, 1971, Eskimo Capitalists, 1981; author, editor: The Nationalization of the Social Sciences, 1986; also articles. With USAAC, 1943-45; with Israel Air Force, 1947-48. Ford Found. area rsch. fellow, 1952-53; Fulbright scholar, 1983. Mem. APA, AAAS, Am. Sociol. Assn., Assn. Sociol. Study of Jewry (pres. 1980), Soc. Sci. Study of Religion (v.p. 1974), Am. Vets. Israel (pres. 1951, 98-2000, newsletter editor 1998—). Jewish. Home: 7055 Greenhill Rd Philadelphia PA 19151-2322 Personal E-mail: sklausner@comcast.net. *My ideals of social conduct have not been designed to assist in attaining professional success. Judaism is a central guiding reference and though I may deviate from its principles in my daily behavior for reasons of good sense and self interest, they remain normative. My professional station arises from an obsession with the requirements of scholarship. A willingness to be critical of current social institutions has brought social attention but not professional advancement.*

KLAUSS, KENNETH KARL, composer, music educator; b. Parkston, SD, Apr. 8, 1923; s. Christian and Paulina (Engel) Klauss. MusB in Composition, U. So. Calif., 1946. Tchr. composition and piano, LA, 1946-50; composer Lester Horton Theater, LA, 1949-50; tchr. music San Francisco, 1950-61; composer, educator LA, 1961—; lectr. in music for dance Idyllwild (Calif.) Sch. Music and Arts, 1967-74; lectr. in music history So. Calif. Inst. Architecture, Santa Monica, 1970-76. Composer in residence Perry/Mansfield Camp, Steamboat Springs, Colo., 1966; guest performer, composer, lectr. Libr. Congress, Am. U., Washington, 1996; guest lectr. U. S.D., Vermillion, 2002. Composer: (opera) Fall of the House of Usher, 1952, harpsichord/violin composition commd. by U. S.D., 2001; author, composer: (poetry/music orchestration) Story of the World Vols. I to VIII, 1952-86; performances by Rawlins Trio of U. S.D., Mpls., Omaha and Vermillion, 2005, Sonata Orch., Vermillion, Yankton, Sioux Falls, Brookings, SD, Worthington, Minn., 2007. Founder, patron Klauss/James Archive and Art Mus., Parkston, 1995—. Recipient hon. mention opera competition Ohio U., Athens, 1954. Democrat. Avocations: history, poetry. Home: 440 Wren Dr Los Angeles CA 90065-5040 Office Phone: 605-928-3366. Personal E-mail: kklauss@earthlink.net. Business E-Mail: musicart@santel.net.

KLAVITER, HELEN LOTHROP, magazine editor; b. Lima, Ohio, Mar. 5, 1944; d. Eugene H. and Jean (Walters) Lothrop; m. Douglas B. Klaviter, June 7, 1969 (div. 1982); 1 child, Elizabeth. BA, Cornell Coll., Mt. Vernon, Iowa, 1966. Communication specialist Coop. Extension Service, Urbana, Ill., 1969-71; mng. editor The Poetry Found. Poetry Mag., Chgo., 1973—. Editorial cons. Harper & Row, N.Y.C., 1983-87. Bd. dirs. Ill. Theatre Ctr., 1989—95, St. Clement's Open Pantry, 1990—, Episc. Diocese of Chgo. Hunger Commn., 1992—. Episcopalian. Office: Poetry Mag The Poetry Found 444 N Michigan Ave Ste 1850 Chicago IL 60611 Office Phone: 312-799-8004. Business E-Mail: hklaviter@poetrymagazine.org.

KLAWE, MARIA MARGARET, academic administrator, engineering and computer science educator; b. Toronto, Ontario, Can., July 5, 1951; d. Janusz Josef and Kathleen Wreath (McCaughan) K.; m. Nicholas John Pippenger, May 12, 1980; children: Janek, Sasha. BSc in math., U. Alberta, 1973; PhD, U. Alberta, Edmonton, Can., 1977; PhD (hon.), Ryerson U., 2001, U. Waterloo, 2003, Queens U., 2004. Asst. prof. dept. math. sci. Oakland U., Rochester, Mich., 1977-78; asst. prof. dept. computer sci. U. Toronto, Canada, 1979-80; rsch. staff mem. IBM Rsch., San Jose, Calif., 1980-89, mgr. discrete math., 1984-88, mgr. dept. math., related computer sci., 1985-87; prof., head dept. computer sci. U. BC, Vancouver, 1988-95, v.p. student and acad. svcs., 1995—98, dean sci., 1998—2002; dean Sch. Engring & Applied Sci. Princeton U., 2003—07, prof. dept. computer sci., 2003—07; pres. Harvey Mudd Coll., Claremont, Calif., 2007—. Spkr. in field; mem. adv. bd. univ. rels. IBM Toronto Lab., 1989; mem. sci. adv. bd. Dimacs NSF Sci. Tech. Ctr., New Brunswick, NJ, 1989-95; mem. adv. bd. Geometry Ctr., 1991-95; mem. BC Premier's Adv. Coun. on Sci. and Tech., 1993—2001, Provincial Adv. Com. on Edn. Tech., 1993; founder, dir. E-GEMS project U. BC, 1992-2002; Chair for Women in Sci. and Engring. Nat. Sciences and Engring. Rsch. Coun. of Can.(NSERC)-IBM, 1997-2002; co-founder, chmn. bd. Silicon Chalk, Vancouver.; bd. trustees Math. Sciences Rsch. Inst., Berkeley, chair bd. trustees Anita Borg Inst. Women and Tech. Palo Alto Calif.; trustee Inst. Pure and Applied Math. LA. Editor: (jours.) Combinatorica, 1985—, SIAM Jour. on Computing, 1986-93, SIAM Jour. on Discrete Math., 1987-93; contbr. articles to profl. jours. Named Can. New Media Educator of Yr., 2001, BC Sci. Coun. Champion of Yr., 2001; recipient Women of Distinction Award in Sci. and Tech., Vancouver YWCA, 1997, Can. Wired Woman Pioneer Award, 2001, Disting. Alum. Award, U. Alberta, 2003, Nico Habermann award, 2004; INCO scholar, 1968—71, NRC Can. fellow, 1973—77. Fellow Assn. Computing Machinery (mem. coun. 1998-2000, v.p. 2000-02, pres. 2002-04); mem. Am. Math. Soc. (bd. trustees 1992-97, chmn. 1995-96), Can. Math. Assn., Can. Heads Computer Sci. (pres. 1990-91), Assn. Women Math., Computing Rsch. Assn. (mem. bd. 1990-96), Soc. Indsl. and Applied Math. Math. Assn. Am. Avocations: running, painting, kayaking, windsurfing. Office: Harvey Mudd Coll Kingston Hall, Rm 201 301 Platt Blvd Claremont CA 91711 Office Phone: 909-621-8120. E-mail: klawe@hmc.edu.*

KLAWITER, DONALD CASIMIR, lawyer; b. Phila., Feb. 26, 1950; s. Joseph C. and Frances J. (Koniecki) K.; m. Marie M. Gabuzda, Jan. 2, 1982; children: Joseph, Jeffrey. BA, MA, U. Pa., Phila., 1972, JD, 1975. Bar: Pa. 1975, US Supreme Ct. 1979, DC 1987, US Dist. Ct. DC 1987, US Ct. Appeals (4th and 8th crcts.) 1988, US Ct. Appeals (9th crct.) 1993. Trial atty. antitrust div. US Dept. Justice, Phila., 1975-78, spl. asst. operations antitrust div. Washington, 1978-80, chief antitrust Dallas, 1980-82, sr. trial atty. Washington, 1982-86; of counsel Morgan, Lewis & Bockius LLP, Washington, 1986-88; ptnr. Morgan, Lewis & Bockius, Washington, 1988—. Chair bd. dirs. Pinecrest Sch., Annandale, Va., 1998-2004; chair bd. trustees Commonwealth Acad., Alexandria, Va., 2001-07; mem. bd. trustees Browne Acad., Alexandria, 2005-. Mem. ABA (litig., antritust law and bus. law sects., chair criminal practice and procedure com. sect. antitrust law 1995-97, mem. governing coun. sect. antitrust law 1997—, sec. sect. antitrust law 2000-01, program officer sect. antitrust law 2001-03, vice chmn. 2003-04, chair-elect 2004-05, chair 2005-06, immediate past chair 2006-), Internat. Bar Assn. (legal practice divsn., antitrust coms). Roman Catholic. Home: 5930 Munson Ct Falls Church VA 22041-2443 Office: Morgan Lewis & Bockius 1111 Pennsylvania Ave NW Washington DC 20004 Home Phone: 703-931-1731; Office Phone: 202-739-5222. Business E-Mail: dklawiter@morganlewis.com.

KLAYMAN, BARRY MARTIN, lawyer; b. Montclair, NJ, Sept. 26, 1952; s. Max M. and Sylvia (Cohen) K.; m. Anna Kornbrot, June 8, 1975; children: Alison Melissa, Matthew Daniel. BA magna cum laude, Columbia U., 1974; JD cum laude, Harvard U., 1977. Bar: Pa. 1977, Del. 1998, US Dist. Ct. (ea. dist.) Pa. 1977, US Dist. Ct. Del. 1998, US Ct. Appeals (3d cir.) 1978. From assoc. to ptnr. Wolf, Block, Schorr & Solis-Cohen LLP, Phila., 1977—. Contbr. articles to profl. jours. Bd. dirs. Akiba Hebrew Acad., 1991—, sec., 1994-95, v.p., 1995-96, 98-2000, treas. 1996-98, pres. 2000-03; dir. B'nai B'rith Youth Orgn. Inc., 2002—; mem. cmty. planning and allocations com. Jewish Fedn. Greater Phila., 1997-2003, trustee, 2000-06, mem. com. nat. svcs., 1991-2003, chair, 1998-2003, mem. com. formal Jewish edn., 2000-03, mem. policy com., mem. strategy and funding com., 2003—; exec. com. United Jewish Cmtys. Nat. Funding Coun., 2002-06. Mem. ABA (litig. sect., torts and ins. practice sect.), Del. Bar Assn., Phila. Bar Assn., Pa. Bar Assn., Assn. Trial Lawyers Am., B'nai B'rith Youth Orgn. (bd. dirs. Phila. region 1984-2001, chmn. 1991-95, mem. Internat. Youth Commn. 1991-2001, exec. com., 1996-2001), B'nai B'rith (coun. v.p. 1996-97, mem. Justice Lodge 1992-2003), Phi Beta Kappa. Office: Wolf Block Schorr & Solis-Cohen LLP 1100 N Market St Ste 1001 Wilmington DE 19801 Home Phone: 610-667-0358; Office Phone: 302-777-0313. Business E-Mail: bklayman@wolfblock.com.

KLAYMAN, LARRY ELLIOTT, lawyer, legal association administrator; b. Phila., July 20, 1951; s. Herman Klayman. AB with honors, Duke U., 1973; JD, Emory U., 1977. Bar: Fla. 1977, D.C. 1980, U.S. Ct. Internat. Trade 1982, U.S. Ct. Appeals (fed. cir.) 1983. Assoc. atty. Blackwell, Walker, Gray et al, Miami, Fla., 1977-78; trial atty. U.S. Dept. Justice Antitrust Div., Washington, 1979-81; assoc. atty. Busby, Rehm & Leonard, P.C., Washington, 1981-83; pvt. practice Washington, 1984-85; pres., chief exec. officer Klayman & Gurley, P.C., Washington, 1985-89, Klayman & Assocs., P.C., Washington, 1989—2002; founder The Klayman Law Firm, 2002—; founder, gen. counsel, chmn. Judicial Watch, 1994—2003. Pres., chief exec. officer Free Trade Enterprises, Ltd., Washington, Internat. Design Enterprises, Ltd., Internat. Food Enterprises, Ltd. Contbr. article to profl. jour. Rep. candidate US Senate, Fla., 2004. Mem. Nat. Press Club, Capitol Hill Club.

KLEBANOFF, SEYMOUR JOSEPH, medical educator; b. Toronto, Ont., Can., Feb. 3, 1927; s. Eli Samuel and Ann Klebanoff; m. Evelyn Norma Silver, June 3, 1951; children: Carolyn, Mark. MD, U. Toronto, 1951; PhD in Biochemistry, U. London, 1954. Intern Toronto Gen. Hosp., 1951—52; postdoctoral fellow dept. path. chemistry U. Toronto, 1954—57; postdoctoral fellow Rockefeller U., NYC, 1957—59, asst. prof., 1959—62; assoc. prof. medicine U. Washington, Seattle, 1962—68, prof., 1968—2000, prof. emeritus, 2000—. Mem. adv. coun. Nat. Inst. Allergy and Infectious Diseases, NIH, 1987—90. Author: The Neutrophil, 1978; contbr. over 200 articles to profl. jours. Recipient Merit award, NIH, 1988, Mayo Soley award, Western Soc. for Clin. Investigation, 1991, Bristol-Myers Squibb award for Disting. Achievement in Infectious Disease Rsch., 1995, Disting. Rsch. Biomed. Sci. award, Assn. Am. Med. Coll., 2007. Fellow: AAAS; mem.: NAS, Am. Acad. Arts and Scis., Inst. of Medicine, Soc. for Leukocyte Biology (Marie T. Bonazinga rsch. award 1985), Endocrine Soc., Infectious Diseases Soc. Am. (Bristol award 1993), Assn. Am. Physicians, Am. Soc. Biol. Chemists, Am. Soc. Clin. Investigation. Home: 509 Mcgilvra Blvd E Seattle WA 98112-5047 Office: U Wash Dept Medicine Div Al & Infectious Disease PO Box 357185 Seattle WA 98195-7185 Office Phone: 206-685-1876. Business E-Mail: seym@u.washington.edu.

KLEBBA, RAYMOND ALLEN, property manager; b. Chgo., Apr. 16, 1934; s. Raymond Aloysius and Marie Cecelia (Tobin) K.; m. Barbara Ann Gurbal, Oct. 7, 1961; children: Anne, Daniel, Mary, Theresa. Student, Loyola U., Chgo., 1954-56; cert. property mgr., Inst. Real Estate Mgmt., 1970. Corr., rep. Western R.R. Assn., Chgo., 1956-61; pres. Midland Warehouses, Chgo., 1961-68; v.p., gen. mgr. Strobeck, Reiss Sch. Mgmt. Co., Chgo., 1968-70, real estate mgr., broker, 1970—83; v.p., dir. Mid-Am. Nat. Bank, Chgo., 1983-90; br. mgr. Bank of Highwood/Deerfield, Ill., 1990-94; v.p. sales First Colonial Mortgage Corp., Chgo., 1994-95; bus. mgr. St. Matthias Parish, Chgo., 1995-98; real estate broker Tempo Real Estate, Inc., Chgo., 1998—. Chicagoland individual casting champion 1999—. Mem. Chgo. Bd. Realtors (vice chmn. comml. and indsl. leasing and property mgmt. coun.), Inst. Real Estate Mgmt. (life; chmn. chpt. of yr. com. 1975-76), Rotary, Moose, KC. Avocations: bowling, golf, gardening, fishing. Home: 4933 N Leavitt St Chicago IL 60625-1308 Office Phone: 773-271-3200.

KLEBER, HERBERT DAVID, psychiatrist, educator; b. Pitts., June 19, 1934; s. Max J. and Dorothea (Schulman) K.; m. Joan Louise Fox, Sept. 9, 1956 (div. Jan. 1988); children: Elizabeth, Marc, Pamela; m. Marian W. Fischman, 1989 (dec. Oct. 2001); m. Anne B. Lawver, Oct. 2004. BA in Psychology cum laude, Dartmouth Coll., 1956; MD, Jefferson Med. Coll., 1960; MA (hon.), Yale U., 1975; PhD (hon.), N.Y. Med. Coll., 1990. Lederle rsch. fellow Jefferson Med. Coll., 1959-60; rotating intern Health Ctr. Hosps. of U. Pitts., 1960-61; resident in psychiatry Yale U., New Haven, 1961-64; surgeon, chief receiving svc. USPHS Hosp., Lexington, Ky., 1964-66; asst. chief Hill-West Haven divsn. Conn. Mental Health Ctr., 1966-67, outpatient and admissions coord., 1967-68, dir., founder drug dependence unit, 1968-75, dir. substance abuse treatment unit, 1975-89; exec. dir. psychiatry emergency rm. svc. Yale-New Haven Hosp., 1967-68; from asst. prof. to assoc. prof. Yale U. Sch. Medicine, New Haven, 1966-75; prof. Yale U., 1975-91; exec. v.p., med. dir. Ctr. on Addiction and

Substance Abuse Columbia U., 1992—2001; prof., dir. divsn. substance abuse N.Y. State Psychiat. Inst., 1991—; prof. psychiatry Columbia U. Coll. Phys. and Surg., NYC, 1991—; attending psychiatrist Columbia-Presbyn. Med. Ctr., 1992—. Mem. nat. adv. coun. Nat. Inst. Drug Abuse, Alcohol, Drug Abuse and Mental Health Adminstrn., 1975-79, NIMH, 1977-79, mem. exec. instns. rev. groups; presdl. appointee US Office Nat. Drug Control Policy, dep. dir., 1989-91; founder APT Found., Inc., 1970, CEO, 1982-89; dir. NIDA Clin. Rsch. Ctr. Treatment of Opioid and Cocaine Abuse, Yale U., 1986-89, dir. rsch. tng. fellowship in substance abuse, 1988-89; mem. drug abuse adv. com. FDA, 1987-90; mem. bd. of sci. counselors Addiction Rsch. Ctr, Nat. Inst. on Drug Abuse, 1982-85; Nolan D.C. Lewis vis. prof. Carrier Found., 1985; dir. Nat. Inst. Drug Abuse Medication Devel. Ctr., 1994—, Columbia U., Rsch. Training Fellowship program, Columbia U., 1993—; bd. dirs. Coll. on Problems of Drug Dependence, Partnership for Drug-free America, Phoenix House Found., Betty Ford Inst.; lectr. and presenter in field. Contbr. chpts.: Opiate Addiction: Origins and Treatment, 1973, Treatment Aspect of Drug Dependence, 1978, Clinical Psychiatric Medicine, 1981, Cocaine: Scientific and Social Dimensions, 1992, Drugs, Alcohol and Tobacco: Making the Science and Policy Connections, several others; editor: APA Treatment Manual for Substance Abuse Disorders, APA Textbook of Substance Abuse Treatment, edits. 1-3, Clinician's Guide to Cocaine Abuse Treatment; (with others) APA Textbook-Treatment of Psychiatric Disorders: Treatment of Substance Abuse; assoc. editor Am. Jour. Drug and Alcohol Abuse and Addictive Behaviors, mem. edit. bd.; rsch. editor Jour. Substance Abuse Treatment, mem. edit. bd. Am. Jour. Addictions, Advances in Alcohol Actions/Misuse, Harvard Rev. of Psychiatry; edit. cons. Archives Gen. Psychiatry, Med. Letter, Jour. Maintenance in the Addictions, Sci.; contbr. over 250 articles to profl. jours. Co-chmn. NYC Task Force; mem. adv. bd. Rand Drug Policy Rsch. Ctr.; mem. Gov.'s Drug Adv. Coun., State of Conn., 1970-76; mem. NY State Adv. Coun. to Office of Alcohol & Substance Abuse Svcs., 1998-2004, Nat. Adv. Coun. Nat. Inst. Drug Abuse, 2003-. Recipient Meritorious Svc. award Lapides Found., 1979, Nyswander and Dole award, 1986, Alcohol, Drug Abuse, Mental Health Agy. award for pub. svc., 1986, Gov.'s award for outstanding svc. in field of substance abuse State of Conn., 1987, Jellinek award Yale U, 1994, Families in Action Drug Prevention award, 1990, Albert Biele Meml. award Jefferson Med. Coll., 2000, Disting. Alumni award Yale U., 2000, Disting. Sci. award Am. Soc. Addiction Medicine, 2005, Charles Burlingame award Inst. Living, 2005. Fellow ACP, Am. Psychiat. Assn. (mem. coun. on addiction, cons. joint commn. on pub. affairs, task force on benzodiazepine dependency, chair practice guidelines for treatment of substance use disorders 2002-06, Gold award 1975, Found.'s Fund prize 1981), Am. Coll. Neuropsychopharmacology (Eddy award of Coll. on Problems of Drug Dependence 1995), N.Y. Acad. Medicine, Am. Acad. Psychiatrists in Alcoholism and Addictions (founding, Founders award 1987); mem. Inst. of Medicine (substance abuse coverage com., medication devel. for substance abuse com.). Republican. Jewish. Avocations: swimming, walking, travel. Office: Columbia U Coll Phys/Surgns 1051 Riverside Dr New York NY 10032-1013 Home Phone: 212-580-9340; Office Phone: 212-543-5570. Business E-Mail: hdk3@columbia.edu.

KLECK, ROBERT ELDON, psychology professor; b. Archbold, Ohio, Aug. 3, 1937; AB in Philosophy, Denison U., 1959; PhD in Social Psychology, Stanford U., Calif., 1963. Postdoctoral fellow Stanford U., 1963-64; asst. prof. Williams Coll., Williamstown, Mass., 1964-66; asst. to assoc. prof. Dartmouth Coll., Hanover, NH, 1966-75, prof. psychology, 1975—, John Sloan Dickey Third Century Prof. of Social Scis., 1985-90, chmn. dept. psychology, 1993-99. Vis. rsch. prof. Boy's Town Ctr. Study of Youth Devel., Stanford U., 1974-75; cons. VA Stroke Project, 1983-86, Disadvantaged Children in N.H., 1974, Bur. Devel. Disabilities, Concord, N.H., 1975-80, Crotchet Mountain Rehab. Ctr., 1973, Abilities, Inc., Albertson, N.Y., 1979-81, Can. Rsch. Coun., NSF, USPHS; faculty sponsore USPHS Post-doctoral fellowship, 1977-78. Cons. editor Jour. Personality and Social Psychology, 1974-78, assoc. editor 1971-72; mem. editorial bd. Jour. Nonverbal Behavior, 1990-93; mem. editorial adv. bd. Action for Children's TV, 1975-79; editorial cons.various jours.; contbr. articles to profl. jours. Danforth fellow, 1959-63; Gen. Motors scholar, 1955-59. Mem. Am. Psychol. Soc., Internat. Soc. Rsch. on Emotion, Soc. Experimental Social Psychology, New Eng. Psychol. Assn., Soc. Kent and Danforth Fellows, Sigma Xi, Phi Beta kappa. Home: 6207 Moore Hall Hanover NH 03755-3578 Office: Dartmouth Coll Dept Of Psychology Hanover NH 03755 Office Phone: 603-646-2056. Business E-Mail: r.kleck@dartmouth.edu.

KLECKER, BEVERLY MCCAULEY, academic administrator; d. Robert Francis and Dorothy (Camden) McCauley. PhD, Ohio State U., 1996. Lic. Profl. Clin. Counselor Ky., 2005. Grad. rsch. assoc. Ohio State U., Columbus, Ohio, 1992—95; asst. prof. Ea. Ky. U., Richmond, Ky., 1996—99. Rschr., evaluator, grants Morehead State U., Morehead, Ky., 2001—. Ky. rep. Mid-South Ednl. Rsch. Assn., Gatlinburg, Tenn., 2003—05; bd. mem. Cath. Social Svcs., Columbus, Ohio, 1987—90. Recipient Outstanding Dissertation, Phi Delta Kappa, 1996. Office: Morehead State U 503 Ginger Hall Morehead KY 40351 Home Phone: 606-783-2536; Office Phone: 606-783-2536.

KLECKNER, ROBERT GEORGE, JR., retired lawyer; b. Reading, Pa., Mar. 14, 1932; s. Robert George and Elizabeth (Endlich) K.; m. Carol Espie, June 15, 1955; children: Anthony Savage, Susan Duffield. BA, Yale U., New Haven, Conn., 1954; LLB, U. Pa., Phila., 1959. Bar: Pa. 1960, NY 1964. Pvt. practice, Reading, 1960-63; assoc. Sullivan & Cromwell, NYC, 1963-70; house counsel Goldman, Sachs & Co., NYC, 1970-78; cons. NYC, 1978-80; house counsel Johnson & Higgins, NYC, 1980-97; sr. atty. legal dept. Marsh & McLennan Cos., Inc., NYC, 1997; ret., 1997. 1st lt. USAR, 1955-57, Korea. Mem. ABA, Assn. Bar City of NY, Berks County Bar Assn., Union Club, Univ. Club, Mill Reef Club, Phi Beta Kappa. Republican. Lutheran. Home: 80 East End Ave New York NY 10028-8004

KLEE, ANN RENEE, lawyer; BA in Ancient History with high honors, Swarthmore Coll., 1983; JD, U. Pa., 1986. Assoc. Crowell & Moring LLP, Washington, 1986—90; ptnr., chair environ. group Preston, Gates, Ellis & Rouvelas Meeds, Washington, 1990—95; environ. counsel to Senator Dick Kempthorne US Senate, Washington; chief counsel Senate Environment and Pub. Works Com., Washington, 1995—2001; counselor, spl. asst. to sec. US Dept. Interior, Washington, 2001—04; asst. adminstr., gen. counsel EPA, Washington, 2004—06; ptnr. Crowell & Moring LLP, Washington, 2006—, co-chair environ., nat. resources group. Office: Crowell & Moring LLP 1001 Pennsylvania Ave NW Washington DC 20004 E-mail: aklee@crowell.com.

KLEE, CLAUDE BLENC, medical researcher; MD, U. Marsailles, France, 1959. Chief lab. chemistry, chief protein biochemistry sect. Nat. Cancer Inst., 1974—. Recipient Women's Excellence in Scis. award, Fedn. Am. Soc. for Exptl. Biology, 1997. Fellow: AAAS; mem.: Inst. Medicine, Nat. Acad. Sci. Office: Nat Cancer Inst-Biochem Lab 9000 Rockville Pike Bethesda MD 20892-0001

KLEE, VICTOR LA RUE, mathematician, educator; b. San Francisco, Sept. 18, 1925; s. Victor La Rue and Mildred (Muller) K.; BA, Pomona Coll., 1945, DSc (hon.), 1965; PhD, U. Va., 1949; Dr. honoris causa, U. Liège, Belgium, 1984, U. Trier, Germany, 1995. Asst. prof. U. Va., 1949-53; NRC fellow Inst. for Advanced Study, 1951-52; asst. prof. U. Wash., Seattle, 1953-54, assoc. prof., 1954-57, prof. math., 1957-97, adj. prof. computer sci., 1974—98, prof. applied math., 1976-84; prof. emeritus, 1998—. Vis. asso. prof. UCLA, 1955-56; vis. prof. U. Colo., 1971, U. Victoria, 1975, U. Western Australia, 1979; cons. IBM Watson Research Center, 1972; cons. to industry; mem. Math. Scis. Research Inst., 1985-86; sr. fellow Inst. for Math. and its Applications, 1987. Co-author: Combinatorial Geometry in the Plane, 1963, Old and New Unsolved Problems in Plane Geometry and Number Theory, 1991, Convex Polytopes, 2003; contbr. more than 200 articles to profl. jours. Recipient Rsch. prize U. Va., 1952, Vollum award for disting. accomplishment in sci. and tech. Reed Coll., 1982, David Prescott Burrows Outstanding Disting. Achievement award Pomona Coll., 1988, Max Planck rsch. prize, 1992; NSF sr. postdoctoral fellow, Sloan Found. fellow U. Copenhagen, 1958-60, fellow Ctr. Advanced Study in Behavioral Scis., 1975-76, Guggenheim fellow, Humboldt award U. Erlangen-Nürnberg, 1980-81, Fulbright fellow U. Trier, 1992. Fellow AAAS (chmn. sect. A 1975), Am. Acad. Arts and Scis.; mem. Am. Math. Soc. (assoc. sec. 1955-58, mem. exec. com. 1969-70), Math. Assn. Am. (pres. 1971-73, L.R. Ford award 1972, Disting. Svc. award 1977, C.B. Allendoerfer award 1980, 99), Soc. Indsl. and Applied Math. (mem. coun. 1966-68), Internat. Linear Algebra Soc., Phi Beta Kappa, Sigma Xi (nat. lectr. 1969). Home: 13706 39th Ave NE Seattle WA 98125-3810 Office: U Wash Dept Math PO Box 354350 Seattle WA 98195-4350 Office Phone: 206-363-1850. E-mail: jmklee@att.net.

KLEEBLATT, NORMAN L., museum curator; AB in Art History, Rutgers U., 1971; diploma in conservation, NYU, 1975, MA, 1975. Conservator The Jewish Mus., NYC, 1975-80, curator collections/conservator, 1981-87, curator collections, 1987-94, Susan and Elihu Rose curator fine arts, 1995—. Mem. sci. coun. Mus. Art and History of Judaism; cons. Montclair (N.J.) Art Mus., 1975. Author: An Expressionst in Paris: the Paintings of Chaim Soutine, 1988; co-author: Treasures of the Jewish Museum, 1986; contbg. author: Gonn Mosny: Atmen und Malen, 1989, Pre-Raphaelite Art in its European Context, 1995, L'Affaire Dreyfus de A & Z: histoire et dictionnaire, 1994, L'Affaire Dreyfus et l'opinion publique en France et à l'étranger, 1995, Diaspora and Modern Visual Culture: Representing African and Jewish Diaspora, 1998; editor: The Dreyfus Affair, 1987; (catalogue) Mirroring Evil: Nazi Imagery/Recent Art, 2001; co-editor: Painting a Place in America, 1991; exhibits include The Paintings of Moritz Daniel Oppenheim: Jewish Life in 19th Century Germany, 1981, Too Jewish? Challenging Traditional Identities, 1996, Mirroring Evil: Nazi Imagery/Recent Art, 2002; reviewer in field. Recipient Hon. Mention, Henry Allen Moe Prize, 1985, 88, Nat. Jewish Book award, 1992, Second prize Henry Allen Moe Prize, 1992, Présidence d'honneur Com. Sci. Soc. Internat. d'Histoire de l'Affaire Dreyfus, 1994—; post-grad. fellow Nat. Mus. Fellowship Act, 1975-76; fellow mus. profls. Nat. Endowment Arts, 1996. Mem. Internat. Assn. Art Critics (Am. sect.), Am. Assn. Mus., Coll. Art Assn. Office: The Jewish Mus 1109 5th Ave New York NY 10128-0118

KLEEMAN, CHARLES RICHARD, nephrologist, educator, researcher; b. LA, Aug. 19, 1923; m. 1945; 3 children. BS, U. Calif., 1944, MD, 1947. Rotating intern San Francisco City Hosp., 1947-48; asst. resident pathology Mallory Inst.-Boston City Hosp., 1948-49; resident in medicine Newington VA Hosp., 1949-51; from instr. to asst. prof. metabolism (renal endocrine & diabetes), dept. medicine & metabolic diseases Yale U. Sch. Medicine, 1953-56; chief divsn. metabolic disease UCLA Med. Ctr., 1956—60; assoc. prof. UCLA Sch. Medicine, 1956—60, prof. medicine Cedars-Sinai Med Ctr., 1961—72, prof., dir. dept. internal medicine, 1972—94, prof. emeritus, 1994—. Nephrologist VA Med. Ctr., West L.A., 1993—; prof. medicine, dept. chief Hadassah Med. Sch.-Hebrew U., Israel, 1972-75; vis. prof. Beilinson Hosp.-Tel Aviv U., 1968, St. Francis Hosp., Honolulu, 1968, U. Queensland, 1966; chief metabolic sect. VA Hosp., L.A. 1956-60, cons., 1962—; chief metabolic sect. Wadsworth VA Med. Ctr., L.A., 1956-60. Upjohn-Endocrine Soc. scholar U. London, 1960-61. Mem. AMA, Am. Physiol. Soc., Inst. Medicine-NAS, Am. Soc. Clin. Investigation, Endocrine Soc., Am. Assn. Physicians. Office: VAMC West LA Med Divsn Nephr W111L 11301 Wilshire Blvd Los Angeles CA 90073 Office Phone: 310-794-1795. Business E-Mail: ckleeman@ucla.edu.

KLEIMAN, ALAN BOYD, artist; b. Bklyn., Feb. 20, 1938; s. Louis and Alfreda (Belowsky) K.; m. Audrey Barbara Code, Feb. 9, 1963; 1 dau., Andrea Kristin. B.F.A., Va. Commonwealth U., 1951; M.F.A., Cranbrook Acad. Art, 1953; student, Oscar Kokoska's Sch. of Seeing, 1956. Asst. publicity dir. Artist Tenents Assn., 1960-67; v.p. Grand St. Artist Group, 1970-75; chmn. Soho Artifacts, 1971-75. Author: Painting Provincetown Water, 1961, Investigations into the Light of Red Color, 1968, Light, Dazzle and Glow, 1970; one-man shows include Mich. State Coll., 1952, Sun Gallery, Provincetown, Mass., 1959, Nexus Gallery, Boston, 1959, Elizabeth Harris Gallery, N.Y.C., 1995, Ohara Gallery, N.Y.C., 1996, Robert Steel Gallery, N.Y.C., 1997, 2003, 04, 06, Kouros Gallery, N.Y.C., 2000; group shows include Nexus Gallery, Boston, 1959, Betty Parsons Gallery, N.Y.C., 1961; 79, Sun Gallery, 1962, New Gallery, Provincetown, Mass., 1961-62, Marino, N.Y.C., 1966, Warren Benedek, N.Y.C., 1972, Landmark Gallery, N.Y.C., 1975-76, Renaissance Soc., Chgo., 1979, Art U.S.A. '80, U.S., Can., Sweden, Siegel Gallery, N.Y.C., 1983, Michael Walls Gallery, N.Y.C., 1989, Robert Steel Gallery, N.Y.C., 1997, 2003-04, 05, 06; represented in permanent collections Mus. Modern Art, Whitney Mus., Am. Arts, Met. Mus. Art, N.Y.C., Carnegie Mus., Pitts., Boston Mus. Fine Arts, William Patterson Coll., Wayne, N.J.; 169 self portraits at Clocktower, N.Y.C., 1985—; retrospective 1960-86 at P.S.I., N.Y.C., 1986; traveling exhbn., China, 1988; with traveling acting group including Harvey Firestein, 1971-76; performer last production of AIDA, Old Met. Opera, 1962. Served with U.S. Army, 1953-55. Recipient 1st prize Boston Arts Festival, 1954; N.Y. State Council Arts grantee, 1977-78; Curtral Council Found. awardee, 1978; grantee Esther and Adolph Gottleib Found., 1985, Pollack-Krasner Found., 1987, NEH, 1989-90. Mem. Theatre of Artists League (v.p. 1972), Orgn. Ind. Artists, Am. Abstract Artists. *My creative drive has at times thrived on procrastination, anger, jealousy, rage, talent and plain hard work. Balancing emotion and intelligence make the tension expressed in my painting. I want to make more and better art.*

KLEIMAN, GARY HOWARD, broadcast, advertising and cellular communications consultant; b. Phila., Jan. 24, 1952; s. Leon and Martha (Rubin) K.; m. Annette Suzanne Vranich, Sept. 23, 1978; children: Aaron Jay, Jared Adam. Diploma, Am. Acad. Broadcasting, Phila., 1969, Pa. State Fire Sch., Media, 1969; BS, Temple U., 1972. Cert. radio mktg. cons., Radio Advt. Bur., NYC; cert. cmty. emergency response team, Md., 2005. Gen. mgr. Sta. WFEC, Harrisburg, Pa., 1974-75; local sales mgr. Sta. WYSP-FM, Phila., 1976-79; pres. A.S.K. Advt., King Prussia, Pa., 1976-80; v.p., gen. mgr. Sta. WGLU-FM, Johnstown, 1980-82, Sta. WAJE, Edensburg, Pa., 1982-84, Sta. WSBY-WQHQ-AM-FM, Salisbury, Md., 1984-86; mgr. Sta. WJDY, Salisbury, 1986-87; pres. IDEAS Unltd. Mktg. and Advt. Co., Salisbury, 1986—; gen. mgr. Sta. WACS-FM, Schenectady, 1988-89; v.p., gen. mgr. Sta. WDLE-FM, Federalsburg, Md., 1989-91; area mgr. Bell Atlantic Mobile Sys., 1992—93; pres. CellComm Mobile, 1993—; gen. mgr. Shore-Trade Exchange, LLC, 2005—06; mng. ptnr. Signfixers LLC, Salisbury, Md., 2006—. Media cons. Sta. WMDT-TV, Salisbury, 1988; dir., tchr. Am. Acad. Broadcasting, Phila., 1976-79. Contbr. articles to profl. publs. Com. chmn. Salisbury Revitalization, 1984—; mem. Bennett Mid. Sch. Parents, Tchrs., Students Assn., pres., 1994-95; bd. dirs. Salisbury Regional Urban Design Action Team, 1984-89, Deers Head Hosp. Found., Am. Heart Assn.; co-sponsor projects Lower Shore Easter Seals, Salisbury, 1985, Am. Cancer Soc., 1984-85, Kidney Found., 1985, Epilepsy Assn., 1985, Johnstown Area Regional Industries, 1981-84; promotion coord. Salisbury Festival com., 1985, 87-91, vice chmn., 1985-90; exec. com. Lower Shore chpt. March Dimes, 1984-89; scout leader Boy Scouts Am., 1988-90; adult leader 4-H, 1988-2001; mgr. area Little League; active campaigner Cambria County Dem. Com., 1982-84, Wicomico County Dem. Com., 1991-2004. Squadron comms. officer, pub. affairs officer, air crew ground team search rescue MDWG USAF aux./CAP, 1997-2003; adv. bd. Wicomico Mentoring Project, 1994-2004, co-chair, 1996-2001, chmn. 2000-01; vice chmn. bd. dirs. Jr. Achievement, 2000-01; mem. Cmty. Emergency Response Team, 2004—. Recipient numerous awards from local civic orgns., 1981—. Mem. Downtown Salisbury Assn. (bd. dirs., v.p. 1997-98, pres. 1999-00), Fruitland C. of C. (bd. dirs. 1996-2000, v.p. 1999-2000), Salisbury Area C. of C. (bd. dirs. 1989-92, 98-2001), Caroline County C. of C. (bd. dirs. 1989), Salisbury Jaycees (Springboard award 1985), Johnstown Jaycees, Salisbury State U. Athletic Club (pres. 1985), Tall Timber Park Assn. (pres. 1992-94). Democrat. Jewish. Avocations: photography, camping, skiing, softball, volleyball. Home: 115 Tall Timber Ln Fruitland MD 21826-1318 Office: Signfixers LLC CellComm Mobile 2205 Northwood Dr Ste 15 Salisbury MD 21801 Office Phone: 410-546-0500. Business E-Mail: gary@signfixers.com. *To me success is not measured in money, it's measured in how others perceive you in your community. To me, a business day starts at 7:30 and ends when all of my clients and customers are happy and all problems have been solved.*

KLEIMAN, MARY MARGARET, lawyer; b. Norfolk, Va., May 26, 1959; d. William Edward and Patricia Mae Holste; m. David James Kleiman, June 29, 1991; children: Amanda Grace, Amy Elizabeth. BA in History summa cum laude, Marian Coll., Indpls., 1981; JD cum laude, Ind. U., Indpls., 1984. Bar: Ind. 1985, U.S. Dist. Ct. (no. and so. dists.) Ind. 1985. Bailiff, law clk. Marion County Mcpl. Ct., Indpls., 1983-84; counsel Am. Fletcher Nat. Bank (now Bank One, Ind. N.A.), Indpls., 1985-88; assoc. Krieg DeVault Alexander & Capehart, Indpls., 1989-95; ptnr. Krieg Devault Alexander & Capehart, Indpls., 1995-2000; v.p. and assoc. gen. counsel Federal Home Loan Bank of Indianapolis, 2000—. Bd. dirs. Ind. Bus. Devel. Corp., 1994-97; spkr. at banking confs. Contbr. articles to profl. jours. Pro bono atty. Cmty. Orgns. Legal Assistance Project, Indpls., 1994—; vol. com. chair, mem. client programs com. Ind. chpt. Nat. Multiple Sclerosis Soc., 1997-2001, trustee Ind. chpt., 1999-2001; mem. mission com. Castleton United Meth. Ch., Indpls., 1993-2000, acolyte coord., mem. worship com., 1998-99, mem. chancel choir, 1999—, chair staff-parish rels. com., 2000-02; bd. dirs. Circle Area Comm. Devel. Corp., 2000—, Downtown Area Comm. Devel. Corp., 2000—, Mass. Ave. Comm. Devel. Corp., 2000—, Naval Air Warfare Center Reuse Planning Authority. Recipient Leadership award Nat. Multiple Sclerosis Soc., 1998, Nat. Vol. of Yr. award Nat. Multiple Sclerosis Soc., 1999, Outstanding Vol. award Ind. Ronald McDonald House, 1990; named to Outstanding Young Women in Am., 1981, 87. Mem. ABA, Ind. State Bar Assn., Indpls. Bar Assn. (chair printed forms com. 1987), Phi Delta Phi. Democrat. Avocations: gardening, cross-stitch, reading science fiction, calligraphy. Office: Federal Home Loan Bank 8250 Woodfield Crossing Blvd Ste 210 Indianapolis IN 46240-4348 E-mail: mkleiman@fhlbi.com.

KLEIN, ARNOLD SPENCER, lawyer; b. NYC, Mar. 10, 1951; s. Paul and Ethel (Cooper) K.; m. Arlene Sandra Feinberg, Aug. 14, 1977; children: Jeffrey Daniel, Rachel Pauli. BA, SUNY, Stony Brook, 1974; JD cum laude, N.Y. Law Sch., 1977. Bar: N.Y. 1978, Fla. 1984, U.S. Dist. Ct. (so. and ea. dists.) N.Y., U.S. Dist. Ct. (so. dist.) Fla., U.S. Ct. Appeals (2d cir.), U.S. Supreme Ct. Mem. Kelley, Drye & Warren, NYC, 1977-85, ptnr., 1986-94, Meltzer, Lippe & Goldstein, LLP, Mineola, NY, 1994—2004; atty. The Law Offices of Kenneth Koopersmith, LLC, Garden City, NY, 2004—. Mem. ABA, N.Y. State Bar Assn., Nassau County Bar Assn. Office: Law Offices of Kenneth Koopersmith LLC 200 Garden City Plz Garden City NY 11530 Office Phone: 516-354-0800. Business E-Mail: aklein@kklawllc.com.

KLEIN, ARNOLD WILLIAM, dermatologist; b. Mt. Clemens, Mich., Feb. 27, 1945; s. David Klein; m. Malvina Kraemer. BA, U. Pa., 1967, MD, 1971. Intern Cedars-Sinai Med. Ctr., LA, 1971—72; resident in dermatology Hosp. U. Pa., Phila., 1972—73, UCLA, 1973—75; pvt. practice Beverly Hills, Calif., 1975—. Prof. dermatology/medicine U. Calif. Ctr. Health Scis.; mem. med. staff Cedars-Sinai Med. Ctr.; asst. clin. prof. dermatology Stanford U., 1982—89; from asst. clin. to prof. dermatology/medicine UCLA, trustee David Geffen Sch. Medicine, 2003—; mem. adv. bd. Botox, Allergan Inc.; retained cons., investigator Elan Pharms.; cons., investigator Inamed Aesthetics, Q-Med, Medicis, Skin-Medica, Ortho-Neutrogena; presenter seminars in field. Assoc. editor: Jour. Dermatologic Surgery and Oncology, reviewer: Jour. Sexually Transmitted Diseases, Jour. Am. Acad. Dermatology; mem. editl. bd. Men's Fitness mag., Shape mag., Archives Dermatology; contbr. articles to profl. jours. Mem. CAlif. State Adv. Com. Malpractice, 1983—89; med. adv. bd. Skin Cancer Found., Lupus Found. Am.; founder R. Tarlow/Dr. Arnold Klein Fund Breast Cancer Treatment. Mem.: AFTRA, AMA, Am. found. AIDS Rsch. (founder, bd. dirs.), Soc. Cosmetic Chemists, Am. Venereal Disease Assn., Jennifer Jones Simon Found. (trustee), Hereditary Disease Found. (bd. dirs.), Discovery Fund Eye Rsch. (bd. dirs.), Lupus Found., Internat. Psoriasis Rsch. Inst., Scleroderma Found., Dermatology Found., Am. Acad. Dermatology, Met. Dermatology Soc., Am. Coll. Chemosurgery, LA Med. Assn., Assn. Sci. Advisors, Am. Assn. Cosmetic Surgeons, Internat. Soc. Dermatologic Surgery, Am. Soc. Dermatologic Surgery, Calif. Med. Assn., Children's Mus. LA (founder), Dance Gallery LA (founder), LA Mus. Contemporary Art (founder), Friars Club, Delphos, Phi Beta Kappa, Sigma Tau Sigma. Office: 435 N Roxbury Dr Ste 204 Beverly Hills CA 90210-5004 Office Phone: 310-275-5136. Personal E-mail: awkleinmd1@aol.com. *The sincerest form of respect is trust. Being a Physician is all about serving this trust. Also, it is about dedication, observation, obsession and creative intelligence. Who and what I am.where I begin and where I end.is all about being a physician.*

KLEIN, BARBARA A., information technology executive; BS magna cum laude, Marquette U.; MBA, Loyola U., Chgo., 1977. CPA. Former exec. Pillsbury, Sears, Roebuck and Co.; former v.p., corp. contr. Ameritech Corp.; former v.p. fin., CFO Dean Foods Co.; sr. v.p., CFO CDW Corp., Vernon Hills, Ill., 2002—. Bd. dir. Corn Products Internat. Bd. mem. Tax Assistance Prog. Mem.: Chgo. Fin. Exchange, Fin. Executives Inst., Chgo. Network, Ill. Soc. CPAs, AICPA. Office: CDW 200 N Milwaukee Ave Vernon Hills IL 60061*

KLEIN, BENJAMIN, economics professor, consultant; b. NYC, Jan. 29, 1943; s. Hyman and Beartha (Kristel) K.; m. Lynne Schneider; children: Franz, Emily, Amanda. ABA in Philosophy, Bklyn. Coll., 1964; MA in Econs., U. Chgo., 1967, PhD in Econs., 1970. Asst. prof. UCLA, 1968-72, assoc. prof., 1973-78, prof. econs., 1978—; faculty rsch. fellow Nat. Bur. Econs., NYC, 1971-72, rsch. assoc., 1976-77; pres. Econ. Analysis Corp., LA, 1980—2004; dir Law and Econs. Consulting Group, 2004—. Vis. prof. U. Wash., Seattle, 1978; cons. FTC, Washington, 1976-86, bd. govs. FRS, Washington, 1973-75. Contbr. articles to profl. jours. Ford Found. fellow, 1967-68, Scaiffe Found. fellow, 1975-76, Law and Econs. fellow U. Chgo. Law Sch., 1979; grantee Sloan Found., 1981-87; recipient ann. prize for disting. scholarship in law and econs. U. Miami Law and Econ. Ctr., 1978-79. ann. award for best articles Western Econ. Assn., 1979. Mem. Am. Econs. Assn. Office: UCLA Dept Econs 405 Hilgard Ave Los Angeles CA 90095-9000 Office Phone: 310-556-0709. Business E-Mail: bklein@lecg.com.

KLEIN, BENJAMIN GARRETT, mathematics professor, consultant; b. Durham, NC, Jan. 24, 1942; s. James Raymond and Lenetta Mae (Garrett) K.; m. Rosemary Therese McAndrew, June 19, 1971; children: David Garrett, Peter Raymond. BA, U. Rochester, 1963; MA, Yale U., 1965, PhD, 1968. Lectr., asst. prof. NYU, NYC, 1967-71; asst. prof. to prof. math. Davidson Coll., NC, 1971—, vice chmn. faculty NC, 1985-88, appt. Dana prof. math. NC, 1990-93, appt. Dolan prof. math. NC, 1993—, chair dept.

math. NC, 1994-98, mem. advanced placement calculus devel. com., 1999—2003; gov. southeastern sect. Math. Assn. Am., 2003—06. Cons. N.C. Dept. Pub. Instrn., Raleigh, 1981-85, 90—. Mem. editl. bd. The Coll. Math. Jour. Elder Davidson Coll. Presbyterian Ch., 1981-83, 87-89, 94-96. Named NC Prof. of Yr., Coun. Advancement and Support Edn., 1991; recipient Thomas Jefferson award, 1990, Hunter-Hamilton Love of Tchg. award, 2004. Mem.: N.C. Assn. Advanced Placement Math. Tchrs., N.C. Coun. Tchrs. Math., Nat. Coun. Tchrs. Math., Math. Assn. Am. (chair S.E. sect. 1993—95, gov. S.E. sect. 2003—06), Am. Math. Soc. Democrat. Office: Davidson Coll PO Box 6937 Davidson NC 28035-6937 Home Phone: 704-892-8306; Office Phone: 704-894-2318. Business E-Mail: beklein@davidson.edu.

KLEIN, BENNETT, lawyer; BA, Oberlin Coll., 1982; JD, Boston U. Atty. Gaston & Snow, 1987—90, Kotin, Crabtree & Strong, 1990—94; AIDS law project dir. Gay and Lesbian Advs. & Defenders (GLAD), 1994—. Mem. AIDS Action Com. Mass., Boston Alliance Gay and Lesbian Youth. Mem.: Mass. Lesbian & Gay Bar Assn. (bd. mem.). Office: Gay and Lesbian Advocates and Defenders Ste 800 30 Winter St Boston MA 02108*

KLEIN, BERNARD, publishing executive; b. NYC, Sept. 20, 1921; s. Joseph J. and Anna (Wolfe) K.; m. Betty Stecher, Feb. 17, 1946; children: Cheryl Rona, Barry Todd, Cindy Ann. BA, CCNY, 1942. Founder, pres. U.S. List Co., Boca Raton, Fla., 1946—; founder, pres., chief editor B. Klein Publs., Delray Beach, Fla., 1953—. Cons. in field. Author: all biennials Ency. of American Indian, 1954—; Guide to American Directories. Served with AUS, 1942-45, ETO. Mem. Direct Mail Advt. Assn. Lodges: Masons. Home: 12727 Coral Lakes Dr Boynton Beach FL 33437-4143 Office Phone: 561-496-3316.

KLEIN, CALVIN RICHARD, fashion designer; b. Bronx, Nov. 19, 1942; s. Leo and Flore (Stern) K.; m. Jayne Centre, Apr. 26, 1964 (div. 1974); 1 dau., Marci; m. Kelly Rector, Sept. 1986 (div. 1996). AA, Fashion Inst. Tech., 1962. Founder, pres., designer Calvin Klein Ltd., NYC, 1968—2003; designer Calvin Klein (a Phillips-Van Heusen company), NYC, 2003—. Critic Parsons Sch. Design; critic, cons. Fashion Inst. Tech.; launched fragrance lines for men and women, Obsession, Eternity, Escape, Contradiction, Truth Calvin Klein. Recipient Coty award, 1973, 74, 75, Woolmark award for Career Achievement, 1987, FIT Pres. award, 2002; named Outstanding Am. talent in women's fashion design Coun. Fashion Designers of Am., 1982, 83, 86, America's 25 Most Influential People, Time, Womenswear/Menswear Designer of the Year, Coun. Fashion Designers of Am., 1993, Lifetime Achievement award, 2001. Mem. Council Fashion Designers, Mus. Modern Art, Met. Mus. Art, Whitney Mus., Guggenheim Mus. Office: Calvin Klein Inc 205 W 39th St 4 New York NY 10018-3102 Address: Calvin Klein Europe Via Montenapoleone 29 20121 Milan Italy*

KLEIN, CHARLOTTE CONRAD, public relations executive; b. Detroit, June 20, 1923; d. Joseph and Bessie (Brown) K. BA, UCLA, 1945. Corr. UPI, Los Angeles, 1945-46; staff writer CBS, Los Angeles, 1946-47; publicist David O. Selznick Studios, Culver City, Calif., 1947-49, Foladare and Assocs., Los Angeles, 1949-51; publicist to v.p. Edward Gottlieb & Assocs., NYC, 1951-62; v.p. to sr. v.p. Harshe Rotman & Druck, NYC, 1962-78; dir. press/govt. affairs Sta. WNET-TV, NYC, 1978-79; pres. Charlotte C. Klein Assocs., NYC, 1979-84; sr. v.p., group supr. Porter Novelli, NYC, 1984-89; prin. Charlotte Klein Assocs., NYC, 1989—2002. Adj. prof. pub. rels. NYU; bd. dirs. U.S. Trademark Assn., 1959-62, Am. Arbitration Assn., 1970-80 (exec. com. 1980-82); mem. adv. bd. Coll. and Cmty. Fellowship Grad. Ctr., CUNY, 2002-06; cons. Ctr. for Advancement of Women, 2003-04. Contbr. articles to profl. jours. Bd. dirs. Manhattan chpt. Am. Cancer Soc., 1988-92; trustee Murray Hill Neighborhood Assn., 2006—. Recipient Cine Golden Eagle, 1977, Matrix award Women in Comms., 1975, Honor award Coll. and Cmty. Fellowship, 2004, Keeper of the Flame award Nat. Women's Hall of Fame, 2005. Mem. Pub. Rels. Soc. Am. (accredited; pres. N.Y. chpt. 1985-86, Silver Anvil award 1978, John Hill award 1988), Women's Forum (bd. dirs. N.Y. chpt. 1986-87, 96-98), Internat. Women's Forum (leadership com. chair dialogue for democracy 1993-98, co-chair task force on violence against women globally, 1998-2001), Women Execs. in Pub. Rels. (pres. 1965), N.Y. Women in Comm. Avocations: painting, stamp collecting/philately. Home Phone: 212-683-3543; Office Phone: 212-683-3543. Personal E-mail: bettlott@earthlink.net.

KLEIN, CHARLOTTE FEUERSTEIN, art consultant; b. Stoneham, Mass., June 3, 1931; d. Harold and Esther B. (Franks) Feuerstein; m. Philipp Hillel Klein, June 21, 1953; children— Joshua David, Daniel William, Jonathan Henry. BS, Boston U., 1953. Tchr. pub. schs., Scotia, Schenectady, Niscayuna, NY, 1953-56, Newton, Mass., 1974-75; ptnr., art cons. Washington Graphics, Washington, 1979-82; dir., art adviser CFK Assocs., Washington, 1982—; mem. Trust for Pub. Land; Mem. AAUW, LWV, Washington Opera Soc., The Phillips Collection, Friends of Kennedy Ctr., Washington, Nat. Symphony Orch. Assn., Holocaust Mus., Smithsonian Assn. Mem. Nat. Bldg. Mus., Am. for Arts Action Fund, Nat. Trust Hist. Preservation, Nat. Mus. Women, US Holocaust Meml. Mus., Nat. Parks Conservation Assn.

KLEIN, CHRISTOPHER CARNAHAN, economist; b. Anniston, Ala., July 5, 1953; s. Wallace Carnahan and Frances Luvona (Meaders) K.; m. Vicki Lynn Brown, May 7, 1983; children: Hannah Marie Brown, Colin Christopher Brown. BA in Econs., U. Ala., 1976; PhD in Econs., U. N.C., 1980. Economist FTC, Washington, 1980-86, Tenn. Pub. Svc. Commn., Nashville, 1986-93, rsch. dir., 1993-94, dir. utility rate div., 1994-95; chief utility rate divsn. Tenn. Regulatory Authority, Nashville, 1995-97, chief econ. analysis divsn., 1997—2002; assoc. prof. econ. and fin. dept. Mid. Tenn. State U., Murfreesboro, 2002—. Mem. adj. faculty Mid. Tenn. State U., Murfreesboro, 1990-94; adj. assoc. prof. Vanderbilt U., 1998-2002; mem. Fed.-State Joint Bd. Staff, 1994-96; mem. rsch. adv. com. Nat. Regulatory Rsch. Inst., Columbus, Ohio, 1990-95, chmn., 1993-95; mem. staff subcom. on gas Nat. Assn. Regulatory Utility Commrs., 1990-94. Editor: Jour. for Econ. Educators, 2007—; contbr. articles to profl. jours. Recipient cert. of commendation FTC, 1985. Mem. Am. Econ. Assn., So. Econ. Assn., Indsl. Orgn. Soc., Transp. and Pub. Utilities Group, Alpha Pi Mu. Avocations: poetry, tube hi-fi, photography. Office: Econ and Fin Dept Middle Tenn State U PO Box 27 Murfreesboro TN 37132 Office Phone: 615-904-8570. E-mail: cklein@mtsu.edu.

KLEIN, CHUCK, retired private investigator, writer; b. Cin., 1942; s. Charles H. and Ruth Emily Klein; m. Annette Margolis Levine, Aug. 18, 1996; children: Trey, Jay, Todd, Amy, Brad. LLB, Blackstone Law Sch., 1972. Cert. police officer, Ohio; cert. fire fighter, Ind.; cert. firearms instr. NRA; lic. pvt. investigator; cert. instinct shooting instr. Tactical Def. Inst., Ohio. Firearms editor P.I. Mag., Toledo, 1988—2002. Author: (fiction) Circa 1957, 1990, (non-fiction) Instinct Combat Shooting, 1986, Klein's Firearm Manual, 1997, Klein's C.C.W. Handbook, 1998, (fiction) The Power of God, 1999, (non-fiction) Lines of Defense, 2000, The Way it Was, 2003, Guns in the Workplace, 2006, Klein Family History, 1771-2006, 2007. Mem. Internat. Assn. Law Enforcement Firearms Instrs., Kiwanis Club of Cin. (pres. 2002-03). Avocations: golf, skeet.

KLEIN, CYNTHIA, art appraiser; BA in Art History, U. Mass., Amherst, BS in Bus. Adminstrn., Mktg. with honors; grad. studies in Art History, Rutgers U. Specialist, paintings dept. to dir., prints dept. C.G. Sloan & Co. Auctioneers, N. Bethesda, Md., 1991—2000; v.p., dir., prints dept. Doyle New York, 2000—. Prints appraiser Antiques Roadshow, WGBH-PBS. Mem.: Am. Hist. Prints Collectors Soc., Soc. for Japanese Arts, Phi Beta Kappa. Office: Doyle New York 175 E 87th St New York NY 10128 Office Phone: 212-427-4141 ext. 246. Office Fax: 212-369-0892. Business E-Mail: prints@doylenewyork.com.

KLEIN, DALE EDWARD, federal agency administrator, engineering educator; b. Cooper County, Mo., July 6, 1947; BS, U. Mo., 1970, MS, 1971, PhD in Nuclear Engring., 1977. Design engr. Procter & Gamble Co., 1970-72; teaching and rsch. asst. nuclear engring. U. Mo., Columbia, 1973-77; asst. prof. U. Tex., Austin, 1977-82, assoc. prof., 1982-90, prof., 1990—, dir. nuclear engring. teaching program, 1988-94, assoc. dean rsch. coll. engring.; asst. to sec. def for nuclear, chem. and bio. defense programs US Dept. Def., Washington, 2001—06; chmn. US Nuclear Regulatory Commn, Rockville, Md., 2006—. Named Young Engr. of Yr., Travis chpt. Tex. Soc. Profl. Engring., 1982, Engr. of Yr., 1990, Tex. Engr. of Yr., 1992, U. Mo. Faculty-Alumni award, U. Mo. Honor award for Disting. Svc. in Engring., Joe J. King Profl. Engring. Achievement award Mem. ASME (Edwin F. Church award 1988, Gustus L. Larson Meml. award 1990). Achievements include research in thermal analysis of nuclear shipping containers, heat transfer augmentation for flow over rough surfaces, liquid metal flows through a packed bed under the influence of a transverse magnetic field, and nuclear waste disposal. Office: US Nuclear Regulatory Commn One White Flint N Bldg 11555 Rockville Pike Rm 18G1 Rockville MD 20852

KLEIN, DAVID P., painter; b. West Bend, Wis., Nov. 13, 1950; s. Lee Joseph and May Klein; m. Mary Elizabeth Kuester, July 25, 1948; children: Eric John, Angela Marie, Bridget Elizabeth. Painter self employed. Exhibitions include West Bend Art Mus., Wis., Charles Allis/Villa Terrace Art Mus., Neville Pub. Mus., Milw. Pub. Mus., Judith Racht Gallery, Peolple's Choice Gallery, Mason St. Art Gallery, Bilhenry Gallery, Fort Morgan Mus., Colo., Barrister's Gallery, La., Franklin Square Gallery, NC, Tamarack Craftsmen Gallery, Mich., Kleine Galerie-Almut Helmert, Germany, exhibitions include galleries, cafes and auctions. Mem.: Wis. Painter and Sculptors, Wis. Artists of all Media, League of Milw. Artists, Knights of Columbus. Home: N2156 Hwy W Campbellsport WI 53010 Office Phone: 920-266-2174. Personal E-mail: maryklein@peoplepc.com. E-mail: demarcationartstudio@hotmail.com.

KLEIN, DEBORAH RAE, nurse; b. Detroit, Mar. 29, 1951; d. Chester Anthony and E. Jacquelyn (Hollenbeck) Simpson; m. Robert Joseph Klein, Apr. 15, 1977; 1 child, Jeffrey. BS in Nursing, Mich. State U., 1974; MS in Health Adminstrn., U. Houston, 1984. Grad. nurse St. Mary's Hosp., Livonia, Mich., 1974; RN U.S. Army, Ft. Polk, La., 1974-78; DON Byrd Meml. Hosp., Leesville, La., 1978-79, Alvin (Tex.) Cmty. Hosp., 1979-83; adminstrn. resident Katy (Tex.) Med. Ctr., 1983-84, DON, 1984-85, COO, DON, 1985-90; v.p. Doctors' Hosp., Tulsa, 1990-97; dir. ops. improvement Okla. divsn. Columbia HCA, 1997-98; v.p., COO SouthCrest Hosp., Tulsa, Okla., 1998—2001; chief nursing officer Vaughn Regional Med. Ctr., Selma, Ala., 2002—03; dir. Tulsa Regional Med. Ctr., Tulsa, Okla., 2000—01; v.p. clin. integration Hillcrest HealthCare Sys., Tulsa, 2000—01; nurse mgr. VAMC, Salem, Va., 2003—. Cons. in field; adj. faculty Bartlesville Wesleyan Coll., 1999-2001. Sec., treas. Sam Houston coun. Boy Scouts Am., 1984-88. Capt. U.S. Army, 1972-78. With U.S. Army Nurse Corps, 1974—78. Recipient Commendation medal, U.S. Army. Mem.: Sigma Thete Tau. Republican. Roman Catholic. Avocations: reading, crafts. Home: 532 Santee Rd Roanoke VA 24019-4928 Office Phone: 540-982-2463 ext. 2485.

KLEIN, EDWARD, writer; b. Yonkers, NY, Oct. 19, 1936; s. Meyer I. and Gertrude (Axelrod) K.; m. Emiko Oshikiri, June 25, 1963 (div. 1975); children: Karen, Alec; m. Tessa Namuth, Mar. 20, 1978 (div. 1981); m. Dolores Jones Barrett, Oct. 24, 1987. BS, Columbia U., 1960, MS, 1961. Copy boy, feature writer N.Y. Daily News, NYC, 1957-60; reporter World Telegram & Sun, NYC, 1960-61; reporter, editor Japan Times, Toyko, 1961-63; fgn. corr. UPI, Tokyo, 1963-64; editor The Shipping and Trade News, Toyko, 1964-65; assoc. editor Newsweek Mag., NYC, 1965-69, fgn. editor, 1969-76, asst. mng. editor, 1976-77; editor N.Y. Times Mag., NYC, 1977-87; contbg. editor Vanity Fair, NYC, 1988—, Parade, NYC, 1991—; columnist Walter Scott's Personality Parade, 1991—. Author: (with Robert Littell and Richard Chesnoff) If Israel Lost the War, 1969, The Parachutists, 1981, All Too Human: The Love Story of Jack and Jackie Kennedy, 1996, Just Jackie: Her Private Years, 1998, The Kennedy Curse: Why Tragedy Has Haunted America's First Family for 150 Years, 2003, Farewell, Jackie: A Portrait of Her Final Days, 2004, The Truth About Hillary: What She Knew, When She Knew It, and How Far She Will Go to Become President, 2005, Katie: The Real Story, 2007; editor: (with Don Erickson) About Men. Mem. Coun. on Fgn. Rels., PEN Am. Ctr., Am. Motorcyclist Assn., The Oversease Press Club N.Y. Office Phone: 212-831-0231. E-mail: meiji@aol.com.

KLEIN, ELEAZER, lawyer; s. Bernard and Shirley Klein; m. Sarah Gotlib-Klein, Aug. 26, 1993; children: Michael, Yakira, Noa. BS, Bklyn. Coll., 1987; JD, Yale Law Sch., 1991. Assoc. Davis Polk & Wardwell, NYC, 1991—96, Schulte Roth & Zabel LLP, NYC, 1996—99, ptnr., 2000—. Sr. editor Yale Law Jour., New Haven, 1989—91; mem. securities regulation com. Assn. N.Y. Bar, 2002—04; dir. Yeshiva Ketana of Manhattan, 2004—. Author: (book/treatise) PIPEs: A Guide to Private Investments in Public Companies; panelist (television show) Street Signs with Ron Insana, chmn. (seminar) 5th Annual Industry Summit on PIPES, 4th Annual Industry Summit on PIPES, panel chair The PIPEs Conf., 2004, 2005, chmn. INSIder Trading Pitfalls, panelist Overview of Restructurings. Leader Congregation Biyan, NYC, 1993—. Mem.: Assn. Bar N.Y., ABA, Alpha Sigma Lambda. Office: Schulte Roth & Zabel LLP 919 Third Ave New York NY 10022 Office Phone: 212-756-2000. Office Fax: 212-593-5955.

KLEIN, ERIC A., lawyer; b. NYC, July 3, 1959; AB, Princeton, 1981; JD, Boston U., 1985. Bar: Calif. 1986. Ptnr. corp. group, leader west coast mergers and acquisitions and securities practices Katten Muchin Zavis Rosenman, LA. Mem.: ABA (mem. Intellectual Property Law Sect., Intellectual Tech. Transfer). Office: Katten Muchin Zavis Rosenman Ste 2600 2029 Century Park E Los Angeles CA 90067 Office Phone: 310-788-4640. Office Fax: 310-712-8482. E-mail: eric.klein@kmzr.com.

KLEIN, EUGENE, lawyer; b. Grondo, June 12, 1963; arrived in US, 1990; 1 child, David. MA, U. Belorus, 1985, PhD, 1987; JD, William Mitchell Coll. Law, 1994. Bar: Minn. 1994, Ill. 2002, Russia. Legal coun. Caterpillar, Inc., Geneva, 1994—98; European coun. Dell Computers, London, 1998—99; atty. Bingham Dana Law Firm, Ill., 1999—2000, Klein Law Offices, Chgo., 2002—. Spkr. Russian immigrant cmty. events, 2002—. Vol. Polish Legal Clinic, Chgo., 2002—04. Mem.: Minn. Bar Assn. Avocations: reading, history. Office Phone: 773-714-1648. Office Fax: 773-714-1649.

KLEIN, GABRIELLA SONJA, retired communications executive; b. Chgo., Apr. 11, 1938; d. Frank E. Vosicky and Sonja (Kosner) Becvar; m. Donald J. Klein. BA in Comm. and Bus. Mgmt., Alverno Coll., 1983. Editor, owner Fox Lake (Wis.) Rep., 1962-65, McFarland (Wis.) Comty. Life and Monona Cmty. Herald, 1966-69; bur. reporter Waukesha (Wis.) Daily Freeman, 1969-71; cmty. rels. staff Waukesha County Tech. Coll., Pewaukee, Wis., 1971-73; pub. rels. specialist JI Case Co., Racine, Wis., 1973-75, corp. publs. editor, 1975-80; v.p., bd. dirs. publs. Image Mgmt. Valley View Ctr., Milw., 1980-82; pres. Comm. Concepts Unltd., Racine, 1983-98; ret., 1998. Past pres. Big Bros./Big Sisters Racine County; past v.p. devel. Girl Scouts Racine County, bd. dirs. Recipient award Wis. Press Assn., Nat. Fedn. Press Women, Silver medal Ad Club Racine, 1998, Outstanding Alumna award Alverno Coll., 1999, Edn. Cmty. Leader of Yr., Racine Area Mfrs. and Commerce, 2000, Thanks Badge award Girl Scouts of Racine County, 2000, Cmty. Trustee award Leadership Racine, 2004, Thanks Badge II award Girl Scouts Racine County, 2005, Oustanding Youth Adv. award Racine County Youth as Resources, 2006; named Wis. Woman Entrepreneur of Yr., 1985, Vol. of Yr. Racine Area United Way, 1994, Woman of Distinction Bus., Racine YWCA, 1995. Home: 3045 Chatham St Racine WI 53402-4001

KLEIN, GARNER FRANKLIN, cardiologist, internist; b. San Pedro, Calif., June 21, 1933; s. John William and Anna Louise K.; m. Nancy Shank, Aug. 19, 1985; children: Kevin Wayne, Samuel Kyle, Lisa K., Garner F. BA in Biology, North Tex. State U., 1953; MA in Anatomy, U. Tex. Med. Br., Galveston, 1956, MD, 1958. Diplomate Am. Bd. Internal Medicine. Intern U.S. Naval Hosp., Camp Pendleton, Calif., 1958—59; resident in internal medicine VA Hosp./Southwestern Med. Sch., Dallas, 1962—66; cardiologist Valley Diagnostic Clinic, Harlingen, Tex., 1966—2002, Valley Bapt. Med. Ctr., Harlingen, 1966—, chief dept. medicine, 1982—84, 1992—94, 2002—04, chief med. staff, 1994—96; pres. Valley Diagnostic Med. and Surg. Clinic, 1992—96; med. dir. Valley Health Plans, Harlingen, 2002—05; exec. dir. Valley Health Care Network, 2005—. Cons. in cardiology Dolly Vinsant Meml. Hosp., San Benito, Tex., 1966-2000, South Tex. Hosp., Harlingen, 1966-2000; med. dir. South Tex. Emergency Care Found., 1991—, Valley Diagnostic Clinic, 1996-99, Los Fresnos Rural Health Clinic, 1996-2000; clin. prof. medicine U. Tex. Health Sci. Ctr., San Antonio, 1999—, Regional Acad. Health Ctr., Harlingen, Tex. Mem. Wesley United Meth. Ch., Harlingen. Lt. comdr. M.C., U.S. Navy, 1958-66. Named Profl. Vol. of Yr., Tex. affiliate Am. Heart Assn., 1983. Fellow ACP, Am. Coll. Cardiology, Acad. for Healthcare Mgmt.; mem. AMA, Tex. Med. Assn., Nat. Assn. EMS Physicians, Air Med. Physician Assn., Nat. Assn. Managed Care Physicians, Am. Coll. Managed Care Medicine, Tex. Soc. Internal Medicine (Amb. Leadership award 1998), Am. Heart Assn. (pres. Tex. affil. 1980-81), Am. Stroke Assn., Am. Coll. Physician Execs., Cameron-Willacy County Med. Soc. (pres. 1978), Sigma Xi, Alpha Omega Alpha. Avocations: hunting, fishing, gardening. Office: Valley Health Care Network 2101 Pease St Harlingen TX 78550 Business E-Mail: garner.klein@valleybaptist.net.

KLEIN, GERHART LEOPOLD, public relations executive; b. Phila., July 24, 1948; s. Joseph G. and Liselotte M. (Peschke) K.; m. Anne Sceia, July 19, 1976. BS cum laude, Temple U., 1970, JD, 1980. Bar: Pa. 1980, N.J. 1980, U.S. Dist. Ct. (ea. dist.) Pa. 1980, U.S. Dist. Ct. N.J. 1980, U.S. Ct. Appeals (3d cir.) 1982, U.S. Supreme Ct. 1985, U.S. Tax Ct. 1985. News anchor WAMS, Wilmington, Del., 1967-68; news anchor, disc jockey WRCP AM & FM, Phila., 1968-70, news dir., 1970; editor, writer, reporter, news anchor WCAU (CBS) Radio, Phila., 1970-72; dir. pub. info., press sec. Pa. Dept. Pub. Welfare, Harrisburg, 1972-73; freelance journalist Phila., 1973-75; asst. editor Focus Mag., Phila., 1974-75; editor, writer, reporter, news anchor KYW Newsradio, Phila., 1975-77; atty. Montgomery, McCracken, Walker & Rhoads, Phila., 1980-85; v.p., gen. mgr. to exec. v.p. Anne Klein & Assocs., Inc., Marlton, NJ, 1985—. Mem. Environ. Commn., Mt. Laurel Twp., NJ, 1988-92; mem. water quality com. Old Taunton Colony Club, 1995—, mem. bd. trustees, 2006-. Recipient Phila. Trial Lawyers Assn. Barrister award, 1980. Mem. Pub. Rels. Soc. Am. (chmn. task force on ethics bd. confidentiality 1991-92, mem. body of knowledge bd. 1994-98, author PR Law Sect. of Accreditation Handbook 1990, Phila. chpt. Pepperpot awards, Presdl. citation 1991, 92), Pub. Rels. Soc. Am. Counselors Acad. (chmn. tech. com.), Pub. Rels. Profls. So. N.J. (treas. 1990-92), Soc. Profl. Journalists, Broadcast Pioneers (v.p. 2006-), Pinnacle Worldwide (treas. 1994-96, pres.-elect 1996-98, pres. 1998-2000, chmn. 2000-02, chmn. emeritus 2002-). Office: Anne Klein & Assocs Inc 10 Lake Ctr Ste 108 Marlton NJ 08053-3424 Office Phone: 856-988-6560. E-mail: gklein@akleinpr.com.

KLEIN, GERSHON A., pediatrician; b. Wilmington, Del., May 6, 1939; s. Maurice and Frances Klein; m. Goldie Klein, June 23, 1963; children: Philip, Sandra, Theodore. BA, U. Del., Newark, 1961; MD, Hahnemann Med. Coll., 1965. Intern Del. Hosp., Wilmington, 1965—66, dir. pediat. outpatient, 1969; resident in pediats. Wilmington Med. Ctr., 1966—68, fellow in genetics, 1968—69; pvt. practice Newark Pediats., Del., 1969—2002; preceptor pediat. outpatient Wilmington Hosp., Christiana Care Health Systems, 1995—. Clin. instr. pediats. Jefferson U., Phila., 1973—; med. officer to comdr. of 116th MASH to state surgeon Del. Army N.G., 1965—96. Founder, v.p., pres. Albert Einstein Acad., Wilmington, 1969—79; ct. appointed spl. advocate CASA New Castle Family Ct., Wilmington, 2003—05; bd. dirs. Prevent Child Abuse Del., Wilmington, 2001—07. Brig. gen. Del. Army N.G., 1996, ret. Mem.: Am. Acad. Pediats., Wilmington New Castle Pediat. Assn. (treas. 1980—2004, Cmty. Svc. award 2005), Med. Soc. Del. Avocations: tennis, kayaking, walking, travel. Home: PO Box 231 Bethany Beach DE 19930 Personal E-mail: gershonklein@verizon.net.

KLEIN, GORDON LESLIE, pediatrician, educator; b. NYC, Aug. 26, 1946; s. Hyman David and Ruth Harriet (Katz) K.; m. Joann Pamela Schulz, July 1, 1973; children: Andrew Howard (dec.), Adrienne Lindsay. BA, Columbia U., 1967; postgrad., Cambridge U., 1970-71; MD, Albert Einstein Coll. Medicine, 1971; MPH, UCLA, 1980. Cert. Am. Bd. Pediat., 1976, in pediat. gastroenterology and nutrition Am. Bd. Pediat., 1990. Intern, resident in pediat. Stanford U. Med. Ctr., Calif., 1971-74; postdoctoral fellow pediat. nutrition Johns Hopkins U. Med. Sch., Balt., 1976-78; postdoctoral fellow in pediat. gastroenterology UCLA, 1978-80, adj. asst. prof. pediat., 1980-82; asst. prof. pediat. Tulane U. Med. Sch., New Orleans, 1982-84; pediat. gastroenterologist City of Hope Med. Ctr., Duarte, Calif., 1984-86; assoc. prof. pediat. and preventative medicine U. Tex. Med. Br., Galveston, 1986-95, prof. pediat., 1995—. Mem. com. revision US Pharmacopeia, Rockville, Md., 1990-2000, chmn. gastroenterology adv. panel, 1990-2000, exec. com. rev., 1995-2000; cons. Nicaraguan Ministry Health, 1992, FDA, NICHD aluminum toxicity in infants; mem. spl. rev. panel osteoporosis NIH; spl. govt. cons., FDA, 1998-2006; vis. prof. Okayama U., Kyushu U., Japan, 1996, Baylor Coll. Medicine, Houston, 1997, U. Sheffield, Eng., 2000; invited lectr. Hosp. Necker, Paris, 1991, Columbia U., 1993, Harvard U., 1994, 99, U. Melbourne, U. Sydney, Australia 1995, Japan, 1996, 2003, China, 1997, 99, 2002, Cambridge U., 2004, 06, Am. Soc. Bone and Mineral Rsch., 2004, Pediat. Acad. Soc., 2005, NIH, 2005, Oxford U., 2005, US Army Inst. Surg. Rsch., 2006, Johns Hopkins U., 2006, 4th Internat. Conf. on Children's Bone Health, 2007, sci. adv. com., 2007; organizing com. pharmacology and pediat. bone workshop NIH and Am. Soc. for Bone and Mineral Rsch., 2005; combined expert adv. panel Internat. Conf. Children's Bone Health and Internat. Soc. Clin. Densitometry, 2007. Editor: Metabolic Bone Disease in Total Parenteral Nutrition, 1985; co-editor: Current Opinion in Pharmacology: Endocrine and Metabolic Diseases, 2005; mem. internat. adv. bd. Jour. of Bone and Mineral Metabolism, 2005, mem. editl. bd. Jour. Burns and Wounds, 2006; contbr. articles to profl. jours. Lt. comdr. USN, 1974—76. Named Clin. Assoc. Physician NIH, 1980-82; recipient Nat. Rsch. Svc. award, 1979-80, Travel award Internat. Conf. Calcium Regulating Hormones, Melbourne, 1995; nominee Howard Hughes Investigatorship in Translational Rsch., 2001; Nutrition Program fellow Project HOPE Nicaragua, 1992. Fellow Am. Acad. Pediat.; mem. N.Am. Pediat. Bone and Mineral Working Group (founder, sec.-treas. 1984-85), Soc. for Pediat. Rsch., Am. Soc. Bone and Mineral Rsch. (lectr. 2004), Am. Soc. Nutrition, Am. Gastroent. Assn., Am. Pediat. Soc., Princeton Club NY Achievements include development of the Pediatric Bone Disease Initiative with the

American Society for Bone and Mineral Research and the NIH; FDA rule governing aluminum contamination of intravenous solutions used for nutrition of hospitalized patients; characterization of the toxic damage of aluminum to bones and liver; characterization of bone loss following burn injury including abnormalities in vitamin D, calcium, parathyroid hormone and treatment for the bone loss. Avocations: travel, reading, horseback riding, music. Office: U Tex Med Br Dept Pediat 301 University Blvd Galveston TX 77555-0352 Home Phone: 281-337-3981; Office Phone: 409-772-1689. Business E-Mail: gklein@utmb.edu.

KLEIN, HARVEY, medical educator; b. NYC, Aug. 29, 1937; s. Emanuel and Rose (Sanderman) K.; m. Phyllis Levine, Sept. 22, 1963; children: Laura, Daniel. SB, U. Chgo., 1959; MD, Harvard U., 1963. Diplomate Am. Bd. Internal Medicine. Intern N.Y.-Cornell, NYC, 1963-64, asst. resident, 1964-65, sr. resident, 1967-68, chief resident, 1968-69, fellow in medicine, 1969-70; asst. prof. medicine Cornell U. Med. Coll., NYC, 1970-75, assoc. prof., 1975-88, William S. Paley prof. clin. medicine, 1992—. Capt. USAF, 1965-67. Office: Cornell U Med Coll 525 E 68th St New York NY 10021-4870 Office Phone: 212-746-4101.

KLEIN, HENRY, lawyer; b. N.Y.C., Oct. 6, 1949; s. Leo Herman and Florence (Silver) K.; m. Ann Laura Hallasey, July 30, 1972; children: Lauren Jennifer, Benjamin Jason. BA, SUNY, Albany, 1971; JD, U. San Diego, 1975. Bar: Calif. 1975, U.S. Ct. Customs and Patent Appeals 1976, U.S. Ct. Appeals (Fed. cir.) 1985, U.S. Dist. Ct. (cen. dist.) Calif. 1986. Trademark atty. U.S. Patent Office, Washington, 1975-77; ptnr. Ladas & Parry, Los Angeles, 1978—2002; private practice 2002-. Mem. San Diego Law Rev., 1974-75; editor-in-chief Trademark Soc. Newsletter, 1977. Mem. U. San Diego Civil Legal Clinic, 1974, Civil Rights Research Council, San Diego, 1974, Calif. Pub. Interest Research Group, San Diego, 1975. N.Y. State scholar, 1967-71; Tex. State legal scholar State of Tex., 1972; recipient Am. Jurisprudence award Bancroft-Whitney Co. and Lawyer Co-Op. Pub. Co., Lubbock, Tex., 1972; Patent Trademark Spl. Achievement awards U.S. Dept. Commerce, Washington, 1976, 77. Mem. U.S. Trademark Assn. (v.p. 1976, pres., chmn. 1977), Los Angeles Patent Law Assn., Phi Delta Phi. Republican. Jewish. Home: 10427 Vivienda St Alta Loma CA 91737-1755 Office: Law Offices of Henry Klein 10427 Vivienda St Alta Loma CA 91737-1755 E-mail: henrykleinlaw@aol.com.

KLEIN, HENRY, architect; b. Cham, Germany, Sept. 6, 1920; came to U.S., 1939; s. Fred and Hedwig (Weiskopf) K.; m. Phyllis Harvey, Dec. 27, 1952; children: Vincent, Paul, David. Student, Inst. Rauch, Lausanne, Switzerland, 1936-38; BArch, Cornell U., 1943. Registered architect, Oreg., Wash. Designer Office of Pietro Belluschi, Architect, Portland, Oreg., 1948-51; architect Henry Klein & Assoc., Architects, Mt. Vernon, Wash., 1952—78; pvt. practice architect Henry Klein Partnership, 1978—. Bd. dirs. Wash. Pks. Found., Seattle, 1977-92, Mus. N.W. Art, 1988-95. With U.S. Army, 1943-46. Recipient Louis Sullivan award Internat. Union Bricklayers and Allied Craftsmen, 1981; Presdl. Design award Nat. Endowment Arts, 1988; George A. and Eliza Howard Found. fellow. Fellow AIA (Seattle chpt. medal 1995). Jewish. Home: 21625 Little Mountain Rd Mount Vernon WA 98274-8003 Office: Henry Klein Partnership 314 Pine St Mount Vernon WA 98273-3852

KLEIN, HERBERT GEORGE, newspaper editor; b. LA, Apr. 1, 1918; s. George and Amy (Cordes) K.; m. Marjorie Galbraith, Nov. 1, 1941; children: Joanne L. (Mrs. Robert Mayne), Patricia A. (Mrs. John Root). AB, U. So. Calif., 1940; PhD (hon.), U. San Diego, 1989, U. So. Calif., 2006. Reporter Alhambra (Calif.) Post-Advocate, 1940-42, news editor, 1946-50; spl. corr. Copley Newspapers, 1946-50, Washington corr., 1950; with San Diego Union, 1950-68, editl. writer, 1950-52, editl. page editor, 1952-56, assoc. editor, 1956-57, exec. editor, 1957-58, editor, 1959-68; mgr. comm. Nixon for Pres. Campaign, 1968-69; dir. comm. Exec. Br., U.S. Govt., 1969-73; v.p. corp. rels. Metromedia, Inc., 1973-77; media cons., 1977-80; editor-in-chief, v.p. Copley Newspapers, Inc., San Diego, 1980—2003; nat. fellow Am. Enterprise Inst., 2004—; cons. Copley Newspapers, Inc., San Diego, 2004—. Publicity dir. Eisenhower-Nixon campaign in Calif., 1952; asst. press sec. V.P. Nixon campaign, 1956; press sec. Nixon campaign, 1958; spl. asst., press sec. to Nixon, 1959-61; press sec. Nixon Gov. campaign, 1962; dir. comm. Nixon presdl. campaign, 1968; mem. Advt. Coun., N.Y. Author: Making It Perfectly Clear, 1980. Trustee U. So. Calif.; past chmn. Holiday Bowl; bd. dirs. Greater San Diego Internat. Sports Coun.; mem. com. Super Bowls XXII, XXIII, and XXXVII; active Olympic Tng. Site Com.; trustee U. So. Calif.; trustee U. Calif. San Diego Found; bd. dirs. San Diego Econ. Devel. Com. With USNR, 1942-46; comdr. Res. Recipient Fourth Estate award U. So. Calif., 1947, Alumnus of Yr. award U. So. Calif., 1971, Gen. Alumni Merit award, 1977, Spl. Svc. to Journalism award, 1969, Headliner of Yr. award L.A. Press Club, 1971, San Diego State U. First Fourth Estate award, 1986, Golden Man award Boys and Girls Club, 1994, Newspaper Exec. of Yr. award Calif. Press Assn., 1994; named Cmty. Champion, Hall of Champions, 1993, Mr. San Diego, 2001. Fellow Am. Enterprise Inst.; mem. Am. Soc. Newspaper Editors (past dir.), Calif. Press Assn., Pub. Rels. Seminar, Gen. Alumni U. So. Calif. (past pres.), Alhambra Jr. C. of C. (past pres.), Greater San Diego C. of C. (mem. exec. com.), Bohemian Club, Fairbanks Country Club, Kiwanis, Rotary (hon.), Sigma Delta Chi (chmn. nat. com., chmn. gen. activities nat. conv. 1958), Scripps Inst. (dir.'s cabinet Oceanography), Delta Chi. Presbyterian. Home: 3890 Nobel Dr Apt 407 San Diego CA 92122 Office: 1855 First Ave Ste 300A San Diego CA 92101-2685 Office Phone: 619-702-1141. Office Fax: 619-702-1145. Business E-Mail: hklein@sandiegocoxmail.com. *As I look back on a lifetime in journalism and politics, the thesis which has most effected my career has been a desire to be a thoughtful "man in the arena". To leave a legacy, you cannot be bland. I believe one must develop a philosophy endowed with principle which allows him to take a stand, popular or not, on issues in which he or she believes.*

KLEIN, HOWARD BRUCE, lawyer, educator; b. Pitts., Feb. 28, 1950; s. Elmer and Natalie (Rosenzweig) K.; m. Lonnie Jean Wilets, Dec. 12, 1977; children: Zachary B., Eli H. Student, Northwestern U., 1968-69; BA, U. Wis., 1972; JD, Georgetown U., 1976. Bar: Wis. 1976, Pa. 1981, U.S. Ct. Appeals D.C., 1978, U.S. Dist. Ct. Pa. 1981, U.S. Ct. Appeals (3rd cir.) 1982, U.S. Supreme Ct. 1983. Law clk. to justice Robert Hansen Wis. Supreme Ct., Madison, 1976-77; asst. atty. gen. dept. justice State of Wis., 1977-80; chief criminal divsn. U.S. Atty.'s Office, Phila., 1980-87; ptnr. Blank, Rome LLP, Phila., 1987-96, chmn. litigation dept., 1991-94; prin. Law Offices of Howard Bruce Klein PC, Phila., 1996—; dir. in house tng. Am. Law Inst.-ABA, 1996—. Regional, nat. instr. Nat. Inst. Trial Advocacy, Phila. and Boulder, Colo., 1987-98; adj. prof. evidence and trial advocacy Temple U. Law Sch., 1984—; instr. Atty. Gen. Advocacy Inst., Washington, 1983-87; lectr. pub. corruption and trial advocacy; cons. Pa. Valley Neighborhood Assn., 1984—. Contbr. to profl. jours. Advisor Phila. Police Dept. Reform Commn., 1986—; campaign issues dir. Pa. Atty. Gen. campaign, Phila., 1988, 92; bd. dirs. Citizens Crime Commn. Delaware Valley, Phila. Mem. Fed. Bar Assn. (chmn. criminal law com.), Phila. Bar Assn., Wis. Bar Assn., D.C. Bar Assn., U.S. Attys. Alumni Assn. (co-founder, exec. bd.), Vesper Club (Phila.). Democrat. Jewish. Avocations: golf, basketball, hiking. Office: Ste 3025 1700 Market St Philadelphia PA 19103-3903 Office Phone: 215-972-1411. Business E-Mail: klein@hbklein.com.

KLEIN, IRWIN GRANT, lawyer; b. Bklyn., June 6, 1949; s. Melvin Morton and Gladys (Mandel) K.; m. Charlene Elena Perez, July 31, 1988; children: Robert Matthew Perez, Gabriella Margaux Perez. BS, U. Wis., 1971; JD, Vt. Law Sch., 1977. Bar: N.Y., 1977, U.S. Dist. Ct. (so. & ea. dist.) N.Y., 1977, Vt., 1977, U.S. Supreme Ct., 1988. Assoc. atty. Hein, Waters, Klein & Zurkow, Far Rockaway, N.Y., 1977-78; asst. dist. atty. Queens County Dist. Atty., Kew Gardens, N.Y., 1979-82; ptnr. Hein, Waters & Klein, Cedarhurst, NY, 1982—89, Lapp & Klein, Cedarhurst, 1989-91, Hein, Waters & Klein, Cedarhurst, 1991—. Mem. Vt. Law Rev., N.Y. State Defenders Assn., N.Y. State Bar Assn., Nassau County Bar Assn., Queens County Bar Assn., Phi Delta Phi. Office: Hein Waters & Klein 123 Grove Ave Cedarhurst NY 11516-2302 E-mail: igkny@earthlink.net.

KLEIN, JAMES EDGAR, actor; b. Beach Grove, Ind., Feb. 22, 1932; s. Charles Raymond and Edna Marie (Pollack) K.; m. Phyliss Dawn Schneider, Nov. 8, 1952; children: Timson, James Jr., Peggy, Daniel, Andrew, Mary, Jon. Lectr. in field; judge Nat. Prospectors and Treasure Convention, 1989-90. Appeared in films (as James Kline) Coming Home, 1978, Comes A Horseman, 1979, Electric Horseman, 1980, China Syndrome, 1981, Tom Horn, 1982, Weekend in the Country, 1997, It's My Party, 1997, City of Angels, 1998, various other films, TV programs, comms.; screenwriter, exec. prodr., actor motion picture Father Dad; author (as James Klein): Where to Find Gold in Southern California, 1975, Where to Find Gold in the Desert, 1977, Where to Find Gold in Nevada, 1985, How to Find Gold, 1997, Gold Rush (childrens), 1998, Follow the Padres (childrens), 1999; other mag. articles and short stories. With U.S. Army, 1952-53. Recipient Cert. of Achievement, Am. Cancer Soc., 1977, Disneyland, 1983, City of Anaheim, 1984, also various schs. Office Phone: 818-769-9111. Personal E-mail: jklein49er@juno.com.

KLEIN, JASON EVAN, publishing executive; b. NYC, May 11, 1960; s. William Louis and Bernice Carol (Tick) K.; m. Robin Fern Nash, July 23, 1989; children: Michael Louis, Jill Lauren. AB, Dartmouth Coll., 1982; MBA, Harvard U., 1986. Assoc. cons. Bain & Co., Palo Alto, Calif., 1982-84; sr. engagement mgr. McKinsey & Co., NYC, 1986-93; dir. strategy Times Mirror, NYC, 1993-95; pres., group pub. Field & Stream/Outdoor Life and Today's Homeowner, NYC, 1995—99; pres., CEO, Times Mirror Mags., NYC, 1999—2001, Healthy Living Media, NYC, 2001—03, Newspaper Nat. Network, NYC, 2003—. Mem. editl. bd.: Dartmouth Alumni Mag. Trustee N.Y.C. Police Found.; bd. dirs. Am. Advt. Found.; bd. dirs. emeritus Recreation Roundtable. Mem. Phi Beta Kappa. Office: Newspaper Nat Network 20 W 33d St 7th Fl New York NY 10001 Business E-Mail: jklein@mba1986.hbs.edu.

KLEIN, JEFFREY PETER, investor; b. NYC, June 29, 1943; s. Seymour M. and Ruth (Liberman) Klein. BA, Colgate U., 1965; MBA, Columbia U., 1967. Exec. Mr. Ephram, Inc., NYC, 1967—69; account exec. Thomson-Leeds Co., 1969—79; officer M.K.B. Group, Inc., NYC, 1979—2000. Trustee, com. chmn. Collegiate Sch., NYC, 1976—85, 1991—98, pres. bd. trustees, 1994—98; bd. dirs., com. chmn. 92d St. YMHA, 1980—; chmn. bd. dirs. NY Chamber Symphony, 1993—2002; pres. Bertha & Isaac Liberman Found., 1983—. Mem.: Mus. Modern Art, Conservation Com., Contemporary Arts Coun., Arch. and Design Com., Colgate Club (N.Y.C.), Harmonie Club (bd. dirs. exec. com. 2002—), Sunningdale Country Club (Scarsdale, N.Y.) (bd. dirs. 1980—85). Avocations: golf, photography, travel, reading. Home: 480 Park Ave New York NY 10022-1613 Office: 200 Park Ave S Ste 1311 New York NY 10003-1503 Personal E-mail: jpk480@aol.com.

KLEIN, JEFFREY S., lawyer, media executive; b. LA, Apr. 15, 1953; s. Norman and Shirlee Klein; m. Karyn Kitson, Sept. 29, 1984; 3 children. BA suma cum laude, Claremont Mens Coll., 1975; M in Journalism, Columbia U., 1978; JD, Stanford U., 1980. Assoc. Kaplan, Livingston, Goodwin, Berkowitz & Selvin, Beverly Hills, Calif., 1980-81, Garey, Mason & Sloane, Santa Monica, Calif., 1981-83; weekly contbr. UPI-Radio, LA, 1983-84; sr. staff counsel Times Mirror, 1983-87, asst. to pres., 1987-90; asst. to pub. L.A. Times, 1989-91; pres. L.A. Times Valley and Ventura County edits., 1991-96; v.p. L.A. Times, 1991-96, sr. v.p. consumer mktg., 1996-97, sr. v.p., gen. mgr. news, 1997-98; pres., COO 101 Comms. LLC, 1999—2001, CEO, 2002—06; chmn. bd. 1105 Media, 2006—07. Pres., CEO Calif. Cmty. News Corp., 1995-97; adj. prof. journalism U. So. Calif., 1985-87, 2002; adv. Gov. Bruce Babbitt, Phoenix, 1980. Author: (weekly column) Legal View, L.A. Times, 1985-93, various book revs.; columnist: Folio mag., 2004-05; contbr. Online Journalism Rev., 1999, Columbia Journalism Rev., 2000. Bd. dirs. Meet Each Need With Dignity, Gould Ctr. for Humanities, Claremont McKenna Coll. Recipient Angel award Vol. League of San Fernando Valley, Disting. Cmty. Svc. award Anti-Defamation League, 1994, Visionary award United Way North Angeles Region, 1995, Premiere Parents award March of Dimes, 1996. Mem. Calif. Bar Assn. Office: 101 Comm 9121 Oakdale Ave Ste 101 Chatsworth CA 91311-6517

KLEIN, JERRY EMANUEL, insurance planning and financial planning executive; b. Cin., Apr. 4, 1933; s. Milton H. and Ida S. (Dunsker) K.; m. Arlene Ruth Rosen, July 3, 1957 (dec. Nov. 1974); children: Marjorie (dec. Sept. 2005), Bradley, Amy; m. Nancy Cohen Hahn, Aug. 7, 1982. BMech. Engring., Cornell U., 1956; MBA, Ohio State U., 1959. CLU, ChFC. Fin. engring. Avco Electronics, Cin., 1959-61; fin. rep. Northwestern Mut. of Milw., Cin., 1961—. Vice chmn. Am. Jewish Com., 1978; pres. Social Health Assn., 1964—66; bd. dirs. Jewish Vocat. Svc., 1964—92, pres., 1978—80, Cancer Family Care, 1981—83; chmn. fin. com. Jewish Fedn., 1981—83, treas., mem. exec. com., 1981—84; bd. dirs. Children Psychiat. Ctr., 1973—86, Jewish Family Svc., 1984—94, Cin. Jewish Fedn., 1972—92, Halom Ho., 1992, treas., 1998—; chmn. HILB Scholarship Com., 1985—; bd. dirs. Radio Reading Svc., 1997, Cin. Assn. Blind, 1999—, TriCounty Parkinson Wellness Assn., 2004—05. 1st lt. USAF, 1956—58. Recipient Kate S. Mack award Jewish Fedn., 1975, Human Rels. award NCCJ, 1992. Mem. Million Dollar Round Table (life), Nat. Assn. Life Underwriters, Estate Planning Coun. Cin., Assn. CLUs. Jewish. Office: Northwestern Mut Fin Network Rookwood Tower 2d Fl 3805 Edwards Rd Cincinnati OH 45209 Office Phone: 513-366-3667.

KLEIN, JOEL IRWIN, school system administrator; b. NYC, Oct. 25, 1946; s. Charles Samuel and Claire (Hofstein) K.; m. Linda Kay Davis, June 26, 1971 (div. May 1977); m. Harriet Howard Davis, Mar. 8, 1980; 1 child, Julia. BA magna cum laude, Columbia Coll., 1967; JD magna cum laude, Harvard U., 1971. Rsch. asst. Ctr. for Advance Study of Behavior Scis. Stanford U., 1971-72; Fredrick Sheldon traveling fellow Harvard U., 1972-73; law clk. U.S. Ct. Appeals, D.C. cir., 1973-74, U.S. Supreme Ct., 1974-75; with Mental Health Law Project, Washington, 1975-76; mem. Rogovin, Stern & Huge, Washington, 1976-81; ptnr. Klein, Farr, Smith & Taranto, Washington, 1981-93; dep. counsel to pres. Exec. Office of the Pres., Washington, 1993-95; prin. dep. asst. atty. gen. antitrust div., U.S. Dept. Justice, Washington, 1995—96, acting asst. atty. gen., 1996—97, asst. atty. gen., antitrust div., 1997—2001; chmn., CEO Bertelsmann, Inc., 2001—02; chancellor NYC Dept. Edn., 2002—. Vis. and adj. prof. law Georgetown U. Law Ctr., 1987—; lectr. Stanford U. Law Sch., 1972; treas. World Fedn. Mental Health, 1985-87. Contbr. articles and book revs. to profl. jours. Mem. U.S. Dept. of State, Office of Human Rights, Delegation to Rev. Psychiat. Abuse in the Former Soviet Union, 1989; active D.C. Big Bros. program, 1990—; mem., ex-officio mem., chairperson. The Green Door, 1976—. Named one of NY Influentials, NY Mag., 2006; recipient Vol. Recognition award Nat. Assn. Attys. Gen., 1993, Isaac Ray award Am. Psychiat. Assn., 1994. Mem. ABA, Am. Law Inst., Am. Psychiat. Assn. Avocations: tennis, reading. Office: NYC Dept Edn 52 Chambers St New York NY 10007*

KLEIN, JOHN JACOB, retired economist; b. Chgo., Aug. 30, 1929; s. John and Mathilda (Keller) K.; m. Sylvia Elvine Knauss, Nov. 25, 1953; children: Leslie Klein Funk. BA cum laude, Northwestern U., 1950; MA, U. Chgo., 1952, PhD, 1955. Asst. prof. econs. Okla. State U., Stillwater, 1957-60; assoc. prof. econs. Fordham U., NYC, 1960-67; prof. econs. Ga. State U., Atlanta, 1967—94, prof. econs. emeritus, 1994—. Author: (with M. Friedman) Studies in the Quantity Theory of Money, 1956, (with Leftwich, Trenton, Poole) The Oklahoma Economy, 1963; author: Money and the Economy, 6th edit. 1986; contbr. articles to profl. jours. With U.S. Army, 1955-57. Mem. Am. Econ. Assn., So. Econ. Assn., Phi Beta Kappa, Pi Mu Epsilon. Republican. Avocation: music. Home: 855 Oakhaven Dr Roswell GA 30075-1248

KLEIN, JONATHAN, broadcast executive; BA magna cum laude, Brown U., 1990. News writer, editor CBS Nightwatch; exec. v.p. CBS News, 1996—98; founder, CEO FeedRoom Inc., 1999—2004; pres. CNN/U.S., 2004—. Prodr.: CBS Morning News, CBS Weekend News, 48 Hours, Coast to Coast, Public Eye with Bryant Gumbel; writer: (TV films) The Buffalo Soldiers, 1997; writer, dir., prodr. Before Your Eyes: One Last Chance, 1998. Recipient 2 Peabody awards, 3 Emmy awards. Office: CNN One CNN Ctr Atlanta GA 30303 Office Phone: 404-827-1500.

KLEIN, JONATHAN D., finance company executive; Various Hambros Bank Ltd., 1983-93; co-founder Getty Investment Holdings L.L.C., 1993-95; joint chmn., co-founder Getty Commns. plc, 1995-96, CEO, dir., 1996-98; co-founder, CEO, dir. Getty Images, 1998—. Dir. Hambros Bank Ltd., 1989-98; bd. dir. Getty Investments L.L.C., A Contemporary Theatre, Realnetworks. Office: Getty Images 601 N 34th St Seattle WA 98103

KLEIN, JOSEPH MARK, retired mining executive; b. NYC, Nov. 9, 1921; s. Erwin Wolffe and Ada (Black) K.; m. Betty Evelyn Northington, Dec. 24, 1948; children: Kathryn Ann Zornes (dec.), Elizabeth Ellen Scahill, Joseph Mark, Jr., Timothy Northington. Certificate in fgn. trade, Am. Grad Sch. Internat. Mgmt., 1947; D Internat Laws (hon.), Thunderbird Am. Grad. Sch. Internat. Mgnt., 1993. Vice pres. internat. ops. Clary Corp., San Gabriel, Calif., 1948-60, dir., 1967-70; dir. internat. ops. Remington Rand Corp., NYC, 1961-62; pres. NBC Internat. Ltd.; v.p. NBC News, NYC, 1962-66; exec. v.p., dir. Cyprus Mines Corp., Los Angeles, 1966-79; chmn. bd. Hawaiian Cement Corp., 1969-79; ret. pres., dir. Pluess-Staufer Industries, Inc., Los Angeles, 1979-91, sr. fin. cons., bd. dirs., 1991-99. Dir. Mission Ins. Group, Inc.; mem. Pres. Export Expansion Council, 1971-74; vice-chmn. bd. trustees Thunderbird Am. Grad. Sch. Internat. Mgmt., 1975-83, chmn. bd. trustees, 1983-88 Served pvt. to capt. U.S. Army, 1940-46. Decorated Silver Star, Bronze Star with oak leaf cluster, Purple Heart, Combat Inf. Badge, Croix de Guerre; recipient Jonas B. Mayer Outstanding Alumni award, Thunderbird Am. Grad. Sch. Internat. Mgmt., 1974, So. Calif. Alumni Assn. award, 1974. Mem. AIME, The Ret. Officers Assn. (pres. dir. west L.A. area chpt.), Town Hall, Mil. Order Purple Heart (comdr. Ariz. 1949-50, Hollywood chpt. 1987-88), Am. Legion (post comdr. 1990-91, trustee 1991—2004), Elks. Republican. Presbyterian. Home: 718 Calle Mandarinas Thousand Oaks CA 91360-2222 Home Phone: 805-375-6181. Personal E-mail: jmk6500@aol.com.

KLEIN, JULIA MEREDITH, freelance journalist; b. Phila., Dec. 11, 1955; d. Abraham and Murielle (Pollack) Klein. BA magna cum laude, Harvard U., 1977. Copy editor J.B. Lippincott, Phila., 1977; features reporter The Oakland Press, Pontiac, Mich., 1978; reporter, critic and editor The Phila. Inquirer, 1983-2000. Nat. Arts Journalism Program fellow, 1996-97, John J. McCloy fellow in journalism, 1998, Alicia Patterson Found. fellow, 2000, Western Knight Ctr. fellow for Specialized Journalism, 2001; Fulbright German Studies Seminar, 2004. Mem. Soc. Profl. Journalists (2d pl. award for criticism 1998, 2003, 3d pl. award for criticism 1999, 1st pl. award for criticism 2006), Am. Soc. Journalists and Authors, N.Am. Travel Journalists Assn., Journalism and Women Symposium, Nat. Book Critics Cir., Phi Beta Kappa Home and Office: 307 Monroe St Philadelphia PA 19147-3211 Home Phone: 215-733-0761; Office Phone: 215-733-0761. Personal E-mail: julklein@verizon.net.

KLEIN, LAURA COLIN, publishing executive; With Levine, Huntley, Schmidt & Beaver Advt., NYC, 1985—86; nat. sales mgr. Andrew's Mag., 1986—89; acct. mgr. ELLE Mag., 1989—92; Ea. sales mgr. Woman's Day, NYC, 1992—96, v.p., ad dir., 1996—2000, v.p., pub., 2002—; pub. Family Life, 2000. Office: Womans Day Mag Hachette Filipacchi Mags Inc 1633 Broadway 42d Fl New York NY 10019 Office Phone: 212-767-6000. Office Fax: 212-767-5610.*

KLEIN, LAWRENCE ALLEN, finance educator; b. Harrisburg, Pa., Jan. 14, 1946; s. Samuel Edward and Ella Violet (Loeb) K. AB, Franklin and Marshall Coll., 1969; MBA, Pa. State U., 1974, PhD, 1978. Adminstrv. asst. dept. acctg. and mgmt. info. sys. Pa. State U., State College, 1975-76; asst. prof. acctg. U. Houston, 1978-79, U. Wyo., Laramie, 1982-84; asst. prof. bus. adminstrn. Franklin and Marshall Coll., Lancaster, Pa., 1979-82; assoc. prof. accountancy Bentley Coll., Waltham, Mass., 1984—. Vis. prof. econ. and mgmt. Vesalius Coll., Brussels, 1996; presenter in field. Author study guides for books in field; co-editor conf. procs., 1976. Program/conf. coord. N.E. Am. Acctg. Assn., State College, 1976; small bus. coun. Laramie Area C. of C., 1973-74. With USAF, 1969-70. Grantee Am. Acctg. Assn., Hasking & Sells Found. Mem. AAUP, NRA (life), AARP, Nat. Retired Tchrs. Assn., Inst. Mgmt. Accts. (I. Wayne Keller award, Ray E. Longnecker award 1980, Cert. Merit Manuscript award), Am. Acctg. Assn. (Sectional Best Paper award 1987), Decision Scis. Internat. (chmn. acctg. track N.E. sect. 1992), Mass. Soc. CPAs (acad. assoc.), Am. Legion (life), Am. Inst. Physics, U.S. Golf Assn., U.S. Tennis Assn. (life), Elks (permanent benefactor), Marine Meml. Club (perpetual benefactor), Jewish War Vets. (life), Beta Gamma Sigma, Beta Alpha Psi, Omicron Delta Kappa. Republican. Jewish. Avocations: tennis, golf, reading, swimming. Home: 521 Katahdin Dr Lexington MA 02421-6452 Office Phone: 781-891-2776. E-mail: lklein@bentley.edu.

KLEIN, LAWRENCE ROBERT, economist, educator; b. Omaha, Sept. 14, 1920; s. Leo Byron and Blanche (Monheit) Klein; m. Sonia Adelson, Feb. 15, 1947; children: Hannah, Rebecca, Rachel, Jonathan. BA, U. Calif.-Berkeley, 1942; PhD, MIT, 1944; MA, Lincoln Coll., Oxford U., 1957; LLD (hon.), U. Mich., 1977, Dickinson Coll., 1981; ScD (hon.), Widener Coll., 1977, Elizabethtown Coll., 1981, Ball State U., 1982, Technion, 1981, U. Nebr., 1983; D (hon.), U. Vienna, 1977; EdD, Villanova U., 1978; D (hon.), Bonn U., 1974, Free U. Brussels, 1979, U. Paris, 1979, U. Madrid, 1980; DSc, Nat. Central Univ. Taiwan, 1985; DHC, So. Helsinki Sch. Econs., 1986; Dr. Humane Letters, Bard Coll., 1986, Bilkent U., 1989, St. Norbert Coll., 1989; DHC, Univ. Lodz, 1990; D. Litt, Univ. Glasgow, 1991; DSc, Rutgers U., 1992; PhD (hon.), Bar Ilan U., 1994; D. honors (hon.), Carleton Univ., 1997; DHC, U. Piraeus, 1999, Acad. Economic Studies, Romania, 1999, U Toronto, 2002, Konan U., Japan, 2002, Keio U., 2002, U del Estaod de Mex., 2004, U. Costa Rica, 2005, U. Slovenia, 2005; LLD (hon.), U. Pa., 2006. Faculty U. Chgo., 1944—47; research assoc. Nat. Bur. Econ. Research, 1948—50; faculty U. Mich., 1949—54; research assoc. Survey Research Center, 1949—54, Oxford Inst. Stats., 1954—58; faculty U. Pa., Phila., 1958—, prof., 1958—, Univ. prof., 1964—, Benjamin Franklin prof., 1968—, prof. emeritus; vis. prof. Osaka U., Japan, 1960, U. Colo., 1962, CUNY, 1962-63, 82, Hebrew U., 1964, Princeton U., 1966, Stanford U., 1968, U. Copenhagen, 1974; Ford vis. prof. U. Calif. at Berkeley, 1968, Inst. for Advanced Studies, Vienna, 1970, 74; hon. prof. Shanghai Jiao Tong Univ., 1984; honorary prof. Nankai Univ., 1993, Shanghai Acad. Soc. Sci., 1994; dir. and chmn. econ. policy com. W.P. Carey & Co., 1984—; adv. State Information Ctr., Beijing, 1992—; hon. chmn. Pa. Inst. for Econ. Rsch. Adv. Bd., 2002—. Cons. Can. Govt., 1947, UNCTAD, 1966, 75, 77, 80, McMillan Co., 1965—74, E.I. du Pont de Nemours, 1966—68, State of N.Y., 1969, AT&T, 1969, Fed. Res. Bd., 1973, UNIDO, 1973—75, Congl. Budget Office,

1977—, Coun. Econ. Advisers, 1977—80; chmn. bd. trustees Wharton Econometric Forecasting Assocs., Inc., 1969—80, chmn. profl. bd., 1980—; trustee Maurice Falk Inst. for Econ. Rsch., Israel, 1969—75; adv. coun. Inst. Advanced Studies, Vienna, 1977—; chmn. econ. adv. com. Gov. of Pa., 1976—78; mem. com. on prices Fed. Res. Bd., 1968—70; prin. investigator econometric model project Brookings Instn., 1963—72, Project LINK, 1968—; sr. adviser Brookings Panel on Econ. Activity, 1970—; mem. adv. com. Inst. Internat. Econs., 1983; hon. mem. Chinese Bd. Soc. Scis., 1997, Romanian Acad., 1999—; coord. Jimmy Carter's Econ. Task Force, 1976; mem. adv. bd. Strategic Studies Ctr., Stanford Rsch. Inst., 1974—76; corr. fellow Brit. Acad., 1991—. Author: The Keynesian Revolution, 1947, Textbook of Econometrics, 1953, An Econometric Model of the United States, 1929-1952, 1955, Wharton Econometric Forecasting Model, 1967, Essay on the Theory of Economic Prediction, 1968, An Introduction to Econometric Forecasting and Forecasting Models, 1980; author, editor: Brookings Quar. Econometric Model of U.S., Ecometric Model Performance, 1976, Lectures in Econmetrics, 1983; editor: Internat. Econ. Rev., 1959—65; assoc. editor:, mem. editl. bd.: Empirical Econs., 1976—. Recipient William F. Butler award, N.Y. Assn. Bus. Economists, 1975, Golden Slipper Club award, 1977, Pres.'s medal, U. Pa., 1980, Alfred Nobel Meml. prize in econs., 1980; hon. fellow, Lincoln Coll., Oxford U., 2004. Fellow: Nat. Assn. Bus. Economists, Am. Acad. Arts and Scis., Econometric Soc. (past pres.), Brit. Acad. (corr.); mem.: NAS, Russian Acad. Sci. (fgn.), Ea. Econ. Assn. (pres. 1974—76), Am. Econ. Assn. (exec. com. 1966—68, pres. 1977, John Bates Clark medalist 1959), Social Sci. Rsch. Coun. (fellow 1945—46, 1947—48, com. econ. stability, dir. 1971—76), Am. Philos. Soc. Achievements include creation of econometric models and the application to the analysis of economic fluctuations and economic policies. Office: U Pa Mc Neil Bldg Rm 335 3718 Locust Walk Philadelphia PA 19104-6209 Address: WP Carey 50 Rockefeller Plaza New York NY 10020

KLEIN, LINDA ANN, lawyer; d. Gerald Ira Klein and Sandra Florence Fishman; m. Michael S. Neuren. BA cum laude, Union Coll., 1980; JD, Washington and Lee U., Lexington, Va., 1983. Bar: Ga. 1983, DC 1984, US Dist. Ct. (no. and mid. dist.) Ga. 1985, US Ct. Appeals (11th cir.) 1986. Assoc. Nall & Miller, Atlanta, 1983—86, Martin, Cavan & Andersen, Atlanta, 1986—90, ptnr., 1990—93; mng. ptnr. Gambrell & Stolz, 1993—. Instr. Nat. Ctr. Paralegal Tng., Atlanta, 1986 Mem.: ABA (editor Trial Techniques newsletter 1989, vice chmn. trial techniques com. 1989—90, chair 1991—92, vice chair fidelity and surety com. 1994—97, chair ann. meeting 1996—97, coun. tort and ins. practice sect. 1998—2005, ho. of dels. 1998—, chair tort and ins. practice sect. 2003—04, chair com. rules & calendar 2006—, chair coalition for justice 2006—, Margaret Brent Women Lawyers of Achievement award 2004), Am. Law Inst., Coun. of Superior Cts. Judges (ex-officio uniform rules com.), Atlanta Bar Assn. (chair commn. on uniform rules of ct. 1986, bd. dirs. Atlanta Coun. on Young Lawyers 1986—89), Inst. for CLE (chair Ga. br. 1998—2000), Nat. Conf. Bar Pres. (exec. coun. 1998—2001), State Bar of Ga. (chair study com. on rules of practice 1987—94, bd. govs. 1989—, exec. com. 1992—99, sec. 1994—96, pres. 1997—98, vice chair profl. liability com.), Pi Sigma Alpha, Phi Alpha Delta. Office Phone: 404-577-6000. Business E-Mail: lklein@gambrell.com.

KLEIN, LLOYD WILLIAM, cardiologist, researcher; b. NYC, Sept. 29, 1952; s. Julian and Zali (Heimlich) K.; m. Barbara Joyce Visocan, Sept. 4, 1982; children: Laura, Jenny. AB cum laude with honors in Chemistry, Kenyon Coll., 1973; MD, U. Cin., 1977. Diplomate Am. Bd. Internal Medicine with subspecialty in cardiovascular disease, Nat. Bd. Med. Examiners; cert. Interventional Cardiology, 1997. Intern/resident Albert Einstein Coll. Medicine/Bronx Mcpl. Hosp. Ctr., 1977-80; clin. fellow in cardiology Mt. Sinai Med. Ctr./CCNY, NYC, 1980-82; attending physician emergency rm. Bronx Mcpl. Hosp. Ctr., 1980-83; assoc. dir. cardiac catheterization labs. Phila. Heart Inst./Presbyn.-U. Pa. Med. Ctr., 1983-88; dir. interventional cardiology, dir. rsch./edn. Cardiac Catheterization Labs., Northwestern Meml. Hosp., Chgo., 1988-90; dir. divsn. cardiology VA Lakeside Med. Ctr., Chgo., 1989-90; med. dir. Rush Heart Inst./Oak Park Hosp./Rush Sys. for Health, Oak Park, Ill., 1998—2001; dir. interventional cardiology Rush-Presbyn.-St. Luke's Med. Ctr., Chgo., 1990—2001, co-dir. Cardiac Catheterization Labs., 1990—2004, assoc. dir. cardiology sect., dir. clin. svcs., 2001—04; dir. rsch. Gottlieb Meml. Hosp., Melrose Pk., Ill., 2004—, dir. prof. devel., 2004—. Instr. medicine, clin. assoc. cardiology Mt. Sinai Sch. Medicine/CCNY, 1982-83; asst. prof. clin. medicine U. Pa., Phila., 1983-88; assoc. prof. medicine Northwestern U., Chgo., 1988-90, Rush U. Med. Sch., Chgo., 1990-97, prof., 1997—. Editor: Quick Reference to Internal Medicine, 1994, Coronary Stenosis Morphology: Analysis and Clinical Implication, 1997, Resource Utilization in cardiac Disease, 1998; contbr. numerous articles and abstracts to profl. jours., chpts. to books; editl. review cons. Annals of Internal Medicine, Circulation, Am. Heart Jour., Archives of Internal Medicine, Jour. of Heart and Lun Transplantation, Critical Care Medicine, Chest; editl. bd. Jour. Am. Coll. Cardiology, 1990-94, 95-98, 2000-04, Am. Jour. Cardiology, 1989—, Catheterization and Cardiovascular Diagnosis, 1994—, Cardiac Chronicle, 1990-94, Cardiovascular Therapeutics, 1997; contbg. editor: Year Book of Critical Care Medicine, 1990-94; assoc. editor Jour. Invasive Cardiology, 2001— Mem. Tobacco Free Ill. Named One of Best Cardiologists in Chgo., Chgo. Mag., 1995, 2004, 06; recipient award Am. Chem. Soc., AMA Physician's Recognition award; George Gund scholar; grantee N.Y. Heart Found., 1982-83, Am. Heart Assn. Southeastern Pa., 1984-85, ADAC Labs., Inc., 1985-87, Glaxo Inc. G.B., 1986-87, Philips, Inc., 1990-92, Boston Sci., Inc., 1990-92, Baxter, Inc., 1994-96, Rush U. Com. on Rsch., 1996-98, SmithKlein, 1997-2000, Robert Wood Johnson Found., 1994-98. Fellow ACP, Am. Coll. Cardiology (mem. database com., database devel. and outcomes assessment subcom. 1996—, Ill. chpt. bd. councilors 1997-2006, mem. program com. 1995-2005, rsch. presentation evaluation com. 1995-2004), Coun. on Clin. Cardiology of Am. Heart Assn., Soc. for Cardiac Angiography and Interventions (registry, program and interventional cardiology com. 1995—, chair 2000—), Coun. on Circulation of Am. Heart Assn.; mem. Am. Fedn. Clin. Rsch., Am. Heart Assn. of Met. Chgo. (chmn. tobacco issues com. 1993-96, pub. policy and gove. rels. com. 1991-2004, vice chair 1995-97), Am. Heart Assn. (West Suburban divsn. founding pres. 1998), Philander Chase Soc., Alpha Omega Alpha, Sigma Chi. Avocations: reading, skiing, chess, classical music. Office: Clinical Cardiology Assocs Gottlieb Meml Hosp Profl Bldg Room 314 701 North Ave Melrose Park IL 60160 Office Phone: 708-681-7878. Business E-Mail: lklein@rpslmc.edu. E-mail: lloydklein@comcast.net.

KLEIN, LYNN ELLEN, artist; b. San Francisco, Apr. 14, 1950; BA in Studio Arts, U. Minn., 1974, MFA in Design, 1976. Instr. art edn. U. Minn., Mpls., 1976-78, lectr. in design, 1974-84; vis. artist U. Iowa, Ames, 1984—, Textile Ctr. of Minn., 2003. Resident Cité Internat. des Arts, Paris, 1984-86, summer 1998. One-woman shows include Rochester (Minn.) Fine Arts Ctr., 1976, Northrup Gallery, U. Minn., Mpls., 1976, Allrich Gallery, San Francisco, 1982, 1988, Coffman Gallery, U. Minn., 1982, The Print Club, Phila., 1985, Foster-White Gallery, Seattle, 1989, Carolyn Ruff Gallery, Mpls., 1994, Robert Green Fine Arts, 2000, exhibited in group shows at Mpls. Inst. Arts, 1976, 1988, 2006, Franklin Inst. Sci. Mus., Phila., 1984, Minn. Mus. Art, St. Paul, 1990, Textile Arts Internat., 1990, 1992, San Francisco Bay Area Women Artists Mentors, 1994, USART San Francisco Internat. Art Expo, I. Wolk Gallery, St. Helena, Calif., 1996, Robert Green Fine Arts, Mill Valley, Calif., 1996, 2002, Craftsman's Guild and Calif. Heritage Gallery, 1998, Ren Brown Collection, Bodega Bay, Calif., 1998, Gensler Architecture-Material Matters, San Francisco, 1998, San Jose Mus. Art, Visible Rhythm, 2001, 2003, Kala Art Inst., 2002, Pyramid Atlantic Book Arts Fair, Wash., 2002, Brave New World Print Portfolio, NY Print Fair, 2004, Neomodern Calif. Abstraction Crocker Art Mus. to Monterey Mus., Sacramento, 2005, Represented in permanent collections Mpls. Inst. Arts, Oakland (Calif.) Mus., Bibliotéque Nat., Dept. des Estampes et de lá Photographie, Paris, Phila. Mus. Art, Walker Art Ctr., Mpls., Achenbach Found., Fine Arts Mus. San Francisco, San Jose Mus. Art., Calif., NY Pub. Libr., Rutgers Univ. Ctr. for Innovative Prints, Crocker Art Mus., Sacramento, San Diego Mus. Art, Libr. Congress, Washington, Toledo Mus., print publs., Double/Absent, edit. 15, 1983 (Calif. Phelan award for printmaking), Untitled, edit. 10, 1992, Wild Women Portfolio, edit. 20, 2002, Brave New World, edit. 20, 2004, commns., Miami Internat. Airport, 2000, Caesar's Palace, Las Vegas, 2001, Fairmount, Cancun, Mex., 2004, Ritz Carelton, Palm Beach, Fla., 2005, numerous others, bibliography, Memory on Cloth, 2002, exhibitions include Catalogue Raisonne, Vermillion Edits. Ltd. 1977-1992, Mpls. Inst. Arts, 2006. Recipient J.D. Phelan award World Print Coun., 1983; Minn. State Arts Bd. Grantee, 1978; Photography fellow, St. Paul, 1984; Rockefeller Found. fellow, Am. Ctr., 1984-86, Jerome Found. Printmaking fellow, Kala Inst., Berkeley, 1989; Amity Art Found. grant, Woodbridge, Conn., 2003. Mem.: Achenbach Graphic Arts Coun.

KLEIN, MARC S., editor, publishing executive; b. Feb. 16, 1949; married; 2 children. BA in Journalism, Pa. State U., 1970. Bur. chief Courier-Post, Camden, N.J., 1970-75; asst. mng. editor Phila. Bull., 1975-81; editor Jewish Exponent, Phila., 1981-83; editor, pub. Jewish Bull. of No. Calif., San Francisco, 1984—. Pub. j. the Jewish news weekly of No. Calif.; mem. exec. com. Jewish Telegraphic Agy. Past pres. Temple Israel, Alameda; former bd. dirs. Oakland-Piedmont Jewish Community Ctr. Recipient 1st place awards Phila. Press Assn., 1973, 1st place award N.J. Press Assn., 1973; Wall St. Jour. Newspaper Fund intern, fellow, 1969. Mem. Am. Jewish Press Assn. (pres.), Soc. Profl. Journalists (past bd. dirs.). Office: 225 Bush St Ste 1480 San Francisco CA 94104-4216 E-mail: marc@jweekly.com.

KLEIN, MARTIN, ocean engineering consultant; b. NYC; s. Allen and Muriel Klein. SBEE, MIT, 1962. Program mgr. sonar systems EG&G Internat., Bedford, Mass., 1962-67; pres. Klein Assocs., Inc., Salem, NH, 1968-89; cons. Andover, Mass., 1989—. Mem. mgmt. coun. Project Urquhart (Loch Ness), London, 1992-2000; mem. bd. advisors B.Engring. Tech. program U. N.H., Durham, 1988-2003; mem. adv. bd. MIT Sea Grant, Cambridge, 1989—; adv. bd. U N.H. Sea Grant, Durham, 1999-2005; bd. dir. Marine Archaeol. and Hist. Rsch. Inst., Elliot, Maine, 1990-98; pres. The Bear Trap Investment Co., 1995-96; mem. vis. com. R.S. Peabody Mus. Archaeology, 1995-98; assoc. mem. Adv. Coun. Underwater Archaeology, 1992-2002. Contbr. articles to mags. Mem. min. search com., publicity dir. Unitarian Universalist Ch., Andover, 1990-91, chair publicity com., 1991-93; trustee Andover Pub. Libr., 1992-98; founding dir. Parent-to-Parent, Andover, 1989-91; mem. collections com. MIT Mus., 2002—. Named to A.B. Davis H.S. Hall of Fame, Mt. Vernon, NY, 1984; recipient Small Bus. Person of Yr. award, SBA, 1983, Merit award, Soc. Hist. Archeology, 2003, Compass Disting. Achievement award, Marine Tech. Soc., IEEE, 2007. Fellow Marine Tech. Soc. (dir. budget and fin. 1991-93, chair fellows com. 1998-99), Explorers Club (emeritus); mem. IEEE (life, Disting. Achievement award 2006), NAE, Instrument Soc. Am. (sr. life), Acoustical Soc. Am., Am. Bonsai Soc. (v.p. 1993-95, pres. 1995-97). Achievements include patents in field; development of first commercially successful side scan sonar; designed and manufactured sonar that helped locate most famous shipwrecks, including Titanic; found famed Loch Ness Wellington bomber; design of first side scan sonar for deep submersible. E-mail: nielk@aol.com.

KLEIN, MARTIN I., lawyer; b. NYC, Nov. 12, 1947; m. Diane Levbarg. BA, Lehigh U., Bethlehem, Pa., 1969; JD, Am. U., Washington, DC, 1972. Bar: NY 1973, Fla. 1978, Calif. 1981, DC 1981; solicitor Supreme Ct. Eng., 1996—. Mem. profl. staff U.S. Senate Com. on Labor and Pub. Welfare, 1969-72; legis. aide U.S. Senator Jacob K. Javits, 1969-72; ptnr., head creditors' rights dept. Dreyer & Traub, NYC, 1980-93; ptnr., head dept. bankruptcy Shea & Gould, NYC, 1993—95; pvt. practice Martin I. Klein, P.C., 1995—. Lectr. Am. Law Inst.-ABA Com. on Continuing Profl. Edn., 1975—, The Practising Law Inst., 1975—, Mathematica, 1981—; adj. assoc. prof. law Benjamin Cardozo Sch. Law, Yeshiva U., 1980—; lectr. Columbia U. Sch. Law, 1980—; mem. med. malpractice mediation panel appellate div. Supreme Ct. State NY 1980—; trustee, treas., pres. Cen. Synagogue, NYC, 1986-98; arbitrator, NYC Small Claims Ct. Contbr. articles on fin. real estate and comml. law to profl. jours. Del. White House Conf. on Youth, 1971; chmn. Town of Palm Beach Zoning Commn., 1994-2001; land devel. regulation bd. Palm Beach County, 2004-, code enforcement bd. Town of Palm Beach, 2006-. Mem. ABA, NY State Bar Assn., Fla. Bar Assn., Calif. Bar Assn., DC Bar Assn., NY County Lawyers Assn. (mem. com. on bankruptcy), Am. Arbitration Assn. (mem. comml. panel). Office: 350 E 79th St 34th Fl New York NY 10021

KLEIN, MARTIN JESSE, physicist, science historian, educator; b. NYC, June 25, 1924; s. Adolph and Mary (Neuman) K.; m. Miriam June Levin, Oct. 28, 1945 (div. 1973); children: Rona F., Sarah M. Klein Zaino, Nancy R. Klein; m. Linda L. Booz, Oct. 8, 1980 (div. 2005); 1 child, Abigail M.; m. Joan Warnow-Blewett, July 9, 2005. AB, Columbia U., 1942, MA, 1944; PhD, MIT, 1948. With OSRD for USN, 1944-45; research assoc. in physics MIT, Cambridge, 1946-49; instr. physics Case Inst. Tech., Cleve., 1949-51, asst. prof., 1951-55, assoc. prof., 1955-60, prof., 1960-67, acting dept. head, 1966-67; prof. history physics Yale U., New Haven, 1967-74, Eugene Higgins prof. history physics and prof. physics, 1974-91, 95-99, Bass prof. history sci., prof. physics, 1991-95, chmn. dept. history sci., 1971-74, William Clyde De Vane prof., 1978-81, prof. emeritus, 1999—. Van der Waals guest prof. U. Amsterdam, 1974, Pieter Zeeman guest prof., 1993; vis. prof. Harvard U., 1989-90, Rockefeller U., 1975, adj. prof. 1976-79. Author: Paul Ehrenfest, Vol. I: The Making of a Theoretical Physicist, 1970; editor: Collected Scientific Papers of Paul Ehrenfest, 1959; sr. editor The Collected Papers of Albert Einstein, 1988-97; editorial adviser Ency. Brit, 1956-76; translator: Letters on Wave Mechanics, 1967; contbr. articles to profl. jours. NRC fellow Dublin (Ireland) Inst. Advanced Studies, 1952-53; Guggenheim fellow Leyden, Netherlands, 1958-59; Guggenheim fellow Yale, 1967-68 Fellow Am. Acad. Arts and Scis., Am. Phys. Soc.; mem. NAS, AAUP, History of Sci. Soc., Am. Assn. Physics Tchrs., Internat. Acad. History of Sci., Phi Beta Kappa, Sigma Xi. Home: 1 Carolina Meadows Apt 104 Chapel Hill NC 27517-8508

KLEIN, MARTIN SAMUEL, management consultant; b. NYC, Dec. 8, 1932; s. David and Dorothy (Manheim) K.; m. Elizabeth Jann Perks, Dec. 19, 1964 (dec. Aug. 1994); children: Sarah Madeline, Dorothy Ann. AB, Harvard U., 1954, MBA, 1962. V.p. United Rsch., Cambridge, Mass., 1962-69, Boston Cons. Group, 1969-73; pres. Instnl. Strategy Assocs., Belmont, Mass., 1973—2005. Cons. Brookings Instn., Washington, 1963-64. Author: (with others) Impact of Transportation on Development, 1964, Combining Public Health Nursing Agencies, 1964; contbr. articles to profl. jours. Bd. dirs. Vis. Nurse Assn., Boston, 1972-82, Harvard Cmty. Health Plan, Boston, 1978-93; vice chmn. Harvard Cmty. Health Plan Found., 1986-93, Cambridge Ctr. for Adult Edn., 1983-85; sec.-treas. Ctr. for Effective Philanthropy, Cambridge, 1982-98; trustee Mt. Auburn Hosp., Cambridge, 1995-2006, overseer, 1994—; trustee Big Sister Assn. Greater Boston, 1996-99, Walter E. Fernald Corp., 2005—; counselor to bd. trustees Aga Khan U., Karachi, 1993-2002. Sr. fellow Cheswick Ctr., 1980—, trustee; Harvard Coll. scholar, 1954, Fulbright scholar, Australia, 1954-55, George F. Baker scholar Harvard Bus. Sch., 1962. Mem. Am. Hosp. Assn. (com. on governance 1998-2001), Mass. Hosp. Assn. (trustee adv. coun. 2002-06), Harvard Club (N.Y.C. and Boston), Belmont Hill Club (treas. 1979-80), Harvard Travellers Club (Boston), Kirribilli Club (Sydney, Australia). Jewish. Office: Instl Strategy Assocs Inc 43 Village Hill Rd Belmont MA 02478-2117

KLEIN, MARY ANN, special education educator; b. Ridgewood, NJ, Jan. 31, 1956; d. Julius R. and Nancy M. Pascuzzo; m. Thomas F. Klein, July 16, 1983. B in Elem. Edn. & Spl. Edn., Adelphi U., Garden City, NY, 1978; M in Spl. Edn. & Reading, Adelphi Univ., Garden City, NY, 1980. Cert. in spl. edn. Learning disabilities specialist Merrick UFSD, Merrick, NY, 1978—. Swimming instr. disabled children and adults Village of Garden City, 1974—79; pvt. piano instr., NY, 1978—82; clinician & diagnostician Adelphi U. Reading Clinic, Garden City, 1980—84; ednl. cons. BOCES of Nassau County, Merrick, NY, 1993—94, SETRC of Nassau County, Westbury, NY, 1995—96; founder peer tutoring program Birch Sch., Merrick, NY; spl. edn. rep. Birch Child Study Team, Merrick, NY. Co-author: (curriculum guide) Foundations for Learning, 1991; author: (resource guide) Strategies to Assist Learning Disabled Children in the Classroom Setting, 1995. Mem. Merrick PTA, 1978—, tchr. liaison, 1994—97; mem. Merrick SEPTA, 1983—, Com. on Spl. Edn., 1983—, Nassau Reading Coun., 1996—; co-founder Students Against Destructive Decision-Making, Birch Sch., Merrick, NY; apptd. Crisis Mgmt. Team, Birch Sch. Mem.: State Congress of Parents & Tchrs. (hon.), Coun. for Exceptional Children, Kappa Delta Pi. Avocations: piano, travel. E-mail: beachbum7777777@aol.com.

KLEIN, MELVYN NORMAN, lawyer, investment executive; b. Chgo., Dec. 27, 1941; s. Harry H. and Bertha M. (Gleicher) K.; m. Annette Lorraine Grossman, Mar. 13, 1976; children: Jacqueline Anne, Jenna Katherine. Student, London Sch. Econs. and Polit. Sci., 1962; BA in Econs. with highest honors, Colgate U., 1963; JD, Columbia U., 1966; postgrad., Johns Hopkins Sch. Advanced Internat. Studies, 1966-67; LHD (hon.), Tex. A&M U., Corpus Christi, 1997. Bar: D.C. 1968, Tex. 1980. Legis. asst. Rep. Sidney Yates, Washington, 1966; assoc. McKinsey & Co., Washington, 1967-68; sr. v.p. Donaldson, Lufkin and Jenrette, Inc., NYC, 1969-77; counsel Brownstein, Zeidman & Schomer, Washington, 1978-93; pvt. practice, Corpus Christi, 1979—. Spl. counsel United Techs. Corp., 1985; bd. dirs. Anixter Internat., Hanover Compressor Corp.; sr. investment adv. Sprout Capital Group III, 1977-87; gen. ptnr. GKH Ptnrs., L.P., 1987—; adj. prof. bus. Tex. A&M., Corpus Christi; mem. adv. com. internat. econ. policy, U.S. Sec. State, 1999-2002; pres. JAKK Holding Co. Guest columnist Corpus Christi Caller-Times newspaper, 1980—. Staff mem. V.P. Hubert Humphrey Presdl. Campaign, 1968; chmn. Corpus Christi Bus. Devel. Comm., 1979-86; chmn. bd. govs. Art Mus. South Tex.; bd. dirs. S. Tex. Ednl. Broadcasting System, 1984-86; mem. exec. com. Pres.'s Pvt. Sector Study of Cost Control in Fed. Govt.; mem. internat. bd. advisors Columbia U. Sch. Internat. Affairs, M.D. Anderson Cancer Ctr. Mem. ABA, World Pres.'s Orgn., Horatio Alger Assn. Disting. Ams., Am. Bus. Conf. (founding mem., chmn. capital formation and tax policy com. 1980-86), D.C. Bar Assn., State Bar Tex., Philos. Soc. Tex., Corpus Christi Yacht Club, Corpus Christi Country Club, River Oaks Country Club (Houston), Std. Club (Chgo.), Rotary. Home: 210 Jackson Pl Corpus Christi TX 78411-1216 Office: 615 N Upper Broadwat Ste 1940 Corpus Christi TX 78477 Office Phone: 361-883-7205.

KLEIN, MICHAEL D., lawyer; b. Wilkes-Barre, Pa., June 9, 1951; BA magna cum laude, King's Coll., 1973; JD, Dickinson Sch. Law, 1976. Bar: Pa. 1976, US Ct. Appeals (3rd cir.) 1984, US Dist. Ct. (mid. dist.) Pa. 1984, US Dist Ct. (ea. dist.) Pa. 1994, Ct. Appeals (DC) 2006. Asst. atty. gen. Commonwealth of Pa., Harrisburg, 1976-82; mgr. corp. affairs, corp. sec. Pa. Am. Water Co., Hershey, 1982-89; ptnr. LeBoeuf, Lamb, Greene & MacRae LLP, Harrisburg, Pa., 1991—, mng. ptnr. Harrisburg office, 1991—. Mem. Pa. Bar Assn., Am. Water Works Assn. Office: LeBoeuf Lamb Greene & MacRae LLP 200 N Third St Ste 300 Harrisburg PA 17108-2108 Home Phone: 717-697-3818; Office Phone: 717-232-8196. Office Fax: 717-232-8720. Business E-Mail: mklein@llgm.com.

KLEIN, MICHAEL ELIHU, physician; b. NYC, Apr. 6, 1946; s. Leo and Edith (Rigrod) K.; m. Elizabeth Angela McGehee, Oct. 8, 1988; children: Michael, Debra, Daniel. BA, Wesleyan U., Middletown, Conn., 1967; MD, MPH, Yale U., 1972. Diplomate Am. Bd. Internal Medicine. Asst. dir. hematology U. Md., Balt., 1979-83; sr. investigator U. Md. Cancer Ctr., Balt., 1979-83; cons. in hematology, oncology Cowley Assocs., Camp Hill, Pa., 1983—87, Spirit Hosp., Camp Hill, 1983—2007, Ctrl. Pa. Hematology & Oncology, Lemoyne, 1997—2007, Jefferson U. Hosp., Phila., 2007—, Pinnacle Health Sys., Harrisburg, 1983—. Chmn. blood usage com. Holy Spirit Hosp., Camp Hill, Pa., 1998—2000, Camp Hill, 2003—06; chief hematology Pinnacle Health Sys., 2002—07, chmn. blood utilization com., 1988—2007; assoc. clin. prof. U. Pa., Hershey, 2004—07; asst. clin. prof. Pa. Coll. Osteopathic Medicine, Phila., 2004—07. Author: Political Dynamics National Health Insurance in New York, 1972; contbr. articles to profl. jours., chpts. to books. Founder, bd. dirs. Number Nine, New Haven, 1971. Comdr. lt. USPHS, 1974-77. Fellow Internat. Acad. Clin. and Applied Thrombosis/Hemostasis; mem. AMA, Am. Soc. Clin. Research, Am. Soc. Clin. Oncology, Am. Soc. Hematology, Am. Legion, Balt. Blood Club (pres. 1979-83). Avocations: stamp collecting/philately, baseball, reading. Office: Jefferson Univ Hosp Sheridan Bldg Ste 801 125 9th Ave Philadelphia PA 19107 Personal E-mail: orioledh@aol.com.

KLEIN, MICHAEL J., pathologist, surgeon; AB, Rutgers U., 1969; MD, Temple U., Phila., 1973. Diplomate in anatomical and clin. pathology Am. Bd. Pathology, 1978. Resident NYU Sch. Medicine, 1973—78, assoc. prof. surg. pathology, 1984—87; attending pathology NYU, 1978—80, asst. prof. pathology, 1979—80, Mt. Sinai Sch. Medicine, 1980—84, prof. pathology and orthopedics NY, 1987—2003; adj. assoc. prof. surg. pathology, 1987—2007; head sect. surg. pathology U. Ala., Birmingham, 2003—, prof. pathology, 2003—07; assoc. dir. labs. Hosp. Joint Diseases Orthop. Inst., NY. Contbr. articles to profl. jours. Fellow: Coll. Am. Pathologists, Am. Soc. Clin. Pathology; mem.: Internat. Skeletal Soc., US/Can. Assn. Pathologists. Avocations: photography, music. Home and Office: Univ Ala Birmingham 619 19th St S Birmingham AL 35249 Home Phone: 205-975-8323. Business E-Mail: thehog@uab.edu.

KLEIN, MICHAEL LAWRENCE, research chemist, educator; b. London, Mar. 13, 1940; s. Julius and Bessie (Bloomberg) K.; m. Brenda May Woodman, June 3, 1962; children— Paula Denise, Rachel Anne B.Sc., Bristol U., Eng., 1961; PhD, Bristol U., 1964. Research fellow CIBA-GEIGEY, Genoa, Italy, 1964-65; research fellow Imperial Chem. Industries (UK), Bristol, England, 1965-67; research assoc. Rutgers U., New Brunswick, NJ, 1967-68; research officer NRC of Can., Ottawa, Ont., 1968-87; prof. chemistry U. Pa., Phila., 1987—91, William Smith prof. chemistry, 1991—93, Hepburn prof. phys. scis., 1993—, dir. Lab. for Rsch. on the Structure of Matter. Part-time prof. chemistry Mc Master U., Hamilton, Ont., 1977-89; mem. internat. relations comm. Natural Scis. and Engring. Research Council, Ottawa, 1982-84, mem. NSERC chem. panel, 1985-86, NSF panels, 1993—, NIH panels, 1996—; mem. FDA Panel, 1999; vis. prof., Paris, Lyon, France, Kyoto, Japan, Amsterdam, Canberra, Australia, Florence, Italy; fellow commoner Trinity Coll., Cambridge, Eng., 1985-86; dir. NSF Materials Rsch. Lab., 1993-96, NSF MRSEC, 1996—; Miller prof. U. Calif., Berkeley, 1997, Linnett prof. U. Cambridge, 1998; fellow Sydney-Sussex Coll., Cambridge, U.K., 1998. Editor: Rare Gas Solids, Vol. I, 1976, Vol. II, 1977, Inert Gases, 1984; mem. editl. bd. Chem. Physics, 1986—, Physics Reports, 1986—, Jour. Phys. Chemistry, 1990-95, Molecular Physics, 1992-99, Computational Materials Sci., 1992—, Jour. Chem. Soc. Farady Trans., 1993-98, Jour. Phys. Condensed Matter, 1994-97, Phys. Chemistry Chem. Physics, 1999—, Accounts of Chem.

Rsch., 2004—, Chem. Physics Letters, 2003—, Jour. Chem. Physics, 2003—; contbr. numerous articles to profl. jours. Recipient Alder prize CECAM, 2004; IBM World Trade fellow, 1970, Guggenheim fellow, 1989, Humboldt fellow, 1995; grantee Natural Scis. and Engring. Rsch. Coun., 1979-89, NSF, 1988—, NIH, 1988—. Fellow Royal Soc. Can., Royal Soc. London, Inst. Physics, Chem. Inst. Can., Am. Phys. Soc. (Rahman prize 1999), Am. Acad. Arts and Scis.; mem. Am. Chem. Soc. (Phila. Sect. award 1998), Royal Soc. Chemistry (U.K.), Indian Acad. Sci. (Hon. fellowship), Acad. Developing World (Hon. fellowship). Office: Univ Pa 141 CHEM/6323 Philadelphia PA 19104 E-mail: klein@lrsm.upenn.edu.

KLEIN, MICHAEL ROGER, investor, foundation administrator; b. NYC, Apr. 10, 1942; s. Jesse and Stephanie (Siegel) K.; m. Joan Ilona Fabry, Feb. 19, 1977; children: Nicholas Jesse, Alexander Fabry. BBA, U. Miami, Coral Gables, Fla., 1963, JD, 1966; LLM, Harvard U., 1967. Bar: Fla. 1966, D.C., 1969, U.S. Dist. Ct. (D.C. cir.) 1970, U.S. Supreme Ct., 1970. Asst. prof. law La. State U., Baton Rouge, 1967-69; assoc. Wilmer, Hale, Washington, 1969—74, ptnr., 1974—2005, sr. counsel, 2006—. Chmn. Zenith Gallery, Inc., Washington, 1978—, LePavillon of D.C., Washington, 1983-89; co-founder, chmn. bd. CoStar Group Inc., 1988—, vice-chmn. bd. dirs. Perini Corp. 1991—, lead dir.; bd. dirs. SRA Internat. Inc.; co-founder, chmn. bd. Precept Corp., 1999—; co-founder, chmn., CEO Le Paradou, LLC, 2003-; co-owner, dir. Astar Air Cargo, Inc., 2003—, chmn. Sunlight Found., 2005-. Author: Eminent Domain, 1969; contbr. articles to profl. jours. Trustee Ctr. for Law in the Pub. Interest, L.A., 1975-91, Am. Himalayan Found., 1996—; chmn. and pres. Sunlight Found., 2005-; chmn. bd. trustees Advocates for Pub. Interest, Washington, 1986-89; dir. Support Ctr. of D.C., Inc., 1991-95. Mem. Am. Law Inst. Jewish. Office: Sunlight Found 2001 K St NW Ste 206 Washington DC 20006

KLEIN, MICHAEL S., diversified financial services company executive; 2 children. Grad. cum laude, Wharton Sch. Bus., 1987. With mergers and acquisitions group Salomon Bros. (now Citigroup), 1987—; CEO Citigraoup Corp. and Investment Bank, 2000—03; co-head global investment banking Salomon Smith Barney divsn. Citigroup, 2000—03; CEO global corp. and investment bank for Europe, the Middle East and Africa Citigroup Inc., NYC, 2003—04; vice chmn. Citigroup Internat. PLC, 2004—06; CEO global banking Citigroup Inc., NYC, 2004—06, co-pres. global corp. & investment banking group, 2007, co-chmn., co-CEO Citi Markets & Banking, 2007—. Mem. supervisory bd. Thyssen Bornemisza Group; internat. coun. mem. Belfer Ctr. Named Investment Banker of Yr., Investment Dealers Digest, 2001; named one of 25 Global Leaders to Watch, Fortune Mag., 2001. Office: Citigroup Inc Global Corp and Investment Banking Group 399 Park Ave New York NY 10043*

KLEIN, MILES VINCENT, physics professor; b. Cleve., Mar. 9, 1933; s. Max Ralph and Isabelle (Benjamin) K.; m. Barbara Judith Pincus, Sept. 2, 1956; children: Cynthia Klein-Banai, Gail. BS, Northwestern U., 1954; PhD, Cornell U., 1961. NSF postdoctoral fellow Max Planck Inst., Stuttgart, Germany, 1961; prof. U. Ill., Urbana, 1962—. Co-author: Optics, 1986; contbr. articles to profl. jours. A.P. Sloan Found. fellow, 1963. Fellow AAAS, Am. Phys. Soc. (Frank Isakson prize 1990), Am. Acad. Arts and Scis.; mem. IEEE (Sr.), Nat. Acad. Scis. Office: Materials Rsch Lab 104 S Goodwin Ave Urbana IL 61801-2902 Business E-Mail: mvklein@uiuc.edu.

KLEIN, NAOMI, journalist; b. Montreal, Canada, 1970; d. Michael and Bonnie Klein; m. Avi Lewis. Intern Globe & Mail, Toronto; editor This Mag.; internat. syndicated columnist. Author: (books) No Logo, 2000 (Can. Nat. Bus. Book award, 2001, Prix Médiations, 2001), Fences & Windows, 2002; syndicated columnist Toronto Star, The Nation, NY Times, In These Times, Chgo., Globe & Mail, Toronto, This Mag., The Guardian, UK; co-dir.(with Avi Lewis): (documentaries) The Take, 2004. Miliband Fellow, London Sch. Econ., 2002, Freda Kirchway Fellow, Nation Inst., 2005. Office: The Nation 8th Fl 33 Irving Pl New York NY 10003 Office Phone: 212-209-5400. Office Fax: 212-982-9000.

KLEIN, NEIL CHARLES, physician; b. NYC, Jan. 6, 1935; s. Martin and Jeannette F. (Pazow) K.; divorced; children: Lisa, Susie, David; m. Phyllis Klein, Nov. 26, 1989. AB, Columbia U., 1956; MD, Cornell U., 1960. Diplomate Am. Bd. Internal Medicine, Am. Bd. Gastroenterology, Nat. Bd. Med. Examiners. Intern N.Y. Hosp., 1960—61, resident, 1964—67; fellow in medicine Cornell Med. Coll., 1965—67, clin. instr. in medicine, 1967—70, asst. clin. prof. medicine, 1970—77; assoc. clin. prof. medicine N.Y. Med. Coll., 1977—84, clin. prof. medicine NYC, 1984—98, Columbia U., NYC, 1998—; asst. clin. attending physician N.Y. Hosp., 1970—77, St. Joseph's Hosp., Stamford, Conn., 1967—72; from asst. to assoc. attending physician Stamford Hosp., 1967—, assoc. chief medicine, 1972—75, chief divsn. gastroenterology, 1978—84. Bd. dirs. Conn. Med. Ins. Co., 1988-2002, fin. com., 1988-2002, sec., 1990-2002; bd. dirs. Stamford Health Network, 1987-93, chmn. fin. com., 1994-2001; mem. sci. adv. coun. Fairfield-Westchester Ileitis-Colitis Found., 1982—; mem. Commn. of Aging, Stamford, 1971-82. Fellow ACP, Am. Coll. Gastroenterology, Royal Soc. Tropical Medicine and Hygiene; mem. Fairfield County Med. Assn. (trustee 1980-87, chmn. bd. trustees 1984-85, pres. 1985-86), Conn. State Med. Assn., Am. Soc. Gastrointestinal Endoscopy, Am. Gastrointestinal Assn., Cornell Med. Coll. Alumni Assn. (pres. 1976-78, sr. advisor 1978—), Stamford Med. Soc. (pres. 1990-91). Office: Shoreline Med Group 1450 Washington Blvd Stamford CT 06902-2451 Office Phone: 203-327-9321. Business E-Mail: neilklein@shorelinemedicalllp.com.

KLEIN, NORA J., pediatrician; d. William and Suzanne Avins; children: Sebastian Avins Gray, Samuel Jacob Jr. BS, CCNY, 1966; MD, Albert Einstein Coll. Medicine, 1970. Pediatrician, Geneva, NY, 1973—83; pediatrician, chair CIGNA Health Care, Houston, 1984—2000, Christus Health Care, Houston, 2000—02; pediatrician Maryam Taghadosi and Assocs., Houston, 2003—. Spkr. in field. Contbr. articles to profl. jours.; editl. asst.: Dmitri Shostakovich. Active Drs. Orch. Houston; bd. dirs. Houston Friends of Music, 1996. Fellow: Acad. Breast Feeding Medicine, Am. Acad. Pediatricians; mem.: Houston Pediat. Soc., Tex. Pediat. Soc. Avocation: music. Office: Maryam Taghadosi and Assocs 1213 Herman Dr Houston TX 77004 Office Phone: 713-807-8921.

KLEIN, OTTO GEORGE, III, lawyer; b. Berkeley, Calif., Dec. 7, 1950; BA, U. Wash., 1973; JD, Yale U., 1976. Bar: Wash. 1976. Atty. Perkins Coie, 1976-81; ptnr. Syrdal, Danelo, Klein, Myre & Woods, 1981—88, Heller Ehrman, 1988-97; mem. Summit Law Group, Seattle, 1997—. Office: Summit Law Group Ste 1000 315 5th Ave S Seattle WA 98104-282 Office Phone: 206-676-7000. Business E-Mail: ottok@summitlaw.com.

KLEIN, PAUL E., lawyer; b. NYC, Apr. 26, 1934; AB, Cornell U., 1956; JD, Harvard U., 1960. Bar: Mich. 1960, Ill. 1965, N.Y. 1967, U.S. Supreme Ct. 1977, U.S. Ct. Appeals (2d cir.) 1980. Atty. Dow Chem. Co., Midland, Mich., 1960-65; assoc. Gunther & Choka, Chgo., 1965-66; atty. Esso Rsch. & Engring. Co., Linden, N.J., 1966-67; sr. mng. editor Matthew Bender & Co., NYC, 1967-72; assoc. gen. counsel N.Y. Life Ins. Co., 1972-80, v.p., assoc. gen. counsel, 1980-84; v.p., counsel Huggins Fin. Svcs., Inc., 1984-86; exec. corp. tax. div. Ernst & Young, 1986-95; pvt. practice White Plains, 1995—2004; ret., 2004. Adj. asst. prof. L.I. U., 1972-79, adj. assoc. prof., 1979-80; adj. assoc. prof. acctg. and taxation, Fordham U. at Lincoln Ctr. grad. sch. of bus. adminstrn., 1995-2003. Former columnist Jour. Real Estate Taxation; writer; editor. Mem. Assn. Life Ins. Counsel (sec.-treas. 1979-83, bd. govs. 1983-87), N.Y. State Bar Assn.

KLEIN, PHILIP ALEXANDER, economist; b. Austin, Tex., Oct. 8, 1927; s. David Ballin and Rose (Schaffer) Klein; m. Margaret A. McCormack, May 20, 1961 (dec. Apr. 28, 2004); children: Kathleen Monico, Alan Schaffer. BA, U. Tex., 1948, MA, 1949; PhD, U. Calif., Berkeley, 1958. Instr. Carleton Coll., Northfield, Minn., spring 1955; mem. faculty Pa. State U., State College, 1955—, prof. econs., 1965—2000, emeritus prof. econs., 2000—; rsch. assoc. Nat. Bur. Econ. Rsch., 1955-70, 73-79, Ctr. Internat. Bus. Cycle Rsch., Columbia U., 1979-96, Econ. Cycle Rsch. Inst., 1996—. Vis. prof. San Francisco State U., 1963, U. Hawaii, 1967, Inst. Europeen D'Aminstrn. des Affairs, Fontainbleau, France, 1963—67, U. Osijek; acad. visitor London Sch. Econs., 1973—74; disting. Fulbright fellow U. Siena, Italy, 1989; adj. scholar Am. Enterprises Inst., Washington, 1976—; cons. UN, Ctr. Devel. Planning Projections Policies, 1973, OECD, Paris, 1978—81, EEC, Brussels, 1979—82, World Bank, Washington, 1986—88. Mem. editl. bd. Internat. Jour. Forecasting, 1986—, Jour. Econ. Issues, 1976—81, 1985—87; author: books in field; contbr. chapters to books, articles to profl. jours. With M.C. US Army, 1946—47. Recipient Distinction in Social Scis. award, Pa. State U., 1981, Veblen-Commons award, Assn. Evolutionary Econs., 1990; Fulbright fellow, France, 1963, Yugoslavia, 1970, Italy, 1989. Mem.: Assn. Comparative Econs., Assn. Evolutionary Econs. (pres. 1977, Veblen-Commons award 1990), Econs. Assn., Phi Beta Kappa (pres. chpt. 1981). Home: 719 S Sparks St State College PA 16801-4114

KLEIN, RICHARD S., lawyer; b. NYC, Nov. 27, 1947; BA, CUNY, 1968; JD, Bklyn. Law Sch., 1973. Bar: NY 1974, US Dist. Ct. Ea. Dist. NY, US Dist. Ct. So. Dist. NY. Ptnr. Wilson, Elser, Moskowitz, Edelman & Dicker LLP, NYC. Mem.: ABA, NY State Bar Assn. Office: Wilson Elser Moskowitz Edelman & Dicker LLP 23rd Fl 150 E 42nd St New York NY 10017-5639 Office Phone: 212-490-3000 ext. 2280. Office Fax: 212-490-3038. Business E-Mail: kleinr@wemed.com.

KLEIN, ROBERT, comedian, actor; b. NYC, Feb. 8, 1942; s. Benjamin and Frieda (Moskowitz) K.; m. Brenda Boozer, Apr. 29, 1973 (div.); 1 child, Alexander Stewart. BA, Alfred U., NY, 1962; student, Yale U. Sch. Drama, 1962-63; DHL (hon.), Alfred U., 1980. Mem. Second City Theatrical Co., Chgo., 1965-66. Stage appearances include 20,000 Frozen Grenadiers with Second City Theatrical Co., Chgo., 1965 (debut); Broadway appearances include The Apple Tree, 1966, New Faces of 1968, 1968, Morning, Noon and Night, 1969, They're Playing Our Song, 1979 (Tony award nomination best actor in a musical 1979), The Robert Klein Show! 1985-86, The Sisters Rosensweig, 1993; film appearances include The Landlord, 1970, The Owl and the Pussycat, 1970, Rivals, 1972, Hooper, 1978, The Bell Jar, 1979, Nobodys Perfekt, 1981, The Last Unicorn (voice), 1982, Tales from the Darkside-The Movie, 1990, Radioland Murders, 1993, Mixed Nuts, 1994, Jeffrey, 1995, Next Stop Wonderland, 1996, One Fine Day, 1997, Primary Colors, 1997, Suits, 1998, Goosed, 1998, Labor Pains, 1998; records include Child of the Fifties, 1973 (Grammy award nominee), Mind Over Matter, 1974 (Grammy award nominee), New Teeth, 1975, Let's Not Make Love; frequent TV and concert appearances including (video) Tax Attack 87, (HBO spl.) Robert Klein on Broadway, 1987; TV series include Comedy Tonight, 1970 (host), TV's Bloopers and Practical Jokes, 1984 (host), Robert Klein Time, Dead Comics Society, Stand-Up/Sit Down Comedy, A&E Rev., Sisters, 1993-96; TV movies include Your Place of Mine?, 1983, Poison Ivy, 1985, This Wife for Hire, 1985: radio work includes The Robert Klein Radio Show; videos include Robert Klein: Child of the 50s, Man of the 80s, 1984, Robert Klein on Broadway, 1986, Tax Attack, 1987; author: (memoir) The Amorous Busboy of Decatur Avenue, 2005 (made into HBO spl.). Mem. Actors Equity Assn., Screen Actors Guild, AFTRA, Am. Guild Variety Artists, Writers Guild. Office: c/o Mel Berger William Morris Agy 1325 6th Ave New York NY 10019-6026

KLEIN, ROBERT NICHOLAS, II, real estate developer; 3 children. BA in History with honors, Stanford U., JD. Pres. Klein Fin. Corp., Palo Alto Calif., Klein Fin. Resources. Bd. dirs. Global Security Inst.; participated in drafting of legis. to create the Calif. Housing Fin. Agy., past bd. dirs.; co-author Proposition 71, Calif., 2004; chmn. Yes on Proposition 71 campaign for the Calif. Stem Cell Rsch. & Cures initiative, 2004; interim pres. Calif. Inst. for Regenerative Medicine, 2004—05, chmn. ind. citizens oversight com., 2004—. Named one of 100 Most Influential People of 2005, Time mag. Office: Klein Fin Corp Ste 330 550 Calif Ave Palo Alto CA 94306

KLEIN, ROGER A., lawyer; BA, Washington U., 1971; JD, Georgetown U., 1974. Bar: DC Bar 1975, Md. State Bar 1980, registered: US Supreme Ct., US Ct. Appeals, fourth cir., US Ct. Appeals, DC cir., US Dist. Ct., DC, UD Dist. Ct., Md., US Tax Ct. Ptnr., gen. coun. Howrey LLP, Washington, chmn. Corp & Transactional Group. Author: Polit. Expenditures. Tax Mgmt. Portfolios. 231. 2nd ed., 1985. Gen. counsel Spl. Ops. Warrior Found.; former vice-chmn. Bd. Profl. Responsibility. Mem.: ABA. Office: Howrey LLP 1299 Pennsylvania Ave NW Washington DC 20004-2402 Office Phone: 202-383-6846. Office Fax: 202-383-6610. Business E-Mail: kleinr@howrey.com.

KLEIN, RONALD JAY, congressman, former state legislator, lawyer; b. Cleve., July 10, 1957; s. Marvin Alfred and Beverly Joyce Klein; m. Dori Lynn Dragin, Oct. 23, 1982; children: Brian, Lauren. BA Polit. Sci., Ohio State U., 1979; JD, Case Western Res. U., 1982. Bar: Ohio 1982, Fla. 1986. Assoc. Ulmer, Berne et al., Cleve., 1982-85; assoc. to ptnr. Broad & Cassel, Boca Raton, Fla., 1985-92; ptnr. Sachs, Sax & Klein, P.A., Boca Raton, Fla., 1992—2007; mem. Fla. Ho. of Reps., 1993—96, Fla. State Senate, 1996—2006, US Congress from 22nd Fla. dist., 2007—, mem. fin. svcs. com., fgn. affairs com. Bd. dirs. World Trade Ctr. Palm Beach County; mem. Fla. Atlantic U. internat. bus. adv. bd., Boca Raton, 1995—; commr. Fla. Internat. Affairs Commn., Tallahassee, 1995-96. Bd. dirs. South Palm Beach County Jewish Fedn., Boca Raton, 1991-96; mem. exec. com. Jewish Cmty. Rels. Coun., Boca Raton, 1991-95, 96—; mem. Fla. Holocaust Curriculum Task Force, Tallahassee, 1994—; mem. hon. bd. dirs. Holocaust Rsch. Collection, Fla. Atlantic U., Boca Raton, 1994—; mem. Fla. Atlantic U. Holocaust Commn., 1994—; mem. sch. adv. com., Omni Mid. Sch., Boca Raton, 1996-97. Fleming Fellows Inst. fellow, Washington, 1995-96, Wexner Heritage Found. fellow, N.Y.C., 1997—; recipient Outstanding Contbn. to Edn. award Plumosa Elem. Sch., Boca Raton, 1993, Holocaust Documentation and Edn. Ctr. award, Miami, 1994, Outstanding Support of D.A.R.E. award, Palm Beach County sheriff's office, 1994, Man of Yr. United So. County Dem. Club, 1995, Legislator of Yr. award Fla. Econ. Devel. Coun., Tallahassee, 1996, Legislator of Yr. Am. Electronics Assn. Fla. Coun., 1996, Inaugural Founder's award Am. Jewish Congress, 1996, Outstanding Legislator award Am. Heart Assn., West Palm Beach, 1996, Dist. Cmty. Svc. Anti Defamation League, 1997, Captain of the Industry Fla. Maritime Industry, 1997, Courageous Legislator Nat. Org. for Women, 1998, Legislator of Yr. Alliance of Delray, 1998. Mem. Fla. Bar Assn. (bus. and health care sects.), Palm Beach County Bar Assn. (bus. and health care sects.). Democrat. Jewish. Avocations: outdoor sports, exercise, travel, reading. Office: 313 Cannon House Office Bldg Washington DC 20515 also: 800 E Broward Blvd Ste 300 Fort Lauderdale FL 33301*

KLEIN, ROSEMARY L., lawyer; BS in Acctg., U. Ill., 1989; JD, Wash. U. Sch. Law, 1992. CPA. Atty. Bryan Cave, LLP, 1995—99; corp. tax cons. Price Waterhouse Coopers, 1992—95; former sec., asst. gen. counsel Arch Coal, Inc.; asst. gen. counsel, corp. sec. Premcor, 1999—2003; asst. gen. counsel Solutia Inc., 2003—04, v.p., sec., gen. counsel, 2004—. Office: Solutia Inc PO Box 66760 Saint Louis MO 63166-6760*

KLEIN, SAMI WEINER, librarian; b. Worcester, Mass., July 6, 1939; d. Phillip and Barbara Rose (Ginsburg) Weiner; m. Eugene Robert Klein, Oct. 22, 1961; children: Pamela, Jeffrey, Elizabeth. BS, Simmons Coll., 1961; MLS, U. Md., 1973; postgrad., Johns Hopkins U., 1976-78. Chemist Hercules, Wilmington, Del., 1961-62, FDA, Washington, 1965-66; libr. NSWC, White Oak, Md., 1973-78; chief Hdqs. Libr. EPA, Washington, 1978-82; chief rsch. info. svcs. Nat. Inst. Svcs. and Tech., Gaithersburg, Md., 1982-95; chief rsch. libr. and info. program, rsch. libr. Nat. Inst. Stds. and Tech., Gaithersburg, Md., 1995-99; retired Nat. Inst. Svcs. and Tech., Gaithersburg, Md., 1999. Cons. in field; mem. librs. exec. coun. Met. Washington Coun. of Govts., 1981-82; elected mem. com. Fed. Libr. Info. Ctr., 1993-95, chair, budget and fin. working group, 1994-98. Editor OIS Sci.-Tech Info, 1982-95; mem. editorial bd. Assn. Ofcly. Analyt. Chemists, 1985-92, Sci. and Tech. Librs., 1996—. Chmn. Howard County Holocaust Remembrance Program, 2003; fed. govt. rep. Inst. for Sci. Info. Internat. Users Group, 1985—86; 2d v.p. Bet Aviv Congregation, 2002—04, pres., 2004—06; info. tech. com. Candlelight Concert Soc., bd. mem., 2007—; edn. com. Fed. Libr. and Info. Ctr. Com., 1987—91. Recipient Gold medal Am. Soc. Chemists, 1961, Engring. award Govt. Inidustry Data Exch. Program, 1997. Mem. ALA (sec.-treas. Fed. Librs. Round Table 1983-84, rep. to NTIS 1984-90, bd. dirs. 1986-89, v.p. 1991, pres. 1991-92, nominations chair 1992-93, scholar 1994-96, chair privatization com. 1995-97, chair co-awards com. 1996—, 1st FLRT Disting. Svc. award 1995), Spl. Librs. Assn. (treas. info.-tech. group 1986-87, student loan com. 1984-85), D.C. Law Librs. Soc. (NIST v.p. standards com. for women 1988, pres. 1989, bd. dirs. Comstar Credit Union 1994-2000), Fed. Libr. and Info. Network (exec. adv. com. 1989-91, sec. 1989, vice chair 1990-91), Jewish Mus. Md. (bd. dirs. 1999-2004), Beta Phi Mu. Democrat. Jewish. Home: 11041 Wood Elves Way Columbia MD 21044-1002 Personal E-mail: swklein@verizon.net.

KLEIN, SOPHIA H., entrepreneur; b. Dayton, Ohio, Aug. 17, 1915; d. Felix Frank Borkowski, Helen Marie Sichujainska; children: Helen Marie, Betty Jean. Owner Oak Hill Optical, Dayton, Town & Country Water Softener, Dayton, Klein Enterprises, Dayton, Country Squire Supper Club, Dayton, Bagel Connection, Dayton, Exquisitely Yours Jewelers, Dayton. Initiator rosary ministry various chs. worldwide; program creator Radio Rosary Hour Sta. WGXM-FM; promoter Pope John Paul II Cultural Ctr., Washington, 2000. Mem.: Dayton Cath. Bus. Women's Club (pres., Dayton Woman of Yr. 1988), Holy Seplecher (Lady of the Cross 1987—, U.S. Rep. Millennium visit to Vatican 2000). Democrat. Roman Catholic. Avocation: golf. Home: 4542 Cooper Rd Cincinnati OH 45242-5617

KLEIN, STEPHEN THOMAS, performing arts executive; b. Cleve., Mar. 9, 1947; s. Howard B. and Lilly (Gatchell) K.; m. Mary Ussery, Nov. 19, 1972; children— William Howard, Sarah Katherine. B.F.A., Boston U., 1970. Orch. Mgr. Cleve. Orch., 1978-82; exec. dir. Denver Symphony Orch., Colo., 1982-85, Nat. Symphony Orch., Washington, 1985-94; mng. dir. Pitts. Pub. Theater, 1994—. Office Phone: 502-562-0112. E-mail: sklein@kentuckycenter.org.

KLEIN, SUSAN ELAINE, librarian; b. Cedar Falls, Iowa, Aug. 5, 1952; d. Elmo Calvin and Mabel Audrey Boone; m. Richard Joseph Klein II, Oct. 16, 1982; children: Michael Joseph, Christopher James. BA, U. No. Iowa, 1974. Reporter The No. Iowan, Cedar Falls, summer 1972; res. desk clk. U. No. Iowa Libr., Cedar Falls, summer 1974; paralegal for migrant action program VISTA, Muscatine, Iowa, 1975-76; office asst. Cedar Falls Pub. Libr., 1976-77, libr. asst., 1977—79, cataloger, 1978-86, libr. asst., 1986-87, young adult libr., 1988—. Mem. Iowa Libr. Assn. (cert.). Democrat. Avocations: cooking, bicycling, gardening, canoeing, reading.

KLEIN, T(HEODORE) E(IBON) D(ONALD), writer; b. NYC, July 15, 1947; s. Richard and Norma (Kashins) K. AB, Brown U., 1969; M.F.A., Columbia U., 1972. Asst. story editor Paramount Pictures, NYC, 1972-75; editor-in-chief Twilight Zone Mag., NYC, 1981-86; editor CrimeBeat mag., NYC, 1991-93; editor mag. Sci-Fi Entertainment, Herndon, Va., 1995. Author: (novel) The Ceremonies, 1984, (story collection) Dark Gods, 1985, Reassuring Tales, 2006; screenwriter: (feature film) Trauma, 1994; contbr. fiction to anthologies; author articles in mags., newspapers. Recipient novel award Brit. Fantasy Soc., 1985, novella award World Fantasy Soc., 1986. Mem. Phi Beta Kappa Home: 210 W 89th St New York NY 10024-1805 Home Phone: 212-362-4371. Personal E-mail: metronetwork@hotmail.com.

KLEIN, WARD M., consumer products company executive; With Ralston Purina Co., 1979, Energizer Holding, 1986—, vice-pres. mktg., 1992—94, vice-pres., gen. mgr. global lighting prods., 1994—96, v.p. Asia Pacific & Latin Am., 2000—02, pres., internat., 2002—04, pres., COO, 2004—05, CEO, 2005—. Chmn. various foreign divisions Energizer Holdings. Office: Energizer HQ 533 Marryville University Saint Louis MO 63141 Office Phone: 800-383-7323.*

KLEINBARD, EDWARD D., lawyer; b. NYC, Nov. 6, 1951; s. Martin L. and Joan K.; m. Norma F. Cirincione, Oct. 17, 1947. BA, MA, Brown U., 1973; JD, Yale U., 1976. Bar: N.Y. 1977. Assoc. Cleary, Gottlieb, Steen & Hamilton, NYC, 1977—84, ptnr., 1984—. Book rev., article editor Yale Law Jour., 1975-76; contbr. articles to profl. jours. Fellow Am. Coll. Tax Counsel; mem. ABA, N.Y. State Bar Assn. (co-chmn. fin. instruments com. 1989-91), Assn. Bar City of N.Y., Internat. Assn. Fin. Engrs., Internat. Fiscal Assn. Office: Cleary Gottlieb Steen & Hamilton LLP 1 Liberty Plz Fl 38 New York NY 10006-1470 E-mail: ekleinbard@cgsh.com.

KLEINBAUM, SHARON, rabbi; BA cum laude, Barnard Coll., 1981; studied, Hebrew U, Jerusalem, Oxford U Ctr Post-Graduate Hebrew and Yiddish. Ordained Rabbi. Asst. dir. Nat. Yiddish Book Ctr., Amherst, Mass., 1982—85; student rabbi Congregation Beth Haverim, Atlanta, 1987—90; sr. educ. National Federation of Temple Youth, Jerusalem, 1988—89; dir. congregational rels. Religious Action Center of Reform Judaism, Wash., DC, 1990—92; sr. rabbi Congregation Beth Simchat Torah, NYC, 1992—. Named one of The Top 50 Rabbis in America, Newsweek Mag., 2007; recipient Jewish Fund for Justice Woman of Valor award. Mem.: Nat. Religious Leadership Roundtable (founding mem.), Ctrl. Conf. Am. Rabbis, Reconstructionist Rabbinical Assn. Office: CBST 57 Bethune St New York NY 10014 Office Phone: 212-929-9498. Office Fax: 212-620-3154.*

KLEINBERG, HOWARD J., newswriter; b. NYC, Oct. 23, 1932; s. Benjamin and Ruth (Wile) K.; m. Natalie Bernstein, Feb. 22, 1953; children: Linda Kleinberg Landy, Eliot, Eileen Kleinberg Newmark, David. Student pub. schs. Mem. staff Miami (Fla.) News, 1950-65, 66-88, mng. editor, 1968-76, editor, 1976-88; nat. columnist Cox Newspapers, Miami, 1988—; history columnist Miami Herald, 1989—. Author: Miami, The Way We Were, 1985, The Great Florida Hurricane and Disaster, 1993, Miami Beach, A History, 1994. Mem. Orange Bowl Com. Served with AUS, 1953-55, Korea. Recipient 1st pl. award Fla. Edn. Assn., 1985, Miami Urban League Black Awareness award, 1975, 1st pl. awards for column writing, Cox Newspapers, 1987, 88.

KLEINBERG, JON M., computer scientist, educator; AB, Cornell U., 1993; SM, Mass. Inst. Tech., 1994, PhD, 1996. Rsch. positions, theory and computation group IBM, 1995—96, rsch. positions, computer sci. principles and methodologies group, 1996—97; mem. vis. faculty program IBM Almaden Rsch. Ctr., 1998—; prof. dept. computer sci. Cornell U., 1996—. Mem. visiting faculty program IBM Almaden Rsch. Ctr., 1998—. Contbr. articles to profl. jours. Named a MacArthur fellow, John D. and

Catherine T. MacArthur Found., 2005; recipient NAS award for Initiatives in Rsch., 2001, Rolf Nevanlinna prize, Internat. Math. Union, 2006. Fellow: Am. Acad. Arts & Scis. Office: Cornell Univ Dept Computer Sci Upson Hall Ithaca NY 14853 Office Phone: 607-254-8948, 607-255-3600, 607-255-5331, 607-255-7316. E-mail: kleinber@cs.cornell.edu.*

KLEINBERG, LAWRENCE H., investor, consultant; b. NYC, Dec. 20, 1943; s. Paul and Gertrude (Voron) Kleinberg; m. Lois Helene Kass, June 10, 1967; children: Brian Andrew, Rachel Adele. BA in Econs., Adelphi U., 1965, MBA, 1969. Analyst, Pfizer, Inc., NYC, 1965-69; various fin. mgmt. positions Beech-Nut, Inc., NYC, 1969-73; v.p., controller Life Savers, Inc., NYC, 1973-79, sr. v.p. fin., 1979-83, exec. v.p., 1983, pres., 1984, divsn. pres. Nabisco Brands, Inc., 1984-87; v.p., corp. controller Nabisco Brands, Inc., Parsippany, NJ, 1987-88; sr. v.p. fin. Nabisco Foods Group, Parsippany, 1988-94; sr. v.p. planning Nabisco, Inc., Parsippany, 1995-96; pvt. investor, cons., 1996—. Home: 13285 Verdun Dr Palm Beach Gardens FL 33410 E-mail: lhk43@aol.com.

KLEINBERG, NORMAN CHARLES, lawyer; b. Phila., July 18, 1946; s. Frank and Mildred Brosnan (Hill) K.; m. Marcia Sue Topperman, Jan. 31, 1971; children: Lauren Blythe, Joanna Leigh. AB, Tufts U., 1968; JD, Columbia U., 1972. Bar: N.Y. 1973, U.S. Supreme Ct., U.S. Ct. Appeals (1st, 2d, 3d, 5th, and fed. cirs.), U.S. Dist. Ct. (so. and ea. dists.) N.Y., U.S. Tax Ct., U.S. Dist. Ct. (ea. dist.) Wis., U.S. Dist. Ct. (no. dist.) Calif., U.S. Dist. Ct. (ea. dist.) Mich. Law clk. to judge U.S. Dist. Ct. (so. dist.) N.Y., NYC, 1972-74; assoc. Hughes Hubbard & Reed, NYC, 1974-80, ptnr., 1980—. Articles editor Columbia Jour. Law and Social Problems, 1971-72. Served to staff sgt. USAR, 1968-74. Fellow Am. Coll. Trial Lawyers; mem. ABA, Fed. Bar Coun., Assn. Bar of City of N.Y. (com. on state cts. of superior jurisdiction, com. profl. responsibility, com. profl. and jud. ethics., com. on jud., coun. on jud. adminstrn.), Internat. Bar Assn., N.Y. State Bar Assn., Def. Rsch. Inst. Home: 460 E 79th St New York NY 10021-1443 Office: Hughes Hubbard & Reed 1 Battery Park Plz Fl 12 New York NY 10004-1482 Business E-Mail: kleinber@hugheshubbard.com.

KLEINDORFER, DAWN OLSON, medical educator, neurologist; b. Dec. 8, 1970; BS in Biology (with high honors), Ind. U.; MD, Washington Univ. Sch. Medicine, 1997. Med. residency, dept. neurology U. Mich., 1998—2001; fellowship, cerebrovascular disease divsn., dept. neurology U. Cinn., Coll. Medicine, 2001—02; chief resident, dept. neurology U. Mich., 2000—01; asst. prof., neurology U. Cinn. Selected participant Early Career Women in Academic Medicine Profl. Develop. Seminar, 2004. Contbr. articles to profl. jours. Recipient Top Enrollment award, PROFESS study, Platinum Level, Outstanding Resident Rsch. award, Mich. Neurological Assn., Am. Heart Assn. Health Initiatives Vol. award, 2004; Nat. Stroke Assn. Rsch. Fellowship award, 2002. Mem.: AMA, Am. Stroke Assn., Phi Beta Kappa. Recipient of the Hazel K. Goddess Scholar grant for stroke research in women, 2004-2006. In a two-year study running concurrently in Atlanta and Cincinnati, African American beauticians will be educated about the signs of a stroke, and they will then educate their clientele during their appointments. Office: Univ Neurology Inc 222 Piedmont Ave # 3200 Cincinnati OH 45219-4217 Office Phone: 513-475-8730, 513-558-5328. Office Fax: 513-475-8033. Business E-Mail: dawn.kleindorfer@uc.edu.*

KLEINE, HERMAN, economist; b. NYC, Mar. 6, 1920; s. Max and Fannie (Schechter) K.; m. Paula Stein, June 16, 1962; children— Joseph, Michael. BS, State U. N.Y. at Albany, 1941; MA, Clark U., 1942, PhD, 1951. Researcher for Nat. Indsl. Conf. Bd., 1946; instr. to asst. prof. Worcester Polytech. Inst., 1946-49; economist ECA, Mut. Security Agy., The Hague, Netherlands, 1949-53; internat. relations and econs. FOA, ICA, Washington, 1953-57; dir. U.S. Ops. Mission to Ethiopia, ICA, 1957-59, asst. dep. dir. for ops., 1959-61; Nat. War Coll., 1961-62; AID adviser U.S. Mission to UN, NYC, 1962-64; dep. asst. adminstr. for Africa AID, Washington, 1964-67; dep. dir. U.S. AID mission to Brazil, 1967-69; asso. U.S. coordinator Alliance for Progress, 1969-70; dep. U.S. coordinator, asst. adminstr. Latin Am. Bur. AID, Washington, 1971-76; advisor to controller Interam. Devel. Bank, 1976-84; dir. internship programs Ctr. Immigration Policy and Refugee Assistance, Georgetown U., 1984-86; cons., mediator, 1986—. Mem. U.S. delegation UN Gen. Assembly, 1962, 63 Served from pvt. to capt. USAAF, 1942-46. Recipient AID Distinguished honor award, 1973, Adminstrs. Distinguished Career Service award, 1976, Superior Honor award Dept. State, 1976, Distinguished Alumnus award State U. N.Y. at Albany, 1977; duPont fellow, 1948; named to Hempstead, N.Y. Sch. Dist. Hall Fame, 1986. Mem. Kappa Phi Kappa. Jewish. Home and Office: 100 Hilary Cir Fairfield CT 06825

KLEINE, ROBERT J., state official; m. Judy Karandjeff. BA, We. Md. Coll.; MA, Mich. State U. Dir. office revenue and tax analysis Dept. Mgmt. and Budget, Mich.; editor Pub. Sector Reports Pub. Sector Consultants, Inc., sr. economist, v.p.; pres. Kleine Consulting; state treas. State of Mich., Lansing, 2006—. Office: Treasury Bldg 430 W Allegan St Lansing MI 48922 E-mail: mistatereasurer@michigan.gov.*

KLEINER, DIANA ELIZABETH EDELMAN, art historian, educator, academic administrator; b. NYC, Sept. 18, 1947; d. Morton Henry and Hilda Rachel (Wyner) Edelman; m. Fred S. Kleiner, Dec. 22, 1972; 1 child, Alexander Mark. BA magna cum laude, Smith Coll., 1969; MA, MPhil, Columbia U., 1970-74, PhD, 1976; MA (hon.), Yale U., 1989. Lectr., asst. prof. U. Va., Charlottesville, 1975-76, 76-78; vis. asst. prof. U. Mass., Boston, 1979; Mellon faculty fellow Harvard U., Cambridge, Mass., 1979-80; asst. prof. Yale U., New Haven, 1980-82, assoc. prof., 1982-89, fellow Whitney Humanities Ctr., 1984—87, master Pierson Coll., 1986—87, dir. grad. studies dept. history of art, 1988-90, prof. history of art and classics, 1989-95, dir. grad. studies dept. classics, 1991-94, chair dept. classics, 1994-95, Dunham prof. classics and history of art, 1995—, dep. provost for the arts, 1995—2003, prin. investigator open ednl. resources video lectr. project, 2006—; liason Faculty Programs, AllLearn, 2001—06. Adv. bd. Archaeol. News, Tallahassee, 1980-2000, Am. Jour. Archaeology, Boston, 1985-98; chair program for ann. meetings com. Archaeol. Inst. Am., Boston, 1988-93. Author: Roman Group Portraiture, 1977, The Monument of Philopappos in Athens, 1983, Roman Imperial Funerary Altars with Portraits, 1987, Roman Sculpture, 1992, paperback edit., 1994, Cleopatra and Rome, 2005; editor: I, Clavdia: Women in Ancient Rome, 1996, I Clavdia II: Women in Roman Art and Society, 2000. Bd. dirs. Westville Cmty. Nursery Sch., New Haven, 1989-90, Foote Sch., New Haven, 1994-2000; regional rep. Deerfield (Mass.) Acad., 2001-06, parent's com., 2002-04, trustee, 2004-. Grantee Am. Coun. Learned Socs., 1979, NEH, 1980, 95, Am. Philos. Soc. 1982, John Paul Getty Trust, 1992, William and Flora Hewlett Found., 2006—. Mem. Archaeol. Inst. Am., Coll. Art Assn. Home: 102 Rimmon Rd Woodbridge CT 06525-1941 Office Phone: 203-432-2673. Business E-Mail: diana.kleiner@yale.edu.

KLEINER, FRED SCOTT, art historian, archaeologist, educator, editor; b. NYC, Apr. 29, 1948; m. Diana Elizabeth Edelman, Dec. 22, 1972; 1 child, Alexander Mark. BA with honors, U. Pa., 1968; MA, Columbia U., 1969, PhD, 1973. Agora fellow Am. Sch. Classical Studies, Athens, Greece, 1973-75; asst. prof. art history and archaeology U. Va., Charlottesville, 1975-78; asst. prof. Boston U., 1978-81, assoc. prof., 1981-86, prof., 1986—, dir. grad. studies dept. art history, 1979-81, 99, chmn. dept. art history, 1981-85, 2005—, sr. fellow Soc. Fellows Humanities, 1985-86, 2006—07. Excavator, Cosa, Italy, 1969-70; vis. prof. Yale U., New Haven, 1997. Author: Greek and Roman Coins in the Athenian Agora, 1976, The Early Cistophoric Coinage, 1977, Medieval and Modern Coins in the Athenian Agora, 1978, The Arch of Nero in Rome, 1985, Art Through the Ages, 1996, Art Through the Ages--The Western Perspective, 2002, Art Through the Ages, 12th edit., 2005 (Texty prize, 2001, McGuffey prize, 2001), Art Through the Ages--Non-Western Perspectives, 2005, Art Through the Ages--A Concise History, 2005, A History of Roman Art, 2006 (Texty prize, 2007); editor-in-chief: Am. Jour. Archaeology, 1985—98; contbr. articles to profl. jours., chapters to books. Bd. dirs. Yale Youth Hockey Assn., 1994-97, v.p., 1996-97; co-founder, mgr. Conn. Ice Dogs, 1997-2001. Grantee Am. Philos. Soc., 1971, 80, Am. Coun. Learned Socs., 1978, 82; Guggenheim fellow, 1988-89; Asian Cultural Coun. fellow, 2004. Mem.: Tex. and Acad. Authors Assn. (awards com. 2002—), Coll. Art Assn. (Morey Book award com. 1999—2000, chair 2001—03), Archaeol. Inst. Am. (chmn. fellowship com. 1985, publs. com. 1985—98, numismatics com. 2000—03). Home: 102 Rimmon Rd Woodbridge CT 06525-1941 Office: Boston U Dept Art History Boston MA 02215 Home Phone: 203-389-1378; Office Phone: 617-353-1455. Business E-Mail: fsk@bu.edu.

KLEINER, JOHN PHILIP, cardiologist; b. Sept. 22, 1944; AB, Ripon Coll., Wisc., 1966; MD, U. Wisc. Med. Sch., 1970. Cert. Internal Medicine, Pediatric Critical Care Medicine, Interventional Disease, Cardiovascular Disease. Intern, internal medicine Fitzsimons Army Med. Ctr., Denver, 1971, resident, cardiology, 1973, fellow, 1978; cardiology svc. Dwight D. Eisenhower Army Med. Ctr., Ga., 1976—78; cardiologist Colo. Springs Cardiologists, P.C., Colo. Springs Health Partners, P.C., 2004—. Asst. clin. prof. U. Health Scis. Ctr., 1980. Very active with Pikes Peak YMCA, Cheyenne Mountain Zoo, Colo. Springs Fine Arts Ctr. Named one of Best Doctors in Am., Top Doctors, Colo. Springs Bus. Jour., 2004. Mem.: ACP, Am. Coll. Nuclear Cardiology, Assn. Army Cardiology, Colo. Med. Soc., Am. Coll. Chest Physicians, Am. Heart Assn., Am. Coll. Cardiology, El Paso County Heart Unit. Office: Colo Springs Health Partners PC 209 S Nevada Ave Colorado Springs CO 80903 Office Phone: 719-475-7700. Office Fax: 719-475-8963.*

KLEINER, MADELEINE A., lawyer, hotel executive; b. 1951; Grad., Cornell U.; JD, Yale Law Sch. Clk. to Hon. William P. Gray U.S. Dist. Ct. for Ctrl. Dist. of Calif.; assoc. Gibson, Dunn and Crutcher, LA, 1977—83, ptnr., 1983—95; sr. exec. v.p., chief adminstrv. officer, gen. counsel H.F. Ahmanson & Co., 1995—2001; exec. v.p., gen. counsel, corp. sec. Hilton Hotels Corp., Beverly Hills, Calif., 2001—. Bd. advisors UCLA Med. Ctr. Asst. sec. Performing Arts Coun., L.A. Music Ctr. Office: Hilton Hotels Corp 9336 Civic Ctr Dr Beverly Hills CA 90210 Office Phone: 310-205-4656.*

KLEINFELD, ANDREW J., federal judge; b. 1945; BA magna cum laude, Wesleyan U., 1966; JD cum laude, Harvard U., 1969. Law clk. Alaska Supreme Ct., 1969—71; U.S. magistrate US Dist. Ct. Alaska, Fairbanks, 1971—74; pvt. practice law Fairbanks, 1971—86; judge US Dist. Ct. Alaska, Anchorage, 1986—91, US Ct. Appeals (9th cir.), San Francisco, 1991—. Contbr. articles to profl. jours. Mem.: Tanana Valley Bar Assn. (pres. 1974—75), Alaska Bar Assn. (pres. 1982—83, bd. govs. 1981—84), Phi Beta Kappa. Republican. Office: US Ct Appeals 9th Cir Courthouse Sq 250 Cushman St Ste 3-A Fairbanks AK 99701-4665*

KLEINFELD, ERWIN, mathematician, educator; b. Vienna, Apr. 19, 1927; came to U.S., 1940; s. Lazar and Gina (Schönbach) K.; m. Margaret Morgan, July 2, 1968; children— Barbara, David. BS, CCNY, 1948; MA, U. Pa., 1949; PhD, U. Wis., 1951. Instr. U. Chgo., 1951-53; asst. prof. Ohio State U., 1953-56, asso. prof., 1957-60, prof., 1960-62; prof. math. Syracuse U., 1962-67, U. Hawaii, 1967-68, U. Iowa, 1968—2002, prof. emeritus, 2002—. Vis. lectr. Yale, 1956-57; cons. Nat. Bur. Standards, 1953; rsch. specialist U. Conn., 1955; research mathematician Bowdoin Coll., 1957; rsch. asso. Cornell U., summer 1958, U. Calif., LA, 1959, Stanford, 1960, Inst. Def. Analysis, 1961-62, AID-India, 1964-65; vis. prof. Emory U., 1976-77; Cons. Edn. IX Project, World Bank, U. Indonesia, 1985-86, Mucia/Ind. U.-(ITM) Shah Alam, Malaysia Project, 1988-89. Editorial bd. Jour. Algebra-Academic Press; cons. editor, Merrill Pub. Co.-Div. Bell & Howell. Contbr. articles research jours. Served with AUS, 1945-46. Wis. Alumni Rsch. Found. fellow, 1949-51, vis. rsch. fellow U. New Eng., Australia, 1992; grantee U.S. Army Rsch. Office, 1955-70, NSF, 1970-75. Mem. Am. Math. Soc., Sigma Xi. Home: 1555 N Sierra 120 Reno NV 89503 Home Phone: 775-337-0196; Office Phone: 775-337-0196. Business E-Mail: mkleinfd@math.uiowa.edu.

KLEINFELD, KLAUS, metal products executive, former electronics executive; b. Bremen, Germany, Nov. 6, 1957; s. Klaus Joachim and Elisabeth Berta (Freier) K.; m. Birgit Henriette Müeller, July 27, 1982; children: Hannah, Lena. MBA, U. Goettingen, 1982; PhD, U. Wuerzburg, 1992. Researcher U. Muenster, Germany, 1980-82; cons. Inst. Prof. Bergler, Nuernberg, Germany, 1982-85; product strategy Ciba-Geigy, Basle, Switzerland, 1985-86; cons. Siemens AG, Munich, 1987, corp. strategies mgr., personnel dept. corp. planning and devel., 1988—94, head corp. projects, corp. planning and devel., 1994, head corp. cons., 1995, head fluoroscopy & imaging, angiogrpahy div., med. engr. group, 1998—2000, exec. v.p. med. solutions group, 2000—02; COO Siemens Corp. (USA), 2001—02, CEO, 2002—03; mem. corp. exec. com. Siemens AG, Munich, 2004—05, pres., CEO, 2005—07; pres., COO Alcoa Inc., Pitts., 2007—. Bd. dir. Alcoa Inc., Bayer AG, Citigroup Inc., Internat. Bus. Council, World Econ. Forum; former bd. dir. Nokia Siemens Networks B.V. Author: Argwohn, 1980, Strategic Management and Corporate Identity, 1992; contbr. articles to profl. jours. Dir. Metropolitan Opera, NYC. Avocations: skiing, running, tennis, art. Office: Alcoa Inc 390 Park Ave New York NY 10022*

KLEINGARTNER, ARCHIE, dean, educator, academic administrator; b. Gackle, ND, Aug. 10, 1936; s. Emanuel and Ottile (Kuhn) K.; m. Dorothy Jean Hanselmann, Sept. 21, 1957; children: Elizabeth, Thomas. BA, U. Minn., 1959; MS, U. Oreg., 1961; PhD, U. Wis., 1965. Asst. and assoc. prof. UCLA, 1964-69, assoc. dean, chmn., 1969-71, prof., 1971-75, 83—, dir. entertainment mgmt. program, 1988—, founding dean Sch. Pub. Policy and Social Rsch. Berkeley, 1994—; v.p. U. Calif. Sys., Berkeley, 1975-83. Cons. in field, 1967—; arbitrator in field, 1971—; chmn. Global Window Ptnrs., Inc., 1998—. Mem. labor mgmt. disputes panel City of L.A., 1978—. With U.S. Army, 1954-56. Mem. London Sch. Econs., Alpha Kappa Psi. Republican. Methodist. Avocations: tennis, biking, gardening. Home: 12258 Montana Ave #103 Los Angeles CA 90049 Office: UCLA Sch Pub Policy Social Rsch PO Box 951656 Los Angeles CA 90095-1656 Home Phone: 310-979-6089; Office Phone: 310-206-1589. Business E-Mail: akleinga@ucla.edu.

KLEINHANS, FREDERICK WILLIAM, biophysicist, educator; s. John Ashmore and Sylvia Kleinhans; children: Deborah Jane Moore, Cheryl Moore Gueib, Jill Leslie Moore. BS, U. Mich., Ann Arbor, 1965; PhD, Ohio State U., Columbus, 1971. Asst. prof. physics Dension U., Grandville, Ohio, 1970—72, Ind. U.-Purdue U. Indpls., 1972—77, assoc. prof. physics, 1977—, adj. assoc prof geology, 1997—. Mem. faculty med. biophysics program Ind. U. Med. Ctr, Indpls., 1977—2002; biophysicist Meth. Hosp. Ind., Indpls., 1977—95; vis. scientist Oak Ridge Nat. Labs., Tenn., 1996—99, Smithsonian Instn., Nat. Zoo, Washington, 1998, U. Tenn., Knoxville, 1999—. Contbr. articles to profl. jours. Recipient Outstanding Undergraduate Tchg. award, Amoco Found., 1985, Tchg. Excellence Recognition award, Ind. U., 1999, Trustee's Tchg. award, 2001; grad. fellow, Battelle Meml. Inst., Columbus, Ohio, 1968—70. Mem.: AAAS, Am. Phys. Soc., Biophysical Soc., Soc. Cryobiology (mem. editl. bd. Jour. Cryobiology 2001—), Internat. Dark Sky Assn. (life). Unitarian. Avocations: astronomy, outdoors activities. Office: Ind U-Purdue U 402 North Blackford St Indianapolis IN 46202 Office Phone: 317-274-6900. Office Fax: 317-274-2393. Business E-Mail: starman@iupui.edu.

KLEINHENZ, CHRISTOPHER, foreign language educator, researcher, director; b. Indpls., Dec. 29, 1941; m. Margaret Ellen Zechiel, Aug. 1, 1964; children: Steven Russell, Michael Thomas. BA, Ind. U., 1964, MA, 1966, PhD, 1969. Asst. prof., dir. Bologna program Ind. U., 1970-71; instr. U. Wis., Madison, 1968-69, asst. prof., 1969-70, asst. prof., dept. French and Italian, 1971-75, assoc. prof., 1975-80, chmn. medieval studies program, 1975—80, 1981—84, 1989—95, 1996—2003, prof., 1980—2007, chmn. dept., 1985-88, Carol Mason Kirk prof. Italian, 2000—07, dir. honors program, 2005—07. Dir. devel. grant NEH, Madison, 1976-79, co-dir. rsch. tools grant, 1980-84. Author: The Early Italian Sonnet, 1986, Movement and Meaning in the Divine Comedy, 2005; editor: Medieval Manuscripts and Textual Criticism, 1976, Medieval Studies in North America, 1982, Routledge Studies in Medieval Literature, 1986-2002, Dante Studies, 1988-2003, Medieval Italy: An Encyclopedia, 2004; co-editor: Saint Augustine the Bishop: A Book of Essays, 1994, Routledge Medieval Casebooks, 1991—, Fearful Hope: Approaching the New Millennium, 1999, Courtly Arts and the Art of Courtliness, 2006; assoc. editor: Dante Ency., 2000; chmn. editl. bd. Medieval Acad. Reprints for Teaching, 1981-93; bibliographer MLA, NYC, 1981-88, BIGLLI, Rome, 1994—, Dante Studies, 1984-2002, ICLS, 2002-2006; book rev. editor Italica, 1984-93; co-translator: Dante Alighieri, Il Fiore and the Detto d'Amore, 2000. Chmn. com. on ctrs. and regional assns. Medieval Acad., 1993-99. Recipient Chancellor's Disting. Tchg. award, 2004, Leonard Covello Lifetime Achievement award, 2005, Hilldale award, 2006, Disting. Svc. to the Profession award Assn. Depts. Fgn. Langs., 2006; Newberry Libr./NEH grantee, 1988-89. Mem. Medieval Assn. of Midwest (pres. 1984-85, 2003-04), Dante Soc. Am. (mem. coun. 1985-91), Am. Boccaccio Assn. (v.p. 1987-93, pres. 1993-97), Am. Assn. Tchrs. of Italian (v.p. 1993-98, pres. 1999-03, Disting. Svc. award 2006). Avocations: sports, stamp collecting/philately, photography, travel. Home: 2247 Fox Ave Madison WI 53711-1922 Office: U Wis Dept French and Italian 1220 Linden Dr Madison WI 53706-1525 Office Phone: 608-262-3941. Business E-Mail: ckleinhe@wisc.edu.

KLEINKNECHT, KENNETH SAMUEL, retired air transportation executive; b. Washington, July 24, 1919; s. Christian Frederick and Nell May (Barr) K.; m. Patricia Jean Todd, May 24, 1947; children: Linda May, Patricia Ann, Frederick William. BSM.E., Purdue U., 1942. Project engr. NACA Lewis Research Center, Cleve., 1942-51; aero. research scientist NASA Flight Research Ctr., Edwards AFB, Calif., 1951-59; successively mgr. Mercury Project, dep. mgr. Gemini Program, mgr. command and service modules NASA Johnson Space Ctr., 1959-70, mgr. Skylab Program, 1970-74, dir. flight ops. Houston, 1974-76, asst. mgr. Orbiter Project, 1976-77; head constrn. space shuttle orbiter NASA Johnson Space Center, 1979-81; dep. assoc. adminstr. for space transp. systems European ops. to European Space Agy., Paris NASA Hdqrs., Washington, 1977-79; mgr. program engring., sr. space transp. system tech. adviser Denver div. Martin Marietta Aerospace, 1981-83, mgr. mfg. procurement and testing, 1983-84, dir. design to cost/productivity Space Sta. Project, 1984-88; mgr. laser project Zenith Star Program, 1988-90, ret., 1990. Exec. bd. Sam Houston Area council Boy Scouts Am., Houston, 1972-77. Recipient (with others) Group Achievement award for Mercury Project NASA, 1962, NASA medal for outstanding leadership Pres. of U.S., 1963, 81, John J. Montgomery award San Diego chpt. Nat. Soc. Aerospace Profls., 1963, (with others) Group Achievement award for X-15 Rsch. Airplane Flight Test Orgn., 1964, for Gemini Program, 1966, Exceptional Svc. medal NASA, 1969, Disting. Svc. medal NASA, 1969, 73 Fellow Am. Astron. Soc. (W. Randolph Lovelace II award 1975), AIAA (assoc.); mem. Internat. Acad. Astronautics, Kiwanis, Masons (33rd degree) Home: 825 Front Range Rd Littleton CO 80120-4005 Personal E-mail: ksklein@worldnet.att.net. *As a member of the team that made lunar and space shuttle missions successes, I believe that my "formula for success" is one part high goal and one hundred parts persistence. I have always believed in establishing principles, high ideals of conduct as structures to direct our lives. It is voluntary total dedication to valid ideals, attention to detail, discipline and accepting accountability that will bring success on every level. To reach beyond one's present grasp is to assure ever higher attainments in the future.*

KLEINKORT, JOSEPH ALEXIUS, physical therapist, ergonomist, consultant; b. Bronxville, NY, Jan. 28, 1946; s. Joseph P. and Marie C. (Richter) Kleinkort; m. Kathleen J. Kleinkort, Oct. 23, 1953; children: Pat, Mike, Kelly, Kristin, Kevin. BS in Phys. Therapy, St. Louis U., 1968; MA in Psychology, Ball State U., Muncie, Ind., 1977; PhD (hon.), Medicina Alternativa, Copenhagen, 1983; PhD in Safety Mgmt., Western States U., 1998. Registered safety dir. World Safety Orgn.; registered phys. therapist, Tex., Fla.; cert. indsl. ergonomist; diplomate Am. Acad. Pain Mgmt. Dir. phys. therapy Phys. Therapy, Inc., Ft. Lauderdale, Fla., 1970—72; commd. officer USAF, 1972; dir. phys. therapy USAF Hosp.-Barksdale, Bossier City, La., 1972-74, USAF Hosp.-Torrejone, Madrid, 1974-78; asst. dir. Wilford Hall Med. Ctr., San Antonio, 1980-83; res. at rank of maj. USAF, 1983; pres. Chronic Pain Assn., Inc., San Antonio, 1983-88; exec. dir. Ft. Worth Back Inst., 1988-90; pres. Joseph A. Kleinkort, P.C., Roanoke, Tex., 1983—. Sr. v.p., 1995—96; exec. v.p., 1996—; COO, 1997—; bd. dirs. Sci. Cons. Magnetherapy, Avazzia Med., Inc., Avazzia Corp.; mem. Applied Biomed. Rsch. Inst., 1996—2001; v.p. clin. rsch. Health Rsch. and Clin. Assoc., 1996—; COO Worksteps Inc., 1997—; pres. Ergosteps, 1999—; liaison officer UN for World Safety Orgn.; vis. prof. St. Eustatius Med. Sch. Author: Therapeutic Medical Devices, 1983, Thermal Agents Rehabilitation, 1985, Laser Application Technology, 1986. Precinct judge, San Antonio, 1988; precinct chmn. Denton County Rep. Party, 1996—98; sr. elder First Bapt. Ch., Roanoke, 2001—03; active healing, deliverance and altar ministry Gateway Ch., 2006—; bd. dirs. Arlington Philharm. Symphony, 1993—94, Avazzia Inc. Recipient Alumni Merit award St. Louis U., 1983; named Outstanding Phys. Therapist of Tex., Tex. Phys. Therapy Bd., 1985. Fellow Am. Coll. Orthopedics (membership sec. 1988-90); mem. Internat. Soc. Lasers in Medicine and Sci., Am. Assn. Phys. Medicine and Rehab., Am. Coll. Occupl. and Environ. Medicine, Am. Phys. Therapy Assn. (pres. pain mgmt., orthop. sect.), Am. Acad. Pain Mgmt., Tex. Phys. Therapy Assn., Am. Platform Soc. Avocations: sailing, gospel teaching. Home and Office: 303 Inverness Dr Roanoke TX 76262-5561 Personal E-mail: indusrehab@aol.com.

KLEINLEIN, KATHY LYNN, training and development executive; b. S.I., NY, May 2, 1950; d. Thomas and Helen Mary (O'Reilly) Perricone; m. Kenneth Robert Kleinlein, Oct. 30, 1983. BA, Wagner Coll., 1971, MA, 1974; MBA, Rutgers U., 1984; MA in Theology, Barry U., 1998; EdD, Grad. Theol. Found., 2004. Cert. secondary tchr., N.Y., N.J., Fla. Tchr. English N.Y.C. Bd. Edn., SI, 1971-74, Matawan (N.J.) Bd. Edn., 1974-79; instr. English Middlesex County Coll., Edison, NJ, 1978-81; med. sales rep. Pfizer/Roerig, Bklyn., 1979-81, mgr. tng. ops. NYC, 1981-86; dir. sales tng. Winthrop Pharms. divsn. Sterling Drug, NYC, 1986-87; dir. tng. Reuters Info. Sys., NYC, 1987—90; pres., dir. tng. Women in Transition, 1990—98; pastoral min., dir. religious edn. St. Raphael's Ch., 1998—2001; diocesan dir. catechetical ministry Diocese of Venice, Fla., 2001—. Pres. Kleinlein Cons.; pers. mgmt. officer USAR, NJ, 1981-86; cons. Concepts & Prodrs., NYC, 1981-85; bd. regents Blessed Edmund Rice Sch. for Pastoral Ministry; bd. dirs. Campaign for Human Devel. Trainer United Way, 1982-83, polit. action com., 1982—85; mem. Rep. Presdl. Task Force, Washington, 1983—; chair Sarasota Library Adv. Bd.; sec. Intracoastal Civic Assn.; reinventing govt. coun. Sarasota County Planning Commn., exec. bd. Edn. Found., St. Joseph Bon Secours Hosp.; grievance com. Fla. Bar; bd. regents Blessed Edmund Rice Sch. for Pastoral Ministry. Mem. Sarasota County Sch. Bd., 2002—. Capt. US Army, 1974—78. First woman in N.Y. N.G., 1974; first woman instr. Empire State Mil. Acad.,

Peekskill, N.Y., 1976. Mem.: Sarasota Women's Alliance, Rep. Women's Club, Alpha Omicron Pi. Republican. Roman Catholic. Office Phone: 941-484-9543. Business E-Mail: kleinlein@dioceseofvenice.org.

KLEINMAN, ARTHUR MICHAEL, medical anthropology and psychiatry educator; b. NYC, Mar. 11, 1941; s. Marcia F. (Kaplan) K.; m. Joan Andrea Ryman, Mar. 20, 1965; children: Peter John, Anne Simone. AB, Stanford U., 1962, MD, 1967; MA, Harvard U., 1974. Diplomate Nat. Bd. Med. Examiners, Am. Bd. Neurology and Psychiatry. Med. intern Yale-New Haven Hosp., 1967-68; surgeon USPHS, Bethesda, Md., 1968-70; resident in psychiatry Mass. Gen. Hosp., Boston, 1972-75; assoc. prof. U. Wash., Seattle, 1976-79, prof. psychiatry and anthropology, 1979-82; prof. med. anthropology and psychiatry Harvard Med. Sch., Boston, 1982—; chmn. dept. social medicine, prof. anthropology Harvard U., Cambridge, Mass., 1991-2000, Maude and Lillian Presley prof. med. anthropology and psychiatry, 1993—2002, Esther and Sidney Rabb prof. anthropology, 2002—, chair dept. anthropology, 2004—. Co-chair com. on culture, health and devel. Social Sci. Rsch. Coun., 1990. Author: Patients and Healers in the Context of Culture, 1980 (Wellcome medal Royal Anthrop. Inst.), Social Origins of Distress and Disease, 1986, The Illness Narratives, 1988, Rethinking Psychiatry, 1988, Writing at the Margin, 1995, What Really Matters, 2006; co-editor: Relevance of Social Science for Medicine, 1981, Culture and Depression, 1985, Pain as Human Experience, 1992, Social Suffering, 1997, Remaking a World, 2001, Violence and Subjectivity, 2000, Science and Ethics of the Placebo, 2002, Reducing Suicide, 2002, SARS in China, 2005, Global Pharmaceuticals, 2006, AIDS in China, 2006; editor-in-chief: Culture, Medicine and Psychiatry: A Jour. of Internat. Cross-Cultural Rsch., 1976-86. Recipient Rsch. award NIMH, 1977-79, Rockefeller Found., 1983-86, 89-91, NSF, 1983-86, R.W. Johnson Found., 1989, 94; grantee NIMH, 1984—, Carnegie Corp., 1990-92, 95, MacArthur Found., 1992-94, Rockefeller Found., 1992-94, Russell Sage Found., 1998-2001, others; NIH fellow, 1968-70, Guggenheim fellow, 1992. Fellow AAAS, Am. Psychiat. Assn. (disting. life; vice chmn. coun. on global psychiatry 2002-05), Am. Anthrop. Assn., Inst. Medicine of NAS (chmn. com. on chronic pain, illness behavior and disability, co-chmn. com. preventing suicide), Royal Anthrop. Inst., Am. Acad. Arts and Scis. (Franz Boas award), Am. Anthrop. Assn. Office: Harvard U 330 William James Hall 33 Kirkland St Cambridge MA 02138-2019 Home Phone: 617-661-1584. Business E-Mail: Kleinman@wjh.harvard.edu.

KLEINMAN, KATIE (KATHERINE MILLER KLEINMAN), public television editor; d. David and Donna Miller. BA cum laude, Ohio Univ., 2001. Traffic asst., announcer WOUB-PBS TV, Athens, Ohio, 1999; ops. intern WCMH-NBC affiliate, Columbus, Ohio, 2000; with Online NewsHour with Jim Lehrer PBS, Arlington, Va., 2004—. Co-recipient AAAS Sci. Journalism award for online reporting, 2006. Office: Online NewsHour 2100 Crystal Dr Arlington VA 22202

KLEINPETER, AMY E. CLARK, lawyer; b. Hardin County, Ky., 1970; BS, Hiram Coll., 1992; MS, Univ. Calif., Riverside, 1994; JD, Univ. So. Calif., 2002. Bar: Calif. 2002, Tex. 2004, US Dist. Ct. Ctrl. Calif., US Ct. Appeals Ninth Cir. Atty. pvt. practice, Pasadena, Calif. Bd. mem. Univ. So. Calif. Public Interest Law Found. Editor: Univ. So. Calif. Rev. Law & Women's Studies. Named a Rising Star, So. Calif. Super Lawyers, 2005—06. Mem.: ABA, LA County Bar Assn., Assn. Trial Lawyers Am., Women's Law Assn. LA, Phi Beta Kappa. Office: Law Offices of Amy E Clark Kleinpeter Ste 306 260 S Los Robles Ave Pasadena CA 91101 Office Phone: 626-507-8090. Office Fax: 626-737-6030. Business E-Mail: amykleinpeter@earthlink.net.

KLEIN-SEETHARAMAN, JUDITH, biochemist; b. Cologne, Nord-Rhein Westfalen, Germany, May 30, 1971; d. Clementine Klein; m. Sridhar Seetharaman, Mar. 5, 1971; 1 child, Roshan. PhD, MIT, 1996—2000. Humboldt fellow Goethe Universitaet Frankfurt, Frankfurt/Main, Germany, 2001—; rsch. scientist Carnegie Mellon U., Pittsburgh, 2001—; asst. prof. U. Pitts., Pa., 2002—. Co-director Ctr. Biol. Lang. Modeling, Pittsburgh, 2002—; vis. rschr. Forschungsinstitut Juelich, Nordrhein-Westfalen, Germany, 2002—. Author: (computer game) Biomedical Problem Solving Environment. Recipient Sofja Kovalevskaja Prize, Humboldt-Found. and Bundesregierung Deutschland, 2001; fellow Predoctoral Fellowship, Howard Hughes Med. Inst., 1996-2000; grantee Computational Learning and Discovery in Biol. Sequence, Structure and Function Mapping, NSF, 2002-2007. Mem.: Biophysical Soc., Protein Soc. Achievements include research in analysis of conformational changes in g protein coupled receptors and other signaling proteins using biochemical, biophysical and computational approaches; use of analogy between language and biology for the mapping of sequence to structure, function and dynamics of proteins.

KLEINSINGER, STUART, retired lawyer, music producer; b. NYC, Aug. 1, 1936; s. Harold Kleinsinger and Frieda Feldman. BS, U. Wis., Madison, 1957; JD, St. John's U., NYC, 1959. Bar: NY 1960. Tchr. NYC Bd. Edn., Bronx, 1957—59; asst. corp. counsel City of NY Law Dept., 1966—70; asst. atty. gen. State of NY Law Dept., NYC, 1970—91; prodr. Highlights in Jazz, NYC, 1973—. Vol. tchr. NYC Bd. Edn., 1985—94; Dem. candidate NY State Assembly, Bronx, 1964. Served with US Army N.G., 1959—65. Jewish. Home and Office: Highlights in Jazz 7 Peter Cooper Rd Apt 11E New York NY 10010 Office Phone: 212-982-3697.

KLEINSMITH, BRUCE JOHN See NUTZLE, FUTZIE

KLEINSORGE, WILLIAM PETER, metallurgical engineer; b. San Francisco, Feb. 10, 1941; s. William P. Kleinsorge; m. Kathryn Deane Vincent, Nov. 14, 1966; children: Elizabeth Louise, Victoria Anne. BS in Metall. Engring., U. Nev.-Reno, 1964. Registered profl. engr., S.C., Calif. Welding engr. Mare Island Naval Shipyard, Vallejo, Calif., 1965—69, Charleston-Naval Shipyard, 1969—70; supervisory welding engr. U.S. Naval Ship Repair Facility, Subic Bay, Philippines, 1970—72; head welding engr. Charleston Naval Shipyard, 1972—79; metall. engr. U.S. Nuc. Regulatory Commn., Atlanta, 1979—99; ret., 1999. With Nat. Guard US Army, 1965—72. Mem.: Am. Soc. Mil. Engrs., Am. Welding Soc., Am. Soc. Metals, Masons.

KLEJNOT, GETHA JEAN, school nurse practitioner, music educator; b. Stroudsburg, Pa., July 28, 1950; d. Robert Roger and Betty Wilson Snyder; m. Gerald Francis Klejnot, Sr., Feb. 14, 1986 (div. Apr. 2, 1998); 1 child, Andrew Robert. AA in nursing, C.C. Balt., 1976; MusB, Peabody Conservatory, 1980. RN Md., 1976, CPR, Am. Heart Assn., 1976. Oncology and bone marrow transplant nurse Johns Hopkins Hosp., Balt., 1976—80; head nurse Balt. City Hospitals, 1980—84; home health nurse Bay Area Home Health, Annapolis, 1984—85; icu-ccu nurse SRT Med Staff, Balt.; pvt. piano tchr. for large studio Annapolis, 1987—; sch. health nurse Anne Arundel County Health Dept, 1995—. Tchg. asst. pre-sch. music theory Eastman Sch. Music, U. Rochester, NY, 1968—70. Mem.: Nat. Guild Piano Tchrs. Achievements include Piano study with Maria Luisa Faini, Julio Esteban, Alexander Paskanov; Harpsichord study with Shirley Matthews; Piano pedagogy with Tinka Knopf; Master classes with Eugene List and Ignor Kipnis. Avocation: kayaking. Home: 1217 Plateau Pl Annapolis MD 21401 Home Phone: 410-757-6485; Office Phone: 410-222-7134. Personal E-mail: gesny@comcast.net.

KLEM, CHRISTOPHER A., lawyer; b. Morristown, NJ, Nov. 1, 1952; s. Walter and Mary Elizabeth (Jacoby) K.; m. Susan Mary Morser, Aug. 21, 1976; children: Eric Christopher, Catherine Mary. AB magna cum laude, Harvard U., 1974, JD magna cum laude, 1977. Bar: Mass. 1977. Assoc. Ropes & Gray, Boston, 1977-85, ptnr. corp. dept., 1985—, head ednl. inst practice group & co-head securities & pub. co. practice group. Contbr. articles to profl. jours. Commr. Conservation Com., Lincoln, Mass., 1989-95; trustee, v.p. Fenn Sch., 1996-98; chmn. Lincoln Cmty. Preservation Action Com., 2000-02; trustee Rural Land Found., 1998-2002, St. Mark's Sch., 2002-06; trustee, mem. coun., dir. Mass. Audubon Soc., 2003-; advisor Chewonki Found., 2006—; mem. town planning com. Lincoln, 2006—; overseer DeCordova Mus., 2006-. Mem. ABA (chmn. com. ins. regulation sect. adminstrv. law 1989-91, vice chmn. 1985-89), Boston Bar Assn., Belmont Hill Club, Boston Econs. Club, Phi Beta Kappa. Office: Ropes & Gray One International Pl Boston MA 02110 Home Phone: 781-259-9304; Office Phone: 617-951-7410. Office Fax: 617-951-7050. Business E-Mail: christopher.klem@ropesgray.com, cklem@ropesgray.com.

KLEMA, DONALD DAVID, architect; b. Oak Ridge, Tenn., June 28, 1956; s. Ernest Donald and Virginia Clyde (Carlock) Klema; m. Martha Louise Wetherill, May 22, 1994; 1 child, Madeleine Wetherill. BA with honors, Princeton U., 1978; postgrad., Rice U., 1978-79; MArch, MIT, 1982. Registered arch., Mass. Intern Morris-Aubry Architects, Houston, 1979-80; arch. Ann Beha Assocs., Boston, 1982-86; assoc. William Rawn Assocs., Boston, 1986-89; sr. assoc. Kallmann, McKinnell & Wood Architects, Boston, 1989—2004; assoc. prin. DiMella Shaffer, Boston, 2004—. Design studio instr. Boston Archtl. Ctr., 1989—90, thesis advisor, 1990, vis. archtl. critic, MIT, Mass. Coll. Art, Roger Williams Coll., Wentworth Inst. Tech., 1982—. Prin. works include Charlestown Navy Yard Rowhouses (AIA Honor award, 1994), Marx Hall, Princeton (N.J.) U. (Boston Soc. Archs. award, 1996), Miller Performing Arts Ctr., Alfred U. (AIA/Brick Inst. Am. award, 2001, Boston Soc. Archs. award, 1999), Ewing Marion Kauffman Found. Hdqs., Kansas City, Mo., World Trade Ctr. W., Boston (award Assoc. Gen. Contr. Am., 2003, Boston Soc. Archs. award, 2004), New Gables Residence Hall, U. NH, Durham. Travel grantee, Aga Khan Found., 1982. Mem.: AIA (found. scholar 1981—82), Design Build Inst. Am. (bd. dirs. New England chpt.), Boston Soc. Archs., Phi Beta Kappa. Democrat. Home: 26 Butman St Beverly MA 01915-4649 Office: DiMella Shaffer 281 Summer St Boston MA 02210 Office Phone: 617-426-5004. Business E-Mail: dklema@dimellashaffer.com.

KLEMA, ERNEST DONALD, nuclear physicist, educator; b. Wilson, Kan., Oct. 4, 1920; s. William W. and Mary Bess (Vopat) K.; m. Virginia Clyde Carlock, May 23, 1953; children: Donald David, Catherine Marion. AB in Chemistry, U. Kans., 1941, MA in Physics, 1942; postgrad., Princeton U., 1942, U. Ill., 1946-49; PhD in Physics, Rice U., 1951. Staff scientist Los Alamos Sci. Lab., 1943-46; sr. physicist Oak Ridge Nat. Lab., 1950-56, prin. physicist, 1958; assoc. prof. nuclear engring. U. Mich., 1956-58; prof. nuclear engring. Northwestern U., 1959-68, chmn. dept. engring. scis., 1960-66; prof. engring. sci. Tufts U., 1968-86, dean Coll. Engring., 1968-73, adj. prof. internat. politics Fletcher Sch. Law and Diplomacy, 1973-83, dean emeritus, prof. emeritus Coll. of Engring., 1987—. Vis. scholar physics Harvard U., 1985-86; chmn. subcom. on neutron standards and measurements NRC, 1958-62; del. Internat. Atomic Energy Agy. symposium neutron detection, dosimetry and standardiazation, Harwell, Eng., 1962; cons. Oak Ridge Nat. Lab., Argonne Nat. Lab. Author articles fission cross-sects., gamma-gamma angular correlations, empirical nuclear models, thermal neutron measurements, semi-conductor radiation detectors.;patentee purification hydrogen-argon mixtures. Fellow Am. Phys. Soc., Am Nuclear Soc.; mem. IEEE (sr.), Phi Beta Kappa, Sigma Xi, Pi Mu Epsilon, Alpha Chi Sigma. Clubs: Harbor (Seal Harbor, Me.).

KLEMAN, KIMBERLY C., editor-in-chief; Grad., U. NC-Chapel Hill Sch. Journalism and Mass Communication. Editor St. Petersburg Times, Fla.; dep. editl. dir. Consumer Reports, editor-in-chief, dep. editl. dir., 2007—. Office: Consumer Reports Consumers Union 101 Truman Ave Yonkers NY 10703-1057*

KLEMANN, GILBERT LACY, II, lawyer; b. New Rochelle, NY, July 26, 1950; s. N. Robert and Rosemary Virginia (Gerard) K.; m. Patricia Louise Hild, June 16, 1973; children: Tricia Rosemary, Gilbert Hild. AB, Coll. Holy Cross, 1972; JD, Fordham U., 1975. Bar: N.Y. 1976, U.S. Dist. Ct. (so. and ea. dists.) N.Y. 1976, Conn. 1988, U.S. Supreme Ct. 1991. Assoc. Chadbourne & Parke, NYC, 1975-83, ptnr., 1983-90, of counsel, 2000; sr. v.p., gen. counsel Fortune Brands, Inc. (formerly Am. Brands Inc.), Old Greenwich, Conn., 1991-97, exec. v.p. strategic and legal affairs, 1998, exec. v.p. corp., mem. bd. dirs., 1999; sr. v.p., gen. counsel Avon Products, Inc., NYC, 2001—. Bd. dirs. N.Am. Galvanizing and Coatings, Inc., Alliance One Internat., Inc., NY Lawyers Pub. Interest, Inc. Editor Fordham Law Rev., 1974-75. Mem. Conn. Bar Assn., Greenwich (Conn.) Country Club, Nassau Club (Princeton, N.J.), Longboat Key Club (Fla.). Republican. Roman Catholic. Avocation: golf. Home: 25 Hope Farm Rd Greenwich CT 06830-3331 also: 415 L'Ambiance Dr Longboat Key FL 34288 Office: Avon Products Inc 1345 Ave of the Americas New York NY 10105-0196 Personal E-mail: gilbert.klemann@avon.com.

KLEMENS, PAUL GUSTAV, physicist, researcher; b. Vienna, May 24, 1925; came to U.S., 1959, naturalized, 1968; s. Walter and Ida (Klug) K.; m. Ruth Hannah Wiener, July 30, 1950; children: Michael Walter, Susan Margaret. BSc, U. Sydney, 1946, MSc, 1948; PhD, Oxford U., 1950. With Nat. Standards Lab., Sydney, Australia, 1950-59, research officer, 1950-52, sr. research officer, 1952-57, prin. research officer, 1957-59; physicist Westinghouse Research Lab., Pitts., 1959-64, mgr. transport properties of solids dept., 1964-67; prof. physics U. Conn., 1967-91, prof. emeritus, 1991—, head dept. physics, 1967-74. Vis. prof. Leiden (The Netherlands) U., 1963-64, City U., London, 1989, U. Nottingham, Eng., 1992; mem. adv. bd. on heat Nat. Bur. Standards, 1967-70, mem. adv. bd. on cryogenics, 1974-79; mem. governing bd. Internat. Thermal Conductivity Confs., 1973—; mem. adv. bd. associateship program NRC, 1983-87; mem. standing com. on accreditation Conn. Bd. Higher Edn., 1980-86; cons. Los Alamos Nat. Lab., 1972-97. Contbr. articles to sci. jours. Recipient Y.S. Touloukian award Heat Transfer div. ASME, 1988. Fellow Am. Phys. Soc.; mem. Conn. Acad. Sci. and Engring. (fin. com. 1998-2002) Clubs: Cosmos Washington. Achievements include The Internat. Conference on Phonon Scattering in Condensed Matter decided in 2001 to name its trienniel award the Klemens Award, to recognise his early work in the field. Home: 21 Timber Dr Storrs Mansfield CT 06268-1210 Office: U Conn Dept Physics Storrs Mansfield CT 06269-3046 Office Phone: 860-429-6137. Personal E-mail: klemens@rcn.com.

KLEMENS, RUDOLF HENRYK, mechanical engineer; b. Cracow, Poland, Oct. 1, 1942; s. Jan Ferdynand and Eugenia (Plaza) K.; m. Barbara Jadwiga Krysztopik, Aug. 21, 1976; children: Bartosz, Jacek. MSc, Warsaw U. of Tech., 1968, PhD, 1978, DS, 1994. Asst. Warsaw U. of Tech., 1968-78, asst. prof., 1978-94, assoc. prof., 1994-2001, prof., 2001—. Dep. head of divsn. aircraft engines Warsaw U. of Tech., 1974-86, head combustion group, 1983-88, head postgrad. study in combustion, 1981, 84, head dept. election com., 1996; chmn. adminstrn. Clean Combustion Found., Warsaw, 1994-96; dep. chmn. Clean Combustion Found. Coun., 2000-04; sec. supervisory bd. Polish Combustion Inst., 2001-05; dep. dir. Inst. Heat Engring, Warsaw U. Tech., 2005; mem. Polish Combustion Inst., 2005-; presenter in field. Author: more than 100 publications in field. Recipient Silver medal for merits in fire fighting, 1980, 2 awards Ministry Edn., 1972, 82, Golden Cross of Merit Pres. of Polish Republic, 1990, award Head Nat. Labour Safety Inspectorate, 1996, 2002, Com. Nat. Edn. medal, 2003; named Concurrent Prof., Northeastern U., China, 2002. Mem. AIAA, Internat. Group of Experts on the Explosion Risks of Unstable Substances, Polish Acad. of Scis. (mem. combustion sect.), Polish Astronautical Soc. (dep. chmn. 2001). Roman Catholic. Achievements include research in explosion parameters determination and explosion suppression study; patents for powder extinguisher. Avocations: history, classical music. Office: Warsaw U Tech Dept Power/Aero Engr Nowowiejska 21/25 00-665 Warsaw Poland Office Phone: 0048-22-234-5280. Business E-Mail: klemrud@itc.pw.edu.pl.

KLEMENS, THOMAS LLOYD, editor; b. Pitts., Mar. 28, 1952; s. Robert F. and Ann E. (Lacy) K.; m. Norreen McLellan, Aug. 4, 1973; children: Jonathan, Zachary. BFA, Carnegie-Mellon U., 1974; BSCE, U. Pitts., 1983; postgrad., Roosevelt U., Chgo., 1990-91. Registered profl. engr., Ill. Choir dir., tchr. Wellsville (Ohio) H.S., 1975-76; asst. band dir., tchr. North Hills H.S., Ross Twp., Pa., 1976-79; field engr. S.J. Groves & Sons, Pitts., 1983; structural engr. Sargent & Lundy, Chgo., 1983-87; field engr. Structural Preservation Systems, Inc., Margate, NJ, 1987; project mgr. Northwest Group, Inc., West Chicago, Ill., 1987; engr., purchasing agt. L.J. Keefe Co., Mt. Prospect, Ill., 1987-89; from assoc. editor to editor Hwy. & Heavy Constrn. Cahners Pub., Des Plaines, Ill., 1989-91, editor Hwy. & Heavy Constrn. Products, 1991-93, sr. editor Consulting/Specifying Engr., 1993-94; co-owner Wordwright, Palatine, Ill., 1993—. Instr. Motorola U., 1996-98; com. on constrn. equipment Transp. Rsch. Bd., Washington, 1991-93 adj. faculty William Rainey Harper Coll., Palatine, 1997—. Author Hwy. and Heavy Constrn., 1989-91, editor, 1991-92; author, editor Infrastructure, 1992-93; sr. editor Cons./Specifying Engr., 1993-94; editor PM Engr., Bus. News Pub., 1994-96, Plumbing Engr., TMB Pub., 1996-2003; sr. editor engring. HanleyWood LLC, 2003—. Mem. ASCE, Am. Concrete Inst., Am. Soc. Testing and Materials. Office: Hanley Wood Bus Media 8725 W Higgins Rd Ste 600 Chicago IL 60631 Home Phone: 847-934-8298; Office Phone: 773-824-2511. Business E-Mail: tklemens@hanleywood.com.

KLEMENT, VERA, artist; b. Gdansk, Dec. 14, 1929; d. Klement and Rose (Rakovchik) Shapiro; div.; 1 son, Max Klement Shapey. Cert. in fine arts, Cooper Union Sch. Art and Architecture, 1950. Prof. art U. Chgo., 1969—95. Residency and stipend Camargo Found., Cassis, France. One woman shows include RoKo Gallery, N.Y.C., 1958, 60, Bridge Gallery, N.Y.C., 1965, Artemisia Gallery, Chgo., 1974, Chicago Gallery, 1976, Marianne Deson Gallery, 1979, 81, Goethe Inst., 1981, CDS Gallery, N.Y.C., 1981, 84, Roy Boyd Gallery, Chgo., 1983, 85, 87, 89, 90, 91, 92, 93, Spertus Mus., Chgo., 1987, retrospective exhbn., 1953-86, Renaissance Soc., Chgo., 1987, Brody's Gallery, Washington, 1992, Fassbender Gallery, Chgo., 1994, 95, 96, 97, Chgo. Cultural Ctr., 1999, retrospective exhbn., 1965-99, Fassbender, 1999, 2001, Ft. Wayne (Ind.) Mus. Art, 2001, Block Mus., Northwestern U., Evanston, Ill., 2001, U. Ariz. Mus. Art, Tucson, 2001, Tarble Arts Ctr., Ea. Ill. U., Charleston, 2002, Brauer Art Mus., Valparaiso (Ind.) U., 2002, Eric Yake Kenagy Gallery, Goshen (Ind.) Coll., 2003, Miami U. Mus. Art, Oxford, Ohio, 2004, Maya Polsky Gallery, Chgo., 2004, Frederick Baker, Chgo. 2004, Printworks, Chgo., 2004, Daum Mus. Contemporary Art, Sedalia, Mo., 2004, CDS Gallery, N.Y.C., 2005, Metcap, Chgo., 2005, Alfedena Gallery, Chgo., 2007; group shows include Mus. Modern Art, N.Y.C., 1954, 55, Bklyn. Mus., 1950-60, Dallas Mus. Fine Arts, 1954, Tate Gallery, London, 1956, Museo de Arte Moderno, Barcelona, Spain, 1955, Musee d'Arte Moderne, Paris, 1955, U. Ky., 1959, Art Inst. Chgo., 1967, Walker Art Ctr., Mpls., 1977, U. Mo., 1978, Detroit Inst. Arts, 1978, Ukrainian Inst. Art, Chgo., 1978, Jewish Mus., N.Y.C., 1982, Kunstverein, Munich, Germany, 1987, Amerika Haus, Berlin, 1987, Terra Mus. Am. Art, Chgo., 1988, Corcoran Gallery, Washington, 1994, Cultural Ctr., Chgo., 1994, former IBM Gallery, N.Y.C., 1995, Virginia Beach Ctr. Arts, 1995, Fischer Art Gallery U. So. Calif., 1995, Portland (Oreg.) Mus. Art, Evanston Art Ctr., Mus. Contemporary Art, Chgo., 1996, Block Gallery Northwestern U., Evanston, 1996, Riva Yares Gallery, Santa Fe, 2002, Klein Artworks, Chgo., 2002, Maya Polsky Gallery, Chgo., 2002; represented in permanent collections Mus. Modern Art, N.Y.C., Phila. Mus. Art, Print Club, Phila., Ill. State Mus., Springfield, U. Tex., Nat. Mus. Am. Art, Washington, Jewish Mus., N.Y.C., Art Inst. Chgo., Philip Morris, N.Y.C., Smart Mus. U. Chgo., Sch. Social Svc. Adminstrn. U. Chgo., Mus. Contemporary Art, Chgo., Mary and Leigh Block Mus., Evanston, Mus. Art U. Ariz., Tucson, Union Club League Chgo., Daum Mus. Contemporary Art, Sedalia, Mo., Kresge Mus. Art, East Lansing, Mich., U. Miami Mus. Art, Oxford, Ohio, Davis Mus., Wellesley, Conn., Clay Ctr. Arts, Charleston, W. Va.; also pvt. collections. Recipient Pollock/Krasner Found. award, 1998; Louis Comfort Tiffany Found. fellow, 1954, Guggenheim fellow, 1981-82, Nat. Endowment for the Arts fellow, 1987; Ill. Arts Coun. grantee, 1988, Camargo Found., Cassis, France, 2006. Personal E-mail: veraklement@aol.com.

KLEMENZ, CHRISTINE F., science educator, researcher; b. Estavayer-le-Lac, Switzerland; arrived in US, 2001, permanent resident; d. Heinz H. Klemenz and Irene D. Felchlin; m. Stephen D. Rivenbark, Oct. 11, 2003. Med. lab asst., Coll. for Med. Professions, Lausanne, Switzerland, 1980; chem. engr., U. of Applied Scis., Fribourg, Switzerland, 1990; PhD, U. of Tokyo, 2000. Rsch. engr. Swiss Fed. Inst. of Tech., Lausanne, 1990—2001; rsch. scholar U. Ctrl. Fla., Orlando, 2001—02, faculty, 2002—. Co-organizer 34th Course of Assn. Vaudoise Chercheurs Physique, Grimentz, Switzerland, 1992, First Internat. Sch. on Crystal Growth Tech., Beatenberg, Switzerland, 1998; lectr. Internat. Sch. on Advanced Materials, Madras, India, 1994, 10th Internat. Summer Sch. on Crystal Growth-10, Rimini, Italy, 1998. Recipient Young Scientist award, Internat. Union of Crystallography, 1994, Best Thesis award, Fribourg Industries Group, 1990, Outstanding Achievement award, Swiss Fed. Inst. of Tech., 1999, 2000. Mem.: IEEE, Am. Assn. for Crystal Growth, Am. Ceramics Soc., Materials Rsch. Soc., Air Force Assn. Achievements include research in First single-crystalline high-temperature superconducting NdBCO and YBCO films by LPE; First colorless transparent anatase single-crystals by CTR - enabled for first time photoelectrochemical investigations (for Graetzel solar cells development); Nitride films by LPE; LGS, LGT, LGN (langasite-type) films by LPE and Czochralski technique for high-precision resonators. Avocations: horses, travel, history, music. Office: U Ctrl Fla 4000 Central Florida Blvd Orlando FL 32816 Office Phone: 407-823-6065. Office Fax: 407-882-1462. Business E-Mail: cklemenz@mail.ucf.edu.

KLEMIN, LAWRENCE R., lawyer; b. New Rockford, ND, Mar. 31, 1945; s. Lawrence R. Klemin and Carol M. (Cook) Roaldson; m. Rita R. DiPalma, Sept. 2, 1970; children: Laura K., Peter L. BA in English, U. N.D., 1967, JD with distinction, 1978. Bar: N.D. 1978, U.S. Dist. Ct. N.D. 1978, U.S. Ct. Appeals (8th cir.) 1987, U.S. Supreme Ct. 1988. Hearing officer N.D. Employment Security Bur., Bismarck, 1971-75; assoc. Atkinson & Dwyer, Bismarck, 1978-81; ptnr. Atkinson, Dwyer & Klemin, Bismarck, 1981-82, Dwyer & Klemin, Bismarck, 1982-86; pres. Lawrence R. Klemin, P.C., Bismarck, 1986-92, Bucklin & Klemin, P.C., Bismarck, 1992-96, Bucklin, Klemin & McBride, P.C., Bismarck, 1996—. Pres. Title and Escrow Co., Bismarck, 1988-98, Litig. Svcs., Inc., Bismarck, 1995—; state rep. N.D. legis. assembly, 1998—; mem. state adv. coun. N.D. Office Adminstrv. Hearings, Bismarck, 1993-98; commr. Nat. Conf. of Commrs. on Uniform State Laws, 1999—; arbitrator Nat. Arbitration Forum, BBB Auto Line. Author: Small-Case Litigation Forms, 2004, 2d edit., 2006; author, editor Civil Practice of North Dakota, 1993— Bd. dirs. N.D. March of Dimes, Bismarck, 1994-2002, Burleigh-Morton chpt. Am. Red Cross, 2002—, chair, 2006-; mem. adv. coun. RSVP-Ctrl. N.D., 2005—; mem. Corpus Christi Parish Coun., Bismarck, 1996-2002, chair, 2000-01. With U.S. Army, 1967-70, Vietnam. Mem. State Bar Assn. N.D. (chair adminstrv. law com. 1996-98), N.D. Land Title Assn. (legis. com. 1990-99), Bismarck Mandan C. of C. (bd. dirs. 1996-98), Optimist Internat. (bd. dirs. 1985-86), Elks, Eagles, Am. Legion, Optimist Club. Home: 1709 Montego

Dr Bismarck ND 58503-0856 Office: Bucklin Klemin & McBride PC 400 E Broadway #500 PO Box 955 Bismarck ND 58502-0955 Home Phone: 701-222-2577; Office Phone: 701-258-8988. Business E-Mail: lklemin@bkmpc.com.

KLEMPERER, WILLIAN, chemistry professor; b. NYC, Oct. 6, 1927; s. Paul and Margit (Freund) K.; m. Elizabeth Cole, Jan. 12, 1949; children: Joyce Hillary, Paul, Wendy Judith. AB, Harvard U., 1950; PhD, U. Calif., Berkeley, 1954; DSc, U. Chgo., 1996. Instr. chemistry Harvard U., Cambridge, Mass., 1954-57, asst. prof., 1957-61, assoc. prof., 1961-65, prof., 1965—. Asst. dir. NSF, Washington, 1979-81; vis. scientist Bell Tel. Lab., 1963-83; Evans lectr. Ohio State U., 1981, Pratt lectr. U. Va., 1984, Rollefson lectr. U. Calif., 1985, Oesper lectr. U. Cin., 1987, Kolthoff lectr. U. Minn., 1987, Mary E. Kapp lectr. Va. Commonwealth U., 1987, Linus Pauling Disting. lectr. Oreg. State U., 1988, Harry Emmett Gunning lectr. U. Alta., Can., 1988, Fritz London Meml. lectr. Duke U., 1989, Hinshelwood lectr. Oxford U., Eng., 1989, Neckers lectr. So. Ill. U., 1990; George C. Pimentel meml. lectr. U. Calif., Berkeley, 1992, vis. Miller prof., 1998; Joe L. Franklin meml. lectr. Rice U., 1994, E.K.C. Lee Fellowship lectr. U. Calif., Irvine, 1994; Richard C. Lord lectr. MIT, Cambridge, Mass., 1997; Bernstein lectr. UCLA, 1997. Served with A.C., USN, 1944-46. Recipient Wetherill medal Franklin Inst., 1978, Disting. Svc. medal NSF, 1981, Bomem Michelson award Coblentz Soc., 1990, Faraday Medal and Lectureship Royal Soc. Chemistry, 1995, Ioannes Marcus Marci medal Prague, 2004; named hon. citizen City of Toulouse, France, 2000. Fellow Am. Phys. Soc. (Earle Plyler prize 1983); mem. NAS, Am. Acad. Arts and Scis., Am. Chem. Soc. (Irving Langmuir award 1980, Peter Debye award in phys. chemistry 1994, E. Bright Wilson award in spectroscopy 2001, Remsen award Md. sect. 1992). Achievements include research in molecular structure, energy transfer and intermolecular forces using experimental spectroscopic methods; modelling molecule formation and detection in the interstellar medium. Home: 53 Shattuck Rd Watertown MA 02472-1310 Office: Harvard U Dept Chemistry and Chem Biology 12 Oxford St Cambridge MA 02138-2902 Office Phone: 617-495-4094. Business E-Mail: klemperer@chemistry.harvard.edu.

KLENK, JAMES ANDREW, lawyer; b. Evergreen Park, Ill., July 18, 1949; s. Paul Theodore and Joan (Launspach) K.; m. Carol Evans, Aug. 26, 1972; children: Paul Andrew, Matthew Evans. BA, Beloit Coll., 1971; JD, U. Wis., 1974. Bar: Ill. 1974, Wis. 1974, U.S. Supreme Ct. 1978. Law clk. to Judge Thomas E. Fairchild U.S. Ct. Appeals (7th cir.), Chgo., 1974-75; assoc. Kirkland & Ellis, Chgo., 1975-78; ptnr. Reuben & Proctor, Chgo., 1978-86, Isham, Lincoln & Beale, Chgo., 1986-88, Sonnenschein, Nath & Rosenthal, Chgo., 1988—. Articles editor Wis. Law Rev. Mem. ABA (litigation sect., torts and ins. practice sect., bus. law sect.), Ill. Bar Assn., Media Law Ctr., Order of Coif, Phi Beta Kappa. Office: Sonnenschein Nath & Rosenthal 8000 Sears Tower Chicago IL 60606 Office Phone: 312-876-8062. Business E-Mail: jklenk@sonnenschein.com.

KLENK, TIMOTHY CARVER, lawyer; b. Glen Cove, NY, Apr. 29, 1939; s. Horace I. and Laura (Dugan) K.; m. Ann Ruth Schuessler, 1961 (dec. 1966); 1 child, Carolyn; m. Margaret Jo Garrett, Aug. 30, 1969. AB, Wheaton Coll., 1961; JD, Northwestern U., 1967. Bar: Ill. 1967, U.S. Dist. Ct. (no. dist.) Ill. 1968, U.S. Dist. Ct. (cen. dist.) Wis. 1976, U.S. Dist. Ct. (cen. dist.) Ill. 1981, U.S. Ct. Appeals (7th cir.) 1979, U.S. Supreme Ct. 1980. Systems engr. IBM, NYC, 1961-62; assoc. Kirkland & Ellis, Chgo., 1967-70, Pope, Ballard, Shepard & Fowle Ltd., Chgo., 1970-74, ptnr., 1974-77, dir., 1977-94, mng. dir., 1993-94; ptnr. Ross & Hardies, Chgo., 1994—2003, McGuireWoods LLP, 2003—. Bd. dirs. Living Bibles Internat. U.S., Naperville, Ill., 1983-91, also v.p. 1st lt. U.S. Army, 1962-64. Mem. ABA, Ill. Bar Assn., 7th Cir. Bar Assn., Am. Judicature Soc., Christian Legal Soc. (bd. dirs. 1986—, pres. 1988-90), Am. Arbitration Assn. (arbitrator), Order of Coif. Republican. Avocations: flying, water sports, skiing. Office: Ross & Hardies 150 N Michigan Ave Ste 2500 Chicago IL 60601-7567 E-mail: tklenk@mcguirewoods.com.

KLEPINGER, JOHN WILLIAM, trailer manufacturing company executive; b. Lafayette, Ind., Feb. 7, 1945; s. John Franklin and R. Wanda (North) K.; m. Mary Patricia Duffy, May 1, 1976; 1 child, Nicholas Patrick. BS, Ball State U., 1967, MA, 1968. Sales engr. CTS Corp., Elkhart, Ind., 1969-70; exec. v.p. Woodlawn Products Corp., Elkhart, 1970-78; v.p. Period Ind., Henderson, Ky., 1976-78, Sotebeer Constrn. Co., Inc., Elkhart, 1978-81; gen. mgr. Wells Industries Inc., Ogden, Utah, 1981—2000; regional mgr. Wells Cargo, Inc., Phoenix, 1995—, Carbondale, Pa., 1999—2003. Regional dir. Zion's First Nat. Bank, Ogden, 1986-99. Bd. dirs. St. Benedict's Hosp., Ogden, 1986-94, chmn., 1987-94; bd. dirs. Weber County Indsl. Devel. Corp., Nat. Job Tng. Partnership Inc., 1986-89; active Weber-Morgan Pvt. Industry Coun., 1983-96, Utah Job Tng. Coordinating Coun., 1988-96, chmn. 1993-94; co-chmn. Surge Brake Coalition, 1999—, Trailer Safety Industry Coalition, 2004—; active Tech. and Maintenance Coun. Task Force, 1999—. Named Ogden Bus. Man of Yr., Weber County Sch. Dist., 1984. Mem. Nat. Assn. Trailer Mfrs. (bd. dirs. 1993—, sec.-treas. 1993-94, 98-99, v.p. 1994-95, pres. 1995-97), Weber County Prodn. Mgrs. Assn. (pres. 1984-85, 92-93), Nat. Assn. Pvt. Industry Couns. (bd. dirs. 1986-96, pres. 1988-92), Nat. Alliance Bus. (bd. dirs. 1987-90), Soc. Automotive Engrs. (trailer com. 1999—), Trailer Safety Ind. Coalition (co-chmn. 2004—), Ogden Area C. of C. (bd. dirs. 1986-96, treas. 1986-89), Phoenix C. of C., Exch. Club (bd. dirs. Ogden 1984-86). Roman Catholic. Avocations: finance, community service, leadership, sports, travel. Office: Wells Cargo Inc 6902 W Hadley St Phoenix AZ 85043-4300

KLEPNER, JERRY D., federal agency administrator; b. St. Louis, Dec. 4, 1944; s. Philip and Theresa (Smith) K.; m. Bonnie Klepner, July 1, 1966 (div. 1980); children: Robert, Melissa; m. Karetta Hubbard, June 6, 1981. BA, Washington U., 1967, postgrad., 1966—67. Nat. exec. v.p., dir. legislation Nat. Treasury Employees Union, Washington, 1971-84; ptnr. Anderson, Benjamin, Read & Haney, Washington, 1986-87; staff dir. U.S. Ho. of Reps. Subcom. on Compensation and Employee Benefits, Washington, 1984-86; dir. legislation Am. Fedn. State, County and Mcpl. Employees, Washington, 1987-93; asst. sec. legislation Dept. Health and Human Svcs., Washington, 1993-96; sr. v.p. Ketchum Pub. Rels., Washington, 1996-98; mng. dir. Black, Kelly, Scruggs & Healey, Washington, 1998—. Commr. Va. Statewide Health Coordinating Coun., Richmond, 1986-87; dir. No. Va. Health Systems Agy., Fairfax, 1984-87. Democrat. Jewish. Achievements include boating, fishing, swimming, photography, hist. non-fiction and fiction. Office: Black Kelly Scruggs & Healey 1801 K St NW Ste 901-l Washington DC 20006-1301

KLEPPE, JOHN ARTHUR, electrical engineer, educator, company executive; b. Oakland, Calif., Feb. 21, 1939; s. Arthur William and Musa (Anderson) K.; m. Julianna Marie Galli, Aug. 12, 1961; children: John Frederick, Johanna Beth, Judith Anne. BSEE, U. Nev., 1961, MSEE, 1967; PhD, U. Calif., Davis, 1970. Registered profl. engr., Nev., Calif. Prof. elec. engring. U. Nev., Reno, 1970—2006, prof. emeritus, 2006—, dir. Engring. Research and Devel., 1976-88; pres., research cons. Sci. Engring. Instruments, Inc., Reno, 1968-97; pres. Klepco, Inc., 1976—. Cons.; chief engr. NSF weather expdn. to Antarctica, 1977; del. White House Conf. Small Bus., 1980 Author: (textbook) Engineering Applications of Acoustics, 1989; contbr. articles, papers to publs. and confs. around the world. Served to lt. C.E. USN, 1961-65. Recipient Outstanding Engring. Achievement award for Nev., 1981, 84; Inventor of Yr. award, 1985, Olympus Lifetime award, 2006, Nev. Tech. Hall of Fame, 2006. Mem. IEEE (life), Nev. Innovation and Tech. Coun. (pres. 1981-93, pres. 1996-97), Sigma Xi, Tau Beta Pi. Home: 2776 Spinnaker Dr Reno NV 89519 Office: U Nev Dept Elec and Biomed Engring MS 260 Reno NV 89557-0260 Business E-Mail: kleppe@ee.unr.edu.

KLEPPE, LARS W., retired pathologist; s. Lars and Luise Elizabth Kleppe; m. Marlys A. Miller, May 17, 1958; children: Todd William, Lynn Elizabeth Jacob. BS, No. State Tchrs. Coll., 1951; BS in Medicine, U. Nebr., 1951; MD, U. Nebr., Omaha, 1955. Diplomate Am. Bd. Pathology, 1962. Intern Madison Gen. Hosp., Wis., 1955—56, pathology resident, 1956—60; pathologist, dir. labs. Beloit Meml. Hosp., Wis., 1959—70, Burns Clinic Med. Ctr. P.C., Petoskey, Mich., 1971—93, No. Mich. Hosp., Petoskey, 1971—93. Former dir. schs. med. tech., Beloit and Petoskey; bd. dirs. Burns Clin. Med. Ctr., P.C., Harbor Hall Ctr. for Substance Abuse. Chmn. budget com. United Givers, Beloit, 1961—63. Fellow: Am. Soc. Pathologists, Coll. Am. Pathologists. Home: 920 Glen Haven Cir Apt 2 Petoskey MI 49770

KLEPPER, CAROL HERDMAN, mental health therapist; b. Wagner, SD, July 17, 1933; d. Forrest Glenwood and Augusta Wilhamina (Mills) Herdman; m. Albert Raymond Klepper, May 14, 1955; children: James David, Leesa Lynn, Krista Patrice. BS in Psychology cum laude, South Oreg. State Coll., 1987; MS in Counseling, Oreg. State U., 1989. Nat. cert. counselor, lic. profl. counselor; cert. diplomate in psychotherapy. Dir. counseling Klamath Hospice, Klamath Falls, Oreg., 1990-91; staff therapist Klamath Mental Health Ctr., 1991-94; in-house counselor Wednesday's Child, 1995-2001, title 19 supv., 1996-99; pvt. practice Klamath Falls, Oreg., 2000—. Data rschr. Rich Pickett and Co., Klamath Falls, 1986—90; pre-commitment investigator Klamath Mental Health Ctr., 1991—94; EPSDT coord. County of Klamath, 1991—94; affil. Big Sage Counseling, 2000—02. Mem. youth svcs. team local mid-schs, Klamath Falls, 1992—94; juv. fire-setters network Klamath Falls Fire Dist. #1, 1992—95; head start health bd. Klamath Falls, 1991—2001; del. People to People Program, 2004, del. to South Africa, 2006, amb. to Rwanda, 2007; adv. bd. Klamath Falls Gospel Mission, 2000—; RAPP Team Mem., 1995—; program therapist KAP, 1995—2000; abuse therapist Klamath County Juvenile Dept., 2000—02; child and family counselor Head Start, 2000—01. Mem. Psi Chi. Home and Office: 8926 Highway 66 Klamath Falls OR 97601-9519 E-mail: klepper@cvc.net.

KLEPPER, ELIZABETH LEE, retired physiologist; b. Memphis, Mar. 8, 1936; d. George Madden and Margaret Elizabeth (Lee) K. BA, Vanderbilt U., 1958; MA, Duke U., 1963, PhD, 1966. Rsch. scientist Commonwealth Sci. and Indsl. Rsch. Orgn., Griffith, Australia, 1966-68, Battelle Northwest Lab., Richland, Wash., 1972-76; asst. prof. Auburn U., Ala., 1968-72; plant physiologist USDA Agrl. Rsch. Svc., Pendleton, Oreg., 1976-85, rsch. leader, 1985-96; ret., 1996. Assoc. editor Crop Sci., 1977-80, 88-90, tech. editor, 1990-92, editor, 1992-95; mem. editl. bd. Plant Physiology, 1977-92, Irrigation Sci., 1987-92; mem. editl. adv. bd. Field Crops Rsch., 1983-91; contbr. articles to profl. jours., chpts. to books. Mem. Umatilla Basin Watershed Coun., 2005—, Umatilla County Critical Groundwater Taskforce, 2005—. Marshall scholar Brit. Govt., 1958-59; NSF fellow, 1964-66; Recipient First Citizen award, Pendleton, 2005, White Rose award, March of Dimes, Portland, 2005. Fellow: AAAS, Am. Soc. Agronomy (monograph com. 1983—90, bd. dirs. 1995—98), Soil Sci. Soc. Am. (fellows com. 1986—88), Crop Sci. Soc. Am. (fellows com. 1989—91, pres.-elect 1995—96, pres. 1996—97, Monsanto Disting. Career award 2004, Presdl. award 2006); mem.: Agronomic Sci. Found. (bd. dirs. 1993—99), Sigma Xi. Home: 1454 SW 45th Pendleton OR 97801 Home Phone: 541-276-8416. E-mail: klepperb@uci.net.

KLEPPER, KENNETH O., healthcare executive; Various exec. mgmt. positions Cigna Healthcare, WellChoice, Inc. (formerly Empire BlueCross BlueShield); pres., COO Medco Health Solutions, Inc., Franklin Lakes, NJ, 2003—. Mem. USN Corp. Exec. Panel. Office: Medco Health Solutions Inc 100 Parsons Pond Dr Franklin Lakes NJ 07417 Office Phone: 800-631-7780.*

KLEPPNER, DANIEL, physicist, researcher; b. NYC, Dec. 16, 1932; s. Otto and Beatrice (Taub) Klepper; m. Beatrice Spencer; children: Paul, Sofie, Andrew. BS, Williams Coll., 1953; BA, Cambridge U., Eng., 1955; PhD, Harvard U., 1959. Asst. prof. physics Harvard U., Cambridge, Mass., 1962-66; assoc. prof. MIT, Cambridge, 1966-73, prof., 1974, prof. emeritus, Lester Wolfe prof. physics, 1986, Lester Wolfe prof. physics emeritus, assoc. dir. Rsch. Lab. of Electronics, 1987—2000, interim dir., Rsch. Lab Electronics, 2001. Author: Introduction to Mechanics, 1973, Quick Calculus, 1986. Named 2006 Nat. Medal Sci. Laureate, NSF, 2007; recipient Wolf prize in physics, Wolf Found., Israel, 2005. Fellow: Am. Acad. Arts and Sciences, Optical Soc. Am. (William F. Meggars award 1991, Frederic Ives medal 2007), AAAS, Am. Phys. Soc. (Davisson-Germer prize 1986, Julius Edgar Lilienfeld prize 1991); mem.: Am. Assn. Physics Teachers (Oersted medal 1996), NAS. Office: MIT Dept Physics 77 Mass Ave Rm 26-237 Cambridge MA 02139-4307 Office Phone: 617-253-6811. Office Fax: 617-258-4876. E-mail: kleppner@mit.edu.*

KLERMAN, LORRAINE VOGEL, public health educator; d. Jacob Vogel and Ethel Avidan; children: Jacob A., Elizabeth B., Karen P, Daniel M. BA, Cornell U., Ithaca, NY, 1950; MPH, Harvard U., Cambridge, Mass., 1953, D in Public Health, 1962. Prof. Yale U. Sch. Medicine, New Haven, 1984—92, U. Ala. Sch. Public Health, Birmingham, 1992—2001, Brandeis U. Heller Sch., Waltham, Mass., 2001—. Recipient Martha May Eliot award, APHA, 1996. Office: Brandeis U 415 South St Waltham MA 02454-9110 Office Phone: 781-736-3715. Business E-Mail: klerman@brandeis.edu.

KLESIUS, PHILLIP HARRY, microbiologist, researcher; b. Phila., Mar. 1, 1938; s. Phillip M. and Mary Hoagen (Plummer) K.; m. Patricia Ann Wood, Oct. 31, 1969; children— Stephen, Patrick BS, Fla. So. U., Lakeland, 1961; MS, Northwestern State U., Natchitoches, La., 1963; PhD, U. Tex., Austin, 1966; postgrad., U. Calif.-San Francisco, 1967. Hon. diplomate Am. Coll. Vet. Microbiologists. Asst. prof. microbiology U. Tex., Austin, 1967-68; asst. prof microbiology U. Ariz., Tucson, 1968-72; asst. chief strep sect. USPHS, Fort Collins, Colo., 1972-73; research microbiologist U.S. Dept. Agr., Auburn, Ala., 1973-82, dir., 1982—. Adj. prof. Auburn U., 1974—; adj. assoc. prof. Med. Coll. S.C., Charleston, 1975—; visting prof. Tuskegee Inst., Ala., 1974— Contbr. articles to profl. jours. Recipient Technology Transfer award USDA, 1999; named USDA Scientist of Yr., 1994, 99. Fellow Am. Acad. Microbiology, Am. Assn. Vet. Immunologists (dir. 1985—), Am. Assn. Vet. Pathologists, Am. Assn. Vet. Parasitologists, Am. Soc. Microbiologists. Office: Aquatic Animal Disease Rsch Lab PO Box 952 Auburn AL 36831-0952 Home: 2009 Hillbrook Cir Auburn AL 36830-7657 Business E-Mail: klesiph@vetmed.auburn.edu. E-mail: klesiph@charter.net, pklesius@ars.usda.gov.

KLESKO, RYAN, professional baseball player; b. Westminster, Calif., June 12, 1971; Right field Atlanta Braves, 1992—99, San Diego Padres, 2000—. Spokesperson Make-A-Wish Found. Avocations: hunting, fishing.

KLESSE, WILLIAM R. (BILL KLESSE), energy executive; BS in Chemical Engring., U. of Dayton, 1968; MBA, West Texas State U., 1973. With Diamond Shamrock (now Valero Energy Corp.), 1969—; sr. v.p./Group Executive Diamond Shamrock Corp., 1989—95, exec. v.p., 1995—96; exec. v.p., Refining, Product Supply and Logistics Ultramar Diamond Shamrock Corp., San Antonio, 1996—98, exec. v.p., operations, 1999—2001; chmn. Shamrock Logistics GP, LLC, 1999—2001; exec. v.p., COO Valero Energy Corp., 2001—05, vice chmn., CEO, 2006—.*

KLETT, EDWIN L., lawyer; b. Clearfield, Pa., Dec. 8, 1935; s. John L. and Gertrude Elizabeth (Larson) K.; m. Janis Lynn Gibson; children: David, Lauren, Krista, Kirklin, Keenan. BS in Commerce and Finance, Bucknell U., 1957; JD, Dickinson Sch. Law, Carlisle, Pa., 1962. Bar: Pa. 1963, U.S. Dist. Ct. (we. dist.) Pa. 1963, U.S. Dist. Ct. (mid. dist.) Pa. 1995, U.S. Dist. Ct. (ea. dist.) Pa. 2000, U.S. Ct. Appeals (3d cir.) 1967, U.S. Ct. Appeals (6th cir.) 1985, U.S. Ct. Appeals (11th cir.) 2001, U.S. Supreme Ct. 1983. Assoc. Eckert, Seamans, Cherin & Mellott, Pitts., 1962, ptnr., 1969; sr. ptnr., chmn. Klett Rooney Lieber & Schorling P.C., Pitts., 1989—2006, Buchanan Ingersoll & Rooney P.C., Pitts., 2006—. Trustee Dickinson Sch. Law, 1982-2005, mem. bd. counselors, 2005; trustee Bucknell U., 2004-2008; mem. Pa. Judicial Contract Bd., 2006-; mem. civil procedural rules com. Pa. Supreme Ct., 1986-99, vice chair, 1989-92, chair, 1993-99; mem. jud. conduct bd. Pa., 2006—. Mem. Pa. State Transp. Adv. Bd., Harrisburg, Pa., 1985—88, Rep. State Fin. Com., Harrisburg, Pa., 1986—91, Allegheny County Rep. Fin. Com., Pitts., 1987—92. Fellow Internat. Acad. Trial Lawyers, Am. Coll. Trial Lawyers (Pa. state com. 1994-99, state chair 1996-98), Am. Bd. Trial Advs., Am. Bar Found., Am. Bar Inst., Pa. Bar Found., Alletheny County Bar Found.; mem. ABA (ho. dels. 1999-2000), Am. Bd. Trial Advs., Acad. Trial Lawyers Allegheny County (bd. govs. 1986-89, pres. 1988-89), Am. Judicature Soc., Allegheny County Bar (bd. govs. 1989-92, 99-02, pres. 1999-01). Home: 151 Ordale Blvd Pittsburgh PA 15228-1525 Office: Buhanan Ingersoll & Rooney PC 1 Oxford Ct Fl 40 Pittsburgh PA 15219-1407 Home Phone: 412-561-3670; Office Phone: 412-392-2178. Business E-Mail: edwin.klett@bipc.com.

KLETT, GORDON A., retired savings and loan association executive; b. Galva, Iowa, Apr. 29, 1925; s. Ernest and Frieda (Gutknecht) K.; m. Edna Mae Klett, June 11, 1950; children: Joel G., Kristin F., Andrea E. BA, Valparaiso U., 1949; MA, UCLA, 1951. With U.S. Weather Bur., St. Paul, 1941—42; vis. lectr. U. Ceylon, Colombo, 1951—52; fgn. svc. officer U.S. Dept. State, Mexico, 1956—58; with Glendale Fed. Savs. and Loan Assn., Calif., 1953—56, 1959—84; pres., chief operating officer Glendale (Calif.) Fed. Savs. and Loan Assn., 1980-84. Served with USAAF, 1943-46.

KLEVINSKY, THOMAS JASON, information technology executive; b. Baltimore, June 11, 1973; s. Walt and Dorene Klevinsky; m. Kristy J. Breslin, Apr. 2, 2005. BS, U. Md., College Park, 1996; MBA, Wilmington Coll., New Castle, Del., 2005. Computer specialist US Army Corps Engrs., Balt., 1994—96; security cons. Axent Technologies, Rockville, Md., 1996—97; mgr. Ernst & Young LLP, Balt., 1997—2002; v.p. security ops. MBNA Am., Newark, 2002—06, Bank of Am., Newark, Del., 2006; v.p. security arch. JPMorgan Chase, Newark, Del., 2006—. Author: (computer security reference book) Hack I.T. Security Through Penetration Testing, 2001. Mem.: Fin. Svc. Info. Sharing Analysis Ctr., Internat. Info. Systems Security Consortium (cert. info. sys. security profl.), Am. Mensa. Republican. Office: JPMorgan Chase 500 Stanton Christiana Rd Newark DE 19713-2107 Home Phone: 410-287-8326; Office Phone: 302-552-0201. Business E-Mail: t.j.klevinsky@jpmorgan.com.

KLEY, JOHN ARTHUR, banker; b. Jericho, NY, Oct. 24, 1921; s. John and Annie (Upton) K.; m. Florence Elizabeth Cannon, Sept. 1, 1945 (dec. Apr. 1983); 1 dau., Martha Anne; m. Edna C. Dornhoefer, June 1984 (div. June 1987); m. Lorelei W. Lasecki. Apr. 1989. Grad., Rutgers U., 1952; B.P.S., Pace U., 1974. With Washington Irving Trust Co. (and successor County Trust Co.), White Plains, N.Y., 1937-76, asst. treas., asst. v.p., v.p., 1947-57, exec. v.p., 1957-60, pres., 1960-72, chmn. bd., 1972-76; v.p. Bank N.Y. Co., 1968-74, vice chmn., 1974-77; dir. Bank of N.Y., 1973-77. Past chmn. bd. trustees, trustee emeritus Westchester C.C.; past pres., chmn. Westchester C.C. Found.; past pres. Legal Aid Soc. West County; past chmn. bd. regents Stonier Grad. Sch. Banking, Rutgers U. Served from pvt. to maj. USAAF, 1942-46; lt. col. Res., 1946-51. Recipient Leffinqwell medal, 1960 Mem. ABA (com. on mechanization of check handling, chmn. tech. com. 1954-64, NY State Bankers Assn. (pres. 1969-70), Imperial Golf Club (Naples), Whippoorwill Club (Armonk, N.Y.). Episcopalian. Home: 7515 Pelican Bay Blvd Apt 3C Naples FL 34108-6518

KLIAVKOFF, GEORGE, sports association executive; BS in Jour., Boston Univ.; JD, Univ. Va. Sr. mgr., consumer divsn. RealOne Networks; sr. v.p., bus. devel. Major League Baseball Advanced Media, NYC. Office: Major League Baseball Advanced Media 5th Fl 75 9th Ave New York NY 10011*

KLIBANOFF, HANK, journalist; m. Laurie Leonard; children: Caroline, Eleanor, Corinne. BA in English, Wash. U., St. Louis, Mo.; MS in Jour., Northwestern U., Chgo., 1972. Journalist Daily Herald Newspaper, Biloxi, Miss., 1973—82; exec. editor Phila. Enquirer, 1982—2002; mng. editor Atlanta Journal-Constitution, 2002—. Co-author: (history book) The Race Beat: The Press, The Civil Rights Struggle, and the Awakening of a Nation, 2006 (The Pulitzer Prize for History, 2006). Office: Cox Comm 6205 Peachtree Dunwoody Rd Atlanta GA 30328*

KLICK, JONATHAN, law educator; s. Raymond and Monica Klick; m. Rebecca Tice; children: Jacob, Samuel, Noah, Benjamin. BS, Villanova U., Pa., 1997; MA, U. Md., College Park, 1999; JD, George Mason U. Sch. Law, Arlington, Va., 2003; PhD, George Mason U., Fairfax, Va., 1999—2002. Jeffrey A. Stoops prof. law Fla. State U., Tallahassee, 2004—. Vis. prof. law U. Pa., Phila., 2007. Office: Fla State Univ Coll Law 425 West Jefferson St Tallahassee FL 32306-1601 Office Phone: 850-644-5714. Office Fax: 850-644-5487. Business E-Mail: jklick@law.fsu.edu.

KLICPEROVA-BAKER, MARTINA, psychologist, researcher; b. Prague, Czech Republic, Oct. 13, 1956; d. Milan and Klára (Rindtová) K.; m. James Gregory Baker. PhD, Karlova U., Prague, 1982; CSc, Inst. Psychology/Czech Acad Sc, 1986. Diplomate in psychology, 1980. Rsch. fellow in biology of learning Inst. Physiology, Czech Acad. Scis., Prague, 1976-77; clin. psychologist Child Psychiatry and Drug Dependence Ctrs., Prague, 1980-81; rsch. scholar Rsch. Inst. Psychiatry, Prague, 1986-88; head fgn. rels. office Sch. of Arts, U. Karlova, Prague, 1990-91; sr. rsch. scholar in social and polit. psychology Inst. Psychology, Czech Acad. Scis., Prague, 1991—, chair of sci. com., 1993-97; rsch. psychologist San Diego State U., 1998—. Vis. lectr. Ariz. State U., Stanford U., San Diego State U.; cons. Mn. of Health, Nat. Ethics Bd., Prague, 1990, Pers. Office/State Dept., Prague, 1991-92; convenor of symposium on polit. psychology World Congress of Psychology, Stockholm. Author: Political Psychology: Psychology of Transition to Democracy, 1997; editor: Ready for Democracy?, 1999; contbr. articles to profl. jours. Rsch. grantee Czech Acad. Scis., 1992-94, 95-97, IREX, 1994, Open Soc. Rsch. Support Scheme, 1996-98, Grant Agy. of Czech Republic, 1998—. Mem. Internat. Soc. Polit. Psychology, Internat. Soc. for Rsch. on Aggression, Czech and Moravian Psychol. Assn. Avocations: languages, travel, arts, astronomy, gardening and nature. Office: San Diego State U Polit Sci Dept 5500 Campanile Dr San Diego CA 92182-0002 E-mail: martina@rohan.sdsu.edu.

KLIEBARD, HERBERT MARTIN, education educator, writer; b. NYC, July 24, 1930; s. Morris and Yetta Kliebard; widowed; children: Diane J. Silverberg, Kenneth M. BS in Edn., City Coll. NY, NYC, 1952, MA, 1953; EdD, Tchrs. Coll. Columbia U., NYC, 1963. Tchr. English Bronx Vocational HS, NYC, 1952—53, 1955—56; reading specialist Nyack Pub. Schs., Nyack, 1956—62; rsch. assoc. Tchrs. Coll. Columbia U., NYC, 1962—63; asst. prof. curriculum, instrn., ednl. policy studies U. Wis.,

Madison, 1963—67, assoc. prof. curriculum, instrn., ednl. policy studies, 1967—70, prof. curriculum, instrn., ednl. policy studies, 1970—99, prof. emeritus, 1999—. V.p. divsn. B curriculum studies Am. Ednl. Rsch. Assn., 1986—88. Author (with A. Bellack): The Language of the Classroom, 1966; author: Religion and Education in America: A Documentary History, 1969; editor (with S. Fishman and A. Kazamias): Teacher, Student and Society: Perspectives in Education, 1974; editor: (with A. Bellack) Curriculum and Evaluation, 1977; author: The Struggle for the American Curriculum: 1893-1958, 1986, 3d edit., 2004, Forging the American Curriculum: Essays in Curriculum History and Theory, 1992, Schooled to Work: Vocationalism and the American Curriculum, 1876-1946, 1999, Changing Course: American Curriculum Reform in the Twentieth Century, 2002; contbr. monographs, book reviews, chapters to books, articles to encys., to profl. jours. With MC US Army, 1953—55. Recipient Disting. Work in Area of Curriculum History award, Am. Ednl. Rsch. Assn., 1991, Lifetime Achievement award, 1991, Disting. Alumni award, Tchrs. Coll. Columbia U., 1993, Disting. Faculty Achievement award, U. Wis., Madison, 1996, Outstanding Achievement award, John Dewey Soc., 1999, Mary Ann Raywid Disting. Achievement award, Soc. Profs. Edn., 2000. Mem.: Kappa Delta Pi (laureate chpt. 2000).

KLIEBENSTEIN, DON, retired lawyer; b. Marshalltown, Iowa, May 3, 1936; s. Donald B. and Gertrude E. (Skeie) K.; m. Mary L. Delfs, June 11, 1960; 1 child, Julie Ann. Student, Grinnell Coll., 1953-55; BA, U. Iowa, 1957, JD, 1961. Bar: Iowa 1961, U.S. Dist. Ct. (no., so. dists.) Iowa 1961, U.S. Supreme Ct. 1971. Pvt. practice, Grundy Center, Iowa, 1961-67; ptnr. Kliebenstein & Heronimus, Grundy Center, 1967-77, Kliebenstein, Heronimus & Schmidt, Grundy Center, 1977-98, Kliebenstein Heronimus Schmidt and Harris, Grundy Center, 1999—2003; of counsel Kliebenstein, Heronimus, Schmidt and Harris, 2004—; ret., 2005. County atty. Grundy County, 1965-98. Mem. ABA, Iowa State Bar Assn., Grundy County Bar Assn. (pres. 1979-80), 1st Jud. Dist. Bar Assn. (pres. 1975-76). Republican. Methodist. Home: 701 9th St Grundy Center IA 50638-1238 Home Phone: 319-824-6180; Office Phone: 319-824-6951.

KLIEBHAN, SISTER M(ARY) CAMILLE, academic administrator; b. Milw., Apr. 4, 1923; d. Alfred Sebastian and Mae Eileen (McNamara) K. Student, Cardinal Stritch Coll., Milw., 1945-48; BA, Cath. Sisters Coll., Washington, 1949; MA, Cath. U. Am., 1951, PhD, 1955. Joined Sisters of St. Francis of Assisi, Roman Catholic Ch., 1945; legal sec. Spence and Hanley (attys.), Milw., 1941-45; instr. edn. Cardinal Stritch Coll., 1955-62, assoc. prof., 1962-68, prof., 1968—, head dept. edn., 1962-67, dean students, 1962-64, chmn. grad. div., 1964-69, v.p. for acad. and student affairs, 1969-74, pres., also bd. dirs., 1974-91, chancellor, 1991—. Mem. TEMPO, 1982—2001, bd. dirs., 1986—89; bd. govs. Wis. Policy Rsch. Inst., 1987—97; bd. dirs. Goals for Milw. 2000, 1980—83; treas. Wis. Found. Ind. Colls., 1974—79, 1987—90, v.p., 1979—81, pres., 1981—83; bd. dirs. DePaul Hosp., 1982—91, Sacred Heart Sch. Theology, 1983—2004, dir. emerita, 2004; bd. dirs. Viterbo Coll., 1990—98, Milw. Cath. Home, 1991—2001, St. Ann Ctr. for Intergenerational Care, 1991—99, Wis. Psychoanalytic Found., 1989—96, St. Coletta's of Mass., 1995—98, Internat. Inst. Wis., 1984—94, Milw. Achiever Program, Inc., 1983—2003, dir. emerita, 2004; bd. dirs. Franciscan Pilgrimage Programs, Inc., 1997—2007, Friends of Internat. Inst. Wis., 1994—, Mental Hea.th Assn. Milwaukee County, 1983—87, Pub. Policy Forum, 1987—90, Better Bus. Bur. of Wis., Inc., 1989—2001, YWCA Greater Milw., 1996—2001, St. Camillus Campus, 1996—2001, mem. adv. bd., 1989—96. Mem. Am. Psychol. Assn., Rotary Club of Milw. (v.p., pres. elect 1992-93, pres. 1993-94), St. Mary's Acad. Alumnae Assn., Phi Delta Kappa, Delta Epsilon Sigma, Psi Chi, Delta Kappa Gamma, Kappa Delta Pi. Business E-Mail: ckliebhan@stritch.edu. *It is because of my faith that I can meet every condition with courage.*

KLIEFOTH, A. BERNHARD, III, neurosurgeon; b. San Antonio, Nov. 1, 1942; S. Arthur Bernhard, Jr. and Pauline (Gray) K.; m. Ingrid R. Kunde, Apr. 22, 1968; children: Karena, Tanya. AB in Chemistry, Princeton U., 1965; MD, U. Tex. Med. Br., Galveston, 1970. Diplomate Am. Bd. Neurol. Surgery, 1980. Intern Naval Hosp., Oakland, Calif., 1970-71, resident gen. surgery San Diego, 1972-73; neurosurg. tchr. Washington U., St. Louis, 1973-78, chief resident, 1976—77, instr. in neurosurg., 1976—78, rsch. fellow dept. radiation scis., 1977-78; commd. ensign USN, 1969, advanced through grades to comdr., 1977; staff neurosurgeon Naval Regional Med. Ctr., Oakland, 1978-81; capt. USNR, 1985; practice medicine specializing in neurosurgery Knoxville, Tenn., 1981—; mem. staff U. Tenn. Hosp., St. Mary's Hosp.; chmn. dept. surgery, 1989-90; clin. assoc. prof. surgery U. Tenn. Bd. dirs. Tenn. Donor Svcs., Cole Neurosci. Found., Knoxville Donor Svcs., Epilepsy Found. Ea. Tenn., vis. prof. Bethesda Naval Hosp./Nat. Naval Med. Ctr. Pres., treas/ Princeton Alumni Assn. Knoxville and Ea. Tenn.; mem. exec. com. West Hills Assn.; treas. Westborough Assn. Commd. ensign USN, 1969—81, with USNR, 1981—96, officer in charge of reserve unit of doctors and nurses. Recipient Disting. Southern Neurosurgeon award, So. Neurosurgery Soc., 2003—. Fellow ACS, Stroke Coun. Am. Heart Assn.; mem. AMA, Am. Assn. Neurol. Surgeons, Am. Soc. Stereotactic and Functional Neurosurgery, Tenn. Neurosurg. Soc., World Soc. Stereotactic and Functional Neurosurgery, Congress Neurol. Surgeons, So. Neurosurg. Soc., So. Med. Assn., Tenn. Med. Assn., Knoxville Acad. Medicine, San Francisco Neurol. Soc., Soc. Med. Cons. to Armed Forces, Assn. Mil. Surgeons U.S., Soc. Neurosci. Avocations: photography, coin collecting/numismatics, stamp collecting/philately, computers, travel. Office: 6901 Office Park Cir Knoxville TN Address: PO Box 51648 Knoxville TN 37950-1648 Office Phone: 865-524-9400.

KLIEMAN, RIKKI JO, lawyer, legal analyst; b. Chgo., May 13, 1948; d. Ben and Jeannette (Wiener) K.; m. Philip A. Brady, Sept. 20, 1987 (div.); m. William J. Bratton, April 30, 1999 BS, Northwestern U., Evanston, Ill., 1970; JD, Boston U., 1975. Bar: Mass. 1975, Colo. 1977, U.S. Dist. Ct. Mass. 1975, U.S. Ct. Appeals (1st cir.) 1976, U.S. Ct. Appeals (11th cir.) 1984. Law clk. to Hon. Walter J. Skinner U.S. Dist. Ct., Boston, 1975-76; asst. dist. atty. Middlesex County, Cambridge, Mass., 1977-79, Norfolk County, Dedham, Mass., 1979-81; assoc. Choate, Hall & Stewart, Boston, 1981-84; ptnr. Friedman & Atherton, Boston, 1984-89, Klieman & Lyons, Boston, 1989—94; of counsel Klieman, Lyons, Schindler & Gross (formerly Klieman & Lyons), Boston, 1994—; anchor Court-TV, 1994—2003, legal analyst, 2003—, The Today Show, 2003—. Instr. Bosto U. Sch. Law, 1977-79, 86-, tchr. Continuing Legal Edn., 1979—, adj. prof. Columbia Law Sch., 1996-2003 Author:(autobiography) Fairy Takes Can Come True-How A Driven Woman Changed Her Fate, 2003; Author/editor: Woman Trial Lawyers, 1987—; editor Mass. Lawyers Weekly, 1981-85; contbr. articles to profl. jours.; Film appearances include The Cable Guy, 1996, A Civil Action, 1998, 15 Minutes, 2001; TV appearances include The D.A., 2004, Dr. Vegas, 2004, Las Vegas, 2005, NYPD Blue, 2005; TV miniseries An American Tragedy, 2000 Exec. com. for civil rights Anti Defamation League, Boston, 1991—; dir., clk. Shepherd Ho., Boston, 1986—. Named One of Top Five Female Trial Attys. in U.S.A., Time Mag., 1983. Mem. ABA, Nat. Assn. of Criminal Def. Lawyers (bd. dirs. 1983-88), Boston Bar Assn., Mass. Bar Assn. (criminal justice coun. 1982-84), Women's Bar Assn., Mass. Assn. of Women Lawyers, Mass. Acad. of Trial Attys. Avocations: jogging, aerobics, theater, films. Office: Klieman Lyons Schindler & Gross 21 Custom House St Boston MA 02110

KLIGER, MILTON RICHARD, diversified financial services company executive; b. NYC, Sept. 26, 1922; s. David and Sadie (Zelikow) K.; m. Ruth Salkind, Jan. 30, 1944 (dec. July 1991); children: Alan S., Sandra F.; m. Gladys Duarte, Sept. 26, 1992. BBA, Bernard Baruch Coll., 1947. Acct. Shipowners Agy. Inc., NYC, 1946-48; chief acct. Am.-Israeli Shipping Co. Inc., NYC, 1948-53; exec. v.p. Maritime Overseas Corp., NYC, 1953-87, also bd. dirs.; CFO, sr. v.p., treas. Overseas Shipholding Group Inc., NYC, 1970-87, also bd. dirs.; pres. OSG Internat. Inc., 1980-87; sr. v.p. Argent Group, Ltd., NYC, 1988-89; pres. Milton Kliger Mgmt. Svcs., Inc., NYC, 1989-93, Marine Equity Corp., NYC, 1990—. Home: 7000 Island Blvd Apt 909 Aventura FL 33160

KLIGERMAN, THOMAS ALEXANDER, architect; s. Morton M. Kligerman; m. Kristin Loraine McMahon, Apr. 24, 1993. Grad., Columbia U., NYC; MArch, Yale U., New Haven, 1982. Ptnr. Ike Kligerman Barkley Archs. P.C., NYC. Bd. dirs. Sir John Soane's Mus. Found. Office: Ike Kligerman Barkley Archs PC 330 W 42nd St New York NY 10036 Office Phone: 212-268-0128. Office Fax: 212-268-5679. E-mail: tkligerman@ikba.com.*

KLIMA, ROGER RADIM, physiatrist; b. Prague, Czechoslovakia; came to U.S., 1982, naturalized, 1988; s. Josef and Radka Klima. BA, Zatlanka Coll., Prague, 1971; MD, Charles U., Prague, 1978. Diplomate Am. Bd. Phys. Medicine and Rehab., Am. Bd. Electrodiagnostic Medicine. Resident in surgery Charles U., 1978-79, resident in orthopedic surgery, 1979-81; fellow, clin. clk. Beverly Hills Med. Ctr. and Cedars-Sinai Med. Ctr., LA, 1984-86; resident in surgery U. Medicine and Dentistry-N.J. Med. Sch., Newark, 1986-87; resident in phys. medicine and rehab. U. Medicine and Dentistry-N.J. Med. Sch./Kessler Inst., Newark and West Orange, 1987-90; mem. phys. medicine and rehab. faculty Stanford (Calif.) U. and affiliated hosps., 1990—; dir. phys. medicine and rehab. outpatient svcs. Palo Alto (Calif.) VA Health Care Sys., 1992—, also co-dir. comprehensive pain mgmt. Clin. instr. in phys. medicine and rehab. U. Medicine and Dentistry-N.J.Med. Sch., 1989-90; clin. instr. in phys., medicine and rehab. Stanford U. Sch. Medicine, 1990-96, asst. prof., 1996—. Contbr. articles to profl. jours. Recipient first ann. Thompson Humanitarian award Stanford U. Phys. Medicine and Rehab., 1994, 97, 2000, 07. Mem. Am. Acad. Phys. Medicine and Rehab. (liaison resident physician coun. 1989-90), Assn. Acad. Physiatrists, Am. Assn. Electrodiagnostic Medicine. Office: Stanford U Med Ctr Divsn Phys Medicine and Rehab Rm NC 104 Stanford CA 94305

KLIMANTOV, ALEXIUS GEORGE, engineering executive; b. Samara, Russia, Nov. 4, 1976; s. Yury Vladimirovich Klimantov and Olga Viktorovna Klimantova; m. Natalya Dvorson, Mar. 29, 2000. BS in Computer Sci., Nayanova U., Samara, Russia, 1997. Sys. programmer CommWorks Divsn. 3COM, Reston, Va., 1998—2000; solutions arch. e-tegral Ptnrs., Mclean, Va., 2002; team lead Kernan Sys., College Park, Md., 2002—03; dir. tech. Idocuments, Inc, Balt., 2003—07, v.p. engring., 2007—. Achievements include patents pending for document management system. Home: 13611 Pine View Ln Rockville MD 20850 Office: Idocuments Inc 1301 Warner St Baltimore MD 21230 Home Phone: 301-294-2423.

KLIMCZUK, STEPHEN JOHN, business executive, foundation director; b. North Hollywood, Calif., Jan. 14, 1963; s. Leon and Wanda (Kotowicz) K.; m. Iris C.B. Massion, Sept. 6, 1991; children: Caroline, Julia, Christina, Isabella (dec.). BA in Econs., UCLA, 1983; MBA, Harvard U., 1987. Assoc. cons. Bain & Co., Palo Alto, Calif., 1983-84; fin. analyst John Nuveen & Co. Inc., San Francisco, 1984-85; assoc. Goldman, Sachs & Co., NYC, 1987-88; mgr. Nat. Review Inc., NYC, 1988-89; dir., mem. bd. World Economic Forum, Geneva, 1989-95; dir. global bus. policy coun. A.T. Kearney, Inc., Alexandria, Va., 1996—2005; v.p. strategy and evaluation John Templeton Found., Phila., 2006—. Mng. dir. World Link Publs. S.A., Geneva, 1991-92. Freeman, City of London, 1998. Recipient Cavaliere, S.M.O. Constantiniano di San Giorgio, 1987; named officer Most Venerable Order of St. John, 1994; invested Knight of Malta, 1996. Fellow: Salzburg Seminar, Royal Soc. Arts (London); mem.: Travellers Club (London), Harvard Club of N.Y.C., Phi Beta Kappa. Roman Catholic. Avocations: travel, history, visual arts, mountain walking. Office: John Templeton Found 300 Conshohocken State Rd Ste 500 West Conshohocken PA 19428 Business E-Mail: sklimczuk@templeton.org.

KLIMEK, JOSEPH JOHN, physician, educator; b. Wilkes-Barre, Pa., Sept. 14, 1946; s. Joseph John and Frances Carol (Pavloski) K.; m. Jane Marie Stout, June 26, 1971 (div.); 1 child, Adam. AB cum laude, Princeton U., 1968; MD, Pa. State U., 1972. Diplomate Am. Bd. Internal Medicine, Am. Bd. Infectious Diseases. Intern, resident in internal medicine Hartford U., Conn., then fellow in infectious disease, 1972—76, chief epidemiology, 1976—87, dir. subsplty. medicine, 1985—87, assoc. dir. medicine, 1987—90, assoc. dir. dept. medicine and chmn. AIDS program, 1987—90, dir. dept. medicine, 1990—2005, v.p. for med. affairs, 2006—, chmn. AIDS task force, 1985—90, assoc. chmn. dept. medicine, 1995—; asst. prof. medicine U. Conn., Farmington, 1977—84, assoc. prof., 1984—90, prof., 1990—; assoc. chmn. dept. medicine U. Conn. Sch. Medicine, 1995—. Conn. mem. numerous faculties pharm. industry. Sr. assoc. editor Am. Jour. Infection Control, 1980-95; med. editor Asepsis, The Infection Control Forum; also mem. numerous editl. bds. in field; contbr. articles to med. jours. Recipient Disting. Alumnus award, 1978, ARC award, 1986. Fellow ACP, Infectious Disease Soc. Am.; mem. APHA, AAAS, Am. Profls. in Infection Control, Am. Soc. Microbiology, Am. Fedn. Clin. Rsch., Soc. Hosp. Epidemiologists Am., Am. Venereal Disease Assn., Am. Med. Writers Assn. Achievements include integrated internal medicine residency of Hartford Hospital with University of Connecticut School of Medicine; developed hospital community linkage network for AIDS care in Greater Hartford; introduced primary care medicine practice model to all ambulatory services; expanded care to indigent with two bilingual satellite practices; developed hospital cardiac services product line; developed hospital-wide Program in Integrative Medicine; initiated formal hospitalist program for care of inpatients; facilitated hospital-wide program in palliative medicine; initiated a formal approach to patient safety and quality with a new vice president position. Home: 31 Main St Farmington CT 06032-2229 Office: Hartford Hosp 80 Seymour St Hartford CT 06115-2701 Home Phone: 860-677-6145; Office Phone: 860-545-3501. Business E-Mail: jklimek@harthosp.org.

KLIMENT, ROBERT MICHAEL, architect; b. Prague, Czechoslovakia, June 9, 1933; came to US, 1950; s. Felix and Sophie (Baltinester) K.; m. Janet McClure, Sept. 12, 1959 (div. 1968); 1 child, Nicholas McClure; m. Frances Halsband, May 1, 1971; 1 child, Alexander Halsband. BA, Yale U., 1954, MArch, 1959. Registered architect Penn., NY, NJ, Mass., Conn., Ohio, Va., DC, NC, NH, Md., Ill., Miss.; cert. Nat. Coun. Archtl. Registration Bds. Arch. Mitchell/Giurgola Archs., Phila., 1961-66, arch., assoc. NYC, 1967-71; ptnr. R.M. Kliment Arch., NYC, 1972-78, R.M. Kliment & Frances Halsband Archs., NYC, 1978—. Instr. U. Pa., Phila., 1963-66, vis. prof., 1972-73; asst. prof. Columbia U., NYC, 1966-70, vis. prof., 1977, 84; vis. prof. MIT, Cambridge, Mass., 1970, Yale U., New Haven, 1972-74, NC State U., Raleigh, 1978, Rice U., Houston, 1979, U. Va., Charlottesville, 1979-80, Harvard U., Cambridge, 1980-81. Works include Computer Sci. Bldg. Princeton U. (Nat. Honor award AIA 1994), U. Va. Life Scis. Bldg., Columbia U. Computer Scis. Bldg. (Nat. Honor award AIA 1987, award NYSAA 1985, Tucker award Bldg. Stone Inst. 1985, other awards), Mercantile Exch. Bldg., NY (Bard award for excellence in architecture City Club NY 1989), Burke Chemistry Bldg., Dartmouth Coll., Adelbert Adminstrn. Bldg., Case Western Res. U. (AIA Nat. honor award 1994), Sudikoff Computer Sci. Bldg., Dartmouth Coll., MTA/L.I. R.R. Entrance Bldg., Penn Sta., NY (Bard award for excellence in architecture City Club NY 1995, AIA nat. honor award 1996, NYSAA & NYC AIA awards 1995), Ebert Art Ctr., Coll. of Wooster, US Courthouse and post office, Bklyn., US Courthouse Gulfport, Miss., Yale Divinity Sch., Franklin and Marshall Coll. Roschel Performing Arts Ctr., NYC Primary Sch. 54, NYC Priamry Sch. 178, NYC Monroe High Sch.; exhibited in group shows at Bklyn. Mus., 1977, The Drawing Ctr., 1977, Cooper Hewitt Mus., 1977-78, Mus. Finnish Arichitecture, Helsinki, Finland, 1980, Harvard Grad. Sch. Design, 1981, NAD, 1981, 87, Smith Coll. Mus. Art, 1981, Rice U. Farrish Hall Gallery, 1983, Columbia U. Low Libr., 1986, Parrish Art Mus., 1987, German Architecture Mus., Frankfurt, 1989, Rotunda Gallery, Bklyn., 1995. With US Army, 1955-57. Fulbright scholar, Italy, 1959-60; AIA Archtl. Firm award, 1997, Medal of Honor NYC AIA, 1998. Fellow AIA, Century Assn. Office: R M Kliment & Frances Halsband Architects 255 W 26th St New York NY 10001-8001

KLIMENT, STEPHEN ALEXANDER, architect, editor, journalist; b. May 24, 1930; s. Felix and Sophia (Baltinester) K.; m. Felicia Drury, Dec. 24, 1957; children: Pamela Drury, Jennifer Anne. Student, Ecole Speciale d'Architecture, Paris, 1948-49; BArch, MIT, 1953; MFA in Arch., Princeton U., 1957. Draftsman Jean Labatut, Princeton, NJ, 1957; designer Skidmore, Owings & Merrill, NYC, 1957-59, Reeb-Draz Assos., Cleve., 1959-60; editor Archtl. and Engring. News, 1961-69; v.p. Caudill Rowlett Scott, NYC, 1969-72; architect, cons., 1972-78; editor in chief Advt. & Pub. News, 1978-80; exec. editor Whitney Libr. of Design, 1981-85; v.p., editl. dir. Practice Mgmt. Assocs., Ltd., 1985-87; editor sci. and tech. div. John Wiley & Sons, 1987-90; editor-in-chief Archtl. Record, 1990-96; arch., journalist, 1996—. Adj. prof. Sch. Architecture, Urban Design and Landscape Architecture, City Coll. of CUNY, 1997—; lectr. U. Oreg., Carnegie-Mellon U., U. Ariz., Yale U., Harvard U., Washington U., St. Louis, U. Tex., U. Nebr., Ariz. State U., N.C. State U., Tex. A&M U., Miss. State U. Author: Writing for Design Professionals, 1998, 2d edit., 2006, Creative Communications for a Successful Design Practice, Into the Mainstream: Syllabus for a Barrier-Free Environment, Architectural Sketching and Rendering: Techniques for Designers and Artists; (with R.H. McNulty) Neighborhood Conservation; editor: Design Principal's Report, 1998—; founding editor Building Type Basics Series, John Wiley & Sons, Inc.; contbr. articles to profl. jours., including Architecture, Archtl. Digest, Planning, NY Times. Chmn. adv. coun. Princeton U. Sch. Architecture and Urban Planning, 1973-84. With AUS, 1953-55. Fellow AIA (chmn. OCULUS adv. bd. NY chpt. 2002-05). Anglican. Home and Office: 1255 5th Ave New York NY 10029-3850 Office Phone: 212-426-4800.

KLIMSTRA, DAVID S., pathologist; s. Paul D. and Lois A. Klimstra; m. Sibel Akyol Klimstra, Apr. 17, 1999. BA in Biology, Carleton Coll, Northfield, Minn., 1984; MD, Yale U., New Haven, Conn., 1988. Lic. NY, 1991, bd. cert. Am. Bd. Pathology, 1992. Attending pathologist Meml. Hosp. Cancer and Allied Diseases, NYC, 2003—; chief surg. pathology Meml. Sloan-Kettering Cancer Ctr., 2005—. Prof. pathology and lab. medicine Weill Med. Coll., Cornell U., NY, 2005—. Author: (medical textbook) Tumors of the Gallbladder, Extrahepatic Bile Ducts, and Ampulla of Vater, Tumors of the Pancreas. Recipient Peter F. Curran prize, Yale U. Sch. Medicine, 1988. Mem.: Gastrointestinal Pathology Soc., US and Canacian Acad. Pathology. Achievements include research in characterization of the pathology of pancreatic neoplasms. Office: Memorial Sloan-Kettering Cancer Center 1275 York Avenue New York NY 10021 Office Phone: 212-639-2410. Office Fax: 646-422-2016.

KLINCK, CYNTHIA ANNE, library director; b. Salamanaca, NY, Nov. 1, 1948; d. William James and Marjorie Irene (Woodruff) K.; m. Andrew Clavert Humphries, Nov. 26, 1983. BS, Ball State U., 1970; MLS, U. Ky., 1976. Reference/ young adult libr. Bartholomew County Libr., Columbus, Ind., 1970-74; dir. Paul Sawyier Pub. Libr., Frankfort, Ky., 1974-78, Washington-Centerville Pub. Libr., Dayton, Ohio, 1978—. Libr. bldg. cons.; libr. cons., trainer OPLIN Task Force. Contbr. articles to profl. jours. Bd. dirs. Bluegrass Comty. Action Agy., Frankfort, Ky., 1971-73; founder, bd. dirs. FACTS, Inc., Frankfort, 1972-74; co-founder, bd. dirs. Seniors, Inc., Dayton, Ohio, 1980-81, 91—; trustee, officer South Comty., Inc. Mental Health Ctr., Dayton, 1980-89; pres. Miami Valley Librs.; govt. affairs com., ann. conf. planning com., fin. resources task force conf. presenter Ohio Libr. Coun.; program presenter Ohio Libr. Coun. Confs.; del. to Am. Libr. Assn. Congress on Profl. Edn.; mem. Create-The-Vision Cmty. Planning Task Force, com. chair. Named one of Dayton's Top Ten Women, Dayton Daily News, 2005; recipient Vol. of Yr., So. Metro Regional C. of C. Mem. ALA, Am. Soc. for Info. Sci., Am. Soc. for Pers. Adminstrn., Ohio Libr. Assn. (chmn. legis. com.), South Metro Regional C. of C. (exec. com., bd. dirs., chmn. edn. com., chair), Rotary (bd. dirs.), Pub. Libr. Assn. Mng. for Results (trainer). Office: Washington-Centerville Pub Libr 111 W Spring Valley Rd Dayton OH 45458-3761 Office Phone: 937-435-7375.

KLINE, ALLEN HABER, JR., lawyer; b. Houston, June 17, 1954; s. Allen H. Sr. and Maude Rose (Brown) K.; m. Barbara Ann Byrd, July 24, 1982; children: Allison Ashley, Allen III. BA, U. Denver, 1976; JD, U. Miami, 1979. Bar: Tex. 1980, U.S. Dist. Ct. (so. dist.) Tex. 1980, U.S. Ct. Appeals (5th cir.) 1980, U.S. Ct. Appeals (11th cir.) 1983, U.S. Supreme Ct. 1985; bd. cert. personal injury trial law Tex. Bd. Legal Specialization. Pvt. practice, Houston, 1980—. Mem. Houston Bar Assn., Coll. of the State Bar of Tex., City Wide Club (Houston) (life). Avocations: tennis, water, skiing. Office: 650 N Sam Houston Pkwy E Ste 105 Houston TX 77060 Office Phone: 713-224-3101.

KLINE, DAVID ADAM, lawyer, educator, writer; b. Keota, Okla., Sept. 27, 1923; s. David Adam and Lucy Leila (Wood) K.; m. Ruthela Deal, Aug. 25, 1947; children: Steven, Timothy, Ruthanna. JD, Okla. U., 1950. Bar: Okla. 1949. Law clk., spl. master U.S. Dist. Ct. Okla., 1952-61; 1st asst. U.S. atty. We. Dist. Okla., 1961-69; judge We. Dist. Okla. U.S. Bankruptcy Ct., Oklahoma City, 1969-82; sr. shareholder Kline Kline Elliott & Bryant, PC, Oklahoma City, 1983—. Pres. Nat. Conf. Bankruptcy Judges 1977-78; mem. arbitration panel program U.S. Dist. Ct. (we. dist.) Okla., 1985—mem. faculty Fed. Jud. Ctr., Washington, Nat. Seminar Bankruptcy Judges, 1971-86; adj. prof. law Oklahoma City U., 1980-84; cons. Norton Bankruptcy Law and Practice, 1986, Callaghan & Co.; bd. dirs. Consumer Credit Counseling Svc. Ctr., Okla., 1973-2001, chmn., 1992. Author: A Little Book (A New Thing in the Earth), 1993, A Little Book II (The Blood of the Lion), 1995, A Little Book III (The Revelation), 1997, A Little Book IV (A Still Small Voice), 1998, A Little Book V (Law and Liberty), 2003, The Little Books Collection, electronic edit., 2004; co-author: Briefcase, 1988—2000; mem. editl. bd. Am. Bankruptcy Law Jour., 1974—77, contbg. author Cowan's Bankruptcy Law and Practice, 1983, 2d edit., 1986. Fellow: Am. Coll. Bankruptcy Class II. Office: Kline Kline Elliott & Bryant PC Kline Law Bldg 720 NE 63rd St Oklahoma City OK 73105-6405 Home Phone: 405-396-8731; Office Phone: 405-848-4448. Business E-Mail: dkline@klinefirm.org.

KLINE, DAVID GELLINGER, neurosurgery educator; b. Phila., Oct. 13, 1934; s. David Francis and Lois Ann (Gellinger) K.; m. Carol Anne Loewen, Mar. 1, 1958 (div.); children: Susan, Robert, Nancy. AB in Chemistry, U. Pa., 1956, MD, 1960. Diplomate Am. Bd. Neurol. Surgery (sec.-treas. 1978-83, chmn. 1983-84, adv. bd. 1984-90, chmn. 50th anniversary celebration 1990). Intern and resident in gen. surgery U. Mich., Ann Arbor, 1960-62; research investigator Walter Reed Army Inst. Research and Walter Reed Gen. Hosp., 1962-64; resident in neurosurgery and teaching instr. U. Mich., Ann Arbor, 1964-67; instr. neurosurgery and surgery Sch. Medicine La. State U., New Orleans, 1967-68, asst. prof., 1968-70, assoc. prof., 1970-75, prof., 1976, head sect. of neurosurgery, 1971, chmn. dept. neurosurgery, 1976—, Boyd prof., chmn. neurosurgery, 1995—2006, Boyd prof. neurosurgery, 2006—. Cons. USPHS Health Center Hosp., New Orleans VA Hosp., Kessler AFB Hosp.-Lederle Labs.; vis. investigator Delta Regional Primate Center, Covington; mem. Am. Bd. Med. Specialists, 1978-86, mem. residency rev. com., 1977-84; lectr. in field. Contbr. articles to sci. jours., also mem. numerous editorial bds. Capt. M.C. AUS, 1962-64. Recipient Frederick Coller Surg. prize, 1967; numerous grants. Mem.: ACS, AMA, Soc. Univ. Surgeons, Assn. Acad. Surgery, Congress Neurol. Surgeons, Soc. Univ. Neurosurgeons, Am. Assn. Neurol. Surgeons (bd. dirs. 1985—89, Harvey Cushing medal 2006), So. Neurol. Surgery Soc. (sec. 1976—79, pres. 1985—86), Soc. Neurol. Surgeons (treas. 1986—91, v.p. 1994—95, pres. 1996—97), Am. Acad. Neurol. Surgery, New Orleans Neurol. Soc., La. State Med. Soc., Orleans Parish Med. Soc., Am. Assn. Hand Surgery (hon.), German Neurosurg. Soc. (hon.), Can. Neurosurg. Soc. (hon.), Sunderland Soc. (pres. 1981), Surg. Biol. Club II, Phi Chi, Phi Beta Kappa, Alpha Omega Alpha, Kappa Sigma. Episcopalian (vestry and lay reader). Office: La State U Med Ctr Dept Neurosurgery 1514 Jefferson Hwy New Orleans LA 70121 Home: 307 Fairway Dr New Orleans LA 70124 Home Phone: 504-486-7030, 504-296-0158. Office Fax: 504-568-6127. E-mail: dkline@lsuktc.edu. *Success, whether defined by the individual who believes he or she has achieved it or 'granted' by others has little meaning unless it is accompanied by happiness. To have both, one must not only enjoy his or her life's work but also life as a whole and particularly people and specifically working hard with and interacting well with others. Honesty about one's own efforts as well as those of others, a large measure of perseverance, a sense of humor, and a degree of courage as well as a certain amount of realistic optimism are very necessary to survive let alone flourish.*

KLINE, DONALD, food company executive; b. Chgo., July 6, 1948; s. Ralph Waldo and Theresa (Donato) K.; m. Christine Janet Kennedy, Aug. 23, 1972; children: Bethany Amber, Torah-Ann Shiloh, Nathaniel Darwin Kennedy, Abraham Newton Kennedy, Seth-Andrew Brigham Kennedy. AA, South Suburban Coll., 1969; AS, Kishwaukee Coll., 1971; BS, Roosevelt U., 1974, No. Ill. U., 1974; cert. thermal process control of low-acid canned foods, U. Wis., 1974. Quality control chemist Syntex Labs., Elgin, Ill., 1972-75; quality control mgr. Gt. China Food Products Co., Chgo., 1975; quality assurance mgr. TV Time Foods, Inc. subs. McCormick & Co., Inc., Bremen, Ind., 1975-80; pres. Abinadi Enterprises Internat. Corp., Nappanee, Ind., 1980-82; quality assurance/rsch. and devel. mgr. Snyder's of Hanover, Inc., Hanover, Pa., 1982-92; sr. rsch. assoc. Nabisco Biscuit Co., East Hanover, N.J., 1992-94; dir. quality assurance and tech. svcs. Hanover Foods Corp., Pa., 1994-95; dir. quality assurance UTZ Quality Foods, Inc., Hanover, 1995—2002, dir. tech. svcs., 2002—. Elder Ch. Jesus Christ of Latter-day Saints, 1976—, pres. Sunday sch., 1979-80, project coord., purchasing agt. ch. fund raising projects, 1980-82, exec. sec., 1981-82, pub. rels. dir., 1982-83, 91-92, mission leader for Gettysburg-Hanover, Pa., 1983-85, Gettysburg ward mission leader, 2000-03, Gettysburg ward fin.clk., 2003-04; chmn., pack and troop treas. Boy Scouts of Am., 1985-92, Webeloes leader, 1987-89, merit badge counselor, 1988-92; citizen adv. coun. Spring Grove Area Sch. Dist., 1988-92, ch. employment dir., 1991-92, ch. phys. facilities fin. clk. for York, Pa., 1992-93; dir. Hanover/Gettysburg, Pa. Church Family History Ctr., 1996-2000; sustaining mem. Rep. Nat. Com. Mem. Inst. Food Technologists (profl. emeritus), Snack Food Assn. (sci. rev. 1996—), Am. Assn. Nutritional Cons. (cert. nutritional cons.), Nat. Assn. Cert. Natural Health Profls. (cert. nat. health profl.). Republican. Achievements include development of one hundred different snack foods marketed in U.S. and fgn. countries; development of first product line of flavored sour-dough pretzels. Office: Utz Quality Foods Inc 900 High St Hanover PA 17331-1639 Home: 10 Kevin Dr New Oxford PA 17350-9186 Home Phone: 717-624-3288; Office Phone: 800-367-7629 ext. 367. E-mail: donald.kline@yahoo.com, dkline@utzsnacks.com.

KLINE, EUGENE MONROE, lawyer; b. NYC, May 22, 1914; s. Lewis R. and Hattie (Wachter) K.; m. Harriet Meyer, July 2, 1939; children: Robert A., Thomas R. AB, Columbia U., 1933, LLB, 1935. Bar: N.Y. 1935, U.S. Dist. Ct. (so. dist.) N.Y. 1945, U.S. Dist. Ct. (ea. dist.) N.Y. 1955, U.S. Supreme Ct. 1973. Atty. Charter Rev. Commn., NYC, 1935; assoc. Greenbaum, Wolf & Ernst, NYC, 1935-37, Wagner, Quillinin and Rifkind, NYC, 1937-40; atty. SEC, NYC and Washington, 1941-43; from assoc. to ptnr. Phillips Nizer LLP, NYC, 1943—. With U.S. Army, 1943. Office: Phillips Nizer LLP 666 5th Ave New York NY 10103-0084 Home Phone: 914-939-1418; Office Phone: 212-977-9700. E-mail: ekline@phillipsnizer.com.

KLINE, EVA JANE, library services administrator, educator; b. Duncannon, Pa., Oct. 11, 1942; d. Stanley L. and Grace (Louden) Peters; m. Glenn N. Kline, Sept. 24, 1963 (div. 1971); 1 child, Kent K. Kline. BS in Edn., Kutztown U., Pa., 1963; MLS, U. Pitts., 1978. Libr., tchr. West Perry High Sch., Elliottsburg, Pa., 1963-64; libr. Westerly Pkwy. High Sch., State College, Pa., 1964-65, various 13 schs., State College, 1965-66, Susquenita High Sch., Duncannon, Pa., 1966-68, McConnellsburg Elem. Schs., Pa., 1970-71; dir. libr. svcs. Somerset State Hosp., Pa., 1971—96; tchr. speech, lit. and composition Mt. Aloysius Jr. Coll., Cresson, Pa., 1989—91; libr. Crown Am., Johnstown, Pa., 1997—2000; adminstr. Somerset County Federated Libr. Sys., 1999—; dir. Somerset County Libr., 1999—. Cons. N.W. Ga. Regional Hosp., Rome, Ga., 1990-92, Killam Assocs., Somerset, 1994-97; consortium dir. HI RESCUE, Somerset, 1978-95. Recipient Cert. of Merit award Pa. Libr. Assn., 1996, 1997; named Outstanding Instl. Librarian, Pa. Spl. Librs., Pa. Mental Health Librs., 1983. Mem. Med. Libr. Assn. (Pitts. regional chair 1994-95, Scroll of Exemplary Svc. 2002).Dist. mem, Acad. of Health Infor. Profl. Avocations: taxidermy, reading, travel. Home: PO Box 47 Sipesville PA 15561 Office: Somerset County Federated Libr Sys 6022 Glades Pike Ste 120 Somerset PA 15501-4300 Business E-Mail: ekline@somersetcountypalibraries.org.

KLINE, FRANK MENEFEE, psychiatrist; b. Cumberland, Md., May 14, 1928; s. Frank Huber and Margaret (Menefee) K.; m. Shirley Steinmetz, June 27, 1953; children: Frank F., Margaret L. BS, U. Md., 1950, MD, 1952; PhD, So. Calif. Psychoanalytic Inst., 1977. Diplomate Am. Bd. Psychiatry and Neurology (examiner 1970—). Intern Cin. Gen. Hosp., 1952-53; resident Brentwood VA Med. Ctr., West L.A., 1955-58; regional chief West Ctrl. Mental Svc., L.A. County Dept. Mental Health, LA, 1967—68; assoc. dir. adult psychiatry out-patient dept. L.A. County, U. So. Calif. Med. Ctr., 1968—77, acting dir. adult psychiat. dept., 1977; chief psychiatry VA Med. Ctr., Long Beach, Calif., 1977-91. Clin. prof., vice-chair U. Calif., Irvine, 1978—91, prof. emeritus, 1995—, U. So. Calif.; clin. prof. Drew King, 1992—2004; reviewer Hosp. Cmty. Psychiatry, 1978—, Am. Jour. Psychiatry, 1978—, Readings, 1995—2002; cons. Los Angeles County Dept. Mental Health, 1992—. Editor: A Handbook of Group Psychotherapy, 1983. 1st lt. M.C., U.S. Army, 1953-55. Office: San Pedro Cmty Mental Health Ctr 150 W 7th St San Pedro CA 90731 Personal E-mail: frank.kline1@cox.net.

KLINE, HOWARD JAY, cardiologist, educator; b. White Plains, NY, Nov. 5, 1932; s. Raymond Kline and Rose Plane; divorced; children: Michael, Ethan; m. Ellen Sawamura, June 13, 1987; 1 child, Christopher. BS, Dickinson Coll., 1954; MD, N.Y. Med. Coll., 1958. Intern San Francisco Gen. Hosp., 1958—59; resident Mt. Sinai Hosp., NYC, 1959—61; sr. resident U. Calif. Med. Ctr., San Francisco, 1961—62; cardiology fellow Mt. Sinai Hosp., NYC, 1962—64; dir. cardiology tng. program St. Mary's Hosp., San Francisco, 1970—90, Calif. Pacific Med. Ctr., San Francisco, 1992—. Clin. prof. medicine and cardiology U. Calif. Med. Ctr., San Francisco, 1984—; vis. prof. Nihon U., Tokyo, 1986; dir. cardiology Valley Forge Gen. Hosp. Cardiology editor Hosp. Practice, Cardiology, 1992—; contbr. articles to profl. jours. Lt. col. U.S. Med. Corps, 1967-69. Fellow ACP, Am. Heart Assn., Am. Coll. Cardiology, Am. Coll. Chest Physicians; mem. Golden Gate Tennis Club, U. San Francisco Masters Swim Team. Avocations: painting, reading, running, skiing, tennis, swimming. Office: 2100 Webster St Ste 516 San Francisco CA 94115-2382 Office Phone: 415-561-1625. Personal E-mail: hkline@cpcmg.com.

KLINE, JAMES EDWARD, lawyer; b. Fremont, Ohio, Aug. 3, 1941; s. Walter J. and Sophia Kline; m. Mary Ann Bruening, Aug. 29, 1964; children: Laura Anne Kline, Matthew Thomas, Jennifer Sue. BS in Social Sci., John Carroll U., University Heights, Ohio, 1963; JD, Ohio State U., Columbus, 1966; postgrad., Stanford U., Calif., 1991. Bar: Ohio 1966, NC 1989, US Tax. Ct. 1983. Assoc. Eastman, Stichter, Smith & Bergman, Toledo, 1966-70; ptnr. Eastman, Stichter, Smith & Bergman (name now Eastman & Smith), Toledo, 1970-84, Shumaker, Loop & Kendrick, Toledo, 1984-88; v.p., gen. counsel Aeroquip-Vickers, Inc. (formerly Trinova Corp.), Toledo, 1989-99; exec. v.p. Cavista Corp., 2000—01; dir. devel. Toledo Mus. Art, 2002—03; v.p., gen. counsel, sec. Cooper Tire and Rubber Co., Findlay, Ohio, 2003—. Corp. sec. Sheller-Globe Corp., 1977—84; adj. prof. U. Toledo Coll. Law, 1988—94; bd. dirs. Plastic Techs., Inc.; trustee Promedica Health Edn. and Rsch. Corp., 2002—07. Author: (with Robert Seaver) Ohio Corporation Law, 1988. Trustee Kidney Found. of Northwestern Ohio, Inc., 1972-81, pres., 1979-80; bd. dirs. Toledo Botanical Garden (formerly Crosby Gardens), 1974-80, pres., 1977-79; bd. dirs. Toledo Zool. Soc., 1983-96, 99—2004, pres., 1991-93; bd. dirs. Toledo Area Regional Transit Authority, 1984-90, pres., 1987-88; bd. dirs. Home Away From Home, Inc. (Ronald McDonald House NW Ohio), 1983-88; trustee Toledo Symphony Orch., 1981—, St. John's H.S., 1988-91; trustee Lourdes Coll., 1988-96, chmn., 1994-96; trustee Ohio Found. Ind. Colls., 1991-2007, ProMedica Health Edn. and Rsch. Corp., 2002-07, Toledo Opera, 2003-2005, ProMedica Found., 2006-07. Fellow Ohio Bar Found.; mem. ABA, Nat. Assn. Corp. Dirs., Ohio Bar Assn. (corp. law com. 1977—, chmn. 1983-86), NC Bar Assn., Mfrs. Alliance (chair Law Coun. II 1997-99), Toledo Area C. of C. (trustee 1994—, chmn. 2000-01), Confrerie des Chevealiers du Tastevin, Inverness Club, Toledo Club (trustee 1990-97), Stone Oak Country Club, Ottawa Skeet Club, Fiddlers Creek Club, Answer Club Roman Catholic. Home: 216 Treetop Pl Holland OH 43528-8451 Office: Cooper Tire & Rubber Co 701 Lima Ave Findlay OH 45840 Office Phone: 419-427-4757. Personal E-mail: jektreetop@sbcglobal.net. Business E-Mail: jekline@coopertire.com.

KLINE, JERRY ROBERT, retired administrative judge, ecologist; b. Mpls., May 20, 1932; s. Frederick Andrew and Margaret (Wicklund) K.; m. Alice Nell Reed, Sept. 4, 1954; children: Steven, Jennifer, Robert, Neil, Daniel. BS, U. Minn., 1957, MS, 1960, PhD, 1964. Postdoctoral rsch. assn. Argonne Nat. Lab., Ill., 1964-65, group leader rsch. Ill., 1968-74; scientist, dir. Rainforest Project P.R. Nuclear Ctr., 1965-68; sr. scientist Nuclear Regulatory Commn., Washington, 1974-80, adminstrv. judge, 1980-98. Contbr. articles to profl. jours., chpts. to books. Bd. dirs., chmn. Cedar Lane Unitarian Ch. Served with U.S. Army, 1950-53. Recipient NRC Spl. Achievement award, 1979. Mem. Nature Conservancy, Sigma Xi. Avocations: travel, gardening. Home: 13624 Middlevale Ln Silver Spring MD 20906-2123 Personal E-mail: KJerry@verizon.net.

KLINE, JOHN, congressman; b. Allentown, Pa., Sept. 6, 1947; m. Vicky Kline; children: Kathy, Dan. BA in Biology, Rice U., 1969; MPA, Shippensburg U. Pa., 1988. Mem. US Congress from Minn. 2nd dist., 2003—. Military aide to Pres. Carter; military aide to Pres. Reagan. Active USMC, 1969—94, retired as Colonel USMC. Recipient Hero of the Taxpayer award, Small Bus. Adv. award, Spirit of Enterprise award, True Blue award, Family Rsch. Coun. Republican. Responsibilities while military aide to pres. included carrying "nuclear football" — package containing launch codes for nuclear attack. Office: US Ho Reps 1429 Longworth Ho Office Bldg Washington DC 20515-2302*

KLINE, JOHN WILLIAM, retired military officer, management consultant; b. Zanesville, Ohio, June 26, 1919; s. Gerry William and Lillian Elizabeth (Scheiderer) K.; m. Katherine Edmond Winton, Oct. 24, 1942; children: Susan Isabel (Mrs. John Farris Morehead), Flora Edmond (Mrs. Richard Crandall Creighton), Elizabeth Gerry (Mrs. Paul Sweeney). Student, Ohio U., 1937-40; grad., Primary, Basic and Advanced Flying Schs., 1941, Air Command and Staff Sch., 1949, Air War Coll., 1959; BA, La. Tech. U., 1971. Commd. 2d lt. USAAF, 1941; advanced through grades to maj. gen. USAF, 1968; comdr. (2d Bomb Wing), Hunter AFB, Ga., 1961-63, (397th Bomb Wing), Dow AFB, Maine, 1963-64; dir. operations, chief staff Hdqrs. 8th Air Force, Westover AFB, Mass., 1964-66; vice comdr. 3d Air Div., Andersen AFB, Guam, 1966-68; asst. dep. chief staff ops. Hdqrs. SAC, Offutt AFB, Nebr., 1968-69; vice-comdr. 2d Air Force, Barksdale AFB, La., 1969-72; ret., 1972; v.p., mgmt. cons. Paul R. Ray, Inc., Ft. Worth, 1972—; pres. Mapotec, Inc., Daytona Beach, Fla., 1974, Precision Aerial Surveys, Inc., 1975-85; v.p. ops. Aero Service, Houston, 1976-80, v.p. new ventures and planning, 1980-82. Decorated D.S.M., Legion of Merit with 3 oak leaf clusters, Air medal with oak leaf cluster, Air Force Commendation medal; Air Force Distinguished Service Order Republic Vietnam). Mem. Oak Hills Golf Club, Guadalajara Golf Club, Beta Theta Pi. Presbyterian. Home: One Towers Park Ln # 912 San Antonio TX 78209-

KLINE, KEVIN DELANEY, actor; b. St. Louis, Oct. 24, 1947; s. Robert Joseph and Peggy (Kirk) K.; m. Phoebe Cates, Mar. 5, 1989; 2 children: Owen, Greta. BA in Speech and Theatre, Ind. U.; adv. program diploma, Juilliard Sch. Drama Divsn., NYC, 1972. Founding mem. The Acting Co., NYC, 1972-76. Apptd. artistic assoc. N.Y. Shakespeare Festival, 1993. Actor (Broadway) On the Twentieth Century, 1978 (Tony award), Loose Ends, 1979, Pirates of Penzance, 1980 (Tony award, Obie award), Arms and the Man, 1985, The Play What I Wrote, 2003; (off-Broadway) Richard III, 1983, Henry V, 1984, Hamlet, 1986 (Obie award), Much Ado About Nothing, 1988, Measure for Measure, 1993, The Seagull, 2001, Mother Courage, 2006, King Lear, 2007; actor, dir. (off-Broadway) Hamlet, 1990; actor (Broadway) Ivanov, 1997, Henry IV, Parts I & II, 2003 (Tony nom. best actor in a play, 2004, Drama Desk award best actor, 2004); (films) Sophie's Choice, 1982, Pirates of Penzance, 1983, The Big Chill, 1983, Silverado, 1985, Violets are Blue, 1985, Cry Freedom, 1987, A Fish Called Wanda, 1988 (Acad. award best supporting actor 1989), The January Man, 1989, I Love You To Death, 1989, Soapdish, 1991, Grand Canyon, 1991, Consenting Adults, 1991, Chaplin, 1992, Dave, 1993, George Balanchine's The Nutcracker (voice only), 1993, Princess Caraboo, 1994, French Kiss, 1995, The Hunchback of Notre Dame (voice only), 1996, Fierce Creatures, 1997, In & Out, 1997, The Ice Storm, 1997, A Midsummer Night's Dream, 1999, Wild Wild West, 1999, The Road to El Dorado (voice), 2000, The Anniversary Party, 2001, Life as a House, 2001, The Emperor's Club, 2002, De-lovely, 2004, As You Like It, 2005, The Pink Panther, 2006, A Prairie Home Companion, 2006; dir. (TV movie) Hamlet, 1990; actor, dir. (TV spl.) Hamlet, 1990. Kevin Kline awards to recognize outstanding achievement in profl. theatre in greater St. Louis, Mo. area, named in his honor, 2006; recipient Lifetime Achievement award Lucille Lortel Awards, 2007. Office: William Morris Agy 1325 Avenue Of The Americas New York NY 10019-6026

KLINE, LOWRY F., beverage company executive, lawyer; b. Louden, Tenn., 1940; m. Jane Kline; 3 children. BA, Univ. Tenn., 1962, JD, 1965. Atty. & ptnr. Miller & Martin, 1970—95; gen. counsel Johnston Coca-Cola Bottling Group, 1981—91; sr. v.p., gen. counsel Coca-Cola Enterprises Inc., Atlanta, 1996-97, exec. v.p., gen. counsel, 1997-99, exec. v.p., chief adminstrv. officer, 1999-2001, vice chmn., 2000—02, CEO, 2001—04, 2005—06, chmn., 2002—. Bd. dirs. Dixie Group, Jackson Furniture Industries. Fellow: Chattanooga Bar Found.; mem.: Tenn. Bar Found. (past chmn.), Chattanooga Bar Assn. (past pres.). Office: Coca-Cola Enterprises Inc 2500 Windy Ridge Pkwy SE Atlanta GA 30339-5677*

KLINE, MARK WENDEL, pediatric medicine educator; b. Corpus Christi, Tex., Jan. 31, 1957; s. William Marshall and Elsie Marie (Ford) K. BA, Trinity U., 1978; MD, Baylor Coll. Medicine, Houston, 1981. Diplomate Am. Bd. Pediat., Pediatric Infectious Diseases. Intern, resident pediat. Baylor Coll. Medicine, 1981-85, postdoctoral fellow infectious diseases, 1985-87, asst. prof. pediat., 1990-92, assoc. prof. pediat., 1993-97, prof. pediat., 1997—; asst. prof. pediat. St. Louis U., 1987-89. Assoc. dir. Gen. Clin. Rsch. Ctr., Baylor Coll. Medicine, Tex. Children's Hosp., Houston, 1992—; dir. AIDS Internat. Tng. and Rsch. Program, 1999—. Contbr. chpts. to books and articles to profl. jours. Named One of Five Outstanding Young Texans, Tex. Jr. C. of C., 1993. Fellow Am. Acad. Pediat., Infectious Disease Soc. Am., Am. Pediatric Soc., Soc. for Pediatric Rsch.; mem. Am. Soc. for Microbiology. Office: Baylor Coll Med Dept Peds MC1-4000 6621 Fannin St Houston TX 77030-2303

KLINE, NANCY MATTOON, librarian; b. Providence, Oct. 9, 1937; d. Donald Potter and Lillian Hortense (Groux) Mattoon; m. Kenneth Ernest Kline, June 20, 1959. BS, U. Conn., 1959, MS, 1961; MLS, U. R.I., 1973; PhD, U. Conn., 1994. Map libr. U. Conn. Libr., Storrs, 1970-79, dept. head, 1979-88, asst. to dir. libr., 1989-90, reference librarian, 1991-93, reference collection coord., 1993—, acting reference dept. head, 1995-96, library liaison, 2005—. Contbr. articles to profl. jours., 1973—. Bd. dirs. Mansfield (Conn.) Libr., 1978-83; libr. Mansfield Hist. Soc., 1969-79; com. mem. Planning for Year 2002, Mansfield, 1989-92 Mem. ALA, Spl. Librs. Assn. (assoc. editor bulletin 1973-77, editor 1976-79), Conn. Libr. Assn. (pres. 1980-81), Assn. Coll. and Rsch. Librs. (New Eng. chpt., chair collection devel. interest group 1995—), New Eng. Libr. Assn., Beta Phi Mu, Phi Kappa Phi, Phi Delta Kappa. Office: U Conn Libr 369 Fairfield Storrs Mansfield CT 06269-6016 Home: PO Box 577 Storrs Mansfield CT 06268-0577

KLINE, NORMAN DOUGLAS, retired judge; b. Lynn, Mass., Dec. 28, 1930; s. Samuel and Ida (Luff) K.; m. Betty Toba Feldman, Feb. 27, 1966; children: Sarah, Samuel. AB, Harvard Coll., 1952, postgrad., 1952-53; JD, Boston U., 1959. Bar: Mass. 1959. Pvt. practice, Boston, 1959-60; atty. U.S. Dept. Army, Cleve., 1960; trial atty. FMC, Washington, 1960-72, adminstrv. law judge, 1972-92, chief adminstrv. law judge, 1992—2005. With U.S. Army, 1953-55. Mem. Fed. Adminstrv. Law Judges Conf. Avocations: classical music, collecting cds.

KLINE, PHILLIP D., prosecutor; b. Kansas City, Kans., Dec. 31, 1959; s. James R. and Janet S. (Shirley) K.; m. Deborah Suzanne Shattuck, July 22, 1989; 1 child, Jacqueline Hillary. BS in Pub. Rels. and Polit. Sci., Cen. Mo. State U., 1982; JD, U. Kans., 1987. Bar: Kans. 1987, U.S. Ct. Appeals (10th cir.), U.S. Dist. Ct. Kans. News reporter WHB Radio, Kansas City, Mo., 1981-82; pub. rels. rep. Mid-America, Inc., Kansas City, Mo., 1982-84; assoc. Blackwell, Sanders, Matheny, Weary & Lombardi, Overland Park, Kans., 1987—95; legislator State of Kans., 1992—2000, atty. gen., 2003—06; dist. atty. Johnson County, Kans., 2006—. Nominee Kans. 2d Congl. Dist., 1986; former chmn. taxation com.; fin. chmn. Johnson County Reps., 1990-91; chmn. Shawnee Reps., 1991-92; chmn., co-chmn. Corp. Woods Charity Jazz Festival, Overland Park, 1991-95; bd. dirs. Shawnee Mission Edn. Found., 1994-95, Rep. Ho. Campaign Com. Mem. Johnson County Bar Assn., Kans. Bar Assn., Rotary (bd. dirs., v.p. 1991-93, pres. 1994-95, Disting. Svc. award 1991). Republican. Methodist. Avocations: history, reading, athletics. Office: Johnson County Dist Atty 100 N Kansas Olathe KS 66061*

KLINE, RAYMOND ADAM, professional organization executive; b. New Ringgold, Pa., Sept. 14, 1926; s. Raymond Adam and Helen Marie (Herb) K.; m. Jeanelle Batley, Apr. 26, 1958; children— Robin Jeanelle, Raymond Ashley. AB, Lebanon Valley Coll., 1950, LLD (hon.), 1990; LLB, George Washington U., 1957, JD (hon.), 1982. Bar: DC 1958. Mgmt. analyst Army Missile Command, Huntsville, Ala., 1958-61; chief mgmt. devel. office Marshall Space Flight Ctr., Huntsville, 1961-66; asst. assoc. adminstr. for systems mgmt. NASA Hdqrs., Washington, 1967-75, asst. adminstr. instl. mgmt., 1975-77, assoc. adminstr. mgmt. ops, 1977-79; dep. adminstr. GSA, 1979-84, acting adminstr., 1981, 1984-85; pres. Nat. Acad. Pub. Adminstrn., 1985-92. Instr. in polit. sci. U. Ala., 1958-63 Trustee The Kerr Found., Inc., Okla. City, Okla., 1993-. Served with US Army, 1944-46, 50-51. Mem. D.C. Bar, Phi Delta Phi, Pi Gamma Mu. Home: 15432 Carrolton Rd Rockville MD 20853-1703

KLINE, RICHARD C., oncologist; b. New Martinsville, W.Va., Jan. 29, 1954; MD, La. State U. Sch. Medicine, 1980. Cert. Obstetrics/Gynecology, Oncology. Resident, obstetrics and gynecology Ochsner Found., New Orleans, 1980—84; fellow, gynecological oncology MD Anderson Hosp. and Tumor Inst., Houston, 1984—86; hosp. appointment Ochsner Found. Hosp., New Orleans, 1986—, sect. head, gynecologic oncology; hosp. appointment Leonard J. Chabert Hosp., Maine, 1986. Researcher, investigator Nat. Cancer Inst. Gynecologic Oncology Group. Contbr. articles to profl. jours., chapters to books. Named one of Top Gynecologic Oncologists, New Orleans Mag.*

KLINE, RICHARD STEPHEN, communications and public affairs executive; b. Brookline, Mass., June 20, 1948; s. Paul and Helen (Chartoff) K.; m. Carroll Potter, (dec. Apr. 1984); m. Sharon Tate, June 16, 1985; stepchildren: Allison, Kevin. BA, U. Mass., 1970. Reporter, photographer Worcester (Mass.) Telegram & Gazette, 1970-71; account exec. Wenger-Michael Advt., LA, 1971; pub. rels. dir. Oakland (Calif.) Symphony Orch., 1972; asst. v.p., dir. promotions Gt. Western Savs. and Loan, Beverly Hills, Calif., 1972-75; v.p., dir. mktg. Union Fed. Savs. and Loan, LA, 1975-78; chmn. bd. dirs. Berkhemer & Kline, LA, 1978-88, Berkhemer Kline Golin/Harris, LA, 1988-93; COO Golin/Harris Comm., Chgo., 1992-95; pres. Shandwick U.S.A., NYC, N.Y., 1995-96, Kline Consulting Group, L.A., 1997; regional pres., sr. ptnr. Fleishman-Hillard, Inc., L.A., 1997—2007; v.p. comms. and pub. affairs Occidental Petroleum Corp., L.A., 2007—. Former instr. Am. Savs. and Loan Inst.; bd. dirs. Golin/Harris Communications; exec. com. Santa Barbara Old Spanish Days Fiesta Rodeo, 1992. Past pres., mem. exec. com. Big Bros. L.A.; bd. dirs. Am. Cancer Soc., L.A., Solvang (Calif.) TheatreFest; mem. Town Hall Forum, L.A.; commr. Parks and Recreation, City of Oakland, 1973-74; bd. dirs. United Way, 1988-93, TheaterFest, 1990-94, LA's Best, LA C. of C.; exec. com. Ctrl. City Assocs. Recipient Pres.'s Club award Big Bros. Greater L.A., 1987, 88, Best in West Pub. Svc. award Am. Advt. Fedn., San Francisco, 1975, Commitment to Youth award Big Bros. Greater L.A., 2001. Mem. Nat. Investor Rels. Inst., Pub. Rels. Soc. Am. (Disting. Cmty. Svc. award 1987), Internat. Assn. Bus. Communicators, Newcomen Soc., Nat. Cattlemen's Assn., Arthur W. Page Soc., Calif. Cattlemen's Assn., Am. Quarter Horse Assn., Rancheros Visitadores, Vaqueros de Los Ranchos, Jonathan Club. Avocations: horseback riding, fishing. Office: Occidental Petroleum Corp 10889 Wilshire Blvd 7th Fl Los Angeles CA 90024 Office Phone: 310-443-6249. Business E-Mail: richard_kline@oxy.com.

KLINE, SUSAN ANDERSON, medical educator, internist; b. Dallas, June 4, 1937; d. Kenneth Kirby and Frances Annette (Demorest) Anderson; m. Edward Mahon Kline, Dec. 26, 1964 (dec. July 1990). BA, Ohio U., 1959; MD, Northwestern U., 1963. Diplomate Am. Bd. Internal Medicine, Nat. Bd. Med. Examiners (bd. dirs. 1977-81). Asst. physician NY Hosp., 1967—68, physician-to-outpatients, 1968—69, electrocardiographer, 1968—70, asst. attending physician, 1969—76, physician-in-charge cardiopulmonary lab., 1970—71, dir. adult cardiac catheterizaion lab., 1970—71, dir. adult cardiac catheterization lab., 1971—79, assoc. attending physician, 1976—85, emeritus attending physician, 1985—, emeritus dir. adult cardiac catheterization lab., 1985—; assoc. dean student affairs Cornell U. Med. Coll., NYC, 1974—78; assoc. dean admissions and student affairs Cornell Med. Sch., Ithaca, NY, 1978—80; mgr. occupl. med. programs GE Co., 1980—84; sr. assoc. dean student affairs NY Med. Coll.,

Valhalla, 1984—94, interim dean, v.p. med. affairs, 1994—96, exec. vice dean acad. affairs, vice provost univ. student affairs, 1996—. Mem. test com. Ednl. Commn. on Fgn. Med. Grads., Phila., 1985—92; mem. U.S. Med. Licensing Exam test accommodations com. Nat. Bd. Med. Examiners, Phila., 1992—97; chmn. unmatched student com. Nat. Residency Matching Program, 1998—2000, mem. exec. com., 2003—, chair second match com., 2003—05, pres.-elect, 2004—05, pres., 2005—06, chair nominating com., 2005—06, bd. dirs.; mem. Liaison Com. Med. Edn., 1998—2004, chair ad hoc subcom. rev. accreditation stds., 2000—01, exec. com., 2002—04, policy com., 2003—04; chmn. adv. com. Electronic Residency Application Svc., 1996—2001. Bd. visitors Coll. Arts, Ohio U., Athens, 1981—91; bd. dirs. Burke Rehab. Hosp., White Plains, 1997—2006. Recipient Leaders of the Future award, Nat. Coun. Women, N.Y.C., 1978, Cert. of Appreciation, Ohio U., 1978. Fellow: ACP, Am. Soc. Internal Medicine, Am. Coll. Cardiology; mem.: Phi Kappa Phi, Am. Assn. Med. Colls. (chmn. 1989—93, mem. sr. mgmt. adv. com. 2001—05, chmn. N.E. group on student affairs), N.Y. Cardiologists Soc., Am. Heart Assn. (fellow coun. on clin. cardiology), Cruising Club Am., Alpha Omega Alpha, Phi Beta Kappa. Avocation: sailing. Home: 561 Pequot Ave Southport CT 06490-1366 Office: NY Med Coll Sunshine Cottage Valhalla NY 10595 Personal E-mail: sakline@attglobal.net. Business E-mail: kline@nymc.edu.

KLINE, THOMAS R., lawyer; b. NYC, 1947; AB, Columbia Coll., 1968; JD, Columbia U., 1975. Bar: DC 1976, NY 1976, Md. 1996. Trial atty. US Dept. Justice, Civil Divsn., Fed. Program Branch, 1979—81; ptnr., Litig. Andrews Kurth LLP, Washington. Adj. lectr. Am. U., 1977—81, George Mason U., 1986; adj. asst. prof. George Washington U., 2000—. Mem., editl. bd. Columbia Law Rev., 1974—75. Vol. mediator Alternate Dispute Resolution Program, USDC, Washington, 1996—; bd. dir. Washington Coun. Lawyers, 1984—. James Kent Scholar, 1974—75, Harlan Fiske Stone Scholar, 1972—73, 1973—74. Mem.: CPR Inst. Dispute Resolution (regional panal of disting. neutrals for Washington DC 1999—), ABA (co-chmn. energy resources law com. 1989—98, Tort & Ins. Practice Sect.), NY State Bar, Md. State Bar, DC Bar. Fluent in French. Office: Andrews Kurth LLP Ste 1000 1350 I St NW Washington DC 20005-7205 Office Phone: 202-662-2716. Office Fax: 202-974-9512. Business E-Mail: tkline@andrewskurth.com.

KLINE, THOMAS RICHARD, lawyer; b. Hazleton, Pa., Dec. 18, 1947; children: Hilary, Zachary. AB, Albright Coll., 1969; MA, Lehigh U., 1971; JD, Duquesne U., 1978. Bar: Pa., NY, U.S. Supreme Ct., U.S. Dist. Ct. (ea. dist.) Pa., U.S. Dist. Ct. (we. dist.) Pa., U.S. Ct. Appeals (3rd cir.). Tchr. Hazleton Area Sch. Dist., 1969-74; lectr. Lehigh U., Bethlehem, Pa., 1974; law clk. to Hon. Thomas W. Pomeroy Pa. Supreme Ct., Pitts., 1978; atty. Beasley Casey Colleran Erbstein Thistle & Kline, Phila., 1980-94; ptnr. Kline & Specter, 1995—. Adj. prof. sch. law Temple U.; chmn. fed. jud. nominations com. Ea. Dist., U.S. Dist. Ct. of Pa. Fellow: Internat. Acad. Trial Lawyers, Am. Coll. Trial Lawyers; mem.: ATLA, U. Pa. Inn of Cts., Inner Circle of Advocates, Phila. Trial Lawyers Assn., Pa. Trial Lawyers Assn., Phila. Bar Assn., Pa. Bar Assn., ABA. Office: 1525 Locust St Philadelphia PA 19102-3732 Home Phone: 215-772-1363; Office Phone: 215-772-1371. Business E-Mail: tkline@klinespecter.com.

KLINEDINST, JOHN DAVID, lawyer; b. Washington, Jan. 20, 1950; s. David Moulson and Mary Stewart (Coxe) K.; m. Cynthia Lynn DuBain, Aug. 15, 1981. BA cum laude in History, Washington and Lee U., 1971, JD, 1978; MBA in Fin. and Investments, George Washington U., 1975. Bar: Calif. 1979, U.S. Dist. Ct. (so. dist.) Calif. 1979, U.S. Ct. Appeals (9th cir.) 1987. With comml. lending dept. 1st Nat. Bank Md., Montgomery County, 1971-74; assoc. Ludecke, McGrath & Denton, San Diego, 1979-80; ptnr. Whitney & Klinedinst, San Diego, 1980-83, Klinedinst & Meiser, San Diego, 1983-86; CEO Klinedinst PC, San Diego, 1986—. Trustee Phi Kappa Psi Endowment Fund, 2004—. Mem. law coun. Washington and Lee U., 1993-97, vice chmn. law campaign, 1991-94, trustee, 2001—; vice chmn. bd. dirs. ARC of San Diego/Imperial, 1991-97; pres. House Corp. Calif. Lambda, Phi Kappa Psi, 1999—2006. Recipient Disting. Alumnus award Washington and Lee U., 1993. Mem. ABA (standing com. on legal profl. liability), Order of the Coif (hon.), Calif. Bar Assn., San Diego Bar Assn., San Diego Def. Lawyers, San Diego/Tijuana Sister Cities Soc., Washington Soc. (bd. dirs. 1997—), Washington and Lee U. Alumni Assn. (bd. dirs. 1986-90, pres. 1989-90), Washington and Lee U. Club (pres. San Diego chpt. 1980-87, San Diego Dialogue of U. Calif. San Diego), La Jolla Beach and Tennis Club, Fairbanks Ranch Country Club, Bohemian Club, Phi Kappa Psi. Republican. Episcopalian. Home: 6226 Via Dos Valles Rancho Santa Fe CA 92067-9999 Office: Klinedinst PC 501 W Broadway Ste 600 San Diego CA 92101-3584 Office Phone: 619-239-8131. Business E-Mail: jklinedinst@klinedinstlaw.com.

KLINEFELTER, ANNE, law librarian, educator; BA, U. Ala., 1981, MLS, 1986, JD, 1992. Clin. prof. law U. NC Sch. Law, Chapel Hill, assoc. dir, interim dir. Katherine R. Everett Law Libr. Office: U NC Sch Law Van Hecke-Wettach Hall 100 Ridge Rd, CB #3380 Chapel Hill NC 27599-3380 Office Phone: 919-962-6202. Office Fax: 919-962-1193. E-mail: klinefel@email.unc.edu.

KLINEFELTER, HYLDA CATHARINE, retired obstetrician, gynecologist; b. Gettysburg, Pa., Sept. 28, 1929; d. Roscoe Emanuel and Sara Catherine (Wagner) K.; m. Edward Ralph Kohnstam, June 18, 1955; children: Charles, Kathryn. Student, Gettysburg Coll., 1947-48; AB, U. Pa., 1951; MD, Med. Coll. Pa., 1955. Diplomate Am. Bd. Ob-Gyn. Rotating intern Phila. Gen. Hosp., 1955-56; resident in ob.-gyn. Presbyn. U. Pa. Med. Ctr., Phila., 1956-59; mem. teaching staff Med. Coll. Pa., Phila., 1959-62; staff ob-gyn. Riddle Meml. Hosp., 1962—99; rsch. asst. maternal and child health Pa. Hosp., Phila., 1964-66; co-supr. family planning clinic Presbyn. Hosp./U. Pa. Med. Ctr., 1967-68; ptnr. Media (Pa.) Clinic, 1969-81; pvt. practice, 1981-86; ptnr. Granite Run Ob.-Gyn. Assocs., Media, 1986—99; ret., 1999. Mem. staff Riddle Meml. Hosp., vice chmn. ob-gyn., 1989-93, chmn. ob-gyn., 1993-99. Contbr. articles to med. jours. Fellow ACOG; mem. AMA, Am. Med. Womens Assn. (past treas. dist. 25), Reproductive Medicine Assn., Am. Assn. Gyn. Laparoscopists, Internat. Soc. Gynecology Endoscopy, Delaware County Med. Soc., Pa. Med. Soc., Fox Valley Civic Assn., Soroptimist, Alpha Xi Delta. Republican. Lutheran. Avocations: singing, gardening, needlecrafts, painting. Home: 930 Hidden Hollow Dr Gap PA 17527-9562

KLINEFELTER, JAMES LOUIS, lawyer; b. LA, Oct. 8, 1925; s. Theron Albert and Anna Marie (Coffey) K.; m. Joanne Wright, Dec. 26, 1957 (div.); children: Patricia Anne, Jeanne Marie, Christopher Wright; m. Mary Lynn S. Klinefelter, Aug. 19, 1971; 1 child, Mary Katherine. BA, U. Ala., Tuscaloosa, 1949, LLB, 1951. Bar: Ala. 1951, US Dist. Ct. (no. dist.) Ala. 1959, US Ct. Appeals (11th cir.) 1983. Regional claims rep. State Farm Mut. Auto Ins. Co., Anniston, Ala., 1951-54; ptnr. Burnham & Klinefelter, Anniston, 1954—2003; mem. Sides, Oglesby, Held and Dick, Anniston, 2003—. Mem. adv. com. Supreme Ct. Ala. Mem. Svc. Core of Retired Execs., Ala. Dem. Exec. Com., 1964—, chmn. legis. rev. com., 1964—; past chmn. Calhoun County Dem. Exec. Com., 1964—; mem. Anniston City Sch. Bd. Lt. (j.g.) USNR, 1943-46. Mem. ABA, Assn. Def. Trial Attys., Ala. Bar Assn. (mem. task force on jud. selection, mem. long-range planning task force), Calhoun County Bar Assn., Ala. Def. Lawyers Assn. (past pres.), Ala. Law Inst. (bd. dirs.), Ala. Sch. Bd. Attys. (past pres.), Internat. Assn. Def. Counsel, Kiwanis (past pres.), Anniston Country Club, Phi Kappa Sigma, Phi Alpha Theta. Avocations: tennis, swimming, reading. Home: 1412 Christine Ave Anniston AL 36207-3924 Office: Sides Oglesby Held and Dick 1310 Leighton Ave PO Box 1849 Anniston AL 36202-1849 Personal E-mail: jlk1412@cableone.net. *When obligations or obnoxious tasks are accepted gratefully as opportunities, one's life can be turned about, and bitterness and resentment changed into joyful satisfaction. Hard tasks are the food of growth.*

KLINEFELTER, SARAH STEPHENS, retired dean, broadcast executive; b. Des Moines, Jan. 30, 1938; d. Edward John and Mary Ethel (Adams) Stephens; m. Neil Klinefelter. BA, Drake U., Des Moines, 1958; MA, U. Iowa, Iowa City, 1968; postgrad., Harvard U., Cambridge, Mass., 1984, U. Wis., Madison, 1987, Vanderbilt U., Nashville, Tenn., 1991-92. Chmn. humanities dept. High Sch. Dist. 230, Orland Pk., Ill., 1958-68; chmn. communications and humanities div. Kirkwood Community Coll., Cedar Rapids, Iowa, 1968-78; prof. English Sch. of the Ozarks, Point Lookout, Mo., 1978-86; gen. mgr. Sta. KSOZ-FM, Point Lookout, 1986-90; dean div. of performing and profl. arts Coll. of the Ozarks, Point Lookout, 1989-2001. Commr. Skaggs Cmty. Hosp., Branson, Mo., 1986—; chmn. Branson Planning and Zoning Commn., 1983—2004; project dir. Mo. Humanities Bd.; commr., examiner North Ctrl. Assn. Higher Edn., 1978—85; commr. Iowa Humanities Bd., 1971—78; chair Taney County Planning and Zoning Commn., 1989—98, 2005—; pres. Branson Arts Coun., 1997—2002; co-chair Taney County Bd. Adjustment; FDA norovirus grant coord. Branson City Health Dept., 2003—04; elderhostel instr. Ozark Adventures, 2001—. Democrat. Presbyterian. Home: 182 Hensley Rd Forsyth MO 65653-5137 Personal E-mail: klinefelter@centurytel.net.

KLING, CARL ANDREW, music educator; b. Ft. Worth, June 18, 1968; s. Alvin Andrew and Karen Elaine Kling; m. Jennifer Rae Milles, June 14, 2003. B in Music Edn., Tex. We. U., 1991; MA in Music, Stephen F. Austin State U., 1993; postgrad., Ind. U., 2001. Asst. dir. bands Georgetown Jr. H.S., Tex., 1993—94; assoc. dir. bands Cleburne H.S., Tex., 1994—2000; dir. bands H.F. Stevens Mid. Sch., Crowley, Tex., 2000—01; asst. instr. Ind. U., Bloomington, 2001—04; dir. bands N.W. Mo. State U., Maryville, 2004—, dir. summer music camp, 2004—. Contbr. chapters to books. Grantee, N.W. Mo. State U., 2004. Mem.: Music Educators Nat. Conf., Coll. Band Dir. Assn., Nat. Band Assn., Kappa Kappa Psi, Pi Kappa Lambda. Avocations: camping, hiking, model railroading. Home: 609 S Buchanan St Maryville MO 64468 Office: NW Mo State Univ 800 University Dr Maryville MO 64468 Office Phone: 660-562-1794.

KLING, LEWIS M., multi-industry executive; BSEE, Rensselaer Polytechnic Inst.; MBA, Stetson U. From computer engr. to several managerial positions Apollo div. (later Simulation and Control Systems) GE, 1966—90; v.p., gen. mgr. electronic systems div. Harris Corp., Melbourne, Fla., 1990—95; sr. v.p., gen. mgr. Commercial Avionics Systems Allied-Signal Aerospace, Ft. Lauderdale, Fla., 1995—97, chmn. bd. Am. Russian Integrated Avionics JV; pres. Dielectric Comms. Gen Signal (merged with SPX Corp. 1998), Raymond, Maine, 1997; corp. v.p., officer SPX Corp., 1999—2004; COO Flowserve Corp., Irving, Tex., 2004—05, CEO, pres., mem. bd. dirs., 2005—. Office: Flowserve Corp 5215 N O Connor Blvd Ste 2300 Irving TX 75039 Home Phone: 972-386-3336; Office Phone: 972-443-6505. Business E-Mail: lkling@flowserve.com.*

KLING, MERLE, retired political scientist, retired university official; b. Russia, June 15, 1919; came to U.S., 1921, naturalized, 1927; s. Saul and Dina (Hoffman) K.; m. Ann Ruth Yasgur, Jan. 1, 1948 (dec. June 1976); 1 child, Arnold Saul; m. Sandra Perlman, Aug. 26, 1978 (dec. Aug. 1990). AB, Washington U., St. Louis, 1940, MA, 1941, PhD, 1949, DHC (hon.), 1983; LLD (hon.), Mercy Coll., Dobbs Ferry, NY, 1985. Mem. faculty Washington U., 1946—, asst. prof. polit. sci., 1950-54, asso. prof., 1954-61, prof., 1961-83, prof. emeritus, 1983—; dean Washington U. (Faculty Arts and Scis.), 1966-69, 73-76, provost, 1976-79, exec. vice chancellor, provost, 1979-83, acting chmn. dept. polit. sci., 1970-71; ret., 1971; pres. Mercy Coll., Dobbs Ferry, NY, 1984-85. Vis. prof. U. Ill., 1961; research assoc. Center Internat. Studies, Princeton U., 1964-65 Author: The Soviet Theory of Internationalism, 1952, A Mexican Interest Group in Action, 1961; contbr. articles to profl. jours. Served with AUS, 1942-45. Merle Kling professorship of Modern Letters established in honor, Washington U., 1983. Mem. Am. Polit. Sci. Assn. (council 1967-69), Midwest Polit. Sci. Assn. (editor jour. 1965-66, pres. 1969-70), Phi Beta Kappa, Alpha Kappa Delta, Omicron Delta Kappa. Home: 20 N Kingshighway Blvd Saint Louis MO 63108-1366

KLING, PHRADIE (PHRADIE KLING GOLD), small business owner, educator; b. NYC, July 2, 1933; d. Samuel A. and Mary Leah (Cohen) Kling; m. Lee M. Gold, Sept. 5, 1955 (div. 1976); children: Judith Eileen, Laura Susan, Stephen Samuel, James David. BA, Cornell U., 1955; MA in Human Genetics, Sarah Lawrence Coll., 1971. Genetic counselor assoc. Coll. Medicine and Dentistry N.J., Newark, 1970—73; assoc. genetic counselor Sarah Lawrence Coll., Bronxville, NY, 1970—73; genetic counselor N.Y. Fertility Rsch. Found., NYC, 1971—73; staff assoc., genetic counselor depts. pediatrics, ob-gyn and neurology Columbia U. Coll. Physicians and Surgeons, NYC, 1973—78; asst. in genetics St. Luke's Hosp. Ctr., NYC, 1977—79; health program assoc. Conn. Dept. Health Svcs., Hartford, 1978—84; edn. cons. Conn. Traumatic Brain Injury Assn., Rocky Hill, 1984—85; office mgr. Anderson Turf Irrigation Inc., Plainville, Conn., 1986—92; owner, mgr. KlingWorks, contract adminstrn., Avon, Conn., 1992—. Spkr., instr. health and health ethics issues, Conn., NY, NJ, 1971—85; dir. confs. genetics and traumatic brain injury, 1980—85; project dir. ednl. field testing Biol. Scis. Curriculum Study, 1981—83; scientist AAAS Sci.-by-Mail, 1991—2000. Active Farmington River Watershed Assn., Simsbury, Conn., 1988—; docent Sci. Mus. Conn., West Hartford, 1989—90. Recipient citation for dedicated svc., Conn. Safety Belt Coalition, 1985. Mem.: Conn. Assn. Jungian Psychology (bd. dirs.), Bus. and Profl. Microcomputer Users Group (bd. dirs.), Am. Human Genetics Soc., Am. Mensa (chpt. coord. gifted children 1985—), Cornell Club Greater Hartford. Home and Office: 33 Hunter Rd Avon CT 06001-3618

KLING, S(TEPHEN) LEE, banker; b. St. Louis, Dec. 22, 1928; m. Ann Hemingway (div. 1958); m. Rosalyn H. Kling, May 3, 1962; children: Stephen L., Frank Frederick, Lee C., Allan B. BBA, Washington U., St. Louis, 1950. Chmn. bd., CEO Landmark Bancshares Corp., St. Louis, 1971—91; asst. spl. counselor on inflation White House, Washington, 1978—79; adv. vice-chmn. bd. U.S. divsn. Reed Stenhouse, Inc., 1978—79; chmn. bd. Kling Rechter & Co., 1991—2001, The Kling Co., 2002—. Bd. dirs. Bernard Chaus Inc., NYC, Nat. Beverage Co., Ft. Lauderdale, Fla., Electro Rent Corp., LA. Chmn., trustee Barnes-Jewish Found.; trustee Truman Libr. Inst., Independence, Mo., St. Louis Zoo Found., Chancellors Coun. Washington U., St. Louis, Mo. Botanical Garden, St. Louis, NY Mil. Acad., Cornwall, NY; chmn. Wyman Ctr.; co-chmn. Citizens Com. for Ratification of Panama Canal Treaties;, 1977; apptd. to Def. Base Closure and Realignment Commn., 1995; co-chmn. Coalition for Enactment of Caribbean Basin Initiative Legis., 1982—83; treas. Dem. Nat. Conv., 1976; nat. treas. Carter-Mondale Re-election Com., Gephardt for Pres. Com.; U.S. econ. advisor representing pvt. sector during peace negotiations between Israel and Egypt; apptd. to Mo. State Hwy. and Transp. Commn., 1995, apptd., 1995, chmn., 1997. Mem. Burning Tree Club, Westwood Country Club, St. Louis Club. Home: 17 Country Life Saint Louis MO 63131 also: 9940 Old Olive Rd Saint Louis MO 63141 Office Phone: 314-963-2501. Personal E-mail: sleekling@aol.com.

KLING, WILLIAM HUGH, broadcast executive; b. St. Paul, Apr. 29, 1942; s. William Conrad and Helen A. (Leonard) Kling; m. Sarah Margaret Baldwin, Sept. 25, 1976. BA in Economics, St. John's U., 1964; MA in Comm., Boston U. Pres. Minn. Pub. Radio, Inc., St. Paul, 1966—, Greenspring Co., 1986—, Am. Pub. Media Group, 1999—; founding dir. Nat. Pub. Radio, 1968-70, dir., 1977-80; chmn., founding pres. Pub. Radio Internat., 1982-86, vice chmn., 1986-93; regent St. John's U., 2005—. Co-founder, chmn. Gather.com, 2005—; bd. dirs. Wenger Corp., Irwin Fin.; mem. fund bds. Capital Group Am. Funds, chmn. New Economy Fund, chmn. Small Cap World Fund. Bd. dirs. Minn. Orch., 1987—93; trustee J. L. Found., 1988—2006; bd. dirs., chmn. Fitzgerald Theater Corp., 1983—; James Madison coun. Libr. of Congress, 1992—94. Named Disting. Minnesotan, 1995; named one of 100 Disting. Minnesotans of the Century, Mpls. Star Tribune, 2000; named to Minn. Broadcasters Hall of Fame, 2004; recipient Edward R. Murrow award, 1981, award for Excellence, Channels Mag., 1987. Mem.: Woodhill Country Club, Mpls. Club. Office: Am Pub Media Group 480 Cedar St Saint Paul MN 55101-2274

KLINGBIEL, PAUL HERMAN, retired information scientist; b. Watertown, Wis., Nov. 3, 1919; s. Herman Carl and Elsa Helen (Zilisch) K.; m. Mildred Louise Wells, Nov. 30, 1968; stepchildren: Alice J. Blessley, Jo Ann Grayson. PhB, U. Chgo., 1948, BS, 1950; MA, Am. U., 1966. Abstractor Armed Svcs. Tech. Info. Agy., Dept. Def., Washington, 1953-58; editor Tech. Abstract Bull., 1958-60; dir. Office of Lexicography, 1960-66; phys. sci. adminstr., linguistics rsch. Def. Documentation Ctr., 1966-79; sr. cons. Aspen Systems Corp., 1979-81; systems analyst PRC Data Svcs. Co., Linthicum Heights, Md., 1981-82; lectr. Am. U., Washington, 1966-69; cons. divsn. med. scis. NAS, 1969-70; ret., 1981. Contbr. articles to profl. jours. Pres. Mease Manor Residents Found., Inc. With AUS, 1943-46. Recipient Meritorious Civilian Svc. award, 1974, Disting. Career award, 1979. Fellow AAAS; mem. Assn. Computational Linguistics, N.Y. Acad. Scis. Lutheran. Achievements include research in the field of computational linguistics. Home: 700 Mease Plz Apt 417 Dunedin FL 34698-6629 Personal E-mail: phk19@ij.net.

KLINGELHOFER, STEPHAN E., lawyer; b. Fond du Lac, Wis., June 17, 1943; BA, Yale Univ., 1964; JD, Duke Univ., 1967; MDiv, Va. Theol. Sem., 1979. Bar: D.C. 1968, Ill. 1970, Md. 2001. Atty. corp. tax practice; dir. Devel. Office City Lights Sch., Washington; v.p. & COO Internat. Ctr. for Not-For-Profit Law, Washington, 1994—2001, pres. & CEO, 2001—04, sr. v.p., 2004—; of counsel Hoon & Associates, Md. Priest Episc. Church. Mem.: ABA, Md. Bar Assn. Episcopalian. Office: ICNL Suite 400 1126 16th St NW Washington DC 20036 Office Phone: 202-452-8600. Business E-Mail: sklingel@icnl.org.

KLINGENBERG, BEATE, management educator, director; d. Joachim Walter and Inge Bertha Elise Klingenberg; m. Tom Geerd Geurts, Apr. 8, 1996. MS in Chemistry, Friedrich-Alexander U. of Erlangen-Nuernberg, Germany, 1990; PhD in Phys. Chemistry, Friedrich-Alexander U. of Erlangen-Nuernberg, 1993; MBA, Marist Coll., Poughkeepsie, NY, 2004. Sr. mgr. Infineon Techs., Hopewell Junction, NY, 1999—2003; asst. prof. mgmt. Marist Coll. Sch. of Mgmt., 2003—. Dir. MS in tech. mgmt. Marist Coll. Sch. of Mgmt., 2006—. Contbr. articles to profl. jours. Fin. chair Camerata Chorale, Poughkeepsie, 2006. Feodor Lynen fellow, Alexander-von-Humboldt Found., Germany, 1994—96. Mem.: IAMOT, IEEE, Am. Real Estate Soc., German Soc. Phys. Chemistry, Am. Chem. Soc., Acad. of Mgmt., Alexander-von-Humboldt Assn. of Am., Beta Gamma Sigma. Office: Marist Coll Sch of Mgmt North Rd Poughkeepsie NY 12601 Office Phone: 845-575-3000. Business E-Mail: beate.klingenberg@marist.edu.

KLINGENSMITH, MICHAEL, publishing executive; BA, Univ. Chgo., 1975, MBA, 1976. Pres., pub. Entertainment Weekly Mag. Time Inc., NYC, 1990—96, pres. Entertainment Weekly, 1996—98, pres. Sports Illustrated, 1998—2001, exec. v.p., 2001—. Trustee Univ. Chgo., amfAR; dir. YMCA of Greater NY. Office: Time Inc 1271 Avenue of the Americas New York NY 10020-1300

KLINGER, ALAN MARK, lawyer; b. Bklyn., July 19, 1956; s. David and Gloria (Feldman) K.; m. Susan Debra Wagner, Aug. 29, 1982; children: Zachary, Jesse, Emily. AB, Princeton U., 1978; JD, NYU, 1981. Bar: N.Y. 1982, N.J. 1982, U.S. Dist. Ct. N.J., U.S. Dist. Ct. (so., ea. and we. dists.) N.Y. 1982, U.S. Ct. Appeals (2d cir.) 1985, U.S. Supreme Ct. 1989. Law clk. to judge NJ Supreme Ct., Trenton, 1981-82; assoc. Stroock & Stroock & Lavan, NYC, 1982-90, ptnr., 1990—, mem. operating exec. com., exec. ptnr., 2006—. Bd. dirs. Partnership with Children; trustee Lawyers Com. for Civil Rights Under Law. Mem. ABA, N.Y. State Bar Assn., Fed. Bar Council, Assn. of Bar of City of N.Y., ACLU. Avocations: chess, ping pong/table tennis, basketball. Office: Stroock & Stroock & Lavan LLP 180 Maiden Ln New York NY 10038-4982 Office Phone: 212-806-5818. Office Fax: 212-806-6006. Business E-Mail: aklinger@stroock.com.

KLINGER, GAIL GREAVES, art educator, illustrator; b. Evanston, Ill., Dec. 21, 1953; d. Harold and Darlene Peterson Greaves; m. Richard William Klinger, II, Aug. 14, 1976; children: Kimberly, Kurt, Kristen. BS in Edn. (cum laude), No. Ill. U., DeKalb, 1972—75; M in Curriculum Devel., Nat. Louis U., Wheaton, Ill., 1991. K-12 art instr. Avon Cmty. Unit Dist. 176, Ill., 1976—79; 6-8 home mgmt. Oak Brook Sch. Dist. 53, 1979—83; 6-8 art instr. Butler Sch. Dist. 53, Oak Brook, 1979—. Arts & crafts instr. Elk Grove Village Dist., Ill., 1968—76, Elk Grove Village Park Dist., 1980—85, Oak Brook Pk. Dist., 1977—80; art exhibit coord. Butler Sch. Dist. 53, 1976—, stage set designer, builder, 1976—2002, 2007—, art club sponsor, 1976—2002, yearbook adv., 1981—92, Washington trip coord. & planner, 1981—99, cheerleading coach, 1983—88, art club sponsor, 2007—. Book, Verses for Dad's Heart, 2004, Verse's for Mom's Heart, 2005. Troop leader Girl Scouts Am., Wheaton, 1995—2005; summer arts and crafts dir. Global Outreach to Ojibway Native Ams., Wheaton Bible Ch., 2000—; mem. steering com. Friends of Elk Grove Village Pub. Libr., 1882—1984. Mem.: NEA, Ill. Edn. Assn., Soc. Children's Book Writers & Illustrators, Nat. Art Edn. Assn. Republican. Mem. Christian Ch. Avocations: scuba diving, gardening, interior decorating. Office: Butler Jr HS 2801 York Rd Oak Brook IL 60523-2334 Office Phone: 630-573-2760 ext. 153. Business E-Mail: gklinger@butler53.com.

KLINGER, MARILYN SYDNEY, lawyer; b. NYC, Aug. 14, 1953; d. Victor and Lillyan Judith Klinger. BS, U. Santa Clara, 1975; JD, U. Calif., Hastings, 1978. Bar: Calif. 1978. Assoc. Chickering & Gregory, San Francisco, 1978-81, Steefel, Levitt & Weiss, San Francisco, 1981-82, Sedgwick, Detert, Moran & Arnold, San Francisco and L.A., 1982-87, ptnr. San Francisco, 1988-98, LA, 1998—. Guest lectr. Stanford U. Sch. Engring. Vol. atty. Lawyers Commn. on Urban Affairs, San Francisco, 1978-80. Mem. ABA (tort and ins. practice sect., chair surety and fidelity com. 2003-04, constrn. forum, pub. contracts sect.), Internat. Assn. Def. Counsel (chmn. fidelity and surety com. 1996-98), Nat. Bond Claims Assn. (spkr.), Surety Claims Inst. (spkr.), No. Calif. Surety Underwriters Assn., No. Calif. Surety Claims Assn. (lectr., pres. 1989-90), Surety Assn. L.A. (spkr.). Avocations: reading, hiking, golf. Home: 939 15th St # 10 Santa Monica CA 90403-3146 Office: Sedgwick Detert Moran & Arnold 801 S Figueroa St Fl 18 Los Angeles CA 90017-2573 Home Phone: 310-899-4494; Office Phone: 213-615-8038. Business E-Mail: marilyn.klinger@sdma.com.

KLINGER, STEVEN J., paper company executive; b. Atlanta, Mar. 5, 1959; BBA in Acctg., Ga. State U., 1982. Payroll acct. corp. acctg. Ga.-Pacific Corp., Atlanta, 1982—83, gen. acctg. mgr. distbn., 1983—87, sr. auditor internal audit dept., 1987—88, asst. to contr./ops. contrs. dept., 1988—90, mgmt. trainee softwood lumber, 1991—92, mgr. bus. planning forest resources, 1992—93, dir. acquisition and divestiture fin. dept., 1993—94, divsn. contr. pkg., 1994—95, divsn. contr. containerboard and pkg., 1995—96, regional mgr. J&J corrugated, 1996—98, regional mgr. S.E. pkg. ops., 1998—2000, v.p. pkg. ops., 2000—01, pres. packaging,

2001—03, exec. v.p. and pres. packaging, 2003—05; pres., COO Smurfit-Stone Container Corp., Chgo., 2006—. Past. chmn. Fibre Box Assn.; bd. mem. Internat. Corrugated Case Assn. Mem. bd. adv. Ga. State Univ.; bd. mem. Carr Alliance, Atlanta Acad. Office: Smurfit-Stone Container Corp 150 N Michigan Ave Chicago IL 60601*

KLINGHOFFER, JUDITH APTER, historian, consultant; b. Sept. 4, 1946; d. Abraham Apter and Rachel (Preisler) Basch; m. Arthur Jay Klinghoffer, May 18, 1969; 1 child, Joella. BA, Hebrew U., 1967; MA in Pub. History, Rutgers U., 1986, PhD in History, 1994. Pub. historian, Cherry Hill, 1986-90; asst. prof. Rowan U., Glassboro, N.J., 1991-92; staff mem. Ctr. Hist. Analysis, Rutgers U., New Brunswick, N.J., 1994-95; pres. Global Perspectives, Cherry Hill, 1997—. Vis. lectr. Beijing, China, 1992-93; Fulbright prof., Aarhus, Denmark, 1996. Co-author: Israel and the Soviet Union, 1985, International Citizens' Tribunals: Mobilizing Public Opinion to Advance Human Rights, 2002; author: The Citizen Planner, 1989, Vietnam, The Jews and The Middle East: Unintended Consequences, 1999; contbr. articles to profl. jours., to online jours. E-mail: klinghof@crab.rutgers.edu, judith.klinghoffer@gmail.com.

KLINGLE, PHILIP ANTHONY, law librarian; b. Bklyn., July 24, 1950; s. Lorin Russell and Therese Margaret (Meehan) K.; m. Rachelle Phyllis Miller, Nov. 20, 1977; children: David Adam, Michael Matthew, Anne Elizabeth. BA, Fordham U., 1971; MA, NYU, 1973; MS, Columbia U., 1976. Asst. reference libr. N.Y. Hist. Soc., NYC, 1973-77; libr. Bklyn. Pub. Libr., 1977-78; reference libr., asst. prof. John Jay Coll. Criminal Justice CUNY, 1978-81; libr. Inst. Jud. Adminstrn. Sch. of Law NYU, 1981-82; sr. law libr. ct. libr. N.Y. State Supreme Ct., SI, 1982—. Editor: jour. The Literature of Criminal Justice, 1980-81, IJA Report, 1981-82. Mem. ALA, Am. Assn. Law Librs., Law Libr. Assn. Greater N.Y., Libr. Assn. CUNY (mem. exec. coun. 1978-81). Office: NY State Supreme Ct Libr Richmond County Courthouse Staten Island NY 10301 Office Phone: 718-390-5291.

KLINGLER, GWENDOLYN WALBOLT, state representative; b. Toledo, May 28, 1944; d. L. Byron and Elizabeth (Brown) Walbolt; m. Walter Gerald Klingler, June 11, 1966; children: Kelly Michelle, Lance, Jeffrey. BA, Ohio Wesleyan U., 1966; MA, U. Mich., 1969; JD, George Washington U., 1981. Bar: Ill. Rsch. assoc. U. Mich., Ann Arbor, 1966-71; abstractor Year Book Med. Pub., Chgo., 1972-75; law clk. FDA, Rockville, Md., 1980; atty. Atty. Gen.'s Office State of Ill., Springfield, 1981-84, appellate prosecutor, 1984-92; ptnr. Boyle, Klingler & McClain, Springfield, 1992-95. Mem. Springfield Bd. of Edn., 1987-91, pres., 1988; alderman Springfield City Coun., 1991-95; Rep. Ill. Ho. of Reps., 100th Dist., 1995-2003. Recipient Woman of Achievement award in Govt., Women-in-Mgmt., 1994, Disting. Alumni award Leadership Springfield, 1996. Mem. AAUW, Cen. Ill. Women's Bar Assn. (chair membership com.), Sangamon County Bar Assn., Greater Springfield C. of C., Women-in-Mgmt. Republican. Presbyterian (elder). Home: 1600 Ruth Pl Springfield IL 62704-3362 E-mail: klingler@housegopmail.state.il.us.

KLINGMAN, CHARLES DAVID, health services researcher; m. Charlotte Ann Johnson, Aug. 19, 1966; children: Jeffrey David, Justin Michael. BA, U. Tex., Austin, 1966; MA, U. Wis., Milw., 1967; PhD, Mich. State U., East Lansing, 1973. Instr., asst. prof. social sci. Mich. State U., East Lansing, 1971—74; asst. prof. polit. sci. U. So. Calif., LA, 1974—81; assoc. prof. polit. sci. George Washington U., Washington, 1981—84; rsch. mgr. SysteMetrics/McGraw-Hill, Inc., Washington, 1984—92; sr. analyst Office of Tech. Assessment, U.S. Congress, Washington, 1992—95; dir. outcomes rsch. Parexel Internat., Inc., Alexandria, Va., 1996—2000; sr. dir. health econ. ValueMedics Rsch., LLC, Falls Church, Va., 2000—. Co-author (with William W. Lammers): (book) State Policies for the Aging, 1984, govt. reports; contbr. articles to profl. jours. Fellow, NSF, 1966—67, Haynes Found., L.A., 1975; grantee, Nat. Inst. Aging, NIH, 1978—83. Mem.: Internat. Soc. Pharmacoeconomics and Outcomes Rsch. Office: ValueMedics Rsch LLC 300 N Washington St Ste 303 Falls Church VA 22046 Home Phone: 703-743-1027; Office Phone: 703-286-2900. Business E-Mail: info@valuemedics.com.

KLINGMAN, JOHN PHILIP, architect, educator; b. Phila., July 31, 1947; s. John Philip and Ethel Iva (Serfas) K. BSCE, Tufts U., 1969; postgrad., Stanford U., 1969-70; MArch, U. Oreg., 1983. Registered architect, La. Constrn. coord., project mgr. Payette Assocs., Inc., Boston, 1972-81; mem. design team Fairchild Biochemistry Bldg. Harvard U., 1977—78; project architect LaBouisse & Waggonner Inc. Architects, New Orleans, 1986-89; cons. architect Waggonner & Ball, Inc. Architects, New Orleans, 1990-96; design, planning and preservation U.S. Customhouse, New Orleans, 1996—. Asst. prof. Sch. Architecture Tulane U., New Orleans, 1983-90, assoc. prof., 1990-96, prof., 1996—, Favrot prof., 2002—, assoc. dean, 1991-93; chmn. archtl. rev. com. Historic Dists. Landmarks Commn., 1995—; mem. sustainability subcom., urban planning com. Mayor's Bring New Orleans Back Commn., 2005-06. Author: New New Orleans Architecture, New Orleans Mag., annually, 1997-; co-editor: Talk About Architecture: A Century of Architectural Education at Tulane, 1993. Recipient GSA Honor award for customhouse projects, 1996. Avocation: wood sculpture. Home: 1309 Harmony St New Orleans LA 70115-3424 Office: Tulane U Sch Architecture New Orleans LA 70118 Office Phone: 504-314-2339. Business E-Mail: jklingm@tulane.edu.

KLINGSBERG, DAVID, lawyer; b. NYC, Feb. 4, 1934; m. Fran Sue Morganstern, Aug. 16, 1959; 3 children. LL.B., Yale U., 1957; BS, NYU, 1954. Bar: N.Y. 1958. Law clk. to U.S. Dist. Judge, NY, 1957-58; atty. U.S. Dept. Justice, Office Dep. Atty. Gen., Washington, 1958-59; asst. U.S. atty. criminal div. So. Dist. N.Y., 1959-61; chief appellate atty. U.S. Atty. Office, NY, 1961-62; assoc. Kaye Scholer LLP, NYC, 1962—65, ptnr., 1966—2004, chmn. exec. com., 1996—2004, spl. counsel, 2005—. Adj. faculty Rutgers Sch. Law, 2005—. Contbr. articles to legal jours.; mem. editorial bd. Yale Law Jour, 1956-57. Recipient Pub. Interest Leadership award, Legal Aid Soc., 2001, 2001, Pro Bono Svc. award, 2005. Fellow Am. Coll. Trial Lawyers; mem. ABA, Assn. Bar City N.Y. (chmn. anti-trust and trade regulation com. 1986-89, Thurgood Marshall award for representation in death sentence cases 1998), N.Y. State Bar Assn., Legal Aid Soc. NY (bd. dirs. 2001-06, bd. advisors 2006—). Office: Kaye Scholer LLP 425 Park Ave New York NY 10022-3598 Office Phone: 212-836-8281.

KLINK, FREDRIC J., lawyer; b. NYC, Oct. 4, 1933; s. Frederick Carl and Sophia Adelaide (Wolf) K.; children: Christopher, Charles; stepchildren: Kirsten Morehouse, Trina Morehouse. AB, Columbia U., 1955, LL.B., 1960. Bar: N.Y. 1960. Practiced in, NYC; ptnr. firm Dechert, Price & Rhoads, 1989—2001, of counsel, 2001—. Editor: Columbia U. Law Rev, 1959-60. Served as lt. (j.g.) USNR, 1955-57. Mem. Am. Law Inst., Am., Internat., N.Y. C. bar assns. Office: Dechert LLP 4675 McArthur Ct Newport Beach CA 92660 Home: 23655 Tampico Bay Dana Point CA 92629 Office Phone: 949-442-6012. Business E-Mail: fredric.klink@dechert.com.

KLINKE, LOUISE HOYT, volunteer; b. Rochester, NY, Nov. 16, 1933; d. Martin Breck Hoyt and Evelyn Louise Moone; children: Geoffrey P., David H., Debra L. Stall. AA, Rochester Bus. Inst., 1952. Dir. fin. and pers. Landmark Soc. Western N.Y., Rochester, 1965—85; ret., 1985. Vol. Landmark Soc. Preservation Issues Com., Nathaniel Rochester Soc., Rochester Inst. Tech., Arts and Cultural Coun. Devel. Com.; mem. Meml. Art Gallery, Eastman House, Strong Mus., Nat. Trust for Hist. Preservation, Preservation League N.Y. State, Smithsonian Inst., Met. Mus., Rochester Area Cmty. Found.; treas. Rochester Contemporary; mem. adv. bd MECA, 2005—; bd. dirs. Art Walk, Race and Reconciliation; trustee emeritus. Keuka Coll., 1982—; bd. dirs. Hillside Children's Ctr., 1982—, treas.; past v.p. Hillside Children's Found.; past bd. dirs. Women's Found. Genesee Valley, Friends Eastman Opera; bd. dirs. Rochester Hist. Soc., 1984—, past treas.; bd. dirs. Alzheimer's Assn., past treas.; bd. dirs. Pyramid Arts Ctr., past treas.; bd. dirs. Opera Theatre Rochester, treas.; bd. dirs. Garth Fagan Dance, 2001—. Mem.: BOA, Rochester City Ballet, Geva Theatre, Assn. Fund Raising Profls., Chatterbox Club. Democrat. Episcopalian. Home: 1400 East Ave #203 Rochester NY 14610 Personal E-mail: weesie702@frontiernet.net.

KLINKMAN, MICHAEL SCOTT, medical educator; b. Cass City, Mich., Oct. 31, 1955; s. Keith Harvey Klinkman and Doris Alice Golding; m. Lisa Sanderson, May 19, 1984; children: Andrew Scott, Emily Krista, Hannah Marie. BS in Zoology, U. Mich., Ann Arbor, 1978; MD, U. Mich., 1982; MS in Family Medicine, Case We. Res. U., Cleve., 1987. Diplomate Am. Bd. Family Medicine, 1985, Am. Bd. Family Medicine, 1992, Am. Bd. Family Medicine, 1999, Am. Bd. Family Medicine, 2006. Residency family practice U. Mich., 1982—85, chief resident, dept. family medicine, 1984—85; asst. prof., assoc. residency dir., dept. family medicine Case We. Res. U., 1987—89, assoc. residency dir., dept. family medicine, 1989—91; lectr. dept. family medicine, U. Mich., 1989—91, asst. prof., 1991—98, assoc. prof., 1998—, dept. psychiatry, U. Mich., 2001—. Chair mental health working grp. N.Am. Primary Care Rsch. Grp., 1998—; assoc. dir. med. mgmt. ctr. U. Mich. Health Sys., 1999—2003, dir. disease mgmt. programs, 1999—2003; mem. spl. emphasis panel interventions rev. com. NIMH, Bethesda, Md., 2002—06, mem. study sect., 2006; vis. prof., dept. cmty. medicine & gen. practice Norwegian U. Sci. & Tech., Trondheim, 2003; vis. prof., dept. gen. practice U. So. Denmark, Odense, 2003; dir. primary care programs U. Mich. Depression Ctr., 2003—; bd. mem. nat. alliance for primary care informatics Am. Med. Informatics Assn., 2005—; mem. snomed-ct primary care working grp. SNOMED Internat., 2005—; mem. med. adv. bd. Cielo Med Solutions, LLC, Ann Arbor, 2005—; co-chair Wonca Internat. Classification Com., 2005—; mem. future of family medicine task force N.Am. Primary Care Rsch. Grp., 2006—, mem. info. tech. task force, 2006—; mem. depression & anxiety clin. cons. bd. Wyeth Pharmaceuticals, Collegeville, Pa., 2006—; advisor primary health care classification WHO, Geneva, 2006—; scholar Robert Graham Ctr. Policy Studies in Family Medicine, DC, 2006—. Contbr. chapters to books, articles to profl. jours. Vol. physician Hope Med. Clinic, Ypsilanti, Mich., 1990—2004; deacon bd. Huron Hills Bapt. Ch., Ann Arbor, 2006—07. Recipient Kenneth G. Reeb award for excellence in clin. tchg., Case We. Res. U., 1987—88, Outstanding Clin. Tchr. award, U. Mich. Med. Sch., 1991—92, 1994—95, Vol. Physician of Yr. award, Hope Med. Clinic, 1998; grantee, NIH, 2001—06, HHS, 2002—07, Eli Lilly Found., 2005—. Mem.: Wonca Internat. Classification Com. (co-chair 2005—07), N.Am. Primary Care Rsch. Grp., Phi Beta Kappa. Achievements include invention of ClinfoTracker computer software, a clinical prompt system designed to provide point-of-care clinical decision support for preventive care and disease management; research in mental health problems, particularly depressive disorders, in primary health care, with a focus on competing demands and patient priorities for care; projects designed to create sustainable systems to support primary care treatment of mental health problems, from individual practice-based to community interventions; development of Michigan depression outcomes and collaborative care software, for use by clinical care managers. Office: Univ Mich 1018 Fuller St Ann Arbor MI 48109-0708 Office Fax: 734-998-7335. Business E-Mail: mklinkma@umich.edu.

KLINMAN, JUDITH POLLOCK, biochemist, educator; b. Phila., Apr. 17, 1941; d. Edward and Sylvia Pollock; m. Norman R. Klinman, July 3, 1963 (div. 1978); children: Andrew, Douglas. BA, U. Pa., 1962, PhD (hon.), 1966, degree (hon.), 2006; PhD (hon.), U. Uppsala, Sweden, 2000, U. Penna, 2006. Postdoctoral fellow Weizmann Inst. Sci., Rehovoth, Israel, 1966—67; postdoctoral assoc. Inst. Cancer Rsch., Phila., 1968—70, rsch. assoc., 1970—72, asst. mem., 1972—77, assoc. mem., 1977—78; asst. prof. biophysics U. Pa., Phila., 1974—78; assoc. prof. chemistry U. Calif., Berkeley, 1978—82, prof., 1982—, Miller prof., 1992, 2003—04, prof. molecular and cell biology, 1993—, chair chem. dept., 2000—03, Joel Hildebrand chair, 2002—03. Mem. ad hoc biochemistry and phys. biochemistry study sects. NIH, 1977—84, phys. biochemistry study sect., 1984—88. Mem. editl. bd.: Jour. Biol. Chemistry, 1979—84, Biofactors, 1991—98, European Jour. Biochemistry, 1991—95, Biochemistry, 1993—, Ann. Rev. Biochemistry, 1996—2000, Accts. Chem. Res., 1995—98, Current Opinion in Chemical Biology, 1997—, Chemical Record, 2000—, Advances in Physical Organic Chemistry, 2003—; contbr. articles to profl. jours. Fellow, NSF, 1964, NIH, 1964—66, Guggenheim, 1988—89. Mem.: NAS, Am. Philos. Soc., Am. Soc. Biochemistry and Molecular Biology (membership com. 1984—86, pub. affairs com. 1987—94, program com. 1995, pres.-elect 1997, pres. 1998, past pres. 1999, Merck award 2007), Am. Acad. Arts and Scis., Am. Chmn. Soc. (exec. coun. biol. divsn. 1982—85, chmn. nominating com. 1987—88, program chair 1991—92, Repligen award 1994, Remsen award 2005), Sigma Xi. Office: U Calif Dept Chemistry Berkeley CA 94720-0001 Office Phone: 510-642-2668.

KLIPPEL, JOHN H., physician, medical association administrator; B, Bowling Green State U.; MD, U. Cin. Coll. Medicine. Bd. cert. in rheumatology. Resident in internal medicine Yale-New Haven Hosp.; fellow in rheumatology Nat. Inst. Health, U. Calif., San Diego; clinical dir. Nat. Inst. Arthritis and Musculoskeletal and Skin Diseases (component of Nat. Inst. Health, NIH); med. dir. Arthritis Found., Atlanta, 1999—2003, pres., CEO, 2003—. Author numerous sci. and clinical publ. Recipient Burroughs-Wellcome Vis. Prof. award, Royal Soc. Medicine, London. Fellow: ACP, Am. Coll. Rheumatology; mem.: Am. Bd. Internal Medicine (diplomat). Office: Arthritis Found PO Box 7669 Atlanta GA 30357-0669 Home Phone: 301-652-0992; Office Phone: 404-965-7671. E-mail: jklippel@arthritis.org.

KLIPPERT, RICHARD HOBDELL, JR., engineering executive; b. Oakland, Calif., Jan. 25, 1940; s. Richard Hobdell and Carol Ione K.; m. Penelope Ann Barker, Sept. 5, 1979; children: David, Deborah, Candice, Kristina. BS in Bus., Oreg. State U., Corvallis, 1962; postgrad. in Polit. Sci., U. Calif., Berkeley, 1968—69; postgrad. in Mgmt., George Wash. U., Washington, DC, 1972—73; grad., Naval War Coll., Newport, RI, 1973. Cert. Program Mgr. IBM, 1993, Program Mgr. III SAIC, 2002, Answer Group Mgr. SAIC, 2003. Commd. ensign USN, 1962, advanced through grades to comdr., ret., 1982, expert Antisubmarine Warfare; mem. Combat Search and Rescue Southeast Asia, 1964—67; exec. officer H.S. Squadron, 1974; mem. Flag Staff, 1974—79; chief engr. Light Airborne Multipurpose Sys. MK-III IBM, Washington, 1979—82, mgr. HH-60 sys. engring., 1984—85, mgr. V-22 engring., 1985—88, program mgr. Document Mgmt. Sys. Integration, 1988—, dir. publ. solutions, 1990—; program mgr. USDA SCOAP/ASCS Programs, 1992; capture mgr. WARSIM Program, 1994; dir. USDA FSA programs Unisys Fed. Sys., 1995—97; account mgr. Sci. Applications Internat. Corp., 1997—, divsn. mgr., dir. instrnl. tech., mgr. divsn. Acct. exec. FDA, State of Nev., 2003—07. *Over twenty years of successfully managing large, diversified, organizations by stressing teamwork, customer satisfaction, and quality in all areas. Technical background founded in performance as Chief Engineer for the Navy's LAMPS MKIII program prior to leaving government service, followed by successive engineering, software development, and management positions within IBM. In leading these $100M+ programs, Mr. Klippert had responsibility for the performance of hundreds of technical personnel and dozens of subcontractors and received the "Qualified to Practice in the IBM Federal Program Management Profession" in 1994. On his retirement from IBM, Mr. Klippert joined Science Applications International Corporation and as a Division Manager, focused on Education Technology bringing the benefits of remote managed services and standards-based courseware to the education community. Mr. Klippert is currently Science Applications International Corporation Account Executive for the State of Nevada working as the state's Information Technology Partner.* Author: The Moon Book, 1971; contbr. articles to profl. jours. Loaned exec. Boulder County United Way, 1993; pres. Dayton Valley Cmty. Assn., 2006—. Decorated Silver Star USN. Mem. Soc. Naval Engrs., Assn. Image and Info. Mgmt., Soc. Automotive Engrs., Project Mgmt. Inst., Naval Inst., Sigma Chi. Republican. Congregationalist. Avocations: golf, tennis, photography, bridge. Personal E-mail: rklippert@earthlink.net.

KLIPSTEIN, ROBERT ALAN, lawyer; b. NYC, Sept. 23, 1936; s. Harold David and Hyacinth (Levin) K. AB, Columbia U., 1957, JD, 1960; LLM in Taxation, NYU, 1965. Bar: N.Y. 1960, U.S. Supreme Ct. 1964. Practice of law, assoc. Saxe Bacon & O'Shea, NYC, 1961—; assoc. Rosenman, Colin, Kaye, Petschek & Freund, NYC, 1962—63; law sec. to justice N.Y. County Supreme Ct., 1963-64; assoc. Bernays & Eisner, 1965-70; ptnr. Eisner, Klipstein & Klipstein, 1971-77, Danziger, Bangser, Klipstein, Goldsmith, Greenwald & Weiss, NYC, 1977-92; counsel Sullivan & Donovan, 1992—2001; ptnr. Ballon, Stoll, Bader & Nadler, NYC, 2002—. Arbitrator City of N.Y. Small Claims Ct., 1971—. With US Army, 1960—62. Mem. ABA, N.Y. State Bar Assn., Assn. Bar City of N.Y., N.Y. County Lawyers Assn., Am. Immigration Lawyers Assn., Westchester County Bar Assn., Am. Judges Assn., Univ. Glee Club (N.Y.C.), Phi Alpha Delta. Home: 401 E 74th St Apt 6G New York NY 10021-3931 Office: Ballon Stoll Bader & Nadler 1450 Broadway New York NY 10018 Office Phone: 212-575-7900. Personal E-mail: raklip@aol.com.

KLIR, GEORGE JIRI, systems science educator; b. Prague, Czechoslovakia, Apr. 22, 1932; arrived in U.S., 1966, naturalized, 1972; s. Jan and Emilie (Přitasilová) K.; m. Milena Řeholová, Jan. 26, 1962; children: Jane, John. MSEE, Czech Tech. U., Prague, 1957; PhD, Czechoslovak Acad. Scis., Prague, 1964; D (hon.), Prague U. Econs., 1994, Tech. U. in Brno, 1997, Czech Tech. U., 1998, U. Ostrava, 2003, U. Western Bohemia, 2004; D, Inst. Advanced Studies in Systems Rsch. and Cybernetics, Baden-Baden, Germany. Rsch. fellow Inst. Computer Research, Prague, 1960-64; lectr. U. Baghdad, Iraq, 1964-66, UCLA, 1966-68; assoc. prof. Fairleigh Dickinson U., 1968-69, Sch. Advanced Tech., SUNY, Binghamton, 1969-72, prof. systems sci., 1972—, disting. prof. T.J. Watson Sch., 1984—, chmn. dept. systems sci., 1977-94. Dir. Internat. Conf. Applied Gen. Systems Rsch., 1977, Ctr. for Intelligent Systems, T.J. Watson Sch., 1995-2000. Author: Cybernetic Modelling, 1967, An Approach to General Systems Theory, 1969, Methodology of Switching Circuits, 1972, Architecture of Systems Problem Solving, 1985, 2d edit., 2003, Fuzzy Sets, Uncertainty, and Information, 1988, Facets of Systems Science, 1991, 2d edit., 2001, Fuzzy Measure Theory, 1992, Fuzzy Sets and Fuzzy Logic, 1995, Uncertainty-Based Information, 1998, 2d edit, 1999, Fuzzy Sets, 2000, Uncertainty and Information, 2006 (Book of Yr. award), Uncertainty Modeling and Analysis in Engineering and the Sciences, 2006; author, co-author or editor other books; editor-in-chief: Book Series on Basic and Applied General Systems Research, 1978-82, Book Series on Frontiers in System Science: Implications for the Social Sciences, 1978-84, International Jour. Gen. Systems, 1974—, IFSR Book Series on Systems Science and Engineering, 1984—; mem. editl. bds. other profl. jours.; contbr. numerous articles to profl. jours. Recipient award for outstanding contbns., Austrian Soc. Cybernetics, 1976, award, Netherland Soc. Sys. Rsch., 1976, Bernard Bolzano gold medal in math. scis., Czech Acad. Scis., 1994, Lotfi A. Zadeh Best Paper award, 1994, award for highest achievement in scholarship, Simon Bolivar U. in Caracas, 1997, Arnold Kaufmann's Gold Medal prize for excellence in uncertainty rsch., 2000, CASYS award for outstanding work on anticipatory and intelligent sys., 2001, Chancellor's award excellence in scholarship, creative activities., SUNY, 2005; fellow rsch., IBM, 1969, Netherlands Inst. Advanced Studies, 1975—76, 1982—83, Japan Soc. for Promotion of Sci., 1980. Fellow: IEEE (life Computational Intelligence Soc. Fuzzy Systems Pioneer award 2007), Internat. Fuzzy Systems Assn. (pres. 1993—95, Outstanding Achievement award 2005); mem.: AAAS, N.Am. Fuzzy Info. Processing Soc. (pres. 1988—91), Internat. Fedn. Sys. Rsch. (pres. 1980—84), Internat. Soc. Sys. Scis. (mng. dir., v.p. 1978—80, pres. 1980—81, Disting. Leadership award 1994). Home: 401 Manchester Rd Vestal NY 13850-3606 Office: SUNY/Dept Sys Sci/Indsl Eng Thomas J Watson Sch Engring and Applied Sci Binghamton NY 13902-6000 Business E-Mail: gklir@binghamton.edu. *The main force behind my intellectual development has been my passion for discovery and integration in science and technology. The most precious values in professional life are for me scientific honesty and tolerance.*

KLISZUS, EDWARD A., JR., school system administrator; b. Elizabeth, NJ, Aug. 8, 1953; s. Edward Anthony and Irene Kliszus; m. Lisa L Ippolito, Feb. 14, 2004; children: Erika Anne, Jeffrey Edward. MusB, Nyack Coll., 1971—75; MusM, Manhattan Sch. of Music, 1975—76; PhD, NY U., 1993—2000. Teacher of Music NJ., 1976, NY, 1976, Principal/Supervisor NJ, 1992. Tchr. of music Twp. of Union Pub. Schools, Union, NJ, 1977—86, dir. of music, 1986—2000, dir. of k-8 gifted & talented and computer edn., 1990—94, elem. sch. prin., 1994—2003; supt. of schools Belleville Twp. Bd. of Edn., Belleville, 2004—. Adj. prof. of music Kean U., Union, NJ, 2000—03; dir. and ceo Union Music Sch., NJ, 1986—2000; condr. & music dir. Union Symphony Orch., NJ, 1986—2000; adj. prof. of music Bergen C.C., Paramus, NJ, 1999—2000; coord. union h.s. alternative h.s. Twp. of Union Pub. Schools, Union, NJ, 1992; supt. of schools Denville Twp. Bd. of Edn., Denville, NJ, 2003—04. Author: (educational horizons) Politics and Educational Policy: A School Survival Kit; composer: Fanfare for Chamber Ensemble, 1993, Eclipse, 1994, Light & Shadows, 1994, Ballade for Alto Saxophone & Piano, 1996, Scherzo & prestissimo, 1997, Synapse for C Flute and Piano, 1997, Three Short Pieces for Doublebass & Piano, 1998, Flying. Pres. NJ. Music Administrators Assn., 1994—96. Mem.: Am. Assn. Composers, Authors and Pubs., Pi Lambda Theta (assoc.), Phi Delta Kappa (assoc.). Home Phone: 973-697-6468; Office Phone: 973-450-3500.

KLITZKE, THEODORE ELMER, arts consultant, retired college dean; b. Chgo., Nov. 4, 1915; s. John Frederick and Edith (Bachmann) K.; m. Margaret Bridget Gaughan, Feb. 23, 1946; children: Annetta, Margaret. B.F.A., Chgo. Art Inst., 1940; BA, U. Chgo., 1941, PhD, 1953; D.F.A. (hon.), Kansas City Art Inst., 1980, Md. Inst., Coll. Art, 1982. Instr. art history U. Chgo., 1946-47; edn. adviser U.S. Armed Forces in Germany, Nurnberg, 1948-51; asst. prof. art history N.Y. State Coll. Ceramics, SUNY, Alfred, 1953-59; prof. art history, chmn. dept. U. Ala., 1959-68; v.p. acad. affairs, dean Md. Inst., Coll. Art, 1968-82, pres., 1977-78, Balt. News Network, 1989-97; mem. accessions com. Balt. Mus. Art, 1979-82. Juried art exhbn. Art Inst. of Chgo. & Univ. Chgo., 1938—41. Author: Melville Price Retrospective, 1970; contbg. author: Festschrift Ulrich Middeldorf, 1968, Lothar Strauch: 1907-91, Plastik und Graphik, 1993; contbr. articles to profl. jours. and ency. Bd. dirs. Ala. chpt. ACLU, 1965-68; bd. dirs. S.W. Ala. Self-Help Housing, 1966-68. Served with AUS, 1942-46. Recipient First Annual Peace and Freedom award Democratic Student Orgn., U. Ala., 1968, first prize design competition for altar symbols, Rockefeller Meml. Chapel, Univ. Chgo., 1941; citation Civil Liberties Union Ala. Mem. AAUP, Southeastern Coll. Art Conf. (pres. 1961-62), Coll. Art Assn., Nat. Assn. Schs. Art (dir. 1971-74, mem. commn. on accreditation 1975-78, treas. 1980-82, fellow 1981), Print and Drawing Soc. of Balt. Mus. Art (pres. 1974-76), Union Ind. Colls. Art (chmn. planning com. 1977-80), Am. Studies Assn., Coll. Art Assn. Am., Johns Hopkins Club (Balt.). Home: 7918 Sherwood Ave Baltimore MD 21204-3600 Office Phone: 410-828-0735. E-mail: tklitzke@bcpl.net.

KLITZMAN, BRUCE, physiologist, plastic surgery educator, researcher; b. Dayton, Ohio, Nov. 4, 1951; m. Hardee Burt Brown; children: Rachel Hardee, Page Hardee. BS in Biomed. Engring. cum laude, Duke U., 1974; PhD, U. Va., 1979. Rsch. assoc. physiology U. Ariz. Coll. Medicine, Tucson, 1979-81; asst. prof. physiology, biophysics La. State U. Sch. Medicine, Shreveport, 1981-85; assoc. prof., 1985; sr. dir. Kenan plastic surgery rsch. labs., asst. rsch. prof. surgery and biomed. engring., assoc. prof. cell biology and biochem. engring. Duke U. Med. Ctr., Durham, NC, 1985—2005, assoc. rsch. prof., 2005—. Adj. prof. biomed. engring. La. Tech. U., Ruston, 1982-86; session chmn. Third, Fourth and Fifth World Congresses for Microcirculation, 1984, 87, 91; speaker, lectr. various symposia and seminars. Contbr. articles to profl. jours., chpts. to books; assoc. editor Jour. Reconstructive Microsurgery; editl. bd. Cell Transplantation, Am. Jour. Physiology, Jour. Reconstructive Microsurgery, Microvascular Rsch., Microcirculation. Recipient Instl. Nat. Rsch. Svc. award NIH, 1974-81, Machiko-Kuno Med. Student Rsch. award, U. N.C. at Chapel Hill, 1992, first prize investigator category, Plastic Surgery Ednl. Found., 1988; fellow U. Va., 1979, NATO, 1980; grantee Am. Heart Assn., 1982-85, NIH, 1985—. Mem. Am. Physiol. Soc., Am. Heart Assn. (circulation coun. 1984, grantee 1982-85, rsch. com. La. chpt. 1985), Am. Soc. Reconstructive Microsurgery (chmn. sci. session), Microcirculatory Soc. (sec. 1993-97, program com. 1983-84, mem. com. 1984-87, pres. 1998-99), Soc. Biomaterials, Plastic Surgery Rsch. Coun. (sci. adv. bd. 1998), European Soc. Microcirculation (travel award 1980), Internat. Soc. Oxygen Transport to Tissue, Controlled Release Soc. Home: 3015 Wade Rd Durham NC 27705-5630 Office: Duke U Med Ctr Plastic Surgery Rsch Lab PO Box 3906 Durham NC 27710-0001 Office Phone: 919-684-3929. E-mail: Klitz@duke.edu.

KLOB, HANS RUDOLPH, economist, consultant; b. Windischgarsten, Austria, Nov. 11, 1945; s. Olav M. and Maria A. Klob; m. Adelheid Klob, June 2, 1971; children: Verena-Maria, Bernhard O.R. BS in Applied Econs., U. San Francisco, 1986; PhD, U. Vienna, Austria, 1970. Rsch. asst. Dept. Minerology Vienna Nat. Hist. Mus., 1970—71; expert minerologist German Tech. Asst. to Turkey, Ankara, 1971—72; govt. advisor, project dir. Austrian Tech. Asst. to Rwanda, Kigali, 1973—77; sr. exploration geologist OMV-AG, Vienna, 1978—81; sr. geologist, mgr. devel. Sohio Petroleum Corp., San Francisco, 1981—84; prin. cons., geologist HRK Internat. Geological Cons. Svcs., San Francisco, 1984—; gen. mgr., pres. Argosy Mining Ltd., Vienna, 1995—; gen. mgr., ptnr. M2TL Multimedia Telecomm. Cons., San Francisco, 2003—; sr. v.p., exploration Empire Gold Corp., Vancouver, B.C., Canada, 1997—2002. Author: (novels) Lost in the Yellow Room, 2000. Fellow, U. Edinburgh, 1970—71. Avocations: music, painting, writing, skiing. Office Phone: 415-681-7753. Personal E-mail: hrkinter@aol.com.

KLOBASA, JOHN ANTHONY, lawyer; b. St. Louis, Feb. 15, 1951; s. Alan R. and Virginia (Yager) Klobasa. BA in Econs., Emory U., 1972; JD, Wash. U., 1975. Bar: Mo. 1975, U.S. Dist. Ct. (ea. dist.) Mo. 1975, U.S. Ct. Appeals (8th cir.) 1976, U.S. Supreme Ct. 1979, U.S. Tax Ct. 1981, U.S. Ct. Appeals (9th cir.) 1990, U.S. Ct. Appeals (10th cir.) 1993. Assoc. Kohn, Shands, Elbert, Gianoulakis & Giljum LLP, St. Louis, 1975—80, ptnr., 1981—. Spl. counsel City of Town and Country, Mo., 1987; spl. counsel City of Des Peres, Mo., 1987, alderman, 1989-91. Mem.: ABA, Met. St. Louis Bar Assn., Mo. Bar Assn., Order of Coif, Phi Beta Kappa. Republican. Office: Kohn Shands Elbert Gianoulakis & Giljum LLP One US Bank Plz Ste 2410 Saint Louis MO 63101-1643 Office Phone: 314-241-3963. Business E-Mail: jklobasa@ksegg.com.

KLOBE, TOM, retired art gallery director; b. Mpls., Nov. 26, 1940; s. Charles S. and Lorna (Effertz) K.; m. Delmarie Pauline Motta, June 21, 1975. BFA, U. Hawaii, 1964, MFA, 1968; postgrad., UCLA, 1972-73. Vol. peace corps, Alang, Iran, 1964-66; tchr. Calif. State U., Fullerton, 1969-72, Santa Ana (Calif.) Coll., 1972-77, Orange Coast Coll., Costa Mesa, Calif., 1974-77, Golden West Coll., Huntington Beach, Calif., 1976-77; art gallery dir. U. Hawaii, Honolulu, 1977—2006; ret., 2006. Acting dir. Downey Mus. Art, Calif., 1976; exhibit design cons. Honolulu Acad. Arts, 1998-2005, Mission Houses Mus., 2003, Hawaii State Art Mus., 2002; exhibit designer John Young Mus., U. Hawaii, 1998; cons. Judiciary History Mus., Honolulu, 1982-96, Maui (Hawaii) Arts and Cultural Ctr., 1984-94, curator Keia Wai Ola: This Living Water, 1994; exhbn. coord. Schaefer Portrait Challenge, 2003; exhibit designer Inst. for Astronomy, Honolulu, 1983-86; exhibit design cons. Japanese Cultural Ctr. Hawaii, 1993—; juror Print Casebooks; project coord. Crossings '97: France/Hawaii, Crossings 2003: Korea/Hawaii. Recipient Best in Exhbn. Design award Print Casebooks, 1984, 86, 88, Vol. Svc. award City of Downey, 1977, Chevalier l'Ordre des Arts et des Letters, France, 2000, Robert W. Clopton award for Disting. Cmty. Svc., 2003; named Living Treasure of Hawaii, Honpa Hongwanji Mission of Hawaii, 2005; grantee NEA, 1979-93, State Found. Culture and the Arts, 1977—. Mem.: Am. Assn. Mus., Hawaii Mus. Assn. Roman Catholic. Business E-Mail: globetom@hawaii.edu. *Personal philosophy: Nothing is impossible. Believe in yourself and in each other. Each of us has the ability to shape our destiny.*

KLOBUCHAR, AMY JEAN, senator, lawyer; b. Plymouth, Minn., May 25, 1960; d. Jim and Rose Klobuchar; m. John Klobuchar, 1993; 1 child, Abigail. BA, Yale U., 1982; JD, U. Chgo. Law Sch., 1985. Assoc. ptnr. Dorsey & Whitney LLP, 1985—93; ptnr. Gray Plant Mooty LLP, 1993—98; mem. Minn. Supreme Ct. Jury Task Force; atty. Hennepin County, 1999—2007; US Senator from Minn., 2007—. Bd. dir. Campfire, AMICUS, Big Brothers, Big Sisters; mem., Adv. Com., Youth Coordinating Bd. PACER. Named Super Lawyer, Minn. Law & Politics; named one of 10 Attorneys of Yr., Minn. Lawyer, 2001; recipient 40 Under 40 award, CityBusiness, 1996, Alumni of Yr. award, Wayzata High Sch., 1999, Leadership award, MADD, 2001, Achievement and Leadership award, Ann Bancroft, 2004. Mem.: Minn. County Attorneys Assn. (pres. 2002—03). Democrat. Avocation: cross-country bicycling. Office: US Senate Courtyard Russell Senate Office Bldg Washington DC 20510*

KLOCK, JOHN HENRY, lawyer; b. Gouverneur, NY, Mar. 29, 1944; s. John F. and Patricia M. (Chateau) K.; m. Connie E. McLaughlin, May 31, 1969; children: Thomas, Jacqueline. BA, St. Bonaventure U., 1966; postgrad., U. Va., 1967; MA, NYU, 1970; JD, Rutgers U., 1976. Bar: NJ 1976, US Dist. Ct. NJ 1976, NY 1977, US Ct. Appeals (3d cir.) 1979, US Dist. Ct. (ea. dist.) NY 1981, US Supreme Ct. 1981, US Dist. Ct. (so. dist.) NY 1982, US Dist. Ct. (no. dist.) NY 1988, US Dist. Ct. (we. dist.) NY 2002; cert. civil trial atty. NJ. Law clk. to judge US Dist. Ct. NJ, Newark, 1976-77; assoc. Gibbons PC, Newark, 1977-83, ptnr., 1983—. Author: New Jersey Practice Court Rules (5th edit.), vol. 1, 1A, 2, 2A, 2000, New Jersey Practice Evidence Rules, 4th edit., 2002, New Jersey Practice Trial Lawyers Manual, vol. 2E, 2007; contbr. articles to profl. jours. Active Scotch Plains Hist. Commn.; exec. com. no. dist. Boy Scouts Am., NJ. Named Super Lawyer constrn. law, NJ Mag., 2005, 2006, 2007. Mem. ABA, NJ Bar Assn., NY Bar Assn., US Supreme Ct. Hist. Soc., NJ Hist. Soc., Plainfield Country Club. Roman Catholic. Achievements include patents for quick release automatic chaulk gun. Avocations: golf, gardening. Home: 1800 Lake Ave Scotch Plains NJ 07076-2920 Office Phone: 973-596-4757. E-mail: jklock@gibbonslaw.com.

KLOCK, JOSEPH PETER, JR., lawyer; b. Phila., Mar. 14, 1949; s. Joseph Peter and Mary Dorothy (Fornace) K.; children: Susan Elizabeth, Kathleen Marie, Robert Charles, Peter Joseph II. BA in Philosophy with honors, LaSalle Coll., 1970; JD cum laude, U. Miami, Fla., 1973; DHL (hon.), LaSalle U., 1999. Bar: Fla. 1973, Pa. 1973, D.C. 1978. Ptnr. Steel, Hector & Davis LLP, Miami, Fla., 1977-79, adminstrv. ptnr., 1978-82, chmn., mng. ptnr., 1982—2004, chmn., 2004—05; gen. counsel, chief legal officer Flo-Sun, Inc., 1991—; ptnr. Squire, Sanders & Dempsey, LLP, 2005—07; shareholder Epstein Becker Green, PC, 2007—. Adj. prof. U. Miami Law Sch., 1974-84; bd. dirs. Nat. Beverage Corp., Premier Hotel Corp., Fla., St. Thomas Human Rights Inst.; chmn. bd. dirs. Baypoint Sch., Inc., 1987-92; Fed. Jud. Nominating Com. of Fla., 1993-97. Trustee Belen Jesuit Prep. Sch., St. Joseph's Preparatory Sch., 1998-04, Barry U., Miami Art Mus., Fundacion Mir, New Hope Charities, Inc.; chmn. bd., trustee Carrollton Sch., 1982-98. Fellow Am. Bar Found.; mem. ABA (chmn. Caribbean law com. internat. law sect. 1991-92), Fla. Bar (chmn. civil procedure rules com. 1979-82), D.C. Bar, Dade County Bar Assn., Assn. Bar City of N.Y., Am. Law Inst., Am. Assn. Sovereign Mil. Order Malta, Iron Arrow Honor Soc., Miami City Club (pres. 1994-97), Phi Alpha Delta, Phi Kappa Phi, Omicron Delta Kappa. Democrat. Roman Catholic. Home: 5095 SW 82nd St Miami FL 33143-8503 Office: 200 S Biscayne Blvd Fl 21 Miami FL 33131 also: Ste 200 One North Clematis St West Palm Beach FL 33401 Office Phone: 305-577-2877. Business E-Mail: jklock@ebglaw.com.

KLOEPFER, MARGUERITE FONNESBECK, writer; b. Logan, Utah, Nov. 13, 1916; d. Leon and Jean (Brown) Fonnesbeck; m. Lynn William Kloepfer, Aug. 6, 1937; children: William Leon, Kenneth Lynn, Kathryn Kloepfer Ellis, Robert Alan. BS, Utah State U., 1937. Legal sec. Lynn W. Kloepfer, Atty., Ontario, Calif., 1958-74; freelance writer, novelist Ontario, Calif., 1974—. Author: (novels) Bentley, 1979, Singles Survival, 1979, But Where is Love, 1980, The Heart and the Scarab, 1981, Schatten in der Wuste, 1983, In A Pickle, 2003, Hope's Beat, 2003; contbr. short stories, articles. Pres. Foothill chpt. Nat. Charity League Inc., Ontario, 1965-67, nat. pres., 1968-70; pres. Interfraternity Mother's Clubs council U. So. Calif., Los Angeles, 1971-72. Clubs: Friday Afternoon (West San Bernardino County) (pres. 1986-87). Home: 306 E Hawthorne St Ontario CA 91764-1749

KLOEPFER, WILLIAM, JR., retired public relations executive; b. Evanston, Ill., June 14, 1923; s. William John and Alma Mary (Koch) Kloepfer; m. Nancy Lee Henninger, Nov. 26, 1958; children: Joan Helen, Elizabeth Koch. BS, Northwestern U., Evanston, 1949. Reporter Washington Times-Herald, 1950—51; asst. publicity dir. Rep. Natl. Com., 1952—54; admin. asst. US Congress, 1954—55; pub. info and congl. liason dir. US Civil Aeronautics Bd., 1955—59; pub. rels. dir. Pharm. Mfrs. Assn., 1959—67; comm. dir. Tobacco Inst., 1967—88; ret., 1988. Cons., diplomatic suite US Dept. State, 1979—80. Vol. DC Libr. for Blind, 1989—90; pres. Rehoboth Art League, Del., 2001—04. Sgt. US Army, 1943—46. Named to Hall of Fame, DC Cptr. Pub. Rels. Soc. Am. Mem.: Sci. Writer Assn. Avocations: gardening, cooking, ceramics. Personal E-mail: wkloepfer@aol.com.

KLOEPPER, DAVID ALAN, retired management consultant; b. Colby, Kans., Dec. 8, 1945; s. Robert Mayer and Justine (Peterson) Kloepper; m. Evelyn Maria Gritzbach, June 27, 1969. BS in Metallurgy, MIT. Process devel. engr. Grumman Aerospace, Bethpage, N.Y., 1968-72; mgr. svc. engring. Hilti, Inc., Stamford, Conn., 1972-79; nat. sales mgr. F & S Cen. Mfg., Bklyn., 1979-82; v.p. ops. and adminstrn. Imperial Bolt & Mfg. Co., South Plainfield, N.J., 1982-85; nat. sales mgr. Indsl. Bolt & Nut, Irvington, N.J., 1985-86, T.A. & D.A. Troy, Fairfield, N.J., 1986-87; project mgr. Don Aux Assocs., Hasbrouck Heights, NJ, 1987—2001, practice leader, 1992—2001; ret., 2001. Pres. Van Vorst Pk. Neighborhood Assn., Jersey City, 1981—82; v.p., bd. dirs. Los Alamos Concert Assn., N.Mex., 2002—06; mem. Los Alamos Planning and Zoning Commn., 2002—03; mem. adv. com. Los Alamos Comprehensive Plan, 2002—03; v.p., bd. dirs. Citizen Support Civic Ctr., Inc., 2003—05; mem. fin. stability task force Los Alamos Pub. Schs., 2004—05; bd. dirs. Santa Fe Symphony Orch. and Chorus Found., 2007—. Republican. Avocations: movies, classical music. Home: 570 Rim Rd Los Alamos NM 87544 E-mail: d.kloepper@losalamos.com.

KLOER, PHILIP BALDWIN, critic; b. Honolulu, Sept. 13, 1955; s. Baldwin Ernest and Betty Louise (Burger) K.; m. Heather Ann Windsor, May 14, 1976; 1 child, Amanda Cynthia. BA, Ind. U., 1976. Writer Stillwater (Okla.) News-Press, 1976-78; film critic, columnist Fla. Times-Union, Jacksonville, 1978-85; arts editor Atlanta Constitution, 1985—87, TV critic, 1987—2001, pop culture critic, 2001—. Recipient Olive Br. award Ctr. for War, Peace & Media, NYU, 1991, finalist Green Eyeshade award Sigma Delta Chi, 1986, Feature Writing award Am. Assn. Sunday and Feature Editors, 2004; named TV Critic of Yr., Nat. TV Movie Festival, 1990, Critic of Yr., Fla. Soc. Newspaper Editors, 1985. Office: Atlanta Constitution 72 Marietta St NW Atlanta GA 30303-2804 E-mail: pkloer@ajc.com.

KLOESS, LAWRENCE HERMAN, JR., retired lawyer; b. Mamaroneck, NY, Jan. 30, 1927; s. Lawrence H. and Harriette Adelia (Holly) K.; m. Eugenia Ann Underwood, Sept. 27, 1952; children: Lawrence H. III, Price Mentzel, Branch Donelson, David Holly. AB, U. Ala., 1954, JD, 1956; grad., Air Command & Staff Coll., 1974, Air War Coll., 1976; grad. Indsl. Coll. of the Armed Forces, Nat. Def. U., 1977. Bar: Ala. 1956, U.S. dist. Ct. (no. dist.) Ala. 1956, U.S. Ct. Appeals (5th cir.) 1957, U.S. Ct. Mil. Appeals 1971, U.S. Supreme Ct. 1971, U.S. Ct. Appeals (11th cir.) 1981. Sole practice, Birmingham, Ala., 1956-60, 62-66; corp. counsel Bankers Fire and Marine Ins. Co., 1961-62; dist. counsel for Ala. Office Dist. Counsel U.S. Dept. Vets. Affairs, Montgomery, 1966-95. Contbr. articles to profl. jours. Vice chmn. Salvation Army adv. bd., 1981, bd. dirs., 1978-81; adminstrn. bd. Frazer Meml. United Meth. Ch., 1987-90, 92—; adv. coun. Ret. and Sr. Vol. Program, Montgomery, 1997—; active Montgomery Symphony League, 2000—; bd. dirs., sec. Air Force Judge Adv. Gen. Sch. Found., 1996—. Col. Judge Adv. Gen. USAFR, 1954-86, ret. Decorated Legion of Merit, Meritorious Svc. medal with oak leaf cluster, USAF Commendation medal; named Outstanding Judge Advocate USAFR, 1977, 79 Mem.: ABA (pres. nat. conf. bar 1981—), VFW (life), Wynlakes Residential Homeowners Assn. (bd. dirs), English Speaking Union (bd. dirs. 1997), Ala. Spl. Camp for Children and Adults (bd. dirs. 1999), Svc. Corps of Ret. Execs. Assn. (bd. dirs. 1996—), Farrah Law Soc., Citizens Conf. on Criminal and Juvenile Justice (staff mem. 1974), Citizens Conf. on Ala. Ct. (exec. com., sponsor new jud. article to state constitution 1973), Fed. Bar Assn. (pres. Montgomery chpt. 1973), Montgomery County Bar Assn. (chmn. law day com. 1972, chmn.state bar liason com. 1975, chmn. bd. dirs. 1977, bd. dirs. 1979, chmn. and editor Montgomery County Bar Jour. (ABA Merit award) 1979—80, v.p. 1980, pres. 1981), Ala. Law Found. (trustee), Ala. State Bar Assn. (editl. bd. 1970—82, chmn. law day com. 1973, chmn.citizen edn. com. 1974, chmn. editl. adv. bd. Ala. Lawyer 1975—79, mem. adv. com. CLE 1983, character and fitness com.), Am. Legion, Air Force Assn., Mystic Soc. (krewe of phantom host), Blue-Gray Cols. Assn., Montgomery Country Club, Maxwell-Gunter Officers, Montgomery, Res. Officers Assn. of U.S. (chpt. pres. 1978, state pres. 1982), Ret. Officers Assn. (life), Air War Coll. Alumni Assn. (life), Air Force Ret. Judge Advocate Assn., Capital City Club, The Club, Inc Birmingham, Montgomery Rotary Club (v.p. 1996, pres. 1998), Montgomery Capital Rotary Club (pres. 1979, Paul Harris fellow), Hon. Order Ky. Cols., Theta Chi (Outstanding Alumni award 1976), Sigma Delta Kappa (pres. U. Ala. chpt.). Republican. Home: 7157 Pinecrest Dr Montgomery AL 36117-7413 Personal E-mail: kloess2@aol.com.

KLOHN, EARLE JARDINE, retired engineering company executive, consultant; b. Winnipeg, Man., Can., Aug. 14, 1927; s. August Frank and Florence (McLeod) K.; m. Beryl MacRae, Aug. 8, 1950 (dec. Nov. 19, 1963); children: James Kimberley, Douglas Alan, Barbara Marjorie; m. Lorna Charles, Oct. 2, 1964; 1 child, Michael. BSCE with distinction, U. Alta., Edmonton, Can., 1950, MSCE, 1952. Registered profl. civil engr., Can. Found. engr. O.J. Porter & Co. Ltd., Sacramento, Calif., 1950, R.M. Hardy and Assocs. Ltd., Edmonton, 1951, Klohn Leonoff Ltd., Vancouver, 1952-55, sr. engr., 1955-60, ptnr. Richmond, B.C., Can., 1960, pres., 1970-87, chmn., CEO, 1987-93; pres., CEO Klohn-Crippen Cons. Ltd., Vancouver, B.C., 1988-97, chmn. emeritus, 1997-2000; ret., 2000. Past chmn. Can. Nat. Com. on Large Dams; past mem. com. on tailing dams Internat. Commn. on Large Dams; mem. numerous cons. rev. bds. for earthfill dams; geotech. cons. Revelstoke Dam, Site C Dam, Stikine-Iskut devel. for BC Hydro, numerous others; internat. cons. design and constrn. tailing dams; past chmn. Vancouver Geotech. Group; presenter papers at various seminars, profl. meetings and confs. Contbr. numerous articles to profl. publs. Recipient Alfred A. Raymond award Raymond Internat., 1960, award Vancouver Geotech. Soc., 1998, Legget award Can. Geotech. Soc., 1990, McPartland Meml. medal, 1992, Pub. Paper award Can. Dam Safety Assn., 1995, Meritorious Achievement award Cons. Engrs. of B.C., 2002. Fellow: ASCE, Can. Acad. Engring., Engring. Inst. Can. (past chmn. Vancouver br., Leonard medal 1972); mem.: Internat. Soc. Soil Mechanics and Found. Engring., Assn. Profl. Engrs. BC (Meritorious Achievement award 1982), Can. Inst. Mining and Metallurgy, Assn. Cons. Engrs. Can. Mem. United Ch. Can. Home Phone: 604-531-9198. Personal E-mail: ejklohn@hotmail.com.

KLONOFF-COHEN, HILLARY SANDRA, epidemiologist; d. Harry and Mary Klonoff; m. Randy Earl Cohen, Aug. 31, 1981; 1 child, Auroraleigh Camillia Klonoff. BA in Psychology, U. B.C., Vancouver, 1976; MS in Biology, U. Bridgeport, 1985; PhD in Epidemiology, U. of NC, Chapel Hill, 1987. Cert.Human Nutrition U. of Bridgeport, Conn., 1984. Staff epidemiologist Eisenhower Med. Ctr., Rancho Mirage, Calif., 1988—89; prof. U. of Calif., San Diego, La Jolla, Calif., 1990—. Cons. San Bernardino County Med. Ctr., Calif., 1989—91, Infant Mortality Rev. Program Adv. Com., San Diego, 1994—96; com. mem. Office of Environ. Health Hazard Assessment, Devel. and Reproductive Toxicants Identification Com., Sacramento, 1999—; com. mem., sys. wide cancer rsch. coord. com. U. Calif. Office Pres., Calif., 1994—. Contbr. articles to med. and sci. jours. Recipient Career Devel. award, Calif. Tobacco-Related Disease Program, 1992—94; grantee Calif. Breast Cancer Rsch. Program, 2005—, U. of Calif. Acad. Senate award, 1996, Calif. Tobacco-Related Disease Rsch. Program. Supplemental Minority Tng. grant, 1993-1994, Calif. Tobacco-Related Disease Rsch. Program. New Investigator award, 1990-1992, EPA -Biomarkers for the Assessment of Exposure and Toxicity in Children — STAR award, 2003—, Calif. Tobacco-Related Disease Rsch. Program, 2003—, Save Our Children's Sights, Mobile Pre-school Eye Care, First Five Commn. of San Diego, 2003—05, Calif. Breast Cancer Rsch. Program. Translational Rsch. Collaboration award, 1999-2003, Calif. Tobacco-Related Disease Rsch. Program, 1998—2003, 1993-1999. Mem.: APHA, Soc. for Reproductive Endocrinology and Infertility, Am. Soc. for Reproductive Medicine, Pub. Health Alumni Assn. U. NC Chapel Hill, Assn. for Women in Sci., Soc. Epidemiologic Rsch., So. Calif. Pub. Health Assn. Office: Univ Calif San Diego Dept Family & Preventive Medicine 9500 Gilman Drive La Jolla CA 92093-0607 Office Phone: 858-822-2966. Business E-Mail: hklonoffcohen@ucsd.edu.

KLONTZ, BRADLEY T., psychologist, consultant; b. Farmington, Mich., Feb. 14, 1971; s. Ted Klontz and Wanda Turner, Margie Zugich (Stepmother) and James Turner (Stepfather); life ptnr. Joni Aiko Wada. PsyD, Wright State U., Dayton, Ohio, 1999. Cert. substance abuse counselor Hawaii, 2001. Pres. Coastal Clinics, Inc., Kapaa, Hawaii, 2001—; prin. Klontz Coaching & Consulting, LLC, Forest Park, Ill., 2006; co-founder Klontz Kahler Inst., LLC, Rapid City, SD, 2004—. Author: (book) The Financial Wisdom of Ebenezer Scrooge: 5 Principles to Transform Your Relationship with Money, 2006; prodr.: (audio cd) Relationship Toolkit: Negotiating Your Way to a Successful Relationship, 2005, Relationship Toolkit II: 10 Commandments for Extraordinary Relationships, 2006; contbr. articles to profl. jours. Rsch. grant, Onsite Workshops, 2004—06, Turtle-Wolf Enterprises, 2004, Possibilities!, Inc., 2004—05. Mem.: Hawaii Psychol. Assn. (pres.-elect 2007). Office: Coastal Clinics Inc PO Box 529 Kapaa HI 96746 Home: 2815 Kanani St Lihue HI 96766 Office Phone: 808-346-0605. E-mail: brad@klontzcoaching.com.

KLOPFENSTEIN, REX CARTER, electrical engineer; b. Pittsfield, Mass., Mar. 3, 1938; s. Glenn A. and Jasmine V. (Carter) Klopfenstein; m. Linda Gilgore, Oct. 6, 1962; children: Mark W., Eric G. BSEE, U. Conn., 1959; MEE, Syracuse U., NY, 1963. Engr. GE, Syracuse, 1959-63; lab. mgr. Melpar Divsn. E Sys., Falls Church, Va., 1963-70; mgr. hardware engring. Logicon Inc., Fairfax, Va., 1977-78; software and test mgr. Acuity Sys. Inc., Reston, Va., 1978-81; engring. mgr. AMF Electronic Rsch. Lab., Sterling, Va., 1981-82; tech. staff MITRE Corp., McLean, Va., 1970-77, lead engr., 1982-96, Noblis, Inc. (formerly Mitretek Sys., Inc.), McLean, 1996—. Sec. tech. com. X3K5 Am. Nat. Stds. Inst., Washington, 1992-94. Co-author: Microcomputer Design and Application, 1977; contbr. articles to profl. jours. Mem. Rep. Nat. Com., chmn. honor roll, 1997. Named Engr. of Yr., DC Coun. Engring. and Archtl. Socs., 2000. Fellow: Washington Acad. Scis. (bd. mgrs. 1996—98, pres.-elect 1998, pres. 1999—2000, v.p. adminstrn. 2004—); mem.: IEEE (sr., life) (No. Va. sect. sec. 1991—92, vice-chmn., treas. 1992—93, chmn. 1993—94, nat. area coun. vice-chmn. 1994—95, chmn. 1995—96, web site mgr. 1997—, editor 1998—99, bd. dirs. 2002—05, assoc. editor, Third Millennium medal 2000), Assn. Computing Machinery, Chi Phi, Tau Beta Pi. Avocation: photography. Home: 4224 Worcester Dr Fairfax VA 22032-1140 Office: Noblis Inc 3150 Fairview Pk Dr S Falls Church VA 22042-4519 Office Phone: 703-610-1534. Personal E-mail: r.klopfenstein@ieee.org.

KLOPMAN, GILLES, chemistry professor; b. Brussels, Feb. 24, 1933; came to U.S., 1965; s. Alge and Brana Klopman; m. Malvina Pantiel, Sept. 5, 1957. BA, Athenee d'Ixelles, Belgium, 1952; lic. chemistry, U. Brussels, 1956, D in Chemistry, 1960. Rsch. scientist Cyanamid European Rsch. Inst., Geneva, 1960-67; postdoctoral fellow U. Tex., 1964-65; assoc. prof. Case Western Res. U., Cleve., 1967-69; prof. chemistry Case We. Res. U., Cleve., 1969—, chmn. dept., 1981—86, interim dean sci. and math., 1986—88, C.F. Mabery prof. of rsch., chmn. dept., 1988—2003, C.F. Mabery prof. rsch. emeritus, 2003—. V.p. Biofor, Ltd., PA, 1986-95; pres. Discovery Software Inc., 1991-93, Multicase, Inc., 1995—. Author: All Valence Electrons SCF Calculations, 1970, Chemical Reactivity and Reaction Paths, 1974; contbr. articles to profl. jours. Recipient Kahlbaum prize, Swiss Chem. Soc., 1971; grantee NSF, NIH, EPA, PRF, ONR. Mem. AAUP, Am. Chem. Soc. (Morley medal 1993, Patterson-Crane award, 2005), Brit. Chem. Soc., Belgium Chem. Soc., Sigma Xi. Office: Case Western Res U 10900 Euclid Ave Cleveland OH 44106-1712 Office Phone: 216-831-3740. E-mail: klopman@po.cwru.edu, klopman@multicase.com.

KLOS, JEROME JOHN, lawyer, director; b. La Crosse, Wis., Jan. 17, 1927; s. Charles and Edna S. (Wagner) K.; m. Mary M. Hamilton, July 26, 1958; children— Bryant H., Geoffrey W. BS, U. Wis., 1948, JD, 1950. Bar: Wis. 1950. Pres. Klos, Flynn and Papenfuss, La Crosse, 1950—. Bd. dirs. Union State Bank, West Salem, Wis. Mem. LaCrosse County Bd., 1957-74, vice chmn., 1972-74; pub. adminstr. La Crosse County, 1962-73; bd. dirs. West Salem Area Growth, Inc., La Crosse Area Growth, Inc.; trustee Sander and McKinly Scholarship Funds of West Salem Sch. Dist. Fellow Am. Coll. Real Estate Lawyers, Am. Coll. Probate Counsel, Wis. Law Found.; mem. Wis. Bar Assn., Elks, KC. Office: 800 Lynn Tower Bldg La Crosse WI 54601 E-mail: kfpatts@aol.com.

KLOSE, KEVIN, broadcast executive; b. Toronto, Ont., Can., Sept. 1, 1940; came to U.S., 1942; s. Willard and Virginia Taylor K.; m. Eliza Kellogg, Sept. 1964; children: Nina, Brennan, Chandler. BA in English Lit., Harvard U., 1962; DHL (hon.), Union Coll., 2000, Marist Coll., 2007.

Staff reporter Washington Post, 1967-77, Moscow bur. chief, 1977-81, midwest corr. Chgo., 1983-87, deputy nat. editor, 1987-91; dir. Radio Free Europe/Radio Liberty, Munich, 1992-94, pres. Prague, Czech Republic, 1994-97; dir. U.S. Internat. Broadcasting Bur., Washington, 1997-98; assoc. dir. U.S. Info. Agy., Washington, 1997-98; pres. Nat. Pub. Radio, Washington, 1998—, CEO, 1998—2006. Bd. dirs. E, Independent Sector, Washington; trustee Arthur F. Burns Fellowship Program, 1999-2002; mem. Internat. Rsch. & Exchs. Bd., Washington, 1999—. Author: Russia and The Russians, 1984; co-author: I Will Survive, 1962, The Typhoon Shipments, 1974, Surprise! Surprise!, 1977, Freedom's Child, 1987. With USN, 1962—64. Woodrow Wilson Nat. fellow, 1983-87. Avocations: skiing, sailing. Office: Nat Pub Radio 635 Massachusetts Ave NW Washington DC 20001-3753 Office Phone: 202-513-2000. Business E-Mail: kklose@npr.org.

KLOSS, LINDA L., medical association administrator; B, Coll. St. Scholastica, Minn., 1968. Former sr. mgr. MediQual Systems, Inc., Mass., InterQual, Inc., Chgo.; exec. v.p., CEO Am. Health Info. Mgmt. Assn., Chgo., 1995—. Bd. dirs. Am. Health Info. Mgmt. Assn., 1980—86, pres. bd. dirs., 1985; bd. dir. Nat. Alliance for Health Info. Tech., 2004—. Recipient Sr. Alice Lamb award for achievement, Coll. St. Scholastica, 1984. Office: Am Health Info Mgmt Assn 233 N Michigan Ave Ste 2150 Chicago IL 60601-5519 Business E-Mail: lkloss@ahima.org.

KLOSSNER, WINDY, food products executive; b. Lowville, NY, Nov. 17, 1978; d. Gary P. and Elaine M. Rosiczkowski; m. Matthew J. Klossner, Sept. 9, 2000. AS, SUNY, Morrisville, 1998; BS, Cornell U., 2000. Farm hand Garylaine Farm, Turin, NY, 1988—98; intern Lewis County Soil and Water Conservation Dist., Lowville, 1997—98; field scout Agway, Castorland, NY, 1999; prodn. supr. Kraft Foods, Lowville, 2000—01, sanitation mgr., 2002—06, processing supr., 2006—. Mem. Turin Rep. Com., 2002—; sec. Lewis County Dairy Princess Com., NY, 2004—; mem. Dairy Enhancement Com., Lewis County, 2004—. Mem.: Nat. Environ. Health Assn. (cert. food safety profl.). Avocations: showing dairy cattle, snowmobiling, crafts, skiing. Home: 5030 State Rte 26 Turin NY 13473

KLOSSON, MICHAEL, public policy director; b. Washington, Aug. 22, 1949; s. Boris Hansen and Harriet Fraser (Cheston) K.; m. Bonita L. Bender; children: Emily C., Karen Lee Bender. BA, Hamilton Coll., 1971; M.P.A., Woodrow Wilson Sch., Princeton U., 1974; MA, Princeton U., 1975. Asst. lectr. Hong Kong Baptist Coll., 1971-72; commd. fgn. service officer Dept. State, 1975, staff asst. to asst. sec. of state for East Asian affairs Washington, 1975-77; Chinese Lang. trainee Fgn. Service Inst., Taichung, Taiwan, 1977-78; polit. officer Am. embassy, Taipei, Taiwan, 1978-80; polit. officer office Japanese affairs Dept. State, Washington, 1980-81, spl. asst. to sec. of state, 1981-83; Pearson fellow U.S. Senate, 1983-84; dep. dir. for polit. affairs Office European Security and Polit. Affairs Dept. State, Washington, 1984-87, dir., secretariat staff, 1987-90; dep. chief of mission Am. Embassy, Stockholm, 1990-92, chargé d'affaires, 1992-93, charge d'affaires The Hague, 1993-94, dep. chief of mission, 1994-96; dep. asst. sec. of state for legis. affairs Dept. of State, Washington, 1996-99; cons. genl. U.S. Consulate, Hong Kong, 1999—2002; amb. Republic of Cyprus, 2002—05; internat. affairs advisor ICAF Commandant, Nat. Defense U., 2005—06; Sol. M. Linowitz vis. prof. internat. affairs. Hamilton Coll., NY, 2006; assoc. v.p., chief policy officer Save the Children, 2007—. Decorated Joint Svc. commendation, 2006; recipient Presdl. Meritious Svc. award, 2007; Herbert H. Lehman fellow, 1971, Winston Churchill fellow, 1972-74. Mem. Am. Fgn. Svc. Assn., Phi Beta Kappa. Home: 15437 Narcissus Way Rockville MD 20853 Home Phone: 301-929-1282; Office Phone: 202-685-4771. Personal E-mail: mklosson@hotmail.com.

KLOSTER, CAROL GOOD, wholesale distribution executive; b. Richmond, Va., Aug. 18, 1948; d. David William and Lucy (McDowell) Good; m. John Kenneth Kloster III, Feb. 15, 1975; children: John Kenneth IV, Amanda Aileen. AB, Coll. William and Mary, 1970. Personnel supr. Charles Levy Circulating Co., Chgo., 1974-75, warehouse supr., 1976-77, warehouse mgr., 1978-80, dir. sales, 1980-83, asst. v.p., dir. mktg., 1984; v.p., gen. mgr. Video Trend of Chgo., 1985-86; v.p. gen. mgr. Levy Home Entertainment, 1986-92; pres., CEO Chas Levy Co., 1992—. Mem. bd., Family Focus Inc. Recipient Algernon Sidney Sullivan award Coll. William and Mary, 1970. Presbyterian. Home: 619 W North St Hinsdale IL 60521-3152 Office: Chas Levy Company 1930 George St Ste 1 Melrose Park IL 60160-1501

KLOTMAN, ROBERT HOWARD, retired music educator; b. Cleve., Nov. 22, 1918; s. Louis Klotman and Pearl (Warshawsky) Kaplan; m. Phyllis Helen Rauch, Apr. 4, 1943; children: Janet Lynn, Paul Evan. BS in Music Edn., Ohio No. U., 1940; MA in Music, Case-Western Res. U., 1950; EdD, Columbia U., 1956; MusD (hon)., Ohio No. U., 1984. Supr. music pub. schs., Dola, Ohio, 1940-42; tchr. instrumental, vocal music pub. schs. Euclid, Ohio, 1942, 46; tchr. instrumental music pub. schs. Cleveland Heights, Ohio, 1946-59; dir. music edn. pub. schs. Akron, Ohio, 1959-63; divisional dir. music edn. pub. schs. Detroit, 1963-69; prof., chmn. dept. music edn. Ind. U., Bloomington, 1969-83, prof. emeritus, 1987—. Vis. prof. Shanghai Conservatory of Music, 1985, U. Alta., Edmonton, Can., summer 1991; guest lectr. U. Bar-Ilan, Israel, 1984; ednl. dir. firm Scherl & Roth (string importers), Cleve., 1956-70; mem. adv. bd. Contemporary Music Project, Ford Found., 1964-65; ednl. cons. Summy-Birchard Co. (music pubs.); mem. bicentennial com. J. C. Penney Co., 1974-76. Condr.: Akron Youth Symphony Orch., 1959—63, Oak Park (Mich.) Symphony, 1967—69, Bloomington Youth Symphony Orch., 1969—75, Terre Haute Youth Symphony, 1992, Great Lake Music Camp Orch., 1982—96; author: Learning to Teach Through Playing: String Techniques and Pedagogy, 1971, The School Music Administrator and Supervisor: Catalysts for Change in Music Education, 1973, Teaching Strings, 1996; author: (with others) Humanities Through the Black Experience, Foundations of Music Education, 1983, 1988; co-author: Administrating and Supervising Music, 1991; contbg. author: Ency. of Edn., 1971; editor: Orch. News, 1959—70; mem. editl. bd.: Music Educators Jour., 1962—64, Instrumentalist, 1974—91; editor (with others): Scheduling Music Classes, 1968; editor, contg. author: Music Performance Trust Funds Guide; composer: Action with Strings, 1962, Renaissance Suite, 1964, String Literature for Expanding Technique, 1973. Bd. dirs., sec. Ind. U. Credit Union, 1974-87; chmn. ednl. com. Chamber Music Am., 1993-95. With inf. AUS, 1942-46, ETO, PTO. Recipient citation Nat. Assn. Negro Musicians Inc., 1966, citation Black Music Caucas, 1978, Outstanding Hoosier Musician award, 1986, Disting. Service award Am. String Tchrs. Assn., 1987, Sagamore of the Wabash Govs. award, 1991, medal of honor Midwest Orch./Band Conf., 2003; named to MENC Hall of Fame, 2004; Lowell Mason fellow, 2005. Mem. Chamber Music Am. (chair edn. com. 1993-95), Am. String Tchrs. Assn. (pres. 1962-64, dir. pubs. 1985-94, chmn. past pres. coun. 1998-2000), Music Educators Nat. Conf. (chmn. commn. on tchr. edn. 1968-72, pres. 1976-78, Disting. Svc. award 1989, chmn. Hall of Fame com. 1996-2002, Hall of Fame 2004), Rotary, Phi Mu Alpha Sinfonia, Phi Delta Kappa. Democrat. Jewish. Avocations: tennis, swimming, reading. Business E-Mail: Klotman@indiana.edu.

KLOTSCHE, CHARLES MARTIN, real estate company executive, photographer, writer, financial columnist; b. Milw., Jan. 30, 1941; s. J.M. and Roberta; m. Christine Klotsche, Feb. 13, 1972; children: Lyna, Kelly, Kay. BA in Econs., Babson Coll., 1962; postgrad., U. Wis., Madison, 1963—64; grad., NY Inst. Finance, 1965; MBA in Fin., U. Wis., Milw., 1968. Account exec. Harris-Upham and Co., 1963-65; head, mgr. Real Estate Comml. Divsn., 1966—68; cons. N.Mex. Dept. Indsl. Devel., 1975—77; chmn. bd. First Equity Corp., 1980—; pres. N.Am. Yachtshares, Inc., 1981—, Pan Am. Publs., Inc., 1982—, Trans Pacific Investments, Inc., 1986—; chmn. bd., CEO Klotsche Properties, Inc., 1983—; pres., CEO Pacific Continental Holdings, Inc., 1992—, Blue Moon Charter Co., 1992—; CEO Pan Am. Press, Inc., 1996—. Adv. dir. Bank of Santa Fe; bd. dirs. Visa Internat. Bank, Granada; lectr. Marquette U., 1967, U. New Mex., 1986, Babson Coll., 1991, U. Calif., Irvine, 1992, Santa Monica Coll., 1993, Fla. Atlantic U., 2002, Explorers Club, 2001, Barnes and Noble Bookstores, Palm Beach, 2001-2003, Four Arts Soc., 2003; featured on NBC Evening News, Dateline, Hardcopy, Voice of Am. Author: The Encumbered Perceptive and the Intrepid, 1978, The Real Estate Revolution, 1979, Real Estate Investing, A Practical Guide to Wealth Building Secrets, 1980, Real Estate Syndications, the Complete Handbook, 1983, Real Estate Development and Fin. Handbook, 1986, The 49th Vibration, 1989, Color Vibrational Healing, 1993, Omega Point, 1993, Delta Raven Four, 1994, The Silent Victims, 1997, Continents in the Mist, 1997, How Wall Street Makes Money the Old Fashion Way: They Steal it-, 2004; (screenplays) Capture, 1996, Providence, 1997; (travel) Journeys, 1999, Crossings, 2000, Passages, 2002, Travels with Charlie, 2003, 2d edit., 2005, Good Time Charlie, 2006; travel writer Christian Sci. Monitor, 1988, Gannet and Cox Newspapers; fin. columnist Cox Newspapers; featured in popular mags. Bd. dirs. N.Mex. Spl. Olympics for Mentally Retarded, Orch. Santa Fe, Santa Fe Assn. Retarded Citizens, St. Elizabeth Shelter, UN Assn., Fla., U. Wis.-Milw. Found.; pres. Santa Fe Bus. Cmty. for Arts, 1986—, Palm Beach Sailing for the Disadvantaged, Inc., 2003; active Arthritis Found., Mayors for Peace, Music at Bethesda, Palm Beach, Palm Beach Crime Watch, Adopt-A-Minefield, Palm Beach Symphony; active Boys and Girls Club Palm Beach; exec. dir. Globetrotter Marathon Program, Achilles Found., Freedom Team. With Officer Corps USMC, 1964-67. Recipient 3 nat. awards for excellence Nat. Assn. Homebuilders. Mem. US Mortgage Brokers Assn., Nat. Assn. Realtors, Fla. Assn. Realtors, Urban Land Inst., N.Mex. Gen. Contractors Assn., Rocky Mountain Outdoor Writers and Photographers Assn., Nat. Gallery Art, Smithsonian, Memorial Sloan, Internat. Assn. Resort Developers, Timesharing Internat., Rotary, Gentlemen of the Garden Soc., Palm Beach Zool. Soc., Palm Beach Civic Assn., Palm Beach Preservation Soc., Vets. for Peace, Am. Vets. Disabled for Life, UN Assn. (pres. Palm Beach chpt.), Circumnavigators Club Internat.(pres. Palm Beach chpt.), Palm Beach Sailing Club, Palm Beach Yacht Club, Palm Beach Theater Guild, Southshore Yacht Club, Milw. Athletic Club, Palm Beach Pundits Club, Sons of Civil War Vets. Club, Soc. of Colonial Wars, World Affairs Coun. of Palm Beach, Fla. Cracker Trail Assn., Humane Farming Assn., Miami Press Club, South Fla. Internat. Press Club, Palm Beach Maritime Mus., The Lord's Place of Palm Beach, Habitat for Humanity, Marines Palm Beaches, Boys and Girls Club Palm Beach County, Explorers Club, Sierra Club, Audubon Soc., Nat. Inst. Social Scis., Sci. Mus. Palm Beach, Mental Health Assn. Palm Beach, Arthur Marshall Found., Miami Internat. Press Club, Everglades Found., Heifer Project Internat., Hospice of Palm Beach County, Scripps Inst. Fla. Republican. Lutheran. Office: PO Box 2603 Palm Beach FL 33480-2603 Office Phone: 561-803-0000. Personal E-mail: charlesklotsche@aol.com.

KLOTT, DAVID LEE, lawyer; b. Vicksburg, Miss., Dec. 10, 1941; s. Isadore and Dorothy (Lipson) Klott; m. Maren J. Randrup, May 25, 1975. BBA summa cum laude, Northwestern U., 1963; JD cum laude, Harvard U., 1966. Bar: Calif. 1966, U.S. Ct. Claims 1968, U.S. Supreme Ct. 1971, U.S. Tax Ct. 1973, U.S. Ct. Appeals (fed. cir.) 1982. Ptnr. Pillsbury Winthrop Shaw Pittman LLP, San Francisco, 1966—2000. Mem. tax adv. group to sub-chpt. C J and K, Am. Law Inst.; instr. Calif. Continuing Edn. Bar, Practising Law Inst., Hastings Law Sch.; exec. v.p., sec. Global Ctr. Inc., 2000—01; vice-chmn. HL Ventures, LLC, 2000—05; pvt. investor, 2005—. Commentator Calif. Nonprofit Corp. Law. Mem.: ABA, Calif. State Bar Assn., Internat. Wine and Food Soc. (bd. dir., exec. com., sr. vice chmn., bd. govs. Ams. emeritus), Am.-Korean Taekwondo Friendship Assn. (1st dan-black belt), Harbor Point Racquet and Beach Club, Olympic Club, Northwestern Club, Harvard Club, Beta Alpha Psi, Beta Gamma Sigma (pres. local chpt.).

KLOTTER, JAMES C., historian, educator; b. Lexington, Ky., Jan. 17, 1947; s. John Charles K. and Marjorie Virginia (Gibson) Gabbard; m. Freda Jean Campbell, Dec. 28, 1966; children: Karen, Christopher, Katherine. BA, U. Ky., 1968, MA, 1969, PhD, 1975; LittD, Ea. Ky. U., 1997, Union Coll., 1998. Rsch. analyst Ky. Hist. Soc., Frankfort, 1973-75, asst. editor, 1975-78, mng. editor, 1978-80, state historian, 1980-88, asst. dir., 1988-90, dir., state historian, 1990-98; state historian, prof. history Georgetown Coll., 1998—. Chmn. bd. dir. Farmers State Bank, Booneville, Ky.; bd. dir. Hyden Middlefork Fin., Ky.,Collaborative Tchg. and Learning. Author: William Goebel: Politics of Wrath, 1977, co-author: A New History of Kentucky, 1997; editor: Our Kentucky: Study of Blue Grass State, 2000. Sec. Ky. Civil War Roundtable, Lexington, 1984-94, pres. 1994-2007. Mem. So. Hist. Assn., Ky. Assn. Tchrs. History (pres. 1986-87), Ky. Coun. on Archives (chmn. 1980-81), Ky. Oral History Commn. Bd., Ky. Hist. Soc. Found., U. Ky. Libr. Assn. (pres. 1984-85). Office: 400 E College St # 244 Georgetown KY 40324-1628 Business E-Mail: james_klotter@georgetowncollege.edu.

KLOTTER, JOHN CHARLES, retired law educator; b. Louisville, Nov. 6, 1918; s. John J. and Lillie R. (Fischer) K.; m. Jane Riddle, Nov. 2, 1954 (dec.); children: James C., Douglas A., Ronald L. AB, Western Ky. U., 1941; JD, U. Ky., 1948. Bar: Ky. 1948, U.S. Supreme Ct. 1967. Tchr. pub. schs., Louisville, 1941-42; spl. agt. FBI, 1948-50; legal officer Ky. State Police, 1951-52; dir. divsn. probation and parole State of Ky., Frankfort, 1952-56; assoc. dir. So. Police Inst., U. Louisville, 1957-71, dir. So. Police Inst., prof., dean Sch. Justice Adminstrn., So. Police Inst., 1971-81. Editorial dir. criminal justice text series W.H. Anderson Co., 1970-76; chmn. Louisville-Jefferson County Criminal Justice Commn., 1974-76; mem. Ky. Crime Commn., 1971-75, Ky. Law Enforcement Coun., 1971-81, Atty. Gen.'s Prosecutors Adv. Coun., 1970-82. Author: Techniques for Police Instructors, 1963; (with Kanovitz) Constitutional Law, 1968, 9th edit., 2001, Criminal Evidence, 1971, 8th edit., 2004, Legal Guide for Police, 1978, 6th edit., 2002, Criminal Justice Instructional Techniques, 1979, Legal Aspects of Private Security, 1981, Criminal Law, 1983, 8th edit., 2003. Capt. U.S. Army, 1942-46; col. Res. ret. Ford Found. grantee, 1968 Mem. Ky., Louisville bar assns., Res. Officers Assn., Soc. Former Spl. Agts. FBI. Home: 2103 Starmont Rd Louisville KY 40207-1140 Personal E-mail: jk40207@aol.com.

KLOTZ, CHARLES RODGER, water transportation and investment company executive; b. Englewood, NJ, Apr. 14, 1942; s. George Edward and Beryl Edith (Cullingford) K.; m. Deborah Goodwin, June 25, 1966; children: Christine, Suzanne. BS, Trinity Coll., Hartford, Conn., 1964; MBA, Dartmouth Coll., 1966. Officer Bank of Boston Corp., 1969—85; pres., chief exec. officer Gulf Resources & Chem. Corp., Boston, 1985—89, also bd. dirs.; chmn. bd., CEO Spartan Madison Corp., 1991—2002. Chmn. bd. G.L. Holdings Corp., 1988-2006; CEO, chmn. bd. Gotaas Larsen Shipping Corp., 1988-97, also bd. dirs.; pres., bd. dirs. Tec Capital Ltd., 2000—; bd. dirs., dep. chmn. Trigen Holding AG, 1997-2006. Lt. USCGR, 1966—69. Mem. Flyfisher's Club (London), Wellesley Country Club (bd. trustees 2007—), Coral Beach and Tennis Club (Bermuda), Woods Hole Golf Club. Episcopalian. Office: Bingham McCutchen 150 Federal St Fl 15 Boston MA 02110-1726

KLOTZ, LOUIS HERMAN, structural engineer, educator, engineering executive, consultant; b. Elizabeth, NJ, May 21, 1928; s. Herman Martin and Edna Theresa (Kloepfer) K.; m. Virginia Helen Roll, Apr. 3, 1966 (dec. Oct. 1995); Emily Louise, Jennifer-Claire Virginia. BSCE, Pa. State U., 1951; MCE, N.Y.U., 1956; PhD, Rutgers U., 1967. Registered profl. engr., N.J., N.H. Structural engr. various firms, NY, NJ metro area, 1951-65; asst. prof. civil engring. U. N.H., Durham, 1965-69, assoc. prof. civil engring., 1969-86, chmn. dept. civil engring., 1971-74; spl. projects dir. ASCE, NYC, 1986-87; cons. Klotz Assocs., Inc., New Castle, N.H., 1987-88; project mgr. Universal Engring. Corp., Boston, 1988-91; exec. dir. New Eng. States Earthquake Consortium, 1991-94; pres. Klotz Consultants Group, Inc., New Castle, N.H., 1994—; reservist FEMA, 1999—2002. Cons., evaluator Office of Energy Related Inventions, Gaithersburg, Md., 1978—; mem. energy policy adv. group N.H. Ho. of Reps., Concord, 1979-82; founding mem. N.H. Legis. Acad. Sci. & Tech., Concord, 1980-83. Editor: Energy Sources, The Promises and Problems, 1980; author: Users Manual Small Hydroelectric Financial/Economic Analysis, 1983; (monograph) Water Power, Its Promises and Problems; contbr. articles to Procs. of 1st Internat. Conf. on Computing in Civil Engring., Hydro Rev. Advisor Environ. Protection div. N.H. State Atty. Gen.'s Office, Concord, 1972-76; mem. New Castle (N.H.) Budget Com., 1977-79; tech. reviewer N.E. Appropriate Tech. Small Grants program Dept. Energy, Boston, 1979-80; bd. dirs. Family Svcs. Assn. Portsmouth, 1995-98, Seacoast Hospice, 1996-98. Ford Found fellow, 1962-65, Ford Found. grant, 1968, Systems Design fellow, NASA, Assn. for Engring. Edn., Houston, 1975; named Gen. Acctg. Office Faculty Fellow, U.S. Gen. Acctg. Office, Washington, 1975-76. Mem. AAAS, ASCE (com. on coordination outside ASCE 1978-86), Am. Assn. Engring. Edn., N.Y. Acad. Scis. Republican. Episcopalian. Home: 90 Mainmast Cir New Castle NH 03854-0204 Office: Klotz Consultants Group Inc PO Box 204 New Castle NH 03854-0204 Office Phone: 603-436-5697. Personal E-mail: lhk90@verizon.net.

KLOTZ, MARTIN B., lawyer; b. 1950; BA, Yale U., 1971, PhD, 1976, JD, 1981. Bar: NY 1982. With Paul, Weiss, Rifkind, Wharton & Garrison; asst. US atty. So. Dist. NY, 1988—91; ptnr., litig. dept. Willkie Farr & Gallagher LLP, NYC. Office: Willkie Farr & Gallagher LLP 787 Seventh Ave New York NY 10019 Office Phone: 212-728-8688. Office Fax: 212-728-9688. E-mail: mklotz@willkie.com.

KLOWDEN, MICHAEL LOUIS, think-tank executive; b. Chgo., Apr. 7, 1945; s. Roy and Esther (Siegel) K.; m. Patricia A. Doede, June 15, 1968; children: Kevin B., Deborah C. AB, U. Chgo., 1967; JD, Harvard U., 1970. Bar: Calif. 1971. From assoc. to ptnr. Mitchell, Silberberg & Knupp, LA, 1970-78; mng. ptnr. Morgan, Lewis & Bockius, LA, 1978-95; vice chmn. Jefferies & Co., Inc., LA, 1995-96; pres., COO Jefferies Group, Inc. and Jefferies Co., Inc., LA, 1996-2000, vice chmn., 2000—01; pres., CEO Milken Inst., 2001—. Trustee U. Chgo., 1986—. Office: Milken Institute 1250 Fourth St Santa Monica CA 90401 E-mail: mklowden@milkeninstitute.org.

KLUEMPKE, PATRICK M., energy and food products executive; BS with honors in Fin. and Acctg., St. Cloud State U., Minn. Grain procurement and merchandising positions Gen. Mills; export mktg. position Louis Dreyfus Corp.; with Harvest States, 1983, sr. v.p. corp. planning and bus. devel., 1993—2000; exec. v.p. corp. adminstrn. and shared svcs. CHS Inc. (merger of Cenex and Harvest States), 2000—. Bd. dirs. Ventura Foods, LLC. Aide to Gen. J. Guthrie US Army, Vietnam and Korea. Office: CHS Inc PO Box 64089 Saint Paul MN 55164-0089 Office Phone: 651-355-6000. Office Fax: 651-355-5073.*

KLUG, AARON, molecular biologist; b. Aug. 11, 1926; s. Lazar and Bella (Silin) Klug; m. Liebe Bobrow, 1948; 2 children. B.Sc., U. Witwatersrand; M.Sc., U. Cape Town; PhD, DSc, Cambridge U.; DSc (hon.), U. Chgo., 1978, Columbia U., 1978; D (hon.), U. Strasbourg, 1978; DSc (hon.), Stockholm U., 1980, U. Witwatersrand, 1984, Hebrew U., Jerusalem, 1984, Hull U., 1985, U. St. Andrews, 1987, U. Western Ont., 1991, Warwick U., 1994, Capetwon U., 1997; D Litt, Cambridge U., 1998, Stirling U., 1998; DSc (hon.), London, 2000, Oxford, 2001. Jr. lectr., 1947-48; rsch. student Cavendish Lab. Cambridge (Eng.) U., 1949-52; Rouse-Ball rsch. student Trinity Coll., 1949-52; Colloid Sci. dept., 1953; Nuffield rsch. fellow Birkbeck Coll., London, 1954-57, dir. virus structure rsch. group, 1958-61; mem. staff Med. Rsch. Coun. Lab. Molecular Biology, Cambridge U., 1962—, joint head div. structural studies, 1978-86, dir., 1986-96. Leeuwenhoek lectr. Royal Soc., 1973; Dunham lectr. Harvard U. Med. Sch., 1975; Harvey lectr., N.Y.C., 1979, Lane lectr. Stanford U., 1983; Silliman lectr. Yale U., 1985; Cetus lectr. Berkeley U., 1986; Pauli lectr., Zürich, 1986; Nishina Meml. lectr., Tokyo, 1986; J. T. Baker lectr. Cornell U., 1987; Jean Weigle lectr., Geneva, 1989, Steenbock lectr. U. Wis., Madison, 1989; Innovators in Biochem. lectr. U. Va., Richmond, 1990; Calbiochem. lectr. U. Calif., San Diego, 1991; Neurath lectr. U. Wash., Seattle; Blackett lectr. Delhi, 1997. Contbr. articles to sci. jours. Recipient Heineken prize Royal Netherlands Acad. Sci., 1979, Louisa Gross Horwitz prize Columbia U., 1981, Nobel prize in chemistry, 1982, Gold medal of Merit, U. Cape Town, 1983, Copley medal Royal Soc., 1985, Harden medal Biochem. Soc., 1985; Knight, 1988, Order of Merit, 1995. Fellow Royal Soc. (pres. 1995-2000), Peterhouse (Cambridge hon.), Royal Coll. Physn. (hon., Baly medal 1987), Royal Coll. Pathologists (hon.), Trinity Coll. (Cambridge, hon.), Birkbeck Coll. (London, hon.); mem. Am. Acad. Arts and Scis. (fgn. hon.), French Acad. Scis. (fgn. assoc.), Max-Planck-Gesellschaft (fgn. assoc.), NAS (fgn. assoc.), Am. Philos. Soc. (fgn. mem.), Japan Acad. (hon.). Office: Med Rsch Coun Lab Molecular Biology, Hills Rd Cambridge CB2 2QH England

KLUG, SCOTT LEO, former congressman; b. Milwaukee, Wis., Jan. 16, 1953; s. Ralph William Klug and Josephine (Farrell) Weber; m. Tess Summers, Mar. 4, 1978; children: Keefe, Brett, Collin Phillip. BA, Lawrence U., 1975; MS in Journalism, Northwestern U., 1976; MBA, U. Wis., 1990. Reporter TV sta., Wausau, Wis., 1976-78; reporter Sta. KING-TV, Seattle, 1978-81; investigative reporter Sta. WJLA-TV, Washington, 1981-88; anchor, reporter Sta. WKOW-TV, Madison, Wis., 1988-90; v.p. pub. fin. dept. Blunt, Ellis & Loewi, Madison, 1990; mem. 102nd-105th U.S. Congress from 2d Wis. dist., Washington, D.C., 1991-98, mem. commerce com.; publ., CEO Trails Media Group Inc., Madison, 1999—; pub. affairs counsel Foley and Lardner, Washington, 1999—. Reporter, producer documentaries (Emmy awards 1989, 90). Named Nat. Humanitarian of Yr., Humane Soc., 1986; John McCloy fellow Columbia U. Sch. Journalism, 1987. Republican. Avocations: tennis, basketball, cooking. Office: Trails Media Group PO Box 317 Black Earth WI 53515 also: Foley and Lardner Verex Plaza 150 E Gilman St Madison WI 53703

KLUGE, JOHN WERNER, broadcast and advertising executive; b. Chemnitz, Germany, Sept. 21, 1914; s. Fritz Kluge and Gertrude Donj; m. Theodora Thomson, 1946 (div.); m. Yolanda Zucco, 1969 (div.); children: Samantha, Joseph; m. Patricia Rose Gay, 1981 (div.); 1 child, John W. II; m. Maria Kluge. Student, Wayne U.; BA (4 year honor scholar), Columbia, 1937. Vice pres., sales mgr. Otten Bros., Inc., Detroit, 1937-41; pres., dir. radio sta. WGAY, Silver Spring, Md., 1946-59, St. Louis Broadcasting Corp., Brentwood, Mo., 1953-58, Pitts. Broadcasting Co., 1954-59; pres., treas., dir. Capitol Broadcasting Co., Nashville, 1954-59, Asso. Broadcasters, Inc., Ft. Worth-Dallas, 1957-59; partner Western N.Y. Broadcasting Co., Buffalo, 1957-60; pres., dir. Washington Planagraph Co., 1956-60, Mid.-Fla. Radio Corp., Orlando, 1952-59; treas., dir. Mid-Fla. Television Corp., 1957-60; owner Kluge Investment Co., Washington, 1956-60; partner Nashton Properties, Nashville, 1954-60, Texworth Investment Co., Ft. Worth, 1957-60; chmn. bd. Seaboard Service System, Inc., 1957-58; chm. bd., pres., CEO Metromedia Inc., Secaucus, NJ, 1959-86; former gen. ptnr., chm. bd., pres., CEO Metromedia Co.; now pres., chmn. bd. Benale Holdings Corp., Dallas; also chmn., dir. LDDS Comm., Jackson, Miss.; investor, operator NY/NJ Metro Stars, Secaucus, NJ, 1995. Pres. New Eng. Fritos, Boston, 1947-55, NY Inst. Dietetics, NYC, 1953-60; chmn. bd., pres., dir. Metromedia, Inc., NYC, Metromedia, Inc. (including met. broadcasting div., world wide broadcasting div. and Foster & Kleiser div., outdoor advt.), Bear Stearns Co., Inc.; chmn. bd., treas., dir. Kluge, Finkelstein & Co. (food brokers), Balt.; chmn. bd., treas. Tri-Suburban Broadcasting Corp., Washington, Kluge & Co., Belding Hemingway Co., Inc.; chmn. bd., pres., treas. Washington, Silver City Sales Co., Washington; dir. Marriott-Hot Shoppes, Inc., Chock Full O' Nuts Corp., Nat. Bank Md., Waldorf Astoria Corp., Just One Break, Inc., Belding Heminway Co., Inc.; mem. adv. council Mfrs. Hanover Trust Co.; Mem. Washington Bd. Trade. Bd. dirs. Brand Names Found., Inc., Shubert Found.; v.p., bd. dirs. United Cerebral Palsy Research and Ednl. Found., 1972—; trustee Strang Clinic Miliken U.; bd. govs. N.Y. Coll. Osteo. Medicine. Served to capt. U.S. Army, 1941-45. Named one of Forbes Richest Americans, 1999—, Forbes Richest People, 1999—. Mem. Nat. Food Brokers Assn., Washington Food Brokers Assn. (pres. 1958), Grocery Wheels Washington, Grocery Mfrs. Reps. Washington, Advt. Club Washington, Nat. Assn. Radio and Television Broadcasters, Advt. Council N.Y.C., Nat. Sugar Brokers Assn. Clubs: Army and Navy (Washington), University (Washington), Figure Skating (Washington), National Capital Skeet and Trap (Washington), Broadcasters (Washington); Metropolitan (N.Y.C.), Columbia Associates (N.Y.C.), University (N.Y.C.); Olympic (San Francisco); Marco Polo (N.H. gov.). Office: Metromedia One Meadowlands Plz East Rutherford NJ 07073*

KLUGE, LEN H., director, actor, theater educator; b. Lakeview, Mich., Oct. 28, 1945; s. Leonhard H. and Edna Alvena (Paris) Kluge; m. Heather Lenartson, 2002. Diploma, Am. Acad. Dramatic Arts, 1967; student, Actors Studio, NYC, 1968—69; BFA, Ctrl. Mich. U., 1977, MA in Counseling, 1978. Actor various mediums, NY and Calif., 1967—75; therapist Ionia County Mental Health Dept., Mich., 1978—79; exec. dir. Nat. Coun. on Alcoholism, Lansing, Mich., 1979—81; artistic dir. Spotlight Theatre, Grand Ledge, Mich., 1982—2005; prof. theater Spring Arbor Coll., 1993—95. Dir. The Actors Workshop and Ensemble Acting Co., Lansing, 1986—2005; theatre critic Lansing City Pulse, 2005—. Appeared in: (soap opera) Another World, 1968-69, (off-Broadway play) Man with the Flower in His Mouth, 1969, (film) Rennaisance Man, 1994, spl. performance as Clarence Darrow for Do the Right Thing program, Punta Gorda, Fla., 1996, 97, 98; performed for Boarshead Pub. Theatre, 1997-2001. Mem. Ctr. for the Arts, Lansing; bd. dirs. Child Abuse Prevention Svcs., 1993—; spl. Recipient Obie award, 1969, Thespie X award Lansing State Jour., 1982, 84, 86-90, 2001, Decade of Excellence award for body of work, 1993, Barney award Okemos Barn Theatre, Lansing, 1984, Riverwalk Theater, 91, 95, 96, 99, Star X award Spotlight Theatre, 1984-97, Lifetime Achievement award, Lansing City Pulse, 2003. Lutheran. Avocations: baseball, writing, teaching, lecturing, travel, cigars. Home: 1937 Byrnes Rd Lansing MI 48906-3402 Personal E-mail: wilieloman@aol.com.

KLUGER, JEFFREY, reporter, author; Licensed atty.; adj. instr., sci. journalism NYU; writer, editor NY Times Bus. World Mag.; staff writer Discover Mag.; contbr. Time Mag., 1996—98, sr. writer, 1998—. Co-author (with Jim Lovell): Lost Moon: The Perilous Voyage of Apollo 13 (basis for movie, Apollo 13), 1994; co-author: (with Ron Howard) The Apollo Adventure: The Making of Apollo Space Program and the Movie Apollo 13, 1995; author: Journey Beyond Selene, 1999, Splendid Solution: Jonas Salk and the Conquest of Polio, 2005. Co-recipient First Place, Whitman Bassow award, Overseas Press Club, 2002. Office: Sr Writer Time Mag 1271 Ave of Americas New York NY 10020-1393 Office Phone: 212-522-1212.

KLUGER, RICHARD, writer, editor; b. Paterson, NJ, Sept. 18, 1934; s. David and Ida (Abramson) K.; m. Phyllis Schlain, Mar. 23, 1957; children— Matthew Harold, Leonard Theodore. AB cum laude, Princeton, 1956. Copy editor Wall St. Jour., 1956-57; editor, pub. County Citizen, New City, NY, 1958-60; staff writer N.Y. Post, 1960-61; asso. editor Forbes mag., 1962; gen. books editor N.Y. Herald Tribune, 1962-63, book editor, 1963-66; editor Book Week, 1963-66; sr. editor Simon and Schuster, 1966-68, mng. editor, 1968, exec. editor, 1968-70; editor-in-chief Atheneum Pubs., 1970-71; pres., pub. Charterhouse Books, 1971-73. Author: When the Bough Breaks, 1964, National Anthem, 1969, Simple Justice: A History of Brown v. Board of Education, 1976, Members of the Tribe, 1977, Star Witness, 1979, Un-American Activities, 1982, The Paper: The Life and Death of the New York Herald Tribune, 1986, The Sheriff of Nottingham, 1992, Ashes to Ashes: America's Hundred-Year Cigarette War, 1996, Seizing Destiny: How America Grew from Sea to Shining Sea, 2007; co-author: (with Phyllis Kluger) Good Goods, 1982, Royal Poinciana, 1988. Recipient George Polk award, 1987, Pulitzer prize Gen. Non-Fiction, 1997; Nat. Am. Book Non-Fiction award finalist, 1976, 86; finalist Nat. Book Critics Cir. award, 1997. Home: 1307 Acton St Berkeley CA 94706 Personal E-mail: dickkluger@aol.com.

KLUGHART, TONI ANNE, musician, educator, singer; b. Detroit, Dec. 5, 1964; d. Eugene Stanley McGuire Jr. and Rose Marie (Williams) McGuire; m. Charles Edward Klughart, Dec. 5, 1998; 1 child, Nathaniel Edward. AA Fine Arts, No.Va. C.C., 1983. Piano and voice instr., owner Ten Fingers Piano Studio, Fairfax, Va., 1986—96; asst. mgr. Music & Arts, Springfield, Va., 1986—88; piano instr., accompanist Comm. Music Sch., Richmond, Va., 1996—97; owner Klughart Music Sch., Atlanta, 1998—2003; office asst. Mobility Products Unlimited, LLC, Sparta, Tenn., 2003—07; piano, guitar, voice performer Klughart Music Sch., Sparta, Tenn., 2003—. Author: (lesson book) Music for Little People: Piano Lessons for 4-8 Year Old Children, 2007; singer, composer: CD Christmas and Lullabyes and Mary's Arms, 2004. Organ Study scholarship, Am. Guild Organists, 1995. Avocations: exercise, reading, crocheting, composing.

KLUGHEIT, MARK A., lawyer; b. Phila., Mar. 18, 1948; s. Sam L. and Rose (Deutsch) K.; m. Marianne Nebel, Dec. 15, 1975; 1 child, Richard. AB magna cum laude, Yale U., 1969, JD, 1972. Bar: NJ 1972, US Dist. Ct. NJ 1972, US Dist. Ct. (ea. dist.) Pa. 1974, US Ct. Appeals (3rd cir.) 1975, US Supreme Ct. 1988. Asst. pub. defender State of N.J., Union County, 1972-74; asst. atty. gen. Office Spl. Prosecutor for Phila. County, Commonwealth of Pa., Phila., 1974-75; assoc. Dechert, Price & Rhoads, Phila., 1975-80, ptnr., 1980; gen. counsel Office of US Senator Arlen Specter, 1994—95; ptnr. Dechert, Phila., 1996. Adj. prof. trial advocacy Rutgers Law Sch., Camden, N.J., 1977-79; chmn. Criminal Practice Group, 1982-92; counsel to U.S. Senate Impeachment Trial Com., 1989; cert. mediator U.S. Dist. Ct. (ea. dist.) Pa., 1991. Contbg. author: Antitrust Counseling and Litigation Techniques, 1983; mem. editorial bd. Jour. of Asset Protection and Fin. Crime. Trustee Citizen's Crime Commn. of Del. Valley., Phila., 1984—. Mem. Phila. Bar Assn., Fed. Bar Assn., Phi Beta Kappa, Wissahickon Skating Club. Office: Dechert 2929 Arch St Philadelphia PA 19104 Office Phone: 215-994-2862. Office Fax: 215-994-2222. Business E-Mail: mark.klugheit@dechert.com.

KLUGMAN, STEPHAN CRAIG, newspaper editor; b. Fargo, ND, May 11, 1945; s. Ted and Charlotte (Olson) K.; m. Julie Sue Terpening, Sept. 18, 1971; children: Josh, Carrie. BA in Journalism, Ind. U., 1967. Copy editor Chgo. Sun-Times, 1967-68, asst. telegraph editor, 1968-72, telegraph editor, 1972-74, city editor, 1974-76, asst. mng. editor features, 1976-78; asst. prof. Medill Sch. Journalism, Northwestern U., Evanston, Ill., 1978-79, dir. undergrad. studies, 1979-82; editor Jour.-Gazette, Ft. Wayne, Ind., 1982—. Mem. Am. Soc. Newspaper Editors. Office: Jour-Gazette 600 W Main St Fort Wayne IN 46802-1408 Home Phone: 260-744-4396; Office Phone: 260-461-8853. Business E-Mail: cklugman@jg.net.

KLUKAN, JOSEPH FRANK, aerospace transportation executive, manufacturing executive; b. Cleve., Feb. 26, 1967; s. Ronald Joseph and Rose Mary Klukan; m. Joanna Marie Samardge, Nov. 29, 2003. Degree in mech. engring., Akron U., Ohio, 1989. Cert. ISO auditor Cleve. State U., 2007. V.p. mfg. Dunham Products, Inc., Bedford, Ohio, 1987—. Recipient award, Dale Carnegie and Assocs., 1989. Mem.: North Coast Fastener Assn. (pres. 2003, 2005—06). Independent Thinkers. Achievements include patents in field. Avocations: scuba diving, skiing, auto racing. Office: Dunham Products Inc 6 Industry Dr Bedford OH 44146 Office Phone: 440-232-0885. Office Fax: 440-232-1011. Business E-Mail: jklukan@dunhamproducts.com.

KLUM, HEIDI, model, actress; b. Bergisch-Gladbach, Germany, June 1, 1973; d. Gunther and Erna Klum; m. Ric Pipino, Sept. 6, 1997 (div. Nov. 2002); 1 child, Leni; m. Seal, May 10, 2005; children: Henry Guenther, Johan Rily. Model Victoria's Secret Fashion Show, 2001, 2002, 2003; appeared on covers of major mags. including Elle, Sports Illustrated (Swimsuit Edit.), Mademoiselle, Glamour, Bride's, Cosmopolitan; appeared in campaigns including Bonne Bell, Finesse, Gerry Webber, Givenchy, Amerige, INC, Am. Express, Kathleen Madden, Katjes, Nike, Otto, Peek&Cloppenburg, Swatch, Victoria's Secret; launched line of perfume, 2002; co-creator jewelry collection The Heidi Klum Collection for Mouawad, 2007—; designer of a line of Birkenstocks. Actor: (films) 54, 1998, Blow Dry, 2001, Ella Enchanted, 2004, The Life and Death of Peter Sellers, 2004, Perfect Stranger, 2007; (TV films) Spin City, 1998—99; exec. prodr., host (TV series) Project Runaway, 2004—, TV appearances include Sex and the City, 2001, Malcolm in the Middle, 2002, Yes, Dear, 2002, CSI: Miami, 2003; author (with Alexandra Postman): Heidi Klum's Body of Knowledge: 8 Rules of Model Behavior (To Help You Take off on the Runway of Life), 2004. Charity involvements include ARC, Elizabeth Glazer Pediatric AIDS Found. Named one of World's Richest Model (#3), Forbes, 2007. Office: William Morris Agy One William Morris Pl Beverly Hills CA 90212*

KLUNZINGER, THOMAS EDWARD, writer, actor, film director; b. Ann Arbor, Mich., Sept. 11, 1944; s. Willard Reuben Klunzinger and Katherine Eileen (McCurdy) Klunzinger Scholtz. BA in Advt. cum laude, Mich. State U., 1966. Copywriter Campbell-Ewald Advt. Co., Detroit, 1966-70; travel cons. Moorman's Travel Svc., Detroit, 1973-74; media dir. Taylor for Congress Campaign, East Lansing, Mich., 1974; comms. specialist House Republican Staff, Lansing, Mich., 1975-80; trustee Meridian Twp., Ingham County, Mich., 1980-84; vice chmn. Econ. Devel. Corp., 1982-84; compliance officer The Eyde Co., Lansing, 1985-88; legis. aide Mich. Ho. of Reps., Lansing, 1988-90; comm. officer Ingham Regional Med. Ctr., 1994—96, 2000—03, Schultz Investment Advisors, 2003, Eaton Rapids med. Ctr., 2004—. Author: Chester!, 1981, Heavy Lady, 1983, Double Standards, 1985, A Villa in Unadilla, 1985, Losing It, 1987, The Wizards of Kyshtym/Deine Kleine Beine, 1988, Lounge Lizards/Managing Gran, 1989, Like A Brother, 1989, Loose Dogs Will Bite, 1990, Beloved Friend, 1990, To Be Announced, 1991, Okemos Passing, 1992, Song of the Whale, 1993, Mimsy Borogroves and the Tooth Fairy, 1993, What About the Hungarian?, 1995, The Passion of Richard II, 1996, The Hunchback of Notre Dame, 1997, Out at Home, 1998, The Real Boy's Pirate Show, 1998, As I Was Saying.., 1999, Breakfast in Berlin, 1999, Folles, 2000, Blond Ambition, 2000, Rock the Cradle, 2000, In Pain, 2001, Butterknife, 2002, Better Than Never, 2003, American Burkha, 2003, Rush Limbaugh in Hell, 2003, Not My Baby, 2004, Abe Lincoln on Speed, 2005, Something Wonderful, 2005, The Hero's Song, 2006, Prime Rib, 2006. Mem. Ingham County Bd. Canvassers, 1993—96; treas. Meridian Twp., 1996—2000; pres. Riverwalk Theatre, 1990—92, sec., 1993—95; mem. Ingham County Rep. Com., 1976—2004, sec., 1986—88, 1991—92, 1996, treas., 2001—02, Mich. Rep. State Com., 1981—85, 6th Dist. Rep. Com. sec., 1989—93; bd. dirs. Capital Area Transp. Authority, 1999—2001. Mem.: Mich. Numis Soc. (sec. 1991—96, editor 1993—2004, 1st v.p. 2003—04, 50th ann. coord. 2004—06), Am. Numis. Assn. (region 4 coord. 1997—2006), Dramatists Guild. Address: PO Box 585 Okemos MI 48805-0585 E-mail: teklunzinger@yahoo.com.

KLURFELD, JAMES MICHAEL, journalist; b. NYC, May 15, 1945; s. Herman and Jeanette (Garfield) K.; m. Judith E. Freiband, July 23, 1967; children: Jennifer, Jason. BA, Syracuse U., 1967. Tchr. N.Y. Bd. Edn., 1967-68; reporter Newsday, Melville, N.Y., 1968-73, Albany bur. chief, 1973-76, Washington bur. chief, 1981-86, assoc. editor, 1986-87, editor editorial pages, 1987—, v.p., 1998—. Recipient Pulitzer prize, 1969, Award for Nat. Corr. Sigma Delta Chi, 1983, Disting. Writing award Am. Soc. Newspapers Editors, 1987. Office: Newsday Inc 235 Pinelawn Rd Melville NY 11747-4250

KLUTTS, WILLIAM ALONZO, newspaper editor; b. Ripley, Tenn., June 26, 1928; s. Alonzo and Helen (Given) K; B.A. with honors, U. Chgo., 1947, postgrad. 1947-49. With Chgo. bur. AP, 1945-49; editor The Lauderdale Co. Enterprise, Ripley, Tenn., 1949—; co-pub., 1949-65, pub., 1965—; v.p., dir. Ripley Devel. Corp.; vice chmn. Ripley Housing Authority, 1962-66, chmn. 1966-72; exec. dir. 1972-84; N.Am. membership sec., council mem., Pvt. Libraries Assn., 1978—. Mem. nat. council Boy Scouts Am., 1957; mem. West Tenn. Council, 1955-67; pres. 1958; pres. Consol. Charities, Inc., 1955—; trustee Lauderdale Co. Library, chmn., 1982—; trustee Union U., Jackson Tenn., 1960-65; mem. adv. council Tenn. Civil War Centennial Commn., 1960-65. Served with U.S. Army, 1950-52, capt. USAR; served to lt. comdr. USNR, 1966-78. Coroner Lauderdale County, 1956-79; exec. sec. W. Tenn. Mayors Conf., 1961-79. Winner 24 U. Tenn. press awards. Mem. Am. Hist. Soc. (life), West Tenn. Hist. Soc. (life, v.p.), Tenn. Press Assn., Tenn. Future Farmers (hon.), Ripley C. of C. (pres. 1954). Baptist (deacon, trustee). Lodge: Rotary (pres. 1957, Paul Harris fellow 1983—). Contbr. hist. articles to profl. jours. Office: 145 E Jackson Ave Ripley TN 38063-1556

KLUTZOW, FRIEDRICH WILHELM, neuropathologist; b. Bandoeng, Dutch East Indies, Aug. 6, 1923; arrived in US, 1953; s. Rudolph F.W. and Pauline (Van Thiel) K.; m. Apr. 2, 1954; children: Judith A., Michael J.; m. Merlene Hutto Byars, Dec. 10, 1999. MD, U. Utrecht, Netherlands, 1951. Diplomate Am. Bd. Neuropathology and Anatomic Pathology. Chief of staff Cmty. Meml. Hosp., Oconto Falls, Wis., 1965-68; pathology resident U. Wis., Madison, 1968-71, Armed Forces Inst. Pathology, Washington, 1971—72; neuropathologist VA Hosp., Mpls., 1972-75, dir. pathology dept. Brockton, Mass., 1975-83, Wichita, Kans., 1983-87, chief of staff Bath, N.Y., 1987-90, neuropathologist Bay Pines, Fla., 1991—. Clin. assoc. prof. pathology U. Rochester (N.Y.) Sch. Medicine, U. South Fla., Tampa; cons. in neuropathology Minn. Bd. Med. Practice, 1998—; spkr. in field. Prin. author: Neuropathology Manual: The Practical Approach, 1996; contbr. articles to profl. jours. Col. USAR, 1979-85. Named to Hall Fame, Am. Biog. Inst., 2002; recipient Paul Harris fellowship, Rotary Internat., Bath, NY, 1990, Outstanding Career award, Dept. Vet. Affairs, Washington, 1990. Fellow: Coll. Am. Pathologists; mem.: Internat. Soc. Neuropathology, Am. Assn. Neuropathologists. Republican. Achievements include research in persistent vegetative state; practical approach to lesions in neuropathology. Home: PO Box 3387 West Columbia SC 29171-3387 Office Phone: 727-398-9309. Home Fax: 803-794-4869. Personal E-mail: needle1@msn.com.

KLYATIS, LEV MATUSOVICH, test and reliability scientist; b. Kiev, Ukraine, Mar. 4, 1933; arrived in US, 1993, naturalized, 2000; s. Matus I. Klyatis and Dina Sifry; m. Nellya V. Klyatis, Aug. 31, 1956; children: Irina, New York, Evgeny, Karmiel MS Engring. Tech., Agrl. Inst., 1958; PhD Engring. Tech., Belorussia State U., 1963; DSc Tech. Scis., Leningrad Agrl. U., 1982; Habilitated D Engring., Latvia State U., 1993. Over 20 cert., Am. Soc. Quality, SAE Internat., IEEE. Test engr. Govtl. Test Ctr., Kiev, 1958—62, prin. engr. Kalinin, Russia, 1962—65; prin. specialist Ministry of Agr., Moscow, 1965—68, head dept., 1968—73; lead scientist, head dept. All-USSR Agrichem. Inst., Moscow, 1973—86; head dept. All-USSR Industry Inst., Moscow, 1986—90; prof. U. Agrl. Engring., Moscow, 1988—90; chmn. State Enterprise Testmash, Moscow, 1990—93; head dept. ECCOL Inc., NYC, 1997—. Bd. dirs. Internat. Assn. Arts and Scis. Inc., NYC; academician Acad. for Quality Russian Fedn., 1998—; expert U.S. tech. adv. group to Internat. Electrotech. Commn., 2000—; mem. World Quality Coun., 2002—; expert ISO/IEC Joint Study Group Safety Aspects of Risk Assessment, 2004—; bd. of reviewers Quality Press Pub., 2003—; mem. Elmer A. Sperry Bd. Award, 2006—; cons. in field. Author: Methods of Accelerated Testing, 1969, Foundation of Farm Machinery Accelerated Testing, 1980, Accelerated Evaluation of Farm Machinery, 1985, Trends in the Development of Testing Technique, 1991, Step-by-Step Accelerated Testing, 1999, Successful Accelerated Testing Part 1, 2002, Accelerated Quality and Reliability Solutions, 2006, others; over 30 patents in field; contbr. over 200 articles to profl. books, papers and jours. Recipient Aerospace Outstanding Contbn. award, Tech. Stds. Bd., 2003. Fellow: Am. Soc. Quality (exec. bd. 2002—, rsch. grant 1998, special svc. award 2002, Allen Chop award in reliability 2003); mem.: Soc. Reliability Engrs., Soc. Automotive Engrs. Internat. (governing bd. 2003—). Achievements include development of 15 advanced technological systems of simulation of field input influences; 12 new types of testing equipment; new methodology of accelerated reliability testing; invention of cost-effective technology of accelerated quality improvement, including high correlation between accelerated testing results and field results; new approach in accurate physical simulation of field input influences in the laboratory; integrated quality and reliability solutions. Avocation: running. Home: 72 Montgomery St Apt 701 Jersey City NJ 07302-3827

KLYBERG, ALBERT THOMAS, historical society administrator; b. Hackensack, NJ, Aug. 8, 1940; AB, Coll. Wooster, 1962; MA in History, U. Mich.; LHD (hon.), R.I. Coll., 1985. Asst. curator manuscripts William L. Clements Libr., Ann Arbor, Mich., 1963-68; libr. R.I. Hist. Soc., Providence, 1968-69, exec. dir., 1969-99, Heritage Harbor Mus., Providence, 1999—2003; dir. mus. and programs Heritage Harbor, Providence, 2001; seasonal interpretive ranger/site mgr. Capt. Wilbur Kelly House Mus., Blackstone River State Park, 2003—. Adj. prof. history U. R.I., 1974-93, Providence Coll., 1986-93; project mgr. Woonsocket Visitors Ctr., Mus. Work and Culture. Compiler, bibliographer March of America series Univ. Microfilms, Inc., 1966; editor R.I. History; project dir. Papers of Gen. Nathanael Greene. Mem. R.I. Hist. Soc. Office: Heritage Harbor 222 Richmond St Providence RI 02903

KLYOSOV, ANATOLE ALEX, biochemist, researcher; b. Chernyakhovsk, Russia, Nov. 20, 1946; arrived in US, 1990, naturalized; s. Alexey Ivan and Tamara Michael (Kuz) K.; m. Gail Michael Muratov, Dec. 28, 1967; children: Svetlana, Yuri. MS, Moscow State U., 1969, PhD, 1972, DSc, 1978. Scientist Moscow State U., 1969—72, asst. prof., 1972—75, sr. scientist, 1975—79, prof., 1979—81; prof., head Carbohydrate Rsch. Lab. Acad. Sci. USSR, Moscow, 1981—92; prof. biochemistry Harvard Med. Sch., Boston, 1990—; mgr. biochem. rsch., v.p. LDI Composites (formerly Kadant Composites), 1996—; chief scientist Pro-Pharmaceuticals, Inc., Boston, 2000—. Vis. lectr. biochemistry Harvard U., 1974-75; adv. bd. Coun. Biotech. Acad. Sci. USSR, 1981-90, chmn. commn. cellulose bioconversion, 1982-90; expert panel Biofocus Found., Stockholm, Washington, 1991—. Author: The Practical Course of Chemical and Enzyme Kinetics, 1976, Enzyme Catalysis, 1980, Enzymatic Degradation of Polymers, 1984, Enzyme Engineering at the Industrial Level, 1989, Carbohydrate Drug Design, 2006, Wood-Plastic Composites, 2007. Recipient Lenin Komsomol Nat. prize USSR in Sci. USSR Govt., Moscow, 1978, Nat. prize in Sci., 1984, Sci. and Tech. Gold medal, 1988. Mem.: World Acad. Arts and Scis., Internat. Orgn. Biotech. Bioengring., Am. Chem. Soc. Avocations: science, tennis, running. Home: 36 Walsh Rd Newton MA 02459-3529 Office: Pro-Pharmaceuticals 7 Wells Ave Newton MA 02459 Home Phone: 617-964-3679; Office Phone: 617-559-0033. Personal E-mail: aklyosov@comcast.net. Business E-Mail: klyosov@pro-pharmaceuticals.com, anatoleklyosov@ldicomposites.com.

KMIEC, EDWARD URBAN, bishop; b. Trenton, NJ, June 4, 1936; s. John and Thecla (Czupta) K. Student, St. Charles Coll., Catonsville, Md., 1956, St. Mary's Sem., Balt., 1958; STL, Gregorian U., Rome, 1962. Ordained priest Roman Cath. Ch., 1961. Ordained titular bishop Simidicca and aux. bishop Trenton, 1982-92; bishop of Nashville, 1992—; bishop of Buffalo, 2004—. Roman Catholic. Address: The Catholic Center 795 Main St Buffalo NY 14203 Office Phone: 716-847-5500.

KNABE, GEORGE WILLIAM, JR., pathologist, educator; b. Grand Rapids, Mich., June 29, 1924; s. George William and Dorothy Emma (Fischofer) K., m. Lorine Jeanette Moffit, Jan. 16, 1954; children: Katharine J., Elizabeth J., Ann C., Dorothy M. Student, Mich. State U., 1942-43, The Citadel, Charleston, SC, 1943-44, Johns Hopkins U., 1944-45; MD, U. Md., 1949. Diplomate Am. Bd. Pathology. Intern Balt. City Hosp., 1949-50; resident pathology Cleve. Clin. Found., 1950-51, Henry Ford Hosp., Detroit, 1953-54; chief lab. svc. VA Ctr., Dayton, Ohio, 1955-57; vis. prof. pathology U. El Salvador Sch. Medicine, 1957-59; asst. prof. pathology U. P.R. Sch. Medicine, 1959-60; prof., chmn. dept. pathology Sch. Medicine, U. S.D., 1960-68, dean., 1967-72; dir. med. edn. St. Luke's Hosp., Duluth, 1972-78; prof. pathology U. Minn.-Duluth Sch. Medicine, 1972—, assoc. dean clin. affairs., 1972-76; chief. dept. pathology Virginia (Minn.) Regional Med. Ctr., 1978-98; pres. Range Pathology, 1998—. Bd. dirs Health Sys. Agy. of Western Lake Superior, Duluth 1975-82, No. Lakes Health Care Consortium, 1984—, U. Minn. Health and Med. Sch. Adv. Groups 1972—. 1st lt. to capt. M.C., USAF, 1951-53; surgeon to capt., USPHS Res., 1957—. Mem. AMA, U.S. and Can. Acad. Pathology, Am. Soc. Clin. Pathologists, Coll. Am. Pathologists. Avocations: art, horticulture, photography. Home: 1008 S 7th Ave Virginia MN 55792-3151 Office: Range Pathology 1008 7th Ave S Virginia MN 55792-3151 Home Phone: 218-749-3341; Office Phone: 218-749-3341. Personal E-mail: knabejr@yahoo.com.

KNABLE, MICHAEL, medical researcher; BS, DO, Ohio U. Clin. instr. dept. psychiatry George Wash. U. Med. Ctr.; dep. med. dir. Nat. Inst. Mental Health, 1992—98; med. dir. Stanley Med. Rsch. Inst., 1998—2003, exec. dir., 2003—. Bd. dir. Ahead with Autism Found., Psychiatric Genomics, Inc., DarPharma, Inc. Co-author (with E. Fuller Torrey): Surviving Manic Depression, 2001.

KNACHEL, PHILIP ATHERTON, librarian; b. Indpls., June 23, 1926; s. Firman F. and Mary Esther (Atherton) K.; m. Pierrette Annie Roy, July 1, 1955; children— Sylvette, Eric BS, Northwestern U., 1948; cert., Institut de Tours, France, 1951; MA, Johns Hopkins U., 1952, PhD, 1954; MSLS, Syracuse U., 1959; LittD (hon.), Amherst Coll., 1984. Instr. history Hunter Coll., NYC, 1954-57; historian Rome (NY) Air Devel. Ctr., 1957-59; chief tech. svcs. Folger Shakespeare Libr., Washington, 1959-61, asst. dir., to 1969, assoc. dir., 1969-93; freelance French translator, 1993—. Adj. prof. history U. Md., College Park, 1967-69; French translator cons. Author: England and the Fronde, 1967; editor: Eikon Basilike, 1966, The Case of the Commonwealth of England Stated, 1967 Served with USN, 1944-46 Avocations: piano, travel. Home: 5807 Phoenix Dr Bethesda MD 20817-3401

KNACKSTEDT, MARY V., interior designer; b. Harrisburg, Pa., Oct. 26, 1940; d. Harry and Veronica Knackstedt. Student, Pratt Inst., 1957-59, Cooper Union, Phila. Coll. Art. Pres. Knackstedt Inc., Harrisburg, NYC,

1958—. Adv. bd. PNC Bank, N.A., Camp Hill, Pa., 1981—; lectr. bus. practices Harvard U., 1988—; cons., spkr. in field. Author: Interior Design for Profit, 1980, Profitable Career Options for Designers, 1985, The Interior Design Business Handbook, 1988, 4th edit., 2005, Marketing and Design Services: The Designer Client Rlationship, 1993, Interior Design and Beyond, 1995; prin. works include Hershey Med. Ctr., Milton Hershey Sch., founder's Hall, Hershey, Pa., Hershey Pub. Libr. Bus. devel. program founder Riverfront Peoples Park, Harrisburg, 1980-90; bd. dirs. Harrisburg Symphony Assn., 1983-89; founder, pres. Profl. Cath. Women's Forum; devel. coun. Bishop McDevitt Sch., Harrisburg. Fellow Internat. Interior Design Assn., Am. Soc. Interior Designers (past officer); mem. Internat. Furnishings and Design Assn., Illuminating Engring. Soc. N.Am., Interior Design Soc., Pres.'s Assn., Am. Mgmt. Assn. Home and Office: 2901 N Front St Harrisburg PA 17110-1223 Address: 161 E 61st St New York NY 10021-8125 Home Phone: 212-262-0752; Office Phone: 717-238-7548. Personal E-mail: maryknackstedt@aol.com.

KNAG, PAUL EVERETT, lawyer; b. Flushing, NY, Feb. 26, 1948; s. Howard Alf and Charlotte (Rausch) Knag; m. Maryann McCaffrey, June 27, 1970; children: Paul Everett, Peter, Kathleen, John. BA magna cum laude, Queens Coll., 1967; JD cum laude, Harvard U., 1970. Bar: N.Y. 1970, Conn. 1971, DC 1983. Law clk. U.S. Ct. Appeals (2nd cir.), NYC, 1970-71; ptnr. Cummings & Lockwood, Stamford, 1979—2002, Murtha Cullina LLP, New Haven, 2002—. Author: HIPAA: A Guide to Healthcare Privacy and Security Law, 2002. Mem.: Conn. Health Lawyers Assn., Am. Health Lawyers Assn., Regional Bar Assn., Conn. Bar Assn., Boston Bar Assn., Mass. Bar Assn., Quinnipiack Club, Harvard Club Fairfield County, Middlesex Club Darien, Dunes Club (Naragansett, R.I.), Officer's Club Hartford. Republican. Office: 99 High St Boston MA 02110-2320 Office Phone: 203-653-5407. Business E-Mail: pknag@murthalaw.com.

KNAPP, ALBERT BRUCE, gastroenterologist; b. NYC, Aug. 9, 1955; s. Russell Sage and Bettina K.; m. Alice Anne Cohen, Sept. 7, 1986. BA, Columbia U., 1975, MD, 1979. Intern, resident Albert Einstein Med. Ctr., NYC, 1979-82; fellow in gastroenterology Brigham & Women's Hosp. and Harvard Med. Sch., Boston, 1982-85; attending Lenox Hill Hosp., NYC, 1985—, St. Vincent's Hosp., NYC, 1985—; asst. clin. prof. medicine NYU Med. Sch., NYC, 1990—2004; asst. attending NYU Med. Ctr., NYC, 2002—, assoc. clin. prof. medicine, 2005—. Author textbook in field, 1982; contbr. numerous articles to profl. jours. Trustee N.Y. Police Found., N.Y.C., 1991—. NIH rsch. grantee, 1982. Fellow ACP (jour. reviewer Annals of Internal Medicine 1985—); mem. Am. Gastroenterol. Assn. (jour. reviewer Gastroenterology 1985—), Am. Assn. Gastrointestinal Endoscopy, Am. Assn. for Study of Liver Disease (Rsch. award 1984). Office: 21 E 79th St New York NY 10021-0125 E-mail: albert@knappmd1.com.

KNAPP, CHARLES BOYNTON, economist, former university president, educator; b. Ames, Iowa, Aug. 13, 1946; s. Albert B. and Anne Marie (Taff) K.; m. Lynne Vickers, Aug. 25, 1967; 1 dau., Amanda. BS, Iowa State U., 1968; MA, PhD, U. Wis., 1972. Asst. prof. econs., research assoc. Ctr. for Study of Human Resources, U. Tex., Austin, 1972-76; spl. asst. to Sec. of Labor Dept. Labor, Washington, 1977-79, dep. asst. sec. labor, 1979-81; assoc. prof. pub. policy George Washington U., 1981-82; assoc. prof. econs. Tulane U., New Orleans, 1982-87, sr. v.p., 1982-85, exec. v.p., 1985-87; pres., prof. econs. U. Ga., Athens, 1987-97, pres. emeritus, 2005—; pres. Aspen Inst., 1997-99; ptnr. Heidrick & Struggles Internat., Inc., Atlanta, 2000—04; dir. ednl. devel. CF Found., Inc., Atlanta, 2004—. Bd. dirs. AFLAC Inc. Contbr. articles to profl. jours. Office: CF Found Inc 3445 Peachtree Rd NE Ste 175 Atlanta GA 30326 Business E-Mail: cknapp@cffdn.org.

KNAPP, CHARLES LINCOLN, law educator; b. Zanesville, Ohio, Oct. 22, 1935; s. James Lincoln and Laura Alma (Richardson) K.; m. Beverley Earle Trott, Aug. 23, 1958 (dec. 1995); children: Jennifer Lynn, Liza Beth. BA, Denison U., 1956; JD, NYU, 1960. Bar: N.Y. 1961. Assoc. Paul, Weiss, Rifkind, Wharton & Garrison, NYC, 1960-64; asst. prof. law NYU Law Sch., NYC, 1964-67, assoc. prof., 1967-70, prof. law, 1970-88, Max E. Greenberg prof. contract law, 1988-98, Max E. Greenberg prof. emeritus contract law, 1998—, assoc. dean, 1977-82. Vis. prof. law U. Ariz. Law Sch., Tucson, 1973, Harvard U. Law Sch., Cambridge, Mass., 1974—75, Bklyn. Law Sch., 2003, U. Copenhagen, 2004, Hastings Coll. Law, San Francisco, 1996—97, disting. prof. law, 1998—2000, Joseph W. Cotchett Disting. prof. law, 2000—. Author: Problems in Contract Law, 1976; author: (with N. Crystal and H. Prince) 6th edit., 2007; editor-in-chief: Commercial Damages, 1986. Mem. Am. Law Inst., Order Coif, Phi Beta Kappa. Office: Hastings Coll Law 200 McAllister St San Francisco CA 94102-4707 Business E-Mail: knappch@uchastings.edu.

KNAPP, CHRISTIAN JAKOB, lawyer; b. Speyer, Rheinland Pfalz, Germany, Sept. 12, 1967; s. Hans Juergen and Edda Knapp. BA, Calif. State U., 1991; JD, U. Pacific, McGeorge Sch. Law, 1994; grad. with honors, Judge Adv. Gen.'s Sch., 1997; LLM in Taxation, Wash. Sch. Law, 1998. Bar: Calif. 1994, U.S. Supreme Ct., U.S. Dist. Ct. (cen. dist.) Calif. Real estate agt. Sun View Realty, Helendale, Calif., 1987—91; law clk. Calif. EPA, Sacramento, 1993; assoc. atty. Thompson and Thompson Law Office, Victorville, 1994—95; legal specialist US Army, Ft. Hood, Tex., 1996—97, staff judge adv. and legal assistance atty. Ft. Monmouth, NJ, 1997—98, claims judge adv. and mil. magistrate, 1998—99; assoc. atty. Pursley and Glaeser Law Offices, 1999—2000; staff atty. Social Security Adminstrn., Office Hearings and Appeals, Stockton, 2000—01, supervisory atty., 2001—. Capt. US Army, 1995—99. Recipient Judge Paul W. Brosman award highest class standing criminal law, US Ct. Appeals armed forces, 1997. Office: Social Security Adminstrn 401 N San Joaquin St Stockton CA 95202 Home Phone: 916-207-8855.

KNAPP, CLEON TALBOYS, publishing executive; b. LA, Apr. 28, 1937; s. Cleon T. and Sally (Brasfield) K.; m. Elizabeth Ann Wood, Mar. 17, 1979; children: Jeffrey James, Brian Patrick, Aaron Bradley, Laura Ann. Student, UCLA, 1955-58. With John C. Brasfield Pub. Corp. (purchased co. in 1965, changed name to Knapp Comm Corp. 1977, sold to Condé Nast Publs. in 1993); pres. Talwood Corp., Knapp Found., LA. Bd. visitors John E. Anderson Grad. Sch. of Mgmt., UCLA; chmn. bd. trustees Art Ctr. Coll. Design. Mem. Bel Air Country Club, Regency Club, Country Club of the Rockies, Eagle Springs Golf Club. Office: Talwood Corp 10100 Santa Monica Blvd Los Angeles CA 90067-4003

KNAPP, CRAIG BRIAN, musician, educator; b. Rockville Centre, NY, Feb. 4, 1975; s. Howard Lee and Miriam Gertrude Knapp. AA, Suffolk CC, 1997; MusB in Edn., SUNY Potsdam, 1998; MA, SUNY Stonybrook, 2002. Level I cert. Tech. Inst. for Music Educators, 2004, Orff-Schulwerk cert., levels I, II, III Hofstra U., 2005, level I, II cert. Choral Music Experience Inst., Ithaca Coll., 2006, cert. public sch. tchr. in music, K-12 NY State Edn. Dept. Music tchr., choral conductor Rocky Point Pub. Sch. Dist., Rocky Point, NY, 1998—. Pres. Ants Marching Entertainment, LLC. Named Educator of Month, Dowling Coll./News 12 LI, 2005. Mem.: Orgn. Am. Kodaly Educators, Tech. Inst. Music. Educators, Nat. Assn. Music. Edn., Assn. Tech. in Music Instrn., Am. Music Conf., NY State United Tchrs., NY State Sch. Music Assn., Nassau County Music Educator's Assn., Nat. Assn. Tchrs. of Singing, Music Tchrs. Nat. Assn., Internat. Soc. Music Educators, Internat. Fedn. Choral Music, Internat. Assn. Jazz Edn., Gordon Inst. for Music Learning, Chorus Am., Am. Recorder Soc., Am. Music Therapy Assn., Am. Choral Dir. Assn., LI Am. Orff-Schulwerk Assn. (exec. program dir. for Orff-Schulwerk, Hofstra U. 2005—, exec. liason, program coord. tchr. training 2005—), Kodaly Orgn. NY (exec. bd. mem. 2004—05), Suffolk County Music Educator's Assn. (chair, all county divsn. I east elem. chorus 2003—04, asst. to v.p. for east festivals 2004—05, exec. bd. mem. 2004—07, exec. v.p. for festivals 2005—07), NY State Sch. Music Assn., Music Educators Nat. Conf., Rocky Point Friends of Music, Music Friends, Ams. for Arts, Dalcroze Soc. Am., Kappa Delta Pi (tchr. classroom grant 2007). Home: 124 Lakeside Trail Ridge NY 11961 Office: Rocky Point Schools Joseph Edgar Bldg 525 Route 25 A Rocky Point NY 11778 Home Phone: 631-929-8255; Office Phone: 631-744-1600 ext. 3168, 631-744-1600 3168.

KNAPP, DAVID ALLAN, pharmaceutical educator, researcher, dean; b. Cleve., Feb. 25, 1938; s. Frederick Allan and Ethel R. (Ogden) K.; m. Deanne Evander, June 2, 1962; 1 child, Wendy Kay Knapp Steagall. BS, Purdue U., 1960, MS, 1962, PhD, 1965. Lic. pharmacist. Asst. prof. Coll. Pharmacy Ohio State U., Columbus, 1964-67, assoc. prof., 1967-71; assoc. prof. to prof. U. Md. Sch. Pharmacy, Balt., 1971—, assoc. dean grad. edn. and rsch., 1981-83, chmn. dept. pharm. practice and adminstrn. sci., 1987-91, dir. Ctr. on Drugs and Pub. Policy, 1987-96, acting dean, 1989-91, dean, 1991—. Vis. scholar U. Mich. Sch. Pub. Health, 1970-71, Agy. Healthcare Rsch. and Quality, HHS, 2001-02; intramural researcher Nat. Ctr. for Health Svc. Rsch., Dept. HHS, Hyattsville, Md., 1978; scholar in residence Am. Assn. Colls. Pharmacy, Alexandria, Va., 1986-87. Author: Pharmacy Drugs and Medical Care, 5 edits., 1972-92; contbr. articles to profl. jours. Recipient numerous grants and contracts; named Disting. Alumnus, Purdue U., 1986. Fellow AAAS, APHA, Am. Assn. Pharm. Scientists, Am. Found. Pharm. Edn. (bd. dirs. 1994-96, exec. com. 1995-96), Am. Assn. Colls. Pharmacy (bd. dirs. 1986-89, 93-96, Volwiler Rsch. Gold medal 1986, pres. 1994-95, commn. to stimulate change in pharm. edn. 1989-95, commn. future grad. edn. pharm. scis. 1996-98, chair Argus commn. 1993-99), Am. Pharms. Assn. (rsch. achievement award 1984); mem. Am. Soc. Hosp. Pharmacists (commn. on goals 1996, com. credentialing 1996-99), Soc. Fellows and Scholars (charter class), Sigma Xi, Rho Chi. Unitarian Universalist. Office: Sch Pharmacy U Md 20 N Pine St Baltimore MD 21201-1142 Business E-Mail: dknapp@rx.umaryland.edu.

KNAPP, DAVID HEBARD, retired banker; b. NYC, May 22, 1938; s. Alfred John and Doris (Hebard) K.; m. Letitia Lykes, Aug. 18, 1959; children— Genevieve, Christopher, Breckenridge. BA, Williams Coll. With Rotan, Mosle, Houston, 1960-62; asst. cashier, mgr. credit dept. Fannin Bank, Houston, 1962-64, asst. v.p. comml. loans, 1964-66, v.p. comml. loans, 1968-70, vice chmn. bd., 1970-82; co-chmn. exec. com. Interfirst Bank Fannin, 1982-83; ret. Devel. loan officer AID, Rio de Janeiro, Brazil, 1966-68; pres. Penta Internat., Inc., Houston, 1979-82; dir. Lykes Bros. Inc., Tampa, Fla., First Fla. Banks, Tampa, Interocean Steamship Co., Tampa, Lykes Bros. Steamship Co., New Orleans Trustee St. Lukes Episcopal Hosp., Houston, St. John's Sch., Urban Affairs Corp.; trustee Armand Bayou Nature Center, Pasadena, Tex., pres., 1977-79. Mem.: Houston Country (Houston). Office: 2807 Bammel Ln Houston TX 77098-1105 Home: 3227 Huntingdon Pl Houston TX 77019-3925

KNAPP, GEORGE GRIFF PRATHER, retired insurance executive; b. New Rochelle, NY, June 26, 1923; s. Griff Prather and Lucy Chadbourne (Norvell) K.; m. Eva Witte, May 30, 1953; children: Edward, Wesley, Helen, Elizabeth. BA, Harvard U., 1945; postgrad., Law Sch., 1946. With Chubb & Son, NYC, 1947-88, mgr. personal lines dept., 1966-73, asst. to pres., 1973, Can. zone officer, 1974-78, N.Y. zone officer, 1978-83, sr. v.p., 1968-88, nat. producer liaison, 1984-88; sr. v.p. Fed. Ins. Co., 1968-88, dir., 1970-88; exec. dir. Excess Line Assn. N.Y., 1988-90; cons. ins. advisor Westchster County vol. hosp. Arbitrator for major property/casualty ins. co. Gov. Lawrence Hosp., 1968-75. Served with U.S. Army, 1943-46. Mem.: Harvard Club NYC, Phi Beta Kappa. Republican. Roman Catholic. Home: 23500 Cristo Rey Dr Unit 312D Cupertino CA 95014-6527 Personal E-mail: george.knapp@aceweb.com.

KNAPP, GEORGE M., lawyer; b. Inglewood, Calif., June 19, 1954; BA magna cum laude, UCLA, 1975; JD, George Washington U., 1978. Bar: Calif. 1978, D.C. 1979. Law clk. to Hon. Jon G. Lotis Fed. Energy Regulatory Commn., 1978-79, dep. asst. gen. counsel, 1980; sr. atty. FPL Energy, LLP, Juno Beach, Fla. Mem. ABA (vice chmn. alt. energy sources com. sect. of environ., energy, and resources, 1980-85, chmn. 1985-89, mem. coun. 1989-92, chmn. membership com. 1992-94, chmn. strategic planning com. 1994-96, vice chmn. sect. 1996-97, chmn.-elect sect. 1997-98, chmn. sect. 1998-99), State Bar Calif., D.C. Bar, Energy Bar Assn. (chmn. program com. 1991-92, chmn. internat. energy transactions com. 1995-97), Phi Beta Kappa. Office: FPL Energy LLC 700 Universe Blvd Juno Beach FL 33408 Home Phone: 561-659-9733; Office Phone: 561-304-5146. Business E-Mail: george_knapp@fpl.com.

KNAPP, HOWARD RAYMOND, internist, clinical pharmacologist; b. Red Bank, NJ, Oct. 5, 1949; s. Howard Raymond and Jane Marie (Ray) K.; m. Brenda Louise Carr, 1984; 1 child, Matthew. AB in Biology, Washington U., St. Louis, 1971; MD, Vanderbilt U., 1977, PhD in Pharmacology, 1984. Diplomate Am. Bd. Internal Medicine, cert. clin. densitometrist. Asst. prof. medicine and pharmacology Vanderbilt U., Nashville, 1984-89, assoc. prof., 1990; assoc. prof. internal medicine and pharmacology U. Iowa, Iowa City, 1990-97, prof. internal medicine and pharmacology, 1997-2000, assoc. dir. NIH Clin. Rsch. Ctr., 1997-2000; exec. dir. Billings Clin. Res. Divsn., Mont., 2000—05, v.p. rsch. Mont., 2006—. Mem. NIH Nutrition Study Sect., Bethesda, Md., 1994—96; cons. pharm. firms, grant orgns. and govtl. entities; mem. applied pharmacol. task force Nat. Bd. Med. Examiners, 1997—2000; mem. expert panel on cardiovasc. and renal drugs U.S. Pharmacopeia, 2000—05. Editor-in-chief Lipids, 1995-2006; contbr. numerous articles to profl. jours., chpts. to books. Grantee NIH, Am. Heart Assn., others. Fellow ACP, Am. Heart Assn. (vascular biol. rsch. rev. com. 1993-95, arteriosclerosis coun.); mem. Ctrl. Soc. for Clin. Rsch. (chair clin. pharmacol. sect. 1992-95), Am. Soc. for Clin. Pharmacology and Therapeutics, Am. Oil chemists Soc. (gov. bd., 2002-04, v.p., 2005-06, pres., 2006-07), Am/ Diabetes Assn., NY Adad. Sci., Am. Chem. Soc. Achievements include first demonstration that calcium ionophores stimulate eicosanoid synthesis; first evidence that N-3 fatty acids reduce platelet activation and blood pressure in patients; first demonstration of the effects of 5-lipoxygenase inhibition in humans. Office: Billings Clinic Rsch Ctr 1045 N 30th St Billings MT 59101-0733 Office Phone: 406-255-8475. Business E-Mail: hknapp@billingsclinic.org.

KNAPP, JAMES IAN KEITH, judge; b. Bklyn., Apr. 6, 1943; s. Charles Townsend and Christine (Grange) K.; m. Joan Elizabeth Cunningham, June 10, 1967 (div. Mar. 1971); 1 child, Jennifer Elizabeth; m. Carol Jean Brown, July 14, 1981; children: Michelle Christine, David Michael Keith AB cum laude, Harvard U., 1964; JD, U. Colo., 1967; M in Law in Taxation, Georgetown U., 1989. Bar: Colo. 1967, Calif. 1968, U.S. Supreme Ct. 1983, D.C. 1986, Ohio 1995. Dep. dist. atty. County of L.A., 1968-79; head dep. dist. atty. Pomona br. office, 1979-82; dep. asst. atty. gen. criminal divsn. U.S. Dept. Justice, Washington, 1982-86, dep. assoc. atty. gen., 1986-87, dep. asst. atty. gen. tax divsn., 1988-89, acting asst. atty. gen. tax divsn., 1989, acting dep. chief organized crime sect. criminal divsn., 1989-91, dep. dir., asset forfeiture office criminal divsn., 1991-94; adminstrv. law judge Social Security Adminstrn., 1994—. Editor: California Uniform Crime Charging Standards and Manual, 1975 Vice chmn. Young Reps. Nat. Fedn., 1973-75; pres. Calif. Young Reps., 1975-77; mem. exec. com. Rep. State Ctrl. Com., Calif., 1975-77; pres. Miami Valley Episc. Russian Network, 2004-06. Mem.: DC Bar Assn., Calif. Bar Assn. Episcopalian. Avocations: travel, reading. Office: Office of Disability Adjudication and Review 110 N Main St Ste 800 Dayton OH 45402-1786

KNAPP, MARK LANE, communications educator, consultant; b. Kansas City, Mo., July 12, 1938; s. Herbert H. and Mary Ellen (Coleman) K.; m. Cynthia Lackie Dennis, Jan. 27, 1963 (div. Aug. 1974); children: Hilary A. Cellard, Eric C.; m. Lillian J. Davis, Aug. 8, 1975 (div. July 2002; 1 child, Avery K. Davis. BS, U. Kans., 1962, MA, 1963; PhD, Pa. State U., 1966. From instr. to asst. prof. U. Wis., Milw., 1965-70; from assoc. prof. to prof. Purdue U., West Lafayette, Ind., 1970-80; prof. SUNY, New Paltz, NY, 1980-83; disting. vis. prof. U. Vt., Burlington, 1983; vis. prof. U. Tex., Austin, 1983-85, sr. lectr., 1985-87, prof., 1987-89, Jesse H. Jones Centennial prof. in comm., 1989—, U. Tex. Disting. Tchg. prof., 1999—2007, prof. emeritus, 2007—. Cons., lectr. in field. Author: Nonverbal Communication in Human Interaction, 1972, 6th edit. (with J. Hall), 2005, Japanese edit., 1979, Spanish edit., 1980, Chinese edit., 1999, Portuguese edit., 1999, Polish edit., 2000, Russian edit., 2004, Social Intercourse: From Greeting to Goodbye, 1978, Essentials of Nonverbal Communication, 1980, Interpersonal Communication and Human Relationships, 1984, 5th edit. (with A. Vangelisti), 2005, (with J.C. McCroskey and C.E. Larson), An Introduction to Interpersonal Communication, 1971; editor: (with G.R. Miller) Handbook of Interpersonal Communication, 1985, 2d edit., 1994, 3d edit. (with J.A. Daly), 2002, Lying and Deception in Human Interaction, 2007; contbr. articles to profl. jours., chpts. to books. With U.S. Army, 1957-59. Recipient Outstanding Young Tchr. award Ctrl. States Speech Assn., 1969; Ea. Comm. Assn. scholar, 1982-83. Fellow Internat. Comm. Assn. (pres. 1975-76); mem. Nat. Comm. Assn. (pres. 1989-90, Golden Anniversary award 1974, Disting. Scholar award 1993, Robert J. Kibler Meml. award 1993, Ecroyd award 2004), Assn. Comm. Adminstrs. (pres. 1997), Coun. Comm. Assns. (vice chair 1997). Achievements include research in interpersonal communication, nonverbal communication, communication in developing and deteriorating relationships, lying and deception, communication and the process of aging, communication behavior in organizational settings. Office: U Tex Dept Comm Studies Austin TX 78712 Office Phone: 512-471-3787. Business E-Mail: mlknapp@mail.utexas.edu.

KNAPP, MILDRED FLORENCE, retired social worker; b. Detroit, Apr. 15, 1932; d. Edwin Frederick and Florence Josephine (Antaya) K. BBA, U. Mich., 1954, MA in Cmty. and Adult Edn., 1964, MSW, 1967. Dist. dir. Girl Scouts Met. Detroit, 1954-63; planning asst. Coun. Social Agys. Flint and Genessee Counties, 1965; sch. social worker Detroit Pub. Schs., 1967-98, ret., 1998. Field instr. Alumnae bd. govs. U. Mich., 1972-75, scholarship chair, 1969-70 76-80, chair spl. com. women's athletics, 1972-75, class agt. fund raising Sch. Bus. Adminstrn., 1978-79; active Founders Soc. Detroit Inst. Art, 1969—, Friends Children's Mus. Detroit, 1978— Women's Assn., Detroit Symphony Orch., 1982-89, Mich. Humane Soc., 1991—; vol. Coun. Detroit Symphony Orch., 1990—; trustee, fin. chmn. Children's Mus.; charter mem. World War II Meml. Recipient Appreciation cert.; fellow, Mott Found., 1964; grantee, HEW, 1966. Mem. NASW, Acad. Cert. Social Workers, Nat. Cmty. Edn. Assn. (charter), Sch. Social Work Assn. Am. (charter), Outdoor Edn. and Camping Coun. (charter), Mich. Sch. Social Workers Assn. (pres. 1980-81), Detroit Sch. Social Workers Assn. (past pres.), Detroit Assn. U. Mich. Women (pres. 1980-82), Detroit Fedn. Tchrs., Madame Alexander Doll Club, WWII Meml. (charter mem.). Methodist. Home: 702 Lakepointe St Grosse Pointe Park MI 48230-1706

KNAPP, PAUL RAYMOND, think-tank executive; b. Long beach, Calif., Sept. 8, 1945; s. Franklin L. and Ella Jo (Andrews) K.; m. Shirley K. Wheeler, July 16, 1967 (div. 1987); children: Michele Ann, Erica Elizabeth, Matthew Gary; m. Nancy Jane Gift, May 1, 1988. BS, Calif. State U., Chico, 1970; MBA magna cum laude, U. Chgo., 1977. With Kemper Corp., various locations, 1969-77; sr. v.p., cFO Kemper Fin. Svcs., Inc., Chgo., 1977-87; pres., CEO Kessler Asher Group, Chgo., 1988-90; dir., chmn., pres., CEO, Catalyst Inst., Chgo., 1991—. Bd. dirs. Berger Mut. Funds, Denver, Futures Industry Inst., Washington, 1992—, Internat. Fedn. for Bus. Edn., Kansas City, Mo., 1993—. U.S. nat. com. for Pacific Econ. Cooperation, Washington, 1995—; bd. dirs. Allendale Assn., Lake Villa, Ill., 1988—. Home: 1410 N State Pkwy Chicago IL 60610-1512

KNAPP, RICHARD MAITLAND, association executive; b. Hartford, Conn., July 23, 1941; s. Maitl K.; m. Elizabeth Burgoyne, Apr. 1969; children: Heather, Peter. BA, Marietta Coll., 1963; MA, U. Iowa, 1965, PhD in Hosp. and Health Adminstrn., 1968. Trainee USPHS, 1964-65; project dir. Tchg. Hosp. Info. Ctr., Coun. of Tchg. Hosps., Assn. Am. Med. Colls., Washington, 1968-69; dir. divsn. tchg. hosps. Assn. Am. Med. Colls., Washington, 1969-73, dir. dept. tchg. hosps., 1973-87, sr. v.p., 1987-93, exec. v.p., 1994—; mem. adv. com. ambulatory dental svcs. program Robert Wood Johnson Hosp., 1978-83. Bd. dirs. Nat. Assn. Biomed. Rsch., chmn. exec. com. 1993-95; chmn. exec. com. Ad Hoc Group for Med. Rsch., 1992—. Contbr. articles to profl. jours.; mem. editl. bd. Inquiry, 1983-88. Bd. dirs. Hosp. Fund, Inc., 1984-2000; adv. com. The Commonwealth Fund Exec. Nurse Devel. Program, 1984-93; trustee Inova Health Sys. Bd., 1986-2005, chmn., 1999-2003; trustee Inova Health Care Svcs. Bd., 1982-98, chmn. 1993-98; mem. oper. bd. Fairfax Hosp., 1987-92, sec. bd., 1987-89, chmn. bd., 1990-92; mem. vestry St. Anne's Episc. Ch., Reston, Va., 1979-83. Mem.: Va. Hosp. and Health Care Assn. (bd. dirs. 2001—03), Inst. Medicine of NAS, Am. Hosp. Assn., W.Va. Thoroughbred Breeders Assn., Md. Horse Breeders Assn., Throughbred Owners and Breeders Assn., Hidden Creek Country Club, Cosmos Club, Delta Upsilon. Office: Assn Am Med Colls 2450 N St NW Washington DC 20037-1167 Office Phone: 202-828-0410. Business E-Mail: rmknapp@aamc.org.

KNAPP, ROBERT CHARLES, retired obstetrics and gynecology educator; b. NYC, Jan. 19, 1927; s. Jack and Hilda (Knapp); m. Miriam Hermanos, Nov., 1955; children: Louise, Jennifer, Michael. AB, Columbia U., 1949; MD, SUNY Downstate Med. Center, Bklyn., 1953; MA, Harvard U., 1982; DSc (hon.), SUNY, Bklyn., 2003. Diplomate Am. Bd. Ob-Gyn. Intern Kings County Hosp., Bklyn., 1953-54, resident, 1954-58; instr. ob-gyn SUNY, Bklyn., 1958-62, Am. Cancer Soc. fellow, 1962-63, asst. prof. ob-gyn, 1962-63; asst. prof. Cornell U., 1963-69, assoc. prof., 1969-70, vis. scholar ob-gyn. Weill Med. Coll., 1998—; chmn. dept. ob-gyn. Nassau County Med. Center, East Meadow, NY, 1967-70; assoc. prof. ob-gyn. Harvard Med. Sch., Boston, 1970-75, William H. Baker prof. gynecology, 1975-93, William H. Baker prof. emeritus, 1993—; assoc. chief of staff Boston Hosp. for Women, 1975—80; dir. gynecology surgery and oncology Brigham and Women's Hosp., Boston, 1980-89. Dir. gynecology Sidney Farber Cancer Inst., 1975-89; vis. scholar Weill Med. Coll., Cornell U., 2000-. Served with U.S. Army, 1944-46. Fellow ACOG, ACS; mem. AAAS, Am. Soc. Clin. Oncology, Am. Fedn. Clin. Rsch., Obstet. Soc. Boston, Am. Radium Soc., Boston Surg. Soc. Soc. Gynecologic Oncology, Am. Assn. for Cancer Rsch., Soc. Surg. Oncologists, Internat. Soc. Gynecologic Oncologists. Home: 20 Sutton Pl S New York NY 10022-4165 Business E-Mail: robert_knapp_ma82@post.howard.edu.

KNAPP, ROSALIND ANN, lawyer; b. Washington, Aug. 15, 1945; d. Joseph Burke and Hilary (Eaves) K. BA, Stanford U., 1967, JD, 1973. Bar: Calif. 1973, D.C. 1980. Atty. US Dept. Transp., Washington, 1973—74, spl. asst. to dep. sec., 1974—77, atty.-adv, 1977—79, asst. gen. counsel legislation, 1979-81, dep. gen. counsel, 1981—, acting gen. counsel, 2006—. Mem. D.C. Bar Assn., Calif. Bar Assn. Office: US Dept Transp Office of the General Counsel 400 7th St SW Washington DC 20590-0003 Office Phone: 202-366-4713. Business E-Mail: lindy.knapp@dot.gov.

KNAPP, SYLVIA CLARE, retired language educator; b. Schenectady, NY, Apr. 13, 1937; d. Theodore Karl and Margaret Blann Knapp. BS in Music Edn., Bob Jones U., SC, 1959; MS, Radford U., Va., 1992. Cert.

secondary tchr. Fla., 1959. Missionary OMS Internat., Inc., 1961—2002, Taichung, Taiwan, 1961—2002; tchr. and curriculum dir. Jian Hua Sch. Fgn. Langs., Weihai, China, 2003—05; ret., 2005. Tour accompanist Taiwan Men's Choir OMS Internat., Inc., USA, Can., 1969; dir. Chung Tai English Inst., Taichung, Taiwan, 1970—97; tchr. broadcaster The Chungtai English Broadcast, 1970—89. Author: (bilingual textbooks) Correcting Common Mistakes in English, 1984, The Parables of Jesus, 1992, My Offering, 2002; performer: (recordings) Youth Choruses Vol 3, 1984; contbr. articles to OUTREACH mag. Vol. tchr. English to Chinese restaurant workers, 2006—. Recipient First prize 5th Ann. Music Festival, Schenectady Fedn. Women's Orgn. Mem.: TESOL (assoc.). Avocations: piano, Chinese musical instruments, singing, travel. Home: 889 Ravenwood Dr Greenwood IN 46142-1840 Office: OMS Internat Inc 941 Fry Rd Greenwood IN 46142 Office Phone: 317-881-6751 ext. 348. Personal E-mail: scknapp2003@yahoo.com.

KNAPP, THOMAS JOSEPH, lawyer; b. Chgo., Aug. 27, 1952; s. William Bernard and Jeannette Cecilia (Zarnowiecki) K.; m. Lee Ann Schiller, Sept. 27, 1980; children: Brian Thomas, Terrence Joseph, Christopher Ryan, Katharine Cannon. BA, U. Ill., 1974; JD, Loyola U., Chgo., 1977. Bar: Ill. 1977, Fla. 1979, D.C. 1979, Tex. 1987, U.S. Dist. Ct. (no. and cen. dists.) Ill., U.S. Ct. Appeals (5th, 7th, 8th and 9th cirs.), U.S. Supreme Ct. 1986. Law clk. to presiding justice Cir. Ct. Cook County, Chgo., 1977-78; asst. atty. gen. consumer protection div. Atty. Gen. Ill., Chgo., 1978-80; atty. Burlington No. R.R. Co., Chgo., 1980-83, asst. gen. solicitor, 1983-85, asst. gen. counsel Ft. Worth, 1985-86, assoc. gen. counsel, 1986-88, labor counsel, 1988-95; of counsel Paul, Hastings, Janofsky & Walker, L.L.P., Washington, 1996-98, 2000—02; asst. gen. counsel The Boeing Co., Seattle, 1998—2002; v.p., gen. counsel and sec. Northwestern Corp., Sioux Falls, SD, 2002—. Commr. Village of Wilmette, Ill., 1985; mem. cable TV adv. bd. City of Bedford, 1992-94. Mem. ABA, Assn. Trial Lawyers Am., Nat. Assn. R.R. Trial Counsel, Ill. Trial Lawyers Assn., Chgo. Council of Lawyers, Commn. of Airline R.R. Labor Lawyers. Clubs: Tavern (Chgo.), Union League of Chgo. Roman Catholic. Avocations: sailing, golf, photography. Home: 7116 Darby Rd Bethesda MD 20817-2914 Office: Northwestern Corp 125 S Dakota Ave Sioux Falls SD 57104-6403 Office Phone: 605-978-2930. Business E-Mail: tom.knapp@northwestern.com.

KNAPPENBERGER, PAUL HENRY, JR., science museum director; b. Reading, Pa., Sept. 5, 1942; s. Paul Henry and Kathryn (Medrick) K.; m. Naomi Knappenberger; children— Paul Charles, Timothy Alan, Shannon Rose Lalor, Heidi Kathrin. AB in Math, Franklin and Marshall Coll., 1964; MA in Astronomy (NASA fellow), U. Va., 1966, PhD in Astronomy, 1968. Astronomer Fernbank Sci. Center, Atlanta, 1968-72; instr. Emory U. and Ga. State U., Atlanta, 1970-72; dir. Sci. Mus. of Va., Richmond, 1973-91; pres. The Adler Planetarium, Chgo., 1991—. Asst. prof. Va. Commonwealth U., U. Richmond, 1973-81; bd. dirs. Assn. Sci. and Tech. Centers, pres., 1985-87; instr. astronomy Yellowstone Inst.; former v.p. Midlothian Athletic Assn.; mem. council Nat. Mus. Act, 1984-86. Former mem. bd. dirs. Mus. Film Network, Exhibit Research Collaborative; co-founder Planetarium Show Network; dir. Informal Sci. Instructional Services, Ltd. NSF Sci. Edn. grantee, 1971-72; grantee NEH, Inst. Mus. Services. Mem. Am. Astron. Soc., AAAS, Internat. Planetarium Soc., Va. Acad. Sci., Va. Assn. Museums (council 1979-91), Am. Assn. Museums, Great Lakes Planetarium Assn. Home: 6n488 Splitrail Ct Saint Charles IL 60175-6928 Office: Adler Planetarium 1300 S Lake Shore Dr Chicago IL 60605-2403

KNAUER, GEORG NICOLAUS, philologist; b. Hamburg, Germany, Feb. 26, 1926; came to US, 1975. s. Georg A. and Ilse M. (Groothoff) K.; m. Elfriede Regina Overhoff, Aug. 3, 1951; 1 child, Georg Lorenz. DrPhil, U. Hamburg, 1952. Rsch. asst. Thesaurus Linguae Latinae, Munich, 1952-54; asst. Freie U., Berlin, 1954—61, privatdozent, 1961-64, assoc. prof., 1964-66, prof., 1966-74; prof. classical studies U. Pa., Phila., 1975-88, prof. emeritus, 1988—, chmn. dept. classical studies, 1978-79, 80-82, 85-88; resident Rockefeller Found., Bellagio Study and Conf. Ctr., Como, Italy, 1989. Brit. Coun. scholar U. London, 1957-58; vis. prof. Yale U., 1965-66; Nellie Wallace lectr. Oxford (Eng.) U., 1969; mem. Inst. Advanced Study, Princeton, NJ, 1973-74; vis. prof. Columbia U., fall 1976; mem. Notgemeinschaft für eine freie Universität, Berlin, 1969-90; mem. Bund Freiheit der Wissenschaft, Bonn, 1970—; mem. Internat. Coun. on Future of Univ., NYC. Author: Psalmenzitate in Augustins Konfessionen, 1955, 2d edit. under title Three Studies, 1987, Die Aeneis und Homer, 1964, 2d edit. 1979. Served with German Army, 1944-45. Guggenheim fellow, 1979-80, NEH fellow, 1984-85, Herzog August Bibliothek fellow, Germany, 1991, 97, 2002, 06; vis. scholar Am. Acad., Rome, 1979-80, 90, 97, 2003, 05, resident in classics, 1985 Mem. Am. Philol. Assn., Berliner Wissenschaftliche Gesellschaft, Am. Renaissance Soc. Home: The Quadrangle Apt 3314 3300 Darby Rd Haverford PA 19041-1070 Office: U Pa Dept of Classical Studies Logan Hall Philadelphia PA 19104-6304 Home Phone: 610-649-1857. Business E-Mail: gknauer@sas.upenn.edu.

KNAUER, JAMES PHILIP, physicist; b. Sandusky, OH, May 12, 1950; s. William David Sr. and Alice Roselyn (Mowry) Knauer; m. Susan Diana Holmes, Apr. 8, 1974. BS, MIT, 1972; MS, U. Hawaii, 1974, PhD, 1977. Rsch. asst. MIT, Cambridge, Mass., 1971-72; grad. tchg. asst. U. Hawaii, Honolulu, 1972-74, 74-77, jr. researcher, 1978-79; rsch. investigator U. Pa., Phila., 1977-78; assoc. rsch. scientist Lockheed Missiles & Space Co., Palo Alto, Calif., 1979-86, rsch. scientist, 1979-86; scientist Lab. Laser Energetics U. Rochester, NY, 1986-99, sr. scientist, 1999—. Mgr. Nat. Laser Users Facility, Rochester, 1986—96. Leader 4-H Club, Monroe County, NY, 1987—. Mem.: Carriage Assn. Am., Am. Driving Soc., Am. Phys. Soc. (Excellence in Plasma Physics Rsch. award 1995), N.Y. State Horse Coun., Sigma Xi. Republican. Avocation: riding and driving horses. Office: Lab for Laser Energetics Univ of Rochester 250 E River Rd Rochester NY 14623-1212 Home Phone: 585-359-3065; Office Phone: 585-275-2074. Business E-Mail: jkna@lle.rochester.edu.

KNAUER, VIRGINIA HARRINGTON, advocate, retired federal agency administrator; b. Phila., Mar. 28, 1915; d. Herman Winfield and Helen (Harrington) Wright; m. Wilhelm F. Knauer, Jan. 27, 1940; children: Wilhelm F., Valerie H. (Mrs. I. Townsend Burden III). BFA, U. Pa., 1937; grad., Pa. Acad. Fine Arts, 1937; postgrad., Royal Acad. Fine Arts, Florence, Italy, 1938-39; LL.D. (hon.), Phila. Coll. Textiles and Sci., St. Francis de Sales, Widener Coll., Chester, Pa., Tufts U.; Litt.D. (hon.), Drexel U.; L.H.D. (hon.), Russell Sage Coll., Pa. Coll. Podiatric Medicine; L.H.D., Jacksonville U.; LLD (hon.), U. Pa., 1971. Dir. Pa. Bur. Consumer Protection, 1968-69; spl. asst. to Pres. for consumer affairs The White House, 1969-77; dir. U.S. Office Consumer Affairs, Washington, 1971-77, 81-88; spl. adv. to Pres. for consumer affairs The White House, 1981-88; chair ABRH Inc., Washington, 1988-91; consumer cons. Haney and Knauer, Inc., Washington, 1991-93. Pres. Virginia Knauer & Assocs., Inc., Washington, 1977-81; chmn. Coun. for Advancement of Consumer Policy, 1979-81; U.S. rep., vice chmn. consumer policy com. OECD, 1970-77, 81-88; mem. Coun. Wage and Price Stability, 1974-77; vice-chmn. Philadelphia County Rep. Com., 1958-77; pres. Phila. Congress Rep. Women's Councils, 1958-77; dir. Pa. Coun. Rep. Women, 1963-80; founder N.E. Phila. Coun. Rep. Women, pres., 1956-68 Bd. dirs. Hannah Penn House, 1956—, v.p., 1971; chmn. Knauer Found. Hist. Preservation, 1963—; nat. chmn. to promote no fault automobile ins. Project New Start, 1988-91; bd. dirs. Nat. Coalition for Cancer Survivorship; mem. city coun., Phila., Pa., 1960-68. Recipient Gimbel-Phila. award, 1977, Ind. Achievement in Govt. award Soc. Consumer Affairs Profls., 1983; named Disting. Dau. Pa., 1969; named to Disting. Women's Com., Northwood U., 1997. Mem. Nat. Trust Hist. Preservation, Am. Assn. Ret. Persons, Internat. Neighbors Club, Exec. Women in Govt., Penn Women (trustees coun.), Consumers for World Trade (bd. dirs.), Zeta Tau Alpha, Kappa Delta Epsilon (hon.). Episcopalian.

KNAUSS, DONALD R., consumer products company executive; b. 1951; m. Ellie Knauss. BA, Ind. U. Brand mgr. Procter & Gamble; mktg. & sales mgmt. positions Frito-Lay & Tropicana div. PepsiCo Inc.; sr. v.p. mktg. The Minute Maid Co., 1994—96, sr. v.p., gen. mgr. retail ops., 1996—98, pres., CEO, 2000—04; sr. v.p., mgr. so. Africa The Coca-Cola Co., 1998—2000, pres., COO No. Am., 2004—06; chmn. CEO The Clorox Co., Oakland, Calif., 2006—. Trustee USMC Univ. Found., Morehouse Coll. Officer USMC. Office: The Clorox Co 1221 Broadway Oakland CA 94612*

KNAUSS, JOHN ATKINSON, retired federal agency administrator, oceanographer, educator, retired dean; b. Detroit, Sept. 1, 1925; s. Karl Ernst and Loise (Atkinson) K.; m. Marilyn Mattson, Sept. 6, 1954; children: Karl, William. BS, MIT, 1946; MS, U. Mich., 1949; PhD, U. Calif., 1959; DSc (hon.), U R.I., 1992. Oceanographer Navy Electronics Lab, San Diego, 1947, Office Naval Rsch., 1949-51, Scripps Instn. Oceanography, 1951-52, 55-62; prof. Grad. Sch. Oceanography, U. R.I., Narragansett, 1962-90, dean, 1962-87, provost for marine affairs, 1969-82, v.p. marine programs, 1982-87, prof., dean emeritus, 1990—; undersecretary for oceans and atmosphere Dept. Commerce, Washington, 1989-93; adminstr. Nat. Oceanic and Atmospheric Adminstrn., Washington, 1989-93; U.S. commr. Internat. Whaling Commn., 1991-93; rsch. assoc. Scripps Inst. Oceanography U. Calif., San Diego, 1993—2004. Leader 10 oceanographic expdns. to study oceanic circulation, 1955-65; chair US phys.-chem. panel Internat. Indian Ocean Expdn., 1959-62; mem. Pres's. Commn. on Marine Scis., Engring. and Resources, 1967-68; mem. State Dept. Pub. Adv. Com. on Law of Sea, 1970-82; chair sr. adv. com. on environ. scis. Ctr. for Energy and Environ. Rsch., U. PR, 1977-80; mem. Nat. Adv. Com. on Oceans and Atmosphere, 1978-85, vice chair, 1979-81, chair 1981-85; chair bd. govs. Joint Oceanographic Instns., Inc., 1978-80; co-founder Law of Sea Inst., mem. exec. bd. 1965-76, 82-87; bd. dirs. Coun. for Ocean Law, 1983-89, 94-01; chair marine divsn. Nat. Assn. State U. and Land Grant Colls., 1984-85; chair Joint Oceanographic Instns. for Deep Earth Sampling, 1984-86; bd. dirs. Harbor Br. Oceanographic Instn., 1987-89; 1st vice chmn. Intergovernmental Oceanographic Commn., 1991-93; mem. bd. trustees Bermuda Biological Sta. Rsch., 1995-05, life trustee, 2005-; mem. ocean rsch. adv. panel Nat. Oceanographic Rsch. Leadership Coun., 1998-02, chair, 1998-02, Sea Grant adv. com., 2003-05. US Congress renamed its Sea Grant fellowship the Dean John A. Knauss Fellowship program in 1987. With USNR, 1943-46, 53-54. Named to RI Heritage Hall of Fame, 1983; recipient Albatross award Am. Miscellaneous Soc., 1959, Nat. Sea Grant award, 1974. Fellow AAAS (v.p. 1972-73), Am. Geophys. Union (pres. oceanography sect. 1965-67, pres-elect 1996-98, pres. 1998-2000, Ocean Sci. award 1988); mem. Am. Meteorol. Soc. (hon., coun. 1980-82). Home: 126 Willett Rd Saunderstown RI 02874-3810 Business E-Mail: jknauss@gso.uri.edu.

KNAUSS, ROBERT H., lawyer; b. 1953; m. Marcy Knauss. BA, St. Joseph's U.; JD, Temple U. Sch. of Law, 1982. Bar: Pa. 1982. Atty. Ballard, Spahr, Andrews & Ingersoll, Phila.; assoc. counsel UGI Corp., 1985—2003, v.p., gen. counsel, 2003—; group counsel AmeriGas Propane, Inc. (subsidiary of UGI Corp.), 1985—96, v.p. law, gen. counsel, 1996—; gen. ptnr. AmeriGas Partners (subsidiary of UGI Corp.), 2003—. Office: UGI Corp PO Box 858 Valley Forge PA 19482

KNAUSS, ROBERT LYNN, corporate financial executive; b. Detroit, Mar. 24, 1931; s. Karl Ernst and Loise (Atkinson) K.; m. Angela Tirola Lawson, Feb. 21, 1973; children by previous marriage: Robert B., Charles H., Katherine E.; 1 stepson, Ian T. Lawson. AB, Harvard U., 1952; JD, U. Mich., 1957. Bar: Calif., Tenn., Tex. Assoc. Pillsbury, Madison & Sutro, San Francisco, 1958-60; prof. law U. Mich., 1960-72, v.p. student svcs., 1970-72; dean, prof. law Vanderbilt U., Nashville, 1972-79; dean U. Houston Law Ctr., 1981-93, disting. univ. prof., 1981-95. Vis. prof. Vt. Law Sch., South Royalton, Amos Tuck Sch. Bus. Adminstrn., Dartmouth Coll., Hanover, NH, 1979—81; chmn., CEO Baltic Internat. USA/Inc., 1994—2003; chmn., prin. exec. officer Phillips Svcs. Corp., 2002—03; bd. dirs. Mex. Fund, Equus Total Return, Inc., XO Comm. Inc., Westpoint Internat. Editor: Small Business Financing, 4 vols., 1966, Securities Regulation Sourcebook, 1970-71, (with others) Cases and Materials on Enterprise Organizations, 1987; contbr. articles to profl. jours. Regent Nat. Coll. Dist. Attys., 1981-95. Lt. (j.g.) USN, 1952-55. Fellow Tex. Bar Found., Am. Bar Found; mem. Calif. Bar Assn., Tenn. Bar Assn., Tex. Bar Assn. (chmn. corp. coun. sect. 1991), Am. Law Inst. (life), Order of Coif. Home: PO Box 40 5580 FM 1697 ThreeCreek Ranch Burton TX 77835-0040 Office Phone: 979-289-4000. Personal E-mail: BOBKNAUSS@CS.COM.

KNEALE, JAMES C., gas company executive; CPA. V.p. energy ops. ONEOK Inc., Tulsa, Okla., 1981—92; exec. mgmt. positions Okla. Natural Gas Co. div. ONEOK, 1992—97; pres. Okla. Natural gas Co. div. ONEOK, 1997—99; v.p. through exec. v.p., CFO, treas. ONEOK Inc., Tulsa, Okla., 1999—2007, pres., COO, 2007—. Bd. dir. YMCA Greater Tulsa, Tulsa Boys Home. Mem.: Am. Inst. CPAs, Okla. Soc. CPSa. Office: Oneok Inc 100 W Fifth St Tulsa OK 74103*

KNEAVEL, ANN CALLANAN, humanities educator, communications consultant; b. Balt., Oct. 29, 1946; d. James Michael and Ann (Ijams) Callanan; m. Thomas Charles Kneavel, Jr., Dec. 18, 1970; children: Meredith Elizabeth, Thomas Charles III, Rebecca Ann. BA, Coll. Notre Dame Md., 1968; MA in Am. Lit., U. Md., 1970; PhD in Modern Brit. Lit., U. Ottawa, 1979. Instr. U. Md., College Park, 1968—71, U. Ottawa, 0971—1972, Wilmington Coll., Del., 1976—79, Del. Tech. and C.C., Dover, 1975—79; asst. prof. Widener U., Chester, Pa., 1981—82; prof. Goldey-Beacom Coll., Wilmington, 1981—; dir. satellite campuses Total Quality Master's Program, Falmouth, Mass., 1995—. Contbr. articles to profl. jours. Trustee Hockessin (Del.) Pub. Libr., 1981-93, Alpha Tau Omega Fraternity, Wilmington, 1994—; mem. Friends of Hockessin Libr., 1981—. Mem. MLA, Nat. Coun. Tchrs. English, Conf. on Christianity and Lit., Am. Culture Assn., C.C. Humanities Assn., Alpha Chi (faculty sponsor, Svc. award 1994, v.p. region VI 2000-02, pres. region VI, 2002-04, nat. coun. 2003—), Nat. Coun. 2003-. Roman Catholic. Home: 7 Arthur Dr Hockessin DE 19707-1012 Office: Goldey-Beacom Coll 4701 Limestone Rd Wilmington DE 19808-1927 Business E-Mail: kneavela@gbc.edu.

KNEAVEL, THOMAS CHARLES, JR., psychologist, educator; b. Balt., Oct. 30, 1941; s. Thomas Charles and Caroline Frances (Noha) K.; m. Ann Callanan, Dec. 18, 1970; children: Meredith, Thomas, Rebecca. BS, Loyola Coll., Balt., 1963, MEd, 1968; PhD, U. Ottawa, 1979. Diplomate Am. Bd. Forensic Examiners; lic. psychologist, Del. Tchr. Ridge Sch., Towsen, Md., 1961-65; psychologist Balt. City Schs., 1965-69; clin. psychologist D.C. Children's Ctr., Laurel, Md., 1969-70; psychology intern Child Study Ctr. U. Ottawa, 1970-71; psychology intern Child Diagnostic and Devel. Clinic Children's Hosp. of Ea. Ont., Ottawa, 1971-72; sch. psychologist Cape Henlopen Sch. Dist., Nassau, Del., 1972-79; psychologist Comty. Mental Health Clinic, Beebe Hosp., Lewes, Del., 1973-79; program dir. child crisis unit Terry Children's Psychiat. Ctr., New Castle, Del., 1979-86, chief psychologist, 1982-86; pvt. practice, 1983—; psychologist Christina Sch. Dist., 1986—98; clin. dir. adolescent programs Meadow Wood Hosp., New Castle, Del., 1993—94; dir. psychol. svcs. Med. Ctr. Del. Dept. Adolescent Medicine 1st State Sch., 1995—99; psychologist Thomas A. Edison Charter Sch., Wilmington, 2000—03; cons. psychologist United Spine Ctr., 2005—06, Woodmill Corp. Ctr., Wilmington, 2006—. Cons. on compulsive gambling to dir. Del. Divsn. Mental Health; cons. Joseph Ho., Balt., 1969—70; mem. citizens adv. bd. Cmty. Mental Health Clinic Beebe Hosp., 1974—79; adj. faculty dept. psychiatry and human behavior Thomas Jefferson U. Med. Sch., 1980—86; frequent nat. presenter on treating oppositional disorders in children and adolescents, 1980—82; apptd. by Gov. DuPont and Gov. Castle Del. Devel. Disabilities Planning Coun., 1982—84, vice chmn., 1983—85, chmn., 1985—87; state rep. Nat. Assn. Devel. Disabilities, Washington, 1984—87, mem. child devel. com.; mem. state genetics adv. coun. A.I. DuPont Inst. and State of Del., 1986—94; clin. cons. Turnabout Counseling Ctr., Seaford, Del., 1987—91; apptd. by Gov. Castle State Bd. Psychol. Examiners, 1989, v.p., 1991—92, pres., 1992—94; adj. prof. Widner U., 1995—99. Mem. APA, Del. Psychol. Assn., Nat. Assn. Sch. Psychologists (charter), Del. Sch. Psychologists Assn. (pres. 1976-77), Del. Psychol. Inc. (bd. dirs. 1987-89), Nat. Grad. Sch. for Quality Mgmt. (bd. dirs. 1997- , bd. chair 2003—), Nat. Eagle Scout Assn. Roman Catholic. Home: 7 Arthur Dr Hockessin DE 19707-1012 Office: Woodmill Corp Ctr 5235 Westwoodmill Dr Ste 47 Wilmington DE 19808 Personal E-mail: dockneavel@yahoo.com.

KNEBEL, DONALD EARL, lawyer; b. Logansport, Ind., May 26, 1946; s. Everett Earl and Ethel Josephina (Hultgren) K.; m. Joan Elizabeth Vest, June 5, 1976 (div. 1980); 1 child, Mary Elizabeth; m. Jennifer Colt Johnson, Sept. 25, 1999. BEE with highest distinction, Purdue U., 1968; JD magna cum laude, Harvard U., 1974. Bar: Ind. 1974, U.S. Ct. Appeals (7th cir.) 1980, U.S. Ct. Appeals (3rd cir.) 1986, U.S. Ct. Appeals (6th cir.) 1987, U.S. Ct. Appeals (fed. cir.) 1988, U.S. Ct. Appeals (4th cir.) 2005. Assoc. Barnes, Hickam, Pantzer & Boyd, Indpls., 1974—81; ptnr. Barnes & Thornburg LLP, Indpls., 1981—. Contbr. articles on intellectual property, antitrust and distbn. law to profl. publs. Trustee Indpls. Civic Theatre, 1986—95, chmn., 1988—91, hon. trustee, 1995—2002, trustee, 2002—, chmn., 2002—05; chair United Way Tocqueville Soc., 2005—07. Fellow: Am. Coll. Trial Lawyers; mem.: ABA, TechPoint (dir.), TechLaw Group (v.p. 2002—03, pres. 2004—05), 7th Cir. Bar Assn., Indpls. Bar Assn., Ind. Bar Assn., Columbia Club, Kiwanis (pres. 1991—92). Presbyterian. Office: Barnes & Thornburg LLP 11 S Meridian St Indianapolis IN 46204-3535 Home Phone: 317-873-0335; Office Phone: 317-231-7214. Business E-Mail: dknebel@btlaw.com.

KNEBEL, JOHN ALBERT, lawyer, retired government agency administrator; b. Tulsa, Oct. 4, 1936; s. John Albert and Florence Julia (Friend) K.; m. Zenia Irene Marks, June 6, 1959; children— Carrie, John Albert III, Clemens. BS, U.S. Mil. Acad., 1959; MA in Econs, Creighton U., 1962; JD, Am. U., 1965. Bar: D.C. bar 1966, U.S. Ct. Appeals bar 1966. Asst. to Rep. J.E. Wharton of N.Y., Washington, 1963-64; assoc. mem. law firm Howrey, Simon, Baker & Murchison, Washington, 1965-68; asst. counsel Com. on Agr., U.S. Ho. Reps., Washington, 1968-71; gen. counsel SBA, Washington, 1971-74, U.S. Dept. Agr., Washington, 1973-75; under sec. Dept. Agr., 1975-76, sec. of agr., 1976-77; ptnr. firm Baker & McKenzie, Washington, 1977-86; pres. Am. Mining Congress, Washington, 1986-95; exec. v.p. Nat. Assn. Broadcasters, Washington, 1995—2006. Served to 1st lt. USAF, 1959-62. Mem. Fed. Bar Assn. (past pres.), Am., D.C. bar assns., Delta Theta Phi, Omicron Delta Gamma. Home: 1418 Laburnum St Mc Lean VA 22101-2523

KNECHT, BEN HARROLD, retired surgeon; b. Rapid City, SD, May 3, 1938; m. Jane Bowles, Aug. 27, 1961; children: John, Janelle. BA, U. S.D., 1960; MD, U. Iowa, 1964; cert. total quality mgmt., U. Wash., 1998. Diplomate Am. Bd. Surgery. Intern L.A. County Gen. Hosp., 1964—65; resident in surgery U. Iowa Sch. Medicine, Iowa City, 1968—72; surgeon Wenatchee Valley Clinic, Wash., 1972—; med. dir. Wenatchee Valley Hosp., 1997—; chmn. med. informatics Wenatchee Valley Clinic, 1995—2000, chmn. gen.-vasc. surg. dept., 1996—2001; mem. risk mgmt. commn. Wenatchee Valley Med. Clinic., 1999—, med. dir. group, 2004—07; ret., 2006. Dir. emergency rm. Ctrl. Wash. Hosp., Wenatchee, 1972-79, chmn. libr., 1976-86, chief surgery, 1983-86, mem. risk mgmt. com., 2000-; chmn. claims rev. panel Wash. State Med. Assn., Seattle, 1979-82, prof. liability com. risk mgmt., 1985-90; clin. prof. surgery U. Wash.; mem. adv. risk mgmt. com. Wash. State Physicians Ins. Subscribers, 1990-98, regional adv. com. Nat. Libr. Medicine, 1991-93. Fundraiser Ctrl. Wash. Hosp. Found., 1987; del. Gov.'s Conf. on Libr., 1991; bd. dir. United Way, 1974-77; chmn. North Ctrl. Healthcare Skills Panel, 2003—; mem. founding bd. Cascade Unitarian Fellowship, 1986-88; mem. ad hoc com. on tchg./learning Wenatchee H.S., 1999-2002, mem. prin.'s adv. com., 2002—, chmn. sch. dist. bldg. bond com., 2007; post leader Med. Explorers, 1973-76; mem. Wash. State Healthcare Personnel Shortgage Task Force, 2005-, chair bond campaign Wenatchee Sch. Dist., 2007. Lt. comdr. USN, 1965-68, Vietnam. Recipient AMA Physicians Recognition Award, 1992—2006, WSMA Disting. Svc. award, 1997, Chelan-Douglas County Med. Soc. Appreciation award, 1997. Mem. AMA (alt. del. 1985-87, del. 1988-98, surg. caucus exec. com. 1991-94, group practice adv. com. 2004—), ACS (bd. dir. Wash. chpt. 1981-84), Am. Coll. Physician Exec., Am. Soc. Quality, Am. Med. Group Assn. (chief med. officer panel 2004—), North Pacific Surg. Assn., Wash. State Med. Assn. (trustee 1979-98), Chelan-Douglas County Med. Soc., Am. Soc. Gen. Surgery (founding bd. 1994-2001, bd. dir. 1992-2001), Henry A. Harkins Surg. Soc., Rotary (chmn. youth com. 1976-78), Wenatchee C. of C. (Greater Wenatchee and Cmty. Devel. 2000-02), Alpha Tau Omega. Avocations: snow and water skiing, reading, hiking, computing.

KNECHT, DAVID FREEMONT, pastor; b. Wimbeldon, ND, Aug. 20, 1926; s. Herman F. and Viola Irene (Chist) Knecht; m. Jane Sheldon, Aug. 12, 1951; children: Kathleen Margaret, Jeanne, Christine, Jonathan, Timothy, Laurie. BA, U. ND, Grand Forks, 1950; MDiv, Garrett Evangellical Theol. Seminary, Evanston, Ill., 1953; D of Ministry, St. Paul Sch. Theology, Kansas City, Mo., 1976; D of Divinity (hon.), Dakota Weslayan U., Mitchell, SD, 1987. Cert. elder United Meth. Ch., 1953. Pastor United Meth. Ch., Fairmont, ND, 1953—57, Faith United Meth. Ch., Fargo, ND, 1957—66, McCabe United Meth. Ch., Bismarck, ND, 1966—79, dist. supr., 1979—81; adminstrv. asst. to Bishop Dakotas Area United Meth. Ch., 1981—87; pastor United Meth. Ch., Fargo, 1987—91. Chaplain ND Air Nat. Guard, Fargo, ND, 1960—86. Contbr. articles to profl. jours. With USN, 1944—46, lt. col. USAF, 1960—86. Decorated Air Force Commendation medal with bronze star USAF. Mem.: Kiwanis Club (pres. Bismark chpt. 1974—75, pres. Fargo chpt. 1987—88). Methodist. Avocations: stamp collecting/philately, gardening.

KNECHT, GLEN CHARLES, minister; b. Ogdensburg, NY, Mar. 19, 1930; s. Robert B. and Wilma P. Rosenbaum Knecht; m. Betty Jane Greenwald, Aug. 21, 1951; children: Thomas Robert, Elizabeth Anne Myers, Wendy Jane Higgins, Janet Lynn Dick, Glen Charles Jr., Amy Carol Frierson. BA, Maryville Coll., Maryville, Tenn., 1950; BD, ThM, Princeton Theol. Sem., NJ, 1963; DD (hon.), Covenant Coll., Lookout Mountain, Tenn., 1986. Ordained Presbyn. Ch. USA, 1954, cert. pastoral specialist Am. Assn. Pastoral Counselors. Pastor Union Presbyn. Ch., Kirkwood, Pa., 1954—57, Oxford Presbyn. Ch., Oxford, Pa., 1963—71; missionary evangelist Presbyn. Ch. Mission Agy., Tabriz, Iran, 1957—62; sr. pastor Wallace Meml. Presbyn. Ch., Hyattsville, Md., 1971—83, 1st Presbyn. Ch., Columbia, SC, 1983—97; assoc. pastor 4th Presbyn. Ch., Bethesda, Md., 1997—2007; pastor Christ Reformed Evang. Ch., Annapolis, Md., 2007—. Author: The Day God Made, 2003; contbr. chapters to books.

Co-founder Citizens Advocating Decency, Righteousness and Ethics, Columbia, 1990—97. Named to Order of Palmetto, Gov. SC, 1997. Home: 500 4th St Laurel MD 20707 Home Phone: 301-776-1202. Personal E-mail: knecht500@comcast.net.

KNECHT, JAMES HERBERT, retired lawyer; b. LA, Aug. 5, 1925; s. James Herbert and Gertrude Martha (Morris) K.; m. Margaret Paton Vreeland, Jan. 3, 1953 (dec. 1994); children— Susan, Thomas Paton, Carol. BS, UCLA, 1947; LLB, U. So. Calif., 1957. Bar: Calif. bar 1957, U.S. Supreme Ct. bar 1969. Mem. firm Forster, Gemmill & Farmer, Los Angeles, 1957-84; sole practice, 1985—2005; ret., 2005. Chmn. bd. Templeton (Calif.) Nat. Bank, 1992-95. Fellow Am. Bar Found. (life); mem. ABA, Legion Lex, Caltech Assocs., L.A. Area C. of C. (dir. 1979-83), Beta Theta Pi. E-mail: jknecht@ccaccess.net.

KNECHT, RICHARD ARDEN, family practitioner; b. Grand Rapids, Mar. 7, 1929; s. Fredrick William and Eva Rae (Blakley) K.; m. Joan Matson, Dec. 26, 1951 (div. 1975); children: Richard Arden, Karrie Jo, Jeffrey Paul; m. Patricia Irene Gilmore, Aug. 14, 1976; 1 child, Kimberly Kahler. BS, U. Mich., 1951, MD, 1955. Diplomate Am. Bd. Family Practice, Am. Bd. Geriatric Medicine; cert. med. dir. Intern St. Mary Hosp., Grand Rapids, Mich., 1955-56; pvt. practice, Fife Lake, Mich., 1956—. Fellow Am. Acad. Family Physicians, Am. Geriatric Soc., Royal Soc. Medicine; mem. Mich. Med. Soc. (com. on aging 1988—), Mich. Acad. Family Practice (chmn. com. on aging 1986-88, pub.'s award 1988), Mich. Med. Dirs. Assn. (pres. 1996-97). Avocations: archaeology, motorcycling, geology, hunting, fishing. Home and Office: PO Box 130 125 Morgan St Fife Lake MI 49633 Personal E-mail: r.knecht@charter.net.

KNECHT, WILLIAM L., lawyer; b. Lock Haven, Pa., Jan. 15, 1946; s. Clair N. and Betty R. (Harter) K.; m. Margaret E. O'Malley, June 10, 1972; children: William E., Jennifer M. BA, Pa. State U., 1967; JD, Dickinson Sch. Law, 1970. Bar: Pa. 1970, U.S. Supreme Ct. 1976, U.S. Tax Ct. 1981, U.S. Dist. Ct. (middle dist.) Pa. 1973, Ct. Common Pleas 1970. Assoc. McCormick, Lynn, Reeder, Nichols & Sarno, Williamsport, Pa., 1973-76; ptnr. McCormick, Reeder, Nichols, Bahl, Knecht & Person, Williamsport, 1976-96; ptnr. McCormick Law Firm, Williamsport, 1996—. Bankruptcy trustee U.S. Justice Dept., Williamsport, Pa., 1978-91. Editor Lycoming Reporter, 1976—. 1st lt. US Army, 1971—73. Fellow Pa. Bar Found. (life); mem. ABA, Pa. Bar Assn., Lycoming County Law Assn. (exec. com. 1976—), Lycoming Law Assn. (pres. 1995), Ross Club. Republican. United Ch. of Christ. Avocation: stamps and first day cover collecting. Home: 253 Lincoln Ave Williamsport PA 17701-2237 Office: McCormick Law Firm 835 W 4th St Williamsport PA 17701 Office Phone: 570-326-5131. Business E-Mail: bknecht@mcclaw.com.

KNECHTMANN, JAMES ALLEN, archivist, researcher; b. Tucker, Ga., Nov. 11, 1966; s. James Allen Nechtman and Katherine Gail Henry Nechtman; m. Jennifer Ann Ravet, May 17, 1998. BA, Ga. State U., 1988, MA, 1992; MLIS, San Jose State U., 2005. Cert. archivist Acad. Cert. Archivists/N.Y., 2005. Propr. The Gen. Staff Libr., Alameda, Calif., 1998—; archivist U.S. Naval Hist. Ctr., Washington, 2006—. Archivist Alameda Naval Air Mus., 2005—06. Author: (master's thesis) The German Replacement Army of World War II: Its Origins, Development, and Operation, (manuscript) The Military Career of Brig. Gen. Claudius Charles Wilson, P.A.C.S.; translator: (book) The Battle in Lorraine and the Vosges: Baptism of Fire of the Bavarian Army, 1914, The Battle of St. Quentin, 1914, The Conquest of Novo Georgievsk, 1915; author: (manuscript) The Encounter at St. Quentin on 29 August 1914, The Political and Judicial Career of Justice James Kollock Hines of Georgia, The Military and Political Career of Brig. Gen. George Paul Harrison, Jr., P.A.C.S., 1861-1897, The Military and Political Career of Brig. Gen. George Paul Harrison, Sr., Georgia Militia, The Military Career of Col. William S. Harrison, Georgia Militia, 1807-1830. Mem. Alameda Breakfast Lions Club, 1998—2000. Staff sgt. Ga. Army N.G., 1984—90, Stone Mountain, Ga. Mem.: Mil. Order of the Stars & Bars, SCV (camp comdr. 2004—05). Conservative-R. Episcopalian. Avocations: historical research, stamp collecting/philately, coin collecting/numismatics. Home Phone: 510-332-6215. Personal E-mail: jamesknechtmann@hotmail.com.

KNEE, MICHAEL J., science librarian, consultant; s. Teddy and Minerva Knee; m. Karen R. Kirchofer; children: Margaux, Amber. BA, Montclair State U., 1971, MA, 1975; MLS, Rutgers U., 1977. Serials, reference libr. Rutgers U., Piscataway, NJ, 1977—78; info. scientist Knoll Pharm. Co., Whippany, NJ, 1978—79; pub. services libr. U. N.D., Grand Forks, 1979—81; sci. bibliographer U. Albany, SUNY, 1981—. Author: The Reference Librarian, 1987, Collection Management, 1990, Hypertext/Hypermedia: An Annotated Bibliography, 1990, Library Acquisitions: Theory & Practice, 1992, Reference Services Review, 1995, Wolves: A Bibliography and Guide to the Literature, 1968-1987, 1995, Issues in Science & Technology Librarianship, 1997, College & Research Libraries News, 2001, Computer Science and Computing: A Guide to the Literature, 2006, Journal of Library Administration, 2006; contbr. articles to profl. jours. Recipient Pres.' Librarianship Excellence award, Chancellor's Librarianship Excellence award. Mem.: SUNY Libr. Assn., Am. Chem. Soc., Spl. Libr. Assn. Office: Univ Albany SUNY Sci Libr Albany NY 12222 E-mail: knee@albany.edu.

KNEE, RUTH IRELAN, social worker, health care consultant; b. Sapulpa, Okla., Mar. 21, 1920; d. Oren M. and Daisy (Daubin) Irelan; m. Junior K. Knee, May 29, 1943 (dec. Oct. 1981). BA, U. Okla., Norman, 1941, cert. social work, 1942; MA in Social Svcs. Adminstrn., U. Chgo., 1945. Psychiat. social worker, asst. supr. Ill. Psychiat. Inst., U. Ill., Chgo., 1943-44; psychiat. social worker USPHS Employee Health Unite, Washington, 1944—49; social work assoc. Army Med. Ctr., Walter Reed Army Hosp., Washington, 1949-54; psychiat. social work cons. HEW, Region III, Washington, 1955-56; with NIMH, Chevy Chase, Md., 1956-72; chief mental health care adminstrn. br. Health Svcs. and Mental Health Adminstrn., USPHS assoc. dep. adminstr., 1972-73; dep. dir. Office of Nursing Home Affairs, 1973-74; long-term mental health care cons.; mem. com. on mental health and illness of elderly HEW, 1976-77; mem. panel on legal and ethical issues Pres.'s Commn. on Mental Health, 1977-78; liaison mem. Nat. Adv. Mental Health Coun., 1977-81. Mem. edtl. bd. Health and Social Work, 1979-81. Bd. dirs. Hillhaven Found., 1975-86, governing bd. Cathedral Coll. of the Laity, Washington Nat. Cathedral, 1988-94, Cathedral Fund Com., 1997—,bd. of visitors sch. of social work, Univ. of Okla., 2000— Recipient Edith Abbott award, U. Chgo. Sch. Social Svc. Adminstrn., 2001, Disting. Alumna award, U. Okla. Coll. Arts and Scis., 1999. Fellow APHA (sec. mental health sect. 1968-70, chmn. 1971-72), Am. Orthopsychiat. Assn. (life), Gerontol. Soc. Am., Am. Assn. Psychiat. Social Workers (pres. 1951-53); mem. Nat. Conf. Social Welfare (nat. bd. 1968-71, 2d v.p. 1973-74), Inst. Medicine/NAS (com. study future of pub. health 1986-87), Coun. on Social Work Edn., Nat. Assn. Social Workers (sec. 1955-56, nat. dir. 1956-57, 84-86, chmn. competence study com., practice and knowledge com. 1963-71, presdl. award for exemplary svc. 1999), Acad. Cert. Social Workers (NASW Found. co-chair social work pioneers 1993—), Am. Pub. Welfare Assn., DAR, U. Okla. Assocs., Woman's Nat. Dem. Club (mem. gov. bd. 1992-95, ednl. found. bd. 1992-2000), Cosmos Club (Washington, chair program com. 1998-2001), Phi Beta Kappa (fellow), Psi Chi. Address: 8809 Arlington Blvd Fairfax VA 22031-2705

KNEEDLER, EDWIN S., federal agency administrator; b. 1946; BS, Lehigh U.; JD, U. Va. Bar: Oreg. 1975. Asst. to the solicitor gen. US Dept. Justice, Washington, 1979—93, dep. solicitor gen., 1993—. Professor law George Washington U. Office: US Dept Justice 950 Pennsylvania Ave NW Ste 5143 Washington DC 20530

KNEEDLER, (ALVIN) RICHARD, academic administrator; b. Ruffsdale, Pa., Apr. 8, 1943; s. Alvin Raymond and Louise (Mac Innes) Kneedler; m. Suzette Gallagher, June 17, 1967; children: Eric, Rebecca. AB, Franklin and Marshall Coll., 1965; MA in French Lang. and Lit., U. Pa., 1967, PhD in French Lang. and Lit., 1970; cert. in Ednl. Mgmt., Harvard U., 1975; DHL (hon.), Tohoku Gakuin U., 1993; LHD (hon.), Franklin and Marshall Coll., 2002. Instr. French Franklin and Marshall Coll., Lancaster, Pa., 1968—70, asst. prof. French, 1970—72, asst. to. dean, 1971—74, asst. to pres., 1974—77, sec. coll., 1977—79, v.p. adminstrn., 1979—84, v.p. devel., 1984—88, sec. bd. trustees, 1974—88, pres., 1988—2002; cons. Coun. of Ind. Colls., 2002—05; pres. emeritus Franklin and Marshall Coll., 2002—; interim pres. Rockford Coll., Ill., 2006—. Mem. exec. com. Assn. Ind. Colls. and Univs. Pa., 1989—98, 2000—02, chmn., 1996—97; exec. com. Nat. Assn. Ind. Colls. and Univs., 1999, chair policy and pub. rels. com., 99, mem. coun. ind. coll. dir., 2000—02; chair Pa. Gov.'s Tng., Am.'s Tchrs. Commn., 2005—06. Mem. Lancaster City Planning Commn., 1980—85, chmn., 1983—85; v.p., bd. dirs. Hist. Preservation Trust, Lancaster, 1984—87; sec., bd. dirs. Pa. Sch. Arts, Lancaster, 1985—89; bd. dirs. St. Joseph Hosp., 1991—95, Lancaster Area Arts Coun., 1987—91, Louise Von Hess Found. for Med. Edn., 1990—2006, Urban League Lancaster County, 1991—93, United Way, 1993—98, Urban Alliance, 1998—2002; chmn. Cmty. Cultural Planning Com., 1989—90; mem. Downtown Task Force, 1989—90; trustee Kiski Sch., 1988—95; chmn. exec. bd. Commonwealth Partnership, 1997—98; mem. adv. bd. PRIME, Inc., 1991—98; bd. dirs. Lancaster-York Hist. Region, 2001—06. Mem.: Lancaster Pa. Soc., Mid. States Assn. Schs. and Coll. (vol. evaluator 1986—), Sons of Revolution (mem. exec. com. 2005), Lancaster C. of C. and Industry (bd. dirs. 1990—92, mem. exec. com.), Phi Alpha Theta, Phi Beta Kappa. Democrat. Presbyterian. Home: 1416 Newton Rd Lancaster PA 17603-2461 Home Phone: 815-226-8904; Office Phone: 815-226-4010. Business E-Mail: rkneedler@rockford.edu.

KNEELAND, DOUGLAS EUGENE, retired newspaper editor; b. Lincoln, Maine, July 27, 1929; s. Vernis Bruce and Sadie Jane (Curtis) K.; m. Anne Packard Libby, Sept. 8, 1951 (dec. Nov. 1989); children: Debra Jo Kneeland Wentz, Libby Kneeland Williams, Bruce, Wayne; m. Barbara Jordan Lees, May 24, 1997. BA in Journalism, U. Maine, 1953, LittD (hon.), 2005. Reporter Bangor Daily News, Maine, 1951-53, Worcester Telegram, Mass., 1953-56; city editor, news editor Lorain Jour., Ohio, 1956-59; copy editor, nat. corr., dep. nat. editor N.Y. Times, NYC, Kansas City, San Francisco and Chgo., 1959-81; nat.-fgn. editor Chgo. Tribune, 1981-82, assoc. mng. editor, 1982-87, assoc. editor, 1987-90, pub. editor, 1990-93; vis. lectr. journalism U. Maine, Orono, 1993—2003. Columnist Lincoln News, Maine, 1995—2001. Served with AUS, 1947-49, Korea, Japan. Home: 31 Albert Dr Lincoln ME 04457-4221 E-mail: dougk@midmaine.com.

KNEELAND, MICHAEL J., rental company executive; Pres. Freestate Industries, Inc., 1995—96; gen. mgr. Rylan Rents dba Freestate Industries divsn. Equipment Supply Co., 1996—98; dist. mgr. United Rentals, 1998, v.p. aerial ops., 2000—01, v.p. SE region, 2001—03, exec. v.p. ops., 2003—07, exec. v.p., COO, 2007—, interim CEO, 2007—. Office: United Rentals Inc Five Greenwich Office Park Greenwich CT 06830 Office Phone: 203-622-3131. Office Fax: 203-622-6080.*

KNEESE, CAROLYN CALVIN, retired education educator; b. Austin, Sept. 16, 1941; d. Elmer Ben and Agnes Standlee Calvin; children: Kyle Calvin, Reagan Scott. BA, U. Tex., Austin, 1962; MA, Houston Baptist U., 1990; EdD, U. Houston, 1994. Cert. real estate broker Tex., 1988. Tchr. Austin Sch. Dist., Tex., 1963—64, Highland Park Sch. Dist., Dallas, 1964—67; translator, rschr. Methodist Hosp., Houston, 1969—70; rsch. asst. U. Houston, 1993—94; rsch. assoc. Tex. A&M U., College Station, 1994, asst. prof. dept. ednl. adminstrn. Commerce, 1998—2002, assoc. prof. dept. ednl. adminstrn., 2003—04, ret., 2004. Co-author: School Calendar Reform: Learning in All Seasons, 2006; author: numerous jour. articles and publs. Bd. mem. Partnership Baylor Coll. Medicine, Houston, 2006; past bd. mem. Houston Symphony. Mem.: AAUW, Tex. Real Estate Commn., Phi Delta Kappa. Home: 1100 Uptown Park Blvd Houston TX 77056 Personal E-mail: cckneese@aol.com.

KNEESE, KYLE CALVIN, lawyer; s. Victor Scott and Carolyn Calvin Kneese. BA, U. Tex., 1992; JD/MBA, U. Houston, 1995. Bar: Tex. 1996, U.S. Dist. Ct. (so. dist.) Tex. 2001, U.S. Mil. Cts. 1998. Atty. DeHay & Elliston, LLP, Dallas, 2002—; judge adv. USNR, JAGC, Naval Air Station, J.R.C.-Fort Worth, Tex., 2002—06; assoc. mcpl. judge City Dallas, 2006—. Lt. USN, capt. USMC, 1997—2001, lt. comdr. USNR, 2005—. Decorated Rear Adm. Hugh Howell award of Excellence USN. Mem.: Okinawa Bar Assn., Dallas Young Lawyers (vice chair 2003—), Rotary Club Internat. Avocations: running, golf, basketball. Office: DeHay & Elliston LLP 901 Main St Dallas TX 75202 Home: 3535 Gillespie 405 Dallas TX 75219 Home Phone: 214-282-0553; Office Phone: 214-210-2411. Office Fax: 214-210-2500. Personal E-mail: kckneese@hotmail.com. Business E-Mail: kkneese@dehay.com.

KNEIPPER, RICHARD KEITH, lawyer; b. Kenosha, Wis., June 18, 1943; s. Richard F. and Esther E. (Beaster) K.; m. Sherry Hayes, Dec. 16, 1977; children: Ryan Hayes, Lindsey Merrill. BS, Washington and Lee U., 1965; JD, Cornell U., 1968. Bar: Tex. 1982, U.S. Dist. Ct. (so. dist.) N.Y. 1968, U.S. Ct. Appeals (2d cir.) 1971. Atty. Chadbourne & Parke, NYC, 1968-81, Jones Day, Dallas, 1981-99; chief adminstrv. officer PHNS, Dallas, 1999—. Mem. Bd. Mgrs. Parkland Health and Hosp. Sys. Contbr. numerous articles to profl. jours. Mem. profl. adv. group Save Outdoor Sculpture!; chmn., co-founder Dallas Adopt-a-Monument; bd. dirs., mem. adv. coun. Appalachian Coll. Assn., Inc., Sch. Visual Arts, U. North Tex.; former mem. adv. com. Nat. Arts Edn. Initiative, Nat. Mus. Am. Art, Smithsonian Instn. Mem. ABA, N.Y. Bar Assn., Tex. Bar Assn., Tex. Sculpture Assn., Assn. of Bar of City of N.Y. Episcopal. Office: PHNS Inc 5400 LBJ Freeway Ste 200 Dallas TX 75240

KNEISEL, EDMUND M., lawyer; b. Atlanta, Feb. 21, 1946; s. John F. and Mary E. (Moore) K.; m. Leslie A. Jones, June 19, 1976; 1 child, Mary Kathleen. AB, Duke U., 1968; JD, U. Ga., 1974. Bar: Ga. 1974, U.S. Dist. Ct. (no. and mid. dists.) Ga., U.S. Ct. Appeals (1st, 2d, 4th, 5th, 6th and 11th cirs.), U.S. Supreme Ct. 1984. Law clk. to Hon. R.C. Freeman U.S. Dist. Ct. (no. dist.) Ga., Atlanta, 1974-76; assoc. Kilpatrick & Cody, Atlanta, 1976-82; ptnr. Kilpatrick Stockton LLP, 1982—. Mng. editor Ga. Law Rev., Athens, 1973-74; contbr. articles to profl. jours. Lt. USNR, 1968-71. Mem. ABA, Lawyers Club Atlanta, Druid Hills Golf Club. Office: Kilpatrick Stockton LLP 1100 Peachtree St NE Ste 2800 Atlanta GA 30309-4530 Office Phone: 404-815-6500. Business E-Mail: ekneisel@kilpatrickstockton.com.

KNEISER, RICHARD JOHN, accountant; b. Milw., Nov. 20, 1938; s. Frank Edward and Esther (Sobek) K.; m. Caroline Irene Stahl, Aug. 22, 1959; children: Richard J. Jr., Ronald V., Robert C. BS in Acctg., Marquette U., 1960. CPA. Staff mem. Arthur Andersen & Co., Milw., 1960-65, audit mgr., 1965-73, ptnr., 1973-94. Mem. exec. bd. Wis. Pub. Utility Inst., Madison, 1982-94; advisor acctg. practices com. U.S. Cath. Conf., 1989-2001; mem. adv. bd. Biltmore Investors Bank, 1995-97, N.Am. Clutch Corp., dir.and sec., 2003—; pres. The Carowoods Corp., 1990—. Dir. Skylight Opera Theatre, Milw., 1987-95; active Marquette U. Pres. Exec. Senate, Milw. 1987-94; trustee Village of Oconomowoc Lake, Wis., 1991-95, 97—, mem. planning commn., 1989-93, 97—, chmn. fin. com., 1991-93, pres., 2007—; bd. dirs. Oconomowoc Meml. Hosp. Found., Inc., 1996-99, treas., 1997-98, v.p., 1998-99. Mem. AICPA, Wis. Inst. CPA, Oconomowoc Lake Club (bd. dirs. 1988-97, officer, 1989-95, commodore 1994-95), Beta Gamma Sigma, Beta Alpha Psi. Avocations: antiques, fishing, tennis, golf, gardening. Home: 35920 Pabst Rd Oconomowoc WI 53066-4519 Office Phone: 262-567-6461. Business E-Mail: rkneiser@execpc.com.

KNELLER, JOHN WILLIAM, academic administrator, retired literature and language educator; b. Oldham, Eng., Oct. 15, 1916; s. John William and Margaret Ann (Truslove) K.; m. Alice Bowerman Hart, Apr. 30, 1943; 1 dau., Linda Hart. AB, Clark U., 1938, LittD, 1970; AM, Yale U., 1948, PhD, 1950; French Govt. and Fulbright fellow, U. Paris, France, 1949-50. Asst. in instrn. Yale U., 1947-49; instr. French Oberlin Coll., 1950-52, asst. prof., 1952-55, assoc. prof., 1955-59, prof. French, 1959-65, chmn. dept. Romance langs., 1958-65, dean Coll. Arts and Scis., 1967-68, provost, 1965-69; pres. Bklyn. Coll., CUNY, 1969-79, pres. emeritus, 1979—. Univ. prof. humanities and arts Hunter Coll. and Grad. Ctr., CUNY, 1979-95, prof. emeritus, 1995—; mng. editor French Rev., 1962-65, editor-in-chief, 1965-68; co-chair bd. dirs. Henri Peyre Inst. for the Humanities, 1980-2001; cons. NEH; chmn. subcom. on enrollment goals and projections N.Y. State Edn.; Commr.'s Adv. Coun. on Higher Edn., Adv. Coun. on Higher Edn. Co-author: Initiation au francais, 1963, Introduction a la poesie francaise, 1962; assoc. editor Yale French Studies, 1948-50, gen. editor, Henri Peyre: His Life in Letters, 2005; contbr. articles to jours. in field. Bd. dirs. Independence Savs. Bank, 1973-93. Sgt. AUS, 1942-46. Decorated comdr. Ordre des Palmes Académiques (France). Mem. Am. Assn. Tchrs. French (exec. council 1962-68), Modern Lang. Assn. (exec. council 1965-69), Yale Grad. Sch. Assn. (exec. com. 1967, 71), Bklyn. C. of C. (dir.), Kappa Delta Pi (hon.), Alpha Sigma Lambda (hon.) Clubs: Century (N.Y.C.), Yale (N.Y.C.), Southport Racquet. Personal E-mail: jkneller@optonline.net.

KNELLER, MICHAEL K., transportation services executive; m. Andrea DeFlorio. BA, Yale U., 1996; JD, Stanford U., 2000. V.p., gen. counsel, sec. Landstar Sys. Inc., Jacksonville, Fla., 2005—. Mem.: ABA, Fla. Bar Assn., NY State Bar Assn. Office: Landstar Sys Inc 13410 Sutton Pk Dr S Jacksonville FL 32224 Office Phone: 904-398-9400. Office Fax: 904-306-2539.

KNEPP, CHRISTOPHER A., lawyer; b. Balt., Sept. 22, 1954; BA, U. N.C., 1976; JD cum laude, Harvard U., 1979. Bar: Tex. 1979, U.S. Supreme Ct. 1984. Mem. Hughes & Luce LLP, Austin, Tex.; ptnr. Vinson & Elkins LLP, Austin, Tex. Mem. ABA, State Bar Tex., Phi Beta Kappa. Office: Vinson & Elkins LLP Ste 100 2801 Via Fortuna Austin TX 78746 Office Phone: 512-542-8437. E-mail: cknepp@velaw.com.

KNEPPER, GEORGE W., historian, educator; b. Akron, Ohio, Jan. 15, 1926; s. George W. and Grace (Darling) K.; m. Phyllis Watkins, Aug. 21, 1949; children: Susan Lynne, John Arthur. BA, U. Akron, 1948; MA, U. Mich., 1950, PhD, 1954. Mem. faculty U. Akron, 1948-49, 54-92, assoc. prof. history, head dept., 1959-62; dean U. Akron (Coll. Liberal Arts), 1962-67, prof. history, 1964-88, disting. prof. history, 1988-92. Author: New Lamps for Old, One Hundred Years of Urban Higher Education at the University of Akron, 1970, An Ohio Portrait, 1976, Akron: City at the Summit, 1981, Ohio and Its People, 1989, Summit's Glory: Sketches of Buchtel Coll. and the University of Akron, 1990, Ohio Lands Book, 2002; editor: Travels in the Southland; The Journal of Lucius Verus Biérce 1822-23, 1966. Served to ensign USNR, 1943-46. Fulbright fellow U. London, Eng., 1953-54 Mem. Am., So. hist. assns., Orgn. Am. Historians, Ohio Acad. History, Omicron Delta Kappa, Alpha Tau Omega, Phi Alpha Theta, Alpha Sigma Lambda. Office: Univ Akron Coll Liberal Arts Dept History Akron OH 44325-0001 Home: 1199 Inverness Ln Stow OH 44224

KNERLY, STEPHEN JOHN, JR., lawyer; b. Lakewood, Ohio, Dec. 15, 1949; s. Stephen John Sr. and Mary Louise (Johnson) K.; m. Catherine Arion de Bravura; 1 child, Alexandra M. C. AB summa cum laude, Bowdoin Coll., 1972; AM, Fletcher Sch. Law & Diplomacy, 1973; JD, Case Western Res. U., 1976. Bar: Ohio 1976. Law clk. Stephen J. Knerly and Assocs., Cleve., 1973-74, Hahn, Loeser, Freedheim, Dean et al, Cleve., 1975-76, assoc., 1976-83; ptnr. Hahn, Loeser & Parks, Cleve., 1984—; CEO, mng. ptnr. Hahn, Loeser & Parks, LLP, Cleve., 1993—. James Bowdoin scholar Bowdoin Coll., 1972; named Consul Honoraire de France, Cleve. Mem. French-Am. C. of C. (trustee), Am. Red Cross, Phi Beta Kappa. Home: 10390 Mitchells Mill Rd Chardon OH 44024-8613 Office: Hahn Loeser & Parks LLP 200 Public Sq Ste 3300 Cleveland OH 44114-2301

KNERR, ANTHONY DAVID, financial consultant; b. Bellefonte, Pa., Dec. 7, 1938; s. Henry William Knerr and Catherine Margaret Conner; m. Katrina Ely Carter, June 22, 1963 (div. July 1974); children: Christopher Hamilton, Theodore Gabriel, Sidonie Nagoly; m. Susanne E. Kastler, Apr. 20, 2002. BA magna cum laude, Yale U., 1960, MA cum laude, 1964; PhD, NYU, 1978. Tchr. Milton (Mass.) Acad., 1961-63; program officer Internat. Exchange Program, NYC, 1965-67; assoc., cons. Booz Allen & Hamilton, NYC, 1967-70; vice chancellor for budget and planning CUNY, NYC, 1970-77; spl. asst. to acting pres. Yale U., New Haven, 1977-78; exec. v.p. fin., treas. Columbia U., NYC, 1978-88; pres. Publ. Group Inc., NYC, 1988-90; mng. dir. Anthony Knerr & Assocs., NYC, 1990—. Lectr. Columbia U., N.Y.C., 1986-88; pres. emeritus Caribbean Conservation Corp., 2001—; bd. dirs. Del. Mut. Funds. Author: Shelley's Adonais: A Critical Edition, 1984. Bd. dirs. N.Y. Soc. Libr., 1983—,; pres. emeritus United Neighborhood Houses, 1994—; vice chmn. Humanity in Action, 1997—. Mem. The Century Assn., Keats-Shelley Assn. (bd. dirs. 1983—), Grolier Club, Phi Beta Kappa. Office: Anthony Knerr & Assocs 295 Madison Ave Ste 400 New York NY 10017

KNESEK, MICHAEL JOHN, energy executive; b. Corpus Christi, Tex., July 11, 1954; s. Johnny Louis and Peggy Lou (Rektorik) K.; m. Ellen Clarissa Waters, June 19, 1976; children: Brian Michael, Kristin Marie. CPA Tex. Acctg. supr. Union Tex. Petroleum Corp., Houston, 1976-81; acctg. mgr. to contr. Enterprise Cos., Inc., Houston, 1981—90, v.p., contr., 1990; v.p., contr., prin. acctg. officer Enterprise Products GP and EPCO, Houston, 2000—05, sr. v.p., contr., prin. acctg. officer, 2005—, Enterprise GP Holdings LP, Houston, 2005—. Freelance acct., Houston, 1986. Mem. AICPA, Tex. Soc. CPAs. Republican. Lutheran. Avocations: water-skiing, skiing, jogging, racquetball. Office: Enterprise GP Holdings LP PO Box 4323 Houston TX 77210-4323 Office Phone: 713-381-6500.*

KNESEL, ERNEST ARTHUR, JR., health facility administrator, chemicals executive; b. New Orleans, Dec. 11, 1945; s. Ernest Arthur and Catherine Charlotte (Maier) K.; m. Lavina Lynn Menge, June 2, 1968; children: Eric Ernest, Tami Lynn, Bradley William. Student, Armstrong Coll., 1963—64; BS, Fairleigh Dickinson U., 1968, MS, 1970. Cert. clin. chemist. Technologist Am. Biol. Control Lab., Tenefly, NJ, 1966—68; sr. technologist Englewood Hosp., NJ, 1968—69; founder, v.p. Biomed. Reference Labs., Inc., Burlington, NC, 1969—82; sr. v.p. Roche Biomed. Labs., Inc., Burlington, 1982—95; pres., founder Roche Image Analysis Sys., Inc., Elon College, NC, 1989—96; exec. v.p., founder Autocyte, Inc., Elon College, 1996—99; v.p., founder TriPath Imaging, 1999—2000; cons. True North Group, 2000—01; founder, pres. Select Diagnostics Inc.,

2001—; co-founder, pres. Synermed Select Ptnrs., Inc., 2003—. Founder, mgr. CellSolutions LLC. Inventor serum filter/dispenser vial, automated aliquoting system, cyto-rich automated cytology preparation system and simultaneous machine and human interactive cytology evaluation system. Mem. Am. Assn. Clin. Chemistry, Am. Soc. Clin. Pathologists (assoc.). Roman Catholic. Avocation: magic. Office: Select Diagnostics Inc 1100 Revolution Mill Dr # 1 Greensboro NC 27405

KNETTER, MICHAEL MARK, dean; b. Rhinelander, Wis., Apr. 8, 1960; s. Edmund David and Margaret Helen Knetter; m. Karen Joy Goedewaagen, July 31, 1988; children: Maxine, Lillian. BA in math and economics, U. Wis., Eau Claire, 1983; PhD, Stanford U., 1988. Asst. prof. economics Dartmouth Coll., Hanover, NH, 1988—94, assoc. prof., vice chair dept. economics, 1994—97; assoc. dean MBA program, prof. internat. economics Dartmouth Coll. Tuck Sch. Bus., 1997—2002; dean U. Wis. Sch. Bus., Madison, 2002—, prof. fin., investment, and banking, 2002—. Rsch assoc. Nat. Bur. Econ. Rsch., 1992-; trustee Lehman Bros./First Trust Income Opportunity Fund, Lehman Bros. Liquid Assets trust; former sr. staff economist Pres.' Coun. Econ. Advisors for George H.W. Bush and Bill Clinton. Rsch. fellow German Marshall Fund, 1991; Pub. Policy grantee Lynde and Harry Bradley Found., 1991. Mem. Am. Econ. Assn. Office: Univ Wis School of Business 5110 Grainger Hall 975 University Ave Madison WI 53706 Office Phone: 608-262-1758. Office Fax: 608-265-3121. Business E-Mail: mknetter@bus.wisc.edu.*

KNEUER, JOHN M.R., federal agency administrator; b. 1968; BA, JD, Cath. U. Am. Bar: DC. Atty. advisor comml. wireless divsn. wireless telecomm. bur. FCC, 1996—97; dir. govt. rels. Indsl. Telecomm. Assn., 1997—98; sr. assoc. DLA Piper Rudnick, LLP; dep. asst. sec. for comm. & info. US Dept. Commerce, 2004—05, acting asst. sec. for comm. & info., 2006, asst. sec., 2006—; counselor to asst. sec. Nat. Telecom. & Info. Adminstrn., 2003—04, dep. adminstr., 2004—05, adminstr., 2006—. Office: US Dept Commerce Herbert Clark Hoover Bldg 1401 Constitution Ave NW Rm 4898 Washington DC 20230 Office Phone: 202-482-1840. Office Fax: 202-501-0536.*

KNICKEL, CARIN S., oil industry executive; b. Powell, Wyo. BA in Mktg. and Stats., U. Colo.; M.Mgmt., MIT. Mktg. account mgr. Conoco-Phillips, 1979—87, area dir. light oil sales product supply and trading, 1987, gen. mgr. bus. develop. for refining and mktg. in Europe London, gen. mgr. refining, mktg., and transp., pres. specialty bus. divsn., 2001—03, v.p. human resources Houston, 2003—. Chmn. rodeo run com. ConocoPhillips; bd. dirs. Colo. Spl. Olympics. Office: ConocoPhillips 600 N Dairy Ashford Rd Houston TX 77079*

KNICKERBOCKER, ROBERT PLATT, JR., lawyer, consultant; b. Hartford, Conn., Sept. 23, 1944; s. Robert P. and Audrey Jane (Stempel) K.; m. Kathleen A. Sakal (div. May 1985); children: Sarah, Abigail, Jonathan; m. Barbara Denise Whinnem, Oct. 3, 1987. BA, Cornell U., 1966; JD, U. Conn., 1969. Bar: Conn. 1969, US Dist. Ct. Conn. 1969, US Ct. Appeals, (2d cir.), Fla., 2004. Law clk. to presiding justice Conn. Supreme Ct., Hartford, 1968-69; ptnr. Day, Berry & Howard, Hartford, 1969—2005, legal cons., 2006—. Mem. State Implementation Plan Regulation Adv. Commn., 1979-90; cons. in field. Chmn. Town Plan and Zoning Commn., Glastonbury, Conn., 1975-79, Glastonbury Bd. Edn., 1982-86. Mem. ABA, Fla. Bar Assn. Republican. Episcopalian. Office: 4919 Sabal Lake Cir Sarasota FL 34238 Office Phone: 941-923-7221. Business E-Mail: knicker2@verizon.net.

KNICKERBOCKER, VICKY ANN, academic administrator; b. Duluth, Minn., Feb. 1, 1956; d. Vernon John Knickerbocker and Elma Mae Knicherbocker. BA in Sociology and Criminology, U. Minn., Duluth, 1978; MSW, U. Minn., Mpls., 1991; postgrad., Hamline U., St. Cloud State U., U. Minn. Youth agt. 4-H, 1978—79; fin. worker, 1980—83; accounting clerk, 1983—86; adj. instr. Ctrl. Lakes Coll., Brainerd, Minn., 1992—2002; instr. St. Cloud State U., 1997—99, 2002; outreach coord. Ctr. Holocaust and Genocide Studies, U. Minn., Mpls., 2002—; adj. instr. sociology Inver Hills CC, Inver Grove Heights, Minn., 2004—07, instr., human svcs. and sociology, 2007—. Instr. SW State U., Marshall, Minn., 1998—2000; tchr. participant Summer Inst. Yad Vashem, Jerusalem, 2001; tchr. participant Summer Seminar on Holocaust and genocide studies Jewish Labor Com., Poland and Czech Republic, 2005. Recipient state award for social change agt. in edn., AAUW, 2000; Grad. Recruitment scholar, U. Minn., Duluth, 1988, Will Dodge Cmty. Orgn. scholar, 1990, Ednl. scholar, AAUW, 1997. Mem.: AAUW, Am. Legion Aux., Phi Kappa Phi. Home: 15534 Crocus Ln Eden Prairie MN 55347

KNICKREHM, GLENN ALLEN, management executive; b. LA, Mar. 27, 1948; s. Allen F. and Evelyn Knickrehm. BA magna cum laude, Occidental Coll., 1971; BS, Columbia U., 1971, MBA, 1973. Analyst Exxon Co., NYC and L.A., 1971-72; cons. Boston Cons. Group, Boston and Munich, 1973-77, mgr. Boston, 1977-83; pres., chmn. Our Market Supermarket, Inc., 1980-81; pres. Bay Resource Corp., 1983—2002. Chmn. Apex Internat. Alloys, Inc., 1986-89; pres. Mashamoquet Holdings, Inc., 1995—; adv. Beach Brook Prodns., 1995—; pres. Constellation Prodns., Inc., 1996—; dir. Scuola il Bisonte, Florence, Italy, 1998—; bd. dirs. Am. Repertory Theatre, Mus. Fine Arts, New Eng. Conservatory; trustee Westfield Ctr. for Early Keyboard Studies, 1999—. Dir. New Eng. Theater Guild, Inc., 1985-89, Samuel Bronfman fellow, 1972; pres. Constellation Charitable Found., 2001--. Mem. Boston Anthenaeum, Columbia U. Faculty Club, Phi Beta Kappa, Tau Beta Pi, Beta Gamma Sigma, Sigma Pi Sigma, Pi Mu Epsilon, Kappa Mu Epsilon. Office: Constellation Productions Inc 161 First St Cambridge MA 02142 Office Phone: 617-939-1900.

KNIESNER, JOHN THOMAS, librarian; b. Berea, Ohio, Dec. 19, 1949; s. Albert Henry and Elizabeth (Leonard) K.; m. Patti-Jo Samo, Sept. 8, 1979; children: Janet Deborah, Joseph David. BA, Kent State U., 1971; MLS, U. Mich., 1972. Profl. libr. I Columbus (Ohio) Met. Libr., 1972-76, profl. libr. II, 1977-78, profl. libr. III, 1979-85; dir. Bellaire (Ohio) Pub. Libr., 1986—. Computer cons. Toledo-Lucas County Pub. Libr., Ohio, 1979. Contbr. articles to jours. Mem. steering com. Always a River, 1991; water safety instr. ARC, Columbus and Bellaire, 1984-04. Recipient Civitan award PTA, Bellaire, 1992, 97, plaque for saving lives, Am. Red Cross, Wheeling, W.Va., 1987. Mem. Ohio Libr. Coun. (facilitator 1981-82, 92), S.E. Ohio Libr. Orgn. (pres. 1988-89, 2000-2001, chair compact disc com. 1990-98), Pi Sigma Alpha. Republican. Roman Catholic. Avocations: ice skating, swimming, reading, theater. Office: Bellaire Pub Libr 330 32nd St Bellaire OH 43906-1571 Home Phone: 740-676-4620; Office Phone: 740-676-9421. Personal E-mail: jkniesner@hotmail.com.

KNIFFEL, LEONARD JOHN, editor, librarian; b. Mt. Clemens, Mich., Aug. 25, 1947; s. John and Lucia Helen (Brodacki) K.; m. Judith Worthen, Aug. 22, 1969 (div. Apr. 1977). Ba, Oakland U., 1970; MA, Wayne State U., 1972, MLS, 1975. Libr. Detroit Pub. Libr., 1971-88; editor Am. Librs. Mag. Am. Libr. Assn., Chgo., 1988—. Co-founder, bd. dirs. Poetry Resource Ctr. Mich., 1980-85; photographer, freelance writer. Publisher Fallen Angel Press, 1975-82; editor PRC Newsletter, 1980-85. Mem. Acad. Am. Poets, Gerber/Hart Libr. Archives (bd. dirs. 1994-95), Polish Inst. Arts & Scis. Democrat. Roman Catholic. Avocation: travel. Home: 2743 N Greenview Ave Chicago IL 60614-1117 Office: Am Libr Assn 50 E Huron St Chicago IL 60611-5295

KNIFFEN, DONALD AVERY, astrophysicist, educator, researcher; b. Kalamazoo, Mich., Apr. 27, 1933; s. Frederick Bowerman and Eva Virginia (Arp) Kniffen; m. Janis Kay Nesom, June 14, 1952; children: Karyol Kniffen Poole, Donald Avery Jr., Kimberly Kniffen Giesbrecht. BS magna cum laude, La. State U., 1959; AM, Washington U., St. Louis, 1960; PhD, Cath. U. Am., 1967. Astrophysicist Goddard Space Flight Ctr., Greenbelt, Md., 1960-91; lectr. physics U. Md., College Park, 1978-87; project scientist Compton Gamma Ray Obs., 1979-91; William W. Elliott prof., chmn. dept. physics and astronomy Hampden-Sydney Coll., Va., 1991-2001; rsch. prof. George Mason U., 2002—05; sr. rsch. scientist NASA Hdqrs., 2005—, USRA program mgr., 2006—. Vis. scientist NASA/USRA, Greenbelt, 1997—98; astrophysics cons. NASA/HSTX, NASA/USRA, 1991—98; program scientist NASA Hdqrs., 1999—2005; sr. rsch. scientist NASA/USRA, 2005—; program dir. USRA, 2006—. Contbr. articles to profl. jours. Served with USN, 1952-56. Recipient Medal for Outstanding Leadership NASA, 1992, Laurel award Space/Missiles, Aviation Week & Space Tech., 1991. Fellow Royal Astron. Soc.; mem. AAUP, Am. Phys. Soc., Am. astron. Soc., Internat. Astron. Union, Sigma Xi. Democrat. Avocations: travel, reading, gardening. Home: 2814 Andy Ct Crofton MD 21114-3157 Office: Code 661 NASA Goddard Space Flight Ctr Greenbelt MD 20771-0001 Personal E-mail: dkniffen1@verizon.net. Business E-Mail: dkniffen1@milkyway.gsfc.nasa.gov.

KNIFFIN, PAULA SICHEL, insurance sales executive; b. NYC, Oct. 2, 1941; d. Harold M. and Edith (Sachnoff) Sichel; m. Richrd G. Kniffin, Aug. 3, 1963; children: Douglas, Kelly. BA, Bucknell U., 1963. CLU, cert. fin. planner. Tchr. New Cumberland (Pa.) Jr. High Sch., 1963-64, Meadowbrook Jr. HS, East Meadow, NY, 1964—67; real estate salesperson Claire Sobel Real Estate, Syosset, N.Y., 1979-80; sales force recruiter Mut. of N.Y. Life Ins. Co., Jericho, 1981-82; head of life and health ins. dept., employee benefit cons. The Viking Agy., Inc., Syosset, N.Y., 1983—. Mem. Soc. Fin. Svc. Profls., Fin. Planning Assn., Women Life Underwriters Conf. (pres. 1988-89), Nat. Assn. Ins. and Fin. Advisors (bd. dirs. 1988-89), Nat. Assn. Ins. and Fin. Advisors, Ladies Golf Com. (chair 1990-93), Nassau Country Club, Mayacoo Lakes Country Club. Republican. Avocations: golf, tennis, bridge, reading. Office: The Viking Agy 117 Oak Dr Syosset NY 11791-4625 Office Phone: 516-496-7711. E-mail: paula@vikingagency.com.

KNIGHT, ATHELIA WILHELMENIA, journalist; b. Portsmouth, Va., Oct. 15, 1950; d. Daniel Dennis and Adell Virginia (Savage) K. BA with honors in English, Norfolk State Coll., 1973; MA with honors in Journalism, Ohio State U., 1974. Cert. tchr. Va. Aide D.C. Coop. Extension Service, 1969-72; sub. tchr. Portsmouth Pub. Schs., 1973; reporter Virginian Pilot, Norfolk, 1973, Chgo. Tribune, 1974; met. desk reporter Washington Post, 1975-81, investigative reporter, 1981-94, sports writer, 1994-2000; asst. dir. Washington Post Young Journalists, 2000—03, dir., 2003; adj. prof. Georgetown U., 2002—. Vis. prof. journalism Hampton U., 2001. Mem. Herb Block Found. Recipient Mark Twain award, 1982, 87, Front Page award Washington-Balt. Newspaper Guild, 1982, Nat. award for edn. Edn. Writers Assn., 1987, Pub. Svc. award Md.-Del.-D.C. Press Assn., 1990, 93, 1st Pl. award for spot news, 1997; Ohio State U. fellow, 1974, Nieman fellow Harvard U., 1985-86. Maynard Mgmt. at the Kellogg Sch. of Mgmt. N.W. U., 2003. Mem.: Investigative Reporters and Editors, Nat. Assn. Black Journalists. Methodist. Office: Washington Post 1150 15th St NW Washington DC 20071-0002

KNIGHT, BILLY (WILLIAM R. KNIGHT), professional sports team executive; b. Braddock, Pa., June 9, 1952; m. Danita Edwards; children: Olivia, Erika. Grad., U. Pitts. Draft pick LA Lakers, 1974; player Ind. Pacers, 1974—77, 1979—83, positions up to sr. v.p. basketball ops.; player Buffalo Braves, 1977—78, Boston Celtics, 1978—79, Kans. City Kings, 1983—84, San Antonio Spurs, 1984—85; gen. mgr. Vancouver/Memphis Grizzlies, 2000—01; dir. basketball ops. Atlanta Hawks, 2002—03, exec. v.p., gen. mgr., 2003—. Named to Am. Basketball Assn. All-Rookie Team, 1975, Am. Basketball Assn. All-Star Team, 1976, NBA All-Star Team, 1977. Office: Atlanta Hawks Centennial Tower 101 Marietta St NW Ste 1900 Atlanta GA 30303*

KNIGHT, BOBBY (ROBERT MONTGOMERY KNIGHT), men's college basketball coach; b. Massillon, Ohio, Oct. 25, 1940; s. Carroll and Hazel (Henthorne) K.; m. Nancy Lou Knight, Apr. 17, 1963 (div. 1985); m. Karen Edgar, 1988. BS, Ohio State U., 1962. Asst. coach Cuyahoga Falls (Ohio) High Sch., 1962-63; freshman coach U.S. Mil. Acad., West Point, NY, 1963-65, head basketball coach, 1965-71, Ind. U., Bloomington, 1971-2000, Tex. Tech. U., Lubbock, 2001—. Speaker clinics in field; condr. tng. clinics for coaches and players. Performer: (reality show) Knight School, 2006, (films) Hoop Dreams, 1994, Blue Chips, 1994, Anger Management, 2003; co-author (with Bob Hammel): Knight: My Story, 2002. Trustee Naismith Meml. Basketball Hall of Fame. Served US Army. Recipient Big Ten Coach-of-Year award, 1973, 1975, 1976, 1981, 1989, Naismith Outstanding Contbn. to Basketball award, 2007; named unanimously Nat. Coach of Year, 1975, 1976, 1987, 1989, Nat. Coach of Yr. AP and Basketball Weekly; recipient appreciation plaque from team, 1979; elected to Basketball Hall of Fame, 1991. Mem.: Nat. Assn. Basketball Coaches (bd. dirs.). Methodist. Achievements include coaching US Pan-Am. team to gold medal, 1979; coaching US team to gold medal in 1984 Olympics; coached Ind. U. to NCAA Championship, 1976, 81, 87; college basketball's winningest active coach (one of only 12 NCAA coaches to have won 700 or more games); holds NCAA record for most wins among Men's Division I college basketball coaches, 2007. Office: Tex Tech U Mens Basketball United Spirit Ctr Indiana Ave Lubbock TX 79409*

KNIGHT, BRUCE IRVING, federal agency administrator; b. Gann Valley, SD; Attended, SD State U. Served on staff of Senate Majority Leader Bob Dole; legis. asst. Nat. Assn. Wheat Growers; v.p. pub. policy Nat. Corn Growers Assn.; CEO Nat. Resources Conservation Svc., 2002—06; under sec. for mktg. and regulatory programs USDA, 2006—, chmn. agrl. air quality task force. Bd. dirs. Commodity Credit Corp., 2006—. Office: USDA 1400 Independence Ave SW Washington DC 20250

KNIGHT, CHRISTOPHER L., medical educator; MD, U. Wash., Seattle, 1996. Diplomate Am. Bd. Internal Medicine, 1999. Asst. prof. medicine U. Wash., 2004—. Fellow: ACP; mem.: Soc. Gen. Internal Medicine. Office: U Wash 4245 Roosevelt Way NE Seattle WA 98105 Office Phone: 206-598-3408.

KNIGHT, CHRISTOPHER NICHOLS, lawyer; b. New Haven, Sept. 7, 1946; s. Douglas Maitland and Grace Wallace (Nichols) K.; m. Emily Byrn Turner, Oct. 20, 1979; children: Ethan Douglas, Benjamin Walker Lester, Christopher N. Jr. BA, Yale U., 1968; JD, Duke U., 1971. Bar: Wis. 1971, U.S. Dist. Ct. (ea. dist.) Wis. 1973, U.S. Ct. Appeals (7th cir.) 1977, N.C. 1979, U.S. Dist. Ct. (mid. dist.) N.C. 1979, Minn., 1980, U.S. Supreme Ct. 1980, U.S. Ct. Appeals (4th, 8th cirs.) 1980, U.S. Dist. Ct. Minn. 1980, Ill. 1982, N.Y., 1996. Assoc. Quarles & Brady, Milw., 1971-78, ptnr., 1978-79, Smith & Moore LLP, Greensboro, NC, 1979—80, Kutak Rock, Mpls., 1980-82, Isham Lincoln & Beale, Chgo., 1982-88, Hopkins & Sutter, Chgo., 1988-2001, Foley & Lardner LLP, Chgo., 2001—, mng. ptnr., 2003—04. Bd. dirs. Lyric Opera Chgo., 2003—06, Chgo. Humanities Festival, 2005—, vice chmn., 2006—; bd. trustees Writers' Theatre, 2004—, pres., 2006—. Mem. ABA, Ill. State Bar Assn., Minn. State Bar Assn., NY State Bar Assn., NC State Bar Assn., State Bar Wis., Am. Bar Found., Nat. Assn. Bond Lawyers, Chicagoland C. of C. (bd. dirs. 2004-07), Econ. Club of Chgo. Congregationalist. Office: Foley & Lardner LLP Ste 2800 321 N Clark St Chicago IL 60610-4764 Office Phone: 312-832-4515. E-mail: cknight@foley.com.

KNIGHT, CRANSTON S., history professor; b. Chgo., Sept. 10, 1950; m. J. Dolores Anderson, Aug. 5, 1978; children: Jason J., Illya A., Ashiyrah H. Ramirez-Knight de Torres. BA, So. Ill. U.; MA, Northeastern Ill. U., Chgo., 1990; PhD, Loyola U., Chgo., 2005. Adj. prof. history Loyola U., Chgo., 1992—95; prof. history Columbia Coll., Chgo., 2000—02, Chgo. City Colls., 2001—. Cons. Chgo. Pub. Schs., 1992—93; mem. coun. ethics and internat. affairs Carnegie. Author: (poetry) La Brigada; Spain 1936-1939, On the Borders of Hiroshima: I heard a Rumor of War, In the Garden of the Beast: Vietnam Cries A Love Song, Freedom Song; editor: (anthology) Tour of Duty: Vietnam in the Words of Those Who Were There. Assoc. mem. Pritzer Mil. Libr.; organizer Orgn. of N.E., Chgo., 1998—2003. Recipient Creative Arts award, Benjamin Henry Matchett Found. for Creative Arts, 1989, Humanities and Letters award, U. Ill., 1997, Edn. Excellence award, Henry Horner Alumni and Assocs.: Youth Acad., 1999; Writers Completion grant, Ill. Arts Coun., 1996, 1998. Mem.: Internat. Polit. Sci. Assn., Acad. Political Sci., Assn. Asian Studies, Chgo. Coun. Fgn. Rels., Phi Beta Delta Honor Soc. Internat. Scholars. Roman Catholic. Avocations: writing, travel, movies, photography. Home: 1300 W Hood Chicago IL 60660 Office: Chgo City Colls 1900 W Van Buren Chicago IL 60612 Personal E-mail: savingnet2@yahoo.com. Business E-Mail: cknight@ccc.edu.

KNIGHT, DOUGLAS A., mechanical engineer; b. Athol, Mass., Nov. 1, 1961; s. Robert G. Knight and Janet M. Wilson-Knight; m. Reneé M. Caduie, Dec. 23, 1999; 1 child, Tess A. B, Northeastern U., Boston, 1986. Cert. engring. cons. Knight Engring., Bolton, Mass., 1996—2006; project mgr. Xcellerex, Marlborough, Mass., 2006—. Singer, songwriter: various songs. Republican. Roman Catholic. Achievements include design of Advanced BioPharmaceutical Processes. Home: 307 Harvard Rd Bolton MA 01740 Office: Xcellerex 170 Locke Dr Marlborough MA 01752 Home Phone: 978-779-6775; Office Phone: 508-480-9235 238. Personal E-mail: knightmogul@msn.com. Business E-Mail: dknight@xcellerex.com.

KNIGHT, EDWARD R., judge, psychologist, law educator; b. Milw., Oct. 5, 1917; s. Harry and Lillian (Bachman) K.; m. Judith A. Weidberg, July 6, 1941; 1 child, Barbara Jane. AB, U. Wis., 1940, JD, 1941; AM, NYU, 1942, PhD, 1943. Bar: Wis. 1941, N.J. 1976; diplomate Am. Bd. Profl. Psychology. Master Oxford Acad., Pleasantville, NJ, 1941, psychologist, 1942, head psychologist, 1943, asst. headmaster, 1945-47, headmaster, 1947-73, emeritus, 1973—. U.S. magistrate judge, 1976—; judge Mcpl. Ct., Margate City, N.J., 1976-81; ptnr. Fox, Rothschild, Atlantic City, N.J., 1976—; dir. First Fidelity Bank, 1950-90. Pres., bd. govs. Atlantic City Med. Ctr., 1973-87, chmn. emeritus, 1987—; chmn. Master Planning Bd., Egg Harbor Twp., N.J., 1961-73; chmn. Atlantic County (N.J.) Charter Study Commn., 1973-74. Author: Self-Discipline and Academic Failure; mem. editl. bd. Parental Delinquency; contbr. articles on edn. and psychology to profl. jours. Capt., USAAF, 1943-45; personnel com., personnel div. ATSC, Wright Field. Named Trustee of Century, Atlantic City Med. Ctr., 1998. Fellow APA (sch. psychologists div.); mem. Ea. N.J. psychol. assns., Nat. Assn. Ind. Schs., N.J. Assn. Sch. Psychologists, Interam. Soc. Psychology, Boarding Sch. Headmasters Assn. Mid. States (pres. 1966-67), Wis. Alumni Assn., U. Wis. Mem. Union (life), Atlanticare Health Sys. (vice-chmn. bd.), Phi Delta Kappa, Kappa Delta Pi. Home: 7 N Thurlow Ave Margate City NJ 08402-1213 Office: US Dist Ct 1301 Atlantic Ave Fl 3 Atlantic City NJ 08401-7207

KNIGHT, ERIC A., aerospace executive, entrepreneur, inventor; V.p., assoc. creative dir., sr. copywriter Mintz & Hoke, Inc.; founder, pres. The Imagination Ctr.; v.p., dir. mktg. Brainbug/Outrider; founder, pres. Remarkable Technologies, Inc., 1994—; CEO UP Aerospace, Inc., Conn., 2004—. Spkr. in field; provided creative services, branding and mktg. guidance for a wide range of major well-known businesses. Guest appearance Late Night with David Letterman. 37 inventions and patents/patents pending in field; selected as a top American inventor by both US Patent and Trademark Office and Intellectual Property Owners for "Para-Shirt" invention; one of the early pioneers in online marketing and e-commerce; created The Download America BBS, a dial-up bulletin board system in 1985; avionics team leader for The Civilian Space eXploration Team, which built and launched the first amateur rocket into space in 5/2004; UP Aerospace, Incorporated is the world's premier supplier of low cost space-access services. The company provides the general public, private enterprise and educational institutions with round trip space flights for any kind of payload.

KNIGHT, FRANKLIN W., historian, educator; b. Mile Gully, Manchester, Jamaica, Jan. 10, 1942; came to U.S., 1964; s. Willis Jefferson and Irick May (Sanderson) K.; m. Ingeborg Bauer, June 11, 1965; children: Michael, Brian, Nadine. BA with honors, U. West Indies, Jamaica, 1964; MA, U. Wis., 1965, PhD, 1969. From asst. to assoc. prof. SUNY, Stony Brook, 1968-73; assoc. prof. Johns Hopkins U., Balt., 1973-77, prof., 1977-91, Stulman prof. History, 1991—, dir. Latin Am. Studies Program, 1992-95; v.p. Latin Am. Studies Assn., 1997-98; pres., 1998-00. Author: Slave Society in Cuba, 1970 (Black Acad. award 1971), The Caribbean, 1990; co-editor: The Modern Caribbean, 1989, Atlantic Port Cities, 1991; editor: Caribbean Slave Societies, 1997. Active Md. Quincentenary Com., 1992. Named Disting. Grad. U. West Indies, Jamaica, 1992. Mem. The Hist. Soc. (pres. 2004—), Latin Am. Studies Assn., Assn. Caribbean Historians. Office: Johns Hopkins U 3400 N Charles St Baltimore MD 21218-2680 Office Phone: 410-516-7591. Business E-Mail: fknight@jhu.edu.

KNIGHT, GARY, lawyer, writer, educator; b. St. Joseph, Mo., Dec. 8, 1939; s. Herbert S. and Iris (Crawford) K.; m. Rebecca Emelie Forrester, Nov. 24, 1962; children: Kevin Crawford, David Forrester, Jonathan Gary. Student, Westminster Coll., 1957-59; AB in Polit. Sci., Stanford U., 1961; JD, So. Meth. U., 1964. Bar: Calif. 1965. Assoc. Nossaman, Thompson, Waters and Moss, LA, 1964-68; mem. faculty La. State U. Law Center, Baton Rouge, 1968-85, assoc. prof., 1971-75, prof. law, 1975-85, Campanile prof. marine resources law, 1971-85; owner Jonathan Pub. Co., 1981—. Adv. com. on law of sea Nat. Security Council Inter-Agy. Law of Sea Group, 1972-81; cons. CIA, 1977-85; mem. Gulf of Mex. Fishery Mgmt. Coun., 1981-84. Author: The Future of International Fisheries Management, 1975, Managing the Sea's Living Resources, 1977, The International Law of the Sea: Cases, Documents and Readings, 1991, Marine Fisheries Management Reporter, 1981-94; assoc. editor: Ocean Development and International Law: A Jour. of Marine Affairs, 1972-85. Trustee Wimberley Village Libr. Dist., 2005—, pres., 2007—; bd. dirs. Wimberley Edn. Found., 2006, pres., 2007—. Mem. ABA (com. on law of sea 1971-80, com. marine resources 1967-71), Am. Soc. Internat. Law (bd. rev. and devel. 1975-80, panel on law of sea 1972-80), Internat. Law Assn. (com. on law of sea 1974-81), Law of Sea Inst. (exec. bd. 1975-81), Order of Coif, Phi Alpha Delta, Omicron Delta Kappa, Beta Theta Pi.

KNIGHT, GLADYS (GLADYS MARIA KNIGHT), singer; b. Atlanta, May 28, 1944; d. Merald and Elizabeth (Woods) Knight, Sr.; m. James Newman, June 1961 (div. 1974); children: Kenya Newman, James Newman III; m. Barry Hankerson, Oct. 1974; 1 child, Shanga Hankerson; m. William McDowell, Apr. 2001. Grad. coll.; degree (hon.), Shaw U. Author: lyrics Way Back Home, others; first pub. recital, Mt. Mariah Bapt. Ch., Atlanta, 1948; toured with Morris Brown Choir, 1950-53, recitals local chs. and schs., 1950-53; winner grand prize Ted Mack's Amateur Hour 1952; jazz vocalist, Lloyd Terry Jazz Ltd., 1959-61, mem. Gladys Knight and the Pips (formerly Pips Quartet), 1953—, concert appearances in Eng., 1967, 72, 73, 76, Australia, Japan, Hong Kong, Manila, 1976; rec. artist, Brunswick, 1957-61, Fury, 1961-62, Everlast, 1963, Maxx and Bell, 1964-66, Motown, 1966-73, Buddah, Capitol, Columbia, MCA, 1988; albums with the Pips include Best of Gladys Knight and the Pips, All the

Great Hits, If I Were Your Woman, 1989, Soul Survivors: The Best of Gladys Knight and the Pips 1973-1988, 1990, Blue Lights in the Basement, 1996, Imagination, 1996, The Lost Live Albums, 1996; solo albums include Good Woman, 1991, One Voice, 2005; TV appearance Charlie & Co., 1985; produced, appeared in HBO film Sisters in the Name of Love, 1986. Winner 6 gold Buddah records, 1 gold, 1 platinum Buddah album; 4 Grammy awards; named Top Female Vocalist, Blues and Soul mag. 1972; spl. award Washington City Coun. for inspiration to youth in city, 1972; other awards include Clio, AGVA, NAACP Image, Ebony Music, Cashbox, Billboard, Record World, Rolling Stone, Ladies Home Jour., Am. Music award (with Pips), 1984, 1988, Core award B'nai B'rith award; inducted into Rock and Roll Hall of Fame, 1996. Address: Care Shakeji Inc 3221 LaMirada Ave Las Vegas NV 89120 Personal E-mail: kenyajacks@aol.com.

KNIGHT, GREG, professional sports team executive; m. Carrie Knight, 2004. Student, U. Denver Sch. Law; grad. in Bus., Kutztown U., Pa. Positions up to mgr. Denver Nuggets, 1999—2006, dir. basketball ops., 2006—. Mem.: U. Denver Sports and Entertainment Law Soc. Office: Denver Nuggets 1000 Chopper Cir Denver CO 80204

KNIGHT, H. STUART, law enforcement official, consultant; b. Sault St. Marie, Ont., Can., Jan. 6, 1921; s. Alexander G. and Muriel C. (Breathwaite) K.; m. Betty Cooley, June 29, 1946; children: Suzanne Cawley, Bill, Bob, John, Barbara Powell. BS, Mich. State U., 1948; postgrad., Princeton U., 1965-66. Police officer, Berkeley, Calif., 1949; with U.S. Secret Svc., 1950-82, dir., 1973-82. Vice chmn. Guardsmark Inc., Memphis, 1984—; v.p. Interpol, Paris, 1974-81; disting. faculty fellow Fed. Execs. Inst., Charlottesville, Va., 1981; mem. adv. bd. Am. Products Devel. Co.; mem. steering com. Ctr. for Strategic and Internat. Studies. Bd. dirs. Falls Church (Va.) Homeowners Assn., 1982-84; bd. dirs., pres. INKODE Govt. Sys.; mem. lottery bd. State of Va. Staff sgt. U.S. Army, 1942-46, PTO. Decorated Silver Star, Bronze Star, Purple Heart; named original mem. Gallery of Fame, Mich. State U., to Wall of Fame, 2001, Fed. Exec. of Yr., 1982; recipient Mr. Sam award, Touchdown Club, Washington, 1979. Mem. Internat. Assn. Chiefs of Police (life, mem. bd. officers 1974-81), Nat. Sheriffs Assn. (life), Civitan. Avocations: bicycling, golf, puzzles. Office: Guardsmark Inc 22 S 2nd St Memphis TN 38103-2695

KNIGHT, JAMES ATWOOD, manufacturing executive; b. Providence, Apr. 26, 1954; s. Richard Brayton and Louise (Atwood) K.; m. Cynthia Forbes Olney, June 11, 1983; children: Hilary Atwood, James Atwood Jr., Remington Forbes, William Olney, Elsie Lawson. BS, Boston U., 1975; MBA, Dartmouth Coll., 1984. Sr. assoc. Strategic Decisions Group, Menlo Park, Calif., 1984-88; mgr. Apple Computer, Cupertino, Calif., 1988-90; with Holt, Chgo., 1990, Boston Cons. Group, Chgo., 1991-95; v.p. SCA Consulting L.L.C., Chgo., 1995-97, mng. ptnr., 1997—2001; ptnr. Mercer Cons., 2001—02; chmn., CEO Knight Industries, Northfield, Ill., 2002—; chmn. Knight-Celotex, 2002—; chmn., CEO Knight-Rikett, LLC, 2002—; chmn. Internat. Constrn. Supplies, LLC, 2003—, Freightsource LLC, 2003—, Rikett Global BV, Rikett Tech. AS; CEO Rikett Asia LTD. Bd. dirs. Stay Focused, LLC, Chgo. Metallic Corp. Author: Value Based Management, 1997; contbr. chpt. to book. Avocations: skiing, squash. Office: Knight Industries LLC One Northfield Plz Ste 400 Northfield IL 60093 Home: 11 Downing Rd Hanover NH 03755 E-mail: jknight@aknightcompany.com.

KNIGHT, JEFFREY ALAN, corporate financial executive; b. Bay City, Mich., Aug. 6, 1951; s. Dean Leroy and Mary Margaret (McLeod) K.; m. Ramona Margo Robins, Aug. 30, 1980; 1 child, Alexis. BBA in Acctg., Western Mich. U., 1973. CPA, Mich. Staff auditor Coopers & Lybrand, Detroit, 1973-75, supr., 1976-77; mgr. acctg. systems Guardian Industries Corp., Northville, Mich., 1978, asst. controller, 1979-80, corp. controller, 1981-83, v.p. fin., CFO, 1984—, now group v.p. fin., CFO. Mem. Fin. Execs. Inst., Am. Inst. CPA's, Mich. Assn. CPA's. Office: Guardian Industries Corp 2300 Harmon Rd Auburn Hills MI 48326*

KNIGHT, KAREN ANNE MCGEE, artist, educator, educational research administrator; b. Florence, Ala., July 5, 1956; d. Glenn Houston and Juanita May (Fowler) McGee; m. Charles Ronald Knight, June 3, 1980; 1 child, Lara-Elizabeth. AA, Fla. Coll., 1976; BS, U. N. Ala., 1978, MA in Edn., 1994. Cert. tchr., Tenn., Ala. Title I reading aide Florence City Schs., 1978—79, 1st grade tchr., 1980—83; pre-kindergarten tchr. Belmont Weekday Sch., Nashville, 1984—85; kindergarten tchr. Metro-Davidson County Schs., Nashville, 1985—87; freelance watercolorist Shoals Artist's Guild, Florence, 1992—, Westat/quality control monitor, 1997—98, Westat/assessment adminstr., 1998—2001, Westat/field supr., 2001—. Chair Shoals Artists Guild, 1993—, v.p., 1996, pres., 1998. Sunday sch. tchr. Placed in watercolor competition N. Ala. State Fair, 1993. Mem. Nat. Mus. Women in Arts, Watercolor Soc. Ala. (N.W. Ala. area rep. 1996-2000), Tenn. Valley Art Assn., So. Watercolor Soc., Tenn. Valley Art Assn. Guild Avocations: herb and perennial gardening, genealogy. Home: 111 Snell Dr Florence AL 35630-6257

KNIGHT, KENNETH HUGH, conductor; s. John Hugh and Nola Hobbs Knight; life ptnr. Richard M. Morehead. BA, Yale U., 1969. Mem. Norman Luboff Choir, NYC, 1974—77, Roger Wagner Chorale, LA, 1977—96; instr. of voice Mt. St. Mary's Coll., LA, 1980—90, Calif. Luth. U., 1987—96; dir. of music St. Clare Cath. Ch., Santa Clarita, Calif., 1988—96; instr. of voice Calif. Inst. of the Arts, 1989—91, Occidental Coll., LA, 1994—96; dir. of music Petaluma (Calif.) United Meth. Ch., 1996—2001; founder, music dir. Sonoma County Men's Chorus, Rohnert Park, Calif., 1997—2001; choir dir. United Ch. of Santa Fe, 2002—05; music dir. Santa Fe Men's Camerata, 2002—, Zia Singers, Santa Fe, 2003—; co-founder, music dir. Canticum Novum Chamber Orch. and Chorus, Santa Fe, 2004—. Mem.: Nat. Assn. Tchrs. of Singing, Am. Choral Dirs. Assn., Am. Guild of Mus. Artists (life; bd. dirs. 1980—95). Home and Office: 3 Ladera Rd Santa Fe NM 87508 Home Phone: 505-466-3637; Office Phone: 505-466-3637.

KNIGHT, NORMAN, volunteer, retired broadcast executive; b. July 24, 1924; LLD (hon.), Northeastern U.; DBA (hon.), Nathaniel Hawthorne Coll.; DCS (hon.), Merrimack Coll.; DHL (hon.), Suffolk U.; DCC (hon.), Anna Maria Coll. News reporter, scriptwriter Sta. WEW, WIL, WTMV, 1938-41; Announcer, host-producer Sta. WTMV, 1942; announcer, promotion mgr., news reporting continuity dir. Sta. KTHS, 1943; announcer Sta. WMC, 1943; announcer, news writer, reporter, salesman Sta. WMMN, 1944; gen. mgr. Sta. WAJR, 1944-46; Eastern dir. sta. relations MBS, 1946-49; v.p. sales, advt. and promotion Sponsor Publs., Inc., 1950-53; gen. mgr. Sta. WABD (now WNYW-TV), 1953-54; exec. v.p., gen. mgr. Yankee Network div. RKO Teleradio Pictures, Inc. (operating Yankee Network WNAC, WRKO, WNAC-TV); also dir. Yankee Network; v.p. RKO Teleradio Pictures, 1954-60; pres. Yankee div. RKO Teleradio Pictures, Inc., 1957-60, Yankee div. RKO Gen., Inc., 1958-60; treas., chmn. Knight Sales, Inc.; chmn., treas. Knight Radio, Inc. (WEZF, WGIR and WGIR-FM), Knight Broadcasting N.H, Inc. (WHEB-FM, WXHT, WTMN); pres., treas. Knight Communications Corp. (WTAG and WSRS). Chmn. Caribbean Communications Corp.; tv and radio advisor John F. Kennedy. Established first complete TV sta.: pub. affairs film unit which produced Brotherhood Series: River of Life, Wershmeitz (only film 1956 Hungarian revolt), Suffer the Little Children, Breast Cancer, over 100 programs Dangers of Apathy; TV documentaries, 1953-60; Author: (sales techniques radio/TV) The Cause of All Mankind, (film and TV) A Storm is Always a Challenge, Awake America, others. Radio-TV chmn. United Fund Greater Boston, Mass. Cancer Soc., ARC chpt. Met. Boston, Met. Boston chpt. ARC; bus. chmn. Easter Seal Soc.; radio chmn. Salvation Army; dir. Strawberry Banke; bd. dirs. New Eng. Nephrosis Found.; pres., founder New Eng. Kidney Disease Found.; founder, chmn. Nat. Kidney Disease Found.; pres. Norman Knight Charitable Found.; trustee Mass. Bd. Regional Community Colls., Agassiz Village Camps, Crippled Children's Non-Sectarian Fund, Boys and Girls Camps, Inc.; mem. nat. council, exec. com. New Eng. council Boy Scouts Am.; exec. com., dir. Rescue, Inc.; exec. com. The Jimmy Fund; exec. com., trustee Children's Cancer Research Found., Dana Farber Cancer Inst.; mem. fin. com. Com. Econ. Devel.; mem. devel. council Boston U.; mem. pres.'s council Boston Coll.; bd. dirs. Freedoms Found.; also nat. co-chmn. Am. Freedom Ctr.; chair, pres. Mass. Fallen Firefighters Meml. Fund, 2001. Recipient Americanism award Am. Heritage Com., 1959, awards from VFW, Am. Legion, Amvets, Am. Legion Aux., 1959-60, award for contbn. to radio and TV industry Alpha Epsilon Rho; Golden Mike award Broadcasters Found., 1996; named one of ten Outstanding Yougn Men, Boston Jr. C. of C., 1956, Man of Yr., Italian-Am. Police Assn., Humanitarian award ARC, 1998; Norman Knight Camping Fund for less priviledged established in his honor, 1958, Norman Knight Hyperbaric Medicine Ctr., Mass. Eye and Ear Infirmary established in his name, 1999, Norman Knight Endowment Fund for batter women and children established in his honor, 1999, chair and pres. Mass. Fallen Firefighters Meml., Inc., 2001—; established Knight Nursing Ctr. at Mass. Gen. Hosp., 2004-05. Mem. Radio-TV Execs. Sec., Young Pres.'s Orgn., Broadcast Pioneers, AIM, Alpha Epsilon Rho. Clubs: Variety (Boston); Broadcasting Execs. New Eng, 100 of Mass. (co-founder, pres., dir.), 100 of N.H. (life), 100 of Vt. (life). Office: 63 Bay State Rd Boston MA 02215-1802

KNIGHT, PATRICIA MARIE, biomedical engineer, consultant; BS in Engring. Sci., Ariz. State U., MSChemE; PhD in Biomed. Engring., U. Utah. Teaching and rsch. asst. Ariz. State U., Tempe; product devel. engr. Am. Med. Optics, Irvine, Calif., mgr. materials rsch.; rsch. asst. U. Utah, Salt Lake City; dir. materials rsch. Allergan Surg. Products, Irvine, dir. rsch., v.p. rsch., devel. and engring., 1991—2002; v.p. rsch., devel. Advanced Med. Optics, Santa Ana, Calif., 2002—03; cons. biomed. product rsch. and devel. Laguna Niguel, Calif., 2003—. Contbr. articles to profl. jours. Mem. Soc. Biomaterials, Am. Chem. Soc., Soc. Women Engrs., Assn. Rsch. in Vision and Opthalmology, Biomed. Engring. Soc. E-mail: pkbiomed@cox.net.

KNIGHT, PHILIP HAMPSON, apparel executive; b. Portland, Oreg., Feb. 24, 1938; s. William W. and Lota (Hatfield) Knight; m. Penelope Parks, Sept. 13, 1968; 3 children. BSBA, U. Oreg., Eugene, 1959; MBA, Stanford U., Calif., 1962. CPA Oreg. Asst. prof. bus. adminstrn., 1964—69; co-founder Nike, Inc. (formerly Blue Ribbon Sports, Inc.), 1962, chmn. Beaverton, Oreg., 1967—, CEO, 1967—2004, pres., 1968—90, 2000—04. Bd. dirs. US-Asian Bus. Coun., Washington. 1st lt. AUS, 1959—60. Named Oreg. Businessman of Yr., 1982; named one of 1988's Best Mgrs., Bus. Week Mag., Forbes Richest Ams., 1999—, Forbes Richest People, 1999—. Mem.: AICPA. Republican. Episcopalian. Avocations: tennis, running, golf. Office: Nike Inc One Bowerman Dr Beaverton OR 97005-6453 Office Phone: 503-671-6453.*

KNIGHT, ROBERT EDWARD, bank executive, educator; b. Alliance, Nebr., Nov. 27, 1941; s. Edward McKean and Ruth (McDuffee) K.; m. Eva Sophia Youngstom, Aug. 12, 1966. BA, Yale U., 1963; MA, Harvard U., 1965, PhD, 1968. Asst. prof. U.S. Naval Acad., Annapolis, Md., 1966—68; lectr. U. Md., 1967—68; fin. economist Fed. Res. Bank Kansas City, Mo., 1968—70, rsch. officer, economist, 1971—76, asst. v.p., sec., 1977, v.p., sec., 1978—79; pres. Alliance Nat. Bank, 1979—94, chmn., 1983—94; pres. Robert E. Knight & Assocs., banking and econ. cons., Cheyenne, Wyo., 1979—. Chmn., CEO Eldred Found., 1985—; vis. prof., chmn. banking and fin. East Tenn. State U., Johnson City, 1988; faculty Stonier Grad. Sch. Banking, 1972-2002, Colo. Grad. Sch. Banking, 1975-82, Am. Inst. Banking, U. Mo., Kansas City, 1971-79, Prochnow Grad. Sch. Banking, U. Wis., 1980-84; extended learning faculty Park Coll., 1996-2005; mem. Coun. for Excellence for Bur. Bus. Rsch. U. Nebr., Lincoln, 1991-94, mem. Grad. Sch. Arts and Scis. Coun. Harvard, 1994—; chmn. Taxable Mcpl. Bondholders Protective Com., 1991-94. Contbr. articles to profl. jours. Bd. dirs. Stonier Grad. Sch. Banking, 1979-82, Nebr. Com. for Humanities, 1986-90, People of Faith (Royal Oaks) Found., 2000-04; trustee Knox Presbyn. Ch., Overland Park, Kans., 1965-69; bd. regents Nat. Comml. Lending Sch., 1980-83; mem. Downtown Improvement Com., Alliance, 1981-94; trustee U. Nebr. Found., 1982-94; fin. com. United Meth. Ch. Alliance, 1982-85, trustee, 1990-93; mem. Box Butte County Indsl. Devel. Bd., 1987-94; bd. mem., treas. Sun City Homeowners Found., Sun City, Ariz., 2005-; chmn., CEO, Knight Mus. Found., 1994—. Woodrow Wilson fellow, 1963—64. Mem. Am. Econ. Assn., Am. Fin. Assn., So. Econ. Assn., Nebr. Bankers Assn. (com. state legis. 1980-81, com. comml. loans and investments 1986-87), Am. Inst. Banking (state com. for Nebr. 1980-83), Am. Bankers Assn. (econ. adv. com. 1980-83, cmty. bank leadership coun.), We. Econ. Assn., Econometric Soc., Rotary, Masons. Home and Office: 429 W 5th Ave Cheyenne WY 82001-1249

KNIGHT, ROBERT G., mayor, investment banker; b. Wichita, Kans., July 31, 1941; s. Edwar G. and Melba (Barbour) K.; m. Jane Carol Benedick, Aug. 12, 1967; children— Jennifer, Amy, Kristin BA, Wichita State U. Rep. First Securities Co., Wichita, Kans., 1970-76, v.p., 1984—, Mid-Continent Mcpls., Wichita, Kans., 1977-82, Ranson & Co., Wichita, Kans., 1982-84; mayor City of Wichita, 1980-81, 84—. Trustee Salvation Army, Wichita, 1980—, Urban Ministeries, Wichita, 1980—, Southwestern Coll., Winfield, Kans., 1980—; bd. dirs. Kans. Water Authority, Topeka, 1983—; commr. City of Wichita, 1979—. Served with USMCR, 1962-66 Recipient award of honor Concerned Citizens for Community Standards, 1982 Mem. Nat. League Cities, Kans. League Municipalities Republican. Methodist. Avocation: sports. Office: Mayors Office City Hall 1st Fl 455 N Main St Wichita KS 67202-1600

KNIGHT, ROBERT M., JR., rail transportation executive; m. Julie Knight; 3 children. BBA, Kans. St. U.; MBA, So. Ill. U. With Union Pacific Corp., Omaha, 1980—, various positions in audit, acctg., fin., human resources, quality and mktg. and sales, v.p. quality Omaha, 1996—99, v.p., gen. mgr. energy, 1999—2000, v.p., gen. mgr. automotive, 2000—02, sr. v.p. fin., 2002—04, exec. v.p., CFO, 2004—. Bd. dir. Grupo Ferroviario Mexicana, TTX Co. Office: Union Pacific Corp 1400 Douglas St Omaha NE 68179 Office Phone: 402-544-5000.*

KNIGHT, ROBERT MICHAEL, music educator, department chairman; b. Bloomington, Ill., Sept. 21, 1955; s. Clyde Hubert and Emma Lorraine Knight; m. Mary Martha Bante, Nov. 27, 1982; children: Adam Robert, Jonathan Michael, Matthew Conrad, Justin Arthur. MusB in Edn., Ill. State U., Normal, 1976; MusM, Ind. U., Bloomington, 1978; MusD, Northwestern U., Evanston, Ill., 1988. Prof. U. Wis., Eau Claire, 1988—, chmn. dept. music and theatre arts, 1988—. Office: Univ Wis Eau Claire 105 Garfield Ave Eau Claire WI 54702-4004 Home Phone: 715-836-9823; Office Phone: 715-836-4954. Business E-Mail: knightrm@uwec.edu.

KNIGHT, SHIRLEY, actress; b. Goessel, Kans., July 5, 1936; d. Noel Johnson and Virginia (Webster) K.; m. Eugene Persson, 1959 (div., 1969) m. John R. Hopkins, 1969 (dec. July 23, 1998); children: Kaitlin, Sophie. D.F.A., Lake Forest Coll., 1978. Actress theatre and films. Theater debut in Look Back in Anger, Pasadena (Calif.) Playhouse, 1958, N.Y.C. debut in Journey to the Day, 1963; other N.Y.C. theater appearances include The Three Sisters, 1964, Rooms, 1966, We Have Always Lived in the Castle, 1966, The Watering Place, 1969, Kennedy's Children, 1975 (Tony award), Happy End, 1977; with Bristol (Eng.) Old Vic Theatre in And People All Around, 1967; other appearances in Eng. include A Touch of the Poet, 1970, Antigone, 1971, Economic Necessity, 1973; other U.S. theater appearances include A Streetcar Named Desire, Princeton, N.J., 1976, Happy End, N.Y.C., 1977, Landscape of the Body, Chgo., then N.Y.C., 1977, A Lovely Sunday for Creve Coeur, Charleston, S.C., then N.Y.C., 1979, Losing Time, N.Y.C., 1979, I Won't Dance, Buffalo, 1980, Come Back Little Sheba, N.Y.C., 1984, Women Heroes, N.Y.C., 1986, The Depot, N.Y.C., 1987, Cycling Past the Matterhorn, (off-Broadway), 2005; film appearances include: Five Gates to Hell, 1959, Ice Palace, 1960, The Dark at the Top of the Stairs, 1960, The Couch, 1962, Sweet Bird of Youth, 1962, House of Women, 1962, Flight from Ashiya, 1964, The Group, 1966, Petulia, 1966, Dutchman, 1967, The Rain People, 1969, Secrets, 1971, The Counterfeit Killer, 1970, Juggernaut, 1974, Beyond the Poseidon Adventure, 1979, Prisoners, 1981, Endless Love, 1981, The Sender, 1982, The Secret Life of Houses, 1994, Benders, 1994, Color of Night, 1994, Stuart Saves His Family, 1995, Death In Venice, CA, 1994, Diabolique, 1996, As Good as it Gets, 1997, The Man Who Counted, 1998, 75 Degrees in July, 2000, Angel Eyes, 2001, The Salton Sea, 2002, P.S. Your Cat is Dead, 2002, Divine Secrets of the Ya-Ya Sisterhood, 2002, Fly Cherry, 2003, A House on a Hull, 2003, Sexual Life, 2005, To Lie in Green Pastures, 2005, Locked In, 2005, Grandma's Boy, 2006; TV films include: The Outsider, 1967, Shadow Over Elveron, 1968, The Counterfeit Killer, 1968, Majesty, 1968, The Lie, 1971, The Country Girl, 1973, Friendly Persuasion, 1975, Medical Story, 1975, Return to Earth, 1976, 21 Hours at Munich, 1976, The Defection of Simas Kudirka, 1978, Champions: A Love Story, 1979, Playing for Time, 1980, With Intent to Kill, 1984, Sweet Scent of Death, 1984, Billionaire Boys Club, 1987, Bump in the Night, 1991, Shadow of a Doubt, 1991, To Save a Child, 1991, A Mother's Revenge, 1993, Hoggs' Heaven, 1994, Baby Brokers, 1994, The Yarn Princess, 1994, A Part of the Family, 1994, Fudge-A-Mania, 1995, Dad, the Angel & Me, 1995, Children of the Dust, 1995, Indictment: The McMartin Trial, 1995 (Emmy award), Stolen Memories: Secrets From the Rose Garden, 1996, A Promise to Carolyn, 1996, Somebody Is Waiting, 1996, Little Boy Blue, 1997, The Wedding, 1998, If These Walls Could Talk, 1996, The Univited, 1996, Mary & Time, 1996, Dying to be Perfect: The Ellen Hart Pena Story, 1996, Convictions, 1997, A Father for Brittany, 1998, A Marriage of Convenience, 1998, My Louisiana Sky, 2001, Shadow Realm, 2002, Mrs. Ashboro's Cat, 2003; (TV series) Buckskin, 1958, Angel Falls, 1993, Maggie Winters, 1998; (TV mini series) When Love Kills: The Seduction of John Hearn, 1993; guest appearances includeRawhide, 1959, The Fugitive, 1964, 1965, 2001, Marcus Welby, M.D., 1974, Barnaby Jones, 1975, Spenser: For Hire, 1985, 1987, thirtysomething, 1987, Murder She Wrote, 1990, Matlock, 1990, Law & Order, 1991, 2001, Law & Order: Special Victims Unit, 2003, L.A. Law, 1993, NYPD, 1995, Ally McBeal, 2002, ER, 2002, Crossing Jordan, 2004, Cold Case, 2004, House, M.D., 2005, Desperate Housewives, 2005 and several others. Active Com. for Handgun Control, nat. civil rights orgns., worker for peace. Recipient Tony award (Antoinette Perry for Supporting or Featured Actress), 1976, Emmy award for Outstanding Guest Performer in Comedy Drama or Series, 1988, Emmy award for Outstanding Guest Performer in a Drama Series (NYPD Blue), 1995.

KNIGHT, THEODORE RAYMOND (T.R. KNIGHT), actor; b. Mpls., Mar. 26, 1973; Actor: (plays) Ah, Wilderness!, Amadeus, This Lime Tree Bower, Scattergood; (Broadway plays) Noises Off, 2001—02, Tartuffe, 2003; (films) Garmento, 2002, The Last Request, 2006; (TV series) Charlie Lawrence, 2003, Grey's Anatomy, 2005— (SAG award for Outstanding Perfornace by an Ensemble in a Drama Series, 2007). Office: c/o The Gersh Agency 232 N Canon Dr Beverly Hills CA 90210*

KNIGHT, TIMOTHY P., publishing executive; b. Flint, Mich., Aug. 24, 1965; BA in Acctg., Marquette U., 1987; JD, DePaul U., 1990. Sr. corp. assoc. Skadden, Arps, Slate, Meagher & Flom, Chgo. and London, 1992—96; mergers and acquisitions counsel Tribune Co., Chgo., 1996—97; v.p. affiliates and bus. devel. Classified Ventures, Chgo., 1997—98; v.p. strategy and devel. Tribune Pub. Co., Chgo., 1998—2001; head interactive ops. Chgo. Tribune, 2001—03, v.p. strategic mktg., devel. and fin., 2001—03; exec. v.p., gen. mgr. Newsday, Melville, NY, 2003—04, COO, 2004, pres., 2004—, pub., CEO, 2004—. Chmn.'s coun. Heckscher Mus. Art, Huntington, NY. Office: Newsday 235 Pinelawn Rd Melville NY 11747 Office Phone: 631-843-2365.*

KNIGHT, T.R. See KNIGHT, THEODORE

KNIGHT, W. H., JR., (JOE KNIGHT), law educator, former dean; m. Susan Mask; children: Michael, Lauren. BA in Econs., Speech and Polit. Sci., U. N.C., 1976; JD, Columbia U. Adj. prof. U. Bridgeport Sch. Law, Bridgeport, Conn., 1981—83; assoc. counsel, asst. sec. Colonial Bancorp, Waterbury, Conn., 1979—83; visiting prof. Duke U. Law Sch., 1991, Washington U. Law Sch., St. Louis, Miss., 1992; prof. U. Iowa Coll. Law, 1988—2001; assoc. prof. U. Iowa Coll. Law, 1983—88, acting dean, 1991—93, vice provost, 1997—2000; prof. U. Wash. Law Sch., 2001—, dean, 2001—07. Vis. prof. Washington U., St. Louis, Duke U. Schs. Law; assoc. counsel, asst. sec. Colonial Bancorp. Mem.: ABA, Nat. Bar Assn., Nat. Conf. on Black Lawyers, Soc. Am. Law Tchrs., Am. Law Inst., N.Y. Bar Assn., State Farm Mut. Automobile Ins. Co. (dir.). Office: U Washington Sch Law William H Gates Hall Box 353020 Seattle WA 98195-3020 Office Phone: 206-543-2586. Office Fax: 206-616-5305. Business E-Mail: whknight@u.washington.edu.

KNIGHT, WALKER LEIGH, publishing executive, minister; b. Henderson, Ky., Feb. 6, 1924; s. Cooksey Bennett and Rowena (Henderson) K.; m. Iva Nell Moseley, Nov. 10, 1943; children: Walker Leigh, Kenneth Wayne, Nelda Denise, Emily Jill. BA, Baylor U., 1949. Ordained min. Bapt. Ch., 1948. Reporter Henderson Gleanor and Jour., 1942; pastor in Dale, Tex., 1948-49; editor Falls County Record, Marlin, Tex., 1948-49; assoc. editor Bapt. Std., Dallas, 1950-59; editl. dir. So. Bapt. Home Mission Bd., Atlanta, also editor Missions U.S.A. mag. and Atlanta bur. chief Bapt. Press News Service, 1959-83; editor, pub. Bapts. Today (formerly SBC Today), 1983-89, pub., 1989-93, pub. emeritus, 1994—. Author: Panama, The Land Between, 1965, Struggle for Integrity, 1969, See How Love Works, 1971, Seven Beginnings, 1976, Chaplaincy, Love on the Line, 1978, Tell the People, 1986; contbr.: Southern Baptists Observed, 1992, Struggle for the Soul of the SBC, 1993; editor: The Whitsitt Jour., 1995-98. With USAAF, 1943-45. Home and Office: 1008 Forrest Blvd Decatur GA 30030-4732 Personal E-mail: wleighknight@comcast.net.

KNIGHTEN, CHRISTOPHER BLAIR, conductor, educator; s. Jack Buford Knighten and Monteene Rachel Tanner; m. Janet Whitman. MusB Edn., Baylor U., Waco, Tex., 1986; MusM, U. Colo., Boulder, 1991, D in Musical Arts, 2000. Assoc. dir. bands Baylor U. Sch. Music, Waco, 1992—93; dir. symphonic band and marching band East Carolina U. Sch. Music, Greenville, NC, 1993—. Office: East Carolina Univ Sch Music Greenville NC 27858 Home Phone: 252-714-2416. Business E-Mail: knightenc@ecu.edu.

KNIGHTEN, LATRENDA, elementary school educator, consultant; d. Randolph and Dianne Judson Knighten. BA in Early Childhood Edn. and Psychology, Tulane U., 1987. Cert. tchr. La., 1987. From tchr. kindergarten to specialist math. elem. sch. East Baton Rouge (La.) Parish, 1987—2003, specialist math. elem. sch., 2003—. Contractor La. State Dept. Edn., 01, 2003; cons. in field; mem. numerous coms. East Baton Rouge (La.) Parish; presenter in field. Contbr. lessons for teacher training. Finalist Elem. Tchr. of Yr., East Baton Rouge (La.) Parish, 1996, State Tchr. of Yr. award, La., 1997, Tchr. of Yr. award, CPB Nat. Tchr. Tng. Inst., 1998; named Tchr. of Yr., Wildwood Elem., 1997; recipient Elem. Tchr. of Yr., East Baton Rouge (La.) Parish, 1997; grantee, Friends of Environmental Edn., 1994—95,

Quality Sci. and Math. Equipment Fund, 1994—96, Academic Distinction Fund, 1994—96. Mem.: Nat. Sci. Educators Leadership Assn., Nat. Sci. Tchrs. Assn. (sci. program key leader La. 1997—), Nat. Coun. Tchrs. Math. (chmn. conf. program 2004, profl. devel. com. 2004—, presenter), La. Sci. Tchrs. Assn. (co-chmn. conf. program 2000, regional rep. 2003—), La. Assn. Sci. Leaders, La. Assn. Computer Using Educators, La. Fedn. Tchrs., La. Assn. Tchrs. Math. (sec. 1997—99, co-chmn. conf. program 2000, rep. 2000—01, pres.-elect 2001—02, pres. 2002—04, chmn. conf. 2003, 2003, past pres. 2004—), Baton Rouge (La.) Area Coun. Tchrs. Math. (pres. 2003—, 2000—01, pres.-elect 1999—2000, v.p. elem. 1994—96), Assn. Supr. and Curriculum Devel., Phi Delta Kappa.

KNIGHTLEY, KEIRA, actress; b. Teddington, Middlesex, Eng., Mar. 26, 1985; d. Will Knightley and Sharman Mcdonald. Actor: (films) A Village Affair, 1994, Innocent Lies, 1995, Star Wars: Episode I - The Phantom Menace, 1999, The Hold, 2001, Deflation, 2001, New Year's Eve, 2002, Bend it Like Beckham, 2002, Thunderpants, 2002, Pure, 2002, The Seasons Alter, 2002, Pirates of the Caribbean: The Curse of the Black Pearl, 2003, Love Actually, 2003, King Arthur, 2004, Stories of Lost Souls, 2005, The Jacket, 2005, Pride and Prejudice, 2005, Domino, 2005, Pirates of the Caribbean: Dead Man's Chest, 2006 (Movies-Choice Hissy Fit and Choice Scream, Teen Choice Awards, 2006), Pirates of the Caribbean: At World's End, 2007 (Choice Movie Actress: Action Adventure, Teen Choice Awards, 2007); (TV films) Royal Celebration, 1993, Treasure Seekers, 1996, Coming Home, 1998, Princess of Thieves, 2001; (TV miniseries) Oliver Twist, 1999, Doctor Zhivago, 2002. Named Favorite On-Screen Matchup with Johnny Depp, People's Choice Awards, 2007; named one of 50 Most Powerful People in Hollywood, Premiere mag., 2006, 100 Most Powerful Celebrities, Forbes.com, 2007. Office: PFD Drury House 34-43 Russell St London WC2B 5HA England Office Phone: 020 7344 1010. Office Fax: 020 7836 9544.*

KNIGHT-MCDOWELL, VICTORIA, former elementary school educator, health products executive; m. Rider Knight-McDowell; 1 child, Errol. Former 2nd grade tchr. Spreckels Elementary Sch.; founder, pres. Airborne, Inc., Carmel, Calif., 1997—; owner with CEO husband Knight-McDowell Labs, Calif., 1997—. While teaching developed own preventative remedy which include vitamins, herbal extracts, antioxidents, electrolytes and amino acids called Airborne to combat airborne germs and viruses that are all around in classrooms, offices, stores and airplanes. The product has had celebrity endorsements by Oprah Winfrey and Howard Stern and celebrity commercials including Barry Williams, Butch Patrick and Johnny Whitaker. Office: Airborne Inc 26811 S Bay Dr Ste 300 Bonita Springs FL 34134 also: Knight-McDowell PO Box 2884 Carmel CA 93921 Office Phone: 239-948-8545. Office Fax: 239-948-8551.*

KNIGHTS, EDWIN MUNROE, pathologist; b. Providence, Dec. 25, 1924; s. Edwin Munroe and Viola Ruth (Koreb) K.; m. Ruth Lindsay Currie, Sept. 23, 1961; children: Edwin B., Jessie B., Ross D., David J. (dec. 1979). AB, Brown U., 1948; MD, Cornell U., 1948. Intern Bellevue Hosp., NYC, 1948-49; resident in pathology R.I. Hosp., Providence, 1949-50, Henry Ford Hosp, Detroit, 1952-54; assoc. pathologist Harper Hosp., Detroit, 1954; dir. labs. Hurley Hosp., Flint, Mich., 1957-62, Providence Hosp., Southfield, Mich., 1963-75; dir. Northland Oakland Med. Labs., Southfield, Mich., 1964-75, Bio Sci. Labs., Detroit, 1975-85, Smith Kline Bio-Sci. Labs., Detroit, 1985-89; dir. labs. Kern Hosp., Warren, Mich., 1977-81; pres. Coll. Terr. Inc., Flint, Mich., 1968—2003; dir. Performance Assurance Profls., Bloomfield Hills, Mich., 1988-94; pres. Life Sci. Inc., Flint, 1971-72, Vet. Med. Labs., 1973-75; clin. prof. pathology Mich. State U., 1974-75; rep. Comprehensive Health Planning Coun. S.E. Mich., 1973-85, trustee, 1986-87; mem. lab. peer rev. com. Mich. Dept. Social Svcs., 1979-84; med. dir. Smith Kline Beecham Labs., Detroit, 1990-92, Nat. Health Labs., Flint, 1992-94. Pres. Life Sci. Inc., Grantham, 1996-98; pathologist Project Hope, Indonesia and Vietnam, 1961, Peru, 1962, Ecuador, 1964; bd. dirs. GeneSaver DNA Preservation Svcs., 1996—. Author: Ultramicro Methods for Clinical Laboratories, 1957, 2d edit., 1962; editor: Minicomputers in the Clinical Laboratory, 1970, Lifelines, 1971-75, For Want of an "A" Confusion Reigns. The Day Nature Goofed, 2004, Harvesting Health from your Family Tree, 20017; contbg. editor Jour. Foot Surgery, 1983-89; contbr. articles to profl. jours. and mags. Emeritus mem. adv. coun. New Eng. Hist. Geneal. Soc., trustee, 2001—07; mem. long range planning com. Eastman Cmty. Assn., 1997-2003; bd. overseers USS Constn. Mus., 2005—; bd. dirs. Thomas Jefferson Heritage Soc., 2005—. Lt. MC USNR, 1943-46, 50-52, ETO, Korea. USPHS grantee, 1957-66. Fellow ACP, Coll. Am. Pathologists, Am. Soc. Clin. Pathology (Mich. councillor 1966-68); mem. AMA, Am. Coll. Med. Genetics (affil. doctoral mem. 2005-06), Oakland County Med. Soc. (pres. 1974), Mich. Soc. Pathologists (pres. 1970, del. Mich. State Med. Soc. 1986-93), Internat. Acad. Pathology, Mich. State Med. Soc., Assn. Clin. Scientists, Gen. Soc. Mayflower Descs., Roger Williams Family Assn., Wardroom Club (Boston). Achievements include patents in field. Home and Office: 125 Hawthorne Village Rd Nashua NH 03062

KNILANS, MICHAEL JEROME, retired food products executive; b. Columbus, Ohio, Mar. 3, 1927; s. Alfred Sidney and Bernice (Meyers) K.; m. Anne Eberhardt, June 15, 1947; children: Michael, Kyleen, Christine, Timothy, Suzanne. BS, Ohio State U., 1949. With Big Bear Stores Co., Columbus, 1942-89, mdse. mgr., 1952-61, v.p., 1961-70, exec. v.p., 1970-76, pres., 1976-89, dir., 1976—89; ret., 1989. Bd. dirs. Price Chopper Supermarkets, Schenectady, N.Y. Chmn. bd. Ohio Workers Compensation Bd., 1989-95; bd. dirs. Children's Hosp., Columbus, Mt. Carmel Coll. Nursing, Columbus; v.p. East Ctr. region Boy Scouts Am. With USNR, 1944-46, PTO. Mem. Ohio Coun. Retail Mchts. (treas.), Better Bus. Bur. (pres. 1978), C. of C., Masons, Shriners, Jesters, Rotary (pres. 1981—, dist. gov. 1993-94). Republican. Home and Office: 1119 Kingsdale Ter Columbus OH 43220-4946 Office Phone: 614-451-1293. Personal E-mail: mknilans@aol.com.

KNISELY, RALPH FRANKLIN, retired microbiologist; b. Altoona, Pa., Mar. 30, 1927; s. Calvin Ross and Frieda Pauline (Neher) K.; m. Joan Marie Fitzgerald, Jan. 29, 1949 (div. 1955); 1 child, Patricia Ann; m. Ann Martin, May 21, 1960. BS, postgrad., Pa. State U., 1953. Bacteriologist Altoona Hosp., 1953—56, adminstrv. asst. to pathologist, 1957—59; microbiologist Chem. Corps Dept. Army, Ft. Detrick, Md., 1959—72; rsch. microbiologist Edgewood Arsenal, Aberdeen Proving Ground, Md., 1972—86. Contbg. author: Rapid Identification of Biological Agents, 1966; contbr. articles to profl. jours. Pres. Eastview Civic Assn., Frederick, Md., 1968-69; mem. Srs. and Lawmen Together Coun., Frederick City Police and Frederick County Sheriffs Office. With USN, 1945-46, 50-51; capt. Res. ret., 1945-87. Mem.: AARP (bd. dirs. chpt. 636 1990—92, chpt. pres. 1995—96, bd. dirs. chpt. 636 1997—98), Rsch. Soc. Am. (emeritus), Am. Soc. for Microbiology (emeritus), N.Y. Acad. Sci. (life), Assn. Mil. Surgeons U.S. (life), Philalethes Soc., Knisely Reunion Assn. (historian 1993—, pres. 1994—95), Fleet Res. Assn., Sampson WWII Vets. (life; Md. dir.), Nat. Assn. Ret. Fed. Employees (life; pres. chpt. 409 1995—97, bd. dirs. 1997—98), Am. Legion (life), Am. Philatelic Soc. (life), Ret. Officers Assn. (chpt. v.p. 1969—70, pres. 2002—03), Nat. Sojourners (pres. chpt. 354 1965, 1981, sec. 1986—), Masonic Rsch. Soc., Legion of Honor (comdr. 2002—03), Korean Vets., Quatour Coronati Corr. Cir. (London), Keystone Kopps (pres. 2002), George Washington Masonic Stamp Club (pres. 1978—80, sec. 1988—98), KT, Scottish Rite, Order of Quetzalcoatl, Tall Cedars of Lebanon, Shriners, Masons, Elks (life). Republican. Lutheran. Avocations: amateur radio, genealogy. Home: 7400 Skyline Dr Frederick MD 21702-3652

KNITOWSKI, DAVID ALAN, civil engineer, urban planner; b. Bridgewater, NJ, June 10, 1967; s. Thaddeus and Margaret Knitowski. BS in Civil Engring., Rensselear Poly. Inst., Troy, NY, 1989; M of Urban Planning, NY U., NYC, 1994. Cert. profl. engr., NY, Oreg., Wash., Idaho; Am. Inst. Cert. Planners. Civil engr. Vollmer Assoc., NYC, 1989—97, David Evans & Assoc., Portland, Oreg., 1997—98, Bend, 1998—2003; sr. planner City of Bend, 2003—. Mem.: Profl. Engrs. Oreg., Am. Planning Assn., Inst. Transp. Engrs. Avocations: skiing, hiking, mountain biking, travel, photography. Home: 574 NW Sean Ct Bend OR 97701-2400 Office: City of Bend 710 NW Wall St Bend OR 97701

KNITTEL, CHRISTOPHER ROLAND, economics professor, consultant; b. Rapid City, SD, July 11, 1972; s. Carl Andrew Knittel and Crystal Julie Kreps; m. Allison Elaine Offholter, Dec. 20, 1973. BA in Econs. and Polit. Sci., Calif. State U., Stanislaus, Turlock, 1994; MA in Econs., U. Calif., Davis, 1996; PhD in Econs., U. Calif., Berkeley, 1999. Asst. prof. fin. and econs. Boston U., 1999—2002; assoc. prof. econs. U. Calif., Davis, 2002—. Cons. in field, 1999—. Contbr. articles to profl. jours. Grantee, Net Inst., 2005, 2006; CSEM grantee, UC Energy Inst., 2004. Home: 3785 Castaic Ct West Sacramento CA 95691 Office: Univ Calif Davis One Shields Ave Davis CA 95616 Home Phone: 916-371-8105; Office Phone: 530-752-3344. Personal E-mail: crknittel@ucdavis.edu.

KNIZE, DAVID MAURICE, plastic surgeon; b. Ennis, Tex., Apr. 2, 1938; s. Joseph Fred and Mary Elizabeth (Vavra) K. BA, Tex. U., 1959; MD, Southwestern Med. Coll., 1963. Resident in Orthopedic surgery Duke U., Durham, NC, 1964-66; resident gen. surgery U. Colo., Denver, 1966-68; resident plastic surgery N.Y.U., 1970-74; assoc., prof. surgery U. Colo., Denver, 1974--. Contbr. articles to profl. jours. Lt. comdr. USN, 1969—71. Mem.: AMA, Colo. State Soc., Am. Soc. Plastic and Reconstructive Surgeons. Republican. Avocations: bicycling, windsurfing, scuba diving. Home: 4545 S Monaco St 446 Denver CO 80237-3463 Office: 3701 S Clarkson St Englewood CO 80110-3909

KNOBBE, LOUIS JOSEPH, lawyer, educator; b. Carroll, Iowa, Apr. 6, 1932; s. Louis C. and Elsie M. (Praeger) Knobbe; m. Jeanette M. Sganga, Apr. 3, 1954; children: Louis, Michael, Nancy, John, Catherine. BSEE, Iowa State U., 1953; JD, Loyola U., LA, 1959. Bar: Calif. 1960, U.S. Supreme Ct. 1963, U.S. Patent and Trademark Office. Tech. staff Bell Tel. Labs., 1953-54; patent engr. GE, Washington, 1955—56, N.Am. Aviation, Downey, Calif., 1956-59; patent lawyer Beckman Instruments, Fullerton, Calif., 1959-62; co-founder, ptnr. Knobbe, Martens, Olson & Bear, Newport Beach, Calif., 1962—2002, of counsel, 2003—. Lectr. Computer Law Assn., Inc., LA, L.A. Intellectual Property Law Assn., San Diego Bar Assn.; adj. prof. Sch. Law San Diego U., 1987—2003; mem. engring. adv. bd. U. Calif., Irvine. Co-author: (book) Attorney's Guide to Trade Secrets, 1972, 2d edit., 1996, update, 2002, How to Handle Basic Patent, 1992; contbg. author (book) Using Intellectual Property Rights to Protect Domestic Markets, 1986; contbr. articles to profl. jours. Bd. dirs. Orange County (Calif.) Performing Arts Ctr., 1975—83; past pres. Philharm. Soc. Orange County; past bd. mem., past v.p. Opera Pacific, Orange County; bd. visitors Loyola Law Sch., 2000—. Recipient Jurisprudence award, Anti-Defamation League, 1998, Lifetime Contbn. award, Forum for Corp. Dirs., 2005, Lifetime Achievement award, Am. Jewish Com., 2007. Fellow: Inst. Advancement Engring.; mem.: IEEE (past chmn. Orange County sect., Centennial medal 1984), ABA, Licensing Execs. Soc., Orange County Patent Law Assn. (lectr.), Orange County Bar Assn., State Bar Calif., Am. Arbitration Soc. (panel neutrals), Am. Intellectual Property Law Assn. (lectr.), Pacific Club, First Friday Friars, Santa Ana North Rotary, Eta Kappa Nu, Tau Beta Pi, Phi Kappa Phi. Avocations: boating, still and video photography, travel and exploration in lake powell, death valley, deserts of Arizona and Baja California. Office: 2040 Main St Fl 14 Irvine CA 92614 Home Phone: 714-838-1392; Office Phone: 949-760-0404. Business E-Mail: LKnobbe@kmob.com.

KNOBEL, DALE THOMAS, historian, educator, university president; b. East Cleveland, Ohio, Sept. 14, 1949; s. Harry Spencer and Gwynne Ann K.; m. Tina Jamieson, June 19, 1971; children: Allison. BA, Yale U., 1971; PhD, Northwestern U., 1976. Asst. prof. history Northwestern U., Evanston, Ill., 1976-77, Tex. A&M U., College Station, 1977-84, assoc. prof. history, 1984-96, dir. univ. hons. prog., 1987-92, exec. dir. honors programs and acad. scholarships, 1992-95, assoc. provost for undergrad. programs, 1995-96; provost, dean of faculty, prof. history Southwestern U., Georgetown, Tex., 1996-98; pres., prof. history Denison U., Granville, Ohio, 1998—. Author: America for the Americans: The Nativist Movement in the United States, 1996, Paddy and the Republic: Ethnicity and Nationality in Antebellum America, 1985; co-author: Prejudice, 1982; contbr. Immigrant America, 1994, Fleeing the Famine, 2003, University Presidents as Moral Leaders, 2006; book rev. editor Jour. of Early Republic, 1987-89; contbr. articles to profl. jours. Chmn. Bryan Hist. Landmark Commn., 1987-93; trustee Bryan Tex. Pub. Libr., 1989-92, Brazos Valley Mus. Natural History, 1994-96, Inst. for Internat. Edn. Students, Chgo., 1999—, Newark Midland Theater Assn., 1999-2005, The Works: Ohio Ctr. for History, Art, and Tech.; pres. Denison Univ. Rsch. Found., 1998—, North Coast Athletic Conf., 2004-06, Five Colls. Ohio, Inc., 2004-06; vice chmn. Ohio Found. Ind. Colls., 2002-06; chmn. Ohio Campus Compact, 2001—; sec. Assn. Ind. Colls. and Univs. Ohio, 2006-; chmn. Lakeside Chautauqua Found., 2006—; trustee Lakeside Assn., 2006—; pres. coun. NCAA, 2003-06. Am. Assn. State and Local History grantee, 1984; NEH grantee, 1978; NSF grantee, 1972-74; W.K. Kellogg Found. grantee, 1985-87. Mem. Nat. Collegiate Honors Coun., Orgn. Am. Historians, Immigration History Soc., Soc. for Hist. of the Early Am. Republic, Great Lakes Colls. Assn. (treas. 2004—), Union Club Cleve., Univ. Club Chgo., Rocky Fork Hunt and Country Club, Phi Beta Kappa, Phi Alpha Theta, Omicron Delta Kappa, Phi Kappa Phi, Phi Beta Delta. Methodist. Home: 204 Broadway W Granville OH 43023-1120

KNOBLER, PETER STEPHEN, magazine editor, writer; b. NYC, Dec. 4, 1946; s. Alfred E. and Selma (Frankel) K.; m. Jane Dissin, May 16, 1982;1 child, Daniel Carlyle. BA, Middlebury Coll., 1968; postgrad. creative writing, Columbia U. Reporter Liberation News Svc., NYC, 1969; editor Zygote mag., NYC, 1970; assoc. editor Crawdaddy mag., NYC, 1971-72; editor, 1972-79; pres. Knobler Mgmt. Inc., NYC, 1983-89. Co-author: Giant Steps: The Autobiography of Kareem Abdul-Jabbar, 1983; (with Thomas Henderson) Out of Control, 1987, (with Ann Richards) Straight from the Heart, 1989, (with Peggy Say) Forgotten, 1991, (with Remo Franceschini) A Matter of Honor, 1993, (with James Carville and Mary Matalin) All's Fair, 1994, (with Hakeem Olajuwon) Living the Dream, 1996, (with William Bratton) Turnaround, 1998, (with Daniel Petrocelli) Triumph of Justice, 1998, (with Sumner Redstone) A Passion to Win, 2001, (with Rikki Klieman) Fairy Tales Can Come True, 2003, (with Donny Deutsch) Often Wrong, Never in Doubt, 2005; editor: (with Greg Mitchell) Very Seventies, 1995; screenwriter: Vintage Champions, 1982, That Championship Feeling, 1983, U.S. Open championship matches, 1983, 84, Pride and Passion, 1984; composer songs recorded by The Oak Ridge Boys, Chris Hillman, The Desert Rose Band. Home: 800 W End Ave New York NY 10025-5467

KNOBLOCH, FERDINAND J., psychiatrist, educator; b. Prague, Czech Republic, Aug. 15, 1916; emigrated to Can., 1970; s. Ferdin and Marie (Verunac) K.; m. Susana Hartman (dec. 1944 victim of Holocaust); m. Jirina Skorkovska, Sept. 5, 1947; children: Katerina, Yohana. Maturity degree, Realgymnasium, Prague, 1935; student, Charles U. Med. Sch., Prague, 1935—46; psychoanalytic tng., Charles U. Med. Sch., 1945-53, 1945—53. Successively lectr., asst. prof., assoc. prof. psychiatry Charles U., Prague, 1946-70; mem. faculty U. B.C., Vancouver, Canada, 1970—, prof. psychiatry, 1971-83, prof. emeritus, 1983—; clin. dir. Day House Univ. Hosp., 1972-90. Vis. prof. U. Havana, 1963, U. Ill., Chgo., 1968-69, Columbia U., 1969-70, Albert Einstein Med. Coll., 1970; pres. European seminar mental health and family WHO, 1961, 3d Internat. Congress Psychodrama, 1968; co-chmn. Internat. Symposium Non-Verbal Aspects and Techniques of Psychotherapy, 1974; hon. dir. psychodrama Moreno Inst., NYC, 1974. Author: (with Jirina Knobloch) Forensic Psychiatry, 1967 (award Czechoslovak Med. Soc. 1968), Psychotherapy, 1968, Neurosis and You, 1962, 63, 68, Integrated Psychotherapy, 1979 (transl. into German 1983, Japanese 1984, Czech 1993, Chinese, 1995), Integrated Psychotherapy in Action, 1999; contbr. articles on psychotherapy integration, psychology of music and evolutionary psychology to profl. jours. Polit. prisoner of Gestapo, 1943-45. Fellow Am. Psychiat. Assn. (disting. life), Czechoslovak Soc. Advancement Psychoanalysis and Integration of Psychotherapy (pres. 1968-72), Am. Acad. Psychoanalysis, Polish Psychiat. Assn. (corr.), Can. Psychiat. Assn., Am. Group Psychotherapy Assn., Can. Soc. for Integrated Psychotherapy and Psychoanalysis (pres. 1972—), World Psychiat. Assn. (co-chmn. sect. psychotherapy 1983-93, chmn. 1993-96).

KNOBLOCH, MARCIA M. (MARTA KNOBLOCH), writer; b. Montgomery, Ala., July 7, 1939; d. Kenneth Floyd Musick and Mary Cherry Phelps; m. William W. Knobloch; children: Charles Wayne, Mark David. Student, Coll. Notre Dame of Md., Balt. Vis. poet Fondazione Il Fiore, Florence, Italy, 2003, Festival of Poetry and Poets, St. Mary's Coll. of Md., 1992, Gunston Day Sch. Book and Authors Day, 1999; lectr. and condr. workshops in field; judge poetry contests; curator Emmina Verzella's personal exhbn., NYU and Instituto Italiano di Cultura, 1993; writing instr. Writer's Ctr., Bethesda, Md., 1998—99. Author: (fables) Tales of Five Continents, 1999, (play) La Virago, 2001, (artist book) Quetzal, 2001; contbr. poetry, short stories, critical essays and revs. numerous lit. mags. and anthologies including Balt. Rev., Md. Poetry Rev., numerous others.; guest editor Lite, 2002; contbr.: Md. Poetry Rev., 1988—98; one of founding editors Chesapeake mag., 1993, Passager: A Jour. of Remembrance and Discovery, 1990; editl. asst.: The Spirit of Italy in American Art 1716-1945, 1990, The Shaping Hand of Italy in American Art; A Dictionary of American Artists of Italian Heritage 1776-1945, 1993; co-editor: Margaret, Remembering A Life That Was Poetry, 1998; assoc. editor East of the Bay, A Chester River Anthology, 1999. Asst. to exec. dir. fundraising campaign Lyric Found.; bd. dirs. ARTSCAPE Lit. Arts Com. of Mayor's Adv. Com. on Arts and Culture of Balt., 1989—91, Balt. City Arts Grants Com., 1990, The Sun A.D. Emmart Award Co., Balt.; exec. bd. Balt. Heritage, Balt. Planning Com., Theatre of Nations Festival, Christine di Pizan Soc. for Humanities Steering Com., Coll. Notre Dame of Md., The Women's Assn. of Balt. Symphony, Women's Com. of Balt. Mus. Art, Young Assocs. of Balt. Symphony. Recipient Premio Donna, Lions Castello Ferrara, 1995, Columbia Book award, 1993, Il Premio Nazionale di Arti e Ambiente di Italia, 1991, Lit. Arts award, Balt. ARTSCAPE, 1988. Mem.: Acad. Am. Poets, Poetry Soc. Am., Nat. League of Am. PEN Women, Writers Ctr. Bethesda, Balt. Bibliophiles, Hamilton St. Club, Johns Hopkins Club.

KNODT, JEAN AMELIA SAUSELE, artist, educator; b. Elizabeth, NJ, Apr. 16, 1956; d. George J.H. and Murielene Dorsey Sausele; m. Richard Paul Knodt, June 2, 1984; 1 child, Nicholas Sausele. Student, Brandeis U., Waltham, Mass., 1978; Student, Skowhegan Sch. Painting and Sculure, Maine, 1983; BS in Studio Art, Skidmore Coll., Saratoga Springs, NY, 1978; MFA in Painting, U. Pa., Phila., 1984. Cert. tchr. art K-12 Mass., 1978, tchr. Va., 1997. Graphic designer Addison-Wesley Pub., Reading, Mass., 1979—81; free lance graphic design and illustration, 1978—93; dir. open-inquiry thinking skills lab. The Think Tank Kent Gardens Elem., McLean, Va., 1995—2003. Instr. art Montgomery Coll., Rockville, Md., 1986, 87, 90, Md. Coll. Art and Design, Silver Spring, Md., 1986, Bowie State Coll., Md., 1987; instr. open inquiry learning U. Va., Falls Ch., Va., 2001; presenter in field; cons. in field. Exhibitions include various, 1978—, one-woman shows include Clin. Ctr. Galleries NIH, Bethesda, Md., 2006; contbr. articles to profl. jours. Recipient Sr. Art Exhbn. honors, Dept. Art, Skidmore Coll., 1978; Skowhegan scholar, Dept. Fine Arts U. Pa., 1983. Independent.

KNOEBEL, SUZANNE BUCKNER, cardiologist, educator; b. Ft. Wayne, Ind., Dec. 13, 1926; d. Doster and Marie (Lewis) Buckner. AB, Goucher Coll., 1948; MD, Ind. U.-Indpls., 1960. Diplomate: Am. Bd. Internal Medicine. Asst. prof. medicine Ind. U., Indpls., 1966-69, assoc. prof., 1969-72, prof., 1972-77, Krannert prof., 1977—. Asst. dean rsch. Ind. U., Indpls., 1975-85; assoc. dir. Krannert Inst. Cardiology, Indpls., 1974-90; asst. chief cardiology sect. Richard L. Roudebush VA Med. Ctr., Indpls., 1982-90; editor-in-chief ACC Current Jour. Rev., 1992-2000. Fellow Am. Coll. Cardiology (v.p. 1980-81, pres. 1982-83); mem. Am. Fedn. Clin. Research, Assn. Univ. Cardiologists Office: Krannert Inst 1701 N Senate Ave Indianapolis IN 46202 Home Phone: 317-841-9233; Office Phone: 317-962-0061. Business E-Mail: sknoebel@iupui.edu.

KNOELKER, MICHAEL T.F., science observatory director; b. Feb. 9, 1953; Diploma in Physics, U. Göttingen, Germany, 1978; PhD in Physics, Freiburg U., Germany, 1983. Asst. prof. U. Göttingen, 1983—90; astronomer Kiepenheuer-Intitut Sonnenphysik, Freiburg, 1990—; vis. scientist High Altitude Obs. Nat. Ctr. Atmospheric Rsch., Boulder, Colo., 1987—94, affiliate scientist High Altitude Obs., 1994—95, sr. scientist, dir. High Altitude Obs., 1995—. Mem., steering com. Solar Magnetism Initiative, 1995—; mem. Assn. of Univs. for Rsch. in Astronomy (AURA) Observatory Vis. Com., 1996—. Office: High Altitude Obs Nat Ctr Atmospheric Rsch PO Box 3000 Boulder CO 80307-3000

KNOELL, MICHAEL DAVID, health facility administrator, military officer; b. San Francisco, Oct. 27, 1967; s. David Leo and Connie Jean Knoell; Sharon W. Knoell (Stepmother); m. Amy Denean Sipes, Aug. 14, 1994; children: Katie Francis, Evan Michael. M in Healthcare Adminstrn., Baylor U., San Antonio, 2006. Diplomate Am. Coll. Healthcare Execs., 2005. Joined USN, 1984; deckhand, signalman USS Ark. (CGN 41), Calif., 1985—90; mil. policeman Sigonella, Italy, 1990—94; leading signalman USS La Salle (AGF 3), Gaeta, Italy, 1994—97; chief petty officer; Navy recruiter Pa., 1998—2001; leading chief naval dept. USS Shiloh (CG 67), Calif., 2001—04; Lt. j.g.; dept. head healthcare ops. Naval Hosp. Cherry Point, NC, 2005—. Office: Naval Hosp Cherry Point PSC 8023 Cherry Point NC 28533 Business E-Mail: mcknoell@ec.rr.com.

KNOEPFLMACHER, ULRICH CAMILLUS, literature educator; b. Munich, June 26, 1931; U.S. citizen; s. George A. and Hilde (Weiss) K.; married; 4 children. AB, U. Calif., Berkeley, 1955, MA, 1957; PhD, Princeton U., 1961. From instr. to assoc. prof. U. Calif., Berkeley, 1961-69, Humanities Rsch. prof., 1966-67, 77; asst. dean U. Calif. Coll. Letters and Sciences, Berkeley, 1967-71; prof. U. Calif., Berkeley, 1969-79; prof. English Princeton U., 1979—, now William and Annie S. Paton Found. prof. ancient and modern lit. Vis. prof. Harvard U., 1971; Grad. prof. Tulsa U., 1979, Bread Loaf Sch. English, 1981, 83, 85, 87, NYU, 1982, Johns Hopkins U., 1983; adv. bd. Publs. MLA, 1977-81, SEL, 1979— VIJ, 1982—, Children's Lit., 1987—; dir. NEH summer seminars, 1975, 84, 86, 89, 90, 91, 95, 99. Author: Religious Humanism and the Victorian Novel, 1965, George Eliot's Early Novels: The Limits of Realism, 1968, Laughter and Despair: Readings in Ten Novels of the Victorian Era, 1971, Emily Bronte's Wuthering Heights, 1988, Wuthering Heights: A Study, 1994, Ventures into Childland: Victorians, Fairy Tales, and Femininity, 1998; editor: Francis Newman: Phases of Faith, 1970, George MacDonald's Fairy Tales, 1999, Frances Hodgson Burnett's A Little Princess, 2002; co-editor: Nature and the Victorian Imagination, 1977, The Endurance of Frankenstein: Essays on Mary Shelley's Novel, 1978, Forbidden Journeys: Fairy Tales and Fantasies by Victorian Women Writers, 1992, Cross-Writing the Child and the Adult, 1997; cons. editor Teaching Children's Literature: Issues, Pedagogy, Resources, 1992; edit. bd. publs. MLA, 1981-83. Recipient Disting. Tchg. award Acad. Senate U. Calif., 1977; Am. Coun. Learned Soc. fellow, 1965, Guggenheim fellow, 1969-70, 87-88, sr. fellow NEH, 1972-73, 91-92, sr. fellow Humanities Coun., Princeton U., 1975, Rockefeller Found. sr. fellow, 1983-84, Nat. Humanities Ctr. fellow, 1996. Mem. MLA, Nat. Coun. Tchrs. English, N.E. Victorian Assn., N.Am. Victorian Studies Assn., Children's Lit. Assn. Office: Princeton U Dept English McCosh Hall Princeton NJ 08544-1016 Office Phone: 609-258-4070. E-mail: uknopf@princeton.edu.

KNOKE, DAVID HARMON, sociology educator; b. Phila., Mar. 4, 1947; s. Donald Glenn and Frances Harriet (Dunn) Knoke; m. Joann Margaret Robar, Aug. 29, 1970; 1 child, Margaret Frances. BA, U. Mich., 1969, MSW, 1971, PhD, 1972; MA, U. Chgo., 1970. Asst. prof. sociology Ind. U., Bloomington, 1972-75, assoc. prof., 1975-81, prof., 1981-85, dir. Inst. Social Rsch. and Ctr. for Survey Rsch., 1982-84; prof. sociology U. Minn., Mpls., 1985—, chmn., 1989-92, undergrad. dir., 1995-98, grad. dir., 1998—2002. Mem. sociology program rev. panel NSF, 1981-83; mem. sociology rev. panel Fulbright Scholars, 1993-95; mem. sociology com. Grad. Records Exams., 1998-2000. Author: Change and Continuity in American Politics, 1976, (with Peter J. Burke) Log-Linear Models, 1980, (with James R. Wood) Organized for Action, 1981, (with George W. Bohrnstedt and Alisa Potter Mee) Statistics for Social Data Analysis, 1982, 4th edit., 2002, (with James H. Kuklinski) Network Analysis, 1982, (with Edward O. Laumann) The Organizational State, 1987, Organizing for Collective Action, 1990, Political Networks, 1990, (with George W. Bohrnstedt) Basic Social Statistics, 1991, (with Franz Pappi, Jeffrey Broadbent and Yutaka Tsujinaka) Comparing Policy Networks, 1996, (with Arne Kalleberg, Peter Marsden and Joe Spaeth) Organizations in America, 1996, (with Peter Capelli, Laurie Bassi, Harry Katz, Paul Osterman and Michael Useem) Change at Work, 1997, Changing Organizations, 2001, (with Song Yang) Social Network Analysis, 2007. Recipient NIMH Rsch. Scientist Devel. award, 1977-82, 14 rsch. grants NSF; Nat. Merit scholar, 1965-69, Fulbright Sr. Rsch. scholar, Germany, 1989, scholar, U. Minn. Coll. Liberal Arts, 1996-99; Ctr. Advanced Study Behavioral Scis. fellow, 1992-93. Mem. Am. Sociol. Assn. (chair orgns. and occupation sect. 1992-93), Sociol. Rsch. Assn., Acad. of Mgmt., Internat. Network for Social Network Analysis, European Group for Orgnl. Studies. Unitarian Universalist. Home: 7305 Wooddale Ave S Minneapolis MN 55435-4157 Office: U Minn Dept Sociology Minneapolis MN 55455 Office Phone: 612-624-4300. Business E-Mail: knoke@atlas.socsci.umn.edu.

KNOLES, GEORGE HARMON, history educator; b. LA, Feb. 20, 1907; s. Tully Cleon and Emily (Walline) K.; m. Amandalee (Barker), June 12, 1930; children: Ann Barker (Nitzan), Alice Laurane (Simmons). AB (hon.), Coll. of Pacific, 1928, AM, 1930; PhD, Stanford U., 1939. Instr. history Union High Sch., Lodi, Calif., 1930-35; history asst. Stanford, 1935-36; history instr., 1937-41; asst. prof., 1942-46; assoc. prof., 1946-51; prof. history, 1951-72; Margaret Byrne, prof. Am. history, 1968-72; emeritus, 1972—; chmn. history dept., 1968-72. Dir. Inst. Am. History, 1956-72; prof. history; chmn. div. social sci. State Coll. Edn., Greeley, Colo., 1941-42; summer tchr. Central Wash. Coll. Edn., Ellensburg, 1939, State Coll., Flagstaff, Ariz, 1940, 1941, U. Calif. at Los Angeles, 1947; Stanford U., Tokyo U.; Am. Studies Seminars, Tokyo, 1950-52, 56, U. Wyo., 1955; cons. acad. history Hdq. USAF, 1950-52; dir. summer Inst. Tchrs. Am., Alpach, Austria, 1965; Blazer lectr. U. Ky., 1961; Throchmorton lectr. Lewis an Clark Coll., 1965; Fulbright distinguished lectr., Japan, 1971 Author: The Presidential Campaign and Election of 1892, 1942; Readings in Western Civilization, (with Rixford K. Snyder), 1951; The Jazz Age Revisited, 1955, The New United States, 1959; Editor: The Crisis of The Union, 1860-61, 1965; Sources in American History, 10 vols, 1965-66, The Responsibilities of Power, 1900-1929, 1967; Essays and Assays: California History Reappraised, 1973; Contbg. articles to profl. jour. Lt., USNR, 1944-46. Mem. Am. So. Hist. Assn.; Orgn. Am. Historians (exec. com. 1950-54, bd. editors rev. 1955-58); Am. Studies Assn. (council 1952-54); Soc. of Am. Historians. Clubs: Commonwealth. Methodist. Home: 850 Webster St Apt 220 Palo Alto CA 94301-2878

KNOLL, ANDREW HERBERT, biology professor; b. West Reading, Pa., Apr. 23, 1951; s. Robert Samuel and Anna Augusta (Meyer) K.; m. Marsha Craig, June 22, 1974; children: Kirsten C., Robert A. BA with highest honors, Lehigh U., 1973; MA, Harvard U., 1974, PhD, 1977; PhD (hon.), Uppsala U., Sweden, 1996; DSc (hon.), Lehigh U., 1998. Asst. prof. geology Oberlin Coll., Ohio, 1977-82; assoc. prof. Harvard U., Cambridge, Mass., 1982-85, prof. biology, 1985-2000, curator bot. mus., 1985—, prof. earth and planetary sci., 1985—, chmn. dept. organismic and evolutionary biology, 1992-98, 2004—05, Fisher prof. natural history, 2000—, assoc. dean faculty Arts and Scis., 2000—03. Mem. com. on planetary biology U.S. Space Sci. Bd., 1982-88, NRC Bd. on Earth Scis., 1987-88, 92-95, space studies bd., 1989-90, 97-2000; Crosby vis. lectr. MIT, 1999; mem. sci. team NASA MER 2003 Mars Mission. Assoc. editor Paleobiology, 1980-92, Precambrian Rsch., 1985—, Trends in Ecology and Evolution, 1987-92, Rev. of Palaeobotany and Palynology, 1987—, Am. Jour. Sci., 1990—, Geology, 1992-98, Palaios, 1996-2002, Palaeography Palacoclimatology Palaeocology, 1997—, Internat. Jour. Plant Scis., 1998—; contbr. articles to profl. publs. Bd. dirs. U.S. Nat. Mus. Nat. Hist., 1993-97. Named one of Time/CNN America's Best Scientists, 2002; recipient Walcott medal, Nat. Acad. Scis., 1987, Chang prize in paleontology, Am. Mus. Natural History, 2001, Moore medal, Soc. Sedimentary Geology, 2005, Bownocker medal, Ohio State U., 2005, medal, Paleontological Soc., 2005, Wollaston medal, Geol. Soc. London, 2007; fellow, Geol. Soc. Am., Linnean Soc., London, Am. Acad. Arts and Scis., 1987, Guggenheim, 1987; Vis. fellow, Gonville and Caius Coll., Cambridge, Eng., 1991—92. Fellow AAAS, European Union Geoscis. (hon.); mem. NAS, Bot. Soc. Am., Am. Philos. Soc., Paleontol. Soc. (Schuchert award 1987, medal, 2005), Soc. Study Evolution, Phi Beta Kappa (book award in sci. 2003), Sigma Xi. Avocations: travel, reading, cooking, choral music. Office: Harvard Univ Botanical Museum 26 Oxford St Cambridge MA 02138-2902 E-mail: aknoll@oeb.harvard.edu.

KNOLL, GLORIA JEAN, music educator; b. Bismarck, ND, Mar. 6, 1947; d. Gustav and Edna Kosanke; m. James L. Pearson (div.); children: Kristin Pearson, James K. Pearson, Erik Pearson, Erin Pearson; m. Marvin P. Knoll, June 15, 1991. BS, Minn. State U., Moorhead, 1969. Cert. tchr. ND, 1969. Vocal and instrumental instr. Grandin HS, ND, 1970—73, Prairie Rose Elem. Sch., Bismarck, 1979—89, Hagen Jr. HS, Dickinson, ND, 1989—99, Horizon Mid. Sch., Bismarck, 1999—; vocal music instr. Nathan Twining Jr. HS, Grand Forks, ND, 1973—76. Site chmn. Western Dakota Assn. Music Festival, Bismarck, 2006—; mem. Oahe Women's Orgn., Bismarck, 2004—06; mem. mission outreach McCabe United Meth. Ch., Bismarck, 2000—06. Mem.: Am. Choral Dirs. Assn. (ND state pres. 2003—, ND state membership chmn. 2000—03). Office: Horizon Mid Sch 500 Ash Coulee Dr Bismarck ND 58503 Business E-Mail: gloria_knol@educ8.org.

KNOLL, JAMES LEWIS, lawyer; b. Chgo., Oct. 5, 1942; AB, Brown U., 1964; JD, U. Chgo., 1967. Bar: Ill. 1967, Oreg. 1971, Wash. 1984, Alaska 1993. Mediator, arbitrator, Portland, Oreg. Adj. prof. law Northwestern Sc. Law, Lewis and Clark Coll., 1982-91. Mem. ABA (mem. TIPS coun. 1989-92, chair property ins. com. 1984-85, mem. fidelity surety com., chair comml. tort com. 1985-86), Oreg. State Bar (editor 2 vol. text on ins. 1983, 96), Wash. State Bar, Oreg. Assn. Def. Coun. (pres. 1984). Office: 1500 SW Taylor St Portland OR 97205-1819 E-mail: jim@hamiltonmediation.com.

KNOLL, JEANNETTE THERIOT, state supreme court justice; b. Baton Rouge; m. Jerold Edward Knoll; children: Triston Kane, Eddie Jr., Edmond Humphries, Blake Theriot, Jonathan Paul. BA in Polit. Sci., Loyola U., 1966; JD, Loyola U. Sch. of Law, 1969; LLM in Jud. Process, U. Va. Sch. of Law, 1996; studied with Maestro Adler, Mannes Coll. of Music, 1962-63. Criminal defense atty., first asst. dist. atty. Twelfth Jud. Dist. Ct. Avoyelles Parish, 1972-82; gratuitous atty., advisor U.S. Selective Svc., Marksville, La.; judge (3d cir.) U.S. Ct. of Appeal, 1982-93; assoc. justice La. Supreme Ct., 1997—. Instr. La. Jud. Coll.; chair CLE La. Ct. of Appeal Judges; former mem. state bd. of La. Commn. on Law Enforcement & Criminal Justice; former mem. Past pres. Bus. and Profl. Women's Club; Marksville C. of C.; active Am. Legion Aux.; dir. Arts & Humanities Council of Avoyelles, Inc.; former chmn. La. March of Dimes. Named La. Crimefighters' Outstanding Jurist of Yr., 2000; named to La. Political Hall of Fame, 2000; recipient Met. Opera Assn., New Orleans Opera Guild Scholarship, Outstanding Jud. award, Victims & Citizens Against Crime, Inc., 1995, 2002. Mem.: La. State Bar Assn. Office: La Supreme Ct 400 Royal St New Orleans LA 70130*

KNOLL, MICHAEL STEVEN, law educator; b. Bronx, NY, Apr. 23, 1957; s. Alvin D. and Donna A. (Miller) K. AB, U. Chgo., 1977, AM, 1980, PhD in Econs., 1983, JD, 1984. Bar: Ill., N.Y., D.C. Law clk. to hon. Alex Kozinski US Ct. Appeals (9th cir.), Pasadena, Calif., 1986; legal advisor to vice chmn. US Internat. Trade Commn., Washington, 1984-87; assoc. Debevoise & Plimpton, NYC, 1987-89; of counsel, assoc. Irell & Manella, L.A., LA, 1989-95; asst. prof. U. So. Calif. Law Ctr., LA, 1990-92, assoc. prof., 1992-95, prof., 1995-2000; prof. real estate Wharton Sch., U. Pa., Phila., 2000—; prof. law U. Pa. Law Sch., Phila., 2000—04, assoc. dean, 2004—06, Earle Hepburn prof., 2005—06, Theodore Warner prof., 2006—. Contbr. articles to profl. jours. Mem. Am. Fin. Assn., Am. Econ. Assn. Fin. Mgmt. Assn., Order of Coif. Office: U Pa Law Sch 3400 Chestnut St Philadelphia PA 19104 Office Fax: 215-573-2025. Business E-Mail: mknoll@law.upenn.edu.

KNOLLENBERG, JOSEPH CASTL (JOE KNOLLENBERG), congressman; b. Mattoon, Ill., Nov. 28, 1933; m. Sandie (Moto) Knollenberg; children: Martin, Stephen. BS in Social Sci., Eastern Ill. U., 1955. CLU. Agent, owner ins. co., 1960-93; mem. US Congress from 9th Mich. Dist. (formerly 11th), 1993—, mem. budget com. appropriations, mem. stds. of offcl. conduct coms. Past chmn., Birmingham Cable TV Community Adv. Bd., 18th Dist. Rep. Com., Rep. Com. Oakland County, 1978-86; past pres. St. Bede's Parish Coun., Evergreen Sch. PTA (Birmingham Sch. Dist.), Bloomfield Glens Homeowner's Assn., Cranbrook Homeowner's Assn.; past coord. Southfield Ad Hoc Park and Recreation Devel. Com.; past mem. Southfield Mayor's Wage and Salary Com.; chmn. Candidate Assistance Com./State Com., Oakland County Campaign, 1978; former regional/vice chair 17th Dist. Com., 1975-77; mem. Rep. State Com; exec. com. mem. and fin. com. Rep. Com. Oakland County; founder, mem. Rep. Leadership Com. Oakland County, 1984—; mem. Allstate Ins. Co's P.A.C.; del. Rep. Nat. Conv., 1980; del. to every state convention since 1974. Served as CPL US Army, 1955—57. Recipient Baltic Freedom award, Baltic Am. Freedom League, 2000, Legis. of Yr., Am. Small Manufactures Coalition, 2004. Mem. Am. Soc. Chartered Life Underwriters, Detroit Assn. Life Underwriters, Oakland County Lincoln Rep. Club, Troy C. of C. (current vice chmn.). Republican. Roman Catholic. Office: US Congress 2349 Rayburn HOB Washington DC 20515-2211 also: District Office 30833 Northwestern Hwy Ste 100 Farmington Hills MI 48334 Office Phone: 202-225-5802, 248-851-1366. Office Fax: 202-226-2356.*

KNOLLER, GUY DAVID, lawyer; b. NYC, July 23, 1946; s. Charles and Odette Knoller; children: Jennifer Judy, Geoffrey David. BA cum laude, Bloomfield Coll., NJ, 1968; JD cum laude, Ariz. State U., 1971. Bar: Ariz. 1971, U.S. Dist. Ct. Ariz. 1971, U.S. Supreme Ct. 1976. Trial atty. atty. gen.'s hons. program Dept. Justice, 1971-72; atty., adv. NLRB, 1972-73, field atty. region 28 Phoenix, 1972-74; assoc. Powers, Ehrenreich, Boutell & Kurn, Phoenix, 1974-79; ptnr. Froimson & Knoller, Phoenix, 1979-81, Fannin, Terry & Hay, Phoenix, 1981—85; sole practice Phoenix, 1985—; of counsel Burns & Burns. Mem. bd. visitors Ariz. State U. Coll. Law, 1975-76; pres. Ariz. Theatre Guild, 1990, 91. Fellow Ariz. Bar Found.; mem. ABA, State Bar Ariz. (chmn. labor rels. sect. 1977-78), Ariz. State U. Coll. Law Alumni Assn. (pres. 1977). Office: 2828 N Central Ave Ste 1110 Phoenix AZ 85004-1028 Home Phone: 602-801-9071; Office Phone: 602-230-1099. Business E-Mail: gdkpc@pcslink.com.

KNOPF, ALFRED, JR., retired publisher; b. White Plains, NY, June 17, 1918; s. Alfred A. and Blanche (Wolf) K.; m. Alice Laine, July 27, 1952; children— Alison, Susan, David. Grad., Phillips Exeter Acad., 1937; AB, Union Coll., Schenectady, 1942. With Atheneum Pubs., NYC, 1959-88, chmn. bd., 1964-88. Vis. chmn. Scribner Book Cos.; sr. v.p. MacMillan Pub. Co. (ret.). Capt. USAAF, 1941-45. Mem. Delta Upsilon. Clubs: Dutch Treat (N.Y.C.); Tavern (Chgo.). Home: 530 E 72nd St Apt 18F New York NY 10021-4864

KNOPF, BARRY ABRAHAM, lawyer, educator; b. Passaic, NJ, May 11, 1946; s. Edward and Sonia (Sameth) K.; children: Elisa, Scott. Student, Rutgers U., 1968, JD, 1972. Bar: N.J. 1972, U.S. Dist. Ct. N.J. 1972, U.S. Tax Ct. 1975, U.S. Supreme Ct. 1975, U.S. Ct. Appeals (3d cir.) 1981; cert. civil trial atty., NJ Supreme Ct. Assoc. Cohn & Lifland, Saddle Brook, N.J., 1972-75, ptnr., 1975—. Instr. N.J. Inst. for Continuing Legal Edn., 1982—, Nat. Inst. Trial Advocacy, 1989—; adj. faculty Hofstra U. Sch. of Law, 2000. Co-author: Professional Negligence, Law of Malpractice in New Jersey, 1979, 5th edit., 2001, Personal Injury Litigation Practice in New Jersey, 1990, Civil Trial Preparation, Practical skills Series, 1992, 2d edit., 1996, New Jersey Product Liability Law, 1994; editor, author: Lexus Nexus Practice Guide, New Jersey Personal Injury Litigation, 2007. V.p. Temple Beth Tikvah, Wayne, NJ, 1985—93, pres., 1993—95. Mem. Morris Pashman Inn of Ct. (master 1998-), Trial Lawyers Care. Home: 1014 Smith Manor Blvd West Orange NJ 07052-4227 Office: Cohn Lifland Pearlman Herrmann & Knopf Park 80 West 1 Saddle Brook NJ 07663 Office Phone: 201-845-9600. Business E-Mail: bak@njlawfirm.com.

KNOPF, CLAIRE, editor, writer; b. Passaic, NJ, Apr. 22, 1939; d. Isadore and Helen Knopf. Student, Mich. State U., 1957—59, U. Calif., Berkeley, 1960—61, Columbia U., NYC, 1962—63, Parsons Sch. Design, 1995—96. Freelance copy editor Massada Pub. Co., The Magnes Press, The Hebrew U., Israel, 1970—79; writer Edrei-Sharon Publs., Israel, 1970—79; copy editor Time Mag., Time Warner, Inc., NYC, 1980—96; freelance copy editor New Woman Mag., Vogue Mag., 1997—2000, US Weekly, BabyTalk, Smart Money, In Touch Weekly, Marie Claire, Food & Wine, Ladies' Home Jour., Psychology Today Mag., NYC2012, U.S. Candidate City for Olympic Games; copy editor, writer, reporter Salt Lake Olympic Winter Games and Paralympic Winter Games, Salt Lake City, 2000—02; writer, reporter, rschr. Internat. Figure Skating Mag., 2002—. Mem.: Soc. Children's Book Writers and Illustrators, Time-Life Alumni Soc., NY Press Club, Inc. Avocations: art, writing children's books, ice skating, cross country skiing. Home: Apt 14M 6040 Boulevard East West New York NJ 07093 Personal E-mail: claireknopf@earthlink.net.

KNOPF, KENYON ALFRED, economist, educator; b. Cleve., Nov. 24, 1921; s. Harold C. and Emma A. (Underwood) K.; m. Madelyn Lee Siddy Trebilcock, Mar. 28, 1953 (dec. June 1999); children— Kristin Lee, Mary George. AB magna cum laude with high honors in Econs., Kenyon Coll., 1942; MA in Econs.; PhD, Harvard U., 1949; LLD (hon.), Kenyon Coll., 1993. Mem. faculty Grinnell Coll., 1949-67, prof. econs., 1960-67, Jentzen prof., 1961-67, chmn. dept., 1958-60, chmn. div. social studies, 1962-64, chmn. faculty, 1964-67; dean coll. Whitman Coll., Walla Walla, Wash., 1967-70, prof. econs., 1967-89, Hollon Parker prof. econs., 1985-89, prof. emeritus, 1989—, provost, 1970-81, dean faculty, 1970-78, acting pres., 1974-75; pub. interest dir. Fed. Home Loan Bank, Seattle, 1976-83. Mem. council undergrad. assessment program Ednl. Testing Service, 1977-80 Author: (with Robert H. Haveman) The Market System, 4th edit, 1981; A Lexicon of Economics, 1991; editor: Introduction to Economics Series (9 vols.), 1966, 2d edit., 1970-71; co-editor: (with James H. Strauss) The Teaching of Elementary Economics, 1960. Mem. youth coun. City of Grinnell, 1957—59; mem. Walla Walla County Mental Health Bd., 1968—75, Walla Walla Civil Svc. Commn., 1978—84, chmn., 1981—84; mem. Grinnell City Coun., 1964—67; pres. Walla Walla County Human Svcs. Adminstrv. Bd., 1975—77; mem. Ia. adv. coun. SBA; tax aide AARP/IRS Tax Counseling for Elderly, 1987—98, local coord., 1990—91, assoc. dist. coord. S.E. Wash., 1991—94, assoc. dist. coord. tng., 1994—98; bd. dirs. Skagit County Boys & Girls Club, 2001—, Walla Walla United Fund, 1968—76, pres., 1973; bd. dirs. Shelter Bay Cmty., Inc., 1995—2003, v.p., 1995—97, pres., 1997—2003; bd. dirs. La Conner Cmty. Scholarship Found., 1997—, La Conner Unit Boys and Girls Club, 1999—, pres., 2001—03. With USAF, 1942—46, PTO. Social Sci. Rsch. Coun. grantee, 1951-52. Mem.: Am. Conf. Acad. Deans (exec. com. 1970—77, chmn. 1975), Am. Assn. Ret. Persons, Kiwanis (pres. LaConner club 2003—04), Delta Tau Delta, Phi Beta Kappa. Office: 223 Skagit Way La Conner WA 98257-9602

KNOPF, MATTHEW J., lawyer; b. 1956; BA summa cum laude, SUNY, Stony Brook, 1981; JD, Univ. Chgo., 1986. Bar: Ill. 1986, Minn. 2000. Sr. v.p., gen. counsel County Seat Stores, Inc; atty. Skadden, Arps Law, NYC; ptnr., mergers, acquisitions corp. group Dorsey & Whitney LLP, Mpls., and co-chair, bus. restructuring practice group. Bd. dir. Minnetonka Ctr.Arts. Office: Dorsey & Whitney LLP Ste 1500 50 S Sixth St Minneapolis MN 55402-1498 Office Phone: 612-340-5603. Office Fax: 612-340-2868. Business E-Mail: knopf.matthew@dorsey.com.

KNOPF, PAUL MARK, immunologist; b. Trenton, NJ, Apr. 4, 1936; s. David and Beatrice Knopf; m. Carol Lois Harrison, June 29, 1958; children: Jeffrey William, Steven Harrison, Rachel Analiese. BSc, MIT, 1958, PhD, 1962. Postdoctoral fellow MRC Lab. Molecular Biology, Cambridge, Eng., 1962-64; spl. research assoc. Salk Inst., La Jolla, Calif., 1964-72; prof. med. sci. Brown U., Providence, 1972—2003, Charles A. and Helen B. Stuart prof. med. sci., 1992—2003, chmn. sect. molecular, cellular and devel. biology, 1990-94, chmn. dept. molecular microbiology and immunology, 1994-97, Stuart prof. emeritus med. sci., 2003—. Program dir. ACS Inst. Rsch. Grant, 1976—85; mem. study sect. on parasitic disease NIH, 1985—87; mem. sci. rev. com. Progeria Rsch. Found., 2002—; cons. EpiVax, Inc., 2003—, Ctr. for Internat. Health Rsch., 2005—. Recipient Career Devel. award NIH, 1966-72; named Tchr. of Yr. in Life Scis., Brown U., 1998; grantee NIH, 1966-76, 84-88, 91-99, Rockefeller Found., 1972-80, Edna McConnell Clark Found., 1976-85, WHO, 1979-94, MS Soc., 1989-90; Fulbright-Hays sr. fellow, 1978-79, Fogarty sr. internat. fellow, 1986-87. Mem. AAAS, Am. Assn. Immunologists, Am. Soc. Tropical Medicine and Hygiene, Soc. Neurosci., Am. Soc. Microbiology, New Eng. Assn. Parasitology. Office: Brown U Divsn Biology and Medicine PO Box G-B6 Providence RI 02912-9107 Office Phone: 401-863-1607. Business E-Mail: Paul_Knopf@Brown.edu.

KNOPMAN, DAVID S., neurologist; b. Phila., Oct. 6, 1950; AB, Dartmouth Coll., 1972; MD, U. Minn., 1975. Diplomate Am. Bd. Psychiatry and Neurology. Intern Hennepin County Med. Ctr., 1975-76; resident U. Minn., 1976-79, asst. prof. neurology Mpls., 1980-86, assoc. prof. neurology, 1986-98, prof., 1998—2000; cons. dept. neurology Mayo Clinic, Rochester, Minn., 2000—; prof. Mayo Clinic Coll. Medicine, Rochester, 2000—. Office: Mayo Clinic Dept Neurology Rochester MN 55905 Office Phone: 507-284-2511.

KNOPMAN, DEBRA SARA, environmental scientist, director, hydrologist, policy analyst; b. Phila., Aug. 13, 1953; d. Harold L. and Minnette (Smulyan) Knopman; m. Donald Weightman, Sept. 29, 1985; children: Leah Alana, David Atwood. BA, Wellesley Coll., 1975; MSCE, MIT, 1978; PhD, Johns Hopkins U., 1986. Sci. writer and editor, Washington, 1975-78; legis. asst. Daniel P. Moynihan, Washington, 1979-80; prof. staff mem. U.S. Senate Com. on Environ. and Pub. Works, Washington, 1980-83; student asst., office of groundwater U.S. Geol. Survey, Reston, Va., 1984-85, rsch. hydrologist, nat. rsch. program, 1985-86, hydrologist, br. of systems analysis, 1987-91, chief, br. or systems analysis, 1991-93; dep. asst. sec. water and sci. Dept. Interior, 1993-95; dir. Progressive Policy Inst. Ctr. for Innovation and Environ., 1995—. Mem. Nuclear Waste Tech. Rev. Bd., 1997—. Editor: Scientific Research in Israel, 1976; editor Geophysics News, 1990-92; contbr. articles to profl. jours. Mem. commn. on geoscis., environment and resources NRC, 1995-98. Henry R. Luce Found. scholar, Taiwan, 1978-79. Mem. Am. Geophys. Union (chair pub. info. com. 1990-92). Democrat. Jewish. Address: Progressive Policy Inst 600 Pennsylvania Ave SE Ste 400 Washington DC 20003-4350

KNOPP, ALEX, lawyer, mayor; b. Manchester, Conn., Sept. 23, 1947; m. Betty L. Bono, 1984. BA, Wesleyan U., 1969; JD, George Washington U., 1981. Bar: 1981. Councilman-at-large Common Coun., Norwalk, Conn., 1983-85, pres., 1985-86; mem. Conn. Ho. of Reps., 1987—2001; pvt. practice Norwalk, 1981—; mayor of Norwalk, 2001—05. Mem. Order of Coif, Phi Beta Kappa. Address: 35 5th St Norwalk CT 06855-2402 Personal E-mail: alexknopp@aol.com.

KNOPP, MARVIN ISADORE, mathematics professor; b. Chgo., Jan. 4, 1933; s. Mitshel and Minnie (Israel) K.; m. Josephine Zadovsky, June 9, 1957 (div. 1998); children: Seth David, Yudah Benjamin, Abby Alissa, Elana Melissa. BS, U. Ill., 1954, A.M., 1955, PhD, 1958. Rsch. mathematician Space Tech. Labs., LA, 1958-59; NSF postdoctoral fellow Inst. Advanced Study, Princeton, NJ, 1959-60; asst. prof. U. Wis., 1960-62, assoc. prof., 1962-67, prof., 1967-72; mathematician Nat. Bur. Standards, Washington, 1963-64; vis. prof. U. Basel, Switzerland, 1968-69; prof. U. Ill., Chgo., 1970-76, Temple U., Phila., 1976—, Bryn Mawr (Pa.) Coll., 1988-89. Mem. Inst. Advanced Study, Princeton, N.J., 1975, 78, 88; vis. prof. Ohio State U., spring 1979 Author: Theory of Area, 1969, Modular Functions in Analytic Number Theory, 1970, 2d edit., 1993, Hecke's Theory of Modular Forms and Diricblet Series, 2007; editor Ill. Jour. Math., 1971-78, The Ramanujan Jour., 1995—, Procs. of Conf. in Analytic Number Theory, 1981, others; contbr. articles to profl. jours. NSF grantee, 1960-90, Fulbright-Hays grantee NRC, 1975-76, Nat. Security Agy. grantee, 1990-93. Mem. Am. Math. Soc., London Math. Soc. Democrat. Jewish. Home: 923 Hagys Ford Rd Narberth PA 19072-1419 Office: Temple U Dept Math Philadelphia PA 19122 Home Phone: 610-664-3534; Office Phone: 215-204-7589.

KNORR, PATRICK, communications executive; b. 1973; BS in Social Sci., Kans. State U. Sr. mgmt. positions Internet Companies; internet mgr. Sunflower Broadband, 1998, gen. mgr.; dir., Strategic Planning The World Wide Co. Named one of 40 Executives Under 40, Multichannel News, 2006. Mem.: Am. Cable Assn. (vice chmn. 2004—). Office: Sunflower Broadband One Riverfront Plz Lawrence KS 66044 Office Phone: 785-841-2720. Business E-Mail: pknorr@sunflowerbroadband.com.

KNOSPE, WILLIAM HERBERT, medical educator; b. Oak Park, Ill., May 26, 1929; s. Herbert Henry and Dora Isabel (Spruce) K.; m. Adris M. Nelson, June 19, 1954. BA, U. Ill., Chgo. and Urbana, 1951; BS, U. Ill., 1952; MD, U. Ill., Chgo., 1954; MS in Radiation Biology, U. Rochester, 1962. Diplomate Am. Bd. Internal Medicine and Subspecialty Bd. on

Hematology. Rotating intern Upstate Med. Ctr. Hosps-SUNY-Syracuse, 1954-55; resident in medicine Ill. Central Hosp., Chgo., 1955-56, VA Research Hosp-Northwestern U. Med. Sch., Chgo., 1956-58; investigator radiation biology Walter Reed Army Inst. Research, Washington, 1962-64, investigator hematology, asst. chief dept. hematology, 1964-66; attending physician med. service Walter Reed Gen. Hosp., Washington, 1963-64, fellow in hematology, 1964-65; asst. chief hematology service, chief hematology clinic Walter Reed Army Inst. of Rsch., Washington, 1964-66; asst. attending staff physician Presbyn. St. Luke's Hosp., Chgo., 1967-68, asst. dir. hematology radiohematology lab., 1967-74, assoc. attending staff physician, 1968-74, sr. attending staff physician, 1974—; asst. prof. medicine U. Ill.-Chgo., 1967-69, assoc. prof., 1969-72; assoc. prof. medicine Rush Med. Coll., Chgo., 1971-74, prof. medicine, 1974—; dir. sect. hematology Rush-Presbyn.-St. Luke's Med. Ctr., Chgo., 1974-93; Elodia Kehm prof. hematology Rush-Med. Coll., Chgo., 1986-94, prof. emeritus, 1994—; prof. medicine U. N.Mex., Albuquerque, 1994—2002, emeritus, 2002—. Speaker at profl. confs. U.S. and abroad; vis. prof. medicine dept. hematology U. Basel, Switzerland, 1980-81, Cancer Ctr., U. N.Mex., 1992-93. Contbr. numerous articles to profl. publs. Trustee Ill. chpt. Leukemia Soc. Am., 1977-88, v.p., 1979-80; trustee Bishop Anderson House (Rush-Presbyn.-St. Luke's Ctr.), 1980-94. Served to capt. M.C., USAR, 1958-61, to lt. col., U.S. Army, 1961-66. Fellow ACP; mem. Am. Fedn. Clin. Research, AMA, Am. Soc. Hematology, Am. Soc. Clin. Oncology, Central Soc. Clin. Research, Chgo. Med. Soc., Inst. Medicine Chgo., Internat. Soc. Exptl. Hematology, Radiation Research Soc., Southeastern Cancer Study Group, Polycythemia Vera Study Group, Eastern Coop. Oncology Group, Ill. State Med. Soc., Assn. Hematology-Oncology Program Dirs., Sigma Xi, Chgo. Literary Club. Office: 310 Big Horn Ridge Dr NE Albuquerque NM 87122-1455

KNOTEK, CRYSTAL, air transportation executive; married; 4 children. BS, Concordia Coll., Moorhead, Minn.; M in Mktg. Edn., U. Minn. Reservation sales agt. NW Airlines Corp., 1985, various mgmt. positions in reservations and human resources depts., mng. dir. reservations sales and svc., v.p. reservations sales and svc., v.p. reservations and customer care, 2005—06, sr. v.p. customer svc. and ground ops., 2006—. Bd. mem. Wishes and More Found. Office: NW Airlines Corp 2700 Lone Oak Pky Eagan MN 55121 Office Phone: 612-726-2111.*

KNOTEK, ROBERT FRANK, retired management consultant, educator; b. Racine, Wis., May 10, 1945; s. Joseph Anthony and Josephine Marie (Lauer) K.; m. Janet Ilene Odegaard, Sept. 18, 1965; children: Kristine Margaret, Mikal Jon. LLB, LaSalle U., Chgo., 1973; MBA in Gen. Mgmt. with honors, Calif. Pacific U., 1987, MA in Human Behavior, 1988; postgrad., Harvard U., 1988, U. Autonoma Barcelona, Barcelona, 1997, Oxford U., 2002. Cert. profl. cons.; cert. econ. devel. fin. profl. Mdse. mgr. Schmitt Music Co., Mpls., 1966-74; founder, CEO Met. Music Corp., Richfield, Minn., 1974-87; prin. RFK-Bus. Cons., Eden Prairie, Minn., 1984-97; CEO Kaes Analytics, Inc., Eden Prairie, 1997—2003; ret., 2003. Adj. faculty Hennepin Tech. Coll., Plymouth, Minn., 1985-92, U. Minn. Extension Svc., Mpls., 1990-92, Normandale C.C., Bloomington, Minn., 1992-95, U. St. Thomas, St. Paul, 1995-98, U. Iowa, Iowa City, 1996-99, Nat. Am. U., Bloomington, Minn., 1999-02; adj. prof. LaSalle U., Mandeville, La., 1995-96; vis. scholar U. Tver, Russia, 1994; hosted del. Universitat de La Habana, Cuba, 1998; CIEE guest U. Western Cape, U. Pretoria, 1999. Author: Cash Flow Paradox, 1990, Entrepreneurship Lite, 1998; host (TV series) QCTV: Business Profiles, 1987-88; co-anchor (TV series) Normandale News; contbr. articles to profl. jours. Mem. Eden Prairie Pub. Schs. Com., 1989-91, Hennepin Tech. Coll. Adv. Bd., Plymouth, 1989-91; nominee U.S. Peace Corps, Ea. Europe, 1994. Recipient Cert. Appreciation Minn. Bd. of Vocat. Edn., 1990, Minn. Bd. Tech. Colls., 1991, Am. Soc. for Indsl. Protection, 1992, Golden Apple award C. of C., 1992, Group Study Exch. to Australia Rotary Internat. Found., 1996. Mem. Am. Booksellers Assn., Upper Midwest Booksellers Assn., Internat. Coun. Small Bus., Acad. Entrepreneurship (charter), Nat. Assn. Music Mchts., NY Acad. Scis., Mensa, Alpha Psi Omega, Iota Omega Chi. Libertarian. Lutheran. Avocations: gourmet cooking, jazz guitar. Home: 7614 Bristol Village Curv Bloomington MN 55438-2567 Personal E-mail: rknote19@skypoint.com.

KNOTT, DOUGLAS RONALD, dean, agricultural sciences educator, researcher; b. Fraser Mills, BC, Can., Nov. 10, 1927; s. Ronald David and Florence Emily (Keeping) K.; m. Joan Madeline Hollinshead, Sept. 2, 1950 (dec.); children: Holly Ann, Heather Lynn, Ronald Kenneth, Douglas James (dec.); m. Pat Decker, June 1, 2002 (dec.); m. Irene Sosulski, July 8, 2005. BSA, U. B.C., 1948; MS, U. Wis., 1949, PhD, 1952. Asst. prof. U. Sask., Saskatoon, 1952-56, assoc. prof., 1956-65, prof., 1965-93, head dept. crop sci., 1965-75, assoc. dean rsch. Coll. Agr., 1988-93; prof. emeritus, 1993—. Author: The Wheat Rusts—Breeding for Resistance, 1989; also numerous papers. Named to Saskatchewan Agr. Hall of Fame. Fellow Am. Soc. Agronomy, Agrl. Inst. Can.; mem. Can. Soc. Agronomy, Genetics Soc. Can., Order of Can. Mem. United Ch. of Can. Avocation: tennis. Office: U Sask Dept Plant Scis 51 Campus Dr Saskatoon SK Canada S7N 5A8 Office Phone: 306-966-5004. E-mail: dougknott@shaw.ca.

KNOTT, JENNIFER W., lawyer; b. Irving, Tex., May 9, 1974; BA cum laude, So. Meth. U., 1996; JD cum laude, So. Meth. U. Dedman Sch. Law, 2000. Bar: Tex. 2000, US Dist. Ct. (no. and ea. dists. Tex.). Assoc. McElree, Savage & Smith, P.C., Dallas. Comments editor: So. Meth. U. Law Rev., 1999—2000. Named a Rising Star, Tex. Super Lawyers mag., 2006. Mem.: Dallas Assn. Young Lawyers (mem. freedom run com. 2004, 2005), Dallas Bar Assn. Office: McElree Savage & Smith PC Plz of the Americas Ste 1600 600 N Pearl St Lock Box Number 175 Dallas TX 75201-2809 Office Phone: 214-979-0681. E-mail: jknott@mspc.com.*

KNOTT, JOHN RAY, JR., language educator; b. Memphis, July 9, 1937; s. John Ray and Wilma (Henshaw) K.; m. Anne Percy, Dec. 5, 1959; children: Catherine, Ellen, Walker, Anne. AB, Yale U., 1959, Carnegie fellow, 1960; PhD, Harvard U., 1965. Instr. Harvard U., 1965-67; mem. faculty U. Mich., Ann Arbor, 1967—2006, prof. English, 1976—2006, prof. emeritus English, 2006—, chmn. dept., 1982-87, assoc. dean Coll. Arts and Scis., 1977-80, acting dean Coll. Arts and Scis., 1980-81, interim dir. Inst. for Humanities, 1987-88, interim dir. Program in the Environment, 2001—02; ret., 2006. Dir. region IV Mellon Fellowship Selection Com., 1989-94. Author: Milton's Pastoral Vision, 1971, The Sword of the Spirit, 1980, Discourses of Martyrdom in English Literature, 1563-1694, 1993, Imagining Wild America, 2002; editor: The Triumph of Style, 1967, Mirrors: An Introduction to Literature, rev. edit., 1987, The Huron River: Voices From the Watershed, 2000, Reimagining Place, 2001; contbr. articles on Abbey, Berry, Browne, Bunyan, Fox, Foxe, Haines, Milton, and Spenser to scholarly jours. Woodrow Wilson fellow, 1960-61; NEH fellow, 1974 Mem.: MLA, Nature Conservancy. Office: Univ Mich Dept English Ann Arbor MI 48109

KNOTT, KENNETH, industrial engineering educator, consultant; b. Dudley, Worcestershire, Eng., Mar. 6, 1929; arrived in U.S., 1977; s. John Peter Grainger and Sarah (Turner) K.; m. Margaret Knott, Apr. 22, 1957; children: DiLwyn John, Tracy James. Diploma in Grad. Studies, Engring. Prodn., U. Birmingham at Edgbaston, Eng., 1956; MS in Indsl. Engring., Pa. State U., 1966; PhD in Engring. Prodn., Tech. U. Loughborough, Eng., 1983. Apprentice British Thompson Houston Co. Ltd., Birmingham, 1944-48, Coventry, Eng., 1948-50; design draftsman New Conveyor Co. Ltd., Smethwick, Eng., 1952-53; tech. asst. to gen. mgr. N. Hingley and Sons, Netherton, Eng., 1953-55; prodn. engr. Chubb and Sons, Ltd., Wolverhampton, Eng., 1955-56; plant mgr. John Morris Electrical Engring., Bilston, Eng., 1956; lectr. in prodn. engring. Dudley and Staffordshire Tech. Coll., Dudley, Eng., 1956-63; instr. in indsl. engring. Pa. State U., State College, 1963-66; mng. dir. Maynard Tng. Ctr., Birmingham, 1966-70, Kenneth Knott Ltd., Birmingham, 1966-77, Work Study Contract Svcs., Birmingham, 1970-77; asst. prof. indsl. and mgmt. systems engring. Pa. State U., 1977-84, assoc. prof. indsl. and mgmt. engring., 1984-87, prof. indsl. and mgmt. engring., 1987-95, emeritus prof. indsl. engring., 1996—. Mem. editorial bd. Internat. Jour. Prodn. Rsch., Loughborough, 1984—; mem. robotics sub-com. Welding Rsch. Coun., N.Y.C., 1977-79, welding processes sub-com., 1977-83; mem. com. maintenance in mfg. Nat. Mfg. Engring. Ctr., Ann Arbor, Mich., 1989-90. Author: Job Analysis Procedure Manual, 1970, (with others) A Comparison of Alternative Time Slotting Systems for Indirect Time Standards Work Measurement, 1986, An Analytical Approach to Designing and Testing Time Slotting Systems, 1986; co-author: Laboratory Manual Manufacturing Processes, 1965, Principles and Practice of MTM-2, 1970, Principles and Practice of MTM-3, 1971, Manufacturing Processes Associate Degree Program, 1980; editor Metods Time Measurement Jour., 1982-90; contbr. tech. papers to profl. jours. Recipient AT&T Found. Outstanding Teaching award Am. Soc. Engring. Edn., 1991, Lenhard Teaching fellowship Lenhardt Ctr. Innovative Teaching Pa. State U., 1992. Fellow Inst. Indsl. Engrs. (panel rsch. in work measurement work measurement and methods engring. divsn. 1981-83, assoc. editor IIE Transactions 1982-92, program chmn. 1983-87, rsch. chmn. 1984-89, reorganization com. 1988, divsn. dir. 1982-83, honors chmn. 1991—, pres. Ctrl. Pa. chpt. 1982-83, Phil Carroll award 1986, Tech. Innovation in Indsl. Engring. award 1993), World Acad. Productivity Sci., Soc. Am. Magicians, Pa. Soc. Profl. Engrs., Fedn. Productivity Scis. (hon., London), Methods Time Measurement Assn. (editor Methods Time Measurement Jour., chmn. midland region United Kingdom divsn. 1967-72, internat. com. investigation into Application Handbook Requirements 1970, tech. panel United Kingdom divsn. 1969-77, tng. and qualifications com.), Soc. Mfg. Engrs. (continuing edn. chmn. Ctrl. Pa. chpt. 1987, sec. 1993—), Internat. Brotherhood Magicians, Inner Magic Cir. (decorated Silver Star), Kano Soc., Sigma Xi, Alpha Pi Mu. Avocations: magic, Judo. Home: PO Box 234 Pine Grove Mills PA 16868-0234 Office: Pa State U 207 Hammond Bldg University Park PA 16802-1401 Office Phone: 814-234-2713. Personal E-mail: k.knott@fimexpert.com. Business E-Mail: kok@psu.edu.

KNOTT, WILEY EUGENE, retired electronics engineer; b. Muncie, Ind., Mar. 18, 1938; s. Joseph Wiley and Mildred Viola (Haxton) K.; 1 child, Brian Evan. BSEE, Tri-State U., 1963; postgrad., Union Coll., 1970-73, Ga. Coll., 1987. Assoc. aircraft engr. Lockheed-Ga. Co., Marietta, 1963-65; tech. publs. engr. GE, Pittsfield, Mass., 1965-77, sr. publs. engr., 1977-79, group leader, 1967-79; specialist engr. Boeing Mil. Airplane Co., Wichita, Kans., 1979-81, sr. specialist engr., 1981-84, 89-90, logistics mgr., 1984-85, customer support mgr., 1985-89, base mgr. Castle AFB, 1990-91; facilities plant ops. and maintenance engr. Boeing Comml. Airplane Co., Everett, Wash., 1991-92, lead engr., 1992-93, prin. engr., 1993-95, ret., 1995; part-time bus. cons., 1972—2003. Active Jr. Achievement, 1978-79, Am. Security Coun., 1975-90, Nat. Rep. Snatori al Com., 1979-86 , Nat. Rep. Congl. Com., 1979-87, Rep. Nat. Com., 1979-87 , Rep. Presdl. Task Force, 1981-86, Joint Presdl./Congl. Steering Com., 1982-86, Rep. Polit. Action Com., 1979-86, Mus. of Aviation, 1987-95; state advisor U.S. Congl. Adv. Bd., 1981-86; adviser Jr. Achievement, 1978-79. Mem. Sr. Coalition, Traditional Values Coalition. With AUS, 1956—59. Mem.: NRA, Nat. Army Mus. (founding sponsor), Judicial Watch, Assn. U.S. Army, Amvets, Nat. Def. Indsl. Assn. (life), Air Force Assn. (life), Golf Clubmakers Assn., Srs. Coalition, Overseas Brats, Mil. Brats, Heidelberg Am. H.S. Alumni Assn., Christian Srs. Assn., Am. Conservative Union, Amateur Radio Relay League, Am. Family Assn., Conservative Caucus, Ga. State Golf Assn., Nat. Audubon Soc., Gun Owners Am., The Heritage Found., Ocmulgee Audubon Soc., Ill. Rlwy. Mus., U.S. Golf Assn., PGA Tour Ptnrs. (life), Perry Country Club. Conservative. Presbyterian. Avocations: model building, golf, stamp collecting/philately, coin collecting/numismatics, railroading. E-mail: wileyknott@cox.net.

KNOTT, WILLIAM ALAN, library director; b. Muscatine, Iowa, Oct. 4, 1942; s. Edward Marlan and Dorothy Mae K.; m. Mary Farrell, Aug. 23, 1969; children: Andrew Jerome, Sarah Louise. BA in English, U. Iowa, 1967, MA in L.S., 1968. Asst. dir. Ottumwa (Iowa) Pub. Libr., 1968-69; libr. cons. Iowa State Libr., Des Moines, 1968-69; dir. Hutchinson (Kans.) Pub. Libr., S. Cen. Kans. Libr. Sys., 1969-71, Jefferson County Pub. Libr., Lakewood, Colo., 1971—. With USAR, 1965—67. Mem.: ALA, Urban Librs Coun., Colo. Libr. Assn. Office: Jefferson County Pub Libr 10200 W 20th Ave Lakewood CO 80215-1402 Home Phone: 303-423-3160; Office Phone: 303-275-2200. Business E-Mail: wknott@jefferson.lib.co.us.

KNOTTS, ROBERT SPENCER (BOB KNOTTS), writer, playwright; b. Detroit, Dec. 9, 1952; s. John William and Elizabeth Jeanette Knotts. Writer various Vt. newspapers, Burlington, Vt., 1980—83; reporter, anchor WJOY Radio, Burlington, 1983—86; reporter WCAX-TV, Burlington, 1986—89; writer, reporter South Fla. Sun-Sentinel, Fort Lauderdale, Fla., 1989—94; writer Fort Lauderdale, Fla., 1994—. Author: (book) Super Eight: Today's Hottest Sports Stars, 1999, The Summer Olympics, 2000, Pocket Guide to the 2000 Olympics, 2000, Martial Arts, 2000, Equestrian Events, 2000, Weightlifting, 2000, Track and Field, 2000, Hard News, 2001, Florida History, 2002, Florida Plants and Animals, 2002, Florida Native Peoples, 2002, All Around Florida, 2002, Uniquely Florida, 2002, People of Florida, 2002, (plays) Never Nothin' Again No More, 2001, In Mordant Whispers, 2003, Empath 52 Equals You, 2004, This (Bleep)ing World, 2005; author: (under pen name M.D. Spenser) 10 juvenile novels; So. Arts Fedn., 2005, 2006—07; contbg. editor: Arthur Frommer's Budget Travel, 1999—2005; contbr. articles to mags. including Sports Illustrated, Travel & Leisure, USA Weekend, N.Y. Times, Family Circle, Reader's Digest. Pres., founder Humanity Project, 2007—. Recipient Various Writing & Journalism awards, Fla. Mag. Assn., 2001, Associated Press, 1984, 1985, 1986, Vt. Broadcasters Assn., 1984, 1985, 1986. Mem.: PEN Fla. (sec., treas.), Poets, Playwrights, Editors, Essayists, Novelists, Dramatists Guild of Am., Authors Guild. Avocations: music, auto racing, weightlifting. Office Phone: 954-205-2722. Personal E-mail: rsk1writer@bellsouth.net. Business E-Mail: rsk@thehumanityproject.com.

KNOUS, PAMELA K., wholesale distribution executive; b. Minn. Student, Carleton Coll.; BA in Math., U. Ariz., BS in Bus. Adminstrn. Ptnr. KPMG Peat Marwick, LA, 1977—91; group v.p. finance The Vons Companies, Inc., 1991—94; sr. v.p., CFO The Vons. Companies, Inc., 1994; exec. v.p., CFO The Vons Companies, Inc., 1995—97, treas.; exec. v.p., CFO Supervalu Inc., Mpls., 1997—. Bd. dir. Tennant Co., Twin Cities Pub. Television. Office: Supervalu Inc 11840 Valley View Rd Eden Prairie MN 55344 Office Phone: 952-828-4000. Office Fax: 952-828-8998.*

KNOWLES, BEYONCÉ GISELLE See BEYONCÉ

KNOWLES, CHARLES TIMOTHY, lawyer, state legislator, military officer, educator; b. Providence, Aug. 21, 1949; s. Charles Timothy and Olga (Dower) K.; m. Sandra J. Bellem; children: Justin, Jennifer. BA, U. R.I., 1971; JD cum laude, New Eng. Sch. Law, 1977; MA, US Army War Coll., 2000. Bar: R.I., U.S. Dist. Ct. (R.I.), U.S. Supreme Ct. Assoc. Robinson & Resnick, Warwick, RI, 1977—79, Haronian & Paquin, Warwick, 1979—84; ptnr. Knowles & Bissonnette, Warwick, 1984—; mem. R.I. Ho. of Reps., Providence, 1989—97, chmn. jud. com., 1993—97; ret.; legal counsel corp. com. R.I. Ho. of Reps., 2000—; adj. prof. Johnson and Wales U., 2001—06; pvt. practice, 2006—. Sec. Narragansett (R.I.) Dem. Ctrl. Com., 1982-93; vice-chmn. Narragansett Zoning Bd., 1982-88; coach Narragansett Little League, 1982-88. 1st lt. U.S. Army, 1971-73; Col. R.I. ARNG, 1974-99, brig. comdr., 1997-99; comdr. 1021st civil affairs group, 1999-2001. Decorated Legion of Merit, Meritorious Svc. medal (3), Master Parachutist Wings, Spl. Forces Tab; named to St. Andrew's Hall of Fame, 2002. Mem. ACLU, RI Bar Assn., Am. Legion, Save the Bay, Common Cause, St. Andrew's Alumni Assn. Episcopalian. Home and Office: 56 Fowler St North Kingstown RI 02852-5010 Office Phone: 401-667-7990. Personal E-mail: ctkcolinf@aol.com.

KNOWLES, ELIZABETH PRINGLE, museum director; b. Decatur, Ill., Jan. 9, 1943; d. William Bull and Elizabeth E. (Pillsbury) Pringle; m. Joseph E. Knowles; 1 child, Elizabeth Bakewell. BA in Humanities with honors, Stanford U., 1964; MA in Art History, U. Calif., Santa Barbara, 1968; grad., Mus. Mgmt. Inst., 1984; MBA, Rensselaer Poly. Inst., 1999. Cert. jr. coll. tchr. Calif. Instr. art history Murray State U., Murray, Ky., 1967-68; instr. Santa Barbara Art Inst., 1969, Santa Barbara City Coll., 1969-70, 76-78, instr. cont. edn., 1973-86; from staff coord. docents to curator edn. Santa Barbara Mus. Art, 1974-86; assoc. dir. Meml. Art Gallery, Rochester, NY, 1986-88; instr. mus. studies Calif. State U., Long Beach, 1989; exec. dir. Lyman Allyn Art Mus., New London, Conn., 1989-95; pres. Only In Conn. Spl. Interest Tours, Chester, 1995-97; supr. mus. edn. programs Mystic (Conn.) Seaport Mus., 1996-2001; exec. dir. Wildling Art Mus., Los Olivos, Calif., 2001—. Instr. continuing edn. Santa Barbara City Coll., 1973—86, 2002—. Contbr. essays to art catalogues. Bd. dirs., chmn. Met. Transit Dist., Santa Barbara, 1978—80; commr. Santa Barbara City Planning Commn., 1975—77; founding pres. Santa Barbara Contemporary Arts Forum, 1976—78. Fellow Kellogg Found., Smithsonian Inst., 1985. Mem.: New Eng. Mus. Assn. (v.p. 1993—95), Coll. Art Assn., Am. Assn. Mus. (treas. edn. com. 1986—88). Home Phone: 805-686-4640; Office Phone: 805-688-1082. E-mail: Penny@wildlingmuseum.org.

KNOWLES, HARRY JAY, internet personality, blogger, film critic; b. May 12, 1971; s. Jay and Helen Knowles; m. Patricia Jones, July 15, 2007. Founder, owner website Ain't It Cool News, 1996—. Salesman vintage film memorabilia. Author: Ain't It Cool?: Hollywood's Redheaded Stepchild Speaks Out, 2003; film critic, Penthouse mag., 2006-; film appearances: Ballad of the Sad Cafe, 1991, Colin Fitz, 1997, The Faculty, 1998, Monkeybone, 2001, Ghosts of Mars, 2001, Texas Chainsaw Massacre, 2003, No Pain, No Gain, 2005, Pathogen, 2006. Named No. 82 of 100 Best Things to Happen to Hollywood, Movieline mag., 1997, No. 25 on Forbes Power List, 2000, No. 1 Entertainment News Site in World, London Times, 2005; named one of Top 25 Web Celebs, Forbes mag., 2007, named to Top 50 Influence List of high impact media players, Brill's Content, 2000. Office: PO Box 180011 Austin TX 78718-0011 Business E-Mail: harry@aintitcool.com.*

KNOWLES, JAMES KENYON, applied mathematician, educator; b. Cleve., Apr. 14, 1931; s. Newton Talbot and Allyan (Gray) K.; m. Jacqueline De Bolt, Nov. 26, 1952; children: John Kenyon, Jeffrey Gray, James Talbot. SB in Math., MIT, 1952, PhD, 1957; DSc (hon.), Nat. U. Ireland, 1985. Instr. math. MIT, Cambridge, 1957-58; asst. prof. applied mechanics Calif. Inst. Tech., Pasadena, 1958-61, assoc. prof., 1961-65, prof. applied mechanics, 1965—, William R. Kenan Jr. prof., 1991—, William R. Kenan Jr. prof. emeritus, 1996—. Vis. prof. MIT, 1993-94; cons. in field. Contbr. articles to profl. jours. Recipient Eringen medal, Soc. Engring. Sci., 1991, Goodwin medal, MIT, 1955. Fellow: AAAS, ASME (Koiter medal 2002), Am. Acad. Mechanics. Office: Calif Inst Tech Divsn Engrng & Applied Sci 104-44 1201 E California Pasadena CA 91125-0001 Office Phone: 626-395-4135. Business E-Mail: knowles@caltech.edu.

KNOWLES, JEFFREY D., lawyer; b. Washington, Apr. 22, 1949; BA, Columbia Univ., 1971; JD, NY Law Sch., 1975. Bar: NY 1976, DC 1977. Co-founder, gen. counsel Electronic Retailing Assn., 1990—2003; ptnr., govt. divsn. Venable LLP, Washington, and head, advt., mktg. practice group. Mem.: ABA, Promotion Mktg. Assn., Direct Mktg. Assn., Electronic Retailing Assn. (bd. dir.). Office: Venable LLP 575 Seventh St NW Washington DC 20004 Office Phone: 202-344-4860. Office Fax: 202-344-8300. Business E-Mail: jdknowles@venable.com.

KNOWLES, JEREMY RANDALL, chemist, educator, dean; b. Rugby, England, Apr. 28, 1935; came to U.S., 1974; s. Kenneth Guy Jack Charles and Dorothy Helen (Swingler) K.; m. Jane Sheldon Davis, July 30, 1960; children: Sebastian David Guy, Julius John Sheldon, Timothy Fenton Charles. BA, Balliol Coll., Oxford U., Eng., 1958; MA, D.Phil., Christ Ch., 1961; Doctor honoris causa, U. Edinburgh, 1992, ETH, Switzerland, 2001. Rsch. fellow Calif. Inst. Tech., 1961-62; fellow Wadham Coll., Oxford U., 1962-74, univ. lectr., 1966-74; vis. prof. Yale U., 1969, 71; Sloan vis. prof. Harvard U., 1973, prof. chemistry, 1974—, Amory Houghton prof. chemistry and biochemistry, 1979—, dean faculty of arts and scis., 1991—2002, interim dean faculty of arts and scis., 2006—07, disting. svc. prof., 2003—. Newton-Abraham vis. prof. Oxford U., 1983-84; hon. fellow Balliol Coll., Oxford U., Wadham Coll., Oxford U.; trustee Howard Hughes Med. Inst. Author papers, revs. bioorganic chemistry. Served as pilot officer RAF, 1953-55. Recipient Prelog medal ETH, Switzerland, CBE award (Queen's Birthday Honours), Eng., 1993, Welch award Robert A. Welch Found., 1995, Harvard medal, 2002. Fellow: Royal Soc. (Davy medal 1991), Am. Acad. Arts and Scis., Royal Chem. Soc. London (hon. Charmian medal); mem.: NAS (fgn. assoc.), Am. Philos. Soc., Am. Soc. Biol. Chemists, Am. Chem. Soc. (Nakanishi award 1999, Bader award 1989, Cope Scholar award 1989, Repligen award 1992), Biochem. Soc. London. Home: 67 Francis Ave Cambridge MA 02138-1911 Office: Harvard U Dept Chemistry 12 Oxford St Cambridge MA 02138-5722 Office Phone: 617-495-1566.

KNOWLES, JULIE NALL, secondary school educator; b. Webb, Ala., Nov. 5, 1941; d. Eolie Edward and Creola (Carter) Nall; m. William Durwood Knowles, Jan. 17, 1970. BS in Edn. magna cum laude, Troy State U., Ala., 1965; MA in English, Samford U., Birmingham, Ala., 1969; PhD in English, Auburn U., Ala., 1980; AA in Music, Chattahoochee Valley CC, Phenix City, Ala., 1999. Cert. tchr. Ala., Ga., Fla. Tchr. Ahrens H.S. Jefferson County Schs., Louisville, 1975—76; instr. Auburn U., Ala., 1981—82; assoc. prof. Stillman Coll., Tuscaloosa, Ala., 1983—85; asst. prof. Mercer U., Macon, Ga., 1986—87; prof. Troy State U., Phenix City, Ala., 1987—99; tchr. Camden County HS Camden County Schs., Kingsland, Ga., 1999—2000; tchr. Paxon Sch. Advanced Studies Duval County Sch. Sys., Jacksonville, Fla., 2000—04; prof. Bapt. Coll. of Fla., Graceville, 2005—. Editor, creator: The Chariot, 1988-91; contbr. articles to mags. Ch. pianist Turners Station Bapt Ch., Ky., 1973—76, Union Grove Bapt. Ch., Opelika, Ala., 1976—82, Hatchechubbee Bapt. Ch., Ala., 1988—95; mem. choir Folkston Bapt. Ch., Ga., 2000—. Rsch. grantee Troy State U., 1992; recipient Woodrow Hale Meml. Prize # 1 Green River Writers, 1996. Mem. Profl. Assn. Ga. Educators, Phi Theta Kappa, Phi Kappa Phi, Kappa Delta Pi (counselor Rho Phi chpt. 1989-92, Point of Excellence award 1993). Democrat. Southern Baptist. Avocations: motorcycling, piano, fishing. Home: 10076 E State Hwy 52 Webb AL 36376 Office Phone: 850-263-3261 ext. 467.

KNOWLES, MARIE L., transportation executive; Sr. fin. analyst Arco Transp. Co., Long Beach, Calif., 1972-1986; asst. treas. for banking, 1986-1988; v.p. of fin., planning and control ARCO Internat. Oil and Gas Co., 1988-90; v.p. and controller ARCO, 1990-93; sr. v.p. and pres. ARCO Transp. Co., 1993-96, exec. v.p., CFO LA, 1996—. Office: Atlantic Richfield 4 Centerpointe Dr La Palma CA 90623-2502

KNOWLES, MARJORIE FINE, law educator, dean; b. Bklyn., July 4, 1939; d. Jesse J. and Roslyn (Leff) Fine; m. Ralph I. Knowles, Jr., June 3, 1972. BA, Smith Coll., 1960; LLB, Harvard U., 1965. Bar: Ala., N.Y., D.C. Teaching fellow Harvard U., 1963-64; law clk. to judge U.S. Dist. Ct. (so. dist.), NY, 1965-66; asst. U.S. atty. U.S. Atty.'s Office, NYC, 1966-67; asst. dist. atty. N.Y. County Dist. Atty., NYC, 1967-70; exec. dir. Joint Found. Support, Inc., NYC, 1970-72; asst. gen. counsel HEW, Washington, 1978-79; insp. gen. U.S. Dept. Labor, Washington, 1979-80; assoc. prof. U. Ala. Sch. Law, Tuscaloosa, 1972-75, prof., 1975-86, assoc. dean, 1982-84; law prof., dean Ga. State U. Coll. Law, Atlanta, 1986-91, law prof., 1986—, mem. bd. internat. corp. governance network, 2007—. Cons. Ford Found., NYC, 1973-98, 2000-03, trustee Coll. Retirement Equities Fund, NYC, 1983-2002; exec. com. Conf. on Women and the Constn., 1986-88; com. on continuing profl. edn. Am. Law Inst.-ABA, 1987-93; bd. dirs. Internat. Corp. Governance Network, 2007. Contbr. articles to profl. jours. Am. Council Edn. fellow, 1976—77, Aspen Inst. fellow, Rockefeller Found., 1976. Mem. ABA (chmn. new deans workshop 1988), Ala. State Bar Assn., N.Y. State Bar Assn., D.C. Bar Assn., Am. Law Inst., Tchrs. Ins. Annunity Assn. (trustee 2003-). Office: Ga State U Coll Law University Plz Atlanta GA 30303 Office Phone: 404-413-9181.

KNOWLES, PATRICIA MARIE, science educator; d. Richard Lance and Alice Kay Knowles; children: Jason Zow, Ki-jana Zow, Khalitri Zow. BS in Elem. Edn., Western Oreg. U., Monmouth, 1987; MS in Secondary Edn. Health, Western Oreg. U., 1997; Cert. tchr. Fla. Dept of Edn., 2001. Tchr. Orange County Pub. Schs., Orlando, Fla., 1999—. Team leader Orange County Pub. Schs., Orlando, Fla., 2000—, sci. dept. chairperson, 2004—, athletic dir., 2005—, girls basketball coach, 2000—, girl's track coach, 2000—. Named Tchr. of the Yr., Orange County Pub. Schs., 2006; named to Athletic Hall of Fame, Western Oreg. U., 2004. Mem.: Orange County Classroom Tchrs. Assn. (assoc.), NEA (assoc.), Fla. Edn. Assn. (assoc.). Office: Walker Middle School 150 Amidon Ln Orlando FL 32809 Home Phone: 321-217-4593; Office Phone: 407-858-3210 289. Office Fax: 407-858-3218; Home Fax: 407-858-3218. E-mail: knowlep2@ocps.net.

KNOWLES, RICHARD ALAN JOHN, language educator; b. Southbridge, Mass., May 17, 1935; s. Clarence Fay and Mildred Elizabeth (Branniff) K.; m. Jane Marie Boyle, Sept. 1, 1958; children: Jonathan Edwards, Katherine Mary. BA magna cum laude, Tufts U., 1956; MA, U. Pa., 1958, PhD, 1963. Physics asst. Tufts U., Medford, Mass., 1954-56; asst. instr. English U. Pa., Phila., 1956-60; from asst. prof. to prof. U. Wis., Madison, 1962-90, Dickson-Bascom prof. humanities, 1990—. Vis. lectr. U. Pa., 1967, George Washington U., Am. U., 1969, Cath. U., Washington, 1985; manuscript reader various univs., 1965—; cons. Am. Players Theater, Spring Green, Wis., 1980-83; poetry judge Brittingham Poetry Prize, Madison, 1986—, NEH referee, panelist, Washington, 1988—. Author: (with others) Shakespeare Variorum Handbook, 1971; author: Shakespeare Variorum Handbook, rev., 2003; editor: (with others) English Renaissance Drama, 1978; editor: New Variorum As You Like It, 1977; co-editor New Variorum Shakespeare, 1978—; mem. editl. bd. Shakespeare Notes, 1996—. Officer, prodr. Madison Savoyards, Wis., 1978—; pres. Friends U. Wis. Librs., Madison, 1982—84. Folger Libr. fellow, Washington, 1968, Guggenheim fellow, N.Y., 1976-77; NEH fellow 1983-87; Rsch. fellow Humanities Rsch. Inst., Madison, 1990. Mem. MLA, Shakespeare Assn. Am., Internat. Assn. Univ. Profs. English, Assn. Lit. Scholars and Critics, Nakoma Country Club. Democrat. Avocations: theater, chamber music, opera, gardening, carpentry. Home: 2226 Commonwealth Ave Madison WI 53726-5302 Office: U Wis Dept English 600 N Park St Madison WI 53706-1403 E-mail: rknowles@facstaff.wisc.edu.

KNOWLES, RICHARD NORRIS, chemist; b. Wilmington, Del., Aug. 8, 1935; s. Francis and Dorothy Edith Knowles; m. Alice Keith Pfohl, Aug. 30, 1957 (div. May 1987); children: Elizabeth Nelson, Dorothy Lawrence, Cynthia Norris; m. Claire Elaine Frerichs, Dec. 31, 1988; 1 stepchild, Christine J. Stoelting. BS, Oberlin Coll., 1957; PhD, U. Rochester, 1961. With DuPont Co., Wilmington, Del., 1960-96; asst. works mgr. Chambers Works, NJ, 1980-83; mgr. Niagara Falls Plant, NY, 1983—87, Belle Plant, W.Va., 1987-95; dir. cmty. awareness emergency response & industry outreach Wilmington, 1995-96; with Chem. Mfrs. Assn. in Responsible Care, 1985—96; assoc. Dalmau Network; prin. Richard N. Knowles & Assocs.; advisor to mayor Niagara Falls, 1999—2004; founder, dir. Ctr. Self-Orgnl. Leadership, 2001—; ptnr. Soliance Group. Author: The Leadership Dance, Pathways to Extraordinary Organizational Effectiveness, 2002; (feaures include) The New Pioneers, 1998, The Soul at Work, 2000; contbr. articles to profl. jours. Mem. adv. bd. Inst. Sustainable Enterprise at Fairleigh Dickinson U.; elder Presbyn. Ch.; bd. dirs. Nat. Inst. Chem. Studies, Du Versity, Inst. for the Study of Coherence and Emergence, World Bus. Acad. Recipient Chem. Emergency Planning and Preparedness Ptnr. award, EPA, 1995, 1996. Mem.: Almost Heaven Hammered Dulcimer Soc., Nature Conservancy (DuPont Agrl. Products Crystal award 1991), Am. Chem. Soc. Achievements include 40 patents in field. Office: 6989 Rebecca Dr Niagara Falls NY 14304-3050 Office Phone: 716-622-6467. Personal E-mail: rnknowles@aol.com.

KNOWLES, TONY, former governor; b. Tulsa, Jan. 1, 1943; m. Susan Morris; children: Devon, Lucas, Sara. BA in Econs., Yale U., 1968. Co-owner Downtown Deli, Anchorage, 1976—; mayor Municipality of Anchorage, 1981-87; gov. State of Alaska, 1994—2002. Dem. candidate for Alaska U.S. Senate seat, 2004. Mem. citizen's com. to develop comprehensive plan for growth and devel., Anchorage, 1972; mem. Borough Assembly, Anchorage, 1975—79. With 82d Airborne US Army, 1961—65, Vietnam. Named Child Advocate of the Yr., Child Welfare League Am., 1999; recipient Silver Medal of Merit, VFW, 2001. Democrat. Home: 1146 S Street Anchorage AK 99501

KNOWLES, WILLIAM LEROY (BILL KNOWLES), television news producer, journalism educator; b. LA, June 23, 1935; s. Leroy Edwin and Thelma Mabel (Armstrong) K.; children from previous marriage: Frank, Irene, Daniel, Joseph, Ted; m. Sharon Weaver, Dec. 28, 1990. BA in Journalism, San Jose State Coll., 1959; postgrad., U. So. Calif., 1962—63. Reporter, photographer, prodr. KSL-TV, Salt Lake City, 1963-65; prodr., editor, writer WLS-TV, Chgo., 1965-70; news writer ABC News, Washington, 1970-71, assoc. prodr., 1971-75, ops. prodr., 1975-77, So. bur. chief Atlanta, 1977-81, Washington bur. chief, 1981-82, West Coast bur. chief, 1982-85; prof. U. Mont., Missoula, 1986—2006, prof. emeritus, 2006—; jazz writer and historian; chair radio-TV dept. U. Mont., 2000—03. Advisor U. Mont. Student Documentary Unit; chair faculty senate, 2003-04; lectr. in field. Served with U.S. Army, 1959-62. Decorated Commendation medal; Gannett fellow Ind. U., 1987; Media Mgmt. fellow Poynter Inst. Media Studies, 1988; scholar Fulbright Found., 2007—. Mem. Assn. for Edn. in Journalism (head radio-TV divsn. 1995-96). Office Phone: 406-549-9032. Business E-Mail: bill.knowles@umontana.edu.

KNOWLES, WILLIAM STANDISH, retired chemist; b. Taunton, Mass., June 1, 1917; married; 4 children. BS in Chemistry, Harvard U., 1939; PhD in Steroid Chemistry, Columbia U., 1942. Postdoct. fellow Harvard U., Cambridge, Mass., 1951; chemist Monsanto, St. Louis, 1942—86, emeritus chemist, 1986. Recipient St. Louis award, St. Louis sect. ACS, 1978, IR 100 awards for Asymmetric Hyrogenation, 1974, Monsanto Thomas and Hochwalt award, 1981, ACS Award for Creative Invention, 1982, Paul N. Rylander award, Organic Reactions Catalysis Soc., 1996, Nobel Prize in Chemistry, Royal Swedish Acad., 2001. Mem.: Organic Reactions Catalysis Society (Paul N Rylander award 1996), NAS. Avocations: fly fishing, hiking, bicycling. Home: PO Box 71 Kelly WY 83011-0071

KNOWLTON, KEVIN CHARLES, lawyer; b. Syracuse, NY, Oct. 19, 1957; s. Erwin Leslie and Arlene Grace (Morgan) K.; m. Lois Jean Clair, July 21, 1979; children: Andrew, Keith, Lauren. BA cum laude, Houghton Coll., 1979; JD, Syracuse U., 1982. Bar: Fla. 1982, U.S. Dist. Ct. (mid. dist.) Fla. 1982, U.S. Ct. Appeals (11th cir.) 1982, U.S. Supreme Ct. 1986. Law clk. to judge 2nd Dist. Ct. Appeals, Lakeland, Fla., 1982-85; sr. shareholder Peterson & Myers P.A., Lakeland, 1985—, mgmt. com. Treas. Phoenix (NY) Rep. Com., 1980-82, Planning Bd., 1980-82, Town of Schroeppel Planning Bd., 1980-82; chmn. bd. dirs. Lakeland Christian Sch.; chmn. pres.'s adv. bd. Houghton Coll., 1991-2003, bd. trustees, 2003—; vice-chmn. Fla. Bar 10th Jud. Cir. Grievance Com., 2000-03; instnl. rev. bd. Lakeland Regional Med. Ctr., ethics com.; chmn. exec. bd. dirs. Lake Morton Cmty. Ch., 1995-99, also elder; trustee Houghton Coll., 2003—; chmn. bd. Houghton Coll. Found., 2003—; mem. bd. deacons Heritage Bapt. Ch., 2005—. N.Y. State Regents scholar 1975-79. Mem. ABA, Fla. Bar Assn., Lakeland Bar Assn. (chmn. law day legal forum 1986), Fla. Acad. Healthcare Attys., Am. Health Lawyers Assn., Christian Legal Soc., Houghton Coll. Alumni Assn. (pres. Orlando, Fla. chpt. 1985, 91—), Willson Inn of Ct., Lakeland Yacht and Country Club, Phi Alpha Theta. Avocations: basketball, skiing. Home: 1143 E Highland Dr Lakeland FL 33813-1774 Office: Peterson & Myers PA 225 E Lemon St ste 300 Lakeland FL 33801-4655 Office Phone: 863-683-6511.

KNOWLTON, THOMAS A., retired dean, food products executive; b. Toronto, Ont., Can., June 16, 1946; s. William George and Grace K.; m. Janice Elizabeth Knowlton, June 8, 1968; children: Kimberly, Tricia, Jeffrey, Andrea. BA, U. Windsor, Ont., 1968, MBA, 1970. Brand mgr. Colgate Palmolive, Toronto, 1970-73; product mgr. Gen. Foods, Toronto, 1973-75; v.p., dir. client services Leo Burnett, Toronto, 1975-79; sr. v.p. mktg. and sales Kellogg Salada Can. Inc., Rexdale, Ont., 1979-82, pres., chief exec. officer, 1983-88; v.p. Kellogg Co., 1984—; mng. dir. Kellogg Co. of Gt. Britain Ltd., 1989-90, chmn., 1990-94, exec. v.p., area dir. Europe, 1992-94; corp. exec. v.p., pres. Kellogg N.Am., 1994-99; ret., 1998; dean faculty bus. Ryerson U., Toronto, 2000—05. Bd. dirs. Wm. Wrigley Jr. Co., AIM Trimark Funds Mgmt., Toronto, Sun Rype Products, Cadillac Fairview Corp. Mem. Young Pres.'s Orgn., York Downs Golf and Country Club (Unionville, Ont.), Sanctuary Golf Club (Sanibel, Fla.). Home: 123 Cheltanham Ave Toronto ON Canada M4N 1R1

KNOWLTON, WILLIAM ALLEN, federal agency administrator, educator; b. Weston, Mass., June 19, 1920; s. Frank Warren and Isabelle (Riese) K.; m. Marjorie Adams Downey, Nov. 27, 1943; children: William Allen, Davis Downey, Timothy Riese, Hollister Knowlton Petraeus. BS, U.S. Mil. Acad., 1943; MA, Columbia U., 1957; grad., Nat. War Coll., 1960; LLD (hon.), Akron U., 1972. Commd. 2d lt. U.S. Army, 1943, advanced through grades to gen., 1976; with 7th Armored Div., World War II, Army Gen. Staff, 1947-49, SHAPE, France, 1951-54; assoc. prof. social scis. U.S. Mil. Acad., 1955-58, supt., 1970-74; bn. comdr. 3d Armored Cav. Regt., 1958-59, mil. attache Tunisia, 1961-63; brig. comdr. Ft. Knox, Ky., 1963-64; with Office Chief Staff U.S. Army, 1964-65; mil. asst. to spl. asst. to sec. and dept. sec. def. Office Sec. Def., 1965-66; sec. Joint Staff, dir. pacification support, dep. asst. chief staff for civil ops. revolutionary devel. support U.S. Mil. Assistance Command, Vietnam, 1966-67; asst. div. comdr. 9th Inf. Div., Vietnam, 1968; sec. gen. staff Office Chief Staff U.S. Army, 1968-70; chief staff hdqrs. U.S. European Command, Stuttgart, W.Ger., 1974-76; comdr. Allied Land Forces Southeast Europe, Izmir, Turkey, 1976-77; U.S. rep. NATO Mil. Com., Brussels, 1977-80; ret., 1980; cons. on internat. affairs and strategic intelligence R & D Assocs., Marina del Rey, Calif.; sr. assoc. Burdeshaw Assocs. Ltd., 1981-91; dir. Aeronca Inc., 1982-86, Chubb Corp., Fed. Ins. Co., Vigilant Ins. Co., Chubb Life Am., 1983-93; sr. fellow CAPSTONE course Nat. Def. U., 1984-95, sr. fellow emeritus CAPSTONE course, 1995—. Sr. rsch. fellow Inst. Advanced Technology U. Tex., Austin, 1998—; lectr. Am. U., 1995—1998 Contbr.: Ency. Americana and nat. mags. Trustee Davis and Elkins Coll., 1982-90. Decorated Def. D.S.M., Army D.S.M., Silver Star with 2 oak leaf clusters, Legion of Merit with oak leaf cluster, D.F.C., Bronze Star with V device, Air medal with 9 oak leaf clusters, Army Commendation medal with oak leaf cluster, knight comdr. cross Order Merit W. Ger., officer Legion of Honor France, Vietnamese Nat. Order and Gallantry Cross with palm; recipient George Washington honor medal Freedoms Found., Valley Forge, 1957, 58, Lemnitzer award, 1994, Disting. Grad. award, U.S. Mil. Acad., 2004; named Hon. Col. Regiment, 40th armor Berlin. Mem. Am. Mil. Inst., 7th Armored Divsn. Assn. (hon. pres.), Coun. Fgn. Rels., Soc. Mayflower Descs., Washington Inst. Fgn. Affairs (v.p. 1998), S.R., Soc. Colonial Wars, Univ. Club (N.Y.C.), Army and Navy Club (Washington), Phi Kappa Phi. Home: Goodwin House #452 4800 Fillmore Ave Alexandria VA 22311 Personal E-mail: genbill@aol.com.

KNOX, CHARLES GRAHAM, lawyer; b. Erie, Pa., June 10, 1948; s. William Wallace and Agnes Ruth (Graham) K.; m. Jill Ann Poole, Mar. 22, 1975; children: Stephanie Marie, William Wallace II. BA, Williams Coll., 1970; JD, U. Mich., 1973. Bar: Pa. 1973, U.S. Dist. Ct. (we. dist.) Pa. 1973. Assoc. Buchanan Ingersoll P.C., Pitts., 1972-81, shareholder, 1981-97; ptnr. Marcus & Shapira, LLP, Pitts., 1997—2007; shareholder Buchanan Ingersoll and Rooney P.C., Pitts., 2007—. Pres., bd. trustees Parkwood United Presbyn. Ch., Allison Pk., Pa., 1991, treas., bd. dirs. Wildwood Golf Club, Allison Pk., Pa., 2001-06. Mem.: ABA, Allegheny County Bar Assn., Pa. Bar Assn. Home: 4230 Wembleton Dr Allison Park PA 15101-1564 Office: 301 Grant St Ste 20 Pittsburgh PA 15219-1407 Business E-Mail: charles.knox@bipc.com.

KNOX, HELENE MARGRETHE, poet, editor; b. Sacramento, Calif., May 1, 1943; d. James Dale and Helen Margrete K. BA with honors, U. Calif., 1965, MA, 1968, PhD, 1979; MDiv, Starr King Sch. for Ministry, Berkeley, Calif., 1994. Assoc., instr., sect. leader dept. English U. Calif., Berkeley, 1972-74, 77-78; Fulbright lectr. in Am. studies U. Perpignan, France, 1972-73, U. Augsburg, Fed. Republic Germany, 1980-81; lectr. English U. San Francisco, 1979; vis. asst. prof. humanities Drexel U., Phila., 1981-82; asst. prof. English and creative writing Muhlenberg Coll., Allentown, Pa., 1982-86; prin., owner KnoxProEditing, Oakland, Calif., 1987—; instr. Starr King Sch. for Ministry, 1991. Presenter pub. readings of original poetry, U.S., Europe and Tunisia, 1970—; lectr. on lit., U.S. and Europe, 1972-89; presenter papers at profl. meetings. Contbr. poetry to lit. mags. and anthologies; contbg. editor Standing Before Us: Unitarian Universalist Women and Social Reform, 1776-1936, 2000, The Role of the Dissenter in Western Christianity: From Jesus Through the 16th Century, 2004; contbr. stories, scholarly articles to various publs. Recipient Feminist Theology award Unitarian Universalist Women's Fedn., Boston, 1991. Mem.: PEN West, Nat. Writers Union. Mem. Green Party. Unitarian Universalist. Avocations: music, organic gardening. Office: 2625 Alcatraz Ave #181 Berkeley CA 94705-2702 Office Phone: 510-654-1667. Personal E-mail: hknox@juno.com.

KNOX, JAMES EDWIN, lawyer; b. Evanston, Ill., July 2, 1937; s. James Edwin and Marjorie Eleanor (Williams) Knox; m. Rita Lucille Torres, June 30, 1973; children: James Edwin III, Kirsten M., Katherine E., Miranda G. BA in Polit. Sci., State U. Iowa, 1959; JD, Drake U., 1961. Bar: Iowa 1961, Ill. 1962, Tex. 1982. Law clk. to Hon. Tom C. Clark, U.S. Supreme Ct., Washington, 1961-62; assoc., then ptnr. Isham, Lincoln & Beale, Chgo., 1962-70; v.p. law N.W. Industries, Inc., Chgo., 1970-80; exec. v.p., gen. counsel Lone Star Steel Co., Dallas, 1980-86; sr. v.p. law Anixter Internat. Inc., Chgo., 1986—2002. Instr. contracts and labor law Chgo. Kent Coll. Law, 1964—69; arbitrator Nat. Rlwy. Adjustment Bd., 1967—68; ptnr. Mayer, Brown & Platt, Chgo., 1992—96; gen. counsel Arris Group, Inc., 1996—2002. Mem.: ABA, Ill. Bar Assn., Phi Beta Kappa, Order of Coif. Republican. Office: Anixter Internat Inc 2301 Patriot Blvd Glenview IL 60025-8020 Home Phone: 773-935-0425; Office Phone: 224-521-8796.

KNOX, JAMES MARSHALL, lawyer; b. Chgo., Jan. 12, 1944; s. Edwin John and Shirley Lucille (Collett) K.; m. Janine Foster, July 18, 1964; children: Erik M., Christian S. BA, U. Ill., 1968; MA in Libr. Sci., Rosary Coll., 1973; JD, DePaul Coll. Law, 1979. Bar: Ill. 1979, U.S. Dist. Ct. (no. dist.) Ill. 1979, U.S. Ct. Appeals (7th cir.) 1980. Head reference Northbrook (Ill.) Pub. Libr., 1973-76; asst. dir. hdqrs. Jackson (Miss.) Met. Libr. Sys., 1976-77; assoc. Fishman & Fishman, Ltd., Chgo., 1979-91; prin. Law Office James M. Knox, 1991—. Gen. counsel Deerfield Pub. Libr., Ill., 1994—2006. Commr. Evanston Preservation Commn., 1991-98; sustaining mem. Miss. Hist. Soc. Mem. ABA, Ill. State Bar Assn., Ill. Trial Lawyer's Assn., Chgo. Bar Assn., U. Ill. Alumni Assn. (dir. 1986-91). Home: 121 W Chestnut #3104 Chicago IL 60610 Office: Chestnut Tower 121 W Chestnut Chicago IL 60610 Office Phone: 312-587-1356. Personal E-mail: KawOxford@aol.com.

KNOX, LANCE LETHBRIDGE, venture capitalist; b. Hartford, Conn., Sept. 25, 1944; s. Robert Chester and Leonice Katherine (Merrels) K.; children: Michele Merrels, Elizabeth McVarish; m. Mary E. Lambert, 1981. BA, Williams Coll., 1966; MBA, NYU, 1970. Asst. cashier Citibank, N.C., NYC, 1968-70, asst. v.p., 1970-72, v.p., 1972-74, sr. credit officer, 1973-74; v.p. fin. GATX Corp., Chgo., 1974-77; pvt. investor venture capital, 1978—. Pres. Bistrot Zinc, Chgo.

KNOX, MICHAEL DENNIS, medical educator, research center administrator; b. Wyandotte, Mich., May 9, 1946; s. Harold L. and Mary (Latta) K.; children: John M.P., James R.S. BA, Ea. Mich. U., 1968; MSW, U. Mich., 1971, MA Psychology, 1973, PhD Psychology, 1974. Lic. clin. psychologist, Fla., Va. Dir. Applied Sci., Inc., Ann Arbor, Mich., 1974—76; clin. dir. Cmty. Mental Health Ctr., Inc., Huntington, W.Va., 1976—78; clin. instr. Marshall U. Sch. Medicine, Huntington, 1977—78; dir. We. Tidewater Mental Health Ctr., Suffolk, Va., 1978—86; dir. Ctr. for HIV Edn. and Rsch. U. South Fla., Tampa, 1988—. Adj. prof. psychology Marshall U., 1977-78; asst. prof. Ea. Va. Med. Sch., Norfolk, 1979-86; chmn., bd. dirs. Applied Sci. Corp., Tampa, 1985-1999; assoc. prof., chmn. dept. cmty. mental health U. South Fla., 1986-91, disting. prof., 1991-2001, disting. prof. psychology, 1991-, disting. prof. medicine dept. internal medicine Coll. Medicine, U. South Fla., 1994—, exec. com. faculty senate, 1992-99, pres. faculty senate, 1995-97, disting. prof. gerontology, 2002-05, disting. prof. cmty. and family health Coll. Pub. Health, 1997-2004, disting. prof. global health coll. pub. health, 2004—; disting. prof. dept. mental health law and policy Louis de la Parte Fla. Mental Health Inst., 2001—, courtesy disting. prof. aging studies, 2005—; chmn. adv. coun. faculty senate Fla. State U. Sys., 1996-98; cons. USPHS, Bethesda, Md., 1990-96, NIMH, Rockville, Md., 1990-98; tech. advisor state and local govts.; dir. Fla./Caribbean AIDS Edn. and Tng. Ctr., 1999-; vis. scholar dept. psychiatry Oxford (Eng.) U., 1999; lectr. in field. Author books including: Last Wishes: A Handbook to Guide Your Survivors, 1995, HIV and Community Mental Healthcare, 1998; editor: US Peace Registry, 2006; contbr. more than 60 articles on AIDS and psychology; invited reviewer 5 acad. jours., internat. spkr. 1982—. Adv. Joint Commn. on Accreditation of Hosps., Chgo., 1982-84; co-chair Am. Found. for AIDS Rsch. Nat. HIV/AIDS Update Conf., 2004; mem. steering com. S.E. Region STD/HIV Prevention Tng. Ctr., 2004—; chmn., CEO, US Peace Meml. Found., Inc., 2005—. Recipient Disting. Svc. award Nat. Coun. Cmty. Mental Health Ctrs., 1984, resolution of appreciation, 1993, Millennium Appreciation award, Tampa General Hosp. Infectious Disease Ctr., 2000, Million Dollar Rschr. Award, gold mem., USF, 2005-2006; grantee Emory U., 1988-91, NIMH, 1991-93, U. Miami, 1991-99, U. Calif. 2001, HHS, 1999—, Fla. Dept. Health 2001—. Fellow APA, Am. Psychol. Soc.; mem. Internat. AIDS Soc., U. Mich. Alumni Assn., Nat. Assn. Aids Edn. and Tng. Centers, U.S. Power Squadron (bd. dirs. 1983-84), Sigma Xi. Achievements include research in HIV/AIDS risk factors for the seriously mentally ill, HIV/AIDS risk reduction, AIDS prevention, knowledge and attitudes regarding AIDS among treatment providers. Avocations: boating, swimming. Office: U South Fla Fla Mental Health Inst MHC 1700 13301 Bruce B Downs Blvd Tampa FL 33612-3807 Business E-Mail: knox@fmhi.usf.edu.

KNOX, ROBERT SEIPLE, physicist, researcher; b. Franklin, NJ, July 13, 1931; s. Harvey Stoll and Laura (Seiple) K.; m. Myrta I. Borges, Sept. 1, 1954; children: Bruce Robert, Wayne Harvey, Lee Benjamin. BS in Engring. Physics, Lehigh U., 1953; PhD in Physics and Optics, U. Rochester, 1958. Rsch. assoc. U. Ill., 1958-59, rsch. asst. prof., 1959-60; mem. faculty U. Rochester, NY, 1960—, assoc. prof. dept. physics, 1963-68, prof., 1968-97; sr. scientist Lab. for Laser Energetics, 1985—; chmn. dept. physics and astronomy U. Rochester, 1969-74, assoc. dean spl. programs Coll. Arts and Scis., 1982-87, faculty sr. assoc., 1997-2001, prof. emeritus, 1997—. Cons. solid state sci. divsn. Argonne Nat. Lab., 1959—69, Naval Rsch. Lab., 1960—70; NSF sr. fellow U. Leiden, 1967—68. Author: Theory of Excitons, 1963, (with A. Gold) Symmetry in the Solid State, 1964, (with D.L. Dexter) Excitons, 1965; also articles. Japan Soc. Promotion of Sci. fellow Kyoto U., 1979, Royal Soc. Guest Rsch. fellow, Fulbright fellow Imperial Coll. (London), 1993. Fellow Am. Phys. Soc. (Biol. Physics prize 1994), Am. Soc. Photobiology, Am. Assn. Physics Tchrs., Biophys. Soc., Internat. Soc. Photosynthesis Rsch. Achievements include research in atomic spectra and structure, absorption and luminescence spectra ionic and molecular crystals, photosynthesis theory, picosecond spectroscopy. Office: U Rochester Dept Physics & Astronomy Rochester NY 14627-0171 Business E-Mail: rsk@pas.rochester.edu.

KNOX, SIMMIE LEE, artist; b. 1936; BFA magna cum laude, Temple U. Tyler Sch. of Art, Phila., MFA. Staff mem. Museum of African Art, Washington; portrait artist, 1981—. Portrait commissions include, Martin Luther King, Jr., Bowie State Coll., 1974, Frederick Douglass, Mus. African Art, Washington, DC, 1975, Judge H. Carl Moultrie, The H. Carl Moultrie Courthouse, 1985, Supreme Court Justice Thurgood Marshall, 1989, Dorothy Height, Nat. Coun. Negro Women, 1989, David & Joyce Dinkins, The Schomburg Collection, 1993, Col. Rosemary McCarthy, US Army Nurse Corp., 1994, John V. Atanasoff, Cosmos Club, 1995, Muhammad Ali, 1995, Hank & Billye Aaron, 1996, Melvin Sabshin, Am. Psychiatric Assn., 1997, Official White House portrait, Pres. William Clinton & First Lady Hillary Clinton, 2004, exhibitions include Biennial Contemporary Am. Painting, Corcoran Gallery Art, Washington, DC, 1971.

KNOX, THOMAS ISAAC, cardiologist; b. Danbury, Conn., Dec. 28, 1970; s. Thomas Isaac Knox and Ruthan Baldouf; m. Jennifer Russell, June 17, 1995; children: Thomas Isaac, William Montgomery, Bridget Belle. BA magna cum laude, West. Conn. State U., Danbury, 1992; MD, Tufts U., Boston, 1996. Intern, resident U. Conn. Health Ctr., Farmington, 1996—99; cardiologist St. Francis Hosp., Hartford, Conn., 2002—. Clin. dir. U. Conn. Health Ctr., Farmington, 2000—. Mem. Conn. Tchr. Retirement Bd., Hartford, Conn., 2005—; vice chmn. West Hartford Rep. Town Com., Conn., 2005—. Recipient Chemistry and Biology Achievement award, West. Conn. State U., 1990, 1992; fellow, Baylor Med. Ctr., Springfield, Mass., 1999—2002; K. Gregory Elliot MD scholar. Master: Am. Bd. Hosp. Physicians; fellow: Am. Coll. Ethical Physicians, Am. Coll. Chest Physicians, Am. Coll. Physicians, Am. Coll. Cardiology; mem.: AMA, Hampden County Med. Soc., Hartford County Med. Assn., Conn. State Med. Soc., Am. Assn. Exercise Physiologists, Am. Coll. Nutrition, Am. Soc. Bariatric Physicians, N.Am. Assn. Study Obesity, Am. Heart Assn. (mem. coun. arteriosclerosis, thrombosis and vascular biology), Am.

Soc. Echocardiography, Am. Soc. Nuc. Cardiology, Mass. Med. Soc., Nat. Lipid Assn. Avocations: music, exercise, politics. Office: Smith and Knox Cardiology 310 Collins St Hartford CT 06105

KNOX, WILLIAM ARTHUR, judge; b. Fargo, ND, Jan. 8, 1945; BS, N.D. State U., 1966; JD, U. Minn., 1968. Law specialist USCG, Boston, 1968—69, Juneau, Alaska, 1970—72; prof. Law Sch., U. Mo., Columbia, 1972—85; magistrate judge U.S. Cts., Jefferson City, Mo., 1985—. Author: West's Federal Criminal Forms, 2002, West's Missouri Criminal Practice, 2005. Office: 131 W High St Jefferson City MO 65101-1557 Home Phone: 573-634-4952; Office Phone: 573-634-3418. Business E-Mail: william.knox@mow.uscourts.gov.

KNOX, WYCKLIFFE AUSTIN, JR., lawyer; b. Augusta, Ga., Nov. 1, 1940; s. Wyckliffe Austin Knox Sr. and Byrnece (Purcell) Swanson; m. Shell Hardman, Apr. 15, 1967; children: Wyckliffe Austin III, Dorothy Shell, John Hardman, Davis Purcell. BBA, U. Ga., 1962, JD, 1964. Bar: Ga. 1964, U.S. Dist. Ct. (so. dist.) Ga. 1964, U.S. Ct. Appeals (5th cir.) 1966, U.S. Ct. Claims 1973, U.S. Supreme Ct. 1973, U.S. Ct. Appeals (11th cir.) 1981, U.S. Ct. Appeals (4th cir.) 1983. Assoc. Hull, Towill & Norman, Augusta, 1964-67; ptnr. Hull, Towill, Norman, Barrett & Johnson, Augusta, 1967-76, Knox & Zacks, Augusta, 1976-77, pres., 1977—94; ptnr. Kilpatrick & Cody, 1994—97; ptnr., litig. practice Kilpatrick Stockton LLP, Augusta & Atlanta, 1997—, past chmn. exec. com. Chmn. bd. dirs. 1st Union Nat. Bank of Ga., Augusta, Knox-Rivers Constrn. Co., Thomson, Ga. Mem. bd. visitors sch. law U. Ga., Athens, 1973-76, bd. dirs. athletic assn., 1975-85, emeritus dir. 1985-; mem. jud. com. Bus. Council Ga., Atlanta, 1986—; pres. Ga. council Boy Scouts Am., Augusta, 1974-75; pres.Richmond/Columbia County unit Am. Cancer Soc., Augusta, 1985, chmn. bd. dirs. 1986—; trustee Richard B. Russell Found., Atlanta, 1971—; pres. Georgians for Better Transp.; founding dir. & past chmn. Ga. Lottery Corp.; mem Met. Atlanta Olympic Games Auth.; mem. Commn. for a New Ga.; dir. Ga. C. of C. Fellow Am. Bar Found., Ga. Bar Found; mem. Augusta Bar Assn. (pres. 1984), Ga. Bar Assn., Ga. Acad. Hosp. Attys. (bd. dirs. 1979-80), Am. Acad. Healthcare Attys., Ga. Def. Lawyers Assn. (bd. dirs. 1973-76), YPO. Clubs: Piedimont Driving (Atlanta), Augusta Country (pres. 1988), Pinnacle (Augusta). Lodges: Rotary (pres. local club 1979-80). Methodist. Avocations: fishing, skiing, golf. Office: Kilpatrick Stockton LLP Ste 1400 Wachovia Bank Bldg 699 Broad St Augusta GA 30901-1453 also: Kilpatrick Stockton LLP Ste 2800 1100 Peachtree St Atlanta GA 30309-4530 Office Phone: 706-823-4200, 404-815-6387. Office Fax: 706-828-4461. Business E-Mail: wknox@kilpatrickstockton.com.

KNOXVILLE, JOHNNY (PHILIP JOHN CLAPP), actor; b. Knoxville, Tenn., Mar. 11, 1971; s. Phil and Lemoyne; m. Melanie Lynn Cates, May 15, 1995 (separated July 17, 2006); 1 child, Madison. Student, Am. Acad. Dramatic Arts. Actor: (films) Desert Blues, 1995, Coyote Ugly, 2000, The Tree, 2001, Life Without Dick, 2001, Don't Try This at Home, 2001, Big Trouble, 2002, Deuces Wild, 2002, Men in Black 2, 2002, Grand Theft Parsons, 2003, Walking Tall, 2004, A Dirty Shame, 2004, Lords of Dogtown, 2005, The Dukes of Hazzard, 2005, Daltry Calhoun, 2005, The Ringer, 2005; writer, prodr., actor: Jackass: The Movie, 2002; Jackass Number Two, 2006; creator, writer, prodr.: (TV series) Jackass, 2000—02. Office: Creative Artists Agy 9830 Wilshire Blvd Beverly Hills CA 90212

KNUDSEN, DOUG, food products executive; B, Ill. State U., Normal. Sales rep. Hunt-Wesson, various sr. positions including v.p. and nat. sales mgr. and sr. v.p. sales; pres. Grocery Sales ConAgra Grocery Products Co. (formerly Hunt-Wesson); pres. Retail Sales ConAgra Foods, Inc., 2001—05, pres. ConAgra Foods Sales, 2005—. Mem. sales vanguard com. Grocery Mfrs. Assn.; mem. adv. bd. Computer Sci. Corp. Office: ConAgra Foods Inc 1 ConAgra Dr Omaha NE 68102-5001 Office Phone: 402-595-4000.*

KNUDSON, ALFRED GEORGE, JR., medical geneticist; b. LA, Aug. 9, 1922; s. Alfred George and Mary Gladys (Galvin) Knudson; m. Anna T. Meadows, June 20, 1977; children from previous marriage: Linda, Nancy, Dorene. BS, Calif. Inst. Tech., 1944, PhD, 1956; MD, Columbia U., 1947; DSc (hon.), Thomas Jefferson U., 1992; MD (hon.), U. Oslo, 2000. Chmn. dept. pediat. City of Hope Med. Ctr., Duarte, Calif., 1956—62, chmn. dept. biology, 1962—66; assoc. dean Health Sci. Ctr., SUNY, Stony Brook, 1966—69; dean Grad. Sch. Biomed. Scis., U. Tex. Health Sci. Ctr., Houston, 1970—76; dir. Inst. Cancer Rsch., Fox Chase Cancer Ctr., Phila., 1976—83, sr. mem., 1976—, disting. sci., 1992—, pres., 1980—82. Mem. Assembly Life Scis. NRC, 1975—81. Author: Genetics and Disease, 1965; contbr. articles to profl. jours. Recipient Charles S. Mott prize, GM Cancer Rsch. Found., 1988, medal of honor, Am. Cancer Soc., 1989, Charles Rodolphe Brupbacher Found. prize, 1995, Gairdner Found. Internat. award, 1997, Albert Lasker Clin. Med. Rsch. award, Lasker Found., 1998, John Scott award, City of Phila., 1999, Lila Gruber Meml. Cancer Rsch. award, Am. Acad. Dermatology, 2000, Kyoto prize, 2004, Bristol-Myers-Squibb Cancer award, 2005. Fellow: AAAS; mem.: NAS, Am. Soc. Pediatric Hematology/Oncology (Disting. Career award 1999), Am. Assn. Cancer Rsch. (Lifetime Achievement award 2005), Am. Pediat. Soc., Assn. Am. Physicians, Am. Soc. Human Genetics (pres. 1978, Allan award 1991), Internat. Soc. Pediatric Oncology, Am. Acad. Arts and Scis., Am. Philos. Soc. Achievements include research in genetics of human cancer. Office: Fox Chase Ctr 333 Cottman Ave Philadelphia PA 19111 Business E-Mail: ag_knudson@fccc.edu.

KNUDSON, KEVIN PATRICK, mathematics professor; b. Wausau, Wis., Oct. 7, 1969; s. Margaret Peters and Stephen Knudson; m. Ellen Wall, June 6, 1992; 1 child, Gustav. PhD in Math., Duke U., Durham, NC, 1996. Assoc. prof. Miss. State U., Mississippi State, 2002—. Author: (monograph) Homology of Linear Groups. Recipient Ralph Powe Jr. Faculty Enhancement award, Oak Ridge Assoc. U., 2003—04; fellow, NSF, 1996—99; grantee Std. Grant, 1999—2003. Mem.: Am. Math. Soc. Avocations: tennis, yoga, bicycling. Office: Miss State Univ Dept Math Mississippi State MS 39762 Office Phone: 662-325-7146.

KNUDSON, RUTHANN, environmental consultant, anthropologist, archaeologist; b. Milw., Oct. 24, 1941; d. Sidney Olaus and Clara Ruth (Tappe) K. BA Liberal Arts, Hamline U., St. Paul, 1959—61; BA in anthropology magna cum laude, U. Minn., 1961—63, MA in anthropology, 1963—66; PhD in anthropology, Wash. State U., 1968—73; postgrad. hydrogeology, U. Idaho, Moscow, 1988—88. Cert. profl. archaeologist. Seasonal ranger Bandelier Nat. Monument Nat. Park Svc., N.Mex., 1963; instr. U. No. Colo., Greeley, 1966—68; asst. rsch. prof. U. Idaho, Moscow, 1974—79, assoc. rsch. prof., 1979—81; dir. cultural resource svcs. Woodward Clyde Cons., San Francisco, 1981—86, v.p., shareholder, 1985—88; arch. Nat. Park Svc., Washington, 1990—96; supr. Agate Fossil Beds Nat. Monument, 1996—2005; prin. Knudson Assoc. (formerly Paleo-Designs), 1974—; rsch. assoc. Calif. Acad. Sci., 1986—; exec. dir. Friends of the Mus. of the Plains Indian, 2006—; vice chmn. North Ctr. (MT) RC&D, 2007—. Vis. asst. prof. Wright State U., Dayton, Ohio, 1974; cons. Am. Folklife Ctr., Washington, 1981-83, NRC, Washington, 1982-83; resource cons. Calif. Heritage Task Force, 1983-94, Office Tech. Assessment, Washington, 1986; Woodward lectr., 1985; chmn. bd. dirs. No. Great Plains Inventory and Monitoring Program, 2004-05; affiliate faculty Mont. State U., Bozeman, Mont., 2005—. Author: Cambria Village Ceramics, 1967, Organizational Variability in Late Paleo-Indian Assemblages, 1983, Contemporary Cultural Resource Management, 1986, The Upper Missouri National Wild and Scenic River Cultural Resource Management Plan, 1983; co-editor: The Public Trust and the First Americans, 1995; editor: Plains Artifacts, 2006—; contbr. Sec.-treas. Idaho NOW, 1977—78; exec. dir. Friends of the Mus. of the Plains Indian, 2006—; co-chmn. Nebr. Panhandle Tourism Coalition, 1996—2005, 1998—2000; mem. Bridges to Buttes Scenic Byway Mgmt. Team, 1999—2005, Friends of the Intertribal Gathering, 2003—, Indians & Pioneers Tourism Mktg. Com., 2003—05, Friends of Mo. Breaks, 2005—; vol. Nat. Pk. Svc., 2005—; bd. dirs. Preservation Action, Washington, 1980—85, 1989—90, Californians for Preservation Action, 1981—82, Gt. Falls Pks. and Recreation Bd., 2006—, North Ctrl. RC&D Inc., 2005, v.p., 2007—. Recipient Preservation award Nat. Conf. State Historic Preservation Officers, 1981, Conservation award Am. Soc. Conservation Archaeology, 1981; Frison Inst. vis. sr. fellow, 2004. Mem. Plains Anthropol. Soc. (bd. dirs. 2003—), Soc. Applied Anthropology, Am. Anthropol. Assn. (Margaret Mead award 1983), Soc. Am. Archaeology (exec. bd. 1979-81, exec. com. 1983-85, legis. coord. 1979-82, chmn. com. pub. archaeology 1980-82, 84-85), Mus. of the Plains Indian Artist Assn., Friends of Plains Indian Mus., Women's Coun. Energy and Environ. (bd. dirs. 1994-96), Geol. Soc. Am., Phi Beta Kappa. Methodist. Home and Office: 3021 Fourth Ave S Great Falls MT 59405-3329 Home Phone: 406-216-2676; Office Phone: 406-216-2676. Personal E-mail: paleoknute@3rivers.net.

KNUEPFER, ROBERT CLAUDE, JR., lawyer; b. Oak Park, Ill., Feb. 23, 1952; s. Robert Claude Sr. and Suzanne (White) K.; m. Nancy Jo Bauderer, Aug. 20, 1977; children: Robert Claude III, Jennifer Jo, Lauren Elizabeth, Joseph James. BA, Denison U., Granville, Ohio, 1974; MBA, JD, Northwestern U., Evanston, Ill., 1978. Bar: Ill. 1978, U.S. Dist. Ct. (no. dist.) Ill. 1978, U.S. Ct. Appeals (7th cir.) 1980, U.S. Dist. Ct. (no. dist.) Ill. 1983, U.S. Supreme Ct. 1989. Law clk. to hon. judge William J. Bauer US Ct. Appeals (7th cir.), Chgo., 1978-80; asst. US atty. criminal divsn. Office of US Atty., Chgo., 1980-83; assoc. Baker & McKenzie, Chgo., 1983-87, ptnr., 1987-92, 1995—, mng. ptnr. Budapest, Hungary, 1992-95. Pres. Am. C. of C., Budapest, 1994-95; chmn., bd. dirs. Nat. Svc. League, Budapest, 1994-95; founding dir., bd. dirs. Leadershape, Inc., 1986-02; adj. prof. Northwestern U. Law Sch., Kellogg Bus. Sch., 1995—, chair Kellogg adv. bd., 2003-05, mem. dean's adv. bd., 2006—. Active Chgo. Coun. on Fgn. Rels., 1984—, Hinsdale Plan Commn., Ill., 1990-92; chmn. Glen Ellyn (Ill.) Zoning Bd. Appeals, 1983; past chair Hinsdale Village Caucus; chmn. bd. ATO Nat. Frat., Champaign, Ill., 1986-92, nat. pres., 1990-92; chmn. ATO Found., Indpls., 1995-2002; bd. dirs. Met. Family Svcs. Assn., 1986—, chmn. bd. 2002-05, Chgo. 1996, pres. bd. DuPage, 1997-99, chmn. bd., 2002; mem. exec. bd. Des Plaines Valley Coun. Boy Scouts Am., 1998-2002; trustee The Cmty. Ho. Hinsdale, 2002—; chair Paul and Jean Harris Home Found., 2005—; trustee Alder Panetarium, 2007—. Recipient Kellogg Schaffner award, Northwestern U., 2003, Alumni Svc. award, 2006. Mem. ABA, Fed. Bar Assn., Ill. Bar Assn. (corp. and securities sect. coun. 1990, 1996—, chmn. 2006—), Chgo. Bar Assn., DuPage County Bar Assn., Lawyers Club Chgo., Execs. Club Chgo., Chicagoland C. of C. (bd. dirs. 1995—), Rotary Club (founding pres. Budapest City 1995, Chgo. 1983, Centennial pres. 2004-05), Econ. Club Chgo., Execs. Breakfast Club (bd. dirs. 2003—, chair 2007—), Phi Beta Kappa, Omicron Delta Epsilon, Omicron Delta Kappa. Office: Baker & McKenzie LLP 130 E Randolph St Ste 3500 Chicago IL 60601-6314 also: Baker & McKenzie LLP Andrassy ut 102 H-1062 Budapest Hungary

KNUEPPEL, HENRY W., manufacturing executive; m. Susan Knueppel; 4 children. BS, Ripon Coll.; MBA, Univ. Wis. Mgmt. positions Regal-Beloit Corp., Beloit, Wis., 1979—82, v.p. power transmission group, 1982—85, v.p. ops., 1985—87, exec. v.p., 1987—2002, bd. dir., 1987—, pres. Marathon Electric subs., 1997—99, pres., COO, 2002—05, pres., CEO, 2005, chmn., CEO, 2006—. Office: Regal-Beloit Corp 200 State St Beloit WI 53511*

KNUST, DANIEL MAX, lawyer; b. Brazil, Ind., Oct. 18, 1947; s. Max Richard and Harriet L. (Emmert) K.; m. Carolyn Sue Essig; children: Nathaniel C.M., Ian Webster. AB, Earlham Coll., 1969; JD, Ind. U., 1972. Bar: Mo. 1972, Ind. 1974. Sole practice, Springfield, Mo., 1972-78, Marshfield, Mo., 2007—; assoc. circuit judge State of Mo., Marshfield, 1979—2006. Adj. prof. Drury U., Springfield, Mo., 1977-78 Mem. Mo. Bar Assn. Office: Knust Law LLC PO Box 777 Marshfield MO 65706 Office Phone: 417-859-6061.

KNUTH, DEAN LESLIE, research and development company executive, golf consultant, writer; b. Eau Claire, Wis., Apr. 29, 1947; s. Herbert LaVerne and Betty Lou Knuth; m. Suzanne Yavorsky, May 15, 1998; children: Alison Stewart Brown, Gregory Scott, Stephen Matthew. BS, U.S. Naval Acad., 1970; MS in Engring., U.S. Naval Postgrad. Sch., 1978. Commd. ensign USN, 1970, advanced through grades to capt., 1990; sr. dir. US Golf Assn., Far Hills, NJ, 1981—97; bus. develop. exec. Northrop Grumman Corp., San Diego, 1997—; ret. USN, 1998. Cons. Callaway Golf, 1999—2002. Author: USGA Handicap and Course Rating manuals; contbg. editor: Golf Digest Mag., 1999—. Decorated Legion of Merit Pres. of the U.S.; named one of Greatest Inventions in 25 Years, Golf Digest Mag., 2002. Mem.: Golf Writers Assn. Am., Royal and Ancient Golf Club of St. Andrews, Century Club San Diego. Achievements include first to golf handicap course rating and slope rating system used worldwide; invention of golf handicap system; patents for golf club heads. Avocation: golf. Home: 4392 Colling Rd E Bonita CA 91902 Office: Northrop Grumman Corp 9326 Spectrum Ctr Blvd San Diego CA 92123 Home Phone: 619-421-8322; Office Phone: 858-514-9816. Personal E-mail: dknuth@cox.net. E-mail: dean.knuth@ngc.com.

KNUTH, DONALD ERVIN, computer sciences educator; b. Milw., Jan. 10, 1938; s. Ervin Henry and Louise Marie (Bohning) Knuth; m. Nancy Jill Carter, June 24, 1961; children: John Martin, Jennifer Sierra. BS summa cum laude, Case Inst. Tech., 1960, MS, 1960; PhD in Math., Calif. Inst. Tech., 1963; DSc (hon.), Case Western Res. U., 1980, Luther Coll., Decorah, Iowa, 1985, Lawrence U., 1985, Muhlenberg Coll., 1986, U. Pa., 1986, U. Rochester, 1986, U. Paris-Sud, Orsay, 1986, SUNY, Stony Brook, 1987, Oxford U., Eng., 1988, Brown U., 1988, Valparaiso U., 1988, Grinnell Coll., 1989, Dartmouth Coll., 1990, Concordia U., Montréal, 1991, Adelphi U., 1993, Masaryk U., Brno, 1996, Duke U., 1998, St. Andrews U., 1998, Williams Coll., 2000, U. Tubingen, 2001, Athens U. Econ., 2001, U. Oslo, 2002, Harvard U., 2003, U. Thessaloniki, 2003, U. Antwerp, 2003, U. Montréal, 2004, Armenian Acad. Sci., 2005, Eth Zurich, 2005, Republic of Armenia Nat. Acad. Scis., 2006; D Tech., Royal Inst. Tech., Stockholm, 1991; Pochetnogo Doktora, St. Petersburg U., Russia, 1992; DLitt (hon.), U. Waterloo, 2000, Concordia U., Wis., 2006. Asst. prof., math. Calif. Inst. Tech., Pasadena, Calif., 1963—66, assoc. prof., math., 1966—68; prof., computer sci. Stanford U., Calif., 1968—77, prof., elec. engring. (by courtesy) Calif., 1977—, Fletcher Jones prof., computer sci. Calif., 1977—89, prof., Art of Computer Programming Calif., 1990—92, prof., Art of Computer Programming, emeritus Calif., 1993—. Cons. Burroughs Corp., Pasadena, Calif., 1960—68; staff mathematician Inst. for Def. Analysis-Comm. Rsch. Divsn., 1968—69; guest prof., math. U. Oslo, 1972—73; vis. prof., computer sci. U. Oxford, 2002—06; invited lectr. in field. Author: The Art of Computer Programming, 1968 (Steele prize, 1987), Computers and Typesetting, 1986, 3:16 Bible Texts Illuminated, and several others; mem. editl. bd. Jour. Computer and System Sciences, 1969—, Jour. Algorithms, 1979—2004, Software-Practice and Experience, 1979—, Applied Mathematics Letters, 1987—, Combinatorica, 1985—, Discrete and Computational Geometry, 1986—, Jour. Computer Sci. and Tech., 1989—, Mathematica Jour., 1990—, Random Structures & Algorithms, 1990—, Electronic Jour. Combinators, 1994—, Jour. Exptl. Algorithmics, 1996—, Jour. Graph Algorithms and Applications, 1996—, Japan Jour. Indsl. and Applied Math., 1997—, Theory of Computing, 2004—. Recipient Nat. medal of Sci., Pres. James Carter, 1979, Disting. Alumni award, Calif. Inst. Tech., 1978, Priestley award, Dickinson Coll., 1981, Golden Plate award, Am. Acad. Achievement, 1985, Franklin medal, 1988, J.D. Warnier prize, 1989, Gold Medal award, Case Alumni Assn., 1990, Adelsköld medal, Swedish Acad. Sci., 1994, Harvey prize, Israel Inst. Tech., 1995, Kyoto prize, Inamori Found., 1996, Fellow award, Computer History Mus., 1998; fellow, Guggenheim Found., 1972—73; Woodrow Wilson Fellow, 1960, NSF Fellow, 1960, Hon. Fellow, Magdalen Coll., Oxford U., 2005—. Fellow: Brit. Computer Soc. (Disting. Fellow 1980), Assn. for Computing Machinery (chmn., subcommittee on ALGOL 1963—64, nat. lectr. 1966—67, vis. scientist 1966—67, mem. gen. tech. achievement awards subcommittee 1975—79, mem. editl. bd. Tranactions on Algorithms 2004—, Grace Murray Hopper award 1971, Alan M. Turing award 1974, Computer Sci. Edn. award 1986, Software Sys. award 1986), Am. Acad. Arts and Scis., The Computer Mus.; mem.: NAS, IEEE (hon.; mem. editl. bd., Transactions on Software Engring. 1975—79, W. Wallace McDowell award 1980, Computer Pioneer award 1982, John von Neumann medal 1995), Soc. Indsl. and Applied Math., Math. Assn. Am. (Lester R. Ford award 1975, 1993), French Acad. Sciences (assoc.), Am. Math. Soc. (mem. com. on composition tech. 1978—81, Steele prize for Expository Writing 1986), Acad. Sci. (fgn. assoc. Paris, Oslo, Munich, London), NAE, Royal Soc. London for Improving Natural Knowledge (fgn. mem. 2003), Am. Guild Organists. Lutheran. Achievements include patents in field. Avocations: playing pipe organ, reading, writing. Office: Stanford Univ Computer Scis Dept Gates Bldg 4B Stanford CA 94305-9045

KNUTH, ELDON LUVERNE, engineering educator; b. Luana, Iowa, May 10, 1925; s. Alvin W. and Amanda M. (Becker) K.; m. Marie O. Parrat, Sept. 10, 1954 (div. 1973); children: Stephen B., Dale L., Margot O., Lynette M.; m. Margaret I. Nicholson, Dec. 30, 1973. BS, Purdue U., 1949, MS, 1950; PhD (Guggenheim fellow), Calif. Inst. Tech., 1953. Aerothermodynamics group leader Aerophysics Devel. Corp., 1953-56; asso. research engr. dept. engring. UCLA, 1956-59, asso. prof. engring., 1960-65, prof. engring. and applied sci., 1965-91, prof. emeritus, 1991—, head chem., nuclear thermal div. dept. engring., 1963-65, chmn. energy kinetics dept., 1969-75, head molecular-beam lab., 1961-88. Gen. chmn. Heat Transfer and Fluid Mechanics Inst., 1959; vis. scientist, von Humboldt fellow Max-Planck Inst. für Strömungsforschung, Göttingen, Fed. Republic Germany, 1975-76; mem. Internat. Adv. Com. Internat. Symposium Rarefied Gas Dynamics., 2000—. Author: Introduction to Statistical Thermodynamics, 1966, Who Wrote Those Letters?, 2005, Auf den Spuren von Jürnjakob Swehn, 2005; also numerous articles; patentee radial-flow molecular pump Served with AUS, 1943-45. Recipient Fritz Reuter medal, Landsmannschaft, Mecklenburg, 2002. Mem. AIAA, Am. Soc. Engring. Edn., Am. Inst. Chem. Engrs., Combustion Inst., Soc. Engring. Sci., AAAS, Am. Phys. Soc., Am. Vacuum Soc., Sigma Xi, Tau Beta Pi, Gamma Alpha Rho, Pi Tau Sigma, Sigma Delta Chi, Pi Kappa Phi. Clubs: Gimlet (Lafayette, Ind.). Home: 18085 Boris Dr Encino CA 91316-4350

KNUTSEN, ALAN PAUL, pediatrician, immunologist, allergist; b. Mpls., July 21, 1948; s. Donald Richard and Shirley Marie (Erickson) K.; m. Kim A.; children: Laura Joelle, Brian A., Benjamin C., Elizabeth G., Katherine M., Amy S., Summer A. BA in Biology, U. Calif., 1971; MD, St. Louis U., 1975. Resident pediatrics St. Louis U. Med. Ctr., 1975-78; fellow allergy Duke U. Med. Ctr., Durham, NC, 1978-80;, 1980-93; dir. dept. allergy and immunology St. Louis U. Med. Ctr., 1985—; prof. St. Louis U., 1993—, 1993—. Mem. credentials com. St. Louis U. Med. Ctr., 1980—, infectious disease com., 1980—; dir. pediatric immunology lab, 1983—; dir. pediatric allergy/immunology trng. program. Contbr. articles to profl. jours. Mem. Am. Acad. Allergy/Immunology, Clin. Immunology Soc., Phi Beta Kappa, Alpha Omega Alpha. Democrat. Lutheran. Office: St Louis U Pediatric Rsch Inst 1465 S Grand Blvd Saint Louis MO 63104-1003 Home: 44 S Gore Ave Saint Louis MO 63119-2910 Home Phone: 314-961-3179; Office Phone: 314-268-4014. Business E-Mail: knutsenm@slu.edu.

KNUTSON, DAN, food products executive; BS, MBA, Minn. State Univ., Mankato. CPA, CMA. Fin. mgmt. positions Land O'Lakes Inc., Saint Paul, Minn., 1978—2000, sr. v.p., CFO, 2000—. Mailing: Land O'Lakes Inc PO Box 64101 Saint Paul MN 55164-0101*

KNUTSON, MARK THOMAS, sculptor, architectural firm executive; s. Erling Norman Knutson and Betty Fae Weldon; m. Sara Lynn Cummings, Mar. 29, 2000. BArch in Design, U. Ill., Chgo., 1989; MFA in Sculpture, Cranbrook Acad. Art, Bloomfield Hills, Mich., 1994. Archtl. designer David Chipperfield & Assocs., London, 1984—85; pres. Kason Group Inc., Tijeras, N.Mex., 1995—. Archtl. juror U. N.Mex., Albuquerque, 2001—. Contbr. articles to profl. jours. Avocations: scuba diving, kayaking, bicycling, skiing, martial arts. Office: Kason Group Inc PO Box 2121 Tijeras NM 87059

KNUTZEN, MARTHA LORRAINE, lawyer; b. Bellingham, Wash., Aug. 28, 1956; BA in Polit. Sci., Scripps Coll., 1978; MA in Polit. Sci, Practical Politics, U. San Francisco, 1981, JD, 1981. Bar: Calif. 1981. Lawyer, mgr. legal computer support svcs., San Francisco, 1981—. Mem. San Francisco Citizens' Adv. Com. on Elections, 1994-96; 3d vice chair Dem. Party, San Francisco, 1996-2000, treas., 1996-2000; mem. Resolution Com., Calif. Dem. Party, 2001—2005; chair San Francisco Human Rights Commn., 1996-2005; cmty. organizer. Recipient Civil Rights Leadership award Calif. Assn. Human Rights Commn., 1996. Office: San Francisco Dist Atty 850 Bryant # 322 San Francisco CA 94103 Home: Apt 44 601 Van Ness Ave San Francisco CA 94102-3263

KO, JANG WAN, research scientist, educator; b. Muju, Republic of Korea, Dec. 23, 1967; s. Sungtae Ko and Duksoon Lee; m. Mikyong Minsun Kim, June 14, 2003. BA, Sung Kyun Kwan U., Seoul, Republic of Korea, 1992, EdM, 1994; PhD, U. Mo., 2003. Cert. Assn. Instl. Rsch. Rschr. Korean Ednl. Devel. Inst., Seoul, Republic of Korea, 1995—96; sr. rsch. analyst George Mason U., Fairfax, Va., 2005—. Computer cons. U. Mo., Columbia, 2000—01. Author: Curriculum and Instructional Strategies, 1999, 2003; contbr. articles to profl. jours. Mem.: Assn. Career and Tech. Edn., Korean Soc. Econ. and Fin. of Edn., Korean Soc. Studies of Ednl. Adminstrn., Assn. for Study of Higher Edn., Am. Ednl. Rsch. Assn., Assn. Instl. Rsch. Avocations: tennis, soccer. Office: George Mason U 4400 University Dr 2F2 Fairfax VA 22030 Home: 8305 Elm Grove Ct Vienna VA 22182 Office Phone: 703-993-8840. Office Fax: 703-993-8835. Business E-Mail: jko1@gmu.edu.

KO, KYUNGDUK, statistician, educator; PhD, Tex. A&M U., College Station, 2004. Asst. prof. stats. Boise State U., Idaho, 2004—. Mem.: Inst. Math. Stats. Office Phone: 208-426-1123.

KO, WEN-HSIUNG, electrical engineering educator; b. Shang-Hong, Fukien, China, Apr. 12, 1923; came to U.S., 1954, naturalized, 1963; s. Sing-Ming and Sou-Yu (Kao) K.; m. Christina Chen, Oct. 12, 1957; children: Kathleen, Janet, Linda, Alexander. BSEE, Nat. Amoy U., Fukien, China, 1946; MS, Case Inst. Tech., Cleve., 1956, PhD, 1959. Engr., then sr. engr. Taiwan Telecommunication Adminstrn., 1946-54; mem. faculty Case Inst. Tech., Cleve., 1956-93; prof. elec. and biomed. engring. Case Western Res. U., Cleve., 1967-93, prof. emeritus, 1994—. dir. engring. design center, 1970-82; pres., prin. Wen H. Ko & Assocs., Cleve., 1996—. Cons. NSF, N.Am. Mfg. Co., NIH, 1966-82; pres. Transducer Rsch. Found., 1986-2004; rschr. in med. implant electronics, telemetry and stimulation, microsensors and microactuators, micro-electro-mech.-sys. Recipient career achievement award Transducer Internat. Conf., Chgo., 1997. Fellow IEEE,

AIMBE; mem. Instrument Soc. Am., Bio-Med. Engring. Soc., Sigma Xi, Eta Kappa Nu. Home: 1356 Forest Hills Blvd Cleveland OH 44118-1359 Office: Case Western Res U EECS Dept Cleveland OH 44106 Business E-Mail: whk@cwru.edu.

KOBAK, ALFRED JULIAN, JR., obstetrician, gynecologist; b. Chgo., Feb. 10, 1935; s. Alfred J and Rose B (Baron) Kobak; m. Sue B Stein, May 3, 1959; children: William, Steven, Jane, Deborah. BS, U. Ill., 1957, MD, 1959. Diplomate Am Bd Ob-Gyn. Intern Michael Reese Hosp., Chgo., 1959-60; resident Cook County Hosp., 1960-62, 64-65; practice medicine specializing in ob-gyn. Valparaiso, Ind., 1965—; physician in charge Kobak Ctr. Women's Health, Valparaiso, 2007—. Mem. med. staff Porter Hosp., Valparaiso, 1965—, chmn. dept. OB/GYN, pres. med. staff, 1981—82; clin. assoc. prof. ob-gyn. Ind. U. Sch. Medicine; with Ob-Gyn. Assocs., 1970—2006. Contbr. articles to profl jours. Bd. dirs. N.W. Ind. Jewish Fedn., 1970—84, Porter County Bd. Health, 1991—, pres., 1997; bd. dirs., past pres. Porter County Health Dept. Capt USAF, 1962—64. Fellow: ACS, Am. Coll. Ob-Gyn., Internat. Coll. Surgeons; mem.: AMA, Chgo. Gynecol. Soc. (v.p. 1998—99), Porter County Med Soc (pres. 1979, 1986), Ctrl. Assn. Obstetricians and Gynecologists, Ind. Med. Assn., Am. Soc. Reproductive Medicine, Sand Creek Club. Office Phone: 219-531-7500. Personal E-mail: sakobak@comcast.net. Business E-Mail: drk@thekobakcenter.com.

KOBAK, JAMES BENEDICT, management consultant; b. St. Louis, Mar. 4, 1921; s. Edgar and Evelyn (Hubert) K.; m. Hope McEldowney, June 13, 1942; children: James Benedict, John D. (dec.), Thomas M. BS, Harvard U., 1942; postgrad., Pace Coll., 1946—49. CPA, NY, La., Union S.Africa. Assoc. J.K. Lasser & Co., NYC, 1946-71, partner, 1954-64, adminstrv. partner, 1964-71; internat. adminstrv. partner Lasser, Harmood Banner, Dunwoody, NY, 1964-71; pres. James B. Kobak & Co., Darien, Conn., 1971—. Ptnr. James B. Kobak Bus. Models Co., 1972-82; founder Kobak Open. Author: How to Start a Magazine and Publish It Profitably, 2002. Chmn. mag. com., mem. bus. com. nat. coun. Boy Scouts Am.; co-founder, sec.-treas. John D. Kobak Appalachian Edn. Found., Darien; trustee Hill Sch., Pottstown, Pa.; pres. St. George Village Bot. Garden, St. Croix, US VI. Served to capt., F.A AUS, 1942—46. Mem. AICPA, NY State Soc. CPAs, Transvall Soc. Accts., Harvard Club (NYC), Wee Burn Country Club (Darien), Hapenny Bay Beach Club (St. Croix), Carambola Golf Club, St. Croix Country Club. Home and Office: 2136 Meadow Ridge Redding CT 06896 Home: Sweet Lime Village # 29 Kingshill VI 00850 Personal E-mail: jimkobak@aol.com.

KOBAK, JAMES BENEDICT, JR., lawyer, educator; b. Alexandria, La., May 2, 1944; s. James Benedict and Hope (McEldowney) K.; m. Carol Johnson, June 11, 1966; children: James Benedict III, Katherine Jean, Marcie Ann. BA magna cum laude, Harvard U., 1966; LLB, U. Va., 1969. Bar: U.S. Dist. Ct. (so. and ea. dists.) N.Y. 1972, U.S. Supreme Ct. 1977, U.S. Ct. Appeals (2nd cir.) 1973, (5th cir.) 1982, U.S. Dist. Ct. (no. dist.) Calif. 1983, N.J. 1996. Asst. prof. U. Ala., 1969-70; assoc. Hughes Hubbard & Reed LLP, NYC, 1970-77, ptnr., 1977—. Lectr. in law U. Va., 1986-2000; adj. assoc. prof. Fordham U., 1986—; arbitrator Am. Arbitration Assn.; pres. NY County Lawyers Assn. Found., 2005-. Editor: Misuse: Licensing and Litigation, 2000; mem. bd. editors Va. Law Rev., 1967-69, assoc. editor, 1968-69; contbr. articles to profl. jours., mags., treatises and newspapers. Trustee Morristown-Beard Sch., 1995—2001, Jersey City Mus., 2002—. Recipient 18th Rossman Meml. award, Jour. of Patent and Trademark Office Soc., 1991. Mem. ABA (antitrust sect., former chair intellectual property com.), Assn. Bar City NY, NY County Lawyers Assn. (bd. dirs. 1988-93, 95-97, 2001—, chmn. trade regulation com. 1987-88, chmn. com. on changing trends in the profession 1990-93, chmn. com. on law reform 1994-98, exec. com. 1996-98, chair libr. com. 1998—, Boris Kostelanetz Pres. award 2006), Order of Coif, Am. Law Inst., Adirondack 46ers Club, Keene Valley Country Club (trustee 1995-98), Harvard Club NY. Home: 206-95 W Shearwater Ct Jersey City NJ 07305 Office: Hughes Hubbard & Reed 1 Battery Park Plz Fl 12 New York NY 10004-1482 Business E-Mail: kobak@hugheshubbard.com.

KOBASHIGAWA, JON AKIRA, internist, cardiologist, researcher, educator; b. Honolulu, Sept. 25, 1954; s. Eikichi and Alice K. BS, Stanford U., 1976; MD, Mt. Sinai Sch. Medicine, 1980. Diplomate Am. Bd. Internal Medicine, Am. Bd. Cardiology. Intern, resident, cardiology fellow UCLA Med. Ctr., 1980-86; from clin. instr. medicine to clin. prof. UCLA, 1986-99, clin. prof. medicine, 1999—, med. dir. heart transplant program, 1994—, chief divsn. clin. faculty medicine, 1998—. Contbr. articles to profl. jours. Upjohn clin. scholar, 1980; grantee in field. Mem. AAAS, Am. Coll. Cardiology (past chmn. heart failure and transplant com.), Internat. Soc. Heart Lung Transplantation (bd. dirs., program chair 1999—, pres. 2004), Am. Soc. Transplantation, Am. Heart Assn. (chair 1998—), Alpha Omega Alpha. Office: Univ Cardiovasc Med Group 100 UCLA Med Plz Ste 630 Los Angeles CA 90095-0001 Office Fax: 310-794-1211. Business E-Mail: jonk@mednet.ucla.edu.*

KOBASUK, MARK G., lawyer, pharmaceutical executive; BA summa cum laude, Hiram Coll.; MA in Econs., Georgetown U., JD; studied at, Fletcher Sch. Law and Diplomacy. Intelligence officer CIA, 1981—88; law clk. US Dist. Ct., LA, 1988—89; assoc. Litig. Dept. Taft, Stettinius & Hollister LLP, Cin., 1989—98, ptnr., 1998—2006; v.p., gen. counsel Omnicare, Inc., Covington, Ky., 2006—. Mem.: Fed. Bar Assn. (pres. Cin.-No. Ky. Chap.). Office: Omnicare, Inc 1600 RiverCenter II 100 East RiverCenter Blvd Covington KY 41011*

KOBAYASHI, ALBERT SATOSHI, mechanical engineering educator; b. Chgo., Dec. 9, 1924; s. Toshiyuki and Taka (Torii) K.; m. Elizabeth Midori Oba, Sept. 24, 1953; children: Dori Kobayashi Ogami, Tina, Laura. BS in Engring., U. Tokyo, 1947; MSME, U. Wash., 1952; PhD, Ill. Inst. Tech., 1958. Position II engr. Konishiroku Photo Industry, Tokyo, 1947-50; design engr. Ill. Tools Works, Chgo., 1953-55; rsch. engr. Armour Rsch. Found., Ill. Inst. Tech., Chgo., 1955-58; from asst. prof. to assoc. prof. dept. mech. engring. U. Wash., Seattle, 1958-64, prof., 1964-97, Boeing Pennell prof. structural mechanics, 1988-95, prof. emeritus, 1997—. Coll. faculty assoc.The Boeing Co. Seattle, 1958—76; cons. Math. Sci. Northwest, Bellevue, Wash., 1962—82, UN Devel. Program, NY, 1984; vis. scholar U. Tokyo, 1969, 77; program dir. mech., structural and materials engring. divsn. NSF, 1987—88, expert, structural and materials program, 2005. Contbr. over 490 papers to Fracture Mechanics, Exptl. Mechanics Biomechanics and numerical analysis. Decorated Order of Rising Sun, gold rays with neck ribbons Emperor of Japan, 1997; recipient F. G. Tatnall award Soc. Exptl. Stress Analysis, 1973, B.J. Lazan award, 1981, R. E. Peterson award, 1983, William Murray Lecture medal, 1983, Burlington Resources Found. Faculty Achievement award, 1992, M. M. Frocht award, 1995, G. E. Sr. Rsch. award Am. Soc. Engring. Edn., 1995, Disting. Alumni award Univ. Student Club, U. Wash., 1997; named to Mech. Engring. Hall of Fame, U. Wash., 2006. Fellow ASME (Daniel C. Drucker medal 2007), Soc. Exptl. Mechanics (hon. life mem., pres. 1989-90), Internat. Congress on Fracture (hon.). Home: 15420 62nd Pl NE Kenmore WA 98028-4312 Office: U Wash Dept Mech Engring Box 352600 Seattle WA 98195-2600 Home Phone: 425-488-1869; Office Phone: 206-543-5488. Business E-Mail: ask@u.washington.edu.

KOBAYASHI, BERT TAKAAKI, JR., lawyer; b. Honolulu, Feb. 4, 1940; s. Bert Takaaki Sr. and Victoria Ruth (Tsuchiya) K.; m. Harriet Sanae Ishimine, Aug. 11, 1962; children: Christopher T., Jonathan A., Matthew H., Jennifer Sanae. Student, U. Hawaii, 1958—60; BA, Gettysburg Coll., Pa., 1962; JD, U. Calif., Hastings, 1965. Bar: Hawaii 1965, U.S. Dist. (fed. dist.) Hawaii 1965. Assoc. Chung, Vitousek, Chuck & Fujiyama, Honolulu, 1967-69, Kono, Ariyoshi, Honolulu, 1969-71; sr. ptnr. Kobayashi, Sugita & Goda, Honolulu, 1971—. Bd. dirs. First Hawaiian Bank, Honolulu, Western Air Lines, Schuler Homes, Am. Law Inst.; exec. com. Bancwest Corp. Honolulu; mem. State Jud. Selection Commn., Honolulu, 1985-01, chmn., 1987-89. Mem. ABA, ATLA, Am. Coll. Trial Lawyers, Hawaii Bar Assn., Am. Bd. Trial Advs., Am. Law Inst., Japan-Hawaii Econ. Coun., Am. Judicature Soc. (nat. bd. dirs. 2000—, exec. com. of bd. dirs. 2003—). Office: Kobayashi Sugita & Goda 999 Bishop St Ste 2600 Honolulu HI 96813-4430 Office Phone: 808-539-8700. E-mail: btk@ksglaw.com.

KOBAYASHI, HERBERT SHIN, electrical engineer; b. Webster, Tex., Feb. 6, 1929; s. Mitsutaro and Moto Kobayashi; m. Haruko Orita; children: June, Naomi, Ken. *To my 6th grade teacher, Miss Madison, I mentioned numbers could represent letters, she said that would never work. To my assistant principal who let me look at all the popular mechanics magazines. To T.A. Olson who taught us how to fix things and work with lathe. To U.S. Army drafted in 1954 and sent to Anti—aircraft school (guided missile). To University of Michigan to study automatic controls. To S.I.E., Boeing, Locheed, and NASA for work experience. To TRW from Al Law, Bob Godfried, Dr. Dunbridge, Milty for teaching about how to build BIT synchronizers. To Department of Transportation for requesting help on doppler radar. To my dad and mom for making me wealthy.* BSEE, U. Houston, 1951; MSEE, U. Mich., 1958, MS in Indsl. Engring., 1969. Design engr. SIE, Houston, 1960-61, Boeing Aerospace, Huntsville, Ala., 1961-62, New Orleans, 1962, Lockheed Electronics, Houston, 1963; aerospace technologist NASA, Houston, 1963—2002; pres. Kobayashi Inc., Webster, Tex., 1960—. *My father, Mirsutaro Kobayashi, with a college degree, left Japan for America in 1904. My mother, Moto, came from Japan in 1913. They had three daughters and five sons. We were vegetable farmers for 70 years and still farm. Hope, sister was high school salutorian in 1933 and graduated from Rice Institute in 1937. Ricki, brother, was high school valedictorian in 1940 and got a PHD from University of Michigan in 1950. Mitsu, sister, was high school valedictorian in 1945 and graduated from Rice Institute in 1951. June, daughter, was valedictorian in high school in 1985 and graduated from Rice University in 1990. Naomi, my daughter, was high school valedictorianin 1986 and got a Law Degree from Yale University in 1994. My mother, MOTO, was high school valedictorian in Japan in 1907.* Patentee in field. Mem. planning and zoning commn., Webster, 1993-94. With U.S. Army, 1954-56. Mem. IEEE, AIAA. Achievements include development of technique to make stronger concrete slabs, pulse width modulation for servo loop (closed or open) more efficiency; patents for rotary adjustable dirt, sand, rock seperator. Home: 1428 NASA Pkwy Webster TX 77598-4702 Office Phone: 281-332-3349. Personal E-mail: herbkooo@verizon.net.

KOBAYASHI, HISASHI, computer scientist, dean; b. Tokyo, June 13, 1938; arrived in U.S., 1965; m. Masaye Okubo. BS, U. Tokyo, 1961, MS, 1963; MA, Princeton U., 1966, PhD, 1967. Radar system designer Toshiba, Kawasaki, Japan, 1963-65; mem. rsch. staff IBM, Yorktown Heights, NY, 1967-86; dir. Japan Sci. Inst. IBM Japan Ltd., 1982-86; Sherman Fairchild U. prof. elec. engring., computer sci. Princeton (N.J.) U., 1986—, dean Sch. Engring. and Applied Sci., 1986-91. Vis. asst. prof. UCLA, 1969—70; vis. prof. U. Hawaii, 1975, Tech. U. Darmstadt, Germany, 1979—80, U. Victoria, Canada, 1998, U. Tokyo, 1991—92; cons. prof. Stanford U., 1976; internat. prof. U. Libre de Bruxelles, Belgium, 1980; mem. computer sci. panel NRC, 1981—82; mem. adv. bd. Inst. Sys. Sci., Nat. U. Singapore, 1986—2001, Advanced Sys. Found., Vancouver, Canada, 1986—98; mem. adv. bd. dep. elec. engring. U. Pa., 1986—91; mem. sci. adv. com. Stanford Rsch. Inst. Internat., Menlo Park, Calif., 1986—91; sci. adv. bd. NASA, Washington, 1990—92; external examiners rev. bd. Ctr. Sys. Sci. Simon Fraser U., 1990—92; mem. Premier's Coun., Ont., Canada, 1990—91; bd. advisors Bower award and prize Franklin Inst., Phila., 1990—; bd. dirs. gov. Internat. Coun. Computer Comms., Washington, 1992—2005; internat. adv. bd. Advanced Inst. Sci. and Tech. Ministry Economy, Trade and Industry, Japan, 2001—05; exec. com. 21st Century Ctr. of Excellence Program Ministry Culture and Edn., Japan, 2001—. Author: (book) Modeling and Analysis, 1978; assoc. editor: IEEE Trans Info. Theory, 1980—83, editor-in-chief: Performance Evaluation, 1981—86; contbr. articles to profl. jours. Recipient David Sarnoff RCA award, 1960, Invention award, IBM, 1971, 1973, Outstanding Contbn. award, 1975, 1984, Humboldt award, 1979, Silver Core award, IFIP, 1980, Edward Rhein Tech. award, 2005. Fellow: IEEE (life; chmn. Richard Hamming award 1990—91), Inst. Electronic, Info. and Comms. Engrs. Japan, Engring. Acad. Japan; mem.: Internat. Coun. Computer Comm. (gov. 1993—2005), Internat. Fedn. Info. Processing (chmn. working group 1982—86), Internat. Union Radio Sci. (vice chmn. commn. C 1978—81). Achievements include patents in field. Home: 347 W 57th St # 33B New York NY 10019 Office: Princeton U B323 Engring Quadrangle Princeton NJ 08544-5263 Home Phone: 212-977-1897; Office Phone: 609-258-1984. Business E-Mail: hisashi@princeton.edu.

KOBAYASHI, NORITAKE, business educator; b. Tokyo, Feb. 23, 1932; s. Daijyo and Makiko (Tadokoro) K.; m. Mieko Mary Margaret Nishino, May 21, 1960; children: Norikazu, Sumiko, Kumiko. AB cum laude, Harvard U., 1953, postgrad., 1953-54; LLB, Keio U., Japan, 1954, PhD, 1973. Lectr. Keio U., 1956-62, assoc. prof. Yokohama, 1962-73, prof. Grad. Sch. Bus. Adminstrn., 1973-96, dir. sch. bus., 1980-83, dean Grad. Sch. Bus. Adminstrn., 1987-91, Mitsubishi chair, prof. Tokyo, 1991-96, prof. emeritus, 1996—; dean Shukutoku U. Coll. of Cross-Cultural Comm. and Bus., Saitama, 1996—2000, Shukutoku U. Grad. Sch. Internat. Bus. and Culture, 2000—02; prof. Shukutoku U., 2002—03. Vis. prof. Ind. U., Bloomington, 1968, Asian Inst. Mgmt., Philippines, 1970, Internat. Mgmt. Inst., Geneva, 1974, UCLA, Anderson Sch. Mgmt., LA, 2004; corp. auditor Fuji Xerox Co., Ltd., 2002-03, adviser, 2003-04 Author: Joint Venture in Japan, 1967, The World of Japanese Business, 1969, International Business, 1972, Japanese Multinational Enterprises, 1980, Management, A Global Perspective, 1997, Japanese International Corporations: Internationalization and Performance, 2007. Trustee emeritus Brown U.; bd. dirs. Inst. for Internat. Studies and Training, 2005—. Recipient Mgmt. Sci. Pub. Prize Nihon Keiei Kyokai, 1981. Fellow Acad. Internat. Bus.; Workshop to Study Multinat. Enterprises (hon. pres.); mem. Comparative Law Assn. Japan, Mgmt. Assn. Japan, Am. Acad. Polit. and Social Sci., Japan-Am. Soc., Keio U. Alumni Assn., Tokyo-Am. Club, Harvard Club, Tokyo Club. Home: 304 5-17-1 Higashi gotauda Shinagawa-ku Tokyo 141-0022 Japan Personal E-mail: n.kobayashi@alea.ne.jp.

KOBAYASHI, RIKI, retired chemical engineer, educator; b. Webster, Tex., May 13, 1924; s. Mitsutaro and Moto (Shigeta) K.; m. Barbara Joan Stevens, June 1, 1957; children: James Brock, Alec Stevens; m. Lee Mary Parker Lovejoy, Nov., 1971; children: Susan, Anne. BSChemE, Rice U., 1944; MS, U. Mich., 1947, PhD in Chem. Engring., 1951. Faculty dept. chem. engring. Rice U., Houston, 1951-94, Louis Calder prof., 1967-94, prof. emeritus, 1994—; ret. D.L. Katz disting. lectr. U. Mich., 1975; hon. chmn., honoree Symposia on Thermodynamics, Chromatography & Transport Phenomena, Am. Inst. Chem. Engrs. Spring Meeting, 1987; plenary lectr. Chemicon '89 Trivandrum, India; Lindsay disting. lectr. Tex. A&M U., 1985; cons. in field. Author (with others): Handbook of Natural Gas Engineering, 1959; contbr. articles to profl. jours. Served with AUS, 1945-46. Recipient Meritorious award Cyrogenic Engring. Conf. Com., 1966, 1st Donald L. Katz award Gas Processors Assn., 1985, Outstanding Engring. Alumni award Rice U., 1985; Japan Soc. Promotion of Sci. fellow, 1985. Fellow AICE, Am. Inst. Chemists; mem. AIME, NAE, Am. Inst. Physics, Am. Chem. Soc., Japan Inst. Chem. Engring. (hon.), Tex. Acad. Engring., Sci. and Medicine, Sigma Xi, Alpha Chi Sigma, Tau Beta Pi, Phi Lambda Upsilon, Phi Kappa Phi. Unitarian Universalist. Achievements include co-invention of diffl. kinetics. Home: 348 Piney Point Rd Houston TX 77024-6506

KOBAYASHI, SUSUMU, retired computer company executive; b. Kumamoto, Japan, Apr. 3, 1939; s. Senkichiro and Michiko Kobayashi. BS, Tokyo Inst. Tech., 1963. Programmer Osaka (Japan) Gas Co., Ltd., 1963-65, C. Itoh Computing Svcs. Co., Ltd., Tokyo, 1965-67; applications analyst, systems engr. Control Data Far East, Inc., Tokyo, 1967-75; asst. gen. mgr. systems dept. JMA Sys., Inc., Tokyo, 1975-79; dir. Nuc. Data Corp., Tokyo, 1979-89, Yokogawa Supertek Corp., Tokyo, 1989-90; tech. advisor sales divsn. Yokogawa Cray ELS Ltd., Tokyo, 1990-92; tech. advisor Cray Rsch. Japan Ltd., Tokyo, 1990-96; advisor Tsukuba Press Ltd., Tsukuba-shi, Japan, 1996-97; pres. Tera Computer Japan (now called Cray Japan, Inc.), Tokyo, 1997—2000, 2000—02, chief scientist Tsukubashi, 2002—04, rep., 2004—05; ret. Translator, editor: book Fortran 4 (D. D. McCracken), 1968, Lisp 1.5 Primer (C. Weissman), 1970, A Few Good Men from Univac (D. E. Lundstrom), 1992, The Official Computer Widow's (and Widower's) Handbook (by Experts on Computer Widow/Widowerhood), 1992, Future Computer Opportunities (Jack Dunning), 1993, Enabling Technologies for Petaflops Computing (T. Sterling, P. Messina, P. H. Smith), 1997, The Supermen (Charles J. Murray), 1998; contbr. articles to electronic mags. Mem.: IEEE, AIAA, Astron. Soc. Pacific, Am. Assn. Artificial Intelligence, Japan Info. Processing Soc., Japan Math. Soc., Assn. Computing Machinery. Avocations: motoring, audio/visual. Home: 85-2-206 Migawa 2-chome Mito 310-0912 Japan Home Phone: +81-29-241-3543.

KOBDISH, GEORGE CHARLES, lawyer; b. Casper, Wyo., June 30, 1950; s. Richard Matthew and Jo Earl (Uttz) K.; m. Mary Ellen Griffith, Jan. 24, 1969; children: George Charles, Jr., Kelly Rebecca, Kimberlee Nelle. BBA with honors, U. Tex., 1971, JD, 1974. Bar: Tex. 1974, U.S. Dist. Ct. (no. dist.) Tex. 1975. Asst. atty. gen. State of Tex., Austin, 1974—76; assoc. McCall, Parkhurst & Horton LLP, Dallas, 1976—80, ptnr., 1981—. Bd. dirs. North Dallas Shared Ministries, 1993—2000, pres., 1996—98; lay gen. chairperson Cath. Cmty. Appeal, 2000—01; bd. dirs. Notre Dame of Dallas Schs, Inc., 2000—06, pres., 2004—06; mem. adv. coun. The Cath. Found., 2006—. Mem. Am. Coll. Bond Counsel, Nat. Assn. Bond Lawyers, Tex. Bar Assn., Dallas Bar Assn., Royal Oaks Country Club, Tower Club, Serra Internat. (Dallas bd. dirs., pres. 1998-99, U.S.A. coun., gov. Dist. 46, 2002-03), Phi Delta Theta. Roman Catholic. Office: McCall Parkhurst & Horton LLP 717 N Harwood St Ste 900 Dallas TX 75201-6586 Office Phone: 214-754-9236. Business E-Mail: ckobdish@mphlegal.com.

KOBER, ARLETTA REFSHAUGE (MRS. KAY L. KOBER), supervisor; b. Cedar Falls, Iowa, Oct. 31, 1919; d. Edward and Mary (Jensen) Refshauge; m. Kay Leonard Kober, Feb. 14, 1944; children: Kay Mary, Karilyn Eve. BA, State Coll. Iowa, 1940; MA, U. No. Iowa. Tchr. HS, Soldier, Iowa, 1940—41; tchr. Montezuma HS, Iowa, 1941—43, East Waterloo HS, 1943—50; coord. Office Edn. Waterloo (Iowa) Cmty. Schs., 1967—84; head dept. coop. career edn. West HS, Waterloo, 1974—84. Mem. Waterloo Sch. Health Coun.; mem. nominating com. YWCA, Waterloo; Black Hawk County chmn. Tb Christmas Seals; ward chmn. ARC, Waterloo; co-chmn. Citizen's Com. Sch. Bond Issue; pres. Waterloo PTA Coun., Waterloo Vis. Nursing Assn., 1956—62, 1982—94, Kingsley Sch. PTA, 1959—60; v.p. Waterloo Women's Club, 1962—63, pres., 1963—64, trustee bd. clubhouse dirs., 1957—58; mem. Gen. Fedn. Women's Clubs, Nat. Congress Parents and Tchrs.; bd. dirs. United Svcs. Black Hawk County, Broadway Theatre League, St. Francis Hosp. Found., Black Hawk County Rep. Women, 1952—53; del. Iowa Rep. Convs., 1996, 1998; Presbyterial world svc. chmn. Presbyn. Women's Assn.; deacon Westminister Presbyn. Ch., 1995—98. Mem.: LWV (dir. Waterloo 1951—52), NEA, AAUW (v.p. Cedar Falls 1946—47), Black Hawk County Hist. Soc. (charter), Internat. Platform Assn., Town Club (dir.), PEO, Elklets, Dleta Kappa Gamma, Delta Pi Epsilon (v.p. 1966—67). Home: 3436 Augusta Cir Waterloo IA 50701-4608

KOBER, JOHN A., lawyer; b. LaCrosse, Kans. s. John B. and Dotty Kober; m. Norma Kober, Sept. 28, 1985; children: Kersten, Colin. BS, Kans. State U., 1980; JD, Washburn U., 1982; LLM, U. Mo., 1984. Bar: Tex., Nebr., Kans., U.S. Dist. Ct. (no. dist.) Tex. Ptnr. Morgan Lewis, Dallas. Lectr. in field; cons. in field. Contbr. articles to profl. jours. Mem.: ABA, Dallas Bar Assn., Tex. Soc. CPAs, Atty.-CPA Assn., AICPAs, Tarrant County Bar Assn., Tex. Bar Assn., Employee-Owned S Corps. of Am. (mem. tech. legis. adv. bd. ESOP S corp. legis.), Nat. Ctr. of Employee Ownership (bd. dirs.), ESOP Assn. (immediate past chair nat. fin. adv. com.). Office: Morgan Lewis & Bockius 1717 Main St #3200 Dallas TX 75201 Home Phone: 214-507-9790; Office Phone: 214-466-4105. Business E-Mail: jkober@morganlewis.com.

KOBETZ, RICHARD WILLIAM, criminologist, consultant; b. Chgo., Oct. 23, 1933; s. Nestor Joseph and Mary (Zurek) K.; m. Eleanore Marian Sever, Oct. 8, 1960 (div. Dec. 1995); children: Kevin, Kimberly and Candice (twins). AA, Chgo. City Jr. Coll., 1959; student, Ill. Tchrs. Coll., 1964-66; MS in Pub. Adminstrn., Ill. Inst. Tech., 1968; D of Pub. Adminstrn., Nova U., 1978. Diplomate Am. Bd. Forensic Examiners; cert. personal protection specialist. Police officer Winnetka (Ill.) Police Dept., 1954-55; from police officer to sgt. to lt. Chgo. Police Dept., 1955-68; asst. dir. Internat. Assn. Chiefs of Police, Washington, 1968-79; capt. Gretna (La.) Police Dept. Exec. dir., trainer, cons. Exec. Protection Inst., Berryville, Va., 1979—; dir., trainer, cons. North Mountain Pines Tng. Ctr., Winchester, Va., 1979—; security cons. numerous U.S. corps., 1979—; active various security and enforcement agys., 1979—; del. Interpol; spkr. UN, Vienna; cons. security Olympic Games Author: The Police Role and Juvenile Delinquency, 1971, Juvenile Justice Administration, 1973, Target Terrorism: Providing Protective Services, 1979, Providing Executive Protection, 1990, Vol. II, 1994; contbr. articles to profl. jours., chpts. to books. Acad. Security Educators and Trainers disting. fellow, 1987. Mem. Acad. Security Educators and Trainers (pres., v.p. 1982—), Internat. Assn. Chiefs of Police (Achievement award 1979), Am. Soc. Indsl. Security, Am. Soc. Criminology, Am. Soc. for Pub. Adminstrn. Clubs: Nine Lives Assocs. (Berryville) (exec. sec. 1978—). Republican. Roman Catholic. Avocations: shooting, camping, travel. Home and Office: Highlander Lodge 276 Journeys End Ln Bluemont VA 20135-1862 Home Phone: 540-554-2540; Office Phone: 540-554-2540. E-mail: rwk@crosslink.net.

KOBI, DANIEL CASEY, lawyer; b. Ft. Wayne, Ind., June 26, 1975; s. Neil H. and Deborah J. Kobi. BS, Ind. U., 1997, JD, 2001. Assoc. Sidley Austin LLP, NYC, 2001—05; v.p. Investment Banking Divsn. Legal Lehman Bros. Inc., NYC, 2005—. Author: Staying True to Purpose: Including Corporate Debtors Under 362 (h) of the Federal Bankruptcy Code, 2001, Wall Street v. Main Street: The SEC's New Regulation FD and Its Impact on Market Participants, 2002. Mem.: ABA, Federalist Soc., NY Bar Assn. Office: Lehman Bros Inc 745 7th Ave New York NY 10019 Office Phone: 212-526-6259. Business E-Mail: ckobi@lehman.com.

KOBLENTZ, ROBERT ALAN, lawyer; b. Columbus, Ohio, Aug. 20, 1946; m. Kathryn Anderson, Oct. 20, 1973; children: Maureen, Robert. BA, Ohio State U., 1967, JD, 1970. Bar: Ohio 1970, U.S. Dist. Ct. (so. dist.) Ohio 1971, U.S. Supreme Ct. 1992; bd. cert. family rels. law specialist. Legal rsch. Bancroft-Whitney Co., San Francisco, 1970-71; atty. Tracy, DeLibera, Lyons & Collins, Columbus, 1971-78, DeLibera, Lyons, Koblentz & Scott, Columbus, 1978-80, Scott, Koblentz & Binau, Columbus, 1980-86; pvt. practice Columbus, 1986—. Bd. dirs. Friends of WOSU,

Columbus, 1982-88, Opera Columbus, 1984-87, Upper Arlington Civic Assn., Columbus, 1988-90. Named OH Super Lawyer, Law Politics Cin. Mag., 2005, 2006, 2007. Mem. ABA, Ohio State Bar Assn. (cert. family rels. specialist, del. family law sect. 1979—), Ohio Acad. Trial Lawyers (chmn. family law sect. 1983), Columbus Bar Assn. (chmn. family law com. 1976-78), Franklin County Trial Lawyers (pres. 1985-86). Office: 35 E Livingston Ave Columbus OH 43215-5762 Office Phone: 614-461-6666.

KOBLENZ, MICHAEL ROBERT, lawyer; b. Newark, Apr. 9, 1948; s. Herman and Esther (Weisman) Koblenz; m. Bonnie Jane Berman, Dec. 22, 1973; children: Adam, Alexander, Elizabeth. BA, George Washington U., 1969, LLM, 1974; JD, Am. U., 1972. Bar: NJ 1972, U.S. Dist. Ct. NJ 1972, DC 1973, U.S. Dist. Ct. DC 1973, U.S. Ct. Appeals (7th cir.) 1976, U.S. Ct. Claims 1973, U.S. Mil. Ct. Appeals 1974, NY 1980, U.S. Dist. Ct. (so. dist.) NY 1980. Atty. U.S. Dept. Justice, Washington, 1972—75; lectr. Am. U., 1975—78; spl. asst. U.S. atty. Office of U.S. Atty., Chgo., 1976—78; atty. Commodity Futures Trading Commn., Washington, 1975—77, spl. counsel, 1977, asst. dir., 1977—78, regional counsel NYC, 1978—80; assoc. Rein, Mound & Cotton, NYC, 1980—82; ptnr. Mound, Cotton & Wollan (and predecessor firms), NYC, 1983—. Contbr. articles to legal jours. Bd. appeals Village of Flower Hill, Manhasset, NY, 1983—84, trustee, 1984—86; dep. mayor Village of East Hills, NY, 1993—94, mayor, 1994—; active Roslyn Little League, 1991—2001, bd. dirs., 1992. Recipient Cert. of Appreciation for Outstanding Svc., U.S. Commodity Futures Trading Commn., 1977. Home: East Hills 20 Hemlock Dr Roslyn NY 11576-2303 Office: Mound Cotton Wollan & Greengrass 1 Battery Park Plz New York NY 10004-1405 Home Phone: 516-484-9144; Office Phone: 212-804-4247. Business E-Mail: mkoblenz@moundcotton.com.

KOBLIK, STEVEN S., academic administrator; Pres. Reed Coll., Portland, Oreg., 1992—2001, The Huntington Library, Art Collections, and Botanical Gardens, San Marino, Calif., 2002—. Office: Reed Coll Office Pres 3203 SE Woodstock Blvd Portland OR 97202-8199

KOBRIN, LAWRENCE ALAN, lawyer; b. NYC, Sept. 14, 1933; s. Irving and Hortense (Freezer) K.; m. Ruth E. Freedman, Mar. 5, 1967; children: Jeffrey, Rebecca, Debra. AB in History summa cum laude, Columbia U., NYC, 1954, JD, 1957. Bar: NY 1957, US Dist. Ct. (so. dist.) NY 1958, US Dist. Ct. (ea. dist.) 1958, US Ct. Appeals (2d cir.) 1959, US Supreme Ct. 1966. Assoc. Cahill, Gordon, Reindel & Ohl, NYC, 1958-59, Arthur D. Emil, 1959-63; ptnr. Emil & Kobrin, 1963-79, Milgrim, Thomajan, Jacobs and Lee, 1979-83, Cahill Gordon & Reindel LLP, 1984—2006, sr. counsel, 2007—. Bd. dirs. Wurzweiler Sch. Social Work, vice-chmn., 1994-98; treas. The Jewish Week, NYC, 1992-96, chmn., 1996-2006, chmn. emeritus, 2006-; trustee North European Oil Royalty Trust, 2006-. Notes editor Columbia U. Law Rev.; mng. editor Tradition, 1961-64, editl. com. 1964—; contbr. articles to profl. jours. V.p., assoc. treas., chmn. dist. com. Fedn. Jewish Philanthropies, NYC, 1981-84, com. long range planning, 1985-86; chmn. Ramaz Sch., NYC, 1978-83; sec. to bd. Bar Ilan U., NYC, 1972-80; pres. The Jewish Ctr., NYC, 1987-90, NYC UJA-Fedn., chmn. communal planning com., 1988-91; v.p. Union Orthodox Jewish Congregations, 1968-74; chmn. campus com., 1962-66, Israel com., 1967-72, pub. com., 1972-78; pres. Massad Camps, 1971-77; bd. dirs. Am. Friends Pardes, 1991-96, Histadrut Ivrit., 1991-2003; mem. exec. com. Orthodox Caucus, 1995-2007, Columbia Barnard Hillel, 1995—2007; bd. exec. com. Edah, 1994-2006; dir. Columbia Coll. Alumni Assn., 1990-96, v.p., 1992-94. Kent scholar, 1954-55, Stone scholar, 1954-57. Mem. Nat. Assn. Coll. and Univ. Attorneys (1973-80), Am. Coll. Real Estate Lawyers. Home: 15 W 81st St New York NY 10024-6022 also: 8 Popple Swamp Rd Cornwall Bridge CT 06754-1135 Office Phone: 212-701-3337. Personal E-mail: kobrinL@mindspring.com. Business E-Mail: Lkobrin@cahill.com. E-mail: lak56@columbia.edu.

KOBS, JAMES FRED, direct marketing consultant; b. Chgo., June 27, 1938; s. Fred Charles and Ann (Ganser) K.; m. Nadine Schumacher, May 18, 1963; children: Karen, Kathleen, Kenneth BS in Journalism, U. Ill., 1960. Copywriter Rylander Co., Chgo., 1960—62; mng. dir. Success Mag., Chgo., 1963—65; mail order mgr. Am. Peoples Press, Westmont, Ill., 1966—67; exec. v.p. Stone & Adler Advt., Chgo., 1967—78; chmn. Kobs & Brady Advt., Inc. (now Draft Fcb), Chgo., 1978—88, vice chmn., 1988; chmn. Kobs Gregory & Passavant, Chgo., 1989—2001; pres. Kobs Strategic Cons., Chgo., 2002—. Guest lectr. U. Wis., U. Ill., NYU; adj. prof. direct mktg. Northwestern U. Medill Sch. Journalism Grad. Program; instr. U. Chgo. Strategic Direct Mktg. Cert. Program; internat. lectr. in field Author: Profitable Direct Marketing, 2d edit., 1991, 24 Ways to Improve Your Direct Mail Results, 99 Proven Direct Response Offers; contbr. articles to periodicals Past chmn. Direct Mktg. Ednl. Found Recipient numerous local and nat. advt. awards; named to Direct Mktg. Hall of Fame Mem. Direct Mktg. Assn. (dir., sec., exec. com., recipient Silver and Gold Mailbox, Gold Medallion, Gold Echo, Ed Mayer award), Chgo. Assn. Direct Mktg. (past pres., Direct Marketer of Yr.), Boys and Girls Clubs of Chgo. (corp. bd.), Alpha Delta Sigma Office: Kobs Strategic Consulting 222 N Columbus Dr Ste 2202 Chicago IL 60601

KOBUS, RICHARD LAWRENCE, architect; b. Chgo., Nov. 19, 1952; BS in Architecture, U. Ill., 1974; MArch, Harvard U., 1978. Registered architect, Mass., N.H., Maine, Ill., Pa., R.I., Ohio, N.J., Conn., Wash., Mo., N.Y., Vt. Designer Metz, Train, Olsen & Youngren, Chgo., 1974-75, Shepley, Bulfinch, Richardson & Abbott, Boston, 1978-79; assoc. Skidmore, Owings and Merrill, Boston, 1979-83; pres., prin., founder Tsoi/Kobus & Assocs., Inc., Cambridge, Mass., 1983—. Archtl. prin. healthcare acad., corp., and rsch. facilities U.S., Europe, Asia. Mem. permanent bldg. com. Town of Belmont, 1999—2003; bd. trustees Buckingham, Browne and Nichols, 1999—2005, Mass. Eye and Ear Infirmary, 1999—; pres. Major's Cove Assn., Edgartown, Mass., 1997—2001. Julia Amory Appleton fellow Harvard U., 1978-79; recipient Gov. Design award, 1986, Modern Healthcare Nat. Design award, 1988, 94, 98, AIA.Boston Soc. Architects Healthcare Assembly Design award, 1997, 98, 99, 2001, 06, PCI Design award, 1995, 98, AIA Honor Design award, 1994, 97, 98, 99, Am. Sch. and Univ. Archtl. Portfolio award, 1989, 90, Small Bus. of Yr. award Greater Boston C. of C., 2000, Golden Travel award IMI New England Region, 2002, Cost Effectiveness award St. Louis Coun. Constrn. Consumers, 2004, Constrn. award Acad. Gen. Contractors St. Louis, 2004. Mem.: AIA (mem. Acad. on Arch. for Health 1997—, Healthcare Assembly Design award 1997, 1998, 1999, 2001), Soc. Campus and Univ. Planning, Urban Land Inst., Boston Soc. Archs. (sec. bd. dirs. 2000—01), Am. Coll. Healthcare Archs. (founding mem. and fellow), Nat. Assn. Indsl. and Office Parks. Avocations: sailing, rowing, photography, auto racing. Office: Tsoi/Kobus & Assocs Inc PO Box 9114 One Brattle Sq Cambridge MA 02238-9114 E-mail: rkobus@tka-architects.com.

KOBZA, DENNIS JEROME, architect; b. Ullysses, Nebr., Sept. 30, 1933; s. Jerry Frank and Agnes Elizabeth (Lavicky) K.; m. Doris Mae Riemann, Dec. 26, 1953; children: Dennis Jerome, Diana Jill, David John. BS, Healds Archtl. Engring., 1959. Draftsman, designer B.L. Schroder, Palo Alto, Calif., 1959-60; sr. draftsman, designer Ned Abrams, Architect, Sunnyvale, Calif., 1960-61, Kenneth Elvin, Architect, Los Altos, Calif., 1961-62; ptnr. B.L. Schroder, Architect, Palo Alto, Calif., 1962-66; pvt. practice architecture Mountain View, Calif., 1966—. Served with USAF, 1952-56. Recipient Solar PAL award, Palo Alto, 1983, Mountain View Mayoral award, 1979. Mem. C. of C. (dir. 1977-79, Archtl. Excellence award Hayward chpt. 1985, Outstanding Indsl. Devel. award Sacramento chpt., 1980), AIA (chpt. dir. 1973), Constrn. Specifications Inst. (dir. 1967-68), Am. Inst. Plant Engrs., Nat. Fedn. Ind. Bus. Orgn., Rotary (dir. 1978-79, pres. 1986-87). Home: 3840 May Ct Palo Alto CA 94303-4545 Office: 2083 Old Middlefield Way Mountain View CA 94043-2465 Office Phone: 650-961-6103. Business E-Mail: dkarch@kobza.com. E-mail: dkobza@kobza.com.

KOC, LORRAINE K., lawyer; b. Gulfport, Miss., Jan. 29, 1958; BA magna cum laude, Univ. Pa., 1979, MA, 1979, JD, 1983. Bar: Pa. 1983. Gen. counsel Deb Shops, Inc., Phila., 1985—. Mem. adj. faculty Pa. State Univ., Abington, 1989—, mem. bd. advisors, 1989—. Mem.: Assn. Corporate Counsel, Pa. Bar Assn. (mem. employment law com.), Nat. Assn. Women Lawyers (pres. 2006—), ABA (chair corp. counsel com. gen. practice sect. 2004), Soc. Human Resource Mgmt., Phila. Bar Assn. (Disting. Svc. award 1988). Office: Deb Shops Inc 9401 Bluegrass Rd Philadelphia PA 19114 Office Phone: 215-676-6000 ext. 217. Business E-Mail: lkoc@debshops.com.

KOCAOGLU, DUNDAR F., engineering management educator, industrial engineer, civil engineer; b. June 1, 1939; came to U.S., 1960; s. Irfan and Meliha (Uzay) K.; m. ALev Baysak, Oct. 17, 1968; 1 child, Timur. BSCE, Robert Coll., Istanbul, Turkey, 1960; MSCE, Lehigh U., 1962; MS in Indsl. Engring., U. Pitts., 1972; PhD in Ops. Rsch., 1976. Registered prof. engr., Pa., Oreg. Design engr. Modjeski & Masters, Harrisburg, Pa., 1962-64; ptnr. TEKSER Engring. Co., Istanbul, Turkey, 1966-69; project engr. United Engrs., Phila., 1964-71; rsch. asst. U. Pitts., 1972-74; vis. asst. prof., 1974-76; assoc. prof. indsl. engring., dir. engring. mgmt., 1976-87; prof., chmn. engring. and tech. mgmt. dept. Portland State U., 1987—. Pres., CEO TMA-Tech. Mgmt. Assocs., Portland, Oreg., 1973—; pres, CEO Portland Internat. Conf. Mgmt. Engring. and Tech., 1990—. Editor: Management of R&D and Engineering, 1992; co-editor: Technology Management-The New International Language, 1991, Innovation in Technology Management-The Key to Global Leadership, 1997, chnology and Innovation management, 1999, Technology Management in the Knowledge Era, 2001, Technology Management for Reshaping the World, 2003; series editor: Wiley Series in Engring, and Tech. Mgmt., 1984-98; contbr. articles on tech. mgmt. to more than 100 profl. jours. Lt. C.E., Turkish Army, 1966-68. Fellow IEEE (Centennial medal 1984, Millennium medal, 2000); editor-in-chief trans. on engring. mgmt. 1986—2002, Millennium medal, 2000); mem. Informs (chmn. Coll. Engring. Mgmt. 1979-81), Am. Soc. Engring. Edn. (chmn. engring. mgmt. div. 1982-83), IEEE Engring. Mgmt. Soc. (fellow, publs. dir. 1982-85), ASCE (mem. engring. mgmt. bd. govs. 1988-93), Muhendis, Ilim Adamlari ve Mimarlar Dernegi Soc. Turkish Engrs. and Scientists (hon.), Am. Soc. Engring. Mgmt. (dir. 1981-86), Omega Rho (pres. 1984-86). Office: Portland State U Engring & Tech Mgmt Program PO Box 751 Portland OR 97207-0751 Office Phone: 503-725-4660. Business E-Mail: kocaoglu@etm.pdx.edu.

KOCEL, KATHERINE MERLE, psychology professor, researcher; d. Benjamin Frances and Alice Marie Kocel; m. Robert M. Loew (dec.); 1 child, Rebecca M. Loew; m. John K. Kleinjans. BA in Psychology, Antioch U., 1968; PhD in Social Psychology, U. Hawaii, 1978. Rsch. asst. U. Calif. Med. Ctr., San Francisco, 1969—71; instr., rsch. asst. U. Hawaii, Honolulu, 1972—78, instr. II, 1990—92; rsch. assoc. U. Calif.-LA, 1979—81; comm. Loew Broadcasting, Honolulu, 1982—89; prof. psychology Jackson State U., Miss., 1993—2000, Berkeley City Coll., Berkeley, Calif., 2000—. Cons. Media Rsch. Group, Honolulu, 1983—88; spkr. in field, 1995—99. Author: (book) Cognitive Abilities, 1977, Treatment Delivery System & Alcohol Abuse in Women, 1982; contbr. chapters to books, articles to profl. jours.; prodr., dir., bd. dirs. (TV show) League of Women Voters, Honolulu, 1986—90. Bd. dirs. Am. Assn. U. Women, Palo Alto, Calif., 2001—02. Recipient Tchr. of Year, Miss. Psychological Assn., 1999. Mem.: APA, Sci. Rsch. Soc. Am., Sigma Xi, Psychology Tchrs. CCs, Nat. Sci. Found. (panelist Instrumentation & Lab. Improvement Program 1996—97, panelist grad. rsch. fellowship program 1998—2000, 2004), Stanford Parents & CAL Alumni. Avocations: hiking, swimming, cooking, reading. Personal E-mail: kkocel@gmail.com.

KOCH, CHARLES DE GANAHL, industrial company executive; b. Wichita, Kans., Nov. 1, 1935; s. Fred Chase and Mary Clementine (Robinson) Koch; m. Liz Koch; 2 children. BS in Gen. Engring, MIT, 1957, MS in Mech. Engring., 1958, MSChemE, 1959; DSc (hon.), George Mason U.; JD (hon.), Babson Coll.; PhD in Commerce (hon.), Washburn U. Engr. Arthur D. Little, Inc., Cambridge, Mass., 1959-61; v.p. Koch Engring. Co., Inc., Wichita, 1961-63, pres., 63-71, chmn., 1967-78; pres. Koch Industries, Inc., Wichita, 1966-74, chmn., CEO, 1967—. Bd. dirs. Intrust Bank, N.A., Mercatus Ctr. Chmn. Inst. Humane Studies, Claude R. Lambe Charitable Found., Charles G. Koch Charitable Found. Named one of World's Richest People, Forbes mag., 1999—, Forbes Richest Ams., 2006; recipient Entrepreneurial Leadership award, Nat. Found. for Tchg. Entrepreneurship, Adam Smith award, Am. Legis. Exch. Coun., Brotherhood/Sisterhood award, Nat. Conf. Christians and Jews, Disting. Citizen award, Boy Scouts of Am., Free Enterprise award, Coun. Nat. Policy, Spirit of Justice award, Heritage Found., Dir.'s award for global vision in energy, NY Merc. Exch., 1999, Nat. Disting. Svc. award, Tax Found., 2000. Mem.: Flint Hills Nat., Mt. Pelerin Soc., The Vintage Club. Office: Koch Industries PO Box 2256 4111 E 37th St N Wichita KS 67220

KOCH, CHARLES JOHN, credit agency executive; Pres., COO, CEO Charter One Bank FSB, 1976—; pres. Charter One Fin. Inc., Cleve., First Fed. Savings Ball. Office: Charter One Fin Inc 1215 Superior Ave E Cleveland OH 44114-3249

KOCH, CHRISTOF, biologist, educator; b. Kansas City; m. Edith Koch; children: Alexander, Gabriele. BS, Lycée Descartes, Rabat, Morocco, 1974; MS magna cum laude in Physics, Univ. Tübingen, Germany, 1980; PhD magna cum laude in Physics, Max-Planck-Inst. für biologische Kybernetik, Tübingen, Germany, 1982; postdoctoral fellow, MIT, 1982—84. Rsch. scientist MIT, 1984—86; asst. prof., computation and neural sys. Calif. Inst. Tech., 1986—91, assoc. prof., 1991—93, prof., 1994—2000, Lois and Victor Troendle prof. cognitive, behavioral biology, 2000—. Recipient Young Investigator award, Office Naval Rsch., 1987, Presdl. Young Investigator award, NSF, 1988, Alexander von Humboldt Rsch. Prize, 1997. Fellow: Am. Acad. Arts & Scis.; mem.: AAAS, IEEE, NY Acad. Sciences, Optical Soc. Am., Am. Assn. Artificial Intelligence, Assn. Rsch. in Vision and Ophtalmology, European Soc. Neuroscience, Soc. Neuroscience. Achievements include holding 6 patents. Avocation: mountain climbing. Office: Koch Lab Divsn Biology 216-76 Calif Inst Tech Pasadena CA 91125 Business E-Mail: koch@klab.caltech.edu.*

KOCH, CHRISTOPHER A., school system administrator; Grad., So. Ill. U.; MA, PhD in Ednl. Policy and Leadership, George Washington U. Adminstr. Office of Vocational and Adult Edn. US Dept. Edn.; dir. spl. edn. Ill. State Bd. Edn. (ISBE), Springfield, 2001—06, chief edn. officer, 2002—03, interim state supt., 2006—07, state supt., 2007—. Mem.: Nat. Assn. of Dirs. of Spl. Edn. Office: Ill State Bd Edn 100 N 1st St Springfield IL 62777 Office Phone: 866-262-6663.*

KOCH, CRAIG R., automobile rental company executive, automobile leasing company executive; b. Nov. 1946; m. Debra Koch. BS, Lehigh U., 1968, MBA, 1971. Mktg. assoc. RCA Corp., 1971-72; mgr. fleet planning Hertz Corp., 1972-73, mgr. fleet ops. adminstrn., 1973-77, div. v.p. fleet ops. adminstrn., 1977-78; div. v.p. Hertz Europe Ltd., 1978-80; v.p. Rent-A-Car div. Hertz Corp., 1980-83, exec. v.p. Rent-A-Car div., 1983-87, pres., Rent-A-Car div., 1988—93, pres., COO, 1993—2000, CEO, 2000—06, chmn., 2006—. Office: Hertz Corp 225 Brae Blvd Park Ridge NJ 07656-1888

KOCH, CYNTHIA M., library director; BA, Pa. State U.; MA, U. Pa., PhD in Am. Civilization. Dir. Old Barracks Mus., Trenton, NJ, 1979—93; exec. dir. NJ Coun. for the Humanities, 1993—97; assoc. dir. Penn Nat. Commn. on Society, Culture and Cmty., U. Pa., 1997—99; dir. Franklin D. Roosevelt Presdl. Libr. and Mus., Hyde Park, NY, 1999—. Ex-officio dir. Franklin and Eleanor Roosevelt Inst. Mem.: Phi Beta Kappa. Office: Franklin D Roosevelt Presdl Libr and Mus 4079 Albany Post Rd Hyde Park NY 12538-1990 Office Phone: 845-486-7752. E-mail: cynthia.koch@nara.gov.*

KOCH, DAVID HAMILTON, chemical company executive; b. Wichita, Kans., May 3, 1940; m. Julia Koch; children: David Jr., Mary Julia, John Mark. BSChemE, MIT, 1962, MSChemE, 1963. Rsch. engr. and process design engr. Amicon Corp., Cambridge, 1963-64, Arthur D. Little, Inc., Cambridge, Mass., 1964-67, Halcon Internat., Inc., NYC, 1967-70, Sci. Design Comp. (affiliate of Halcon Internat., Inc.), NYC; with Koch Industries, Inc., Wichita, Kans., 1970—, exec. v.p., 1981—, bd. dirs.; chmn. bd. dirs., CEO Chem. Tech. Grp., LLC (subs. Koch Industries, Inc.). Bd. dirs. Hosp. for Spl. Surgery, NYC. Bd. trustees Meml. Sloan Kettering, NYC (also mem. bd. overseers and managers), House Ear Inst., LA, Johns Hopkins U., Prostate Cancer Found., LA; gov. NY Presbyn. Hosp., NYC, Deerfield Acad., Mass.; bd. dirs. Am. Mus. Natural Hist., NYC, Aspen Inst., Colo., Inst. Human Origins, Phoenix, Ariz., Rockefeller U., NYC, MIT (life mem. of corp.), Reason Found., Santa Monica, Calif., CATO Inst., Washington, TV Sta. WNET, NYC; bd. overseers, tV Sta. WGBH, Boston; bd. visitor, M.D. Anderson Cancer Adv. Bd., Houston, Tex.; bd. assoc., Whitehead Inst., Cambridge, Mass.; bd. advs. John Hopkins Med. Ctr.; chmn.'s coun. Met. Mus. Art, NYC; mem. Libertarian Party Candidate for V.P. US, 1980; vice-chmn., bd. dir Am. Ballet Theatremem; nat. dinner chmn. Rep. Gov.'s Assn., 1999; active Nat. Cancer Adv. Bd., James Madison Coun., Libr. Congress, Washington. Named a honoree, NY Acad. Medicine's 10th Ann. Gala, 2004; named in honor David H. Koch Bldg., MIT; named one of World's Richest People, Forbes mag., 2001—, Forbes Richest Ams., 2006; recipient Businessman of Yr., Manhattan Rep. Party, 2002, Corp. Citizenship award, Woodrow Wilson Internat. Ctr. Scholars, 2004, Entrepreneurial Leadership award, Nat. Found. for Tchg. Entrepreneurship, Award for Excellence in Corp. Leadership, Soc. Meml. Sloan-Kettering, 2005. Mem. River Club (NY), Racquet & Tennis Club (NY), Explorers Club (NY), numerous others. Avocations: skiing, tennis, golf. Office: Koch Industries, Inc 667 Madison Ave 22nd Fl New York NY 10021-8029 also: Koch Industries, Inc 4111 E 37th St N Wichita KS 67220 Office Phone: 212-319-1100, 316-828-5500. Business E-Mail: david.koch@kochchemtech.com.*

KOCH, ED (EDWARD IRVING KOCH), lawyer, former mayor; b. NYC, Dec. 12, 1924; s. Louis and Joyce Koch Student, Coll. City N.Y.; LLB, NYU, 1948. Bar: N.Y. State 1949. Pvt. practice, NYC, 1949-64; democratic dist. leader Greenwich Village, 1963-65; sr. partner firm Koch Lankenau Schwartz & Kovner, NYC, 1965-69; mem. N.Y.C. Council, 1967-68, 91st-92nd Congresses from 17th Dist. N.Y., 1969-72, 93d-95th congresses from 18th Dist. N.Y., 1973-77, mem. appropriations com., sec. N.Y. Congl. del.; mayor N.Y.C., 1978-89; ptnr. Bryan Cave LLP, NYC, 1990—. Author: Politics, 1985, All the Best, Letters from a Feisty Mayor, 1990, Ed Koch on Everything: Movies, Politics, Personalities, Food, and Other Stuff, 1994, Giuliani: Nasty Man, 1999; co-author (with William Rauch) Mayor, 1984, (with John Joseph O'Connor) His Eminence and Hizzoner: A Candid Exchange, 1989, (with Daniel Paisner) Citizen Koch, 1992,(with Wendy Corsi Staub) Murder on 34th Street, 1997, Murder on Broadway, 1996, The Senator Must Die, 1998, (with Herbert Resnicow) Murder at City Hall, 1995, (with Daniel Paisner) I'm Not Done Yet!: Keeping at It, Remaining Relevant, and Having the Time of My Life, 1999, (with Pat Koch Thaler) Eddie, Harold's Little Brother, 2004; judge (TV series) The People's Court, 1997-99 Served with AUS, World War II. Recipient: NY Fed. Bar Coun. Emory Buckner medal for Outstanding Pub. Svc., 2004 Office: Bryan Cave LLP 1290 Ave Americas Fl 33 New York NY 10104-3300 Business E-Mail: eikoch@bryancave.com.*

KOCH, EDGAR FRANK, protective services official; b. Balt., Feb. 10, 1949; s. Frank Marion and Blanche Koch; m. Lynda Marie Grunder, Sept. 16, 1967; children: Edgar Frank II, Adam Alan. BS, Towson U., Md., 1974; MS, U. Balt., 1988. Cert. McCrone Microscopy Inst. Dep. chief Anne Arundel County Police, Millersville, Md., 1970—95; dir. crime lab. Balt. Police Dept., 1997—; prof. forensic sci. U. Balt., 2002—. Mem. Gov.'s Exec. Adv. Coun., Annapolis, Md., 1990—94; presenter in field. Mem. Gov.'s Exec. Coun., Annapolis, 1990—94, Gov.'s Coun. Volunteerism, Annapolis, 1994—2000; v.p. Take Back Our Sts. Found., Anne Arundel County, 1994—. Recipient Unit citation, Chief of Police Anne Arundel, 1993, Balt. Police Dept., 2002, Gov.'s citation, Gov. Md., 1994. Mem.: Am. Acad. Forensic Sci., Am. Soc. Crime Lab. Dirs., Police Futurist Internat., FBI Nat. Acad. (cert.), Nat. Inst. Justice (peer reviewer 2002—). Avocations: golf, Karate. Home: 210 Coronet Dr Linthicum MD 21090 Office: Balt Police Dept 242 W 29th St Baltimore MD 21211-2908

KOCH, EDNA MAE, lawyer, nurse; b. Terre Haute, Ind., Oct. 12, 1951; d. Leo K. and Lucille E. (Smith) K.; m. Mark D. Orton. BS in Nursing, Ind. State U., 1977; JD, Ind. U., 1980. Bar: Ind. 1980, U.S. Dist. Ct. (so. dist.) Ind. 1980. Assoc. Dillon & Cohen, Indpls., 1980-85; ptnr. Tipton, Cohen & Koch, Indpls., 1985-93, LaCava, Zeigler & Carter, Indpls., 1993-94, Zeigler Cohen & Koch, Indpls., 1994—. Leader seminars for nurses, Ind. U. Med. Ctr., Ball State U., Muncie, Ind., St. Vincent Hosp., Indpls., Deaconess Hosp., Evansville, Ind., others; lectr. on med. malpractice Cen. Ind. chpt. AACCN, Indpls. "500" Postgrad. Course in Emergency Medicine, Ind. Assn. Osteo. Physicians and Surgeons State Conv., numerous others. Mem. ABA, ANA, Ind. State Bar Assn., Indpls. Bar Assn., Am. Soc. Law and Medicine, Ind. State Nurses Assn. Republican. Office: Zeigler Cohen & Koch Ste 104 9465 Counselors Row Indianapolis IN 46240-3816 Home Phone: 317-843-0978; Office Phone: 317-844-5200. Business E-Mail: ekoch@zcklaw.com.

KOCH, EDWARD RICHARD, lawyer, accountant; b. Teaneck, NJ, Mar. 25, 1953; s. Edward J. and Adelaide M. K.; m. Cora Susan Koch, Apr. 12, 1997; children: Edward Peter, William John. BS in Econs. magna cum laude, U. Pa., 1975; JD, U. Va., 1980; LLM in Taxation, NYU, 1986. Bar: N.J. 1980, U.S. Dist. Ct. N.J. 1980, U.S. Tax Ct. 1981, U.S. Ct. Claims 1981. Staff acct. Touche Ross & Co. (now Deloitte & Touche), Newark, 1975-77; assoc. Winne, Banta & Rizzi, Hackensack, N.J., 1980-82; tax atty. Allied Corp. (now Honeywell Internat. Inc.), Morristown, 1982-87; asst. v.p. ChemBank (now JP Morgan Chase), NYC, 1987-90; tax mgr. Paul Scherer & Co. LLP, NYC, 1990-97, ptnr., 1998—. Chmn. law and legis. com. U.S.A. Track and Field, Indpls., 1989-2000, chmn., 1989-2000, chmn. ins. com., 1984-88, bd. dirs., 1989—, treas., 2000—; pres. N.J. Athletics Congress, Red Bank, 1986-90; mem. Jury of Appeals, 1988, U.S. Olympic Men's Marathon Trials, Holy Family Sch. Edn. Coun., 1992-96; Olympic Track and Field ofcl., 1996. Mem. AICPA, N.J. Soc. CPAs, Am. Assn. Attys.-CPAs, N.J. State Bar Assn., N.J. Striders Track Club (chmn. 1981-96), Magazine Publishers Am. (chair tax comm., 2002-). Republican. Roman Catholic. Avocation: running track and field. Home: 130 Grant St Haworth NJ 07641-1951 Office: Paul Scherer & Co 335 Madison Ave Fl 9 New York NY 10017-4605 Personal E-mail: edrkoch@yahoo.com. Business E-Mail: ekoch@pscherer.com.

KOCH, EDWIN ERNEST, artist, interior designer; b. Bronx, NY, Feb. 21, 1915; s. Henry Koch and Elsie Ziegenbalg. One-man shows include Mus. of Hudson Highlands, 1986; exhibited in group shows at Met. Mus. Art, 1952, Bklyn. Mus., 1953, Pa. Acad., 1953, NAD, 1958, Am. Watercolor Soc.; represented in permanent collections Butler Art Inst.,

Youngstown, Ohio. With AUS, 1942-46. Recipient Top Best in Show awrd Middle Town Art Soc., 1980's, Nat. Arts Club, 1989. Mem. Audubon Artists Am., Nat. Soc. Painters in Casein and Acrylic (bd. dirs. 1975-76), Painters and Sculptors Soc. N.J. (v.p. 1978), Knickerbocker Artists, Artists Equity. Home: 109 Old Hoagerburgh Rd Wallkill NY 12589-3430 Personal E-mail: eek@frontier.net.

KOCH, JAMES VERCH, academic administrator, economist; b. Springfield, Ill., Oct. 7, 1942; s. Elmer O. and Wilma L. K.; m. Donna L. Stickling, Aug. 20, 1967; children: Elizabeth, Mark. BA, Ill. State U., 1964; PhD, Northwestern U., 1968. From asst. prof. to prof. econs. Ill. State U., 1967-78, chmn. dept., 1972-78; dean Faculty Arts and Scis., R.I. Coll., Providence, 1978-80; prof. econs., provost, v.p. acad. affairs Ball State U., Muncie, Ind., 1980-86; pres. U. Mont., Missoula, 1986-90, Old Dominion U., Norfolk, Va., 1990-2001, prof. econs., 2001—. Author: Industrial Organization and Prices, 2d edit, 1980, Microeconomic Theory and Applications, 1976, The Economics of Affirmative Action, 1976, Presidential Leadership, 1996, The Entrepreneurial President, 2003. Mem. Am. Econ. Assn. Lutheran. Office: Old Dominion U Dept Econs Norfolk VA 23529 Home Phone: 757-683-3458; Office Phone: 757-683-3458. Business E-Mail: jkoch@odu.edu. *Survival in the 21st century, whether in higher education or in automobile production, demands and requires quality. Excellence must be our goal in all that we undertake. This is an attitude that must be instilled in the home, in our schools, and throughout society so that it permeates our lives.*

KOCH, JOHN MICHAEL, psychiatrist; b. June 5, 1967; MD, U. Wis., Madison, 1995. Psychiatrist Prevea Clinic, Green Bay, Wis., 2004—. Fellow: Am. Assn. Neuromuscular and Electrodiagnostic Medicine, Am. Acad. Phys. Medicine & Rehab.; mem.: AMA.

KOCH, KARL R., policy advisor; BA, U. South Fla., Tampa, 1988; JD, Stetson U., DeLand, Fla. Chief of staff to Gov. Buddy MacKay State of Fla.; Fla. dir. Clinton/Gore presdl. reelection campaign, 1996; v.p., prin. Dewey Square Group, 1997—2002; chief of staff to US Rep. Jim Davis US Ho. of Reps., 2002—07; sr. policy advisor Pub. Policy & Regulation Group Holland & Knight LLP, Tampa, 2007—. Office: Holland & Knight LLP 100 N Tampa St, Ste 4100 Tampa FL 33602-3644 Office Phone: 813-227-6473. Office Fax: 813-229-0134. Business E-Mail: karl.koch@hklaw.com.

KOCH, KATHLEEN DAY, lawyer; b. St. Louis, Nov. 27, 1948; d. Edward J. and Margaret (Beckmeier) D.; children: Stefan, Martha, Rebecca. Student, Concordia Coll., River Forest, Ill., 1966-69; BS in Edn., U. Mo., 1971; JD, U. Chgo., 1977. Bar: Ill. 1977, D.C. 1978. Atty. HUD, Washington, 1977-79, U.S. Merit Sys. Protection Bd., Washington, 1979-84; sr. atty., personal law divsn. U.S. Dept. Commerce, Washington, 1984-87; assoc. counsel to pres. White House, Washington, 1987-88; gen. counsel Fed. Labor Rels. Authority, Washington, 1988-91; spl. counsel Office Spl. Counsel, Washington, 1991-97; chief OEEOA FBI, Washington, 1997—; dep. gen. coun., equal opportunity & adminstr. law U.S. Dept. Housing and Urban Development, Washington. Recipient Disting. Alumni award U. Mo., St. Louis, 1990. Office Phone: 202-708-3250. Office Fax: 202-708-3389. Business E-Mail: kathleen_d._koch@hud.gov.

KOCH, MARGARET RAU, writer, artist, historian; b. Sacramento; d. George James Rau and Callista Marie Martin; children: Edward James, Kathleen, Thomas C. Student, U. Calif., Berkeley, 1936-38. Mem. editl. staff Santa Cruz (Calif.) Sentinel, 1958-76. Author: Santa Cruz County, Parade of the Past, 1973, 74, 77, 81, 91, 99, They Called It Home, 1974, Walk Around Santa Cruz, 1978, Going To School in Santa Cruz County, 1978, The Pasatiempo Story, 1990, Santa Cat-Behind the Lace Curtains, 2001; exhibited in group shows at Sedona Arts Ctr., Yavapai County Arts Fair, Ft. Verde Art Show, 1997, 98, 99, 2000. Organizer, first pres. Santa Cruz Hist. Soc. Recipient 3 Mixed Media Watercolor awards Yavapai County Art Fair, Ariz., 2 Watercolor awards Fort Verde Art Show, Ariz. Mem. No. Ariz. Watercolo Soc., Pen Women, Santa Cruz Art League, Sedona Art Ctr. Home: 2307 Town Center Dr Klamath Falls OR 97601-7142

KOCH, MOLLY BROWN, retired parent educator; b. Phila., Pa., Nov. 20, 1927; d. Harry and Sarah Potash Brown; m. William Koch, June 22, 1947; children: Jessica Robin Jones, Andrea Leslie London, Richard Andrew. Continuing edn., Balt. Hebrew U., 1957—67. Tchr. Balt. Hebrew Congregation Religious Sch., 1966—74, Temple Oheb Shalom, 1979, Reform Jewish Acad., Youth Inst.; parent educator Balt. City and Balt. County Boards of Edn., 1956—65; tchr., prin. Columbia Jewish Family Sch., 1975—78. Dir. Project Yedid, Balt., 1980—87. Author: 27 Secrets to Raising Amazing Children, 2007. Pub. edn. Personal Freedom Found. and Project Yedid, Balt., 1975—87; pres. Jews for Judaism, Balt., 1999—2004; bd. mem. Prisoners' Aid, Balt., 1960—62, Robert Lindner Found., Balt., 1958—62; pres., co-founder Personal Freedom Found., 1975—80; dir. Project Yedid, 1980—87. Recipient Hon. Outstanding Woman award, Woman's Day Mag., 1979, Disting. Svc. award, Mid. Atlantic-Great Lakes Organized Crime Law Enforcement Network, 1987, Ofcl. Recognition, Senate of the State of Md., 1987, 2002, Balt. County Coun., 2002, First Ann. Lipsetts award, Bd. of Jewish Edn., 1979. Avocations: public speaking, writing. Home Phone: 410-653-3999. Personal E-mail: mabko18@bcpl.net.

KOCH, ROBERT CHARLES, lawyer, community activist; b. Berwyn, Ill., Apr. 7, 1947; s. Eugene William and Ellen Marie (Hudec) K.; m. Sharon Smith, June 27, 1970; children: Jason, Ryan, Lindsay. BS, Ill. Inst. Tech., 1969; JD, Coll. William and Mary, 1972. Bar: Ill. 1972, Okla. 1978, N.Y. 2003, Fla. 2003. Assoc. Bell, Boyd & Lloyd, Chgo., 1972-78; staff atty. Phillips Petroleum Co., Bartlesville, Okla., 1978-81, sr. atty., 1986-90, sr. counsel, 1990—2002; counsel Phillips Petroleum Co. Europe & Africa, London, 1981-86; mng.ptnr. Koch Law Office, 2002—. Author of Sunday sch. curriculums. Chmn. Washington County Dem. Party, Bartlesville, 1993-97; pres., dir. Westside Cmty. Assn., Bartlesville, 1997—2002. Mem.: ATLA, ABA, Okla. Bar Assn., N.Y. State Bar Assn., Fla. Bar, Am. Legion. Democrat. Presbyterian. Avocations: church youth ministry, travel. Home: 839 Berkeley St Boca Raton FL 33487 Office: 7401 N Federal Hwy Boca Raton FL 33487 Mailing: PO Box 81041 Boca Raton FL 33481-0841 E-mail: BobKoch@KochLawOffice.com.

KOCH, ROBERT LOUIS, II, manufacturing company executive, mechanical engineer; b. Evansville, Ind., Jan. 6, 1939; s. Robert Louis and Mary L. (Bray) K.; m. Cynthia Ross, Oct. 17, 1964; children: David, Kevin, Kristen, Jennifer. BSME, U. Notre Dame, 1960; MBA, U. Pitts., 1962; D of Tech. (hon.), Vincennes U., 1992. Registered profl. engr., Ind. V.p. Ashdee Corp., Evansville, 1962-68, pres., 1968-82; ptnr. Fesk Partnership, Evansville, 1964—; chmn., CEO Gibbs Die Casting Corp., Henderson, Ky., 1976—; pres., CEO Koch Enterprises, Inc., Evansville, 1982—; chmn., dir. UNISEAL, Inc., Evansville, 1984—2005; v.p., dir. Brake Supply Co., Evansville, 1986—; chmn. bd. Marco Sales, Inc., St. Louis, 1997—. Exec. in residence U. So. Ind., Evansville, 1967; bd. dirs. Fifth-Third Bancorp, Cincinnati, Ohio, Bindley Western Industries, Indpls., So. Ind. Properties, Inc., Evansville, So. Ind. Minerals, Inc., N.Am. Green, Inc., Audubon Metals LLC, Ind. Econ. Devel. Corp.; lead dir. Vectren Corp.; chmn. bd. dirs. Uniseal Rubber Products, Inc., Arnold, Mo., 1988-95. Inventor, patentee water purifier, drying oven, powder coating booth, electro painting system. Contr., dep. mayor City of Evansville, 1976-80; active Gov.'s Fiscal Policy Adv. Com., Indpls., 1978-89, Pres. Adv. Coun. Indiana Univ., 1992—, Purdue U., 1992—, parents exec. com., West Lafayette, 1985-88, sch. bd. nominating com., 1987-89; vice-chmn. bd. trustees U. Evansville, 1985-92, chmn. bd. trustees, 1993-96; pres. Signature Sch. Found. Inc., Evansville, 1994—, pres. bd. dirs., 2001; vice-chmn. bd. trustees Evansville Mus. Arts and Scis., 1982-92; bd. dirs. SW Ind. Pub. Broadcasting, 1985-89, Pub. Edn. Found., Evansville, 1986-88, Hoosiers for Higher Edn., 1991-98, Commit, Inc., Cmty. Alliance Found., 1991—, Ind. Colls. Ind., 1992—, Found. for Ind. Higher Edn., 1996-2000, Project E, 2000-04; treas. Vanderburgh County Rep. Com., Evansville, 1984-88; pres. Cath. Edn. Found., Evansville, 1978-82; chmn. Ind. Econ. Devel. Coun., 1991-92, Ind. Humanities Coun. Bus. Forum, 1999, United Way of Southwestern Ind. Campaign, 1998; co-chmn. Ind. Bus. Higher Edn. Forum, 1991-96; pres. Cath. Found. Southwestern Ind., 1992—; v.p. Ind. Acad., Indpls., 1999--; pres. Evansville Regional Bus. Com., 2002--. 1st lt. USAR, 1961-67. Recipient Challenger award Nat. Assn. Woodworking Machinery Mfrs., Louisville, 1980, Boy Scout's Disting. Citizen's award, 1991, Rotary Club Citizenship award, 1991, Sagamore of the Wabash, 1999; named Exec. of Yr. Profl. Secs. Assn., 1984, Knight of the Order of the Holy Sepulchre, 1996, Entrepreneur of Yr., Ind. Mfg., 1998, Ind. Bus. Leader of Yr. Ind. C. of C., 2002. Mem. Metro Evansville C. of C. (bd. dirs. Met. 1983-96, named Bus. Person of Yr. 1998), Ind. C. of C. (bd. dirs., chmn. 1991—), Young Pres. Orgn., World Pres. Orgn., Evansville Country Club, Victoria Nat. Golf Club. Avocations: golf, tennis, skiing. Office: Koch Enterprises Inc 10 S 11th Ave Evansville IN 47744-0001

KOCH, ROBERT MICHAEL, research scientist, consultant, educator; b. Mineola, NY, Apr. 19, 1964; s. Roy Arthur and Ellen Anne (Trimble) K.; m. Laureen Theresa Chase, July 6, 1991. BSME, Poly. U., Bklyn., 1986, PhD in Applied Mechanics, 1991. Profl. engr., R.I. Mech. engr. Vernitech Corp., Deer Park, N.Y., 1983-85; instr. Poly. U., Bklyn., 1986-91; chief rsch. scientist Naval Undersea Warfare Ctr., Newport, RI, 1991—. Cons. Beltran, Inc., Bklyn., 1988-91; adj. prof. Roger Williams U., Bristol, R.I., 1993—. Teaching fellow Poly. U., 1986-90, rsch. fellow, 1987, 90, Fed. Engr. of Yr. NSPE, 2005. Mem. AIAA, ASME, Acoustical Soc. Am., N.Y. Acad. Scis., Sigma Xi. Republican. Roman Catholic. Achievements include research in undersea propulsion, underwater shock analysis, underwater structural acoustics, adaptive procedures in h-and p-version finite element analysis, rapid prototyping with stereolithography, probabilistic structural mechanics, ultrasonic wave propagation in elastic solids. Home: 304 White Horn Dr South Kingstown RI 02881-1829 Office: Naval Undersea Warfare Ctr Code 8232 Bldg 1302 Newport RI 02841-0001

KOCH, STEPHEN BAYARD, writer, language educator; b. St. Paul, May 8, 1941; s. Robert Fulton and Edith (Bayard) K.; m. Frances Bernard Cohen, Apr. 25, 1987. BA, CCNY, 1962; MA, Columbia U., 1963, postgrad., 1963-66. Instr. English dept. SUNY, Stony Brook, 1965-70; adj. prof. Columbia U., NYC, 1978-89, acting chmn., then chmn. writing div. Sch. Arts, 1989—98. Lectr. creative writing program Princeton (N.J.) U., 1979-86. Author: Night Watch, 1970, Stargazer: Andy Warhol's World and His Films, 1973, 3d edit., 1991, The Bachelors' Bride, 1986, Double Lives, 1994, revised edit., 2004, The Modern Library Writer's Workshop: A Guide to the Craft of Fiction, 2003, The Breaking Point: Hemingway, Dos Passos, and the Murder of Jose Robles, 2005; contbr. articles to numerous pubs. Democrat. Episcopalian. Office: Inkwell Mgmt Inc 521 Fifth Ave 26th Fl New York NY 10175 Office Phone: 212-249-7199. Personal E-mail: stephenkoch41@msn.com.

KOCH, STEVEN, lawyer, investment banker, finance company executive; b. Evanston, Ill., Feb. 9, 1956; s. David and Sylvia (Kurtzon) K.; m. Ellen Liebman, May 17, 1986 (dec. Dec. 2005). BA, Hampshire Coll., Amherst, Mass., 1977; MBA, JD, U. Chgo., 1982. Bar: Ill. 1982. Law clk. to judge U.S. Ct. Appeals (7th cir.), 1982—83; assoc. Lehman Bros. Kuhn Loeb, NYC, 1983—85; joined First Boston (now Credit Suisse), 1985, mng. dir., 1989—93, co-head mergers and acquisitions group, 1993—2000, co-chmn. mergers and acquisitions group, 2000—; vice chmn. Credit Suisse, 2000—. Bd. mem. Mount Sinai Hosp. Med. Ctr., Chgo., Greater Chgo. Food Depository. Office: Credit Suisse Securities USA LLC 227 W Monroe St Chicago IL 60606-5016 Office Phone: 312-750-3000. Business E-Mail: Steven.Koch@credit-suisse.com.

KOCH, THOMAS FREDERICK, lawyer; b. Hackensack, NJ, Nov. 24, 1942; s. Elmer J. and Evelyn (Zombeck) K.; m. Sally J. Tucker, June 6, 1970; children: Christine E., Donald T. AB, Middlebury Coll., 1964; JD, U. Chgo., 1967. Bar: Vt. 1967, U.S. Dist. Ct. Vt. 1971. Assoc. firm Free and Bernasconi, Barre, Vt., 1970-74; ptnr. Bernasconi & Koch, Barre, 1974—. Mem. jud. nominating bd. State of Vt., 1979-81; mem. Vt. Ho. of Reps., 1977-80, 97—, mem. mcpl. corps and elections, judiciary, house rules and joint rules coms. health and welfare, chmn., 2001-04, human svcs. com., instn. and corrections coms., joint com. on health access oversight, co-chair, 2004; moderator Town of Barre, 1984-; chmn. Vt. Rep. Platform Com. 1984. Del. nat. convs. of Assn. of Evang. Luth. Chs., 1978, 84, 86; del. to constrn. conv. of Evang. Luth. Ch. in Am., 1987-94; mem. churchwide assemblies, 1991, 97, 99; mem. New Eng. synod coun. Evang. Luth. Ch. Am., 1987-94; mem. churchwide assemblies, 1991, 97; scoutmaster Boy Scouts Am., Barre, 1989-93, dist. chmn. 1993-96, 98-2000; mem. exec. bd. Green Mountain Coun., 1997—, v.p. for dist. ops., 2002-03, v.p. for adminstrn., 2004—. Mem. Vt. Bar Assn., Washington County Bar Assn., Barre Lions Club (pres. 1977-78). Republican. Home: 326 Lowery Rd Barre VT 05641-9090 Office: 107 N Main St PO Box 892 Barre VT 05641-0892 E-mail: tfklaw@sover.net.

KOCH, THOMAS L, engineering educator; AB, Princeton U., 1977; PhD in Applied Physics, Calif. Inst. Tech., 1982. Prof. physics and elec. and computer engring. Lehigh U., Bethlehem, Pa., dir. Ctr. for Optical Tech., 2003—, Daniel E. '39 and Patricia Smith chair, 2003—. V.p. tech. platforms Agere Sys. Contbr. articles to profl. jours. Fellow: IEEE (William Streifer Award for Scientific Achievements), Optical Soc. Am.; mem.: NAE, Lasers and Electro-Optics Soc. Office: Lehigh U 19 Memorial Dr W Bethlehem PA 18015 Office Phone: 610-758-2601.

KOCH, VIRGINIA GREENLEAF (VIRGINIA M. GREENLEAF), painter; b. Chgo., Aug. 28, 1925; d. William Henry and Henrietta Irene (Moser) Greenleaf; m. Aley Allan, 1945 (div.); m. William Greenough, 1951 (dec.); m. Henry Koch, Aug. 20, 1962 (dec.); children: Diedra G., William G. Pupil of Ivan Olinsky, 1941-42; student, Yale U., 1943-45; pupil of Robert Brackman, 1946; student, Am. U., Washington; postgrad., Am. U., 1956-57; pupil of Gene Davis, 1968-70. One-woman shows include Studio Gallery, Washington, 1970, 72, 74, 76, Haslem Gallery, Madison, Wis., 1971, In Town Gallery, Cleve., 1973, World Bank, Washington, 1972, Art League No. Va., 1973, Main St. Gallery, Boston, 1976-81, 83, 87-89, Nantucket, 1977, 82-89, 91-93, 95-98, Gallery 124, NYC, 1983, Gallery at Essex Meadows, 2001, Christy Lawrence Gallery, Old Lyme, Conn., 2003; exhibited in group shows at Maritime Mus., 1990-91, Newport News, Va., 1971-72, U. No. Va., 1973, U. Richmond, Va., 1972, U. Md., 1975, Parsons Drefyss Gallery, NYC, 1976-77, Phillips Collection, Washington, 1989, Corcoran Gallery, 1975, 92-93, Cooley Gallery, 2003, 04, 05, Old Lyme, 1991-2002, Alva Gallery, New London, Conn., 2001, Rittenhouse Fine Arts Gallery, Phila., 2002, Cooley Gallery, 2005, 06, Pet Connections Old Lyme, 2005, 06, Diane Birdsall Gallery, Old Lyme, 2007; represented in permanent collections Dept. of State, Washington, Lyme Acad. of Fine Arts, Old Lyme, various ambassadors' residences. Active Olde Town Citizens' Com., Alexandria, Va., 1964-73, Georgetown Citizens' Assn., Washington, 1971-75, Hosp. Thrist Shop, Nantucket, Mass., 1968-71, Nat. Symphony of Washington, DC Com., 1970—; bd. dirs. Arts Council of Nantucket. Mem. Studio Gallery, Foundery Group Women Painters, Artists' Equity, Art League Va., Art Found. Nantucket Hist. Found., Old Lyme Hist. Found. Office Phone: 860-434-3272.

KOCH, WILLIAM C., JR., state supreme court justice; b. Honolulu, Sept. 12, 1947; married. BA, Trinity Coll., Hartford, Conn., 1969; JD, Vanderbilt U., Nashville, 1972; LLM, U. Va., Charlottesville, 1996. Asst. atty. gen. State of Tenn., 1972—76, sr. asst. atty. gen., 1976—77, dep. atty. gen., 1977—78, counsel to Gov. Lamar Alexander, 1981—84; commr. Tenn. Dept. Pers., 1979—81; judge Tenn. Ct. Appeals, 1984—2007; assoc. justice Tenn. Supreme Ct., 2007—. Adj. instr. Vanderbilt U., 1988—95; instr. constl. law Nashville Sch. Law, 1997—. Mem. Harry Phillips Am. Inn of Ct., 1990—, Am. Inns of Ct. Found., 2000—; bd. trustees United Way Met. Nashville, 1981—; mem. instl. rev. com. Baptist Hosp., 1991—94, mem. ethics com., 1994—2003; co-chair Tenn. Supreme Ct. Adv. Commn. Tech., 1997—2001; bd. trustees Cmty. Found. Mid. Tenn., 2005—. Mem.: ABA, Scribes, Am. Judicature Soc., Nashville Bar Found., Tenn. Bar Found., Nashville Bar Assn., Tenn. Bar Assn., Nashville Rotary. Episcopalian. Office: Tenn Supreme Ct 203 Supreme Ct Bldg 401 Seventh Ave N Nashville TN 37219 Office Phone: 615-741-1529.*

KOCH, WILLIAM I., energy company executive; CEO Oxbow Carbon & Minerals, West Palm Beach, Fla. Named one of Forbes Richest Americans, 2006. Office: Oxbow Corp 1601 Forum Pl West Palm Beach FL 33401-8101

KOCHANEK, PATRICK MICHAEL, pediatrician, educator; b. Detroit, July 1, 1954; s. Julius E. and Stella A. (Mrowiec) K.; m. Denise Marie Kochanek; children: Ashley, Stanton, Jillian. BS, U. Mich., 1976; MD, U. Chgo., 1980. Intern, then resident U. Calif., San Diego, 1980-83; fellow pediatric critical care medicine Children's Hosp. Nat. Med. Ctr., Washington, 1983-86; guest scientist Naval Med. Rsch. Inst., Bethesda, Md., 1983-86; from asst. prof. to prof. U. Pitts., 1986—2002, prof., 2002—, dir. Safar Ctr. for Resuscitation Rsch., 1994—; dir. pediatric critical care medicine rsch. Children's Hosp. Pitts., 1992—. Editor in chief Pediatric Critical Care Medicine, 2000—. Recipient Investigator award Soc. Critical Care Medicine, 1994—. Office: Safar Ctr Resuscitation Rsch 3434 5th Ave Pittsburgh PA 15260 Home Phone: 412-561-5987; Office Phone: 412-383-1900. Business E-Mail: kochanekpm@ccm.upmc.edu.

KOCHEMS, ROBERT GREGORY, lawyer; b. Cleve., Aug. 6, 1951; s. Roy George and Virginia Mae (Budniak) Kochems; 1 child, Alane Carin. BA cum laude, John Carroll U., Univ. Heights, Ohio, 1973; JD, St. Louis U., 1976. Bar: Pa. 1976, US Dist. Ct. (we. dist.) 1978. Sole practice, Mercer, Pa., 1976-81, 88-92; ptnr. Bogaty, McEwen, Sparks, & Kochems, PC, Mercer, 1981-87, Nelson, Ryan & Kochems, 1992—2002; pvt. practice Mercer, 2004—. Asst. pub. defender Mercer County, 1977-88; asst. dist. atty., 1988—; sub-com. chairperson Mercer County Juvenile Ct. Adv. Com., 1986-88, chair child death rev. com., 1999-2004, leader dist. atty.'s child abuse prosecution unit, 1996-2001; solicitor Mercer County Regional Planning Commn., 1991—; law enforcement coord. Sharon/Farrell Weed and Seed Program, 2001--. Assoc. editor St. Louis U. Law Jour., 1975-76. Bd. dirs. Transfer Harvest Home Assn., 1986-88; solicitor Mcpl. Corp., 1996—; co-chairperson Mercer County Sexual Assault Response Team, 2000-2004. Mem. Pa. Bar Assn., Mercer County Bar Assn. (sec. 1977-79, bench bar com. 1982, 84), KC (adv. 1978-88). Democrat. Home: 1188 Center Town Rd Grove City PA 16127 Office Phone: 724-662-3270. Business E-Mail: rkochems@mcc.co.mercer.pa.us.

KOCHER, JUANITA FAY, retired auditor; b. Falmouth, Ky., Aug. 9, 1933; d. William Birgest and Lula (Gillespie) Vickroy; m. Donald Edward Kocher, Nov. 18, 1953. Grad. high sch., Bright, Ind. Cert. internal auditor and compliance officer. Bookkeeper Mchts. Bank and Trust Co., West Harrison, Ind., 1952-56, teller, asst. cashier, 1962-87, br. mgr., 1979-87, internal auditor, 1987-96, ret., 1996; bookkeeper Progressive Bank, New Orleans, 1956-58; with proof dept. 1st Nat. Bank, Cin., Ohio, 1958-59, teller Harrison, Ohio, 1959-62. Bookkeeper Donald E. Kocher Constrn., Harrison, 1981—. Mem. Am. Bankers Assn., Ind. Bankers Assn. Home: 11277 Biddinger Rd Harrison OH 45030

KOCHER, MININDER SINGH, pediatric orthopaedic surgeon, epidemiologist; b. Rochester, NY, Dec. 23, 1966; s. Haribhajan Singh and Ranjit Kaur Kocher; m. Michele Mary Dupre, June 4, 1994; children: Sophia Dupre, Isabelle Dupre, Calvin Dupre, Ava Dupre. AB, Dartmouth Coll., 1989; MD, Duke U., 1993; MPH, Harvard U., 2000. Bd. cert. Am. Bd. Orthopaedic Surgeons, 2002. Intern Beth Israel Hosp./Harvard Med. Sch., 1993—94; resident Harvard Combined Orthop. Surgery Residency program, 1994—98; fellow pediat. orthop. surgery Boston Children's Hosp., 1998—99; fellow sports medicine Steadman Hawkin's Clinic, 1999—2000; pediatric orthop. surgeon Children's Hosp. Boston, 2000—; asst. prof. orthop. surgery Harvard Med. Sch., Boston, 2000—06, assoc. prof. orthop. surgery, 2006—; cons. Steadman Hawkins Sports Medicine Found., Vail, Colo., 2000—. Dir. Children's Hosp. Orthop. Inst. for Clin. Effectiveness, Boston, 2000—; asst. dir. divsn. sports medicine Children's Hosp., Boston, 2005—. Sci. adv. com. Steadman Hawkins Sports Medicine Found., Vail, Colo., 2000; med. adv. com. LeadingMD.com, LA, 2001. Recipient Wilburt Davidson award, Duke U. Sch. Medicine, 1993, Harris Yett award, Harvard Combined Orthop. Program, 1994, Von Meyer award, Children's Hosp. Boston, 1998, Zimmer award, Am. Orthop. Assn., 1999, Richard Kilfoyle award, New Eng. Orthop. Soc., 1999, Clin. Rsch. prize, Arthroscopy Assn. N.Am., 2000, 2001, Vernon Thompson award, Western Orthop. Assn., 2000, Kappa Delta award, Otherpedic Rsch. and Edn. Found., 2005; Nat. Honor Soc. scholar, LG Balfour, 1985—89, Nat. Merit Scholarship, 1985—89, Rufus Choate scholar, Dartmouth Coll., 1988—99. Fellow: Am. Acad. Orthop. Surgeons (Kappa Delta Clin. Rsch. award 2005); mem.: Am. Orthop. Soc. for Sports Medicine, Anterior Cruciate Ligament Study Group, Pediat. Orthop. Soc. N.Am. (clin. effectiveness com. 2002—, bd. dirs. 2005, Angela Kuo award 2004), Phi Beta Kappa. Office: Childrens Hosp Boston 300 Longwood Ave Boston MA 02135 Home Phone: 508-785-1430; Office Phone: 617-355-7497. Business E-Mail: mininder.kocher@childrens.harvard.edu.

KOCHHAR, KALPANA, economist; m. Rakesh Kochhar, Oct. 27, 1988; children: Shivani, Mihir Naresh. PhD in Econ., Brown U., Providence, 1987. Asst. dir. IMF, Washington, 2003—05, sr. advisor, 2005—. Office: International Monetary Fund 700 19th St NW Washington DC 20431 Office Phone: 202-623-8770. Office Fax: 202-589-8770. Business E-Mail: kkochhar@imf.org.

KOCHI, JAY KAZUO, chemist, educator; b. LA, May 17, 1927; s. Tsuruzo and Shizuko (Moriya) K.; m. Marion Kiyono, Mar. 1, 1959; children: Sims, Julia. Student, Cornell U., 1945; BS, UCLA, 1949; PhD, Iowa State U., 1952. Faculty Harvard U., 1952-55; NIH fellow Cambridge U., Eng., 1956; mem. faculty Iowa State U., 1956; with Shell Devel. Co., 1957-61; mem. faculty dept. chemistry Case Western Res. U., Cleve., 1962-69, prof., 1966-69; prof. chemistry Ind. U., Bloomington, 1969-74, Earl Blough prof. chemistry, 1974-84; Robert A. Welch Disting. prof. chemistry U. Houston, 1984—. Cons. chemist, 1964—. Mem. Am. Chem. Soc., Chem. Soc. (London), Nat. Acad. Scis., Sigma Xi. Achievements include research on mechanism of catalysis of organic reactions, organometallics, electrochemistry and photochemistry, time-resolved spectroscopy, and x-ray crystallography of reactive intermediates. Home: 4372 Faculty Ln Houston TX 77004-6601 Office: U Houston Dept Chemistry 4800 Calhoun Rd Houston TX 77204-5003 Office Phone: 713-743-3293. Business E-Mail: jkochi@uh.edu.

KOCH JOHNS, PATRICIA A., theater educator; b. Nebr. BA, Kearney State Univ. (now Univ. Nebr. Kearney). Tchr., Ark., Cozad (Nebr.) H.S., 1976—2001, Lincoln (Nebr.) H.S., 2001—. Named Nebr. Tchr. of Yr., 2006. Office: Lincoln High Sch 2229 J St Lincoln NE 68510 Business E-Mail: pkoch@lps.org.*

KOCIENIEWSKI, DAVID, journalist; Bur. chief Trenton Bur. NY Times. Author: The Brass Wall: The Betrayal of Undercover Detective #4126, 2003; editor: Two Seconds Under the World: Terror Comes to America, 1994. Office: NY Times Trenton Bur PO Box 021 Trenton NJ 08625 also: NJ State House 125 W State St Trenton NJ 08625-2521 Office Phone: 609-292-5173 ext. 1. E-mail: davidk@nytimes.com.

KOCIS, JANET KAY, elementary school educator; b. Litchfield, Ill., May 6, 1951; d. Thomas Dewey Allan and Loeta Joyce Jones; m. Peter Anthony Kocis, Apr. 12, 1975; children: Nichol Antonacci, Amanda. MusB, So. Ill. U., 1973; M in Tchr. Leadership, U. Ill., Springfield, 2004. Tchr. music Sch. Dist. #7, Gillespie, Ill., 1973—76; tchr. 5th and 6th grades Sts. Simon and Jude, 1979—84; tchr. music St. ALoysius Sch., Springfield, 1986—93; tchr. 6th grade sci. Enos Sch., 1997—2002; tchr. 6th grade math., lang. arts Grant Mid. Sch., 2002—03, tchr. 7th and 8th grade math., 2003—06, coach math., 2005—; tchr. 8th grade math. Franklin Mid. Sch., 2006—. Mem.: ASCD, Nat. Suprs. Math., Nat. Coun. Tchrs. Math. Office: Franklin Middle Sch 1500 Outer Park Dr Springfield IL 62704 Office Phone: 217-525-3164.

KOCIUBES, JOSEPH LEIB, lawyer; b. Frankfurt, Fed. Republic, Germany, June 16, 1947; s. Max and Rachel (Ackermn) Kociubes; m. Peggy Ann Roth, May 18, 1969; children: Lisa Roth, Adam Roth. BA, U. Pitts, Pitts., Pa., 1969; JD, Harvard U., 1974. Bar: Mass./ US Dist. Ct. 1974, Mass./ US Ct. Appeals (1st cir.) 1974, US Supreme Ct. 1981, Mass./ US Ct. Appeals (6th cir.) 1987, Mass./ US Ct. Appeals (4th cir.) 1988. Assoc. Bingham, Dana & Gould, Boston, 1974—81, ptnr., 1981, mem. mgmt. com., 1984—96; faculty various programs Mass. continuing Legal Edn., 1989—; trial practice adv. Harvard Law Sch., 1985—; adj. prof. Northeastern Law Sch., 2001—. Gen. counsel, dir. ACLU of Mass., 1999—; dir., mem. exec. com. Greater Boston Legal Svc., 1989; dir. Vol. Lawyers Project, 1985—95. Fellow: Internat. Acad. Trial Lawyers, Am. Coll. Trial Lawyers; mem.: Boston Bar Assn. (v.p. 2000—01, pres.-elect 2001—02, pres. 2002—03, dir. lawyers com. for civil rights under law 2004—), Mass Bar Found., Am. Bar Found., Mass. State Com., Boston Bar Found. (trustee 1997—2005), Mass. State Com., Am. Coll. Trial Lawyer. Office: Bingham McCutchen 150 Federal St Boston MA 02110-1726 Office Phone: 617-951-8337. E-mail: joe.kociubes@bingham.com.

KOCSIS, JAMES PAUL, artist; b. Buffalo, Apr. 27, 1936; Grad., U. of the Arts, 1958. Illustrator children's books, 1961-68; illustrator, designer Random House Publ., 20th Century Fox, 1967; pub. Kocsis catalogues, books, color prints and posters. Instr. drawing and pictorial composition, lectr. U. of Arts, Phila., 1965-67; lectr. Kutztown State Tchrs. Coll., civic and social grps. Works included in pub. collections: Lessing J. Rosenwald, Nat. Gallery Art, Washington, Library of Congress, Washington, Albright-Knox Art Gallery, Buffalo, Victoria and Albert Mus., London, Kendal (Eng.) Mus., Bodleian Library Oxford U., Eng.; pvt. collections Her Royal Highness Elizabeth Queen of Eng., His Royal Highness Charles, Prince of Wales, Right Hon. Lord Kenneth Clark, Nancy and Ronald Reagan Presdl. Collection, White House, Lehigh Valley (Pa.) Hosp., 1989, Lehigh Valley Internat. Airport, Allentown, Pa., others; one-man shows include Igneous Man Exhbn.I, Columbia (S.C.) Mus. Art, 1974, Crucifixion Exhbn.-Memory of Phila. Scourge Period 1972, U. of Arts, 1976, Igneous Man Exhbns. 2-41, Harvard U., 1976, Sydney (Australia) Opera House, 1979, Dhahran (Saudi Arabia) Cen. Library, 1982, Jilin U., Changchun, China, 1982, 13th Ann. Festival Arts, United World Coll SE Asia, 1984, Italsider Steel Co., Genoa and Alessandria, Italy, 1985, United World Coll. Adriatic, Trieste, Italy, 1985, United World Coll. So. Africa, Mbabane, 1985, Internat. Music & Art Festival, Glamorgan, Wales, 1985, U.S. Internat. U.-Europe, London, 1985, U. Glasgow, Scotland, 1985, James Joyce Mus., Dublin, Ireland, 1985, Kendal (Eng.) Mus., 1986, Internat. Pub. Rels. Conv., Harare, Zimbabwe, 1987, Trinity Coll. Oxford U., 1988, Imo State Libr., Owerri, Nigeria, 1989, Progress Bank of Nigeria Ltd., Lagos, 1989, Nat. Arts Theatre, Lagos, 1989, Freedom Hall, Martin Luther King, Jr. Ctr. Nonviolent Social Change and Atlanta-Fulton Pub. Libr., Atlanta, 1990, U.S. Mission to the UN, N.Y.C., 1991, UN, N.Y.C. (first Am. honored with one-man exhbn., 1991), Sopot, Poland, 1991, Gdansk, Poland, 1991, German-Am. Inst., Saarbrucken, Germany, 1992, Amerika Haus, Frankfurt, Germany, 1992, Zentral-Bibliothek, Cologne, Germany, 1993, Freie Universitat Berlin, Universitatbibliothek, Berlin, 1994, Igneous Man Exhbn./India, Gandhi Peace Found., New Delhi, 1995, Internat. India Ctr., New Delhi, 1995, Nat. Mus. and Libr. Casa de la Cultura Ecuatoriana Benjamin Carrion, Quito, Ecuador, South Am., 1998, Benjamin Franklin Libr., Mexico City, 1998, Inst. de Investigaciones Estetícas, U. Nacional de Mex., Mexico City, 1998, La Casa de Cultura, Jesus Reyes Heroles, Coyoacan, Mex., 1999, Libr. of Nat. Acad. Athens, 2003, Elefterios Venizelos Internat. Airport, 2003, Vikelaia Libr., Crete, 2003, Acad. Athens (Greece) U., 2003, The Hermitage Mus., St. Petersburg, Russia, 2005, Dostoevsky Mus., St. Petersburg, Russia, 2005, Russian Acad. Arts, St. Petersburg, Russia, 2005. Recipient Biannual award Am. Inst. Graphic Arts, 1968, Letters of Recognition Lord Kenneth Clark, 1981, Her Royal Highness Elizabeth, The Queen of Eng., His Royal Highness, Charles, Prince of Wales, 1983. Achievements include inventing new art form: Psychic Impressionism. Home and Office: PO Box 905 Allentown PA 18105-0905 Personal E-mail: cvjpk@earthlink.net.

KOCSIS, JOAN BOSCO, elementary school educator; b. Phillipsburg, NJ, Feb. 6, 1941; d. Frederick B. and Frances (Marina) Bosco; m. Gerald S. Kocsis Sr., Dec. 30, 1961; children: Gerald S. Jr., Jacqueline Kocsis Morgan. BA, Trenton State Coll., 1962; MEd, U. N.C., Charlotte, 1987. Cert. kindergarten-4 tchr., early childhood edn., lang. arts kindergarten-12, social studies 7-12, adminstrn., supervision and curriculum, N.C. Tchr. grades kindergarten, 1, 3 Hamilton Twp. (N.J.) Bd. Edn., 1962—68; tchr. grades kindergarten, talented and gifted Hopewell Valley Bd. Edn., Pennington, 1976—79; tchr. grades 4, 2, 3 Union County Pub. Schs., Monroe, 1981—88; tchr. grade 1 Charlotte (N.C.)-Mecklenburg Pub. Schs., 1988—89; tchr. grades 1, 2 Union County Pub. Schs., Monroe, 1989—. Presenter (TV show) "Positively for Parents", 1992. Recipient Presdl. award for excellence in tchg. sci. and math. NSF, 1994. Mem. NEA, NSTA, N.C. Sci. Tchrs. Assn., Assn. Presdl. Awardees in Sci. Tchg., Internat. Reading Assn. (Union-Monroe coun. treas. 1993—). Home: 309 Auckland Ln Matthews NC 28104-7867

KOCUR, SEAN EDWARD, lab administrator; b. Beverly, Mass., Nov. 19, 1971; s. Edward Marshall Kocur and Carol Ann Marie Keith; m. Tara Lee Kocur, Dec. 30, 1994; children: Benjamin Aaron, Jonathan Patrick, Adam Matthew, Alyssa Grace. BS in Chemistry, Salem Coll., Mass., 2002; MS in Toxicology, Northeastern U., Mass., 2007. Cert. auto glass technician, Mass. Bd. of Registry, chemist, Am. Soc. Clin. Pathologists. Asst. mgr. Best Friends Pet Care, Boxford, Mass., 1988—95; preload supr. United Parcel Svc., Lynnfield, Mass., 1990—94; auto glass technician J.N. Philips Glass, Salem, 1995—98; auto glass shop mgr. New Angle Glass, Lynn, Mass., 1998—2002; forensic toxicologist Willow Labs and Med. Ctr., Lynn, Mass., 2002—. Pvt. 1st class USMC, 1994-95. Mem. Am. Chem. Soc., Soc. Toxicology, Internat. Assn. Forensic Toxicology, New Eng. Assn. Forensic Scientists, Phi Kappa Phi. Republican. Congregationalist. Avocations: book collecting, basketball, football, baseball, kenpo karate (green belt). Home: 61 Collins St Danvers MA 01923 Office Phone: 781-268-2400 ext 1114. Personal E-mail: sekocur@comcast.net.

KODALI, DHARMA RAO, engineering educator; s. Seetharamaiah and Venkata Subbamma Kodali; m. Suseela Karlapudi, Dec. 25, 1982; children: Harsha Sitharam, Sithara. PhD, Kurukshetra Universtiy, 1974—80. Asst. prof. biophysics Boston U. Sch. Medicine, Boston, 1989—91; R&D mgr. Cargill, Inc., Mpls., 1991—2003; corp. sr. prin. scientist Gen. Mills, Mpls., 2003—04; mng. dir. Global Agritech, Inc., 2004—; adj. prof. dept. bioproducts and bio-systems engrng. U. Minn., 2005—. Mem., tech. adv. com. Ctr. Interfacial Engrng., U. Minn., Minneapolis, 1993—98; mem., instl. rev. bd. Abbott Northwestern Hospitals, Minneapolis, 2003—. Recipient Chmns. Innovation award, Cargill, Inc., 2001; fellow, Am. Inst. Chemists, 1986; Whitaker Rsch. grantee, Whitaker Health Scis. Fund, 1989. Mem.: FSCT, STLE, Indian Sci. Congress Assn., Am. Chem. Soc. (Innovation award 2002), Am. Oil Chemists Soc. (chair-person, indsl. oil products divsn. 2001—04, TL Mounts award 2003). Achievements include patents for 21 US issued patents; research in pubs. more than 60 papers published. Home: 710 Olive Ln Plymouth MN 55447 Business E-Mail: kodali@globalagritech.us.

KODAMA, KENNETH PHILIP, science educator, academic administrator; b. New Brunswick, NJ, July 31, 1951; s. Sidney Philip Kodama and Harriet Edna Peterson; m. Anna Brownell Carr, July 10, 1980; children: Emily Ann, Alice Brownell, Peterson Kashiro. BA, BA, U. Pa., Phila., 1973; MS, PhD, Stanford U., Calif., 1977. Asst. prof. Lehigh U., Bethlehem, Pa., 1978—83, assoc. prof., 1983—89, prof., 1989—, assoc. dean Coll. Arts and Scis., 1996—99, chair earth and environ. sci. dept., 1991—94, assoc. chair earth and environ. sci. dept., 2004—. Mem. com. sci. and arts Franklin Inst., Phila., 1997—. Assoc. editor: Jour. Geophys. Record; contbr. articles to sci. jours. Recipient NSF grants, 1988—. Fellow: Geol. Soc. Am. (George P. Woollard award 2006); mem.: Am. Geophys. Union (assoc. editor GSA Bull 2000—), Sigma Xi. Moravian. Avocation: music. Office: Lehigh U Dept Earth and Environ Sci 31 Williams Dr Bethlehem PA 18015

KODAT, CATHERINE GUNTHER, literature and language professor; b. Ocala, Fla., July 7, 1957; d. Donald George and Joan Bennett Gunther; m. Alexander William Kodat, Oct. 18, 1986; children: Axel Nofz, Madeleine Gunther, Dexter Bennett. BA, U Balt., 1980; PhD, Boston U., 1994. Metro desk reporter The Balt. Sun, 1981—87; lectr. English Boston Coll., Chestnut Hill, Mass., 1992—92, Tufts U., Medford, Mass., 1994—95; asst. prof. English, Am. studies Hamilton Coll., Clinton, NY, 1995—2001, assoc. prof. English, Am. studies, 2001—. Fellow, Rothermere Am. Inst., U. Oxford, 2004; grantee, Coun. Internat. Exch. Scholars, Fulbright Scholars Program, 2005; Millicent C. McIntosh Flexible fellow, Woodrow Wilson Nat. Fellowship Found., 2002—04, Angela J. and James J. Rallis scholar, Boston U. Humanities Found., 1992—93. Mem.: MLA, Am. Studies Assn. Office: Hamilton College 198 College Hill Rd Clinton NY 13323 Office Phone: 315-859-4341. E-mail: ckodat@hamilton.edu.

KOEDEL, JOHN GILBERT, JR., retired metal products executive; b. Pitts., June 25, 1937; s. John Gilbert and Elizabeth Marie (Kramer) K.; m. Fay Birren, Dec. 21, 1963; 1 son, John III. BS in Commerce, Washington and Lee U., 1959. V.p. Pitts. Nat. Bank, 1960-68; various positions up to pres. Nat. Forge. Co., 1968-95. Bd. dirs. The RCR Group, Inc. Served to sgt., U.S. Army, 1960-65. Mem. Fishing Bay Yacht Club, Conenango Club, Masons. Republican. Presbyterian. Avocations: sailing, woodworking. Home: PO Box 877 Deltaville VA 23043-0877

KOEDEL, ROBERT CRAIG, minister, historian, educator; b. Tarentum, Pa., July 1, 1927; s. Theodore and Evelyn (Dagan) K.; m. Barbara Ellen Wood, Jan. 6, 1962. BA, Wheaton Coll., Ill., 1949; M.Div., Pitts. Theol Sem., 1953; MA, U. Pitts., 1964; postgrad., Temple U., 1964-70. Ordained to ministry Presbyn. Ch. U.S.A., 1953. Pastor Monaghan Presbyn. Ch., Dillsburg, Pa., 1956-59; asst. pastor Mt. Calvary Presbyn. Ch., Corapolis, Pa., 1959-60; assoc. pastor Dormont Presbyn. Ch., Pitts., 1960-64; mem. faculty Atlantic Community Coll., Mays Landing, NJ, 1966-92, prof. social sci., history, religion, 1978-92, chmn. dept. history, 1969-70, 78-79, asst. dean instrn., 1970-72; lectr. in history Stockton State Coll., 1985-86; clergyman Pitts. Presbytery. Author: South Jersey Heritage: A Social, Economic and Cultural History, 1977, God's Vine in This Wilderness: Religion in South Jersey to 1800, 1980, Following the Water: The Shellfish Industry in South Jersey, 1983, Becoming a Presbyterian, 1993, Letters from Wheaton by a Forty-Niner, 1997, The Sky Pilot Said It: Memoires of an Air Force Chaplain, 2001; contbr. articles to profl. jours., articles to newspapers. Mem. Atlantic County Cultural and Heritage Adv. Bd., 1991. Served as chaplain USAF, 1953-56. N.J. Hist. Commn. research grantee, 1974, 84. Mem. United Teaching Professions, N.J. Hist. Soc. (trustee 1985-88), Atlantic County Hist. Soc. (editor jour. 1983-91), Gloucester County Hist. Soc., Pitts. Presbytery, Hist. Soc. Western Pa. (rsch. historian). Home: 1 Unger Ln Pittsburgh PA 15217-1018

KOEGEL, WILLIAM FISHER, lawyer; b. Washington, Aug. 18, 1923; s. Otto Erwin and Rae (Fisher) K.; m. Barbara Bixler, Feb. 2, 1946 (dec. 1968); children: John Bixler, Robert Bartlett; m. Ruth Swan Boynton, June 21, 1969 (dec. 1983); m. Irene Lawrence, Aug. 4, 1984. BA, Williams Coll., 1944; LL.B., U. Va., 1949. Bar: N.Y. 1950. From assoc. to ptnr. Clifford Chance US LLP (formerly Rogers & Wells), NYC, 1949—88, head litigation dept., 1977-88, sr. counsel, 1989—. Chmn. Scarsdale (N.Y.) Republican Town Com., 1965-71; pres. trustees Hitchcock Presbyn. Ch., Scarsdale, 1970-73, 78-79, 82-83. Served with AUS, 1943-45, ETO. Fellow ACTL; mem. ABA, N.Y. State Bar Assn., Bar Assn. City N.Y., Order of Coif. Clubs: Town (Scarsdale) (pres. 1976-77); Williams (N.Y.C.); Shenorock Shore, Fox Meadow Tennis, The Moorings. Office: Clifford Chance US LLP 31 West 52nd St New York NY 10014 Home: 704 Heritage Hills Somers NY 10589 E-mail: bkoegel7@aol.com.

KOEGEN, ROY JEROME, lawyer; b. Spokane, Wash., Mar. 1, 1949; s. Frank J. and Jeanne (Bardsley) K.; m. Ann Martinelli, Aug. 28, 1970; children: Jennifer, Christopher. BA, Gonzaga U., 1971; JD, U. Calif., San Francisco, 1974. Bar: Calif. 1974, Wash. 1979, U.S. Supreme Ct. 1982. Assoc. Wilson, Jones, Morton & Lynch, San Mateo, Calif., 1974-78, Blair & Koegen, Spokane, 1978-80; ptnr. Preston, Thorgrimson, Ellis & Holman, Spokane, 1980-90, Perkins Coie LLP, Seattle, Spokane, 1990—2002, Lukins & Annis, PS, Spokane, 2002—05, Koegen Edwards LLP, 2005—. Author: Washington Municipal Financing Deskbook, 1992. Chmn. exec. com. Cmty. Alcohol Ctr., Spokane, 1982—84, Century II Park Dist., Spokane, 1982—84; bd. dirs. Nature Conservancy, Wash. Nat. Pk. Found. Mem. ABA, Wash. Bar Assn., Calif. Bar Assn., Nat. Assn. Bond Lawyers, The Nature Conservancy (bd. dirs.). Roman Catholic. Office: Koegen Edwards LLP Bank of America Financial Ctr 601 W Riverside Ave Ste 840 Spokane WA 99201 Office Phone: 509-747-4040. Business E-Mail: roy@koegenedwards.com.

KOEHLER, MYRON, retired secondary school educator; b. Kirby, Tex., Oct. 28, 1927; s. Otto Albert and Annie (Biesenbach) Koehler; m. Marie Sherwood, May 14, 1954; children: Carol Ann, Sharon Marie, Carrie Lynn, Rene Lee. BS, SW Tex. State U., San Marcos, 1950, MEd, 1955; EdD, Tex. A&M U., College Station, 1972. Jr. HS tchr. San Antonio Sch. Dist., 1950—53; HS tchr. NE Sch. Dist., San Antonio, 1954—62, 1967—68, HS vice prin., 1962—67; rschr., prof. Tex. A&M U., 1972—79; HS prin. Somerset Sch. Dist., Tex., 1979—81; HS tchr. Bryan Sch. Dist., Tex., 1982—86; ret., 1986. Driver edn. cons. SW Tex. State U., San Marcos, 1976, Prairie View A&M U., 1977, USAF, 1978. Contbr. rsch. reports, article to profl. publs. Mem. Coulter Airfield adv. com. City of Bryan, Tex., 1997—2004; coordinator Habitat for Humanity, Bryan, 2002; asst. scoutmaster Boy Scouts Am., Bryan, 1997—2006, mem. Order of Arrow Vigil, 1997—2006; mem. Brotherhood of St. Andrews, Episc. Ch., Bryan, 2002—05. With USAAC, 1946—47, lt. col. USAFR, 1951—52, lt. col. USAFR, 1958—87. Named Disting. Commr., Boy Scouts Am., Houston, 1987; recipient Silver Beaver award, 1977, Meritorious Svc. medal, Nat. Security Agy., Ft. Meade, Md., 1980; James West fellow, Boy Scouts Am., Irving, Tex., 1999. Mem.: Tex. Ret. Tchrs. Assn. (life; pres. 2000—02), VFW, Am. Legion (life), Lions Club (dist. gov. 2003—04, pres. Bryan Breakfast club, Tex. Lions Found. 2005, co-chmn. dist. convention 1998, co-chmn. state convention 1999, Melvin Jones fellow 1992—2004, Jack Wiech fellow Tex. Lions Camp, Kerrville 2002, Lion of Yr. Bryan Breakfast club 1984, Pres.' Silver award 1989, Pres.s award 2002). Republican. Episcopalian. Achievements include invention of carrier lock automatic mechanism for plegias. Avocations: hunting, fishing, camping, travel, stamp collecting/philately. Home: 2107 Wilkes St Bryan TX 77803-6021 Personal E-mail: mmkoehler@juno.com, mmkoehler0906@peoplepc.com.

KOEHLER, REGINALD STAFFORD, III, lawyer; b. Bellevue, Pa., Dec. 29, 1932; s. Reginald S. and Esther (Hawken) K.; m. Ann Ellsworth Rowland, June 15, 1956; children: Victoria Elizabeth Clark, Cynthia Rowland, Robert Steven. BA, Yale U., 1956; JD, Harvard U., 1959. Bar: N.Y. 1960, Calif., Fla., D.C. 1979, Wash. 1984, Oreg. 1985, Alaska 1985, U.S. Supreme Ct. 1973. Assoc. Davis Polk & Wardwell, NYC, 1959-68; ptnr. Donovan Leisure Newton & Irvine, NYC, 1968-84, Perkins Coie, Seattle, 1984—. Author: The Planning and Administration of a Large Estate. Fellow Am. Coll. Trust and Estate Counsel; mem. N.Y. State Bar Assn., Calif. Bar Assn., D.C. Bar Assn., Wash. Bar Assn., Oreg. Bar Assn., Alaska Bar Assn., Chi Psi. Episcopalian. Office: Perkins Coie 1201 3rd Ave Fl 48 Seattle WA 98101-3029 Office Phone: 206-359-8632. Business E-Mail: rkoehler@perkinscoie.com.

KOEHLER, ROBERT BRIEN, priest; b. Hastings, Nebr., Aug. 26, 1950; s. Robert Joseph and Melba Deloris (Morey) K.; m. Terry Ellen Collins; children: Gregory, Michael, Louisa. BA cum laude, U. Dallas, 1972; postgrad., U. Wis., 1973; MDiv, Nashotah Ho., 1976. Chaplain DeKoven Found., Racine, Wis., 1976-81; Curate Emmanuel Ch., Rockford, Ill., 1978-81; Rector St. Raphael's Ch., Ft. Myers Beach, Fla., 1981-84; Vicar Ch. Holy Cross, Burleson, Tex., 1984-87; Canon to the Ordinary, Diocese of Ft. Worth, 1987-93; Rector St. Luke's Ch., Ft. Myers, Fla., 1993—2001, Baton Rouge, 2001—. Exec. dir. Episc. Synod Am., Ft. Worth, 1991-93. Dist. chmn. Boy Scouts Am., Ft. Myers, 1993-96; trustee Nashotah (Wis.) House, 1994—; bd. dirs. Interfaith Vol. Care Givers, 1996-99, Goodwill Industries, S.W. Fla., 1999-2001; instl. review com. Lee Meml. Health Sys., 1999-2001. Mem. SAR, Soc. Holy Cross, Soc. Colonial Wars. Office: St Luke's Episc Ch 8833 Goodwood Blvd Baton Rouge LA 70806 E-mail: frkoehler@stlukesbr.org.

KOEHLER, ROBERT H., lawyer; b. Kansas City, Kans., Sept. 22, 1941; AB, Marquette Univ., 1963; JD, Univ. Kans., 1966. Bar: Kans. 1966, DC 1973, Va. 1999, DC Ct. Appeals, Va. Supreme Ct., US Ct. Mil. Appeals, US Ct. Appeals (1st, 4th, 5th, 6th, 10th, DC, Fed. cir.), US Supreme Ct. 1973. Ptnr., Govt. Contracts, Def. & Nat. Security Affairs practices, mem. mgmt. com., office mng. ptnr. Patton Boggs LLP, McLean, Va. Dir., mem. exec. com., former chmn. USO of Metro. Washington. Served US Army, 1967—73. Decorated Bronze Star, Meritorious Svc. award, Army Commendation medal, Vietnam Svc. medal. Office: Patton Boggs LLP 9th Fl 8484 Westpark Dr Mc Lean VA 22102-5117 Office Phone: 703-744-8005. Office Fax: 703-744-8001. Business E-Mail: rkoehler@pattonboggs.com.

KOEHN, ENNO, engineering educator, researcher; b. Flushing, NY, Apr. 29, 1936; s. Theodore J. and Anna M. (Sievers) K.; m. Carol Ann Butcher, Nov. 25, 1967; children: William Enno, James Frederick. BCE, CUNY, 1958; MS, Columbia U., 1960; PhD, Wayne State U., 1975. Registered profl. engr., Tex., Ind., Ohio. Engrng. inspector Bd. Water Supply, NYC, 1957; rsch. engr. N.Am. Rockwell, Columbus, Ohio, 1958-59; asst. prof. L.I. U., Greenvale, NY, 1960-66; specialist IBM, Burlington, Vt., 1966-67; prof. civil engrng. Ohio Northern U., Ada, 1967-79; assoc. prof. civil engrng. Purdue U., West Lafayette, Ind., 1979-84; prof., chair dept. civil engrng. Lamar U., Beaumont, Tex., 1984—2003, prof., 2003—. Rsch. cons. Atomic Internat., Canoga Park, Calif., 1962, GM Corp., Warren, Mich., 1973, Bechtel Corp., Ann Arbor, Mich., 1978-81, U.S. Army Rsch. Lab., Champaign, Ill., 1983-88; program evaluator Accreditation Bd. for Engrng. and Tech. Contbr. articles to profl. jours. Active Alumni Rep. Com. Columbia U., N.Y.C., 1990—; sustaining mem. Boy Scouts Am. Troop Com., 1980—; pres., campaign chairperson United Way, Ada, 1975-77, Lamar Engrng., Beaumont, 1984-86. Fellow ASCE (Best Paper nomination); mem. NSPE, Am. Soc. Engrng. Edn. (Best Paper nomination), Assn. Advancement Cost Engrng. Internat., Rotary Internat. (dir. 1970-73), Tau Beta Pi (chpt. adviser), Sigma Xi (Membership award), Chi Epsilon (Honor Membership award). Episcopalian. Avocations: reading, gardening, walking, travel. Office: Lamar U Civil Engrng Dept PO Box 10024 Beaumont TX 77710-0024

KOEHN, WILLIAM JAMES, lawyer; b. Winterset, Iowa, Mar. 24, 1936; s. Cyril Otto and Ilene L. (Doop) K.; m. Francia C. Leeper, Sept. 6, 1958; children: Cynthia Rae, William Fredric, James Anthony. BA, U. Iowa, 1963, JD cum laude, 1963. Bar: Iowa 1963, U. S. Ct. Appeals (8th cir.) 1971, U.S. Ct. Appeals (10th cir.) 1972, U.S. Ct. Appeals (2d cir.) 1972, U.S. Ct. Appeals (5th cir.) 1977, U.S. Supreme Ct. 1971. Of counsel Davis, Brown, Koehn, Shors & Roberts, P.C., Des Moines, 1963—. Prof., lectr. in U.S., Can., Europe. Bd. editors Iowa Law Rev., 1961-63; contbr. articles to profl. jours. Co-founder Big Bros.-Sisters of Greater Des Moines, 1969, pres., 1976-77; chmn. Des Moines Friendship Commmn., 1970-71; bd. dirs. Greater Des Moines YMCA, 1983-90; co-chmn. Des Moines Bicentennial Commn., 1975-76; chmn. Environ. and Pub. Works Commn.; mem. adv. com. civil justice reform act, 1990; chmn. worldwide dispute resolution com., Lex Mundi, 1989-94, bd. dirs., 1992-96; arbitrator AAA Comml. Sect., 2004—, DRCS, 2007—. Lt. USNR, 1958-61. Mem. ABA (environ. litigation sub-com., construction com., internat. lit. environ. commn.), Iowa Bar Assn. (environ. coun. 1989-92, 1999-2001, litigation com. 1992-95, proflism. com. 1994-2002, chmn. internat. law sect. 2005-06), Polk County Bar Assn., Iowa Trial Lawyers Assn., Order of Coif. Independent. Office: Fin Ctr 666 Walnut St Des Moines IA 50309-3904 Home: 29980 Nantucket Dr PO 669 Pacific City OR 97135 Office Phone: 515-288-2500. Business E-Mail: wjk@davisbrownlaw.com.

KOEL, BRUCE EDWARD, chemist, educator, researcher; b. Norton, Kans., June 30, 1955; BS in Chemistry with highest honors, Emporia State U., 1976, MS in Chemistry, 1978; PhD in Chemistry, U. Tex., 1981. Miller Inst. postdoctoral fellow U. Calif., Berkeley, 1981-83; asst. prof. chemistry and biochemistry U. Colo., Boulder, 1983-89, assoc. prof. chemistry and biochemistry, 1989, fellow Coop. Inst. for Rsch. in Environ. Scis., 1983-89; assoc. prof. chemistry U. So. Calif., 1990-93, prof. chemistry, 1993—2005, chmn. dept. of chemistry, 1998—2005; prof. chemistry Lehigh U., 2005—. Cons. Chemistry and Laser Sciences, Los Alamos Nat. Lab., 1984-92, Hewlett-Packard, 1985-89, J&A Assocs., 1986, Chemistry and Laser Scis.-1 Los Alamos Nat. Lab., 1992-94, Burge and Assocs., 1992-95, Chem Alert Corp., 1993-95; reviewer for proposals to Am. Chem. Soc.-Petroleum Rsch. Fund, Army Rsch. Office, Dept. Energy, ISF, NSF; adj. prof. material sciences, U. So. Calif., 1995-2005, founder Lab. for Molecular Robotics, 1994; mem., Ctr. for Advanced Materials and Nanotechnology, Lehigh U.; lectr., spkr. in field. Mem. editorial adv. bd.: Langmuir; referee Applied Surface Sci., Catalysis Letters, Chemistry of Materials, Internat. Conf. on Metall. Coatings and Thin Films, Jour. Catalysis, Jour. Chem. Physics, Jour. Electron Spectroscopy and Related Phenomena, Jour. Phys. Chemistry, Jour. Am. Chem. Soc., Jour. Vacuum Sci. and Tech., Langmuir, Sci., Surface Sci.; contbr. articles to profl. jours. Recipient Dreyfus Found. grant for New Faculty, 1983, Exxon Edn. Found. award, 1987, Union Carbide Innovation Rsch. awards, 1990, 91; U. fellow U. Tex., Austin, 1978, NSF Energy Related trainee, 1978, Alfred P. Sloan Rsch. fellow, 1990. Fellow Am. Phys. Soc.; mem. Am. Chem. Soc. (divsn. colloid and surface chemistry Proctor and Gamble fellowship 1980, various com. positions, George A. Olah award in Hydrocarbon or Petroleum Chemistry, 2007), Am. Phys. Soc., Am. Vacuum Soc., Materials Rsch. Soc. Office: Lehigh U Dept Chemistry Sinclair Lab Rom 305C 6 E Packer Ave Seeley G Mudd Bldg Bethlehem PA 18015 Office Phone: 610-758-5650. Business E-Mail: brk205@lehigh.edu.*

KOELBL, JAMES J., dean; Faculty mem. U. Ill., Loyola U., U. Louisville; group assoc. dir. profl. svc. ADA; dean Sch. Dentistry W.Va. U., 1999—. Mem.: W.Va. State Dental Assn. (v.p. 2004—). Office: W Va Univ Sch Dentistry Robert C Byrd Health Sci Ctr Med Ctr Dr Morgantown WV 26506-9400 Office Phone: 304-293-2521. Office Fax: 304-293-5829. Business E-Mail: jkoelbl@hsc.wvu.edu.

KOELLER, ROBERT MARION, lawyer, director; b. Quincy, Ill., Apr. 8, 1940; s. Marion Alfred and Ruth (Main) K.; m. Marlene Meyer, June 1962; children: Kristin, Katherine, Robert. AB, MacMurray Coll., 1962; LLB, Vanderbilt U., 1965. Bar: Ind. 1968. Asst. gen. counsel Nat. Homes Acceptance Corp., Lafayette, Ind., 1967-70; gen. counsel, sec. Herff Jones Co., Indpls., 1970-74; ptnr. Warren, Snider, Koeller & Warren, Indpls., 1974-76; pvt. practice Indpls., 1976—; mem. Coons, Maddox & Koeller, Indpls., 1993-96, Maddox, Koeller Hargett & Caruso, 1996—2002, Ittenbach Johnson Trettin & Koeller, Indpls., 2002—. Dir. various cos. Mem. ABA, Ind. Bar Assn., Indpls. Bar Assn., Hillcrest Country Club. Republican. Methodist. Office: Ste 4 6350 N Shadeland Ave Indianapolis IN 46220 Office Phone: 317-842-5235. Business E-Mail: rkoeller@ijtklaw.com.

KOELLING, THOMAS WINSOR, lawyer; b. Jefferson City, Mo., Oct. 10, 1951; s. Oscar Alvin and Helen Louise (Shields) K.;m. Rebecca Ann Nentwig, Nov. 24, 1973; children: Zachary Thomas, Mathew Garret. BS in Criminal Justice Adminstrn., Ctrl. Mo. State U., Warrenburg, 1978; JD, U. Mo., 1981. Bar: Mo. 1981, Colo. 1982, U.S. Dist. Ct. (we. dist.) Mo. 1981, U.S. Dist. Ct. Colo. 1981, U.S. Ct. Appeals (8th cir.) 1982, U.S. Ct. Appeals (10th cir.) 1981, U.S. Supreme Ct. 1992. Assoc. Tinsley, Frantz et al, Lakewood, Colo., 1981-82, Rex Johnson Law Office, Colorado Springs, Colo., 1982-85; ptnr. Koelling & Crawford, P.C., Kansas City, Mo., 1985—. Legal advisor Kansas City Ski Club, 1987, Competitors Assn., Kansas City, 1995—; adj. prof. dept. criminal justice and legal studies Mo. Western State Coll., St. Joseph, Mo., 1998-2001. With USAF, 1972-76. Mem. Am. Coll. Legal Medicine, Am. Soc. Law, Medicine Ethics, Am. Trial Lawyers Assn., Mo. Assn. Trial Lawyers, Clay County Bar Assn. Roman Catholic. Avocations: skiing, fly fishing, backpacking. Home: 9617 N Campbell St Kansas City MO 64155-2056 Office: Koelling & Crawford PC 5950 N Oak Trfy Ste 202 Kansas City MO 64118-5164 Office Phone: 816-452-2468. Personal E-mail: kclaw@msn.com.

KOELLNER, LAURETTE, aerospace transportation executive; b. Bklyn., Oct. 21, 1954; B in Bus. Mgmt., U. Ctrl. Fla.; MBA, Stetson U. Cert. contracts mgr. Nat. Contracts Mgmt. Assn. Analyst contracts, advanced to various positions McDonnell Douglas, 1978—86, mgr. contracts and pricing missle sys. co. Titusville, Fla., 1986—88, bus. mgr. Tomahawk Cruise Missle prog., 1988—89, dir. strategic and bus. planning, 1989—90, head internal support and svcs. ops. missle prodn. facility, 1990—92; budget mgr. McDonnell Douglas Aerospace, St. Louis, 1992—94, dir. human resources divisn., 1994—96, v.p., gen. auditor, 1996—97, Boeing Co. (formerly McDonnell Douglas), St. Louis, 1997—99, v.p., corp. controller, 1999—2004, exec. v.p., 2004—; pres. Connexion by Boeing, 2004—06, Boeing Internat., 2006—. Bd. dirs. Sara Lee Corp., Exostar, Chgo. Coun. Fgn. Rels., Chicagoland C. of C.; mem. bd. regents U. Portland; mem. dean's exec. coun. coll. bus. adminstrn. U. Ctrl. Fla. Named to Hall of Fame, U. Ctrl. Fla., 2003. Mem.: Economic Club Chgo. Office: Boeing World Hdqs 100 N Riverside Chicago IL 60606 Office Phone: 312-544-2000.*

KOELMEL, JOHN R., finance company executive; Grad., Coll. Holy Cross. Mng. ptnr. KPMG LLP, Buffalo; chief adminstrv. officer Fin. Instns. Inc., 2000—02; exec. v.p., CEO First Niagara Fin. Group, Inc., 2004—06, exec. v.p., COO, acting CEO, 2006—07, pres., CEO, 2007—. Office: First Niagara Fin Group Inc 6950 S Transit Rd Lockport NY 14095-0004 Office Phone: 716-625-7500. Office Fax: 716-625-8416. E-mail: john.koelmel@fnfg.com.*

KOELMEL, LORNA LEE, data processing executive; b. Denver, May 15, 1936; d. George Bannister and Gladys Lee Steuart; m. Herbert Howard Nelson, Sept. 9, 1956 (div. Mar. 1967); children: Karen Dianne, Phillip Dean, Lois Lynn; m. Robert Darrel Koelmel, May 12, 1981; stepchildren: Kim, Cheryl, Dawn, Debbie. BA in English, U. Colo., 1967. Cert. secondary English tchr. Substitute English tchr. Jefferson County Schs., Lakewood, Colo., 1967—68; sec. specialist IBM Corp., Denver, 1968—75, pers. administr., 1975—82, asst. ctr. coord., 1982—85, office systems specialist, 1985—87, backup computer operator, 1987—; computer instr. Barnes Bus. Coll., Denver, 1987—92; owner, mgr. Lorna's Precision Word Processing and Desktop Pub., Denver, 1987—89; computer cons. Denver, 1990—. Editor newsletter Colo. Nat. Campers and Hikers Assn., 1992-94. Organist Christian Sci. Soc., Buena Vista, Colo., 1963-66, 1st Ch. Christ Scientists Thornton-Westminster, Thornton, Colo., 1994—; chmn. bd. dirs., 1979-80. Mem. NAFE, Nat. Secs. Assn. (retirement ctr. chair 1977-78, newsletter chair 1979-80, v.p. 1980-81), Am. Theatre Organ Soc. (Rocky Mountain chpt.), Am. Guild Organists, U. Colo. Alumni Assn., Avon Ind. Sales Rep and Pres. Club, Alpha Chi Omega (publicity com. 1986-88). Clubs: Nat. Writers. Lodges: Job's Daus. (recorder 1953-54). Republican. Avocations: quilting, piano, bridge, logic problems, golf.

KOELTL, JOHN GEORGE, federal judge; b. NYC, Oct. 25, 1945; s. John J. and Elsie (Bender) K. AB summa cum laude, Georgetown U., 1967; JD magna cum laude, Harvard U., 1971. Bar: N.Y. 1972, U.S. Dist. Ct. (so. and ea. dists.) N.Y. 1975, U.S. Ct. Appeals (2d cir.) 1975, U.S. Supreme Ct. 1978, U.S. Ct. Appeals (5th and 11th cirs.) 1981, U.S. Ct. Appeals (4th cir.) 1992, U.S. Dist. Ct. (no. dist.) N.Y. 1982. Law clk. to Judge U.S. Dist. Ct. (so. dist.), NYC, 1971-72; law clk. to Justice Potter Stewart U.S. Supreme Ct., Washington, 1972-73; asst. spl. prosecutor Watergate Spl. Prosecution Force, Dept. Justice, Washington, 1973-74; assoc. Debevoise & Plimpton, NYC, 1975-78, ptnr., 1979-94; judge U.S. Dist. Ct. (so. dist.), NYC, 1994—. Adj. prof. law NYU Law Sch., 1999—. Mem. bd. editors Manual for Complex Litigation 4th edit.; contbr. articles to profl. jours. Mem.: ABA (bd. editors jour. 1991—97, vice chmn. securities com. adminstrv. law sect. 1979—81, co-dir. divsn. publs. litigation sect. 1982—84, coun. mem. litigation sect. 1984—87, assoc. editor Litigation jour. 1975—78, exec. editor 1978—80, editor-in-chief 1980—82, chmn. 1st amendment com. 1987—89, chmn. spl. pubs. com. 1989—92, dir. divsn. publs. litigation sect. 1992—93), Am. Law Inst., Harvard Law Sch. Assn. N.Y. (v.p. 1993—94), N.Y. County Lawyers Assn. (mem. fed. cts. com. 1984—87), N.Y. State Bar Assn., Assn. Bar N.Y.C. (mem. com. on fed. legislation 1976—78, sec. 1978—81, mem. com. profl. and jud. ethics 1981—84, fed. cts. com. 1984—86, chmn. 1986—89, mem. com. on profl. responsibility 1991—94, mem. com. on internat. dispute resolution 2000—). Office: US Courthouse 500 Pearl St Rm 1030 New York NY 10007-1316

KOEN, BILLY VAUGHN, mechanical engineering educator; b. Graham, Tex., May 2, 1938; s. Ottis Vaughn and Margaret (Branch) Koen; m. Deanne Rollins, June 3, 1967; children: Kent, Douglas. BA in Chemistry, U. Tex., 1961, BS in Chem. Engring., 1961; S.M. in Nuclear Engring., MIT, 1962, Sc.D. in Nuclear Engring., 1968; Diplome d'ingenieur en Genie Atomique, L'institut National des Scis. et Techniques Nucleaires, France, 1963. Registered profl. engr., Tex. Asst. prof. mech. engring. U. Tex., Austin, 1968-71, assoc. prof., 1971-80, Minnie S. Piper prof., 1980, prof., 1981—; dir. Bur. Engring. Teaching U. Tex.-Austin, 1973-76. Prof. Ecole Centrale, Paris, 1983; undergrad advisor mech. engring., 1988-92; vis. prof. Tokyo Inst. Tech., 1994 (summer), 1998-99, 2001 (summer); cons., lectr. in field. Author: Definition of the Engineering Method, 1985, Discussion of the Method, 2003; contbr. articles to profl. jours. Bd. dirs. Oak Ridge Associated Univs., 1975-76. Recipient Standard Oil Ind. award, 1970, W. Leighton Collins Distinguished and Unusual Service awd., Am. Soc. for Engineering Education, 1992. Fellow Am. Soc. Engring. Edn. (v.p. 1987-93, Chester Carlson award 1980, Ben Dasher best paper award 1985, 86, Helen Plants award 1986, William Elgin Wickenden best paper award 1986, Olmsted award, dir. 1982-84, W. Leighton Collins award 1992, Centennial medallion 1993), Am. Nuc. Soc.; mem. N.Y. Acad. Sci., Association des Ingenieurs en Genie Atomique, Rotary Club (Austin; Internat. fellow 1962), Phi Beta Kappa, Sigma Xi (disting. lectr. 1981-83), Tau Beta Pi. Mem. Soc. Of Friends. Achievements include development of computer algorithm for calculation of nuclear system reliability. Office: U Tex Dept Mech Engring Etc 5160 Austin TX 78712 Business E-Mail: koen@uts.cc.utexas.edu.

KOEN, ROBERT G., lawyer; b. 1946; BA with honors, U. Wis., 1968; JD, Georgetown U., 1972. Bar: NY 1973, US Tax Ct. 1974, NJ 1974. Ptnr. Akin Gump Strauss Hauer & Feld LLP, NYC; ptnr., comml. real estate DLA Piper US LLP, NYC, 2004—. Editor Real Estate Fin. Jour.; contbr. articles to profl. jours. Law fellow Georgetown Law Sch., 1971-72. Mem.: ABA, Commercial Real Estate Secondary Market and Securitization Assn., NY State Bar Assn., Assn. of Bar of NYC. Office: DLA Piper US LLP 1251 Ave of the Americas New York NY 10020-1104 Office Phone: 212-335-4987. Office Fax: 212-884-8487. Business E-Mail: robert.koen@piperrudnick.com.

KOENIG, ALLEN EDWARD, higher education consultant; b. Feb. 11, 1939; s. Edward and Eva (Barnes) Koenig; m. Judy Lynn Gill, June 8, 1969; children: Wendy, Jody, Mark. BA, U. So. Calif., 1961; MA, Stanford U., 1962; PhD, Northwestern U., 1964. Asst. prof. speech Ea. Mich. State U., Ypsilanti, 1964—65, U. Wis.-Milw., 1965—67, Ohio State U., Columbus, 1967—69; dir. comm. AAUP, Washington, 1969—70; v.p. devel. Capital U., Columbus, 1970—74; exec. v.p. Marycrest Coll., Davenport, Iowa, 1974—75; assoc. dir. U. So. Calif.-Idyllwild Campus, 1975—76, exec. dir., 1976—79; pres. Emerson Coll., Boston, 1979—89, Chapman U., Orange, Calif., 1989—91; sr. assoc. Thomas H. Langevin & Assoc., 1992—2002; sr. cons. R.H. Perry & Assocs., 1993—. Prof. cons. radio TV stas. Appalachia Ednl. Lab., Charleston, W.Va., 1967—69; mem. commn. on leadership devel. Am. Coun. on Edn., Washington, 1984—86; cofounder Registry Coll. and U. Pres., 1992, vice chmn., 2003—; vis. prof. mass comm. Boston U., 1991—92. Sr. editor: The Farther Vision: Educational Television Today, 1967; editor: Broadcasting and Bargaining: Labor Relations in Radio and Television, 1970, Jour. Ednl. Broadcasting Rev., 1967—69; contbr. articles to profl. jours. Bd. mem., v.p., treas., pres. Profl. Arts Consortium, Boston, 1981—89; exec. bd. dirs. pres.'s steering com. Boston Pub. Schs., 1982—86; trustee Marycrest Coll., Davenport, 1982—86. Recipient Broadcast Preceptor award, San Francisco State Coll., 1969, 1971. Mem.: NATAS (bd. govs. New Eng. chpt. 1980—84, pres. 1988—89), Mass. Corp. for Ednl. Telecomm. (chmn. 1989), Assn. Ind. Colls. and Univs. in Mass. (exec. com. 1983—89), Alpha Kappa Delta, Alpha Epsilon Rho. Office Phone: 614-798-0538. E-mail: akoenig@columbus.rr.com.

KOENIG, HAROLD MARTIN, former United States Navy surgeon general; b. Salinas, Calif., Feb. 28, 1940; m. Deena Prescott; children: Steven Fillmore, Scott Osborne, Grant Matthew. BS, Brigham Young U., 1962; MD, Baylor U., 1966. Diplomate Am. Acad. Pediatrics, Pediatric Hematology and Oncology. Commd. lt. USN, 1958, advanced through grades to vice adm.; gen. med. officer Fleet Activities, Sasebo, Japan, 1967-69; resident, fellow Naval Hosp., San Diego, 1969-73, head pediatric, hematology-oncology div., 1973-80; chief pediatrics Naval Regional Med. Ctr., Oakland, Calif., 1980-83; dir. med. svcs. Naval Hosp., Oakland, 1983-84, exec. officer Portsmouth, Va., 1984-85, comdg. officer San Diego, 1985-87, Naval Health Scis. Edn. and Tng. Command, Bethesda, Md., 1987-88; dir. health care ops. div. Office of Surgeon Gen./Naval Medicine, Washington, 1988-90; dep. asst. sec. def. Health Svcs. Ops., Office of Sec. Def., Washington, 1990-94; surgeon gen. USN, Washington, 1994-98, ret., 1998. Contbr. articles to profl. jours. Decorated Def. Superior Svc. medal, Legion of Merit (2); recipient 4 other personal awards, Navy disting. svc. medal. Fellow Am. Acad. Pediatrics (chmn. mil. sect. 1982-84), Am. Soc. Hematology; mem. AMA, other med. socs. Home: 4933 Marlborough Dr San Diego CA 92116-2346 Personal E-mail: eaglesct@cox.net.

KOENIG, HAROLD PAUL, management consultant, ecologist, evangelist, writer; b. Mason City, Iowa, Apr. 22, 1926; s. Reuben Harold and Dorothea (Paule) K.; m. Barbara Anne Rucker, June 29, 1974; children: Kimberley Anne, Joseph Paul, Liberty U. Student, Ohio Wesleyan U., 1944-45; BS, Iowa State U., 1947; MS, Ill. Inst. Tech., 1956. Registered profl. engr., Iowa, Minn., Ill., Ind., Fla.; ordained to ministry Bapt. Ch., 1994. Chief engr. Grain Processing Corp., Muscatine, Iowa, 1948-50; engr. mgr. Standard Oil Co. Ind., Whiting, Ind., 1953-56; with Booz, Allen & Hamilton, Chgo. and Genoa, Italy, 1956-64; v.p. Dresser Industries, Inc., Dallas, 1964-67; founder, chmn., pres., CEO Ecol. Sci. Corp., Miami and Lugano, Switzerland, 1967-73, Tele-Optics, Inc., West Palm Beach, Fla., 1986-90; chmn., pres., CEO Unionam., Inc. subs. Windham Power Lifts, Elba, Ala., 1974-76; dir. gen., CEO Matisa, S.A., Lausanne, Switzerland, 1977-78; dir. gen. Canron Pipe & Hydraulics, Montreal, Que., Can., 1978-80; COO Tel-Tech Devices, Inc., Ft. Lauderdale, Fla., 1984-86; chmn. H.P. Koenig Mgmt. Cons., Miami, 1980-84, Jupiter, Satellite Beach, Melbourne, Fla., 1990—. Cert. trainer Evang. Explosion Internat., Ft. Lauderdale, 1981—, cert. Evang. Explosion lectr., West Palm Beach, 1991—; advisor Citizens Democracy Corps, Russia, 1996-97, Ukraine, 1998; lectr. in field. Author: Winning Against Satan-Applying Military Principles to Spiritual Warfare, 1991; contbr. articles to profl. jours. Witness on environ. and ecol. matters U.S. Congress, Washington, 1969-71; adv. for founding Earth Day, 1970; mem. Citizens Democracy Corps, Khabarovsk, Sakhalin Island, Russia, 1996, Velikie Luki, Russia, 1997, Odessa and Nikolaev, Ukraine, 1998; adv. for Drug Treatment Fla., 1998-; mem. Pres. Nixon's Com. on Environ. Quality, 1969-72; deacon Bapt. Ch., missionary to Kenya; founder, pres., CEO H.E.A.R.T. (Help Early Addicts Receive Treatment), 1999-; scoutmaster, Iowa, 1949-50. Lt. comdr. USNR, 1943-46; PTO Seabees, 1951-53. Recipient Eagle Scout award with bronze, silver, gold palms, Boy Scouts Am., 1942, Meritorious Svc. award, Govt. of Italy, 1962, Ziegenhein award, PREVENT of Brevard, 2005. Mem. Phi Gamma Delta (Golden Owl award), Gideon. Republican. Avocations: tennis, bridge, golf. Home and Office: 705 Palmer Way Melbourne FL 32940 Home Phone: 321-752-4485, 321-544-8455; Office Phone: 321-752-4485.

KOENIG, JACK L., chemist, educator; b. Cody, Nebr., Feb. 12, 1933; s. John and Lucille (Ewart) K.; m. Jeanus Brosz, July 5, 1953; children: John, Robert, Stan, Lori. BS, Yankton Coll., 1955; MS, U. Nebr., 1957, PhD, 1959. Chemist E. I. DuPont, Wilmington, Del., 1959-63; prof. Case Western Res. U., Cleve., 1963—. Program officer NSF, Washington, 1972-74. Author: Chemical Microstructure of Polymer Chains, 1982, Spectroscopy of Polymers, 1992; co-author: Physical Chemistry of Polymers, 1985, Theory of Vibrational Spectroscopy of Polymers, 1987. With U.S. Army, 1953-55. Recipient Disting. Lectr. award BASF, 1990, Internat. Rsch. award Soc. Plastics Engrs., 1991, Disting. Svc. award Cleve. Tech. Socs. Coun., 1991, Pioneer in Polymer Sci. award Polymer New Mag., 1991, ACS award in applied polymer sci. Am. Chem. Soc., 1997. Fellow Am. Physics Soc.; mem. NAE, Am. Chem. Soc. (award in applied polymer sci. 1997), Soc. Applied Spectroscopy. Achievements include research in characterization of polymers by spectroscopic methods. Office: Case Western Res U 10900 Euclid Ave # 7202 Cleveland OH 44106-1712 Home Phone: 440-338-3213; Office Phone: 216-368-4176. Business E-Mail: Jack.Koenig@case.edu, jlkg@case.edu.

KOENIG, KRISTI L., emergency physician; MD, Mt. Sinai Sch. Medicine, NYC. Diplomate Am. Bd. Emergency Medicine. Nat. dir., emergency mgmt. office Fed. Dept. Vets. Affairs, Washington, 1999—2004; dir. pub. health preparedness, dept. emergency medicine U. Calif. at Irvine, Orange, Calif., 2004—. Inivted spkr. and lectr. in field. Contbr. numerous articles to profl. jours. Achievements include expert in the fields of Homeland Security, disaster and emergency medicine, emergency management, and emergency medical services (EMS). Office Phone: 714-456-5239. Business E-Mail: kkoenig@uci.edu.

KOENIG, MAUREEN CATHERINE, science educator; b. LA, June 11, 1949; d. Robert Curtis and Lucille Catherine Martin; m. William Richard Koenig, Sept. 12, 1970; children: Kristin Maureen, Ryan Patrick. BS in Biology, Loyola Marymount U., 1971; MS in Edn., U. So. Calif., 2001. Clear single subject tchg. credential in life sci. Commn. on Tchr. Credentialing, State of Calif., 1992. Med. technologist, bacteriologist specialist, co-dept. head bacteriology, edn. coord. sch. of med. tech. Daniel Freeman Hosp., Ingelwood, Calif., 1971—78; tchr. sci., math, computer St. Anthony Claret Sch., Anaheim, Calif., 1987—2001; 7th & 8th grade sci. tchr. Yorba Linda Mid. Sch., Calif., 2002, sci. dept. chair, 2004—. Presenter in field. Recipient ExploraVisions awards Competition - US Western Regional Winner, Nat. Sci. Tchrs. Assn., Toshiba, 1998, Innovation in Edn. award, Project Tomorrow, 2006. Mem.: NSTA (assoc.), Orange County Sci. Educators Assn. (assoc.), Calif. Sci. Tchrs. Assn. (assoc.), Phi Kappa Phi (life). Avocations: hiking, dinosaur excavation, ATV riding, snowmobiling, skiing. Home Phone: 714-779-0905; Office Phone: 714-528-7090. Office Fax: 714-996-2752. Personal E-mail: mo_koenig@hotmail.com. E-mail: mkoenig@pylusd.org.

KOENIG, ROBERT AUGUST, minister, educator; b. Red Wing, Minn., July 14, 1933; s. William C. and Florence E. (Tebbe) Koenig; m. Pauline Louise Olson, June 21, 1962. BS cum laude, U. Wis., Superior, 1955; MA in Ednl. Adminstrn., U. Minn., 1965, PhD, 1973; MDiv magna cum laude, San Francisco Theol. Sem., 1969; postgrad. (John Hay fellow), Bennington Coll., summer, 1965. Ordained to ministry Presbyn. Ch., 1970. Supr. music Florence (Wis.) H.S., 1955—56; dir. instrumental music Chetek (Wis.) Pub. Schs., 1958—62; tchr. instrumental music and humanities Palo Alto (Calif.) Sr. H.S., 1962—65; asst. to min. St. John's Presbyn. Ch., San Francisco, 1964—65; min. Sawyer County (Wis.) larger parish, 1969—74; tchr. gen. music Jordan Jr. H.S., Palo Alto, 1966—69; instr. Coll. Edn. U. Minn., 1969—71; adminstv. asst. to pres. Lakewood State C.C., White Bear Lake, Minn., 1971—72; asst. to exec. dir. Minn. Higher Edn. Coord. Bd., St. Paul, 1972, coord. commn. and pers. svcs., 1972—74; instr. Inver Hills C.C., Inver Grove Heights, Minn., 1974; pastor First Presbyn. Ch. of Chippewa Falls (Wis.), 1974—85; sr. pastor Grove Presbyn. Ch., Danville, Pa., 1985—88, First Presbyn. Ch., South St. Paul, Minn., 1988—98; stated supply pastor Couderay and Radisson Presbyn. Chs., Wis., 1999—. Mem. study com. Presbytery of Chippewa, 1973—74, mem. min. rels. com., 1974—77; adj. asst. prof. ednl. adminstrn. U. Minn., Mpls., 1976—77; mem. faculty U. Wis. Ext., Eau Claire, 1977; chmn. 3d Ann. Bibl. Sem., 1977; mem. faculty Communiversity, 1977—85; mem. ministerial rels. com. Presbytery of No. Waters, 1977—82, chmn., 1981—82, moderator, 1983; mem. internat. coord. com. ch. mission Synod Lakes and Prairies, 1978—79; chmn. Synod Designation Pastor Plan Cabinet, 1982—84, Presbytery Coun., 1982—84, mem., 1987—88; chairperson Christian edn. com. Presbytery of Northumberland, 1987—88; mem. Christian edn. com. Synod of the Trinity, 1987—88; mem. com. ministry Presbytery of Twin Cities Area, 1999—2001, Danville-Riverside Area Ministerial Assn., 1985—88, pres., 1987—88; mem. South St. Paul Ministerial Assn., 1988—98, pres., 1989—90. Contbr. articles to profl. jours. Bd. dirs. N. Ctrl. Career Devel. Ctr., Mpls., 1978—84, chmn. fin. com., 1979—84, bd. dirs. devel. found., 1983—85; pres. Chippewa Valley Ecumenical Housing Assn., 1984—85; bd. dirs. Coll. Edn. and Human Devel. Alumni Soc. U. Minn., 1999—2005, mem. exec. com., 2001—05, v.p., 2001—02, pres., 2002—04. With US Army, 1956—58, Korea. Nominee One of 100 Most Disting. Alumni of U. of Minn.'s Coll. Edn. and Human Devel., 2006. Mem.: Heritage Soc., Pres. Club U. Minn., Elks (Danville chpt.), Masons (grand chaplain Wis. chpt. 1977—80, 1983—85), Phi Delta Kappa. Home: 6045 Bowman Ave E Inver Grove Heights MN 55076-1502 Office Phone: 651-552-1175.

KOENIG, ROBERT EMIL, clergyman; b. St. Louis, Aug. 31, 1919; s. Hermann Emil and Martha Ida (Baur) K.; m. Norma Caroline Evans, July 18, 1943; children: Elsa Koenig Weber, Robert, Richard, Martha Koenig Stone, Thea Koenig Burton, Laura Koenig Godinez. BS, U. Chgo., 1941; BD, Chgo. Theol. Sem., 1945; PhD, U. Chgo., 1953; DD, Elmhurst Coll., 1987. Pastor St. John's Evang. & Reformed Ch., Hinsdale, Ill., 1943-46; from instr. to assoc. prof. religion Elmhurst (Ill.) Coll., 1946-54; dir. curriculum Bd. Christian Edn., Phila., 1954-61; editor-in-chief United Ch. Bd. for Homeland Ministries, Phila., 1961-84; interim pastor St. Paul's United Ch. Christ, Fort Washington, Pa., 1985-87, Bethany United Ch. Christ, Phila., First United Ch. of Christ, Quakertown, Pa., St. Vincent United Ch. of Christ, Phoenixville, Pa., Collenbrook United Ch., Brownback's United Ch. of Christ, Spring City, Boehm's United Ch. of Christ, 1988—2003; adj. prof. Christian edn. Lancaster (Pa.) Theol. Sem., 1988-89; cons., dir. Koenig Ch. Edn. Cons., Inc., Havertown, Pa., 1988—2006; ret., 1984. Adj. instr. Defiance Coll., 1995-2000. Mng. editor PRISM Mag., 1990—. Pres. Ardmore (Pa.) Jr. High Home and Sch. Assn., 1962-63; mem. Penn Wynne (Pa.) Libr. Bd., 1985-89; pres. Univ. Glee Club of Phila., 1987-88; mem. ElderNet, Lower Merion, Pa., 1986—, pres., 1988-89, treas., 1994-96. Mem. Haverford Twp. Clergy Assn. (treas. 1990-2006). Democrat. Avocations: singing, playing violin, hiking. Home and Office: Phoebe Berks Village #69 1 Reading Dr Wernersville PA 19565

KOENIG, ROBERT LOUIS, writer; b. Honolulu, Oct. 18, 1951; m. Mary Ellen Noonan, May 25, 1979; children: Laura Ann, Mark Robert, Christopher James, Claire Ellen. BA in English, Wash. U., St. Louis, 1973; MA in English, Tulane U., New Orleans, 1974; MA in Journalism, U. Mo., Columbia, 1975. Corr. St. Louis Post-Dispatch, DC, 1987—94; Germany corr. Sci., Berlin, 1995—97, ctrl. European corr. Bern, Switzerland, 1997—2001; publications dir. Inst. Genomic Rsch., Rockville, Md., 2002—05; contbg corr. Sci. jour., DC, 2005—. Author: (book) The Fourth Horseman, 2007. Recipient Wash. Corr. award, Nat. Press Club, 1994. Mem.: U. Rsch. Mags. Orgn., Nat. Assn. Sci. Writers. Personal E-mail: rob.koenig@gmail.com.

KOENIG, RODNEY CURTIS, lawyer, rancher; b. Black Jack, Tex., Nov. 21, 1940; s. John Henry and Elva Marguerite (Oeding) K.; m. Mary Mishler, May 1, 1993; children: Erik Jason, Jon Todd. BA, U. Tex., 1962, JD with honors, 1969; postgrad., Auburn U., 1965-67. Bar: Tex. 1969, U.S. Dist. Ct. (so. dist.) Tex. 1970, U.S. Ct. Appeals (5th cir.) 1970, U.S. Tax Ct. 1980, U.S. Ct. Mil. Appeals 1986. Ptnr. Fulbright & Jaworski, LLP, Houston, 1969—. Asst. prof. Auburn U., 1965-67; lectr. in field Contbr. articles to profl. jours. Pres. Houston Navy League, 1979-81; mem. Battleship Texas Commn.; bd. dirs. Houston divsn. Am. Heart Assn., Fayette Heritage Mus., St. Mark's Med. Ctr. Found.; dir. Advanced Estate Planning and Probate Course, 1988, Crawford & Hattie Jackson Found.; trustee Luck and Loessin Collection Trust, Luth. Found. of the S.W., treas., exec. com.; active Tex. Luth. U. Corp.; co-chair Planned Giving Adv. Coun., U. Tex., 2005—. With USN, 1962—67, capt. JAGC USNR, 1967—89. Recipient Fed. Republic of Germany Order of Merit, 1994. Fellow Am. Coll. Trust and Estate Counsel, Coll. State Bar Tex. (charter); mem. ABA, Internat. Acad. Estate and Trust Law (academician, exec. com.), Tex. Judge Adv. Res. Officers Assn., German Texan Heritage Soc. (pres. 1997-2000), Tex. German Soc. (founding dir.), Res. Officers Assn., Sons of Republic of Tex., Wednesday Tax Forum (past chmn.), German Gulf Coast Assn. (pres. 1989-93), Bach Soc. (bd. dirs., v.p. 2005—), English Speaking Union (bd. dir., v.p.), Houston Early Music (pres. 2000-04), Houston Karneval Verein (prince 1994-95), USS San Jacinto Com. (treas.), Houstonian Club, Frisch Auf Valley Country Club, Order of Coif, US Naval Order, U.T. NROTC Alumni Assn. (pres. 2000-02), Houston Saengerbund (pres. 2006—), Phi Delta Phi, Omicron Delta Kappa. Lutheran. Home: 2720 University Blvd Houston TX 77005-3440 Office: Fulbright & Jaworski LLP 1301 Mckinney St Fl 51 Houston TX 77010-3031 Office Phone: 713-651-5333. Business E-Mail: rkoenig@fulbright.com.

KOENIG, WILLIAM S., sports association executive; m. Melinda Witmer; children: Stephen, Samantha. B with honors in Econs., Harvard U., 1983; M in Econs. and Indsl. Rels., London Sch. Econs., 1984; JD, U. Pa. Sch. Law, 1987. Atty. Proskauer, Goetz & Mendelsohn; staff atty. NBA, 1990, asst. gen. counsel, gen. counsel, 1994—99; exec. v.p. bus. affairs, gen. counsel NBA Entertainment, 1999—. Office: NBA Entertainment 450 Harmon Meadow Blvd Secaucus NJ 07094*

KOENIGER, ALFRED CASH, history professor; b. Little Rock, Mar. 16, 1949; s. Alfred William and Mary Tom Koeniger; m. Rachel Lynn Flora, July 5, 1980; 1 child, Anderson Cash. AB with honors, Washington & Lee U., 1971; MA, Vanderbilt U., 1974, PhD, 1980. Vis. instr. Murray (Ky.) State U., 1979—80; vis. asst. prof. Miss. State U., Starkville, 1980—81; asst. prof. U. So. Miss., Natchez, 1981—86; assoc. prof. Va. Mil. Inst., Lexington, 1986—90, prof., 1990—. Coord. social studies U. So. Miss., Natchez, 1981—86; vis. prof. Washington & Lee U., Lexington, Va., 2003—04; exec. dir. Alumni Coll. at Va. Mil. Inst., Inc., Lexington, 1996—2007, pres. bd. dirs., 2004—07. Contbr. articles to profl. jours., chapters to books. Mem. adv. com. Brownsburg Mus., Va., 2006; elder New Providence Presbyn. Ch., Brownsburg, 1991—. Rsch. grantee, Am. Philos. Soc., 1982, AASLH/NEH, 1984. Mem.: So. Hist. Assn., Sigma Chi (v.p. bd. dirs. ho. corp. Zeta chpt. 1995—2006). Avocation: gardening. Office: Dept History Va Mil Inst Lexington VA 24450 Office Phone: 540-464-7470. Office Fax: 540-464-7246. E-mail: koenigerac@vmi.edu.

KOENIGSKNECHT, ROY A., dean; b. Fowler, Mich., Dec. 27, 1942; s. Joseph I. and Katherine (Zimmermann) K.; m. Marilie A. Dani, Aug. 20, 1966; children: John, Adam, Amanda. AB in Psychology, Central Mich. U., 1964; MA in Speech and Lang. Pathology, Northwestern U., 1965, PhD in Communicative Disorders, 1968. Head speech and lang. pathology Northwestern U., Evanston, Ill., 1973-78, prof. speech and lang. pathology, 1975-85, chair communicative disorders, 1978-81, assoc. dean Grad. Sch., 1981-85; prof. speech and hearing sci. Ohio State U, Columbus, 1985—; dean Grad. Sch. Ohio State U., Columbus, 1985-95; v.p. Ohio State U. Rsch. Found., Columbus, 1985-95. Mem. Grad. Record Exams. Bd., 1991-95, NIH adv. bd. on deafness and other communicative disorders, 1990-95; cons. evaluator Commn. on Instns. Higher Edn., 1996—. Author: Developmental Sentence Analysis, 1974; Interactive Language Development, 1975. Contbr. articles to profl. jours. Mem. adv. coun. on grad. study Ohio Bd. Regents, Columbus, 1985-95; bd. dirs. Friends of Evanston Pub. Libr., 1984, Evanston Pub. Libr., 1985. Recipient Disting. Alumni award Central Mich. U., 1977; Fulbright fellow, 1982. Fellow Am. Speech-Lang. Hearing Assn. (exec. bd. 1986-91, pres. 1990), AAU Assn. Grad. Schs.), Com. on Instnl. Cooperation Grad. Deans (chair 1985-86), Nat. Assn. State U. and Land Grant Colls.- Coun. Rsch. Pol. and Grad. Edn. (exec. com. 1995-96), Torch Club Columbus (pres. 2005-2006). Avocations: golf, skiing. Home: 720 Gatehouse Ln Columbus OH 43235-1732 Office: Ohio State U 105 Pressey Hall Columbus OH 43210-1335 Home Phone: 614-888-8339; Office Phone: 614-292-8118. Business E-Mail: koenigsknecht.1@oso.edu.

KOENKER, DIANE P., history professor; b. Chgo., July 29, 1947; m. Roger Koenker; 1 child. AB in History, Grinnell Coll., 1969; AM in Comparative Studies in History, U. Mich., 1971, PhD in History, 1976. From asst. prof. to assoc. prof. in history Temple U., Phila., 1976-83; asst. prof. history U. Ill., Urbana-Champaign, 1983-86, assoc. prof., 1986-88, prof. history, 1988—, dir. Russian and East European Ctr., 1990-96, editor Slavic Rev., 1996—2006. Vis. lectr. history U. Ill., Urbana-Champaign, 1975; vis. fellow Australian Nat. U., 1989, Fulbright-Hays Faculty Rsch. Abroad, 1993; lectr. in field. Author: Moscow Workers and the 1917 Revolution, 1981, paperback edit., 1986, (with William G. Rosenberg) Strikes and Revolution in Russia 1917, 1989, Republic of Labor: Russian Printers and Soviet Socialism, 1918-1930, 2005; editor: Third All-Russian Trade Union Conference 1917, 1982, (with William G. Rosenberg and Ronald Grigor Suny) Party, State and Society in the Russian Civil War: Explorations in Social History, 1989, (with Ronald D. Bachman) Revelations from the Russian Archives, 1997, (with Anne E. Gorsuch) Truizm: The Russian and East European Tourist under Capitalism and Socialism, 2006; editor, translator: (with S.A. Smith) Notes of a Red Guard, 1993; mem. editl. bd. Cambridge Soviet Paperbacks; mem. adv. bd. Soviet Studies in History, 1986-89; book reviewer to numerous jours.; contbr. articles to profl. jours. Fellow Temple U., 1977, 82, Russian Inst.-Columbia U., 1977-78, NEH, 1983-84, NEH, 1984-85, 94-95, MUCIA Exch. fellow Moscow State U., 1991, Guggenheim Found., 2006; grantee Am. Coun. Learned Socs.-Social Sci. Rsch. Coun., 1977-78, Temple U., 1979-81, 82-83, William and Flora Hewlett Internat. Rsch. grant, 1986, 91, Nat. Coun. for Soviet and East European Rsch., 1989, Arnold O. Beckman Rsch. Bd. grant, 1990-91, 2002—, IREX Travel grant, 1993, 2006, Nat. coun. Eurasian and East European Rsch. grant, 2007; recipient Fulbright-Hays Faculty Rsch. award for USSR, 1989. Mem. Am. Hist. Assn. (mem. membership com. 1996-98, European History sect. chair 2001, Chester Higby prize European sect. 2003), Am. Assn. Advancement Slavic Studies (bd. dirs. 1996—), Midwest Workshop of Russian and Soviet Historians, Assn. Women in Slavic Studies. also: U Ill Dept History 810 S Wright St Urbana IL 61801-3644

KOEPFINGER, JOSEPH LEO, retired utilities executive; b. Sewickley, Pa., May 6, 1925; s. Joseph P. and Mary M. (O'Hanlon) K.; m. Genevieve C. Strobel, Oct. 1, 1955; children: Nancy, Joseph, Margaret, Patricia, James, Paul. BSEE, U. Pitts., 1949, MSEE, 1953. Jr. devel. engr. Duquesne Light Co., Pitts., 1949-52, devel. engr., 1952-54, sr. devel. engr., 1954-57, project engr., 1957-61, sr. project engr., 1961-64, projection and comml. engr., 1964-80, dir. project and comml. dept., 1980-85, dir. sys. studies and rsch., 1985-2000, ret., 2000, ind. cons., 2000—. Chmn. accredited std. com. C62, Am. Nat. Std. Inst.; bd. dirs. Mehta Tech. Inc.; U.S. tech. adv. Internat. Electrotech. Commn., 1979—2007, post sec. for IEC C37, 1996—2007; advisor to Lane dept. computer sci. and elec. engring. acad. W.Va. U., IEEE Power Engring. Soc. disting. lectr. Prin. writer standard Guide for Surge Withstand Capability Test, 1974 Pres. Moon Area Sch. Dist., Moon Twp., Pa., 1978-79. With U.S. Army, 1943-45, ETO. Fellow IEEE (mem. emeritus stds. bd., Charles P. Steimetz award 1989), IEEE Power Engring. Soc. (Excellence in Power Distbn. Engring. award 1998, IEC 1906 award 2006). Democrat. Roman Catholic. Home: 119 Windy Willow Dr Coraopolis PA 15108-2945

KOEPKE, ALLEN HENRY, music educator, composer; b. Chgo., Apr. 20, 1939; s. Henry Emil and Dorothy Laura Frieda (Theel) Koepke; m. Sherril Lynn Head, June 8, 1986; children: Scott, Amy Koepke Hanisch, Ann, Stephen stepchildren: Amy Reedy Davis, Chad Reedy, Ryan Reedy. BA, Luther Coll., Decorah, Iowa, 1960; MA, U. Northern Iowa, Cedar Falls, 1967. Cert. permanent tchg. Iowa Dept. Edn., 1967. Dir. choral activities Clear Lake Cmty. Schs., Clear Lake, Iowa, 1960—67, Jefferson H.S., Cedar Rapids, 1967—80, Kirkwood C.C., 1980—96; choir dir. Springfield Luth. Ch., Decorah, 1957—58, Calmar Luth. Ch., 1958—60, First Congregational Ch., Clear Lake, 1960—67, St. Stephens Luth. Ch., Cedar Rapids, 1967—72, Trinity Meth. Ch., 1972—83, All Saints Cath. Ch., 1983—85, St. John's Christ Episcopal Ch., 1985—97, St. Mark's Luth. Ch., Iowa, 1998—. Musical and tour dir. The Young Americans, LA, 1969; mem. artistic com. Cedar Rapids Symphony Orch., 1998—; bd. dir. Heuer Publs., Iowa. Composer: Missa Brevis, 1995, In Praise of Music, 1996, A Vision, A Dream, 1996, over 60 published works. Initiator Show Choir, Iowa, 1968, Collegiate Jazz Choir, Iowa, 1983; musical dir. Cedar Rapids Follies, 1979—83, NAACP prodn. Kismet, Cedar Rapids, 1982. Recipient Iowa Prof. of Yr., Carnegie Found. Advancement of Tchg., 1996, Innovator of Yr., League for Innovation, 1996. Mem.: Am. Choral Dirs. Assn., Iowa Choral Dirs. Assn. (Robert M. McCowen Meml. award 1997). Lutheran. Avocations: reading, golf, crossword puzzles. Personal E-mail: ahkoepke@aol.com. E-mail: allen@koepkemusic.com.

KOEPKE, JOHN ARTHUR, hematologist, clinical pathologist; b. Milw., Mar. 25, 1929; s. Elmer Paul and Meta Clara (Jennrich) K.; m. Evelyn Mae Lovekamp, June 18, 1955; children: Mary Evelyn, John Frederick, Mark David, James Robert. BA, Valparaiso U., 1951; MD, U. Wis., 1956; MS, Marquette U., 1964. Intern, resident in clin. pathology and internal medicine Milw. Hosp., 1956-60; mem. faculty U. Ky. Coll. Medicine, 1961-71, assoc. prof., 1965-71; dir. clin. pathology, prof. pathology U. Iowa, Iowa City, 1972-79, vice chmn. dept., 1972-79; prof. pathology, assoc. prof. internal medicine Coll. Medicine, Duke U., Durham, NC, 1979-94; dir.clin. transfusion svc. hematology lab. Duke U. Med. Ctr., 1979-88, prof. emeritus, 1994—. Vis. scientist Karolinska Inst., Stockholm, 1967-68, Royal Postgrad. Med. Sch., London, 1978. Author 7 books in field; editor 6 books; bd. editors Am. Jour. Clin. Pathology, 1976—, Clin. and Lab. Hematology, 1978-94, Blood Cells, 1985-98; assoc. editor Cytometry, 1993-1998, Comms. in Clin. Cytometry, 1994-99, Lab. Hematology, 1994—; contbr. over 250 articles to profl. jours., 25 chpts. to books. Recipient Pres.'s award Valparaiso U., 1951, also Disting. Alumnus award, 1980. Fellow Am. Soc. Clin. Pathology, Coll. Am. Pathologists; mem. AMA, Internat. Coun. for Standards in Hematology (secretariat 1978—, v.p. 1990-92, pres. 1992-94). Lutheran. Home: 3924 Saint Mark's Rd Durham NC 27707-5015 Personal E-mail: nckoepke@mindspring.com.

KOEPKE, TRACEY LYNN, marketing professional, writer; b. Willimantic, Conn., Aug. 1, 1969; d. Alan John and Barbara Ann (Savitsky) Koepke. BA, U. Conn., Storrs, 1992; postgrad., Duke U., Durham, NC, 2006—. Asst. sales mgr. Filene's, West Hartford, Conn., 1992—93; substitute tchr. Coventry Pub. Schs., Conn., 1993—94; pub. rels. asst. U. Conn., Storrs, 1994—96; rschr. and story coord. InSight Productions, Inc., Durham, 1996—98; rsch. office mgr. Sch. Pharmacy, U. NC, Chapel Hill, 1998—99; sr. pub. info. officer Duke U. Med. Ctr. News Office, Durham, 1999—2007; mktg. mgr. Duke U. Health Sys., 2007—. Vol. Durham Rescue Mission, 1998—2004, Immaculate Conception Ch., Durham, 1998—2007, ARC, Chapel Hill, 1997—99. Recipient High Flyer award, Duke Emergency Svcs. Dept., 2001. Mem.: Nat. Assn. Sci. Writers, Kappa Kappa Gamma. Office: Univ Tower 3100 Tower Blvd Rm 1006B Durham NC 27707 Home Phone: 919-419-0187; Office Phone: 919-419-5012. Personal E-mail: tracey.koepke@gmail.com. Business E-Mail: koepk002@mc.duke.edu.

KOEPP, DONNA PAULINE PETERSEN, librarian; b. Clinton, Iowa, Oct. 8, 1941; d. Leo August and Pauline Sena (Outzen) Petersen; m. David Ward Koepp, June 5, 1960 (div. June 1984). BS in Edn., U. Colo., 1967; MA in Libr., U. Denver, 1974; postgrad., U. Colo., 1984-85. Subject specialist govt. publs., map dept. Denver Pub. Libr., 1967-85; head govt. documents, map libr. U. Kans., Lawrence, 1985-2000, map and geomedia svcs. libr., 2000—02. Head govt. document, microforms, reference instrn. Soc. Sci. Program Harvard U., 2002-; apptd. Fed. Depository Libr. Coun. to Pub. Printer, 1998-2001. Prodn. mgr. Meridian Jour., 1988-93, 96-99; editor: Index and Carto-Bibliography of Maps, 1789-1969, 1995. Recipient Documents to the People award Congl. Info. Svc./Govt. Documents Round Table/ALA, 1999. Mem. Map & Geography Round Table of Am. Libr. Assn. (chmn. 1986-87, Outstanding Contbn. to Map Librarianship 1991), Govt. Documents Round Table of Am. Libr. Assn., Western Assn. Map Librs. (sec. 1983-84). Office: Govt Documents Microforms Libr Lamont Libr Lower Level U Harvard College Libr Cambridge MA 02138- Office Phone: 617-495-2105. Business E-Mail: koepp@fas.harvard.edu.

KOEPP, STEPHEN, editor; b. Wis., 1956; BA in journalism, U. Wis. Eau Claire, 1978. News reporter, city editor Waukesha Freeman, Wis., 1978—81; with letters dept. Time mag., NYC, 1981, bus. reporter, 1981—83, staff writer, 1983—86, assoc. editor, 1986—88, sr. editor, 1988—94, asst. mng. editor, 1994—2001, dep. mng. editor, 2001—; editor Time.com, 2006. Office: Time & Life Bldg Rockefeller Ctr 1271 Ave of the Americas New York NY 10020-1393 Office Phone: 212-522-3575. Office Fax: 212-522-0003. E-mail: stephen_koepp@timemagazine.com.

KOEPPEL, GARY MERLE, publishing executive, art gallery owner, writer; b. Albany, Oreg., Jan. 20, 1938; s. Carl Melvin and Barbara Emma (Adams) K.; m. Emma Katerina Koeppel, May 20, 1984. BA, Portland State U., 1961; MFA, State U. Iowa, 1963. Writing instr. State U. Iowa, Iowa City, 1963-64; guest prof. English U. P.R., San Juan, 1964-65; assoc. prof. creative writing Portland (Oreg.) State U., 1965-68; owner, operator Coast Gallery, Big Sur, 1971—, Pebble Beach, Calif., 1986—, Maui, Hawaii, 1985—, Hana, Hawaii, 1991—, Carmel, Calif., 2003—; owner Coast Pub. Co., Coast Seri Graphics, Coast Advt., Coast Lic., 1991—. Editor, pub. Big Sur Gazette, 1978-81; producer, sponsor Maui Marine Art Expo., 1984-95, Calif. Marine Art Expo., Paris Marine Art Expo., Hawaiian Cultural Arts Expo., 1993; founder, pres. Global Art Expos1994, Planet Big Sur, 1996, Coast Constrn., 1998; founder ideasbank.com, 1999, investmentart.com, 2001; co-founder Automotive Expo, 2004. Author: Sculptured Sandcast Candles, 1974, Henry Miller, The Paintings, 1991. Founder Big Sur Vol. Fire Brigade, 1975; founder, pres. Enduring Freedom Found., 2006; chmn. coordinating com. Big Sur Area Planning, 1972-75; chmn. Big Sur Citizens Adv. Com., 1975-78. Mem. Am. Soc. Appraisers, Big Sur C. of C. (pres. 74-75, 82-84), Big Sur Grange, Phi Gamma Delta, Alpha Delta Sigma. Address: Coast Gallery PO Box 223519 Carmel CA 93922-3519 Business E-Mail: gary@coastgalleries.com.

KOEPPEL, HOLLY KELLER, electric power industry executive; b. Pitts., May 17, 1958; married; 2 children. BS in Bus., Ohio State U., Columbus; MS in Bus., Ohio State U. From mgr. to v.p. Asia-Pacific Ops. Consolidated Natural Gas, Sydney, Australia, 1984—2000; v.p. new ventures for corp. devel. Am. Electric Power Co., Columbus, Ohio, 2000—02, exec. v.p. comml. ops., 2002—04, exec. v.p. AEP Utilities East, 2004—06, exec. v.p., CFO, 2006—. Office: Am Elec Power Co 1 Riverside Plz Columbus OH 43215-1000 Office Phone: 614-716-1000.*

KOEPPEL, JOHN A., lawyer; b. Jersey City, Aug. 9, 1947; s. A.J. and Florence (McDonald) K.; m. Susan Lynn Rothstein, Nov. 12, 1972; children: Adam, Leah. BA in Govt. cum laude, U. Notre Dame, 1969; MA in Internat. Law, Tufts U., 1970; JD, U. Calif., San Francisco, 1976. Bar: Calif. 1976, D.C. 1980, U.S. Dist. Ct. (no. dist.) Calif. 1976, U.S. Supreme Ct. 1980. Assoc. Barfield, Barfield, Dryden & Ruane, San Francisco, 1976-80; from assoc. to shareholder Ropers, Majeski, Kohn & Bentley, San Francisco, 1980—, resident dir., 1992-95, 97-99; mediator San Francisco Superior Ct., 1993—. Arbitrator San Francisco Superior Ct., 1979—; legal counsel San Francisco Jaycees, 1980-81, Friends of the Americas, San Francisco, 1982-84; bd. dirs. ST. Francis Homes Assn., 1985-88; instr. Hastings Coll. Advocacy, San Francisco, 1988-91; lectr. U. Calif., San Francisco, 1990-95; sec. San Francisco Casualty Claims Assn., 1993-95; bd. dirs. and legal counsel Or Shalom, 2002—05; bd. dirs. Ropers Majeski Kohn & Bentley, 1992-99, 2003—. Active Youth Sports Coaching, 1990—2000; bd. dirs. San Francisco Sch., 1998—2000, San Francisco Food Bank, 2005—. Mem. Nat. Bd. Trial Advocacy, Calif. State Bar (certificate of recognition for pro bono legal work, 1989), D.C. Bar, San Francisco Bar Assn. (Outstanding Vol. 2004, 05). Avocations: running, skiing, hiking, rowing, travel. Office: Ropers Majeski Kohn & Bentley 201 Spear St Ste 1000 San Francisco CA 94105 Home Phone: 415-664-8453; Office Phone: 415-543-4800. Business E-Mail: jkoeppel@ropers.com.

KOEPPEL, NOEL IMMANUEL, financial planner, securities broker, real estate broker; b. NYC, Apr. 30, 1930; s. Eziel and Anna (Bodian) K.; divorced; children: Thomas Joseph, Elizabeth Mansfield, Roberta Sharon. BA, U. Wis., 1952; MBA, Wharton U. of Pa., 1957. CFP. V.p. E. Koeppel, Inc., Jamaica, N.Y., 1956-77; account exec. First Investors Corp., NYC, 1977-79, Ross Stebbins Co., NYC, 1980-82; account exec., CFP Advest Inc., Forest Hills, N.Y., 1982-83, Donald & Co. Securities Inc., Jersey City, N.J., 1983-90, Stuart Coleman Co. Inc., NYC, 1990-97; account exec. Brill Sec. Inc., NYC, 1998—. Lt. (j.g.) USN, 1952-56. Mem.: Fin. Planners Assn. N.Y., Inst. CFPs, Penn Club N.Y. Avocations: skiing, sailing, hiking, classical music and art. Home: 130 E End Ave New York NY 10028-7553 Office: Brill Sec Inc 152 W 57th St Fl 16 New York NY 10019-3310 Office Phone: 212-439-1523.

KOEPPEL, PETER STAFFORD, advertising executive; s. Eugene L. and Marilyn Koeppel; m. Deborah Koeppel, May 24, 1986; 2 children. BA in Psychology magna cum laude, SUNY, Albany, 1975; MBA, U. Pa., Phila., 1980. Assoc. product mgr. H.J. Heinz, Pitts., 1980—82; product mgr. Ben Hogan Co., Ft. Worth, 1982; account supr. Richards Group, Dallas, 1983—86; ptnr. Joiner Rowland Serio Koeppel, Dallas, 1986—95; pres. Koeppel Direct, Dallas, 1995—. Adv. bd. Electronic Retailing mag., Washington, 2004—07. Contbr. articles to profl. jours. Sole sponsor FBLA Invention Showcase Scholarship Program for Young Inventors, Washington, 2006; plan competition mentor Wharton Sch. Bus., 2007—; judge bus. plan competition Wharton Sch., 2007—; hon. com. mem. Wheelchair Found., 2007—. Mem.: Electronic Retailer Assn., Direct Mktg. Assn. (broadcast coun. 2005—07, pharm. coun. 2005—07). Avocations: golf, reading, travel. Office: Koeppel Direct 16200 Dallas Pkwy 270 Dallas TX 75248 Office Phone: 972-732-6110. Business E-Mail: pkoeppel@koeppelinc.com.

KOERBER, ERICA, photographer; b. 1970; Owner, chief photographer Evon Photography; ops. mgr. Ventana Rsch. Corp. Involved with Susan G. Komen Race for the Cure, Women's Found. Southern Ariz., Youth On Their Own, Brewster Ctr. Domestic Violence Services, Angel Charity for Children, Tucson Indian Ctr., Arts for All & Third St. Kids, Humane Soc. Southern Ariz., Child Protective Services. Named one of 40 Under 40, Tucson Bus. Edge, 2006. Office: Ventana Research Corporation 2702 S4th Ave Tucson AZ 85713 Office Phone: 520-882-8772. Office Fax: 520-882-8762.

KOERNER, BRENDAN I., columnist; BA, Yale Univ. Sr. editor U.S. News & World Report; contbg. editor Wired mag.; columnist New York Times, Slate mag., Gizmodo.com. Markle fellow New America Found. Contbr. articles to New Republic, Mother Jones, Washington Monthly, Village Voice, Christian Science Monitor. Mailing: New York Times 229 W 43d St New York NY 10036 Office Phone: 212-556-7395. Business E-Mail: tips@gizmodo.com.

KOERNER, WENDELL EDWARD, JR., lawyer, mediator; b. Mexico, Mo., July 22, 1938; s. Wendell Edward and Dorothy Irene Koerner; m. Mary Jo Maday, Sept. 29, 1973 (dec. Jan. 1998); children: Jennifer L. Wolfe, R. John Maday, Greg S. Maday, Ryan E. Koerner. BS in Indsl. Mgmt., U. Kans., 1960; JD, U. Mo., Columbia, 1968. Bar: Mo. 1968, U.S. Dist. Ct. (we. dist.) Mo. 1968, U.S. Ct. Appeals (8th cir.) 1973, U.S. Dist. Ct. Kans. 1998. Assoc. Brown, Douglas & Brown, St. Joseph, Mo., 1968-71, ptnr., 1972-98, Franke & Schultz, P.C., Kansas City, Mo., 1999—. Vol. legal counsel YWCA, St. Joseph, 1983-92; temple atty. Moila Shrine Temple, St. Joseph, 1993-97; spkr. in field. Bd. dirs. Ecumenical Corp. for Housing Opportunity, St. Joseph, 1997—; vol. in probation and parole The Mo. Bar, 1971-73. Named Lawyer of Year Ben Ely Jr. award, Mo. Org. Def. Lawyers, 2006; recipient Lon O. Hocker Meml. Trial Lawyer award, Mo. Bar Found., 1973. Fellow Am. Coll. Trial Lawyers; mem. Mo. Bar, St. Joseph Bar Assn. (pres. 1985), Mo. Orgn. Def. Lawyers (pres. 1995-96), Internat. Assn. Def. Counsel, Am. Bd. Trial Advocates, Masons, Shriners. Mem. Chjistian Ch. (Disciples of Christ). Avocations: golf, fishing. Home: 4005 Miller Rd Saint Joseph MO 64505-1541 Office: 8900 Ward Pky Kansas City MO 64114 Business E-Mail: wkoerner@fsmlawfirm.com.

KOERNIG, STEPHEN K., marketing professional, educator; s. Sharon Beck and Neil Koernig. BS, U. Ill., 1989, PhD, 2000; MBA, DePaul U., Chgo., 1994. Assoc. prof. Calif. State U., Fullerton, 1999—2002; asst. prof. DePaul U., Chgo., 2002—. Contbr. articles to jours. including Jour. Advt., Psychology and Mktg., Jour. Tchg. in Internat. Bus., Quar. Jour. Electronic Commerce. Doctoral Consortium fellow, Am. Mktg. Assn., 1997. Mem.: Mktg. Educators Assn., Acad. of Mktg. Sci., Am. Mktg. Assn. Office: DePaul Univ Ste 7500 1E Jackson St Chicago IL 60604 Office Phone: 312-362-5282. Business E-Mail: skoernig@depaul.edu.

KOESSEL, DONALD RAY, retired bank executive; b. Grand Rapids, Mich., May 15, 1929; s. Fred Christian and Erna Wilhelmina (Grein) K.; m. Jeannine C. Koessel; children: Martin, Kathryn. BA, Yale U., 1951; MBA, Harvard U., 1955. Copywriter Grand Rapids Press, 1951-52; public relations rep. Smith Kline & French Labs., 1952-53; money market analyst Nat. Shawmut Bank of Boston, 1955-58; asst. sec. 1st Bank System, Mpls., 1958-62, asst. v.p., 1962-65; with 1st Nat. Bank Mpls., 1965-85, exec. v.p., 1975-85, chmn. trust com., 1979-85. Home: 18064 N Somerset Dr Surprise AZ 85374-6446

KOESTER, FREDERICK. H., aviation systems engineer; b. Mt. Vernon, NY, Aug. 28, 1932; s. Frederick H. and Frances A. (Moore) K.; m. Eileen R. Bobb, Dec. 30, 1961; children: Robert J., John M., Thomas E. BS in Naval Sci., US Naval Acad., 1955; BSEE, Naval Postgrad. Sch., Monterey, Calif., 1962; MS in Adminstrn., Systems Mgmt., George Washington U., 1967. Commd. ensign USN, 1955, advanced through grades to lt. comdr., ret., 1975; sr. engr. Booz-Allen & Hamilton, Bethesda, Md., 1975-79, ManTech Internat., Washington, 1979-82, Raytheon Svc. Co., Washington,

1982-84, 86-90; task mgr., sr. engr. Quest Rsch. Corp., McLean, Va., 1984-86; sr. systems engr. MiTech Inc., Rockville, Md., 1990-93; knowledge strategist, systems engr. Titan Systems Corp., Washington, 1993—. Editor: Digital Symposium Proceedings, 1966; contbr. articles to profl. jours. Mem. Soc. Competitive Intelligence Profls. Republican. Roman Catholic. Avocations: golf, investing, history. Home: 7601 Gaylord Dr Annandale VA 22003 Office: Fed Aviation Adminstrn Fed Office Bldg 10-A 800 Independence Ave Washington DC 20005

KOESTER, HELMUT HEINRICH, history professor; b. Hamburg, Germany, Dec. 18, 1926; came to U.S., 1958; s. Karl and Marie-Luise (Eitz) K.; m. Gisela G. Harrassowitz, July 8, 1953; children: Reinhild, Almut, Ulrich, Heiko. ThD, U. Marburg, Germany, 1954; Privatdozent, U. Heidelberg, Germany, 1956; ThD (hon.), U. Geneva, U. Berlin. Ordained to ministry Luth. Ch., 1956; asst. pastor Hannover, Germany, 1951-54; teaching asst., then asst. prof. U. Heidelberg, 1954-56, 56-58, 59; mem. faculty Harvard U. Div. Sch., 1958-98, John H. Morison prof. N.T. studies, 1964-98, Winn prof. ecclesiastical history, 1968-98, rsch. prof., 2000—. Vis. prof. U. Heidelberg, 1963, Drew U., 1966, U. Minn., 1990, Free U. Amsterdam, 1992, Boston U., 2000, Williams Coll., 2001. Author: Synoptische Ueberlieferung bei den Apostolischen Vaetern, in Texte und Untersuchungen, 1957, (with James M. Robinson) Trajectories through Early Christianity, 1971, Einfuehrung in das Neue Testament, 1979, Introduction to the New Testament, 1982, Ancient Christian Gospels, 1990, (with Francois Bovon) Genèse de l'écriture chrètienne, 1991, History, Religion and Culture of the Hellenistic Age, 1995, History and Literature of Early Christianity, 2000, (CD-Rom) The Cities of Paul, 2004, Paul and His World, 2007; editor Harvard Theol. Rev., 1975-99, Hermeneia, Archaeol. Resources for New Testament Studies. Asso. trustee Am. Schs. Oriental Research, 1974-75; trustee William F. Albright Inst. Archaeol. Research, 1974-80. Served with German Navy, 1944-45. Guggenheim fellow, 1964-65; Am. Coun. Learned Socs. fellow, 1971-72, 78-79. Fellow Am. Acad. Arts and Scis.; mem. Soc. Bibl. Lit. (pres. 1990-91), Soc. Novi Testamenti Studiorum. Home: 12 Flintlock Rd Lexington MA 02420-1704 Office: 45 Francis Ave Cambridge MA 02138-1911 Office Phone: 617-495-5926. Business E-Mail: helmut_koester@harvard.edu.

KOESTER, JOLENE, academic administrator; BA magna cum laude, U. Minn., 1970; MA in Communication Arts, U. Wis., Madison, 1971; PhD in Speech Communications, U. Minn., 1980. Asst. prof. speech and drama U. Mo., Columbia, 1980—83; asst. prof. communication studies Calif. State U., Sacramento, 1983—85, assoc. prof. communication studies, 1985—89, dept. chair communication studies, 1986—89, prof. communication studies, 1989—2000, asst. v.p. academic affairs, 1989—91, assoc. v.p. academic affairs, 1991—93, v.p. academic affairs, 1993—2000, provost, 1996—2000; pres. Calif. State U. Northridge, 2000—. Office: Calif State U UN 200 18111 Nordhoff St Northridge CA 91330-8230

KOETTER, CORNELIA M., lawyer; b. Durham, NC, Apr. 25, 1958; BA cum laude, Loyola Coll., 1980; JD, U. Md., 1985. Bar: Md. 1986, DC 1990. Assoc. Nolan, Plumhoff & Williams, Chartered, Towson, Md. Mem.: Comml. Real Estate Women, Md. Bar Assn. Office: Nolan Plumhoff & Williams Chartered Ste 700 Nottingham Ctr 502 Washington Ave Towson MD 21204-4528 Office Phone: 410-823-7800. Office Fax: 410-296-2765. E-mail: ckoetter@nolanplumhoff.com.*

KOETTER, DIRK J., professional and former college football coach; b. Pocatello, Idaho, Feb. 5, 1959; m. Kim Koetter; 4 children. BS in Physical Edn., Idaho State U., 1981, MA in Athletic Adminstrn., 1982. Offensive coord. San Francisco State, 1985; offensive coord. & quarterback coach Texas-El Paso, 1986—88, U. Missouri, 1989—93, Boston Coll., 1994—95, U. Oreg., 1996—97; head coach Boise State, 1998—2000, Ariz. State U., 2000—06; offensive coord. Jacksonville Jaguars, 2007—. Recipient Big West Conf. Coach of the Year, 1999, 2000. Achievements include with Boise State: three winning seasons, two conference titles, two Humanitarian Bowl wins (1999, 2000); with Arizona State U.: three winning seasons, Holiday Bowl (2002), Sun Bowl (2004), Insight Bowl (2005). Office: Jacksonville Jaguars 1 ALLTEL Stadium Pl Jacksonville FL 32202*

KOFF, FRED WILLIAM, retired research chemist; b. Haapsalu, Estonia, July 21, 1922; s. Fritz and Matilde (Lindström) K.; m. Annemarie Fehmel, June 13, 1947 (div. Apr. 1989). Degree in marine navigation, Merchant Marine Acad., Tallinn, Estonia, 1944. Rsch. chemist Chem. Rsch. Ctr. Allied Chem. Corp., Morristown, NJ, 1959-84. Contbr. articles to profl. jours. including Hydrometallurgy, Jour. Am. Chem. Soc.; patentee in field. Freedom fighter against Russian encroachment into the affairs of the Baltic States, Ctrl. and East European Coalition in U.S., N.Y.C., 1994—. Lutheran. Avocations: sailing, classical music. Home: 19804 Rhea See Dr Lutz FL 33548-4281

KOFF, HOWARD MICHAEL, lawyer; b. Bklyn., July 25, 1941; s. Arthur and Blanche Koff; m. Linda Sue Bright, Sept. 10, 1966; 1 son, Michael Arthur Bright. BS, NYU, 1962; JD, Bklyn. Law Sch., 1965; LLM in Taxation, Georgetown U., 1968. Bar: NY 1965, DC 1966, US Supreme Ct. 1969, US Ct. Appeals (2d, 3d, 4th, 5th, 7th, 9th and DC cirs.), US Dist. Ct. (no. dist.) NY 1981. Appellate atty. tax divsn. US Dept. Justice, Washington, 1965-69; tax supr. Chrysler Corp., Detroit, 1969-70; chief tax counsel Conn. Gen. Life Ins. Co., Hartford, Conn., 1970-77, Rohm & Haas Co., Phila., 1977-78; ptnr. Dibble, Koff, Lane, Stern and Stern, Rochester, 1978—81; pres. Howard M. Koff, P.C., Albany, NY, 1981—. Lectr. tax matters. Editor-in-chief Bklyn. Law Rev., 1964—65, charter mem. editl. adv. bd. Jour. Real Estate Taxation; contbr. articles to legal jours. Chmn. pub. adv. coun. N.Y. State Ethics Commn. Recipient Founders Day award, NYU, 1962, Lawyers Coop. award for gen. excellence, Lawyers Coop. Pub. Co., 1965. Mem. ABA (past chmn. subcom. on partnerships tax sect.), FBA (past pres. Hartford County chpt.), Albany County Bar Assn. Republican. Home: 205 W Bernhard Ct Albany NY 12203-4905 Office: 600 Broadway Albany NY 12207-2205 Office Phone: 518-463-5530.

KOFF, ROBERT HESS, academic administrator, adult education educator; b. Chgo., June 5, 1938; s. Arthur Karl and Dorothy (Hess) K. BA, U. Mich., 1961; MA, U. Chgo., 1962, PhD, 1966. Lic. psychologist, Calif. Instr., counselor S. Shankman Orthogenic Sch. U. Chgo., 1961—64; tchr. U. Chgo. Lab. Sch., 1963—64; instr. U. Ill., Champaign, 1964, U. Chgo., 1964—66; vis. scientist, Lab. for Hypnosis Rsch., asst. prof. Stanford U., Calif., 1966—72; prof., dean Roosevelt U., Chgo., 1972—79; univ. dean SUNY, Albany, 1979—92; program dir., sr. v.p. Danforth Found., St. Louis, 1992—2003; prof., asst. vice chancellor Ctr. Advanced Learning Washington U., St. Louis, 2003—. Vis. scholar Oxford U., Eng., 1965; chmn. N.Y. State Ednl. Cert. Bd., Albany, 1981-92. Mem. Nat. Adv. Coun. on Edn. of Disadvantaged Children, Washington, 1979-82, Gov.'s Adv. Commn. on Children and Youth, Albany, 1981-92. Mem. APA (com. chmn.), Am. Ednl. Rsch. Assn., Nat. Register Health Svc. Providers in Psychology. Office: Ctr for Advanced Learning/Washington U Campus Box 1135 Saint Louis MO 63130 Office Phone: 314-935-5946.

KOFF, SHIRLEY IRENE, writer; b. Oakland, Calif., Aug. 31, 1948; d. Lawrence Ray and Stella Pauline (Durham) Butler; m. Robert Allen Koff, June 12, 1971; children: Jennifer, Katherine. BA, Calif. State U., 1971, MA, 1972. Adj. prof. Pellissippi State U., Knoxville, 1989-93; asst. mgr. Adolfo II, Pigeon Forge, Tenn., 1994-98. Poet, writer; tchr. adult religious edn. classes and seminars; expert info. provider internet resource AskAnything.com. Tchr., lay min., bd. dirs. First Assembly of God Ch., Sevierville, 1996-99; core group leader, founding mem. Wellspring Congregation, United Meth. Ch., 1999-2001. Mem.: AAUW, Knoxville (Tenn.) Writers Guild, Tenn. Writers Alliance, Appalachian Writers Assn., Mensa. Democrat. Avocations: writing, speaking, teaching. Home: 1214 Amber Ln Sevierville TN 37862-6101 E-mail: sikoff@chartertn.net.

KOFFEL, MARTIN M., engineering company executive; b. 1939; MS, MBA, Stanford U., 1971. With Homestake Mining Co., 1974-81, Cooper Labs., Inc., 1981-84, Gilette Corp., 1984-86, Cooper Vision Inc., 1986-88; chmn. bd., pres., CEO URS Corp., San Francisco, 1989—. Bd. dir. McKesson Corp., San Francisco, 2000—02, James Hardie Industries N.V., Mission Viego, Calif., 2001—02. Adv. coun. McLaren Sch. Bus., U. San Francisco; trustee Am. Enterprise Inst. Pub. Policy, Washington. Office: URS Corp 600 Montgomery St 25th Fl San Francisco CA 94111-2727 Office Phone: 415-774-2700. Office Fax: 415-398-1905.*

KOFFLER, WARREN WILLIAM, lawyer; b. NYC, July 21, 1938; s. Jack and Rose (Conovich) K.; m. Barbara Rose Holz, June 11, 1959; m. Jayne Audri Goetzel, May 15, 1970; children: Kevin, Kenneth, Caroline. BS, Boston U., 1959; JD, U. Calif., Berkeley, 1962; LLD, NYU, 1972. Bar: D.C. 1962, N.Y. 1963, U.S. Dist. Ct. D.C. 1963, Fla. 1980, Va. 1981, Pa. 1982. Atty. FAA, Washington, 1964; pvt. practice law Washington, 1964, 78—, Hollywood, Palm Beach, Miami, Fla., 1978—; atty. Fed. Home Loan Bank Bd., Washington, 1964-66; ptnr. Koffler & Spivack, Washington, 1967-77. Mem. ATLA, ABA, FBA, Inter-Am. Bar Assn., D.C. Bar Assn., Fla. Bar Assn., Va. Bar Assn., Brit. Inst. Internat. and Comparative Law, Univ. Club (Washington), Bankers Club (Miami), Membership Club PGA Nat. (Palm Beach), City Club (Palm Beach), Circumnavigator's Club (N.Y./Palm Beach). Office: 4521 PGA Blvd Ste 361 West Palm Beach FL 33418 also: 1730 K St NW Washington DC 20006-3868 Office Phone: 561-694-6665. Personal E-mail: wwkvip@msn.com.

KOFMAN, LEONID, consumer products company executive; b. Ukraine; Pres., CEO Chocolate Printing Co., Inwood, NY, 1998—. Achievements include development of Food Imaging System (FISCO), the world's first commercial, high-volume system for reproducing any image directly onto edible products. Office: Chocolate Printing Co 600 Bayview Ave Inwood NY 11096 Office Phone: 866-371-0030. Business E-Mail: info@chocolography.com.

KOFORD, STUART KEITH, electronics executive; b. North Hollywood, Calif., Oct. 25, 1953; s. Kenneth Harold and Theresa (Sutton) K.; m. Gail Anne Joerger, Dec. 28, 1985; 1 child, Michelle Anne. BSME, Mich. Tech. U., 1976. Engr. Motorola, Schaumburg, Ill., 1976-77, sr. engr., 1977-79; engring. project mgr. Amphenol, Cicero, Ill., 1979-80, mgr. R & D, 1980-82, mgr. engring. Broadview, Ill., 1982—91; pres. Koford Engring., Lisle, Ill., 1982-2001; product gen. mgr. MK-Koford, Des Plaines, Ill., 2001—04; ptnr., sec.-treas. Micro-Lungo, 1998—; pres. Koford Engring., Winchester, Ohio, 2004—. Contbr. articles to profl. jours.; patentee in field. Mem. IEEE (program com. Electronic Components Conf. 1979-91), Soc. Plastic Engrs., ASME, Electronic Connector Study Group (program chmn. 1982-84). Republican. Avocation: slot car racing (world champion 1989). Office: Koford Engring LLC 1441 Dorcey Rd Winchester OH 45697

KOGA, ROKUTARO (ROCKY KOGA), physicist; b. Nagoya, Japan, Aug. 18, 1942; came to U.S., 1961, naturalized, 1966; s. Toyoki and Emiko (Shinra) K.; m. Cordula Rosow, May 5, 1981; children: Evan A., Nicole A. BA, U. Calif., Berkeley, 1966; PhD, U. Calif., Riverside, 1974. Rsch. fellow U. Calif., Riverside, 1974-75; rsch. physicist Case Western Res. U., Cleve., 1975-79, asst. prof., 1979-81; physicist Aerospace Corp., LA, 1981-96, sr. scientist, 1996-2000, dsting. scientist, 2000—. Contbr. articles to profl. confs. Mem. IEEE, Am. Phys. Soc., Am. Geophys. Union, N.Y. Acad. Scis., Sigma Xi. Achievements include research on gamma-ray astronomy, solar neutron observation, space sciences, charged particles in space and the effect of cosmic rays on microcircuits in space. Office: Aerospace Corp Space Scis Lab Los Angeles CA 90009 Business E-Mail: rocky.koga@aero.org.

KOGAN, ESTHER, education educator, director; d. Noma and Fanny Kogan; m. Ruben Niesvizky, Oct. 12, 1985; children: Itamar Niesvizky-Kogan, Tanya Niesvizky-Kogan. D, Columbia U., 1988—97. Asst. prof. Adelphi U., Garden City, NY, 1998—2003, dir., grad. early childhood program, 2003—, assoc. prof., 2003—. Cons. Hunter Coll., NYC, 1994—; cons. admissions assoc. Hollingworth Preschool, Teachers Coll. Columbia U., NYC, 1994—. Author: (book) Gifted Bilingual Students: A Paradox? (Gabino Barreda medal (Mex.), 1988); editor: Pathways to Inclusion: Voices from the Field. Grantee Internat. Student scholarship, Teachers Coll., Columbia U., 1991—96, Profl. Devel. (President's) fellowship, Adelphi U., 2003—04. Mem.: ECELI, NAGC, NAEYC. Office Phone: 516-877-4474.

KOGAN, PAVEL, conductor; b. Moscow, June 6, 1952; s. Leonid and Elizaveta (Gilels) K.; m. Ljubov Kazinskaja, Dec. 21, 1977 (div. Sept. 1984); 1 child, Dmitri. M, Moscow Conservatory, 1976. Condr. Leningrad Philharm. Orch., 1974, USSR State Symphony Orch., State Symphony Orch. of USSR Radio and TV, Moscow Philharm. Orch., Bolshoi Theater Symphony Orch.; music dir., chief conductor Zagreb (Yugoslavia) Philharm. Orch., 1988—90, Moscow State Symphony Orch., 1989—; prin. guest condr. Utah Symphony Orch., Salt Lake City, 1998—. Guest condr. music festivals, Helsinki, Dubrovnik, Montreux, Prague, Villach, Vancouver Symphony, Houston Symphony, Toronto Symphony, Nat. Arts Ctr. Orch., Indpls. Symphony, Oregon Symphony, Kansas City Symphony, NJ Symphony, Fla. Orch. Condr. (recordings) Tchaikovsky symphonies, Prokofiev's symphonies 1, 5, 6. Recipient First prize, Gold medal, Sibelius Internat. Violin Competition, Helisinki, 1970, Nat. prize, Russian Fedn., 1977; Named People's Artist of Russian Fedn., 1994. Mem.: Russian Acad. Arts. Achievements include opened Bolshoi Operas, 1988-1989. Office: Moscow State Symphony Orch 1/2 Spartakovskaja Sq 103009 Moscow Russia

KOGAN, RICHARD J., former pharmaceutical company executive; b. NYC, June 6, 1941; s. Benjamin and Ida K.; m. Susan Linda Scher, Aug. 29, 1965. BA, CCNY, 1963; MBA, NYU, 1968. V.p. planning and adminstrn. pharm. divsn. Ciba-Geigy Ltd., Summit, NJ, 1975-76, pres. Can. pharm. ops., 1976—79, pres. U.S. pharm. divsn., 1979—82; exec. v.p. pharm. ops. Schering-Plough Corp., Kenilworth, NJ, 1982—86, pres., COO, 1986—96, pres., CEO, 1996—2003, chmn. bd. dirs., 1998—2002. Bd. dirs. Colgate-Palmolive Co., The Bank of NY Co., Inc.; trustee St. Barnabas Corp. and Med. Ctr. Trustee NYU, bd. overseers Stern Sch. Bus. Mem.: Coun. Fgn. Rels. Office Phone: 973-379-6560. Personal E-mail: rjk@rjkogan.com.

KOGELNIK, HERWIG WERNER, electronics company executive; b. Graz, Austria, June 2, 1932; came to U.S., 1960; naturalized, Jan. 1992; s. Sepp and Siglinde K.; m. Christa Muller, Mar. 7, 1964; children: Christoph N., Florian A., Andreas M. Dipl.-Ing., Tech. U. Vienna, 1955, Dr.techn., 1958; D.phil., Oxford U., 1960. Mem. research staff Bell Labs., Murray Hill, N.J., 1961-67, head coherent optics research dept. Holmdel, N.J., 1967-76, dir. electronics research lab., 1976-83; dir. photonics research lab. Bell Labs. Lucent Techs., Holmdel, 1983-97, adj. photonic sys. rsch. v.p., 1997—. Contbr. articles in field to profl. jours.; patentee in field of lasers, holography, electronics and optical comm. Chmn. Monmouth (N.J.) Arts Found., 1973-76; past trustee N.Y. Mus. Holography Recipient Johann Joseph Ritter von Prechtl medal Tech. U., Vienna, Austria, 1990; hon. fellow St. Peter's Coll., Oxford U., 1992; named 2006 Nat. Medal Tech. Laureate. Fellow: NAE, NAS, IEEE (David Sarnoff award 1989, Quantum Electronics award 1991, Medal of Honor 2001), Optical Soc. Am. (pres. 1989, Frederic IVES medal 1984); mem.: AAAS, Am. Inst. Physics (past gov.), Am. Phys. Soc., Seabright Lawn Tennis & Cricket Club (pres. 1994—2000). Office: Bell Labs Lucent Techs Photonics Rsch Lab 791 Holmdel Keport Rd RM L-215 Holmdel NJ 07733-0400 E-mail: herwig@lucent.com.*

KOGER, MICHAEL PIGOTT, physician, writer; b. Balt., Jan. 20, 1953; s. Linwood Jr. and Margaret (Pigott) K.; children: Michael Pigott Koger Jr. Student, Morgan State U., 1970, Fisk U., 1971-73, MIT, 1973-74; MD, Meharry Med. Coll., 1979; BA Journalism, Ga. State U., 2001, BA in Spanish, 2002; MA in Health Sci., U. Ala., 2003, postgrad., 2002—06. Internal med. resident Franklin Sq. Hosp., Balt., 1979—82; attending physician Provident Hosp., Balt., 1982-85, VA Hosp., Marion, Ill., 1986-88, Central State Hosp., Milledgeville, Ga., 1988—92, Northwest Ga. Regional Hosp., Rome, 1992—96, Complete Wellness Med. Ctr., Atlanta, 1997; news dir. Sta. WRAS, Ga. State U., Atlanta, 2000—02; with Applied Rsch. Ctr., Ga. State U., 1999—2002; announcer WVUA FM Tuscaloosa New Rock 90.7 FM, 2002—03. Chmn. dept. quality assurance and utilization review Hancock Meml. Hosp., Sparta, Ga., 1985-86; mem. sci. adv. bd. Nutrition Superstore.com, 1999-2001. Columnist Sparta Ishmaelite, 1985-86, Signal (Ga. State U.), 2000. Vol. com. Olympic Games, Atlanta, 1996, Hands on Atlanta, 1996-97, Atlanta Cmty. Food Bank, 1996-97, organizing com. Atlanta Paralympic, 1996, Am. Heart Assn., Marietta, Ga., 1996. Mem. AMA, Soc. Profl. Journalists, Journalism History Soc. Home: 321 W Charleston St #1011A Lincoln NE 68528 Business E-Mail: mkoger@alum.mit.edu.

KOGGE, PETER MICHAEL, computer scientist, educator; b. Washington, Dec. 3, 1946; s. Roy and Louise (McGrath) K.; m. Mary Ellen Clarke, June 12, 1971; children: Peter Michael, Mary Elizabeth, Timothy McGrath. BSEE, U. Notre Dame, 1968; MS in Systems Info. Scis., Syracuse U., 1970; PhDEE, Stanford U., 1973. Jr. engr. IBM, Owego, NY, 1968-72, staff engr., 1972-74, adv. engr., 1974-76, sr. engr., 1976-81, mem. sr. tech. staff, 1981-93; IBM fellow, 1993; McCourtney prof. computer sci. U. Notre Dame, Ind., 1994—, interim dept. chair computer sci. dept. Ind., 2000—01, prof. elec. engring., assoc. dean rsch. Coll. Engring Ind., 2001—. Adj. prof. computer scis. SUNY, Binghamton, 1977—94; past mem. rev. com. NSF Computing Divsn.; program chair 6th Symposium on Frontiers of Massively Parallel Computation, 1996; disting. vis. scientist NASA Jet Propulsion Lab., 1997; program com. Supercomputing, 1998, 99, 2000, 02, 03, 04, 05, Internat. Symposium on Computer Arch., 1999, Micro, 2005, Internat. Solid State Circuits Conf., 2003, 04, 05, 06, Internat. Conf. Supercomputing, 2003, 04, 05; program vice chair 7th Symposium on Frontiers of Massively Parallel Computation, 1999; program co-chmn. Great Lakes Conf. on VLSI, 2002. Author: Architecture of Pipelined Computers, 1980, Architecture of Symbolic Computers, 1991; editor conf. proc. Internat. Conf. on Parallel Processing, 1988. Recipient IBM Outstanding Innovation awards for Space Shuttle, IOP, 3838 Array Processor, AI Parallel Processor, Pres.'s award for patents, Daniel L. Slotnick award for most original paper Internat. Conf. Parallel Processing, 1994, Outstanding Computer Sci. and Engring. Dept. Instrn., 1999. Fellow IEEE; mem. Assn. for Computing Machinery, Am. Assn. Artificial Intelligence, IBM Acad. Tech. Roman Catholic. Office: U Notre Dame Dept Computer Sci and Engring 384 Fitzpatrick Hl Engrng Notre Dame IN 46556-5637 Business E-Mail: kogge@cse.nd.edu.

KOGLIN, TERRY LEE, mechanical engineer, consultant; b. Janesville, Wis., May 6, 1948; s. Charles Leroy and Patricia Ann (Dean) Koglin; m. Jane Ann Oakey (div.). BS, U. Wis. Madison, 1975. Cert. profl. engr., NJ, Pa., Fla., NY, Wash., Ohio. Mchanical engr. Finnish Nat. Railways, Helsinki, Finland, 1975; mech. engr. Airpax Electronics, Cambridge, Md., 1976—78, Earle Gear and Machine, Phila., 1978—82; cons. Steinman Boynton Gronquist and Birdsall, NYC, 1982—99, Parsons Brinckerhoff Quade and Douglas, NYC, 1999—2003. Author: Financing High Speed Rail System: High Speed Rail Association Symposium, 1992, Preserving Williamsburg's Cables Civil Engineering, 1996, High Speed Rail Project for New York City: Symposium on Urban Transportation, 2000, Movable Bridge Engineering, 2003. Com. mem. Am. Railway Engring., Wash., DC, 1999—; lectr. Princeton U., Princeton, NJ, 1997—99. Mem.: Heavy Movable Structures Inc., Am. Railway Engring. and Maintenance Way Assn., Internat. Assn. for Bridges and Structural Enging. Republican. Achievements include invention of railroad-highway crossing; movable bridge ctr. lock; development of cable repair techniques and mechanisms for suspension bridges; coal burning process for internal combustion engines. Avocations: travel, writing, reading, politics, history. Business E-Mail: koglintl@yahoo.com.

KOGOD, ROBERT P., philanthropist, former real estate company executive; b. 1931; m. Arlene R. Kogod, 1956; 3 children. BS, Am. U., 1962, LLD (hon.), 2000. Joined Charles E. Smith Companies, 1959; co-chmn. & co-CEO Charles E. Smith Residential Realty Inc., 1967—2001; merged with Archstone Communities Trust to become Archstone-Smith Trust, 2001, bd. trustees, 2001—; co-chmn. & co-CEO Charles E. Smith Comml. Realty LP, 1997—2001; merged with Vornado Realty Trust, 2002, bd. trustees, 2002—. Bd. regents Smithsonian Instn., 2005—; advisor to pres., mem. bd. trustees Am. U., 2003—; has contbd. to Smithsonian Instn., Signature Theatre, Wooly Mammoth Theatre, Am. U., U. Md. Clarice Smith Performing Arts Ctr., many others. Named one of Top 200 Collectors, ARTnews mag., 2004. Avocation: Collector modern and contemporary art, especially Am. Office: Vornado Realty Trust 888 7th Ave New York NY 10019

KOGUT, JOHN ANTHONY, wholesale distribution executive; b. Lackawanna, NY, Dec. 8, 1942; s. John J. and Rose J. (Gaj) K.; m. Deborah A. Hillman; children: David J., Robert J., Katherine A., Lindsey A., Kimberly M. BS in Pharmacy, U. Buffalo, 1965; MBA, Syracuse U., 1978. Pharmacist, mgr. Fay's Drug Co., Liverpool, NY, 1969-75, v.p., 1975-82, sr. v.p., 1982-89, pres., 1989-95; pres. Health Mart divsn., v.p. Franchise Svcs. FoxMeyer Corp., 1995-96; pres. Health Mart Divsn., v.p. mktg. McKesson Corp., 1996-99; pres. pharmac ops. Cmty. Health Svcs., Inc., Chgo., 1999—. Mem. N.Y. State Bd. Pharmacy, 1987-95. Served to capt. U.S. Army, 1966-69 Mem. Am. Pharm. Assn., Pharm. Soc. of State N.Y., Am. Mgmt. Assn., Nat. Assn. Chain Drug Stores (pharmacy affairs com. chmn. 1982-83), N.Y. State Bd. Pharmacy. Republican. Roman Catholic. Home Phone: 315-595-6670; Office Phone: 315-595-6170. Business E-Mail: jkogut@pharmacyaide.com.

KOGUT, KENNETH JOSEPH, engineer, consultant; b. Chgo., Dec. 3, 1947; s. Joseph Henry and Estelle Theresa (Swiercz) K.; m. Darlene Agnes Jedlicka, June 15, 1974. Student, Lewis Coll., Detroit, 1966—68; BME, U. Detroit, 1971, ME, postgrad., U. Detroit, 1972—. Registered profl. engr., Ill., cert. energy mgr., green bldg. engr. Mech. engr. Fluor Pioneer Inc., Chgo., 1972-73, cons. engr., 1973-75; project mgr. Engring. Corp. Am., Chgo., 1976-77; sr. cons. pub. utilities DeLoitte, Haskins & Sells, Chgo., 1977-79; individual practice as energy and mgmt. cons., 1979—. Author: Energy Management for the Community Bank. Alfred P. Sloan fellow, 1971-73; reciepient award Pres.'s Program for Energy Efficiency, Corp. Energy Mgmt. award, 1981, Regional Energy Profl. Devel. award, 1984, Regional Energy Engr. of Yr. award, 1987, Ill. Energy award, 1988, Illiana Energy Mgmt. Exec. of Yr. award Assn. Energy Engrs., 1992, 96, Disting. Svc. award Assn. Energy Engrs., 1999, Excellence in Engring. award Am. Soc. Heating Refrigeration and Air-Conditioning Engrs. Ill. chpt., 1994, Energy Mgrs. Hall of Fame, 2002. Mem. Am. Nuclear Soc., Nat., Ill. socs. profl. engrs., Assn. Energy Engrs. (pres. Chgo. chpt. 1985, pres Ill. chpt. 1990-93, regional v.p. 1993-95, dir. chpt. devel., 1996, internat. pres-elect

1997, internat. pres. 1998, energy policy com.), Environ. Engrs. and Mgrs. Inst., Demand-Side Mgmt. Soc., Exec. Hosp. Engrs. Soc. Ill., Energy Svcs. Mktg. Soc., Blue Key, Tau Beta Pi, Pi Tau Sigma, Polish Nat. Alliance. Address: 5232 170th Pl Oak Forest IL 60452-4450

KOGUT, LIOR, mechanical engineer, researcher; b. Haifa, Israel, Nov. 3, 1973; s. Judith and Shlomo Kogut; m. Merav Avital, Apr. 22, 1973; children: Dean, Daniella. BS, Technion - Israel Inst. of Tech., 1991—95, MS, 1997—98, PhD, 1999—2002. R&d engr. Israeli Def. Force, Tel-Aviv, Israel, 1995—99; post-doctoral fellow U. of Calif. at Berkeley, 2002—. Sec., contact mechanics com. of theASME tribology divsn. ASME, 2002. Mem.: ASME. Business E-Mail: kogut@newton.berkeley.edu.

KOH, HAROLD HONGJU, dean, law educator; b. Cambridge, Mass., Dec. 8, 1954; s. Kwang Lim and Hesung (Chun) Koh; m. Mary-Christy Fisher, Feb. 19, 1984; children: Emily J.Y., William H.W. BA cum laude, Harvard U., 1975, JD, 1980; BA, Magdalen Coll., Oxford U., 1977; MA (hon.), Yale U., 1990; LLH (hon.), CUNY-Queens Law Sch., 1998, Suffolk Law Sch., 1999, U. Conn., 2000, Conn. Coll., 2001, Skidmore Coll., 2002; LHD (hon.), Albertus Magnus Coll., 1999, Dickinson Coll., 2000. Bar: N.Y. 1981, D.C. 1981, U.S. Dist. Ct. D.C. 1981, U.S. Ct. Appeals (D.C. cir.) 1981, U.S. Ct. Claims 1982, Conn. 1985, U.S. Supreme Ct. 1985, U.S. Dist. Ct. Conn. 1987. Law clk. to judge U.S. Ct. Appeals (D.C. cir.), Washington, 1980-81; law clk. to Justice Harry A. Blackmun U.S. Supreme Ct., Washington, 1981-82; assoc. Covington & Burling, Washington, 1982-83; atty.-advisor Office of Legal Counsel, Dept. Justice, Washington, 1983-85; assoc. prof. law Yale Law Sch., New Haven, 1985-90, prof., 1990-93, dir. Orville H. Schell Jr., Ctr. Internat. Human Rights, 1993—98, Gerald C. and Bernice Latrobe Smith Prof. internat. law, 1993—, dean, 2004—. Adj. asst. professorial lectr. law George Washington U. Nat. Law Ctr., 1982—85; vis. prof. internat. law U. Toronto, 1990, 2002; vis. prof. Hague Acad. Internat. Law, 1993; vis. fellow All Souls Coll., Oxford U., 1996—97; Waynflete Lectr. Magdalen Coll., Oxford U., 1996—97; asst. sec. state for Democracy, Human Rights and Labor U.S. Dept. State; commr. Commn. for Security and Cooperation in Europe; U.S. delegate UN Gen. Assembly (Third Com.), UN Human Rights Commn., Orgn. Am. States, Coun. Europe, Orgn. for Security and Cooperation in Europe, UN Com. Against Torture, 1998—2001, Inaugural Cmty. of Democracies Meeting, Warsaw, 2000, UN Conf. on New and Restored Democracies, Cotonou, Benin, 2000. Author: The National Security Constitution, 1990, Transnational Legal Problems, 1994, International Business Transactions in United States Courts, 1998, (with Ronald C. Slye) Deliberative Democracy and Human Rights, 1999, The Human Rights of Persons with Intellectual Disabilities: Different But Equal, 2003, Transnational Business Problems, 2003; bd. editors Am. Jour. Internat. Law, Human Rights Quarterly, Foundation Press; contbr. articles to profl. jours. Bd. dirs. Human Rights Watch, Arms Control Assn. Co-recipient Human Rights Award, Am. Immigration Lawyers' Assn., 1992, Trial Lawyer of Yr. Award, Trial Lawyers for Pub. Justice, 1995; named Public Sector 45, American Lawyer mag., 1997; recipient Richard E. Neustadt Award, Am. Polit. Sci. Assn., 1991, Justice in Action Award, Asian-Am. Legal Defense & Edn. Fund, 1993, Korean Am. Coalition Pub. Service Award, 2001, John Quincy Adams Freedom Award, Amisad Am., 2002, Arthur J. Goldberg Award, Jacob Fuchsberg Law Ctr., Touro Law Sch., 2000, Wolfgang Friedmann Award, Columbia Jour. Transnational Law, 2003, Villanova Medal, Villanova Law Sch., 2000, Louis B. Sohn Award, Am. Bar Assn., 2005; grantee Marshall scholar, Oxford U., 1977. Fellow: Am. Acad. Arts and Scis; mem.: Am. Soc. Internat. Law., Am. Law Inst., Twentieth Century Fund. Office: Yale Law Sch PO Box 208215 New Haven CT 06520-8215 E-mail: harold.koh@yale.edu.*

KOH, HOWARD KYONGJU, academic administrator, educator, former public health commissioner; b. Cambridge, Mass., Mar. 15, 1952; s. Kwang Lim and Hesung (Chun) K.; m. Claudia Anne Arrigg; children: Steven, Daniel, Katherine. BA, Yale U., 1973, MD, 1977; MPH, Boston U., 1995. Prof. schs. medicine and pub. health Boston U., 1994-97; dir. cancer prevention and control Boston U. Med. Ctr., 1997-97; commr. pub. health State of Mass., 1997—2003; assoc. dean pub. health practice Harvard Sch. Pub. Health, Boston, 2003—, dir. divsn. pub. health practice, 2003—, Harvey V. Fineberg prof. pub. health practice, 2005—. Chmn. Mass. Coalition Healthy Future, Boston, 1995-97; apptd. mem. Nat. Cancer Adv. Bd., 2000. Contbr. over 200 articles to profl. jours. Bd. dirs. Am. Cancer Soc., Mass., 1986-97. Recipient Preventive Oncology Acad. award Nat. Cancer Inst., 1988-93. Mem.: Inst. Medicine. Office: HSPH Divsn Pub Health Practice Landmark Bldg 677 Huntingdon Ave Boston MA 02115 Office Phone: 617-495-4000. Office Fax: 617-495-8543. E-mail: hkoh@hsph.harvard.edu.

KOH, STEVE Y., lawyer; b. Seattle, Aug. 20, 1967; BBA magna cum laude, U. Wash., 1989; JD, Yale U., 1992. Bar: Wash., US Supreme Ct., US Ct. Appeals (5th Cir.), US Ct. Appeals (9th Cir.), US Dist. Ct. (We. Dist.) Wash. Intern to Hon. Jose A Cabranes US Dist. Ct., (Dist. Conn.), 1990; summer assoc. Cravath Swaine & More, NY, 1991; law clk. to Hon. Patricia Wald US Ct. Appeals (DC Cir.), 1992—93; atty. US Dept. Justice, Fraud Sect., 1993—95; ptnr., mem exec. com. Perkins Coie LLP, Seattle, chmn. hiring com. Articles editor Yale Law Jour. Bd. trustees Childhaven. Named a Super Lawyer, Wash. Law& Politics; named to best lawyers under 40, Nat. Asian-Pacific ABA. Mem.: Fed. Bar Assn. (trustee), Wash. State Bar Assn., Asian Bar Assn. Office: Perkins Coie LLP Ste 4800 1201 Third Ave Seattle WA 98101-9000 Office Phone: 206-359-8530. Office Fax: 206-359-9000. Business E-Mail: skoh@perkinscoie.com.*

KOHAN, BETSY BURNS, lawyer; b. La Mesa, Calif., Jan. 24, 1949; d. William Richard and Winifred Marion Burns; m. Dennis Lynn Kohan, Mar. 8, 1986; children: Toni Kick, Bart, Elyse, David Karowsky. BA, Stanford U., Calif., 1971; JD, U. Colo., 1974. Bar: Colo. 1974, Calif. 1985, Tenn. 2006. Ptnr. Karowsky, Witwer & Oldenburg, Greeley, Colo., 1974-82; pvt. practice, Greeley, 1983-84; v.p., assoc. gen. counsel Sun Savs., San Diego, 1985-86; v.p., asst. gen. counsel Imperial Savs. & Loan Assn., San Diego, 1986-88, Am. Real Estate Group, Irvine, Calif., 1988-90, Columbia Savs. & Loan Assn., Irvine, 1990-91; staff atty. FDIC, Irvine, 1991-94; prof. Anhui Inst. Fin. and Trade, Bengbu, China, 1994, Guangzhou Inst. Fgn. Trade, China, 1995; sr. counsel Nissan N.Am., Inc., Nashville, 1996—. Mem. Commn. on Legal and Jud. Edn., Colo. Supreme Ct., Denver, 1983-84. Contbr. articles to legal publs. Chmn. Colo. Commn. on Women, Denver, 1978-80; vice chmn. bd. trustees U. No. Colo., 1980-84. Named Outstanding Coloradoan, Colo. Jaycees, 1980, Outstanding Young Lawyer, Colo. Bar Assn., 1979. Mem. LA Bar Assn. (comml. law com. 1997-2006), Tenn. Bar Assn., Nashville Bar Assn. Home: 230 Gardenridge Dr Franklin TN 37069-4022 Office: Nissan N Am Inc 333 Commerce St 7th Fl Nashville TN 37201 Office Phone: 615-725-1282. Business E-Mail: betsy.kohan@nissan-usa.com.

KOHAN, DENNIS LYNN, finance educator; b. Kankakee, Ill., Nov. 22, 1945; s. Leon Stanley and Nellie K.; m. Julianne Johnson, Feb. 14, 1976 (dec. Sept. 1985); children: Toni, Bart, Elyse; m. Betsy Burns, Mar. 8, 1986; 1 child, David. BA, Ill. Wesleyan U., 1967; postgrad., John. Marshall Law Sch., 1971—74; MPA, Gov.'s State U., 1975. Police officer Kankakee County, 1967-75; loan counselor, security officer Kankakee Fed. Savs. & Loan, Kankakee, 1975-76; mgr. Bank Western, Denver, 1976-85; mgr. real estate lending dept. Ctrl. Savs., San Diego, 1985-87; maj. loan work-out officer Imperial Savs., San Diego, 1987-88; cons. Equity Assurance Holding Corp., Newport Beach, Calif., 1987-88; compliance officer Am. Real Estate Group and New West Fed. Savs. and Loan, Irvine, Calif., 1988-90; co-founder Consortium-Real Estate Asset Cons., Costa Mesa, Calif., 1990-91; investigator, criminal coord. Resolution Trust Corp., Newport Beach, 1991-94; instr. for Internat. Trade Anhui Inst. Fin. and Trade, Bengbu, China, 1994-95; instr. Guangzhou Inst. Fgn. Trade, China, 1995—; owner Kohan Internat. Bus. Forensics, 1995—; investigator Office Insp. Gen. LA Unified Sch. Dist., 2000—. Instr. U. No. Colo. Coll. Bus., Greeley, 1981-85; chmn. bd. North Colo. Med. Ctr., Greeley, 1983-85; pres. bd. Normedco, Greeley, 1984-85; part-time prof. bus. pub. adminstrn. So. Calif. Internat. Coll., 1998—. Vol. cons., chmn. ARC, Colo., 1979-85; campaign mgr. Donley Senatorial campaign, Colo., 1982, Kinkade City Coun. campaign, Colo., 1983; chmn. Weld County Housing Authority, 1981. Staff sgt. U.S. Army, 1969-71, Vietnam. Mem. Nat. Assn. Realtors, Shriners, Kiwanis. Personal E-mail: dkohan@earthlink.net.

KOHAN, LOIS RAE, community health nurse; b. Paterson, NJ, Feb. 2, 1945; d. Raymond Cornelius and Margaret Gavina (Phillips) Englishman; m. Raymond Roy Kohan, Oct. 16, 1966; children: Jeffrey, Glenn, Sharon, Kevin, Craig. Diploma, Hackensack Hosp., NJ, 1966. Substitute sch. nurse Hillsdale (NJ) Pub. Schs., 1976-80; phys. assessment nurse Phys. Measurements, Inc., Caldwell, NJ, 1978-81; pvt. duty nurse Charles Blando Family, Oradell, NJ, 1980-85, At Home Nursing Agy., Thells, NY, 1985-87; pub. health nurse Dumont (NJ) Bd. Health, 1987-91, Hillsdale (NJ) Bd. Health, 1992—; pediat. nurse Bergen Cmty. Health Care Nursing Agy., 1992—; parish nurse Hillsdale United Meth. Ch., 2003—. Den leader Boy Scouts Am., Hillsdale, 1975-85; counselor, dir., founder Helping Hand Food Pantry, Hillsdale, 1992—; mem. Drug Alliance Force, Hillsdale, 1996-97; adv. bd. Bergen County Juvenile Fire Prevention Program, Paramus, N.J., 1994-97; active ch. choir. Recipient Hillsdalean award Mayor and Coun. Hillsdale, 1992, Mayor's award Mayor and Coun. Hillsdale, 1995, Gov. Nurses award, 1993, N.Y. Times Job Market Nursing award, 2003, Citizen of Yr. award Greater Pascack Valley C. of C., 2005; finalist Volvo For Life award 2004. Mem. N.J. State Nurses Orgn., Nurses Alumni Hackensack Med. Ctr., Bergen County Mcpl. Nurses Assn., Hillsdale Woman's Club. Methodist. Avocations: walking, hiking, tennis, gardening, crafts. Home: 45 Carlyle Pl Hillsdale NJ 07642-2805 Office Phone: 201-666-4800 ext. 5028.

KOHARCHIK, THOMAS DAVID, music educator; b. Johnstown, Pa., June 21, 1981; s. Thomas John and Linda Susan Koharchik. BS in Music Edn., Ind. U. Pa., 2003. Cert. tchg. Pa. Dept. Edn. Music dir. North Hills Chorale, Pitts., 2004—; dir. vocal music Freeport Sch. Dist., Pa. Dir., musical prodr. Freeport (Pa.) Sch. Dist., 2005—, musical advisor, 2005—06. Composer: Gentle Mary, 2002, Forever, 2003. Dir. music liturgy St. Mary's Roman Cath., Freeport, 2003—, dir. musical activity, 2003—06. Staff sgt. USAR, 1998—2006, Iraq. Mem.: Pa. Music Educators Assn., Am. Choral Dirs. Assn., Music Educator's Nat. Conf., VFW, Phi Kappa Phi. Home: 324 Juniper Ln Box 184 G Tarentum PA 15084

KOHART, MARY BETH, real estate company executive; BS in Fin. and Real Estate, Ind. U., 1992, student in Spanish. Cert. comml. investment mem. Mem. staff valuation svcs. Sturges, Griffin, Trent & Co. (now CB Richard Ellis); with Hines; mem. staff to prin. office svcs., v.p. Colliers Turley Martin Tucker, Indpls., 1999. Bd. mem. Kappa Alpha Theta Alumni Assn. Mem.: Comml. Real Estate Women Network (pres. 2005), Soc. Indsl. and Office Realtors, Therapy Dogs Internat., Indpls. Jr. League. Office: Colliers Turley Martin Tucker 1 American Sq Ste 1300 Indianapolis IN 46282 Office Phone: 317-639-0487. Office Fax: 317-639-0504. E-mail: mkohart@ctmt.com.*

KOHEN, ELLI, science educator; b. Istanbul, Turkey, Oct. 2, 1930; arrived in US, 1969; s. Yasef and Vida Kohen; m. Cahide Bahar Kohen, June 21, 1957; 1 child, Dahlia Kohen-Gordon. MD, U. Istanbul, 1954; D in Clin. Psychology, Karolinska Inst., Stockholm, 1973. Resident in pathology Springfield (Mass.) Hosp., 1956—57, Westfield (Mass.) State Sanat., 1958—60; house physician in pathology Sarafand Hosp., Israel, 1957—58; fellow in pharmacol. Baylor Sch. Med., Houston, 1960—61; from fellow in biophysics to rsch. assoc. U. Pa. Johnson Found. Sch. Med., Phila., 1961—66; vis. scientist Karolinska Inst., Stockholm, 1966—69; sr. scientist, disting. scientist Cancer Rsch. Inst., Miami, Fla., 1969—84; prof. biology U. Miami, Coral Gables, Fla., 1981—2001, prof. emeritus, 2002—. Workshop dir. in field. Author: Cell Structure and Function By Microspectrofluorometry, 1989, Analytical Use of Fluorescent Probes in Oncology, 1996, Histological Correlates of Cellular Detoxification, 1997, Applications of Optical Engineering To The Study of Cellular Pathology, Vol. I, 1997, Ladino/English-English/Ladino Dictionary, 2000, La Concierge, 2001, Fluorescence Probes in Oncology, 2002, Atlas of Cell Organelles Fluorescence, 2003, World History and Myths of Cats, 2003; contbr. chapters to books, articles to profl. jours. 1st lt. MC Turkish Army, 1954—55. Grantee, NIH, Am. Cancer Soc., Cystic Fibrosis Found., Nat. Sci. Found. on Metabolism. Mem.: European Acad. Sci., Arts and Letters (corr.). Jewish. Achievements include research in microspectrofluorometry and microinjection of single living cells; first to subdisciplines of cell biology, cell biochemistry, cellular pathology and cellular pathopharmacology. Avocations: history, travel, coin collecting/numismatics, cruising, linguistics. Office: Univ Miami Nano Method Lab Dept Chemistry 1320 Campo Sano Coral Gables FL 33146 Business E-Mail: ekohen@umiami.ir.miami.edu.

KOHEN, MARTHA, architecture educator; Grad., U. de la Republica, Montevideo, Uruguay; postgrad. diploma, Cambridge U., Eng. Arch., tchr., Paysandu, Uruguay, 1971—76; arch., cons. Matto Grosso, Brazil, 1976—84, Sao Paulo, Brazil, 1976—84; asst. prof. Sommer and Sprechmann Studio, Sch. Arch., 1985—94; assoc. prof. Otero Studio, Sch. Arch., Montevideo, 1994—98; dir. acad. cooperation unit faculty arch. Univ. de la Republica, Uruguay, 1998—2003; dir. and prof. Sch. Arch., Coll. Design, Constrn. and Planning U. Fla., 2003—; founding mem. Kohen-Otero Archtl. Studio, Montevideo, 1989—. Dep. bd. mem. Internat. Coun. Urban Planners, 1994, nat. mem., 1995—2000; vis. prof. Internat. Seminars Arch. e Citta U. degli Studi di Napoli Federico II, Italy, 1991—93; vis. lectr. Sch. Arch., Rosario, Argentina, 1992, Rosario, 1996—98, NYU Internat. Ctr. for Advanced Studies, 2000; mem. jury Fourth Internat. Seminary, Napoli, Italy, 1992; vis. prof. 7th Internat. Seminary, Napoli, Italy, 1998; vis. prof. dept. arch. U. Hong Kong, 2002. Recipient First prize, Barao de Rio Branco Square, Rio de Janeiro, 1995, Meml. of the Disappeared Detained Citizens, City of Montevideo, 1996, Hdqrs. of URAGUA, 2000, Spl. Mention, The Cerrillos Masterplan, Portal del Bicentenario, Santiago de Chile, 2001, First prize landscape arch., Quito Internat. Biennale, 2002, First prize, Sao Paulo Biennal of Arch., 2003. Mem.: Uruguayan Archtl. Assn. (mem. Coll. Cons., mem. Coll. Juries 1995—), Soc. for Internat. Devel. (Uruguayan chpt.). Office: Univ Fla Sch Arch PO Box 115702 Gainesville FL 32611-5702

KOHL, BENEDICT M., lawyer; b. 1931; AB, Brown U., 1952; LL.B. cum laude, Harvard U., 1955. Bar: D.C. 1955, U.S. Supreme Ct. 1962, N.J. 1963. Partner Lowenstein, Sandler, Kohl, Fisher & Boylan, Roseland, NJ; atty. interpretative div. Office Chief Counsel, IRS, 1957-60, Office of Tax Legis. Counsel, U.S. Treasury Dept., 1960-62. Nat. v.p. Am. Jewish Com., former N.J. pres.; former trustee Overlook Hosp. Mem. ABA, N.J. State, Essex County bar assns. Office: Lowenstein Sandler Kohl et al 65 Livingston Ave Ste 9 Roseland NJ 07068-1725

KOHL, BENJAMIN GIBBS, historian, educator; b. Middletown, Del., Oct. 26, 1938; s. Victor Philip and Catherine B. (Carpenter) K.; m. Judith Ann Cleek, Jan. 2, 1961; children: Benjamin Gibbs, Laura Ann Kohl Ball. AB with honors, Bowdoin Coll., 1960; MA, U. Del., 1962; PhD, Johns Hopkins U., 1968. Adj. instr. Franklin and Marshall Coll., Lancaster, Pa., 1961-62; instr. history Johns Hopkins U., Balt., 1965-66, Vassar Coll., Poughkeepsie, NY, 1966-68, asst. prof., 1968-74, assoc. prof., 1974-81, prof., 1981-2001, chmn. dept. history, 1979-82, 88, 1993-96, Andrew W. Mellon prof. of humanities, 1994-2001, prof. emeritus, 2001—. Pres. Am. Friends of Warburg Inst., NYC, 1994-96; adv. bd. Renaissance Studies, 1988—; pres., Hedgelawn Found., Worton, Md., 2003—. Author: Renaissance Humanism, Bibliography of Materials in English, 1985, Padua Under the Carrara, 1998, The Records of the Venetian Senate on disk 1335-1400, 2000, Culture and Politics in Early Renaissance Padua, 2001; co-author: (with A.A. Smith), Major Problems in the History of the Italian Renaissance, 1995, (with A. Mozzatto and M. O'Connoll) Rulers of Venice, 1332-1524, 2007; co-editor: (with R.G. Witt) The Earthly Republic, 1978; co-editor Centennial Directory of the American Academy in Rome, 1995, Weyer on Witchcraft, 1998; contbr. more than 20 scholarly essays and more than 50 books revs. on medieval and Renaissance history to profl. jours Historian City of Poughkeepsie, 1971—77; sec. planning commn. Betterton, Md., 2005—; bd. visitors and govs. Washington Coll., Chestertown, Md., 2006—. Fulbright fellow, Padua, Italy, 1964-65; Am. Acad. fellow, Rome, 1970-71; Delmas fellow, Venice, 1978, Mellon Found. Emeritus fellow, 2006—. Fellow Royal Hist. Soc.; mem. AAUP (pres. chpt. 1987-89, 95-98, Medieval Acad. Am. (life), Renaissance Soc. Am. (life), Am. Hist. Assn. (life). Democrat. Episcopalian. Avocations: reading, walking, gardening. Home: PO Box 166 One Bayview Rd #8 Betterton MD 21610-0166 Office Phone: 410-348-5858. Personal E-mail: kohlinmd@dmv.com.

KOHL, HERBERT H., senator, professional sports team owner; b. Milw., Feb. 7, 1935; BA, U. Wis., Madison, 1956; MBA, Harvard U., 1958. Pres. Kohl's Grocery and Dept. Stores, 1970—79, Herbert Kohl Investments; owner, pres. NBA Milw. Bucks, 1985—; US Senator from Wis., 1989—. State chmn. Dem. Party, Wis., 1975-77; ranking minority mem. jud. subcommittee on terrorism, tech. & govt. info.; mem. com. appropriations, com. judiciary, spl. com. aging. Served with USAR, 1958—64. Recipient Nat. Boys and Girls Club award, 2000, Honored Cooperator award, Nat. Cooperative Bus. Assn., 2001, Silvio O. Conte award, Pub. Awareness and Edn., Brain Injury Assn. Am., 2002, Disting. Svc. to Agr. award, Wis. Farm Bur. Fedn., 2002, Friend of Farm Bur., Am. Farm Bur., 2002, Friend of Public Power award, Mcpl. Electric Utilities of Wis., 2002, Disting. Svc. award, Food Rsch. and Action Ctr., 2003, Charles Dick Medal of Merit, Nat. Guard Assn. US, 2003, Nat. Leadership award, Coalition Juvenile Justice, 2004, Leadership award, Family Svcs. N.W. Wis., 2004, Children's Champion award, Nat. Child Support Enforcement Assn., 2004. Democrat. Jewish. Office: US Senate 330 Hart Senate Office Bldg Washington DC 20510-0001 also: US Senator Herb Kohl Ste 950 310 W Wisconsin Ave Milwaukee WI 53203-2205 Office Phone: 202-224-5653, 414-297-4451. Office Fax: 202-224-9787, 414-297-4455.*

KOHL, JOHN PRESTON, finance educator, consultant; b. Allentown, Pa., Dec. 26, 1942; s. Claude Evan and Edna Lenoir (Woodland) Kohl; m. Nancy Ann Christensen, Mar. 11, 1967; children: John P. Jr., Mark C. BA, Moravian Coll., 1964; MDiv, Yale U., 1967; MS in Mgmt., Am. Tech. U., 1974, MS in Counseling, 1976; PhD in Bus. Adminstrn., Pa. State U., 1982. Ordained to ministry United Ch. of Christ, 1967. Min. Christ Congl. Ch., New Smyrna Beach, Fla., 1968-71, First Congl. Ch., Hutchinson, Minn., 1971-73; instr. Pa. State U., University Park, 1978-82; asst. prof. mgmt. U. Tex., El Paso, 1982-85; assoc. prof. San Jose State U., 1985-87; prof., chmn. dept. mgmt. U. Nev., Las Vegas, 1988-99; dean Grad. Sch. Internat. Trade & Bus. Adminstrn. Tex. A&M Internat. U., Laredo, 1999—2003, interim provost, v.p. acad. affairs, 2002; dean Coll. Bus. and Econs., Calif. State U.-East Bay, Hayward, 2005—07. Cons. in field. Co-author: Personnel Managment, 1986; contbr. articles to profl. jours. Capt. US Army, 1973—78, col. USAR, 1993—99. Decorated Nat. Def. Svc. medal, Meritorious Svc. medal, Army Commendation medal. Mem.: Am. Acad. Mgmt. Home: 3030 Deer Meadow Dr Danville CA 94506 Office: State Univ East Bay Dean Coll Bus and Econs Hayward CA 94542-3066 Office Phone: 510-885-3291. Business E-Mail: john.kohl@csueastbay.edu.

KOHL, ROBERT L., lawyer; b. NYC, Mar. 19, 1944; s. Sol and Mimi K.; m. Enid H. Kohl, Aug. 26, 1967; children: David, Lauren. BA, Queens Coll., 1965; JD, Harvard U., 1968. Bar: NY 1968, US Dist. Ct. (ea. dist.) NY 1971. Assoc. Beekman & Bogue, NYC, 1968-75, ptnr., 1975-81, Gaston & Snow, NYC, 1981-91, Rosenman & Colin, NYC, 1991—2002, Katten Muchin Rosenman LLP, NYC, 2002—. Mem. ABA (com. on fed. regulation of securities, subcom. on 33 Act gen.). Avocations: skiing, tennis, running, biking. Office: Katten Muchin Rosenman LLP 575 Madison Ave New York NY 10022 Office Fax: 212-940-8776. Business E-Mail: robert.kohl@kattenlaw.com.

KOHLBERG, IRA, physicist, mathematician; d. Samuel Kohlberg and Helen Schan; m. Betty Beacon (div.); children: Curt, Aileen, Kenneth; m. Margaret Tynes Gillespie, May 26, 2002. BEE, City U. N.Y., 1956; MS in Physics, U. Pitts., 1960; PhD in Physics, Boston U., 1966. Project engr. Foster Wheeler Corp., 1956—58; fellow in physics Joint Westinghouse-U. Pitts., 1958—61; math. physicist Ion Physics Corp., 1961—65; sr. scientist Tech. Ops., Inc., 1965—66; chief physics sect. Keystone Computer Assoc., 1966—70; v.p. rsch. Analytical Sys. Engring. Corp., 1970—71; mem. tech. staff MITRE, 1971—76; cons., owner Energy Electromagnetics, 1975—77; tech. dir. govt. programs GTE Labs., 1977—86, sr. staff strategic sys., 1977—86, mgr. radio sci. comm. sys. divsn., 1977—86; pres. Kohlberg Assoc., Inc., 1985—. Cons. Air Force Electronic Sys. Divsn., 1976; adj. rsch. staff mem. Inst. Def. Analysis, 1986—, Ctr. Naval Analysis, 1997—2006. Contbr. articles to numerous profl. jours.; reviewer: Electromagnetics Jour., IEEE Trans. Elec. Insulation, IEEE Trans. Power Electronics, IEEE Trans. Indsl. Applications; contbr. scientific papers. Chmn. U.S. nat. com. Internat. Union Radio Sci. Commn. E Noise and Interference Control, 2003—06; mem. Internat. Electrotech. Commn., Army Sci. Bd. Recipient Citation Cons. Effort on AWACS Program, Air Force, 1978, Citation for Outstanding Tech. Performance in Sci. Svc. Program, Battelle, 1988, Citation for Tech. Accomplishments in Mil. Critical Tech. Program, Undersec. of Def., 1990, Citation for Outstanding Paper, Internat. Union of Radio Sci., Lille, France, 1996, Citation for Invaluable Contbns. to Mil. Critical Tech. Program in Weapons Effects Tech., Def. Threat Reduction Agy., 2004. Fellow: Energy Sys. Inst., Electromagnetic Pulse Soc.; mem.: IEEE (tech. com. electromagnetic compatibility), AIAA (sr.). Avocation: skiing. Office: Kohlberg Assoc Inc PO Box 23077 Alexandria VA 22309 Office Phone: 703-834-0363. Office Fax: 703-931-7792. Business E-Mail: ikohlberg@ida.org.

KOHLBERG, JAMES A., venture capitalist; BA, Golden Gate U.; MBA, NYU. With Merrill Lynch, Kohlberg Kravis Roberts & Co., NYC, 1984—87; co-founder, mng. prin. Kohlberg & Co., Mt. Kisco, NY, 1987—. Bd. dirs. Allied Aerospace Engring., Inc., Applied Graphics Tech., Inc., CUSA Busways, LLC, Holley Performance Products, Inc., Innotek, Inc., Katy Industries, Inc., Nancy's Specialty Foods, Inc., Nevamar Co., LLC, Orion Food Sys. LLC, Simplicity Mfg. Inc., Tinnerman Palnut Engineered Products LLC, KTTI Holding Co., Inc., AGY Holding Corp., Coach America Group Inc., Invisible Technologies, Inc., Nielson & Bainbridge Inc., SVP Holdings, Ltd., Stanadyne Corp., Packaging Dynamics Inc.; mem. mgmt. com. Katonah Debt Advisors. Office: Kohlberg & Co 111 Radio Cir Mount Kisco NY 10549 Office Phone: 914-241-7430. Office Fax: 914-241-7476.

KOHLBERG, JEROME, JR., (JERRY KOHLBERG), venture capitalist, lawyer; b. NYC, 1925; married; 4 children. BA, Swarthmore Coll., 1946; MBA, Harvard Bus. Sch.; LLM, Columbia U. Sch. Law, 1950. Bar: N.Y. Formerly with Bear Stearns & Co., Inc.; sr. founding ptnr. Kohlberg, Kravis, Roberts & Co., NYC, 1976-87; chmn. Houdaille Industries, Inc., Fort Lauderdale, Fla., exec. com.; chmn., co-founder Kohlberg & Co., Mt. Kisco, NY, 1987—94, spl. limited principal, 1994—. Bd. dirs. Sterndent

Corp. Founder Kohlberg Found., Campaign for America, Campaign Reform Project; bd. managers Swarthmore Coll. Named one of Forbes' Richest Americans, 2006; named to Private Equity Hall of Fame, 1994. Fellow: Am. Acad. Arts & Sciences. Achievements include forming the Campaign Reform project which was pivotal in passing The McCain-Feingold campaign finance reform bill. Office: Kohlberg & Co 111 Radio Circle Mount Kisco NY 10549

KOHLER, HERBERT VOLLRATH, JR., diversified manufacturing company executive; b. Sheboygan, Wis., Feb. 20, 1939; s. Herbert Vollrath and Ruth Miriam (DeYoung) Kohler; m. Natalie Black; children: Laura Elizabeth, Rachel DeYoung, Karger David. Grad., The Choate Sch., 1957; BS in Indsl. Adminstrn., Yale U., 1965. With Kohler Co., Wis., 1965—, gen. supr. warehouse div., 1965-67, factory systems mgr., 1967-68, v.p. operations, 1968-71, exec. v.p., 1971-72, chmn. bd., chief exec. officer, 1972—, pres., 1974—, dir., 1967. Ret. chmn. Kohler Found.; dir. emeritus Harnischfeger Corp.; dir. Nat. Assn. Manufacturers. Dir. Nat. Outward Bound, Inc.; trustee Lawrence U., Appleton, Wis.; dir. Friendship House, Sheboygan, Wis. With US Army, 1957—58. Named one of Forbes' Richest Americans, 2000—, World's Richest People, Forbes mag., 2002—; named to Nat. Kitchen and Bath Hall of Fame, 1989, Nat. Housing Hall of Fame, 1993, Morgan Horse Hall of Fame, 1996; recipient Ellis Island Medal of Honor, 1997. Mem.: Am. Morgan Horse Assn., Am. Horse Show Assn., Sheboygan Economic (pres. 1973—74). Republican. Episcopalian. Achievements include patents for over 200 design and utility innovations. Avocation: breeding Morgan show horses. Office: Kohler Co 444 Highland Dr Kohler WI 53044*

KÖHLER, HORST, President of Federal Republic of Germany; b. Skierbieszów, Poland, Feb. 22, 1943; m. Eva Luise Köhler; two children. PhD in Econs. and Polit. Scis., U. Tübingen, Germany, 1977. Rsch. asst. Inst. for Applied Econ. Rsch., 1969—76; various positions German Ministries Econs. and Fin., 1976—93; German dep. min. fin., 1990-93; pres. German Savings Bank Assn., 1993-98, European Bank for Reconstruction and Devel., 1998-2000; mng. dir., chmn. exec. bd. Internat. Monetary Fund, 2000—04; pres. Fed. Republic Germany, 2004—. Rep. fed. chancellor preparation Group Seven Econ. Summits, Houston, 1990, London, 1991, Munich, 1992, Tokyo, 1993; hon. prof. U. Tübingen, 2003. Office: Bundespraesidialamt 11010 Berlin Germany

KOHLER, LAURA E., human resources executive; married; 3 children. Grad., Duke U., 1984; MFA, Cath. U., 1987. Past tchr. Chgo. Pub. Schs.; past corp. team facilitator; past mgr. Nat. Players, Washington; past residence mgr. Olney (Md.) Theatre; founder Chgo.; past exec. dir. Kohler Found., Inc.; v.p. human resources Kohler Co., 1990—, past v.p. comm., 1994—99, sr. v.p. human resources, also bd. dirs. Office: Kohler Co 444 Highland Dr Kohler WI 53044-1500

KOHLER, PETER OGDEN, retired academic administrator, internist, educator; b. Bklyn., July 18, 1938; s. Dayton McCue and Jean Stewart (Ogden) K.; m. Judy Lynn Baker, Dec. 26, 1959; children: Brooke Culp, Stephen Edwin, Todd Randolph, Adam Stewart. BA, U. Va., 1959; MD, Duke U., 1963; PhD in Pub. Svc. (hon.), U. Portland, 2003. Diplomate Am. Bd. Internal Medicine and Endocrinology. Intern Duke U. Hosp., Durham, NC, 1963-64, fellow, 1964-65; clin. assoc. Nat Cancer Inst., Nat Inst. Child Health and Human Devel., NIH, Bethesda, Md., 1965-67, sr. investigator, 1968-73, head endocrinology service, 1972-73; resident in medicine Georgetown U. Hosp., Washington, 1969-70; prof. medicine and cell biology, chief endocrinology divsn. Baylor Coll. Medicine, Houston, 1973-77; prof., chmn. dept. medicine U. Ark., 1977-86, interim dean, 1985-86; chmn. Hosp. Med. Bd., 1980-82, chmn. council dept. chmn., 1979-80; prof., dean Sch. Medicine, U. Tex., San Antonio, 1986-88; pres. Oreg. Health & Sci. U., Portland, 1988—2006; vice chancellor NW U. Ark. for Med. Scis., 2007—. Cons. endocrinology merit rev. bd. VA, 1985—86; mem. bd. sci. counselors NICHD, 1987—92, chair, 1990—92; chair task force on health care delivery AAHC, 1991—92; Inst. Medicine bd. dirs. Stds. Ins. Co.; bd. dirs. Portland br. Fed. Res. Bank of San Francisco; chair Task Force on Improving Quality of Long-Term Care, 1994; mem. adv. bd. Loaves and Fishes, 1989—99; mem. Gov.'s adv. com. Commn. on Tech. Edn., 1989—92; chair Oreg. Health Coun., 1993—95; various positions Am. Bd. Internal Medicine, 1987—93, NIH; mem. numerous bd. dirs. and adv. bds. Editor: Current Opinion in Endocrinology and Diabetes, 1994-97, Diagnosis and Treatment of Pituitary Tumors, (with G. T. Ross), 1973, Clinical Endocrinology, 1986; assoc. editor: Internal Medicine, 1983, 87, 90, 94, 98; contbr. articles to profl. jours. Mem. campaign cabinet United Way, 1999—2004. With USPHS, 1965-68. NIH grantee, 1973—; Howard Hughes Med. Investigator, 1976-77; recipient NIH Quality awrds, 1969, 71, Disting. Alumnus award Duke Med. Sch., 1992, MRF Mentor award, Med. Rsch. Found., 1994, Humanitarian award Am. Lung Assn., 1996, Jewish Nat. Fund Tree of Life award, 1998, Internat. Citizens award Oreg. Consular Corps., 1999, Human Rels. award Am. Jewish Com., 2002, Leadership award Coun. for Advancement and Support of Edn., 2004, Hope award Nat. Multiple Sclerosis Soc., 2005; named Honored Citizen, Archl. Found. Oreg., 2002; named one of Twenty Leaders of Change, The Bus. Jour., 2004, Nat. Multiple Sclerosis Soc. Hope award, 2005. Master ACP; mem. AMA (William Beaumont award 1988), Inst. Medicine, Am. Soc. Clin. Investigation, Am. Fedn. Clin. Rsch. (nat. coun. 1977-78, pres. so. sect. 1976), So. Soc. Clin. Investigation (coun. 1979-82, pres. 1983, Founder's medal 1987), Am. Soc. Cell Biology, Assn. Acad. Health Ctrs. (chmn. 1998-99, bd. dirs.), Assn. Am. Physicians, Am. Diabetes Assn., Endocrine Soc. (coun. 1990-93), Raven Soc., Phi Beta Kappa, Sigma Xi, Alpha Omega Alpha, Omicron Delta Kappa, Phi Eta Sigma. Methodist. Office Phone: 479-521-8269. Business E-Mail: pkohler@uams.edu.

KOHLER, TIMOTHY A., social sciences educator; s. E. Lawrence and Roberta Graham Kohler; m. Marilyn K. Von Seggern, Oct. 21, 1951; children: Claire L., Sander V.S. AB, New Coll., Sarasota, Fla., 1972; PhD in Anthropology, U. Fla., Gainesville, 1978. Regents prof. dept. anthropology Wash. State U., Pullman, 1978—, dir. igert program evolutionary modeling, 2006—. External prof. Santa Fe Inst., 1995—. Editor (author): (book) Village Formation on the Pajarito Plateau, New Mexico: Archaeology of Bandelier National Monument, 2004, Model-Based Archaeology of Socionatural Systems, 2007. Grantee Village Ecodynamics Project, NSF, 2001—06. Mem.: Soc. for Am. Archaeology (editor Am. Antiquity 2000—04), AAAS. Achievements include research in archaeology of the U.S. Southwest. Avocations: hiking, gardening. Office: Dept Anthropology Wash State Univ College Hall Pullman WA 99164-490 Business E-Mail: tako@wsu.edu.

KOHLHEPP, ROBERT J., apparel executive; BS, Thomas More Coll.; MBA, Xavier Univ., 1971. Mgmt. positions through v.p. fin. Cintas Corp., Cin., 1967—79, exec. v.p., 1979—84, bd. dir., 1979—, pres., COO, 1984—95, pres., CEO, 1995—97, CEO, 1997—2003, vice-chmn., 2003—. Bd. dir. Parker Hannifin Corp. Office: Cintas Corp 6800 Cintas Blvd Mason OH 45040 Mailing: Cintas Corp PO Box 625737 Cincinnati OH 45262-5737*

KOHLI, GURMANDER SINGH, plastic surgeon; b. Quetta, India, Oct. 27, 1945; s. Asa Singh Kohli and Jaswant Kaur Sethi; m. Maninder Kaur Dutta, Apr. 13, 1975; children: Sanjivan, Moneet, Manpreet, Harjivan, Sukhjivan. MBChB, U. Glasgow, 1973. Diplomate Am. Bd. Plastic Surgery, 1984, lic. Mass., Calif., England, Lithuania. Resident Boston Med. Ctr., 1975—79, 1979—81; plastic surgeon pvt. practice, Boston, 1981—2004; chief plastic surgery Boston Regional Med. Ctr., Stoneman, 1989—99, Whidden Meml. Hosp., Everett, 1992—2001; asst. clin. prof. surgery Tufts U. Sch. Medicine, Boston, 2002—; asst. clin. prof. plastic surgery U. Calif., San Diego, 2004—; plastic surgeon pvt. practice, Irvine, Calif., 2004—; asso. prof. divsn. plastic surgery Loma Linda U. Sch. Medicine, 2006—. Fellow, Plastic Surgery Ednl. Found., 2002—, Nat. Endowment Plastic Surgery, 2002—. Fellow: Am. Coll. Surgeons; mem.: Am. Soc. Plastic Surgeons. Sikh. Home: 3 Hollinwood Irvine CA 92618-4070 Office Phone: 909-558-2100. Personal E-mail: gsk@kohli.com.

KOHLMANN, SUSAN J., lawyer; b. Jan. 15, 1958; BA, Yale Univ., 1979; JD, Columbia Univ., 1982. Bar: NY 1983. Ptnr., chmn. Intellectual Property dept., office mng. ptnr. Pillsbury Winthrop Shaw Pittman, NYC. Editor (Casenote & Comment): Columbia Jour. Transnational Law. Mem. bd. legal adv. NOW Legal Def. & Edn. Fund. Mem.: Internat. Trademark Assn., Assn. Bar City of NY (co-chmn. Com. on Women & the Law 1999—2001, mem. exec. com.). Office: Pillsbury Winthrop Shaw Pittman 1540 Broadway New York NY 10036 Office Phone: 212-858-1707. Office Fax: 212-858-1500. Business E-Mail: susan.kohlmann@pillsburylaw.com.

KOHLMEIER, LOUIS MARTIN, JR., newspaper reporter; b. St. Louis, Feb. 17, 1926; s. Louis Martin and Anita (Werling) K.; m. Barbara Anne Wilson, Nov. 15, 1958; children— Daniel Kimbrell, Ann Werling. B.Journalism, U. Mo., 1950. Staff writer Wall St. Jour., St. Louis and Chgo., 1952-57, Washington, 1960—; staff writer St. Louis Globe-Democrat, 1958-59. Author: The Regulators Watchdog Agencies and the Public Interest, 1969. Served with AUS, 1950-52. Recipient Nat. Headliners Club award nat. reporting, 1959, Sigma Delta Chi award Washington corr., 1964, Pulitzer prize nat. reporting, 1964 Home: # 105 11400 Strand Dr Apt 105 Rockville MD 20852-2942

KOHLMEYER, JASON C., lawyer; b. Moorhead, Minn., May 5, 1972; BA, Concordia Coll., 1995; JD, Hamline U., 2000. Bar: Minn. 2000, US Dist. Ct. (dist. Minn.) 2002, US Ct. Appeals (8th cir.) 2005, US Supreme Ct. 2006. Shareholder Manahan, Bluth & Kohlmeyer, Law Office, Mankato, Minn. Served in USAR, 1989—95. Named a Rising Star, Minn. Super Lawyers mag., 2006; named one of Top Ten Up and Coming Attys., Minn. Lawyer, 2002. Mem.: Amdahl Inn of Cts., Assn. Trial Lawyers of Am. (chair criminal law sect. 2006—07), Minn. Trial Lawyers Assn., 6th Dist. Bar Assn. (pres. 2004—05), ABA (chair family law com.-young lawyers divsn. 2003—05, YLD Family Law Fellow 2004—06), Minn. State Bar Assn. (chair new lawyers sect. 2004—05). Office: Manahan Bluth & Kohlmeyer Law Office 110 S Broad St PO Box 287 Mankato MN 56002 Office Phone: 507-387-5661. E-mail: Kohlmeyer@manahanbluth.com.*

KOHLOSS, FREDERICK HENRY, retired engineer; b. Ft. Sam Houston, Tex., Dec. 4, 1922; s. Fabius Henry and Rowena May (Smith) K.; m. Margaret Mary Grunwell, Sept. 9, 1944; children: Margaret Ralston, Charlotte Foster, Eleanor. BS in Mech. Engring., U. Md., 1943; M in Mech. Engring., U. Del., 1951; JD, George Washington U., 1949. Engring. faculty George Washington U., Washington, 1946-50; devel. and stds. engr. Dept. Def., 1950-51; chief engr. for mech. contractors Washington, 1951-54, Cleve., 1954-55, Honolulu, 1955-56; cons. engr., 1956-61; pres. Frederick H. Kohloss & Assocs., Inc., Cons. Engrs., Honolulu, 1961-91; chmn. Lincolne, Scott & Kohloss Inc, Cons. Engrs., Honolulu, 1991-97, sr. cons., 1997-2001, cons. engr., 2001—03, ret., 2003. Contbr. articles to profl. jours. Served with AUS, 1943-46. Fellow ASME, ASHRAE, Chartered Inst. Bldg. Svcs. Engrs., Instn. Engrs. Australia, Australian Inst. Refrigeration, Air Conditioning, Heating; mem. IEEE (sr.), NSPE, Soc. Fire Protection Engrs. Home: 2500 N Rosemont Blvd #433 Tucson AZ 85712 Office Phone: 520-325-4753. E-mail: fredpeg@cox.net.

KOHLSTEDT, DAVID LEE, geophysicist, educator; b. Mitchell, SD, Nov. 19, 1943; s. Guido Christian and Ruth Catherine (Eckstein) K.; m. Sally Gregory, Dec. 27, 1966; children: Kristian Gregory, Kurt Frederick. BS, Valparaiso U., Ind., 1965; MS, U. Ill., 1967, PhD, 1970. Rsch. assoc. Cambridge (Eng.) U., 1970-71, MIT, Cambridge, 1971-75; from asst. prof. to prof. materials sci. Cornell U., Ithaca, N.Y., 1975-89, prof., 1983-89; prof. geophysics U. Minn., Mpls., 1989—, chair dept. geology and geophysics, head Winchell Sch. Earth Scis., 2006—. Vis. prof. MIT, 1982-83, Australian Nat. U., 1983, Hannover (Germany) U., 1984, U. Bayreuth, 1993-94. Contbr. articles to Jour. Geophys. Rsch., Earth Planetary Sci. Letters, Solid State Comm., Jour. Applied Physics, Phys. Rev., Jour. Material Sci., Sci., others. Fulbright fellow, 1970-71, Guggenheim fellow, 1982-83; recipient Alexander von Humboldt award, 1993-94, AGU Hess medal, 2003, EGU Neël medal, 2005; named disting. lectr. Mineral. Soc. U.K., 1997, disting. lectr. Japanese Soc. for Promotion Sci., 1999. Fellow AAAS, Am. Geophys. Union; mem. Am. Ceramic Soc. Achievements include research in rheology of partially molten rocks, water solubility in nominally anhydrous minerals, flow in Earth's upper mantle. Office: U Minn Dept Geology Dept Head Pillsbury Hall Minneapolis MN 55455-0219 Office Phone: 612-624-7311. Business E-Mail: dlkohl@umn.edu.

KOHLSTEDT, JAMES AUGUST, lawyer; b. Evanston, Ill., June 1, 1949; s. August Lewis and Deloris (Weichelt) K.; m. Patricia Ann Lang, Oct. 8, 1977; children: Katherine, Matthew, Lindsey, Kevin. BA, Northwestern U., 1971; JD, MBA, Ind. U., 1976. Bar: U.S. Dist. Ct. (no. dist.) Ill. 1976, U.S. Tax Ct. 1978. Tax specialist Peat Marwick, Mitchell & Co., Chgo., 1976-77; assoc. Bishop & Crawford Ltd., Oak Brook, Ill., 1977-83, 1984-85; ptnr. Arnstein, Gluck, Lehr & Milligan, Oak Brook, 1985-87, Keck, Mahin and Cate, Oak Brook, 1987-96, McBride Baker & Coles, 1996-2001, mem. mgmt. com., 1997; chair McBride Baker & Coles Trade and Profl. Assn. Practice Group; sr. ptnr. The Kohlstedt Law Firm LLC, 2001—. Bd. dir. Nat. Entrepreneurship Found., Bloomington, Ind., 1981-92, Camp New Hope Devel. Bd., Oak Brook, 1983; mem. sch. bd. Lyons Twp. H.S. Dist. 204, La Grange, Ill., 1985—, v.p., 2005—; mem. Hinsdale (Ill.) Cmty. House Coun., 1991-94; mem. area leadership com. Superconducting Super Collider, 1987-88; mem. citizens adv. com. on edn. to U.S. Congressman Harris Fawell, 1986-93; bd. dir. Ill. Corridor Partnership for Excellence in Edn., 1988-94, DuPage Conv. and Visitors Bur., 1997-2001; mem. exec. bd. Visit Ill., 1997-2003; mem. planned giving com. Elmhurst Coll., 1986—; mem. citizens adv. panel U.S. Army ROTC Cadet Command, 1991-94; bd. dir. Ill. Math and Sci. Acad. Alliance, 1989—; del. White House Conf. Travel and Tourism, 1995; mem. allied adv. bd. midwest chpt. Am. Soc. Travel Agents, 1995; Collegiate Edn. adv. com. Dept. Def., 1995. Recipient Outstanding Young Citizen of Chgo. award 1987, award of excellence Nat. Sch. Pub. Rels., 2005. Mem. ABA, Ill. Travel and Tourism Assn., Ill. Bar Assn., DuPage Estate Planning Coun., Oak Brook Jaycees (pres. 1984—, chmn. bd. 1985, trustee 1985-86), Beta Gamma Sigma. Republican. Lutheran. Office Phone: 630-571-0793. Business E-Mail: jim@ktlawpro.com.

KOHLSTEDT, SALLY GREGORY, historian, educator; b. Ypsilanti, Mich., Jan. 30, 1943; BA, Valparaiso U., 1965; MA, Mich. State U., 1966; PhD, U. Ill., 1972. Asst. prof. Simmons Coll., Boston, 1971-75; assoc. prof. to prof. Syracuse (N.Y.) U., 1975-89; prof. history of sci. U. Minn., Mpls., 1989—; dir. Ctr. for Advanced Feminist Studies, 1997-98. Vis. prof. history of sci. Cornell U., 1989, Amerika Inst. U. Munich, 1997; vis. assoc. Calif. Inst. Tech., 2004, lectr. in field. Author: The Formation American Scientific Community: AAAS, 1848-1860, 1976; editor: (with Margaret Rossiter) Historical Writing on American Science, Osiris, 2d Series, 1, 1985, (with R.W. Home) International Science and National Scientific Identity: Australia between Britain and America, 1991, The Origins of Natural Science in the United States: The Essays of George Brown Goode, 1991, (with Barbara Haslett et al.) Gender and Scientific Authority, 1996, (with Helen Lonino) The Women, Gender, and Science Question, 1997, The History of Women in Science: An Isis Reader, 1999, (with Bruce Leavenstein and Michael Sokal) The Establishment of Science in America: The American Association for the Advancement of Science, 1999; contbr. articles to profl. jours.; mem. editl. bd. Signs, 1980-88, 90-93, Sci., 1980-81, News and Views: History of Am. Sci. Newsletter, 1980-86, Sci., Tech. and Human Values, 1983-90, Syracuse Scholar, 1985-88, chair, 1988, Minerva, 2000—, Isis, 2002—; assoc. editor Am. Nat. Biography, 2d edit., 1988-98, consulting edit., 1993-99; Gruphon Press Reprints in the History of Science, 1993-98; reviewer books, articles, proposals for NSF, NEH, U. Chgo. Press, others; editor sci. biography series Cambridge U., 1997-2003. Grantee NSF, 1969, 78-79, 84, 93-95, 2002, 06, Smithsonian Instn. predoctoral fellow, 1970-71, Danforth Assoc., 1975-82, Syracuse U. grantee, 1976, 82, Am. Philos. Soc. rsch. grantee, 1977, Haven fellow Am. Antiquarian Soc., 1982, Fulbright Sr. fellow U. Melbourne, Australia, 1983, Woodrow Wilson Ctr. fellow, 1986, Smithsonian Instn. Sr. fellow, 1987. Fellow AAAS (nominating com. 1980-83, 96-98, sect. chair 1986, bd. dirs. 1998-2002, chair divsn. on sci., ethics and religion 2003—, coun. 2004—), Am. Hist. Assn. (profl. com. 1974-76, rep. U.S. Nat. Archives Adv. Coun. 1974-76), Berkshire Conf. Women Historians (program com. 1974), Forum on the History Sci. in Am. (coord. com. 1980-86, chair 1985, 86), History of Sci. Soc. (sec. 1978-81, coun. 1982-84, 89-91, 94-96, com. on publs. 1982-87, chair nominating com. 1985, 99, women's com. 1972-74, vis. lectr. 1988-89, chair edn. com. 1989, pres. 1992, 93, Pfizer prize com. 2006—), Internat. Congress for History of Sci. (U.S. del. 1977, 81, vice chair 1985) Orgn. Am. Historians (chair com. on status of women 1983-85, endowment fund drive, auction subcom. 1990-91). Lutheran. Home: 108 Pillsbury Run SE Minneapolis MN 55455 Business E-Mail: sgk@umn.edu.

KOHN, A. EUGENE, architect; b. Phila., Dec. 12, 1930; s. William Bernard and Hannah (Steinberg) K.; m. Barbara S. Kohn; children: Brian, Steve, Laurie. BArch, U. Pa., 1953, MArch, 1957. Registered architect Ala., Calif., Colo., Conn., Del., D.C., Fla., Ga., Idaho, Ill., Kans., Ky., Md., Mass., Mich., N.J., N.Y., N.C., Ohio, Okla., Pa., Tenn., Tex., Va., Wis., Minn., U.K., Japan; lic. profl. planner, N.J. With Nolan Swinburne, 1957-60; project designer, project mgr. Nolan & Swinburne, Architects, Phila., 1958-60; project designer, studio designer head Vincent G. Kling Architects, Phila., 1960-64; designer Kahn & Jacobs Architects, NYC, 1964-65; dir. design Welton, Becket & Assocs., NYC, 1965-67; pres., prin. John Carl Warnecke & Assocs., NYC, Los Angeles, San Francisco, 1967-76; founder, pres. Kohn Pedersen Fox Assocs. PC, Architects and Planners, NYC, 1976—. Mem. archtl. rev. panel N.Y. Port Authority; guest lectr. Bucknell U., U. Ky., UCLA, U. Pa., Miami U., Oxford, Ohio, Kent State U., U. Tenn., N.Y. Inst. Tech., Clemson U., Pa. State U., U. Fla., Washington U., St. Louis, U. Chgo., Ill. Inst. Tech., U. Wis., Pratt U., Harvard U., Kuala Lumpur, Australia, New Zealand, Japan, Russia, Hong Kong; spkr. in field; archtl. critic various univs.; exec. fellow Harvard Design Sch. Former bd. dirs. Sheltering Arms Children Svc., Archtl. League, Chgo. City Ballet; chmn. bd. overseers Grad. Sch. Fine Arts, trustee U. Pa., adv. bd. MS in Real Estate Devel.; trustee Columbia U. Grad. Sch. Arch. and Planning, Silvermine Art Guild; mem. bd. advisors com. on the Art Gallery and Brit. Arts Ctr. Yale U.; bd. trustees Mus. African Art, NYC, Nat. Bldg. Mus. Lt. comdr. USN, 1953—56. Recipient Receiving the Flame of Truth award, Fund for Higher Edn., 1987, GSA award, Ellis Island Medal of Honor, 1998; Theopolis Parsons Chandler fellow. Fellow: AIA (pres. N.Y. chpt. 1987—88, internat. steering com., honor design awards 1962, 1984, 1987); mem.: Mcpl. Art Soc. N.Y., Nat. Coun. Archtl. Registration Bds., N.Y. State Assn. Archs., N.Y. Bldg. Congress, Urban Land Inst. (trustee), Royal Inst. Brit. Architects, Octagon Soc. of the AIA, University (N.Y.C.), City Club N.Y., TAu Sigma Delta. Avocations: painting, music, tennis, golf, skiing. Home: 570 Park Ave New York NY 10021 Office: Kohn Pedersen Fox Assocs PC 111 W 57th St New York NY 10019-2211 Home Phone: 212-688-8995; Office Phone: 212-237-3330. E-mail: gkohn@kpf.com.

KOHN, ALAN CHARLES, lawyer; b. St. Louis, Feb. 14, 1932; s. William Kohn and Rose Kohn (Steinberg) K.; m. Joanne J. Kohn, Aug. 29, 1954; children: Tom, Jim, John. AB, Washington U., 1953, LLB, 1955. Law clk. to assoc. justice Charles E. Whittaker U.S. Supreme Ct., 1957-58; assoc. William Kohn, St. Louis, 1958-59, Coburn, Croft & Kohn, St. Louis, 1959—70, ptnr., 1962-70, Kohn, Shands, Elbert, Gianoulakis & Giljum, St. Louis, 1970—. Mem. Mo. Bd. Law Examiners, 1974-79, pres., 1975-79; mem. U.S. Dist. Ct. (ea. dist.) Mo. Bd. Admissions, 1969-75, chmn., 1970-72; mem. fed. practice com. U.S. Dist. Ct. (ea. dist.) Mo., 1987-2003. Editor-in-chief Washington U. Law Quarterly, 1955; contbr. articles to profl. jours. Chmn. Mo. Housing Devel. Com., 1975-79; treas. University City (Mo.) Bd. Edn., 1970-71. 1st lt. U.S. Army Security Agy., 1955-57. Fellow Am. Coll. Trial Lawyers; mem. ABA, ABA Found., Am. Law Inst., Mo. Bar Assn., St. Louis Bar Assn., Am. Bd. Trial Advocates (advocate), Order of Coif, Phi Beta Kappa, Omicron Delta Kappa, Phi Eta Sigma. Republican. Avocation: tennis. Home: 40 Upper Ladue Rd Saint Louis MO 63124-1630 Office: Kohn Shands Elbert Gianoulakis & Giljum LLP One US Bank Plaza Suite 2410 Saint Louis MO 63101 Office Phone: 314-241-3963. E-mail: akohn@kseeg.com.

KOHN, DONALD L., federal official, economist; b. Phila., Nov. 7, 1942; m. Gail Kohn; children: Laura, Jeffrey. BA in Econ., Coll. Wooster, 1964; PhD in Econ., U. Mich., 1971; LLD (hon.), Coll. Wooster, 2006. Fin. economist Fed. Res. Bank Kans. City, 1970—75; economist, divsn. rsch. statistics Fed. Res. Sys., Washington, 1975—78, chief capital markets, 1978—81, assoc. dir., 1981—83, dep. staff dir. for monetary & fin. policy, 1983—87, dir., divsn. monetary affairs, 1987—2001, sec. fed. open market com., 1987—2002, adv. to bd. monetary policy, 2001—02, mem. bd. govs., 2002—, vice chmn., 2006—. Contbr. articles to profl. jours. Recipient Disting. Alumni award, Coll. Wooster, 1998, Disting. Achievement award, Money Marketeers of NYU, 2002. Office: Fed Res Sys Marriner S Eccles Fed Res Bd Bldg 20th St and Constitution Ave NW Rm 2022 Washington DC 20551*

KOHN, IMMANUEL, lawyer; b. Jerusalem, Dec. 6, 1926; arrived in US, 1934; s. Hans and Yetty (Wahl) Kohn; m. Vera Sharpe, July 22, 1950; children: Gail, Peter, Sheila, Robert. Grad., Deerfield Acad., 1944; BA summa cum laude, Harvard U., 1949; LL.B cum laude, Yale U., 1953. Bar: NY 1955, US Dist. Ct. (Ea. Dist.) NY 1955, US Dist. Ct. (So. Dist.) NY 1957, US Ct. Appeals (2nd Cir.) 1966, US Supreme Ct. 1972. Assoc. Cahill Gordon & Reindel LLP, NYC, 1953-62, ptnr., Corp. Practice Area, 1962, mem. exec. com., 1972—, chmn. exec. com., 1991—2005, sr. counsel, 2006—. Trustee Inst. Advanced Study, Princeton, NJ, 1997—. Editor: Yale U. Law Jour., 1951—53. Ensign US Maritime Svc., 1946. Sheldon travelling fellow, 1949—50. Mem.: Order of Coif, Downtown Assn., Beden Brook Club (NJ), Met. Opera Club, Phi Beta Kappa. Office: Cahill Gordon & Reindel LLP 80 Pine St Fl 17 New York NY 10005-1790 Office Phone: 212-701-3803. Office Fax: 212-378-2232. Business E-Mail: ikohn@cahill.com.

KOHN, JEAN GATEWOOD, retired health facility administrator, pediatrician; b. Chgo., July 8, 1926; d. Gatewood and Esther Lydia (Harper) Gatewood; m. Martin M. Kohn, Feb. 10, 1951; children: Helen, Joel, Michael, David. BS, U. Chgo., 1948, MD, 1950; MPH, U. Calif., Berkeley, 1973. Diplomate Am. Bd. Pediatrics. Physician Permanente Med. Group, San Leandro, Calif., 1953-60; pediatric cons. Calif. Children Svcs., 1961-72; lectr. maternal and child health U. Calif., 1973-91; med. advisor rehab. engring. ctr. Packard Children's Hosp. at Stanford, Calif., 1976-97, med. dir. child prosthetic clinic Calif., 1977-97, ret. Calif., 1997, pediatrician Mary L. Johnson Infant Devel. Unit, 2000—. Asst. neurologic diagnostic ctr. U. Calif., San Francisco, 1960-72; pediatric cons. Project HOPE, Nicaragua, 1966, Peru, 1962; pediatric cons. sch. pub. health U. Hawaii, Okinawa, 1975. Contbr. chpts. to books and articles to profl. jours.

Mem. adv. panel State of Calif. Dept. Spl. Edn., Calif. Children Svcs.; bd. dirs. Mental Health Assn., United Cerebral Palsy Assn., Head Start, San Mateo County, 1993—. Recipient Lyda M. Smiley award Calif. Sch. Nurses Orgn., 1987. Fellow Am. Acad. Pediats., Am. Acad. Cerebral Palsy and Devel. Medicine; mem. Project HOPE Alumni Assn. (pres. 1988-92). Office Phone: 650-725-8995.

KOHN, MARY LOUISE BEATRICE, nurse; b. Yellow Springs, Ohio, Jan. 13, 1920; d. Theophilus John and Mary Katherine (Schmitkons) Gaehr; m. Howard D. Kohn, 1944; children: Marcia R., Marcia K. Epstein. AB, Coll. Wooster, 1940; M in Nursing, Case Western Res. U., 1943. Nurse, 1943-44, Atlantic City Hosp., 1944, Thomas M. England Gen. Hosp., U.S. Army, Atlantic City, 1945-46, Peter Bent Brigham Hosp., Boston, 1947, Univ. Hosps., Cleve., 1946-48; mem. faculty Frances Payne Bolton Sch. Nursing Case Western Res. U., Cleve., 1948-52; vol. nurse Blood Svc. ARC, 1952-55; office nurse Cleve., 1955—94; freelance writer. Author: Berry and Kohn's Operating Room Technique, 1951, 11th edit., 2007; asst. editor: Cleve. Physician Acad. Medicine, 1966-71. Bd. dirs. Aux. Acad. Medicine Cleve., 1970-72, officer, 1976; active Cleve. Health Mus. Aux., Am. Cancer Soc. vol.; women's com. Cleve. Orch., 1970, Sta. WVIZ-TV. Mem.: ANA, Soc. Prevention of Cruelty to Animals, Assn. Oper. Rm. Nurses, Assn. Oper. Rm. Nurses of Greater Cleve. (charter, plaque 2004), Greater Cleve. Nurses Assn., Nat. Wildlife Fedn., Cleve. Zool. Soc., Coun. World Affairs, Friends of Cleve. Ballet, Alumni Assn. Wooster Coll., Frances P. Bolton Sch. Nursing Alumni Assn. (pres. 1974—75, bd. dirs. 1997—2000), Western Res. Hist. Soc., Am. Heart Assn., Cleve. Playhouse, Internat. Fund for Animal Welfare, Cleve. Animal Protective League, U.S. Humane Soc., Smithsonian Instn., Cleve. Children's Mus., Alzheimer's Assn., Sierra Club, Antique Automobile Assn. Am., Women's City Club (Jewel award 1992), Cleve. Racquet Club (social com. 1999—2000), Sigma Theta Tau Internat. Home: 28099 Belcourt Rd Cleveland OH 44124-5615

KOHN, PAUL FRANKLIN, mathematician; b. Mpls., Mar. 26, 1958; s. Wilbur and Lois Kohn; m. Fumie Ise Kohn, July 16, 1988. BA in Math., U. Minn., Duluth, 1981, BA in Computer Sci., 1981; MA in Math., U. Ariz., Tucson, 1987. Tchr. Seisen Internat. Sch., Tokyo, 1981—82; translation supr. Inter-Cultural Commn., Tokyo, 1982—83; flight analyst Space Shuttle, 45th Space Wing, Patrick AFB, Fla., 1988—, advisor to comdr., 1988—. Mem.: Math. Assn. Am. Office: 45th Space Wing/SELF Patrick Afb FL 32925 Office Phone: 321-494-5845. Personal E-mail: panda1963@msn.com.

KOHN, RICHARD H., historian, educator; b. Chgo., Dec. 29, 1940; s. Henry L. and Kate K.; m. Lynne Holtan, Aug. 15, 1964; children: Abigail, Samuel. AB, Harvard U., 1962; MS in History, U. Wis., 1964, PhD in history, 1968. Asst. prof. history CCNY, 1968-71; from asst. prof. to prof. Rutgers U., New Brunswick, NJ, 1971-84; Harold Keith Johnson vis. prof. mil. history U.S. Army Mil. History Inst., Army War Coll., Carlisle Barracks, Pa., 1980-81; chief of Air Force history USAF, Washington, 1981-91; adj. prof. Nat. War Coll., Washington, 1985-90; from assoc. prof. to prof. history U. NC, Chapel Hill, 1991—, chair curriculum in peace, war and defense, 1992—2006; Omar N. Bradley chair strategic leadership US Army War Coll. Dickinson Coll, 2006—07. Expert witness U.S. Indian Claims Commn., Washington, 1974; cons. to various def. and hist. agys. and orgns., 1972—; vis. scholar strategic studies Johns Hopkins U. Sch. Advanced Internat. Studies, 1991; dir. Triangle Inst. for Security Studies, 1992-2000; bd. visitors Air Univ. USAF, 1996-2001. Author: Eagle and Sword: The Federalists and the Creation of the Military Establishment in America, 1783-1802, 1975; co-author: The Exclusion of Black Soldiers from the Medal of Honor in World War II, 1997; editor (reprint series) The American Military Experience, 1979; editor: The U.S. Military under the Constitution of the United States, 1789-1989, 1991; co-editor: (books) Air Superiority in World War II and Korea, 1983, Air Interdiction in World War II, Korea, and Vietnam, 1986, Strategic Air Warfare, 1988, Soldiers and Civilians, 2001; contbr. articles to profl. jours., chpts. to books. Recipient cert. for patriotic civilian service Dept. of Army, 1981, 96, Orgnl. Excellence award Dept. Air Force, 1990, Exceptional Civilian Svc. award Dept. Air Force, 1991, Edward F. Miller History prize Naval War Coll., 2005. Mem. Air Force Hist. Found. (Pres.' award 1987), Am. Antiquarian Soc., Am. Hist. Assn. (coun. 1986-89), Orgn. Am. Historians (Binkley-Stephenson award 1973, pub. history com. 1989-92, chair 1991-92), Soc. for Mil. History (trustee 1981-89, 95-99, parliamentarian 1982-89, pres. 1989-93, chair nom. com. 2000-2003), World War II Studies Assn. (bd. dirs. 1985-88, 91-97, 2000-06). Office: U NC Curriculum in Peace War Def CB 3200 Chapel Hill NC 27599-3200

KOHN, ROGER ALAN, surgeon; b. Chgo., May 1, 1946; s. Arthur Jerome and Sylvia Lee (Karlen) K.; m. Barbara Helene, Mar. 30, 1974; children: Bradley, Allison. BA, U. Ill., Urbana, 1967; MD, Northwestern U., Evanston, Ill., 1971. Diplomate Am. Bd. Ophthalmology. Internship UCLA, 1971-72; residency Northwestern U., Chgo., 1972-75; fellowship U. Ala., Birmingham, 1975, Harvard Med. Sch., Boston, 1975-76; chmn. dept. ophthalmology Kern Med. Ctr., Bakersfield, Calif., 1978-87; asst. prof. UCLA Med. Sch., 1978-82, assoc. prof., 1982-86, prof., 1986—. Vice chmn. dept. ophthalmology Santa Barbara Cottage Hosp., Calif., 2004—05, chmn. dept. ophthalmology, 2006—, dir. Author: Textbook of Ophthalmic Plastic and Reconstructive Surgery, 1988; contbr. numerous articles to profl. jours.; author chpts. in 16 additional textbooks; patentee in field. Bd. dirs. Santa Barbara Symphony, Calif., 1990—. Capt. USAR, 1971-77. Name applied to med. syndrome Kohn-Romano Syndrome. Mem. Am. Soc. Ophthalmic Plastic and Reconstuctive Surgery (cert.), Am. Acad. Ophthalmology (Honor award 1995), Santa Barbara Ophthalmologic Soc. (pres. 1998), Pacific Coast Ophthal. Soc. (bd. dirs. 1986—, 1st v.p. 1990). Jewish. Avocations: guitar, tennis. Office: 525 E Micheltorena St Ste 201 Santa Barbara CA 93103-4212

KOHN, SHALOM L., lawyer; b. Nov. 18, 1949; s. Pincus and Helen (Roth) K.; m. Barbara Segal, June 30, 1974; children: David, Jeremy, Daniel. BS in Acctg. summa cum laude, CUNY, 1970; JD magna cum laude, Harvard U., 1974, MBA, 1974. Bar: Ill. 1975, U.S. Dist. Ct. (no. dist.) Ill. 1975, U.S. Ct. Appeals (7th cir.) 1976, U.S. Supreme Ct. 1980, N.Y. 1988, U.S. Dist. Ct. (so. dist.) N.Y. 1988, others. Law clk. to chief judge US Ct. Appeals (2d cir.), NYC, 1974-75; assoc. Sidley Austin LLP, Chgo., 1975-80, ptnr., 1980—. Exec. com. Adv. Coun. Religious Rights in Eastern Europe and Soviet Union, Washington, 1984-86; bd. dirs. Brisk Rabbinical Coll., Chgo. Contbr. articles to profl. jours. Mem. ABA, Chgo. Bar Assn. also: 787 Seventh Ave New York NY 10019 Office: Sidley Austin LLP One South Dearborn Chicago IL 60603 Home Phone: 847-933-9223; Office Phone: 312-853-7756, 212-839-5440. Business E-Mail: skohn@sidley.com.

KOHN, STEPHEN MARTIN, lawyer; b. Plainfield, NJ, Sept. 6, 1956; s. Arthur and Corinne Kohn; m. Leslie M. Rose, Oct. 23, 1988; children: Nataleigh Rose, Max Simon. BS magna cum laude, Boston U., 1979; MA, Brown U., 1981; JD, Northeastern U., Boston, 1984. Bar: Pa. 1985, N.J. 1986, D.C. 1988, U.S. Supreme Ct. 1987. Student law clk. U.S. Ct. Appeals (3d cir.), Phila., 1983-84; dir., corp litigation Govt. Accountability Project, Washington, 1984-88; ptnr. Kohn, Kohn & Colapinto, Washington, 1988—. Adj. prof., clin. supr. Antioch Sch. Law, Washington, 1984-88; chmn. bd. Nat. Whistleblower Ctr., Washington, 1988—. Author: Protecting Environmental and Nuclear Whistleblowers: A Litigation Manual, 1985, Jailed for Peace: The History of American Draft Law Violators, 1986, The Whistleblower Litigation Handbook: Environmental, Health and Safety Claims, 1990, American Political Prisoners: Prosecutions Under the Espionage & Sedition Act, 1994, Concepts and Procedures in Whistleblower Law, 2001; co-author: (with Michael D. Kohn) The Labor Lawyer's Guide to the Rights and Responsibilities of Employee Whistleblowers, 1988, Federal Whistleblower Laws and Regulation, 2003, Whistlebower Law: A Guide to Legal Protections and Procedures for Corporate Employees, 2004; contbr. articles to profl. jours. Fellow Nat. Endowment Humanities, 1981, Pub. Interest fellow Northeastern U. Sch. Law, 2006. Mem. DC Bar Assn. Office: Kohn Kohn & Colapinto LLP 3233 P St NW Washington DC 20007-2756 Office Phone: 202-342-6980. Business E-Mail: mjw@kkc.com.

KOHN, STEVEN M., lawyer; b. Chgo., June 19, 1942; m. Dorine Kohn; 3 children. BA, UCLA, 1965, MBA in fin., 1967; JD, U. San Francisco, 1974. Bar: Calif. 1974. With Crosby Heafey Roach & May (combined with Reed Smith in 2003), 1977—2003, chair products liability practice group; ptnr. Reed Smith LLP, Oakland, Calif., 2003—, practice group leader products liability group, 2003—. Mem.: ABA, Def. Rsch. Inst. (mem. drug and med. device litig. steering com., chair warnings subcom.), Internat. Assn. Def. Counsel, Alameda Bar Assn., San Francisco Bar Assn. Avocations: reading, photography, endurance sports. Office: Reed Smith LLP 1999 Harrison St, Ste 2400 Oakland CA 94612-3572 Office Phone: 510-466-6727. Office Fax: 510-273-8832. Business E-Mail: skohn@reedsmith.com.

KOHN, WALTER, physicist, retired educator; b. Vienna, Mar. 9, 1923; m. Mara Schiff; children: J. Marilyn, Ingrid E.Kohn Katz, E. Rosalind. BA, U. Toronto, Ont., Can., 1945, MA, 1946, LLD (hon.), 1967; DSc (hon.), U. Paris, 1980; PhD (hon.), Hebrew U. Jerusalem, 1981; DSc (hon.), Queens U., Kingston, Can., 1986, Fed. Inst. of Tech., Zurich, 1994, U. Wuerzburg, 1995, Tech. U. Vienna, 1996, Carnegie Mellon U., 1999, Rutgers U., 2001, Oxford U., 2001, U. Sherbrooke, Canada, 2002, Free U., Berlin, 2003; DSc, Tech. U., Dresden, 2003; PhD in Physics, Harvard U., 1948; PhD (hon.), Brandeis U., 1981, Weizmann Inst., Israel, 1997, Tel Aviv U., 1999. Indsl. physicist Sutton Horsley Co., Canada, 1941—43; geophysicist Koulomzine, Que., Canada, 1944—46; instr. physics Harvard U., Cambridge, Mass., 1948—50; asst. prof. physics Carnegie Mellon U., Pitts., 1950—60, assoc. prof. physics, 1953—57; prof. physics U. Calif., San Diego, 1960—79, chmn. dept. physics, 1961—63; dir. Inst. for Theoretical Physics, U. Calif., Santa Barbara, 1979—84; prof. dept. physics U. Calif., Santa Barbara, 1984—, prof. of physics emeritus, rsch. prof. of physics, 1991—; rsch. physicist Ctr. for Quantized Electronic Structures, U. Calif., Santa Barbara, 1991—. Vis. scholar U. Pa., U. Mich., U. Wash., U. Paris, U. Copenhagen, U. Jerusalem, Imperial Coll., London, ETH, Zurich, Switzerland; cons. Gen. Atomic, 1960—72, Westinghouse Rsch. Lab., 1953—57, Bell Telephone Labs., 1953—66, IBM, 1978; mem. or chmn. rev. coms. Brookhaven Nat. Labs., Argonne Nat. Labs., Oak Ridge Nat. Labs., Ames Lab., Tel Aviv U. (physics dept.), Brown U., Harvard U., U. Mich., Simon Frazer U., Tulane U., Reactor Divsn. NIST, Gaithersburg, Md.; chmn. S.D. divsn. Acad. Senate, 1968—69; dir. NSF Inst. Theoretical Physics U. Calif. Santa Barbara, 1979—84; mem. senate rev. com. U. Calif. Mgmt. Nat. Labs., 1986—89; adv. bd. Statewide Inst. Global Conflict and Cooperation, 1982—92; mem. bd. govs. Weizmann Inst. Sci., 1996—. Contbr. over 200 sci. articles and revs. to profl. jours. With Can. Army Inf., 1944—45. Recipient Buckley prize, 1960, Davisson-Germer prize, 1977, Nat. medal of Sci., 1988, Feenberg medal, 1991, Niels Bohr/UNESCO Gold medal, 1998, Nobel prize in Chemistry, 1998; fellow Lehman, Harvard U., 1946, NRC, 1950—51, sr., NSF, 1958, Guggenheim, 1963, sr. postdoctoral, NSF, 1967; grantee Oersted Fellow, Copenhagen, 1951—52. Fellow: AAAS, 1993, Am. Phys. Soc. (counselor-at-large 1968—72); mem.: NAS, 1969, Bavarian Acad. Scis. (corr. mem. 2003—), Royal Soc. of London, 1998, Am. Philos. Soc., Internat. Acad. Quantum Molecular Scis., 1991. Achievements include research in electron theory of solids and solid surfaces. Office: U Calif Dept Physics Santa Barbara CA 93106

KOHN, WILLIAM IRWIN, lawyer; b. Bronx, NY, June 27, 1951; s. Arthur Oscar and Frances (Hoffman) K.; m. Karen Mindlin, Aug. 29, 1974; children: Shira, Kinneret, Asher. Student, U. Del., 1969—71; BA with honors, U. Cin., 1973; JD, Ohio State U., 1976. Bar: Ohio 1976, US Dist. Ct. (no. and so. dists.) Ohio 1976, Ind. 1982, US Dist. Ct. (no. and so. dists.) Ind. 1982, DC 1992, US Supreme Ct., 1992, Ill. 1994, US Dist. Ct. (no., ctrl., and so. dists.) Ill., NY 2006, US Dist. Ct. (so. dist.) NY 2007; cert. Bus. Bankruptcy Law Am. Bankruptcy Bd. Cert. Ptnr. Krugliak, Wilkins, Griffith & Dougherty, Canton, Ohio, 1976-82, Barnes & Thornburg, Chgo., 1982—2001, Sachnoff & Weaver Ltd., Chgo., 2002, Schiff Harden LLP, Chgo., 2002—06, Benesch Friedlander Coplan & Aronoff, LLP, Cleve., 2006—. Adj. prof. law U. Notre Dame, Ind., 1984—90; bd. dirs. Ctr. for Disability and Elder Law, 2006. Author: West's Indiana Business Forms, West's Indiana Uniform Commercial Code Forms; contbr. articles to profl. jours. Bd. dirs. Family Svcs., South Bend, 1985—94, Jewish Fedn., Highland Park United Way, Jewish Family and Cmty. Svcs., 2000—05. Named Vol. of Yr., Ctr. for Disability and Elder Law, 2006; recipient Excellence in Pub. Interest Svc. award, US Dist. Ct. (no. dist.) Ill. and Fed. Bar Assn., 2006. Mem. ABA (bus. bankruptcy subcom.), Am. Bankruptcy Inst. (insolvency sect.), Ill. Bar Assn., Chgo. Bar Assn., Comml. Law League, Am. Bd. Certification (treas.). Office: Benesch Friedlander Coplan & Aronoff LLP 2300 BP Tower 200 Public Sq Cleveland OH 44114-2378 Office Phone: 216-363-4182. Business E-Mail: wkohn@bfca.com.

KOHNE, HEIDI ANN, church musician; b. Salem, Oreg., Sept. 15, 1974; d. Wilmar Allison and Karen Lee Kohne. MusB in organ performance, DePauw U., 1997; MusM in organ and ch. music, Ind. U., 1999. Organist St. Paul's Cath. Ch., Greencastle, Ind., 1994—97; concert office employee Interlochen Ctr. for the Arts, Interlochen, Mich., 1996—97, stage crew employee, 1998; organist Covenant Presbyn. Ch., Gresham, Oreg., 1999—2001; Kresge auditorium stage mgr. Interlochen Ctr. for the Arts, 1999—2003; organist Mt. Tabor Presbyn. Ch., Portland, Oreg., 2001—02, dir. music ministries, organist, 2003—. Program com. mem. Am. Guild Organists, Portland, Oreg., 2001—02, sub dean, 2002—04, dean, 2004—07, webmaster, 2005—. Computer graphics: Interlochen Stage Charts, 2003. Stage hand Portland Baroque Orch., Portland, Oreg., 2003—; accompanist Mt. Tabor Mid. Sch. Choir, Portland, Oreg., 2003—06. Mem.: PEO, Presbyn. Assn. Musicians, Am. Guild Organists (cert. svc. playing). Presbyterian. Home: 1917 NE 77th Ave Portland OR 97213 Office: Mt Tabor Presbyn Ch 5441 SE Belmont Portland OR 97215 Office Phone: 503-234-6493. E-mail: hkohne@theinter.com.

KOHNSTAMM, ABBY E., marketing executive; b. LA; married; 2 children. BA, Tufts U.; MA in Edn., NYU, MBA. Various mktg. positions including sr. v.p. cardmember mktg. Am. Express, 1979—93; v.p. corp. mktg. IBM, Armonk, NY, 1993—98, sr. v.p. corp. mktg., 1998—2006, cons., 2006—. Bd. of overseers Arts & Sci. Tufts U., NYU Stern Sch. of Bus.; bd. dirs. IBM Credit Corp., Tiffany & Co. Mem. Assn. Nat. Advertisers. Avocations: music, theater. Office: IBM Corp New Orchard Rd Armonk NY 10504-1722 Office Phone: 914-765-1900. E-mail: abby@us.ibm.com.

KOHR, HOWARD A., lobbyist; b. 1955; m. Sherri Kohr; 3 children. Mgmt. fellow US Dept. Def.; dep. dir. Nat. Jewish Coalition; asst. Wash. rep. Am. Jewish Com.; various sr. staff positions Am. Israel Pub. Affairs Com., exec. dir., 1996—. Office: Am Israel Pub Affiars Com 440 1st St NW Ste 600 Washington DC 20001*

KOHRING, VICTOR H., state legislator; b. Waukegan, Ill., Aug. 2, 1958; s. Heinz H. and Dolores E. Kohring. AAS in Bus. Adminstrn., Matanuska-Susitna C.C., Palmer, Alaska, 1985; BA in Mgmt. Sci., Alaska Pacific U., 1987, MBA, 1989. State legislator Ho. of Reps., Dist. 26 Wasilla and Peters Creek/Chugiak, AK, 1994, re-elected 1996, 98—; mem. ho. fin. com. Ho. of Reps., 1994, 96, 98—. Chmn. house budge subcoms. for dept. edn., 1995-96, adminstrn., 1995-96, environ. conservation, 1997-98, cmty. and regional affairs, 1997-98, commerce and econ. devel., 1997-98, law, 1999—, natural resources, 1999—; constn. exec., 1978—; real estate developer, 1978-82. Bd. dirs. Alaska Housing Fin. Corp., Anchorage, 1991-94; vice chmn., mem. Iditarod Trail Com.; mem. Matanuska-Susitna Borough Econ. Devel. Commn., 1993-94; mem. Wasilla Planning and Utilities Commn., 1991-94; chmn., mem. Alaska del. Rep. Nat. Conv., Dallas, 1984, dist. del. rep., 1984, 86, 90, 92; treas. Rep. Party Alaska, Mat-Su, 1990, fin. chmn., 1990-91. Mem. NRA, Christian Businessman's Assn., Greater Wasilla C. of C., Chugiak-Eagle River C. of C., Anthony J. Dimond H.S. Alumni Assn., Pioneers of Alaska. Republican. Home: PO Box 870515 Wasilla AK 99687-0515 Office: Alaska Ho of Reps State Capitol Bldg Juneau AK 99801

KOHRMAN, ARTHUR FISHER, pediatrics educator; b. Cleve., Dec. 19, 1934; s. Benjamin Myron and Leah (Fisher) K.; m. Claire Hoffenberg, Nov. 10, 1955; children: Deborah, Benjamin, Ellen, Rachel. BA, BS, U. Chgo., 1955; MD, Western Res. U., 1959. Diplomate Am. Bd. Pediatrics. Lic. Ill., Ind. Intern Cleve. Met. Gen. Hosp., 1959-60; resident in pediatrics Case Western Res. U., Cleve., 1960—62; post doctoral fellow Stanford U., Palo Alto, Calif., 1965-68; from asst. prof. to prof. Mich. State U., East Lansing, 1968—81, assoc. chmn. dept. human devel., 1968—78, assoc. dean Coll. Human Medicine, 1977—81; prof., assoc. chmn. dept. pediatrics U. Chgo., 1981-96; pres. La Rabida Children's Hosp. and Research Ctr., Chgo., 1981-96; prof. pediatrics, assoc. chmn. Northwestern U. Sch. Medicine and Children's Meml. Hosp., Chgo., 1997—2002; prof. preventive medicine Sch. Medicine, Northwestern U., Chgo., 2000—02, prof. emeritus pediatrics and preventive medicine, 2003—. Congl. fellow Office Tech. Assessment, U.S. Congress, 1980-81; pres. Children's Hospice Internat., 1983-86; chmn. instl. rev. bd. U. Chgo., 1986-96. Contbr. numerous scholarly articles to profl. jours. Served to capt. USAF, 1962-65. Recipient Outstanding Service award Am. Diabetes Assn. Mich. chpt., 1977. Fellow Am. Acad. Pediatrics (chmn. com. on bioethics 1990-94); mem. Am. Pediatric Soc., Ambulatory Pediatric Assn., Soc. Pediatric Rsch., Lawson Wilkins Pediatric Endocrine Soc., Alpha Omega Alpha.

KOHRT, CARL FREDRICK, research and development company executive; b. Normal, Ill., Dec. 18, 1943; s. Carl Fred and Catherine Elizabeth (Traughber) K.; m. Margaret Lynne McCartney; children: Kristopher Alan, Brian Douglas, Jason Ivor. BS, Furman U., 1965; PhD, U. Chgo., 1971; MS, MIT, 1991. Postdoctoral fellow James Franck Inst., U. Chgo., 1970—71; sr. scientist rsch. labs. Eastman Kodak, Rochester, NY, 1971-76, rsch. lab. head, 1977-79, asst. div. dir. rsch. labs., 1979-84, asst. to vice chmn. Kodak office, 1984-85, div. dir. electronic rsch. labs., 1985-87, dir. rsch. photographic rsch. labs., 1987-90; Kodak's mem. of Sloan fellow program MIT, Cambridge, 1990—91, gen. mgr. health scis. divsn., 1991-95; exec. v.p., asst. COO, 1995-98; exec. v.p., asst. COO, chief tech. officer, 1998-2000; pres., CEO Battelle Meml. Inst., Columbus, Ohio, 2001—. Vice chmn., bd. dirs. Battelle Energy Alliance LLC, Brookhaven Sci. Assocs.; chair bd. trustees COSI Columbus; bd. trustees Furman U.; bd. dirs. Pharos LLC, Battelle Energy Alliance, LLC; chair bd. govs. UT-Battelle LLC, mem. coun. competitiveness. Contbr. articles to profl. jours.; patentee in field. Chmn. sustaining membership Boy Scouts Am., Rochester, 1988, scoutmaster, Pittsford, NY, 1976-88, mem. exec. bd. Otetiana coun., 1997; chair Cmty. Needs Study, Greece, NY, 1973; bd. dirs. Greater Columbus C. of C; trustee Ohio Bus. Roundtable. Woodrow Wilson fellow (hon.), 1965, NSF Grad. fellow, 1965—70. Mem.: Indsl. Rsch. Inst. (alt. rep.). Presbyterian. Avocations: backpacking, whitewater canoeing, music. Office: Battelle Mem Inst 505 King Ave Columbus OH 43201

KOHUT, JOHN WALTER, corporate executive; b. NYC, Nov. 13, 1946; s. Walter and Stelle (Dudar) K.; m. Linda Susan Ram, Jan. 3, 1987; 1 child, Katherine Grace. BBA in Fin. and Econs., U. Miami, Coral Gables, Fla., 1969. Mgmt. trainee Bankers Trust Co., NYC, 1969-73, asst. treas. in comml. banking, 1973-76, asst. v.p. spl. loans, 1976-79, v.p. European Energy London, 1979-82, v.p. Global Aerospace, 1982-85; mng. dir. Pvt. Equity B.T. Securities Corp., NY, 1985-90; pres., chief exec. officer W. Atlee Burpee Co., Warminster, Pa., 1990-91, Ramko Venture Mgmt., Inc., NYC, 1991—. Bd. dirs. U.S. Automotive Mfg., Inc., Richmond, Va., chmn., prin. fin. officer, 1997-2000; v.p. Pyramid Investors, N.Y.C., 1988-90. Bd. dirs. 309 E. 49th St. C.A., N.Y.C., 1985-91; elected committeeman Rep. County, Somerset, N.J., 1976-79; mem. adv. com. on comml. aspects of space NASA, 1984-87; bd. adv. St. Bartholomew Community Preschool, N.Y.C., 1992-97. Mem. AIAA (bd. dirs. 1987-91), Turnaround Mgmt. Assn., Am. Bankruptcy Inst., Tau Kappa Epsilon. Roman Catholic. Office: Ramko Venture Mgmt Inc 711 5th Ave New York NY 10022-3111 Home: 111 E 80th St Apt 4D New York NY 10021-0350 Office Phone: 212-223-2451. E-mail: ramko@earthlink.net.

KOHUT, ROBERT IRWIN, otolaryngologist, educator; b. Chgo., Nov. 29, 1932; s. Emil and Ruth Irene Kohut; m. Joanne Kay Hughes, Dec. 26, 1953 (dec. Oct. 1982); children: James, Paul, Robert, John; m. Frances Irene Speas, June 6, 1983 (div. 1999). BA, Wittenburg Coll., 1956; MD, U. Chgo., 1960. Diplomate Am. Bd. Otolaryngology (bd. dirs. 1979). Intern U. Chgo., 1961—62, resident in otolaryngology, 1962—65, NIH fellow, 1965—66, instr. in otolaryngology, 1965—66; asst. prof. U. Fla., Gainesville, 1966—68, assoc. prof., 1968-71, assoc. prof., acting chmn., 1971—72; prof., chief otolaryngology U. Calif., Irvine, 1972—79; prof., chmn. otolaryngology Wake Forest U. Sch. Medicine, Winston-Salem, NC, 1979—99, emeritus prof., chair, 1999—. Mem. study sect. Nat. Insts. Neurol. and Communicative Disorders and Stroke/NIH, Bethesda, Md., 1981—86; cons. NASA, 1982—84; mem. adv. bd. Nat. Inst. Deafness and Other Comm. Disorders, 1991—94; exec. v.p. med. affairs, med. dir. Deafness Rsch. Found., 1999—2001. Contbr. numerous chpts. to books and articles to profl. jours.; editor otology divsn. Head and Neck Surgery-Otolaryngology; mem. editorial bd. Am. Jour. Otology, 1992-2000, Am. Jour. Otolaryngology, 1982-2000, Archives of Otolaryngology, 1980-2000, Laryngoscope, 1976-2000. With USAF, 1950-53. Recipient Norvel Pierce award Chgo. Laryngological Soc., 1965, Basic Rsch. award Acad. Ophthalmology and Otolaryngology, 1968. Mem. ACS, Soc. Univ. Otolaryngologists (pres. 1978-79), Barany Soc., Am. Laryngological, Rhinological and Otological Soc. (exec. coun. 1987-90, Edmund Fowler award 1974, Guest of Honor, So. sect. 1996), Am. Broncho-Esophagological Ass., Am. Neurotology Assn., Otosclerosis Study Group, Am. Otological Soc. (sec.-treas. 1987-92, pres.-elect 1992-93, pres. 1993-94), Assn. Acad. Depts. Otolaryngology, Pacific Coast Oto-Ophthalmol. Soc., Forsyth County Med. Soc., N.C. Med. Soc., N.C. Soc. Otolaryngology Head and Neck Surgery (v.p. 1985, pres. 1986-87), Assn. for Rsch. in Otolaryngology, Am. Acad. Otolaryngology-Head and Neck Surgery, Am. Soc. Head and Neck Surgery, Internat. Fedn. Oto-Rhino-Laryngological Soc. (chmn. emeritus standing com. edn. 2004), others. Avocations: fishing, hunting, sailing. Office: Wake Forest U Sch Medicine Dept Otolaryngology Medical Center Blvd Winston Salem NC 27157-0001 Personal E-mail: rikohut@hughes.net.

KOIDE, FRANK TAKAYUKI, electrical engineering educator; b. Honolulu, Dec. 25, 1935; s. Sueichi and Hideko (Dai) K.; children: Julie Anne M., Cheryl Lynne K. BSEE, U. Ill., 1958; MEE, Clarkson U., Potsdam, NY, 1961; PhD, U. Iowa, 1966. Publs. engr. to electronics engr. Collins Radio Co., Cedar Rapids, Iowa, 1958-61; tchr. Cedar Rapids Adult Edn. Sch., 1960-61; lab. instr. U. Iowa Coll. Medicine, 1963-64; asst. prof. Iowa State U., 1966-69; prin. biomed. engr. Tech., Inc., San Antonio, 1968-69; mem.

faculty U. Hawaii, 1969—2002, prof. elec. engring. and physiology, 1974—95, prof. emeritus, 2002—. Cons. in field. Author papers, reports in field. NIH predoctoral fellow, 1966; NASA-Am. Soc. Engring. Edn. Space systems Design Inst. fellow, 1967; NSF Digital and Analogue Electronics Inst. fellow U. Ill., 1972. Mem. IEEE. Office: U Hawaii Dept Electrical Engring 2540 Dole St Honolulu HI 96822-2303 Office Phone: 808-956-7406. Business E-Mail: koide@spectra.eng.hawaii.edu.

KOIVU, SAKU, professional hockey player; b. Turku, Finland, Nov. 23, 1974; m. Hanna Koivu; 1 child, Ilona. Center Montreal Canadiens, 1995—, capt., 1999—. Player NHL All-Star Game, 1998, 2003. Recipient King Clancy Meml. Trophy, NHL, 2002, 2007, Bill Masterton Trophy, NHL, 2002. Achievements include being a member of the Bronze medal Finnish Hockey Team, Lillehammer Olympics, Norway, 1994, Nagano Olympics, Japan, 1998 and the Silver medal Torino Olympics team, Italy, 2006. Avocation: golf. Office: Montreal Canadiens 1275 St Antoine St W Montreal PQ Canada H3C 5L2*

KOJAIAN, C. MICHAEL, real estate company executive; b. Highland Pk., Mich., Nov. 25, 1930; s. Charles Kojaian; m. Elizabeth Ann Kojaian. Pres. Kojaian Companies; chmn. Grubb & Ellis Co., 2002—. Bd. dirs. Flagstar Bank and Ascet; chmn. Dott Industries. Pres. Armenian Apostolic Soc.; mem. Armenian Gen. Benevolent Union. Mailing: Grubb & Ellis Co 500 W Monroe St Ste 2800 Chicago IL 60661*

KOJEVNIKOV, BORIS OLEG, lawyer, consultant; b. Rome, Oct. 16, 1950; came to U.S., 1977; s. Oleg Vladimir and Oxana (Artem) K.; m. Irina Maxim Baranova, Aug. 8, 1974; children: Oxana, Oleg. Law Degre, Inst. Fgn. Rels., Moscow, 1972, Cand Legal Scis., 1984. Legal adviser USSR Ministry Fgn. Trade, Moscow, 1972-77, Amtorg Trading Corp., NYC, 1977-82, Comecon, Moscow, 1982-84; dir. legal dept. Chamber Commerce and Industry, Moscow, 1984-91; v.p. Prosystem GmbH, Vienna, 1991-96; v.p., mem. Golubov & Tiagai, NYC, 1996—; mng. dir. Inhorn GmbH, Vienna, 1999—. Arbitrator Internat. Comml. Arbitration ct., Moscow, 1984—, Internat. Arbitration Ctr., Vienna, 1989-94. Author 4 books; contbr. more than 20 articles to U.S., Russian and German periodicals. Fellow Chartered Inst. of Arbitrators; mem. Assn. Bar City N.Y., U.S.-USSR Trade and Econ. Coun. Inc. (USSR co-chmn. legal com. 1989-91), Canada-USSR Bus. Coun. (USSR co-chmn. legal com. 1989-91), Internat. Chamber of Commerce (USSR coord. ICC-USSR joint task force, 1989-90). Avocations: tennis, squash. Office: Golubov & Tiagai LLC 49 W 45th St #12 New York NY 10036-4603 Home: PO Box 1131 Englewood Cliffs NJ 07632-0131

KOJIMA, SHERI S., high school business educator; married; 3 children. BA, Univ. Hawaii, Manoa; M in Occupational Studies, Univ. Calif., Long Beach. Bus. tchr., 1990—; career, tech. edn. tchr. Waiakea H.S., Hilo, Hawaii, 1994—; and lead instr. Waiakea H.S. Bus. Acad. Named Secondary Educator of Yr., Hawaii Bus. Edn. Assn., 2002, Hawaii Tchr. of Yr., 2006. Office: Waiakea High Sch 155 West Kawili St Hilo HI 96720 Office Phone: 808-974-4888 ext. 245. Business E-Mail: Sheri_Kojima/WAIAKEAH/HIDOE@notes.k12.hi.us.*

KOJIMA, TAKESHI, law educator, arbitrator, writer, dean; b. Yokohama, Japan, Sept. 1, 1936; s. Buzaemon and Maki Kojima; m. Shigeko Niwa, May 3, 1966; children: Natsuko, Haruka. BA, Chuo U., Tokyo, 1959, LLM, 1961, LLD, 1978; qualified lawyer, Inst. Legal Tng. and Rsch., Tokyo, 1963. Rschr. U. Mich., Ann Arbor, 1966-68; asst. prof. law Chuo U., 1960-64, assoc. prof., 1964-71, prof., 1971—2006, councilor, 1995—, chmn. grad. sch., 1997—, hon. prof. law, 2006—; dean Toin Yokohama U., Japan, 2006—, prof. law, chmn. grad. sch. law. Vis. prof. U. Florence, Italy, 1974, Columbia U., N.Y.C., 1988; guest prof. Aix-Marseille (France) U., 1983, Frankfurt (Germany) Goethe U., 1991-92; examiner nat. jud. exam. Ministry Justice, Tokyo, 1984-90, acting chmn. Study Commn. on Issue Fgn. Lawyers (with Ministry Justice, Japan Fedn. Bar Assns.), 1992-94, chmn. Study Commn. on Representation in Internat. Arbitration (with Ministry Justice, Japan Fedn. Bar Assns.), 1994-95; chmn. Study Commn. on Fgn. Lawyers (with Ministy Justice, Japan Bar Assns.), 1996—, acad. councillor Ctr. Internat. Civil & Comml. Law, 1996—; trustee Ctr. Automobile Product Liability, 1995—; chmn. study commn. on issue fgn. lawyers Ministry of Justice, Japan Fedn. Bar Assns., 1996—; legis. coun. Ministry of Justice, 1997—; expert mem. coun. for screening newly founded univs. and other schs., Ministry Edn., 1990-95; dir. Japan Inst. Comparative Law, Tokyo, 1987-90. Co-author: Access to Justice, Vol. I, 1978, Small Claims Courts, 1991; editor: Perspectives on Civil Justice and ADR, 1990, The Grand Design of America's Justice System, 1995; contbr. articles to profl. jours. Spl. arbitrator Ctrl. Tribunal, Ministry Constrn., Tokyo, 1990—; spl. mem. coun. on indsl. structure Ministry Internat. Trade and Industry, Tokyo, 1991-94; mem. Nat. Tribunal Constrn. Procurement, Office of Prime Min., Tokyo, 1991-96; insp. Govtl. Sch. Insp., Ministry Edn., Tokyo, 1993—, chmn. collaborators conf. for rsch. legal edn. reform; coun. legis. on civil procedure, Ministry Justice, 1997—. Mem. Japanese Assn. Civil Procedure Law (pres. 1995-98), Japanese Assn. Pvt. Law (bd. dirs. 1983-87), Japan Legal Aid Assn. (mng. trustee 1993—), Japan Negotiation Assn. (v.p. 1993—), Japan Assn. Lawyers (trustee 1975—), Japanese-Am. Assn. for Legal Studies (councilor 1991-). Buddhist. Avocations: golf, travel.

KOK, FRANS JOHAN, investment banker; b. Zaandam, Netherlands, May 14, 1943; came to U.S., 1963; s. Cornelis and Aaf K.; m. Mary M. Shirley, Dec. 23, 1971. BA in Econ., Occidental Coll., LA, 1967; MA in Econs., Calif. State U., LA, 1969; MBA, Insead, Fontainebleau, France, 1971, Harvard U., 1972. Assoc. Booz, Allen & Hamilton, Washington, 1974-78; chief economist EPA, Washington, 1978-80; CFO, co-founder Long Lake Energy Corp., NYC, 1980-83; mng. dir. Ferris, Baker-Watts, Inc., Balt., 1983-89, 1st Nat. Bank Md., Balt., 1989-94; chmn., CEO, Johan Hekelaar, Inc., Chevy Chase, Md., 1994—; chmn. MarinaLife LLC, Balt. Bd. dirs. MaxPitch Media, Inc., Richmond, Va. Home: PO Box 423 Philomont VA 20131 Home Phone: 540-554-8625; Office Phone: 301-656-7870.

KOK, HANS GEBHARD, consulting engineer; b. Potshausen, Germany, Apr. 5, 1923; came to U.S., 1951, naturalized, 1959; s. George J. and Anitina K. (Janssen) K.; m. Roselle V. Venier, June 22, 1960; Children: George H., Karen R. Student, Suderburg Engring. Coll., Germany, 1940-42, Hamburg Engring Coll., 1945-46; Dipl.Ing, Technische Hochschule, Aachen, Germany, 1950. Registered profl. engr., N.Y., Pa., Ind., Mich., Calif., Fla., N.J., Ariz., Md. Design engr. Lummus Co., NYC, 1951-53; structural engr. M.H. Treadwell Co., NYC, 1953-56, head structural engring. sect., 1956-62, chief structural engr., 1962-63; mgr. plant design divsn. Treadwell Corp., NYC, 1963-69, asst. v.p. engring., 1969-73, v.p. engring., 1973-83; pres. Treadwell Corp. Mich., Inc., 1974-83; dir. BassetMiller Treadwell Pty. Ltd., 1973-83; cons. engr., 1983—. Chmn. exec. com. Coun. Engring. Laws, 1976. Contbr. articles to profl. jours. Recipient 1st award James F. Lincoln Arc Welding Found., 1966. Fellow ASCE; mem. Nat. Soc. Profl. Engrs., N.Y. State Soc. Profl. Engrs., Am. Inst. Mining, Metall. and Petroleum Engrs. (chmn. materialshandling com.), Am. Mining congress, Am. Mgmt. Assn. Home: 4438 Meager Cir Port Charlotte FL 33948-9495

KOKA, PRASAD S., biomedical researcher; s. Satyanarayana Rao and Saraswathy Koka; m. Trishla Gupta; children: Shipra Saraswathi, Anshul, Ankit. PhD, Tex. Tech U., 1977. Postdoctoral fellow Cold Spring Harbor (N.Y.) Lab., 1982—84; postdoctoral assoc. MIT, Cambridge, 1984—85; rsch. fellow, instr. Harvard Med. Sch., Boston, 1985—89; asst./assoc. rschr. U. Calif. Geffen Sch. of Medicine, LA, 1989—2005; assoc. mem. Torrey Pines Inst. for Molecular Studies, San Diego, 2005—. Editor, jour. stem cells Nova Sci. Publishers, Hauppauge, NY, 2005—. Grantee RO-1, NIH, 2005—. Office: Torrey Pines Inst for Molecular Studies 3550 General Atomics Ct San Diego CA 92121 Office Phone: 858-455-3786. Office Fax: 858-455-3804. Business E-Mail: pkoka@tpims.org.

KOKALJ, JAMES EDWARD, retired aerospace administrator; b. Chgo., Oct. 29, 1933; s. John and Antoinette (Zabukovec) K. AA in Engring., El Camino Coll., Torrance, Calif., 1953. Dynomometer lab. technician U.S. Electric Motors, LA, 1953-54; devel. lab. technician AiResearch divsn. Garrett, LA, 1956-59; tech. rep. McCulloch, LA, 1959-65; dist. mgr. Yamaha Internat., Montebello, Calif., 1965-67; salesman Vasek Polak BMW, Manhattan Beach, Calif., 1967-68; sr. svc. rep. Stratos-We. div. Fairchild, Manhattan Beach, 1968-70; asst. regional mgr. we. states J.B.E. Olson div. Grumman, LA, 1970-71; gen. mgr. Internat. Kart Fedn., Glendora, Calif., 1971-73; logistics support data specialist Mil. Aircraft divsn. Northrop Grumman, Hawthorne, Calif., 1974-95; ret., 1995. Author: Technical Inspection Handbook, 1972; contbr. articles to profl. jours. With USN, 1954-56. Mem. U.S. Naval Inst., Internat. Naval Rsch. Orgn., Nat. Maritime Hist. Soc., So. Calif. Hist. Aircraft Found., Found. L.A. Maritime Mus. Republican. Roman Catholic. Avocations: woodworking, ship modeling, history, auto restoration. Home: 805 Bayview Dr Hermosa Beach CA 90254-4147

KOKE, RICHARD JOSEPH, writer, curator; b. NYC, Sept. 19, 1916; s. Joseph and Emily Josephine (Chevrolet) K.; m. Mary A. Kimbley, Jan. 1, 1955. Student, Art Students League, 1935, Cooper Union Art Inst., 1935-37; AB, NYU, 1941; MA, Columbia U., 1947. Historian, Bear Mountain (N.Y.) Trailside Hist. Mus., 1935-37; curator Stony Point (N.Y.) Battlefield Mus., summers 1937-41; research cons. Hudson Valley Survey, 1946-47; historian Saratoga Nat. Hist. Park, 1947; curator mus. N.Y. Hist. Soc., 1947-83, curator emeritus, 1983—. Conducted archaeol. investigations on Revolutionary War mil. sites in Highlands of the Hudson, N.Y., 1935-41 Author: Accomplice in Treason; Joshua Hett Smith and the Arnold Conspiracy, 1973, Corridor Through the Mountains, 1998; editor: Scenic and Historic America, 1938; contbr. mags. and revs.; compiler American Landscape and Genre Painting in the New York Historical Society, 3 vols., 1982. Served with AUS, 1942-45; art dir, in charge cartographic dept. M.C. 1942-44; battlefield history research analyst. hist. sect. Hdgrs. 1944-45; engaged in collection and editing of mil. data pertaining to tactical operations Am. forces, preparation ofcl. army histories of Services of Supply, 1st, 3d, 7th, 9th, 15th armies World War 11, Western European Front. Recipient 1st prize hist. essay contest sponsored by Colonial Dames of N.Y., 1940 Home: PO Box 700 Peru NY 12972-0700 Office: 170 Central Park W New York NY 10024-5152

KOKEN, M. DIANE, former state official, insurance company executive; b. Lancaster, Pa., Dec. 29, 1952; d. James E. Koken and Helen Sotiro; m. John K. Herr III; children: Kathryn, Rebecca. BS magna cum laude, Millersville U., 1972; JD, Villanova U., 1975. Counsel, v.p., corp. sec. Provident Mutual Ins. Co., Phila., 1975-97; commr. Pa. Ins. Dept., Harrisburg, 1997—2007. Pres. Nat. Assn. Ins. Commissioners, 2004—05; bd. dirs. Nationwide Mutual Ins. Co./Nationwide Mutual Fire Ins. Co., 2007—. Mem. ABA, Phila. Bar Assn., Internat. Claims Assn.*

KOKKELER, FAY ESTHER, music educator; d. Ray Lorraine-Frank and May Ida Herzog. BS in Music Edn., U. Mo., Columbia, 1969; MusM, So. Ill. U., Edwardsville, 1971. Cert. music tchr. Music tchr. Wohlwead Elem. Sch., St. Louis, 1969—71, Plantation Mid. Sch., Fla., 1971—72; chorus/drama tchr. Seminole Mid. Sch., Plantation, 1972—, chmn. unified arts dept.; percussion instr. Broward CC, Pompano Beach, Fla., 1973—84. Prin. timpanist, percussionist Fla. Grand Opera, Miami, 1971—86, Miami, 2000—, Miami City Ballet, 1986—; prin. timpanist Symphony of Americas, Ft. Lauderdale, Fla., 1988—2005. Author drama curriculum. Named Tchr. of Yr., Seminole Mid. Sch., 1983, 1984, 1993, Arts Tchr. of Yr., Broward County Sch. Dist., 1995. Mem.: Broward Tchrs.' Union, Am. Fedn. Musicians, Broward Vocal Tchrs. Assn. Democrat. Avocations: flower arranging, furniture refinishing, stained glass. E-mail: fkokkeler@bellsouth.net.

KOKONAS, NICK J., restaurant owner; b. 1968; m. Dagmara Cepuritis; 2 children. BA, Colgate U., 1990. Derivatives trader Chgo. Merc. Exch., 1990—94; founder Third Moment Trading LLC, Chgo., 1996—2002; co-founder & ptnr. Alinea, Chgo., 2005—; mng. ptnr. Achatz LLC, Chgo. Named one of 40 Under 40, Crain's Chgo. Bus., 2006. Office: Alinea 1723 N Halsted Chicago IL 60614 Office Phone: 312-867-0110. E-mail: info@alinearestaurant.com.

KOKOTOS, WILLIAM J., cardiothoracic surgeon; b. NYC; BA in Chemistry, NYU, 1986, MD, 1990. Resident in gen. surgery NYU Med. Ctr., NYC, 1990—95, thoracic surgery fellow, 1995—97; attending surgeon Heart Lung Inst., Pitts., 1997—2003; attending surgeon, dir. arrhythmia surgery Winthrop U. Hosp., Mineola, NY, 2003—. Fellow: ACS, Soc. Thoracic Surgeons; mem.: AMA. Office: 120 Mineola Blvd Ste 300 Mineola NY 11501 Office Phone: 516-663-4400.

KOKOTOVIC, PETAR V., electrical and computer engineering educator; b. Mar. 18, 1934; Dipl.Eng., U. Belgrade, Yugoslavia, 1958, Magistar (Elec. Engring.), 1963; Candidate of Tech. Scis., Russian Acad. Scis., Moscow, 1965. Prof. elec. engring. U. Ill., Urbana, 1966-91, Grainger prof. emeritus, 1991—; prof. elec. and computer engring. U. Calif., 1991—; dir. Ctr. for Control Engring. and Computation. Recipient Quazza medal Internat. Fedn. Automatic Control, 1990, IEEE Control Sys. Field award, 1995. Fellow: IEEE (Engring. Outstanding AC Transactions Paper award 1982—83, Axelby Outstanding Paper award 1991—92, H. Bode Prize lecture 1991, James H. Mulligan, Jr. Edn. medal 2002, Richard E. Bellman Control Heritage award 2002); mem.: NAE. Office: U Calif Electrical & Comp Eng Dept Santa Barbara CA 93106

KOLA, ARTHUR ANTHONY, lawyer; b. New Brunswick, NJ, Feb. 16, 1939; s. Arthur Aloysius and Blanche (Raym) K.; m. Jacquelin Lou Draper, Sept. 3, 1960; children— Jill, Jean, Jennifer; m. Anna Molnar, Apr. 15, 1977 AB, Dartmouth Coll., 1961; LLB, Duke U., 1964. Bar: Ohio 1964, U.S. Dist. Ct. (no. dist.) Ohio 1969, U.S. Ct. Appeals (6th cir.) 1971, U.S. Supreme Ct. 1972. Assoc. Squire, Sanders & Dempsey, Cleve., 1964-65, assoc., 1968-74, ptnr., 1974-94; pvt. practice Kola Law Office, Cleve., 1994—. Asst. prof. law Ind. U., Bloomington, 1967-68; instr. labor law Case Western Res. U., Cleve., 1976 Bd. visitors Duke U. Sch. Law, 1985—. Served to capt. U.S. Army, 1965-67 Mem. Ohio Bar Assn., Cleve. Bar Assn. (chmn. labor and employment law sect. 1993-94), Am. Arbitration Assn. (bd. dirs. 1991-97). Office: Kola Law Office 6100 Oak Tree Blvd Ste 200 Independence OH 44131-6914 Office Phone: 216-328-2009.

KOLA, RAMESH, oncologist; MD, Osmania Med. Coll., Hyderabad, 1982. Lic. bd. cert. oncology, hematology and internal medicine. Resident Grant Hosp.-Rush, Chgo., 1985—88; fellow oncology-hematology U. Ill., Chgo., 1988—91; oncologist, hematologist Dreyer Med. Clinic, Aurora, Ill., 1991—2005, chmn. oncology, 1999—2005; oncologist, hematologist Midwest Ctr. for Cancer, Sandwich, Ill., 2005—. Med. dir. Vis. Nurse Assn. Hospice, Aurora, 1993—2005; med. dir. oncology rsch. Rush Copley Med. Ctr., Aurora, 2003—05. Cancer liaison physician Am. Cancer Soc., Aurora, 1999—2004, sponsor Relay for Life Sandwich, 2006. Named Top Doctor, Castle Connolly, 2001; recipient Milestone award, Dreyer Med. Clinic, 2003, Pres. award, Vis. Nurse Assn., 2004. Office: Midwest Ctr for Cancer and Blood 15 W Pleasant Ave Sandwich IL 60548

KOLAKOWSKI, DIANA JEAN, county commissioner; b. Detroit, Aug. 28, 1943; d. Leo and Genevieve (Bosh) Zyskowski; m. William Francis Kolakowski, Jr., Oct. 22, 1966; children: Wiliam Francis III, John. BS, U. Detroit, Mich., 1965. Lab. asst. chemistry dept. U. Detroit, 1961-65; rsch. chemist Detroit Inst. Cancer Rsch., Mich. Cancer Found., 1965-70; substitute tchr. Warren (Mich.) Consol. Schs., 1979-81; mem. Macomb County Bd. Commrs., Mt. Clemens, Mich., 1983—2006, vice chmn., 1993-95, chmn., 1995-97; econ. devel. dir. City of Warren, 2006—. Dir. S.E. Mich. Transp. Authority, Detroit, 1983—85; trustee Macomb County Ret. System, Mt. Clemens, 1988—91, 1992—95, 2003—06; del. S.E. Mich. Coun. Govts., Detroit, 1987—2006, vice chmn., 1995—99, chmn., 1999—2000, Regional Transit Coord. Coun., 1995—97; bd. dirs. Creating a Healthier Macomb, 1996—2001, Macomb Bar Found., 1996—2006. Contbr. articles to sci. jours. Trustee Myasthenia Gravis Found., Southfield, Mich., 1964-71; dir. Otsikita coun. Girl Scouts Am., 1995-96; mem., sec. Sterling Heights (Mich.) Bd. Zoning Appeals, 1978-83; mem. Macomb County Dem. Exec. Com., Mt. Clemens, 1982—, 10th and 12th Dem. Congl. Dist. Exec. Com., Warren, 1982—, del. 1996 Dem. Nat. Conv.; mem. behavioral medicine adv. coun. St. Joseph Hosp., Warren Cmty. Chorus Named Woman of Distinction, Macomb County Girl Scouts U.S.A., 1996, Woman of Yr., Am. Fedn. State, County and Mcpl. Employees 411, 2004; recipient Leadership award, Cath. Social Svcs. Macomb, 1997, Polish Pride award, Polish Am. Citizens for Equity, 1997, Excellence in County Govt. award, 1997, Regional Ambassador award, S.E. Mich. Coun. Govt., 2005; GM scholar, U. Detroit, 1961—65. Mem.: Warren Hist. Soc., Polish Am. Congress, Alpha Sigma Nu. Roman Catholic. Avocations: singing, piano, crossword and jigsaw puzzles. Home: 33488 Breckenridge Dr Sterling Heights MI 48310-6082 Office: Mayor's Office City of Warren 29500 Van Dyke Warren MI 48093 Office Phone: 586-574-4519.

KOLANDER, DAVID J., retired chemicals executive; b. Slayton, Minn., Aug. 27, 1935; s. Irwin E. and Viola G. Kolander; m. Patricia L. Devereaux-Williams, Feb. 16, 1963; children: Kristen L. Boe, Robert J., James D. BChE, U. Minn., Mpls., 1958. Process devel. engr. Procter & Gamble, Cin., 1958—59; analyst product and market Gen. Mills, Inc., Mpls., 1961—63; mgr. sales ops. Lindsay Co., St. Paul, 1963—66; various mgmt. positions 3M. Co., St. Paul, 1966—90; v.p. divsn., gen. mgr. 3M Co., 1990—97, ret., 1997. Vol. fundraiser Mayo Clinic, Phoenix, 2000—06. Fellow, Kaiser Aluminum, 1960—61. Mem.: Indsl. Safety Equipment Assn. (bd. dirs. 1991—97), Am. Guild Organists. Republican. Lutheran. Avocations: music, golf. Home: 41466 N 109th Pl Scottsdale AZ 85262 Home Phone: 480-595-8617. Personal E-mail: dave@koly.com.

KOLAR, ERIK E., real estate company executive; married; 3 children. BS in Econs., U. Del. Sr. v.p. CB Comml.; pres., prin. Preferred Real Estate Investments; founding ptnr., pres., CEO Patriot Equities, Wayne, Pa. Cap. US Army. Named one of 40 Under 40, Phila. Bus. Jour., 2006. Office: Patriot Equities Ste 115 1200 Liberty Ridge Dr Wayne PA 19087 Office Phone: 484-615-1201. Office Fax: 610-993-2624. E-mail: ekolar@patriotequities.com.

KOLAR, MARY JANE, trade and professional association executive; b. Benton, Ill., Aug. 9, 1941; d. Thomas Haskell and Mary Jane (Sanders) Burnett; m. Otto Michael Kolar, Aug. 13, 1966; children: Robin Lynn, Deon Michael. BA with high honors, So. Ill. U., 1963, MA with highest honors, 1964. Tchr. pub. schs., Benton and Zeigler, Ill., 1960-63; grad. asst. and grad. fellow So. Ill. U., Carbondale, 1963-64; instr. Ridgewood High Sch., Norridge, Ill., 1964-67, Maine Twp. High Sch., Des Plaines, Ill., 1967-70; freelance writer plumbing, heating & cooling industry couns. Chgo., 1970-71; edni. coord. Am. Dietetic Assn., Chgo., 1971-72; dir. profl. devel. Am. Dental Hygienists Assn., Chgo., 1972-78; dir. Learning Ctr. div. Am. Coll. Cardiology, Bethesda, Md., 1978-80; dir. edn. Nat. Moving and Storage Assn., Alexandria, Va., 1980-82; exec. dir. Women in Communications, Inc., Austin, Tex., 1982-84, Altrusa Internat., Chgo., 1984-87, Assn. Govt. Accts., Alexandria, Va., 1987-90, Bus./Profl. Advt. Assn., Alexandria, 1991-92, Am. Assn. Family and Consumer Scis., Alexandria, 1992-96, dir. Project Taking Charge Adolescent Pregnancy Prevention Program, 1993-95; pres., CEO The Alexandria Group, Inc. (charter accredited co., Am. Soc. Assn. Execs.), 1996—. Mem. Accreditation Commn. for Assn. Mgmt. Cos., 2005—06; cons. spkr. various profl., philanthropic and trade assns., ednl. instns. and fed agys. Contbr. articles to profl. jours. and assn. mags., chapters to books. Mem. adv. council Accrediting Commn., Assn. of Ind. Colls. and Schs., 1980-88; treas. Pub. Employees Roundtable, 1988-90, Hollin Hills Civic Assn., 1989-90. Fellow Am. Soc. Allied Health Professions (dir. 1978-79), Am. Soc. Assn. Execs. (life, charter accredited; commr. accreditation commn. for assn. mgmt. cos. 2002-07, Key Profl. Assn. coun. 1994-96, peer rev. com., 1997-2000, rsch. com. 1996-2000, strategic leadership forum com. 1996-97, awards com. 1992-93, univ. affairs commn. 1986-92, chair 1990-91, found. bd. 1987-91, chmn. edn. sect. 1982-83, bd. dirs. 1983-86, chair higher edn. task force 1990-91, chair fellows 1987, Educator of Yr. award 1978, Key award 1990); mem. Greater Washington Soc. Assn. Execs. (edn. com. 1979-82, CEO com. 1990-92, 94-96, vice chair 1995-96, strategic planning com. 1994-95, exec. search com. 1994-96), Future Home Makers Am. (bd. dirs. 1992-96), Alexandria C. of C. (assn. coun. 1990-96, steering com. 1993-96), Women in Comm. (newsletter editor, legis. and career re-entry chair, chair ERA task force, dir. Washington profl. chpt. 1981-83, program com. Chgo. chpt. 1984-86), So. Ill. U. Alumni Assn. (bd. dirs. 1984-89, v.p. 1986-89, presdl. search com. 1986-87). Office: PO Box 142089 Austin TX 78714-2089 also: 8309 Cross Park Dr Austin TX 78754 Home Phone: 512-278-9250; Office Phone: 512-973-0040. Business E-Mail: mjkolar@alexandriagroup.com. *Being a professional means many things. It means adhering to an ethical code, having high standards of quality, striving toward excellence through basic and ongoing preparation for the profession I have chosen to practice. It means having goals and being willing to contribute to solving the social, economic and political problems of the society of which I am a part. Professionalism is more than acceptance of responsibility, more than doing one's duty, more than being good at what one does. Professionalism requires a commitment to what you do and to the future. It carries with it obligation and risk. It necessitates service to the profession— a willingness to be a leader— and a desire to meet the needs of others.*

KOLARIK, WILLIAM JOEL, II, accountant; b. Stillwater, Okla., July 19, 1977; s. William Joel and Yvonne Claudia Kolarik. BBA, MPA, U. Tex., Austin, 2000; postgrad., La. State U., Baton Rouge, 2006—. CPA Calif. Grad. assoc. The Walt Disney Co., Burbank, Calif., 1999, supr. corp. tax, 2000—. Mem.: ASCAP, ABA, Mensa.

KOLASKY, WILLIAM JOSEPH, JR., lawyer; b. Springfield, Vt., Mar. 26, 1946; s. William J. Sr. and Valentina (Stankiewicz) K.; m. Mary L. Coyne, Jan. 16, 2001; children: Robert, Caroline, Ethan. AB magna cum laude, Dartmouth Coll., 1968; JD magna cum laude, Harvard U., 1971. Bar: Mass. 1971, D.C. 1975, U.S. Dist. Ct. D.C. 1975, U.S. Ct. Appeals (D.C. cir.) 1976, U.S. Supreme Ct. 1976. Law clk. Chief Judge Bailey Aldrich, US Ct. Appeals (1st cir.), Boston, 1971—72; asst. to gen. counsel U.S. Dept of Army, Washington, 1972—75; assoc. Wilmer, Cutler & Pickering, Washington, 1975-78, ptnr., 1979—2001, 2002—04; dep. asst. atty. gen., internat. enforcement antitrust divsn. U.S. Dept. Justice, Washington, 2001—02; ptnr., co-chmn. antitrust and competition dept. Wilmer Cutler Pickering Hale & Dorr LLP, Washington, 2004—. Instr. Am. Univ.

Washington Coll. Law. Note editor Harvard Law Rev., 1969-70; contbr. legal articles to profl. jours. Capt. US Army, 1972—75. Mem. ABA (antitrust sect.), D.C. Bar Assn., Phi Beta Kappa, Omicron Delta Epsilon. Office: Wilmer Cutler Pickering Hale & Dorr LLP 1875 Pennsylvania Ave NW Washington DC 20006 Office Phone: 202-663-6000. Office Fax: 202-663-6363. Business E-Mail: william.kolasky@wilmerhale.com.

KOLATA, DAVID, advocate; b. 1969; BA, U. Notre Dame, 1991; MA in polit. sci., U. Toronto, 1993; PhD in polit. sci., Vanderbilt U., 2002. Policy analyst Environ. Law & Policy Ctr., Chgo.; sr. policy analyst & exec. dir. Citizens Utility Bd., Chgo., 2001—; columnist Daily Southtown, Chgo., 2005—. Named one of 40 Under 40, Crain's Chgo. Bus., 2006. Office: Citizens Utility Bd Ste 1760 208 S LaSalle St Chicago IL 60604 Office Phone: 800-669-5556, 312-263-4282. Office Fax: 312-263-4329. E-mail: dkolata@CitizensUtilityBoard.org.

KOLATA, GINA, journalist; b. Balt., Feb. 25, 1948; d. Arthur and Ruth Lillian (Aaronson) Bari; m. William George Kolata; children: Therese Bari, Stefan Matthew. BS in Microbiology, U. Md., 1969, MA in Applied Mathematics, 1973; postgrad., MIT, 1969-70. Copy editor Sci. Mag., Washington, 1973-74, writer, 1974-87; columnist GQ, Bild der Wissenschaft, 1984—87, Jour. Investigative Dermatology, 1985—87; reporter, sci. and medicine N.Y. Times, NYC, 1987—. Spkr. in field. Co-author: The Baby Doctors: Probing the Limits of Fetal Medicine, 1991; author Sex in America, 1995, Flu: The Story of the Great Influenza Pandemic, 2001, Clone: The Road to Dolly and the Path Ahead, 2001, Ultimate Fitness: The Quest for Truth About Exercise and Health, 2003. Named finalist, Pulitzer prize, 2000; recipient Statis. Reporting Excellence award, Am. Statis. Assn., 2004. Avocations: bicycling, running. Office: NY Times Sci Times Sect 229 W 43rd St New York NY 10036-3959

KOLATCH, MYRON, magazine editor; b. Bklyn., Sept. 26, 1929; s. Philip S. and Rebecca (Langberg) K.; m. Francine Ruth Miller, Jan. 28, 1951; children: Barry Steven, Jonathan Lee, Sari Elana. B.A, N.Y. U., 1950, postgrad in English, 1950-51. Mem. staff New Leader, 1953, mng. editor, 1960-61, exec. editor, 1961—. Bd. dirs. Tamiment Inst. Served with AUS, 1951-53. Home: 18622 Radnor Rd Jamaica NY 11432-5829 Office: Columbia U Butler Libr 535 W 114th St Rm 521A New York NY 10027 Office Phone: 212-854-1640. Business E-Mail: mkolatch@thenewleader.com.

KOLATTUKUDY, PAPPACHAN ETTOOP, medical center executive, biochemist, educator; b. Cochin, Kerala, India, Aug. 27, 1937; came to the U.S., 1960; m. Marie M. Paul. BS, U. Madras, 1957; B in Edn., U. Kerala, 1959; PhD, Oreg. State U., 1964. Prin. jr. HS, India, 1957-58; HS chemistry tchr., 1959-60; asst. biochemist Conn. Agrl. Experiment Sta., New Haven, 1964-69; assoc. prof. Wash. State U., Pullman, 1969-73, prof. biochemistry, 1973-80, dir. inst. biol. chemistry, 1980-86; dir. Ohio State Biotech. Ctr., Columbus, 1986-95, dir. Neurobiotech. Ctr., dir. med. biotech., 1995—2003; dir. Biomolecular Sci. Ctr. , chair dept. molecular biology and microbiology U. Ctrl. Fla., Orlando, 2003—04, Dean, Burnett Coll. Biomed. Scis., 2004—. Cons. Analabs, New Haven, Allied Chem. Corp., Solvay, N.Y., Genencor Corp., South San Francisco, Calif., Monsanto Co., St. Louis; mem. Overseas Adv. Com., India; mem. Edison Bio-Tech. Ctr., Cleve., trustee; mem. adv. com. to MUCIA on Sci. and Tech., Nat. Agrl. Biotech. Consortium; Ohio rep. to Midwest Plant Biotech. Consortium. Contbr. over 300 articles to profl. jours.; patentee in field. Recipient Golden Apple award Wash. State Apple Commn., President's Faculty Excellence award Wash. State U.; grantee NIH, NSF, Am. Heart Assn., Am. Cancer Soc., DOE. Mem. Fedn. Am. Socs. for Exptl. Biology, Am. Soc. Plant Physiologists, Am. Soc. Microbiology. Home: 1112 Cherry Valley Way Orlando FL 32828 Office: U Ctrl Fla Coll Biomed Scis Biomolecular Sci Bldg Rm 136 4000 Central Florida Blvd Orlando FL 32816 Home Phone: 407-273-1555. E-mail: pk@mail.ucf.edu.

KOLB, CHARLES CHESTER, foundation administrator; b. Erie, Pa., Sept. 4, 1940; s. John Christian and Edna Lucille (Church) Kolb; m. Joy Bilharz, June 3, 1972 (div. Mar. 1991); 1 child, Nancy Gwenyth; m. P. Jean Drew, July 20, 1991; 1 child, Catherine Claire Fraley. BA in History, Pa. State U., 1962, PhD in Archaeology and Anthropology, 1979. Instr. anthropology Pa. State U., University Park, 1966-69, Bryn Mawr (Pa.) Coll., 1969-73; from instr. to asst. prof. anthropology Pa. State U., Erie, 1973-84; dir. rsch. and grants Mercyhurst Coll., 1984-89, asst. dir. Hammermill Libr., 1989; humanities adminstr. program officer divsn. state programs NEH, Washington, 1989-91, program officer divsn. preservation and access, 1991-96, sr. program officer, 1997—, Recovering Iraq's Past Initiative, 2003—, Rediscovering Afghanistan Initiative, 2004—. Manuscript reviewer Holt, Rinehart and Winston, Inc., 1977—89, Prentice-Hall, Inc., 1979—85, William C. Brown, Pubs., 1982—85, U. Tex. Press, 1988—, U. Utah Press, 1991—, U. Press Fla., 1994—, AltaMira Press/Sage, 1995—, U. Pa. Mus. Applied Sci. Ctr. Archaeology, 1996—, Dover Pub., 1996—, U. Press Colo., 2003—, Centro de Estudios Arqueológicos el Colegio de Michoacán, Mexico, 2004—, U. Ariz. Press, 2005—; grant proposal reviewer NEH, 1981—89, NSF, 1982—, Wenner-Gren Found. Anthropol. Rsch., 1987—89, Social Sci. Humanities Rsch. Coun. Can., Canada, 2003—, Can. Found. Innovation, 2004—, Nat. Geog. Soc. Rsch., Conservation and Exploration Grants, 2005—; co-founder, ann. symposium co-organizer Ceramic Studies Interest Group, 1986—. Author: Marine Shell Trade and Classic Teotihuacan, 1987; editor: A Pot for All Reasons, 1988, Ceramic Ecology, 1988, 1989, 1997; contbr. articles to profl. jours., chapters to books; book and film reviewer: sci. books and films, 1977—, manuscript reviewer: Am. Antiquity, 1978—, Current Anthropology, 1979—, Ancient Mesoamerica, 1990—, Ethnohistory, 1995—, Jour. Material Culture, 1995—, Hist. Archaeology, 1995—, L.Am. Antiquity, 1995—, H-Net Revs., 1996—, Jour. Archeol. Sci., 1998—, Jour. Am. Inst. Conservation, 2001—, Geoarchaeology, 2007—, abstractor: Ceramic Abstracts, 1990—96, Art and Archaeology Tech. Abstracts, 1996—, regional editor: La Tinaja: Newsletter Archeol. Ceramics, 1991—, N.Am. corr.: Old Potter's Almanack, 1992—, reviewer: CHOICE, 1992—, ScienceNETLinks, 1999—, Transoxiana: E-Jour. de Estudios Orientales, 2003—, Ctrl. Asian Rsch. Rev., 2003—; co-author: Ency. Modern Asia, 2002, Ency. World's Minorities, 2003, Dictionary Am. History, 2002, Ency. Modern Mid. East and N. Africa, 2d edit., 2004, Ency. Developing World, 2005, Ency. World Geography, 2005. Mem. Commonwealth of Pa., Gov.'s Conf. Librs. and Info. Sys., 1989. Fellow: AAAS (Panelist Sci. Journalism awards 2003—), Am. Anthrop. Assn., Royal Anthrop. Inst. Gt. Britain and Ireland; mem.: ALA, Mid-Atlantic Regional Archives Conf. Archivists Soc. S.W. Archivists, Assn. Recorded Sound Collections, Soc. Clay Pipe Rsch., Am. Inst. Afghanistan Studies, Ctrl. Eurasian Studies Soc., Naval Hist. Found., Assn. Moving Image Archivists, Paleopathology Assn., NY State Archeol. Assn., Soc. Pa. Archeology, Register Profl. Archeologists, Soc. Am. Archivists, Soc. Hist. Archeology, Soc. Am. Archeology, Prehistoric Ceramic Rsch. Group, Materials Rsch. Soc., Coun. Mus. Anthropology, Soc. Archeol. Scis. (life; assoc. editor Archeol. Ceramics Bull. 1997—, bd. dirs. 1998—), Pearl Harbor History Assocs. (life), Assn. Field Archaeology, Archeol. Inst. Am., Am. Soc. Ethnohistory, Am. Ethnological Soc., Am. Chem. Soc., Am. Ceramic Soc., Internet 2: Archaeology Spl. Interest Group, US Naval Inst. (life), Sigma Xi, Pi Gamma Mu, Phi Kappa Phi, Alpha Kappa Delta. Home: 1005 Pruitt Ct SW Vienna VA 22180-6429 Office: NEH Divsn Preservation & Access 1100 Pennsylvania Ave NW Washington DC 20506-0001 Office Phone: 202-606-8250. Business E-Mail: ckolb@neh.gov.

KOLB, CHARLES EDWARD MEALEY, federal government official, lawyer; b. Salisbury, Md., Nov. 6, 1950; s. Stanley Denmead and Kathryn Beatrice (East) K.; m. June Joelynn Fletcher, July 25, 1976 (div. 1983); m. Ingrid Ann Christner, Aug. 27, 1988. AB, Princeton U., 1973; BA with honors, Balliol Coll. Oxford U., Eng., 1975, MA, 1980; JD, U. Va., 1978. Assoc. Cahill, Gordon & Reindel, NYC, 1978; law clk. to Hon. Joseph H. Young U.S. Dist. Ct. Md., Balt., 1978-79; assoc. Covington & Burling, Washington, 1979-82, Foreman & Dyess, Washington, 1982-83; asst. gen. counsel U.S. Office Mgmt. and Budget, Washington, 1983-86; dep. gen. counsel for regulations and legis. U.S. Dept. Edn., Washington, 1986-88, dep. under sec. for planning, budget and evaluation, 1988-90; dep. asst. for domestic policy to the Pres. of U.S. The White House, 1990—. Bar: D.C. 1978, Md. 1978. Contbr. articles to profl. jours. Sec. bd. dirs. Internat. Human Rights Law Group, Washington, 1983-91. Mem. Soc. of the Cincinnati, Princeton Club N.Y. Republican. Episcopalian. Office: The White House Office Policy Devel 2nd Fl W Wing Washington DC 20500

KOLB, CHARLES EUGENE, research and development company executive; b. Cumberland, Md., May 21, 1945; s. Charles Eugene and Doris Helen (McFarland) Kolb; m. Susan Marie Foote, Aug. 19, 1965; children: Craig E., Amy C. BS, MIT, 1967; MA, Princeton U., 1968, PhD, 1971. Sr. rsch. sci. Aerodyne Rsch. Inc., Burlington, Mass., 1971-74, prin. rsch. sci. Bedford, Mass., 1975-76, dir. Ctr. Chem. and Environ. Physics, 1977-79, tech. dir. applied scis. divsn., 1979-80, dir. applied scis. divsn., v.p., 1981-84, exec. v.p. and dir. rsch. Billerica, Mass., pres., CEO, 1985—. Assoc. atmospheric chemistry Harvard U., 1976—85; rsch. affiliate Spectroscopy Lab. MIT, 1981—92, rsch. affiliate dept. aeronautics and astronautics, 1993. Editor: Geophys. Rsch. Letters, 1996—99; mem. editl. bd. Internat. Jour. Chem. Kinetics, 1990—92; contbr. chapters to books, articles to profl. jours. Fellow: AAAS, Am. Geophys. Union, Am. Phys. Soc., Optical Soc. Am.; mem.: Union Concerned Scientists, Combustion Inst., Am. Chem. Soc. (chmn. northeastern sect. 1991, trustee northeastern sect. 1994—96, com. environ. improvement 2002—, chair 2005—, Creative Advances in Environ. Sci. and Tech. award 1997, Harry A. Hill award northeastern sect. 2005), MIT Alumni Assn. (Lobdell award 1981, Bronze Beaver award 1987). Home: 8 Stearns Rd Bedford MA 01730-1077 also: 46 Oak Grove Ave East Falmouth MA 02536-7431 Office: Aerodyne Rsch Inc 45 Manning Rd Billerica MA 01821-3976 Home Phone: 781-687-9094; Office Phone: 978-663-9500 290. E-mail: kolb@aerodyne.com.

KOLB, DAVID ALLEN, psychologist, educator; b. Moline, Ill., Dec. 12, 1939; s. John August and Ethel May (Petherbridge) K.; m. Alice Yoko; 1 son, Jonathan Demian. AB cum laude, Knox Coll., 1961; PhD, Harvard U., 1967; ScD (h.c.), U. N.H., 1984; PhD (h.c.), Internat. Mgmt. Ctr., Buckingham, 1988; LittD (h.c.), Franklin U., 1994; DHL (h.c.), SUNY, 1996. Asst. prof. organizational psychology MIT, Cambridge, 1965-70, assoc. prof., 1970-75; prof. organizational behavior and mgmt. Case Western Res. U., Cleve., 1976—, deWindt Prof. Leadership and Enterprise Devel. Weatherhead Sch. Mgmt., 1992-97, chmn. dept., 1984-90. Vis. prof. mgmt. London Grad. Sch. Bus., 1971; dir. Devel. Research Assos., 1966-80; mgmt. cons., U.S., Australia, N.Z., Indonesia, Singapore, Malaysia, Thailand, Japan. Author: Experiential Learning: Experience as the source of learning and development, 1984, Kolb Learning Style Inventory 3.1, 2005; co-author: Organizational Behavior: An Experiential Approach, 8th edit, 2007, Organizational Behavior: A Book of Readings, 8th edit, 2007, Changing Human Behavior: Principles of Planned Intervention, 1974, Innovation in Professional Education: Steps on Journey from Teaching to Learning, 1995, Conversational Learning: An Experiential Approach to Knowledge Creation, 2002. Woodrow Wilson fellow, 1962. Mem. Internat. Assn. Applied Social Scientists (charter), Soc. Intercultural Edn., Tng. and Rsch. (charter), Coun.l Advancement of Experiential Learning (Research Excellence award 1984, Morris T. Keaton Adult and Experiential Learning award 1991, Case Weatherhead Rsch. Recognition award 2002-03). Office: Case Western Res U Dept of Orgn Behavior Cleveland OH 44106 Office Phone: 216-368-2050. E-mail: dak5@msn.com.

KOLB, DOROTHY GONG, elementary school educator; b. San Jose, Calif. d. Jack and Lucille Gong; m. William Harris Kolb, Mar. 22, 1970. BA with highest honors, San Jose State U., 1964; postgrad., U. Hawaii, Calif. State U., LA; MA in Ednl. Tech., Pepperdine U., 1992. Cert. in elem. edn., edn. for mentally retarded, edn. for learning handicapped pre-sch., adult classes, resource specialist, English lang. devel., specially designed acad. instrn. in English, 2000, 2003. Tchr. Cambrian Sch. Dist., San Jose, 1964-66, Ctrl. Oahu Sch. Dist., Wahiawa, Hawaii, 1966-68, Montebello (Calif.) Unified Sch. Dist., 1968—. Recipient Very Spl. Person award, Calif. PTA, 1998, Hon. Svc. award, 2003; Walter Bachrodt Meml. scholar. Mem.: Tau Beta Pi, Pi Tau Sigma, Kappa Delta Pi, Pi Lambda Theta.

KOLB, FELIX OSCAR, physician; b. Vienna, Nov. 12, 1921; arrived in US, 1938; s. Leon and Hilde (Grunwald) K.; m. Susan L. Goldberger, July 1, 1966; children: Lisa F., Marc E. AB, U. Calif., Berkeley, 1941; MD, U. Calif., San Francisco, 1943. Diplomate Am. Bd. Internal Medicine, Am. Bd. Endocrinology and Metabolism. Intern San Francisco Gen. Hosp., 1943-44; clin. asst. U. Calif. Med. Ctr., San Francisco, 1946-47; med. resident VA Hosp., U. Calif., San Francisco, 1947-49, New Eng. Ctr. Hosp., Boston, 1949-50; grad. asst. endocrine svc. of Dr. Fuller Albright Mass. Gen. Hosp., Boston, 1950-51; attending physician U. Calif. Hosp., San Francisco, 1952—; asst. chief, assoc. chief, sr. dept. of medicine Mt. Zion Hosp., San Francisco, 1952-98, emeritus, 1998—; asst. assoc. dir. metabolic rsch. unit U. Calif., San Francisco, 1952-85, clin. prof. medicine, 1969-99, clin. prof. medicine emeritus, 1999—, asst. assoc. dir. metabolic rsch. unit, 1952-85; pvt. practice in endocrinology and metabolism San Francisco, 1952-99; retired. Cons. physician Shriners Hosp., San Francisco, VA Hosp., San Francisco, Children's Hosp., San Francisco, Letterman Hosp., San Francisco, Marshal Hale Hosp., San Francisco, Calif. Pacific Med. Ctr., San Francisco. Author: Surviving a Health Crisis, 2006; contbr. articles to profl. jours., chapters to books; mem. editl. bd. Metabolism, Reviewer for Ann. and Arch. Internal Medicine, Calcified Tissue Internat. Capt. US Army, 1944-46. Fellow ACP; mem. AMA, Calif. Med. Assn., San Francisco Med. Assn., Am. Diabetes Assn., Endocrine Soc., Am. Fedn. for Clin. Rsch., We. Soc. for Clin. Rsch., Am. Soc. Internal Medicine, Calif. Soc. Internal Medicine, San Francisco Soc. Internal Medicine, Am. Soc. for Bone and Mineral Rsch., Alpha Omega Alpha (sec.-treas. 1955-56), Phi Delta Epsilon. Democrat. Jewish. Avocations: piano, golf. Home: 9 Starboard Ct Mill Valley CA 94941-3210 Fax: 415-383-1013. E-mail: FOKolbmd@yahoo.com.

KOLB, GLORIA RO, medical products executive; BS in Mech. Engring., MIT, 1994; MS in Mech. Engring., Stanford U., 1995; MBA in Entrepreneurship, Babson Coll., 2001. Founder, pres. Fossa Med., Inc., 2001—. Named one of Top 100 Young Innovators, MIT Tech. Review, 2004.

KOLB, HAROLD HUTCHINSON, JR., language educator; b. Boston, Jan. 16, 1933; BA in English with honors, Amherst Coll., 1955; MA in Am. Studies, U. Mich., 1960; PhD in British and Am. Lit., Ind. U., 1968. Instr. English Valparaiso U., 1960-62; teaching assoc. Ind. U., 1962-65; from asst. prof. to prof. English U. Va., Charlottesville, 1967-99, prof. emeritus, 2000—, dir. Ctr. for Liberal Arts, 1984-99. Project dir. NEH, 1972-76, 85-99; dir. Canadian Judicial Writing Program, 1981-84; guest prof. Am. studies U. Bonn, 1982; chmn. MLA Delegate Assembly Steering Com., 1984-85. Author: The Illusion of Life-American Realism as a Literary Form, 1969, A Field Guide to the Study of American Literature, 1976, A Writer's Guide: The Essential Points, 1980; co-author: A Handbook for Research in American Literature and American Studies, 1994; contbr. articles to scholarly and other publs. Naval aviator USN, 1955—59. Recipient Armstrong prize in English, Amherst Coll., 1952, James A. Work prize, Ind. U., 1965, Guggenheim fellowship, 1970-71, Faculty Leadership award Am. Assn. Higher Edn., Carnegie Found. for Advancement of Teaching and Change mag., 1986, Citation for Leadership in Rejuvenation of Secondary and Elem. Edn., Va. Bd. Edn., 1987, Phillip E. Frandson award for Innovation and Creative Programming, Nat. U. Continuing Edn. Assn., 1988, Outstanding Faculty award, Va. Coun. Higher Edn., 1988. Business E-Mail: hhk6s@virginia.edu.

KOLB, JAMES A., science foundation director, writer; b. Berkeley, Calif., May 31, 1947; s. James DeBruler and Evelyn (Thomas) K.; m. Mary Catherine Eames; children: Thomas, Catherine Mary. BA in Zoology, U. Calif., Berkeley, 1970, BA in Biol. Sci., Ecology, 1970, MS in Wildland Resource Sci., 1972. Rsch. asst. Sagehen Creek Rsch. Sta. U. Calif., Berkeley, 1970, tchg. asst. dept. wildlife & fisheries, 1970-71, rsch. assoc. air pollution resource ctr. Berkeley, Riverside, 1971; tchr. secondary sci. Hayward (Calif.) Unified Sch. Dist., 1972-77; dir. Marine Sci. Ctr., Poulsbo, Wash., 1981-92; exec. dir. Marine Sci. Soc. Pacific Northwest, Poulsbo, 1992-95, For Sea Inst. Marine Sci., Indianola, Wash., 1995—98; dir. academic studies West Sound Academy, Poulsbo, 1998—. Project dir. Marine Sci. Project FOR SEA, Poulsbo, 1978-81; mem. Wash. State Environ. Edn. Task Force, Olympia, 1986—, Puget Sound Water Quality Authority Edn. & Pub. Involvement, Olympia, 1987-91, Marine Plastics Debris Task Force, Olympia, 1987; dir. acad. studies, West Soun Acad., Poulsbo, 1998-; cons., tchr., trainer Hood Canal Wetlands Project, Hoodsport, Wash., 1990. Author: Marine Science Activities, 1979 (NSTA award 1986), Marine Biology and Oceanography, 1979, 80, 81 (NSTA award 1985, 86), Marine Science Career Awareness, 1984 (NSTA award 1985), The Changing Sound, 1990, Puget Soundbook, 1991, Life in the Tidal Zone, 1995, The Sea Around Us, 1995, Life in the Estuary, Begining in the Watershed, 1995, Life With Pagoo, 1995, Investigating the Ocean Planet, 1995, Ocean Studies, Ocean Issues, 1995, Marine Biology and Oceanography, 1995, Marine Explorations CD-ROM, 1997, The Tuna/Dolphin Controversy CD-ROM, 1998, Marine Science Clip Art Portfolio CD-ROM, 1998, Marine Biology and Oceanography CD-ROM, 2000, Ocean Studies, Ocean Issues CD-ROM, 2001; co-author: A Salmon in the Sound, 1991, Discovering Puget Sound, 1991, The Puget Sound Book CD-Rom, 2003, The Electronic Whale Gray Whale Migration Simulation CD-ROM, 2004. Mem. NSTA, ASCD, Internat. Reading Assn., Nat. Marine Educators Assn. (Marine Edn. award 1997), Northwest Assn. Marine Educators (past pres.), Wildlife Soc., People for Puget Sound (v.p.).

KOLB, KEITH ROBERT, architect, educator; b. Billings, Mont., Feb. 9, 1922; s. Percy Fletcher and Josephine (Randolph) K.; m. Jacqueline Cecile Jump, June 18, 1947; children: Brooks Robin, Bliss Richards. Grad. basic engring., Rutgers U., 1944; BArch cum laude, U. Wash., 1947; MArch, Harvard U., 1950. Registered arch., Wash., Mont., Idaho, Calif., Oreg., Nat. Coun. Archtl. Registration Bds. Draftsman, designer various archtl. firms, Seattle, 1946-54; draftsman, designer Walter Gropius and Archs. Collaborative, Cambridge, Mass., 1950-52; prin. Keith R. Kolb, Arch., Seattle, 1954-64, Keith R. Kolb Arch. & Assocs., Seattle, 1964-66; ptnr. Decker, Kolb & Stansfield, Seattle, 1966-71, Kolb & Stansfield AIA Archs., Seattle, 1971-89; pvt. practice Keith R. Kolb FAIA Archs., Seattle, 1989—. Instr. Mont. State Coll., Bozeman, 1947-49; asst. prof. arch. U. Wash., Seattle, 1952-60, assoc. prof., 1960-82, prof., 1982-90, prof. emeritus, 1990—. Design arch. Dist. II Hdqrs. and Comm. Ctr., Wash. State Patrol, Bellevue, 1970 (Exhbn. award Seattle chpt. AIA), Hampson residence, 1970 (nat. AIA 1st honor 1973, citation Seattle chpt. AIA 1980), Acute Gen. Stevens Meml. Hosp., 1973, Redmond Pub. Libr., 1975 (jury selection Wash. coun. AIA 1980), Tolstedt residence, Helena, Mont., 1976, Herbert L. Eastlick Biol. Scis. Lab. bldg. Wash. State U., 1977, Redmond Svc. Ctr., Puget Sound Power and Light Co., 1979, Computer and Mgmt. Svcs. Ctr., Paccar Inc., 1981 (curatorial team selection Mus. History and Industry exhbn. 100th anniversary of AIA 1994), Seattle Town House, 1960 (curatorial team selection Mus. History and Industry exhbn. 100th anniversary of AIA 1994), Comm. Tower, Pacific N.W. Bell, 1981 (nat. J.F. Lincoln bronze), Forks br. Seattle 1st Nat. Bank, 1981 (commendation award Seattle chpt. AIA 1981, nat. jury selection Am. Architecture, The State of the Art in the '80's 1985, regional citation Am. Wood Coun. 1981), Reg. ops. Control Ctr. Sacramento Dist. Corps Engrs. McChord AFB, Wash., 1982, Puget Sound Blood Ctr., 1983-88, expansion vis./dining/recreation facilities Wash. State Reformatory, Monroe, 1983, Univ. Sta. P.O., U.S. Postal Svc., Seattle, 1983, Guard Towers, McNeil Island Corrections Ctr. Wash., 1983, Magnolia Queen Anne Carrier Annex, U.S. Postal Svc., Seattle, 1986, Tolstedt residence, Seattle, 1987, Maxim residence, Camano Island, Wash., 1991, Carmean residence alterations/additions, Seattle, 1995, 96, 97, 2001, 02, Susanna Burney and Bliss Kolb residence, Seattle, 2001-04; subject of articles. Pres. Laurelhurst Cmty. Club, Seattle, 1966. Served with U.S. Army, 1943-45, ETO. Decorated Bronze Star medal ETO; recipient Alpha Rho Chi medal; selected Am. Archs., Facts on File, Inc., 1989. Fellow AIA (dir. Seattle chpt. 1970-71, sec. Seattle chpt. 1972, Wash. state coun. 1973, pres. sr. coun. Seattle chpt. 1994-96, trustee Seattle Archtl. Found. 1994-96, Citation award Seattle chpt. for a Seattle 1960 Town House, 1990, honored Living Legends Series 2002); mem. U. Wash. Archtl. Alumni Assn. (pres. 1958-59), Phi Beta Kappa, Tau Sigma Delta. Home and Office: 3379 47th Ave NE Seattle WA 98105-5326 Office Phone: 206-527-7544.

KOLB, KEN LLOYD, writer; b. Portland, Oreg., July 14, 1926; s. Frederick Von and Ella May (Bay) K.; m. Emma LaVada Sanford, June 7, 1952; children: Kevin, Lauren, Kimrie. BA in English with honors, U. Calif., Berkeley, 1950; MA with honors, San Francisco State U., 1953. Cert. jr. coll. English tchr. Freelance fiction writer various nat. mags., NYC, 1951-56; freelance screenwriter various film and TV studios, LA, 1956-81; freelance novelist Chilton, Random House, Playboy Press, NYC, 1967—. Instr. creative writing Feather River Coll., Quincy Calif., 1969; min. Universal Life Ch. Author: (teleplay) She Walks in Beauty, 1956 (Writers Guild award 1956); (film) Seventh Voyage of Sinbad, 1957, Snow Job, 1972; (novel) Getting Straight, 1967, The Couch Trip, 1970, Night Crossing, 1974; represented in permenant collections Gotlieb Archival Rsch. Ctr.; contbr. articles to profl. jours., popular mags. Foreman Plumas County Grand Jury, Quincy, 1970; chmn. Region C Criminal Justice Planning Commn., Oroville, Calif., 1975-77; film commr. Plumas County, 1986-87. Served with USNR, 1944-46. Mem. Writers Guild Am. West, Authors Guild, Plumas Ski Club (pres. 1977-78), Mensa, Phi Beta Kappa, Theta Chi. Democrat. Avocations: skiing, tennis, travel. Home and Office: PO Box 30022 Cromberg CA 96103-3022 Office Phone: 530-836-2332. *The true measure of success is not the attainment of great wealth or a position of power over others, but the quality of one's own life. I'm grateful for the money and honors I've had from writing, but more important to me is my ongoing love affair with my wife and the loving friendship of my grown children. I believe in God and a sense of humor as guiding principles, but I can't explain either one.*

KOLB, LISA MARIE, music educator; b. Flushing, NY, Aug. 6, 1979; d. Robert James and Vita Marie Toolan; m. Erick James Kolb, Aug. 13, 2004. MusB, Nyack Coll., 2001; MSEd, Queens Coll., 2006. Public School Teacher State Edn. Dept./New York, 2002. Music tchr. Elmont Meml. HS, NY, 2002—06, New Hyde Pk. Meml. HS, NY, 2003—06; music tchr., jr. high jazz band advisor Floral Pk. Meml. HS, 2006—. Ch. organist Bellerose Bapt. Ch., NY, 1999—; sr. musical prodr. Elmont Meml. HS, NY, 2002—; tri-m music honor soc. advisor New Hyde Pk. Meml. HS, 2002—06; all-dist. festival accompanist Sewanhaka Ctrl. HS Dist., Floral Park, NY, 2004—06; piano tchr., Floral Park, NY, 2002—; performer New Hyde Pk. Adult Band Program, 2004—; asst. dir. Sr. High Drama Prodn., Elmont, NY, 2005—; sr. musical orch. dir. Floral Pk. Meml., 2006—. Named one of Outstanding Am. Tchrs., Nat. Honor Rolls, 2006—07; recipient Excellence in Tchg. award, Nyack Coll., 2001—02, Model Student Tchr. award, 2001—02. Mem.: NY State Band Dirs. Assn., Am. Guild Organists, Nassau Music Educators Assn., Music Educators Nat.

Conf. R-Consevative. Avocations: hiking, photography, running. Office: Floral Park Meml HS 210 Locust St Floral Park NY 11001 Home Phone: 516-354-0945; Office Phone: 516-488-9327. Personal E-mail: mistic17@aol.com.

KOLB, RICHARD MAURICE, sports writer, sportscaster; b. Washington, Feb. 17, 1951; s. Maurice Woodrow and Dorothy Evelyn (Taylor) K.; 1 child, Michael Richard. Student, U. Md., 1969-71; AA, Prince George's Coll., 1971; AS, No. Va. Coll., 1978. Lic. radio operator, D.C. Pub. info. news specialist USDA, Washington, 1977-78; sports writer Tampa (Fla.) Tribune, 1988-89; pub. rels. dir. Brewster Tech. Ctr., Tampa, 1991; editor Sports Tampa Bay, 1993; sports columnist Bowl Mag., Washington, 1990—, Bowling World, Dublin, Calif., 1991—, Pinbuster, St. Petersburg, Fla., 1993—, Across the Lanes, San Antonio, 1996—; radio sports anchor WTAN, Clearwater, Fla. Writer-photographer Bowling Digest, Chgo., 1998—. Columnist Sports Time mag., 1999—; radio sports talk show host Sta. WWBA, St. Petersburg, Fla. Mem. Young Dems. of Am., College Park, Md., 1970-79. Recipient Best Sports Writer and Sportscaster, Tampa Tribune's Top Ten Award, 1994, Best Feature Story award Bowling Mag., 1998, Gen. Excellence award Pro Bowlers Assn Tour, 2000. Mem. Bowling Writers Assn. Am. (Bowler of Mo. com. 1997—), Young Am. Bowling Alliance (mem. collegiate bowling poll 1995—), Bowling Writers Assn. Am. (Bowler of Year com. 2001-), Fla. Press Club. Democrat. Avocations: photography, videos, exercising, bowling, golf. Home: 5677 Sailfish Dr Lutz FL 33558-7108 E-mail: ferguson@api.org.

KOLB, SHARON MARIE, education educator, director, consultant; b. Kenosha, Wis., Sept. 6, 1966; d. Darrell Anthony and Colleen Faith Kolb; life ptnr. Britta Jan Johnson; 1 child, Kelly Kolb-Johnson; 1 child, Shelby Kolb-Johnson. BS, U Wis. Eau Claire, Eau Claire, 1988; MS, U Wis. Whitewater, 1993; PhD, U Wis., 2000. Tchr. Beaver Dam Unified Sch., Wis., 1988—2000; lectr. U. Wis., Whitewater, 2000—01, asst. prof., coord. cognitive disabilities program, 2001—05, assoc. prof. spl. edn., licensure and field experience coord., 2005—. Cons. Statewide Transition Consortium"Wis. Healthy and Ready to Work Project", Madison, 2002—; spkr. in field. Contbr. chapters to books A Practitioner's Guide to Facilitating the Role of Families in the Transition Process, 2003, articles profl. jours., rsch. papers to numerous confs. Mem. Am. Legion Auxiliary, Wis., 1973—, Rainbow Families of Wis., Madison, Wis., 1997—. Recipient Transition:18-21 Age Group, Dept. of Pub. Instr., 2002—03. Mem.: Coun. Exceptional Children, Phi Kappa Phi. Democrat. Lutheran. Avocations: parent volunteer, volleyball, softball, guitar. Home: 335 Huntsville Ridge Sun Prairie WI 53590 Office: Dept of Special Education 800 West Main Street Whitewater WI 53190 Office Phone: 262-472-4831. Business E-Mail: kolbs@uww.edu.

KOLB, VERA M., chemist, educator; b. Belgrade, Yugoslavia, Feb. 5, 1948; arrived in U.S., 1973; d. Martin A. and Dobrila (Lopicic) Kolb; m. Cal Y. Meyers, 1976 (div. 1986); m. Michael S. Gregory, 1997 (div. 1999). BS, Belgrade U., 1971, MS, 1973; PhD, So. Ill. U., 1976. Fellow So. Ill. U., Carbondale, 1977-78, vis. faculty lctr., 1978-85; assoc. prof. chemistry U. Wis., Parkside, 1985-90, prof. chemistry, 1990—, dept. chair, 1995-97. Vis. scientist Salk Inst. Biol. Studies U. Calif., San Diego, 1992—94; instr. San Francisco State U., 1997; vis. scholar Northwestern U., 2002—03. Editor: (book) Teratogens, Chemicals which Cause Birth Defects, 2nd edit., 1993, 1988; contbr. articles to profl. jours.; musician (violinist): Racine Symphony Orch., Parkside Cmty Orch., 2002—05. Assoc. dir. higher edn. Wis. Space Grant Consortium, 1995—97, assoc. dir. for special initiatives, 2002—05; violinist Racine (Wis.) Symphony Orch., Parkside Cmty. Orch. Recipient Rsch. and Higher Edn. awards, Wis. Space Grant Consortium, 1999—, Hall of Fame, Southeastern Wis. Educators, 2002; grantee, NIH, 1984—87, Am. Soc. Biochemistry and Molecular Biology, 1988; Fulbright grantee, 1973—76, NASA fellow, 1992—94. Mem.: Am. Chem. Soc. (task force occupl. safety and health 1980—94). Achievements include patents in field. Office: Univ Wis Parkside Dept Chemistry PO Box 2000 Kenosha WI 53141-2000 Office Phone: 262-595-2133.

KOLB, VICTORIA L., retired mathematics educator; b. Glen Ellyn, Ill., Feb. 14, 1925; d. Ferdinand L. and Lucile D. Larson; m. Guenther F. Kolb, June 26, 1954; children: Wendy K. Harris, Deborah K. Magee, Katherine M. BA in Math., Lake Forest Coll., Ill., 1946; MA in Edn., U. Ill., Champaign, 1949. Math. tchr. Sch. Dist. #71, Champaign, 1946—48, Deerfield (Ill.) H.S., 1965—66, Sch. Dist. #109, Deerfield, 1966—87; math. tchr., counselor Waukegan (Ill.) Twp. H.S., 1948—50; math. tchr. Lago Cmty. H.S. Std. Oil N.J., Island of Aruba, Netherlands Antilles, 1950—52; cons. guidance svcs. Evanston (Ill.) Twp. H.S., 1952—54; coll. counselor, dean of girls North Chicago (Ill.) H.S., 1954—56. Sectional spkr. 10th summer meeting Nat. Coun. of Teachers of Math., Madison, Wis., 1950; exhibit chairperson Nat. Assn. of Deans of Women Conv., Chgo., 1953, info. chairperson, 55; mem. youth divsn. Evanston Coun. of Social Agys., 1953—54; regional judge Ill. Jr. Acad. of Sci., Northbrook, 1978—80, state judge, Champaign, 1979; adviser Ill. Math. League Contest, Deerfield, 1982—83. Participant Women's Health Initiative Study, Madison, 1996—2004; mem. alumni bd. of govs. Lake Forest (Ill.) Coll., 1960—63, 1982—88; sec. Iowa County Libr. Planning Com., Dodgeville, Wis., 1994—98; pres. Am. Field Svc., Deerfield, 1972—73; dir. supervisory bd. Deer Pk. Fed. Credit Union, Deerfield, 1984—87. Recipient Disting. Svc. citation, Lake Forest Coll., 1996. Mem.: Ill. Ret. Tchrs. Assn. (assoc.), Wis. Woodland Owners Assn. (assoc.). Republican. Lutheran. Avocations: digital photography, computer projects, gardening, swimming. Home: 7496 Knutson Rd Barneveld WI 53507-9702 Home Phone: 608-924-1911. Personal E-mail: akedew@mhtc.net.

KOLBAS, ROBERT MICHAEL, electrical engineering educator; b. Syracuse, NY, Nov. 13, 1953; s. John Michael and Frances C. Kolbas; children: Michael Thomas, Daniel Robert, Sarah Anne, Mary Chen; m. Dahua Zhang (dec.). BS in Engring., Cornell U., 1975; MS in Physics, U. Ill., 1977, PhD, 1979. Rsch., teaching asst. U. Ill., Urbana, 1975-79; prin. rsch. scientist Honeywell, Inc., Bloomington, Minn., 1979-83, sr. prin. rsch. scientist, 1983-85; assoc. prof. N.C. State U., Raleigh, 1985-90, prof. elec. and computer engring., 1990—, head elec. and computer engring. dept., 1995-2000. Contbr. articles to profl. pubs.; patentee in field. Mentor to high sch. students, N.C. Sch. Sci. and Math., Durham, 1988-91. Kodak doctoral fellow U. Ill./Kodak, 1978. Fellow IEEE; mem. Tau Beta Pi, Sigma Xi. Office: N C State U PO Box 7911 Raleigh NC 27695-0001 Home Phone: 919-821-4676; Office Phone: 919-515-5257. Business E-Mail: kolbas@eos.ncsu.edu.

KOLBE, JIM (JAMES THOMAS KOLBE), retired congressman; b. Evanston, Ill., June 28, 1942; s. Walter William and Helen (Reed) K. BA in Polit. Sci., Northwestern U., 1965; MBA in Econs., Stanford U., 1967. Asst. to coordinating architect Ill. Bldg. Authority, Chgo., 1970-72; spl. asst. to Gov. Richard Ogilvie State of Ill., Chgo., 1972-73; v.p. Wood Canyon Corp., Tucson, 1973-80; mem. Ariz. State Senate from Dist. 14, 1977-83, majority whip, 1979-80; mem. U.S. Congress from 8th dist. Ariz., 1985—2007; mem. appropriations com.; chmn. appropriations subcom. treasury, postal svc., gen. gov. Trustee Embry-Riddle Aero. U., Daytona Beach, Fla.; bd. dirs. Community Food Bank, Tucson; Republican precinct committeeman, Tucson, 1974—. Served as lt. USNR, 1968-69, Vietnam. Republican. Methodist.

KOLBEN, DEBORAH, editor; Grad., U. Mich., Johns Hopkins U. Reporter Bklyn. Papers, NY Daily News, 2004—06; edn. reporter, city editor NY Sun, 2006—07; mng. editor Village Voice, NYC, 2007—. Recipient 2 Nat. Newspaper Assn. awards. Office: Village Voice 36 Cooper Sq New York NY 10003*

KOLBER, SUZY, sportscaster; b. Phila., May 14, 1964; BA, U. Miami, 1986. Prodr. WTVJ-TV, Miami, 1985—89; videotape coord. CBS Sports, NYC, 1986; prodr. Greyhound Racing Am., 1988—90; sports specials prodr. WPLG-TV, Miami, 1989—90; prodr. Cowboys Special Edition, 1990—91; former anchor WPEC-TV, West Palm Beach, 1991—93; co-host ESPN2's SportsNight & ESPN2's SportsFigures, 1993—95; anchor Fox Sports, 1996—99; host NFL Match-Up, 1999—2003, ESPN's X Games and Winter X Games, 2000—01; reporter ESPN's Sunday Night Football, 2001—05; host ESPN's tennis coverage of Wimbledon, 2003—, ESPN's tennis coverage of French Open, 2004—, ESPN's NFL Draft telecast, 2004—06; anchor SportsCenter; reporter ESPN's Monday Night Football, 2007—. Named one of Sports Business Daily's 10 favorite sports TV personalities of past 10 years, 2004; recipient Maxwell Club's Sports Broadcaster of Yr. award, 2006. Office: ESPN Plaza 935 Middle St Bristol CT 06010*

KOLBERT, JACK, language educator; b. Perth-Amboy, NJ, Apr. 25, 1927; s. Robert and Sophie (Burstein) Kolbert- Kroop; m. Ruth M. Katz (dec. June 2003); children: Harry Jules, Shelley Robert. BA magna cum laude, U. So. Calif., 1948, MA; postgrad., U. Calif., Berkeley, 1949-51; PhD, Columbia U., 1957. Lectr. French Columbia U., NYC, 1951-52; instr. French, Spanish Wesleyan U., Middletown, Conn., 1954-55; from asst., assoc. prof. to prof. Romance langs. U. Pitts., 1955-65, chmn. dept. of Romance and Modern langs., 1960-65; prof. U. N.Mex., Albuquerque, 1965-77; vis. prof. Pomona Coll., Claremont, Calif., 1970-71; pres. Monterey (Calif.) Inst. of Internat. Studies, 1977-80; dir. external rels. Calif. Acad. of Scis., San Francisco, 1980-82; div. chmn. Piedmont Community Coll., Charlottesville, Va., 1982-85; dept. chmn. Susquehanna U., Selinsgrove, Pa., 1985-92, prof., 1992-96, prof. emeritus, 1996—. Cons. City of Pitts. and Forest Hills Schs., Allegheny County, Pa., 1956-66; cons. Bucknell U. Press, Greenwood Friends Sch., Pa.; hon. fellow, mem. bd. advisors Inst. of Am. Univs., Aix-en-Provence, France; vis. prof. U. Kansas, 1968, Calif. State U., L.A., 1971, Am. Inst. Univs., Aix-En-Provence, France, 1995; cons. Dept. Edn. Commonwealth of Pa., 1985-96; mem. adv. bd. for French Lit., Contemporary Authors, Gale Rsch. Pubs., 2002—. Author: Edmond Jaloux, Critique Littéraire, 1962, The World of A. Maurois, 1986 (Choice Book award 1987); co-author: L'Art de Michel Butor, 1970, Vols. I and II French for Elementary Teachers, 1958, 60, The Worlds of Elie Wiesel, 2001; editl. bd. profl. jours.; contbr. more than 500 articles and reviews to profl. jours. Hon. Consul Gen. French Republic, N.Mex., No. Calif., 1965-80; pres. City Coun. Albuquerque, 1974-77; bd. dirs. St. Joseph's Med. Ctr., Albuquerque, 1974-77, Albquerque C. of C., 1974-77; co-chmn. Commonwealth of Va. Lang. Com., Richmond, 1983-85. Fulbright fellow, Pre, Post Doctoral Fulbright fellow, Paris, 1953-54, 63-64, Ford fellow, Ford Found., 1954-55, Camargo Found. fellow, France, 1992-93, fellow Cerisy-La-Salle Found. Elie Wiesel, 1995; hon. fellow Inst. Am. Univs., Aix-en-Provence, France; decorated knight and officer Acad. Palms, French Govt., Paris, knight Nat. Order of Merit, French Govt., Paris; named Pa. Lang. Prof. of Year, 1987. Mem. MLA (hon., life), Am. Assn. Tchrs. of French (bd. mem. 1967-75, hon. life). Democrat. Jewish. Avocations: classical music, gymnastics, travel, lecturing. Office Phone: 570-374-0101. E-mail: jackkolbert@hotmail.com.

KOLBERT, KATHRYN, lawyer, educator; b. Detroit, Apr. 8, 1952; d. Melvin and Rosalie Betty (Frank) K.; children: Samuel Kolbert-Hyle, Kate Kolbert-Hyle. BA, Cornell U., 1974; JD, Temple U., 1977. Bar: Pa. 1977, U.S. Dist. Ct. (ea. dist.) Pa. 1977, U.S. Ct. Appeals (3d cir.) 1977, U.S. Supreme Ct. 1985, U.S. Dist. Ct. N.D. 1991, U.S. Ct. Appeals (5th cir.) 1991, U.S. Ct. Appeals (10th cir.) 1994, U.S. Ct. Appeals (8th cir.) 1994. Atty. Community Legal Svcs., Phila., 1977-79, Women's Law Project, Phila., 1979-88; co-founder, dir. policy Women's Agenda, Phila., 1984-88; atty. pvt. practice, Wyndmoor, Pa., 1997. Cons. Planned Parenthood Fedn., N.Y.C., 1988-89, Nat. Abortion Rights Action League, Washington, 1987; cons. reproductive freedom project ACLU, N.Y.C., 1988-89, state coordinating counsel, 1989-92; v.p. Ctr Reproductive Law & Policy, N.Y., 1992-97; lectr. dept. women's studies U. Pa., 1978-86, 90-91, lectr. Sch. Law, 1989-91, sr. rsch. adminstr. Annenberg Pub. Policy Ctr., 1998—; Open Soc. Inst. fellow, 1998-2000. Exec. prodr. (radio series on constnl. law) Justice Talking; contbr. chpts. to books. Founder, Commn. to Elect Women Judges, Women Judges Pac, Phila, 1984; bd. dirs. Com. to Elect the Casey 5, Phila. Recipient Dedicated Advocacy award Nat. Abortion Rights Action League Pa., 1986, Pa. Coalition Against Domestic Violence, 1986, Luth. Settlement House Women's Program, 1987, Am. Dem. Action award, 1989, honoree Women's Way, 1991; named One of 100 Most Influential Lawyers in Am., Nat. Law Jour. Democrat. Jewish. Business E-Mail: KKOLBERT@asc.upenn.edu.

KOLDA, THOMAS JOSEPH, non-profit organization executive; b. Chgo., Dec. 1, 1939; s. Amos Joseph and Cecilia Marie (Baxa) K.; m. Gail Judith Kettler, June 30, 1962; children: Brian Joseph, Jeffrey Thomas. BA, Coe Coll., 1961, MA, 1984; PhD in Adminstrn. and Fin. Mgmt., Columbia Pacific U., 1986. Cert. fund raising exec. Dir. devel./pub. rels. Mt. Mercy Coll., Cedar Rapids, Iowa, 1965-69; v.p. delve. St. Mary's Coll., Orchard Lake, Mich., 1969-71; dir. devel. Roman Catholic Diocese, Tucson, 1971-74; dir. devel./pub. rels. The Pontifical Coll. Josephinum, Columbus, Ohio, 1975-77; dir. trusts and estates Ohio State U. Devel. Fund, Columbus, 1977-85; v.p. devel. Coe Coll., Cedar Rapids, Iowa, 1985-87; dir. trusts and estates Marquette U., Milw., 1987-92; pvt. practice cons. fin. and charitable gift planning, 1992-98; dir. Coll. Edn. Advancement and Univ. Planned Giving U. Wis., Whitewater, 1999—2004; dir. gift planning Case Western Res. U., Cleve., 2005—. V.p. Whitewater City Coun., Wis. Mem. Nat. Soc. Fund Raising Execs. (past pres. Ctrl. Ohio chpt.), Internat. Assn. Fin. Planning (bd. dirs. 1991-95), Coun. Advancement and Support Edn., Nat. Com. on Planned Giving. Office: Adelbert Hall 409 10900 Euclid Ave Cleveland OH 44106 E-mail: koldat@case.edu, koldat@adelphia.net.

KOLDENHOVEN, DEAN, former mayor; m. Ruth Koldenhoven; 4 children. Mem. Zoning Bd. Appeals, Palos Heights, Ill.; mayor Palos Heights, Ill., 1997—2001; brick salesman Tri-State Brick Co. Chmn. Ill. Dollars for Scholars. Recipient Profile in Courage award, John F. Kennedy Libr. Found., 2002. Mem.: Local 21 Bricklayers.*

KOLE, JANET STEPHANIE, lawyer, writer; b. Washington, Dec. 20, 1946; d. Martin J. and Ruth G. (Goldberg) K. AB, Bryn Mawr Coll., 1968; MA, NYU, 1970; JD, Temple U., 1980. Bar: Pa. 1980, N.J. 1994, N.Y. 2000. Assoc. editor trade books Simon & Schuster, NYC, 1968-70; publicity dir. Am. Arbitration Assn., NYC, 1970-73, freelance photojournalist, 1973-76; law clk. Morgan Lewis & Bockius, Phila., 1977-80; assoc. Schnader, Harrison, Segal & Lewis, Phila., 1980-85; ptnr. Cohen, Shapiro, Polisher, Shiekman & Cohen, Phila., 1985-95; ptnr., chmn. environ. practice group Klehr, Harrison, Harvey, Branzburg & Ellers, Phila., 1995-97; pvt. practice, 1997-2001; chmn. environ. dept. Cooper, Levenson, April, Niedelman & Wagenheim, Atlantic City/Cherry Hill, NJ, 2001—03; chmn. environ. dept., shareholder Flaster Greenberg, PC, Cherry Hill, NJ, 2003—. Chmn. environ. practice group Flaster Greenberg, PC. Author: Post Mortem, 1974; editor Environmental Litigation, 1991, 99; contbr. numerous articles to profl. jour.; past mem. editl. bd. New Am. Rev. Mem. Mayor's Task Force on Rape, NYC, 1972-77; adv. Support Ctr. Child Advs., Phila., 1980—; mem. Phila. Vol. Lawyers for Arts, NJ Vol. Lawyers for the Arts. Fellow Acad. Advocacy, Am. Bar Found.; mem. ABA (former co-chair individual and small firm, former co-chair environ. litigation com., former dir., publs., former coun. mem. sect. litigation, dir. publs., former co-divsn. dir. substantive areas litigation, former editor litigation news, former chmn. com. monographs and unpublished papers, com. spl. pubs., former co-chair electronic publ. com., co-chmn. book pub. bd.), ATLA. Office: 3d Fl 1810 Chapel Ave West Cherry Hill NJ 08002 Home Phone: 215-413-0858; Office Phone: 856-382-2230. Business E-Mail: janet.kole@Flastergreenberg.com.

KOLEK, ROBERT EDWARD, lawyer; b. Chgo., June 1, 1943; s. Joseph and Mary Kolek; m. Linda L. Bernicchi, Aug. 27, 1966; children: Kimberley M. Szalkus, Robert E. Jr. BBA, Loyola U., Chgo., 1965, JD, 1968. Bar: Ill. 1968. Law clk. to Hon. Thomas Kluczynski, Ill. Supreme Ct., Chgo., 1968-70. Mem. ABA, Chgo. Bar Assn. Roman Catholic. Avocation: photography. Office: Schiff Hardin LLP 6600 Sears Tower Chicago IL 60606 Office Phone: 312-258-5500. E-mail: rKolek@schiffhardin.com.

KOLENDA, JOANNE L., elementary school educator, secondary school educator, volunteer; b. Des Moines; d. Ralph J. and Marian L. Schindler; m. David J. Kolenda; children: Christopher, Daniel, Mark, Laura Reilly. BA, Creighton U., Omaha, 1964; MA, Nebr. U., 1984. Cert. tchg. English, History, French, Iowa, Nebr. Tchr. English Omaha Pub. Schs., Nebr.; tchr. U. Nebr., Omaha No. H.S., Omaha Tech H.S., Omaha Ctrl. H.S. Author: The Theory of Transcendence, 1984, Testing, Testing: One, Two, Three, 1985. Recipient Rsch. award, Sorbonne U., 1995. Mem.: Act II Playhouse Guild (life), Joslyn Art Mus. Assn. (life), Am. Lawyers Aux. (life), Opera Vols. Internat. (life), Alpha Sigma Alpha (life), Alpha Sigma Nu (life).

KOLESNIKOV, ALEXANDER IVANOVICH, physicist; arrived in US, 2000; s. Ivan M. Kolesnikov and Maria V. Kolesnikova; m. Tatiana K. Bazhenova, Nov. 21, 1974; children: Svetlana A. Kolesnikova, Yury A., Vasily A. Diploma, Moscow Engring. and Physics Inst., 1977; PhD, Inst. Solid State Physics, Russian Acad. Scis., Chernogolovka, Russia, 1983. Scientist, sr. scientist Inst. Solid State Physics, Russian Acad. Scis., Chernogolovka, 1977—99; Humboldt fellow Inst. Festkoerperforschung der Forschungcentrum Juelich, Juelich, Germany, 1987—89; rsch. fellow U. Manchester Inst. Sci. and Tech., England, 1996—99; vis. scientist Argonne Nat. Lab., Ill., 2000—02, physicist, instrument scientist, 2003—. Recipient Gold medal, Krasnodar dist. Slavyansk HS, Russia, 1961—71; Rsch. fellow, Alexander von Humboldt Found., Germany, 1987—89. Achievements include research in structural and dynamical properties of metal hydrides; fullerenes and carbon nanotubes; crystalline and amorphous forms of ice; water in confinement. Office: Argonne National Laboratory 9700 S Cass Ave Bldg 360 C-209 Argonne IL 60439 Home Phone: 630-985-2189; Office Phone: 630-252-3555.

KOLESNIKOV, EVGENI, surgeon, scientist, consultant; b. Uchkeken, Russia, June 16, 1949; arrived in US, 1990; s. Boris Kolesnikov and Zinaida Don; m. Tatiana Bondarenko, Jan. 26, 1979; children: Angela Kolesnikova, Oleg Kolesnikov. MD, Odessa State Med. U., Ukraine, 1976; PhD, Med. Acad. Advanced Studies, Kiev, Ukraine, 1982; DMedSc, Kiev Nat. Med. U., Ukraine, 1988. Lic. Surgeon Odessa State Med. U., 1977, cert. in cardio-pulmonary perfusion Northeastern U., Mass. Gen. Hosp., Harvard Med. Sch., Boston, 1992, lic. surg. laser specialist SLT, Pa., 1994, cert. laparoscopic surgery specialist Inst. Surgery and Transplantology, Kiev, Ukraine, 1999. Surgeon nat. inst. clin. and exptl. surgery, 1977—82; asst. prof. Kiev Nat. Med. U., 1982—96; prof., cons. Kiev Med. Inst., 1996—, prof. surgery, 1998—2000, vice-rector, 1998—2000. Physician Obesity Surgery Ctr., Woodbridge, Va., 2000—07; founder, pres. Intermed, 1994—; cons. in field; 18 presentations in field. Author: Sorption Detoxification in Surgical Clinic, Low Temperatures in Medicine; contbr. numerous articles to profl. jours. Recipient Nat. Laureate prize, Ukraine, 1986. Fellow: Internat. Coll. Surgeons; mem.: Am. Acad. Cosmetic Surgery, NY Acad. Sci., Va. Acad. Sci., Internat. Fedn. Surgery Obesity, Am. Soc. Bariatric Surgery, Nat. Assn. Plastic and Reconstructive Surgeons (v.p. 1999—), Harvard Med. Sch. Postgrad. Assn. Achievements include 14 patents in field; development of mini-open roux-en-y gastric bypass and "tightening jacket" abdominoplasty after weight loss surgical procedures; new methods of treatment of acute pancreatitis, including laparoscopic approach and regional perfusion of the pancreas with sorption detoxication. Personal E-mail: kyevgeni@yahoo.com.

KOLEVAR, KEVIN M., federal agency administrator; b. 1967; Grad., U. Mich. Staff mem. to Senators Spencer Abraham and Connie Mack US Senate, 1993—2003; chief of staff to dep. sec. US Dept. Energy, 2003—05, sr. policy adv. to sec., 2003—05, asst. sec. for energy delivery and reliability, 2005—07, dir. energy delivery & reliability, 2007—. Office: Office Electricity Delivery & Energy Reliability US Dept Energy 1000 Independence Ave SW Washington DC 20585 Office Phone: 202-586-1411. Office Fax: 202-586-1472.*

KOLEY, GOUTAM, science educator; b. Deshapara, West Bengal, India, Jan. 9, 1976; s. Nimai Chandra and Manju Koley; m. Soma Nayak, July 17, 2005. BTech, Indian Inst. of Tech., Kharagpur, India, 1998; MS, U. of Mass., Lowell, 1999; PhD, Cornell U., Ithaca, NY, 2003. Asst. prof. U. of S.C., Columbia, 2003—. Cons., founder, shareholder Widetronix, Inc., Ithaca, NY, 2003—. Grantee Investigation of GaN nanowire devices and device integration, U. of S.C. Nanocenter, 2005—06. Mem.: IEEE, Materials Rsch. Soc. Achievements include development of Scanning Kelvin Probe Microscopy techniques to wide bandgap semiconductor materials and devices charcaterization. Office: 3A12 Swearingen Ctr Dept of EE 301 S Main St Columbia SC 29208 Home Phone: 803-772-5160; Office Phone: 803-777-3469. Office Fax: 803-777-8045. E-mail: koley@engr.sc.edu.

KOLFF, WILLEM JOHAN, retired internist, medical educator; b. Leiden, Holland, Feb. 14, 1911; arrived in U.S., 1950, naturalized, 1956; s. Jacob and Adriana (de Jonge) Kolff; m. Janke C. Huidekoper, Sept. 4, 1937; children: Jacob, Adriana P., Albert C., Cornelis A., Gualtherus C.M. Student, U. Leiden Med. Sch., 1930—38; MD summa cum laude, U. Groningen, 1946; MD (hon.), U. Turin, Italy, 1969, Rostock U., Germany, 1975, U. Bologna, Italy, 1983; DSc (hon.), Allegheny Coll., Meadville, Pa., 1960, Tulane U., 1975, CUNY, 1982, Temple U., 1983, U. Utah, 1983; D. of Tech. Scis. (hon.), Tech. U. Twente, Enschede, The Netherlands, 1986; DSc (hon.), U. Athens, 1988, Aix-Marseille II, 1993. Internist, head med. dept. Mcpl. Hosp., Kampen, Holland; dir. divsn. artificial organs Cleve. Clinic Found., 1950—67; privaat docent, dept. medicine U. Leiden, 1950—67; prof. surgery U. Utah Coll. Medicine, Salt Lake City, 1967—, Disting. prof. medicine and surgery, 1979—, prof. internal medicine, 1981—, dir. Kolff's Lab., 1986—, dir. Inst. Biomed. Engring., dir. divsn. artificial organs, 1967—86, prof. emeritus, 1986—. Decorated commandeur Order Van Oranje Netherlands, Orden de Mayo al Merito en el Grade de Gran Official Argentina; named one of Utah's Most Disting. Achievers, 1996, 100 Most Important Americans in the 20th Century, Life mag.; named to, Nat. Inventors Hall of Fame, 1985, 1995, On the Shoulders of Giants Hall of Fame, Cleve., 1989; recipient Landsteiner medal for establishing blood banks during German occupation in Holland, Netherlands Red Cross, 1942, Cameron prize, U. Edinburgh, Scotland, 1964, Gairdner prize, Gairdner Found., 1966, Valentine award, N.Y. Acad. Medicine, 1969, 1st Gold medal, Netherlands Surg. Soc., 1970, Leo Harvey prize, Technion, Israel, 1972, Sr. U.S. Scientist award, Alexander Von Humboldt Found., 1978, Austrian Gewerbeverein's Wilhelm-Exner award, 1980, John Scott medal, City of Phila., 1984, Japan prize, Japan Found. Sci. and Tech., 1986, Rsch. prize, Netherlands Royal Inst. Engrs., 1986, 1st Jean Hamburger award, Internat. Soc. Nephrology, 1987, 1st Edwin Cohn-De Laval award, World Apheresis Assn., 1990, Fed. prize, Fedn. Sci. Med. Assn., 1990, Father of Artificial Organs award and medal, Internat. Soc. Artificial Organs, 1992, Christopher Columbus Discovery award in biomed. rsch., NIH, 1992, Legacy of Life award, LDS Deseret

Found., 1995, Lifetime Achievement award, Ahmedabad, India, 1996, Russ prize, Ohio U. and Nat. Acad.of Engring., 2003, The Lasker Award, 2002. Mem.: ACP, NAE (City of Medicine award 1989), AAUP, AAAS, AMA (Sci. Achievement award 1982), European Dialysis and Transplant Assn., Nat. Kidney Found., Am. Soc. Artificial Internal Organs, N.Y. Acad. Scis., Soc. Exptl. Biology and Medicine, Am. Physiol. Soc., Academia Nacional de Medicine (hon.; Colombia), Austrian Soc. Nephrology (hon.), Rotary. Achievements include patents for ventricular assist device and method of manufacturing; collapsible artificial ventricle and pumping shell; ventricular assist device with volumne displacement chamber; electrohydraulic heart with septum mounted pump; muscle and air powered left ventricular assist device; development of artificial kidney for clinical use, 1943; heart-lung machine, 1949; first membrane oxygenator, 1955; disposable twin-coil kidney, 1956; balloon pump, 1962; wearable artificial kidney (WAK), 1981; artificial heart, 1958; human implantation, Dr. Barney Clark, 1982.

KOLINSKY, MICHAEL ALLEN, emergency physician; b. Phila., Dec. 23, 1947; s. Maurice and Lenore (Rose) K.; m. Barbara Victorine, June 20, 1981; children: Nicole, Daniel, Samuel. BA, U. Wis., 1970; MD, Rush U., 1979. Diplomate Am. Bd. Emergency Medicine. Staff physician emergency dept. River Parishes Hosp., LaPlace, La., 1982-85, Rutland Regional Med. Ctr., Vt., 2005—; co-med. dir. emergency dept. Meadowcrest Hosp., Gretna, La., 1985-92; co-med. dir. City of New Orleans Emergency Med. Svcs., 1987—2004; med. dir. emergency dept. Tulane U. Med. Ctr., New Orleans, 1992—. Fellow Am. Acad. Emergency Medicine. Office: Tulane Med Ctr Emergency Dept 1415 Tulane Ave New Orleans LA 70112-2600 E-mail: kolinsky@tulane.edu.

KOLITZ, JONATHAN ELIANHU, hematologist, oncologist; b. Tel Aviv, July 20, 1953; MD, Yale U., 1979. Diplomate Am. Bd. Internal Medicine, Am. Bd. Hematology, Am. Bd. Oncology. Intern North Shore U. Hosp., Manhasset, N.Y., 1979-80, resident in internal medicine, 1980-82; fellow in med. oncology Meml. Sloan Kettering Cancer Ctr., 1982-85; mem. staff North Shore U. Hosp., Manhasset, 1995—2005, assoc. prof., 2005—. Asst. prof. Cornell U. Med. Coll., 1990-95; asst. prof. NYU Sch. Medicine, 1996—. Mem. ACP, Am. Assn. Cancer Rsch., Am. Soc. Clin. Oncology, Am. Soc. Hematology (cancer and leukemia group B), Soc. Biol. Therapy. Office: North Shore Hosp 450 Lakeville Rd New Hyde Park NY 11042 Office Phone: 516-734-8970. Business E-Mail: kolitz@nshs.edu.

KOLKER, ADAM ROSS, plastic surgeon, educator; s. Paul and Susan Kolker; m. Lauren Pia Silverman, Jan. 27, 2001. BS in Bio Arts, Union Coll., NY, 1988; MD cum laude, Albany Med. Coll., 1990. Diplomate Am. Bd. Plastic Surgery, Am. Bd. Surgery, Nat. Bd. Med. Examiners. Clin. asst. prof. surgery Mt. Sinai Sch. Medicine. Attending plastic surgeon St. Vincent's Hosp. and Med. Ctr., NYC, Manhattan Eye, Ear and Throat Hosp., The Mt. Sinai Hosp. Fellow, Harvard Med. Sch., U. Melbourne, Australia. Fellow: ACS; mem.: Am. Soc. Aesthetic Plastic Surgeons, Am. Soc. Plastic Surgeons. Office: Mt Sinai Sch Medicine 710 Park Ave New York NY 10021 Office Phone: 212-744-6500. Business E-Mail: drkolker@kolkermd.com.

KOLKER, ALLAN ERWIN, ophthalmologist; b. St. Louis, Nov. 2, 1933; s. Paul P. and Jean Kolker; m. Jacquelyn Krupin, Dec. 8, 1957; children: Robin, Marci, David, Scott. AB, Washington U., St. Louis, 1953, MD, 1957. Diplomate Am. Bd. Ophthalmology (dir. 1994-98). Intern St. Louis Children's Hosp., 1957-58; resident in ophthalmology Washington U./Barnes Hosp., St. Louis, 1960-65; glaucoma fellow Washington U., St. Louis, 1963—64, staff, faculty, 1964—, prof. ophthalmology, 1974-96, clin. prof. ophthalmology, 1996—. Med. dir. The Glaucoma Inst., pvt. practice; mem. glaucoma com. Prevent Blindness Am. Author: (with J. Hetherington) Becker and Shaffer's Diagnosis and Therapy of the Glaucomas, 3d, 4th, 5th edit., 1983, (with T. Krupin) Complications in Ophthalmic Surgery, 1999; contbr. numerous articles to profl. jours., chpts. to books. Served with USPHS, 1958-60. NIH spl. fellow, 1963-65; grantee, 1969-80; 1st Disting. Eye Alumni award Washington U., 1990, Alumni/Faculty award Washington U. Sch. Medicine, 2002. Mem. AMA, Assn. Rsch. in Vision and Ophthalmology, Am. Acad. Ophthalmology (mem. coun. 1986-92, trustee 1994-98, Life Achievement award 2002), Am. Bd. Ophthalmology (dir. 1994-98), Am. Ophthal. Soc., Am. Glaucoma Soc. (founding mem., pres. 1992-94, Spl. Honor award 2002), Mo. Ophthal. Soc. (pres. 1986-87), St. Louis Med. Soc. Home: 176 Plantation Dr Saint Louis MO 63141-8352 Office: Glaucoma Cons Midwest 12601 Olive Blvd Saint Louis MO 63141-6313 Office Phone: 314-878-7962.

KOLKEY, DANIEL MILES, former judge, lawyer; b. Chgo., Apr. 21, 1952; s. Eugene Louis and Gilda Penelope (Cowan) K.; m. Donna Lynn Christie, May 15, 1982; children: Eugene, William, Christopher, Jonathan. BA, Stanford U., 1974; JD, Harvard U., 1977. Bar: Calif. 1977, U.S. Dist. Ct. (ea. dist.) Calif. 1978, U.S. Dist. Ct. (cen. dist.) Calif. 1979, U.S. Ct. Appeals (9th cir.) 1979, U.S. Dist. Ct. (no. dist.) Calif. 1980, U.S. Supreme Ct. 1983, U.S. Dist. Ct. Ariz. 1992, U.S. Dist. Ct. (so. dist.) Calif. 1994. Law clk. U.S. Dist. Ct. judge, NYC, 1977-78; assoc. Gibson Dunn & Crutcher, LA, 1978-84, ptnr., 1985-94; counsel to Gov., legal affairs sec. to Calif. Gov. Pete Wilson, 1995-98; assoc. justice Calif. Ct. Appeal, 3rd Appellate Dist., Sacramento, 1998—2003; ptnr. Gibson, Dunn & Crutcher, San Francisco, 2003—. Arbitrator bi-nat. panel for U.S.-Can. Free Trade Agreement, 1990—94; commr. Calif. Law Revision Commn., 1992—94, vice chair, 1993—94, chair, 1994; mem. Blue Ribbon Commn. on Jury Sys. Improvement, 1996; adj. prof. McGeorge Sch. Law, 2001—04; mem. Calif. State-Fed. Jud. Coun., 2001—03. Co-editor: Practitioner's Handbook on International Arbitration and Mediation, 2002; contbr. articles to profl. jours. Co-chmn. internat. rels. sect. Town Hall Calif., LA, 1985—90; chmn. internat. trade legis. subcom., internat. commerce steering com. L.A. Area C. of C., 1983—91, law and justice com., 1993—94; adv. coun., exec. com. Asia Pacific Ctr. for Resolution of Internat. Bus. Disputes, 1991—94; mem. L.A. Com. on Fgn. Rels., 1983—95, Pacific Coun. Internat. Policy, 1999—; gen. counsel Citizens Rsch. Found., 1990—94; assoc. mem. ctrl. com. Calif. Rep. Party, 1983—94, 2005—, mem. ctrl. com., 1995—98; dep. gen. coun. credentials com. Rep. Nat. Conv., 1992, alt. Calif. Delegation, 1992, Calif. del., 1996; bd. dirs. L.A. Ctr. for Internat. Comml. Arbitration, 1986—94, treas., 1986—88, v.p., 1988—90, pres., 1990—94. Master Anthony Kennedy Inns. of Ct., 1996-99. Mem. Am. Arbitration Assn. (panel of arbitrators, arbitrator large complex case dispute resolution program 1993-94), Am. Law Inst., Chartered Inst. Arbitrators, London (assoc. 1986-94), Friends of Wilton Park So. Calif. (chmn. exec. com. 1986-94, exec. com. 1986—). Office: Gibson Dunn & Crutcher LLP One Montgomery St 31st Fl San Francisco CA 94104-4505 Office Phone: 415-393-8240.

KOLKIN, MITCHELL, lawyer; b. Mar. 12, 1950; BA, U. Pa., 1971; JD, Duke U., 1976. Bar: Calif. 1976, Md. 1981. Ptnr., transactional bus. Venable LLP (formerly Venable, Baetjer & Howard), Balt. Note, comment editor Duke Law Jour., 1975-76. Mem. ABA, Md. State Bar Assn., Bar Assn. Balt. City, State Bar Calif., Phi Beta Kappa. Address: Venable LLP 1800 Mercantile Bank & Trust Blg 2 Hopkins Plz Baltimore MD 21201-2930 Office Phone: 410-244-7656. Office Fax: 410-244-7742. Business E-Mail: mkolkin@venable.com.

KOLKO, GABRIEL, historian, educator; b. Paterson, NJ, Aug. 17, 1932; s. Philip and Lillian Kolko; m. Joyce Manning, June 11, 1955. BA, Kent State U., 1954; MS, U. Wis., 1955; PhD, Harvard U., 1962. Assoc. prof. U. Pa., 1964-68; prof. history SUNY-Buffalo, 1968-70, York U., Toronto, Ont., Canada, 1970-92, Disting. research prof., 1986-92, prof. emeritus, 1992—. Author: Wealth and Power in America, 1962; The Triumph of Conservatism, 1963; author: Railroads and Regulations, The Politics of War, 1968, The Roots of American Foreign Policy, 1969, The Limits of Power, 1972, Main Currents in Modern American History, 1976, Anatomy of a War, 1985, Confronting the Third World, 1988, Century of War, 1994, Vietnam, Anatomy of a Peace, 1997, Another Century of War?, 2002, The Age of War, 2006, After Socialism, 2006; contbr. articles to profl. jours. Fellow Social Sci. Research Council, 1963-64; Guggenheim fellow, 1966-67; fellow Am. Council Learned Socs., 1971-72; Killam fellow, 1974-75, 82-84 Fellow Royal Soc. Can. Home: Wittenburgergracht 53 1018 MX Amsterdam Netherlands E-mail: kolko@chello.nl.

KOLLAER, JIM C., real estate executive, architect; b. Amarillo, Tex., Jan. 5, 1943; s. Walter W. and Margaret M. Kollaer; 1 child, Andrew N. Student, Amarillo Coll., 1960-62, La. State U., 1962-65; BArch, Tex. Tech. U., 1969. Lic. architect, Tex.; lic. broker, Tex. V.p., dir. urban design RKA Inc. Assoc., Dallas, 1969-75; with CRS Inc., Houston, 1975—80, v.p., dir. mktg., 1977-80; pres. Houston divsn. Henry Miller Co., Houston, 1980-85; pres. Henry S. Miller/Grubb & Ellis, 1985-89, Kollaer Internat., 1989-90; pres., CEO Greater Houston Partnership, 1990—2005; exec. v.p., ptnr. Staubach Co. Houston, Corp. Svc., 2005—. Past chmn. Tex. Bus. Hall of Fame; past bd. dirs. Ctr. Houston's Future; cons. and lectr. in field. Sr. fellow Am. Leadership Forum. Fellow AIA; mem. Tex. Soc. Archs., Urban Land Inst., Tex. Assn. Realtors, Nat. Assn. Realtors, Houston Wilderness (bd. dirs.), U.S. C. of C. (bd. dirs. 1999-2005), Chamber Found. (bd. dirs.), Coronado Club, Houston Realty Breakfast Club. Republican. Presbyterian. Office: The Staubach Co 2500 One Riverway Houston TX 77056 Home Phone: 713-844-3601. E-mail: jim.kollaer@staubach.com.

KOLLAR, EDWARD JAMES, retired biology educator; b. Forest City, Pa., Mar. 3, 1934; s. I. J. and Mary (Zaverl) K.; m. Catherine Ann Tobin, Feb. 23, 1963; children: Michelle, Elizabeth, Rachael, Brian, Rebecca. BS, U. Scranton, 1955; MS, Syracuse U., 1959, PhD, 1963. Instr., zoology, rsch. assoc. U. Chgo., 1963-66, asst. prof., biology, rsch. assoc., zoology, 1966-67, asst. prof., anatomy, biology, 1967-69, asst. prof., anatomy, 1969-71; assoc. prof., oral biology U. Conn. Health Ctr., 1971-76, prof., oral biology, 1976-97, prof. emeritus, 1998—, acting head, dept. oral biology, 1985-86, 96-98, oral biology grad. program dir., 1983-88, assoc. dean acad. affairs, 1988-98, program dir., dentist sci. award program, 1990-97. Vis. prof. Guy's Hosp. Med. Sch., London, 1978, Inst. Molecular Biology, Salzburg, Austria, prof., 1971-90; presenter in field. Editor-in-chief Archives of Oral Biology, 1978-97; mem. editl. bd. Saudi Dental Jour., Epithelial Cell Biology. Numerous exec. positions various ednl. coms. Grantee NIH; recipient Quantrell award, U. Chgo., 1968, Issac Schour Meml. Basic Sci. award, 1981, City of Paris medal, 1986. Mem. Am. Soc. Zoologists, Internat. Soc. Devel. Biologists, Cranofacial Group Internat. Assn. (pres. 1983), Internat. Soc. Differentiation, Devel. Biology, Tissue Culture Assn., Bone Tooth Soc., Sigma Xi (treas. Chgo. chpt. 1969, sec. 1970). Democrat. Roman Catholic. Business E-Mail: kollar@nso.uchc.edu.

KOLLÁR, JÁNOS, mathematics professor; b. Budapest, Hungary, June 7, 1956; came to U.S., 1981. BS, Eötvös U., Budapest, 1980; PhD, Brandeis U., Waltham, Mass., 1984. Jr. fellow Harvard U., Cambridge, Mass., 1984-87; assoc. prof. math. U. Utah, Salt Lake City, 1987-90, prof. math., 1990-94, disting. prof. math., 1994—99; prof. math. Princeton U., 1999—. Author: Rational Curves on Algebraic Varieties, 1996, Shafarevich Maps and Automorphic Forms, 1996; editor: Current Topics in Algebraic Geometry, 1995, Internat. Jour. Math., Singapore, 1990-96, Inventiones Math., Berlin, 1995—; assoc. editor Duke Math. Jour., Durham, N.C., 1990-96, Annals of Math., Princeton, N.J., 1992-98, European Jour. Math., 1998-2001. Fellow A.P. Sloan Found., N.Y.C., 1992; named Presdl. Young Investigator, NSF, Washington, 1991; recipient Frank Nelson Cole prize in Algebra Am. Math. Soc., 2006. Mem. Hungarian Acad. Scis., US NAS Office: Princeton U Dept Math 605 Fine Hall Washington Rd Princeton NJ 08544-1000 Office Phone: 609-258-4200. Office Fax: 609-258-1367. Business E-Mail: kollar@math.princeton.edu.*

KOLLAR-KOTELLY, COLLEEN, federal judge; b. Apr. 17, 1943; m. John T. Kotelly. BA, Cath. U., 1965, JD, 1968. Law clerk to Hon. Catherine Kelly, Dist. Columbia Ct. Appeals, 1968—69; atty. criminal divsn. US Dept. Justice, 1969-72; chief legal counsel St. Elizabeth's Hosp., 1972-84; judge DC Superior Ct., 1984-97, dep. presiding judge, criminal divsn., 1995—97; dist. judge US Dist. Ct. DC, 1997—; presiding judge Fgn. Intelligence Surveillance Ct., 2002—. Apptd. mem. Judicial Conf. Com. Fin. Disclosure by Chief Justice Rehnquist, 2000—02; adj. prof. joint tchg. program on mental health and the law Georgetown U. Sch. Medicine, chair bd. art trust for superior ct. Fellow: ABA; mem.: Thurgood Marshall Inn of Ct. (founding mem.). Office: 333 Constitution Ave NW Washington DC 20001-2802*

KOLLAS, CHAD D., medical educator; b. Carlisle, Pa., Sept. 14, 1963; s. William C. and Dianne L. Kollas; m. Beth Boyer, June 10, 1989; children: Paul W., Sarah E. MD, Pa. State U., Hershey, 1989. Assoc. physician New London Internal Medicine, Snellville, Ga., 1992—93, Geisinger Clinic, Danville, Pa., 1993—98; asst. dir. med. edn. Orlando Regional Med. Ctr., Fla., 1998—2000; sect. leader, palliative medicine M.D. Anderson Cancer Ctr. Orlando, 2000—. Chair bioethics com. Orlando Regional Healthcare, 2001—07. Contbr. articles to profl. jours. Bd. mem. Dr. Phillips Little League, Orlando, 2005—06. Recipient Spirituality Curricula award, John Templeton Found., 2000; grantee, AMA Rsch. & Edn. Found., 1998. Fellow: ACP (govs. adv. coun. 1999—2000), Am. Assn. Hospice & Palliative Medicine, Am. Coll. Legal Medicine (pubs. com. 1999—2001). Avocations: hiking, travel, writing. Office: MD Anderson Cancer Ctr Orlando 1400 S Orange Ave MP-760 Orlando FL 32806 Office Phone: 407-648-3800. Office Fax: 407-425-5203. E-mail: chad.kollas@orhs.org.

KOLLATZ, REBECCA LYNN, music educator; b. St. Francis, Wis., Mar. 4, 1978; d. Kenneth Donald and Debra Lou Kollatz. MusB, Butler U., Indpls., 2001; MA in Edn., Viterbo U., La Crosse, Wis., 2007. Pool mgr., water safety instr. New Berlin Pk. and Recreation, New Berlin, Wis., 1992—2005; band, choral dir. Williams Bay Sch. Dist., Wis., 2001—02; voice instr. White Ho. of Music, Waukesha, Wis., 2002; dir. orchs. John Bullen Middle Sch., Kenosha, Wis., 2002—. Coord. sch.-wide enrichment John Bullen Mid. Sch., Kenosha, Wis., 2003—05; internship Indpls. Children's Choir, 2000; treas. Butler U. Chorale, Indpls., 1998—2000. Presenter (rsch. conf.) Luca Morenzio, Masque of the Red Death; musician: (opera) Cosi fan Tutti (2d pl. Nat. Assn. Tchrs. Singing competition, 2001). Leader Weight Watchers, 2005—; music ministry Newman Ctr., Indpls., 1998—2001. Named Outstanding Sophomore, Pi Kappa Lambda, 1998, Gus Poulimas Outstanding Prospective String Tchr., Butler U., 2001; recipient Alta. Denk String award, Mu Phi Epsilon, 2000, Gerke Meml. Performance award, 2000; Pressor scholar, Butler U., 1998. Mem.: ASTA (assoc.), MENC (assoc.), Phi Kappa Phi, Pi Kappa Lambda, Mu Phi Epsilon (sec. Kappa chpt. 1998—2000, v.p. Kappa chpt. 2000—01). Achievements include research in correlation between instrumental music lessons and the academic achievement of low-income middle school students. Avocations: swimming, knitting, philosophy, music. Home: 15980 W Allison Dr New Berlin WI 53151 Office: John Bullen Middle Sch 2804 39th Ave Kenosha WI 53144 Personal E-mail: bkollatz@sbcglobal.net.

KOLLER, DAPHNE, computer scientist; m. Dan Avida. BS in Math. and Computer sci., Hebrew U., Jerusalem, Israel, 1985, MSc in Computer Sci., 1986; PhD in Computer Sci., Stanford U., Calif., 1993. Postdoctoral fellow, computer sci. divsn. U. Calif., Berkeley, 1993—95; asst. prof., computer sci. Stanford U., Calif., 1995—2001, assoc. prof., computer sci. Calif., 2001—. Author: published in jour. such as Games and Economic Behavior, Artificial Intelligence, Science, and Nature Genetics. Named a MacArthur Fellow, 2004; recipient Young Investigator award, Office of Naval Rsch., 1999, Presdl. Early Career award for Scientists and Engineers, 1999, Fellow Internat. Joint Conf. on Artificial Intelligence Computers and Though award, 2001; Rothschild Grad. Fellowship, 1989—90, U. Calif. President's Postdoctoral Fellowship, 1993—95, Sloan Found. Rsch. Fellowship, 1996. Avocations: reading, music, hiking, sailing, scuba diving. Office: Computer Sci Dept Rm 142 Gates Bldg 1A Stanford U 353 Serra Mall Stanford CA 94305-9010 Office Phone: 650-723-6598. Office Fax: 650-725-1449. Business E-Mail: koller@CS.stanford.edu.

KOLLER, LOREN D., veterinary medicine educator; b. Pomeroy, Wash., June 16, 1940; s. Edwin C. and Doris K. (Shelton) K.; m. Kathleen Noel Ringness, Sept. 7, 1963; children: Susan E., Michael D., Christopher L. DVM, Wash. State U., 1965; MS, U. Wis., 1969, PhD, 1971. Head diagnostic and comparative pathology Nat. Inst. Environ. Health Scis., Research Triangle Park, NC, 1971-72; rsch. assoc. dept. vet. medicine Oreg. State U., Corvallis, 1972-76, assoc. prof., 1976-78, prof., 1995—2001, dean Coll. Vet. Medicine, 1985-95; assoc. prof. dept. vet. medicine, asst. dean U. Idaho, Moscow, 1978-81, assoc. prof., assoc. dean, 1981-82, prof., assoc. dean, 1982-85; owner Loren Koller & Assocs., LLC, 2001—. Rsch. asst. dept. vet. sci. U. Wis., Madison, 1968-71; assoc. veterinarian Blue Cross Vet. Clinic, Corvallis, 1965-66; mem. Nat. Adv. Com. to Establish Acute Exposure Guidelines for Hazardous Substances Commn.; chair expert consultation panel provisional adv. levels Nat. Homeland Security Rsch. Ctr. Office Rsch. and Devel. US EPA. Contbr. articles to profl. jours., chpts. to books. Served to capt. M.C., U.S. Army, 1966-68. Grantee NIH, USDA, Dow Chem. Co., EPA, WHO, FDA, Merck Sharp & Dohme, Warner-Lambert, Pew Found. Fellow Acad. Toxicol. Sci.; mem. AVMA, NAS (mem. com. toxicology and Inst. of Medicine). Personal E-mail: kollerl@pacifier.com.

KOLLER, SHIRLEY LEAVITT, sculptor; b. Youngstown, Ohio, Apr. 6, 1921; d. Benjamin Harrison and Rose (Cohen) Leavitt; m. Herbert Richard Koller Mar. 7, 1943 (dec. June 1988); children: Donald Lee, Susan Koller Van Horne, Laura Frances. Diploma, Cleve. Inst. Art, 1942; BS, Western Res. U., Cleve., 1942; MFA, Am. U., 1972. Lectr. No. Va. C.C., Alexandria, 1977-92; curator art program AAAS, 1997—. Lectr. sr. citizens Jewish Cmty. Ctr. of Greater Washington, Rockville, Md., 1990, 95, Washington Hebrew Congregation, Washington, 1995, Georgetown, 2001; appearance on Peter Jennings/ABC World News Tonight, 1991, Arlington Cable, 1990, Voice of Am. Radio, 1992; adj. faculty Md. Coll. of Art & Design, 1991-93; vis. artist Fairfax County Pub. Schs., 1982-85; visual art specialist, Fillmore Arts Ctr., Washington, 1977-81; spkr. in field. Artist: (3-D wall installation) The Joy of Transportation, 1989-93 (comm. 1989); writer: (newsletter) Eye Wash, 1990-92; curator Tri-State Ednl. Assn. exhibits, Washington, Jewish Cmty. Ctr. Greater Washington, 2006, Tri State Sculptors Edn. Assn. exhibit, 2007; one-woman shows include Watkins Gallery, Am. U., 1972, AAAS/Atrium Gallery, Washington, 1989-90, O Street Studios, Washington, 1990, Friedholm Fine Arts Gallery, Asheville, NC, 1991, Mansion Art Gallery, Rockville, 1993, Gate House Gallery, Washington, 1994, Artisans of Va. Invitational, 2004—, Artistans Ctr. Va., 2006, Imago Gallery, Warren, RI, 2006, Washington Sq., 2007, others; exhibited in group shows at Gallery 10, Washington, 1998, Tri-State Sculptors Ednl. Assn., Washington, 1997, Associated Artists of Winston-Salem, NC, 1996, 99, Tri-State Sculptors Conf., U. SC, Spartenburg, 1996, ARTS 901 E Street, Washington, 1996, AAAS, Washington, 1995-96, Newhouse Ctr. for Contemporary Art, S.I., NY, 1995-96, Mill River Gallery, Ellicott City, Md., 1999, Tysons Galleria II, Vienna, Va., 1999, Washington Sculptors Group, 1998-00, Coastal Carolina U., Myrtle Beach, 1999, Grounds for Sculpture, Hamilton, NJ, 2000, 02, Mus. Art, Beijing, 2001, Brookside Gardens, 2002-03, Meridith Coll., Raleigh, NC, 2003, Artists In Our Midst, Washington, 2003, Capetown (South Africa) U., 2003, Washington Scultors Group Ann. Exhbn., Washington, 2004, Tri-State Sculptors Conf., Winston-Salem, NC, 2004, Am. Ctr. for Physics, College Park, Md., 2004-05, Arlington Art Ctr., 2006, Sculpture Now 06 Washington, 2006, Arlington Art Ctr., Va., 2006, Imago Gallery, Warren, RI, 2006, others; work collected at Ballston Metro Sta., Arlington, Va., First Am. Bank, Va. Commonwealth U., U. Md., AAAS/Washington, Akin Group, Law Offices, Washington, IBM Rsch. Hdqrs., Durham, NC, Internat. Sculpture Ctr., Hamilton NJ, Tri State Sculptors Edn. Assn., U. NC, Brevard, Am. Ctr. for Physics, 2004-05, others; curator Tri State Sculptors Edn. Assn. Exhibit, Washington Sq., Washington, 2007. Finalist Best Pub. Art Sculpture award, Rockville, 2004; named to Hall of Fame, Shaker Heights (Ohio) H.S., 2001; recipient Editor's Choice award, Internat. Libr. Photography, 1998. Mem. Tri-State Sculptors Ednl. Assn. (life), Washington Sculptors Group. Democrat. Jewish. Avocations: travel, lecturing, gourmet cooking. Home: 2700 Virginia Ave NW Washington DC 20037-1908 E-mail: shirleyartkoller@metronets.com.

KOLLIAS, JIM HARRY, music educator; b. Laguna Beach, Calif., Jan. 4, 1966; s. Harry D. and Linda Kollias; m. Doris C. Kateyiannis, Aug. 20, 1989; 1 child, Christina Eleftheria; 1 child, Harrison James. BA in Music, UCLA, 1987; MS in Music Edn., U. Ill., Champaign-Urbana, 1996. Cert. profl. clear single subject instrn. credential, music Calif. Instrumental music dir. Vina Danks Mid. Sch., Ontario, Calif., 1988—94, Columbus Tustin Mid. Sch., Tustin, 1994—2004, C. E. Utt Mid. Sch., Tustin, 1994—96; orch. dir. Tustin H.S., Calif., 2000—05; dir. bands and orch. Beckman H.S., 2004—. Guest condr. San Bernardino County H.S. Honor Orch., Calif., 1998, San Bernardino County Concert Orch., Calif., 2000; mentor tchr. Ontario Montclair Sch. Dist., Ontario, 1993—94, Tustin Unified Sch. Dist., 1996—97; chairperson Tustin Unified Sch. Dist. Facilities Com., 1995—96; presenter in field. Composer: (music) Everyone Can Play in Twelve Keys, 1990; contbr. articles to profl. jours. Named Tchr. of Yr., Columbus Tustin Mid. Sch., 1998, Beckman H.S., 2006, Toast of the Town, Town & Country Com., Orange County Philharm. Soc., 2001; recipient Pied Piper award, So. Calif. Sch. Band & Orch. Assn., 1996, PTSA Hon. Svc. award, Vina Danks Mid. Sch. PTSA, 1992; grantee, Orange County Philharm. Soc., Tustin Pub. Schs. Found. Mem.: Calif. Music Educators Assn., San Bernardino County Music Educators Assn. (secondary orch. rep. 1993—94), So. Calif. Sch. Band & Orch. Assn. (v.p. elem. & mid. sch. edn. 1999—2001). Personal E-mail: jhkollias@yahoo.com. Business E-Mail: jkollias@tustin.k12.ca.us.

KOLMIN, KENNETH GUY, lawyer; b. NYC, Oct. 22, 1951; s. Frank William and Edith Kolmin; m. Suzan L. Frumm, Sept. 3, 1978; children: Stephen Todd, Jennifer Dana, Robert Scott. BS summa cum laude, SUNY, Albany, 1973; MS, Syracuse U., 1975, JD cum laude, 1975. Bar: Ill. 1976, U.S. Dist. Ct. (7th dist.) Ill. 1976, U.S. Tax Ct. 1980, U.S. Supreme Ct. 1985; CPA, Ill. Tax cons. Arthur Young and Co., Chgo., 1976-79; atty. Shefsky Saitlin & Froelich, Chgo., 1979-81; ptnr. Rooks Pitts & Poust, Chgo., 1981-84, Schwartz & Freeman, 1984-96, Sonnenschein, Nath & Rosenthal, Chgo., 1996—. Contbr. articles to profl. jours. Mem. ABA, AICPA, Ill. Bar Assn., Ill. Soc. CPAs. Home: 975 Eastwood Rd Glencoe IL 60022-1122 Office: Sonnenschein Nath & Rosenthal 8000 Sears Tower Chicago IL 60606

KOLODEY, FRED JAMES, lawyer; b. LaCoste, Tex., Mar. 5, 1936; s. Raymond and Mamie V. (Newman) K.; children: Trecia Anne Estep, Michele Leigh Winn; m. Helen Gable McIntosh, June 10, 1989. BA, Tex. Christian U., Ft. Worth, 1962; LLB, So. Meth. U., Dallas, 1964. Bar: Tex. 1964. Since practiced in Dallas; ptnr. Kolodey & Thomas, 1975-83, of counsel, 1983-94, Thomas, Sheehan & Culp, 1994—2001, Kolodey, Thomas & Blackwood, 2001—05; prin. Law Office of Fred Kolodey,

Dallas, 2005—. Pres. Dallas Jr. Bar Assn., 1969 Comments editor: Southwestern Law Jour, 1963-64. Mem. dist. hearing office panel Dallas Community Coll., 1974, Democratic precinct chmn., 1968-73. Mem. Tex., Dallas bar assns., Delta Theta Phi (pres. 1963, Nat. award 1964), Alpha Chi, Pi Sigma Alpha. Home: 107 Shepherd's Glen Rd Heath TX 75032 Office Phone: 214-782-1610.

KOLODNER, RICHARD DAVID, biochemist, educator, director; b. Morristown, NJ, Apr. 3, 1951; s. Ignace Izack and Ethel (Zelnick) Kolodner; m. Karin Ann Gregory, Aug. 6, 1983 (div. May 1991); m. Jean Y.J. Wang, Dec. 2, 2004. BS, U. Calif., Irvine, 1971, PhD, 1975; MS (hon.), Harvard U., 1988. Rsch. fellow Harvard U. Med. Sch., Boston, 1975-78; from asst. prof. to prof. biochemistry Dana Farber Cancer Inst. and Harvard U. Med. Sch., Boston, 1978—97; chmn. divsn. cellular molecular biology Dana-Farber Cancer Inst., 1991-94, head x-ray crystallography lab., 1991-97, chmn. divsn. of human cancer genetics, 1995-97; prof. medicine, mem. Cancer Ctr. U. Calif. Med. Sch., San Diego, 1997—; mem. Ludwig Inst. Cancer Rsch., San Diego, 1997—, assoc. dir. NYC, 2004—05, exec. dir. lab. sci. and tech., 2006—. Editor: PLASMID Jour., 1986—95; assoc. editor: Cancer Rsch. Jour., 1995—2000, Cell jour., 1996—; mem. editl. bd. Molecular Cellular Biology Jour., 1999—, Jour. Biol. Chemistry, 2000—05, DNA Repair Jour., 2003—; contbr. articles to sci. jours. Recipient Jr. Faculty Rsch. award, Am. Cancer Soc., 1981, Faculty Rsch. award, 1984, Merit award, NIH, 1993, Charles S. Mott prize, GM Cancer Rsch. Found., 1996; grantee, NIH, 1978—; rsch. grantee, Am. Cancer Soc., 1980—82. Fellow: Am. Acad. Microbiology; mem.: NAS, Am. Assn. Cancer Rsch. (Kirk Landon award 2007), Genetic Soc. Am., Am. Soc. Microbiology, Am. Soc. Biochemistry and Molecular Biology. Home: 13468 Kibbings Rd San Diego CA 92130-1231 Office: Ludwig Inst for Cancer Rsch 9500 Gilman Dr CMME 3058 La Jolla CA 92093-0669 Home Phone: 858-259-9027. Business E-Mail: rkolodner@ucsd.edu.

KOLODNER, ROBERT M., federal agency administrator, health information technology executive; Undergraduate Degree, Harvard Coll., 1970; MD, Yale Univ. Sch. Medicine, 1974. Cert. Psychiatry. Clin. fellowship, medicine Harvard Univ. Sch. Medicine, 1975; psychiatric residency Washington Univ. Sch. Medicine, 1975—78; chair, mental health spl. interest user group Veterans Health Adminstrn., Dept. Veterans Affairs, 1983—89, acting co-chair, clin. record spl. interest user group, 1989—91, chair, clin. applications requirements group, 1991—93, dir., med. info. resources mgmt. office, 1993—96, assoc. chief info. officer for enterprise strategy (formerly bus. enterprise solutions and tech.), Office of Info., 1996—2005, chief health informatics officer (CHIO), 2005—06; interim nat. health info. tech. coord. US Dept. Health and Human Svc., Washington, 2006—07, nat. health info. tech. coord., 2007—. Lectr. on med. informatics throughout the US. Mem. of several editl. boards; contbr. articles to several med. jours., chapters to books. Achievements include involvement with the development and oversight of VistA, Veterans Affairs electronic health records system and My HealtheVet, Veterans Affairs personal health records for veterans; establishment of the Federal Health Information Exchange (FHIE) program. Office: US Dept Health and Human Svcs 200 Independence Ave SW Washington DC 20201*

KOLODNY, EDWIN HILLEL, neurologist, geneticist, director; b. Boston, Mar. 15, 1936; s. Myer Zeman and Naomi Lillian (Zalkind) K.; m. Roselyn Leinwand, May 31, 1958; children: Nancy, Leonard Benjamin, Robin, Noah Jacob. AB in Econs. cum laude, Harvard Coll., 1957; MD with honors, NYU, 1962. Diplomate Am. Bd. Psychiatry and Neurology, Am. Bd. Med. Genetics. Intern, resident in internal medicine Bellevue Hosp., NYC, 1962-64; resident in neurology Mass. Gen. Hosp., Boston, 1964-67; spl. fellow lab. neurochemistry Nat. Inst. Neurol. Diseases, Bethesda, Md., 1967-70; asst. prof. neurology Harvard Med. Sch., Boston, 1970-76, assoc. prof., 1976-85, prof., 1985-91; Bernard and Charlotte Marden prof., chmn. dept. neurology NYU Med. Ctr., NYC, 1991—. Vice-chmn. exec. com. Med. Bd. Tisch Hosp., NY, 1993-97, chmn., 1997-99; vis. prof. Weizmann Inst. Sci., Rehovot, Israel, 1988, 90; assoc. dir. Eunice Kennedy Shriver Ctr., Mental Retardation, Inc., Waltham, Mass., 1976-83, acting dir., 1983-84, dir., 1984-90; assoc. neurologist Mass. Gen. Hosp., Boston, 1976-87, neurologist, 1988-91; chmn. com. Rsch. Ctrs. Forward Planning Mental Retardation, Nat. Inst. Child Health and Human Devel., 1983-84; cons. pres.'s com. Mental Retardation, 1982; adv. genetic svcs. Dept. Pub. Health Mass., 1977-80; mem. Mass. Nat. Inst. Health Centennial Com., 1987-88, profl. adv. bd. Internat. Rett Syndrome Assn., 1986-94, sci. adv. bd. United Leukodystrophy Found., 1986-94, sci. med. adv. com. Canavan Found., 1994—; mem. expert com. Gaucher Initiative Project Hope, 2000—; mem. steering com. Global Orgn. for Lysosomal Diseases, 2002—06. Mem. editl. bd. Annals of Neurology, 1984-89; contbr. articles to profl. jours. Mem. sci. adv. bd. Nat. Tay Sachs and Allied Diseases Assn., 1970—; mem. med. adv. bd. Dysautonomia Found., 2001—; v.p., trustee Temple Emanuel, Newton, Mass., 1983—89; trustee Hebrew Coll., Brookline, Mass. Recipient Solomon A. Berson Med. Alumni Achievement award clin. sci. NYU Sch. Medicine, 1993, Above and Beyond award Nat. Tay Sachs and Allied Diseases Assn., 2003, Disting. Svc. award ROFEH Internat., 2004, Art of Listening award Genetic Alliance, 2006. Fellow Am. Coll. Med. Genetics, Am. Acad. Neurology (S. Wier Mitchell award 1970); mem. Am. Assn. Neuropathology (Moore award 1975), Am. Neurol. Assn., Am. Soc. Human Genetics, Am. Soc. Neurochemistry, Child Neurology Soc., Harvard Varsity Club (Cambridge), Assn. for Rsch. in Nervous and Mental Diseases (bd. dirs. 1993—), Alpha Omega Alpha. Avocations: judaica, photography. Home: 110 Bleecker St Apt 24D New York NY 10012-2106 Office: NYU Med Ctr 550 1st Ave New York NY 10016-6402 Home Phone: 212-677-9500; Office Phone: 212-263-6347. Personal E-mail: ekolc@yahoo.com. Business E-Mail: edwin.kolodny@med.nyu.edu.

KOLODNY, STANLEY CHARLES, oral surgeon, retired military officer; b. NYC, Feb. 22, 1923; s. Aaron and Lea (Stern) K.; m. Mary Kathryn Leigh, Feb. 22, 1947; children: Kathleen Susan, Carter Leigh, Stanley Charles. BA, U. Tex., 1944; D.D.S., Baylor U., 1947; MS, U. Ill., 1961. Diplomate: Am. Bd. Oral and Maxillofacial Surgery. Commd. 1st lt. USAF, 1951, advanced through grades to maj. gen., 1981; cons. in oral surgery Surgeon Gen. U.S. Air Force, 1966; chmn. dept. oral surgery Wilford Hall USAF Med. Center, San Antonio, 1969-75, dir. dental services, 1975-77; asst. surgeon gen. for dental services Bolling AFB, Washington, 1979-82. Clin. prof. dept. surgery U. Tex. Dental Br., Houston, 1969-77; clin. asso. prof. dept. surgery U. Tex. Med. Sch., San Antonio, 1969-77 Contbr. chpt. to book, articles to profl. jours. Bd. dirs. Am. Cancer Soc., 1970-77. Decorated D.S.M., Legion of Merit with oak leaf cluster, Air Force Commendation medal; recipient cert. of achievement for outstanding oral surgery USAF. Fellow Am. Coll. Dentists, Am. Assn. Oral and Maxillofacial Surgeons; mem. ADA, Soc. Air Force Clin. Surgeons. Home: 6401 Red Bud Dr Flower Mound TX 75022-5859 Personal E-mail: hgenkolodny@comcast.net.

KOLODNY, STEPHEN ARTHUR, lawyer; b. Monticello, NY, 1940; BA in Bus. Adminstrn., Boston U., 1963, JD, 1965. Bar: Calif., 1966; U.S. Dist. Ct. (cen. dist.) Calif. 1966, U.S. Supreme Ct. 2004; cert. family law specialist. Sole practice, LA, 1966—95; partner Kolodny and Anteau, LA, 1995—. Lectr. family law subjects; adj. prof. U. Houston; ABA Trial Advocacy Inst., 1989—, co-chair, 1997—. Author: Evidence ABA Adv., 1996, (ann. publ.) Family Law Contempts; co-author: The Divorce Trial Manual, 2003 Named Number One Family Law Trial Lawyer, Calif. Lawyer Mag., Aug. 1999; named one of Top 10 Lawyers in U.S.A., Town and Country Mag., 1998, Worth Mag., 2002; recipient Silver Shingle award for disting. svc. to profession Boston U. Sch. Law, 2003. Mem. Am. Acad. Matrimonial Lawyers (past pres. So. Calif. chpt.), Am. Coll. Family Trial lawyers (founding dir., diplomate, exec. v.p.), Internat. Acad. Matrimonial Lawyers (bd. gov., past pres. U.S.A. chpt.), Calif. State Bar Assn. (cert. family law specialist 1980—; lectr. State Bar panel, CEB programs, family law sect., article author), L.A. County Bar Assn. (lectr., past chmn. family law sect.), Beverly Hills Bar Assn. (lectr., family law sect.). Office Phone: 310-271-5533. Office Fax: 310-271-3918. Business E-Mail: kolodny@kolodny-anteau.com.

KOLODZEI, NATALIA A., art association administrator, art historian, curator; b. Moscow, Jan. 8, 1974; d. Tatiana A. and Alexander D. Kolodzei; m. Marc David Miller. BA in Art History with honors, State U. N.J., 1998. Exec. dir. Kolodzei Art Found., Inc., Highland Park, NJ, 1991—; curator Bergen Mus. Art and Sci., Chelsea Art Mus., NYC, 2005. Mem. adv. bd. Russian Am. Forum, N.Y., 1995—. Contbr. articles to exhbn. catalogs, art mags. Art Chronika, Iskusstvo; editor: (catalogs and books) Oleg Vassiliev; Memory Speaks. Themes and Variations, 2004, Art Constitution, Vadim Voinov: The State Hermitage Under a Full Moon, 2005. Named Hon. Citizen of State of Okla., Gov. of Okla., 1993. Mem. Am. Assn. Advancement Slavic Studies, Internat. Salon Soc. (amb. 1996—), Internat. Assn. Art Critics (Russian sect.), Assn. Art Historians, Jr. Assn. Mus. Modern Art, Young Collectors Coun. Guggenheim Mus., Internat. Art Fund, Print Club NY (bd. dirs.), NY Russian Club (bd. dirs.), Golden Key Nat. Honor Soc., Phi Beta Kappa. Avocation: collecting Russian and eastern European art. Home: 123 S Adelaide Ave Apt 1N Highland Park NJ 08904-1615 Office Phone: 732-545-8425. Home Fax: 732-545-8428. Personal E-mail: kolodzei@kolodzeiart.org.

KOLOKYTHAS, ANTONIA, oral surgeon, oncologist; m. George Sotiropoulos, Dec. 28, 1998. DDS, Aristotle U. Thessaloniki, Greece, 1995. Cert. AAOMS. Head and neck cancer fellow U. Md., Balt., 2004—05; oral oncologist U. San Francisco, 2005—06, asst. clin. prof., 2005—06; maxillofacial surgeon Oral Maxillofacial Surgeons Lake County, Gurnee, Ill., 2006—. Recipient 2nd position award, Internat. Congress Oral Oncology, 2005. Fellow: Internat. Acad. Oral Oncology; mem.: Ill. Soc. Oral and Maxillofacial Surgeons. Achievements include research in identification of molecular markers in squamous cell carcinoma or the oral tongue. Home Phone: 847-390-9895; Office Phone: 847-623-2830.

KOLOPAJLO, LAWRENCE HUGH, chemistry professor; BS, Muskingum Coll., New Concord, Ohio, 1973; MS, Pa. State U., University Park, 1976; PhD, Western Mich. U., Kalamazoo, 1982. Cert. tchr. secondary edn. Ohio, 1986. Asst. prof. chemistry Ea. Mich. U., Ypsilanti, Mich., 2002—. Contbr. articles to profl. jours. Mem.: Mich. Sci. Tchrs. Assn., Am. Chem. Soc. Roman Catholic. Office: Ea Mich Univ 202 Mark Jefferson Hall Ypsilanti MI 48197 Home Phone: 419-824-4552; Office Phone: 734-487-0100. Office Fax: 734-487-1496. Business E-Mail: lkolopajl@emich.edu.

KOLSHAK, JOSEPH C., air transportation executive; BS in Acctg., Marquette U., Milw. With Delta Air Lines, Inc., Atlanta, 1988—, spl. assignment supr. to v.p. flight ops., 1991—93, flight ops. coord., 1993—94, flight ops. mgr., asst. chief pilot, 1994—96, gen. mgr. flight ops., 1996—98, dir. investor rels., 1998—2001, v.p. flight ops., 2001—02, sr. v.p. flight ops., 2002—04, sr. v.p., chief ops., 2004—05, exec. v.p., chief ops., 2005—06, exec. v.p. ops., 2006—. Officer USMC. Office: Delta Air Lines Inc PO Box 20706 Atlanta GA 30320-6001 Office Phone: 404-715-2600.*

KOLSON, ANN J., editor; Staff writer Phila. Inquirer, 1984—94; Sunday Times editor NY Times, 1997—. Office: NY Times Arts and Leisure 229 W 43rd St New York NY 10036 Office Phone: 212-556-3679.

KOLTNOW, PETER GREGORY, engineer, consultant; b. NYC, Apr. 14, 1929; s. Harry George and Fay (Richman) Koltnow; m. Dorothy D. Witter, Oct. 27, 1950; children: Nan Koltnow Chase, Nina. BS, Antioch Coll., 1951; MS, U. Calif., Berkeley, 1956. Engr. City of Dayton, Ohio, 1953-55; traffic engr. County of Fresno, Calif., 1956-62, Auto Club of So. Calif., 1962-67; dir. urban div. Automotive Safety Found., Washington, 1967-69, Hwy. Users Fedn., 1970-71, v.p., 1971-74, pres., 1974-84; counselor to pres. Am. Trucking Assns., 1985-90. Guest lectr. various univs., 1965—; chmn. Transp. Rsch. Bd., 1979. Contbr. articles to profl. jours. Pres. Candlelighters, 1970—71. With Ordnance Corps US Army, 1951—53. Recipient Disting. Svc. award, Transp. Rsch. Bd., 1982. Mem.: ASCE (James Laurie prize 1984), Nat. Acads. (nat. assoc.). Unitarian Universalist. Home and Office: 3100 N Leisure World Blvd Apt 401 Silver Spring MD 20906

KOLTUN, FRANCES LANG, editor, publisher, broadcaster; b. NYC; d. Samuel and Rebecca (Lang) K. BA magna cum laude, Bklyn. Coll.; MA, Columbia U. Editor Am. Girl Mag., NYC, Charm Mag., NYC, Mademoiselle Mag., NYC; owner, pres. Frances Koltun Enterprises Ltd., NYC, 1972—; radio and TV broadcaster NBC, NYC. Writer and performer Travel Today, a radio syndicated program with 400 stas.; bd. dirs. Travel Industry Assn., Washington. Author: Frances Koltun's Complete Book for the Intelligent Woman Traveler; editor, pub. ann. supplement A Fifth Avenue Christmas, other spl. newspaper supplements; pub., editor A Matter of Wit mag., 1998—; creator Beautiful Flowers-Beautiful Walls, 2002-03. Named as A Woman of Accomplishment Wings Club, N.Y.C.; recipient Lifetime Achievement award Bklyn. Coll., 2002. Mem. Trends, Women's Forum.

KOLVE, V. A., English literature educator; b. Taylor, Wis., Jan. 18, 1934; s. Amos and Gunda (Lien) K. BA, U. Wis., 1955; BA with honors, Oxford U., 1957, MA, DPhil, Oxford U., 1962. From asst. prof. to assoc. prof. English Stanford (Calif.) U., 1962-69; prof. English U. Va., Charlottesville, Va., 1969-78, Commonwealth prof. English, 1979-86, chmn. dept. English, 1979-81; found. prof. English UCLA, 1986—2001, prof. emeritus, 2001—. Ednl. adv. bd. Guggenheim Found., 1988—, Alexander Lectures, U. Toronto, 1993, Clark Lectures, Cambridge U., 1994 Author: The Play Called Corpus Christi, 1966, Chaucer and The Imagery of Narrative, 1984; author, editor: (with Glending Olson) Norton Critical Edition: Chaucer: The Canterbury Tales, 1989, 2d expanded edit., 2005. 1st lt. U.S. Army, 1959. Recipient Brit. Coun. Humanities prize, 1985, Harbison Teaching award Danforth Found., 1972, UCLA Disting. Teaching award, 1995, Disting. Faculty award, 1999; Jenkins Rsch. fellow Oxford U., 1958-62, Guggenheim fellow, 1968, Sr. fellow Ctr. Advanced Studies in Visual Arts, Nat. Gallery, 1984, fellow Ctr. Advanced Study in Behavioral Scis., Stanford U., 1985; Rhodes scholar, 1955-58. Fellow Medieval Acad. Am. (pres. 1992), Am. Acad. Arts and Scis.; mem. MLA (chair exec. com. Chaucer divsn. 1973-77, 86-90, James Russell Lowell prize 1985), New Chaucer Soc. (trustee 1988-92, pres. 1994-96), Early English Text Soc., AAUP, Phi Beta Kappa. Democrat. Home: 2034 Outpost Dr Los Angeles CA 90068-3726 E-mail: kolve@ucla.edu.

KOLVENBACH, PETER HANS, priest, religious order superior; b. Druten, The Netherlands, 1928. Student U. Nijmegen (Netherlands), theology St. Joseph U., Beirut, linguistics, Paris, 1963-67. Joined Jesuit Order Netherlands; ordained priest Roman Cath. Ch., 1961; prof. linguistics St. Joseph U., Beirut, 1968-81; provincial superior Beirut, 1974-81; rector Pontifical Oriental Inst., Rome, 1981-83; superior-gen. Soc. of Jesus, 1983—; consultor Congregation for Oriental Chs., mem. Congregation for Evangelization of Peoples, mem. Orthodox-Cath. dialogue, 1983—. Author: In Cammino Verso La Pasqua, 1988, Men of God: Men for Others, 1990, El Padre Kolvenbach en Colombia, 1990, Kolvenbach en México, 1990, Fedeli Adio E All Uomo, 1990, Cinco mensajes universitarios, 1991, Seleccion de escritos 1983-90, Folli Per Cristo, 1999, Faubourg Du Saint Espirit, 2004, also various articles and revs. in field of linguistics and spiritual theology; mem. of commns. Cath. Orthodox dialogue books. Address: Borgo Santo Spirito 4 00193 Rome Italy Office Phone: 39-06-689-771-288. Business E-Mail: infosj@sjcuria.org.

KOLYER, JOHN MCNAUGHTON, materials scientist, retired chemist; b. East Williston, NY, June 30, 1933; s. John and Mildred (McNaughton) K.; children: Scott McNaughton, Paul Franklin, Craig David, Jeffrey John. BA, Hofstra U., 1955; PhD, U. Pa., 1960. Technician Olin-Mathieson Chem. Corp., Port Washington, NY, 1955-56; rsch. chemist FMC Corp., Princeton, NJ, 1960-62; tech. supr. Allied Chem. Corp., Morriston, NJ, 1964-71; mem. tech. staff Rockwell Internat., Anaheim, Calif., 1973-96; scientist, engr. Boeing Co., Anaheim, 1997—2006; ret. Author: many technical articles and works of fiction and verse; patentee in field; author: Engaged to be Dead, 2004. Mem.: NY Acad. Scis., Soc. Advancement Materials Processing and Engring., Am. Chem. Soc., Phi Lambda Upsilon, Kappa Mu Epsilon, Sigma Kappa Alpha. Office: 1455 Superior Ave Apt 124 Newport Beach CA 92663-6107

KOLZIG, OLAF, professional hockey player; b. Johannesburg, Apr. 6, 1970; Goalie Washington Capitals, 1989—. Player NHL All-Star Game, 2000. Co-recipient Harry Holmes Meml. Trophy, 1994; recipient Jack Butterfield Trophy, 1994, Vezina Trophy, 2000, King Clancy Meml. Trophy, 2006. Avocations: golf, fishing. Office: Washington Capitals Ste 750 401 Ninth St NW Washington DC 20004

KOMAKI COX, RITSUKO U., medical educator; arrived in U.S., 1970; d. Isao and Yukiko Ueda; m. Senichiro Komaki, Apr. 20, 1970 (div. June 1978); m. James D. Cox, Jan. 28, 1980; children: Christoph, Lara. BS, Hiroshima U., Japan, 1965, MD, 1969. Intern St. Mary's Hosp., Milw., 1972—73; hematology fellow VA Hosp., Milw., 1973—74; radiology and oncology resident Milw. County Hosp., 1974—79, radiation oncology fellow, 1979—80, asst. and assoc. prof., 1980—85; assoc. prof. Columbia Presbyn. Hosp., NYC, 1985—88; tenured prof. radiation oncology MD Anderson Cancer Ctr., Houston, 1988—. Named Alumna of Yr., Med. Coll. Wis., 2005, Gloria Lipton Tennison Disting. Prof. Lung Cancer Rsch., U. Tex., 2006; recipient Golden Apple award, 2004. Mem.: Internat. Assn. Study Lung Cancer (bd. dirs. 2005—06), Am. Radium Soc. (pres.-elect 2006), Am. Assn. Women Radiologists (pres. 2001, Marie Curie award 2005). Avocations: travel, Japanese gardens. Office: U Tex MD Anderson Cancer Ctr Unit 97 1515 Holcombe Houston TX 77030

KOMANDURI, KRISHNA V., physician, research scientist; b. Hyderabad, Andhra Pradesh, India, Oct. 17, 1965; s. Sesha C. and Vijaya L. Komanduri; m. Cheryl Lynn Fahrner, Aug. 6, 2000; children: Arjun H., Kiran A., Malini G., Jaya L. BS, MIT, 1983; MD, U. Minn., 1991. Lic. Tex., 1999. Asst. prof. medicine M.D. Anderson Cancer Ctr., Houston, 1999—2006, assoc. prof. medicine dept. stem cell transplantation and cellular therapy, 2006—. Dir. M.D. Anderson Cancer Ctr. Bone Marrow Transplant Fellowship Program, Houston, 2001—; assoc. dir. M.D. Anderson Cancer Ctr. Hematology/Oncology Fellowship Program, Houston, 2005—; med. editl. bd. mem. Nexcura, Inc., Seattle, 2002—. Recipient President's Student Leadership and Svc. award, U. Minn., 1990, Outstanding Student award, Minn. Med. Found., 1991; grantee, Leukemia and Lymphoma Soc. of Am., 2000—03, 2005—, NIH, 2005—; Nat. Merit Scholar, 3M, 1983—87. Mem.: Am. Soc. Blood and Marrow Transplantation, Am. Soc. Hematology. Achievements include research in in human T cell immunology; patents pending for method of measuring de novo T cell production in adult humans; method to specifically deplete a population of alloreactive or antigen-specific T cells. Office: MD Anderson Cancer Ctr 1515 Holcombe Blvd Unit 900 Houston TX 77030 Home Phone: 713-436-3970; Office Phone: 713-563-3324.

KOMAR, VITALY, artist; b. Moscow, Sept. 11, 1943; Student, Stroganov Inst. Art and Design, Moscow, 1967. Ptnr. Former Komar & Melamid Archive, NYC, 1973—2003. Instr. visual art Moscow Regional Art Sch., 1968-76. Exhibitions include Wadsworth Atheneum, Hartford, Conn., 1978, Mus. Modern Art, Oxford Eng., Mus. Decorative Art, Paris, 1985, Neuen Gesellschaft für Gildende Kunst, Berlin, 1988, Bklyn. Mus., 1990, Alternative Mus., NYC, 1994, Storefront for art and architecture, NYC, 1995, Ukraine State Mus., Kiev, 1995, Mus. Modern Art, Cologne, Germany, 1997, Kunsthalle, Vienna, Austria, 1998; exhibited in group shows at Met. Mus. Art, NYC, 1982, 84, Chrysler Mus., Norfolk, Va., 1983, Sydney, Australia, 1986, Kassel, Documenta 8, Germany, 1987, Solomon R. Guggenheim Found., 1987, FIAC, Paris, 1989, Bklyn. Mus., 1990, Venice Bienalle, 1997, 99, Yeshiva U. Mus., NYC, 2002-03, Cooper Union, NYC, 2005, Feldman Gallery, NYC, 2005, Moscow Bienalle, 2007; represented in permanent collections Whitney Mus. Am. Art, NYC, Stedeliyk Mus., Amsterdam, The Netherlands, Guggenheim Mus., Mus. Modern Art, Met. Mus. Art; commns. include mural Unity, 1st Interstate Bank Bldg., LA, 1993, murals Liberty as Justice, NY, Bronx Housing Ct., 1994-98. Grantee Nat. Endowment Arts, 1982. Fax: 212-777-6653. E-mail: v.komar@yahoo.com.

KOMAROFF, ANTHONY LEADER, physician; b. Milw., June 7, 1941; s. Michael I. and Lillian J. (Leader) K.; m. Lydia Villa, June 18, 1970. AB, Stanford U., 1963; MD, U. Wash., 1967. Intern Cambridge Hosp., Cambridge, 1967-8; resident Beth Israel Hosp., Boston, 1970-72, asst. physician, 1971-79; sr. physician Brigham & Women's Hosp., Boston, 1992—, chief div. gen. medicine, 1982-97; Simcox-Clifford-Higby prof. medicine Harvard Med. Sch., Boston, 1993—; editor-in-chief Harvard Health Publs., Boston, 1997—. Mem. nat. adv. coun. Reg. Med. Programs, Dept. HEW, Washington, 1971-76. Editor: Harvard Medical School Family Health Guide, 2005; contbr. over 270 articles to profl. jours. Lt. col. USPHS, 1968-70. Grantee, HEW, Dept. Health and Human Svcs., 1976—. Achievements include development of field of clinical algorithms; applications of computers in medical care; studies of common illnesses. Office: Harvard Health Publs 10 Shattuck St Boston MA 02115-6011 Office Phone: 617-432-4714.

KOMAROFF, STANLEY, lawyer; b. Bklyn., Apr. 1, 1935; s. William Ralph and Fanny (Wein) K.; m. Rosalyn Steinglass, Dec. 25, 1960; children: William Charles, Andrew Steven. BA, Cornell U., Ithaca, NY, 1956, JD, 1958. Bar: NY 1959. Assoc. Proskauer Rose LLP, NYC, 1958-68, ptnr., 1968—, chmn., 1991-99; sr. advisor Henry Schein, Inc., Melville, NY, 2004—. Mem. hosp. rev. and planning coun. NY State, 1982-92; trustee Beth Israel Med. Ctr., 1984—, vice chair, 1999-2007; trustee St. Lukes-Roosevelt Hosp. Ctr., Continuum of Health Ptnrs. Inc.; mem. bd. regents LI Coll. Hosp., 2001—; bd. dirs. Edmond de Rothschild Found., Club Med, Inc., 1984-95, Overseas Shipholding Group, Inc., NYC Econ. Devel. Corp., Westhampton Beach Performing Arts Ctr.; chmn. ann. fund Cornell U. Law Sch., 1991-93, mem. adv. coun. 1st lt. USAR, 1958. Fellow Am. Bar Found.; mem. NY State Bar Assn., Assn. Bar City of NY, NY County Lawyers Assn., Order of Coif, Sunningdale Country Club, Phi Kappa Phi. Home: 910 Park Ave Apt 5-s New York NY 10021-0255 Office: Henry Schein Inc 135 Duryea Rd Melville NY 11747 Business E-Mail: Stanley.Komaroff@Henryschein.com.

KOMAROV, ANDREI M., biophysicist, educator, research scientist; b. Frunze, Russia, Sept. 22, 1961; arrived in US, 1992; s. Mikhail I. Komarov and Emma G. Komarova; m. Natalia V. Kouznetsova; 1 child, Valeria. MD, Russian State Med. U., 1984; PhD, Inst. of Chem. Physics, Acad. of Scis., Russia, 1988. Vis. scientist Med. Coll. of Wis., Milw., 1992—94; sr. rsch. scientist George Washington U., Washington, 1994—97, asst. rsch. prof.,

1998—. Ad hoc referee numerous jours.; presenter in field; lectr. in field. Contbr. articles to profl. jours., chapters to books. Recipient Diploma of Sr. Scientist in Biophysics award, State Attestation Commn., Russia, 1992, Faculty Rsch. award, George Wash. U., 1998, Rsch. award, TRUE Rsch. Found., 2006. Mem.: Oxygen Club of Greater Washington. Achievements include development of nitric oxide trapping agents for nitric oxide detection and scavenging; research in the role of nitric oxide and iron in inflammation. Office: George Washington U Dept Biochemistry 2300 Eye St NW Ross Hall 441 Washington DC 20037

KOMISAR, ARNOLD, otolaryngologist, educator; b. NYC, Nov. 27, 1947; s. Samuel and Sonia (Schwartz) K.; children: Alexandra Danielle, Jonathan Reed. BS, Bradley U., Peoria, Ill., 1968; DDS, NYU, 1972, MS in Health Care Mgmt., 2004; MD, Hahnemann Med. Coll., Phila., 1975. Diplomate Am. Bd. Otolaryngology, Nat. Bd. Med. Examiners, Nat. Bd. Dental Examiners. Resident in surgery Beth Israel Med. Ctr., NYC, 1975-76; resident in otolaryngology Mt. Sinai Med. Sch., NYC, 1976-79; asst. prof. otolaryngology Albert Einstein Coll. Medicine, NYC, 1979-85, assoc. prof., 1985-86, assoc. clin. prof., 1986-90; assoc. dir. head and neck surgery Albert Einstein Affiliated Hosps., NYC, 1982-86; attending otolaryngologist Montefiore Hosp. and Med. Ctr., NYC, 1979-90, Bronx Mcpl. Hosp. Ctr., NYC, 1979-90, North Ctrl. Bronx Hosp., NYC, 1979-90, N.Y. Hosp.-Cornell U. Med. Ctr., NYC, 1997—; clin. assoc. prof. otolaryngology Cornell U. Med. Coll., NYC, 1994—98, clin. prof., 1998—2000; attending otolaryngologist N.Y. Hosp.-Cornell U. Med. Ctr., NYC, 1997—2000; clin. prof. otolaryngology NYU, 2000—. Otolaryngologist Lenox Hill Hosp., NYC, 1986—, asst to dir. resident edn. dept. otolaryngology, 1986—, adj. otolaryngologist, 1987—, attending otolaryngologist, 1989—, assoc. dir. otolaryngology, 1990—, vice-chmn., 2003-2005, acting chmn., 2006-07; cons. otolaryngology NY Eye and Ear Infirmary, NYC, 1986-89; courtesy staff surgery-otolaryngology Drs. Hosp., NYC, 1986-90; attending staff Manhattan Eye Ear and Throat Hosp., 1995—; attending otolaryngologist NY Hosp. Cornell U. Med. Ctr., 1997-2000; presenter in field. Contbr. articles to profl. jours., chpts. in books. Recipient Centurion award Bradley U., 1997, Resident Tchg. award, Manhattan Eye Ear Throat Hosp., 1999, Stanley M. Blaugrund Tchg. award NYU, 2003. Fellow ACS, Am. Soc. Head and Neck Surgery, Am. Acad. Facial Plastic and Reconstructive Surgery, Am. Acad. Otolaryngology/Head and Neck Surgery (Honor award 1998), Triological Soc. (Mosher award 1989), Am. Bronchoesophalogical Soc., NY Acad. Medicine, Am. Laryngol. Assn.; mem. AMA, Am. Acad. Anti-Aging Medicine, Pan-Am. Soc. Brochoesophagology, Soc. Univ. Otolaryngologists, NY Head and Neck Soc., Med. Soc. NY, NY Laryngol. Soc., NY County Med. Soc. Avocations: reading, travel. Office: 1317 3d Ave New York NY 10021-2995 Office Phone: 212-861-8888. Business E-Mail: axk2@aol.com.

KOMISAR, DAVID DANIEL, retired academic administrator; b. NYC, July 20, 1917; s. Jacob and Yetta (Jacobson) K.; m. Beatrice Liebman, Aug. 15, 1940 (dec. Sept. 1981); children— Jack Lloyd, June Diana; m. Molly Komisar, Nov. 1984 BSS., Coll. City N.Y., 1937, MS, 1940; postgrad., U. Glasgow, 1945, Sorbonne, 1946; PhD, Columbia U., 1953. With Civil Service, NYC, 1939-42; indsl. personnel work, 1943-44; counselor vocational rehab. U.S. Army, 1943-46; dir. guidance Mohawk Coll., 1946-48; dir. guidance, chmn. dept. psychology Champlain Coll., State U. N.Y., Plattsburg, 1948-53; chmn. dept. psychology U. Hartford, 1953—, pres. univ. faculty senate, 1964-65; dean U. Hartford (Sch. Arts and Scis.), 1966-67, dean of faculties, 1967-70, v.p. acad. affairs, 1970-71, provost, 1972-80, Univ. prof., 1980-84, prof. and provost emeritus, 1984—; mem. Conn. Civil Service Commn., 1980-84; pres. Emeriti Assn., 1989-91; cons. Palm Beach County Mental Health Assn., 1991—. Project dir. research in mental retardation Office Vocat. Rehab., Dept. Health, Edn. and Welfare, 1964-65, psycho-social com. social rehab. services, 1968-74; head New Eng. Conf. Mental Retardation, 1960, Conn. Task Force on Mental Retardation, 1960-61; Conn. rep. Nat. Def. Edn. Act, 1960-61; research fellow U.S. Office Vocational Rehab., 1962-63; Conn. Citizens Com. on State Welfare, 1967-69; mem. standing com. accreditation Conn. Commn. High Edn., 1969-75. Contbr. articles on testing, therapy, vocational selection to profl. jours. Co-chmn. Citizens Charter Com. Hartford, 1959; mem. bd. Hartford Jewish Cmty. Ctr., 1955-63, v.p., 1963-78, life officer 1978—; mem. bd. Mental Health Assn., 1959-62; bd. dirs. Inst. of New Dimensions, Palm Beach Cmty. Coll., 1994—. Recipient rsch. grant for study residential care retarded children HEW, 1965-69, Disting. Svc. medal U. Hartford, 1990, Univ. medal U. Hartford, 1991; elected to Townsend Harris Hall of Fame, 1998. Mem. Conn. Valley Assn. Psychologists (past pres.), Am. Psychol. Assn., Conn. Psychol. Assn. (council; pres.), Nat. Vocational Guidance Assn., Am. Personnel and Guidance Assn., Sigma Xi. Clubs: Connecticut Valley Torch (past pres.), Probus (past pres.) (Hartford).

KOMISAR, KEN, recording industry executive; b. New Haven, Conn. With promotion, A&R & dance depts. Atlantic Records; sr. dir. A&R Epic Records, LA, 1989; gen mgr. MJJ Records, 1995—2000; v.p. A&R Sony BMG Music Entertainment, 2000—07; pres. Tennman Records, Beverly Hills, Calif., 2007—. Office: Tennman Records PO Box 18765 Beverly Hills CA 90209*

KOMISARJEVSKY, CHRISTOPHER P.A., retired public relations executive; b. Feb. 16, 1945; BS in Polit. Sci., MBA; postgrad. German Lit./Internat. Affairs, U.S./Europe. Hill and Knowlton, Inc., 1972-92, pres., CEO Europe, Mid. East and Africa ops., CEO Carl Byoir & Assocs.; pres., CEO Gavin Anderson & Co. Omnicom, 1992-95; pres., CEO Burson-Marsteller U.S., NYC, 1995-99, Burson-Marsteller Worldwide, NYC, 1998—2004. Chmn. Burson-Marsteller Global Corp. Practice, 1995-99. Co-author: Peanut Butter and Jelly Management, 2000; contbr. articles to profl. jours.; lectr. at Spain's Instituto de Empresa, Switzerland's Internat. Inst. for Mgmt. Devel., N.Y.U. Grad. Sch. Bd. dirs. several non-profit orgs.; trustee EQ Advisors Trust. Capt. U.S. Army, 1967-72 (Vietnam). Recipient Ellis Island Medal of Honor, 1996. Personal E-mail: chris.komisarjevsky@gmail.com.

KOMISKE, BRUCE KING, hospital administrator; b. June 22, 1948; BS in Biology, U. Pitts., 1970; M in Hosp. Adminstrn., Duke U., 1972. Asst. adminstr. Suburban Hosp., Bethesda, Md., 1974-77; v.p. Yale/New Haven Hosp., 1977-83; adminstr., CEO Norwood (Mass.) Hosp., 1983-86; pres. RIH Ventures, Providence, 1986-93; v.p. planning, mktg., bus. devel. R.I. Hosp., Providence, 1986-93; exec. dir. Hasbro Children's Hosp. and R.I. Hosp./Women & Infants Hosp., Providence, 1986—97, Children's Hospital Found., 1997—2004; exec. dir. clinical facilities devel. U. Calif., San Francisco, 2004—07; project dir. KEO Internat. Consultants, 2006; chief new hospital design & construction Children's Meml. Hospital, Chgo., 2007—. Lectr. Yale U., George Washington U., Providence Coll., R.I. Health Industries Coun., New Eng. Healthcare Assembly, Conn. Hosp. Assn., Am. Hosp. Assn., others. Author: Family Partnership in Hospital Care - The Cooperative Care Concept. Bd. dirs. R.I. March of Dimes, Providence Ronald McDonald House, R.I. Assn. for Cardiac Children; grad. Leadership R.I., 1988. 1st lt. U.S. Army, 1972-74. Recipient Health Care Forum and 3M 1988 Orgnl. Innovator award-Silver medal. Fellow Am. Coll. Healthcare Execs. (regent for R.I. 1990-94). Office: Children's Meml Hospital 2300 Children's Plz Chicago IL 60614

KOMMEDAHL, THOR, plant pathology educator; b. Mpls., Apr. 1, 1920; s. Thorbjørn and Martha (Blegen) K.; m. Faye Lillian Jensen, June 2, 1924; children: Kris Alan, Siri Lynn, Lori Anne. BS, U. Minn., 1945, MS, 1947, PhD, 1951. Instr. U. Minn., St. Paul, 1946-51, asst. prof. plant pathology, 1953-57, assoc. prof., 1957-63, prof., 1963-90, prof. emeritus, 1990—; asst. prof. plant pathology Ohio Agrl. Research and Devel. Ctr., Wooster, 1951-53, Ohio State U., Columbus, 1951-53; prof. Univ. Coll., U. Minn., St. Paul, 1990—. Cons. botanist and taxonomist Minn. Dept. Agr., 1954-60, Sci. Mus. Minn., 1990—; 7th A.W. Dimock lectr. Cornell U., 1979; external assessor U. Pertanian Malaysia, 1994-97. Author: Pesky Plants, 1994; co-author: Scientific Style and Format, 1994; editor Minn. Fulbright newsletter, 1995—2002, Procs. IX Internat. Congress Plant Protection, 2 vols., 1981, Corn Disease newsletter, 1970—76, assoc. editor The Boghopper, 1996—, cons. editor McGraw Hill Ency. Sci. and Tech., 1972—78, editor-in-chief Phytopathology, 1964—67;. 7th edit., 2006; sr. editor: Challenging Problems in Plant Health, 1982, Plant Disease Reporter, 1979; contbr. articles to profl. jours. Bd. mem. Park Bugle, 1998—2007. Recipient Elvin Charles Stakman award, 1990, award of merit, Gamma Sigma Delta, 1994, Ed Stevens Vol. award, Roseville, 2007; Guggenheim fellow, 1961, Fulbright scholar, 1968. Fellow AAAS, Am. Phytopathol. Soc. (councilor 1958-60, pres. 1971, publs. coord. 1978-84, Disting. Svc. award 1984, 93, sci. adv. 1984—, adv. bd. office internat. programs 1987-93, editor Focus 1981—); mem. Am. Inst. Biol. Scis., Bot. Soc. Am., Coun. Sci. Editors, Internat. Soc. Plant Pathology (councilor 1971-78, sec.-gen. and treas. 1983-88, treas. 1988-93, editor newsletter 1983-93), Mycol. Soc. Am., Minn. Acad. Sci., N.Y. Acad. Scis., Weed Sci. Soc. Am. (award of excellence 1968), Fulbright Assn. (editor newsletter Minn. chpt. 1995-2002). Baptist. Home: 1666 Coffman St Apt 322 Saint Paul MN 55108-1340 Office: U Minn Dept Plant Pathology 495 Borlaug Hall 1991 Upper Buford Cir Saint Paul MN 55108-6030 Office Phone: 612-625-3164. Office Fax: 612-625-9728. Business E-Mail: thork@umn.edu.

KOMOLA, CHRISTINE T., corporate financial executive; BS in Acctg., Miami U. CPA 1992. With Ernst & Young LLP; asst. contr. Staples, Framingham, Mass., 1997, v.p. planning & control, 1997—99, CFO Staples.com, 1999—2001, sr. v.p., gen mdse. mgr. furniture and wholesaler, 2001—04, sr. v.p., contr., 2004—. Mem.: AICPA, Mass. Soc. CPA. Office: Staples 500 Staples Dr Framingham MA 01702*

KOMOROSKI, LEN, professional sports team executive; m. Denise Komoroski; children: Kristin, Kelly, Jamie, Zachary. Grad. cum laude, Duquesne U., 1982. With Maj. Indoor Soccer League Pitts. Spirit, 1982; mgmt. position NHL Pitts. Penguins; with Maj. Indoor Soccer League Minn. Strikers; regional mgr. sports mktg. Miller Brewing Co.; v.p. sales, sr. sales and mktg. ofcl. NBA Minn. Timberwolves, 1988—94; sr. v.p., COO Internat. Hockey League Cleve. Lumberjacks; sr. v.p., chief bus. ops. NFL Phila. Eagles; pres. NBA Cleve. Cavaliers/Quicken Loans Arena. Bd. dirs. Cleve. chpt. City Year, ARC, United Way; bd. mem. Greater Cleve. Conv. and Visitors Bur. Office: Cleve Cavaliers One Center Ct Cleveland OH 44115-4001*

KOMPASS, EDWARD JOHN, consulting editor; b. Jersey City, Dec. 22, 1926; s. Edward F. and Margaret A. (Doran) K.; m. Amelia M. Heubel, Sept. 22, 1951; children: Christine (Mrs. Kevin Scully), Daniel E., Andrew J., Timothy M., Matthew P., Julie A. (Mrs. Matthew Wilhm). Degree in mech. engring., Stevens Inst. Tech., 1951. Jr. engr. Intelectron Inc., NYC, 1951-52; engr. De Florez Co., NYC, 1952-54; asst. editor control engring., McGraw-Hill Pub. Co., NYC, 1954-60, assoc. editor, 1960-65; mng. editor control engring., Dun-Donnelley Pub. Corp., NYC, 1965-72; editor control engring., Tech. Pub., Barrington, Ill., 1972-86; editorial dir. control engring. Cahners Publ., 1986-87, cons. editor, 1987—, forum discussions moderator, control engring online, 1997. Co-organizer ann. advanced control confs. Purdue U., Lafayette, Ind., 1974-77, 79-93; conf. dir. Internat. Control. Engring. Expn. and Conf., Chgo., 1992-94; mem. adv. coun. Indsl. Automation Conf., 1994, 95, 96. Editor, contbr. profl. articles and editorials to jours.; editorial advisor Detroit Engr. With USNR, 1944-46. Recipient 19th Ann. Crain award Assn. Bus. Pubs., 1987. Mem. IEEE, Am. Soc. Bus. Paper Editors, Instrument Soc. Am., Engring. Soc. Detroit, Am. Legion, VFW, Rotary Internat., Beta Theta Pi. Roman Catholic. Home and Office: 678 Cobb Hill Rd Lincoln VT 05443-9699 E-mail: ekompass@gmavt.net.

KONA, MARTHA MISTINA, librarian; b. Banovce, Slovakia; came to U.S., 1950; d. Albert and Anna (Kubrican) Mistina; m. William Kona, Aug. 6, 1955 (dec. Dec. 1989); children: Olivia, Lindy Anne. Student, U. Salzburg, 1950; BA, Rosary Coll., 1953, MA, 1958; postgrad., Roosevelt U., 1980. Libr. instr., prof. Univ. Ill., Chgo., 1958-63; rsch. libr. Cen. Soya Chemurgy, Chgo., 1965-73; asst. dir. Rush Univ. Libr., Chgo., 1973-78; pvt. practice cons., info. specialist Wilmette, Ill., 1980; pvt. practice author and lectr., 1985—. Cons., liaison Matica Slovenska, Slovak Nat. Libr. and Archives, Martin, Slovak Republic, Slovak World Congress, 1991-98. Author: Soybean Proteins, 1969, Multi Media Catalog, 1975, Health Science Librarians of Illinois, 1977, Slovak Americans and Canadians, 1985; co-author, editor: Archbishop Dr. Karol Kmetko, 1989, PhD Dissertations in Slovakiana in the Western World: Bibliography, 1996; contbr. articles to profl. jours. Bd. dirs. Slovak Am. Found. Edn. and Sci., Inc., 1994; Slovak rep. European-Am. adv. bd. Archdiocese Chgo. Mem. AAUW, AAUP (chair bylaws com. 1975-77), Health Sci. Librs. Ill. (co-founder, archivist 1970-77), Slovak World Congress (chair heritage and culture commn. 1990—), First Slovak League of Am., Slovak Cath. Falcon, Ill. Audio Visual Assn. (pres. 1975-77), Sovereign Mil. Order of Temple of Jerusalem (Grand Cross, 1975, Order of Merit in Grade and Rank of Grand Comdr., 1999—, Grand Magistral Liaison, 1989-96), Slovak Inst. (Rome), Imperial Order of Constantine the Great and St. Helen (bd. dirs. 1977—), Dames of the Order in the U.S.A. (Lady Comdr.), Order St. John Jerusalem, Woman's Club Wilmette Philanthropy (chair 1991-93), Pi Gamma Mu. Avocations: reading, travel, classical music, physical fitness, beachcombing. Home: 2335 Middlesex Dr Toledo OH 43606-3143

KONAN, DENISE, academic administrator, economics professor; BA, Goshen Coll.; MA, PhD, Univ. Colo., Boulder. Prof. econ. Univ. Hawaii, Manoa, 1993—, asst. vice chancellor, 2002—05, interim chancellor, 2005—07. Contbr. articles in profl. jours., chapters to books. Office: U Hawaii Manoa Dept Econ 2424 Maile Way Honolulu HI 96822

KONATE, DIALLA, mathematician, educator; b. Bafoulabe, Mali, Sept. 10, 1953; s. Zegue Konate and Morimoussou Dansira; m. Habsatou Ba, Sept. 24, 1977; children: Ramata, Mariam, Aicha, Ibrahim. DEA, U. Lyon, France, 1978; Doctorate, U. Lyon, 1979. Lectr. U. Grenoble, France, 1976-78; sr. lectr. U. Lyon, 1978-80; asst. prof. ENIG, Gabes, Tunisia, 1980-83, chair dept. math., 1980-84; dir., sci. rschr. LICIA, Paris, 1984-96, ICTA, Washington, 1998—; prof. UAG, France; prof. math. dept. Va. Polytechnic Inst. State U., Blacksburg, Va.; dir. inst. high performance computing applications Winston-Salem State U., SC. Chair sci. program INTI, Africa, 1998—; mem. anti-corruption forum World Bank Mali Govt., 1998-2000; UNDP vis. prof. U. Mali, 1998—; devel. project supr. World Bank, Africa, 1999—. Editor Techinche-Technique-Development, 1987. Achievements include research in singular perturbation; developing a new technique in singular perturbation that is now considered as an appreciable advance in field. Business E-Mail: dkonate@vt.edu, konated@wssu.edu.

KONCHITSKY, ALON, electronics engineer, communications executive; PhD, Bournemouth U., Eng., MA in Mgmt.; BSc in Computer Sci., Tel Aviv U.; degree in Elec. Engring., Tel Aviv Inst. Tech. Rschr. DSP Comm., Tel Aviv; tech. leader Nokia, San Diego; chief wireless arch. Advanced Radio Solutions, Cupertino, Calif., 2002—05, chief tech. officer. Cons. Goldman Sachs, Fidelity, VCs, San Diego; dir. Digital Comm. Sys., v.p. engring. tech. rsch. Recipient Tech. award, USAF, 1995. Mem.: IEEE, U. Calif. San Diego Connect. Constitution. Achievements include development of digital radio. Office Phone: 408-480-3186. Personal E-mail: dr.alon.konchitsky@ieee.org.

KONDAS, NICHOLAS FRANK, retired shipping company executive; b. Eger, Hungary, Sept. 26, 1929; arrived in US, 1957; s. Miklos and Ilona (Racz) K.; m. Elfriede O. Strauss; children: Walter, Nicolette. MS in Econs., Karl Marx U., Budapest, Hungary, 1952. Mgr. Szovosz Cent., Budapest, 1952-56; assembler S. Goldberg Inc., Hackensack, N.J., 1957-67; supr. Alfred Industries, Richfield Park, N.J., 1967-68; mgr. C.R. Bard, New Providence, N.J., 1968-69; v.p. Seatrain Lines Inc., NYC, 1969-81; gen. mgr. Harper Robinson Co., San Francisco, 1981-82; ret. v.p. Farrell Lines Inc., NYC, 1982-2000; pres. Dionic Resources Inc., 1994; ret., 2001. V.p. Transp. Sys. Internat., Washington, 1980-2001, Pacific Enterprises Inc., 1992-05. Served to lt. Hungary Army Res., 1952-56. Avocation: photography. Personal E-mail: graynick@aol.com.

KONDRACKE, MORTON MATT, journalist; b. Chgo., Apr. 28, 1939; s. Matthew and Genevieve Marta (Abrams) K.; m. Millicent Martinez, Oct. 7, 1967 (dec. July 2004); children: Alexandra, Andréa; m. Marguerite Sallee, May 6, 2006. AB, Dartmouth Coll., 1960. Corr. Chgo. Sun Times, Chgo. and Washington, 1963-77; exec. editor The New Republic, Washington, 1977-85; columnist Wall Street Jour., Washington, 1980-85, United Features Syndicate, Washington, 1983-85; Washington bur. chief Newsweek Mag., Washington, 1985-86; sr. editor The New Republic, Washington, 1986—91; exec editor & columnist Roll Call, 1991—; TV commentator, co-host The Beltway Boys, Fox News Channel, 1996—. Radio commentator Nat. Pub. Radio and Sta. WRC-AM, Washington, 1978-83; TV commentator McLaughlin Group, Washington, 1981—96, PBS; author Saving Milly, 2001. Panelist presdl. debate, Kansas City, Mo., 1984. Served with U.S. Army, 1960-63 Mem.: Michael J. Fox Found. for Parkinson's Rsch, Parkinson's Action Network. Office: Roll Call Suite 700 50 F St NW Washington DC 20001 E-mail: mmk@rollcall.com.

KONDRACKI, EDWARD JOHN, lawyer; b. Elizabeth, NJ, Sept. 27, 1932; s. John and Catherine Chudio (Saas) K.; m. Barbara Terese Caruso; children: Carol Ann, Maryanne, Christopher. BSEE, NJ Inst. Tech., Newark, 1959; JD with honors, George Wash. U., Washington, DC, 1963. Bar: Va. 1964, DC 1964, US Dist. Ct. DC 1964, US Ct. Appeals (fed. cir.) 1983, US Ct. Claims 1976, US Ct. Customs and Patent Appeals 1976, US Dist. Ct. (ea. dist.) Va. 1964, pro hac vica US Dist. Ct. (ctrl. dist.) Calif., US Dist. Ct. (so. dist.) Ala., US Dist. Ct. (no. dist.) Fla., US Dist. Ct. (no. dist.) Ga., US Dist. Ct. (we. dist.) La., US Dist. Ct. (ea. dist.) Mich., US Dist. Ct. (no. dist.) Okla., US Dist. Ct. (ea. dist.) Pa., US Dist. Ct. (no. dist.) NY, US Dist. Ct. (ea. dist.) Tex., US Dist. Ct. (no. dist.) Tex. Patent atty. Gen. Electric Co., Washington, 1959-63; assoc. Kerkam, Stowell Kondracki & Clarke, P.C. and predecessor, Arlington, Va., 1963-65; dir., prin. Kerkam, Stowell Kondracki & Clarke, P.C., Arlington, 1965-99; prin. Miles & Stockbridge, McLean, Va., 2000—. Owner, dir. Patmark Paralegal Svcs., 1975—90; chmn. Structured Occupl. Ctr., 1999—, gen. counsel, 2003—. Author: Proper Use of Trademarks and Servicemarks, 1982, Common Pitfalls Encountered in Patenting Inventions, 1983, Copyright Protection of Computer Software, 1989, Intellectual Property, Rights Acquisition and Protection Conference World Trade Assn. NJ, 1989, Trademarks-Servicemarks, Use, Usage and Protection, 1990; contbr. article to Voice of Tech. Bd. dirs. The Amadeus Concerts, Inc., 2003—. With USN, 1951—55. Mem. ABA, Am. Intellectual Property Law Assn., Internat. Assn. Protection Indsl. Property, Fed. Bar Assn., Va. Bar Assn., Internat. Trademark Assn., Washington Patent Lawyers Club, North Va. Patent Lawyers Club, DC Bar Assn. (chmn. com. internat. affairs 1973), Va.'s Elite Lawyers of No. Va., Gt. Falls Hist. Soc., Marmota Farm Assn., KC, Tau Beta Pi, Eta Kappa Nu, Omicron Delta Kappa, Phi Eta Sigma. Office: 1751 Pinnacle Dr Ste 500 Mc Lean VA 22102-3833 Office Phone: 703-903-9000. Business E-Mail: ekondracki@milesstockbridge.com.

KONDRUP, JOHN THOMAS, retired research scientist; b. NYC, May 24, 1925; s. James John and Anna Kondrup; m. Anna Rabinowitz (div.); children: Bella, David, Gloria, James; m. June B. Graham, May 15, 1976. BS, MS. Dir., oper., mgr. Acasian Resume & Writing, Baton Rouge, 1982—99; sales rep., cashier Wal-Mart, Zachary, La., 1999—2006; ret., 2006. With USN, 1943—59. Independent. Home: La War Vets Home 4739 La Hwy 10 Jackson LA 70748

KONDRUP, STEVEN W., state agency administrator; BA in Bus. Adminstrn. Pers. adminstr. Western Mortgage Corp., Utah; ops. mgr. leasing divsn. Nev. First; v.p., banking ctr. mgr. Bank of Am.; dep. commr. Nev. Divsn. Fin. Instns., 2005—06, acting commr., 2006—. Ret. master sgt. US Army. Office: Office of Commr Nev Divsn Fin Instns 2785 E Desert Inn Rd Ste 180 Las Vegas NV 89121 Office Phone: 702-486-4120. Office Fax: 702-486-4563. E-mail: skondrup@fid.state.nv.us.

KONECK, JOHN MICHAEL, lawyer; b. Mpls., Aug. 16, 1953; s. Robert W. and Bernice V.; m. Debra K. Plotz, Aug. 16, 1980; 1 child, Robert John. BS, N.D. State U., 1975; JD, Yale Law Sch., Mpls., 1978. Bar: N.D. 1978, Minn. 1979. Jud. law clk. N.D. Supreme Ct., Bismarck, 1978-79; ptnr., pres. Fredrikson & Byron, Mpls., 1979—. Real property law specialist, mem. Minn. Bd. Legal Cert., Supreme Ct. Minn., 1994-99, chmn., 1996-99; mem. Vol. Lawyers Network; assoc. prof. William Mitchell Coll. Law, 1997—. Mem. ABA (chair litig. and dispute resolution, com. of sect. real property, probate and trust law 1995-98, chief editor newsletter of litig. and dispute resolution com. 1991-93, vice chair 1991-95), Am. Coll. Real Estate Lawyers, Minn. State Bar Assn. (co-chair real property cert. coun. 1990—, mem. rules of profl. conduct com.), State Bar Assn. N.D., Hennepin County Bar Assn. (co-chair rules of profl. conduct com. 1994-96). Office: Fredrikson & Byron 200 S 6th St Ste 4000 Minneapolis MN 55402-1425 Home Phone: 651-483-3198; Office Phone: 612-492-7038. Business E-Mail: jkoneck@fredlaw.com.

KONECNI, VLADIMIR J. J. CH. S. (GRAF KONECNI), psychologist, educator, writer; b. Belgrade, Yugoslavia, Oct. 27, 1944; s. Josip J. and Dora D. (Vasic) Konecni; m. Daiva K. Stasiulis, Jan. 3, 1973 (div. Apr. 7, 1977); m. Marie Gabrielle Frey, May 11, 1987 (dec. Oct. 1, 1989); m. Mirjam Christina Dolman, Nov. 27, 1993; 1 child, Dusan A. V. C. B. BSc magna cum laude, Belgrade U., Yugoslavia, 1968; MA, U. Toronto, Can., 1971, PhD, 1973. Asst. prof. U. Calif. San Diego, La Jolla, 1973—78, assoc. prof., 1978—82, prof. psychology, 1982—; prof. methodology in psychology Belgrade U., Serbia and Montenegro, 1994—. Vis. prof. Sydney U., 1979, U. Western Australia, Perth, 1979, Pontifica U. Catolica, Rio de Janeiro, 1980, London Sch. Econs., 1980—81, Free U. Berlin, 1986, Hebrew U., Jerusalem, 1986, U. Cape Town, South Africa, 1987, U. Amsterdam, Netherlands, 1991, Tartu U., Estonia, 2002—; fellow John Simon Guggenheim Meml. Found., NYC, 1979—80; vis. scientist Russian Acad. Scis., St. Petersburg, 1993. Author, producer, director: (performance pieces) Paat (The Boat), 2001; author, director, producer (performance pieces) Beckett v. Duchamp, 2002, author, producer, director Dvojnost (Duality), 2003; one-man shows include Of Nuns, Spices, and Boiling Mud, 1982, West Hollywood Art Galleries, 1986, Blue and brown, Tallinn City Mus., Estonia, 1999; poet (prin. works) Port-au-Prince, 1996, Door, 1997. Fellow, John Simon Guggenheim Meml. Found., 1979—80. Mem.: Internat. Informatization Acad., European Psychology-Law Assn., Internat. Assn. Aesthetics. Libertarian. Serbian Orthodox. Avocations: mountain climbing, horseback riding, swimming, chess, fencing.

KONENKAMP, JOHN K., state supreme court justice; b. Oct. 20, 1944; m. Geri Konenkamp; children: Kathryn, Matthew. JD, U. S.D., 1974. Dep. state's atty., Rapid City; pvt. practice, 1977-84; judge SD Cir Ct. (7th cir.), 1984—88, presiding judge, 1988-94; assoc. justice SD Supreme Ct., Pierre, 1994—. Bd. dirs. Alt. Dispute Resolution Com., Adv. Bd. for Casey Family

Program. Served in USN. Mem. Am. Judicature Soc., State Bar S.D., Pennington County Bar Assn., Nat. CASA Assn., Am. Legion. Office: SD Supreme Ct 500 E Capitol Ave Pierre SD 57501-5070*

KONERKO, PAUL, professional baseball player; b. Providence, Mar. 2, 1976; First baseman Chgo. White Sox, 1999—. Host Starlight Children's Found., Comiskey Park. Achievements include mem. Major League Baseball World Champions, 2005. Office: Chgo White Sox 333 W 35th St Chicago IL 60616

KONETY, BADRINATH R., surgeon, researcher; s. R. S. and Prabha R. Konety; m. Suma H. Murthy, Oct. 1992; children: Isha R., Arjun S. BA, St. Joseph's Coll., Bangalore, India, 1984; MD, Bangalore U., 1990; MBA, U. Pitts., 2000. Diplomate Am. Bd. of Urology, 2003. Asst. prof. U. of Iowa, 2001—; chief, sect. of urology Vets. Adminstrn. Med. Ctr., 2002—. Recipient Resident Essay Contest, Am. Urologic Assn. NE Sect., 1998, Pfizer Scholars in Urology award, Pfizer Inc., 1998, Frederick N. Schwentker Endowment award, U. Pitts., 1998; fellow Jahnigen Rsch. scholar, Am. Geriat. Soc., 2004—; grantee New Investigator award, Dept. of Def., 2004—. Fellow: ACS (assoc.); mem.: Soc. for Basic Urologic Rsch., Soc. of Urologic Oncology, Am. Urologic Assn. Achievements include development of Urinary tumor marker BLCA-4 for bladder cancer; EAU-AUA Exchange Fellow year 2004; research in American Foundation for Urologic Disease Research Scholar Award; Ferdinand Valentine Fellowship. Office: Univ Iowa Dept of Urology 3236 RCP 200 Hawkins Dr Iowa City IA 52242 Office Phone: 319-356-1974.

KONETZNI, ALBERT H., JR., career officer; b. NYC, Nov. 16, 1944; s. Albert H. Sr. and Adeline E. (Gergel) K.; m. Shirley A. Lane, Nov. 21, 1995; children: Albert H. III, Kristen, Kiera, Kyle. BS, U.S. Naval Acad., Annapolis, Md., 1966; MS in Pers. Adminstrn., George Washington U., 1972. Commd. ensign U.S. Navy, 1966, advanced through grades to vice adm., 2001; submarine office, comdr. U.S.S. Grayling, Charleston, SC, 1981-84; comdr. Submarine Squadron 16, Kingsbay, Ga., 1987-89; asst. chief pers. for policy, plans, career progression U.S. Navy, Washington, 1994-95; comdr. Submarine Group Seven, Yokosuka, Japan, 1995-98; comdr. submarine force U.S. Pacific Fleet, Harbor, Hawaii, 1998-2001; dep. commdr. in chief, chief of staff U.S. Atlantic Fleet, 2001—; sr. v.p. Wash. Group Internat., Inc. Co-author: Command At Sea, 1980. Office: USN 562 London Hill Rd W Woodbine GA 31569 Office Phone: 803-507-8111. Personal E-mail: konetzniah@myway.com.

KONG, ADAMS WAI KIN, electrical engineer, researcher; b. Hong Kong, Dec. 1, 1974; s. Hon Sum Kong and Po Chu Li; m. Wai Lan Kwong. BS in Math. Sci., Hong Kong Bapt. U., 1998; MPhil in Computing, Hong Kong Poly U., 2001; PhD in Elec. and Computer Engring., U. Waterloo, Canada, 2007. Tchr. Caritas Inst. for Further and Adult Edn., Tuen Mun Night Sch., Hong Kong, 1997; project asst. dept. math. Hong Kong Bapt. U., 1998; part-time vis. lectr. dept. computing Hong Kong Poly. U., 2000—01, rsch. asst. dept. computing Biometrics Rsch. Ctr., 2001—02, rsch. assoc. dept. computing Biometric Rsch. Ctr., 2002—03; cons. Knowledge Funds Ltd., Waterloo, 2007; asst. prof. Nanyang Tech. U., Singapore, 2007—. Reviewer 16th Internat. Conf. on Computers and Their Applications, 2001—01, Pattern Recognition, 2001—01, Optical Engring., 2003—03, Internat. Jour. Image and Graphics, 2003—05, Second Internat. Conf. on Machine Learning and Cybernetics, 2003—03, IEEE Transactions on Systems, Man and Cybernetics (Part C), 2003—05, Internat. Conf. on Image Analysis and Recognition, 2004—04, Internat. Conf. on Biometric Authentication, 2004—04, Pattern Recognition Letters, 2005—05, IEEE Systems, Man, and Cybernetics Conf., 2005—05, Asia-Pacific Workshop on Visual Info. Processing, 2005—05, Internat. Jour. Computers and Applications, 2005—06, IEEE Transactions on Systems, Man and Cybernetics (Part B), 2005—05. Contbr. articles to profl. jours. in field. Named to President's Honour Roll, Hong Kong Bapt. U., 1995—96, 1996—97, 1997—98; recipient Sir Edward Youde Meml. prize, Sir Edward Youde Meml. Fund Coun., 1993, Scholastic award, Hong Kong Bapt. U., 1998, Hon. Mention of Math. Contest in Modeling, Consortium for Math. and its Applications, 1998, Internat. Doctoral Student award, U. Waterloo, 2004, Internat. Grad. Student award, 2004, Internat. Doctoral Student award, 2005, 2006; scholar, City U. Hong Kong, 1998, Hong Kong Poly. U., 1999, 2000; Taipei Trade Ctr. scholar, Hong Kong Bapt. U., 1996, Zheng Ge Ru Found. scholar, 1997, Grad. scholar, U. Waterloo, 2005, Faculty Engring. Grad. scholar, 2006. Mem.: IEEE. Achievements include patents pending for palm print identification using palm line orientation; first to using orientation field for palmprint identification; identifying the genetically related features in palmprints for personal identification; analyzing the current iris recognition systems; patents pending for method of palmprint identifcation; apparatus for capturing a palmprint image; patents for method of print identification using geometry, line and/or texture feature; invention of effective palmprint algorithm for real-time large scale personal identification; discovery of correlation features in identical twins palmprints. Avocations: soccer, travel. Office: Nanyang Technol Univ Sch Computer Engring Block N4 Nanyang Ave Singapore 639798 Singapore Personal E-mail: adamskong@ieee.org.

KONG, JIN AU, electrical engineering educator; b. Kiangsu, China, Dec. 27, 1942; s. Chin-Hwu and Shue C. Kong; m. Wen-Yuan Yu, June 27, 1970; children— Shing, David S. BS, Taiwan U., Taipei, 1962; MS, Chiao Tung U., Hsinchu, Taiwan, 1965; PhD, Syracuse U., 1968. Research engr. Syracuse U., N.Y., 1968-69; Vinton Hayes postdoctoral fellow engring., asst. prof. elec. engring. MIT, Cambridge, 1969-71, asst. prof., 1969-73, assoc. prof., 1973-80, prof., 1980—, chmn. area IV on energy and electromagnetic systems, 1984—. Vis. scientist Lunar Sci. Inst., Houston, summers 1971, 72; vis. prof. elec. engring. U. Houston, 1981-82; cons. UN, 1977-80, Raytheon Co., 1979-82, Hughes Aircraft Co., 1981, Lockheed Missile and Space Co., 1984, Schlumberger-Doll Research, 1985, MIT Lincoln Lab., 1979—; pres. Electromagnetics Acad., 1989—; lectr. in field. Author: Theory of Electromagnetic Waves, 1975, Electromagnetic Wave Theory, 1986; co-author: Applied Electromagnetism, 1983, Theory of Microwave Remote Sensing, 1985; editor: Research Topics in Electromagnetic Wave Theory, 1981, Wiley Series in Remote Sensing, 1985—; editor-in-chief Jour. of Electromagnetic Waves and Applications, 1986—, Progress in Electromagnetics Research, 1989—; contbr. numerous articles to profl. jours.; reviewer numerous jours., govt. orgns., book cos. Recipient Teaching award Grad. Student Council, MIT, 1985 Fellow IEEE; mem. Internat. Union Radio Sci., Am. Phys. Soc., Am. Geophys. Union, Optical Soc. Am., Sigma Xi, Phi Tau Phi, Tau Beta Pi Home: 9 Kitson Park Dr Lexington MA 02421-8109 Office: 77 Massachusetts Ave Rm 26-305 Cambridge MA 02139-4301 Business E-Mail: kong@emwave.org.

KONG, LAURA S. L., geophysicist; b. Honolulu, July 23, 1961; d. Albert T.S. and Cordelia (Seu) K.; m. Kevin T.M. Johnson, Mar. 3, 1990. ScB, Brown U., 1983; PhD, MIT/Woods Hole Oceanog. Inst., 1990. Grad. rschr. Woods Hole (Mass.) Oceanog. Instn., 1984-90; postdoctoral fellow U. Tokyo, 1990-91; geophysicist Pacific Tsunami Warning Ctr., Ewa Beach, Hawaii, 1991-93; seismologist U.S. Geol. Survey Hawaiian Volcano Obs., 1993-95; rschr. U. Hawaii, Honolulu, 1996-99; environ. specialist Dept. Transp., Honolulu, 2000—05; dir. Internat. Tsunami Info. Ctr., Honolulu, 2005—. Chair Hawaii Earthquake Adv. Bd., 1994—; tsunami advisor State of Hawaii, 1999—; mem. equal opportunity adv. bd. Nat. Earth Svc. Pacific Region, Honolulu, 1992-93, Asain-Am.-Pacific Islander spl. emphasis program mgr., 1992-93; mem. steering com. U.S. Nat. Tsunami Hazard Mitigation Program; mem. Hawaii State Hazard Mitigation Forum, Hawaii Multi-Hazard Sci. Adv. Com.; legis. rschr. Hawaii Senate, 1996-98. Contbr. articles to profl. jours.; spkr., editl. reviewer in field. Rsch. fellow Japan Govt.-Japan Soc. for Promotion of Sci., 1990; recipient Young Investigator grant Japan Soc. for Promotion of Sci., 1990. Mem. Am. Geophys. Union, Seismol. Soc. Am., Hawaii Ctr. for Volcanology, Assn. Women in Sci., Sigma Xi. Avocation: sports. Office: Nat Weather Svc Internat Tsunami Info Ctr 737 Bishop St Ste 220 Honolulu HI 96813 E-mail: laura.kong@fhwa.dot.gov.

KONG, XUAN, electrical engineer, educator; b. Chengdu, Sichuan, China, May 25, 1965; s. Fancheng and Wenlin (Bai) K.; m. Ning Zhuang, Dec. 17, 1988; children: Albert, Alissa. BSc, Sichuan U., Chengdu, 1984; MSc, U. Man., Winnipeg, Can., 1986; PhD, Johns Hopkins U., 1991; MBA, Boston U., 2006. Software engr. LCC Inc., Arlington, Va., 1993; asst. prof. elec. engring. No. Ill. U., De Kalb, 1993-98, assoc. prof. elec. engring., 1998—2000; v.p. rsch. Neurometrix, Inc., Waltham, Mass., 1999—. Author: Adaptive Signal Processing Algorithms: Stability and Performance, 1995; contbr. articles to sci. procs. Rsch. grantee NIH, 1995, 1998, Office of Naval Rsch. Mem. IEEE, Eta Kappa Nu, Beta Gamma Sigma, PRMIA. Office Phone: 781-314-2722.

KÖNIG, PETER, pediatrician, educator; b. Cluj, Romania, Feb. 14, 1938; came to U.S., 1976; s. Rudolf and Irina (Grünwald) K.; m. Lea Schiffer, Sept. 30, 1965; 1 child, Orly. Graduate, Timisoara Med. Sch., Romania, 1959; MD, Hebrew U., Jerusalem, 1966; PhD, U. London, 1974. Resident Hadassah Hosp., Jerusalem, 1969—70, Bikur Cholim Hosp., Jerusalem, 1970-71, staff, 1974-76; fellow in pulmonary diseases Brompton Hosp., London, 1971-74; asst. prof. child health U. Mo., Columbia, 1976-80, assoc. prof. child health, 1980-84, prof. in child health, 1984—. Fellow Am. Acad. Allergy; mem. Am. Thoracic Soc., Acad. Allergy, Soc. Pediatric Research, Chilean Asthma Found., Sigma Xi. Home: 1310 Vintage Dr Columbia MO 65203-4878 Office: U Mo Child Health 1 Hospital Dr Columbia MO 65212-5276 Office Phone: 573-882-6978. Business E-Mail: KonigP@health.missouri.edu.

KONIGSBERG, ALLEN STEWART See ALLEN, WOODY

KONIGSBURG, ELAINE LOBL, writer; b. NYC, Feb. 10, 1930; d. Adolph and Beulah (Klein) Lobl; m. David Konigsburg, July 6, 1952; children— Paul, Laurie, Ross. BS, Carnegie Mellon U., 1952; postgrad., U. Pitts., 1952-54; DHL (hon.), U. North Fla., 2001. Author: juveniles Jennifer, Hecate, Macbeth, William McKinley and Me, Elizabeth, 1967 (Newbery Honor Book), From The Mixed-Up Files of Mrs. Basil E. Frankweiler, 1967 (Newbery medal 1968), About the B'nai Bagels, 1969, (George), 1970, Altogether, One at a Time, 1971, A Proud Taste for Scarlet and Miniver, 1973 (Nat. Book award nominee), The Dragon in the Ghetto Caper, 1974, The Second Mrs. Giaconda, 1975, Father's Arcane Daughter, 1976, Throwing Shadows, 1979 (Am. Book award nominee), Journey to an 800 Number, 1981, Up From Jericho Tel, 1986, Samuel Todd's Book of Great Colors, 1990, Samuel Todd's Book of Great Inventions, 1991, Amy Elizabeth Explores Bloomingdale's, 1992, T-backs, T-shirts, COAT and Suit, 1993, TalkTalk, 1995, The View From Saturday, 1996 (Newbery medal 1997), Silent to the Bone, 2000, The Outcasts of 19 Schuyler Place, 2004. Recipient Regina medal, Cath. Libr. Assn., 2001; named to State of Fla. Hall of Fame, 2000.

KONING, PAUL MATTHEW, lawyer; b. Port Washington, NY, Sept. 25, 1956; s. Paul A.J. and Ursula Koning; m. Patricia Sonders, June 21, 1981; children: Daniel, John. AB with distinction, Cornell U., 1978; JD cum laude, So. Meth. U., Dallas, 1981. Bar: Tex. 1981, US Supreme Ct., US Ct. Appeals (5th cir.), US Dist. Ct. (all dists. Tex.). Assoc. Hughes & Luce, LLP, Dallas, 1982-88, ptnr., 1989—. Named a Tex. Super Lawyer, Law % Politics mag. and Tex. Monthly, 2005—06; named one of Best Lawyers in Dallas, D Mag., 2005. Master: William Taylor Jr. Am. Inn Ct.; mem.: Dallas Bar Assn. (mem. Bus. Litig. Sect. Coun.), ABA, Dallas Bar Found., Tex. Bar Found., State Bar Tex. (mem. Standing Com. Professionalism 2003—, past mem. and panel chair Dist. 6A Grievance Com.). Office: Hughes and Luce LLP 1717 Main St Ste 2800 Dallas TX 75201-7342 Office Phone: 214-939-5564. Office Fax: 214-939-5849. E-mail: paul.koning@hughesluce.com.*

KONISHI, MASAKAZU, neuroscientist, educator; b. Kyoto, Feb. 17, 1933; BS, Hokkaido U., Japan, 1956, MS, 1958; PhD in Zoology, U. Calif., Berkeley, 1963; degree (hon.), Hokkaido U., 1991; LLD (hon.), Hokkaido U., Japan, 1991. Postdoctoral fellow Alexander von Humboldt Found., 1963-64; fellow Internat. Brain Rsch. Orgn. and UNESCO, 1964-65; asst. prof. zoology U. Wis., 1965-66; asst. to assoc. prof. biology Princeton U., NJ, 1970-75; prof. biology Calif. Inst. Tech., Pasadena, 1975-79, Bing prof. behavioral biology, 1979—. Mem. Salk Inst., 1991—. Assoc. editor Jour. Neurosci., 1980-89, sect. editor, 1990-93; mem. editl. adv. bd. Jour. Comparative Physiology. Recipient Elliot Coues award, Am. Ornithologists Union, 1983, F.O. Schmitt prize, 1987, Internat. prize for biology Japan Soc. for Promotion Sci., 1990, David Sparks award in Integrative Neurophysiology U. Ala., 1992, Charles A. Dana award for Pioneering Achievements in Health and Edn., 1992, Sci. Writing prize Acoustical Soc. Am., 1994, Found. Ipsen prize, 1999, Kresge/Mirmelstein award for Excellence in Auditory Rsch., 2001, Lewis S. Rosenstiel award for Disting. Work in Basic Med. Sci., Brandeis U., 2004, Edward M. Scolnick prize in Neuroscience, McGovern Inst., MIT, 2004, Gerard prize, Soc. Neuroscience, 2004, Karl Spencer Lashley award, Am. Philos. Soc., 2004. Mem.: Internat. Soc. Neuroethology (pres. 1986—89), Am. Acad. Arts and Scis., Nat. Acad. Scis. Office: Calif Inst Tech Divsn Biology 1200 E California Blvd Pasadena CA 91125-0001

KONNER, JOAN WEINER, academic administrator, writer, educator, television producer and retired executive; b. Paterson, NJ, Feb. 24, 1931; d. Martin and Tillie (Frankel) Weiner; children: Rosemary, Catherine (dec.); m. Alvin H. Perlmutter. Student, Vassar Coll., 1948—49; BA, Sarah Lawrence Coll., 1951; MS, Columbia U., 1961. Editl. writer, columnist, reporter Hackensack (N.J.) Record, 1961-63; prodr., reporter WNDT Ednl. Broadcasting Corp., NYC, 1963-65; prodr., writer, reporter NBC News, NYC, 1965-77; exec. prodr. nat. pub. affairs programs WNET Ednl. Broadcasting Corp., NYC, 1977-78, exec. prodr. Bill Moyers Jour., 1978-81, v.p. met. programming, 1981-84; exec. prodr., pres., co-founder Pub. Affairs TV with Bill Moyers PBS; dean, prof. Columbia U. Grad. Sch. Journalism, NYC, 1988—97; pub. Columbia Journalism Rev. Columbia U., NYC, 1988-99, dean emerita Grad. Sch. Journalism, 1997—; ret. Prof. emeritus Grad. Sch. Journalism, Columbia U., N.Y.C., 1988-2006. Prodr., editor, author (documentaries and numerous books). Bd. dirs. Hudson River Found., Contemplative Mind in Society, Florence and John Schumann Found.; past trustee Providence Jour., Columbia U., Rockland Ctr. for Arts, Sarah Lawrence Coll., Religion Writers Found., Radio and TV News Dirs. Found., Pulitzer Prize Bd.; mem. Hudson River Found. Recipient 16 Emmy awards NATAS, Columbia-du Pont award, Peabody award, Gavel award ABA, Edward R. Murrow award, others. Mem. Dirs. Guild, Writers Guild, Soc. Profl. Journalists, Newspaper Women's Club of N.Y.C., Century Assn., Cosmopolitan Club. E-mail: jk25@columbia.edu.

KONNEY, PAUL EDWARD, health products executive, lawyer; b. Hartford, Conn., June 24, 1948; s. William Frederick and Dorothy (Dittmer) K.; m. Elizabeth Buhl Wright Temple, July 27, 1968 (div. 1979); m. Barbara Jean Greaves, June 2, 1979; children: Gretchen Blair Konney Blanchard, Tyler Wingard. AB cum laude, Harvard U., 1966; JD, U. Pa., 1969. Bar: NY 1973. Law clk. to Hon. Chief Judge William Hastie U.S. Ct. Appeals, Phila., 1969-70; assoc. Debevoise & Plimpton, NYC, 1971-81; v.p., gen. counsel Tambrands Inc., Lake Success, NY, 1982-83, v.p., gen. counsel, sec. White Plains, NY, 1983-89, sr. v.p., gen. counsel, sec., 1989-93; v.p., gen. counsel Quaker State Corp., Oil City, Pa., 1994, v.p., gen. counsel, sec. Irving, Texas, 1995, sr. v.p., gen. counsel, sec., 1996-98, Estee Lauder Cos. Inc., NYC, 1999—2004; gen. counsel. head worldwide regulatory affairs Metagenics Inc., San Clemente, Calif., 2005—. Bd. dirs. Taylor & Dodge Inc., NYC; mem. US Del. US/USSR Legal Exchange, Russia, 1988; internat. policy com. US C of C, Washington, 1989—; forum for US-EU Legal and Econ. Affairs, 1999-. Article and book rev. editor U. Pa. Law Rev., 1968-69. Bd. dir. Visiting Nurse Assn., Dallas, 1996-99. Mem. U.S. delegation to 1st U.S.-USSR legal seminar. Mem. ABA (com. of corp. gen. counsel 1999-, exec. com. 2001-04), Am. Soc. Corp. Secs., U.S. C. of C. (internat. policy com.). Episcopalian. Office: Metagenics Inc 100 Avenida La Pata San Clemente CA 92673

KONNYU, ERNEST LESLIE, former congressman; b. Tamasi, Hungary, May 17, 1937; arrived in US, 1949; s. Leslie and Elizabeth Konnyu; m. Lillian Muenks, Nov. 25, 1959; children: Carol, Renata, Lisa, Victoria. Student, U. Md., 1960-62; BS in Acctg., Ohio State U., 1965. Mem. Calif. Assembly, Sacramento, 1980-86, 100th Congress from 12th Calif. dist., 1987-89; CEO Konnyu Financials and Taxes, Inc. Chmn. Assembly Rep. Policy Com. of State Assembly, Sacramento, 1985-86; vice chmn. Assembly Human Svcs., Sacramento, 1980-86; vice chmn. Policy Rsch. Com., Sacramento, 1985-86. Mem. Rep. State Cen. Com., Calif., 1977-88, Rep. Cen. Com., Santa Clara County, Calif., 1980-88; mem. adv. bd. El Camino Hosp., Mountain View, Calif., 1987-89. Served to maj. USAF, 1959-69. Recipient Nat. Def. Medal, 1968, Disting. Service award U.S. Jaycees, 1969, Nat. Security award Am. Security Council Found., 1987; named lifetime senator U.S. Jaycees, 1977. Mem. Am.- Hungarian C. of C. (v.p. 1995-97). Republican. Roman Catholic. Avocations: politics, golf. Office Phone: 408-244-3299. Personal E-mail: konnyu@sbcglobal.net. E-mail: goernie@sbcglobal.net.

KONOLA, CLAUDETTE JUNE, finance company executive, consultant; b. Deadwood, SD, Sept. 2, 1948; d. Donald John Konola and Rose Marie Larive-Konola. BSc, Univ. Colo., 1981. Mgmt. trainee Am. Nat. Bank, Denver, 1974-80; training coord. loan analysis United Bank Denver, 1980-81; asst. v.p. Canadian Commercial Bank, Denver, 1981-83, First Interstate Bank Denver, 1983-88; v.p. Ctrl. Bank Denver, 1988-93; revolving loan fund adminstr. Mesa county Western Colo. Bus. Devel. Corp., Grand Junction, Colo., 1994-96; southwest regional dir. Cmty. Reinvestment Fund, Inc., Mpls., 1996—2002, nat. dir. tng. and assistance, 2002—. Pres. Downtown Denver Bus. and Profl. Women, 1985—87; treas. Women's Bean Project, Denver, 1991—93; sec., treas. Riverside Task Force, Grand Junction, 1995—98; co-founder Colo. Women's Hall of Fame, 1986. Democrat. Office: Cmty Reinvestment Fund PO Box 552 Clifton CO 81520-0552 Office Phone: 970-434-5318. Personal E-mail: claudette@crfusa.com.

KONOPINSKI, VIRGIL JAMES, retired industrial hygienist, safety consultant; b. Toledo, July 11, 1935; BSChemE, U. Toledo, 1956; MSChemE, Pratt Inst., 1960; MBA, Bowling Green State U., 1971. Registered profl. engr., Ind., Calif., cert. safety profl. Assoc. engr. Owens Ill., Toledo, 1956, 60; real estate developer Grand Rapids, Ohio, 1961; chem. engr. USPHS, Cin., 1961-64; sr. environ. engr. Vistron Corp., Lima, Ohio, 1964-67; environ. specialist, asst. to dir. environ. control Owens Corning Fiberglas, Toledo, 1967-72; gen. mgr. Midwest Environ. Mgmt., Maumee, Ohio, 1972-73; staff specialist, indl. hygienist Williams Bros. Waste Control, Tulsa, 1973-75; dir. divsn. indsl. hygiene and radiol. health Ind. State Bd. Health, Indpls., 1975-87; exec. v.p. ACT Ind., Indpls., 1987-89; sr. cons. Occusafe, Chgo., 1990-91; regional safety engr., human resources analyst/safety U.S. Postal Svc., Bloomingdale, Ill., 1991—2003; cons. in field, 2003—. Bd. dirs. IOSHA Indsl. Hygiene, 1975—83; cons. indoor air, occupl. health abd safety, Zionsville, 1987—91; cons. indoor air, safety, Cary, 1991—2003, Maumee, Ohio, 2003—. Contbr. articles to profl. jours. With USNR, 1956—59. Mem.: Am. Soc. Safety Engrs., Mil. Officers Assn. Republican. Roman Catholic. Home and Office: 7206 Longwater Dr Maumee OH 43537 Office Phone: 419-878-3158.

KONOWIECKI, JOSEPH SAMUEL, lawyer, health facility administrator; b. Albany, NY, May 17, 1953; BA in polit. sci. magna cum laude, UCLA, 1975; JD, U. Calif. Hastings Coll. Law, San Francisco, 1978. Bar: Calif. 1978, DC. Ptnr. K & R Law Group (formerly Konowiecki & Rank LLP), LA, 1980—2001; gen. counsel PacifiCare Health Systems, Inc., Calif., 1989—, sec. Calif., 1993—, exec. v.p. Calif., 1999—, full-time exec. v.p., gen. counsel, sec. Calif., 2002—. Adv. bd. ForestWeb Inc., 2000—. Founding editor Hastings Comm. and Entertainment Law Jour.; contbr. articles to Practicing Law Inst., law journals. Mem.: LA County Bar Assn. Office: Pacificare Health Systems Inc 3120 Lake Center Dr Santa Ana CA 92704 Office Phone: 714-825-5200.*

KONSTAN, DAVID, classics and comparative literature professor, researcher; b. NYC, Nov. 1, 1940; s. Harry and Edythe (Wahrman) K.; m. Pura Nieto; children: Eve Anna, Geoffrey Theodore. Instr. Bklyn. Coll., 1965-67; prof. Wesleyan U., Middletown, Conn., 1967-87; prof. classics and comparative lit. Brown U., Providence, 1987—. Author: Epicurean Psychology, 1973, Roman Comedy, 1983, Simplicius Physics 6, 1989, Sexual Symmetry, 1994, Greek Comedy and Ideology, 1995, Friendship in The Classical World, 1997, Philodemus on Frank Criticism, 1998, Pity Transformed, 2001, The Emotions of the Ancient Greeks, 2006, (with J. Ramelli) Term for Eternity, 2007. Mem. Am. Philol. Assn. (pres. 1999). Avocation: cooking. Office: Brown U 48 College St Providence RI 02912-1856 Office Phone: 401-863-3140. Business E-Mail: dkonstan@brown.edu.

KONSTANTINOVA, IRINA VITAL'EVNA, immunologist, researcher; b. Tomsk, USSR, Mar. 2, 1930; d. Vitaly Mikhailovich Konstantinov and Margarita A. Gromova; m. Boris Borisovich Fuks; 1 child, Alexandr. BS in Gen. Medicine, Novosibirsk Med. Inst., USSR, 1954; MD, Novosibirsk Med. Inst., 1959; Full Doctor of Sci., Inst. Biomed. Problems, Moscow, 1974. Head lab. immunology Inst. Exptl. Biology and Medicine, Novosibirsk, 1960-64; head lab. space immunology Inst. Biomed. Problems, Moscow, 1964-96; co-investigator internat. immunological program NASA L.B. Johnson Space Ctr., Houston, 1992-96. Prin. investigator Russian nat. immunological res. program in the manned space flights Inst. Biomed. Problems, Moscow, 1968-96. Author: Immune System in Extreme Conditions. Space Immunology., 1988, Immune System in Space and Other Extreme Conditions, 1991. Recipient prize Internat. Sci. Found., 1993, prize Russian Acad. Med. Scis., Moscow, 1994. Mem. N.Y. Acad. Sci. Achievements include inventions of Method of Stimulation of Immunity; development of a new branch of biological science, named Space Immunology.

KONTIO, PETER, lawyer; b. Fitchburg, Mass., Jan. 7, 1948; AB in Econ. cum laude with high honors, Clark Univ., 1970; JD, Univ. Chgo., 1973. Bar: Ga. 1973. Ptnr., trial and litig., internat. litig., telecom. groups Alston & Bird LLP, Atlanta. Mem. Chgo. Law Rev. Mem.: ABA, Atlanta Bar Assn., Federal Defender Program, Inc. (pres.), Univ. Chgo. Law Sch. Atlanta Area Alumni Assn. (pres.), Lawyers Club Atlanta, Phi Beta Kappa, Omicron Delta Epsilon, Psi Chi. Office: Alston & Bird LLP One Atlantic Ctr 1201 W Peachtree St NW Atlanta GA 30309-3424 Office Phone: 404-881-7172. Office Fax: 404-881-7777. Business E-Mail: pkontio@alston.com.

KONTNY, VINCENT L., rancher, retired engineering executive; b. Chappell, Nebr., July 19, 1937; s. Edward James and Ruth Regina (Schumann) K.; m. Joan Dashwood FitzGibbon, Feb. 20, 1970; children: Natascha Marie, Michael Christian, Amber Brooke. BSCE, U. Colo., 1958,

DSc honoris causa, 1991. Operator heavy equipment, grade foreman Peter Kiewit Son's Co., Denver, 1958-59; project mgr. Utah Constrn. and Mining Co., Western Australia, 1965-69, Fluor Australia, Queensland, Australia, 1969-72; sr. project mgr. Fluor Utah, San Mateo, Calif., 1972-73; sr. v.p. Holmes & Narver, Inc., Orange, Calif., 1973-79; mng. dir. Fluor Australia, Melbourne, 1979-82; group v.p. Fluor Engrs., Inc., Irvine, Calif., 1982-85, pres., chief exec. officer, 1985-87; group pres. Fluor Daniel, Irvine, Calif., 1987-88, pres., 1988-94, Fluor Corp., Irvine, 1990-94, vice chmn., 1994; ret., 1994; bd. dirs. Chgo. Bridge & Iron Co., Plainfield, Ill., 1997—; COO Washington Group Internat., Inc., Boise, Idaho, 2000—03. Purchased Last Dollar Ranch, Ridgway Co. 1989, Centennial Ranch, Colona Co., 1992, owner Double Shoe Cattle Co. Contbr. articles to profl. jours. Mem. engring. devel. coun., U. Colo.; mem. engring. adv. coun., Stanford U. Lt. USN, 1959-65. Mem.: Nat. Acad. Constrn. (pres. 2007, v.p. 2006), Center Club (Costa Mesa, Calif.). Republican. Roman Catholic. Avocations: skiing, hunting, fishing. Home and Office: 35000 S Highway 550 Montrose CO 81401-8477 Personal E-mail: vincekontny@starband.net.

KONTOS, GEORGE JOHN, JR., surgeon; b. Chgo., May 26, 1958; s. George John and Sherry Knox Kontos; m. Sherry Knox Reed, Aug. 24, 1991; children: Alexis Reed, Nicholas John. BA, Northwestern U., 1979; MD, Loyola U., Maywood, Ill., 1982. Diplomate Am. Bd. Thoracic Surgery, 1992, Am. Bd. Surgery, 1988. Resident, gen. surgery Mayo Clinic, Rochester, Minn., 1982—88; resident, cardiac surgery U. Ala., Birmingham, 1988—91; cardiovasc. and thoracic surgeon Midwest Cardiovasc. Ctr., Sioux Falls, SD, 1992—94, Ctrl. Ala. Thoracic and Cardiovasc. Surgery, Montgomery, 1994—2002; surgeon U. Tenn., Memphis, 2002—03; thoracic, cardiovasc. surgeon Helena Surgery Assoc., Ark., 2004—07; thoracic surgeon Genesis Health Group Surg. Assocs., Silvis, Ill., 2007—. Guest reviewer Jour. Applied Physiology, Houston, 1991—92, Transplantation, Boston, 1991—97, Am. Jour. Cardiology, Dallas, 2001, 2002, 2004. Mem. Am. Hellenic Philanthropic Orgn., Montgomery, Ala., 1994—2002. Grantee, Am. Heart Assn., 1992. Fellow: Am. Coll. Chest Physicians, Am. Coll. Cardiology, Southeastern Surg. Congress, Am. Coll. Surgeons; mem.: Johns Hopkins Med. and Surg. Assn., Priestly Soc., Mayo Clinic, N.Y. Acad. Scis., Soc. Thoracic Surgeons. Greek Orthodox. Avocations: fountain pen collector, water sports, sailing. Home: 3392 Valleywynds Dr Bettendorf IA 52722 Office: Genesis Health Group Surg Assn 855 Illini Dr Ste 401 Silvis IL 61282 Office Phone: 309-792-6355.

KONVICKA, JASON WADE, lawyer; b. Houston, May 9, 1969; s. Albert Joe and Rebecca Anne Konvicka; m. Karen Elizabeth Dunivan, Sept. 5, 1998; children: Charles Barner, Sidney Rowe. BS, U. Richmond, 1991, JD, 1994. Bd. cert. civil trial adv.: Nat. Bd. Trial Advocacy 2006. Law clk. Ct. of Appeals of Va., Chesapeake, 1994—95; assoc. Emroch & Kilduff, LLP., Richmond, Va., 1995—2000; shareholder Allen, Allen, Allen & Allen, P.C., Richmond, 2000—. Executive editor U. Richmond Law Rev.; contbr. articles to profl. jours. Mem.: Am. Bd. Trial Advocates, ATLA, Richmond Bar Assn., Va. Trial Lawyers Assn (editor jour.). Avocations: running, travel, food, wine. Office: Allen Allen Allen & Allen PC 1809 Staples Mill Rd Richmond VA 23230 Office Phone: 804-257-7528.

KONWIN, THOR WARNER, financial executive; b. Berwyn, Ill., Aug. 17, 1943; s. Frank and Alice S. (Johnson) K.; m. Carol A. Svitak, Aug. 2, 1967 (div. Feb. 1990); 1 child, Christopher Vernon; m. Virginia Colburn, May 21, 1993 (div. Mar. 2002). AA, Morton Jr. Coll., 1966; BS, No. Ill. U., 1967; MS, Roosevelt U., 1971. Acct. Beckerman & Terrill, CPA's, Chgo., 1967-68; cost acct. Sunbeam Corp., Chgo., 1968-72; CFO Gen. Molded Products, Inc., Chgo., 1972-75; controller Sunbeam Appliance Co., Chgo., 1975-81; chief fin. officer Bear Med. System, Inc., Riverside, Calif., 1981-84, Bird Products Corp., Palm Springs, Calif., 1984—, gen. ptnr., 1985—2001; pres. B&B Ventures Ltd., Riverside, 1987—; chief exec. officer Med One Fin. Group, Salt Lake City; pres. Tags Antiques, Inc., Palm Springs; owner, founder Branford House Antiques, Brandon, Vt., 2005—. Bd. dirs. Bird Med. Techs., Inc., Palm Springs, Bird Products Corp., Palm Springs, Bird Internat., Inc., Riverside, B&B Ventures, Inc., Riverside, Equilink, Inc. Riverside, Stackhouse, Inc., Riverside, Med One Fin. Group, Salt Lake City; CEO Equitable Inc., Palm Springs, Calif., 1990—; adv. coun. U. Calif. Grad. Bus. Sch., Riverside, 1988—; CEO Entertainment Leader Inc., Cathedral City, Calif., 1995-2000; CEO, founder Safety Systems, Inc., 2002—. Served with U.S. Army, 1969-71. Home: 6691 US Route 7 Brandon VT 05733 Office Phone: 802-483-2971. Personal E-mail: thorkonwin@aol.com.

KONWINSKI, JACQUELINE MARIE KORALEWSKI, secondary school educator; b. Toledo, Apr. 11, 1943; d. Michael Joseph and Anne Rose (Drabik) Koralewski; m. James Robert Konwinski, June 25, 1966; children: John Robert, Mary Jacqueline (dec.) BA, Mary Manse Coll., 1965; MA, U. Toledo, 1986. Cert. tchr., Ohio. Tchr. Summerfield High Sch., Petersburg, Mich., 1965-66, Ctrl. Cath. High Sch., Toledo, 1966-67, McAuley High Sch., Toledo, 1979-83, Notre Dame Acad., Toledo, 1987—. Recipient Platinum award, Doors to Diplomacy, 2005. Mem. Nat. Coun. Social Studies, Ohio Coun. Social Studies, Polish Geneal. Soc. Mich., Friends Lathrop House. Democrat. Roman Catholic. Office: Notre Dame Acad 3535 W Sylvania Ave Toledo OH 43623-4479 Home Phone: 419-882-5045; Office Phone: 419-475-9359. Business E-Mail: jkonwinski@nda.org.

KONZ, GERALD KEITH, retired manufacturing executive; b. Racine, Wis., Apr. 3, 1932; m. Marianne Bubolz; children: Richard C., Brenda S. BS in Econs., U. Wis., 1957, LLB, 1960. V.p. in charge corp. tax dept. S.C. Johnson & Son, Inc., Racine, 1982-98, chmn. bd. trustees pension trust, employee profit sharing and savs. plan, 1982-98. Bd. dirs. Johnson Family Funds, Inc., Racine, Wis. Pub. Expenditure Survey, Madison, 1982-92; mem. adv. bd. Venture Investors, Inc., Madison, Wis., 1997—98. Treas. St. Catherines H.S. Found., Racine, 1994—97, pres., 1997—2001; bd. dirs. YMCA, Racine, 1988—98. Mem. ABA, Tax Execs. Inst. (pres. Wis. chpt. 1972), Wis. Bar Assn., Racine-Kenosha Estate Planning Coun. (pres. 1980). Office: 3515 Taylor Ave Racine WI 53405-4727 Home Phone: 262-554-7796; Office Phone: 262-554-7796. E-mail: gkonz@wi.rr.com.

KOO, ANTHONY YING CHANG, economist, educator; b. Shanghai, Nov. 22, 1918; came to U.S., 1940; s. Vee-Sing and Tseng (Soo) K.; m. Delia Zung-Fung Wei, June 6, 1943; children: Victoria M., Margery E., Emily D. BA, St. John's U., Shanghai, 1940; MS, U. Ill., Urbana, 1941; MA, Harvard U., Cambridge, Mass., 1943, PhD, 1946. Prof. econs. U. Mich., Ann Arbor, 1964-67; from asst. prof. to prof. Mich. State U., East Lansing, 1950-64, prof. econs., 1967—. Cons. The East-West Ctr., Honolulu, 1963, Internat. Labor Orgn., Geneva, 1965-66, U.S. Dept. Energy, Washington, 1980-82; vis. prof. Nat. Taiwan U., 1969-70, Indonesia 2d U. Project, 1989, Wuhan U. and Zhongshan U., China, 1990; adj. prof. econs. Fla. State U., 1990—. Author: Land Market Distortion and Tenure Reform, 1982; editor: Selected Essays of Gottfried Haberler, 1986; editor/author: The Liberal Economic Order, 1993; contbr. articles to profl. jours. Grantee, Soc. Sci. Coun., 1953, 1957, 1964, 1968, Ford Found., 1956—57, 1961—62, NSF, 1965—67. Mem. Am. Econ. Assn., Econometric Soc., Acad. Sinica. Office: Mich State U Dept Of Econs East Lansing MI 48824 also: Fla State U Dept Econs Tallahassee FL 32306 Office Phone: 517-355-7583. Business E-Mail: koo@msu.edu.

KOO, BENJAMIN HAI CHANG, structural engineer, educator; b. Shanghai, Apr. 4, 1920; came to U.S., 1941; s. Vee-Sing and Tseng (Soo) K.; m. Gretchen Hsu, Aug. 15, 1951. BS in Civil Engring., St. John's U., Shanghai, 1941; MS, Cornell U., 1942, PhD, 1946. Engr. Carter Constrn. Co., Toronto, 1946—48; engr., designer Corbett & Tingnir Co., Inc., NYC, 1950—54; structural engr. Tippett-Abbett-McCarthy-Stratton, NYC, 1954—56; structural and found. engr. W.H. Treadwell Co., NYC, 1956—61; devel. engr. ACF Industries, St. Charles, Mo., 1961—64; prof. civil engring. U. Toledo, 1965—90, prof. emeritus engring., 1990—. Contbr. articles to profl. jours. Recipient Outstanding Tchr. award U. Toledo, 1974. Fellow ASCE (life); mem. Am. Soc. Engring. Edn. (life). Achievements include patents for low level piggyback trailer-train freight car and cushioned underframe system for piggyback trailer-train freight car; two US patents. Office: U Toledo Civil Engring Dept 2801 W Bancroft St Toledo OH 43606-3328

KOO, GEORGE PING SHAN, business consultant; b. Changting, China, June 4, 1938; came to the U.S., 1949, naturalized, 1955; s. Ted Swei Yen and Pei-Fen (Yang) K.; m. May Jen, May 5, 1962; children: Denise, Douglas, Alyssa. BS, MIT, 1960, MS, 1962; DSc, Stevens Inst. Tech., 1969; MBA, U. Santa Clara, 1975. Mgr. Allied Chem. Corp., 1963-71; assoc. dir. SRI Internat., 1972-78; v.p. Chase Manhattan Bank, 1978-79; mng. dir. Bear-Stearns China Trade, 1979-82; v.p. Bear-Stearns & Co., 1982-83; pres. Microelectronic Bus. Internat., Inc., Mountain View, Calif., 1983-85; v.p. Tiara Computer Sys., Inc., 1985-86; mng. dir. internat. svcs. H&Q Tech. Ptnrs., Inc., 1987; mng. dir., CEO Internat. Strategic Alliances, Inc., 1988-99; dir. Chinese svcs. group Deloitte & Touche LLP, San Jose, Calif., 1999—. Cons., chair on Asian Fin. and Alliances, Santa Clara, Calif., 1990-93. Human rels. commr. City of Mountain View, 1994-98. Mem. Asian Am. Mfrs. Assn. (chmn. 1996-97), mem. com. of 100 (dir. 1998-2006, vice chair, 2003-06). Home: 1819 Van Buren Cir Mountain View CA 94040-4054 Office Phone: 650-255-6902. Personal E-mail: geopkoo@yahoo.com.

KOO, JOHN YING MING, psychiatrist, dermatologist; b. Tokyo, Jan. 9, 1955; arrived in U.S., 1967; s. Kwang Ming Koo and Amy Tsai Ma; m. Nancy Chiang, July 7, 1978; children: Kathie, Jennifer, Jocelyn, Jonathan, Karina. BA in Biochemistry, U. Calif., Berkeley, 1977; MD, Harvard U., 1981. Cert. psychiatry and dermatology. Intern UCLA Ctr. Health Scis., 1981—82; resident in psychiatry UCLA Neuropsychiatric Inst., 1982—85; resident in dermatology U. Calif.-San Francisco Med. Ctr., 1985—88; dir. Psoriasis and Skin Treatment Ctr., U. Calif., San Francisco, 1988—; prof. and vice chmn. dept. dermatology, prof. U. Calif., San Francisco, 1989—. Med. adv. bd. Nat. Psioriasis Found., Portland, Oreg., 1995; cons. in field. Mem. editl. bd.: Jour. Am. Acad. Dermatology, 1994; editor: Dermatology and Psychosomatics, 1999. Scholar Harvard Nat. scholar, Harvard Med. Sch., Boston, 1981. Mem.: Am. Psychiat. Assn., Am. Acad. Dermatology, Assn. for Psychocutaneous Medicine N.Am. (founder). Avocations: philosophy, military history. Office: U Calif San Francisco Psoriasis and Skin Treatment Ctr 515 Spruce St San Francisco CA 94118 Office Phone: 415-476-4701. Office Fax: 415-502-4126.

KOO, MICHELE, plastic surgeon; b. Shanghi, China, Sept. 30, 1956; Grad., Stanford U., 1978; MD, Washington U., 1986. Cert. Am. Bd. Plastic Surgery. Internship gen. surgery Washington U./Barnes Hosp., 1986—89, resident, 1989—90; fellow U. Kans., 1991—92, resident plastic surgery, 1992—93; surgeon Aesthetic Surgery Inst., Ltd. Featured in New Beauty Mag. Recipient Outstanding Pub. award for young electrophysiologists, Heart Rhythm Soc. Fellow: Am. Coll. Surgeons; mem.: St. Louis Met. Med. Soc., St. Louis Soc. Plastic & Reconstructive Surgeons, Am. Soc. Plastic Surgeons, Am. Soc. Aesthetic Plastic Surgery, Am. Med. Women Assn., Stanford Alumni Assn. Office: 333 S Kirkwood Ste 203 Saint Louis MO 63122 Office Phone: 314-984-8331. Office Fax: 314-821-8377.*

KOO, YIDO, electronics executive; b. Seoul, Republic of Korea, Jan. 11, 1973; s. Youngjo Koo and Junghee Lee; m. Naehee Kim, Aug. 29, 1973. BS, Seoul Nat. U., 1996, MS, 1998, PhD, 2003. Part time staff Hyundai Electronics Corp. (now Hynix), Kyounggi-Do, Republic of Korea, 1996—97, Samsung Electronics Corp., Kyounggi-Do, 1999—2000; mgr. GCT Semiconductor, Inc., Seoul, 2003—. Contbr. articles to profl. jours. Mem.: IEEE (assoc. Best Student award Solid-State Cirs. Soc. Seoul Chpt. 2003). Achievements include patents for LC oscillator with wide tuning range and low phase noise; output driver having output current compensation and method of compensating output current; patents pending for integrated circuit package having inductance loop formed from a bridge interconnection; research in comparison frequency doubling and charge pump matching techniques for dual-band Delta Sigma fractional-N frequency synthesizer; 0.25-um CMOS quad-band GSM RF transceiver using an efficient LO frequency plan. Office: GCT Semiconductor Inc 2121 Ringwood Ave San Jose CA 95131 E-mail: ydkoo92@gmail.com.

KOO, YONGHOI, investment banker; b. Seoul, Republic of Korea, Oct. 2, 1964; s. SoonKi Koo and KwiByung Lee; m. Hyejung Cho, June 1, 1991. PhD in Math., U. Minn., Mpls., 1998. Cert. gen. securities rep. Nat. Assn. Securities Dealers, 2005. Rschr. Max Planck Inst., Leipzig, Germany, 1998—99, U. Conn., Storrs, 2001; dir. R & D Fist Global, Seoul, Republic of Korea, 2002—03; quantitative analyst Morgan Stanley, NYC, 2004—05; v.p. Citigroup, NYC, 2005—. Lectr., organizer Korean Assn. Risk Profl., Seoul, 2003. Discovery mathematical properties of interface problems. Lt. Republic of Korea Army, 1989—90. Recipient Outstanding Tchg. award, 1998; scholar, Korean Govt., 1992—94. Mem.: Am. Math. Soc. Home: 22 Ave at Port Imperial Apt 311 West New York NJ 07093 Home Phone: 201-388-4954.

KOOB, CHARLES EDWARD, lawyer; b. Kansas City, Mo., Aug. 31, 1944; s. Charles H. and Adeline (Meinert) K.; m. Pamela Ann (Nabseth), June 26, 1971; children: Jason Wyeth, Peter Nabseth. BA, Rockhurst Coll., 1966; JD, Stanford U., 1969. Bar: Calif. 1970, N.Y., 1972 U.S. Dist. Ct. (so. and ea. dist.) N.Y. 1973, U.S. Ct. Appeals (2d cir.) 1975, U.S. Ct. Appeals (5th cir.) 1979, U.S. Supreme Ct. 1988, U.S. Ct. Claims 1988, U.S. Ct. Appeals (3d cir.) 1985. Assoc. Simpson, Thacher, and Bartlett, NYC, 1970—76, ptnr., 1976—, co-head litig. group. Mem. ABA, N.Y. State Bar Assn., Calif. State Bar Assn. Office: Simpson Thacher and Bartlett 425 Lexington Ave Fl 15 New York NY 10017-3954 Office Phone: 212-455-2970. Office Fax: 212-455-2502. Business E-Mail: ckoob@stblaw.com.

KOOB, ROBERT DUANE, chemistry professor, academic administrator; b. Graetinger, Iowa, Oct. 14, 1941; s. Emil John and Rose Mary (Slinger) Koob; m. E. Yvonne Ervin, June 9, 1960; children: Monique, Gregory, Michael, Eric, David; children: Angela, Julie. BA in Edn., U. No. Iowa, 1962; PhD in Chemistry, U. Kans., 1967. From asst. prof. to prof. chemistry ND State U., Fargo, 1967—90, chmn. dept. chemistry, 1974—78, 1979—81, dir. Water Inst., 1975—85, dean Coll. Sci. and Math., 1981—84, v.p., 1985—90, interim pres., 1987—88; v.p. for acad. affairs, sr. v.p. Calif. Poly. State U., San Luis Obispo, 1990—95; pres. U. No. Iowa, Cedar Falls, 1995—, prof., 1995—. Cons. TransAlta, Edmonton, Alta., Canada, Alta. Rsch. Coun., Mitre Corp., Washington; bd. dirs. State Bank Fargo, Fargo Cass County Econ. Devel. Corp.; chair bd. dirs. Cal Poly Found.; chair Iowa Coordinating Coun. for Post-H.S. Edn., 1996—97. Contbr. articles to profl. jours. V.p. Crookston Diocesan Sch. Bd., Minn., 1982; pres. elem. sch. bd., St. Joseph's Ch., Moorhead, Minn., 1982, parish coun., Moorhead, Minn., 1983; pres. bd. Shanley H.S., Fargo, 1985; serves on Cedar Valley Promise, Cedar Valley Alliance, Cedar Valley United Way, Opportunity Works, Am. Coun. Edn., Am. Assn. of States Colls. and Univs. Named to Cedar Valley Bus. Hall of Fame; grantee in field. Mem.: Iowa Assn. Coll. Pres. (pres. 1996). Roman Catholic. Avocations: reading, flying, sailing, sports, bicycling. Office: Univ of Northern Iowa 1227 W 27th St Cedar Falls IA 50614-0002 Office Phone: 319-273-2566. E-mail: bob.koob@uni.edu.

KOOGLE, TIMOTHY K., communications executive; MS in Engr., Stanford U. Pres. Intermec Corp.; corp. v.p. Western Atlas Inc.; with Motorola Inc.; chmn., CEO Yahoo! Corp., Santa Clara, Calif., 1999—. Chmn. bd. dirs. AIM. Office: Yahoo Inc 701 First Ave Sunnyvale CA 94089-1019

KOOIJMANS, PIETER HENDRIK, former judge; b. Heemstede, The Netherlands, July 6, 1933; m. A. Kooijmans-Verhage; 4 children. Degree, Free U., Amsterdam, The Netherlands, 1964. Mem. Faculty of Law Free U. of Amsterdam, 1960-65, prof. European law and pub. internat. law, 1965-73; state sec. for fgn. affairs Govt. of The Netherlands, 1973-77; prof. pub. internat. law U. Leiden, The Netherlands, 1978-92, 95-97; minister of fgn. affairs Govt. of The Netherlands, 1993-94; judge Internat. Ct. of Justice, The Hague, Netherlands, 1997—2006. Author textbooks in field; contbr. articles to profl. jours. Head Netherlands del. to UN Commn. on Human Rights, 1982-85, 92, chair commn., 1984-85, spl. reporter on questions relevant to torture, 1985-92; mem. various UN and Orgn. on Security and Coop. in Europe missions to former Yugoslavia, 1991-92.

KOOKEN, JOHN FREDERICK, retired bank holding company executive; b. Denver, Nov. 1, 1931; s. Duff A. and Frances C. K.; m. Emily Howe, Sept. 18, 1954; children: Diane, Carolyn. MS, Stanford U., 1954, PhD, 1961. With Security Pacific Nat. Bank-Security Pacific Corp., LA, 1960-92; exec. v.p. Security Pacific Corp., LA, 1981-87, CFO, 1984-92, vice chmn. Los Angeles, 1987-92; ret., 1992. Bd. dirs. Golden State Bancorp., 1992-2002, ACE Ltd., 1985-91 Centris Group, 1986-99, Pacific Gulf Properties, 1994-2001, East West Bancorp, 2002-; lectr. Grad. Sch. Bus. U. So. Calif., 1962-67; chmn. Bank Adminstrn. Inst., 1989-90. Pres. bd. dirs. Children's Bur., L.A., 1981-84; bd. dirs. United Way, L.A., 1982-89, Huntington Meml. Hosp., Pasadena, 1985—, chmn., 1999—2002; bd. dirs. So. Calif. Healthcare Systems, 1993—2005, chmn. 2001—2005. Lt. (j.g.) USNR, 1954-57. Mem.: Fin. Execs. Inst. (pres. LA chpt. 1979—80, dir. 1981—84).

KOOL, ERIC T., chemist, educator; b. 1960; BS, Miami U., Ohio, 1982; PhD, Columbia U., 1988. Prof. dept. chemistry Stanford (Calif.) U. Contbr. articles to profl. jours. Recipient faculty awad Am. Cyanamid, 1994, Pfizer award Am. Chem. Soc., 2000; named Young Investigator, Office Naval Rsch., 1992, Young Investigator, Beckman Found., 1992, Young Investigator, Army Rsch. Office, 1993; Dreyfus Found. Tchr.-scholar, 1993, Arthur C. Cope scholar Am. Chem. Soc., 2000; Alfred P. Sloan Found. fellow, 1994. Achievements include research on design, synthesis and study of molecules that mimic complex biological functions such as replication. Office: Stanford U Dept Chemistry Stauffer I Rm 103 Stanford CA 94305-5080 E-mail: kool@leland.stanford.edu.

KOOLURIS DOBBS, LINDA KIA, artist, photographer; b. Orange, NJ, 1949; m. Kildare Dobbs, 1981. AA, Pine Manor Coll., 1968; Cert., Sorbonne, 1968-69; BFA with honors, Sch. Visual Arts, 1972. Tchg. staff various colls., 1975—; tchg. staff fashion dept/ Ryerson U., 1980—2003; tchg. staff Avenue Rd. Art Sch., 1999—. Exhibitions include Mus. of Textiles, Toronto, Bronxville Art and Frame Gallery, Atrium Gallery, Chubb Group of Ins. Cos., Warren, N.J., Vancouver Art Gallery, Newbury Fine Arts, Boston and Edgartown, Mass., Art Gallery of Hamilton, Toronto Watercolour Soc., Vancouver Maritime Mus., Ceperley House of Visual Arts Burnaby, B.C., Sutton Gallery, The Granary, Port Hope, Ont., Hummingbird Centre, Carrier Gallery, Columbus Ctr., First Canadian Pl. Gallery, Toronto, U. Toronto, Regis Coll., U. Toronto, Zwicker's Gallery, Halifax, N.S., Represented in permanent collections AT&T, Artform, Norway, Glaxo Wellcome Inc., Inland Pacific Enterprises, Temple Scott & Assocs., Uniglobe, Goodman & Goodman, Advance Travel, AGF Mgmt. Ltd., Toronto Stock Exch., Ont. Govt. Art Collection, Parliament Bldg., Queen's Park, Pine Manor Coll., U.S., Mt. Sinai Hosp., Merrill Lynch, Aon Reed Stenhouse, U. Toronto, Harry Ransom Humanities Rsch. Ctr., U. Tex., Austin, Law Soc. Upper Can., Scotia McLeod, Probyn & Co., Munk Ctr. Internat. Studies, Massey Coll. Faculties of Law and Dentistry, U. Toronto, others, prin. works include portrait commns. the Hon. Henry N. R. Jackman, the Hon. Edwin A. Goodman, the Hon. Barbara McDougall, others, the Hon. David Peterson, Prof. Vern Krishna, Dr. Syvia Ostry, Brian Moore, Judge Ronald St. John MacDonald, Richard B. Wright, Karen Kain, others, Splash 3, 4, 5 & 8, Can. Bus. Mag.; contbr. photographs to popular mags. and newspapers including Nat. Post, Fin. Post, Verve Mag., Can. Bus. Mag., Irish Times Mag. Recipient Ann. Art Purchase prize Pine Manor Coll., 1968, 2d prize Fin. Post Ann. Reports awards, 1981, Hon. Mention Ann. Fall Show Toronoto Watercolour Soc., 1991, Best in Architecture award Toronto Watercolour Soc. 1994. Home Phone: 416-960-8984; Office Phone: 416-960-8984.

KOOMULLIL, ROY PAULOSE, mechanics and engineering educator; arrived in U.S., 1993; s. Paulose Chacko Koomullil and Saramma Paulose; m. Betty Susan Mathew, Apr. 27, 1998. B in Tech., Mar Athanasius Coll. Engring., Kothamangalam, Kerala, India, 1990; M in Tech., Indian Inst. Tech., Madras, India, 1992; PhD, Miss. State U., 1997. Scientist Indian Space Rsch. Orgn., Trivandrum, Kerala, India, 1992—93; post-doctoral fellow Miss. State U., Starkville, 1997—98, vis. rsch. asst., 1998—99, asst. rsch. prof., 1999—2002; Berkeley rsch. assoc. Naval Rsch. Lab., Washington, 1998—98; asst. prof. U. Ala., Birmingham, 2002—. Summer faculty fellow Wright Patterson AFB, Dayton, Ohio, 2004, Dayton, 05. Grantee Numerical Contaminant Transport Model Applicable to an Urban Regime Simulation, Miss. Space Commerce Initiative, 2000, Integrated Multidisciplinary Simulation Environment for Analysis and Testing of Rocket Based Combustion Cycle, NASA, 2001—03, Focus Project on CFD Demonstration Tool, Maj. Shared Resource Ctr., Dept. Def., 2000—01, Validation, Verification and Certification by Analysis, 2003—06, 6 DOF Libr. and Std. Interface, 2002—03, Multi-Disciplinary Analysis of Chem. Dispersion in an Urban Environment, 2003—04, Parallel Code Coupling Interface DAKOTA, 2004—05, Multidisciplinary/MultiComponent Data Exch. Specification, 2004—05, Unstructured Overset Grid Framework for Moving Body Applications, Arnold Engring. Devel. Ctr. /Aerospace Testing Alliance, 2003—04. Mem.: AIAA, Soc. for Indsl. and Applied Math. Office: Univ Ala Birmingham BEC 257 1530 3rd Ave South Birmingham AL 35294-4461 Home Phone: 205-823-1892; Office Phone: 205-934-0832. Office Fax: 205-975-7217. Business E-Mail: rkoomul@uab.edu.

KOON, THERESA HELEN, voice educator, singer; b. Rumford, Maine, Apr. 6, 1955; d. Charles Marvin and Elizabeth Ann (Ashe) Koon. BA in Humanities, Maryhurst U., Portland, 1977; MusM in Voice, U. Victoria, Can., 1996. Voice tchr., coach Pvt. Studio and CC's, Germany, 1978—; adj. voice faculty PCC and MHCC, 1980—; soloist Thuringer landes Theater, Rudolstadt, Germany, 1990—93; founder, dir. Opera for Heritage, Pacific Northwest, 1995—2000. Composer: (Operas) Promise, 2003, performer operas, cabaret, theater and symphonies. Grantee Fellowship, U. Victoria, 1994—96. Mem.: Oreg. Coun. for Humanities, Nat. Opera Assn., Nat. Assn. Tchrs. Avocations: writing, poetry, dance, hiking, skiing. Home: 805 SE Lexington St Portland OR 97202

KOONCE, CALVIN SCOTT, brokerage firm executive, physicist; b. Columbus, Ga., Dec. 9, 1937; s. Loftin Burns and Virginia (Scott) K.; m. Janet Elizabeth Bell, July 22, 1967; children: Elizabeth Ann, Kathleen Sharon, Franklin Scott. BS, MIT, 1960; PhD, U. Calif., Berkeley, 1967. Physicist Nat. Bur. Standards, Gaithrsburg, Md., 1967-75; pres. Koonce Securities, Inc., Bethesda, Md., 1979-99, chmn., 1999—; pres. Montgomery Investment Mgmt., Bethesda, 1989—. Contbr. articles to profl. jours. Recipient Disting. Young Scientist award Md. Acad. Scis., 1969; fellow NSF, 1963. Mem. Am. Phys. Soc., Security Traders Assn. of Washington (pres. 1987), Beta Theta Pi. Republican. Presbyterian. Home: 9101 Kendale Rd Potomac MD 20854-4512 Office: Koonce Securities Inc 6550 Rock Spring Dr Ste 600 Bethesda MD 20817-1185 Business E-Mail: calvin@koonce.net.

KOONCE, NEIL WRIGHT, lawyer; b. Kinston, NC, July 8, 1947; s. Harold Wright and Edna Earle (Regan) K.; m. Virginia Gayle Evans, Feb. 27, 1993; children: Channing, Carl Younger, Ginny Younger. AB, U. N.C., 1969; JD, Wake Forest U., 1974; postgrad. exec. program, U. Va., 1983. Bar: N.C. 1973, U.S. Dist. Ct. (mid. dist.) N.C. 1975, U.S. Ct. Appeals (4th cir.) 1978, U.S. Supreme Ct. 1981. Atty. Cone Mills Corp., Greensboro, N.C., 1974-81, sr. atty., 1981-85, asst. gen. counsel, 1985-87, gen. counsel, 1987—, v.p., 1989—, v.p., gen. counsel, corp. sec., 1999—2004; v.p. Internat. Textile Group, Inc., Greensboro, 2004—, gen. counsel, 2004—. Bd. dirs. Family and Children's Svcs., Greensboro, 1981-89, S.C. Energy Users Com., Columbia, S.C., 1984-89, Carolina Utility Customer's Assn., Raleigh, 1983-90, 94—, N.C. Found. for Rsch. and Econ. Edn., 1986-87, 93—, Electricity Consumers Resource Coun., Washington, 1987, 92—, vice chmn., 1990, chmn., 1991; bd. dirs. N.C. Citizens for Bus. and Industry, Raleigh, 1991-96, Met. YMCA, Greensboro, 1991-95, Salvation Army Boys and Girls Clubs, Greensboro, 1996-2004, S.C. Mfrs. Alliance, 1998-2003. With AUS, 1970-71. Mem. ABA, N.C. Bar Assn., N.C. Mfrs. Assn. (bd. dirs. 1998—, vice chmn. 2004-06, chmn. 2006—), Greensboro Bar Assn., Rotary (sec. 1983-86, bd. dirs. 1985-90, pres. 1988). Democrat. Presbyterian. Home: 200 Irving Pl Greensboro NC 27408-6510 Office: International Textile Group Inc 804 Green Valley Rd 300 Greensboro NC 27408-7020

KOONCE, PAUL D., energy executive; Grad., U. Tenn., 1982. With Transcontinental Gas Pipeline, Sonat Energy Svcs., Consol. Natural Gas; sr. v.p. comml. ops. Dominion, Richmond, sr. v.p. portfolio mgmt. Va. Power, 2000—02, CEO transmission Va. Power, 2003, CEO energy Va. Power, 2004—06, pres., COO energy Va. Power, 2006—, exec. v.p., CEO Dominion Energy, 2006—. Office: Dominion PO Box 26532 Richmond VA 23261-6532*

KOONS, IRVIN LOUIS, graphics designer, consultant, marketing professional; b. Harrisburg, Pa., Mar. 14, 1922; s. Frank and Rose (Silver) K.; m. Leah Fay, Dec. 25, 1949; children: Adam, Jonathan, Joshua. Grad., Pratt Inst., 1942, New Sch., NYC, 1946; student and instr., Ecole Des Beaux Arts, Fontainebleau, France, 1948-50; student, others schs. in France, Switzerland and Italy, 1947-49. Designer, chief exec. officer Irv Koons Assocs. (subs. Saatchi and Saatchi Worldwide, since 1983), NYC, 1950-89; sr. advisor to adminstr. UN Devel. Program, NYC, 1989—. Sr. advisor Div. for Pvt. Sector in Devel. and UNISTAR, UNDP; founder, co-dir. Internat. Design Assistance Commn., 1984—; sr. advisor to adminstr. UN Devel. Programme, 1989—; past cultural attache, spl. cons. U.S. Dept. State, India; dir. 1st internat. packaging exhbn. USIA; tchr. various art schs.; advisor Inferential Focus Forum; lectr. mktg. NYU, U. Pa., Columbia U., U. Tel Aviv, Northwestern U. and others in Eng., Holland, France, Switzerland, Brazil, China, India; expert legal witness corp. and product image/identity. Exhibited paintings and drawings in group shows in U.S. and France, represented in permanent collections including Mus. Modern Art, Cooper Hewitt Nat. Design Mus., the Jewish Mus., Yeshiva U. Mus.; complete collection of works on 7,000 slides plus several thousand sketches and finished itmes at Hagley Mus. and Libr., Wilmington, Del.; slides also available on CD-Rom; prin. works include Life of Moses series, 1975-78, stained glass wall for Fedn. Jewish Philanthropies, 1975, series coord. Torah ornaments for Temple Emmanuel, N.J., 1986; designed stage sets for traveling shows of original broadway casts: Harriette, Three Sisters, Blythe Spirit, Springtime for Henry, others; illus. many books and mags. including Ladies Home Jour., Good Housekeeping, Fortune, Seventeen, Sports Illustrated; designer 1st Daily offset newspaper in world, Middletown Daily Record, 1956 (Ayer Cup best design 1957, 58), redesign Washington Star, 1969; cons. editor Graphis Packaging, Switzerland, 1970; art critic The Statesman newspaper, India, 1946; contbr. articles on mktg. to profl. jours.; subject one-man articles in mags. including Graphis, Idea, 1976, others; 40-min. multi-image show of life and work produced by PDC, 1982. Founder, co-dir. Internat. Design Assistance Commn.; bd. dirs., exec. com. Found. for Future Generations; past bd. dirs. Am.-Israel Cultural Found.; bd. dirs., trustee Temple Emanuel, Englewood N.J., 1987; trustee Art Ctr. No. N.J., Englewood, 1960-68; artist in residence Melton Orgn., 2003; contbr. logo and trade mark designs and graphic comms. to non-profit civic orgns. including Am. Cancer Soc., Fedn. Jewish Philanthropies, World Hunger, Sloan-Kettering Meml. Hosp., United Cerebral Palsy, Jewish Theol. Sem., many others. With inf. U.S. Army, 1942-46, CBI. Recipient Best Ann. Report Design, 1957, 59, 61, Silver award Variety Store Merchandisers, 1967, Gold award Variety Store Merchandisers, 1970, Gold award Internat. Folding Carton Competition, 1964, Gold award Paperboard Packaging Council, 1974, awards N.Y. Art Dir.'s Club, 1958, 59, 63, 76, 77, 79 (2), awards Am. Inst. Graphic Arts, 1955, 58, 59, 60 (3), 61, 65 (2), 72, awards Soc. Illustrators, 1959, 68, Communication Arts awards, 1960, 64, 66, 67, 71, awards N.J. Art Dir.'s Club, 1962, 65 (3), 68, awards Package Design Mag., 1963-68, 70 (3),Indsl. Design awards, 1968, 75, Package of Yr. award, 1968, awards NYU, 1973, 74, Best Bottle of Yr. award, 1975, Clio award, 1976, 77, 81, Gold awards Package Design Council, 1977, 79, 80 (2), 87 (2), Gold Clio award, 79, 84, 88, Nat. Printing award, 1981, Desi award 1981, Best of Best 1985, Pratt. Inst. Alumni Achievement award, 1998; named one of 2000 Outstanding Designers and Artists of 20th Century, Cambridge Internat. Biographical Ctr., 2005, (2)others. Mem. Package Designers Coun. (Person of Yr. 1982, bd. dirs. 1962—), Indsl. Design Soc. Am., Packaging Inst., Am. Inst. Graphic Arts. Avocations: collecting historical packages, rewriting and illustrating legends, fables and fairy tales from India. Home: 213 Engle St Tenafly NJ 07670-2139 Office: Irv Koons Assocs 213 Engle St Tenafly NJ 07670-2139 Home Phone: 201-568-7387; Office Phone: 201-568-7387. Personal E-mail: ikadesign@aol.com.

KOONS, JEFF, artist; b. York, Pa., 1955; Attended, Sch. Art Inst. Chgo., 1975—76; BFA, Maryland Inst. Coll. Art, 1976. One person shows include New Mus. Contemporary Art, N.Y., 1980, Internat. With Monument, N.Y., 1985, Feature Gallery, N.Y., 1985, Daniel Weinberg Gallery, L.A., 1986, MCA, Chgo., 1988, Sonnabend Gallery, N.Y., 1988, 91, Max Hetzler Gallery, Cologne, Germany, 1988, 91, Donald Young Gallery, Chgo., 1988, Venster Gallery, Rotterdam, The Netherlands, 1989, Lehmann Gallery, Lausanne, Switzerland, 1992, Christophe Van de Weghe, Brussels, 1992, San Francisco Mus. Modern Art, 1992, 93, Walker Art Ctr., Mpls., 1992, Stedelijk Mus., Amsterdam, 1992, Mus. Contemporary Art, Sydney, 1996, Per Skarstedt Fine Art Gallery, N.Y.C., 1996, Guggenheim Mus., Bilbao, Spain, 1997, Sonnabend Gallery, N.Y.C., 1999, Rockefeller Ctr., 2000, New Paintings, 2001, Easyfun-Ethereal, Fruitmarket Gallery, Guggenheim Mus., Edinburg, 2001, Kunsthaus Bregenz, 2001, Shopping, Tate Liverpool, 2002, La Part de l'autre, Musée d'art Contemporain, 2002, Museo Archeologico Nazionale, Naples, 2003, Sonnabend Gallery, 2003, Backyard, Galarie Max Hetzler, Berlin, 2004, others; exhibited in group shows at P.S. 1, Long Island City, N.Y., 1981, Annina Nosei Gallery, N.Y., 1981, Barbara Gladstone Gallery, N.Y., 1981, Renaissance Soc., Chgo., 1982, 85, Espace Lyonnais d'Art Contemporain, Lyon, France, 1982, Artists Space, N.Y., 1983, LACE, L.A., 1983, White Columns, N.Y., 1984, Hallwalls, Buffalo, 1984, Features Gallery, Chgo., 1985, Whitney Mus., N.Y., 1985, 87, 89, 90, Michael Kline Gallery, N.Y., 1985, Galerie Crousel-Hussenot, Paris, 1985, New Mus., N.Y., 1985, Fundacion Caixa de Pensiones, Madrid/Barcelona, 1985, ICA, Boston, 1985, 88, Prospect Gallery, Frankfurt, Germany, 1985, Centro Reina Sofia, Madrid, 1987, Saatchi Collection, London, 1987, 88, LACMA, L.A., 1987, Centre Pompidou, Paris, 1987, John & Marble Ringling Mus. Art, Sarasota, Fla., 1987, Carnegie Internat., Pitts., 1988, Ctr. Nat. des Art Plastiques, Paris, 1988, MCA, Chgo., 1988, Kunsthalle, Dusseldorf, Germany, 1988, Roseum, Malmo, 1988, MOCA, L.A., 1989, Kunstverein, Hamburg, 1989, Kunsthalle, Basel, Switzerland, 1989, Mus. Modern Art, N.Y.C., 1989, 90, Biennale, Venice, Italy, 1990, Mus. Haus Lange and Mus. Haus Esters, Krefeld, 1990, Pharmakon, Tokyo, 1990, Biennial, Sydney, 1990, Thaddaeus Ropac Gallery, Salzburg, Austria, 1990, Stedelijk Mus., Amsterdam, 1990, Israel Mus., Tel Aviv, 1990, Deste Found., Athens, Greece, 1990, Mus. Art, Indpls., 1991, Martin-Gropius-Bau, Berlin, 1991, Mus. voor Hedendaagse Kunst, Hertogenbosch, The Netherlands, 1992, Anthony d'Offay Gallery, London, 1992, Musee d'Art Contemporain Pully/Lausanne, 1992, Ctr. Curatorial Studies Mus., Bard Coll., Annondale-on-Hudson, N.Y., 1996-97, Mus. Modern Art, 1997-98, Whitney Mus. Am. Art, N.Y.C., 1990-2000, James Cohan Gallery, 2000, Mus. Contemporary Art, Chgo., 2000, Royal Acad. Arts, London, 2000, Sonnabend Gallery, N.Y., 2001, Give & Take, Serpentine Gallery and Victoria & Albert Mus., 2001, Points of Departure II: Connection with Contemporary Art, San Francisco Mus. Modern Art, 2001, Marianne Boesky Gallery, 2002, James Cohan Gallery, 2003, 04, Mori Art Mus., Tokyo, 2003, Deste Found., Athens, 2004, others; author: (book) The Jeff Koons Handbook, 1993; co-author: (with Thomas Kellein) Jeff Koons: Pictures 1980-2002, 2003 (with Robert Rosenblum and David Sylvester) Jeff Koons: Easy Fun Ethereal, 2003. Studio: Jeff Koons Prodns Inc 600 Broadway Fl 2 New York NY 10012-3206 Mailing: c/o Gagosian Gallery 980 Madison Ave New York NY 10021

KOONS, KENNETH EDWARD, historian, educator, historian, consultant; b. Waynesboro, Pa., Oct. 10, 1954; s. John Henry and Doris Elaine Koons; m. Deborah Jean Kocher, July 2, 1955; children: Jacob Wesley, Elizabeth Marie. BA in History, Shippensburg State Coll., 1976, MA in History, 1978; ArtsD in History, Carnegie Mellon U., 1982. Asst. prof. history Va. Mil. Inst., Lexington, 1982—88, assoc. prof. history, 1988—92, prof. history, 1992—, Gen. Edwin Cox '20 Inst. prof. history, 2002—, assoc. head history dept. Scholar/curator Mus. Shenandoah Valley, Winchester, Va., 2000—05; guest lectr./cons. Frontier Culture Mus., Staunton, Va., 1990—2004; mem. nat. adv. coun./cons. Stonewall Jackson Ho., Lexington, 2004—; cons./editor Va. Cattlemen's Found. and Dairy Found. Va., Daleville, 2002—04; cons. McGraw Hill Pub., New York, NY, 2003—04; scorer advance placement examinations in world history Ednl. Testing Svc., Princeton, NJ, 2002. Editor: (collection essays) After the Backcountry: Rural Life in the Great Valley of Virginia, 1800-1900; contbr. essay; editor: (book) Virginia's Cattle Story: The First Four Centuries; contbr. articles to profl. jours. Wrote essay in support of hist. photog. and artifact display Augusta County Cultural and Hist. Commn., Verona, Va., 1994—95; rec. sec./mem. books com. Augusta County Hist. Soc., Staunton, 2003—06. Recipient Maury Rsch. Award, Va. Mil. Inst., 2001, Wilbur Hinman, Jr. Rsch. Award, 1990; fellow Jessie Ball duPont Seminar, The Cultural Politics of the Family, Nat. Humanities Ctr., 1997; Fellowship, Problems of Modernization: History and the Social Sciences, Nat. Endowment Humanities, 1976, Mellon Rsch. Fellowship, Va. Hist. Soc., 1991, 1992, Discretionary and Implementation grant for Conf.: After the Backcountry: Rural Life and Soc. in the 19th Century Valley Va., Va. Found. Humanities and Pub. Policy, 1993, Discretionary and Implementation grant for conf. After the Backcountry: Rural Life and Society in the 19th Century Valley Va., 1995, Travel fellowship, Scots-Irish Historians' Tour of No. Ireland, Brit. Coun., 1994. Mem.: Appalachian Studies Soc., Popular Culture Assn., World History Assn., Orgn. Am. Historians, So. Hist. Assn., Va. Hist. Soc. Avocations: gardening, woodworking, fly-fishing. Office: Virginia Military Institute Dept History Scott Shipp Hall Lexington VA 24450 Home Phone: 540-377-2872. E-mail: koonske@vmi.edu.

KOONTZ, ALFRED JOSEPH, JR., financial analyst, consultant; b. Balt., Mar. 6, 1942; s. Alfred J. and Mary Agnes K.; m. Kay Francis Frank, Aug. 4, 1962; children— Debbie Kay, Denise Marie, Stacey Lynn, Alfred Joseph, III. BSBA, Pa. State U., 1964. CPA, Md. Mgr. Price Waterhouse & Co., Balt., 1964-73, sr. mgr. NYC, 1973-74, Morristown, NJ, 1974-75; v.p. fin Piper Aircraft Corp., Lock Haven, Pa., 1975-80, sr. v.p. fin., 1980-85, sr. v.p. fin., treas., 1985-86, exec. v.p., chief operating officer Vero Beach, Fla., 1987-88; pres., dir. Piper Acceptance Corp., Lakeland, Fla., 1985-88; sr. v.p. fin. and adminstrn., treas., bd. dirs. Todd Shipyards Corp., Seattle, 1988-91; exec. v.p., CFO Pay'N Pak Stores Inc., Bellevue, Wash., 1992-93; pres. Alfred J. Koontz & Assoc., Vero Beach, 1993—; co-owner, CFO Pub. Telecomm. Providers, Inc., Vero Beach, 1993-97; co-owner, operator A&K Enterprises of Vero, Inc., 1994—. Client rels. exec. Diamond Cluster Internat., Chgo., 1998-2003; CFO Wannabe's, LLC, 1999, acting CFO TEF, Inc, 2004-05. Mem.: AICPA. Home: 1790 Sand Dollar Way Vero Beach FL 32963-2723 Personal E-mail: akeovi@aol.com.

KOONTZ, CARL LENNIS, II, retired investment counselor; b. Oct. 28, 1942; s. Carl Lennis and Jessie Marie (Rhodes) K.; m. Rose Marie Catalano, May 6, 1978. BS, U. Tenn., 1964, MS magna cum laude, 1968. Quality control analyst Ford Motor Co., Cin., 1965-66; mgmt. trainee Abbott, Procter & Paine, Richmond, Va., 1968-70; v.p. pension cons. Paine, Webber, NYC, 1970-76; asst. v.p. Scudder, Stevens & Clark, NYC, 1976-78, v.p. investments, 1978-85, mng. dir., 1985-87; v.p. Scudder, Stevens & Clark of Can., Toronto, Ont., 1984-87, Smith Barney Capital Mgmt., 1987-92; v.p. investment policy com. Capital Mgmt. Assocs., NYC, 1992, sr. v.p., 1993; pres. Capital Mgmt. Mid-Cap Fund, 1994, co-head equity investments, 1996, co-chief investment officer, mng. dir., 1998; pres. Capital Mgmt. Small-Cap Fund, 1998; mng. dir. Weiss, Peck & Greer, 2000—03, head Large Cap Growth Group, 2001—03, mgr. Large-Cap Growth Fund, 2001—03; mng. dir. asset mgmt. Bank of NY, 2004—06, chief investment officer Large-Cap Growth, 2004—06, mgr. Hamilton Large Cap. Growth Fund, 2005—06; ret., 2006. Mem. dean's adv. coun. Col. of Bus., U. Tenn. With U.S. Army ANG, 1965-70. Fellow Fin. Analysis Fedn. (chartered fin. analyst); mem. Investment Counsel Assn. Am. (chartered investment counselor), N.Y. Soc. Security Analysts, Madison Ave. Sports Car Driving and Chowder Soc., Holland Lodge, Univ. Club, Antique Automobile Club Am., Pontiac Oakland Club Internat., Bond Club N.Y. Avocations: antique cars, model building, photography, swimming, tennis. Home: 373 Middlesex Rd Darien CT 06820-2518

KOONTZ, DEAN RAY, writer; b. Everett, Pa., July 9, 1945; s. Raymond and Florence (Logue) K.; m. Gerda Ann Cerra, Oct. 15, 1966. BS, Shippensburg U., 1966, LittD (hon.), 1989. Tchr. Appalachian Poverty Program, Saxton, Pa., 1966-67, Mechanicsburg (Pa.) Sch. Dist., 1967-69; freelance writer Orange, Calif., 1969—. Author of over 59 novels including Star Quest, 1968, The Fall of the Dream Machine, 1969, Fear That Man, 1969, Anti-Man, 1970, Beastchild, 1970 (Hugo award nomination 1971), Dark of the Woods, 1970, The Dark Symphony, 1970, Hell's Gate, 1970, The Crimson Witch, 1971, A Darkness in My Soul, 1972, The Flesh in the Furnace, 1972, Starblood, 1972, Time Thieves, 1972, Warlock, 1972, A Werewolf Among Us, 1973, Hanging On, 1973, The Haunted Earth, 1973, Demon Seed, 1973, rev. edit., 1997, After the Last Race, 1974, Nightmare Journey, 1975, Night Chills, 1976, The Vision, 1977, Whispers, 1980, Phantoms, 1983, Darkfall, 1984, Twilight Eyes, 1985, Strangers, 1986, Watchers, 1987, Lightning, 1988, Servants of Twilight, 1989, The Bad Place, 1990, Cold Fire, 1991, Hideaway, 1992, Dragon Tears, 1993, Mr. Murder, 1993, Winter Moon, 1994, Dark Rivers of the Heart, 1994, Strange Highways, 1995, Intensity, 1996, Santa's Twin, 1996, Fear Nothing, 1997, Tick Tock, 1997, Sole Survivor, 1997, From the Corner of His Eye, 2000, Icebound, 2000, False Memory, 2000, One Door Away from Heaven, 2001, By the Light of the Moon, 2002, The Face, 2003, The Taking, 2004, Life Expectancy, 2004, Velocity, 2005 (Publishers Weekly bestseller list), Odd Thomas, 2005; (with Kevin Anderson) Dean Koontz's Frankenstein: Book One: Prodigal Son, 2005, Forever Odd, 2006, Brother Odd, 2006, The Husband, 2006, The Good Guy, 2007; (children's books) Robot Santa: The Further Adventures of Santa's Twin, 2004; others under pseudonyms David Axton, Brian Coffey, Deanna Dwyer, K.R. Dwyer, John Hill, Leigh Nichols, Anthony North, Richard Paige, and Owen West. Mailing: PO Box 9529 Newport Beach CA 92658-9529*

KOONTZ, LAWRENCE L., JR., state supreme court justice; b. Roanoke, Va., Jan. 25, 1940; BS, Va. Polytech. U., 1962. Asst. commonwealth's atty., Roanoke, 1967—68; judge Va. Juvenile & Domestic Rels. Dist. Ct., 1968—76, Va. Cir. Ct. (23rd cir.), 1976—85, Ct. Appeals of Va., 1985—95; justice Va. Supreme Ct., 1995—. Mem.: ABA. Office: Va Supreme Ct PO Box 1315 Richmond VA 23218-1315 Office Phone: 540-387-6082.

KOOP, C. EVERETT (CHARLES EVERETT KOOP), former Surgeon General of the United States, educator; b. Bklyn., Oct. 14, 1916; s. John Everett and Helen (Apel) K.; m. Elizabeth Flanagan, Sept. 19, 1938; children: Allen van Benschoten, Norman Apel, David Charles Everett, Elizabeth. AB, Dartmouth Coll., 1937, DSc (hon.), 1989; MD, Cornell U., 1941; DSc in Medicine, U. Pa., 1947, DSc (hon.), 1990; LLD (hon.), Ea. Bapt. Coll., 1960, Phila. Coll. Osteo. Medicine, 1979, LaSalle Coll., 1983, Colby-Sawyer Coll., 1988, Princeton U., 1989, Hahnemann U., 1989, U. Miami, 1991, U. Cin., 1991; MD (hon.), U. Liverpool, Eng., 1968; LHD (hon.), Wheaton Coll., 1973, Phila. Theol. Sem., 1980, Chgo. Med. Sch., 1988, Brown U., 1990; DSc (hon.), Gwynedd Mercy Coll., 1978, Washington and Jefferson Coll., 1979, Marquette U., 1983, Ea. Mich. U., 1985, N.Y. Med. Coll., 1985, Ball State U., 1987, Kirskville Coll. Osteo. Med., 1988, Albany Med. Coll., 1988, Colby Coll., 1988, Yeshiva U., 1988, Phila. Coll. Pharmacy and Sci., 1988, Baylor Coll. Medicine, 1988, U. Mass., Boston, 1989, Brandeis U., 1990, Northwestern U., 1990, U. New England, 1991; D. Pub. Svc. (hon.), George Washington U., 1991; DPH, Cedar Crest Coll., 1995; D in Humanities, So. Utah U., 1997; LLD, Med. Coll. Pa., 1997. Diplomate Am. Bd. Surgery, Nat. Bd. Med. Examiners. Intern Pa. Hosp., Phila., 1941-42; fellow in surgery U. Pa. Hosp., Phila., 1942-47; fellow in pediat. surgery Children's Hosp., Boston, 1946; surgeon-in-chief Children's Hosp. of Phila., 1948-81; with U. Pa. Sch. Medicine, 1942-85, prof., 1959-85; former dep. asst. sec. for health HHS; surg. gen. of U.S. US Dept. Health & Human Services, 1981-89; former dir. internat. health USPHS, from 1982; chair Safe Kids Nat. Campaign, Washington; dir. Elizabeth De Camp McInery prof. surgery C. Everett Koop Inst. Dartmouth-Hitchkock Med. Ctr., Hanover, NH, 1993—. Cons. USN, 1964—81; sr. scholar C. Everett Koop Inst. at Dartmouth; dir. Ready to Learn Program Carnegie Found., 1993—95; McEnerny prof. surgery Dartmouth Med. Sch. Author: Visible and Palpable Lesions in Children, The Right to Live, The Right to Die, 1976, The Right to Live, The Right to Die, rev. edit., 1980, Smoking: The New Book of Knowledge, 1989; author: (with E. Koop)) Sometimes Mountains Move, 1979; author: (with F. A. Schaeffer)) Whatever Happened to the Human Race?, 1979; author: Koop: The Memoirs of America's Family Doctor, 1991; author: (with T. Johnson)) Let's Talk, 1992; editor: surgery sect. Jour. Clin. Pediatrics, 1961—64; mem. editl. bd.: Zeitschrift fur Kinderchirurgie and Grenzqebiete, 1964—81, editor-in-chief: Jour. Pediatric Surgery, 1965—77, editl. cons.: Japanese Jour. Pediatric Surgery and Medicine, 1970—81, chmn. editorial bd.: PHS Reports, 1982—89, mem. editorial adv. bd.: Tobacco Control: An Internat. Jour.; contbr. publs. in surg. physiology, biomed. ethics, physiology of surg. neonate, tech. advances in pediatric surgery. Bd. dirs., pres. Nat. Health Mus. Inc.; bd. dirs., chmn. sci. adv. com. Biopure; chmn. Patient Med. Edn., 1993—96, Patient Med. Record, Inc., 1997—; Bd. dirs. Med. Assistance Programs, Inc., Brunswick, Ga., Friends Nat. Libr. of Medicine. Decorated chevalier Legion of Honor France, Order Duarte, Sanchez and Mella Dominican Republic, Chevalier French Legion of Honor; named Hon. Citizen, City of Balt., 1985; recipient medal, City of Marseille, Presbyn. Man of Yr. award, Presbyn. Social Union Phila., 1975, Super Achiever of Yr. award, Phila. chpt. Juvenile Diabetes Found., 1975, Man of Yr. award, Jewish Community Chaplaincy Svc. Phila., 1975, Copernicus medal, Polish Surg. Soc., 1977, Gold medal, Children's Hosp. Phila., 1981, Sec. of Health of Commonwealth of Pa. award, 1981, Thomas Linacre award, Nat. Fedn. Cath. Physicians Guild, 1981, Key to City of St. Louis, 1985, Award of Distinction, Alumni Assn. Cornell U. Med. Coll., 1988, Humanitarian Svc. award, City of Boston, 1989, Harry S. Truman award, City of Independence, Mo., 1990, Daniel Webster award, Dartmouth Coll., 1990, John Wiley Jones Disting. Lectr. award, Rochester Inst. Tech., 1990, NAS Public Welfare medal, 1990, Tyler prize, U. So. Calif., 1991, Albert Schweitzer prize, Johns Hopkins U., 1991, Person of Yr. award, Nat. Hosp. Orgn., 1991, C. Everett Koop Hon. Lectr. medal named in his honor, Anchor & Caduceus Soc., 1991, C. Everett Koop Health Adv. award named in his honor, Am. Soc. for Health Care Mktg. and Pub. Rels., Gustav O. Lienhard award, Inst. Medicine, 1992, Presdl. medal of Freedom, 1995, Heinz Found. award, 1995, Medal of Honor, Am. Cancer Soc., 2000, Presdl. Medal of Freedom; scholar Disting. scholar to Carnegie Found. for advancement of teaching. Fellow: ACS, Am. Acad. Pediatrics (William E. Ladd Gold medal), Royal Coll. Physicians and Surgeons of Glasgow (hon.), Royal Coll. Surgeons Eng. (hon.); mem.: AMA, Societé Suisse De Chirurgie Infantile, Deutschen Gesselschaft für Kinderchirugi, Societé Française de Chirurgie Infantile, Assn. Mil. Surgeons U.S. (pres. 1982, 1987, Founders medal), Internat. Soc. Surgery, Brit. Assn. Pediatric Surgeons (Dennis Browne Gold medal), Soc. U. Surgeons, Royal Soc. Medicine, Am. Surg. Assn., Sigma Xi. Office: Dartmouth Coll Dartmouth-Hitchcock Ctr C Everett Koop Inst Hanover NH 03755

KOOPERSMITH, KIM, lawyer; b. Lake Success, NY, Aug. 11, 1959; d. Kenneth and Marcia Ilene (Shapiro) K.; m. William J. Borner, June 19, 1983; children: Meredith Lee, Charlotte Jane. BA cum laude, U. Pa., 1981; JD, Fordham U., 1984. Bar: NY 1985, US Dist. Ct. (so. and ea. dists.) NY 1985, US Ct. of Appeals (2nd cir.). Ptnr. Anderson Kill Olick & Oshinsky, P.C., NYC, 1984; now ptnr. litig. and mem. mgmt. com. Akin Gump Strauss Hauer & Feld LLP, NYC. Contbr. articles to profl. pubs. Mem. NY State Bar Assn., Assn. of Bar NYC Office: Akin Gump Strauss Hauer & Feld LLP 590 Madison Ave New York NY 10022-2524 Office Phone: 212-872-1060. Business E-Mail: kkoopersmith@akingump.com.

KOOPMAN, RICHARD NELSON, engineer, consultant; b. Buffalo, Nov. 26, 1945; s. Richard John Walter and Nellie Elkins (Wisbrock) K.; m. Mary Margaret Blume, July 17, 1970; Anthony Blake (dec.), Laura Nicole. BSME, Washington U., 1968; MSME, U. Minn., 1969, PhD, 1975. Registered profl. engr., Ill., Minn. Engr. Honeywell, Inc., Mpls., 1973-75, Argonne (Ill.) Nat. Lab, 1975-80; mem. tech. staff, supr. Bell Labs, Naperville, Ill., 1980-85; dir. McDonald's Corp., Oak Brook, Ill., 1985—96; v.p. Fla. Plastics Internat., Inc., Evergreen Park, Ill., 1999—2001; sr. cons. Engring. Sys. Inc., Aurora, 1996—2002, dir. mech. and elec. engring., 2002—06, pres., 2006—. Contbr. articles to profl. jours.; patentee in field. Mem. Hinsdale (Ill.) Planning Commn., 1992-95, Zoning Bd. Appeals, 1995-96; bd. dirs. Bradley U. Parents Orgn., 1995-99, career com. chair, 1996-98; bd. dirs. Graue Mill Mus., 1984-91. Named Supr. of Yr., INROADS-Chgo., 1991. Mem. ASME (section chmn. 1980-81), Nat. Soc. Profl. Engrs., Hinsdale Jaycees (treas. 1980-83), Woodlands Home Owners Assn. (treas. 1998—), Visage Internat., Tau Beta Pi, Omicron Delta Kappa, Pi Tau Sigma. Mem. United Ch. of Christ. Office: Engring Sys Inc 3851 Exchange Ave Aurora IL 60504 Office Phone: 630-851-4566. E-mail: rnkoopman@esi-il.com.

KOOPMAN, WILLIAM JAMES, medical educator, internist, immunologist; b. Lafayette, Ind., Aug. 19, 1945; s. William James and Barbara Mary (Morehouse) K.; m. Lilliane Kathryn Desimone, June 15, 1968; children: Benjamin, Anna, Rebecca, Steven. BA, Washington and Jefferson U., 1967; MD, Harvard U., 1972. Diplomate Am. Bd. Internal Medicine. Intern/resident in medicine Mass. Gen. Hosp., Boston, 1972-74; rsch. fellow NIH, Bethesda, Md., 1974-77; from asst. prof., assoc. prof. to prof.

medicine specializing in rheumatology and clin. immunology U. Ala., Birmingham, 1977—, Howard L. Holley prof. medicine, 1988-95, dir. Multipurpose Arthritis Ctr., 1983-96, chmn. Dept. Medicine, 1995—2005, chmn. emeritus, 2005—. Mem. nat. adv. coun. Nat. Inst. Arthritis, Musculo-skeletal and Skin Diseases, 1987-90; chmn. bd. sci. counselors, NIH, NIAMS, 1991-95. Editor: Arthritis and Rheumatism jour., 1985—90, Arthritis and Allied Conditions, 14th edit.; contbr. more than 250 articles to profl. jours. Recipient Carol Nachman Rsch. prize Fed. Republic Germany, 1982. Fellow ACP (master), Am. Coll. Rheumatology (pres. Southeastern region 1986-87, treas. 1992-94, 2nd v.p. 1994-95, pres.-elect 1995-96, pres. 1996-97); mem. ACP (master), Am. Soc. Clin. Investigation (pres. 1990-91), Assn. Am. Physicians, Am. Assn. Immunologists, Inst. of Medicine, Birmingham Area C. of C. Presbyterian. Avocations: fishing, gardening. Office: U Ala Sch Medicine 1530 3rd Ave S Birmingham AL 35294-3408 Office Phone: 205-934-5305. E-mail: wkoopman@uab.edu.*

KÖÖRNA, ARNO, economist, educator; b. Tallinn, Estonia, Feb. 2, 1926; s. Artur and Anna-Helena (Schultz) K.; m. Eha Lind, Dec. 28, 1946; children: Silvia, Vello. PhD, Tartu U., Estonia, 1955; academician, Estonian Acad. Scis., Tallinn, 1973, PhD in Econs., 1970. Prof. Tartu U., 1972-75; sec. gen. Estonian Acad. Scis., 1973-82, v.p., 1982-91, pres., 1991-94, ex-pres., 1995. Author: Economic Motivation of Quality, 1978, Science in Estonia, 1993, Estonian Science in Transition, 1994; contbr. articles to profl. jours. Mem. Mem. Estonian Parliament, Tallinn, 1985—90; chmn. Estonian Sci. Coun., Estonia, 1992—94. Mem. Internat. Assn. IUS Primi Viri (mem. standing com.), World Futures Studies Fedn., Russian Acad. Humanities, Ctrl. European Acad. Sci. and Art (hon.). Home: Kapi 9-22 10136 Tallinn Estonia Office: Estonian Acad Scis Kohtu 6 10130 Tallinn Estonia Office Phone: 6115801. E-mail: arno.koorna@mail.ee.

KOOSER, TED (THEODORE J. KOOSER), poet; b. Ames, Iowa, Apr. 25, 1939; s. Theodore B. and Vera (Moser) Kooser; m. Kathleen Rutledge. BS, Iowa State U., 1962; MA, U. Nebr., 1968. Former v.p. Lincoln Benefit Life; 13th Poet Laureate Cons. in Poetry to the Libr. of Congress, 2004—05; founder Am. Life in Poetry project, 2005—. Vis. prof. English U. Nebr., Lincoln. Author: (poetry collections) Official Entry Blank, 1969, A Local Habitation and a Name, 1974, Not Coming to Be Barked At, 1976, Sure Signs, 1980 (Soc. of Midland Authors Poetry Prize, 1980), One World at a Time, 1985, The Blizzard Voices, 1986, Weather Central, 1994, Winter Morning Walks: One Hundred Postcards to Jim Harrison, 2000 (Nebr. Book Award for poetry, 2001), Delights & Shadows, 2004 (Pulitzer Prize for poetry, 2005); co-author (with Jim Harrison): Braided Creek: A Conversation in Poetry, 2003 (Soc. Midland Authors Poetry Prize, 2004); author: (chapbooks/spl. editions) Grass County, 1971, Twenty Poems, 1973, Shooting a Farmhouse/So This is Nebraska, 1975, Old Marriage and New, 1978, Etudes, Bits Press, 1992, A Book of Things, 1995, A Decade of Ted Kooser Valentines, 1996, Flying at Night: Poems, 1965-1985, 2005; co-author (with Harley Elliott): Voyages to the Inland Sea, 1976; co-author: (with William Kloefkorn) Cottonwood County, 1979; author: (essay collection) Local Wonders: Seasons in the Bohemian Alps, 2002 (Nebr. Book Award for nonfiction, 2003, Gold Award for Autobiography, Fore-Word mag. Book of Yr. Awards), (non-fiction) The Poetry Home Repair Manual: Practical Advice for Beginning Poets, 2005. Recipient Prairie Schooner Prize in Poetry, 1976, 1978, Stanley Kunitz Poetry Prize, Columbia Mag., 1984, Pushcart Prize, 1984, Nebr. Governor's Art Award, 1988, Mayor's Art Award, Lincoln, Nebr., 1989, Richard Hugo Prize, Poetry N.W., 1994, James Boatwright Award, Shenandoah, 2000, Merit Award in Poetry, Nebr. Arts Coun., 2000, Mari Sandoz Award, Nebr. Libr. Assn., 2000; writing fellowship, Nat. Endowment Arts, 1976, 1984. Address: care Copper Canyon Press Bldg 313 Ft Worden State Pk PO Box 271 Port Townsend WA 98368

KOOYMAN, GERALD LEE, physiologist, researcher; b. Salt Lake City, June 16, 1934; s. Albert John and Virginia L. (Monson) K.; m. Melba Mae Bingham, July 6, 1962; children: Carsten, Tory. AB, UCLA, 1957; PhD, U. Ariz., 1966. Postdoctoral fellow NSF, London, 1966-67; asst. rsch. physiologist U. Calif. San Diego, La Jolla, 1967-94, rsch. prof. to prof. emeritus biology, 1994—. Author: Weddell Seal, Consummate Diver, 1981; editor: Fur Seals: Maternal Behavior On Land and At Sea, 1986, Diverse Divers, Physiology and Behavior, 1989; contbr. articles to sci. jours. Recipient Antarctic medal NSF. Fellow AAAS, London Zool. Soc., Explorers Club (Finn Ronne Meml. award, Polar Field Sci. and Exploration 2007); mem. Am. Physiol. Soc., Am. Soc. Zoologists, Sigma Xi. Office: Scripps Instn Oceanography U Calif San Diego 9500 Gilman Dr La Jolla CA 92093-0225 E-mail: gkooyman@ucsd.edu.

KOPE, SHANE BRIEN, lawyer; b. Ft. Lauderdale, Fla., Aug. 2, 1974; s. Davis Brien and Georgia Kay Kope. JD, Dickinson Sch. Law, 2002. Lic.: Pa. (atty.) 2004. Law clk. Cumberland County Cts., Carlisle, Pa., 2001—04. CLE Web devel. asst. Pa. Bar Inst., Mechanicsburg, 2003—. Vol. Harrisburg Soup Kitchen, Pa., 2002—. Fellow Cherie T. Millage fellowship, for law clerking for the Cherokee Nation, Okla., 1999. Mem.: Cumberland County Bar Assn., ABA, Pa. Bar Assn., Dauphin County Bar Assn. Liberal. Office Phone: 717-761-7573. Office Fax: 717-761-7572. Business E-Mail: sbkope@kopelaw.com.

KOPEL, DAVID BENJAMIN, lawyer; b. Denver; s. Gerald Henry and Dolores B. Kopel; m. Deirdre Frances Dolan, 1987. BA in History, Brown U., 1982; JD, U. Mich., 1985. Bar: Colo. 1986, N.Y. 1986, U.S. Dist. Ct. (ea. and so. dists.) N.Y. 1986, U.S. Ct. Appeals (2d cir.) 1988, U.S. Dist. Ct. Colo. 1988, U.S. Ct. Appeals (10th cir.) 1988, U.S. Ct. Appeals (D.C. cir.) 1997, U.S. Ct. Appeals (5th cir.) 1999, U.S. Ct. Appeals (4th cir.) 2003. Assoc. Sullivan & Cromwell, NYC, 1985-86; asst. dist. atty. Manhattan Dist. Atty., NYC, 1986-88; asst. atty. gen. Colo. State Atty. Gen., Denver, 1988-92; rsch. dir. Independence Inst., Golden, Colo., 1992—. Adj. prof. NYU Sch. of Law, 1998-99. Democrat. Avocations: skiing, golf, amateur radio. Office: Independence Inst 13952 Denver West Pkwy Ste 400 Golden CO 80401

KOPELL, BRIAN HARRIS, neurosurgeon, director; b. NYC, Oct. 20, 1970; BA, U. Pa., Phila., 1992; MD, NYU, 1996. Lic. NY, 1996, Ohio, 2003, Wis., 2004. Fellow Cleve. Clinic Found., 2003—04; asst. prof. Med. Coll. Wis., Milw., 2004; dir. restorative neuroscience program Froedtert Hosp., 2004—. Office: Med Coll Wis 9200 W Wisconsin Ave Milwaukee WI 53226 Office Phone: 414-805-5483. Office Fax: 414-955-0115. Business E-Mail: bkopell@mcw.edu.

KOPELMAN, IAN STUART, lawyer; b. Chgo., Oct. 11, 1949; s. Ted and Norma (Hyman) K.; m. Nancy Henriette Stamp, Mar. 18, 1984; children: Meredith Samantha, Jason Lee. BA cum laude, Knox Coll., 1971; JD with distinction, U. Iowa, 1974. Bar: Ill. 1974, U.S. Dist. Ct. (no. dist.) Ill. 1974, U.S. Tax Ct. 1974. Ptnr. Arnstein & Lehr, Chgo., 1979-88; prin. Shefsky & Froelich Ltd., Chgo., 1988-96; ptnr., chair employee benefits/exec. compensation group Altheimer & Gray, Chgo., 1996-99, Rudnick & Wolfe, Chgo., 1999-2000; ptnr., chair employee benefits/exec. compensation dept. Piper, Marbury, Rudnick & Wolfe (now DLA Piper US LLP), Chgo., 2000—. Adj. prof. law John Marshall Law Sch., 2004—; lectr. in field. Contbr. articles to profl. publs. Pres. Chgo.-Knox Coll. Alumni Assn., Chgo., 1978-79. Recipient commendation Internat. Acad. Trial Lawyers, 1974, award Iowa Acad. Trial Lawyers. Mem. ABA, Ill. Bar Assn., Chgo. Bar Assn. (chmn. employee benefits com. 1981-82, commendation 1986), Profit Sharing/401k Coun. Am. (legal counsel 2005—, legal and legis. com. 1990—, bd. dirs. 1997-2005), Midwest Benefits Coun. (chmn. legal and legis. com. 1991-93), Chgo. Assn. Commerce and Industry, Phi Sigma Alpha, Omicron Delta Kappa, Phi Delta Phi. Jewish. Avocations: theater, history, reading, sports. Office: DLA Piper US LLP Suite 1900 203 N La Salle St Chicago IL 60601-1293 Office Phone: 312-368-2161. Office Fax: 312-236-7516. Business E-Mail: Ian.Kopelman@dlapiper.com.

KOPELMAN, LEONARD, lawyer; b. Cambridge, Mass., Aug. 2, 1940; s. Irving and Frances Estelle (Robbins) K.; m. Carol Hunsberger. BA cum laude, Harvard U., 1962, JD, 1965. Bar: Mass. 1966. Assoc. Warner & Stackpole, Boston, 1965-73; sr. ptnr. Kopelman and Paige, Boston, 1974—. Lectr. Harvard U., 1965—; permanent master Mass. Superior Ct., 1971—; gen. counsel Emerson Coll.; hon. consul gen. of, Finland, Mass., 1975—; U.S. del. Soc. for Internat. Devel.; Chmn. Mass. Jud. Selection Com. for the Fed. Judiciary, 1971—; chief counsel AAUP; dean consular corps of Boston, 2001—. Trustee Cathedral of the Pines, 1972; pres. Hillel Found. of Cambridge, Inc., 1973—; trustee Faulkner Hosp., 1974— , Parker Hill Med. Ctr., 1976—; dir. gen. Consular Corps Coll. Named a Super Lawyer in Govt. Law and Politics Media, Boston Mag., 2007; named one of the 12 most powerful lawyers in Mass. Nat. Law Jour.; NEH grantee, 1975. Mem. ABA (exec. coun. 1969—), Mass. Bar Assn. (chmn. mcpl. law sect.), Am. Judges Assn., Mass. C. of C. (pres. 1974-77), Harvard Faculty Club, Algonquin Club (pres.), Orgn. Consular Corps. Ams. (exec. v.p. 2002—), Harvard Club, Union Club, Hasty Pudding Club, St. Botolph Club. Home: 33 Yarmouth Rd Chestnut Hill MA 02467-2815 Office: Kopelman and Paige 101 Arch St Boston MA 02110-1134

KOPELMAN, MILTON, retired secondary school educator, principal; b. NYC, Jan. 19, 1927; s. Jacob Kopelman and Sophia Herman Kopelman; m. Harriet Ressler, Dec. 25, 1949; children: Steven, Kenneth, Donna. BS, CCNY, 1946; MA, Columbia U., NYC, 1948. Tchr. biology Bronx HS Sci., NYC, chmn. biology dept., 1961—77, prin., 1977—90. Adj. instr. tchrs. coll. Columbia U., 1955—70; adj. instr. CUNY, 1971—73, Hunter Coll., Lehman Coll.; adj. NY State Dept. Edn., 1991—96; adj. instr. Yonkers Bd. Edn., NY, 1997—98; cons. in field; mem. summer inst. NSF, U. Colo., Pa. State U., SUNY, 1971—73. Pres., founder Bronx HS Sci. Endowment Fund, NYC, 1978—89; cons. Ronald Lauder Found. Support and Enrichment Edn. in Ea. Europe. With US Army, 1946—47. Recipient Excellence in Tchg. award, SUNY, Albany, 1987, Torch of Liberty award, Antidefamation League B'nai B'rith, 1989, Congl. award, US Congress, 1990; Milton Kopelman Scholarship Fund named in his honor. Mem.: Coun. Supers. and Adminstrs., Hymark Vets. Assn. Avocations: photography, golf, music, nature, physical fitness. Home: 6 Gerri Ln Yonkers NY 10703

KOPELMAN, RICHARD ERIC, management educator; b. NYC, May 31, 1943; s. Seymour H. and Leona L. (Quint) K.; m. Carol Fialkov, June 7, 1970; children: Joshua Marc, Michael Adam. BS, U. Pa., 1965, MBA, 1967; DBA, Harvard U., 1974. Instr. bus. C.C. Phila., 1967-69; instr. mgmt. Baruch Coll./CUNY, NYC, 1973-74, asst. prof., 1974-77, assoc. prof., 1978-80, prof., 1981—. Cons. in field; corp. dir. Aleph Null Corp., 1979-88, Applied Photonics, Inc., 1986-91, Infodex Sys., Inc., 1986-88, EMS Devel. Corp., 1992-96; pres. Cube One, Inc., 1998—; acad. co-dir. MS in Indsl. Rels. program Baruch/Cornell U., 1985-97, acad. co-dir. Baruch exec. MS in Indsl. Rels. program, 1994-2000; acad. dir. Baruch exec. MS in Indsl. and Labor Rels. program, 2000—, faculty co-dir. Zicklin Svc. Excellence Initiative, 2003—. Author: The Management of Productivity: A Practical People-Oriented Perspective, 1986; mem. editl. rev. bd. Jour. Social Behavior and Personality, 1985-89, Nat. Productivity Rev., Jour. Orgnl. Behavior Mgmt., Perceptions, 1991-94, Jour. Psychology, 1999—, Jour. Orgnl. Excellence, 2000—; contbr. numerous articles to profl. and acad. jours. Bd. dirs. Day Care Coun., Nassau County, 1979-82; Nassau Symphony Orch., 1984-85. Recipient Pres. award for excellence in tchg. Baruch Coll., 1987, Pres. award for excellence in scholarship, 2005, Tchg. Excellence award, 1989, 91, 92, 93, CUNY Excellence Award for Rsch., Sch. Bus. and Pub. Adminstrn. Tchg. and Svc., 1999; William B. Harding fellow Harvard U. Mem. APA, Acad. Mgmt., Decision Scis. Inst., Soc. for Human Resource Mgmt. (accredited pers. diplomate, sr. profl. in human resources), Am. Compensation Assn., Met. N.Y. Assn. for Applied Psychology (sec. 1986-87, treas. 1987-88, v.p. 1988-89, pres. 1989-90), Sigma Iota Epsilon (faculty advisor Baruch Coll. chpt. 2003-). Home: 65 Colgate Rd Great Neck NY 11023-1501 Office: Baruch Coll Zicklin Sch Bus/Dept Mgmt 1 Bernard Baruch Way New York NY 10010-5518 Home Phone: 516-466-4667; Office Phone: 646-312-3629. Personal E-mail: rekopelman@managingperformance.com. Business E-Mail: richard_kopelman@baruch.cuny.edu.

KOPELOFF, IRIS HOPE, dermatologist; d. Arnold and Marcia Kopeloff; m. Michael Rahmin; children: Samantha, Austin, Gabrielle. BA summa cum laude, Wellesley Coll., Mass., 1985; MD, Mt. Sinai Sch. Medicine, NYC, 1989. With Dermatology Ctr. Ridgewood, NJ. Fellow: Am. Acad. Dermatology; mem.: Phi Beta Kappa. Office: Dermatology Ctr Ridgewood 140 Chestnut Ridgewood NJ 07450

KOPELSON, ARNOLD, film producer; b. NYC, Feb. 14, 1935; BS, NYU; JD, NY Law Sch., 1959. Founder Kopelson Entertainment. Bd. dirs. CBS Corp., 2007—; exec. com. producers branch Acad. Motion Pictures Arts and Sciences. Prodr. (film) Foolin' Around, 1980, Dirty Tricks, 1981, Gimme an F, 1984, Platoon, 1986 (Acad. award Best Picture, Golden Globe, and an Independent Spirit award), Triumph of the Spirit, 1989, Out for Justice, 1991, Falling Down, 1993, The Fugitive, 1993 (Acad. award nom Best Picture), Outbreak, 1995, Seven, 1995, Eraser, 1996, Murder at 1600, 1997, Mad City, 1997, The Devil's Advocate, 1997, U.S. Marshals, 1998, A Perfect Murder, 1998, Don't Say A Word, 2001, Joe Somebody, 2001, Twisted, 2004; exec. prodr. (film) Lost and Found, 1979, The Legacy, 1979, Night of the Juggler, 1980, Final Assignment, 1980, Dirty Tricks, 1981, Model Behavior, 1984, Warlock, 1989, Fire Birds, 1990; exec. prodr. (TV) Past Tense, 1994, The Fugitive, 2000, Thieves, 2001. Mem. advisory bd. Rand Corp. Ctr. Middle East Public Policy.*

KOPENHAVER, PATRICIA ELLSWORTH, podiatrist; Student, Columbia U., 1950-53; BA, George Washington U., 1954; MA, Columbia U., 1956; Dr. Podiatric Medicine, N.Y. Coll. Podiatric Medicine, 1963, postgrad., 1980; LLD (hon.), Barry U., 1998; MD (hon.) (hon.), Internat. U. Health Scis. Sch. Medicine, 2001; MD (hon.), Internat. Univ. of the Hlth. Sci., 2001. Diplomate Nat. Bd. Podiatry Examiners. Pvt. practice podiatry, Greenwich, Conn., 1964—; staff podiatrist Havenhealth Care Ctr., Greenwich, 2003—. Mem. staff Laurelton Convalescent Hosp., Greenwich; trustee N.Y. Coll. Podiatric Medicine, 1998. Bd. dirs. Monmouth Opera Guild, 1965; trustee Monmouth Opera Festival, 1966, v.p., 1964; mem. Greenwich Arts Coun.; program chmn. Greenwich Women's Rep. Club, 1983-84, 4th dist. rep., 1984-85, 87—; trustee N.Y. Coll. Podiatric Medicine, 1998—. Recipient Hosp. Fund award for med. research translations ARC, Alumni award of distinction N.Y. Coll. Podiatric Medicine, 1997; scholarship named in her honor N.Y. Coll. Podiatric Medicine, 1997. Mem. AAUW (v.p. 1991, pres. Greenwich br. 1992-94, bd. dirs. 1996), NOW, Conn. Podiatric Med. Assn., Hist. Soc., Asian Soc., Fairfield Podiatry Assn., Am. Assn. Women Podiatrists (founding charter pres. 1969-78), Acad. Podiatry, Am. Podiatry Coun., UN Assn. U.S.A., Acad. Podiatric Medicine (chmn. nominating com. 1981, 1st v.p. 1983-84, chmn. fundraising 1984-85, chmn. women's issues 1985, chmn. cmty. edn. 1989), NY Coll. Podiatry Med. (bd. amb.), Am. Acad. Sports Medicine, Am. Acad. Podiatric Sports Medicine (assoc. 1989), George Washington U. Alumni Assn., Columbia Alumni Assn., Fairfield County Alumni Assn. Columbia U., Coast Soc. Founders Barry U. (treas. 1998), Nat. Fedn. Rep. Women, Bruce Mus., Nature Conservancy, Federated Garden Clubs Conn., St. Mary Ladies Guild, Greenwich Gardeners, Womans' Club (ways and means com. 1989, pres.), English Speaking Union, Soroptimists Internat. Am. (pres. Greenwich br. 1990—, bd. dirs. 1997-98), Inc. (vice chmn. program com. 1985—, regional med. scholarship chmn. 1987, med. scholarship chmn. N.E. region 1988, program dir. 1988—, pres. Greenwich br. 1990-92), Toastmasters, Travel Club (program com. 1984—), Soroptimist (bd. dirs. 1997, 2000—), Greenwich Woman's Club (chair gardeners judges 2001—), Pi Epsilon Chi. Home: 2 Sutton Pl S New York NY 10022-3070 also: 8 Dearfield Dr Greenwich CT 06831-5348 Office Phone: 203-661-9311. Office Fax: 203-869-5096.

KOPES-KERR, COLIN P., physician, publishing executive; b. Washington, Jan. 31, 1950; s. Walter Frances and Jean Bridget Kerr; m. Diane Maria Kopes, Jan. 20, 1996; children: Oliver Scott, Colin Jamison, Liam Connor, Anna Lorraine. BA in Classics, Harvard U., Cambridge, Mass., 1971; MD, U. Pa., Phila., 1977; MPH, U. Calif., Berkeley, 1979, JD, 1983. Diplomate Am. Bd. Family Medicine, 1986. Intern pediatrics Children's Hosp. Nat. Med. Ctr., Washington, 1977—78; intern, resident family medicine Case Western Res. U./Univ. Hosp., Cleve., 1983—86; program dir. Coll. Medicine Pa. State U., Hershey, 1988—92; pub. Primary Care Press, Granite Bay, Calif., 1986—; vice chmn., program dir. dept. family medicine SUNY, Stony Brook, NY, 2001—05; med. dir. Sacramento Family Physicians, 2005—06; pub., author Kopes-eHealth.com, Santa Rosa, Calif., 2007—; program dir. Santa Rosa Family Medicine Residency Program, 2007—. Bd. dirs. Sutter Med. Group Redwoods, Santa Rosa. Bd. dirs. Sonoma County Acad. Found. Excellence Medicine, 2007—. Fellow: Am. Acad. Family Physicians (licentiate). Democrat. Unitarian. Avocations: computers, tennis, reading, travel. Office: Santa Rosa Family Medicine Residency 3324 Chanate Rd Santa Rosa CA 95404 Office Phone: 707-576-4079. Office Fax: 707-540-6224.

KOPF, GEORGE MICHAEL, retired ophthalmologist; b. Chilton, Wis., Oct. 20, 1935; s. George and Mary (Schmid) K.; m. Sandra Mary Nolte, Dec. 29, 1962; children: Karen, Jennifer, Nancy. BS, U. Wis., 1958, MD, 1961. Diplomate Am. Bd. Ophthalmology. Intern Luther Hosp., Eau Claire, Wis., 1961-62; resident Milw. County Hosp., 1962-63, Detroit Gen. Hosp., 1965-68; ophthalmologist pvt. practice, Zanesville, Ohio, 1968—; ret., 1999. Mem. med. staff Bethesda Hosp., Zanesville; mem. med. Staff Good Samaritan Med. Ctr., Zanesville, pres., 1978, sec. bd. dirs., 1986-96. Capt. USAF, 1963-65. Fellow ACS, Am. Acad. Ophthalmology; mem. Ohio Ophthalmology Soc. (pres. 1976-77), Muskigum County Acad. Medicine (pres. 1983), Ohio State Med. Assn., Rotary. Republican. Roman Catholic. Avocations: tennis, swimming, hiking, reading, travel. Home: 22030 Longleaf Tr Bonita Springs FL 34135

KOPF, RICHARD G., federal judge; b. 1946; BA, U. Nebr., Kearney, 1969; JD, U. Nebr., Lincoln, 1972. Law clk. to Hon. Donald R. Ross US Ct. Appeals (8th cir.), 1972-74; ptnr. Cook, Kopf & Doyle, Lexington, Nebr., 1974-87; U.S. magistrate judge, 1987-92; fed. judge US Dist. Ct. (Nebr. dist.), 1992—, chief judge, 1999—2004. Mem. ABA, ABA Found., Nebr. State Bar, Nebr. State Bar Found. Office: US Dist Ct 586 US Courthouse 100 Centennial Mall N Lincoln NE 68508-3859 Office Phone: 402-437-5252. Business E-Mail: richard_kopf@ned.uscourts.gov.

KOPIELSKI, CAMILLE ANN, counseling administrator, volunteer; b. Chgo., Dec. 25; d. John Louis and Martha Ann Filar; m. Stanley Bernard Kopielski, May 14, 1966 (dec.). BA in History, Polit. Sci., St. Mary of the Woods, Ind., 1959; MA in History, Govt., Boston Coll., 1961. Cert. counseling and guidance Northeastern Ill. Nat. Bd. Cert. Counselors Assn., Chgo. Counselor, tchr. Carl Schurz HS, Chgo., 1960—93. Sec. Secondary Sch. Counselors Assn., Chgo., 1980—97; chmn. North Ctrl. Accrediting Assoc. Sch. Cmty. Team, Chgo., 1986—93; Eucharistic minister coord. Our Lady of Wayside, Arlington Heights, 1989—; trustee Holy Trinity High Sch., Chgo., 1998—; bd. mem. Gordon Tech. H.S. Judge nat. spelling bee Polish Nat. Alliance, 1994—; v.p. ill. divsn. Polish Am. Congress, 1985—2004, 2006—, nat. dir., 1990—2004, 2006, bd. mem., Am. Coun. Polish Culture, 2004—; page Nat. Polit. Conv., Ill., 1952—56; chair Chgo. Intercollegiate Coun. Scholarship Com., 1960—; treas. Polish Mus. Am., Chgo., 1989—; dir. Copernicus Found., Chgo., 1998—2000, Legion Young Polish Women, Chgo., 1999—2000; pres. Coalition Polish Am. Women, Polit. Advancement, Chgo., 1998—2000; bd. mem. Lira Ensemble, Chgo., 2002—. Bishop Abramowicz Sem. Bd., Chgo., 2003—; adv. council Polish Nat. Alliance Dist. 12,13, Chgo., 1999—; adv. State Congl. Ethic Cmty., Chgo., 2001—; audit mem. PNA Women's Div. Dist. 13, Chgo., 1998—, PNA Welfare Assoc, Chgo., 2000—; audit com. Polish Constn. Day Parade, Chgo., 2001—; pres. Polish Women's Civic Club, 1994—98, 2002—; bd. mem. Polish Am. Leadership Assn.; treas. Coun. 91 PNA, 1991—; nat. dir. Polish Am. Congress, Chgo., 2006—; bd. mem. Pope John Paul II Jubilee, Chgo., 2003; judge nat. spelling bee Polish Women's Alliance, 2000; mem. White House Conf. Drugs Edn., Chgo., 1995. Mem.: Am. Assn. Friends Kosciuszco, Windows Wayside, Coun. Educator Polonia, Ill. Congress Parent Tchrs. (life), Polish Falcons, Polish Women's Alliance, Polish Roman Catholic Union Am., Polish Nat. Alliance (vice chmn. book conv. 1994, judge 1998—2003, pres. Love of Fatherland Soc. 2001—), Polish Arts Club Chgo., St. Mary of the Woods Coll. Chgo. Club (bd. mem. 1997—), Order Malta (dame). Roman Catholic. Achievements include development of 1st Polish Bilingual program, Carl Schurz HS, 1975; Polish Am. Heritage Month, 1985-2002; coordinating Youth career conference, U. Ill., 1998; founder Polish Honor Soc., 2001.

KOPKO, KIMBERLY ANN, psychologist, researcher; d. Michael Francis and Gloria Jean Kalman; m. Edward Eugene Kopko, Aug. 9, 1992; 1 child, Spencer Randall. BA, Brown U., 1998; MEd, Harvard U., 2000; PhD, Cornell U., 2005. Tchg. asst. Brown U., Providence, 1995; rsch. asst. Butler Psychiat. Hosp., Providence, 1995, E.P. Bradley Hosp. Devel. Psychopathology Rsch. Ctr., Providence, 1996—98, Harvard Family Rsch. Project, Cambridge, Mass., 1999, Cornell U., Ithaca, NY, 2000, tchg. asst., 2000—05, rsch. supr., 2003—04; fellow Cornell Employment and Family Careers Inst., Ithaca, 2001—03; predoctoral fellow Cornell Inst. Rsch. on Children, Ithaca, 2004; rsch. asst. Columbia U., NYC, 2005—; asst. prof. Ithaca Coll., NY, 2006—. Cons. Dr. Kopko Parenting, Ithaca, 2005—; parenting educator Cornell Coop. Ext., Ithaca, 2005—. Parent rep. Immaculate Conception Sch., Ithaca, 2000—. Grantee, Cornell U., 2004. Mem.: APA (assoc.; mem. divsn. 7 devel. psychology), Assn. Family and Conciliation Cts., Soc. Rsch. in Child Devel. (assoc.), Harvard Club (life), Sigma Xi (assoc.), Phi Beta Kappa (life). Home Phone: 607-256-7459; Office Phone: 607-273-1811. Personal E-mail: kak33@cornell.edu. E-mail: kak@drkopkoparenting.com.

KOPLAN, STEPHEN, former federal official; m. Harriet Koplan; children: Michael, Bruce, David, Adam. BA, Brandeis U., 1957; JD, Boston U.; LLM in Taxation, NYU. Bar: Mass., DC. Prosecutor tax divsn. US Dept. Justice, atty. civil rights divsn; legislative rep. tax and internat. trade issues AFL-CIO; staff atty. US Senator Lee Metcalf; gen. counsel post office and civil svc. com. US Senate; v.p. governmental affairs Joseph E. Seagram & Sons, Inc.; principal Bayh & Connaughton, Washington, McNair Law Firm, Washington; dir. governmental and conservation affairs Safari Club Internat.; commr. US Internat. Trade Commn., 1998—, chmn., 2000—02, 2004—06. Democrat.

KOPLEWICZ, HAROLD SAMUEL, child and adolescent psychiatrist; b. Bklyn., Jan. 12, 1953; s. Joseph and Romana (Magid) K.; m. Linda Jane Sirow, June 22, 1980; children: Joshua, Adam, Sam. BS, U. Md., 1973; MD, Albert Einstein Coll. of Medicine, 1978. bd. cert. Psychiatry, Neurology in Psychiatry; Diplomate Am. Bd. Psychiatry and Neurology, 1983, Am. Bd. Child Psychiatry, 1984. Med. dir. preschool hyperactivity program NY State Psychiat. Inst., NYC, 1982-85, med. dir. children's anxiety clinic, 1983-86; dir. gen. residency tng. child psychiatry Columbia Coll. Physicians and Surgeons, NYC, 1985-86; chief divsn. child and adolescent psychiatry Schneider Children's Hosp. and Hillside Hosp. of

L.I. Jewish Med. Ctr., NYC, 1986-96; editor Youth Mental Health Update, 1989-96; assoc. prof. psychiatry Albert Einstein Coll. Medicine, NYC, 1991-96; dir. child and adolescent psychology divsn. NYU Med. Ctr./Bellevue Hosp. Ctr., NYC, 1996—; prof. clin. psychiatry and pediatrics, vice chmn. psychiatry NYU Sch. Medicine, 1996—2006, founder, dir. NYU Child Study Ctr., 1997—, Arnold and Debbie Simon prof. child and adolescent psychiatry, prof. pediatrics, 2000—, chmn., dept. child and adolescent psychiatry, 2006—. Cons. Riverdale Cmty. Ctr., 1981-86, The Dalton Sch., 1991-96, The N.Y. Infirmary, 1991, The Family Acad., 1991-96, Jewish Child Care Assn., 1992-96, Health Edn. Task Force, Roslyn Sch. Dist., 1993-96; dir. Nat. Child Mental Health Inst., 1999—; Richard B. Richter vis. prof. in child psychiatry Ind. U., 2005. Author: It's Nobody's Fault: New Hope and Help for Difficult Children and Their Parents, 1996, Childhood Revealed: Art Expressing Pain, Hope and Discovery, 1999, Trubulent Times Prophetic Dreams, 2000, More Than Moody: Recognizing and Treating Adolescent Depression, 2002; editor NYU Child Study Ctr. Letter, 1996—; editor-in-chief: Jour. Child and Adolescent Psychopharmacology, 1997—; mem. adv. bd. Parents Mag., 1996—, Parents In Action, 1996—; mem. profl. adv. bd. Big Apple Parent Paper, 1995—, NYC chpt. Nat. Alliance for Mentally Ill, 2001—. Bd. dirs. Raoul Wallenberg New Leadership Soc., 1983-87, Cmty. Mainstreaming Assocs., 1990; chmn. Simon Wiesenthal Ctr., 1984-86; commr. NY State Commn. for Study of Youth Crime and Violence and Reform of the Juvenile Justice Sys., 1993-96; prin. investigator Developing Innovative Mental Health Care Delivery for Adolescents, Hewlett-Woodmere Sch. Dist., 1992; adv. bd. Our Children's Found., 1996-97. Recipient Hulse award NY Coun. Child and Adolescent Psychiatry, 1995, Exemplary Psychiatrist award Nat. Alliance Mentally Ill, 1997, Contbns. to Humanity award Marymount Manhattan Coll., 1999, Am. Grand Hope award 2000. Fellow Am. Acad. Child and Adolescent Psychiatry (Reiger award 1997), Am. Psychiat. Assn.; mem. Soc. Profs. Child and Adolescent Psychiatry, Am. Bd. Psychiatry and Neurology (examiner 1988-98), Nat. Bd. Med. Examiners (mem. psychiatry com. 1993-96), Nat. Found. Depressive Illness (nat. bd. dirs. 1992—), Mental Health Assn. of N.Y. (profl. adv. bd. 1997—). Office: NYU Child Study Ctr 577 1st Ave New York NY 10016 Fax: 212-263-0484. E-mail: harold.koplewicz@nyumc.org.

KOPLIK, MICHAEL R., sales representation company executive; s. Perry H Koplik. Sales mgr. Castle & Overton Inc., NYC, 1957—60; dir., v.p. Perry H. Koplik & Sons Inc., NYC, 1960—78, pres., CEO, 1978—2001, 2003—. Office: Perry H Koplik & Sons Inc 450 Park Ave New York NY 10022-2605

KOPLIN, BERNICE J., lawyer; b. Lynn, Mass., Oct. 6, 1943; d. Harold and Rita (Cohen) Berzof; m. Joseph K. Koplin, June 4, 1972; children: Jonathan, Joshua. BA, Douglass Coll., 1965; MA, Brandeis U., 1970; MS, Simmons Coll., 1972; JD, Temple U., 1981, LLM in Taxation, 1984, LLM in Trial Advocacy, 1994. Bar: Pa. 1981, U.S. Dist. Ct. (ea. dist.) Pa. 1982, U.S. Tax Ct. 1982, U.S. Ct. Appeals (3d cir.) 1982, U.S. Ct. Claims 1986, U.S. Supreme Ct. 1986, D.C. 1987, Fla. 1987, N.J. 1987, N.Y. 1993. Assoc. Meltzer & Schiffrin, Phila., 1981-82; sole practice Phila., 1982-83, 86-88; ptnr. Goldman, Koplin & Marshall, P.C., Phila., 1983-86, Levine and Koplin, Phila., 1988-91, Schachtel, Gerstley, Levine & Koplin, Phila., 1991—. Enrolled agt. IRS. Contbr. articles to profl. jours. Mem. Ctl. Women's Com., Phila. Orch., 1978—, chmn., 2001—; bd. dirs. Settlement Music Sch., Phila., 1985-1987. Mem. ABA, Pa. Bar Assn., N.J. Bar Assn., Fla. Bar Assn., Phila. Bar Assn., Camden County Bar Assn., Cosmopolitan Club (Phila., bd. govs. 1985-87, chmn. fin. com. 1985-1987). Jewish. Avocation: bird watching. Home: 251 Saint Josephs Way Philadelphia PA 19106-3806 Office: 1288 Rt 73 S Ste 301 Mount Laurel NJ 08054 also: 123 S Broad St Ste 2170 Philadelphia PA 19109

KOPLOVITZ, KAY, television network executive; b. Milw., Apr. 11, 1945; d. William E. and Jane T. Smith; m. William C. Koplovitz Jr., Apr. 17, 1971. BS, U. Wis., 1967; MA in Comms., Mich. State U., 1968. Radio and TV producer, dir. Sta. WTMJ-TV, Milw., 1967; editor Comm. Satellite Corp., Washington, 1968-72; dir. cmty. svc. UA Columbia Cablevision, Oakland, NJ, 1973-75; v.p., exec. dir. UA Columbia Satellite Services Inc., Oakland, NJ, 1977-80; founder, chmn., CEO USA Networks and Sci-Fi Channel, NYC, 1977—98; CEO Koplovitz & Co., NYC, 1998—; chmn. Reality Central, 2003—; non-exec. chmn. Liz Claiborne Inc., NYC, 2006—. Founder Springboard 2000; bd. dirs. Springboard Enterprises, Liz Claiborne Inc., 1992—, Instinet. Mem. bd. overseers NYU Grad. Sch. Bus., 1984-90; bd. dir. Nat. Jr. Achievement, 1986-1996. Named to Entrepreneur Hall of Fame, Babson Coll., 2001, Cable Hall of Fame, 2001, Broadcasting Mag. Hall of Fame, 1992; recipient Outstanding Alumnus award, Mich. State U. Grad. Sch. Bus., 1985, Oustanding Corp. Social Responsibility, CUNY, 1986, Women Who Run the World award, Sara Lee Corp., 1987, Muse award, N.Y. Women in Film and TV, 1992, Ellis Island medal of honor, 1993, Crystal award, Women in Film, 1993. Mem.: Com. of 200, Nat. Acad. Cable Programming (bd. dirs. 1984—87), Cable Advt. Bur. (bd. dirs., exec. com., treas. 1981—87, Chmn.'s award for leadership 1987), Women in Cable (founding bd. dirs., membership chmn. 1979—80, v.p. 1981—82, pres. 1982—83), Nat. Acad. TV Arts and Scis. (chmn. 1994—97, bd. dirs. 1984—93), Internat. Coun., Advt. Coun. Inc. (chmn. 1992—93, bd. dirs. 1985—94), Nat. Cable TV Assn. (bd. dirs. 1984—98), N.Y.C. Partnership (bd. dirs. 1987—), Womens Forum. Avocations: tennis, skiing, travel. Office: Koplovitz & Co 30 Rockefeller Ctr 27th Fl New York NY 10112 E-mail: kay@koplovitz.com.*

KOPLOW, ELLEN, lawyer, brokerage house executive; BA, Univ. Md.; JD cum laude, Univ. Balt. Mng. principal Miles & Stockbridge, Columbia, Md.; dep. gen. counsel Ameritrade Holding Corp., Omaha, 1999—2000, acting gen. counsel, 2000—01, exec. v.p. & gen. counsel, 2001—. Office: Ameritrade Corp First Floor 132 National Business Pkwy Annapolis Junction MD 20701 Office Phone: 402-331-2744. Office Fax: 402-597-7789. Business E-Mail: ekoplow@ameritrade.com.

KOPLOWITZ, STEPHAN, choreographer; b. 1956; Choreographer and dance dir. Packer Collegiate Inst., 1983—2006; dean dance Calif. Inst. the Arts, 2006—. Founding mem. Webbed Feats. Choreographer (multimedia works) seen at Grand Ctr. Terminal, Lincoln Ctr., Bryant Pk., N.Y.C., Nat. History Mus., London, Brit. Lib., Germany. Recipient N.Y. Dance and Performance award for Sustained Achievement in Choreography, 2000, Alpert award, 2004; fellowship, John Simon Guggenheim Meml. Found., 2003.

KOPP, CHARLES GILBERT, lawyer; b. Hartford, Conn., Jan. 10, 1933; s. Henry and Grace (Goldberg) K.; m. Ann Weiss, June 10, 1962 (div. 1963) BA, Amherst Coll., 1955; JD, U. Pa., 1960. Bar: Pa. 1961. Sr. counsel Wolf, Block, Schorr and Solis-Cohen LLP, Phila., 1960—. Vis. lectr. Villanova (Pa.) Univ., 1981. Contbr. articles to profl. jours. Commr. Delaware River Port Authority, 1986-87; co-chmn. select com. of U.S. Embassy, Bern, Switzerland, 1985; mem. Pa. Gov.'s Spl. Tax Commn., 1980; mem. fin. com. Rep. State Com., 1984-98, mem. leadership com.; bd. dirs. Pennsylvanians for Effective Govt., Harrisburg, 1987-99; mem. Pa. Electoral Coll., 1988; mem. adv. bd. region I, Resolution Trust Corp., 1990-93; mem. coun. The Pa. Soc., 1991-98; trustee Thomas Jefferson U. Hosp., 1988—, Pop Warner Little Scholars; mem. adv. bd. PNC, Phila., 1992-2000. 1st lt. USAF, 1955-57. Recipient Pop Warner Gold Football award, 1988. Mem.: ABA, Phila. Bar Assn., Pa. Bar Assn., Greater Phila. C. of C. (exec. com. 1988—96), Vesper Club, Pyramid Club. Republican. Jewish. Home: 210 W Rittenhouse Sq Apt 3306 Philadelphia PA 19103-5780 Office: Wolf Block Schorr and Solis Cohen LLP 1650 Arch St Fl 22 Philadelphia PA 19103-2003

KOPP, EUGENE HOWARD, communications and electrical engineer, consultant; b. NYC, Oct. 1, 1929; s. Jacob and Fanny (Lipschitz) K.; m. Claire Bernstein, Aug. 31, 1950; children: Carolyn, Michael, Paul. B.E.E., CCNY, 1950, M.E.E., 1953; PhD in Engring, UCLA, 1965. Registered profl. engr., Calif. Project engr. Polarad Electronics Corp., Long Island City, NY, 1950-53, Kaye Halbert Corp., Culver City, Calif., 1953-55; chief engr. Precision Radiation Instruments, Inc., Los Angeles, 1955-58; mem. faculty sch. engring. Calif. State U., Los Angeles, 1958-74, assoc. prof., 1962-66, prof., 1966-74, dean engring. Sch., 1967-73; v.p. acad. affairs West Coast U., Los Angeles, 1973-79; sr. scientist Hughes Aircraft Co., 1980-85, mgr. R & D, 1985-93, dir. advanced programs, 1994-95; v.p. mobile satellites Boeing Satellite Sys., 1996-97, chief scientist comml. satellites, 1998—2002; chief scientist homeland security The Boeing Co., 2003—05, chief engr. joint programs, 2006, consulting comm. engr., 2006—. Lectr. evening divsn. CCNY, N.Y.C., 1950-53; lectr. UCLA, 1979-91. Vis. research fellow U. Leeds, Eng., 1966-67 Fellow AIAA (assoc.); mem. IEEE, Tau Beta Pi, Eta Kappa Nu, Pi Tau Sigma. Avocation: flying. Office: PO Box 1351 South Pasadena CA 91031-1351

KOPP, EUGENE PAUL, lawyer; b. Charleston, W.Va., Nov. 20, 1934; s. Eugene Alexander and Virginia Elizabeth (King) K.; m. Katherine Patricia Rogers, July 1, 1967; 1 son, Eugene Paul. BA, U. Notre Dame, 1957, MA, 1958; JD, W.Va. U., 1961. Ba: W.Va. 1961, D.C. 1977, Tex. 1980. Law clk. U.S. Dist. Ct. W.Va., 1961-62; trial atty. Dept. Justice, Washington, 1962-69; dep. dir. USIA, 1973-77, acting dir., 1976-77; assoc. gen. counsel Champlin Petroleum Co., Ft. Worth, 1977-81; v.p. Washington affairs Union Pacific Corp., Washington, 1981-87; dep. dir. U.S. Info. Agy., 1989-93; exec. dir. MFJ Task Force, 1993-94; of counsel Clarendon Assocs., Inc., 1995-97, Ruddy and Muir, 1998—2004; vice chmn. Nexphase Comms., Inc., 2000—01; ptnr. Kopp, Kramer, Quinn LLC, Wash., DC, 2004—; of counsel Sale and Quinn, 2004—. Cons. nat. Security Council, Washington, 1981, mem. transition team, 1980. Mem.: Washington Inst. Fgn. Affairs, DC Bar Assn., Tex. Bar Assn., W.Va. Bar Assn., Dacor Club (Washington), Met. Club (Washington), Belle Haven Country Club. Roman Catholic. Home: 508 Cathedral Dr Alexandria VA 22314-4706 Office Phone: 202-833-4170. Personal E-mail: kopponbeat@aol.com.

KOPP, NANCY KORNBLITH, state official; b. Coral Gables, Fla., Dec. 7, 1943; d. Lester and Barbara M. (Levy) Kornblith; m. Robert E. Kopp, May 3, 1969; children: Emily, Robert E. III. BA with honors, Wellesley Coll., 1965; MA in Govt, U. Chgo., 1968; LittD (hon.), Hood Coll., 1988; LHD (hon.), Towson U., 2001; JD (hon.), U. Md., Balt., 2001. Instr. polit. sci. U. Ill., 1968-69; staff spl. subcom. on edn. U.S. Ho. of Reps., Washington, 1970-71; legis. staff Md. Gen. Assembly, Annapolis, 1971-74; mem. Md. Ho. of Dels., 1974—2002, spkr. pro tem, 1991-93, chmn. appropriations subcom on edn. and devel., chmn. spending affordability joint com.; state treas. State of Md., Annapolis, 2002—. Chmn. Md. Coll. Savings Plans; appointed to Nat. Assessment governing governing; treas. So. Regional Edn. Bd., chair, commn. on ednl. quality, mem. exec. com., Nat. Conf. of State Legis. Mem. State Retirement and Pension Bd.; vice chmn. Capital Debt Affordability Com., chmn.; mem. Nat. Assessment Governing Bd., Md. Supplemental Retirement Bd., Md. Higher Edn. Investment Bd. Mem.: Nat, Assn. State Auditors, Comptrollers and Treasurers (treas.), N.E. State Treas. Assn. (chmn. capital debt affordability com., vice chmn. state ret. and pension bd.). Democrat. Jewish. Office: Goldstein Treasury Bldg 80 Calvert St Annapolis MD 21401 Office Phone: 410-260-7160. E-mail: nkopp@treasurer.state.md.us.*

KOPP, RICHARD EDGAR, electrical engineer; b. Bklyn., July 12, 1931; s. Edgar A. and Anna M. (Barto) K.; m. Elaine Hecker, June 14, 1953; children: Debra, Richard (dec.), Lisa, Barbara. BEE, Poly. Inst. Bklyn., 1953, MS, 1957, DEE, 1960. Rsch. engr. Grumman Aerospace Corp., Bethpage, NY, 1953-58, head computing rsch. group, 1958-65, head systems rsch. lab., 1965-70, dir. systems scis. rsch., 1970-89, dir. sci. adv. bd., 1989-90, pvt. cons., 1990—. Mem. adv. com. Poly. Inst. Imaging Scis.; adj. prof. Poly. Inst. Bklyn., 1961-70. Contbr. articles to profl. jours. Fellow AIAA (assoc.); mem. IEEE (sr.). Home: 119 Constantine Way Mount Sinai NY 11766 Personal E-mail: rekopp@aol.com.

KOPP, STEPHEN JAMES, academic administrator; m. Jane Kopp; children: Adam, Elizabeth. BS, U. Notre Dame, 1973; PhD in Physiology and Biophysics, U. Ill., Chgo., 1976. Postdoctoral fellow dept. physiology St. Louis U., 1976-77; rsch. assoc. dept. biol. chemistry U. Ill. Med. Ctr., Chgo., 1977-78, NIH postdoctoral fellow, 1979-85; asst. dir. Magnetic Resonance Lab. Chgo. Coll. Ostepathic Medicine, 1979-85, acting dean Allied Health Programs Downers Grove, Ill., 1991-92, dean Coll. Allied Health Professions, 1992-97, chmn. dept. physiology, 1983-94; dean Herbert H. and Grace A. Dow Coll. Health Professions Ctrl. Mich. U., Mt. Pleasant, 1997; founding dean Coll. Allied Health Professions Midwestern U.; provost Ohio State U., Athens, 2002—04; spl, asst. to chancellor Ohio Bd. Regents; pres. Marshall U., Huntington, W.Va., 2005—. Cons. MITRE Corp., McClean, Va., 1980-81. Contbr. articles to profl. jours. Named Outstanding Young Men Am., 1980; Granite City Steel Rsch. fellow, 1975. Mem. Am. Osteopathic Assn. (evaluator 1996-98). Office: Marshall U Office of Pres One John Marshall Dr Huntington WV 25755 Office Phone: 304-696-2300. E-mail: kopp@marshall.edu.*

KOPP, WENDY, educational association administrator; b. Austin, Tex., June 29, 1967; m. Richard Barth; 3 children. BA, Princeton U., 1998, degree (hon.), 2000, Conn. Coll., 1995, Drew U., 1995, Smith Coll., 2001, Pace U., 2004, Mercy Coll., 2004. Founder, pres. Teach For America, NYC, 1989—. Mem. Pres. Coun. on Svc. and Civic Participation, 2003—; adv. bd. mem. Ctr. Pub. Leadership, Kennedy Sch. Govt., Harvard U., 2003—, Nat. Coun. on Tchr. Quality; bd. dirs. New Tchr. Project, Learning Project, Kipp Acad. Author: One Day, All Children: The Unlikely Triumph of Teach For America and What I Learned Along the Way, 2001. Named Woman of Yr., Glamour mag., 1990; named to Time Mag. Roster of Am. Most Promising Leaders Under 40, 1994; recipient Jefferson Award for Pub. Svcs., 1991, Kilby Young Innovator award, 1991, Woodrow Wilson award, 1993, Aetna's Voice of Conscience award, 1994, Citizen Activist award, Gleitsman Found., 1994, Children's Champion Award, Child mag., 2003, Clinton Ctr. Award for Leadership and Nat. Svc., 2003, Outstanding Social Entrepreneur Award, Schwab Found., 2003, Golden Plate award, Acad. Achievement, 2006; Nat. Acad. fellow, 1990. Office: Teach For America 315 W 36th St 7th Fl New York NY 10018-6404 Office Phone: 212-279-2080. Office Fax: 212-279-2081.*

KOPPEL, MICHAEL G., retail executive; B in acctg., Univ. Conn. Fin. mgmt. positions May Dept. Stores, 1984—88, v.p., controller G. Fox div., 1988—93, v.p., controller Filene's div., 1993—97; CFO Lids Corp., 1997—98; COO CML Group, 1998—99; v.p., controller, prin. acctg. officer Nordstrom Inc., Seattle, 1999—2001, exec. v.p., CFO, 2001—. Office: Nordstrom Inc 1617 6th Ave Seattle WA 98101*

KOPPEL, ROSS, sociology professor, researcher; b. NYC, Aug. 18, 1946; s. Noah and Nita Koppel; m. Margaret Lee Shope, Dec. 15, 1990; children: Tobias Noah, Jonah Andreas. BA, MA, Ph.D, Temple U., Phila, 1964—80. Cert. clin. sociologist Am. Assn. for Applied and Clin. Sociologists, 1998. Rsch. dir. Temple U., Phila., 1981—83, PNR and Assoc., Roslyn, Pa., 1983—85; adj. prof. sociology dept. U. Pa., Phila., 1994—; prin. investigator: study of hospitals and medication errors Sch. of Medicine, Univ. of Pa., Phila., 2001—. Pres. Social Rsch. Corp., Phila., 1985—. Contbr. articles to profl. jours. Recipient Sociol. Practice award, Soc. of Applied Sociology, 2002, William F. Whyte award, Am. Sociology Assn.; fellow, NIMH, 1968—72, NSF, 1966. Mem.: Sociol. Practice Assn. (pres. 2002—), Am. Sociol. Assoc. Achievements include development of new ways of understanding costs of Alztheimer's Disease; research in information technology and medical errors. Office: Social Research Corporation PO Box 15 Wyncote PA 19095 Office Phone: 215-576-8221.

KOPPEL, TED, newscaster; b. Lancashire, Eng., Feb. 8, 1940; arrived in US, 1953; m. Grace Anne Dorney, 1963; children: Andrea, Deirdre, Andrew, Tara. BA in speech, Syracuse U., 1960; MA in mass comm. rsch. & polit. sci., Stanford U., 1962. News corr., writer Sta.-WMCA, NYC, 1963; with ABC News, 1963—2005, former gen. assignment corr., former Vietnam war correspondent, Miami bur. chief, 1968—69, Hong Kong bur. chief, 1969—71, chief diplomatic corr., 1971—80, anchor The ABC Saturday Night News, 1975—77, anchor Nightline, 1980—2005, former mng. editor; mng. editor The Discovery Channel, 2006—; and op-ed page contbr. NY Times, 2006—. Corr. for TV spls. including The People of People's China, 1973, Kissinger: Action Biography, 1974, Second to None, 1979, The Koppel Reports, 1988—90; contbr. columnist NY Times, 2006—. Co-editor: The Wit and Wisdom of Adlai Stevenson, 1965; co-author (with Marvin Kalb): In The National Interest, 1977; author: Nightline: History in the Making and the Making of Television, 1996. Named best interviewer on radio or TV, Washington Journalism Review, 1987, Chevalier de l'Ordre des Arts et des Lettres, Republic of France, 1994, Broadcaster of Yr., Internat. TV and Radio Soc.; named to Broadcasting Hall of Fame; recipient George Polk Awards for TV reporting, 1981, George Polk Awards for network TV reporting, 1985, Gold Baton, du-Pont Columbia awards, 1985, Sol Taishoff Award for Excellence in Broadcast Journalism, Nat. Press Found., 1984, Fred Friendly First Amendment award, Quinnipiac Coll., 1997, 41 Emmy awards, Acad. TV Arts and Scis., 8 George Foster Peabody awards, 10 duPont-Columbia Awards, 9 previous Overseas Press Club awards, plus President's award for dedication and support of foreign news coverage, 2006, 2 Sigma Delta Chi awards, Soc. Profl. Journalists, Goldsmith Lifetime Achievement award for Excellence in Journalism, Joan Shorenstein Barone Ctr. on the Press, Politics and Pub. Policy, Harvard Univ., Gabriel Personal Achievement award, Nat. Catholic Assn. of Broadcasters and Communicators, numerous others. Office: Discovery Communications 1 Discovery Pl Silver Spring MD 20910

KOPPELMAN, ANDREW MARTIN MAYER, law educator; b. Nyack, NY, Aug. 29, 1957; s. George Irving and Ruby Etta (Lee) K.; m. Valerie Jane Quinn, June 24, 1989; children: John Miles Isidore, Georgina Isabella, Emme Sophia. AB, U. Chgo., 1979; MA in Polit. Sci., Yale U., 1986, JD, 1989, PhD, 1991. Bar: Conn. 1990, NY 1991. Law clk. to Chief Justice Ellen A. Peters conn. Supreme Ct., 1991—92; asst. prof. politics Princeton U., NJ, 1992—97; asst. prof. law and polit. sci. Northwestern U., Chgo., 1997—2000, assoc. prof., 2000—03, George C. Dix prof. constitutional law, 2000—01, prof. law, 2003—07, John Paul Stevens prof. law and polit. sci., 2007—. Vis. prof. law U. Tex. at Austin, 1997. Author: Antidiscrimination Law and Social Equality, 1996 (Myers Center Award, 1997), The Gay Rights Question in Contemporary American Law, 2002, Same Sex, Different States: When Same-Sex Marriages Cross State Lines, 2006; contbr. articles to profl. jours. Summer rsch. fellow Ctr. for Studies in Law, Econs. and Pub. Policy Yale U., 1988, 90, 91, NEH summer rsch. stipend fellow, 1993, Harvard U. Program in Ethics and Professions fellow, 1994-95. Office: Northwestern U Sch Law 357 E Chicago Ave Chicago IL 60611 Business E-Mail: akoppelman@northwestern.edu.

KOPPELMAN, CHAIM, artist, educator; b. Bklyn., Nov. 17, 1920; s. Samuel and Sadie (Mondlin) K.; m. Dorothy Myers, Feb. 13, 1943; 1 child, Ann. Student, Bklyn. Coll., 1938, Am. Artists Sch., 1939; student Aesthetic Realism, with Eli Siegel, 1940-78; student, Art Coll. Western Eng., Bristol, 1944, Ecole des Beaux-Arts, Rheims, 1945, Art Students League, 1946, Amedée Ozenfant Sch., 1946-49; student Aesthetic Realism, with Ellen Reiss, 1978—. Art instr. N.Y. U., 1947-55, N.Y. State U., New Paltz, 1952-58; instr. Sch. Visual Arts, NYC, 1959—. Cons. Aesthetic Realism Found., N.Y.C., 1971— Author: This is the Way I See Aesthetic Realism, 1969; illustrator: Damned Welcome, Aesthetic Realism Maxims (by Eli Siegel), 1972; contbr. articles to profl. jours.; Bibliographies of his work The Indignant Eye (Ralph Shikes), 1969, The New Humanism (Barry Schwartz), 1974, The Art of the Print (Fritz Eichenberg), 1976, American Prints and Printmakers (Una Johnson), 1980, Hilla Rebay: In Search of the Spirit in Art (Joan Lukach), 1983; one man shows include Asso. Am. Artists Gallery, 1973, Terrain Gallery, N.Y.C., 1974, 83, Warwick (Eng.) Gallery, 1975, Merida Rapp Graphics, Louisville, 1985, Print Club, Phila., Beatrice Conde Gallery, 2000, others; group shows include Purdue U., 1972, Utah State U., 1972, Arte Fiera, Bologna, 1978, NAD, N.Y.C., 1983, Print Club, Phila., 1988, Alternative Mus., N.Y.C., 1988, Art Mus., Bogota, 1996; represented in permanent collections Victoria and Albert Mus., London, Mus. Fine Arts, Caracas, Venezuela, Mus. Modern Art, N.Y.C., Met. Mus. Art, N.Y.C., Library of Congress, Washington, Los Angeles County Mus. Art, Phila. Mus. Art, Guggenheim Mus., others; sculptor Eli Siegel Meml., Druid Hill Park, Balt., 2002. Served with USAF, 1942-45. Decorated Bronze Star; recipient N.Y. State Creative Artists Pub. Svc. award, 1976, prize Soc. Am. Graphic Artists, Fabri prize Nat. Acad. Ann., 1989, Cook prize, 1998, Lifetime Achievement award Soc. Am. Graphic Artists, 2004, Peace Tower award Whitney Biennial, 2006; Louis Comfort Tiffany grantee, 1956, 59, Documenta II, Kassel, 1961. Mem. Nat. Acad. Design. Home and Office: 498 Broome St New York NY 10013-2213 Office Phone: 212-966-0015. Personal E-mail: pierodella@aol.com. *I learned from Eli Siegel, the great American poet and critic, the most important thing an artist can know-this Aesthetic Realism statement: "All beauty is a making one of opposities and the making one of opposites is what we are going after in ourselves." Every artist is trying to put together opposites such as sameness and difference, warm and cool, freedom and order, and every person and artist is trying to put these same opposites together in his life.*

KOPPELMAN, CHARLES A., record company executive; Chmn. O.Y., NYC; chmn., CEO EMI Records Group, NYC, 1994—97, EMI Music Publishing, 1990—94, CAK Entertainment Co.; former dir., chmn. Steve Madden Ltd., 2000—04; cons. Martha Stewart Living Omnimedia, Inc., 2003—, vice chmn., 2003—05, chmn., 2005—. Bd. trustees Hofstra U. Dean's Coun. Hofstra Law Sch. Recipient Abe Olman Publishers award, Songwriters Hall of Fame, Humanitarian of the Year, T.J. Martell Found. Leukemia, Cancer and AIDS Rsch. Achievements include formerly singer with trio Ivy; song previewer, then with Don Kirshner as dir. of music pub. co. Office: Martha Stewart Living Omnimedia Inc 11 W 42nd St New York NY 10036 Office Phone: 212-827-8000. Office Fax: 212-827-8204.

KOPPELMAN, DOROTHY MYERS, artist, consultant; b. NYC, June 13, 1920; d. Harry Walter and May (Chalmers) Myers; m. Chaim Koppelman, Feb. 13, 1943; 1 child, Ann. Student, Bklyn. Coll., 1938-42, Am. Artists Sch., 1940-42, Art Students League, 1942; student of Aesthetic Realism, with Eli Siegel, 1942-78, with Ellen Reiss, 1978—. Instr. art Bklyn. Coll., 1952-75; dir. Terrain Gallery, NYC, 1955-83, Visual Arts Gallery., Sch. Visual Arts, 1961-62; pres. Aesthetic Realism Found., 1973-85, cons., 1973—. Instr. Nat. Acad. Sch. of Design, 1988—89, 1996, 98. One-woman shows include Terrain Gallery, 1961, Rina Gallery, Jersey City, 1961, Atlantic Gallery, 1999; exhibited in group shows at Mus. Modern Art, N.Y.C., 1962, Balt. Mus., 1962, Bklyn. Mus., 1962, N.J. State Mus., Jersey City, 1959, San Francisco Art Inst., 1961-62, 65, Butler Art Inst., Youngstown, Ohio, 1965, 1966, Nat. Acad. of Design Juried Ann., 1986, 90, 2000, Swiss Inst., N.Y.C., Susan Teller Gallery, N.Y.C., 1993, 95, Drawing Ctr., N.Y.C., Audubon Soc. ann., N.Y.C., 1995-96, 98, Chuck Levitan Gallery, N.Y.C., 1996, Puffin Room, 1996, Washington Square East Gallery, N.Y.C., 1992, 96, Am. Soc. Contemporary Artists Anns., 1994-2006, Atlantic Gallery, 1998-2006, Beatrice Conde Gallery, 2000, Terrain

Gallery, 2001, 02, 03,04, 05, Sarah Lawrence Gallery, 2001, Denise Bibro Gallery, 2001, Peace Tower Whitney Mus. Am. Art, 2006; represented in permanent collections Hampton U., Nat. Mus. Women in the Arts, Washington, Rosenzweig Mus., Durham, NC, Savannah Coll. Art and Design, Washington County Mus. Art, Md., Libr. Congress, Washington, N.Y. Hist. Soc.; author Poems and Prints, 2000; co-author: Aesthetic Realism: We Have Been There - Six Artists, 1969; illustrator Children's Guide to Parents (by Eli Siegel), 1971, 2d edit., 2003. Recipient Theresa Lindner award for painting ASCA, 1996, Clara Shainness award for painting, 1999; Tiffany grantee for painting, 1965. Home: 498 Broome St New York NY 10013-2213 Office: Aesthetic Realism Found Inc 141 Greene St New York NY 10012-3201 Personal E-mail: pierodella@aol.com.

KOPPELMAN, LEE EDWARD, regional planner, educator; b. NYC, May 19, 1927; s. Max and Madelyn Judith (Eisenberg) K.; m. Constance E. Lowinger, June 18, 1948; children: Leslie, Claudia, Laurel, Keith. BEE, CCNY, 1950; MS, Pratt Inst., 1964; D in Pub. Adminstrn., NYU, 1970; LLD, L.I. U., 1978; DHL, Dowling U., 1991. Cert. landscape architect, NY; cert. profl. planner, NJ. Cons. on site planning and landscape architecture, 1950-60; dir. planning Suffolk County Planning Dept., 1960-88; exec. dir. LI Regional Planning Bd., 1965—; leading prof. polit. sci., dir. ctr. regional policy studies SUNY, Stony Brook, 1967—. Adj. prof. environ. sci. Syracuse U., 1976-83; cons. US Dept. Housing and Urban Devel., 1972-78, UN on Land Use and Coastal Zone Planning; mem. Coastal Zone Mgmt. Adv. Com., 1973-75, Nassau/Suffolk Comprehensive Health Planning Council, Melville, NY, 1973-76, Nat. Shoreline Erosion Adv. Panel, 1974-81; exec. dir. tax relief on LI Bi-County State Commn., 1991-92; adv. coun. Sch. of Art, Architecture and Planning Cornell Univ., 1995—. Co-author: Planning Design Criteria, 1968 (3rd edit. 1981), Housing: Planning and Design, 1974, A Methodology to Achieve the Integration of Coastal Zone Science and Regional Planning, 1974, The Urban Sea: Long Island Sound, 1976, Site Planning Criteria, 1978, Long Island Comprehensive Waste Treatment Management Plan, Vol. 1 and 2, 1979, Time Saver Standards for Site Planning, 1982, Long Island Segment of the Nationwide Urban Runoff Program, 1982, Financing Government on Long Island, 1992, The Long Island Comprehensive Special Groundwater Protection Area Plan, 1992, Airport Joint Use Feasibility Study: Calverton Airport, 1993, Financing Government on Long Island, working paper, vols. 1, 2, and 3, 1993, Groundwater and Land Use Planning Experience from North Am., 1996, Town of East Hampton comprehensive Plan, 2002, Fire Island National Seashore-1964-2004: An Adminstrative History, 2005, Third Nassau-Suffolk Comprehensive Land Use Plan 2000-2030, 2007. Recipient cert. of tribute Temp. State Commn. on Water Resources Planning, 1964, career achievement medal Engring. and Archtl. Alumni CCNY, 1977, Disting Alumnus award NYU, 1985, medal of honor LI Assn., 1987, Lone Eagle award Pub. Rels. Soc. Am., 1987, Disting. Leadership award nat. honors program Am. Planning Assn., 1989, Disting. Svc. award NY met. chpt. Am. Planning Assn., 2000, Disting. Svc. medal Found. for LI State Parks, 2001, Career Achievement medal, Pratt Inst. Sch. of Arch.; Paul Harris fellow, 2002; named Citizen of Yr. LI chpt. NSPE, 1983; nominee Pres.'s Medal of Freedom, Congressman Steve Israel, 2005. Mem. Am. Inst. Architects (hon.), Am. Inst. Planners, NY State County Planners Assn. (pres. 1967-68), Internat. Fedn. Planning and Housing, Assn. Architecture and Engr., Sigma Xi. Home: 2 Dune Ct East Setauket NY 11733-1527 Office: SUNY Ctr Regional Policy Studies Stony Brook NY 11794-0001 Office Phone: 631-632-9021.

KOPPERUD, MARILYN SUE, music educator; b. Windom, Minn., Aug. 6, 1948; d. William Vaupel and Doris Niffenegger; children: Bryce, Joel. MusB in Edn., Morningside Coll., 1970; cert. in Orff-Schulwerk, U. Denver, 1982; MusM in Edn., U. No. Colo., 1991. Lic. tchr. Colo. Tchr. music Storden-Jeffers (Minn.) Schs., 1972—74, Fulda (Minn.) Pub. Schs., 1974—82, Adams Sch. Dist., Northglenn, Colo., 1982—. Asst. prof. music U. No. Colo., Greeley, Colo., 1990—91; organist Northglenn (Colo.) Meth. Ch., 1988—91; dir. music, organist United Ch. Christ, Denver, 1992—98, St. John Luth. Ch., Thornton, 1998—2003, Messiah Luth. Ch., Denver, 2003—; freelance pianist, accompanist, Denver, 1988—. Vol. Habitat for Humanity, Denver, 1994. Mem.: NEA, Am. Guild Organists, Am. Choral Dirs. Assn., Phi Kappa Lambda. Democrat. Avocations: hiking, bicycling, reading, travel, shopping. Home: 11284 Decatar Cir Westminster CO 80234 E-mail: mskopperud@msn.com.

KOPPES, CLAYTON R., academic administrator; s. Clinton and Effie Koppes. Grad., Bethel Coll., 1967; MA, Emory Coll., 1968; PhD, U. Kans., 1974. Sr. rsch. fellow Calif. Inst. Tech.; mem. faculty Oberlin Coll., 1978—. Irvin E. Houck prof. humanities, 1986—91, dean Coll. Arts and Scis., 1996—2004, v.p. acad. affairs, provost, 2004—05, prof. hist. dept., 2005—. Author: JPL and the American Space Program, 1982 (Dexter prize Soc. for the History of Tech.); co-author: Hollywood Goes to War: How Politics, Profits & Propaganda Shaped World War II Movies, 1987. Office: Oberlin Coll Rice Hall 305 Oberlin OH 44074 Office Phone: 440-775-8317.*

KOPPLE, JOEL D., medical educator; s. Louis A. and Evelyn I. Kopple; m. Madelynn G. Kopple; children: David, Michael, Deborah, Joshua. BS, Northwestern U., 1958; MD, U. Ill., 1962; Doctorate (hon.), P.J. Sfarik U., Kosice, Slovak Republic, 1995, U. Szeged, Hungary, 2002. Diplomate Am. Bd. Internal Medicine, 1969, subspecialty of nephrology Am. Bd. Internal Medicine, 1974, clin. nutrition Am. Bd. Nutrition, 1980, cert. specialist in clin. hypertension Am. Soc. for Hypertension, 2001. Assoc. prof. medicine and pub. health UCLA Sch. Medicine, Torrance, Calif., 1976—78, prof. medicine and pub. health, 1978—; med. investigator VA Wadsworth Med. Ctr., LA, 1976—81; chief divsn. nephrology and hypertension Harbor-UCLA Med. Ctr., Torrance, 1982—. Co-editor: (book) Nutritional Management of Renal Disease; contbr. articles to profl. jours. Past pres. Nat. Kidney Found., 1998—2000; pres. Coun. Am. Kidney Socs., 1998—99, Am. Soc. for Parenteral and Enteral Nutrition, 1990—91, Internat. Soc. for Renal Nutrition and Metabolism, 1991—94, Internat. Fedn. Kidney Foundations, 2000—03; mem. Am. Bd. Nutrition, 1984—90. Recipient David M. Hume Meml. award, Nat. Kidney Found., 1983, Louis Pasteur medal and award, U. Strasbourg, France, 1988, Malpighi medal, U. Messina, Italy, 2000, Robert H. Herman award, Am. Soc. Clin. Nutrition, 2004, Sandor Koranyi award, Hungarian Soc. Nephrology, 2005. Office: Harbor-UCLA Medical Center 1000 W Carson St Box 406 Torrance CA 90509 Office Phone: 310-222-3891. Office Fax: 310-782-1837. Business E-Mail: jkopple@labiomed.org.

KOPPUS, BETTY JANE, retired savings and loan association executive; b. Toledo, June 14, 1922; d. Carl Emerson and Hilda Sarah (Semlow) Koppus. Student, pub. schs. With United Savs. and Loan Assn. (now Sky Bank), Toledo, 1940—, asst. sec., 1943—62, treas., 1962—73, sec., 1973—78, v.p., 1978-84, ret., 1984. Former trustee, sec. Luth. Social Svcs.; mem. St. Mark Luth. Ch. Mem.: Zonta Toledo I, River Rd. Garden Club, Beta Sigma Phi. Address: 5709 Chardonnay Dr Toledo OH 43615-7312

KOPROSKI, ALEXANDER ROBERT, real estate company executive; b. Stamford, Conn., Apr. 6, 1934; s. Alexander J. and Gladys J. (Kryger) Koproski; m. Patricia A. Velliquette; children: Lisa, Susan, Gregory, Beth. Student, U. Conn., 1952-54; BS in Mktg. and Fin., Tri-State U., Angola, Ind., 1959. Lic. real estate broker Conn., N.Y. Comml. and indsl. broker S.H. Silberman, Inc., Stamford, 1960-73; owner, CEO, comml. and indsl. broker Al Koproski Realty, Stamford, 1973—. Mem. Coastal Mgmt. Adv. Com. Nat. v.p. Polish Nat. Youth Baseball Found., 1997; co-chmn. nat. coun. Kosciuszko Found.; past pres. Holy Name Home and Sch. Assn.; past chmn. Kosciuszko Pk. Meml. Com., Stamford Pulaski Meml. Com., Hartford; past mem. Stamford Bicentennial Com., Resource Recovery Task Force, Polish Am. Affairs Coun., Mayor's South End. Adv. Com., Stamford C.E.T.A. Manpower Program; mem. South End Revitalization Com., Stamford, 1996—; treas., fund raiser Am. Ctr. Polish Culture, Washington; chmn. Little League, Dzialdowo, Poland; grand marshal N.Y.C. Pulaski Parade, 2000; mem. com. dedication of Pope John Paul II statue, Stamford; past chmn. Poles for Ford Com.; mem. Poles for Bush, 2000; past chmn. lay adv. bd., past chmn. 75th ann. yr. book Holy Name of Jesus Cath. Ch., Stamford, lay adv. bd., mem. 100th anniversary com., 2002—03; mem. com. statue dedication Pope John Paul II statue, Stamford, Conn., 2004; past bd. dir. Polish Am. Congress Conn., Polish Am. Ctrl. Com. Stamford; bd. dir. Polish Slavic Info. Ctr., Stamford, 1975—, Am. Ctr. Polish Culture, Inc., Washington, 1990—, chmn. bd. dir.; mem. Polish studies adv. com. Ctrl. Conn. State U., 1994. With US Army, 1955—57. Named Citizen of Yr., Polish Am. World, N.Y.C., 1978, Layman of Yr., Stamford Kiwanis Club, 1979; recipient Krzyzem Kawwalerskim Orderu Zaslugi Rzeczypospolitej Polskeij medal, Govt. of Poland, 1994, Ellis Island Medal of Honor, 1998, Excellence award Inst. for Religious Edn. and Pastoral Studies, Sacred Heart U., 2001, Polish Govt. medal, 2001, Urzad Kultury Fizcznej i Sportu award, Govt. of Poland, 2001, REAPS award for excellence, Sacred Heart U. Bapt. Ct., 2001, Baseball field in Dzialdowo, Poland named "Al Koproski Stadium", 2003. Mem.: Stamford Bd. Realtors, Stamford Hist. Soc., Stamford Old Timers Athletic Assn. (v.p. 2005—, pres. 2007), Polish Am. Cultural Soc. (historian, pres. 2002—, Citizen of the Yr. 1975), St. Davids Bluff Homeowners Assn. (pres.), Oceanview Beach and Tennis Club (past pres.), Polish Am. Bus. and Profl. Club (past pres.), Holy Name Athletic Club (pres., CEO, past pres., Citizen of the Yr. 1982), Exch. Club, Am. Coun. Polish Cultural Club (nat. fundraising chmn. Washington project), Am. Assn. Mil. Order of Malta. Republican. Roman Catholic. Achievements include honor by dedication of Al Koproski Little League Baseball Stadium, Dzialdowo Poland. Avocations: swimming, fundraising, travel. Home: 222 Ocean Dr E Stamford CT 06902-8134 Office: Polish Slavic Info Ctr PO Box 631 Stamford CT 06904-0631 Office Phone: 203-323-9944.

KOPROWSKI, HILARY, microbiologist, educator; b. Warsaw; s. Pawel and Sonia (Berland) Koprowski; m. Irena Grasberg; children: Claude Eugene, Christopher Dorian. BA, Nikolaj Rej Gymnasium of Luth. Congregation, Warsaw; MD, U. Warsaw; grad., Warsaw Conservatory Music and Santa Cecilia Acad., Rome; DSc (hon.), Ludwig-Maximilian U., Munich, Widener Coll.; D in Medicine and Surgery, U. Helsinki, Finland; MD (hon.), U. Uppsala, Sweden; LittD (hon.), Thomas Jefferson U.; DMS (hon.), U. Lublin, Poland, Univ. Coll. Dublin, U. Poznan, Poland, U. Warsaw Acad. Medicine, La Salle U. Rsch. asst. dept. exptl. and gen. pathology U. Warsaw, 1936—39; staff Yellow Fever Rsch. Svc., Rio de Janeiro, 1940—44; staff rsch. divsn. Am. Cyanamid Co., 1944—46; asst. dir. viral and rickettsial rsch. Lederle Lab., Pearl River, NY, 1946—57; dir. Wistar Inst., Phila., 1957—91, prof., 1957—93, prof. laureate, 1993—; Wistar Inst. prof. of rsch. medicine U. Pa., 1957—; prof. microbiology and immunology Thomas Jefferson U., Phila., 1992—; dir. Ctr. Neurovirology, Biotech. Found. Labs., 1992—. Cons. WHO, 1950—; mem. microbiology study sect. NIH, 1956—60; mem. PAHO; mem. adv. com. Nat. Multiple Sclerosis Soc., 1970—78; mem. immunobiology adv. com. NIH, USPHS, 1975—76; mem. bd. sci. counselors divsn. cancer etiology Nat. Cancer Inst., 1982—86, chmn., 1987—90; mem. biol. response modifiers program deicision network com. NIH, 1985—87. Co-editor: Methods in Virology, Viruses and Immunity, Current Topics in Microbiology and Immunology, 1965—. Hon. trustee Kosciuszko Found., 1993—. Decorated commandeur Order du Mérite pour la Rsch. et l'Invention, chevalier Order Royal De Lion Belgium, officer Order of the Polish Republic, comdr. Order of The Lion of Finland, chevalier Legion d'honneur (France), Greater Order of Merit Poland; named hon. trustee, Kosciuszko Found., 1993; recipient Alvarenga prize, Coll. Physicians Phila., 1959, Alfred Jurzykowski Found. Polish Millenium prize, 1966, Felix Wankel Tierschutz prize, 1979, Phila. Cancer Rsch. award, Phila. Cancer Club, 1989, San Marino award, 1989, Nicolaus Copernicus medal, Polish Acad. Scis., 1989, The Phila. award, 1990, John Scott award, 1990, Andrzeja Drawicza award, Presidents of Poland, 2005, Lifetime Achievement award, Monte Jade Sci. and Tech. Assn. Mid-Atlantic, Alexander von Humboldt Sr. U.S. Scientist award; scholar Fulbright scholar, Max Planck Inst. für Verhaltensphysiologie, Seewiesen, Fed. Republic Germany, 1971. Fellow: AAAS, Phila. Coll. Physicians, N.Y. Acad. Medicine; mem.: NAS, N.Y. Acad. Scis. (pres. 1959, trustee 1960—72), Finnish Acad. Arts and Scis., Russian Acad. Med. Scis., Polish Acad. Scis., Yugoslavian Acad. Scis., Nat. Acad. Arts and Scis., Order of the Smile (Andrzeja Drawicza award 2005). Achievements include development of first oral polio vaccine which ultimately led to elimination in 1992 of polio from the Americas; new rabies vaccine for humans, reducing the number of injections and of oral vaccine in bait for immunization of wildlife; research in mechanism of damage of cells in brain in neurotropic virus infection; development of first monoclonal antibody for treatment and cure of colorectal cancer. Office: Thomas Jefferson U Dept Microbiology and Immun JAH-M85 1020 Locust St Philadelphia PA 19107 Home Phone: 610-649-1327; Office Phone: 215-503-4761. Business E-Mail: hilary.koprowski@jefferson.edu.

KORAL, ALAN MAX, lawyer; b. NYC, July 10, 1941; s. Max and Sylvia (Stoffman) K. AB with highest honors, U. Rochester, NY, 1962; postgrad., Princeton U., NJ, 1962-65; JD, U. Chgo., 1975. Bar: Ill. 1975, NY 1977, US Dist. Ct. (no. dist.) Ill. 1975, US Dist. Ct. (so. dist.) NY 1978, US Dist. Ct. (no. dist.) NY 1981, US Dist. Ct. (ea. dist.) NY 1986, US Ct. Appeals (11th cir.) 1987, US Ct. Appeals (2nd cir.) 1990, US Ct. Appeals (3d and 4th cirs.) 1995. Assoc. Vedder, Price, Kaufman & Kammholz, Chgo., 1975-76, Vedder, Price, Kaufman, Kammmholz & Day, NYC, 1976-81, ptnr., 1982-2000, Vedder, Price, Kaufman & Kammholz, NYC, 2000—03, voting shareholder, 2003—. Author: Conducting the Lawful Employment Interview, 1st edit., 1984, 4th edit., 1992, Employee Privacy Rights, 1988. Mem. N.Y. State Human Rights Adv. Coun., NYC, 1985. Recipient Cmty. Svc. award Bar Assn. Human Rights Greater NY, 1988. Mem. ABA, NY State Bar Assn. (chmn. elect 2007-, co- chmn. CLE com., mem. exec. com. labor and employment sect.), Assn. Bar City NY, Coll. Labor and Employment Lawyers. Office: Vedder Price Kaufman & Kammholz 1633 Broadway New York NY 10019 Home Phone: 212-496-8283; Office Phone: 212-407-7750. Business E-Mail: akoral@vedderprice.com.

KORALESKI, JOHN J., rail transportation executive; m. Stephanie Koraleski; 4 children. BBA, MBA, U. Nebr., Omaha. Various positions in info. techs., real estate and adminstrv. depts. Union Pacific RR Union Pacific Corp., contr., exec. v.p. fin., CFO Union Pacific RR, chmn. Union Pacific Distbn. Svcs., exec. v.p. mktg. and sales, 1999—. Bd. dirs. Insight Network Logistics, LLC, Bridges Investment Fund. V.p. fin., mem. bd. trustees Union Pacific Found.; chmn. nat. adv. com. U. Nebr. Coll. Bus. Adminstrn., Omaha; mem. adv. bd. YWCA; hon. mem. bd. dirs. Nebr. Meth. Hosp. Bd. and Nebr. Meth. Hosp. Found. Office: Union Pacific Corp 1400 Douglas St Omaha NE 68179 Office Phone: 402-544-5000.*

KORANYI, ADAM, mathematics professor; b. Szeged, Hungary, July 13, 1932; came to U.S., 1957, naturalized, 1963; s. Jeno and Vilma (Szigethy) K.; m. Anna Eiben, Mar. 16, 1968; children— Peter, Daniel. Diploma, U. Szeged, 1954; PhD, U. Chgo., 1959. Instr. Harvard, 1959-60; asst. prof. U. Calif. at Berkeley, 1960-64; vis. asst. prof. Princeton, 1964-65; faculty Belfer Grad. Sch. Sci., Yeshiva U., NYC, 1965-79, prof. math., 1968-79, Washington U., St. Louis, 1979-85; Disting. prof. Lehman Coll. CUNY, 1985—. Contbr. articles to profl. jours. Mem. Am. Math. Soc., Acad. Scis. Hungary. Home: 26 Royden Rd Tenafly NJ 07670-1010 Office: CUNY Lehman Coll Bronx NY 10468

KORB, CHRISTINE ANN, music therapist, researcher, educator; b. Milw., Aug. 9, 1943; d. Carl William and Lucille (Bell) Knoernschild; m. Mark Lee Korb, June 3, 1967 (div. May 1991); children: Tracy Lee, Amy Elizabeth. BS, Mt. Mary Coll., Milw., 1965; MMus in Music Therapy, Colo. State U., Ft. Collins, 1988. Registered and bd. cert. music therapist. Field dir. Girl Scouts of Am., Ill, Wis., 1965-69; contractual swimming tchr. YMCA, Janesville, Wis., 1970-76; contractual music tchr. YWCA, Janesville, Wis., 1971-76; music therapist inpatient/outpatient psychiat. unit Poudre Valley Hosp., Ft. Collins, 1989-92; music therapist Mary Hill Retirement Ctr., Milw., 1992-93, VA Med. Ctr., Milw., 1992-98; vis. asst. prof. music therapy Willamette U., Salem, Oreg., 1998—2003; dir of music therapy Marylhurst Univ., Oreg., 2000—. Composer (musical works) Namasté, 1988 (Art of Peace award 1985), We Are Your People of Love, 1981 (hon. mention Am. Song Festival 1981), Windseeker, 1988, Merry Christmas Day, 1994. Founding mem. Women in the Arts, Ft. Collins, 1987-88. Rsch. for music therapy grantee Helen Bader Found., Milw., 1994-95. Mem. AAUW, Am. Music Therapy Assn., Music Tchrs. Nat. Assn., Amnesty Internat., Mu Phi Epsilon. Democrat. Avocations: reading, spirituality, hiking, cross country skiing, canoeing. Home: 13538 SW 63rd Pl Portland OR 97219-8122 Office Phone: 503-636-8141. Business E-Mail: ckorb@marylhurst.edu.

KORB, DONALD L., federal agency administrator, lawyer; b. Cleve., Apr. 29, 1948; s. Max E. and Frances A. (Wright) K.; m. Patricia A. Krawulski, June 24, 1972; children: Patrick, Laurel. BA, John Carroll U., 1970; JD, Case Western Res. U., 1973; LLM in Taxation, Georgetown U., 1977. Bar: Ohio 1973, DC 1978. Atty.-advisor Office Chief Counsel, IRS, Washington, 1974-77, asst. to IRS commr., 1984-86; assoc. Thompson, Hine and Flory, Cleve., 1978-81, ptnr., 1981—84, Thompson, Hine and Flory LLP, Cleve., 1986—97, Thompson Hine LLP, 1998—2004; tax ptnr. Cooper & Lybrand, Cleve., 1997—98; chief counsel, IRS, asst. gen. counsel US Dept. Treasury, Washington, 2004—. Spkr. in field. Contbr. articles to profl. jours. Mem. exec. com. Cuyahoga County Republican Orgn., 1998—2004, mem. fin. com., 1994, 2003—04; chair, Long-Range Strategic Planning Com. of the Bd. Trustee Cleve. Opera, 2001, trustee, 1999—2004. 1st lt. US Army, 1973. Fellow Am. Coll. Tax Counsel (regent 2001-04); mem. ABA (mem. 1978-, tax sect., chmn. adminstrv. practice com. 1992-94, vice chair com. ops. 2000-02, coun. dir. 1996-99, LMSB Divsn. Coord. 2003-04), Cleve. Bar Assn., Cleve. Tax Club, Soc. Am. Baseball Rsch. Republican. Roman Catholic. Avocations: collecting recordings and librettos of Broadway musicals; US Commemorative and airmail postage stamps and US postal stationary; lionel trains; books about subjects such as baseball, presdl. elections, Cleve. history, H.L. Mencken, passenger trains and 20th century US History; political board/computer games. Office: 1111 Constitution Ave NW Washington DC 20224 Office Fax: 202-622-4277. Business E-Mail: donald.l.korb@irscounsel.treas.gov.

KORB, WILLIAM BROWN, JR., retired manufacturing executive; b. Warren, Pa., Apr. 27, 1940; s. William Brown and Helen (Haslett) K.; m. Dorothy Wendell Trout, June 11, 1962; children: Karen Michel, David Wendell, Christine Leigh. BS in Indsl. Engring, Pa. State U., 1962; grad. advanced mgmt. program, Harvard U., 1979. With Reliance Electric Co. div. Exxon, 1962-86, gen. mgr. mech. group, Mishawaka, Ind., 1977-79, operating v.p., Cleve. Elec., 1979-86; pres., CEO, bd. dirs. Gilbarco, Inc., Greensboro, NC, 1987-99, Marconi Commerce Systems, Inc., 1999—2001; ret., 2001. Bd. dirs. Cambrex Corp., Premier Farnell plc. Mem.: Kiawah Island Club. Home: 60 Surfsong Rd Kiawah Island SC 29455

KORBER, BETTE TINA MARIE, chemist; b. Long Beach, Calif., 1958; d. George Korber. BS in chemistry, Calif. State U., 1981; PhD in chemistry in the field of immunology, Calif. Inst. Tech., 1988. Postdoctoral fellow Los Alamos Nat. Lab., 1990, tech. staff scientist theoretical biology and biophysics (T10) group, 1993—. Elizabeth Glaser scientist Pediatric AIDS Found., 1997—2003; external faculty Santa Fe Inst., N.Mex. Nominee Rave award in Medicine, WIRED, 2005; recipient Los Alamos Nat. Achievement award, 1996, 2002, Elizabeth Glaser Scientist for the Pediatric AIDS Found., 1997—2003, Outstanding Alumnus award for Sch. Natural Scis., Calif. State U., Long Beach, 2001, Ernest Orlando Lawrence award, US Dept. Energy, 2004; fellow, Leukemia Soc., Harvard U., 1988—90, Dir. Funded Postdoctoral Fellow, Los Alamos Nat. Lab, 1990—92; grantee Los Alamos Nat. Lab. Fellow, 2002. Achievements include publishing over 100 sci. papers that have been cited over 3,700 times; conducting pioneering studies delineating the genetic characteristics of the virus population; developing the Los Alamos HIV database, a foundation for HIV research for scientific community; internationally recognized AIDS researcher. Office: Los Alamos Nat Lab MS K710 T 10 Theoretical Divsn Los Alamos NM 87545 Office Phone: 505-665-4453. Office Fax: 505-665-3493. Business E-Mail: btk@lanl.gov.

KORBER, LOUISE ANN, artist; b. Wilmington, Del., Oct. 23, 1934; d. Stanley Kasmir and Margaret Helen (Kelly) Czajkowski; m. Ernest Andrew Korber, Oct. 28, 1961; children: Edward Andrew, Jonathan Paul, Ann Louise. BA, U. Del., 1956, MA, 1962; postgrad., U. Pa., 1959-60, Pa. Acad. Fine Arts, 1960-61, 62-63. Elem. art instr. Oak Grove Sch., Elsmere, Del., 1956-57; elem. and middle sch. art instr. Wilmington Friends Sch., 1957-60. Recipient Winsor Newton '89 Award. Exhibited in juried shows Pa. Watercolor Soc., Harrisburg, 1982, Galerie Triangle, 1982, 96, and Martin Luther-King Meml. Libr., Washington, 1983, Ctr. for the Creative Arts, Hockessin, Del., 1985, Sketch Club, Phila., 1993, 95, Chester County Art Assn., West Chester, Pa., 1987, 88, 89, 90, 91, 94, 95, 96, 97, 98, West Chester U., 1987, Balt. Watercolor Soc., 1987, 88, 89, 96, Mayflower Hotel, Washington, 1988, J. Low Art Gallery, 1989; represented in permanent collections Univ. Del., Del. Trust Co., Prudential Savs. Bank, Hotel duPont, Wilmington Trust Co., Hempt Bros., Inc., Chem. Bank, Skadden, Arps, Slate, Meagher & Flom, Texaco, AmeriHealth Inc., others. Mem. Studio Group (pres. 1996-98), Balt. Watercolor Soc., Phila. Watercolor Club, Pa. Watercolor Soc. (signature). Roman Catholic. Home: 212 Unami Trl Newark DE 19711-7509

KORBITZ, BERNARD CARL, retired oncologist, hematologist, educator, consultant; b. Lewistown, Mont., Feb. 18, 1935; s. Fredrick William and Rose Eleanore (Ackmann) K.; m. Constance Kay Bolz, June 22, 1957; children: Paul Bernard, Guy Karl. B.S. in Med. Sci., U. Wis.-Madison, 1957, M.D., 1960, M.S. in Oncology, 1962; LL.B., LaSalle U., 1972. Asst. prof. medicine and clin. oncology, U. Wis. Med. Sch., Madison, 1967-71; dir. medicine Presbyn. Med. Ctr., Denver, 1971-73; practice medicine specializing in oncology, hematology, Madison, 1973-76; med. oncologist, hematologist Radiologic Ctr. Meth. Hosp., Omaha, 1976-82; practice medicine specializing in oncology, hematology, Omaha, 1982-95, ret., 1995; sci. advisor Citizen's Environ. Com., Denver, 1972-73; mem. Meth. Hosp., Omaha, 1977—; dir. Bernard C. Korbitz, P.C., Omaha, 1983-96; bd. dirs., pres. B.C. Korbitz P.C., ret., 1996. Contbr. articles to profl. jours. Webelos leader Denver area Council, Mid. Am. Council of Nebr. Boy Scouts Am.; bd. elders King of Kings Luth. Ch., Omaha, 1979-80; bd. elders St. Mark Luth. Ch., Omaha, 1993-98; mem. People to People Del. Cancer Update to People's Republic China, 1986, Eastern Europe and USSR, 1987; mem. U.S. Senatorial Club, 1984, Republican Presdl. Task Force, 1984. Served to capt. USAF, 1962-64. Named Medford (Wis.) H.S. Athletic Hall of Fame, 1997. Fellow ACP, Royal Soc. Health; mem. Am. Soc. Clin. Oncology, Am. Soc. Internal Medicine, AMA, Nebr. Med. Assn., Omaha Med. Society, Omaha Clin. Soc., Phi Eta Sigma, Phi Beta Kappa, Phi Kappa Phi, Alpha Omega Alpha. Avocations: photography, fishing, travel. Home: 9024 Leavenworth St Omaha NE 68114-5150

KORCHAGIN, VLADIMIR, astrophysicist; b. Frunze, Russia, July 23, 1950; s. Ivan and Anna Korchagin; m. Elena Langueva, Dec. 5, 1990; children: Andrey, Ivan, Marya. MD in physics, Rostov U., 1972, PhD in Theoretical Astrophysics, 1976; DS in Theoretical Astrophysics, Moscow U., 1991. Jr. sr. leading rschr. Inst. Physics, Rostov-on-Don, Russia, 1976—; rsch. scientist Yale Astron. Dept., New Haven, 2001—. Sec. sci. coun. Inst. Physics, 1989—97. Grantee, NSF. Mem.: Internat. Astron. Union, European Astron. Soc. Achievements include research in galactic dynamics, nonlinear processes in astrophysics. Mailing: Yale U Dept Astron 260 Whitney Ave New Haven CT 06520 Office Phone: 203-432-9887. Business E-Mail: vik@astro.yale.edu.

KORCHIN, JUDITH MIRIAM, lawyer; b. Kew Gardens, NY, Apr. 28, 1949; d. Arthur Walter and Mena (Levisohn) Goldstein; m. Paul Maury Korchin, June 10, 1972; 1 son, Brian Edward. BA with high honors, U. Fla., Gainesville, 1971, JD with honors, 1974. Bar: Fla. 1974, US Ct. Appeal (2d, 5th and 11th cirs.), US Dist. Ct. (so., mid. and no. dists) Fla. Law clk. to judge U.S. Dist. Ct., 1974-76; assoc. Steel, Hector & Davis, Miami, Fla., 1976-81, ptnr., 1981-87, Holland and Knight, Miami, 1987—. Author, exec. editor U. Fla. Law Rev., 1973—74; contbr. chapters to books, articles to profl. jours. Mem. U. Fla. Law Ctr. Coun., 1980-83; pres. alumni bd. U. Fla. Law Rev., 1983; bd. dirs. Fla. Film & Rec. Inst., 1982-84, Am. Jewish Com., 2007-. Named Best of the Bar, So. Fla. Bus. Jour., 2004—06; named one of Fla. Trend's Legal Elite, 2004, 2005, 2006, 2007, Fla. Super Lawyers, 2006, 2007, Best Lawyers in Am., 2006—07; recipient Trail Blazer award, The Women's Com. of 100, 1988. Fellow: Fla. Bar Found. (subcom. legal assistance for poor 1988—90), Am. Bar Found.; mem.: ABA (sect. alternative dispute resolution, vice chmn. 1994—95, co-chmn. fed. ct. mediation com. 1995, sect. labor and employment law, sect. litig.), Fla. Bar Assn. (vice chmn. jud. nominating procedures com. 1982, civil procedure rules com. 1984—89, 1993—95), Nat. Assn. Bank Women (TV panelist greater Miami chpt. 1987), Nat. Assn. Women Bus. Owners (adv. coun. 1987—88), Dade County Bar Assn. (bd. dirs. 1981—82, treas. 1982, sec. 1983, 3d v.p. 1984, 2d v.p. 1985, 1st v.p. 1986, pres. 1987), CPR Inst. Dispute Resolution (nat. panelist 1994—, exec. com. 2003—), Am. Arbitration Assn. (employment law panel, s.e. complex litig. panel 1993—, comml. law panel 1993—), Greater Miami C. of C. (com. profl. devel. 1988—90), Rabbinical Assn. Greater Miami (TV panelist Still Small Voice 1987), City Club (bd. dirs. 1988—93), Phi Kappa Phi, Phi Beta Kappa, Order of Coif. Office: Holland & Knight PO Box 015441 701 Brickell Ave Ste 3000 Miami FL 33131-2898 Office Phone: 305-789-7764. Business E-Mail: judith.korchin@hklaw.com.

KORCHYNSKY, MICHAEL, metallurgical engineer; b. Kiev, Ukraine, Apr. 11, 1918; arrived in U.S., 1950, naturalized, 1956; s. Michael and Jadwiga (Zdanowicz) K.; m. Taisija Lapin, Nov. 22, 1951; children: Michael, Marina, Roksana Dipl. Ing. in Metals Tech., Tech. U. Lviv, 1942. Lectr. Tech. U. Lviv, 1942-44; chief engr. C.E., U.S. Army, Germany, 1945-50; rsch. metallurgist Union Carbide Co., Niagara Falls, NY, 1951-61; rsch. supr. Jones & Laughlin Steel Corp., Pitts., 1962-68, dir. product rsch., 1969-72; dir. alloy devel. metals divsn. Union Carbide Co., NYC, 1973-77, Pitts., 1978-86; cons., prin. Korchynsky and Assocs., Pitts., 1986—. Metall. cons. Strategic Minerals Corp.-STRATCOR, 1986—; lectr. Niagara U., 1957—58, Sanya, Hainan, China, 2005, Ekaterinburg, Russia, 06, Kolkata, India, 07; keynote spkr. internat. confs. Recipient Achievement award, Vanadium Internat. Tech. Com., 2003, China Fgn. Specialist award, Govt. of China, 2004, Leadership award, Ctr. for Tech. Studies and Rsch., San Sebastian, Spain, 2005, Materials Sci. medal, Krakow U., 2003; Sr. fellow, Union Carbide, 1979. Fellow Am. Soc. Metals Internat. (Andrew Carnegie lectr. 1973, W.H. Eisenman medal 1984, F.C. Bain award 1986); mem. AIME (Howe meml. lectr. 1983, Robert Earll McConnell engring. achievement award 1991) Iron and Steel Soc., SAE Internat., Am. Iron and Steel Inst. (medalist), Acad. Engring. Scis. of Ukraine, Ukrainian Technol. Soc., Polish Metall. Assn. (hon.). Achievements include patents for alloy design and processing tech. of a family of micro-alloyed high-strength low alloy steel; research in advances in metallurgy of high strength steels. Home: 2770 Milford Dr Bethel Park PA 15102-1763 Office Phone: 412-787-4703. Business E-Mail: mike.korchynsky@stratcor.com.

KORD, VICTOR GEORGE, artist, educator; b. Satu Mare, Romania, Sept. 16, 1935; came to the U.S., 1943; s. Joseph and Clara (Steuer) K.; m. Elizabeth Mary Boyd, Aug. 11, 1971; children; Emily, Tyler. Student, Cleve. Inst. Art, 1953-57; BFA, Yale U., 1958, MFA, 1960. Instr. U. Ill., Champaign, 1960-65; asst. prof. U. Wis., Madison, 1965-67, assoc. prof., 1967-75, prof., 1975-81, prof., dept. chair, 1979-81, Va. Commonwealth U., Richmond, 1981-86, prof., 1986-87, Cornell U., Ithaca, N.Y., 1987-93, dept. chair, 1987-93. Bd. dirs. Federated Arts Coun., Richmond, 1983-85. With U.S. Army, 1960. Guggenheim fellow, 1962-63. Mem. Coll. Art Assn. Democrat. Jewish. Avocations: ice hockey, golf.

KORDECKI, DON HARRY, theater director; b. Chgo., Nov. 12, 1931; s. Harry and Helen Kordecki; m. Melissa Ollene Cornett, Oct. 15, 1969; children: Adam Cornett, Patricia Stringer, Coral Lane Ethridge; m. Margaret Cook, Aug. 21, 1954 (div.). Radio sta. owner WKRW Radio, Cartersville, Ga., 1961—81; theatre dir. The Grand Theatre, 1988—. Chmn. Conv. and Visitors Bur., Cartersville, 2004. Sr. master sgt. USAF, 1991. Decorated Ga. Commendation medal Ga. Dept. Def., Air Force Commendation medal USAF. Mem.: US Inst. Tech. Theatre, Rotary Club the Etowah. Presbyterian. Avocations: reading, magic, hiking. Office: The Grand Theatre 7 Wall St Cartersville GA 30120 Home Phone: 770-382-2180; Office Phone: 770-386-7343. Personal E-mail: dkordecki@hotmail.com. Business E-Mail: dkordecki@thegrandtheatre.org.

KORDESTANI, OMID, information technology executive; BSEE, San Jose State U., Calif.; MBA, Stanford U. Former positions in mktg., product mgmt., and bus. devel. 3DO Co., Go Corp., and Hewlett-Packard; dir. OEM sales Netscape, 1996—97, v.p. bus. devel. sales, 1998—99; sr. v.p. worldwide sales and field ops. Google Inc., Mountain View, Calif., 1999—. Named one of 100 Most Influential People, Time Mag., 2006, Forbes Richest Americans, 2006. Office: Google Inc 1600 Amphitheatre Pky Mountain View CA 94043

KORDISH, HEIKE CHRISTIANE, library director; MS, Grad. Sch. Libr. Sci., Columbia Univ.; MBA, Columbia Univ. Libr. Yale Univ. Libr., 1967—68; libr. positions through asst. univ. libr. for budget & planning Columbia Univ. Libraries, 1968—87; dep. dir. rsch. libraries NY Pub. Libr., NYC, 1987—2003, dir. Humanities & Social Sci. Libr., 2003—. Bd. dir., mem. exec. com. METRO, Nat. Info. Standards Org. Office: NY Pub Library 5th Ave and 42d St New York NY 10018 Business E-Mail: hkordish@nypl.org.

KORDONS, ULDIS, lawyer; b. Riga, Latvia, July 9, 1941; arrived in U.S., 1949; s. Evalds and Zenta Alide (Apenits) Kordons; m. Virginia Lee Knowles, July 16, 1966. AB, Princeton U., 1963; JD, Georgetown U., 1970. Bar: N.Y. 1970, Ohio 1978, Ind. 1989. Assoc. Whitman, Breed, Abbott, NYC, 1970-77, Anderson, Mori & Rabinowitz, Tokyo, 1973-75; counsel Armco Inc., Parsippany, NJ, 1977-84; v.p., gen. counsel, sec. Sybron Corp., Saddle Brook, NJ, 1984-88, Hillenbrand Industries Inc., Batesville, Ind., 1989-92; pres. Plover Enterprises, Cin., 1992—96, Kordons & Co., LPA, Cin., 1996—. Lt. USN, 1963—67. Mem.: ABA, Ind. Bar Assn., Ohio Bar Assn., N.Y. Bar Assn. Office: 8238 Wooster Pike Cincinnati OH 45227-4010 Home Phone: 513-272-2836; Office Phone: 513-272-1636. E-mail: ukordlaw@aol.com.

KOREMAN, DOROTHY GOLDSTEIN, physician, dermatologist; b. Bklyn., Nov. 1, 1940; d. Benjamin and Ida (Krenick) Goldstein; m. Neil M. Koreman, Aug. 16, 1964; children: Elizabeth Koreman Landau, Robert Stephen. BA, Bklyn. Coll., 1961; MD, SUNY, Bklyn., 1965. Diplomate Am. Bd. Dermatology. Intern pediatrics Kings County Hosp. Ctr., Bklyn., 1965-66; resident dept. dermatology Wayne State U. Sch. Medicine, Detroit, 1966-69; clin. instr. dermatology Sch. Medicine Wayne State U., Detroit, 1969-71; asst. clin. prof. dermatology U. Miami, 1971-75, assoc. clin. prof. dermatology, 1975-82, clin. prof. dermatology and cutaneous surgery, 1982—. Mem. Miami Dermatol. Soc. (pres. 1978-79). Avocations: travel, cooking, reading, skiing, needlepoint. E-mail: skinkor40@aol.com.

KOREN, EDWARD BENJAMIN, cartoonist, educator; b. NYC, Dec. 13, 1935; s. Harry L. and Elizabeth (Sorkin) K.; m. Catherine Curtis Ingham; children: Nathaniel, Alexandra, Benjamin. BA, Columbia U., 1957; student, Atelier 17, Paris, 1957-59; M.F.A., Pratt Inst., 1964; D.H.L. (hon.), Union Coll., 1984. Cartoonist, staff artist New Yorker mag., NYC, 1962; mem. faculty Brown U., 1964—, assoc. prof. art, 1969-77, adj. assoc. prof., 1977—2006. Disting. visitor Am. Acad. in Berlin, 2003. One-man traveling exhbn. Art Gallery, SUNY, Albany, 1982; exhibited in group shows including Expn. Dessins d'Humeur, Soc. Protectrice d'Humeur, Avignon, France, 1973, Biennale Illustration, Bratislav, Czechoslovakia, 1973, Art from the New York Times, Soc. Illustr., N.Y.C., 1973, Art from the New Yorker, Grolier Club, 1975, Terry Dintinfass Gallery, N.Y.C., 1975-77, 79, 91, Virginia Lynch Gallery, 1992, 94, 00, 02, Wash. Art Assn., Conn., 2004, Middlebury Mus. of Art, 2006; work appears in Fogg Mus., Princeton U. Mus., RISD Mus., Fitzwilliam Mus., Swann Collection Cartoon and Caricature, Libr. of Congress; contbr.: drawings to various publs. including The Nation, Time mag., Newsweek mag., Fortune mag., N.Y. Times, Sports Illustrated mag., Vogue mag., Vanity Fair mag.; illustrator: Don't Talk to Strange Bears, 1969, The People Maybe, 1974, Cooking for Crowds, 1975, Noodles Galore, 1977, How to Eat Like a Child, 1978, Dragons Hate to be Discrete, 1978, Teenage Romance, 1981, Do I Have to Say Hello?. 1989, A Dog's Life, 1995, Dear Bruno, 1996, Pet Peeves, 2000, The New Legal Seafoods Cookbook, 2003, Travelling While Married, 2003, Thelonius Monsters Sky-High Fly Pie, 2006; author, illustrator: Behind The Wheel, 1972; author: Do You Want to Talk About It?, 1977, Are You Happy?, 1978, Well, There's Your Problem, 1980, Caution, Small Ensembles, 1983, What About Me?, 1989, Quality Time, 1995, The Hard Work of Simple Living, 1998, Very Hairy Harry, 2003. John Simon Guggenheim fellow, 1970-71; named disting. visitor Am. Acad., Berlin, 2003. Mem. Author's League, Soc. Am. Graphic Artists. Home Phone: 802-276-3103. Personal E-mail: eddo@sover.net.

KOREN, EDWARD FRANZ, JR., lawyer; b. Eustis, Fla., Aug. 6, 1946; s. Edward Franz Sr. and Frances (Boyd) K.; m. Louise Poole, June 19, 1970; children: Daniel Edward, Susan Louise. BSBA in Acctg., U. Fla., 1971, JD with high honors, 1974. Bar: Fla. 1975, US Dist. Ct. (mid. dist. Fla.) 1977, US Supreme Ct. 1980, US Ct. Appeals (11th cir.) 1981, US Tax Ct. 1985, US Ct. Claims 1986. Instr. tax U. Fla., Gainesville, 1974-75; assoc. Holland & Knight, Lakeland, Fla., 1975-79, ptnr. Tampa, Fla., 1980—, chmn. trusts and estates dept., 1983—2004, chair pvt. wealth svcs. dept., 2004—. Adj. prof. grad. tax prog. U. Fla., Gainesville, 1996; adj. prof. grad. estate planning prog. U. Miami Law Sch., 2000-. Contbr. articles to profl. jours.; exec. editor U. Fla. Law Rev., 1973—74, lead author, editor Estate and Personal Fin. Planning (West), 1988—2007. Capt. US Army, 1971—72. Named Gerald T. Hart Outstanding Tax Atty., 2002—03; named one of Top 100 Attys., Worth mag., 2005—07; recipient Robert C. Scott Meml. award, 1991. Fellow: Am. Bar Found., Am. Coll. Tax Counsel (bd. cert. estate planning & probate lawyer, Fla. bar bd. legal specialization and edn.); mem.: ABA (chmn. marital deduction com. 1991—95, supervisory coun. 1995—2001, mem. exec. coun. 1995—2006, rep. to the Nat. Conf. Attys. and Corp. Fiduciaries 1998—, vice chmn. probate and trust divsn. 2001—03, real property, probate and trust law sect. 2001—, chair, real property, probate and trust law sect. 2004—05), Am. Judicature Soc., Hillsborough County Bar Assn., Lakeland 10th Jud. Cir., Fla. Inst. CPA, Am. Assn. Attys. and CPA, Fla. Bar Assn. (chmn. 1982—84, vice-chmn. bd. certification, designation and advt. 1984—88, chmn. real property, probate and trust law sect. 1988—89, chmn. tax sect. 1990—91, active various sects. and coms., continuing legal edn. com.), Am. Coll. Trust and Estates Counsel (mem. bus. planning com. 1994—, regent 1997—2003, past chmn. estate and gift tax com. 2001—04), Fla. Blue Key, Centre Club, Tampa Club, Lakeland Yacht and Country Club, Phi Delta Phi, Phi Kappa Phi, Order of Coif. Republican. Presbyterian. Office: Holland & Knight LLP PO Box 1288 100 N Tampa St Ste 4100 Tampa FL 33602-3644 Office Phone: 813-227-6655, 863-499-5314. Business E-Mail: ed.koren@hklaw.com.

KOREN, MICHAEL, elementary school educator; b. Milw., May 22, 1958; s. Seymour and Betty Koren; m. Tova Walder, June 29, 2003. B, U. Wis., Milw., 1980, M, 1985. Tchr. Herman Consolidated Sch., Mayville, Wis., 1980—82, Maple Dale Sch., Fox Point, Wis., 1982—. H.S. basketball ofcl. Mem.: Nat. Coun. Social Studies (bd. dirs. 2004—), Wis. Coun. Social Studies (mem. exec. bd. 1992—, treas. 2000—). Avocations: cooking, travel. Office Phone: 414-351-7380.

KOREN, NORMAN LEE, computer company executive; s. David and Jane Koren; m. Louise Elliott Marks, June 30, 2001; children: Nathan Lee, Henry David. AB, Brown U., Providence, 1965; MA, Wayne State U., Detroit, 1969. Engr. Honeywell, Waltham, Mass., 1967—70, Sperry Univac, Blue Bell, Pa., 1970—73; sci. programmer ISS Sperry Univac, Santa Clara, Calif., 1973—82; sr. engr. Applied Info. Memories, Milpitas, Calif., 1982—85; rsch. assoc. Kodak Rsch. Labs., San Diego, 1985—98; sr. adv. engr. Storagetek, Louisville, Colo., 1998—2001; pres., founder Imatest LLC, Boulder, 2004—. Author: www.normankoren.com. Mem.: IEEE, Soc. Imaging Sci. and Tech. Jewish. Achievements include patents for write equalization for partial response channels, a method for increasing data density on magnetic tape. Avocations: photography, hiking. Home and Office: 3478 16th Cir Boulder CO 80304 Business E-Mail: norman@imatest.com.

KOREN, YORAM, mechanical engineering educator; b. Tel Aviv, Aug. 1, 1938; came to U.S., 1985; s. Shlomo and Bathia (Rabinowitz) Shterwzis; m. Aliza Halina Palyard, Apr. 3, 1963; children: Shlomik, Esther. BS, Israel Inst. Tech., MS in Elec. Engring., PhD in Mech. Engring. Founding dir. NSF Engring. Rsch. Ctr. for Reconfigurable Mfg. Systems, 1996—; Paul G. Goebel prof. engring. U. Mich., Ann Arbor. Cons. Ford, Coldy Internat., Cybernet System, Metcut, SKF, Frat, 1980—. Author: Computer Control of Manufacturing Systems, 1983, Robotics for Engineers, 1985, Numerical Control of Machine Tools, 1978; contbr. articles to profl. jours.; patentee in field. Sgt. maj. USAF, 1957-61. Fellow SME, ASME; mem. IEEE (sr.), CIRP, NAE. Home: 4101 Thornoaks Dr Ann Arbor MI 48104-4255 Office: U Mich 2238 GG Brown Bldg Ann Arbor MI 48109-2125 Office Phone: 734-936-3596. E-mail: ykoren@umich.edu.

KORENAGA, JUN, geophysicist, educator; BSc, U. Tokyo, 1992, MSc, 1994; PhD in Marine Geology and Geophysics, MIT/Woods Hole Oceanog. Instn., 2000. Miller rsch. fellow U. Calif., Berkeley; asst. prof. dept. geology and geophysics Yale U., New Haven, 2003—. Contbr. articles to sci. jours.; mem. editl. bd.: Geophys. Jour. Internat., 2005—. Recipient James B. Macelwane medal, Am. Geophys. Union, 2006. Office: Dept Geology and Geophysics Yale U PO Box 208109 New Haven CT 06520-8109 Office Phone: 203-432-7381. Office Fax: 203-432-3134. E-mail: jun.korenaga@yale.edu.*

KORENGOLD, GEORGE MATTHEW, physician; b. NYC, Dec. 16, 1946; s. Marvin Curtis and Edna (Gerler) K.; m. Barbara Lynn Korengold, Aug. 23, 1970; children: Adam Stuart, Erin Carol. BA, U. Pa., Phila., 1968; MD, George Washington U., 1992. Diplomate Am. Acad. Pediatrics. Pediatric resident Children's Nat. Med. Ctr., Washington, 1972-75; pediatrician Korengold, Mayol, Deutsh, Walters & Gatto, MDs, Bethesda, Md., 1975—. Mem. Montgomery County Med. Soc., Montgomery-Prince George's Pediatric Soc. (pres. 1990). Office: Ste 238 11325 Seven Locks Rd Potomac MD 20854-3205 Home Phone: 301-657-0770; Office Phone: 301-299-8930. E-mail: gmbpk@aol.com.

KORENIC, LYNETTE MARIE, librarian; b. Berwyn, Ill., Mar. 29, 1950; d. Emil Walter and Donna Marie (Harbutt) K. m. Jerome Dennis Reif, Dec. 31, 1988. BS in Art, U. Wis., 1977, MFA, 1979, MA in LS, 1981, MA in Art History, 1984; PhD in Art History, U. Calif., Santa Barbara, 2006. Asst. art libr. Ind. U., Bloomington, 1982-84; art libr. U. Calif., Santa Barbara, 1984-88, head Arts Libr., 1988-99; art libr. U. Wis., Madison, 1999—. Author articles. Mem. Art Librs. Soc. N.Am. (sec. 1983-84, v.p. 1989, pres. 1990), Beta Phi Mu. Office Phone: 608-263-2256. E-mail: lkorenic@library.wisc.edu.

KORENKOV, MICHAEL, surgeon; b. Moscow, July 29, 1962; arrived in Germany, 1992; s. Igor and Tatjana (Leschinskaja) K.; m. Marina Pak, Oct. 28, 1983; children: Leonid, Michael. MD, 1st Med. Inst., Moscow, 1985; PhD, Ctrl. Inst. for Med. Edn., Moscow, 1990. Surg. ho. officer Ctrl. Inst. for Med. Edn., Moscow, 1985-87; surg. resident Botkin Hosp., Moscow, 1987-90; staff surgeon dept. surgery Ctrl. Inst., Moscow, 1990-92; surgeon 2d dept. surgery U. Cologne, Germany, 1993—. Contbr. articles to profl. jours., chpts. to books. Mem. European Assn. Endoscopic Surgery, German Surg. Soc. Avocations: literature, travel. Office: Dept Surgery 2 U Cologne Ostmerheimer St 200 51109 Cologne Germany E-mail: michaelkorenkov@unikoeln.edu.

KORETSKY, ALEXANDER, entrepreneur; b. Ukraine, 1982; Grad., Pace U., NYC. Fin. advisor, NYC; co-founder & co-pres. MetroHorse.com, Hackensack, NJ, 2006—. Named one of Best Entrepreneurs Under 25, Bus. Week, 2006. Office: MetroHorse 1 University Plz Dr Hackensack NJ 07601 Office Phone: 201-441-9696.

KORF, BRUCE RICHARD, clinical geneticist, neurologist; b. Bklyn. AB, Cornell U., 1974, MD, 1980; PhD in Genetics and Cell Biology, Rockefeller U., 1979. Diplomate Am. Bd. Psychiatry and Neurology, 1986, Am. Bd. Pediatrics, 1988; diplomate in clin. genetics, cytogenetics and molecular genetics Am. Bd. Med. Genetics, 1984; registered, Mass. Bd. Registration in Medicine, 1983, am. Bd. Med. Genetics, 1993. Intern in pediatrics Children's Hosp., Boston, 1980-81, jr. asst. resident in pediatrics, 1981-82, jr. asst. resident in neurology, 1982-83, sr. asst. resident in neurology, 1983-84, chief resident in neurology, 1984-85, fellow in genetics, 1982-85, asst. in neurology, 1985, asst. in medicine and genetics, dir. clin. genetics program, 1986; clin. fellow in pediatrics Harvard Med. Sch., Boston, 1980-82, clin. fellow in neurology, 1982-85, instr. neurology, 1985-86, asst. prof. neurology, 1986-93, assoc. prof. neurology, 1993, med. dir. Harvard-Partners Ctr. Genetics; dir. clin. genetics program Beth Israel Hosp., Boston, 1991; chmn. Dept Genetics U. Ala., Birmingham, Wayne H. Finley and Sara Crews Finley chmn. med. genetics. Invited lectr. in field. Sect. editor genetics Current Opinion in Pediatrics, 1991; field editor Am. Jour. Med. Genetics, 1992; mem. editorial bd. Jour. Clin. Dysmorphology, 1987, Current Protocols in Human Genetics, 1992, Genetics in Medicine, Am. Jour. Human Genetics; contbr. articles and reviews to med. and sci. journals. Bd. dirs. Mass. chpt. March Dimes Birth Defects Found., 1990—. Recipient Clin Investigator Devel. award NINCDS; Bodman scholar, 1970; Cornell Nat. scholar, 1970; Von Meyer Traveling fellow, 1983; grantee NIH, 1986-89, Muscular Dystrophy Assn., 1992—. Fellow Am. Coll. Med. Genetics (founding fellow, former v.p.); mem. Am. Genetics Assn., Genetics Soc. Am., Am. Acad. Neurology (steering subcom. Continuum series 1992-93), Am. Soc. Human Genetics, Am. Acad. Pediatrics, Nat. Neurofibromatosis Found. (clin. care adv. bd. 1985, co-chmn. 1988, chmn. med. policy com. 1988, rsch. adv. bd. 1990, adv. bd. dirs. Mass. chpt. 1985, chmn. med. affairs com., 2003-; Von Recklinghausen award 1989, Pres.'s award, 1991, Courtemanche award, 1993), Assn. Professors Human and Med. Genetics (pres.), Child Neurology Soc., Teratology Soc., Phi Beta Kappa, Phi Kappa Phi, Sigma Xi. Office: Genetics Dept Univ Alabama Kaul Human Genetics BldgRm 230 720 20th St S Birmingham AL 35294-0024 Office Phone: 205-934-9411. Office Fax: 205-934-9488. E-mail: bkorf@uab.edu.

KORF, GENE ROBERT, lawyer; b. Greenville, SC, June 2, 1952; s. Norman and Paula (Heller) K.; m. Madeline Jane Hammer, June 20, 1976; children: Scott, Neil. BA summa cum laude, Hunter Coll., 1974; JD, Bklyn. Law Sch., 1977; LLM in Taxation, NYU, 1983. Dir. Korf & Rosenblatt, Morristown, NJ. Prodr. (mus. rev.) And the World Goes Round (Drama Desk award 1990, 91, Outer Critics Cir. award 1990, 91), The Kentucky Cycle, 1993 (Tony award nominee 1994), The Crucible, 2002 (Tony award nominee 2002). Long Day's Journey Into Night, revival, 2003 (Tony award 2003). Trustee Roundabout Theatre Co., 1993—, Harold Wetterberg Found., 1991—, Blanche and Irving Laurie Found., 1991—, Schulman Family Found., 1993, George A. Ohl, Jr. Charitable Trust. Recipient City Ctr./Leonard Harris award 2001. Jewish. Office: Korf & Rosenblatt 89 Hdqrs Plz North Tower 14th Fl Morristown NJ 07960-1734 Office Phone: 973-993-1743.

KORF, JEAN PRINZ, retired theater educator; b. New Albany, Ind., Oct. 28, 1925; d. Winfield Henry and Waneta Sadler Prinz; m. Leonard Lee Korf, Aug. 15, 1949; children: Kerry Lee, William Milton, Geoffrey Leonard. BA, UCLA, 1947, MA, 1953; MS in Edn., U. So. Calif., 1963. Theater prodn. mgr. Whittier (Calif.) H.S., 1949-52; drama tchr. Calif. H.S., Whittier, 1953-66; theater arts prof. Rio Hondo Coll., Whittier, 1966-90. Founder TheaterCreations Unltd., 1990—; guest dir. La State U., Baton Rouge, 1990, 91, St. Barts Playhouse, N.Y.C., 1992, U.S. State Dept. Arts Am., Bialystok, Poland, 1993. Commr. Whittier Cultural Arts Commn., 1993-2004; bd. dirs. Whittier Cultural Arts Found., 1990-2006. Fellow Coll. Fellows Am. Theater (dean 1994-96), Rio Hondo Coll.; mem. Los Angeles County Mus. Art, Ams. for the Arts, UCLA Theater Film & TV Alumni Assn. (bd. dirs. 1991-2000), Nat. Theatre Conf., Nature Conservancy, World Wildlife Fund, Save the Children. Democrat. Unitarian Universalist. Avocations: theatre going, attending cultural events, conservation, travel, genealogy. Home: 9811 Pounds Ave Whittier CA 90603-1616 Personal E-mail: jeankorf@aol.com.

KORF, RICHARD PAUL, mycology educator; b. Bronxville, NY, May 28, 1925; s. Frederick and Evelyn F. (Krug) K.; m. Kumiko Tachibana, June 27, 1959; children: Noni, Mia, Ian, Mario. BSc, Cornell U., 1946, PhD, 1950. Lectr. botany U. Glasgow, Scotland, 1950-51; asst. prof. Cornell U., Ithaca, NY, 1951-55, assoc. prof., 1955-61, prof. mycology, 1961-92, chmn. theatre arts, 1985-86, prof. emeritus, 1992—. Fulbright rsch. prof. Yokohama (Japan) Nat. U., 1957-58; cons. prof. U. Ryukyus, Ryukyu Islands, 1969; adjunktvikar U. Copenhagen, 1973; Fulbright rsch. scholar U. Louvain, Belgium, 1972-73; dir. Exe Island Biol. Sta., Portland, Ont., 1973—; mem. sci. coun. Academia Sinica, Beijing, China, 1985-90. Editor Mycotaxon, 1974-91; book rev. editor Mycologia, 1972-80; corr. editor Mycological Rsch., 1996-98; mem. editl. bd. Persoonia, 1987—, Mycosystema, 1988-94. State vice chair Liberal party, NY, 1968. Sr. postdoctoral fellow NSF, Yokohama, 1957; recipient SUNY Chancellor's award for excellence in teaching, 1992. Fellow Br. Mycol. Soc. (Centennial); mem. Internat. Mycol. Assn. (nomenclature chmn. 1971-84), Internat. Assn. Plant Taxonomy (mem. gen. com. 1975-91); Mycol. Soc. Am.

(pres. 1971, Disting. Mycologist Award 1991). Avocations: acting, contract bridge, naturism. Home: 316 Richard Pl Ithaca NY 14850-3129 Office: Cornell U Plant Pathology Plant Sci Bldg Ithaca NY 14853 Office Phone: 607-280-5645. E-mail: info@mycotaxon.com.

KORFIATIS, GEORGE, academic administrator, engineering educator; BS, Rutgers U., 1978, MS in Water Resources Engring., 1980, PhD in Water Resources/Environ. Engring., 1984. Founding dir. Ctr. Environ. Engring., prof. civil, environ. and ocean engring. Stevens Inst. Tech., Hoboken, NJ, dean Charles V. Schaefer, Jr. Sch. Engring. at, 2002—, provost, univ. v.p., 2006—. Contbr. articles to profl. jours. Mem.: Greek Hydrotechnical Assn., Hazardous Materials Control Rsch. Inst., Air & Waste Mgmt. Assn., Am. Water Well Assn., Am. Water Resources Assn., Internat. Water Resources Assn., Am. Geophysical Union, Am. Soc. Engring. Edn., Am. Soc. Testing and Materials, Internat. Assn. of Hydraulic Rsch., Internat. Soc. Soil Mechanics and Foundation Engring., Am. Soc. Civil Engrs., Technical Chamber of Greece. Office: Stevens Inst Tech Sch Engring 404 Edwin A Stevens Hall 1 Castle Point on Hudson Hoboken NJ 07030 Office Phone: 201-216-5263. Office Fax: 201-216-8909. E-mail: gkorfiat@stevens.edu.*

KORFMACHER, WALTER AVERILL, chemist, researcher; b. St. Louis, Nov. 6, 1951; s. William Charles and Louise Trowbridge (Averill) K.; m. Madeleine Marie Deutsch, June 1, 1974; children: Mary Averill, Joseph Deutsch. BS in Chemistry, St. Louis U., 1973; MS in Chemistry, U. Ill., 1975, PhD in Chemistry, 1978. Lab. instr. St. Louis U., 1970—72; tchg. asst. U. Ill., Urbana, 1973—75; grad. rsch. asst. Colo. State U., Ft. Collins, 1976—78; rsch. chemist Nat. Ctr. for Toxicol. Rsch., Jefferson, Ark., 1976—91; dir. Dept. Drug Metabolism Schering-Plough Rsch. Inst., Kenilworth, NJ, 1991—. Adj. assoc. prof. U. Tenn. Coll. Pharmacy, Memphis, 1988-91; adj. asst. prof. dept. chemistry U. Ark., Little Rock, 1983-91; adj. assoc. prof. dept. toxicology U. Ark. Med. Scis., Little Rock, 1991. Contbr. more than 100 articles to profl. jours. Recipient Plaque award USPHS, 1989, Commendable Svc. award FDA, 1990, Regional Achievement award N.J., 2002. Mem. AAAS, Am. Chem. Soc., Am. Soc. Mass Spectrometry, Assn. Ofcl. Analytical Chemists, N.Y. Acad. Scis., Phi Beta Kappa, Sigma Xi. Roman Catholic. Achievements include research in area of analytical methods development, particularly trace organic analysis, utility of GC-MS and LC-MS as well as tandem mass spectrometry. Office: Schering Plough Rsch Inst Dept Drug Metabolism 2015 Galloping Hill Rd Dept Drug Kenilworth NJ 07033-1300 Business E-Mail: walter.korfmacher@spcorp.com.

KORG, JACOB, English literature educator; b. NYC, Nov. 21, 1922; s. Reuben and Mary (Lehrman) K.; m. Cynthia Stewart, Jan. 21, 1952; 1 dau., Nora Francis. BA, CCNY, 1943; MA, Columbia U., 1947, PhD, 1952. Instr. English Bard Coll., 1947-49, CCNY, 1950-55; from asst. prof. to prof. U. Wash., Seattle, 1955-68, prof. English, 1970-91, prof. emeritus, 1991—; prof. English U. Md., 1968-70. Vis. prof. Nat. Taiwan U., 1960. Author: George Gissing, A Critical Biography, 1963, Dylan Thomas, 1965, Language in Modern Literature, 1979, rev. edit., 1992, Browning and Italy, 1983, Ritual and Experiment in Modern Poetry, 1995, Winter Love: Ezra Pound and H.D., 2003, also articles, revs.; editor: London in Dickens' Day, 1960, George Gissing's Commonplace Book, 1962, The Force of Few Words, 1966, Twentieth Century Views of Bleak House, 1968, Poetry of Robert Browning, 1971; co-editor: George Gissing on Fiction, 1978; mem. editl. bd. Victorian Poetry, 1979-2002, Nineteenth-Century Lit., 1983-95, Rivista di Studi Vittoriani. Served with AUS, 1943-46. Mem.: MLA, Assn. Literary Scholars and Critics. Office: Univ Wash Dept English Seattle WA 98195-0001 Home: 900 University St Apt 14-0 Seattle WA 98101 Business E-Mail: korg@u.washington.edu.

KORHONEN, FAWNA J., geologist, researcher; b. Las Vegas, Nev., Mar. 26, 1975; d. Joel A. Korhonen and Debra L. Swanson. BA in Geology, Carleton Coll., Northfield, Minn., 1997; PhD, U. Minn., Mpls., 2006. Geologist Barr Engring. Co., Bloomington, Minn., 1997—2000; rsch. assoc. U. Md., College Park, 2006—. Fulbright fellow, Inst. Internat. Edn., 2004—05, NSF Postdoctoral Rsch. fellow, 2006—. Office: U Md Dept Geology College Park MD 20742 Home Phone: 301-405-8653. Personal E-mail: korhonen@geol.umd.edu.

KORIEH, CHIMA J., history professor; BA in History with 1st class honors, U. Nigeria, Nsukka, 1991; MA in Edn., U. Helsinki, Finland, 1994; MPhil in Edn., U. Bergen, Norway, 1996; PhD in History, U. Toronto, Canada, 2002. Prof. African history Ctrl. Mich. U., Mt Pleasant, 2002—04, Rowan U., Glassboro, NJ, 2004—. Editor: Missions, States, and European Expansion in Africa (Rockefeller Found. African Dissertation Internship award, 1999); co-editor: Gendering Global Transformations: Gender, Culture, Race, and Identity, The Aftermath of Slavery: Transitions and Transformations is Southeastern Nigeria, Religion, History, and Politics in Nigeria; associate editor Encyclopedia of Western Imperialism and Colonialism since 1450; contbr. articles to profl. jours. Vis. rsch. fellow, African Rsch. Ctr., Leiden, Netherlands, 2006, postdoctoral fellow, West African Rsch. Assn., 2007. Home: 10 Franklin Rd Glassboro NJ 08028 Office: Rowan U 201 Mullica Hill Rd Glassboro NJ 08028 Home Phone: 1-856-256 4500 ext 3994. Business E-Mail: korieh@rowan.edu.

KORMAN, BARBARA, sculptor; b. NYC, Apr. 8, 1938; d. David and Rose (Katz) K. BFA cum laude, N.Y. State Coll. Ceramics, 1959, MFA, 1960. Sculptor Barbara Korman Design Studio, NYC, 1960—. Educator sculpture and design N.Y.C. Bd. Edn., 1961-91; photographer, prodr. audio-visual ednl. packages, N.Y.C., 1973-89; designer, producer wearable sculpture, 1992—. One-woman shows include Overseas Press Club, N.Y.C., 1988, Tiffany & Co. Windows, 1992, U.S. Mil. Acad., West Point, N.Y., 1996, Westchester C.C., Valhalla, N.Y., 2003, Krause Gallery, Providence, 2003, Piero Gallery, South Orange, N.J., 2004, Gallery Yellow, Cross River, N.Y., 2006, exhibited in group shows at Met. Mus. Art, N.Y.C., 1976, Nat. Arts Club, 1976, Hudson River Mus., Yonkers, N.Y., 1978, Queens Mus., Flushing, N.Y., 1981, Heckscher Mus., Huntington, N.Y., 1996, Grounds for Sculpture, Hamilton, N.J., 2001, Yosemite Gallery, Yosemite Nat. Park, Calif., 2002, Hammond Mus., North Salem, N.Y., 2004, Arts Exch., Westchester Arts Coun., White Plains, N.Y., 2004, Katunah Mus., N.Y., 2006. Recipient Excaliber Foundry award for bronze casting, 1998, BRIO award for sculpture, 1997-98, Jeffrey Childs Willis Meml. prize for Sculpture, 1984, Outstanding Art Educator award Sch. Art League, 1977, Internat. Woman's Yr. award for Outstanding Cultural Contbns., 1975, 76, House of Heydenryk prize for Sculpture, 1974, Yosemite Renaissance XVII award, 2002, Coun. Am. Artist Socs. award, 2002; materials grantee Formica Corp., 1985. Mem. Internat. Sculpture Ctr., Katonah Mus. Artist Assn. (bd. dirs., pres.), Bronx Coun. of Arts. Studio: 357 E 201st St Bronx NY 10458-2205 E-mail: kormanstudio@aol.com.

KORMAN, CAN E, engineering educator, department chairman; DSc, U. Md., College Park. Prof., chair George Washington U., Washington, 2005—. Office: George Washington Univ 801 22nd St NW Washington DC 20052 Office Phone: 202-994-6083. Office Fax: 202-994-0227. Business E-Mail: korman@gwu.edu.

KORMAN, EDWARD R., federal judge; b. NYC, Oct. 25, 1942; s. Julius and Miriam Korman; m. Diane R. Eisner, Feb. 3, 1979; children: Miriam M., Benjamin E. BA, Bklyn. Coll., 1963; LLB, Bklyn. Law Sch., 1966; LLM, NYU, 1971. Bar: NY 1966, admitted to practice: US Supreme Ct. 1972. Law clk. to judge NY Ct. Appeals, 1966—68; assoc. Paul, Weiss, Rifkind, Wharton and Garrison, 1968-70; asst. US atty. Eastern Dist. NY, 1970—72; asst. to solicitor gen. of US, 1972—74; chief asst. US atty. Eastern Dist. NY, 1974—78, US atty., 1978—82; ptnr. Stroock & Stroock & Lavan, NYC, 1982-84; prof. Bklyn. Law Sch., 1984-85; US dist. judge Eastern Dist. NY, 1985—, chief judge, 2000—07. Chmn. Mayor's Com. on NYC Marshals, 1983—85; mem. Temporary Commn. of Investigation of State of NY, 1983—85. Jewish. Office: US Dist Ct US Courthouse 225 Cadman Plz E Brooklyn NY 11201-1818 Office Phone: 718-613-2470.

KORMAN, JAMES WILLIAM, lawyer; b. Washington, Apr. 29, 1943; s. Milton D. and Bernice (Rosensweig) K.; m. Barbara Dale Lewis, June 11, 1967; 1 child, Katherine Korman Frey. AB, Coll. William & Mary, 1965; JD, George Washington U., 1968. Bar: Va. 1968, D.C. 1970, U.S. Supreme Ct. 1972, U.S. Ct. Appeals (4th cir.) 1974, U.S. Dist. Ct. (ea. dist.) Va. 1975. Assoc. Kinney, Smith and Barham, Arlington, Va., 1968-73, ptnr., 1973-78; pres. Bean, Kinney & Korman, Arlington, 1979—. Mem. Va. Bar Coun., 1983-89, 98-2004, 10th dist. grievance com., 1978-81; mem. adv. bd. Bank of Arlington, Va., 1977-78; lectr. various civil litgation topics continuing legal edn.; contbg. atty. Mathew Bender's Fed. Practice Forms, 1978; panelist Va. Conf. Nat. Assn. Bank Women, 1984; adj. prof. George Mason U. Law Sch., 1996—; neutral case evaluator, Fairax Circuit Ct., 1995-; mem. faculty Va. State Bar Profl. Course, 1998-2001; mem. bd. govs. family law sect. Va. State Bar, 2005-. Contbr. articles to profl. jours. Bd. dirs. No. Va. Jewish Cmty. Ctr., 1985-91; adv. bd. Sch. Contemporary Edn., Springfield, Va., 1985-91; Va. Commn. on Women and Minorities in the Law, 1988-92. Capt. JAG USAR, 1972—74. Recipient Meritorious Svc. award Legal Aid Bur., 1968, Adult Leadership award Boy Scouts Am., 1972; named One of 50 Top Divorce Lawyers Washingtonian Mag., 2000, 04, Washington's Best Lawyers, 2004, One of Best Lawyers in Am., 1995, 97, 99, 2001, 03, 05, 06; named to Va. Super Lawyers, 2006, Va. Legal Elite, Va. Bus. Mag., 2007-. Fellow: Am. Bar Found., Va. Law Found., Am. Acad. Matrimonial Lawyers (Va. chpt. v.p. 1996—99, pres. 2001—03, cert. arbitrator); mem.: ATLA, ABA, Plaintiffs Bar Ltd., Va. Trial Lawyers Assn. (jud. task force 1998—, 2002), Arlington Bar Found. (bd. dirs. 1990—, pres. 2000—01), Arlington Bar Assn. (bd. dirs. 1977—81, pres. 1981—82, Robert J. Arthur Disting. Svc. award 2002), Va. State Bar (pro bono steering com. 1992—93, bd. govs. family law sect. 2005—). Democrat. Avocation: collecting political buttons. Home: 2450 N Wakefield Ct Arlington VA 22207-3554 Office: Bean Kinney & Korman 2300 Wilson Blvd 7th Fl Arlington VA 22201 Office Phone: 703-525-4000. Business E-Mail: jkorman@beankinney.com.

KORMAN, MARTIN, lawyer; b. Phila., Oct. 10, 1963; AB, Stanford U., 1985; JD, Yale U., 1989. Bar: NY 1990, Calif. 1994. Ptnr. Wilson Sonsini Goodrich & Rosati. Named one of 45 Under Forty-Five, Am. Lawyer, 2003. Office: Wilson Sonsini Goodrich & Rosati 650 Page Mill Rd Palo Alto CA 94304-1050 Office Phone: 650-493-9300.

KORMAN, NATHANIEL IRVING, research and development company executive; b. Providence, Feb. 23, 1916; s. William and Tillie (Jacobs) K.; m. Ruth C. Kaplan, Apr. 6, 1941; children: Michael, Robert. BS summa cum laude, Worcester Poly. Inst., 1937; MS (Coffin fellow), MIT, 1938; PhD, U. Pa., 1958. Dir. advance mil. systems RCA Corp., 1958-67. Chmn. radar panel U.S. R&D Bd., 1948-56; lectr. U. Pa. Evening Grad. Sch., 1967-68; cons. in field Color Sci., 1968-83; pres. Ventures R&D Group. Author: The Evolution of Human Society, 1998; patentee in field. Mem. Citizens Com. for Better Schs., Moorestown, N.J., 1958. Recipient Merit award RCA, 1951. Fellow IEEE; mem. Sigma Xi. Home: 5700 Teakwood Trl NE Albuquerque NM 87111-6225

KORMES, JOHN WINSTON, lawyer; b. NYC, May 4, 1935; s. Mark and Joanna P. Kormes; m. Frances W. Kormes, Aug. 19, 1978; 1 child, Mark Vincent. BA in Econs., U. Mich., 1955, JD, 1959. Bar: Pa. 1961, DC 1961, US Supreme Ct. 1968. With License and Inspection Rev. Bd. Phila., 1972-73; asst. dist. atty. City of Phila., 1973-74; pvt. practice Phila., 1961—. Moot ct. advisor. Mem. staff Re-elect the Pres. Com., 1972, Rizzo for Mayor Com., 1971, 1975, Phila. Flag Day Assn., 1965—. With USAF, 1956—57. Recipient NY Intercoll. Legis. Assmebly award, 1954, RI Model Congress award, 1954, Queens Coll. Speech Guild award; Eminent Wisdom fellow Wisdom Hall of Fame. Fellow Lawyers in Mensa (charter), Triple Nine Soc. (elections officer 1992-93, legal officer, new mem. welcome program officer 1993—, com. to revise constitition 1993—, ombudsman 1994—), Internat. Soc. Phlos. Enquiry (sr. fellow, pub. Best Telicom 1986-87, legal officer 1986-91, v.p. 1990-91), Wisdom Soc.; mem. Am. Legion (life), Phila. Bar Assn., Phila. Trial Lawyers Assn., NY State Trial Lawyers Assn., Am. Arbitration Assn., Fed. Bar Assn., Pitts. Inst. Legal Medicine, Assn. Trial Lawyers Am., Intertel, Internat. Platform Assn., Cincinnatus soc., Top One Percent Soc., Collegium Soc. 99.5 (charter), Poetic Genius Soc. 99.5 (charter), Masons, Shriners, KP, Lions, Delta Sigma Rho. Republican. Home: 1070 Edison Ave Philadelphia PA 19116-1342 Office: 8122 Lister St Philadelphia PA 19152 Office Phone: 215-338-3658. Personal E-mail: markvkormes@yahoo.com.

KORMONDY, EDWARD JOHN, retired academic administrator, science educator; b. Beacon, NY, June 10, 1926; s. Anthony and Frances (Glover) Kormondy; m. Peggy Virginia Hedrick, June 5, 1950 (div. 1989); children: Lynn Ellen, Eric Paul, Mark Hedrick. BA in Biology summa cum laude, Tusculum Coll., 1950, DSc (hon.), 1997; MS in Zoology, U. Mich., 1951, PhD in Zoology, 1955. Tchg. fellow U. Mich., 1952-55; instr. zoology, curator insects Mus. Zoology, 1955-57; from asst. prof. to assoc. prof. Oberlin Coll., Ohio, 1957—67, prof., 1967—69, acting assoc. dean, 1966—67; dir. Commn. Undergrad. Edn. Biol. Scis., Washington, 1968-72; dir. Office Biol. Edn. Am. Inst. Biol. Scis., Washington, 1968-71; mem. faculty Evergreen State Coll., Olympia, Wash., 1971-79, interim acting dean, 1972-73, v.p., provost, 1973-78; sr. profl. assoc., directorate sci. edn. NSF, 1979; provost, prof. biology U. So. Maine, Portland, 1979-82; v.p. acad. affairs, prof. biology Calif. State U., LA, 1982-86; sr. v.p., chancellor, prof. biology U. Hawaii-West Oahu and U. Hawaii, Hilo, 1986-93, chancellor emeritus, 2000—; pres. U. West LA, 1995-97; pro bono spl. asst. to pres. Pacific Oaks Coll., Pasadena, Calif., 2000—05; acting pres. Tusculum Coll., Greeneville, Tenn., 2007. Acting pres. Tusculum Coll., Greeneville, Tenn., 2007. Author: Introduction to Genetics: A Program for Self Instruction, 1964, Readings in Ecology, 1965, General Biology, A Book of Readings, 1966, Concepts of Ecology, 1969, 4th edit., 1996, General Biology: The Integrity and Natural History of Organisms, 1977, Handbook of Contemporary World Developments in Ecology, 1981, International Handbook of Pollution Control, 1989, Biology, 1984, 1988, Fundamentals of Human Ecology, 1998, University of Hawaii-Hilo: A College in the Making, 2001; contbr. articles to profl. jours. With USN, 1944—46. Postdoctoral fellow, U. Ga., 1963—64, Vis. Rsch. fellow, Georgetown U., 1978—79, Rsch. grantee, NAS, Am. Philos. Soc., NSF. Fellow: AAAS; mem.: NSF (rsch. grantee), So. Calif. Acad. Scis. (bd. dirs. 1985—86, 1993—97, v.p. 1995—96), Nat. Assn. Biology Tchrs. (pres. 1981), Ecol. Soc. Am. (sec. 1976—78), Sigma Xi. Personal E-mail: ekor@aol.com.

KORN, DAVID, pathologist, educator; b. Providence, Mar. 5, 1933; s. Solomon and Claire (Liebman) Korn; m. Phoebe Richter, June 9, 1955 (div. Dec. 1993); 1 adopted child, Joanna M. Fiduccia children: Stephen James, Daniel Clair, Michael Philip; m. Carol Scheman, Dec. 24, 1997. BA, Harvard U., 1954, MD, 1959. Intern Mass. Gen. Hosp., Boston, 1959—60, resident in Pathology, 1960—61; rsch. assoc. NIH, 1961—63, asst. pathologist, 1963—68; mem. staff Lab. Biochem. Pharmacology; prof. pathology Sch. Medicine, Stanford (Calif.) U., 1968—97, chmn. dept. pathology Sch. Medicine, 1968—84; physician-in-chief pathology Stanford Hosp., 1968—84, dean Sch. Medicine, 1984—85, v.p., dean, 1986—95; cons. pathology Palo Alto VA Hosp., 1968—84; sr. v.p. biomed. and health scis. rsch. Assn. Am. Med. Colls., 1997—. Sr. surgeon USPHS, 1961—66; cell biology study sect. NIH, 1973—77, chmn., 1976—77; bd. sci. counselors, divsn. cancer biology and diagnosis Nat. Cancer Inst., 1977—82, chmn., 1980—82; chair Nat. Cancer Adv. Bd., 1984—91; disting. scholar-in-residence Assn. Am. Med. Colls., 1995—97; sr. fellow sci. and health policy Assn. Acad. Health Ctrs., 1995—97. Mem. editl. bd. Human Pathology, 1969—74, assoc. editor, 1974—88, mem. editl. bd. Jour. Biol. Chemistry, 1973—79. Founding mem., chmn. bd. Calif. Transplant Donor Network, 1987—95. Recipient Disting. Young Scientist award, Md. Acad. Sci., 1967. Fellow: AAAS, Am. Soc. Clin. Pathology (hon.); mem.: Inst. Medicine, Assn. Pathology Chmn. (Disting. Svc. award 1999), Fedn. Am. Soc. Exptl. Biology (bd. dirs., exec. com.), Am. Soc. Investigative Pathology (Gold-headed Cane award 2003), Am. Soc. Biochemistry and Molecular Biology. Home: 3827 Cathedral Ave NW Washington DC 20016 Office: AAMC 2450 N St NW Washington DC 20037-1167 Home Phone: 202-686-2067; Office Phone: 202-828-0509. Business E-Mail: dkorn@aamc.org.

KORN, EDWARD DAVID, biochemist; b. Phila., Aug. 3, 1928; s. Joel and Carrie (Goldman) K.; m. Muriel Evelyn Fisher, June 23, 1950; children: Elizabeth Gail, Sarah Harris Korn Gilchrist. BA, U. Pa., 1949, PhD, 1954. Scientist Nat. Heart, Lung, Blood Inst., Bethesda, Md., 1954-69; vis. scientist Cambridge (Eng.) U., 1958-59, 69-70; prof. FAES Grad. Program, Bethesda, 1966-76; head sect. on cell biology Nat. Heart Lung and Blood Inst., Bethesda, 1969—, chief lab. of cell biology, 1974—, sci. dir., 1989-99. Editor: (book series) Methods in Membrane Biology, 1974-79; assoc. editor Jour. Biol. Chemistry, 1977-93; contbr. numerous sci. articles to jours. in field, 1953—. Recipient Superior Svc. award USPHS, 1980, Presdl. Meritorious Exec. Rank award, 1987; Mider lectr. NIH, 1985. Mem. NAS, Am. Soc. for Biochemistry and Molecular Biology, Biophys. Soc., Am. Soc. Cell Biology, Found. Advanced Edn. in Scis. (bd. dirs. 1977-92). Office: NIH 9000 Rockville Pike Bldg 50 Bethesda MD 20892-0001 E-mail: edk@nih.gov.

KORN, JESSICA SUSAN, research scientist, educator, program manager; b. LA, Aug. 16, 1968; d. Lester B. and Carolbeth (Goldman) K. BA in Sociology, UCLA, 1990, MA in Edn., 1992, PhD in Philosophy, 1996. Actor Curb-Esquire Films, Burbank, Calif., 1984; exec. asst. Korn Capital Group, Inc., LA, 1991; tchg. asst. Grad. Sch. Edn. and Info. Studies UCLA, 1995, rsch. analyst Grad. Sch. Edn. and Info. Studies, 1992—96, postdoctoral fellow Higher Edn. Rsch. Inst., 1996—97, tchg. assoc., 1997, rsch. scientist, project mgr. Higher Edn. Rsch. Inst. grad. Sch. Edn., 2006—; rsch. scientist, affiliate asst. prof. U. Wash., 1997—99; v.p. instnl. rsch. Eckerd Coll., St. Petersburg, Fla., 1999—2005; rsch. scientist, assoc. dir. instnl. rsch. Loyola U. Chgo., 2005—06; program mgr., rsch. scientist Higher Edn. Rsch. Inst., 2006—. Internat. election observer Orgn. for Security and Cooperation in Europe, 1997, 98, 2000, 02. Contbr. articles to profl. jours. Jr. assoc. Big Sisters Am., LA, 1994-98. Mem. AAUW, Am. Ednl. Rsch. Assn., Assn. Study of Higher Edn., Assn. for Instnl. Rsch., Nat. Coun. Rsch. on Women, Screen Actors Guild Am. Avocations: working with rape and other trauma survivors, international/humanitarian aid/advocacy work, travel, yoga. Office Phone: 310-825-1925. Business E-Mail: jskorn@ucla.edu.

KORN, LAURENCE, health products executive; PhD, Stanford U. Hellen Hay Whitney postdoctoral fellow Carnegie Instn. of Washington; staff scientist MRC Lab. of Molecular biology, Cambridge, England; asst. prof. Stanford U., Calif., head rsch. lab., 1981—86; dir., chmn. bd. Protein Design Labs, Inc., Fremont, Calif., 1986—, CEO, 1987—. Office: Protein design Labs Inc 34801 Campus Dr Fremont CA 94555

KORN, MICHAEL JEFFREY, lawyer; s. Howard Leonard and Joyce Ellen K.; m. Pamela Ann, May 29, 1983; children: David Harold, Suzanne Faye. BA, U. Va., 1976; JD, U. Fla., 1979. Bar: Fla. 1980, U.S. Dist. Ct. (no. and mid. dist.); U.S. Ct. Appeals (5th and 11th cir.). Jud. law clk. Fla. 1st Dist Ct. Appeal, Tallahassee, 1980-81; assoc. Boyer, Tanzler, and Boyer, Jacksonville, Fla., 1981-84; pvt. practice Jacksonville, Fla., 1984-87; ptnr. Prom, Korn, and Zehmer, P.A., Jacksonville, Fla., 1987-95, Korn and Zehmer, P.A., Jacksonville, Fla., 1995—. Rules com., Fla. Appellate Ct., 1991-2002, 2006-. Bd. dirs. North Fla. coun. Camp Fire, 1983—86; bd. dirs. Jacksonville Jewish Fedn., 1985—2007, v.p., 1994—99, 2003—07, treas., 1999—2003; bd. dirs. Youth Leadership Jacksonville, 1989—93, Jacksonville Cmty. Coun., 1989—94, 1996—98, pres., 1995; bd. dirs. Mandarin Cmty. Club, Jacksonville, 1988—91; cmty. adv. bd. WJCT-TV, Jacksonville, 1996—2004, chmn., 1999—2000; bd. dirs. United Way of N.E. Fla., 1999—2007, chmn., 2005—07, bd. trustees, 2007—; bd. dirs. Nonprofit Ctr. of N.E. Fla., Inc., 2003—, pres., 2006—; trustee North Fla. Family Housing Found., 1999—2003. Recipient Young Leadership award Jacksonville Jewish Fedn., 1992, Tree of Life award Jewish Nat. Fund, 2001; named Vol. of Yr. WJCT Pub. Broadcasting, 2004, Vol. Leadership award Jacksonville, 2005. Mem. Fla. Bar (litig., appellate and health law sect., grievance com. 2001, chair 2003), Jacksonville Bar Assn. (fee arbitration com. 1987-90, chair 1995-99, chair appellate practice sect. 2003-2004), Acad. Fla. Trial Lawyers. Jewish. Avocations: running, reading, golf.

KORN, PETER A., arbitrator, mediator, educator; b. NYC, Sept. 16, 1939; s. Samuel S. and Sylvia Korn; m. Marian Bell, Dec. 24, 1967; 1 child, Sheryl Robin. BBA, CCNY, 1961; M.G.A., U. Pa., 1962. Exec. asst. City of Rochester, NY, 1962-64, budget dir. NY, 1964-69, city mgr. NY, 1980-85; mgr. City of Long Beach, NY, 1970-71; adminstr. Jersey City, 1972-75, Broward County, Fla., 1975-76; prof., asst. to pres. Nova U., Ft. Lauderdale, Fla., 1976-80; v.p. electronic tng. divsn. Kodak Corp., Rochester, 1986-87, cons. state and local services, electronic tng. div., 1987-89; prof. pub. adminstrn. SUNY, Brockport, 1987-90; city mgr. City of Peoria, Peoria, Ill., 1990-96, City of New Rochelle, 1996—2002; labor arbitrator, 2002—. Adj. prof. polit. sci. Iona Coll., 2003—. Author: Financing City and Schools in Yonkers NY, 1976 Mem.: Indsl. Rels. Rsch. Assn., Am. Arbitration Assn. Avocation: boating.

KORNBERG, ALAN WILLIAM, lawyer; b. NYC, Dec. 11, 1952; s. Peter and Selma (Borden) K. AB, Brandeis U., 1974; JD, NYU, 1977. Bar: N.Y. 1978, D.C. 1993. Assoc. Milbank, Tweed, Hadley & McCloy, NYC, 1977-86, ptnr., 1986-90, Paul, Weiss, Rifkind, Wharton & Garrison, LLP, NYC, 1990—. Adj. instr. law Yeshiva U., N.Y.C., 1984-85. Bd. dirs. Lubovitch Dance Found., Inc., 1988-98, Photographers & Friends United Against AIDS, 1989-92, Classical Action, 1993-98; trustee Bennington Coll., Vt., 2004—. Fellow Am. Coll. Bankruptcy; mem. ABA, Am. Coll. Bankruptcy Found. (dir. 2006—), N.Y. Bar Assn., Assn. of Bar of City of N.Y., Akin Hall Assn. Home: 975 Park Ave New York NY 10028 Office: Paul Weiss Rifkind Wharton & Garrison LLP 1285 Avenue Of The Americas New York NY 10019-6064 Office Phone: 212-373-3209. Business E-Mail: akornberg@paulweiss.com.

KORNBERG, ARTHUR, biochemist, educator; b. Bklyn., Mar. 3, 1918; s. Joseph and Lena (Katz) Kornberg; m. Sylvy R. Levy, Nov. 21, 1943 (dec. 1986); children: Roger David, Thomas Bill, Kenneth Andrew; m. Charlene Walsh Levering, 1988 (dec. 1995); m. Carolyn Frey Dixon, 1998. BS, CCNY, 1937, LLD (hon.), 1960; MD, U. Rochester, 1941, DSc (hon.), 1962, U. Pa., U. Notre Dame, 1965, Washington U., 1968, Princeton U., 1970, Colby Coll., 1970; LHD (hon.), Yeshiva U., 1963; MD honoris causa, U. Barcelona, Spain, 1970. Intern in medicine Strong Meml. Hosp., Rochester, NY, 1941—42; commd. officer USPHS, 1942, advanced through grades to med. dir., 1951; mem. staff NIH, Bethesda, Md., 1942—52, nutrition sect., div. physiology, 1942—45; chief sect. enzymes and metabolism Nat. Inst. Arthritis and Metabolic Diseases, 1947—52;

guest research worker depts. chemistry and pharmacology coll. medicine NYU, 0466; dept. biol. chemistry med. sch. Washington U., 1947; dept. plant biochemistry U. Calif., 1951; prof., head dept. microbiology, med. sch. Washington U., St. Louis, 1953—59; prof. biochemistry Stanford U. Sch. Medicine, 1959—88, chmn. dept., 1959—69, prof. emeritus dept. biochemistry, 1988—. Mem. sci. adv. bd. Mass. Gen. Hosp., 1964—67, Regeneron Pharmaceuticals Inc., Maxygen, XOMA Corp.; bd. govs. Weizmann Inst., Israel. Author: For the Love of Enzymes, 1989, The Golden Helix: Inside Biotech Ventures, 1995; contbr. sci. articles to profl. jours. Lt. (j.g.), med. officer USCGR, 1942. Co-recipient Nobel prize in Physiology or Medicine, Nobel Found., 1959; named Arthur Kornberg Med. Rsch. Bldg. at U. Rochester in his honor, 1999; recipient Paul-Lewis award in enzyme chemistry, 1951, Max Berg award prolonging human life, 1968, Sci. Achievement award, AMA, 1968, Lucy Wortham James award, James Ewing Soc., 1968, Borden award, Am. Assn. Med. Colls., 1968, Nat. medal of sci., 1979, Gairdner Found. Internat. Awards, 1995. Mem.: NAS, Am. Philos. Soc., Am. Acad. Arts and Scis., Royal Soc., Harvey Soc., Am. Chem. Soc., Am. Soc. Biol. Chemists (pres. 1965), The Japan Soc. (hon.), Alpha Omega Alpha, Sigma Xi, Phi Beta Kappa. Office: Stanford U Sch Med Dept Biochemistry Beckman Ctr Rm B400 Stanford CA 94305-5307 Business E-Mail: akornberg@stanford.edu.

KORNBERG, FRED, electronics executive; b. Lemberg, Poland, Jan. 28, 1936; s. Karl Kalman and Edith (Keller) K.; m. Rowena Birnbach, June 15, 1958; children: Michelle Caren, Matthew Eric, Tara Kim. BSEE, NYU, 1958, MSEE, 1959. Staff rsch. scientist Coll. Engring. NYU, Bronx, NY, 1958-59; sr. staff engr. Radio Engring. Labs., LI, NY, 1956-62, dir. rsch., 1962-69; gen. mgr., v.p. Nardcom Group, Melville, NY, 1969-71; exec. v.p. Comtech Telecommunications Corp., Melville, NY, 1971-76, pres., 1976—; also bd. dirs. Mem. IEEE (sr. mem.), Armed Forces Communication and Electronics Assn. (sr. mem.). Republican. Jewish. Avocations: jogging, reading, swimming. Home: 17 Palatine Ct Syosset NY 11791-1105 Office: Comtech Telecommunications Corp 105 Baylis Rd Melville NY 11747 Office Phone: 516-777-8900. Business E-Mail: fkornberg@comtechtel.com.

KORNBERG, SIR HANS LEO, biochemist, educator; b. Herford, Germany, Jan. 14, 1928; s. Max and Margarete (Silberbach) K.; m. Monica Mary King, Oct. 6, 1956 (dec. June 1989); children: Julia Margaret, Rachel Elizabeth, Jonathan Paul, Simon Alexander; m. Donna Haber, July 28, 1991. BSc, U. Sheffield, Eng., 1949, PhD, 1953, DSc (hon.), 1979; MA, Oxford U., Eng., 1959, DSc, 1961; ScD, Cambridge U., Eng., 1975; DSc (hon.), Warwick U., Eng., 1975, Leicester U., 1979, Bath U., 1980, Strathclyde U., 1985, South Bank U., 1994, Leeds U., 1995, La Trobe U., 1997; D.U. (hon.), Essex U., 1979; MD (hon.), Leipzig U., 1984; LLD (hon.), Dundee U., 1999. Mem. sci. staff M.R.C. cell metabolism rsch. unit Oxford, 1955—60; prof. biochemistry U. Leicester, 1960—75; Sir William Dunn prof. biochemistry Cambridge U., England, 1975—95, fellow Christ's Coll., 1975—, Master, 1982—95; prof. Boston U., 1995—. Lectr. Worcester Coll. Oxford, 1958-60; Leeuwenhoek lectr. Royal Soc., 1972; Weizmann Meml. lectr., Rehovot, 1975; mem. Sci. Rsch. Coun., 1967-72, chmn. sci. bd., 1969-72; mem. U.G.C. Biol. Sci. Com., 1967-76; UK rep. NATO-ASI Panel, 1970-76, chmn., 1974-75; chmn. Royal Commn. on Environ. Pollution, 1976-81; mem. Agrl. Rsch. Coun., 1981-84; mem. Priorities Bd. for Rsch. and Devel. in Agr., 1984-90; chmn. adv. com. on Genetic Modification, 1986-95. Author: (with Hans Krebs) Energy Transformations in Living Matter, 1957; contbr. articles to profl. jours. Mng. trustee Nuffield Found., 1972-93; gov. Hebrew U. Jerusalem, 1976-97, hon. gov., 1997—; sci. gov. Weizmann Inst. Sci., Rehovot, Israel, 1981-90, emeritus gov., 1990—; trustee Marine Biol. Lab., Woods Hole, Mass., 1982-87, 88-93, Wellcome Trust, 1990-92; gov. Wellcome Trust Ltd., 1992-95; bd. dir. UK Nirex Ltd., 1986-95. Recipient Colworth medal Biochem. Soc., 1963, Otto Warburg medal German Biochem. Soc., 1973; created knight bachelor, 1978; John Stokes rsch. fellow U. Sheffield, 1951-53, Commonwealth Fund fellow Yale U., U. Calif. Berkeley, Pub. Health Rsch. Inst., NY, 1953-55; hon. fellow Worcester Coll., Oxford, 1981, Brasenose Coll., Oxford, 1982, Wolfson Coll., Cambridge, 1990. Fellow Royal Soc. (coun. 1975-77), Inst. Biology (hon., v.p. 1970-72), Royal Soc. Arts, Royal Coll. Physicians (hon.), Am. Acad. Microbiology; hon. mem. Am. Soc. Biochemistry and Molecular Biology, Am. Acad. Arts and Scis. (fgn. assoc.), German Soc. Biol. Chemists, Japanese Biochem. Soc., Biochem. Soc. UK (pres. 1990-95), Brit. Assn. Advancement Sci. (hon., pres. 1984-85); mem. NAS (fgn. assoc.), Am. Philos. Soc., German Acad. Scis. (Leopoldina), Italian Nat. Acad. Sci. (Lincei), Phi Beta Kappa. Office: The University Professors Boston U 745 Commonwealth Ave Boston MA 02215-1401 also: Biology Dept Boston Univ 5 Cummington St Boston MA 02215 Home Phone: 617-739-6103; Office Phone: 617-353-1691. Business E-Mail: hlk@bu.edu.

KORNBERG, ROGER DAVID, biochemist, structural biologist; b. St. Louis, Apr. 24, 1947; s. Arthur and Sylvy Ruth (Levy) K.; m. Yahli Deborah Lorch, Sept. 18, 1984; children: Guy Joseph, Maya Lorch, Gil Lorch.adr BS, Harvard U., 1967; PhD, Stanford U., 1972. Mem. sci. staff MRC Lab. Molecular Biology, Cambridge, Eng., 1974-75; asst. prof. biol. chemistry Harvard Med. Sch., Cambridge, Mass., 1976-77; prof. cell/structural biology Stanford (Calif.) U., 1978—, chmn. dept., 1984-92, Winzer prof. Structural Biology. Contbr. articles to profl. jours. Recipient Eli Lilly award, 1981, Passano award, 1982, Ciba-Drew award, 1990, Harvey prize Technion, 1997, Gairdner Found. Internat. award, 2000, Welch award in Chemistry, 2001, Le Grand prix Charles-Leopold Mayer, Academie des Sciences, France, Alfred P. Sloan, Jr. award, GM Cancer Rsch. Found., 2005, Nobel Prize in Chemistry, Nobel Found., 2006. Mem. NAS, Am. Acad. Arts and Sciences. Office: Stanford U Dept Structural Biology Fairchild Bldg 1st Fl 299 Campus Dr Stanford CA 94305-5126 E-mail: kornberg@stanford.edu.*

KORNBERG, WARREN STANLEY, journalist; b. NYC, June 21, 1927; s. Murray and Helen (Blumberg) K.; m. Felice Sher, June 15, 1952; children: Lisa Kornberg, Jena Talarico, Eva Polston. BA, Adelphi Coll., 1950; MA, Columbia, 1952; postgrad., U. Mo., 1954-55. Reporter Fall River (Mass.) Herald News, 1955-58, Boston Herald, 1958-59, Washington Post, 1960-61; Washington corr.-sci. editor McGraw Hill Publs., Washington, 1962-66; editor Sci. News, Washington, 1966-70; writer syndicated column Warren Kornberg on Science, 1969-70; sci. editor pub. affairs NSF, Washington, 1970-75; editor NSF mag. Mosaic, Washington, 1975—93; book rev. editor Physics Today, 1993—2003. Home: 11017 Kenilworth Ave Garrett Park MD 20896-0153

KORNBLATT, M. DAVID, corporate financial executive; BS, Drexel U. CPA. Sr. tax mgr. KPMG, 1987—93; dir. taxes The Gillette Co., London, 1998—2002; from dir. taxes to CFO York (Pa.) Internat., 1993—2003, v.p., CFO, 2002—06; sr. v.p., CFO Carpenter Technology Corp., Wyomissing, Pa., 2006—07.

KORNBLAU, BARBARA L., physical therapist, educator; BS in Occupl. Therapy, U. Wis., Madison, 1977; JD, U. Miami Sch. Law, 1984. Admitted to practice: Fla., US Ct. Appeals, 11th cir., US Dist. Ct., So. Dist. Fla.; diplomate Am. Acad. Pain Mgmt., Am. Bd. Disability Analysts; lic. Occupl. Therapist Fla., Tex., rehab. svcs. provider/rehab. counselor, cert. disability mgmt. specialist, case mgr., disability analysis: sr. disability analyst. Occupl. therapist Kuakini Med. Ctr., Honolulu, 1978, Rock County Health Care Ctr., Janesville, Wis., 1978—79, Coop. Edn. Svc. Agy. #17, Janesville, Wis., 1979—80; contract occupl. therapist Prince George County Pub. Health Dept., Md., 1980; asst. to coord. disabled students affairs Cath. U., Washington, 1980; occupl. therapist South Miami Hosp., 1980—85; dir. clin. svcs., owner Innovative Therapeutics, 1985—87; assoc. dir. Occupl. Therapy Resource Svcs., Inc., 1985—87; chief occupl. therapy Bapt. Hosp. of Miami, Fla., 1986—87; atty. for various law firms in the areas of personal injury, asbestos litigation and workers' compensation, 1987—89; pres. ADA Cons., Inc., 1991—; pvt. practice law, 1985—; adj. prof. Fla. Internat. U., Sch. Health Sciences, 1986, adj. prof. occupl. therapy, 1992, vis. lectr. occupl. therapy, 1992—93; prof. occupl. therapy and pub. health Nova Southeastern U., Ft. Lauderdale, Fla., 1994—, adj. prof., Shepard Broad Law Ctr., 2003—. Cons. in field, 1982—; invited presenter in field. Contbr. numerous articles to profl. jours., chpts. to books, chapters to books; co-author (with Karen Jacobs): Principle and Practices of Work, 2001; co-author: (with Shirley Starling) Ethics in Rehabilitation, 2000; mem. editl. bd. Am. Jour. Pain Mgmt., Occupl. Therapy in health Care, Prevention Plus Newsletter, Advance for Occupl. Therapists, peer rev. panel mem. Jour. of Care Mgmt., guest appearances for TV, radio print & web-based media. Founder, former dir. Pro Bono Law Project for the Deaf; program participant Put Something Back; mem. attorney's divsn. ACLU; vol. Dade County Bar Assn. Vol. Lawyers Program; numerous other civic activities; mem. instnl. rev. bd. and ethics com. Deering Hosp.; past bd. dirs. Bus. Coalition for Americans with Disabilities; former edn. com. mem. Multiple Sclerosis Soc.; bd. dirs., chair S.E. br. Fla. chpt. Arthritis Found., 1998—2000, sec., 1999—2000, chpt. del. to nat. ho. of dels., 1999—2000, exec. bd. mem. Fla. chpt., 1999—2000; past steering com. ann. jud. reception Greater Miami Jewish Fedn.; former exec. bd. mem. Am. Occupl. Therapy Found.; former profl. adv. bd. mem. Asperger Syndrome Coalition of US; founding pres., chair bd. dirs. Friends of Occupl. Therapy, Inc.; immediate past-pres., chair bd. dirs. Fund for the Promotion of Awareness of Occupl. Therapy; former mem. bus. adv. coun., projects with industry Abilities, Inc. Named Young Achiever, Wis. State Jour., 1976, Disting. Lectr., Maine Tech. Coll. Sys., 1993, Outstanding Alumni, U. Wis.-Madison Sch. Edn., 1999; recipient Outstanding Sr. award, U. Wis., 1977, Presdl. Recognition Award for outstanding svc. to families and communities, Rotary Internat., 1995, 1996, Cmty. Advocate award, Deaf Services Bur., 1996, Vol. of the Yr. award, Arthritis Found. (Fla. Chpt.), 1998, Vanderkooi Lectureship, Tex. Women's U., 2003, Ellen Garms Lectureship, Wayne State U., 2004; fellow DeWitt Wallace fellow, NYU Inst. Rehab. Medicine, 1973; scholar Wis. State Legis. scholar, 1974—77, Henry B. Herman Meml. scholar, 1975; Robert Wood Johnson Health Policy Fellow, IOM, 2006. Fellow: Am. Occupl. Therapy Assn. (chair, work programs spl. interest sect. 1993—96, chair, commn. stds. and ethics comm. 1998—2000, immediate past pres., chair bd. dirs. 2001—04, pres.-elect, exec. bd. dirs., chair stds. and ethics commn., past chair work programs spl. interest sect., paper reviewer ann. conf., mem. adminstrn., edn., tech., & work programs spl. interest sect., former mem. governance taskforce, former mem. collaboration taskforce, former mem. representative assembly, Svc. award 1996, 2000, 2004); mem.: Internat. Assn. Rehabilitation Professionals, Am. Pub. Health Assn., Am. Soc. Pain Educators (mem. adv bd.), U. Wis. Alumni Assn. (former pres. and founding mem. S. Fla. chpt.), Fla. Bar Assn. (employment, workers' compensation and elder law sects., co-chair, com. on phys. and comm. access to the legal cmty.), Am. Soc. for Law, Medicine and Ethics, ABA (labor sect.), Nat. Assn. Rehab. Providers in the Pvt. Sector, Case Mgmt. Soc. Am., N.Am. Cervicogenic Headache Soc., Fla. Occupl. Therapy Assn. (legal cons., conf. planning com. mem., paper peer reviewer, legis. impact team capt., Svc. award 1994—97, Award of Excellence 1998), Autism Soc. Am., APHA, Am. Bd. Disability Analysts, Am. Acad. Pain Mgmt. (adv. bd. edn. com. mem., adv. bd.), U. Wis. Alumni Assn. (South Fla. chpt.) (former pres. & founding mem., organized ann. founder's day events, past alumni judge for homecoming floats in Madison), U. Miami Alumni Assn., U. Miami President's Club, South Miami Rotary Club (Paul Harris fellow, sec. and pres.-elect, numerous other com. positions), U. Miami Hurricane Club, Pi Theta Epsilon. Office: Nova Southeastern Univ 3200 S University Dr Fort Lauderdale FL 33328 Office Phone: 954-262-1238. Office Fax: 305-667-6211. E-mail: kornblau@nova.edu.

KORNBLET, DONALD ROSS, communications company executive; b. St. Louis, Nov. 7, 1943; s. Louis Yale and Mildred Fayette (Levey) K.; m. Ann Louise Vogel, Dec. 30, 1973; children: Ben Michael, David, Sarah. BA, Yale U., 1966. Dir. pub. info. Urban League St. Louis, 1968—71; midwestern dir. Coro Found., 1971—76; v.p., ptnr. Fleishman-Hillard, Inc., 1976—84; pres., co-owner USA-800, Inc., Kansas City, Mo., 1984—86; pres., owner BRI, St. Louis, 1986—2002; sr. v.p. Americall Group, Inc., 2002—05, Kornblet Consulting, 2006—. Instr. edn. St. Louis CC. Prodr.: (radio show) Daily Essentials for Bus. Success. Mem. chancellor's coun. U. Mo., St. Louis, 1982-85; bd. dirs. Zelda Epstein Day Care Ctr., St. Louis, 1989; pres. Wellington Way Condominium, 1989; bd. dirs. Better Bus. Bur. Ea. Mo., 1990-2000, chmn., 1994-95, Coun. Better Bus. Burs., 1997-2005, The Nat. Conf., 1990, Coro Found., Midwestern Ctr., 1992, bd. trustees Coro Found., 1998; trustee Laumeier Sculpture Park, St. Louis County. Recipient merit award Opportunities Industralization Ctr., St. Louis, 1984; named One of Top 25 Small Bus. Owners, St. Louis U., 1988. Mem. Direct Mktg. Assn. (Direct Marketer of Yr. 1995), Bus. Mktg. Assn., Univ. Club (Washington), Yale Club. Jewish. Office: 6147 Lindell Saint Louis MO 63112 Home Phone: 314-862-2089. E-mail: drkornblet@yahoo.com.

KORNBLUTH, JESSE, editor, writer; b. 1946; s. Samuel Kornbluth; m. Katherine Ann Johnson, May 26, 1984. BA magna cum laude, Harvard Coll. Prof. screenwriting NYU Tisch Sch. Arts; co-founder Bookreporter-.com, 1996; editl. dir. America Online, 1997—2002; founding editor HeadButler.com, 2004—. Mem. adv. bd. Darkness2Light, The Community. Author: (books) Notes from the New Underground, 1968, Pre-Pop Warhol, 1988, Highly Confident: The Crime & Punishment of Michael Milken, 1993, Airborne Again!: The Triumph and Struggle of Michael Jordan, 1996; co-author: The Other Guy Blinked, 1987, Because We Are Americans: What We Discovered on September 11, 2001, 2001, author screenplays, (blogs) Swami Uptown, 2005—; cultural concierge Men's Health, contbg. editor Topic, Vanity Fair, New York, Architectural Digest, Departures, contbr. New Yorker, NY Times; editor: (books) Now You Know: Reactions After Seeing Saving Private Ryan, 1999. E-mail: HeadButlerNYC@AOL.com.

KORNEL, LUDWIG, medical educator, physician, scientist; b. Jaslo, Poland, Feb. 27, 1923; came to U.S., 1958, naturalized, 1970; s. Ezriel Edward and Ernestine (Karpf) K.; m. Esther Muller, May 27, 1952 (div. 1996); children: Ezriel Edward, Amiel Mark; m. Barbara Konaszewska, Mar. 18, 1997. Student, U. Kazan Med. Inst., USSR, 1943-45; MD, Wroclaw Med. Acad., Poland, 1950; PhD, U. Birmingham, Eng., 1958. Intern Univ. Hosp., Wroclaw, 1949-50, Hadassah-Hebrew U. Hosp., Jerusalem, 1950-51, resident medicine, 1952-55; Brit. Council scholar, Univ. research fellow endocrinology U. Birmingham, 1955-57, lectr. medicine, 1956-57; fellow endocrinology U. Ala. Med. Ctr., 1958-59, from asst. prof. to prof. medicine, 1961-67; dir. steroid sect. U. Ala. Med. Center, 1962-67, assoc. prof. biochemistry, 1965-67; postdoctoral trainee in steroid biochemistry U. Utah, 1959-61; prof. medicine U. Ill. Coll. Medicine, Chgo., 1967-71; dir. steroid unit Presbyn.-St. Lukes Hosp., Chgo., 1967-93, assoc. biochemist, 1967-70, sr. biochemist on sci. staff, 1970-71, attending physician, 1967-71; prof. medicine and biochemistry Rush Med. Coll., 1970-93, prof. emeritus of internal medicine and biochemistry Chgo., 1993—; sr. attending physician, sr. scientist Rush-Presbyn.-St. Lukes Med. Ctr., 1971-96, dir. steroid hypertension rsch. lab., 1971-95; sr. endocrinologist KHK Endocrinology and Diabetes Outpatient Clinic, Jerusalem, Israel, 1996-98. Hon. guest lectr. Polish Acad. Sci., Warsaw, 1965; vis. prof. Kanazawa (Japan) U., 1973, 82, 88, 93. Mem. editl. bd. Clin. Physiol. Biochemistry, 1975-94, Endocrinology, 1994-98; co-editor: Yearbook of Endocrinology, 1986-90; co-author: Ency. of Human Biology, 1991, 96; contbr. articles to profl. jours.; contbr. chpts to books. Recipient Physicians Recognition award AMA, 1969, 73, 76, 81, 86, Outstanding New Citizen award Citzenship Council Met. Chgo., 1970 Fellow Am. Coll. Clin. Pharmacology and Chemotherapy, Nat. Acad. Clin. Biochemistry (bd. dirs. 1982-86), Royal Soc. health; mem. AMA, AAAS, AAUP, Endocrine Soc., Am. Fedn. Clin. Rsch., N.Y. Acad. Scis., Am. Physiol. Soc., Cen. Soc. Clin. Rsch., Israel Soc. for Biochemistry and Molecular Biology, Am. Acad. Polit. and Social Scis., Fedn. Am. Socs. for Exptl. Biology (nat. corr. 1975—), Fedn. Israel Socs. for Exptl. Biology, Am. Soc. Hypertension, Israel Soc. Hypertension, Sigma Xi. Achievements include research in endocrinology and steroid biochemistry. *Nothing can be accomplished without a sense of purpose. A long-term goal in life is a sine qua non for creative productivity. When the latter is channeled towards achieving a better understanding of various phenomena around us, the process of learning is at its best and a progress in scientific investigation ensues.*

KORNETCHUK, ELENA, curator, art dealer; b. Berlin, June 10, 1948; d. Lev A. Kornetchuk and Tatiana G. Berg. BA, U. Md., College Park, 1970; MA, U. Iowa, Iowa City, 1972; PhD, Georgetown U., Washington, 1977. Instr. U. Iowa, 1970—72, U. Md., College Park, 1972—76; pres., dir. Internat. Images Ltd., Sewickly, Pa., 1977—. Bd. dirs. Russian Hist. Preservation, NYC, 1980—. Contbg. author: books From Gulag to Glasnost, 1995; author: The Quest For Self-Expression, 1996, Evengii, 2007. Contbr. Ocean Conservancy, Nat. Wildlife, Williamsburg Found. Recipient Excellence in Arts award, Pitts. Mag., 2000. Mem.: Advanced Global Tech., Pitts. Tech. Inst., Pitts. Airport C. of C. Avocations: scuba diving, travel, cooking, gardening, animals. Office: Internat Image Ltd 514 Beaver St Sewickley PA 15143

KORNFELD, NEIL S., lawyer; b. June 12, 1963; BS, Northwestern U., 1985; JD, Boston U., 1988. Bar: NY 1989, US Dist. Ct. Ea. Dist. NY, US Dist. Ct. So. Dist. NY. Asst. dist. atty. NY County Dist. Atty.'s Office, NYC, 1988—93; ptnr. Wilson, Elser, Moskowitz, Edelman & Dicker LLP, NYC. Mem. faculty NY Coll. Podiatric Medicine. Mem.: NY County Law Assn., NY State Bar Assn. Office: Wilson Elser Moskowitz Edelman & Dicker LLP 23rd Fl 150 E 42nd St New York NY 10017-5639 Office Phone: 212-490-3000 ext. 2505. Office Fax: 212-490-3038. Business E-Mail: kornfeldn@wemed.com.

KORNFELD, ROBERT JONATHAN, playwright, photographer; b. Newtonville, Mass., Mar. 3, 1919; s. Lewis Felix and Lillian (Seiferth) K.; m. Celia Seiferth Kornfeld, Aug. 23, 1945; 1 child: Robert J. Jr. AB, Harvard Coll., 1941. Script writer Sta. XEQ, Mexico City, 1938-39; editor Fed. Writers Project, New Orleans, 1941-42; reporter The Examiner, San Francisco, 1942-43; copy writer Conner Co., San Francisco, 1944, Albert Frank Agy., NYC, 1945-47, Agrl. Adv. & Rsch., NYC, 1947-50, Knox Kornfeld & Smith, NYC, 1950-60; writer Robert Kornfeld Assoc., NYC, 1961-78, playwright, 1979—. Vis. artist Am. Acad. in Rome, 1996; adviser Classic Stages of La.; play reader, 2004—05. Author: Landmarks of the Bronx, 1990, (plays) The Art of Love, 1988 (1st prize San Francisco Playwrights Ctr., 1988), 2006, Three ByK, 1993, Nadezhda, 1994, 616 Royal Street, 1994, Matisse, 1995, 2007, The Hanged Man, 1996, Acting Out, 1996, Queen of Carnival, 1997, Father New Orleans, 1997, Hot Wind from the South, 1998, The Celestials, 1998, Retrospective, 1999, Passage in Purgatory, 2000, The Celestials, 2005, The Gates of Hell, 2000; photographer (group shows) The Mask, 2000, Photographs, 2001, The Gates of Hell, 2002, Starry Night, 2003; dir.: (plays) Theater for the New City; author (libretto): (Operas) A Dream Within a Dream, 1985, Music for St. Nicholas, 2006, Ligeia, 1990. Chmn. Riverdale Hist. Dist., 1975—, Toscanini Collection, 1984—87, Landmarks Task Force, 1975—99; bd. dirs. Hist. Dist. Coun., 1978—; mem. Time Sq. Playwrights, 2005—; bd. dirs. Riverdale Nature; active Bronx County Dem. Com.; mem. Banjamin Franklin Dem Club, Dem. County Com., 2004—; bd. dirs. Riverdale Neighborhood Ho., 1968—90, Theater for the New City, NYC, 1992—2005, Met. Historic Structures Assn. Pvt. US Army, 1939—40. Recipient proclamation of thanks NY City Coun. for Toscanini Collection, 1984, Preservation award Met. Hist. Structures Assn., 1989, award for establishing Riverdale Hist. Dist. NY City Coun., State Assembly, Riverdale Neighborhood House, 1990, Bronx Landmarks Guardian award Bronx Borough pres., 1995, First prize Sanfrancisco Playwrites Ctr., 1988. Mem. Dramatists Guild, NY Theatre League, PEN (freedom to write com.), Harvard Club (NYC), Riverdale Yacht Club, Nat. Arts Club (co-chair lit. com.), Harvard Ind. Film Group, Sierra Club, Times Square Playwrights. Home: Withers Cottage 5286 Sycamore Ave Bronx NY 10471-2838 Personal E-mail: rojokosr@aol.com.

KORNFELD, STUART A., hematology educator; b. St. Louis, Mo., Oct. 4, 1936; AB, Dartmouth Coll., 1958; MD, Washington U., 1962. Rsch. asst. biochemistry dept. sch. medicine Washington U., St. Louis, 1958-62, from instr. to asst. prof. medicine, 1966-70, from asst. to assoc. prof. biochemistry, 1968-72, prof. medicine dept. internal medicine, 1972—, prof. biochemistry, co-dir. divsn. hematology and oncology, 1976—, dir. divsn. oncology, 1973-76; intern med. ward Barnes Hosp., 1962-63, asst. resident, 1965-66; rsch. assoc. nat. inst. arthritis and metabolic disease NIH, 1963-65. Faculty rsch. assoc. Am. Cancer Soc., 1966-71; mem. cell biology study sect. NIH, 1974-77; mem. bd. sci. counselors Nat. Inst. Arthritis, Diabetes & Digestive & Kidney Disease, 1983-87; mem. sci. rev. bd. Howard Hughes Med. Inst., 1986—; mem. bd. sci. advisers Jane Coffin Childs Meml. Fund. Res., 1987—; Jubilee lectr. Biochemistry Soc., 1989. Assoc. editor Jour. Clin. Investigation, 1977-81, editor, 1981-82; assoc. editor Jour. Biol. Chemistry, 1982-87; author 145 publs. Recipient Borden award, 1962, Rsch. Career Devel. award NIH, 1971-76; named Harden Medallist, Biochemistry Soc., 1989, Passano Found. laureate, 1991. Mem. NAS (mem. inst. medicine), Am. Soc. Clin. Investigation (counselor 1972-75), Am. Soc. Hematology, Am. Soc. Biol. Chemists, Assn. Am. Physicians (sec. 1986—), Am. Acad. Arts and Sci., Am. Chem. Soc., Sigma Xi. Achievements include research in the structure, biosynthesis and function of glycoproteins, especially those which are found on the surface of normal and malignant cells, targeting of newly synthesized acid hydroloses to lysosomes. Office: 8826 Clin Scis Res Bldg PO Box 8125 Saint Louis MO 63156-8125

KORNGOLD, GERALD, law educator, former dean; b. Aug. 20, 1952; BA, U. Pa., 1974, JD, 1977. Bar: Pa. 1977, D.C. 1979, Ohio, 1995. Atty. Wolf, Block, Schorr & Solis-Cohen, Phila., 1977-79; asst. prof. N.Y. Law Sch., NYC, 1979—81, assoc. prof., 1981—84, assoc. dean for acad. affairs, 1984-86, prof., 1984—87, Case Western Res. U. Sch. Law, Cleve., 1987—, Everett D. and Eugenia S. McCurdy prof., 1994—, dean, 1997—2006, Case Western Res. U. Sch. Mgmt., Cleve., 2004. Author: Private Land Use Arrangements: Easements, Covenants, and Equitable Servitudes, 1990, (with Paul Goldstein) Real Estate Transactions, 1993. Named Prof. of the Yr., NY Law Sch., 1982—83, Case Western Reserve U. Sch. Law, 1989—90, 1995—96, 1996—97. Mem. Am. Law Inst., Phi Beta Kappa Office: Case Western Res U Sch Law 11075 East Blvd Cleveland OH 44106-5409 Office Phone: 216-368-3283. E-mail: slb11@case.edu.

KORNHABER, DONNA MARIE, theater educator; b. New Haven, Conn., Dec. 16, 1979; d. Donna Marie Fusco; m. David Deren Kornhaber, Jan. 9, 2005. BFA in Film and TV, NYU, NYC, 1999, MFA in Dramatic Writing, 2001; MA in English and Comparative Lit., Columbia U., NYC, 2003, MPhil in Theatre, 2005, postgrad., 2005—. Asst. to dean, artistic dir. Yale Sch. Drama/Yale Repertory Theatre, New Haven, 2001—02; faculty fellow Columbia U., NYC, 2003—. Presenter in field. Contbr. articles to profl. jours., columns in newspapers. Mem.: MLA, Mensa. Avocations: writing, music, travel. Personal E-mail: dmf2004@columbia.edu.

KORNHAUSER, BARRY PAUL, playwright, theater director; b. Newark, Oct. 29, 1952; s. Arthur Alan and Florence Kornhauser; m. Carol Anne Jacobs, June 1975; children: Max, Samuel, Ariel. BA, Franklin & Marshall Coll., Lancaster, Pa., 1974. Stage mgr., playwright Fulton Opera Ho., Lancaster, 1982—98, playwright-in-residence, dir. theater for young audiences, 1999—. Panelist state arts couns., Pa., NJ, Ohio, 1988—. Author: (plays) Cyrano, 2000 (Helen Hayes Best Play award, 2005), Reeling, 2005 (Ivey award for playwriting, 2006), Sowing the Wind, 2006 (Pennpat New Dirs. grantee, 2006). Mem. adv. bd. 21st Century Cmty. Learning Ctr., Lancaster, 2004—, South Ctrl. Ptnrs., Lancaster, 2005—; v.p. Jewish Cmty. Ctr., Lancaster, 1998—2000; mem. Shaarai Shomayim Brotherhood, 1998—; bd. dirs. Theatre Young Audiences, 2006—, Lancaster Found. Ednl. Enrichment, 2006—. Recipient Bonderman Playwriting prize, 1st Ednl. Theater award, Pa. Coun. Arts, 1994, Cmty. Svc. award, Lancaster Deaf Svcs., 2001; grantee Pa. Coun. Arts, Mid-Atlantic Arts Found.; Creativity grantee, Nat. Endowment Arts, 2005. Mem.: Dramatists Guild, Phi Beta Kappa. Democrat. Avocations: reading, sculpting, hosting Fresh Air Fund children. Home: 1065 Columbia Ave Lancaster PA 17603 Office Phone: 717-394-7133 x105. Office Fax: 717-397-3780. Business E-Mail: bkornhauser@thefulton.org.

KORNICKER, LOUIS SAMPSON, museum curator; b. NYC, May 23, 1919; s. Howard and Lena (Cohen) K.; m. Beatrice Nyman; children: Lance, Steven, William. BS, U. Ala., 1941; BSChemE, 1942; MA, Columbia U., 1954; PhD, 1957. Tech. group supr. Hercules Powder Co., Chattanooga, Tenn., 1942-45; sr. process engr., pilot plant supt. Cities Svc. Refining Co., Lake Charles, La., 1945-48; sec., treas. Uncle Sam Chem. Co., NYC, 1948-57; asst. dir. Inst. Marine Sci. U. Tex., Port Aransas, 1957-60; geologist Office Naval Rsch., Chgo., 1960-61; prof. oceanography Tex. A&M U., College Station, 1961-64; curator dept. invertebrate zoology Smithsonian Inst., Washington. Adj. prof. biology George Washington U., 1968—. Author: Antarctic Ostracoda (Myodocopina), 1975, Research: Revision, Distribution, Ecology and Ontogeny of the Ostracode Subfamily Cyclasteropinae, 1981, Antarctic and Subantarctic Myodocipina (Ostracoda), 1993; assoc. editor: Biology and Paleobiology of Ostracoda, 1975; mem. editl. bd. Palaeogeography, Palaeoclimatology and Palaeocology, 1960-87; mem. bd. assoc. editors Antarctic Research Series Am. Geophys. Union, 1978-90. Mem. Soc. Systematic Zoology, Crustacean Soc., Sigma Xi. Office: Smithsonian Instn Nat Mus Natural History Washington DC 20560-0001 Business E-Mail: kornicker.l@si.edu.

KORNOWSKI, ROBERT RICHARD, engineer, science educator; b. Green Bay, Wis., June 1, 1943; m. Georgiana Nistor, Mar. 3, 2004; children: Robert Merrill, Jenny Lynn, Jane Ann, Mircea Manoila, Veronica Manoila. B in Electronics Engring. Tech., DeVry Inst. Tech., 1972. Employed Motorola, 1965, microcircuits new product group leader land mobile products sector Schaumburg, Ill., 1981-86, microcircuits staff engr. Land Mobile Products Sector, 1986-89, materials orgn. prin. staff engr./inventor with Component Tech. Engring. Group, comml. govt. and indsl. solutions sector, 1989—. Instr. and tech. curriculm cons. electronics William Rainey Harper Coll., Palatine, Ill., 1972—, mem. electronics and mfg. adv. com., 1995—; lectr. in field. Mem. Internat. Microelectronics and Pkg. Soc. Achievements include research in modelling structures to derive new or improved design equations, primarily in support of advanced component development; patentee in field. Office: Motorola Comml Govt and Indsl Solutions Sector 1301 E Algonquin Rd Rm 3025 Schaumburg IL 60196-1078

KORNREICH, EDWARD SCOTT, lawyer; b. Bklyn., Apr. 18, 1953; s. Lawrence and Selma K.; m. Shirley (Werner), Feb. 28, 1982; children: Mollie, Davida, Lawrence. BA magna cum laude (hon.), Columbia U., 1974; JD, Harvard U., 1977. Bar: NY 1978, US Dist. Ct., NY, Southern & Eastern Dist., US Ct. Appeals, Second Circuit. Appellate atty. Legal Aid Soc., NYC, 1977-79; assoc. atty. Rosenman and Colin, NYC, 1979-84; v.p., legal affairs, gen. counsel St. Luke's-Roosevelt Hosp. Ctr., NYC, 1984-87; mem. Garfunkel, Wild, and Travis, P.C., Gt. Neck, NY, 1987-90; ptnr., co-chair health care law dept. Proskauer Rose, LLP, NYC, 1990—. Joint com. on health care decisions near end of life ABA and Hastings Ctr., 1992-95; sr. adv. com. Robert Wood Johnson N.Y. Acad. Medicine Project. Trustee, post grad. Ctr. Mental Health, N.Y.C., 1992-99. Fellow NY Acad. Medicine; mem. Am. Health Lawyers Assn.,; N.Y. State Bar Assn. (chair provider's com. health law sect. 2002—, treas. 2006, sec. 2007),; Assn. Bar City N.Y. (com. on medicine and law 1985-88, chmn. health law com. 1991-94, AIDS com. 1986-97), Phi Beta Kappa. Avocation: running. Office: Proskauer Rose LLP 1585 Broadway Fl 27 New York NY 10036-8299 Office Phone: 212-969-3395. Business E-Mail: ekornreich@proskauer.com.

KORNS, LEOTA ELSIE, writer, mountain land developer, insurance broker; b. Canton, Okla., Jan. 19, 1916; d. James Abraham and Ida Agnes (Engel) Klopfenstine; m. Richard Francis Korns, July 1, 1943 (wid. Dec. 17, 1988); 1 child, Michael Francis. BS, Pitts. State U. of Kans., 1966. Sec. various firms, Kans. City, Mo., 1937-45; cons. Electrolux Corp., St. Paul, 1946-49; sec. health, safety and waste IAEA, Vienna, Austria, 1959-60; tchr. Montezuma-Cortez H.S., Cortez, Colo., 1966-67; ins. agent Korns Ins. Agy., Durango, Colo., 1968—; owner, pres. Korns Investments, Inc., Durango, Colo., 1970—. Bd. dirs. LaPlata County Landowners Assn., Durango, 1981-87; writer, instr. women's history course U. N.Mex., Albuquerque, Ft. Lewis Coll., Durango, Colo., and Mesa (Ariz.) C.C., 1970-75; also spkr. in field. Author: (novels) Yesterday Should Have Been Over, 1965, Somewhere Out in the West, 2002; (play) Angry Young Men, 1957; writer numerous short stories including The Combine, 1947. Convenor, mem. NOW, Durango, 1970—; precinct capt. La Plata County Rep. Party, 1981—. Mem. Unity Sch. Christianity, Trimble Hot Springs. Avocations: mountain walking, swimming, piano, cross country skiing. Home: 519 Hickory Ridge Bayfield CO 81122

KORNSTEIN, SUSAN G., medical educator; d. Arnold I. and Esta S. Kornstein; m. Lee B. Krumbein, Sept. 6, 1987. ScB, Brown U., Providence, MD, 1983. Diplomate Am. Bd. Psychiatry and Neurology, 1988. Prof. psychiatry and ob-gyn. Va. Commonwealth U., Richmond, 1988—, exec. dir. Inst. Women's Health. Editor: Women's Mental Health: A Comprehensive Textbook; editor-in-chief Jour. Women's Health, 2005—. Fellow: Am. Psychiat. Assn.; mem.: Am. Coll. Psychiatrists, Internat. Assn. Women's Mental Health (pres.-elect 2004—). Achievements include research in depression, anxiety disorders, premenstrual syndrome; gender differences in depression. Office: Va Commonwealth U PO Box 980710 Richmond VA 23298-0710 Office Phone: 804-828-5637. Office Fax: 804-828-5644. Business E-Mail: skornste@vcu.edu.

KOROBKIN, BARRY JAY, architect; b. NYC, Dec. 9, 1949; s. Raymond Lawrence and Leanore Anne (Kaplan) K.; m. Laura Hanft, Aug. 27, 1977; children: Rachel Tess, Robert Benjamin. BA magna cum laude, Williams Coll., 1971; MArch, Harvard U., 1976. Registered architect, Mass., N.Y., Fla. Planner M. Paul Friedberg and Assocs., NYC, 1972; architect Herman Hertzberger, Amsterdam, The Netherlands, 1976-77; lectr. Harvard Grad. Sch. Design, Cambridge, Mass., 1977-79; ptnr. KJA Architects, Somerville, Mass., 1979-89, Linden Properties Inc., Somerville, 1983—; prin. Korobkin Assocs., Somerville, 1990—. Author: Images for Design, 1974; prin. works include Eldridge House, 1981 (AIA award 1982, Mass. Gov.'s award 1987), Maxim House, 1984 (New England AIA award 1987). Recipient AIA medal Harvard U. Grad. Sch. Design, 1976; Sheldon fellow Harvard U., 1977. Mem. AIA (chmn. housing com. 1987-90, rsch. fellow 1973), Boston Soc. Architects (bd. dirs. 1990-92), Phi Beta Kappa. Democrat.

KOROLOGOS, ANN MCLAUGHLIN, communications executive, former secretary of labor; b. Newark, Nov. 16, 1941; d. Edward Joseph and Marie (Koellhoffer) Lauenstein; m. John McLaughlin, 1975 (div. 1991); m. Tom C. Korologos, 2000. Student, U. London, 1961-62; BA, Marymount Coll., 1963; postgrad., Wharton Sch., 1987. Supr. network comml. schedule ABC, NYC, 1963-66; dir. alumnae relations Marymount Coll., Tarrytown, NY, 1966-69; account exec. Myers-Infoplan Internat. Inc., NYC, 1969-71; dir. comm. Presdl. Election Com., Washington, 1971-72; asst. to chmn. and press sec. Presdl. Inaugural Com., Washington, 1972-73; dir. Office of Pub. Affairs, EPA, Washington, 1973-74; govt. rels. & comm. exec. Union Carbide Corp., NYC and Washington, 1974-77; pub. affairs, issues mgmt. counseling McLaughlin & Co., 1977-81; asst. sec. for pub. affairs US Dept. Treasury, Washington, 1981-84; under sec. US Dept. Interior, Washington, 1984-87; cons. Ctr. Strategic and Internat. Studies, Washington, 1987; sec. US Dept. Labor, Washington, 1987-89; vis. fellow Urban Inst., 1989-92; pres., CEO New Am. Schs. Devel. Corp., 1992-93; ret., 1993. Mem. def. adv. com. Women in the Svcs., 1973—74; mem. Am. Coun. Capital Formation, 1976—78; mem. environ. edn. task force HEW, 1976—77; chair Pres.'s Commn. Aviation Security and Terrorism, 1989—90; bd. dirs. Kellogg Co., Host Hotels & Resorts, Inc., Am. Airlines, AMR Corp., Harman Internat. Industries, Inc., Vulcan Materials Co., 1990—2004, 2007—, Fannie Mae, 1994—2006, Microsoft Corp., 2000—06; pres. Fed. City Coun., 1990—95; vice-chair Aspen Inst., 1996, chair, 1996—2000; chmn. bd. trustees RAND Corp. Bd. dirs. The Dana Found. Mem.: Sulgrave Club, Met. Club, Cosmos Club. Republican. Roman Catholic.

KOROLOGOS, TOM CHRIS, former ambassador; b. Salt Lake City, Apr. 6, 1933; s. Chris T. and Irene (Kolendrianos) K.; m. Carolyn Joy Goff, June 16, 1960 (dec. Jan. 1997); children— Ann, Philip Chris, Paula; m. Ann McLaughlin, Dec. 9, 2000. BA, U. Utah, 1955; MS (Grantland Rice Meml. fellow 1957; Pulitzer traveling fellow 1958), Columbia, 1958. Reporter Salt Lake Tribune, 1950-56, 59-60; reporter N.Y. Herald Tribune, 1958; account exec. David W. Evans & Assos., Salt Lake City, 1960-62; asst. to Senator Wallace Bennett of Utah, Washington, 1962-71; dep. asst. Pres. Nixon, 1971-74; asst. to Pres. Ford, 1974-75; cons. Timmons and Co., Washington, 1975—2003; sr. advisor to Bob Dole, 1996; sr. counselor to Amb. Paul Bremer Office of Coalition Provisional Authority, Baghdad, Iraq, 2003; US amb. to Belgium US Dept. State, Brussels, 2004—07. Dir. congl. rels. Pres.-Elect Reagan; former chmn. U.S. Adv. Commn. Pub. Diplomacy. Former chmn. bd. trustees Am. Coll. of Greece; former mem. bd. dirs. Internat. Media Fund; mem. Internat. Broadcasting Bd. Govs., 1995-2002. With USAF, 1956-57. Recipient Disting. Alumnus award U. Utah, 1989, Hon.Doctorate in Human Letters, 2003. Mem. Ahepa. Greek Orthodox.

KOROMA, ABDUL G., judge; b. Freetown, Sierra Leone, Sept. 29, 1943; Student, Kings Coll., U. London, Kiev State U. Bar: Lincoln's Inn, High Ct. Sierra Leone, Rep. of Korea. Joined Govt. of Sierra Leone, 1964, various positions, 1964-69, dep. permanent rep. to UN, 1978-81, permanent rep. to UN, 1981-85, permanent rep. to UNESCO, 1985—88, amb. to Ethiopia and Orgn. African Unity, 1988—92, former amb. to EEC; judge Internat. Ct. of Justice, The Hague, Netherlands, 1994—. With Ministry Fgn. Affairs, 1969; high commr. to Zambia and Tanzania, 1988, Barbados, Jamaica, Trinidad and Tobago, 1988; del. UN Gen. Assembly; mem. Internat. Law Com., chair 43d session; mem. dels. to 3d UN Conf. on Law and Sea, UN Conf. on Succession of States in Respect to Treaties, UN Commn. on Internat. Trade Law, Spl. Com. on Rev. of UN Charter and on Strengthening Role of Orgn. Com. on Peaceful Uses of Outer Space; vice chair UN Charter Legal Com., 1978; chmn. UN Spl. Com. of 24, UN 6th Com. (legal); lectr. numerous univs.; mem. internat. planning legal coun. Internat. Ocean Inst.; mem. com. experts on application of convs. and recommendations, Internat. Labour Office, Geneva. Contbr. articles to profl. jours. Pres. Henry Dunant Ctr., Geneva. Decorated insignia Comdr. of Rokel; recipient Internat. Inst. Humanitarian Law prize Promotion, Dissemination and Tchg. Internat. Humanitarian Law. Mem.: Lincoln's Inn (hon. bencher), Am. Soc. Internat. Law, Inst. Internat. Law (assoc.). Office: Internat Ct of Justice Peace Palace Carnegieplein 2517 KJ The Hague Netherlands*

KORONES, SHELDON BERNARR, pediatrician, educator; b. NYC, Apr. 26, 1924; s. Samuel Aaron and Estelle (Goldstein) K.; m. Judith Ann Kest, June 15, 1952; children: David N., Susan Gifford. BS, U. Tenn., 1944; MD, U. Tenn., Memphis, 1947. Diplomate Am. Bd. Pediatrics, Am. Bd. Neonatal/Perinatal Medicine. Intern Boston City Hosp., 1948-49; asst. resident pediat. Babies Hosp., NYC, 1950-51, 53-54; asst. in pathology Children's Med. Ctr., Boston, 1949-50; asst. clin. prof. pediat. U. Tenn., 1961-68, assoc. prof. newborn svcs. dept. pediats., 1968-72, prof. pediats., dir. newborn svcs., 1972-89, prof. ob-gyn., 1982-89, alumni disting. svc. prof. pediat. ob-gyn., 1989—. Project dir., prin. investigator collaborative perinatal project NIH, Bethesda, 1960-75; dir. newborn ctr. Regional Med. Ctr. Memphis, 1968-2004; perinatal adv. com. State Tenn., 1974—, chmn. subcom. standards regionalization perinatal care, 1975—, subcom. liaison, legis. funding and cmty. edn., 1979—, subcom. perinatal transp., 1979-86, gov.'s task force prevention mental retardation, 1980-83, gov.'s task force healthy children, 1983-86, subcom. follow-up, 1983-86, subcom. evaluation, 1983-86, subcom. med. home., 1983-86, task force child devel. standards dept. human svcs., 1984-86; med. svc. adv. com. March of Dimes, 1974-78, edn. adv. com., 1979-1987, exec. com. west Tenn. chpt., 1986-92; bd. examiner oral exams maternal and fetal medicine Am. Bd. Ob-Gyn., Chgo., 1975; study panel bur. med. devices diagnostic products FDA, 1976-93; prin. investigator Nat. Heart, Lung, Blood Inst., Bethesda, Md., 1976-83, Coop. Multictr. Network Neonatal Intensive Care Rsch., Bethesda, 1986-2001; profl. edn. rsch. com. Am. Lung Assn. Tenn., 1977-81; pres.-elect med. staff Regional Med. Ctr. Memphis, 1982-83, pres. 1983-84; adv. bd. Office Drug Policy, Memphis, 1991; subcom. ob-gyn. newborn svcs. TLC Family Care Healthplan, Memphis, 1994—; mem. perinatal com. devel. clin. practice guidelines TennCare, First Mental Health, Inc., 1996; spkr., cons. in field. Author: High Risk Newborn Infants: The Basis for Intensive Nursing Care, 1972, 4th edit., 1986, Spanish translation, 1979, Russian translation, 1981; co-author: Neonatal Decision Making, 1993; author, co-author: (chpts.) Synopsis of Pediatrics, 1963, 6th edit., 1984, Resuscitation of the Newborn, 3d edit., 1973, Iatrogenic Problems in Neonatal Intensive Care, 1976, Current Diagnosis, 1977, Standards and Recommendations for Hospital Care of Newborn Infants, 6th edit., 1977, Current Therapy in Obstetrics and Gynecology, 1980, 83, Assisted Ventilation of the Newborn, 1981, The Use of Computers in Perinatal Medicine, 1982, Parent-Baby Attachment in Premature Infants, 1983, Infant Stress under Intensive Care, 1985, Gynecology and Obstetrics, Vol. 2, 1985, Teratogen Update: Environmentally Induced Birth Defect Risks, 1986, Assisted Ventilation of the Neonate, 1988, 4th edit., 2003, Comprehensive Pediatrics, 1990; author: (introduction) Planning and Design for Perinatal and Pediatric Facilities, 1977; editor Ross Labs., Columbus, Ohio, 1975-82, Perinatal Press, U. Tenn., Memphis, 1976-78, Brentwood Pub. Corp., L.A., 1977-88, Am. Baby Hosp. Network Adv. Bd., 1984—, Jour. Perinatology-Neonatology, 1988—, Am. Baby Mag., 1992—; reviewer C.V. Mosby Co., 1976-77, 81, 83, J.B. Lippincott Co., 1979, Williams and Wilkins Co., 1981, Polymorph films, 1985, Pediats., 1974—, New Eng. Jour. Medicine, 1975—, Am. Jour. Ob-gyn., 1979, 92, 97, Jour. Pediats., 1997, Pediat. Nephrology, 1997-2004, Pediat. Infectious Disease Jour. 1997-2000, 2003-04, Arch. Pediat. and Adolescent Medicine, 1999, Jour. Perinatology, 2001-04, Acta Paediatrica, 2003; contbr. over 300 articles to profl. publs. Bd. dirs. Memphis Orch. Soc., 1961-70. With USPHS, 1951-53. Named Citizen of Yr. Newspaper Guild Memphis, 1974, Who's Who in Medicine, Memphis Mag., 1984-88, Top Doctors, 1996; recipient Myrtle Wreath award Hadassah, 1976, Contribn. to Perinatal Medicine commendation Commr. Pub. Health Tenn., 1978, Cmty. Svc. award Nat. Conf. Christians and Jews, 1982, City Coun. Memphis, 1982, L.M. Graves Meml. Health award Mid-South Med. Ctr. Coun., Inc., 1984, Cert. Appreciation, Gov. Lamar Alexander, 1986, Key to City Memphis, Mayor Richard Hackett, 1988, Alumni Svc. award U. Tenn. Nat. Alumni Assn., 1989, Themis award March of Dimes, 1991, Meritorious Svc. commendation State Tenn. Ho. of Reps., 1992, Person of Vision award Alliance for Blind Visually Impaired, 1994, Meritorious Svc. award Tenn. Hosp. Assn., 1995; Sheldon B. Korones Chair Neonatology U. Tenn. Coll. Medicine named in his honor, 1989, Sheldon B. Korones Newborn Ctr. named in his honor, 2004; grantee NIH, 1960-75, 1971-75, 1985-2001, Merck, Sharpe and Dohme, 1970-73, Tenn. Dept. Health, 1970—, Memphis Regional Med. Program, 1972-75, Tenn. Dept. Human Svcs., 1972—96, March of Dimes, 1973-80, Nat. Heart, Lung, Blood Inst., 1976-83, Nat. Inst. Child Health Human Devel., 1986-91, 91-96, 96—, Tenn. Dept. Children's Svcs., 1996-2001. Fellow Am. Coll. Ob-Gyn. (assoc.); mem. So. Soc. Pediat. Rsch., Am. Acad. Pediats. (com. fetus and newborn 1969-75, liaison com. perinatal health Am. Coll. Ob-Gyn. 1965-74, rep. to joint com. newborn hearing Am. Speech Hearing Assn., Am. Acad. Ophthalmology Otolaryngology 1969-75, task force on circumcision 1973-74), Tenn. chpt. Pediatrician of Yr. 1994), Tenn. Pediat. Soc., Memphis Pediat. Soc., Am. Pediat. Soc., Tenn. Perinatal Assn. (bd. dirs. 1983—), Russian Perinatologists Assn. (hon. pres. 1996), Nat. Assn. Perinatal Social Workers (hon. 1980), Sigma Xi, Alpha Omega Alpha. Office: U Tenn 853 Jefferson Ave Rm 201 Memphis TN 38103-2807 Home Phone: 901-682-3692; Office Phone: 901-448-5950. Business E-Mail: skorones@utmem.edu.

KOROS, WILLIAM JOHN, chemical engineering educator; b. Omaha, Aug. 31, 1947; s. William Alexander and Mary Ellen (Roth) K.; m. Ann Marie Teahan, Dec. 19, 1970. BSChemE, U. Tex., 1969, MSChemE, 1975, PhDChemE, 1977. Registered profl. engr., Tex. Chem. engr. E.I. DuPont, Wilmington, Del., 1969-71, cons., 1982—, engr. Camden, SC, 1971-73; research asst. U. Tex., Austin, 1973-77; asst. prof. chem. engring. N.C. State U., Raleigh, 1977-80, prof., 1980-83; prof. chem. engring. U. Tex., Austin, 1983—2001, B.F. Goodrich prof. material engring., 1986—2001, chmn. chem. engring., 1993-97, Roberto C. Goizueta chair in chem. engring., 2001—. Editor in chief Jour. Membrane Sci. Recipient Sigma Xi Research award, 1980, Young Investigators award NSF, 1983, Alcoa Found Research award N.C. State U., 1983. Fellow AIChE (Inst. award for excellence in indsl. gas separations 1995, Gerhold award 1999), AAAS; mem. Am. Chem. Soc., Nat. Acad. Engring. Home Phone: 404-352-9979. Business E-Mail: wjk@che.gatech.edu.

KOROT, BERYL, artist; b. NYC, Sept. 17, 1945; d. George and Frieda (Braunstein) K.; m. Steve Reich, May 30, 1976; 1 child, Ezra. Student, U. Wis., 1963-65; BA, Queens Coll., 1967. Chief, co-founder Radical Software, 1970-73; co-editor Video Art, 1976. Exhibitions include 4 channel video work Dachau 1974, 5 channel video work, weavings, drawings, Text and Commentary: Three Tales and the Cave:, Kitchen, N.Y.C., 1975, Everson Mus. Art, Syracuse, N.Y., 1975, 1977, Documenta 6, Kassel, Germany, 1977, Videopoints, Mus Modern Art, N.Y.C., 1978, Mickery Theatre, Holland, 1978, Whitney Mus., N.Y.C., 1980, San Francisco Art Inst., 1981, Leo Castelli Gallery, N.Y.C., 1977, Mus. Fine Arts, Montreal, 1979, John Weber Gallery, 1986, Jack Tilton Gallery, 1987, Carnegie Mus. Art, 1990, Long Beach Mus. Art, 1988, Jewish Mus., N.Y.C., 1988, Video Skuptur, Kunstverein, Koln, 1989, The Cave, 1993, Reina Sofia Mus., Madrid, 1993—94, Dusseldorf Kunsthalle, Whitney Mus. Am. Art, N.Y.C., Carnegie Mus. Art, ICC Gallery, Tokyo, 1997, Hindenburg, 1998, Bklyn. Acad. Music, 1998, Spoleto Festival, 1998, Mass. Coll. Art, 1999, Historischen Mus., Frankfurt, 2000—01, Whitney Mus., NYC, 2000—01, Jewish Mus. Paris, 2002—03, short commd. work, Art 21, PBS, 2002, Apex Gallery, N.Y.C., 2004, DM2, 2005, Seoul, Korea, 2005, web project, Auschwitz, 2005—. Fellow, N.Y. State Coun. on Arts, 1978, Creative Artist Pub. Svc., 1975, 1979; grantee, Rockefeller Found., 1989, 1998, Andy Warhol Found., 1991, NEA, 1991—92; artist fellow, 1975, 1977, 1979, Guggenheim fellow, 1994, Montgomery fellow, Dartmouth Coll., 2000. Personal E-mail: bkorot@aol.com.

KOROTKIN, FRED, writer, philatelist; b. Duluth, Minn., Oct. 25, 1917; s. Morris and Ethel (Billert) K. BA, U. Minn., Mpls., 1949. Writer-instr. Palmer Writers Sch., Mpls., 1961-66; editor Finance & Commerce, and Daily Market Record, Mpls., 1966-67; stamp editor Mpls. Star, 1970-74, White Bear Press, 1976, Minn. Suburban Newspapers, Inc., 1983-85, The Enterpri$e, 1988-89, Post Publs. Weekend, 1989-91. Mem. philatelic adv. panel Am. Revolution Bicentennial Commn., 1971-74, Am. Revolution Bicentennial Adminstrn., 1974, philatelic advisor, 1974-76; regional rep. Interphil '76, 1974-76, USO, AARP, So. Poverty Law Ctr./Klanwatch Project. Contbr. revs., articles to popular mags., newspapers. Pres. North High Alumni Assn., Mpls., 1946-47; mem. nat. adv. bd. The Generation After; assoc. Simon Wiesenthal Ctr. for Holocaust Studies; mem. St. Louis Park Centennial Commn., 1985-86; charter mem. US Holocaust Meml. Mus., US World War II Meml., Air Force Meml. Found., Nat. WWII Mus.; founding mem. F.D.R. Meml., Nat. Campaign for Tolerance, William J. Clinton Presdl. Found. Recipient Disting. Topical Philatelist Hall of Fame award, medal, 2004, and invited to sign Disting. Topical Philatelist scroll of honor, 1962, Silver medal for Keeping Posted column in Mpls. Star Am. Philatelic Soc.-Chgo. Philatelic Soc. Conv., 1974, Silver award for Keeping Posted column in Post Publs. Weekend, sponsored by Coun. Philatelic Orgns., 1989, True Grit award Grit Mag., 1997, 98. Mem.: MADD, DAV (life; comdr. Mpls. chpt. No. 1 1986), Internat. Assn. Philatelic Journalists, Internat. Philatelic Press Club (gov.), Am. Philatelic Soc. (life; writers unit), Civil War Preservation Trust, Nat. Trust for Hist. Preservation, Srs. Coalition, City of Hope, Hebrew Immigration Aid Soc., Nat. Assn. for the Repeal of Abortion Laws, Minn. Sr. Fedn., American Values, Life Extension Found., Ret. Sr. Citizens' League, Father Solanus Guild, People for the Am. Way, Internat. Platform Assn., Jerusalem Instn. for the Blind, Keren Or, Inc., Camera, Holocaust Survivors Assn. USA (nat. adv. bd.), Alliance Ret. Ams., Am. United for Separation of Ch. and State, Nat. Com. to Preserve Social Security, Statue of Liberty-Ellis Island Found. Inc. (charter), Mid. East Media Rsch. Inst., Am. Topical Assn. (founding pres. chpt. 1957—61, nat. pres. 1968—70, 1970—72, dir., nat. adv. com.), Paralyzed Vets. Am. (hon.), Manuscript Soc., Collectors Club NY, Royal Philatelic Soc. New Zealand, Christchurch Philatelic Soc., Inc., New Zealand Stamp Collector's Club (hon.; anonymously donated ann. Fred Korotkin Cup for best thematic entry 1966—). Home: Apt 512 4925 Minnetonka Blvd Minneapolis MN 55416-2271 also: PO Box 11053 Minneapolis MN 55411-0053 *Ever since I was a youngster I've tried to determine what character traits help make a person successful. I've come to believe that the most important combination is still confidence in self, stick-to-itiveness, and that other winning ingredient which can be called aim, direction or goal.*

KOROTKIN, MICHAEL PAUL, lawyer; b. NYC, Oct. 5, 1937; m. Marcia Ellen, Aug. 28, 1960; children: Darryl, Alan, Alyssa. AB, Duke U., 1959; LLB, NYU, 1962. Bar: N.Y. 1963. Ptnr. Kramer Levin Naftalis & Frankel LLP, NYC, 1973—. Named a Superlawyer, 2007; named one of Best Lawyers in Am., 2006, 2007. Office: Kramer Levin Naftalis & Frankel LLP 1177 Ave of the Americas New York NY 10036 Office Phone: 212-715-9155. E-mail: mkorotkin@kramerlevin.com.

KOROTKOV, ROMAN Y., engineer, research scientist; PhD, Northwestern U., 2001. Engr. Lucent Technologies, Reading, Pa., 2001; scientist Arkema, King of Prussia, Pa., 2001—06. Mem.: Materials Rsch. Soc.

(assoc.). Achievements include patents in field. Office Phone: 610-878-6454. Office Fax: 610-878-6261. Personal E-mail: rkorotkov@yahoo.com. Business E-Mail: roman.korotkov@arkemagroup.com.

KORS, MICHAEL (KARL ANDERSON JR.), fashion designer; b. LI, NY, Aug. 9, 1959; s. Joan Kors. Student, Fashion Inst. Tech., 1977. Designer, buyer, display dir. Lothar's Boutique, NYC, 1978-81; founder Kors by Michael Kors, 1981—. The first women's ready-to-wear designer House of Celine, Divsn. Moët Hennessy Louis Vuitton, 1997, creative dir., 99; released signature fragrance for women, Michael Kors, 2000; released signature fragrance for men, Michael Kors, 01. Named Womenswear Designer of Yr., Coun. Fashion Designers Am., 1999, Menswear Designer of Yr., 2003; recipient First Am. Original award, DuPont, 1983, Elle/Cadillac Fashion award for Excellence, 1995, Lifetime Achievement award, Lighthouse Internat., 1999, NY award, NY Mag., Golden Hanger award for best designer, E! TV Networks, Women's Fragrance Star of Yr. for MICHAEL, Fragrance Found., 2000, Men's Fragrance Star of Yr. for MICHAEL for Men, Best New Women's Fragrance for MICHAEL, Cosmetic Exec. Women, Best New Men's Fragrance for MICHAEL for Men. Mem.: Coun. Fashion Designers Am. (exec. v.p., bd. dir.). Office: Michael Kors USA Inc 11 W 42 St New York NY 10036 Business E-Mail: inquiries@michaelkors.com.*

KORS, R. PAUL, search company executive; b. Pontiac, Mich., June 12, 1935; s. Ralph Dewey and Lydia Elizabeth (Shavlik) K.; m. Carol Jayne Kullick, July 17, 1966; children: Kristen Patricia, Shannon Elizabeth. BBA, U. Mich., 1958; MBA, U. So. Calif., 1965. Salesman Nalco Chem. Co., LA, 1958-66; investment mgr. Dean Witter & Co., LA, 1966-73; sr. assoc. Korn Ferry Internat., LA, 1973-74, v.p. Houston, 1974-77, v.p., mgr., 1977-78; founder, pres., CEO Kors Montgomery Internat., Houston, 1978—. Chmn. ITP Worldwide, 2003—. Served to 1st lt. U.S. Army, 1958. Mem.: Palmas del Mar Country Club. Avocations: skiing, golf, tennis, films, reading. Home: 14306 Heatherfield Dr Houston TX 77079-7407 Office: R Paul Kors 14306 Heatherfield Dr Houston TX 77079-7407 Home Phone: 281-493-4730; Office Phone: 713-840-7101. Business E-Mail: pkors@korsmontgomery.com.

KORSCHOT, BENJAMIN CALVIN, retired investment company executive; b. LaFayette, Ind., Mar. 22, 1921; s. Benjamin G. and Myrtle P. (Goodman) K.; m. Marian Marie Schelle, Oct. 31, 1941; children: Barbara E. Korschot Haehlen, Lynne D. Korschot Gooding, John Calvin. BS, Purdue U., 1942; MBA, U. Chgo., 1947. V.p. No. Trust Co., Chgo., 1947-64; sr. v.p. St. Louis Union Trust Co., 1964-73; exec. v.p. Waddell and Reed Co., Kansas City, Mo., 1973-74, pres., 1974-79, vice-chmn. bd., 1979-85; pres. Waddell & Reed Investment Mgmt. Co., 1985-86; chmn. bd. Waddell & Reed Asset Mgmt. Co., 1973-86, retired, 1986. Pres. United Group of Mut. Funds, Inc., Kansas City, Mo., 1974-85, chmn., 1985-86; vice-chmn. Roosevelt Fin. Group, St. Louis, 1968-91, chmn. adv. bd., 1991-92; treas. Helping Hand of Goodwill Industries, 1993-95, chmn. investment com., 1995-2004; bd. dirs. Mo. United Meth. Found., 1995-2004, chmn. investment com., 2001-2004; chmn. bd. govs. Investment Co. Inst., 1980-82; chmn. bd. Fin. Analyst Fedn., 1978-79. Contbr. articles on investment fin. to profl. publs.; author autobiography, 1997. Mem. Civic Coun. Greater Kansas City, Mo., 1974-85; chmn. fin. com. ARC Retirement Sys., 1986-87. With USN, 1942-45, 50-52. Mem. Inst. CFAs, Fin. Execs. Inst., Kansas City Soc. Fin. Analysts, Lakewood Oaks Golf Club. Republican. Home: 101 NW Hackberry St Lees Summit MO 64064-1477 Personal E-mail: bckorschot@yahoo.com. *A happy Christian home environment, the adversity of the depression of the 30's, the challenges of competitive sports, the desire to achieve knowledge, recognition and responsibilities, a devoted wife and three children who made our marriage most meaningful have been the dominant influences of my life.*

KORSHUNOV, VYACHESLAV SLAVA A., pharmacist, educator; s. Anatoly E. Korshunov and Raisa V. Korshunova; m. Olga N. Vasilyeva, Mar. 5, 2002; 1 child, Alexander V. Diploma with honors in Pharmacy, Pyatigorsk State Acad. Pharmacy, Russia, 1997; MS in Biology, Pushchino State U., Russia, 1999; PhD in Pharmacy and Pharmacology, Pyatigorsk State Acad. Pharmacy, Russia, 2000. Lic. pharmacist Russia, 1998. Rsch. asst. prof. U. Rochester, NY, 2004—06, asst. prof., 2006—. Contbr. chapters to books, articles to profl. jours. Recipient Young Scientists Competition award, 1996, 1999, Young Scientist Travel award, 2000; grantee, Soros Found., 1999. Mem.: Am. Physiol. Soc. (Young Investigator award 2003), Am. Heart Assn. (Irvine H. Page Young Investigator Rsch. award 2005), N.Am. Vascular Biology Orgn. (Jr. Investigator award 2006). Avocation: Judo. Home Phone: 585-359-8166; Office Phone: 585-273-1914.

KORST, CHRISTOPHER A., lawyer, rental company executive; V.p., asst. gen. counsel Thorn Americas, 1992—96, v.p. bus. devel., 1996, v.p. Thorn Auto, 1996—97; COO AdvantEdge Quality Cars, 1997—99, prin., owner, 2000—01; sr. v.p., gen. counsel Rent A Ctr., Plano, Tex., 2001—. Office: Rent A Center 5700 Tennyson Pkwy Plano TX 75024*

KORST, HELMUT HANS, mechanical engineer, educator; b. Vienna, Jan. 4, 1916; came to U.S., 1948; married, 1942; 4 children. Diploma in Engring., Vienna Tech. U., 1941, Dr. Tech. Sci., 1947, Golden Dr. diploma, 1997. Rsch. engr. Maschinenfabrik Augsburg-Nurnberg AG, Germany, 1941-45; asst. prof. mech. engring. Vienna Tech. U., 1945-48, vis. lectr. gas dynamics, 1948-49; from assoc. prof. to prof. mech. engring. U. Ill., Urbana, 1949-84, head dept. mech. and indsl. engring., 1962-74, prof. emeritus, 1984—; chair naval air power engring. USN Postgrad. Sch., Monterey, Calif., 1979; Ebaugh Chair Mech. Engring. U. Fla., Gainesville, 1984; pvt. practice cons. Urbana, 1956—. Vis. prof. Kans. State U., Manhattan, 1950, Va. Poly. Inst. and State U., Blacksburg, 1954; design specialist Gen. Dynamics Convair, Ft. Worth, 1955; propulsion specialist Rocketdyne div. N.Am. Aviation, 1960, 65-68; cons. GE, 1959, Adv. Group Aeronautical R & D NATO, 1964, U.S. Missile Command, 1971—. Sr. postdoctoral fellow NSF, 1957; recipient ASEE Centennial medal 1993, Daniel Guggenheim medal in aviation, 1994. Fellow: AIAA, ASME; mem.: ASME Internat. (hon.), Am. Soc. Engring. Edn., Sigma Xi. Achievements include research on internal and external aerodynamics, jet and rocket propulsion, and heat transfer. Address: 3 Eton Ct Champaign IL 61820-7602 Business E-Mail: h-korst@uiuc.edu.

KORSTEN, SUSAN SNYDER, science educator; b. Cherry Hill, NC, July 28, 1944; d. Eugene Ralph and Beatrice Roggen Snyder; m. Mark Allen Korsten, Dec. 18, 1974; children: Eric Robert, Caroline Messer. AB, U. Pa., Phila., 1966; MA, Tchrs. Coll. Columbia U., NYC, 1967. Cert. tchr. grades 1-6 N.Y.C. Tchr. math. Riverside Sch., NYC, 1967—68; tchr. 5th grade Downtown Cmty. Sch., NYC, 1968—71; tchr. math. and computer Dalton Sch., NYC, 1971—94; tchr. sci. Calhoun Sch., NYC, 1994—. Mem. sch. bd. Downtown Cmty. Schs., 1968—71; spkr. elem. sch. sci. Assn. Tchrs. Ind. Schs., NYC, 1996—2005. Author: articles in sch. newspapers, poems in sch. archive. Mem. bd. Hastings Creative Arts Coun., Hastings-on-Hudson, 1979—87; nature guide Hastings Elem. Sch., 1981—87; founder, co-dir. Help-A-Child Program, Hastings-on-Hudson, 1992—. Named Outstanding Tchr. of Yr., Calhoun Sch., 2000; recipient Prin.'s Excellence award, Prin. Dalton 1st Program, 1993. Mem.: Assn. Tchrs. Ind. Schs. Democrat. Jewish. Achievements include first educator invited to teach at Dalton Schools in Tokyo and Nagoya; taught Japanese teachers how to instruct computer, science and mathematics; created and taught in one of the first computer laboratories for young children, 1978. Avocations: ballroom dancing, singing, travel, poetry, aerobics. Home: 2 Edgewood Ave Hastings On Hudson NY 10706 Office: Calhoun Sch 433 West End Ave New York NY 10024 Office Phone: 212-497-6500. Business E-Mail: susan.korsten@calhoun.org.

KORT, WESLEY ALBERT, religious studies educator, writer; b. Hoboken, NJ; s. Arthur Henry Kort and Jantina Schrik; m. Phyllis May Hoekstra, Dec. 17, 1960; children: Anne Catherine Rankowitz, Eva Deane, Alexander Wesley. BA, Calvin Coll., 1956; BD, Calvin Theol. Sem., 1959; MA, U. Chgo., 1961, PhD, 1965. Instr. Princeton U., NJ, 1963—65; asst. to assoc. prof. Duke U., Durham, NC, 1965—77, prof., 1977—. Author: Shriven Selves: Religious Problems in Recent American Fiction, 1972, Narrative Elements and Religious Meaning, 1975, Moral Fiber: Character and Belief in Recent American Fiction, 1982, Modern Fiction and Human Time: A Study in Narrative and Belief, 1985, Story, Text, and Scripture: Literary Interests in Bibical Narrative, 1988, Bound to Differ: The Dynamics of Theological Discourses, 1992, Take, Read: Scripture, Textuality and Cultural Practice, 1996, C.S. Lewis Then and Now, 2001, Place and Space in Modern Fiction, 2004; contbr. essays and reviews to profl. jours. Fellow: Soc. of Arts, Religion and Contempory Culture, Erasmus Inst.; mem.: Ctr. Theol. Inquiry. Home: 308 Old Buggy Tr Hillsborough NC 27278 Office: Duke Univ Dept Religion Box 90964 Durham NC 27708 Office Phone: 919-660-3514. Office Fax: 919-660-3530. Business E-Mail: wkort@duke.edu.

KORTEN, DAVID C., writer; b. Longview, Wash., July 30, 1937; AB in Psychology, Stanford U., 1959, MBA, 1961, PhD, 1968. Asst. dean, Fulbright asst. prof., Coll. Bus. Adminstrn. Haile Sellassie I U., Addis Ababa, Ethiopia, 1963-66; program mgr., asst. behavioral and social scis. Office of Sec. of Def., Washington, 1969-70; vis. assoc. prof. Ctrl. Am. Inst, Bus. Adminstrn., Managua, Nicaragua, 1970-73, Harvard U. Grad. Sch. Bus., Cambridge, Mass., 1970-75; inst. assoc. Harvard Inst. Internat. Devel., Cambridge, Mass., 1975-77; lectr. population studies Harvard Sch. Pub. Health, Cambridge, Mass., 1976-78; coord. Mgmt. Insts. Working, Manila, The Philippines, 1977-83; vis. prof. Asian Inst. Mgmt., Manila, The Philippines, 1977-85; project specialist Ford Found., Manila, The Philippines, 1978-81; Asia regional advisor on devel. mgmt. (Manila and Jakarta) Agy. Internat. Devel., Washington, 1981-88; v.p. for Asia Inst. Devel. Rsch., Boston, 1988-89; founder, pres. People-Centered Devel. Forum, Bainbridge Island, Wash., 1990—. Co-founder, bd. chair The Positive Futures Network, Bainbridge Island, 1996—; bd. dirs. Context Inst., Bainbridge Island, 1994-96, Bus. Alliance for Local Living Econs., 2004—, Bainbridge Grad. Inst., 2005-06. Author: The Great Turning: From Empire to Earth Community, 2006, The Post-Corporate World: Life After Capitalism, 1999, Globalizing Civil Society, 1998, When Corporations Rule the World, 1995 (Tomorrow's 10 Best award 1998), 2d edit., 2001, Getting to the 21st Century: Voluntary Action and the Global Agenda, 1990, Planned Change in a Traditional Society: Psychological Problems of Modernization in Ethiopia, 1972; co-author: Casebook for Family Planning Management, 1977; Editor: Community Management: Asian Experience and Perspectives, 1986, People-Centered Development: Contributions Toward Theory and Planning Frameworks, 1984, Bureaucracy and the Poor: Closing the Gap, 1981; contbr. numerous articles to profl. jours. and mags.; mem. editl. adv. bd. Devel., 1998—, Environment and Urbanization, 1993—, World Bus. Acad. Perspectives, 1997-99; mem. editl. adv. bd. Kumarian Press, Inc., 1991—. Chair ACLU N.W. Fla., 1968. Capt. USAF, 1968-70. Mem.: Club of Rome.

KORTH, FRITZ-ALAN, lawyer; b. Ft. Worth, Aug. 29, 1938; s. Fred and Vera (Connell) K.; m. Penne Percy, Dec. 15, 1965 (div. 1997); children: Fritz-Alan Jr., Maria Eleanor, James Frederick. AB, Princeton U., 1961; LLB cum laude, U. Tex., 1964; HHD (hon.), U. Americas, 1982. Bar: Tex. 1964, D.C. 1964. Asst. sec. OKC Corp., Dallas, 1964-65; ptnr. Korth & Korth, Washington, 1965—; pres. Wilmar Corp., Port Chester, NY, 1980—. Founder, sec., bd. dirs. Women's Nat. Bank, Washington, 1978-85, chmn. bd. First WNB Corp., 1982-85; bd. dirs. Trans Leisure Corp., N.Y.C., 1970-75, chmn. bd., 1973-75; bd. dirs. Del Norte Tech., Inc., Dallas., 1969—, chmn., 1982-98, vice chmn. bd. dirs., 1998—; bd. dirs. Del Norte Tech. Ltd., Swindon, Eng.; trustee Meridian Internat. Ctr., 2003—. Registrar St. John's Episcopal Ch., Washington, 1968-70, vestryman, 1970-74, treas., 1973-77; chmn. fin. com., mem. diocesan coun. Episcopal Diocese Washington, 1973-77; trustee, treas. Cathedral chpt. Washington Nat. Cathedral, 1977-84; pres. U. Americas Found., 1969-84; bd. assocs. U. Americas, Puebla, Mex., 1969—; bd. dirs. Travelers Aid Soc. Washington, 1969-86, pres., 1973-75; dir. Southwestern Exposition and Livestock Show, 1987—; charter commr. U.S.-Mex. Commn. for Ednl. and Cultural Exch., 1991-97; pres. AMMA Found., Inc., 1994—, dir. 1989. Mem. ABA, Inter-Am. Bar Assn., D.C. Bar, Tex. Bar Assn., Am. Law Inst., Am. Soc. of Most Venerable Order of Hosp. of St. John of Jerusalem, Phi Delta Phi. Clubs: Met. (Washington), Chevy Chase (Washington); Argyle (San Antonio); Steeplechase (Ft. Worth); Princeton (N.Y.C.); Gymkhana Club (Mauritius). Mailing: PO Box 65482 Washington DC 20035-5482 also: 888 17th St NW Ste 608 Washington DC 20006-3313

KORTHALS, CANDACE DURBIN, lawyer; b. Tampa, Fla., Oct. 3, 1948; d. Robert F. and Geraldine B. Durbin; children: John Kristofor, Kathryn Elizabeth. BA in Internat. Studies, Ohio State U., 1969, BS in Edn., 1970; JD cum laude, Nova U., 1982. Bar: Fla. 1982. Tchr. Palatka (Fla.) Mid. Sch., 1970-72, Dillard H.S., Ft. Lauderdale, Fla., 1974-79; atty. Broward County Pub. Defenders, 1982-84, Grimmett & Korthals, 1984-90, Gunther & Whittaker, 1990-94, Law Office of John Camillo, 1994-99, Neale & De Almeida, 1999-2000, Heinrich, Gordon, Hargrove, Weihe & James, 2000—02, Barnett & Barnard, Hollywood, 2002—. Staff mem. Nova Law Rev., 1981, 82. Office: Barnett & Barnard 4601 Sheridan St #505 Hollywood FL 33021 Office Phone: 954-463-3449. Business E-Mail: ckorthals@bbslawfirm.com.

KORTLANDER, SUSAN ELIZABETH, psychologist; b. Austin, Tex., Oct. 29, 1956; d. William Clark and Elizabeth F. Kortlander; m. Bruce A. Harvey, Sept. 18, 1982; children: Aaron Kortlander Harvey, Jason Leonard Harvey. BA summa cum laude in History, Ohio U., 1978; MA in History of Art, U. Pa., 1984; MS in Clin. Psychology, San Jose State U., Calif., 1988; PhD in Clin. Psychology, Temple U., 1994. Lic. psychologist Dept. Health Divsn. of Med. Quality Assurance, Fla., 1998. Psychology intern Belmont Ctr. Comprehensive Treatment, Phila., 1992—93; resident psychology Children's Psychiat. Ctr., Miami, Fla., 1995—98; interventionist Teen Intervention Project Nova Southeastern U., Ft. Lauderdale, Fla., 1997—98, Fla. Internat. U., North Miami, 1999—2001, clin. supr., co-investigator ATTAIN program, 1999—2001; clin. dir. Susan B. Anthony Ctr., Inc., Lauderdale Lakes, Fla., 2001—02; pvt. practice Weston Psychcare P.A., Weston, Fla., 2003—, Pines Psychol. Assn. PA, Pembroke Pines, Fla., 2006—. Co-author: Anxiety Disorders in Youth:Cognitive Behavioral Interventions, 1992; contbr. chapters to books, articles to profl. jours. Fellow, U. Pa., 1980—81; grantee, Temple U., 1994. Mem.: APA, South Fla. Soc. Trauma Based Disorders, Fla. Psychol. Assn. (bd. mem. Fla. initiative for suicide prevention), Phi Beta Kappa. Avocations: art, reading, swimming. Office: Weston PsychCare PA 2771 Executive Park Drive Suite #4 Weston FL 33331 also: Pines Psychological Assoc PA 700 N Hiatus Rd Ste 213 Pembroke Pines FL 33026 Home Phone: 954-920-8938; Office Phone: 954-431-0411. Office Fax: 954-431-0413. Personal E-mail: harv2774@bellsouth.net.

KORZENSKI, ROBERT M., manufacturing executive; b. 1954; V.p. ops. Scott Paper Co., v.p. sales & mktg.; pres., COO Fonda Group Inc., 1998—2002; pres. Hoffmaster brand Sweetheart Cup Co., 2002—04; sr. v.p. integration Solo Cup Co., Highland Park, Ill., 2004—05, exec. v.p. sales & mktg., 2005—06, pres., COO, 2006, pres., CEO, 2006—. Office: Solo Cup Co 1700 Old Deerfield Rd Highland Park IL 60035*

KOS, PAUL, artist; b. Rock Springs, Wyo., Dec. 23, 1942; BFA, San Francisco Art Inst., 1965, MFA, 1967. One-man shows include Jernigan Wicker Fine Arts, San Francisco, 1995, Berkeley Art Mus., U. Calif., 2003, Grey Art Gallery, NYU, 2003, San Diego Mus. Contemporary Art, Cin., 2003, exhibited in group shows at Frederick Weisman Mus. Art, Malibu, 1998, Lance Fung Gallery, NYC, 1999, Gallery Paule Anglim, San Francisco, 2003, The Katzen Am. U. Mus., 2005, San Francisco Art Inst., 2006. Fellow, Nat. Endowment Fellowship, 1974, 1976, 1982, 1993, Western States Art Fellowship, 1983, 1987, Louis Comfort Tiffany Found. Fellowship, 1986, Rockefeller Found. Fellowship, 1987, John Simon Guggenheim Meml. Fellowship, 1990; Grant, Nat. Endowment Media Arts, 1986, Nat. Endowment for Arts, 1997, Flintridge Found., 1999—2000.

KOSAKOW, JAMES MATTHEW, lawyer; b. New London, Conn., Apr. 12, 1954; s. Leonard Louis and Lois Ann (Rosen) K.; 1 child, Jonathan Daniel. BA, Conn. Coll., 1976; JD, Yeshiva U., 1984. Bar: N.Y. 1985, Conn. 1985, D.C. 1985, Fla. 1991, U.S. Dist. Ct. (so. and ea. dists.) 1985, U.S. Tax Ct. 1993. Assoc. Vittoria & Forsythe, NYC, 1986-92, Gregory and Adams, Wilton, Conn., 1992-94; pvt. practice NYC and Westport, Conn., 1994-97; ptnr. Kove & Kosakow, LLC, 1997—2005, McLaughlin & Stern, LLP, NYC, 2005—. Adj. asst. prof estate and gift taxation and planning NYU Sch. Continuing and Profl. Studies; lectr. in field. Co-author: Handling Federal Estate and Gift Taxes, 6th edit., 2000; asst. editor Insights and Strategies; contbr. articles to profl. jours. Fellow Am. Coll. of Trust and Estate Coun., trustee, bd. dirs. Internat. Nursery Sch., Queens, N.Y., 1987-89; mem. estates & trusts specialty group lawyers divsn. United Jewish Appeal-Fedn. Jewish Philanthropies of N.Y., Inc., 1990-94; commr. Wilton Water Commn., 1995-96, Wilton Fire Commn., 1996-2000; chmn. membership com. Mid-Fairfield Substance Abuse Coalition, 1995-96; dir. Thee Art Tree Source, Inc., 1995—; adv. com. The Unicorn Archive. Mem. N.Y. Bar Assn. (legis. com., trusts and estates sect. 1987—). Office: McLaughlin & Stern LLC 260 Madison Ave New York NY 10016 Office Fax: 212-448-0066. Business E-Mail: jkosakow@mclaughlinstern.com.

KOSARIN, JONATHAN HENRY, lawyer, consultant; b. Bklyn., Aug. 13, 1951; s. Lester and Norma (Higger) K.; m. Gayle C. Skarupa, Nov. 27, 1982. BA in History magna cum laude, Syracuse U., 1973; JD, Bklyn. Law Sch., 1976; LLM in Govt. Contract Law, George Washington U., 1984; postgrad., U.S. Army Command and Gen. Staff Coll., 1990, U.S. Army War Coll., 1997. Bar: N.Y. 1977, D.C. 1978, U.S. Supreme Ct. 1980, U.S. Ct. Claims 1981, U.S. Ct. Appeals (Fed. cir.) 1982. Commd. 2d lt. U.S. Army, 1973, advanced through grades to col., 1997, prosecutor trial counsel Ft. McClellan, Ala., 1977-78, adminstrv. law officer, 1978-79, instr. law, 1979-80, trial atty. contract appeals div. Washington, 1980-84; contracts atty. U.S. Army Hdqrs., Heidelberg, Fed. Rep. Germany, 1985-87; assoc. gen. counsel, dir. procurement law Fed Home Loan Bank Bd., Washington, 1987-89; assoc. counsel USN, Washington, 1989-94, dep. counsel, 1994—. Adj. asst. prof. contract law JAG Sch., Charlottesville, Va., 1988—93, adj. assoc. prof., 1993—95, adj. prof., vice chmn., 1995—99, adj. prof., chmn., 1999—2002; dep. gen. counsel def. prisoner of war Missing Pers. Office, 2002—07; acting chief contract law U.S. Army Europe, Heidelberg, Germany, 2003; adj. faculty contract law U. Va., Charlottesville, 1989—; mem. faculty Fed. Publs. Seminars, 1995—, ESI Internat., 1999—2002. Vol. info. specialist Smithsonian Instn. Washington, 1993—, pres. Temple Rodef Shalom, Falls, Church, Va., 2000-02; mem. Mid-Atlantic coun. Union Reform Judaism, 2002-, v.p., 2006-; para-Rabinnic fellow Temple Rodef Shalom, Falls Church, 1998—. Mem. ABA, D.C. Bar Assn., Titanic Hist. Soc., No. Va. Football Ofcls. Assn. (bd. dirs. 2005—), No. Va. Football Officers Assn, Nat. Assn. Sports Ofcls., Phi Alpha Delta, Phi Beta Kappa, Phi Kappa Phi, Phi Delta Kappa Democrat. Office: USN Office of Gen Counsel Box 26256 Arlington VA 22215 Personal E-mail: kosarin9426@verizon.net.

KOSASKY, HAROLD JACK, fertility researcher; b. Winnipeg, Man., Can., Oct. 19, 1927; s. Jack and Lillian (Resnick) K.; m. Shirley Anne Johnston, Sept. 3, 1955; children: Julia, Leah, Robert. BA, U. Manitoba, Can., 1948; MD, U. Manitoba, 1953. Diplomate Am. Bd. Ob-gyn.; lic. Coll Physicians and Surgeons Can., Med. Coun. Can., Ky. State Bd. Health, Idaho State Bd. Health, Mass. Bd. Registration in Medicine. Intern Deer Lodge VA and Grace Hosps., Winnipeg, Man., Canada, 1952-53; resident in gen. surgery Col. Belcher Hosp., Calgary, Alta., Canada, 1953-54; resident in psychiatry Warren (Pa.) State Hosp., 1955-56; jr. asst. resident, asst. resident, sr. resident in ob-gyn. Chgo. Lying-In Hosp., 1956-59; exch. fellow in ob-gyn. Newcastle Gen. Hosp., U. Durham, England, 1959-60; asst. and assoc. prof. U. Louisville Sch. Med., 1961-65; asst. and assoc. in ob-gyn. various hosps., Boston, 1966-81; gynecologist, obstetrician Boston Hosp. for Women, 1965-81; gynecologist Brigham & Women's Hosp., Boston, 1981—; instr. ob-gyn. Harvard U., 1965—; pres., CEO Boston Rheology, 2000—05. Cons. Ovutime, Boston, 1972-82; pres. Saltime Co., 1994, chmn. 1999-2000; asst. vis. surgeon Boston City Hosp., 1967-69; mem. Ky. Govs. Task Force on Mental Retardation, 1964-65; chmn. Com. on Malignancy, 1963-65. Contbr. articles to profl. jours.; co-inventor Ovutime; inventor Saltime Ovulation group of instruments. Fellow: ACS, Boston Obstetric Soc. (emeritus), Royal Soc. Health, Royal Coll. Surgeons Can. (cert.); mem.: AAAS, Louisville Med. Forum (v.p.), Louisville Obstet. and Gynecol. Soc. (sec., treas. 1962—65), Assn. Prof. Ob-gyn., Royal Coll. Obstetricians and Gynecologists, Gen. Med. Coun. Can. (lic.), Harvard Club. Episcopalian. Office: Box 67506 Chestnut Hill MA 02467 Office Phone: 617-556-6680.

KOSCIELAK, JERZY, research scientist; b. Lodz, Poland, Sept. 6, 1930; s. Jozef and Regina (Pokrzywa) K.; m. Anna Kitaszewska, 1969 (div. 1974); 1 child, Katarzyna. MB, Med. Acad., Warsaw, Poland, 1953, MD, 1960, DrSci, 1966. Asst. dept. physiol. chemistry Med. Acad., Warsaw, 1950-51; asst. and sr. asst. dept. biochemistry Inst. of Hematology, Warsaw, 1951-67; rsch. fellow Harvard Coll., Cambridge, 1964-65; head immunochem. lab. Inst. of Hematology, Warsaw, 1968-69, head dept. biochemistry, 1969—2002. Sci. sec. Inst. of Hematology, Warsaw, 1969-97, dir., rsch. 1997—, prof., 1973—. Editor-in-chief Acta Haematologica Polonica jour., 1976-85; contbr. articles to profl. jours. Mem. Polish Biochem. Soc. (chmn. Warsaw divsn. 1967-69), Forum of Carbohydrates Coming of Age (FCCA), Polish Acad. Sci., Internat. Glycoconjugate Orgn. (Polish rep. 1988—, pres. 1993-95), Found. for Glycobiology Glyco XII (founder, pres. 1993—). Avocation: history. Office: Inst of Hematology Chocimska 5 00957 Warsaw Poland Office Phone: 004822 8489515. Business E-Mail: kosci@atos.warman.com.pl.

KOSEL, RENÉE, state representative; b. Chgo., Apr. 03; m. Alfred Kosel; 3 children. BS in Edn., Western Ill. U. Bd. dirs. Lincoln-Way H.S. Dist. Recipient numerous awards. Mem.: local cmty. orgns. Republican. Lutheran. Office: 200 N Stratton Office Bldg Springfield IL 62706 Address: 19201 S LaGrange Rd Ste 204B Mokena IL 60448 Office Phone: 708-479-4200. E-mail: rkosel@aol.com.

KOSHALEK, RICHARD, academic administrator, former museum director, consultant; b. Wausau, Wis., Sept. 20, 1941; s. H. Martin and Ethel A. (Hochtritt) K.; m. Elizabeth J. Briar, July 1, 1967; 1 child, Anne Elizabeth. Student, U. Wis., 1960-61, MA, 1965-67; BA, U. Minn., 1965. Curator Walker Art Ctr., Mpls., 1967-72; asst. dir. NEA, Washington, 1972-74; dir. Ft. Worth Art Mus., 1974-76, Hudson River Mus., Westchester, NY, 1976-80, Mus. Contemporary Art, LA, 1980-99, dir. emeritus,

1999—; dir. Pasadena Design Ctr., 1999; pres. art ctr. Coll. of Design, Pasadena, Calif., 1999—. Mem. Pres.' Coun. on Arts, Yale U., New Haven, Conn., 1989-94; mem. internat. bd. Biennale di Venezia, Italy, 1992-93; mem. internat. adv. bd. Wexner Ctr., Ohio State U., Columbus, 1990—; mem. com. of assesors The Tate Gallery of Art, London; mem. internat. jury Philip Morris Art award, 1996; commr. Kwangju Biennale, 1997; mem. screening com. Osaka Triennale, 1997; selection com. Museo de Art Contemporaneo de Monterrey prize, 1997-98; panel chair Phila. Exhbns. Initiative, 1998, fed. adv. com. for internat. exhbns. Nat. Endowment for the Arts, 1997; bd. mem. Am. Fedn. of Arts, 2001—, Internat. Design Conf., Aspen, 2001; juror Chrysler Design awards, 2002, La Biennale De Venezia, 2002; del., panelist, World Econ. Forum, 2002, 2003; cons. in field. Co-curator (exhibitions and books) Panza Collection, 1986, Ad Reinhardt, 1991, Arata Isozaki, 1991, Louis I. Kahn, 1992, Robert Irwin, 1993, At the End of the Century: One Hundred Years of Architecture, 1998, Richard Serra, 1998. Mem. Chase Manhattan Bank Art Com., NYC, 1986-99; chmn. architect selection Walt Disney Concert Hall, LA, 1988-90; mem. adv. Neighborhood Revitalization Bd. for Pres. Clinton, Little Rock, Ark., 1993; bd. dirs. Am. Ctr. in Paris, 1993—. Recipient Parkinson Spirit of Urbanism award U. So. Calif. Archtl. Guild, 1996, Outstanding Achievement award U. Minn., 2007; NEA fellow, 1972, Durfee Found. fellow, 1992, Design fellow IBM, 1984; Chevalier Des Arts et Lettres, French Govt., 1999. Mem. Am. Assn. Mus. Dirs. Office: Office of the President Art Center Coll of Design 1700 Lida St Pasadena CA 91103 Office Phone: 626-396-2200. Business E-Mail: richard.koshalek@artcenter.edu.

KOSHIBA, MASATOSHI, physicist, educator; b. Toyohashi, Aichi, Japan, Sept. 19, 1926; m. Kyoko Kato, Oct. 5, 1959. BS in physics, U. Tokyo; PhD, U. Rochester, 1955. Prof. dept. physics U. Tokyo, 1970—87; prof. Tokai U., 1987—97; prof. emeritus Internat. Ctr. Elem. Particle Physics, U. Tokyo, 1987—. Recipient Der Grosse Verdienstkreutz, Pres. of West Germany, Order of Cultural Merit, Emperor of Japan, Wolf prize in physics, Wolf Found., Israel, 2000, W.K.H. Panofsky prize, 2002, Nobel prize in physics, 2002. Mem.: NAS, The Japan Acad., Japanese Astron. Soc., Physical Soc. Japan, Am. Physical Soc. Office: Univ Tokyo 7-3-1 Hongo Bunkyo-ku Tokyo 113-0033 Japan

KOSHKIN-YOURITZIN, VICTOR, art educator; b. NYC, Dec. 20, 1942; s. Basil and Tatiana Y.; m. Glenda Allen Green (div. 1980); m. Cynthia Lee Kerfoot (div. 1997). BA in Art History cum laude with honors, Williams Coll., 1964; cert., Columbia U., 1965; MA in Art History, NYU, 1967, cert. in Mus. Tng., 1969. Instr. art history Vanderbilt U., Nashville, 1968-69, Newcomb Coll., Tulane U., New Orleans, 1969-72; asst. prof. art history U. Okla., Norman, 1972-80, assoc. prof., 1980-94, prof., 1994-97, David Ross Boyd disting. prof. history of art, 1997—. Lectr. in field; panelist program art on film Met. Mus. Art and J. Paul Getty Trust, N.Y.C., 1987, NEH, 1984; trustee Mabee-Gerrer Mus. Art, Shawnee, Okla., 1995-02, chmn. bd. trustees, 1996-99, mem. adv. bd., 2002-; mem. coun. advisors Ogden Mus. So. Art, U. New Orleans, 1995-03; trustee Okla. Mus. Art, Oklahoma City, 1978-84; mem. acquisitions com. Oklahoma City Art Mus., 1992-96; guest lectr. South African Dept. Nat. Edn., 1986; lectr. Met. Mus. Art, Art Students League N.Y., Dallas Mus. Art, The Pentagon, other instns. in Eng., France, Africa, the Caribbean; cruise guest lectr. masterpieces of French impressionist and post impressionist painting Cunard Line, 1993. Author: Oklahoma Treasures, 1986, Five Contemporary Russian Artists, 1992, Twentieth-Century Russian Art, 1994, Paintings, Drawings, and Prints from the Late 19th and Early 20th Centuries, 1996, Twentieth-Century Russian Drawings, 1997, Pavel Tchelitchew, 2002, Photographs By Charles Henri Ford, 2006; author introduction: American Watercolors from The Metropolitan Museum of Art, 1991 (Book of Month Club Selection); contbr. articles to profl. jours. including Arts, Art Jour. and Gazette des Beaux-Arts; represented in collections including Nat. Libr. France, Paris, Beinecke Libr., Yale U., Wallach Divsn. Art, Prints, and Photographs, NY Pub. Libr., Wadsworth Atheneum Mus. Art, The Andy Warhol Mus. Ford Found. fellow Inst. Fine Arts, NYU, 1967-69, IBM and Noble fellow Columbia U., 1964-65; recipient Gov.'s Arts and Edn. award, Oklahoma City, 1992, Hon. citation State of Okla. House Reps., 1993, Outstanding Pub. award, Okla. Mus. Assn., 2003. Mem. Koussevitzky Recs. Soc., Inc. (v.p. 1992—). Avocations: tennis, music. Home: 1721 Oakwood Dr Norman OK 73069-4449 Office: U Okla 520 Parrington Oval Rm 202 Norman OK 73019-3011 Office Phone: 405-325-2691. Business E-Mail: vky@ou.edu.

KOSIK, EDWIN MICHAEL, federal judge; b. 1925; BA, Wilkes Coll., Wilkes-Barre, Pa., 1949; LLB, Dickinson Sch. Law, Carlisle, Pa. Asst. U.S. atty. Pa. State Workmen's Compensation Bd., 1953-58, chmn., 1964-69; pvt. practice Needle, Needle & Needle, 1958-64; pres. judge 45th Jud. Dist. Ct. Common Pleas, 1979-86; judge U.S. Dist. Ct. (mid. dist.) Pa., Scranton, 1986—, now sr. judge. Office: US Dist Ct US Courthouse PO Box 856 Scranton PA 18501-0856 Office Phone: 570-207-5730. E-mail: chambers_of_edwin_m._kosik@pamd.uscourts.gov.

KOSINSKI, EDWARD JOHN, cardiologist, educator; b. Springfield, Mass. BA, U. Pa.; MS, Wake Forest U. Sch. Medicine, MD, 1973. Cert. Internal Medicine, 1976, Cardiovascular Disease, 1979, lic. Conn. and Mass. Intern, medicine Columbia-Presbyn. Med. Ctr., NYC, 1973—74, resident, cardiology, 1974—76; fellow Peter Bent Brigham Hosp., Boston, 1976; former chairperson, cardiovascular medicine and interventional cardiology St. Vincent's Med. Ctr.; assoc. clin. prof. Yale Med. Sch., Columbia U., NY Med. Coll.; private practice Conn. Mem.: Am. Heart Assn., Am. Coll. Cardiology. Office: 4675 Main St Bridgeport CT 06606*

KOSKINEN, JOHN ANDREW, foundation executive; b. Cleve., June 30, 1939; s. Yrjo Alfred and Irja (Danska) K.; m. Patricia Salz, June 15, 1963; children: Jeffrey, Cheryl. BA magna cum laude, Duke U., 1961; JD cum laude, Yale U., 1964; postgrad., Cambridge U., Eng., 1964-65. Bar: Calif. 1965, Conn. 1972. Clk. to presiding judge U.S. Ct. Appeals, Washington, 1965-66; lawyer Gibson, Dunn & Crutcher, LA, 1966-67; spl. asst. to dep. exec. dir. Nat. Adv. Commn. Civil Disorders (also known as Kerner Commn.), Washington, 1967-68; legis. asst. to Mayor John Lindsay NYC, 1968-69; adminstrv. asst. to Senator Abraham Ribicoff Conn., 1969-73; v.p. Palmieri Co., Washington, 1973-77, pres., chief operating officer, 1977-79, pres., chief exec. officer, 1979-94; dep. dir. for mgmt. Office of Mgmt. and Budget, Washington, 1994-97; asst. to Pres., chmn. President's Coun. on Year 2000 Conversion, Washington, 1998-2000; dep. mayor, city adminstr. Washington, 2000—03; pres. U.S. Soccer Found., Washington, 2004—; bd. dirs. Capital Strategies, 2007—. Bd. dirs. AES Corp., 2004—. Mem. Pres.'s Mgmt. Improvement Coun., 1979-80; bd. dirs. Nat. Captioning Inst., 1979-91, chmn., 1986-87, vice-chmn., 1979-86; trustee Coop. Assistance Fund, 1982-93; trustee Duke U., 1985-97, vice chmn. 1993-94, chmn. 1994-97; chmn. Washington 1994 World Cup Commn., 1989-94, Washington Olympic Football Organizing Com., 1993-96; vice chmn. Am. Soccer League, 1987-91; dir. U.S. Soccer Found., 1993-94, 2001—; pres. Washington Met. Area Coun. Govt., 2003. Fellow Nat. Acad. Pub. Adminstrn., Phi Beta Kappa; mem. Duke U. Gen. Alumni Assn. (pres. 1980-81), Soccer Hall of Fame, Va. Avocations: soccer, tennis, music. Office: US Soccer Foundation Ste 210 1050 17th St NW Washington DC 20036 Home Phone: 202-723-4020; Office Phone: 202-872-6657. Personal E-mail: johnkosk@aol.com.

KOSLOW, JONATHAN L., lawyer; b. NYC, 1953; BA magna cum laude, NYU, 1974; JD, Boston U., 1977; LLM in Estate Planning, U. Miami, 1978. Bar: NY 1978. Ptnr.-in-charge trusts and estates Skadden, Arps, Slate, Meagher & Flom LLP, NYC. Contbr. articles to profl. publs. Mem.: NY State Bar Assn. (mem., trusts and estates law sect.), ABA (mem., real property, probate and trust law sect.). Office: Skadden Arps Slate Meagher & Flom LLP 4 Times Sq New York NY 10036 Office Phone: 212-735-2810. Office Fax: 917-777-2810. Business E-Mail: jkoslow@skadden.com.

KOSLOW, STEPHEN HUGH, health science association administrator, pharmacologist, neuroscientist; s. Julius and Lillian Koslow; m. Diane Heisler, Aug. 18, 1962; children: Karin, James. BS, Columbia U., 1962; PhD, U. Chgo., 1967. Internat. postdoctoral fellow Swedish Med. Rsch. Coun., Karolinski Inst., 1968-69; pharmacologist, chief neurobiology unit St. Elizabeth's Hosp., Washington, 1970-77; chief biol. rsch. sect. Clin. Rsch. br. NIMH, Rockville, Md., 1975-81, chief Neurosci. Rsch. br., 1981—85, chief Basic Scis. Neurosci. Rsch., 1985—88, dep. dir. divsn. Basic Brain and Behavioral Scis., 1989—90; dir. divsn. Basic and Clin. Neurosci. Rsch. NIMH-NIH, Rockville, 1990—99; assoc. dir., dir. office neuroinformatics NIMH, Rockville, 1999—2004; dir. external rels. Allen Inst. Brain Sci., Seattle, 2005—, Biomedical Consulting, 2006—. Project dir. NIHM-CRB Collaborative Program on Psychobiology of Depression-Biol. Study, 1975-85; mem. adv. bd. Tourette Syndrome Assn., Bayside, NY, 1984; chair fed. coordinating com. on the Human Brain Project, 1991—; chair neuroinformatics subgroup of Office Econ. Coop. & Devel., Megasci. Forum, Biol. Working Group, 1996-99; co-chair US/EC com. on neuroinformatics, 1998—, chair global sci. forum neuroinformatics working group, 2000-02. Mem. editl. bd. Neuropsychopharmacology, 1987-92, Critical Revs. in Neurobiol., 1991-2004, Human Brain Mapping, 1993-2004, Psychopharm. Bull., 1989-99, Neuroimage; series editor Progress in Neuroinformatics Rsch., 1996-2001, Neuroimage, 1995-2001, CNS Drug Revs., 1995-99, Biomednet, 1999-2003; editor: Databasing the Brain From Data to Knowledge, 2005; assoc. editor Jour. Integrative Neurosci. Recipient NIMH Quality Increase award, 1977-78, Health Adminstr.'s award for Meritorious Achievement, 1986, Pub. Health Svc. Spl. Recognition award, 1992, Alumni Achievement award U. Chgo. Club of Washington, 1995, two Dir.'s awards NIH, 1996, Pres. award Internat. Neural Network Soc., 2001; Swedish Med. Rsch. Coun. internat. postdoctoral fellow, 1968-69, Spl. NATO fellow, 1969. Fellow AAAS, Am. Coll. Neuropsychopharmacology, Am. Coll. Med. Informatics; mem. Am. Soc. for Neurochemistry, Am. Soc. Pharmacology and Exptl. Therapeutics, Collegium Internat. Neuro Psychopharmacologium, Soc. for Neurosci., Soc. Biol. Psychiatry. Home and Office: 8642 Falcon Green Dr West Palm Beach FL 33412 E-mail: stevekoslow@gmail.com.

KOSNER, EDWARD A(LAN), editor; b. NYC, July 26, 1937; s. Sidney and Annalee (Fisher) Kosner; m. Alice Nadel, Feb. 1, 1959; children: John Robbins, Anthony William; m. Julie Baumgold, Nov. 19, 1978; 1 child, Lily. BA, CCNY, 1958. CCNY corr. NY Times, NYC, 1957—58; rewriteman, asst. city editor NY Post, NYC, 1958—63; assoc. editor Newsweek Mag., NYC, 1963—67, gen. editor, 1967—69, nat. affairs editor, 1969—72, mng. editor, 1972—75, editor, 1975—79, NY Mag., NYC, 1980—93, editor, pub., 1986—91, editor, pres., 1991—93; editor-in-chief Esquire Mag., NYC, 1993—97, NY Daily News, NYC, 2000—03; editor NY Sunday Daily News, NYC, 1998—99. Author: It's News To Me, 2006. Recipient various journalism awards. Mem.: Am. Soc. Mag. Editors (pres. 1984—86, exec. com.), Century Club. Personal E-mail: edsquire@aol.com.

KOSS, LEOPOLD G., pathologist, educator; b. Gdansk, Poland, Oct. 2, 1920; arrived in U.S., 1947, naturalized, 1952; s. Abram and Rose (Merenholc) Kon; m. Lydia Palla; children: Michael S., Andrew C., Richard P. MD, U. Berne, Switzerland, 1946; Doctorate (hon.), Pomeranian Med. Acad., Poland, 2002. Intern Lincoln Hosp., NYC, 1947-48; tng. pathology St. Gallen, Switzerland, 1946-47, Kings County Hosp., Bklyn., 1949-52; instr. pathology LI U. Coll. Medicine, NY, 1949-52; mem. staff Meml. Hosp. Cancer and Allied Diseases, NYC, 1952-70, attending pathologist, 1961-70, chief cytology svc., 1961-70; pathologist-in-chief Sinai Hosp. Balt., 1970-73; prof., chmn. dept. pathology Montefiore Hosp., Med. Ctr. Albert Einstein Coll. Medicine, Bronx, NY, 1973-92, prof., chair emeritus, 1993—. Hon. prof. pathology Severance Med. Coll., Seoul, Korea, 1956; assoc. mem. Sloan-Kettering Inst. Cancer Research, NYC, 1957-70; assoc. prof. pathology Sloan-Kettering div. Postgrad. Sch. Med. Sci., Cornell U., 1957-70; prof. pathology Jefferson Med. Coll., Phila., 1970-73; clin. prof. pathology U. Md. Med. Sch., 1971-73; vis. pathologist James Ewing Hosp., NYC, 1952-60; former cons. pathologist NY State Dept. Health, Hosp. Spl. Surgery, NYC; cons. pathologist Walter Reed Army Med. Ctr., Nassau County Med. Ctr.; Frost lectr., Balt., 1999. Author: Diagnostic Cytology and Its Histopathologic Bases, 5th rev. edit. 2006, Tumors of the Urinary Bladder, 1975, Supplement, 1984, Aspiration Biopsy: Cytologic Interpretation and Histologic Bases, 2d rev. edit. 1992, Introduction to Gynecologic Cytology, 1999; editor: Advances in Clinical Cytology, Vol. I, 1981, Vol. II, 1984, Papillomaviruses and Human Diseases, 1987, Errors and Pitfalls in Diagnostic Cytology, 1997; contbr. more than 390 articles to profl. jour. and 40 chpts. to books also monographs. Served to maj. M.C., AUS, 1955-57. Decorated officer Order of Merit, Polish Republic, 2004; recipient Wien award Papanicolaou Cancer Inst., 1963, Alfred P. Sloan award cancer rsch., 1964, Fred Stewart award, 1984, Vandenberge-Hill award, 1984, Meritorious medal U. Brussels, 1987, Jurzykowski award, 1991, Disting. Pathologist award US and Can. Acad. Pathology, 2001, Disting. Pathologist award Assn. Pathology Chairs, 2002. Fellow: AAAS, Internat. Acad. Cytology (Goldblatt award 1962, Kazumasa Masubuchi Life-Time Achievement award in clin. cytology 1995), Coll. Am. Pathologists, Am. Soc. Clin. Pathology, Royal Coll. Pathologists (hon. Found. lectr. 1997), Royal Coll. Pathologists (hon.); mem.: AMA, Am. Soc. for Colposcopy and Cervical Pathology (Disting. Svc. award 1996), Internat. Soc. of Urol. Pathology (F.K. Mostofi Disting. Svc. award 1995), German Acad. Sci. (Leopoldina), Peruvian Soc. Ob-Gyn., Polish Soc. Pathology, Japanese Soc. Pathology, Argentinian Soc. Cytology, Mex. Soc. Cytology, Brit. Soc. Clin. Cytology (hon.), Royal Acad. Medicine Spain (corr.), Korean Med. Assn., NY State Soc. Pathology (Lansky-Ratner award 1989), NY Pathology Soc. (pres. 1985—87, Middleton-Goldsmith lectr. 1992), Internat. Acad. Pathology (Maude Abbott lectr. 1989), Am. Soc. Cytology (pres. 1962, Papanicolaou award 1966), James Ewing Soc., Am. Soc. Exptl. Pathology (Gold Cane award 1993), Order of Merit Republic of Poland (officer, medal 2004). Office: Montefiore Med Ctr 111 E 210th St Bronx NY 10467-2401 Office Phone: 718-920-5185. Business E-Mail: lkoss@montefiore.org.

KOSS, TAMARA, dermatologist, educator; b. San Jose, Costa Rica, Mar. 6, 1971; d. Jaime Koss and Jaya Tischler; m. Michael A. Bender, May 31, 1998. BA in Psychology magna cum laude with highest honors, Harvard U., Boston, 1993; MD cum laude, Yale U., New Haven, 1999. Diplomate Am. Bd. Dermatology, 2003. Fellow Boston Laser & Dermatology Ctr., 2003—04; hon. clin. observer St. John's Inst. Dermatology, London, England, 2004—05; assoc. dermatologist Dr. Phillis Smith, Huntington, NY, 2005, Dr. Tina K. Funt, Garden City, NY, 2005—, Dr. Marina I. Peredo, Smithtown, NY, 2005—. Instr. dermatology Coll. Physicians & Surgeons Columbia U., NYC, 2006—. Contbr. articles to profl. jours. Recipient Gordon W. Allport prize, Harvard U., 1993; Merck/Mass. Gen. Hosp. Minority fellow, 1995. Fellow: Am. Acad. Dermatology; mem.: Women's Dermatologic Soc., Alpha Omega Alpha, Phi Beta Kappa. Achievements include research in first isolation of the Rickettsia akari organism since 1940s. Office: Marina I Peredo MD PC 260 Middle Country Rd Ste 208 Smithtown NY 11787

KOSSAR, RONALD STEVEN, lawyer; b. Ellenville, NY, May 30, 1948; s. Emanuel and Helen (Panken) K.; m. Sandra Perlman, Aug. 25, 1973. BA cum laude, Boston U., 1970; JD, Am. U., 1973. Bar: N.Y. 1974, D.C. 1974, U.S. Dist. Ct. (no. dist.) N.Y. 1974, U.S. Tax Ct. 1974, U.S. Ct. Appeals D.C. 1974. Tax law specialist Office Asst. Commr. (Tech.), IRS, Washington, 1973-75; sole practice Middletown, NY, 1976—. Dir. Newburgh (N.Y.) Realty Corp. Mem. ABA, N.Y. State Bar Assn., Orange County Bar Assn., Middletown Bar Assn., D.C. Bar. Jewish. Office: 402 E Main St Middletown NY 10940-2516 Office Phone: 845-343-5111. Office Fax: 845-343-5222. Business E-Mail: rsklaw@warwick.net.

KOSSEFF, JEFF, reporter, news correspondent; married. BA, MA, U. Mich. Tech. reporter The Oregonian, Portland, reporter Washington, DC bur., 2004—; corr. Newhouse News Svc., Washington. Co-recipient George Polk award for Nat. Reporting, 2006. Office: The Oregonian 1320 SW Broadway Portland OR 97201 also: Newhouse News Svc 1101 Connecticut Ave NW, #300 Washington DC 20036 Office Phone: 503-294-7605. E-mail: jeff.kosseff@newhouse.com.*

KOSSLYN, STEPHEN M., psychologist, educator; b. Santa Monica, Calif., Nov. 30, 1948; s. S. Duke and Rhoda Kosslyn; m. Robin S. Rosenberg, Mar. 28, 1982; children: Justin Lewis Rosenberg, David Alan Rosenberg, Nathaniel Solté Rosenberg. BA in Psychology, UCLA, 1970; PhD in Psychology, Stanford U., 1974. Asst. prof. psychology The Johns Hopkins U., 1974-77; assoc. prof. psychology Harvard U., 1977-81; rsch. affiliate of the Ctr. for Cognitive Sci. MIT, 1980-94; assoc. prof. psychology Brandeis U., 1981-82; prof. psychology Harvard U., 1983—, chmn. dept. psychology, 2005—; co-dir. James S. McDonnell Found. Summer Inst. in Cognitive Neuroscience, 1987; assoc. psychologist in neurology Mass. Gen. Hosp., 1990—. Vis. asst. prof. psychology U. Calif., Berkeley, 1976; cons. Consulting Statisticians, Inc., 1977—83; vis. prof. Johns Hopkins U., 1982—83, Maitre de Conf. Coll. de France, 1997—98; mem. governing bd. Cognitive Sci. Soc., 1989—95. Author: Image and Mind, 1980, Ghosts in the Mind's Machine, 1983, Wet Mind: The New Cognitive Neuroscience, 1992, Image and Brain, 1994, Elements of Graph Design, 1994; author: (with R. Rosenberg) Psychology: The Brain, The Person, The World, 2001, Psychology in Context, 2006; author: The Case for Mental Imagery, 2006; editor (with others): Tutorials in Learning and Memory: Essays in Honor of Gordon H. Bower, 1983, Quantitative Analyses of Behavior, Vol. 9: computational and Clincial Approaches to Pattern Recognition and Concept Formation, 1989, An Invitation to Cognitive Science: Visual Cognition and Action, 1990, Essays in Honor of William K. Estes, 1992, Frontiers in Cognitive Neuroscience, 1992, The Neuropsychology of Mental Imagery, 1996; editor: Graph Design for the Eye and Mind, 2006; editor: (with Smith) Cognitive Psychology: Mind and Brain, 2006; contbr. articles to profl. jours. Recipient Boyd R. McCandless Young Scientist award, divsn. 7 APA, 1978, Initiatives in Rsch. award, NAS, 1983, Cattell award, 1991, J-L Signoret prize, Fondation Ipsen/Am. Acad. Arts and Scis., 1995; Guggenheim fellow. Mem.: APA, AAAS, Soc. Exptl. Psychologists, Am. Acad. Arts and Scis., Soc. Neuroscience, Psychonomic Soc., Cognitive Sci. Soc., Mass. Neuropsychol. Soc., Am. Psychol. Soc. Avocations: classical music, French, bass. Home Phone: 617-864-8468; Office Phone: 617-495-3932. Business E-Mail: smkosslyn@wjh.harvard.edu.

KOSTELANETZ, RICHARD, writer, artist; b. NYC, May 14, 1940; s. Boris and Ethel (Cory) K. AB with honors, Brown U., 1962; postgrad. (Fulbright scholar), King's Coll., U. London, 1964-65; MA, Columbia U., 1966. Program assoc. thematic studies John Jay Coll. CUNY, 1972-73; sr. staff Ind. U. Writers' Conf., 1976; vis. prof. English and Am. studies U. Tex. at Austin, 1977; vis. prof. of theater Hunter Coll., CUNY, 2002; guest Mishkenot Sha'ananim, Jerusalem, 1979, 86, DAAD Berliner Kunstlerprogramm, 1981-83; master artist Atlantic Ctr. for the Arts, 2001. Co-propr. Assembling Press, 1970-82; lit. dir. The Future Press, 1976—; propr. Wordsand Music (ASCAP), 1982—; Archae Editions, 1978— guest artist WXXI-FM, Rochester, 1975-76, Synapse, Syracuse U., 1975, Cabin Creek Ctr. for Work and Environ. Studies, 1978, Electronic Music Studio of Stockholm, 1981, 83-84, 86, 88, Bklyn. Coll. Ctr. for Computer Music, 1984, Dennis Gabor Lab. Mus. Holography, 1985, 89, Exptl. TV Lab., Owego, NY, 1985-87, 89-91, 2006, Real Art Ways, 1988, Film/Video Arts, 1989, Inst. Electronic Arts, Alfred U., 2004. Author: Music of Today, 1967, The Theatre of Mixed Means, 1968, 2d edit., 1981, Master Minds: Portraits of Contemporary American Artists & Intellectuals, 1969, Visual Language, 1970, In the Beginning, 1971, The End of Intelligent Writing, 1974; 2d edit. as Literary Politics in Am, 1977; I Articulations/Short Fictions, 1974, Recyclings, vol. 1, 1974, complete text, 1984, Openings & Closings, 1975, Extrapolate, 1975, Come Here, 1975, Modulations, 1975, Portraits from Memory, 1975, Constructs, 1976, Rain Rains Rain, 1976, Numbers: Poems and Stories, 1976, Numbers Two, 1977, Illuminations, 1977, One Night Stood, 1977, Grants & the Future of Literature, 1978, Constructs Two, 1978, Tabula Rasa, 1978, Inexistences, 1978, Wordsand, 1978, Twenties in the Sixties, 1979, "The End" Appendix, 1979, "The End" Essentials, 1979, And So Forth, 1979, Exhaustive Parallel Intervals, 1979, More Short Fictions, 1980, Metamorphosis in Arts, 1980, The Old Poetries and the New, 1981, Autobiographies, 1981, Reincarnations, 1982, Turfs/Arenas/Fields/Pitches, 1983, American Imaginations, 1983, Epiphanies, 1983, Autobiographien New York Berlin, 1986, Prose Pieces/After Texts, 1987, The Old Fictions and the New, 1987, The Grants-Fix, 1987, Conversing with Cage, 1988, rev. edit., 2002, On Innovative Music(ian)s, 1989, Unfinished Business, 1990, The New Poetries and Some Olds, 1991, Politics in the African-American Novel, 1991, Constructs Three, 1991, Constructs Four, 1991, Constructs Five, 1991, Constructs Six, 1991, Fifty Untitled Constructivist Fictions, 1991, Intermix, 1991, Flipping, 1991, Published Encomia, 1991, Solos, Duets, Trios & Choruses, 1991, On Innovative Art(ist)s, 1992, A Dictionary of the Avant-Gardes, 1993, 2d edit., 1999, Wordworks: Poems New & Selected, 1993, On Innovative Performance(s), 1994, One Million Words of Booknotes 1958-1993, 1996, Minimal Fictions, 1994, Crimes of Culture, 1995, Fillmore East: Recollections of Rock Theater Twenty-Five Years After, 1995, Radio Writings, 1996, Openings, 1997, Thirty Years of Critical Engagements with John Cage, 1997. An ABC of Contemporary Reading, 1995, John Cage (Ex)plain(ed), 1996, 3-Element Stories, 1998, Vocal Shorts: Collected Performance Texts, 1998, Which Witch?, 1999, Political Essays, 1999, 3 Canadian Geniuses, 2001, More Wordworks, 2005, 35 Years of Visible Writing, 2004, SoHo: The Rise and Fall of an Artists Colony, 2003, Autobiographies at 60, 2004, Contagion: A Novel, 2004, Reimagining Rockaway Postcards, 2004, Erotic Minimal Fictions, 2005, The East Village, 1969-70, 2004, Autobiographies at 50, 2005, Film & Video: Alternative Views, 2005, Ghosts, 2006, Kaddish and Other Audio Writings, 2006, More Wordworks, 2006, Autobiographies at 50, 2006, Home & Away Travel Essays, 2006, Book-Art, Anthologies & Alternative Publishing, 2006, On Sports & Sportsmen, 2006, The Maturity of American Thought, 2006, Jewish Writings So Far, 2006, Archae's Alphabet, 2006, Furtherest Fictions, 2007, Fields, Pitches/Turfs/Arenas, 2007, others; editor, contbr.: On Contemporary Literature, 1964, 69, The New American Arts, 1965, Twelve from the Sixties, 1967, The Young American Writers, 1967, Beyond Left & Right: Radical Thought for Our Times, 1968, Imaged Words & Worded Images, 1970, Moholy-Nagy, 1970, 91, John Cage, 1970, 91, Possibilities of Poetry, 1970, Social Speculations, 1971, Human Alternatives: Visions for Us Now, 1971, Future's Fictions, 1971, Seeing Through Shuck, 1972, BreakthroughFictioneers, 1973, The Edge of Adaptation, 1973, Essaying Essays, 1975,Language & Structure, 1975, Younger Critics in North America, 1976, Esthetics Contemporary, 1977, 88, Assembling Assembing, 1978, Visual Literature Criticism, 1979, Text-Sound Texts, 1980, Scenarios, 1980, The Yale Gertrude Stein, 1980, A Critical Assembling, 1980, Aural Literature Criticism, 1981, American Writing Today, 1981, The Avant-Garde Tradition in Literature, 1982, Gertrude Stein Advanced, 1990, Merce Cunningham, 1992, 98, John Cage: Writer, 1993, Writings AboutJohn Cage, 1993, 2000, Nicolas Slonimsky: The First 100 Years, 1994, A Portable Baker's Biographical Dictionary of

Musicians, 1995, AnOther E.E. Cummings, 1998, Writing on Glass, 1997, Classic Essays on 20th Century Music, 1996, A B.B. King Companion, 1997, 2005; A Frank Zappa Companion, 1997, Virgin Thomson: A Reader, 2002, The Gertrude Stein Reader, 2002, An Aaron Copland Reader, 2003, others; composer: Praying to the Lord, 1977, 81, Invocations, 1981, 84, The Gospels/Die Evangelien, 1982, The Eight Nights of Hanukah, 1983, New York City, internat. version, 1984, Am. version, 1987, A Special Time, 1985, Baseball: Americas' Game, 1988, 2nd edit., 1998, Onomatopoeia, 1988, Kaddish, 1990, Acoustic Fiction I: Ululation, 1992, No, I'm Not Richard Kostelanetz, 1993; producer numerous audiotapes, films, videotapes, extended radio features for stas. in Australia, Fed. Republic Germany, Sweden, U.S.; filmmaker: (with others) Openings & Closings, 1978, Constructivist Fictions, 1978, Epiphanies, 1981-94, Ein Verlorenes Berlin/A Berlin Lost/Berlin Perdu/Ett Forlorat Berlin/El Berlin Perdido/Berlin Sche-Einena Jother, 1984-88 (prizewinner Ann Arbor, Mich., Film Festival); video art: Three Prose Pieces, 1975, Kinetic Writings, 1989, Video Strings, 1989, Stringsieben, 1989, Turfs/Grounds/Lawns, 1989, Invocations, 1988, Seductions, 1988, The Gospels Abridged, 1988, Relationships, 1988, Two Erotic Videotapes, 1988, Two Sacred Texts, 1988, Partitions, 1986, Onomatopoeia, 1989, Kaddish, 1991, Openings & Closings, 1975, Video Writing, 1987, Declaration of Independence, 1979, Epiphanies, 1980, Home Movies Reconsidered, 1992, Americas' Game. 2001, Video Poems, 2004, Video Stories, 2004, Secret Stories, 2004, Infinities, 2006; contbg. editor: Pushcart Prize; writer, narrator: Camera Three, WCBS-TV, 1974; co-founder, compiler Assembling, 1970-82; co-pub., editor: Precisely, A Critical Jour., 1977—; contbr. articles, poems, revs., photographs and essays to mags.; numerous group exhbns. visual poetry, visual fiction, audiotapes, videotapes, films, holograms and numerical art; comprehensive exhbn.: Wordsand, at Simon Fraser U., U. Alta., Cornell Coll., Vassar Coll., U. ND, Calif. State U., Bakersfield, Dade County CC, Miami, Fla., 1978-81; retrospectives of video art: Anthology Film Archives, 1994, Bumbershoot, Seattle, 1991, Festival de la Baite, Geneva, 1989, U. of SC, 1978. Woodrow Wilson fellow, 1962-63, Pulitzer fellow in critical writing, 1965-66, fellow Guggenheim Meml. Found., 1967-68, Fund for Investigative Journalism, 1980, Vogelstein Found., 1980, Internat. fellow Columbia U., 1963-64, Editors fellow CCLM, 1983, Ivri-Nasawi fellow, 2000—; Visual Arts grantee Nat. Endowment of Arts, 1976, 78, 79, 85, 86, 90, Media Arts grantee Nat. Endowment of Arts, 1981, 82, 84, 91; N.Y. State Regents scholar, 1963-64, Am. Pub. Radio Program Fund, 1984; Pollock-Krasner fellow, 2001; recipient Standard award ASCAP, 1983-92, 94— (annually). Mem. Nat. Coalition Ind. Scholars, Internat. Assn. Art Critics, Soc. for Origination of Horspiel in Am., Phi Beta Kappa. Address: PO Box 444 Prince St New York NY 10012-0008 *To do what has not been done in several domains and in the course of that adventure to discover new possibilities in art, in writing, and in myself.*

KOSTELNIK, MICHAEL CHARLES, commissioner, retired military officer; b. Harlingen, Tex., May 15, 1946; s. Michael and Nita Louise K.; m. Barbara Lynn Brychta, Dec. 23, 1966; 1 child, Khristine Lynn Kostelnik Carlson. BS in Mech. Engring., Tex. A&M U., 1969; MS in Indsl. and Mgmt. Engring., U. Iowa, 1970; grad., USAF Test Pilot Sch., 1977; post grad., U. Fla., 1980; grad., Nat. Def. U., 1981, USAF Instrument Pilot Instrs. Sch., Indsl. Coll. of Armed Forces, 1986, Def. Sys. Mgmt. Coll., 1989; grad. sr. exec. devel. program, U. NH, 1993; grad., Syracuse U., 1996. Lic. commercial pilot, multi-engine, instrument FAA, level III cert. Dept. Defense Acquisition Program Mgr. Commd. 2nd lt. USAF, 1969, advanced through grades to maj. gen., 1994; pilot trainee Vance AFB, Okla., 1970-71; with 18th Tactical Reconnaissance Squadron, Shaw AFB, SC, 1971-72; aircraft comdr., instr. pilot, wing flight examiner 10th Tactical Reconnaissance Wing, Alconbury, England, 1972-75; ctr. test project pilot 4485th Test Squadron, Tactical Air Warfare Ctr., Eglin AFB, Fla., 1975-76; squadron ops. officer 3246th Test Wing, Eglin AFB, 1977-81; tactical fighter requirements officer Office Dep. Chief of Staff for Rsch., Devel. and Acquisition, Washington, 1981-85; dir. combined test forces Edwards AFB, Calif., 1986-87; comdt. USAF Test Pilot Sch., Edwards AFB, 1987-89; dep. program dir. F-16 Sys. Program Office, Wright-Patterson AFB, Ohio, 1989-91; program dir. Short Range Attack Missile II, SRAM-Tactical Sys. Program Office Aero. Sys. Divsn., Air Force Sys. Command, Wright-Patterson AFB, 1991-92; First Sys. Program dir., Aircraft Sys. Program Office Aero. Sys. Ctr., Air Force Material Command, Wright-Patterson AFB, 1992-93; vice comdr. Warner Robins Air Logistics Ctr., Robins AFB, Ga., 1993-94; dir. spl. programs Office Under Sec. of Def., The Pentagon, Washington, 1994-95; dir. plans Hdqs. Air Force Materiel Command, Wright-Patterson AFB, Ohio, 1995—97; vice comdr. Air Force Materiel Command, Wright Paterson AFB, 1997—98, comdr. Air Force Devel. Test Ctr. Eglin AFB, Fla., 1998—99, comdr. Air Armament Ctr., 1999—2002; dep. assoc. adminstr. for space shuttle and internat. space sta. Hdqrs. NASA, Washington, 2002—05; asst. commr. US Customs and Border Protection Air and Marine Dept. Homeland Security, 2005—. Assoc. editor Whispering Wind, 1992—; contbr. articles to profl. mags.; TV appearances. Decorated Def. Disting. Svc. medal, Air Force Disting. Svc. medal with oak leaf cluster, Legion of Merit, Meritorious Svc. medal with two oak leaf clusters, Air Force Commendation medal with oak leaf cluster; recipient Marie Radice award Am. Indianist Soc., 1985, Les Bircher award, 1987, Nat. Def. Indsl. Assoc. gold medal, 2001, Air Force Assoc. Jerry Waterman award, 2001, NAACP Cleophs McIntosh Armed Svcs. award, 2000, NDIA Moseley Munitions Mgmt. award, 2000, Computer Week Fed. 100 award, 2004; named 1st Disting. Grad. of Mary Carroll H.S., Corpus Christi, 2004; named to Acad. Dist. Grads., Mech. Engring., Tex. A&M U., 2004. Mem. NASA (Outstanding Leadership award 2005), Soc. Exptl. Test Pilots (sect. chmn.), Order of Daedalions. Roman Catholic. Avocations: golf, alpine skiing, Native American crafts and culture, fishing. Office: US Customs and Border Protection Air and Marine Dept Homeland Security 1300 Pennsylvania Ave NW Rm 6 4A Washington DC 20229 Office Phone: 202-344-3899. Business E-Mail: michael.kostelnik@dhs.gov.

KOSTELNY, ALBERT JOSEPH, JR., lawyer; b. Phila., July 11, 1951; s. Albert Joseph and Margaret (Naile) K. BA, U. Pa., 1973, MA, 1974; JD, Fordham U., 1979. Bar: NY 1980, U.S. Dist. Ct. (so. dist.) NY 1983, U.S. Ct. Claims 1983, U.S. Supreme Ct. 1983, U.S. Ct. Internat. Trade 1985, U.S. Ct. Appeals (2d cir.) 1985. Atty. NY State Divsn. Human Rights, NYC, 1980-81, sr. atty., 1981-89, acting chief adminstrv. law judge, 1989-91, adjudication counsel to commr., 1991—, dir. prosecutions unit, 1998—2001, assoc. atty., 2001—. Mem. ABA, NY State Bar Assn., NY County Lawyers Assn., ATLA. Republican. Roman Catholic. Office: NY State Divsn Human Rights One Fordham Plz Bronx NY 10458-5871 Home Phone: 215-922-4373; Office Phone: 718-741-8404. Business E-Mail: akostelny@dhr.state.ny.us.

KOSTEN, THOMAS R., psychiatrist, educator; b. Bklyn., Feb. 16, 1951; s. Richard Kosten; m. Therese Kosten, Aug. 12, 1978; children: Molly, Neal. MD, Cornell, NYC, 1977. Lic. Psychiatry Am. Bd. Psychiatry And Neurology, 1984, Addiction Psychiatry Am. Bd. Of Psychiatry And Neurology, 1993. Chief of psychiatry VA Conn., West Haven, Conn., 1996—2000; prof. Yale U., New Haven, 1983—2006, Baylor Coll. Medicine, Houston, 2006—. Congl. fellow, u.s. ho. of rep. Ho. Subcommittee on Human Resources (Christopher Shays, Chair), Washington, 1998—99. Recipient America's Top Drs., Second Edit.; Top Doctors: N.Y., Sixth Edit., Castle Connolly Med. Ltd., 2002. Fellow: Am. Acad. of Addiction Psychiatry (pres. 1998—2000). Achievements include research in 1993 Joel Elkes Internat. award for outstanding contrb. to Psychopharmacology, American Coll. of Neuropsychopharmacology 2000-on Sr. Scientist Award, Nat. Inst. on Drug Abuse. Avocations: tennis, ice skating. Office: Baylor College Medicine Michael E DeBailey VA Med Ctr 2002 Holcombe Blvd Houston TX 77030 Business E-Mail: kosten@bcm.tmc.edu.

KOSTER, BARBARA, insurance company executive; Acct. Chase Manhattan Bank, 1976—87, v.p. fin. sys., 1980—85, v.p. info. svcs., 1985—88, pres., Chase Access Svcs., 1988—95; v.p., policy adminstrn. and mgmt. info. systems Prudential Financial, 1995—97, v.p., Individual Fin. Svcs., 1997—2000, chief info. officer, individual life ins. systems Newark, 2000—03, sr. v.p., chief info. officer, 2004—. Recipient award Women in Sci. & Tech., 1999. Office: Prudential Ins Co Am 751 Broad St Newark NJ 07102-3714

KOSTER, ELAINE, publishing executive; b. NYC; BA, Barnard Coll. Pres., pub. Dutton Signet, NYC; head Elaine Koster Literary Agy. LLC, NYC. Office: Elaine Koster Literary Agy LLC 55 Central Park W Ste 6 New York NY 10023-6003 Personal E-mail: elainekost@aol.com.

KOSTER, EMLYN HOWARD, geologist, educator; b. Suez Canal Zone, Egypt, Mar. 18, 1950; arrived in Eng., 1953, Canada, 1971, came to U.S., 1996; s. Douglas Albert and Dorothy Muriel (Roberts) Koster; m. Maryse Rémillard Koster, May 22, 1974; children: Véronique Justina, Simon Emlyn. BSc with spl. honours in Geology, U. Sheffield, Eng., 1971; PhD in Geology, U. Ottawa, 1977. Rsch. scientist terrain scis. divsn. Geological Survey of Can., Ottawa, 1973-74; cons. Geo-Analysis Ltd., Ottawa, 1975-76; asst. prof. dept. geology Concordia U., Montreal, Canada, 1976-77; asst. prof. dept. geol. scis. U. Sask., Saskatoon, Canada, 1977-80; rsch. officer, project mgr. Alta. Geol. Survey, Alta. Rsch. Coun., Edmonton, Canada, 1980-86; dir. Royal Tyrrell Mus. of Palaeontology, Drumheller and Field Sta., Dinosaur Provincial Park, UNESCO World Heritage Site, Alta., 1986-91; dir. gen. Ont. Sci. Centre, Agy. Govt. Ontario, Toronto, Canada, 1991-96; pres., CEO Liberty Sci. Ctr., NJ, 1996—. Mem. Challenger Ctr. for Space Sci. Edn., Va., 1993—2002, Can.-China Dinosaur Expdn. to Gobi Desert, China, 1987; vis. prof. U. Buenos Aires, 1988; pres. Geol. Assn. Can., 1996—97; mem. adv. com. Mus. Mgmt. Inst., Getty Leadership Inst., Calif., 1997—99; bd. dirs. Assn. Sci.-Tech. Ctrs., Washington, 1993—2001; v.p. Giant Screen Theatre Assn., Minn., 2003—; mem. Interdisciplinary Planning Com. for Liberty State Park, NJ, 1999—; Prin.-for-a-Day NY Pub. Schs., 2001; mem. sr. adv. bd. Flandrau Sci. Ctr., Ariz., 2002—; vis. prof. Inst. Marine and Coastal Studies, Rutgers U., NJ, 2002—; bd. dirs. Prosperity N.J.; mem. adv. coun. Met. Waterfront Alliance for N.Y. Harbor; advisor Coll. Sci. and Math., Montclair State U., 2004—; keynote spkr. Internat. Forum on Culture of Sci., Tech. and Innovation in Soc., Bogota, Colombia, 2004. Contbr. papers in sci. jours.; author numerous field guidebooks, book reviews; many interviews in field; internat. spkr. at more than 125 sci. confs., assn. events, convs., workshops. Mem. leadership council UNA of the USA; advisor NJ Gov.'s Commn. on Victims Meml. to the World Trade Ctr. disaster, 2001; bd. dirs. Hudson County C. of C., 1997—, Save Ellis Island! Found., NJ, 2000—; mem. bd. regents St. Peter's Coll., NJ, 1998—2003. Decorated chevalier Ordre des Palmes Academiques (France); recipient Tracks award Can. Soc. Petroleum Engrs., 1984, John Cotton Dana award N.J. Assn. Mus., 2003. Fellow: Explorers Club; mem.: AAAS (com. on pub. awareness of sci. 2003—), N.Y. Soc. Assn. Execs. (bd. dirs. 2004—). Avocations: ecology, culture, tourism. Office: Liberty Sci Ctr Liberty State Pk 251 Phillip St Jersey City NJ 07305-4600 Business E-Mail: ekoster@lsc.org.

KOSTERE, KIM MARTIN, psychologist, consultant; b. Detroit, Jan. 22, 1954; s. Walter Thomas and Shirley Marian (Goebel) Kostere. BA, Mercy Coll., Dobbs Ferry, NY, 1977; MA, Ctr. Humanistic Studies, Detroit, 1983, PsyS, 1986; PhD, Union Inst., Cin., 1989. Therapist Metro T.A.G., Livonia, Mich., 1978-81, Highland Waterford Ctr., Waterford, Mich., 1981-83; psychologist, v.p. substance abuse svcs. Square Lake Counseling Ctr., Bloomfield Hills, Mich., 1983-90; psychologist, co-dir. Counseling Ctr., P. C., Bloomfield Hills, Mich., 1991-99; cons., 1999—. Co-founder, dir. Ont. NLP Inst., Can., 1979-80; adj. faculty psychology Edison C.C., Naples, Fla., 1999—, Capella U., Mpls. Author: A Brief Account of the Center for Humanistic Studies, 1987; co-author: Get the Results You Want, 1987, Maps, Models and the Structure of Reality, 1989, Utilizing the Metaphor: An Ericksonian/NLP Approach, 1992. Democrat. Roman Catholic. Personal E-mail: kimk@cyberisle.com.

KOSTERLITZ, J. MICHAEL, physics professor; BA, MA, Cambridge Univ.; PhD in theoretical physics, Oxford Univ., 1969. Royal Soc. Exchange fellow Instituto di Fisica Teorica, Torino, Italy, 1969—70; rsch. fellow Birmingham Univ., 1970—73, lectr., math. physics, 1974—78, sr. lectr., 1978—80, reader, math. physics, 1980—81; postdoctoral fellow Cornell Univ., 1973—74; prof., physics Brown Univ., Providence, 1982—. Recipient Maxwell Medal, Inst. Physics, 1980. Fellow: Am. Phys. Soc. (Lars Onsager Prize 2000), Am. Acad. Arts & Scis. Office: Dept Physics Brown Univ Providence RI 02912 Office Phone: 401-863-3193. Business E-Mail: J_Kosterlitz@Brown.EDU.*

KOSTIC, DINA, musician, music educator; b. Belgrade, Serbia, Jan. 18, 1977; d. Lana Peck. MusB, So. Meth. U., Dallas, 1996; MusM, Northwestern U., Evanston, Ill., 1998. Concertmaster New World Symphony, Miami Beach, Fla., 1999—2002; lectr. violin Barry U., Miami Shores, Fla., 2002—; violinist Fla. Philharm., Fort Lauderdale, 2002—03, Palm Beach Chamber Music Festival, Fla., 2003—; concertmaster Orlando Philharm., Fla., 2003; violinist Palm Beach Opera, West Palm Beach, Fla., 2004—. Digital reviewer Insight for the Blind, Fort Lauderdale, 2003—. Scholar, So. Meth. U., 1992—96, Civic Orch. Chgo. Mem.: Am. String Tchrs. Assn. Avocations: skiing, travel. Home Phone: 773-368-8772. Personal E-mail: sobeviolin@aol.com.

KOSTIS, JOHN BASIL, cardiologist; b. Yannina, Greece, June 14, 1936; came to US, 1964; s. Basil John and Vasiliki Ilia (Masouras) K.; m. Barbara Charleston, June, 1969; children: William Jason, Steven Lawrence. MD, U. Salonica, Greece, 1960; student, USAF Sch. Aerospace Medicine, 1963. Diplomate Am. Bd. Internal Medicine, subspecialty cardiovascular disease, specialty clin. hypertension, Am. Bd. Clin. Lipidology. Resident internal medicine Evangelismos Hosp., 404 Gen. Hosp., Athens and Larissa, Greece, 1963-64; intern Bklyn.-Cumberland Med. Ctr., 1964-65, med. resident, 1965-67; fellow cardiology Phila. Gen. Hosp., 1967-69; instr. physiology and aviation medicine Sch. Aviation Medicine, Athens, 1969-70; assoc. clin. medicine, asst. prof. medicine U. Pa., Phila., 1971-72; assoc. prof. Coll. Medicine and Dentistry NJ-Rutgers Med. Sch., New Brunswick, 1972-76; chief cardiology Robert Wood Johnson U. Hosp., New Brunswick, 1980—97. Adj. prof. biomed. engring. Rutgers U. Coll. Engring., Piscataway, NJ, 1975—, Grad. Sch. Biomed. Engring., 1976—; prof. medicine U. Medicine and Dentistry NJ-Robert Wood Johnson Med. Sch., New Brunswick, 1976—, chief div. cardiovascular disease, 1982-84, chief div. cardiovascular disease and hypertension, 1984-97, prof. pharmacology, 1986—, John G. Detwiler prof. cardiology, 1987—, chmn. dept. medicine, 1990—; cons. pharm. industry. Co-editor: Essentials of Cardiovascular Diagnosis, 1984, Beta Blockers in the Treatment of Cardiovascular Disease, 1984, The Pharmacological Treatment of Cardiovascular Diseases, 1986, Angiotensin Converting Enzyme Inhibitors, 1987, The Prevention of Sudden Cardiac Death, 1990; assoc. editor Cardiology, mem. editl. bd. Am. Jour. Cardiology, Clin. Therapeutics, Cardiovasc. Drug Revs., others, co-inventor device noninvasive diagnostic system for coronary artery disease. Grantee pharm. industry, NHLBI, NIH, NIA. Fellow ACP, Am. Heart Assn. (disting. leadership in rsch. award 1986), mem. Am. Coll. Cardiology, Assn. U. Cardiologists, Am. Soc. Hypertension, Internat. Soc. Hypertension, Assn. Profs. of Medicine. Office: U Med and Dentistry NJ Robt Wood Johnson Med Sch PO Box 19 New Brunswick NJ 08903-0019 Office Phone: 732-235-7685. Business E-Mail: kostis@umdnj.edu.

KOSTKA, ROBERT RAYMOND, social studies educator, department chairman; b. Taunton, Mass., Apr. 17, 1949; s. Stanley Andrew and Agnes Elizabeth Kostka; m. Lynne Spence, Dec. 1, 1947; children: Andrew Spence, Allison Spence. BS, Salem State Coll., Mass., 1970, MA in Tchg., 1975. Tchr. Bridgewater-Raynham Regional HS, Mass., 1970—90, chair social studies, tchr., 1990—. Chair, Kingston bd. water commrs., Mass., 1991. Mem. Kingston Master Plan Com., 1996—98, Kingston Dem. Town Com., 1976; bd. mem. Mass. Coun. for the Social Studies, Boston, 2005; founding mem. South Shore Social Studies Suprs., Mass. Mem.: Mass. Tchrs. Assn. (assoc.). Democrat. Unitarian Universalist. Avocations: sports, reading, politics, bridge, fishing. Home: 55 South St Kingston MA 02364 Office: Bridgewater-Raynham Regional HS 166 Mt Prospect St Bridgewater MA 02324 Home Phone: 781-585-9898; Office Phone: 508-697-6902. Business E-Mail: rkostka@bridge-rayn.org.

KOSTKA, RONALD WAYNE, marketing consultant; b. Chgo., Sept. 13, 1931; s. James V. and Marie (Zvolanek) K.; m. Madonna Lou Miller, June 8, 1957 (div. Dec. 1980); children: Paul, Daniel, Jane; m. Irene Mary Harnett, Sept. 14, 1991. BS in journalism, U. Ill., Urbana, 1957. Reporter Champaign News Gazette, Champaign, Ill., 1956-57; copy editor Mpls. Tribune, Mpls., 1957-58; pub. rels. mgr. 3M Co., St. Paul, Minn., 1958-92; cons. mktg. Pub. Rel., Minnetonka, Minn., 1992—. Contbr. articles to profl. jours. Firearms safety instr. State of Minn., Minnetonka, 1967-77. Staff Sgt. USAF, 1951-55, Korea. Decorated Air medal (4 OLC), Purple Heart, Hwarang (Republic of Korea). Mem.: NRA, DAV, Soc. Profl. Jours. (cert. 1957), Nat. Muzzle Loading Rifle Assn. Avocations: canoeing, hunting, skeet shooting. Home: 12800 Marion Ln W Apt 805 Minnetonka MN 55305

KOSTOVA, ELIZABETH, writer; b. New London, Conn., 1964; m. Georgi Kostova, 1990. BA in Brit. Studies, Yale Univ.; MFA, Univ. Mich., 2004. Author: (novels) The Historian, 2005 (debuted #1 NY Times Bestseller list, Debut Author of Yr. Quills Book awards, 2005). Mailing: Author Mail Little Brown Co 1271 Ave of the Americas New York NY 10020

KOSTOW, KATHRYN E., conservation biologist; d. Peter and Colleen Kostow. BS, Coll. Idaho, Caldwell, 1978; MS, U. Minn., Mpls., 1981. Conservation biologist utility industry, Portland, Oreg., 1985—89, Oreg. Dept. Fish and Wildlife, Clackamas, 1990—. Painting and graphic arts for confs., publs.; contbr. articles to profl. publs. Recipient Gipson scholarship, Coll. Idaho, 1974—78, Webster fellowship, Delta Waterfowl Rsch. Sta., 1979, rsch. grant, 1980—81, awards for svc., Oreg. Dept. Fish and Wildlife, 1995, Oreg. Dept. of Fish and Wildlife, 2000, 2005. Fellow: Pacific Fisheries Biologists (life), Gilbert Ichthyologic Soc. (life). Democrat. Achievements include research in Fish Population Status And Risk Assessment. Avocations: graphic arts, gardening, and antique collecting, travel. Office: Oreg Dept Fish and Wildlife 17330 SE Evelyn St Clackamas OR 97015 Home Phone: 503-655-2177; Office Phone: 971-673-6025. Personal E-mail: kostow@onemain.com. Business E-Mail: kathryn.e.kostow@state.or.us.

KOSTYO, JACK LAWRENCE, physiology educator; b. Elyria, Ohio, Oct. 1, 1931; s. Louis and Matilda (Thomasko) K.; m. Shirlianne Guth, June 10, 1953; children: Cecile A., Louis C. AB, Oberlin Coll., 1953; PhD, Cornell U., 1957; MD (hon.), U. Göteborg, 1978. NRC fellow Harvard Med. Sch., Boston, 1957-59; asst. prof., then prof. physiology Duke U., 1959-68; prof., chmn. dept. physiology Emory U., Atlanta, 1968-79; prof. physiology U. Mich. Med. Sch., Ann Arbor, 1979-94, chmn. dept. physiology, 1979-85, active prof. emeritus in internal medicine, 1995—; assoc. dir. Mich. Diabetes Rsch. and Tng. Ctr., Ann Arbor, 1986-97, dir. grants program, 1997—. Mem. endocrinology study sect. NIH/USPHS, 1967-71, internat. and coop. projects study sect., 1992-96; mem. physiology test com. Nat. Bd. Med. Examiners, 1974-77, mem. comprehensive part II com., 1986-91, U.S. Med. Licensure Examination Step 2 Com., 1990-91. Editor in chief Endocrinology, 1978-82; sect. editor Ann. Rev. Physiology, 1982-86; mem. editorial bd. Growth Regulation, 1990-97; contbr. articles to profl. jours. Mem. adv. bd. Searle Scholars, 1982-85. Recipient Lederle Med. Faculty award, 1961, Ernst Oppenheimer Meml. award Endocrine Soc., 1969 Mem. Endocrine Soc. (editl. bd., coun., chmn. awards com.), Am. Physiol. Soc. (editl. bd., coun., chmn. standing com. on edn., mem. coun. of endocrinology and metabolism sect., chmn. endocrinology and metabolism sect. 1990-91, rep. to Coun. Acad. Socs. of Assn. Am. Med. Colls., mem. AAAS sect. on med. scis., editor Handbook of Physiology sect. 7, Endocrinology, vol. 5), Soc. for Exptl. Biology and Medicine (editl. bd.), Internat. Union Physiol. Scis. (commn. on med. edn.), Assn. Chmn. Depts. Physiology (pres. 1979, coun.), Am. Diabetes Assn., Coun. Acad. Socs. (adminstrv. bd. 1983-86), Sigma Xi. Office: Mich Diabetes Rsch-Tng Ctr U Mich Med Sch 1331 E Ann St 0580 Ann Arbor MI 48109 Office Phone: 734-763-5730. E-mail: jkostyo@umich.edu.

KOSTYO, JOHN FRANCIS, lawyer; b. Findlay, Ohio, Feb. 9, 1955; s. Albert Robert and Mary Agnes (Welsh) K.; m. Shirley Ann Allgyre, June 9, 1984. BA in Polit. Sci. and Philosophy magna cum laude, John Carroll U., 1978; JD, Case Western Res. U., 1981. Bar: Ohio 1981, U.S. Dist. Ct. (no. dist.) Ohio 1982, U.S. Dist. Ct. (ea. dist.) Mich. 1991, U.S. Supreme Ct. 1991, U.S. Dist. Ct. (so. dist.) Mich. 1992, U.S. Dist. Ct. (we. dist.) Mich. 1992, U.S. Dist. Ct. (6th cir.) Calif. 2001. Assoc. Weasel & Brimley, Findlay, 1981-89; ptnr. Brimley, Kostyo & Elliott, L.P.A., Findlay, 1989-91, Brimley & Kostyo Co., L.P.A., Findlay, 1991, Brimley, Kostyo & Lather Co., L.P.A., 1991-93, Brimley & Kostyo Co. L.P.A., 1993-99; v.p. Mid-Am. Title Agy., Inc., Findlay, Ohio, 1989—; mem. Kostyo & Clark, PLL, Findlay, Ohio, 1999—, Fuller & Henry, Ltd., 2001—04; pvt. practice Findly, 2004—. Lectr. contracts and negotiable instruments U. Findlay, 1981-84, sr. lectr. 1984-96. Mem. ABA (corp. banking and bus. law, litigation div.), Ohio Bar Assn., Toledo Bar Assn., William Taft Am. Inn of Ct., Alpha Sigma Nu. Clubs: Rockwell Springs Trout. Lodges: Elks, K.C. (4th degree). Roman Catholic. Avocations: sports, reading, theater. Home: 462 Penbrooke Dr Findlay OH 45840-7472 Office: Law Office John F Kostyo Riverside Executive Suites 1100 East main Cross Ste 200 Findlay OH 45840 also: MidAm Title Agy Inc 100 E Main Cross St Findlay OH 45840-4861 Office Phone: 419-422-7700. Business E-Mail: jfk@kostyolaw.com.

KOSUB, JAMES ALBERT, lawyer; b. San Antonio, Jan. 8, 1948; s. Ernest Pete and Lonie (Doege) K.; divorced; 1 child, James Jr.; m. Jane Stevens Cain, Aug. 11, 1979; children: Kathryn, Nicholas (dec.). Student, East Carolina U., 1970, San Antonio Coll., 1971-72; BS, Tex. State U., 1974; JD, St. Mary's U., San Antonio, 1977. Bar: Tex. 1978, US Dist. Ct. (we. dist.) Tex. 1980, US Ct. Appeals (5th cir.) 1981, US Dist. Ct. (so. dist.) 1986, US Supreme Ct. 1988, US Dist. Ct. (no. and ea. dists.) Tex. 1990. Ptnr. Kosub & Langlois, San Antonio, 1978-79, Kosub, Langlois & Van Cleave, San Antonio, 1979-83; mng. ptnr. Kosub & Langlois, San Antonio, 1983-86; sr. ptnr. James A. Kosub, San Antonio, 1986-94; pvt. practice Eldorado, Tex., 1994—2002; sr. ptnr. Kosub & Griffin, 2002—05; sr.ptnr., LLP Kosub, Griffin & Elkins, 2006—. Bd. dirs. Judson Ind. Sch. Bd. Trustees, Converse, Tex., 1975-81, Bexar County Fedn. Sch. Bds., San Antonio, 1977-80. Sgt. USMC, 1966-70. Fellow: San Antonio Bar Found., Tex. Bar Found.; mem.: ABA (EEOC liaison com. San Antonio chpt. 1987—93), State Bar Tex. (coun. labor and employment sect. 1993—97, sec. 1997—98, vice chair 1998—99, chair 1999—2000), Coll. State Bar Tex., 5th Cir. Bar Assn., Fed. Bar Assn., San Antonio Bar Assn. (bd. dirs.

1990—92, sec. 1992—93), Schleicher County C. of C. (pres. 1998—2000), Schleicher County Lions Club (v.p. 2003—04). Episcopalian. Avocations: carpentry, gardening, golf. Office: 105 S Main Eldorado TX 76936-0460 Office Phone: 325-853-2711. Business E-Mail: jkosub@kgelaw.com.

KOSZARSKI, RICHARD, art historian, curator; b. NYC, Dec. 18, 1947; s. Casimir and Janina (Orzechowski) K.; m. Diane Kaiser, 1975; 1 child, Eva. BA, Hofstra U., 1969; MA, NYU, 1974, PhD, 1977. Lectr. Sch. Visual Arts, NYC, 1974-84, NYU, 1976, 97, Columbia U., NYC, 1980-86; historian Astoria Motion Picture & TV Found., NYC, 1977-81; curator of film Am. Mus. Moving Image, NYC, 1981-92, exhbn. curator Masterpieces of Moving Image Tech., 1988, head collections and exhbns., 1992-96, sr. historian, 1996-97; assoc. prof. English Rutgers U., 1998—. Author: (books) Hollywood Directors 1914-40, 1976, The Rivals of D.W. Griffith, 1976, Hollywood Directors 1941-76, 1977, Universal Pictures: 65 Years, 1977, The Man You Loved to Hate, 1983, The Astoria Studio and Its Fabulous Films, 1983, An Evening's Entertainment: The Age of the Silent Feature Picture, 1915-1928, 1990, Von: The Life and Films of Erich von Stroheim, 2001, Fort Lee: The Film Town, 2004; (documentary films) Roger Corman, Hollywood's Wild Angel, 1978, The Man You Loved to Hate, 1979; editor-in-chief Film History, An Internat. Jour., N.Y.C., 1986—. Mem. Ft. Lee Film Commn. Rsch. associateship Am. Film Inst., 1971, 72; rsch. grantee Am. Coun. Learned Socs., 1978; recipient Nat. Film Book award Nat. Film Soc., 1984, award Prix Jean Mitry, 1991; NEH fellow, 2003. Mem. Polish Inst. Arts and Scis., Antique Wireless Assn., Kosciuszko Found., Assn. Moving Image Archivists.

KOSZEGI, KATHLEEN A., elementary school educator; d. Arnold S. and Gladys Roxbury; m. Donald G. Koszegi, July 17, 1971; children: Donald Koszeg Jr., David Koszeg. BS in Edn., Kent State U., 1969; MA in Edn., Ea. Mich. U., 1989. Cert. tchr. Mich. Tchr. St. Damian Sch., Westland, Mich., St. Dunstan Sch., Garden City. Named Tchr. of Yr., VFW post 9665, Westland, 2005, 4th Dist., 2005. Mem.: Internat. Reading Assn.

KOTABE, MASAAKI, business educator; b. Mito, Ibaraki, Japan, Jan. 5, 1954; arrived in U.S., 1978; s. Torin and Tomeko Kotabe; m. Sylvia Donnelly-Kotabe; children: Akihiro, Euka, Hiroki. BSS, U. Chiba, Japan, 1976; MBA, Mich. State U., East Lansing, 1980; PhD, Mich. State U., 1987. Prof. internat. bus. and mktg. U. Tex., Austin, 1990—98, Temple U., Phila., 1998—. Author: Global Sourcing Strategy, 1992, Marketing Management, 2005, Global Marketing Strategy, 2007. Mem.: Acad. of Mgmt., Am. Mktg. Assn. (Hans B. Thorelli 5 Yr. award 2005, S. Tamer Cavausgil Best Paper award 1998), Acad. Internat. Bus. (v.p. 1997—98). Office: Temple U Fox Sch Bus 349 Speakman Hall Philadelphia PA 19122-6023

KOTAS, ROBERT VINCENT, pediatrician, educator; b. Buffalo, Nov. 26, 1938; s. Vincent John and Regina K.; m. Ilona Rae Fielding, Mar. 2, 1968; children: Nicole, Timothy, Robert, Rebecca. BS, Canisius Coll., 1959; MD, U. Buffalo, 1963. Diplomate: Am. Acad. Pediatrics. Research assoc. McGill U., 1969-70; intern Buffalo Children's Hosp., 1963-64; resident in pediatrics Johns Hopkins Hosp., Balt., 1964-66; asst. prof. pediatrics U. Okla. Med. Sch., 1970-72, dir. newborn services, 1970-72; dir., div. devel. physiology; career investigator W.K. Warren Med. Research Center, Tulsa, 1972-76, sci. dir., 1976-80; dir. William and Natalie Warren Med. Inst., Tulsa, 1980-83; chief pediatrician Ella Austin Health Ctr., San Antonio, 1989-95, med. dir., 1993-95; lab. dir., 1993-95; pediatrician UTHSC-SA Primary Care Cmty. Pediat., San Antonio, 1995-98, Minor Emergency Ctr., San Antonio, 1998-99; assoc. Fernando A. Guerra, MD, San Antonio, 1998-99, Lonestar Pediats., Kaufman, Tex., 1999—2002; lead staff physician Cmty. Outreach Clinic/Bluitt-Flowers, Dallas, 2003; pvt. practice, 2006—. Clin. prof. pediats. U. Okla. Med. Sch., Tulsa, 1977-99; clin. instr. pediats. U. Tex. Southwestern Med. Ctr., Dallas, 2002; assoc. prof. pediats. U. Tex. Health Sci. Ctr., San Antonio, 1983-98, dir. rsch. devel., 1993-94, also med. dir.; guest scientist Nat. Inst. Child Health and Human Devel., Bethesda, Md., 1975-77, also cons.; cons. Am. Lung Assn., others; cons. pediatrician San Antonio Ind. Sch. Dist. Contbr. articles to profl. jours. and books. Served as capt. USAF, 1966-68. Recipient continuing edn. awards AMA; Best M.D. Written Book award Am. Med. Writers Assn., 1980; Mosby scholar, 1963; grantee NIH, 1969-70, 75-79, 84-88; grantee USPHS, 1968-69, 91-95; others. Fellow Am. Coll. Obstetricians and Gynecologists (assoc.); mem. Johns Hopkins Med. and Surg. Assn., So. Soc. Pediatric Rsch., Soc. Pediatric Rsch., Am. Physiol. Soc., Soc. Gynecol. Investigation. Home: 604 Courageous Dr Rockwall TX 75032-5768 *Grateful for the excitement of impending discovery which characterizes my work with its promise of surprise in the midst of daily routine, I am indebted for the guidance and inspiration that my present and past associates have given me to deal effectively with the diversity and perversity of experience.*

KOTCHER, SHIRLEY J.W., lawyer; b. June 6, 1924; m. Harry A. Kotcher; children: Leslie Susan, Dana Anne. BA, NYU; JD, Columbia U. Bar: N.Y. In-house counsel Booth Meml. Med. Ctr., Flushing, N.Y., 1975-83, gen. counsel, 1983-91; v.p., gen. counsel the N.Y. Hosp. Med. Ctr. Queens, 1991-97; advisor health care Borough Pres. Queens, 1978. Author: Hidden gold and Pitfalls in New Tax Law, 1970. Mem. North Hempstead Sr. Citizen Commn., Manhasset, NY, 1999—; mem. affordable sr. housing endowment adv. com. Town of North Hempstead, 1999—; bd. dirs. Denton Green Housing Co. Inc., Garden City Park, NY, 1999—. Mem. ABA (health law forum com.), Nat. Health Lawyers Assn., Am. Acad. Hosp. Attys., Am. Soc. Law and Medicine, Am. Soc. Health Care Risk Mgmt., Assn. for Hosp. Risk Mgmt. N.Y., Greater N.Y. Hosp. Assn. (legal adv. com. 1976-97).

KOTCHKA, CLAUDIA B., consumer products company executive, accountant; b. July 11, 1951; married; 1 child. BBA, Ohio Univ., 1973. CPA. With Arthur Anderson & Co., 1973—78; mktg. & brand mgmt. positions with Proctor & Gamble Co., Cin., 1978—97, v.p. art & package design, 1997—98, v.p. design & mktg. knowledge, 1998—99, v.p., feminine care mktg., 1999—2000, v.p. eBus. ventures, 2000—01, v.p., design innovation and strategy, 2001—. Mem. adv. bd. New Zealand Trade and Investment; spkr. in field. Featured in or quoted in numerous publications, guest appearance Today Show. Named one of Best Leaders of 2005, BusinessWeek, 25 Masters of Innovation, 20 Masters of Design, Fast Company Mag., 2005. Office: Proctor & Gamble Co 1 Proctor & Gamble Plz Cincinnati OH 45202

KOTECKI, KEVIN, beer company executive; MBA, Northwestern Univ. Kellogg Sch. Bus., 1988. Formerly with ConAgra Foods Co., P&G; brand dir. Coors Brewing Co., Golden, Colo.; pres., COO Brach's Candy Co., 2000—02; CEO Pabst Brewing Co., Chgo., 2005—. Office: Pabst Brewing Co PO Box 792627 San Antonio TX 78279

KOTEFF, ELLEN, editor; b. Harvey, Ill. d. Walter Peter and Florence (Walz) Koteff. BS in Journalism, U. Fla. Editor Palm Beach (Fla.) Daily News; met. editor Daily Record, Parsippany, NJ; exec. editor Nation's Restaurant News, NYC, editor-in-chief, 2004—. Former v.p. Internat. Foodservice Editl. Coun.; mem. jury IFMA Silver Plate; bd. mem. Elliot Leadership Inst. Bd. dirs. Women's Foodservice Forum, 2003. Named Innovator, Media Bus. Mag., 2007; recipient Jesse H. Neal award, 2002, 2004, 2006; McAllister Editl. fellow, 2002. Office: Nations Restaurant News 425 Park Ave New York NY 10022-3506 Office Phone: 212-756-5186. Business E-Mail: ekoteff@nrn.com.

KOTELLY, GEORGE VINCENT, editor, writer, electrical engineer; s. James Visar and Pauline (Plaha) K.; m. Shirley Elizabeth Mullo, June 14, 1959; children— Kenneth James, William John, Douglas George, Joanne Elizabeth BSE.E., Tufts U., 1953. Publs. engr. Raytheon, Burlington, Mass., 1970-73; tech. writer USM Corp., Beverly, Mass., 1973-75; engrng. writer Analogic, Wakefield, Mass., 1975-77; tech. editor Computer Design Mag., Littleton, Mass., 1977-79; sr. editor Edn. Mag., Boston, 1979-83; editor-in-chief Mini-Micro Systems Mag., Cahners Pub. Co., Boston, 1983-88; mng. editor Lightwave Jour. PennWell Pub. Co., Westford, Mass., 1988-89; sr. editor Lincoln Lab. MIT, Lexington, 1989-91; editor COMDEX Preview and Show Daily The Interface Group, Needham, Mass., 1991-93; exec. editor Lightwave Jour. PennWell Pub. Co., Nashua, NH, 1993-97; editor-in-chief Vision Systems Design Mag., 1997—2003; tech. editor Advanced Imaging Mag., Cygnus Pub., Melville, NJ, 2004—05; pres. Koty Assocs., 2005—. Contbr. numerous articles to tech. jours. Sgt. U.S. Army, 1954-56. Mem. IEEE. Republican. Mem. Albanian Orthodox Ch. Avocations: golf, bowling, chess, jogging, baseball. Home: 8 Dornoch Cir North Chelmsford MA 01863 Office Phone: 978-323-9881. Personal E-mail: geoshirl1@msn.com.

KOTEN, JOHN F., editor-in-chief; b. Dec. 8, 1954; With Wall St. Jour., 1977—92, reporter, sr. writer, Chgo. bureau chief, sr. editor; editor Worth mag., 1992—2002; editor-in-chief Inc Mag., 2002—, Fast Company Mag., 2005—; CEO Mansueto Ventures, 2005—. Regular guest CNBC. Contbg. editor: Smart Money mag. Named one of 100 Most Influential Journalists, Journalist and Fin. Reporting Group. Office: Inc Magazine 375 Lexington Ave New York NY 10017*

KOTHARI, HEMRAJ, mechanical engineer, management consultant; b. Sujangarh, Rajasthan, India, Nov. 10, 1933; s. Khoobchand and Gulab (Singhee) Kothari. BSc, Calcutta U., 1953; DWP, Woolwich (Eng.) Poly., 1959; advance cert. in planning and estimating, City & Guilds, London, 1959; PhD (hon.), World U., Ariz., 1991. Registered and chartered profl. engr., London, U.S., India, Europe; cert. mgmt. cons. Prin. Kothari Cons., Calcutta, 1961—, Kothari Orgn., Calcutta, 1961—. Owner, editor Kothari Pubs., Calcutta, 1961—; dir., editor India Internat. News Svc., Calcutta, 1961—; founder, organizer 1st All India Engr.'s Conf., 1st and 2d All India Dirs. Conf., 1st All India Specialized Pubs. Conf. and Exhbn.; Indian del. to various internat. confs. Editor, dir.: The Dir., Profl. Engr., Compact Weekly, What's On in Calcutta, Films and Femme, Sci. and Engring., other jours. and mags., founder, editor: Who's Who Indian series, other reference works; contbr. articles to profl. jours. Apptd. assessor municipalities Gov. of West Bengal. Fellow: Inst. Dirs. (London), Royal Soc. Health (London), Royal Soc. Arts, Commerce and Mfg., Inst. Mech. Engrs. London (life), Indian Coun. Arbitration (life; past mem. governing coun.), Inst. Valuers (life), Assn. Engrs. (life), Instn. Stds. Engrs. (life), Royal Asiatic Soc. London (life), Brit. Interplanetary Soc. (life), Inst. Commerce (London) (life), Inst. Engrs. (life), Geol., Mining and Metallurgical Soc. (life), Inst. Plant Engrs. (life); mem.: AAEI (life), ASME (life), NAS (life), IASLIC (life), Am. Arbitration Assn. (panelist), Assn. Indian Engrs. UK (founder), Asian Media Info. and Communication Centre (Singapore), Nat. Geographic Soc. U.S.A., Assn. Food Scientists and Technologists (life), Bhartiya Vidhya Bhawan (life), Indian Coun. World Affairs (life), Indian Inst. Pub. Adminstrn. (life), Indian Libr. Assn. (life), Bombay Nat. History Soc. (life), Indian Nat. Trust Art and Cultural Heritage (life), Asiatic Soc. Bengal (life), Indian Soc. Tng. and Devel. (life), Indian Soc. Tech. Edn. (life), Computer Soc. India (life), N.Y. Acad. Scis. (life), Agr.-Hort. Soc. India (life), Indian Inst. Metals (life), Geo Met. Inst. India (life), Indian Sci. Congress Assn. (life), Indian Soc. Soil Sci. (life), Computer Soc. India (life), Fedn. Karnataka Chambers Commerce and Industry (patron), Assn. Engrs. (former v.p.), Engring. Coun. U.K., Nat. Forensic Coun. U.S.A. (special panelist), Inst. Mgmt. Cons. India (former com. mem.), Internat. C. of C. Mem. Jain Ch. Avocations: films, reading, journalism. Home: 3D Rajhans 6 Hastings Park Rd Alipore Kolkata 700027 India Office: Kothari Orgn 12 India Exchange Place Calcutta 700001 India Office Phone: 2230-9563.

KOTHARI, RAJESH UJAMLAL, investment company executive; b. Pontiac, Mich., Dec. 4, 1967; s. Ujamlal and Kumud (Choksi) K. BA in Econ., U. Mich., 1989, MBA, 1992. CFA Assn. Investment Mgmt. and Rsch. Assoc. Zaske, Sarafa & Assoc., Bloomfield Hills, Mich., 1984-89; portfolio mgr. Masco Corp., Taylor, Mich., 1989—94; founder, treasurer, dir. internat. investing Cranbrook Capital Mgmt., Detroit, 1994—96; dir. GMA Capital, Farmington Hills, 1996; bd. dirs. Amicas, Inc., VerNova, Inc.; investment officer ProVen Pvt. Equity, London; co-founder, mng. dir. Seneca Partners Inc., Birmingham, 2002—. Dep. comdr. CAP, USAF Aux., Pontiac, 1981—. Recipient Comdrs. Commendations CAP, 1991, 92, 93, named on of 40 Under 40, Crain's Detroit Bus., 2006. Mem. Fin. Analyst soc. Detroit, Nat. Assn. Security Profls. (treas. Detroit chpt. 1995—), Mich. Venture Capital Assn. (bd. mem., exec. com.). Avocations: fencing, camping, jet skiing. Office: Seneca Partners Inc 300 Park St Ste 400 Birmingham MI 48009 Office Phone: 248-723-6650. Office Fax: 248-723-6651.

KOTHARY, PIYUSH C., research scientist; b. Yangon, Myanmar, Sept. 4, 1940; s. Chamanlal D. and Labhuben C. Kothary; m. Sarla P. Parekh, Feb. 21, 1943; children: Shilpa, Priya. PhD magna cum laude, La Salle U., 1994. Demonstrator St. Xavier's Coll., Bombay, 1963—71; sr. rsch. assoc. U. Mich., Ann Arbor, 1971—. Dir. rsch. Skillman Lab. Kellogg Eye Ctr., Ann Arbor, 1994—. Grantee, NIH, 1990—95, 1993. Mem.: Assn. for Rsch in Vision and Ophthalmology (presenter 1994—2005). Office: 521 Kellogg Eye Ctr 1000 Wall St Ann Arbor MI 48105 Office Phone: 734-936-9254. Personal E-mail: piyush0940@aol.com. Business E-Mail: kotha@umich.edu.

KOTHS, KIRSTON EDWARD, biochemist; b. Lafayette, Ind., Dec. 24, 1948; s. Jay Sanford and Margaret Louise (Edwards) K.; m. Catherine Elizabeth Lutes, Aug. 24, 1985. BS, Amherst Coll., 1971; PhD, Harvard U., 1979. Scientist Cetus Corp., Emeryville, Calif., 1979—82, dir. protein chemistry, 1982—91, sr. scientist, 1984—89, sr. dir. discovery rsch., 1989—91; dir. protein therapeutics rsch. Chiron Corp., Emeryville, 1991—2001, biotech. rsch. and patent cons., 2002—. Achievements include more than 40 US patents. Avocations: gold prospecting, documentary video, photography, fly fishing, teaching dance. Home: 2646 Mira Vista Dr El Cerrito CA 94530 Office Phone: 510-932-8642. E-mail: koths@sbcglobal.net.

KOTIN, PAUL, pathologist; b. Chgo., Aug. 13, 1916; s. Elias and Rose (Spunt) K.; m. Pauline H. Stephan, Dec. 12, 1970; children: Joel Tepper, David Bernard. BS, U. Ill., 1937, MD, 1940. Intern Deaconess Hosp., Chgo., 1939-40, resident pathology, 1940-41; pvt. practice pathology and internal medicine San Luis Obispo, Calif., 1946-48; researcher pathology U. So. Calif., 1949-50; med. microbiologist Los Angeles County Hosp., 1950-51, attending staff pathologist, 1951-62; mem. faculty U. So. Calif., 1951-62, prof. pathology, 1959-60, Paul Pierce prof. pathology, 1960-62; chief carcinogenesis studies br. Nat. Cancer Inst., 1962-63, asso. dir. for field studies, 1963-64, sci. dir. for etiology, 1964-66; dir. div. environ. health scis. NIH, 1966-69; dir. Nat. Inst. Environ. Health Scis., 1969-71; v.p. for health scis., dean Sch. Medicine, Temple U., Phila., 1971-74; sr. v.p. health, safety and environment Johns-Manville Corp., 1974-81. Edgar Allen Meml. lectr. Yale Sch. Medicine, 1957; vis. prof. oncology U. Wis., 1959-60; vis. prof. pathology U. N.C., also Duke U., 1967-71; Harry Shay Meml. lectr. Temple U., 1964; Sappington Meml. lectr. Am. Occupational Medicine Assn., Anaheim, Calif., 1979, Gehrmann lectr., Nashville, 1981; chmn. Gordon Research Conf. Cancer, 1965, Beryllium Industry Sci. Adv. Com., 1995—; adj. prof. pathology U. Colo., 1974—; Cons. air pollution med. program, div. spl. health service USPHS, 1958-62; mem. sci. adv. bd. Council Tobacco Research-U.S.A., 1952-65; adv. com. r.r. diesel gases and dust Calif. Pub. Utilities Commn., 1956-62; adv. com. research pathogenesis cancer Am. Cancer Soc., 1962-65; pathology study sect. NIH, 1962-66, lung cancer task force, 1967-68; corr. mem. permanent European com. Research Chronic Hazards, 1960—; cancer prevention com. UICC, 1962-66, com. on exptl. design and methodology in carcinogenesis, 1967-70; sci. com. Inst. Occupational and Environ. Health, Quebec. Asbestos Mining Assn., 1966-75; mem. Fed. Com. Pest Control, 1964-71; program com. Tenth Internat. Congress, 1967-70; mem. Expert Panel on Carcinogenicity, 1962-70, Nat. Environ. Health Scis. Center, 1965, Nat. Adv. Com. Occupational Safety and Health, 1975-78, Armed Forces Epidemiol. Bd., 1976-80; chmn. Beryllium Industry Sci. Adv. Com., 1990—. Editorial adv. bd.: Cancer Research, 1957-61, Internat. Rev. Exptl. Pathology, 1968—; editorial bd.: AMA Archives Pathology, 1965-71, Environ. Research, 1966—, Am. Jour. Pathology, 1971-82; Contbr. articles to med. jours. Served with AUS, 1941-46. Recipient Superior Service award HEW, 1966, Disting. Service award, 1969; Sr. postdoctoral fellow NSF, 1959-60; named Alumnus of Yr. U. Ill. Coll. of Medicine, 1990. Fellow Coll. Am. Pathologists, N.Y. Acad. Scis., Am. Acad. Occupational Medicine; mem. AMA (com. research on tobacco and health 1966-78), Am. Assn. Cancer Research (dir.), Am. Assn. Pathologists and Bacteriologists, AAAS, Am. Indsl. Hygiene Assn. (hon.), Am. Occupational Medicine Assn. (Knudsen award 1981), Sigma Xi, Alpha Omega Alpha. Office Phone: 505-984-8064.

KOTKIN, DAVID See COPPERFIELD, DAVID

KOTLARCHUK, IHOR O.E., lawyer; b. Ukraine, July 31, 1943; came to U.S., 1946, naturalized, 1957; s. Emil and Lidia N. (Maceluch) K. BS in Fin., Fordham U., 1965, JD, 1968; LLM, Georgetown U., 1974, MA in Govt., 1982; MEd, Mary Washington Coll., 2003. Bar: N.Y. 1969, D.C. 1972, Va. 2001, U.S. Ct. Mil. Appeals, U.S. Tax Ct., U.S. Supreme Ct. Sr. trial atty. criminal sect. tax divsn. U.S. Dept. Justice, Washington, 1973-78, civil sect. tax divsn., 1978-80, fraud sect. criminal divsn., 1980-84, internal security sect. criminal divsn., 1984-97; ret., 1999; sr. internat. law enforcement adv. on tax policy/enforcement U.S. Treasury Dept., 2000—; pvt. practice law Alexandria, Va., 2001—. Tchr. social studies, Stafford, Va., 2003—. Pres. Washington Group, 2000-05, also bd. dirs.; bd. dirs. Alexandria Times; pres. DC br., Ukrainian Congress Com. Am., 2006-; With U.S. Army, 1969-73, Vietnam, JAG, ret. col. USAR. Decorated Bronze star, Legion of Merit. Mem.: ABA, Ukrainian Am. Bar Assn. (bd. dirs., bd. govs. 2006—), DC Bar Assn., Va. Trial Lawyers Assn., Va. State Bar Assn., NY State Bar Assn., Ukrainian Assn. Washington, DC (pres. 2000—01), Res. Officers Assn., Phi Alpha Delta. Ukrainian Catholic. Address: 205 S Lee St Alexandria VA 22314-3307 Office: 109 S Fairfax St Alexandria VA 22314-3307 Fax: 703-548-1861.

KOTLER, MILTON, marketing company executive; b. Chgo., Mar. 15, 1935; s. Maurice and Betty (Bubar) K.; m. Greta Smith, July 11, 1976; children: Anthony, Joshua, Jonathan, Rebecca. BA, U. Chgo., 1954, MA in Polit. Sci., 1957, postgrad. (Jane Morton fellow), 1957-59. Asst. prof. Chgo. City Coll., 1961-63; resident fellow Inst. for Policy Studies, Washington, 1963-77; exec. dir. Inst. Neighborhood Studies, Washington, 1972-75, Nat. Assn. Neighborhoods, Washington, 1975-81; v.p. Ctr. for Responsive Governance, Washington, 1981—, treas., 1980—; pres. Kotler Mktg. Group, Washington, 1984—, Beijing, Shenzhen, Shanghai. Vis. prof. U. Calif., Berkeley, 1968, George Washington U., 1985; adj. prof. Am. U., Washington, 1976—, U. Md., 1980— Author: Neighborhood Government, 1969, 2d edit., 2005, Building Neighborhood Organization, 1983; co-editor: Clear Sighted View of Chinese Marketing, 2005; co-editor Jour. Community Action, 1981—; contbr. chpts. to books. V.p. Alliance for Voluntarism, 1979-80; chmn. bd. Washington Symphony Orchestra, 1992—. Office: 925 15th St NW 4th Flr Washington DC 20005 Office Phone: 202-415-5941. Business E-Mail: mkotler@kotlermarketing.com.

KOTLER, PHILIP, marketing educator, writer; b. Chgo., May 27, 1931; s. Maurice and Betty (Bubar) K.; m. Nancy Ruth Kellum, Jan. 30, 1955; children: Amy Elizabeth, Melissa Eve, Jessica Kellum. Student, DePaul U., 1948-50; MA, U. Chgo., 1953; PhD, MIT, 1956; postgrad., U. Chgo., 1957, Harvard, 1960; PhD (hon.), DePaul U., 1988, U. Zurich, Switzerland, 1989, Athens U. Econs. and Bus., 1995, Stockholm U., 1998, Crackow U. Econs., 1998; PhD (hon.), Budapest Sch. Econ. Sci. and Pub. Policy, B.I. Norwegian Sch. Mgmt. Sch. analyst Westinghouse Corp., Pitts., 1953; asst., then assoc. prof. Roosevelt U., Chgo., 1957-61; from asst. prof. to prof. marketing Northwestern U., Evanston, Ill., 1962-69, A. Montgomery Ward prof. marketing, 1969-73, Harold T. Martin prof. marketing, 1973-88, S.C. Johnson & Son disting. prof. internat. mktg., 1989—. Adv. mktg. editor Holt, Rinehart and Winston, 1965-78; chmn. Coll. on Mktg., Inst. Mgmt. Scis., 1968; mem. adv. bd. Yankelovich Ptnrs. Author: Simulation in Social and Administrative Science, 1971, Creating Social Change, 1971, The New Competition, 1985, Marketing for Health Care Organizations, 1986, Marketing Models, 1992, Marketing for Congregations: Serving People More Effectively, 1992, Strategic Marketing for Education Institutions, 1995, High Visibility, 1997, Standing Room Only: Strategies for Marketing the Peforming Arts, 1997, The Marketing of Nations, 1997, Museum Strategy and Marketing, 1998, Kotler on Marketing, 1999, Marketing Places Europe, 1999, Marketing Asian Places, 2001, Marketing Moves, 2002, Repositioning Asia, 2002, Marketing Professional Services, 2002, Social Marketing: Improving the Quality of Life, 2002, A Framework for Marketing Management, 2003, Marketing Places: Attracting Investment, Industry and Tourism to Cities, States, and Nations, Marketing for Hospitality and Tourism, 2003, Marketing Global Biobrands, 2003, Rethinking Marketing, 2003, Marketing Insights A to Z, 2003, Lateral Marketing, 2003, Strategic Marketing for Nonprofit Organizations, 2003, Ten Deadly Marketing Sins, 2004, Attracting Investors, 2004, Corporate Social Responsibility: Doing the Most Good for Your Company and Your Cause, 2005, Principles of Marketing, 2005, Marketing Management: Analysis, Planning and Control, 2005, According to Kotler, 2005, The Elusive Fan: Reinventing Sports in a Crowded Marketplace, 2006. Bd. govs. Sch. of Art Inst. Chgo., 1985-2004. Mem. Am. Mktg. Assn. (bd. dirs. 1970-72, First Disting. Mktg. Educator 1985), Inst. Mgmt. Scis., Marketing Sci. Inst. (trustee 1974-84), Phi Beta Kappa. Office: Northwestern U Kellogg Sch Mgmt Evanston IL 60208-0001

KOTLER, RICHARD LEE, lawyer; b. LA, Apr. 13, 1952; s. Allen S. Kotler and Marcella (Fromberg) Swartz; m. Cindy Jasik, Dec. 9, 1990; children: Kelsey Elizabeth, Charles Max. BA, Sonoma State Coll., 1976; JD, Southwestern U., 1979. Bar: Calif. 1980, U.S. Dist. Ct. (cen. dist.) Cal. 1980; cert. family law specialist. Sole practice, Newhall, Calif., 1980-83, 88—; sr. ptnr. Kotler & Hann, Newhall, 1983-88; pvt. practice Law Offices of Richard L. Kotler, Newhall, 1984-86. Judge pro temp Municipal Ct., 1981-84, Superior Ct., 1985—. Chmn. Santa Clarita Valley Battered Women's Assn., Newhall, 1983-87; bd. dirs. Santa Clarita Valley Hotline, Newhall, 1981-83. Recipient Commendation award L.A. County, 1983; named SCV Paintball champion. Mem. Santa Clarita Valley Bar Assn. (v.p. 1985—), L.A. Assn. Cert. Family Law Specialtists, Los Angeles Astronomy Soc., Newhall Astronomy Club. Avocations: astronomy, classic cars, stamp collecting/philately, fishing. Office: Ste 204 24881 San Fernando Rd Santa Clarita CA 91321-4172

KOTLER, ROBERT, cosmetic surgeon; b. Chgo., Ill., Sept. 16, 1942; Attended, U. Wisconsin, 1960—63; BS in Medicine, Northwestern U., Chgo., 1964; MD, Northwestern U. Med. Sch., 1967; completed specialty tng., Northwestern U. and U. Ill., 1973, and several others. Lic. Calif., Ill., Va., diplomate Nat. Bd. Med. Examiners, Am. Bd. Otolaryngology/Head and Neck Surgery, 1973, Am. Bd. Cosmetic Surgery, 1980. Student rsch. fellow, dept. medicine Northwestern U. Med. Sch., 1966, tchr. asst., dept. anatomy, 1966; lab. rsch., rsch. lab. VA Adminstrn. Hosp., Chgo., 1966; intern Kaiser Found. Hosp., San Francisco, 1967—68; resident, gen. surgery Cook County Hosp., Chgo., 1968—69; resident, head and neck surgery Northwestern U., Chgo., 1969—70, U. Ill., Chgo., 1971—73; fellowship, cosmetic and reconstructive surgery of the face, head and neck Am. Acad. of Facial Plastic and Reconstructive Surgery; clin. instr., divsn. head & neck surgery, dept. surgery UCLA Med. Sch.; cons., attending surgeon VA Med. Ctr., LA; private practice Beverly Hills, Calif., 1977—. Chief, head and neck dept. DeWitt Army Hosp., Fort Belvoir, Va.; cons., residency program instr. Walter Reed Army Med. Ctr., Washington; founder, pres. Am. Nasal and Facial Surgery Inst., Inc.; commr., reg. cons. Med. Bd. Calif., Dept. Consumer Affairs; cons. City of LA, County of LA; spkr. in field. Author: Chemical Rejuvenation of the Race, Secrets of a Beverly Hills Cosmetic Surgeon, 2002, The Consumer's Guidebook to Cosmetic Facial Surgery, The Expert's Guide to Safe, Successful Surgery, The Essential Cosmetic Surgery Companion, Don't Consult A Cosmetic Surgeon Without This Book!, 2005; contbr. to several med. publs. and presentations, to several med. and lay books; guest appearances Dr. 90210, Access Hollywood, EXTRA, Oprah, Deborah Noville Tonight, Entertainment Tonight. Maj. med. corps. US Army, 1973—75. Mem.: Am. Soc. Outpatient Suregeons (fmr. head and neck sect. chmn.), AMA, Calif. Med. Assn., LA County Med. Assn., Am. Acad. Cosmetic Surgery, Pan-Pacific Surgical Soc., Calif. Soc. Specialty Plastic Surgeons, Canadian Soc. Facial Plastic Surgery, Am. Soc. Outpatient Surgeons, European Soc. Facial Surgery, Am. Soc. for Laser Medicine & Surgery, Internat. Coll. Surgeons, Am. College Surgeons, Am. Soc. for Dermatologic Surgery, Internat. Soc. Cosmetic Surgeons, Karl Meyer Surgical Soc., Am. Acad. Ophthalmology and Otolaryngology, Soc. Mil. Head and Neck Surgeons, Assn. Mil. Surgeons, Am. Acad. Facial Plastic Surgery and Reconstructive Surgery. Office: 436 N Bedford Dr Ste 201 Beverly Hills CA 90210 Office Phone: 310-278-8721. Office Fax: 310-278-0114.

KOTLER, STEVEN, investment banker; b. NYC, Jan. 9, 1947; s. Louis and Etta (Smeltzer) K.; m. Carolyn Miller, Sept. 26, 1973; children: William, Thomas. BBA, CCNY, 1967. V.p. N.Y. Hanseatic Corp., NYC, 1967-74; with Schroder Wertheim & Co. Inc., NYC, 1974—, gen. ptnr., 1979—, mng. dir., 1981—, pres., 1987—, CEO, 1996-99; vice chmn. Gilbert Global Equity Capital, LLC, NYC. Bd. dirs. Birch Telecom, CPM Holdings; bd. dirs., co-chmn. True Temper Sports; bd. govs. Am. Stock Exch., 1992-97; coun. pres. The Woodrow Wilson Internat. Ctr. for Scholars, 1999-02; mem. infrastructure and housing task force NYC Partnership, NYC C. of C.; bd. overseers Calif. Inst. Arts. Served with USAR, 1967-72. Mem.: Coun. on Fgn. Rels.

KOTLOWITZ, ALEX, writer, journalist; Student, Wesleyan U. Former prodr. segments TV series MacNeil/ Lehrer NewsHour; former reporter The Wall Street Jour.; former contbr. NPR. Writer-i-residence Northwestern U.; Welch chmn. in Am. studies U. Notre Dame, South Bend, Ind. Author: There Are No Children Here: The Story of Two Boys Growing Up In the Other America, 1991 (Helen Bernstein award Excellence Journalism N.Y. Pub. Libr. 1992), The Other Side of the River: A Story of Two Towns, a Death and America's Dilemma, 1998 (Heartland prize for nonfiction Chgo. Tribune 1998), Never a City So Real, 2004; contbr. The N.Y. Times Mag., This Am. Life. Recipient George Polk award TV reporting Long Island U. Journalism dept. work on MacNeil/Lehrer NewsHour, 1984, Robert F. Kennedy award Coverage of Disadvantaged, George Foster Peabody award 2003. Office Phone: 708-445-8805. E-mail: akotlowitz@aol.com.

KOTLOWITZ, ROBERT, writer, editor; b. Paterson, NJ, Nov. 21, 1924; s. Max and Debra (Kaplan) K.; m. Carol Naomi Leibowitz, Oct. 15, 1950; children— Alexander William, Daniel Justin. BA, Johns Hopkins, 1947; preparatory diploma, Peabody Conservatory Music, 1941. Asso. editor Pocket Books, Inc., 1950-55, Discovery, 1952-55; mgr. press and information RCA Victor Records, 1955-60; sr. editor Show mag., 1960-64, Harper's mag., 1965-67, mng. editor, 1967-71; sr. v.p., dir. programming Sta. WNET/ Channel 13, NYC, 1971-91, editorial advisor, 1991—. Guest lectr. Queen's Coll., 1954-55; author monthly column Performing Arts, 1966— Author: novel Somewhere Else, 1972, The Boardwalk, 1977, Sea Changes, 1986, His Master's Voice, 1992, (memoire) Before Their Time, 1997; Contbg. editor: Atlantic Monthly, 1971-74; Contbr. nat. publs. Served with inf. AUS, 1943-46. Recipient Edward Lewis Wallant award for novel, 1972, Nat. Jewish Book award, 1972, Nat. Emmy award, 1973; sr. fellow Freedom Forum, Columbia U., 1993; fellow Am. Acad., Berlin, 1998. Mem. Century Assn. Home: 54 Riverside Dr New York NY 10024-6509 Office Phone: 212-787-0239.

KOTOSKE, ROGER ALLEN, artist, educator; b. South Bend, Ind., Jan. 4, 1933; s. Michael and Louise (Gallo) K.; 1 child, Tamara. Student, U. Notre Dame, 1950-52; BFA, U. Denver, 1955, MA, 1956. Instr. Fitzsimons Army Hosp., Denver, 1956-58, U. Denver, 1958-68; mem. faculty U. Ill., 1968—; now assoc. prof. Vice pres., artist Denver Nat. Sculpture Symposium, 1968 One man shows James Yu Gallery, N.Y.C., 1974, Hiestand Gallery, Miami U., Oxford, Ohio, 1978, Hilton Center for Performing Arts, St. Louis, 1979, group shows include, Galex Nat. 23, Galesburg, Ill., 1989, Greater Midwest Internat. III, Warrensburg, Mo., 1988, SUNY, Potsdam, 1975, Grey Gallery, N.Y.C., 1976, Illinois Painters III, 1980; exhibited in group show U. Del., Newark, 1986, U. of Ill. Faculty Internat. Exchange Exhbn., Chinese Fine Arts Mus., Beijing, China, 1987, Art Yard, Denver, 1996, Vanguard Art in Colo. 1940-1970, Boulder Mus. Contemporary Art, 1999; represented in permanent collections Rock Hill Nelson Gallery, Kansas City, Mo., SUNY, Oswego, Denver Art Mus., others. Ford Found. grantee, 1975-78 Home: 1611 W White St Champaign IL 61821-3017

KOTOV, OLEG VALERIEVICH, cosmonaut; b. Simferopol, Oct. 27, 1965; s. Valeri Efimovich and Elena Ivanovna Kotov; m. Svetlana Nikolayevna Bunyakina; 2 children. Grad., Kirov Mil. Med. Acad., 1988. Dep. lead test doctor and lead test doctor. Gagarin Cosmonaut Tng. Ctr., 1988—96, cosmonaut candidate, 1996—98, test cosmonaut, 1998—; rep. Gagarin Cosmonaut Tng. Ctr. Johnson Space Ctr., 1999; CAPCOM Expedition-3 & 4 in MCC-M, 2001—02, Moscow Support Group in MCC-H, 2001—02; chief CAPCOM Branch, Cosmonaut Office, 2004. Rsch. cosmonaut Soyuz TM-28 Mission; flight engr. and Soyuz comdr. Expedition-15 Mission, Soyuz TMA10, 2007. Avocations: diving, computers, photography. Office: NASA Johnson Space Ctr c/o Astronaut Office/CB Houston TX 77058

KOTRLA, MIROSLAV, physicist; b. Pribram, Czech Republic, Dec. 28, 1957; s. Miroslav and Gizela (Danisovska) K.; m. Jindřiška Röschová, Mar. 31, 1982; children: Jakub, Jan. RNDr, Charles U., 1982, PhD, 1988. Rsch. worker Inst. of Physics/ASCR, Prague, 1982-89, 91, 1993—; postdoctoral fellow Internat. Sch. for Advanced Studies, Trieste, Italy, 1990, U. Genova, Italy, 1992. Referee Phys. Rev. jour., Jour. Physics, 1997—; external tchr. faculty of maths. and physics, Charles U., Prague, 1994—. Contbr. articles to profl. jours. Rsch. grantee Acad. Sci. of Czech Republic, Prague, 1993-94, 95-97, Dept. Edn. Czech Republic, 1999-2001, Grant Agy. of Czech Republic, 2001-03, 06—, European Commn., 2006—. Mem. Union of Czechoslovak Mathematicians and Physicists (phys. sci. sect.), Middle European Cooperation in Statis. Physics (mem. internat. adv. bd. 2001-), CSNMT (sect. nanosci. and nanotechs.). Avocations: yoga, stamp collecting/philately, strategic games, gardening. Office: Inst of Physics/Acad Sci of Czech Rep/Na Slovance 2 CZ 18221 Prague 8 Czech Republic Office Phone: 420-266-052-904. Business E-Mail: kotrla@fzu.cz.

KOTSAY, MARK STEVEN, professional baseball player; b. Woodler, Calif., Dec. 2, 1975; Student, Calif. State U., Fullerton. Ctr. field, right field Fla. Marlins, 1996—2000, San Diego Padres, 2000—03, Oakland Atheletics, 2004—. Named Most Outstanding Player Coll. World Series, 1995; recipient Golden Spikes award, USA Baseball, 1995. Achievements include being a mem. of U.S. Olympic Baseball Team, 1996; being tied for Ea. League for double plays by outfielder with four, 1997. Mailing: care Oakland Atheletics Network Assoc Coliseum 7000 Coliseum Way Oakland CA 94621

KOTSOVOS, JERRY FRANK, retired secondary school educator; b. Portland, Oreg., May 20, 1946; s. John Gerald and Bernice Marie Kotsovos; m. Sharon Irene Brumfield, Aug. 5, 1967; children: Darren Wade, Laura Eve. BS, U. Oreg., 1968; MS, So. Oreg. U., 1971. Cert. tchr. Oreg. Social studies tchr. Marshfield H.S., Coos Bay, Oreg., 1968—2003; ret., 2003. Cons. advanced placement program Coll. Bd., Princeton, NJ, 1984—2001. Author: Comfortable Lies and Uncomfortable Truths, 2005. Mem. walkathons March of Dimes, Coos Bay; mem. Tchr. Participation in Presdl. Classroom, Washington, 1974; campaign worker Dem. Party, Coos Bay, 1972. Recipient Tchr. Recognition award, U.S. Dept. Edn., 1999. Mem.: NEA, Coos Bay Edn. Assn. (rep. 1970). Achievements include topic of Time mag. article, 1977. Avocations: travel, distance running. Home: 5508 NW Jackson St Camas WA 98607 E-mail: jskots@comcast.net.

KOTT, DAVID RUSSELL, lawyer; b. Trenton, NJ, Jan. 22, 1952; s. Maurice G. and Ruth (Shulman) K.; m. Lauren Handler, Aug. 24, 1980; children: Emily R., Adam J. BA, Am. U., 1973; JD, Rutgers U., 1977. Bar: N.J. 1977, U.S. Dist. Ct. N.J. 1977, U.S. Ct. Appeals (3d cir.) 1980, N.Y. 1984, U.S. Dist. Ct. (so. and ea. dists.) N.Y. 1985; cert. civil trial atty. Law clk. to justice N.J. Supreme Ct., Morristown, 1977-78; from assoc. to ptnr. McCarter & English LLP, Newark, 1978—. Sustaining mem. Product Liability Adv. Coun. Fellow Am. Coll. Trial Lawyers (elected one of top 100 N.J. Super Lawyers), 2006; mem. ABA, Am. Bd. Trial Advocates, N.J. Bar Assn., Essex County Bar Assn., Assn. Def. Trial Lawyers Attys., Trial Lawyers N.J., Fedn. Ins. and Corp. Attys., Def. Rsch. Inst., The Newark Club. Republican. Jewish. Office: McCarter & English LLP 4 Gateway Ctr 100 Mulberry St Newark NJ 07102-4004 Business E-Mail: dkott@mccarter.com.

KOTTAMASU, MOHAN RAO (K.V.R. MOHAN RAO), physician, health facility administrator; b. Gudivada, India, Jan. 13, 1947; arrived in U.S., 1973; s. Janardana Rao and Kanthamma (Maddi) Kottamasu; m. Sarada Devi Vusirikala, Dec. 20, 1992; children: Pallavi, Aamani. MBBS, Gulbarga Med. Coll., 1972. Diplomate Am. Bd. Internal Medicine, 1977, in pulmonary disease Am. Bd. Internal Medicine, 1980. House surgeon Govt. Gen. Hosp., Gulbarga, India, 1971-72; intern St. Vincent's Med. Ctr. Richmond, SI, NY, 1973-74, resident, 1974-76, chief resident, 1976-77; pulmonary diseases fellow Lahey Clinic and Deaconess Hosp., Boston, 1977-79; clin. fellow Harvard Med. Sch., Boston, 1978-79; assoc. Valley Pulmonary and Med. Assocs., Springfield, Mass., 1979-81, ptnr., v.p., 1981—. Adj. asst. prof. clin. pharmacy Mass. Coll. Pharmacy and Allied Health Scis., 1984—; pres. med. staff Mercy Hosp., Springfield, 1989—91. Pres. house staff St. Vincent's Med. Ctr., 1976; founding pres. Indian Assn. Greater Springfield, 1985—86. Fellow: ACP, Am. Coll. Chest Physicians; mem.: AMA, Hampden Dist. Med. Soc. (pres.-elect 1999, pres. 2000—01, Cmty. Clinician of the Yr. 2001), Mass. Med. Soc., Am. Thoracic Soc. Hindu. Avocations: chess, gardening. Home: 112 Twin Hills Dr Longmeadow MA 01106-2952 Office: Valley Pulmonary Med Assocs 222 Carew St Springfield MA 01104-4103 Office Phone: 413-739-5661. Personal E-mail: mohan_kottamasu@hotmail.com.

KOTTAS, JOHN FREDERICK, business administration educator; b. Hampton, Va., Apr. 18, 1940; s. Harry and Johnny (Edwards) K.; m. Betty Ann Hokenson, Aug. 7, 1965; children: John Bohlin, Ellen Elizabeth, Katherine Caroline, Paul Frederick. BS, Purdue U., 1962; MS, Northwestern U., 1964, PhD, 1968. Lectr. Wharton Sch., U. Pa., Phila., 1966-68; asst. prof. Sch. Bus. Adminstrn., U. N.C., Chapel Hill., 1968-73; adj. assoc. prof. Boston U. Overseas Grad. Program, Heidelberg, W. Ger., 1973-74; asso. prof. coordinator mgmt. sci. and info. systems Sch. Bus. Adminstrn., U. Mo., St. Louis, 1974-79; Zollinger prof. bus. adminstrn. Coll. William and Mary, Williamsburg, Va., 1979—. Presented three-day mgmt. seminar on Inventory Mgmt. and Control at numerous univs., U.S. and Can., 1976-78; cons. in field. Co-author: Production/Operations Management: Contemporary Policy of Managing Operating Systems, 1972, Cases and Applications in Lotus 1-2-3 (for DOS), 1995, Cases and Applications in Lotus 1-2-3 (for Windows), 1996, Cases and Applications in Microsoft EXCEL 5.0, 1996; contbr. articles to various publs. NDEA fellow, 1962-65; Walter P. Murphy fellow, 1962 Home: 109 Maxwell Pl Williamsburg VA 23185-5523 Office: Coll of William and Mary Mason Sch Bus Williamsburg VA 23187 Office Phone: 757-221-2868. Personal E-mail: jfkott@cox.net. Business E-Mail: john.kottas@mason.wm.edu.

KOTTER, JOHN PAUL, organizational behavior educator, management consultant; b. San Diego, Feb. 25, 1947; s. Paul Henry and Louise (Churchill) K.; m. Nancy Dearman; children: Jonathan, Caroline. BS, MIT, 1968, MS, 1970; D.BA, Harvard U., 1972. Rsch. fellow Harvard Bus. Sch., Boston, 1972-73, asst. prof., 1973-77, assoc. prof., 1977—80, prof., 1980—90, named Konosuke Matsushita Prof. of Leadership, 1990; ret. Cons. in field. Author: The General Managers, 1982, Power and Influence, 1985, The Leadership Factor, 1988, A Force for Change, 1990, Corporate Culture and Performance, 1992, The New Rules, 1995, Leading Change, 1996, Matsushita Leadership, 1997 (Fin. Times/Booz-Allen and Hamilton Global Bus. Book Award for biography/autobiography, 1998), John P. Kotter on What Leaders Really Do, 1999, The Heart of Change, 2002, Our Iceberg is Melting, 2006, others. Named #1 "leadership guru" in Am., Bus. Week mag., 2001; recipient Exxon Award for Innovation in Grad. Bus. Sch. Curriculum Design, Johnson, Smith and Knisely Award for New Perspectives in Bus. Leadership. E-mail: jkotter@hbs.edu.

KOTTER, RITA JOAN, theatre educator, design consultant; b. Superior, Wis., Aug. 6, 1934; d. Edward Kotter and Mernnie Geraldine Bellino; children: Rebekah West, Laura Majors, Richmond Majors. BA, U. of Wis., 1952—56; MA, U. of Colo., 1959—69. Teacher Certification Colo., 1959. Tchr., theatre, speech, English Beloit Pub. Schools, Wis., 1956—57, Roseville Pub. Schs., Mich., 1957—58, Canon City Pub. Schs., Colo., 1959—60, Brighton Pub. Schs., Colo., 1960—64, Boulder Valley Schs., Colo., 1964—91; fine arts dept. chair Fairview H.S., Boulder, Colo.; parliamentarian U. of Colo. Bd. of Regents, 1999—. Pub. speaking trainer Boulder Bus. & Profl. Women, Boulder, Colo., 1993—2006; theatre cons. Carousel Dinner Theatre, Ft. Collins, Colo., 1992—94; master artist-in-residence Deer Creek Elem. Sch., Bailey, Colo., 1993—93; student tchr. supr. U. of No. Colo., 1993—94. Pres. Secondary Sch. Theatre Assn., Washington, 1983—85; bd. of nominations chair Am. Theatre Assn., DC, 1973—85; pres. Arts & Humanities Assembly of Boulder County, 1965—2005; chair Leadership Boulder-C. of C., 1993—97; parliamentarian Alliance for Colo. Theatre, Denver, 1984—97; treas. Rocky Mountain Theatre Assn., Denver, 1989—93; adjudicator Am. Coll. Theatre Festival, 1972—92, Festival of Am. Cmty. Theatres, Denver, 1980—90. Recipient Women Who Light up the Cmty., Boulder C. of C., 1999, Inaugural Hall of Fame, Colo. Thespian Soc., 2000, AMOCO Gold Medallion of Excellence, Rocky Mountain/Am. Coll. Theatre Festival, 1984, Alpha Psi Omega Outstanding Theatre Student, U. of Wis. at Superior, 1956, Disting. Svc. award, Alliance for Colo. Theatre, 1993. Mem.: Boulder Bus. & Profl. Women (parliamentarian 1994—2000), Am. Alliance for Theatre & Edn. (dir. of stds. 1987—91), Colo. Alliance for Arts Edn (v.p. 2003—04). Avocations: reading, theatre, skating, tennis, dance. Home: 1407 Bradley Dr Boulder CO 80305 Home Phone: 303-499-9260.

KOTTICK, EDWARD LEON, musician, educator; b. Jersey City, June 16, 1930; s. Hyman W. and Frieda M. (Stoller) K.; m. Gloria Astor, May 10, 1953; children: Judith, Janet AB, NYU, 1953; MA, Tulane U., 1959; PhD, U. N.C., Chapel Hill, 1962. Trombonist New Orleans Philharm., 1955-57; asst. prof. music Alma Coll., Mich., 1962-65; vis. prof. music U. Kans., Lawrence, 1965-66; assoc. prof. music U. Mo.-St. Louis, 1966-68; prof. music U. Iowa, Iowa City, 1968-92, prof. emeritus, 1992. Author: The Unica in the Chansonnier Cordiforme, No. 42 of Corpus Mensurabilis Musicae, 1967, Tone and Intonation on the Recorder, 1974, The Collegium: A Handbook, 1977, The Harpsichord Owner's Guide, 1987; author: (with G. Lucktenberg) Early Keyboard Instruments in European Museums, 1997; contbr. articles to profl. jours.; author: A History of the Harpsichord, 2003. With US Army, 1953—55. Recipient Edward S. Allen award, AAUP Iowa Conf., 1993, Michael Brody Faculty Excellence award, U. Iowa, 1998; grantee, 1975, 1980, 1985, 1990; summer fellow, 1976. Mem. Am. Mus. Instrument Soc. (bd. govs. 1986-90,Curt Sachs Lifetime Achievement in Musical Instruments award 2006), Am. Musicol. Soc. (chpt. sec. 1961-62, chpt. program com. 1964-66, chair com. 1972-73, 96-97, mem. nat. com. Collegium Musicum 1973-75), Fellowship Makers and Restorers of Hist. Instruments, Galpin Soc. (grantee, 1976), Guild Am. Luthiers, Midwestern Hist. Keyboard Soc. (bd. dir. 1980-90, 94-97). Home: 502 Larch Ln Iowa City IA 52245-3434 Personal E-mail: ed@kottick.com.

KOTTKAMP, JEFFREY DEAN, lieutenant governor, lawyer; b. Indpls., Nov. 12, 1960; s. Donald D. and Cecilia A. (Webber) K. BS in Polit. Sci., Fla. State U., Tallahassee, 1984; JD, U. Fla., 1987. Bar: Fla. 1988, US Dist. Ct. (so. and mid. dists.) Fla. 1989, US Ct. Appeals (11th cir.) 1991, US Supreme Ct. 1995; cert. cir. ct. mediator. Assoc. Kimbrell & Hamann, P.A., Miami, Fla., 1988-90; law clk. to Hon. Joe Eaton US Dist Ct. (so. dist.) Fla., Miami, 1990, law clk. to Hon. Sidney Aronovitz, 1990-91; assoc. Henderson, Franklin, Starnes & Holt, P.A., Ft. Myers, Fla., 1991—; atty. Morgan & Morgan, P.A., Cape Coral, Fla.; rep. Fla. State Ho. of Reps, 2001—; lt. gov. State of Fla., 2006—. Mem. editorial bd. Fla. Bar Jour., 1989—. Mem. Dade County Bar Assn. (editor-in-chief bar bull. 1989-91, bd. dirs. young lawyers sect. 1990-91, Cert. of Merit 1991), S.W. Fla. Fed. Bar Assn. (v.p. 1995), Lee County Bar Assn. (pres. 1998). Republican. Office Phone: 850-488-4711. Office Fax: 850-921-6114.*

KOTUK, ANDREA MIKOTAJUK, public relations executive, writer; b. New Brunswick, NJ, Oct. 19, 1948; d. Michael and Julia Dorothy (Muka) Mikotajuk. BA, Rutgers U., 1970. Pub. relations asst. Wall St. Jour. Newspaper Fund, Princeton, NJ, 1970; editorial asst. Redbook mag., NYC, 1970-71; asst. pub. relations dir. Children's Aid Soc., NYC, 1971-75; assoc. pub. relations dir. Planned Parenthood, NYC, 1975-80; pres. Andrea & Assocs., NYC, 1980—. Contbg. editor Arts Mag., 1970-75. Office: Andrea & Assocs 5th Floor 112 E 23rd St New York NY 10010-4518 Office Phone: 212-353-9585. Personal E-mail: andreapr@earthlink.net.

KOTULA, MICHAEL ANTHONY, lawyer; b. Rockville Centre, NY, Aug. 17, 1965; s. Michael Stanley and Rosemary Therese Kotula. BA, Emory U., 1987; JD with honors, George Washington U., 1990. Bar: N.J. 1990, D.C. 1991, N.Y. 1995, U.S. Dist. Ct. N.J. 1990, U.S. Dist. Ct. D.C. 1992, U.S. Dist. Ct. (ea. and so. dists.) N.Y. 1998, U.S. Ct. Appeals (3rd cir.) 1992. Law clk. Hon. Curtis E. von Kann U.S. Superior Ct. (D.C.), Washington, 1990-91; assoc. Carr, Goodson, Lee & Warner, Washington, 1991-94, Rivkin, Radler, LLP, Uniondale, NY, 1994-98, ptnr., 1998—. Contbg. author: The Law of Liability Insurance, 1999; contbr. articles to profl. jours.; conf. lectr. Recipient Outstanding Advocate award Met. Washington Trial Lawyers Assn., 1990, Gold Achiever's award, Mentoring Partnership, LI, 2006; named to 40 Under 40, LI Bus. News, 2004. Mem. ABA (vice chair excess, surplus lines and reinsurance gen. com. tort trial and ins. practice sect., 2007-), NY State Bar Assn. (exec. com. young lawyers sect. 1997-2001, liaison to the environ. law sect. 1997-2001). Avocations: running, weightlifting, travel, sports, kayaking. Office: Rivkin Radler 926 Rex Corp Plz Uniondale NY 11556-0926 Office Phone: 516-357-3000. Business E-Mail: michael.kotula@rivkin.com.

KOTWAL, RUSS STEVEN, military officer, physician; b. Birmingham, Ala., Sept. 16, 1964; m. Bari Marie Petree, Feb. 16, 1985; children: Ashley Russell, Aaron Steven, Kirstyn Marie. BS, Tex. A&M U., Coll. Sta., Tex., 1985; MD, Uniformed Svcs. U. of the Health Scis., Bethesda, Md., 1996; M in Pub. Health, U. of Tex. Med. Br., Galveston, Tex., 2004. Fellow Am. Acad. of Family Physicians, 2003, Diplomate Am. Bd. of Family Physicians, 1999. Residency in family practice Martin Army Cmty. Hosp., Fort Benning, Ga., 1996—99; ranger bn. surgeon 3d Bn., 75th Ranger Rgt., Fort Benning, 1999—2003; residency in aerospace medicine Inst. Naval Operational Medicine, Pensacola, Fla., 2004—05; ranger regimental surgeon 75th Ranger Regiment, 2005—. Adj. asst. prof. Dept. Mil. and Emergency Medicine, Uniformed Svcs. Univ. of Health Sci., 2004—07. Contbr. articles pub. to profl. jour. Lt. col. US Army, 1985—2007, Tex., Hawaii, Md., Ga., Fla., med. platoon leader, logistician 25th infantry divsn. US Army, 1986—90. Decorated 3 Bronze Stars, 1 Meritorious Svc. medal, 1 Joint Svc. Commendation medal with valor device, 3 Army Commendation medals, 4 Army Achievement medals US Army; recipient Chmn. of Joint Chiefs of Staff award for Excellence in Mil. Medicine, Dept. Def., 2000. Mem.: AMA (us army surgeon gen. rep. 1992—96), 75th Ranger Regiment Assn., Uniformed Svcs. Acad. of Family Physicians, Spl. Ops. Med. Assn., Assn. of the US Army, Aerospace Med. Assn., Assn. of Mil. Surgeons of the US, Am. Acad. of Family Physicians, Soc. of US Army Flight Surgeons (life). Achievements include research in malaria, combat parachute injuries and pain control in combat; six short combat tours, four in Afghanistan and two in Iraq; Sr. mil. parachutist with two combat jumps, one into Afghanistan in October 2001 and one into Iraq in March 2003. Avocations: travel, parachuting, hunting. Office: Hdqs 75th Ranger Regiment 6420 Dawson Loop Fort Benning GA 31905 Office Phone: 706-545-4545.

KOTYNEK, GEORGE ROY, mechanical engineer, educator, marketing executive; b. Lake Forest, Ill., Apr. 18, 1938; s. Anton Joseph and Zdenka K.; m. Virginia Jean Hyde, Sept. 4, 1965 (div. 1973); children: John Anton, Joseph George. BSME, Ill. Inst. Tech., 1960. Registered profl. engr., Ill. Efficiency engr. Commonwealth Edison Co., Chgo., 1959-63; instr. physics Glenbard East High Sch., Lombard, Ill., 1963-67; systems engr. Sargent and Lundy, Chgo., 1967-77; prin. engr. Fluor Corp., Chgo., 1977-85; mgr. fossil tech. Stearns Catalytic World Corp., Oak Brook, Ill., 1985-86; mgr. mktg. Volund USA Ltd., New Providence, NJ, 1986-94; tech. cons. VECTRA Techs., Inc., Lincolnshire, Ill., 1994-96; sr. tech. cons. Duke Engring. & Svcs., Inc., Naperville, Ill., 1996—2002, AREVA Framatome ANP, Naperville, 2002—05, Sigma Energy Solutions, 2005—. Mem. hazardous materials adv. com. Waubonsee C.C., Sugar Grove, Ill., 1992—. Contbr. articles to profl. publs. Mem. People to People Internat. Conventional and Nuclear Power Engring. Delegation to People's Republic of China, 1987. Mem. ASME (newsletter editor 1980-82, vice chmn. membership 1982-83, vice chmn. programs 1983-84). Achievements include the design of 2,700-MW electric generating station for Sargent & Lundy. Office: Sigma Energy Solutions 1245 E Diehl Rd Ste 304 Naperville IL 60563 Home Phone: 708-484-6639.

KOTZ, NATHAN KALLISON (NICK KOTZ), news correspondent, author; b. San Antonio, Sept. 16, 1932; s. Jacob and Tybe (Kallison) K.; m. Mary Lynn Booth, Aug. 7, 1960; 1 child, Jack Mitchell. AB magna cum laude in Internat. Relations, Dartmouth Coll., 1955; student, London Sch. Econs., 1955-56. Reporter, Des Moines Register, 1958-64, Washington corr., 1964-70; also for other Cowles Publs. (newspapers); nat. corr. Washington Post, 1970-73; adj. prof. Sch. Communication, Am. U., Washington, 1978-86; sr. journalist in residence Duke U., 1983; corr. PBS Frontline, 1992. Farmer, Broad Run, Va., 1980— Free-lance writer, 1973; author: Let Them Eat Promises: The Politics of Hunger in America, 1969, Wild Blue Yonder: Money, Politics, and the B-1 Bomber, 1988, Judgment Days: Lyndon Baines Johnson, Martin Luther King, Jr., and the Laws That Changed America, 2005; co-author: The Unions, 1971, A Passion for Equality: George Wiley and the Movement, 1977. Bd. dirs. Iowa Bds. Internat. Edn., 1962-64, Suburban Md. Fair Housing, 1966-72, Black Student Fund, 1976-86—, Penn-Faulkner, 1986—; bd. dirs. Fund for Investigative Journalism, 1977-86, chmn., 1978-82. Served to 1st lt. USMCR, 1956-58. Recipient Pulitzer prize for nat. reporting, 1968; Raymond Clapper Meml. award, 1966, 68, 2d pl., 1973, Disting. Service award Sigma Delta Chi, 1966, Robert F. Kennedy Journalism award, 1968, Spl. Merit award Am. U., 1981, award for pub. svc. Nat. Mag., 1985, Adj. Faculty award Am. U., 1985, Olive Branch award NYU Ctr. War, Peace and News Media, 1989, Iowa Author award, 2005, Martin Luther King Jr. Social Justice award Dartmouth Coll., 2006, Robert F. Kennedy Meml. Book High Honor award, 2006. Mem. Nat. Press Club, Cosmos Club, Phi Beta Kappa.

KOTZ, SAMUEL, statistician, educator, translator, editor; b. Harbin, China, Aug. 28, 1930; s. Boris and Guta (Kahana) K.; m. Roselyn Greenwald, Aug. 6, 1963; children: Tamar Ann, Harold David, Pauline Esther. MSc with honors, Hebrew U., Jerusalem, 1956; PhD, Cornell U., 1960; Dr. honoris causa, U. Athens, 1995, Harbin Inst. Tech., 1984, Bowling Green State U., 1997. Rschr. Israel Meteorol. Svc., 1954-58; lectr. Bar-Ilan U., Israel, 1960-62; postdoctoral Ford fellow U. NC, 1962-63; assoc. prof. U. Toronto, 1963-67; prof. math. Temple U., 1967-79; prof. stats. U. Md., College Park, 1979-97, disting. scholar-tchr., 1984-85. Disting. vis. prof. Bucknell U., 1977, Guelph (Can.) U., 1987; hon. prof. Harbin Inst. Tech., 1987; Eugene Lukacs disting. rsch. prof. Bowling Green (Ohio) State U., 1992; vis. prof. U. Luleå, Sweden, 1993, 95, Hong Kong U., 1994, U. Copenhagen, summer 1996, U. South Brittany, Vannes, France, 1998; vis. prof. econs. and fin. St. Petersburg (Russia) U., summer 1995; vis. rschr. Internat. Statis. Inst., The Hague, summer 1996, U. Paul Sabatier, Toulouse, France, summer 1998, U. York, Eng., 1999, U. Salford, Eng., 1999, 2000, Athens U. Econs., 1999, U. Lund, Sweden, 2000; vis. sr. rsch. scholar George Washington U., 1997—, U. Trento, Italy, summers, 2001, 02, U. Padua, 2002, U. Bologna, 2002. Author, editor 30 books, 4 Russian-English profl. dictionaries, over 135 rsch. papers; translator 18 books; co-editor-in-chief: Encyclopedia of Statistical Sci., 9 vols. and supplement, 1982-89, editor-in-chief up-date vols. 1-3, 1994-98, 2d edit., 16 vols., 2005; co-editor: Breakthroughs in Statistics, 3 vol., 1995-98; editor: Leading Statistical Personalities, 1997; co-author: Process Capability Indices, 1993, 98, Applied Bayesian Statistics (in Chinese), 2000, 2d edit., 2001, Extreme Value Distributions, 2000, 3d edit., 2005, Correlation and Dependence, 2001, Laplace Distributions and Applications, 2001, Strength-Stress Models, 2003, Statistical Size Distributions in Economics, 2003, Multivariate T-distributions and Applications, 2004, Beyond Beta, 2005, Handbook of Capability Indices, 2006; mem. editl. bd. Jour. Quality Rsch. and Tech.; coord. editor AIEE Transactions; editor-in-chief: Quality Management and Control. Served with Israeli Army, 1950-52. Fellow Am. Statis. Assn., Inst. Math. Stat., Royal Statis. Soc., Washington Acad. Sci. (hon.); mem. Internat. Statis. Inst. (elected mem.). Office: George Washington U Dept Engring Mgmt and Sys Analysis Washington DC 20052-0001 Office Phone: 202-994-7187. Business E-Mail: kotz@gwu.edu.

KOTZWINKLE, WILLIAM, writer; b. Scranton, Pa., Nov. 22, 1938; s. William John and Madolyn (Murphy) K.; m. Elizabeth Gundy. Student, Rider Coll., Pa. State U. Author: The Fireman, 1969, The Ship That Came Down the Gutter, 1970, Elephant Boy: The Story of the Stone Age, 1970, The Day the Gang Got Rich, 1970, The Oldest Man, and Other Timeless Tales, 1971, Elephant Bangs Train, 1971, The Return of Crazy Horse, 1971, Hermes 3000, 1972, The Supreme, Superb, Exalted and Delightful, One and Only Magic Building, 1973, Up the Alley with Jack and Joe, 1974, The Fat Man, 1974, Night-Book, 1974, Swimmer in the Secret Sea, 1975, The Leopard's Tooth, 1976, Doctor Rat, 1976 (World Fantasy award best novel 1977), Fata Morgana, 1977, Herr Nightingale and the Satin Women, 1978, The Ants Who Took Away Time, 1978, Dream of Dark Harbor, 1979, The Nap Master, 1979, Jack in the Box, 1980 (pub. as Book of Love, 1982), Christmas at Fontaine's, 1982, (novelization of screenplay) E.T., The Extra-Terrestrial, 1982 (N.D. Children's Choice award 1983, Buckeye award 1984), (novelization of screenplay) Superman III, 1983, Great World Circus, 1983, Queen of Swords, 1983, Trouble in Bugland: A Collection of Inspector Mantis Mysteries, 1983, E.T., The Book of the Green Planet, 1985, Seduction in Berlin, 1985, Jewel of the Moon, 1985, Heart of Wood, and Other Timeless Tales, 1986, The World Is Big and I'm So Small, 1986, The Exile, 1987, The Midnight Examiner, 1989, Hot Jazz Trio, 1989, The Empty Notebook, 1990, The Game of Thirty, 1994, The Million Dollar Bear, 1995, Tales from the Empty Notebook, 1996, The Bear Went Over the Mountain, 1996, The Amphora Project, 2005; screenwriter: (films) A Nightmare on Elm Street 4: The Dream Master, 1988, Book of Love, 1991; co-author (with Glenn Murray and Audrey Colman) Walter the Farting Dog, 2001, Walter the Farting Dog: Trouble at the Yard Sale, 2004. Recipient Nat. Mag. award for fiction, 1972, 75; O'Henry prize, 1975. Office: Doubleday 1540 Broadway New York NY 10036-4039

KOU, VICTORIA, medical educator; BA in Econs., Northwestern U., Evanston, Ill., 1988; MD, George Washington U., Washington, 1997. Rsch. assoc. Prudential, Newark, 1989—91; resident Mt. Sinai Hosp., NYCc, 2002—05; asst. prof. UMDNJ, NJ Med. Sch., Newark, 2005—. Lt. comdr. USN, 1997—. Scholar, US Navy, 1993. Mem.: Am. Coll. Emergency Physicians. Office: UMDNJ University Hospital 150 Bergen St Newark NJ 07101 Home Phone: 908-277-0995; Office Phone: 973-972-5128. Personal E-mail: vwkou@aol.com. E-mail: kouvw@umdnj.edu.

KOUCHOUKOS, NICHOLAS THOMAS, surgeon; b. Grand Rapids, Mich., Dec. 26, 1936; s. Thomas Paul and Antoinette (Karver) K.; m. Judith Buell, Aug. 24, 1966; children— Nicholas Thomas, Robert Buell, Thomas Paul. Student (James B. Angell scholar), U. Mich., 1954-57; MD cum laude, Washington U., 1961. Diplomate Am. Bd. Thoracic Surgery (bd. dirs. 1989-96). Intern Barnes Hosp., Washington U. Med. Ctr., St. Louis, 1961-62, asst. resident in surgery, 1962-65, chief adminstrv. resident, 1965-66; sr. clin. trainee in surgery USPHS, 1966-67; asst. in surgery Sch. Medicine Washington U., St. Louis, 1961-65, instr. surgery, 1965-67, John M. Shoenberg prof. cardiovascular surgery, 1984-96, vice chmn. dept. surgery, 1993-96; research fellow surgery Sch. Medicine, U. Ala., Birmingham, 1967-68, instr. surgery, 1967-69, advanced trainee thoracic and cardiovascular surgery, 1968-70, asst. prof. surgery, 1969-71, assoc. prof., 1971-74, prof., vice-dir. div. thoracic and cardiovascular surgery, 1974-81, John W. Kirklin prof. cardiovascular surgery, 1981, clin. prof., 1981-84; cardiovascular surgeon-in-chief Jewish Hosp. of St. Louis, 1984-96, surgeon in chief, 1988-96; mem. cardiovascular research study com. Am. Heart Assn., 1977-79; surgery study sect. USPHS, Bethesda, Md., 1977-80; vice chmn. dept. surgery Washington U. Sch. Medicine, St. Louis, 1991-96. Ad hoc cons. Specialized Centers in Research Arteriosclerosis, Nat. Heart and Lung Inst., Bethesda, 1971-72, mem. ad hoc rev. com. for collaborative studies on coronary artery surgery, 1973-75, surgery A study sect., 1976-77; mem. merit rev. bd. in cardiovascular studies VA, Washington, 1976-78 Editorial bd. Jour. Cardiac Rehab., 1979-84, Current Topics in Cardiology, 1977-92, Circulation, 1978-81, 86-88, Cardiology Update, 1979-92, Annals Thoracic Surgery, 1980-89, Cardiosat, 1984-92; assoc. editor Jour. Thoracic and Cardiovascular Surgery, 1994-98. Fellow: ACS, Am. Coll. Cardiology (asst. treas. 1997—99, sec. 1999—2000, finalist Young Investigators award 1962); mem.: AAUP, AMA, Internat. Cardiovascular Soc., Soc. Vascular Surgery, Soc. Univ. Surgeons, So. Surg. Assn., So. Thoracic Surg. Assn., St. Louis Thoracic Surg. Soc. (pres. 1993—95), Soc. Thoracic Surgeons (treas. 1992—97, v.p. 1998, pres. 1999—2000, historian 2007—), John Kirklin Soc., St. Louis Met. Med. Soc., Internat. Surg. Soc., Assn. Acad. Surgery, Assn. Clin. Cardiac Surgeons, Am. Surg. Assn., Am. Assn. Thoracic Surgery, Alpha Omega Alpha, Phi Beta Kappa. Home: 25 Picardy Ln Saint Louis MO 63124-1606 Office: Missouri Baptist Hosp 3009 N Ballas Rd Ste 360C Saint Louis MO 63131-2308 Office Phone: 314-996-5287. Personal E-mail: ntkouch@aol.com.

KOUCKY, JOHN RICHARD, metallurgical engineer, manufacturing executive; b. Chgo., Sept. 21, 1934; s. Frank Louis and Ella (Harshman) K.; m. Beverly Irene O'Dell, Aug. 16, 1958 (dec. May 1990); children: Deborah, Diane; m. Beverly Kay Cummins, Apr. 27, 1991 (dec. Jan. 1996); m. Mary Ann Hubbard, Jan. 4, 1997. BSMetE, U. Ill., 1957; MBA, Northwestern U., 1959. Metallurgist, asst. plant mgr. Fansteel Metall. Corp., North Chicago, Ill., 1957-64; supr. production engring. cen. foundry div. Gen. Motors Corp., Saginaw, Mich., 1964-67; asst. gen. mgr. Marion (Ind.) Malleable Iron, 1967-68; mgr. production engring. tech., plant mgr., v.p. engr. Wagner Castings Co., Decatur, Ill., 1968-79, 83-91; v.p., gen. mgr. Pa. mall iron div. Gulf & Western, Lancaster, 1979-82; v.p. tech. Wagner Laser Techs., 1989-94; v.p. Decatur Mfg. Co., 1993-95, 300 Below, Inc., Decatur, 1993—. Bd. dirs. Little Theater. 1st lt. US Army, 1957—58. Mem. Am. Soc. Metals (local chmn. 1976—), Am. Foundrymans Soc. (local vice chmn. 1968—), Ductile Iron Soc. (nat. bd. dirs. 1983—), Iron Castings Soc., Soc. Automotive Engrs., U. Ill. Dept. Materials Sci. Alumni Assn. (bd. dirs. 1983-98, Loyalty award 1986), Gray Iron Founders Assn., Soc. for Advancement Material and Process Engring., Country Club Decatur, Decatur Tennis Club (pres. 1976-78), Decatur Racquet Club. Republican. Avocations: tennis, golf, bridge, gardening. Home: 510 Greenway Ln Decatur IL 62521-2533 Office: 300 Below Inc 2999 Parkway Dr Decatur IL 62526 Office Phone: 217-423-3070. E-mail: jkoucky@300below.com.

KOUGIANOS, ELIAS, engineering educator, consultant; m. Diane M. Kwiatkowski. BSEE, U. Patras, Greece, 1985; MSEE, La. Sate U., Baton Rouge, 1987; MS in Physics, La. State U., Baton Rouge, 1988, PhD in Elec. Engring., 1997. Software applications engr. Computer Ventures Inc., Baton Rouge, 1988—89; mem. tech. staff -rsch. Tex. Instruments, Inc., Dallas, 1989—98; asst. prof. DeVry U., Irving, Tex., 1998—99; corp. cons. Avant! Corp (now Synopsys, Inc.), Phoenix, 1999—2000; sr. methodology arch. Cadence Design Systems, Inc., Dallas, 2000—04; asst. prof. U. North Tex., Denton, 2004—. Design Automation Conf. fellow, IEEE and Assn. Computing Machinery, 2005. Mem.: IEEE. Office: U North Tex 3940 N Elm St Denton TX 76207-7102 Home Phone: 940-891-6708; Office Phone: 940-891-0678.

KOUL, DIMPY, biology professor, cell biologist, researcher; d. Poushker Nath and Krishna Koul; m. Anil Garyali; children: Arnav Garyali, Anvi Garyali. PhD, Post Grad. Inst. Med. Edn., Chandigarh, 1996. Rsch. assoc. MD Anderson Cancer ctr., Houston, 1999—2000, instr., 2000—03, asst. prof., 2003—. Recipient Gold medal and Honor of Distinction, U. Kashmir, India, 1989, Nat. prize for Best Young Scientist, Indian Immunology Soc., 1994, Award for Excellence in Basic Rsch., Amgen, 1999, Young Investigator award, Am. Assn. Indian Scientists, 2000; fellow, U. Kashmir, India, 1986—87, Post Grad. Inst. Med. Edn., 1990—94, Internat. Union of Immunological Soc., 1995. Achievements include research in tumor suppressor gene PTEN and the phosphatidylinositol 3 kinase (PI3K)-AKT signaling. Office: MD Anderson Cancer Cter 1515 Holocomb Blvd Box 1002 Houston TX 77030 Home Phone: 713-799-2869; Office Phone: 713-834-6202. Business E-Mail: dkoul@mdanderson.org.

KOUL, HARI KRISHEN, surgery professor, scientist; b. Anantnag, Kashmir, India, Sept. 14, 1963; s. Soom Nath and Shyama (Dulari) K.; m. Sweaty Koul, Apr. 29, 1994; children: Neil, Kashyap. BS in Biology and Chemistry, Kashmir U., 1984, MS in Biochemistry, 1986; PhD in Biochemistry, Postgrad. Inst. Med. Edn and Rsch., Chandigarh, India, 1990. Jr. rsch. fellow Postgrad. Inst. Med. Edn. and Rsch., 1986-88, sr. rsch. fellow, 1988-90, tutor in biochemistry, 1990-91; postdoctoral fellow in surgery and physiology U. Mass. Med. Sch., Worcester, 1991-94, sr. rsch. assoc. in surgery and physiology, 1994-96, instr. urologic and transplantation surgery, 1996-97; sr. staff scientist, prin. investigator Henry Ford Health Scis. Ctr., Detroit, 1997—2003; prof., dir. rsch. divsn. urology U. Colo. Health Scis. Ctr., Denver, 2003—, program dir. urosciences, 2004—. Pres. Assn. Basic Med. Scientists, Chandigarth, India, 1990-91; mem. Vet's Health Adminstrn. Rev. Bd., 2004—, various emphasis and rev. panels; mem. rsch. adv. coun., U. Colo. Sch. Medicine, 2003—, mem. clin. translational rsch. adv. coun., 2004—, mem. Cancer Ctr.; mem. internal adv. com. Clin. Transitional Rsch. Ctr. UCDHSC, 2007; vis. prof. Morgan State U., Balt., 2004; spkr. and lectr. in field. Author: (chpt.) Kidney Stones Medical and Surgical Management, 1996; editl. bd. (journal) Urol. Rsch., 2001; contbr. articles to profl. jours. Founding exec. dir. Save Kashmir Movement, 1999; mem. Am. Friends India, 2000, India Think Tank, 2000; coord. Panun Kashmir, 2000. Recipient Jr. Rsch. fellowship Coun. Sci. and Indsl. Rsch., New Delhi, 1987, Internat. Scientist of Yr., 2002; Sr. Rsch. fellow Coun. Sci. and Indsl. Rsch., 1988, Postdoctoral fellow U. Mass. Med. Sch., 1991; Rsch. grantee NIH, 1997—. Fellow: Am. Soc. Nephrology, Am. Coll. Nutrition; mem.: NIH (program dir. urolithiasis rsch. project 1997—2003, mem. site visit com. U. Chgo. program project Bethesda, Md. 1999, mem. gen. medicine B-study sect. and urology spl. emphasis panel 2000, charter mem. urology kidney and genitourinary diseases study Sect. 2004—), AAAS, ACLU, Internat. Cell Death Soc., Sexual Medicine Soc. N.Am., Oxalosis and Hyperoxaluria Found. (mem. sci. adv. bd. 2006—), Soc. Baric Urologic Rsch., Am. Urological Assn. (south ctrl. sect.), Soc. Am. Asian Scientists in Cancer Rsch. (bd. dir. 2004—), Am. Soc. Nephrology, Am. Soc. Biochemistry Molecular Biology, Molecular Medicine Soc., ROCK Soc. (pres. 2005—06), Urolithiasis Soc. India, NY Acad. Sci., Am. Chem. Soc., Kashmir Overseas Assn. (bd. dir. Mich. chpt. 2003, pres.). Avocations: cricket, soccer, international public policy analysis, reading, thinking. Office: Divsn Urology Dept Surgery U Colo Sch Medicine 4200 E Ninth Ave Box C317 Denver CO 80262 Home: 5645 S Havana Ct Englewood CO 80111 Office Phone: 303-315-2383. Personal E-mail: harikoul@yahoo.com. Business E-Mail: hari.koul@uchsc.edu.

KOURI, DONALD JACK, chemist, educator; b. Hobart, Okla., July 25, 1938; s. Eddie and Theresa LaJuan (Williams) K.; m. Shirley Ann Stewart, Apr. 9, 1965; children: Lisa Renee, David Matthew. BA, Okla. Bapt. U., 1960; MS, U. Wis., 1962, PhD, 1965. Postdoctoral fellow Joint Inst. Lab Astrophysics, U. Colo., 1965-66; asst. prof. chemistry Midwestern U., Wichita Falls, 1966-67, U. Houston, 1967-71, assoc. prof., 1971-73, prof., 1973—, Disting. Univ. prof., 1987-96, Cullen Disting. prof. chemistry and physics, dir. Inst. for Digital Informatics and Analysis. Vis. lectr. U. Ill., 1972; vis. scientist Inst. for Strömungsforschung, Göttingen, Fed. Republic Germany, 1973-74; bd. dirs. Inst. for Digital Informatics and Analysis. Recipient U.S. Sr. Scientist award Alexander von Humboldt Found., 1973-74, Southwestern Tex. sect. award Am. Chem. Soc., 1981, Sigma Xi Rsch. award, 1995; fellow A.P. Sloan Found., 1972-74, Weizmann Inst., 1973, Inst. for Advanced Studies, Hebrew U. Jerusalem, 1978-79, Guggenheim Found., 1978-79. Fellow Am. Phys. Soc. (exec. com. mem., sec.-treas. Few Body Topical group); mem. IEEE, ASCAP, Am. Chem. Soc., Am. Assn. Physics Tchrs. Democrat. Baptist. Office: U Houston Dept Chemistry 4800 Calhoun Rd Houston TX 77204-5003 Business E-Mail: kouri@uh.edu.

KOURIDES, IONE ANNE, endocrinologist, researcher, educator; b. NYC, Sept. 1, 1942; d. Peter T. and Anne E. (Spetseris) K.; m. Charles G. Zaroulis, Nov. 30, 1974; children: Anna Larisa, Andrew, Christina, Peter. BA, Wellesley Coll., 1963; MD, Harvard U., 1967. Diplomate Am. Bd. Internal Medicine, Am. Bd. Endocrinology and Metabolism. Intern Jewish Hosp., Washington U., St. Louis, 1967-68; resident Montefiore, Albert Einstein Med. Sch., Bronx, NY, 1968-69; fellow Beth Israel, Harvard U., Boston, 1970-72; assoc. prof. medicine Cornell U. Med. Coll., NYC, 1981—; sr. med. dir., worldwide team leader endocrine care Pfizer Inc., NYC, 1990—. Mem. editl. bd. Endocrinology, Jour. Clin. Endocrinol Metabolism, also others; contbr. over 100 articles to sci. jours., chpts. to books. Mem. nat. campaign Harvard Med. Sch., Boston, 1986-92; nat. bd. dirs. Philoptochos Soc. Greek Orthodox Archdiocese. Grantee NIH, 1979-84. Fellow ACP; mem. Am. Soc. Clin. Investigation, Am. Assn. Physicians, Am. Thyroid Assn. (coms.), Endocrine Soc. (coms.). Achievements include discovery of alpha-secreting pituitary tumors; measurement of amniotic fluid thyroid stimulating hormone that can be used to diagnose hypthyroidism in utero; development of insulin secretagogue Glucotrol XL. Home: 1070 Park Ave New York NY 10128-1000 Office: Pfizer Inc 235 E 42nd St New York NY 10017-5755 Office Phone: 212-573-2178. Business E-Mail: kourii@pfizer.com.

KOURIDES, PETER THEOLOGOS, lawyer; b. Istanbul, Turkey, July 24, 1910; arrived in US, 1912, naturalized, 1931; s. Theologos and Zafiro (Gurlides) Kourides; m. Anna E. Spetseris, Aug. 4, 1938; children: Ione A., P. Nicholas. BA, Columbia, 1931, JD, 1933; HHD (hon.), Hellenic Coll., 1985. Bar: NY 1933. Mem. firm Seward, Raphael & Kourides, NYC, 1935—; gen. counsel Greek Archdiocese N.Am. and S.Am., 1938-96; trustee Hellenic Cathedral City NY, 1938-98; trustee, counsel St. Basil's Acad., Garrison, NY, 1946-97; United Greek Orthodox Charities, 1965-70; counsel World Conf. Religion Peace, 1970-82, Consultate Gen. Greece, NYC, 1963-90. Rep. at enthronement of Athenagoras I Greek Archdiocese of N.Am. and S.Am., Istanbul, 1949. Author: The Evolution of the Greek Orthodox Church in America and Its Current Problems, 1959, The Centennial History of the Archdiocesan Cathedral of the Holy Trinity, 1992. Nat. v.p. Order of Ahepa, 1960; counsel Columbia U. Cancer Clinic, Greece, 1965—70; mem. gen. bd. Nat. Coun. Chs., 1960—82, v.p., 1969—72; del. 3d Assembly World Coun. Chs., New Delhi, 1961, del. 4th Assembly Uppsala, Sweden, 1968, del. 5th Assembly Nairobi, Kenya, 1975, mem. internat. affairs com., 1968—74; del. World Conf. Religion on Peace, Kyoto, 1971; trustee Hellenic Coll., Brookline, Mass., 1968—97. Decorated grand comdr. Knights of Holy Sepulchre Jerusalem, Golden Cross Order of Phoenix King Constantine II of Greece, Titular Archon Megas Nomophylax Ecumenical Patriarchate of Ea. Orthodox Ch. Mem.: ABA, Am. Judicature Soc., Consular Law Soc., NY Bar Assn., Columbia Alumni Assn., Hellenic Am. C. of C. (dir., counsel 1955—). Home: 46 Groton St Forest Hills NY 11375-5921 Home Phone: 718-268-6991.

KOURILSKY, FRANÇOIS MICHEL, research scientist; b. Paris, Dec. 28, 1934; s. Raoul and Simone (Develay) Kourilsky; m. Colette Lucienne Bellegarde, Nov. 7, 1956 (div. Dec. 1985); children: Laurent, Michel; m. Françoise Marie-Noël Gauthier, Aug. 20, 1988. Cert. in Psychophysiology, Faculty Scis., Paris, 1961; Cert. in Immunology, Pasteur Inst., Paris, 1962; MD, Faculty Medicine, Paris, 1966; D (hon.), U. Buenos Aires, 1992. Sr. resident Paris Hosp., 1960-66; rsch. fellow Sch. Medicine, NYU, 1962-63; chef de clinique-attache Faculty Medicine, Paris, 1966-68; rschr. Nat. Inst. Health and Med. Rsch., France, 1967—88, emeritus rsch. dir., 2000—; dir. gen. Nat. Ctr. Sci. Rsch., France, 1988-94; hon. dir. rsch. Inst. Gustave Roussy, Villejuif, France, 1995—2002, emeritus dir. rsch., 2001—. Dir. unit of tumor immunology Nat. Inst. Health and Med. Rsch., U. Paris 7, 1974-76; dir. Inst. Immunology Marseille, France, 1976-85; chmn. sci. coun. coord. Inst. Curie, Paris, 1983-87; dir. Federative Rsch. Inst., Inst. Gustave Roussy, 1996-2000; chmn. sci. coun. firms Immunotech SA, 1982, Epigene SA, 2000-01, IPSOGEN S.A., 2001—. Contbr. over 100 articles to profl. jours. V.p. superior coun. rsch. tech. French Ministry Rsch., 1983-87; chmn. commn. Plan Recherche, 1985; chmn. Rsch. Obs. Midi, Pyrenees, France, 2000-2003; pres. Mediterranean Techs., Provence, Alpes, Cote D'Azur, 2000-2003. Decorated officer Nat. Order of Merit (France), officer Legion D'Honneur (France), comdr. Order of Merit (Germany). Home: 21 Blvd Du Montparnasse 75006 Paris France Personal E-mail: kourilsky.francois@wanadoo.fr.

KOURLIS, REBECCA LOVE, director, former state supreme court justice; b. Colorado Springs, Colo., Nov. 11, 1952; d. John Arthur and Ann (Daniels) Love; m. Thomas Aristithis Kourlis, July 15, 1978; children: Stacy Ann, Katherine Love, Aristithis Thomas. BA with distinction in English, Stanford U., 1973, JD, 1976; LLD (hon.), U. Denver, 1997. Bar: Colo. 1976, D.C. 1979, U.S. Dist. Ct. Colo. 1976, U.S. Ct. Appeals (10th cir.) 1976, Colo. Supreme Ct., U.S. Ct. Appeals (D.C. cir.), U.S. Claims Ct., U.S. Supreme Ct. Assoc. Davis, Graham & Stubbs, Denver, 1976-78; sole practice Craig, Colo., 1978-87; judge 14th Jud. Dist. Ct., Craig, Colo., 1987-94; arbiter Jud. Arbiter Group, Inc., 1994-95; justice Colo. Supreme Ct., 1995—2006; exec. dir. Inst. Advancement Am. Legal Sys. U. Denver, 2006—. Water judge divsn. 6, 1987-94; lectr. to profl. groups. Contbr. articles to profl. jours. Chmn. Moffat County Arts and Humanities, Craig, 1979; mem. Colo. Commn. on Higher Edn., Denver, 1980-81; mem. adv. bd. Colo. Divsn. Youth Svcs., 1988-91; mem. com. civil jury instructions, 1990-95, standing com. gender and justice, 1994-97, chair jud. adv. coun., 1997-2002, chair com. on jury reform, 1996—, chair com. family issues, 2002—; co-chair com. on atty. grievance reform, 1997-2002; mem. long range planning com. Moffat County Sch., 1990; bd. visitors Stanford U., 1989-94, Law Sch. U. Denver, 1997-2002; trustee Kent Denver Sch., 1996-2002, Graland Sch., 2004—. Named N.W. Colo. Daily Press Woman of Yr., 1993; recipient Trailblazer award AAUW, 1998, Mary Lathrop award Colo. Women's Bar Assn., 2001, Jud. Excellence award Acad. Matrimonial Lawyers, 2002, Champion for Children award Rocky Mountain Children's Law Ctr., 2003, Friend of Children award Adv. for Children, 2003. Fellow: Colo. Bar Found., Am. Bar Found.; mem.: N.W. Colo. Bar Assn. (Cmty. Svc. award 1993—94), Dist. Ct. Judges' Assn. (pres. 1993—94), Colo. Bar Assn. (bd. govs. 1983—85, mineral law sect. bd. dirs. 1985, sr. v.p. 1987—88), Rocky Mountain Mineral Found. Office: 2044 E Evans Ave Ste 307 Denver CO 80208 Office Phone: 303-871-6600. Business E-Mail: legalinstitute@du.edu.

KOUROUPAS, PAUL, telecommunications industry executive, lawyer; s. George Kouroupas and Katherine Taylor Adams; m. Carolyn Corona, Aug. 28, 1999; children: Samuel Grayson, Aidan Paul, Nolan George, Madelyn Rose. BA, Temple U., Phila., 1988; JD, Cath. U. Columbus Sch. Law, Washington, 1992. V.p., regulatory and external affairs Teleport Comm. Group, SI, 1992—99; v.p., regulatory affairs Global Crossing Ltd., Florham Park, NJ, 1999—. Mem.: Pa. Bar Assn. Achievements include expert witness in numerous regulatory and legislative forums. Office: Global Crossing Ltd 200 Park Ave Ste 300 Florham Park NJ 07932 Office Phone: 973-937-0243. Business E-Mail: paul.kouroupas@globalcrossing.com.

KOUSSA, HAROLD ALAN, insurance account executive; b. Central Falls, RI, June 20, 1947; s. Harold Albert and June Joann (John) K. BSEngring. Sci., U. R.I., 1969; MBA Fin., U. Hartford, 1975; MS in Engring. Sci. Nuclear Engring., Rensselaer Poly. Inst., 1977. Lic. property and casualty ins. prodr., Conn. Reactor engring. asst. Conn. Yankee Atomic Power Co., Haddam Neck, 1969-75, reactor engr., 1975-77; staff nuclear engr. Am. Nuclear Insurers, Farmington, Conn., 1977-79, sr. staff nuclear engr., 1979-81, prin. engr., 1981-82, mgr. ops., 1982-89, account exec., 1989-93, cons., 1993-94; account exec. Indsl. Risk Insurers, Hartford, Conn., 1994-97; account mgr., sen. account exec. Arkwright, Waltham, Mass., 1997-99, FM Global (formerly Arkwright), Norwood, Mass.,

1999—. Mem East Hampton Rep. Town Com., 1982-88; del. Conn. Rep. Conv., 1982, 84, 86; mem. East Hampton Water Pollution Control Authority, 1982-88, vice chmn., 1984-85, chmn., 1985-88. Capt. USNR, 1982—. Decorated Meritorious Svc. medal, Navy Commendation medal, Navy Achievement medal (4), Nat. Def. Svc. medal, Mil. Outstanding Vol. Svc. medal, Armed Forces Res. medal, Global War on Terrorism Svc. medal. Mem. ASME, Am. Nuc. Soc., Am. Soc. Naval Engrs., U.S. Naval Inst., Navy League U.S., Naval Res. Assn., Res. Officers Assn., Masons, U. R.I. Fast Break Club. Home: 105 Sheldonville Rd North Attleboro MA 02760 Office Phone: 781-440-8385. E-mail: harold.koussa@fmglobal.com.

KOUSSER, J(OSEPH) MORGAN, historian, educator; b. Lewisburg, Tenn., Oct. 7, 1943; s. Joseph Maximillian and Alice Holt (Morgan) K.; m. Sally Ann Ward, June 1, 1968; children: Rachel Meredith, Thaddeus Benjamin. AB, Princeton U., 1965; M.Phil., Yale U., 1968, PhD, 1971; MA, Oxford U., Eng., 1984. Instr. Calif. Inst. Tech., Pasadena, 1969-71, assoc. prof. Padadena, 1975-79, prof., 1979—. Vis. prof. U. Mich., Ann Arbor, 1980, Harvard U., Cambridge, Mass., 1981-82, Oxford U., 1984-85, Claremont Grad. Sch., 1993; expert witness Minority Voting Rights Cases; researcher. Author: Shaping of Southern Politics, 1974, Colorblind Injustice: Minority Voting Rights and the Undoing of the Second Reconstruction, 1999. Recipient Lillian Smith award So. Regional Coun., 1999, Ralph J. Bunche award Am. Polit. Sci. Assn., 2000; Guggenheim Found. fellow, 1984-85, Woodrow Wilson Ctr. fellow, 1984-85; grantee NEH, 1974, 82. Mem. Orgn. Am. Historians, Am. Hist. Assn., Social Scis. History Assn., So. Hist. Assn. Democrat. Avocation: running. Office: Calif Inst Tech 228-77 Caltech Pasadena CA 91125-7700 Office Phone: 626-395-4080. E-mail: kousser@hss.caltech.edu.

KOUTS, HERBERT JOHN CECIL, retired physicist; b. Bisbee, Ariz., Dec. 18, 1919; s. Oliver Allen and Lillian (Niemeyer) K.; m. Hertha Pretorius, Feb. 2, 1942; children: Anne Elizabeth, Catherine Jennifer; m. Barbara Stokes, Mar. 27, 1974; stepchildren: Francis Spitzer, Michael Spitzer, Daniel Spitzer. BS, La. State U., 1941, MS, 1946; PhD, Princeton U., 1952. With Brookhaven Nat. Lab., Upton, L.I., NY, 1950-73, 77-89, sr. scientist, asso. div. head, 1958-73, chmn. dept. nuclear energy, 1977-88; mem. Def. Nuclear Facilities Safety Bd., U.S. Govt., Washington, 1989-2000; ret. Dir. div. reactor safety rsch. AEC, Washington, 1973-75; dir. Office Nuclear Regulatory Rsch., U.S. Nuclear Regulatory Commn., Washington, 1975-76; mem. adv. com. reactor physics AEC, 1956-63, mem. adv. com. reactor safeguards, 1962-66; mem. European Am. Adv. Com. for Reactor Physics to European Nuclear Energy Agy., 1962-68; mem. internat. nuclear safety adv. group to IAEA, 1985-92. Served with USAAF, 1942-45. Recipient E. O. Lawrence award AEC, 1963, Disting. Service award, 1975; Disting. Service award NRC, 1976, Sec. Energy's Gold medal for achievement, 1999. Mem. Am. Nuclear Soc. (Theos Thompson award in nuclear reactor safety 1983), N.Y. Acad. Scis., Center Moriches Audubon Soc., Nat. Acad. Engring. Home: 249 S Country Rd Brookhaven NY 11719-9704 E-mail: hjckouts@erols.com.

KOUTSKY, DEAN ROGER, advertising executive; b. Omaha, Nov. 17, 1935; s. John Lewis and Ann Helen (Swan) K.; m. Kathryn Junette Strand; children: Linda, Lisa. BFA, Mpls. Coll. Art and Design, 1957. Art dir. Knox Reeves Advt., Inc., Mpls., 1958-65; v.p., exec. art dir. BBDO, Inc., Mpls., 1965-70; v.p., assoc. creative dir. Campbell-Mithun, Inc., Mpls., 1970-80, sr. v.p., creative dir., 1980-83, exec. v.p., exec. creative dir., 1983-85, vice chmn., 1985-89; exec. cons. Campbell-Mithun Esty, Inc., Mpls., 1989-90; ptnr., mgr. Harmon Ct., 1991-97. Bd. trustees Mpls. Coll. Art and Design, 1982-90, chmn., bd. trustees, 1985-89, adj. prof. advt./design divsn., 1995-2005. Office: 2005 James Ave S Minneapolis MN 55405-2404

KOUTSOFTAS, DEMETRIOUS CHARLES, geotechnical engineering consultant; b. Famagusta, Cyprus, May 10, 1946; came to U.S., 1969; s. Charles M. and Christena (Panteli) K.; m. Ellen Cheng, Aug. 20, 1971 (div. 1977); m. Rita Hui Lai See, Aug. 20, 1983. BS in Engring., Technion, Israel Inst. Techn., Haifa, 1968; MSCE, U. Mass., Boston, 1971; postgrad., MIT, 1972. Registered profl. civil engr., Calif., chartered engr., U.K. Staff engr. Dames & Moore, Cranford, NJ, 1973-74, project engr., 1974-76, sr. engr., 1976-78, Chgo., 1978-81, assoc. engr. Hong Kong, 1981-83, mng. prin., 1983, assoc. engr. San Francisco, 1984; prin., v.p. URS, San Francisco; assoc. prin., geotechnical group leader Ove Arup + Ptnrs., San Francisco. Contbr. articles on geotech. engring. to profl. jours. Mem. ASCE (Middlebrooks award, 1988, Martin S. Kapp Found. Engring. Award, Ralph B. Peck Award, 2004), NAE, Can. Geotech. Soc., Internat. Soc. Soil Mech. and Found. Engring. Inst. Civil Engring. Avocation: photography. Home: 60 Joost Ave San Francisco CA 94131-3239 Office: Ove Arup + Ptnrs Ste 260 901 Market St San Francisco CA 94103

KOUVEL, JAMES SPYROS, physicist, educator; b. Jersey City, May 23, 1926; s. Spyros and Ifegenia (Cassianos) K.; m. Audrey Lumsden, June 26, 1953; children: Diana, Alexander. B.Engring., Yale U., 1946, PhD, 1951. Research fellow U. Leeds, Eng., 1951-53, Harvard, 1953-55; physicist Gen. Electric Co. Research and Devel. Center, 1955-69; prof. physics U. Ill.-Chgo., 1969—2007. Vis. scientist Atomic Energy Rsch. Establishment, Harwell, Eng., 1967-68; vis. prof. U. Paris, Orsay, France, 1981; cons. Argonne (Ill.) Nat. Lab., 1969-89, mem. rev. com., 1970-72, vis. scientist, 1973-74; mem. materials rsch. adv. com. NSF, 1980-82, mem. materials rsch. groups spl. emphasis panel, 1993; mem. evaluation panel NRC, 1981-85. Author papers in field.; Editor: Magnetism Conf. proc, 1965-67; editorial bd.: Jour. Magnetism and Magnetic Materials, 1975—. Served with USNR, 1944-46. Guggenheim fellow, 1967-68; NSF rsch. grantee, 1973-96. Fellow Am. Phys. Soc., AAAS Home: 223 N Euclid Ave Oak Park IL 60302-2107 Office: U Ill Physics Dept Chicago IL 60607-7059 Office Phone: 312-996-5348. Business E-Mail: kouvel@uic.edu.

KOUWENHOVEN, GERRIT WOLPHERTSEN, retired museum director; b. Mt. Kisco, NY, May 8, 1939; s. John Atlee and Eleanor Warren (Hayden) K.; m. Ellen Mather Davis, June 17, 1961; children: Derek Gerritsen, Kirsten Elizabeth. BA in English, U. Colo., 1962, postgrad., 1962—64, Seattle Pacific U., 1975—76, Antioch, 1981—82. Human rights intern Eleanor Roosevelt Meml. Found., 1964—65; field rep., investigator equal opportunities divsn. State of Wis. Indsl. Commn., 1964—66; from employment specialist to asst. dir. Seattle Urban League, 1966—73; pvt. practice campaign cons., 1973—75; tchr. English, chair dept. English LaConner H.S., Wash., 1976—78; tchr. English Arlington Meml. H.S., Vt., 1978—79; pvt. practice rschr., 1979—80; dean Ethan Allen C.C., Manchester Center, Vt., 1981—82; with Friends of Hildene, Inc., Manchester, 1983—2001, exec. dir., 1986—2001, exec. dir. emeritus, 2002—. Mem. allocations com. United Way Bennington County, 1992—95; mem. adv. coun. Merck Forest & Farmland Ctr., 2002—05, trustee, 2005—, v.p., 2005—; bd. dirs. Manchester Hist. Soc., 2004—06, pres., 2005—06; mem. chancel choir First Congl. Ch., Manchester, 1979—, chair stewardship, 1980—82, 1991—93, bd. trustees, 1981—84, 1991—94, 2004—05, co-chair bicentennial steering com., 1983—84, bd. deacons, 1985—88, 1996—99, chair, 1986, chair search com., 1986—88, 1996—98; mem. exec. com. Vt. Conf. United Ch. of Christ, 1999—, chmn., bd. of dirs., 2002—06, treas., 2006—07; trustee Dorset Players, Inc., Vt., 1983—91, treas., 1986—91; bd. trustees Long Trail Sch., Dorset, 1988—98, vice chair, 1989—90, 1996—97, chair, 1990—96; bd. trustees Am. Theatre Works, Inc., Dorset, 1990—94, chair fin. com., 1992—94; bd. dirs. Preservation Trust Vt., Burlington, 1991—, v.p., 1993, 2005—, pres., 1994—2004; bd. trustees United Counseling Svc. Bennington County, Inc., 1992—, sec., 1994—, v.p., 1995, pres., 1996—; bd. trustees Coll. St. Joseph, Vt., 1999—2002; bd. dirs. Vt. Conf. United Ch. of Christ, 1998—2006, 2007—, Vt. Alliance of Conservation Voters, 2001—02, Rutland Vis. Nurse Assn. and Hospice, 2006—. Recipient Cmty. Svc. award Manchester C. of C., 1994, Cleveland E. and Phyllis B. Dodge award for Outstanding Cmty. Svc., United Counseling Svc. Bennington County, 2000, Preservation Trust of Vt. award, 2005. Mem. Dorset Nursing Assn. (bd. dirs. 1997-, sec. 1997-2000, 05-06, pres. 2000-03, v.p. 2003-05), Lions (Manchester chpt., bd. dirs. 1984-94, sec. 1984-88, pres. 1991-93). Office: 95A Elm St PO Box 1233 Manchester VT 05254

KOUYMJIAN, DICKRAN, art historian, educator; b. Tulcea, Romania, June 6, 1934; (parents Am. citizens); s. Toros S. and Zabelle I. (Calusdian) K.; m. Angèle Kapoïan, Sept. 16, 1967. BS in European Cultural History, U. Wis., 1957; MA in Arab Studies, Am. U., Beirut, 1961; PhD in Near East Lang. and Culture, Columbia U., 1969; D (hon.), Nat. Acad. Scis., Republic of Armenia, 2005. Instr. English and gen. edn. depts. Am. U. Beirut, 1959—61; instr. English Columbia U., NYC, 1961-64; dir. Am. Authors, Inc., NYC, 1965-67; asst. prof. and asst. dir. Ctr. for Arabic Studies Am. U., Cairo, 1967-71; prof., chmn. Armenian Studies dept. Haigazian U., Beirut, 1971-72; assoc. prof. history Am. U. Beirut, 1971-75; prof. art history Am. U., Paris, 1976-77; prof. history and art, dir. Armenian Studies program Calif. State U., Fresno, 1977—. Dir. Ctr. for Armenian Studies, Calif. State U., Fresno, 1990—; Fulbright disting. lectr., prof. Armenian and Am. Lit. Yerevan (Armenia, USSR), 1987; cons. archaeology UNESCO, Paris, 1976; prof., chairholder Armenian Sect., Inst. Nat. des Langs. et Civilisations Orientales, U. Paris, 1988—91; 1st incumbent Haig & Isabel Berberian endowed chair Armenian studies Calif. State U., Fresno, 1989—; 2nd incumbent William Saroyan endowed chair of Armenian studies U. Calif., Berkeley, 1996—97; vis. prof. Oriental Inst. U. Louvain-la-Neuve, Belgium, 2001. Author: Index of Armenian Art, part I, 1977, part II, 1979, The Armenian History of Ghazar P'arpetzi, 1986, Arts of Armenia, 1992; co-author: (with A. Kapoïan) The Splendor of Egypt, 1975, (with M. Stone, H. Lehmann) Album of Armenian Paleography, 2002, Armenian edit., 2006, (with Giusto Traina, Carlo Franco, Cecilia Veronese Arslan) History of Alexander of Macedonia: An Illustrated Armenian Manuscript of the 14th Century, 2003; author and editor: William Saroyan: An Armenian Trilogy, 1986, William Saroyan: Warsaw Visitor and Tales of the Vienna Streets, 1990; editor: (books) Near Eastern Numistatics, Iconography, Epigraphy and History, 1974, Essays in Armenian Numismatics in Honor of C. Sibilian, 1981, Armenian Studies: In Memoriam Haïg Berbèrian, 1986, Movses of Khoren and Armenian HIstoriography from its Beginnings, 2000; editl. bd. Armenian Rev., 1974—, Ararat Lit. mag., 1975—, Revue des Etudes Armèniennes, 1978—, NAASR Jour. Armenian Studies, Jour. of the Soc. for Armenian Studies, 1995—; contbr. articles to profl. jours. With US Army, 1957. Recipient St. Sahag and St. Mesrob medal His Holiness Karekin I, Catholics of All Armenians, 1996, Outstanding Prof. award Am. U., Cairo, 1968-69, 69-70, Hagop Kevorkian Disting. Lectureship in Near Eastern Art and Civilization, NYU, 1979, Arthur H. Dadian Armenian Heritage award Armenian Students Assn. Am., 2003; voted Outstanding Prof. of Yr., Faculty Senate, Calif. State U., Fresno, 1986-87; Fulbright fellow, USSR, 1986-87, Michael Dukakis fellow Am. Coll. Thessaloniki, 2003; grantee NEH, Paris, 1980-81, 95, Bertha & John Garabedian Charitable Found., 1994—; chosen Scholar of U. Phi Beta Phi Calif. State U., 1999; named Man of Yr. Armenian Nat. Com. Calif., 2000. Mem. Am. Oriental Soc., Am. Numismatic Soc., Mid. East Studies Assn. (charter), Coll. Arts Assn., Soc. Armenian Studies (charter, pres. 1985-86, 92-94), Sociéte asiatique (Paris), Internat. Assn. of Armenian Studies, Mid. East Medievalist, Assn. Paléographique Internat., Phi Kappa Phi (nat. scholar Fresno chpt. 1998, Univ. Scholar award chpt. 962 1999). Achievements include selected to serve on jury for annual Francqui Fund Prize, Brussels, 2001. Avocations: music, films, bibliophile. Home: 54 rue Boussingault 75013 Paris France Office: Calif State U Armenian Studies Program 5245 N Backer Ave # PB4 Fresno CA 93740-8001 Office Phone: 559-278-2669. Business E-Mail: dickrank@csufresno.edu.

KOUZMITCHEVA, GALINA A., molecular biologist, researcher; arrived in US, 1997; d. Aleksandr N. Kouzmitchev and Valentina M. Kouzmitcheva; m. Nikolay V. Boltovskiy, Jan. 17, 1998. BS with hons., Kuibishev State U., Samara, 1978, MS with honors, 1978; degree, Moscow State U., Russia, 1983; PhD, Vector, Novosibirsk, Russia, 1991. Sr. scientist SRC Vector, Novosibirsk, Russia, 1980—92; scientist, head biochemical lab. Novosibirsk Serpentry, 1992—94; sr. scientist SRC Vector, Novosibirsk, 1994, State Rsch. Ctr. Vector, Novosibirsk, 1994; postdoctoral fellow U. of Columbia-Missouri, Columbia, Mo., 1997—99, U. Oreg., Eugene, 2000—01, Auburn U., Ala., 2001—06, rsch. fellow, 2006—. Contbr. articles to profl. jours. Recipient Merit cert., Inst. BioEngineering, SRC Virology and Biotechnology Novosibirsk , Russia, 2003; fellow, Cancer Rsch. Ctr., Columbia, Mo., 1997—98, Dept. Biol. Scis., U. Columbia, Mo., 1998—99, Inst. Molecular Biology, U. Oreg., Eugene, 2000—01. Mem.: AAAS, Russian Soc. Biotechnologists, Am. Inst. Biol. Scis. Achievements include invention of device for electro elution; patents in field; patents pending in field. Office: Auburn Univ Dept Pathobiology 252 Greene Hall Auburn AL 36849 Home Phone: 334-887-6417; Office Phone: 334-844-2675.

KOVAC, SHIRLEY ANN, retired elementary school educator; b. Sharon, Pa., Feb. 7, 1950; d. Peter and Stella Antos; m. Donald Edward Kovac; children: Shelly, Karen, Donald Jr. BS in Edn., Slippery Rock U., 1972. Libr. aide Sharon City Schs., Pa., 1972—75, substitute tchr., 1975—76; tchr. 1st grade Hadley Elem. Sch., 1976—82, Musser Elem. Sch., 1982—83; tchr. 1st and 2d grade West Hill Elem. Sch., 1983—90; tchr. 5th grade Case Ave. Elem. Sch., 1990—93, tchr. 2d grade, 1993—2005; ret., 2005. Recipient Tchg. and Spl. Student Activities award, Adminstrn. and Bd. Edn., Sharon, 1999. Mem.: NEA, Pa. State Tchrs. Assn., Sharon Tchrs. Assn. Office: Ednl Svc Ctr 215 Forker Blvd Sharon PA 16146

KOVACEVIC, RADOVAN, mechanical engineering educator; b. Niksic, Yugoslavia, July 17, 1947; came to U.S., 1987; s. Bozo and Zagorka (Vujicic) K.; m. Ljiljana Sokic, Dec. 10, 1972; children: Ivana, Jelena. BS, U. Belgrade, Yugoslavia, 1969, MS, 1972; PhD, U. Titograd, Yugoslavia, 1978. From asst. prof. to prof. U. Titograd, Titograd, 1975-86; assoc. prof. Syracuse (N.Y.) U., 1987-90, U. Ky., Lexington, 1991-95, prof., 1995-97; Herman Brown chair prof. So. Meth. U., Dallas, 1997—. Cons. prof. Harbin (China) Inst. Tech., 1994. Co-author: Principles of Abrasive Waterjet Technology, 1998; contbr. over 100 articles to profl. jours. Recipient Taylor Rsch. medal, Soc. Mfg. Engrs., 2000, Adams Meml. Membership award, Am. Welding Soc., 1997. Fellow: ASME. Achievements include patents for high-pressure waterjet-assisted cooling/lubrication system in machining, method of monitoring and control for the 3D shape of wld pool based on vision system, new control of gas metal arc welding. Office: So Meth Univ PO Box 750335 Dallas TX 75275-0335 E-mail: kovacevi@smu.edu.

KOVACEVICH, RICHARD M., bank executive; b. Oct. 30, 1943; BA in Industrial Engring., Stanford U., 1965, M in Industrial Engring., 1966, MBA, 1967. Exec. v.p. Kenner div. Gen. Mills, Inc., Mpls., 1967-72; prin. Venture Capital, 1972-75; v.p. consumer services Norwest Corp., Mpls., from 1975, then sr. v.p. N.Y.C. banking group, then exec. v.p., mgr. N.Y.C. bank div., then exec. v.p. mem. policy com., vice-chmn., chief operating officer banking group, 1986—89, pres., COO, vice chmn., 1989—93, CEO, 1993—96, chmn., 1995—96; chmn., CEO Wells Fargo & Co. (merged with Norwest Corp.), 1996—98; pres., CEO Wells Fargo & Co., San Francisco, 1998—2001, chmn., pres., CEO, 2001—05, chmn., CEO, 2005—07, chmn., 2007—. Mem. bd. dirs. Cargill, Inc., Cisco Systems, Inc., Target Corp.; mem. Federal Reserve's Federal Advisory Council, Calif. Bus. Roundtable, Calif. Commn. for Jobs and Economic Growth; chmn. San Francisco Com. on Jobs. V.p., bd. of govs. San Francisco Symphony; vice chmn., bd. trustees San Francisco Museum of Modern Art. Recipient Banker of the Year, Am. Banker, 2003. Office: Wells Fargo & Co 420 Montgomery St San Francisco CA 94163-1205 Office Phone: 415-396-4928.*

KOVACEVICH, ROBERT EUGENE, lawyer; b. Nov. 9, 1933; s. John Edward and Katrina Margaret K.; m. Yvonne R. Stokke; children: Tawni, Mark, Phillip, Bernhard. Grad., St. Martin's Coll., Lacy, Wash., 1955; JD with honors, Gonzaga U., Spokane, Wash., 1959; LLM in Taxation, NYU, 1960. Bar: Wash., 1960; U.S. Ct. Appeals (9th cir.) 1963, U.S. Ct. Appeals (fed. cir.) 1982, U.S. Ct. Appeals (11th cir.) 1988, U.S. Ct. Appeals (10th cir.) 1993, U.S. Dist. Ct. (ea. dist.) Wash. 1960, U.S. Dist. Ct. (we. dist.) Wash., 1976, U.S. Ct. Claims, 1973, U.S. Tax Ct., 1982, Wash. Supreme Ct., 1959, U.S. Supreme Ct., 1975, Coeur d'Alene, Kalispel, Spokane, Puyallup, and drafting committee IRS Indian Tribes, 2005, Swinomish Tribal Bars, 2001-03. Lawyer U.S. Supreme Ct., Spokane, 1963-72; ptnr. Kovacevich & Algeo, Spokane, 1972-80; pvt. practice Spokane, 1980—. Instr. Gonzaga U. Sch. Bus., 1967-84; mgr. leasing co.; expert witness U.S. Senate Com. Appropriations, 1976. Mem. ABA, Assn. Trial Lawyers, Fed. Bar Assn. Ea. Wash., Spokane Co. Bar. Assn., Spokane Club. Office: 818 W Riverside Ave Ste 715 Spokane WA 99223-6453 Home Phone: 509-448-2677; Office Phone: 509-747-2104. E-mail: KovarevichRobert@Qwest.net.

KOVACH, ANDREW LOUIS, human resources specialist, consultant; b. Greensboro, Pa., Feb. 4, 1948; s. Andrew and Pauline (Nassar) K.; m. Cindy Juliani, Nov. 28, 1970; 1 child: Courtney. BS in Indsl. Engineering, W.Va. U., 1969. Engr. DuPont, Martinville, Va., 1970—73; supt. engr. Allied Corp., Syracuse, NY, 1973—75, mgr. employee rels. Morristown, NJ, 1976—80, mgr. orgnl. devel., 1980, dir. human resources NYC, 1981—82, dir. comml. devel., 1983—87; sr. v.p. human resources, info. sys. Morristown Meml. Hosp., 1988—96; v.p. human resources and chief adminstrv. officer Atlantic Health Sys., Morristown, 1996—. Bd. dirs. AOS Acquisition Group, Morristown Surg. Ctr., NJ; ethics com. Morris Twp., Morristown. Mem.: Park Ave. Club, Morristown Club (bd. dir.). Presbyterian. Home Phone: 973-267-2383. Business E-Mail: andy.kovach@atlantichealth.org.

KOVACH, BILL, educational foundation administrator; b. Greeneville, Tenn., Sept. 16, 1932; s. John and Olga (Sicos) K.; m. Lynne Marie Stamm, Jan. 11, 1956; children: Teresa, David, Charles, John. BS, East Tenn. State U., 1959; LLD (hon.), Colby Coll., 2000; PhD (hon.), Boston U., 2007. Gen. assignment Press-Chronicle, Johnson City, Tenn., 1959-61; reporter Nashville Tennessean, 1961-68, N.Y. Times, NYC, 1968-79, Washington bur. chief Washington, 1979-86; editor Atlanta Jour.-Constitution, 1986-88; curator Nieman Found., Harvard U., 1989-2000; chmn. Com. of Concerned Journalists, Washington, 1997—; John Seigenthaler chair of excellence in First Amendment studies Middle Tenn. State U., 2004, lectr. journalism, 2006—. Lectr. Ball State U., Muncie, Ind., 1981; chair adv. bd. Internat. Consortium Investigative Journalists; bd. dirs. Ctr. for Pub. Integrity, Harvard Mag. Co-author: The Elements of Journalism, 2001, Warp Speed: America in the Age of Mixed Media, 1999; contbg. author: Assignment America, 1984, The Art of Writing Non-Fiction, 1986, Profiles in Courage for Our Time, 2002. With USN, 1951—55. Stanford Profl. Journalism fellow, 1967-68. Mem. AAAS. Home Phone: 301-718-2508; Office Phone: 202-419-3651. Business E-Mail: bkovach@journalism.org.

KOVACH, ROBERT LOUIS, geophysics educator; b. LA, Feb. 15, 1934; s. Nicholas Arthur and Stefania Teresa (Rüssler) K.; m. Linda Elly Heyn, Dec. 23, 1960; children: Denise Lynn, Dianne Yvonne, John Robert, Robert John. Geophysical Engring Degree, Colo. Sch. Mines, 1955; MA, Columbia U., 1959; PhD, Calif. Inst. Tech., 1962. Registered geophysicist, Calif. Sr. scientist Jet Propulsion Lab., Pasadena, Calif., 1961-63; asst. prof. Calif. Inst. Tech., Pasadena, 1963-65, Stanford (Calif.) U., 1965-66, assoc. prof., 1966-70, prof. geophysics, 1970—. Prin. investigator Apollo Moon Seismic Expts., 1996-76; cons. DOE, 1996-97. Author: Earth's Fury, 1995, Conflict with the Earth, 1997. Lt. U.S. Army, 1956-58. Fellow John Simon Guggenheim Found., 1971; recipient Exceptional Sci. Achievement award NASA, 1973. Fellow Geol. Soc. Am.; mem. Am. Geophysical Union (pres. seismology sect. 1976-78), Can. Well Logging Soc., Seismol. Soc. Am., Soc. Exploration Geophysicists. Office: Dept Geophysics Stanford University Stanford CA 94305 Office Phone: 415-723-4827. Business E-Mail: kov@pangea.stanford.edu.

KOVACHY, EDWARD MIKLOS, JR., psychiatrist, consultant; b. Cleve., Dec. 3, 1946; s. Edward Miklos and Evelyn Amelia (Palenscar) K.; m. Susan Eileen Light, June 21, 1981; children: Timothy Light, Benjamin Light. BA, Harvard U., 1968, JD, MBA, Harvard U., 1972; MD, Case Western Reserve U., 1977. Diplomate Nat. Bd. Med. Examiners. Resident in psychiatry Stanford U. Med. Ctr., Stanford, Calif., 1977-81; pvt. practice psychiatry, mediation, exec. coaching Menlo Park, Calif., 1981—. Presenter ann. meeting Am. Psychol. Assn., 1998, Calif. Assn. Marriage and Family Therapists, 1999. Co-prodr. Jolson and Company, Century Ctr. for the Performing Arts, N.Y.C., 2002; columnist The Peninsula Times Tribune, 1983-85. Trustee Mid-Peninsula H.S., Palo Alto, Calif., 1990-2001, mem. bd. advisors, 2001—; mem. gift com. Harvard Coll. Class of 1968, 25th reunion chmn. participation, San Francisco, 1993, 30th reunion chmn. participation, West Coast, 1998, nat. co-chmn. participation and assocs. giving, 1999—, nat. co-chmn. participation, 35th reunion, 2003. Recipient Albert H. Gordon award Harvard U., 2000, 05, Joseph R. Hamlen award Harvard U., 2003; named to Hall of Fame, Shaker Heights Alumni Assn., 2003. Mem. Am. Psychiat. Assn. (presenter annual meetings 1984, 98), Physicians for Social Responsibility, Assn. Family and Conciliation Cts., No. Calif. Psychiat. Soc., Harvard Alumni Assn. (dir. 2006—). Presbyterian. Avocations: personal activism, musical comedy, athletics. Office: 1187 University Dr Menlo Park CA 94025-4423 Office Phone: 650-329-0600. Personal E-mail: edkovachy@aol.com.

KOVACIC, WILLIAM EVAN, commissioner, law educator; b. Poughkeepsie, NY, Oct. 1, 1952; s. Evan Carl and Frances Katherine (Crow) K.; m. Kathryn Marie Fenton, May 18, 1985. AB with honors, Princeton U., 1974; JD, Columbia U., 1978. Bar: NY 1979. Law clk. to Hon. Roszel C. Thomsen U.S. Dist. Ct. Md., Balt., 1978—79; atty. planning office bur. competition FTC, Washington, 1979—82, atty. advisor to commr. George W. Douglas, 1983, gen. counsel, 2001—04, commr., 2006—; assoc. Bryan, Cave LLP, Washington, 1983—86; prof. George Mason U. Sch. Law, Arlington, Va., 1986—99; E.K. Gubin Prof. Govt. Contracts Law George Washington U. Law Sch., Washington, 1999—. Mem. U.S. Senate Judiciary Subcom. on Antitrust and Monopoly, Washington, 1975—76; commr. US FTC, 2006—. Contbr. legal articles to profl. jours. Harlan Fiske Stone fellow, Columbia U., 1976—78. Mem. ABA (antitrust law and pub. contract law sects.), Fed. Bar Assn. Roman Catholic. Office: George Washington U Law Sch 720 20th St NW Washington DC 20052-0001 also: FTC 600 Pennsylvania Ave NW Rm 540 Washington DC 20580 Business E-Mail: wkovacic@ftc.gov.

KOVACS, DORA MARTA, neuroscientist, researcher, educator; b. Budapest, Hungary, June 28, 1962; arrived in US, 1986; d. Zoltan Vajna and Caterina Deseo; m. Peter Kilbridge, Apr. 30, 1994 (div. 1996); m. Rudolph Emile Tanzi, May 24, 2002. MS, BS summa cum laude, U. Bologna, Italy, 1986; PhD in Pharmacology and Toxicology, U. Padova, Italy, 1991. Rsch. assoc. Case Western Res. U., Cleve., 1986-88; from rsch. assoc. to sr. fellow U. Pitts., 1989-93; joined Genetics and Aging Rsch. Unit Mass. Gen. Hosp., Charlestown, 1993, assoc. prof. neurology, dir. Neurobiology of Disease Lab.; rsch. fellow Harvard Med. Sch., Boston, 1993-96, instr. Charlestown, 1996, assoc. prof. neurology. Contbr. articles to profl. jours. Grantee Nat. Rsch. Svc. Tng. grant, 1996—97; Britton fellow for rsch. on alzheimers, 1988—89, John Douglas French Alzheimers Found. fellow, 1995—98. Mem.: Soc. for Neurosci. Achievements include research in transcription factors of the Alzheimer amyloid precursor protein; first to characterize the Alzheimer associated presenilin proteins. Office: Genetics and Aging Rsch Unit MassGen Inst Neurodegenerative Disease Bldg 114, 16th St Charlestown MA 02129 Office Phone: 617-726-3668. Office Fax: 617-724-1823. E-mail: kovacs@helix.mgh.harvard.edu.*

KOVACS, WILLIAM JOSEPH, physician, educator; s. John Joseph and Elizabeth Mary Kovacs; m. Nancy Josephine Olsen; children: Daniel John, Andrew Norman. AB, U. Chgo., 1970—73, MD, 1973—77. Diplomate internal medicine Am. Bd. Internal Medicine, 1980, endocrinology & metabolism Am. Bd. Internal Medicine, 1983. From asst. prof. to prof. medicine Vanderbilt U., Nashville, 1985—2004; Diana & Richard C. Strauss prof. biomedical rsch. U. Tex., Southwestern Med. Ctr., Dallas, 2004—.

KOVACS, WILLIAM LAWRENCE, lawyer; b. Scranton, Pa., June 29, 1947; s. William Lawrence and Jane Claire (Weiss) K.; m. Mary Katherine Maras, Dec. 2, 1979; children: Katherine Elizabeth, William Lawrence III, Margaret Ellen, Tyler Alexander. BS magna cum laude, U. Scranton, 1969; JD, Ohio State U., 1972. Bar: Pa. 1972, D.C. 1973, U.S. Ct. Appeals (D.C. cir.) 1974, U.S. Supreme Ct. 1976, Va. 1981. Legis. asst., staff atty. Congressman Fred B. Rooney, Washington, 1972-74; chief counsel U.S. Ho. of Reps. Subcom. on Transp. and Commerce, Washington, 1975-77; assoc. Liebert, Short, FitzPatrick & Lavin, Phila., 1977-78; environ., litigation atty. Nat. Chamber Litigation Ctr., Washington, 1979; ptnr. Abrams, Kovacs, Westermeier & Goldberg, Washington, 1980-84, Kovacs & Bury, Fairfax, Va., 1984-85, Jaeckle, Fleischmann & Mugel, Washington, 1986-87, Eckert, Seamans, Cherin & Mellott, Washington, 1987-89, Dunn, Carney, Allen, Higgins & Tongue, Portland, Oreg., 1990, Keller & Heckman, Washington, 1991-97; pres. Clean States Found., Inc., 1997-98; dir. legal affairs Worldwide Sunshine Makers, Inc., Washington, 1997-98; v.p. environ. tech. and regulatory affairs U.S. C. of C., Washington, 1998—. Contbr. articles to profl. jours. Mem. Hazardous Waste Facilities Siting Bd., Richmond, Va., 1984-86; vice chmn., 1984-85, chmn., 1985-86. Mem. ABA (vice chmn. energy resources law com. sect. on torts and ins. practice 1981-83, chmn. 1983-84), U.S. C. of C. (mem. environ. law adv. com. 1986-92). Roman Catholic. Home: 9805 Arnon Chapel Rd Great Falls VA 22066-3908 Office: 1615 H St NW Washington DC 20062-0001 Home Phone: 703-759-4511; Office Phone: 202-463-5457. Business E-Mail: wkovacs@uschamber.com.

KOVAL, KENNETH JOSEPH, orthopedist, surgeon; b. NYC, Oct. 20, 1958; s. Raymond and Gloria Koval; m. Mary Reynolds; children: Courtney, Michael, Lauren. BS in Chemistry, Tufts U., Boston, 1980; MD, NYU Sch. Medicine, 1984. Prof. dept. orthops. NYU Sch. Medicine, NYC, 2002, Dartmouth Med. Sch., Lebanon, NH, 2002—. Office: Dartmouth Med Sch 1 Medical Center Dr Lebanon NH 03756

KOVALCHUK, ILYA, professional hockey player; b. Tver, Russia, Apr. 15, 1983; Right wing Atlanta Thrashers, 2001—. Mem. Team Russia, Olympic Games, Salt Lake City, 2002, Torino, Italy, 06; player NHL YoungStars Game, 2002, NHL All-Star Game, 2004. Named to All-Rookie Team, NHL, 2002, Second All-Star Team, 2004; recipient Maurice Richard Trophy, 2004. Achievements include the first Russian player to be selected first in an NHL Entry Draft; being a member of bronze medal Russian Hockey team, Salt Lake City Olympic Games, 2002. Office: Atlanta Thrashers Centennial Tower, Ste 1900 101 Marietta St NW Atlanta GA 30303

KOVALEV, ALEXEI, professional hockey player; b. Togliatti, Russia, Feb. 24, 1973; m. Eugenia Kovalev; children: Nikita, Ivan. Right wing NY Rangers, 1992—98, 2003—04, Pitts. Penguins, 1998—2003, Montreal Canadiens, 2004—. Mem. Unified Team, Olympic Games, Albertville, France, 1992, Team Russia, Olympic Games, Salt Lake City, 2002, Torino, Italy, 06; player NHL All-star game, 2001, 03. Recipient Olympic Gold medal, 1992. Achievements include being a member of gold medal Unified Hockey Team, Albertville Olympic Games, 1992; being a member of Stanley Cup Champion NY Rangers, 1994. Avocations: golf, flying. Office: c/o Montreal Canadiens 1275 St Antoine St W H3C 5L2 Montreal PQ Canada*

KOVARIK, MADELINE, education educator; EdD, U. of Ctrl. Fla., Orlando, 1986. Lic. tchr. Fla., 1976. Adminstr./tchr. Brevard County Pub. Schs., Viera, Fla., 1978—2002; asst. prof. of edn. Rollins Coll., Winter Park, Fla., 2002—. Problem capt. Odyssey of the Mind, Viera, Fla., 1995—2006. Recipient Christa McAuliffe Tchg. award, Rollins Coll., 2004. Master: Kappa Delta Pi (assoc.; co-chapter advisor 2002—06). Office Phone: 407-646-2304.

KOVATCH, JAK GENE, artist; b. LA, Jan. 17, 1929; s. Jack and La Vinia Blanche (Abernathy) K.; m. Carol Jean Wilhelm, Dec. 24, 1967; 1 son by previous marriage, Jason. Student, UCLA, 1946, Chouinard Art Inst., 1947-49, Calif. Sch. Art, LA, 1949-50, U. So. Calif., 1951, L.A. City Coll., 1955-56, Art Students League, NYC, 1972-75. Student asst. Lynton Kistler Studio, LA, 1952-53; staff animation dept. Walt Disney Prodns., Inc., Burbank, Calif., 1953. Instr. drawing and anatomy Famous Artists Schs., Westport, Conn., 1957-59; tchr. Roger Ludlowe H.S., Fairfield, Conn., 1959-60; extension instr. NYC Coll., 1959-60; instr. sculpture Fairfield U., 1967; faculty U. Bridgeport, Conn., 1962-94, Ethyl prof. design, 1988-94, assoc. prof. dept. design, 1978-88, prof. design, 1988-94; faculty Silvermine Sch. Art, New Canaan, Conn., 1994—; vis. faculty Aldrich Mus. Contemporary Art, Ridgefield, Conn., 1999; fellow Mellon Found.; vis. faculty Yale U., 1979-80, 82-83; lectr. in field. Stage designer for, Benjamin Zemach, L.A., 1953-54, freelance illustrator, NYC, 1957-58; one-man show Monroe C. Gutman Libr., Harvard U., 2000; exhibited in group shows including Taipei Fine Arts Mus., Taiwan, R.O.C., 1987, 91, Tokyo Met. Mus., Japan, 1985-87, Barbican Arts Ctr., London, 1989, Legislative and State Office Bldgs., Hartford, 1991, Salford Mus., Eng., 1989, Inst. Tech. Aeroespacial, Sao Jose dos Campos, Brasil, 1987, U. Hawaii, 1985, Mus. Modern Art, Wakayama, Japan, 1987, Northeastern U., Boston, 1999, Butler Inst. Am. Art, Youngstown, Ohio, 2002, Boston Printmakers, 2002; represented in permanent collections Fogg Mus. Art, Cambridge, Mass., Libr. Congress, Joseph Hirshhorn Mus., Smithsonian Instn., Wash., D.C., Fairfield Art Collection, John Slade Ely House Collections, New Haven, Bicentennial Art Collection, Westport (Conn.) Town Hall, U. Miss., Albert Dorne Collection, NYC, others; artist project grant from Conn. Commn. on Arts, Hartford, 1984-85. Selection com. State of Conn. Commn. on Arts, Percent for Art Program, Hartford, 1987-88. Recipient award Boston Mus. Fine Arts, 1954, Wadsworth Atheneum, Hartford, Conn., 1958, 79, Mus. Art, Sci. and Industry, Bridgeport, 1962-63, 65-66, 75, 77, 79, 81-84, 22 awards Fairfield (Conn.) U., 1973-95, award New Haven Paint and Clay Club, 1976, 78, 81, 89-90, 97-98, 2002, 05, spl. recognition award Print Club Albany, Schenectady Mus., 1992, John Taylor Arms Meml. award Audubon Artists, Inc., Nat. Arts Club, N.Y.C., 1993, etching award Stamford (Conn.) Mus., 1994, Painting award New Britain Mus. Am. Art, 1997, awards Brush and Palette Club, New Haven, 2000, 02, George W. McClellan award Greenwich Art Soc., 2006, Louis M. Hipp Jr. Meml. award, 2006 and more than 180 others. Mem. Soc. Am. Graphic Artists, Boston Printmakers, Audubon Artists (bd. dirs. for graphics 1995), Conn. Acad. Fine Arts, Greenwich Art Soc., LA Printmaking Soc., Phila. Print Club, Silvermine Guild Artists (trustee 1979-83), Westport-Weston Arts Coun. Home: 34 Sasco Creek Rd Westport CT 06880-6341 Office: Silvermine Sch of Art Inc 1037 Silvermine Rd New Canaan CT 06840-4398 Office Phone: 203-259-9461. Personal E-mail: jakkovatch@sbcglobal.net. *I consider my concept of Image Continuum to be a significant consequence of 50 years of painting and printmaking. Six basic components form the foundation of this concept: 1. Use of former images to create new ones; 2. Repetition of a theme (subject matter and symbols repeated); 3. Use of modules; 4. Use of storyboards and grids; 5. Structuring forms transparently; 6. Use of abstraction, animation, distortion. An integral part of Image Continuum is persistent use of multiple images. This means of expression may be directly related to my personal impatience with dwelling too long on one image or idea. I have been able to temper this drive for immediacy and rapid image development by using images in a series or storyboard format.*

KOVE, MIRIAM, psychotherapist; b. Chotin, Romania, Feb. 17, 1941; came to U.S., Sept. 12, 1962; d. Avrum and Riva (Nussenbaum) Wolkove; m. Marc L. Kouffman, Aug. 16, 1964 (div. Oct. 24, 1989); children: Avra, Paulette. BA in English Lit., Sir George Williams U., 1962; MA in Early Childhood, Hunter Coll., 1975; Cert. in Psychoanalytic Psychotherapy, New Hope Guild, NYC, 1979; MSW, Adelphi U., 1983. Tchr. various pub. schs., Montreal, Can., 1957-58; actress NYC, 1962—; tchr. early childhood Emanuel Nursery Sch., NYC, 1964-74; adj. lectr. early childhood Cmty. Coll., Bklyn., 1974-75; psychotherapist, clinician New Hope Guild Ctr., NYC, 1979-81; intake dir., clinician Insts. of Religion and Health, NYC, 1983-84; pschotherapist NYC, 1984—; faculty, supr. New Hope Guild Ctr., NYC, 1990—; dir. day care on-site therapy program C.I.S. Counseling Ctr., NYC, 1992-94. Author: (book) Myths and Madness, 2007. Mem. People for the Am. Way, Warsaw Gathering of Holocaust Survivors. Recipient Hebrew prize Sir George Williams U., 1962; recommended for English prize Concordia U. Fellow Nat. Orgn. Social Work, Soc. for Clin. Social Work Psychotherapists (edn. com.); mem. New Hope Grad. Soc. (steering com.), Am. Bd. Examiners in Clin. Social Work. Jewish. Home and Office: 320 E 25th St Apt 8ee New York NY 10010-3100 Home Phone: 212-685-2090; Office Phone: 212-689-1442. Personal E-mail: miriamkove@hotmail.com.

KOVEL, RALPH MALLORY, writer, antique expert; b. Milw. s. Lester and Dorothy K.; m. Terry Horvitz; children: Lee R., Karen. Attended, Ohio State U. Pres., chmn. U.S. Brands, Inc.; pres. Lucayan Aquaculture, Freeport, Bahamas. V.p., treas. Antiques, Inc.; trustee WVIZ-TV, Western Res. Hist. Soc., Cleve., Cleve. Pops Orch., Inc., Sara Lee Foods; Hiram fellow, former tchr. course in antiques Western Res. U., John Carroll U. Writer: (with Terry Kovel) syndicated column Kovels Antiques and Collecting, 1955—, Ask the Experts, House Beautiful, 1979-2000, Medio, CD-Rom Mag., 1995, The Kovels on Collecting, Forbes Mag., 2000-02; editor: monthly newsletters Kovels on Antiques and Collectibles, 1974—, Kovels Sports Collectibles, 1992-97; Know Your Antiques, Pub. TV, 1969-70; syndicated TV series Kovels on Collecting, 1981, 87, Collector's Journal TV, 1989-93, Flea Market Finds with the Kovels HGTV, 2000-04; numerous appearances on radio and TV talk shows; author: (with Terry Kovel) Kovels' Dictionary of Marks-Pottery and Porcelain, 1953, rev. edit., 1995, Directory of American Silver, Pewter and Silver Plate, 1958, American Country Furniture, 1780-1875, 1963, Kovels' Know Your Antiques, rev. edit., 1993, Kovels Antiques and Collectibles Price List, 39th edit., 2007, Kovels' American Art Pottery, 1993, Kovels' Bid, Buy & Sell Online, 2001, The Kovels' Bottle Price List, 13th edit., 2006, Kovels' Price Guide for Collector Plates, Figurines, Paperweight and Other Ltd. Editions, 1978, Kovels' Collector's Guide to American Art Pottery, 1974, Kovels' Collector's Guide to Limited Editions, 1974, Kovels' Know Your Collectibles, 1981, 1992, Kovels' Book Antique Labels, 1982, Kovels' Depression Glass and Dinnerware Price List, 8th edit. 2004, Kovels' Illustrated Price Guide to Royal Doulton, 2d edit., 1984, Kovels' Organizer for Collectors, rev. edit., 1983, Kovels' Collectors' Source Book, 1983, Kovels' New Dictionary of Marks Pottery and Porcelain, 1850 to the Present, 1986, Kovels' Advertising Collectibles Price List, 1986, 05, Kovels' Guide to Selling Your Antiques and Collectibles, rev. edit., 1990, Kovels' American Silver Marks 1650 to Present, 1989, Kovels' Antiques and Collectibles Fix-It Source Book, 1990, Kovels' Quick Tips: 799 Helpful Hints on How to Care For Your Collectibles, 1995, Kovels' Guide to Selling, Buying and Fixing Your Antiques and Collectibles, 1995, The Label Made Me Buy It, 1998, Kovel's Yellow Pages 2d edit., 2003, Kovel's American Antiques 1750-1900, 2004, Kovels American Collectibles 1900-2000, 2007; (video tape series) Collecting With the Kovels, Art Pottery I, Art Pottery II, 1995, Kovels' Page-A-Day Collectibles Calendar 1990, 1991, Kovels' Antiques and Collectibles 2003 Day-At-A-Time Calendar; contbr. numerous articles on antiques to publs, chapt. to books. Former mem. rev. and allocations com. United Torch Fund, Cleve.; past pres. E. End Neighborhood Settlement House; past chmn. adv. com. Woodhill Homes; past bd. dirs. Soc. Collectors, Silver Mus. Religious Art. Recipient Lane Bryant award, 1966; Peirce Award for Outstanding Cmty. Svc. Sta. WVIZ-TV, 1980, Cleve. Emmy award best entertainment, 1971, Cleve. Emmy award cultural affairs programming, 1987, Cleve. Pops Orch. Star award, 2005. Mem.: Union League Club (Chgo.), Oakwood Club (Cleve.). Office: PO Box 22200 Cleveland OH 44122-0200

KOVEL, TERRY HORVITZ, writer, antiques authority; b. Cleve. d. Isadore and Rix Horvitz; m. Ralph Kovel; children: Lee R., Karen. BA, Wellesley Coll., 1950. Tchr. math. Hawken Sch. for Boys, Shaker Heights, Ohio, 1961-71; now pres. Antiques Inc.; past tchr. course in antiques Western Res. U., John Carroll U. Writer: (with Ralph Kovel) syndicated column Kovels Antiques and Collecting, 1955—, Ask the Experts, House Beautiful, 1979-00, Medio, CD-ROM mag., 1995, The Kovels on Collecting, Forbes Mag., 2000-02; editor: monthly newsletters Kovels on Antiques and Collectibles, 1974-, Kovels Sports Collectibles, 1992-97; TV series Know Your Antiques, Pub. TV, 1969-70; syndicated TV Series Kovels on Collecting, 1981, 87, Collector's Journal TV, 1989-93, Flea Market Finds with the Kovels HGTV, 2000-04; numerous appearances on radio and TV talk shows; author: (with Ralph Kovel) Kovels' Dictionary of Marks-Pottery and Porcelain, 1953, rev. edit., 1995, Directory of American Silver, Pewter and Silver Plate, 1958, American Country Furniture, 1780-1875, 1963, Kovels' Know Your Antiques, rev. edit, 1993, Kovels' American Art Pottery, 1993, Kovels' American Antiques 1750-1900, 2004, Kovels American Collectibles 1900-2000, 2007, Kovels' Antiques and Collectibles Price List, 39th edit., 2007, Kovels' Know Your Collectibles, 1981, 92, Kovels Bottle Price List, 13th edit., 2006, Kovels' Organizer for Collectors, 1978, revised, 1983, Kovels' Price Guide for Collector Plates, Figurines, Paperweights and Other Limited Editions, 1978, Kovels' Collector's Guide to American Art Pottery, 1974, Kovels' Collector's Guide to Limited Editions, 1974, Kovels' Depression Glass and Dinnerware Price List, 8th edit., 2004, Kovels' Illustrated Price Guide to Royal Doulton, 2d edit., 1984, Kovels' Collectors' Source Book, 1983, Kovels' New Dictionary of Marks Pottery and Porcelain, 1850 to the Present, 1986, Kovels' Advertising Collectibles Price List, 1986, 05, Kovels' Guide to Selling Your Antiques and Collectibles, 1987, 2d edit., 1990, Kovels' Book of Antique Labels, 1982, Kovels' American Silver Marks 1650 to the Present, 1989, Kovels' Antiques and Collectibles Fix-It Source Book, 1990, Kovels' Guide to Selling, Buying and Fixing Your Antiques and Collectibles, 1995, Kovels' Quick Tips: 799 Helpful Hints on How To Care for Your Collectibles, 1995, The Label Made Me Buy It, 1998, Kovels' Yellow Pages, 2d. edit., 2003, Kovels' Bid, Buy and Sell Online, 2001; (Video tape series) Collecting With the Kovels, 1995, Art Pottery I, Art Pottery II, Kovels' Page-A-Day Collectibles Calendar 1990, 1991, Kovels' Antiques and Collectibles 2003 Day-At-A Time-Calendar; contbr. numerous articles on antiques to publs, chapt. to books. Trustee Hiram Coll., 1989—99, hon. trustee, 2000; bd. mem. Shaker Hist. Soc. Hiram fellow; recipient Peirce award for outstanding cmty. svc. Sta. WVIZ-TV, 1980, Cleve. Emmy award for best entertainment, 1971, Cleve. Emmy award for cultural affairs programming, 1987; Laurel Sch. Alumanae of Yr. Office: PO Box 22200 Cleveland OH 44122-0200

KOVNER, BRUCE S., investment company executive; b. NYC, 1945; 3 children. BA, Harvard Coll., 1966; student, John F. Kennedy Sch. Govt., 1970. Cons. US Congress, Nat. Sci. Found., Coun. Environ. Advisors for State of NY, Fels Ctr. Govt., U. Pa., 1970—76; v.p. to sr. v.p. Commodities Corp., Princeton, NJ, 1977—83; founder, chmn. Caxton Associates LLC, 1983—. Founder, chmn. Sch. Choice Scholarships Found.; chmn., bd. dirs. Juillard Sch.; bd. dirs. Am. Enterprise Inst., Manhattan Inst., Philharmonic-Soc., NY, Lincoln Ctr. for the Performing Arts; chmn. Am. Enterprise Inst. Named one of Richest Americans, Forbes, 1999—, World's Richest People, 2001—. Office: Caxton Assocs LLC 500 Park Ave New York NY 10022*

KOWALCHICK, EDWARD M., headmaster; b. Phila. m. Patricia Perri Kowalchick; 2 children. AB, St. Joseph's U., 1971; MA, Villanova U., 1975. Teacher and sch. administrator Hill Sch. & Rosemont Sch., Pa., 1971—; v.p. for enrollment Lynn University in, Boca Raton, Fla.; head of sch. Brother Rice High Sch., Bloomfield Hills, Mich., 2002—04; headmaster Georgetown Prep, Bethesda, Md., 2004—07. Co-founder Internat. Boys' Schools Coalition, 1991—.*

KOWALCZYKOWSKI, STEPHEN CHARLES, microbiologist, cellular and molecular biologist, educator; b. Dec. 18, 1950; BS in Chemistry, Rensselaer Poly. Inst., Troy, NY, 1972; PhD in Chemistry, Georgetown U., Washington, 1976. Am. Cancer Soc. postdoctoral fellow molecular biology U. Oreg., Eugene, 1976—81; asst. prof. molecular biology Northwestern U. Med. Sch., Chgo., 1981—87, assoc. prof., 1987—91; prof. microbiology and molecular and cellular biology U. Calif., Davis, 1991—, chmn. sect. microbiology, 1992—99, dir. Ctr. Genetics and Devel., 2000—, disting. prof. microbiology and molecular and cellular biology, 2005—. Contbr. articles to sci. jours.; mem. editl. bd.: Jour. Biol. Chemistry, 2003—, mem. editl. adv. bd.: Am. Chem. Soc. Chem. Biology, 2006—. Recipient MERIT award, NIH, 2000—. Fellow: AAAS, Am. Acad. Arts & Scis., Am. Acad. Microbiology; mem.: NAS, Biophysical Soc., Am. Soc. Microbiology, Am. Chem. Soc. (biol. chemistry divsn.), Am. Soc. Biochemistry and Molecular Biology. Achievements include patents in field. Office: U Calif Davis Microbiology Sect Briggs Hall Rm 310 1 Shields Ave Davis CA 95616-8665 Office Phone: 530-752-5938, 530-752-5939. E-mail: sckowalczykowski@ucdavis.edu.

KOWALSKI, DEBRA ATKISSON, physician; d. Thomas and Patricia Atkisson; m. Roger Geer, June 22, 2002; 1 child, Katherine. MD, Tex. Tech U. Sch. of Medicine, Lubbock, 1986. Board Certification Am. Bd. of Psychiatry and Neurology, 1991, Board Certification, Child and Adolescent Psychiatry Am. Bd. of Psychiatry and Neurology, 1993. Assoc. med. dir. Cook Children's Med. Ctr., Ft. Worth, 1992—96; med. dir. The Excel Ctr., Ft. Worth, 1996—2001, Sundance Behavioral Health Care, Ft. Worth, 2005—. Cons. Early Childhood Intervention, Ft. Worth, 2000—, CorpHealth, Ft. Worth, 1999—. Tchr. Tex. Girl's Choir, Ft. Worth, 2006, Elem. Sunday Sch. Class, Ft. Worth, 2005—06; cons. Early Childhood Mental Health Com., Ft. Worth, 2005; troop leader Girl Scouts, Ft. Worth, 2001—06. Named one of Ft. Worth Tex. Top Docs, Tarrant County Med. Soc., 2002—04, 2006, Tex. Super Docs, Tex. Monthly, 2006; Seeley fellowship, Karl Menninger Sch. of Psychiatry, 1991. Fellow: Am. Psychiat. Assn. (rep. public affairs com.); mem.: Tex. Soc. of Psychiat. Physicians. Avocations: travel, cooking, reading. Office: Debra Atkisson Kowalski MD PA 6410 Southwest Blvd Ste 205 Fort Worth TX 76109 Office Phone: 817-735-4430. Office Fax: 817-735-4565.

KOWALSKI, KENNETH LAWRENCE, physicist, researcher; b. Chgo., July 24, 1932; s. Florian Lawrence and Emily Helen (Sinoga) K.; m. Audrey Bellin; children: Eric Clifford, Claudia Gail. BS, Ill. Inst. Tech., 1954; PhD, Brown U., 1963. Aero. rsch. scientist Lewis Rsch. Ctr., NACA, 1954-57; rsch. assoc. in physics Brown U., summer 1962, Case Inst. Tech., Cleve., 1962-63, asst. prof. physics, 1963-67, assoc. prof., 1967-73, Case Western Res. U., 1967-73, prof., 1973—, exec. officer dept. physics, 1970-71, chmn. dept. physics, 1971-76. Vis. prof. Inst. Theoretical Physics U. Louvain, Belgium, 1968-69; scientist-in-residence Argonne Nat. Lab., 1986-87, User Fermilab, 1993—. Author: (with S.K. Adhikari) Dynamical Collision Theory and It's Applications, 1991; editor: (with W.J. Fickinger) Modern Physics in America, 1988; contbr. articles to profl. jours. NSF grantee, 1972-96. Mem. Am. Phys. Soc. Achievements include research on theoretical physics. Home: 2172 Bellfield Ave Cleveland Heights OH 44106 Office: Case Western Res U Dept Physics 10900 Euclid Ave Dept Physics Cleveland OH 44106-1712 Office Phone: 216-368-4011. Business E-Mail: klk3@po.cwru.edu.

KOWALSKI, MICHAEL J., retail products executive; Various positions including group v.p. mktg. Tiffany & Co., NYC, 1983-92, exec. v.p. merchandising & mktg., 1992—96, pres., 1996—99, COO, 1997—99, CEO, 1999—2002, chmn., CEO, 2002—. Bd. dirs. Fairmont Hotels and Resorts, Bank of New York, Tiffany & Co., 1995—. Office: Tiffany & Co 727 5th Ave New York NY 10022*

KOWARSKI, ALLEN AVINOAM, endocrinologist, educator; b. Tel Aviv, Dec. 30, 1927; s. Hanoch and Sima (Tkazh) K.; m. Hanna Rose Zas, Mar. 24, 1950; children: David, Ruth. Student, Hebrew U., Jerusalem, 1946—47, MD, 1955; student, U. Lausanne Med. Sch., Switzerland, 1949—52. Acad. physician Hebrew U., 1955-62; instr., fellow Johns Hopkins U., Balt., 1962-68, asst. prof., 1968-72, assoc. prof., 1972-81; prof. U. Md., Balt., 1981—; pres. Kay Labs., Inc., 1974—. Patentee in field; contbr. over 170 articles to profl. jours. Grantee NIH, 1979-97, McNeil Pharm., 1984-86, DuPont Critical Care, 1985-90, Genentech Found. for Growth & Devel., 1994-95, Lilly Rsch. Lab. 1996-98. Mem. Am. Pediat. Soc., Soc. Pediat. Rsch., Lawson-Wilkins Pediat. Endocrine Soc., The Endocrine Soc., Am. Fedn. Clin. Rsch., Am. Diabetes Assn. (Diabetes Rsch. award 1983, Charles H. Best medal for disting. svc. 1994). Achievements include invention of nonthromogenic blood withdrawal sys., nonthrombogenic glucose monitor; discovery of DAWN phenomenon in diabetes and bioinactive growth hormone syndrome (Kowarski syndrome); integrated concentration of growth hormone method for diagnosis of growth hormone deficiency. Office: Kay Labs Inc 5801 Nicholson Ln Unit 1135 Rockville MD 20852-5734

KOWEL, STEPHEN THOMAS, electrical engineer, educator; b. Phila., Nov. 20, 1942; s. Abraham and Anna K.; m. Janis Zoltan, June 7, 1970; children: Ann, Eugene, Rose. BSEE, U. Pa., 1964; PhD in Elec. Engring., 1968; MSEE, Poly. Univ., 1966. Rsch. assoc. U. Pa., Phila., 1968-69; asst. prof. elec. and computer engring. Syracuse (N.Y.) U., 1969-74, assoc. prof., 1974-79, prof., 1979-84; prof. elec. engring. and computer sci. U. Calif., Davis, 1984-90, vice-chair dept., 1986-90, dir. organized rsch. program on polymeric ultrathin film systems, 1988-90; chmn. elec. and computer engring. U. Ala., Huntsville, 1990-97, dir. PhD program in optical sci. and engring., 1992-97, interim dean engring., 1997—98, dir., lab. for integrated computing and optoelectric systems, 1998-99, prof elec. and computer engring., 1998-99; dean engring. U. Cin., 1999—2004, prof. elec. engring., 2004—. Vis. prof. Cornell U., Ithaca, N.Y., 1982-83; cons. in field. Contbr. articles to profl. jours.; patentee in field. Grantee NASA, USAF, U.S. Army,

NSF, Advanced Rsch. Projects Agy. Fellow OSA, IEEE (Centennial medal 1984); mem. AAUP, Am. Soc. Engring. Edn., Sigma Xi. Home: 3787 Brighton Manor Ln Cincinnati OH 45208-1965 Business E-Mail: stephen.kowel@uc.edu.

KOZA, JOHN R., medical educator, writer; BA in Computer Sci., U. Mich., 1964, MA in Math., 1966; MS in Computer Sci., U.Mich., 1966; PhD in Computer Sci., U. Mich., 1972. Chmn., CEO, co-founder Scientific Games, Inc. (now ASE Co.), Atlanta, 1973—87; pres. Third Millennium Venture Capital Ltd., 1987—, Genetic Programming Inc., 1998—, Third Millennium On-Line Products, Inc., 2000—; tchr, computer sci. (genetic algorithms and genetic programming) Stanford U., 1988—2003, tchr. computer sci. (artificial life), 1993—94, co-taught med. info. sci., 1995—2000, lectr., computer sci. dept., sch. engring., 1988—91, cons. assoc. prof., computer sci. dept., 1991—92, cons. prof., computer sci. dept., sch. engring., 1992—98, cons. prof., Stanford BioMedical Informatics, dept. medicine, sch. medicine, 1998—2005, cons. prof., dept. elec. engring., sch. engring., 1999—2005. Bd. trustee Sante Fe Inst., 1999—2002, mem. sci. bd., 1995—98; chair Genetic Programming Conf., 1996—98; mem. bus. com. Genetic and Evolutionary Computation Conf., 1995—2005; mem. program policy com. Genetic Programming, 1999—2005; invited spkr. in field. Cons. editor Book Series on Genetic Programming, Kluwer Academic Publishers, mem. adv. bd. Genetic Programming and Evolvable Machines, mem. editl. bd. Evolutionary Computation, Artificial Life and Evolutionary Optimization, assoc. editor IEEE Transactions on Evolutionary Computation, 1997—2000; co-author: Genetic Programming III: Darwinian Invention and Problem Solving, 1999, Genetic Programming IV: Routine Human-Competitive Machine Intelligence, 2003, Every Vote Equal: A State-Based Plan for Electing the President By National Popular Vote, 2006; originator Agreement Among the States to Elect the President by National Popular Vote; author: Genetic Programming: One the Programming of Computers by Means of Natural Selection, 1992, Genetic Programming II: Automatic Discovery of Reusable Programs, 1994; author and co-author (tech. reports) Computer Sci. Dept. and Stanford Biomedical Informatics program, Dept. Medicine, Stanford U. Mem.: Internat. Soc. for Genetic and Evolutionary Computation (mem. exec. bd. 1999—). Achievements include being the co-inventor of the rub-off instant lottery game ticket used by state lotteries since 1974; inventor of the 1966 board game Consensus concerning the electoral coll. Mailing: PO Box K Los Altos CA 94023 Office: Sect on Med Informatics Dept Medicine Sch Med Stanford U Med Sch Office Bldg Mail Code 5479 251 Campus Dr Stanford CA 94305-5479 Office Phone: 650-960-8180. Office Fax: 650-941-9430. Business E-Mail: koza@stanford.edu. E-mail: john@johnkoza.com.

KOZAK, ALEXANDER L., engineer; b. Kiev, Ukraine, June 16, 1951; arrived in US, 1996; s. Leonid Kozak and Evgenia Gerasimova; m. Evgenia I. Chakshova, Feb. 10, 1973; children: Natalia, Dmitry. MS in Structural Mechanics, Kiev Civil Engring. Inst., 1973, PhD in Structural Mechanics, 1981, DSc in Structural Mechanics, 1995. Sun cert. programmer Java platform. Engr., rschr., sr. rschr., prin. rschr. Struct. Mech. Inst. Kiev State Tech. U. Constrn. and Arch., 1973-95; sr. engr., prin. engr. SC Solutions, Inc., Sunnyvale, Calif., 1996—. Contbr. articles to profl. jours. Avocation: stamp collecting/philately. Business E-Mail: kozak@scsolutions.com.

KOZAK, HARLEY JANE, actress, writer; b. Wilkes-Barre, Pa., Jan. 28, 1957; d. Joseph Aloysius and Dorothy (Taraldsen) K.; m. Gregory Aldisert, 1997; children: Audrey, Lorenzo and Gianna. Cert., NYU, 1980. Appeared in films Parenthood, 1989, Arachnophobia, 1990, The Taking of Beverly Hills, 1990, The Favor, 1990, Necessary Roughness, 1991, All I Want for Christmas, 1991, Magic in The Water, 1995, TV series Harts of the West, 1993-94, Bringing Up Jack, 1995, You Wish, 1997; author: (novels) Dating Dead Men, 2004 (Agatha, Anthony and Macavity awards for Best First Mystery Novel, Nebr. Book award for Best Fiction, 2005), Dating is Murder, 2005. Office: Renee Zuckerbrot Lit Agy 115 W 29th St 10th Fl New York NY 10001 Home Phone: 310-455-2111.

KOZAK, JOHN W., lawyer; b. Chgo., July 25, 1943; s. Walter and Stella (Palka) Kozak; m. Elizabeth Mathias, Feb. 3, 1968; children: Jennifer, Mary Margaret, Suzanne. BSEE, U. Notre Dame, 1965; JD, Georgetown U., 1968. Bar: Ill. 1968, DC 1968. Patent advisor Office Naval Rsch., Corona, Calif., 1968-69; assoc. Leydig, Voit & Mayer, Ltd. and predecessor firms, Chgo., 1969-74, ptnr., 1974—, chmn. mgmt. com., 1982-91, pres., 2001—. Mem. United Charities Legal Aid Soc., 1989—2002. Fellow: Am. Coll. Trial Lawyers; mem.: ABA, Chgo. Intellectual Property Law Assn., Licensing Execs. Soc., Am. Intellectual Property Law Assn., Orchid Island (Fla.) Golf and Beach Club, Knollwood Club (Lake Forest), Winter Club (Lake Forest, Ill.), Lawyers Club Chgo., Univ. Club (Chgo.). Office: Leydig Voit & Mayer Ste 4900 2 Prudential Pla Chicago IL 60601 Office Phone: 312-616-5600. Business E-Mail: jkozak@leydig.com.

KOZBERG, DONNA WALTERS, rehabilitation services professional; b. Milford, Del., Jan. 1, 1952; d. Robert Glyndwr and Gailey Ruth (Bedorf) Walters; m. Ronald Paul Kozberg, June 8, 1974; 1 child, Mariel Gailey. BA, U. Fla., 1973, M in Rehab. Counseling, 1974; MFA, CUNY, 1979; MBA, Rutgers U., 1986. Cert. rehab. counselor. Rehab. counselor Office Vocat. Rehab., NYC, 1975-81; area dir. Lift, Inc., Staten Island, NY, 1981-83, ea. region dir. pub. relations, advt. Mountainside, NJ, 1983-85, v.p., 1985—, v.p., chief fin. officer, 1988, exec. v.p., 1991-93, pres., 1993; co-founder, mng. dir. Expert Strategies, Inc., Mountainside, NJ, 1992—; self-employed writer, editor, 1975—. Adv. bd. Rutgers Exec. Master Bus. Adminstrn. Contbr. articles to profl. jours.; assoc. editor Parachute mag., 1978; editor-in-chief (newsletter) Counselor Adv, 1980. Pres. Com. on Employment of People with Disabilities; trustee Ctr. for Creative Living; bd. dirs. N.J. Adv. Coun. for Independent Living, adv. panel NYU. Mem. Nat. Rehab. Assn. (Spl. citation 1974, grantee 1973), Nat. Rehab. Adminstrs. Assn., Nat. Rehab. Counselors Assn., N.J. Rehab. Counselors Assn. (pres. 1996), Poets and Writers. Avocations: Tennis, English lit., Tae Kwon Do. Home: 45 Dug Way Watchung NJ 07069-6011 Office: Lift Inc PO Box 4264 Warren NJ 07059-0264 E-mail: dwkozberg@aol.com.

KOZBERG, JOANNE CORDAY, public affairs consultant; b. Edmonton, Alta., Can., July 4, 1944; d. Eliot and Marian (Lipkind) Corday; m. Roger A. Kozberg, May 25, 1968; children: Lindsey, Anthony. BA in history, U. Calif., Berkeley, 1966; MA in pub. policy, Occidental Coll., 1969. Assoc. prodr. KCET Cmty. Affairs Dept., LA, 1967-68; dir. So. Calif. NAACP Legal Def. and Edn. Fund, LA, 1975-77; acting exec. dir., dir. pub. affairs and the arts program CORO Found., LA, 1978-81; sr. policy cons. to US Senator Pete Wilson, LA, 1984-88; chair Calif. Arts Coun., 1988—91, exec. dir., 1991-93; sec. state and consumer affairs State of Calif., 1993-98; pres., COO Music Ctr. of LA County, 1999—2002; now ptnr. Calif. Strategies, LA. Mem. Nat. Hwy. Adv. Commn., Washington, 1980-86; dir. Western States Arts Fedn., Santa Fe, 1991-94, Nat. Assembly of State Arts Agys., Washington, 1992-94. Pres. The Blue Ribbon, LA, 1988—91; trustee Calif. Cmty. Found.; bd. dirs. Ctr. Theatre Group, LA, 1994—99; bd. regents U. Calif., 1998—; bd. trustees J. Paul Getty Trust, LA, 2005—. Recipient Rosalie M. Stern award U. Calif., Berkeley, 1984, Crystal Eagle award for pub. affairs excellence, Coro Found., 1998; CORO fellow, 1967. Mem. Calif. Club, Hillcrest Country Club. Republican. Jewish. Avocations: bicycling, tennis. Office: Calif Strategies Ste 1025 1875 Century Pk E Los Angeles CA 90067

KOZBERG, RONALD PAUL, health and human services administrator; b. NYC, Apr. 8, 1951; s. Raymond and Muriel (Tolmas) K.; m. Donna Lynn Walters, June 8, 1974; 1 child, Mariel Gailey. BA, Queens Coll., 1973; M of Rehab. Counseling, U. Fla., 1974; M of Pub. Health, Columbia U., 1986. Cert. rehab. counselor. Program dir. South Beach Psychiat. Ctr., SI, N.Y., 1974-76; dir. rehab. svcs. Bklyn. Developmental Ctr., 1976-85; dir. stds. and compliance Bronx Developmental Svcs., 1985-91; pres. Expert Strategies, Inc., Warren, N.J., 1991—. Technology com. chairperson Union County Edn. Coun., Westfield, N.J., 1993—. Author: The Do's and Dont's of Interviewing, 1992. Recipient Dean's Coun. award Dean of Health Related Professions, 1974. Mem. Nat. Rehab. Adminstrs. Assn. (N.E. regional bd. mem. 1982), Nat. Rehab. Counselors Assn. (N.Y. state sec., treas. 1981-82), Nat. Rehab. Assn. (pres., Spl. Citation 1974), Am. Pub. Health Assn. Avocations: golf, tennis, photography. Home: 45 Dug Way Watchung NJ 07069-6011 Office: Expert Strategies Inc PO Box 4264 Warren NJ 07059-0264 E-mail: rpkozberg@aol.com.

KOZHEVNIKOV, VLADIMIR F., physicist, researcher, educator; b. Neustrelitz, Germany, Nov. 14, 1947; arrived in US, 1997, naturalized, 1997; s. Feodor M. Kozhevnikov and Klara Ja Grossman; m. Yelena P. Spivak, Sept. 20, 1980; children: Polina, Asya. MSc, Gorky U., Russia, 1971; PhD, Moscow Aviation Inst., 1977; DSc, Kurchatov Inst. Atomic Energy, Moscow, 1990. Jr. rschr. Moscow Aviation Inst., 1978-84, sr. rschr., 1984-90, leading rschr., 1990-97, prof., 1991-97; exptl. physicist, educator U. Utah, Salt Lake City, 1997—2004; vis. prof. Katholieke U., Leuven, Belgium, 2004—06, guest prof., 2007—; prof. U. Tulsa, Okla., 2007—. Vis. rschr. Kuratov Inst. Atomic Engring., Moscow, 1979—97. Contbr. articles to profl. jours. Recipient Kurchatov prize Russian Rsch. Ctr. Kurchatov Inst., 1996; Japan Soc. for Promotion Scis. fellow, 1997. Mem. Am. Chem. Soc., Am. Phys. Soc., Moscow Phys. Soc. Avocations: music, literature, sports. Office: Univ Tulsa Dept Physics and Engring Physics 600 S College Ave Tulsa OK 74104 Business E-Mail: vladimir.kozhevnikov@fys.kuleuven.be.

KOZIARA, EUGENE HARRY, retired aerospace engineer; b. Hamtramck, Mich., Dec. 20, 1929; s. Frank Joseph and Angela (Zur) Koziara; m. Laura Ann Bomarito, June 21, 1958; children: Eugene H. Jr., Ann E. Castro, Frank J. II, Linda M. Frassrand. BS in Physics and Math., U. Mich., Ann Arbor, 1951, postgrad., 1954; MS in Physics and Electronics, Wayne State U., Detroit, 1954, MBA in Mgmt. and Econs., 1964, postgrad., 1964—65, Ohio State U., Columbus, 1968—69. Rsch. analyst U. Mich., Ypsilanti, 1951—53; physics fellow Wayne State U., Detroit, 1953—54; grad. in tng. GM Rsch., Detroit, 1954; electronics engr. Hughes Aircraft Co., Culver City, Calif., 1954—56; fire control sys. engr. Chrysler Missile divsn. Chrysler Corp., Sterling Heights, Mich., 1956—58; group engr. Martin Co., Balt., 1958—59; staff engr. Sparton Corp., Jackson, Mich., 1959—60, Bendix Corp., Bendix Sys. Divsn., Ann Arbor, 1960—63; engring. specialist Ling Tomco Vought, Mich. Divsn., Warren, 1963—65; mem. tech. staff V N.Am. Rockwell Corp., Columbus, 1965—70; engring. sys. analyst Corp. Offices Teledyne Continental Motors Corp., Warren, 1970—71; sr. sys. analyst Ford Motor Co., World Hdqs., Dearborn, Mich., 1972—77, Mt. Clemens, Mich., 1972—77; ret., 1977. Co-author: Linear Programming, 1955. Mem.: Sigma Pi Sigma. Achievements include first to technical schematics for US satellite launch.

KOZIEL, JACEK, agricultural engineer, educator; PhD, U. Tex., Austin, 1998. Asst. prof. Tex. Agrl. Expt. Sta., Amarillo, 2000—04, Iowa State U., Ames, 2004—. Contbr. articles to profl. jours. Recipient Agrl. Engr. of the Yr., Am. Soc. of Agrl. Engineers - Tex. Sect., 2003. Mem.: Am. Soc. Agrl. and Biol. Engrs. (Agrl. Engr. of Yr. Tex. sect. 2003), Air and Waste Mgmt. Assn., Am. Chem. Soc., Sigma Xi. Achievements include patents pending for ethanol purification. Office: Iowa State U 3103 NSRIC Ames IA 50011 Office Phone: 515-294-4206.

KOZINN, ALLAN, music critic, reporter; Contbg. editor High Fidelity, Opus, Keynote; music critic NY Observer, 1987—88; with NY Times, NYC, 1991—, classical music critic. Author The Guitar: The History, the Players, The Music, 1984, Mischa Elman and the Romantic Style, 1989, The Beatles, 1995, The New York Times Essential Library: Classical Music, 2004. Recipient ASCAP-Deems Taylor award, 1981, 1989. Office: NY Times Culture Desk 229 W 43rd St New York NY 10036 Office Phone: 212-556-4133. Office Fax: 212-556-1516. E-mail: kozinn@nytimes.com.

KOZINSKI, ALEX, federal judge; b. Bucharest, Romania, July 23, 1950; came to US, 1962; s. Moses and Sabine (Zapler) K.; m. Marcy J. Tiffany, July 9, 1977; children: Yale Tiffany, Wyatt Tiffany, Clayton Tiffany. AB in Econs. cum laude, UCLA, 1972, JD, 1975. Bar: Calif. 1975, DC, 1978. Law clk. to Hon. Anthony M. Kennedy US Ct. Appeals (9th Cir.), 1975-76; law clk. to Chief Justice Warren E. Burger US Supreme Ct., 1976-77; assoc. Covington & Burling, Washington, 1979-81; dep. legal counsel Office Pres-elect, Washington, 1980; asst. counsel to Pres. The White House, Washington, 1981; spl. counsel Merit Systems Protection Bd., Washington, 1981-82; chief judge US Claims Ct., Washington, 1982-85; judge US Ct. Appeals (9th cir.), Pasadena, Calif., 1985—. Lectr. law U. So. Calif., 1992. Office: US Ct Appeals Ste 200 125 S Grand Ave Pasadena CA 91105*

KOZIOL, JOHN CRAIG (CRAIG KOZIOL), career military officer; b. Jan. 1954; m. Virginia R. Koziol; children: Ryan, Tyler. BA, Norwich U., 1976; MS in Bus. Adminstrn., Troy State U., 1981; grad., Squadron Officer Sch., Maxwell AFB, 1981, Air Command and Staff Coll., 1988, Air War Coll., 1995, Joint and Combined Warfighting Sch., Armed Forces Staff Coll., 1996; grad. Nat. Security Mgmt. Course, Syracuse U., 2000; grad. Exec. Program for Gen. Officers, Harvard U. Joined USAF, 1976, advanced through grades to maj. gen., 2006, flight comdr. 6931st Electronic Security Squadron Iraklion Air Force Station, Greece, 1977—79, chief exploitation mgmt. 6911th Electronic Security Group Hahn Air Base, West Germany, 1979—80, asst. dir. ops., 1981—82, intelligence staff officer Air Staff Training Program Washington, 1982—83, unit dir. command post ops. 6944th Electronics Security Squadron Ft. George G. Meade, Md., 1983—84, comdr. Detachment 1, 6912th Electronic Security Group Berlin, 1984—87; consolidated cryptologic program element monitor Directorate of Policy, Plans and Programs, USAF, Washington, 1988—89, exec. officer to dir., 1989—90; exec. officer to asst. chief of staff for intelligence USAF, Washington, 1990—91, chief program devel. and integration Directorate of Resource Mgmt., 1991—92; chief Intelligence Policy, Plans and Programs Div., Directorate of Intelligence N.Am. Aerospace Defense Command, US Space Command, Peterson AFB, Colo., 1995—96, comdr. Combined Intelligence Ctr., 1996—97; comdr. 17th Training Group USAF, Goodfellow AFB, Tex., 1997—99, dir. intelligence Air Combat Command Langley AFB, Va., 1999—2000, vice comdr. 8th Air Force Barksdale AFB, La., 2000—02, dep. dir. Intelligence, Surveillance and Reconnaissance, dep. chief staff Air Space Ops. Washington, 2002—03, comdr. 55th Wing Offutt AFB, Nebr., 2003—05, comdr. Air Intelligence Agency, 8th Air Force dep. comdr. Info. Ops., comdr. Joint Info. Ops. Ctr. Lackland AFB, Tex., 2005—. Decorated Defense Superior Svc. Medal, Legion of Merit, Meritorious Svc. Medal, Aerial Achievement Medal, Commendation Medal USAF, Meritorious Unit Award, Outstanding Unit Award, Orgnl. Excellence Award, Joint Meritorious Unit Award, Nat. Defense Svc. Medal, S.W. Asia Svc. Medal, Global War on Terrorism Svc. Medal, Armed Forces Svc. Medal, NATO Medal, Kuwait Liberation Medal. Office: Air Intelligence Agy 2 Hall Blvd, Ste 201 San Antonio TX 78243

KOZITKA, RICHARD EUGENE, retired consumer products company executive; b. Staples, Minn., Apr. 30, 1934; s. Michael V. and Luella H. (Drews) K.; m. Mary Elizabeth Juneau, Sept. 27, 1969; children: Michael Arthur, Laura Juneau Hensley. BA in Journalism, U. Minn., 1956. Program dir. Jr. Achievement of Chgo., 1961-63; mgr. publ./employee communications The Quaker Oats Co., Chgo., 1963-72, dir. employee and audio visual communications, 1972-78, v.p. corp. adminstrv. svcs., 1978-95. Trustee Luth. Social Svcs. Ill. Served with U.S. Army, 1957-61. Mem. Westmoreland Country Club (Wilmette, Ill.), Chgo. Curling Club (Northbrook, Ill.), Univ. Club Chgo., Pelican Strand Country Club (Naples, Fla.), La Playa Beach Club (Naples). Lutheran. Home: 9790 Gulf Shore Dr Unit 205 Naples FL 34108

KOZLOFF, JESSICA S., academic administrator; b. San Antonio, Mar. 29, 1941; d. Robert John and Ann (Acklen) Sledge; m. Stephen R. Kozloff, June 12, 1965; children: Kyle Schaller, Rebecca Esther. BS, U. Nev., 1963, MA, 1964; PhD, Colo. State U., 1983. Prof. polit. sci. U. Northern Colo., Greeley, 1976-89, exec. asst. to pres., 1985-89; v.p. acad. affairs State Colls. in Colo., Denver, 1989-94; pres. Bloomsburg U., 1994—. Mem. Middle States Commn. on Higher Edn., 2000—, chair 2006-; bd. dirs. Geisinger Health Plan, 2004— Bd. dirs. United Way, Bloomsburg, 1994—2000, Boy Scouts Am., Bloomsburg, 1994—2000. Acad. Adminstrn. fellow Am. Coun. on Edn., 1985. Mem.: Pa. Compact (bd. dirs. 1998—2001), Bloomsburg C. of C., Nat. Collegiate Athletics Assn. (mem. pres. commn. 1996—2001), Am. Assn. State Colls. and Univs. (bd. dirs. 2004—), Bloomsburg Rotary Club. Avocations: golf, tennis, skiing, biking, travel. Office: Bloomsburg U 400 E 2nd St Bloomsburg PA 17815-1399 Home Phone: 570-389-4695; Office Phone: 570-389-4526. Business E-Mail: jkozloff@bloomu.edu.

KOZLOFF, LLOYD M., dean, microbiologist, educator; b. Chgo., Oct. 15, 1923; s. Joseph and Rose (Hollobow) K.; m. Judith Bonnie Friedman, June 16, 1947; children: James, Daniel, Joseph, Sarah BS, U. Chgo., 1943, PhD, 1948. Asst., then assoc. prof. biochemistry U. Chgo., 1949-61, prof., 1961-64; prof. microbiology U. Colo., Denver, 1964-80, chmn. dept. microbiology, 1966-76, assoc. dean, prof., 1976-80; dean, prof. U. Calif., San Francisco, 1981-91, prof., dean emeritus, 1991—. Career investigator USPHS, U. Chgo., 1962 Founding editor Jour. Virology, 1966-76; contbr. articles to profl. jours., chpts. to books. Chmn. bd. dirs. Proctor Fund., 1981-91; v.p. San Francisco Alliance for Mental Illness, 1993-96; pres. emeritus U. Calif. San Francisco Faculty Assn., 1996-2000. With USN, 1944-46. Commonwealth Fund fellow, 1953, Lederle Found. fellow, 1954; recipient Disting. Svc. award U. Chgo., 2004. Fellow AAAS, Am. Acad. Microbiol. (hon.); mem. Am. Soc. Biol. Chemistry, Am. Soc. Microbiology (head virology sect. 1974-76), Am. Chem. Soc., N.Y. Acad. Sci. Home: 43000 Lyndon Ln Fort Bragg CA 95437 Office: U Calif Grad Divsn San Francisco CA 94114-2732

KOZLOFF, THEODORE J., lawyer; b. Reading, Pa., 1941; BA, U. Pa., 1964, MA in Econ., 1964, LLB cum laude, 1967. Bar: Calif. 1967, N.Y. 1968. Mem. Comm. on Securities Regulation, Assoc. of the Bar of the City of New York, 1981—84, Skadden, Arps, Slate, Meagher & Flom, San Francisco; Board of Overseers University of Pennsylvania Law School, 1986—90; bd. trustees The Hill School, Pottstown, Pa., 1987—96. Editor U. Pa. Law Rev., 1966-67. Office: Skadden Arps Slate Meagher & Flom 4 Embarcadero Ctr San Francisco CA 94111-4106

KOZLOV, VIKTOR, professional hockey player; b. Togliatti, Russia, Feb. 14, 1975; Center San Jose Sharks, 1994-98, Fla. Panthers, Sunrise, 1997—2004, NJ Devils, 2004—06, NY Islanders, 2006—07, Washington Capitals, 2007—. Player NHL All-Star game, 2000; mem. Team Russia, Olympic Games, Tornio, Italy, 2006. Office: Washington Capitals Ste 890 627 Glebe Rd Arlington VA 22203

KOZLOVSKY, TIMOTHY FRANCIS, music educator; b. Green Bay, Wis., Dec. 27, 1965; s. Robert James and Margaret Adele Kozlovsky; m. Eileen Ryana Harty, Nov. 19, 1973; children: Nolan Grant, Ellis Victor, Adele Nadine. BA in Music Edn., U. Wis., Green Bay, 1989; MA in Music Edn., U. Wis., Stevens Point, 2005. Lic. instrumental, choral and gen. music tchr. Wis. Dept. Pub. Instrn., 1989. Band dir. Suring Pub. Schs., Wis., 1990—2000, Pulaski Cmty. Mid. Sch., Wis., 2000—. Dir. Pulaski Area Cmty. Band and Jazz Ensemble, 1999—. Recipient Disting. Employee award, Pulaski Cmty. Sch. Dist., 2004, 2007. Mem.: Nat. Band Dirs. Assn., Music Educators Nat. Conf. (pres. collegiate chpt. 1988—89), Am. Sch. Band Dirs. Assn. Roman Catholic. Home: 3941 Big Sky Dr Pulaski WI 54162 Office: Pulaski Cmty Middle School 911 South Saint Augustine St Pulaski WI 54162 Home Phone: 920-865-3941; Office Phone: 920-822-6580.

KOZLOW, RICHARD, artist; Author, illustrator book Of Man's Inhumanity to Man, 1964. Represented in permanent collections Chrysler Corp., William Kessler Assocs., Archs., Mich. Nat. Bank Corp. hdqs., Weight Watchers Internat., others, Detroit Inst. Arts, Smithsonian Nat. Mus. Am. Art, Washington, State of Mich. Libr. Mus., Lansing, others, Wayne State U., one-man shows include Detroit Artists Market, 1950, Instituto Allende, Mex., 1960—61, Raymond Burr Gallery, L.A., Calif., 1963, Arwin Galleries, Detroit, 1963, Rehn Galleries, N.Y.C., 1958, 1967, Foster Harmon Gallery of Am. Art, Sarasota, Fla., 1983, Arwin Gallery, 1973, Shweyer-Galdo Galleries, Birmingham, Mich., 1983, Malton Gallery, Cin., 1985, Rubiner Gallery, West Bloomfield, Mich., 1990, Posner Gallery, Farmington Hills, Mich., 1983, 1984, Birmingham, 1999, Mex. Nat. Inst. de Bellas Artes, 1994, U. Mich. Holocaust Series, 1998, exhibited in group shows at Butler Art Inst., Youngstown, Ohio, 1950, 1952, Detroit Scarab Club, 1952, 1953, Provincetown (Maine) Arts Festival, 1958, Hudsons Salutes to the Detroit Artists Market, 1963, Mus. of Art of Ogunquit Maine, 1964, Am. Embassy, London, 1966, Lithografias de la Collecion Mourlot, P.R., 1971, Birmingham Temple, West Bloomfield, 1988, featured in publs. With USN, 1944—46. Recipient Socrates award for outstanding advt., Detroit Art Dirs. Awards, Nat. Outdoor Advt. 1st award for best painted billboard, Mich. Founders award, Detroit Inst. Arts, 10-Yr. Retrospective award, Lois and Alvin Spector Found. for Arts award for outstanding achievement. Home: 176 Suffield Birmingham MI 48009 Office Phone: 248-642-5512.

KOZLOWSKI, CHERYL M., fixed income analyst; b. Boston, July 19, 1974; d. Leo Dennis and Angeles Zenaida. BA, Middlebury Coll., 1996; postgrad., Harvard Bus. Sch., 2000—02. Lic. pilot. Fin. analyst Merrill Lynch, NYC, 1996-1998; prin. Clayton, Dubilier & Rice, Inc., NYC, 1998-2000; equity analyst Am. Express, 2002—04; fixed income analyst Airlie Opportunity Fund, 2004—. Treas. The Friends of Tolstoy Found., 1998—2002; chmn. Young New Yorkers of N.Y. Philharmonic, 1999—2002; bd. dirs. Shackleton Schs., 2000—05. Avocation: skiing. Home: 610 Park Ave Apt 14A New York NY 10065-7025 E-mail: ckozlowski@mba2002.hbs.edu.

KOZLOWSKI, DAMIAN MARK, diversified financial services company executive; b. Sept. 16, 1964; MS, Boston U.; MBA, Wharton Sch. Fin. and Strategic Mgmt. Mng. dir. Banc of Am. Securities; global COO Citigroup Private Bank, 2000—02, pres. U.S. region, 2002—05, global CEO, 2005—07. Mem. Citigroup Mgmt. com., 2005—07.*

KOZLOWSKI, RONALD STEPHAN, retired librarian; b. Chgo., Oct. 18, 1937; s. Stephan James and Helen Marie Beck (Tancula) K.; m. Barbara Hartlein, Aug. 8, 1964; children: Ann, Keith, Ellen, Brent. BS in Edn, Ill. State U., 1961; MA in LS, Rosary Coll., 1968. Audiovisual libr. Triton Jr. Coll., River Grove, Ill., 1968-69; br. libr. Evansville (Ind.) Pub. Librs., 1969-70, asst. dir., 1971-74; head reference and acquisitions dept. Ind. State U., Evansville, 1970-71; dir. West Fla. Regional Libr., Pensacola, 1974-77, Louisville Free Pub. Libr., 1977-83, Pub. Libr. Charlotte and Mecklenburg County, NC, 1983-86; exec. dir. Cuyahoga County Pub. Libr., Cleve., 1986-89; dir. Miami-Dade Pub. Libr. Sys., Miami, Fla.,

1989-1993; adminstr. Anne Arundel County Pub. Libr., Annapolis, Md., 1993—2002; ret., 2002. Del. White House Conf. on Librs.; bd. trustees State Libr. Va., 2006—. Mem. ALA, Md. Libr. Assn. Home: 1731 Timberly Waye Richmond VA 23233 Home Phone: 804-740-0418. Personal E-mail: rskozlowski@comcast.net.

KOZLOWSKI, THOMAS JOSEPH, JR., lawyer, wealth management executive; b. Norristown, Pa., July 29, 1950; s. Thomas Joseph Kozlowski, Jr. and Mary Elisa (Alvarez) Kozlowski; m. Michelle Mary Champagne, Jan. 9, 1971; children: Brian Christopher, Scott Michael, Mark Daniel. BSBA in Acctg., Georgetown U., 1971, JD, 1979; MBA, George Washington U., 1975. CPA Va.; bar: D.C. 1979, Va. 1980. Sr. acct. Touche Ross & Co., Washington, 1972-75; dir. internal audit Pentagon Fed. Credit Union, Arlington, Va., 1975-77; supr. acct. Snyder, Newrath & Co., Washington, 1977-79; v.p., sec. Owens & Co., Inc., Arlington, 1979-86; sr. v.p. fin. Realty Investment Co., Inc., Silver Spring, Md., 1986-89; sr. v.p., treas. The Selzer Group, Inc., NYC, 1989-93; pres. The Collector's Gallery of Va. Inc., Alexandria, 1992-96; exec. v.p. dir. Family Office Group Merrill Lynch Trust Co., Princeton, NJ, 1993—2005; pres. AFIOS, Inc., Newtown, Pa., 2005—. Bd. dirs. Sciens Internat. Fund of Hedge Funds, Sciens Global Opportunity Fund; bd. advisors Cachet Media Inc., NY. Editor: Jour. Law and Policy in Internat. Bus., 1976—79. Arbiter Fairfax County Consumer Protection Commn., Va., 1977—95; treas. Commonwealth Found., Inc., Silver Spring, 1986—89; bd. dirs. Resdl. Youth Svcs., Inc., Alexandria, 1981—89, treas., 1982—84, v.p., 1984—85; treas. Coplex Found., NYC, 1989—93; planned giving adv. coun. Pa. State U., 2000—, mem. external adv. bd. Schreyer Honors Coll., 2006—; alumni admissions program Georgetown U., 2003—. Mem.: AICPA, ABA, Inst. Mgmt. Acctg. (cert. mgmt. acctg., cert. disting. performance 1975), Va. State Bar Assn., D.C. Bar Assn., D.C. Inst. CPA. Democrat. Roman Catholic. Avocations: reading, photography. Office: AFIOS Inc PO Box 1013 Washington Crossing PA 18977 Home Phone: 215-860-3355; Office Phone: 215-860-7472. Personal E-mail: tomkozlowski@comcast.net.

KOZMA, ADAM, electrical engineer; b. Cleve., Feb. 2, 1928; s. Desire and Vera (Nagy) K.; m. Eileen Marie Somogyi, Oct. 24, 1956 (dec. Jan. 1978); children: Paul A. (dec.), Peter A.; m. Rebecca Chelius, Feb. 6, 1993. BSME, U. Mich., 1952, MS in Engring.-Instrumentation Engring., 1964; MS in Engring. Mechanics, Wayne State U., 1961; PhD in Elec. Engring., U. London, 1968; diploma of membership, Imperial Coll., 1969. Design engr. US Broach Co., Detroit, 1951-57; rsch. engr. Inst. Sci. & Tech., Willow Run Labs. U. Mich., Ann Arbor, 1958-69; gen. mgr. Electro Optics Ctr. Harris, Inc., Ann Arbor, 1969-73; sr. rsch. engr. radar div. Environ. Rsch. Inst. Mich., Ann Arbor, 1973-75, mgr. elec. and electromagnetics dept., 1975-76, mgr. tech. staff, 1976-77, v.p., dir. radar div., 1977-85, v.p., corp. devel., 1985-86; v.p., dir. def. electronics engring. div. Syracuse (N.Y.) Rsch. Corp., 1986-88; head intelligence systems dept. MITRE Corp., Bedford, Mass., 1988-89, head advanced systems dept., 1990-93; adj. prof. Coll. Engring. U. Mich., Ann Arbor, 1993—2002, vis. scholar, 2003—06. Cons. Conductron Corp., Ann Arbor, 1966, IBM, Endicott, N.Y., 1967-68, U.S. Army Missile Command, Huntsville, Ala., 1974-76, MITRE Corp., 1993-2001, Veridian-ERIM-Internat., Inc., 1998-2001; lectr. various univs.; engring. cons., 1993-2005. Co-author: Hologram Visual Displays (Motion Picture TV Engrs. honorable mention 1977); patentee in field. With US Army, 1946—47, with USAR, 1947—51, with reserve USAF, 1953—61. Fellow IEEE (life), Optical Soc. Am.; mem. Aero. and Electronics Systems Soc. of IEEE (radar sys. panel 1984-2006, emeritus, 2006- bd. govs. 91-93), Geosci. and Remote Sensing Soc. of IEEE, Am. Def. Preparedness Assn. (chmn. various coms. avionics sect. 1975-88, Ordnance medal 1984), Soc. Photo-Optical Instrumentation Engrs., Sigma Xi. Lutheran. Avocations: tennis, skiing, bicycling. Home and Office: 2996 Appleway Ann Arbor MI 48104-1808 Business E-Mail: akozma@umich.edu.

KOZOL, JONATHAN, writer; b. Boston, Sept. 5, 1936; s. Harry Leo and Ruth (Massell) K. BA, Harvard U., 1958; Rhodes scholar, Magdalen Coll., Oxford U., 1958-59. Tchr. Boston pub. schs., 1964-65, Newton pub. schs., 1966-68; dir., trustee Store-front Learning Center, 1968-74; prof. edn. Trinity Coll., 1980. Cons. U.S. Office Edn., 1965-66; vis. lectr. Yale U., 1969, others; instr. Ctr. for Intercultural Documentation, Cuernavaca, Mex., 1969, 70, 74. Author: Death At An Early Age, 1967 (Nat. Book award, 1968), Free Schools, 1972, The Night Is Dark and I Am Far From Home, 1975, Children of the Revolution, 1978, Prisoners of Silence, 1980, On Being A Teacher, 1981, Illiterate America, 1985, Rachel and Her Children, 1988 (Robert F. Kennedy Book award, 1989), Savage Inequalities, 1991 (New Eng. Book award, 1992, Amazing Grace, 1995 (Anisfield-Wolf Book award, 1996), Ordinary Resurrections, 2000 (Christopher award, Harry Chapin award, 2001, Wilbur award, 2001), The Shame of the Nation 2005 (Nation/Puffin award 2005), Letters to a Young Teacher, 2007; corr.: Los Angeles Times, USA Today, 1982-83; contbr. to N.Y. Times Book Rev., 1968-85; reporter-at-large The New Yorker mag., 1988, Harper's mag., 2005. Trustee New Sch. Children, Roxbury, Mass.; bd. dirs. Nat. Literacy Coalition, 1980-83. Recipient Olympia Thousand Dollar award, 1962, Lannan Literary award, 1994; Saxton fellow in creative writing Harper & Row, 1964; Guggenheim fellow, 1970, 84; Field Found. fellow, 1972; Ford Found. fellow, 1974; Rockefeller Found. fellow, 1978, fellow in humanities, 1983. Mem. Nat. Coalition for the Homeless, Fellowship of Reconciliation. Address: PO Box 145 Byfield MA 01922-0145 Office Fax: 978-462-8577. Personal E-mail: jonathankozol@gmail.com. *My concerns are the education, health and housing of low income children.*

KOZOLCHYK, BORIS, law educator, consultant; b. Havana, Cuba, Dec. 6, 1934; came to U.S., 1956; s. Abram and Chana (Brewda) D.; m. Elaine Billie Herman, Mar. 5, 1967; children: Abbie Simcha, Raphael Adam, Shaun Marcie. DCL, U. Havana, 1956; Diplome, Faculte Internat. de Droit, Luxembourg, 1958; LLB, U. Miami, 1959; LLM, U. Mich., 1960, SJD, 1966. Teaching asst. Sch. of Law U. Miami, Fla., 1957-59; asst. prof. law Sch. of Law So. Meth. U., Dallas, 1960-64; resident cons. The Rand Corp., Santa Monica, Calif., 1964-67; dir. Law Reform Project USAID, San Jose, Costa Rica, 1967-69; prof. law Coll. of Law U. Ariz., 1969—. Tchg. asst. Faculte Internat. de Droit Campare, 1958; vis. prof. law Nat. U. of Mex., 1961; vis. exch. prof. law Nat. U. of Chile, Santiago, 1962; guest lectr. Latin Am. Law seminar Stanford (Calif.) U., 1964; guest lectr. extension grad. seminar on Latin Am. law UCLA, 1965; Bailey vis. prof., Tucker lectr. La. State U., 1979; vis. prof. U. Aix en Provence, France, 1985; cons. on legal sys. U.S. Agy. Internat. Devel., 1974-77; legal cons. Overseas Pvt. Investment Corp., 1974; cons. uniformity of comml. laws Orgn. Am. States and U.S. State Dept., 1974-77; expert witness on banking and comml. law and custom issues; advisor Libr. Congress Law divsn.; Joseph Bernfeld Meml. lectr. L.A. Bankruptcy Forum, 1989; magisterial lectr. Nat. U. Mex. Sch. Law, 1989; advisor Project Lao, 1991; lectr. in field. Author of books; bd. mem. Am. Jour. of Comparative Law; mem. editl. bd. Internat. Banking Law Jour.; founder, faculty advisor Ariz. Jour. of Internat. and Comparative Law, 1982-86; reporter Ency. Comparative Law, 1989; contbr. articles to profl. jours. and publs. Selected Nat. U. Mex. rep. First Mexican congress Comml. Law, 1974; pres. Ariz. Friends of Music, 1975-76; hon. chmn. community rels. com. Jewish Fedn. So. Ariz.; mem. adv. com. Ariz.-Mex. Commn. Govs.; legal advisor Ariz.-Mex. Banking com.; del U.S. Coun. on Internat. Banking to ICC; adv. mem. U.S. del. to UNCITRAL Internat. Contract Law, 1989-95; dir., pres., bd. dirs. Nat. Law Ctr. for InterAm. Free Trade, 1992—. NSF grantee, 1973-75; recipient Extraordinary Tchg. and Rsch. Merit award Coll. Law, U. Costa Rica, 1969, Cmty. Svc. award Tucson Jewish Cmty. Coun., 1979, Man of Yr. award, 1982, Commendation award U.S. Dept. Justice, 1979, Disting. Svc. award Law Coll. Alumni Assn., 1990, Commendation award U.S. Dept. State, 1990, Ptnrs. in Democracy award Am.-Israel Friendship League, 2003, cert. of Honor Outstanding Contbn. Civil Rights and Social Justice, Tucson Human Rels. Commn., 2003, Excellence in Internat. Edn. award U. Ariz. Ctr. for ESL, 2004; named to Hall of Fame Profs. of Comml. Law, Nat. U., Mex., 1987; named One of Most Influential Hispanics, Hispanic Bus. Mag., 1991, Man of Yr., Hispanic Profl. Action Com., 1995; Guadalajara chpt. Mex. and US Student Bar Assn. was named the Boris Kozolchyk chpt., Guadalajara br. The Inst. Legal Rsch. of Tech. Monterrey named the Boris Kozolchyk Inst. Mem. ABA (task force for the revision of UCC article 5, Leonard J. Theberge award 2004), State of Ariz. Bar (Honoree at 100 Women and Minority Lawyers Dinner), Inter-ABA (co-chmn. comml. law and procedure sec. 1973-78, Best Book award 1973), Am. Soc. of Internat. Law, Internat. Acad. Comml. and Consumer Law (pres. 1988-90), Am. Acad. Fgn. Law (founding), Am. Law Inst. (consultative com. to UCC articles 3, 4, 4a and 5), Nat. Mexican Notarial Bar Assn. (hon. life 1982), Internat. Acad. Comml. and Consumer Law (elected pres. 1988), Sonora Bar Assn. (1st Disting. Svc. award 1989). Home: 7401 N Skyline Dr Tucson AZ 85718-1166 Office: U Ariz Coll Of Law Tucson AZ 85721-0001 Home Phone: 520-297-1642. Personal E-mail: b.kozolchyk@natlaw.com.

KOZUSKO, DONALD D., lawyer; b. 1945; BA, Villanova U., 1967; JD, Harvard Law Sch., 1970. Bar: Ohio 1970, DC 1974. Ptnr. Jones Day, Bryan Cave, Kozusko Harris Vetter Warch LLP, Washington. Dir. Shaking the Tree: Interactive Productions, US Friends of Cayman HospiceCare, Inc. Served in JAG Office USN. Named one of Top 100 Attys., Worth mag., 2005. Fellow: Am. Coll. Trusts Estates Counsel; mem.: Soc. Trust Estate Practitioners. Office: Kozusko Harris Vetter Wareh LLP 1666 K St NW Ste 400 Washington DC 20006 Office Phone: 202-457-7211. Office Fax: 202-318-4444.*

KRA, PAULINE SKORNICKI, French language educator; b. Lodz, Poland, July 30, 1934; arrived in US, 1950, naturalized, 1955; d. Edward and Nathalie Skornicki; m. Leo Dietrich Kra, Mar. 10, 1955; children: David Theodore, Andrew Jason. Student, Radcliffe Coll., 1951-53; BA, Barnard Coll., 1955; MA, Columbia U., 1963, PhD, 1968; MA, Queens Coll., 1990. Lectr. Queens Coll., CUNY, 1964-65; asst. prof. French Yeshiva U., NYC, 1968-74, assoc. prof., 1974-82, prof., 1982-99, prof. emerita, 1999—; sr. programmer analyst Dept. Biomed. Informatics Columbia U., NYC, 1998—. Author: Religion in Montesquieu's Lettres Persanes, 1970; co-editor: Montesquieu, Lettres Persanes, 2004; contbr. articles to profl. jours. Mem. MLA, Am. Assn. Tchrs. French, Am. Soc. 18th Century Studies, Société Française d'étude du XVIII Siècle, Soc. Montesquieu, Assn. for Computers and Humanities, Assn. for Lit. and Linguistic Computing, Phi Beta Kappa. Achievements include invention of methods for extracting information on interactions between biological entities from natural language text data. Home: 10914 Ascan Ave Forest Hills NY 11375-5370

KRAAY, MATTHEW JOSEPH, orthopedist, educator; s. Dick and Zora A. Kraay; m. Christine R. Restifo, Sept. 5, 1987; children: Matthew N., Michelle A., Richard J. BS, Mich. State U., East Lansing, 1977; MS, U. Mich., Ann Arbor, 1978; MD, Wayne State U., Detroit, Mich., 1983. Diplomate Am. Bd. of Orthop. Surgery, 1993. Dir. divsn. of joint reconstruction and arthritis surgery U. Hosps. of Cleve., 1995—; K.G. Heiple and Fred A. Lennon prof. orthop. surgery Case Western Res. U., Cleve., 2006—. Reviewer Jour. of Bone and Joint Surgery, 2004—; mis adv. task force AAOS/AAHKS, 2004—. Bd. dirs. Arthritis Found. of NE Ohio, Cleve., 2003—06; shands cir. Orthop. Rsch. and Edn. Found., 2003—06; med. and sci. com. Arthritis Found. of Northeastern Ohio, Cleve., 2002—06. Recipient Otto Aufranc award, Hip Soc., 2006; Allen Surg. Rsch. fellowship, Case Western Res. U., 1984-1985, Adult Reconstruction fellowship, U. Hosps. of Cleve., 1989-1990, Comprehensive Arthritis Program fellowship, The Hosp. for Spl. Surgery, 1990-1991. Fellow: Am. Acad. Orthop. Surgeons; mem.: Am. Assn. Hip and Knee Surgeons, Cleve. Orthop. Soc. (pres.), Am. Orthop. Assn., Cleve. Yachting Club (life). Office: Univ Hosps of Cleve 11100 Euclid Ave Cleveland OH 44106 Office Phone: 216-844-8372. Business E-Mail: matthew.kraay@uhhospitals.org.

KRABBE, JEROEN AART, actor; b. Amsterdam, Dec. 5, 1944; s. Maarten and Margreet (Reiss) K.; m. Herma van Geemert, Dec. 31, 1965; children: Martyn, Jasper, Jakob. Student, Acad. of Fine Arts, Amsterdam, 1980, Acad. of Dramatic Arts, 1965. Actor Rosenberg (Marion) Office, LA. Actor: (films) Soldier of Orange, 1978, The Fourth Man, 1982 (Best Actor award), No Mercy, 1987, The Living Day Lights, 1987, A World Apart, 1988, Crossing Delancey, 1988, Melancholia, 1989, Till There Was You, 1990, Kafka, 1991, The Prince of Tides, 1991, Robin Hood, 1991, Kakda, King of the Hill, 1992, The Fugitive, 1993, Farinelli, 1994, Immortal Beloved, 1994, Blood of a Poet, 1995, Dangerous Beauty, 1998, The Disappearance of Garcia Lorca, 1997, Ever After, 1998, An Ideal Husband, 1999, The Sky is Falling, 2000, The Discovery of Heaven, 2001, Fogbound, 2002 (also assoc. prodr., dir.), Ocean's Twelve, 2004, Off Screen, 2005, Deuce Bigalo: European Gigolo, 2005, (TV films) Family of Spies, 1990, Robin Hood, 1991, Dynasty: The Reunion, 1991, Stalin, 1992, The Odyssey, 1997, Business for Pleasure, 1997, Only Love, 1998, Jesus, 1999; dir.: (films) The Discovery of Heaven, 2001; dir., prodr. (films) Left Luggage, 1998; autobiography: Jeroen Krabbé-Painter, 2005. Recipient Imagfic '84 award, Madrid, 1984, Vittorio de Sica prize, Sorrento, 1983, Anne Frank prize, Amsterdam, 1985, Rotterdams Golden Heart award, 1986-87, Golden Calf award for life achievement Dutch Film Festival, 1996, The Rembrandt award for life achievement Veronica Broadcasting Corp., 1998, Berlin, Blue Angel award, 1998, Emden, Best Film of Festival; comdr. Order of the Dutch Lion. Office: Marion Rosenberg 8428 Melrose Pl Ste C West Hollywood CA 90069-5308

KRABBE, THOMAS JOSEPH, music educator; b. Appleton, Wis., Apr. 8, 1967; s. Ralph Joseph and Germaine Judith (Jandrin) Krabbe. MusB, St. Norbert Coll., DePere, Wis., 1989; MusM, Ariz. State U., Tempe, 1991. Cert. tchr. Wis. Music tchr. Kyrene Sch. Dist., Tempe, 1991—94, Neenah Sch. Dist., Wis., 1994—98, Verona Area Sch. Dist., Wis., 1998—99, Madison Met. Sch. Dist., Wis., 1999—. Mem.: Pi Kappa Lambda, Delta Epsilon Sigma. Roman Catholic. Avocations: singing, composing, songwriting, arranging. Personal E-mail: tjkrabbe@juno.com.

KRABILL, ROBERT ELMER, osteopathic physician; b. Wayland, Iowa, June 4, 1934; s. Robert H. and Amanda (Wyse) K.; m. Ellen Savage, Sept. 1, 1963; children: Keith Andrew, Angela Kay, Valerie Ann, Kelly Dawn. BS, Iowa Wesleyan Coll., 1961; DO, Kirkville Coll. Osteo. Medicine, 1966. Diplomate Am. Bd. Family Practice. Intern Cuyahoga Falls Gen. Hosp., Ohio, 1966—67, mem. staff, 1967—; gen. practice osteo. medicine Uniontown, Ohio, 1967—. Sec., treas. gen. practice dept. Cuyahoga Falls Gen. Hosp., 1985-86. Named one of Outstanding Young Men of Am., U.S. Jaycees, 1969. Mem. Am. Osteo. Assn., Ohio Osteo. Assn., Am. Coll. Gen. Practitioners Osteo. Medicine and Surgery. Mennonite. Home: 3733 N Vista St NW Uniontown OH 44685-8496 Office: PO Box 399 Uniontown OH 44685-0399

KRACH, DALE JAMES, science educator, athletic trainer; b. Phila., Jan. 12, 1947; s. James and Laura Abel Krach; m. Donna Rae Davis, Aug. 1, 1970; children: Joshua Dale, Nathan Jarrett, Amy Meredith. AB in Psychology, W.Va. U., 1970; MS in Environ. Sci., Drexel U., 1977; Postgrad. in sports medicine, Pa. State U., 1984; Cert. sci. tchr., U. West Ga., 1999, Cert. in ednl. leadership, 2002. Cert. athletic trainer Nat. Athletic Trainers Assn., master athletic adminstr. Nat. Interscholastic Administrators Assn., EMT Pa. Field supervising environ. protection specialist Bucks County Dept. of Health, Doylestown, Pa., 1971—77; health edn. instr., emergency care program asst. Pa. State U., State College, 1977—84; athletic trauma and rehab. specialist PAPP Clinic, Newnan, Ga., 1984—92; sci. tchr., head athletic trainer Northgate H.S., Newnan, 1996—. Sports medicine cons. U.S. Women's Olympic Weightlifting, Marietta, Ga., 1990—95; sports medicine staff 11th Pan Am. Games, Indpls., 1987; asst. chief athletic trainer, EMT Centennial Olympic Games, Atlanta, 1996. Mem. med. staff Boy Scouts of Am. Nat. Jamboree, Fort A.P. Hill, Va., 1989—2001; athletic trainer, mem. med. staff Ga. State Games, Atlanta and Augusta, 1990—2000; 2d v.p. Lambda Omicron chpt. Alpha Phi Omega, Morgantown, W.Va., 1969—70. Named Eagle Scout, Boy Scouts Am., 1963; recipient Silver Beaver award, 1995. Mem.: AAHPERD (corr.), Ga. Athletic Trainers Assn. (corr.), Nat. Interscholastic Athletic Adminstrs. Assn. (corr.), Nat. Athletic Trainers Assn. (corr.), Nat. Assn. Secondary Sch. Prins. (assoc.), Kappa Delta Pi, Eta Sigma Gamma. Avocations: camping, outdoor sports, military memorabilia, reading, travel. Home: 145 Marsha Way Sharpsburg GA 30277-3377 Office: Northgate HS 3220 Fischer Rd Newnan GA 30265 Home Phone: 770-251-9658; Office Phone: 770-463-5585. Office Fax: 770-463-4982. Personal E-mail: dkrach@charter.net. E-mail: dale.krach@cowetaschools.org.

KRACKE, ROBERT RUSSELL, lawyer; b. Decatur, Ga., Feb. 27, 1938; s. Roy Rachford and Virginia Carolyn (Minter) K.; m. Barbara Anne Pilgrim, Dec. 18, 1965; children: Shannon Ruth, Robert Russell, Rebecca Anne, Susan Lynn. Student, Birmingham So. Coll.; BA, Samford U., 1962; JD, Cumberland Sch. Law, 1965. Bar: Ala. 1965, U.S. Tax Ct. 1971, U.S. Supreme Ct. 1971. Individual practice law, Birmingham, Ala., 1965—; founding ptnr. Kracke and Thompson, Birmingham, 1980—. Editor: Birmingham Bar Bull, 1974—; mem. bd. editors: Ala. Lawyer, 1980-86, 2003—07; contbr. articles to profl. jours. Coordinating com. Nat. Conv. of ARC of U.S., 1999—; pres., treas. Nov. Organ Recital Series, 1999—, chief adminstrv. officer, 1970—99; pres. Housing Agy. Retarded Citizens; pres. Ala. chpt. Nat. Voluntary Health Agys., 1988—89; exec. com. legal counsel Birmingham Opera Theatre, 1983—95; active Dem. Exec. Com., 1970—98; deacon Ind. Presbyn. Ch., Birmingham, 1973—76, elder, 1999—2003, trustee I.P.C. Found., 2004—, pres. adult choir, 1968—99, bd. dirs., Ala. Assn. Retarded Citizens, Jefferson County Assn. Retarded Citizens, 1983—91, pres.-elect, 1994—96, pres., 1996—98; bd. dirs., founding pres. Ala. chpt. Juvenile Diabetes Rsch. Found. Internat.; bd. dirs. ARC of Ala., 1996—98, Found.of ARC; v.p., bd. dirs. Mental Retardation/Devel. Disabilities Health Care Authority of Jefferson County, 2003—. With USNR, 1955—61. Mem.: ABA (award merit law day 1976), US Supreme Ct. Hist. Soc., Am. Judicature Soc., Ala. Bar Assn., Birmingham Bar Assn. (exec. com., law libr. chmn., law day 1976, bull., history and archives com.), Birmingham-Jefferson Hist. Soc. (bd. dirs., editor newsletter), Ala. Hist. Assn., So. Hist. Assn., Rotary (pres. Shades Valley club 1988—89, sec. dist. 6860 1990—91, dir. 2005—, dist. coord. comm., bd. dirs., sec. ednl. found., Paul Harris fellow), The Club, Sigma Alpha Epsilon, Phi Alpha Delta (pres. chpt. 1964—65). Home: 4410 Briar Glen Dr Birmingham AL 35243-1743 Office: Kracke and Thompson 2204 Lakeshore Dr Ste 306 Lakeshore Park Plz Birmingham AL 35209 Business E-Mail: rkracke@ktlegal.com.

KRACOV, DANIEL A., lawyer; b. NYC, June 30, 1963; BA magna cum laude, Univ. Md., 1985; JD, Univ. Va., 1988. Bar: Va. 1988, DC 1989. Ptnr., Food & Drug Law, Health Care practices, dep. dir. Public Policy & Regulatory dept. Patton Boggs LLP, Washington. Mem. editl. bd. Va. Jour. Internat. Law; contbr. articles to profl. jours. Home: Patton Boggs LLP 2550 M St NW Washington DC 20037-1350 Office Phone: 202-457-5623. Office Fax: 202-457-6315. Business E-Mail: dkracov@pattonboggs.com.

KRAEHE, ENNO EDWARD, history professor; b. St. Louis, Dec. 9, 1921; s. Enno and Amelia Roth (Henckler) K.; m. Mary Alice Eggleston, May 25, 1946; children: Laurence Adams, Claudia. BA, U. Mo., 1943, MA, 1944; PhD, U. Minn., 1948. Instr. history U. Del., 1946-48; asst. prof. history U. Ky., 1948-50, asso. prof., 1950-63, prof., 1963-64, U. N.C., 1964-68, U. Va., 1968-71, Commonwealth prof., 1971-77, William W. Corcoran prof., 1977-91, William W. Corcoran prof. emeritus, 1991—. Vis. prof. U. Mo., 1946, U. Va., 1955, U. Tex., 1955, U. Minn., 1963; U.S. Dept. State Specialist in, Germany, 1953; mem. regional selection com. Woodrow Wilson fellowship Found., 1959-60; mem. Sr. Fulbright-Hayes History Screening Com., 1970-73 Author: Metternich's German Policy Volume I: The Contest with Napoleon 1799-1814, 1963; author: Volume II: The Congress of Vienna, 1814-1815, 1983; editor: The Metternich Controversy, 1971; mem. editl. bd. Ctrl. European History, 1967-72, Austrian History Yearbook, 1969-74; contbr. entries and articles to encys. and hist. jours., U.S. and Europe. Active Charlottesville Com. on Fgn. Rels.; mem. Nat. Coordinating Com. for Promotion of History, mem. policy bd., 1985-88; mem. Met. Opera Guild, Friends of Ky. Ctr. Recipient Best Book award Phi Alpha Theta; Fulbright scholar Austria, 1952-53; Guggenheim fellow, 1960-61, Am. Coun. Learned Socs. fellow, 1969, 73, resident fellow Rockefeller Ctr. in Bellagio, 1983; grantee NEH, 1973, 80, 83, NEH Libr. Preservation Screening Com., 1988 Mem. Am. Hist. Assn., Conf. Group for Ctrl. European History (mem. exec. bd. 1966-68), German Studies Assn. (mem. exec. coun. 1985—), So. Hist. Assn. (chmn. European sect. 1974, 75, Disting. Svc. award European sect.), Charlottesville Com. on Fgn. Rels., Colonnade Club, Blue Ridge Swimming Club, Phi Beta Kappa. Episcopalian. Home: 500 Crestwood Dr Apt 2107 Charlottesville VA 22903-4879

KRAEMER, ALFRED ROBERT, school librarian; b. NYC, Dec. 25, 1948; s. Philip George and Bernadette (Klein) K.; children: Sarah McCall, Philip Joseph. BA, Beloit Coll., 1973; MSLS, U. N.C., 1978; MA, N.C. State U., 1983; PhD, U. N.C., Greensboro, 1997. Cert. pub. libr., N.C.; lic. elem. and secondary tchr., N.C. Libr. asst. Duke Med. Ctr., Durham, N.C., 1976-78; English tchr. Patterson Sch., Lenoir, N.C., 1978-80; asst. prof. English St. Mary's Coll., Raleigh, N.C., 1980-88; asst. dir. tchg. fellows N.C. State U., Raleigh, 1989-92; sch. libr. Guilford County Schs., Greensboro, N.C., 1995--. Author: Malory's Grail Seekers and 15th Century English Hagiography, 1999. With USN, 1967-70. Mem. MLA, ALA. Democrat. Episcopalian. E-mail: jack_kraemer@yahoo.com.

KRAEMER, HARRY M. JANSEN, JR., investment and former medical products executive; BA in Math. and Econs. summa cum laude, Lawrence U., Wis., 1977; M in fin. and acctg., Northwestern U. Kellogg Sch., 1979. CPA Ill. With N.W. Industries, Bank of Am.; dir. corp. devel. Baxter Internat. Inc., Deerfield, Ill., 1982, various positions in domestic and internat. ops., sr. v.p., CFO, 1993-97, mem. Office Chief Exec., 1995—, pres., 1997, CEO, 1999—2004, bd. dirs., 1995, chmn., 2000; exec. ptnr. Madison Dearborn Partners, Chgo., 2005—. Bd. dirs. Sci. Applications Internat. Corp., Evanston Northwestern Healthcare; mem. Bus. Roundtable, Healthcare Leadership Coun. Bd. trustees, deans' adv. bd. Northwestern U. J.L. Kellogg Grad. Sch. Mgmt.; bd. trustees Lawrence U. Recipient Schaffner award, Northwestern U. Kellogg Sch., 1996. Mem.: Chgo. Club, Comml. Club Chgo. Office: Madison Dearborn Partners 9 W 57th St # 42 New York NY 10019-2701

KRAEMER, HELENA ANTOINETTE CHMURA, psychiatry educator; Degree, Stanford U., 1963. With Stanford U., 1964—, prof. biostats. in psychiatry, Dept. Psychiatry and Behavioral Scis., 1991—, mem. Comprehensive Cancer Ctr. Mem. editorial bd. Jour. Child & Adolescent Psychopharmacology. Co-author: How Many Subjects?: Statistical Power Analysis in Rsch., 1987, Evaluating Medical Tests: Objective & Quantitative Guidelines, 1992, To Your Health: How to Understand What Research Tells Us About Risk, 2005. Recipient Harvard award in psychiat. epidemiology and biostats., 2001. Mem.: Inst. Medicine. Office: Stanford U Dept

Psychiatry and Behavioral Scis 300 Pasteur Dr Stanford CA 94305 also: Stanford Comprehensive Cancer Ctr 875 Blake Wilbur Dr Stanford CA 94305 Business E-Mail: hck@stanford.edu.

KRAEMER, IRA B., symphony conductor; b. Newark, Mar. 25, 1942; s. Alex Kraemer and Rae Warshawski; m. Janet Lynda Ericson, July 7, 1974; children: Erik, Kris, Daryll, Lyndyn. Advanced conducting studies with, Pierre Monteux, 1960—61, Carl Bamberger, 1962—66; BS in Conducting, Mannes Coll. Music, NYC, 1966; PhD in Music, Buxton U., London, 1994. Music dir., conductor Little Symphony of Newark, 1965—69, Suburban Symphony, Cranford, NJ, 1979—80, Summit Symphony, NJ, 1980—83, Performing Arts Ensemble, Red Bank, NJ, 1991—2002, Young Players Philharmonic, Somerset, NJ, 2001—. Composer: (saxophone quartet) Petite Suite, 1987 (world broadcast, 1988), (for early electronic musical instruments) Suite for Ondes Martenot, Harp, Celeste and String Orch., 2002, (viola sonata) Sonata for Viola & Piano, 1988. Supporter Young Players Philharmonic, Somerset, 2001—. Recording grantee, Union County Cultural Commn., 1984. Mem.: ASCAP. Avocation: antiques. Office: 467 Grant Ave Scotch Plains NJ 07076 Office Phone: 908-322-4469. Personal E-mail: ira@eclipse.net. E-mail: info@ypphilharmonic.org.

KRAEMER, KENNETH LEO, architect, urban planner, educator; b. Plain, Wis., Oct. 29, 1936; s. Leo Adam and Lucy Rose (Bauer) K.; m. Norine Florence, June 13, 1959; children: Kurt Randall, Kim Rene. BArch, U. Notre Dame, Ind., 1959; MS in City and Regional Planning, U. So. Calif., 1964, M of Pub. Adminstrn., 1965, PhD, 1967. From instr. to asst. prof. U. So. Calif., LA, 1965-67; from asst. prof. to rsch. prof. U. Calif., Merage Sch. Bus., Irvine, 1967—, dir. Pub. Policy Rsch. Orgn., 1974-92, dir. Ctr. Rsch. Info. Tech. and Orgns., 1992—2007, dir. Ctr. Study Personal Computing Industry, 2004—, Taco Bell chair in IT for mgmt. Cons. Office of Tech. Assessment, Washington, 1980, 84-85; pres. Irvine Research Corp., 1978—. Author: Management of Information Systems, 1980, Computers and Politics, 1982, Dynamics of Computing, 1983, People and Computers, 1985, Modeling as Negotiating, 1986, Data Wars, 1987, Wired Cities, 1987, Managing Information Systems, 1989, Asia's Computer Challenge, 1998, Globalization of E-Commerce, 2006. Mem. Blue Ribbon Data Processing Com., Orange County, Calif., 1973, 79-80, Telecomm. Adv. Bd., Sacramento, 1987-92. Fellow Assn. for Info. Sys.; mem. Am. Soc. for Pub. Adminstrn. (Disting. Research award 1985), Internat. Conf. on Info. Systems, Am. Planning Assn., Assn. for Computing Machinery, Notre Dame Club. Democrat. Roman Catholic. Office: U Calif Ctr Rsch Info Tech & Orgns Berkley Pl N Ste 3200 Irvine CA 92697-0001 E-mail: kkraemer@uci.edu.

KRAEMER, LILLIAN ELIZABETH, retired lawyer; b. NYC, Apr. 18, 1940; d. Frederick Joseph and Edmee Elizabeth (de Watteville) K.; m. John W. Vincent, June 22, 1962 (div. 1964). BA, Swarthmore Coll., 1961; JD, U. Chgo., 1964. Bar: N.Y. 1965, U.S. Dist. Ct. (so. dist.) N.Y. 1967, U.S. Dist. Ct. (ea. dist.) N.Y. 1971. Assoc. Cleary, Gottlieb, Steen & Hamilton, NYC, 1964-71, Simpson Thacher & Bartlett, NYC, 1971-74, ptnr., 1974-99, of counsel, 2000—06; ret., 2007. Mem. vis. com. U. Chgo. Law Sch., 1991-94; bd. dirs. Legal Momentum. Bd. mgrs. Swarthmore Coll., 1993—2005; warden St. Francis Episcopal Ch., Stamford, Conn., 2001-05; bd. dirs. Turtle Bay Music Sch., 2005—. Fellow Am. Coll. Bankruptcy; mem. Lawyers Alliance for N.Y. (bd. dirs. 1996-2001, co-chair capital campaign 2003-05), Assn. Bar City N.Y. (mem. various coms.), Order of Coif, Phi Beta Kappa. Democrat. Avocations: travel, reading, word games. Home: 2 Beekman Pl New York NY 10022-8058 Address: 46 Saddle Rock Rd Stamford CT 06902 E-mail: lkraemer@stblaw.com.

KRAEMER, MICHAEL FREDERICK, lawyer; b. NYC, Jan. 21, 1947; s. Jerome W. and Honey (Dunner) K.; m. Ross Shepard, June 21, 1970; 1 child, Jordan Harriet. BA cum laude, Amherst Coll., 1969; JD, U. Pa., 1972. Bar: Pa. 1972, N.J. 1973, Mass. 2003, RI 2003, U.S. Dist. Ct. (ea. dist.) Pa. 1972, U.S. Dist. Ct. N.J. 1973, U.S. Ct. Appeals (3d cir.) 1974, U.S. Ct. Appeals (2d cir.) 1980, U.S. Ct. Appeals (4th and 7th cirs.) 1981, U.S. Ct. Appeals (6th cir.) 1990, U.S. Ct. Appeals (1st cir.) 2001, U.S. Dist. Ct. Mass. 2003, U.S. Dist. Ct. RI 2003. Assoc. Astor & Weiss, Phila., 1972-75, Pechner, Sacks, Dorfman, Rosen & Richardson, Phila., 1975-76; ptnr. Kleinbard, Bell & Brecker, Phila., 1976-85, White and Williams LLP, Phila., 1985—2002, Hinckley, Allen & Snyder LLP, Providence, 2002—. Bd. dirs. Ctr. City Residents Assn., Phila., 1976-78; Served to 2d lt. USAR, 1972-73. Recipient Disting. Svc. award Amherst Coll. Alumni Coun., 1994. Mem. Amherst Alumni Assn. Phila. (pres. 1977-79), Indsl. Rels. Rsch. Assn., Univ. Club, Providence. Office: Hinckley Allen & Snyder LLP 1500 Fleet Ctr Providence RI 02903

KRAEMER, PHILIPP, manufacturing company executive, inventor; b. Hahn, Germany, Jan. 17, 1931; s. George Heinrich and Anna Erna K.; m. Rosemarie Sandner, June 2, 1956; children: Lynda, Irene, Sandra. Student vocat. sch., Darmstadt, Germany. Tool and die maker, 1956-61; tool maker Quality Tool & Massey Ferguson, 1961-64; founder Kraemer Tool & Mfg. Co. Ltd., Brampton, Ont., Can., 1964, pres., gen. mgr. Mem. Pollution Control Assn., Can. Mfg. Assn. Lutheran. Patentee oil-sand separator, 8 other patents; co-inventor Sound Perfection, Spadafora violine bow-guide. Home: 34 Kendleton Dr Rexdale ON Canada M9V 1V4 Office: Devon Rd Brampton ON Canada L6T 5A4 Office Phone: 905-458-0400. E-mail: p.kraemer@kraemertool.com.

KRAETZER, MARY C., sociologist, educator, consultant; b. NYC, Sept. 12, 1943; d. Kenneth G. and Adele L. Kraetzer; m. Kestas E. Silunas. AB, Coll. New Rochelle, 1965; MA, Fordham U., 1967, PhD, 1975. Instr. Mercy Coll., Dobbs Ferry, NY, 1969—70, asst. prof., 1970—75, assoc. prof., 1975—79, prof., 1979—, program dir. behavioral sci., 1997—, program dir. MPA program in health svc. mgmt., 2000—01, program dir. grad. programs in health svc. mgmt., 2001—. Rsch. asst. Fordham U., Bronx, N.Y., 1965-67, tchg. asst., 1967-68, tchg. fellow, 1968-69, adj. instr., 1971-75, adj. asst. prof., 1975-76; adj. assoc. prof. L.I. U. Grad. br. Campus Mercy Coll., 1976-79, adj. prof., 1979-81, coord. MS in Cmty. Health Program, 1976-81, adj. prof. Westchester campus, 1988-94; rsch. cons. elem. schoolbooks Nat. Coun. Chs./Ch. Women United Task Force on Global Consciousness, N.Y.C., 1971; mem. adv. com. edn. and society div. Nat. Coun. Chs., 1975-78; mem. evaluation team Middle States Assn. Colls. and Secondary Schs. Commn. on Higher Edn., Monmouth, N.J., 1976; presenter in field. Contbr. chapters to books, articles to profl. jours. Recipient Tchg. Excellence award Mercy Coll., 1999; Bd. Regents scholar, 1961-65, 65-69; Fordham U. scholar, 1965-68; Fordham U. fellow, 1968-69; Mercy Coll. grantee, 1984, 85, 86, 88, 92; Mercy Coll. Faculty Devel. grantee, 1999; NSF summer intern, 1967. Mem. APHA (conf. presenter), Am. Sociol. Assn. (presenter). Office: Mercy Coll 555 Broadway Dobbs Ferry NY 10522-1134 Office Phone: 914-674-7341. Business E-Mail: mkraetzer@mercy.edu.

KRAEUTLER, ERIC, lawyer; b. Newark, Oct. 9, 1954; s. John Howard and Marie (Bevere) K.; m. Jacqueline Maykranz, May 18, 1985; children: Matthew John, Caroline Ann. BA, Princeton U., 1976; JD, U. Va., 1980. Bar: Pa., US Dist Ct. (ea. dist.) Pa., US Ct. Appeals (3d cir.), US Ct. Appeals (9th cir.), US Ct. Appeals (fed. cir.), US Disst. Ct. (no. dist.) Ind., US Supreme Ct. Assoc. Morgan, Lewis & Bockius, LLP, Phila., 1980-84, 1987-90; ptnr. Morgan, Lewis & Bockius, Phila., 1990—, co-leader, intellectual property litigation practice, 1999—, chair firmwide profl. recruiting com., 2000—; asst. U.S. atty. U.S. Atty.'s Office, Phila., 1984-87; spl. dep. atty. gen. Commonwealth of Pa., 1992-94. Trustee Princeton Tower Club, 1980—, Nat. Multiple Sclerosis Soc., 1993—2006, sec., 1994—96, vice chmn., 1996—98, chmn., 1998—2000; mem. Swarthmore Zoning Hearing Bd., Pa., 2003—, chair, 2007—; mem. Princeton Alumni Coun., 1984—87, Com. of Seventy, 2001—, exec. com., 2002—. Mem. ABA, Fed. Bar Assn., Phila. Bar Assn., Intellectual Property Owner Assn. Presbyterian. Avocation: running. Home: 35 Wellesley Rd Swarthmore PA 19081-1232 Office: Morgan Lewis & Bockius LLP 1701 Market St Philadelphia PA 19103-2903 Home Phone: 610-543-3893; Office Phone: 215-963-4840. Business E-Mail: ekraeutler@morganlewis.com.

KRAFKA, MARY BAIRD, lawyer; b. Ottumwa, Iowa, Jan. 4, 1942; d. Glenn Leroy and Alice Erna (Krebill) B.; m. Jerry Lee Krafka, Oct. 14, 1962; children: Lisa Krafka Piper, Gregory D., Jeffrey A., Amy Krafka Pittman. BA in English and Human Rels., William Penn Coll., Oskaloosa, Iowa, 1990; JD, U. Iowa, 1993. Bar: Iowa 1993. Vol. lawyer Legal Svcs. Corp., Ottumwa, 1993-94; pvt. practice, Ottumwa, 1994—. Mem. AAUW, ABA, Iowa Bar Assn., Wapello County Bar Assn., PEO Sisterhood (Iowa chpt. HC 1973). Lutheran. Avocations: sewing, reading, walking, running, people. Home: 931 W Mary St Ottumwa IA 52501-4904 Office: 101 S Market St Ste 203 Ottumwa IA 52501-2933 Office Phone: 641-683-7515. Business E-Mail: mbkrafka@lisco.com.

KRAFT, ARTHUR, dean; b. Eden, NY, May 7, 1944; s. Arthur Brauer and Mary Jane (Forti) K.; m. Joan Marie Brown, Sept. 3, 1966; children: Arthur G., Stephen Michael, Leigh Judith. BS, St. Bonaventure U., 1966; MA, SUNY, Buffalo, 1969, PhD, 1970. Asst. prof. Ohio U., Athens, 1969—72, assoc. prof., 1972—75; prof. U. Nebr., Lincoln, 1975—77, assoc. dean Coll. Bus., 1977—83; dean Coll. Bus. and Econs. W.Va. U., Morgantown, 1983—87; dean sch. bus. Rutgers U., New Brunswick, NJ, 1987—93; dean Sch. Mgmt. Ga. Inst. Tech., Atlanta, 1993—97; dean Coll. Commerce, Charles H. Kellstadt Grad Sch. Bus. DePaul U., Chgo., 1997—2005; dean Robert J. and Carolyn A. Waltos, Jr. chair in bus. and econs. George L. Argyros Sch. Bus. and Econs. Chapman U., Orange, Calif., 2006—. Mem. pension adv. com. Monongalia County Hosp., Morgantown, 1985-87., 1985—87. Recipient NASA fellowship Stanford U., 1973, fellow Sears-Roebuck Fellowship Found., Washington, 1974-75; named Outstanding Young Individual Jaycees, Lincoln, 1978 Mem. Am. Econ. Assn., Am. Assembly of Collegiate Schs. of Bus. (chmn. bd. 2006-07, visitation com. 1977—, continuing accreditation com. 1987, bus. accreditation com. 1995—), North Ctrl. Assn. (evaluator 1986-87), Beta Gamma Sigma. Avocations: trivia, sports. Office: Chapman Univ George L Argyros Sch Business Economics Beckman Hall One University Dr Orange CA 92866 Office Phone: 714-628-2839. Personal E-mail: artkraft07@yahoo.com.

KRAFT, DONALD EUGENE, architecture and engineering company executive; b. Rochester, NY, Aug. 10, 1929; s. Nicholas Raymond and Rosella Theresa (Miller) K.; m. Rosemarie Ursula Kraus, April 24, 1965; children: Eva Maria, Christian Martin, Donald Alexander Nicholas. Student, U. Rochester, NYC, 1948—51; BS in Engring., Bus. Adminstrn., Econs., Empire State Coll., 1977. Registered profl. engr., N.Y. Engr. stds. dept. Kodak Park, 1950-52; sales rep. C.A. Brewer, Inc., 1952-56; civil and san. engr. design Lozier Engrs. and Morrison & Morrison, 1956-61; v.p. gen. mgr. Profl. Chem. Corp. Dental Equipment, 1962-65; project engr. new product devel. Caldwell Mfg. Co., Inc., 1965-71; applications engr. Schlegel Corp., 1971-72; pres. Don Kraft Co., Penfield, NY, 1973—; sales, design, R&D and project mgr. turnkey automated prodn. equipment Alliance Tool Corp., 1978-81; gen. ptnr. Arens Assoc. Architecture and Engring. Svcs., Penfield, NY, 1986—. Cons. in field. Patentee in hydraulics, pneumatics, dental equipment, window hardware, weather seals, automotive & bus. equipment. With USN, 1947-48, USNR, 1947, 48-49, 54-58. Mem. Rochester C. of C., Civic Music Assn., Meml. Art Gallery, Rochester Yacht Club. Republican. Roman Catholic. Achievements include beyond state-of-the-art products, (pumps, meters, scales, dental equipment, window hardware, weather seals, gas balance, copiers, business equipment, electronic packaging), automated production equipment & systems (automotive parts, hand saws, military equipment), trisected an angle using only a straight edge and a compass, solving a 2400 year old problem, and working on gravity machine research and development and up-to-date formulas. Office: 1930 Harris Rd Penfield NY 14526-1822 Office Phone: 585-377-9190. Home Fax: 585-377-7505. E-mail: arens@bluefrog.com.

KRAFT, GEORGE HOWARD, physician, educator; b. Columbus, Ohio, Sept. 27, 1936; s. Glen Homer and Helen Winner (Howard) K.; children: Jonathan Ashbrook, Susannah Mary. AB, Harvard U., 1958; MD, Ohio State U., 1963, MS, 1967. Diplomate Am. Bd. Phys. Medicine and Rehab. (subspecialty in spinal cord injury medicine), Am. Bd. Electrodiagnostic Medicine. Intern U. Calif. Hosp., San Francisco, 1963—64, resident in phys. medicine and rehab., 1964—65, Ohio State U., Columbus, 1965—67; assoc. U. Pa. Med. Sch., Phila., 1968—69; asst. prof. U. Wash., Seattle, 1969—72, assoc. prof., 1972—76, prof., 1976—, Alvord prof. MS rsch., 2005—; chief of staff U. Wash. Med. Ctr., Seattle, 1993—95. Dir. electrodiagnostic medicine U. Wash. Hosp., 1987—, dir. Multiple Sclerosis Ctr., 1982—; co-dir. Muscular Dystrophy Clinic, 1974—; bd. dirs. Am. Bd. Electrodiagnostic Medicine, 1993-2000, chmn., 1996-2000 Co-author: Chronic Disease and Disability, 1994, Living with Multiple Sclerosis: A Wellness Approach, 2000, The M.S. Workbook, 2006; cons. editor: Phys. Medicine and Rehab. Clinics, 1990—, EEG and Clin. Neurophysiology, 1992-96; assoc. editor Jour. Neurol. Rehab. and Neurol. Repair, 1988-2000, Muscle and Nerve, 1998-2000; contbr. articles to profl. jours. Sci. peer rev. com. C Nat. Multiple Sclerosis Soc., N.Y.C., 1990-96, chmn., 1993-96, med. adv. bd., 1991—; bd. sponsors Wash. Physicians for Social Responsibility, Seattle, 1986—. Rsch. grantee Rehab. Svcs. Adminstrn., 1976-81, Nat. Inst. Handicapped Rsch., 1984-88, Nat. Multiple Sclerosis Soc., 1990-92, 94-95, 2005—Nat. Inst. Disability and REhab. Rsch., 1998—. Fellow Am. Acad. Phys. Medicine and Rehab. (pres. 1984-85, Zeiter award 1991, Krusen award 2002); mem. Am. Assn. Electrodiagnostic Medicine (pres. 1982-83. Lifetime Achievement award 2004), Assn. Acad. Physiatrists (pres. 1980-81), Am. Acad. Clin. Neurophysiology (pres. 1995-97), Am. Acad. Neurology, Internat. Rehab. Medicine Assn., Alpha Omega Alpha. Episcopalian. Office: Dept Rehab Med U Wash PO Box 956490 Seattle WA 98195 Home Phone: 206-467-0206; Office Phone: 206-543-7272.

KRAFT, GERALD, economist; b. Detroit, July 1, 1935; s. Jule and Shirley (Schwartz) K.; m. Sandra Doris Johnson, Aug. 7, 1955; children: Michael Stanton, Lynn Barbara. Student, U. Chgo., 1951-52; BA, Wayne U., 1955; MA, Harvard U., 1957. Mng. dir. Harvard U. Statis. Lab., Cambridge, Mass., 1957-58; prin. United Rsch. Inc., Cambridge, 1958-61; sr. rsch. assoc. Sys. Analysis and Rsch. Corp., Boston, 1961-64, Regional and Urban Planning Implementation, Inc., Cambridge, 1964-65; pres., CEO, chmn. Charles River Assocs. Inc., Boston, 1965-92; CEO The GSK Group, Ltd., 1994—; chmn. Modern Broadcast Prodns. Lectr. MIT, Harvard U., U. Pa., Northeastern U.; mem. planning com., dir. Maritime Transp. Rsch. Bd., NRC, 1976-79; mem. Group I Coun., mem. coms. Transp. Rsch. Bd., 1977-80, NRC v.p. program pres. Transp. Rsch. Forum, 1977; chmn. 2nd Internat. Tungsten Symposium, 1982. Author: (with others) The Role of Transportation in Regional Economic Development, 1971; co-author: Report of Task Force on Transp. to Sci. Adv. panel to Com. on Pub. Works, U.S. Ho. of Reps, 1974; contbr. articles to profl. jours. Trustee, dir., fin. com., exec. com., former chmn. budget subcom., asst. treas. Beth Israel Hosp.; past dir. Beth Israel Corp.; trustee, fin. com., patient care and quality com., audit and compliance com. Beth Israel Deaconess Med. Ctr.; past dir. Med. Care Boston, Inc.; fin. com. Commonwell, Inc.; mem. Harvard U. Grad. Sch. Arts & Scis., adv. com. grad. student life Harvard U.; adv. bd. Medifile, Inc.; mem. allocation subcom. United Way. Mem. AAAS, Am. Econ. Assn., Econometric Soc., Am. Statis. Assn., Inst. Mgmt. Scis., Ops. Rsch. Soc. Am. (Boston Branch), Internat. Wine and Food Soc. (past treas., past pres., past chmn.), Confrerie des Chevaliers du Tastevin, Sous-Commanderie de Mass.(officier commandeur), Grand Senechal (past chef du protocole), Harvard Club Boston, Univ. Club, Rotary (past bd. dirs., trustee student aid fund, Paul Harris fellow), Fine Wine Coun. Mass. (bd. dirs.), Beefeater Club, Chaine des Rotisseurs (vice echanson), L'ordre Mondial, Confraternita Enogastronomica Toscana, Phi Beta Kappa. Home: 60 Scotch Pine Rd Weston MA 02493-1405 Home Phone: 781-237-2427. Business E-Mail: gkraft@gskgroup.com.

KRAFT, HENRY ROBERT, lawyer; b. LA, Apr. 27, 1946; s. Sylvester and Freda (Shochat) K.; m. Terry Kraft, July 21, 1968; children: Diana, Kevin. BA in History, San Fernando Valley State Coll., 1968; JD, U. So. Calif., 1971. Bar: Calif. 1972, U.S. Dist. Ct. (ctrl. dist.) Calif. 1985, U.S. Ct. Appeals (9th cir., fed. cir.) 1998, U.S. Dist. Ct. (so., ctrl. and no. dists.) Calif 1998. Dep. pub. defender San Bernardino (Calif.) County, 1972-78; pvt. practice, Victorville, Calif., 1979-96; city atty. Victorville, 1987—2002; of counsel Best Best & Krieger LLP, Victorville, 1996-98; assoc. Parker, Covert & Chidester, Tustin, Calif., 1999-2000; ptnr. Parker & Covert LLP, Tustin, 2000—. Atty. City of Barstow, Calif., 1980-97; instr. Victor Valley Coll., Victorville, 1986—. Atty. Barstow Community Hosp., 1980-88. Mem. FBA, San Bernardino Bar Assn. (fee dispute com., jud. evaluation com.), High Desert Bar Assn. (pres., v.p., sec. 1979-81), Calif. Soc. Health Care Attys., League Calif. Cities, Am. Arbitration Assn. (panel neutral arbitrators). Democrat. Jewish. Avocations: bicycling, travel, wine enthusiast. Office Phone: 714-573-0900. Business E-Mail: hkraft@parkercovert.com.

KRAFT, IRVIN ALAN, psychiatrist; b. Huntington, W.Va., Nov. 20, 1921; m. Shirley Goldin, July 4, 1951; children: Karen Kraft Pennebaker, Joanna Kraft Katz, Elizabeth Kraft Schmachtenberger, Mark. BS, NYU, 1943, MD, 1949. Diplomate Am. Bd. Psychiatry and Neurology, Am. Bd. Child Psychiatry. Chief psychiatry Tex. Children's Hosp., Houston, 1958-65; prof. mental health U. Tex. Sch. Pub. Health, Houston, 1975-91; emeritus prof. mental health U. Tex., Houston, 1991—; assoc. clin. prof. pediatrics Baylor Coll. Medicine, Houston, 1977—, clin. prof. psychiatry, 1977—, U. Tex. Sch. Medicine, Houston, Galveston. Med. dir. Tex. Inst. Family Psychiatry, Houston, 1964-79; dir. Houston Heart Assn., 1969-70; med. dir. Adult Adolescent Rehab. Ctr., Houston, 1982-85; chmn. subcom. Mental Health Needs Coun., Houston, 1988-89. Author: (with others) Adolescent Group Psychotherapy, 1989, Bibliography of Child and Adolescent Psychiatry, 1990; co-editor: Child Group Psychotherapy: Future Tense, 1986; mem. editorial bd. Jour. Child and Adolescent Group Therapy, 1989—. Mem. drug prevention com. High Sch. for Health Professions, Houston, 1989-90; mem. Tex. House Rep. Com. on Edn., 1974. N.Y. Acad. Scis. fellow, 1971—; recipient Gold award Am. Acad. Pediatrics, 1969, cert. of award Am. Group Psychotheraphy Assn., 1970. Fellow Am. Acad. Child and Adolescent Psychiatry (life), Am. Group Psychotherapy Assn. (life), Am. Acad. Psychoanalysis (life), Am. Psychiat. Assn. (life), Houston Group Psychotherapy Soc. (life), Southwestern Group Psychotherapy Soc. (life), Houston Psychiat. Soc. (life), Tex. Soc. Psychiat. Physicians (life), Tex. Soc. of Child and Adolescent Psychiatry (life), Am. Orthopsychiatry Assn. (life). Home: 2423 Gramercy Blvd Houston TX 77030-3105 Office: 4545 Post Oak Pl # 375 Houston TX 77027 Office Phone: 713-668-1971. Office Fax: 713-668-2555. Personal E-mail: irvkraft@houston.rr.com.

KRAFT, JAMES ALLEN, lawyer; b. Seattle, Mar. 8, 1955; s. Warren Earl and Barbara Anne (Allen) K.; m. Dominique Patricia Posy, Aug. 4, 1984. AB in East Asian Studies cum laude, Harvard U., 1978, JD, 1982. Bars: N.Y. 1982, Wash. 1984. Assoc. Milbank, Tweed, Hadley & Mc Cloy, NYC, 1982-84; assoc. corp. counsel Burlington Northern, Inc., Seattle, 1984-88; sr. corp. counsel Burlington Resources, Inc., Seattle, 1988, asst. v.p. law, 1989; v.p. law and corp. affairs Plum Creek Timber Co., Seattle, 1989—2002, sr. v.p., gen. counsel and sec., 2002—. Contbr. articles to profl. jours. Mem. bd. trustees Pacific Northwest Ballet Co., Seattle, 1986—. Mem. ABA, Wash. State Bar Assn., N.Y. State Bar Assn., Japan Am. Soc. State Wash., (trustee 1987—). Clubs: Lincoln's Inn Soc. (Cambridge, Mass.) (co-chmn. 1981-82). Republican. Avocations: squash, gardening. Office: Plum Creek Timber Co 999 3rd Ave Ste 4300 Seattle WA 98104-4096

KRAFT, JOHN, dean; BS in Math., St. Bonaventure U., 1966; MA in Economics, U. Pitts., 1970, PhD in Economics, 1971. Asst. prof. economics U. Fla., 1970—74, prof. fin., 1980—86, assoc. dean, dir. Bur. Econ. and Bus. Rsch.; prof. fin., dean Ariz. State U. Coll. Bus., 1986—90; prof. U. Fla. Warrington Coll. Bus., Gainsville, Fla., 1990—, dean, 1990—. Dir. Inroads/Phoenix, Economics Club Phoenix, Ariz. State Univ. Rsch. Ctr., Univ. Fla. Found., Divsn. Sponsored Rsch. Econ. Policy Fellow, Brookings Instn., 1970—73. Office: U Fla Warrington Coll Bus 100 Bryan Hall PO Box 117150 Gainesville FL 32611-7150 Office Phone: 352-392-2397. E-mail: john.kraft@cba.ufl.edu.

KRAFT, KENNETH HOUSTON, JR., insurance agency executive; b. Chgo., Apr. 2, 1934; s. Kenneth Houston and Elizabeth (Preston) K.; m. Ruth Neely, Aug. 11, 1956 (div. Sept. 1979); children: Katherine Elizabeth, Carolyn Ruth, Kenneth Houston III; m. Kathleen Hartung, Mar. 16, 1985. BS in Fin., Purdue U., 1956. Pres., chmn. bd. Kraft Ins. Agy., Inc., Winter Park, Fla., 1960—, KHK Fin. Corp., Winter Park, 1974—; chmn. bd. Echo Pub. Co., Sulfur Springs, Tex., 1970—2000; owner Kraft Cattle Co., 1981—86. Sr. mem., exec., fin., comml. loan, audit and exam. coms. Barnett Bank Cen. Fla., Orlando, 1965-98; founding dirs. Goodings Groceries of Fla., Altamonte Springs, Fla., Schwartz Electro-Optics, Orlando, Internat. Laser Sys., Orlando, KHK Fin. Corp., Carson City, Nev., Princeton Fin. Corp., Orlando, Falcon Aviation, Orlando, TV-9 Inc., ABC affiliate, Orlando, First Ctrl. Corp., Orlando, Inglewood Daily News, Inglewood Citizen Co., LA. Bd. dirs. Winter Park C. of C., 1965-70, Orange County chpt. ARC, Orlando, 1963-65, Orange County chpt. United Way, Winter Park, 1970-72, Winter Park YMCA, 1972-75, citrus grower Kraft Groves, 1966-2000; mem. Fla. Citrus Mut., Lakeland, 1966-2000, Com. of 100 of Orange County, Inc., Orlando, 1983—; bd. trustees Winter Park Meml. Hosp., 1969-88, also exec. com., compensation com., chmn. long range planning com.; chmn. Winter Park Cmty. Trust Fund, 1981-92; mem. grievance com. 9th Jud. Cir., 1987-90; active Boy Scouts Am., Rollins Coll. Fiat Lux Soc., Corp. Coun., Crummer Grad. Sch. Bus., Winter Park, Fla.; mem. selection com. COMPUSA Fla. Citrus Bowl, 1999. Lt. (j.g.) USNR, 1956-58. Named Outstanding Young Man of Winter Park, Winter Park Jaycees, 1970, Citizen of the Yr., Winter Park, Fla., 2002. Mem.: US Navy League, US Naval Inst., So. Grand Bank Owners Assn., Nat. Assn. Ins. Agts., Fla. Assn. Ins. Agts., Ctrl. Fla. Assn. Ins. Agts. (pres. 1963—64), Purdue U. Alumni Assn. (pres. coun., dirs. cir. Krannert Grad. Sch. Mgmt., Deans Club Sch. Sci.), Indian Creek Y and Country Club (Kilmarnock, Va.), Country Club of Orlando (pres. 1994—95), Gold Club Purdue Mus. Orgn., All-Am. John Purdue Club, U. Club, Rotary (bd. dirs. Winter Park Club 1968—74), Useppa Island Club, Captiva Island Yacht Club, Masons, Delta Delta (chpt. pres. 1956, ctrl. Fla. alumni chpt.pres. 1960), Sigma Chi (Significant SIG award for achievement in profl. career and civic endeavors, presented to few Sigma Chi frat. alumni 2004). Republican. Presbyterian. Home: 231 Chelton Cir Winter Park FL 32789-6004 also: 1765 Venus Dr Sanibel FL 33957-3427 Office: Kraft Ins Agy Inc PO Box 1443 Winter Park FL 32790-1443: 328 Deep Water Drive White Stone VA 22578

KRAFT, RICHARD LEE, lawyer; b. Lassa, Nigeria, Oct. 14, 1958; m. Tanya Kraft, July 14, 1984; children: Devin, Kelsey. BA in Fgn. Svc., Baylor U., 1980, JD, 1982. Bar: N.Mex. 1982, U.S. Dist. Ct. N.Mex., U.S. Ct. Appeals, U.S. Supreme Ct. Assoc. Sanders, Bruin & Baldock, Roswell, N.Mex., 1982-87, ptnr., 1987-98, Kraft & Stone, LLP, Roswell, 1998-2000; owner The Kraft Law Firm, 2000—. Vol. lawyer Ea. N.Mex. U., Roswell,

1984-98; bd. dirs. Roswell YMCA, 1983-87, Crimestoppers, 1991-94; pres. Roswell Mens Ch. Basketball League; participant Roswell Mens Ch. Softball League; asst. chair legal div. United Way Drive, 1990; pres. sch. bd. Valley Christian Acad., 2003—. Recipient Outstanding Contbn. award N.Mex. State Bar, 1987, 2000. Mem. N.Mex. Bar Assn. (bd. dirs. young lawyers div. 1983-91, pres. 1986-87, chmn. membership com., bar commr. 1986-87, 91-2003, pres. 1998-99, Outstanding Young Lawyer award 1990), Chaves County Bar Assn. (chair law day activities, chair ann. summer picnic com., rep. bench and bar com.), Roswell Legal Secs. Assn. (hon.), Roswell C. of C. (participant and pres. Leadership Roswell, exec. dir., bd. dirs. 1991-), Sertoma (bd. dirs. Roswell club 1989-91) Valley Christian Acad. (pres., bd. dirs., 2003-). Baptist. Office: Kraft & Hunter LLP 111 W Third St Roswell NM 88201-4783 Office Phone: 505-625-2000. Business E-Mail: rkraft@krafthunter.com.

KRAFT, ROBERT ARNOLD, retired medical educator, physician; b. Seattle, Mar. 27, 1924; s. Vincent Irving and Blanche (Palmer) K.; m. Robby Lee Roberson, June 12, 1949 (dec. Aug. 2002); children: Angela Kraft Cross, Peter, Darius. BA, U. Wash., 1948, MD, 1954. Diplomate Am. Bd. Pathology, Am. Bd. Nuclear Medicine. Intern USPHS Hosp., Staten Island, N.Y., 1954-55; resident in Pathology Tacoma (Wash.) Gen. Hosp, 1958-60, U. Calif., San Francisco, 1960-62; staff pathologist Peninsula Hosp., Burlingame, Calif., 1962-90, dir. nuclear medicine, 1965-90; asst. clin. prof. nuclear medicine and pathology U. Calif., San Francisco, 1962-90. Bd. dirs. Am. Bd. Nuclear Medicine, L.A., 1990-95. Capt. USAF, 1943-45, ETO. Decorated DFC. Fellow Am. Coll. Nuclear Physicians (regent 1985-91), Coll. Am. Pathologists; mem. Am. Coll. Nuclear Physicians (pres. Calif. chpt. 1972-73), Soc. Nuclear Medicine (trustee 1982-85), South Bay Pathology Soc. (pres. 1966-67). Avocations: golf, astronomy, history, gardening. Home: 971 Baileyana Rd Hillsborough CA 94010-6173

KRAFT, ROBERT K., professional sports team executive; b. Brookline, Mass., July 5, 1941; m. Myra Kraft; 4 children. Grad., Columbia U., NYC; MBA, Harvard U. Owner Foxboro Stadium, Mass.; chmn. Chestnut Hill Mgmt.; founder Internat. Forest Products, 1972; pres. New Eng. TV Corp., 1986-91; with Rand-Whitney Group, Inc., Worcester, Mass.; pres. Internat. Forest Products Group Cos.; chmn. Carmel Container Systems, Ltd., Israel; owner New Eng. Patriots, 1994—. Mem. exec. com. Dana Farber Cancer Inst.; trustee Columbia U.; bd. dirs. Harvard Sch. Bus., Viacom Inc. Mem. bd. overseers Boston Symphony Orch., Boston Mus. Sci. Named one of Forbes Richest Ams., 2006. Avocations: golf, tennis. Office: New Eng Patriots Gillete Stadium One Patriots Pl Foxboro MA 02035-1388*

KRAFT, ROBERT PAUL, astronomer, educator; b. Seattle, June 16, 1927; s. Victor Paul and Viola Eunice (Ellis) K.; m. Rosalie Ann Reichmuth, Aug. 28, 1949; children: Kenneth, Kevin. BS, U. Wash., 1947, MS, 1949; PhD, U. Calif.-Berkeley, 1955; DSc (hon.), Ind. U., 1995. Postdoctoral fellow Mt. Wilson Obs., Carnegie Inst., Pasadena, Calif., 1955-56; asst. prof. astronomy Ind. U., Bloomington, 1956-58, Yerkes Obs., U. Chgo., Williams Bay, Wis., 1958-59; staff Hale Obs., Pasadena, 1960-67; prof., astronomer Lick Obs., U. Calif., Santa Cruz, 1967-92; astronomer, prof. emeritus, 1992—. Acting dir. Lick Obs., 1968-70, 71-73, dir., 1981-91; dir. U. Calif. Observatories, 1988-91; chmn. Fachbeirat, Max-Planck-Inst., Munich, Fed. Republic Germany, 1978-88; bd. dirs. Cara corp. (Keck Obs.), Pasadena, 1985-91; bd. dirs. AURA, 1989-92. Contbr. articles to profl. jours. Jila vis. fellow U. Colo., Nat. Bur. Stds., Boulder, 1970; Fairchild scholar Calif. Inst. Tech., Pasadena, 1980, Tinsley prof. U. Tex., 1991-92; Henry Norris Russell lectr. Am. Astron. Soc., 1995; recipient Disting. Alumnus award Coll. Arts and Scis., U. Wash., 1995, Catherine Wolfe Bruce Gold medal Astron. Soc. Pacific, 2005. Mem. Nat. Acad. Sci., Am. Acad. of Arts and Scis., Am. Astron. Soc. (pres. 1974-76, Warner prize 1962, Russell prize lectr. 1995), Internat. Astron. Union (v.p. 1982-88, pres.-elect 1994-97, pres. 1997-2000), Astron. Soc. Pacific (bd. dirs. 1981-87), Royal Astron. Soc. (fgn. assoc.). Democrat. Unitarian Universalist. Avocations: contract bridge, art appreciation, classical music, opera, eonology. Office: U Calif Lick Observatory Santa Cruz CA 95064 E-mail: kraft@ucolick.org.

KRAFT, SCOTT COREY, news correspondent; b. Kansas City, Mo., Mar. 31, 1955; s. Marvin Emanuel and Patricia (Kirk) K.; m. Elizabeth Brown, May 1, 1982; children: Kate, Kevin. BS, Kans. State U., 1977. Staff writer AP, Jefferson City, Mo., 1976-77, Kansas City, 1977-79, corr. Wichita, Kans., 1979-80, nat. writer NYC, 1980-84; nat. corr. L.A. Times, Chgo., 1984-86, bur. chief Nairobi, Kenya, 1986-88, Johannesburg, South Africa, 1988-93, Paris, 1993-96, dep. fgn. editor, 1996-97, nat. editor, 1997—. Recipient Disting. Reporting in a Specialized Field award Soc. of the Silurians, 1982, Peter Lisagor award Headline Club Chgo., 1985, Feature Writing finalist Pulitzer Prize Bd., 1985, Sigma Delta Chi award, 1993. Office: LA Times Nat Editor 202 W 1st St Los Angeles CA 90012

KRAFT, YVETTE, art educator; b. Washington, Jan. 17, 1945; d. Alvin Abraham and Rena Zlotnick Kraft. Studies with Master Painter Leon Berkowitz, 1982—87; student, Corcoran Coll. of Art and Design, 1992—2004. Art dir. after-sch. program Georgetown Montessori Sch., 1988; art instr. Washington Home, Sr. Citizen Care Facility, 1989—90; art instr. students with spl. needs Horace Mann Elem. Sch., 1990; art instr. Southeast Asian Refugee Children, 4-H, Arlington, Va., 1989—90; pvt. art instr. ages 2-17, 1990—92; art instr. Janney Elem. Sch., 1991, 1998, 1999, Ben Murch Elem. Sch., 1991; artist-in-residence Anne Beers Elem. Sch., 1992—93; art instr. children and adolescents with emotional disorders Clara Aisenstein, MD, Child Psychiatrist, 1993—96; art instr. Randle Highlands Elem. Sch., 1994, Naylor Rd. Elem. Sch., 1997, Bethany Woman's Shelter, 1998—2000, S.E. Vets. Svc. Ctr., Washington, 2005—; condr. art classes N St. Village, Washington, 2003—04. Fine arts com. Washington Hebrew Congregation, 1979—82; adv. bd. New Art Examiner Mag., Washington, 1985—86; asst. mgr. Americana West Gallery; founder, dir. Project City People, 1992, 93; edn. dir. Fondo del Sol Visual Arts Ctr., 1992—93. One-woman shows include Maret Sch., Washington, 1987, Georgetown Montessori Sch., 1988, Horace Mann Sch., 1989, Fillmore Sch. of Arts, 1991, NIH, Clin. Ctr. Gallery, Bethesda, Md., 1995, Fondo de Sol Visual Arts Ctr., Washington, 1996, DC Arts Ctr., 1999, Nat. Coalition for Homeless, 2001, exhibited in group shows at Am. Art League, 1982—85, Highlights of the Yr. Exhbn., Martin Luther King Libr., 1986—87, Washington Hebrew Congregation, 1986—87, 2002—03, Capricorn Gallery, Bethesda, Md., 1987, Ctr. for Collaborative Art and Visual Edn., Washington, 1999, Capital Children's Mus., 1999, Eight Is An Octive, Nat. Theatre, 2000, Am. Oh Yes Folk Art Gallery, 2000—03, Joy of Motion, 2001, Rockville Arts Pl., Md., 2003. Grantee grant, Cafritz Found., 1990, 1991, Hattie M. Strong Found., 1991, George Preston Marshall, 1991. Independent. Jewish. Avocations: jazz, walking, art museums, sketching, clothing design and coordination. Office Phone: 202-332-0535.

KRAGTHORPE, STEVE, college football coach; b. Missoula, Mont., Apr. 28, 1965; m. Cynthia Kragthorpe; 1 child, Chris; children: Brad, Nik. B in Bus. Admin., West Tex. A & M Univ., 1988; MBA, Ore. State Univ., 1989. Asst. coach No. Ariz. U., 1990—93; off. coord. No. Tex. U., 1994—95; quarterbacks coach Boston Coll., 1996; asst. coach Texas A & M U., Lubbock, Tex., 1997—2000; quarterbacks coach Buffalo Bills, 2001—02; head coach Tulsa U., 2003—06, U. Louisville, 2007—. Recipient Coach Yr., Western Athletic Conf., 2003, FWAA/Scripps First Coach Yr. award, 2003. Office: Athletics Dept SAC Bldg U Louisville 2100 S Floyd St Louisville KY 40292*

KRAHL, ENZO, retired surgeon; b. Fiume, Italy, Apr. 22, 1924; came to U.S., 1951, naturalized, 1955; s. Massimiliano and Camilla (Aub) K.; m. Anne Katharine Ferbstein, June 14, 1958; children— Edward Alexander, Katharine Frances MD, U. Florence, Italy, 1948. Diplomate Am. Bd. Surgery. Asst. dept. surgery U. Rome, 1948-51; fellow in vascular surgery Columbia Presbyn. Med. Ctr., NYC, 1951-52, fellow in surgery, 1954-55; resident in surgery St. Vincent's Hosp., NYC, 1952-54; chief resident in surgery Akron City Hosp., Ohio, 1957-58; dir. grad. edn. Akron Gen. Hosp., 1959-60; practice medicine specializing in surgery Akron, 1958-60, Superior, Wis., 1960-84; ret., 1984. Mem. staff Superior Meml. Hosp., also bd. dirs.; founder Superior Clinic, 1964; past dir. Blue Cross-Blue Shield United of Wis. Author: Life is a Fatal Disease (Reflections on a Lifetime), 2005; contbr. articles to med. jours. Past v.p. Duluth-Superior Symphony; past mem. exec. com. bd. dirs. Health Systems Agy. Western Lake Superior. Served as capt. M.C., U.S. Army, 1955-57 Recipient United Fund award, 1965, cert. of merit N.Y.C. CD, 1953 Mem. Wis. State Med. Soc., Italian Heritage Soc., Am. Bridge League, The Landings Club Jewish. Home: 15 Cotton Xing Savannah GA 31411-2504 Personal E-mail: anneande@bellsouth.net.

KRAHMER, DONALD LEROY, JR., lawyer; b. Hillsboro, Oreg., Nov. 11, 1957; s. Donald L. and Joan Elizabeth (Karns) Krahmer; m. Suzanne M. Blanchard, Aug. 16, 1986; children: Hillary, Zachary. BS, Willamette U., 1981, MBA, 1987, JD, 1987. Bar: Oreg. 1988, Wash. 2003. Fin. analyst U.S. Bancorp, Portland, 1977-87; intern U.S. Senator Mark Hatfield, 1978; legis. aide State Sen. Jeannette Hamby, Hillsboro, 1981-83, State Rep. Delna Jones, Beaverton, 1983; bus. analyst Pacificorp, Portland, 1987; mgr. mergers/acquisitions Pacificorp Fin. Svcs., Portland, 1988-89, dir., 1990; CEO, pres. Atkinson Group, Portland, 1991—2002; ptnr. Black Helterline, LLP, Portland, 1991—2001; shareholder Schwabe Williamson & Wyatt, P.C., Portland, 2002—, chmn., tech. and bus. practice. Bd. dir. Portland Bus. Alliance, Self-Enhancement, Inc., Pacific Continental Bank; chmn. Willamette Forum; with Oreg. Entrepreneur Forum, 1993, chmn. adv. bd., 95, chmn. bd., 98; founder, co-chmn. Oreg. Emerging Bus. Initiative, 1997—2005, New Economy Coalition, 2001—05; founder, chmn. Oreg. Tech. Alliance, 2002—03; chmn. audit com. Pacific Continental Bank, 2003—, chmn. corp. gov. com., 2003—04. Founder Needle Bros., 1994; chmn. Atkinson Grad. Sch. Devel. Com., Salem, Oreg., 1989—92; adv. bd. Ctr. for Law and Entrepreneurship U. Oreg. Sch. Law, 1997—2002; founder Conf. of Entrepreneurship, Salem, 1984; chmn. Entrepreneurship Breakfast Forum, Portland, 1993; chmn., founder Oreg. Conf. on Entrepreneurship and Awards Dinner, 1994—99, sr. v.p., 1999—2005; exec. com., bd. dir. Boy Scouts Am. (Cascade Pacific Coun.), chmn. cmty. fund dir., 1997, chmn. Scoutrageous, 2000; co-chair Com. for Oreg.'s Future, 2002; steering com. Oreg. Opportunity; tech. advisor Oreg. Coun. on Knowledge and Econ. Devel., 2002—05; mem. Greater Portland Innovation Network, 2002—05; tech. advisor Oreg. Innovation Coun., 2005—; bd. trustees Jesuit HS, 2006—; treas. Com. to Re-Elect Jeannette Hamby, 1986; vice-chmn. Gov.'s Coun. on Small Bus. State of Oreg.; mem. Gov.'s Econ. Devel. Joint Bds. Working Group, 1999—2002; mem. ch. coun. Our Savior Luth. Ch., 2000—01; bd. dir. fin. com., devel. com. Am. Diabetes Assn., Portland, 1990—96; bd. visitors Coll. Law Willamette U., 1997—2002; bd. dirs. ONAMI, 2004—. Named one of Top 50 Leaders to Watch, Oreg. Bus. Mag., 2003; recipient Pub.'s award, 1987, Founders award, Willamette U., 1987, award, Scripps Found., 1980, 40 Under 40 award, Bus. Jour., 1996. Mem.: RAINS, ABA, Oreg. Tech. Alliance, Micro2Nano Collaborative, Am. Electronics Assn. (Oreg. coun.), Portland Soc. Fin. Analysts, Multnomah County Bar Assn., Software Assn. of Oreg., Oreg. Biotech. Assn., Japan-Am. Soc. Oreg., Oreg. Biosci. Assn., Oreg. Bar Assn. (sec. 1998, chmn. 1999, chmn. exec. com., fin. instns. com. sec., exec. com., bus. law sect., Pres.'s award 1999, James B. Castles Leadership award 2002), Assn. for Corp. Growth, Assn. Investment Mgmt. and Rsch., Arlington Club (treas. 2002, 1st v.p. 2003, bd. dirs., pres. 2004), Multnomah Athletic Club, City Club. Republican. Lutheran. Home: 16230 SW Copper Creek Dr Portland OR 97224-6500 Office: Schwabe Williamson & Wyatt 1211 SW 5th Ave Ste 1800 Portland OR 97204-3718 Office Phone: 503-796-2882. Business E-Mail: dkrahmer@schwabe.com.

KRAICHNAN, ROBERT HARRY, physicist, consultant; b. Phila., Jan. 15, 1928; s. Robert Maxwell and Anna (Maximon) Kraichnan; m. Carol Gebhardt, May 22, 1954 (div. 1988); 1 child, John; m. Judy Ellen Moore, June 30, 1989. BS in Physics, MIT, 1947, PhD in Theoretical Physics, 1949. Mem., asst. to Albert Einstein Inst. Advanced Study, Princeton, NJ, 1949-50; mem. tech. staff Bell Tel. Labs., 1950-52; rsch. assoc. Columbia U., NYC, 1952-56; rsch. assoc. Courant Inst. NYU, NYC, 1956-58, sr. rsch. scientist Courant Inst., 1958-62; pvt. practice physicist, 1962-80; pres., prin. Robert H. Kraichnan, Inc., Santa Fe, 1980—. Adj. assoc. prof. dept. grad. physics NYU, 1956—57; cons. Naval Rsch. Lab., 1957—59, Inst. Def. Analyses, 1967—70, Los Alamos Nat. Lab., 1979—, Princeton U., 1987—; cons. Inst. Space Studies NASA, 1961—69, contractor, 1967—69; assoc. in physics Woods Hole (Mass.) Oceanographic Inst., 1960—70; contractor Office Naval Rsch., 1962—80; rsch. affiliate meteorology MIT, 1963—. Contbr. articles to sci. jours. Recipient ADION medal, Observatoire de Nice, Dirac prize, Internat. Ctr. Theoretical Physics, 2003; grantee, NSF, 1970—. Fellow: AAAS, Am. Phys. Soc. (Otto Laporte award 1993, Lars Onsager Meml. prize 1997); mem.: NAS. Avocations: mountain hiking, violin, carpentry.

KRAINES, MERRILL M., lawyer; b. NYC, Aug. 3, 1955; BA magna cum laude, Dartmouth Coll., 1976; JD, Columbia U., 1979. Bar: NY 1980. Ptnr. and co-head tech. and emerging companies dept. Fulbright & Jaworski, LLP, NYC. Mem. ABA (sect. corp. banking and bus. law, small bus. com., subcom. emerging growth ventures), NY State Bar Assn. Office: Fulbright & Jaworski LLP 666 5th Ave Fl 31 New York NY 10103-3198 Office Phone: 212-318-3000. Office Fax: 212-318-3400. Business E-Mail: mkraines@fulbright.com.

KRAININ, JULIAN ARTHUR, film director, producer, cinematographer, writer; b. NYC, Jan. 24, 1941; s. David A. and Anne N. (Wineblatt) K.; m. Martha Wineblatt, June 17, 1967; 1 child, Todd Philip. BS, Allegheny Coll., 1962, HHD (hon.), 1993; MFA, Columbia U., 1965. Prodr. spl. projects Westinghouse Broadcasting Co., NYC, 1967-69, also prodr., dir., writer, 1967—; v.p., exec. prodr. Krainin/Sage Prodns., Inc., NYC, 1969-80, also dir., writer, 1969-80; pres. Krainin Prodns., Inc., NYC, 1976—. Nat. lectr. motion pictures at various univs. and colls., 1967—; cons. on films U. Mass., 1973; juror Mid-West Film Makers and Graphic Arts Festival, 1971-72, Nat. Emmy Awards, 1975-82, 85-90, Dirs. Guild of Am. Awards, 1987-90; mem. journalism adv. bd. Queens Coll., 1987-90; bd. dirs. Bklyn. Ctr. for Families in Crises, 1986-90; journalism adv. bd. Queens Coll. Films include: The Reluctant Revolution, 1968, Exit to Nowhere, 1967, Promises to Keep, 1967, The March, 1965, Nowhere Fast, 1968, Hide and Seek, 1966, (with Jacques Cousteau) Oceans: The Silent Crisis, 1972, Art is (Acad. award nominee, hon. screenings White House, Mus. Modern Art), 1972, The Other Americans (Emmy award), 1969, Princeton: A Search for Answers (Acad. award), 1973, The American Experiment, 1974, Going Metric, 1975, To America, 1976, The Broken Silence, 1976, The World of James Michener: Hawaii Revisited, 1977, The World of James Michener: The South Pacific, End of Eden? (hon. screening Mus. Modern Art), 1978, (with Ed Asner) The Writer, 1980, The Making of an Opera, 1980, Luciano Pavorotti At Home, 1980, La Gioconda miniseries, 1980, Heritage: Civilization and the Jews (Peabody, Emmy, Christopher awards), 1981-82, PBS series, CBS Reports: Don't Touch that Dial!: The Making of a Television Series (Emmy nominee, TV Guide citation, 1982, The Smithsonian Quadrangle: A View from the Castle, 1984, America Undercover: The Wrong Man, 1985-86, (with Tom Peters) The Power of Excellence, 1987; (with Abba Eban) Heritage: Civilization and the Jews, Disaster at Silo 7, 1988, Memory and Imagination, New Pathways to the Library of Congress, 1990; documentary film: The Television Quiz Show Scandal, 1991, Queen's College, 1993, (feature film) Quiz Show, 1994 (4 Acad. award nominations including Best Picture), The Unabomber: Deadly Mail!, 1996, The Thousand Acre Universe, 1996, George Wallace (Golden Globe, Humanitas, Cable Ace, Peabody awards), The John Glenn Story: Return to Space and Return of the Hero, 1998-99, Something the Lord Made, 2004 (Emmy, 9 Nominations, 3 awards including Best TV Movie, Peabody, Am. Film. Inst., Dir. Guild Am., Christopher, NAACP Image, Freddie, TV Critics Assn. awards and nominations). Recipient numerous awards and citations including Acad. Award, 1973, Emmy Award, 1969, 2004, Chgo. Internat. Film Festival award, 1969, 77, 78, Florence Internat. Film Festival award, 1969, Cine Golden Eagle awards, 1969, 72, 73, 74, 76, 78, Photog. Soc. Am. award, 1968, Venice Film Festival award, 1970, Moscow Internat. Film Festival award, 1970, Cindy award Prodrs. Assn. Am., 1971, 76, San Francisco Internat. Film Festival award, 1972, Am. Film Festival award, 1974, 76, 78, Tel Aviv Internat. Film Festival award, 1970, Atlanta Internat. Film Festival award, 1969, 72, Festival of Ams. award, 1976, N.Y. Internat. Film and TV Festival award, 1969, 72, Gabriel award, 1968-70, Oberhausen Internat. Film Festival award, 1969, Columbus Film Festival award, 1973, Manheim Internat. Film Festival award, 1969, U.S. Indsl. Film Festival award, 1973, Ohio State award, 1967, N.Y. Film Festival at Lincoln Center award, 1970. Mem. Writers Guild Am. (awards), Acad. Motion Picture Arts and scis., Photog. Soc. Am., Dirs. Guild Am. (award 1973). Office: 25211 Summerhill Ln Stevenson Ranch CA 91381-2262 Office Phone: 661-259-9700. Business E-Mail: krainin@ca.rr.com.

KRAJEWSKI, MICHAEL, conductor; b. Detroit; m. Darcy Krajewski. Grad, Wayne State U., U. of Cinn. Coll. Conservatory of Music. Music dir. Modesto Symphony Orch.; asst. condr. Detroit Symphony Orch.; music dir. Detroit Symphony Civic Orch.; resident condr. Fla. Symphony Orch.; prin. pops condr. Houston Symphony Orch., 2000—, New Mex., Long Beach and Jacksonville Symphonies. Fellowship condr. Detroit Symphony; artist intern Mich. Opera Theatre. Performed with Boston Pops Orch., San Francisco, St. Louis, Detroit, Balt., Atlanta, Minn., Oreg. et al. Recipient awards, Am. Soc. of Composers, Authors and Publishers. Office: Houston Symphony 615 Louisiana St Ste 102 Houston TX 77002

KRAKAUER, SARAH YAEL, psychologist; b. Princeton, NJ, Apr. 24, 1950; d. Cyrus Herzl and Joan Kendall Gordon; m. Henry Krakauer, Oct. 16, 1971; children: Ilana Deborah, Mark Mendel, Benjamin Samuel. BA in English and Am. Lit. magna cum laude, Brandeis U., 1972; D in Psychology, Va. Consortium Profl. Psychology, 1991. Lic. Clin. Psychology Bd. Psychology, Va., 1993. Staff psychologist Ea. State Hosp., Williamsburg, Va., 1991—94; clin. psychologist, ind. contractor Psychol. Assoc. Williamsburg, Va., 1993—97; clin. psychologist pvt. practice, Williamsburg, 1997—. Adj. asst. prof. psychology Coll. William and Mary, Williamsburg, Va., 1992—2000, adj. assoc. prof. psychology, 2002—. Author: Treating Dissociative Identity Disorder: The Power of the Collective Heart; contbr. articles to profl. jours. Mem.: APA, Internat. Soc. Study of Trauma and Dissociation, Tidewater Acad. Clin. Psychologists, Va. Acad. Clin. Psychologists, Va. Psychol. Assn., Phi Beta Kappa, Phi Kappa Phi. Achievements include development of cautious, respectful, and empowering therapy model for treating dissociative survivors of childhood trauma. Preliminary clin. observations support the efficacy of this model. Office: 333 McLaws Cir Ste 1 Williamsburg VA 23185 Office Phone: 757-220-4943.

KRAKAUR, LINDA E., language educator; b. Silver Spring, Md., Dec. 12, 1965; m. Keith A. Schur, June 16, 2002. BA in English Edn., U. Md., College Park, 1985—89; Postgraduate Diploma in Drama in Edn., U. Ctrl. Eng., Birmingham, 2001—03; Master of Studies in Drama in Edn., Trinity Coll., Dublin, 2003—05. Cert. secondary English & drama tchr. Md. English and drama tchr. Fairfax County Pub. Schs., Falls Church, Va., 1992—2004; English tchr. Montgomery County Pub. Schs., Olney, Md., 2004—. Adj. prof. Arts Integration Inst. Towson U., Towson, Md., 2004—; mem. review bd. arts and learning jour. Am. Ednl. Rsch. Assn., 2004; art educator Ctr. for Renaissance and Baroque Studies, College Park, Md., 2006, Crossing Borders/Breaking Boundaries. Grantee Four Texts and Japanese Culture fellow, Nat. Endowment Humanities, 1992, Breaking Down Boundaries Incorporating Latino Lit. & Culture in Classroom fellow, 1999; Impact II Rsch. grant, Fairfax County Pub. Schs., 2004, fellowship, Woodrow Wilson Nat. Fellowship Found., 2007. Mem.: Am. Alliance for Theatre and Edn., Am. Assn. Theatre Edn. Home Phone: 301-445-2228. Personal E-mail: dramaties@aol.com.

KRAKOFF, REED D., apparel designer; b. Feb. 20, 1965; s. Sandra and Robert L. Krakoff; m. Amy Jedlicka, Aug. 7, 1993. AAS Fashion Design, Parsons Sch. Design; BA in Econ. & Art History, Tufts U., 1993. Sr. designer Polo/Ralph Lauren, 1988—92; head designer, sportswear Tommy Hilfiger USA, Inc., 1992—93, sr. v.p., mktg., design & comm., 1993—96; sr. v.p., exec. creative dir. Coach Inc., 1996—99, pres., exec. creative dir., 1999—. Recipient Am. Fashion Award, Accessories Designer of the Year, 2001, 2004. Office: Coach Inc 516 W 34th St New York NY 10001 Office Phone: 212-594-1850. Office Fax: 212-594-1682.*

KRAKOSKY, NORAH, historic site staff member; b. Kingston, Pa., Nov. 11, 1981; d. Ronald and Ruth Krakosky. BA in Nonfiction Writing and Art History summa cum laude, U. Pitts., 2004; MA in Cultural Heritage with distinction, U. East Anglia, Norwich, Eng., 2006. Asst. lang. tchr. Japan Exch. and Tchg., Kumanoto, Japan, 2004—05; curatorial intern Wolterton Hall, Norwich, 2006; comm. asst. Heinz History Ctr., Pitts., 2006—. Mem.: Nat. Trust Hist. Preservation, Phi Beta Kappa. Avocations: reading, movies, cooking, embroidery, writing.

KRAKOWER, BERNARD HYMAN, management consultant; b. NYC, May 11, 1935; s. David and Bertha (Glassman) K.; m. Sondra Joan Fishbein, Apr. 14, 1968; children: Lorna, Victoria, Ariela Shauna. BA in Advt., UCLA, 1959; cert. in real estate, 1966, cert. in indsl. rels., 1972; MBA, Pepperdine U., 1979. Loan officer Lytton Fin. Corp., LA, 1961-65; mgmt. cons. James R. Colvin & Assocs., LA, 1965-67; sr. indsl. rels. rep. Sci. Data Systems (Xerox), 1967-68; dir. ops. Tratec, Inc., LA, 1968-70; chmn. Krakower/Brucker Internat., Inc., LA, 1970-88; sr. ptnr. Krakower Finnegan Assocs., LA, 1988-90; pres. Krakower Group, Inc., 1990—. Bd. dirs. Columbia Nat. Bank, Santa Monica, Calif., Elings Park, Santa Barbara, Calif.; mem. adv. bd. Private Financing Group, 2000. Mem. citizens liaison com. LA Dept. Recreation and Parks, 1973; apptd. commr., v.p. LA Countywide Citizens Planning Coun. by LA County Bd. Suprs., 1988-97, v.p., 1991-93, pres. 1993-97; pres., bd. dirs. LA Bus. Coun.; mem. bd. visitors Pepperdine U. Graziadio Sch. Bus. and Mgmt., 1997—; leadership mem. Santa Barbara Region Econ. Cmty. Project, 1997; v.p. bd. dirs. Santa Barbara Newcomers, 1999; mem. adv. bd. Calif. Coast Venture Forum, 1999, co-chmn. Santa Barbara Region Tech. Coun., 1999; bd. dirs. Santa Barbara Regional C. of C., 2001, pres., 2006, chmn. bd., 2006—; sec. Elings Pk. Bd., 2006-. Mem. So. Calif. Tech. Coast Angels, Santa Barbara Region C. of C. (bd. dirs. 2001—, mem. fin. com. 2001—, mem. exec. com. 2003—, bd. dir. Elings Pk. chpt. 2003—, chmn. bd. 2006, chmn. emeritus 2007). Personal E-mail: kgi@krakower.net.

KRAKOWER, TERRI JAN, biochemist, researcher; b. Houston, Mar. 09; d. Sidney and Delores K. BS in Biochemistry and Biophysics, U. Houston, 1979; postgrad., U. Calif., Davis, 1980; PhD in Chemistry, U. Tex., 1990. Grad. student asst. State of Calif. Air Resources Bd., Sacramento, 1981, 82; environ. quality specialist State of Tex. Air Control, Austin, summer 1984; predoctoral fellow, tchg. and rsch. U. Tex., Austin,

1987-90; staff fellow Boston Biomed Rsch. Inst., Boston, 1990-92; postdoctoral rsch. fellow Harvard Med. Sch., Boston, 1990-91; rsch. assoc. Baylor Coll. Medicine, Houston, 1993-94; postdoctoral fellow dept. biochemistry U. Tex. Health Sci Ctr., San Antonio, 1994-96; sci. com. specialist and coord. IBIDS database Offices Dietary Supplements and Dir. NIH, Bethesda, 1998-00; nutritional biochemist Wellness Works, Marble Falls, 2003—. Major contbr. to Calif. document leading to first U.S. regulation of air emissions from class I hazardous waste disposal in State of Calif. Air Resources Bd., Sacramento, 1981, 1982; organic and biochem. lab. instr. U. Tex., Austin, 1986. Vol. Mus. of Sci., Boston, 1992, Alexandria Archaeology, 1998, Red Cross Hurricane Relief, 2005; vol. radio prodr., 1998-00, v.p. Radio Prodrs. Guild, 1999, WEBR, Fairfax Pub. Access Corp., 1998—. Recipient scholarship U. Calif, Davis, 1980; grantee: Tex. Pub. Edn. grants, U. Tex., 1986-89; named predoctoral rsch. fellow Nat. Inst. Alcohol and Alcohol Abuse, through Inst. for Neurosci., U. Tex., Austin, 1988-89. Mem. Am. Chem. Soc., Am. Soc. Biochemistry and Molecular Biology. Achievements include isolation of monoclonal antibody that recognizes monoamine oxidase A and B in human tissue, and first monoclonal antibody that recognizes rodent monoamine oxidase A.

KRAKOWSKI, JANE, actress; b. Parsippany, NJ, Oct. 11, 1968; Actor: (TV films) No Big Deal, 1983, When We Were Young, 1989, Women & Men 2: In Love There are No Rules, 1991, CatDog: The Great Parent Mystery, 2001, Just a Walk in the Park, 2002, A Christmas Carol, 2004, Mom at Sixteen, 2005; (films) Vacation, 1983, Fatal Attraction, Stepping Out, 1991, Mrs. Winterbourne, 1996, Hudson River Blues, 1997, Dance With Me, 1998, Go, 1999, The Flinststones in Viva Rock Vegas, 2000, Ice Age, 2002, Marci X, 2003, When Zachary Beaver Came to Town, 2003, Alfie, 2004, (voice) Open Season, 2006,: (TV series) Search For Tomorrow, 1984—86, Another World, 1989, Due South, 1995, Ally, 1999, Rocket Power, 2002, Ally McBeal, 1997—2002, Everwood, 2002—03, Hack, 2004, Law & Order, 2004; (TV films) 30 Rock, 2006—; (Broadway plays) Nine, 2003 (Tony award for Best Performance by a Featured Actress in a Musical, Best Actress, 2003, Drama Desk award for Best Actress, 2003, Outer Critic's award for Best Actress, 2003), Grand Hotel, Starlight Express; (plays) Guys and Dolls, 2005 (Laurence Olivier award for Best Actress in a Musical, 2006). Office: c/o All American Celebrity and Talent Network Ste 200 4717 Knights Arm Dr Durham NC 27707*

KRAKOWSKI, RICHARD JOHN, lawyer, public relations executive; b. Meppen, Fed. Republic of Germany, Apr. 3, 1946; came to U.S., 1951, naturalized, 1962; s. Feliks and Maria (Chilinski) K. MBA, DePaul U., 1979; JD, John Marshall Law Sch., 1983. Bar: Ill. 1984. Personnel dir. Andy Frain, Inc., Chgo., 1973-78; pub. rels. dir. Chgo. Health Sys. Agy., 1978-84; assoc. firm Mangum, Smietanka & Johnson, Chgo., 1984-87; asst. atty. gen. Ill. Atty. Gen.'s Ofc., 1987-96. Bd. dirs., St. Mary of Nazareth Hosp., Holy Trinity H.S.; lectr. in field. Co-author: Health Care Financing and Policy Making in Chicago and Illinois, 1982. Fundraising and pub. rels. dir. Cabrini-Green Sandlot Tennis Program, Chgo., 1979-83; sustaining mem. Rep. Nat. Com., 1981—; bd. dirs. Internat. Latino Cultural Ctr. Capt. U.S. Army, 1969-72. Mem. ABA, Nat. Advs. Soc., Ill. Bar Assn., Chgo. Bar Assn., Chgo. Coun. Fgn. Rels., Lyric Opera Guild, Art Inst. Chgo., Chgo. Soc. Polish Nat. Alliance, Publicity Club (Chgo.). Roman Catholic. Office: Cook County Human Resources Divsn 118 N Clark St Ste 824 Chicago IL 60602-1312 Home: 1550 N Lake Shore Dr Apt 16e Chicago IL 60610-6600 Personal E-mail: rjkrak1350@hotmail.com.

KRALEMANN, WILLIAM JOSEPH, retired chemistry educator; b. St. Louis, Sept. 21, 1948; s. William C. and Dorothy L. Kralemann; m. Catherine A. Kralemann, Nov. 8, 1975; children: Laurie A. Brikenmeier, Matthew W. BA in Sci., U. Mo., Columbia, 1974; MA in Sci. Edn., Webster U., St. Louis, 1990. Chemist Warner_Jenkinson Co., St. Louis, 1975—77; tchr. chemistry Chaminade, St. Louis, 1978—83, Hazewood Ctrl. HS, Florissant, Mo., 1983—2005, ret., 2005. Coach Cath. Youth Coun. Athletic League, Overland, Mo., 1984—90; coach football and track Hazelwood Ctrl. HS, 1979—90, writer sci. curriculum, 1984—87, adv. chemistry hons. program, 1990—2004, sponsor sci. fair, 1990—2004. With US Army, 1967—70, Vietnam. Decorated Vietnam Gallentry Cross U.S. Army; named Influential Tchr., Mo. Scholars Acad., 2000, Truman State U., 2001, Sci. Tchr. of Yr., Hazelwood Ctrl. HS, 2004, Tchr. of Month, Hazelwood Ctrl. HS Student Coun., 2005. Mem.: ACS (mem. edn. group), Nat. Assn. Biology Tchrs., Mizzou Alumni Assn. Roman Cath. Avocations: travel, reading, dog training. Home: 135 Sally Dr Florissant MO 63031

KRALL, DIANA, musician, singer; b. Nanaimo, BC, Can., Nov. 16, 1964; m. Elvis Costello, Dec. 2003; children: Dexter Henry Lorcan, Frank Harlan James. Student, Berklee Coll. Music, 1982—84; degree (hon.), U. Victoria. With Justin Time Records, Montreal, Que., Canada, 1993, GRP, Verve Records. Musician: (albums) Stepping Out, 1993, Only Trust Your Heart, 1995, All For You, 1996, Love Scenes, 1997, When I Look In Your Eyes, 1999 (Grammy award for Best Jazz Vocal Performance, 2000, Grammy award nomination for Album of Yr., 2000, Cert. Platinum, U.S. and Portugal, Double Platinum in Can., Gold, France, Juno award Best Vocal Jazz Album), The Look of Love, 2001 (Quadruple Platinum, Can., Platinum, Australia, New Zealand, Poland and Portugal, Gold, France, Singapore, Eng., Juno award for Best Artist, Best Album, Best Vocal Jazz Album, Record of Yr. award Nat. Jazz Awards), Live in Paris, 2002 (Grammy award for Best Jazz Vocal Album, 2002), Heartdrops: Vince Benedetti Meets Diana Krall, 2003, The Girl in the Other Room, 2004, Xmas Songs featuring the Clayton/Hamilton Jazz Orchestra, 2005, From This Moment On, 2006. Named Musician of Yr., Nat. Jazz Awards, Internat. Musician. Office: Macklam/Feldman Mgmt 1505 W 2d Ave Ste 200 Vancouver BC Canada V6H 3Y4 E-mail: management@mfmgt.com.*

KRALL, LISA KRISTINA, education educator; d. Wesley James and Marja-Leena Bodin; m. Peter Joseph Krall, Mar. 29, 2003; 1 child, Luke Wesley. BS in Elem. Edn., U. Minn. Twin Cities, Mpls., 1992, MEd in Elem. Edn., 1997, postgrad., 1999—. Cert. Nat. Bd. Profl. Tchg. Stds., 1998. Elem. edn. tchr. Minnetonka Pub. Schs., Minn., 1992—2005; asst. prof. Bemidji State U., Mpls., 2005—06, adj. prof., 2006—; grad. rsch. asst. U. Minn. Twin Cities, Mpls., 2006—. Presenter in field. Recipient Child Centered Excellence in Tchg. award, Minnetonka Sch. Dist., 2005. Mem.: ASCD, Edn. Minn., Children's Lit. Network, Twin Cities Area Reading Coun., Pi Lambda Theta, Nat. Coun. Tchrs. English, Internat. Reading Assn., Phi Kappa Phi.

KRALL, TODD, program manager; b. Lorain, Ohio, Apr. 30, 1971; s. Joseph and Bonnie Krall; m. Shannon Milligan, Oct. 12, 2002. Student, Kent State U., Ohio, 1989—94. Program mgr. Ryder, Cleve., 1999—. Home Phone: 440-670-3071; Office Phone: 440-333-2967. Office Fax: 443-331-0307; Home Fax: 443-331-0307. Personal E-mail: tek208@yahoo.com.

KRALL, VITA, psychologist; b. New Haven, July 9, 1923; d. Moses Adam and Jennie (Alper) K. BA, Antioch Coll., Yellow Springs, Ohio, 1944; MA, U. Iowa, 1945; PhD, Rochester U., NY, 1951. Lic. psychologist, Conn. Instr. U. Rochester, 1948-51, Mich. State U., East Lansing, 1951-53; sr. clin. psychologist Topeka, 1953-58, Kans. Neurol. Inst., Topeka, 1959-60; staff psychologist Child Guidance Clinic of Greater Bridgeport (Conn.), Inc., 1961-62; psychologist, dir. tng. Michael Reese Hosp., Chgo., 1963-88; rsch. psychologist Hartford (Conn.) Hosp., 1989-90. Author: Developmental Psychodiagnostic Assessment of Children and Adolescents, 1989, Play Therapy Primer, 1989, Psychological Development of High Risk Multiple Birth Children, 1991. Recipient Saft award for outstanding instr. Michael Reese Hosp., Chgo., 1983, 87, Disting. Svc. award, Am. Bd. Profl. Psychologists, 1987, Disting. Psychologist, Ill. Psychol. Assn., 1983. Fellow Am. Orthopsychiatric Assn., APA; mem. Soc. for Personality Assessment. Avocation: painting. Home and Office: 18 Atwater St Milford CT 06460-7662 Office Phone: 203-874-2947.

KRALLINGER, JOSEPH CHARLES, entrepreneur, consultant, writer; b. Lancaster, Pa., May 29, 1931; s. Ferdinand and Mathilde (Meyer) K.; m. Hilde Eisenhauer, Oct. 1, 1955; children— Joanne, Diane, Robert BS in Econs. cum laude, Franklin and Marshall Coll., 1953. CPA. Auditor GAO, Denver, 1953; auditor Army Audit Agy., 1953-55; ptnr. Arthur Andersen & Co., Phila., 1955-76; v.p. strategic planning and acquisitions, chief fin. officer Berwind Corp., Phila., 1976-88; cons. Palm Desert, Calif., 1988—. Dir., bus. advisor and investor various indsl., health care, mining, oil and gas cos., 1976—; cons. in field. Author: An Auditor's Approach to Statistical Sampling, 5 vols., 1967-72, Strategic Planning Workbook, 1989, 2d edit., 1993, How to Acquire the Perfect Business for Your Company, 1991; Planeacion Estrategica Practica, 1991; Mergers and Acquisitions: Managing the Transactions, 1997, Chinese and Spanish edits., 2000; contbr. articles to profl. jours. Bd. dirs. alumni coun. Franklin and Marshall Coll., Lancaster, 1969-75; pres., tchr. religious edn. St. Genevieve Cath. Ch., Flourtown, Pa., 1971-76; bd. dirs. Whitemarsh Twp. Citizens Coun., Plymouth Meeting, Pa., 1972-75; hon. life mem., past chmn. bd. dirs. Phila. chpt. Am. Cancer Soc. Recipient Nat. Vol. award Am. Cancer Soc., 1985, Crusade award Am. Cancer Soc., 1985, Teaching award St. Genevieve Ch., 1985, Cert. Merit Inst. Mgmt. Accts., 1998. Mem. AICPA (statis. sampling com.), Pa. Inst. CPAs, Nat. Assn. Accts. (past pres. Phila. chpt.), Planning Forum (past pres. Phila. chpt.), Soc. Children's Book Writers and Illustrators, Ironwood Country Club (bd. dirs. 1991-93). Avocations: golf, racquet sports, writing, reading. Home and Office: 636 McLendon Hills Dr West End NC 27376

KRAM, SHIRLEY WOHL, federal judge; b. NYC, 1922; Student, Hunter Coll., 1940-41, CUNY, 1940-47; LLB, Bklyn. Law Sch., 1950. Atty. Legal Aid Soc. N.Y., 1951-53, 1962-71; assoc. Simons & Hardy, 1954-55; pvt. practice law, 1955-60; judge Family Ct., NYC, 1971-83, U.S. Dist. Ct. (So. Dist.), NYC, 1983—93, sr. judge, 1993—. Author: (with Neil A. Frank) The Law of Child Custody, Development of the Substantive Law Office: 2101 US Courthouse 40 Centre St New York NY 10007-1581

KRAMARSKY, WERNER H., art collector; b. Amsterdam; s. Siegfried and Lola Kramarsky; m. Sarah-Ann Kramarsky; children: Stephen Mortimer, Daniel Jacob, Ann. NY State Commr. Human Rights, 1975—82. Bd. trustees Mus. Modern Art, NYC, 1998—, life trustee, 2003—, mem. drawing com., 1994—, vice chmn., 1998—, mem. com. on archives, library and rsch., 1997—; chmn. bd. Andy Warhol Found.; bd. dirs. UCLA Hammer Mus. Named one of Top 200 Collectors, ARTnews mag., 2004. Avocation: Collector modern and contemporary drawings, especially Am. Home: 560 Broadway New York NY 10012 Office Phone: 212-966-6601.

KRAMER, ALAN SHARFSIN, lawyer; b. NYC, Apr. 28, 1934; s. Michael and Alene (Sharfsin) K. BA, Dickinson Coll., 1956; LL.B., Columbia, 1962, JD, 1969. Bar: N.Y. 1962. Practice in, NYC, 1962-69, 73—; sr. v.p. Am. Medicorp, Inc., NYC, 1969-72; individual practice, 1974-78; pres. Alan S. Kramer (p.c.), 1978—; sr. mng. dir. Bear, Stearns & Co., Inc., 1990-96. Editor: Columbia Law Rev, 1960-62. Mem. nat. coun. Salk Inst.; mem. bd. visitors Columbia Law Sch. Served with M.I. AUS, 1956-58. Mem. Assn. of Bar of City of N.Y. Home: 315 E 86th St New York NY 10028-4714 Office: 500 Marmaroneck Ave Ste 405 Harrison NY 10528

KRAMER, ALLAN FRANKLIN, II, researcher, botanical garden official; b. NYC, Dec. 10, 1950; s. Walter Frederick and Dorothea (Russell-Hurley) K. AB, Coll. of Holy Cross, 1972; MS, Pratt Inst., 1979. Sr. document analyst Aspen Systems Corp., NYC, 1979-81, team leader analyst, 1981-83, mgr. rsch. staff, 1983-86; sr. editor Bus. Guides, Inc. div., sr. rsch. mgr. Lebhar-Friedman, Inc., NYC, 1987-91; trustee Bklyn. Botanic Garden, 1995-97, 2000—. Mem. exec. com. Bklyn. Bot. Garden Aux., 1991—, v.p., 1993-95, pres. 1995-97, dir., 1997—; mem. pres.'s coun. Coll. Holy Cross, class chmn.; dir.Youth Svcs. Opportunities Project; dir., treas. Park Slope Vol. Ambulance Corps.; dir. CAMBA; dir. Park Slope Neighborhood Family Ctr.; vice chair, dir., treas. Reel Works Teen Filmaking, 2003—; dir. Prospect Park YMCA. Gager fellow, 1991—. Mem. Am. Assn. Bot. Gardens and Arboreta, New Eng. Soc. in City of Bklyn. (v.p., dir.), Hundred Yr. Assn. N.Y., Royal Oak Found., Friendly Sons of St. Patrick (chmn.), Soc. Old Bklyn. (life), Battle of Bklyn. Conservancy (dir.), Assn. St. George the Martyr (Knight), Greek Order of St. Dennis of Zante (Knight), Montauk Club (dir.), Mcpl. Club Bklyn., Bklyn. C. of C., Surf Club of Quogue, English Speaking Union, Steuben Soc. Am., French-Am. Friendship Found., Beta Phi Mu (life). Avocations: sailing, travel, antiques. Home: 35 Prospect Park W Brooklyn NY 11215-2370

KRAMER, ANDREA S., lawyer; b. Chgo., Mar. 15, 1955; BA summa cum laude with high distinction, U. Ill., 1975; JD cum laude, Northwestern U., 1978. Bar: Ill. 1978, U.S. Tax Ct. 1980, U.S. Ct. Fed. Claims 1982, Ill. Ct. Appeals (no. dist., 7th cir.). With Coffield, Ungaretti & Harris, Chgo.; ptnr. McDermott Will & Emery LLP, Chgo. Adj. law prof. Northwestern U. Sch. Law. Author: Financial Products: Taxation, Regulation and Design, 2000; mem. editorial bd. Jour. Criminal Law and Criminology, 1976-78; contbr. articles to profl. jours., chpts. to books. Founding bd. mem. The Women's Treatment Ctr., Chgo., chmn. bd. dirs.; bd. dirs. Dance Art. Named one of The 50 Most Influential Women Lawyers in Am., Nat. Law Jour., 2007; recipient Bronze Tablet, U. Ill., 1975, Unsung Heroine Award, Cook County Bd. Commrs., 2004. Mem. Anti-Defamation League, Internat. Bar Assn., Chgo. Bar Assn. (sect. taxation), Chgo. Fin. Exchange, Alpha Lambda Delta, Phi Alpha Theta, Phi Beta Kappa, Phi Kappa Phi. Office: McDermott Will & Emery LLP 227 W Monroe St Chicago IL 60606-5096 Office Phone: 312-372-2000, 312-984-6480. Office Fax: 312-984-7700. Business E-Mail: akramer@mwe.com.*

KRAMER, ANDREW MICHAEL, lawyer; b. NYC, Nov. 2, 1944; s. Irving and Ida (Kaplan) K.; m. Cheryle Lynn Safran, June 21, 1966; children: Howard, Jennifer; m. Nita Lynne Albert, Mar. 13, 1983; children: Samantha, Stephanie. BA cum laude, Mich. State U., 1966; JD cum laude, Northwestern U., 1969. Bar: Ill. 1969, D.C. 1977, U.S. Ct. Appeals (4th cir.) 1977, U.S. Ct. Appeals (5th cir.) 1972, U.S. Ct. Appeals (6th cir.) 1972, U.S. Ct. Appeals (7th cir.) 1970, U.S. Ct. Appeals (11th cir.) 1982, Ohio 1990. Assoc. firm Seyfarth, Shaw, Fairweather & Geraldson, Chgo., 1969-73, ptnr. Washington, 1974-83; ptnr. client affairs Jones Day, Washington and Cleve., 1983. Exec. dir. Ill. Office Collective Bargaining, Springfield, 1973-74. Contbr. articles to profl. jours. Mem.: ABA, D.C. Bar Assn., Chgo. Bar Assn., Pepper Pike Club (Cleve.), Firestone Country Club, Congl. Country Club (Md.). Office: Jones Day 51 Louisiana Ave NW Washington DC 20001-2113 Office Phone: 202-879-4660. Business E-Mail: akramer@jonesday.com.

KRAMER, BARNETT SHELDON, oncologist; b. Balt., July 29, 1948; s. Mervin and Muriel Hannah (Woolf) K.; m. Ruth Solomon, June 25, 1972; 1 child, Jeremy. Student, Johns Hopkins U., 1966-69, MPH, 1991; MD, U. Md., 1973. Intern Washington U., St. Louis, 1973-74, med. resident, 1974-75; fellow Nat. Cancer Inst., Bethesda, Md., 1975-78, sr. investigator, 1986-90, assoc. dir., 1990-96, dep. dir. Divsn. Cancer Prevention and Control, 1996-97, dep. dir., Divsn. Cancer Prevention, 1997-2000; asst. prof. U. Fla., Gainesville, 1978-83, assoc. prof., 1983-86; editor-in-chief Jour. Nat. Cancer Inst., Bethesda; dir. Office Med. Applications of Rsch. NIH, 2000—, assoc. dir. for disease prevention, 2001—. Prof. medicine Uniformed Svcs. U. Health Scis., Bethesda, Md., 1989-90, clin. prof. medicine, 1990—. Co-editor: (with P. Greenwald and D. Weed) Cancer Prevention and Control, 1995; (with J. Gohagan and P. Prorok) Cancer Screening Theory and Practices, 1999, (with C. Allegra) Understanding Clinical Trials, 2000; assoc. editor Jour. Nat. Cancer Inst., 1988-94, editor-in-chief, 1994—; mem. editl. bd. Physicians Data Query, 1988—, chmn. bd. cancer prevention and screening, 1992—; contbr. articles to profl. publs., chpts. to books. With USPHS, 1975-78. Fellow ACP; mem. Am. Soc. Clin. Oncology (mem., chair cancer prevention com. 2006—), Alpha Omega Alpha, Delta Omega. Avocation: fountain pen collecting. Office: NIH Office Disease Prevention Rm 2B-03 6100 Executive Blvd MSC 7523 Bethesda MD 20892-2082 Business E-Mail: kramerb@od.nih.gov, bk76p@nih.gov.

KRAMER, BARRY ALAN, psychiatrist, educator; b. Phila., Sept. 9, 1948; s. Morris and Harriet (Greenberg) K.; m. Paulie Hoffman, June 9, 1974; children: Daniel Mark, Steven Philip. BA in Chemistry, NYU, Bronx, 1970; MD, Hahnemann Med. Coll., Phila., 1974. Resident in psychiatry Montefiore Hosp and Med. Ctr., Bronx, N.Y., 1974-77; practice medicine specializing in psychigary, NYC, 1977-82; staff psychiatrist L.I. Jewish-Hillside Med. Ctr., Glen Oaks, N.Y., 1977-82; asst. prof. SUNY, Stony Brook, 1978-82; practice medicine specializing in psychiatry, LA, 1982—; asst. prof. psychiatry U. So. Calif., 1982-89, assoc. prof. clin. psychiatry, 1989-94, prof. clin. psychiatry, 1994-98; ward chief L.A. County/U. So. Calif. Med. Ctr., 1982-98. Med. dir. ECT, Cedars Sinai Med. Ctr., 1998—; cons. Little Neck Nursing Home (N.Y.), 1979-82, L.I. Nursing Home, 1980-82; dir. ECT U. So. Calif. Sch. Medicine, 1990; adj. asst. prof. U. So. Calif., Sch. Pharmacy, 2004—. Reviewer Am. Jour. Psychiatry, Hosp. and Cmty. Psychiatry; mem. editl. bd. Convulsive Therapy; contbr. articles to profl. juors., papers to sci. meetings. Grantee NIMH, 1979-80, UCLA/U. So. Calif. Long-Term Gerontology Ctr., 1985-86, NARSAD, 2001—; named one of Am.'s Top Doctors, Castle Connolly Med. Ltd., 2001-06, Am.'s Top Psychiatrists, Consumers Rsch. Coun. Am., 2007. Fellow Am. Psychiat. Assn., Assn. Convulsive Therapy (editl. bd.); mem. AMA, Soc. Biol. Psychiatry, Calif. Med. Assn., L.A. Med. Assn., Am. Assn. Geriatric Psychiatry, Gerontol. Soc. Am., So. Calif. Psychiat. Soc. (chair ETC com.). Jewish. Office: Cedars Sinai Med Ctr Thalians 306-C 8730 Alden Dr Los Angeles CA 90048 also: PO Box 5792 Beverly Hills CA 90209-5792 Office Phone: 310-423-4014. Personal E-mail: barryakramer@yahoo.com. Business E-Mail: krameb@cshs.org.

KRAMER, BURTON, graphic designer, educator; b. NYC, June 25, 1932; s. Sam and Ida (Moore) K.; m. Irene Margarite Therese Mayer, Feb. 22, 1961; children: Gabrielle Kimberly, Jeremy Jacques. BS in Graphic Design, Ill. Inst. Tech., Chgo., 1954; postgrad. (Fulbright scholar), Royal Coll. Art, London, 1955-56; M.F.A., Yale U., 1957; D (hon.), Ontario Coll. Art and Design, 2003. Designer Will Burtin, NYC, 1957-58; asst. art dir. Arch. Record, NYC, 1959; pres., creative dir. Kramer Design Assoc., Ltd., Toronto, Canada, 1967—2001; designer Geigy Chem. Corp., NYC, 1959-61; dir. corp. graphics Clairtone Sound Corp., Toronto, Canada, 1967; chief designer Halpern Advt., Zurich, Switzerland, 1961-65; instr. Ont. Coll. Art & Design, Canada, 1978—99. Guest lectr. Rochester Inst. Tech., 1976, 81, designer-in-residence, 1981; vis. lectr. U. Cin., 1980; guest lectr., Arnhem, The Netherlands, 1994, Mexico City U. Autonoma, 1995; spkr. 1st Internat. Biennial of Symbols/Logotypes, Ostend, Belgium, 1994; mem. faculty Seneca Coll. Book designer The Art of Norval Morrisseau, 1979, Passionate Spirits, 1980; author Can. sect. Trademarks and Symbols of the World, 1973; co-author: Report on Canadian Road Sign Graphics, 1968; work pub. in numerous nat. and internat. jours., annuals and books; contbr. articles to profl. jours.; major works include signing-info. sys. CBC Broadcast Ctr., Toronto, IBM Tng. Ctr., Centenary Hosp., Scarborough, St. Lawrence Ctr. for Arts, Eaton Ctr., Erin Mills New Town, Mississauga, Metro Ctrl. YMCA, Copps Coliseum, Union Sta.; designer visual identity programs for CBC, N.Am. Life Assurance, Can. Imperial Bank Commerce, Reed Paper, ONEX Packaging Inc., Gemini, Vincor Internat., Can. Sys. Group, Nat. Rsch. Coun. Can., Centrestage, Royal Ont. Mus., Teknion Furniture Sys., Inc., Decoustics, Chartwell I.R.M., Scarborough Bd. Edn., Ont. Edn. Comm. Authority, Can. Crafts Coun., Ont. Guild Crafts, Zoomit Corp.; exhbns.include Pekao Gallery, Toronto, 1999, Peak Gallery, 2002, Kabat Wrobel Gallery, Toronto, 2003, Found. for Constructive Art, Calgary, 2002, Galerie Wolfgang Exner, Vienna, 2004-05, Gallery Carrion Vivar, Bogota, 2005, Arta Gallery, Toronto, 2005, Siano Gallery, Phila., 2006, Oeno Gallery, Prince Edward County, 2006, 07; work shown on websites Canadian Ctr. for Contemporary Art, www.ccca.ca, 2002, www.geoform-.net, www.art-exchange.com. Decorated Order of Ont.; recipient gold medal Internat. Typographic Composition Assn., 1971, gold medal Art Dir. Club Toronto, 1973, medal Leipzig BookFair, Toronto Arts Lifetime Achievement award 1999. Fellow Soc. Graphic Designers Can. (past pres.); mem. Alliance Graphique Internat., Royal Can. Acad. Arts. Home: 101 Roxborough St W Toronto ON Canada M5R 1T9 Office: 103 Dupont St Toronto ON Canada M5R 1V4 Office Phone: 416-921-1078 ext. 23. Business E-Mail: burton@kramer-design.com.

KRAMER, CECILE EDITH, retired medical librarian; b. NYC, Jan. 6, 1927; d. Marcus and Henrietta (Marks) K. BS, CCNY, 1956; MS in L.S., Columbia U., 1960. Reference asst. Columbia U. Health Scis. Library, NYC, 1957-61, asst. librarian, 1961-75; dir. Health Scis. Libr. Northwestern U., Chgo., 1975-91, asst. prof. edn., 1975-91, prof. emeritus, 1991—. Instr. library and info. sci. Rosary Coll., 1981-85; cons. Francis A. Countway Library Medicine, Harvard U., 1974. Pres. Friends of Libr., Fla. Atlantic U., Boca Raton. Fellow Med. Libr. Assn. (chmn. med. sch. librs. group 1975-76, editor newsletter 1975-77, instr. continuing edn. 1966-75, mem. panel cons. editors Bull. 1987-90, disting. mem. Acad. Health Info. Profls. 1993—); mem. Biomed. Comm. Network (chmn. 1979-80). Home: Homewood at Boca 9591 Yamato Rd Boca Raton FL 33434

KRAMER, DALE VERNON, retired language educator; b. Mitchell, SD, July 13, 1936; s. Dwight Lyman and Frances Elizabeth (Corbin) K.; m. Cheris Gamble Kramarae, Dec. 21, 1960; children: Brinlee, Jana. BS, SD State U., Brookings, 1958; MA, Case Western Res. U., Cleve., 1960, PhD, 1963. Instr. English Ohio U., Athens, 1962-63, asst. prof., 1963-65, U. Ill., Urbana, 1965-67, assoc. prof., 1967-71, prof. English, 1971-96; prof. emeritus, 1997—; acting head English dept. U. Ill., Urbana, 1982, 86-87, assoc. dean Coll. of Arts & Scis., 1992-95. Chmn. bd. editors Jour. English and Germanic Philology, 1972-95; mem. bd. editors Cambridge Edit. of the Works of Joseph Conrad, 1995—; assoc. vice provost, prof. English, U. Oreg., 1990. Author: Charles Robert Maturin, 1973, Thomas Hardy: The Forms of Tragedy, 1975, Thomas Hardy: Tess of the d'Urbervilles, 1991; editor: Critical Approaches to the Fiction of Thomas Hardy, 1979, Thomas Hardy, The Woodlanders, 1981, 85, Thomas Hardy, The Mayor of Casterbridge, 1987, Critical Essays on Thomas Hardy: The Novels, 1990, The Cambridge Companion to Thomas Hardy, 1999. Served to capt. US Army, 1958-66. Mem. Ctr. Advanced Study, 1971; Am. Philos. Soc. grantee, 1969, 86, NEH grantee, 1986. Mem.: Thomas Hardy Assn. (v.p. 2007—). Congregationalist.

KRAMER, DANIEL JONATHAN, lawyer; b. Cin., Dec. 20, 1957; BA magna cum laude, Wesleyan U., Middletown, Conn., 1980; JD, NYU, 1984. Bar: N.Y. 1985, U.S. Dist. Ct. (so. and ea. dists.) N.Y. 1985, U.S. Ct. Appeals (2d cir.) 1989. Assoc. Cravath, Swaine & Moore, NYC, 1985-86; law clk. to Chief Judge Wilfred Feinberg, U.S. Ct. Appeals for 2d Cir., NYC, 1986-87; assoc. Schulte Roth & Zabel LLP, NYC, 1987-92, ptnr., 1993—2002, Paul, Weiss, Rifkind, Wharton & Garrison, LLP, NYC, 2002—. Mem. pro se discretionary panel U.S. Ct. Appeals for 2d Cir., 1988—. Author: Federal Securities Litigation: Commentary and Forms, A

Deskbook for the Practitioner, 1997, Regulation of Market Manipulation, Federal Securities Exchange Act of 1934, 2002; contbr. articles to law jours. and newspaper. Bd. dirs. Leukemia Soc., N.Y.C., 1995-98; Big Apple Greeter, 2001-03. Mem. ABA, Assn. Bar City N.Y., N.Y. Lawyers for Pub. Interest. Office: Paul Weiss Rifkind Wharton & Garrison LLP 1285 Avenue of the Americas New York NY 10019

KRAMER, EDWARD GEORGE, lawyer; b. Cleve., July 15, 1950; s. Archibald Charles and Katherine Faith (Porter) K.; m. Roberta Darwin, June 15, 1974. BS in Edn., Kent State U., 1972; JD, Case Western Res. U., 1975. Bar: Ohio 1975, U.S. Dist. Ct. (no. dist.) Ohio 1975, U.S. Ct. Appeals (6th cir.) 1980, U.S. Supreme Ct. 1980, U.S. Dist. Ct. (so. dist.) Ohio 2005. Assoc. dir. The Cuyahoga Plan of Ohio, Cleve., 1975-76; exec. dir. The Housing Advs., Inc., Cleve., 1976—; sr. ptnr. Kramer & Assocs., LPA, Cleve., 1981—. Spl. counsel atty. gen. State of Ohio, Columbus, 1983-95; pres. Atty. Svcs., Inc., 1987-2002, ASI Info. Sys.; dir. Housing Law Clinic, 1989-95; dir. Fair Housing Law Clinic, 1995—; adj. lectr. Cleve. State U., 1991-94, adj. prof., 1994—; alt. consumer rep., FTC, Washington, 1976-77; cons. HUD, Washington, 1978-80, joint select com. sch. desegregation, Ohio Gen. Assembly, Columbus, 1979; visitors com., Case Western Res. U. Sch. Law, Cleve., 1977-83; chmn. Ford Motor Consumer Appeals Bd., 1989-93; bd. advisors Brownstone Pub. Author: How to Settle Small Claims: A Guide to The Use of Small Claims Courts, 1973, (with others) A Guide to Regional Housing Opportunities, 1979, (with Buchanan) Mobile Home Living: A Guide to Consumers' Rights, 1979; contbr. articles to legal jours. Chmn. Ohio Protection and Advocacy System for Developmentally Disabled, Columbus, 1978-80; trustee Muscle Disease Soc., Cleve., 1979-81; sec. Cuyahoga County Housing and Econ. Devel. com., Cleve., 1983—; mem. Cleve. Mayor's Com. on Employment of Handicapped, 1978-79; mem. fair housing adv. bd. John Marshall Law Sch. Named Disting. Recent Grad. Case Western Reserve U. Law Alumni Assn., 1985; Roscoe Pound fellow; recipient Fair Housing Pioneer Award Cuy. County Commisioners, 2001, Trustee award Legal Aid Soc. Cleve., 2004 Mem.: ATLA (chair fair housing litig. group 2004—, employment rights sect. chair 2001—02, chair sections leaders coun. 2002—03, chair civil rights sect. 2003—, newsletter editor, Outstanding Section Newsletter award 2005), ACLU (litigation com.), ABA (sect. on urban state and local govt. law, com. on housing and urban devel., forum on constrn. industry), Trial Lawyers for Pub. Justice, Am. Arbitration Assn., Ohio State Bar Assn., Million Dollar Adv. Panel, Planetary Soc., Assn. Am. Law Schs. (com. on clin. legal edn.), Nat. Employment Lawyers Assn., Cleve. Bar Assn. (trustee 1995—98, com. on homeless, chmn. law sch. liaison), Am. Coll. Barristers (life), Masons (Tyrian worshipful master 1989, 1991), Old River Yacht Club, Palm Beach Club (London), Cleve. Grays, Order of Ea. Star (James A. Garfield chpt.). Democrat. Mem. United Ch. Christ. Avocations: softball, scuba diving, collecting coins and stamps, chess, reading. Office: Kramer & Assocs LPA 3214 Prospect Ave E Cleveland OH 44115-2614 Office Phone: 216-431-5300 106. Personal E-mail: kramere7@aol.com.

KRAMER, EDWARD JOHN, materials engineering educator; b. Wilmington, Del., Aug. 5, 1939; s. Edward Noble and Irma (Nemetz) K.; m. Gail Allen Woodford, Aug. 24, 1963; children: Eric Woodford, Jeanne Noble. BChemE, Cornell U., 1962; PhD, Carnegie-Mellon U., 1967. Asst. prof. dept. materials sci. and engring. Cornell U., Ithaca, NY, 1967-72, assoc. prof., 1972-79, prof., 1979-88, Samuel B. Eckert prof. materials sci. and engring., 1988-97; prof. dept. materials & chem. engring. U. Calif., Santa Barbara, 1997—. Vis. scientist Argonne (Ill.) Nat. Lab., 1974-75; vis. prof. Akademie der Wissenschaften Inst. Metallphysik, Göttingen, Germany, 1979, Ecole Poly. Federale de Lausanne, Switzerland, 1982, Johannes Gutenberg U., Mainz, Germany, 1987-88. Contbr. over 300 articles to sci. jours. Recipient U.S. Sr. Scientist award Alexander von Humboldt Stiftung, 1987-88, Swinburne award Inst. Materials, U.K., 1996; NATO fellow, 1966-67, John Simon Guggenheim Found. fellow, N.Y.C., 1988. Fellow AAAS, Am. Phys. Soc. (High Polymer Physics prize 1985); mem. NAE, Materials Rsch. Soc., Am. Chem. Soc., Böhmische Phys. Soc. Avocation: masters swimming. Office: Univ Calif Materials Dept Engring II Santa Barbara CA 93106 Office Phone: 805-894-4999. Business E-Mail: edkramer@mrl.ucsb.edu.

KRAMER, ELEANOR, retired real estate broker, tax specialist, financial consultant; b. NYC, Feb. 18, 1939; d. Herman I. Kramer and Fay (Berger) Kramer-Levy; m. Richard H. Fitz-Gerald III, Dec. 24, 1959 (div.); m. Gregory F. Navarro, Oct. 1, 1975 (div. Mar. 1996); children: Brad, Cindy. BA in Speech and Theater, Bklyn Coll., 1975; MS in Urban Affairs, CUNY, Hunter Coll., 1976. Tchr. cultural arts Bronx (N.Y.) Bd. Edn., 1966-70; real estate broker, pres. Tritown Realty Corp., Mamaroneck, NY, 1978-83; pvt. practice tax cons. Mamaroneck, 1983—2000. Adj. prof. sociology Rockland CC, Suffern, N.Y., 1979-85, Westchester CC, Valhalla, NY, 1979-85; founder dance therapy St. Vincent's Hosp., NYC; lectr., demonstrator NYC Pub. Schs., author, prodr., performer, co-creator child edn. programs, 1967-77; ombudsman Bklyn. Coll., 1974-75. Mem. pub. rel. com. Bicentennial commn. Village of Mamaroneck, 1976; bd. dirs. Cmty. Action Program, Mamaroneck, 1977-79. Mem.: LWV (bd. dirs. 1977—80), NOW (ad hoc chmn. 1970, co-chair, co-author women's ednl. seminar Libr. of Congress), Nat. Soc. Tax Preparers, Lions (Larchmont, NY). Avocations: puzzles, tennis, antiques, jazz, theater. Mailing: 616 Clearwater Park Rd Ste 313 West Palm Beach FL 33401 Office Phone: 561-832-3506.

KRAMER, EUGENE LEO, lawyer; b. Barberton, Ohio, Nov. 7, 1939; s. Frank L. and Portia I. (Acker) Kramer; m. JoAnn Stockhausen, Sept. 19, 1970; children: Martin, Caroline, Michael. AB, John Carroll U., 1961; JD, U. Notre Dame, 1964. Bar: Ohio 1964. Law clk. U.S. Ct. Appeals (7th cir.), Chgo., 1964-65; ptnr. Squire, Sanders & Dempsey, Cleve., 1965-91, Roetzel & Andress, A Legal Profl. Assn., Cleve. and Akron, Ohio, 1992-97; spl. counsel Ohio Atty. Gen., 2003—06. Cons. Ohio Constl. Revision Commn., Columbus, 1970—74. Trustee Regina Health Ctr., 1997—, pres., 2001—04; past pres. HELP Found., Inc., HELP, Inc., Cleve., 1981—92, Playhouse Sq. Assn., Cleve., 1980—84; pres. N.E. Ohio Transit Coalition, 1992—; mem. policy com. Build-Up Greater Cleve. Program, 1982—98; mem. Greater Cleve. Partnership; trustee Consultation Ctr. Diocese Cleve., 1990—96; mem. Future Ch. Leadership Coun., 2005—; trustee Citizens League Greater Cleve., 1984—90, 1993—, Citizens League Rsch. Inst., 1995—97, Lyric Opera Cleve., 1995—2006, Beck Ctr. for the Arts, 2007—, St. Ann Found., 1990—92. Recipient Disting. Leadership award, HELP, Inc., 1986, Pioneer Achievement award, HELP-Six Chimneys, Inc., 1986, Disting. Svc. award, Assn. Retarded Citizens, 1990, Vol. Svc. award, City of Lakewood, 2001. Mem.: ABA, Cleve. Bar Assn., Ohio State Bar Assn. (chmn. local govt. law com. 1986—90), Club Key Tower. Democrat. Roman Catholic. Avocations: music, theater, sports, travel. Home and Office: 1422 Euclid Ave Ste 1162 Cleveland OH 44115-2001 Home Phone: 216-228-7442; Office Phone: 216-621-7974. Personal E-mail: elkramer5@aol.com.

KRAMER, FRANKLIN DAVID, lawyer; b. Liberty, NY, Nov. 13, 1945; s. Solomon and Carolyn Bertha (Cohen) C.; m. Noël Anketell, May 30, 1970; children: Katherine Anketell, Christopher Anketell. BA cum laude, Yale U., 1967; JD magna cum laude, Harvard U., 1971. Bar: N.Y. 1972, D.C. 1972, Supreme 1976. Law clk. assoc. judge U.S. Ct. Appeals (2d cir.), NYC, 1971-72; assoc. Shea & Gardner, Washington, 1972-77, ptnr., 1982—; spl. asst. to asst. sec. def. Dept. Def., Washington, 1977-79, prin. dep. asst. to asst. sec. def. for internat. security affairs, 1979-81; dep. asst. sec. European and NATO Affairs, 1996—96; asst. sec. Def. Internat. Security Affairs, 1996—2001; disting. rsch. fellow Ctr. for Tech. and Nat. Security Policy, Wash., DC, 2001—. Capstone prof. George Wash. U. Elliott Sch. Internat. Affairs; chmn. bd. World Affairs Coun., Wash., DC; chmn. com. Asian and Global Security Atlantic Coun. Contbr. articles to profl. jours. Mem. ABA, Internat. Inst. Strategic Studies, Am. Arbitration Assn. (comml. arbitrator). Democrat. Jewish. Office: Ctr for Tech and Nat Security Policy Nat Def U 300 5th Ave SW Fort Lesley J McNair Washington DC 20319 Office Phone: 202-685-2529. Office Fax: 202-685-3581.

KRAMER, GORDON, mechanical engineer; b. Bklyn., Aug. 1937; s. Joseph and Etta (Grossberg) K.; m. Ruth Ellen Harter, Mar. 5, 1967 (div. June 1986); children: Samuel Maurice, Leah Marie; m. Eve Burstein, Dec. 17, 1988. BS, Cooper Union, 1959; MS, Calif. Inst. Tech., 1960. With Hughes Aircraft Co., Malibu, Calif., 1959-63; sr. scientist Avco Corp., Norman, Okla., 1963-64; asst. divsn. head Batelle Meml. Inst., Columbus, Ohio, 1964-67; sr. scientist Aeroject Electrosystems, Azusa, Calif., 1967-75; chief engr. Beckman Instrument Co., Fullerton, Calif., 1975-82; prin. scientist McDonnell Douglas Microelectronics Co., 1982-83, Kramer and Assocs., 1983-85; program mgr. Hughes Aircraft Co., 1985-96, ret., 1996; fin. advisor Ameriprise Fin., 1999—. Cons. Korea Inst. Tech. NSF fellow, 1959-60. Mem. IEEE. Democrat. Jewish. Home: 153 Lake Shore Dr Rancho Mirage CA 92270-4055 Office Phone: 760-340-3903. Personal E-mail: gordeve@aol.com. Business E-Mail: gordon.x.kramer@ampf.com.

KRAMER, KEITH ALLAN, music educator, composer; b. Balt., Mar. 19, 1968; D Musical Arts, U. Miami, 1999. Grad. asst. U. Miami, Coral Gables, Fla., 1995—98; prof. music Harford C.C., Bel Air, Md., 1998—. Composer: (chamber work for clarinet and piano) Uncertainty Principle, 1998 (Winner of the College Music Society Mid-Atlantic Chapter Student Composer Competition, 1999), (concerto for soprano saxophone) Limits of Reason, 1996 (Winner of the University of Miami Symphony Orchestra Composition Competition, 1998), (chamber work for piano) Spatial Extremes, 2003; composer, condr.: Beyond Sonic Boundaries, 2006. Recipient prize in Symphony Orch. Composition Competition, U. Miami, 1998. Mem.: BMI, Coun. for Higher Edn. in Music (CHEM), Soc. for Music Theory, Coll. Music Soc., Am. Composers Forum, Soc. Composers Inc. Office: Harford CC 401 Thomas Run Road, Harve de Grace Hall Bel Air MD 21015 Office Phone: 410-836-4000 ext. 7706. Personal E-mail: kkramer@keithkramer.org.

KRAMER, KENNETH BENTLEY, retired federal judge, former congressman; b. Chgo., Feb. 19, 1942; s. Albert Aaron and Ruth (Pokrass) K.; m. Louise Kotoshirodo; children: Kenneth Bentley, Kelly J. BA magna cum laude in Polit. Sci., U. Ill., 1963; JD, Harvard U., 1966. Bar: Ill. 1966, Colo. 1969. Dep. dist. atty. El Paso County, Colo., Colorado Springs, 1970-72; pvt. practice law Colorado Springs, 1972-78; mem. Colo. Ho. of Reps., 1973-78, US Congress from 5th Colo. Dist., 1978-86; asst. sec. Dept. Army, Washington, 1988-89; judge US Ct. Appeals Vets. Claims, Washington, 1989-2000, chief judge, 2000—04. Chmn. com. on vets. benefits ABA, 1990-94. Bd. visitors U.S. Air Force Acad., 1979-86; bd. dirs. Pikes Peak Mental Health Ctr., 1976-78, Mountain Valley chpt. March of Dimes, 1983-85, US Space Found., 1983— (founder), US Assn. Former Mem. of Congress, 2006-; commr. Nat. Coun. on Uniform State Laws, 1977-78. Capt. U.S. Army, 1967-70. Recipient Disting. Civilian Svc. medal. Mem. Phi Beta Kappa.

KRAMER, LARRY, dean, lawyer, educator; b. Chgo., June 23, 1958; m. Sarah Delson, 1996; 1 child, Veronika. BA magna cum laude, Brown U., 1980; JD cum laude, U. Chgo., 1984. Clerk to Judge Henry J. Friendly U.S. Ct. Appeals for the Second Cir., 1984—85; to Justice William J. Brennan, Jr. U.S. Supreme Ct., 1985—86; asst. prof. U. Chgo., 1986—90, prof., 1990—91; vis. prof. U. Mich., 1990—91, prof., 1991—94; vis. prof., Golieb Fellow NYU, 1993—94, Russell D. Niles Prof. Law, 2001—04, assoc. dean Rsch. and Academics, 2002—04; dean, Richard E. Lang Prof. Law Stanford Law Sch., 2004—. Reporter Fed. Cts. Study Com., 1989—90; cons. Mayer, Brown, Rowe & Maw, New York, NY, 1991—2004; assoc. dir., instr. Inst. Judicial Adminstrn., NYU, 1994—98; dir. English-Lang. Studies The Hague Acad. Internat. Law, 1994. Co-author: Conflict of Laws: Cases-Comments-Questions, 1993, 2001; editor: Reforming the Civil Justice System, 1996; author: The People Themselves: Popular Constitutionalism and Judicial Review, 2004. Recipient L. Hart Wright Award for Excellence in Teaching, U. Mich. Law Sch., 1991, Award for Best Teacher, Assn. Am. Law Schools, 2000, Order of the Coif, U. Chicago Law Sch. Fellow: Am. Acad. Arts & Sciences; mem.: ABA, Chgo. Coun. Lawyers (bd. govs. 1989—91), Brennan Ctr. for Jusice (bd. mem. 1995—2004), Am. Assn. Law Schs. (chair Conflict Laws Sec. 1992—93, chair Fed. Cts. Sec. 1996—97), Judicature Soc., NY Bar Assn., Am. Law Inst., Phi Beta Kappa. Office: Stanford U Sch Law Crown Quadrangle 559 Nathan Abbott Way Stanford CA 94305-4985 Office Phone: 650-723-4985. E-mail: deans.office@law.stanford.edu.

KRAMER, LAWRENCE STEPHEN, journalist; b. Hackensack, NJ, Apr. 24, 1950; s. Abraham and Ann Eve (Glasser) K.; m. Myla F. Lerner, Sept. 3, 1978; children: Matthew Lerner, Erika. BS in Journalism, Syracuse U., 1972; MBA, Harvard U., 1974. Reporter San Francisco Examiner, 1974-77, exec. editor, 1986-91; reporter Wash. Post, 1977-80, asst. to exec. editor, 1982, asst. mng. editor, 1982-86; exec. editor Trenton Times, NJ, 1980-82; founder, pres., exec. editor DataSport Inc. (acquired by Data Broadcasting Corp.), San Mateo, Calif., 1991-94; v.p. news, sports, mktg. Data Broadcasting Corp., San Mateo, 1994-97; founder, pres., CEO CBS.Marketwatch.com., San Francisco, 1997—2005, CBS pres. digital media, 2005—. Guest lectr. Harvard Bus. Sch.; mem. Pulitzer Prize Jury, 1987—88; founding bd. mem. Online Pub. Assn., 2001. Recipient W.R. Hearst Found. award 1971-72, Gerald Loeb award 1977, Nat. Press Club award; named one of 100 Most Influential Bus. Journalists 20th Century, 2000 Mem. Soc. Profl. Journalists Achievements include created SporTrax; created DBC News, predecessor co. to MarketWatch.com. Home: 8 Auburn Ct Belvedere Tiburon CA 94920-1349

KRAMER, LINDA KONHEIM, curator, art historian; b. NYC, Nov. 8, 1939; d. Clarence John and May (Sternberg) Konheim; m. Samuel R. Kramer, Apr. 24, 1977; 1 child, Nicholas Clarence. BA in Fine Arts and Art History, Smith Coll., 1961; BFA in Painting and Graphic Design, Yale U., 1963; MA in 19th and 20th Century European and Am. Art, NYU, 1968, PhD, 2000. Curator asst. Solomon R. Guggenheim Mus., 1963—66, program adminstr., 1966—76; cataloger modern drawings Sotheby Park-Bernet, NYC, 1980-82; expert in modern drawings Sotheby's N.Y., 1982-85; curator prints and drawings, dept. head Bklyn. Mus., 1985-94. Tchr. Sch. Visual Arts, N.Y.C., 1977-80, Manhattanville Coll., summer 1995, 96; exec. dir. Nancy Graves Found., N.Y.C., 1996—; mem. adv. bd. Coll. Fine Arts, West Wash. U., Bellingham, 1987-95. Author: books, pamphlets and catalogs; contbr. articles to profl. jours. Grantee Nat. Mus. Act, 1976, 78; Jane and Morgan Whitney fellow Met. Mus. Art, 1995-96. Mem.: Am. Assn. Mus., Print Coun. Am., Art Table, Coll. Art Assn. Home: 372 Central Park W New York NY 10025-8240 Office: Nancy Graves Found 450 W 31st St 2d Fl New York NY 10001-4608 Office Phone: 212-560-0602. Business E-Mail: mail@nancygravesfoundation.org.

KRAMER, MARC Z., publishing executive; Grad., SUNY, Albany, N.Y. Law Sch. Lawyer labor dept. N.Y.C. Bd. Edn.; dep. gen. counsel, gen. counsel Mayor's Office Labor Rels., 1985—90; labor assoc. Proskauer Rose Goetz & Mendelsohn, NY, 1990—93; v.p., gen. counsel NY Daily News, 1993—98; v.p. labor rels. NY Times, NYC, 1998—99, prodn. supr., 1999—2001, sr. v.p. production, 2001—04, sr. v.p. circulation, 2004—06; CEO Daily News, NYC, 2006—. Office: Daily News 450 W 33d St New York NY 10001

KRAMER, MARY ELIZABETH, ambassador, former state legislator; b. Burlington, Iowa, June 14, 1935; d. Ross L. and Geneva M. (McElhinney) Barnett; m. Kay Frederick Kramer, June 13, 1958; children: Kent, Krista. BA, U. Iowa, 1957, MA, 1971. Cert. tchr., Iowa. Tchr. Newton (Iowa) Pub. Schs., 1957-61, Iowa City Pub. Schs., 1961-67, tchr., asst. supt., 1971-75; dir. pers. Younkers, Inc., Des Moines, 1975-81; v.p. Wellmark, Inc., Des Moines, 1981-99; mem. Iowa Senate from 37th dist., Des Moines, 1990—2004; pres. of the senate, 1997—2004; US amb. to Barbados and Ea. Caribbean, 2004—06. Mem. Olympic adv. com. Blue Cross and Blue Shield Assn., Chgo., 1988—92; presdl. appointee White House Commn. on Presdl. Scholars, 2001, now chmn.; Bd. dirs. Polk County Child Care Rsch. Ctr., Des Moines, 1986—96, YWCA, Des Moines, 1989—94. Named Mgr. of Yr. Iowa Mgmt. Assocs., 1985, Woman of Achievement YWCA, 1986, Woman of Vision Young Women's Resource Ctr., 1989. Mem. Soc. Human Resource Mgmt. (Profl. of Yr. 1996), Iowa Mgmt. Assn. (pres. 1988), Greater Des Moines C. of C. (bd. dirs. 1986-96), Nexus, Rotary Internat. Republican. Presbyterian. Avocations: music, public speaking.

KRAMER, MICHAEL STUART, pediatric epidemiologist; b. NYC, July 8, 1948; arrived in Can., 1978; s. George and Beatrice (Jacobs) K.; m. Claire Yael Sasportas, June 14, 1981; children: Eric, Elise, Philippe. BA, U. Chgo., 1969; MD, Yale U., 1973. Diplomate Am. Bd. Pediatrics, Am. Coll. Epidemiology. Intern in pediat. Yale New Haven (Conn.) Hosp., 1973-74, resident in pediat., 1974-76; fellow clin. epidemiology Yale U., 1976-78; asst. prof. faculty medicine McGill U., Montreal, Que., Canada, 1978-82, assoc. prof., 1982-87, prof., 1987—. Com. mem. U.S. Inst. Medicine/NAS, Washington, 1986—; vis. scientist Nat. Perinatal Epidemiology Unit, Oxford, England, 1991—92; cons. WHO, Geneva, 1984—, Nat. Health R&D Program Can., 1992—97; Nat. Health Scientist, 1992—97; disting. scientist Can. Inst. Health Rsch., 1997—2002, sr. investigator, 2002—, sci. dir. Inst. Human Devel. and Child and Youth Health, 2003—. Author: Clinical Epidemiology and Biostatistics, 1988, Nutrition During Pregnancy, 1990, Adverse Events Associated With Childhood Vaccines, 1994, Improving Birth Outcomes, 2003, Reducing Birth Defects, 2003. Violinist:New Haven Symphony, 1969-73, I Medici di McGill, Montreal, 1990-94. Nat. Health Rsch. scholar, 1982-88; recipient Prix d'excellence Insvc. Clubs Coun. Que., Montreal, 1987, Chercheur Boursier Sr. FRSQ, Que., 1988-91, Rsch. award Ambulatory Pediatric Assn., 1993, Sanofi Pasteur award for pediat. rsch. Can. Pediat. Soc., 2006. Mem.: Soc. Pediat. and Perinatal Epidemiol. Rsch. (pres. 1997—98), Soc. Epidemiol. Rsch. (John Cassel Meml. lectr. 2004), Soc. Pediat. Rsch. (coun. 1986—89). Avocations: chamber music (violin), skiing, hiking, tennis, squash. Office: McGill U 2300 Tupper St Montreal PQ Canada H3H 1P3 Office Phone: 514-412-4400 ext. 22687. Business E-Mail: Michael.Kramer@mcgill.ca.

KRAMER, NOËL ANKETELL, judge; b. Bay City, Mich., Nov. 22, 1945; d. Thomas Jackson and Ruth Genevieve (LeRoux) Anketell; m. Franklin D. Kramer, May 30, 1970; children: Katherine, Christopher. BA with honors, Vassar Coll., 1967; JD with honors, U. Mich., 1971. Bar: D.C. 1972, U.S. Supreme Ct. 1975. Assoc. Wilmer, Cutler & Pickering, Washington, 1971-76; asst. U.S. atty. D.C. US Dept. State, Washington, 1976-84; judge D.C. Superior Ct., Washington, 1984—2005, dep. presiding judge, criminal div., 1999—2003, presiding judge, criminal div., 2000—05; assoc. judge D.C. Ct. Appeals, Washington, 2005—. Recipient Judge Robert A. Shuker award, 2004. Mem. ABA., Nat. Assn. Women Judges, Women's Bar Assn. D.C. (Woman Lawyer of Yr., 2005), D.C. Bar (chair person cts., lawyers and adminstrn. justice div. 1982-84), U. Mich. Law Club Washington (pres. 1976-78). Office: DC Ct Appeals 500 Indiana Ave NW Rm 6000 Washington DC 20001-2131 Office Phone: 202-879-2786.*

KRAMER, ORIN STUART, investment services company executive; b. Maplewood, NJ, June 27, 1945; s. Julian Saul and Ruth (Tantleff) K.; m. Hilary Meg Ballon, Jan. 7, 1989; children: Sophia, Charles. BA, Yale U., 1967; JD, Columbia U., 1970. Atty. Simpton, Thacher & Bartlett, NYC, 1970-71; exec. dir. N.Y. State Commn. on Economy, NYC, 1973-74; assoc. dir. White House Domestic Policy Staff, Washington, 1977-81; cons. McKinsey & Co., NYC, 1981-83, Kramer Assoc., NYC, 1984—; gen. ptnr. Boston Provident Partners, 1992; gen ptnr. Kramer Spellman LP, Fort Lee, NJ, 1995—. Vice chair, exec. dir. N.Y. State Commn. on Liability Ins. and Tort Reform, N.Y.C., 1986, Calif. Workers Compensation Ratemaking Commn., Sacramento, 1986. Author: Rating the Risks, 1990, Rate Suppression and its Consequences, 1991. Home: 261 Glenwood Rd Englewood NJ 07631-1910

KRAMER, PAUL R., lawyer; b. Balt., June 6, 1936; s. Philip and Lee (Labovitz) K.; m. Janet Amitin, Sept. 1, 1957; children: Jayne, Susan, Nancy. BA, Am. U., 1959, JD, 1961. Bar: Md. 1961, D.C. 1962, U.S. Supreme Ct. 1965, U.S. Ct. Appeals (6th cir.) 1992, U.S. Dist. Ct. 1963, U.S. Ct. Appeals (4th cir.) 1964, U.S. Ct. Appeals (9th cir.) 1996. Staff atty., dep. dir. Legal Aid Agy. Fed. Pub. Defender's Office, Washington, 1962-63; asst. U.S. atty. Dist. Md., 1963-69; dep. U.S. atty. Md. Balt., 1969-83; exec. bd. Balt. area coun. Boy Scouts Am., 1970-83, coun. adv. bd. Balt. area, 1983—, N.E. regional adv. bd., 1999—. Mem.-at-large Boy Scouts of Am. Nat., 1992—; instr. CLE U. Md. Sch. Law, 1975-80; assoc. prof. law Villa Julie Coll., 1976-80; assoc. professorial lectr. George Washington U., 1979; instr. Nat. Coll. Dist. Attys., 1979; permanent mem. 4th cir. fed. jud. conf. Fellow Md. Bar Found.; mem. ABA, Fed. Bar Assn. (pres. Md. chpt. 1973-74, nat. dep. sec. 1981-82, nat. sec. 1982-83, nat. cir. v.p. 1973-81, 86-87, cir. officer 4th cir. 1992-93, v.p. 4th cir. 1996-02, chmn. nat. cir. v.p. 1978-80, nat. coun. 1973-2005, jud. selection com. 1971-79, 88-90, faculty Fed Practice Inst. 1981-86, strategic long range planning com. 1995-96, found. charter life fellow 2002—), Md. Bar Assn. (subcom. litig. dist. ct. 1990—, found. fellow 1996—, bd. govs. 2005-07, jud. adminstrv. com. 2006—), Balt. Bar Assn. (criminal law com., dist. ct. com. 1990—, jud. selection com. 1992-2006, chair judiciary sub-com. on policy 1993-94, atty. grievance commn. of Md., inquiry com. Balt. City, 1993—, chair criminal law com., drug ct. com. 1994-95, jud. adminstrn. com. 2006-), Balt. County Bar Assn., Nat. Assn. Criminal Trial Attys., Md. Trial Lawyers Assn., Md. Criminal Def. Attys. Assn., U.S. Atty. Alumni Assn. (bd. dirs. 2003—), Barrister's Law Club (pres. 2003) Masons (past master). Office Phone: 410-727-5531, 800-794-8095. Personal E-mail: paulkramer11@aol.com.

KRAMER, PETER DAVID, psychiatrist, psychology professor; m. Rachel M. Schwartz, June 29, 1980; children: Sarah Elizabeth, Jacob Aaron, Matthew Charles. AB, Harvard Coll., 1970; postgrad., Univ. Coll., London, 1970-72; MD, Harvard Med. Sch., 1976. Diplomate in psychiatry and in adolescent psychiatry Am. Bd. Psychiatry and Neurology. Resident in internal medicine U. Wis. Hospitals, Madison, 1976-77; resident in psychiatry Yale U., New Haven, 1977-80; acting dir. divsn. sci. Alcohol, Drug Abuse, Mental Health Adminstrn., Rockville, Md., 1980-82; outpatient dir. R.I. Hosp., Providence, 1982-84; asst. prof. dept. psychiatry Brown U., Providence, 1982-91, assoc. prof., 1991-95, prof., 1995—; asst. prof. psychiatry George Washington U., 1981-82. Author: Moments of Engagement, 1989, Listening to Prozac, 1993, Should You Leave?, 1997, Spectacular Happiness, 2001, Against Depression, 2005, Freud: Inventor of the Modern Mind, 2006; mem. editl. bd. Psychiat. Times, 1985—, The Psychodynamic Letter, 1990-92, Am. Jour. Psychotherapy, 1996—; contbr. articles to profl. jours.; host syndicated pub. radio show The Infinite Mind, 2005-06. Mem. Am. Psychiat. Assn. (pvt. practice com. 1988-94, chmn. 1992-94), R.I. Med. Soc., R.I. Psychiat. Soc. (pres. 1990-91). Office: 196 Waterman St Providence RI 02906-2212

KRAMER, PETER ROBIN, computer company executive; b. NYC, Sept. 29, 1951; s. Morris and Ruth (Soloway) K.; m. Gerry Festo, Aug. 25, 1985. BA in Fine Arts, SUNY, Stony Brook, 1973; MFA, L.I. U., 1975. Dir., gen. ptnr. Doll & Richards Gallery, Boston, 1979-81; exec. v.p. and dir. Zoom Telephonics, Inc., Boston, 1977—. Mem. nat. adv. bd. Coll. Arts and Scis., SUNY, Stony Brook, 1999—2003. Bd. dirs. Cambridge Art Assn., 1983-86, pres. 1986-88; mem. nat. adv. bd. Coll. Arts and Scis. SUNY, Stony Brook, 1999-; dir. Intermute, Inc., 2000-05. Avocations: old houses, fine arts, antiques, tennis, golf.

KRAMER, PHILIP JOSEPH, lawyer; b. Binghamton, NY, May 1, 1936; s. Donald W. and Gladys M. (Dorion) K.; m. Barbara E. Fisher, July, 1960; children: Perry, Donald, Matthew, Sharon. BA, Yale U., 1958; LLB, Cornell U., 1961. Bar: NY 1961, US Dist. Ct. (no. dist.) NY 1961. Assoc. Kramer, Wales & Robinson, Binghamton, 1961-64, ptnr., 1964-78; justice, 6th Jud. Dist. NY Supreme Ct., 1978; ptnr. Kramer, Wales & McAvoy, Binghamton, 1979-84, Kramer, Wales & Wright, Binghamton, 1984-95, Kramer & Kenyon, 1996-98; spl. counsel Hinman, Howard & Kattell. Pres. Binghamton Local Devel. Agy., 1982-87. Fellow Am. Coll. Trial Lawyers; mem. NY State Bar Assn., Broome County Bar Assn. (pres. 1982). Democrat. Roman Catholic. Avocations: fishing, hunting. Office: 700 Security Mut Bldg 80 Exchange St PO Box 5250 Binghamton NY 13902-5250 Office Phone: 607-231-6893. Fax: 607-723-6605. E-mail: pkramer@hhk.com.

KRAMER, PHILLIP D., oil industry executive; Various positions Plains All American Pipeline, Houston, CFO, 1992—, sr. v.p., 1997-98, exec. v.p., 1998—. Office: Plains All American Pipeline Ste 1600 333 Clay St Houston TX 77002*

KRAMER, RICHARD J., manufacturing executive; b. Cleve., Oct. 30, 1963; married; 4 children. BS in Bus. Adminstrn., John Carroll U., 1986. CPA. With PricewaterhouseCoopers, 1987—2000, ptnr.; v.p. corp. fin. Goodyear Tire & Rubber Co., 2000, v.p. fin. North American Tire, 2002—03, sr. v.p. strategic planning & restructuring, 2003—04, exec. v.p., CFO, 2004—. Office: Goodyear Tire & Rubber Co 1144 East Market St Akron OH 44316*

KRAMER, RICHARD JAY, gastroenterologist, educator; b. Morristown, NJ, Mar. 31, 1947; s. Bernard and Estelle (Mishkin) K.; m. Leslie Fay Davis, June 28, 1970; children: Bryan Jeffrey, Erik Seth Davis. Student, UCLA, 1965-68; MD, U. Calif., Irvine, 1972. Diplomate Am. Bd. Internat. Med., Am. Bd. Gastroenterology. Intern Los Angeles County Harbor Gen. Hosp., Torrance, Calif., 1972-73; resident Santa Clara Valley Med. Ctr., San Jose, Calif., 1973-76; fellow gastroent. Stanford (Calif.) U. Hosp., 1976-78; pvt. practice San Jose, 1978—2003; tchr. gastroenterology Santa Clara Valley Med. Ctr., San Jose, 2003—. Clin. assoc. prof. of medicine Stanford (Calif.) U., 1984—; chmn. med. dept. Good Samaritan Hosp., San Jose, 1988-90. Pres. Jewish Family Service Bd., San Jose, 1974. Recipient Regents scholarship U. Calif., 1965, 68, Mosby Book award, Mosby Books, Inc., Irvine, Calif., 1972. Fellow Am. Gastroent. Assn.; mem. Am. Coll. Physicians, Calif. Med. Soc., Santa Clara County Med. Soc., No. Calif. Soc. Clin. Gastroenterologists, Internat. Brotherhood Magicians, Mystic 13 (pres. 1986-87, San Jose), Masons, Alpha Omega Alpha. Jewish. Avocations: magic, travel.

KRAMER, SIDNEY B., publishing executive, literary agent, lawyer; b. NYC, 1915; s. Louis and Mildred (Hindin) K.; m. Esther Schlansky, Nov. 23, 1939; children: Wendy Beth Kramer Posner, Mark William. BS, NYU, 1936; JD, Bklyn. Law Sch., St. Lawrence U., 1939. Bar: N.Y. 1940, Conn. 1962, U.S. Supreme Ct. 1975. Practice in, NYC, 1940-45, Westport, Conn., 1963—; founder (1945), sr. v.p. Bantam Books, Inc., NYC, 1945-67; founder (1950), mng. dir. Corgi Books, London, 1960-62; pres., dir. Remarkable Bookshop, 1960-95; pres. New Am. Library, NYC, 1967-72, MEWS Books Ltd., Westport, Conn., 1975—. Mng. dir., cons. Cassell & Collier Macmillan Pubs. Ltd., London, 1973-74. Chmn. Democratic Town Com., also justice peace, Westport, 1960—; chmn. Save Westport Now, 1981—. Recipient Westport Arts Heritage award for Lit., 2001. Mem. Conn. Bar Assn. Office: 20 Bluewater Hill Westport CT 06880-6504 Personal E-mail: mewsbooks@aol.com.

KRAMER, SIMON PAUL, writer; b. Cin., Aug. 17, 1914; s. Simon Pendleton and Minnie (Halle) K.; m. Marie Louise Belden, Jan. 5, 1955 (div. 1968); 1 child, Theresa. BA, Princeton U., 1935; MLitt, Trinity Coll., Cambridge, Eng., 1938. Spl. asst. coord. Inter-Am. Affairs, Washington, 1940-43; staff CIA, Washington, 1947-51; ptnr. Auerbach, Pollak and Richardson, NYC, 1954-57; pres. Conporacion Industrial, Panama, 1954-57, Panama Coop. Fisheries, 1957-60; staff cons. IGY-Nat. Acad. Scis., Washington, 1956-57, 60-62. Author: The Last Manchu, 1967, 2d edit. 1987, Latin American Panorama, 1968, The City in American Life, 1970, Nelson Rockefeller and British Security Coordination in Sage Readers in 20th Century History, 1982, Memories of a Secret Agent, 2007. Lt. USNR, 1943-46. Republican. Avocations: politics, gardening, bridge. Home and Office: 3023 Dent Pl NW Washington DC 20007-2916 Personal E-mail: sptk@erols.com.

KRAMER, WILLIAM DAVID, lawyer; b. Anniston, Ala., Feb. 2, 1944; s. John Robert and Janice Marian (Dye) K.; m. Johanna Scalzi, Dec. 1, 1973; children: Elizabeth Annemarie, David MacLaren. Student, Case Western Res. U., 1959-60; AB in Govt. with honors magna cum laude, Oberlin Coll., 1965; JD, M in Pub. Adminstrn., Harvard U., 1969. Bar: Mass. 1969, D.C. 1973, U.S. Ct. Appeals (D.C. cir.) 1974, U.S. Dist. Ct. D.C. 1976, U.S. Ct. Appeals (10th cir.) 1978, U.S. Ct. Internat. Trade 1983, U.S. Ct. Appeals (fed. cir.) 1983. Assoc. dir. Gov.'s Com. on Law Enforcement and Adminstrn. Criminal Justice, Boston, 1969-71, dep. dir., 1971-73; assoc. Squire, Sanders & Dempsey, Washington, 1973-79, ptnr., 1979-92, Baker Botts LLP, Washington, 1992-2000; mem. Verner, Liipfert, Bernhard, McPherson and Hand, Chartered, Washington, 2000—02; ptnr., fed. regulatory matters, internat. trade DLA Piper US LLP, 2002—. Founding pres., chmn. bd. dirs. Children's Chorus of Washington, 1995-97, mem. adv. bd., 1997—. Mem. Phi Beta Kappa. Office: DLA Piper US LLP Ste 700 1200 19th St NW Washington DC 20036-2412 Home Phone: 301-654-8527; Office Phone: 202-861-6203. Office Fax: 202-689-8557. Business E-Mail: bill.kramer@dlapiper.com.

KRAMISH, ARNOLD, physicist, historian, writer; b. Denver, June 6, 1923; m. Vivian Ruth Raker, Aug. 19, 1952; children: Pamela, Robert. BS, U. Denver, 1945; A.M., Harvard U., 1947. With Manhattan Project, 1944-46, AEC, 1946-51; sr. staff mem. Rand Corp., Santa Monica, Calif., 1951-68; v.p. Inst. for the Future, Washington, 1968-70; sci. attache U.S. Mission to UNESCO, Paris, 1970-73; counselor for sci. and tech. affairs U.S. Mission to OECD, Paris, 1974-76; sci. research R & D Assocs., Arlington, Va., 1976-81; ind. tech. cons., 1981—; tech. dir. White House Study preliminary to Strategic Def. Initiative, 1981—84; advisor Under-secretary of Def. for Policy, 1984—91; assoc. Global Bus. Access Ltd., 1991—. Prof. UCLA, 1965-66, London Sch. Econs., 1967-68; adj. prof. internat. studies U. Miami, Fla., 1969; fellow Woodrow Wilson Internat. Ctr. for Scholars, 1982-83; Rockefeller scholar, Bellagio, Italy, 1984; pres. Tech. Analysis Internat., 1983—. Author: Atomic Energy for Your Business, 1956, Atomic Energy in the Soviet Union, 1959, The Peaceful Atom in Foreign Policy, 1963, The Future of Non-Nuclear Nations, 1970, The Griffin, 1986; also numerous articles, book chpts.; patentee nuclear radiometer. Sci. advisor European Cmty., 1960-62. With AUS, 1943-46. Carnegie fellow Coun. on Fgn. Rels., 1958-59; John Simon Guggenheim fellow, 1966-67; Rsch. fellow Inst. for Strategic Studies, London, 1966-67; Sr. fellow Global Access Inst., 1994—. Mem. PEN, Authors Guild. Office: PO Box 2621 Reston VA 20195-0621 Business E-Mail: kramish@post.harvard.edu.

KRAMLICH, C(HARLES) RICHARD (DICK), venture capitalist; b. Green Bay, Wis., Apr. 27, 1935; m. Debra Durbrow, Apr. 26, 1961 (div.); m. Lynne Kramlich (dec. 1980); m. Pamela Kramlich; children: Mary, Richard Squire, Peter Ward, Christina. BS in History, Northwestern U., 1957; MBA, Harvard U., 1960. With Kroger Co., Cin., 1960—64; joined Gardner & Preston Moss, Boston, 1964, exec. v.p., 1968—69; gen. ptnr. Arthur Rock & Assocs., 1969—78; co-founder & gen. ptnr. New Enterprise Assocs., Menlo Park, Calif., 1978—. Bd. dirs. Fabric7Systems, Financial Engines, Force10 Networks, Foveon, Informative, Zhone Technologies, Visual Edge Tech., Silicon Valley Bancshares, 2005—, Tabula, Kor Electronics, Xoom, IPunity, Sierra Monsoon. Vice chmn. bd. dirs. San Francisco Exploratorium; bd. dirs. UCSF Found., Bay Area Video Coalition; founder New Art Trust, 1997—. Named one of Top 200 Collectors, ARTnews mag., 2004; recipient Lifetime Achievement Award in Entrepreneurship & Innovation, Lester Ctr. for Entrepreneurship & Innovation, Haas Sch. Bus., U. Calif. Berkeley, 2005. Fellow: World Tech. Network (World Tech. award (Finance) 2005); mem.: Nat. Venture Capital Assn. (pres. 1992—93, chmn. 1993—94, Lifetime Achievement Award 2001). Avocation: collector video and new media art. Office: New Enterprise Associates 2490 Sand Hill Rd Menlo Park CA 94025 Office Phone: 650-854-9499. Office Fax: 650-854-9397. Business E-Mail: dkramlich@nea.com.

KRAMM, DEBORAH ANN, information technology executive; b. Pasadena, Calif., June 24, 1949; d. Donald F. and Mary (Roach) Coonan; m. Kenneth R. Kramm, Dec. 20, 1969; children: Deidre Lyn, Jonathan Russel. BA, U. Calif., Irvine, 1971; MS, Mich. Tech. U., 1981. Cert. mgmt. cons. Math. asst. NASA-Jet Propulsion Lab., Pasadena, 1967-70; libr. asst. U. Calif. Irving Libr., 1967-71; rsch. assoc. animal behavior lab. Mich. Tech. U., Houghton, 1971-80; programmer, analyst Shell Oil Co., Houston, 1981-85; corp. auditor EDP, 1985-87; team leader SLA, 1988-90, supr. resource planning adminstrn., 1990-91, adminstrv. coord. product devel. ctr.-design ctr., 1991-93, bus. analyst sr. systems analyst, 1993-96, engagement mgr., 1996-97, mgr. engagement svc., 1998-99, mgr. sales and contract support, 1999—2001; prin. cons. Shell IT Internat., 2001—03; sr. learning cons., regional svc. leader Shell Learning, 2003—. Chmn. bd. MMARK, Houston, 1983-85. Contbr. articles to profl. jours.; designer (program application software) Shell Point-of-Sale Terminal, 1982-85. Treas. KFHS Orch., 1986-88; co-leader Boy Scouts Am., Houston, 1981-83. AAUW scholar, 1980, Calif. State scholar, 1967-71. Mem.: AAUW (pres. br. 1975—81), Inst. Mgmt. Cons., CMC (v.p., bd. dirs.), Shell Data Processors Club, Houston Bus. Forum (pres. bd. dirs.), Assn. for Women in Computing (membership bd. dirs.). Home: 5814 Pinewilde Dr Houston TX 77066-2324 Office: Shell Oil Co PO Box 2463 Houston TX 77252-2463

KRAMM, GERHARD, meteorologist, researcher; b. Cologne, Germany, July 9, 1946; arrived in US, 2001; s. Wilhelm and Anna Kramm; m. Carmen Nicole Moelders, Aug. 13, 1992. BE in Indsl. Engring., U. Applied Scis., Cologne, 1973; BS in Meteorology, U. Cologne, Cologne, 1975, MS in Meteorology, 1980; PhD in Meteorology, Humboldt U., Berlin, 1994; ME in Indsl. Engring. (hon.), U. Applied Scis., Cologne, 2000. Mem. rsch. faculty Geophys. Inst., U. Alaska, Fairbanks, 2001—. Mem.: Am. Geophys. Union. Office: U Alaska - Fairbanks Geophys Inst 903 Koyukuk Dr Fairbanks AK 99775-7320 Office Phone: 907-474-5992. E-mail: ffgk@uaf.edu.

KRAMNICZ, ROSANNE, freelance writer; b. Binghamton, NY, Mar. 26, 1948; d. Peter W. and Helena T. (Piotrowski) K.; m. Colin Douglas Anable, Dec. 10, 1990. BA/BS, Reed Coll., 1970. News columnist The Am., Deer River, Minn., 1976-78, Western Itasca Rev., Bemidji, Minn., 1977-78; news feature writer Va. Pilot, Virginia Beach, 1979; film script rschr. Warner Bros., Phoenix, 1980-81; poetry contbr. Dreams, 1981; clog dance instr., 1989—; feature writer Bangor (Maine) Daily News, 1985; columnist, feature writer Peninsula Daily News, Port Angeles, Wash., 1990-92; freelance writer Nordland, Wash., 1992—. Sailed with sextant (celestial navigation) from Wash. to Hawaii, 1980, 88; writing tchr. Maine Women in the Arts, 1982, Bangor, 1985, Oahu (Hawaii) Arts, 1982; co-author: (poetry) Stylus, 1984 (Libr. award); massage therapist, 1989—, shaman healing therapist and spkr., 2001—. Contbr. articles and stories to numerous jours., periodicals, and other publs. Mem. Jefferson County Dem. Club, Port Townsend, Wash., 1996-, Marrowstone Island Cmty. Assn., Nordland, 1991-; vol. EMT and CPR instr. Squaw Lake (Minn.) Ambulance, Virginia Beach, 1979, Chimacun (Wash.) Food Bank, 1989-93; crisis clinic vol., 1969-70. Recipient Merit award Famous Poets Soc., 1995; named Select Poetry Reader/Writer, Minn. Arts Coun., 1977, USMC Platoon Queen, Parris Island, NC, 1965. Avocations: swimming, gardening, dance, travel. Home: 281 Nolton Rd Nordland WA 98358-9539

KRAMON, GLENN, newspaper business editor; m. Alison Gwinn; 1 child, Caitlin. BA with honors, Stanford U., 1975. Copy editor, reporter The Kansas City Star, 1975-77; from reporter to bus. editor The San Francisco Examiner, 1977-86, bus. editor, 1986-87; health care reporter, copy editor The NY Times, NYC, 1987—92, Sunday bus. editor, 1992—94, dep. bus. editor, 1994—97, bus. editor, 1997—2004, assoc. mng. editor for career devel., 2004—06, asst. mng. editor for enterprise, 2006—. Recipient Minard Editor award, UCLA Anderson Sch. Mgmt., 2003. Avocations: keeping daily journal, travel, running, hiking, skiing. Office: NY Times 229 W 43rd St New York NY 10036-3959

KRAMP, SUZAN MARIE, systems programmer; MusB in Music Edn., Susquehanna U., 1975; MusM, Ohio State U., 1977; AS in Bus. Data Processing, Columbus State CC, 1987. Cert. database adminstr. IBM, solutions expert IBM, specialist IBM. Programmer, analyst Franklin County Data Ctr., Columbus, Ohio, 1986—90, Nationwide Ins., Columbus, 1990—94, database adminstr., 1994—97, DB2 systems programmer, 1997—. Mem., fundraiser Nat. Audubon Soc., Columbus chpt., Ohio, 1988—2006. Mem.: Ctrl. Ohio DB2 Users Group, Am. Birding Assn., U.S. Chess Fedn., Nat. Mus. Am. Indian, Nat. Wildlife Fedn., Hawk Mountain Sanctuary, Cornell Lab. Ornithology, Columbus Zoo Colo Club, Mensa. Home Phone: 614-759-9201; Office Phone: 614-249-5864.

KRANE, HILARY K., lawyer, apparel executive; b. Chgo. m. Kelly Bulkeley; children: Dylan, Maya, Conor. Bachelor's degree, Stanford U., 1986; JD, U. Chgo., 1989. Law clk. to U.S. Dist. Judge Milton I. Shadur, 1989—90; litig. assoc. Skadden, Arps, Slate, Meagher & Flom, 1990—94; various positions including asst. gen. counsel, ptnr. PricewaterhouseCoopers, San Francisco, 1994—2005; sr. v.p., gen. counsel Levi Strauss & Co., 2006—. Office: Levi Strauss & Co 1155 Battery St San Francisco CA 94111*

KRANE, STEPHEN MARTIN, rheumatologist, educator; b. NYC, July 15, 1927; s. Daniel Golden and Bessie (Berman) K.; m. Cynthia Ramin, June 28, 1952; children: David Alan, Peter Jay, Ian Matthew, Adam. AB, Columbia U., 1946, MD, 1951; A.M. (hon.), Harvard U., 1968; MD (hon.), U. Geneva, 1989, U. Paris, 2003. Intern to chief resident in medicine Mass. Gen. Hosp., Boston, 1951-57, chief arthritis unit, 1961, physician, 1969—2001; research fellow Washington U., St. Louis, 1956; asst. in medicine Harvard U. Med. Sch., Boston, 1958, prof., 1972-87, Persis, Cyrus and Marlow B. Harrison Disting. prof. clin. medicine, 1987—. Contbr. articles to profl. jours. Served with USNR, 1945-46. Recipient Kappa Delta award Orthopedic Rsch. Soc., 1977, Herberden medal Herberden Soc., London, 1980; named Guggenheim fellow Oxford U., 1973-74. Fellow ACP, AAAS, Am. Acad. Arts and Scis., Am. Coll. Rheumatology (master, Disting. Investigator award 1995); mem. Am. Soc. Clin. Investigation, Assn. Am. Physicians, Am. Soc. Biol. Chemistry, Molecular Biology, Soc. Bone Mineral Rsch., Endocrine Soc. Home: 101 Windsor Rd Newton MA 02468-1121 Office: Mass Genl Hosp Boston MA 02114 Business E-Mail: krane.stephen@mgh.harvard.edu.

KRANE, STEVEN CHARLES, lawyer; b. Far Rockaway, NY, Jan. 20, 1957; s. Harry and Gloria (Christle) Krane; m. Faith Marston, Oct. 1, 1983; children: Elizabeth Jordan, Cameron Marston. BA in Polit. Sci. with honors, SUNY, Stony Brook, 1978; JD, NYU, 1981. Bar: NY 1982, US Dist. Ct. (so., no. and ea. dists.) NY 1982, US Ct. Appeals (1st, 2d, 3d, 6th and DC cirs.) 1987, US Supreme Ct. 1987. Law clk. to Assoc. Judge Judith S. Kaye NY Ct. Appeals, NYC and Albany, 1984-85; assoc. Proskauer Rose LLP, 1981—84, 1985—89, ptnr. NYC, 1989—. Chair adv. practice group Proskauer Rose LLP, chair com. profl. stds., ethics ptnr.; lectr. law Columbia U. Sch. Law, NYC, 1989-92; vis. prof. Ga. Inst. Tech., 1994-96; departmental disciplinary com. Appellate divsn. 1st Jud. dept. Supreme Ct. NY, 1996-2000, spl. trial counsel, 1991-93, Appellate divsn. 2d Jud. dept.; mem. grievance com. 9th Jud. Dist. NY, spl. referee, 2006-. Editor articles, NYU Jour. Internat. Law and Politics, 1980-81. Securities Inst. NYU fellow, 1980-81; recipient Vol. Counsel award Legal Aid Soc., 1984. Fellow Am. Bar Found. (chmn. NY state), NY Bar Found. (dir. 2004—); mem. ABA (standing com. ethics & profl. responsibility 2004-06, chmn. 2006—, Gramm-Leach-Bliley task force 2002—, ho. dels. 2000—, liaison task force on atty.-client privilege 2005-, mem. com. transnat. legal practice 2006-, adv. task force internat. trade in legal svcs. 2006-), NY Bar Assn. (com. on stds. of atty. conduct, chmn. 1999-, com. on profl. ethics 1990-94, spl. com. to rev. the code of profl. responsibility 1992-95, chmn. 1995-99, vice chair spl. com. on future of profession 1997-2000, ho. dels. 1996—, com. on mass disaster response 1997-2003, com. on multidisciplinary practice and legal profession 1998-99, exec. com. 1998-2003, mem.-at-large, exec. com. 1998-2000, spl. com. on law gov. firm structure and ops., vice chair 1999-2003, chair, spl. com. on multidisciplinary practice, 2003-06, pres. 2001-02, pres. com. on access to justice, co-chair 2000-01, co-chair spl. com. to rev. attorney fee regulation, 2003-05, spl. assn. ho. com. chair 2000-05, vice chair sect. internat. law and practice 2003-, chair spl. com. on cross-border legal practice 2004—, spl. com. for student loan assistance for public interest 2005—), Assn. of Bar of City of NY (com. on profl. and jud. ethics 1990-93, chmn. 1993-96, sec. 1985-88, com. on profl. responsibility, chmn. subcom. provision legal svcs. 1985-88, com. on fed. cts. 1996-99, chmn. del. to NY State Bar Assn. ho. dels. 1997-98, Thurgood Marshall award for death row inmate representation 1998, internat. security affairs 2001-03), Am. Law Inst., NY State Jud. Inst. Professionalism in Law, Federalist Soc. (profl. responsibility practice group exec. com. 1999-2003), Hist. Soc. Cts. of State of NY (trustee 2001-2003), Phi Beta Kappa, Pi Sigma Alpha. Republican. Avocations: military history, meteorology, Boston Red Sox baseball. Office: Proskauer Rose LLP 1585 Broadway New York NY 10036-8299 Office Phone: 212-969-3435. E-mail: skrane@proskauer.com.

KRANE, SUSAN, museum director, curator; b. Gary, Ind., June 8, 1954; BA, Carleton Coll., 1976; MA, Columbia U., 1978; MBA, U. Colo., 2000. Rockefeller Found. intern Walker Art Ctr., Mpls., 1978-79; curator Albright-Knox Art Gallery, Buffalo, 1979—87, High Mus. Art, Atlanta, 1987-95; adj. faculty Emory U., 1988-95; dir. U. Colo. Art Mus., 1996—2001; adj. prof. U. Colo., Scottsdale Mus. Contemporary Art, Ariz., 2001—. Author catalogues: Judy Pfaff, 1982, Surfacing Images: The Paintings of Joe Zucker, 1982, Mario Merz, 1984, Jan Kotik: The Painterly Object, 1984, Hollis Frampton: Recollections Recreations, 1984, The Wayward Muse, 1987, Albright-Knox Art Gallery: The Paintings and Sculpture Collection, 19877, Creighton Michael, 1987, Sherrie Levine, 1988, Houston Conwill, 1989, Ida Applebroog, 1989, Lynda Benglis: Dual Natures, 1991, Joel Otterson, 1991, Max Weber: The Cubist Decade 1910-1920, 1991, Barbara Ess, 1992, Ray Smith, 1993, Alison Saar, 1993, Equal Rights and Justice, 1994, Tampering Artists and Abstraction Today, 1995; contbr. Striking Out: Another American Road Show, 1991, Graven Images, 1991, Conversations at the Castle: Changing Audiences and Contemporary Art, Out of Order: Mapping Social Space, 2000, Lesley Dill: A 10-Year Survey, 2002, Let's Walk West: Brad Kahlhamer, 2004 Office: Scottsdale Mus Contemporary Art 7380 E Second St Scottsdale AZ 85251 Business E-Mail: susank@sccarts.org.

KRANE, VIKKI, psychology educator; d. Mark and Penny Krane. PhD, Univ. of N.C., Greensboro, 1990. Prof. sport psychology Bowling Green State U., Bowling Green, Ohio, 1990—, dir. women's studies program, 2003—. Editor: The Sport Psychologist, 2000—04, Women in Sport & Physical Activity Jour., 2005—06; contbr. articles to profl. jours. Fellow Rsch. consortium fellow, AAHPERD, 1992. Fellow: Assn. for the Advancement of Applied Sport Psychology (cert. cons. 1993, secretary-treasurer 1994—97, cert. cons., 2000, 2005, Dorothy Harris Young scholar 1995); mem.: Am. Alliance of Health, Phys. Edn., Recreation, and Dance (pres. 2005—, Mabel Lee Young Profl. award 1997), N.Am. Soc. for the Psychology of Sport and Phys. Activity. Office: Bowling Green State U Women's Studies 226 East Hall Bowling Green OH 43403 Office Phone: 419-372-2620.

KRANICH, MARGARET MANSLEY, artist; d. Walter Edward and Elsie Katherine (Kerth) Mansley; m. Wilmer LeRoy Kranich, July 1, 1950; children: Laurence Wilmer, Deborah Margaret, Gary Richard. BS, West Chester U., 1946; MS, U. Pa., 1949; postgrad., Pa. State U., 1949, Worcester State Coll., 1961, Sch. the Worcester Art Museum, 1978-84. Cert. secondary tchr., English, social studies, guidance counseling. English tchr. Bristol (Pa.) H.S., 1946-48; tchr. Phila. Sch. System, 1948-50; yoga tchr. Worcester (Mass.) Polytechnic Inst., 1972-78; pvt. practice portrait artist pvt. practice, Worcester, Mass., 1982-85; pvt. practice portrait artist Chapel Hill, N.C., 1985-92; pvt. practice Shrewsbury, Mass., 1992—. Named artist-in-residence Southgate at Shrewsbury, Mass., 2006. Represented in permanent collections Dr. Robert H. Goddard Rocket Pioneer Scientist, 1984, The Rev. Michael Scrogin, Four WPI Presidents, Lee Bracegirdle and French Horn, Sydney Philharm. Symphony Orch., Dr. Richard Cartwright, Rocket Scientist, Dr. Benjamin Griffin, Pres. Andover-Newton Theol. Sch., others; exhibited at Southgate at Shrewsbury, Mass., 1994. V.p., bd. dirs. Child Guidance Assn. of Worcester, Mass., 1966-70; bd. dirs. The Children's Friend of Worcester, Mass., 1966-70, Merrifield House of Worcester, Mass., 1966-70; working vol. Child Guidance Assn. Nursery Sch. for Retarded, Worcester, Mass., 1962; mem. founding com. Worcester Internat. House; chorus dir Southgate at Shrewsbury, 2002, yoga instr, 1996—. Recipient First prize portrait Cen Mass. Art Assn., 1982, U. Mass. Med. Ctr. Solo Art Show, Worcester, 1984, 3 Person Art Exhibit Worcester Poly. Inst., 1985. Mem. AAUW, Nat. Mus. Women in the Arts (charter mem.). Baptist. Avocations: travel, genealogy, music, reading. Home: 30 Julio Dr Apt 615 Shrewsbury MA 01545-3047 Personal E-mail: mkranich@townisp.com.

KRANIS, MICHAEL DAVID, lawyer, judge; b. NYC, Aug. 17, 1955; s. Herbert and Mildred (Swartz) K.; m. Patricia Ann Pagano, Sept. 29, 1989. BA, SUNY, Albany, 1977; JD, Union U., 1980. Bar: N.Y. 1981, U.S. Dist. Ct. (so. and ea. dists.) N.Y. 1983. Law clk. to hon. judge Robert C. William N.Y. Supreme Ct., Monticello, 1980-82; prin. Michael D. Kranis, P.C., Poughkeepsie, N.Y., 1982-88; ptnr. Coombs, Kranis & Wing, Poughkeepsie, 1988-94; sole practitioner Poughkeepsie, 1995—. Asst. corp. counsel City of Poughkeepsie, 1983-85, hearing officer, 1994—; adj. prof.

D.C. C.C., Poughkeepsie, 1984-87; judge Town of Pleasant Valley, N.Y., 1988-97; gen. counsel Grace Smith House, Inc., Poughkeepsie, 1983-95; adj. prof. Marist Coll., 1993. Mem. exec. com. Dutchess County Rep. Com., Pleasant Valley, 1997-2000, 01-03, Jud. Nominating Com., Dutchess County, 1987, 97-2000; mem. DC Rep. Com., 1985-87, 97—; mem. Pleasant Valley Planning Bd., 1984-86; bd. dirs., chmn., vice chmn. Task Force for Child Protection, Inc., 1992-2000, 2003-06; bd. dirs. Dutchess County Econ. Devel. Corp., 1994-2003, Child Abuse Prevention Ctr., Inc., 1994-2006, Arlington Band Boosters Inc.; bd. dirs. Pleasant Valley Little League, v.p., 2001-06; mem. Town of Pleasant Valley Rep. Com., 1984-87, 97—, chmn., 2001-03; bd. counselors Children's Home of Poughkeepsie. Mem. N.Y. State Bar Assn. (ho. of dels. 2000—), Dutchess County Bar Assn. (pres. 1998-99, treas., v.p. 1996, pres.-elect 1997, chmn. fee dispute com., chmn. bar endowment, v.p.), Dutchess County Magistrates Assn., N.Y. State Magistrates Assn., Rotary (pres., bd. dirs. Pleasant Valley chpt. 1985-97, Paul Harris fellow 1987). Office: 40 Garden St Poughkeepsie NY 12601 Office Phone: 845-454-1123. Personal E-mail: kranislaw@aol.com.

KRANITZ, THEODORE MITCHELL, lawyer; b. St. Joseph, Mo., May 27, 1922; s. Louis and Miriam (Saferstein) K.; m. Elaine Shirley Kaufman, June 11, 1944; children: Hugh David, Karen Gail and Kathy Jane (twins). Student, St. Joseph Jr. Coll., 1940-41; BS in Fgn. Svc., Georgetown U., 1948, JD, 1950. Bar: Mo. 1950, U.S. Supreme Ct. 1955. Pres., sr. ptnr. Kranitz & Kranitz, PC, St. Joseph, 1979—. Author: articles in field. Pres. St. Joseph Comty. Theatre, Inc., 1958-60; bd. dirs. United Jewish Fund St. Joseph, 1957—, pres., 1958-63; sec. Boys' Baseball St. Joseph, 1964-68; trustee Temple Adath Joseph, 1970-74, 77-80; bd. dirs. Temple B'nai Sholem, 1976—, Lyric Opera Guild Kansas City, 1980-91; founder, pres. St. Joseph Light Opera Co., Inc., 1989-90; mem. St. Joseph Postal Customers Adv. Coun., 1993-2005, chmn., 1993-95; mem., sec. St. Joseph Downtown Assn., 1995-97 Mem. Mo. Bar, St. Joseph Bar Assn. (pres. 1977-78), Am. Legion, Air Force Assn., B'nai B'rith (dist. bd. govs. 1958-61). Home: 2609 Gene Field Rd Saint Joseph MO 64506-1615 Office: Kranitz & Kranitz PC Boder Bldg 107 S 4th St PO Box 968 Saint Joseph MO 64502-0968 Office Phone: 816-232-4409. Office Fax: 816-232-8558. Business E-Mail: tkranitz@kranitzlaw.com.

KRANKING, MARGARET GRAHAM, artist, retired educator; b. Dec. 21, 1930; d. Stephen Wayne and Madge Williams (Dawes) Graham; m. James David Kranking, Aug. 23, 1952; children: James Andrew, Ann Marie Kranking Eggleton, David Wayne. BA summa cum laude (Clendenin fellow), Am. U., Washington, DC, 1952. Asst. to head publs. Nat. Gallery Art, Washington, 1952-53. Tchr. art Woman's Club, Chevy Chase, Md., 1976-88, 98-2006; guest instr. Amherst Coll., 1985, The Homestead, Hot Springs, Va., 1997; judge The Miniature Painters, Sculptors and Gravers Soc. Washington, 69th Ann. Internat. Exhbn., 2002, Bethesda, Md. One-woman shows include Spectrum Gallery, Washington, 1974, 76, 78-79, 83, 85, 87, 90, 92, 95, 97, 2000, Philip Morris, U.S.A., Richmond, Va., 1982-83, 86, Forence Mus., SC, 1991, Lombardi Cancer treatment Ctr., Washington, 1992, Capital Gallery, Frankfort, Ky., 1993, Acad. Arts, Easton, Md., 1999, Warm Springs Gallery, Va., 1997-98, NIH, 2006, 07; exhibited in group shows at Balt. Mus., 1974, 76, Corcoran Gallery Art, Washington, 1952, 72, USIA Traveling Exhbt., C.Am., 1978-79, AARP Traveling Exhbn., 1986; represented in permanent collections U. Va., Philip Morris U.S.A., USCG, AT&T, Freddie Mac, Florence Mus., SC, Navy Fed. Credit Union Hdqs., Vienna, Va., Marsh and McClennan Co., Washington, The Washington Hilton, DC, USCG Hall Heroes; traveling exhbn. Nat. Watercolor Soc., Watercolor U.S.A., Am. Watercolor Soc., Am. Artist mag., North Light mag., Adirondacks Nat. Exhbn. of Am. Watercolor, Artitude Internat. Art Competition, N.Y., Shada Gallery, Riyadh, Saudi Arabia, Belle Grove Plantation Invitational, Middletown, Va., Strathmore Hall Arts Ctr., North Bethesda, Md., Wash. Woman mag., Am. Speech-Lang. Hearing Assn., mag., Govt. House, Annapolis, Md. Invitational, 1997-99, Strathmore Hall Arts Ctr., North Bethesda, Md., Montgomery Coll. Invitational, Md., Glen View Mansion Invitational, Rockville, Md., 2000, Art in Embassies, NYC, 2005-07; ofcl. artist USCG; commd. to do painting of mil. funeral of Lt. Jack Rittichier for USCG Hall of Heroes, 2004; art in embassies, Residence of John Bolton Amb. to UN and U.S. Mission, NY, 2005-07, U.S.A. Mission Office, UN; contbr. reprodns. and text to numerous books. Recipient George Gray award USCG Art Program, N.Y., 1991, 98. Mem.: Western Colo. Watercolor Soc., Ala. Watercolor Soc., Balt. Watercolor Soc., Western Fedn. Watercolor Socs., Watercolor Art Soc. Houston, Transparent Watercolor Soc. Am., Am. Watercolor Soc., Washington Soc. Landscape Painters, Potomac Valley Watercolorists (pres. 1981—83), Washington Watercolor Assn., So. Watercolor Soc., Ga. Watercolor Soc., Southwestern Watercolor Soc., Nat. Watercolor Soc. Roman Catholic. Home: 3504 Taylor St Chevy Chase MD 20815-4022

KRANS, MICHELLE M., publishing executive; b. Chgo. m. Michael Krans; 1 child, Sarah. With McCord Ins. Services, Studio City, Calif., 1985—90; mktg. & promotions mgr. Desert Sun, Palm Springs, Calif., 1990—2001, advt. & mktg. dir., 2001—05, pres., pub., 2005—. Named Advt. Exec. of Yr. for 2005, Gannett Co. Inc.; recipient 4 Pres.'s Rings for outstanding work in advt. & mktg., Chmn.'s Ring, 2006. Office: The Desert Sun PO Box 2734 Palm Springs CA 92263 Office Phone: 760-322-8889.

KRANSELER, LAWRENCE MICHAEL, lawyer; b. Newton, Mass., Oct. 28, 1958; s. Arthur Sheldon and Barbara Joan (Siegel) K.; m. Wendy Kranseler; children: Alex, Jenna, Lucas. BS in Econs., Boston Coll., 1980; MBA, JD, U. Pa., 1984; postgrad., Dartmouth U., 2004. Bar: Mass. 1985, U.S. Dist. Ct. Mass. 1985. Assoc. Hale and Dorr, Boston, 1984-89; supervising sr. counsel Hasbro, Inc., Pawtucket, R.I., 1989-95, mng. atty., 1995-2000; v.p. Hasbro Inc., Pawtucket, R.I., 2001—; v.p., sec. Hasbro Interactive, Inc., Pawtucket, 1997—2000. Mem. children's advertising review unit advisory bd. Better Bus. Bur.; vol. mentor UCAP Mentoring Program; mem. Caru Supporters Coun. Bd. dirs., treas., chmn. fin. com., mem. exec. com., vol. Big Brother/Big Sister Assn.; fundraising capt. Am. Heart Assn., Combined Jewish Philanthropies; coach Town of Sharon Baseball, Town of Sharon Soccer, Town of Sharon Basketball; coord. Town of Sharon Softball; mem. adv. bd. children's advt. unit BBB. Recipient James E. Shaw Meml. award Pres. Boston Coll., 1980. Mem. ABA, Mass. Bar Assn., Boston Bar Assn., Phi Delta Phi. Home: 30 Sentry Hill Rd Sharon MA 02067-1522 Office: Hasbro Inc 1027 Newport Ave Pawtucket RI 02861-2500 E-mail: LKranseler@hasbro.com.

KRANTZ, JUDITH TARCHER, novelist; b. NYC, Jan. 9, 1928; d. Jack David and Mary (Brager) Tarcher; m. Stephen Falk Krantz, Feb. 19, 1954 (dec. Jan. 4, 2007); children: Nicholas, Anthony. BA, Wellesley Coll., 1948. Fashion publicist, Paris, 1948-49; fashion editor Good Housekeeping mag., NYC, 1949-56; contbg. writer McCalls, 1956-59, Ladies Home Jour., 1959-71; contbg. west coast editor Cosmopolitan mag., 1971-79. Author: Scruples, 1978, Princess Daisy, 1980, Mistral's Daughter, 1982, I'll Take Manhattan, 1986, Till We Meet Again, 1988, Dazzle, 1990, Scruples Two, 1992, Lovers, 1994, Spring Collection, 1996, The Jewels of Tessa Kent, 1998, Sex & Shopping: Confessions of a Nice Jewish Girl, 2000. Office: St Martin Press 175 5th Ave New York NY 10010

KRANTZ, LINDA LAW, librarian; b. Princeton, NJ, June 19, 1943; d. Harold Bell and Ruth Workman Law; m. David Walter Krantz, July 29, 1967. Student, Mt. Union Coll., 1961-63; BA in French Lit., U. Rochester, 1965; MLS, Rutgers State U., 1967. Libr. asst. Fine Hall Libr. Math. and Physics Princeton U., 1962—66; reference libr. Princeton Pub. Libr., 1966-67; cataloger NASA Lewis Rsch. Ctr., Cleve., 1967; reference libr. sci.-tech. Cleve. Pub. Libr., 1968-69; reference libr. Wright State U. Libr., Dayton, Ohio, 1969-73; libr. dir. Rockbridge Regional Libr., Lexington, Va., 1974—. Bd. dirs. Kendal Corp. Musician (violinist): Rockbridge Orch., 1975—96, 1999—, Allegheny-Highlands Symphony Orch., 1997—. Mem.: ALA, Va. Pub. Libr. Dirs. Assn. (pres. 2002—03), Va. Libr. Assn. (legis. co-chair 1997—99, George Mason award 1995), Lexington Rotary Club (bd. dirs. 1997, 2005—, pres. 2006—07, Paul Harris fellow 1996), Omicron Delta Kappa. Avocations: music, nature, reading, cats. Home: 151 Elliots Hill Ln Lexington VA 24450-7203 Office: Rockbridge Regional Libr 138 S Main St Lexington VA 24450-2316 Office Phone: 540-463-4324 100. Personal E-mail: lkrantz@cfw.com. E-mail: lkrantz@rrlib.net.

KRANTZ, MICHAEL SCOTT, protective services official, educator; BA, Rutgers U., New Brunswick, NJ, 1987; MA, Seton Hall U., Sout Orange, NJ, 1995, PhD, 2004. Cert. EMT St. Barnabas Hosp., NJ, 1989; basic police tng. County Essex, Dept. Pub. Safety, 1990, police officer Police Tng. Commn., NJ, 1990, instr. Somerset County Police Acad., 1991, trainer, cons. Anti-Defamation League, NJ, 1992, incident command sys. State NJ, Divsn. State Police, 1993, diversity trainer Panel Ams., Diversity Tng. Inst., 1994, human resource tng. devel. SHU, NJ, 1995, first responder, critical incident mgmt. State NJ Dept. Health, 1995. Prof. nat. and corp. security NJ City U., Jersey City, 2002—. Security and human capital cons. ARK Cons. LLC, NJ, 1992—. Recipient Svc. award, Police Benevolent Assn., 1990—2000. Mem.: Honor Legion Police Depts.State NJ (hon. Courage Under Fire award 1995), Am. Soc. Indsl. Security, NJ State Police Benevolent Assn., Fraternal Order Police, Kappa Delta Pi. Office Phone: 732-249-3361.

KRANTZ, STEVEN GEORGE, mathematics professor, writer; b. San Francisco, Feb. 3, 1951; s. Henry Alfred and Norma Oliva (Crisafulli) K.; m. Randi Diane Ruden, Sept. 7, 1974. BA, U. Calif., Santa Cruz, 1971; PhD, Princeton U, 1974. Asst. prof. UCLA, 1974-81; assoc. prof. Pa. State U., University Park, 1981-84, prof., 1984-86; prof. dept. math. Washington U., St. Louis, 1986—, chmn. dept. math., 1999—, divsn. head for sci. depts., 2002—. Adv. bd. Am. Inst. Math., Am. Math. Soc. book series; mng. editor Jour. Math. Analysis and Applications. Founder, mng. editor Jour. Geometric Analysis; editor-in-chief Jour. of Math. Analysis and Apps.; Author: Function Theory of Several Complex Variables (monograph), 1982, 2d edition, 1992, Complex Analysis: The Geometric Viewpoint, 1990, Real Analysis and Foundations, 1991, Partial Differential Equations and Complex Analysis, 1992, A Primer of Real Analytic Functions, 1992, Geometric Analysis and Function Spaces, 1993, How to Teach Mathematics, 1993, 2nd edit., 1999, A Tex Primer for Scientists, 1995, The Elements of Advanced Mathematics, 1995, 2d edit., 2002, Techniques of Problem Solving, 1996, Function Theory of One Complex Variable, 1997, A Primer of Mathematical Writing, 1996; (with H. R. Parks) The Geometry of Domains in Space, 1999, Contemporary Issues in Mathmatics Education, 1999, A Handbook of Complex Variables, 1999, A Panorama of Harmonic Analysis, 1999, Handbook of Typography for the Mathematical Sciences, 2000, The Implicit Function Theorem, 2002, Mathematical Apocrypha, 2002, Graduate School and Careers in Mathematics: A Survival Guide, 2003; cons. editor Birkhäuser Pub., 2002-, McGraw-Hill, 2002-; contbr. numerous rsch. articles to profl. publs. Recipient Disting. Tchg. award, UCLA Alumni Found., 1979:NSF rsch. grantee, 1975—, Kemper grantee, 1994; Richardson fellow Australian Nat. U., 1995. Mem. Am. Math. Soc. (prin. organizer summer rsch. inst. 1989), Math. Assn. Am. (Chauvenet prize, Beckenbach prize 1994), Am. Inst. Math. (dep. dir. 2006—), Textbook Authors Assn. Office Phone: 650-845-2072. Business E-Mail: sk@math.wustl.edu.

KRANWINKLE, CONRAD DOUGLAS, lawyer, broadcast executive; b. Elgin, Ill., Oct. 27, 1940; s. Conrad David and Helen Elvira (Walgren) K.; m. Susan Hall Warren, Aug. 24, 1962; children: Mark Conrad, Jane Shafer. BA, Northwestern U., 1962; JD, U. Mich., 1965. Bar: Calif. 1966, U.S. Dist. Ct. (ctrl. dist.) Calif. 1966, U.S. Ct. Appeals (9th cir.) 1966, N.Y. 1995. Law clk. to chief justice U.S. Supreme Ct., Washington, 1966-67; ptnr. Munger, Tolles & Olson, LA, 1967-88, O'Melveny & Myers, 1989—2000, mng. ptnr., 1996—2000; exec. v.p., gen. counsel Univision Comms., Inc., 2000—. Vis. prof. law U. Mich., winter 1993. Pres. Poly. Sch. Bd. Trustees, Pasadena, Calif., 1986-88; mgr. Rep. Gubernatorial campaign, Calif., 1973-74; chmn. U.S. Senate campaign, Calif., 1978. Mem. Am. Law Inst., Coun. on Fgn. Rels., Calif. C. of C. (bd. dirs. 1990-94), Calif. Club, Valley Hunt Club, River Club. Office: Univision Comms Inc Ste 3050 1999 Avenue of the Stars Los Angeles CA 90067 Home Phone: 626-799-9468; Office Phone: 310-556-7655. E-mail: dkranwinkle@univision.com, drankwinkle@chartwell.com.

KRANZ, KIMBERLY RENEE, elementary music educator; b. Mesa, Ariz., Dec. 30, 1980; d. Robert Allen and Connie Lee Huff; m. Elliott Gregory Kranz, Dec. 31, 2004. BA, Luther Coll., Decorah, Iowa, 2003. Instr. 7-12 vocal music Starmont Cmty. Schs., Arlington, Iowa, 2003—05; tchr. K-5 elem. music Caledonia (Minn.) Area Schs., 2005—. Mus. dir. Caledonia Area Schs., 2005—; speech coach Starmont Cmty. Schools, Arlington, Iowa, 2003—05. Mem. Caledonia Area Arts Coun., 2005—06. Mem.: NEA, Profl. Educators of Iowa, Caledonia Edn. Assn. Home: 619 North Kingston St Caledonia MN 55921 Office: Caledonia Elem Sch 511 W Main St Caledonia MN 55921 Home Phone: 507-724-1029; Office Phone: 507-725-5205.

KRANZOW, RONALD ROY, lawyer; b. Chgo., Aug. 4, 1931; s. Roy Ludwig and Elsie Emma (Hennig) K.; m. Joan Carole Stromberg, June 7, 1952; children: Susan, Kenneth, Jill. Student, De Paul U., 1949-52, Syracuse U., 1952-53, Trinity U., 1953-54, Roosevelt U., 1956, John Marshall Law Sch., 1956-59; JD, Golden Gate U., 1961. Bar: Calif. 1961, Tex. 1977, U.S. Ct. Appeals (9th cir.) 1961, U.S. Ct. Appeals (2d cir.) 1969, U.S. Ct. Appeals (8th cir.) 1976, U.S. Ct. Appeals (fed. cir.) 1982. Sales corr. Internat. Cellucotton Products Co., Chgo., 1949-52; sales asst. Kaiser Aluminum & Chem. Corp., Oakland, Calif., 1956-61, trademark counsel, 1961-68, PepsiCo Inc., Purchase, NY, 1968-74, asst. gen. counsel, 1976-86, assoc. gen. counsel, 1986-96; v.p., legal counsel Frito-Lay Inc., Dallas, 1974-89, sr. v.p., legal counsel, 1989-95; assoc. gen. counsel Frito-Lay, Inc., Dallas, 1995-96. Contbr. articles to profl. jours. Trustee Grace Presbyn. Village, Dallas, 1995-96. Mem. ABA, Dallas Bar Assn. (chmn. antitrust and trade regulation sect. 1990-91), Am. Intellectual Property Law Assn., U.S. Trademark Assn. (chmn., com. mem. 1965—, pres., chmn. bd. dirs. 1977-78), Internat. Trademark Assn. Republican. Presbyterian. Avocations: church teaching, sports, reading.

KRAPF, KEITH ALAN, science educator; b. Urbana, Ill., June 2, 1959; s. Robert Donald and Bertha Fay Krapf; m. Susan Marie Gerling, Aug. 12, 1983; children: Kayla Rose, Kara Sue. AS in Biology, Parkland Coll., Champaign, Il., 1979; BS in Edn., So. Ill. U., Carbondale, 1981, MS in Biol. Sci., 1987. Tchr. biology, drivers edn. Armstrong HS, Ill., 1981—83; sci. tchr. Carbondale Jr. High, 1988—89; forensic scientist Ill. State Police, Carbondale, 1989—91; asst. prof. life sci. John A. Logan Coll., Carterville, Ill., 1991—, chair life sci. dept., 2006—. Fin. officer U. Ill. Ext. Coun., Franklin County, 2005—06, pres., 2006—. Treas. First Christian Ch., Benton, 2006—; dir., bd. dirs. Taste of Freedom 4th July Festival, Benton, Ill., 1996—2006. Named Biology Grad. Tchr. of Yr., So. Ill. U., Carbondale, 1983—86. Home: 10816 Bunny Hop Rd Benton IL 62812 Office: John A Logan Coll 700 Logan College Dr Carterville IL 62918-2501

KRARAS, GUST C., hotel executive; b. Terpsithea, Greece, Mar. 4, 1921; came to U.S., 1938; s. Christ I. and Ypapanti (Contos) K.; m. Stella Dialectos, Apr. 28, 1946; children: Christ, Angel, Ypapanti. Owner-operator Lorraine Hotel & Restaurant, Wildwood, NJ, 1955-73, White Star Motel, Wildwood, 1972—; owner-operator Nantucket Motel, Wildwood, 1973—, White Star Tours, Reading, Pa., 1975—; owner Two Mile Landing, Wildwood, 1982—; owner-operator Beach Terrace Motor Inn, Wildwood, 1985—, Rusty Rudder Restaurant, Wildwood, 1985—, Mansion Heights Assocs., Birdsboro, Pa., 1986—. Owner-operator G.C.M., Reading, 1980—, Hopewell Heights, Birdsboro, 1988—. Editor hist. jours., 1954, 70, 75, 89. Pres. St. Constantine Ch., St. Helen Ch., Reading, 1958-59, 77, chpt. 61 Am. Hellenic Ednl. Progressive Assn., Reading, 1957; dist. gov. 5th dist. AHEPA, N.J., Del., 1981-82. With OSS, 1943-45, ETO. Mem. Nat. Tour Assn., Archon Depoutatos of Ecumenical Patriarchate of Constantinople, Masons, Shriners. Republican. Greek Orthodox. Office: White Star Tours Inc 26 E Lancaster Ave Reading PA 19607-2632 E-mail: gkraras@whitestartours.com.

KRASEAN, THOMAS KARL, historian; b. South Bend, Ind., Feb. 21, 1940; s. William Henry and Rose Ercelia (Mariottini) K.; m. Arleen Ruth Llewellyn, June 19, 1965 (div. Oct. 1970); children: Thomas Karl, David William, Elizabeth Rose; m. Liliane Siahou, Nov. 4, 1972. AA, Kellogg Community Coll., 1960; student, U. Ala., 1960-61; BA, East Mich. U., 1963; MA, Western Mich. U., 1965. Cert. in fund raising mgmt., 1996. Field rep. Ind. State Libr., Indpls., 1965-69, state archivist, 1969-70; dir. Byron Lewis Libr., Vincennes (Ind.) U., 1970-77; field rep. Ind. Hist. Soc., Indpls., 1977-82, dir. field svcs. divsn., 1982-92, dir. cmty. rels. divsn., 1992-97, dir. devel. and membership svcs., 1997—2001, spl. asst. to the pres., 2001—02, dir. planned giving, 2002—05. Rep. Ind. Am. Revolution Bicentennial Commn., 1971-77; mem. Adv. Com. Historic Preservation, 1972-73, Adv. Com. Ind. Hist. Bur., 1980-2000; chmn. George Rogers Clark Trail Found., 1972-74; founder, pres. Old N.W. Corp., 1973-77; bd. dirs. Ind. Adv. Com. Nat. Hist. Publs. and Records Commn., 1979-97. Mem. White River Park Task Force, Indpls., 1981-83; bd. dirs. Friends of the State Archives, 2000—, sec.-treas., 2005-06. Named Sagamore of the Wabash; recipient Lifetime Achievement award, Eli Lilly, 2005. Mem. Am. Assn. State and Local History (state chmn. awards com. 1981-92, regional chmn. awards com. 1988-92, nominating com. 1992-95), Soc. Am. Archivists, Midwest Archives Conf. (charter), Ind. Hist. Soc. (adv. coun. Ind. Jr. Hist. Soc. 1971-2001), Ind. Oral History Roundtable (charter), Soc. Ind. Archivists (founder, sec., treas. 1972-92), Civil War Roundtable (pres. 1970-71, 79-80, 93-94), Battle Creek (Mich.) Indpls. Civil War Roundtable (life), Indpls. Lit. Club (pres. 1989, treas. 1991—), Contemporary Club Indpls. (bd. dirs. 1998-2000, pres. 2001-02), Devonshire Neighborhood Assn. (pres. 1998-2000). Republican. Roman Catholic. Avocations: travel, book collecting. Home: 6038 Castlebar Cir Indianapolis IN 46220-4107 Office: Ind Hist Soc 450 W Ohio St Indianapolis IN 46202-3269 E-mail: tkrasean@indianahistory.org.

KRASHESKY, ALAN, newscaster; married; 3 children. BS in Comm. Mgmt., Ithaca Coll., NYC, 1981. Weekend sports anchor, weathercaster and reporter WBNG-TV, Binghamton, NY, 1981; weathercaster and reporter KTBC-TV, Austin, Tex., 1982; reporter WLS-TV, Chgo., 1982—89, co-anchor morning news, 1989—94, co-anchor 5pm news, 1994—98, co-anchor 6pm news, 1998—, co-anchor 4pm news, 2005—, host NewsViews. TV Journalist Francis Cardinal George: Journey of Hope, 1999 (Silver Angels award, 1999), Pilgrimage of Peace: The Pope in the Holy Land, 2000 (Chgo. Emmy award, 2000). Named Alumnus of Yr., Milton Hershey Sch., 2005; recipient Outstanding Young Alumni award, Ithaca Coll., 1992, Father of Yr., Chgo. Father's Day Coun., 1996, Communicators award, Archdiocese of Chgo., 1997, Heritage Media award, Polish Am. Congress, 1997, Outstanding Achievement in Broadcast Journalism award, Milton Hershey Sch., 1997. Mem.: NATAS (Chgo. chpt.), Chgo. Headline Club. Office: WLS-TV 190 N State St Chicago IL 60601

KRASIK, CARL, lawyer, bank executive; b. Pitts., May 26, 1944; BA, Yale U., 1966; JD, Harvard U., 1969. Bar: Pa. 1970. Atty., mem. mgmt. and exec. coms. Reed, Smith, Shaw & McClay, Pitts., 1970—95; with Mellon Fin. Corp., Pitts., 1995—, asst. gen. counsel, sec., assoc. gen. counsel, corp. sec., gen. counsel, corp. sec. Mem. Allegheny County Bar Assn. (counsel corp. law sect. 1991—), Phi Beta Kappa. Office: Mellon Fin Corp 1 Mellon Ctr Pittsburgh PA 15258-0001 Office Phone: 412-234-1537. Office Fax: 412-234-8417.*

KRASINSKI, JOHN, actor; b. Newton, Mass., Oct. 20, 1979; AB in Literatures in English, Brown U., 2001; grad., Nat. Theater Inst. Script intern Late Night with Conan O'Brien. Actor: (TV series) Ed, 2003, Law & Order: Criminal Intent, 2004, CSI: Crime Scene Investigation, 2005, Without a Trace, 2005, The Office, 2005— (Outstanding Performance by an Ensemble in a Comedy Series, SAG, 2007); (films) Doogal, 2004, Kinsey, 2004, Taxi, 2004, Duane Hopwood, 2004, Jarhead, 2005, For Your Consideration, 2006, Dreamgirls, 2006, The Holiday, 2006, License to Wed, 2007, (voice) Shrek the Third, 2007. Named one of Five Hot New Stars, People Mag.*

KRASINSKI, NICOLE, chef; Attended, DeAnza Coll., Cupertino, Calif.; grad., Art Inst. Chgo. Pastry chef Red Hen Bakery, Chgo., Tapawingo, Ellsworth, Mich., 2000, Rubicon, San Francisco, 2004—. Named one of San Francisco's Rising Stars, StarChefs.com, 2007. Office: Rubicon 558 Sacramento St San Francisco CA 94111 Office Phone: 415-434-4100.*

KRASLOW, DAVID, retired publishing executive, writer, consultant, reporter; b. NYC, Apr. 16, 1926; s. Frank and Goldie (Sirota) K.; m. Bernice Schonfeld, Sept. 18, 1949; children: Ellen Anne, Karen Leah, Susan Beth. BA in Journalism, U. Miami, Fla., 1948. Washington corr. L.A. Times, 1963-66, news editor Washington bur., 1966-70, chief Washington bur., 1970-72; asst. mng. editor Washington Star-News, 1972-74; chief Washington bur. Cox Newspapers, 1974-77; pub. Miami News, 1977-88, sports writer, 1947-48; successively sports writer, reporter, Washington corr. Miami Herald, 1948-63; panelist news program Sta. WPBT-TV, Miami, 1979-91; v.p. Cox Newspapers, Miami, 1989-91. Co-author: A Certain Evil, 1965, The Secret Search for Peace in Vietnam, 1968. Life trustee, acad. affairs com., Sch. Medicine com., athletic adv. com. U. Miami; mem. Orange Bowl Com.; founding pres. Ctr. Fine Arts (now Miami Art Mus.), Miami, 1979-84. With USAAF, 1944-46. Recipient George Polk award, 1969; Raymond Clapper award, 1969; Dumont award, 1969; Nieman fellow Harvard U., 1961-62 Mem.: Gridiron Club (Washington). Jewish. Personal E-mail: dkgables@aol.com.

KRASNA, ALVIN ISAAC, biochemist, educator; b. NYC, June 23, 1929; s. Selig and Esther (Finer) K.; m. Elaine C. Cohen, Feb. 27, 1955; children— Susan Roni, Gary Marc, Allen Selig. BA, Yeshiva Coll., 1950; PhD, Columbia U., 1955. Mem. faculty Columbia U., 1956—, prof. biochemistry, 1970—, acting chmn., 1977-78, 88-90, vice chmn., 1978-88, 90—. Contbr. to profl. jours. Predoctoral fellow NSF, 1953; Guggenheim fellow, 1962; research grantee NSF; research grantee NIH; research grantee Am. Cancer Soc.; research grantee AEC, Dept. Energy Mem. Am. Chem. Soc., Am. Assn. Biol. Chemists, AAAS, Harvey Soc., Am. Soc. Microbiology, Sigma Xi. Home: 6 Arbor Dr New Rochelle NY 10804-1101 Office: 630 W 168th St New York NY 10032-3702

KRASNER, DANIEL WALTER, lawyer; b. NYC, Mar. 18, 1941; s. Nathan and Rose Krasner; m. Ruth Pollack, Dec. 20, 1964; children: Jonathan, Lisa, Noah, Rebecca. BA, Yeshiva Coll., 1962; LLB, Yale U., 1965. Bar: N.Y. 1966, U.S. Dist. Ct. (so. dist.) N.Y. 1967, U.S. Dist. Ct. (ea. dist.) N.Y. 1968, U.S. Supreme Ct. 1978, U.S. Ct. Appeals (1st, 2d, 3d, 5th, 6th, 8th-11th dists.). Assoc. Pomerantz Levy Houdek & Block, NYC, 1965—76; sr. ptnr. Wolf Haldenstein Adler Freeman & Herz, NYC, 1977—. Vice chmn. Westchester Day Sch., Mamaroneck, N.Y., 1979-86; v.p., trustee Bd. Jewish Edn., N.Y.C., 1981—. Democrat. Avocations:

tennis, golf, sailing. Office: Wolf Haldenstein Adler Freeman & Herz 270 Madison Ave New York NY 10016-0601 Office Phone: 212-545-4600. Business E-Mail: krasner@whafh.com.

KRASNER, STEPHEN DAVID, federal agency administrator, political science educator; b. NYC, Feb. 15, 1942; s. Jack and Lillian Rhoda (Weiss) K.; m. Joan Beverly Karliner, Sept. 3, 1967 (div. Sept. 1987); children: Daniel J., Rachel L.; m. Patricia L. Brandt, Feb. 13, 1999. BA, Cornell U., 1963; M in Internat. Affairs, Columbia U., 1967; PhD, Harvard U., 1972. Asst. prof. Harvard U., Cambridge, Mass., 1971-75; from asst. to assoc. prof. UCLA, 1976-81; prof. Stanford U., Calif., 1981—, chair polit. sci. dept., 1984—91, Graham H. Stuart prof. internat. rels., dep. dir. Inst. for Internat. Studies. Sr. fellow Hoover Inst.; mem. policy planning staff US Dept. State, Washington, 2001, dir. Policy Planning, 2005—; dir. governance and devel. Nat. Security Coun., 2002. Author: International Regimes, 1982, Structural Conflict, 1985, Sovereignty: Organized Hypocrisy, 1999. Fellow Am. Acad. Arts and Scis.; mem. Coun. on Fgn. Rels., Am. Polit. Sci. Assn., Am. Econs. Assn. Office: Stanford U Dept Polit Sci Stanford CA 94305-2044 also: US Dept State 2201 C Street NW Washington DC 20502

KRASNEWICH, KATHRYN, water transportation executive; b. 1973; BS, U. Ill., 1995. Investment banker Arthur Andersen & cO., 1995—2000, Deutsche Bank, 2000—03; dir. mergers and acquisitions Brunswick Corp., Chgo., 2003—. Named one of 40 Under Forty, Crain's Bus. Chgo., 2005. Office: Brunswick Corp 1 Northfield Ct Lake Forest IL 60045-4811 Office Phone: 847-735-4700. Office Fax: 847-735-4765.*

KRASNEY, RINA SUSAN, school librarian; b. Phila., Mar. 15, 1950; d. Myron and Lillian (Shiman) K. BA, Douglass Coll., 1971; MLS, Rutgers U., 1973. Libr. Austin C.C., Tex., 1977-80, U. Mo., St. Louis, 1980-85, St. Louis Pub. Libr., 1985-86, Ferguson-Florissant Sch. Dist., St. Louis, 1986—. Fellow St. Louis Tchrs.' Acad., 1998—; cons. for reading programs Gackstatter Found., 2000—; cons. in field. Dir. choice reading grant program Gackstatter Found., 2000—. Mem. NEA (bldg. rep.). Home: 8260 Audrain Dr Saint Louis MO 63121-4504 Office Phone: 314-506-9825. Personal E-mail: krasneyrina@aol.com. Business E-Mail: rkrasney@fergflor.k12.mo.us.

KRASNO, RICHARD MICHAEL, foundation executive, educator; b. Chgo., Jan. 20, 1942; s. Louis R. K. and Adeline G. (Glassman) Kaplan; children: Jeffrey Patrick, Eric Peter; m. Carin Blucher. BS, U. Ill., 1965; PhD, Stanford U., 1970; LittD (hon.), Coll. St. Rose, 1983; LLD (hon.), Sacred Heart U., 1984. Asst. prof. ednl. psychology U. Chgo., 1970-74; program advisor Brazil Ford Found., Rio de Janeiro, 1974-77, program advisor Latin Am. NYC, 1977, program advisor Mid.-East & Africa, 1978-80; deputy asst. sec. of edn. U.S. Dept. Edn., Washington, 1980-81; exec. v.p. Inst. Internat. Edn., NYC, 1981-83, pres., CEO, 1983-98; pres. Monterey (Calif.) Inst. Internat Stud, 1998-99, Kenan Charitable Trust, Chapel Hill, NC, 1999—. Commr. U.S.-Brazil Fulbright Commn., 1975-77, U.S. Nat. Commn. UNESCO, 1983; chmn. Internat. Transition Team Dept. Edn., 1979, 80; mem. U.S.-Mex. Bilateral Commn., 1980, 84; sr. Fulbright lectr., 1973-74. Contbr. articles to profl. jours. Trustee Laspau, Cambridge, Mass., 1980—82, Eisenhower Exch. Program, 2002—; chmn. Rhodes Scholars Selection Com., 2001—04; dir. U. NC Healthcare, 2004—. Nat. Defense Edn. fellow U.S. Govt., 1967-68. Mem. Coun. Fgn. Rels., Century Assn., Cosmos Club. Office: The Kenan Ctr PO Box 3858 Chapel Hill NC 27515-3858 Business E-Mail: richard_krasno@unc.edu.

KRASNOFF, ERIC, health products executive; s. Abraham Krasnoff; m. Robin Krasnoff; 2 children. BA in Anthropology, Columbia Univ. Various exec. positions, including v.p., sr. v.p., group v.p., exec. v.p., pres., COO Pall Corp., East Hills, NY, 1975—94, chmn, CEO, 1994—2006, chmn., pres., CEO, 2006—. Chmn. bd. Nat. Blood Found., 2001—; Presdl. adv. bd. Nat. Ctr. for Disability Svcs.; vice chmn. Am. Bus. Conf.; bd. dir. Nassau Healthcare Corp., 2004—. Bd. trustees Long Island Univ., 1992—. Office: Pall Corp 2200 Northern Blvd Greenvale NY 11548-1289 Office Phone: 516-484-5400.*

KRASNOW, ERWIN GILBERT, lawyer; b. Bklyn., Jan. 8, 1936; s. Charles and Etta (Simowitz) K.; m. E. Judith Levine, Sept. 6, 1960 (dec. July 1994); children: Michael Andew, Catherine Beth; m. Jane Gasperini, Nov. 25, 1995. AB summa cum laude, Boston U., 1958; JD, Harvard U., 1961; LLM, Georgetown U., 1965. Bar: Mass. 1961, US Dist. Ct. Mass. 1961, DC 1963, US Ct. Appeals (DC cir.) 1963, US Supreme Ct. 1965, US Ct. Appeals (4th cir.) 1978, US Ct. Appeals (5th and 11th cirs.) 1982. Rsch. asst. Harvard U. Law Sch., Cambridge, Mass., 1961; adminstr. asst. to Congressman Torbert H. Macdonald, US Ho. of Reps., Washington, 1962—64; ptnr. Kirkland and Ellis, Washington, 1964—76; sr. v.p., gen. counsel Nat. Assn. Broadcasters, Washington, 1976—84; ptnr. Verner, Liipfert, Bernhard, McPherson & Hand, Washington, 1984—2001, Shook, Hardy & Bacon, Washington, 2002—03; owner Garvey Schubert Barer, Washington, 2004—. Vis. prof. Ohio State U., 1974; disting. vis. lectr. Temple U., 1976; adj. prof. Am. U., 1975, Law Ctr., Georgetown U., 1984; professorial lectr. Grad. Sch. Arts and Scis., George Washington U., 1982, 83, adj. prof., 1998; professorial lectr. Sch. Law, Cath. U. Am., 1982; bd. dirs. Broadcast Capital Fund, Inc. (formerly Minority Broadcast Investment Fund), 1978—, treas., 1979-92, vice chmn., 1993—; mem. govt. industry adv. coun. Ctr. for Telecom. Studies, George Washington U., 1980-84; mem. adv. bd. Inst. for Comm. Law, Sch. Law, Cath. U. Am., 1982—; mem. bd. advisors Comm. Media Ctr., NY Law Sch., 1982—; mem. adv. com. comm. law program UCLA, 1983-85. Co-author: A Candidate's Guide to the Law of Political Broadcasting, 1977, 3d edit., 1984, Buying and Building a Broadcast Station, 3d edit., 1987, 100 Ways To Cut Legal Fees and Manage your Lawyer, 1988, Radio Financing: A Guide for Lenders and Investors, 1990, Insider's Guide to Radio Acquisition Contracts, 1992; co-author: FCC Lobbying A Handbook of Insider Tips and Practical Advice, 2001; editor: National Assosication of Broadcasters Legal Guide to FCC Broadcast Rules, Regulations and Policies, 1977; bd. editors Fed. Comm. Bar Jour., 1973-75; mem. editl. adv. bd. Jour. Broadcasting, 1972-85, Telematics and Informatics, 1982—; mem. adv. com. COMM/ENT Law Jour., 1983—; contbr. articles to legal publs. Mem. ABA (vice chmn. agy. adjudication com. 1974-77, chmn. comm. law com. adminstrv. law sect. 1980-81), FBA (pres. Capitol Hill chpt. 1963-64, dep. co-chmn. comm. law com. 1967-69, co-chmn. 1970-71), Fed. Comm. Bar Assn. (exec. com. 1976-79, 84-85, treas. 1984-85), Capitol Hill Bar Assn. (past pres.), Boston U. Alumni Club Washington (pres. 1967-70), Boston U. Nat. Alumni Assn. (bd. dirs. 1966-68, regional v.p. 1971, 73), Phi Beta Kappa. Home: 3307 Q St NW Washington DC 20007-2717 Office: Garvey Schubert Barer Flour Mill Bldg 5th fl 1000 Potomac St NW Washington DC 20007-3501 Office Phone: 202-298-2161. Business E-Mail: ekrasnow@gsblaw.com.

KRASNOW, KENNETH, real estate company executive; married; 2 children. BBA, Emory U. Various positions including exec. mng. dir. Cushman & Wakefield, NYC, 1986—2005; exec. v.p., dir. brokerage svcs. Trammell Crow Co., 2005—. Lectr. in field; mem. Real Estate Bd. NY, Bus. Coun. Fairfield County, Real Estate Fin. Assn. Contbr. articles to newspapers. Named one of Top 50 Leaders in Comml. Real Estate, Real Estate Weekly mag., Top 40 under 40, Real Estate NY; recipient award, Friends of Island Acad.

KRASNOW, RICHARD P., lawyer; b. Bklyn., Feb. 12, 1947; s. Nathan A. and Doris (Pearson) Krasnow; m. Nancy Meyrich, Oct. 3, 1982. AB, U. Chgo., 1968; JD, NYU Sch. Law, 1972. Bar: NY, US Supreme Ct., US Cts. of Appeal (2nd and 3rd cirs.), US Dist. Ct. (no., so. and ea. dists. NY), US Dist. Ct. (no. dist. Tex.). Assoc. Shereff, Friedman, Huffman & Goodman, NYC, 1972-73; ptnr. bus. financing and restructuring dept. Weil, Gotshal & Manges, NYC, 1972—. Mem. ABA, NY State Bar Assn., Assn. Bar City of NY Office: Weil Gotshal & Manges 767 5th Ave New York NY 10153-0119 E-mail: richard.krasnow@weil.com.

KRASNY, MICHAEL P., investment company executive; BS in Fin., U. Ill., 1975. Founder, chmn., CEO, sec. CDW Computer Ctrs., Vernon Hills, Ill., 1984—2001, pres., 1984—90, bd. mem. emeritus, 2001—; pres. Sawdust Investment Mgmt. Corp. Bd. mem. Kellogg Sch. of Mgmt., Northwestern U. Bd. dirs. Ctr. for Enriched Living, The Anti-Defamation League, B'nai Brith Beber Camp. Named one of Forbes' Richest Americans, 2006; recipient Entrepeneur of Yr., Ernest and Young, 1993, CEO of Yr., Fin. World, 1996, Torch award for marketplace ethics, Nat. BBB, 2000. Mem.: Young Pres. Orgn., Econ. Club of Chgo. Office: CDW 200 N Milwaukee Ave Vernon Hills IL 60061-1577

KRASUSKI, RICHARD, cardiologist; s. Andrew and Barbara Krasuski; m. Renee Krasuski; children: Michael, Matthew. M.D., Harvard U., Boston, 1994. Diplomate Am. Bd. Internal Medicine, 1997. Dir. heart failure svcs. Wilford Hall Med. Ctr., San Antonio, dir. noninvasive cardiology, 2003—05, dir. cardiovasc. rsch., 2002—05; dir. adult congenital heart disease svcs. Cleve. Clinic, Cleve., 2005—. Contbr. articles to profl. jours. Maj. USAF, 1990—2005. Recipient Rschr. of Yr., Wilford Hall Med. Ctr., 2003—04. Fellow: Am. Coll. Cardiology. Office: The Cleveland Clinic 9500 Euclid Ave Cleveland OH 44195 Office Phone: 216-445-7430. Office Fax: 216-636-0616.

KRATCHE, RICHARD P., physician; b. Aug. 27, 1961; BA, Harvard U., Cambridge, Mass., 1983; MD, Ohio State U., Columbus, Ohio, 1987. Diplomate Am. Bd. Family Medicine. Med. dir. Solon and Chagrin Falls Family Health Ctrs., Cleve. Clinic, 2002—; vice chmn. divsn. regional med. practice Cleve. Clinic, 2006—. Recipient Raymond A. Kinala Tchg. award, Case Western U., Cleve., 1994. Fellow: Am. Acad. Family Physicians; mem.: Soc. Tchrs. Family Medicine. Office: 29800 Bainbridge Rd Solon OH 44139

KRATHWOHL, DAVID READING, retired education educator; b. Chgo., May 14, 1921; adopted s. Marie (Reimold) Krathwohl; m. Helen Jean Abney, Dec. 20, 1943; children: James D.(dec.) , David A., Ruth Anne Krathwohl Cleghorn, Kristin Jeanne. BS, U. Chgo., 1943, MS, 1947, PhD, 1953. Asst. dir. unit on evaluation Bur. Ednl. Research, Coll. Edn., U. Ill., 1949-55, instr., 1949-53; asst. prof., 1953-55; asso. prof. Mich. State U., 1955-58, prof., 1958-65, research coordinator, 1955-63; chmn. Psychol. Found. Edn., 1960-63; dir. Bur. Ednl. Research, 1963-65; dean Sch. Edn., Syracuse, 1965-76, prof., 1965-91, Hannah Hammond prof. edn., 1982-91, Hannah Hammond prof. emeritus, 1991—; ret., 1991. Chmn. bd. trustees Ea. Regional Inst. Edn., 1966—71. Author (with others): Taxonomy of Educational Objectives: Cognitive Domain, 1956; author: Affective Domain, 1964, Social and Behavioral Science Research: A New Framework for Conceptualizing, Implementing and Evaluating Research Studies, 1985, How to Prepare a Research Proposal, 3d edit., 1988, Methods of Educational and Social Science Research: An Integrated Approach, 2d edit., 1998; author: (with N.L. Smith) How to Prepare a Dissertation, 2005; editor (with L. W. Anderson): A Taxonomy for Learning, Teaching and Assessing: A Revision of Bloom's Taxonomy of Educational Objectives, 2001. With USAAF, 1943—46. Fellow, Ctr. Advanced Study Behavioral Scis., 1980—81. Fellow: APA (v.p. ednl. psychology divsn.), AAAS; mem.: Am. Psychol. Soc., Am. Ednl. Rsch. Assn. (pres.). Home: 9 Thornwood Ln Fayetteville NY 13066-2529

KRATOCHVIL, BYRON GEORGE, chemistry educator, researcher; b. Osmond, Nebr., Sept. 15, 1932; came to Can., 1967; s. Frank James and Mabel Louise (Schneider) K.; m. Marianne Spain; children: Susan, Daniel, Jean, John. BS, Iowa State U., 1957, MS, 1959, PhD, 1961. Asst. prof. chemistry U. Wis.-Madison, 1961-67; assoc. prof. chemistry U. Alta., Edmonton, Canada, 1967-71, prof. chemistry, 1971-98, prof. emeritus, 1998—, dept. chmn., 1989-95, assoc. v.p. rsch., 1996-98, sr. advisor, v.p. rsch., 1998-2001; dir. planning and ops. Alta. Synchrotron Inst., 2002—04. Co-author: (with W.E. Harris) Chemical Analysis, 1969, Chemical Separations and Measurements, 1974, Introduction to Chemical Analysis, 1981; analytical editor Can. Jour. Chemistry, Ottawa, Ont., 1985-88, sr. editor, 1988-93; contbr. articles to profl. jours. Recipient Merit award Iowa State U. Alumni, 1990. Fellow AAAS, Chem. Inst. Can. (bd. dirs. 1977-80, Fisher Lectr. award 1990); mem. Am. Chem. Soc. Office: U Alta Dept Chemistry Chemistry Centre Edmonton AB Canada T6G 2G2 Office Phone: 780-492-4665. E-mail: ron.kratochvil@ualberta.ca.

KRATOCHVIL, L(OUIS) GLEN, lawyer; b. Highland, Wis., Oct. 11, 1922; s. John A. and Emma (Pusch) K.; m. Evelyn Gregory, Sept. 12, 1946; 1 son, Louis Glen Jr. LLB, U. Wis., 1951; JD, U. Wis., Madison, 1951. Bar: Wis. 1951, Tex. 1952, U.S. Dist. Ct. (so. dist.) Tex. 1956, U.S. Ct. Appeals (5th cir.) 1956, U.S. Supreme Ct. 1956, U.S. Dist. Ct. (ea. dist.) Tex. 1961. Landman Shell Oil Co., Houston, 1951-52; assoc. firm Murphy & Crystal, Houston, 1953-55; asst. U.S. atty. So. Dist. Tex., 1955-57; pvt. practice Houston, 1957—99. Pres. McGregor Terr. Civic Club, Houston, 1954, Young Rep. Club U. Wis., 1950. Lt. USNR, 1941-46, PTO. Mem.: FBA, ABA, U. Wis. Alumni Assn. (pres. Houston chpt. 1972—73), Maritime Law Assn., Houston Bar Assn., Wis. Bar Assn., Tex. Bar Assn., Brazos River Club (treas. 1970—99), Lions (pres. 1955), Phi Alpha Delta (chief justice 1950). Home: 302 Kickerillo Dr Houston TX 77079-7412 Office: Kratochvil and Powell 3303 Main St Ste 207 Houston TX 77002-9321

KRATOVIL, JANE LINDLEY, think tank associate, not-for-profit developer; b. Boston, Nov. 25, 1952; 1 child, Lindley. BA, Lynchburg Coll., 1974. Various positions U.S. Ho. of Reps., Washington, 1974-77, The Pittston Co., Greenwich, Conn., 1977-79; assoc. dir. City Sports Mgmt. Inc., Washington, 1979-82; adminstrv. asst. to spl. asst. to pres. for adminstrn. The White House, Washington, 1982-85; exec. asst. to gen. and dep. gen. counsel U.S. Dept. Treasury, Washington, 1985-88; exec. dir., sec. Eisenhower World Affairs Inst., Washington, 1988-2000; pres. Lindley & Assoc., Alexandria, Va., 2000—. Office: 2230 Candlewood Dr Alexandria VA 22308-1505 E-mail: jkratovil@earthlink.net.

KRATT, PETER GEORGE, lawyer; b. Lorain, Ohio, Mar. 7, 1940; s. Arthur Leroy and Edith Ida (Dietz) K.; m. Sharon Amy Maruska, June 15, 1968; children: Kevin George, Jennifer Ivy. BA, Miami U., Oxford, Ohio, 1962; JD, Case Western Res. U., 1966. Bar: Ohio 1966. Atty. Cleve. Trust Co., 1966-74; assoc. counsel AmeriTrust Co., 1974-84, sec., assoc. counsel, 1985-87, sec., sr. assoc. counsel, 1987-92; ret. v.p., mgr. personal trust adminstrn. Huntington Trust Co., 1993-99. Mem. Ohio Bar Assn., Lions. Methodist. Avocations: hiking, gardening. E-mail: pkratt@centurytel.net.

KRAUS, DAVID ROBERT, lawyer; b. Pitts., July 1, 1960; BA, Dickinson Coll., 1982; JD, Boston U., 1985. Bar: Pa. 1985, U.S. Dist. ct. (mid. dist.) Pa. 1987. Counsel Pa. Bd. Fin. and Revenue, Harrisburg, 1985-87; mng. ptnr. Dechert LLP (formerly Dechert Price & Rhoads), Harrisburg, 1987—. Office: Dechert LLP 30 N 3rd St Harrisburg PA 17101-1703 E-mail: david.kraus@dechert.com.

KRAUS, GARY EDWARD, neurosurgeon; b. NYC, Dec. 19, 1960; s. John H. and Gusti Kraus. BS in Physics and Elec. Engring., Rensselaer Polytechnic Inst., Troy, NY, 1982; MD, SUNY, Stony Brook, 1986. Diplomate Am. Bd. Neurol. Surgery. Resident in neurosurgery St. Louis U., Sch. Medicine, 1986—92; fellow Barrow Neurol. Inst., Phoenix, 1992—93; co-founder Wallace Kettering Neurosci. Inst., Dayton, 1994, assoc. med. dir., 1994—2004, med. dir gamma knife ctr., 1999—2004; med. dir. neurosci. ctr. West Houston Med. Ctr., 2004—. Mem. credintialing bd. United Health Care, Dayton, Ohio, 1995—2000; with Neurosurgery PA, Houston, 2004—; founder Houston Back and Neck Pain Support Group, 2005—; cons. Houston Radio Fitness Program, 2006—. Mem. edit. bd.: Total Body Mag., 2007—; author: Microsurgical Anatony of the Brain, 1994; contbr. chapters to books, articles to profl. jours. Mem.: Harris County Med. Soc., Tex. Med. Assn., Am. Assn. Neurol. Surgeons. Achievements include patents in field. Avocations: weightlifting, running, writing. Office: Neurosurgery PA-Kraus Back and Neck Inst 12121 Richmond Ave Ste 324 Houston TX 77082

KRAUS, HERBERT MYRON, public relations executive; b. Cleve., Sept. 21, 1921; s. Joseph Emil and Eva (Meyers) K.; m. Barbara Cohen, Sept. 9, 1945 (div. Jan. 1, 1955); 1 child, Gale Ann Kraus Reinitz; m. Catherine Eugenia Capraro, Mar. 5, 1955; 1 child, Claudia Willa Kraus Piper. BA, U. Ill., 1941. Pub. rels. assoc. Nat. Jewish Hosp., Denver, 1948—51; dir. pub. rels. State of Israel Bond Dr., 1951—54; pvt. practice, 1954—73; pres. Manning, Selvage & Lee of Chgo., 1973—82; pvt. practice, 1982—85; pres. Kraus Dunham Nikolich P.R., 1986—88; sr. counselor Weiser Walek Group, 1989—92, Herbert M. Kraus & Co., 1990—, Fin. Rels. Bd., 1992—2001. Instr. pub. rels. Columbia Coll., Chgo., 1990-2007 adj. prof. pub. rels. Stuart Grad. Sch. Bus., Ill. Inst. Tech., Chgo. Co-chmn. John Fischetti Cartoon Awards Com., Chgo., Comms. Chgo. XV, 1989; pres. Friends of WFMT, Inc., 1989-90; bd. dir. Victory Gardens Theatre, Chgo., 1978-95, Am. Jewish Com., Chgo., 1989—; del. Rep. Nat. Conv., Detroit, 1980; columnist: Chgo. Journalist; bd. dir. Emanuel Congregation, 2000-04. Recipient Alschuler award for comty. svc. Am. Jewish Com., 1995. Fellow: Pub. Rels. Soc. Am.; mem.: Chgo. Headline Club, Chgo. TV Acad., Publicity Club Chgo. (pres. 1989—90, Lifetime Achievement award 2006), Chgo. Journalists Assn. (bd. dirs. 2000—), Am. Friends of Czech Republic. Avocations: theater, travel, humor writing, poker. Home: 415 W Aldine Ave Apt 7A Chicago IL 60657-3601 Home Phone: 773-472-1587; Office Phone: 312-578-9114. E-mail: hkraus921@sbcglobal.net.

KRAUS, JILL GANSMAN, former jewelry industry marketing executive; b. Phila., Oct. 25, 1952; d. Lester David and Lois (Singer) Gansman; m. Peter Steven Kraus, July 20, 1980; 2 children, Jason Andrew, Benjamin Michael. BFA, Carnegie Mellon U., 1974; MFA, RISD, 1977. Designer Accesocraft, NYC, 1977-78, Cadoro, NYC, 1978-79; asst. to dir. of design Monet Jewelry, NYC, 1979-81; sr. designer Swank Inc., NYC, 1981-85; named product mktg. mgr. Marvella, NYC, 1985; cons. Liz Claiborne; named v.p. design & training Swarovski Jewelry US Ltd., NYC, 1992. V.p. associates divsn. Jewish Guild for the Blind, NYC, 1983—87; bd. trustees Carnegie Mellon U.; bd. dirs. World Studio Found., NYC; co-chair Friends of the Carnegie Internat.; commd. Kraus Campo garden for Carnegie Mellon U. campus, 2004. Named one of Top 200 Collectors, ARTnews mag., 2004. Democrat. Avocation: Collector Contemporary Art.

KRAUS, JOSEPH ROLAND, reference librarian; b. Fond du Lac, Wis., July 22, 1967; BS in Physics, Beloit Coll., Beloit, Wis., 1989; MLS, U. Md., College Pk., Md., 1995. Libr. engring. George Mason U., Fairfax, Va., 1995—98; libr. Penrose Libr. U. Denver, 1998—. Mem.: ALA, AAAS, Am. Soc. for Engring. Edn. (Digital Libr. award 1997), Spl. Librs. Assn. (chmn. physics, astronomy, math. divsn. 2007—, Travel award 1995). Office: University of Denver Penrose Library 2150 E Evans Ave Denver CO 80208 Home Phone: 303-933-4399. Business E-Mail: jokraus@du.edu.

KRAUS, MARGERY, management consultant, communications company executive; b. Franklin, NJ, May 20, 1946; d. Soland Lily (Cvern) Rosen; m. Stephen Kraus, Sept. 4, 1966; children: Lisa, Evan, Mara. BA in Polit. Sci., Am. U., 1967, MA in Govt., 1970. With Close Up Found., Arlington, Va., 1971-84, v.p., 1976-84; exec. v.p. APCO, Inc., Washington, 1984—88; pres., CEO APCO Worldwide (formerly APCO, Inc.), Washington, 1988—. Bd. dirs. Internat. Mgmt. and Devel. Inst., Northwestern Mutual Govt'l Rels. Com., chair, Coun. of PR Firms, Pub. Affairs Coun., Catherine B. Reynolds Found., Inst. for Public Rels., Creative Coalition, Meridian Internat. Ctr.; cons., speaker in field; adv. bd. Kellogg Sch. Mgmt. Bd. dirs. Close Up Found. Named Washington Businesswoman of the Year, 1998, Pub. Rels. Profl. of Yr., Pub. Rels. Week, 1997, 2004, Internat. Pub. Rels. Profl. of Yr., 2001. Mem., Adv. Bd., Terry Sanford Inst. of Public Policy, Duke Univ, Coun. on Am. Politics, George Washington Univ. Grad. Sch. of Political Mgmt. Home: 9609 Whitecedar Ct Vienna VA 22181-5423 Office: APCO Worldwide 700 12th St NW Ste 800 Washington DC 20005 Home Phone: 703-281-9638. Business E-Mail: mkraus@apcoworldwide.com.

KRAUS, NAOMI, retired biochemist; b. Budapest, Hungary, July 4, 1933; came to U.S., 1965; d. Jacob and Vilma (Schwartz) K.; (div.); 1 child, Daphna. MS, Hebrew U., Jerusalem, Israel, 1960; PhD, Hebrew U., 1966. Instr. U. Pa., Phila., 1968-74; asst. prof. U. Tex. Sch. Medicine, Houston, 1974-76, assoc. prof., 1976-86, prof., 1986—2000; ret., 2000. Editor: Hormonal Control of Gluconeogenesis, 1986. Pres. Gulf Coast chpt. Assn. Women in Sci., 1974-76, v.p., 1989-90. Recipient grants from NIH, NSF. Mem. AAAS, Am. Soc. Cell Biology. Achievements include rsch. in role Ca 2+ plays in the transduction of hormonal signals.

KRAUS, PETER STEVEN, diversified financial services company executive; b. Aug. 12, 1952; B in Econs., Trinity Coll., Hartford, Conn., 1974. Named ptnr. Goldman, Sachs & Co., NYC, 1994, co-head fin. institutions group, investment banking divsn., 1998—2001, co-head pvt. wealth mgmt., 2001, co-head investment mgmt. divsn., 2001—, also mng. dir. & mem. mgmt. com. Charter trustee Trinity Coll., 1998—; bd. overseers Calif. Inst. Arts; co-chair Friends of the Carnegie Internat.; commd. Kraus Campo garden for Carnegie Mellon U. campus, 2004. Named one of Top 200 Collectors, ARTnews mag., 2004. Avocation: Collector Contemporary Art. Office: Goldman, Sachs & Co 85 Broad St New York NY 10004

KRAUS, ROZANN B., performing company executive; b. Dayton, Ohio, Oct. 7, 1952; m. Daniel Michael Epstein, Oct. 25, 1970; children: Jennah Buckaroo EpsteinKraus, Connor Bagel EpsteinKraus. MA, SUNY, Brockport, 1973. Pres./founder The Dance Complex, Cambridge, Mass., 1991—. Artistic dir./choreographer KRAUSAND., Cambridge, Mass., 1974—98. Performer (concert dance) Paul Robeson award (Creative and Concerned Participation in the Arts in the Cmty., 1982). Democrat. Avocations: running, swimming, bicycling, political activism, writing. Office: The Dance Complex 536 Massachusetts Ave Cambridge MA 02139 Office Phone: 617-547-9363. Business E-Mail: rozann@dancecomplex.org.

KRAUS, RUBY JEAN, art educator; d. Grady Joseph Reese and Verna Mae White; m. Ruby Jean White, Feb. 7, 1970; 1 child, Mathew Tyson. BS in Edn., SW Mo. State U., Springfield, 1976. Cert. visual arts specialist Tenn., 1987. Title I math./lang. arts tchr. Tenn. Prep. Sch., Nashville, 1987—96; visual arts specialist Bradley County Pub. Schs.-Walker Valley H.S., Cleveland, Tenn., 1999—; art tchr. grades 1-5 Jefferson Elem. Sch., Jefferson City, Tenn., 2006—. Art cons. Lee U., Cleveland, 1999—2006. Recreational art dir. Ch. of God, Ardmore, Okla., 1981—86, pres. women's group. Recipient Mayoral award for Tchr. Excellence, City of Nashville Mayor, 1993. Mem.: NEA (bldg. rep. 1992—94). Achievements include development of Church Program for families with Special Needs. Avocation: community service. Office: Bradley County Public Schools Keith St Cleveland TN 37312 Home Phone: 423-312-7490; Office Phone: 855-475-4712. Personal E-mail: vernruby@charter.net. Business E-Mail: rkraus@k12tn.net.

KRAUS, SHERRY STOKES, lawyer; b. Richmond, Ky., Aug. 11, 1945; d. Thomas Alexander and Callie (Ratliff) Stokes; m. Eugene John Kraus, Aug. 27, 1966. Student, U. Ky., 1962-64; BS, Roosevelt U., 1966; JD cum laude, Albany Law Sch., 1975; LLM in Taxation, NYU, 1981. Bar: N.Y. 1976, U.S. Dist. Ct. (we. dist.) N.Y. 1976, U.S. Tax Ct. 1986. Law clk. U.S. Tax Ct., Washington, summer 1974; law clk. 4th dept. appellate divsn. N.Y. State Supreme Ct., Rochester, 1975-77; assoc. Nixon, Hargrave, Devans & Doyle, Rochester, 1977-81, 83-84, Harter, Secrest & Emery, Rochester, 1984-86; pvt. practice Rochester, 1986—. Faculty grad. tax program Sch. Law, NYU, N.Y.C., 1981-82; prin. tech. adv. to assoc. chief counsel - tech. IRS, Washington, 1983-84; mem. N.Y. State Tax Appeals Adv. Panel on Practice & Procedure, 1998—. Articles editor ABA Tax Articles Periodical, The Tax Lawyer, 1984-88; mng. editor NYU Tax Articles Periodical, NYU Tax Law Rev., 1981-82; lead articles editor Tax Articles Periodical, Albany Law Rev., 1973-75; contbr. articles to profl. jours. David J. Brewer scholar Albany Law Sch., 1973. Mem. ABA, N.Y. State Bar Assn. (tax sect. exec. com. 1984—), Monroe County Bar Assn. (treas. 1990-92), Monroe County Bar Found. (pres. 1994-95), Justinian Soc. Avocations: watercolors, guitar, dulcimer. Office: 513 Times Square Bldg Rochester NY 14614-2078 Office Phone: 585-262-3360. Business E-Mail: sskraus@frontiernet.net.

KRAUS, STEVEN GARY, lawyer; b. Newark, Aug. 22, 1954; s. Leon Judah Kraus and Rose (Cohen) Turchin; m. Jane Susan Sukoneck, June 29, 1980; children: Adam. AB, Brandeis U., 1976; JD, Rutgers U., 1979, MA, 2004; student in Ins. Law, U. Conn., 2005—07. Bar: N.J. 1979, Pa. 1979, U.S. Dist. Ct. N.J. 1979, U.S. Supreme Ct. 2002. Jud. law sec. to assignment judge Charles A. Rizzi, Superior Ct. N.J., Camden, 1979-80; assoc. Kavesh & Basile, Vineland, N.J., 1980-81, Bennett & Bennett, West Orange, N.J., 1981-82; pvt. practice, Warren, N.J., 1982—. Mem. ABA, N.J. State Bar Assn., Nat. Assn. Subrogation Profls. (cert. subrogation recovery profl.). Home: 17 Regent Cir Basking Ridge NJ 07920-1900 Office: 122 Mount Bethel Rd Warren NJ 07059-5127 Home Phone: 908-604-2293; Office Phone: 908-561-4240. Business E-Mail: steven.kraus@subrogationlawyer.com.

KRAUSE, CHARLES JOSEPH, otolaryngologist; b. Des Moines, Apr. 21, 1937; s. William H. and Ruby I. (Hitz) Krause; m. Barbara Ann Steelman, June 14, 1962; children: Sharon, John, Ann. BA, State U. Iowa, 1959, MD, 1962. Diplomate Am. Bd. Otolaryngology. Intern Phila. Gen. Hosp., 1962—63; resident in surgery U. Iowa, 1965—66, resident in otolaryngology, 1966—69; fellow dept. plastic surgery Marien Hosp., Stuttgart, Germany, 1970; asst. prof. otolaryngology U. Iowa, 1969—72, asso. prof., 1972—75, vice chmn. dept. otolaryngology, 1973—77, prof., 1975—77; prof., chmn. dept. otolaryngology U. Mich. Med. Sch., Ann Arbor, 1977—92; pres. Am. Bd. Otolaryngology, Houston. Prof. dept. otolaryngology U. Mich., 1977—2000, emeritus prof., 2000—, asst. dean for clin. affairs, 1986—89, sr. assoc. dean med. sch., 1992—96, chief clin. affairs, 1992—95, sr. assoc. hosp. dir., 1995—96; chief clin. affairs U. Mich. Hosps., Ann Arbor, 1986—89; bd. dirs. Am. Bd. Otolaryngology, 1984—2002, pres., 1998—2000. Author: book in field; contbr. chapters to books, articles to profl. jours. Capt. USAF, 1963—65. Fellow: Am. Soc. Head and Neck Surgery (coun. 1980—83, chmn. rsch. com. 1980—83, pres. 1987—88); mem.: Am. Bd. Otolaryngology (bd. dirs. 1984—, exam. com. chair 1993—, pres.-elect 1996—98, pres. 1998—2000), Centurions of Deafness Rsch. Found., Am. Laryngol. Assn., Am. Laryngol., Rhinol. and Otol. Soc., Am. Cancer Soc. (med. adv. com. Washtenaw County unit), Walter P. Work Soc. (pres. 1987), Soc. United Otolaryngologists, Am. Acad. Depts. Otolaryngology, Mich. Otolaryngol. Soc., Mich. State Med. Soc., Washtenaw County Med. Soc. (exec. com. 1979—82), Assn. Rsch. in Otolaryngology, Am. Assn. Cosmetic Surgeons, Assn. Head and Neck Oncologists, ACS (adv. coun. otolaryngology 1979—83), Am. Acad. Facial Plastic and Reconstructive Surgery (regional v.p. 1977—80, chmn. rsch. com. 1977—80, pres. 1981—82), Am. Acad. Otolaryngology Head and Neck Surgery (bd. dirs. 1987—93, sec.-treas. 1987—93, pres.-elect 1995, pres. 1996), AMA. Republican. Presbyterian. Home and Office: 880 Sea Dune Ln Marco Island FL 34145-1840 E-mail: cjkrause1@aol.com.

KRAUSE, CHESTER LEE, publishing executive; b. Iola, Wis., Dec. 16, 1923; s. Carl and Cora E. (Neil) K. Grad. high sch., Iola. Ind. contractor, 1946-52; chmn. bd. Krause Publs., Inc., Iola, 1952-95. Co-editor: Standard Catalog of World Coins 1975-80; chmn. bldg. fund drive Iola Hosp., 1975-80; active Village Bd., 1963-72, Assay Commn., 1961, Marshfield Clinic Nat. Adv. Coun., 1992-96. With AUS, 1943-46 Named Wis. Small Businessman of Yr. Wis. Small Bus. Adminstrn. Adv. Coun., 1990; Melvin Jones fellow, 1990; recipient Meguiar award, 1995, Friend of Automotive History award Soc. Automotive Historians, 1995, Marshfield Clinic Heritage Found. award, 2001. Mem. Soc. of Automobile Historians (Friends of Automobile Historians 1995), Am. Numis. Assn. (medal of merit, Farren Zerbe award, Hall of Fame, Lifetime Achievement award, Exemplary Svc. award 2005, Profl. Numis. Guild Lifetime Achievement award, 2007, Amb. Numis. award, 2007), Can. Numis. Assn. Home: 290 E Iola St Iola WI 54945-9620 Office: 160 N Chet Krause Dr Iola WI 54945 Office Phone: 715-445-5570. E-mail: ckrause@athenet.net. *To publish on time, all the time.*

KRAUSE, DAVID JOHN, aerospace engineer; b. Beaver Dam, Wis., Jan. 4, 1956; s. Edward N. and Lucille (Hoinacki) K.; m. Catherine Piercecchi, Mar. 2, 1987. BS in Engring. Mechanics, U. Wis., 1986. Comml. diver Oceaneering Internat., Morgan City, La., 1978-81; aerospace engr. Space Data Corp., Tempe, Ariz., 1987—99; project engr. Orbital Sci. Corp., Chandler, Ariz., 1988—99; chief engr. NASA Sounding Rocket Ops./Orbital Scis. Corp., Wallops Flight Facility, Va., 1999—. With USAF, 1975-77. Mem. AIAA, SAE. Office: NASA Sounding Rocket Ops Wallops Flight Facility PO Box 99 Wallops Island VA 23337 Business E-Mail: david.j.krause.1@gsfc.nasa.gov.

KRAUSE, EDWARD CHARLES, priest, educator; b. Worcester, Mass., Sept. 11, 1940; s. Edward Krause and Elizabeth Linden. BA, Notre Dame U., 1963; STL, Gregorian U., Rome, 1967; PhD, Boston U., 1975. Priest Congregation of the Holy Cross. Prof., chaplain Stonehill Coll., North Easton, Mass., 1970—75, St. Mary's Coll., Notre Dame, Ind., 1975—80; prof., pastor Gannon U., Erie, Pa., 1980—. Mem. adv. bd. Scholars for Social Justice, St. Louis, Confraternity of Cath. Clergy. Author: (book) Democracy and J.C. Muray, 1975; contbg. editor: Nat. Cath. Register Newspaper, Ency. Cath. Sch. Doctrine; editor: Social Justice Rev.; author: (13-part series) Forming a Catholic Consience, Becoming Catholic: The RCIA; contbr. essays to publs. Med. moral advisor St. Mary's Nursing Home, Erie, 1980—, St. Vincent's Hosp., Erie, 1982—96, Diocese of Erie, 1986—. Recipient Pro Ecclesia award, The Vatican, 1994; fellow, NEH, 1987. Mem.: Am. Soc. Christian Ethics, Am. Acad. Religion, Fellowship of Cath. Scholars, Soc. Cath. Social Scientists (bd. dirs.). Achievements include numerous appearances and two 13-part series on EWTN, the Catholic TV/radio network. Office Phone: 814-871-7545. Business E-Mail: Krause001@gannon.edu.

KRAUSE, GLORIA ROSE, music educator; b. Milw., Oct. 30, 1922; d. Carl Fred and Rose (Bremeier) Runge; m. George Tanner Krause Jr., June 24, 1960; 1 child, George Henry. MusB, U. Rochester, 1946; MusM, Northwestern U., 1954. Music tchr. Livington Manor (N.Y.) Cen., 1946-59, Monticello (N.Y.) Cen. Sch., 1959-61, Liberty (N.Y.) Cen. Sch., 1966-67, Livingston Manor Sch., 1968-79, Narrowsburg (N.Y.) Ctrl. Sch., 1979-87. Dir. Ill. Winds Chamber Ensemble, Narrowsburg, N.Y., 1975—; gen. mgr. Delaware Valley Opera, Narrowsburg, 1986—. Music dir.: (operas) HMS Pinafore, Mikado, Pirates of Penzance, Princess Ida, Patience, Amahl and Night Visitors, The Medium, Gondoliers, Marriage of Figaro, Don Pasquale, Die Fledermaus, Gypsy Baron, The Beggars Opera, La Traviata, Madame Butterfly, La Boehme, The Medium, The Merry Widow, The Barber of Seville (Rossini), Student Prince, Orphans in the Underworld, Hansel and Gretel; bassoonist with Highland Symphony Orch., Middletown, NY, 1986-90, New Sussex Cmty. Orch., Sparta, NJ, 1984-90. Pres. Del. Valley Arts Alliance, 1980—; bd. dirs. Tusten-Cochecton Libr., Narrowsburg, 1988—. Recipient Svc. award Siddha Meditation Ashram Found., South Fallsburg, NY, 1990, Recognition award Alliance NY State Arts Coun., 1995; named Woman of Yr., Catskill Mountain Bus. and Profl. Women, 1995; Gloria R. Krause Recital Hall named in her honor Del. Valley Arts Alliance, 2002 Office: Del Valley Opera PO Box 188 Narrowsburg NY 12764-0188 Office Phone: 845-252-3136. Business E-Mail: dvo@citlink.net.

KRAUSE, HARRY DIETER, law educator; b. Germany, 1932; naturalized, 1954; m. Eva Maria Disselnkötter, 1957; children: Philip Renatus, Thomas Walther, Peter Herbert. Student, Freie U., Berlin, 1950-51; BA, U. Mich., 1954, JD, 1958. Bar: Mich. 1959, D.C. 1959, Ill. 1963, U.S. Supreme Ct. 1963. With firm Covington & Burling, 1958-60; with Ford Motor Co., Dearborn, Mich., 1960-63; asst. prof. to prof. law U. Ill., Champaign, 1963-82, Alumni Disting. prof. law, 1982-89, Max L. Rowe prof. law, 1989-94, tchg. prof. emeritus, 1994—. Fulbright prof. U. Bonn, Germany 1976-77; vis. assoc. Ctr. Socio-Legal studies, 1977; vis. fellow Wolfson Coll. Oxford U., Eng., 1984; US Del. to Hague Conf. on Pvt. Internat. Law Treaty on Internat. Adoptions, 1990-93; commr. Uniform State Laws, Ill., 1991-97; reporter Uniform Parentage Act, 1969-73, Rev. Uniform Adoption Act, 1979-84, Uniform Putative Fathers Act, 1985, Nat. Conf. Commr. on Uniform State Laws; mem. Internat. Acad. Comparative Law Rapporteur US, Uppsala, 1966, Teheran, 1974, Budapest, 1978, Caracas, 1983, Sydney, 1986, Brisbane, 2002, Utrecht, 2006; gen. rep. Athens, 1994; cons. on family law and social legis. to fed. and state legis., jud. and exec. commns.; vis. prof. law U. Mich., 1981, U. Miami, 1987; Culverhouse prof. Stetson U., 1991. Author: Illegitimacy: Law and Social Policy, 1971, Family Law: Cases and Materials, 1976, 5th edit., (with Elrod, Garrison,Oldham), 2003, Kinship Relations, 1976, Family Law in a Nutshell, 1977, 4th edit. (with D. Meyer), 2003, Child Support in America: The Legal Perspective, 1981; law editor: (with R. Walker et. al.) Inclusion Probabilities in Parentage Testing, 1983, (with D. Meyer) Family Law (Thomson-West's Blackletter Series), 1988, 3d edit., 2004, International Library of Essays in Law and Legal Theory: Family Law I: Society and Family, 1992, Family Law II: Cohabitation, Marriage and Divorce, 1992, Child Law: Parent, Child and State, 1992; bd. editors Mich. Law Rev., 1957-58, Family Law Quar., 1971—, Jour. Legal Edn., 1988-91, Am. Jour. Comparative Law, 1991-2004, and others. With US Army, 1954-56. Recipient von Humboldt Found. rsch. prize, 1992, 2004; Guggenheim fellow, 1969-70; assoc. Ctr. Advanced Study U. Ill., 1970, 79; German Marshall Fund US fellow, 1977-78; Hewlett fellow, Australia, 1984; German Acad. Exch. Svc. fellow, 1985. Mem. ABA (past mem. coun. sect. family law, com. chmn.), Am. Law Inst. (life; adviser family law project 1990-2001), Ill. Bar Assn. (past mem. coun. sect. on family law, internat. law), Am. Assn. Comparative Study of Law (dir. 1980-2000), Internat. Soc. Family Law (v.p. 1973-77, exec. coun. 1977-97), Order of Coif. Office: U Ill Coll Law Champaign IL 61820 Business E-Mail: hkrause@law.uiuc.edu.

KRAUSE, HELEN FOX, retired otolaryngologist; b. Boston, Mar. 20, 1932; d. Nathan and Frances Lena (Rich) Fox; children: Merrick Eli, Beth Riva Harper, Kim Debra Codd. BS, U. Maine, 1954; MD, Tuft U., 1958. Diplomate Am. Bd. Otolaryngology. Intern Health Ctr. Hosps. Pitts., 1958-59; resident Eye & Ear Hosp., Children's Hosp., VA Hosp., 1959-62; pvt. practice Pitts., 1962—2003; ret., 2003. Mem. otolaryngology adv. bd. U.S. Pharmacopea, 1991-96, 00—, chmn., 1995-00; prof. U. Pitts. Sch. Medicine; vis. prof. Pan Hellenic Otorhinolaryngology Soc., Crete, Greece, 1993, Panama, Argentina, 1998, China, Hong Kong, 1999, Thailand, China, Taiwan, 2000, Pan Am. Otolaryn. Soc., 2000; pres., dir. 1st World Congress of Otorhinolaryngologic Allergy, Endoscopy and Laser Surgery, Athens, 1998, 01; bd. dirs. Bayer Pharm. Women's Health Initiative; vis. prof. Thailand, Singapore; lectr. 2nd World Congress Otolaryngology, Allergy and Immunology, 2001; chairperson Nat. Hadassah Physicians Coun. Author, editor: Otolaryngic Allergy and Immunology, 1989; lectr., vis. prof. Singapore, Bangkok, Hong Kong (multiple tng. programs 1990); contbr. chpts. to books and articles to profl. jours. Pres. North Hills Jewish Cmty. Ctr., Pitts., 1973-74; cons. North Allegheny Sch. Bd., Pitts., 1977; lectr. North Allegheny Sr. High Sch., Wexford, 1979-84; chmn. Desert Storm Project, North Hills Bus. and Profl. Women, 1991. Recipient Disting. Svc. award, Pa. Acad. Otolaryngology, 1993, Hon. Achievement award, Am. Acad. Otolaryngology Head and Neck Surgery, 1993, Bd. Govs. Chair award, 2000, Bd. Govs. award, Practioner of Excellence, 2003, Presdl. citation, 2004, Bd. Govs. Volunteerism award, 2004, Bd. Govs. Vounteerism award, 2005, Recognition award, Panhellenic Soc. ORL-HNS, 2001, Lifetime Achievement award, Am. Acad. Otolaryngic Allergy, 2002; scholar Jackson Meml. Labs., Bar Harbor, Maine, 1954. Fellow ACS, Am. Acad. Otolaryngology Head and Neck Surgery (bd. govs. 1982-89, 90—, Practitioner Excellence award 2003, Presdl. citation 2004, Volunteerism award 2004, 05, 06), Am. Acad. Otolaryngologic Allergy (pres. 2984-85, Lifetime Achievement award 2002, Svc. award 1990, cert. appreciation 1991, Pres.'s award 1997, Spl. Achievement award 1997), Am. Acad. Facial Plastic and Rsch. Surgery; mem. Pa. Acad. Otolaryngology (pres. 1989-90), Internat. Soc. Otorhinolaryngic Allergy and Immunology (pres. 1995-98), Pitts. Otological Soc. (pres. 1983-85), Phi Beta Kappa, Phi Kappa Phi. Office: 1301 Aviara Pl Gibsonia PA 15044-8042 Personal E-mail: hfk@zoominternet.net.

KRAUSE, JAMES R., mercantile exchange executive; BS in computer sciences, Mich. State U.; MBA in fin. and acctg., So. Ill. U. Positions with MCC Powers, Pullman Inc., Shure Bros.; joined Chgo. Merc. Exch., Inc., 1985, named dir. clearing, regulatory, adminstrn. systems/sys. devel., 1986, v.p. clearing systems, v.p. systems devel., 1990—98, sr. v.p. systems devel., 1998—99, sr. v.p. enterprise computing, 1999—2000, mng. dir. enterprise computing, 2000—01, mng. dir. ops. and enterprise computing, 2001—04, mng. dir., chief info. officer, 2004—07; mng. dir., chief info officer CME Group Inc. (formerly Chgo. Merc. Exch., Inc.), 2007—. Named one of Premier 100 IT Leaders, Computerworld, 2005. Office: CME Group Inc 20 S Wacker Dr Chicago IL 60606 Office Phone: 312-930-1000.*

KRAUSE, JOHN L., retired optometrist; b. Portland, Oreg., Oct. 26, 1917; m. Nancy D., Sept. 30, 1942; children: Diana L., Karen L., Ronald L. Student, Northwestern U., 1935—37; OD, Ill. Coll. Optometry, 1947. Practice optometry, Niles, Ill., 1978—87; ret., 1987. USAF Med. Service liaison officer, Northwestern U. Med. Sch., Chgo., 1964-91. Author: Sight Check Your Child, 1961, Holiday Fax, 1991, 3d edit., 2006, Win-Win, Inc., 1994; contbr. articles to nat. mags.; patentee card holder, 1967. Bd. overseers S.E. Univ. Coll. Optometry, North Miami Beach, Fla., 1993; liaison to optometry Nat. Alliance Mental Health, 1993; mem. ins. coun. City Tamarac, Fla., 1995—, chmn., 2002—; ombudsman State of Fla., Broward County, 1996-2000. Served with U.S. Army, 1941-45, to lt. col. USAF, ret., 1970. Decorated Bronze Star with cluster, Combat Medic badge; named to Sr. Hall of Fame, Broward County Fla., 2000; recipient hon. award, Armed Forces Optometric Soc., 2002. Mem. Am. Optometric Assn., Ill. Optometric Assn., Fla. Optometric Assn. Armed Forces Optometric Soc. (Honor award 2002), Air Force Assn., Fla. Pub. Health Assn. (chmn.-elect vision sect. 1992), Fla. Ret. Optometrists Assn. (pres. 1993-95, editor 1995—2007), Kappa Phi Delta, Phi Theta Upsilon, Phi Mu Delta. Achievements include patents for eyedrop transport apparatus, 2002, 2004. Avocations: golf, stamp collecting/philately, autographs. Home: 7270 Fairfax Dr Tamarac FL 33321-4305 Personal E-mail: dockrause@webtv.net.

KRAUSE, MANFRED OTTO, physicist; b. Stuttgart, Germany, Mar. 11, 1931; came to U.S., 1960, naturalized, 1970; s. Friedrich Bernhard and Friedel Ernstine K.; m. Josephine Winifred Cammer, Dec. 26, 1963; m. C. Denise Caldwell, Sept. 15, 2001. BS, Technische Universität Stuttgart, 1954, diploma in physics, 1957, PhD, 1960. Sr. physicist Wm. H. Johnston Labs., Inc., Balt., 1960-63; sr. scientist Oak Ridge Nat. Lab., 1963-95; exch. prof. U. Paris, 1975. Cons. Oak Ridge, 1995—, U. Ctrl. Fla. Contbr. articles to profl. jours., chapters to books. Recipient Alexander von Humboldt award, 1975-76. Fellow Am. Phys. Soc.; mem. AAAS, Smithsonian Instn., Audubon Soc., Nature Conservancy. Achievements include discovery of x-ray spectrometry based on photoelectric effect. Home: 125 Baltimore Dr Oak Ridge TN 37830-7837 Business E-Mail: mok@ornl.gov.

KRAUSE, MARJORIE N., biochemist; b. Chgo., July 25, 1937; d. Robert Mortimer Krause and Eleanor Driese. BS, Mich. State U., 1959; MS, Cleve. State U., 1986. Cert. tchr., Mich.; cert. medical technologist in hematology Am. Soc. Clinical Pathologists. Technician Dartmouth Coll., Hanover, N.H., 1960-66, U. Vt., Burlington, 1966-70; technologist Case We. Res. U., Cleve., 1971-75, 89-93, U. Hosps., Cleve., 1975-79; lab technologist, med. technologist Cleve. Clinic Found., 1979-89; computer lab technician Lakeland C.C., Kirtland, Ohio, 1996-97, 99; narrator Sea World Ohio, Aurora, 1998, info. technologist, 2000. Judge youth sci. fair Ohio Acad. Scis., Columbus, Ohio, 1995, 96. Vol. Cleve. Orch., 1972—, Playhouse Sq. Found., 1988—2004, Hunter Jumper Classic, 1999—2002, Internat. Children's Games, 2004. Recipient cert. recognition, Playhouse Sq. Found., 1995, 1996, 1998, 2004. Avocations: natural history, bird watching, opera, theater, classical music. Home: 27500 Bishop Park Dr Apt 316 Wickliffe OH 44092-2757

KRAUSE, PETER, actor; b. Alexandria, Minn., Aug. 12, 1965; 1 child, Roman. Student, Gustavus Adolphus Coll., St. Peter, Minn.; MFA, NYU. Actor: (films) Blood Harvest, 1987, LoveLife, 1997, Melting Pot, 1997, The Truman Show, 1998, My Engagement Party, 1998, It's a Shame About Ray, 2000, We Don't Live Here Anymore, 2004, Civic Duty, 2006; (TV series) Carol & Company, 1990, Cybill, 1995, The Great Defender, 1995, If Not For You, 1995, Sports Night, 1998—2000, Six Feet Under, 2001—05; TV appearances include Seinfeld, 1992, Beverly Hills 90210, 1992, Party of Five, 1997. Office: c/o Creative Artists Agy 9830 Wilshire Blvd Beverly Hills CA 90212-1825

KRAUSE, RICHARD MICHAEL, medical scientist, government official, educator, researcher; b. Marietta, Ohio, Jan. 4, 1925; s. Ellis L. and Jennie Mae (Waterman) Krause. BA, Marietta Coll., 1947, DSc (hon.), 1978; MD, Case Western Res. U., 1952; DSc (hon.), U. Rochester, 1979, Med. Coll. Ohio, Toledo, 1981, Hahnemann Med. Coll. and Hosp., 1982; LLD (hon.), Thomas Jefferson U., 1982. Rsch. fellow dept. preventive medicine Case Western Res. U., 1950—51; intern Ward Med. Svc., Barnes Hosp., St. Louis, 1952—53, asst. resident, 1953—54; asst. physician to hosp. Rockefeller Inst., 1954—57, asst. prof., assoc. physician to hosp., 1957—61; prof. epidemiology Sch. Medicine, Washington U., St. Louis, 1962—66, assoc. prof. medicine, 1962—65, prof. medicine, 1965—66; assoc. prof., physician to hosp. Rockefeller U., 1966—68, prof., sr. physician, 1968—75; dir. Rockefeller U. (Animal Rsch. Ctr.), 1974—75, Nat. Inst. Allergy and Infectious Diseases, NIH, HEW, Bethesda, Md., 1975—84; USPHS surgeon, 1975—77; asst. surgeon gen., 1977—84; dean Emory U. Sch. Medicine, Atlanta, 1984—89, Robert W. Woodruff prof. medicine, 1984—89; mem. program com. Inst. Medicine, 1986—87; sr. sci. adv. Fogarty Internat. Ctr. NIH, Bethesda, 1989—; sr. investigator NIAID NIH, Bethesda, 2000—. Bd. dirs. Mo.-St. Louis Heart Assn., 1962—66, mem. rsch. com., 1963—66; mem. exec. com. coun. on rheumatic fever and congenital heart disease Am. Heart Assn., 1963—66, chmn. coun. rsch. study com., 1963—66, mem. assn. rsch. com., 1963—66, mem. policy com., 1966—70; mem. commn. streptococcal and staphylococcal diseases U.S. Armed Forces Epidemiol. Bd., 1963—72, dep. dir., 1968—72; bd. dirs. N.Y. Heart Assn., 1967—73, chmn. adv. coun. on rsch., 1969—71, mem. dirs. coun., 1973—75; cons. WHO, 1967—, mem. coccal expert com., 1967—; mem. steering com. Biomed. Sci. Scientific Working Group, WHO, 1978; mem. infectious disease adv. com. Nat. Inst. Allergy and Infectious Disease, NIH, 1970—74; bd. dirs. Royal Soc. Medicine Found., Inc., 1971—77, treas., 1973—75; bd. dirs. Allergy and Asthma Found. Am., 1976—77, Lupus Found. Am., 1977—79. Assoc. editor: Jour. Immunology, 1963—71, sect. editor: Viral and Microbial Immunology, 1974—75; editor: Jour. Exptl. Medicine, 1973—75; adv. editor:, 1976—84, mem. editl. bd.: Bacteriological Revs., 1969—73, Infection and Immunity, 1970—78, Immunochemistry, 1973—80, Clin. Immunology and Immunopathology, 1976—78; contbr. articles to profl. jours. With US Army, 1944—46. Decorated Gumhuria medal Egypt; recipient DSM, HEW, 1979, C. William O'Neal Disting. Am. Svc. award, Robert Koch Medal in Gold, Berlin, 1985, Sr. U.S. Scientist award, Alexander Von Humboldt Found., Fed. Republic Germany, 1986. Mem.: AAAS, Am. Epidemiol. Soc., Practitioner's Soc. N.Y., Royal Soc. Medicine, Infectious Diseases Soc. Am., Am. Coll. Allergists, Harvey Soc., Am. Soc. Microbiology, Am. Assn. Immunologists, Am. Soc. Clin. Investigation, Am. Soc. Biol. Chemists, Am. Acad. Allergy, Assn. Am. Physicians, Inst. Medicine, U.S. Nat. Acad. Scis., Cosmos (Washington), Century Assn. (N.Y.C.). Achievements include research in pathogenesis and epidemiology of streptococcal diseases; immunochem. studies on streptococcal antigens; immunogenetics; recognition of rabbit antibodies with molecular uniformity, genetics of immune response. Home: 4000 Cathedral Ave NW Apt 413B Washington DC 20016-5268 Office: NIAID NIH Rm 202 16 Center Dr Bldg 16 Bethesda MD 20892-0001 E-mail: richard_krause@nih.gov.

KRAUSE, ROY G., office staffing firm executive; BS in Acctg., Ohio State U.; MBA, Ga. State U. Acct. KPMG Peat Warwick, LLP, 1973—80; CFO HomeBanc Mortgage Corp., Atlanta, 1980—95; exec. v.p., CFO Spherion Corp., Ft. Lauderdale, Fla., 1995—2003, pres., COO, 2003—04, pres., CEO, 2004—. Office: Spherion Corp 2050 Spectrum Blvd Fort Lauderdale FL 33309*

KRAUSE, SONJA, chemistry professor; b. St. Gall, Switzerland, Aug. 10, 1933; arrived in US, 1939, naturalized; d. Friedrich and Rita (Maas) K.; m. Walter Walls Goodwin, Nov. 27, 1970 BS, Rensselaer Poly. Inst., 1954; PhD, U. Calif., Berkeley, 1957. Sr. phys. chemist Rohm & Haas Co., Phila., 1957-64; vol. U.S. Peace Corps, Nigeria, 1964-65; asst. lectr. Lagos U.; asst. prof. Gondar Health Coll. U.S. Peace Corps, Ethiopia, 1965-66; vis. asst. prof. U. So. Calif., LA, 1966-67; chemistry faculty Rensselaer Poly. Inst., Troy, NY, 1967—2004, prof., 1978—2004, prof. emeritus, 2004—. Mem. coun. Gordon Rsch. Conf., 1981-83; mem. com. on polymers and engring. NRC, 1992-94; sabbatical Inst. Charles Sadron, Ctr. Rsch. on Macromolecules, Strasbourg, France, 1987. Author: (with others) Chemistry of Environment, 1978, 2d edit., 2002; editor: Molecular Electro-Optics, 1981; mem. editorial adv. bd. Macromolecules, 1982-84 Bd. dirs. Nat. Plastics Ctr. and Mus., Leominster, Mass., 1996-2000. Fellow Am. Phys. Soc. (coun. divsn. biol. physics 1980-93); mem. IUPAC (assoc.), Am. Chem. Soc. (chmn. ea. N.Y. sect. 1981-82, councillor 1991-95, adv. bd. petroleum rsch. fund 1979-81, assoc. mem. com. on edn. 1993-95, assoc. mem. internat. com. 1996), Biophys. Soc. (coun. 1977), N.Y. Acad. Scis., Sigma Xi (pres. Rensselaer Poly Inst. chpt. 1984-85). Business E-Mail: krauss@rpi.edu.

KRAUSE, WILLIAM AUSTIN, engineering executive; b. Lennox, Calif., Nov. 16, 1930; s. William August and Grace Olive (Davies) K.; m. Judith M.; children: Kenneth R., Michael W., Richard R., William R. AA, Pasadena City Coll., 1950; BS in Engring., U. Calif.-Berkeley, 1952. Registered profl. engr., Mont., La., N.Mex., Fla., Miss., Tex., Calif., Del., Ky., Okla., Ala., Colo., Ill., Kans., Mich., W.Va.; also The Netherlands. Supt., mgr. constrn. operations C.F. Braun Co., Alhambra, Calif., 1952-63; gen. mgr. Lummus Co., Bloomfield, N.J., 1963-69; pres., chief exec. officer J.F. Pritchard & Co., Kansas City, Mo., 1969-73, Internat. Systems and Controls Process Group, Houston, 1969-73; pres. Sigma-Chapman, Inc., Houston, 1973-86; chmn. Omnipure, Inc., Houston, 1975-86; pres. Chapman Engrs. Inc., 1973-90, also bd. dirs.; chmn. Chapman Engrs. Internat. Inc., 1988-89; pres. Krause, Inc., 1990—. Dir., mem. audit and exec. coms. Camco, Inc., Houston, 1970-98; dir. Velocys A subsidiary of Battelle Meml. Inst., Columbus, Ohio, 2001-. Patentee in field. Mem. Young Pres.'s Orgn. (dir. 1973-77, chmn. exec. com. 1975-76, sec. Kansas City chpt. 1971-72), World Pres. Orgn., ASME, Am. Inst. Chem. Engrs. (lectr. project mgmt.), AIME, Nat., Calif., Tex. socs. profl. engrs., Calif. Alumni Assn., Univ. Club (Houston, bd. govs.). Home and Office: 10 S Briar Hollow Ln Unit 93 Houston TX 77027-2891 Personal E-mail: wakjmk@sbcglobal.net.

KRAUSER, ROBERT STANLEY, healthcare executive; b. NYC, Aug. 24, 1937; s. Benjamin and Eva (Ferester) K.; m. Mary Kay Edwards, June 12, 1977 (dec. May 1999); children: Robert Edwards, Kathryn Edwards. BA, U. Vt., 1958; MS, Columbia U. Grad. Sch. Bus., 1959. Rschr., portfolio analyst Merrill, Lynch, Pierce et al, NYC, 1961-63; dir. spl. situations rschr. Orvis Bros., NYC, 1964-66; dir. rsch. Amott, Baker, NYC, 1966-69; v.p. rsch. counsel Bruns, Nordemann & Rea, NYC, 1970-75; v.p. rsch. assoc. Rosenkrantz, Ehrenkrantz, NYC, 1976-77; investment banker Herzfeld & Stern, Stamford, Conn., 1978-82; chmn., pres. Viral Response Sys., Inc., Greenwich, Conn., 1983—. Patentee in field. With USAR, 1959. Recipient Cert. of Recognition Eli Whitney Mus., 1987. Mem. Nat. Assn. Chain Drug Stores, Am. Mensa (Philanthropic award 1987), Inventors Assn. Conn. (Inventor of Yr. 1988), U.S. Tennis Assn. (ranked 1995), The Wimbledon Soc., Landmark Club, East Hampton Tennis Club (mixed doubles champ 1972), Armonk Tennis Club, Grand Slam Tennis Club (singles champ 1977, 78), San Diego Tennis and Racquet Club, Balboa Tennis CLub. Avocations: tennis, skiing, swimming, travel, medical reading. Home and Office: 444 Taconic Rd Greenwich CT 06831-2850

KRAUSHAR, JONATHAN POLLACK, communications and media consultant; b. Kew Gardens, NY, Apr. 26, 1948; s. Leo and Evelyn (Pollack) K.; m. Linda Marie Pekarski, Apr. 20, 1980; children: Matthew, Elizabeth. BA in English, U. Wis., 1969; MBA in Mktg. and Internat. Bus., NYU, 1981. Reporter The Hudson Dispatch, Union City, NJ, 1970, The Record, Hackensack, NJ, 1970-72; assoc. prodr. Sta. WPIX-TV News, NYC, 1973, Sta. WCBS-TV News, NYC, 1974-76; spl. projects supr. Philip Morris Internat., NYC, 1976-82; v.p. Ailes Comms., Inc., NYC, 1982, sr. v.p., 1984, pres. corp. comms. group, 1990, pres., 1991-95, Jon Kraushar and Assocs., Inc., NYC, 1996—. Freelance writer N.Y. Times, N.Y.C., 1972-76, Washington Post, Washington, 1972-76. Author: (with Roger Ailes) You Are the Message, 1988; inventor (video) Electronic Resume, 1982. Media adviser Reagan/Bush Campaign, N.Y.C., 1984, Bush/Quayle Campaign, N.Y.C., 1988, Forbes for Pres., 1996, 2000; debate coach Dick Cheney, 2000. Recipient Feature Writing award N.J. Press Assn., 1972; pub. affairs reporting fellow Washington Journalism Ctr., 1974; fed. grantee U. Wis. Dept. Behavioral Disabilities, 1969. Mem. Internat. Assn. Bus. Communicators (bd. dirs. N.Y. chpt., chmn. main event spkrs. program 1983-85), Econ. Club. Republican. Jewish. Avocations: in-line skating, swimming, water sports. Office: Jon Kraushar and Assocs Inc 10 E 40th St Ste 1308 New York NY 10016-0201

KRAUSS, ALISON, country musician; b. Champaign, Ill., July 23, 1971; m. Pat Bergeson, Nov. 8, 1997. Albums (with Union Sta.) So Long So Wrong, 1997, Too Late to Cry, 1987, Two Highways, 1989, I've Got That Old Feeling, 1990, Every Time You Say Goodbye, 1992, I Know Who Holds Tomorrow, 1994 (Grammy award Best Southern, Country or Bluegrass Gospel album), Now That I've Found You, 1995, Forget About It, 1999, New Favorite, 2001, Alison Krauss and Union Sta. Live, 2002, Lonely Runs Both Ways, 2002 (3 Grammy awards: Best Country Group Performance, Best Country Instrumental Performance, Best Country Album, 2006). Co-recipient with Brad Paisley, Music Video of Yr., "Whiskey Lullaby", Country Music Assoc., 2004, with Brad Paisley, Musical Event of Yr. "Whiskey Lullaby", 2004, with Brad Paisley, Video of Yr., Vocal Event of Yr., "Whiskey Lullaby", Acad. Country Music, 2005; named to Grand Ole Opry, 1993; recipient Female Vocalist of Yr. award, Internat. Bluegrass Music Assn., 1990—91, 1993, 1995, Entertainer of Yr. award, 1991, 1995, Rising Video Star of Yr.-Europe award Country Music TV, 1995, Single of Yr. award, Country Music Assn, 1995, Vocal Event of Yr., 1995, Horizon award, 1995, Female Vocalist of Yr., 1995, Best New Country Artist Tour award Pollstar, 1995, Americana Artist of Yr. award Gavin, 1995, Country Artist of Yr. Rolling Stone, 1995, Grammy award Best Bluegrass Recording, 1992, Grammy award Best Country Collaboration with Vocals, 1995, Grammy award Best Female Country Vocal Performance, 1996, Bluegrass/Old-Time Music Album award, 1996, Best Female Vocalist, 1996, Grammy award Best Country Instrumental Performance, 1998, Grammy award Best Bluegrass Album, 1998, Grammy award Best Country Performance by a Duo or Group with Vocals, 1998. Office: Ds Management PO Box 121499 Nashville TN 37212-1499

KRAUSS, GEORGE, metallurgist; b. Phila., May 14, 1933; s. George and Berta (Reichelt) K.; m. Ruth A. Oeste, Sept. 10, 1960; children: Matthew, Jonathan, Benjamin, Thomas. BS in Metall. Engring., Lehigh U., Bethlehem, Pa., 1955; MS, MIT, Cambridge, 1958, ScD, 1961. Registered profl. engr., Colo., Pa. Devel. metallurgist Superior Tube Co., Collegeville, Pa., 1955-56; prof. Lehigh U., Bethlehem, Pa., 1963-75, Colo. Sch. Mines, Golden, 1975—; dir. Advanced Steel Processing and Products Research Ctr., 1984-93; Amax Found. prof., 1975-90; prof. dept. metall. engring. Colo. Sch. Mines, Golden, 1990-92, John Henry Moore prof., 1992-97, Univ. prof. emeritus, metallurg. cons., 1997—. Author: Principles of Heat Treatment of Steel, 1980, Steels: Heat Treatment and Processing Principles, 1990, Tool Steels, 5th edit., 1998, Steels: Processing Structure and Performance, 2005; editor: Deformation Processing and Structure, 1984, Carburizing: Processing and Performance, 1989; editor Jour. Heat Treating, 1978-82; co-editor Fundamentals of Microalloying Forging Steels, 1987; contbr. articles profl. jours. NSF fellow Max Planck Inst. fur Eisenforschung, 1962-63; recipient Adolf Martens medal, Wiesbaden, 1990, Disting. Alumni award Lehigh U., 1993, George R. Brown Gold medal, 1998; named Outstanding Educator, Colo. Sch. Mines, 1990 Fellow ASM, The Metals Soc., Internat. Fedn. Heat Treatment and Surface Engring., Japan Soc. Promotion Sci.; mem. AIME, Iron and Steel Soc.-AIME (disting. mem. 1993, Howe lectr. 2003), Iron and Steel Inst. Japan (hon.), Am. Soc. Materials Internat. (hon.; trustee 1991-94, v.p. 1995-96, pres. 1996-97, C.S. Barrett silver medal 1998, Bodeen Heat Treating Achievement award 1999, A.E. White Disting. Tchr. award 1999, Campbell lectr. 2000), Internat. Fedn. Heat Treatment (pres. 1989-91, medal, 2007), ASM Materials Edn. Found. (trustee 2004-07). Home: 3807 Ridge Rd Evergreen CO 80439-8517 Office: Colo Sch Mines Dept Metall Engring Golden CO 80401 Office Phone: 303-674-0670. Business E-Mail: gkrauss@mines.edu.

KRAUSS, HENRY FREDERICK, JR., optometrist; b. Sewickley, Pa., Apr. 10, 1952; s. Henry Frederick and Mirella Anna (Guerrieri) K.; m. Sally Winston Miller, July5, 1975; children: Molly Anne, Henry Neil, Malinda Paige, Michael Winston. BS, Centre Coll., Ky., 1976; OD, U. Houston, 1980. Optometrist, owner Eye Care Assocs., Richardson, Tex., 1980—. V.p. ProComp Systems Inc., Albuquerque, 1983-86; ptnr. K-W Distbrs., Dallas, 1983-86, Summit Seminars, Richardson, 1985—; owner, operator Profl. Enhancement Strategies, 1997—; pres. Simplified Web Solutions, 2004-. Bd. dirs. Found. for Edn. and Rsch. in Vision, 1988-89, S.W. Vision Svc. Plan, 1982-84. Fellow Am. Acad. Optometry; mem. Am. Optometric Assn., Tex. Optometric Assn. (Young Optometrist of Yr. award 1985), North Tex. Optometric Assn. (pres. 1983-84), Am. Pub. Health Assn. (vision care sect.). Republican. Mem. Lds Ch. Avocations: golf, tennis, photography, horsemanship, sailing, scuba diving. Office: Eye Care Assocs 660 W Campbell Rd Richardson TX 75080-3301 Home Phone: 972-235-4314; Office Phone: 972-231-9595. E-mail: drkrauss@ecarichardson.com, hkrauss@ecatexas.net.

KRAUSS, HERBERT HARRIS, psychologist; b. Phila., June 13, 1940; s. Leon and Ethel Sarah (Cohen) K.; m. Beatrice Joy Osgood, Aug. 26, 1965; children: Michael Conal, Daniel Avram. BS, Pa. State U., 1961, MS, 1962; PhD, Northwestern U., 1966. Lic. psychologist, N.Y. Intern in med. psychology U. Oreg. Med. Sch., 1962-63; asst. prof. psychiatry, psychology U. Kans. Med. Sch., Kansas City, Kans., 1966-67; asst. prof. psychiatry, psychology, chief psychologist in child psychiatry Ohio State U. Coll. Medicine, Columbus, 1967-69; assoc. prof. psychology U. Ga., Athens, 1969-71; prof. psychology Hunter Coll., CUNY, NYC, 1971-2001, chmn. dept. psychology, 1992-99; dir. rehab. rsch. and outcomes mgmt. Internat. Ctr. for the Disabled, NYC, 1984—2002; prof., chmn. dept. psychology Pace U., NYC, 2001—. Cons. Managed Health Network, N.Y.C., 1979-90, PhD Program, NYU, rehab. counselling, 1991—; adj. assoc. prof. psychiatry Cornell Med. Sch., N.Y.C., 1978—; assoc. attending psychologist Payne Whitney Clinic, N.Y. Hosp., 1978—; ptnr. Health Resources Mgmt. Co-author: Living with Anxiety and Depression, 1974; co-editor: Between Survival and Suicide, 1976, A Provider's Guide to Psychiatric Services in the General Hospital, 1986, The Aging Workforce: A Guide for University Administrators, 1992, Violence in the Schools: Cross-National and Cross-Cultural Perpsectives, 2005, Violence and Exploitation against women and girls, Vol. 1087 N.Y. CAcad. Scis.; co-editor Internat. Jour. Group Tensions, 1995-2000, assoc. editor, 2000—; cons. editor Jour. Individual Psychology, 1996—. Cons. Irvington, N.Y. Drug Coun., 1983; coach football and wrestling Irvington Sunnysiders, 1978-83, soccer Am. Youth Soccer Orgn., Houston, 1976-78. Named Outstanding Teacher Psychology, N.Y. Psychol. Assn., 1972. Fellow APA; mem. N.Y. Acad. Scis., Ea. Psychol. Assn., Internat. Orgn. for Study of Group Tensions (v.p., co-pres. 1999—), Am. Coun. on Germany, Am. Evaluation Assn., Cornell Club, Sigma Xi. Home: 520 Grand Ave Newburgh NY 12550-1929 Office: Pace Univ Dept Psychology 41 Park Row Rm 1313 New York NY 10038-1598 Home Phone: 845-565-7063; Office Phone: 212-346-1434. Business E-Mail: hkrauss@pace.edu.

KRAUSS, JUDITH BELLIVEAU, nursing educator; b. Malden, Mass., Apr. 11, 1947; d. Leo F. and Dorothy (Conners) Belliveau; m. Ronald L. Krauss, Sept. 5, 1970; children: Jennifer Leigh, Sarah Elizabeth. BS, Boston Coll., 1968; MSN, Yale U., 1970. RN, Conn. Clin. specialist Conn. Mental Health Ctr., New Haven, 1971-73; clin. instr. Yale Sch. Nursing, New Haven, 1971-73; asst. prof. rsch. Yale U. Sch. Nursing, New Haven, 1973-78, assoc. dean, 1978-85, prof., dean, 1985-98, prof., 1998—; master Yale U. Silliman Coll., 2000—, chair coun. of masters, 2004—. Cons. pharm. and pub. cons., sch., govt. agys. Author: The Chronically Ill Psychiatric Patient and the Community, 1982 (Am. Jour. Nursing Book of Yr. 1982); editor Archives of Psychiat. Nursing, 1986-2005; mem. editl. bd. Psychiat. Rehab., Psychiat. Svcs.; contbr. articles to profl. jours Trustee Boston Coll., 1991-99, trustee assoc., 2000—; bd. dirs. Josiah Macy Jr. Found., 2007—. Am. Nurses Found. scholar, 1978; recipient Chamberlain award Soc. Edn. and Rsch. in Nursing, 1994, Alumni Achievement award Boston Coll., 2004, medal Yale U. Sch. Nursing, 2005; named Disting. Alumna Yale Sch. Nursing, 1984; scholar Am. Acad. Nursing/Inst. Medicine, 1998-99. Mem. ANA (Disting. Contbn. to Psychiat. Nursing award 1992, Leadership citation 2002), Am. Acad. Nursing, Conn. Nurses Assn. (mem. cabinet on edn. 1987-89, bd. dirs. 1988-91, rep. to ANA house of dels. 1988-91, Josephine Dolan award 1989), Sigma Theta Tau (Disting. Lectr. award 1987), Delta Mu (Founders award 1987). Avocations: tennis, golf, hiking, skiing. Office: Yale U Sch Nursing Ste 200 100 Church St S New Haven CT 06536-0740 Home Phone: 203-432-0682. Business E-Mail: judith.krauss@yale.edu.

KRAUSS, LAWRENCE MAXWELL, physicist, astronomy educator, researcher, author; b. NYC, May 27, 1954; s. Alfred and Geraldine (Title) Krauss; m. Katherine Anne Kelley, Jan. 19, 1980; 1 child. BSc with first class honours in Math. and Physics, Carleton U., Ottawa, Ont., Can., 1977; PhD in Physics, MIT, Cambridge, 1982; DSc (hon.), Carleton U., Ottawa, Ont., Can., 2003. Jr. fellow Harvard Soc. Fellows, Cambridge, Mass., 1982-85; asst. prof. depts. physics and astronomy Yale U., New Haven, 1985-88, assoc. prof., 1988-93; Ambrose Swasey prof. physics, prof. astronomy Case Western Res. U., Cleve., 1993—. Assoc. European Orgn. Nuc. Rsch. (CERN), 1983, sci. assoc., 1996—97; vis. rschr. Smithsonian Astrophysy. Obs., 1984—88, Inst. Theoretical Physics, Santa Barbara, Calif., 1984, 85, 88, 89, 92, 2002, 03, U. Chgo., 1989, Inst. Nuc. Theory, Seattle, 1994, Lawrence Berkeley Lab. Inst. Nuc. and Particle Astrophysics, 1995, 96, 98, Institut des Hautes Études Scientifiques, Bures-sur-Yvette, France, 1997—98, Cambridge U. Isaac Newton Inst., 1999, Perimeter Inst., 2003; vis. scientist Boston U. and Smithsonian Astrophysy. Obs., 1985—86, Harvard-Smithsonian Ctr. Astrophysics, Cambridge, Mass., 1986—89; assoc. dept. physics Harvard U., 1987—95; mem. panel astronomy and astrophysics survey com. NRC, Washington, 1989—90; chmn. dept. physics Case Western Res. U., 1993—2005, dir. Ctr. Edn. and Rsch. in Cosmology and Astrophysics, 2002—, dir. office of sci., pub. policy and bio-entrepreneurship Sch. Medicine, 2005; Hooker disting. vis. prof. McMaster U. Origins Inst., 2005; mem. Inst. Advanced Study, 2005. Contbr. articles to profl. jours., to popular media; author: The Fifth Essence, 1989, Fear of Physics, 1993, Physics of Star Trek, 1995, Quintessence: The Mystery of the Missing Mass, 2000, Atom: A Single Oxygen Atom's Journey from the Big Bang to Life on Earth.and Beyond, 2002 (Am. Inst. Physics Sci. Writing award, 2002), Hiding in the Mirror: The Mysterious Allure of Extra Dimensions, from Plato to String Theory and Beyond, 2005; mem. adv. bd.: Odyssey Mag., 1997—; editor: Modern Physics Letter A, 1998—2000, Internat. Jour. Modern Physics, 1998—2000. Trustee Cleve. Mus. Natural History, 2002—; bd. advisors Def. of Constutution, 2005; bd. advisors, mem. guidance com. Sci. Fiction Experience, Seattle, 2003; trustee, mem. exec. com. Great Lakes Sci. Ctr., 1998—2004; mem. internat. adv. com. Internat. Conf. on Dark Matter Detection, 2000; mem. Aspen Ctr. Physics, 1998—; bd. dirs. Faststart Found., 2003—. Recipient First Prize award, Gravity Rsch. Found., 1984, Prize award, 1989, 1991, 1995, 1999, Presdl. Young Investigator award, 1986, Glover award, Distinction in Physics Achievement and Physics Edn., Dickenson Coll., Pa., 1997, Andrew R. Gemant award, Am. Inst. Physics, 2001, Humanism award, Free Inquirers of N.E. Ohio, 2003, Oersted medal, Am. Assn. Physics Tchrs., 2004, No. Ohio Live award of Achievement, Sci. and Tech., 2004; Vis. scholar, Phi Beta Kappa, 2007—. Fellow: AAAS (chmn.-elect physics divsn. 2006—, Award for Pub. Understanding of Sci. and Tech. 2000), Am. Phys. Soc. (mem. exec. com. divsn. astrophysics 1997—2000, chair forum physics and soc., Julius Edgar Lilienfeld prize 2001, Joseph A. Burton Forum award 2005); mem.: Bulletin Atomic Scientists (bd. sponsors), Am. Astron. Soc., Skeptics Soc. (bd. advisors 2001—). Office: Case Western Res U Physics Dept 10900 Euclid Ave Cleveland OH 44106-7079 E-mail: krauss@cwru.edu.

KRAUSS, RONALD MAXWELL, research scientist, endocrinologist, educator; b. NYC, May 12, 1943; s. Theodore Coleman Krauss and Lisbeth Hauser Rock; m. Sharon Anne Wald, May 11, 1969; children: Daniel Kalman, Jeffrey Aaron. AB magna cum laude, Harvard U., Cambridge, Mass., 1964; MD cum laude, Harvard Med. Sch., Boston, 1968. Lic. Am. Bd. of Endocrinology and Metabolism, 1977. Sr. investigator Nat. Heart and Lung Inst., Bethesda, Md., 1973—74; adj. prof., dept. nutritional scis. and toxicology U. Calif., Berkeley, 1993—, asst. clin. prof. medicine San Francisco, 1974—82, assoc. adj. prof. medicine, 1982—; assoc. dir. endocrine and metabolic svc. Alta Bates Hosp., Berkeley, Calif., 1976—85; sr. scientist and dir., atherosclerosis rsch. Children's Hosp. Oakland Rsch. Inst.; staff scientist Lawrence Berkeley Nat. Lab., Berkeley, Calif., 1976—84, sr. scientist, 1984—2003, head, molecular medicine rsch. program, 1989—92, head, dept. of molecular medicine, 1992—2003, co-director lipoprotein rsch. program, dep. dir. rsch. medicine and radiation biophysics divsn. Chmn. nutrition com. Am. Heart Assn., Dallas, nat. spokesperson panel, 1998—, founder and chmn. coun. on nutrition, phys. activity, and metabolism, 2000—04, mem. bd. dir.; mem. macronutrient panel Food and Nutrition Bd. of Inst. of Medicine, Washington, 1999—2002; sr. sci. adviser Nat. Cholesterol Edn. Program, NIH, Bethesda, Md., 1999—2001; mem. steering com. Nat. Lipid Edn. Coun., NYC, 1999—. Lead author: Am. Heart Assn Dietary Guidelines, 1996, 2000. Lt. comdr. U.S. Pub. Health Svc., 1970—74. Recipient Detur Prize, Harvard U., 1961, Spl. Recognition award, Am. Heart Assn. Coun. on Arteriosclerosis, Thrombosis, and Vascular Biology, 2001; grantee, NIH, 1976—. Fellow: Am. Heart Assn. (Disting. Achievement award 2001); mem.: Am. Fedn. Clin. Rsch., Fedn. of Am. Societies Exptl. Biology, Am. Soc. of Clin. Investigation, Alpha Omega Alpha, Phi Beta Kappa. Achievements include discovery of atherogenic lipoprotein phenotype as most common genetically influenced trait associated with premature heart disease risk; patents in field; first to demonstrate genetic influence on cholesterol and lipoprotein response to low fat diets; to demonstrate protection from atherosclerosis in genetically engineered mice. Avocations: jogging, singing, crossword puzzles. Office: Children's Hosp Oakland Rsch Inst 5700 Martin Luther King Jr Way Oakland CA 94609 Office Phone: 510-450-7908. Business E-Mail: rkrauss@chori.org.

KRAUSZ, MICHAEL, philosopher, educator; b. Geneva, Sept. 13, 1942; s. Laszlo and Susan Beate (Strauss) K.; m. Constance Frances Costigan. BA, Rutgers U., 1965; spl. studies, London Sch. Econs., 1963; MA, Ind. U., 1966; PhD, U. Toronto, 1969; postgrad., Oxford U., 1969—70. Acting chmn. dept. Bryn Mawr Coll., Pa., 1983-84, chmn. dept. Pa., 1993—2003, Milton C. Nahm prof. Pa., 2003—. Vis. asst. prof. Am. U., Washington, 1973-74; vis. prof., lectr. Georgetown U., 1977-79, Hebrew U., Jerusalem, 1978, Swarthmore Coll., 1980-81, Haverford Coll., 1981-82, U. Nairobi, 1985; disting. vis. prof. Am. U., Cairo, 1980; spl. lectr. U. Oxford, 1987, 89; instr. Curtis Inst. Music, 2002, 04, 06—; chmn. external rev. com. dept. philosophy Swarthmore Coll., 1987, Smith Coll., 1990; rsch. assoc. to vice prin. Linacre Coll., Oxford U., 1988, vis. sr. mem., 1986-90; vis. sr. mem. Linacre Coll., 1986-90, 98, 99; vis. prof. Indian Inst. Advanced Studies, Shimla, India, 1992, U. Ulm, 1997; co-dir. Confs. on Philosophy of Human Studies, 1981-88, co-founder, chmn., 1988-94, Greater Phila. Philosophy Consortium; mem. emeritus fellowship selection panel Andrew W. Mellon Found., 2003-07; overseas lectr. Indian Coun. Philos. Rsch., 2003. Referee: NEH, 1978, 1982, Jour. Aesthetics and Art Criticism, 1986, Nous, 1996; author: Rightness and Reasons: Interpretation in Cultural Practices, 1993, Limits of Rightness, 2000, Interpretation and Transformation: Explorations in Art and the Self, 2007; co-author (with Rom Harré): Varieties of Relativism, 1995; editor: Critical Essays on the Philosophy of R. G. Collingwood, 1972, Relativism: Interpretation and Confrontation, 1989, The Interpretation of Music, 1993, Greater Phila. Philosophy Consortium Series, Philosophy in the Global Context, 1995, Is There a Single Right Interpretation?, 2002, Interpretation and Its Objects: Studies in the Philosophy of Michael Krausz, 2003, Andreea Ritivoi; co-editor: The Concept of Creativity in Science and Art, 1981, Relativism: Cognitive and Moral, 1982, Rationality, Relativism, and the Human Sciences, 1986, Jewish Identity, 1993, Interpretation, Relativism & the Metaphysics of Culture, 1999; editor: (series) Philosophy of History and Culture, E.J. Brill, 1986—, Greater Philadelphia Philosophy Consortium, 1992—, Philosophy and the Global Context, 1995—, Interpretation and Translation, 2007—; co-editor: Greater Philadelphia Philosophy Consortium, 1985—92; author: revs., papers; 20 one-man exhibitions. Bd. dirs. Solisti N.Y., 1987—88; founder, pres., assoc. artistic dir. Phila. Chamber Orch., 1984; artistic dir., condr. The Great Hall Chamber Orch., 2005—; guest condr. Pleven Philharm. Orch., Bulgaria, 1999, 2000, Vratsa Philharm., Bulgaria, 2001, Plovdiv Philharm., Bulgaria, 2002, 2004. Fellow Royal Soc. Arts, London, 1973—, Andrew Mellon, Aspen Inst. Humanistic Studies, 1977—78, Ossabaw Found., 1978, 1980, Ctr. for Study of Developing Soc., 1998—99; grantee Ford Found., 1971, Bryn Mawr Coll., 1973—74, 1976, 1985—86, 1989, Alfred Sloan Found., 1986; hon. fellow, Tata Energy Rsch. Inst., New Delhi. Fellow Ctr. Study Developing Soc.; mem. Am. Philos. Assn., Am. Soc. Aesthetics (program chmn. ea. divsn. 1987—, chmn. steering com. ea. divsn. 1989-90, program chmn. nat. divsn. 1991, mem. Am. steering com.), World Congress Philosophy. Jewish. Avocation: conducting music. Office: Bryn Mawr Coll Dept Philosophy Bryn Mawr PA 19010 Office Phone: 610-526-5332. Business E-Mail: mkrausz@brynmawr.edu. E-mail: mkrausz@earthlink.net.

KRAUTHAMMER, CHARLES, columnist, editor; b. NYC, Mar. 13, 1950; s. Shulim and Thea K.; m. Robyn Trethewey; 1 child, Daniel. BA, McGill U., 1970; postgrad., Balliol Coll. Oxford U., 1970-71; MD, Harvard U., 1975. Diplomate Am. Bd. Psychiatry and Neurology. Resident in psychiatry Mass. Gen. Hosp., Boston, 1975-78; sci. advisor Dept. HHS, Washington, 1978-80; speech writer V.P. Walter Mondale, Washington, 1980-81; sr. editor The New Republic, Washington, 1981-88; essayist Time Mag., 1983—; syndicated columnist The Washington Post, 1984—. Author: Cutting Edges, 1985; contbr. sci. articles to psychiat. jours. Recipient Nat. Mag. award Am. Soc. Mag. Editors, 1984, Pulitzer prize for commentary, 1987, Bradley prize, 2003; Commonwealth scholar British Coun., Oxford, 1970-71.

KRAVATH, ALAN WOLFE, retired education evaluator; b. NYC, Sept. 27, 1939; s. Reuben and Fanny (Tannenbaum) K.; m. Carla Friedman, June 11, 1967; children: Gabriel, Daniel (dec.). BA in English, CCNY, NYC, 1965; MS in Spl. Edn., L.I. U., Bklyn., 1993. Cert. tchr. spl. edn., tchr. English, N.Y. Assoc. editor RSI Mag., NYC, 1963-67; account exec. Creamer-Dickson-Basford Pub. Rels., NYC, 1967-71; nat. dir. pub. info. United Svc. Orgns., Washington, 1971-77; evaluation educator, tchr. N.Y.C. Bd. Edn., 1987—2005; ret., 2005. Founder, pub. (booklet) Westchester Media Directory, 1984. Pub. rels. advisor pub. rels. adv. com. New Rochelle (N.Y.) Bd. Edn., 1977. Mem. East Yonkers Kiwanis (sec. 1984-87). Home: 1245 California Rd Eastchester NY 10709 Personal E-mail: alankravath@msn.com.

KRAVEKA, JACQUELINE MARIA, pediatrician, oncologist, researcher, scientist; b. Velasco, Cuba, July 29, 1966; arrived in U.S., 1971, naturalized; d. Luis R. and Glenda J. Kraveka; m. Ernesto Mario Barros, July 17, 1999; children: Alejandro Mario Barros children: Emily Marie Barros. BA, Columbia U., 1989; DO, Nova Southeastern U., 1994. Diplomate Am. Bd. Pediat., Am. Bd. Pediat. Hematology-Oncology, Nat. Bd. Osteo. Med. Examiners. Resident in pediat. Miami (Fla.) Children's Hosp., 1994—97; fellow pediat. hematology oncology Med. U. SC, Charleston, 1997—2000, asst. prof. of pediat., 2000—, dir., pediatric bone marrow transplant program, 2002—. Study chmn. Children's Oncology Group. Contbr. articles to profl. publs. Recipient Pediatric Loan Repayment Program award, NIH, 2002—; grantee Mentored Career Devel. award, 2003—; Carl Storm Under-represented Minority fellowship, 2006. Fellow: Am. Coll. Osteo. Pediatricians, Am. Acad. of Pediat.; mem.: AAAS, Soc. Pediat. Rsch., Am. Osteo. Assn., Am. Soc. Pediat. Hematology Oncology, Am. Soc. Hematology, Am. Soc. Clin. Oncology, Am. Assn. Cancer Rsch.

(Minority Scholar award in cancer rsch. 2000, 2002), Children's Oncology Group. Roman Catholic. Office: Med U SC 135 Rutledge Ave PO Box 250558 Charleston SC 29425 Business E-Mail: kravekjm@musc.edu.

KRAVETZ, KATHARINE, education educator; b. Houston, July 18, 1947; d. Frederick and Emily (Hollander) Kunreuther; m. Eric Stuart Kravetz, Aug. 25, 1974; children: Rachel, Daniel. BA, Harvard U., 1968; JD, Georgetown U., 1975. Bar: D.C. 1975, Md. 1981. Placement specialist TransCentury Corp., Washington, 1971—72; atty. Pub. Defender Svc. D.C., 1975—79, Law Offices of Katharine Kravetz, Washington, 1979—91; adj. prof. justice Am. U., Washington, 1979—82, 1988—91, asst. prof. justice, law and soc., 1991—94, academic dir. study abroad, 1994—98, asst. prof. justice, law and soc., 1998—. Mem. faculty senate Am. U., 2001—02, asst. prof. Transforming Communities, 2000—; mem. steering com. on ex-offenders D.C. Govt./Non-Profit Coalition, Washington, 2000—02. Contbr. articles to profl. jours. Vol. U.S. Peace Corps, Rezaiyeh, Iran, 1968—70; mem., study circles D.C. Prisoners Legal Svcs. Project, 2000. With US Peace Corps., 1968—70.

KRAVIS, HENRY R., investment banker; b. Tulsa, Jan. 6, 1944; s. Raymond Kravis and Bessie Roberts; m. Helene-Diane (Hedi) Shulman (div.); children: Robert S., Kimberly R., Harrison S.(dec.); m. Carolyn Roehm, 1985 (div. 1993); m. Marie-Josée Drouin, Feb. 19, 1994. BA in Econs., Claremont-McKenna Coll., 1967; MBA, Columbia U., 1969. Ptnr. Bear Stearns; co-founder Kohlberg Kravis Roberts & Co., NYC, 1976, sr. ptnr., 1987—. Bd. dirs. PRIMEDIA Inc., 1991—. Founder NYC Investment Fund; co-founder Rep. Leadership Coun.; bd. trustees Claremont-McKenna Coll., Met. Mus. Art, NYC, Mount Sinai Hosp., NYC; co-chair Partnership for NYC; chair Columbia Bus. Sch. Adv. Bd.; vice chmn. Rockefeller U. Named one of Top 200 Collectors, ARTnews mag., 2004, Forbes' Richest Ams., 2006. Mem.: Coun. Fgn. Rels. Achievements include historic billion dollar buyout of Wometco Companies in 1984; $25 billion RJR Nabisco buyout in 1989. Avocation: Collector Old Master drawings and paintings, Impressionist art, 20th-century art, French furniture. Office: Kohlberg Kravis Roberts & Co Ste 4200 9 W 57th St New York NY 10019*

KRAVIS, MARIE-JOSEE DROUIN, economist; b. Ottawa, Ont., Can., Sept. 11, 1949; d. Gaëtan and Anne Drouin; m. Henry R. Kravis, 1994. BA in Econs, U. Que., Montreal, 1970; MA, U. Ottawa, 1973; LLD (hon.), Univ. Windsor, Laurentian Univ., Canada. Fin. analyst Power Corp. Can. Ltd., 1969-70; spl. asst. to solicitor gen. Can., also to minister supply and services Govt. of Can., 1971-73; sr. economist Hudson Inst., 1973—76; exec. dir. Hudson Inst. Canada, Montreal, 1976—94; sr. fellow Hudson Inst., 1994—, bd. mem. & exec. com. mem. Mem. Canadian Council for Rsch. on Social Sci. & Humanities, 1982—86, Canadian Govt. Comm. Adv. Bd., 1982—89, Consultative Com. on Fin. Inst., Govt. Quebec, 1984—90; vice chmn. Royal Canadian Commn. on Nat. Passenger Transp., 1990—92; bd. dir. Ford Motor Co., 1995—, Vivendi Universal, 2001—, Interactive Corp., 2001—. Co-author: Canada HAS a Future, 1978, Quebec 1985, 1980, Western European Adjustment to Structural Economic Problems; contr. articles to profl. jours.; former weekly columnist for National Post, Canada; former host of weekly Canadian TV show on economics. Bd. trustees Mus. Modern Art, NYC; trustee Inst. for Advanced Study, Princeton, NJ; chmn. Robin Hood Found. Named one of Top 200 Collectors, ARTnews Mag., 2004. Fellow: Council on Fgn. Rels.; mem.: Forest and Stream (Dorval, Que.) (sr. fellow). Avocation: collector of Old Masters, Impressionism, 20th century art & French furniture. Office: Hudson Institute 1015 15th St NW Ste 600 Washington DC 20005-2605 Office Phone: 202-223-7770. Office Fax: 202-223-8537.

KRAVITCH, PHYLLIS A., federal judge; b. Savannah, Ga., Aug. 23, 1920; d. Aaron and Ella (Wiseman) K. BA, Goucher Coll., Balt., 1941, LLD (hon.), 1981; LLB, U. Pa., Phila., 1943; LLD (hon.), Emory U., Atlanta, 1998. Bar: Ga. 1943, US Dist. Ct. 1944, US Supreme Ct. 1948, US Ct. Appeals (5th cir.) 1962. Practice law, Savannah, 1944—76; judge Superior Ct., Eastern Jud. Circuit of Ga., 1977—79, US Ct. Appeals (5th cir.), Atlanta, 1979—81, US Ct. Appeals (11th cir.), 1981—96, sr. judge, 1996—. Mem. Jud. Conf. Standing Com. on Rules, 1994—2000. Trustee Inst. Continuing Legal Edn. in Ga., 1979—82; mem. Bd. Edn., Chatham County, Ga., 1949—55; mem. coun. Law Sch., Emory U., Atlanta, 1985—; mem. vis. com. Law Sch., U. Chgo., 1990—93; bd. visitors Ga. State U. Law Sch., 1994—; mem. regional rev. panel Truman Scholarship Found., 1993—2000; mem. vis. com. Goucher Coll., 2000—. Recipient Hannah G. Solomon award, Nat. Coun. Jewish Women, 1978, James Wilson award, U. Pa. Law Alumni Soc., 1992, Trailblazer award, Greater Atlanta Hadassah, 2000, Kathleen Kessler award, Ga. Assn. Women Lawyers, 2001, Shining Star award, Atlanta Women's Found., 2002, J. Ben Watkins award, Stetson Coll. Law, 2005. Fellow: Am. Bar Found.; mem.: ABA (Margaret Brent award 1991), Nat. Assn. Women Lawyers (Arabella Babb Mansfield award 1999), U. Pa. Law Soc., Am. Law Inst., Am. Judicature Soc. (Devitt award com. 1998—99), State Bar Ga., Savannah Bar Assn. (pres. 1976). Office Phone: 404-335-6300.*

KRAVITT, JASON HARRIS PAPERNO, lawyer; b. Chgo., Jan. 19, 1948; s. Jerome Julius and Shirley (Paperno) K.; m. Beverly Ray Niemeier, May 11, 1974; children: Nikola Wedding, Justin Taylor Paperno. AB, Johns Hopkins U., 1969; JD, Harvard U., 1972; diploma in comparative legal studies, Cambridge U., Eng., 1973. Bar: Ill. 1973, N.Y. 2002, U.S. Dist. Ct. (no. dist.) Ill. 1973, U.S. Dist. Ct. (so. dist.) N.Y. 2002. Assoc. Mayer, Brown Rowe & Maw (formerly Mayer, Brown & Platt), Chgo., 1973-78, ptnr., 1979—, co-chmn., 1998-2001. Adj. prof. law Northwestern U., Evanston, Ill., 1994—, adj. prof. fin. Kellogg Sch. Mgmt., 1998—. Editor: Securitization of Financial Assets, 2d edit., 1996. Bd. dirs. Chgo. Met. YMCA, 1998—2001, Mus. Contemporary Art, Chgo., 1974—75; dir., chmn. The Cameron Kravitt Found., 1984—; sec., chair legal, regulatory tax and acctg. com. Am. Securitization Forum, 2001—. Fellow Am. Coll. Comml. Lawyers; mem. ABA, Chgo. Coun. Lawyers, Chgo. Bar Assn., NY State Bar Assn., NYC Bar Assn., Econ. Club of Chgo., Execs. Club Chgo. Home: 250 Sheridan Rd Glencoe IL 60022-1948 Office: Mayer Brown Rowe & Maw 190 S La Salle St Ste 3100 Chicago IL 60603-3441 Office Phone: 212-506-2622. Business E-Mail: jkravitt@mayerbrown.com.

KRAVITZ, ELLEN KING, musicologist, educator; b. Fords, NJ, May 25, 1929; d. Walter J. and Frances M. (Prybylowski) Kokowicz; m. Hilard L. Kravitz, Jan. 9, 1972; children: Julie Frances, Heather Frances stepchildren: Kent, Kerry, Jay. BA, Georgian Ct. Coll., 1964; MM, U. So. Calif., 1966, PhD, 1970. Tchr. 7th and 8th grade music Mt. St. Mary Acad., North Plainfield, NJ, 1949-50; cloistered nun Carmelite Monastery, Lafayette, La., 1950-61; instr. Loyola U., LA, 1967; asst. prof. music Calif. State U., LA, 1967-71, assoc. prof., 1971-74, prof., 1974—99, emeritus prof., 1999—. Founder Friends of Music Calif. State U., LA, 1976. Mem. editl. adv. bd.: Jour. Arnold Schoenberg Inst., 1977—87; editor: Jour. Arnold Schoenberg Inst., Vol. I, No. 3, 1977, Jour. Arnold Schoenberg Inst., Vol. II, No. 3, 1978; author (with others): Catalog of Schoenberg's Paintings, Drawings and Sketches; author: (book) Music in Our Culture, 1996. Guest lectr. Schoenberg Centennial Com., 1969—, mem., 1974. Mem.: Hist. Assn. L.A. Music Ctr., Am. Musicol. Soc., L.A. County Mus. Art, Pi Kappa Lambda, Mu Phi Epsilon.

KRAVITZ, LEE, editor; BA, Yale U.; MA in Journalism, Columbia U. Editl. dir. Scholastic Inc.; editor React (subs. Parade Pubs.), 1995—2000; v.p. Parade Pubs., 1995—2000, sr. v.p., 2000—; editor Parade Magazine, NYC, 2000—. Office: Parade 711 3rd Ave New York NY 10017-4014 Office Phone: 212-450-0920. Office Fax: 212-450-7284. E-mail: lee_kravitz@parade.com.*

KRAVITZ, RUBIN, chemist; b. Framingham, Mass., Mar. 22, 1928; s. Abe and Lillian (Cohen) K. m. Geraldine Pudaim, Aug. 20, 1950 (dec.); children: Richard Alan, Steven Jay, Stuart Paul; m. Annabelle S. Durieux, July 16, 1978; 1 child, Michelle Pearl. BS, Northeastern U., 1952, D in Pharm, 1982. Analytical chemist FDA, HEW, Boston, 1956-61; analytical chemist Alcohol and Tobacco div. U.S. Treasury Dept., Boston, 1961-65; supr. phys. testing lab. plastic div. Am. Hoechst Corp., Leominster, Mass., 1967-78, rsch. chemist plastic div., 1978-83; sr. devel. engr. EPS, 1983-85; pres. Nat. Plastics Mus. Inc., 1981-85; dir., pres. T.H.E. Hypnosis Ctr., Virginia Beach, Va., 1986-89; staff pharmacist MacDonald Army Hosp., Ft. Eustis, Va., 1987-89; chief pharmacist U.S. Army Health Clin., Fort Monroe, Va.; pres., chief exec. officer Cadet Labs., Virginia Beach, 1984—; chief pharmacist U.S. Army Health Clinic, Ft. Monroe, 1989—. Del. Va. Pharm. Assn., 1988; mem. Mid-Atlantic Cholesterol Coun. Cubmaster Boy Scouts Am., Worcester, Mass., 1967-68; trustee, founding pres. Nat. Plastics Ctr. and Mus., 1985—. With USAAF, 1946-48. Recipient Hygeia Bowl award, Wyeth Ayerst, 2002. Mem. Assn. Mil. Surgeons U.S., Soc. Plastic Engrs. (newsletter editor 1969-71, treas. Pioneer Valley sect. 1972-73, v.p. 1973-74, chmn. tech. com. 1973, pres. Pioneer Valley sect. 1975-76, chmn. sect. museum 1979-85, achievement award 1981), ASTM (chmn. compression molding 1969-70, vice chmn. publicity and papers com. D-20 on plastics 1972-76, chmn. subcom. specimen preparation, chmn. sect. plastic furniture, chmn. specimen preparation 1976, chmn. task group Kravitz impact test method 1976, chmn. D 20.12 Olefin Plastics com., mem. exec. com. 1982-85), Assn. Analytical Chemists, Assn. to Advance Ethical Hypnosis, Am. Soc. Rsch. and Clin. Hypnosis, K.P. (chancellor comdr. 1963-64).

KRAVITZ, STEVEN J., lawyer; b. Bklyn., Mar. 26, 1946; AB magna cum laude, U. Miami, 1967; JD cum laude, Harvard U., 1970. Bar: Fla. 1970, U.S. Tax Ct. 1971, U.S. Dist. Ct. (so. dist.) Fla. 1971. Mem. Greenberg, Traurig, Hoffman, Lipoff, Rosen & Quentel P.A., Miami, Fla.; of counsel. Greenberg Traurig, LLP, Miami, Fla. Mem. v.p. Hillel Cmty. Day Sch., Latin Am. Jewish Cmty. Miami; nat. vice chmn. United Jewish Appeal, chmn. Greater Miami Jewish Fedn., gen. campaign chmn. Greater Miami Jewish Fedn., 1991-92; past pres. Greater Miami Jewish Fedn., 1993-94. Grantee Woodrow Wilson fellow in Polit. Sci., 1967. Mem. ABA, Fla. Bar, Dade County Bar Assn., Phi Kappa Phi, Omicron Delta Kappa, Phi Sigma Alpha. Office: Greenberg Traurig LLP 221 Brickell Ave Miami FL 33131 Office Phone: 305-579-0500. Office Fax: 305-579-0717.

KRAW, GEORGE MARTIN, lawyer, writer; b. Oakland, Calif., June 17, 1949; s. George and Pauline Dorothy (Herceg) K.; m. Sarah Lee Kenyon, Sept. 3, 1983 (dec. Nov. 2001). BA, U. Calif., Santa Cruz, 1971; student, Lenin Inst., Moscow, 1971; MA, U. Calif., Berkeley, 1974, JD, 1976. Bar: Calif. 1976, U.S. Supreme Ct. 1980, D.C. 1992. Pvt. practice, 1976—; ptnr. Kraw & Kraw, San Jose, 1988—. Mem. adv. com. Pension Genefit Guaranty Corp., 2002—05. Mem. ABA, Internat. Soc. Cert. Employee Benefit Specialists, Nat. Assn. Health Lawyers, Inter-Am. Bar Assn. Office: Kraw & Kraw 1754 Technology Dr Ste 106 San Jose CA 95110 Business E-Mail: gkraw@kraw.com.

KRAWCHECK, SALLIE L., diversified financial services company executive; b. Charleston, SC, Nov. 28, 1964; d. Leonard and Towning Krawcheck; m. Gary Appel; 2 children. BA, U. N.C., Chapel Hill, 1987; MBA, Columbia U., NYC, 1992. Fin. analyst Salomon Brothers, Inc.; assoc. corp. fin. dept. Donaldson, Lufkin & Jenrette; sr. rsch. analyst Sanford C. Bernstein & Co., 1994—98, dir. rsch., 1999—2001; exec. v.p. Alliance Capital Mgmt. L.P., 2001—02; chmn., CEO Sanford C. Bernstein & Co., 2001—02, Smith Barney, NYC, 2002—04; exec. v.p. fin., ops. & strategy, CFO Citigroup Inc., NYC, 2004—07, chmn., CEO Global Wealth Mgmt. divsn., 2007—. Mem. Citigroup Mgmt. com., Citigroup Bus. Heads com. Bd. dirs. U. N.C. at Chapel Hill Foundations, Inc., Carnegie Hall; bd. overseers Columbia Bus. Sch. Named Most Influential Person Under the Age of 40, Fortune mag., 2003; named one of Global Business Influentials, Time mag., 2002, Most Powerful Women in Bus., Fortune mag., 2002, 2003, 2004, 2006, World's 100 Most Powerful Women, Forbes mag., 2005—06, 25 Most Powerful Women in Banking, US Banker, 2006, Next 20 Female CEOs, Pink Mag. & Forté Found., 2006. Office: Citigroup Inc 399 Park Ave New York NY 10022*

KRAWETZ, ARTHUR ALTSHULER, chemist, science administrator; b. Chgo., Oct. 30, 1932; s. John and Grace (Altshuler) K. BS in Chemistry, Northwestern U., Evanston, Ill., 1952; MS in Phys. Chemistry, U. Chgo., 1953, PhD in Phys. Chemistry, 1955. Cert. profl. chemist; chartered chemist, chartered scientist Royal Soc. Chemistry. V.p. Phoenix Chem. Lab., Inc., Chgo., 1950-73, tech. dir., 1958—, pres., 1974—. Contbr. articles to profl. jours. 1st Lt. USAF, 1956—58, capt. Res. USAF. Fellow Am. Inst. Chemists, Royal Soc. Chemistry (chartered chemist); mem. ASTM (chmn. sub-com. D02.11 engring. scis., sub-com. N-VI fire resistance 1974-84, sub-com. IX-D oxidation 1974-81, task force on precautionary statements for hazardous material and lab. ops. 1976-84, com. mem.), Am. Chem. Soc., Instrument Soc. Am., Air & Waste Mgmt. Assn., Soc. for Applied Spectroscopy, Soc. Automotive Engrs., Soc. Tribologists and Lubrication Engrs., Nat. Lubricating Grease Inst., The Coblentz Soc., Nat. Fire Protection Assn. (com. on classification and properties of hazardous chemical data, phys. and chem. data consistency adv. com.), Chgo. Gas Chromatography Discussion Group, Phi Beta Kappa, Sigma Xi, Phi Lambda Upsilon, Pi Mu Epsilon. Achievements include patents for temperature control apparatus and method, method of determining acid content of oil sample, automatic oxygen measuring system, viscometers, measurement of bulk modulus and pressure viscosity, corrosion rate evaluation procedures; registered copyrights for various software. Office: Phoenix Chem Lab Inc 3953 W Shakespeare Ave Chicago IL 60647-3497 Office Phone: 773-772-3577. Personal E-mail: pclinc@exnet.com.

KRAWETZ, STEPHEN ANDREW, molecular medicine and genetics scientist, educator; b. Fort Frances, Ont., Can., Sept. 17, 1955; s. Stephen and Michaelene (Medynski) K.; m. Lorraine Ruth St. John, Aug. 19, 1977; children: Rhochelle Tairaesa, Alexandra Renée. BSc, U. Toronto, Ont., 1977, PhD, 1983. Tchr. Scarborough Bd. Edn., Ont., 1976-77; Alberta Heritage Found. Med. Rsch. postdoc. fellow U. Calgary, Alta., Canada, 1983-89; asst. prof. rsch. ctr. for molecular biology Wayne State U., Detroit, 1989, asst. prof. molecular biology and genetics, 1989-92, asst. prof. obstetrics and gynecology and molecular biology and genetics, 1992-94, assoc. prof. ob/gyn. and molecular medicine and genetics, 1994-2000, prof. ob-gyn. and molecular medicine and genetics Inst. Sci. Computing, 2000, Charlotte B. Failing prof. ob-gyn. and molecular medicine and genetics and Inst. Sci. Computing, 2001—07, dir. Bioinformatics Node Mich. Life Scis. Corridor, 2001—, dir. Ctr. of Excellence for Combating the Paternal Impact of Toxicol. Waste on the Next Generation, dir. translational reproductive sys., 2007—. Biotech. cons., Calgary, 1985-89, Grosse Pointe Woods, Mich., 1989—; co-founder Genetic Imaging, Inc., 1988. Mem. editl. bd. BioTechniques, Ag Biotech News and Info., Cellular and Molecular Biology Letters, Gene Therapy and Molecular Biology, Archives Andrology: Jour. Reprodn. Sys.; contbr. numerous articles to scholarly jours. Recipient B.C. Childrens Hosp. Rsch. award, Vancouver, 1984, Computer Applications in Molecular Biology award IntelliGenetics Inc., Mountain View, Calif., 1988, others, Bd. of Govs. award Wayne State U., 2004; named Outstanding Basic Scientist, C.S. Mott Ctr., 1999; Alta. Heritage Found. Med. Rsch. fellow, 1985-88. Mem. AAAS, Am. Soc. Human Genetics, Soc. for the Study of Reprodn. Achievements include development of a computer-based imaging system for biological data, of the basis of biological sequence alignment algorithm; first definition of sequence interpretation errors in the GenBank database; first to define a genic domain in human sperm; research in gene therapy targeted to the amelioration of human disease; showed that selective potentiation of our genome mediates cell-phenotype.

KRAWINKLER, HELMUT, engineering educator, consultant; b. Innsbruck, Austria, Apr. 6, 1940; s. Hans and Anna Krawinkler; m. Michele Marie Krawinkler, Apr. 18, 1975; 1 child, Marcus Alexander. Degree in Civil Engring., Tech. U., Vienna, Austria, 1964; PhD, U. Calif., Berkeley, 1971. Registered profl. engr., Bd. Profl. Engrs., Calif., 1975. Prof. civil engring. Stanford U., Calif., 1973—. Cons. in field. Dir. NEES, Davis, Calif., 2003—06. Mem.: Network for Earthquake Engring. Simulation, Structural Engrs. Assn. Calif. (hon.). Home: 245 Galli Drive Los Altos CA 94022 Office: Stanford University Dept of Civil Engineering Stanford CA 94305-4020 Home Phone: 650-714-2065; Office Phone: 650-723-4129. Office Fax: 650-723-7514. Business E-Mail: krawinkler@stanford.edu.

KRAYNAK, HELEN, special education consultant; b. Jersey City, Mar. 28, 1936; d. Stephen and Irene (DanKovich) Ozimok; m. John Kraynak, June 23, 1956; children: Deborah Mary Fiocco, Lorie Elizabeth Kraynak. BS in Edn., Jersey City State Coll., 1958; student, Rutgers U., 1985-87; learning disabilities cert., Nova U., 1991. Cert. Elem., N.J., Fla., Specific Learning Disabilities, Fla. Kindergarten tchr., Old Bridge, N.J., 1962-63; 2nd grade tchr., 1963-65; 3rd grade tchr., 1965-66; resource tchr., 1966-67; reading tchr., 1968-89; learning disabilities tchr. Palm City, Fla., 989-92; mainstream cons. Palm City Elem. Sch. and Hidden Oaks Mid. Sch., Palm City, Fla., 1992—; cons. Felix A. Williams Elem. Sch., Stuart, Fla., 2002—05. Mentor, student tchr. supr. Fla. Atlantic U., 2002-05. Bd. dirs. Old Bridge (NJ) Cath. Youth Orgn., 1972-75; Christian Cath. Doctrine tchr. Nativity of Our Lord Ch., 1972-85, Sts. Cyril and Meth. Ch., Ft. Pierce, Fla., 1995-05; leader Girl Scouts US, East Brunswick, NJ, 1966-72. Mem. NEA, Coun. Exceptional Children, Am. Fedn. Tchrs., N.J. Tchrs. Edn. Assn., Alpha Delta Kappa (pres. 1990-92). Avocations: world travel, walking on the beach, reading. Home: 9500 S Ocean Dr Apt 207 Jensen Beach FL 34957-2327

KRAYNAK, MARCELLE GEORGEANN, not-for-profit developer; b. NYC, Apr. 3, 1944; d. Richard A. and Bernice (Weinberg) Kane; m. Anthony Walter Kraynak, Sept. 27, 1989; children: Marylin Kotansky, Joseph Kossmann, Bobbi Dempsey, William Kossmann. AAS in Human Svcs. magna cum laude, Lackawanna Jr. Coll., Hazleton, Pa., 1996. LPN, Pa. Buyer cosmetics F. W. Woolworth, Jamaica, NY, 1964—65; asst. dir., group supr. YMCA/YWCA; staff nurse St. Joseph's Med. Ctr., Hazleton, 1989—90; dir. Children's Rainbow Found., Hazleton, 1990—92; founder, exec. dir. Silent Santa, Hazleton, 1992—. Co-chair Vietnam Relocation Com., Wilkes-Barre, Pa., 1974; v.p. Vine Manor Resident Coun., Hazleton, 1993—. Named Nurse of Hope, Am. Cancer Soc., 1989; recipient Sam-Son award, Sam-Son Prodns. Avocations: reading, writing. Home and Office: 320 W Mine St #204 Hazleton PA 18201

KRAYZIE BONE, (ANTHONY HENDERSON), rap artist; b. Cleveland, June 3, 1974; Mem. Bone Thugs-N-Harmony, 1993; co-founder Bone Thug Records. Musician: (albums) (with Bone Thugs-N-Harmony) E 1999 Eternal, 1995, The Art of War, 1997, BTNHResurrection, 2000, Thug World Order, 2002, Thug Stories, 2006, Everyday Thugs, 2006, (solo) Thug Mentality, 1999, Thug on da Line, 2001, Gemini: Good vs. Evil, 2005, Thugline Soldiers, 2007, (songs) Tha Crossroads, 1996 (Grammy award, Best Group Rap Performance, 1997), (with Chamillionaire) Ridin', 2006 (MTV Video Music award, Best Rap Video, 2006, Grammy award, Best Group Rap Performance, 2007). Co-recipient Favorite Rap Artist award, Am. Music Awards, 1998. Office: Bone Thug Records PO Box 857 North Hollywood CA 91603 Office Phone: 818-755-0744. E-mail: info@bonethugaffiliated.com.*

KREBS, ARNO WILLIAM, JR., lawyer; b. Dallas, July 7, 1942; s. Arno W. and Lynette (Linnstaedter) K.; m. Peggy Sharon Stagg, Dec. 17, 1966; 1 child, Kirsten; m. Barbara Lyn Craig, Dec. 28, 1973 BA, Tex. A&M U., 1964; LL.B., U. Tex., 1967. Bar: Tex. 1967, US Dist. Ct. (so. dist.) Tex. 1968, US Ct. Appeals (5th cir.) 1971, US Ct. Appeals (11th cir.) 1981, US Dist. Ct. (we. and no. dists.) Tex. 1981, US Supreme Ct. 1983, US Dist. Ct. (ea. dist.) Tex. 1984. Assoc. Fulbright & Jaworski, Houston, 1967-75, ptnr., 1975—2006, of counsel, 2006—. Contbr. articles to profl. jours. Mem. Houston Bar Assn., Tex. Aggie Bar Assn. (pres. 1978-79), Tex. Bar Found., Houston Bar Found., Tex. A&M U. 12th Man Found. (pres. 1988). Lutheran. Office: Fulbright & Jaworski 1301 Mckinney St Fl 51 Houston TX 77010-3031 Office Phone: 713-651-5522. Personal E-mail: akrebs@fulbright.com.

KREBS, CARL F., architectural firm executive; b. Phila., Aug. 27, 1959; AB, Harvard U., 1981; MArch, Columbia U., 1985. Ptnr. Davis Brody Bond Aedas, 1984—. Ptnr.-in-charge Health Scis. Learning Ctr., U. Wis.; ptnr.- in-charge Lang. Resource Ctr., Columbia U., World Trade Ctr. Meml. Mus. Recipient Arch. Record award, Bus. Week, 2000. Office: Davis Brody Bond Aedas 315 Hudson St 9th Fl New York NY 10013

KREBS, EDWIN GERHARD, biochemistry educator; b. Lansing, Iowa, June 6, 1918; s. William Carl and Louise Helena (Stegeman) K.; m. Virginia Frech, Mar. 10, 1945; children: Sally, Robert, Martha. AB in Chemistry, U. Ill., 1940; MD, Washington U., St. Louis, 1943; DSc (hon.), U. Geneva, 1979; degree (hon.), Med. Coll. Ohio, 1993; DSc (hon.), U. Ind., 1993; doctorate (hon.), U. Nat. De Cuyo, 1993; DSc (hon.), U. Ill., 1995, Washington U., St. Louis, 1995. Intern, asst. resident Barnes Hosp., St. Louis, 1944-45; rsch. fellow biol. chemistry Wash. U., St. Louis, 1946-48; prof., chmn. dept. biol. chemistry Sch. Medicine U. Calif., Davis, 1968-76; from asst. prof. to prof. biochemistry U. Wash., Seattle, 1948-66, prof., chmn. dept. pharmacology, 1977-83, prof. biochemistry and pharmacology, 1984-91, emeritus prof., biochemistry and pharmacology, 1991—; investigator, sr. investigator Howard Hughes Med. Inst., Seattle, 1983-90, sr. investigator emeritus, 1991—. Mem. Phys. Chemistry Study Sect. NIH, 1963-68, Biochemistry Test Com. Nat. Bd. Med. Examiners, 1968-71, rsch. com. Am. Heart Assn., 1970-74, bd. sci. counselors Nat. Inst. Arthritis, Metabolism and Digestive Diseases, NIH, 1979-84, Internat. Bd. Rev., Alberta Heritage Found. for Med. Rsch., 1986, external adv. com. Weis Ctr. for Rsch., 1987-91; mem. subgroup interconvertible enzymes IUB Spl. Interest Group Metabolic Regulation; internat. adv. bd. Advances in Second Messenger Phosphoprotein Rsch.; external adv. com. Cell Therapeutics Inc., Seattle; adv. bd. Kinetek, Vancouver, B.C. Mem. editorial bd. Jour. Biol. Chemistry, 1965-70; mem. editorial adv. bd. Biochemistry, 1971-76; mem. editorial and adv. bd. Molecular Pharmacology, 1972-77; assoc. editor Jour. Biol. Chemistry, 1971-93; mem. internat. adv. bd. Advances in Cyclic Nucleotide Rsch., 1972—; editorial advisor Molecular and Cellular Biochemistry, 1987—. Recipient Gairdner Found. award, Toronto, 1978, J.J. Berzelius lectureship, Karolinska Institutet, 1982, George W. Thorn award for sci. excellence, 1983, Sir Frederick Hopkins Meml. lectureship, London, 1984, Rsch. Achievement award Am. Heart Assn., Anaheim, Calif., 1987, 3M Life Scis. award FASEB, New Orleans, 1989, Albert Lasker Basic Med. Rsch. award, 1989, CIBA-GEIGY-Drew award Drew U., 1991, Steven C. Beering award, Ind. U., 1991, Welch award in chemistry Welch Found., 1991, Louisa Gross Horwitz award Columbia U., 1989, Alumni Achievement award Coll. Liberal Arts and Scis. U. Ill., 1992, Nobel prize in physiology or medicine, 1992, Kaul Found. award for excellence, 1996; John Simon Guggenheim fellow, 1959, 66. Mem. NAS, Am. Soc. Biol. Chemists (pres. 1986, ednl. affairs com. 1965-68, councillor 1975-78), Am. Acad. Arts and Scis., Am. Soc. Pharmacology and Exptl. Therapeutics. Achievements include lifelong study of the protein phosphorylation process. Office: U Wash HSB K540E PO Box 357750 Seattle WA 98195-7750 Home Phone: 206-325-8176; Office Phone: 206-543-8500. Business E-Mail: egkrebs@u.washington.edu.

KREBS, HERMANO IGO, research scientist; BS in Naval Engring., Escola Politecnica da Universidade de Sao Paulo, Brazil, 1980, MS in Naval Engring., 1987; MS in Ocean Engring., Yokohama Nat. U., Japan, 1989; PhD in Engring., MIT, 1997. Tchr., elec. design Escola Técnica Federal de Sao Paulo, Brazil, 1977—78, rsch. asst., 1978—79; surveyor, ships, offshore platforms, container cranes Am. Bur. Shipping, Sao Paulo, Brazil, 1980—86; vis. researcher, high speed containership Sumitomo Heavy Industry, Hiratsuka, Japan, 1989; engr., container crane design & construction Casper, Phillips & Assocs., Tacoma, 1993—96; rsch. asst., robot-aided neuro-rehabilitation and functional imaging MIT, Cambridge, Mass., 1989—96, prin. rsch. scientist, lectr., 1997—. Contbr. scientific papers, articles to profl. jours. Achievements include patents in field. Office: MIT 77 Massachusetts Ave Rm 3-137 Cambridge MA 02139-4307 Office Phone: 617-253-8112. Office Fax: 617-258-7018. Business E-Mail: hikrebs@mit.edu.*

KREBS, JOHN RICHARD, zoologist, science administrator; b. Sheffield, Yorkshire, Eng., Apr. 11, 1945; s. Hans Adolf and Margaret Cicely (Fieldhouse) Krebs; m. Katharine Anne Fullerton, Aug. 3, 1968; children: Emma Helen, Georgina Clare. BA, Oxford U., Eng., 1966, MA, PhD, Oxford U., Eng., 1970; DSc (hon.), Sheffield U., Eng., 1993; DSc (hon.), U. Wales, 1997, U. Birmingham, Eng., 1997, U. Exeter, 1998; DUniv (hon.), U. Stirling, Scotland, 2000; DSc (hon.), U. Warwick, Eng., 2000, Cranfield U., 2001; DSc (hon.), U. Kent, Eng., 2001, U. Plymouth, 2001, South Bank U., 2003, Heriot-Watt U., 2002, Queen's U., Belfast, Northern Ireland, 2002, Lancaster U., 2005, U. Guelph, Can., 2006. Departmental demonstrator ornithology Edward Grey Inst. Field Ornithology, Oxford U., 1969-70, lectr. zoology, 1976-88, Pembroke Coll., Oxford U., 1969-70, E.P. Abraham fellow zoology, 1981-88, ofcl. fellow, 1988—2005, hon. fellow, 2005—; asst. prof. Inst. Animal Resource Ecology U. B.C., Vancouver, 1970-73; lectr. zoology U. Coll. North Wales, Bangor, 1973-74; SRC rsch. officer animal behavior rsch. group dept. zoology Oxford U., 1975-76, Royal Soc. rsch. prof., 1988—2005; chief exec. United Kingdom Natural Environ. Rsch. Coun., Swindon, England, 1994-99. Mem. Agrl. and Food Rsch. Coun., U.K., 1989—94; chmn. U.K. Food Stds. Agy., 2000—05; prin. Jesus Coll., Oxford, 2005—. Author: (with N.B. Davies) An Introduction to Behavioural Ecology, 1981, 3rd edit., 1993, (with D.W. Stephens) Foraging Theory, Princeton Monographs in Behavior and Ecology, No. 4, 1987; editor: (with N.B. Davies) Behavioural Ecology: An Evolutionary Approach, 1978, 4th edit., 1997; (with A. Kamil and H.R. Pulliam) Foraging Behavior, 1987; (with G. Horn) Behavioural and Neural Aspects of Learning and Memory, 1991. Sci. fellow Nuffield Found., London, 1981; recipient Sci. medal Zool. Soc., London, 1981, Frink medal Zool. Soc., 1996, London, 1981, Bicentenary medal Linnaean Soc., London, 1983, Elliot Coues award Am. Ornithologists Union, 1999, medal Assn. of Study of Animal Behavior, 2000, Benjamin Ward Richardson gold medal Royal Soc. for Promotion of Health, 2002, Wooldridge medal Brit. Vet. Assn., 2003, Outstanding Achievement award Soc. for Food Hygiene Tech., 2005, Low Rayner Meml. medal Royal Coll. Physicians, 2005, Harben Gold medal Royal Inst. Pub. Health, 2006; hon. fellow U. Cardiff, Wales, 1999, U. Wales Inst., Cardiff, 2006, Zool. Soc. London, 2006; named Knight Bachelor, Britain, 1999, Life Peer Lord Krebs of Wytham, Oxfordshire, 2007. Fellow: Royal Soc. (Croonian lectr. and medal 2004), Acad. Med. Scis.; mem.: Am. Acad. Arts and Scis. (fgn.), Acad. Europaea, Brit. Ecol. Soc. (hon.), NAS (fgn. hon.), Max Planck Soc., Assn. for Study Animal Behaviour (pres. 1992—94, medal 2000), Am. Philos. Soc. (fgn.). Avocations: gardening, violin, running, tennis. Office: The Principals Lodgings Jesus College Oxford OX1 3DW England

KREBS, KEITH ERVIN, minister; b. Castle Rock, Va., July 18, 1932; s. Ervin E. and Ruth H. (Johnson) Krebs; m. Ruth H. Krebs, Apr. 27, 1929; children: Sandra, Kurt, Karla, Erik, Brock, Stephanie, Rachel. BA, Columbia U., NYC, 1954. Pastor Chelan Luth. Ch., Wash., 1960—64, First Luth. Ch., Seattle, 1964—67, Resurrection Luth. Ch., Springfield, Oreg., 1967—72, Emmanuel Luth. Ch., Walla Walla, Wash., 1997. Lt. j.g. USN, 1954—56, Korea. Lutheran. Home: 404 S Palouse Walla Walla WA 99362

KREBS, LEO FRANCIS, lawyer; b. Botkins, Ohio, June 9, 1937; s. Eugene L. and Velma L. K.; m. Paula Anne Calvert, Nov. 4, 1961; children: Matthew, Mark, Thomas, Peter. BA, U. Dayton, 1959; JD, Georgetown U., 1965. Bar: Ohio 1966, U.S. Dist. Ct. (so. dist.) Ohio 1966, U.S. Ct. Appeals (6th cir.) 1974, U.S. Supreme Ct. 1975. Legal dep. Montgomery Probate Ct., 1966-68; assoc. Bieser, Greer & Landis, Dayton, Ohio, 1968-74, ptnr., 1974—. Assoc. editor Georgetown Law Rev., 1964-65. Chmn. fin. com. Holy Angels, 1986-98, former chmn., bd. dirs. parish coun.; former bd. dirs. Cath. Social Svcs. Dayton, 1987-90; former mem. Oakwood YMCA Baseball Commn.; coach YMCA baseball. 1st lt. U.S. Army, 1959-62. Fellow Am. Coll. Trial Lawyers, Ohio State Bar Found.; mem. ABA, Ohio State Bar Assn., Ohio Assn. Trial Attys., Dayton Bar Assn., Phi Delta Phi. Avocations: hiking, bicycling. Office: Bieser Greer & Landis 6 N Main St Ste 400 Dayton OH 45402-1914 Business E-Mail: lfk@bgl.com.

KREBS, MEIKEN, chemicals executive; CFO several German and Italian companies; v.p. corp. auditing, risk mgmt. Merck KGaA, Darmstadt, Germany, 2003—06; pres., CEO EMD Chem. Inc. (subs. Merck KGaA), Gibbstown, NJ, 2006—. Office: EMD Chemicals 480 S Democrat Rd Gibbstown NJ 08027 Office Phone: 856-423-6300. Office Fax: 856-423-4389. Business E-Mail: emdinfo@emdchemicals.com.

KREBS, ROBERT ALAN, lawyer; b. Pitts., Dec. 12, 1958; s. James Arthur and Helen Marie (McGrogan) K.; m. Elizabeth Ann Bedford, Apr. 20, 1985; children: Stephen Vladimir, Diane Kathleen. BA, Pa. State U., 1981; student, U. Exeter, UK, 1981; JD, Capital U., 1984. Bar: Pa. 1984, DC 1989, US Dist. Ct. (ea. dist.) Pa. 1990, US Dist. Ct. (we. dist.) Pa. 1984, US Dist. Ct. (no. dist.) Ohio 1990, US Dist. Ct. (DC) 1989, US Ct. Appeals (DC cir.) 1989, US Ct. Appeals (3d cir.) 1986, US Supreme Ct. 1988. Assoc. Henderson & Goldberg, Pitts., 1985-87, Messer Shilobod & Crenney, Pitts., 1987-89, Klett Lieber Rooney & Schorling, Pitts., 1989-91, Conte, Melton & D'Antonio, Conway, Pa., 1992—2002, Morella & Assocs., Pitts., 2002—04, of counsel, 2004—. Articles editor Capital Law Rev., 1983-84. Mem. com. on jud. issues Pa. Gov.-Elect Edward G. Rendell Transition Team, 2003; commr. Pa. Workers Compensation Appeal Bd., 2004—; mem. Pa. Dem. State Com., 37th Dist., 1994—2006, Allegheny County Dem. Com., Pitts., 1991—2006. Recipient Am. Jurisprudence award Lawyers Coop. Pub. Co., 1982. Mem.: ABA, Western Pa. Trial Lawyers Assn. (chair edn. com. 1994—95, bd. govs. 1994—2004, co-chair comeback award com. 2001—04, co-chair pres.'s scholarship com. 2001—04), Allegheny County Bar Assn. (fed. ct. sect. coun. 1996—99, chair, appellate practice com. 2004—06, workers' compensation sect. coun. 2006—), Pa. Trial Lawyers Assn. (amicus curiae com. 1996—2004), DC Bar Assn., Capital U. Law Sch. (bd. visitors 2001—05). Democrat. Roman Catholic. Home: 3235 Comanche Rd Pittsburgh PA 15241-1138 Office: Manor Oak One Ste 310 1910 Cochran Rd Pittsburgh PA 15220 Office Phone: 412-531-2680. E-mail: bobkrebs@verizon.net, rkrebs@state.pa.us.

KREBS, ROCKNE, artist; b. Kansas City, Mo., Dec. 24, 1938; s. Arthur Sanford and Lorine (Fisher) Krebs; m. Nizette Brennan, Oct. 30, 1991; children: Heather, Rockne Brennan, Nizette Cameron. BFA, U. Kans., 1961. Exhbns. include Gallery of Modern Art, Washington, 1968, Corcoran Gallery Art, Washington, 1969, U.S. Pavilion Expo 70, Osaka, Japan, 1970, Art Inst. Chgo., 1970, L.A. County Mus., 1970, New Orleans Mus., 1971, Phila. Mus. Art, 1973, Omni-Internat. Complex, Atlanta, 1973-76, Walker Art Ctr., Mpls., 1974, Art Prk, Lewiston, N.Y., 1975, U.S. Bicentennial Expo Sci. and Tech. Kennedy Space Ctr., Cape Canaveral, Fla., 1976, Balt. Inner Harbor, 1977, Fort Worth Art Mus., 1978, Disneyland Hotel, Anaheim, Calif., 1979, The Mall, Washington, 1980, Cin. Contemporary Art Ctr., 1985, Meml. Art Gallery, Rochester, N.Y., 1987, U. Rochester (N.Y.), 1987, Okla. Art Ctr., 1988; executed laser and neon artwork Urban Scale-Pine Ave. and City of Long Beach, Calif., 1992, laser artwork Pegasus Cloud Projection at Downtown Plz., City of Sacramento, 1993, neon, laser, fiber optic and search lights artwork Red River Bridge, Shreveport, La., 1993-95, animated laser projection Olympics CNN Ctr., Atlanta, 1996, laser art, The Universe Exhbn. at Armory Art Ctr., Pasadena, Calif., 2001; pioneer use of lasers in art; rschr, author: The Laserman Letters to Myself, 1996-99; patentee in field. Lt. USN, 1961-64. Mem.: SAR. Office: PO Box 292 194 Old Mill Ln Burgess VA 22432 Office Phone: 202-246-4190. Business E-Mail: rockne@crosslink.net.

KREBS, WILLIAM HOYT, industrial hygienist, health science association administrator; b. Detroit, Apr. 6, 1938; s. William Thomas and Mary Louise (Hoyt) K.; m. Susan Kathryn Bartholomew, Aug. 8, 1964 (div. July 1976); children: Elizabeth Louise, William Thomas II; m. Jane Germer Meikle, June 18, 1983 (dec. May 2004); stepchildren: David Andrew, Sarah Elizabeth. BS, U. Mich., 1960, MPH (IH), 1963, MS, 1965, PhD, 1970. Rsch. asst. U. Mich., Ann Arbor, 1962-63; indsl. hygienist Lumbermens Mut. Casualty Co., Chgo., 1963-64, GM Corp., Detroit, 1970-77, mgr. toxic materials control activity, 1977-81, dir. toxic materials control activity, 1981-90, dir. indsl. hygiene activity, 1990-93; v.p. Indsl. Health Scis., Inc., Grosse Pointe Park, Mich., 1993—94, pres., 2004—. Mem. asbestos adv. com. Mich. Occupational Health Standards Commn., Lansing, 1984—. Contbr. articles to profl. jours. Mem. Grosse Pointe Meml. Ch., Grosse Pointe Farms, 1954; mem. health and safety com. Detroit Area coun. Boy Scouts Am., 1980; mem. environment and energy com. Detroit Regional Chamber. Fellow Am. Indsl. Hygiene Assn. (hon. mem.; bd. dirs. 1976-79, v.p. 1986-87, pres. 1988-89); mem. AAAS, APHA, Mich. Indsl. Hygiene Soc. (pres. 1980-81), Brit. Occupational Hygiene Soc., Internat. Occupational Hygiene Assn. (v.p. 1990-91, pres. 1992-93), Internat. Commn. on Occpl. Health, Soc. Automotive Engrs. Presbyterian. Home: 1014 Bishop Rd Grosse Pointe Park MI 48230-1421 Office: Indsl Health Scis Inc 1014 Bishop Rd Grosse Pointe Park MI 48230-1421 Office Phone: 313-885-8225.

KRECHETNIKOV, ROUSLAN, mathematician, educator; s. Vitaly Krechetnikov and Valentina Krechetnikova. BS, Moscow Inst. Physics & Tech., MS with honors, 1992—98, PhD, 2003. Postdoctoral scholar U. Calif., Santa Barbara, 2002—04, Calif. Inst. Tech., Pasadena, Calif., 2004—06; asst. prof. Carleton U., Ottawa, Ontario, Canada, 2006—. Contbr. articles to profl. jours. Office: Carleton U Sch Math & Stats Herzberg Labs 1125 Colonel By Dr Ottawa ON Canada K1S 5B6 Office Fax: 613 520 3536. Business E-Mail: rkrechet@math.carleton.ca.

KRECZKO, ALAN JAMES, lawyer, insurance company executive; b. May 7, 1951; s. Steve Henry and Martha Helen (Shoda) Kreczko; m. Joan Latimer, Apr. 30, 1983. BA magna cum laude, Boston Coll., 1972; JD magna cum laude, Univ. Mich., 1976. Bar: Ohio. Atty. U.S. Dept. State, Washington, 1976—79, legal adv. to Camp David negotiations, 1979—83, asst. legal adv. Near East & So. Asian Affairs, 1983—87, asst. legal adv. Oceans, Environ. & Sci., 1987—88, dep. legal adv. Oceans, Environ. & Sci., 1988—93; spl. asst. to Pres., legal adv. Nat. Security Council, 1993—96; sr. dep. asst. sec. Population, Refugees & Migration U.S. Dept. State, 1996—2001, acting asst. sec. Population, Refugees & Migration, 2001—03; sr. v.p., dep. gen. counsel Hartford Fin. Services Group, Hartford, Conn., 2003—07, exec. v.p., gen. counsel, 2007—. Vis. prof. Georgetown Univ. Law Ctr. Contbr. articles to profl. jours. Recipient Younger Fed. Lawyer of the Yr., Fed. Bar Assn., 1984, Distinctive Honor award, U.S. Dept. State, 1986, Presdl. Meritorious Exec. award, 1987, 1991, Presdl. Disting. Exec. award, 1989, Tom Clarke award, Fed. Bar Assn., 1992. Mem.: Phi Beta Kappa. Office: Hartford Fin Svcs Group Hartford Plz 600 Asylum Ave Hartford CT 06115*

KREEK, MARY JEANNE, physician; b. Washington; d. Louis Francis and Esperance (Agee) K; m. Robert A. Schaefer, Jan. 24, 1970; children: Robert A., Esperance Anne BA, Wellesley Coll., 1958; MD, Columbia U., Coll. Physicians and Surgeons, 1962; D (hon.), Uppsala U., Sweden, 2000, Tel Aviv U., 2007. Med. rschr. NIH, Bethesda, Md., 1957—62; intern, resident Cornell N.Y. Hosp. Med. Ctr., NYC, 1962—65, fellow, 1965—67; instr. medicine Cornell Med. Coll., 1966—67; clinician specializing in internal medicine, endocrinology, gastroenterology, hepatology, pharmacology, neurosci., molecular genetics NYC, 1966—. Mem. staff N.Y.-Presbyn. Hosp.-Weill Sch. Medicine of Cornell U., 1968—77, clin. asst. prof., asst. attending physician, now assoc. attending physician, adj. assoc. prof.; asst. prof. Rockefeller U., 1967—72, sr. rsch. assoc., physician, 1972—83, assoc. prof., physician, 1983—94, prof., sr. physician, head of lab., 1994—; head Ind. Lab. on Biology of Addictive Disease, 1975—94, head of lab., 1994—; sr. physician Rockefeller U. Hosp., 1994—; adj. prof. Beijing Med. U., 1996—2000, Peking U., 2000—, Karolinska Inst., 2001; mem. gen. medicine study sect. NIH, 1973—77; co-chmn. John E. Fogarty (NIH) Internat. Conf. Hepatotoxicity Due to Drugs and Chems., 1977, charter mem. peer rev. oversight group, 1996—2000; vis. prof. Pahlavi U., Shiraz, Iran, 1977; spl. adv. Nat. Inst. Drug Abuse, 1976—86, mem. nat. adv. coun., 1991—95, mem. molecular genetics consortium, 1999—; prin. investigator Rsch. Ctr. Biol. Basis Addictive Diseases, 1987—; mem. gastroenterology adv. com. FDA, 1975—79, 1992—96, NIH Gen. Clin.; mem. gen. rsch. ctr. study sect. NIH, 1979—83, chmn., 1982—83; mem. exec. com. Coll. Problems Drug Dependence, 1982—87, 1989—94, chmn. exec. com., 1985—87, chair sci. program com., 1991—96; fellow CPDD, 1992—; dir. NIH-Nat. Inst. Drug Abuse Rsch. Ctr., 1987—. Recipient Borden Rsch. award, 1962, Career Scientist award Health Rsch. Coun. City NY, 1974-75, Dole/Nyswander award, 1984, Rsch. Scientist award NIH Gen. Clin. sect., 1978—, Mentor of Mentors award Am. Soc. Addiction Medicine, 1995, Assn. for Med. Edn. and Rsch. in Substance Abuse-Betty Ford award for outstanding rsch., 1996, R. Brinkley Smithers Disting. Scholar award Am. Soc. Addiction Medicine, 1999, Nathan B. Eddy award, Lifetime Rsch. award Coll. on Problems of Drug Dependence, 1999, Gold Medal Lifetime Excellence award Columbia U. Coll. Physicians and Surgeons Alumni Assn., 2004, Marian Fischman award, Coll. Ptnrs., 2005, Founders award, Intenat. Narcotic Rsch. Conf., 2005 Fellow: ACP (life), Am. Coll. Psychiatry, Harvey Soc., NY Acad. Scis., Am. Fedn. for Clin. Rsch., Assn. Am. Physicians (life), Am. Coll. Neuropsychopharmacology (mem. coun. 2004—); mem.: Soc. on Neurosci., Rsch. Soc. on Alcoholism, Coun. Fgn. Rels. (life), Internat. Narcotic Rsch. Conf. (exec. com. 1993—97, pres.-elect 2001—03, pres. 2003—06, past pres. 2006—), Internat. Assn. Study Liver, Am. Assn. Study Liver Diseases, Endocrine Soc., N.Y. Gastroent. Assn. (pres. 1987), Am. Gastroent. Assn., Shakespeare Soc. of Wellesley, Phi Beta Kappa, Sigma Xi. Office: Rockefeller U New York NY 10021

KREER, IRENE OVERMAN, association and meeting management executive; b. McGrawsville, Ind., Nov. 11, 1926; d. Ralph and Laura Edith (Sharp) Overman; m. Henry Blackstone Kreer, Dec. 22, 1946 (dec.); children: Laurene (dec.), Linda Kreer Witt. BS in Speech Pathology, Northwestern U., 1948. Speech pathologist Ill. pub. schs., 1947-49; staff asst., lectr. Art Inst. Chgo., 1962—; pres. Irene Overman Kreer & Assocs., Inc., 1962—. TV appearances representing Art Inst. edn. programs; lectr. in field. Past bd. dirs. Glenview (Ill.) Pub. Libr.; mem. The Art Inst. Chgo., Glenview Cmty. Ch., Field Mus., Chgo. Architecture Found., Smithsonian Assocs. Mem. Nat. Trust Hist. Preservation, Assn. Alumnae Northwestern U. (bd. dirs. 1975—), Delta Delta Delta. Republican. Avocations: travel, archaeology, tennis.

KREGEL, KEVIN R., astronaut; b. Amityville, NY, Sept. 16, 1956; s. Alfred H. and Frances T. Kregel. BS in Astronautical Engring., USAF Acad., Colo. Springs, Colo., 1978; MPA, Troy State U., 1988. Commd. 2d lt. USAF, 1978, student pilot Williams AFB, Ariz., 1978—79; exchange officer RAF, Lakenheath, England, 1980—83, USN, Whidbey Island Seattle, 1984—86; student USN Test Pilot Sch., Patuxent River, Md., 1987—88; test pilot Eglin AFB, Fla., 1988—90; resigned USAF, 1990; aerospace engr., instr. pilot NASA Shuttle Flights, 1990—92; astronaut trainee Johnson Space Ctr., Houston, 1992—93; space flight crew mem., 1995—. Recipient 4 Space Flight medals, NASA, Exceptional Svc. award. Achievements include 4 Space flights; 5000 flight hours in 30 different aircraft; 66 carrier landings. Office: Astronauts Office CB Johnson Space Ctr Houston TX 77058

KREGER, DAVID LAWRENCE, gastroenterologist; b. Portsmouth, Va., Feb. 8, 1946; s. H. Sol and Ruth S. (Silverman) K.; m. Ruth H., Mar. 31, 1974; children: Seth Adam, Senta Lauren. BA, Duke U., 1968; MD, Med. Coll. Va. Intern Med. Coll. Va. Hosp., Richmond, 1972-73, resident, 1973-75; gastroenterologist Gastroen. Assocs. Tidewater, Norfolk, Va., 1978—. Gastroenterology fellow, Duke U. Med. Ctr., Durham, N.C., 1975—77. Office: Gastroen Assocs Tidewater 160 Kingsley Ln Ste 200 Norfolk VA 23505-4600 Home Phone: 757-440-0705; Office Phone: 757-889-6800.

KREGER, MELVIN JOSEPH, lawyer; b. Buffalo, Feb. 21, 1937; s. Philip and Bernice (Gerstman) K.; m. Patricia Anderson, July 1, 1955 (div. 1963), children: Beth Barbour, Arlene Roux; m. Renate Hochleitner, Aug. 15, 1975. JD, Mid-valley Coll. Law, 1978; LLM in Taxation, U. San Diego, 1988. Bar: Calif. 1978, US Dist. Ct. (cen. dist.) Calif. 1979, US Tax Ct. 1979, US Supreme Ct. 1995; cert. specialist in probate law, trust law and estate planning law, taxation law, Calif. Life underwriter Met. Life Ins. Co., Buffalo, 1958-63; bus. mgr. M. Kreger Bus. Mgmt., Sherman Oaks, Calif., 1963-78, enrolled agt., 1971—; pvt. practice North Hollywood, Calif., 1978—. Mem. Nat. Assn. Enrolled Agts., Calif. Soc. Enrolled Agts., State Bar Calif., LA Bar Assn., San Fernando Valley Bar Assn. (probate sect., tax sect.). Jewish. Avocations: computers, travel. Office: 11424 Burbank Blvd North Hollywood CA 91601-2301 Office Phone: 818-506-4723. Business E-Mail: mel@meltaxlaw.com.

KREHBIEL, FREDERICK AUGUST, II, electronics executive; b. Chgo., June 2, 1941; s. John Hammond and Margaret Ann (Veeck) K.; m. Kay Kirby, Dec. 21, 1973; children: William Veeck, Jay Frederick. BA, Lake Forest Coll., 1963. Advt. and human resources mgr. Molex, Inc., Lisle, Ill., 1965—67, export mgr., 1967—69, v.p. internat., 1970—75, exec. v.p., dir., from 1976, vice chmn., CEO, 1988-93, chmn., CEO, 1993—98, co-chmn., co-CEO, 1998—2001, co-chmn., 2001—, CEO, 2004—05. Bd. dirs. Tellabs Inc., Molex, Inc., DeVry, Inc. Trustee Rush Med. Ctr., Chgo., Lyric Opera, Chgo., Chgo. Hist. Soc., Mus. Sci. and Industry, Chgo., Chgo. Orch. Assn., Sch. of Art Inst., Chgo., Trinity Found., Ireland; trustee, chmn. Chgo. Zool. Soc. Mem. Hinsdale (Ill.) Golf Club, Chgo. Club, Casino Club (Chgo.), Racquet Club Chgo., Everglades Club, Bath and Tennis Club Palm Beach. Home: 505 S County Line Rd Hinsdale IL 60521-4725 Office: Molex Inc 2222 Wellington Ave Lisle IL 60532-3820 Business E-Mail: fkrehbiel@molex.com.

KREHBIEL, JOHN H., JR., retired electronics company executive; b. 1937; BA, Lake Forest Coll., 1959. With Molex Inc., Lisle, Ill., 1959—75, pres., 1975—99, COO, 1996—99, co-CEO, 1999—2001, co-chmn., 1999—. Named one of 400 Richest Ams., Forbes mag., 2006. Office: Molex Inc 2222 Wellington Ct Lisle IL 60532-3820*

KREIDER, CLEMENT HORST, JR., neurosurgeon; b. Annville, Pa., Oct. 14, 1932; s. Clement Horst and Eleanor Lucille (Etter) K.; m. Yvonne Maria Vignone, Mar. 6, 1983; children: Clement H. III, John William H., George E. Etter (dec. Jan. 2001); stepchildren: Michael A. Ketcham (dec. July 1997), David C. Ketcham. Student, Yale U., 1949-51, 53-54; BS, Bethany Coll., W.Va., 1957; MD, Temple U., 1963. Lic. physician, Pa., N.J. Intern Pa. Hosp., Phila., 1963-64; resident in gen. surgery Temple U. Hosp, Phila., 1964-65, resident in neurosurgery, 1965-69; pvt. practice neurosurgery Harrisburg, Pa., 1969-72, Ocean, N.J., 1972-99; chief sect. neurosurgery Jersey Shore Med. Ctr., Neptune, N.J., 1972-96, attending neurosurgeon, 1996-99, emeritus, 2000—. Sr. attending Monmouth Med. Ctr., Long Branch, N.J., 1972-99, emeritus attending, 2000—; full attending Riverview Med. Ctr., Red Bank, N.J., 1972-99, emeritus, 2000; cons. emeritus CentraState Med. Ctr., Freehold, N.J.; courtesy staff emeritus Med. Ctr. of Ocean County, Point Pleasant, N.J., Kimball Med. Ctr., Lakewood, N.J., Bayshore Cmty. Hosp., Holmdel, N.J.; clin. instr. surgery Hershey (Pa.) Med. Ctr., 1970-72, Hahnemann Med. Ctr., Phila., 1970-72. Contbr. articles to profl. jours.; mem. com. on pub. N.J. Medicine, Lawrenceville, 1985-99. With U.S. Army, 1951-53. Fellow Stroke Coun., Am. Heart Assn.; mem. Congress of Neurol. Surgeons, Am. Assn. Neurol. Surgeons Joint Sect. on Cerebrovasc. Surgery, Med. Soc. N.J., N.J. Neurosurg. Soc., Monmouth County Med. Soc., Acad. Medicine of N.J. Avocation: cooking. Office Phone: 732-280-7374.

KREIDLER, CHARLES W(ILLIAM), linguist, educator; b. Frankfort, Ky., Aug. 5, 1924; s. Christopher George and Elizabeth Allen (Best) K.; m. Carol Jane Kardos, Aug. 15, 1959; children: James Christopher, Julia Frances Hickey. AB in Spanish, U. Cin., 1948; MA in Linguistics, U. Mich., 1951, PhD, 1957. Teaching fellow U. Mich., Ann Arbor, 1953-54, asst. prof. English, 1959-63; instr., then asst. prof. modern langs. St. Peter's Coll., Jersey City, 1954-58; Fulbright lectr. in English Ctrl. Univ. Ecuador and U. Guayaquil, Ecuador, 1958-59; assoc. prof., then prof. linguistics Georgetown U., Washington, 1963-93, prof. emeritus, 1993—; Fulbright Prof. U. Sao Paulo, Brazil, 1990, Cath. U. of Asuncion, Paraguay, 1994. Lectr. U. P.R., 1965, U. So. Calif., 1968; guest prof. U. Regensburg, Germany, 1975; cons. in field. Author: (with Allen Glatthorn and Ernest Heiman) The Dynamics of Language, 1971, The Pronunciation of English: A Course Book, 1989, 2d edit., 2003, Describing Spoken English, 1997, Introducing English Semantics, 1998; editor: Phonology: Critical Concepts, 2000; contbr. articles to profl. jours. With USNR, 1943-46. Home: 4512 Verplanck Pl NW Washington DC 20016-2432 E-mail: chak321@aol.com.

KREIDMAN, PERRY L., lawyer; b. Rockville Centre, NY, June 11, 1951; BA cum laude, Colgate U., 1973; JD, NYU, 1976. Bar: NY 1977, US Dist. Ct. Ea. Dist. NY, US Dist. Ct. So. Dist. NY. Ptnr. Wilson, Elser, Moskowitz, Edelman & Dicker LLP, NYC. Mem.: ABA (tort & ins. practice sect., litig. sect.), NY State Bar Assn. (ins. & negligence sect.), Phi Beta Kappa. Office: Wilson Elser Moskowitz Edelman & Dicker LLP 23rd Fl 150 E 42nd St New York NY 10017-5639 Office Phone: 212-490-3000 ext. 2226. Office Fax: 212-490-3038. Business E-Mail: kreidmanp@wemed.com.

KREIG, ANDREW THOMAS, trade association executive; b. Chgo., Feb. 28, 1949; s. Albert Arthur and Margaret Theresa (Baltzell) K. AB, Cornell U., 1970; MSL, Yale U., 1983; JD, U. Chgo., 1990. Bar: D.C. 1991, Mass. 1991, Ill. 1991. Writer, editor Hartford Courant, Conn., 1970—84; media dir. Conn. House Spkr., Hartford, 1994; freelance author, journalist, lectr. Hartford and Chgo., 1985—89; law clk. U.S. Dist. Judge

Mark L. Wolf, Boston, 1990—91; assoc. Latham & Watkins, Washington, 1991—93; v.p., comm. dir. Wireless Comm. Assn. Internat., Inc., Washington, 1993—96, v.p., gen. counsel, 1996, pres., CEO, 1997—. Ethics com. Soc. Profl. Journalists, 1987-90. Author: Spiked: How Chain Management, 1987, 2d edit., 1988; editor Spectrum, 1994—; bd. editors Pvt. & Wireless Cable, 1994—, Wireless Internat., 1996—; contbr. articles to profl. jours. V.p. Residences Market Square, Washington, 1993-98; co-chair Fixed Wirless Com. Coalition, 2000—. Ford Found. fellow, Yale Law Sch., New Haven, 1982—83. Mem. Fed. Com. Bar Assn. (legis. com.). Home: PH8 701 Pennsylvania Ave NW Washington DC 20004-2608 Office: Wireless Comms Assn Ste 700 W 1333 H St NW Washington DC 20005 Office Phone: 202-452-7823. Business E-Mail: president@wcai.com.

KREIGER, BRUCE D., lawyer; b. Bronx, NY, Dec. 9, 1943; BA with honors, City U. NY, 1965; MBA, U. Calif., 1968, JD, 1971. Bar: Calif. 1972, U.S. Dist. Ct. Calif. (No. dist.) 1974, U.S. Ct. Appeals 1975, U.S. Supreme Ct. 2000. Atty. Dean Witter & Co., Nat. Assn. Securities Dealers; asst. gen. counsel, asst. atty. Shaklee Corp.; former spl. counsel to the Reagan White House, Exec. Office of the Pres. of U.S., 1981; v.p., gen. counsel, sec. Colgate-Palmolive subs., Blyth, Inc., Greenwich, Conn. Adj. prof. Hastings Coll. Law, 1974—75. Contbr. articles to profl. jours. Mem.: ABA (mem. bus. law sect., bilateral investment treaty com.), Am. Corp. Counsel Assn. Office: Blyth Inc One E Weaver St Greenwich CT 06831 Office Phone: 203-552-6621. Office Fax: 203-552-9168.

KREIMER, MICHAEL WALTER, financial planner, investment company executive; b. NYC, Aug. 29, 1963; s. Anthony Kreimer and Frieda (Göebel) Rath; m. Madeline Louise Lawler, Dec. 31, 1992; children: Jillian Marie, Maximilian Walter. BS cum laude, SUNY, Albany, 1985. Lic. ins. agt., N.Y.; CFP. Assoc. v.p. McLaughlin, Piven, Vogel Inc., Jericho, NY, 1985-88; fin. planner, br. mgr. A.G. Edwards & Sons, Smithtown, NY, 1988—. Agt. Ins. Dept. State of NY, 1989—. Cons. (newsletter) Investing, 1992—. Fundraiser Big Bros./Big Sisters Suffolk, Commack, N.Y., 1989; mem. Nat. Parks Conservation Assn., Washington, 1992; coach Bellport Girls Soccer, 2002-04, So. County Youth Soccer League, 2002-. Mem. NASD (lic.), Internat. Bd. Standards and Practices for CFPs (CFP mark 1993), Inst. CFPs (direct pub. awareness program 1994-97, L.I. chpt.), Southampton C. of C., Rotary Internat. (dir. 2003-04, sec. 2004-05, pres. 2005-06). Republican. Roman Catholic. Avocations: tennis, skiing, golf, running. Home: 2 Abets Creek Path East Patchogue NY 11772-5400 Office: A G Edwards Sons PO Box 599 Water Mill NY 11976-0599 Office Phone: 631-726-5100.

KREIMER, SETH F., lawyer, educator; BA magna cum laude, Yale U., 1974, JD, 1977. Law clk. to Hon. Arlin M. Adams US Ct. Appeals, 1977—78; assoc. Fine, Kaplan & Black, Phila., 1978—81; asst. prof. U. Pa. Law Sch., Phila., 1981—85, assoc. prof., 1985—92, prof., 1992—2004, assoc. dean, 2002—04, Kenneth W. Gemmill prof., 2004—. Cons. ACLU, Planned Parenthood Fedn., Cmty. Legal Svcs., Lawyers Com. for Civil Rights under Law, Pub. Interest Law Ctr. of Phila., Phila. Mayor's Com. on Homeless, Phila. Human Rels. Commn., Disabilities Law Project, City of Phila., Juvenile Law Ctr., Women's Law. Office: U Pa Law Sch 3400 Chestnut St Philadelphia PA 19104 Office Phone: 215-898-7447. Office Fax: 215-573-2025. E-mail: skreimer@law.upenn.edu.

KREIN, CATHERINE CECILIA, broadcast and journalism educator; b. NYC, July 2, 1935; d. Timothy T. and Catherine A. Mitchell; m. Robert Krein, Apr. 18, 1970; 1 child, Karyn Elise. BS, Fordham U., 1960; film cert., NYU, 1974; MA, Queens Coll., 1994. Various positions including prodr., editl. dir., writer CBS News, NYC, 1963-86; chief spokesperson Bklyn. Dist. Atty., 1986-87; v.p. external affairs Molloy Coll., Rockville Centre, NY, 1987-99; adj. prof. Hofstra U., 1997—99, prof. journalism Hempstead, 1999—2004; adj. prof. journalism Monmouth U., West Long Br., NJ, 2004—. Mem.: IRTS, NATAS, L.I. Communicators Assn., L.I. Coalition Fair Broadcasting, Profl. Pub. Rels. of L.I., Soc. Profl. Journalists, Pub. Rels. Soc. Am., Radio TV News Dirs. Assn. Home: 904 Jersey Ave Spring Lake NJ 07762-1924

KREIN, PHILIP T., electrical engineer, educator, electronics executive; m. Sheila Fitzgerald. AB, BS, Lafayette Coll., Easton, Pa., 1978; PhD, U. Ill., Champaign-Urbana, 1982. Registered profl. engr., Ill., Oreg. Physicist Tektronix, Inc., Beaverton, Oreg., 1984—87; prof. U. Ill., Urbana, 1987—. Chmn. bd. dirs. SmartSpark Energy Systems, Inc., Champaign. Author: (textbook) Elements of Power Electronics, 1997. Asst. scoutmaster Boy Scouts Am., Champaign, 2004—06. Fellow: IEEE (soc. pres. 1999—2000, Walter E. Newell Electronics award IEEE Power Electronics Soc.). Achievements include patents and patents pending in field. Office: U Ill 1406 W Green St Urbana IL 61801 Office Phone: 217-333-4732. Office Fax: 217-333-1162. Business E-Mail: p.krein@ieee.org.

KREINBERG, ROMEO, chemicals executive; Grad., Nat. U. Architecture and City Planning, Buenos Aires. With Dow Chem. Co., 1977, bus. ops. mgr. latex and new ventures Corp. Product dept. Midland, Mich., regional comml. dir., 1990—92, gen. mgr. Italy, 1992—94, v.p. Europe, 1992—94, v.p. Europe polyethylene and PET/PTA, 1994, global v.p. polyethylene and PET/PTA, 1995—2000, bus. grp. pres. polyolefins and elastomers, 2000, sr. v.p. plastics, 2003, mem. Office of the Chief Exec., 2004—, exec. v.p. performance plastics and chems., 2005—. Bd. mem. Dupont Dow Elastomers, PBB - Polisur, US Coun. Internat. Bus., Univation Tech., LLC; bd. dirs. Dow Corning Corpn., Oman Petrochemical Industries Co., LLC. Office: Dow Chem Co 47 Bldg Midland MI 48067*

KREINDLER, PETER MICHAEL, lawyer; b. Liberty, NY, Mar. 30, 1945; BA in Econ., Harvard U., 1967, JD magna cum laude, 1971. Bar: D.C. 1971, N.Y. 1989. Law clk. to Judge Irving R. Kaufman US Ct. Appeals (2nd cir.), 1971—72; law clk. to Justice William O. Douglas US Supreme Ct., 1972—73; assoc. Hughes, Hubbard & Reed, 1975-77, ptnr., 1977-88; prin., assoc. gen. counsel Coopers & Lybrand, 1988—89; ptnr. Arnold & Porter, 1990-91; sr. v.p., gen. counsel and sec. AlliedSignal, Morristown, NJ, 1992—95; sr. v.p., gen. counsel Honeywell Internat., Morristown, NJ, 1999—. Office: Honeywell Internat Inc 101 Columbia Rd Morristown NJ 07960-4640*

KREINHEDER, HAZEL FULLER, retired genealogist, historian; b. Northampton, Mass., Aug. 27, 1935; d. John Herbert and Hazel Gertrude Fuller; m. Robert Frederick Kreinheder, Nov. 14, 1959; children: John Frederick, Paul Robert. BA, U. Mass., 1957. Lab. asst. dept. chemistry Amherst (Mass.) Coll., 1952-57; rsch. analyst Dept. Def., Fort George G. Meade, Md., 1957-63; libr. staff mem. Columbia Hist. Soc., Washington, 1976-77; hist. rschr. Washington, 1977-81; staff genealogist DAR, Washington, 1981-85, corrections genealogist, 1985-2001, ethnic and minority genealogist, 1997—2007, asst. dir. genealogy divsn., 2001—07; ret., 2007. Hist./geneal. cons. Washington Perspectives, Inc., 1977—90. Co-author/author: 5 booklets. Mem. exec. bd. Capitol Hill Babysitting Coop., 1966—68; mem. Com. 100 Fed. City, 1978—, mem. hist. preservation com., 1978—81; vol. pre-sch. vision screening program Prevention Blindness Soc., 1969—72; mem. Oldest Inhabitants DC, 1999—, Bryan Sch. Neighborhood Assn., 1995—2005, Assn. Preservation of Hist. Congl. Cemetery, Nat. Bldg. Mus., 1999—, Friends of Libr./U. Mass., Cir.-on-the-Hill, treas., 1964—65. Civil air patrol, 1956—57. Named Hon. Ky. Col., 2003; recipient Capitol Hill Citizen of the Yr., Capitol Hill Restoration Soc., 1970. Mem.: DAR (life; nat. vice chmn.'s assn., vice chair patriot index com. 1992—95, Mary Mattoon chpt. libr. 1996—, vice chair minority rsch. lineage rsch. com. 1998—, assoc. mem. Francis Duclos chpt. 2005), Soc. Genealogique Canadienne-Francaise, Soc. Genealogy Que., Nat. Geneal. Soc., Capitol Hill Village, Nat. Assn. Rail Passengers, Washington Rescue League, Friends of Paul Revere, Capitol Hill Restoration Soc. (sec. 1967—68, treas. 1968—70, co-chmn. hist. preservation com. 1979—81, chmn. ho. com. 1979—81), Friends of Emily Dickinson, Friends of Jones Libr., Nat. Assn. Rail Passengers, Nat. Inst. Geneal. Rsch. Alumni Assn., Washington Humane Soc. Republican. Lutheran. Avocations: civic activities, reading. Home: 113 Kentucky Ave SE Washington DC 20003-1447

KREININ, MORDECHA ELIAHU, economics professor; b. Tel Aviv, Jan. 20, 1930; came to U.S., 1951, naturalized, 1960; m. Marlene Miller, Aug. 29, 1956; children: Tamara, Elana, Miriam. BA, U. Tel Aviv, 1951; MA, U. Mich., 1952, PhD, 1954. Asst. prof. econs. Mich. State U., East Lansing, 1957-59, assoc. prof., 1959-61, prof., 1961-90, univ. disting. prof. econs., 1990—. Vis. prof. econs. UCLA, 1969, UN, Geneva, 1971-73, NYU, 1975, 93, 96, U. Toronto, 1978, others; vis. scholar Inst. Internat. Econs. Studies, U. Stockholm, 1978-80, U. B.C., summer, 1983, Monash U., Melbourne, Australia, 1987-94, 2002, NYU, 1993, 96, Copenhagen Bus. Sch., Denmark, 1994-95, Kobe (Japan) U., 1997, Ctr. Southeast Asian Studies, U. Singapore, 1998, Johns Hopkins U., 2002; adj. rsch. assoc. East-West Ctr., Honolulu, 1990—; world lectr. tours on behalf of U.S. Info. Svc., 1974-96; cons. to Dept. Commerce, 1964-66, Dept. State, 1972-74, UN Coun. Fgn. Rels, N.Y.C., 1965-67, Brockings Instn., 1972-75, Ctrl. Am. Common Market, 1972-75, Internat. Monetary Fund, 1976, East-West Ctr., Honolulu, 1987—; mem. internat. econs. rev. bd. NSF, 1981, 85; bd. dirs. Internat. Trade and Fin. Assn., pres. 1993; sr. Fulbright specialist, 2001—. Author: Israel and Africa: A Study in Technical Cooperation, 1964, Alternative Commercial Policies*Their Effects on the American Economy, 1967, International Economics-A Policy Approach, 10th edit., 2005, Trade Relations of the EEC*An Empirical Investigation, 1974, International Commercial Policy: Issues for the 1990's, 1993, Contemporary Issues in Trade Policy, 1995, (with L. Officer) The Monetary Approach to the Balance of Payments: A Survey, 1978, Economics, 1983, 3d edit., 1999, 4th edit., 2003; co-author: Economic Integration on Asia, 2000, Economic Integration and Development, 2002; editor: Can Australia Adjust?, 1988, International Commercial Policy: Issues for the 90's, 1993, Contemporary Issues in Trade Policy, 1995, The U.S.-Canada Free Trade Agreement, 1999, Empirical Modeling in International Trade, 2005; co-editor: Asia-Pacific Economic Linkages, 1997; contbr. articles to profl. jours. NSF fellow, 1964-73, Ford Found. fellow, 1960-61; recipient Disting. Faculty award Mich. State U., 1968, State of Mich. Collegiate award, 1984, Whitefield Winslow Faculty award, 1994; Festschrift in his honor, Washington, 2003; essays pub. in his honor Empirical Models in International Trade, 2005 Mem. AAUP, Am. Econ. Assn., Midwest Econ. Assn., Western Econ. Assn., Royal Econ. Assn., Internat. Trade and Fin. Assn. (bd. dirs. 1991-94, pres. 1992). Jewish. Home: 1431 Sherwood Ave East Lansing MI 48823-1851 Office: Mich State U Dept Econs East Lansing MI 48824 E-mail: kreinin@msu.edu.

KREIPKE, MERRILL VINCENT, civil engineer, consultant; b. Evansville, Ind., Feb. 14, 1916; s. Charles Edwin and Ida Marguerite (Hufnagel) Kreipke; m. Dorothy Louise Neu, July 17, 1937; children: Karen Jean Kreipke Walker, Jane Ann Kreipke Runyon; m. Dorothy Louise Brewer, Dec. 29, 2000. BSCE, Purdue U., West Lafayette, Ind., 1936. Registered profl. engr., Ky., Ind., Va.; cert. ordained deacon/elder; registered land surveyor Ind. Various positions City Engr.'s Office, Evansville, 1936-39; from insp. to asst. engr. Louisville Dist. C.E., 1939-44, 46-51, chief soils and materials engring., 1951-56; civil engr. Chief of Engrs., Dept. Army, Washington, 1956-61; engr. geophys. scis. Chief of R&D, Dept. Army, Washington, 1961-69, chief geophys. scis., 1969-73, acting chief environ. scis., 1973-74; head mil. R&D C.E., Dept. Army, Washington, 1974-75; cons. Falls Church, Va., 1975—. Head US del. NATO Sci. Studies, 1966, 68, 70. Mem. campsite devel. com. No. Va. Girl Scouts Am., 1957—60; mem. retirement cmty. task force Westminster at Lake Ridge, 1978—90, mem. integrated strategic plan com., 2003—; bd. dirs. Westminster-Ingleside Found., 2004—, Westminster Presbyn. Retirement Cmty., 2006—; mem. new site bldg. com. Covenant Presbyn. Ch., 2003—, mem. residents coun., 2004—06, pres. residents coun., 2005—06. Lt. (j.g.) USNR, 1944—46. Fellow: ASCE; mem.: NSPE, Soc. Am. Mil. Engrs., Va. Soc. Profl. Engrs. (No. Va. chpt. pres. 1978—79, Outstanding Svc. award 1979, 1988), Internat. Soc. Terrain-Vehicle Sys. (founding). Presbyterian. Home: Westminster at Lake Ridge 12191 Clipper Dr Apt 403 Woodbridge VA 22192-2240

KREIS, JASON, professional soccer coach, retired professional soccer player; b. Omaha, Dec. 29, 1972; Student, Duke U. Midfielder Dallas Burn, 1998—2005, Real Salt Lake, 2005—07, U.S. Nat. Team, 1999—2007; head coach Real Salt Lake, 2007—. U.S. Nat. Soccer Team debut 1996; finished 9th in MLS scoring, 1996, scored goal in all-star game; 3-time All-Am., Duke U. Office: US Soccer Fedn 1801-1811 S Prairie Ave Chicago IL 60616

KREISBERG, NEIL IVAN, advertising executive; b. NYC, Feb. 1, 1945; s. Leo and Lucille (Levy) K.; children: Andrew Jay, Tracy Michelle (dec.); m. Linda Gering, Sept. 24, 1986; children: William Gering, James Gering. BS,BA, Rider Coll., Trenton, NJ, 1966. With Grey Worldwide, Inc., NYC, 1966—, v.p., mgmt. supr., 1974-79, sr. v.p., account mgmt., 1979-85, exec. v.p., 1985-93, exec. v.p., group dir., 1993-99; group exec. v.p., exec. mng. dir. Grey Global Group, NYC, 2000—. Mem.: Advt. Ednl. Found. (bd. dirs.), Brae Burn Country Club (bd. govs.). Jewish. Office: Grey Advt Inc 777 3rd Ave New York NY 10017-1401 Home Phone: 914-273-2181; Office Phone: 212-546-2683. E-mail: nkreisberg@grey.com.

KREISBERG, ROBERT A., dean, medical educator; Student, U. Ala., U. South Ala.; MD, Northwestern U., 1958. Vice chair dept. medicine U. Ala., Birmingham, prof.; interim dean U. South Ala. Coll. Med., Mobile, 2000, dean, 2001—06, v.p. med. affairs; with Bapt. Health Sys., Ala., 2006—. Fellow Am. Coll. Physicians (gov. Ala., regent, chair scientific program subcom., ednl. policy com., gen. chair, Disting. Tchr. award 1994); mem. Am. Fedn. Clin. Rsch. (pres. 1974-75). Office: Bapt Health Sys 840 Montclair Rd Birmingham AL 35213 Office Phone: 205-592-5135.

KREISER, FRANK DAVID, real estate executive; b. Sept. 20, 1928; s. Harry D. and Olive W. (Quist) K.; m. Patricia Williams, Aug. 23, 1973; children: Sally, Frank David, Susan, Paul, Mark, Patti, Richard. Student, U. Minn., 1948—49. Cert. residential broker. Real estate developer, 1960—. Founder, owner Frank Kreiser Real Estate, Inc., Mpls., 1966-89, pres., 1979—; owner F. & P.K. Properties, 1973—; membership chmn. RELO, 1987-88; br. mgr. Merrill Lynch Realty, 1989-90, br. mgr., v.p. Burnet Realty, 1990-97; broker Coldwell Banker, 1998—; ptnr., founder B & K Properties Co., Mpls., 1976-96; chmn. bd., founder Transfer Location Corp., Atlanta, 1979-84. With U.S. Army, 1946-47, Korea Mem. Mpls. Bd. Realtors (dir. 1972), Minn. Assn. Realtors, Realtors Nat. Mktg. Inst., Minn. Multi Housing Assn., Edina C. of C., 50th France Bus. Assn. (pres. 2000-02), Edina Country Club. Lutheran. Address: 5036 France Ave S Minneapolis MN 55410-2033 Business E-Mail: fkreiser@cbburnet.com.

KREISMAN, ARTHUR, higher education consultant, retired humanities educator; b. Cambridge, Mass., June 7, 1918; s. Louis and Rose (Shechtell) K.; m. B. Evelyn Goulston, Apr. 20, 1940 (dec. July 1992); children: Peter Jon, Steven Alan, Richard Curt, James Bruce; m. Mamie Jewel Liles Tribble, July 17, 1994. AB, Brigham Young U., 1942; student, Harvard U., 1939; AM, Boston U., 1943, PhD, 1952; LittD (hon.), City U., 1988. Grad. asst. in English Boston U., 1942-43; with Signal Corps. U.S. Army, 1943-45, with Signal Corps. overseas, 1944-45; instr. U.S. Armed Forces Inst., 1945, So. Oreg. U., Ashland, 1946, asst. prof., 1947-51, assoc. prof., 1951-55, prof., 1955-81, chmn. dept. English, 1951-63, chmn. humanities div., 1955-69, dir. gen. studies, 1959-66, dean arts and scis., 1966-77, dir. curricular affairs, 1978-80, prof. emeritus, 1981—, appt. ofcl. univ. historian, 1985; co-founder with Evelyn Kreisman Edukon, Inc., 1982—. TV lectr. Network Ednl. TV, 1955-58; dir. Block Teaching Project, U.S. Office Edn., 1957-59, Nat. Def. Edn. Act Inst. for Advanced Study in English, 1966; cons. Fedn. Regional Accrediting Commns. in Higher Edn., 1974-75, Coun. on Postsecondary Accreditation, 1975-79, Chico (Calif.) State U., 1973-76, City U. Seattle, 1975-99, Lincoln Meml. U., 1976, Marylhurst Edn. Center, 1976, Oreg. Inst. Tech., 1977-79, Sheldon Jackson Coll., 1979-83, Council on Chiropractic Edn., 1982, 83, Griffin Coll., 1990-91; mem. Gov.'s Adv. Com. on Arts and Humanities, 1966-69, 71-76; mem. task force human svcs. Oreg. Ednl. Coordinating Council, 1972; mem. steering com. Oreg. Joint Com. for Humanities, 1972-74; chmn. Seminar Coll. Evaluators NW Assn. Schs. and Colls., U. Wash., 1977-84; mem. nat. adv. bd. on quality assurance in experiental learning Coun. on Advancement Experiental Learning, 1978-80; team leader Danforth Found. Workshop on Liberal Arts Edn., Colo. Coll., 1972. Author: Correspondence Courses for State System, American Literature, 1955, World Literature, 1956, Contemporary Literature, 1961, Reader's Guide to the Classics, 1961, Remembering: The History of Southern Oregon University, 2002; editor: Oregon Centennial Anthology, 1959; Contbr. poetry and articles to periodicals. Active Ashland City Coun., 1950-54; co-founder Rogue Valley Unitarian Fellowship, 1953; bd. dirs. Comty. Chest, Inst. Renaissance Studies, 1956-64, Friends of Libr., 1991-96, pres., 1994-96; steering com. Learning in Retirement Program, 1993-94; chmn. bd. trustees Ashland Cmty. Hosp., 1960-64; bd. dirs. So. Calif. U. for Profl. Studies, 1997-99; chmn. bd. dirs. North Ctrl. U., 1998-99; emeritus bd. dirs. Ashland Cmty. Hosp. Found., 2005. Recipient Bicentennial anniversary prize in humanities Columbia U., 1954, Disting. Svc. award Ashland Cmty. Hosp. Found., 1998; prize for excellence in teaching, 1966, Outstanding Svc. award Indsl. Coll. Armed Forces, 1976, Disting. Svc. award Alumni Assn., 1977; Ford Found. fellow in Oriental philosophy and religion Harvard, 1954 Mem. AAUP (past pres. Oreg. coun.), Nat. Coun. Tchrs. English (past pres. Oreg. coun.), Commn. of Pacific Assn. of Schs. and Colls. (elected 1994-95), N.W. Assn. Schs. and Colls. (examiner 1958—, trustee 1976-80, mem. comm. colls. 1972-80), Am. Legion (past post comdr.), Lambda Iota Tau, Phi Kappa Phi, Tau Kappa Alpha. Office: 1880 Green Meadows Way Ashland OR 97520-3683

KREITH, FRANK, research engineer, consultant; b. Vienna, Dec. 15, 1922; s. Fritz and Elsa (Klug) K.; m. Marion Finkels, Sept. 21, 1951; children: Michael, Marcia, Judith. BSME, U. Calif., Berkeley, 1945; MS in Engring., UCLA, 1946; DSc, U. Paris, 1964. Registered profl. engr., Calif., Colo. Rsch. engr. Jet Propulsion Lab. Calif. Inst. Tech., 1945-49; asst. prof. U. Calif., Berkeley, 1951-53; assoc. prof. mech. engring. Lehigh U., Bethlehem, Pa., 1953-59; prof. engring. U. Colo., 1959-77; chief solar thermal rsch. Solar Energy Rsch. Inst., Golden, Colo., 1977-87; sr. fellow Nat. Conf. State Legis., 1987—2001; pres. Environ. Cons. Svcs., 1974-77; cons. NATO, 1980-85, Nat. Renewable Energy Lab, 1990-98. Author: Principles of Heat Transfer, 1958, 2d edit., 1965, 3d edit., 1973, (with C. B. Wrenn) Nuclear Impact, 1975, (with J. F. Kreider) Principles of Solar Engineering, 1980; CRC mech. engr. series editor, 1997-, EPRI, 2005; co-editor: Solar Energy Handbook, 1981; editor-in-chief Handbook of Solid Waste Managmement, 1993, Handbook of Energy Efficiency, 1996, Handbook of Mechanical Engineering, 1997, Ground Transportation for the 21st Century, 1999, Handbook of Thermal Engineering, 2000, Handbook of Energy Efficiency and Renewable Energy, 2007. Mem. Human Rels. Commn., 1963-65, Energy Adv. Com., 1979-82. Recipient First Gen. Achievement award, 1983; Guggenheim fellow, 1950. Mem. ASME (hon. life; heat transfer meml. award 1972, medal, 1998, Washington award 1997, Edwin F. Church medal 2001, Disting. Lectr., 2002-), Internat. Solar Energy Soc.(hon.), Sigma Xi (nat. lectr. 1980-81, Charles Greeley Abbott award 1988), Phi Tau Sigma. Office Phone: 303-443-1406. E-mail: fkreith@comcast.net.

KREITLOW, BURTON WILLIAM, retired adult education educator; b. Howard Lake, Minn., Aug. 14, 1917; s. William Arthur and Esther Ingeborg (Nelson) K.; m. Doris J. Ounsworth, Sept. 13, 1944; children: Karen Neal, Candace Kreitlow. Tchg. cert., Cokato (Minn.) Normal, 1935; BS, U. Minn., 1941, MA, 1948, PhD, 1949. Rural tchr. Dist. 58, Montrose, Minn., 1935-37; county 4-H agt. Minn. Ext. Svc., Mankato, Minn., 1938-39, county agr. agt. Warren, Minn., 1941-42, dist. supr. 4H St. Paul, 1945-46; asst. prof. basic coll. Mich. State U., East Lansing, 1948-49; from asst. prof. to prof. U. Wis., Madison, 1949-81, prof. emeritus, 1981—. Vis. prof. Tex. A&M U., Fla. State U., Alaska-Pacific U., Wash. State U., Nat. Taiwan U., U. Hawaii (Hilo), U. Alaska, Anchorage; Disting. vis. prof. Ohio State U. Grad. Sch., 1975-76; workshop leader, lectr.; chmn. Commn. of Profs., 1961-63; bd. dirs. emeritus Coll. St. Scholastica, Duluth, Minn., 1992-93, Aging Trust Fund, Northland Found., Duluth, 1991-94. Author: Rural Education: Community Backgrounds, 1954, Leadership for Action in Rural Communities, 1960, (series) Steps to Learning, 1966-80; playwright (with others) Under the Stars and Stripes--Stories of World War II, 2002, Conversations on Lifelong Learning, 2005; editor: Examining Controversies in Continuing Education, 1981, Creative Planning for the Second Half of Life, 1997; contbr. column to (jour.) Adult Learning, 1989-91. Mem. Wisconsin Heights Sch. Bd., Mazomanie, Wis., 1959-62; pres. Homestead Coop. of Grand Marais (Minn.), 1992-94. Haight Travel fellow U. Wis. Grad. Sch., 1967; named to Internat. Adult and Continuing Edn. Hall of Fame, Am. Assn. Adult and Continuing Edn., 1996 Mem. NEA (chair publs. com. rural dept. 1965-67), Minn. Gerontol. Soc., Lions (pres. 1959, 85), Phi Delta Kappa. Democrat. Mem. UCC Ch. Avocations: community volunteer, leading memoir writing groups, continued teaching and learning. Personal E-mail: dorburt@boreal.org.

KREITZBURG, MARILYN JUNE, academic librarian; b. Rockford, Ill. d. A.E. and Margaret Louise (Harvey) Kreitzburg. Student, Rockford Coll. for Women, 1948—50; AB magna cum laude, Knox Coll., 1954; MA, U. Va., 1956; cert. in philosophy, U. Edinburgh, Scotland, 1960. Copywriter, broadcaster radio and TV Black Hawk Broadcasting Co., Waterloo, Iowa, 1959—60; freelance promotion NYC, 1957; lectr. on Asia, women and fgn. affairs Ill., Iowa, 1957—59; order libr., asst. to coll. libr. Knox Coll., Ill., 1960—72; faculty libr., asst. prof. history Johnstown Coll., U. Pitts., 1972—93, dir. libr. and overseer of dept. audiovisual instr. svcs., 1972—75, divisional libr. and cataloguer for edn., engring., soc. sci., 1975—77, head of curriculum room, nonprint media, periodicals and reference, 1977—78, head of instr., ref., rsch., 1978—93; exhibits and instr. Urban League Pitts. prog. for Johnstown youth; judge HS regional speech contests; mem. faculty senate com. ednl. policies, 1980—93. Pvt. music instr., 1946—48, 1950—52; presenter tchr. in-svc. meetings Cambria and Somerset counties; cons. in field, 1972—93; spkr. in field. Rescue vol. Richland Twp. Vol. Fire Dept., ARC Disaster Inquiry Svc., 1977; mem. Inter-Svc. Club Coun., 1976—80; leader Girl Scout Songsters, Rockford, Ill., 1948—50; vol. Windber Regional Hospice, Windber Med. Ctr., 2002—; bd. dir., actress Prairie Players Civic Theater, 1960—65. Recipient medal, DAR, 1948, Nichols prize in history, 1954; Helen Lee Wessels fellow, 1954—56, Fulbright fellow at large, in Southeast Asia, 1957—59. Mem.: Johnstown Art League (pres. 2003, 2004, exec. com. 2005—06, mem. archives com. and corr. 2006—), Women's Assn. U. Pitts. (pres. 1978—79, exec. bd.), Inter Nos, Soroptimist Internat. (chpt. pres. 1978—79), Pi Beta Phi, Sigma Alpha Iota, Pi Sigma Alpha, Delta Kappa Gamma Soc. Internat. (chpt. v.p. 1966—68, pres. 1989—91, World Fellowships chmn. 2002—), Phi Beta Kappa.

KREITZER, DAVID MARTIN, artist; b. Ord, Nebr., Oct. 23, 1942; s. David and Norma (Buls) K.; m. Ana Bueno, Apr. 1, 1972 (div. 1978); 1 child, Anatol Christian; m. Jacalyn Bower, Nov. 26, 1987; 1 child, Fredricka Jacalyn. BS, Concordia Coll., Seward, Nebr., 1965; MA, San Jose State U., 1967. Exhibited in group and one-man shows including Maxwell Gallery, San Francisco, 1968-72, Akrum Gallery, L.A., 1970-89, Adele M. Gallery, Dallas, 1972-90, Summa Gallery, N.Y.C., 1988-95, Stary-Sheets Gallery, L.A., 1991-95., Campanile Gallery, Chgo., 1995, Joseph Hirshhorn, Washington D.C., Howard Akmanson Jr., L.A., Santa Barbara Mus. Calif., Sheldon Gallery U. Nebr., Lincoln, Bd. dirs. Music and Arts for Youth, San Luis Obispo, Calif., 1983-85. Recipient Ciba-Geigy award 1971, Gold medal San Francisco Art Dirs. Club, 1970. Home: 1442 12th St Los Osos CA 93402-1711 Business E-Mail: jkreitze@calpoly.edu.

KREITZER, JACALYN BOWER, vocalist, voice educator; b. Silverton, Oreg., Feb. 16, 1956; d. Jack Allen and Coraliss Mae Bower; m. David M. Kreitzer, Nov. 26, 1987; children: Frederica, Anatol. MusB, U. Puget Sound; postgrad., U. So. Calif., 1982—85. Lead role Contessa/Andrea Chenier/San Francisco Opera, 1998, Erda/Das Rheingold/Deutsche Oper Berlin, 1991, Brangane/Tristan und Isolde/Teatro Liceu, Barcelona, 1989, Ericlea/Ritorno di Ulisse/San Francisco Opera, San Francisco, 1986, Urlich & Mahler 2/Prague Radio Symphony, Prague, Czech Republic, 1999, Rossweisse/Die Walkure/Metropolitan Opera, NYC, 1984—87, Mother/The Consul, Spoleto, Italy, Sosostris/Midsummer Marriage/New York City Opera, NYC, Waltraute/Die Walkure/Theatre Chatelet, Utrica/Un Ballo in Maschera/Dublin Grand Opera, Waltraute, Fricka/Die Walkure/Chgo. Lyric Opera, Chgo., Brangane/Tristan Und Isolde/LA Opera, Brangane/Tristan Und Isolde/Barcelona Opera, Erster Magd/Electra/Geneva Opera, Norns/Gotterdammerung/Artpark NY, Norns, Waltraute, Fricka, Erda/Der Ring Des Nibelungen/Seattle Opera, Seattle. Prodr., Marilyn Horne/Frederica von Stade recitals; voice-performance tchr. Cal Poly Music Dept., San Luis Obispo, 1994—; founder, prodr., dir. opera theater Cal Poly State U., San Luis Obispo, 2003—; panelist Opera Am. Recipient Flagstad Young Wagnerian award, Wagner Foundation, NYC, 1987, Sullivan Found., Sullivan Found./ New York, NY, 1988, Liederkranz, Liederkranz/New York, NY, 1988, Outstanding Lectr. Award, Cal Poly State Univ./San Luis Obispo, Calif. Mem.: NATS, AGMA. Republican. Lutheran. Achievements include Master classes with Elizabeth Schwarzkopt. Avocations: outdoors, wilderness. Home: 1442 12th St Los Osos CA 93402 E-mail: jkreitze@calpoly.edu.

KREITZER, LOIS HELEN, investor; b. Pitts., Feb. 2, 1933; d. Franklin and Helen Katherine (Leyda) Maroney; m. William Emil Kreitzer, Nov. 14, 1962. BS, Pa. State U., U. Pk., 1955. Stockbroker Janney Montgomery Scott LLC and predecessor firms, Pitts., 1955—62; cons. Pitts., 1962—68; executrix of estates, 1968—82; personal investor, 1975—; shareholder activist, 1970—. Mem. AAUW (life, jrs. sec., v.p., pres. 1960-62), DAR (jrs. treas.-sec., v.p., pres. 1957-60), Nat. Assn. Investors Corp. (life), Pa. State U. Alumni Assn. (life), Colonial Dames 17th Century (charter treas.), Pa. State Club of Allegheny County (pres. 1963), Pitts. Athletic Assn., Coll. Club Pitts. (life, jr. v.p., pres. 1959-60), Soroptimist Internat. (life, v.p. Pitts. chpt. 1961). Republican. Presbyterian. Avocations: cooking, baking, theater, travel, walking.

KREITZER, MICHAEL N., lawyer; b. Balt., Apr. 5, 1962; s. Milton Kreitzer and Toby Greenberg; children: Kimberly, Amanda, Joshua. BS in Computer and Info. Scis. with high honors, U. Fla., 1984; JD with honors, George Washington U., 1987. Bar: Fla. 1987, U.S. Dist. Ct. (so. dist.) Fla. 1988, U.S. Dist. Ct. (mid. dist.) Fla. 2002, U.S. Dist. Ct. (no. dist.) Fla. 2005; cert. bus. litigator Fla. Bar, 2001. Assoc. atty. Fowler, White & Barnett, PA, Miami, Fla., 1987—92, ptnr., 1992—2003, Bilzin, Sunberg, Baena, Price & Axelrod, LLP, Miami, Fla., 2003—; ptnr., chmn. litigation dept., mem. exec. com. Bilzin, Sunberg et al, Miami, Fla., 2005—. Mem.: ABA, Dade County Bar Assn. Office: Bilzin Sunberg Baena Price 200 S Biscayne Blvd Ste 2500 Miami FL 33131 Office Phone: 305-350-2384. Office Fax: 305-351-2224. E-mail: mkreitzer@bilzin.com.

KREITZMAN, RALPH J., lawyer; b. NYC, Nov. 11, 1945; s. Emanuel M. and Hannah G. (Steinhardt) K.; m. Wendy A. Karpel, Nov. 24, 1968; children: Susan Beth, Emily Meg. BS in Acctg., Rider U., 1967; JD cum laude, Bklyn. Law Sch., 1970. Bar: NY 1971, US Dist Ct. (so. dist.) NY 1971, US Dist. Ct. (ea. dist.) NY 1973, US Ct. of Appeals (2nd cir.) 1975, US Supreme Ct. 1976. Assoc. Hughes Hubbard & Reed LLP, NYC, 1970-80; sr. ptnr. real estate group Hughes Hubbard & Reed LLC, NYC, 1980—. Trustee Village of Great Neck, NY, 2001-07, dep. mayor, 2003-07, mayor, 2007-, former mem. then chair planning bd., former mem. archtl. rev. com.; v.p. Great Neck Village Ofcls. Assn., 2007-; dir Water Authority of Great Neck North, 2007-. With USAR, 1968—74. Mem. ABA (real property law sect. and com. on fgn. investment in U.S. real estate), NY State Bar Assn. (real property law sect., com. on comml. leases and com. on financings), Assn. of Bar of City of NY (com. on real property law, former chair leasing subcom.). Office: Hughes Hubbard & Reed LLP 1 Battery Park Plz New York NY 10004-1482 Office Phone: 212-837-6740. Business E-Mail: kreitzman@hugheshubbard.com.

KREIZINGER, LOREEN I., lawyer; b. Syracuse, NY, Apr. 16, 1959; d. David F. and Blanche L. (Heaney) Mosher; m. Kenneth R. Kreizinger, Aug. 30, 1985; children: Katelyn Rose, Hunter Robert. Grad. in nursing, Crouse-Irving Meml. Hosp., Syracuse, 1981; BS in Bus. with honors, Nova U., 1987, JD, 1990. Bar: Fla. 1990; RN, N.Y., Fla. Nurse ICU and infants neonatal unit, Syracuse, Ft. Lauderdale, Fla., 1979-86; med. malpractice cons. Krupnick, Campbell et al, Ft.Lauderdale, 1986-90, assoc., 1990-92, of counsel, 1992—; pvt. practice, Ft.Lauderdale, 1992—. Instr. adult intensive care Crouse-Irving Meml. Hosp., 1981-82; adj. prof. Nova U., Ft. Lauderdale, 1994—; seminar instr. legal aspects of nursing Fla. Bd. Nursing, 1990-92; guest spkr. TV talk show Med. Malpractice, 1991. Sec., bd. dirs. Shepherd Care Ministries, Hollywood, Fla., 1993, 94; mem. choir 1st Bapt. Ch. Ft. Lauderdale, 1994—. Mem. ABA (law and medicine com. 1990—), FBA, ATLA (spl. L-Trytophen com. 1991-94), Fla. Bar Assn., Fla. Assn. Women Lawyers, Fla. Acad. Trial Lawyers, Broward County Women Lawyers Assn., Broward County Trial Lawyers Assn., Phi Alpha Delta. Republican. Avocations: sailing, skiing, rollerblading.

KREJCI, ROBERT HARRY, not-for-profit developer, consultant; b. Chgo., June 4, 1913; s. John and Johanna (Tischer) K.; m. Marian Hallock, Mar. 28, 1941 (dec. Aug. 1986); 1 child, Susan Ann Krejci Stevens. BS in Forestry with honors, Mich. State U., East Lansing, 1940. Dist. exec. Boy Scouts Am., Chgo., 1940-48, asst. scout exec., 1948-50, scout exec. Herrin, Ill., Huntington, W.Va., 1950-65; devel. cons. The Cumerford Corp., Kansas City, 1965-73, dir. western divsn. Ft. Lauderdale, Fla., 1974-78; devel. cons. in pvt. practice, San Diego, 1978-90. Co-founder, pres. Philanthropy Coun., San Diego, 1987-93; dir. World War II Farm Labor Camp, State of Ill., 1942, 43. Author: How to Succeed in Fund Raising For Your Non-Profit Organization, 1989. Vol. organizer United Way, various cities, Ill., 1955, 56. Recipient George Washington medal Freedoms Found. at Valley Forge, 1953; named Vol. of Yr. Philanthropy Coun., 1996, Exemplar, Rancho Bernardo Rotary Found., 1995. Mem. Rotary Internat. (Paul Harris fellow). Avocations: travel, gardening, writing, collecting humor. Home: 16566 Casero Rd San Diego CA 92128-2743

KRELL, DAVID, stock exchange executive; V.p. Merrill Lynch, 1978—81; first v.p. mktg. & sales divsn. Chgo. Bd. Options Exch., 1981—84; v.p. options and index products NY Stock Exch., NYC, 1984—97; co-founder, chmn. K-Squared Rsch., LLC, 1997—98; founder, pres., CEO Internat. Securities Exch., Inc., NYC, 1998—. Past adj. prof. Rutgers U. Grad. Sch. Mgmt., Baruch Coll. Grad. Sch.; bd. dir. Internat. Fedn. of Tech. Analysts, The Options Clearing Corp.; pres. Market Technicians Assn.; taught, coordinated and directed numerous seminars and workshops New York Inst. of Fin. Office: Internat Securities Exch Inc 60 Broad St New York NY 10004 Office Phone: 212-943-2400. Office Fax: 212-425-4926.*

KRELL, REBECCA DAWN, music educator; b. Springfield, Ill., Mar. 6, 1976; d. Gloria May Keeslar; m. Eric James Krell, June 3, 2000; 1 child, Elia Carolina. MusB in Edn., Ea. Ill. U., Charleston, 1998. Tchr. k-6 gen. music Hawthorne Irving, Rock Island, Ill., 2001—02; dir. k-12 music Rivermont Collegiate, Bettendorf, Iowa, 2002—03; tchr. k-6 gen. music F.V.de Coronado Elem. Sch., Nogales, Ariz., 2003—04; dir. 6-12 dist. choral Nogales Unified Sch. Dist., 2004—. Piano player and nursery asst. First Bapt. Ch., Nogales, 2003—. Mem.: Am. Choral Dirs. Assn. (assoc.), Music Educators Nat. Conf. (assoc.). R-Consevative. Avocations: walking, reading, piano, singing. Home Phone: 520-281-5770; Office Phone: 520-604-2474.

KRELL-MORRIS, CHERI LEE, psychologist; b. Toledo, Mar. 23, 1949; d. Leonard Charles and Doris Leone (Sharples) Krell; B.Ed., U. Toledo, 1975; M.S., U. Nev., 1979; postgrad. Immaculata U., 2003; children—Marci Lynn, Cari Ann. Lic. psychologist, Pa.; cert. sch. psychologist. Health edn. cons. Ohio Dept. Health, Div. Alcoholism, Columbus, 1975-77; dir. social services Cherry Hill (N.J.) Med. Ctr., 1979-80; mgr. StayWell Control Data Corp., Norristown, Pa., 1980-82, edn. and lifestyle change cons., 1982; counselor New Life Youth & Family Svcs., 1985-2003; sch. psychologist Spring-Ford Sch. Dist., 2003—; pvt. practice Innovative Counseling Assocs., 2001—. Dir. Ohio's Am. Teenage Inst. on Alcohol and Other Drugs, Columbus, 1975-77; faculty Midwest Inst. Alcohol Studies, Notre Dame, Ind. and Kalamazoo, Mich., 1977. Served with USAF, 1968-72. Mem. Pa. Psychol. Assn., Nat. Assn. Sch. Psychologists, Eta Sigma Gamma. Mem. United Ch. of Christ. Home: 212 Salford Station Rd Perkiomenville PA 18074-9740 Office: Spring-Ford High Sch 350 South Lewis Rd Royersford PA 19468-2499 Office Phone: 610-326-2728. Business E-Mail: cmorr@spring-ford.org.

KREMEN, RICHARD M., lawyer; b. Balt., 1945; BA with honors, Oberlin Coll., 1968; JD with honors, George Washington U., 1973. Bar: Md. 1973, D.C. 1974. Ptnr. Piper Marbury Rudnick & Wolfe, Balt., 1990—2004; ptnr., co-chmn. Bankruptcy & Bus. Reorganization practice group DLA Piper Rudnick Gray Cary, Balt., 2005—. Past. mem. Rules com., U.S. Bankruptcy Ct., Md. dist.; mem. Panel of Bankruptcy Trustees, Md. Chmn. emeritus Better Bus. Bureau of Greater Md.; bd. mem. Balt. Chamber Orch.; chmn. bd. trustees Beth Tfiloh Congregation. Fellow: Am. Coll. Bankruptcy; mem.: ABA (chmn. subcom. bankruptcy crimes and abuses), Am. Bankruptcy Inst., Turnaround Mgmt. Assn. (past pres., dir. Md. chpt.), Md. Bar Assn. (past chmn. subcom. creditors rights, bankruptcy and insolvency). Office: DLA Piper Rudnick Gray Cary 6225 Smith Ave Baltimore MD 21209-3600 Home Phone: 410-484-3807; Office Phone: 410-580-4191. Office Fax: 410-580-3001. Business E-Mail: richard.kremen@dlapiper.com.

KREMENTZ, JILL, photographer, author; b. NYC, Feb. 19, 1940; d. Walter and Virginia (Hyde) Krementz; m. Kurt, Jr. Vonnegut, Nov. 1979; 1 child, Lily Vonnegut. Student, Drew U., 1958—59; attended Art Students League. With Harper's Bazaar mag., 1959—60, Glamour mag., 1960—61; pub. rels. staff Indian Industries Fair, New Delhi, 1961; reporter Show mag., 1962—64; staff photographer N.Y. Herald Tribune, 1964—65, staff photographer Vietnam, 1965—66; assoc. editor Status-Diplomat mag., 1966—67; contbg. editor N.Y. mag., 1967—68; corr. Time-Life Inc., 1969—70; contbg. photographer People mag., 1974—; chancellor, commr. Nat. Portrait Gallery, DC. Contbr. photography numerous U.S. and fgn. periodicals; photographer (one-woman shows) Madison (Wis.) Art Ctr., 1973, U. Mass., Boston, 1974, Nikon Gallery, N.Y.C., 1974, Del. Art Mus., Wilmington, 1975, Newark Mus., 1994, Staley-Wise Gallery, 1996; one-woman shows include The Margaret Mitchell House, Atlanta, 1999; photographer (one-woman shows) The Nat. Portrait Gallery, 2003—, The Mark Twain House, Hartford, Conn, 2004, (permanent collections) Mus. Modern Art, Libr. of Congress, The Face of South Vietnam (text by Dean Brelis), 1968, Words and Their Masters (text by Israel Shenker), 1974; author: Sweet Pea: A Black Girl Growing Up in the Rural South (foreword by Margaret Mead), 1969, A Very Young Dancer, 1976, A Very Young Rider, 1977, A Very Young Gymnast, 1978, A Very Young Circus Flyer, 1979, A Very Young Skater, 1979, The Writer's Image, 1980, How It Feels When a Parent Dies, 1981, How It Feels to be Adopted, 1982, How It Feels When Parents Divorce, 1984, The Fun of Cooking, 1985, Lily Goes to the Playground, 1986, Jack Goes to the Beach, 1986, Katherine Goes to Nursery School, 1986, Jamie Goes on an Airplane, 1986, Tanya Goes to the Dentist, 1986, Benjy Goes to a Restaurant, 1986, Holly's Farm Animals, 1986, Zachary Goes to the Zoo, 1986, A Visit to Washington, D.C., 1987, How It Feels to Fight for Your Life, 1989, A Very Young Skier, 1990, A Very Young Musician, 1990, A Very Young Gardener, 1990, A Very Young Actress, 1991, How It Feels to Live With a Physical Disability, 1992, The Writer's Desk, 1996, The Jewish Writer, 1998. Recipient Nonfiction award, Washington Post/Children's Book Guild, 1984, ACCH Joan Fassler Meml. Book award, 1990, Equality, Dignity, Independence award, Nat. Easter Seals, 1992. Mem.: PEN. Address: care Alfred A Knopf Inc 201 E 50th St New York NY 10022-7703

KREMER, HONOR FRANCES (NOREEN KREMER), real estate broker, small business owner; came to U.S., 1961; m. Manny Kremer; 1 child, Patrick David. BS, CUNY; MS, Baruch Coll. Group sec. Bentalls, Ltd.; office mgr. Aschner Assocs., NYC, 1961-63; pub. rels. asst. McMaster U., Hamilton, 1963-64; office mgr. Packaging Components, NYC, 1965-67; head acctg. Shaller Rubin Assocs., NYC, 1967-72, v.p. fin. and adminstrn., 1979-82, sr. v.p., 1982—, sec.-treas. multi-media divsn., 1972-75. Pvt. practice bus. cons., 1986-89; sr. v.p., exec. v.p., fin. officer Lewis & Gace Med. Advt., N.Y.C., 1989-91; broker, owner Malone Kremer Realty, Leonia, N.J., 1991—; bus. cons., 1991—. Mem. Nat. Assn. Realtors, N.J. Assn. Realtors, Nat. Fedn. Bus. and Profl. Women (bd. dirs., v.p.), Advt. Fin. Mgmt. Group. Roman Catholic. Home Phone: 212-684-1016; Office Phone: 201-461-1100.

KREMER, MICHAEL, economist, educator; AB in Social Studies magna cum laude, Harvard U., 1985, PhD in Econs., 1992. Tchr., adminstr. Eshisiru Secondary Sch., Kakamega Dist., Kenya, 1985—86; exec. dir., founder WorldTeach, 1986—89; postdoctoral fellow MIT, 1992—93, asst. prof. econs., 1993—94, Pentti Kouri Career Devel. asst. prof. econs., 1994—96, Pentti Kouri Career Devel. assoc. prof. econs., 1996—98, prof. econs., 1998—99, Harvard U., 1999—2003, Gates prof. developing societies, 2003—. Vis. asst. prof. U. Chgo., 1993; faculty rsch. fellow Nat. Bur. Econ. Rsch., 1993—99, rsch. assoc., 1999—, Harvard Inst. Internat. Devel., 1997—2000; faculty fellow Ctr. Internat. Devel., 1998—; sr. fellow The Brookings Instn., 1998—; co-chair, co-founder Bur. Rsch. and Econ. Analysis of Devel., 2001—; cons. devel. econs. rsch. group The World Bank, 2001—; non-resident fellow Ctr. Global Devel., 2002—. Assoc. editor: Quarterly Jour. Econs., 1998—, Jour. Devel. Econs., 1999—; contbr. numerous articles to profl. jours. Recipient Presidential Early career award for Scientists and Engrs., 1996; fellow, Nat. Sci. Found., 1989—92; Nat. fellow, Hoover Instn., Stanford U., 1994—95, Health and Aging fellow, Nat. Bur. Econ. Rsch., 1996—97, MacArthur fellow, MacArthur Found., 1997. Fellow: Am. Acad. Arts and Scis. Office: Harvard U Dept Econs Littauer Ctr 207 Cambridge MA 02138 Office Phone: 617-495-9145. Office Fax: 617-495-7730. Business E-Mail: mkremer@fas.harvard.edu.

KREMER, MICHAEL, surgeon; b. Lich, Germany, Oct. 10, 1975; arrived in US, 2004; s. Norbert Horst and Renate Brigitte Maria Kremer. MD, U. Heidelberg, Germany, 2002. Intern dept. surgery U. Heidelberg, 2002—04; postdoctoral rsch. fellow U. NC, Chapel Hill, 2004—. Mem. editl. bd. World Jour. Gastroenterology, 2007—; contbr. articles to profl. jours. Recipient Young Investigator award, SEBM, 2006, Trainee Travel award, ASIP, 2007, Poster Distinction award, AASLD, 2007. Mem.: Am. Assn. for the Study of Liver Diseases, Soc. for Exptl. Biology and Medicine, Am. Soc. for Investigative Pathology. Achievements include research in immune dysfunction in hepatosteatosis. Office: Univ NC 3013 Thurston Bowles 7178 Chapel Hill NC 27599 Home Phone: 919-960-3543; Office Phone: 919-843-7373. Business E-Mail: mkremer@med.unc.edu.

KREN, JOSEF, physiology professor; arrived in US, 1991; s. Irena Matouskova. BSc in Biology/Chemistry, Masaryk U., Brno, Czech Republic, 1985, DSc, 1988; PhD, U. Nebr., Lincoln, 1996. Prof. human physiology Doane Coll., Lincoln, 2002—, Bryan Lincoln Gen. Hosp. Coll. Health Scis., Lincoln, 2005—. Author: (book) Birds of the Czech Republic, 2000. Recipient Disting. Tchg. award, Midland Luth. Coll., 2006. Mem.: Brit. Ornithologist Union, Am. Ornithologist Union. Office: BryanLGH Coll Health Scis 5035 Everett St Lincoln NE 68506 Home Phone: 402-721-5487; Office Phone: 402-481-8768. Personal E-mail: josef.kren@doane.edu.

KRENDEL, EZRA SIMON, systems and human factors engineering consultant; b. NYC, Mar. 5, 1925; s. Joseph and Tamara (Shapiro) K.; m. Elizabeth Spencer Malany, Aug. 20, 1950 (dec. Nov. 1983); children: David A., Tamara E. Krendel-Clark, Jennifer K. Hall; m. Janet Brownlee Allen, June 27, 1992. AB, Bklyn. Coll., 1945; Sc.M. in Physics, MIT, 1947; A.M. in Social Relations, Harvard, 1949; MA honoris causa, U. Pa., 1971. From research engr. to sr. staff engr. Franklin Inst. Research Labs., 1949-55, lab. mgr., 1955-63, tech. dir., 1963-66, sr. adviser, cons., 1961; dir. Mgmt. Sci. Ctr., Wharton Sch. U. Pa., Phila., 1967-69, prof. ops. research and stats., Wharton Sch., 1966-90, prof. emeritus, 1990—, prof. systems engring. Sch. Engring. and Applied Sci., 1983-93; prin. scientist Systems Tech., Inc., Hawthorne, Calif., 1987—89. Emeritus prof.; rsch. adv. com. on control guidance and nav. NASA, 1964-65; various coms. Hwy. Rsch. Bd., NRC, 1964-74; vis. lectr. NATO, 1968, 71; mem. roster of arbitrators Fed. Mediation and Conciliation Svc.; cons. in field. Author: Unionizing the Armed Forces, 1977; contbr. articles to profl. publs. Mem. Phila. Mayor's Sci. and Tech. Adv. Council. Recipient Louis E. Levy Gold medal Franklin Inst., 1960. Fellow IEEE, AAAS, APA, Am. Psychol. Soc., Human Factors Soc.; mem. Cosmos Club, Sigma Xi. Home: 211 Cornell Ave Swarthmore PA 19081-1933 Office Phone: 610-543-9107. Personal E-mail: krendel@wharton.upenn.edu. Business E-Mail: ezra@krendel.org.

KRENDL, CATHY STRICKLIN, lawyer; b. Paris, Tex., Mar. 14, 1945; d. Louis and Margaret Helen (Young) S.; m. James R. Krendl, July 5, 1969; children: Peggy, Susan, Anne. BA summa cum laude, North Tex. State U., 1967; JD cum laude, Harvard U., 1970. Bar: Alaska 1970, Colo. 1972. Atty. Hughes, Thorsness, Lowe Gantz & Clark, Anchorage, 1970-71; adj. prof. U. Colo. Denver Ctr., 1972-73; from asst. prof. to prof. law, dir. bus planning program U. Denver, 1973-83; ptnr. Krendl, Krendl, Sachnoff & Way, Denver, 1983—. Author: Colorado Business Corporation Act Deskbook, 2003—07; editor: Colorado Methods of Practice, 8 vols., 1983—2007, Closely Held Corporations in Colorado, vols. 1-3, 1981; contbr. articles to profl. jours. Named Disting. Alumna, North Tex. State U., 1985, Super Lawyer, Colo., 2006, 2007, Platinum Author, Thomason West, 2006, 2007. Mem. Colo. Bar Assn. (bd. govs. 1982-86, 88-91, chmn. securities subsect. 1986, bus. law sect. 1988-89, Professionalism award), Denver Bar Assn. (pres. 1989-90). Avocation: reading. Home: 1551 Larimer St Apt 1101 Denver CO 80202-1630 Office Phone: 303-629-2600. E-mail: csk@krendl.com.

KRENDL, KATHY, dean; BA in english, Lawrence U., 1972; MA in journalism, Ohio St. U., 1977; PhD in comm., U. Mich., 1982. Dean Ind. U. , Sch. of Continuing Studies, 1994—96, Ohio U. Coll. Comms., Athens, 1996—. Office: Ohio U Coll Comm RTVC 483B Athens OH 45701-2905

KRENEK, DEBBY, newspaper editor; b. Tex., Dec. 11, 1955; d. Ernest Reed and Elizabeth Pendleton (Brown) K.; m. James C. Roberts Jr., Feb. 28, 1987; children: Christine Elizabeth Roberts, Taylor James Roberts. BJ, Tex. A&M Univ., 1978. Copy editor Corpus Christi (Tex.) Caller-Times, 1978-81; copy editor to news editor Dallas Times Herald, 1981-85, asst. bus. editor, 1985-86, exec. news editor, 1986-87; dep. news editor NY Daily News, 1987-88, dep. mng. editor, 1988-91, mng. editor, 1991-93, exec. editor, 1993-97, editor-in-chief, 1997-2000; assoc. editor Newsday, 2001—03, cross-media editor, 2003—04, mng. editor, 2004—. Chief creative officer Petplace.com, 2000—01. Named to Acad. of Women Achievers YWCA, NY, 1992, named to Texas Twenty (most influential Texans) Tex. Monthly Mag., 1998. Avocations: photography, tennis, home renovation. Office: Newsday 235 Pinelawn Rd Melville NY 11747-4250

KRENEK, MARY LOUISE, political scientist, researcher; b. Wharton, Tex., Dec. 8, 1951; d. George P., Jr. and Vlasta (Zahn) Krenek. AA, Wharton County Jr. Coll., 1972; BA, Tex. A&I U., 1974; MA in Polit. Sci., St. Mary's U., 1992; Czech lang. cert., Charles U., 1994. Cert. secondary and elem. tchr. Tex. Polygraph examiner, San Antonio, 1979—81; ind. contractor market, polit. and social rschr. San Antonio, Houston, 1982—; with S.W. Casting, Houston. Substitute tchr., tchr. San Antonio Ind. Sch. Dist., 1981—82, Houston Ind. Sch. Dist., 1991—98, 2002—; instr. govt. Wharton County Jr. Coll., 1997—99; assoc. J.C. Penney Co., Inc., 1994—2000; with Am. Acad. Excellence, Houston, Southwest Casting, 2006—. Actor(movie productions, TV commercials):. Sec. Egypt Plantation Mus., 2003; del. Tex. Dem. Conv., 1971—72, 2006; precinct chair Dem. Party, Ft. Bend County, Tex. 1st lt. US Army, 1975—78, lt. col. USAR, 1978—2003, ret. USAR, 2003. Mem.: AARP, Tex. Czech Heritage and Cultural Ctr., Am. Polit. Sci. Assn., Nat. Assn. Self-Employed, Point/Counterpoint (Houston chpt.), Res. Officers Assn. (sec.-treas. Alamo chpt., jr. v.p. Dept. Tex., sec. Greater Houston chpt., ROTC coord.), Wharton County Hist. Mus. Assn. (assoc.), Houston Czech Cultural Ctr., Women in Mil. Svc. Am. Meml. Found. (charter), St. Mary's U. Alumni Assn., Am. Legion, Pi Sigma Alpha. Roman Catholic. Avocations: reading, writing, travel. Home: 10502 Fountain Lake Dr Stafford TX 77477-3711 also: PO Box 310 Egypt TX 77436-0310 Personal E-mail: marykrenek01@aol.com.

KRENICKI, JOHN, JR., manufacturing executive; BSME, Univ. Conn., 1984; MS, Purdue Univ. Joined GE, 1984; sales gen. mgr. for structured products GE Plastics; European comml. dir. GE Silicones; v.p. and gen. mgr. of the Americas GE Lighting, Cleve., 1999—2000; v.p. and gen mgr. of super abrasives GE, Worthington, Ohio, 2000; pres. CEO GE Trans. Sys., 2000—03, GE Plastics, Pittsfield, Mass., 2003—04; sr. v.p. GE, 2003—; pres., CEO GE Adv. Materials, 2004—05, GE Energy, 2005—. Mem.: GE Elfun, GE Univ. Exec., U. Mich.*

KRENS, THOMAS, museum director; b. NYC, Dec. 26, 1946; BA in Polit. Economy with honors, Williams Coll., 1969; M in Art, SUNY, Albany, 1971; M in Pub. and Pvt. Mgmt., Yale U., 1984; HHD (hon.), SUNY, Albany, 1989. Asst. prof. art Williams Coll., Williamstown, Mass., 1972-80, asst. prof. history art grad. program, 1977-80, adj. prof.; dir. Mus. Art Williams Coll. Mus. Art, Williamstown, Mass., 1981-88; cons. Solomon R. Guggenheim Mus., NYC, 1986-88; dir. Solomon R. Guggenheim Mus., Guggenheim Mus. SoHo, NYC, 1988—2005, The Peggy Guggenheim Collection, Venice, Italy, 1988—; dir., trustee Solomon R. Guggenheim Found., 1988—2005. Adv. com. mus. project NEA and Am. Fedn. Arts, Washington; adj. prof. art history Williams Coll., 1988-91, dir. artist in residence program, 1976-80; lectr. in field. Mem. Aspen Inst. Italia (bd. dirs.), Soc. Kandinsky/Ctr. Georges Pompidou, Gesellschaft fur Moderne Kunst am Mus. Ludwig (adv. bd.), Coun. Fgn. Rels., Assn. Art Mus. Dirs. (assoc.), AFA (adv. com.), Yale Univ. Coun. (com. on the art gallery and Brit. Art Ctr).*

KRENT, HAROLD J., dean, law educator; BA, Princeton U.; JD, NYU Sch. Law. Clerk for Hon. William H. Timbers Second Cir.; atty. Dept. Justice, Appellate Staff Civil Div.; prof. law Chgo.-Kent Coll. Law, Ill Inst. Tech., 1994—, assoc. dean, 1997—2002, interim dean, 2002—03, dean, 2003—. Cons. Adminstrn. Conf. of U.S. Author: Presidential Powers, 2005; contbr. articles to law jours. Office: Chgo-Kent Coll Law Ill Inst Tech 565 W Adams St Chicago IL 60661-3691 Office Phone: 312-906-5010. E-mail: hkrent@kentlaw.edu.*

KRESA, KENT, retired aerospace executive; b. NYC, Mar. 24, 1938; s. Helmy and Marjorie (Boutelle) K.; m. Joyce Anne McBride, Nov. 4, 1961; 1 child, Kiren BSAA, MIT, 1959, MSAA, 1961, EAA, 1966. Sr. scientist rsch. and advanced devel. divsn. AVCO, Wilmington, Mass., 1959-61; staff mem. MIT Lincoln Lab., Lexington, Mass., 1961-68; dep. dir. strategic tech. office Def. Advanced Rsch. Projects Agy., Washington, 1968-73; dir. tactical tech. office Def. Advanced Rsch. Project Agy., Washington, 1973-75; v.p., mgr. Rsch. & Tech. Ctr. Northrop Corp., Hawthorne, Calif., 1975-76, v.p., gen. mgr. Ventura divsn. Newbury Park, Calif., 1976-82, group v.p. Aircraft Group LA, 1982-86, sr. v.p. tech. devel. and planning, 1986-87, pres., COO, 1987-90; chmn. bd., pres., CEO Northrop Grumman Corp., LA, 1990—2001, chmn. bd., CEO, 2001—03. Bd. dirs. Avery Dennison Corp. 1999-, non exec. chmn. 2005-; bd. dir. Fluor Corp., GM Corp., MannKind Corp. Bd. dirs. John Tracy Clinic for the Hearing-Impaired, W.M. Keck Found.; bd. govs. L.A. Music Ctr.; bd. visitors Anderson Sch. Bus., UCLA; bd. trustees Calif. Inst. Tech. Recipient Henry Webb Salsbury award MIT, 1959, Arthur D. Flemming award, 1975, Calif. Industrialist of Yr. Calif. Mus. of Sci. and Industry and the Calif. Mus. Found., 1996, Bob Hope Disting. Citizen award Nat. Security Indsl. Assn., 1996; Sec. of Def. Meritorious Civilian Svc. medal, 1975, USN Meritorious Pub. Svc. citation, 1975, Exceptional Civilian Svc. award USAF, 1987. Fellow AIAA; mem. Aerospace Industries Assn. (past bd. govs.), Naval Aviation Mus. Found., Navy League U.S., Soc. Flight Test Engrs., Assn. U.S. Army, Nat. Space Club, Am. Def. Preparedness Assn., L.A. Country Club, NAE.

KRESGE, ALEXANDER JERRY, chemistry professor; b. Wilkes-Barre, Pa., July 17, 1926; married; 3 children. BA, Cornell U., 1949; PhD in Chemistry, U. Ill., 1953. Rsch. assoc. Purdue U., West Lafayette, Ind., 1954-55, MIT, 1955-57; assoc. chemist Brookhaven Nat. Lab., 1957-60; from asst. prof. to prof. chemistry Ill. Inst. Tech., Chgo., 1960—68; prof. chemistry U. Toronto, Ont., Canada, 1974-92, chmn. chem. group Ont., 1974-78, prof. emeritus Ont., Canada, 1992—. Guest prof. MIT, 1965; vis. scientist Fritz Haber Inst., 1981, U. Goteborg, 1983; mem. Gordon Rsch. Conf. on Chemistry and Physics of Isotopes, vice chmn., 1967, chmn., 1968; lectr. in field. Mem. editorial adv. bd. Isotopes in Organic Chemistry, Jour. Phys. Organic Chemistry. Fulbright scholar U. London, 1953-54; NSF sr. fellow, 1964-65, Guggenheim fellow, 1964-65, Killam fellow, 1984-86, Yamada fellow, 1985; recipient Morley medal of Cleve. sect. Am. Chem. Soc., Syntex award Chem. Inst. Can. Fellow Royal Soc. Can., Chem. Inst. Can.; mem. AAAS, Am. Chem. Soc., Royal Soc. Chemistry (Ingold lectr. 1995), Argentinian Soc. Organic Chemistry (hon.). Achievements include research in reaction mechanisms, isotope effects, flash photolysis, acid-base catalysis and kinetics. Office: Dept Chemistry Univ Toronto Toronto ON Canada M5S 3H6 Office Phone: 416-978-7259. Business E-Mail: akresge@chem.utoronto.ca.

KRESGE, BRUCE ANDERSON, retired physician; b. Detroit, Dec. 20, 1931; s. Stanley Sebastian and Dorothy Eloise (McVittie) Kresge; m. Peggy Ann Sale, June 14, 1952; children: Deborah Kresge McDowell, Katherine Kresge Lutey, Susan Kresge Drewes, Cynthia Kresge Furlong, Stephen. BA, Albion Coll., 1953; MD, Wayne State U., 1956. Intern Detroit Receiving Hosp., 1956-57; resident U. Mich. Hosp., 1959-60; pvt. practice Rochester, Mich., 1960-90; mem. staff St. Joseph Mercy Hosp., Pontiac, Mich., Pontiac Gen. Hosp., 1960-67, Crittenton Hosp., Rochester, 1967—. Pres. Rochester br. YMCA, 1975—77; trustee Kresge Found., 1960—67, Crittenton Hosp., 1993—99; hon. trustee Albion Coll., 1999—. With M.C. US Army, 1957—59. Mem.: AMA. Republican. Methodist. Home: 1071 N Lake Angelus Rd Lake Angelus MI 48326-1026

KRESGE, CHARLES T., chemicals executive; B in Chemistry, Swarthmore Coll.; PhD in Phys. Chemistry, U. Calif., Santa Barbara. Rsch. chemist catalyst synthesis & devel. grp. Mobil Corp., Paulsboro, NJ, 1979, head exploratory synthesis & characterization grp., 1987—93, head catalyst synthesis, characterization and applications Paulsboro and Princeton, 1993—97, tech. leader, chief scientist exploratory materials chemistry rsch., 1997, sr. mem. tech. leadership strategic rsch. ctr. Mobil Tech. Co.; grp. head fluid catalytic cracking rsch. W.R. Grace & Co., 1985—87; global R & D dir. Dow Chem. Co., Midland, Mich., 1999—2000, global R & D dir. chem. scis., 2000—05, head rsch. and engring. scis., 2005, v.p. R & D. Mem. bd. chem. scis. & tech. NAS. Contbr. articles to profl. publs.; mem. editl. bd.: Advanced Functional Materials. Co-recipient Donald W. Breck award in Molecular Sieve Sci., Internat. Zeolite Conf., 1994; recipient R & D 100 award for Innovation. Mem.: Am. Chem. Soc., NAE. Achievements include patents in field. Office: Dow Chem Co 566 Bldg 2030 Dow Ctr Midland MI 48674 Office Phone: 989-638-8669. Office Fax: 989-638-7572. E-mail: ctkresge@dow.com.*

KRESGE, NICOLE, editor; b. Chgo., June 23, 1972; d. Alexander Jerry and Yvonne Kresge; m. Rene Hayden, June 9, 2001; 1 child, Severin Alexander Hayden. BA, Cornell U., Ithaca, NY, 1994; PhD, Scripps Rsch. Inst., San Diego, 2001. Postdoctoral fellow NIH, Bethesda, Md., 2001—03; regulatory compliance officer Tech. Resources Internat., Bethesda, 2003—04; editor Am. Soc. Biochemistry and Molecular Biology, Bethesda, 2004—. Mem.: NASW, AAAS, Assn. Women in Sci. (editor 2006—07), DC Sci. Writers Assn. Office: Am Soc Biochemistry and Molecular Biology 9650 Rockville Pike Bethesda MD 20814

KRESH, J. YASHA, cardiovascular researcher, educator; b. Russia, July 13, 1948; came to U.S., 1967; m. Myrna Blickman. BSEE, N.J. Inst. Tech., 1971; MSBME, Rutgers U., 1973, PhD, 1976. Rsch. assoc. Beth Israel Med. Ctr., Newark, 1976-79; dir. rsch. Jefferson Med. Coll., Phila., 1979-86; prof. medicine, dir. cardiovascular biophysics and computing Cardiovascular Rsch. Ctr., Phila., 1986—; prof., dir. rsch. cardiothoracic surgery Drexel U. Coll. Medicine, Phila., 1986—. Prof. biomed. and mech. engring. Drexel U., 1984—. Author: Complex Systems Science in Biomedicine, 2006; author more than 190 publs. in physiol. cardiology and bioengring. jours.; patentee in field. Fellow Am. Coll. Cardiology, Biomed. Engring. Soc., Am. Heart Assn., Am. Inst. Med. and Biol. Engring.; mem. IEEE, AAAS, NY Acad. Sci., Am. Soc. Artificial Internal Organs, Sigma Xi, Tau Beta Pi, Eta Kappa Nu. Avocations: theoretical biology, computers, Porsches, biocomplexity. Office: Drexel U Coll Medicine MS # 111 245 N 15th St Philadelphia PA 19102-1192 Office Phone: 215-762-1703. Business E-Mail: jkresh@drexelmed.edu.

KRESS, WILLIAM F., manufacturing executive; s. Jim Kress. Pres. Green Bay (Wis.) Packaging. Bd. dir., Shenandoah Energy Inc., 2000—. Office: Green Bay Packaging 1700 North Webster Ct Green Bay WI 54302-1166

KRESSEL, HENRY, venture capitalist; b. Vienna, Jan. 24, 1934; came to U.S., 1946, naturalized, 1955; s. Aaron and Hudi (Zauderer) K.; m. Bertha Horowitz, Sept. 16, 1956; children: Aron, Kim. BS magna cum laude, Yeshiva U., 1955; MS, Harvard U., 1956; MBA, U. Pa., 1959, PhD (David Sarnoff fellow), 1965. Engr. Solid State div. RCA, 1959-61, engring. leader, 1961-63, 65-66; mem. tech. staff RCA David Sarnoff Research Center, 1966-70, head semicondr. device research, 1970-78, dir. materials research lab., 1978-79, staff v.p. solid state research Princeton, NJ, 1979-83; sr. v.p. E.M. Warburg, Pincus & Co., NYC, 1983-84, mng. dir., 1985—99, sr. mng. dir. NYC, 2000—. Regents lectr. U. Calif., San Diego, 1978-79; bd. dirs. Yeshiva U. Rsch. Inst.; cons. solar energy U.S. ERDA, 1975, USAF; adv. com. engring. NSF, 1996-99; engring. adv. coun. N.C. State U., 1985-88; mem. bd. dirs. several high tech. companies. Author: Semiconductor Lasers and Heterojunction LED's, 1977; editor: Characterization of Epitaxial Semiconductor Films, 1976, Semiconductor Devices for Optical Communication, 1980; Competing for the Future: How Digital Innovations are Changing the World, 2007; assoc. editor: IEEE Jour. Quantum Electronics, 1978-81; chmn. coordinating com. Jour. Lightware Tech., 1981-82; contbr. numerous articles to sci. jours.; patentee in field. Mem. bd. trustees Yeshiva U., 2005-. Served with Fin. Corps U.S. Army, 1959. Recipient David Sarnoff award RCA, 1974, Revel award Yeshiva U., 1980 Fellow IEEE (pres. Lasers and Electro-optics Soc. 1978-79, Centennial award 1984, Millennium award 2000, Sarnoff award 1985, Leos Svc. award 1992), Am. Phys. Soc.; mem. Nat. Acad. Engring. Home: 1056 Fifth Ave New York NY 10028 Office: E M Warburg Pincus & Co 466 Lexington Ave Fl 10 New York NY 10017-3147 Home Phone: 212-876-9621; Office Phone: 212-878-0674. Business E-Mail: hkressel@warburgpincus.com.

KRESSEL, HERBERT YEHUDE, medical educator; b. Bklyn., Nov. 20, 1947; BA, Brandeis U., Waltham, Mass., 1968; MD, U. So. Calif., LA, 1972. Diplomate Am. Bd. Radiology in diagnostic radiology; lic. physician, Calif., Pa., Wis., N.Y., N.J., Mass. Intern in medicine U. Wash. Hosp., Seattle, 1972-73; resident in radiology U. Calif., San Francisco, 1973-74, NIH fellow in diagnostic radiology, 1974-76, clin. instr. radiology, 1976-77, asst. prof., 1977-80, assoc. prof., 1980-85, prof., 1985-93; Miriam H. Stoneman prof. radiology Harvard Med. Sch., Boston, 1993—; attending physician GI radiology sect. dept. radiology Hosp. of U. Pa., 1977-82, dir. continung edn., 1979-93, attending physician, chief MRI sect., 1982-93; radiologist-in-chief Beth Israel Deaconess Med. Ctr., Boston, 1996—, pres., CEO, chief med. officer, 1998-2000, radiologist-in-chief, 2000—. Mem. plan devel. adv. task force on magnetic resonance for 1986 HealthSystems Plan-Health Systems Agy. Southeastern Pa., Inc., 1985-87; dir. R.I. Magnetic Resonance Imaging Network, Providence, 1988-93; mem. sci. adv. com. for rsch. grants Am. Cancer Soc., 1990-93; task force chmn. Com. on Studies Involving Human Beings, U. Pa., 1985-92; mem. coun. for continuing med. edn. U. Pa., 1990-93. Mem. editl. bds. Radiology, 1985-91, Magnetic Resonance in Medicine, 1987—; editor Magnetic Resonance Ann., 1985-88, Magnetic Resonance Quar., 1988-94; patentee in field. Mem. bd. dirs. Coregroup, 1996. Recipient Sylvia Sorkin Greenfield award Am. Assn. Physicists in Medicine, 1993. Fellow Am. Coll. Radiology (Commn. on Magnetic Resonance 1987-90, com. on pub. rels. 1987—, com. MR stds. and accreditation 1987—, chmn. com. on MR clin. applications 1987, Commn. on Govt. Rels. 1992—), Soc. Magnetic Resonance in Medicine (trustee 1987, sci. program com. chmn. 1989-90, pres.-elect 1990-91, pres. 1991-92, Crues Kressel award sect. magnetic resonance technologists 1991, Silver medal 1994), Radiol. Soc. N.Am. (refresher course com. 1992-93), Am. Roentgen Ray Soc., Soc. Gastrointestinal Radiologists, Soc. Computed Body Tomography (rsch. com. 1990-93), Mass. Radiol. Soc., New Eng. Roentgen Ray Soc. Office: Beth Israel Hosp Dept Radiology 330 Brookline Ave Rm Cc483B Boston MA 02215-5491 Office Phone: 617-667-2506. Business E-Mail: hkressel@bidmc.harvard.edu.

KRESSEL, ROBERT J., federal judge; b. St. Paul, June 14, 1947; s. John George and Margery Jane (Roberts) K.; m. Chris Kerper, Aug. 13, 1971; children: Benjamin, Rachel. AB, U. Notre Dame, 1969; JD, Harvard U., 1972. Bar: Minn., 1972, U.S. Dist. Ct., Minn., 1972, U.S. Ct. Appeals (8th cir.), 1972. Assoc. Kressel, Cecere & Seiler, Mpls., 1972-76; ptnr. Nichols, Kressel & Johnson, Mpls., 1976-78; pvt. practice Mpls., 1978-79; asst. U.S. trustee U.S. Dept. Justice, Mpls., 1979-82; bankruptcy judge U.S. Bankruptcy Ct., St. Paul, 1982-83, Mpls., 1984—, chief judge, 1986-93, judge bankruptcy appellate panel 8th cir., 1996—. Hearing examiner State Office of Hearing Examiners, St. Paul, 1977-79; referee Hennepin County Conciliation Ct., Mpls., 1979; adj. prof. Hamline U., 1983-84, William Mitchell Coll. of Law, 1986-94; mem. adv. com. on bankruptcy rules Jud. Conf. U.S., 1994—; mem. bankruptcy judges edn. com. Fed. Jud. Ctr., 1993-96. mem. gender fairness task force 8th Cir., 1993-97, chair bankruptcy com., 1993-97; mem. 8th Cir. Jud. Coun., 1992-96, lectr. numerous seminars, progs. and CLE instns. Author: Calculating The Present Value of Deferred Payments Under A Chapter 12 Plan: A New Twist To An Old Problem, 1988. Mem. Fed. Bar Assn. (bd. dirs. Minn. chpt. 1982—, v.p. Minn. chpt. 1985-88, pres.-elect Minn. chpt. 1988-89, pres. Minn. chpt. 1989-90), Minn. State Bar Assn., Hennepin County Bar Assn., Nat. Conf. Bankruptcy Judge (Gov. 1987-90), Am. Bankruptcy Inst. Office: US Bankruptcy Ct 300 S 4th St 8W US Courthouse Minneapolis MN 55415-1320 Office Phone: 612-664-5250.

KRESSLEY, CARSON, television personality; b. Allentown, Pa., Nov. 11, 1969; B in Fin. and Fine Arts magna cum laude, Gettysburg Coll., 1991. Ind. stylist; stylist men's sportswear div. and nat. advt. campaign Polo Ralph Lauren, NYC; fashion specialist TV series Queer Eye for the Straight Guy, 2003—. Author: Off the Cuff: The Essential Style Guide for Men--And the Women Who Love Them, 2004, (children's books) You're Different and That's Super, 2005; co-author: Queer Eye for the Straight Guy: The Fab 5's Guide to Looking Better, Cooking Better, Dressing Better, Behaving Better, and Living Better, 2004; author: (bi-weekly column) Us Weekly mag., 2003—; actor: (films) The Perfect Man, 2005. Avocation: nationally ranked equestrian (former mem. U.S. World Cup Equestrian Team). Office: ICM 8942 Wilshire Blvd Beverly Hills CA 90211-1934

KRESTY, LAURA ANN, medical researcher, educator; d. Edmund M. and Donna Kresty; m. Charles Mathew Paros, Aug. 28, 1987; children: Morgan Kresty Paros, Devyn Kresty Paros. PhD, Ohio State U., Columbus, 2000. Asst. prof. Ohio Stae U., 2003—. Contbr. articles to profl. publs. Educator, spkr. seed grant dollars for cancer rsch. OCRA, Columbus, 2005—07. Grantee, NCI, 2005, 2007. Mem.: AACR. Roman Catholic. Office: Ohio State U CCC Bldg 410 West 12th Ave Ste 302B Columbus OH 43210 Home Phone: 614-294-2688; Office Phone: 614-688-7787.

KRETCHMAR, LESLIE, medical/surgical nurse; d. Arthur Lockwood Kretchmar and Elaine Edgell Hughes; m. Salah Ghalib Husseini, Mar. 23, 1966 (div. Oct. 21, 1991); children: Ghalib Arthur Husseini, Tarik Salah Husseini, Sharif Salah Husseini. ADN, Coll. of DuPage, Glen Elyn, Ill., 1979; BA, U. Ill., Chgo., 1995. Registered Nurse, Dept. of Profl. Regulation/Ill., 1979. Staff nurse Glen Ellyn Clinic, Ill., 1979—85, Bapt. Hosp., Nashville, 1987—88; program coord. U. Ill., Chgo., 1989—2004; staff nurse Luth. Gen. Hosp., Park Ridge, Ill., 2004—05, HCR Manor Care, Naperville, 2005—. Literacy vol. Literacy Vols. Am., Wheaton, Ill., 1991—94; vol. Med. Reserve Corps, Cmty. Emergency Response Team. Mem.: Rehab. Nurses Assn. (assoc.), Am. Nurses Assoc. (assoc.). Christian - Presbyterian. Home Phone: 630-858-8624. Personal E-mail: lesliekretchmar@netzero.net.

KRETSCHMAR, WILLIAM EDWARD, state legislator, lawyer; b. St. Paul, Aug. 21, 1933; s. William Emanuel and Frances Jane (Peterson) K BS, Coll. St. Thomas, 1954; LLB, U. Minn., 1961. Bar: N.D. 1961, U.S. Dist. Ct. N.D. 1961. Pvt. practice Kretschmar Law Office, Ashley, ND, 1962—; mem. N.D. Ho. of Reps., Bismarck, 1972-98, speaker, 1988-90, 2000—. Mem. N.D. Commn. Uniform State Laws, 1987—; del. N.D. Constl. Conv., Bismarck, 1971-72 Mem. ABA, State Bar Assn. ND, Lions (pres. local club 1972-73, 93-94), Elks, Eagles. Republican. Roman Catholic. Avocations: hunting, swimming, hiking, bicycling, skiing. Home: 201 E 3d St Venturia ND 58413-4015 Office: Kretschmar Law Office 117 1st Ave NW Ashley ND 58413-7037

KRETSCHMER, FRANK FREDERICK, JR., electrical engineer, researcher, consultant; b. Phila., July 31, 1930; m. Shirley J. Kretschmer; children: Frank F. III, John, Diane, Linda, Thomas. BSEE, Pa. State U., 1957; MSEE, Drexel Inst. Tech., 1961; PhD, Johns Hopkins U., 1970. Asst. devel. engr. Burroughs Corp., Paoli, Pa., 1957-58; project engr. Bendix Radio Corp., Towson, Md., 1958-64; rsch. assoc. Johns Hopkins U., Balt., 1964-70; supervisory electronics engr. Naval Rsch. Lab., Washington, 1970-90, 90—. Cons. in field. Author: Aspects of Radar Signal Processing, 1986; contbr. over 35 papers to profl. jours. and confs. With USN, 1948-52. Fellow IEEE (life). Achievements include over 20 patents in field.

KRETSCHMER, KEITH HUGHES, investor; b. Omaha, Oct. 20, 1934; s. John G. and Mary (Hughes) K.; m. Adine Williams, Oct. 1, 1960; children: Hugh, Dara, Kurt. AA, Wentworth Acad., 1954; BS, U. Nebr., 1956; student, UCLA, 1968. With J.G. Kretschmer & Co., Omaha, 1958—60; gen. agt. Lincoln Life & Casualty, 1960—62; exec. v.p., sec.-treas. Automated Mgmt. Sys., Kansas City, Mo., 1962—68; investment exec. Shearson, Hammill & Co., LA, 1968—75; gen. ptnr. Bear Stearns & Co., LA, 1975—85; sr. mng. dir. Bear Stearns & Co. Inc., Boston, 1985—91, spl. assoc. dir., 1991—92; mng. dir. Oppenheimer & Co., Inc., Boston, 1993—94, Oppenheimer Capital, 1995—2001; bd. dirs. Visiphor Corp. Mem. stockholders com. Tosco Corp., LA, 1982; bd. dirs. Cogent Fin. Group dba Medi Credit, 2004-06. Author: Your Option, 1978. Advanceman Rep. Pres.'s Nixon and Ford, 1970-76; trustee Lighthouse Preservation Soc., 1986-88, Wentworth Mil. Acad., Lexington, Mo., 2005—; founding dir. Option Soc. So. Calif., 1974-85; bd. dirs. Pacific Palisades-Malibu YMCA, 1976-86, chmn. bd. dirs., 1980; bd. dirs. South Shore Art Ctr., Cohasset, Mass., 1988-97, pres., 1991-93; bd. dirs. World Affairs Coun. Boston, 1989-96; mem. pres.'s coun. Accion Internat., 1992—. Served to maj. U.S. Army, Airborne Ranger, 1956-58. Mem. The Explorers Club, Aircraft Owners and Pilots Assn., Exptl. Aircraft Assn., Seaplane Pilots Assn., CEO Club, Angel Flight, AERO Club New Eng., Vintage Sports Car Club Am., Masons, Shriners. Congregationalist. Avocation: pilot since 1952. Office: 294 Sunshine Ave Sequim WA 98382 Home: 323 North St Sequim WA 98382 Office Phone: 360-808-7788. Personal E-mail: kkretsc@aol.com.

KRETZSCHMAR, WILLIAM ADDISON, JR., language educator; b. Ann Arbor, Mich., Sept. 13, 1953; s. William Addison and Audrey June (Krauss) K.; m. Claudia Suzanne Miller. AB, U. Mich., 1975; MA in Medieval Studies, Yale U., 1976; PhD in English, U. Chgo., 1980. Instr. English Mundelein Coll., Chgo., 1977-82, dir. summer sch., 1979-81; asst. prof. English U. Wis., Whitewater, 1982-86, U. Ga., Athens, 1986-89, assoc. prof., 1989-95, prof., 1995—, dir. linguistics program, 1996-99, Willson prof. in humanities, 2004—. Author: Introduction to Quantitative Analysis of Linguistic Survey Data, 1996; editor: Dialects in Culture (R.I. McDavid, Jr.), 1979, Handbook of the Linguistic Atlas of the Middle and South Atlantic States, 1993, Oxford Dictionary of Pronunciation for Current English, 2001; editor: Linguistic Atlas Middle and South Atlantic States, Linguistic Atlas North-Central States, 1984—; editor Jour. English Linguistics, 1983-99, Empirical Linguistic Series, 1996-99; contbr. articles to profl. jours. Mem. MLA (regional del. 1983-86), Am. Dialect Soc. (exec. com. 1999-2003, pres. 2007—), Linguistic Soc. Am., Medieval Acad. Am., Assn. Computers Humanities (bd. dir. 1999-2003). Home: 125 Renfrew Dr Athens GA 30606-3936 Office: U Ga Dept English Athens GA 30602 Business E-Mail: kretzsch@uga.edu.

KREUTHER, GABRIEL, chef; Attended, Ecole Hoteliere, Strasbourg, France, 1984—87. Chef de partie Le Caprice, Wash., DC, 1988—90; sous chef Franz Keller's Kronenschlosschen Restaurant, Hattenheim, Germany, 1991—92; chef de partie Le Fer Rouge, Colmar, France, 1992—93; exec. sous chef L'Ermitage de Bernard Ravet, Switzerland, 1993—97; sous chef La Caravelle, NYC, 1997; chef de cuisine Jean Georges Restaurant, NYC, 1999—2002; exec. chef Atelier, Ritz Carlton NY, 2002—04, The Modern, NYC, 2004—. Armed Forces, France. Named Rising Star Chef, StarChefs.com, 2002; named one of Best New Chefs, Food & Wine Mag., 2003; recipient Best Kitchen's Apprentice in France award, 1987, Best New Restaurant award, James Beard Found., 2006. Office: The Modern 9 W 53rd St New York NY 10019 Office Phone: 212-408-6632. Business E-Mail: gkreuther@themodernnyc.com.

KREUTZER, NATALIE RUTH JONES, music educator; b. Washington; d. Berwyn Edgar Jones and Wilda Jones Shafer. M in Music Edn., Ind. U., Bloomington, 1989, PhD, 1997. Second Degree Reiki Usui Ryoko Sys., 2005; cert. profl. tchr. Nebr., 2000. Music tchr. grades K-12 various pub. schs., Webster County, Nebr., 1968—87; grad. tchg. asst. Ind. U., Bloomington, 1987—91; lectr. in music edn. U. Zimbabwe, Harare, 1993; assoc. prof. music edn. U. Idaho, Moscow, 2002—. Faculty advisor African Students' Assn. U. Idaho, Moscow, 1999—2003, supr. and observer student tchrs. in music, 1997—, rsch. advisor for music and spl. needs topics; presenter multicultural music workshops, 1998—. Prodr.: (dvd) Zimbabwe Children's Singing Games; editor, contbr.: web-based curriculum in music edn. Jazzonline; contbr. articles to profl. jours. Chair Bicentennial Com., Bladen, Nebr., 1975—76; editor Centennial Yearbook, Bladen, 1986; founder Cmty. Zimbabwe Marimba Ensemble, Moscow, 2003. Fellow, Social Sci. Rsch. Coun., 1991; grantee, Am. Musicological Soc., 2003. Mem.: Early Childhood Music and Movement Assn., Soc. for Ethnomusicology, Orgn. Am. Kodaly Educators (nat. bd. mem. 2000—02). Achievements include designer and pioneer of the first ever music degree in Zimbabwe. Avocations: palmistry, music and humor for healing, feng shui living space arrangements. Home: 650 N Hayes St Moscow ID 83843 Office: School of Music University of Idaho PO Box 44015 Moscow ID 83844 Home Phone: 208-883-7959; Office Phone: 208-885-6425. Personal E-mail: natalienpaddy@hotmail.com. Business E-Mail: nataliek@uidaho.edu.

KREVANS, JULIUS RICHARD, academic administrator, internist; b. NYC, May 1, 1924; s. Sol and Anita Krevans; m. Patricia N. Abrams, May 28, 1950; children: Nita, Julius R., Rachel, Sarah, Nora Kate. BS Arts and Scis, N.Y. U., 1943, MD, 1946. Diplomate: Am. Bd. Internal Med. Intern, then resident Johns Hopkins Med. Sch. Hosp., mem. faculty, until 1970, dean acad. affairs, 1969—70; physician in chief Balt. City Hosp., 1963—69; prof. medicine U. Calif., San Francisco, 1970—, dean Sch. Medicine, 1971—82, chancellor, 1982—93, chancellor emeritus, 1993—. Contbr. articles on hematology, internal med. profl. jours. With USMC, 1948—50, AUS. Mem. ACP, Assn. Am. Physicians. Address: 32 Birch Bay Dr Bar Harbor ME 04609 E-mail: krevansmaine@adelphia.net.

KREVANS, RACHEL, lawyer; b. Balt., June 15, 1957; d. Julius Richard and Patricia (Abrams) K. BA, Dartmouth Coll., 1979; JD, U. Calif., Davis, 1984. Law clk. hon. Robert Boochever U.S. Ct. Appeals for Ninth Cir., Juneau, Alaska, 1984-85; assoc. Morrison & Foerster LLP, San Francisco, 1985-90, mng. ptnr.-San Francisco office, 1991—. Office: Morrison & Foerster LLP 425 Market St San Francisco CA 94105-2482 Office Phone: 415-677-7178. Office Fax: 415-268-7522. Business E-Mail: rkrevans@mofo.com.

KREY, DEAN MARIE, retired education educator; b. Turtle Lake, Wis., Feb. 18, 1942; d. Henry August and Sophie Otillia Wickboldt; m. Monte Arthur Hansen, June 12, 1965 (div. 1983); m. Robert Dean Krey, Sept. 5, 1987. BS, U. Wis., River Falls, 1964, MS in Tchg., 1969; PhD, U. Minn., Mpls., 1977. Cert. tchr. Wis. 6th grade tchr. New Richmond Pub. Schs., New Richmond, Wis., 1964—65, St. Croix Falls Pub. Schs., Wis., 1965—68; instr., tchr. 2d grade lab sch. U. Wis., River Falls, 1969—71, prof. tchr. edn., 1969—2002, assoc. dean, 1982—88, prof. emerita, 2002—. Coord. Tchg. Methods Block, 1972—2002; mem. curriculum writing team State of Wis. Dept. Pub. Instrn., 1973—2000; co-leader Brit. Exch. Program for Elem. Sch. Children, 1975; social studies children's book cons. Kane Press, NYC, 2003—06; spkr. in field; cons. in field; workshop leader, Taiwan, 1974, Taiwan, 77. Author: Children's Literature in Social Studies: Teaching to the Standards, 1998; contbr. columns, articles to profl. jours. and chpts. to books. Co-chmn. Wis. Gov.'s Writing Team Social Studies Academic Stds., 1994—98; reviewer chmn. notable social studies trade books young people Children's Book Coun., NYC, 1997—2000; curriculum team mem. exploring humanitarian law ARC, Washington, 2002—06, rep. Ea. Europe and exploring humanitarian law workshop Budapest, Hungary, 2003. Named Disting. Tchr. of Yr., U. Wis.-River Falls, 1991, Tchr. Educator of Yr., U. Wis.-River Falls/Wis. Dept. Pub. Instrn., 1992, Outstanding Faculty Mem., U. Wis.-River Falls Coll. Edn., 1993; 18 grants, 1988—2000. Mem.: AAUW (moderator voter forum 2004, vol. book sale, Outstanding Woman Univ. Prof. award 1988), Wis. Coun. Social Studies (pres. 1983—85, Outstanding Svc. award 1988, Snavely award for contbns. in field of social studies 2000), Nat. Coun. Social Studies (Pres. award 1999), Phi Kappa Phi, Phi Delta Kappa. Avocations: choral singing, pastel painting, dance, reading. Home: 724 River Ridge Ct River Falls WI 54022 Personal E-mail: rdkrey@comcast.net.

KREYCHE, GERALD FRANCIS, retired philosophy educator; b. Kenosha, Wis., June 19, 1927; s. Harold Joseph and Henrietta Fredericka (Oteman) K.; m. Eleanor Ann Okon, June 19, 1948. AB, DePaul U., 1949, AM, 1950; PhD cum laude, U. Ottawa, Can., 1958. Mem. faculty DePaul U., 1950-59, chmn. dept. philosophy, 1961-82, prof., 1965-89, prof. emeritus, 1989—; now also Danforth assoc. Aquinas lectr. Alverno Coll., Milw., 1963; vis. prof. St. Mary's Coll., Minn., 1977; bd. advisors Univ. Press Am. Condr.: radio programs What Do You Think?, What's the Big Idea?, 1960; frequent appearances ednl. and comml. TV, also radio, 1958—; Author: Perspectives on God, 1972, Thirteen Thinkers, Heroes of the American West; also articles religious publs.; Co-editor: Harbrace Philosophy series; Visions of the American West, 1988, Heroes of the American West, 2001; sr. editor: Am. Thought; sect. editor: U.S.A. Today; bd. advisors: Philos. Research and Analysis; former editor-in-chief Listening: A Journal of Religion and Culture; referee Archives of Philosophy With AUS, 1945-46. Recipient DePaul U. Distinguished Service award, 1969, Univ. award for excellence, 1984-85, Viam Sapientiae award, 1989 Mem. Am. Metaphys. Soc., Ill.-Ind. Am. Cath. Philos. Assn. (pres. 1960), Am. Cath. Philos. Assn. (pres. 1972-73), Chgo. Lit. Club (pres. 1986-87), Phi Kappa Theta, Phi Eta Sigma. Home: 15881 County Rd 28 Dolores CO 81323 E-mail: ellieok@fone.net.

KREYLING, EDWARD GEORGE, JR., retired railroad executive; b. St. Louis, June 1, 1923; s. Edward George and Mildred (Schroeder) K.; m. Mary Emily Gronemeyer, Sept. 4, 1943; children: Carol (Mrs. Robert D. Knight), Deborah Ann (Mrs. Hugh J. Risseeuw), Edward George III. BSBA, Washington U., St. Louis, 1947, MBA, 1954. Accountant Monsanto Chem. Co., 1947-50; chief statistician White Rodgers Elec. Co., St. Louis, 1950-54; dir. market research Laclede-Christy Co., St. Louis, 1954-55; with St. L.-S.F. Ry., 1955-69, dir. marketing, 1964-65, v.p. traffic and indsl. devel., 1965-69; v.p. traffic I.C. R.R., Chgo., 1969-70; exec. v.p. Penn Central Transp. Co., Phila., 1970-71; v.p. marketing So. Ry., 1971-79, sr. v.p. mktg. service, 1979-80, exec. v.p. mktg., 1981-82; v.p. mktg. services Norfolk So. Corp. (Va.), 1982-87, ret. Active Virginia Beach. Sch. Bd., 1992-94; dir. Seton House, 1995-98, Va. Christian Coalition, 1998-2001, v.p.; dir. Assist Crisis Pregnancy Ctr., 2001—. Served with AUS, 1943-45. Mem. Nat. Freight Traffic Assn. Home: 11307 Stones Throw Dr Reston VA 20194-1044 Personal E-mail: ekreylingj@aol.com.

KRIBEL, ROBERT EDWARD, consultant, retired physicist, academic administrator; b. Pitts., Sept. 17, 1937; s. Joseph P. and Helen M. K.; m. Ruth Ann Gropelli; children— Robert E., Karen A., Mark P., Gary P. BS, U. Notre Dame, 1959; MS, U. Calif., San Diego, 1966, PhD in Physics, 1968. Research scientist Gen. Atomic, Inc., 1965-69; assoc. prof. physics Drake U., 1970-73; vis. assoc. prof. applied physics Cornell U., 1973-74; prof., head dept. physics James Madison U., 1974-78, Auburn (Ala.) U., 1978-87, acting dean scis. and math., 1985-87, prof. physics, 1987-88; v.p. acad. affairs Jacksonville (Ala.) State U., 1988-92, prof. physics, 1992-93; dean natural scis. and math. Mesa State Coll., 1993-99; pres. REK Enterprises, Auburn, Ala., 1999—; chief acad. officer Air U., 2000—02. Contbr. articles to profl. jours. Served with U.S. Navy, 1959-62. Mem. Am. Inst. Physics, Sigma Xi, Phi Kappa Phi. Avocations: amateur radio, electronics. Personal E-mail: bkribel@charter.net. Business E-Mail: trek_ent@charter.net.

KRICORIAN, MARY JO GEYER, biology instructor, environmental scientist, consultant; b. Balt., July 26, 1971; d. Joseph Bennett and Rosemary Brown Geyer; m. Paul Kricorian, Oct. 24, 2004; 1 child, Bennett Paul. BS, Washington and Lee U., Lexington, Va., 1993; MS, U. Va., Charlottesville, 1996. Environ. cons. Perrin Quarles Assocs., Inc., Charlottesville, 1996—; biology instr. Washington and Lee U., 2005—. Avocations: hiking, outdoor activities. Office: Washington and Lee U Howe 411 Lexington VA 24450 Home Phone: 540-886-6229; Office Phone: 540-458-8444.

KRIDEL, RUSSELL WILLIAM HAYES, plastic surgeon, educator; b. NYC, Oct. 12, 1948; m. Cheryl Ann; children: Christopher Brent, Blake Alexander. BA in Polit. Sci., Stanford U., Calif., 1970; MD, U. Cin., 1975. Cert. Am. Bd. Otolaryngology 1981, Am. Bd. Cosmetic Surgery 1987, Am. Bd. Facial Plastic and Reconstructive Surgery 1991, Diplomate Nat. Bd. Med. Examiners. Intern gen. surgery Baylor Coll. Medicine, Houston; resident otolaryngology Baylor Affiliated Hosps., Houston, 1975-77, resident facial plastic surgery, 1977-80; fellow Am. Acad. Facial Plastic and Reconstructive Surgery, Houston, 1980—81; asst. clin. prof. U. Tex. Health Sci. Ctr., 1981—2005, assoc. clin. prof., 2005—. Hosp. staff Spring Br. Med. Ctr., 1981—, Hermann Hosp., 1981—, St. Luke's Episcopal Hosp., 1981—, Meth. Hosp., 1981—, Health South Hosp. for Specialized Surgery, 1994—. Contbr. articles to med. jours., chapters to books; guest: (TV series) CBS Early Show; featured: magazines Vogue. Named Best Plastic Surgeon in Houston for nose surgery, Houston Chronicle, 2003. Fellow ACS, AMA, Harris County Med. Soc., Houston Soc. Otolaryngology; mem. Am. Acad. Facial Plastic and Reconstructive Surgery (nat. pres. 2000-01, fellow 1980-81) Office: Facial Plastic Surgery Assocs 6655 Travis St Ste 900 Houston TX 77030-1336 Office Phone: 713-526-5665. Office Fax: 713-526-5160. Business E-Mail: mailbox@todaysface.com.*

KRIDER, PATRICIA ANN, library director; b. Buffalo, Sept. 4, 1956; d. Alfred J. and Mary M. (Byrns) Mlinarchik; m. Jonathan J. Krider, Aug. 18, 1989. AAS in Legal Secretarial, Trocaire Coll., 1978; Assoc. Applied Bus., Stark Tech. Coll., Canton, Ohio, 1984; BA in Mgmt., Walsh Coll., 1989; MBA, Ashland Univ., 1996. Acctg. clk. U.S. Fidelity & Guaranty Ins., Buffalo, 1974-76; payroll clk. Stitches of Va., Virginia Beach, 1978-79; asst. bookkeeper Ind. Ins. Svcs. Inc., Canton, Ohio, 1979-84; computer programming tech. asst. Stark Tech. Coll., Canton, Ohio, 1984—87, instr., 1987—99; dir. computer services Nat. First Ladies Libr., Canton, Ohio, 1999—2000, exec. dir., 2000—. Mem. AAUP, Coll. Staff Assn. (pres. 1989-91). Democrat. Roman Catholic. Avocations: reading, travel. Office: Nat First Ladies Library Saxton McKinley House 331 S Market Ave Canton OH 44702 Office Phone: 330-452-0876 ext 309. Business E-Mail: pkrider@firstladies.org.

KRIEBEL, CHARLES HOSEY, management sciences educator; b. Tarrytown, NY, Nov. 6, 1933; s. Nelson Stearly and Elizabeth Grace (Hosey) K.; m. Jan Lilly McAuley, June 7, 1961; children: Paul Charles, Susan, James McAuley, Carl Nelson. BS in Econs., U. Pa., 1959, MA in Stats., 1961; PhD in Indsl. Mgmt., MIT, 1964. Instr. Wharton Sch. Fin., U. Pa., Phila., 1959-61; asst. prof. Sloan Sch., MIT, Cambridge, 1963-64, Grad. Sch. Indsl. Adminstrn., Carnegie-Mellon U., Pitts., 1964-67, assoc. prof., 1967-70, prof., 1970-2000, prof. emeritus Pitts., 2000—, head dept indsl. mgmt., 1981-86; dir. strategic tech. Met. Life, NYC, 1987-88. Cons. McKinsey & Co., Inc., N.Y.C., Rand Corp., Santa Monica, Calif., Gulf Oil Corp., Pitts., Imperial Tobacco, Montreal, Que., Can., Mellon Bank (N.A.), Pitts., LTV STeel Co., Inc., Gen. Reins Corp., N.Y.C., Industrikonsulent I.K.O., Copenhagen, Westinghouse Electric Corp., Pitts., U.S. Steel Corp., Pitts., Rockwell Internat., Pitts., Am. Mgmt. Sys., Fairfax, Va., HAL Inst. Computer Tech., Osaka, Japan, other indsl. firms; rep. NAS; mem. adv. bd. NSF, 1985-88. Mem. editl. bd. Internat. Fedn. Info. Processing, 1971—; editl. cons. Prentice-Hall, Inc., 1967-80; contbr. more than 130 articles to profl. jours. With Signal Corps, U.S. Army, 1954-56. Fulbright-Hays advisor, 1965-79; Ford Found. fellow MIT, 1964. Fellow AAAS; mem. Assn. Computing Machinery (nat. lectr.), Inst. Mgmt. Scis. (dept. editor Mgmt. Sci.), Ops. Rsch. Soc. Am., Am. Econ. Assn., Am. Statis. Assn., Econometric Soc., N.Y. Acad. Scis., Info. Systems Rsch. (sr. editor bd.), Delta Kappa Epsilon (pres. 1959). Office: Carnegie-Mellon U Grad Sch Indsl Admin Pittsburgh PA 15213

KRIEG, KENNETH JOSEPH, former federal agency administrator; b. 1961; m. Anne Hurt Krieg. BA, Davidson Coll., 1983; M in Pub. Policy, Harvard U. Various def. & fgn. policy positions, Washington; various mktg. & sales positions including v.p. and gen. mgr. office and consumer papers divsn. Internat. Paper Co., Stamford, Conn., 1990—2001; exec. sec. sr. exec. coun. (SEC) US Dept. Def., Washington, 2001, spl. asst. to sec., dir. program analysis and evaluation, under sec. def. acquisition, tech. & logistics, 2005—07. Recipient Alumni Svc. award, Davidson Coll., 2003.*

KRIEG, NANCY KAY, social worker, poet, musician; b. Jefferson City, Mo., Oct. 11, 1954; d. Arlin Darrell and Doris Lee Basinger; m. Russell Hugh Krieg, Mar. 15, 1975 (div. Aug. 18, 1988). BA in Psychology, Columbia Coll., 1994. Co-owner The Melody Shop, Jefferson City, Mo., 1975—85; co-mgr. Premiere Video, Osage Beach, 1991—94; social worker Miller County Psychol. Svcs., Eldon, 1994—95; substitute tchr. Eldon Pub. Schs., 1995; tchg. counselor, supr. Overland Pk., Kans., 1995—96; substitute tchr. Oak Hill Day Sch., Gladstone, Mo., 1997—98; tchg. counselor Concerned Care, Inc., Kansas City, 1998—. Author poetry. Recipient Mo. Writers' Week award for Poetry, Mo. Writers Guild, 1994, 1995, 1996, 1997. Mem.: Am. Fedn. Musicians, Acad. Am. Poets, The Writers Pl. Avocations: jazz drummer/percussion, mandolin, guitar, songwriting, poetry. Home: 1236 E 25th Ave Kansas City MO 64116

KRIEGEL, ROBIN, medical association administrator; BA, Hofstra U., 1971. Exec. dir. Am. Soc. Parenteral & Enteral Nutrition, Silver Spring, Md., 2000, Am. Assn. Med. Soc. Execs., 1988—2000. Fellow: Am. Soc. Assn. Execs.; mem.: Greater Washington Soc. Assn. Execs., Assn. Forum Assn. Execs., N.Y. Soc. Assn. Execs. Office: Am Soc Parenteral Enteral Nutrition 8630 Fenton St Ste 412 Silver Spring MD 20910-3803

KRIEGER, ALBERT J., lawyer; b. NYC, Nov. 4, 1923; BA, NYU, 1945, LLB, 1949. American Bar Assoc., National Association of Criminal Defense Lawyers, Florida Association of Criminal Defense Lawyers, U.S. Supreme Court 1960, bar: New York 1949, Florida 1976, Michigan 1980. Of counsel Law Offices of Scott A. Srebnick, Miami. Faculty mem. National Criminal Defense College, Mercer Law School, 1985—. Recipient Outstanding Practitioner, Criminal Justice Section, New York State Bar Association, 1977, Criminal Law Committee Commendation, Chicago Bar Association, 1984, Lifetime Achievement Award, National Association of Criminal Defense Lawyers, 1987, Robert C. Heeney Memorial Award, 1995, C. Clyde Atkins Civil Liberties Award, ACLU of Florida, Inc., 2001. Mem.: ABA, Fla. Assn. of Criminal Defense Lawyers, Nat. Assn. of Criminal Defense Lawyers. Office: 2400 South Dixie Highway Ste 200 Miami FL 33133

KRIEGER, ELLIE, chef, dietitian, TV personality; B in Clin. Nutrition, Cornell U.; M in Nutrition Edn., Columbia U. Dir., Nutritional Services La Palestra Ctr. for Preventative Medicine. Model Wilhelmina; adj. prof. NYU, Dept. of Nutrition, Food Studies, Health; spokesperson Calif. Strawberry Commn., Horizon Organic and Boca Foods. Author: Small Changes, Big Results, 2005; host Healthy Appetite, Food Network, 2006—, Living Better, (radio) In Balance with Ellie Krieger; contbr. Your Diet Mag., Parenting Mag., articles Women's Day Mag., Baby Talk Mag., American Baby Mag., Running News Mag.; columnist Rodale's Fitness Swimmer, guest appearances Today, CNN, Saturday Early Show, CBS, Your Total Health, The Other Half, In Food Today. Office: Flutie Entertainment c/o Robert A Flutie 6500 Wilshire Blvd Ste 2240 Los Angeles CA 90048 Office Phone: 310-247-1100. Office Fax: 310-247-1122.

KRIEGER, IRVIN MITCHELL, retired chemistry professor; b. Cleve., May 14, 1923; s. William I. and Rose (Brodsky) K.; m. Theresa Melamed, June 9, 1965; 1 dau., Laura. BS, Case Inst. Tech., 1944, MS, 1948; PhD, Cornell, 1951. Rsch. asst. Case Inst. Tech., Cleve., 1946-47; teaching fellow Cornell U., Ithaca, NY, 1947-49; instr. Case Western Res. U., 1949-51, asst. prof., 1951-55, assoc. prof., 1955-68, prof., 1968-88, prof. emeritus, 1988—; dir. Center for Adhesives, Sealants and Coatings, 1983-88. Vis. prof. U. Bristol, 1977-78; cons. for chem. firms; prof. invité Ecole Nat. Supérieure de Chimie de Mulhouse, 1987, Louis Pasteur U., Strasbourg, France, 1989. Contbr. articles to profl. jours. With USNR, 1943—46. NSF fellow Université Libre De Bruxelles, 1959-60; sr. fellow Weizmann Inst., 1970 Mem. Am. Chem. Soc., Am. Inst. Chem. Engrs., AAUP, Soc. Rheology (pres. 1977-79, Bingham medalist 1989). Home: 3460 Green Rd Apt 101 Beachwood OH 44122-4076 Office Phone: 216-921-6133. E-mail: imk@case.edu.

KRIEGER, MARCIA SMITH, federal judge; b. Denver, Mar. 3, 1954; d. Donald P. Jr. and Marjorie Craig (Gearhart) Smith; m. Michael S. Krieger, Aug. 26, 1976 (div. July 1988); children: Miriam Anna, Matthias Edward; m. Frank H. Roberts, Jr., Mar. 9, 1991; stepchildren: Melissa Noel Roberts, Kelly Suzanne Roberts, Heidi Marie Roberts. BA, Lewis & Clark Coll., 1975; JD, U. Colo., 1979. Bar: Colo. 1979, U.S. Dist. Ct. Colo. 1979, U.S. Ct. Appeals (10th cir.) 1979. Rotary grad. fellow U. Munich, Germany, 1975—76; assoc. Mason, Reuler & Peek, P.C., Denver, 1976-83, Smart, DeFurio Brooks, Eklund & McClure, Denver, 1983-84; ptnr. Brooks & Krieger, P.C., Denver, 1984-88, Wood, Ris & Hames, P.C., Denver, 1988-90; pvt. practice U.S. Bankruptcy Court, 10th Circuit, Denver, 1990-94; judge U.S. Bankruptcy Ct., 10th Circuit, Denver, 1994-2000; chief judge U.S. Bankruptcy Ct., Denver, 2000—02, U.S. Dist. Ct., 2002—. Lectr. U. Denver Grad. Tax Program, 1987—, Colo. Soc. CPA's, Denver, 1984-87, Colo. Continuing Legal Edn., Denver, 1980—, Colo. Trial Lawyers Assn., Denver, 1987—, U. Colo. Law Sch.; adj. instr. U. Colo. Sch. Law, 1999-2001; spkr. in field. Contbr. articles to profl. publs. Vestry person Good Shepherd Episcopal Ch., Englewood, 1986—, judge and coach for H.S. mock trial. Mem. Colo. Bar Assn. (past chair Com. Court Reform; past mem. Professionalism Com.), Arapahoe Bar Assn., Arraj Inn of Ct. (v.p.), Nat. Conf. Bankruptcy Judges (past chair Internat. Law Rels. Com, Ethics Com.; past mem. Newsletter Com., Program Com.), Littleton Adv. Coun. for Gifted and Talented education, Alfred A. Arraj Inn of Court (past pres.), Colo. Jud. Coordinating Coun., Kenya Children Found. (bd. dirs.). Republican. Avocations: international relations, travel, marksmanship. Office: US Dist Ct Dist Colo Alfred J Arraj US Courthouse 901 19th St A-941 Denver CO 80294

KRIEGER, PAUL EDWARD, lawyer; b. Fairmont, W.Va., Mar. 30, 1942; s. Paul Julius Krieger and Martha Frances (Graham) Ralph; m. Nora Elizabeth Krieger, July 28, 2001; children: Andrew, Thomas. BS in Mining Engring., U. Pitts., 1964; postgrad., Pa. State U., 1964-65; LLB, U. Md., 1968; LLM, George Washington U., 1971. Bar: Md. 1968, U.S. Patent and Trademark Office 1970, D.C. 1973, Tex. 1979. Faculty rsch. asst. U. Md., 1967-70; assoc. Brumbaugh, Graves, Donohue & Raymond, NYC, 1970-71; ptnr. Lane, Aitken, Dunner & Ziems, Washington, 1971-78; sr. pat. atty. Dresser Industries Inc., Dallas, 1978-79; ptnr. Pravel, Hewitt, Kimball & Krieger, Houston, 1979-98, Fulbright & Jaworski, Houston, 1998—. Adj. prof. U. Houston Law Ctr., 1985—. Mem. ABA, Am. Bar Found., Am. Pat. Law Assn., Tex. Bar Found., Tex. Bar Assn., Houston Bar Found., Internat. Assn. of Defense Coun. Office: Fulbright & Jaworski 1301 Mckinney St Ste 5100 Houston TX 77010-3031 Home: 4306 Colony W Dr Richmond TX 77469 Office Phone: 713-651-5167. E-mail: pkrieger@fulbright.com.

KRIEGER, ROBERT LEE, JR., human resource/management consultant, educator, writer, travel/meeting planner, political analyst, internet marketing consultant; b. Louisville, Nov. 13, 1946; s. Robert Lee and June Elise (Waters) K. BBA, U. Memphis, 1968, MBA, 1969. Cert. pers. cons., travel planner, mgmt. cons. Adminstrv. asst. to mayor City of Memphis, 1969-72; dir. devel. programs U. Memphis, 1972-74; pvt. cons. practice, Memphis, 1974—95; pres. KR Internat. Inc., Memphis, 1995—. Mem. faculty U. Memphis Coll. Bus., 1984—; worldwide travel cons. and meeting planner, 1962—; keynote spkr. numerous profl. groups. Trustee, life mem. Rep. Presdl. Task Force, Washington, 1980—; mem. Rep. Nat. Adc. Com., Washington, 1972—, Rep. Regional Steering Com.; mem. US Olympic Soc., Boulder, Colo., 1968—; active Make-A-Wish, St. Jude. Recipient US Treasury award US Dept. Treasury, 1971, Nat. Presdl. Medal of Merit, Rep. Presdl. Task Force, 1984, Rep. Legion of Merit, Pres.'s award Memphis Cotton Carnival Assn., 1968-85. Mem. Data Processing Mgmt. Assn., Am. Mgmt. Assn., Soc. Profl. Journalists, Am. Film Guild, Met. Opera Guild, US Navy League, U. Memphis Alumni Assn., Mensa, Alpha Delta Sigma. Episcopalian. Avocations: writing, movies, photography, travel, internet. Home: 964 Wrens Roost #4 Memphis TN 38119 Personal E-mail: german711@hotmail.com.

KRIEGER, SANFORD, lawyer; b. NYC, Nov. 4, 1943; s. Harry and Ruth Krieger; m. Carol B. Bachenheimer, Aug. 19, 1967; 1 child, Paul Matthew. BA cum laude, Cornell U., 1965; JD cum laude, Harvard U., 1968. Bar: N.Y. 1971, U.S. Dist. Ct. (so. dist.) N.Y., U.S. Supreme Ct. 1974.3. Legal adviser to Ethiopian Govt., 1968-70; assoc. Simpson Thacher & Bartlett, NYC, 1970-73, Fried Frank Harris Shriver & Jacobson, London, 1973-75, ptnr. NYC, 1977—; gen. counsel, mng. dir. AEA Investors LLC, NYC, 2003—. Mem. ABA, Assn. Bar City N.Y. Office: Fried Frank Harris Shriver & Jacobson 1 New York Plz Fl 22 New York NY 10004-1980 also: AEA Investors LLC 65 East 55th St New York NY 10022 Office Phone: 212-859-8230. Business E-Mail: kriegsa@ffhsj.com.

KRIEGSMAN, ALAN M., arts critic; b. NYC, Feb. 28, 1928; s. Harry Pickel and May (Cohn) K.; m. Sali Ann Ribakove, Nov. 28, 1957. Student, MIT, 1945—46; BS, Columbia U., 1951, MA, 1953. Lectr. in music Columbia U., NYC, 1955-60; music and performing arts critic San Diego Union, 1960-65; asst. to the pres. Juilliard Sch., NYC, 1965-66; music and performing arts critic Washington Post, 1966-74, dance critic, 1974-96, critic emeritus, 1996—. Advisor-cons. vis. com. on arts and humanities, MIT, 1976-86; vis. lectr. Dance Critics Conf., Am. Dance Festival; adjudicator Pulitzer Prize juries in music, criticism, feature writing, 1980-94; bd. dirs. Choo-San Goh & H. Robert Magee Found., 1996—. Contbr. articles on performing arts to various publs. Mem. leadership group nat. dance/media project UCLA, 1996-2000. With U.S. Army, 1946-47. Fulbright scholar U. Vienna, 1956-57; recipient Pulitzer prize in Criticism, 1976, Metro DC Dance awards, spl. citation for inestimable contbns., 2002, Trustees award Dance/USA, 2004. Mem. Dance Inst. Washington (bd. dirs. 1996—), Dance Critics Assn. (bd. dirs. 1996-98), Cunningham Dance Found. (bd. dirs. 1999—). Democrat. Jewish. Avocations: piano, mathematics, science. Home: 4701 Willard Ave Apt 1013 Chevy Chase MD 20815-4622 Home Phone: 301-657-3695; Office Phone: 301-657-3695. Personal E-mail: amkmike@verizon.net.

KRIEGSMAN, EDWARD MICHAEL, lawyer; b. Bridgeport, Conn., Oct. 29, 1965; s. Irving Martin and Marlene Sonya (Kates) K.; m. Meryl Gail Dennis, June 11, 1989; children: Barry Alan, David Jacob, Rachel Lynn. BS in Biology, MIT, 1986; JD, U. Pa., 1989. Bar: Pa. 1989, U.S. Patent and Trademark Office 1989, Mass. 1990, U.S. Ct. Appeals (Fed. cir.) 1990, U.S. Dist. Ct. Mass. 1992. Assoc. Finnegan, Henderson, Farabow, et al, Washington, 1989-90; ptnr. Kriegsman & Kriegsman, Framingham, Mass., 1990—. Mem. ABA, Am. Intellectual Property Law Assn., Mass. Bar Assn., Fed. Cir. Bar Assn., Boston Patent Law Assn., South Middlesex Bar Assn. Jewish. Avocations: reading, sports. Home: 103 Richard Rd Holliston MA 01746-1213 Office: Kriegsman & Kriegsman 30 Turnpike Rd Ste 9 Southborough MA 01772 Office Phone: 508-481-3500. Business E-Mail: edward.kriegsman@kriegsmanlaw.com.

KRIEGSMAN, SALI ANN, performing arts executive, consultant, writer; b. NYC, Apr. 16, 1936; d. Aaron and Charlotte (Pomeranz) Ribakove; m. Alan M. Kriegsman, Nov. 28, 1957. MA, Goddard Coll., 1976. Rsch. assoc. Scripps Clinic and Rsch. Found., La Jolla, Calif., 1961-65; exec. editor Am. Film Inst., Washington, 1969-74; asst. prof. George Washington U., Washington, 1979-80; dance cons. Smithsonian Instn., Washington, 1979—84; dir. dance program NEA, Washington, 1986-95; exec. dir. Jacob's Pillow Dance Festival, Becket, Mass., 1995-98. Writer An Evening of Dance, In Performance at the White House, Sta. WETA-TV, 1998; mem. arts acad. adv. com. Coll. Bd., 1996-97; mem. nat. dance and media project leadership group UCLA, 1996-2000; mem. steering com. Am. Assembly Art, Tech. and Intellectual Property, 2000-02; sr. advisor Digital Dance Libr., 2002-03. Author: Modern Dance in America: The Bennington Years, 1981; contbr.: Britannica Book Of The Year, 1984-86; contbg. author: International Encyclopedia of Dance, 1998. Bd. dirs. Mass. Mus. Contemporary Art, 1995-97, Meredith Monk/The House Found., 2001—; pres. Dance Heritage Coalition, 1999-2000. Recipient Flo-Bert award N.Y. Com. To Celebrate Nat. Tap Dance Day, 1997, Oklahoma City U. Preservation of Heritage Am. Dance award, 1999, Tap Preservation award, N.Y.C. Tap Festival, 2002, Tradition in Tap award, 2006; fellow Va. Ctr. for Creative Arts, 2003. E-mail: saliann@verizon.net.

KRIENS, SCOTT G., information technology executive; BA, Calif. State U., Hayward. Co-founder StrataCom, Inc., 1986—96; chmn., CEO Juniper

Networks, Inc., Mountain View, Calif., 1996—. Dir. VeriSign, Inc., Equinox, Inc. Office: Juniper Networks Inc 1194 N Mathilda Ave Sunnyvale CA 94089-1206*

KRIER, JAMES EDWARD, law educator, writer; b. Milw., Oct. 19, 1939; s. Ambrose Edward and Genevieve Ida (Behling) Krier; m. Gayle Marian Grimsrud, Mar. 22, 1962 (div.); children: Jennifer, Amy; m. Wendy Louise Wilkes, Apr. 20, 1974; children: Andrew Wilkes-Krier, Patrick Wilkes-Krier. BS, U. Wis., 1961, JD, 1966. Bar: Wis. 1966, U.S. Ct. Claims 1968. Law clk. to chief justice Calif. Supreme Ct., San Francisco, 1966-67; assoc. Arnold & Porter, Washington, 1967-69; acting prof., then prof. law UCLA, 1969-78, 80-83; prof. law Stanford U., Calif., 1978-80, U. Mich. Law Sch., Ann Arbor, 1983—, Earl Warren DeLano prof., 1988—. Cons. Calif. Inst. Tech., EPA; mem. pesticide panel NAS, 1972—75, mem. com. energy and the environment, 1975—77. Author: (book) Environmental Law and Policy, 1971; author: (with Stewart) Environmental Law and Policy, 2d edit., 1978; author: (with Ursin) Pollution and Policy, 1977; author: (with Dukeminier) Property, 1981; author: (with Alexander and Schill) Property, 6th edit., 2006; contbr. articles to profl. jours. Served to lt. US Army, 1961—63. Mem.: Order of Coif, Artus, Phi Kappa Phi. Office: U Mich Law Sch 625 S State St Ann Arbor MI 48109-1215 Office Phone: 734-763-4701. Business E-Mail: jkrier@umich.edu.

KRIESBERG, IRVING, painter; b. Chgo., Mar. 13, 1919; s. Max and Bessie (Turner) K.; m. Ruth Miller, Apr. 5, 1921 (div. 1973); children: Nell, Matthias; m. Barbara Nimri Aziz, Dec. 2, 1974. BFA, Sch. of Art Inst. Chgo., 1941; MA, NYU, 1972. Tchr. Yale U. Grad. Sch., 1962-71; dir. state-wide honors studio program SUNY, 1972-77; tchr. painting Columbia U. Grad. Sch., 1977-79; tchr. painting and ceramics La. State U. Grad. Sch., 1980; Beaumont prof. painting Washington U., St. Louis, 1982; instr. terra-cotta, vis. artist Skidmore Coll., 1989; vis. artist painting Vt. Studio Sch., 1989; instr. sculpture Appalachian Ctr. for Crafts, 1992. Conductor lectrs. and workshops throughout the U.S. and India. Author: Looking at Pictures, 1955, Art, The Visual Experience, 1965, Working with Color, 1987; one-man shows at Guggenheim Mus., 1972, Fairweather-Hardin, Chgo., 1979, Dintenfass Gallery, N.Y.C., 1980-82, Everson Mus., Syracuse, N.Y., 1980, Rose Mus., Brandeis, 1980, Washington U. Art Mus., St. Louis, 1982, Graham Modern Gallery, N.Y.C., 1985, Montclair (N.J.) Art Mus., 1986; represented in permanent collections at Balt. Mus. Art, Cin. Mus. Art, Mus. Modern Art, N.Y.C., Whitney Mus., N.Y.C., Corcoran Gallery, Washington, Rose Mus., Brandeis, Nat. Gallery Am. Art, Washington, Rep. Peter Findlay Gall, N.Y.C. Recipient awards Ford Found., 1965, Fulbright, 1965-66, N.Y. State, 1974, 78, 91, NEA, 1984, Guggenheim, 1976. Mem. NAD (academician, 1994-)

KRIESBERG, LOUIS, sociologist, educator; b. Chgo., July 30, 1926; s. Max and Bessie (Turner) K.; m. Lois Ablin, Aug. 23, 1959; children: Daniel A., Joseph A. PhB, U. Chgo., 1947, MA, 1950, PhD, 1953. Instr. sociology sch. gen. studies Columbia U., NYC, 1953-56; Fulbright rsch. scholar U. Cologne, Germany, 1956-57; sr. fellow in law and behavior scis. U. Chgo., 1957-58; sr. study dir. Nat. Opinion Rsch. Ctr., 1958-62; assoc. prof. dept. sociology, 1962-67, Syracuse (N.Y.) U., 1962-67, prof., 1967-97, prof. emeritus, 1997—, dir. program on analysis and resolution conflicts, 1985-94, Maxwell prof. social conflict studies, 1994-97, Maxwell prof. emeritus social conflict studies, 1997—. Author: Mothers in Poverty, 1970, Social Inequality, 1979, Social Conflicts, 1973, rev. edit., 1982, International Conflict Resolution, 1992, Constructive Conflicts, 1998, 3d edit., 2006; editor: Social Processes in International Relations, 1968, Research in Social Movements, Conflicts, and Change, vols. 1-14, 1978-92; co-editor: Intractable Conflicts and Their Transformation, 1989, Timing the De-escalation of International Conflicts, 1991. Cons., lectr. Syracuse Area Middle East Dialogue Group. Grantee U.S. Inst. Peace, MacArthur Found., Hewlett Found. Fellow Am. Sociol. Assn. (chair peace and war sect. 1990-91, Disting. Career award 1993), Internat. Peace Rsch. Assn. (co-chair internat. conflict resolution 1989-94), Internat. Studies Assn. (chair peace studies sect. 1998-99), Internat. Sociol. Assn. (rsch. com. 1, exec. com. 1982-86), Internat. Soc. Polit. Psychology (governing coun. 1992-94), Soc. for Study Social Problems (pres. 1983-84, Lee Founders award 1990), Ea. Sociol. Soc. (exec. com. 1977-81), Peace Studies Assn. (ann. award 1995), NY State Sociol. Assn. (Disting. Svc. award 1999), Peace and Justice Assn. (Peace Scholar award 2006). Jewish. Avocations: swimming, travel. Office: Syracuse Univ Maxwell Sch Citizenship PARC Eggers 400 Syracuse NY 13244 Business E-Mail: lkriesbe@syr.edu.

KRIESBERG, SIMEON M., lawyer; b. Washington, June 4, 1951; s. Martin and Harriet M. K.; m. Martha L. Kahn, Jan. 9, 1994. AB, Harvard U., 1973; M in Pub. Affairs, Princeton U., 1977; JD, Yale U., 1977. Bar: D.C. 1977, U.S. Dist. Ct. D.C. 1978, U.S. Ct. Appeals (D.C. cir.) 1978, U.S. Ct. Internat. Trade 1979, U.S. Ct. Appeals (Fed. cir.) 1981, U.S. Supreme Ct. 1982. Assoc. Leva, Hawes, Symington, Martin & Oppenheimer, Washington, 1977—83; sr. counsel internat. trade Sears World Trade Inc., Washington, 1983—85, v.p., gen. counsel, 1985—87; ptnr. Mayer Brown Rowe & Maw LLP, Washington, 1987—. Professorial lectr. Nitze Sch. Advanced Internat. Studies, Johns Hopkins U., 1991-93; mem. binat. dispute resolution panel under U.S.-Can. Free Trade Agreement, 1990-92; guest scholar Brookings Inst., 1992-93; mem. roster of dispute resolution panelists under NAFTA, 1996-2004. Mem. editorial adv. com. Internat. Legal Materials, 1991-97; article and book rev. editor Yale Law Jour., 1976-77. Officer or dir. Washington Hebrew Congregation, 1980-94, Jewish Cmty. Rels. Coun. Greater Washington, 1986-94, Interfaith Conf. Met. Washington, 1989—, Wash. D.C. Jewish Cmty. Ctr., 1994-07, Mid-Atlantic coun. Union Reform Judaism, 1994-02; mem. Washington chpt. Am. Jewish Com., 2007—. Recipient Pro Bono Svc. award Internat. Human Rights Law Group, 1991, Lawrence L. O'Connor medal Sears, Roebuck and Co., 1984. Mem. ABA, Am. Law Inst., Am. Soc. Internat. Law, D.C. Bar. Office: Mayer Brown Rowe & Maw LLP 1909 K St NW Washington DC 20006-1101 Business E-Mail: skriesberg@mayerbrownrowe.com.

KRIESEL, DEANNA, education educator; m. Ronald Kriesel, 1959; 1 foster child; 1 child. AA, Chaffey Coll., 1960; BA, LaVerne U., Calif., 1962; MA, Sam Houston State U., 1984. Cert. K-3 reading specialist Calif., tchr. learning disabled, mentally handicapped, other health impaired Okla., elem. edn., mid. sch. math. and social studies, psychometrist Okla. 3d grade tchr. Pomona Sch. Dist., Calif., 1962—66; 3d-4th grade tchr. Upland Sch. Dist., Calif., 1966—70, tchr. learning disabled, 1973—74; pre-sch. tchr. 1st Ch. God, Pomona, 1972—73, sec., treas. Sacramento, 1976—81; tchr. jr. HS learning disabled Klein Sch. Dist., Houston, 1981—85, Moore Sch. Dist., Okla., 1985—90, psychometrist, 1990—99; asst. prof. tchr. edn. Mid-Am. Christian U., Oklahoma City, 1999—. Supporter Angel Tree Prison Fellowship, Oklahoma City, 1996—, Deanna's Early Childhood Devel. Ctr., Kenya; bd. dirs., vol. Godside Ministries to Inner City Youth, Denver, 1998—. Finalist medal for excellence, Okla. Found. for Excellence, 1991. Mem.: Internat. Reading Assn., Coun. for Exceptional Children, Christian Educators Assn. Internat. (chpt. officer 1962—). Republican. Office: Mid-Am Christian U 3500 SW 119th St Oklahoma City OK 73170 Business E-Mail: dkriesel@macu.edu.

KRIFTCHER, NOEL N., humanities educator, director; b. Bklyn., June 14, 1939; s. Irving Sol and Rose Cohen Kriftcher; m. Bernadette M. Russo, Sept. 2, 1983; children: Eric L., Brian S., Dana L. Kriftcher Brancaccio. BS in English, NYU, 1959; MS in Edn., Hofstra U., Hempstead, NY, 1971, profl. diploma in ednl. adminstrn., 1972, EdD in ednl. adminstrn., 1978. Cert. tchr. English NYC, 1959, prin. NY, 1969, sch. adminstr. and supr. NY, 1969, sch. adminstr. NY, 1972. Tchr. Jr. HS 49, Bklyn., 1959—64, Jr. HS 192, Queens, NY, 1964—65, Springfield Gardens HS, Queens, 1965—71; asst. prin. August Martin HS, Queens, 1971—74; exec. asst. to supt. NYC Bd. Edn., Queens, 1974—80; prin. Seward Pk. HS, NYC, 1980—88; supt. high schs. Bklyn. and Staten Island, NY, 1988—96; exec. dir. Packard Ctr. Tech. and Ednl. Alliances, Industry prof. humanities Polytechnic U., Bklyn., 1996—. Pres.-elect HS Prins. Assn. of City of NY, 1985—86, pres., 1986—88; mem. NYC Del. to Austria Ministry of Edn., 1993, 96; supt. Citywide Chair to Increase Sci. Stds. and Achievement, NYC Bd. Edn., 1993—96; coord. Future City Competition, 1998—; dir. Knowledge Workers Ednl. Alliance, 1999—; mem. adv. bd. Acad. Info. Tech., NYC, 1999—; coord. FIRST Robotics Competition, 2002—, FIRST Lego League Competition, 2003—; spkr. in field. Contbr. articles to profl. jours. Mem. adv. bd. Promise Fund, Poly. U., 1997—; vice chmn. policy bd. Staten Island Continuum of Edn., 1988—96; trustee East 55th St. Conservative Synagogue, NYC, 1997—; bd. dirs. NYC Acad. Pub. Edn., 1998—. Recipient Disting. Ednl. Leadership award, Kingsborough CC, Bklyn., 1989, Vienna medal of distinction, City of Vienna, Austria, 1996, Recognition award, ASCE, 2000, Crystal Leadership award in edn., Virtual Enterprises, Internat., 2006; grantee, Consolidated Edison Co., 2003—06, David and Lucile Packard Found., 1995, 1999. Mem.: NY Acad. Pub. Edn., Phi Delta Kappa (Disting. Kappan award 1997). Avocations: book reviewing, golf, travel. Office: Poly U 6 MetroTech Ctr Brooklyn NY 11201 Office Phone: 718-260-3524.

KRIKALEV, SERGEI KONSTANTINOVICH, flight engineer, cosmonaut, researcher; b. Leningrad, Russia, Aug. 27, 1958; s. Konstantin Sergeevich and Nadia Ivanova Krikalev; m. Elena Yurl'vena Terekhina; 1 child, Olga Sergeevna Krikalyova. Degree in Mech. Engring., Leningrad Mech. Inst., 1981. Lab. asst. and sr. lab. asst. Leningrad Mech. Inst., 1980—97; aircraft technician on operation and repair of aircraft and engines All-Union Voluntary Soc. for Assistance to the Army, Air Force and Navy, 1981; with NPO Energia, Russia, 1981—85; cosmonaut Y.A. Gagarin Cosmonauts Tng. Ctr., Russia, 1985—, tng. for flight on Mir space sta., flight engr. Soyuz TM-7 mission, 1988—89, mem. backup crew Mir mission, 1990—92; flight engr. Soyuz TM-12, 1990—91, Soyuz TM-12 and Mir OS, 1991—92; tng. as flight expert of crew No 4 Discovery Orbiter under STS-60 program Johnson Space Ctr., 1992—94; prime mission specialist, mem. crew, STS-60 NASA Space Shuttle Mission, 1994; tng. as back-up cosmonaut of Titov, flight specialist of the Discovery crew-4 under the STS-63 program Johnson Space Ctr., 1994—95; back-up specialist Discovery Orbiter flight 4 under STS-63, 1995; flight engr. ISS-1, 1996; mem. crew STS-88 Endeavor Internat. Space Sta. assembly mission, 1998; mem. Expedition-1 crew, 2000—01; Soyuz and ISS comdr. Expedition 11, 2005. Named Hero of the Soviet Union, Hero of the Russian Fedn., L'Officier de la L'egion d'Honneur (France); recipient Gold Star medal of the Hero of the Soviet Union, Order of Lenin, Order of Friendship of the Peoples, Gold Star medal of the Hero of the Russian Fedn., NASA Spaceflight medal, 1994, 1998, NASA Disting. Svc. medal, Order of Eagle First Class, Assn. of the Russian Manufactuers. Achievements include member of the Soviet and Russian National Aerobatic Flying Teams. Champion of Moscow in 1983 and Champion of the Soviet Union in 1986. Avocations: swimming, bicycling, aerobatic flying, amateur radio operations from space, skiing, windsurfing. Office: Russian Space Agy 42 Shchepkinst 129857 Moscow Russia

KRIKEN, JOHN LUND, architect; b. Calif., July 5, 1938; s. John Erik Nord and Ragnhild (Lund) K.; m. Anne Girard (div.); m. Katherine Koelsch, Aug. 8, 1988. BArch, U. Calif., Berkeley, 1961; MArch, Harvard U., 1968. Ptnr. Skidmore, Owings and Merrill, San Francisco, 1970—2003, cons. ptnr., 2003—. Tchr. Washington U., St. Louis, 1968, U. Calif., Berkeley, 1972, Rice U., Houston, 1979; prof. U. Calif., Berkeley, 2005—; design advisor, chief architect Ho Chi Minh City, Vietnam, 1994—; mem. design rev. bd. Port San Francisco, 1995—. Mem. Bay Conservation and Devel. Commn., Calif., 1984—; mem. Arts Commn. City and County of San Francisco, 1989-95; mem. design rev. bd. Berkeley campus U. Calif., 1986-92; bd. dirs. San Francisco Planning and Rsch., 1995—; vice chair, Eng. and Des. Advisory Panel (EDAP) for the rebuilding pf San Francisco Bay Bridge, 1997—; mem. GSD's alumni coun. Harvard U, 2000—; CED's dean's adv. coun. U. Calif., Berkeley, 2000—; mem. San Francisco Arts Commn., 2006—. Fellow AIA; mem. Am. Inst. Cert. Planners, Sunday Afternoon Watercolor Soc. (founding mem.), Lambda Alpha Internat. Office: Skimore Owings & Merrill 1 Front St San Francisco CA 94111-5303 Office Phone: 415-981-1555.

KRIKORIAN, BLAKE, entrepreneur, consumer electronics company executive; B in Mech. Engring., UCLA, 1989. With General Magic; co-founder, group project mgr. Philips Mobile Computing Group, 1994—98; sr. v.p. Metis Associates (acquired by BSQUARE in 2000), 1998; pres. Mainbrace Corp. (acquired by BSQUARE in 2000), 1998—2000; founder, CEO id8 Group Holdings, Inc., San Mateo, Calif., 2000—04; co-founder, CEO Sling Media, Inc., San Mateo, Calif., 2004—. Spkr. in field. Named one of 50 Who Matter Now, CNNMoney.com Bus. 2.0, 2006. Achievements include with other members of Slingbox Media, Inc., created Slingbox Player, a device that allows a person to watch their own TV from a laptop anywhere in the world; Slingbox Player named one of PC World Innovations in 2006, Business Week Best Products of 2005, Time Best Inventions of 2005, Popular Science Best of What's New 2005 & Laptop Best of CES 2005; Slingbox Player has won awards including Mobile Trax Mobility award-Accessories in 2006 and International Consumer Electronics Show Innovations 2006 Design and Engineering Finalist; Sling Media Inc. was chosen by Fortune as one of the 25 Breakout Companies of 2005 and 2006 ACE award Finalist-Start-up Company of Year. Office: Sling Media Inc 901 Mariners Island Blvd Ste 300 San Mateo CA 94404 Office Phone: 650-293-8000. Office Fax: 650-378-4422.*

KRIKORIAN, JASON, consumer electronics company executive; B in Psychology, U. Calif. Berkeley, 1989; MBA, JD, U. Va. With Hale and Dorr, Boston; with securities law dept. Wilson Sonsini Goodrich & Rosati, Palo Alto, Calif.; with Boston Consulting Group; ptnr., v.p. id8 Group Holdings, Inc., San Mateo, Calif., 2000—04; co-founder, CFO, v.p. bus. develop. Sling Media, Inc., San Mateo, Calif., 2004—. Spkr. in field. Achievements include with other members of Slingbox Media, Inc., created Slingbox, a device that allows a person to watch their own TV from a laptop anywhere in the world; Slingbox Player named one of PC World Innovations in 2006, Business Week Best Products of 2005, Time Best Inventions of 2005, Popular Science Best of What's New 2005 & Laptop Best of CES 2005; Slingbox Player has won awards including Mobile Trax Mobility award-Accessories in 2006 and International Consumer Electronics Show Innovations 2006 Design and Engineering Finalist; Sling Media Inc. was chosen by Fortune as one of the 25 Breakout Companies of 2005 and 2006 ACE award Finalist-Start-up Company of Year. Office: Sling Media Inc 901 Mariners Island Blvd Ste 300 San Mateo CA 94404

KRIKOS, GEORGE ALEXANDER, pathologist, educator; b. Old Phaleron, Greece, Sept. 17, 1922; came to U.S., 1946; s. Alexios and Helen (Spyropoulou) K.; m. Aspasia Manoni, June 22, 1949; children: Helen, Alexandra, Alexios. DDS, U. Pa., 1949; PhD, U. Rochester, 1959; PhD (hon.), U. Athens, Greece, 1981. Asst. prof. pathology U. Pa. Sch. Dentistry, 1958-61, assoc. prof., 1961-67, prof., 1967-68, chmn. dept., 1964-68; assoc. prof. oral pathology U. Pa. Grad. Sch., 1962-68, prof. oral pathology, 1968; prof. pathobiology Sch. Dentistry, U. Colo., Denver, 1968-75, chmn. dept. pathobiology, 1968-73, prof. oral biology, 1975-86, clin. prof. oral biology, 1986-91, prof. oral biology emeritus, 1991—, asst. dean basic sci. affairs, 1973-75, asso. dean oral biology affairs, 1975-76. Vis. prof. Sch. Dentistry, U. Athens, 1980-81; mem. dental study sect. NIH, 1966-70; mem. cancer com. Colo.-Wyo. Regional Med. Program, 1970-72; cons. oral pathology Denver VA Hosp., 1970-72 Served with AUS, 1949-54. Mem. Am. Soc. Investigative Pathology, Internat. Assn. Dental Rsch., Sigma Xi. Home: 350 Ivy St Denver CO 80220-5855

KRILL, KAY (KATHERINE LAWTHER KRILL), apparel executive; b. Wilmington, NC, Mar. 27, 1955; d. James Wyatt and Katherine (King) L.; m. Charles Philip McEvoy III, Sept. 12, 1981 (div. Oct. 1985); 2 children. BA in Psychology and Econs., Agnes Scott Coll., Atlanta, 1977. From asst. buyer to buyer Macy's Dept. Store, Atlanta, 1977-81; buyer Talbot's, Hingham, Mass., 1981-84, dir. catalog merchandising, 1984-88; v.p. merchandising Mark Shale, Burr Ridge, Ill., 1988—90; exec. v.p. gen. merchandising mgr. women's ops. Hartmarx Corp., 1990—92; pres. Carroll Reed, 1992—94; merchandising v.p. separates, dresses and petites Ann Taylor Stores Corp., 1994—96, sr. v.p. gen. merchandise mgr. Ann Taylor Loft, 1996—98, exec. v.p. Ann Taylor Loft, 1998—2001, pres. Ann Taylor Loft, 2001—04, pres., 2004—, mem. bd. dirs., 2004—, CEO, 2005—. Mem. Jr. League Atlanta, 1977-81, Boston, 1981-88, Chgo., 1988; mem. bd. trustees Agnes Scott Coll., 1994-00; chairperson bd. visitors Bolles Sch., Jacksonville, Fla., 1992-98. Mem. Fashion Group Boston, Nat. Assn. Female Execs., Direct Mktg. Assn. Clubs: East Bank (Chgo.). Republican. Episcopalian. Avocations: tennis, aerobics, shopping. Office: Ann Taylor Stores Corp 7 Times Sq New York NY 10036*

KRIM, MATHILDE, medical educator; b. Como, Italy, July 9, 1926; came to U.S. BS, U. Geneva, Switzerland, 1948, PhD, 1953; DSc (hon.), Long Island U., 1987; LLD (hon.), Columbia U., 1988; DSc (hon.), Brandeis U., 1989; DHL (hon.), Southeastern Mass. U., 1990; DSc. (hon.), Tulane U., 1990; DHL (hon.), SUNY, Stonybrook, 1991; DSc (hon.), Columbia Coll., 1992, Dartmouth Coll., 2005. Asst. genetic sect., dept. exptl. biology Weizmann Inst. Sci., Rehovot, Israel, 1953-54, jr. scientist, 1954-57, rsch. assoc., 1957-59; rsch. assoc.divsn. virus rsch. Cornell Med. Coll., NYC, 1959-62; rsch. assoc. Sloan Kettering Inst. Cancer Rsch., NYC, 1962-68, assoc., 1968-75, assoc. mem., 1975-85, co-head interferon evaluation program, 1975-81, head interferon lab, 1981-85; assoc. rsch. scientist dept. pediatrics St. Luke's-Roosevelt Hosp. Ctr. and Columbia U., NYC, 1986-90; adjunct prof. pub. health Columbia U., NYC, 1990—; founding co-chair, chmn. bd., CEO Am. Found. for AIDS Rsch., NYC, 1985—2005, founding chmn., bd. dir., 2005—. Bd. dirs. AIDSFILMS, Am. Com. for Weizmann Inst. Sci., Nat. Biomed. Rsch. Found.; trustee Scientists' Inst. for Pub. Information, Feinberg Grad. Sch. Weizmann Inst. Sci., African-Am. Inst.; mem. adv. panel on higher edn., New York, 1965, President's Com. on Mental Retardation, 1966-69, jury Albert D. Lasker Rsch. awards 1968-71, 78—, adv. bd. Health Profls. for Polit. Action, 1968-70, adv. com. to Sec. of HEW on Health Proteciton and Disease Prevention, 1969-70, Coun. NEH, 1969-73, Panel of Cons. on Cancer, Com. Labor and Pub. Welfare, U.S.Senate, 1970-71, adv. com. Nat. Colorectal Cancer Program NIH, 1971-73, working group develo. rsch. segment Virus Cancer Program NIH, 1971-74, review com. "A" Virus Cancer Program NIH, 1974-77, adv. com. Inst. Internat. Edn., 1974—, adv. com. Program of Sci., Tech., and Human Values NEH, 1974-78, U.S. Nat. Commn. for UNESCO, 1979-80, adv. com. World Rehabilitation Fund, 1978-82, Interferon Clin. Adv. Com. Schering-Plough Corp., 1980-85, Bristol Labs. Adv. Panel on Biological Response Modifiers, 1981-84, sci. adv. com. Am. Found. AIDS Rsch., 1985—, Com. of 100 for Nat. Health Ins., AIDS task force Am. Assn. Sex Educators, Counselors and Therapists, 1985—, rsch. adv. coun. Nat. Orgn. for Rare Disorders Inc., 1985—, AIDS Health Edn. Risk Reduction Consultation, Ctrs. for Disease Control, 1986, task force on Chemotherapeutics, Nat. Inst. of Allergy and Infectious Diseases, NIH, 1986, met. area adv. com. Lower Manhattan AIDS consortium, 1986—, scientific adv. bd. Nat. Coalition on Immune System Disorders, 1986—, adv. com. The Village Nursing Home, 1986—, sect. for the study of ethical, legal and social issues HIV Ctr. for Clin. and Behavioral Studies, 1987—, AIDS Rsch. Ctr., 1987—, bd. advisors Nat. Lawyers Guild AIDS Network, 1987—, AIDS adv. panel Planned Parenthood Fed. Am., 1988—, nat. adv. com. Nat. Communtiy AIDS Partnership, 1988—, adv. com. Women and AIDS Resource Network, 1988—; commr. Pres.'s Commn. for the Study of Ethical Problems in Medicine and Biomedical and Behavioral Rsch., adv. bd. LOVE HEALS, 1989—, adv. bd. Internat. Alliance for Haiti, 1989—, adv. bd. AIDS-AUFKLARUNG, Frankfurt, Germany, 1990—, internat. com. Lottare Informare Formare Educare, Rome, Italy, 1990—, adv. coun. Columbia Sch. Pub. Health, 1990—, AIDS adv. panel, Med. Soc. State of New York, 1992—. Editor (with others) Mediation of Cellular Immunity in Cancer by Immune Modifiers: Progress in Cancer Research and Therapy, 1981;mem. editorial bd. The Aids Record; assoc. editor Cancer Investigation, Interferon Newsletter, Aids Care; contbr. articles to profl. jours. Bd. dirs. Nat. Med. Assn. Found., 1968-69, Inst. of Soc., Ethics, and the Life Scis. (The Hastings Ctr.), 1979-89; trustee Nat. Urban League, 1966-72, The Rockefeller Found., 1971-84, AIDS Med. Found. 1983-89, chairperson; vice chmn. Citizens Organized Against Drug Abuse, 1966; exec. sec. Am. Com for Assistance to Tunisia, 1968-69; dir. at large Am. Cancer Soc., 1970-72. Fellow NAS 1977; scholar, U. Geneva, 1947-52; recipient Spirit of Achievement award Nat. Women's Divsn. Albert Einstein Coll. Medicine, 1972, Humanitarian award Fund for Human Dignity, 1985, award for contbns. to civic life Women's City Club, 1986, John and Samuel Bard award in medicine and sci., 1986, Human Rights Campaign Fund award, 1986, Elizabeth Cutter Morrow award, City of New York YWCA, 1986, Jack Dempsey Humanitarian award St. Clare's Hosp. and Health Ctr., 1986, 10 Ams. Who've Made a Difference award Better Health and Living Mag., 1987, Eleanor Roosevelt Leadership award NOW, 1987, Achievement award Am. Assn. of Physicians for Human Rights, 1987, Humanist Disting. Svc. award Am. Humanist Assn., 1987, Hall of Fame award Internat. Women's Forum, 1987, Commitment to Life award, AIDS project L.A., 1987, Frontrunner award Sara Lee Corp., 1988, Exceptional achievement award, Women's Project and Prodns., 1988, Pres.'s award Am. Equity Assn., 1988, Medical award Hassadah, New York, 1988, award for Pioneering Achievements in Health and Higher Edn. Charles A. Dana Found., 1988, gold medal of honor Casita Maria, 1988, Caring award Stewart McKinney Found., 1988, Outstanding Mother award Nat. Mother's Day Com., 1989, Myrtle Wreath Humantiarian award Nat. Hassadah, 1991, Edwin C. Whitehead award Nat. Ctr. Health Edn., 1991, M. Carey Thomas award Bryn Mawr Coll., 1991, Scientic Freedom and Responsibility award AAAS, 1994; named Woman of Distinction Birmingham (Ala.) So. Coll., 1987, Dallas Cares Benefit honoree, 1989, 100 New York Women Barnard Coll., 1989. Mem. NAS, NAACP, Am. Assn. Advancement of Sci., Soc. Biological Therapy, Am. Soc. Microbiology, Internat. Soc. for Interferon Rsch., Am. Humanists Assn.

KRIMIGIS, STAMATIOS MIKE, physicist, researcher, educator, engineering executive, consultant; b. Chios, Greece, Sept. 10, 1938; s. Michael and Angeliki (Tsetseris) K.; m. Maria Anastasopoulou, 1990; children: Michael, John. BS in Physics, U. Minn., 1961; MS in Physics, U. Iowa, 1963, PhD in Physics, 1965. Rsch. assoc. dept. physics and astronomy U. Iowa, Iowa City, 1965—66, asst. prof., 1966—68; supr. space physics sect. Johns Hopkins U. Applied Physics Lab., Laurel, 1968-74, supr. space physics and instrumentation group, 1974-81, chief scientist space dept., 1980-90, head space dept., 1991—2004, head emeritus, 2004—; mem. Space Sci. Bd., Nat. Acad. Scis. NRC, 1983-86; chmn. com. on solar and space physics, 1983-86; cons. Mem. steering com. space sci. working group Assn. Am. Univs., 1983-85; mem. space sci. and applications adv. com., NASA, 1987-91, mem. solar sys. exploration subcom., 1998-01; prin. investigator several MASA missions, including Voyager 1, 2 and Cassini. Contbr. over 400 articles to sci. jours.; author book chpts. on solar, interplanetary and magnetospheric plasma physics, cosmic rays, magnetospheres of Earth, Jupiter, Saturn, Uranus and Neptune. Recipient Exceptional Sci. Achievement medal NASA, 1981, 86, Acad. prize Am. Hellenic

Ednl. Progressive Assn., 1994, COSPAR Space Sci. award, 2002. Fellow AIAA, AAAS, Am. Geophys. Union, Am. Phys. Soc.; mem. Internat. Acad. Astronautics (Space Sci. award 1994), Athens Acad. Greek Orthodox. Home: 613 Cobblestone Ct Silver Spring MD 20905-5806 Office: Johns Hopkins U Applied Physics Lab Laurel MD 20723-6099 E-mail: tom.krimigis@jhuapl.edu.

KRIMM, SAMUEL, physicist, researcher; b. Morristown, NJ, Oct. 19, 1925; s. Irving and Ethel (Stein) K.; m. Marilyn Marcy Neveloff, June 26, 1949; children: David Robert, Daniel Joseph. BS in Chemistry, summa cum laude, Poly. Inst. Bklyn., 1947; MA in Phys. Chemistry, Princeton U., 1949, PhD in Phys. Chemistry, 1950. Postdoctoral fellow U. Mich., Ann Arbor, 1950-52, mem. faculty, 1952—, prof. physics, 1963-2001, prof. emeritus, 2001—, mem. Macromolecular Rsch. Ctr., 1968—, mem. biophysics rsch. divsn., 1962—, chmn. biophysics rsch. div., 1976-86, dir. program in protein structure and design, 1985-94, assoc. dean research Coll. Lit., Sci. and Arts, 1972-75. Chmn. infrared spectroscopy Gordon Rsch. Conf., 1968; mem. NAS/NRC NBS Polymers divsn. Evaluation Panel, 1973-76, chmn., 1975-76; materials rsch. adv. com. NSF, 1981-86, chmn., 1984; mem. DOE Coun. on Material Scis., 1986-89; program adv. com. Internat. Conf. on Raman Spectroscopy, 1984-86, exec. com., 1988-90; Fraser Price Meml. lectr., 1988; disting. lectr. Inst. Materials Sci. U. Conn., 1995; com. on promoting rsch. collaboration NAS/IOM, 1987-89; cons. B.F. Goodrich, 1956-86, Allied 1963-93, Monsanto, 1987-92; vis. prof. U. Cambridge, 1962-63, Weizmann Inst., 1970, U. Mainz, 1983, U. Paris, 1991. Author papers on vibrational spectroscopy, x-ray diffraction studies of natural and synthetic polymers, potential energy function devel.; mem. editorial bd. Jour. Polymer Sci. Polymer Physics Edn., 1967-99; Biopolymers, 1973-2006; Macromolecules, 1968-71; Jour. Macromolecular Sci.-Rev. Macromolecular Chemistry, 1983-92. Served with USNR, 1944-46. Recipient Humboldt award, 1983; U. Mich. Disting. Faculty Achievement award, 1986; Textile Research Inst. fellow, 1947-50; NSF sr. postdoctoral fellow, 1962-63; sr. fellow U. Mich. Soc. Fellows, 1971-76 Fellow AAAS, Am. Phys. Soc. (High Polymer Physics prize 1977, chmn. div. biol. physics 1979, div. councilor 1981, exec. com. 1983, planning com. 1992); mem. Am. Chem. Soc., Biophys. Soc., Coblentz Soc. (hon., bd. mgr. 1967-70). Office: U Mich Biophysics Rsch Divsn 930 N University Ave Ann Arbor MI 48109 Home Phone: 734-663-1978. Business E-Mail: skrimm@umich.edu.

KRING, TIM (RICHARD TIMOTHY KRING), television producer, writer; b. El Dorado, Calif., July 9, 1957; m. Lisa L. Kring; children: Amelia, Ethan. Studied film, Allen Hancock Jr. Coll.; BA in Religious Studies, U. Santa Barbara; MFA, U. So. Calif. Film Sch. Writer: TV series Knight Rider, 1982, Misfits of Science (1 episode), 1985, writer, co-executive prodr.: TV series L.A. Doctors, 1998, writer: TV series Chicago Hope, 1994 (nominee for Outstanding Drama Series, Emmy award, 1997); prodr.: (TV series) Chicago Hope, 1996—97; supervising prodr. (TV series) Chicago Hope, 1997; writer, co-exec. prodr.: TV series Providence (5 episodes), 1999—2001, writer, exec. prodr.: TV series Crossing Jordan, 2001—07, creator, exec. prodr., writer: TV series Heroes, 2006— (Furure Classic award, TV Land award, 2007, nominee, new series, Writers Guild Awards, 2007), writer: screenplays Teen Wolf Too, 1987, Bay Coven, 1987, Without Consent, 1994, Falling For You, 1995, Sublet, 1998, writer, co-creator: Strange World, 1998; actor: No Regrets, 2003. Recipient Rave award-TV, WIRED Mag., 2007. Avocation: collecting acoustic guitars.*

KRINGEL, JEROME HOWARD, lawyer; b. Milw., Apr. 2, 1940; s. Lester E. and Irene A. (Kreutzer) K.; m. Mary Kathleen McAuliffe, Sept. 8, 1962; children: Anne, Mary Karen, Jennifer, Elisabeth, Katherine. AB, Marquette U., 1962; postgrad., U. Heidelberg, Germany, 1963; LLB, Yale U., 1966. Bar: Wis. 1966, U.S. Dist. Ct. (ea. dist.) Wis. 1966, U.S. Ct. Appeals (7th cir.) 1966. Ptnr., coord. bus. practice Michael, Best & Friedrich, Milw., 1966—. Trustee Shorewood (Wis.) Village Bd., 1974-80. Mem. ABA, Wis. Bar Assn. (chmn. bus. law sect. 1990-91), Milw. Bar Assn. Office: Michael Best & Friedrich LLP 100 E Wisconsin Ave Ste 3300 Milwaukee WI 53202-4108 Business E-Mail: jhkringel@michaelbest.com.

KRINGEN, JOHN A., federal agency administrator; b. 1947; PhD in Polit. Sci., U. Minn. Joined CIA, 1978, with Directorate of Intelligence, 1978, dir. Crime and Narcotics Ctr., dep. dir. for intelligence, 2005—; dir. Office of Imagery Analysis Nat. Imagery and Mapping Agency, 1998—2000. Prof. U. Md. Office: CIA Office of Pub Affairs Washington DC 20505

KRINSKY, CAROL HERSELLE, art historian, educator; b. NYC, June 2, 1937; d. David and Jane (Gartman) Herselle; m. Robert Daniel Krinsky, Jan. 25, 1959; 2 children. BA, Smith Coll., 1957; MA, NYU, 1960, PhD, 1965. Mem. faculty NYU, 1965—, assoc. prof. art history, 1973-78, prof., 1978—; Frederic Lindley Morgan prof. U. Louisville, 2001. Author: Vitruvius de Architectura, 1521. 1969, Rockefeller Center, 1978, Synagogues of Europe, 1985, rev. edit., 1996, Gordon Bunshaft of Skidmore, Owings & Merrill, 1988, Europas Synagogen, 1988, Contemporary Native American Architecture, 1996; contbr. articles to profl. jours. Bd. dirs. Internat. Survey Jewish Monuments, Syracuse, N.Y., 1981—, Soc. Archtl. Historians, 1978-80, 86-89, The Mac Dowell Colony, Inc., 1989—, Jewish Heritage Coun. World Monuments Fund; co-chair seminar on the city Columbia U., 1993-95. Grantee Am. Coun. Learned Socs., 1981, Nat. Endowment for the Arts, 1993; recipient Arnold Brunner award NYC chpt. AIA, 1990. Fellow Soc. Archtl. Historians (pres. 1984-86, pres. NYC chpt. 1977-79); mem. Coll. Art Assn. (Disting. Tchg. of Art History award 2004), Planning History Group, Am. Urban History Assn., Internat. Ctr. Medieval Art, Women's City Club, Phi Beta Kappa. Office: NYU Dept Art History 100 Washington Sq E Rm 303 New York NY 10003-6688 Office Phone: 212-998-8186. Business E-Mail: chk1@nyu.edu.

KRINSKY, FREDDA S., clinical chemist, consultant; b. Bklyn., May 17, 1952; d. Sam and Priscilla Krinsky. BS in Med. Biology, L.I. U., 1975, MS in Med. Biology, 1979; MBA in Corp. Fin., Adelphi U., 1987. Med. technologist Johns Hopkins Hosp., Balt., 1975-78; clin. chemist Smith-Kline Clin. Labs., Lake Success, NY, 1980-83; lab. adminstr. Cen. Gen. Hosp., Plainview, NY, 1983-86; cons. Strategies & Techs., Plainview, NY, 1987-96; corp. tech. staff Grumman Corp., Bethpage, NY, 1988-91, legal and patent staff liaison, 1990-91; adminstrv. ops. staff ROLM, Jericho, NY, 1991-92; cons. Chase Manhattan, NYC, 1993-96; CEO Krinsky & Co. LLC, Highlands Ranch, Colo., 1998—. Clin. adj. instr. Sch. of Med. Biology, L.I. U., Greenvale, N.Y., 1983-86; coord. continuing lab. medicine-edn., Johns Hopkins Hosp., Balt., 1976-78. Grantee HEW, 1978-79. Mem. AAAS, Internet C. of C., Rockies Venture Club, Internat. Leadership Coun., Forum of Women Entrepreneurs, Women in Tech. Achievements include development of a database system for tracking intellectual properties, method for facilitating the technology transfer of the inventions within the appropriate strategic business unit for exploitation both internally and externally. Home and Office: 10073 Charissglen Ln Highlands Ranch CO 80126-5526 E-mail: krinskycompany@msn.com.

KRINSKY, ROBERT DANIEL, consulting firm executive; b. Bklyn., Jan. 24, 1937; s. Milton and Josephine E. (Bachrach) K.; m. Carol M. Herselle, Jan. 25, 1959; children: Alice E., John D. BA, Antioch Coll., 1957. Various actuarial positions The Segal Co., NYC, 1954-65, v.p. to exec. v.p., 1966-82, pres., 1982-93, chmn., 1994—2005, chmn. emeritus, 2006—; bd. dirs. Wiss, Janney, Elster Assocs., Inc., 2003—. Mem. working com. Nat. Coordinating Com. for Multi-employer Pension Plans, Washington, 1982—. Trustee Antioch U., Yellow Springs, Ohio, 1983-02, chmn., 1993-02; trustee Moses L. Parshelsky Found., 1982—; bd. dirs. Harbor Festival Found., N.Y.C., 1983-87, Advs. for Youth, 2005-; chmn. Conf. Bd. Chmn. Small Liberal Arts Colls. and Univs., 2000-02; bd. dirs. Elderhostel, Inc., 2001-, vice chmn., 2003-04, chmn., 2004—. Asst. health svc. officer USPHS, 1959-61. Fellow Conf. Actuaries in Pub. Practice; mem. Am. Acad. Actuaries, Soc. Actuaries (assoc.), Assn. Pvt. Pension and Welfare Plans (bd. dirs. 1982—, chmn. 1988-89), Nat. Dance Inst. (bd. dirs. 1987—, chmn. 1988-89, 93-03), Musica Sacra (bd. dirs. 2003-), Century Assn. Office: The Segal Co 1 Park Ave New York NY 10016-5895 Home Phone: 212-475-1482. Personal E-mail: rdkactbird@aol.com. Business E-Mail: rKrinsky@segalco.com.

KRINSKY, YEHUDA, rabbi; b. 1933; m. Devorah Krinsky; children: Sheine, Chana, David; children: Schmaya, Levi. Ordained Rabbi Ctrl. Lubavitch Yeshiva, Brooklyn. Former second rabbi Chabad Lubavitch Hasidic Movement, rabbi, religious leader, CEO. Spkr. in field. Contbr. articles to numerous profl. jours. Named one of The Top 50 Rabbis in America, Newsweek Mag., 2007. Office: Chabad 770 Eastern Pkwy Brooklyn NY 11213 Fax: 718-774-2718.

KRIPPNER, STANLEY CURTIS, psychologist; b. Edgerton, Wis., Oct. 4, 1932; s. Carroll Porter and Ruth Genevieve (Volenberg) Krippner; m. Lelie Anne Harris, June 25, 1966 (div. 2002). BS, U. Wis., 1954; MA, Northwestern U., 1957, PhD, 1961; PhD (hon.), U. Humanistic Studies, San Diego, 1982. Diplomate Am. Bd. Sexology. Speech therapist Warren Pub. Schs. (Ill.), 1954-55, Richmond Pub. Schs. (Va.), 1955-56; dir. Child Study Ctr. Kent (Ohio) State U., 1961-64; dir. dream lab. Maimonides Med. Ctr., Bklyn., 1964-73; prof. of psychology Saybrook Grad. Sch., San Francisco, 1973—. Adj. prof. psychology Calif. Inst. Human Sci., 1994—; vis. prof. U. P.R., 1972, Sonoma State U., 1972-73, U. Life Scis., Bogota, Colombia, 1974, Inst. for Psychodrama and Humanistic Psychology, Caracas, Venezuela, 1975, State U. West Ga., 1976, John F. Kennedy U., 1980-82, Inst. for Rsch. in Biopsychophysics, Curitiba, Brazil, 1990; adj. prof. Calif. Inst. Integral Studies, 1991-97; lectr. Acad. Pedagogical Scis., Moscow, 1971, Acad. Scis., Beijing, 1981, Minas Gerais U., Belo Horizonte, Brazil, 1986-87. Author: (with Montague Ullman) Dream Telepathy, 1973, rev. edit., 1989, Song of the Siren: A Parapsychological Odyssey, 1975, (with Alberto Villoldo) The Realms of Healing, 1976, rev. edit., 1987, 2003, Human Possibilities, 1980, (with Jerry Solfvin) La Science et les Pouvoirs Psychiques de l'Homme, 1986, (with Alberto Villoldo) Healing States, 1987, (with Joseph Dillard) Dreamworking, 1988, (with David Feinstein) Personal Mythology, 1988, (with Patrick Welch) Spiritual Dimensions of Healing, 1992, (with Dennis Thong and Bruce Carpenter) A Psychiatrist in Paradise, 1993, (with David Feinstein) The Mythic Path, 1997, (with Andre de Carvalho) Sonhos Exoticos, 1998, (with Fariba Bogzaron and Andre de Carvalho) Extraordinary Dreams and How to Work with Them, 2002, (with Stephen Kierulff) Becoming Psychic, 2004; editor: Advances in Parapsychological Research, Vol. 1, 1977, Vol. 2, 1978, Vol. 3, 1982, Vol. 4, 1984, Vol. 5, 1987, Vol. 6, 1990, Vol. 7, 1994, Vol. 8, 1997, Psychoenergetic Systems, 1979, Dreamtime and Dreamwork, 1990; co-editor: Galaxies of Life, 1973, The Kirlian Aura, 1974, The Energies of Consciousness, 1975, (with Susan Powers) Future Science, 1977, Broken Images, Broken Selves, 1997, (with Mark Waldman) Dreamscaping, 1999, (with Etzel Cardeña and Steven J. Lynn) Varieties of Anomalous Experience, 2000, (with Teresa McIntyre) The Psychological Effects of War Trauma on Civilians, 2003; mem. editl. bd. Alternative Therapies in Health and Medicine, Jour. Humanistic Psychology, Jour. Transpersonal Psychology, Jour. Indian Psychology, Dream Network, Humanistic Psychologist; contbr. 1000 articles to profl. jours Mem. Joseph Plan Found.; Bd. dirs., adv. bd. Acad. Religion and Phys. Rsch., Survival Rsch. Found., Hartley Film Found. Recipient Svc. to Youth award YMCA, 1959, Citation of Merit Nat. Assn. Creative Children and Adults, 1975, Cert. Recognition Office Gifted and Talented, US Office Edn., 1976, Volker medal South Africa Soc. Psychical Rsch., 1980, Bicentennial medal U. Ga., 1985, Charlotte and Karl Bühler award, 1992, Dan Overlade Meml. award, 1994, Humanist of Yr. award Ch. of Humanism, 1996, Career Achievement award Parapsychol. Assn., 1998, J.B. Rhine Award, 2002, Ashley Montagu Peace prize, 2003; named to Wisdom Hall of Fame, 2001. Fellow: APA (pres. divsn. 32 1980, pres. divsn. 30 1997, Disting. Contbns. to Profl. Hypnosis award 2002, Disting. Contbns. to Internat. Advancement of Psychology award 2002), Western Psychol. Assn., Soc. Sci. Study Sexuality, Soc. Sci. Study Religion, Am. Psychol. Soc., Am. Soc. Clin. Hypnosis; mem.: ACA, AAAS, Soc. Clin. and Exptl. Hypnosis, Parapsychol. Assn. (pres. 1983), Nat. Soc. Study of Edn., Menninger Found., Internat. Soc. Gen. Semantics, Western Psychol. Assn., Swedish Soc. Clin. and Exptl. Hypnosis, Soc. Gen. Sys. Rsch., Soc. Accelerative Learning and Tchg., Coun. Exceptional Children, Biofeedback Soc. Am., Soc. Sci. Exploration, Sleep Rsch. Soc., Nat. Assn. for Gifted Children, Internat. Soc. for Study of Dissociation, Internat. Soc. Hypnosis, Assn. Transpersonal Psychology, Assn. Humanistic Psychology (pres. 1974—75), Inter-Am. Psychol. Assn., Soc. for the Anthropology Consciousness, Internat. Assn. for Study of Dreams (pres. 1993—94, Lifetime Achievement award 2006), Internat. Coun. Psychologists, Am. Ednl. Rsch. Assn., Am. Soc. Psychical Rsch., World Future Soc. Office: Saybrook Grad Sch 747 Front St 3rd Fl San Francisco CA 94111 Home Phone: 415-456-2153. Business E-Mail: skrippner@saybrook.edu.

KRISCH, ALAN DAVID, physics professor; b. Phila., Apr. 19, 1939; s. Kube and Jeanne (Freiberg) K.; m. Jean Peck, Aug. 27, 1961; 1 child, Kathleen Susan. AB, U. Pa., 1960; PhD, Cornell U., 1964. Instr. Cornell U., 1964; mem. faculty U. Mich., Ann Arbor, 1964—, assoc. prof. high energy physics, 1966-68, prof., 1968—, dir. Spin Physics Ctr., 1994—. Vis. prof. Niels Bohr Inst., Copenhagen, 1975-76; trustee Argonne Nat. Lab., 1972-73, 80-82, chmn. zero gradient syncrotron users group, 1973-75, 78-79, chmn. internat. com. high energy spin physics symposia, 1977-94, past chmn., 1995-2006, mem., 2007—, chmn. organizing com. conf. on particle and nuclear physics intersections, 1983-86, mem., 1987-91, hon. mem., 1994—; chmn.-elect, chmn. IUCF Users Group, 1997-2002; spokesperson NEPTUN-A Expt. at 400 GeV UNK accelerator in Russia, 1989-99, SPIN@FERMI collaboration Fermilab, 1991-95, SPIN@HERA collaboration DESY in Germany, 1996-99, SPIN@U-70 Exp. at 70 Gev IHEP accelerator in Protvino, Russia, 2000—, SPIN@COSY Expt. COSY accelerator, Jülich, Germany, 2002-, SPIN@J-PARC Collaboration, Tokai, Japan, 2003—. Trustee Ann Arbor Hands On Mus., 1999-2005. Fellow NSF, 1963, Guggenheim Found., 1971-72, Denmark Nat. Bank, 1975-76. Fellow Am. Phys. Soc.; mem. AAAS. Achievements include discovery of heavy elementary particles, of structure within the proton, of scaling in inclusive reactions, of spinning core within proton, of large spin forces in violent proton collisions, of precise confirmation of large spin forces; invention of inclusive reactions; development of first high energy spin-polarized proton beam, of first strong focusing spin-polarized proton beam; demonstration of "Siberian snake" technique for accelerating spin-polarized beams; first spin-flipping of polarized boson beam. Office: U Mich Randall Lab Ann Arbor MI 48109-1120

KRISCHE, MICHAEL J., chemistry professor; b. Sept. 16, 1966; BS in Chemistry, U. Calif., Berkeley, 1989; PhD in Chemistry, Stanford U., 1996. NIH post-doctoral fellow Université Louis Pasteur, 1997—99; asst. prof. chemistry U. Tex., Austin, 1999—2004, prof. chemistry, 2004—. Invited lectr. in field; lectureship on organic synthesis Japanese Soc. Synthetic Chemistry, 2005. Contbr. articles to profl. jours. Recipient NSF Career award, 2000, Rsch. Corp., Cottrell Scholar award, 2002, Frasch Found. award in chemistry, 2002, Camille-Dreyfus Tchr.-Scholar award, 2003, Johnson & Johnson Focused Giving award, 2005, Solvias Ligand prize, 2006, Elias J. Corey award, Am. Chem. Soc., 2007; Sigma Xi grantee/vis. researcher, Surrey U., UK, 1991—92, Veatch grad. fellowship, Stanford U., 1995—96, Presidents Undergraduate Fellow, U. Calif. Berkeley, 1987—88, Fulbright Fellow, Helsinki U., Finland, 1989—90, Alfred P. Sloan Rsch. Fellow, 2003. Office: Dept Chemistry and Biochemistry Welch Hall Room 5 146 University of Texas at Austin Austin TX 78712 Office Fax: 512-232-5892, 512-471-8696. Business E-Mail: mkrische@mail.utexas.edu.*

KRISCHER, GORDON EUGENE, lawyer; b. Chgo., Dec. 9, 1946; BS, U. Ill., 1968; JD magna cum laude, Harvard U., 1971. Bar: Calif. 1972, N.Y. 1991. Ptnr. O'Melveny & Myers, LA, Newport Beach. Faculty Exec. Mgmt. Prog. of Claremont Grad. Sch., 1975—92; dir. So. Calif. Chpt. of Industrial Rels. Rsch. Assn., 1980—95. Vol. of Am. LA 1989-. Mem. ABA (labor law sect., mgmt. co-chair com. on Membership and Fin. 1992-, com. on practice & procedure before NLRB 1978-, co-chair 1992-1995); LA County Bar Assn. (exec. com. labor law sect. 1987-88), Assn. Bus. Trial Lawyers, Phi Beta Kappa, fellow Coll. Labor & Employment Lawyers. Mem. bd. editors Harvard Law Review, 1969-71. Office: O'Melveny & Myers 610 Newport Ctr Dr 17th Fl Newport Beach CA 92660 Office Phone: 949-823-7155. Office Fax: 949-823-6994. Business E-Mail: gkrischer@omm.com.

KRISE, THOMAS WARREN, academic administrator, literature and language professor, retired military officer; b. Ft. Sam Houston, Tex., Oct. 27, 1961; s. Edward Fisher and Elizabeth Ann (Bradt) K.; m. Patricia Lynn Love, Sept. 5, 1987. BS, USAF Acad., 1983; MSA, Cen. Mich. U., 1986; MA, U. Minn., 1989; PhD, U. Chgo., 1995; diploma, Air Command and Staff Coll., Maxwell AFB, Ala., 1996, Air War Coll., 2001. Commd. 2d lt. USAF, 1983, advanced through grades to lt. col., ret., 2005; dep. ICBM comdr. 742d Strategic Missile Squadron, Minot AFB, ND, 1983-85, ICBM crew comdr., 1985-86, ICBM flight comdr., 1986-87; instr. English USAF Acad., Colorado Springs, 1989-91, asst. prof., 1991-92, 97-99, assoc. prof., 1999—2002, prof., 2002—05; prof. and chair dept. English U. Ctrl. Fla., 2005—. Sr. mil. fellow Inst. Nat. Strategic Studies, 1995—97; vice-dir. Nat. Def. U. Press, 1995—97; dir. English major program USAF Acad., 1997—2000, deputy head, dept. English and Fine Arts, 2002—03; dir. Air Force Humanities Inst., 1997—2005, pres. faculty senate, 2003—05; vis. prof. U. W.I., Mona, Jamaica, 1999. Asst. editor: War, Lit. and the Arts, 1991—92, assoc. editor:, 1998—2003, mng. editor:, 2003—05; editor: Caribbeana: An Anthology of English Literature of the West Indies 1657-1777, 1999; gen. editor: McNair Papers monograph series, 1995—97; contbr. articles to profl. jours. Adult literacy tutor Coalition for Adult Literacy, Colorado Springs, 1989-91, literacy tutor trainer, Adult Literacy Network, Colorado Springs, 1991-92 Recipient Defense Meritorious Svc. medal, Meritorious Svc. medal, Air Force Commendation medal, Combat Readiness medal; Summer Inst. grantee Nat. Endowment for the Humanities, 1990, Seiler Rsch. grantee F.J. Seiler Rsch. Lab., A.F. Systems Command, 1991, Faculty Rsch Com. grantee, 1998-2004, Salzburg Seminar grantee, 2003, Rsch. grant USAF Inst. Nat. Security Studies, 1998, 99, CBS Bicentennial Narrators scholar, 1994; Fulbright fellow, 1999. Mem.: MLA, SAR (Pikes Peak chpt. pres. 1991—92), Fulbright Assn., Air Force Assn., Assn. Grads. USAF Acad. (bd. dirs. 1991—95, Chgo. chpt. pres. 1993—95), Mil. Officers Assn. Am., Soc. Early Americanists (exec. coord. 2003—05, v.p. 2005—07, pres. 2007—), Soc. 18th Century Am. Studies (sec.-treas. 1995—99), Am. Soc. 18th Century Studies (conf. dir. 2002), Early Caribbean Soc. (pres. 2002—), Colorado Springs Adult Literacy Network (pres. 1991—92), Royal Air Force Club (London), Army and Navy Club (Washington), Toastmasters Internat. (U. Minn. chpt. pres. 1988—89), Sigma Tau Delta, Phi Kappa Phi. Episcopalian. Avocations: travel, sailing, skiing, hiking, scuba diving. Home: 2001 Cove Trl Winter Park FL 32789 Office: Dept English Univ Ctrl Florida Orlando FL 32816-1346 Home Phone: 407-628-1514; Office Phone: 407-823-1159. Personal E-mail: krisetw@hotmail.com. Business E-Mail: tkrise@mail.ucf.edu.

KRISHEN, KUMAR, research technologist; b. Kashmir, India, June 22, 1939; came to U.S., 1964, naturalized, 1976; s. Srikanth and Dhanwate Bhat; m. Vijay Lakshmi Raina, Aug. 6, 1961; children: Lovely, Sweetie, Anjala. BA with highest merit in Math. & Physics, Jammu and Kashmir U., India, 1959; B of Tech., Calcutta U., 1962, M of Tech., 1963; MS in Elec. Engring., Kans. State U., 1966, PhD with distinction, 1969. Asst. prof. elec. engring. dept. Kans. State U., Manhattan, 1968-69; staff scientist and engr. Lockheed Electronics Co., Inc., Houston, 1969-76; mgr. microwave program NASA, Johnson Space Ctr., Houston, 1976-78, mgr. advanced microwave programs, 1978-81, coord. advanced programs expt. sys. divsn., 1981, mgr. advanced programs tracking and comm., 1981-88; asst. for tech. and advanced programs Mission Support Directorate, 1988-89; chief technologist NIO, Johnson Space Ctr., 1990—2001, Tech. Transfer and Commercialization, Johnson Space Ctr., 1994—98; vis. prof. Va. Tech., 2001—04; mem. Innovative Tech. Transfer Partnerships Program NASA Johnson Space Ctr., 2004—. Adj. prof. Rice U., 1986-96; vis. prof. Va. Tech. U., 2001—; rsch. adv. NRC; coord. The Krishen Trio Performers, 1969—; established Krishen Found. for Arts and Scis., 1983—. Author: Why Me?; contbr. articles on radar tech., sensing, comm., tracking, robotic vision, culture, poetry, and human devel. Co-founder pres. Hindu Worship Soc., 1970-72, 74, 79-80, 83; pres. ICC-CL, 1987; program chmn. World Congress on Superconductivity, 1990-96. Recipient Gold and Silver medals Calcutta U., Outstanding Performance and Superior Performance award NASA, 1979, 82, 84-87, NASA/JSC Cert. of Commendation, 1987; Govt. India Merit scholar, 1959-61. Fellow Soc. Design Process Sci.; assoc. fellow AIAA; mem. IEEE (sr., chmn. Galveston Bay sect. 1994), Sigma Xi (pres., founding pres. Clear Lake chpt. 1994-96), Phi Kappa Phi, Eta Kappa Nu. Home: 4127 Long Grove Dr Seabrook TX 77586-4222 Office: NASA Johnson Space Ctr Code AT Houston TX 77058 Business E-Mail: krishen@vt.edu.

KRISHER, BERNARD, foreign correspondent; b. Frankfurt, Germany, Aug. 9, 1931; s. Joseph and Fella (Solnica) K.; m. Akiko Yaginuma, May 1, 1960; children: Deborah, Joseph. BA, Queens Coll., 1953; postgrad., Columbia U., 1961-62. From staffwriter to asst. editor mag. N.Y. World-Telegram & Sun, 1955-61; corr. Newsweek, 1963—, bur. chief Tokyo, 1968-80; corr. Fortune, 1981-83; chief editl. advisor Focus Weekly Mag. Shincho-sha Pub. Co., Tokyo, 1981-97; editl. advisor Dohosha Pub. Co., Kyoto and Tokyo, 1984-98; editor at large Japan Avenue, 1991-94; editor at large Asia Wired mag., 1993-98; founder, pub. The Cambodia Daily, Phnom Penh, 1993—; editl. dir. Future Book series Tachibana Pub. Co., Tokyo, 1998—. Hon. rsch. assoc., vis. scholar East Asian Rsch. Ctr., Harvard U., 1978-79; Far East rep. The Media Lab. MIT, 1987—. Author: (with Alan Levy) Draftee's Confidential Guide, 1957, Interview, 1976, The Plus and Minuses of Being Japanese, 1978, Harvard Diary, 1979, How Harvard Sees Japan, 1979, We Who Lived in Japan, 1986; (with King Norodom Sihanouk) Charisma and Leadership, 1990, (with Cambodia Daily staff) A Vision for a New Asia, 2003. Founder, vol. chmn. Japan Relief for Cambodia, 1992—; vol. chmn. Am. Assistance for Cambodia, 1993—, Internet Appeal for N. Korean Flood Victims, 1995—; chmn. Sihanouk Hosp.- Ctr. of Hope, Phnom Penh, Cambodia, 1996—. Recipient Gleitsman Internat. Activist award, 2001, Iue Asia Pacific Culture prize, 2003, Asia's Hero award Time mag., 2005. Mem Coun. Fgn. Rels. Home: 4-1-7-605 Hiroo Shibuya-ku Tokyo 150-0012 Japan Business E-Mail: bernie@krisher.com.

KRISHNAMURTHY, KATHIRAVAN, research associate; s. Krishnamurthy Duraiswamy and Kasturi Krishnamurthy. BS in Agrl. Engring., Tamilnadu Agrl. U., India, 1999; MS in Agrl. and Biol. Engring., Pa. State U., 2002, PhD in Agrl. and Biol. Engring., 2006. Rsch. asst. Pa. State U., University Park, 2001—06; rsch. assoc. Ala. A&M U., Normal, 2006—. Mem. Univ. Park Allocation Com. Pa. State U., 2003—05, mem. web adv. com., 2003—05, lab safety officer microbiological engring. lab., 2003—05; placement cell sec. Agrl. Engring. Coll. and Rsch. Inst., Tamil

Nadu Agrl. U., 1999. Contbr. articles to profl. jours., chapters to books. Judge Pa. Jr. Acad. Sci. State Meeting, 2001—04, Pa. Gov.'s Sch. Agrl. Scis. Rsch. Symposium, 2002; pres. Vedic Soc., Pa. State U., 2003—04. Mem.: Internat. Assn. for Food Protection, Inst. Food Technologists (mem. com. higher edn. 2005—06), Inst. Biol. Engring., Am. Soc. for Microbiology (mem. internat. mentoring program 2005—), Am. Soc. Agrl. Engrs. (mem. food processing com. 2004—06), Sigma Xi, Gamma Sigma Delta, Alpha Epsilon, Phi Tau Sigma. Hindu. Achievements include research in cost-effective, novel disinfection techniques for inactivation of pathogenic microorganisms to ensure the safety of food. Office Phone: 256-372-4177.

KRISHNAMURTHY, RAMESH SALIGRAMA, environmental scientist, researcher; s. Saligrama RajaRao Krishnamurthy and K. G. Leelavathy; 1 child, Ravi James Cullop. BSc, Bangalore U., 1981—84; BS, Oreg. State U., Corvallis, 1989, MA, 1992, MS, 1994; PhD, U. Oreg., Eugene, 1999; MPH, UCLA, 2005. Rsch. asst. Indian Inst. Sci., Bangalore; radio prodr. Oreg. Pub. Broadcasting, Corvallis, Oreg., 1992—95; rsch. scientist Internat. Inst. Human Evolutionary Rsch., Bend, 1995—99; dir. Linus Pauling collection Oreg. State U., Corvallis; assoc. prof. and asst. dean U. Pacific, Stockton, Calif., 1999—2005; pub. health informatics scientist Ctrs. Disease Control & Prevention, Atlanta, 2005—. Health rsch. scientist and project dir. VA, LA, 2005. Editor: Innovative Environmental Technology Evaluation and Commercialization. Technology, History of Atomic Energy Collection at Oregon State University: A Catalogue of Holdings, Linus Pauling on Peace, Pauling Symposium: A Discourse on the Art of Biography. Gov. UN Assn., NYC, 1994—97; dir. and dep. permanent rep. to the UN Resource Ctr. for the UN, San Francisco, 1999—2004; dir. Ashoka Trust Rsch. in Ecology and the Environ., Boston, 1999—2003. Recipient Clara L. Simerville award, Oreg. State U., 1993, Recognition plaque, Coll. Pharmacy and the Linus Pauling Inst. Oreg. State U., 1998, Outstanding Tchr. of Yr., U. Pacific Sch. Internat. Studies, 2001—02; fellow Fulbright-Hays Seminar Abroad Program - Rwanda, U.S. Dept. Edn., 2004; Betsy Dana scholar, UN Office World Federalist Movement, 1993, Internat. Trade and Devel. Grad. fellow, Oreg. State Sys. Higher Edn., 1992, 1995. Mem.: APHA (assoc.; internat. health sect. 2005—), Hon. Order Ky. Cols. Achievements include research in health Informatics and international public health. Office: Ctrs Disease Control & Prevention Atlanta GA Home: 2010 Chambord Dr Stockton CA 95210-2254 Home Phone: 209-992-1596.

KRISHNAN, KRISHNASWAMY RANGA RAMA R., psychiatry educator; b. Madras, Tamilnadu, India, Apr. 22, 1956; came to U.S., 1981; s. N. Krishnaswamy and Sulochana Krishnaswamy Reddy; m. Sripriya Chitamoor, May 21, 1987; children: Vaishnavi, Prahlad. PUC, Loyola Coll., Madras, India, 1973; MBBS, U. Madras, 1978. Chief resident Duke Med. Ctr., Durham, 1981—83, asst. prof., 1984—89, assoc. prof., 1990—95, prof., 1995—, chmn. psychiatry, 1998—. Vice dean Duke GMS-NUS, Singapore, 2006—. Office: Duke U Med Ctr Box 3950 Durham NC 27710-0001 Office Phone: 919-684-5616. Business E-Mail: krish001@mc.duke.edu.

KRISHNAN, SUNIL, radiologist, educator, oncologist, researcher; s. Krishnan and Padmaja Marar; m. Veena Chandramohan, Nov. 11, 2000. MD, Christian Med. Coll., Vellore, 1995. Cert. Am. Bd. Internal Medicine, 2000, Am. Bd. Radiology, 2005. Intern Christian Med. Coll., Vellore; tumor biology fellow Med. Coll. Onio, Toledo, 1995—97; med. resident Pa. State Geisinger Med. Ctr., Danville, 1997—2000; radiation oncology resident Mayo Clinic, Rochester, Minn., 2000—04; asst. prof., radiation oncology MD Anderson Cancer Ctr., Houston, 2004—. Study sect. mem. Nat. Cancer Inst., Toronto, Ontario, 2006—; co-chair, gastrointestinal translational rsch. com. Radiation Oncology Therapy Group, Phila., 2006—. Minn. Medicine; contbr. chapters to books, articles to profl. jours. Mem-at-large Am. Cancer Soc. Bd., Olmsted County, Rochester, Minn., 2002—04; physician liaison, navigator program Am. Cancer Soc. No. Midwest Zone, Rochester, 2002—04. Recipient Found. Leadership award, AMA, 2002; grantee, Nat. Cancer Inst., 2002, Rsch. grant, Nat. Brain Tumor Found., 2003, Radiation Therapy Oncology Group, 2006, U. Tex. Ctr. Biomed. Engring., 2006, 2007; Mayo Brother's Disting. fellow, Mayo Clinic Grad. Sch. Medicine, 2002, Robert D. and Alma Moreton fellow, Mayo Clinic, Rochester, 2002, Rsch. fellow, Radiol. Soc. N.Am., 2003, Rsch. grant, Hitachi Inc., 2005, Nat. Comprehensive Cancer Network, 2005, Genentech Inc., 2006, 2007. Mem.: Am. Soc. Clin. Oncology, Am. Soc. Therapeutic and Radiation Oncology (chair, gastrointestinal sci. program com. 2005—), Radiation Therapy Oncology Group. Achievements include patents pending for use of nanoparticles in the photodynamic treatment of tumors and non-destructive testing; optimizing molecular imaging of signaling pathways using nanoparticles. Office: MD Anderson Cancer Ctr 1515 Holcombe Blvd Houston TX 77030 Office Phone: 713-563-2300.

KRISHNASWAMY, DILIP, computer architect; s. N. and S. Krishnaswamy. BTech in Electronics and Comm., Indian Inst. Tech., Madras, 1991; MS in Computer Sci., Syracuse U., 1993; PhDEE, U. Ill., 1997. Vis. rschr. Ctr. Theoretical Studies, Indian Inst. Sci., Bangalore, Karnataka, 1990—90; vis. rschr. Thomas J Watson Rsch. Ctr. IBM, Yorktown Heights, NY, 1994; vis. rschr. Cadence Design Sys., San Jose, Calif., 1996; arch. Intel Corp., Folsom, Calif., 1997—; part-time tchg. faculty U. Calif., Davis, 1998—2005. Program com. mem. and session chair High Performace Computing Com., Calcutta, West Bengal, India, 1999; tech. program com. mem. Internat. MultiConf. Computer Sci. and Engring., Las Vegas, 2002—04; program com. mem. Systemics, Cybernetics and Informatics, Orlando, 2002—; vice-chair, design and developers forum, 48th ieee global comm. conf. IEEE Comm. Conf., New York, NY, 2005—; tech. program com. mem., 3G wireless conf. Delson Group, San Francisco, 2002—; session chair design and developers forum IEEE Globecom, San Francisco, 2003, session chair, design and developers forum, Dallas, 04; session chair, tech. program com. mem. IEEE MMNS, San Diego, 2004; tech. program com. mem. Internat. MultiConference in Computer Sci. and Engring., Las Vegas, 2002—04. Contbr. numerous articles to profl. jours., chapters to books. Fellow, Syracuse U., 1991—93. Mem.: IEEE (VLSI Test Symposium Com. Best Paper award 1998), IEEE Comm. Soc. (vice-chair tech. com. on design and devel. 2003—, session chair 56th vehicular tech. conf., co-chair, 49th global comm. conf. expo tech. program 2005—), IEEE Computer Soc. Achievements include design of Intel PXA800F cellular processor, presented at IEEE HotChips Conference at Stanford, 2003; patents pending for adaptive wireless networks and methods for communicating multimedia in a proactive enterprise; network aware cross-layer protocol methods and apparatus. Office: Intel Corp 1900 Prairie City Rd Folsom CA 95630 Home: 3500 Garfield Ave Carmichael CA 95608-3014 Home Phone: 916-768-0939; Office Phone: 916-356-2829.

KRISLOV, MARVIN, academic administrator, lawyer, educator; b. Balt., Aug. 24, 1960; s. Joseph and Evelyn (Moreida) K.; m. Amy Ruth Sheon, Aug. 25, 1993; children: Zachary Jacob, Jesse Harris, Eve Rose. BA in Econs. summa cum laude, Yale U., 1982; BA/MA in Modern History, Oxford U., Eng., 1985; JD, Yale U., 1988. Bar: Calif. 1988, DC 1989, Mich. 1999. Law clk to Judge Marilyn Hall Patel US Dist. Ct. (no. dist.) Calif., San Francisco, 1988-89; trial atty. civil rights divsn. US Dept. Justice, Washington, 1989-93; spl. asst. U.S. atty. US Atty.'s Office, Washington, 1989-90; spl. counsel Office of Counsel to the Pres., Washington, 1993-94, asst. counsel, 1994, assoc. counsel, 1995-96; dep. solicitor US Dept. Labor, Washington, 1996-98, acting solicitor, 1997-98; v.p., gen. counsel U. Mich., Ann Arbor, 1998—2007; pres. Oberlin Coll., Ohio, 2007—. Adj. prof. law, George Washington U. Law Sch., Washington, 1991-93; adj. prof. U. Mich. Law Sch., 2000—, U. Mich. polit. sci. dept., 2001—. Mem. New Haven Bd. Aldermen, 1982-83. Rhodes scholar, 1983. Mem. Phi Beta Kappa. Office: Oberlin Coll Office of Pres 70 N Professor St Oberlin OH 44074 E-mail: Marvin.Krislov@oberlin.edu.*

KRISS, GARY W(AYNE), priest; b. Balt., Dec. 29, 1946; s. Warren B. and Margaret L. (Austin) K. AB cum laude, Dartmouth Coll., 1968; MDiv, Yale U. Div. Sch., 1972; postgrad. studies, The Gen. Theol. Sem., NYC, 1972, St. George Coll., Jerusalem, 1978; DD, Nashotah House, 2001. Ordained to ministry Episcopal Ch. as deacon, 1972, as priest 1972. Chaplain to the congregation Cathedral Ch. of St. Paul, Burlington, Vt., 1972-74; coord. Rock Point (Vt.) Summer Confs., 1973-77; vicar St. Mark's, St. Luke's Parishes, Castleton and Fair Haven, Vt., 1974-78; asst. to dean The Cathedral of All Saints, Albany, N.Y., 1978-79, canon precentor, 1979-84, dir. inst. Christian studies, 1979-84; dean Cathedral of All Saints, Albany, 1984-91; dean and pres. Nashotah (Wis.) House, 1992—2001; interim rector St. Paul's Epis. Ch., Troy, NY, 2001—02, assoc. priest, 2002—04; vicar St. Paul's Ch., Salem, NY, 2003—. Bd. dirs. Brookhaven Home for Boys, Chelsea, Vt., 1975-79, Albany Collegiate Interfaith Ctr., 1982-90, pres. 1984-90; Episcopal campus priest, SUNY, Albany, 1980-84; bd. dirs. Capital Area Coun. of Chs., Albany, N.Y., 1989-91, chmn. of Faith and Learning Commn.; The Living Ch. Found., 1994—. Bd. dirs. Samaritan Shelters, Glenmont, N.Y., 1979-91, The Child's Hosp., Albany, 1986-90, Child's Nursing Home, Albany, 1987-91, pres. 1990-91. Episcopalian. Home and Office: PO Box 26 Cambridge NY 12816

KRISS, ROBERT J., lawyer; b. Cleve., Dec. 15, 1953; BA summa cum laude, Cornell U., 1975; JD cum laude, Harvard U., 1978. Bar: Ill. 1978, U.S. Dist. Ct. (no. dist.) Ill. 1978, U.S. Ct. Appeals (7th cir.) 1983, U.S. Dist. Ct. (no. dist. trial bar) Ill. 1982. Ptnr. Mayer, Brown, Rowe & Maw LLP, Chgo. Presenter in field; adj. prof. trial practice Northwestern U. Law Sch. Author: published short story. Chmn. consent degree task force Chgo. Park Dist., 1986-87; bd. dirs. Chgo. Legal Assistance Found., 1996-2000, Victory Gardens Theater, 2003-04, Chgo. Coun. Sci. Tech., 2007. Named a Leading Lawyer in Ill., Ill. Super Lawyer, 2005. Mem.: ABA (sect. on litigation, bus. law). Avocation: writing. Office: Mayer Brown Rowe & Maw 71 S Wacker Dr Chicago IL 60606-4637 Home Phone: 847-501-3813; Office Phone: 312-701-7165. Business E-Mail: rkriss@mayerbrown.com.

KRISTENSEN, DOUGLAS ALLAN, former state legislator; b. Kearney, Nebr., Jan. 4, 1955; s. Donald M. and Mary Lou (Martin) K.; m. Terri S. Harder; children: Morgan Claire, Paige Nicole. BA, U. Nebr., 1977; JD, Drake U., 1980. Bar: US Supreme Ct. Ptnr. Lieske & Kristensen, 1981—2002; atty. Kearney County, 1982-88; mem. Nebr. Legislature from 37th dist., Lincoln, 1988—; chmn. transp. com. Nebr. Legislature, Lincoln, 1991-98, mem. intergovtl. coop. and revenue coms., mem. exec. bd., chair transp. com., 1991-97, speaker of the legislature, 1998—2002; chancellor U. Nebr., 2002—. Bd. dirs. young lawyers ssect. Nebr. Bar, 1984-88, Nebr. CLE Inc., 1986-90. Pres. Rocky Mountain Athletic Conf., 2005—06. Henry Toll fellow, 1991; recipient Pres.' award Nebr. Assn. County Ofcls., 1987. Mem. Nebr. Bar Assn. (award of spl. merit 2002), Iowa Bar Assn., Nebr. County Atty.'s Assn. (bd. dirs. 1985-88), Rotary Internat., Optimists Club. Office: University of Nebraska at Kearney 905 W 25th St Lincoln NE 68849 Home: 219 N Brown Ave Minden NE 68959-1524

KRISTIANSEN, ERIC W., lawyer; BS, Trinity U., 1996; JD, Tulane U. Law Sch., La., 2000. Bar: Tex. 2000, US Dist. Ct. (so. dist. Tex.) 2000, US Dist. Ct. (ea. dist. Tex.) 2001. Assoc. Baker Hostetler, Houston. Mem.-elect bd. dirs. Big Brothers and Big Sisters of Houston. Named a Rising Star, Tex. Super Lawyers mag., 2006. Mem.: Tex. Bar Assn., Tex. Young Lawyers Assn., Houston Young Lawyers Assn., Houston Bar Assn. Office: Baker Hostetler 1000 Louisiana St Ste 2000 Houston TX 77002 Office Phone: 713-646-1331. E-mail: ekristiansen@bakerlaw.com.*

KRISTIANSEN, KAI DE LANGE, physicist; Doctorate, U. Oslo, Norway, 2005. Rschr. U. Oslo, 2005, U. Calif., Santa Barbara, 2005—. Scholar, Norwegian Rsch. Coun., 2005—. Achievements include research in Physics.

KRISTIANSEN, MAGNE, electrical engineer, educator; b. Elverum, Norway, Apr. 14, 1932; came to U.S., 1958, naturalized, 1967; s. Martin and Ella (Sobye) K.; m. Aud Bohn, July 6, 1957; children: Sonja Bohn, Eric Bohn. BS in Elec. Engring., U. Tex., Austin, 1961, PhD (Ford Found. fellow), 1967. Registered profl. engr., Tex. Rsch. engr. U. Tex., Austin, 1964-66; faculty Tex. Tech U., Lubbock, 1966—, prof., 1971—, dir. plasma lab., 1970—80; dir. pulsed power lab. Tex. Tech. U., 1980—2001, dir. Ctr. Pulsed Power and Power Electronics, 2001—; v.p. rsch. and engring. Enfitek, Inc., Lubbock, 1987-90; v.p. R & D Integrated Tech. Inc., Lubbock, 1990-98. Cons. def. products divsn. Varo, Inc., Garland, Tex., 1970-71; cons. Aerospace Corp., El Segundo, Calif., 1974-76, BDM Corp., Albuquerque, 1975-76, 85-87, Palisades Inst., N.Y. and NRC, 1977, Rockwell Internat., 1978, Maxwell Labs., 1979-83, LaJolla Inst., 1979, NASA, 1979, Norwegian Rsch. Coun., 1980, Sci. Applications, Inc., 1983-88, 91-92, Lawrence Livermore Nat. Lab., 1983-95, McDonnell Douglas, 1986, LTV Missiles and Electronics Group, 1987-89, NEA-Lindberg A/S, 1988, Physics Internat. Co., 1992-97, Rocket Rsch. Co., 1992, Swedish Def. Rsch. Inst., 1992-2005; Hazeltine Ocean Sys., 1995, Lockheed Martin, 1995-96, 2003, 04, Integrated Technologies, Inc., 1998-2001; collaborator Los Alamos Nat. Lab., 1974-95, others; contractor DNA, 1986-97, NASA, 1990-2001, Wright Aeronautical Labs., 1994-96. Co-author: An Introduction to Controlled Thermonuclear Fusion, 1977, Russian, Japanese, Chinese translations, 1980-81, Rotating Mirror Cameras, 1997; co-editor: Advances in Pulsed Power Technology, 1984—. Contbr. articles to profl. jours. Mem. USAF Sci. Adv. Bd., 1981-85. Served with Royal Norwegian Air Force, 1950-58. Recipient Meritorious Civilian Svc. award USAF, 1985, Excellence award Halliburton Found., 1994; grantee State of Tex., 1966-85, 88-94, NSF, 1967-87, AEC, 1968-71, Air Force Office Sci. Rsch., 1968—, Dept. Energy, 1978-79, Army Rsch. Lab., 1994-99, Strategic Missile Command, 2005-; sr. fellow sci. NATO, 1975, fellow Japan Soc. Promotion Sci., 1979. Fellow IEEE (life, Pulsed Power Conf. Peter Haas award 1987, Nuc. and Plasma Sci. Soc. Merit award 1991, Millennium medal), Am. Phys. Soc.; mem. AAAS, Russian Acad. Scis. (fgn. mem., Ural sect.), Am. Soc. Engring. Edn., Sigma Xi, Tau Beta Pi, Eta Kappa Nu, Phi Kappa Phi. Home: 3105 78th St Lubbock TX 79423-1815 Office: Tex Tech U Dept Elec/Computer Engring Lubbock TX 79409-3102 Home Phone: 806-745-1071. Business E-Mail: m.kristiansen@ttu.edu.

KRISTIN, KAREN, artist; b. LA, Aug. 27, 1943; d. Earle Barnard and Ann Maxine (Taylor) Immel; m. Richard Edward Amend, Aug. 21, 1976 (div. Aug. 1981); m. Gary Marchal Lloyd, Oct. 1, 1985 (div. Sept.1989). Student, Art Ctr. Coll. Design, 1961, Valley Jr. Coll., 1962, Pierce Jr. Coll., 1967—68, UCLA, 1969—70. Lectr. UCLA Ext. Program, 1973-76; scenic artist Hollywood, Calif., 1978-83; ptnr., designer, lead painter Sky Art Scenic Art Svcs., Hollywood, Calif., 1983-88; owner, pres., lead painter, designer Sky Art Karen Kristin, Inc., Englewood, Colo., 1989—. Spkr., lectr. in field. Co-author (under Karen Kristin Amend): Handwriting Analysis: The Complete Basic Book, 1980, Achieving Compatbility with Handwriting-Analysis, vol. I, Understanding Your Emotional Relationships, 1992, vol. II, Exploring Your Sexual Relationships, 1992; prin. murals include The Cirque Du Soleil Theater, Las Vegas, 1993, N.Mex. Mus. Natural History, 1989, 90, Forum Shops at Caesars, Las Vegas, 1992, 97, Kansas City Station Hotel and Casino, Kansas City, Mo., 1996, Sunset Station Hotel and Casino, Las Vegas, 1997, Venetian Hotel Grand Canal Shoppes, Las Vegas, 1998, Chaitanya Joti Mus., Puttaparthy, India, 2000, Hyatt Casino, Blackhawk, Colo., 2001, Argosy Casino, Kans. City, Mo., 2003, Rangeeli Mahal, Barsana, India, 2003, Boulder Sta. Casino, Las Vegas, 2004, Charlestown Race and Sports Book, 2005, The Bismarck Airport, 2005, Venetian Grand Canal Shoppes, Macau, China, 2006, 07; sky art backdrops for numerous movies, commls., and TV. Mem. Am. Assn. Handwriting Analysts (spkr. 1991—), Am. Handwriting Analysis Found. (sprk. 1991—), Human Graphics Ctr., Graphex Internat. and Gold NIBS, Universal Soc. of Integral Why (mentor 1994—). Democrat. Avocations: photography, reading, travel, camping, fishing. Office: Sky Art Karen Kristin Inc 125 N Sligo Cortez CO 81321-2939 Home Phone: 303-918-2983. Personal E-mail: skyartkk@aol.com.

KRISTOF, KATHY M., journalist; b. Burbank, Calif., Feb. 4, 1960; d. Joseph E. and Frances S. Kristof; m. Richard R. Magnuson, Jr., Jan. 4, 1986 (div.); 2 children. BA, U. So. Calif., LA, 1983. Reporter L.A. Bus. Jour., 1984-88, Daily News, Woodland Hills, Calif., 1988-89, L.A. Times, 1989—; syndicated columnist L.A. Times Syndicate, 1991—. Author: Kathy Kristof's Complete Book of Dollars and Sense, 1997, Investing 101, 2000, Taming the Tuition Tiger, 2003; contbr. articles to mags. and profl. jours. Recipient John Hancock Fin. Svcs. award, 1992, Personal Fin. Writing award ICI/Am. U., 1994, Consumer Adv. of Yr., Calif. Alliance for Consumer Edn., 1998. Mem. Soc. Bus. Editors and Writers (pres. 2003), Calif. Newspapers Pubs. Assn. (2nd pl. Bus. and Fin. Story award 1999). Office: Los Angeles Times 202 W 1st St Los Angeles CA 90012 E-mail: kathy.kristof@latimes.com.

KRISTOF, LADIS KRIS DONABED, political scientist, writer; b. Cernauti, Romania, Nov. 26, 1918; came to U.S., 1952, naturalized, 1957; s. Witold and Maria (Zawadzki) Krzysztofowicz; m. Jane McWilliams, Dec. 29, 1956; 1 son, Nicholas. Student, U. Poznan, Poland, 1937-39; BA, Reed Coll., Portland, Oreg., 1955; MA, U. Chgo., 1956, PhD, 1969. Regional exec. dir., Sovromlemn, Romania, 1948; sales mgr. Centre du Livre Suisse, Paris, France, 1951-52; lectr. U. Chgo., 1958-59; assoc. dir. Inter-Univ. Project History Menshevism, NYC, 1959-62; mem. faculty dept. polit. sci. Temple U., 1962-64; research fellow Hoover Instn., Stanford U., 1964-67; faculty polit. sci. U. Santa Clara, 1967-68; asso. Studies Communist System, Stanford, 1968-69; mem. faculty polit. sci. U. Waterloo, Ont., Can., 1969-71; prof. polit. sci. Portland (Oreg.) State U., 1971-89, prof. emeritus, 1990—. Vis. prof. U. Wroclaw, Poland, 1990, U. Iasi, Romania, 1991, U. Punjab, India, 1992, U. Bucharest, Romania, 2004. Author: The Nature of Frontiers and Boundaries, 1959, The Origins and Evolution of Geopolitics, 1960, The Russian Image of Russia, 1967, The Geopolitical Contours of the Post-Cold War World, 1992; also articles in Romania; co-author, co-editor: Revolution and Politics in Russia, 1972. Active Internat. YMCA Center, Paris, 1950-52, NAACP, Chgo., 1957-59, Amnesty Internat., Portland, 1975—. Served with Corps Engrs. Romanian Army, 1940-45. Fulbright scholar Romania, 1971, 84 Mem. Am. Polit. Sci. Assn., Assn. Am. Geographers, Am. Assn. for Advancement of Slavic Studies, Internat. Polit. Sci. Assn., Western Slavic Assn. (pres. 1988-90), Am.-Romanian Acad. Arts and Scis. (v.p. 1995-00). Home: 23050 NW Roosevelt Dr Yamhill OR 97148-8336 Office: Portland State Univ Dept Polit Sci Portland OR 97207 Personal E-mail: kristofj@pdx.edu. *War, want and concentration camps, exile from home and homeland, these have made me hate strife among men, but they have not made me lose faith in the future of mankind. Personal experience, including my own unsteady progress through life, has taught me to beware of man's capacity for plain stupid, irrational, as well as consciously evil behavior, but it also has taught me that man has an even greater capacity for recovery from lapses. In a short thrust of planned, wisely guided activity he is able to climb to higher levels of material and intellectual achievement than he ever reached before. In short, I remain a rationalist and an optimist at a time when the prophets of doom have the floor. My query is, if man has been able to create the arts, the sciences and the material civilization we know in America, why should he be judged powerless to create justice, fraternity and peace.*

KRISTOF, NICHOLAS DONABET, journalist; b. Chgo., Apr. 27, 1959; s. Ladis K.D. and Jane (McWilliams) K.; m. Sheryl WuDunn; children: Gregory, Geoffrey, Caroline. BA, Harvard U., 1981; BA and MA in Law, U. Oxford, Eng., 1983; diploma in Arabic, Am. U. in Cairo, 1983-84; student, Taipei Lang. Inst., 1987-88. Econs. reporter NY Times, NYC, 1984-85, fin. corr. LA bur., 1985-86, chief Hong Kong bur., 1986-87, chief Beijing bur., 1988-93, chief Tokyo bur., 1995-99, sr. writer, 1993-2000, assoc. mng. editor, 2000—01, columnist, 2001—. Vis. fellow East-West Ctr., 1993; vis. scholar Linfield Coll., 1994, 99. Author: (with S. WuDunn) China Wakes: The Struggle for the Soul of a Rising Power, 1994, Thunder from the East: Portrait of a Rising Asia, 2000. Recipient Pulitzer prize for fgn. reporting, 1990, George Polk award for fgn. reporting LI U., NY, 1990, Hal Boyle award Overseas Press Club, 1990, Michael Kelly Meml. award for fearless pursuit and expression of truth, Atlantic Monthly, 2005, Pulitzer prize for commentary, 2006; Citations for Excellence, 1994, 96, 2000; Rhodes scholar, 1981-83. Avocations: travel, reading, running. Office: NY Times 229 W 43rd St New York NY 10036-3959

KRISTOFF, KARL W., lawyer; b. Buffalo, Mar. 31, 1942; BA, SUNY, Buffalo, 1965; JD, John Marshall Law Sch., 1968. Bar: Ill. 1968, U.S. Supreme Ct. 1974, N.Y. 1976. Ptnr., v.p. dipute resolution divsn., chair edn. law practice group Hodgson, Russ, LLP, Buffalo. Mem. editorial bd. The John Marshall Jour. Practice and Procedure, 1968, active, 1967. Mem. N.Y. Vets. Affairs Commn., 2002—. Maj. gen. ret. N.Y. Air N.G. Mem. Am. Arbitration Assn. (comml. panel arbitrators), Nat. Pub. Employer Labor Rels. Assn., Nat. Coun. Sch. Attys., N.Y. State Assn. Sch. Attys., N.Y. State Pub. Employer Labor Rels. Assn., Edn. Law Assn. Office: Hodgson Russ LLPr One M&T Plz Ste 2000 Buffalo NY 14203-2391 E-mail: kkristoff@hodgsonruss.com.

KRISTOFFERSON, KRIS, singer, lyricist, actor; b. Brownsville, Tex., June 22, 1936; m. Fran Beir, 1960 (div. 1969), children: Tracy, Kris; m. Rita Coolidge, Aug. 19, 1973 (div. 1980), 1 child, Casey.; m. Lisa Meyers, Feb. 19, 1983-, five children. BA in Creative Lit., Pomona Coll., 1958, D (hon.), 1974; Rhodes scholar, Oxford U., Eng., 1960. Worked at a variety of jobs in Nashville, including comml. helicopter pilot, 1965-69. Appeared at Newport (R.I.) Folk Festival, 1969, and on Johnny Cash TV program, 1970; concert and rec. artist, 1970—; albums recorded include Kristofferson, 1970, The Silver-Tongued Devil and I, 1971, Border Lord, Jesus Was a Capricorn, Spooky Lady's Sideshow, 1974, Big Sur Festival, Songs of Kristofferson, Who's to Bless and Who's to Blame, Easter Island, 1978, Shake Hands With the Devil, 1979, (with Rita Coolidge) Breakaway, Repossession, 1986, Third World Warrior, 1990, (with Highwaymen) Highwayman II, 1990, Singer, Songwriter, 1991, (with Willie Nelson, Rita Coolidge and Larry Gatlin) Live At The Philharmonic, 1992; actor (films): Cisco Pike, 1972, Pat Garrett and Billy the Kid, 1973, Blume in Love, 1973, Bring Me the Head of Alfredo Garcia, 1974, Alice Doesn't Live Here Anymore, 1974, The Sailor Who Fell From Grace With The Sea, 1976, A Star is Born, 1976 (Golden Globe award for Best Motion Picture Actor 1977), Vigilante Force, 1976, Semi-Tough, 1977, Convoy, 1978, Heaven's Gate, 1981, Rollover, 1981, Flashpoint, 1984, Songwriter, 1984, Trouble in Mind, 1985, Big Top Pee-Wee, 1988, Millennium, 1989, Welcome Home, 1989, Sandino, 1990, Night of the Cyclone, 1990, Knights, 1993, Paper Hearts, 1993, Lone Star, 1996, Fire Down Below, 1997, Girls Night, 1998, Blade, 1998, Dance with Me, 1998, Payback, 1999, The Joyriders, 1999, Planet of the Apes, 2001, Blade 2, 2002, Disappearances, 2004, Silver City, 2004, Blade Trinity, 2004, The Jacket, 2005, Dreamer: Inspired by a True Story, 2005, others; actor (TV films): Freedom Road (miniseries), 1979, The Lost Honor of Kathryn Beck, 1984, Stagecoach, 1986, The Last Days of Frank and Jessie James, 1986, Blood and Orchids (miniseries), 1986, Amerika (miniseries), 1987, Miracle in the Wildnerness, 1991, Christmas in Connecticut, 1992, Bob Dylan 30th Anniversary Celebration, 1993, Tad 1995, America's Music: The Roots of Country Music (miniseries), 1996, Blue Rodeo, 1996, Dead Man's Gun, 1997, Two for Texas, 1998, Outlaw Justice, 1999, NetForce, 1999, Perfect Murder, Perfect Town: JonBenet and the City of Bolder, 2000, American Roots Music (miniseries), 2001, Lives of Saints (miniseries), 2004, 14 Hours, 2005; performed (with Rita Coolidge) songs for soundtrack of The Last Movie, 1971; composer songs Sunday Morning Comin' Down, 1970 (Song of Year Country Music Assn.), Help Me Make It Through the Night, Me and Bobby McGee, (both nominated for Grammy award for Best Song 1971), Why Me, Lord, For the Good Times, Jody and the Kid, When I Loved Her. Capt. (helicopter pilot) US Army, 1960—65. Named to Country Music Hall of Fame, Country Music Assn., 2004; recipient Johnny Cash Visionary award, Country Music TV, 2007. Office: One Way Records Inc 4250 Coral Ridge Dr Coral Springs FL 33065-7616

KRISTOL, DANIEL MARVIN, retired lawyer; b. July 7, 1936; s. Abraham Louis and Pearl Cecile (Oltman) K.; m. Katherine Fairfax Chinn, Nov. 4, 1968; children: Sarah Douglas, Susan Fairfax. BA, U. Pa., 1958, LLB, 1961. Bar: Del. 1961, U.S. Dist. Ct. Del. 1962. Assoc., ptnr. Killoran & VanBrunt, Wilmington, Del., 1961-76; dir. Prickett, Jones, Elliott & Kristol, Wilmington, 1976-99; ptnr. predecessor Prickett, Ward Burt & Sanders, Wilmington, 1976-99; dir. Richards, Layton & Finger, Wilmington, 1999—2006, ret., 2006; spl. master Superior Ct. of New Castle County, Wilmington, 2007. Pub. defender Ct. Common Pleas, Wilmington, 1966-69; asst. solicitor City of Wilmington, 1970-73; spl. counsel Div. Housing State of Del., 1972-87, gen. counsel Del. State Housing Authority, 1973-99; special master Superior Ct. New Castle, Del., 2007. With USAR, 1964-67. Mem. ABA, Del. State Bar Assn. (chmn. real and personal property com. 1974-78, chmn. world peace through law com. 1980-81, chmn. sr. lawyers com. 1999—), Am. Coll. Real Estate Lawyers, Wilmington Country Club, Greenville Country Club, Mill Reef Club (Antigua, W.I.), Wilmington Club, Penn Club of N.Y. Republican. Jewish. Office: PO Box 551 Wilmington DE 19899-0551 E-mail: kristol@rlf.com.

KRISTOL, WILLIAM (BILL KRISOL), editor, political analyst; b. NYC, Dec. 23, 1952; s. Irving Kristol and Gertrude Himmelfarb; m. Susan Scheinberg, Dec. 28, 1975; children: Rebecca Louise, Anne Elizabeth, Joseph Max. AB, Harvard U., 1973, PhD, 1979. Instr., then asst. prof. polit. sci. U. Pa., Phila., 1978-83; asst. prof. pub. policy Harvard U., Kennedy Sch. Govt., Cambridge, Mass., 1983-85; spl. asst., chief of staff US Dept. Edn., Washington, 1985-89; campaign mgr. Alan Keyes for Senate, Md., 1988; domestic policy adv. Office of V.P., The White House, Washington, 1989, chief of staff to v.p., 1989-93; dir. Bradley Project of 90s, Washington, 1993; chmn. Project for the Rep. Future, Washington, 1993-95; co-founder, editor The Weekly Standard, Washington, 1995—. Appears regularly FOX News Sunday, FOX News Channel; co-author (with Lawrence Kaplan): The War Over Iraq: America's Mission and Saddam's Tyranny, 2003. Mem.: Washington Speakers Bur. Jewish. Office: Weekly Standard 1150 17th St NW Ste 505 Washington DC 20036-4621

KRITZER, PAUL ERIC, publishing executive, lawyer; b. Buffalo, May 5, 1942; s. James Cyril and Bessie May (Biddlecombe) K.; m. Frances Jean McCallum, June 20, 1970; children: Caroline Frances, Erica Han. BA, Williams Coll., 1964; MS in Journalism, Columbia U., 1965; JD, Georgetown U., 1972. Bar: U.S. Supreme Ct. 1978, Wis. 1980. Reporter, copy editor Buffalo Evening News, 1964, 69, 70; instr. English Augusta Coll., Ga., 1968-69; law clk. Office of FCC Commr., Washington, 1971, MCI, Washington, 1972; counsel US Ho. of Reps., Washington, 1972-77; assoc. counsel Des Moines Register & Tribune, 1977-80; editor, pub. Waukesha Freeman, Wis., 1980-83; legal v.p., sec. Jour. Comm. Inc., Milw., 1983—. Trustee Carroll Co., Waukesha, 1981-89; producer Waukesha Film Festival, 1982; bd. dirs. Des Moines Metro Opera, Inc., 1979-80, Milw. Youth Symphony Orch., 1992-2001, pres. 1994-97; bd. dirs. United Performing Arts Fund, 1994-97, Milw. Symphony Orch., 1997-2004, Waukesha Landmarks Commn., 2005-06; adj. instr. Marquette U., 2007—. With US Army, 1965—68. Presbyterian. Avocations: bridge, gardening. Home: 211 Oxford Rd Waukesha WI 53186-6263 Office: Jour Communications Inc 333 W State St PO Box 661 Milwaukee WI 53201-0661 Home Phone: 262-548-9666; Office Phone: 414-224-2374. Business E-Mail: pkritzer@journalcommunications.com.

KRITZMACHER, JOHN A., telecommunications industry executive; BS in Math and Economics, Dartmouth Coll., 1982; MBA, NYU Stern Sch. Bus. Joined accelerated leadership devel. program Bell Labs, 1982, various positions in fin. planning and analysis, partnership and acquisition planning, moved into mktg. and sales, systems engring. and market unit mgmt., 1989; head fin.planning and analysis team former Network Systems Group Lucent Technologies, 1996, fin. v.p. switching solutions group, 1998, fin. v.p. product lines and supply chain operations, corp. contr., 2001—06, CFO, 2006—. Office: Lucent Technologies 600 Mountain Ave New Providence NJ 07974

KRIVKOVICH, PETER GEORGE, advertising executive; b. Bad Ischl, Austria, Oct. 25, 1946; came to U.S., 1953; s. George M. Krivkovich and Ada (Kalenkiewicz) Bajor; children: Peter A., Alexis C. BS, U. Ill., 1969; postgrad., Loyola U., Chgo., 1972-73. Advt. asst. Kemper Ins. Co., Chgo., 1969-71; account exec. Nader-Lief, Chgo., 1971-72; account mgr. Leo Burnett, Chgo., 1972-73; ptnr. Hackenberg, Normann, Krivkovich, Chgo., 1973-80; pres. Cramer-Krasselt, Chgo., 1981-86, pres., COO, 1987-98, pres., CEO, chmn. bd., 1999—; pres., CEO CKPR, 2002—. Mem. Nat. Advt. Rev. Bd. Bd. dirs. Off The Street Club, 1997—, Prentice Hosp., 1998—, Chgo. Humanities Festival, 2002—03. Named One of 100 Best and Brightest Advt. Execs. of Yr. Advt. Age mag., 1986, Midwest Advt. Exec. of Yr. Adweek mag., 1987. Mem. Am. Assn. Advt. Agys. (chmn. Chgo. chpt. 1992, 93, regional bd. govs. 1996, 97, nat. bd. govs. 1998-2002, 06—, bd. dirs. Ad coun. 2007—), Direct Mktg. Assn., Chgo. Assn. Direct Mktg., Chgo. Advt. Club, Glenview (Ill.) C. of C., Tavern Club, Exec. Club. Office: Cramer-Krasselt 225 N Michigan Ave Ste 800 Chicago IL 60601-7690 E-mail: pkrivkov@c-k.com.

KRIVOSHIA, ELI, JR., lawyer; b. Midland, Pa., Apr. 20, 1935. BA, U. Pitts., 1957; LLB, Harvard U., 1960. Bar: 1961. Assoc., Throp, Reed & Armstrong, Pitts., 1960-69, ptnr., 1970-83; gen. Counsel Nat. Steel Corp., 1983-95, pvt. practice, Pitts., 1995—. Mem. Allegheny County Bar Assn., ABA, Pa. Bar Assn. Office Phone: 412-394-6810.

KRIVOSHIK, ANDREW PETER, engineer, physician; b. Elizabeth, NJ, Feb. 20, 1968; s. Peter Enoch and Elizabeth Elsie Krivoshik; m. Susan Elise Lyon, Aug. 10, 1991; children: Amy, David. BSE with honors, Princeton U., NJ, 1990; MD, U. Ill., 1999, PhD, 2001. Diplomate Am. Bd. of Pediatrics; registered profl. engr. Tech. cons. KEA Inc., Elizabeth, NJ, 1983-90; technician IBM TJ Watson, Yorktown Heights, NY, 1988, 89; resident physician pediat. Mayo Clinic, Rochester, Minn., 1999—2002; fellow pediatric hematology-oncology Duke U. Med. Ctr., 2002—04; assoc. med. dir, physician devel. program Abbott Labs., 2004—06, med. dir. oncology group, 2006—. Elec. item writer NCEES, 1996. Contbr. articles to profl. jours. Fellow U. Ill. at Urbana-Champaign, 1990-91, 98-99, Molecular Biophysics Tng. Grant USPHS, 1991-93, V Found. Cancer Rsch., 2002-2004. Mem. NSPE, IEEE, Biophys. Soc., Cum Laude Soc., Tau Beta Pi. Office: Abbott Labs Oncology Group R48K AP30 200 Abbott Park Rd Abbott Park IL 60064 Business E-Mail: andrew.krivoshik@abbott.com.

KRIVOSHIK, DAVID PETER, lawyer; s. Peter Enoch and Elizabeth Elsie Krivoshik; m. Cindy S. Sousa, Aug. 1, 1992; children: Dawn Marie Hartman, Paula Diane, Laura Amy, Peter David, Danielle Natasha. BS in Engring. and Biol. Scis., Rutgers U., New Brunswick, NJ, 1976; M in Elec. Engring., Stevens Inst. Tech., Hoboken, NJ, 1978; JD, Rutgers Law School-Newark, Newark, NJ, 1990—94. Bar: Pa. 1994, USPTO 1994, NJ 1995, US Dist. Ct. NJ 1995. Dir. data processing City of Elizabeth, 1977—79; profl. engr. Krivoshik Engring., Elizabeth, 1979—94; patent atty. Gibbons Del Deo Dolan Griffinger & Vecchione, Newark, 1994—2000; sr. patent atty. Mathews Shepherd, Princeton, NJ, 2000—06, Lerner David Littenberg Krumholtz & Mentlik, Westfield, NJ, 2006—. Contbr. articles to profl. publs. Mem.: Mensa. Office: Lerner David Littenberg Krumholz Mentlik 600 South Ave West Westfield NJ 07090 Home Phone: 908-788-8705; Office Phone: 908-654-5000. Business E-Mail: dkrivoshik@ldlkm.com.

KRIZ, FRANK KENNETH, JR., surgeon; s. Frank Kenneth and Virginia Mary Kriz; m. Jeanette Elizabeth Kriz; 5 children. BS, U. Md., College Park, 1954; MD, U. Md., Balt., 1958. Diplomate Am. Bd. Orthop. Surgery. Clin. asst. prof. U. S. Fla., Tampa, 1971—. Lt. col. US Army, 1958—69. Fellow: ACS, Am. Acad. Orthop. Surgeons; mem.: N.Am. Spine Soc. Office: 800 Dr M L King Jr Blvd Ste 1 Tampa FL 33603

KRIZ, GEORGE JAMES, retired agricultural research administrator; b. Brainard, Nebr., Sept. 20, 1936; s. George Jacob and Rose Agnes Kriz; m. Patricia Elizabeth Kelly (div. Feb. 1989); children: Rosalie Sue, Richard Patrick, Thomas George; m. Rhoda Mae Whitacre, June 23, 1989. BS in Agrl. Engring., Iowa State U., 1960, MS in Agrl. Engring., 1962; PhD, U. Calif., Davis, 1965. Lectr. U. Calif., Davis, 1965; asst. prof. agrl. engring. N.C. State U., Raleigh, 1965-68, assoc. prof., 1968-72, prof., 1972-99, assoc. dept. head, 1969-73, asst. rsch. dir., 1973-81, assoc. rsch. dir., 1981-99, prof. emeritus, 1999—. Operator bed and breakfast. Fellow Am. Soc. Agrl. Engring. (bd. dirs. 1983-85, found. trustee 1986-94, 96-97, pres. 1995-96, presdl. citation 1988, 91); mem. Coun. Agrl. Scis. and Tech. Avocations: gardening, walking. Office Phone: 540-450-0341. E-mail: house@visuallink.com.

KRIZAN, KELLY JOE, physician, leather craftsman; b. Winner, SD, Jan. 16, 1951; s. Miles Woodrow and Sadie Mae (DeSmet) Kelly; m. Susan Barker Krizan, Aug. 21, 1971 (div. Aug. 1983); children: Nicholas Miles, Jennifer Rebecca; m. Cynthia Lydia Obras, Aug. 6, 1983. BS, SD State U., 1973; BS medicine, U. SD, 1976; MD, Tufts U., 1978. Diplomate Am. Bd. Family Practice, commd. Am. Bd. Radiology. Intern USAF Med. Ctr., Scott AFB, Ill., 1978—79, resident Ill., 1979—81; staff physician USAF Hosp., Hill AFB, Utah, 1981—83, chief emergency svcs., chief family practice Utah, 1983—84, USAF Hosp., Ircirlik AB, Turkey, 1983—84; chmn. dept. family practice USAF Hosp., Hill AFB, 1985—86; resident radiology U. Wash., 1986—90, clin. asst. prof., 1990—; chmn. dept. radiology 13th AF Med. Ctr., Clark AB, Philippines, 1990—91, St. Mary's Health Care Ctr., Pierre, SD, 1993—2005, chief staff, 1997, Walla Walla (Wash.) Gen. Hosp., 2006—; pres. bd. dirs. Oahe Inc., 2001—05. Bd. dirs. St. Mary's Found., Pierre, SD, Walla Walla Gen. Hosp. Leather goods, (various awards). Bd. dir. Pierre Players, Short Grass Art Coun. First active duty capt. USAF, 1978—84, lt. col. USAF, 1984. Named one of Am. Top Radiologists, Rsch. Coun. Am., Am.'s Top Physicians; recipient Winner Regional Healthcare Ctr., St. Mary's Found., 1993—94. Fellow: Am. Acad. Family Physicians; mem.: Radiol. Soc. N. Am., Am. Roentgen Ray Soc., Am. Coll. Radiology (rural econ. com. mem. 2003—), Phi Kappa Phi. Roman Catholic. Office: Walla Walla Gen Hosp 1025 South 2nd Ave Walla Walla WA 99362 Office Phone: 509-527-8000 ext. 1320. Business E-Mail: kellykrizan@mac.com.

KRIZEK, EDWIN JOHN, marketing professional; b. NYC, Dec. 28, 1954; s. Virginia Ruth and Edwin John Krizek; life ptnr. Caroline Leland. BA, U. Pa., 1975, MS, 1976; MBA, Columbia U., 1982, MPH, 1983. Pres. Krizek Mktg., Swarthmore, Pa., 1998—. Author: (chpt.) Threshold, 2002, (short story collection) Afterlife and Other Stories, 2004. Mem. Unitarian Universalist Ch. of Del. County, Media, Pa., 1994—2003. Home and Office: Krizek Mktg 801 Yale Ave #830 Swarthmore PA 19081 Office Phone: 610-328-7593. Personal E-mail: ekrizek@yahoo.com.

KRIZEK, RAYMOND JOHN, engineering educator, consultant; b. Balt., June 5, 1932; s. John James and Louise (Polak) K.; m. Claudia Stricker, Aug. 1964; children: Robert A., Kevin J. BE, Johns Hopkins U., 1954; MS, U. Md., 1961; PhD, Northwestern U., 1963; doctorate (hon.), U. Cantabria, Spain, 2003. Instr. U. Md., College Park, 1957-61; rsch. asst. civil engring. Northwestern U., Evanston, Ill., 1961-63, asst. prof. civil engring., 1963-66, assoc. prof. civil engring., 1966-70, prof. civil engring., 1970—, chmn. dept. civil engring., 1980-92, dir. Master of Project Mgmt. program, 1994—, Stanley F. Pepper chair prof., 1987—. Cons. to industry. Editor books; contbr. numerous articles to profl. jours. Served to lt. U.S. Army Corp Engrs., 1955-57. Decorated Palmes Academiques (France); recipient Hogentogler award ASTM, 1970; named disting. vis. scholar NSF, 1972. Mem.: ASCE (pres. GEO Inst. 1997—98, Huber Rsch. prize 1971, Karl Terzaghi award 1997, Ill. sect. Civil Engr. of Yr. 1999, Hon. mem. 2002, Wallace Hayward Baker award Geo-Inst. 2003, G. Brooks Earnest award 2005, Karl Terzaghi lecture 2006), Internat. Soc. Soil Mechanics and Geotech. Engring., Nat. Acad. Engring., Spanish Royal Acad. Engring. (corr.). Roman Catholic. Home: 1366 Sanford Ln Glenview IL 60025-3165 Office: Dept Civil Engring Northwestern U 2145 Sheridan Rd Evanston IL 60208-3109 Office Phone: 847-491-4040. Business E-Mail: rjkrizek@northwestern.edu.

KROCHALIS, RICHARD F., federal agency administrator; BS in Environ. Sys. Engring., Cornell U.; M in City and Regional Planning, Harvard U. Dir. dept. constrn. and land use City of Seattle, Seattle, 1992-99, dir. dept. design, constrn. and land use, 1999—2001; regional adminstr. Fed. Transit Adminstrn., 2002—. Past pres. Sustainable Seattle, 2002-03; mem. U. Wash. Capital Campaign Cabinet, 2003-; mem. coun. Cornell U., 1991-98; co-chair Cornell U. Coll. of Arch. Art, Planning Adv. Coun., 2005-. Mem. Urban Land Inst., Am. Planning Assn., Am. Inst. Cert. Planners. Office: FederalTransit Adminstrn Ste 3142 915 Second Ave Seattle WA 98174-1002 Office Phone: 206-220-7954. E-mail: rick.krochalis@dot.gov.

KROCK, CURTIS JOSSELYN, pulmonologist; b. Fort Smith, Ark., Oct. 11, 1935; s. Frederick Henry and Hazel Armiger (Josselyn) Krock; m. Ruth Leone Johnson, Apr. 27, 1968; children: Eric Gregory, Lynn Alyson; m. Susan de la Fuente, July 15, 2006. BA, Stanford U., 1957; MD, Johns Hopkins U. Sch. Medicine, 1961. Diplomate Am. Bd. Internal Medicine, Am. Bd. Pulmonary Medicine. Intern Barnes Hosp., St. Louis, 1961-62, resident in internal medicine, 1963-65; resident in pathology Johns Hopkins U. Sch. Medicine, Balt., 1962-63; pulmonary fellow Duke U., Durham, NC, 1965-66; pvt. practice Holt-Krock Clinic, Ft. Smith, Ark., 1968-72, Carle Clinic, Urbana, Ill., 1972-2001, also bd. dirs., 1978-80, chief medicine dept., 1996-99; clin. asst. prof. U. Ill., Urbana, 1976-99, clin. assoc. prof., 2000—; interim chief of medicine UICOM-UC; chief of medicine Carle Found. Hosp., 2003—. Capt. US Army, 1966—68. Fellow: ACP; mem.: Sierra Club, Sigma Xi. Avocations: violin, reading. Home: 2125 Lynwood Dr Champaign IL 61821-6606 Office: Carle Clin Edn Ctr Forum Bldg 611 W Park Urbana IL 61801-2530 Office Phone: 217-383-4617. Personal E-mail: ckrock1935@aol.com. Business E-Mail: curtis.krock@carle.com.

KROEBER, KARL, language educator; b. Oakland, Calif., Nov. 24, 1926; s. Alfred Louis and Theodora Quinn (Kracaw) K.; m. Jean Taylor, Mar. 21, 1953; children— Paul Demarest, Arthur Romeyn, Katharine. AA, Coll. of Pacific, Stockton, Calif., 1945; AB, U. Calif., Berkeley, 1947; MA, Columbia U., 1951, PhD, 1956. Asst. prof. U. Wis.-Madison, 1956-61, asso. prof., 1961-63, prof., 1963-70; asso. dean U. Wis.-Madison (Grad. Sch.), 1963-65; prof. English and comparative lit. Columbia U., NYC, 1970—, chmn. dept. English and comparative lit., 1973-76, Mellon prof. humanities, 1987. Author: Romantic Narrative Art, 1960, The Artifice of Reality, 1964, Studying Poetry, 1965, Backgrounds to British Romantic Literature, 1968, Styles in Fictional Structure, 1971, Romantic Landscape Vision, 1975, Images of Romanticism, 1978, Traditional Literatures of the American Indian, 1981, rev. edit. 1997, Wordsworthian Scholarship and Criticism, 1973-84, 1986, British Romantic Art, 1986, Romantic Fantasy and Science Fiction, 1988, Retelling/Rereading, 1992, Romantic Poetry: Recent Revisionary Criticism, 1993, Native American Persistence and Resurgence, 1994, Ecological Literary Criticism, 1994, Artistry in Native American Myths, 1998, Ishi in Three Centuries, 2003, Native American Storytelling, 2004, Make Believe in Film and Fiction, 2006; emeritus editor Studies in American Indian Literatures; mem. editl. bd. The Wordsworth Circle, Native American Bibiliography Series, Studies in English Lit., Boundary 2. Served with USNR, 1944-46. Named Disting. Scholar, Keats-Shelley Assn., 1991; Fulbright Rsch. grantee Italy, 1960-61, U.S. Office Edn. Rsch. grantee, 1965-66; Guggenheim fellow, 1966-67; NEH fellow, 1991. Mem. MLA, Internat. Assn. Univ. Profs. English, N.Am. Soc. Study of Romanticism, Jane Austen Soc. N.Am., Acad. Lit. Studies, Byron Soc., Assn. for Study of Native Am. Lit., Keats-Shelley Assn. Office: Columbia U Dept English & Comparative Lit New York NY 10027 Office Phone: 212-854-5210. Business E-Mail: kk17@columbia.edu.

KROEGER, CHAD, musician; b. Hanna, Alta., Can., Nov. 15, 1974; Guitarist & lead singer Nickelback, 1995—; signed to Roadrunner Records, NYC; co-founder VI0VI (604) Records, Vancouver, Canada, 2002—. Musician: (albums) Curb, 1996, The State, 2000, Silver Side Up, 2001 (Juno award for Best Album, 2002), The Long Road, 2003, All the Right Reasons, 2005 (Juno award for Best Rock Album, 2006, Favorite Rock Album award, Am. Music Awards, 2006, Billboard Rock Album of Yr., 2006), (songs) How You Remind Me (Juno award for Best Single, 2002, Billboard Top 100 Single, Top 100 Track, Top Hot 40 Track, Top Hot 100 Airplay Track, 2002). Named Top 100 Singles Artist, Billboard, 2002, Favorite Group, People's Choice Awards, 2007; recipient Best New Group award, Juno Awards, 2001, Best Group award, 2002, 2006, Songwriters of Yr. award, 2003, Group of Yr., Billboard Music Awards, 2006, Hot 100 Group of Yr., 2006, World's Best Rock Group, World Music Awards, 2007, Best-Selling Canadian Artist, 2007. Office: c/o Bryan Coleman Union Entertainment Group 1323 Newbury Rd Ste 104 Thousand Oaks CA 91320 also: 604 Records Unit 362 101-1001 W Broadway Vancouver BC V6H 4E4 Canada*

KROELL, DEVI, accessories designer; b. Austria, 1980; Formerly designer Jean-Charles de Castelbajac, Place Vendome jewelers; owner Devi Kroell - East Hampton Store, NY, 2006—. Recipient Swarovski's Perry Ellis award for Accessory Design, Coun. of Fashion Designers of Am., 2006. Achievements include design and portraits featured in Vogue, W, Elle, Town & Country, Harper's Bazaar, People, US Weekly. Office: 670 Broadway, Ste 506 New York NY 10012 Office Phone: 212-228-3201. Office Fax: 212-228-3237.

KROEMER, HERBERT, electrical engineering educator; b. Weimar, Germany, Aug. 25, 1928; Diplom-Physiker, Gottingen U., Germany, 1951, Dr. rer. nat., 1952; Doctorate (hon.), Tech. U. Aachen, Germany, 1985, U. Lund, Sweden, 1998, U. Colo., 2001. Prof. elec., computer engring. U. Calif., Santa Barbara, faculty rsch. lectr., 1985—96, Donald W. Whittier chair in elec. engring., 1986—. Recipient Heinrich Welker medal Internat. Symposium on GaAs and related compounds, 1982, Alexander von Humboldt Rsch. award, 1994, NAE, 1997, Nobel Prize in physics, 2000, Order of merit, Germany, 2001. Mem. NAS, IEEE (J.J. Ebers award Electron Devices Group 1973, Nat. lectr. 1983, Jack Morton award 1986, Medal of Honor, 2002), Am. Phys. Soc. Office: Rm 4107 Elec-Computer Engring Dept Univ Calif Santa Barbara CA 93106-9560

KROENER, WILLIAM FREDERICK, III, lawyer; b. NYC, Aug. 27, 1945; s. William Frederick Kroener Jr. and Barbara (Mitchell) Kroener; m. Evelyn Somerville Bibb, Sept. 3, 1966; children: William F. Kroener IV(dec.) , Mary Elizabeth, Evangeline Alberta, James Mitchell. AB, Yale Coll., 1967; JD, MBA, Stanford U., Calif., 1971. Bar: Calif. 1972, N.Y. 1979, D.C. 1983. Assoc. Davis Polk & Wardwell, NYC, 1971-79, London, 1974—75, ptnr. NYC, 1979-82, 1982-94, Washington, 1982—94; gen. counsel FDIC, 1995—2006; counsel Sullivan & Cromwell LLP, Washington and LA, 2006—. Lectr. Stanford U. Law Sch., 1993—94, George Washington U. Law Sch., 1995—98, Washington Coll. Law, Am. U. Law Sch., Washington, 1997—2003; mem. legal adv. group Fed. Fin. Instns. Exam. Coun., 1995—2006, chmn. legal adv. group, 2001—03. Pres. Kroener Family Found.; gov. bd. mem. St. Albans Sch., 1991—95; fin. com. mem. Protestant/Episcopal Cathedral Found.-Wash. Nat. Cathedral, 1992—95; mem. bd. visitors Stanford U. Law Sch., 1983—92, deans adv. coun., 1992—93; nat. chair Stanford Law Fund, 1990—92; dir., gen. counsel Kenwood Citizens Assn., Inc., 1993—94; governing bd. FDIC Corp. Univ., 2002—06. Mem.: ABA, Assn. Bar City of NY, Am. Law Inst., Lido Isle Yacht Club, Kenwood Golf Club, Yale Club of NYC. Republican. Episcopalian. Office: Sullivan & Cromwell LLP 1701 Pennsylvania Ave NW Washington DC 20006-5605 also: Sullivan & Cromwell LLP 1888 Century Park E Los Angeles CA 90067-1725 Office Phone: 202-956-7095. Business E-Mail: kroenerw@sullcrom.com.

KROENING, K. DUBEAR, biology professor, researcher; b. Elmhurst, Ill., Oct. 20, 1964; s. Ronald and Ann Kroening; m. Cindy Morey, Jan. 6, 2001; children: Riann Kreiling, Nathan Kreiling, Jared Kreiling, Karlee. BS, No. Mich. U., Marquette, 1989; PhD, U. Minn., Twin Cities, 1995. Postdoctoral rschr. U. Wis., Madison, 1995—2000; asst. prof. biol. scis. U. Wis. Fox Valley, Menasha, 2000—. Contbr. articles to profl. jours. Recipient Tchr. Yr. award, Jour. Parasiology, 2006. Mem.: Am. Soc. Microbiology. Achievements include patents pending for an improved method for preserving grain byproducts. Office: Univ Wis Fox Valley 1478 Midway Rd Menasha WI 54952 Office Phone: 920-832-0117. Office Fax: 920-832-2674. Business E-Mail: dubear.kroening@uwc.edu.

KROENKE, E. STANLEY, real estate developer, professional sports team owner; b. Cole Camp, Mo. m. Ann (Walton) Kroenke; children: Whitney, Josh. Grad. in Bus., U. Mo., MBA, 1973. Chmn., owner The Kroenke Grp., Columbia, Mo.; chmn. THF Realty; owner Kroenke Sports Enterprises; vice chmn., co-owner NFL St. Louis Rams, 1995—; owner Pepsi Ctr., Denver, 2000—, NBA Denver Nuggets, 2000—, NHL Colo. Avalanche, 2000—, Arena Football League Colo. Crush, 2002—, Nat. Lacrosse League Colo. Mammoth, 2002—, Maj. League Soccer Colo. Rapids, 2003—. Bd. dirs. Cmty. Investment Partnership Funds I and II, St. Louis, Boone County Nat. Bank, Columbia, Ctrl. Bancompany, Jefferson City; co-owner Screaming Eagle Vineyard, Napa Valley, Calif., 2006-. Trustee Coll. of the Ozarks; mem. bd. Greater St. Louis Area Coun. Boy Scouts of Am., St. Louis Art Mus. Named one of 400 Richest Ams., Forbes mag., 2006. Office: St Louis Rams 1 Rams Way Earth City MO 63045-1525*

KROEPPEL, WARREN, airport terminal executive; BS in Aero. Sci., Embry-Riddle Aero. U., 1976; MBA in Fin., Adelphi U., 1983. Cert. comml. pilot, flight instr. FAA. Comml. pilot; mgr. ops. planning redevel. program JFK Airport Port Authority, Flushing, NY, 1989—96, mgr. airport ops., security and svcs. LaGuardia Airport, 1996—99, dep. gen. mgr. John F. Kennedy Internat. Airport, 1999—2000, gen. mgr. LaGuardia Airport, 2000—. Office: LaGuardia Airport Hangar 7 Ctr 3rd Fl Flushing NY 11371 Business E-Mail: wkroeppel@panynj.gov.

KROESEN, FREDERICK JAMES, retired army officer, consultant; b. Phillipsburg, NJ, Feb. 11, 1923; s. Frederick James K. and Jean Ursula (Shillinger) Kroesen; m. Rowene Wilder McCray, Mar. 4, 1944; children: Karen McCray Kroesen Klare, Frederick J. III, Gretchen McCray Kroesen Tackaberry. BS in Agr., Rutgers U., 1944, LHD (hon.), 1983; BA in Internat. Affairs, George Washington U., 1962, MA in Internat. Affairs, 1966. Enlisted U.S. Army, 1942, commd. 2d lt., 1944, served with 63d Infantry div. WWII, advanced through grades to gen., 1976; served with 187th Airborne Regimental Combat Team, Korean War, 1953-55; instr. U.S. Army War Coll., 1962-65; mem. staff asst. chief of staff for force devel. U.S. Army, 1965-68, 70-71; served with Americal Div. Vietnam War, 1968 and 1971, comdr. Div., 1971; dep. comdr. XXIV Corps. U.S. Army, 1971-72, comdr. 1st Regn. Asst Command, VN, 1972, comdr. 82d Airborne Div., 1972-74, comdr. VII Corps in Europe., 1975-76, comdr. U.S. Army Forces Command, 1976-78, vice chief of staff U.S. Army, 1978-79; comdr.-in-chief U.S. Army, Europe, 1979-83; comdr. NATO Cen. Army Group Heidelberg, Germany, 1979-83; ret., 1983. Pvt. cons. in internat. security affairs; former mem. Army Sci. Bd. Decorated Def. D.S.M., Army D.S.M. with oak leaf cluster, Purple Heart with 2 oak leaf clusters, Silver Star with oak leaf cluster, Legion of Merit with 2 oak leaf clusters, D.F.C., Bronze Star with V and 2 oak leaf clusters, combat inf. badge with two stars; recipient Mil. Order of World War Disting. Svc. medal, 1985, Americanism award Am. Legion, 1993, State of N.J. Disting. Svc. medals, 1983, 95; named to Rutgers Hall Disting. Alumni, Rutgers Loyal Son, Cook Coll. Disting. Alumni award. Fellow Inst. Land Warfare (sr.), Assn. US Army (Creighton W. Abrams medal 2004); mem. US Army War Coll. Alumni Assn. (former pres.), US Army War Coll. Found. (past bd. dirs.), 63d Div. Assn., 82d Airborne Div. Assn., Amcl Div. Vets. Assn., Rakkasan Assn., Soc. French Legion of Honor, Soc. Rhin et Danube, Assn. Grads. US Mil. Acad. (Sylvanus Thayer award 2007), Rutgers Cap & Skull, Delta Upsilon. Home: 1250 S Washington St # 223 Alexandria VA 22314-4455 Personal E-mail: fkroesen@earthlink.net.

KROFT, STEVE, news correspondent, editor; b. Kokomo, Ind., Aug. 22, 1945; s. Fred and Margaret Kroft; m. Jennet Conant, June 29, 1991; 1 child, John Conant. BS, Syracuse U., 1967; MS in Journalism, Columbia U., 1975; DHL (hon.), Ind. U., SUNY; DHL, LI U., 2005. Reporter Sta. WSYR-TV, Syracuse, NY, 1972—74; investigative reporter Sta. WJXT-TV, Jacksonville, Fla., 1975—77; reporter Sta. WPLG-TV, Miami, Fla., 1977—79, CBS News, NYC, 1980—81, corr. S.W. bur. Dallas, 1981—83, corr. Cen. Am. bur. Miami, 1983—84, corr. London, 1984—86, prin. corr. W. 57th program NYC, 1986—89, corr., co-editor 60 Minutes, 1989—. Trustee Syracuse U. Sgt. US Army, 1970—71, Vietnam. Recipient Ohio State award, Ohio State U., 1979, 1992, 1994, Emmy awards, 1982, 1984, 1990, 1993, 1998, 2000, 2002, 2003, Lifetime Achievement Emmy award, 2003, Arents award, Syracuse U., 1992, George Foster Peabody award, 1992, 1998, 2003, Dupont award, Columbia U., 2003. Office: CBS News 60 Minutes 555 W 57th St New York NY 10019-2925

KROFT, STEVEN HOWARD, hematopathologist, medical educator; b. San Antonio, June 2, 1965; s. Arthur Ellis and Roslyn Ann Kroft; m. Laura Renee Field, June 17, 1989; children: Maxwell Alexander, Charles William, Henry Oliver. BS, MIT, 1986; MD, U. Ill., 1991. Cert. anatomic and clinical pathology Am. Bd. Pathology, 1996, hematology Am. Bd. Pathology. Resident in anat. and clin. pathology McGaw Med. Ctr. Northwestern U., Chgo., 1991—96; fellow in hematopathology U. Mich. Med. Sch., Ann Arbor, 1996—97; asst. prof. pathology U. Tex. Southwestern Med. Sch., Dallas, 1997—2002, assoc. prof. pathology, 2002—05, Med. Coll. Wis., 2005—07, prof. pathology, 2007—; dir. hematopathology Dynacare Labs., Froedtert Hosp. and Med. Coll. Wis., Milw., 2005—. Med. dir. hematology lab. Parkland Meml. Hosp., Dallas, 1997—2003; med. dir., clin. flow cytometry Veripath Labs. U. Tex. Southwestern Med. Ctr., Dallas, 2003—05, mem., med. adv. bd., 2003—05. Editor: (textbook) Color Atlas of Hemoglobin Disorders, assoc. editor: Clin. Cytometry, 2002, Lab. Medicine, 2004—07, mem. editl. adv. bd.:, 2007—, mem. editl. bd.: Am. Jour. Clin. Pathology, 2002—, Internat. J. Lab. Hematology, 2007—; contbr. chapters to books, articles to profl. jours including Blood, Am. Jour. Clin. Pathology, Brit. Jour. Hematology, Modern Pathology, Leukemia, Am. Jour. Surg. Pathology. Named one of Best Doctors in Am., 2003—06; recipient Outstanding Tchr. award, U Tex. Southwestern, 1999, Pathology Resident Tchg. award, U. Tex. Southwestern, 1999, 2000. Fellow: Am. Soc. Clin. Pathology (bd. dirs. 2006—), Coll. Am. Pathologists (mem. hematology and clin. microscopy resource com. 1998—2005, chair hematology and clin. microscopy resource com. 2006); mem.: Internat. Soc. Lab. Hematology, Soc. Hematopathology, U.S. and Can. Acad. Pathology, Am. Soc. Hematology, Clin. Cytometry Soc. Office: MCW Dept Pathology 8701 Watertown Plank Rd Milwaukee WI 53226 Home Phone: 262-242-6364; Office Phone: 414-805-8459. Office Fax: 414-805-8444. Business E-Mail: skroft@mcw.edu.

KROGH-JESPERSEN, MARY-BETH, academic administrator; b. Schenectady, NJ, Aug. 10, 1949; d. George Henry and Barbara V. (Norton) Baillie; m. Karsten Krogh-Jespersen, Dec. 20, 1975; children: Erik, Sheila Ann, Michelle Grace. BA in Chemistry, Northeastern U., 1972; MBA, Pace U., 1990; PhD in Chemistry, NYU, 1976. Lectr. in chemistry Rutgers U., New Brunswick, NJ, 1979-81; prof. Pace U., NYC, 1981-92, chair dept. chemistry, 1990-92; dean coll. of sci. Rochester (N.Y.) Inst. Tech., 1992-95; vice provost Rowan Coll., Glassboro, NJ, 1995-96; assoc. v.p. for acad. affairs Richard Stockton Coll., Pomona, NJ, 1996-2000; chancellor Pa. State Worthington Scranton, 2000—. Contbr. articles to profl. jours. Mem. Am. Chem. Soc., Am. Phys. Soc. Roman Catholic. Office: Pa State Worthington Scranton 120 Ridgeview Dr Dunmore PA 18512-1602 Office Phone: 570-963-2539. Business E-Mail: kroghm@psu.edu.

KROHN, KENNETH ALBERT, radiologist, educator; b. Stevens Point, Wis., June 19, 1945; s. Albert William and Erma Belle (Cornwell) K.; 1 child, Galen. BA in Chemistry, Andrews U., 1966; PhD in Chemistry, U. Calif., 1971. Acting assoc. prof. U. Wash., Seattle, 1981-84, assoc. prof. radiology, 1984-86, prof. radiology and radiation oncology, 1986—, adj. prof. chemistry, 1986—. Guest scientist Donner Lab. Lawrence Berkeley (Calif.) Lab., 1980-81; radiochemist, VA Med. Ctr., Seattle, 1982—; affiliate investigator Fred Hutchinson Cancer Rsch. Ctr., 1997—. Contbr. articles to profl. jours.; patentee in field. Recipient Aebersold award, 1996; fellow, NDEA. Fellow AAAS; mem. Am. Assn. for Cancer Rsch., Am. Soc. Clin. Oncology, Am. Chem. Soc., Radiation Rsch. Soc., Soc. Nuclear Medicine, Acad. Coun., Sigma Xi. Home: 550 NE Lakeridge Dr Belfair WA 98528-8720 Office: U Washington Imaging Rsch Lab Box 356004 Seattle WA 98195-6004 Office Phone: 206-598-6245. Business E-Mail: kkrohn@u.washington.edu.

KROHN, TRACY W., oil industry executive, gas industry executive; BS in Petroleum Engring., La. State U., 1978. Petroleum engr., offshore drilling supervisor Mobil Oil Corp.; sr. engr. Taylor Energy; pres., CEO W&T OffShore, Inc., Houston, 1983—, chmn., 2004—, treas., 1997—; chmn., CEO Aviara Energy Corp., Houston, 1996—97. Named one of Forbes' Richest Americans, 2006. Office: W&T Offshore Inc Nive Greenway Plz Ste 300 Houston TX 77046

KROHNFELDT, GRETCHEN ANN, secondary school educator, genealogist; b. Denver, Jan. 7, 1970; d. Howard Glen and Rita Iris (Adomite) Acker; m. Mark Dale Krohnfeldt, Dec. 22, 1996; children: Cara Rhiannon, Caius Alexander, Caxton William. BA in World History, U. Colo., Denver, 1992, MA in Curriculum and Instrn., 2002. Children's photographer, Lakewood, Colo., 1988—94; pvt. genealogist Colo., 1988—; tchr. Jefferson County Schs., Arvada, Colo., 1994—. Mentor tchr. Jefferson County Schs., 1999—, mem. assessment writing team, 2000—01, mem. instrl. advocacy team, 2003—05. Recipient Value award: Teamwork, Jefferson County Bd. Edn., 2002, Value award: Excellence, 2005. Democrat. Episcopalian. Avocations: history, quilting, sports, photography. Office: Arvada Mid Sch 5751 Balsam Stq Arvada CO 80002 Home: 6504 Moss Cir Arvada CO 80007 Personal E-mail: krohnfeldt@msn.com.

KROHNKE, DUANE W., retired lawyer; b. Keokuk, Iowa, June 29, 1939; s. Ward Glenn and Marian Frances (Brown) K.; m. Mary Alyce Luschen, June 25, 1963; children: Alan Duane, Brian Douglas. BA, Grinnell Coll., Iowa, 1961, Oxford U., 1963, MA, 1970; JD, U. Chgo., 1966; DHL, Grinnell Coll., 1999. Bar: N.Y. 1967, Minn. 1970, U.S. Supreme Ct. 1970, U.S. Ct. Appeals (2d cir.) 1967, U.S. Ct. Appeals (8th cir.) 1970, U.S. Ct. Appeals (D.C.) 1974, U.S. Dist. Ct. (so., ea. dists.) N.Y. 1967, U.S. Dist. Ct. Minn. 1970. Assoc. atty. Cravath, Swaine, Moore, NYC, 1966-70, Faegre & Benson, Mpls., 1970-73, ptnr., 1974-2000, of counsel, 2001; ret., 2001. Adj. prof. U. Minn. Law Sch., 2002—. Editl. bd.: U. Chgo. Lit. Rev., 1964—66. Co-chair Bicentennial com. U.S. Dist. Ct. Minn. dist., Mpls., 1986-88; elder Westminster Presbyn. Ch., Mpls., 1985-91; trustee United Theol. Seminary, New Brighton, Minn., 1988-98. Recipient Alumni award Grinnell Coll., 1982; Rhodes scholar Rhodes Trustees, Oxford, Eng., 1961-63; Mecham scholar U. Chgo., 1963-66. Mem. Minn. State Bar Assn. (co-chair antitrust sect. 1982-84, co-chair ethics/standards of practice com. of ADR sect. 1995-96, chair elect ADR sect. 1996-97, chair ADR sect. 1997-98), Minn. Human Rights Advocates (vol. award 1991, 99, 2002), Order of Coif, Phi Beta Kappa. Avocations: reading, exercise.

KROKHIN, ARKADII, physics professor; b. Irkutsk, Russia, Feb. 1, 1956; arrived in U.S., 2003; s. Anatolii Krokhin and Lidiya Smirnova; m. Lyudmila Gumen, Dec. 28, 1979; children: Andrey, Oleg. MS in Physics, Kharkov State U., Ukraine, 1978; PhD, Kiev State U., Ukraine, 1983. Sr. rschr. Inst. Radiophysics and Electronics, Kharkov, 1983—92; prof. physics U. Autonoma de Puebla, Mexico, 1992—2003, U. North Tex., Denton, Tex., 2003—. Sr. assoc. Internat. Ctr. Theoretical Physics, Trieste, Italy, 2001—03. Contbr. articles to profl. jours. Grantee, Dept. Energy CONACyT, 1995—2003. Mem.: Am. Phys. Soc. Avocations: tennis, skiing. Office: Univ North Texas PO Box 311427 Denton TX 76203 Office Phone: 940-565-3968. Business E-Mail: arkady@unt.edu.

KROLICK, MERRILL A., cardiologist; b. NYC, Oct. 14, 1959; s. Stanley David and Barbara Krolick; m. Dana Konopka, Oct. 19, 1989; children: Matthew, Alex. BS, Rensselaer Poly. Inst., 1981; DO, Coll. Osteo. Medicine, NY, 1985. Bd. cert. Internal Medicine, Cardiology, Interventional Cardiology. Cardiologist Prince William Cardiology, Manassas, Va., 1992—94, The Heart and Vascular Inst. of Fla., Largo, Fla., 1994—. Contbr. articles to med. jours. Pres. Am. Heart Assn. Pinellas County, Largo, 1996. Republican. Office: Heart & Vascular Inst of Fla 1345 W Bay Dr Largo FL 33770 Home: 7664 Hunter Ln Pinellas Park FL 33782 Home Phone: 727-546-0952; Office Phone: 727-489-5400. Personal E-mail: mkrolick@tampabay.rr.com.

KROLICKI, BRIAN KEITH, lieutenant governor, former state official; b. Providence, Dec. 31, 1960; s. Thadeus James Krolicki and Gail Carolyn (Gourdeau) Jacaus; m. Kelly Lea DiGiusto, May 21, 1994. BA in Polit. Sci., Stanford U., 1983. Cert. gov. fin. mgr.; lic. securities dealer. Assoc. banker Bankers Trust Co., NYC, 1984-85; sr. acct. exec. First Commodity Boston, Zephyr Cove, Nev., 1985-86; acct. exec. Smith Barney, San Francisco, 1986-87, investment banker Manama, Bahrain, 1987-89; pres. Inter Am. Mktg. Corp., Reno, London, 1989-91; chief dep. state treas. and sec. state bd. fin. State of Nev., Carson City, 1991-99, state treas., 1999—2006, lt. gov., 2007—. Sec. Nev. Master Lease Corp., Carson City, 1992—. Mem. Rep. State Ctrl. Com., Nev., 1990; vice-chmn. planning commn. Douglas County, Minden, Nev., 1991; chmn. support svcs. Am. Cancer Soc., Nev., 1993-96, bd. dirs. Southwestern US divsn.; bd. dirs. found. Lake Tahoe (Calif.) C.C., 1996. Recipient Unruh award, 2004, Gritz award for Excellence in Pub. Fin. Mem. Nev. Govt. Fin. Officer Assn. (pres. 1997—). Avocations: guitar, outdoors. Office: Lieutenant Governor Capitol Complex Carson City NV 89701 Office Phone: 775-684-5637. Office Fax: 775-684-5782.*

KROLIK, JULIAN HENRY, astrophysicist, educator; b. Detroit, Apr. 4, 1950; m. Elaine F. Weiss, Oct. 9, 1983; children: Theodore, Abigail. BS, MIT, 1971; PhD, U. Calif., Berkeley, 1977. Mem. Inst. for Advanced Study, Princeton, NJ, 1977-79; postdoctoral scientist MIT, Cambridge, Mass., 1979-81; rsch. assoc. Harvard U., Cambridge, Mass., 1981-84; asst. prof. Johns Hopkins U., Balt., 1984-86, assoc. prof., 1986-91, prof., 1991—. Office: Johns Hopkins Univ Dept Of Physics Astron Baltimore MD 21218

KROLL, BARRY LEWIS, retired lawyer; b. Chgo., June 8, 1934; s. Harry M. and Hannah (Lewis) K.; m. Jayna Vivian Leibovitz, June 20, 1956; children: Steven Lee, Joan Lois Kroll Dolgin, Nancy Maxine Kroll Richardson. AB in Psychology with distinction, U. Mich., 1955, JD with distinction, 1958. Bar: Ill. 1958. Assoc. firm Jacobs & McKenna, Chgo., 1958-66, Epstein, Manilow & Sachnoff, Chgo., 1966-68, Schiff, Hardin, Waite Dorschel & Britton, Chgo., 1968-69; ptnr. Wolfberg & Kroll, Chgo., 1970-74, Kirshbaum & Kroll, Chgo., 1972-74; of counsel Jacobs, Williams & Montgomery, Ltd., Chgo., 1973-74; ptnr. Jacobs, Williams & Montgomery Ltd., Chgo., 1974-85, Williams & Montgomery Ltd., Chgo., 1985—2001; of counsel Williams Montgomery & John, Ltd., 2002—. Faculty John Marshall Law Sch., Chgo., 1969-73; atty. for petitioner in U.S. Supreme Ct. decision Escobedo vs Ill., 1964; mem. legal and legis. com. Internat. Franchise Assn., 1976-80 Asst. editor: Mich. Law Rev, 1957-58. Chmn. Park Forest Bd. Zoning Appeals, Ill., 1971-78. Served to Capt., Judge Advocate Gen. Corps, US Army, 1959-63. Named Outstanding Young Man, Park Forest Jr. C. of C., 1966. Mem. Ill. Bar Assn., Chgo. Bar Assn. (chmn. legis. com. 1974-75), Ill. Appellate Lawyers Assn. (treas. 1978-79, sec. 1979-80, pres. 1981-82), Bar Assn. 7th Fed. Circuit, Order of Coif, Tau Epsilon Rho, Alpha Epsilon Pi. Jewish (trustee congregation 1966-70, 72-75, 90—, pres. men's club 1965-66). Home: 1440 N State Pkwy Apt 21B Chicago IL 60610-6509 Personal E-mail: jaynabarry@msn.com, blk@willmont.com.

KROLL, CONNIE RAE, librarian, information services consultant; b. Karlstad, Minn., June 12, 1955; d. Rudolph Julius and Irene Eleanor K. AAS, U. Minn., Crookston, Minn., 1975; BA, U. ND, Grand Forks, 1992; MLIS, U. Okla., Norman, 1993; postgrad. studies, Tex. Woman's U., Denton, 1993—96. Circulation svcs. asst. N.W. Regional Libr., Thief River Falls, Minn., 1979-84, br. libr. substitute Warren, Hallock, Minn., 1985-88; libr. rsch. asst. U. ND, Grand Forks, 1988-90; circulation asst. Grand Forks Pub. Libr., 1990-91; supr. interlibr. svcs. U. ND Med. Libr., Grand Forks, 1988-92; grad. asst. reference Bizzell Libr. U. Okla., Norman, 1993; grad. asst., vol. Tex. Woman's U., Denton, 1993-96; libr., dir. LRC Howard Coll., San Angelo, Tex., 1996—; med. libr. Reynolds Army Hosp, Lawton, Okla., 2003—. Grant reviewer LSCA, State of Wash., Olympia, 1994; rsch. cons. Haynes & Boone Law Firm, Dallas, 1995-96; planning com., Tex. Tech. Visions of the Future, Lubbock, Tex., 1996—, instrl. coun. Howard Coll., San Angelo, Tex., 1996—; presenter: How to Avoid Vertical Stripes and an Empty Pocketbook, 1997. Vol. Christmas at Old Ft. Concho, San Angelo, Tex., 1996, 97, 99; catalog sale rep. Concho Kennel Club, San Angelo, 1997, hospitality chair, 1998, chair state employees contbn. campaign, 1998, chair Ann. Dog Show, 1999. Recipient Title IIB fellowship Dept Edn., Norman, Okla., 1993, Title IIB Dept. Edn., Denton, Tex., 1994-96, Mayo Drake scholarship State Employees Contbn. Campaign, Albuquerque, N. Mex., 1997. Mem. ALA, Tex. Libr. Assn. (com. mem.), Assn. Libr. and Info. Sci. Educators, N.D. Libr. Assn., Med. Libr. Assn. (s. ctrl. chpt. 1997). Home: 407 NW 5th St Lawton OK 73507-6934

KROLL, MARTIN N., lawyer; b. NYC, Nov. 30, 1937; s. Jack and Ruth (Strassman) K.; m. Rita Evangeline Grossman, Aug. 14, 1965; children: Spencer, Jonathan, Evan. BA, Cornell U., 1959; JD, U. Pa., 1963. Sr. ptnr. Kroll, Levy, Baron & Feinstein, NYC, 1972-80, Snow, Beeker, Kroll, Klaris & Kraus, NYC, 1980-86, Kroll, Moss and Kroll, LLP, Garden City, N.Y., 1987—. Receiver Chrysler Bldg., N.Y.C., 1975-77; village atty. Village of East Hills (N.Y.), 1988-95; counsel Town of North Hempstead, 1987-2001, counsel Econ. Devel. Agy. Town of North Hempstead, 1992—; bd. dirs. AIPAC Regional Coun.; pres. Jewish Lawyers Assn. of Nassau County, N.Y., 1980. Vice chmn. Nassau County Republican Party, Westbury, N.Y., 1986—2005. Recipient Torch of Liberty, B'Nai Brigh-ADL, 1982; named Master Builder Conf. of Jewish Educators, 1990. Mem. ABA, N.Y. State Bar Assn., Nassau County Bar Assn. Office: Kroll Moss & Kroll 400 Garden City Plz Garden City NY 11530-3322 Office Phone: 516-873-8000. E-mail: mkroll100@aol.com.

KROLL, SOL, lawyer; b. Russia, Aug. 10, 1918; m. Ruth Saslow; children: Gerald, Judy, Elise, Elliott. LLB, St. John's U., 1942. Bar: N.Y. 1942, U.S. Supreme Ct. 1956. Former U.S. counsel Inst. London Underwriters; former U.S. counsel to Assn. Francaise des Socs. D'Assurances Transports; former mem. com. of interfraud task force N.Y. Ins. Dept.; sr. ins. counsel. County atty. Putnam County, N.Y. Contbr. articles on Am. ins. law to various ins. mags. Mem. ABA, Fed. Bar Assn., N.Y. State Bar Assn., N.Y.C. Bar Assn., Internat. Assn. Ins. Counsel, Industry Adv. Com. on Ins., Ins. Fedn. NY (bd. dirs.). Home: 600 Cantitoe St Bedford NY 10506-1107 Office: 1365 York Ave New York NY 10021 Office Phone: 212-750-4470. Office Fax: 212-988-7207. Personal E-mail: skroll@aol.com.

KROLL, SUE, broadcast executive; Pres. internat. mktg. Warner Bros. Pictures. Named one of 100 Most Powerful Women in Entertainment, Hollywood Reporter, 2006. Office: Time Warner 4000 Warner Blvd Burbank CA 91522 Office Phone: 818-954-6000. E-mail: sue.kroll@warnerbros.com.*

KROLOPP, RUDOLPH WILLIAM, retired industrial designer, consultant; b. Chgo., June 7, 1930; s. Rudolph and Emma (Nice) K.; m. Dorcas S. Hall; children: Jacqueline, Mark, Joseph, Sharon, Lizabeth, John, Jennifer. BFA, U. Ill.-Champaign, 1956; postgrad., Lake Forest Coll., Ill., 1974-78. Staff designer Motorola Consumer Products, Chgo., 1956-59, chief designer, 1959-62, mgr. indsl. design communication div., 1962-82, dir. indsl. design, 1982-97, mem. patent com., 1981-97, chmn. corp. graphic standards council, 1983-97. Assoc. prof. indsl. design. U. Ill. Chgo. 1984; interviewed in CNN, MSMBC and Fox TV networks, and various publs., including Newsweek, Chgo. Sun Times, Reuters Am., others. Designer 2d bn. 24th Marines Meml., Chgo., 2005. Instr. phys. fitness Oak Park YMCA, Ill., 1967; instr. cardiovascular health Buehler YMCA, Palatine, Ill., 1968—, bd. dirs., 1980— , chmn. program com., 1980— , sec. bd. dirs., 1983-84. Served with USMC, 1948-52. Recipient Master Design award Product Engring. Mag., 1961, Weson Design award Western Electronic Conv., 1970, Design Excellence award Indsl. Design Mag., 1972, Design Engring. award Nat. Marine Electronics Assn., 1972, Good Design award Hannover Fair, Germany, 1978, Nekkei Design award, 1990, Internat. Design award, 1991, Corp. award for good design, 1992, Design Excellence award, 1996, Idea Design award, 1997, Good Design award Hannover Fair, 1997. Fellow Indsl. Designers Soc. Am. (chmn. fellowship awards com. 1996, program chmn., sec., regional v.p., chmn. nat. nominating com., Spl. award 1993). Clubs: Parkers SAC (Chgo.) (pres. 1962-65). Roman Catholic. Achievements include co-designed the first cellular telephone; patents in field. Home: 103 Golfview Rd Lake Zurich IL 60047-1290

KROMINGA, LYNN, cosmetics executive, lawyer; b. LA, May 16, 1950; d. Dale E. and Phyllis M. Krominga; m. Amnon Shiboleth, Apr. 9, 1992; 1 child, Karen Lee Shiboleth. BA in German, U. Minn., 1972, JD, 1974. Bar: Minn. 1974, N.Y. 1976. Assoc. firms in Mpls. and N.Y.C., 1974-77; assoc. counsel Am. Express Co., NYC, 1977-80; sr. internat. counsel Revlon, Inc., NYC, 1981-92, v.p. law, 1988-92, gen. counsel to exec. com., 1991-92, pres. licensing divsn., 1992-98, mem. exec. com., 1993-94, 97-99, exec. v.p. bus. devel., 1998-99; mem. bd. advisors MakeoverStudio.com, 1999—2001; bd. advisors Salonforce.com., 1999—2002; CEO Fashion Wire Daily, Inc., 2002; ptnr. KLS Mgmt. LLC, 2002—04, Krominga Holdings LLC, 2004—. Bd. dirs. StructuredWeb.com., 2000-01, Avis Budget Group, Inc, 2006—. Mem. ABA, Internat. Bar Assn. Cosmetic, Toiletry and Fragrance Assn. (vice chmn. govt. rels. com. 1991-92), Am. Arbitration Assn. (corp. counsel com. 1986-92, panel of arbitrators for large complex cases 1993-94), Phi Beta Kappa. E-mail: lkrominga@aol.com.

KRONBERG, PHILIPP PAUL, physicist, educator; arrived in U.S., 2002; s. Philipp and Jean Stewart (Davidson) Kronberg; children: Paul Andrew, Martin Thomas, Michael Philipp. BSc in Engring. Physics, Queen's U., Kingston, Ont., 1961, MSc in Physics, 1963; PhD in Physics, Manchester U., Eng., 1967, DSc, 1995. Lectr. U. Manchester, England, 1966—68; asst. to full prof. phys. scis. and astronomy U. Toronto, Canada, 1968—99, prof. emeritus dept. physics, 1999—; disting. Orson Anderson scholar Los Alamos Nat. Lab., N.Mex., 2002—03, vis. scholar, 2003—. Chmn. supercomputer user's group U. Toronto, Canada, 1968—88, chmn. Connaught phys. scis. and engring. rev. panel, 1982—85, mem. rsch. bd., 1985—89, pres.' com. rev. Innovations Found., 1988, provostial search com. dean sch. grad. studies, 89, project leader proposed collaboration with Calif. Tech. in millimetre astronomy, 1990—92; VLA adv. com. Nat. Radio Astronomy Observatory, United States, 1978—80; chmn. VLA adv. com. Assoc. Univs. Inc., DC, 1979—80, vis. com., 1979—82, chmn. vis. com., 1981—82; chmn. steering com. Algonquin Radio Observatory Millimetre Telescope NRC Canada, Ottawa, 1983—86, governing coun., 1987—90, assessment com., 1988—90, co-chmn. rev. com. divsn. physics, 1988—2002; mem. Atlantic Coun., Toronto, 1985—90; mgmt. bd. Ontario Ctr. Large Scale Computation, 1986—90, mem. Ontario Inter-Univ. adv. bd., 1986—90; mem. rev. panel nat. facility function of Assoc. Univs. Inc. and Nat. Radio Astronomy Observatory NSF, United States, 1987, mem. task force assess US radio astronomy facilities, 88, mem. rev. bd. design and constrn. Green Bank Telescope, 1989—90; chmn., scientific organizer Internat. Astronomical Union Symposium No. 140, Heidelberg, Germany, 1988—90; chmn. scientific and tech. rev. com. Sudbury Neutrino Observatory NRC and NSERC, Canada, 1988; bd. mgmt. Mont Mégantic Obs. U. Montreal/U. Laval, 1980—84; mgmt. bd. James Clerk Maxwell Submillimeter Telescope, 1990—91, ISOTRACE U. Toronto, 1990; Canadian rep. and scientific rev. com. Japan Inst. Space and Astronautical Scis./Canadian Space Agy. Very Long Baseline Interferometry Satellite, 1995—97, 2000; scientific organizing com. workshop on cosmological magnetic fields Aspen Inst. Physics, Colo., 1996, co-organizer workshop on astrophysical dynamos, 2000; disting. vis. fellow Commonwealth Sci., Indsl. Rsch. Orgn., Australia, 2007, U. Sydney, Australia, 2007. Pres. The Reserve at Santa Fe, 2005—. Recipient Humboldt award, Max Planck Inst., 1990, 1998, 2007; fellow, Guggenheim Found., 1985, Killiam Found., 1990; Humboldt fellow, Max Planck Inst., 1980. Fellow: Am. Phys. Soc.; mem.: Am. Astron. Soc., Boulevard Club Toronto (comdr. 1998—2000), Sigma Xi (pres. Toronto chpt. 1999—2001). Episcopalian. Avocations:

sailing, tennis, history, international affairs. Home: Unit 1407 941 Calle Mejia Santa Fe NM 87501 Personal E-mail: ppk101010@yahoo.com. Business E-Mail: kronberg@lanl.gov.

KRONE, CHERYL A., research scientist, consultant; b. Renton, Wa., May 25, 1948; d. Wilbur T. and Helen Faye K. BS, U. Washington, Seattle, 1978, MS, 1981, PhD, 1984. Vis. scientist U. Hawaii at Manoa, Honolulu, 1983; lectr. U. Washington, Seattle, 1983-84; rsch. chemist Nat. Oceanic and Atmospheric Adminstrn., Seattle, 1984-98; sr. rsch. scientist Applied Rsch. Inst., Seattle, 1998—. Deputy dir. Applied Rsch. Inst., Seattle, 1998—; cons. CK Consulting Svcs., Renton, Wa., 1998—. Author: (book chpt.) CRC Carcinogens and Mutagens in the Environment, 1982, over 30 articles in peer-reviewed med. sci. jours. Mem. Am. Chem. Soc., Inst. of Food Tech., New Zealand Assn. Scientists, Am. Physical Soc., Phi Beta Kappa, Sigma Xi. Avocations: bicycling, running, hiking. Office: Applied Rsch Inst PO Box 1969 Palmerston North 5301 New Zealand E-mail: cakrone@u.washington.edu.

KRONE, NORMAN BERNARD, real estate developer, lawyer; b. Memphis, Sept. 13, 1938; s. Irving and Eva (Sauer) K.; m. Norma Lee Moon; children: John, Christine, David. LLB, Stetson U., 1964. Bar: Fla. 1964, Ohio 1987, US Dist. Ct. (mid. dist.) Fla. 1965, US Ct. Appeals (7th cir.) 1968; lic. real estate broker, Ohio, Mich., Ala. Atty. Lifsey & Johnston, Tampa, Fla., 1964—65; pvt. practice Tampa, Fla., 1965—66; property mgmt. atty. Ford Motor Co., Dearborn, Mich., 1966—67; audit mgr. Montgomery Ward & Co., Chgo., 1967—68, corp. real estate mgr., 1968—75; exec. v.p. Momtgomery Ward Properties Corp., Chgo., 1970—75; from v.p. to sr. v.p. Walgreen Co., Deerfield, Ill., 1975—85; pres., CEO The Hausman Co., Cleve., 1987—2001; sr. exec. v.p. Henry S. Miller, Grubb & Ellis Comml./Retail Svc., 1985—87; mng. prin. NK Devel. Ltd., 1996—2002; prin. NK Real Estate Adv. Ltd., 2002—; COO Olympia Devel. Group, 2003—05; sr. devel. officer DeBartolo Devel., LLC, 2005—. Trustee Internat. Coun. Shopping Ctr., NYC, 1976-79; dir. Myers Industries, Lincoln, Ill., 1976-83; instr. Intercoun. Shopping Ctr.-Inst. Profl. Devel.; dean U. Shopping Ctr. instructor - Law for Non-Lawyers, ednl. adv. com., small ctr. com., chmn. retail adv. com., 1975-76, cert. leasing specialist, 1995-, cert. constrn. devel. and design profl., 2006-; cons. Krone Group LLC, 2001-03; instr., spkr. in field. Author, editor: The Lease and Its Language, 1996, ICSC Study Lease, 2000, Anatomy of a Lease, 2001; contbr. articles to mags. Acting judge City of Tampa, 1964-66; bd. dir. Met. Housing and Planning Coun., Chgo., 1977-80, New City YMCA, 1976-78; mem. sch. bd. Palisades Cmty. Sch. Dist., 1968-69; mem. strategic planning com. Met. Chgo. YMCA, 1976-77; 1st pres. Cleve. Pops Orch.; bd. dir. Walgreen Hist. Found., 1984-87; co-founder, pres., mem. exec. com. Realty Resources (a network of comml. brokerage firms), 1987-2001. Named Entrepreneur of Yr. Operation Breadbasket, 1977. Mem. Cleve. Bar Assn., Real Estate Inst., Beachwood C. of C. (pres. 1996, exec. com. 1992-2001, life bd. dir.), Acacia Country Club (bd. dir. 1997-99, chmn. planning com. 1998-99, sec. 1998). Avocations: woodworking, golf. Office: DeBartolo Devel LLC 14934 N Florida Ave Tampa FL 33613 Office Phone: 813-676-7683. Personal E-mail: nbkrone@netscape.net. Business E-Mail: nkrone@debartolodevelopment.com.

KRONENBERG, ANDREAS, nuclear chemist, radiochemist, nuclear technology consultant; b. Leipzig, Germany, Mar. 22, 1971; B in chemistry, Tech. U. of Dresden, Germany, 1993; M in chemistry, U. Marburg, Germany, 1997; PhD, U. Mainz, Germany, 2001. Rsch. assoc. Fla. State U., Tallahassee, 2001—02, Los Alamos Nat. Lab., N.Mex., 2003—04; stewardship rsch. assoc. Oak Ridge Assoc. Univs., Tenn., 2004—. Tech. expert IAEA, Geneva. Dir. Ballet Internat. Mem.: Juilliard Assn., Sch. Am. Ballet Assn., Inst. Nuc. Materials Mgmt., Internat. Material Info. Soc., Radiochemistry Soc., Am. Soc. Materials, Material Rsch. Soc., German Phys. Soc., German Nuc. Soc., German Chem. Soc., Am. Nuc. Soc., Am. Phys. Soc., Internat. Nuc. Target Devel. Soc., Am. Chem. Soc. Achievements include research in classical nuclear chemistry techniques and radiochemical methods; isotope production, target preparation and target design; separation and speciation methods, ion exchange chromatography, extraction, tracer-level chemistry, rapid chemistry and tracer applications; on-line and off-line irradiation on accelerator facilities and nuclear research reactors, neutron activation analysis, especially delayed neutron activation analyses; nuclear cross section and decay data measurements; nuclear technology and applications; radioactive ion beam production and experiments for stewardship science; nuclear non-proliferation. Office: Oak Ridge Assoc Univs MS 6374 Bldg 6008 Oak Ridge TN 37831 Home Phone: 202-413-6891; Office Phone: 865-241-1514. Office Fax: 854-576-5780. Personal E-mail: kronenberg@nuc-tec-consult.com. E-mail: kronenberga@ornl.gov.

KRONENBERG, RICHARD SAMUEL, physician, educator; b. Chgo., Aug. 7, 1938; s. Frank Paul and Ruth Ida (Zaretzsky) K.; m. Carole Marie Hurd, Oct. 11, 1963; children: Karen, Marilyn, Brenda. BA, Northwestern U., 1960, MD, 1963. Intern Parkland Meml. Hosp., Mpls., 1967-68, resident in internal medicine, 1968; rsch. fellow Cardiovascular Rsch. Inst. U. Calif., San Francisco, 1968-70; asst. prof. medicine U. Minn., 1970-74, assoc. prof., 1974-79, prof., dir. pulmonary div., 1979-84; prof. U. Tex. Health Sci. Ctr., Houston, 1984—2002; prof. medicine, exec. v.p. for clin. affairs U. Tex. Health Ctr., Tyler, 1984—2002; sr. v.p. Mother Frances Health Sys., 2002—. Reviewer subsplty. programs in internal medicine Accreditation Coun. Grad. Med. Edn., Chgo., 1985—. Mem. editorial rev. bd. The Asbestos Monitor, Nat. Asbestos Coun. Jour., 1990-93; contbr. chpts. to books. Capt. USAF, 1965-67. Recipient Rsch. Career Devel. award NIH, 1973-78. Fellow ACP, Am. Coll. Chest Physicians; mem. Nat. Asbestos Coun. (bd. dirs. 1990-93), Asbestos Disease Assn. (pres. 1990-93), Ctrl. Soc. Clin. Rsch. Avocation: bicycling. Home: 5615 Cedar Hill Cir Tyler TX 75703-3912 Business E-Mail: kronen.r@tmfhs.org. E-mail: kronenr@tmfhs.org.

KRONER, ARNOLD FRIEDRICH, financial consultant, economist; b. Gablonz, Czechoslovakia, May 16, 1939; came to U.S., 1962; s. Arnold and Anna Marie (Gramer) K.; m. Edith Ficklin Crammatte, Aug. 12, 1972; 1 child, Erik. MA, Cornell U., 1966, PhD, 1971. Asst. prof. econs. dept. U. Pitts., 1968-75, Columbia U., NYC, 1973-74; asst. treas. Chase Manhattan Bank, NYC, 1975-76; asst. v.p. Chem. Bank, NYC, 1976-78; sr. v.p., treas. Nat. Australia Bank, NYC, 1984-87; v.p. Algemene Bank Nederland, N.V., NYC, 1978-84, 87-90; pres. Pegasus Econometric Group, Inc., Hoboken, N.J., 1991-92; v.p. ASLK-CGER Bank, NYC, 1992-93; pres. Spectral Inc., White Plains, NY, 1993—. Cons. Intern. Banking Inst., St. Petersburg Russia, 1995-96; cons. to prime min. of Belarus, 1996-97. Editor Portfolio-Internat. Econ. Perspectives, 1972-75. V.p. Silver Lake Civic Assn., S.I., N.Y., 1979-82. Named Richardson fellow, 1960, UN fellow, 1961, U. N.C. fellow, 1962; recipient Andrew Clark fellowship Cornell U., 1966. Mem. Royal Econ. Soc., Am. Econ. Assn. Roman Catholic. Avocations: skiing, camping. Home and Office: PO Box 635 White Plains NY 10603-0635 E-mail: arnkroner@aol.com.

KRONER, FRED L., journalist; b. Champaign, Ill., Nov. 16, 1955; s. James Carlton and Naomi Ruth Kroner; m. Dee Siddens, Aug. 21, 1976 (div. Nov. 1996); 1 child, Devin Richard; m. Emily Sue Moon, June 6, 1999. BS, U. Ill., 1978. Sportswriter Champaign Courier, 1974-78, Bloomington (Ill.) Pantagraph, 1978-81, Champaign News-Gazette, 1981—. Contbg. author: Cascade of Memories, 1998, Nature's Echoes, 2000, Enlightened Shadows, 2001; author: Citizen Pain, Brian Cardinal, 2001, booklets and newspaper series. Coach Little League Baseball, Champaign, 1982—86, Summer League Baseball, Sullivan, Ill., 1990—93; guest commentator WDAN Radio, Danville, Ill., 1995—. Named Newsman of the Yr., Ill. Wrestling Coaches Assn., 1984, 1988, 2000, Sportswriter of the Yr. for Ill., Nat. Sportscasters & Sportswriters Assn., 2001; recipient awards, AP, 1985, 1989. Mem.: Nat. Sportswriters and Sportscasters Assn., Ill. Press Assn., Soc. Profl. Journalists. Methodist. Avocations: gardening, poetry. Office: Champaign-Urbana News-Gazette PO Box 677 Champaign IL 61824-0677 Home: PO Box 778 Mahomet IL 61853-0778

KRONFELD, EDWIN, natural gas company executive; m. Lydia Shepard Ballinger, Feb. 16, 1960; children: Nicholas, Alice, Alexander. Student, Harvard Coll., 1948—51; LLB, Harvard U., 1958; LLM, Georgetown U., 1962. Bar: N.Y., Washington, Okla. Staff atty. Securities & Exch. Commn., Washington, 1958—61; assoc. Lear & Scoutt, Washington, 1961—62; sole practice Washington, 1962—68; ptnr. Neal Siegler & Kronfeld, Washington, 1968—69, Morgan Lewis & Bockius, Washington, 1969—79, Thieman & Kronfeld, Tulsa, 1980—84, Kronfeld & Ribner, Tulsa, 1985—88; pres. Plymouth Resources Inc., Tulsa, 1982—. Lectr. Am. Law Inst.-ABA, Chgo., 1970-78; lectr. Practicing Law Inst., N.Y.C., 1970-78; adj. prof. law Georgetown U., Washington, 1971-78. Chmn. Tulsa Philharm., 1998 Mem. Okla. Ind. Petroleum Assn., Tulsa Assn. Petroleum Landmen, The Summit Club. Home: 2660 S Birmingham Pl Tulsa OK 74114 Office: Plymouth Resources Inc 15 W Sixth St Ste 2300 Tulsa OK 74119 Office Phone: 918-599-1812. Business E-Mail: kronfeld@plymouthgas.com.

KRONGARD, HOWARD J., federal agency administrator, lawyer; b. Dec. 12, 1940; s. Raphael Harris and Rita (Keyser) K.; children: Kenneth, Mara Lynn. BA, Princeton U., 1961; JD, Harvard U., 1964; postgrad., Cambridge U., 1964-65. Bar: Md. 1965, N.Y. 1967, U.S. Dist. Ct. Md. 1965, U.S. Dist. Ct. (so. dist.) N.Y. 1967, U.S. Ct. Appeals (2d cir.) 1973, U.S. Ct. Appeals (8th cir.) 1980, U.S. Supreme Ct. 1991. Assoc. Piper & Marbury, Balt., 1964, Cravath, Swaine & Moore, NYC, 1965, 66-73; law clk. to Hon. Kenneth B. Keating N.Y. Ct. Appeals, Albany, 1966; assoc., gen. counsel Peat, Marwick, Mitchell & Co., NYC, 1973-86; gen. counsel Deloitte, Haskins & Sells, NYC, 1986-89, Deloitte & Touche, LLP, NYC, 1989-95; of counsel Freshfields Bruckhaus Deringer, London/NYC, 1996—2005; insp. gen. US Dept. State, Washington, 2005—. Spkr. in field; bd. dirs. Lacrosse Found., Inc., Balt., 1981—, PCX Equities, Nat. Legal Ctr. Pub. Interest; U.S. rep. to Internat. Lacrosse Fedn.; pub. gov. Pacific Exch. Named Outstanding Player in U.S.A., U.S. Club Lacrosse Assn., 1968, 74; inducted into Lacrosse Hall of Fame, 1985, N.Y. Sports Hall of Fame, 1994; recipient Ames Briefwriting prize Harvard Law Sch., 1962; Frank Knox Meml. fellow, 1965. Mem. Assn. of Bar of City of N.Y., Harvard Club. Office: US Dept State 2121 Virginia Ave NW Rm 8100 Washington DC 20037

KRONICK, SUSAN D., retail executive; b. NYC; Grad., Conn. Coll. Exec. trainee Bloomingdale's Macy's Inc. (formerly Federated Dept. Stores Inc.), 1973—85; operating v.p. , divsn. merchandise mgr. Bloomingdale's Macy's Inc., 1985—88, sr. v.p., divsn. merchandise mgr. Bloomingdale's, 1988—90, exec. v.p., gen. mgr. Bloomingdale's, 1990—91, sr. v.p. dir. stores, Bloomingdale's, 1991—93, pres. RLG Divsn. Atlanta, 1992—97, chmn. Burdines Fla., 1997—2000, group pres. regional dept. stores Cin., 2001—03, vice chmn., 2003—. Bd. dirs. Pepsi Bottling Group. Recipient Nat. Human Rels. award, Am. Jewish Com., 1999. Office: Macy's Inc 7 W Seventh St Cincinnati OH 45202*

KRONMAN, ANTHONY TOWNSEND, dean, law educator; b. 1945; m. Nancy I. Greenberg, 1982 BA, Williams Coll., 1968, PhD, 1972; JD, Yale U., 1975. Bar: Minn. 1975, N.Y. 1983. Assoc. prof. U. Minn., 1975-76; asst. prof. U. Chgo., 1976-79; vis. assoc. prof. Yale U. Law Sch., New Haven, 1978-79, prof., 1979—, Edward J. Phelps prof. law, 1985—2004, dean, 1994—2004, Sterling prof. law, 2004—. Editor: (with R. Posner) The Economics of Contract Law, 1979 (with F. Kessler and G. Gilmore) Cases and Materials on Contracts, 1986; past mem. editorial bd. Yale Law Jour.; author: Max Weber, 1983, The Lost Lawyer, 1993. Decorated comdr. Nat. Order Merit (France); Danforth Found. fellow, 1968-72. Fellow ABA, Am. Acad. Arts and Scis.; mem. Selden Soc., Conn. Bar Assn. (Cooper fellow), Coun. on Fgn. Rels. Office: Yale U Law Sch PO Box 208215 New Haven CT 06520-8215 Business E-Mail: anthony.kronman@yale.edu.

KRONMILLER, JAN E., dean, academic administrator; BS in Chemistry, Ohio State U., DDS, 1978; PhD in biomedical sciences, U. Conn., 1991. Cert. pediatric dentistry and orthodontics. NIH rsch. fellow U. Conn. Health Ctr.; asst. prof. pediatric dentistry U. Pitts.; pvt. practice; head orthodontics section, Coll. Dentistry U. Ky.; prof. and chair. dept. orthodontics, Sch. Dentistry Oreg. Health Scis. U., prof., grad. program, Sch. Medicine; dean, Coll. Dentistry Ohio State U., 2001—. Recipient Nat. Rsch. Svc. award, NIH, Individual Physician Scientist award. Fellow: Internat. Coll. Dentists, Am. Coll. Dentists. Office: 305 W 12th Ave Columbus OH 43210 Office Phone: 614-292-9755. Office Fax: 614-292-7619. Business E-Mail: kronmiller.1@osu.edu.

KROO, ILAN M., aeronautical engineer, educator; BS, Stanford U., 1978, MS, 1979, PhD in Aeronautics and Astronautics, 1983. Rsch. scientist Advanced Aerodynamic Concepts Branch, NASA Ames Rsch. Ctr., Moffett Field, Calif., 1982—85; prof. Dept. Aeronautics and Astronautics Stanford U., 1985—; chief scientist Desktop Aeronautics, Inc., 1986—. Mem. Air Force Sci. Adv. Bd., NRC Aeronautics and Space Engring. Bd. Contbr. articles to profl. jours. Recipient NASA Special Achievement Award, 1985. Fellow: AIAA (mem. Tech. Com. on Aircraft Design); mem.: NAE. Office: Dept Aeronautics and Astronautics Sch Engring, Stanford U Durand Bldg, 496 Lomita Mall Stanford CA 94305-4035 Office Phone: 369-723-2994. E-mail: kroo@stanford.com.

KROP, PAMELA S., lawyer; BA summa cum laude, U. Fla., 1978; JD, Stanford U., 1982. Bar: DC, Minn. Assoc. gen. counsel capital fleet svcs. GE Corp., v.p., gen. counsel medical sys. IT, gen. counsel healthcare bio. sci. div.; gen. counsel, corp. sec. St. Jude Medical Corp., St. Paul, 2006—. Contbr. articles to numerous profl. jours. Mem.: ABA (internat. law and bus. subcom.), Minn. State Bar Assn. Office: St Jude Medical Inc One Lillehei Plz Saint Paul MN 55117 Office Fax: 651-482-8318.

KROPP, EDWARD H., education educator, consultant; b. Reading, Pa., June 13, 1944; s. Karl Gustaf and Erna Mittag Kropp; m. Phyllis Ann Bauman, Nov. 5, 1966; children: Peter Alex, Julie Marie (Kropp) McKenzie. BA, Temple U., 1966; MA, George Mason U., 1994; EdD, U. Va., 2006. Project mgmt. profl. George Washington U. Staff mgr. Chesapeake and Potomac Tel., Roanoke, Va., 1969—81; dist. mgr. A T & T, Basking Ridge, NJ, 1981—96; comml. bids dir. Sci. Application Internat. Corp., San Diego, 1996—2000; sr. mgr. KPMG Cons. (Bearing Point), McLean, Va., 2000—02; prof. U. Va., McLean, 2003—. Pres. E. H. Kropp & Assoc., Vienna, 2002—. Author: (book) A Guide to Repair Svc. Bur. Analysis, 1971, (manual) Land Mine Warfare (USMC), 1983. Exec. bd. Nat. Capital Area Coun., BSA, Wash., DC, 1998—. Col. USMCR, 1966—94. Mem.: Nat. Contact Mgmt. Assn. Avocations: ednl. leadership rsch., in-prison literacy instrn. Home: 3879 Charter Club Dr Doylestown PA 18902

KROPP, JAMES HERBERT, SR., investment manager; b. NYC, Feb. 24, 1949; s. Herbert H. and Agatha (Tell) K.; m. Linda Budziloski, July 4, 1969; children: Jamie, Jody, Jennifer. BBA, St. Francis Coll., 1971; postgrad., NYU Grad. Sch. Bus., 1971-73. CPA, N.Y. Mgr. Arthur Young & Co., CPAs, NYC, 1973—80; v.p., treas.-contr. Morgan Stanley Realty Inc., NYC, 1980—85; exec. v.p. The Harlon Group, Raleigh, N.C., 1985-89; mng. dir. MECA Assocs., LA, 1989-94, Christopher Weil & Co. Inc., San Diego, 1995—2004; sr. v.p. Garit-Globe USA Inc., 2005—. Dir. PS Bus. Parks, CNL Funds. Mem. AICPA, Nat. Assn. Real Estate Investment Trusts. Republican. Office: 1660 NE Miami Gardens Dr North Miami Beach FL 33179 Home: 483 Centre Is Golden Beach FL 33160 E-mail: jkropp@gazitgroup.com.

KROPP, RONALD D., engineering executive; BS in Acctg., No. Ill. U., DeKalb. CPA. With Arthur Andersen, Ill. Tool Works (ITW), Glenview, 1993—, mgr. consol. reporting and analysis, dir. corp. acctg., v.p., contr. fin. reporting, 2002—05, prin. acctg. officer, 2005—06, sr. v.p., CFO, 2006—. Office: Ill Tool Works 3600 W Lake Ave Glenview IL 60026-1215 Office Phone: 847-724-7500. Office Fax: 847-657-4572.*

KROSHL, WILLIAM MARK, operations research specialist; b. Chgo., Mar. 17, 1954; s. William John and Dorothy Grace Kroshl; m. Christina Arlene DisPennett, Dec. 27, 1975; children: Jennifer Nadine Blevins, Heather Elaine Croydon, William James, Mark Christopher. BA in Economics, Northwestern U., 1975; MS in Ops. Rsch., US Naval Postgrad. Sch., Monterey, Calif., 1988. Navigator USS Sellers, 1975—79; ops. officer USS Schenectady, 1980—81; engr. officer USS Truett, 1982—83, USS Seattle, 1983—85; exec. officer USS Detroit, 1988—90; assoc. chmn., dept. math. US Naval Acad., Annapolis, Md., 1990—94; instr. US Naval Postgrad. Sch., 1994—97; ops. rsch. analyst, applied physics lab. Johns Hopkins U., Laurel, Md., 1997—. Comdr. USN, 1975—77. Mem.: Sigma Xi, Inst. Ops. Rsch. and Mgmt. Scis., Mil. Ops. Rsch. Soc. (dir. 2005—). Office: Johns Hopkins Univ Applied Physics Lab 11100 Johns Hopkins Rd Laurel MD 20723 Personal E-mail: billandtina@kroshlfamily.net. Business E-Mail: william.kroshl@jhuapl.edu.

KROSSER, HOWARD S., aerospace transportation executive; b. Bklyn., Dec. 2, 1936; s. Samuel and Celia (Wexler) K.; m. Roslyn Elaine Rosenthal, Apr. 30, 1939; children: Scott A., Barry I. BS in Engring., Rutgers U., 1959; MS in Indsl. Mgmt., Ga. Inst. Tech., 1970; postgrad., Harvard U., 1985. Engr., engring. supr. Picatinny Arsenal, Dover, NJ, 1959-66; br. mgr., engr. Prodn. Modernization Agy., Dover, 1966-73; divsn. engring. mgr. Army Prodn. Agy., Dover, 1973-78; program mgr. Army Tank Command, Warren, Mich., 1978-85; dir. lab. Army Armament R & D Ctr., Dover, 1985-86, tech. dir., 1986-88; v.p., gen. mgr. Hercules Aerospace, Wilmington, Del., 1988-89; pres. Hercules Def. Electronic Systems Inc., Wilmington, 1990-94; chmn. bd. dirs., pres. Alliant Def. Electronics Sys. Inc., Clearwater, Fla., 1994-96; v.p. smart weapons sys. Alliant Techsys., Inc., Mt. Arlington, NJ, 1996—. Mem. Army Sci. Bd., Washington, 1990-93. Recipient Meritorious Civilian Svc. award U.S. Army, 1986, Exceptional Civil Svc. award, 1988. Mem. Assn. of U.S. Army, Am. Def. Preparedness Assn. (Leslie Simon award 1988). Office: Alliant Techsys Inc PO Box 405 Wharton NJ 07885-0405

KROSZNER, RANDALL SCOTT, federal official, economics professor; b. Englewood, NJ, June 22, 1962; AB, ScB magna cum laude, Brown U., 1984; MA in Econs., Harvard U., 1987, PhD, 1990. Teaching asst. dept. econs. Brown U., Providence, 1983-84; tutor Winthrop House, Harvard U., Cambridge, Mass., 1985—, rsch. asst., 1985, teaching fellow, 1986; rsch. asst. Nat. Bur. Econ. Rsch., 1985; jr. staff economist Coun. Econ. Advisors, Exec. Office Pres., Washington, 1987—88; R.C. Hoiles postdoctoral fellow Harvard U., Cambridge, 1989-90; economist Economics Resource Group, Cambridge, Mass., 1989—90; asst. prof. economics. U. Chgo., 1990—94, assoc. prof., 1994—99, prof., 1999—2001, 2003—06; assoc. dir. George J. Stigler Ctr. for Study of the Econ. & the State, 1999—2001, 2003—05, dir., 2005—06; mem. Coun. of Econ. Advisors The White House, Washington, 2001—03; mem. bd. govs. Fed. Res. Sys., Washington, 2006—. Referee Quar. Jour. Econs., Jour. Money, Credit and Banking, Jour. Polit. Economy, Jour. of Bus.; vis. prof., Stockholm Sch. Economics, 1994, Free U., Berlin, 1995, Inst. Internat. Econ. Sudies, Stockholm U., 1996, Bertil Danielson vis. prof. banking & fin., 1998-99; vis. scholar, SEC, 1992, IMF, 1993-95, Rsch. Dept. Fed. Res. Bank St. Louis, 1996, Fed. Res. Bank Kans. City, 1997, Fed. Res. Bank Mnpls., 1999, Am. Enterprise Inst., 2003-; John M. Olin vis. fellow in Law & Economics, U. Chgo. Law Sch., 1999-2000; bd. dirs. Nat. Assn. Bus. Economists, 2005- Co-author (with Tyler Cowen) Explorations in the New Monetary Economics, 1994; Co-editor (with Louis Putterman) The Economic Nature of the Firm: A Reader, 1986; Contbr. articles to profl. jours. NSF fellow, 1984-87, Claude R. Lambe fellow, 1988-89; Richard M. Weaver scholar, 1988-89; Recipient Brattle prize for Best Corp. Fin. Paper , Joun. Fin., 1999 Mem. Am. Econ. Assn., Phi Beta Kapa, Sigma Xi. Office: Fed Res Sys 20th St & Constitution Ave NW Washington DC 20551*

KROTO, HAROLD WALTER, chemistry researcher, educator; b. Wisbech, Cambridgeshire, Oct. 7, 1939; s. Heinz and Edith K.; m. Margaret Henrietta Hunter, 1963; 2 children. BSc in Chemistry, U. Sheffield, 1961, PhD, 1964; PhDHC, U. Stockholm, 1992; DHC, U. Limburg, 1993, U. Sheffield, 1995, U. Kingston, 1995. Postdoctoral fellow NRCC, 1964-66; rsch. scientist Bell Tel. Labs., NJ, 1966-67; lectr. U. Sussex, Brighton Sussex, England, 1968-77, reader, 1977-85, prof. chemistry, 1985-91, Royal Soc. Rsch. prof., 1991—2004; Francis Eppes prof. chemistry and biochemistry Fla. State U., Tallahassee, 2004—. Chmn. Vega Sci. Trust. Mem. editl. bd. Chem. Soc. Reviews, 1990—; contbr. over 280 articles to profl. jours. Created knight, 1996; recipient award Sunday Times Book Jacket Design Competition, 1964, Tilden lectr., 1981-82, Faraday lectr., 2002, medal 2002, Internat. New Materials prize Am. Phys. Soc., 1992, Italgas prize for innovation in chemistry, 1992, Longstaff medal Royal Soc. Chemistry, 1993, Hewlett Packard Europhysics prize, 1994, Science pour L'art prize Moet Hennessy Louis Vuitton, 1994, Copley medal, 2004; co-recipient Nobel prize in chemistry, 1996. Fellow: Royal Soc.; mem.: Academia Europea, NAS (assoc.). Achievements include co-discovery of a form of pure carbon known as buckyballs.

KROTT, JOSEPH P., gas industry executive, comptroller; BS summa cum laude, U. Del., 1985. CPA. Formerly audit mgr. Coopers & Lybrand; comptr. Sunoco Inc., Phila., 1998—, joined, 1990, mgr. consolidation acctg. and spl. projects, 1990—, dir. compensation and benefits, 1998. Mem.: Pa. Inst. CPA, Am. Inst. Pub. Accts. Office: Sunoco Inc Ten Penn Ctr 1801 Market St Philadelphia PA 19103-1699

KROUPA, DIANE LYNN, federal judge; b. Mitchell, SD, Oct. 12, 1955; d. Edwin Raymond and Delores Ilene (Duncan Burg) K.; m. Robert Eugene Fackler, Sept. 12, 1981; children: Erin Elizabeth, Sara Marie. BS in Fgn. Svc., Georgetown U., 1978, postgraduate student, 1981-83; JD, U. SD, Vermillion, 1981. Bar: SD 1981, DC 1984, Minn. 1986. Atty., adv. IRS legis. and regulation divsn. Office of Chief Counsel, Washington, 1981-84; atty., adv. to Judge Joel Gerber US Tax Ct., Washington, 1984-85, judge, 2003—; assoc. Dorsey & Whitney, Mpls., 1985-87, Parsinen Bowman Levy, Mpls., 1987-90, ptnr., 1990-95; judge Minn. Tax Ct., St. Paul, 1995—2001, chief judge, 1998—2001; spl. counsel Faegre & Benson LLP, Mpls., 2001—03. Chair tax sect. Hennepin County Bar, Mpls., 1985—; mem. adv. bd. Hamline U., St. Paul, 1995—. Editor multi-vol. treatises on corps., 1995; contbr. articles to profl. jours. Legal adv. Minn. Women's Polit. Caucus, Minn. Women's Edn. Coun., St. Paul, 1989-91, Jr. League Mpls., 1991-93. Recipient Vol. of Yr. award, Jr. League of Minn., 1993. Mem.: Am. Judicature Soc., Nat. Assn. of Women Judges, Minn. State Bar Assn. (Cmty. Vol. of Yr. 1998, Disting. Service award 2001), ABA. Avocations: children activities, computers, furniture refinishing, reading. Office: US Tax Ct 400 2nd St NW Washington DC 20217 Office Phone: 202-521-0725.

KROUS, HENRY FRANKLIN, pathologist, educator; b. Denver, Sept. 27, 1943; s. Elwyn S. Krous and Elizabeth D. Deffer; children: Tanja E., Timothy F. BS, U. Nebr., 1965, MD, 1969. Cert. Am. Bd. Pathology. Intern Virginia Mason Hosp., Seattle; resident U. Wash., Seattle, fellow; prof. pathology U. Calif. Sch. Medicine, LaJolla, 1985—; dir. pathology Rady Children's Hosp., San Diego, 1985—. Lt. comdr. USN, 1974—76. Recipient Sen. Daniel Boatwright award, Calif. Dept. Health Svcs., Sacramento, 1999. Mem.: U.S. Can. Assn. Pathology, Soc. Pediatric Pathology (pres. 2002—03). Avocations: literature, opera. Office: Childrens Hosp 3020 Childrens Way San Diego CA 92123

KROUSE, GEORGE RAYMOND, JR., lawyer; b. Atlantic City, Sept. 30, 1945; s. George R. and Viola (Rogers) K.; m. Susan Naylor, Aug. 5, 1967; children: Geoffrey, Alison. AB cum laude, Brown U., 1967; JD with distinction, Duke U., 1970. Bar: NY 1971, US Ct. Mil. Appeals 1971, US Dist. Ct. (so. and ea. dists.) NY 1975. Assoc. Simpson Thacher & Bartlett, NYC, 1970-71, 75-78, ptnr., 1978—, chmn. corp. dept., 1991—2002, sr. adminstrv. ptnr., 2002—06, mem. exec. com., 1992—2007. Sr. lectr. fellow Duke U. Sch. Law; dir. Global Capital Markets Ctr., Duke U. Articles editor Duke Law Jour. Mem. bd. visitors Duke Sch. Law, 1986—92, chmn., 1997—2001. Capt. USAF, 1971—75. Decorated Air Force Commendation medal, Meritorious Svc. medal; recipient Duke U. Disting. Alumnus award, 2002, Henry Kessler Soc. Disting. Svc. award, 2004, Chambers Leading Capital Markets and Governance Lawyer. Mem. ABA, N.Y. State Bar Assn., Assn. of Bar of City of N.Y. (com. corps. 1985-88, com. art law 1990-93), Order of Coif, Montclair Golf Club, Cape Cod Nat. Golf Club, Bonita Bay Club. Avocations: golf, art. Office: Simpson Thacher & Bartlett LLP 425 Lexington Ave 18th Fl New York NY 10017-3954 Home Phone: 973-744-6454; Office Phone: 212-455-2730. Office Fax: 212-455-2502. Business E-Mail: gkrouse@stblaw.com.

KROVATIN, GERALD, lawyer; b. 1952; BA, Columbia U., 1974; JD, Rutgers U., 1977. Bar: N.J. 1977. Ptnr. Krovatin & Assocs. LLC, Newark. Adj. faculty crim. trial seminar Rutgers Sch. Law, Newark, 1987-90. Fellow Am. Coll. Trial Lawyers; mem. N.J. State Bar Assn., Assn. Criminal Def. Lawyers N.J. (trustee 1995-99). Office: Krovatin & Assocs LLC 744 Broad St Newark NJ 07102-3802 Office Phone: 973-424-9777. E-mail: gkrovatin@krovatin.com.

KRSUL, JOHN ALOYSIUS, JR., lawyer; b. Highland Pk., Mich., Mar. 24, 1938; s. John A. and Ann M. (Sepich) K.; m. Justine Oliver, Sept. 12, 1958; children: Ann Lisa, Mary Justine. BA, Albion Coll., 1959; JD, U. Mich., 1963. Bar: Mich. 1963. Assoc. Dickinson Wright PLLP, 1963-71, ptnr. Detroit, 1971-99, consulting ptnr., 2000—. Asst. editor: U. Mich. Law Rev, 1962-63. Recipient Disting. Alumnus award Albion Coll., 1984; Sloan scholar, 1958-59; Fulbright scholar, 1959-60; Ford. Found. grantee, 1964 Fellow: Am. Bar Found. (life; chmn. Mich. chpt. 1988—89); mem.: ABA (ho. of dels. 1979—2002, chmn. standing com. on membership 1983—89, exec. coun. 1984—91, chmn. sect. gen. practice 1989—90, tort and ins. practice sect., exec. coun. 1991—94, bd. govs. 1991—99, chmn. fin. com. 1993—94, exec. com. 1993—94, 1996—99, treas. 1996—99, editl. bd. ABA Jour. 1996—99, chmn. audit com. 2003—07), Am. Bar Ins. Cons. Inc. (bd. dirs. sec. 1988—95), Am. Bar Endowment (bd. dirs. 1996—99), Nat. Conf. Bar Pres. (exec. coun. 1986—89), Am. Judicature Soc. (dir. 1971—79, exec. com. 1973—74), Fellows of Young Lawyers Am. Bar (bd. dirs. 1977—86, pres. 1983—84, chmn. bd. 1984—86), Mich. State Bar Found. (trustee 1982—83, 1985—99, chmn. fellows 1986—87), State Bar Mich. (commr. 1973—83, pres. 1982—83), Detroit Bar Assn. Found. (dir. 1971—84, pres. 1979—80), Detroit Bar Assn. (dir. 1971—80, pres. 1979—80), Am. Bar Retirement Funds (bd. dirs. 1999—2005, sec. 2003—05, v.p. 2005—06, pres. 2006—07, bd. dirs. 2007—), Sixth Cir. Jud. Conf. (life), Detroit Club, Orchard Lake Country Club, Delta Tau Delta, Phi Eta Sigma, Omicron Delta Kappa, Phi Beta Kappa. Office: Dickinson Wright PLLC 500 Woodward Ave Ste 4000 Detroit MI 48226-3416 Home: 10048 Weko Dr Bridgman MI 49106-4310

KRUCK, DONNA JEAN, special education educator, consultant; b. Peoria, Ill., Jan. 26, 1930; d. Walter George and Lois Irene (Newburn) Hagemeyer; m. Michael Roy Kruck Jr., June 27, 1948; children: Pamela Ann Kruck Hokanson, Michael Roy III, Quentin Robert; m. Somran Sirironrong, May 19, 1998. BS, Ill. State U., 1961; MEd, U. Ill., 1968. Cert. spl. edn. tchr. and adminstr., Ill. Tchr. New Lenox Dist. 122, Ill., 1956-61; tchr. spl. edn. Lincoln Way Area Joint Agreement, New Lenox, 1961-66; tchr. spl. edn., coord. Joliet Twp. High Sch. Dist. 204, Ill., 1966-86; pvt. practice cons. and diagnostician New Lenox, 1986-92. Child adv. New Lenox Dist. 122, 1986-88; instr. Chapel Christian U., 1994-96; LCMS missionary, ESL tchr., Bangkok, 1997—. Author: Let's Learn to Cook, 1971. Pres. Joliet Twp. Edn. Assn., 1971-76; donar Aurora Area Blood Bank, Joliet, 1974-90; v.p. Island Lakes Homeowners Assn., 1994-96; v.p. Luth. Women's Missionary League, 1993, pres., 1994-97; pres. Aid Assn. for Luths., 1995-97. Mem. AAUW, NEA (life), Nat. Ret. Tchr. Assn., Am. Assn. Ret. Persons, Am. Assn. Mental Retardation, Am. Bus. Women's Assn., Coun. Exceptional Children (life), Coun. Adminstrs. Spl. Edn., Christian Edn. Assn., Ill. Edn. Assn. (life), Ill. Div. Learning Disabilities, Coun. for Ednl. Diagnostic Svcs. (div. learning disabilities), Lutherans for Life, Brandywine Inst. Orthopedics (founder), Kappa Delta Pi, Delta Kappa Gamma. Lutheran. Avocations: travel, presenting travelogues. Personal E-mail: Sirironrong@yahoo.com.

KRUCKEBERG, ARTHUR RICE, botanist, educator; b. LA, Calif., Mar. 21, 1920; s. Arthur Woodbury and Ella Muriel K.; m. Mareen Schultz, Mar. 21, 1953; children— Arthur Leo, Enid Johanna; children by previous marriage— Janet Muriel, Patricia Elayne, Caroline. BA, Occidental Coll., Los Angeles, 1941; postgrad., Stanford U., 1941-42; PhD, U. Calif.-Berkeley, 1950. Instr. biology Occidental Coll., 1946; teaching asst. U. Calif.-Berkeley, 1946-50; mem. faculty U. Wash., Seattle, 1950—, prof. botany, 1964-88, emeritus, 1988—, chmn. dept., 1971-77. Cons. in field. Co-founder Wash. Natural Area Preserves system, 1966. Served with USNR, 1942-46. Mem. Wash. Native Plant Soc. (founder 1976), Calif. Bot. Soc. Rsch. edaphics of serpentines, flowering plants. Home: 20312 15th Ave NW Shoreline WA 98177-2166 Office: U Wash PO Box 351800 Seattle WA 98195-180o Office Phone: 206-543-1976. Business E-Mail: ark@u.washington.edu.

KRUCOFF, MITCHELL WOLFE, cardiologist; b. Washington, Jan. 28, 1954; m. Carol Krucoff, 1974; children: Max, Rae. MD, George Washington U. Sch. Medicine, 1980. Cert. Internal Medicine, Cardiovascular Disease. Intern, internal medicine George Washington U. Hosp., DC, 1980—81, resident, cardiology DC, 1981—83; fellow Georgetown U. Hosp., Washington, 1983—85, hosp. appointment; asst. prof. Georgetown U., Washington; prof. medicine and cardiology Duke U. Med. Ctr.; mem. exec. faculty Duke Clin. Rsch. Inat.; dir. Cardiovascular Devices Unit, eECG Core Lab.; dir., Cardiovascular Lab. Durham VA Med. Ctr., 1995—. Dir. MANTRA Study Project; bd. dir. Sri Satya Sai Inst. Higher Med. Scis., Puttaparthi, India; mem., clin. trials review com. Nat. Heart, Lung and Blood Inst.; mem. adv. panel, circulatory devices FDA. Contbr. articles to publications, chapters to books; sr. editor Journal of Alternative & Complementary Medicine, past editor-in-chief Alternative Therapies in Health and Medicine, lead author MANTRA Pilot Study, Am. Heart Jour., 2001, MANTRA Study Phase II, The Lancet, 2005, featured in O, The Oprah Mag. & Talk and Time Mag., featured on 20/20 & A&E Special Report, The MANTRA Study Project was subject of 1 hr. spl. Can Prayer Heal?, BBC/Discovery Channel, 2004; co-author (with wife): Healing Moves:. How to Cure, Relieve, and Prevent Common Ailments with Exercise, 2004; co-editor: Integrative Cardiology, 2007. Fellow: Am. Coll. Cardiology; mem.: Am. Coll. Chest Physicians. Achievements include being internationally recognized for pioneering research, including Complementary therapies in patients with heart disease, Computer-assisted heart monitoring, New modalities of coronary revascularization. Address: 7423 Erwin Rd Hsp N B 3246 Durham NC 27710 Mailing: Duke U Health Sys 508 Fulton St Rm A3006 Durham NC 27705 Office Phone: 919-286-6860. Office Fax: 919-286-6861. E-mail: helingmoves@aol.com, kruco001@mc.duke.edu.*

KRUEGER, ALAN B., economics professor; b. Sept. 17, 1960; BS in Indsl. & Labor Rels., Cornell U., 1983; MA in Econ., Harvard U., 1985, PhD in Econ., 1987. Chief economist US Dept. Labor, 1994—95; asst. prof. econ. & pub. affairs Princeton U., 1987—91, prof. econ. & pub. affairs, 1992—, Bendheim prof. econ. & pub. policy, 1992—. Bd. trustees Russell Sage Found.; bd. dirs. Am. Inst. Rsch. Co-author: (novels) Myth and Measurement: The New Econ. of the Minimum Wage, 1997, Inequality in Am.: What Role for Human Capital Policies?, 2004; author Edn. Matters: A Selection of Essays on Edn., 2001; editor (mem. editorial bd.): (jour.) Sci.; editor: Jour. of Econ. Perspectives, 1996—2002; co-editor: Jour. of the European Econ. Assn., 2003—05; contbr. articles Econ. Scene column, New York Times, to profl. jours. Co-recipient IZA Prize in Labor Econ., 2006; recipient Kershaw Prize, Assn. for Pub. Policy and Mgmt., 1997, Mahalanobis Meml. Medal, Indian Econometric Soc., 2001; fellow NBER Olin, 1989—90, Sloan Fellow in Econ., 1992, Econometric Soc., 1996, Am. Acad. of Arts & Sci, 2002, Am. Acad. of Polit. and Social Sci., 2003, Soc. of Labor Econ., 2005. Mem.: Exec. Com. of the Am. Econ. Assn. Office: Princeton U Industrial Relations Sect Princeton NJ 08544-2098 Office Phone: 609-258-4046. Office Fax: 609-258-2907. E-mail: akrueger@princeton.edu.*

KRUEGER, ALLAN C., chemist; b. Arcadia, Calif., May 16, 1967; BS in Chemistry, Calif. State U., Chico, 1990; PhD in Organic Chemistry, Wayne State U., Detroit, 1994. Assoc. rsch. investigator Abbott Labs., Ill., 1997—. Fellow Post-Doctoral Fellowship, NIH, 1995—97. Mem.: Am. Chem. Soc. Home: 7260 Presidential Dr Gurnee IL 60031 Office: Abbott Labs 200 Abbott Park Rd Abbott Park IL 60064 Personal E-mail: a.chris.krueger@abbott.com.

KRUEGER, ANNE, economist; b. Endicott, NY; BA, Oberlin Coll., Ohio, 1953; MS, U. Wis., 1956, PhD, 1958, Georgetown U., 1992; PhD (hon.), Hacettepe U., Ankara, Turkey, 1990, Monash U., 1995; D of Bus. (hon.), Melbourne Bus. Sch., 2004. From asst. prof. to prof. econs. U. Minn., Mpls., 1959—82; v.p. econs. and rsch. The World Bank, Washington, 1982-86; art and scis. prof. econs. Duke U., Durham, NC, 1987-93; Herald and Caroline L. Ritch prof arts and scis. in econs. Stanford (Calif.) U., 1993—2003, dir. Ctr. Rsch. Econ. Devel. and Policy Reform, 1996-2001; 1st dep. mng. dir. Internat. Monetary Fund, Washington, 2001—06, spl. adv. to mng. dir., 2006—07; prof. internat. econ. Sch. for Advanced Internat. Studies Johns Hopkins U., Washington, 2007—. Vis. com. dept. econs. Harvard U., 1990-98; sr. non-resident fellow Brookings Inst., 1990-92; rsch. assoc. Nat. Bur. Econs.; hon. prof. Acad. Nat. Economy, Moscow, 2004. Author: Trade Policies and Developing Nations, 1995, Economic Policies at Cross Purposes, 1993, Economic Policy Reform in Developing Countries, 1992, The Political Economy of Agricultural Pricing Policy, Vol. 5: A Synthesis of the Political Economy in Developing Countries, 1992, Economic Policy Reform: The Second Stage, 2000; co-author (with O. Aktan): Swimming Against the Tide: Turkish Trade Reform in the 1980s, 1992; editor: (with R.H. Bates) Political and Economic Interactions in Economic Policy Reform, 1993, The World Trade Organization as an International Institution, 1998, Economic Policy Reform: Second Stage, 2000, A New Approach to Sovereign Debt Restructuring, 2002, Economic Policy Reform and the Indian Economy, 2003, (with Jose Antonio Gonzales, Vittorio Corbo and Aaron Tornell) Latin American Macroeconomic Reform: The Second Stage, 2003, (with Sajjid Z. Chinoy) Reforming India's Economic, Financial and Fiscal Policies, 2003. Mem. N.Y. State Regents Commn. on Higher Edn., 1992-93. Recipient Robertson prize NAS, 1984, Bernhard Harms prize Inst. for World Economy, Kiel, 1990, Enterprise award Kenan Inst., 1990, Seidman prize, 1994; named Hon. Prof., Acad. Nat. Economy, Moscow, 2004. Fellow AAAS, Econometric Soc. (award 1984); mem. NAS, Am. Econ. Assn. (disting. fellow, chmn. com. rsch. 1988-92, chmn. commn. on grad. edn. in econs. 1989-90, v.p. 1977, pres.-elect 1995, pres. 1996, rep. to Internat. Econ. Assn. and mem. IEA exec. com. 1992-98, v.p. Internat. Econ. Assn. 1994-98). Office: Nitze Sch Advanced Internat Studies Johns Hopkins Univ 1717 Massachusetts Ave NW Ste 704 Washington DC 20036 Office Phone: 202-587-3238.

KRUEGER, ARLIN JAMES, physicist; b. Oct. 22, 1933; s. Rudolph August and Mathilda E. (Pooch) K.; m. Susan J. Peacock, Dec. 28, 1978; children: Sandra, Timothy, Terry. BA, U. Minn., 1955, postgrad., 1956—58, Colo. State U., 1976—78. Physicist Naval Weapons Ctr., China Lake, Calif., 1959-69; physicist-astrophysicist Goddard Space Flight Ctr., Greenbelt, Md., 1969-2000; W.H. Elkins prof. physics U. Md., Balt., 2000—01, rsch. prof., 2001—. Developer of rocket and satellite instruments: sensor sci. Nimbus-7 Total Ozone Mapping Spectrometer (TOMS), 1975—93, Rocoz Optical Rocket Ozonesonde, 1961—79, Volcanic Ash Mapper, 1998—2000; mem. com. ext. U.S. Std. Atmosphere; instrument scientist U.S.-USSR Meteor 3/TOMS mission, U.S. Earth Probe/TOMS mission; prin. investigator Japanese ADEOS/TOMS mission, NASA Earth Sys. Scis. Pathfinder, Volcanic Ash Monitor (VOLCAM) Satellite Program, NASA Airborne Antarctic Ozone Experiment/TOMS Real-Time Support, NASA Airborne Arctic Experiment/TOMS Real Time Support; co-investigator Earth Observing Sys. Volcanic Eruption Investigation, Rsch. on Antarctic Ozone Hole; adv. volcanic hazards panel Office Fed. Coord. of Meteorology; invited lectr. Nat. Inst. Polar Rsch., Tokyo, AT&T Bell Labs., U.S. Naval Acad., Goddard Space Flight Ctr. Engring. Colloquium, Gordon Rsch. Conf. on Volcano-Climate, Fermi Sch. Physics, Italy, Russian Acad. Scis., Moscow; Quaternary Rsch. lectr. U. Wash.; invited participant and spkr. sci. workshops and confs. Contbr. articles to profl. publs. Recipient Exceptional Sci. Achievement medal, NASA, Exceptional Svc. medal, 2001, Goddard rsch. and study fellow, Colo. State U., 1976—78, William T. Pecora award, TOMS Sci. Team, 2006. Mem. AAAS, Am. Meteorol. Soc., Internat. Assn. Meteorology and Atmospheric Physics (internat. ozone commn.), Am. Geophys. Union, Sigma Xi. Achievements include research on stratospheric ozone, remote sensing from satellites, volcanic eruptions, volcanic aviation hazards, atmosphere of Mars. Home Phone: 301-384-5549; Office Phone: 410-455-8906.

KRUEGER, BONNIE LEE, editor, writer; b. Chgo., Feb. 3, 1950; d. Harry Bernard and Lillian (Soyak) Krueger; m. James Lawrence Spurlock, Mar. 8, 1972. Student, Morraine Valley Coll., 1970. Adminstrv. asst. Carson Pirie Scott & Co., Chgo., 1969-72; traffic coord. Tatham Laird & Kudner, Chgo., 1973-74, J. Walter Thompson, Chgo., 1974-76, prodn. coord., 1976-78; editor-in-chief Assoc. Pubs., Chgo., 1978—, Sophisticate's Hairstyle Guide, 1978—, Sophisticate's Beauty Guide, 1978—, Complete Woman, 1981—; pub., editorial svcs. dir. Sophisticate's Black Hair Guide, 1983—, Sophisticate's Soap Star Styles, 1994-95. Active Statue of Liberty Restoration Com., NYC, 1983, Chgo. Architecture Found.; campaign worker Cook County State's Atty., Chgo., 1982; poll watcher Cook County Dem. Orgn., 1983. Recipient Exceptional Woman in Pub. award, Women in Periodical Pub., 2000. Mem. Soc. Profl. Journalists, Am. Health and Beauty Aids Inst. (assoc., Communicator of Yr. award), Lincoln Park Zool. Soc., Landmarks Preservation Coun. of Ill., Art Inst. Chgo., Chgo. Hist. Soc., Mus. Contemporary Art, Peta, Headline Club, PAWS (Pets Are Worth Saving), Historymakers, Sigma Delta Chi, City Club Chgo. Lutheran. Office: Associate Pubs 875 N Michigan Ave Chicago IL 60611-1803 Office Phone: 312-266-8680. Business E-Mail: krueger@associatedpub.com. *I approach my life like one would approach the climbing of a mountain— plenty of faith, determination, self criticism, hard work and the joy and knowledge that the top is there for everyone to reach, if you pursue it with a combination of fervor, patience and love.*

KRUEGER, DEBORAH A. BLAKE, school psychologist, consultant; b. Chgo., Aug. 22, 1954; d. Stanley Walter and Maryanne Lois Blake; m. Darrell George Krueger, May 31, 1986; children: Sarah, Joshua. BA, DePaul U., 1976, MEd, 1980; PhD, Loyola U., 1998. Lic. sch. psychologist Ill. Learning disabilities specialist Assocs. in Family Therapy, Lake Bluff, Ill., 1980-85; reading and learning disabilities specialist Proviso West H.S., Hillside, Ill., 1980-82; edn. therapist Hartgrove Hosp., Chgo., 1982-85; dir. spl. edn. Old Orchard Hosp., Skokie, Ill., 1985-87; program coord. One-to-One Learning Ctr., Northfield, Ill., 1995-98; sch. psychologist Winnetka (Ill.) Pub. Schs., 1997—. Cons. Naperville and Woodridge Schs., 1998—; lectr. Loyola U., Chgo., 1997—; pvt. practice, Northbrook, 2000—; third party cons. hartgrove Psychol. Hosp., Chgo., 1985—88, Old Orchard Psychol. Hosp., Skokie, 1987—89; co-founder Baby N'Me Mother-Infant Dyad Groups, 1991; spkr. Resolve Orgn., Good Samaritan Hosp., Downers Grove, Ill., 1991; global initiative del. partipant to Eastern Europe, 2004. Founder Living with Infertility and Experimentation, Evanston, Ill., 1990—96, mem. steering com., 1990—94. Grantee, Loyola U., 1996. Mem.: APA, Ill. Assn. Infant Mental Health, Ill. Sch. Psychol. Assn., Soc. Personality Assessment, Nat. Assn. Sch. Psychologists, Assn. Advancement Therapeutic Edn. Avocations: piano, exercise, reading, local school involvement. Home: 2434 Ridgeway Ave Evanston IL 60201-1858 Office: Winnetka Pub Schs 520 Glendale Ave Winnetka IL 60093-2135 also: 910 Skokie Blvd Northbrook IL 60062 Office Phone: 847-604-4160. Personal E-mail: DbKrueger@aol.com.

KRUEGER, GERALD PETER, psychologist; b. Evanston, Ill., Apr. 3, 1944; s. Albert August and Pauline Mary (Didier) K.; m. Jessica Ann Prendergast, Aug. 26, 1967; children: Michael G., Deborah L., Kevin A. BA in Psychology, U. Dayton, 1966; MA in Exptl. and Engring. Psychology, Johns Hopkins U., 1975, PhD in Exptl. Psychology, 1977; grad., U.S. Army Command and Gen. Staff Coll., 1980, U.S. Army War Coll., 1988. Cert. profl. ergonomist Bd. Certification Profl. Ergonomics. Rschr. engring. psychology Bunker-Ramo Corp., Wright-Patterson AFB, Ohio, 1966—69; human factors rsch. psychologist U.S. Army Human Engring. Lab., Aberdeen, Md., 1969—71; R & D coord. Def. Advanced Rsch. Projects Agy., Saigon, Vietnam, 1971—72; mil. police ops. officer U.S. Army, Ft. Meade, Md., 1972, aviation psychologist Aeromed. Rsch. Lab. Ft. Rucker, Ala., 1976—80; R & D programs staff officer U.S. Army Med. R & D Command, Ft. Detrick, Md., 1980—84; dep. chief dept. behavioral biology Walter Reed Army Inst. Rsch., Washington, 1984—88; dir. biomed. applications rsch. divsn. U.S. Army Aeromed. Rsch. Lab., Ft. Rucker, 1988—90; comdr., sci. tech. dir. U.S. Army Rsch. Inst. Environ. Medicine, Natick, Mass., 1990—94; ret. col. U.S. Army, 1994; v.p. ergonomics R & D svcs. Biomechanics Corp. Am., Melville, NY, 1994—95; prin. rsch. scientist, ergonomist Star Mountain, Inc., Alexandria, Va., 1995—98; pres. Krueger Ergonomics Cons., Inc., 1998—; prin. scientist, ergonomist Wexford Group Internat., Vienna, Va., 2000—06. Tchr. U.S. Armed Forces Inst., Saigon, 1971, Johns Hopkins U., 1974-75, U. So. Calif., 1977-80; adj. asst. prof. med.-clin. psychology Uniformed Svcs. U. Health Scis., Bethesda, Md., 1997—; mem. sci. coun. to UTEK Corp., Plant City, Fla., 1999—.; bd. dirs. Commonwealth Biotechs., Inc., Richmond, Va., 2004-07. Book review editor Ergonomics in Design Mag., 1995—; assoc. editor Mil. Psychology, 1991-2003, mem. editl. bd., 2003—; guest editor jours. in field; contbr. articles to profl. jours. Recipient Richard M. Griffith Meml. award So. Soc. Philosophy and Psychology, 1978, Order of Mil. Med. merit for career contbns. Army Med. Dept., 1992, numerous mil. awards, medals and skill proficiency badges, including Legion of Merit, 1994, Bronze Star U.S. Army, 1972, Meritorious Svc. medals with 2 oak leaf clusters. Fellow APA (pres. divsn. mil. psychology 1995-96, pres. divsn. engring. psychologists 2001-02), Human Factors and Ergonomics Soc. (pres. Potomac chpt. 2003); mem. Soc. for Indsl. Orgnl. Psychologists, Assn. US Army, Nat. Def. Indsl. Assn., Ergonomics Soc., Aerospace Med. Assn., Aerospace Human Factors Assn., Soc. for Human Performance in Extreme Environments, Army War Coll. Alumni Assn., VFW, Am. Legion. Roman Catholic. Avocations: participating in running events, organizing community activities. Office: Krueger Ergonomics Consultants 4105 Komes Ct Alexandria VA 22306-1252 Office Phone: 703-850-6397. E-mail: jerrykrueg@aol.com. *Pick good mentors. Mine taught me to: 1) Try new things, welcome challenges. 2) Develop a high level of competence. 3) Know your customers' needs. 4) Always give them more than they expect.*

KRUEGER, JAMES A., lawyer; b. Sept. 21, 1943; s. A.A. and Margaret E. (Hurley) K.; m. Therese Eileen Connors, Aug. 2, 1968; 1 child, Colleen. BA cum laude, Gonzaga U., 1965; JD, Georgetown U., 1968; LLM, NYU, 1972. Bar: Wash. 1969, U.S. Supreme Ct. 1972, U.S. Tax Ct. 1972, U.S. Dist. Ct. (we. dist.) Wash. 1980, U.S. Ct. Appeals (9th cir.) 1982. Mem. staff U.S. senator from Wash., 1967-68; mem. Vandeberg, Johnson & Gandara (and predecessor firms), 1972—. Spl. dist. counsel Wash. State Bar Assn., 1984-94; adj. prof. law, U. of Puget Sound, 1974-76. Co-author: Representing the Close Corporation, 1979, Partnership Agreements, 1981, Planning for the Small Business Enterprise, 1982, The Partnership Handbook, 1984. Chmn. bd. Cath. Cmty. Svcs. of Pierce and Kitsap Counties, 1983-84; bd. dirs. United Way of Pierce County, 1973-82, 99—. Capt. U.S. Army, 1968-72. Decorated Bronze star. Mem. ABA, Wash. State Bar Assn., Tacoma-Pierce County Bar Assn. Roman Catholic. Office: 1201 Pacific Ave Ste 1900 Tacoma WA 98402-4315

KRUEGER, JOANNA KATHERINE, chemistry professor, researcher; d. Dale Bernard and Ruth Ellen Krueger; m. James Michael Mottonen; children: Nathanael John Mottonen, Frieda Analiese Mottonen. PhD, Princeton U., NJ, 1991. Cardiology fellow U. Tex. Southwestern Med. Ctr., Dallas, 1991—95, Los Alamos Nat. Lab., 1995—99; asst. prof. U. NC, Charlotte, 1999—2005, assoc. prof., 2005—. Contbr. chapters to books. Lay min. Advent Luth. Ch., Charlotte, NC, 2003. Grantee, NIH Nat. Heart Lung and Blood Inst., 1995—98, Biotech award, NC Biotech. Ctr., 2000—02, Jr. Faculty Enhancement award, Oak Ridge Assoc. U., 2001—02, NSF, 2003—, R.C. Cottrell Coll. Sci., 2003—05; F. W. and Elsie L. Heyl scholar, Kalamazoo Coll., 1982—85. Mem.: Am. Soc. Biochemistry and Molecular Biology (mem. editl. bd. 2006—), Advanced Photon Source (proposal adv. committe 2005—07), Nat. Inst. Stds. and Tech. Ctr. Neutron Rsch. (program adv. com. 2004), Biophysical Soc. Home: 5906 Marshbank Ln Charlotte NC 28269 Office: UNC Charlotte Chemistry Dept 9201 University City Blvd Charlotte NC 28223-0001 Home Phone: 704-947-1272; Office Phone: 704-687-4913. Office Fax: 704-687-3151. Business E-Mail: jkkruege@uncc.edu.

KRUEGER, KATHERINE KAMP, lawyer; b. Chgo., Apr. 7, 1944; d. Rudolph Pollay and Josephine Yvette (Marland) Kamp. Student U. Paris, Sorbonne, 1963-64; B.S. magna cum laude, Tulane U., 1965, M.S., 1968; J.D., Northwestern U., 1980. Bar: Tex. 1980, Ill. 1988, Wash. 1996. Micropaleontologist, Gulf Oil Corp., New Orleans, 1967-68; custodian collections geology Field Mus., Chgo., 1968-76, lectr., 1975-76; lectr. earth sci. Northeastern Ill. U., Chgo., 1977; atty. oil and gas Gulf Oil Corp., Houston, 1980-81, Amoco Prodn. Co., Houston, 1981-87, atty. environ. law Amoco Corp., Chgo., 1987-89; atty. litigation Amoco Prodn. Co., Houston, 1989-90; atty. legal dept. Dow Chem. Co., Freeport, Tex., 1990-92; atty. legal dept. City of Houston, Tex., 1992-93, adminstr. dept. pub. works and engring., 1993-94; regulatory analyst Environ. Resource Ctr., Houston, 1994-95; environment atty. Quileute Tribe, 1996—; bd. dirs. The Eureka Soc., Escondido, Calif., 1974—; vol. lectr. Desk and Derrick, Houston, 1983. Contbr. articles to profl. jours. Campaign vol., poll watcher

Ind. Democratic candidate for Ill. Constl. Conv., Chgo., 1968; poll watcher Ind. Democratic candidate for Ill. Rep., Chgo., 1978; del. Dem. Senatorial Dist. 7 Conv., Tex., 1984, Moscow Conf. on Law and Bilateral Econ. Rels., 1990. NSF Student grantee microbiol. dept. U. Miami Marine Lab., 1960-64; grantee La. Heart Found., Sophie Newcomb Coll. Botany Dept., 1962-63, Grad. Sch. Tulane U. Scholars and Fellows Orgn., 1965-66; named Steinmayer Best Geol. Student, Tulane U., 1965; Houston Bar Found. fellow, 1982—. Fellow Houston Bar Found. (life); mem. ABA, State Bar Tex., Houston Bar Assn., Chgo. Bar Assn., Phi Beta Kappa, Sigma Gamma Epsilon, Eta Sigma Phi. Address: PO Box 1607 Forks WA 98331-1607 Office: Quileute Natural Resources PO Box 187 La Push WA 98350 Office Phone: 360-374-2265. Business E-Mail: katie.krueger@quileutenation.org.

KRUEGER, KEITH ROGER, educational association administrator; b. St. Paul, Mar. 27, 1957; s. Richard Ernest and Shirley May (Popp) K. BA, George Washington U., 1979; MAPA, U. Minn., 1981. Fellow V.P. Walter Mondale, Washington, 1980; adminstrv. asst. Minn. Sen. Health Com., St. Paul, 1982; chief legis. asst. Congressman Gerry Sikorski, Washington, 1983—85; dir. govt. rels. Am. Optometric Assn., Washington, 1985—86; pres. Non-Profit Mgmt. Assocs., Washington, 1986—2002; CEO Consortium Sch Networking, Washington, 2002—. Episcopalian. Office: Consortium Sch Networking 1025 Vermont Ave NW Ste 1010 Washington DC 20005 Office Phone: 202-861-2676 ext. 118. Office Fax: 202-861-0888. E-mail: Keith@cosn.org.*

KRUEGER, KENNETH JOHN, nutritionist, educator; b. LA, Jan. 29, 1946; s. Charles Herbert and Adelaide Marie K.; m. Ellen Santucci, June 16, 1979 (div. 1989); children: Kenneth, Michael, Scott, David. BA in Humanities, U. So. Calif., 1968; MS in Edn. (Psychology), Mt. St. Mary's Coll., 1972. Tchr. English Corcoran H.S., Calif., 1968, Charter Oak H.S., Covina, Calif., 1969—90; instr. nutrition and exercise Mt. San Antonio Coll., Walnut, Calif., 1974—80; pres. Mega Group, Ltd., 1990, The Krueger Group, Malibu, Calif., 1991—2000; exec. Overnite Express, LA, 1993, Calif. Parcel Express, Encino, 1994—96; nutritionist Swiss Nat. Team, 1995—99; tchr. phys. edn. Hiram Johnson H.S., Sacramento, 1995—96. Adj. prof. phys. edn. Sierra Coll., Rocklin, Calif., 1996; health instr. L.A. City Coll., 1996-97, West L.A. Coll., 1998; swim coach Mt. San Antonio Coll., Walnut, Calif., 1974-77; coach, v.p. Trojan Swim Club, Newport Beach, Calif., 1976-90; bd. dirs. Nutrition and Exercise Cons., Tustin, Calif.; nutrition and exercise dir. Health Am., 1987-90; chmn., nutrition and fitness com. Internat. Eating Disorders Com., 1988; U.S. nat. team nutritionist for (FINA) World Cup 1988 Champions; recruiter Club Med, Paris, 1976-78; program coord. Pacific Am. Inst., San Francisco, 1983; asst. coach Vevey Natation, Switzerland, 1972-73; asst. swim coach Swiss Nat. Team, 1968, 85; chief marshall U.S. Olympic Swim Trials, Irvine, 1980, linguistics chmn. protocol U. So. Calif. Venue, L.A. Olympic Com., 1983-84; mem.-at-large long distance com. U.S. Swimming, Colorado Springs, 1987-91, coach So. Calif. Long Distance Swimming, 1987-89; del. chief, coach and swimmer So. Calif. Swimming for Internat. Crossing of Lake Geneva, sponsored by Internat. Olympic Com., Switzerland, 1987; meet dir. U.S. 25K Long Distance Swimming Championships/FINA World Cup Trials, Long Beach, Calif., 1988, U.S. 25K Swim Championships, Long Beach, 1989. Author: Reflections and Refractions, 1973; contbr. articles to internat. profl. nutrition and sport jours. Bd. dirs. U.S.A. Athletes Hall of Fame, 1991-92. Recipient NCAA All Am. award U. So. Calif., 1966, NCAA Nat. Champ award, 1966, U.S. Masters Swimming Champion, 1972 and annually 1974-81, Internat. Sr. Olympics Champion, 1972 and annually 1974-85; recipient commendations U.S. Congress, Calif. Senate, L.A. County Bd. Suprs; inducted into U.S.A. Athletes Hall of Fame. Mem. KC. Libertarian. Roman Catholic. Avocations: sports, reading. Mailing: 5435 Vesper Ave Sherman Oaks CA 91411 Personal E-mail: krkrueger@hotmail.com.

KRUEGER, MARLO BUSH, retired lawyer; b. Little Rock, Sept. 5, 1956; d. James Shepherd Bush and Frances Rosannah Davidson; m. James Robert Krueger, Sept. 15, 2001. BS in Pub. Adminstrn., U. Ark., Fayetteville, 1978, JD, 1981. Bar: Ark. 1981. Asst. reporter decisions Ark. Supreme Ct. and Ct. of Appeals, Little Rock, 1982—88, reporter decisions, 1988—95, interim reporter decisions, 2006. Articles editor (jour.) The Saline (Best Edited Document award, 1994, Dale Bumpers award for best Civil War article, 1994, Best Comty. History Pub. in Local Jour. award, 2000). Mem., sec. Saline County History and Heritage Soc., 1994—95, treas., 2006—07; mem. various bds. and coms. 1st Meth. Ch., Benton, 1984—89, 1992—93. Mem.: Ark. Bar Assn., Assn. Reporters of Jud. Decisions (various coms., exec. bd. 1987—94, pres. 1992—93, Devoted Svc. award 1995), Phi Delta Phi (life; clk. 1980—81). Meth. Avocations: genealogy, fishing, computers, photography, history. Home: 4011 Hwy 5 Benton AR 72019-8277 Personal E-mail: krueger@wildblue.net.

KRUEGER, RAYMOND ROBERT, lawyer; b. Portage, Wis., Aug. 29, 1947; s. Earl Andrew and Catherine Virginia (Klenert) K.; m. Barbara Bowen, June 21, 1969; children: Lindsey, Michael. BA in Econs., U. Wis., 1969, JD, 1972. Bar: Wis. 1972. Assoc. Charne, Glassner, Tehan, Clancy & Taitelman S.C., Milw., 1973-79, shareholder, 1979-91; ptnr. Charne Clancy Krueger Pollack & Corris S.C., Milw., 1991—92, Michael, Best & Friedrich LLP, Milw., 1992—. Chmn. Georgia O'Keeffe Found., Abiquiu, N.Mex., 1989—; trustee Village of Whitefish Bay, Wis., 1989—2003; mem. Milwaukee River Revitalization Coun., 1988—, vice chair, 1989—96, chair, 1996—; dir. River Revitalization Found., Inc., 1998—, chair, 2001—03; trustee Milw. Art Mus., 2003—, mem. bldg. com., 1996—2003; chair Whitefish Bay Cmty. Devel. Authority, 2002—. Capt. USAF, 1969—78. Mem. ABA (natural resources sect.), State Bar Wis. (environ. law sect.), Milw. Bar Assn. (environ. law sect.), Environ. Law Inst. Avocation: visual arts. Office: Michael Best & Friedrich LLP 100 E Wisconsin Ave Ste 3300 Milwaukee WI 53202-4108 Office Phone: 414-271-6560. Business E-Mail: rrkrueger@mbf-law.com.

KRUEGER, RICHARD BOHN, psychiatrist; b. Escanaba, Mich., July 23, 1945; s. Harold Ernst and Marvel (Bohn) K.; m. Meg Susan Kaplan, NOv. 25, 1988; 1 child, Molly Kaplan. BA, Albion Coll., 1967; MD, Harvard U., 1977. Diplomate Am. Bd. Internal Medicine, Am. Bd. Psychiat. Neurology with added qualifications in forensic psychiatry. Intern Boston VA Med. Ctr., 1977-78, resident, 1978-80; resident in psychiatry Boston U. Med. Sch., 1980-83; staff psychiatrist Pembroke (Mass.) Hosp., 1983-89, Columbia Presbyn. Hosp., NYC, 1989—. Rsch. psychiatrist N.Y. State Psychiat. Inst., N.Y.C., 1991-94, clin. psychiatrist, 1994—. Mem. Am. Psychiat. Assn., AMA, AAPL. Office: NY State Psychiat Inst Washington Heights Cmty Svc 210 E 68th St Apt 1-h New York NY 10021-6024

KRUEGER, ROBERT CHARLES, former ambassador, congressman, senator; b. New Braunfels, Tex., Sept. 19, 1935; s. Arlon E. and Faye (Leifeste) Krueger; life ptnr. Kathleen Tobin Krueger; children: Mariana, Sarah, Christian. BA, So. Meth. U., 1957; MA, Duke U., 1958; M.Litt., Oxford U., Eng., 1961, D.Phil., 1964; D.Litt. (hon.), U. St. Thomas; D.Pub.Service (hon.), Lycoming U., 2003; DHL (hon.), Tex. Luth. U., 2006. From instr. to assoc. prof. English Duke U., 1961-72; vice provost, dean Trinity Coll. Arts and Scis., Duke U., 1972-73; chmn. bd. Comal Hosiery Mills, 1973-75; ptnr. Krueger Brangus Ranch, 1974-86; mem. 94th-95th Congresses from 21st Tex. dist., 1975-79; U.S. ambassador-at-large, coord. for Mex. affairs, 1979-81; pres. Krueger Assocs., 1981-91; Bentsen prof. govt.-bus. rels. Lyndon B. Johnson Sch., U. Tex., 1985-86; Tsanoff prof. pub. affairs Rice U., 1986-88; Disting. lectr. So. Meth. U., 1991; commr. Tex. R.R. Commn., 1991—93; U.S. senator from Tex., 1993-94; amb. to Burundi, 1994-96; amb. to Botswana, 1996—2000; spl. rep. of sec. of state So. Africa Devel. Cmty., 1998—2000; rsch. fellow Merton Coll. Oxford (Eng.) U., 2000—01; cons. on nat. and internat. bus. and fgn. affairs, 2001—. Spkr. in field; mem. chancellor's bd. advisors U. Ill. Med. Ctr.; bd. dir. Moneygram Corp.; vis. disting. prof. U. Tex., Austin, 2003—05, Tex. State U., San Marcos, 2002—06. Author: The Poems of Sir John Davies, 1975; contbr. articles to profl. jours. and newspapers. Bd. dir. Cath. Charities, San Antonio, 2001—05, South Tex. Kidney Found., 2001—05. Mem.: Tex. Philos. Soc. (pres. 1993), Phi Beta Kappa, Blue Key. Office: PO Box 311717 New Braunfels TX 78131-1717 Office Phone: 830-629-7347. E-mail: kruegerx@swbell.net.

KRUEGER, ROBERT EDWARD, mechanical engineer, manufacturing executive; b. LA, Mar. 26, 1922; s. Edward Jr. and Ida Viola (Herren) K.; m. Elizabeth Westerfors, Sept. 10, 1949; children: Karen Elizabeth, Clarence Frederick (dec.), Roger Carl (dec.), Bruce Wayne, Glen Herren. Student, LA City Coll., 1939-40, Calif. Inst. Tech., 1940-43, 46-47, Yale U., 1943-44, Harvard U., MIT, Army Electronics Tng. Ctr.; BSME, Stanford U., 1950, MBA, 1952. Lic. fed. firearms dealer and ammunition mfr. Bur. Alcohol, Tobacco and Firearms. Trainee Douglas Aircraft Co., Santa Monica, Calif., summers 1941-43; staff mem. Los Alamos (N.Mex.) Sci. Lab., 1947-49; chief engr. Rutishauser Corp., Pasadena, Calif., 1952-53; asst. to pres. Unitek Corp., El Monte, Calif., 1953-55; sales mgr. Donner Sci. Co., Concord, Calif., 1955-57, Shand & Jurs divsn. Gen. Precision Equipment Corp., Berkeley, 1957-58; v.p. sales Advanced Instruments, Richmond, Calif., 1958-60; sales mgr. Gilliland Instruments, Oakland, Calif., 1960-62; ptnr. Krueger & Smith, Berkeley, 1969-72; founder, pres. Tetra Valves, Inc., Berkeley, 1972-78; owner, propr. Krueger Mfg.-Engring., Lafayette, Calif., 1962—. Author or co-author books, manuals, other works; patentee in field. Donor portraits of U.S. Pres. George Bush and Barbara Bush, White Ho., Washington, 1995, portrait of U.S. Pres. George Bush, Nat. Portrait Gallery, Washington, 1995; v.p. Calif. Rep. Assembly, 1983-84. With USAAF, 1942-47; with USAFR, 1947-53. Recipient John Singleton Copley medal Nat. Portrait Gallery, 1999. Mem. IEEE (life), AAAS, ASTM, NRA (life, endowment), Am. Soc. for Metals Internat. (life), Am. Def. Indsl. Assn. (life), James Smithson Soc./Smithsonian Instn. (Patron award Benefactors Cir. 1991), Nat. Mus. Am. Indian (charter), Colonial Williamsburg Found., Raleigh Tavern Soc., USN League (life), Spencer Baird Soc., Calif. Rifle and Pistol Assn. (life), Calif. State Sheriffs Assn., Contra Costa County Sheriffs Posse. Pantheist. Avocations: U.S. national heritage, art collections, politics, travel, photography. Home: 1084 Via Roble Lafayette CA 94549-2925 Office: Krueger Mfg-Engring 1084 Via Roble Lafayette CA 94549-2925

KRUEGER, SAM QUAN, museum administrator; b. Saigon; BA, State U. NY, Columbia U.; MPA, City U. NY. Mgr. cmty. based partnerships Whitney Mus. Am. Art, Nat. Book Found.; strategic planner; mgr. orgnl. and support svcs. United Way NYC; COO Mus. Chinese in the Americas, 2006—. Nat. Svc. Fellowship, U.S. Corp. Nat. and Cmty. Svc., 1998. Office: Mus of Chinese in the Americas 70 Mulburry St 2d Fl New York NY 10013*

KRUEGLER, CATHERINE A., sister, parochial school educator; d. James Lawrence Kruegler and Rose Mary Catherine Maloney. AS, Hudson Valley C.C., 1972; BS cum laude, Coll. St. Rose, 1977; MA, Boston Coll., 1988. Cert. tchr. N.Y. Educator St. Paul's Sch., Norwich, NY, 1972—75, Mechanicville, NY, 1977—79; pastoral minister St. Anthony's Ch., Syracuse, NY, 1979—86, Sacred Heart Ch., Mercedes, Tex., 1986—87, Prince of Peace Ch., Lyford, Tex., 1987—91; dir. religious edn. St. Patrick's Ch., Albany, NY, 1991—97; theology tchr. Cohoes (N.Y.) Cath. Sch., 1997—98, Saratoga (N.Y.) Cath. Sch., 1999—2002; liason labor Free the Children, Albany, 2001—02; svc. learning coord. Acad. of Holy Names, Albany, 2003—05. Bd. dirs. Urban Ministry Bd., Syracuse, 1982—86; del. mem. Witness for Peace, Nicaragua, 1985, 1990, s. ctrl. coord. Brownsville, Tex., 1990, Sisters Coun. Leadership, 1987—91; bd. dirs. St. Casimir's Sch., Albany, 1992—94. Recipient Svc. award, St. Patrick's Ch. and Hispanic Apostolate, N.Y., 1997; scholar, Hispanic Apostolate, N.Y., 1994. Mem.: Pax Christi. Democrat. Roman Catholic. Achievements include internat. observer election, Nicaragua, 1990; mem. del. kidnapped Flotilla for Peace, 1985. Avocations: reading, photography, pottery, gardening, skiing. Office: Acad of Holy Names 1075 New Scotland Rd Albany NY 12208 Office Phone: 518-438-7895. Business E-Mail: sckruegler@ahns.org.

KRUESI, FRANK EUGENE, transportation executive, former federal agency administrator; b. Marblehead, Mass., July 12, 1950; s. William Rogers and Lydia Abigail (Fuller) K.; m. Susan Francis Boyd, Sept. 1, 1971 (div. Jan. 1993); children: Elizabeth Ann, William Shepardson; m. Barbara Grochala, Oct. 16, 1993. BA in Econs. cum laude, Middlebury Coll., 1972; MA in Polit. Sci., U. Chgo., 1979. Lectr. polit. sci. Loyola U., Chgo., 1974, DePaul U., Chgo., 1979, Rosary Coll., Chgo., 1979; rsch. assoc. Ill. Gov.'s Commn. Individual Liberty & Personal Privacy, Chgo., 1975; cons. Ill. Gov.'s Commn. Mental Health Code, Chgo., 1975-77; exec. officer Cook County State's Atty. Office, Chgo., 1980-89; chief policy officer Office of Mayor of City of Chgo., 1989-93; asst. sec. for policy US Dept. Transp., Washington, 1993—97; pres. Chgo. Transit Authority, 1997—2007. Issues dir. Daley for State's Atty. and Mayor campaigns, Chgo., 1980-89. Democrat.

KRUG, EDWARD CHARLES, environmental scientist; b. New Brunswick, NJ, Aug. 24, 1947; s. Edward and Regina (Bartkoviak) K.: m. Nancy Wegner, July 19, 1988. BS in Environ. Sci with highest honors, Rutgers U., 1975, PhD in Soil Sci., 1981. cert. profl. soil scientist. Asst. scientist Conn. Agrl. Expt. Sta., New Haven, 1980-85; assoc. scientist Ill. State Water Survey U. Ill., Champaign, 1985-90; advisor Com. for a Constructive Tomorrow, Washington, 1989-90, dir. environ. projects, 1991-93; ind. environ. cons. Winona, Minn., 1993—. Sci. adv. com. Environ. Issues Coun., U.S.A., 1993—; adv. bd. Media Rsch. Ctr., Alexandria, Va., 1991—; adj. profl. scientist Ill. State Water Survey, U. Ill., Champaign, 1999—; biogeochemist Office of the Chief, Ill. State Water Survey, Champaign, 2000—; tech. adv. group, nutrient sci. com. Ill. EPA. Contbg. author: Encyclopedia for Earth System Science, 1992; contbr. articles to profl. jours. Mem. NJ Ad Hoc Water Quality Control Com., New Brunswick, 1972-73; reviewer, tech. advisor NJ Pub. Interact Rsch. Group, New Brunswick, 1972-75; chmn. ch. and soc. coms. United Meth. Ch., Winona, 1990-91, 2000—; mem. regional tech. adv. group U.S. Environ. Agy., 2001—. With USN, 1967-69. Recipient Frank G. Helyar award Rutgers U., 1973, Excellence in Rev. award Jour. Environ. Quality, 1991. Mem. Am. Geophys. Union, Soil Sci. Soc. Am., Internat. Union Soil Scientists, Ill. Soil Carbon Ptnrs. Working Group, Internat. Union Soil Scientists. Achievements include development of organic acid buffering theory; generalization of Rosenquist land-use theory to include naturally increased acidity of watershed from accelerated loss of bases; unified theory of acid/base biogeochemistry; generalization of nitrogen cycle to more comprehensively address internal cycling. Office: Ill State Water Survey 2204 Griffith Dr Champaign IL 61820 Home Phone: 217-328-0495; Office Phone: 217-244-0877. Business E-Mail: ekrug@uiuc.edu.

KRUG, JOHN CARLETON (TONY KRUG), academic administrator, library director, consultant; b. Evansville, Ind., Nov. 27, 1951; s. John Elmer and Mary Ellen K.; m. Anna Marie Waters, July 3, 1983. BA, Ind. State U., 1972, MLS, 1973; PhD, So. Ill. U., Carbondale, 1985. Lic. to ministry Bapt. Ch. Exec. dir. Olney (Ill.) Carnegie Pub. Libr., 1973-74; assoc. dean Wabash Valley Coll., Mt. Carmel, Ill., 1974-84; mem. Com. for U.S. Depository State Plan, Springfield, Ill., 1982-84; dir. librs. Maryville Coll., St. Louis, 1984-88; dir. info. svcs. Bethany (W.Va.) Coll., 1988-97; dean libr. svcs. Carson Newman Coll., Jefferson City, Tenn., 1997—2002; dir. ctrl. libr. Appalachian Coll. Assn., Berea, Ky., 2002—. Coord. libr. activities, Appalachian Coll. Assn., 1997-2002; sec. pro-tem Ill. Basin Coal Mining Manpower Council, Mt. Carmel, 1974-79; governing bd. exec. com. Higher Edn. Ctr. Cable TV, 1986-88; conf. speaker Kans. State U., 1982. Author: Libraries Using/Planning for Microcomputers, 1986; also computer programs. V.p. bd. dirs. Wabash Area Vocat. Enterprises, Mt. Carmel, 1978-81; bd. edn. Wabash Cmty. Unit, Mt. Carmel, 1980-83; exec. com. Cmty. Edn. and Arts Assn., Carbondale, 1983-84; visual arts adv. com. Ill. Arts Coun., Chgo., 1982-84; pastor Hopewell United Meth. Ch., Bridgeport, Ill., 1976-77; minister Terre Haute (Ind.) 1st Bapt. Ch., 1972—; elder Gateway Christian Ch., 1986-88; bd. dirs. Fair Haven Christian Sch., 1986-88; pres. T3-Tchrs., Tech., Tomorrow. Mem. Assn. Christian Librs. Office: Appalachian Coll Assn 210 Center St Berea KY 40403 Home Phone: 865-621-1282; Office Phone: 865-548-5450. Business E-Mail: krug.tony@gmail.com.

KRUGER, BARBARA, artist; b. Newark, Jan. 26, 1945; Student, Syracuse U., Parsons Sch. Design, NYC, Sch. Visual Arts. Illustrator Condé Nast Publs., NYC, 1967-68, chief designer Mademoiselle mag., 1968-72. Film critic Artforum; vis. artist Calif. Inst. Art, Art Inst. Chgo., U. Calif., Berkeley; prof. art dept. UCLA; arranger collections Pictures and Promises, The Kitchen, N.Y.C., 1981, Artists' Use of Lang., Franklin Furnace, N.Y.C., 1983, Creative Perspectives in Am. Photography, Hallwall's Gallery, Buffalo, 1983. Author: Picture/Readings, 1979, No Progress in Pleasure, 1982; one-woman shows Crousel/Hussenot Gallery, Paris, 1987, Monika Spruth Gallery, Cologne, Germany, 1987, 90, Nat. Art Gallery, Wellington, New Zealand, 1988, Mary Boone Gallery, N.Y.C., 1989, Galerie Bebert, Rotterdam, The Netherlands, 1989, Fred Hoffman Gallery, Santa Monica, Calif., 1989, Duke U. Mus. Art, Durham, N.C., 1990, Whitney Mus. Modern Art, Mus. Contemporary Art, Chgo., Mus. Contemporary Art, L.A., 1999, numerous others; exhibited in group shows Whitney Mus. Am. Art, N.Y.C., 1973, 82, 83, 85, 87, 89, Castello di Rivoli, Turin, Italy, 1989, Pa. Acad. Fine Arts, Phila., 1989, Denver Art Mus., 1989, Mus. 20th Century, Vienna, Austria, 1989, Ctr. Georges Pompidou, Paris, 1989, Mus. Contemporary Art, L.A., 1989, Rheinhalle, Cologne, 1989, Frankfurt (Germany) Kunstverein and Schirn Kunsthalle, 1989, also numerous others; work represented in various publs. Grantee Creative Artists Svc. Program, 1976-77, Nat. Endowment Arts, 1983-84; Golden Lion award lifetime achievement, Venice Biennial, 2005. Office: Mary Boone Gallery 745 5th Ave Ste 405 New York NY 10151-0401 also: UCLA Department of Art Ste 245 11000 Kinross Ave Los Angeles CA 90095

KRUGER, GUSTAV OTTO, JR., retired oral surgeon, educator, department chairman; b. NYC, Sept. 28, 1916; s. Gustav Otto and Anna Charlotte (Mellquist) K.; m. Helyn E. Hollingsworth, Apr. 12, 1947; children: Deborah Ann (Mrs. M. Henry King III), Tristram Coffin, Abigail Hollingsworth Imus. BS, George Washington U., 1938, AM, 1939; DDS, Georgetown U., 1939, ScD (hon.), 1977. Diplomate Am. Bd. Oral and Maxillofacial Surgery (pres. 1964). Intern Johns Hopkins Hosp., 1939-40; fellow Mayo Found., 1940-42, 45-48; mem. faculty Georgetown U. Sch. Dentistry and Grad. Sch., 1948-87, prof. oral surgery, chmn. dept., 1948-87, prof. emeritus, 1987—, assoc. dean, 1966-82; ret., 1987. Chief dental dept. Georgetown U. Hosp., Washington, 1948-82; cons. VA hosps., Martinsburg, W.Va. and Washington, U.S. Naval Hosp., Bethesda, D.C. Gen. Hosp., Washington; cons. to Pres.'s physician, 1960-64; cons. Walter Reed Army Med. Ctr.; mem. cancer tng. com. Nat. Cancer Inst., USPHS, 1967-71, chmn., 1969-71. Author: Textbook of Oral and Maxillofacial Surgery, 1959, 6th edit., 1984; contbr. articles to profl. jours. Capt. Dental Corps AUS, 1942-45, CBI, PTO. Recipient Arnold K. Maislen award N.Y. U., 1970; Simon P. Hullihen award W.Va. Soc. Oral Surgeons and W.Va. Med. Ctr., 1980; named Man of Year Georgetown U. Alumni Assn., 1961, Disting. Svc. award, 1992. Fellow AAAS, Am. Coll. Dentists (chmn. D.C. sect. 1969-71, Disting. Svc. award 2002), Internat. Coll. Dentists (chmn. D.C. sect. 1967-70); mem. ADA (chmn. oral surgery sect. 1961, mem. rev. commn. on advanced edn. in oral surgery 1965-71, chmn. commn. 1969-71), D.C. Dental Soc. (pres. 1960, Sterling V. Mead award 1989), Am. Assn. Oral and Maxillofacial Surgeons (program chmn. 1961, 79th Ann. Meeting dedication 1997), Middle Atlantic Soc. Oral and Maxillofacial Surgeons (pres. 1952), Am. Assn. Dental Schs., Am. Acad. Oral Pathology, Am. Acad. Oral and Maxillofacial Radiology, Internat. Assn. Dental Research, Am. Coll. Oral and Maxillofacial Surgeons (Harry Archer award 1992), Wash. Dental Study Club (pres. 1993), Kiwanis (co-chmn. orthop. com. 1971-86), Xi Psi Phi, Sigma Gamma Epsilon, Omicron Kappa Upsilon. Home: 6806 Bradgrove Cir Bethesda MD 20817-3001

KRUGER, JEROME, materials science educator, consultant; b. Atlanta, Feb. 7, 1927; s. Isaac and Sarah (Stein) K.; m. Mollee Coppel, Feb. 20, 1955; children: Lennard, Joseph. BS, Ga. Inst. Tech., 1948, MS, 1949; PhD, U. Va., 1952. With Naval Rsch. Lab., Washington, 1952-55; with Nat. Bur. Standards, Commerce Dept., Washington, 1955-83, group leader Corrosion and Electrodeposition, 1966-83; prof. Johns Hopkins U., 1984-99, chmn. materials sci. and engring., 1986-88, prof. emeritus, 1999—. Cons. Argonne Nat. Lab., Lockheed, Balt. Gas & Electric, Teletech Thompson, Dalton & DeRose, Mueller Brass, S.W. Rsch. Inst., Dickenson, Wright, Moon, Van Dusen & Freeman, Haineness, Dickey & Pierce, W.O. Snead, H.M. Huber Co., DACCO Sci.; Jerome Kruger vis. scholar U. Va., 1998. Divisional editor Jour. Electrochem. Soc., 1966-83; subject area editor: Ency. of Materials Sci. and Engring.; also editor books; contbr. articles to tech. jours., chpts. to book. DuPont fellow U. Va., 1951-52; recipient Silver medal Commerce Dept., 1962, Gold medal, 1972; Blum award Nat. Capitol sect. Electrochem. Soc., 1966, Foley award, 1999; Samuel Wesley Stratton award Nat. Bur. Standards, 1982; Presdl. rank of Meritorious Exec. of Sr. Exec. Svc., 1982; U.R. Evans award Inst. Corrosion (U.K.), 1991, Hon. fellow, 1996; establishment of Jerome Kruger vis. scholar program at U. Va., 1998, 1st invited scholar, 1999. Fellow Electrochem. Soc. (treas. 1982-86, hon. mem. 1987, Outstanding Achievement award 1977, Olin Palladium medal 1995), fellow Nat. Assn. Corrosion Engrs. (bd. dirs. 1983-86, W.R. Whitney award 1976, Jerome Kruger award in corrosion sci., Balt.-Washington sect., 1997); mem. Am. Inst. Conservation, Internat. Corrosion Coun. (1st v.p. 1984-87, pres. 1987-90), Fedn. Materials Socs. (pres. 1977), Standards Alumni Assoc. (pres. 2004-06) Nat. Inst. Stds. and Tech., Sigma Xi, Tau Beta Pi. Jewish. Home and Office: 619 Warfield Dr Rockville MD 20850-1921

KRUGER, KENNETH, architect; b. Newark, Aug. 13, 1928; s. Rudolph Robert and Clarise Estelle (Goldman) K.; m. Elinor Margaret Kane, July 22, 1978; children: Jonathan, Karen, Kai. BArch, MIT, 1951, MS, 1953, postgrad., 1964; MArch, Harvard U., 1952; postgrad., U. Rome, 1955. Registered arch., Mass., N.J., N.Y., profl. engr., Mass.; cert. Nat. Coun. Archtl. Registration Bds.; lic. constrn. supr., home inspector, real estate broker, Mass. Archtl. designer Carl Koch & Assoc., Cambridge, Mass., 1953-54; structural designer Frank Grad, Paris, 1955; arch. Marcel Breuer & Assocs., NYC, 1956-57; structural engr. Simpson & Stratta, San Francisco, 1959-60, Chin & Hensolt, San Francisco, 1961-62, Internat. Engring. Co., Rio de Janeiro, 1963; arch., engr. Kenneth Kruger, Boston, 1964-68, Kruger Kruger Albenberg Archs. & Engrs., Cambridge, 1969—. Instr. arch. MIT, Cambridge, 1952-53. Mem. Fresh Pond Adv. Bd., Cambridge, 2002, Mass. Designer Selection Bd., 2002-05. Overseas fellow MIT, 1952, Rotch prize, 1951; Fulbright scholar, 1954-55. Fellow ASCE, AIA, Am. Soc. Home Insps. (v.p. 1991, Pres.'s award 1991, exec. com. 1991-93, dir.-at-large 1988-90, 92-94, chmn. bylaws com. 1992-94; dir. New Eng. chpt. 1982), Boston Soc. Archs. (dir., commr. 1974-77), Boston Soc. Civil Engrs., Boston Assn. Structural Engrs. (chmn. mission and membersip com. 2001-05), Constrn. Specification Inst., Sigma Xi, Alpha

Epsilon Pi. Avocations: skiing, tennis, squash, backpacking, biking. Office: Kruger Kruger Albenberg 67 Grozier Rd Cambridge MA 02138-3314 Home Phone: 617-868-0681; Office Phone: 617-661-3812.

KRUGER, KENNETH CHARLES, architect; b. Santa Barbara, Calif., Aug. 19, 1930; s. Thomas Albin and Chleople (Gaines) K.; m. Patricia Kathryn Rasey, Aug. 21, 1955; children: David, Eric. BArch, U. So. Calif., 1953. Registered arch., Calif. Pres. Kruger Bensen Ziemer, Santa Barbara, 1960-90; part-time instr. architecture dept. Calif. Poly., San Luis Obispo, 1993-95; part-time arch., 1993—. Regent Calif. Archtl. Found., 1997-2003. Bd. dirs. United Boys and Girls Club, 2000-. Fellow AIA; mem. Archtl. Found. Santa Barbara (pres. 1987-89). Democrat. Home: 1255 Ferrelo Rd Santa Barbara CA 93103-2101

KRUGER, LON, men's college basketball coach; b. Topeka, Aug. 19, 1952; m. Barbara Miles; children: Angie, Kevin. BS in Bus., Kans. State U., 1975; MS in Phys. Edn., Pittsburg State U., Kans., 1977. Draft pick Houston Astros, 1970, St. Louis Cardinals, Atlanta Hawks, 1974, head coach, 2000—03; asst. coach Pittsburg State U., Kans., 1976-77; grad. asst. coach Kans. State U., 1977-78, asst. coach, 1978-82, head coach, 1986—90, Pan Am. U., 1982-86, athletic dir., 1982-85; head coach U. Fla., 1990—96, U. Ill., 1996—2000, UNLV, 2004—; asst. coach NY Knicks, 2003—04. Asst. coach US Pan Am. Team, 1987; head coach Big Eight Select Team, Beijing, 1987, U.S.A. Jr. World Champion Team, 1991, U.S.A. World U. Games Team, 1995; bd. dirs. Nat. Assn. Basketball Coaches, 1994—2000. Co-chairperson Alachua County's Red Ribbon Campaign, 1991-93. Named Big Eight Player of Yr., 1973, 74, Southeastern Conf. Coach of Yr., 1992, 94, Gainesville Vol. of Yr., 1995, State of Ill. Collegiate Coach of Yr., 1997; named to the Kans. Hall of Fame, 1999, Kans. State U. Hall of Fame, 2003, Topeka and Shawnee County Sports Hall of Fame, 2006. Office: Mens Basketball UNLV Athletics Dept 4505 Maryland Pky Las Vegas NV 89154 Office Phone: 702-895-3295. E-mail: lon.kruger@unlv.edu.*

KRUGER, MOLLEE COPPEL, writer; b. Bel Air, Md., Mar. 28, 1929; d. Benjamin and Mary Coppel; m. Jerome Kruger, Feb. 20, 1955; children: Lennard Gideon, Joseph Avrum. BA, U. Md., 1950. Columnist The Harford Gazette, Bel Air, Md., 1945-47; advt. copywriter Joseph Katz Co., Balt., 1951-55; TV scriptwriter Jewish Community Coun., Washington, 1960-72; columnist, feature writer various newspapers, Washington and NYC, 1967-88; freelance writer various nat. publs., 1980—. Condr. writing workshop Montgomery County Cmty. Svcs., Rockville, Md., 1982; cons. Buddemeir Co., Balt., 1958-59; pres. Maryben Books, Rockville, 1970—; tchr. creative writing Jewish Cmty. Ctr., Rockville, 1974-78, cons. editor sr. adult publs., 1975, 76, 77; cons. editor Stds. Alumni Assn., 1992. Author: Unholy Writ, 1970, More Unholy Writ, 1973, Yankee Shoes, 1975 (Gold Ribbon Bicentennial award 1976), Daughters of Chutzpah, 1983, Admiral of the Mosquitoes, 1990, Ladies First, 1995 (mus. adaptation 1st prize Nat. Music Competition Nat. League Am. Pen Women), A Purse of Humorous Verse for Jewish Women, 2005; editor Std. newsletter Nat. Bur. Stds., 1978-80 (Excellence award 1979); performer one-woman show on Emma Lazarus, Jewish Cmty. Coun., Washington, 1976; playwright (one act plays) The Muted Note: A Pulpit Drama, 1965, Master of Dreams: S.Y. Agnon, 1968, President McKinley is Dead, 1977; playwright, prodr. hist. show for Md. 350 Com., Montgomery County, Rockville, 1982-84, (play script) A Purse of Verse, 2007; contbr. articles to popular mags.; author numerous poems Founding mem. Humanities Commn. Montgomery County, 1984-91; judge Md. Writing Contest for Sr. Citizens, Annapolis, 1987-91, Montgomery County Bd. Elections,l 1990-92. Recipient Cert. of Recognition US Dept. Commerce, Washington, 1979, Alice Sherry Meml. award Poetry Soc. Va., Charlottesville, 1988, Courage award Dystonia Med. Found., 1997, Gov. Arts award Md. Citizens for the Arts Found., 2002, Lifetime Achievement recognition U. Md. Librs., 2003; named Outstanding Md. Woman Writer Md. State Dept. Edn., Md. Commn. for Women, Balt., 1989; Millenium poetry displayed in Montgomery County, Md. Govt. Bldg., 2000-; named Notable Montgomery County Author, Friends of the Libr., 2001, winner Nat. Essay Contest, 2007. Mem. Nat. League Am. Pen Women (Md. state letters chmn. 1990-92, 1999-2001, br. pres.-elect, nat. letters bd. 1992-94, founding mem. Chesapeake Mag., 1993, chmn. nat. letters com., nat. membership chmn. 1994-95, nat. exec. bd. 1994-96, nat. pub. rels. chmn. 1996-98, writing awards 1983, 85, 87, 89, 1st prize Nat. Adult Short Story contest 1994, 1st prize Nat. Catherine Leach Poetry competition 1994, 1st prize Nat. Miriam S. Rogers letters contest, 1995, 2d prize Chesapeake Short Story contest 1996, 2d prize Md. Form Poetry 1999, centennial com. 1997, 1st pl. 1998, millenium planning com. 1999), Mortar Bd. Alumni Club (pres. 1977-78, 50th ann. recognition cert. 2000, 50th Class Reunion com. 2000, Comcast Humanities Achievement award, 2001). Democrat. Jewish. Avocations: walking, travel.

KRUGER, PAULA, telecommunications industry executive; b. Bklyn., July 31, 1950; d. Jean Jacques Kruger and Jo Campione; m. Lawrence C. Heller; children: Michael, Tracy, Jessica. BA in Bus. Adminstrn., C.W. Post, Brookville, NY, 1972; MBA, LI U., 1976. V.p. customer rels. Cablevision, Woodbury, NY, 1994—97; corp. v.p. customer svc. Am. Express, NYC, Citibank, NYC, v.p. devel. divsn.; v.p. consumer svcs. group Republic of Korea; v.p. teleservices Excel Comm., 1997—99, exec. v.p. customer and ind. rep. ops., 1999; gen. mgr. customer relationship mgmt. svc. line Electronic Data Systems Corp., 2002—03; exec. v.p. mass markets group Qwest Comm. Internat., Inc., Denver, 2003—. Office: Qwest Comm Internat Inc 1801 California St Denver CO 80202 Office Phone: 303-992-1400. Office Fax: 303-896-8515.*

KRUGER, STEVEN F., literature educator; b. Natick, Mass., July 3, 1958; s. Stanley I. Kruger and Alice S. Kastenbaum Kruger; life ptnr. Glenn Burger. BA, Williams Coll., Williamstown, Mass., 1980; PhD, Stanford U., Calif., 1988. Prof. English Queens Coll. CUNY, Flushing, NY, 1988—, prof. English and medieval studies The Grad. Ctr. NYC, 1992—, exec. officer PhD Program in English, Grad. Ctr., 2004—. Editor (with Deborah R. Geis): Approaching the Millennium: Essays on Angels in America; editor: (with Glenn Burger) Queering the Middle Ages; contbr. literary criticisms to profl. jours.; author: The Spectral Jew: Conversion and Embodiment in Medieval Europe, AIDS Narratives: Gender and Sexuality, Fiction and Science, Dreaming in the Middle Ages. Recipient President's Excellence in Tchg. award, Queens Coll., CUNY, 1996; grantee, Social Scis. and Humanities Rsch. Coun. Can., 2000—01. Mem.: MLA (mem. exec. com. divsn. on Middle English lang. and lit. 1998—2002), Medieval Club N.Y. (pres. 2003—05), Medieval Acad. Am., New Chaucer Soc. (mem. program com. 1998, mem. local arrangements com. 2006). Democrat. Jewish. Office: Queens College and Graduate Center CUNY 365 Fifth Avenue New York NY 10016 Home Phone: 212-661-8398; Office Phone: 212-817-8315. Office Fax: 212-817-1518. Business E-Mail: skruger@gc.cuny.edu.

KRUGER, TODD M., music educator; s. Niel and Patricia Kruger; m. Paula Kruger; children: Peter, Erin, Jennifer. BS, U. Wis., Stevens Point, 1983; MS, U. Wis., Oshkosh, 1985; MusM, U. Wis., Madison, 1992. Vocal tchr. Iron Mountain schs., Mich., Mayville schs., Wis.; vocal music dir., chmn. dept. Mayville HS, 1988—. Honors dir. Big River Conf., 1999. Named Tchr. of Yr., Mayville Sch. Bd., 1992; recipient Blue and Gold award, Mayville Future Farmers Am. Mem.: Wis. Choral Dirs. Assn. (facilities chmn. 2001—03, co-chmn. facilities 2004—), Lions Club. Office: Mayville HS 500 N Clark St Mayville WI 53050

KRUGMAN, PAUL ROBIN, economics professor; b. Albany, NY, Feb. 28, 1953; s. David Krugman and Anita Alman; m. Robin Wells. BA, Yale U., 1974; PhD, MIT, 1977. Asst. prof. Yale U., New Haven, 1977-80; assoc. prof. MIT, Cambridge, 1980-83, prof. econs., 1983—94, 1996—2000, Stanford, 1994—96; op-ed columnist N.Y. Times, 1999—; prof. internat. trade, internat. economics Princeton U., 2000—. Research assoc. Nat. Bur. Econ. Research, Cambridge, 1979—; economist internat. policy U.S. Council Econ. Advisers, Washington, 1982-83; mem. bd. economists L.A. Times. Author: Exchange Rate Instability, 1988, The Age of Diminished Expectations, 1990, Rethinking International Trade, 1990, Geography and Trade, 1991, Currencies and Crises, 1992, Peddling Prosperity, 1994, Development, Georgraphy, and Economic Theory, 1995, The Self-Organizing Economy, 1996, Pop Internationalism, 1996, The Accidental Theorist, 1998, The Return of Depression Economics, 1999, Fuzzy Math: The Essential Guide to the Bush Tax Plan, 2001, The Great Unraveling, 2003, over 200 jour. articles; co-author: Market Structure and Foreign Trade, 1985, International Economics: Theory and Policy, 1988, Market Structure and Trade Policy, 1989, Foreign Direst Investment in the United States, 1989, The Spatial Economy, 1999; editor: Strategic Trade Policy and The New International Economics, 1986, Exchange Rate Targets and Currency Bands, 1992, Trade with Japan: Has the Door Opened Wider?, 1994, Currency Crises, 2000; co-editor: Empirical Studies of Strategic Policy, 1994. Recipient John Bates Clark Medal, 1991, Eccles Prize for Excellence Econ. Writing, 1991, Adam Smith award, 1995, Nikkei Prize (with M. Fujita and A. Venables), 2001, Alonso Prize, Regional Sci. Assn., 2002. Fellow Econometric Soc., 1987-, Am. Acad. Arts and Sci., 1992-; mem. Group of Thirty, 1988- Office: Princeton U Woodrow Wilson Sch 414 Robertson Hall Princeton NJ 08544

KRUGMAN, RICHARD DAVID, pediatrician, academic administrator, educator; b. NYC, Nov. 28, 1942; s. Saul and Sylvia (Stern) K.; m. Mary Elizabeth Kerber, July 9, 1966; children: Scott, Joshua, Todd, Jordan. AB, Princeton U., 1963; MD, NYU, 1968. Resident U. Colo. Sch. Medicine, Denver, 1968-71; staff assoc. Nat. Inst. Health, Bethesda, Md., 1971-73; asst. prof. U. Colo. Sch. Medicine, 1973-78, assoc. prof., 1978-87, prof. of pediatrics, 1988—, dean, 1992—. Author: The Battered Child, 5th edit., 1997; editor: (jour.) Child Abuse/Neglect, 1986-2001. Chmn. U.S. Adv. Bd. Child Abuse and Neglect, Washington, 1989-91; dir. Kempe Nat. Ctr. for Prevention and Treatment of Child Abuse and Neglect, Denver, 1981-92; trustee Princeton U., 2001-2005. Recipient C. Henry Kempe award Nat. Conf. on Child Abuse, 1989, St. Geme award U. Colo. Sch. Medicine, 1992, 98; Paul Harris fellow Rotary Internat., Sydney, Australia, 1992. Mem. Internat. Soc. Prevention of Child Abuse and Neglect (pres. 1992-94), Am. Acad. Pediatrics (Ray Helfer award 1995, Brandt Steele award 1996), Am. Pediatric Soc., Inst. Medicine. Office: U Colo Sch Medicine 4200 E 9th Ave Denver CO 80262-0001

KRUGMAN, STANLEY LEE, international management consultant; b. NYC, Mar. 2, 1925; s. Harry and Leah (Greenberg) K.; m. Helen Schorr, June 14, 1947; children: Vicky Lee, Thomas Paul; m. Carolyn Schambra, Sept. 17, 1966; children: David Andrew, Wendy Carol; m. Gail Jennings, Mar. 17, 1974. Grad., Remmselaer Poly. Inst., 1945; B Chem. Engring., Rensselaer Poly. Inst., 1947; postgrad., Poly. Inst. Bklyn., Columbia U., 1947-51. Process devel. engr. Merck & Co., Rahway, NJ, 1947-51; sr. process and project engr. C.F. Braun & Co., Alhambra, Calif., 1951-55; with Jacobs Engring. Co., Pasadena, Calif., 1955-76; from chief engr. to v.p. engring. and constrn. to v.p. gen. mgr. to exec. v.p. to pres., and dir.; exec. v.p., dir. Jacobs Engring. Group Inc., Pasadena, Calif., 1974-82; pres., dir. Jacobs Constructors of P.R., San Juan, 1970-82; pres. Jacobs Internat. Inc., 1971-82, Jacobs Internat. Ltd., Inc., Dublin, 1974-82; dep. chmn. Jacobs LTA Engring., Ltd., Johannesburg, 1981-82; pres. Krugman Assocs., 1982—; internat. mgmt. cons. Patentee in field. Served to lt. (j.g.) USNR, 1944-46, PTO. Mem.: Am. Chem. Soc., Am. Inst. Chem. Engrs., U.S. Naval Inst. Presbyterian. Home and Office: 60 Condon Ln Port Ludlow WA 98365

KRUGMAN, STANLEY LIEBERT, science administrator, geneticist; b. St. Louis, June 8, 1932; s. Bernard and Della (Goldberg) Krugman; m. Judith Raechel Alfend, June 28, 1958; children: Mark Bernard, Jeffrey Jon. BS in Forestry, U. Mo., 1955; MF, U. Calif., Berkeley, 1956, PhD in Plant Physiology, 1961. Rsch. aide U. Calif., 1956-61, rsch. assoc., 1961-62; rsch. physiologist U.S. Forest Svc., 1962-64, project leader, 1964-71, staff geneticist Washington, 1971-80, staff dir., 1980-95; sr. for specialist, pvt. cons. World Bank Natural Resources, Washington, 1995—. Cons. in field. Editor: (book) Seeds of Woody Plants, 1974, Advances in Reproductive Biology, 1974, Management Biosphere Reserves, 1979, Advances in Forest Physiology, 1980. Recipient Sci. medal, USSR, 1995, Czech Republic, 1995, Poland, 1997. Fellow: AAAS, Soc. Am. Foresters (William Schlich medal 1990); mem.: Internat. Union Forestry Orgn. Jewish. Office: 6515 Dryden Dr Mc Lean VA 22101-4627 Office Phone: 703-356-9145. Personal E-mail: skrugman@juno.com.

KRUK, JOHN MARTIN, retired professional baseball player, sportscaster; b. Charleston, W.V., Feb. 9, 1961; Student, Allegany C.C. Baseball player San Diego Padres, 1981-89, Philadelphia Phillies, 1989-94; with Chgo. White Sox, 1994—95; baseball analyst ESPN, 2003—. Named to Nat. League All-Star team, 1991-93. mem. World Series Team, 1993. Office: ESPN 935 Middle St Bristol CT 06010

KRUKOWSKI, Mrs. JAN See HARROW, NANCY

KRUKOWSKI, JAN, communications executive; b. Lodz, Poland, Nov. 18, 1930; arrived in U.S., 1941; s. Edward and Alice (Landau) K.; m. Nancy Harrow; children: Damon, Anton. BA, N.Y.U., 1952, MA, 1961. Writer Dem. Nat. Com., NYC, 1952—56; account exec. Alfred Auerbach Assocs., 1957; v.p. Press Release, Inc., 1958; pres. Krukowski and Symington, Inc., 1959—63; exec. v.p. Barton-Gillet Co., 1964—80; pres. Jan Krukowski & Co., 1980—. Trustee Am. Symphony Orch., 2001—, chair trustees, 2005—; trustee Tchrs. Coll., Columbia U., 2002—; bd. dirs. Norman and Rosita Winston Found., 1997—. Mem.: Century Assn. Office: Jan Krukowski & Co 40 Wooster St New York NY 10013 Home Phone: 212-249-4339. Business E-Mail: jkrukowski@jankrukowski.com.

KRULAK, CHARLES CHANDLER, bank executive; b. Quantico, Va., Mar. 4, 1942; s. Victor Harold and Amy (Chandler) K.; m. Zandra Lynn Meyers, June 27, 1964; children: David Chandler, Todd Cameron. BS, U.S. Naval Acad., 1964; MS, George Washington U., 1973; advanced mil. course, Amphib. War Sch., 1968, Army Command and Gen. Staff, Coll., 1976, Nat. War Coll., 1982. Commd. 2d lt. USMC, 1964, advanced through grades to gen., 1995, retired, 1999, rifle co. comdr. Vietnam, 1965-66, 69-70, bn. comdr. Hawaii, 1983-85; mil. asst. Asst. Sec. Def. for Command, Control, Comm. and Intelligence, Washington, 1986-87; dep. dir. White House Mil. Office, Washington, 1987-89; brigade comdr. and asst. divsn. comdr. USMC, N.C., 1989-91, force svc. support group comdr. N.C., 1989-90, force svc. support comdr., brigade comdr., 1990-91; dir. pers. mgmt., pers. procurement Hdqtrs. Marine Corps, 1991-92; comdg. gen. MCCDC, Quantico, Va., 1992-94; comdr. marine forces, Pacific and comdg. gen. Fleet Marine Forces, Pacific, Camp Smith, Hawaii, 1994-95; commandant USMC, 1995-99; sr. vice chmn. MBNA Am. Corp., Wilmington, Del., 1999—2001; chmn., CEO MBNA Europe Bank Ltd., 2001—; exec. vice chmn., chief adminstrv. officer MBNA Corp., 2004—. Contbr. articles to Marine Corps Gazette. Decorated D.S.M. (2), Def. D.S.M. (2), Silver Star, Bronze Star with combat V (3), Purple Heart (2). Avocations: running, reading. Office: MBNA Am 1100 N King St Wilmington DE 19884-0001

KRULAK, VICTOR HAROLD, newspaper executive; b. Denver, Jan. 7, 1913; s. Morris and Besse M. (Ball) K.; m. Amy Chandler, June 1, 1936; children: Victor Harold Jr., William Morris, Charles Chandler. BS, U.S. Naval Acad., 1934; LL.D., U. San Diego. Commd. 2d lt. USMC, 1934; advanced through grades to lt. gen.; service in China, at sea, with USMC (Fleet Marine Forces), 1935-39; staff officer, also bn. regimental and divsn. comdr. World War II, World War II; chief staff (1st Marine Div. Korea); comdg. gen. (Marine Corps Recruit Depot), San Diego; formerly spl asst. to dir., joint staff counterinsurgency and spl. activities (Office Joint Chiefs Staff); comdg. gen. Fleet Marine Force Pacific, Pacific, 1964-68; ret., 1968; v.p. Copley Newspaper Corp., 1968-79; pres. Words Ltd. Corp., San Diego. Trustee Zool. Soc. San Diego. Decorated D.S.M., Navy Cross, Legion of Merit with 3 oak leaf clusters, Bronze Star, Air medal, Purple Heart (2) U.S.; Cross of Gallantry; Medal of Merit Vietnam; Distinguished Service medal (Korea), Order of Cloud and Banner, Republic of China. Mem. U.S. Naval Inst., U.S. Marine Corps Assn., Am. Soc. Newspaper Editors, InterAm. Press Assn., U.S. Strategic Inst. (chmn.). Home: # 307 2404 Loring St San Diego CA 92109 Office: Words Ltd 2404 Loring St San Diego CA 92110-4827

KRULFELD, RUTH MARILYN, anthropologist, educator; m. Jacob Mendel Krulfeld, 1964; 1 child, Michael David. BA cum laude, Brandeis U., 1956; PhD, Yale U., 1974. Field rschr. micro-geog. rsch. farms, Singapore, Malaya, 1951-53; anthrop. rschr., Jamaica, 1957, Costa Rica, Nicaragua, Panama, 1958, Sasak of Lombok, Indonesia, 1960—63, 1993; anthrop. rschr. S.E. Asian refugees to U.S., 1981—; anthrop. rschr., Lombok, Indonesia and N.E. Thailand, 1993; asst. prof. anthropology, dir. grad. students George Washington U., Washington, 1964-72, 93-97, assoc. prof., 1973-76, prof., 1976-2000, chmn. dept. anthropology, 1984-87, founder spl. grad. program in internat. world devel., prof. anthropology, internat. affairs, prof. emeritus anthropology, human scis., internat. affairs, 2000—. Bd. dir. No. Va. Humanities Coun., Internat. Buddhist Com.; rschr. Laotian refugees in U.S., 1981-, also rschr. on culture change in villages in Indonesia; bd. dirs. Newcomers Cmty. Svc. Ctr.; mem. bd. advisors Lao-Am. Women's Assn., Lao Cmty. Forum; mem. faculty Semester At Sea, 1999, 2003, 07; bd. dir. Successful New Ams. Project, S.E. Asian Resource Action Ctr Co-author: Reconstructing Lives, Recapturing Meaning: Refugee Identity, Gender and Culture Change, 1994, Beyond Boundaries: Selected papers on Refugees and Immigrants, 1997, Power, Ethics, and Human Rights: Anthropological Studies of Refugee Research and Action, 1998; contbr. articles to profl. jours.; editl. bd. com. on refugees and immigrants. Recipient Banneker award, Ctr. for Washington Area Studies, 1996, The George Washington U. award for Pedagogical R&D in Edn., The George Washington U. award for outstanding contbns. to univ. and wider soc., 2000; grantee, Found. for Study of Man, 1957, Am. Coun., 1963; Currier scholar, Yale U., 1958, Ford fellow, 1960—62, Cotlow faculty rsch. grantee, 1992—93, faculty rsch. grantee, George Washington U., 1992—93, rsch. grantee, Va. Found. Humanities and Pub. Policy, 1995—96. Mem.: AAAS (Com. on Sci. Freedom and Responsibility), Am. Anthrop. Assn. (nominating com., com. on refugee issues gen. anthropology divsn., vice chair com. on refugee issues 1992—94, gen. anthropology divsn. 1993—94, exec. bd. com. on refugees and immigrants 1994—99, CORI editl. bd. 1998—99, CORI award for best paper on refugee issues 1992, Pedagogical Rsch. and Innovative Devel. in Edn. award 1994, CORI award for leadership and contbn. to refugee studies com. on refugees and immigrants 2000), Anthrop. Soc. Washington. Office: George Washington U Dept Anthropology Washington DC 20052-0001 *Perhaps the major attitudes that have motivated my work have been a deep respect for my fellow human beings, and a need to learn from them, to experience their wondrous creativity, ability and diversity; as an anthropologist, to understand as much about human societies as I could, and as an educator, to ignite this enthusiasm and wonder in my students, to encourage them to go beyond our present understanding and abilities. As an advocate for human rights, I hope to instill in my students the wish to be involved in social action.*

KRULIK, BARBARA S., production manager, curator, art director, writer; b. NYC, June 13, 1955; d. Herbert Arnold and Irene Sylvia K. BA in Art History, Pa. State U., State Coll., 1976; MA in Museology, Reinwardt Acad., Amsterdam, The Netherlands, 2000. Asst. to dir. NAD, NYC, 1976—78, acting dir., 1977-78, coord. exhbns., 1978-83, asst. dir., 1983-89, interim dir., 1989-90, dep. dir., 1990-92; assoc. dir. Forum Gallery, NYC, 1992-94; dir. Grad. Sch. Figurative Art New York Acad. Art, NYC, 1994-97; owner, dir. KCCS (Krulik Cultural Cons. Svs.), 2001—; mgr. Magpie Music Dance Co., Amsterdam, Netherlands, 2003—, Streettheater Co. Warner en Consorten, Amsterdam; mem. steering com. Found. Exhbn. Man, Amsterdam, Netherlands, 2004—; prodn. mgr. No Apology, Amsterdam, 2004—05, Cinedans, 2006, Bodies Anonymous, Amsterdam, 2006. Ind. curator, 1997—; cons., 1997—. Author, editor exhbn. catalogues. Mem. Am. Assn. Mus. (curators and registrars coms.), Internat. Coun. on Mus. Personal E-mail: b.krulik@chello.nl.

KRULITZ, LEO MORRION, financial planner, publishing executive, director; b. Wallace, Idaho, June 15, 1938; s. John Morrion and Myrtle (Parker) K.; m. Donna Eileen Ristau, June 18, 1960; children— Cynthia, Pamela. BA, Stanford U., 1960; JD cum laude, Harvard U., 1963; MBA, Stanford U., 1969. Bar: Idaho 1963, Ind. 1969, DC 1978, U.S. Supreme Ct. 1978. Ptnr. firm Moffatt, Thomas, Barrett & Blanton, Boise, Idaho, 1963-67; v.p., treas. Irwin Mgmt. Co., Columbus, Ind., 1969-77; solicitor Dept. of the Interior, Washington, 1977-79; gen. counsel Cummins Engine Co., Columbus, Ind., 1979-80, v.p., 1980-92; pres. Cummins Fin., Inc., 1984-92, Cummins Cash and Info. Svcs., Inc., 1988-92; pres., CEO Saunders, Inc., Birmingham, Ala., 1992-93; pres., CEO, dir. Parkland Mgmt. Co., Cleve., 1994—2005; endowment trustee Euclid Ave. Christian Ch., 2005—06; dir. Horvitz Newspapers, Inc., Bellevue, Wash., 1994—2005. Trustee Lois U. Horvitz Found., 1998-2005; exec. dir. H.R.H. Family Found., 1994-98; treas. Irwin-Sweeney-Miller Found., Columbus, 1976-77; dir. L'Enfant Plaza Properties, Washington, 1974-77; mem. U.S. delegation Soviet Union Conf. on Environ. Law, 1978 Active Bartholomew Consol. Sch. Bd., 1982-88; trustee Wheelright Mus. of the Am. Indian, 2002—; pres. Wheelright Mus. Endowment Fund, 2005—, Wheelwright Mus., 2007—. Democrat.

KRULL, JEFFREY ROBERT, library director; b. North Tonawanda, NY, Aug. 29, 1948; s. Robert George and Ruth Otilie (Fels) K.; m. Alice Marie Hart, Apr. 12, 1969; children: Robert, Marla. BA, Williams Coll., Williamstown, Mass., 1970; MLS, SUNY, Buffalo, 1974. Cert. profl. libr., NY, Ohio, Ind. Traffic mgr. New Eng. Tel. Co., Burlington, Vt., 1970—71; tchr. English and German, varsity basketball coach Harrisburg Acad., Pa., 1971—72; reference libr. bus. and labor dept. Buffalo and Erie County Pub. Libr., 1973—76; head libr. Ohio U., Chillicothe, 1976—78; dir. Mansfield-Richland County Pub. Libr., Ohio, 1978—86, Allen County Pub. Libr., Ft. Wayne, Ind., 1986—. Mem. exec. com. Ft. Wayne Area Libr. Svc. Authority, 1986-90, v.p., 1989; mem. exec. com. Ind. Coop. Libr. Svcs. Authority, 1992-96, pres., 1994-95; mem. Online Computer Libr. Ctr. Pub. Libr. Adv. Coun., 1994-97; pres. Ft. Wayne Area INFONET, 1995-2001. Pres. Three Rivers Literacy Alliance, 1997—99; trustee Ohionet, Columbus, 1984—86; mem. Ind. Libr. and Hist. Bd., 2006—. Named Sagamore of the Wabash, Gov. Ind., 2001. Mem. ALA, Pub. Libr. Assn. (pres. met. librs. sect. 1990-91, statis. report adv. com.), Libr. Adminstrn. and Mgmt. Assn. (sec. libr. orgn. and mgmt. assn. 1996-97), Ohio Libr. Assn. (bd. dirs. 1985-86), Ind. Libr. Fedn. (vice chmn. legis. com. 1987—), Urban Librs. Coun., Beta Phi Mu, Ft. Wayne Rotary Club. Home: 3017 Oak Borough Run Fort Wayne IN 46804-7808 Office: Allen County Pub Libr 900 Library Plz Fort Wayne IN 46802 Office Phone: 260-421-1252. E-mail: jkrull@acpl.lib.in.us.*

KRULL, STEPHEN KEITH, lawyer; b. Peoria, Ill., Jan. 1965; m. Elizabeth A. Krull. BBA, Ea. Ill. U., 1986; JD with high honors, Chgo.-Kent Coll. Law, 1990. Assoc. atty. Sidley & Austin, Chgo.; corp. counsel A.B. Dick Co., Chgo.; divsn. counsel Roofing Systems Bus. Owens Corning, Toledo, 1996—99, v.p. corp. comm., gen. counsel, 1999—2003, sr. v.p., gen. counsel, sec., 2003—. Chmn. legal adv. bd. Nat. Ctr. Missing and Exploited Children, Washington; mem. assoc. bd. dirs. Boys & Girls Clubs Toledo, 2004—; bd. mem. Habitat for Humanity Ohio, 2005—. Office: Owens Corning 1 Owens Corning Pky Toledo OH 43659 Office Phone: 419-248-8000. Office Fax: 419-248-5337. E-mail: stephen.k.krull@owenscorning.com.*

KRUM, DEE, secondary school educator; b. Maquoketa, Iowa, Jan. 6, 1958; d. Wayne Richard and Marilyn Joyce Williams; m. Roy Leon Krum, Dec. 6, 1980; children: Bobby Lee, Joey Leon. BA in English Edn., Iowa Wesleyan Coll., Mt. Pleasant, 1980, postgrad., 1980. Jr. high lang. arts tchr. St. Joseph Sch., DeWitt, Iowa, 1983—91; English, theater tchr. West Ctrl. HS, Maynard, Iowa, 1991—2005; speech, theater tchr. Maquoketa (Iowa) HS, 2005—. Libr. bd. Maynard Pub. Libr., 1994—98; adv. bd. West Central Sch., Maynard, 1996—2002, sch. to work adv., 1996—2005. Mem.: Iowa HS Speech Assn., Educators of Theater Arts, Nat. Forsenics League. Democrat. Home: 309 W Monroe Maquoketa IA 52060

KRUMBOLTZ, JOHN DWIGHT, psychologist, educator; b. Cedar Rapids, Iowa, Oct. 21, 1928; s. Dwight John and Margaret (Jones) K.; m. Helen Brandhorst, Aug. 22, 1954 (div. Aug. 1986); children: Ann, Jennifer; m. Betty Lee Foster, Nov. 8, 1987. BA, Coe Coll., Cedar Rapids, 1950; MA, Columbia Tchrs. Coll., 1951; PhD, U. Minn., 1955; PhD (hon.), Pacific Grad. Sch. Psychology, 1991. Counselor, tchr. W. Waterloo (Iowa) H.S., 1951-53; from teaching asst. to instr. U. Minn., 1953-55; from asst. prof. ednl. psychology to assoc. prof. Mich. State U., 1957-61; faculty Stanford U. Sch. Edn., 1961-66, prof. edn. and psychology, 1966—. Vis. sr. research psychologist Ednl. Testing Service, 1972-73; fellow Ctr. for Advanced Study in Behavioral Scis., 1975-76, Advanced Study Ctr., Nat. Ctr. for Research in Vocat. Edn., Ohio State U., 1980-81; vis. colleague dept. psychology Inst. Psychiatry, U. London, 1983-84 Author: (with others) Learning to Study, 1960; (with Helen B. Krumboltz) Changing Children's Behavior, 1972; editor: Learning and the Educational Process, 1965, Revolution in Counseling, 1966; (with Carl E. Thoresen) Behavioral Counseling: Cases and Techniques, 1969, Counseling Methods, 1976; (with Anita M. Mitchell and G. Brian Jones) Social Learning and Career Decision Making, 1979; (with Daniel A. Hamel) Assessing Career Development, 1982; contbr. articles to profl. jours. With USAF, 1955-57. Recipient Eminent Career award Nat. Career Devel. Assn., 1994, Living Legend award Am. Counseling Assn., 2004, Outstanding Achievement award, U. Minn., 2006; Guggenheim fellow, 1967-68. Mem. APA (pres. div. counseling psychology 1974-75, award for disting. profl. contbns. to knowledge 2002), Am. Ednl. Rsch. Assn. (v.p. div. E. 1966-68), Am. Pers. and Guidance Assn. (Outstanding Rsch. award 1959, 66, 68, Disting. Profl. Svcs. award 1974, Leona Tyler award 1990). Home: 933 Valdez Pl Stanford CA 94305-1008

KRUMHOLZ, HARLAN MARC, cardiologist, internist, educator; b. St. Louis, Mo., Mar. 21, 1958; BS, Yale Coll., 1980; MD, Harvard Med. Sch., 1985; MSc, Harvard Sch. Pub. Health, 1992. Cert. Internal Medicine, Cardiovascular Disease. Intern & resident, internal medicine U. Calif., San Francisco, 1985—88; chief resident Moffitt Hosp.; fellow, cardiology Beth Israel Hosp., Boston; hosp. affiliation Yale New Haven Hosp., New Haven; asst. prof. medicine (cardiology) and epidemiology and pub. health Yale Sch. Medicine, 1992—97, assoc. prof. medicine (cardiology) and epidemiology and pub. health, 1997—2002, full prof. medicine (cardiology) and epidemiology and pub. health, 2002—05, Harold H. Hines, jr. prof. medicine and epidemiology and pub. health (cardiology), 2005—; founder, dir. Yale-New Haven Hosp. Ctr. for Outcomes Rsch. and Evaluation, 1992—; co-dir. Robert Wood Johnson Clin. Scholars Program, 1996—. Chair steering com. Am. Heart Assn. Ann. Scientific Forum on Quality of Care and Outcomes Rsch. in Cardiovascular Disease & Stroke; co-clinical coord. Nat. Project for Myocardial Infarction, Centers for Medicare & Medicaid Services; chair, cardiovascular conditions clin. adv. panel Joint Commn. on Accreditation of Healthcare Organizations; chair, writing com. to develop performance measures on acute myocardial infarction Am. Coll. Cardiology/Am. Heart Assn.; cardiovascular expert panel of the performance measurement coordinating coun. AMA, Joint Commn. on the Accreditation of Healthcare Organizations, Nat. Com. for Quality Assurance; chair, technical expert panel for pub. reporting Centers for Medicare & Medicaid Svcs.; chair, quality care and outcomes rsch. expert panel Am. Heart Assn.; mem. nat. scientific adv. coun. Am. Fedn. for Aging Rsch.; chair, Nat. Peer Review Com. for Outcomes Rsch. Am. Heart Assn.; mem. exec. coun. Heart Failure Soc. Am.; mem. writing com. to revise the 1999 guidelines for mgmt. of patients with acute myocardial infarction Am. Coll. Cardiology/Am. Heart Assn.; chair, Working Group on Outcomes Rsch. in Cardiovascular Disease Nat. Heart, Lung and Blood Inst. Contbr. articles to profl. jours.; assoc. editor Circulation, editor Journal Watch Cardiology, serves on several editl. bds.; author: The Expert Guide to Beating Heart Disease, 2005. Paul Beeson Faculty Scholar, 1996—99. Mem.: Assn. Am. Physicians, Am. Soc. for Clin. Investigation. Office: Sect Cardiovascular Medicine Yale U Sch Medicine I-Wing Ste 456 333 Cedar St PO Box 208017 1 New Haven CT 06510 Office Phone: 203-785-4114. Business E-Mail: harlan.krumholz@yale.edu.*

KRUMLAUF, ROBERT EUGENE, neuroscientist, educator; B in Chem. Engring., Vanderbilt U., 1970; PhD in Devel. Biology, Ohio State U., 1979. Chief chem. engr. Capital City Products Inc., Columbus, Ohio, 1970—75; fellow dept. biochemistry Ohio State U., 1975—79; postdoctoral fellow Dr A. Balmain Beatson Inst. Cancer Rsch., Glasgow, Scotland, 1979—82, Dr S. Tilghman Inst. Cancer Rsch., Phila., 1982—85; from group leader to adj. group leader NIMR, England, 1985—2000, adj. group leader, 2000; sci. dir. Stowers Inst. Med. Rsch., Kansas City, Mo., 2000—. Prof. oral biology Sch. Dentistry U. Mo., Kansas City, 2000—; prof. oral biology Dept. Anatomy and Cell Biology U. Kans. Med. Sch., Kansas City, 2001—; prof. neuroscience Graduate Program U. Kans., Kansas City, 2002—. Editor: Devel. Biology, 1995—; mem. editl. bd.: New Biologist, 1989—92, Mechanisms of Devel., 1990—, Nucleic Acids Rsch., 1992—, Current Biology, 1993—2000, Portland Press, 1994—2000, Devel., 1994—, Molecular and Cellular Neurobiology, 1995—, Human Molecular Genetics, 1996—98, Genes and Function, 1997—98, InScight, 1998—. Fellow: Acad. Med. Scis.; mem.: Am. Acad. Arts and Scis., Soc. Pathology and Teratology, Acad. Med. Scis. UK, The Genetical Soc., Am. Soc. Microbiology, Am. Assn. Anatomists, Soc. Devel. Biology, Brit. Soc. Devel. Biology, European Molecular Biology Org., European Devel. Biology Org. (sec. 1997—2001). Office: Stowers Inst 1000 E 50th St Kansas City MO 64110 Home: 5407 Mission Dr Mission Hills KS 66208 Home Phone: 913-831-7680; Office Phone: 816-926-4051. Business E-Mail: rek@stowers-institute.org.

KRUMP, GARY JOSEPH, marketing executive, lawyer, judge; b. Breckenridge, Minn., June 27, 1946; m. Mary Kay Chermak; children: Adam, Jonathon. BA, N.D. State U., 1968; JD, U. Minn., 1971, postdoctoral, 1972; cert. in health care, So. Ill. U., Edwardsville, 1978, MBA, 1979; grad. cert., George Washington U., 1981; grad., Fed. Exec. Inst., 1988, U.S. Army Command & Gen. Staff Coll., 1989; grad. sr. mgrs. in govt. program, Harvard U., 1998. Bar: Minn. 1971, U.S. Ct. Mil. Appeals 1972, U.S. Supreme Ct. 1975, D.C. 1977. Commd. 2nd lt. U.S. Army, 1970, advanced through grades to capt., 1971, capt. with JAGC, 1972-76, chief internat. law-Japan, 1974-76; chief adminstrv. law Walter Reed Army Med. Ctr., 1976-77; sr. staff atty. office of gen. counsel VA, Washington, 1978-83, nat. coord. med. care recovery program, 1979, dep. asst. gen. counsel, 1983-87, assoc. dep., asst. sec. for acquisitions, 1988-89; v.p., gen. counsel JSA Healthcare Corp., 1989-91; dir., corp. sec. DKH Healthcare; dir. Office of Real Property Mgmt. Office Real Property Mgmt., U.S. Dept. VA, Washington, 1991-92, dep. asst. sec. acquisitions and material mgmt., 1992—2003, acting asst. sec. acquisitions and facilities, 1992-95; VA environ. exec., 1994—2003; chmn., chief adminstrv. judge VA Bd. Contract Appeals, 2003—06; VA dispute resolution offcl., 2003—06; fed. judge US Dept. VA, Washington, 2003—06; v.p., dir. fed. mktg. The Rhoads Group, Washington, 2006—. Mem. faculty Ctrl. Mich. U., U. Va.; apptd. to career Fed. Sr. Exec. Svc.; gen. counsel, dir. Soccerama Assn., Inc., 1987-93; sec. DKH Healthcare, Inc., 1990-91; prin., dir., gen. counsel ISG, Inc., 1991-97; dir., gen. counsel Am. Health Group, Inc., 1993-97; mem. Interagy. Com. on Supply Mgmt. Steering Group, Nat. Performance Rev. Com. on Reinventing VA; chair Interagy. Procurement Reform Working Group, 1993-95; chair interagy. contracts group GSA; mem. Interagy. Contracts Adv. Group; chair nat. conf. reinventing small bus. partnerships VA, 1993; chair interagy contracts group GSA, mem. adv. group; apptd. Pres.' Com. for Purchase from Blind and Other Severely Disabled, 1992-03, chmn. fed. women's program, 1992-03, mentoring program, 2003, chair, 1996-00; com. chmn. Subcom. on Procurement Reform, 1996-97, pres. com. disting. svc. award, 2000, chmn. subcom. on governance, 2002-03; mem. nat. adv. bd. Fed. Prison Industries, 1995-03, chair subcom. administrn., 1994-03; trustee Leadership VA, 1992-95; mem. Fed. Environ. Execs. Task Force, 1994-03; mem. Interagy. Com. on Stds. Policy, 1995-03, VA Stds. Exec., 1994-03, VA Metrics Exec., 1994-2003; mem. Interagy. Electronic Commerce Task Force, 1994-03; departmental co-chair Combined Fed. Campaign VA, 1994, departmental co-chair, campaign mgr., 1999; chair VA Departmental Environ. Adv. Group, 1994-03; bd. dirs. VA Dept., 1992-95; chmn. bd. dirs. VA Supply Fund, 1993-03; mem. Fed. Procurement Coun., 1991-97; mem. Procurement Execs. Coun., 1997-03, vice chair, 2000-03, chair com. on electronic commerce, 1999-03; mem. Interagy. e-Gov Task Force, Office Mgmt. & Budget, Exec. Office of Pres., 2000-03; mem. VA e-Gov Steering com., 2000-03; Creekmore lectr. on procurement law Judge Advs. Sch., Army, U. Va., 1997; mem. com. on ethics DC Bar, 2001-03; judge VA Dispute Resolution Official, 2003; pres. com. leadership award, 2003; adv. bd. Fed. Procurement Nat. Conf., 2002-03; dir. The Procurement Round Table, 2006-; program mgr. PRT Elmer and B. Staats award, 2006-; spkr. in field. Sec. Vets. Affairs Commendation, 1989, 95; mem. Ctr. for Pub. Resources Nat. Procurement Com., 1986-89, Adminstv. Conf. U.S. Alternative Disputes Resolution Symposium, 1988. Served to lt. col. JAGC, USAR, 1976-2000. Decorated U.S. Legion of Merit; recipient Fed. 100 Info. Tech. award, Fed. Procurement Coun., 1997, Presdl. Rank award, 1997, VA Meritorious Svc. award, 2000, Exceptional Svc. award, U.S. Army, P.R., 2000, Log. Chief award, USAF, 2002, VA Exceptional Svc. award, 2003, Exceptional Svc. award, Procurement Execs. Coun., 2003, U.S. Atty. Gen.'s Certificate, 2004, Disting. Career award, VA, 2006. Fellow Nat. Contract Mgrs. Assn. (bd. advisors 1989-90, 93-2003, com. internat. contracting 1995-2003); mem. ABA (vice chair com. on healthcare contract law 1997-2003, com. on healthcare), VFW (life), Judge's Assn. (bd. contract appeals, 2003), Fed. Bar Assn. (nat. chmn. tort law com., health and human svcs. coun. chmn. 1980-81, chmn. Nat. Tort Conf. 1979, editor Tort Law Newsletter 1978-81, Superior Svc. awards 1979, 81), D.C. Bar Assn. (com. ethics), Nat. Forensic Ctr., Am. Coll.-Legal Medicine (assoc.), Internat. Soc. Mil. Law and Law of War, Internat. Legal Soc., Res. Officers Ass. (life), Mid-Atlantic Token Kai, Japanese Sword Soc. U.S., Fed. Acquisition Inst. Policy Bd., Fed. Procurement Coun., Contract Svcs. Assn. (procurement com. 1989-91), Interagency Med. Procurement Mgmt. Com., Govt. Procurement Tng. (adv. com.), Interagency Procurement Career Mgmt. Com., Fed. Real Property Execs. (interagy. adv. coun. 1991-93), Vets. of Am., Am. Legion (life), Bd. of Contract Appeals Judges Assn. (chmn. ethics seminar 2004), Bd. of Contract Appeals Bar Assn., VFW (life), Res. Officers Assn. (life), Rolls Royce Owners Club, Beta Gamma Sigma, Tau Kappa Epsilon. Home: 13812 Town Line Rd Silver Spring MD 20906-2112 Office: The Rhoads Group Ste 350 700 Thirteenth St NW Washington DC 20005 Office Phone: 202-637-0040. Business E-Mail: gkrump@rhoadsdc.gov.

KRUMP, PAUL J., insurance company executive; BA in Bus. Adminstrn., St. John's U. Underwriting trainee The Chubb Corp., 1982, exec. protection and internat. underwriter Dusseldorf, Germany, 1986, no. zone mgr. dept. fin. instns., US underwriting mgr. dept. fin. instns., exec. v.p. Chubb & Son, 2000, COO Chubb Comml. Ins., 2000—. Attendee exec. edn. program IMD, Lausanne, Switzerland. Office: The Chubb Corp 15 Mountain View Rd Warren NJ 07059 Office Phone: 908-903-2000. Office Fax: 908-903-2027.*

KRUPER, JOHN GERALD (JACK KRUPER), sales and marketing executive; b. Carbondale, Pa., Feb. 10, 1949; s. John Joseph and Evelyn (Bernosky) K.; m. Renee Jane Shugg, Aug. 4, 1973; children: Kevin John, Melissa Lynn, Abbey Renee. BSBA in Acctg., U. Scranton, 1970; postgrad., SUNY, 1974, U. Scranton, 1985. Store mgr. Endicott Johnson Corp., schenectady, 1970-71; retail mdse. distbr. Endicott, 1971-72; asst. mdse. buyer, 1972-74; full line mdse. buyer, 1974-76; dir. corp. advt. and sales promotion, 1976-79; gen. sales mgr. Ranger divsn., 1979-81; v.p. merchandising, 1981-84; v.p. branded footwear divsn., 1984—86; v.p. Continental Mktg. Group, Inc., 1986-90, v.p. sales and mktg. Lehigh divsn., 1990-92, Iron Age divsn. Childs Corp., 1992-94; nat. sales dir. hy-test divsn. Florsheim Shoe Co., 1994—; nat. sales and prodn. devel. mgr. to gen. mgr. Florsheim Work Group, 1996-97, 96-97; brand gen. mgr. John Deere Footwear divsn., 1997-99, John Deere Internat. divsn., 1999—2001; v.p. sales and mktg. Tatra Mfg. Co., Cary, Ill., 2001—02; mng. dir., CEO Occupl. Footwear Co. Am., 2002—. Served with Corps Engrs., U.S. Army, 1970. Office: 3307 South Rte 31 Crystal Lake IL 60012 Office Phone: 815-788-9314. Personal E-mail: jgkruper@aol.com.

KRUPKA, ROBERT GEORGE, lawyer; b. Rochester, NY, Oct. 21, 1949; s. Joseph Anton and Marjorie Clara (Meteyer) Krupka; m. Pamela Banner Krupka; children: Kristin Nicole, Kerry Melissa. BS, Georgetown U., 1971; JD, U. Chgo., 1974. Bar: Ill. 1974, Colo. 1991, DC 1991, Calif. 1998, US Dist. Ct. (no. dist.) Ill. 1974, US Dist. Ct. (ea. dist.) Wis. 1974, US Ct. Appeals (7th cir.) 1976, US Supreme Ct. 1978, US Dist. Ct. (ctrl. dist.) Ill. 1980, US Dist. Ct. (so. dist.) Ill. 1988, US Dist. Ct. (no. dist.) Calif. 1980, US Dist. Ct. (ctrl. and so. dists.) Calif. 1999, US Dist. Ct. Ariz. 1998, US Dist. Ct. Colo. 1998, US Dist. Ct. Md. 2000, US Dist. Ct. (ea. dist.) Tex. 2006, US Dist. Ct. (we. dist.) Wis., 2006, US Ct. Appeals (4th and fed. cirs.) 1982, US Ct. Appeals (6th cir.) 1985, US Ct. Appeals (1st, 2nd, 3rd, 5th, 8th, 9th, 10th and 11th dists.) 1999, US Patent and Trademark Office. Assoc. Kirkland & Ellis LLP, Chgo., 1974—79, ptnr., 1979—. Author: Infringement Litigation Computer Software and Database, 1984, Computer Software, Semiconductor Design, Video Game and Database Protection and Enforcement, 1984. Mem. bd. trustees Francis W. Parker Sch., 1987-98, pres., 1994-97. Named one of Top 10 Trial Lawyers in Am., Nat. Law Jour., 1998, 2005, Leading Practitioners in the Fed. Cir., 2001, Top 100 Most Influential Lawyers, 2006, Top 30 Intellectual Property Lawyers, Daily Jour. Extra, 2005, Top 500 Lawyers in Am., Lawdragon, 2005, Top 100 Attys. in Calif., Daily Jour., 2005, World's Leading Lawyers for Bus. in Intellectual Property, Chambers Global, 2006; recipient Calif. Lawyer Atty. of Yr. award, Calif. Lawyer Mag., 2004. Mem. ABA (chmn. sec. com. 1982-88, chmn. divsn. 1988-90, 98—, coun. 1994-97, chair intellectual property law sect., mem. litig. sect.), LA Bar Assn., Internat. Bar Assn. (co-chair intellectual property and entertainment law com.), Am. Intellectual Property Law Assn. (chmn. subcommittee 1988—), LA Intellectual Property Law Assn., Chgo. Intellectual Property Law Assn., Copyright Soc. US, Fed. Cir. Bar Assn., Internat. Trademark Assn., ITC Trial Lawyers, Nat. Inst. Trial Advocacy (trustee 2002—), Regency Club. Office: Kirkland & Ellis LLP Ste 3700 777 S Figueroa St Los Angeles CA 90017-5800 Office Phone: 213-680-8456. Office Fax: 213-680-8500. E-mail: bkrupka@kirkland.com.

KRUPMAN, WILLIAM ALLAN, lawyer; b. Cleve., Aug. 14, 1936; s. Joel and Betty (Button) K; m. Anne deLemos, June 19, 1960; children: Pamela, Theodore, Sally. BA, Amherst Coll., 1958; LLB, U. Mich., 1961; LLM in Labor Law, NYU, 1962. Bar: Ohio 1961, NY 1962. Ptnr. Jackson Lewis LLP, NYC, 1962—75, mng. ptnr., 1975—2006, chmn. emeritus, 2006—. Author: Winning NLRB Elections, 1997. Chmn. bd. dirs. Children's Village, Dobbs Ferry, NY Mem. NY State Bar Assn. Home: 2 Ponds Ln Purchase NY 10577 Office: Jackson Lewis LLP 59 Maiden Ln New York NY 10038-4502 Office Phone: 212-545-4002.

KRUPNICK, ELIZABETH RACHEL, human resources consulting firm and former insurance company executive; b. NYC, Oct. 21, 1949; d. Julius Michael and Doris (White) K.; children: Tobias Perse, Jacob. BA in Art History, Colby Coll., 1973; MA, U. Mo., 1976. Instr. journalism Emerson Coll., Boston, 1976-78; asst. prof. journalism U. Maine, Orono, 1978-79, Portland Oreg. State U., 1979-83; asst. v.p. Aetna Life & Casualty, Hartford, Conn., 1985-89, v.p. corp. affairs, 1989—92, sr. v.p. corp. affairs; sr. v.p. corp. comm. NY Life; pres. Dewe Rogerson, 1997—98; sr. v.p., US corp. practice dir. Manning, Selvage & Lee, 2000—01; exec. v.p. global corp. comm. Bcom3, 2001—03; sr. v.p. global comm. Mastercard Internat., Purchase, NY, 2003—04; founder TKO Comm. Cons., 2004—07; sr. v.p., chief mktg. officer Heidrick & Struggles Internat., Inc., Chgo., 2007—. Co-author: From Despair to Decision, 1982. Mem. Women in Communications, Ins. Info. Inst. communications com., 1987, pub. relations com., 1986. Office: Heidrick & Struggles Internat Inc 233 S Wacker Dr Sears Tower Ste 4200 Chicago IL 60606

KRUPNICK, JANICE LEE, psychologist, psychotherapist, educator; b. Newark, Mar. 7, 1950; d. Jacob and Betty (Katz) K.; m. Richard Michael Suzman, July 21, 1976; children: Daniel, Jessica. AB, Oberlin Coll., 1972; MSW, U. Mich., 1974; MA, U. Calif., Berkeley, 1985, PhD, 1988. Lic. psychologist, Md., D.C. Social worker Long Beach (Calif.) Neuropsychol. Inst., 1974-75; fellow Mt. Zion Hosp./Med. Ctr., San Francisco, 1975-77; program analyst NIMH, Rockville, Md., 1980-81; asst. clin. prof. U. Calif., San Francisco, 1977-83; cons. NAS, Washington, 1983-84; asst. clin. prof. Georgetown U., Washington, 1984-90; asst. rsch. prof. George Washington U., Washington, 1988-91; assoc. clin. prof. Georgetown U., Washington, 1990-94, clin. prof., 1994—, rsch. prof., 2000—. Cons. NIMH, Bethesda, Md., 1990-91, Am. Psychiat. Assn., 1990-91; tchr. dynamic psychotherapy seminar for advanced psychiat. residents Georgetown U., lectr. interpersonal psychotherapy course. Co-author: Personality Styles and Brief Psychotherapy, 1984; contbr. articles to psychiat. and psychol. jours. Participant rallies for women's rights, Washington, 1986—. Clin. fellow NIMH, 1975-77, rsch. fellow NIMH, 1986-88. Mem. Am. Psychol. Assn., Soc. for Clin. Social Work, Soc. for Psychotherapy Rsch. Jewish. Avocations: reading, movies, travel, swimming. Home: 4100 Oliver St Chevy Chase MD 20815-7120 Office: 5480 Wisconsin Ave Ste 220 Chevy Chase MD 20815-3503 Office Phone: 301-654-2142. Business E-Mail: krupnicj@georgetown.edu.

KRUPP, CLARENCE WILLIAM, lawyer, health facility administrator; b. Cleve., June 20, 1929; s. William Frederick and Mary Mae (Volchko) K.; m. Janice Margaret Heckman, June 28, 1952; children: Bruce, Carolyn. BBA cum laude, Cleve. State U., 1958, LL.B., 1959, LL.M., 1963; LL.D. (hon.), 1974. Bar: Wis. 1972. Dir. pers. Case Tech. U., Cleve., 1960—63; dir. indsl. relations and indsl. engring. Buxbaum Co., Canton, Ohio, 1963-66; mgr. indsl. relations Trane Co., La Crosse, Wis., 1966-73; dir. personnel-labor relations environ. products div. ITT, Phila., 1973; v.p. indsl. relations, gen. counsel G. Heileman Brewing Co., La Crosse, 1973-76; atty., v.p. human resources-risk control, sec. Good Samaritan Hosp., Dayton, Ohio, 1976-80; mgr. compensation and benefits State of Ariz., Phoenix, 1980-83; personnel adminstr., law/land mgmt. divsn. agt. Salt River Project, 1983-94; Indian and sch. land specialist, 1992—; chmn., pres. C.W. Krupp P.C., 1986—. Cons. on labor rels., 1969, 81-83, 88—; elec. line land impact cons., western states, 2000—. Contbr. articles to profl. jours. Mcpl. arbitrator, La Crosse, 1976; pres., mem. La Crosse Bd. Edn., 1969-72; mem. Wis. Gov.'s Task Force on Edn., 1972-73, Ohio Little White House library del.; mem. Ariz. Spinal Injury Panel, 1984-2000. Served with U.S. Army, 1951-53. Named Outstanding Ariz. State Profl. Employee, 1982, Employee of Quarter, 1990, 91. Mem. ABA (forum hosp. law, labor law sect.), Am. Corp. Counsel Assn., Nat. Notary Assn., Wis Bar Assn. (Continuing Edn. award 1972), Am. Assn. Hosp. Attys., Ariz. Assn. Industries (healthcare com. 1983-97, chmn. legis. subcom. 1983-97), Am. Soc. Law and Medicine, Dayton C. of C., Electric League of Ariz. (ins. advisor 1985-97), Internat. Right of Way Assn. (regional cons. Native Am. land rights 1998—), Rotary. Democrat. Roman Catholic. Home and Office: 8701 E Via De La Gente Scottsdale AZ 85258-4040 Home Phone: 480-998-7653; Office Phone: 480-998-7653. Personal E-mail: clarewk@msn.com. *Understand and be tolerant of the views of others. With that insight your decisons will be respected and your judgment both honored and sought.*

KRUPP, EDWIN CHARLES, astronomer; b. Chgo., Nov. 18, 1944; s. Edwin Frederick and Florence Ann (Olander) K.; m. Robin Suzanne Rector, Dec. 31, 1968 (div., 2006); 1 son, Ethan Hembree. BA, Pomona Coll., 1966; MA, UCLA, 1968, PhD (NDEA fellow, 1970-71), 1972. Astronomer Griffith Obs., Los Angeles Dept. Recreation and Parks, 1972—, dir., 1976—. Mem. faculty El Camino Coll., U. So. Calif., extension divs. U. Calif.; cons. in ednl. TV C.C. Consortium; host teleseries Project: Universe. Author: Echoes of the Ancient Skies, 1983, The Comet and You, 1986 (Best Sci. Writing award Am. Inst. Physics 1986), The Big Dipper and You, 1989, Beyond the Blue Horizon, 1991, The Moon and You, 1993, Skywatchers, Shamans & Kings, 1996, The Rainbow and You, 2000; editor, co-author: In Search of Ancient Astronomies, 1978 (Am. Inst. Physics-U.S. Steel Found. award for best sci. writing 1978), Archaeoastronomy and the Roots of Science; editor-in-chief Griffith Obs., 1984—; contbg. editor Sky & Telescope, 1993—. Mem. Am. Astron. Soc. (past chmn. hist. astronomy divsn., solar physics divsn. writing award 2002), Astron. Soc. Pacific (past dir., Klumpke-Roberts Outstanding Contbns. to the Public Understanding and Appreciation of Astronomy award 1989, G. Bruce Blair medal for contbns. to pub. astronomy 1996, Clifford W. Holmes award for contbns. to amateur astronomy 2002), Internat. Soc. Archaeoastronomy and Astronomy in Culture (coun. mem., 2004-), Internat. Astron. Union, Explorers Club, Am. Rock Art Rsch Assn., Sigma Xi. Office: Griffith Observatory 2800 E Observatory Rd Los Angeles CA 90027-1255 Business E-Mail: eckrupp@earthlink.net.

KRUPP, FRED D., lawyer, environmental services administrator; b. Mineola, NY, Mar. 21, 1954; s. Arthur L. and Rosalind (Mehr) K.; m. Laurie Louise Devitt, Aug. 21, 1982; children: Alexander Mehr, Zachary Devitt, Jackson O'Connor. BS, Yale U., New Haven, 1975; JD, U. Mich., Ann Arbor, 1978. Ptnr. Albis & Krupp, New Haven, 1978-83; ptnr. Cooper, Whitney, Cochran & Krupp, New Haven, 1984; pres. Environ. Def., 1984—; gen. counsel Conn. Fund for the Environment, New Haven, 1978-84. Mem. Pres.'s Commn. on Environ. Quality, 1991-92; mem. Pres.'s Coun. on Sustainable Devel., 1993-99; mem. Pres.'s Adv. Com. Trade Policy and Negotiations, 1994-2002; bd. dirs. H. John Heinz III Ctr. for Sci., Econs. and Environment, 1999-2005. Helen De Roy fellow U. Mich. Law Sch. 1986 Office: Environ Def 257 Park Ave S New York NY 10010-7304 Office Phone: 212-616-1234.

KRUPP, JAMES ARTHUR GUSTAVE, management consultant; b. Naples, Italy, Oct. 27, 1944; arrived in U.S., 1945; s. Ralph Gustave and Lydia (Guerroni) Krupp; m. Joyce Ann Draffan, Nov. 5, 1966; children: James Michael Douglas, Matthew Ralph Alexander. Student, U.S. Naval Acad., 1963—66; BSME magna cum laude, U. New Haven, 1971, EMBA, 1981. Cert. fellow in prodn. and inventory. Prodn. control mgr. Sargent & Co., New Haven, 1966-72; prodn. scheduling mgr. Stanley Tools, New Britain, Conn., 1972-75; materials mgr. Whitney Blake, Hamden, Conn., 1975-76; materials control mgr. Burndy Corp., Norwalk, Conn., 1976-79; prodn. and inventory mgr. Picker Corp., Northford, Conn., 1979-81; materials mgr. Carlyle Johnson Machine Co., Manchester, Conn., 1981-84; dir. advanced planning systems ITT Sealectro, New Britain, 1984-89; v.p. materials Echlin Inc., Branford, Conn., 1989-99; dir. materials planning Stanadyne Corp., Windsor, Conn., 1999—2006; prin. project engr. Atlantic Inertial Sys., Sheshire, Conn., 2006—. Mem. editl. bd. Prodn. and Inventory Mgmt. Jour., 1988—; contbr. articles to profl. jours. Chmn. bd. ethics, Wallingford, Conn., 1980—84; mem. Charter Revision Commn., Wallingford, 1988—89; councilman Town of Wallingford, 1984—85. With USN, 1963—67. Mem.: Assn. Internal Mgmt. Cons., Am. Prodn. and Inventory Control Soc. (Romey Everdell award 1998), Mensa. Independent. Roman Catholic. Avocations: youth soccer and special olympics referee, fishing, chess. Office Phone: 203-250-3578. Business E-Mail: jimkrupp@hotmail.com. *Whether in life or business, there are 3 guiding principles whose attainment surpass all measures of success: 1) An unfaltering tradition of the highest sense of personal honor. 2) An absolute respect for the dignity of all those with whom one comes in contact. 3) An unwaivering commitment to excellence in all that one does.*

KRUSE, ANN GRAY, computer programmer; b. Oklahoma City, Jan. 4, 1941; d. Floyd and Bernice Florence (Follansbee) Gray; m. Roy Edwin Kruse, Mar. 20, 1971 (dec.). AB, Randolph Macon Woman's Coll., 1963; MBA, U. Chgo., 1973. Programming mgr. Ind. Info. Controls, Valparaiso, Ind., 1966-67; systems programmer Am. Steel Foundries, Hammond, Ind., 1970-73; engr. applications programmer Bell Helicopter Textron, Fort Worth, 1974-76; lead systems programmer Harris Data Communications, Dallas, 1976-81; sr. systems programmer Lone Star Gas Co., Dallas, 1981-82; sr. software specialist Raytheon, Dallas, 1982—. Republican. Episcopalian. Home: 6128 Black Berry Ln Dallas TX 75248-4909 Office: PO Box 660023 Dallas TX 75266-0023 E-mail: akruse@gsb.uchicago.edu.

KRUSE, F. MICHAEL, judge; b. American Samoa; LLB, Victoria U., Wellington, New Zealand; LLM, George Washington U. Atty., Pago Pago, Am. Samoa, 1972—87; apptd. High Ct. Am. Samoa, Pago Pago, 1987—, now chief justice. Office: The High Ct Am Samoa Courthouse Chief Justice PO Box 309 Pago Pago AS 96799 Office Phone: 011-684-633-1401. Office Fax: 011-684-633-1318.*

KRUSE, JOHN ALPHONSE, lawyer; b. Detroit, Sept. 11, 1926; s. Frank R. and Ann (Nestor) K.; m. Mary Louise Dalton, July 14, 1951 (dec. Apr. 2006); children: Gerard, Mary Louise, Terence, Kathleen, Joanne, Francis, John, Patrick. BS, U. Detroit, 1950, JD cum laude, 1952. Bar: Mich. bar 1952. Ptnr. Alexander, Buchanan & Conklin, Detroit, 1952-69, Harvey, Kruse, PC, Detroit, 1969—. Guest lectr. U. Mich., U. Detroit, Inst. Continuing Legal Edn.; city atty. Allen Park, Mich., 1954-59; twp. atty., Van Buren Twp., Mich., 1959-61. Co-founder Detroit and Mich. Cath. Radio. Past pres. Palmer Woods Assn.; mem. pres.'s cabinet U. Detroit; bd. dirs. Providence Hosp. Found. Named one of 5 Outstanding Young Men in Mich., 1959, Outstanding Alumnus, U. Detroit Sch. Law, 1989; recipient Humanitarian award Neuromuscular Inst. 1988, Voice of Life award Mich. Right to Life, 2006. Mem. Detroit Bar Assn., State Bar Mich. (past chmn. negligence sect.), Assn. Def. Trial Counsel (bd. dirs. 1966-67), Am. Judicature Soc., Internat. Assn. Def. Counsel, Equestrian Order of the Holy Sepulchre. Clubs: Detroit Golf (past pres.). Roman Catholic. Home: 5569 Hunters Gate Dr Troy MI 48098-2342 Office: 1050 Wilshire Dr Ste 320 Troy MI 48084-1526 Home Phone: 248-641-7681; Office Phone: 248-649-7800. Business E-Mail: jkruse@harveykruse.com. E-mail: johnakruse@yahoo.com. *Start each day with a simple petition - Lord help me to do your will today. End each day in thanks for his divine guidance. Prayer is to the soul as exercise is to the body. Neglect neither!.*

KRUSE, LAYNE E., lawyer; b. Emporia, Kans., Aug. 15, 1951; BA, Tex. A&M U., 1973; MSc, London Sch. Econs., 1974; JD, Yale U., 1977. Bar: Tex. 1978, cert.: Tex. Bd. Legal Specialization (civil trial law). Law clk. to Hon. John R. Brown U.S. Ct. Appeals (5th cir.); mem. Fulbright & Jaworski L.L.P., Houston. Past chair antitrust and bus. litigation sect. State Bar Tex. Mem.: ABA, Houston Bar Assn. Office: Fulbright & Jaworski LLP 1301 Mckinney St Ste 5100 Houston TX 77010-3031 Office Phone: 713-651-5194. E-mail: lkruse@fulbright.com.

KRUSE, MARYLIN LYNN, retired language educator; b. Kansas City, Mo., June 26, 1940; d. Mildred Marie Goetsch; m. Richard Lee Weinberg, Dec. 26, 1962 (div. Oct. 1988); children: Eric H., Kerstin I; m. Leon Edward Kruse, Dec. 28, 1998. BA, Cornell Coll., Mt. Vernon, Iowa, 1962; MA, Marycrest Coll., Davenport, Iowa, 1982. Tchr. English Galesburg Cmty. Schs., Ill., 1962—63, Grant Cmty. Schs., Fox Lake, Ill., 1963—64, Saydel Cmty. Schs., Des Moines, 1965—66; instr. English Grandview Coll., Des Moines, 1966—76; behavior disorders cons. We. Ill. Assn., Galesburg, 1976—77; coord. prevocational Knox-Warren Spl. Edn. Dist., Galesburg, 1977—78; tchr. Spanish Winola Cmty. Schs., Viola, Ill., 1979—80; tchr. spl. edn. Pleasant Valley Cmty. Schs., Iowa, 1980—86; instr. English Ea. Iowa C.C. Dist., Davenport, 1983—86; tchr. spl. edn. Davenport Cmty. Schs., 1986—94, tchr. fgn. lang., 1994—2002, ret., 2002. Adj. instr. English Daytona Beach CC, Fla., 2003—. Co-author: Parent Prerogatives, 1979. Recipient Tchr. Incentive award State of Iowa Dept. Edn., 1982; chpt. II grant U.S. Office of Edn., Williams Jr. High, 1988. Mem.: Audubon Soc. Republican. Presbyterian. Avocations: bird watching, reading. Home: 3023 S Atlantic Ave 807 Daytona Beach FL 32118-6157 Personal E-mail: krusel@dbcc.edu.

KRUSE, PAMELA JEAN, lawyer; b. Miami, Fla., June 3, 1950; d. Robert Emil and Irma G. Kruse. BS, Mich. State U., 1973, MA, 1975, PhD, 1979; JD, U. Mich., 1985. Bar: Mich. 1986. Grad. asst. Mich. State U., East Lansing, 1976-77, asst. intramural dir., 1977-79, labor rels. rep., 1979-81, asst. dir. labor rels., 1981-82; resident mgr. 719 Oakland, Ann Arbor, Mich., 1982-83; rsch. asst. Law Sch. U. Mich., Ann Arbor, 1982-85; jud. clk. U.S. Dist. Ct. (we. dist.) Mich., 1985-86; assoc. Clary, Nantz, Wood, Hoffius, Rankin & Cooper, Grand Rapids, Mich., 1986-91; with Village Bike Shops, 1991—. Bd. dirs. Babe Zaharias Golf Tournament, Am. Cancer Soc., 1987-91. Recipient Gold and Silver medals U.S. Pan Am. Team, Winnipeg, Man., Can., 1967, Silver medal U.S. Olympic Team, Mexico City, 1968; holder world records swimming 400 meters freestyle, 1967, 200 meters freestyle, 1967, 440-yard freestyle, 1966; inducted to Greater Fort Lauderdale Sports Hall of Fame, 1979. Mem. ABA, State Bar Mich. (exec. coun. young lawyers sect. 1987-90), Grand Rapids Bar Assn. (chairperson, exec. bd. dirs. young lawyers set. 1987-91), Mich. Pub. Employer Labor Rels. Assn. (bd. dirs. 1981-82, chmn. manual revision com. 1982), Mich. State U. Alumni Assn. (1st v.p., bd. dirs. 1988-89), U.S. Olympians, Phi Delta Kappa, Kappa Alpha Theta. Office: Village Bike Shop Ltd 450 A Baldwin St Jenison MI 49428

KRUSE, RONIA, information technology executive; b. 1970; MS in Taxation, Wayne State U., 1994. Lectr. Wayne State U.; sr. tax cons. Deloitte & Touche L.L.P., 1995—99; pres., CEO OpTech L.L.C., Detroit, 1999—. Named one of 40 Under 40, Crain's Detroit Bus., 2006. Office: OpTech LLC Guardian Bldg 500 Griswold Ste 1690 Detroit MI 48226 Office Phone: 313-962-9000. Office Fax: 313-962-9001.

KRUSE, SCOTT AUGUST, lawyer; b. NYC, July 15, 1947; s. Norman W. and Sarah E. (Doyle) K.; m. Ruth H. Cohnen, Dec. 9, 1975; children: Eric, Marissa, Max. AB, Princeton U., 1969; JD, Harvard U., 1972. Bar: Calif. 1972. Assoc. Gibson, Dunn & Crutcher, Los Angeles, 1972-77; gen. counsel Fed. Mediation and Conciliation Svc., Wash., 1977-79; ptnr. Gibson, Dunn & Crutcher, Los Angeles, 1980—. Contbr. articles on labor law to profl. jours. Capt. USAR, 1969—77. Mem. ABA (com. chmn. 1978-79, com. on equal opportunity law, labor and employment sect., co-chmn. OFCCP liaison subcom.), Calif. Bar Assn., Internat. Bar Assn. (labor com.), Indsl. Relations Research Assn. Democrat. Office: Gibson Dunn & Crutcher 333 S Grand Ave Los Angeles CA 90071-3109 Office Phone: 213-229-7970. Office Fax: 213-229-6970. Business E-Mail: skruse@gibsondunn.com.

KRUSE, STEIN, cruise line executive; m. Linda Kruse; children: Victoria, Alexander. BS, Purdue U. Exec. v.p., COO Radisson Seven Seas Cruises; pres., CEO Seven Seas Cruise Line; sr. v.p., CFO "K" Line Am.; sr. v.p. fleet ops. Holland America Line Inc. & Windstar Cruises, 1999, pres., COO, 2003—04, pres., CEO, 2004—. Bd. govs. World Trade Ctr. Seattle. Bd. dirs. US Coast Guard Found. Mem.: Internat. Coun. Cruise Lines (bd. dirs.), Cruise Lines Internat. Assn. (former chmn.). Office: Holland America Line Inc 300 Elliott Ave W Seattle WA 98119 Office Fax: 206-281-3535.*

KRUTSICK, ROBERT STANLEY, retired science administrator; b. Lansford, Pa., Dec. 6, 1942; s. John Jacob and Mary Ann (Novak) K.; m. Charlotte Ann Harper, Feb. 18, 1977; children: Robert Steven, Laurie, Tracy, Andrew, Daniel. BS, Pa. State U., University Park, 1968; M in Local and State Govt., U. Pa., Phila., 1967. Sr. v.p., treas. Univ. City Sci. Ctr., Phila., 1978-88, acting pres., 1988-90, exec. v.p., 1988-97; ret., 1997. Supr. Upper Merion Twp., King of Prussia, Pa., 1989; pres. Upper Merion Park and Hist. Found., 1997—; bd. dirs., pres. Upper Merion Area Sch. Dist.; chair Upper Merion Twp. Planning Commn.; pres. Lafayette Ambulance Squad, 2002; joint oper. com. Ctr. Tech. Studies. Mem.: Upper Merion Area Edn. Found. (chair), Optimist Club (past pres.). Republican. Roman Catholic. Avocations: tennis, golf, basketball. Home: 210 Cedar Pk Wayne PA 19087-2170 Personal E-mail: bkrutsick@aol.com.

KRUTTER, FORREST NATHAN, lawyer; b. Boston, Dec. 17, 1954; s. Irving and Shirley Krutter. BS in Econs., MS in Civil Engring., MIT, 1976; JD cum laude, Harvard U., 1978. Bar: Nebr. 1978, U.S. Supreme Ct. 1986, NY 1991. Antitrust counsel Union Pacific R.R., Omaha, 1978-86; sr. v.p. law, sec. Berkshire Hathaway Group, Omaha, 1986—; pres. Republic Ins., Dallas, 2000—. Co-author: Impact of Railroad Abandonments, 1976, Railroad Development in the Third World, 1978; author: Judicial Enforcement of Competition in Regulated Industries, 1979; contbr. articles Creighton Law Rev. Mem. ABA, Phi Beta Kappa, Sigma Xi. Office: Berkshire Hathaway Group 4016 Farnam St Omaha NE 68131-3016 Office Phone: 402-536-3214. Business E-Mail: fkrutter@berkre.com.

KRUZAN, JAMES BRENDAN, financial planner; b. Hammond, Ind., Mar. 27, 1959; s. James Francis and Joan (Joyce) K.; m. Dena Lee Payne, Aug. 3, 1985; children: Kaylee, Brendan. BS, BA, Wayne State U., 1981. Cert. fin. planner. Teller, mgmt. trainee Nat. Bank Detroit, Livonia, Mich., 1979-82; registered rep., dist. mgr. IDS/Am. Express, Southfield, Mich., 1982-86; registered rep. Prudential Bache Securities, Inc., Birmingham, Mich., 1986-87; br. mgr. Raymond James Fin. Svcs., Inc., Clarkston, Mich., 1987—; pres., CEO, chief investment strategist Kaydan Group, Inc., Clarkston, Mich., 1996—. Mem.: Fin. Planning Assn. Avocations: golf, travel. Office: Kaydan Group Inc 20 W Washington Ave Ste 14 Clarkston MI 48346-1576 Business E-Mail: james.kruzan@raymondjames.com.

KRYCH, MARGARET A., religious organization administrator, educator; b. Perth, Australia, Apr. 4, 1942; d. Ernest W and Hannah S Sanders; m. Arden L Krych, Sept. 4, 1971; children: Meredyth A. Krych Appelbaum, David A. BA, U. Western Australia, 1963; BD with honors, Melbourne Coll. of Div., Australia, 1965, ThM, 1970; PhD, Princeton Theol. Sem., 1985. Clergy Meth. Ch. Australasia, Perth, Australia, 1966—67, assoc. dir. dept. christian edn., 1968—70; editor Luth. Ch. Am., Phila., 1973—77; Charles Norton prof. of christian edn. and theology Luth. Theol. Sem., Phila., 1977—, assoc. dean grad. edn., 1997—. Cons. Ednl. Ministry with Youth Project, LTSP, Phila., 1999—; mem. ELCA Bd. Augsburg Fortress Publ. House, Mpls., 2003—07. Author: (non-fiction book) Teaching the Gospel Today, 1987, Teaching About Lutheranism, 1993, (non-fiction book, co-authored) Confirmation: Engaging Lutheran Foundations and Practices, 1999; co-author: (non-fiction book) Ministry of Children's Education, 2004; contbr. Named one of, Outstanding Young Women of Am., 1976, 1977; named to Women in Leadership in Theol. Edn. program, Assn. Theol. Schs., 2001; recipient JR Saunders prize in philosophy, U. Western Australia, 1960; grantee Wabash Ctr. for Teaching and Learning, 2005; scholar Hackett competitive scholarship, U. Western Australia, 1963, 1964; Tchg. and Learning grantee, Assn. Theol. Schs., 1999. Mem.: Assn. Profs. and Rschrs. in Religious Edn., Am. Acad. Religion, Assn. for Dr. of Ministry Edn. (steering com. 2001—04), Assn. Luth. Tchg. Theologians (discussion leader 2001—02), Soc. for Rsch. in Child Devel. Evangelical Lutheran. Avocations: music, travel. Office: Luth Theol Sem 7301 Germantown Ave Philadelphia PA 19119-1794 Office Phone: 215-248-6347. Business E-Mail: mkrych@ltsp.edu.

KRYDER, GEORGE M., III, lawyer; b. Akron, Ohio, Sept. 16, 1951; AB, Princeton U., 1974; JD, Vanderbilt U., 1977. Bar: Ohio 1977, Ga. 1978, DC 1978, Tex. 1980. Law clk. to Judge Harry Phillips US Ct. Appeals (6th cir.), 1977-78; ptnr. Carrington, Coleman, Sloman & Blumenthal, LLP, Dallas, Vinson & Elkins, LLP. Mng. editor Vanderbilt Law Rev., 1976-77. Exec. com. Inst. Law and Tech. Named one of Best Lawyers in Dallas, D Mag., 2003, 2005; Patrick Wilson scholar, 1974—77. Mem.: Tex. Ctr. Ethics and Professionalism, Tex. Bar Found., Ctr. Am. and Internat. Law, Ctr. Am. and Internat. Law and Tech., Dallas Assn. Def. Coun., Dallas Bar Assn., Am. Inns Ct., Liaison, ABA (co-chair Profl. Liability Litig. Com. 1999—2003, co-chair Expert Witness Com. Sect. Litig. 2003—04), Standing Com. Lawyers' Profl. Liability. Office: Vinson & Elkins LLP Trammell Crow Ctr 2001 Ross Ave Ste 3700 Dallas TX 75201-2975 Office Phone: 214-220-7719. Office Fax: 214-999-7719. E-mail: gkryder@velaw.com.*

KRYDER, MARK HOWARD, computer and electrical engineering executive, educator, consultant; b. Oct. 7, 1943; BSEE, Stanford U., Calif., 1965, MSEE, 1966; PhD in Elec. Engring. and Physics, Calif. Inst. Tech., 1969. Rsch. fellow Calif. Inst. Tech., 1969—71; vis. prof. U. Regensburg, Germany; rschr., mgr. Exploratory Bubble Devices IBM, 1973—78; assoc. prof. Carnegie Mellon U., 1978—80, prof., 1980—90, dir. Engring. Rsch. Ctr. in Data Storage Systems, 1990—98; sr. v.p., dir. Seagate Rsch., Seagate Tech., Pitts., 1998—, chief tech. officer, 2003—. Contbr. articles to sci. jours. Recipient David L. Lawrence award, Vectors/Pitts., 2003. Fellow: IEEE (Magnetics Soc. Achievement award, Reynold B. Johnson Info. Storage award, Millennium medal), Am. Phys. Soc. (George E. Pake prize 2007); mem.: NAE. Achievements include patents in field. Office: Seagate Tech 1251 Waterfront Pl Pittsburgh PA 15222-4215 E-mail: kryder@ece.cmu.edu.*

KRYGER, JERRI RENEE, elementary school educator; b. Tucson, Oct. 27, 1961; d. Arthur Alex and Donna Lee Elias; m. Richard C. Kryger, June 28, 1986. BA, Ariz. State U., Tempe, 1985. Cert. elem. edn. Ariz., ESL endorsment Ariz. Classroom teacher 1st and 2d grades Gadsden Dist. #32, San Luis, Ariz., 1985—2004; computer tchr. K-6 Ariz. Desert Sch., San Luis, 2004—05; computer tchr. SW Jr. High, San Luis, 2005—. Asst. swim coach Yuma HS, Ariz., 1986—93; head swim coach So. Ariz. Sandsharks, Yuma, 1995—2002; swim coach Kofa HS, Yuma, 1995—2005. Pres. Gadsden Edn. Assn., San Luis, 2004—06. Fellow: Ariz. Edn. Assn. (assoc.). Home: 2218 W Brook St Yuma AZ 85364 Office: SW Jr High 963 N 8th Ave San Luis AZ 85349 Home Phone: 928-782-3155; Office Phone: 928-627-6580.

KRYLOV, DMITRI, biologist; b. Leningrad, Russia, Mar. 24, 1969; s. Mstislav Krylov and Nina Krylova. PhD, U. Wash., Seattle, 2000. Rsch. asst. U. Wash., Seattle, 1995—2000; rsch. scientist Nat. Ctr. for Biotechnology Info., Bethesda, Md., 2001—. Contbr. articles to profl. jours. , Marine Biology Labs. fellow, 1993, U. Oreg. scholar, 1991—93. Mem.: Internat. Soc. for Computational Biology (edn. com. 2001—06). Achievements include a novel method for identifying protein-protein interactions (biochemistry); development of a method for full genome protein sequence comparisons; discovery of the evolutionary history of Cell Cycle Kinases; produced a comprehensive classification of eukoryotic proteins; produced a classification of protein domains. Avocations: travel, volleyball. Business E-Mail: krylov@ncbi.nlm.nih.gov.

KRYS, SHELDON JACK, retired diplomat; b. NYC, June 15, 1934; s. Martin and Anna K.; m. Doris M., May 24, 1964; children— Wendy M., Madeleine S., Susan Jennifer. N.D., U. Md., College Park, 1955; grad., Nat. War Coll., Washington, 1977; PhD (hon.), St. John Fisher Coll., 1996. Newscaster Radio Sta. KRSD, Rapid City, SD, 1955-57; dir., prodr. Radio Sta. WWDC, Washington, 1957-59; prin. Chris Sheldon Pub. Rels., Washington, 1959-61; cons. to dir. FMCS, Washington, 1961-62; ednl. and cultural affairs officer, dir. reception ctrs. Dept. State, Washington, 1962-64, mgmt. officer London, 1965-66, spl. asst. to amb., 1966-69, dir. pers. Latin Am. Washington, 1969-74, adminstrv. counselor Belgrade, 1974-76, fgn. svc. insp. Washington, 1977-79, exec. dir. Bur. Near Eastern and South Asian Affairs, 1979-83, dep. dir. mgmt. ops., 1983-84, exec. asst. to under sec. for mgmt., 1984-85; amb. to Trinidad and Tobago, 1985-88; exec. sec. Laird Commn., 1987; asst. sec. state adminstrn. and info. mgmt., 1988-89; asst. sec. state diplomatic security, 1989-92; diplomat-in-residence George Washington U., Washington, 1992-93; cons. internat. and intergovtl. affairs Fletcher, Heald & Hildreth, P.L.C., Roslyn, Va., 1994—. Co-chmn. ambassadorial seminar Dept. of State, 1992—2003. Mem. bd. George Foster Peabody Awards, 1990-95, chmn. bd. 1993-95, chmn. emeritus 1996, chmn. editl. bd. Fgn. Svc. Jour., 1994-96; bd. dirs. Sr. Living Found., 1997—; bd. dirs., treas. Washington Inst. Fgn. Affairs, 2006—; trustee St. John Fisher Coll., 1997—. Recipient Meritorious Honor award, Dept. State, 1974, Disting. Honor award, 1981, Superior Honor award, 1983, Presdl. Meritorious Svc. award, 1983, Wilbur J. Carr award, 1994. Mem. Armed Forces Comm. and Electronics Assn. (bd. dirs. 1991-92), Nat. War Coll. Alumni Assn., Am. Fgn. Svc. Assn., Am. Broadcast Pioneers, Broadcast Found., City Tavern Club. Avocation: gardening. Office: Fletcher Heald & Hildreth PLC 1300 North 17th St 11th Fl Arlington VA 22209-3801

KRYSTKOWIAK, LARRY BRETT, professional basketball coach; b. Missoula, Mont., Sept. 23, 1964; m. Jan Krystkowiak; children: Cameron, Luc, Ben. Student, U. Mont., 1982—86, BA in Bus. Adminstrn., 1996. Draft pick Chgo. Bulls, 1986, profl. basketball player, 1994—95, San Antonio Spurs, 1986—87, Milw. Bucks, 1987—92, asst. coach, 2006—07, head coach, 2007—; profl. basketball player Utah Jazz, 1992—93, Orlando Magic, 1993—94, Levallois Basketball Club, Paris, 1996, LA Lakers, 1996—97, Continental Basketball Assn. Idaho Stampede, 1997—98, head coach, 2003—04; asst. coach U. Mont., 1998—2000, head coach, 2004—06; asst. coach Old Dominion U., 2001—02, Norfolk Collegiate HS, Va., 2002—03. Mailing: Milw Bucks 1001 N Fourth St Milwaukee WI 53203*

KRYTER, KARL DAVID, retired research scientist; b. Indpls., Oct. 13, 1914; s. George David and Mary Matilda (Christoph) K.; m. Grace Irene Brown, June 21, 1946; children: Dianne, Victoria (Mrs. Myron I. Liebhaber), Kathryn (Mrs. Richard A. Rendon). AB, Butler U., 1939; PhD, U. Rochester, 1942. Rsch. tchr. fellow Harvard U., Cambridge, Mass., 1942-46; asst. prof. Washington U., St. Louis, 1946-48; dir. human resources research labs. Air Force Cambridge Rsch. Ctr., 1948-57; head dept. psychoacoustics Bolt Beranek & Newman, Inc., Cambridge, Mass., 1957-65; dir. Sensory Scis. Rsch. Ctr., Menlo Park, Calif., 1965-76; staff scientist Stanford Rsch. Inst., Menlo Park, 1976-85. Adj. prof. San Diego State U., 1990—; tchr. Colby Coll., 1960—63, MIT, 1958—59; advisor U.S. Pres.'s Office for Sci. and Tech., 1968—70; mem. SST environ. study com. Dept. Interior, 1969; past chmn. coun. com. hearing and bioacoustics NAS/NRC, 1960. Author: The Effects of Noise on Man, 1970-85, Handbook of Hearing and the Effects of Noise, 1994. Recipient Disting. Svc. award in sci. Am. Speech and Hearing Assn., medal U. Liege, Belgium. Fellow APA (coun. reps. 1966-69), Soc. Engring. Psychologists (pres. 1965, Franklin V. Taylor award), Acoustical Soc. Am. (coun., pres. 1972). Home: 5500 Calle Real Apt 326 Santa Barbara CA 93111 Personal E-mail: kdkryter@cox.net.

KRZYSZTOFOWICZ, ROMAN, systems engineering and statistical science educator, consultant; b. Cieszyn, Poland, Sept. 27, 1947; came to U.S., 1974; naturalized, 1985; s. Janusz and Irena (Rogozinska) K.; m. Liana Balayan, May 27, 1995; children: Arman, Nayiri. MS with highest distinction, Cracow Tech. U., Poland, 1970; PhD, U. Ariz., 1978. Rsch. engr. Inst. for Meteorology and Water Resources, Cracow, 1970-72, head computer ctr., 1972-74; lectr. Chief Tech. Orgn., Cracow, 1973-74; asst. prof. systems engring. U. Ariz., Tucson, 1978-79; asst. prof. civil engring. MIT, Cambridge, Mass., 1979-82; assoc. prof. systems engring. U. Va., Charlottesville, Va., 1982-86, prof. systems engring., 1986—, dir. grad. program systems engring., 1984-89, assoc. dir. ctr. for risk mgmt. engring. systems, 1987-88, prof. statistics, 1995—. Vis. scientist Swiss Fed. Inst. Tech., Lausanne, 2002; lectr. George Washington U., 1982-83, NATO Advanced Study Inst., Tucson, 1985, Deauville, France, 1993, Coop. Program for Operational Meteorology, Edn. and Tng., Boulder, Colo., 1993-96; rep. NSF in coop. rsch. initiatives with Brazil and Poland, 1991; reviewer proposals NSF, 1980—, Natural Scis. and Engring. Rsch. Coun. Can., 1987—; rschr. Nat. Weather Svc., 1992, 1995; expert on flood forecasting, Commn. for Hydrology, World Meteorological Orgn., 1997-2000; mem. doctoral examination com. U. Que., 1997, 2000, U. Paris VI, 2002, École Nationale du Génie Rural des Eaux et des Forêts (ENGREF), Paris, 2004; reviewer articles for numerous jours. Editor Jour. of Hydrology, 1996—; mem. editl. bd. Stochastic Hydrology and Hydraulics, 1990-98, Control and Cybernetics, 1994—, Stochastic Environ. Rsch. and Risk Assessment, 1999—, Water Resources Monographs of the Polish Academy of Sciences, 2000—, Jour. Applied Meteorology, 2001—02; contbr. articles to profl. jours., chpts. to books, entries to Systems and Control Ency., Concise Ency. Environ. Systems, Ency. Ops. Rsch. and Mgmt. Sci., Ency. of Sci. and Tech. Recipient Prof. W. Wierzbicki award Polish Soc. Civil Engrs. and Technicians, 1970, Rsch. award NSF, 1978-99, Presdl. Young Investigator award Pres. of U.S., 1984. Mem. IEEE, Am. Statis. Assn., Soc. for Judgment and Decision Making, Internat. Inst. Forecasters, Inst. for Ops. Rsch. and the Mgmt. Scis., Am. Geophys. Union, Am. Water Resources Assn., Am. Meteorological Soc., Tau Beta Pi (Eminent Engr. award 1985). Republican. Armenian Catholic. Avocations: opera, theater, skiing, sailing, hiking. Office: U Va PO Box 400747 151 Engineer's Way Charlottesville VA 22904-4747 Business E-Mail: rk@virginia.edu. *Education is a launchpad to a rewarding life. Research demands passion and endurance. The challenge for me as an academician is to turn learners into thinkers, to bring about in students a transition from* *acquiring knowledge to creating new knowledge, to graduate scientists and engineers who not merely perpetuate today's technology but invent a better one. For it is the creative element that uplifts the individual and benefits mankind.*

KRZYZANOWSKI, RICHARD L., lawyer; b. Warsaw, Mar. 25, 1932; came to U.S., 1967, naturalized, 1972; s. Andrew and Mary K.; children: Suzanne, Peter, Christine. BA, U. Warsaw, 1956; ML, U. Pa., 1960; PhD, U. Paris, 1962. Bar: Pa. With Crown Cork & Seal Co., Inc., Phila., 1967—, dir., exec. v.p. gen. counsel, 1990-2001. Counselor John Paul II Found., Vatican, Rome, Italy; exec. trustee, founder Krzyzanowski Found., Phila. Mem. Int. Bar Assn. (London). Home and Office: 466 Wyndmoor Ln Huntingdon Valley PA 19006 Office Phone: 215-914-2323.

KRZYZEWSKI, MIKE (MICHAEL WILLIAM KRZYZEWSKI), college basketball coach; b. Chgo., Feb. 13, 1947; m. Carol Mickie Marsh; children: Debbie Savarino, Linda Frasher, Jamie Spatola. BS, U.S. Mil. Acad., 1969. Capt. team, 1968—69; capt. second team All-NIT, 1969; capt. North-South game, 1969; head coach svc. teams, 1969—72; head basketball coach U.S. Mil. Acad. Prep Sch., Ft. Belvoir, Va., 1972—74; grad. asst. Ind. U., 1974—75; head basketball coach U.S. Mil. Acad., West Point, NY, 1975-80, Duke U. Blue Devils, Durham, NC, 1980—. Head coach So. team Nat. Sports Festival, 1983; instr. Olympic Trials, 1984. Co-author (with Bill Brill): A Season Is a Lifetime: The Inside Story of the Duke Blue Devils and Their Championships Seasons, 1993; co-author: (with Donald T. Phillips) Leading with the Heart: Coach K's Successful Strategies for Basketball, Business and Life, 2000, 5 Point Play: Duke's Journey to the 2001 National Championship, 2001; co-author: (with Jamie Krzyzewski Spatola) Beyond Basketball: Coach K's Keywords for Success, 2006. Chmn. Children's Miracle Network Telethon; bd. dirs. V Found.; with Comprehensive Cancer Ctr., NABC Coaches vs. Cancer; bd. dirs. K Lab Human Performance; fundraising leader Emily Krzyzewski Ctr. Immaculate Conception Cath. Ch., Durham, NC. Served US Army, 1967—69, officer US Army, 1969—74, ret. capt. US Army, 1974. Named Met. N.Y. Basketball Writer's Coach of Yr., 1977, Coach of Yr., ACC, 1984, 1986, 1997, 1999, 2000, Nat. Coach of Yr., Basketball Times, 1997, CBS/Chevrolet, 1986, 2000, Naismith, 1989, 1992, 1999, Sporting News, 1992, UPI, 1986, Victor awards, 2001, Sportsman of Yr., Sporting News, 1992, Coach of Decade, NABC, 1990, Naismith Meml. Basketball Hall of Fame, 2001, America's Best Coach, Time/CNN, 2001, 3d Best Coach All Time, CBS show; recipient Wooden award, Legends of Coaching, 2000, GTE (now Verizon) Reads with the NABC Lit. Champion award, 2000. Mem.: NCAA (basketball issues com.), Nat. Assn. Basketball Coaches (pres. 1998—99, Dist. Coach of Yr. 1977, 1984, 1992, 1994, 1999, 2000, Nat. Coach of Yr. 1991, 1999). Achievements include coaching team to NCAA Divsn. I Championship, 1991, 92, 2001, 2nd place, 1986, 90, 94, 99, final four, 1986, 88, 89, 90, 91, 92, 94, 99, 2001, 2004; ranked first in the Big Apple NIT Champion, ACC Champion, NCAA Tournament Finalist, equal NCAA record for most victories in a season, 1986; ranked first, ACC Champion, NCAA Champion, team ranked number 1 from start to finish, a first repeat NCAA Champion since 1972-73; ranked first, NCAA Tournament Finalist, ACC regular season champion, ACC Champion, equal for most victories in a season, 1999; ranked first, NCAA Champion, ACC regular season co-champion, ACC Champion, TiVo Preseason NIT champion, 2001; ranked first, ACC Champion, NCAA Tournament Sweet 16, Maui Invitational champion, 2002; only 4th coach in NCAA history to earn 3 or more national championships along with John Wooden, Adolph Rupp, and Bob Knight. Office: Duke Univ Cameron Indoor Stadium Durham NC 27708-0556

KSANSNAK, JAMES EDWARD, diversified financial services company executive, accountant; b. Hazleton, Pa., Mar. 13, 1940; s. Edward J. and Helen (Holodick) K.; m. Valerie M. Anderson, June 9, 1962 (div. 1986); children: Keith, Janet, Linda; m. Suzanne M. Teefy, Feb. 21, 1987. BS magna cum laude in Acctg., St. Joseph's U., Phila., 1962. C.P.A. With Arthur Andersen & Co., Phila., 1962-86, sr. mem. staff, 1964-67, mgr., 1967-71, ptnr., 1971-79, mng. ptnr., 1979-86; sr. v.p. ARAMARK Corp. (formerly ARA Svcs., Inc.), Phila., 1986-87, sr. v.p., CFO, 1987-91, exec. v.p., CFO, 1991-97, vice chmn., 1997—2001. Bd. dirs. CSS Industries, Inc., Aramark Corp.; chmn. Tasty BakingCo., 2003—. Contbr. articles to profl. jours. Mem. Cmty. Leadership Seminar, 1972, trustee, bd. dirs., 1984; treas., bd. dirs. Ambler (Pa.) Youth Svcs., 1974-79; bd. dris., mem. exec. com. Phila. YMCA, 1974-94, chmn. fin. com., chmn. ann. meeting, city fundraising chmn., 1974-83, maj. gifts chmn., 1984-87, chmn. 1987-91; mem. exec. com. Phila. Urban Affairs Coalition, 1978-95; bd. dirs. Greater Phila. Internat. Network, 1980-86, INROADS-Phila., Inc., 1981-90, Am. Cancer Soc., 1994-96, Thomas Jefferson U., 1994—, Main Line Health Sys., 1996-98; mem. Mayor's Com. on Literacy, Phila., 1984-85; mem. fin. com., exec. com. Presbyn.-U. Pa. Med. Ctr., 1981-90, chmn. found., 1986; vice chmn. United Way, 1982; trustee Coll. Bus., St. Joseph's U., 1982-85. Recipient alumni award St. Joseph's U., 1980; named Profl. of Yr., Phi Chi Theta, 1981 Mem. AICPA, Pa. Inst. CPAs (chmn. tech. meetings 1970, chmn. coop. with attys. 1972, exec. comm. Phila. chpt. 1980-82), Planning Execs. Inst. (chmn. bd. 1981, Neil Denen award 1984), Union League, Sunnybrook Golf Club, Loxahatchee Golf Club, Knights of Malta. Republican. Roman Catholic. Home: 205 Echo Dr Jupiter FL 33458 Office: Aramark Corp 1101 Market St Philadelphia PA 19107-2988

KSIENSKI, AHARON ARTHUR, retired electrical engineer; b. Warsaw, June 23, 1924; came to U.S., 1951, naturalized, 1959; s. Isreal and Rebecca K.; married; children: David, Ruth. B.E. in Mech. Engring, Inst. Mech. Engring., London, 1947; M.Sc. in Elec. Engring, U. So. Calif., 1952, PhD, 1958. Sr. staff engr., head antenna dept. research staff Hughes Aircraft Co., Culver City, Calif., 1958-67; prof. elec. engring., tech. dir. communication systems electrosci. lab. Ohio State U., 1967-76, prof. elec. engring., chmn. communication and propagation com. electrosci. lab., 1976-87, prof. emeritus, 1987—; ret., 1987. Bd. dirs. Ohio State U. Research Found., 1975-79; cons. in field. Editor trans., revs. in field. Recipient Brabazon award Inst. Electronic and Radio Engrs., London, 1967, 76 Fellow IEEE; mem. Internat. Union Radio Sci. (chmn. commns. B and C 1972-75) Home: 665 Trafalgar Dr Hagerstown MD 21742 Personal E-mail: aharon@myactv.net.

KSOBIECH, KATE, sociologist, educator; b. Milw., July 17, 1958; d. Richard and Evangeline McGuire; m. Ken Ksobiech, Jan. 24, 1943; children: Shelli, Dana Hanizeski, Laura, Dawn Hanizeski, Danielle Hanizeski. BA, Alverno Coll., Milw., 1986; MA, Marquette U., Milw., 1988; PhD in Urban Studies, U. Wis., Milw., 2001. Postdoctoral fellow Med. Coll. Wis., Milw., 2002—04; sr. rsch. analyst Pub. Policy Forum, Milw., 2004—05; assoc. rschr. U. Wis., Milw., 2006—, lectr. Whitewater, 2007—. Adj. asst. prof. Marquette U., Milw., 2005—06. Coord. spl. events and fundraising Young Dance Acad., Oak Creek, Wis., 2003. Dissertation fellow, U. Wis., Milw., 2000—01, Nat. Rsch. Svc. Award Postdoctoral fellow, NIH, 2002—04, Devel. grantee, NIMH, 2003—04. Mem.: Nat. Comm. Assn. Avocations: crafts, writing. Home: 7819 S Quincy Ave Oak Creek WI 53154 Office: Univ Wisconsin - Milwaukee Ctr Urban Initiatives/Rsch Eng Hall B50 PO Box 413 Milwaukee WI 53201-0413 Home Phone: 414-229-4847; Office Phone: 414-229-4847. Business E-Mail: k8@uwm.edu.

K-TURKEL, JUDITH LEAH ROSENTHAL (JUDI K-TURKEL), writer, editor, publisher; b. NYC, Jan. 3, 1934; d. Samuel S. and Pauline (Turkel) Rosenthal; m. Franklynn Peterson; children: Joseph, Jeffrey Kesselman, David, Kevin Peterson. BA, Bklyn. Coll., 1955. Story and mng. editor Dell Publs., NYC, 1955-58, 62-65; editor-in-chief Sterling, Stearn & KMR Publs., NYC, 1959-62; sr. editor Macfadden-Bartell Publs., NYC, 1966-68; freelance writer NYC and Wis., 1968—2005; pres. P/K Assocs., Inc., Madison, Wis., 1977—. Instr. adult edn. Great Neck (N.Y.) Pub. Schs., 1973-76, U. Wis., Madison, 1977-82; instr. journalism Madison Area Tech. Coll., 1984-87; lectr. nonfiction writing CW Post Ctr., L.I. U., Manhasset, N.Y., 1976-77; tchr.-in-residence Rhinelander (Wis.) Sch. Arts, 1984-86. Author: (writing as Judi Kesselman) Stopping Out, 1976, (writing as Judi Kesselman-Turkel with Franklynn Peterson) The Do-It-Yourself Custom Van Book, 1977, Vans, 1979, (with others) Eat Anything Exercise Diet, 1979, Snowmobile Maintenance and Repair, 1979, I Can Use Tools, 1981, (textbook) Good Writing, 1980—, Test Taking Strategies, 1981, 2d edit., 2004, Study Smarts, 1981, 2004, Homeowner's Book of Lists, 1981, How to Improve Damn Near Everything Around Your Home, 1981, The Author's Handbook, 1982, rev., 1986, 2006, The Grammar Crammer, 1982, 2004, Research Shortcuts, 1982, 2004, Note-Taking Made Easy, 1982, rev. edit. 2004, The Vocabulary Builder, 1982, rev. edit. 2004, Getting it Down: How to Get Your Ideas on Paper, 1983, rev. edit.(as Secrets to Writing Great Papers), 2004, Spelling Simplified, 1983, 2004, The Magazine Writer's Handbook, 1983, rev. edit., 1986, 2006; syndicated computer newspaper columnist, 1983—; editor (newsletter) CPA Micro Report, 1985-92, CPA's PC Network Advisor, 1991-92; pub. CPA Computer Report, 1994-2006; contbr. articles to profl. jours. Chmn. non-partisan Citizens Nominating Com., Great Neck, 1972-75. Recipient Bus. Press. award, 1977, Nat. Press Club award, 1984, 85. Mem. Am. Soc. Journalists and Authors, Coun. Wis. Writers (pres. 1982-85), Authors Guild, Authors League. Avocations: travel, music. Office: P/K Assocs Inc 3006 Gregory St Madison WI 53711-1847 E-mail: info@booksthatteach.com.

KUBA, JOHN ALBERT, mortician; b. Cedar Rapids, Iowa, Apr. 14, 1940; S. Edward Rudolph and Josephine Marie (Barta-Letovsky) K. Student, Coe Coll., Cedar Rapids, 1958-59, Tex. A&I U., 1959-61, Washington U., St. Louis, 1961-62; grad., Wis. Inst. Mortuary Sci., 1963. Ptnr., owner E&J Homes Ltd., Kuba Funeral Homes, Cedar Rapids, 1963-94; pres., CEO Sisley Grove Cemetery, Cedar Rapids, 1966—, E&J, Inc., Cedar Rapids, 1966—; tchr. English in pvt. sch., Pribram, Czech Republic. Trustee Czech Nat Cemetery, Cedar Rapids, 1966-81, fin. sec., 1981-94; owner Velvet Feed Bag Restaurant, 1979-84, Czech Village Shirt, ETC Shop, 1991, founder. Author: Cooking in America, 1971. V.p. Linn County Hist. Mus. Assn., Cedar Rapids, 1966-69, Czech Fine Arts, 1970-75; fin. sec. Linn County Dem. Ctrl. Com., 1970-74; vol. San Antonio AIDS Found.; docent Inst. Texan Cutures, San Antonio Conservation Soc.; mem. Bexar County Czech Heritage Soc., Victoria County Czech Heritage Soc., Unity Found., S.A. Equal Right Polit. Caucus; sec. Minn.-Iowa dist. Civitan Internat. Spl. Olympics, South Bend, Reno-Tahoe, Mpls.-St. Paul. Recipient Outstanding Lt. Gov, Civitan Internat., 1989-90, Outstanding Community Svc. and Humanitarian award Modern Woodmen of Am., 1990 Mem. Czechoslovak Soc. Am. Franternal Life Assn. (pres. 1964-67, sec.-treas. 1971—, Fraternalist of Yr. 1991), Western Fraternal Life (sec. 1986-89), K.C. (past faithful navigator 4 degrees), 16th Ave Merchants Assn. (sec.), Minowa Dist. Civitan (gov. 1980-81, fellow 1991, dist. honor key 1991), Tex. Czech Heritage Soc., Victoria County Czech Heritage Soc., Bexar County Czech Heritage Soc., Lodge Jr. Am. Czech #388 (pres., sec., treas., sec.-treas., fin. sec.), Cath. Order of Foresters, K.C., Moose Lodge, Eagles, Elks, Cath. Workman, Cedar Rapids Sokol, Fedn. of Czech Groups, Czech Heritage Found., Linn County Hist. Soc., Czech Fine Arts, W.F.L.A., Alamo Bus. Coun. San Antonio, Assn. for the Mentally Disabled, Civitan Club. Roman Catholic. Avocations: archaeology, gourmet cooking, travel, gardening, mystery reading. Office: Dhouha 93 261 01 Pribram Czech Republic

KUBALE, BERNARD STEPHEN, lawyer; b. Reedsville, Wis., Sept. 5, 1928; s. Joseph and Josephine (Novak) Kubale; m. Mary Thomas, Apr. 21, 1956 (dec. Jan. 13, 2001); children: Caroline, Catherine, Anne stepchildren: Lauren Ziedonis, Nicholas Ziedonis; m. Karen Robinson, Jan. 23, 2004. BBA, U. Wis., 1950, LLB, 1955; LLD (hon.), St. Norbert Coll., 1985. CPA Wis.; bar: Wis. 1955. Acct. John D. Morrison and Co., Marquette, Mich., 1950-51; atty., ptnr. Foley and Lardner, Milw., 1955—, chmn. mgmt. com., 1985-94. Bd. dirs. Green Bay Packers, E. R. Wagner Mfg. Co., Wausau Homes. Chmn. bd. dirs. St. Norbert Coll., DePere, Wis., 1980—84, Children's Hosp. Wis., Milw., 1982—91. 1st lt. USAF, 1951—53. Mem.: ABA, Milw. Bar Assn., Wis. Bar Assn., Wis. Inst. CPAs, Milw. Club, Chenequa Country Club. Republican. Roman Catholic. Avocations: fishing, skiing. Home: 5935 Monclaire Rd Hartland WI 53029 Office: Foley & Lardner 1st Wisconsin Ctr 777 E Wisconsin Ave Ste 3800 Milwaukee WI 53202-5367 Personal E-mail: bskubale@aol.com.

KUBAS, GREGORY JOSEPH, research chemist; b. Cleve., Mar. 12, 1945; s. Joseph Arthur and Esther Kubas; m. Chrystal Henry, Dec. 22, 1973; children: Kelly Richmond (dec. 1997), Sherry Lopez. BS, Case Inst. Tech., 1966; PhD, Northwestern U., 1970. Postdoctoral fellow Princeton (N.J.) U., 1971-72, Los Alamos (N.Mex.) Nat. Lab., 1972-74, mem. staff, 1974—; lab. fellow, 1987—. Author: Metal Dihydrogen And Sigma Complexes, 2001; contbr. articles to profl. jours.; chpts. to books. Recipient E.O. Lawrence Meml. award US Dept. Energy, 1994. Fellow AAAS; mem. Am. Chem. Soc. (Inorganic Chemistry award 1993). Achievements include patents in field. Office: Los Alamos Nat Lab MS J582 Los Alamos NM 87545-0001 Home: 53 Avenida Las Nubes Santa Fe NM 87508

KUBASIK, CHRISTOPHER E., aerospace transportation executive; b. Cheverly, Md., Mar. 26, 1961; BS in Acctg with honors, U. Md. Sch. Bus., 1983; attended exec. program, Northwestern U. Kellogg Sch. Bus., 1997. CPA. Ptnr. Ernst & Young, 1996; v.p., controller Lockheed Martin Corp., Bethesda, Md., 1999—2001, CFO, 2001—, exec. v.p., CFO, 2004—07, exec. v.p. electronic sys., 2007—. Vice-chmn. Lockheed Martin Diversity Coun.; chmn., Ethics and Bus. Conduct Steering Com. Lockheed Martin; chmn. bd. dirs. Lockheed Martin Investment Mgmt. Co. Office: Lockheed Martin Corp 6801 Rockledge Dr Bethesda MD 20817-1877*

KUBEK, GARY W., lawyer; b. June 4, 1954; BA summa cum laude, Yale U., 1975, JD, 1978. Bar: NY 1979. Law clerk to Judge J. Joseph Smith US Ct. Appeals, Second Cir., 1978—79; litig. ptnr. Debevoise & Plimpton LLP, NYC. Mem.: ABA (vice chair distbn. and franchise com. 2004—07, mem. litig., antitrust and bus. sects.), Assn. Bar of City NY (former mem. antitrust com. and ethics com.). Office: Debevoise & Plimpton LLP 919 Third Ave New York NY 10022 Office Phone: 212-909-6267. Office Fax: 212-909-6836. E-mail: gwkubek@debevoise.com.

KUBIAK, GARY, professional football coach; b. Houston, Aug. 15, 1961; m. Rhonda Kubiak; children: Klint, Klay, Kline. Grad., Texas A&M U., 1982. Quarterback Denver Broncos, 1983—91, offensive coord., 1995—2006; head coach Tex. A&M U., 1992—93; quarterbacks coach San Francisco 49ers, 1994; head coach Houston Texans, 2006—. Achievements include asst. coach, Super Bowl Champion San Francisco 49ers, 1994, Den. Broncos 1997, 1998. Office: c/o Houston Texans 2 Reliant Park Houston TX 77054

KUBIC, CHARLES RICHARD, civil engineer; b. Greensburg, Pa., Dec. 7, 1950; s. William Louis and Josephine Roberta (Mologne) K.; m. Anne Renee Sheroda, July 29, 1972; children: Charles Brian, Kathryn Anne, Andrew William. BSCE, Lehigh U., 1972, MSCE, 1978. Registered profl. engr., Pa., Va. Commd. ensign CEC U.S. Navy, 1972, advanced through grades to rear admiral, 1998, ret., 2005; asst. head constrn. dept. OICC, Bangkok, 1973—75; co-comdr. NMCE Four, Port Hueneme, Calif., 1975—77; assignment officer Naval Mil. Pers. Command, Washington, 1978—80; asst. pub. works officer Nat. Naval Med. Ctr., Bethesda, Md., 1980—82; AOICC for design OICC Mediterranean, Madrid, 1982—85; White House fellow White House Office Policy Devel., 1985—86; dir. Strategic Programs Office Naval Facilities Engring. Command, Alexandria, Va., 1986—89; comdg. officer NMCB Three, Port Hueneme, 1989—91; prodn. officer Navy Pub. Works Ctr., Norfolk, Va., 1991—94; vice comdr. Atlantic Divsn. Navfacengcom, Norfolk, 1994—97; com 22NCR Norfolk, 1997—99; vice comdr. Navfacengcom, 1998—99; comdr. Third Naval Constrn. Brigade and PACNAVFACENGCOM, 1999—2002, First Naval Constrn. Divsn., 2002—05; pres. ECE Internat., 2005—. Contbr. articles to profl. jours. Scoutmaster Boy Scouts Am., Bangkok, 1973-75, cubmaster, Madrid, 1984, Va., 1985-87, 92-94. Decorated 3 Legion of Merit medals, 4 Meritorious Service medals; CNO scholar, 1977-78. Fellow Soc. Am. Mil. engrs.; mem. NSPE, U.S. Naval Inst., Phi Beta Kappa, Tau Beta Pi, Sigma Phi Epsilon. Republican. Roman Catholic. Avocations: golf, skiing, scuba diving, running. Office: 501 Clark St Clarks Green PA 18411 E-mail: kubicfam@worldnet.att.net.

KUBIDA, WILLIAM JOSEPH, lawyer; b. Newark, Apr. 3, 1949; s. William and Catherine (Gilchrist) K.; m. Mary Jane Hamilton, Feb. 4, 1984; children: Sara Gilchrist, Kathleen Hamilton. BSEE, USAF Acad., 1971; JD, Wake Forest U., 1979. Bar: N.C. 1979, U.S. Patent Office 1979, Ind. 1980, U.S. Dist. Ct. (no. dist.) Ind. 1980, U.S. Dist. Ct. (so. dist.) Ind. 1980, U.S. Ct. Appeals (7th cir.) 1981, U.S. Dist. Ct. Ariz. 1982, U.S. Ct. Appeals (9th and fed. cirs.) 1982, Ariz. 1982, Colo. 1990, U.S. Dist. Ct. Colo. 1990, U.S. Ct. Appeals (10th cir.) 1990. Patent and trademark atty. Lundy and Assocs., Ft. Wayne, Ind., 1979-81; patent atty. Motorola, Inc., Phoenix, 1981-85; intellectual property counsel Nippon Motorola, Ltd., Tokyo, 1985-87; ptnr. Lisa & Kubida, Phoenix, 1987-89; engring. law counsel Digital Equipment Corp., Colorado Springs, Colo., 1989-92; of counsel Holland & Hart, Denver, Colorado Springs, 1992-93, ptnr., chmn. intellectual property practice group, 1993-99; ptnr., dir. intellectual property practice group Hogan & Hartson LLP, Colorado Springs, 1999—. Bd. dirs. Colorado Springs Tech Incubator, Bd. dirs. Colorado Springs Tech. Incubator. 1st lt. USAF, 1971—76. Mem. Am. Intellectual Property Law Assn. (computer software sect.), Licensing Exec. Soc. (Pacific Rim subcom.), Country Club Colo., Mensa, Intertel, Federlist Soc., Aston Martin Owners Club, Phi Delta Phi. Republican. Mem. Christ Ch. Of Col. Springs. Office: Hogan & Hartson LLP Two N Cascade Ave Ste 1300 Colorado Springs CO 80903 Office Fax: 719-448-5909. Business E-Mail: wjkubida@hhlaw.com.

KUBIET, LEO LAWRENCE, media consultant; b. Apr. 11, 1924; s. Joseph J. and Laura Agnes (Bucy) Kubiet; m. Mary Jean Metz, Sept. 14, 1946; children: Lawrence Michael, Martin Alan. BA in Journalism and English, Fairmont State U., W. Va., 1949; postgrad., U. Mich., Ann Arbor, 1950, Wayne State U., Detroit, 1952, U. Detroit, 1953. With The News, Detroit, 1950-68; retail advt. mgr. St. Petersburg Times and Evening Ind., Fla., 1968-70, advt. mgr., 1970-75, advt. dir., 1975-76, corp. dir., 1976-89, v.p. advt., 1986-87, sr. v.p., 1987-89; dir. Modern Graphic Arts, Fla. Trend Mags., Inc. divsn. Semit Corp. Charter and hon. life mem. advt. adv. coun. U. Fla., 1978—, hon. life, 1995—; mem. Pres.'s Coun.; bd. dirs. U. Fla. Found., chmn. Embrace Excellence Campaign Fund Coll. Journalism, 1989—93; bd. govs. St. Petersburg Area of C. of C., 1979—83; bd. dirs. Tampa Bay Coun. Nat. Assn. Investors Corp., 1995—2000. Mem. advt. agy. rev. com. Fla. Lottery Commn.; bd. dirs. Fla. Orch., 1988—89, Hall of Fame Bowl, 1987—91; mem. fund raising com. St. Anthony's Hosp. Found., 1991—93; fin. com. vol. St. John Vianney Ch.; bd. dirs. Point Brittany Condo Two Corp., 1998—2003, v.p., 2000—01, treas., 2001—03. With Seabees USN, 1942—46. Mem.: Am. Newspaper Pubs. Assn. (plans com. 1975—89), Newspaper Advt. Bur., St. Petersburg Sales and Mktg. Execs. (pres. 1973—74), St. Petersburg Advt. Fedn. (bd. dirs., Silver medal 1977), Am. Press. Inst. (so. region adv. coun.), Internat. Newspaper Advt. and Mktg. Execs. (hon. life) (past pres.), Point Brittany Men's Round Table (v.p. 2004—, pres. 2005—, Man of Yr. 2004), KC (4th degree), Commerce Club Pinellas County (past pres.), Pt. Brittany Yacht Club (treas. 2001—03, commodore 2004—05, bd. govs. 2000—05), St. Petersburg Yacht Club. Roman Catholic. Avocations: golf, fishing, travel, computers, community service. Home: 5108 Brittany Dr S Apt 308 Saint Petersburg FL 33715-1525 Personal E-mail: LeJeKub@tampabay.rr.com.

KUBIK, TIMOTHY ROBERT WHITE, director, history educator; b. Sandy Point, Nova Scotia, Canada, Mar. 27, 1966; s. Robert William Kubik and Janet Ann Malins; m. Nancy J.M. Matchett, Aug. 17, 1967; children: Kenneth Ian, Sophia Lillian. PhD, Johns Hopkins U., 1997. Asst. dir. upper sch. The Ross Sch., East Hampton, NY, 1998—2002; chair history Kent Denver Sch., Englewood, Colo., 2002—. Curriculum cons. UN Assn. of US, NYC, 1999—2002. Mem.: Am. Hist. Assn., UN Assn. U.S. (pres. 2005—06). Independent. Avocations: fencing, running, historical miniatures, cross country skiing, horseback riding. Home: 5926 S Kenton St Englewood CO 80111 Office: Kent Denver Sch 4000 E Quincy Ave Englewood CO 80113 Home Phone: 720-200-0883; Office Phone: 303-770-7660 506. E-mail: tkubik@kentdenver.org.

KUBILUS, NORBERT JOHN, information technology executive; b. Newark, Oct. 6, 1948; s. Vity Leo and Ursula Eva (Yarusavage) K.; m. Linda J. Ferri, July 23, 1988; 1 child from previous marriage, Jessica Leigh; 1 stepchild, James M. Feigert. ScB cum laude, Seton Hall U., 1970; MS, Rensselaer Poly. Inst., 1973. Cert. data processor Inst. Cert. Computer Profls., 1982, sys. profl. Inst. Cert. Computer Profls., 1982, computing profl. Inst. Cert. Computer Profls., 1982, amb. Inst. Cert. Computer Profls., 1982. Rsch. asst. Rensselaer Poly. Inst., Troy, NY, 1971-72; systems programmer, analyst RAPIDATA, Fairfield, NJ, 1972-76, mgr. quality assurance, 1976-78, mgr. corp. support svcs., 1978-79, dir. software devel., 1979-81, asst. v.p., 1980-81; v.p., COO network svcs. divsn. NDC, Fairfield, 1981-83; v.p. info systems and tech. Ednl. Testing Svc., Princeton, NJ, 1983-86; mng. ptnr. Norda Group, Yardley, Pa., 1986-88; v.p., chief tech. officer Optimal Solutions, Inc., Hoboken, NJ, 1987-91; v.p., chief info. officer BCM, Inc., Plymouth Meeting, Pa., 1991-94; v.p. ops., chief info. officer Leading Hotels of World, Ltd., NYC, 1994-96; pres. DataLEAD Comms. Inc., 1995—96; mng. ptnr. Kubilus Ferri & Assocs., Yardley, Pa., 1996-2000; dir. ops. and fin. Stellcom, Inc., San Diego, 2000—01; ptnr. Tatum Ptnrs., San Diego, 2001—06; chief info. officer Sunterra Corp., North Las Vegas, Nev., 2004—. Reviewer Reston Pub. Co., Va.; adj. prof. NJ Inst. Tech., 1976—84; nat. lectr. Assn. Computing Machinery, 1976—80; prof. computer sci. Coll. NJ, 1997—2001; mem. assoc. faculty US Open U., 2000—01; advisor Ctr. Commercialization of Advanced Tech., 2002—; mem. adv. bd. Zybernetix, Inc., 2002—04, CIO Decisions, 2007—; chair CIO SIG San Diego Telecom Coun., 2003—04; bd. dirs. Teracenter Inc., Seasons At Aliante HOA; trustee Am. Resort Devel. Assn. Author: Developing Computer-Based Accounts Receivable, 1981, Manager's Guide to Distributed Data Processing, 1982, How to Implement Management Information Systems, 1983, How to Select Small Business Computer Software, 1984, Business Use of the Internet, 1997; columnist Computerworld; contbr. articles to profl. jours. Treas. Cedar Grove Jaycees, NJ, 1977; bd. dirs. Gathering Internat. Families Together, 1983—86. Decorated Order of Cross and Crescent, 1970; NSF tng. grantee, 1972; recipient Physics medal Seton Hall U., 1970, Tech. Leadership award Hewlett Packard Corp., 1993; Faculty fellow Coll. NJ, 1998-2001; named one of 100 IT Leaders Computerworld Premier, 2007. Mem.: Women in Tech. Internat. (mem. leadership coun. 2006—, chair tech. for tots), Am. Mgmt. Assn. (info. systems and tech. coun. 1985—, chmn.Year 2000 Forum 1998—2000, editor Mgmt. Handbook, 3d edit.), Assn. Info. Tech. Profls. (legis. network 1985—93, bd. dirs. 1988—91, 2002—, v.p. 2003, pres. 2004, chair legis. affairs com. 2005—, mem. awards com. 2006—, Individual Performance award 1987, 1989, 1990, 1998, 2003), Digital Equipment Computer Users Soc. (US exec. bd. 1977—81), Design Fin. Officers Group (vice chmn. 1992—93, chair

1993—94), Contingency Planning Exch., Assn. Computing Machinery (chair, Info. Mgmt. Working Group 2000—01), Inst. Cert. Computer Profls. (life; NJ state dir. 1989—90), Upsilon Pi Epsilon, Sigma Pi Sigma. Office: Sunterra Corp 3865 W Cheyenne Ave North Las Vegas NV 89032 Office Phone: 702-804-8600. Business E-Mail: nkubilus@sunterra.com.

KUBINA, JUNE M., elementary school educator, music educator; b. Madison, Wis., May 18, 1969; d. Joseph Patrick Sweeney and June Mary Schmidt; m. Wade E. Kubina, Sept. 14, 2002; 1 child, Roman Peter. MusB in Music Edn., U. Wis., 1996; MEd, Nat. Louis U., Chgo., 2002. Cert. tchr. instrumental music preK-12 grade Dept. Pub. Instrn., Wis., 1996, tchr. k-6 grade, 7-12 grade music Bd. Ednl. Examiners Lic. Iowa, 1996. Dir. bands Tri-County Cmty. Sch. Dist., Thornburg, Iowa, 1996—97; substitute tchr. Madison Met. Sch. Dist., Wis., 1997; dir. bands Musical Youth, Inc., Madison, 1998—99; instr. brass Madison Met. Schs., Wis., 1998—99; dir. bands Franklin Mid. Sch., Janesville, Wis., 1999—. Pvt. tchr. instrumental music, Janesville, Wis., 1987—; dir. summer band Wis. Rapids Sch. Dist., 1996; judge various festivals. Named Outstanding Am. Tchr., Nat. Honor Roll, 2006. Mem.: NEA, Nat. Assn. Music Edn., Wis. Youth Band Dir. Assn., Wis. Edn. Assn., Wis. Sch. Music Assn., Nat. Band Assn. (assoc.). Avocations: dogs, motorcycling, nature, camping, philosophy. Home: 3441 Sheffield Dr Janesville WI 53546 Office: Franklin Mid Sch 450 N Crosby Ave Janesville WI 53545 Home Phone: 608-279-8849; Office Phone: 608-743-6142. Office Fax: 608-743-6010. Personal E-mail: bandrocks@charter.net. Business E-Mail: jkubina@janesville.k12.wi.us.

KUBISTAL, PATRICIA BERNICE, educational consultant; b. Chgo., Jan. 19, 1938; d. Edward John and Bernice Mildred (Lenz) Kubistal. AB cum laude, Loyola U., Chgo., 1959, AM, 1964, AM, 1965, PhD, 1968; postgrad., Chgo. State Coll., 1962, Ill. Inst. Tech., 1963, State U. Iowa, 1963, Nat. Coll. Edn., 1974-75. With Chgo. Bd. Edn., 1959-93, tchr., 1959-63, counselor, 1963-65, adminstrv. intern, 1965-66, asst. to dist. supt., 1966-69, prin. spl. edn. sch., 1969-75; prin. Simpson Sch., 1975-76, Brentano Sch., 1975-87, Roosevelt H.S., 1987, Haugan Sch., 1989; prin. Cook County Juvenile Temporary Detention Ctr. Sch. Jones Met. H.S. Bus. and Commerce, 1989-90, adminstr. dept. spl. edn., 1990-93; supr. Lake View Evening Sch., 1982-92, ednl. cons., 1993—. Lectr. Loyola U. Sch. Edn., Nat. Coll. Edn. Grad. Sch., Mundelein Coll., 1982-91, DePaul U., 1998-99; coord. Upper Bound Program of U. Ill. Circle Campus, 1966-68. Book rev. editor of Chgo. Prins. Jour., 1970-76, gen. editor, 1982-90. Active Crusade of Mercy; mem. com. Ill. Constnl. Conv., 1967-69; mem. Citizens Sch. Com., 1969-71; mem. edn. com. Field Mus., 1971; ednl. advisor North Side Chgo. PTA Region, 1975; gov. Loyola U., 1961-87; pres. St. Matthews Parish Coun., 1995-98. Recipient Outstanding Intern award Nat. Assn. Secondary Sch. Prins., 1966, Outstanding Prin. award Citizen's Sch. Com. of Chgo., 1986; named Outstanding History Tchr., Chgo. Pub. Schs., 1963, Oustanding Ill. Educator, 1970, one of Oustanding Women of Ill., 1970, St. Luke's Logan Sq. Cmty. Person of Yr., 1977; NDEA grantee, 1963, NSF grantee, 1965, HEW Region 5 grantee for drug edn., 1974, Chgo. Bd. Edn. Prins.' grantee for study robotics in elem. schs.; U. Chgo. adminstrv. fellow 1984. Mem. Ill. Personnel and Guidance Assn., NEA, Ill. Edn. Assn., Chgo. Edn. Assn., Am. Acad. Polit. and Social Sci., Chgo. Prins. and Adminstrs. Assn. (pres. aux.), Nat. Coun. Adminstrv. Women, Chgo. Coun. Exceptional Children, Loyal Christian Benevolent Assn., Kappa Gamma Pi, Pi Gamma Mu, Phi Delta Kappa, Delta Kappa Gamma (paliamentarian 1979-80, pres. Kappa chpt. 1988-90, Lambda state editor 1982-92, chmn. Lambda state comm. com. 1992, Internat. Golden Gift Fund award), Delta Sigma Rho, Phi Sigma Tau. Home and Office: 5111 N Oakley Ave Chicago IL 60625-1829

KUBLER, FRANK LAWRENCE, lawyer; s. Frank Martin and Esther Helen (Flora) K. AA, Miami-Dade Jr. Coll., 1978; BS in Mech. Engring., U. Miami, Coral Gables, Fla., 1981, BA in History, 1982, JD, 1986. Bar: Fla. 1986, U.S. Cir. Ct. (11th cir) 1988, U.S. Cir. Ct. (fed. cir.) 1989, U.S. Patent Office 1987. Assoc. Dominik, Stein, Saccocio, Reese, Colitz & Van der Wall, Miami Lakes, Fla., 1986-90; pres. Law Office of Frank L. Kubler, Miami Lakes, 1990—; cons. Oltman, Flynn & Kubler, Ft. Lauderdale, Fla., 1990-96, ptnr., 1996—. Mem. Inter-Am. Law Rev., 1985. Mem. Patent Law Assn. South Fla. (v.p. 1993-94, pres. 1994-95), Mensa, Rotary (dir. 1992-94, chmn. scholarship com. 1994-95), Tau Beta Pi. Office: 915 Middle River Dr Ste 415 Fort Lauderdale FL 33304-3561 Office Phone: 305-829-1869. Personal E-mail: frankkubler@msn.com.

KUBO, EDWARD HACHIRO, JR., prosecutor; b. Honolulu, July 9, 1953; s. Edward H. and Rose M. (Coltes) K.; children: Diana K., Dawn M., Edward H. III. BA in Polit. Sci., U. Hawaii, 1976; JD, U. San Diego, 1979. Bar: Hawaii 1979. Legal asst. Legal Aid Soc. Hawaii, 1975-76; law clk. Kobayashi & Watanabe, Honolulu, 1979; dep. pros. atty. Honolulu City Prosecutor's Office, 1980-83, 85-90; assoc. Carlsmith & Dwyer, Honolulu, 1983-85; asst. US atty. Hawaii US Dept. Justice, Honolulu, 1990—2001, US atty. Hawaii, 2001—. Instr. Honolulu Police Dept. Acad., Waipahu, Hawaii, 1986-89; lectr. US Dept. Justice, Lincoln, Neb., 1997, Pearl Harbor Police Acad., 1995, Western State Vice Investigators Assn. Conf., Houston, 1997, Las Vegas, 1998; spkr. teleconf. US Dept. Justice Violence Against Women Act, 1998, Hawaii Bar Assn. H.S. Mock trial adv., 1996-99. Co-author: Concurrent Jurisdiction for Civil RICO, 1987. Recipient Nat. Art medal (France), 1992, Cert. of Appreciation, US Immigration and Naturalization Svc., 1992, Drug Enforcement Adminstrn., 1997, Plaque of Appreciation, US Border Patrol, 1995, cert. appreciation Bureau Alcohol, Tobacco & Firearms, 1999. Mem. Hawaii Bar Assn., Order of Barristers.*

KUBY, RONALD LAWRENCE, lawyer; b. Cleve., July 31, 1956; s. Donald Joseph Kuby and Ruth Miller; m. Marilyn Vasta, Jan. 24, 2006; 1 child, Emma Sojourner Vasta-Kuby. BA, U. Kans., 1979; JD magna cum laude, Cornell U., 1983. Bar: N.Y. 1984. Assoc. Kunstler & Kuby, NYC, 1994—95, Law Office William M. Kunstler, NYC, 1984—94; ptnr. Law Office Ronald L. Kuby, NYC, 1996—2004, Kuby & Percz, LLP, 2004—. Contbr. articles to profl. jours.; guest anchor: (TV series) Ct. TV; WABC Radio. Mem. adv. bd. police misconduct task force N.Y. Civil Liberties Union, 1999—. Named Outstanding On-Air Broadcast Personality, N.Y. State Broadcasters Assn., 2005; recipient Thurgood Marshall award, N.Y. City Bar Assn., 1998, Achievement in Radio Best Talk Show Host award, N.Y. Metro, 2000, 2001, award for excellence in 9/11 broadcasting, UFA/UFOA (N.Y. Firefighters), 2003, Radio and Rec. Industry award for best local talk show host in Am., 2004. Communist. Office: 119 W 23rd St New York NY 10011 Home Phone: 212-677-1740. E-mail: ronkuby@aol.com.*

KUC, JOSEPH A., research scientist; b. NYC, Nov. 24, 1929; s. Peter and Helen (Dubec) K.; m. Karola Ingrid Maywald, July 17, 1991; children: Paul D., Rebecca R., Miriam A. BS, Purdue U., 1951, MS, 1953, PhD, 1955. Asst. prof. Purdue U., West Lafayette, Ind., 1955—59, assoc. prof., 1959—63, prof., 1963—74, U. Ky., Lexington, 1974—95, prof. emeritus, 1995—. Contbr. over 300 articles to profl. jours. Pres. Cen. Ky. ACLU, Lexington, 1977-79. Mem. Am. Chem. Soc., Am. Phytopathol. Soc., Am. Soc. Plant Physiologists, Am. Soc. for Biochemistry and Molecular Biology, N.Y. Acad. Sci., Phytochem. Soc., Ky. Acad. Sci., Sigma Xi. Avocations: hiking, gardening, conversation. Home and Office: 5502 Lorna St Torrance CA 90503

KUCERA, DANIEL WILLIAM, retired bishop; b. Chgo., May 7, 1923; s. Joseph F. and Lillian C. (Petrzelka) K. BA, St. Procopius Coll., 1945; MA, Catholic U. Am., 1950, PhD, 1954. Joined Order of St. Benedict, 1944, ordained priest Roman Cath. Ch., 1949. Registrar St. Procopius Coll. and Acad., Lisle, Ill., 1945—49, St. Procopius Coll., Lisle, Ill., 1954—56, acad. dean, head dept. edn., 1956—59, pres., 1959—65; abbot St. Procopius Abbey, Lisle, 1964—71; pres. Ill. Benedictine Coll. (formerly St. Procopius Coll.), Lisle, 1971—76, chmn. bd. trustees, 1976—78; aux. bishop Joliet, Ill., 1977—80; bishop of Salina Kans., 1980—83; archbishop of Dubuque Iowa, 1983—95; ret., 1995. Mem.: KC (4 degree). Roman Catholic. Personal E-mail: dwkucera@aol.com.

KUCHEMAN, CLARK ARTHUR, philosophy and religious studies educator; b. Akron, Ohio, Feb. 7, 1931; s. Merlin Carlyle and Lucile (Clark) K.; m. Melody Elaine Frazer, Nov. 15, 1986. BA, U. Akron, 1952; BD, Meadville Theol. Sch., 1955; MA in Econs., U. Chgo., 1959, PhD, 1965. Instr., then asst. prof. U. Chgo., 1961-67; prof. Claremont (Calif.) McKenna Coll., 1967—, Claremont Grad. Sch., 1967—. Co-author: Belief and Ethics, 1978, Creative Interchange, 1982, Economic Life, 1988; contbg. editor: The Life of Choice, 1978; contbr. articles to profl. jours. 1st lt. USAF, 1955—57. Mem. Am. Acad. Religion, Hegel Soc. Am., N.Am. Soc. for Social Philosophy. Democrat. Home: 10160 60th St Riverside CA 92509-4745 Office: Claremont McKenna Coll Dept Philosophy Religon Pitzer Hall 850 Columbia Ave Claremont CA 91711-6420 Office Phone: 909-607-7980. Business E-Mail: clark.kucheman@claremontmckenna.edu. *Education and life itself have the same purpose, and, borrowing words from G. W. F. Hegel, ".the final purpose of education is liberation and the struggle for a higher liberation still.".*

KUCHNER, EUGENE FREDERICK, neurosurgeon, educator, neuroscientist; b. NYC, 1945; s. Morton H. and Edna Estelle Kuchner; m. Joan Ruth Freedman, Sept. 2, 1968; children: Marc Jason, Eric Benjamin. AB, Johns Hopkins U., 1967; MD, U. Chgo., 1971. Diplomate Am. Bd. Neurol. Surgery, Am. Bd. Med. Examiners. Resident in surgery Yale U. Sch. Medicine, New Haven, 1971—72; postdoc. fellow Yale U., New Haven, 1972; resident in neurosurgery Montreal Neurol. Inst., McGill U., Que., Canada, 1972—76, spine fellow, 1976; neurosurgeon SUNY Downstate Sch. Medicine, Bklyn., 1976—79, SUNY Sch. Medicine, Stony Brook, 1979—97, assoc. prof., 1983—; cons. neurosurgeon North Shore U. Hosp./NYU Sch. Medicine, 1997—. Mem. staff North Shore U. Hosp.-Cornell Med. Ctr., 1977—97, cons. surgeon, 1992—97; mem. neurosurgery attending staff Univ. Hosp., Stony Brook, 1979—97, Nassau County Med. Ctr., 1977—2000, St. John's Episcopal Hosp., 1976—99, Mt. Sinai-NYU Health Sys., 1997—; clin. assoc. prof. neurosurgery Cornell U. Med. Coll., NY, 1990—97. Contbr. articles to profl. publs.; specialist in microsurgery, magnetic resonance imaging, spinal trauma, pituitary surgery. Recipient K.G. McKenzie Meml. award, Royal Coll. Physicians and Surgeons Can., 1976, Open Scholarship award, Johns Hopkins U., yearly, 1963—66, Scholarship award, U. Chgo., yearly, 1967—70; fellow, NSF, Blackman-Hoffman Found., 1969—70; NSF chemistry fellow, MIT, 1968, USPHS fellowship, Divsn. Epidemiology Columbia U. Sch. Pub. Health, N.Y.C., 1969. Mem. ACS, AMA, Am. Assn. Neurol. Surgeons, Congress Neurol. Surgeons, NY Acad. Scis., LI Neurosci. Acad., Suffolk Acad. Medicine, Montreal Neurol. Ins. Fellows Soc., NY State Neurosurg. Soc., NY State Med. Soc., NY State Soc. Surgeons, Am. Coll. Med. Quality, Healthcare Info. and Mgmt. Sys. Soc., Am. Epilepsy Soc., Am. Soc. Law Medicine and Ethics, Yale Surg. Soc., Yale Club NYC, Sigma Xi. Office: Stony Brook Med Ctr PO Box 721 Stony Brook NY 11790-0721

KUCHNER, MARC JASON, astrophysicist; b. Montreal, Que., Can., Aug. 7, 1972; s. Eugene and Joan Kuchner. AB in Physics, Astronomy and Astrophysics, Harvard U., Cambridge, Mass., 1994; PhD in Astronomy, Calif. Inst. Tech., Pasadena, 2000. Postdoctoral fellow Harvard-Smithsonian Ctr. for Astrophysics, Cambridge, 2000—03, Princeton U., NJ, 2003—05; astrophysicist NASA Goddard Space Flight Ctr., Greenbelt, Md., 2005—. Mem.: BMI, Am. Astron. Soc. Achievements include invention of Band-Limited Masks and Eighth-Order masks, tools for finding extrasolar planets; research in theory of planet formation and planet-disk interactions; discovery of first example of comet dust around a white dwarf star. Office: NASA Goddard Space Flight Ctr Code 667 Greenbelt MD 20771 E-mail: marc.kuchner@nasa.gov.

KUCHTA, RONALD ANDREW, museum director, editor, curator; b. Lackawanna, NY, June 23, 1935; s. Andrew and Clara May (Barnes) K.; m. Sique Stoll, Oct. 1, 1970 (div. 1974). BA, Kenyon Coll., 1957; MA, Western Res. U., 1961; postgrad. in mgmt., Cornell U., 1979. Curator Chrysler Mus., Provincetown, Mass., 1961-68, Santa Barbara (Calif.) Mus. Art, Calif., 1968-74; dir. Everson Mus. Art, Syracuse, NY, 1974-95; editor Am. Ceramics mag., 1995; dir. Loveed Fine Arts, NYC, 1995. Adj. prof. Syracuse U., 1974—95; trustee Fondo del Sol, Washington, 1974—, Nat. Conf. Educators of Ceramic Arts, 1986, Quarry Rd. Sculpture Pk., Cazenovia, NY; founding dir. Syracuse China Ctr. for Study of Am. Ceramics; chmn. Urban Arts Commn., Syracuse, 1992—93; juror Mino '89 Internat. Competition for Ceramics, Gifu, Japan, 1989, Concorso Internat. della Ceramica d'Arte, Faenza, Italy, 1990, Biennale Nat. de Ceramique, Trois Rivieres, Que., Canada, 1992, 2d Cairo Internat. Biennale Ceramics, 1994, Mainline Art Ctr., Phila., 1997, San Angelo (Tex.) Ceramic Nat., 1998, Ariz. Commn. on the Arts, 1999, 1st World Biennale for Ceramics, Ichon, Republic of Korea, 2001, 2d World Biennale for Ichon, 2003, No. Clay Ctr. McKnight Awards, Mpls., 2003; bd. dirs. Watershed Ctr., North Edgecomb, Maine, Longhouse Res., Easthampton, NY, Mus. Ceramic Art, NYC, The Antonia and Vladimer Kulaev Cultural Heritage Fund Inc., LA; lectr. U. Regina, Sask., Canada, Mimar Sinan U., Istanbul, Turkey, Alta. Coll. Art, Calgary, Calif. Conf. Advancement of Ceramic Art, Davis, Nat. Mus. History, Taipei, Taiwan, 1993, Japan Soc., NYC, 1994, Czech Ceramic Design Ctr., Cesky Krumlov, 1996, Internat. Acad. Ceramics, Nagoya, Japan, 1996, Nat. Arts Club, NYC, Bard Coll., NYC, 1997, Cleve. Mus. Art, Stetson U., DeLand, Fla., Washington U., St. Louis, 1997, Santa Barbara City Coll., 1998, Cotta Terra Symposium, Deruta, Italy, 1998, Konstfack U. Coll. Arts, Crafts and Design, Stockholm, 1998, Royal Coll. Art, London, 1998, Oslo (Norway) Internat. Ceramic Symposium, 2003, Arundal Coll., Anapolis, Md., Anne Arundel Coll., Arnold, Md., 2005—; curator Enigmatic Visions/Sublime Forms Contemporary Japanese, 1998, Ceramic Longhouse Res., Easthampton; US commr. World Biennale for Ceramics, Republic of Korea, 2005; spkr. in field. Author: Mayan Figurines, 1971, Interior Vision, 1971, Modern Mexican Art, 1972, Provincetown Painters, 1975, Batuz: Works in Paper, 1981, Robert Beauchamp: An American Expressionist, 1984, The Elegiac and the Primordial: Ceramics at the End of the Twentieth Century, 1997, Consuming Ceramics: Its Classification and Place in the U.S. Art Market, 2001, Norwegian Clay and the Possible Superiority of Ceramics, 2003, Elimination and Affirmation: The Potent Process of the Jury, Alberto Mingotti; pub.: A Century of Ceramics in the U.S., 1979, American Ceramics: Collection of Everson Museum of Art, 1989; author: Sedalia, Missouri Daum Museum of Art, (catalog) Romancing Clay, The Ceramics of Peter Callas, 2007; translator: Pre-Hispanic Art: Time and Culture, 1997; Women Touch: Ceramics. Commr. 3d World CeramicBiennale, Republic of Korea, 2004—. With US Army, 1958—60. Mem.: Assn. Art Mus. Dirs. (emeritus), Nat. Arts Club, Internat. Acad. Ceramics, Phi Kappa Sigma. Democrat. Episcopalian. Home: 60 Sutton Pl S New York NY 10022-4168 Office: Loveed Gallery 575 Madison Ave New York NY 10022 Home Phone: 212-753-9030; Office Phone: 212-661-4397, 212-605-0591. Personal E-mail: ronkuch9876@aol.com.

KUCHYNSKI, MARIE, physician; b. Cleve., Sept. 23, 1964; d. Harry Gregory and Albina (Guarnera) K.; m. K. William Burdick; children: Nicole, Stephanie. BA, Case Western Reserve U., 1986, MD, 1990. Diplomate in internal medicine and in rheumatology Am. Bd. Internal Medicine. Intern U. Hosps. Cleve., 1990-91, resident, 1991-93; pvt. practice Elyria, Ohio, 1995-98, Brunswick, Ohio, 1998—. Mem. utilization mgmt. com. Cleve. Health Network, 1996-98; med. advisor Tri-City Lupus Project, 1997-98. Rheumatology fellow U. Hosps. Cleve., 1993-95. Mem. AMA, Am. Coll. Physicians, Am. Coll. Rheumatology, Cleve. Soc. Rheumatology, Internat. Soc. Clin. Densitometry, Phi Beta Kappa. Democrat. Roman Catholic. Avocations: gardening, crafts, piano. Home: 21503 Brookfield Pl Strongsville OH 44149 Office: Univ Primary Care Practice 3812 Center Rd Brunswick OH 44212-3024 Office Phone: 330-220-8411. Personal E-mail: mkuchynski@aol.com.

KUCIC, JOSEPH, management consultant, industrial engineer, network engineer, information security specialist; b. Mali Losinj, Croatia, Yugoslavia, Dec. 21, 1964; came to U.S., 1967, naturalized, 1974; s. Roman Kucic and Esterina (Karcic) Milevoj; m. Gia Michelle Bonavisa, Sept. 11, 1992; children: Ann Marie, Jillian Michelle. AAS, Coll. of Aeronautics, 1984; BS, Thomas A. Edison State Coll., 1986; B in Tech., N.Y. Inst. Tech., 1986; MBA, St. John's U., Jamaica, NY, 1989. Cert. info. sys. security profl. Internat. Info. Sys. Security Cert. Consortium, 2004, cert profl. Microsoft, 1998, cert. design assoc. CNCO, 1998, network assoc. Cisco, 1998. Workload planner Butler Aviation-Newark, Inc., Newark, 1984-85; tech. planner N.Y. Airlines, Flushing, NY, 1985-86; product support engr. United Techs.-Pratt & Whitney, East Hartford, Conn., 1986; indsl. engr. Montefiore Med. Ctr., Bronx, 1986-88; sr. work mgmt. analyst Bank Leumi Trust Co., NYC, 1988-89; sr. methods analyst Salomon Bros., Inc., NYC, 1989-92; mgmt. cons. United Mgmt. Techs., NYC, 1992-93; sr. sys. analyst Met. Hosp. Ctr. N.Y.C. Health & Hosp. Corp. Metro. Hosp. Ctr., 1993; dir. info. svcs. N.Y.C. Health & Hosp. Corp. Bronx Mcpl. Hosp. Ctr., 1993-94; project mgr. Montefiore Med. Ctr., Bronx, 1994-96, ANS Comms., Inc., Elmsford, NY, 1996; mgr. infrastructure planning, divsn. of Am. Online ANS Comms., Inc., 1996-97; mgr. KPMG Peat Marwick, Hawthorne, NY, 1997-98; sr. mgr. KPMG LLP, NYC, 1998-2000; dir. profl. svcs. Network Assocs., Inc., 1999; mng. dir. Pricewaterhouse Coopers, LLP, NYC, 2000—02; cons. GM Asset Mgmt., NYC, 2002—04; v.p., exec. technology advisor Computer Assocs. Internat., 2004—. Spkr. in field. Contbr. articles to profl. jours. Mem.: Internat. Info. Sys. Security Sys. Cert. Consortium, Info. Sys. Audit and Control Assn., Info. Sys. Security Assn., Asn. Computing Machinery Computer Security Inst., Coll. Aeronautics Alumni Asn. (pres. 1990-92), SAE (affiliate), AIAA, IEEE (assoc.), Inst. Indsl. Engr. (chpt. pres. 1988-89, chmn. bd. N.Y.C. chpt. 1989-90, bd. govs. 1988-92, Cert. of Recognition 1988) (sr.), St. John's Univ. Col. Bus. Admin. Alumni Asn. (bd. dir. 1991-93), Wings Club N.Y., Tau Alpha Pi. Republican. Roman Catholic. Avocation: tennis. Office: 1351 Washington Blvd Ste 800 Stamford CT 06702 Personal E-mail: jkucic@mail.com.

KUCIJ, TIMOTHY MICHAEL, engineer, minister, musician; b. Whittier, Calif., Sept. 2, 1954; m. Paulina V. Jimenez, 1979. Studied with Frank Sanucci, Edward D. Berryman, Thurla Wallis, Kathreen Prout, Eddy L. Manson, Henry Charles Smith, Joseph P. Free, Ronald Gearman, 1965—78; student, Sherwood Music Conservatory, Chgo., 1965—68; BA in Music, Calif. State Poly. U., Pomona, 1978; ThM cum laude, Christian Bible Coll., 1983; grad. studies, Maranatha Bapt. Bible Coll., Ctrl. Bapt. Theol. Sem. Licensed minister Bapt. Ch., 1982. Tech. writer Honeywell Inc., West Covina (Calif.) and Mpls., 1977-84; reliability engr. Advanced Systems divsn. Northrop Corp., Pico Rivera, Calif., 1984-86; sr. engr. quality and reliability Swedlow, Inc., Garden Grove, Calif., 1986-88, mgr., quality assurance, composites divsn., 1988-90, quality assurance staff specialist, 1990-92; div. quality assurance engr. Rexroth Corp. Piston Pump divsn., Fountain Inn, SC, 1992-94; sr. quality engr. Hi-Shear Corp., Torrance, Calif., 1996-98; sr. quality sys. mgr. TRW Automotive, Carson, Calif., 1998—2004; short term assignments, consulting in quality mgmt., 2004—. Lectr. tech. and engring.; tchr. piano, organ and composition, 1971—81; active pulpit supply local Bapt. Chs., Calif., SC. Performer: (organ, piano) Debut, 1966, (pipe organ) Wiltern Theater, 1966—68, Busch-Reisinger Mus. Harvard U., 1972, 1973, 1974; composer: scores of original piano pieces including Persistence and The Storm, Purity, Remembrance, Your Song, Yearning, Compassion, A Little Jingle, A Familiar Song, Images, Paulina, Afterthought, Blue Fragrance, Sunset, Then, Piano Lesson # 1, Chase, Unrest, Nebulae, Distress, Retrograde, Frolic, The Happy Whistler, The Little Toy March, Hope, Teardrops, Reminisce, Wind Chimes, A Place Somewhere, Rainbows, The Bicentennial Rag, The Pulsar Rag, Dazzling Fingers, The Butterfly Rag, Serenity, first 25 original pieces written in honor of Am. bicentennial; music housed in: LA County Libr., Seattle Pub. Libr., Dallas Pub. Libr., Denver Pub. Libr., LA Pub. Libr., St. Louis Pub. Libr., Atlanta-Fulton County Libr., Master's Coll. Libr., Calif. State Poly. U. Libr., Archive Contemporary Music, Phila. Free Libr., Juilliard Sch. Music Libr., Calif. Bapt. Coll. Libr., Biola U. Libr., NY Pub. Libr., Cleve. Pub. Libr., Boston Pub. Libr., Harvard U. Libr., Chicago Pub. Libr., U. Kans. Gorton Music Libr., among others; musician: (recordings) KRC Records, 1993—, A Place Somewhere, 1993, 2003, LifeSongs, 1993, 2003; concertized nationally (piano, pipe organ), scored comprehensive piano arrangements Jesus Loves Me, Over the Rainbow, songwriter Jesus is the Answer, O Jesus; editor: The Golden State Baptist, 1995—96; contbr. articles to various periodicals. Asst. to local pastors Bapt. chs. in Tex., Ga., Wis., Minn., and Calif., 1978—82; pastor Victory Bapt. ch., Pine City, Minn., 1982—83; music dir., Bible tchr. Calvary Bapt. Ch., La Verne, Calif., 1988—92, mem. sch. bd., ch. coun., 1989—92; music dir., youth dir. Covina Bapt. Temple, 1985—87; pastor First Missionary Bapt. Ch., Gardena, Calif., 1994—96; bd. dirs. Garden Grove Symphony Orch., 1989—90. Named one of Outstanding Young Men in Am., US Jaycees, 1980; recipient First prize, So. Calif. Organ Competition, 1966, Performer's cert., 1967, Disting. Alumnus award, Calif. State Poly. U., 1989. Mem.: Christian Fellowship Art Music Composers, Broadcast Music, Inc., Am. Symphony Orch. League, Am. Soc. Quality, Creation Rsch. Soc., Am. Composer's Forum. Republican. Baptist. Personal E-mail: tkucij@ca.rr.com.

KUCINICH, DENNIS JOHN, congressman; b. Cleve., Oct. 8, 1946; s. Frank and Virginia Kucinich; m. Elizabeth Harper, Aug. 21, 2005; 1 child. Student, Cleve. State U.; BA in Speech and Comm., Case Western Res. U., 1973, MA in Speech and Comm. V.p. sales & mktg. Town and Country Printing, Cleve.; mem. city coun. City of Cleve., 1970—75, Ohio, 1981—82, mayor, 1977-79; clk. of cts. Mcpl. Ct., Cleve., 1976—77; pres. K Comm., Cleve., 1985—95; mem. Ohio State Senate, 1994—96, US Congress from 10th Ohio dist., 1997—, mem. edn. and labor com., mem. oversight and govt. reform com., chmn. domestic policy subcommittee. US del. UN Conv. Climate Change, 1998, 2004. Author: A Prayer for America, 2003. Recipient Outstanding Senator of Yr. award NASW, 1996, Green Thumb award, League of Conservation Voters, 1997, Charles Van Riper award, Nat. Coun. Communicative Disorders, 1998, Oak Tree award Ohio PTA, 1999, Congl. Appreciation award, Operation Lifesaver, 2000, Champion for Peace award, Military Families Speak Out, 2007; named Outstanding Pub. Official, Internat. Eagles. Mem.: Internat. Alliance of Theatrical Stage Employees, Moving Picture Technicians, Artists and Allied Crafts of the US. Democrat. Roman Catholic. Office: 14400 Detroit Ave Lakewood OH 44107 Office Phone: 202-225-5871, 216-228-8850. Office Fax: 216-228-6465.*

KUCZWARA, THOMAS PAUL, federal agency administrator, lawyer; b. Dec. 21, 1951; s. Stanley Leo and Eleanore (Pawelko) K.; m. Diana Lynn Rychtarczyk, Sept. 8, 1979; 1 child, Paul Stanley. BA, Loyola U., Chgo., 1973; JD, U. S.C., 1976. Bar: Ill. 1976, U.S. Dist. Ct. (no. dist.) Ill. 1982. Assoc. Doria Law Offices, Chgo., 1977-78; asst. corp. counsel City of Chgo., 1978-80; asst. city atty. City of Aurora, Ill., 1980-82; postal insp. U.S. Postal Inspection Svc., Salt Lake City, 1982-85, regional insp. atty. cen. region Chgo., 1985—. Mem. St. Bartholomew's Parish Coun., Chgo., 1978; vol. atty. Lawyers for Creative Arts, 1978. Ill. state scholar, 1969.

Mem. Sierra Club, Pi Sigma Alpha. Roman Catholic. Office: US Postal Inspection Svc Chgo Divsn 433 W Harrison 6th Fl Chicago IL 60669-2201 Office Phone: 312-983-6227. E-mail: tpkuczwara@uspis.gov.

KUCZYNSKI, PEDRO-PABLO, Prime Minister of Peru; b. Lima, Peru, Oct. 3, 1938; s. Maxime and Madeleine Louise (Godard) K.; married; 4 children. BA, Exeter Coll., Oxford U., Eng., 1959; M.P.A., Princeton U., 1961. Economist World Bank, 1961-67, sr. economist, 1971-73; dep. dir.-gen. Central Res. Bank Peru, 1967-69; sr. economist Internat. Monetary Fund, Washington, 1969-71; v.p., ptnr. Kuhn, Loeb & Co. Internat., NYC, 1973-75; dir. dept. econs. Internat. Finance Corp., Washington, 1975-77; pres., chief exec. officer Halco Mining Inc., Pitts., 1977-80; chmn., mng. dir. First Boston Internat. Co., NYC, 1982-92; former pres., CEO Westfield Capital Ltd., Miami, Fla.; minister of energy and mines Peru, 1980-82; minister of economy and finance, 2001—02, 2004—05; Prime Minister, 2005—. Mem. Univ. Club (Washington), Pitts. Golf Club, Racquet and Tennis Club. Office: Presidencia del Consejo de Ministros Avenida 28 Julio 878 Miraflores Lima Peru Office Phone: 011 511 221 2609.

KUDELKA, JAMES, choreographer, artistic director; b. Newmarket, Ont., Can. Student, Nat. Ballet Sch., Toronto. Dancer Nat. Ballet of Can., Toronto, 1972-81, artist in residence, 1992-96; prin. dancer Les Grands Ballets Canadiens, Montreal, 1981-84, resident choreographer, 1984-90; works created for San Francisco and Joffrey Ballets, Am. Ballet Theatre, Birmingham Royal Ballet; artistic dir. Nat. Ballet Can., Toronto, 1995—2005, resident choreographer, 2005—. Choreographer (ballets) Sonata, Nat. Ballet of Can., 1973, Apples, 1974, A Party, 1976, Washington Square, 1977, 1979, Bach Pas de Deux, 1979, Windsor Pas de Deux, 1979, The Rape of Lucrece, 1980, Playhouse, 1980, All Night Wonder, 1981, Dido and Aeneas, 1982, Unfinished Business, 1984, Death of an Old Queen, 1985, Dracula, 1985, Collisions, 1986, Vers la Glace, 1986, The Heart of the Matter, 1986, Soudain d'Hiver Dernier, 1987, Signatures, 1988, In Camera, 1988, The Wakey Nights, 1989, Scheherazade, 1989, Divertissement Schumann, 1989, There, below, 1989, The Comfort Zone, 1989, Love Dracula, 1989, Pastorale, 1990, Violin Concerto, 1990, Romeo and Juliet Before Painting, 1990, Romance, 1990, Musings, 1991, Desir, 1991, Mixed Program, 1991, Mirror, 1991, This Isn't the End, 1991, The First Dance, 1992, The Miraculous Mandarin, 1993, Vittoria Pas De Deux, 1993, Ghosts, 1993, New York, 1993, Making Ballet, 1993, The Actress, 1994, Spring Awakening, 1994, Gluck Pas De Deux, 1994, Heroes, 1994, The Nutcracker, 1995, Solo for Rex, 1995, Missing, 1995, I'm a Stranger Here Myself, 1996, A Piece for Walter, 1996, Daisy's Dead, 1996, The Four Seasons, 1997, Les Chemins de L'Amour, 1998, Swan Lake, 1999, A Disembodied Voice, 1999, The Firebird, 2000, Nora's Tarantella, 2000, The Contract, Nat. Ballet Can., 2002, Chacony, 2004, Cinderella, 2004, An Italian Straw Hat, 2005, (ballets) Genesis, Les Grands Ballets Canadiens, 1982, In Paradisum, 1983, Alliances, 1984, Le Sacre du Printemps, 1987, La Salle des Pas Perdus, 1988, Concerto Grosso, 1988, Cruel World, Am. Ballet Theatre, 1994, Sin and Tonic, 2002, States of Grace, 1995, Dreams of Harmony, San Francisco Ballet, 1987, The End, 1992, Terra Firma, 1995, Some Women and Men, 1998, Le Baiser de la fée, Birmingham Royal Ballet, The Book of Alleged Dances, Australian Ballet, 1999, Fifteen Heterosexual Duets, Toronto Dance Theatre, Six Tableaus for the Sexually Challenged, Montreal Danse, Gazebo Dances, 2003, Cinderella, 2004, Passage, 1981, Intimate Letter, 1981, Hedda, 1983, Court of Miracles, 1983. Office: Walter Carsen Centre for The Nat Ballet of Can 470 Queens Quay W Toronto ON Canada M5V 3K4 E-mail: info@ballet.ca.

KUDISCH, MARC, actor; b. Hackensack, NJ, Sept. 22, 1966; s. Raymond and Florence Kudisch. BFA, Fla. Atlantic U., 1988. TV spokesperson Toyota, 1999—2000. Actor: (Broadway plays) Joseph and the Amazing Technicolor Dreamcoat, 1993, Beauty and the Beast, 1995—97, The Scarlet Pimpernel, 1997, High Society, 1998, The Wild Party, 2000, Bells Are Ringing, 2001, Thoroughly Modern Millie, 2002, Assassins, 2004, Chitty Chitty Bang Bang, 2005, (nat. tour) Bye Bye Birdie, 1992; (plays) Another Antigone, 1988, Tamara: The Living Movie, Quiet on the Set, Forever Plaid, Phantom of the Opera, Jekyll & Hyde, The Prince and the Pauper, 2001, A Little Night Music, 2002, No Strings, 2003, The Thing About Men, 2003, A Little Night Music, 2004, The Highest Yellow, 2004, See What I Wanna See, 2005, Broadway by the Year: 1926, 2004; actor & dir.: plays Broadway by the Year: 1963, 2004, Broadway by the Year: 1930, 2006; actor: (TV films) Bye Bye Birdie, 1995, (guest appearances) Sex & the City, 1999, One Life to Live, 2005, All My Children, 2005. Mailing: c/o Bauman Redanty & Shaul Talent Agency 250 West 57 St Ste 2223 New York NY 10019

KUDISH, DAVID J., financial executive; b. NYC, Aug. 10, 1943; s. L. Ben and Nellie D. (Kaufman) K.; m. Sheri K. Ross-Kudish; children: Lisa, Seth, Debra, Stephanie, Samantha. BS, U. Rochester, 1965; MS, U. Minn., 1967; postgrad., Harvard. U., 1996. With Dean Witter & Co., Inc., NYC, 1968-73; with Oppenheimer & Co., NYC, 1973-74; ptnr., dir. investment cons. Hewitt Assocs., Lincolnshire, Ill., 1974-82; pres., mng. dir. Stratford Advisory Group, Inc., Chgo., 1982—2001; pres. Stratford Investment Group, Inc., 1983-2000, Advocate Investment Advisors, LLC (now called Advocate Asset Mgmt., LLC), Chgo., 2001—. Asset mgr. pension, endowment and charitable funds. Editor Benefits Quar. Mem. Mayor's Energy Task Force, City of Chgo.; gov. mem. Sustaining Fellows, Art Inst. Chgo., Contemporary Art Cir. of Mus. Contemporary Art; benefactor Lyric Opera of Chgo.; mem. gala com. Chgo. Abused Women's Coalition; bd. dirs. Com. for Accuracy in Mid. East Reporting in Am., Aspen Cmty. Campaign; mem. Jewish Cmty. Rels. Coun., Jewish Fedn. Met. Chgo.; mem. exec. bd. Chgo. chpt. Am. Jewish Com.; bd. govs. The Investigative Projecton Terrorism; mem. adv. bd. Middle East Forum; regent Ctr. Security Policy; lectr (Aspen, Chgo., Cleve.) Terrorism and the Media. With USAF, 1968, Air NG, 1968-73. Minn. Mining and Mgr. fellow U. Minn., 1967; NSF grantee, 1967 Mem. Tau Beta Pi, Sigma Alpha Mu. Clubs: Standard. Republican. Jewish. Office: Advocate Asset Mgmt LLC Ste 1510 10 S Riverside Plz Chicago IL 60606 Office Phone: 312-756-0074. Office Fax: 312-756-0084.

KUDO, TOSHIFUMI, surgeon, researcher; b. Ajisu, Yamaguchi, Japan, Jan. 25, 1968; s. Takao and Kimiko Kudo; m. Sonoe Mitake, July 10, 1994; children: Yukari, Asuka. MD, PhD, Tokyo Med. and Dental U., 1993. Diplomate Japan Surgical Bd., lic. physician Japan. Attending surgeon Tokyo Med. and Dental U. Hosp., 2002—03, 2006—; endovascular rsch. fellow UCLA Gonda Vascular Ctr., 2003—06. Contbr. scientific papers to profl. jours. Recipient World Coll. Vascular Diseases prize, Internat. Congress of the Asian Vascular Soc., 2002. Mem.: Internat. Soc. Vascular Surgery (instl. rep. 2006—), Internat. Soc. Endovascular Specialists. Achievements include development of surgical devices. Office Phone: 81 3 5803 5255. Business E-Mail: t-kudo.srg1@tmd.ac.jp.

KUDRAVETZ, DAVID WALLER, lawyer; b. Sumter, SC, Feb. 2, 1948; s. George and Barbara (Waller) K.; m. Eleanor McCrea Snyder, June 21, 1969; 1 child, Julia McCrea. BS, U. Va., 1971, JD, 1974. Bar: Va. 1974, U.S. Tax Ct. 1974; CPA, Va. Assoc. Robert M. Musselman, Charlottesville, Va., 1974; ptnr. Carwile & Kudravetz, Charlottesville, Va., 1975-78, McClure, Callaghan & McCallum, Charlottesville, Va., 1979-81, McCallum & Kudravetz, P.C., Charlottesville, Va., 1982—. Instr. fed. income taxation U. of Va. Sch. Continuing Edn., 1975-79. Mem. AICPA, Va. State Bar Assn., Charlottesville-Albemarle Bar Assn., Am. Assn. Atty.-CPAs, Va. Soc. CPAs. Office: McCallum & Kudravetz PC 250 E High St Charlottesville VA 22902-5178

KUDRITZKI, ROLF-PETER, astronomer, educator; Grad. in Physics, Tech. U. Berlin, 1971, PhD in Astronomy, 1973; habilitation in Astronomy, U. Kiel, Germany, 1979. Rsch. asst. Inst. Astronomy and Astrophysics Tech. U. Berlin, 1971—76; rsch. asst. U. Kiel Inst. Theoretical Physics and Obs., Germany, 1976—78, lectr., 1979—82; prof. astronomy, dir. Inst. Astronomy and Astrophysics U. Munich, 1982—2000; sci. mem. Max-Planck-Inst. Astrophysics, 1990—; dir. U. Hawaii Inst. Astronomy, 2000—. Dean sch. physics U. Munich, 1999—2000; interim vice chancellor rsch. and grad. edn. U. Hawaii, Manoa, 2003—04. Contbr. articles to sci. jours. Mem.: Am. Astron. Soc., Acad. Scis. North Rhine-Westphalia, Germany, Deutsche Akademie der Naturforscher Leopoldina, Berlin-Brandenburgi Acad. Scis., Max-Planck-Soc., Germany, Internat. Astron. Union, Astron. Soc., Germany. Office: Inst Astronomy U Hawaii 2680 Woodlawn Dr Honolulu HI 96822 E-mail: kud@ifa.hawaii.edu.

KUDRLE, ROBERT THOMAS, economist, educator; b. Sioux City, Iowa, Aug. 23, 1942; s. Chester John and Helen Marguerite Kudrle; m. Venetia Hilary Mary Thomas, July 20, 1970; children: Paul John Reginald, Thomas David Chester. AB, Harvard U., 1964, AM, 1969, PhD, 1974; MPhil., U. Oxford, Eng., 1967. Grad. rsch. assoc. Ctr. Internat. Affairs Harvard U., Cambridge, Mass., 1969-71; instr. Tex. A & M Univ., College Station, 1971-72; asst., assoc. prof. Humphrey Inst. U. Minn., Mpls., 1972-83, asst., assoc. dir. Ctr. Internat. Studies, 1972-82, prof. Humphrey Inst., 1983—, dir. MA program pub. affairs, 1984-86, dir. Freeman Ctr. Internat. Econ. Policy, 1990-97, assoc. dean rsch. Humphrey Inst., 1992-96, Freeman prof. internat. trade and investment policy, 2006—. Cons. U.S. Dept. Justice, U.S. AID, Urban Inst., UN Ctr. Transnat. Corps., Consumer and Corp. Affairs Can., WHO, others. Author: Agricultural Tractors: A World Industry Study, 1975; co-author State Evaluation of Foreign Sales Efforts, 1988; co-editor Reducing the Cost of Dental Care, 1983, The Industrial Future of the Pacific Basin, 1984, Jour. Internat. Studies Quarterly, 1980-84, 85; mem. editorial bd. Internat. Political Economy Yearbook, 1983—, Jour. Health Politics, Policy & Law, 1981-92; contbr. articles to profl. jours., chpts. to texts. 1st v.p. UN Assn. Minn., Mpls., 1976—78, mem. adv. coun., 1978—88. Graduate prize fellow Harvard U., 1967-69, Pew Faculty fellow in Internat. Affairs Harvard U., 1990-91; Nuffield Coll. studentship, Oxford, Eng., 1966-67; Rhodes scholar, Oxford, Eng., 1964-67. Mem. Assn. Pub. Policy Analysis and Mgmt. (instl. rep. 1988-97), Internat. Studies Assn. (v.p. 1998-99), Am. Econ. Assn., Harvard Club Minn. Avocations: running, gardening. Home: 4650 Fremont Ave S Minneapolis MN 55419-2263 Office: Humphrey Inst Pub Affairs 301 19th Ave S Ste 300 Minneapolis MN 55455-0429 Business E-Mail: bkudrle@hhh.umn.edu.

KUDROW, LISA (LISA MARIE DIANE KUDROW), actress; b. Encino, Calif., July 30, 1963; d. Lee and Nedra Kudrow; m. Michael Stern, May 27, 1995; 1 child, Julian Murray. BS in Biology, Vassar Coll., Poughkeepsie, NY, 1985. Actress (TV series) Mad About You, 1991-99, Friends, 1994-2004 (Emmy award outstanding supporting actress, 1998, SAG award outstanding performance female, 2000, Am. Comedy award, 2000, Golden Satellite award best actress, 2000), Hopeless Pictures, 2005; (TV guest appearances) Cheers, 1989, Newhart, 1990, Life Goes On, 1990, Coach, 1993-94, Flying Blind, 1993, Hope & Gloria, 1996, The Simpsons (voice), 1998; (films) The Crazysitter, 1995, Romy and Michele's High School Reunion, 1997, Clockwatchers, 1997, The Opposite of Sex, 1998 (NY Film Critics Circle award, 2000), Hercules (voice) 1998, Analyze This, 1998, Hanging Up, 2000, All Over the Guy, 2001, Dr. Dolittle 2 (voice), 2001, Analyze That, 2002, Marci X, 2003, Wonderland, 2003, Happy Endings, 2005; exec. prodr.: (TV films) Picking Up and Dropping Off, 2003; actress, exec. prodr., writer (TV series) The Comeback, 2005; (music video) The Rembrandts I'll Be There For You, 1995. Named one of 50 Most Beautiful People in World, People mag., 1997. Mem.: Groundlings Improv Group.

KUEBLER, DAVID WAYNE, insurance company executive, private investigator; b. New Orleans, Apr. 18, 1947; s. Royce Matthew and Rosemary (West) K.; m. Gayle Rose Mary Blank Key Kuebler; children: Kira Louise, Krystal Lynn. B. in Bus. Mgmt., Loyola U., New Orleans, 1969. Lic. ins. broker, investment mgr.; lic. investigator, La. Asst. mgr. Winn-Dixie, Inc., New Orleans, 1962-69; account exec. Travelers Ins. Co., St. Louis, 1969-74; sr. account exec. Gen. Am. Life., St. Louis, 1974-76; dist. mgr. Guardian Life Ins., New Orleans, 1976-81; pres. Profl. Planners, Inc., Kenner, La., 1981—. Louisiana-detectives.com, 2001, Pro-Care, Inc., 1983—. Asst. chief of staff civil mil. ops. 377 Taacom, New Orleans, 1987. Coach girls athletics, Metairie, La., 1987. Col. USAR. Mem.: John E. Reid Inst., Bus. Espionage Controls and Countermeasures Assn., Met Plus Group Millionaires. Democrat. Avocation: coaching girls softball and basketball. Home: 29 Chateau Haut Brion Kenner LA 70065 also: 29 Chateau Haut Brion Dr Kenner LA 70065-2062 Office Phone: 504-416-7400. E-mail: dwkuebler@cs.com.

KUECHLE, JOHN MERRILL, lawyer; b. Mpls., Dec. 18, 1951; s. Harry Bronson and Virginia (McClure) K.; m. Nancy Anderson, June 20, 1976; 1 child, David Michael. AB magna cum laude, Occidental Coll., 1974; JD cum laude, Harvard U., 1977. Bar: Calif. 1977. Assoc. Mitchell, Silberberg & Knupp, LA, 1977-83, ptnr., 1983-2000, of counsel, 2001—. Active Culver City Planning Commn. Mem. Phi Beta Kappa. Republican. Episcopalian. Avocations: track and field, orienteering, rock climbing. Home: 10733 Ranch Rd Culver City CA 90230-5458 Office: Mitchell Silberberg & Knupp 11377 W Olympic Blvd Los Angeles CA 90064-1625 Office Phone: 310-312-3139. Business E-Mail: jmk@msk.com.

KUECHLE, SCOTT E., manufacturing executive; BBA, Univ. Wis. Eau Claire; MSIA, Carnegie Mellon Univ. Fin. mgmt. positions Goodrich Corp., Charlotte, NC, 1983—94, dir. fin. & banking, 1994—98, v.p., treas., 1998—2004, v.p., contr., 2004—05, sr. v.p., CFO, 2005—. Office: Goodrich Corp 4 Coliseum Ctr 2730 W Tyvola Rd Charlotte NC 28217-4578*

KUECHMANN, CHRISTOPHER ROBERT, library director; b. Toledo, Ohio, Dec. 1, 1949; s. Robert Jackson and Dorothy May (Piper) Kuechmann; m. Gloria Ann Sandefer, Dec. 31, 1992. BA, Earlham Coll., Richmond, Ind., 1973; MLS, U. Wis., Milw., 1985. Children's libr. Edinburg Pub. Libr., Tex., 1985—90, libr. dir., 1991—98, Starr County Pub. Libr., Rio Grande City, Tex., 1990—91, Matteson Pub. Libr., Ill., 1998—99, Ohio Twp. Pub. Libr. Sys., Newburg, Ind., 1999—2000; regional libr. dir. North Ark. Regional Libr., Yellville, 2000—02; libr. dir. Clewiston Pub. Libr., Fla., 2002—05; parish libr. dir. Tangipahoa Parish Libr., Amite, La., 2005—. Columnist: Ark. Libr., 2001—02. Mem.: ALA (assoc.; Tex. del. to libr. legis. days 1994), La. Libr. Assn. (assoc.), Rotary. Democrat. Methodist. Avocations: travel, stamp collecting/philately, reading. Home: 465 South 4th St Ponchatoula LA 70454 Home Phone: 985-386-9644; Office Phone: 985-748-3465. Business E-Mail: ckuechma@state.lib.la.us.

KUEHL, ALEXANDER EDWARD, physician, health facility administrator, educator, writer; b. St. John, Nfld., Can., Aug. 12, 1944; came to US, 1945; s. Frederick George and Olivia Kendall (Dwyer) K.; children: Kendall Ann Warsaw, Bruce Ongsiako. BA, Johns Hopkins U., 1966, MPH, 1976; MD, Syracuse U., 1970. Bd. cert. in Orthopaedic Surgery; bd. cert. in Emergency Medicine. Intern U. Hosp., Syracuse, 1970-71, resident, 1971-73, Johns Hopkins Hosp., 1974-78; fellow in emergency med. svc. and trauma U. Hosp., Balt., 1978-79; dir. med. affairs Md. Inst. Emergency Med. Svcs., Balt., 1979—81; v.p. med. dir. NYC Health & Hosps. Corp., 1981-89; assoc. prof. surgery and pub. health Cornell U. Med. Sch., 1985—2000; dir. emergency medicine NY Presbyn. Hosp., 1989—97; dir. Le Fleuve Inst., 2000—. Chairperson N.Y.C. Regional Coun., 1988—89, N.Y.C. Med. Adv. Com., 1981—97; med. dir. CVPH Emergency Care Ctr., 1997—2000, Noble Hosp., 2000—05; commr. pub. health St. Lawrence County, 2001—03; mem. adv. bd. WHO, 1985. Author: (textbooks) Medical Director's Handbook, 1989, Prehospital Systems and Medical Oversight, 2002. Chmn. Mayoral Transition (Health), NYC, 1993. Lt. col. USAR. Fellow ACS, Am. Coll. Emergency Dispatch (pres. 1994-99), Am. Coll. Emergency Physicians; mem. Nat. Assn. Emergency Med. Svc. Physicians (founding mem., bd. dirs. 1986-97. Stewart award 1991), Clinton County Med. Soc. (pres. 1998-2002), Pub. Health Honor Soc. Johns Hopkins U. Home: 6 Rocky Edge Rd Morristown NY 13664 Office: Le Fleuve Inst 97 Rock Island Gouverneur NY 13642 Office Phone: 315-287-2056. E-mail: alexanderkuehl@msn.com.

KUEHL, HANS HENRY, electrical engineering educator; b. Detroit, Mar. 16, 1933; s. Henry Martin and Hilde (Schrader) K.; m. Anna Meidinger, July 25, 1965; children: Susan, Michael. BS, Princeton U., 1955; MS, Calif. Inst. Tech., 1956, PhD, 1959. Asst. prof. elec. engring. U. So. Calif., 1960-63, assoc. prof., 1963-72, prof., 1972—2004, prof. emeritus, 2004—, chmn. dept. elec. engring., electrophysics, 1987-98. Cons. Deutsch Co., L.A., 1973, Hughes Aircraft Co., Culver City, Calif., 1975. Contbr. articles to profl. jours. Recipient Tchg. Excellence award U. So. Calif., 1964, Haliburton award U. So. Calif., 1980, Lifetime Achievement award U. So. Calif., 2006; named to Royal Oak Dondero HS Hall Fame, 2006. Fellow IEEE; mem. Am. Phys. Soc., Internat. Sci. Radio Union, Eta Kappa Nu (bd. dirs. 2000-02, Outstanding Faculty award 1977). Avocations: tennis, racquetball. Office: U So Calif Elec Engring Dept PHE 622 Mc 0271 Los Angeles CA 90089-0271 Business E-Mail: kuehl@usc.edu.

KUEHL, SHEILA JAMES, state legislator; b. Tulsa, Feb. 9, 1941; d. Arthur Joseph and Lillian Ruth (Krasner) K. BA, UCLA, 1962; JD, Harvard U., 1978. Actress, 1950-65; assoc. dean of students UCLA, 1969-75; pvt. practice LA, 1978-85; law prof. Loyola U. LA, 1985-89; mng. atty. Calif. Women's Law Ctr., LA, 1989-93; mem. Calif. State Assembly, Sacramento, 1995-2000, spkr. pro tem, 1997-99, chair jud. com., 1999-2000; mem. Calif. State Senate, 2001—. Chair natural resources and water com., Calif. State Assembly, 2001—06, chmn. health com., 2007—. Appeared in TV series Broadside, 1964-65, as Zelda Gilroy in Dobie Gillis, 1959-63, as Jackie Erwin in Trouble with Father, 1950-56. Bd. overseers Harvard U., 1997-05. Named One of 20 Most Fascinating Women in Politics, George Mag., 1996, named One of 100 Most Influential Attys. in Calif., Calif. Law Bus., 1998; recipient Barry Goldwater Human Rights award, 1998, Legislator of Yr., Calif. Pks. and Recreation Soc., 1999, Pub. Svc. award UCLA Alumni Assn., 2000, Liberty award Lambda Legal Def. Edn. Fund, 2002, Women in Govt. award Good Housekeeping, 2003, Courageous Leader award Women Against Gun Violence, 2005, Matthew O. Tobriner Pub. Svc. award Legal Aid Soc., 2005; named Legislator of Yr., Congress Calif. Srs., 2006. Office: State Capitol Sacramento CA 95814-4906 Office Phone: 916-651-4023.

KUEHM, JULIE K., nurse, educator; BS, Concordia U., 2000; MA in Edn., U. Phoenix, 2005. Nurse mgr. West Suburban Midwife Assoc., Oak Park, Ill., 1998—2001; tchr. Christ Luth. Sch., Pitts., 2001—. Lutheran. Office: Christ Lutheran Sch 400 Barclay Ave Pittsburgh PA 15221 Office Phone: 412-271-7173.

KUEHN, BRIAN ALLEN, lawyer; b. Saginaw, Mich., Feb. 27, 1953; s. Hubert and Phyllis Kuehn; m. Luann Louise Melcher, Aug. 17, 1974; children: Christopher Allen, Julia Louise. JD, U. Ill., Champaign-Urbana, 1980. Bar: Ill. 1980. Jr. ptnr. Lester Berry Smith, Ltd., Peoria, Ill., 1980—84; ptnr. Smith, Waters, Kuehn & Huges, Peoria, Ill., 1984—94; litig. atty. Ghantous Law Offices, Peoria, 1995—99, Jim Rochford & Assoc., Peoria, 1999—2004, Carter Law Offices, Peoria, 2004—. Bd. dirs. Willow Hill United Meth. Ch., East Peoria, Ill., 2006—07. Fellow: Inns of Ct. (licentiate; barrister 2006—07). Avocations: photography, flying, hunting, music, vocal and instrumental. Home: 1524 Upper Spring Bay Rd East Peoria IL 61611 Office Phone: 309-673-3517. Office Fax: 309-673-3318. Personal E-mail: kuehn@mtco.com. Business E-Mail: bkuehn@jcarterlaw.com.

KUEHN, COLEEN P., advertising executive; b. 1969; d. Ronald L. and Kathleen Moriarty Kuehn; m. Robert Lassiter Malin; 1 child. BS mgmt., Tulane U.; MBA, U. Mich. With Coca Cola, Am. Express, Procter & Gamble; pres. digital & emerging media bus., MediaCom; exec. dir. leading client services and strategy, MediaCom; exec. v.p., chief strategist MPG, 2003—. Mem bd. of dirs. Advt. Week, 2006. Named a Woman to Watch, Advt. Age, 2007; recipient Pryor Award, U. of Michigan, Bronze "e" integration award, MediaWeek. Mem.: Am. Assn. of Advt. Agencies (AAAA), NY New Media Assn. (NYNMA), Advt. Club in NY. Office: MPG 195 Broadway New York NY 10007 Office Phone: 646-587-5000. Office Fax: 646-587-5005.*

KUEHN, GEORGE E., lawyer; b. NYC, June 19, 1946; m. Mary Kuehn; children: Kristin, Rob, Geoff. BBA, U. Mich., 1968, JD, 1973. Bar: Mich. 1974. Assoc. Hill, Lewis et al, Detroit, 1974-78; ptnr. Butzel, Long et al, Detroit, 1978-81; exec. v.p., gen. counsel, sec. The Stroh Brewery Co., Detroit, 1981-99—; shareholder Butzel Long, Detroit, 2000—. With U.S. Army, 1969-71. Office: Butzel Long 350 S Main St Ste 200 Ann Arbor MI 48104 Office Phone: 734-213-3257. Business E-Mail: Kuehn@butzel.com.

KUEHN, JAMES MARSHALL, newspaper editor; b. Mobridge, SD, May 23, 1926; s. Christ A. and Selma (Brandon) K.; m. Phyllis Yvonne Larson, Apr. 3, 1950; children— Douglas James, Deborah Kay, Diana Lisa. BA, U.S.D., 1949. State editor Rapid City (S.D.) Jour., 1949-54, wire editor, 1954-58, mng. editor, 1958-66, exec. editor, 1966-73, v.p.-editor, 1973-86. Vice pres. Rapid City Library Bd., 1969-73; dir. Mt. Rushmore Nat. Meml. Soc., 1991—; dir. Mt. Rushmore Inst, 2006—. Served with C.E. AUS, 1945-46. Mem. Rapid City C. of C. (v.p. 1970-73), S.D. C. of C. (dir. 1978-81), Lambda Chi Alpha. Lodges: Kiwanis (pres. 1973-74). Republican. Lutheran. Personal E-mail: jmpykuehn@rushmore.com.

KUEHN, KURT P., delivery service executive; BA, Yale Univ.; MBA, Univ. Miami. Mgmt. positions UPS, Atlanta, 1997—, facilities planning mgr., 1986, mgr. strategic cost dept., 1996, v.p. bus. info. analysis, v.p. investor rels., 1999—2003, sr. v.p. worldwide sales & mktg., 2004—. Office: UPS 55 Glendale Pky Atlanta GA 30328*

KUEHN, RICHARD ARTHUR, telecommunications consultant; b. Cleve., Jan. 31, 1939; s. Arthur John and Alice (Schilling) K.; m. Cynthia Louise Shideler, Dec. 31, 1984. BBA, Case Western Res. U., 1960. V.p. Warwick Communications, Cleve., 1957-62; pres. RAK Assocs., Cleve., 1962—. Author: Cost Effective Telecommunications; editor Telecom. Info. Mgmt. Jour., 1999; columnist Bus. Communications Rev., 1974—; contbr. 100 articles to profl. jours. Mem. Soc. Telecommunication Cons. (founder). Home and Office: 12500 Edgewater Dr Ste 1407 Cleveland OH 44107-1027 Personal E-mail: raktel@sbcglobal.net.

KUEHN, RONALD L., JR., natural resources company executive; b. Bklyn., Apr. 6, 1935; m. Allison Spencer, June 7, 1986; children: Kathleen, Kelly, Erin, Coleen, Shannon, Caroline, Ronald L. III. BS, Fordham U., 1957, LL.B., 1964. Bar: N.Y. 1964. Assoc. Hughes, Hubbard & Reed, NYC, 1964-68; exec. v.p., gen. counsel Allied Artists Pictures, NYC, 1968-70; v.p., gen. counsel, sec. So. Natural Resources, Inc., Birmingham, Ala., 1970-79, exec. v.p., 1979-81; COO Sonat Inc., 1982-83, pres., CEO, 1984—99, chmn. bd., 1986-99, ret., 1999; non-exec. chmn. El Paso Corp., 1999—2000, consultant, 2001—03, lead dir., 2002—03, interim CEO,

2003, chmn., 2003—. Bd. dirs. Transocean Offshore, Inc., AmSouth Bancorp., Praxair Inc., The Dun & Bradstreet Corp.; trustee Tuskegee U. 1st lt. U.S. Army, 1958-59. Mem. ABA, N.Y. State Bar Assn., Assn. of Bar of City of N.Y., Fed. Energy Bar Assn., Newcomen Soc. of U.S., Bretton Woods Com. Roman Catholic. Office: El Paso Corporation 1001 Louisiana St Houston TX 77002

KUEHNE, TRACY ELIZABETH, music educator; b. Doylestown, Pa., Jan. 17, 1978; d. Paul Curtis and Karen Elizabeth Kuehne. BS in Bible, Bapt. Bible Coll., 2001, B in Sacred Music, 2001. Organist Springfield (Pa.) Bapt. Ch., 2001—03; dir. Sch. Music, Suzuki piano tchr. Lexington Christian Acad., Line Lexington, Pa., 2001—, choir dir., tchr. music history, 2002—. Pianist Cornerstone Ch. of Skippack, Pa., 2004—06. Mem.: Suzuki Assn. Ams. (cert.), Music Tchr.'s Nat. Assn. Republican. Avocations: reading, cooking, needlecrafts, ballet. Office: Lexington Christian Acad PO Box 10 Line Lexington PA 18932 Office Phone: 215-822-2442. Personal E-mail: tpianok@hotmail.com.

KUEHNER, MARVIN ERNEST, surgeon; b. Pflugerville, Tex., Oct. 12, 1934; s. Ernest Frank and Blanche Annie (Kilian) K.; m. Hope Stephanie Maki, Mar. 31, 1990; children: Mark, Jon, Daryl, Kathryn, Michael, David, Steven, Karolyn, Daniel. BS in Pharmacy, U. Tex., 1957; MD, Washington U., 1961. Diplomate Am. Bd. Surgery. Resident surgery Jewish Hosp., St. Louis, 1961-66; staff surgeon Interstate Med. Ctr., Red Wing, Minn., 1969-74, Marshfield (Wis.) Clinic, 1974—, chmn. salary com, 1983-93; mem. salary com., 1994—. Contbr. articles to profl. jours. With AUS, 1966-69. Fellow ACS; mem. AMA, Soc. Vascular Surgery, Midwestern Vascular Surgery Soc., Midwest Surgical Assn Lutheran. Avocations: electronics, running, skiing, wood working. Office: Marshfield Clinic 1000 N Oak Ave Marshfield WI 54449-5702 Home Phone: 715-389-2870; Office Phone: 715-389-3218. Business E-Mail: kuehner.marvin@marshfieldclinic.org.

KUEHNI, NORMAN ARNOLD, private investigator, researcher; b. New Glarus, Wis., July 17, 1928; s. Arnold Samuel and Amelia (Mani) K.; m. Joanne Beth Voeck, Sept. 4, 1948; children— Kathleen Ann Porta, Barbara Dawn Rector, Pamela Jo Zulzer. Student U. Wis., 1946-49. With Dane County Traffic Dept., Madison, Wis., 1954-63; criminal investigator Bur. Alcohol, Tobacco and Firearms, U.S. Treasury Dept., Chgo., 1963-66, area supr., 1966-70, coordinator organized crime drive, 1970-72, spl. agt. in charge Washington Field Office, 1972-73, regional insp., Washington, 1973-75, dep. asst. dir. inspection, Washington, 1975-79, spl. agt. in charge, St. Paul, 1979-83; pvt. investigator, owner Eagle Eye Detective Agy., Hudson, Wis., 1983—. Served with U.S. Army, 1947-48. Recipient cert. of merit State of Minn., 1983, Badge of Royal Can. Mounted Police, 1983, Albert Gallatin award U.S. Treasury Dept., 1983, Spl. Agt. Retirement award U.S. Dept. of Treasury, 1983, cert. of appreciation Fed. Drug Enforcement Agy., 1983. Mem. Mensa, Fraternal Order Police, Wis. Private Investigators, Wis. Law Enforcement Assn. Lutheran. Club: Westwood Country (Vienna, Va.). Lodges: Masons, Order Eastern Star. Avocations: travel.

KUEHNLE, KENTON LEE, lawyer; b. Chgo., Nov. 10, 1945; s. Robert Louis and Mary Caroline (Recktenwald) K.; m. Sherry L. Esposito, June 6, 1970; children: Robert, Amanda, Matthew. BA, Augustana Coll., 1967; JD, Duke U., Durham, NC, 1970. Bar: Ohio 1970, US Dist. Ct. (so. dist.) Ohio 1971. Assoc. Dunbar, Kienzle & Murphey, Columbus, Ohio, 1970-77; ptnr. Loveland, Callard & Clapham, Columbus, 1977-80, Scott, Walker & Kuehnle, Columbus, 1980-86, Thompson, Hine & Flory, Columbus, 1986—2001, Roetzel & Andress, Columbus, 2001—03, Allen, Kuehnle Stovall & Neuman LLP, Columbus, 2003—. Instr. paralegal program Capital U. Law Sch., 1998-2001. Author: Ohio Real Estate Law, 3 vols., 2003, Ohio Condominium Law, 2005; contbr. articles to profl. jours. Mem. Augustana Coll. Alumni Bd., Rock Island, Ill., 1986-89; elder First Presbyn. Ch., Grove City, Ohio, 1990-93; pres. Computer Users Group, Columbus, 1985-86; mem. exec. bd. CompDrug, Columbus, 1992-, v.p., 2005-. Mem. ABA (sect. real property, probate and trust law 1973—, com. on condominium and coop. housing 1977—), Columbus Bar Assn. (chmn. real property com. 1976-78, chmn. micro computer subcom. 1986-87, 92-94, lectr. for bar assn. seminars), Ohio State Bar Assn. (bd. govs. real property sect. 1979-82, 90—, chmn. 1997-99, editor state real property sect. newsletter 1995-99, chmn. subcom. to rev. condominium statute 1980-81, mem. real property specialization bd. 2004—, lectr. continuing legal edn. programs), Am. Coll. Real Estate Lawyers (vice chair title ins. subcom., mem.condominium subcom.). Avocations: computer programming, baseball, theology. Home: 11325 Big Plain Circleville Rd Orient OH 43146-9301 Office: Allen Kuehnle Stovall & Neuman LLP 21 West Broad St Ste 400 Columbus OH 43215 Home Phone: 614-877-9501; Office Phone: 614-221-8500. Business E-Mail: kuehnle@aksnlaw.com.

KUENN, MARJORIE ASP, music educator; b. Moorhead, Minn., Dec. 26, 1951; d. Robert Louis and Violet Rose Asp; m. Brent Jay Kuenn, Feb. 25, 1978 (div. Jan. 2001). *Grandparents Charles and Inga Asp and Lars and Hannah Foldoe were Swedish and Norwegian immigrants. They brought with them a strong work ethic and a desire for a better life. They believed that education and hard work were the means to accomplish their goals. Charles Asp became an educator. Her father Robert Asp was also an educator and a visionary. He built the Viking longship "Hjemkomst" that sailed from Duluth to Oslo Norway in 1982, and is now on display in Moorhead Minnesota. Robert and Rose Asp instilled in their children the belief that success is an attainable goal.* EdB in Violin, U. So. Miss., 1973, EdM, 1974. Violinist Fargo-Moorhead Symphony, 1967—69, Meridian Symphony, Miss., 1969—79, Jackson Symphony, Miss., 1969—79, Jackson Mini-Orch., 1969—79, Miss. Opera South, 1969—79, Miss. Opera, 1969—79, Gulfcoast Symphony, Miss., 1969—79, Miss. Ballet Orch., 1969—79, Mobile Opera, Ala., 1969—79, Tupelo Symphony, Miss., 1969—79, Greenville Symphony, Miss., 1969—79, Monroe Symphony, La., 1969—79, U. So. Miss. Symphony, Opera, Chamber & Ensemble, 1969—74; tchr. Jackson Symphony Orch., 1974—79; dir. orch. Hickman Mills Sch. Dist., Kansas City, Mo., 1979—; chair dept. music Smith-Hale Mid. Sch., Kansas city, 1990—; choir dir. Grace Bapt. Ch., Lee's Summit, Mo., 2005—. *Marjorie Kuenn has 25 years of experience working in the church music ministry. She has worked with instrumentalists and vocalists, and has taught vocal technique classes to choirs in several churches. She is currently the choir director at Grace Baptist Church in Lee's Summit, Missouri.* Author: Vocal Techniques, vol. I, 1998, Vocal Techniques, vol. II, 2003, Choir Warm-up Exercises, 2002. Music scholar, U. So. Miss., 1969—73, Grad. Music Studies fellow, 1973—74. Mem.: U. So. Miss. Alumni Assn., Am. Fedn. Tchrs., Music Educators Nat. Conf., Mu Phi Epsilon, Alpha Lambda Delta. Avocations: sewing, reading, exercise. Office: Smith-Hale Mid Sch 8925 Longview Rd Kansas City MO 64134 Office Phone: 816-316-7663. Business E-Mail: marjoriek@hickmanmills.org.

KUENNEN, THOMAS GERARD, journalist; b. St. Louis, June 30, 1953; s. George Glennon and Earline (Doherty) K.; m. Anne L. Gillette, Sept. 10, 1988; 1 child, Madeline Livingston. BJ, U. Mo., 1975. Copy editor Macon (Ga.) Telegraph & News, 1976-77; news editor Mascoutah (Ill.) Herald, and related newspapers, 1977-79; pub. rels. assoc. Booker Assocs., Inc., St. Louis, 1979-80, Fru Con Corp., St. Louis, 1980-81; assoc. editor Rock Products Mag., Chgo., 1981-84; editor Roads & Bridges Mag., Des Plaines, Ill., 1984-95; prin., editor Expresswaysonline.com, Buffalo Grove, Ill., 1995—. Mem. editl. com. Am. Bus. Press, N.Y.C., 1984-85. Contbg. editor: Concrete Products, Better Roads, Aggregates Manager. Recipient Jesse H. Neal award Am. Bus. Press, 1983, Svc. award La. Associated Gen. Contractors, 1990, Editl. Excellence award Am. Soc. Bus. Press Editors, 1998, finalist Jesse H. Neal award, 2005. Mem. Constrn. Writers Assn. (bd. dirs. 1985-86, 95-99, Robert F. Boger award 1985, 93, 95, 98, Hon. Mention 2003), The Rd. Info. Program (bd. dirs. 1999—), Road Gang, Nat. Asphalt Pavement Assn. (Hot Mix Hall of Fame), Women in Comm. (treas. 1983-84, Cub's Cup 1985). Roman Catholic. Office: Expresswaysonline.com 251 N Milwaukee Ave Ste 224B Buffalo Grove IL 60089

KUENSTER, JOHN JOSEPH, editor; b. Chgo., June 18, 1924; s. Roy Jacob and Katheryn (Holechek) Kuenster; m. Mary Virginia Maher, Feb. 15, 1947 (dec. Feb. 1983); m. Suely Brazão, July 1, 1995. Editor The Columbian, Chgo., 1948-57; staff writer Chgo. Daily News, Chgo., 1957-65; dir. devel. and pub. rels. Mercy Hosp., Chgo., 1965-66; sr. writer The Claretians, Chgo., 1966—2007; editor Baseball Digest, Evanston, Ill., 1969—; exec. editor Century Pub. Co., Evanston. Author: Cobb to Catfish, 1975; co-author: To Sleep with the Angels, 1996; author: Heartbreakers, 2001, At Home and Away, 2003, How St. Jude Came to Chicago, 2004, The Best of Baseball Digest, 2006, (booklets) The Police, Money, Mission in Guatemala, Honesty, Is it the Best Policy?. Mem.: Baseball Writers' Assn. Am. Roman Catholic. Office: Baseball Digest Lakeside Publishing Co 990 Grove St Evanston IL 60201-6510 Office Phone: 847-491-6440. Business E-Mail: jkuenster@centurysports.net.

KUES, IRVIN WILLIAM, financial planner; b. Balt., Apr. 23, 1936; s. Harry Irvin and Theresa Frances (Seliga) K.; m. Mary Carolyn Gaff, Oct. 24, 1959; Pamela, Janet, Lynne, Leslie. BS in Engring. Sci., Johns Hopkins U., 1957, M in Bus. Sci., 1959. Cert. data processer. Rsch. analyst Am. Newspaper Rsch. Inst., Chgo., 1957-59; mgmt. analyst Western Elec. Co., Balt., 1959-61; asst. supt. E.D.P. Bethlehem (Pa.) Steel Co., 1961-66; v.p. data processing Comml. Credit Corp., Balt., 1966-74; CFO Johns Hopkins Hosp., Balt., 1974-86, Johns Hopkins Health System, Balt., 1986-94; chmn. provider reimbursement rev. bd. U.S. Dept. HHS, Balt., 1994—. Bd. dirs. Francis Scott Key Hosp., Balt., Med. Svcs. Corp., Balt., Dome Corp., Balt., Med. Ctr. Ins. Co., Bermuda; mem. fin. coun. Md. Hosp. Assn., Towson; chmn. Health Svcs. Cost Rev. Commn., 2003—. Co-author: Yearbook of Healthcare Mgmt., 1991—. Advisor Villa Julie Coll., Stevenson, Md., 1991. Fellow Healthcare Fin. Mgmt. Assn.; mem. Healthcare Rate Coun., Ctr. Club. Avocations: tennis, golf, reading. Home: 1214 Brook Meadow Dr Towson MD 21286-1751 Office Phone: 410-321-0109. Business E-Mail: kues1@msn.com. E-mail: ikues@verizon.net.

KUESTER, DENNIS J., diversified financial services company and bank executive; b. Milw., Mar. 7, 1942; m. Sandy Kuester. BBA in Acctg. & Fin., U. Wis.-Milw., 1966, DCS (hon.), 1996. Various sales and sales mgmt. positions IBM Corp., Milw., Mpls., Chgo., 1966—75; v.p. M & I Data Services, Inc. (now Metavante Corp.), Milw., 1976—85, pres, 1985—93, chmn., CEO, 1993—98; chmn. Metavante Corp., 1998—; pres. Marshall & Ilsley Corp., Milw., 1987—2005, CEO, 2002—07, chmn., 2005—; pres. M&I Marshall & Ilsley Bank, 1989—2001, CEO, 2001—07, chmn., 2001—. Mem. adv. coun. FRS, 2004—; bd. dirs. Modine Mfg. Co., Krueger Internat., Super Steel Products Corp., Wausau Paper Corp. Bd. dirs. Froedtert Meml. Lutheran Hosp., Lynde and Harry Bradley Found.; chmn. Christian Stewardship Found.; mem. U. Wis.-Milw., 1994—, pres., 1990—92. Recipient Disting. Alumnus award, U. Wis.-Milw. Alumni Assn., 1988. Office: Marshall & Ilsley Corporation 770 N Water St Milwaukee WI 53202-3509*

KUFFEL, EDMUND, electrical engineering educator; b. Poland, Oct. 28, 1924; s. Franciszek and Marta (Glodowska) K.; m. Alicja, Oct. 4, 1952; children: Anna, John, Richard, Peter. BSc, U. Coll., Dublin, 1953, MSc, 1954, PhD, 1959; DSc, U. Manchester, 1967. Rsch. engr. Met. Vickers Electric Co., Manchester, England, 1954-60; mem. faculty elec. engring. U. Manchester Inst. Sci. and Tech., 1960-68; head of elect. engring. U. Windsor, Ont., Canada, 1970-78; prof. elec. engring. U. Man., Winnipeg, Canada, 1968-70, head of elec. engring., 1978-79, dean of engring., 1979-89, prof. elec. engring., dean emeritus, 1989—. Cons. various mfrs. high voltage cables; bd. dirs. Man. Hydro Elec. Bd., 1978-96; cons. prof. Xi'an Jiaotong U., People's Rep. China, 1986—. Author or co-author 4 textbooks and more than 200 pub. tech. papers on high voltage engring. Fellow IEEE, Can. Acad. Engring. Home: 2661 Knowles Ave Winnipeg MB Canada R2G 2K7 Office: U Manitoba Fac Engring Winnipeg MB Canada R3T 2N2 E-mail: ekuffel@shaw.ca.

KUFORIJI, PAMELA DELOIS, school system administrator; m. Yomi Kuforiji. D, Loyola U., Chgo., 2006. Cert. adminstr. Ill., 2006. Dist./univ. liaison No. Ill. U., DeKalb, 2003—04; dist. instrnl. coach Elgin Sch. Dist., Ill., 2004—. Ednl. cons. Pro-mise Ptnrs., Streamwood, Ill., 2003—. Mem.: ASCD, Ill. Reading Coun., Internat. Reading Assn., Iota Phi Lambda. Office: School District U-46 355 E Chicago St Elgin IL 60120 Home Phone: 630-372-7331; Office Phone: 847-888-5000 4073. Business E-Mail: pamkuforiji@u46.org.

KUH, CHARLOTTE VIRGINIA, economist; b. Apr. 13, 1944; d. Peter Greenebaum and Frederica Angela (Coerr) K.; m. Roy Radner, Jan. 22, 1978; children: Siobhan Frederica, Michael Edwin. BA magna cum laude, Radcliffe Coll., 1967; MPhil (Univ. fellow), Yale U., 1969, PhD (Dept. Labor grantee), 1976. Rec. sec.-treas. Econometric Soc., New Haven, 1970-75; acting asst. prof. engring. econ. systems Stanford U., 1974-76; asst. prof. Harvard U. Grad. Sch. Edn., 1976-79; staff mgr., dist. mgr. AT&T Corp., 1979-87; exec. dir. grad. records exams program Ednl. Testing Svc., 1987-95; exec. dir. Office of Sci. and Engring. Personnel Nat. Rsch. Coun., 1995—2001; dep. exec. dir. policy & global affairs divsn. Nat. Rsch. coun., Washington, 2001—. Mem. rev. panel NSF, 1979, 81, mem. adv. panel policy rsch. and sci. resource studies, 1983-87; mem. rev. panel Nat. Inst. Edn., 1978-85; mem. com. study nat. needs for biomed. and behavioral research pers. NRC, 1980-85, mem. adv. panel Office Sci. and Engring. Pers., 1983-90, mem. panel on stats. on supply and demand for precoll. sci. and math. tchrs., com. on nat. stats., 1986-89, mem. com. Women in Sci. and Engring. NRC, 1991-95, vice chair, 1993-95, mem. com. to study strategies to strengthen excellence of the N.I.H. Intramural Research Program, Inst. of Medicine, 1988; mem. exec. com. of dels. Am. Coun. Learned Socs., 1999—2002, chmn. 2001-02, treas., bd. dirs., 2002—; mem. adv. com. Bunting Inst., Radcliffe Coll., 1998—2001; cons. in field. Author articles in field. Grantee Carnegie Coun. Higher Edn., Ford Found., Spencer Found. Fellow Assn. Women in Sci.; mem. Am. Econ. Assn., Econometric Soc. Office: Natl Research Council 500 5th St Washington DC 20001 E-mail: ckuh@nas.edu, cvkuh@earthlink.net.

KUH, ERNEST SHIU-JEN, electrical engineering educator; b. Peking, China, Oct. 2, 1928; s. Zone Shung and Tsia (Chu) K.; m. Bettine Chow, Aug. 4, 1957; children: Anthony, Theodore. BS, U. Mich., 1949; MS, MIT, 1950; PhD, Stanford U., 1952; DEng (hon.), Hong Kong U. Sci. and Tech., 1997, Nat. Chiao Tung U., Taiwan, 1999. Mem. tech. staff Bell Tel. Labs., Murray Hill, NJ, 1952-56; assoc. prof. elec. engring. U. Calif., Berkeley, 1956-62, prof., 1962—, Miller rsch. prof., 1965-66, William S. Floyd Jr. prof. engring., 1990—, William S. Floyd Jr. prof. engring. emeritus, 1993—, chmn. dept. elec. engring. and computer sci., 1968-72, dean Coll. Engring., 1973-80. Cons. IBM Rsch. Lab., San Jose, Calif., 1957—62, NSF, 1975—84; mem. panel Nat. Bur. Stds., 1975—80; mem. vis. com. Gen. Motors Inst., 1975—79; mem. vis. com. dept. elec. engring. and computer sci. MIT, 1986—91; mem. adv. coun. elec. engring. dept. Princeton (NJ) U., 1986—98; mem. bd. councilors Sch. Engring. U. So. Calif., 1986—91; mem. sci. adv. bd. Mills Coll., 1976—80. Co-author: Principles of Circuit Synthesis, 1959, Basic Circuit Theory, 1967, Theory of Linear Active Network, 1967; Linear and Nonlinear Circuits, 1987. Recipient Alexander von Humboldt award, 1980, Lamme medal Am. Soc. Endring. Edn., 1981, U. Mich. Disting. Alumnus award, 1970, Berkeley citation, 1993, C & C prize Japanese Found. for Computers and Comm. Promotion, 1996, Phil Kaufman award EDAC, 1998; Brit. Soc. Engring. and Rsch. fellow, 1982. Fellow IEEE (Edn. medal 1981, Centennial medal 1984, Circuits and Systems Soc. award. 1988), AAAS; mem. NAE, Acad. Sinica, Chinese Acad. Scis. (fgn. mem.), Sigma Xi, Phi Kappa Phi. Office: U Calif Elec Engring & Computer Sci Berkeley CA 94720-0001 Business E-Mail: kuh@eecs.berkeley.edu.

KUH, RICHARD HENRY, lawyer; b. NYC, Apr. 27, 1921; s. Joseph Hellmann and Fannie Mina (Rees) K.; m. Joyce Dattel, July 31, 1966; children: Michael Joseph, Jody Ellen. BA, Columbia Coll., 1941; LLB magna cum laude, Harvard U., 1948. Bar: N.Y. 1948, U.S. Dist. Ct. (so. dist.) N.Y. 1948, U.S. Dist. Ct. (ea. dist.) N.Y. 1967, U.S. Supreme Ct. 1968. Assoc. firm Cahill, Gordon & Reindel, 1948-53; asst. dist. atty. N.Y. County Dist. Attys. Office, 1953-64, dist. atty., 1974; pvt. practice law NYC, 1966-71; ptnr. firm Kuh, Goldman, Cooperman & Levitt, NYC, 1971-73, Kuh, Shapiro, Goldman, Cooperman & Levitt, P.C., NYC, 1975-78, Warshaw Burstein Cohen Schlesinger & Kuh, NYC, 1978—. Adj. prof. NYU Law Sch. Author: Foolish Figleaves, 1967; mem. bd. editors: Harvard Law Rev, 1947-48; mem. adv. bd.: Contemporary Drug Problems, 1975— , Criminal Law Bull, 1976—; contbr. articles to popular and profl. jours. Trustee Temple Israel, N.Y.C., 1975-84, Grace Ch. Sch., 1981-85. With U.S. Army, 1942-45, ETO. Walter E. Meyer Research and Writing grantee, 1964-65 Mem. ABA (chair criminal justice sect. 1983-84, chair spl. com. on evaluation jud. performance 1983-90, ho. dels. 1988-93, mem. jud. evaluation adv. com. Nat. Ctr. State Cts. 1990-91, chair 1st nat. conf. gun violence 1994), Assn. Bar City N.Y., Am. Bar Found., Harvard Law Sch. Assn. N.Y. (trustee 1989-92), Harvard Club (mem. admissions com. 1998-01), Phi Beta Kappa. Democrat. Jewish. Home: 14 Washington Pl New York NY 10003-6609 Home Phone: 212-982-0982; Office Phone: 212-984-7820. E-mail: jkuh@verizon.net.

KUHBACH, ROBERT GERDES, manufacturing executive; b. New Haven, May 21, 1947; s. Arend Gerdes and Muriel Ruth (Dinger) K.; m. E. Sherrell Andrews, Nov. 5, 1977; children: Allison Meryl, Courtney Heather. BA in Econs., Yale U., 1969; JD, U. Mich., 1972. Bar: N.Y. 1974. Assoc. Breed, Abbott & Morgan, NYC, 1973-79; atty., sr. atty., gen. counsel Gen. Host Corp., Stamford, Conn., 1980-89; sr. v.p., exec. v.p., dir., gen. counsel, sec. Sudbury, Inc., Cleve., 1989-92; v.p., gen. counsel, sec. Dover Corp., NYC, 1993—2002, v.p., treas., 2002—06, v.p. fin., CFO, 2006—. Capt. U.S. Army, 1971-78. Recipient S. Anthony Benton award U. Mich. Law Sch., Ann Arbor, 1972. Mem. ABA, Am. Soc. Corp. Secs., Am. Corp. Coun. Assn., Bar Assn. of City of N.Y. Office: Dover Corp 280 Park Ave New York NY 10017 E-mail: rgk@doverc.com.*

KUHI, LEONARD VELLO, astronomer, academic administrator; b. Hamilton, Ont., Can., Oct. 22, 1936; came to U.S., 1958; s. John and Sinaida (Rose) K.; m. Patricia Suzanne Brown, Sept. 3, 1960 (div.); children: Alison Diane, Christopher Paul; m. Mary Ellen Murphy, July 15, 1989. BS, U. Toronto, 1958; PhD, U. Calif., Berkeley, 1964. Carnegie postdoctoral fellow Hale Obs., Pasadena, Calif., 1963-65; asst. prof. U. Calif., Berkeley, 1965-69, assoc. prof., 1969-74, prof., 1974-89, chmn. dept. astronomy, 1975-76, dean phys. scis. Coll. Letters and Sci., 1976-81, provost, 1983-89; sr. v.p. for acad. affairs, provost U. Minn., Mpls., 1989-91, prof. astronomy, 1989—, chmn. dept. astronomy, 1997—. Vis. prof. U. Colo., 1969, Coll. de France, Paris, 1972-73, U. Heidelberg, 1978, 80-81; bd. dirs. Am. Inst. Physics. Contbr. articles to profl. jours. Recipient Alexander von Humboldt Sr. Scientist award, 1980-81; NSF research grantee, 1966—. Fellow AAAS; mem. Am. Astron. Soc. (treas. 1987, 96—), Astron. Soc. Pacific (pres. 1978-80), Internat. Astron. Union, Assn. Univ. for Rsch. Astronomy (chair bd. dirs. 1998-2001). Office: U Minn Dept Astronomy 116 Church St SE Minneapolis MN 55455-0149 Home Phone: 952-470-0856; Office Phone: 612-624-7053. Business E-Mail: kuhi@astro.umn.edu.

KUHL, DAVID EDMUND, nuclear medicine physician, educator; b. St. Louis, Oct. 27, 1929; s. Robert Joseph and Caroline Bertha (Waldermeyer) Kuhl; m. Eleanor Dell Kasales, Aug. 7, 1954; 1 child, David Stephen. AB, Temple U., Phila., 1951; MD, U. Pa., 1955; LHD (hon.), Loyola U. Chgo., 1992. Diplomate Am. Bd. Radiology, Am. Bd. Nuc. Medicine (a founder; life trustee 1977-). Intern, then resident in radiology Sch. Medicine and Hosp. U. Pa., 1955—56, 1958—63, mem. faculty, 1963—76, chief div. nuc. medicine, 1963—76, prof. radiology, 1970—76, vice chmn. dept., 1975—76; prof. bioengring. Moore Sch. Electrical Engring. U. Pa., 1974—76; prof. radiol. scis. UCLA Sch. Medicine and Hosp., 1976—86, chief div. nuc. medicine, 1976—84, vice-chmn. dept., 1977—86; prof. internal medicine and radiology U. Mich. Sch. Medicine, Ann Arbor, 1986—2000, chief divsn. nuc. medicine, dir. PET Ctr., 1986—2002, prof. radiology, 2000—. Disting. faculty lectr. in biomed. rsch. U. Mich. Med. Sch., 1992, Henry Russel lectr., 98; mem. adv. com. Dept. Energy, NIH, Internat. Commn. on Radiation Units and Measures, Max Planck Soc. Mem. editl. bd.: various jours.; contbr. articles to med. jours. Served as officer M.C. USNR, 1956—58. Recipient Rsch. Career Devel. award, USPHS, 1961—71, Ernst Jung prize for medicine, Jung Found., Hamburg, 1981, Emil H. Grubbe gold medal, Chgo. Med. Soc., 1983, Berman Found. award peaceful uses atomic energy, 1985, Steven C. Beering award for advancement med. sci., Ind. U., 1987, Disting. Grad. award, U. Pa. Sch. Medicine, 1988, William C. Menninger Meml. award, ACP, 1989, Javits Neurosci. Investigator award, NIH, 1989, Charles F. Kettering prize, GM Cancer Rsch. Found., 2001, Hon. Lifetime Mem. award, Einstein Soc. , Nat. Atomic Mus. Found., 2001. Fellow: Nat. Inst. for Med. and Biol. Engring., Am. Coll. Nuc. Physicians, Am. Coll. Radiology; mem.: Inst. Medicine Nat. Aad. Scis., Am. Neurol. Assn. (Foster Elting Bennett Meml. lectr. 1981), Soc. Nuc. Medicine (ann. lectr. 1991, Nuc. Pioneer citation 1976, Disting. Scientist award 1981, Herman L. Blumgart, M.D. Pioneer award 1979, George Charles de Hevesy Nuc. Medicine Pioneer award 1995, Benedict Cassen prize for rsch. 1996), Radiol. Soc. N.Am. (ann. orator 1982, Outstanding Rschr. award 1996), Assn. Univ. Radiologists, Assn. Am. Physicians, Alpha Omega Alpha. Office: U Mich Hosp Divsn Nuc Medicine 1500 E Medical Center Dr Ann Arbor MI 48109-0028 Business E-Mail: dkuhl@umich.edu.

KUHL, PATRICIA K., science educator; b. Mitchell, SD, Nov. 5, 1946; d. Joseph John and Susan Mary (Schaeffer) K.; m. Andrew N. Meltzoff, Sept. 28, 1985; 1 child, Katherine. BA, St. Cloud State U., Minn., 1967; MA, U. Minn., 1971, PhD, 1973. Postdoctoral research assoc. Cen. Inst. for Deaf, St. Louis, 1973-76; from rsch. assoc. to prof. U. Wash., Seattle, 1976—82, prof., 1982—, William P. and Ruth Gerberding prof., 1997—, dept. chair, 1994—, dir. Inst. Learning and Brain Scis., 2003—. Gov. bd. Am. Inst. Physics, 1994-96; trustee Neurosci. Rsch. Found., 1994—; bd. dirs. Wash. Tech. Ctr., U. Wash., 1994-96; invited presenter White House Conf. on Early Learning and the Brain, 1997, Early Childhood Cognitive Devel., 2001. Editor Jour. Neurosci., 1989-96. Recipient Women in Research citation Kennedy Council, 1978, Virginia Merrill Bloedel Scholar award, 1992-94. Fellow AAAS, Am. Psychol. Soc., Acoustical Soc. Am. (assoc. editor Jour. 1988-92, chair medals and awards, 1992-94, v.p. 1997, Silver medal 1997, pres. 1999—); mem. Am. Acad. Arts and Scis. Office: Inst Learning and Brain Sci Dept Speech & Hearing Sciences 357988 Seattle WA 98105-6247 Office Phone: 206-685-1921. Business E-Mail: pkkuhl@u.washington.edu.

KUHL, PAUL BEACH, lawyer; b. Elizabeth, NJ, July 15, 1935; s. Paul Edmund and Charlotte (Hetche) Kuhl; m. Janey Mae Stadheim, June 24, 1967; children: Alison Lyn, Todd Beach. BA, Cornell U., Ithaca, NY, 1957; LLB, Stanford U., Calif., 1960. Assoc. Law Offices of Walter C. Kohn, San

Francisco, 1961-63, Sedgwick, Detert, Moran & Arnold, San Francisco, 1963-73, ptnr., 1973-99, of counsel, 2000—. Pro tem judge, arbitrator San Francisco Superior Ct., 1989—. Served to lt. USCG, 1961. Recipient Def. Atty. of Yr. award, San Francisco (Calif.) Trial Lawyers Assn., 2001. Mem.: ABA, Meditation Soc., Am. Platform Tennis Assn. (regional pres., bd. dirs. 2003—), No. Calif. Assn. Def., Def. Rsch. Inst., Am. Bd. Trial Advs., Am. Coll. Trial Lawyers, Tahoe Tavern Property Owners Assn. (sec. 1979—81, pres. 1981—83, bd. dirs. 2006—), Lagunitas Country Club (v.p. 1995—97, pres. 2006—). Avocations: tennis, reading. Home: PO Box 1434 Ross CA 94957-1434 Office: Sedgwick Detert Moran & Arnold One Market St Steuart Tower 8th Fl San Francisco CA 94105 Office Phone: 415-781-7900. Business E-Mail: beach.kuhl@sdma.com.

KUHL, RANDY (JOHN R. KUHL JR.), congressman, lawyer; b. Bath, NY, Apr. 19, 1943; s. John R. and Myrtle (Wombacker) Kuhl; children: John R. III, Christopher, James Whitney. BS in Civil Engrign., Union Coll., 1966; JD, Syracuse U. Coll. Law, 1969; DHL (hon.), Keuka Coll. Bar: NY 1970, US Supreme Ct. Legal counsel social svc. and hwy. dept. Steuben County, NY, asst. atty. NY; county atty., village atty. Prattsburgh, NY; town atty. Rathbone and Pulteney; mem. NY State Assembly, 1980-86, NY State Senate, 1986—2004, chmn. agr. standing com., 1987-99, asst. majority leader, 1995—2004, chmn. edn. standing com., 1999—2003, chmn. transp. standing com., 2003—04; mem. US Congress from 29th NY dist., 2005—, mem. edn. and the workforce com., mem. agr. com., mem. transp. and infrastructure com., vice chair aviation subcommittee. Mem. adv. com. Five Rivers coun. Boy Scouts Am.; pres. bd. dirs. Reginald Wood Scouting Meml. Recipient NYFB Disting. Svc. award, Frederick L. Zimmerman award Susquehanna River Basin Commn., 2001. Mem. NY Bar Assn., Steuben County Bar Assn., Am. Arbitration Assn., Rotary, Elks, Branchport Rod and Gun Club. Episcopalian. Office: US Ho Reps 1505 Longworth Ho Office Bldg Washington DC 20515-3229 Office Phone: 202-225-3161.*

KUHLA, DONALD E., chemicals executive; b. SI, NY, June 9, 1942; s. Robert Elliot and Dorothy (Ware) K.; m. Sandrra Casstellucci, June 19, 1965; children: Jennifer, Robert. BA in Chemistry, NYU, 1964; PhD in Organic Chemistry, Ohio State U., 1968. Rsch. chemist Pfizer, Groton, Conn., 1968-69, medicinal chemist, 1969-74, project leader, mgr., asst. dir., 1974-81; dir. medicinal chemistry, preclin. scis. Rorer Group, Ft. Washington, Pa., 1989-90, sr. v.p. ops., 1989-90; pres., chief. exec. officer Hybridon, Inc., Worcester, Mass., 1990—. Contbr. articles to profl. jours. Mem. AAAS, Am. Chem. Soc., N.Y. Acad. Scis., Internat. Soc. for the Study of Xenobiotics, Phila. Organic Chemists. Achievements include over 100 patents in field; rsch. on various aspects of organic synthesis. Office: Albany Molecular Research 21 Corporate Cir Albany NY 12212-5098

KUHLENSCHMIDT, MARK STUART, microbiologist, researcher; b. Evansville, Ind., Oct. 31, 1947; s. Ervin Carl and Laura Lucy Kuhlenschmidt; m. Theresa Marie Banet, June 16, 1973; children: Matthew Scot, Michael Stuart. BS, Purdue U., W. Lafayette, Ind., 1969; MS in Medicine, U. Louisville, Ky., 1971; PhD in Medicine, U. Pitts., 1975. Postdoctoral fellow Johns Hopkins U., Balt., 1975—77, rsch. scientist, 1977—83; from asst. prof. vet. medicine to prof. U. Ill., Urbana, Ill., 1983—98, prof., 1998—, asst. head Dept. Pathobiology, 2002—. Dir. Instnl. Animal Care and Use program U. Ill., 2003—, affiliate prof. Dept. Agr. Engring., 2002—. Contbr. articles to profl. jours. Coach baseball Am. Legion, Champaign, Ill., 1999—2006. Recipient Outstanding Rsch. award, U. Ill. Coll. Vet. Medicine, 1994, Recognition for Excellent Tchg. award, U. Ill., 1995—99; grantee, USDA, 1984—2006, NIH, 1999—2002; Olive V. Levin Meml. Postdoctoral fellowship, Leukemia Soc. Am., 1975—77. Mem.: Am. Chem. Soc., Am. Soc. Microbiology, Am. Soc. Biochemistry and Molecular Biology, Ill. State Vet. Med. Assn. (assoc.), Omega Tau Sigma, Phi Zeta. Achievements include research in mechanisms of microbial adhesion and host-pathogen interactions responsible for infectious disease. Home: 1406 Cobblefield Rd Champaign IL 61822 Office: University of Illinois Vet Med 2001 S Lincoln Ave Urbana IL 61802 Home Phone: 217-398-1270; Office Phone: 217-333-9039. Office Fax: 217-244-7421. Personal E-mail: mkuhl6@insightbb.com. Business E-Mail: kuhlensc@uiuc.edu.

KUHLER, DEBORAH GAIL, grief therapist, retired state legislator; b. Moorhead, Minn., Oct. 12, 1952; d. Robert Edgar and Beverly Maxine (Buechler) Ecker; m. George Henry Kuhler, Dec. 28, 1973; children: Karen Elizabeth, Ellen Christine. BA, Dakota Wesleyan U., 1974; MA, U. N.D., 1977. Outpatient therapist Ctr. for Human Devel., Grand Forks, ND, 1975-77; mental health counselor Community Counseling Services, Huron, SD, 1978-88, 91-93; owner, dir. bereavement svcs. Kuhler Funeral Home, Huron, 1978—; adj. prof. Huron U., 1979—83, 1990—2002; mem. from dist. 23 S.D. Ho. Reps., Pierre, 1987-90; mem. House Judiciary com., chair House Health and Welfare Com., Pierre, 1990. Active First United Meth. Ch. Named Young Alumnus of the Yr., Dakota Wesleyan U., 1989, Bus. and Profl. Women, 1989. Mem. ACA, PEO, Am. Mental Health Counselors Assn., Assn. for Death Edn. and Counseling. Avocations: reading, breadmaking, sewing, piano. E-mail: kuhlerdg@yahoo.com.

KUHLER, RENALDO GILLET, retired museum director, medical illustrator; b. Teaneck, NJ, Nov. 21, 1931; s. Otto August and Simonne L. (Gillet) K.; 1 child, Anne Marie Cooper. BA, U. Colo., 1961. Curator of history, illustrator exhibit, miniature diorama preparator Ea. Wash. State Hist. Soc. Mus., Spokane, 1962-67; mus. illustrator NC State Mus. Natural History, Raleigh, 1969—2003, ret., 1999. Designer, executor of art work for sci. illustrations, awards, brochures, pamphlets and periodicals Dept. Agr. and Mus., NC, 1972-74; designer 36 illustrations for Handbook of Reptiles and Amphibians of Florida, Part 1 (Ray E. Ashton), 1981; contbr. many illustrations Atlas of Freshwater Fishes of North America (David Lee), Endangered Threatened and Rare Fauna of North Carolina (Ross, Rohde and Lindquist), Distribution Survey of North Carolina Mammals (Lee, Funderburg and Clark); Endangered Threatened and Rare Fauna of North Carolina, part 1 (Mary K. Clark), Potential Effect of Oil Spills on Seabirds, etc. (Lee and Socci), Poisonous Snakes of North Carolina (William M. Palmer), Reptiles of North Carolina (William M. Palmer and Alvin Braswell), Synopsis of North American Centipede (Rowland Shelley), 2002; gen. illustrator: American Firearms and the Changing Frontier (Waldo E. Rosebush); also contbr. to jours. and bulls. including Then.C-.Naturalist; currently working on skull illustrations for Mammals of North Carolina (Mary Kay Clark); calligrapher; creator wood handicrafts; violin maker, 1949. Appearance as sci. illustrator (TV) Nat. Geog., June 2001; contbr. illustrations to Fishes of Chesapeake Bay, 1997. Mem. Dem. Nat. Com.; life mem. Raleigh Rhinoceros Club, 2000—; vol. sci. illustrator NC State Mus. Natural History, 1999-. Mem. Nat. Trust Hist. Preservation, Nat. Smokers Alliance, Rails to Trails, East Coast Greenway Alliance, Raleigh Rhinoceros Club (life), Raleigh Cardinal Club, Human Rights Campaign. Democrat. Avocations: model building, carburator fittings for pipes, designing suits. Home and Office: Apt 3 510 Tilden St Raleigh NC 27605-1524 Office Phone: 919-833-1067.

KUHLIK, BRUCE NEIL, lawyer; b. Detroit, Sept. 7, 1956; s. Earl Harvey and Barbara (Osterman) K.; m. Robyn Joy Lipton, May 6, 1984; children: Erica, Lauren. AB summa cum laude, Harvard U., 1978, JD magna cum laude, 1981. Bar: DC 1982, US Supreme Ct. 1985, Pa. 2005. Law clk. to Judge Levin H. Campbell, U.S. Ct. Appeals (1st cir.), Mass., 1981-82; assoc. Covington & Burling, Washington, 1982-84, 86-90; asst. & solicitor gen. US Dept. Justice, Washington, 1984-86; ptnr. Covington & Burling, Washington, 1990—2002; sr. v.p. and gen. counsel Pharm. Rsch. and Mfrs. of Am., 2002—05; v.p. and assoc. gen. counsel Merck & Co., Inc., Whitehouse Sta., NJ, 2005—07, sr. v.p., gen. counsel, 2007—. Contbr. articles to profl. jours.; editor: Harvard Law Rev. Mem. D.C. Bar, Phi Beta Kappa. Office: Merck & Co Inc 1 Merck Dr PO Box 100 Whitehouse Station NJ 08889 Office Phone: 908-423-1000.*

KUHLMAN, THOMAS ASHFORD, retired American studies educator, writer; b. Cleve., May 24, 1939; s. Orlyn Lee and Catherine Mary (Ashford) K.; m. Mary Louise Haynes, Aug. 22, 1964; children: John Christopher, Katherine Mary. Honors AB, Xavier U., 1961; AM, Brown U., 1963, PhD, 1967. Teaching fellow Brown U., 1963-64; instr. English Georgetown U., 1964-67; asst. prof. English Creighton U., 1967-70, assoc. prof., 1970—2005, coord. continuing edn., 1973-74; ret., 2005; assoc. prof. emeritus Creighton U., 2006—. Vis. scholar Am. Acad. in Rome, 1981; mem. faculty Inst. Jewish Studies, Omaha, 1974-75; regional dir. Nat. Bicentennial Youth Debates, 1975-76; dir. Copper Hollow Writers Workshop, 1977-78; regional humanist Nebr. Com. Humanities, 1976-78; reg. spkr. Joslyn Art Mus.; participant Attingham Study Tour of Brit. Country Houses, 2002. Playwright Each of These Landlords, 1976, Georgian Punch Bowl, Monteith Design, 1982, Idiots Delete, 1987, Hostages of the Court, 1993, Ambition in Exile, 1997, fiction in Prairie Schooner, Shadows; other literary jours.; author of numerous essays; editor The Beauty of Thy House: The History, Art, and Architecture of St. Cecilia Cathedral, Omaha, 2005, Baroque Nebraska: An Architectural Entertainment, 2007. Mem. Omaha Symphony Coun., 1972-79, mem. exec. com., 1974-77; heritage chmn., bd. dirs. Omaha-Douglas County Bicentennial Commn., 1974-76; sec., bd. dirs. Met. Arts Coun., 1976-78; pres. Landmarks, Inc., 1987-88; bd. dirs. Florence Arts and Humanities Coun., 1979, pres. 1980; bd. dirs. Nebr. Archtl. Foun., 1992-99; mem. cmty. bd. Nebr. Shakespeare Festival, 1992-2004; mem. adv. bd. Joslyn Castle Inst. for Sustainable Cmtys.; v.p. Omaha chpt. Irish-Am. Cultural Inst.; bd. dirs. Irish Arts Coun., Omaha, 2004-06; mem. pastoral coun. St. Cecilia Cathedral, Omaha, 2003-06; cons. Omaha Gold Coast Historic Preservation Assn. Woodrow Wilson fellow, 1961, Andrew W. Mellon fellow, U. Kans., 1984, NEH fellow U. N.C.-Chapel Hill, 1989; grantee Office of Edn. Humanities, 1968, Rsch. grantee Creighton U. Faculty, 1969, grantee Nebr. Arts Coun., 1978, grantee Can. Govt. Faculty Devel. Programme, 1979. Mem. Am. Studies Assn., Omaha Workshop Theater (pres. 1992-97), Nebr. Humanities Coun. (spkrs. bur. 1987-2005), Hist. Soc. Douglas County (dir. 1995-2001), Vasari Soc. (founding fellow), Council Bluffs Country Club, Alpha Sigma Nu. Republican. Roman Catholic. Home: 3650 Burt St Omaha NE 68131-1946

KUHLMANN, FRED MARK, lawyer; b. St. Louis, Apr. 9, 1948; s. Frederick Louis and Mildred (Southworth) K.; m. Barbara Jane Nierman, Dec. 30, 1970; children: F. Matthew, Sarah Ann Morgan. AB summa cum laude, Washington U., St. Louis, 1970; JD cum laude, Harvard U., 1973. Bar: Mo. 1973. Assoc. atty. Stolar, Heitzmann & Eder, St. Louis, 1973-75; from tax counsel to staff v.p. McDonnell Douglas Corp., St. Louis, 1975—87, sr. v.p., gen. counsel, 1991—97; exec. v.p. McDonnell Douglas Health Systems Co., 1987—89; pres. McDonnell Douglas Systems Integration Co., 1989—91; of counsel Bryan Cave, St. Louis, 1997-98; pres. Sys. Svc. Enterprises, St. Louis, 1998—2004, co-CEO, 2004—. Bd. dirs. Republic Health Corp., Dallas, 1988-90, Grace Place Retreats, 2005—; mem. governing bd. Luth. Med. Ctr., 1989-95, chmn., 1990-92. Bd. dirs. Luth. Charities Assn., 1982-91, sec. 1984-86, chmn. 1986-89; elder Luth. Ch. of Resurrection, 1977-80; mem. Regents Coun. Concordia Sem., 1981-84; chmn. cub scout pack 459 Boy Scouts Am., 1984-86; bd. dirs. Luth. H.S. Assn., 1978-84, 91-97, pres. 1992-97, long range planning com. 1990-92, chmn. alumni assn., 1981; chmn. North Star dist. Boy Scouts Am., 1990-93; bd. dirs. Mcpl. Theatre Assn., St. Louis, 1991—; chmn. long range planning com. St. Paul's Luth. Ch., 1988-91, 98-2001, pres., 1996-97, 2002-03; bd. dirs., mem. exec. com. United Way of Greater St. Louis, 1994-97, chmn. Vanguard divsn., 1994-97; mem. amb. coun. Luth. Family and Children's Svcs. of St. Louis, 1998—; bd. dirs. Luth. Found. St. Louis, 1998—, chmn., 2004-06; mem. adv. bd. Webster U. Bus. and Tech. Sch., 1999-2001; mem. bd mgrs. worker benefit plans Luth. Ch.-Mo. Synod, 2001—, vice-chmn., 2006—; bd. dirs. KFUO Radio Arts Bd., 2005—, Thrivent Fin. for Luths., 2006—. Recipient Disting. Leadership award Luth. Assn. for Higher Edn., 1981. Mem. ABA, Mo. Bar Assn., Bar Assn. Met. St. Louis, Bellerive Country Club, Phi Beta Kappa, Omicron Delta Kappa. Republican. Avocations: tennis, golf, racquetball. Home: 1711 Stone Ridge Trails Dr Saint Louis MO 63122-3546 Office: Sys Svc Enterprises 77 Westport Plz Ste 500 Saint Louis MO 63146-3126 Home Phone: 314-821-4833; Office Phone: 314-439-4702. Business E-Mail: fmkuhlmann@sseinc.com.

KUHLMANN-WILSDORF, DORIS, materials scientist, inventor, retired educator; b. Bremen, Germany, Feb. 15, 1922; 1956, naturalized, 1963; d. A. Friedrich and Elsa S. (Dreyer) K.; m. Heinz G.F. Wilsdorf, Jan. 4, 1950; children: Gabriele (dec.), Michael (dec.). BS in Physics, U. Göttingen, Germany, 1944, MS, 1946, PhD in Materials Sci., 1947; DSc in Physics-Materials Sci., U. Witwatersrand, South Africa, 1954; DSc in Physics (hon.), U. Pretoria, South Africa, 2004. Postdoctoral fellow U. Göttingen, 1947-48; postdoctoral fellow in physics U. Bristol, Eng., 1949-50; lectr. physics U. Witwatersrand, Johannesburg, 1950-56; from assoc. prof. metall. engring. to prof. U. Pa., Phila., 1957-63; prof. engring. physics U. Va., Charlottesville, 1963-66, univ. prof. applied sci., 1966—2005; prof. emeritus, 2005—. Co-founder, HiPerCon; founder, owner, Kuhlmann-Wilsdorf Motors LLC; inventor in field. Editor: 4 materials sci. books; contbr. 300 articles to profl. jours. Recipient J. Shelton Horsley award Va. Acad. Sci., 1966, Americanism medal DAR, 1966, Heyn medal German Metall. Soc., 1988, Achievement award Soc. Women Engrs., 1989, Ragnar Holm Sci. Achievement award IEEE, 1991. Fellow Am. Soc. Materials Internat. (life, Edward DeMille Campbell Meml. lectr. 2002), Am. Phys. Soc.; mem. Am. Soc. Women Engrs. (life), Am. Soc. Engring. Edn. (medal for excellence 1965, 66), AIME Metall. Soc. (life), Nat. Acad. Engring. 10 patents in field. Business E-Mail: dwilsdorf@embarqmail.com.

KUHN, ALBERT JOSEPH, language educator; b. Dowell, Ill., Apr. 4, 1926; s. Albert and Elizabeth (Furjes) K.; m. Roberta Marshall, June 12, 1949 (dec. 1993); children— William, Frederick. BA, U. Ill., 1950; PhD, Johns Hopkins, 1954. Mem. faculty Ohio State U., 1954—, chmn. English dept., 1964-71, prof. English, 1965, provost, v.p. acad. affairs, 1971-79, dir. Univ. Honors, 1985-89, professor emeritus, 1989—. Contbr. to Romantic Bibliography, 1963, also articles.; editor: Three Sentimental Novels, 1970, Victorian Literature and Society, 1984 Mem. region VIII Woodrow Wilson Selection Com., 1961-68; mem. research bd. Children's Hosp., 1973-77; trustee Battelle Meml. Inst. Found., 1975-79. Served with USNR, 1944-46. Recipient Disting. Svc. award Ohio State U., 1991. Mem. MLA, North Cen. Assn. Colls. and Schs. (cons.-evaluator), Kit Kat Club (Columbus), Phi Beta Kappa, Phi Kappa Phi. Home: 35 Webster Park Ave Columbus OH 43214-3512

KUHN, BEVERLY THOMPSON, transportation engineer; m. Darrell Lee Kuhn. BSCE cum laude, Tex. A&M U., 1989, M of Civil Engring., 1990; PhD, Pa. State U., 1997. Registered pofl. engr., Tex. Engring. rsch. assoc. Tex. Transp. Inst., Tex. A&M U. Sys., Houston, 1990—91, asst. rsch. scientist, 1991—94, dir. ctr. for profl. devel., assoc. rsch. engr. College Station, 1997—2001, divsn. head, assoc. rsch. engr., 1999—2003, divsn. head, rsch. engr., 2003—07, divsn. head, sr. rsch. engr., 2007—; rsch. asst. Pa. Transp. Inst., Pa. State U., University Park, Pa., 1994—97. Instr. dept. civil and environ. engring. Pa. State U., University Park, 1995—96; instr. dept. civil engring. Tex. A&M U., College Station, 2000—04. Author: Managed Lanes Handbook, 2005 (TxDOT Top Innovations and Rsch. Findings award); contbr. articles to profl. jours. Mentor MentorNet, 2002; block capt. Pebble Creek Owners Assn., College Station, 2002; mentor ATMentors Tex. A&M U., College Station, 2003—; parent coun. rep. Tex. A&M Children's Ctr., College Station, 2005—; role model enigmatic computer class Pa. State Women in Engring. Program, University Park, 2002, role model girls exploring engring., 2002; vol. freshman welcome day Tex. A&M U., College Station, 2000; vol. Brazos Boosting Engring. Sci. and Tech., Tex., 2000; judge Tex. State Sci. and Engring. Fair, Austin, 1999. Recipient Herbert H. Richardson Team award, Tex. Transp. Inst. /Trinity Industries, 2005, Lechner Merit award, Tex. A&M U. Coll. Engring., 1985—86, Outstanding Achievement award, Tex. A&M U. Coll. Engring. Faculty, 1989, Oustanding Student award, Mid-Atlantic Univ. Transp. Ctr., 1997, Rschr. award, Tex. Transp. Inst. / Trinity Industries, 2000, Leadership Tex. award, Found. for Women's Resources, 2003, Top Innovations and Rsch. Findings award, Tex. Dept. Transp., 2005; Royce E. Wisenbaker grad. fellow, Tex. A&M U. Coll. Engring., 1989—90, Dean's Edn. fellow, Pa. State U. Coll. Engring., 1994—97, Grad. Engring. Edn. fellow, NSF, 1994—97, Transp. fellow, Eno Found., 1996, Frank H. Newnam, Jr. scholar, Tex. A&M U. Dept. Civil Engring., 1986—87, Worthington A. Franks scholar, 1987—88, D.C. Greer scholar, 1988—89, Carmen E. Turner sholar, Women's Transp. Seminar, 1996, Rockwell scholar, Intelligent Transp. Soc. Am., 1996, Burton W. Marsh fellow, Inst. Transp. Engineers, 1989. Mem.: Inst. Transp. Engrs. (chair task force on determining vehicle signal change/clearance int 1991—94, tech. com. on establishing guidelines for fwy. svc. patrols 1993—95, mgr. traffic engring. coun. tech. com. 1996—2005, Burton W. Marsh fellowship selection com. 1997—2000, edn. coun. 2000, vice-chair - traffic engring. coun. 2005—07, standing com. on recommended practices 2005, mgr. of traffic engring. coun. website 2005), Am. Soc. for Engring. Edn., Pa. State Women in Engring. Alumnae Soc., Intelligent Transp. Soc. Tex., Intelligent Transp. Soc. Am., Transp. Rsch. Bd. Joint Subcommittee on Managed Lanes, Transp. Rsch. Bd. (sec., com. on user info. sys. 1998—2004, chair com. on user info. sys. 2004—), Leadership Tex. Alumnae Assn., Phi Kappa Phi, Chi Epsilon, Tau Beta Pi (life). Office: Tex Transp Inst 3135 Tamu College Station TX 77843-3135 Home Phone: 979-690-6111; Office Phone: 979-845-1536.

KUHN, EDWIN P., travel company executive; BS in bus. adminstrn., Ohio State U.; grad. work, Wright State U., Dayton, Ohio. Named pres., CEO TravelCenters of Am., Inc., 1992—, now chmn. Mem. Nat. Assn. Truck Stop Operators (chmn. long-range planning com.). Office: TravelCenters of Am Inc 24601 Center Ridge Rd Ste 200 Westlake OH 44145 Office Phone: 440-808-9100.

KUHN, HOWARD ARTHUR, engineering executive, educator; b. Pitts., Dec. 6, 1940; s. Howard E. and Selma W. Kuhn; m. Beverly A. Burke, Dec. 23, 1961; children: Amy, Jeffrey, David, Stephen. BS, Carnegie-Mellon U., 1962, MS, 1963, PhD, 1966. Registered profl. engr., Pa., Fla., SC. Prof. engring. Drexel U., Phila., 1966-74, U. Pitts., 1975-89, adj. prof., 1989-2000, 2004—; v.p., CTO Scienda Bldg. Scis., 2000—02, cons. engr. Irwin, Pa., 2002—; dir. R & D The ExOne Co., 2002—. Dir. freshman engring. program, U. Pitts, 1981-88, indsl. adv. com.; cons. engr. Deformation Control Tech., Pitts., 1980-88; tech. dir. Concurrent Techs. Corp., 1988, tech. v.p., 1989-92, v.p., chief tech. officer, 1992-2000; bd. dirs. Pitts. Tech. Coun. Author: Powder Forging, 1990; editor: Powder Metallurgy Processing, 1978, ASM Handbook on Mechanical Testing, 2000; inventor powder metallurgy forging, aluminum plate rolling improvements. Pres. PTA, Gibsonia, Pa., 1976-77; mem. Civic Adv. Com., Gibsonia, 1978-82; chmn. Laurel Highlands Cancer Program, bd. dirs. Johnstown Chiefs Hockey Team, 1995-2000; dir. advanced tech. programs Cambria County Area C.C., 1994-96, bd. trustees C.C., 1996-2000; bd. dirs. Orangeburg-Calhoun Tech. Coll. Fellow Am. Soc. Materials Internat. (life, chmn. mfg. tech., nominating com., Pitts. chpt. exec. bd. treas., Zay Jeffries award, Edgar C. Bain award, Campbell lecture selection com.); mem. ASME (life), Am. Powder Metallurgy Inst. (life), The Materials Soc. (life), Soc. Mfg. Engrs. (life), Light Gage Steel Engrs. Assn., Richland Athletic Assn. (pres.). Democrat. Methodist. Home: 128 McCaffrey Ln Johnstown PA 15905 Office: 8001 Pennsylvania Ave Irwin PA 15642 Home Phone: 412-334-5520; Office Phone: 724-978-7214. Business E-Mail: howard.kuhn@exone.com.

KUHN, JAMES D., real estate company executive; BA in Fin., Syracuse U., MBA in Real Estate; postgrad., The Wharton Sch., Harvard U. Lender Met. Life Ins. Co.; sr. ptnr. and exec. v.p. acquisitions and devel. The Mendik Co., 1978, owner, mgr., 1990—92; prin., pres., COO Newmark & Co. Real Estate Inc., NYC, 1992—. Chmn. NYU Real Estate Inst.; trustee Nat. Jewish Med. and Rsch. Ctr. Bd. dirs. Kids Found. for Devel. Diseases; bd. trustees, bd. dirs. Nat. Jewish Med. and Rsch. Ctr.; chmn. adv. bd. NYU Real Estate Inst.; adv. bd. Whitman Sch. Mgmt. Syracuse U. Named Young Man of Yr., Real Estate Bd. NY, 1985; recipient Real Estate Svc. Award of Yr., NYU, 1984, Nat. Jewish Humanitarian award, 1994. Mem.: Urban Land Inst. (corp. real estate coun.). Office: Newmark & Co Real Estate Inc 125 Park Ave New York NY 10017 Office Phone: 212-372-2000. E-mail: jkuhn@newmarkkf.com.*

KUHN, JAMES EDWARD, judge; b. Hammond, La., Oct. 31, 1946; s. Eton Percy and Mildred Louise (McDaniel) K.; m. Cheryl Aucoin, Dec. 27, 1969; children: James M., Jennifer L. BA, Southeastern La. U., 1968; JD, Loyola U. of South, 1973; attended, U.S. Army War Coll. Bar: La. 1973, Colo. 1995, U.S. Supreme Ct. 1978. Asst. dist. atty. 21st Jud. Dist., La., 1980-90, judge Livingston, St. Helena, Tangipahoa, 1990-95, Ct. Appeals (1st cir.), Baton Rouge, 1995—. Instr. history, and polit. sci. Southeastern La. U., Hammond, 1991—; past mem. appellate ct. performance and standards com. La. Supreme Ct.; past mem. La. State Bar Assn. com. on profl. and quality of life com., ins., negligence and worker's comp., 1983-90 Founder For Our Youth; past bd. dir. La. Coun. Child Abuse, past sec.-treas. Conf. Ct. Appeal Judges State of La. With Nat. Guard US Army, 1969—74. Recipient Am. Jurisprudence award Loyola Law Sch. Mem. ABA, La. State Bar Assn. (CLE com.), Colo. Bar Assn., 21st Jud. Bar Assn., Am. Judicature Soc., Am. Judges Assn., New Orleans Bar Assn., Baton Rouge Bar Assn., Covington Bar Assn., Fla. Parishes Inns of Ct., Delta Theta Phi, Phi Kappa Phi. Home: 253 W Oak St Ponchatoula LA 70454-3330 Office Phone: 985-386-6082.

KUHN, JAMES PAUL, management consultant; b. Milw., July 11, 1937; s. Clarence George and Genevieve Mary K.; m. Josephine M. Keller, Dec. 27, 1958; children: Christine, Cynthia, George. BME, Marquette U., Milw., 1961; MBA, U. Chgo., 1972. Mfg. mgr. GE Co., Fairfield, Conn., 1961-65; prin. A.T. Kearney, Inc., Chgo., 1966-74, v.p., 1984—2001, Booz Allen & Hamilton, Inc., NYC, 1975-77; pres. Case Mfg. Svcs., Chgo., 1978-83; dir. Case & Co., Inc., NYC, 1980-83; CFO Timeless Designs, Inc., Chgo., 1984—; CEO AKN Properties LLC, Chgo., 2005—. Contbr. articles to profl. jours. Mem.: Marco Island Country Club.

KUHN, KEITH C., library director; BA, Indiana U., Indpls., 1974; MLS, Indiana U., Bloomington, 1976. Libr. svcs. dir. Pub. Libr. Cin. & Hamilton County, Cin. Pres. Indiana U. Sch. Libr. & Info. Sci. Alumni Bd., 2003—07; mgmt. com. YMCA of Greater Cin. Recipient Sullivan award, ALA, 2007. Mem.: Cin. Book Arts Soc. (pres. 2005—06, vice-chmn. 2003—04, chmn. 2004—05), Beta Phi Mu (y.p. Phi ch. 2005—06). Office: Pub Libr Cin & Hamilton County 800 Vine St Cincinnati OH 45202-2009 Office Phone: 513-369-6900. Business E-Mail: keith.kuhn@cincinnatilibrary.org.

KUHN, MATTHEW, retired engineering company executive; b. Sacalaz, Banat, Romania, Mar. 19, 1936; came to U.S., 1967; s. Peter and Katherine (Gerres) K.; m. Betty Jane Ritchie, Aug. 20, 1966; children: Andrew Jason, Andrea Suzanne. BASc in Engring. Physics, Queen's U., Kingston, Ont., Can., 1962; MASc, U. Waterloo, Ont., 1963, PhDEE, 1967, D of Engring.

(hon.), 1985; postgrad., Brown U., 1967-68. Supr. MTS Bell Tel. Labs., Murray Hill, NJ, 1968—73; from mgr. adv. tech. to asst. v.p. BNR Ltd., Ottawa, Ontario, Canada, 1973—85; asst. v.p. BNR Inc., Research Triangle Park, NC, 1985—89; pres. Microelectronics Ctr. of N.C., Research Triangle Park, 1989—94, EconTech Cons. & Rsch. Mgmt. Svcs., 1994—99, ret., 1999. Adj. prof. engring. mgmt. Duke U., 1997-2000; presenter numerous profl. meetings. Contbr. articles to profl. jours. Mem. N.C. Bd. Sci. & Tech., 1991-94; chmn. adv. coun. Queen's U., 1983-84; chmn. engring. adv. coun. Duke U., Durham, N.C., 1989-94. Fellow IEEE (editor spl. issue Electron Devices Jour. Optoelectronics 1975). Roman Catholic. Achievements include discovery of quasi-static method measurement technique for integrated circuit development; co-development first generation fiber optics technology. Home: 11 Piney Point Whispering Pines NC 28327 Personal E-mail: mkuhnet@embarqmail.cm. *It is sometimes necessary to disagree but never to be disagreeable.*

KUHN, PAUL HUBERT, JR., investment advisor; b. Chattanooga, Sept. 7, 1943; s. P. Hubert and Pauline Anna (Byrnes) Kuhn; m. Jeanne Bartlett Elmore, June 7, 1966 (dec. 1996); children: Katherine, Christopher. BA, Vanderbilt U., 1965; MBA, Ind. U., 1971. Chartered investment counselor. V.p., prin. Stein Roe & Farnham, Chgo., 1971-89; v.p. Stein Roe Spl. Fund, Chgo., 1983-89; mng. ptnr. Davidson Ptnrs. Investment Counsel, Nashville, 1989-2000; ptnr. J.C. Bradford & Co., Nashville, 1989-2000; prin. Woodmont Investment Counsel, 2000—. Bd. dirs. Augustana Hosp., Chgo., 1980-83, USO of Chgo.; pres. Lincoln Park Renewal Corp., Chgo.; chmn. investment com. Cath. Diocese Nashville, 2005-; chmn. Major Gifts Campaign, Nashville Cares; pres. Tenn. Fgn. Language Inst. Fund. Lt. USN, 1965-69. Mem. CFA Inst., CFA Soc. Nashville (bd. dirs. 1997-2001, pres. 2001-02), Nat. Orgn. Reform Marijuana Laws (bd. dirs. 1997—), Tavern Club (Chgo.) (bd. govs.), Woman's Athletic Club of Chgo. (hon.), Phi Beta Kappa, Omicron Delta Kappa. Republican. Roman Catholic. Office: Woodmont Investment Counsel 102 Woodmont Blvd Ste 350 Nashville TN 37205 Home Phone: 615-298-2038; Office Phone: 615-297-0673. E-mail: paul@woodmontcounsel.com.

KUHN, TIMOTHY R., communication educator; b. Anniston, Ala., Apr. 7, 1969; s. Richard and Joan Kuhn. BS, U. Minn., Mpls., 1991, MA, 1996; PhD, Ariz. State U., Tempe, 2000. Assoc. prof. dept. comm. U. Colo., Boulder, 2000—. Mem.: Acad. Mgmt., Internat. Comm. Assn., Nat. Comm. Assn. (vice chair orgnl. comm. divsn. 2005—06). Office: University of Colorado at Boulder Department of Communication 270 UCB Boulder CO 80309-0270 Office Phone: 303-492-2986. Business E-Mail: tim.kuhn@colorado.edu.

KUHN, WILLIAM ANDREW, music educator; b. North Tonawanda, NY, June 15, 1971; s. Frederick John and Marie Ann Kuhn; m. Rachelle Corpuz, May 25, 1994; children: Joshua Ryan, Victoria Lynn. AS, Villa Maria Coll., 1991; BMus, U. Ariz., 1994; MA, SUNY, Buffalo, 1999. Cert. tchr. NY. Music tchr. Baker Victory Sch., Lackawanna, NY, 1995—96, Kenmore Mid. Sch., Kenmore, NY, 1996—. Profl. jazz bassist, guitarist. Named Tchr. of Yr., Kenmore Mid. Sch., 2005; scholar Sch. of Music Jazz scholar, U. Ariz., 1991—94. Mem.: Erie County Music Educators Assn. (assoc.), NY State Sch. Music Assn. (assoc.; music performance adjudicator 2001—), Music Educators Nat. Conf. (assoc.), Kenmore Teachers Assn. (assoc.), NY State United Teachers (assoc.). Democrat. Home: 41 Stoneleigh Ave Buffalo NY 14223 Office: Kenmore Mid Sch 155 Delaware Rd Kenmore NY 14217 Home Phone: 716-877-4990; Office Phone: 716-874-8403. Office Fax: 716-874-8650. Personal E-mail: wakuhn1@yahoo.com. E-mail: william_kuhn@kenton.k12.ny.us.

KUHN, WILLIS EVAN, II, lawyer, mediator; b. Indpls., July 20, 1948; s. Theodore Roosevelt and Theresa Anne (Lupinacci) K.; m. Virginia Katherine Williams, Apr. 12, 1983; children: William Franklin, Virginia Anne. BA, Vanderbilt U., 1970; JD with honors, U. Tex., 1973. Bar: Tex. 1973; cert. mediator. Assoc. Johnson & Gibbs, Dallas, 1973-75, Moore & Peterson, Dallas, 1975-80; ptnr. Baker, Smith & Mills, Dallas, 1980-85, Kuhn & Fishman, Dallas, 1985-90, Hopkins & Sutter, Dallas, 1990-93; pvt. practice Dallas, 1993—. Mem. Dallas So. Meml. Assn., 1992—. Mem. State Bar Tex., Dallas Bar Assn., Dallas Athletic Club, Order of Coif, Phi Kappa Psi. Republican. Avocations: golf, history. Office: 15851 N Dallas Pkwy #600 Dallas TX 75001-6030 Home: 6062 Jereme Trl Dallas TX 75252-5130 Office Phone: 972-450-6540.

KUHRAU, EDWARD W., lawyer; b. Caney, Kans., Apr. 19, 1935; s. Edward and Dolores (Hardman) Kuhrau; m. Janiece Christal (div. 1983); children: Quentin, Clayton; m. Sandy Shreve. BA, U. Tex., 1960; JD, U. So. Calif., 1965. Bar: Calif. 1966, Wash. 1968, Alaska 1977. With Perkins Coie (and predecessor firms), Seattle, 1968—, ptnr., 1973—. Editor-in-chief Wash. Real Property Deskbook; contbr. articles to profl. jours. With USAF, 1955—58. Mem. ABA, Wash. Bar Assn., Am. Coll. Real Estate Lawyers, Pacific Real Estate Inst. (pres., founding trustee), Order of Coif, Seattle Yacht Club. Office: Perkins Coie 1201 3rd Ave Fl 40 Seattle WA 98101-3029 E-mail: kuhre@perkinscoie.com.

KUIKEN, TODD ALAN, medical researcher, rehabilitation services professional, educator; b. Champaign, Ill., Mar. 28, 1960; m. Lisa Bierman. BS in Biomedical Engring., Duke U., 1983; PhD in Biomedical Engring., Northwestern U., 1989; MD, Northwestern U. Med. Sch., Chgo., 1990. Diplomate Am. Bd. Of Phys. Medicine And Rehab. Intern, physical medicine and rehab. Evanston Hosp., Ill., 1991; resident, physical medicine and rehab. Rehab. Inst. Chgo./Northwestern U. Med. Sch., 1992—95, Frankel Rsch. fellow Ill., 1992; dir. of amputee svcs. Rehab. Inst. Chgo., 1999—, vice chief staff Ill., 2000—01, chief of staff, 2001—03, dir. neural engring. ctr. for artificial limbs, 2004—; asst. prof., phys. medicine and rehab. Northwestern U. Feinberg Sch. Medicine, Chgo., 1997—2004, assoc. prof., dept. physical medicine and rehab., 2004—, assoc. dean, 2003—; assoc. dean of academic affairs Rehab. Inst. Chgo., Feinberg Sch. Medicine, 2002—; asst. prof., dept. biomedical engring. Northwestern U., 2005—. Bd. dirs. Rehab. Inst. Of Chgo., 2001—03. Named one of Breakthrough Doctors, Chgo. Mag., 2003, Best Doctors in Chgo., 2004, Top Doctors in Chgo., Chgo. Hosp. News, 2004; recipient Sarah Bakin Rsch. award, 1995, Scholl Recognition award for rehab. rsch., 1995, Da Vinci award for Innovated Engring., Nat. Multiple Sclerosis Soc., 2005, Grand award winner for Best Tech. of 2005, Popular Sci. Mag., 2005;, NIH grantee, 2003—. Mem.: Internat. Soc. Prosthetics and Orthotics (Best paper, runner-up IX World Congress, Internat. Soc. for Prosthetics and Orthotics, Amsterdam, Netherlands 1998), IEEE, Assn. Academic Physiatrists, Am. Acad. Physical Medicine and Rehab. (chmn. prosthetics & orthotics, wheelchairs & human biomechanics group 1997—99), Am. Acad. of Orthotists and Prosthetists. Achievements include patents for stand up wheelchair. Home: 1220 Forest Ave Oak Park IL 60302 Office: Rehab Inst Chicago 345 E Superior Ste 124 Chicago IL 60611 also: Northwestern Univ Feinberg Sch Medicine RIC 1309 303 East Chicago Ave Chicago IL 60611-3008 Office Phone: 312-238-8072, 312-238-1315. Office Fax: 312-238-1166. E-mail: tkuiken@rehabchicago.org, tkuiken@northwestern.edu.*

KUJALA, WALFRID EUGENE, musician, educator; b. Warren, Ohio, Feb. 19, 1925; s. Arvo August and Elsie Fannie (Ojajarvi) K.; m. Sherry Henry, Dec. 29, 1989; children by previous marriage: Stephen, Gwen, Daniel. MusB, Eastman Sch. Music, 1948, MusM, 1950. Flutist Rochester Philharm. Orch., 1948—54; soloist, flutist, piccoloist Chgo. Symphony Orch., 1954—2001; prof. flute Northwestern U., Evanston, Ill., 1962—. Vis. prof. of flute Shepherd Sch. Music, Rice U., 1995-97. Author: The Flutist's Progress, 1970, The Flutist's Vade Mecum of Scales, Arpeggios, Trills and Fingering Technique, 1995, Orchestral Techniques for Flute and Piccolo, 2006; consulting editor Flute Talk Mag., 1991—; contbr. articles to profl. jours.; performed world premiere of Concerto for Flute by Gunther Schuller with Chgo. Symphony Orch., conducted by Sir Georg Solti, 1988. Served with AUS, 1943-45, ETO, PTO. Recipient Exemplar of Music Tchg. award, Northwestern U., 1992, Cultural Leadership award, Ill. Coun. Orch., 2007. Mem.: Nat. Flute Assn. (past pres., Lifetime Achievement award 1997). Office: Sch Music Northwestern U Evanston IL 60208-2400 E-mail: walfridkujala@aol.com.

KUJAWA, SISTER ROSE MARIE, academic administrator; b. Detroit; d. Francis and Anne Kujawa. BS in math., Madonna U., Livonia, Mich., 1966; MS in edn. and math., Wayne State U., Detroit, 1971, PhD in higher edn. adminstrn., 1979. Dept. chair math. Bishop Borgess H.S.; asst. prin. and curriculum coord. Ladywood H.S.; prof. Madonna U., Livonia, Mich., 1975, academic dean, academic v.p., acting dean Coll. of Arts and Sci., pres., 2001—. Office: Madonna U 36600 Schoolcraft Rd Livonia MI 48150-1173 Office Phone: 800-852-4951 5315. E-mail: srosemarie@madonna.edu.*

KUJAWSKI, DANIEL, science educator; b. Bujenka, Poland, Feb. 23, 1948; came to U.S., 1996; s. Jan and Czeslawa Kujawska; m. Danuta Radziszewska, July 14, 1974; 1 child, Anna. MSc, Warsaw U. Tech., Poland, 1973, DSc, 1992; PhD, Polish Acad. Scis., 1978. Lectr., sr. lectr. Warsaw Tech. U., 1975-89; lectr., sr. rsch. assoc. U. Alta., Edmonton, Can., 1989-96; from assoc. prof. to prof. Western Mich. U., Kalamazoo, 1996—. Co-chmn. low-cycle fatigue com. Polish Group Fracture, 1987-89. Author: (textbook) Fatigue Life of Metals, 1991, (book) Modeling of the Fatigue Life and Crack Propagation in Metals, 1991. Killam postdoctoral scholar U. Alta., Edmonton, 1983-85. Mem. ASME, SAE. Achievements include research in the mech. behavior of metals and composites, fatigue and fracture mechanics. Avocations: tennis, swimming, walking. Office: Western Mich U Mech and Aero Engring Kalamazoo MI 49008 Office Phone: 269-276-3428. Office Fax: 269-276-3421. Business E-Mail: daniel.kujawski@wmich.edu.

KUJAWSKI, ELIZABETH SZANCER, art curator, consultant; b. NYC, Feb. 7, 1951; d. Henryk and Irene (Zilz) Szancer; children: Melissa, Stephanie. BA cum laude in Art History and Italian, Douglass Coll., 1972; MA in Art History, Queens Coll., 1975. Info. asst. Whitney Mus. Am. Art, NYC, 1972-75; asst. curator Collection of Nelson A. Rockefeller, NYC, 1975-79; asst. dir. SKT Galleries, Inc., NYC, 1979-82; prin., art curator, cons. Elizabeth Szancer Kujawski Art Advisors, NYC, 1982—. Mem. exhbn. com. Internat. Ctr. Photography, NYC. Mem.: Art Table, Inc., Internat. Assn. Profl. Art Advisors (pres. 1998—2000, bd. dirs. 2000—). Avocations: tennis, languages, travel. Office: 767 5th Ave Ste 4200 New York NY 10153-0023 Office Phone: 212-572-3867. Personal E-mail: eartsk@aol.com.

KUKI, ATSUO, pharmaceutical executive; s. Hirondo and Yoko Kuki; m. Martha T. Kuki, June 12, 1982; children: Martin, Ayako. BS in Chemistry, Yale U., 1978; PhD in Phys. Chemistry, Stanford U., Calif., 1985. Asst. prof. chemistry Cornell U., Ithaca, N.Y., 1986-95; dir. computational chemistry Alanex Corp., San Diego, 1995-97, sr. dir. discovery chemistry, 1997—2005; exec. dir. structural and computational biology Pfizer La Jolla, San Diego, 2005—. Author: Long Range Electron Transfer in Biology, 1991; contbr. articles to profl. jours. including Sci., Jour. of Chem. Physics. Recipient Dreyfus Tchr. scholar Camille and Henry Dreyfus Found., 1989; Presdl. Young Investigator award NSF, 1989; Pfizer Global R&D Achievement award, 2005. Mem. Am. Chem. Soc., Am. Phys. Soc., Biophys. Soc. Achievements include development of first application of quantum path integrals to the study of biomolecules, theoretical and computational methods to elucidate the motion of electrons in proteins, methods for the computational design of potential pharmaceuticals which exploit the efficiency of combinatorial chemistry, research in computational biology with emphasis on cancer pathways. Office: Pfizer La Jolla 10614 Science Ctr Dr CB6 San Diego CA 92121 Business E-Mail: atsuo.kuki@pfizer.com.

KUKLA, EDWARD RICHARD, rare books and special collections librarian; b. Detroit, Jan. 31, 1941; s. Stanley Frank and ClaraBelle (Morton) K. BA, Wayne State U., 1962; MA, U. Mich., 1963, MLS, 1973. Asst. instr. Mich. State U., East Lansing, 1970-72; media mobile libr. State Libr. of Mich., 1972; asst. libr. rare books and manuscripts Greenfield Village and Henry Ford Mus., Dearborn, Mich., 1974-78; rare books and spl. collections libr. Wash. State U., Pullman, 1979-86; libr. Mpls. Athenaeum, 1987—2005; head spl. collections dept. Mpls. Pub. Libr., 1987—2003, spl. collections bibliographer, 2004—05; archives processor Fair Oaks Apts., Mpls., 2006—07. Educator, lectr. rare books, history of books and printing, book collecting; reviewer NEH. Author: Un estudio critico sobre Altazor de Vicente Huidobro, 1963, The Scholar and the Future of the Research Library Revisited, 1973, The Struggle and the Glory: A Special Bicentennial Exhibition, 1976. Recipient C. Allen Harlan scholarship, 1958, medal of distinction Fgn. Lang., 1958, Cert. of Appreciation, Mpls. Pub. Libr. Bd., 2004; tchg. fellow U. Mich, Ann Arbor, 1963-66. Mem. ALA, Assn. Coll. and Rsch. Librs. (rare books sect. 1990, local arrangements com.), U. Mich. Sch. Libr. Sci. Alumni Assn. (life), Am. Contract Bridge League, Am. Cut Glass Assn. (life), Am. Film Inst. (charter), English First (life), Haviland Collectors Internationale Found., Minn. Film Arts Founders Club, Pickard Collectors Club (charter), Walker Art Ctr., Mich. Jr. Acad. Sci., Art and Letters (jr. mem.), U. Mich. Union Club (life), Phi Beta Kappa, Sigma Delta Pi, Beta Phi Mu. Home: 1556 Emerald Ct Petoskey MI 49770-7704

KUKLA, WENDY JO, music educator; b. Two Rivers, Wis., Apr. 21, 1964; d. Gerald Charles and Sharon Ann Wojta; m. James Edward Kukla, July 15, 1989; children: Natalie Jo, Cole James, Paige Marie. BA, U. Wis., Green Bay, 1987; MusM, U. Wis., Milw., 1993. Vocal music tchr. Princeton Sch., Wis., 1987—88, Kohler Pub. Schs., Wis., 1988—. Pvt. piano tchr., Kohler, 1988—. Performer Sheboygan Pops Band, Wis., 1996, Kohler HS Band, 2001; music entertainer St. John's Ch., Kohler, 1990—, Am. Club, Kohler, 1989—, Waelder Haus, Kohler, 2006. Mem.: Music Educators Nat. Conf. Roman Catholic. Avocations: weightlifting, swimming, jogging, bicycling. Home: 1713 Ridge Rd Sheboygan WI 53083 Office: Kohler Pub Schs 33 Upper Rd Kohler WI 53044

KUKLENYIK, ZSUZSANNA, chemist, researcher; b. Nyiregyhaza, Hungary, May 15, 1963; d. Ferenc and Zsuzsanna Ferencne Mosolygo; m. Peter Kuklenyik, May 21, 1988; children: Andrea Ester, Elizabeth Clara, Daniel Ernest. MS in Chem. Engring., Tech. U. Budapest, 1987; PhD in Chemistry, Emory U., 1996. Rsch. assoc. Emory U., Atlanta, 1996—98; sr. rsch. scientist Centers for Disease Control and Prevention, Atlanta, 2001—. Mem. Cross Roads Cmty. Ch., Lawrenceville, Ga., 2001—05. Avocation: tennis. Office: Centers for Disease Control and Prev 4770 Buford Highway MS: F-17 Atlanta GA 30341 Home Phone: 678-442-0054; Office Phone: 770-488-7923. Office Fax: 770-488-4609. Business E-Mail: zkuklenyik@cdc.gov.

KUKLIN, SUSAN BEVERLY, lawyer, librarian, educator; d. Albert and Marion (Waller) K. BA in English and History with honors, U. Ariz., 1969, JD, 1973; MLS, Ind. U., 1970; LLM in Taxation, DePaul U., 1981. Bar: Ariz. 1973, Ill. 1980, Calif. 1984, US Dist. Ct. (no. dist.) Ill. 1980. Asst. city atty. City of Phoenix, 1974-75; dep. county atty. County of Pima, Ariz., 1975-76; polit. sci., law libr., asst. prof. Northern Ill. U., 1976-78; law libr., assoc. prof. U. SD, 1978-79; dir. law libr., assoc. prof. DePaul U., 1979-83; law libr., dir. Santa Clara County, San Jose, Calif., 1983—2004; faculty libr. Pima CC, Tucson, 2005—. Editor: Desert Vista Campus Newsletter, 2006—. Sec. bd. trustees Law Library Santa Clara County; sec. exec. bd. dir. Amigos de Pima Found., Pima CC, Tucson, 2007-. Mem. Am. Assn. Law Libr. (cert. law libr.), Coun. Calif. County Law Libr. (newsletter editor 1983-84), Northern Calif. Assn. Law Libr., Ariz. Librs. Assn., Phi Beta Kappa, Phi Kappa Phi, Alpha Lambda Delta, Phi Alpha Theta, Phi Delta Phi. Office: Pima CC West Campus Libr 2202 W Anklam Rd Tucson AZ 85709 Business E-Mail: skuklin@pima.edu.

KUKSI, KRIS M., artist; b. Springfield, Mo., Mar. 2, 1973; s. Letha Mae and Vincent Clupny (Stepfather). MFA, Ft. Hays State U., 2002. Fine art, The Throne of Lucifer (First Pl. Artrom gallery Fantastic 2005 competition, 2005), one-man shows include The Strange and the Fantastic, The Great Passage, The Within, Toward the Within. Finalist 2d Pl. award, Impact Artists Gallery, 2002; recipient award of Merit, Williamsburg Art and Hist. Ctr., 2003, Publ., Slowart Productions, 2003. Mem.: Soc. for the Art of imagination (assoc.). Home: 717 1/2 Main B Hays KS 67601 Office: Kris Kuksi PO Box 1531 Hays KS 67601 Home Phone: 785-625-7502; Office Phone: 785-650-4990. Personal E-mail: kkuksi@hotmail.com.

KULA, IRWIN JAMES, religious education educator; b. NYC, Nov. 29, 1957; s. Morton and Charlotte Helen (Scher) K.; m. Dana Beth Kurzweil, Aug. 29, 1982; children: Gabriella, Talia. BA, Jewish Theol. Sem., 1978, MHL, 1982; BA, Columbia U., 1978. Ordained to ministry Jewish Theol. Sem., 1982. Rabbi Congregation of the Old City, Jerusalem, 1980-81, Congregation B'nai Amoona, St. Louis, 1982-88; dir. edn. Ctr. for Learning and Leadership, NYC, 1988—; faculty Wexner Heritage Found., NYC, 1988—. Bd. dirs. Jewish Fedn. St. Louis, 1986-88; cons. Bronfman Found., Montreal, Que., Can., 1991—; cons., founder Ctr. for Jewish Living, Chgo., 1993—; co-pres., CLAL, 2002- Host: (TV series) Publ. Television Spirituality Show. Exec. bd. Rabbinic Cabinet, United Jewish Appeal, N.Y.C., 1986-88. Named one of 45 Leaders to Watch, Jewish Week, N.Y.C., 1995, Top 50 Rabbis in America, Newsweek Mag., 2007. Democrat. Avocations: basketball, music, art.*

KULAK, CHESTER B., dentist; BA, Seton Hall U., South Orange, NJ, 1960; DMD, Fairleigh Dickinson U. Sch. Dentistry, Teaneck, NJ, 1965; advanced tng. cert. in TMJ, U. Medicine and Dentistry of NJ, Bergen, 1987. Diplomate Am. Acad. Pain Mgmt., cert. med. investigator level V Am. Coll. Forensic Examiners, homeland security level III Am. Coll. Forensic Examiners, forensic cons. Am. Coll. Forensic Examiners. Pvt. practice, Lawrenceville, NJ, 1967—. Tchr. secondary history and econ.; clin. instr. dept. oral radiology and diagnosis Faileigh Dickinson U., Teaneck, NJ; instr. dental asst. tng. program Mercer County CC, guest lectr., NJ Diabetes Assn., NJ Dental Hygiene Assn., NJ Dental Assts. Assn.; guest lectr., facilitator law and ethics Am. Coll. Dentists - U. Medicine and Dentistry NY; cons. NJ State Bd. Dental Examiners, Dental Assisting Nat. Bd., Nat. Assn. Dental Assts. Bd. mem NJ affiliate Am. Diabetes Assn., 1980—87, charter mem. Mercer County chpt., bd. mem. Mercer County chpt., 1978—87. Recipient Achievement award, Am. Acad. Oral Radiology, 1965, C.V. Mosby Achievement award, Fairleigh Dickenson U., 1965, Student Achievement award, NJ Dental Assn., 1965, Alumni Achievement award, Fairleigh Dickenson U., 1982, Disting. Cmty. Svc. award, Kiwanis Internat., 1970. Master: Acad. Gen. Dentistry; fellow: Internat. Coll. Cranio-Mandibular Orthop., Acad. Continuing Edn., Am. Coll. Dentists, Internat. Coll. Dentists, Am. Endodontic Soc. (dir. 1999—2004, Humanitarian award 1982), Pierre Fauchard Acad., NJ Acad. Medicine; mem.: Am. Acad. Forensic Odontology, Am. Acad. Pain Mgmt., Acad. Oral Diagnosis, Radiology and Oral Medicine, Nat. Soc. Dental Practitioners, Acad. Dental Therapeutics and Stomatology, Am. Acad. Oral Medicine, NJ Acad. Gen. Dentistry (pres. mid-state chpt. 1974—2000), NJ Dental Assn. (trustee 1975—78, chmn. peer rev. coun. 1977—78, v.p. 1980—81, pres. 1982—83, chmn. bd. trustees 1982—83, chmn. jud. coun. 1983—84), Mercer Dental Soc. (exec. com. 1971—84, chmn. children's dental health week 1973—76, v.p. 1975—76, trustee 1975—78, contbg. editor jour. 1975—80, Mercer County CC liaison 1975—88, mem. nominating com. 1976, pres. 1977—78, chmn. reference com. 1977—83, registrar continuing edn. program 1977—93), Am. Coll. Forensic Examiners, Omicron Kappa Upsilon. Home and Office: 2796 Princeton Pike Lawrenceville NJ 08648-3221 Office Phone: 609-882-9443.

KULENOVIC, DZAFER JEFF, bank executive, advocate; b. Dusseldorf, Germany, July 1, 1965; arrived in US, 1974; s. Nahid Kulenovic and Marijana Dezelic; m. Selma Kljako, June 21, 1992; 1 child, Jasmina. BBA with honors, Loyola U., Chgo., 1987; MBA, DePaul U., Chgo., 1990. Auditor River Forest Banc Corp, Chgo., 1987—92; loan rev. assoc. First Colonial Bankshares, Chgo., 1991—92; loan rev. officer Bank One Ill., Chgo., 1992—95; v.p. credit adminstrn. GreatBanc, Inc., Chgo., 1995—2005; dep. chief credit officer Bridgeview Bank, Chgo., 2005—06; exec. v.p., chief credit officer Great Banc Ops. Corp., Chgo., 2006—07; chief credit officer, sr. vice provost Del. Place Bank, Chgo., 2007—. Radio commentator Voice of Croatia, Chgo., 1991—93, Voice of Bosniacs, 1993—94; dir. Bosnia United; v.p. and sec. Congress of North Am. Bosniacs, 2002—; mem. governing bd. Party Dem. Action, Sarajevo, Bosnia-Herzegovina, 2002—; bd. dirs. Chgo. Math. & Sci. Acad. Contbr. articles to Bosnian newspapers. Election judge, Chgo., 1998—99; bd. dirs. Islamic Cultural Ctr., Chgo., 1992—95, 2000—, treas., 1992—93, sec., 2001—04, pres., 2004—. Recipient Life Achievement award, Islamic Cultural Ctr., 1995. Mem.: Chgo. Math. and Sci. Acad., Field Mus. Natural History (corr.), Risk Mgmt. Assn. (assoc.), Am. Croatian Soc. (corr.), Bosnian Am. Cultural Assn. (corr.; dir. 1992—2003, sec. 1995—2004, Appreciation award 2004), Dem. Action Party Chgo. (corr.; pres. 1995—99, 2002—04, bd. dirs. 1992—, Life Time Achievement award 1997). R-Conservative. Muslim. Avocations: travel, stamp collecting/philately, coin collecting/numismatics, swimming, golf. Personal E-mail: d.kulenovic@comcast.net.

KULESHA, KEVIN JOHN, investment banker; b. Englewood, NJ, May 15, 1956; s. Kasmier J. and Florence L. (Anguissola) K. BSBA, Georgetown U., 1976; MSIA, Carnegie Mellon U., 1979. Field dir. Bradley for Senate Com., Bethesda, Md., 1975-76; commodity trader Chgo., 1977; assoc. Morgan Stanley & Co., NYC, 1979-83; v.p. Lazard Fréres & Co., NYC, 1983-86, Furman Selz Mager Dietz & Birney, NYC, 1986-87, Merrill Lynch Capital Markets, NYC, 1987-88, dir., 1989-91; mng. dir. The Sandstone Group, Story, 1991—. With Andean Investment Advisors, LLC, Denver, 1998-99; , exec. v.p. Fin. Industries Corp., Austin, 1992; chmn., CEO IncSurance LLC, Story, Wyo., 2001—

KULESZA, CHESTER STEPHEN (BUD KULESZA), financial executive; b. Elizabeth, NJ, Jan. 12, 1947; s. Chester S. and Mary Ellen (Sales) K.; m. Kathleen Marie Hickman, June 14, 1969; children: Kevin Michael, Marie Kathleen. AAS in Acctg., Middlesex County Coll., Edison, NJ, 1969; BS in Commerce, Rider U., 1973. Cert. fin. mgr. With fin./acctg. depts. Johnson & Johnson, New Brunswick, NJ, 1969-73; asst. contr. ITT Morton Frozen Foods, Charlottesville, Va., 1973—81; sr. fin. mgr. RJR Delmonte Frozen Foods, San Francisco, 1981-83; v.p., contr. ITT Bus. & Consumer Comm., Raleigh, NC, 1983—86; CFO, contr. ITT Electromech. Components, Fountain Valley, Calif., 1986—90; sr. v.p. fin. ITT Automotive-Worldwide, Auburn Hills, Mich., 1990—98. Presenter XV World Congress of Accountancy, 1997. Author of book foreword: The Practice Analysis of Management Accounting, 1996; contbr. articles to profl. jours. Chmn. acctg. and fin. adv. bd. Oakland U., Rochester, Mich., 1994—; bus. adv. curriculum com. Detroit Coll. of Bus., Dearborn, Mich., 1996—; acctg. accreditation com. Internat. Assn. Mgmt. Edn., St. Louis, 1997. With U.S. Army, 1964-67. Honoree Beta Gamma Sigma, 1997. Mem. Inst. Mgmt. Accts. (cert., nat. pres. 1999-2000, bd. dirs.), Fin. Execs.

Inst. (chair acad. rels. com. Detroit chpt. 1995—), Beta Alpha Psi (hon.). Republican. Avocations: wine tasting, travel, gourmet cooking, singing. Personal E-mail: bud.kulesza@att.net.

KULICKI, JOHN M., structural engineer; BS, Lafayette Coll., 1965; MS in Civil Engring., Lehigh U., 1967, PhD in Civil Engring., 1974. Cert. Pres., chief engr., CEO Modjeski and Masters Inc., Harrisburg, Pa. Recipient George S. Richardson Medal, 1996. Office: Modjeski and Masters Inc PO Box 2345 Harrisburg PA 17105

KULIK, ROSALYN FRANTA, food company executive, consultant; b. Wilmington, Del., Aug. 29, 1951; d. William Alfred and Virginia Louise (Ellis) Franta. BS in Voc. Home Econs. Edn., Purdue U., 1972, MS in Foods and Nutrition, 1974; postgrad. in advanced mgmt. program, Harvard Bus. Sch., 1990. Registered dietitian. Home economist Kellogg Co., Battle Creek, Mich., 1974-75, nutrition and consumer specialist, 1975-77, mgr. advt. to children, 1977-79, corp. adminstrv. asst., 1979, dir. nutrition, 1979-82, dir. nutrition and analytical services, 1982, v.p. nutrition and chemistry, 1983, v.p. quality and nutrition, 1983-87, v.p., asst. to chmn., 1987-88; exec. v.p., gen. mgr. Fearn Internat., Franklin Park, Ill., 1988-90; cons., 1991—. Adj. faculty U. Tampa, Fla., 2001—05. Contbr. articles on food sci. and nutrition to profl. jours. Tampa Bay regional coord. Camp Invention, Inc., 2004—05; mem. ch. coun. Grace Luth. Ch., Tampa, Fla., 2000—03, 2004—, v.p., 2004—07, pres., 2007—; bd. dirs. State Arthritis Found., County Vol. Ctr., Neighborhood Property Owners Assn., 2002—06. Recipient Ada Decker Malott Meml. scholarship, Purdue U., 1970, disting. alumna award Purdue U. Sch. of Consumer and Family Sci., Excellence in Svc. award Nutrition in Complementary Care Dietetic Practic Group, 2005. Fellow Am. Dietetic Assn. (cofounder, exec. officer nutrition in complementary care dietetic practice group 1998-2004, chair 2002-03, author position statement 2005); mem. Inst. Food Technologists (profl. mem.), Am. Dietetic Assn., Homeowners Property Assn. Avila (bd. dirs. 2002-06), Phi Kappa Phi, Gamma Sigma Delta, Omicron Nu, Alpha Omicron Pi. Republican. Lutheran. Avocations: music, church work, travel, jr. league volunteerism. Personal E-mail: kulikcon@msn.com.

KULIKOWSKI, CASIMIR ALEXANDER, computer scientist, engineer, educator; b. Hertford, Herts, Eng., May 4, 1944; arrived in U.S., 1961; s. Victor A. and Isabel S. (Tuckett) Kulikowski; m. Christine A. Wilk, May 31, 1969; children: Michael Edward, Victoria Anne. BE with honors, Yale U., New Haven, Conn., 1965, MS, 1966; PhD, U. Hawaii, 1970. From asst. prof. to assoc. prof. Rutgers U., New Brunswick, NJ, 1970—77, prof., 1977—97, chmn. dept. computer sci., 1984—90, dir. Lab. Computer Sci. Rsch., 1985—96, bd. govs. prof., 1997—. Mem. bd. sci. counselors Nat. Libr. Medicine, Bethesda, Md., 1984—87; mem. biomed. libr. rev. com. NIH, 1994—99, chair, 1997—99; co-chair sci. program com. World Congress on Med. Informatics, 2004. Author: A Practical Guide to Designing Expert Systems, 1984, Computer Systems that Learn, 1992; editor: Artificial Intelligence Expert Systems and Languages in Modeling & Simulation, 1988; co-editor: Yearbook of Medical Informatics, 2001—; assoc. editor: Artificial Intelligence in Medicine Jour., 2001—; mem. editl. bd. Jour. Am. Med. Informatics Assn., 1993—98, Methods Info. in Medicine, 1999—, Iterations: An Interdisciplinary Jour. Software History, 2001—05. Pres. Highland Park Residents Assn., NJ, 1983—88. Fellow: IEEE, AAAS, Am. Inst. Med. and Biol. Engring., Am. Coll. Med. Informatics, Am. Assn. Artificial Intelligence; mem.: Internat. Med. Informatics Assn. (v.p. 2007—), NAS Inst. Medicine. Office: Rutgers U Dept Computer Sci Hill Ctr Busch Campus New Brunswick NJ 08903 Office Phone: 732-445-2006.

KULIKOWSKI, MICHAEL, history professor; b. Sept. 3, 1970; m. Kathryn Salzer, Aug. 20, 1994. BA, Rutgers U., New Brunswick, NJ, 1991; MA, U. Toronto, Can., 1992, PhD, 1998; Licentiate in Medieval Studies, Pontifical Inst. Mediaeval Studies, Toronto, 1995. Vis. asst. prof. Washington and Lee U., Lexington, Va., 1998—99, Smith Coll., Northampton, Mass., 1999—2001; asst. prof. history U. Tenn., Knoxville, 2001—05, assoc. prof. history, 2005—06, Alvin and Sally Beaman assoc. prof. history, 2006—. Solmsen fellow Inst. for Rsch. in the Humanities, U. Wis., Madison, 2005—06. Author: (scholarly monograph) Late Roman Spain and Its Cities, 2004; co-author: Hispania in Late Antiquity, 2005; author: Rome's Gothic Wars from the Third Century to Alaric, 2006. Mem.: Medieval Acad. Am., Classical Assn. Can., Am. Hist. Assn., Soc. for the Promotion of Roman Studies. Office: Dept History Univ Tenn 915 Volunteer Blvd Knoxville TN 37996

KULISH, NICHOLAS, reporter; b. Arlington, Va. BA in Polit. Sci., Columbia Univ., 1997. Reporter, Washington bur. Wall St. Jour.; editl. bd. mem. NY Times, 2005—. Author: Last One In. Recipient Fulbright Scholar, Berlin, 2003. Office: Editl Bd NY Times 229 W 43rd St New York NY 10036 Office Fax: 212-556-3815.

KULKARNI, BIDY, reproductive endocrinologist, biomedical researcher, consultant; b. Janwa, Maharashtra, India, Apr. 18, 1930; arrived in U.S., 1961; s. Dhondu Y. Kulkarni and Sita Deshpande; m. Suman Sane, May 8, 1957; children: Neela, Bob. BS, Ferguson Coll., Poona, India, 1952; MS, U. Poona, 1956, PhD, 1962. Post doctoral fellow Clark U. and Worcester Found., Shrewsbury, Mass., 1961—64, Nat. Rsch. Coun., Ottawa, Ont., Canada, 1964—66; sect. chief dept. endocrinology S.W. Rsch. Found., San Antonio, 1967—70; asst. prof. ob-gyn. U. Chgo., 1970—73; dir. gynecol. endocrinology Michael Reese U., Chgo., 1970—72; dir. reproductive endocrinology Loyola U. Med. Ctr., Maywood, Ill., 1973—79, assoc. prof. ob-gyn., 1973—79; dir. reproductive endocrinology Cook County Hosp., Chgo., 1980—93; assoc. prof. ob-gyn. Chgo. Med. Sch., N. Chgo., 1981—93; pres. Rsch. and Edn. Svcs., Darien, Ill., 1991—. Cons. in field; dir. perinatal ctr. Loyola U. Med. Ctr., Maywood, 1975—77; hon. attending physician Cook County Hosp., Chgo., 1993—. Contbr. articles to profl. jours., chapters to books. Named Outstanding Citizen of Yr., Met. Chgo., 1973; grantee, Ctr. for Population Rsch., NIH, Agy. for Internat. Devel. Mem.: Internat. Fedn. Fertility Socs., Am. Fertility Soc., Nat. Acad. Biochemistry, Soc. for Study of Reprodn., Endocrine Soc., Chgo. Gynecol. Soc. (life), Chgo. Gynecol. Soc. (life Outstanding Scientist 2000), Soc. Reproductive Medicine (life). Democrat. Avocations: badminton, hiking, travel. Home: 9 S 155 Nantucket Darien IL 60561 Office: Rsch and Edn Svcs RES 9 S 155 Nantucket Darien IL 60561 Office Phone: 630-963-4692.

KULKARNI, KAVITA-VIBHA ARUN, chemist; b. Dharwad, Karnataka, India, Aug. 12, 1945; arrived in U.S., 1971; d. Ratnakar and Chhaya Ratnakar Joshi; m. Arun Pandurang Kulkarni, June 30, 1971 (dec.); children: Arvind Kulkarni, Aparna Kulkarni. BSc, Pune U., India, 1965, MS, 1968, U. South Fla., 1998. Sci. and math. tchr. Adarsha Vidya Bhavan HS, Pune, 1968—69; quality control chemist Dai-ichi-Karkaria Pvt. Ltd., Pune, 1969—71; cashier Roses Dept. Store, Raleigh, NC, 1974—75; lectr. in chemistry NC State U., Raleigh, 1975—80, Ea. Mich. U., Ypsilanti, 1984—85; rsch. tech. in biology U. Tampa, Fla., 1989—90; rsch. asst. in internal medicine U. South Fla., Tampa, 1990—91, tchg. asst. organic chemistry, 1994—95, sci. advisor, 1999—2003; rsch. chemist Belmac Pharm. Co., Tampa, 1991—94. Contbr. articles to profl. jours. Non-backward class scholar, Maharastra State Govt., India, 1961—63, open merit scholar, 1963—65, merit scholar, Pune U., 1966—68. Mem.: Am. Chem. Soc., Phi Lambda Upsilon. Avocations: reading, travel, crocheting. Home: 18422 Dorman Rd Lithia FL 33547

KULKARNI, KISHORE GANESH, economics professor, consultant; b. Oct. 31, 1953; arrived in U.S., 1976; s. Ganesh Y. and Sindhu G. Dhekane; m. Jayu K., Aug. 17, 1980; children: Lina, Aditi. BA, U. Poona, India, 1974, MA, 1976, U. Pitts., 1978, PhD, 1982. Tchg. asst. U. Pitts., 1976—78, tchg. fellow, 1978—80, asst. prof. Johnstown, Pa., 1981—82, U. Ctrl. Ark., Conway, 1982—86; assoc. prof. U. La., Monroe, 1986—89, Met. State Coll., Denver, 1989—93, prof., 1993—. Prof. semester at sea program U. Pitts., 1994; chmn. dept. econs. Met. State Coll., Denver, 1994—97; vis. prof. Sch. Comm. and Mgmt. Sci., Kochi, India, 2007. Author: Principles of Macro Monetary Theory, Simplified Macro Monetary Theory, Readings in International Economics; co-author: Understanding Microeconomics, Understanding Macroeconomics, Economic Development in India and China: New Perspectives on Progress and Change; editor: Indian Jour. of Econs. and Bus.; contbr. articles to profl. jours. Named Outstanding Tchr., Golden Key, 1997; recipient 1st prize, Forum of Free Enterprise, Bombay, India, 1975, Rama Watumull Fund award, Honolulu, 1977, Outstanding Rschr./Scholar award, 2001, Disting. Svc. to the Coll. Faculty Senate, 2004; fellow, Nat. Inst. Bank Mgmt., Pune, India, 1974. Mem.: Assn. Indian Econ. Studies, So. Econ. Assn., Midwest Econ. Assn., Am. Econ. Assn., Golden Key Nat. Hon. Soc. (Outstanding Tchr. award 1997). Avocation: tennis. Home: 2249 S Miller Ct Lakewood CO 80227 Office Phone: 303-556-2675. Business E-Mail: kulkarnk@mscd.edu.

KULL, BRYAN PAUL, business consulting executive; b. Newark, Jan. 23, 1960; s. Paul and Joan Lorraine (Schell) K.; m. Lindsay Fairfield Patton, Nov. 26, 1983; children: Taylor Bryan, Kathryn. BS in Mgmt., Keene State Coll., NH, 1982; MBA in Mktg., So. Ill. U., 1987. Sales rep. Warner-Lambert Co., Morris Plains, NJ, 1982—84; key account mgr. Clorox Co., Oakland, Calif., 1984—86; divsn. mgr. Alberto-Culver Co., Melrose Park, Ill., 1986—89; area mgr. Schering-Plough Corp., Memphis, 1989—90; nat. sales mgr. Shering-Plough Healthcare, Liberty Corner, NJ, 1991—94; v.p. spl. mkts. Sunshine Biscuits, Inc., Woodbridge, NJ, 1994—96; v.p. client svc. Info. Resources, Inc., Fairfield, NJ, 1997—2000; ptnr. Computer Sci. Corp., West Orange, NJ, 2000—01; client ptnr. Cambridge Technology Ptnrs., 2001—03; v.p. Intellinex LLC, NYC, 2003—06; mng. ptnr. The Gallup Orgn., Princeton, NJ, 2006—. Mem. Triathlon Fedn., Davis, Calif., 1988-89. Mem. Assn. MBA Execs., Nat. Assn. Chain Drug Stores (assoc.), Pres.'s Club at Schering-Plough. Republican. Presbyterian. Avocations: golf, tennis, skiing, bicycling, wine collecting.

KULLAS, ALBERT JOHN, management consultant, systems engineer; b. Webster, Mass., May 5, 1917; s. Albert J. and Mary (Piechowiak) K.; m. Joyce M. Gladue, Jan. 31, 1942; children: Michael, Daniel, Mark, James. BS in Civil Engring., Worcester Poly. Inst., 1938; grad., Am. Mgmt. Assn., 1956; MS in Civil Engring., NYU, 1940; grad., Sloan Sch. Mgmt. Sr. Execs., MIT, 1973. Registered profl. engr. With Martin Marietta Corp., 1940-82, structures mgr. Balt., 1955-57, chief engr., 1957, design engring. mgr., 1957-59, tech. devel. mgr., 1959-60, Dyna Soar and Gemini Launch vehicle tech. dir., 1960-62, research and engring. dir. Denver, 1962-65, dir. tech. ops., 1965-66, dir. space sci., research, adv. tech., 1966-67, dir. Voyager program, 1967-68, dir. Planetary Systems, 1968, dir. Viking project, div. v.p., 1969-72, div. v.p. ops. rev., 1972-73, v.p. data systems, 1973-82; mgmt. and systems engring. cons. Littleton, Colo., 1982-98; pres. Albert J. Kullas, Inc. Rsch. and tech. panel space vehicles NASA, 1968-78; chmn. bd. Biax Corp., 1987-90; 1st v.p. Highlands, Inc., 1999-2004; bd. dirs. THI. Contbr. articles to profl. jours. Rsch. adv. coun. Colo. State U., 1971—; treas. Porter Hosp. Found., 1980-85, 1st v.p., 1986-88, pres., 1988-90, v.p., 1990-93, emeritus, 2003—; bd. dirs. Colo. Jud. Inst., 1980-91, chmn., 1984-86; exec. com. Rocky Mountain Sci. Coun., 1964-65; bd. dirs. MIT Alumni Colo., 1990-2002. Recipient Robert H. Goddard award Worcester Poly. Inst., 1962 Fellow AIAA (award 1967); Asso. fellow (chmn. honors and awards com. 1973-81); mem. ASCE, Sigma Xi, Tau Beta Pi. Home: 5088 W Maplewood Ave Littleton CO 80123-6729 *I believe that being thorough, consistent, and persistent in pursuing one's convictions are necessary ingredients for personal and managerial success.*

KULLBERG, DUANE REUBEN, accounting firm executive; b. Red Wing, Minn., Oct. 6, 1932; s. Carl Reuben and Hazel Norma (Swanson) K.; m. Sina Nell Turner, Oct. 19, 1958 (dec. Sept. 1989); children: Malissa Kullberg, Caroline Godellas; m. Susan Turley, Dec. 30, 1992; stepchildren: Betsy Lucas, Jane Magnuson. BBA, U. Minn., 1954. With Arthur Andersen & Co., S.C., 1954-89, ptnr., 1967-89, mng. ptnr., Mpls., 1970-74, dep. mng. ptnr., Chgo., 1975-78, vice chmn. acctg. and audit practice worldwide, 1978-80, mng. ptnr., CEO, 1980-89, ret., 1989. Bd. dirs. Nuveen Investments, Inc., Chgo. Bd. Options Exch. Life trustee Northwestern U., Art Inst. Chgo., U. Minn. Found., chmn. bd. trustees, 1993-95; chair Swedish Coun. Am. Found., 1999-2001. With U.S. Army, 1956-58. Decorated comdr. Royal Order of Polar Star (Sweden), 1989; recipient Legend in Leadership award Emory U., 1992, Regents award U. Minn., 1995, Outstanding Achievement award U. Minn., 1990. Mem. Chgo. Club, Comml. Club, Mpls. Club. Home (Summer): 55 East Erie St Apt 1703 Chicago IL 60611-2247 Home (Winter): 6444 N 79th St Scottsdale AZ 85250-7919 Office Phone: 312-953-3083. Personal E-mail: drkchicago@mac.com, dkullberg@mac.com.

KULLBERG, GARY WALTER, advertising agency executive; b. White Plains, NY, Dec. 15, 1941; s. Walter George and Neva Virginia (Franz) K.; m. Audrey Ellen Greenwald, June 20, 1976; 1 child, Eric Alan. BS, U. R.I., 1963. Contr. WCD, Inc., NYC, 1963-66; v.p., mgmt. supr. Ogilvy & Mather, NYC, 1966-77; sr. v.p., account group head Wells, Rich, Greene, NYC, 1977-83; CEO, CFO, co-founder Fredericks Kullberg Amato Pisacane, Inc., 1983-88; pres. Kullberg Amato Pisacane/ABP, Inc., 1987-89; pres., COO PanCom Internat. Corp., 1989-91; CEO PanCom Comm. Corp., 1991-93, Kullberg Cons. Group LLC, 1993—. Spkr. in field. Greater NY adv. bd., co-chmn. mktg. comm. com. and devel. com. Salvation Army, exec. bd. U. RI Found. Mem.: Am. Mktg. Assn., West Point Soc. N.Y. (career adv. com.), U. R.I. Alumni Assn. (pres., exec. com., govt. rels. com., capital campaign leadership com., fin. com.), N.Y. Athletic Club, Phi Gamma Delta. Home and Office: Kullberg Cons Group LLC 171 Forge Rd North Kingstown RI 02852-1007 Office Phone: 401-886-5001. Business E-Mail: gary@kullbergconsultinggroup.com.

KULLMAN, ELLEN JAMISON, chemicals executive; b. Jan. 22, 1956; m. Michael Kullman; 3 children. BS in Mech. Engring., Tufts U., 1978; MBA, Northwestern U. Various bus. devel., mktg. and sales positions GE; mktg. mgr. med. imaging DuPont, Wilmington, Del., 1988—90, bus. dir. x-ray film, 1990—92, global bus. dir. electronic imaging Printing & Pub., 1992—94, global bus. dir. White Pigment & Mineral Products, 1994—95, v.p., gen. mgr. White Pigment & Mineral Products, 1995—98, v.p., gen. mgr. Safety Resources, 1998—99, v.p., gen. mgr. Bio-Based Materials, 1999—2000, v.p., gen. mgr. DuPont Flooring Systems & DuPont Surfaces, 2001—02, group v.p. DuPont Safety & Protection, 2002—06, exec. v.p. Dupont Safety & Protection; Dupont Coatings & Color Tech.; Mktg. & Sales & Safety & Sustainability, 2006—. Bd. dir. Gen. Motors Corp., 2004—. Trustee Christiana Care Corp.; mem. bd. overseers Tufts U.; bd. dirs. Del. Symphony, Wellness Comty. Named one of 50 Most Powerful Women in Bus., Fortune mag., 2006, 50 Women to Watch, Wall St. Jour., 2006; recipient Aiming High award, 2004. Office: DuPont Bldg 1007 Market St Wilmington DE 19898*

KULNANE, LAURA SHAPIRO, geneticist; b. Cleve., May 19, 1970; d. Paul Y. and Susan Teichman Shapiro; m. Joseph Matthew Kulnane, Mar. 21, 1999; children: Ethan James, Cadence Grace. BS in Psychology, Ind. U., 1992. Rsch. assoc. biol. psychiatry Metrohealth Med. Ctr., Cleve., 1992—93; rsch. asst. II in psychiatry Case Western Res. U., Cleve., 1993—96, rsch. asst. II in genetics, 1996—2000, rsch. asst. III in genetics, 2000—04, rsch. asst. IV, lab mgr. genetics, 2001—, supr. histology core for genetics, 1999—2005. Contbr. articles and abstracts to profl. jours. Democrat. Jewish.

KULOK, WILLIAM ALLAN, entrepreneur, venture capitalist; b. Mt. Vernon, NY, July 24, 1940; s. Sidney Alexander and Bertha (Lembeck) K.; m. Susan B. Glick, June 26, 1965; children: Jonathan, Brian, Stephanie. BS in Econs., U. Pa., 1962. CPA, N.Y. Acct. David Kulok Co., NYC, 1962-67; asst. to pres. Syndicate Mags., NYC, 1967-70; founder Kulok Capital Inc., NYC, 1970, pres., 1970—. Bd. dirs. Listcomp Corp., Mail Mgmt. Corp., Mag. Devel. Fund, Lazard Spl. Equities Fund, ASA Internat. Ltd., N.Y. Import/Export Ctr., Inc., Ctr. for Exec. Edn., Arts & Events, Inc., World Trade Ctr., Palm Beach, Physicians Indemnity RRG, Risk Mgmt. Ctr., Inc.; lectr. Wharton Sch., U. Chgo., NYU. Pres. N.Y. Soc. Ethical Culture, 1978-80; vice chmn. bd. Ethical Culture Schs., 1979, chmn., 1982-86. Mem. AICPA, Sleepy Hollow Country Club, Loxahatchee Club, Tryall Golf and Beach Club (Jamaica, W.I.). Home: 116 Echo Dr Jupiter FL 33458-7716 Office: Risk Mgmt Ctr Inc Ste 304 2300 Palm Beach Lakes Blvd West Palm Beach FL 33409 Personal E-mail: billkulok@hotmail.com.

KULONGOSKI, TED (THEODORE RALPH KULONGOSKI), governor, former state supreme court justice; b. Washington County, Mo., Nov. 5, 1940; married; 3 children. BA, U. Mo., 1967, JD, 1970. Bar: Oreg., Mo., U.S. Dist. Ct. Oreg., U.S. Ct. Appeals (9th cir.). Legal counsel Oreg. State Ho. of Reps., 1973-74; founding and sr. ptnr. Kulongoski, Durham, Drummonds & Colombo, Oreg., 1974-87; deputy dist. atty. Multnomah County, Oreg., 1992; atty. gen. State of Oreg., 1993-97, gov., 2003—; justice Oreg. Supreme Ct., 1997—2001. State rep. Lane County (Oreg.), 1974-77, state senator, 1977-83; chmn. Juvenile Justice Task Force, 1994, Gov.'s Commn. Organized Crime; mem. Criminal Justice Coun.; exec. dir. Met. Family Svc., 1992; dir. Oreg. Dept. Ins. and Fin., 1987-91. Mem. Oreg State Bar Assn., Mo. Bar Assn. Democrat. Office: Gov's Office 254 Capitol Bldg 900 Court St NE Salem OR 97301 Office Phone: 503-378-3111. Office Fax: 503-378-8970.*

KULPA, CHARLES F., microbiologist, educator; s. Charles F. Kulpa, Sr.; m. Loretta May Blanford, Nov. 16, 1984. BS, MS, U. Mich., Ann Arbor, PhD, 1970. Staff fellow NIH, Bethesda, Md., 1971—72; asst. prof. U. Notre Dame, Ind., 1972—78, assoc. prof., 1978—91, prof., 1991—, chair, 2002—. Fellow: Am. Acad. Microbiology; mem.: Gt. Lakes Local Sect. Soc. Indsl. Microbiology (dir. 1999—2006), Am. Soc. Microbiology (Ind. br. pres. 1988—89, Ind. bd. Outstanding Academic Achievement award 2004), Sigma Xi. Office: University of Notre Dame 107 Galvin Life Sciences Notre Dame IN 46556 Office Phone: 574-631-7496.

KULSKI, JULIAN EUGENIUSZ, architect, writer; b. Warsaw, Mar. 3, 1929; came to US, 1948, naturalized, 1950; s. Julian Spitoslav and Eugenia Helena (Solecka) K; children: Julian S., Stefan T.A. Student, Sch. Architecture Oxford U., Eng., 1947-48; BArch, Yale U., 1953, MArch, 1954; PhD, Warsaw Inst. Tech., 1966. Practice architecture, city planning, Conn., 1954-59, Washington, 1959—; prof. architecture U. Notre Dame, South Bend, Ind., 1960-65; prof., dir. urban and regional planning George Washington U., Washington, 1965-67; prof., dir. city and regional planning Howard U., 1967-90. Cons. World Bank, 1964-90; bd. dirs. Nat. Archtl. Accrediting Bd., 1971-76; chmn. accrediting com. Harvard U., 1972, 75, U. PR, 1974, Pratt U., 1975, Carnegie-Mellon U., 1976, U. Va.1978. Author: Land of Urban Promise, 1967 (Book-of-Month award), Evolution of American Urban Systems, 1970, Architecture in a Revolutionary Era, 1971, Dying, We Live, 1979, Legacy of the White Eagle, 2007; contbr. articles to profl. jours. Served with Polish Army, 1941-46. Decorated Home Army Cross, Army Cross (4), Medal of Valor, Silver Cross of Merit with Sivoros (Poland); knight of Malta, Order St. John of Jerusalem; recipient cert. of achievement Nat. Archtl. Accrediting Bd., 1973, 76. Fellow AIA; mem. Am. Planning Assn., Am. Inst. Cert. Planners, AAUP. Office: Ste 31 2139 Wyoming Ave NW Washington DC 20008 *My life has been guided by the following philosophy: It is hard to work for freedom, harder yet to die for it, and hardest of all to suffer for it.*

KULSTAD, GUY CHARLES, public works official; b. Feb. 28, 1930; s. John Marlyn and Anne Mildred (Boyd) Kulstad Ibison; m. Bonnie Jane Sherman, Aug. 28, 1955 (div. Aug. 1996); children: Anne Marie Kulstad Hurst, Mark, Alice Kulstad Krause. BS in Civil Engring., U. Calif., Berkeley, 1958. Registered profl. engr., Calif., Oreg., Wash., traffic engr., Calif., land surveyor, Oreg.; cert. c.c. instr., Calif. Engring. aid County Rd. Dept., LA, 1951, asst. civil engr., 1953-58; dir. pub. wks. Benicia, Calif., 1958-59; dep. dir. pub. wks. Solano County, Calif., 1959-65; dir. pub. wks. Humboldt County, Calif., 1965-92; mgmt. cons., 1992—. Gen. mgr. Humboldt Bay Wastewater Authority 1975, 82-89. Mem. Employer support of N.G. and Res. With AUS, 1951-53. Recipient Outstanding Svc. award North Bay chpt. Calif. Soc. Profl. Engrs., 1964, Boss of the Yr. award Arcata Jaycees, Recognition award Humboldt Toastmaster, Meritorious Leadership award, Surveyor award Calif. Land Surveyors Assn., Illmars Lagzdin award for engring. contbns., Guy C. Kulstad award Humboldt County Dept. Pub. Wks. Fellow ASCE; NSPE, mem. Nat. Soc. County Engrs., Calif. County Engrs., County Engrs. Assn. Calif., Sons of Norway.

KULTERMANN, UDO, architectural and art historian, educator, writer; b. Stettin, Germany, Oct. 14, 1927; came to U.S., 1967, naturalized, 1981; s. Georg and Charlotte (Schultz) K.; m. Judith Danoff, May 10, 1975. Student, U. Greifswald, Germany, 1947—50; PhD magna cum laude, U. Muenster, Germany, 1953; PhD (hon.), Art Acad. Tallinn, Estonia, 2004. Curatorial asst. Kunsthalle, Bremen, Germany, 1954-55; art editor Bertelsmann Pubs., Guetersloh, Germany, 1955-56; program dir. Am. House, Bremen, Germany, 1956-59; dir. city art mus. Schloss Morsbroich, Leverkusen, Germany, 1959-64; dir. Morsbroicher Kunsttage, Leverkusen, 1961; prof. Washington U., St. Louis, 1967-94, prof. emeritus, 1994—. Ednl. leader study tours German architects to Japan, 1965, 67; arch. commn. Biennale Venice, 1979—82; ednl. leader Soviet-Am. Travelling Arch. Seminar, Russia, 1986—87, Nat. Trust for Hist. Preservation, Cruise, Copenhagen, Amsterdam, Rouen, Mont St. Michel, Bordeaux, and Lisbon, 1989; jury Nat. U., Al Ain, United Arab Emirates, 1987, Internat. Open Air Exhbn., Pistany, Czech Republic, 1969; participant 2d Biennale Arab art Govt. of Morocco; lectr. in field; cons. in field. Author: Architecture of Today, 1958, Hans und Wassili Luckhardt-Bauten und Projekte, 1958, Dynamische Architektur, 1959, New Japanese Architecture, 1960, New Architecture in Africa, 1963, Junge deutsche Bildhauer, 1963, Der Schluessel zur Architektur von heute, 1963, New Architecture in the World, 1965, History of Art History, 1966, paperback edit., 1981, English. edit., 1993, Spanish edit., 1994, Croatian edit., 2002, The New Sculpture-Assemblage and Environments, 1967, Architektur der Gegenwart, 1967, Gabriel Grupello, 1968, The New Painting, 1969, rev. edit., 1978, New Directions in African Architecture, 1969, Kenzo Tange-Architecture and Urban Design, 1970, paperback edit., 1978, 1989, Art and Life: The Function of Intermedia, 1970, New Realism, 1972, Die Architektur im 20 Jahrhundert, 1977, English edit., 1993, 6th revised edit., 2003, Ernest Trova, 1977, I Contemporanei, Storia della Scultura nel Mondo, 1979, Architecture in the Seventies, 1980, Architects of the Third World, 1980, Zeitgenoessische Architektur in Osteuropa, 1985, Spanish edit., 1989, Visible Cities-Invisible Cities-Urban Symbolism and Historical Continuity, 1988, A Short History of Art History, 1987, Japanese edit., 1996, Korean edit., 1999, Kunst und Wirklichkeit-Von Fiedler bis Derrida-Zehn Annaeherungen,

1991, Die Maxentius-Basilika.Ein Schluesselwerk spaetantiker Architektur, 1996, Contemporary Architecture in the Arab States-Renaissance of a Region, 1999, Thirty Years After-The Future of the Past, 2002, Architecture and Revolution-The Visions of Boullée and Ledoux, 2003; co-author, (with Werner Hofmann): Modern Architecture in Color, 1970;; editor: Kenzo Tange: Architecture and Urban Design, 1970, paperback edits., 1978, 1989, Architektur der Welt, Verlag und Datenbank fuer Geisteswissenschaften, Weimar, 1996—2005, St. James Modern Masterpieces: The Best of Art, Architecture, Photography and Design Since 1945, 1998, vol. VI Architecture in South and Central Africa in: World Architecture: A Critical Mosaic 1900-2000, 2000; contbr. chapters to books, scientific papers to profl. jours. Recipient Disting. Faculty award, Washington U., 1985. Mem.: Nat. Faculty Humanities, Arts, Scis., Croatian Acad. Scis. and Arts (corr.). Avocation: painting. Personal E-mail: ukulter@rcn.com.

KULYK, KAREN GAY, artist; b. Toronto, Can., July 19, 1950; d. Joseph and Natalie Melanie (Solowski) K. BFA with honors, York U., 1973. Founder, curator Seedlings Gallery, Toronto, 1973-75; established studios worldwide, 1975—. Tchr. various instns., Can., Thailand, Bermuda, Eng., Mexico. One-woman shows include Kitchener-Waterloo Art Gallery, 1994, Rodman Hall, St. Catharines, Ont., 1995, Harbinger Gallery, 1994—, Marianne Friedland Gallery, 1974-1996, Masterworks Found. Gallery, Hamilton, Bermuda, 1997, Henry Dyson Fine Art, London, 1996—, Carnegie Gallery, Dundas, Ont., Can., 1996, Nancy Poole's Studio, Toronto, 1996-99, Gallery on the Bay, Hamilton, Ont., 1997—, Wallack Gallery, Ottawa, Can., 1996—, Zwicker Gallery, Halifax, N.S., Can., 1999—, Nat. Gallery Thailand, Grey Coll. U. Durham, Eng., 2000; exhibited in group shows at Harbinger Gallery, Waterloo, Ont., Touchstone Gallery, Hong Kong, Marianne Friedland Gallery, Fla., Sotheby's, Toronto, Chgo. Internat. Art Exhbn., York U., U. Toronto, Offices of Gov. Gen. of Can., Carleton U. Art Gallery, numerous others; represented in collections at Kitchener-Waterloo Art Gallery, Wilfred Laurier U., Waterloo, Art Gallery of Hamilton, Carleton U., York U., Agnes Etherington Art Gallery, Nat. Gallery of Bermuda, Hartford Coll., Md., Can. Trust, Dominion Trust, Shell Can., Thai Airways Internat., Can. Airlines Internat., Dalhousie U., N.S., Aliant Atlantic Telecom., Can., others, pvt. collections; illustration: Orff, 27 Dragons and a Snarkel, Dalhousie U. Art Gallery, Halifax, Nova Scotia; subject of several newspaper articles. Recipient Grollo d'Oro, award Treviso Internat. Art Competition, 1983; grantee Sheila Hugh Mackay Found., 1996. Home and Office: 5270 Morris St Halifax NS Canada B3J 1B4 Personal E-mail: mgoodyear@dal.ca. E-mail: karenkulyk@hotmail.com.

KUMAKO, KUAMI MAWUNYO, agricultural scientist; b. Cotonou, Benin, Nov. 11, 1963; s. Martin Kouami Kumako and Felicia Kpogo. BS in Agrl. Sci. Engring., U. Bénin, Togo, 1995; MS in Agrl. Econs., U. Ky., 2000. Rsch. asst. devel. program UN, Lomé, Togo, 1994—95; rsch. asst. dept. agrl. econs. U. Ky., Lexington, 1998—2001. Rsch. cons. World Bank, Washington, 2000—01. Mem. Commité Action Renouveau, Togo, 1990—96. Achievements include discovery of principle of rainfall-based index contract application in insurance. Personal E-mail: kumako1@hotmail.com.

KUMALO, DUMISANI SHADRACK, ambassador; b. Sept. 16, 1947; 1 child. BA, U. South Africa; MA, Ind. U., Bloomington. Reporter Golden City Post, South Africa, 1967; feature writer Drum mag., 1969—70; polit. reporter Johannesburg Sunday Times, 1970; mktg. exec. officer Total Oil Co., South Africa, 1976—77; with UN observer mission African Nat. Congress; internat. edn. program coord. Phelps-Stokes Fund, NYC, 1978—80; projects dir. Africa Fund and Am. Com. Africa, 1980—97; dir. US desk South African Dept. Fgn. Affairs, 1997—99, amb., permanent rep. to UN NYC, 1999—. Chair ad hoc adv. group on Burundi and Guinea-Bissau UN Econ. and Social Coun.; chair UN Commn. on Social Devel.; v.p. UN Gen. Assembly. Office: Permanent Mission of South Africa to UN 333 E 38th St Fl 9 New York NY 10016-2772 Office Phone: 212-213-5583. Office Fax: 212-692-2498.*

KUMANYIKA, SHIRIKI K., nutrition epidemiology researcher, educator; b. Balt., Mar. 16, 1945; m. Christiaan B. Morssink; children: Chenjerai, Annoesjka. BA, Syracuse U., 1965; MS in Social Work, Columbia U., 1969; PhD in Human Nutrition, Cornell U., 1978; MPH, Johns Hopkins U., 1984. Asst. prof. nutrition Cornell U., Ithaca, NY, 1977-84; from asst. prof. to assoc. prof. epidemiology Johns Hopkins U. Sch. Hygiene and Pub. Health, Balt., 1984-89, asst. prof. internat. health, 1984-89; assoc. prof. nutritional epidemiology Pa. State U., University Park, 1989-92, prof. epidemiology, 1993-96; assoc. dir. for epidemiology Pa. State U. Coll. Medicine, Hershey, 1992-96; prof. epidemiology, prof. human nutrition and dietetics U. Ill. at Chgo., 1996-99, head dept. human nutrition and dietetics, 1996-99; chief of svc. U. Ill. Hosp. Nutritional Svcs., 1996-99; prof. epidemiology Children's Hosp. Phila., U. Pa. Sch. Med., Phila., 1999—, assoc. dean health promotion and disease prevention, 1999—, dir., grad. program, pub. health studies; dir. Penn-Cheyney Export Ctr. Inner City Health, Phila. Sr. scholar, Ctr. Clin. Epidemiology & Biostatistics (CCEB) U. Pa., sr. fellow, Inst. Aging, Leonard Davis Inst. Health Economics, adj. prof. epidemiology dept. health evaluation scis. Coll. Medicine, Pa. State U., Hershey, 1996-99; mem. adv. bd. Women's Health Alliance. Contbr. articles to profl. jours. Bd. dirs. Nat. Rural Ctr., 1978-82, Nat. Black Women's Health Project, 1994-99; mem. Women's Health Initiative adv. com. 1993-, US Dietary Guidelines Com., 1995, 2000, Nat. Heart, Lung, & Blood Inst. adv. coun., 1996-2000, NIH Obesity Task Force, 2001-, Nat. Children's Study adv. com., 2002-2003; active WHO. NIH grantee; recipient Bolton L. Corson medal Franklin Inst., 1997. Fellow Am. Coll. Epidemiology, Am. Coll. Nutrition; mem. AAUP, APHA, Am. Diabetes Assn., Am. Dietetic Assn., Am. Inst. Nutrition, Am. Soc. for Clin. Nutrition, Assn. Black Cardiologists, Internat. Soc. on Hypertension in Blacks, Nat. Med. Assn., N.Am. Assn. Study of Obesity, Soc. for Epidemiol. Rsch., Soc. for Nutrition Edn., Internat. Soc. and Fedn. Cardiology, Inst. Medicine. Office: Ctr Clin Epidemiology and Biostats U Pa Sch Med 8th Fl Blockley Hall 423 Guardian Dr Philadelphia PA 19104-6021 E-mail: skumanyi@cceb.med.upenn.edu.

KUMAR, BINOD, materials engineer, educator; b. Jamalpur, Bihar, India, Jan. 13, 1946; came to U.S., 1971; s. Rambaran and Ramsunderi (Rai) Singh; m. Shyama Thakur, May 23, 1969; children: Vineet, Sunita. MS, Pa. State U., 1973, PhD, 1976. Glass technologist Seraikella Glass Works, Konnagar, India, 1968-71; rsch. engr. Anchor Hocking Corp., Lancaster, Ohio, 1976-79, U. Dayton, 1980—88, sr. rsch. engr., 1988—2002, dist. rsch. engr., group leader, 2002—, prof., 1992. Cons. Zimmer, Inc., Warsaw, Ind., 1987-90, Mead, Inc., Dayton, 1988, JAFE, Inc., Greenville, Ohio, 1987-90, Rotor Seal Dynamics, Calif., 1995, Tex. Tech. Industries, Maine, 1999. Trustee India Found., Dayton, 1991-95. Mem. Am. Ceramic Soc., Electrochem. Soc., Indian Ceramic Soc. (life). Achievements include 110 publs. and 15 patents contributing to the fields of glass tech., solid state ionics, lithium rechargeable batteries, fuel cells and high temperature superconductivity; also mentoring jr. profls., undergraduate and grad. students. Office: U Dayton 300 College Park Ave Dayton OH 45469-0001 Business E-Mail: kumarb@udri.udayton.edu.

KUMAR, KRISHNA, chemistry professor; b. Madras, India, Nov. 1970; BS in Chemistry, St. Stephen's Coll., 1991; PhD in Organic Chemistry, Brown U., 1996. Skaggs rsch. fellow Scripps Rsch. Inst. & Skaggs Inst. for Chemical Biology, 1996—98; asst. prof. chemistry Tufts U., 1998—2002, assoc. prof. chemistry, 2003—05, prof. chemistry, 2006—, chmn. chemistry, 2006—; assoc. mem. cancer ctr. Tufts Sch. Med. & New England Med. Ctr., 1999—. Recipient Career award, Nat. Sci. Found., 2002, DuPont Young Prof. award, E.I. du Pont de Nemours & Co., 2003, Global Indus Tenovator award, MIT, 2006. Office: Tufts U Chemistry Dept 62 Talbot Ave Medford MA 02155 Office Phone: 617-627-3441. Business E-Mail: krishna.kumar@tufts.edu.

KUMAR, KV, management consultant; s. M.V. and Saraswathi Krishna Murthy; m. Vijaya Srinivasa Murthy, Mar. 23, 1983; children: Sanjay, Vishnu Srinivas. Industrial & Production Engineering, Poly. Inst./India, 1967. CEO Bus. & Strategic Cons. Internat., Inc., Waldorf, Md., 2002—; pres. Kumar Enterprises LLC. Pres. & ceo Am. Systems Internat., Inc., Bethesda, Md., 2000—03; apptd. Nat. Adv. Coun., Small Bus. Adminstrn., 2005. Mem., bd. of governors Internat. Brain Injury Assn., Washington, 1995—2003; mem., round table, mbda U.S. Dept. of Commerce, Washington, 1992—93; mem., round table U.S. SBA, Washington, 1992—93; Ariz. local bd. mem. U.S. SSS, 1998—2004; mem., DC econ. devel. com. D.C. Govt., 1992—93; leader, help the sr. citizen group Sr. Citizen Group of Wash., D.C., 1973—78; coun. mem. Ariz. Governor's Coun. on Spinal & Head Injuries, 1998—2003, Ariz. State Rehab. Coun., 1998—2003; mem., nat. steering com. Bush-Cheney, 2004; nat. chmn. U.S. Indian Am. C. of C., Washington, 2003—05; nat. pres. Nat. Indian Am. C. of C., Washington, 1991—2003; founder/dir. First Liberty Bank Corp., Inc., Washington, 1987—91; mem., exec. bd. Red Means Stop Coalition, Phoenix, 2003—05; chmn, dist. appeals bd. U.S. SSS, Phoenix, 2004—05; mem., franchise alliance com. Internat. Franchise Assn., Washington, 1992—93. Recipient Millenium award, Brain Injury Assn. of USA, 2000, IBIA President's award for Outstanding Achievement, IBIA, Stockholm, Sweden, 2003, Meritorius Svc. award and Bronze medal, U.S. SSS, 2004, Honored Patriots award, U.S. Selective Svc. Svc. Sys., 2000, award for dedicated services to Minority Businesses, U.S. Hispanic C. of C., 1993, 1996, 1997. Mem.: Indian Inst. of Indsl. Engineers (hon.). R-Consevative. Hindu. Avocation: travel. Home: 7272 E Gainey Ranch Rd Unit # 103 Scottsdale AZ 85258 Home Phone: 480-368-5500; Office Phone: 480-368-5500. Office Fax: 480-607-9500; Home Fax: 480-607-9500. Personal E-mail: kvkumarusa@yahoo.com. E-mail: kvkumar@bscii.com.

KUMAR, NISHA, Internet company executive; BA magna cum laude, Harvard Coll.; MBA, Harvard Bus. Sch. Investment banker Morgan Stanley; v.p. corp. devel. Priceline.com; with bus. affairs group AOL LLC, 2001; v.p. mergers and acquisitions Time Warner Inc., v.p. corp. ops.; exec. v.p., CFO AOL LLC, Dulles, Va., 2007—. Term mem. Coun. Fgn. Rels. Dir. Human Care Charitable Trust. Office: AOL LLC 22000 AOL Way Dulles VA 20166*

KUMAR, PANGANAMALA RAMANA, electrical and computer engineering educator; b. Nagpur, Maharashtra, India, Apr. 21, 1952; arrived in U.S., 1973; s. Panganamala Bhavanarayana and Panganamala Kamala (Avasarala) Murthy; m. Devarakonda Jayashree Sundaram, Jan. 22, 1982; children: P. Ashwin, Shilpa P. BTech in Elec. Engring., Indian Inst. Tech., Madras, 1973; MS, Washington U., St. Louis, 1975, DSc, 1977. Asst. prof. dept. math. and computer sci. U. Md., Baltimore County, 1977—82, assoc. prof., 1982—84; assoc. prof. dept. elec. and computer engring. and coordinated sci. lab. U. Ill., Urbana, 1985—87, prof. dept. elec. and computer engring., 1987—, rsch. prof. coordinated sci. lab., 1987—, Franklin W. Woeltge prof. elec. and computer engring., 2000—. Co-author: Stochastic Sys., 1986; assoc. editor: Sys. and Control Letters, 1984-93, Math. of Control Signals and Sys., 1986-2005, SIAM Jour. on Control and Optimization, 1989-93, Jour. Discrete Event Dynamic Systems: Theory and Application, 1993-2004; mem. editl. bd. Jour. on Adaptive Control and Signal Processing, 1986-99, Math. Problems in Engring., 1995—, ACM Trans. on Sensor Networks, 2004-06, Foundations and Trends in Networking, 2004, IEEE Trans. on Mobile Computing, 2005-06; editor Comm. Info. and Sys., 1999; assoc. editor IEEE Trans. on Automatic Control, 1982-83, assoc. editor at large, 1989-97; mem. editl. bd. Sadhana, 2005—, Academy Proceedings in Engineering Sciences, 2005—; contbr. articles to profl. jours., chpts. to books. Recipient Donald P. Eckman award, Am. Automatic Control Coun., 1985. Fellow: IEEE (Field award Control Sys. 2006); mem.: NAE. Avocation: ping pong/table tennis. Office: Univ Ill Urbana Champaign Coord Sci Lab 1308 W Main St Urbana IL 61801-2307 Office Phone: 217-333-7476. E-mail: prkumar@uiuc.edu.

KUMAR, PRADEEP, physics professor, researcher; b. Allahabad, Up, India, Jan. 1, 1949; s. Kali Shankar and Shanti Devi; m. Diana Lynn Tonnessen, Oct. 30, 1987; children: Casey Alok, Vijay Alexander, Ravi Armand. PhD, U. Calif., La Jolla, 1973. Asst. prof. U. So. Calif., LA, 1977—78, U. Fla., Gainesville, 1979—83, assoc. prof., 1983—93, prof., 1993—. Guest prof. NORDITA, Copenhagen, 1978—79. Home: 2390 NW 18th Place Gainesville FL 32605 Office: University of Florida PO Box 118440 Gainesville FL 32611-8440 Home Phone: 352-379-8781; Office Phone: 352-392-6690. Office Fax: 352-846-0295; Home Fax: 352-379-8781. Personal E-mail: pkumar@ufl.edu.

KUMAR, RAJ, medical educator; b. Kanpur, Uttar Pradesh, India, Dec. 15, 1959; s. Sri Lal Chhote and Laxmi Vijay; m. Sangh Mittra, Dec. 1993. BSc, Kanpur U.; MBBS, GSVM Med. Coll., Kanpur, 1980, MS in Surgery, 1985; MCh, AIIMS, New Delhi, 1990. Registered MCI India, 1990. Registered neurosurgeon AIIMS New Delhi, 1991—93; asst. prof. SP Med. Coll., Bikaner, Rajasthan, India, 1995—96; from asst. prof. to prof., head neurosurgery SGPGIMS, Luckow, India, 1996—. Mem.: Nat. Acad. Med. Scis., Nat. Acad. Scis. Home: Type IV 79 SGPGIMS Lucknow India Office: SGPGIMS Dept Neurosurgery Lucknow India Home Phone: 91-522-2668700, 91-522-2668900; Office Phone: 91-522-2668800. Business E-Mail: rajkumar@sggpi.ac.in.

KUMAR, RAJENDRA, electrical engineering educator; b. Amroha, India, Aug. 22, 1948; arrived in US, 1980; s. Satya Pal Agarwal and Kailash Vati Agarwal; m. Pushpa Agarwal, Feb. 16, 1971; children: Anshu, Shipra. BS in Math. and Sci., Meerut Coll., 1964; BEE, Indian Inst. Tech., Kanpur, 1969, MEE, 1977; PhD, U. New Castle, NSW, Australia, 1981. Mem. tech. staff Electronis and Radar Devel., Bangalore, India, 1969-72; rsch. engr. Indian Inst. Tech., Kanpur, 1972-77; asst. prof. Calif. State U., Fullerton, 1981-83, Brown U., Providence, 1980-81; prof. Calif. State U., Long Beach, 1983—, dept. chmn., 2005—. Cons. Jet Propulsion Lab., Pasadena, Calif., 1984-91, Aerospace Corp., El Segundo, Calif., 1995—. Contbr. articles. Recipient Best Paper award Internat. Telemetering Conf., Las Vegas, 1986, 10 New Technology awards NASA, Washington, 1987-91. Mem.: AAUP, AIAA, NEA, IEEE (sr.), Inst. of Navigation, Calif. Faculty Assn., Inst. Navigation, Auto Club So. Calif. (Cerritos), Tau Beta Pi (eminent mem.), Sigma Xi, Eta Kappa Nu. Achievements include patents for efficient detections and signal parameter estimation with applications to hihg dynamic GPS receivers; multiusage estimation of received carrier signal parameters under very high dynamic conditions of the receiver; fast frequency acquisition via adaptive least squares algorithms; Kalman filter ionospheric delay estimator; method and apparatus for reducing multipath signal error using deconvolution; adaptive smoothing system for fading communication channels; others. Avocations: gardening, walking, hiking, reading. Home: 13910 Rose St Cerritos CA 90703-9043 Office: Calif State U 1250 N Bellflower Blvd Long Beach CA 90840-0001 Office Phone: 562-985-1556. Personal E-mail: rajendrakumar@sbcglobal.net. Business E-Mail: kumar@csulb.edu.

KUMAR, RAMYA, academic administrator; d. Brinda Kumar. BA in Psychology, U. Mass., 2001, MS in Biol. Scis., 2003. Cert. rape aggression defense instr. Rape Aggression Defense Sys. Resident advisor U. Mass., Lowell, 1999—2000, asst. resident dir., 2000—02, resident dir., 2002—03, Mich. State U., East Lansing, Mich., 2003—04, assoc. dir. student affairs, Lyman Briggs Sch., 2003—04; hall dir. U. Ariz., Tucson, 2004—06, coord. comm. program, 2006—. Culture fest mktg. chair U. Mass., 2000—01, safety com., 2000—01, yearbook prodn. com., 2000—02; coord. residence hall orientation Mich. State U., 2003—04, advisor, Lyman Briggs ambassadors, 2003—04, com. mem. women's history banquet and conf., 2003—04; advisor, coalition Indian undergrad. students Mich. State. U., East Lansing, Mich., 2003—04; regional conf. programming advisor affiliated coll. and univ. residence halls Inter Mountain, Tucson, 2004—04; freshman seminar instr. U. Ariz., Tucson, 2004—, advisor, residence hall coun., 2004—05, staff selection, tng. com., 2004—, acad. initiatives com., 2004—; adcisor mktg. and design Ariz. Collegiate Leadership Conf., 2006. Vol. tunnel of opression U. Ariz., 2004—, sexual assault awareness marathon organizer, 2004—; yound adult coord., tchr. children's spirituality class Sri Sathya Sai Baba Ctr. Tucson, 2005. Recipient Resident Advisor of Yr., U. Mass., 1999, Programmer of Yr., 1999, Psi Chi Inductee, Psi Chi Nat. Honors Soc. Psychology, 2001. Mem.: Assn. Internat. Mountain Affiliated Housing Ofcrs., Nat. Assn. Student Pers. Adminstrs., Am. Coll. Pers. Assn., Psi Chi. Achievements include research in Alzheimer's using mazes and diet patterns, published in the Journal of Neuromolecular Medicine. Home Phone: 520-621-1680.

KUMAR, ROMESH, chemical engineer; b. Rajpura, India, Oct. 18, 1944; arrived in U.S., 1966; s. Kundan Lal and Pushpa (Wati) Agarwal; m. Kumkum Khanna, Feb. 22, 1976. BS, Panjab U., India, 1965; MS, U. Calif., Berkeley, 1968, PhD, 1972. From postdoctoral appointee to sr. chem. engr. Argonne Nat. Lab., Ill., 1972—2004, sr. chem. engr., 2004—, head fuel cell dept. Chem. Engring. divsn. Tchr. fuel cell power sys. design and analysis for transp. applications. Contbr. to Weissberger's Techniques in Chemistry, 1975; patentee in field. Recipient Silver medal Panjab U., 1965, Medal for Disting. Performance U. Chgo., 2004. Hindu. Home: 1549 Ceals Ct Naperville IL 60565-6148 Office: 9700 Cass Ave Argonne IL 60439-4803 Office Phone: 630-252-4342. Business E-Mail: kumar@cmt.anl.gov.

KUMAR, SANTOSH, medical educator, research scientist; b. Nalanda, Bihar, India, Feb. 26, 1969; s. Shiv Nandan Prasad and Dhanma Devi; m. Namita Sinha, Apr. 16, 1998; 1 child, Sneha Sinha. BS, U. Delhi, India, 1990; MS, Indian Inst. Tech., Bombay, 1993, PhD, 1998. Post-doctoral fellow U. Mo., Kansas City, 1998—2001; rsch. instr. U. Tex. Med. Br., Galveston, 2001—04, asst. prof., 2005—. Contbr. articles various profl. jours. Jr. Rsch. fellowship, Indian Inst. Tech., Bombay, 1993-1995, Sr. Rsch. fellowship, 1995-1998, Post-Doctorate fellowship, U. Mo., 1998-2001, NIEHS Ctr. Pilot grant, Nat. Inst. Environ. Health Scis., U. Tex. Med. Br., 2003. Mem.: AAAS (hon.), Am. Soc. Pharmacology and Exptl. Therapeutics (Post-Doctoral Best Paper award 2003), Am. Soc. Biochemistry and Molecular Biology (hon.). Office: Univ Tex Med Br Pharmacology and Toxicology 301 Univ Blvd Galveston TX 77555-1031 Office Phone: 409-772-9677. Office Fax: 409-772-9642. Business E-Mail: sakumar@utmb.edu.

KUMAR, SURINDER, food products executive; b. Lahore, Panjab, India, Apr. 2, 1944; came to U.S., 1966; s. Kanshi Ram and Kailash (Wanti) Arora; m. Janet Lauer, July 21, 1973; 1 child, Daven Arora. BS, Nat. Dairy Research Inst., Karnal, India, 1965; MS, Ohio State U., 1968, PhD in Food Sci. and Nutrition, 1971; MBA in Mktg. and Fin., U. Chgo., 1979. Group leader Quaker Oats Co., Barrington, Ill., 1972-75, mgr., 1975-81, assoc. dir., 1981-82; dir. Frito Lay, Dallas, 1982-84; v.p. Pepsi Cola Co., Valhalla, NY, 1984; sr. v.p. Pepsicola Co., 1984—92; pres. former Warner Lambert Co., 1992—95; sr. v.p. global r&d Pepsicola Restaurants, Dallas, 1995—98; sr. v.p., global R&D, Mead Johnson divsn. Bristol-Myers Squibb, 1998—2001; with Wm. Wrigley Jr. Co., Chgo., 2001—, chief innovation officer, quality assurance and scientific & regulatory affairs, r&d global engring. Peoria, Ill., 2001—. Mem. nutritional adv. bd. Monell Chem. Senses Ctr.; mem. mgmt. bd. Food Update; spkr. in field; adv. bd. Depaul U. Patentee in field; author Riding The Blue Train; contbr. articles to profl. jours. Pres. India Assn. Ohio State U., 1969; mem. tech. adv. bd. Rutgers U. Named Outstanding Grad., Indian Agriculture Research Inst., 1966; recipient Disting. Alumni award Ohio State U., 1987. Mem. Indsl. Research Inst., Inst. Food Technologists, Sigma Xi, Gamma Tau Delta. Home: PO Box 271065 Flower Mound TX 75027-1065

KUMAR, VERINDER, accountant, financial executive; b. Mirpur, Kashmir, India, Sept. 24, 1932; arrived in U.S., 1979; s. Basheshar Nath and Tara Wanti (Durga Devi) Mahajan; m. Manjula Mehandru, Oct. 31, 1965; children: Monisha, Ayesha. BA, Punjab U., India, 1958. Cert. acct., U.K. Acct. Punjab Nat. Bank, New Delhi, 1958-62, Glenhurst Hayes, Ltd., London, 1963-65, George Cohen Group, London, 1965-68; fin. acct. Nuffield Nursing Homes Trust, London, 1968-79; comptr. Community Nutrition Inst., Washington, 1980-84, treas./cons., 1984—2002; CFO Wilcoxon Constrn., Inc., Rockville, Md., 1984—. Bd. dirs., sec., treas. Md. Pools, Balt., Tyma-Kumar Joint Venture, Rockville; v.p. Avery Corp. Mem.: Woodford Pk. Residents Assn. Republican. Hindu. Avocations: hiking, fishing, cricket, soccer, reading. Home: 8505 Bethany Ct Vienna VA 22182-5060

KUMAR, VIKAS, neuropharmacologist, researcher; b. Palwal, Faridabad, Haryana, India, Feb. 16, 1973; s. Ajit Kumar and Savitri Arya; m. Reena Arora, Oct. 15, 2002. PharmD, Dayananda Sagar Inst. Pharmacy, Bangalore, 1990; B in pharmacy, Gulbarga U., 1995, PharmM, 1997; PhD, Banaras Hindu U., Varanasi, India, 2000. Registered pharmacist State Pharmacy Coun., 1991. Lectr. Hindu Coll. Pharmacy, Sonepat, Haryana, India, 1997—98; sr. rsch. fellow Banaras Hindu U., Varanasi, India, 1998—2000, reader pharmacology dept. pharmaceutics Inst. Tech., 2006—; scientist to sr. scientist Indian Herbs Rsch. & Supply Co. Ltd, Saharanpur, India, 2001—03; rsch. assoc. Lupin Rsch. Pk., Pune, Maharashtra, India, 2003—04, Tex. Tech Sch. Pharmacy, Amarillo, 2004—06. Cons. Indo Phytochem Pharms., Sirmour, India, 2004—05. Recipient Semi Khatib Gold medal, Luqman Coll. Pharmacy, 1996, Servier Young Investigators' award, Inst. Rsch. Internat. Servier, France, 1999; Sr. Rsch. fellow, Indian Coun. Med. Rsch., Govt. of India, New Delhi, 1999, Post Doctoral fellow, So. Ill. U., 2002. Mem.: Internat. Brain Rsch. Orgn., Acad. Pharm. Scientists Gt. Britain, Am. Assn. Pharm. Scientists, Assn. Pharm. Tchrs. India (life), Soc. for Phytomedica (life), Indian Soc. Biomedical Scientists (life), Indian Sci. Congress Assn. (life), Indian Soc. Chemists & Biologists (life), Indian Pharmacy Graduates' Assn. (life), Assn. Physiologists and Pharmacologists India (life), Indian Acad. Neurosciences (life), Indian Pharm. Assn. (life), Soc. Young Scientists (life), Indian Pharmacological Soc. (life). Office Phone: 91-542-2307049. Business E-Mail: vikask@bhu.ac.in.

KUMAR, VIKRAM SHEEL, information technology executive; BS in Indsl. Engring. and Ops. Rsch., Columbia U.; MD, Harvard Med. Sch. Pres., CEO Dimagi, Inc. Mem. adv. bd. Global Emerging Tech. Inst.; founding fellow Media Lab Asia. Named one of Top 100 Young Innovators, MIT Tech. Review, 2004; recipient Tech. in Svc. Humanity award, 2004, Paul and Daisy Soros New Am. Office: Dimagi Inc 390 Commonwealth Ave Ste 605 Boston MA 02215

KUMBLE, STEVEN JAY, lawyer; b. July 3, 1933; m. Barbara Kumble (div.); children: Charles Todd, Roger Glenn; m. Peggy Basten Vandervoort (div.); m. Angela Marie Giguere. BA, Yale U., 1954; JD, Harvard U., 1959; LLD (hon.), L.I. U., 1990. Bar: N.Y. 1960. Ptnr. Finley, Kumble, Wagner, Underberg, Manley & Casey, NYC, 1968-87; of counsel Summit Rovins & Feldesman, NYC, 1988-90; chmn. bd. dirs. Lincolnshire Mgmt., Inc., NYC, 1985—2004; chmn., bd. dirs. Corinthian Capital Group, LLC, 2005—. Mem. adv. bd. Inst. Civil Justice, Rand, 1999—2005; mem. dean's adv. bd. Harvard Law Sch., 2006—. Vice chmn. bd. dirs. LI U., Greenvale,

NY, 1984—; chmn. 1982-94, trustee bd. Gov.'s Com. Scholastic Achievement, NYC, 1981-. 1st lt. US Army, 1955—57. Mem. Assn. of Bar of City of NY, Harvard Club, Wanumetonomy Golf Club (Newport, RI), Yale Club, Breakers Golf Club (Palm Beach), Phi Beta Kappa. Avocations: skiing, golf. Home Phone: 212-759-5221; Office Phone: 212-920-2300. Business E-Mail: skumble@corinthiancap.com.

KUMIN, LIBBY BARBARA, speech language pathologist, educator; b. Bklyn., Nov. 11, 1945; d. Herbert H. and Berniece (Shuch) K.; m. Martin J. Lazar, Jan. 18, 1969; 1 child, Jonathan Kumin Lazar. BA summa cum laude, LIU, 1965; MA, NYU, 1966, PhD, 1969. Lic. speech pathologist, pathology. Asst. prof. speech pathology U. Md., College Park, 1972-76, cons., 1976-80; assoc. prof. Loyola Coll., Balt., 1980-88, prof., 1988—, chmn. dept. speech and lang. pathology, 1983—99, dir. MS program, 1983—2003, dir. grad. programs, 1999—2003. Adj. prof. Loyola Coll., 1976-80; specialist in speech and lang. in Down Syndrome; mem. profl. adv. bd. Nat. Down Syndrome Cong.; leader of parent and profl. seminars; mem. Down Syndrome Med. Interest Group. Author: Aphasia, 1978, Communication Skills in Children with Down Syndrome, 1994, Classroom Language Skills in Children with Down Syndrome, 2001, Early Communication Skills for Children with Down Syndrome, 2003, What Did You Say?, 2006; mem. editl. bd.: Down Syndrome Rsch. and Practice; contbr. articles to profl. jours. Recipient Outstanding Individual of Yr. award Howard County Assn. Retarded Citizens, Nat. Meritorious Svc. award Nat. Down Syndrome Congress, 1987, Rsch. award Christian Pueschel Meml., 2004, The Pres.'s award Nat. Down Syndrome Soc., 2005; grantee Loyola Coll., 1983, 91, 97, 99, 2002, 04, Aaron and Lillie Straus Found., 1983-89, 99-2005, Taishoff Family Found., 2005, 06, Columbia Found., Joseph P. Kennedy Found., 1995, 2002, Shriver Ctr., 1996-98, 2002 Mem. ARC, Nat. Down Syndrome Soc. (Pres.'s award 2005), Nat. Down Syndrome Congress, Am. Speech/Lang./Hearing Assn. (cert.), Md. Speech and Hearing Assn., Taishoff Family Found., Sigma Tau Delta, Pi Lambda Theta. Office: Loyola Coll Dept Speech Pathology 4501 N Charles St Dept Speech Baltimore MD 21210-2601 Business E-Mail: lkumin@loyola.edu.

KUMIN, MAXINE WINOKUR, poet, writer; b. Phila., June 6, 1925; d. Peter and Doll (Simon) Winokur; m. Victor Montwid Kumin, June 29, 1946; children: Jane Simon, Judith Montwid, Daniel David. AB, Radcliffe Coll., 1946, MA, 1948; LHD (hon.), Centre Coll., 1976, Davis and Elkins Coll., 1977, Regis Coll., 1979, New England Coll., 1982, Claremont Grad. Sch., 1983, U. N.H., 1984, Bowdoin Coll., 2002. Instr. Tufts U., Medford, Mass., 1958-61, lectr. English, 1965-68. Scholar Radcliffe Inst. for Ind. Study, 1961-63; vis. lectr. U. Mass., Amherst, 1973, Princeton U., 1977, 79, 81-82; adj. prof. Columbia U., 1975; Fannie Hurst prof. of literature Brandeis U., 1975, Wash. U., St. Louis, 1977; Carolyn Wilkerson Bell vis. scholar Randolph-Macon Woman's Coll., 1978; poet in residence Bucknell U., 1983; vis. prof. MIT, 1984, U. Miami, 1995, Pitzer Coll., 1996; McGee prof. of writing Davidson Coll., 1997; writer in residence Fla. Internat. U., 1998-2000; master artist Atlantic Ctr. for Arts, New Smyrna Beach, Fla., 1984-2002; staff mem. Bread Loaf Writers' Conf., 1969-71, 73, 75, 77; poetry cons. Library of Congress, 1981-82; elector The Poet's Corner, The Cathedral of St. John the Divine, 1990-1996; mem. staff Sewanee Writer's Conf., 1993-94, Bucknell U. visiting poet, 2001. Author: (poetry) Halfway, 1961, The Privilege, 1965, The Nightmare Factory, 1970, Up Country: Poems of New England, 1972 (Pulitzer Prize for poetry 1973), House, Bridge, Fountain, Gate, 1975, The Retrieval System, 1978, Our Ground Time Here Will Be Brief, 1982, Closing the Ring, 1984, The Long Approach, 1985, Nurture, 1989, Looking for Luck, 1992 (Poets' Prize), Connecting the Dots, 1996, Selected Poems 1960-1990, 1997, The Long Marriage, 2001, Bringing Together, 2003, Jack and Other New Poems, 2005; (novels) Through Dooms of Love, 1965, The Passions of Uxport, 1968, The Abduction, 1971, The Designated Heir, 1974; (essays) To Make A Prairie: Essays on Poets, Poetry, and Country Living, 1980, In Deep: Country Essays, 1987, Women, Animals and Vegetables: Essays and Stories, 1994, Inside the Halo and Beyond, 2000, Always Beginning, 2000; (short stories) Why Can't We Live Together Like Civilized Human Beings?, 1982; (juvenile) Sebastian and the Dragon, 1960, Spring Things, 1961, A Summer Story, 1961, Follow the Fall, 1961, A Winter Friend, 1961, Mittens in May, 1962, No One Writes a Letter to the Snail, 1962, Archibald the Traveling Poodle, 1963, (with Sexton) Eggs of Things, 1963, (with Sexton) More Eggs of Things, 1964, Speedy Digs Downside Up, 1964, The Beach Before Breakfast, 1964, Paul Bunyan, 1966, Faraway Farm, 1967, The Wonderful Babies of 1809 and Other Years, 1968, When Grandmother Was Young, 1970, When Great-Grandmother Was Young, 1971, (with Sexton) Joey and the Birthday Present, 1971, (with Sexton) The Wizard's Tears, 1975, What Color Is Caesar?, 1978, The Microscope, 1984; contbr. poems to nat. mags. Recipient Lowell Mason Palmer award, 1960, William Marion Reedy award, 1968, Eunice Tietjens Meml. prize Poetry Mag., 1972, Borestone Mountain award, 1976, Radcliffe Coll. Alumnae Recognition award, 1978, Am. Acad. and Inst. Arts and Letters award for excellence in literature, 1980, Levinson award Poetry mag., 1987, The Poets' prize, 1994, Aiken Taylor Poetry prize, 1995, Centennial award Harvard Grad. Sch. Arts and Scis., 1996, NH Writers Project Lifetime Achievement award, 1998, Ruth Lilly Poetry Prize, 1999, Charity Randall award, 2000, Robert Frost award, Plymouth Coll., 2001, Harvard U. Arts medal, 2005; grantee Nat. Endowment for the Arts, 1966; fellow Nat. Coun. on Arts and Humanities, 1967-68; fellow Acad. Am. Poets, 1986-2002; fellow Woodrow Wilson, 1979-80, 91-93. Mem. Acad. Am. Poets (chancellor), Poetry Soc. Am., PEN Am., Authors Guild, The Writers Union.

KUMMANT, ALEXANDER K., rail transportation executive; b. Aug. 27, 1960; m. Kathleen Regan. BA, Case Western Reserve Univ., 1982; MS, Carnegie Mellon Univ., 1986; MBA, Stanford Univ., 1990. Bus. analyst Timken Co.; with Emerson Elec. Co., SPX Corp.; regional ops. mgr. Union Pacific Railroad Co., regional v.p. ctrl., v.p., gen. mgr. indsl. products, v.p. premium ops.; pres. BOMAG, Germany; exec. v.p., chief mktg. officer Komatsu Am. Corp., 2005—06; pres., CEO Nat. Railroad Passenger Corp. (AMTRAK), Washington, 2006—. Office: AMTRAK 60 Massachusetts Ave NE Washington DC 20002*

KUMMEROW, ARNOLD A., superintendent of schools; b. Framingham, Mass., Mar. 25, 1945; s. Arnold A. Sr. and Elizabeth Patricia (Westfield) K.; m. Constance Booth, July 10, 1971. BME, Eastern Mich. U., 1968, MA, 1975; PhD, U. Mich., 1989. Cert. adminstrn., Mich. Instrumental music dir. Vandercook Lake Pub. Schs., Jackson, Mich., 1968-74; instrumental music dir., asst. prin., prin. L'Anse Creuse Pub. Schs., Mt. Clemens, Mich., 1975-89; asst. supt. curriculum and pers. Lincoln Consol. Schs., Ypsilanti, Mich., 1989-91; asst. supt. Ypsilanti Pub. Schs., 1991-93; mem. curriculum devel. staff Mich. Dept. Edn., 1993-94; supt. Carsonville-Port Sanilac (Mich.) Schs., 1994-97, Armada (Mich.) Area Schs., 1997—. Named Exemplary Sch. Prin., Mich. Dept. Edn. and U.S. Dept. Edn. Mem. AASA, MASA, ASCD. Home: 17201 Knollwood Dr Clinton Township MI 48038-2833 Office: Armada Area Schs 74500 Burk St Armada MI 48005-3314

KUMMINGS, DONALD DALE, language educator; b. Lafayette, Ind., July 28, 1940; s. Herman Wilhelm and Estelle Catherine (Easterwood) K.; m. Gail Nadine Savage, Mar. 23, 1963 (div. Aug. 1978); children: Kevin Scott (dec.), Jeremy William; m. Patricia Finnelly Larson, Mar. 21, 1987. BA, Purdue U., 1962, MA, 1964; PhD, Ind. U., 1971. Tchg. assoc. Purdue U., West Lafayette, Ind., 1963—64; instr. English Adrian Coll., Adrian, Mich., 1964—66; assoc. instr. Ind. U., Bloomington, 1966—70; asst. prof. English U. Wis.-Parkside, Kenosha, 1970—75, assoc. prof. English, 1975—85, prof. English, 1985—, chair dept. English, 1974—76, 1991—94. Book rev. editor Rutgers U., Camden, N.J., 1983-90; panelist, reviewer NEH, Washington, 1992-2005; lectr. in field; book manuscript cons. Harcourt Brace Jovanovich, U. Tenn. Press, Susquehanna U. Press, U. Iowa Press, Houghton Mifflin, W.W. Norton, Oxford (Eng.) U. Press, Blackwell Pub., A.B. Longman, Bedford/St. Martin's. Author: Walt Whitman, 1940-1975: A Reference Guide, 1982, The Open Road Trip: Poems, 1989; editor: Approaches to Teaching Whitman's "Leaves of Grass," 1990, A Companion to Walt Whitman, 2006; co-editor: Walt Whitman: An Encyclopedia, 1998; contbr. numerous articles to profl. jours. Mem. Honor Our Neighbors' Origins and Rights, 1991—. Named Wis. Prof. of Yr., Carnegie Found. for Advancement of Tchg., 1997. Mem. MLA (cons. reader 1993, 94), ACLU, Am. Lit. Assn., Acad. Am. Poets, Wis. Fellow of Poets, Walt Whitman Assn., Walt Whitman Birthplace Assn., Greenpeace. Avocations: travel, photography, jazz, racquetball. Office: U Wis-Parkside Dept English PO Box 2000 Kenosha WI 53141-2000 Office Phone: 262-595-2525. E-mail: kummings@uwp.edu.

KUMMLER, RALPH H., chemical engineer, educator, dean; b. Jersey City, Nov. 1, 1940; m. Jean Evelyn Helge, Aug. 25, 1962; children: Randolph Henry, Bradley Rolf, Jeffrey Ralf. BSChemE, Rensselaer Poly. Inst., 1962; PhD, Johns Hopkins U., 1966. Chem. engr. GE Space Scientist Lab., Valley Forge, Pa., 1965—69; assoc. prof. chem. engring. Wayne State U., Detroit, 1970—75, prof., 1975—, chmn. dept., 1974—93, dir. hazardous waste mgmt. programs, 1986—, assoc. dean rsch., 1997—2001, interim dean, 2001—04, dean, 2004—. Contbr. articles to publs. Bd. dirs., past pres. Kirkwood Lake Assn. Fellow: Engr. Soc. Detroit (Young Engr. of Yr. award 1975, Gold award 1990, Disting. Svc. award 1994, Horace Rackham Humanitarian award 1999, Disting. Svc. award 2004), Am. Inst. Chemists; mem.: AIChE (past pres. Detroit chpt.), Svc. award 1981, Chem. Engr. of Yr. award 1981), Mich. Air and Waste Mgmt. Assn. ((past pres.), Waste Mgmt. award 2002), Am. Chem. Soc., Tau Beta Pi, Sigma Xi. Achievements include co-patentee in chem. innovations. Office: Wayne State U Coll Engring Detroit MI 48202 Business E-Mail: rkummler@wayne.edu.

KUM-NJI, PHILIP, pediatrician, educator; s. Nolbert and Esther NNsen Kum-Nji; m. Stella Yuh Yih, Sept. 9, 1958; children: Nicole Ndum, Germain Nji, George Temfung, Paul Che, Peter Feul. MD, U. of Yaounde Sch. of Medicine, Cameroon, 1971—77; MPH, Tulane Sch. of Pub. Health and Tropical Medicine, 1985—86. Pediatrics Am. Bd. of Pediat., 1994. Med. officer Ministry of Pub. Health, Mbouda, Mbengwi, and Buea, Cameroon, 1978—84; instr. in pub. health U. of Yaounde Med. Sch., Cameroon, 1984—85; asst. prof. pediat. U. of Pitts. Sch. Medicine; asst. prof. VCU Sch. Medicine, Richmond, Va. Med. dir. miss. children's health project Children's Health Fund, Clarksdale, Miss. Author (rsch.) numerous pubs. in med. jours. Fellow: Am. Acad. of Pediat.; mem.: So. Soc. of Pediatric Rsch., Ambulatory Pediatric Assn. Office: Children's Med Ctr VCU Univ Sch Medicine 1001 East Marshal St Richmond VA 23298 Home: 4732 Whitestone Dr Richmond VA 23234 Office Phone: 804-828-0099. Business E-Mail: pkumnji@vcu.edu.

KUMPATY, HEPHZIBAH J., chemistry professor; m. Subha K. Kumpaty. PhD, U. Miss., 1996. Assoc. prof. U. Wis., Whitewater, Wis., 1996—. Rschr. U. Wis., Milw., 2006, dir. women and sci. program, Oshkosh, Wis., 1999—2002. Contbr. articles to profl. jours. Recipient Chancellor's award, U. Wis. Whitewater, 2005. Mem.: Am. Chem. Soc. (advisor local student chpt. 1999—2006, Chemistry Mag. award 2005). Avocations: travel, reading, cooking. Office: UW Whitewater 800 West main st Whitewater WI 800 W Home Phone: 262-472-1097; Office Phone: 262-472-1097. Business E-Mail: kumpatyh@uww.edu.

KUMPFER, KAROL LINDA, research psychologist; b. Neptune, NJ, July 30, 1943; d. Beverly Donald and Mary Belle (Campbell) K.; m. Henry Overton Whiteside, Mar. 6, 1978; 1 child, Jane H. BA, Colo. Women's Coll., 1966; MA, U. Utah, 1970, PhD, 1972; postdoctoral, U. Minn., 1975. Lic. psychologist, Utah. Asst. prof. psychology Oberlin Coll., Ohio, 1971-73; research assoc. Inst. Child Devel. U. Minn., Mpls., 1975-76; asst. prof. Colo. Women's Coll., Denver, 1976-78; psychologist Salt Lake County Mental Health Dept., 1979-80; dep. dir. State Div. Alcoholism and Drugs, Salt Lake City, 1980-84; vis. assoc. prof. Grad. Sch. Social Work U. Utah, Salt Lake City, 1983—88, asst. prof. pyschiatry, 1986—88, assoc. prof. dept. health promotion and edn., 1988—2005, prof. dept. health promotion and edn., 2005—; dir. Ctr. Substance Abuse and Prevention, Washington, 1998—2000; author, dir. Strengthening Families Program, Salt Lake City, 1982—; coordinating scientist Center for Disease Control, 2000—03. Editor/author: Childhood and Chemical Abuse: Prevention and Intervention, 1986. Bd. dirs. Repetory Dance Theatre, Salt Lake City, 1983-87, Western Assn. Concerned Adoptive Parents, Salt Lake City, 1985-90, Utah Alliance for Mentally Ill, Salt Lake City, 1979-80, Utah Mental Health Assn., 2000-03, House of Hope, Salt Lake City, 1994-98, Indian Walk-in Ctr., 2000—05, chair-elect, 2004-05; sec. bd. dirs. Utah Opera Guild, 1994-98; pres. U. Utah. Faculty Women's Club, 1974-75; mem. exec. com., chair Salt Lake City Mayor's Substance Abuse Prevention Coalition, 2000—. Grantee Utah Dept. Social Svcs., Salt Lake City, 1984-1986, Dept. Justice Office Juvenile Justice and Juvenile Delinquency Prevention, 1987-2003, Nat. Inst. on Drug Abuse, 1998-2004, Ctr. for Substance Abuse Prevention, 1997-2002; recipient SAMHSA/CSAP Model Prevention Program award, 2000, White House Office Nat. Drug Control Policy Dirs. award for Disting. Svc., 2000, Luther Terry Lectr. award U.S. Commd. Officers Assn., 2000. Mem.: APHA, AAAS, APA, Soc. for Prevention Rsch. (bd. dirs. 1995—2002, pres. 1997—99), Nat. Inst. Drug Abuse (spl. task force 1985—, grantee 1982—86, 1998—2004), Coun. on Social Work Edn., Nat. Inst. Alcoholism and Alcohol Abuse (spl. task force 1985—, grantee 1980, 2000—06), Am. Acad. Child Psychiatry (spl. task force 1986—88), Utah Psychol. Assn. (bd. dirs. 1985—88), Nat. Coun. Social Work Edn., Am. Pub. Health Assn. (mem. 1996—), Utah Psychologists in Pvt. Practice Assn. (pres. 1985—90), Sigma Xi. Democrat. Unitarian Universalist. Avocations: skiing, sailing, hiking, travel. Office: Health Promotion Edn U Utah 250 S 1850 East Salt Lake City UT 84112-0920 Office Phone: 801-581-7718.

KUMRA, VANDANA, otolaryngologist; d. Ved and Chandra Kumra; m. Navneet Kathuria. BA, Johns Hopkins U., Balt. Lic. NY, 1992. Physician, surgeon Vandana Kumra, MD, NYC, 1992—. Fellow: ACS, Am. Acad. Otolaryngology. Office: Vandana Kumra MD Ste 1H 262 Ctrl Pk W New York NY 10024 Office Phone: 212-873-6036.

KUNDA, DOLORES, marketing executive; b. 1956; BA English Lit., Smith Coll., 1977; MBA Mktg., Northwestern U., 1984. Joined client service dept. trainee, Leo Burnett, 1984; head Hispanic mktg. grp., Leo Burnett, 1993—99; founder, pres., CEO Lápiz Agy., 1999—. Mem. bd. dirs. Old Town Sch. of Folk Music in Chgo., Am. Assn. of Advt. Agencies' Hispanic mktg. steering com., Am. Advt. Federation's Mosaic Ctr. on Multiculturalism. Spkr. in field. Named a Woman to Watch, Crain's Chgo. Bus., 2007; named Chgo. Hispanic Hero, Chgo. Fire Soccer Franchise, 2003, 2004, Woman of the Year, Chgo. Advt., 2007; named one of The Top Latinas in the US, Hispanic Bus. mag., 2004, Vanidades mag., 2004; recipient Outstanding Achievement Award, Hispanic comm. by Hispanic mag., 2004. Office: Lapiz Inc 35 W Wacker Dr Chicago IL 60601 Office Phone: 312-220-5959. Office Fax: 312-220-3259.*

KUNDEL, HAROLD LOUIS, radiologist, educator; b. NYC, Aug. 15, 1933; s. John A. and Emma E. (Tolle) K.; m. Alice Marie Pape, Mar. 28, 1958; children: Jean, Catherine, Peter AB, Columbia U., 1955, MD, 1959; MS, Temple U., 1963; MA (hon.), U. Pa., 1980. Diplomate Am. Bd. Radiology. Asst. to assoc. prof. Temple U., Phila., 1967-73, prof. radiology, 1973-80; Matthew J. Wilson prof. research radiology U. Pa., Phila., 1980—2001, Matthew J. Wilson prof. emeritus radiology, 2001—. Dir. Pendergrass Diagnostic Imaging Labs. U. Pa., Phila., 1980—2001; sr. fellow L. Davis Inst., U. Pa. Contbr. articles to profl. jours. Capt. USAF, 1963—65. Fellow: Am. Coll. Radiology; mem.: SPIE, Am. Roentgen Ray Soc., Radiol. Soc. N.Am. (Honor award 1978), Assn. Univ. Radiologists (Meml. award 1963, Stauffer award 1982), Alpha Omega Alpha. Lutheran.

KUNDER, JAMES R., federal agency administrator; b. Oct. 8, 1948; BS, Harvard U.; MS, Georgetown U. Founder, prin. Kunder/Reali Assocs., Arlington, Va.; dep asst. adminstr. bur. external affairs US Agy. Internat. Devel., Washington, 1987—91, dir. office of US fgn. disaster assistance, 1991—93, dir. for relief and reconstruction in Afganistan, 2002, dep. asst. adminstr. bur. Asia and Near East, 2002—04, asst. adminstr. Bur. Asia & Near East, 2005—, acting dep. adminstr., 2007—. Legis. dir. U.S. Ho. of Reps.; sr. transp. analyst Commonwealth of Pa.; dep. dir. Nat. Rep. Senatorial Com. Contbr. articles to profl. jours. V.p. program devel. Save the Children Fedn. Infantry platoon comdr. USMC, 1970—73. Office: US Agy Internat Devel Ronald Reagan Bldg 1300 Pennsylvania Ave NW Rm 409 034 Washington DC 20523-1000 Office Phone: 202-712-0200.

KUNDIG, TOM, architect; BA magna cum laude in Environ. Design, U. Wash., 1977, MArch, 1981. Lic. Wash., 1982, Alaska, 1983, Idaho, 2000, Fla., 2002, NC, 2003, Oreg., 2004, NY, 2005, Calif., 2005, Colo., 2005. Assoc. C. Cichanski & Assocs., 1977—80; arch. Bruno Inabnit Akitectcuburo, Switzerland, 1980—81, TRA, 1981—83, The Callison Partnership, 1983, MHK Archs., 1984—85; prin. Jochman/Kundig Partnership, 1983—84; ptnr. Olsen Sundberg Kundig Allen Archs., Seattle, 1986—. Design studio instr. U. Wash., 1998—2001, instr. grad. design studio, 1999, lectr. dept. architecture, 99; vis. design critic dept. architecture Wash. State U., 1999; vis. design critic U. Oreg., Kyoto, 2001, vis. instr. dept. landscape architecture, 04; vis. design critic Tex. Tech U. Coll. Architecture, 2004; D. Kenneth Sargent vis. design critic Syracuse U. Coll. Architecture, 2006. Prin. works include Seattle Art Mus. (Blueprint award, 1981), The Meadow House (AIA Seattle Commendation award, 1993, AIA NW & Pacific Region Design Merit award, 1994), Home House (AIA Seattle Conceptual Citation award, 1996), Urban Villa (AIA Seattle Citation award, 1996, AIA NW & Pacific Region Design Honor award, 1997), Chapel of St. Ignacius (AIA Nat. Religious Architecture award, 1997, 1998, AIA Nat. Honor award, 1999), Studio House (AIA Seattle Merit award, 1997, AIA NW & Pacific Region Design Honor award, 1998, AIA Summit 2000 Western Internat. Design Merit award, 2000), The Brain: A Filmmaker's Studio (AIA Seattle Conceptual Honor award, 1999, AIA Seattle Honor award, 2000, AIA NW & Pacific Region Design Honor award, 2001, AIA Nat. Honor award, 2004), Chicken Point Cabin (AIA Seattle Honor award, 2002, AIA NW & Pacific Region Design Honor award, 2003, The Chgo. Athenaeum: Mus. Architecture and Design Am. Architecture award, 2004, AIA Nat. Honor award, 2004, Residential Arch. Grand award, 2005), Lake House (Masonry Inst. Wash. award, 2004), North Seattle Residence (Met. Home Design 100, 2005), Smithsonian's Cooper-Hewitt Nat. Design Mus., Arch.'s Office (Internat. Interior Design Assn. No. Pacific Chpt. INawards, 2005), Delta Shelter (Residential Arch. Grand award, 2006, Record House, Archtl. Record, 2006, AIA Seattle Merit award, 2006), Tyee River Cabin (AIA Seattle Merit award, 2006). Named one of 8 North Am. Emerging Archs., Archtl. League NY, 2004; recipient Architecture award, AAAL, 2007. Fellow: AIA; mem.: Tau Sigma Delta, Phi Beta Kappa. Office: Olson Sundberg Kundig Allen Archs 159 S Jackson St Ste 600 Seattle WA 98104 Office Phone: 206-624-5670. Office Fax: 206-624-3730.*

KUNDU, MUKUL RANJAN, physics and astronomy professor; b. Calcutta, India, Feb. 10, 1930; came to U.S., 1959; s. Makhan Lal and Monoroma K.; m. Sept. 9, 1958; children: Krishna, Rina, Sanjit. BS (with first class honors), U. Calcutta, India, 1949, MS, 1951; DSc, U. Paris, 1957. Assoc. prof. Cornell U., Ithaca, NY, 1962-65, Tata Inst. Fund Rsch., Bombay, 1965-68; prof. U. Md., College Park, 1968—, dir. astronomy, 1978-85. Editor: Radio Physics of the Sun, 1980, Unstable Current Systems and Plasma Instabilities in Astrophysics, 1984, Energetic Phenomena on the Sun, 1989; author: Solar Radio Astronomy, 1965; mem. editorial bd. Solar Physics, 1967—. Named Nat. Acad. Sci. fellow, 1967, 74-75, 86, U.S. Sr. Scientist awardee Humbolt Found., 1978, Am. Phys. Soc. fellow, 1989. Fellow Am. Phys. Soc.; mem. Am. Astron. Soc., Am. Geophys. Union, Internat. Astron. Union, Internat. Union Radio Sci. Office: U Md Dept Astronomy College Park MD 20742-0001 Home Phone: 301-989-3169; Office Phone: 301-405-1524. Business E-Mail: kundu@astro.umd.edu.

KUNER, CHARLES, retired secondary school educator; b. Chgo., July 3, 1938; s. George and Rose Kuner; m. Evelyn Sioc-Kuner, Oct. 11, 1997. BA in History, Roosevelt U., Chgo., 1962; MA in Tchg., Northeastern Ill. State U., Chgo., 1970, MA in Urban Sociology, 1977. Social studies tchr. Funston Elem. Von Steuben, Chgo., 1962—65; social studies, sci. tchr. Farragut Career Acad. HS, Chgo., 1965—2007; ret. Coach sch. debate team, 1990—95; established, supr. David Cerda Legal Clin., Farragut Career Acad. HS Libr., 2003—. Contbr. articles to profl. jours., local newspapers. Active Nat. Conf. Cmty. and Justice, 1960, Facing History and Ourselves, Chgo., 1980—, Close-up Found., Alexandria, Va., 1996—, Constl. Rights Found., Chgo., 1997—, Mikva Challenge Found., Chgo., 2003—; mem. Internat. Platform Assn., 1983—84. Named Amb. for Peace, Interreligious and Internat. Fedn. for World Peace, 2004; recipient Recognition of Excellence, Ill. State Bd. Edn., 1983—84, Tchr. Recognition award, Black Sch. Educators, 1985, Ednl. award, Blum-Kovler Found., 1989, Suave Performance Plus award, 2002, Cmty. Leadership award, Litle Village Cmty. Devel., 2003; Fry Fellowship, U. Chgo. Mem.: Chgo. Tchrs. Union, Nat. Coun. Social Studies. Democrat. Jewish. Avocations: rare books, classical music, history. Home: 6437 N Troy St Chicago IL 60645

KUNES, JAN, physicist; b. Plzen, Czech Republic, May 27, 1974; s. Vladislav Kunes and Marie Kunesova; 1 child, Petr. MSc, Charles U., Prague, 1997; PhD, Charles U., 2002. Postdoctoral fellow U. Calif., Davis, 2002—05; Humboldt fellow U. of Augsburg, Germany, 2006—. Fellow Humbodt Rsch. fellow, Humboldt Found., 2006, NATO Rsch. fellow, NSF, 2002. Mem.: Am. Phys. Soc. Office: Institute for Theoretical Physics University of Augsburg Augsburg Germany Office Phone: 49 821 598 3714. Business E-Mail: jan.kunes@physik.uni-augsburg.de.

KUNES, RICHARD W., cosmetics executive; MBA in Internat. Bus./Fin., Pace U. With Colgate-Palmolive Co.; internat. mfg. contr. internat. ops. group Estée Lauder Companies, Inc., NYC, 1986, regional fin. officer Asia/Pacific markets, v.p., contr. global ops., v.p. ops. fin. worldwide, v.p. fin. adminstrn., corp. contr., 1998—2000, sr. v.p., 2001—04, CFO, 2001—, exec. v.p., 2004—. Office: Estée Lauder Co Inc 767 5th Ave New York NY 10153*

KUNG, CANDIE, professional golfer; b. Kaohsiung, Taiwan, Aug. 8, 1981; Attended, U. So. Calif. Winner U.S. Pub. Links Championship, 2001, State Farm Classic, 2003; Wachovia LPGA Classic, 2003, LPGA Takefuji Classsic, 2003. Two-time NCAA All-Am.; winner Pac-10 Championships, 2000; three-time Am. Jr. Golf Assn. All-Am. Named Am. Jr. Golf Assn. Player of Yr., 1999. Office: c/o LPGA 100 International Golf Dr Daytona Beach FL 32124-1092

KUNG, DOUGLAS C., systems engineer; b. Elkhart, Ind., Feb. 23, 1971; s. Franklin H. and Betty C. Kung; m. Cher V. Andres, Feb. 14, 1999; 1 child, Cadence Fahn Andres. BA, U. Ariz., Tucson, 1995. Tech. sales specialist Pacific Bell, Oakland, Calif., 1997—99; integration sales mgr. SBC Datacomm, Pleasanton, Calif., 1999—2002; systems engr. SBC,

Dublin, Calif., 2002—06; applications engr. Nexus IS, Inc, Pleasanton, 2006—. Bd. dirs., chair Chinese Am. Polit. Assn., Walnut Creek, Calif., 1995—97. Recipient Pres. Club Pinnacle award, SBC, 2000; Nat. Merit scholar, Clorox Corp., 1989. Mem.: IEEE, Am. Mensa (life), Lamba Chi Alpha (pres. 1992—93, Andrew Gustaveson Meml. scholar 1993). Home Phone: 925-560-1414; Office Phone: 925-226-3320. Personal E-mail: d.kung@yahoo.com.

KUNG, LISA, lawyer; b. 1969; Degree in Physics and Philosophy, Emory U.; JD, NYU, 1997. Rockefeller Brother Fund fellow Vera Inst. Justice, NYC; Soros Justice fellow Law Ctr. for Homeless, Atlanta; staff atty. Southern Ctr. for Human Rights, Atlanta, 1999—2006, dir., 2006—. Named one of Litigation's Rising Stars, The Am. Lawyer, 2007. Office: Southern Ctr for Human Rights 83 Poplar St NW Atlanta GA 30303-2122*

KUNG, PANG-JEN, materials scientist, electrical engineer; b. I-Lan, Taiwan, May 13, 1959; s. Ching-Yu and A-Se (Yu) K.; m. Tzyy-Yun Tzeng, May 18, 1986; children: Naihau, Naiwei. MSChemE, Nat. Tsing Hua U., 1983; MSEE, Auburn U., 1988; MMetE, Carnegie Mellon U., 1991, PhD in Materials Sci., 1993; MBA, U. Conn., 1998. Registered profl. engr. Jr. engr. Tatung Co., Taipei, Taiwan, 1979—80; tchg. asst. Nat. Tsing Hua U., Hsin-Chu, Taiwan, 1981—82, rsch. asst., 1982—83; assoc. scientist Indsl. Tech. Res. Inst., Hsin-Chu, 1985—86; tchg. and rsch. asst. Auburn U., Ala., 1986—89; rsch. asst. Carnegie Mellon U., Pitts., 1989—91; staff rsch. asst. Los Alamos Nat. Lab., N.Mex., 1991—92, rsch. fellow, 1993—94; sr. scientist Advanced Fuel Rsch., Inc., East Hartford, Conn., 1995—98; chmn. Pioneer Techs., Inc., West Hartford, Conn., 1996—99; cons. InfiMed, Inc., Liverpool, NY, 1998—2000; product devel. engr. JDS Uniphase, Research Triangle Park, NC, 2001—02; pres. Optotrack, Inc., Cary, NC, 2002—. Chmn. acad. affairs Tatung Inst. Tech., Taipei, 1979-80; tech. info. editor Indsl. Tech. Rsch. Inst., Hsin-Chu, 1985-86; translator tech. articles Super Tech. Books Co., Taipei, 1986; adj. prof. Strayer U., Cary, N.C., 2004—. Author, editor: Unit Operations in Chemical Engineering, 1986; contbr. articles to profl. jours. 2nd lt. Chinese Air Force, 1983-85. Recipient Editor's Choice award Nat. Poetry Assn., 1989, 90; Am.-Chinese Engr. scholar Am.-Chinese Assn. Engrs., 1980; Liang Ji-Duan fellow Carnegie Mellon U., 1991. Mem. AAAS, IEEE, SPIE, Materials Rsch. Soc., Am. Vacuum Soc. (Tech. Paper award 1992), Acad. Am. Poets, Beta Gamma Sigma. Achievements include research in diamond thin films and high Tc superconductors; superconducting quantum interference devices and biomagnetic systems; surface characterization and microstructural analysis; ferroelectric devices, giant magnetoresistive sensors, high-speed microelectronics, epitaxial heterostructures, in-process monitors, pulsed laser deposition, thermal evaporation, sputtering; pyroelectric sensor arrays, gas sensors, plasma-enhanced chemical vapor deposition, x-ray imaging materials, digital radiography and fluoroscopy, microelectromechanical systems (MEMS); optical switches and waveguides; optical communication systems; nanotechnology, microfluidics, biol. and chem. assays. Office: Optotrack Inc PO Box 1242 Cary NC 27512 Home Phone: 919-434-5006; Office Phone: 919-363-2802. Business E-Mail: ckung@optotrack.com.

KUNG, PATRICK CHUNG-SHU, biotechnologist; b. Nanjing, China, July 10, 1947; came to U.S., 1969; s. Tao and Yuing (Li) K.; m. Yie Lu; children: Julia, Calvin, Charles Shen. BS, Fu Jen U., Taiwan, 1968; PhD, U. Calif., Berkeley, 1974. Rsch. fellow MIT, Cambridge, 1974-77; sr. rsch. fellow Ortho Pharm. Co., J & J, Raritan, NJ, 1978—81; v.p. rsch. Centocor Inc., Malvern, Pa., 1982-83; co-founder, exec. v.p., vice chmn. T Cell Sci., Inc./Avant Immunotherapies, Inc., Cambridge, 1984—98; bd. dirs. Phyto-Ceutica, Inc., New Haven. Exec. bd. Coll. Letters and Scis. U. Calif., Berkeley, 1989-91; bd. dirs. PhytoCeutica, Inc., pres., CEO, 1999-2003; bd. dirs. Briglow, Ltd. Contbr. articles to profl. jours. Trustee Park Sch., Brookline, Mass., 1992-95. Recipient Philip Hoffman award Johnson & Johnson Co., 1979, Achievement award Chinese Inst. Engrs., 1988, Discoverers award U.S. Pharm. Mfrs. Rsch. Assn., 1991, Thomas Alva Edison award N.J. Rsch. Coun., 1991. Mem. Soc. Chinese Bioscientists in Am. (pres. bio/pharm. scis. divsn. 1994, 95). Personal E-mail: drpckung@aol.com.

KUNIHOLM, BRUCE ROBELLET, academic administrator, educator; b. Washington, Oct. 4, 1942; s. Bertel Eric and Berthe Eugenie (Robellet) K.; m. Elizabeth Fairbank, June 29, 1968 (div. July 1987); children: Jonathan, Erin; m. Donna Slawson, Jan. 19, 2001. AB in English, Dartmouth Coll., 1964; MA in History, Duke U., 1972, MA in Pub. Policy Sci., 1976, PhD in History, 1976. Instr. English Robert Acad./Robert Coll., Istanbul, Turkey, 1964—67; fellow Coun. Fgn. Rels./NEH Dept. State, Washington, 1979, internat. rels. officer policy planning staff, 1979—80; from instr. to prof. Duke U., Durham, NC, 1975—87, prof. pub. policy studies and history, 1987—, chmn. dept. public policy studies, 1989—94, 2005—, dir. Terry Sanford Inst. Pub. Policy, 1989—94, 2005—. Vis. prof. Internat. Rels. Koc U., Istanbul, Turkey, 1995-96, 2002; vice-provost for acad. and internat. affairs, Duke U., Durham, 1996—2001; chmn. acad. com.Can.-U.S. Fulbright Program, 2000-05; dir. Ctr. for Internat. Studies, 1999—2001; guest scholar Woodrow Wilson Internat. Ctr. Scholars, 1982; cons. NEH, USMC, Dept. State, U.S. Army, United Tech. Corp.; invited lectr. numerous orgns., colls., univs., fgn. countries including U.S. Senate Fgn. Rels.Com., CIA, State Dept., Chase Manhattan Bank, Harvard U., Brown U., Dartmouth Coll., Yale U., Princeton U., France, Eng., Germany, Italy, Kuwait, Saudi Arabia, Sudan, Can., Turkey, also others. Author: Origins of the Cold War in the Near East, 1980 (Stuart L. Bernath prize 1981), The Persian Gulf and United States Policy, 1984, The Palestine Problem and United States Policy, 1986; contbr. articles to profl. jours.; contbr. chpts. books. Bd. dirs., chmn. acad. com. Found. for Ednl. Exch. between Can. and U.S., 2000-05; exec. com. Assn. Profl. Schs. Internat. Affairs, 2007-; ednl. adv. bd. Govt. Accountability Office, 2005-. Capt. USMC, 1967-71, Vietnam. Decorated Bronze Star with V device; recipient Disting. Teaching award Trinity Coll., Duke U., 1989; rsch. grantee Harry S. Truman Libr., 1984, Duke U. Rsch. Coun., 1985-86, Inst. Turkish Studies, 1986-87, travel grantee Ctr. Soviet and East European Studies, 1991; Fulbright sr. rsch. fellow, Turkey, 1986-87, Woodrow Wilson Internat. Ctr. Scholars fellow Smithsonian Instn., 1986-87, sr. fellow Nobel Inst., Oslo, 1994. Mem. Am. Hist. Assn., Fulbright Fellows, Coun. Fgn. Rels., Orgn. Am. Historians, Soc. Historians Am. Fgn. Rels., Mid. East Inst., Mid. East Studies Assn., Internat. Inst. Strategic Studies, Phi Beta Kappa. Democrat. Avocations: triathlons, banjo, wine. Home: 613 Swift Ave Durham NC 27701 Office Phone: 919-613-7309. Business E-Mail: bruce.kuniholm@duke.edu.

KUNIN, MADELEINE MAY, former ambassador to Switzerland, former governor; b. Zurich, Switzerland, Sept. 28, 1933; arrived in U.S., 1940, naturalized, 1947; d. Ferdinand and Renee (Bloch) May; m. John W. Hennessey, Jr., Feb. 12, 2006; children: Julia, Peter, Adam, Daniel. BA, U. Mass., 1956; MS, Columbia U., 1957; MA, U. Vt., 1967. Newspaper reporter Burlington Free Press, Vt., 1957-58; guide Brussels World's Fair, Belgium, 1958; TV asst. producer Sta. WCAX-TV, Burlington, 1960-61; freelance writer, instr. English Trinity Coll., Burlington, 1969-70; mem. Vt. Ho. of Reps., 1973-78; lt. gov. State of Vt., Montpelier, 1979-82, gov., 1985-91; disting. vis. in Pub. Policy Bunting Inst., Cambridge, Mass., 1991-92; Montgomery fellow Dartmouth Coll., Hanover, NH, 1992; dep. sec. edn. Dept. Edn., Washington, 1993-96; U.S. amb. to Switzerland, 1996-99; scholar in residence Middlebury Coll., 1999; disting. vis. prof. St. Michael's Coll. and U. Vt., 2003—. Fellow Inst. Politics, Sch. Govt. Harvard U., 1983, pub. policy fellow Bunting Inst., Radcliffe Coll., 1991—92; lectr. Middlebury Coll., St. Michael's Coll., 1984; disting. pub. policy visitor Rockefeller Ctr., Dartmouth Coll., 1992; mem. Vt. Joint Fiscal Com., 1977—78; mem. exec. com. Nat. Conf. Lt. Govs., 1979—80; founder, pres. Inst. Sustainable Cmtys., Montpellier, 1991—; mem. 3 person com. to recommend v.p. to Bill Clinton; mem. transition team, co-chair nat. com. Women for Clinton, 1992; commentator TV and Pub. RAdio. Author: Living a Political Life: A Memoir, 1994, The Big Green Book, 1976; contbr. articles to profl. jours., mags. and newspapers. Commentator Vt. Pub. Radio. Named Outstanding State Legislator, Eagleton Inst. Politics, Rutgers U., 1975; Montgomery fellow, Dartmouth Coll., 1991, scholar in residence, Middlebury Coll., 1999—. Fellow: Am. Acad. Arts and Scis.; mem.: New Eng. Gov.'s Conf. (chairperson), Nat. Gov.'s Conf. (chair com. energy and environ.), Nat. Gov.'s Assn. (mem. exec. com.). Democrat. Office: Univ Vt Burlington VT 05401 Personal E-mail: madeleine.kunin@uvm.edu.

KUNIN, MYRON, hair care company executive. CEO, vice-chmn. bd. dirs. Regis Corp., Edina, Minn., pres. Curtis Squire Venture Capital, Inc.; Collector Old Masters, contemporary art; lifelong trustee, Minneapolis Inst. Arts. Office: Regis Corp 7201 Metro Blvd Edina MN 55439-2103

KUNIYUKI, KEN TOSHIO, mathematics professor; b. Harbor City, Calif., Aug. 13, 1972; s. Francis T. and Violet Y. Kuniyuki. BS, Stanford U., 1995, MS, 1995—95; MA, U. Calif. San Diego, La Jolla, 1999. Tchg. asst. U. Calif. San Diego, La Jolla, 1995—99; adj. instr. San Diego City Coll., 1999—2000; lectr. U. San Diego, 1999—2000; adj. instr. San Diego Mesa Coll., 2000—00, asst. prof. math., 2001—05, assoc. prof. math., 2005—. Mesa coord. Math Field Day San Diego Mesa Coll., 2001—, mem. acad. senate, 2003—. Mem.: Math. Assn. Am., Calif. Math. Coun. C.C. South, Am. Math. Assn. Two-Yr. Colls., Phi Beta Kappa. Avocation: political analysis. Home: 8933 Lombard Pl #218 San Diego CA 92122-1535 Office: San Diego Mesa College 7250 Mesa College Dr San Diego CA Home Phone: 619-252-4839; Office Phone: 619-388-2396. Personal E-mail: kkuniyuk@yahoo.com.

KUNKEL, GEORGIE BRIGHT, freelance writer, retired counselor; b. Chehalis, Wash. d. George Riley and Myrtia (McLaughlin) Bright; m. Norman C. Kunkel, Apr. 25, 1946; children: N. Joseph D.C.(dec.) , Stephen Gregory, Susan Ann, Kimberly Jane Waligorska. BA in Edn., Western Wash. U., 1944; MEd, U. Wash., 1968. Tchr. pub. schs., Vader, Centralia, Seattle, Wash., 1941-67; counselor Highline Pub. Schs., Seattle, 1967-82. Sch. counselor rep. State of Art Conf., Balt., 1980; spkr. on women's issues, humor, and the Holocaust. Author: You're Damn Right I Wear Purple! Color Me Feminist, 2000; co-author (with Norman C. Kunkel): WWII Liberator's Life: AFS Ambulance Driver Chooses Peace, 2006; editor: Women and Girls in Edn., 1972—75; columnist: West Seattle Herald and Northwest Prime Time; contbr. articles to profl. jours. Organizer Women and Girls in Edn., Wash. State, 1971; pres. Wash. State NOW, 1973; past pres. West Seattle Dem. Women's Club. Grantee Women Adminstrs. Wash. State, 1971, Edn. Svc. Dist., Seattle, 1980; recipient Woman of Achievement award Past Pres. Assembly, 2000; winner essay contest and appeared on Oprah show. Mem. NEA (sec. pub. rels.), ACA (pres. state br. 1982-83), Am. Sch. Counseling Assn. (pres. state divsn. 1980-81), Seattle Counselors Assn. (organizer, past pres. office exec., Counselor of Yr. award 1990). Unitarian Universalist. Avocation: singing. Home and Office: 3409 SW Trenton St Seattle WA 98126-3743 Office Phone: 206-935-8663.

KUNKEL, JOE CARROLL, finance company executive; b. Killeen, Tex., Aug. 10, 1962; s. Melton Leroy and Carol Sue Kunkel. BBA, Howard Payne U., 1984. Sr. unit trainer SallieMae, Killeen, Tex., 1988—93; coord. loan servicing Brazos Higher Edn. Svc. Corp., Waco, Tex., 1993—97; compliance officer Academic Mgmt. Svcs., Swansea, Mass., 1997—2002; corp. compliance officer, ombudsman NextStudent Inc., Phoenix, 2002—. Home: 37 E Woodward Dr Phoenix AZ 85004-1317 Office: 1901 North Black Canyon Hwy Phoenix AZ 85027 Home Phone: 602-274-2279; Office Phone: 602-439-6070. Office Fax: 602-439-6069. E-mail: jkunkel@nextstudent.com.

KUNKEL, NANCY ANGELA, psychologist; b. Iowa; D Psychology, Chgo. Sch. Profl. Psychology, 1995. Clin. psychologist Alexian Bros. Behavioral Health Hosp., Hoffman Estates, Ill., 1996—2005, clin. dir., 1999—2002; pvt. practice clin. psychologist PsychOne, Barrington, Ill., 2004—. Cons. in field. Mem.: APA. Avocations: piano, exercise, travel. Office: PsychOne 130 Harrison Barrington IL 60010 Office Phone: 847-382-5688. Office Fax: 847-382-5699. Personal E-mail: psychone@comcast.net.

KUNKEL, RICHARD LESTER, public radio executive; b. Syracuse, NY, Nov. 12, 1944; s. Lester DeLong Kunkel and Margaret Fanny Ralph; m. Mary Joan Goldsworthy, Aug. 10, 1968; children: Richard J., Charles J., Joseph B. BS, Syracuse U., 1967, MS, 1969. Lic. real estate broker, N.C. Program dir. Sta. WNBI, Northland Broadcasting, Park Falls, Wis., 1969-72; instr., prodn. dir. Sta. WMKY, Morehead (Ky.) State U., 1972-77; radio mgr. Maine Pub. Broadcasting Network, Orono, 1977-78; instr., sta. mgr. Sta. KNTU, U. North Tex., Denton, 1978-84; v.p., dean Southeastern Ctr. for Arts, Atlanta, 1985-88; pres., gen. mgr. Spokane (Wash.) Pub. Radio Inc., 1988—. Cons., 1978—. With Army N.g., 1968-74. Recipient Addy award 1975. Avocations: photography, computers. Office: KPBX/KIBX and KSFC Spokane Pub Radio 2319 N Monroe St Spokane WA 99205-4586 Home Phone: 509-467-4848. Business E-Mail: rkunkel@kpbx.org.

KUNKLE, DAVID M., police chief; b. Nov. 13, 1950; BS, U. Tex., Arlington, 1976, MA, 1994. With Dallas Police Dept., 1972—82; police chief City of Grand Prairie, Tex., 1982—85, Arlington Police Dept., Tex., 1985—99, Dallas Police Dept., 2004—; dep. city mgr. City of Arlington, 1999—2004. Office: Dallas Police Dept 1400 S Lamar St Dallas TX 75215

KUNKLE, WILLIAM JOSEPH, judge, lawyer; b. Lakewood, Ohio, Sept. 3, 1941; s. William Joseph and Georgia (Howe) K.; m. Sarah Florence Nesti, July 11, 1964; children: Kathleen Margaret, Susan Mary. BA, Northwestern U., Evanston, Ill., 1963, JD, 1969. Bar: Ohio 1969, U.S. Dist. Ct. (no. dist.) Ill. 1969, Ill. 1969, U.S. Ct. Appeals (7th cir.) 1991, U.S. Supreme Ct. 1991. Process control engr. Union Carbide Corp., Cleve., 1964-65, prodn. supr. Greenville, SC, 1965-66; assoc. Hauxhurst, Sharp, Mollison & Gallagher, Cleve., 1969-70; asst. pub. defender Cook County Pub. Defender, Chgo., 1970-73; asst. states atty. Cook County States Atty., Chgo., 1973-85; ptnr. Phelan, Cahill & Quinlan, Ltd., Chgo., 1985-96, Cahill, Christian & Kunkle, Ltd., Chgo., 1996—2002, Wildman, Harrold, Allen & Dixon, Chgo., 2002—04; judge Cir. Ct. Cook County, 2004—. Chmn. The Ill. Gaming Bd., 1990—93; dep. spl. outside counsel U.S. Ho. Reps., Washington, 1988—89; adj. prof. I.I.T. Chgo. Kent Sch. Law, 1980—84; instr. Nat. Inst. Trial Advocacy, 1978—82, 1986; lectr. Nat. Coll. Dist. Attys., 1978—85, Nat. Law Enforcement Inst., 1983—85; 1st asst. states atty. of Cook County, 1983—85; spl. state's atty. 18th Jud. Cir., DuPage County, 1995—99. Contbg. author: Punishment Prosecutor's Viewpoint, 1983, 1989, Trial Techniques Compendium, Nat. College of Dist. Attys. (2d, 3rd, 4th, 5th, 6th eds.). Recipient Disting. Faculty award Nat. Coll. Dist. Attys., 1980, Award for Prosecution Svc. Chgo. Assn. Commerce & Industry, 1981. Fellow Am. Coll. Trial Lawyers, ABA; mem. Internat. Soc. Barristers, Nat. Dist. Attys. Assn. (bd. dirs. 1984-85), Assn. Govt. Attys. in Capital Litigation (pres. 1983-84), Chgo. Bar Assn. (bd. mgrs. 1983-84), Ill. State Bar Assn. (LAWPAC trustee 1989-95), Internat. Assn. Gaming Attys., Chgo. Crime Commn. (bd. dirs.). Avocations: golf, softball, carpentry, motorcycling.

KUNKLER, ARNOLD WILLIAM, retired surgeon, educator; b. St. Anthony, Ind., Nov. 18, 1921; s. Edward J. and Selma (Hasenour) K.; m. Muriel Burns, 1954; m. Barbara McElroy, 2004; children: Lisa, Arnold William, Carolyn, Christine, Phillip, Kevin. AB, Ind. U., 1943, MD, 1949. Diplomate Am. Bd. Surgery. Intern Ind. U. Med. Ctr., Indpls., 1949-50, asst. resident in surgery, fellow vascular surg. research, 1950-54, resident in surgery, 1954-55, faculty, 1955—76, clin. prof. surgery, 1976-94, emeritus clin. prof. surgery, 1995—. Individual practice medicine specializing in gen. surgery, Terre Haute, Ind., 1955-94; dir. med. edn. Terre Haute Regional Hosp., 1970-79; staff Terre Haute Center Med. Edn.; chief of staff Terre Haute Regional Hosp., 1989-90. Contbr. articles to profl. jours. Pres. Terre Haute Med. Edn. Found., 1972-73, 78-81, bd. dirs., 1967-86; pres. cmty. adv. coun. Terre Haute Center Med. Edn., 1976-80; treas. Wabash Valley Cmty. Blood Program, 1974-78; trustee Terre Haute Regional Hosp., 1978-84 , chmn. bd., 1981-84, Vigo County Bd. Health, 1990-97. With U.S. Army, 1943-46, ETO. Fellow ACS (pres. Ind. chpt. 1980-81); mem. Ind. State Med. Assn. (com. med. edn. 1986-92), Vigo County Med. Soc., Pam. Am. Med. Assn., Pan Pacific Surg. Assn., Midwest Surg. Assn., Aesculapian Soc. Wabash Valley, Ind. Soc. Chgo., Pres.'s Cir. Ind. U., Dean's Coun. Ind. U. Sch. Medicine, Rotary Club of Terre Haute, Sagamore of the Wabash, Columbia Club, Highland Country Club, Commons Club (Bonita Springs, Fla.). Democrat. Roman Catholic. Home: 5300 W 96th St Indianapolis IN 46268 Personal E-mail: akunkler@msn.com. *Success and service are interdependent.*

KUNOS, GEORGE, pharmacologist; b. Budapest, Hungary, May 14, 1942; came to U.S., 1987; s. Istvan and Gabriella (Kalman) K.; m. Ildiko Vermes, June 11, 1967; children: Anne-Marie, Doreen. MD, Budapest Med. U., 1966; PhD, McGill U., Montreal, Can., 1973. Asst. prof. dept. pharmacology McGill U., 1974-79, assoc. prof., 1979-83, prof. dept. pharmacology and dept. of medicine, 1984-88; lab. chief Nat. Inst. Alcoholism, Bethesda, Md., 1987-92; prof., chmn. dept. pharmacology Va. Commonwealth U., Richmond, 1992—2000; scientific dir. Nat. Inst. Alcohol Abuse and Alcoholism, Nat. Inst. Health, 2000—. Mem. pharmacology task force Nat. Bd. Med. Examiners, 1996-99. Editor monographs in field; contbr. over 150 sci. articles to profl. jours. Recipient Monat-Fraser Associateship award McGill U., 1981-87. Mechoulam award Internat. Cannabinoid RSch. Soc., 2005. Fellow Am. Heart Assn. (coun. on high blood pressure; mem. Am. Soc. Pharmacol. Exptl. Therapy, Am. Soc. Biochem. Molecular Biology, Soc. for Neurosci., Hungarian Acad. Scis. Achievements include identification of role of endogenous opioid peptides of the brain in regulation of blood pressure and in antihypertensive drug action, unique mechanisms in regulation of hormone receptors role of endogenous cannabinoids in cardiovascular appetite and body weight regulation. Office: Nat Inst Alcohol Abuse & Alcoholism Nat Inst Health PO Box 8413 Bethesda MD 20892-9413 Office Phone: 301-443-2069.

KUNOWSKI, HERBERT PETER, lawyer; b. LA, Dec. 7, 1958; AA with honors, El Camino Coll., 1984; BA magna cum laude, UCLA, 1987; JD, Pepperdine U., 1990. Bar: Calif. 1990; U.S. Dist. Ct. (so., ea., no. and cen. dists.) Calif. 1990; U.S. Ct. Appeals (9th cir.) 1990. With Office of City Atty., LA, 1989—90, Wilson, Elser, Moskovwitz, Edelman & Dicker LLP, LA, 1990, ptnr. Judicial arbitrator and mediator LA County Superior Ct., judge pro tem. Mem. Calif. State Bar, LA County Bar Assn., The Federalist Soc., Orange County Bar Assn. Office: Wilson, Elser, Moskowitz, Edelman & Dicker LLP Ste 2700 1055 W 7th St Los Angeles CA 90017 Office Phone: 213-624-3044 429. Office Fax: 213-624-8060. E-mail: kunowskih@wemed.com.

KUNSTADTER, GERALDINE SAPOLSKY, foundation executive; b. Boston, Jan. 6, 1928; d. Harry Herman and Nettie Sapolsky; m. John W. Kunstadter, Apr. 23, 1949; children: John W., Lisa, Christopher, Elizabeth Student, MIT, 1945-48. Draftsman U. Chgo. Cyclotron Project, 1948; engring. asst. Gen. Electric Corp., Lynn, Mass., 1948-49; pres. Capricorn Investments Corp., 1971—; chmn., pres., dir. A. Kunstadter Family Found., NYC, 1966—. Host family program dir. N.Y.C. Commn. for UN, 1971-86; pres. Nat. Inst. Social Scis., 1979-81; adv. coun. hospitality com. UN Delegations; bd. dirs. NYC Global Ptnrs. Mem. internat. hospitality com. Nat. Coun. Women; mem. Com. Mgmnt. of Network 20/20; bd. dirs. Bridge to Asia Found., Atlantic Coun. of U.S., Inst. World Affairs; bd. dirs Nat. Com. on. US-China Rels.; bd. dirs. Network 20/20. Recipient Windham award, 1970, Silver medal, Nat. Inst. Social Sci., 1981, Pres.'s medal, Archtl. Soc. China, 2001. Mem. Inst. Current World Affairs, Nat. Com. US-China Rels., Coun. on Fgn. Rels., Hurlingham Club, Lansdowne Club (London), Cosmopolitan Club N.Y.

KUNTZ, CHARLES, IV, neurosurgeon; b. Oct. 21, 1964; married; 2 children. BA in Chemistry magna cum laude, Holy Cross Coll., 1987; MD in Infectious Disease, Case Western Res. U., 1991. Intern, resident, fellow U. Washington Affiliated Hosps., Seattle, 1991-2000; assoc. prof., vice chmn., dir. spine and peripheral nerve surgery dept. neurosurgery Mayfield Clinic and Spine Inst., U. Cin., 2000—. Contbr. articles to profl. jours. Mem. AMA, Am. Assn. Neurol. Surgeons, Congress Neurol. Surgeons, N.Am. Spine Soc., Phi Beta Kappa, Alpha Omega Alpha. Office: Ste 3100 222 Piedmont Ave Cincinnati OH 45219 Office Phone: 513-475-8667. Office Fax: 513-475-8033. Personal E-mail: charleskuntz@yahoo.com.

KUNTZ, CHARLES POWERS, lawyer; b. LA, May 7, 1944; m. June Emerson Moroney, Dec. 23, 1969; children: Michael Nicholas, Robinson Moroney, Katie Moroney. AB with honors, Stanford U., 1966, JD, 1969; LLM, NYU, 1971. Bar: Calif. 1970, N.Y. 1970, U.S. Dist. Ct. (no. dist.) Calif. 1970, U.S. Ct. Appeals (9th cir.) 1970, U.S. Supreme Ct. 1979. Staff atty. project for urban affairs Office Econ. Opportunity, NYC, 1969-71; dep. pub. defender Contra Costa County Pub. Defender's Office, Martinez, Calif., 1971-75; assoc. Treuhaft, Walker & Brown, Oakland, Calif., 1976-78; ptnr. Hirsch & Kuntz, San Rafael, Calif., 1979-85; pvt. practice San Rafael, 1985-89; ptnr. Coombs & Dunlap, Napa, Calif., 1989—. Mem.: ABA, Napa County Bar Assn., Calif. Attys. Consumer Justice, Inns of Ct. Home: 48 Wild Rye Way Napa CA 94558-7014 Office: Coombs & Dunlap 1211 Division St Napa CA 94559-3372 Office Phone: 707-252-9100. Business E-Mail: ckuntz@coombslaw.com.

KUNTZ, EDWARD LAWRENCE, healthcare executive; b. Phila., Feb. 22, 1945; s. Samuel J. and Mary S. (Shulman) K.; m. Caroline L. Lessner, Aug. 3, 1969; m. Stuart M., David M., Beth. BA, Temple U., 1966, JD, 1969, ML, 1978. Pvt. practice, Phila., 1970-78; asst. gen. counsel ARA Svcs., Phila., 1978-79, sector counsel, 1979-84, assoc. gen. counsel, 1984-85; exec. v.p. ARA Living Ctrs., Houston, 1985-92; chmn., CEO Living Ctrs. Am., Houston, 1992-97, Vencor Inc. (now Kindred Healthcare), Louisville, 1999—2003; pres. Kindred Healthcare, Louisville, 1999—2002, chmn. of bd., 2004—. Dir. Alzheimer's Assn., Houston, 1993—; advisor Woodway Fin. Group, Houston, 1994—; mem. com. Am. Health Care Assn., Washington, 1986—. Co-chmn. fundraising campaign United Way, Med. Ctr., Houston, 1993; bd. dirs. Alley Theater, 1994-97, mem. facilities com., 1994; bd. trustees, adminstrv. and pers. com. Enamu-El, 1996-97. Mem. Thyroid Soc. of Houston (bd. dirs., vice chmn. 1995—), Am. Health Care Assn. (chmn. multifacility steering com., bd. dirs., exec. com., long term financing task force 1997, former mem. numerous coms.), Alzheimer's Assn. (bd. dirs. 1992-97), Thyroid Soc. (vice chmn. bd. dirs., chmn. fund devel. 1996, chmn. bd. 1997), Anti-Defamation League (bd. dirs. 1996-97). Home: 8807 Stable Crest Blvd Houston TX 77024-7035 Office: Kindred Healthcare 680 S Fourth St Louisville KY 40202*

KUNTZ, HAL GOGGAN, petroleum exploration company executive, rancher; b. San Antonio, Dec. 29, 1937; s. Peter A. and Jean (Goggan) K.;

children: Hal Goggan, Peter, Michael B., Vesta. BS in Engring., Princeton U., 1960; MBA, Oklahoma City U., 1972. Line, staff positions Mobil Oil Corp., Dallas, Oklahoma City, and New Orleans, 1963-74; co-founder, pres. CLK Corp., New Orleans and Houston, 1974—, IPEX Co., New Orleans, 1974—, CLK Investments I, II, III, and IV, 1979—; pres. Gulf Coast Exploration Co., New Orleans, 1979—, CLK Producing, CLK Oil and Gas Co., CLK Exploration Co., 1980—; rancher Tex., Mexico. Bd. dirs. North Houston Bank. Mem. Mus. Fine Arts, Houston, 1978—; mem. condrs. cir. Houston Symphony, 1980; mem. governing bd. Houston Opera. With AUS, 1960-63. Mem. Am. Mgmt. Assn., Nat. Small Bus. Assn., Inter-Am. Soc., Soc. Exploration Geophysics, Am. Assn. Petroleum Geologists, Aircraft Owners and Pilots Assn., River Oaks C. of C., Petroleum Club, U. of Houston Club, Argyle Club, Order of Alamo, Coronado Club, Princeton Club, River Oaks Country Club, San Antonio Country Club. Republican. Roman Catholic. Avocations: golf, skiing, birdshooting. Office: 5 Post Oak Park Ste 2330 4400 Post Oak Pkwy Houston TX 77027 Home Phone: 713-622-1433; Office Phone: 713-871-0202. E-mail: Hal_Kuntz@sbcglobal.net.

KUNTZ, JOEL DUBOIS, lawyer; b. Dennis, Mass., Feb. 5, 1946; s. Paul Grimley Kuntz and Harriette (Hunter) Ainsworth; m. Karan Judd, June 29, 1968; children: Matthew Christopher, Kristin Lara. BA, Haverford Coll., 1968; JD, Yale U., 1971; LLM in Taxation, NYU, 1980. Bar: Conn. 1972, Oreg. 1974. Assoc. Stoel, Rives, Boley, Jones & Grey, Portland, Oreg., 1974—79, ptnr., 1979—94; v.p., gen. counsel Entek Internat. LLC, Lebanon, Oreg., 1994—. Author (with James S. Eustice): Federal Income Taxation of S Corporations, 1982, 4th edit., 2001; author: (with James S. Eustice, Charles S. Lewis, Thomas P. Deering) Tax Reform Act of 1986: Analysis and Commentary, 1987; author: (with Robert J. Peroni) U.S. International Taxation, 1992. Capt. USMC, 1971-74. Mem. Am. Coll. Tax Counsel, Internat. Fiscal Assn. Democrat. Home: 3910 Lakeview Blvd Lake Oswego OR 97035-5549 Address: PO Box 39 Lebanon OR 97355-0039 Personal E-mail: jdkuntz@attglobal.net.

KUNTZ, LEE ALLAN, lawyer; b. Nashville, July 9, 1943; s. Irwin and Lucy (Kornman) K.; 1 child, Douglas. BA, Duke U., 1965; LLB, Columbia U., 1968. Bar: N.Y., 1968, U.S. Dist. Ct. (so. dist.) N.Y., 1973, U.S. Tax Ct., 1973. Assoc. Shearman Sterling LLP, NYC, 1968—76, ptnr., 1976—, mng. ptnr., 1994—98, sr. ptnr. real estate group, 1988—93, 2004—. Mem. policy com. Shearman Sterling LLP, 1991—99. Contbr. articles to profl. jours. Bd. visitors Columbia Law Sch., 1998—; dir. Vol. Legal Svc., 2000—, Am. Coll. Real Estate Lawyers, 2002-. Mem.: ABA, Urban Land Inst., Assn. Bar City N.Y. Office: Shearman Sterling LLP 599 Lexington Ave Fl C2 New York NY 10022-6069 Office Phone: 212-848-7392.

KUNTZ, LILA ELAINE, business educator; b. Decorah, Iowa, July 13, 1931; d. Arthur Lloyd and Alice Elene (Thompson) Dahle; m. Darrell Wayne Kuntz, Dec. 26, 1959 (div. 1979); 1 child, Barbara Lynn. BA, Luther Coll., 1954; postgrad., U. Iowa, 1957-58, U. Minn., 1961-75, Mankato State Coll., 1966-76. Cert. tchr., Minn. Tchr. business Flat Rock (Mich.) High Sch., 1954-55, Springville (Iowa) High Sch., 1955-58, Spring Lake Park (Minn.) High Sch., 1958-60, Lincoln High Sch., Bloomington, Minn., 1961-70, Jefferson High Sch., Bloomington, 1970—. Rep. del., Edina, minn., 1979-95; active Norwegian-Am. Mus., Decorah, Iowa, 1987—. Mem. NEA, Minn. Edn. Assn., Minn. Bus. Edn. Assn., Bloomington Edn. Assn., Delta Pi Epsilon. Lutheran. Avocations: concerts, photography, reading, travel. Home: 5221 Abercrombie Dr Edina MN 55439-1466 Office: Jefferson High Sch 4001 W 102nd St Bloomington MN 55437-2699

KUNTZ, MARION LUCILE LEATHERS, classicist, historian, educator; b. Atlanta, Sept. 6, 1924; d. Otto Asa and Lucile (Parks) Leathers; m. Paul G. Kuntz, Nov. 26, 1970; children by previous marriage: Charles, Otto Alan (Daniels). BA, Agnes Scott Coll., 1945; MA, Emory U., 1964, PhD, 1969. Lectr. Latin Lovett Sch., Atlanta, 1963-66; from mem. faculty to prof. Ga. State U., 1966—75, Regents' Prof., 1975—, chmn. dept. fgn. langs., 1975-84, Fuller E. Callaway prof., 1984—, rsch. prof., 1984—. Author: Colloquium of the Seven About Secrets of the Sublime of Jean Bodin, 1975, Guillaume Postel, Prophet of the Restitution of All Things: His Life and Thought, 1981, Jacob's Ladder and the Tree of Life: Concepts of Hierarchy and the Great Chain of Being, 1987, Postello, Venezia e Il Suo Mondo, 1988, Venice, Myth and Utopian Thought, 1999, The Anointment of Dionisio: Prophecy and Politics in Renaissance Italy, 2002; also scholarly articles; mem. editl. bd. Library of Renaissance Humanism. V.p. acad. affairs Am.-Hellenic Found.; patron Atlanta Opera. Named Latin Tchr. of Yr. State Ga., 1965; Am. Classical League scholar, 1966, Gladys Krieble Delmas scholar, 1991; Am. Coun. Learned Socs. grantee, 1970, 73, 76, 81, 87, 90; recipient Alumni Disting. Prof. award Ga. State U., 1994, medal for excellence in Renaissance studies Pres. of Coun. Gen., Tours, France, 1995, Disting. Career Alumna award Agnes Scott Coll., 1995 Master: Soc. Values in Higher Edn., Philosophy and Religion; mem.: Am. Cath. Hist. Assn., Classical Assn. Midwest and South (Semple award 1965), Am. Philol. Assn., Archaeol. Inst. Am., Soc. di Philosophique Medievale, Soc. Medieval and Renaissance Philosophy (exec. bd. 1988—90), Medieval Acad. Soc. de Culture Européenne, Soc. des Seizièmistes, Soc. Christian Philosophers (exec. bd. 1987—), Internat. Soc. Neo-Latin Studies, Internat. Soc. Neo-Platonic Studies, Am. Hist. Assn., Am. Soc. Ch. History, Am. Cath. Philos. Assn., Am. Soc. Aesthetics, Renaissance Soc. Am. (coun. 1994—97, trustee 2003—), Michael C. Carlos Mus. (patron), Friends of the Vatican Libr., Italia Nostra, Fondazione Ambiente Italiana, Am. Friends Vatican Libr. Patron Arts in Vatican Mus., Coun. Amici di Biblioteca Nazionale di San Marco, Italian Cultural Soc., Nat. Trust Hist. Preservation, Atlanta Hist. Soc., High Mus. of Art, Friends of the Warburg Inst., World Monuments Fund, The Atlanta Symphony, The Atlanta Opera, Am. Acad. Rome (sec.-treas. 1970—74), Druid Hills Civitan Club, The Commerce Club, Omicron Delta Kappa, Phi Kappa Phi, Phi Beta Kappa. Roman Catholic. Home: Villa Veneziana 1655 Ponce De Leon Ave Atlanta GA 30307 also: San Marco 4157 Venice Italy Business E-Mail: marion@gsu.edu.

KUNTZ, WILLIAM FRANCIS, II, lawyer, educator; b. NYC, June 24, 1950; s. William Francis I and Margaret Evelyn (Brown) K.; m. Alice Beal, May 20, 1978; children: William Thaddeus, Katharine Lowell, Elizabeth Anne. AB, Harvard U., 1972, AM, 1974, JD, 1977, PhD, 1979. Bar: N.Y. 1978. Assoc. Shearman & Sterling, NYC, 1978-86; mem. Milgrim, Thomajan & Lee, NYC, 1986-94; ptnr. Seward & Kissel, NYC, 1994-2001, The Torys Law Firm, NYC, 2001—04, Constantine Cannon, 2004—05, Baker & Hostetler LLP, NYC, 2005—. Assoc. prof. Bklyn. Law Sch., 1987-2002. Author: Criminal Sentencing, 1988. Bd. dirs. MFY Legal Svcs., Inc., N.Y.C., 1984-90, Boys Brotherhood Republic, N.Y.C., 1986-90, Habitat for Humanity, N.Y.C., 1987-90; chmn. Resources for Children with Spl. Needs, N.Y.C., 1986-89, 2006—; mem. N.Y. Civilian Complaint Rev. Bd., 1987—, chmn., 1994. Mem. ABA, N.Y. State Bar Assn., N.Y. County Lawyers Assn. (bd. dirs. 1991-96), Assn. of Bar of City of N.Y. (chmn. mcpl. affairs com. 1992-95, judiciary com., exec. com. 2002—, chmn. 2005-06, v.p. 2006—), Bklyn. Bar Assn. (judiciary com. 1995—), Met. Black Bar Assn., Practising Law Inst. (bd. dirs. 2006—). Democrat. Roman Catholic. Office: Baker & Hostetler LLP 666 Fifth Ave New York NY 10103 Home Phone: 718-596-2750; Office Phone: 212-589-4229. Business E-Mail: wkuntz@bakerlaw.com.

KUNTZMAN, RONALD, research and development company executive; b. Bklyn., Sept. 17, 1933; s. Herman and Fanny Kuntzman; m. Bernice Russman, May 29, 1955; children: Fred, Gary. BS, Bklyn. Coll., 1955; MS, George Washington U., 1957, PhD in Biochemistry, 1962. Biochemist lab. chem. pharmacology Nat. Heart Inst., NIH, Bethesda, Md., 1955-62; sr. biochemist Wellcome Research Labs.-Burroughs Wellcome & Co. U.S.A. Inc., Tuckahoe, NY, 1962-66, dep. head biochem. pharmacology dept., 1967-70; assoc. dir. dept. biochemistry and drug metabolism Hoffmann-La Roche Inc., Nutley, NJ, 1970-71, assoc. dir. biol. research, 1972-73, dir. therapeutics research, 1973-79, asst. v.p., 1974-81, dir. pharm. R & D, 1980-81, v.p. pharm. R&D, 1981-84, v.p. R&D, 1984-92; adj. prof. dept. chem. biology and pharmacognosy Rutgers U. Coll. Pharmacy, Piscataway, NJ, 1990—; adj. mem. Roche Inst. Molecular Biology, Nutley, NJ, 1992-96. Adv. coun. Nat. Orgn. for Rare Disorders, 1987-91; adj. prof. Rutgers U., 1990—. Mem. editl. bd. Biochem. Pharmacology, 1966-68, Neuropharmacology, 1970-78, Xenobiotica, 1970-84, Archives of Biochemistry and Biophysics, 1971-78, Life Scis., 1973-78; contbr. articles to profl. jours. Mem. AAAS, Am. Soc. Pharmacology and Exptl. Therapeutics (editorial bd. jour. 1968-75, nominating com. 1972, chmn. divsn. nominating com. 1977, chmn. divsn. drug metabolism 1978-81, sec.-treas. 1981-83, coun. 1981-83, chmn. long-range planning com. 1987-92, exec. com. divsn. drug metabolism 1973-76, John Jacob Abel award 1969), Am. Soc. Biol. Chemists, Am. Coll. Neuropsychopharmacology, Soc. Toxicology, George Washington U. Alumni Assn. (Dist. Alumni Achievement award 1988), Roche Inst. Molecular Biology (adj. 1992-96), Sigma Xi. Achievements include research on steroids and other normal body constituents which are metabolized by drug metabolizing enzymes; discovered P448, the hemoprotein inducible by hydrocarbon; demonstrated that DOPA-5HTP decarboxylase are the same enzyme. Address: 16 Reunion Rd Rye Brook NY 10573-1085 E-mail: ronkfun@aol.com.

KUNZ, APRIL BRIMMER, state legislator, lawyer; b. Denver, Apr. 1, 1954; divorced. AA, Stephens Coll., 1974; BS, U. So. Calif., 1976; JD, U. Wyo., 1979. Bar: Wyo. Pres. K and R Enterprises; mem. Wyo. Ho. Reps., Cheyenne, 1985-86, 90-92, Wyo. Senate, Cheyenne, 1992—, chair jud. com., v.p., 1999—2000, majority floor leader, 2001—02, pres., 2003—04. Mem. Laramie County Rep. Women's Club. Mem. Wyo. State Bar Assn, Laramie County Bar Assn. Republican. Home: PO Box 285 Cheyenne WY 82003-0285 Office: Wyo Senate State Capitol Cheyenne WY 82002-0001

KUNZ, HEIDI, healthcare company executive; Grad., Georgetown U., 1977; MBA, Columbia U. Dir. overseas financing, asst. treas., then treas. GM Can.; fin. mgmt. positions through v.p., treas. GM, White Plains, NY, 1979—95; exec. v.p., CFO ITT, 1995-99, Gap Inc., 1999—2003, Blue Shield Calif., San Francisco, 2003—. Bd. dirs. Agilent Technologies, Inc., 2000—. Office: Blue Shield 50 Beale St San Francisco CA 94105-1808

KUNZ, MICHAEL E., court administrator; b. Bristol, Pa., Feb. 13, 1943; s. Frank John Kunz and Mary Margaret Corrigan; m. Marleen Agnes Senkarik, Aug. 10, 1963; children: Catherine, Mary Ann, Joanne, Lisa. BS, St. Joseph's U., 1970, MBA, 1980. Dep. clk. U.S. Dist. Ct. (ea. dist.) Pa., Phila., 1962-75, chief dep. clk., 1976-79, clk. of the ct., 1979—. Adj. prof. Saint Joseph's U., 1998—. Contbr. articles to profl. jours. Active adv. bd. Coll. Bus. Adminstrn., St. Joseph's U., Phila., 1990—; mem. Father Judge H.S. Adv. Bd., 2001-. Recipient Bartholomew A. Sheehan award St. Joseph's U. Law Alumni, 1987, Dir.'s Outstanding Leadership award Adminstrv. Office U.S. Cts., 1992; named for Outstanding Leadership, Fed. Cts. Com. Phila. Bar, 1989. Mem. Am. Judicature Soc., Fed. Cts. Clks. Assn., Capitol Historical Soc., Hist. Soc. USDC, Am. Assn. State and Local History, EDPA (sec.). Office: US Dist Ct 2609 US Courthouse Philadelphia PA 19106

KUNZ, THOMAS R., real estate company executive; Attended, Weber State U., U. Utah. Owner employment agy.; pres. software co.; with Century 21 Real Estate LLC, 1982—, sr. v.p. real estate sales Cendant Real Estate Franchise Group, 2001—02; pres. Century 21 Award, 2002—04; pres., CEO Century 21 Real Estate LLC, 2004—. Served with US Army. Office: Century 21 Real Estate LLC 1 Campus Dr Parsippany NJ 07054

KUNZE, GEORGE WILLIAM, retired soil scientist; b. Warda, Tex., Sept. 16, 1922; s. John Paul and Hermine (Moerbe) K.; m. Flora Mae Rothmann, July 11, 1947; children: Brenda Kay, Wayne Lester. BS, Tex. A&M U., 1948, MS, 1950; PhD, Pa. State U., 1952. Asst. prof. Tex. A&M U., 1952-56, assoc. prof., 1956-60, prof. soil mineralogy, 1960-84, asso. dean Grad. Sch., 1967-68, dean, 1968-84; ret., 1984. Cons. U. Alaska, 1963-66; cons. Bangladesh Agrl. U., 1970, Grad. Sch. Agrl. Scis., Castelar Argentina, 1972; mem. Fed. Adv. Com. on Affirmative Action in Employment Practices in Instns. of Higher Edn.; pres. Conf. So. Grad. Schs., 1980-81 Cons. editor Soil Science, 1958-84. With USAAF, 1943—45. Recipient Faculty Disting. Achievement award in research Tex. A&M U., 1966, in administration Tex. A.&M. U., 1984 Fellow: AAAS, Am. Soc. Agronomy, Mineral Soc. Am.; mem.: Clay Mineral Soc. Am. (councilor). Home: PO Box 107 Warda TX 78960-0107

KUNZE, OTTO ROBERT, retired agricultural engineering educator; b. Warda, Tex., May 27, 1925; s. John Paul and Hermine Amanda (Moerbe) K.; m. Alice Ruth Eifert, Aug. 5, 1951; children: Glenn, Allen, Charles, Karen. BS, Tex. A&M U., College Station, 1950; MS, Iowa State U., Ames, 1951; PhD, Mich. State U., East Lansing, 1964. Registered profl. engr., Tex. Agrl. and indsl. engr. Ctrl. Power and Light Co., San Benito, Tex., 1951-56; rsch. asst. agrl. engring. dept. Mich. State U., East Lansing, 1961-64; assoc. prof. agrl. engring. dept. Tex. A&M U., College Station, 1956-61, 64-69, prof. agrl. engring. dept., 1969-90, prof. emeritus agrl. engring. dept., 1990—. Vis. prof. Nanjing (China) Coll. Food, Grain and Oil Econs., 1993; lectr. Tsukuba U., Japan, 93; cons. and vis. prof. Nat. Chung Hsing U. in Taichung and Nat. Taiwan U. in Taipei, Taiwan, 1994; lectr., cons. Internat. Conf. on Grain Drying in Asia, Bangkok, Thailand, 1995; engring. cons. Advanced Dryer Sys., Inc., Alachua, 1997, Farmers Rice Coop., Sacramento, 1992, Post Harvest Process and Food Engring. Ctr., G.B. Pant U., Pantnagar, India, 1985, Rice Process Engring. Ctr., Indian Inst. Tech., Kharagpur, 1975, Rice Tec, Alvin, Tex., 1996; lectr. on rice harvesting Asian Productivity Orgn., Taichung, Taiwan, 1985, 87; lectr. U. PR, Mayaguez, 1990; keynote spkr. PR sect. Am. Soc. Agrl. Engrs., Añasco, 1990; publ. coord. Rice Tech. Working Group, 1976-90. Contbr. chpts. to 7 books, over 100 articles to profl. jours. Mem. A&M Consol. Bd. Equalization, College Station, 1969-71; mem. Tex. Air Control Bd., Austin, 1979-90; mem. pediatric scholarship com. M.D. Anderson Cancer Ctr., Houston, 1990-2006. With US Army, 1944-46, ETO. Decorated 2 Bronze Stars; recipient Outstanding Svc. award Rice Tech. Working Group, 1990, Outstanding Agrl. Engring. achievement 20th Century, 2000; Faculty fellow NSF, 1961-62. Fellow Am. Soc. Agrl. Engrs. (tech. dir., numerous coms.), Am. Assn. Cereal Chemists (assoc. editor), Sigma Xi (sec. 1969-70, chmn. 1970-71), Phi Kappa Phi (pub. rels. officer 1984-85). Lutheran.

KUNZE, RALPH CARL, retired savings and loan association executive; b. Buffalo, Oct. 31, 1925; s. Bruno E. and Esther (Graubman) K.; m. Helen Hites Sutton, Apr. 1978; children by previous marriage: Bradley, Diane Kunze Cowgill, James. BBA, U. Cin., 1950, postgrad., 1962-63; grad., Ind. U. Grad. Sch. Savs. and Loan, 1956, U. Calif., 1973. With Mt. Lookout Savs. & Loan Co., Cin., 1951-63, sec., mng. officer, 1958-63; with Buckeye Fed. Savs. & Loan Assn., Columbus, Ohio, 1963-77, exec. v.p., sec., 1967-70, pres., sec., vice chmn. bd. dirs., 1970-77; pres., chief operating officer, dir. Gate City Savs. and Loan Assn., Fargo, ND, 1977-81; chief exec. officer, dir. United Home Fed., Toledo, 1981-91, also chmn. bd. dirs., 1985-91; ret., 1991. Former trustee Ohio Savs. and Loan League, Toledo C. of C.; mem. investment adv. com. City of Toledo; mem. media contact group and legis. com. U.S. Savs. League. Mem. Toledo Com. 100, Toledo Zool. Soc., St. Vincent Hosp. Found.; past pres. Toledo Zoo; past pres. coun. Hope Luth. Ch.; pres. Toledo Neighborhood Housing Svcs., 1981-83; pres., chmn. pers. com. United Way Franklin County, Ohio; past pres. Ohio Soc. Prevention Blindness; bd. dirs. Revitalization Corp. Toledo, 1983-84, Bittersweet Farms, Autistic Cmty. of N.W. Ohio, Inc.; past mem., trustee Kidney Found. Northwestern Ohio and Luth. Social Svcs., Wesley Glen Retirement Meth. Ctr., Columbus, 1974-77. Served with USNR, 1944-45. Mem.: Lambda Chi Alpha. Home: 2606 Emmick Dr Toledo OH 43606-2701

KUNZEL, ERICH, JR., conductor, arranger, educator; b. NYC, Mar. 21, 1935; s. Erich and Elisabeth (Enz) Kunzel; m. Brunhilde Gertrud Strodl, Sept. 5, 1965. AB in Music, Dartmouth Coll., 1957; postgrad., Harvard U., 1957—58; AM, Brown U., 1960; LittD, No. Ky. State U., 1973; D of Arts, Coll. Mt. St. Joseph, 1996; D in Musical Arts, U. Cin., 2000. Condr. Sante Fe Opera, 1957, Santa Fe Opera, 1964, 1965; music faculty Brown U., 1958—65; asst. condr. R.I. Philharmonic, 1963—65; resident condr. Cin. Symphony Orch., 1965—77; condr. Cin. Summer Opera, 1966, 1973, Cin. Ballet Co., 1966—68; assoc. prof. U. Cin. Coll.-Conservatory Music, 1965—71, chmn. opera dept., 1968—70; music dir. Philharmonia Orch., 1967—71, New Haven (Conn.) Symphony Orch., 1974—77, San Francisco Art Commn. Pops, 1981—83; condr. Cin. Pops Orch., 1977—; prin. pops condr. Naples Philharm. Orch., 1993—. Guest condr. Boston Symphony, Cleve. Orch., Boston Pops, Phila. Orch., San Francisco Symphony, Buffalo Philharm., Rochester Philharm., Pitts. Symphony, Atlanta Symphony, Chgo. Symphony Orch., Interlochen Arts Festival, Dallas Symphony, Detroit Symphony, Toronto Symphony, Montreal Symphony, St. Louis Symphony, Nat. Symphony, London Symphony, China Nat. Symphony, Can. Opera Co., San Francisco Opera, others. Editor, arranger choral works, recs. for Decca Gold Label, Atlantic Records, Telarc Internat., Vox Records, Caedmon Records, Pro Arte Records, Fanfare, MMG, MCA Classics Gold. V.p. Pierre Monteux Meml. Found., Met. Opera Guild; chmn. Greater Cin. Arts and Edn. Ctr., 1998—. Named Billboard Crossover Artist of Yr., 1988, 1989, 1990, 1991; named to Hon. Order Ky. Cols.; recipient Grand Prix du Disque, 1989, Sony Tiffany award, 1989, Classical Record of Yr. award, Japan, 1989, Grammy nomination, 1989, 1991, 1993, 1995, Ohioana Pegasus award, 2000, Nat. Medal Arts, Nat. Endowment Arts, 2006. Mem.: Am. Symphony Orch. League, Delta Omicron, Phi Mu Alpha Sinfonia, Phi Delta Theta (Disting. Alumnus award 1996). Mailing: c/o Peter Throm Mgmt LLC 2040 Tibbitts Court Ann Arbor MI 48105*

KUO, CHUN-FANG FRANK, counselor, educator; b. Taichung, Taiwan, July 25, 1963; arrived in U.S., 1990; s. Tung-Huan Samuel Kuo and I-Chung Esther Liu. BS Psychology, Nat. Cheng-Chi U., 1986; MS Counseling and Counselor Edn., Ind. U., 1993; PhD Counseling Psychology, U. Mo., 2005. Adminstrv. asst. Chinese Army, Ping-Tung, Taiwan, 1986—88; staff counselor Lee-Ming Inst. Tech., Taipei, Taiwan, 1988—90; adminstrv. intern U. Mo., Kansas City, 1994—97, tchg. and rsch. asst., 1997—2002; intern psychology U. Pitts., 2002—03; staff counselor Counseling Svcs. Truman State U., Kirksville, Mo., 2003—05; counselor, asst. prof. counseling svcs. Old Dominion U., Norfolk, Va., 2005—. Cons. mental health ReStart, Inc. Psychol. Svcs., Kansas City, 1997—2001; supr. Kansas City Family Ct., 2001—02; coord. Chinese Christian fellowship U. Mo., 1995—97. Author: Parent Education for Parents of Teenage Children, 1993, The Influence of Christian Belief on Perceptions of Counselor Empathy, Response Type, and Social Influence, 2005, Academic Procrastination and Anxiety of College Students. Active coll. outreach program Lake Rd. Chapel, Kirksville, 2003—05; mem. visitation team Pitts. Chinese Christian Ch., 2002—03; co-worker evang. com. Emmanuel Chinese Bapt. Ch., Lenexa, Kans., 1994—96, mem. choir, 1994—2002, asst. prin. Sunday Sch., 1999—2001. Chancellor's Non-Resident fellow, U. Mo., 1994—2005, Alumni scholar, Taichung Second H.S., 1979—81. Mem.: ACA, APA, Am. Coll. Pers. Assn. Avocations: tennis, ping pong/table tennis, bowling, volleyball, chinese calligraphy. Office Phone: 757-683-4401. Business E-Mail: ckuo@odu.edu.

KUO, FRANKLIN F., computer scientist, electrical engineer; b. Apr. 22, 1934; came to U.S., 1950, naturalized, 1961; s. Steven C. and Grace C. (Huang) K.; m. Dora Lee, Aug. 30, 1958; children: Jennifer, Douglas. BS, U. Ill., 1955, MS, 1956, PhD, 1958. Asst. prof. dept. elec. engring. Poly. Inst. Bklyn., 1958-60; mem. tech. staff Bell Telephone Labs., Murray Hill, NJ, 1960-66; prof. elec. engring. U. Hawaii, Honolulu, 1966-82; exec. dir. SRI Internat., Menlo Park, Calif., 1982-94; founder, v.p. GWcom, 1994-98; sr. adv. Mtone Wireless Inc., 1998—. Dir. info. systems Office Sec. of Def., 1976-77; liason scientist U.S. Office Naval Research, London, 1971-72; cons. prof. elec. engring. Stanford U., Calif., 1982—96; vis. prof. U. Mannheim, Germany, 1995-96, Nihon U. Global Bus. Sch., 1998-2002; mem. exec. panel Chief of Naval Ops., 1980-85; mentor, Stanford U. Grad. Sch. of Bus., 1999-; advisor China Vest, 2001-03. Author: Network Analysis and Synthesis, 1962, (2d edit.), 1966, Linear Circuits and Computations, 1973; co-author: System Analysis by Digital Computer, 1966, Computer Oriented Circuit Design, 1969, Computer Communications Networks, 1973, Protocols and Techniques in Data Communication Networks, 1981, Multimedia Communications, 1997; cons. editor, Prentice-Hall Inc., 1967—; mem. editorial bd. Future Generations Computer Systems; contbr. articles to profl. jours.; developer Alohanet packet broadcast radio network Mem. Pres. coun. U. Ill.; mem. adv. bd. Beckman Inst.; mem. dean's adv. bd. U. Calif. Santa Cruz, 2002—. Recipient Alexander von Humboldt Found. Rsch. award, 1994. Fellow IEEE; mem. The Internet Soc., Tau Beta Pi, Eta Kappa Nu Home: 824 La Mesa Dr Portola Valley CA 94028 E-mail: ffkuo@mindspring.com.

KUO, JOHN TSUNGFEN, geophysicist, educator, researcher; b. Hangchow, Chejiang, China, Apr. 1, 1922; came to U.S., 1949; naturalized, 1967; s. Lee Kuo; m. Marilyn Dunlap, Apr. 14, 1957; children: Ping Andrea, Sonya Sue, J. David. BS in Geology with Physics and Math., U. Redlands, 1952, ScD (hon.), 1978; MS in Geophysics, Cal. Inst. Tech., 1954; PhD in Geophysics, Stanford U., 1958. Asst. prof. San Jose (Calif.) St. Coll., 1957-60; rsch. assoc. Stanford U., 1958-60; rsch. scientist Columbia U., NYC, 1960-64, assoc. prof., 1964-67, prof., 1967-83, Vinton prof., 1983-85, Ewing and Worzel prof., 1985-92, Ewing and Worzel prof. emeritus, 1992—. Participant DEEPSCAN, 1963; dir. Aldridge Lab. Applied Geophysics, 1964-92, Lamont-Doherty's Underground Geophys. Obs., Ogdensburg, N.J., 1967-77, Columbia U., Project Migration, Inversion, Diffraction and Scattering, 1979-89; disting. sr. vis. scholar U. Cambridge, Eng., 1970-71; vis. prof. U. Tex., Austin, 1977-78, Cornell U., N.Y., 1978, 92-97, Tech. U. Clausthal, Germany, 1987; adj. prof. Cornell U., 1992-98; Columbia U. del. China, 1979; tech. adv. 20th Dist. Congressman, 1983-2004; hon. prof, co-dir. integrated basin studies Chengdu U. Tech., China, 1986; hon. prof. Acad. Sinica, 1979—, China U. Geoscis., Beijing, 1992; hon. sr. rschr., hon. prof. Inst. Geophysics, Chinese Seismological Adminstrn., 1995—, hon. prof., 2006—; expert World Bank, 1982. Mem. editl. bd. Bollettino di Geofisica, Italy, 1985-89; contbr. over 120 articles to profl. jours. Danforth Tchg. fellow, 1957—, Sr. Postdoctoral fellow NSF, 1970; Rsch. grantee NSF, NASA, U.S. Geol. Survey, Office Naval Rsch., Air Force Office Sci. Rsch., Air Force Geophysics, U.S. Bur. Mines; recipient Alexander von Humboldt award for disting. U.S. sr. scientist, Fed. Republic Germany, 1986, Hon. Knight for Life award Knights Round Table Internat., 1993, Alumni Career Achievement award U. Redlands, 2002. Fellow Geol. Soc. Am. (sr.), Royal Astron. Soc. U.K.; mem. Internat. Union Geodesy and Geophysics (fellow Assn. Geodesy, pres. permanent commn. for Earth tides 1979-87), Am. Geophys. Union (life, assoc. editor Geophysics Rev.), Soc. Exploration Geophysicists (rep.-at-large, com. mem., chmn. com.), Seismol. Soc. Am., Petroleum Exploration Soc. NY, Round Table Internat. (hon. life), China Geophys. Soc. (fgn. corr.), Sigma Xi. Home: 11 Hoffman Ln Blauvelt NY 10913-1707 Office: Columbia U New York NY 10027 Business E-Mail: kuojt@ldeo.columbia.edu.

KUO, WINSTON PATRICK, pediatric and oral medicine dentist, biomedical researcher; b. Poughkeepsie, NY; s. Chien and Helen Kuo. BS in Biology cum laude, SUNY, Albany, 1988; DDS, Columbia U., NYC, 1993; MS in Med. Informatics, MIT, Cambridge, Mass., 2001; DMS in Oral Biology, Harvard U., Boston, 2005. Cert. in pediat. dentistry U. So. Calif., in oral medicine Harvard U., in dental informatics Harvard U. Resident gen. practice dentistry Catholic Med. Ctr., Brooklyn, 1993—95; resident pediatric dentistry U. So. Calif. & Rancho Los Amigos Med. Ctr., 1995—97, Rancho Los Amigos Med. Ctr., 1996—97; resident oral medicine U. Medicine and Dentistry NJ, 1997—98; fellow med. informatics Harvard Med. Sch., 1998—2002; resident oral medicine Harvard Sch. Dental Medicine, 1998—2005, fellow dental informatics, 1998—2005, post doctoral devel. biology, 2005—06; post doctoral organismic and evolutionary biology Harvard U., 2006—. Recipient Rsch. Fellowship award, Nat. Libr. Medicine, 1998—2002, Fellowship award, Mucosal Injury in Cancer Conf., 2000, Rsch. Asst. award, MIT, 2001, Brazil/US Internat. Training in Med. Informatics Fellowship award, 2002—04, Poster award, Assn. Bimolecular Resource Facilities, 2006; Travel fellowship, Dept. Energy, 2001, 2002. Mem.: Internat. Soc. for Computational Biology, Am. Med. Informatics Assn., Am. Acad. of Oral Medicine (Lester W. Burket award 2003, Robert I. Schattner award 2002), Am. Acad. of Pediatric Dentistry, Am. Dental Assn. Achievements include research in sequence oriented comparison of gene expression measurements across different hybridization-based technologies; calmodulin pathway and the evolution of elongated beak morphology in Darwin's finches. Office: Harvard Sch Dental Medicine Dept Devel Biology 188 Longwood Ave REB 5th Fl Boston MA 02115 Business E-Mail: wkuo@genetics.med.harvard.edu.

KUO, YING YING, instructional designer; arrived in U.S., 1993; d. Yin-Po Kuo and Hsiu-Shya Kuo Hung; m. Shih-Houng Young, Jan. 1, 1986; children: Tso-Hsuan Jason Young, Pei-Chen Jenny Young. BS, Tsing Hua U., Hsinchu, 1980, MS, 1983; MA, U. Ala., 1998; EdD, W.Va. U., 2003. Web designer W.Va. U., Morgantown, 2004, instrnl. designer, 2004—. Indsl. engr. Gen. Instrument of Taiwan, Taipei, 1980—81; planning specialist Sci. Based Indsl. Pk., Hsinchu, 1983—85; asst. rschr. Chung Shan Inst. of Sci. and Tech., TaoHuan, Taiwan, 1985—93. Co-author: (book) Instructors Manual for Intentional Group Counseling. Recipient Appreciation in Multicuitural and Diversity award, Dean of the Coll. of Human Rsch. and Edn., 2002. Mem.: Am. Ednl. Rsch. Assn. (assoc.), Phi Beta Delta. Buddism. Achievements include design of Learning Traits Questionnaire. Office: W Va U 1 Medical Dr Morgantown WV 26506 Home Phone: 304-291-3113; Office Phone: 304-293-2491.

KUPCHAK, KENNETH ROY, lawyer; b. Forrest Hills, Pa., May 15, 1942; s. Frank V. and Anne B. (Ruzanic) Kupchak; m. Patricia K. Geer, Jan. 27, 1967; children: Lincoln K., Robinson K. AB, Cornell U., 1964; BS, Pa. State U., 1965; JD in Internat. Affairs, Cornell U., 1971. Bar: Hawaii 1971, U.S. Dist. Ct. Hawaii 1971, U.S. Supreme Ct. 1988. Meteorology staff U. Hawaii, Honolulu, 1968; ptnr. Damon Key Leong Kupchak Hastert, Honolulu, 1971—, v.p., 2002—, bd. dir., 1974—. Chief minority counsel 8th legis. Hawaii Ho. Reps., Honolulu, 1974—75; legis. coord. Hawaii State Assn. Counties, Honolulu, 1988; bd. dir. Fletcher Constrn. Co., N.Am. Ltd.; adj. prof. William S. Richardson Sch. Law, U. Hawaii, 1993; mem. Honolulu Common Fgn. Rels., 1995—; vice chair bd. counselors Mid-Pacific Inst., 1993—95, trustee, 1995—, chmn. pers. com., 1998—, chmn. edn. com., 2000—, chmn. pres. evaluation com., 2002—, vice chmn. bd. trustees, 2004—; lectr. on constrn. law. Co-author: Fifty State Construction Lien and Bond Laws, 2000, The Design/Build Process, 1997, A State-By-State Guide to Architect, Engineer and Contractor Licensing, 1998, A State-By-State Guide to Construction and Design Law, 1998; contbr. articles to profl. jours. Chair agenda com. C.Z.M. Statewide Adv. Com., Hawaii, 1980—92; pres., bd. dirs. Hawaii Cmty. Svc. Coun., Honolulu, 1982—88; trustee Moanalua Gardens Found., 1985—88, Operation Raleigh (N.C.) U.S.A., 1986—90; bd. dirs. Hawaii Nature Ctr., 1989—, sec., 2001—02, pres., 2002—; chair Hawaii State Commn. on Korean and Vietnam War Meml., 1992—95. Capt. USAF, 1964—68, Vietnam. Centennial fellow, Pa. State U., 1996. Fellow: Am. Coll. Constrn. Lawyers; mem.: ABA (constrn. industry forum, dispute resolution steering com. 1994—2001, chair 1998—2000, co-chair ann. meeting 2001, governing com. 2002—05, chair membership com. 2003—05, chair mktg. com. 2004—06, nominating com. 2007), USAF Assn. (v.p. Hawaii chpt. 1994—97), Am. Arbitration Assn. (panel arbitrators), Internat. Bar Assn., Hawaii Bar Assn., Cornell Law Alumni Assn. (exec. com. 1990—93), Hawaii Lacrosse Club (founder, dir., sec. 1990—2000), Volcano Golf and Country Club, Oahu Country Club, Cornell Club Hawaii (bd. dirs., chair scholarship com. 1994—2000). Avocations: lacrosse, hiking, photography. Office: 1600 Pauahi Tower 1001 Bishop St Honolulu HI 96813-3429 Office Phone: 808-531-8031. E-mail: krk@hawaiilawyer.com.

KUPCHAK, MITCHELL, professional sports team executive, retired professional basketball player; b. Hicksville, NY, May 24, 1954; m. Claire Kupchak. Student, U. NC; MBA, UCLA, 1987. Player Washington Bullets, 1976—81, LA Lakers, 1981—86, asst. gen. mgr., 1986—94, gen. mgr., 1994—. Mem. US basketball team World Univ. Games, 1973, Olympics, 1976. Recipient Gold medal World Univ. Games, 1973, Olympics, 1976; named to NBA All-Rookie Team, 1977. Achievements include winning NBA Championships as a member of the Bullets, 1978, Lakers, 1982, 85. Office: LA Lakers 555 N Nash St El Segundo CA 90245*

KUPCHELLA, CHARLES EDWARD, academic administrator, author, educator; b. Nanty Glo, Pa., July 7, 1942; s. Charles Francis and Margaret (Bouite) K.; m. R. Adele Kiel, July 20, 1963; children: Richard Charles, Michele Louise, Jason Charles. BS in Edn., Indiana U. of Pa., 1964; PhD, St. Bonaventure U., 1968. Asst. prof. Bellarmine Coll., Louisville, 1968-72, assoc. prof., 1972-73; assoc. dir. cancer rsch. ctr. Sch. of Medicine, assoc. prof. U. Louisville, 1973-79; prof., chmn. dept. biology Murray (Ky.) State U., 1979-85; dean Ogden Coll. Western Ky. U., Bowling Green, 1985-93; provost S. E. Mo. State U., Cape Girardeau, 1993—99; pres. U. N.D., 1999—. Author: Sights/Sounds: Special Senses, 1976, Environmental Science, 1986, 3rd rev. edit., 1993, Dimensions of Cancer, 1987; contbr. chpts. to books, over 50 articles to profl. jours. Bd. dirs. Ky. Ctr. for Pub. Issues, Lexington, 1990-93; mem. cancer edn. rev. com. NIH/Nat. Cancer Inst., 1993-97; mem. inst. rsch. grant rev. com. Am. Cancer Soc., 1993-96; chmn. N.D. Cancer Coalition, 2006—; trustee N.D. Hist. Soc., 2002—; ptnr. Nat. Dialogue Cancer, 2000—. NDEA fellow, 1964-68. Mem. AAAS (nominating com. sect. on sci. and engring. 1995-97), Ky. Acad. Sci. (pres. 1977), Ky. Sci. and Tech. Coun. (sec., treas. Lexington 1988-93), Am. Assn. Cancer Edn. (chair fin. com. 1990-93, treas. 1993-96, pres. 1999-2000, exec. coun., mem. midwest higher edn. commn. 1999-2001, mem. accreditation rev. coun. higher learning commn. 2005-06). Office: U of North Dakota Office of Pres Grand Forks ND 58202 Office Phone: 701-777-2121.

KUPELIAN, LOUISE PAULSON, musician, educator; b. Swarthmore, Pa., Jan. 9, 1922; d. Paul Michael and Annastasia Paulson; m. Vahey S. Kupelian, June 23, 1943; children: Theodore Paul, David Ralph, Diane Louise. Grad., Phila. Conservatory Music, 1941. Master piano tchr. Louise Kupelian Piano Studios, Chevy Chase, Md., 1938—2006, concert pianist, 1940—. Master: Music Tchrs. Nat. Assn. (life; master piano tchr.); mem.: Md. State Music Tchrs. Assn. (life; co-chair program planning 1989—91), Friday Morning Music Club (life; judge 1990—92), Phi Kappa Phi (life). Home Phone: 301-652-0879.

KUPER, ADAM JONATHAN, anthropologist, educator; b. Johannesburg, Republic of South Africa, Dec. 29, 1941; s. Simon Meyer and Gerty (Hesselson) K.; m. Jessica Sue Cohen, Dec. 16, 1966; children: Simon, Jeremy, Hannah. BA, U. Witwatersrand, Johannesburg, 1961; PhD, U. Cambridge, Eng., 1966; D (hons.), U. Gothenburg, Sweden, 1978. Lectr. in social anthropology Makerere U., Kampala, Uganda, 1967-70; lectr. in anthropology Univ. Coll. U. London, 1970-76; prof. African anthropology and sociology U. Leiden, Netherlands, 1976-85; prof. social anthropology, head human scis. dept. Brunel U., Middlesex, England, 1985—. Mem. Inst. for Advanced Study, Princeton, N.J., 1994-95. Author: Kalahari Village Politics: An African Democracy, 1970, Anthropologists and Anthropology: The British School, 1922-72, 1973, 2d rev. ed. 1983, 3rd rev. ed. 1996, Changing Jamaica, 1976, Regionaal Vergelijkend Onderzoek in Afrika, 1977, Wives for Cattle: Bridewealth and Marriage in Southern Africa, 1982, South Africa and the Anthropologist, 1987, The Invention of Primitive Society: Transformations of an Illusion, 1988; editor: The Social Anthropology of Radcliffe-Brown, 1982, The Social Science Encyclopedia, 3d edit., 2004, Current Anthropology, 1985-93, Conceptualizing Society, 1992, The Chosen Primate, 1994, Culture: The Anthropologist' Account, 1999, Among the Anthropologists, 1999, The Reinvention of Primitive Society, 2005; contbr. more than 90 articles to profl. jours. Fellow: British Acad.; mem.: Acad. Europe. Avocation: golf. Home: 16 Muswell Rd London N10 2BG England Business E-Mail: adam.kuper@brunel.ac.uk.

KUPERMAN, ROBERT IAN, retired advertising agency executive; b. Bklyn., Dec. 31, 1941; s. Morris and Gertrude Kuperman; m. Colette Chestnut, Aug. 22, 2004; 1 stepchild, John. BFA, Pratt Inst., 1963. Vice pres., sr. art dir. Doyle Dane Bernbach, NYC, 1963-71; v.p., creative dir. Della Femina Travisano & Ptnrs., NYC, 1971-73; sr. v.p., creative dir. Wells, Rich & Greene, NYC and Los Angeles, 1973-80, BBDO/West, Los Angeles, 1980-82; exec. v.p., exec. creative dir. DDB, LA, 1982—87; exec. v.p., creative dir. chiat/Day, LA, 1987—98, pres., CEO, 1998—2001; chmn. DDB New York, 2001—03, pres., CEO NY, 2001—05; cons. DDB Worldwide, 2005—. Instr. Sch. Visual Arts, N.Y.C., 1968-74, Pratt Inst., Bklyn., 1966-68, Art Ctr., LA, 1975-79; adv. Jackson Lab. Art dir. TV comml. 1949 Auto Show, 1970 (Clio Hall of Fame award 1979), Volkswagen advertisements, (now in Smithsonian Mus. Art), other TV commls. Recipient Gold medals N.Y. Art Dirs. Show, 1969, 71, Andy award Advt. Club N.Y., 1970, Clio awards for excellence in worldwide advt., 1970, 72, 74, 78, 83; Ellis Island Medal of Honor. Mem. Los Angeles Creative Club (co-founder, chmn. bd. dirs.), Los Angeles Advt. Club (bd. dirs. 1979). Office: DDB Worldwide 437 Madison Ave New York NY 10022 Office Phone: 212-415-2525.

KUPERMAN, ROMAN GREGORY, toxicologist, ecologist; b. Moscow, May 20, 1957; arrived in USA, 1986; s. Gregory I. Kuperman and Olga R. Blau; m. Frances L. Pergericht, Feb. 24, 1982; 1 child, Natalie Jill. BSc in Biology and Chemistry, Moscow State Pedagogical U., 1980; PhD, Ohio State U., 1993. Program mgr., sr. scientist Geo-centers, Inc., Aberdeen Proving Ground, Md., 1999—2002; rsch. biol. scientist Edgewood Chem. Biol. Ctr., Aberdeen Proving Ground, Md., 2002—. Leader key tech. area Tech. Coop. Program, 2003—; chmn. contaminated soils adv. group Soc. Environ. Toxicology and Chemistry, Pensacola, Fla., 2002—04; liaison rep. to NAS, U.S. nat. com. for soil sci. Soil Ecology Soc., 2005—. Grantee, Strategic Environ. Rsch. and Devel. Program, 2000—04. Mem.: Soc. Environment Toxicology and Chemistry. Office: Edgewood Chem Biol Ctr AMSRD-ECB-RT-TE E5641 5183 Blackhawk Rd Aberdeen Proving Ground MD 21010-5424 Office Phone: 410-436-4697. Office Fax: 410-612-5399. Business E-Mail: roman.kuperman@us.army.mil.

KUPERMAN, WILLIAM A., oceanographer, educator; BS, Polytechnic Inst. Bklyn.; MS, U. Chgo.; PhD, U. Md. Prof. oceanography, dir. Marine Physical Lab. Scripps Inst. Oceanography, U. Calif., San Diego, Sec. of Navy / Chief of Navel Ops. Oceanography chiar. Co-author: Computational Ocean Acoustics; contbr. articles to profl. jours. Fellow: Acoustical Soc. Am. (ores., Pioneers of Underwater Acoustics Medal 1995); mem.: NAE. Office: Scripps Inst Oceanography U Calif 9500 Gilman Dr La Jolla CA 92093-0701 E-mail: wkuperman@ucsd.edu.

KUPERSMITH, JOEL, internist, medical school dean; b. Nov. 26, 1939; s. Charles Douglas and Sally K.; m. Judith Freidman, June 15, 1969; children: David, Rebecca, Adam. BS, Union Coll., Schenectady, 1960; MD, NY Med. Coll., 9641. Prof., chief clin. pharmacology Mt. Sinai Sch. Medicine, NYC, 1974—86; chief cardiology divsn. Beth Israel Med. Ctr., NYC, 1985-86; prof., chief cardiology divsn. U. Louisville Sch. Medicine, East Lansing, 1986-91, V.V. Cooke prof. medicine Lubbock, 1987-91; prof., chair medicine Mich. State U., East Lansing, 1991-97; dean Sch. Medicine, dean Sch. Biomed. Sci. Tex. Tech U. Sch. Medicine, Lubbock, 1997—2001, v.p. clin. affairs, 1997—2001, prof. internal med., 1997—2004; chief rsch. devel. office Dept. Vets. Affairs, Washington, 2005—. Chief cardiac arrhythmia clinic Mt. Sinai Med. Ctr., 1977—85, assoc. prof. pharmacology, 1979—84; scholar-in-residence Inst. Medicine, Assn. Am. Med. Coll., 2003—05. Author: Clinical Manual of Electrophysiology, 1997, The Pharmacologic Management of Heart Disease, 1993. Recipient Affirmative Action award U. Louisville, 1988, Alumni Assn. Disting. Achievement award NY Med. Coll. Med. Sch., Coun. Deans, 1992. Mem.: AMA (med. sch. sect., governing coun.), Assn. Am. Med. Coll. (Petersdorf scholar-in-residence 2003—05, task force on fraud/abuse), Am. Heart Assn. (exec. com. Coun. on Clin. Cardiology 1991—94), Assn. Profs. Medicine (program com. 1994), Am. Soc. Clin. Investigation (sr.).

KUPFER, DAVID J., psychiatry professor; b. NYC, Feb. 14, 1941; s. Alex and Muriel (Greenfield) Kupferstein; m. Barbara Stern Burstin, June 1963 (div. Mar. 1975); m. Ellen Frank, June 1975; children: Andrea, Jeffrey, Deborah, Nancy, Erica, Tonia. BA magna cum laude, Yale U., 1961, MD, 1965. Diplomate Am. Bd. Psychiatry and Neurology. Med. intern Montefiore Hosp. Ctr., NYC, 1965—66; clin. fellow in psychiatry Yale U. Sch. Medicine, New Haven, 1966—67; postdoctoral fellow, chief resident in psychiatry Dana Psychiat. Clinic, Yale-New Haven Hosp., 1969—70; asst. prof. Yale U. Sch. Medicine, New Haven, 1970—73; assoc. prof. psychiatry U. Pitts., 1973—75, prof., 1975—, chmn. dept., 1983—; dir. rsch. Western Psychiat. Inst. and Clinic Western Psychiat. Inst. and Clinic, Pitts., 1973—, Thomas Detre prof., chmn. dept. psychiatry, 1994—. Office: U Pitts Western Psychiat Inst & Clinic 3811 Ohara St Pittsburgh PA 15213-2593

KUPFERER, JAMES LEO, JR., biotechnologist; b. Richmond Heights, Mo., July 14, 1969; s. James Leo and Patricia Ann Kupferer; m. Paige Maxon Kupferer, Nov. 25, 1995; 1 child, James Alexander. BA, Va. Poly. Inst. & State U., Blacksburg, Va., 1991. Prin. Fluor Global Location Strategies, Greenville, SC, 1999—2004, mng. dir., 2004—. Mem.: CoreNet Global, Biotech. Industry Orgn. Office: Fluor Global Location Strategies 100 Fluor Daniel Dr Greenville SC 29607 Office Fax: 864-676-7633. Business E-Mail: jim.kupferer@fluor.com.

KUPIETZKY, MOSHE JOSEPH, lawyer; b. NYC, May 17, 1944; s. Jacob Harry and Fanny (Dresner) K.; m. Arlene Debra Usdan, June 22, 1966; children: Jay, Jeff, Jacob. BBA cum laude, CCNY, 1965; LLB magna cum laude, Harvard U., 1968. Bar: NY 1969, Calif. 1970. Law clerk to Hon. William B. Herlands U.S. Dist. Ct., NYC, 1968-69; assoc. Mitchell Silberberg & Knupp, LA, 1969-74, ptnr., 1974-80; ptnr., prin. Hayutin Rubinroit Praw & Kupietzky, LA, 1980-87; ptnr. Sidley, Austin LLP, LA, 1987—; mng. partner, LA office and head, corp. and fin. practice group Sidley, Austin, Brown & Wood, LA, mem. exec. com. Editor: Harvard Law Rev., 1967—68. Bd. dirs. Nat. Inst. Jewish Hospice, Beverly Hills, Calif., 1986-98, LA Econ. Devel. Corp.; bd. advisors Graziadio Sch. Bus. and Mgmt. Pepperdine U., LA, 1996-98. Mem. ABA, Beverly Hills Bar Assn., LA County Bar Assn., Calif. State Bar (vice-chair opinions com. 2004-05.). Office: Sidley Austin LLP 555 W 5th St Ste 4000 Los Angeles CA 90013-3000 Home Phone: 310-277-9179; Office Phone: 213-896-6000. E-mail: mkupietzky@sidley.com.

KUPPERMAN, LOUIS BRANDEIS, lawyer; b. Augusta, Ga., Dec. 16, 1946; s. Herbert Spencer and Mollie (Kleven) K.; children: David Evan, Robert Dennis; m. Eileen Spadafina, Oct. 24, 1992. BS, Fairleigh Dickinson U., 1972; JD, Bklyn. Law Sch., 1975. Bar: Pa. 1975, U.S. Dist. Ct. (ea. dist.) Pa. 1978, U.S. Ct. Appeals (3d cir.) 1978, U.S. Supreme Ct. 1982. Jud. law clk. to Judge Jacob Kalish Ct. of Common Pleas of Phila. County, 1975-76, jud. law clk. to Judge Eugene Gelfand, 1976-77; corp. counsel Health Corp. Am., Wayne, Pa., 1977-78; ptnr. Dilworth, Paxson, Kalish & Kauffman, Phila., 1978-86; mem. firm, chmn. real estate dept. Baskin Flaherty Elliott & Mannino, P.C., Phila., 1986-90; ptnr., vice chmn. environ. law dept. Obermayer, Rebmann, Maxwell & Hippel, Phila., 1990—. Lectr. Pa. Bar Inst. Author: Real Estate Tax Assessment Appeals, 1987. Chancellor's del. to Phila. Fairleigh Dickinson U., 1983, 86. Recipient Disting. Alumnus award Fairleigh Dickinson U., 1983. Mem. ABA, Pa. Bar Assn., Phila. Bar Assn., (chmn. real estate litigation com. 1983-85), Pyramid Club of Phila. Home: 80 Delancy Ct Phoenixville PA 19460-5741 Office: Obermayer Rebmann Maxwell & Hippel 1 Penn Ctr 19th Fl 1617 John F Kennedy Blvd Philadelphia PA 19103-1821 Home Phone: 610-933-2905; Office Phone: 215-665-3000. Business E-Mail: Louis.Kupperman@Obermayer.com.

KUPPIREDDI, SIREESH, computer scientist; b. Hyderabad, India, June 7, 1978; s. Ramasubba Reddy and Parvathi Kuppireddi. BS in Elec. Engring., Jawaharlal Nehru Technol. U., Hyderabad, India, 1999; MS in Computer Sci. and Engring., U. Tex., Arlington, 2002. Cons. HCL Infosys., Noida, India, 2003—04; programmer analyst HCL Techs., Parsippany, NJ, 2004—05; cons. Hitachi Consulting, Houston, 2005—06; application integration specialist Transmontaigne Inc., Denver, 2006—. Scholar, Math. Olympiad. Mem.: IEEE (assoc.). Home: 3780 W 112th Ave Apt 301 Westminster CO 80031 Office: Transmontaigne Incs 1670 Broadway Suite 3100 Denver CO 80202 Home Phone: 303-475-3050. Personal E-mail: sireesh235@yahoo.com. Business E-Mail: skuppireddi@transmontaigne.com.

KURATA, PHILLIP CEDOMIR, journalist; b. Coaldale, Pa., Oct. 28, 1946; s. Fred and Virginia May (Mefford) Kurata; m. Chialing Chang, July 5, 1980 (div. Apr. 1995); 1 child, Shana Rebecca. BA, Kans. U., 1968, MA, 1982. Tchr. English Peace Corps, Tunis, Tunisia, 1968—70; tchr. pub. health Project Hope, Tunis, 1970—71; corr. Far Ea. Econ. Rev., Taiwan, 1979—81, Hong Kong, 1979—81, UPI, Hong Kong, 1981—82; editor/translator Agence France-Presse, Paris, 1982—85; journalist Voice of Am., Tokyo, Beijing and Washington, 1985—98; writer U.S. State Dept., Washington, 1998—, Iraq provincial action officer, 2006. Profl. boxer All-Japan Kickboxing Assn., Tokyo, 1972—74. Author: (novels) The Reluctant Agent, 2000 (Fiction prize, Washington Writers' Pub. House, 2000). Recipient Superior Hon. award, State Dept., 2004. Bahai. Home: 3409 Pendleton Dr Silver Spring MD 20902 Personal E-mail: kuratapc@hotmail.com.

KURATKO, DONALD F., entrepreneurial educator, consultant; b. Chgo., Aug. 27, 1952; s. Donald W. and Margaret M. (Browne) K.; m. Deborah Ann Doyle, Dec. 28, 1979; children: Christina Diane, Kellie Margaret. BA in Econs., John Carroll U., 1974; MBA in Mgmt., Benedictine U., 1979; DBA, PhD. in Entrepreneurship, Nova Southea. U., 1984. Lic. funeral dir., Ill. Funeral dir. Kuratko Funeral Home, North Riverside, Ill., 1975-83; prof. bus. Benedictine U., Lisle, 1979-83; prof., exec. dir. entrepreneurship program Ball State U., Muncie, Ind., 1983—2004, disting. prof., 1990—2004; Jack M. Gill chair entrepreneurship, prof. entrepreneurship, exec. dir. Johnson Ctr. for Entrepreneurship and Innovation, Kelley Sch. Bus., Ind. U., Bloomington, 2005—. Cons. Kendon Assocs., Riverside, 1983—88, Intrapreneurial Group, 1989—, Acordia, AT&T, GTE, United Techs., Ameritech, Union Carbide Corp.; dir. PA Labs, Acordia Ctrl. Ind., Ind. monument advisors, Beacon Venture Capital; developed entrepreneurship program Ball State U., Ind. U. Author: Management, 1988, 3d edit., 1991, Effective Small Business Management, 1986, 7th edit., 2001, Entrepreneurship: Theory, Process Practice, 1989, 7th edit., 2007, Entrepreneurship and Innovation in the Corporation, 1987, Entrepreneurial Strategy, 1994, The Entrepreneurial Decision, 1997, The Breakthrough Experience, 1998, Strategic Entrepreneurial Growth, 2001, 2d edit., 2004, Human Resource Function in Emerging Enterprises, 2002, Corporate Entrepreneurship, 2002, FrontLine HR, 2005, Innovation Acceleration, 2005, The Entrepreneurial Planning Guide, 2006, Corporate Entrepreneurship and Innovation, 2007; editor Jour. Small Bus. Mgmt., mem. editl. bd. Mid-Am. Bus. Jour., 1985—95, Jour. Bus. Venturing, cons. editor Entrepreneurship Theory & Practice Jour.; contbr. over 150 articles to profl. jours. Named Outstanding Young Hoosier, Ind. Jaycees, 1985, one of Outstanding Young Men of Am., 1983-84, #1 Entrepreneurship Program Dir. in USA, Entrepreneur Mag., 2003, #2 Entrepreneurship Program Dir. in USA, 2004-05, Disting. Tchg. Professorship, 1990, Stoops Disting Prof. Bus., 1990, Outstanding Univ. Prof., 1996, Entrepreneur of Yr. in Ind., Ernst & Young, Inc. Mag. and Merrill Lynch, 1990; 21st Century Entrepreneurship Rsch. fellow; Disting. scholar U.S. Assn. for Small Bus. and Entrepreneurship, 2003; recipient George Washington medal of honor, 1987, Extrepreneurship Excellence award Leavey Found., 1988, Excellence award N.F.I.B. Found., 1993, Nat. Outstanding Entrepreneurship Educator of Yr. award, 1993, Kauffman Found. Entrepreneurship Educator award, 1994, Entrepreneural World of Differences award, 1998, Thomas W. Binford Meml. award, 2000, Outstanding Rschr. award, 1999; Top 20 Business Week, Top 25 Success Mag., Top 4 Entrepreneur Mag., 2006, No. 1 U.S. News and World Report, 2007, Nat. Innovative Pedagogy award, 2001, Outstanding Educator award Ind. Distance Learning Assn., 2004, John E. Hughes/USASBE award for entrepreneurial advocacy, 2007, Nat. Model MBA Entrepreneurship Program award, 2007. Mem. US Assn. Small Bus. and Entrepreneurship (pres. 1993-94), Nat. Acad. Mgmt., Internat. Coun. Small Bus., Midwest Bus. Adminstrn. Assn. (pres. entrepreneurship divsn. 1992-93), Gobal Consortium Entrepreneurship Ctrs. (exec. dir. 2000—). Roman Catholic. Avocations: weightlifting, jogging. Office: Ind Univ Kelley Sch Bus Bloomington IN 47405-1703 Home: 3781 Sterling Ave Bloomington IN 47401 Business E-Mail: dkuratko@indiana.edu.

KURDZIEL, MICHAEL THOMAS, engineering executive; b. Kenmore, NY, June 4, 1964; s. Thomas Roy and Carol Ann Kurdziel; m. Colleen Irene Coakley; children: Robert Walter, Chistopher Thomas, Alexander Michael. BS in Elec. Engring., SUNY, Buffalo, 1986, MS in Elec. Engring., 1988, PhD in Elec. Engring., 2001. Lic. Profl. Engr., N.Y., 1992. Mem. tech. staff Harris Corp, Rochester, NY, 1994—96, project leader, lead hardware engr., 1996—98; prin. tech. specialist Harris Corp., Rochester, NY, 1999—2002, sr. engring. mgr., chief cryptographer, 2002—. Chmn. IEEE Milcom Comsec Session, 2002—. Asst. Cub Scouts, Rochester, NY, 2004; mem. Parish Coun., Rochester, NY, 1992—93; com. chmn. Ch. Planning Com., Rochester, NY, 1995—99. Recipient Next Level award, Harris Corp., 2001, Excellence award, 2005, Golden Quill award, 2005, 2006; scholar State Regents Scholarship, State of N.Y., 1982—86, Grad. Tchg. Assistantship, SUNY Grad. Sch., 1986—88. Mem.: IEEE (conf. session chair 2003), Am. Mensa. Right To Life Party. Roman Catholic. Achievements include patents for Real-Time Mozer Coding With a Neural Net; Method and Apparatus for Data Encryption; patents pending for

Random number source and associated methods; 2G Method and apparatus for data encryption; Cryptographic device and associated methods; Wireless cryptographic fill system and method. Avocations: exercise, woodworking, travel, gardening. Home: 98 W Forest Dr Rochester NY 14624 Office: Harris Corp 1680 Univ Ave Rochester NY 14610 Office Phone: 585-242-3214. Business E-Mail: mkurdzie@harris.com.

KURFEHS, HAROLD CHARLES, real estate executive; b. Jersey City, Dec. 10, 1939; s. Harold Charles and Matilda Gertrude (Ruschman) Kurfehs; m. Linda Roberta Lepis, Aug. 1, 1964; children: Harold Charles III, Diane E., Robert C. BS (Oaklawn Found. scholar), St. Peter's Coll., 1962; MBA, Wharton Sch. U. Pa., 1964. Product mgr. Am. Brands, Inc., NYC, 1958-62, 64-66; account exec. Benton & Bowles, NYC, 1966—68; account mgr. Wells, Rich, Greene, Inc., NYC, 1968-69; v.p., dir. mktg. Meta-Language Products, Inc., NYC, 1969-70; sr. acct. exec. McCaffrey & McCall, Inc., NYC, 1970-71; dir. advt. Ethan Allen, Inc., NYC, Danbury, Conn., 1971-75; v.p., gen. mgr. retail/franchise divsn. N.Am. ops. Reed Ltd., Toronto, 1975-76; v.p., gen. mgr. fabric divsn. Reed Nat. Drapery Co. and Sanderson Fabrics, Toronto, 1975-76; pres. Fairfield Book Co., Inc., Harlin House, Ltd., Brookfield, Conn., 1977-83; dir. advt. and pub. rels., bd. dirs., mem. mktg. planning bd. Ethan Allen, Inc., Danbury, Conn., 1983-85; sr. comml. investment broker William Raveis Comml. Investment Real Estate, Danbury, Conn., 1985-96; sr. comml. broker Century 21, Scalzo Realty, Inc., Bethel, Conn., 1996—2002; v.p. Coldwell Banker Comml., Scalzo Group, 2002—. Lectr. We. Conn. State U., 1985—86; chmn. Real Estate United Way No. Fairfield County, Conn., 1990, 91, account exec., bus. and industry divsn., 2001; mem. policies and procedures com. lead mgmt. Conn. Econ. Resource Ctr., 1995—96; alt. mem. Brookfield Planning Commn., 1997, 98, elected mem., 1999—, vice chmn., 2002—; mem. Brookfield Econ. Devel. Commn., 2004—, chmn., 2007—; mem. adv. bd. New Mil Bank, Danbury, Conn., 2005—06, Fairfield County Bank, 2006—. Contbr. articles to profl. jours. Del. Rep. State Conv., Conn., 2004; mem. Rep. Town Com., 2005—06. Named Top Prodr., State of Conn., 1988, 1989, Broker of Month, Conn. Real Estate Jour., 1990, Broker of Yr., Scalzo Comml., 1998, Coldwell Banker Comml., 2002—03, 2006, Listing Agt. of Yr., 2001. Mem.: NRA (life), Internat. Coun. Shopping Ctrs., Conn. Assn. Realtors (regl. treas. 1992, state dir. 1993, 1994, state sec. 1994, state v.p. 1995, regional pres. 1995—96, state pres.-elect 1996, state pres. 1997, state dir. 1998, comml. investment divsn.), Wharton Grad. Club NY, Pi Sigma Phi. Home: 42 Obtuse Rd N Brookfield CT 06804-3140 Office: 6 Stony Hill Rd Bethel CT 06801-1028 Office Phone: 203-205-7665. Business E-Mail: kurfehs@coldwellbankerscalzo.com.

KURIAN, GEORGE THOMAS, publisher; b. Changanacherry, Kerala, India, Aug. 4, 1931; came to U.S., 1968; s. Thomas Kurian and Mary (Abraham) George; m. Annie Cyriack, Aug. 22, 1966; 1 child, Sarah Claudine. MA, Madras Christian Coll., India, 1951. Dir. Indian Univs. Press, Madras, 1960-68; editor Clarence L. Barnhart, Bronxville, NY, 1968-71, Macmillan Inc., NYC, 1971-72; pres. George Kurian Reference Books, Baldwin Place, NY, 1972—. Bd. dirs. Fgn. Affairs Info. Svc., Baldwin Place, 1982—. Editor: Ency. of Third World, 1978 (ALA award 1978), World Press Ency., 1982, World Edn. ency., 1988 (ALA award 1988), Ency. of First World, 1990, Ency. of the Future, 1995, World Christian Encyclopedia, 2000, International Encyclopedia of Political Science, Encyclopedia of Christian Civilization, Encyclopedia of Christian Literature; 19 other encys. and 33 reference books. Mem. The Encyclopedists: Internat. Ency. Soc. (pres. 1990—), World Future Soc., Am. Historical Assn., Dictionary Soc. N.Am., Oral History Assn., World Acadamy of Arts and Letters, Am. Political Sci. Assn. Republican. Avocation: carpentry. Home: 3689 Campbell Ct Yorktown Heights NY 10598-1808 Office: George Kurian Reference Books PO Box 519 Baldwin Place NY 10505-0519 Home Phone: 914-962-0164; Office Phone: 914-962-3287. E-mail: gtkurian@aol.com.

KURIAN, PIUS, nephrologist, educator; b. Arpookara, India, May 9, 1959; s. Pylo and Mariamma Kurian; m. Sally Kurian, May 11, 1986; children: Michelle Maria, Matthew Paul, Catherine Tresa. BSc, Kuriakose (India) Elias Coll., 1979; MB, BChir, Kottayam (India) Med. Coll., India, 1986. Diplomate Am. Bd. Internal Medicine, Am. Bd. Nephrology, Am. Bd. Forensic Examiners; specialist clin. hypertension, Am. Soc. Hypertension. Resident in internal medicine Nassau County Med. Ctr., East Meadow, NY, 1988-91, fellow in nephrology, 1991-94; attending physician in nephrology Mercy Med. Ctr. and Cmty. Hosp., Springfield, Ohio, 1994—. Asst. prof. dept. medicine Wright State U., Dayton, Ohio, 1998; chief divsn. internal medicine Mercy Med. Ctr., Springfield, Ohio, 1999, chmn., dir. dept. medicine Mercy Med. Ctr., Springfield, Ohio, 2000; med. dir. Cmty. Physicians Dialysis, Springfield, 2000—; chmn. ethics com. Cmty. Hosp., Springfield; mem. governing bd. Cmty. Mercy Health Ptnrs. Health Sys., Springfield, 2006. Fellow ACP, Am. Soc. Nephrology; mem. AAAS, AMA, Am. Soc. Hypertension (specialist in clin. hypertension), Am. Coll. Physicians Execs., Internat. Soc. Nephrology, Renal Physicians Assn., Am. Soc. Nephrology, NY Acad. Scis., Nat. Kidney Found, Clark County Med. Soc. (pres. 2004). Roman Catholic. Office: 247 S Burnett Rd Springfield OH 45505-2639 Home Phone: 937-390-3144; Office Phone: 937-322-7364. Personal E-mail: piuskurian@doctor.com, hypertensionandnephrology@hotmail.com.

KURIAN, THOMAS, computer software company executive; B summa cum laude in Elec. Engring., Princeton U., NJ; MBA, Stanford U., Calif. Cons. McKinsey & Co., London, Brussels and San Francisco; with Oracle Corp., Redwood City, Calif., 1996, various product mgmt. and devel. positions Oracle Server Techs. Divsn., v.p. e-bus., sr. v.p. Oracle Server Techs. Devel. Office: Oracle Corp 500 Oracle Pky Redwood City CA 94065 Office Phone: 650-506-0024.*

KURIANSKY, JUDY, television and radio personality, reporter, clinical psychologist, writer, educator; b. NYC, Jan. 31, 1947; d. Abraham and Sylvia (Feld) Brodsky; m. Edward Kuriansky, Aug. 24, 1969. BA, Smith Coll., 1968; EdM, Boston U., 1970; PhD, NYU, 1980. Diplomate Am. Bd. Sexology, 2003. Reporter Sta. WABC-TV, NYC, 1980-82, Sta. WBZ-TV, Boston, 1981-82, Sta. WCBS-TV, 1982-86, NYC, 1986-88, Sta. WPIX-TV, NYC, 1987-89, Sta. CNBC-TV, Ft. Lee, NJ, 1989-93; host Total Wellness for Women program Sta. WDBB-TV, Birmingham, Ala., 1988-89; program host Sta. WABC-AM, NYC, 1980-87, Sta. WOR-AM, 1987-88; temp. program host ABC Talk Radio, NYC, 1988-90; host Modern Satellite Network, 1981; TV host J.C. Penney Golden Rule Network, Dallas, 1988-90; feature contbr. Attitudes Show LifeTime, 1992-94; host Love Phones, nat. syndicated Premiere Radio Networks, NYC, 1992-97; host Dr. Judy Show, Winstar Radio, 1998-99. Spokesperson Universal Studios Fla., 1993—94, Church and Dwight, 2000—01; cons. Lily of France, Charles of the Ritz, The Rolland Co., Taylor-Gordon Arons Advt., Clairol, Durex, London Internat., 1995, Organon, 1999—, Ky. Married for Life Survey, 2003—; tchr. Columbia U. Med. Sch., 1974—79, Inst. for Health and Religion, 1980—82; adj. prof. clin. psychology NYU, 1993—95; adj. prof. psychology Columbia U. Tchrs. Coll., 2001—; vis. prof. Beijing U. Health Sci. Ctr., 2002—; judge Most Unforgettable Women contest Revlon, 1990; judge Close-Up N Roll Contest, 1993, Cooney Waters P.R., Herpes Awareness Contest, 1996; therapy coord. Nat. Inst. for Psychotherapists, 1977—79; therapist Ctr. for Marital and Family Therapy, 1986—; cons. Shanghai Inst. Reproductive Health Instrn., China, 1999—; trainer marital cons. China Sexology Assn., 2000—; v.p. Quezon Corp., 1978—79; sr. rsch. scientist N.Y. State Psychiat. Inst., 1970—78; lectr. Blanton Peale Inst., 1979—81; mem. adv. bd. Single Living mag., 1997—98, Lane Bryant, 1997—98; adj. prof. psychology Yeshiva Univ., 2003—; asst. clin. prof. psychiatry Columbia Med. Ctr., 2003—; vis. prof Peking U. Health Scis. Ctr.; instr. dept. psychiatry Hong Kong U.; mem. exec. bd. Internat. Assn. Applied Psychology, 2006—; mem. at large UN Com. Mental Health, 2006—. Author: Sex, Now That I've Got Your Attention, Let Me Answer Your Questions, 1984, How to Love a Nice Guy, 1990, Italian and Japanese transls., Generation Sex, 1995, The Complete Idiots Guide to Dating, 1996, (translations in Polish and Spanish) 3rd edit., 2003, The Complete Idiots Guide to a Healthy Relationship, 1997, Goodbye My Troubles, Hello My Happiness, 1997, The Complete Idiots Guide to Tantric Sex, 2001;: 2d edit., 2004, China Reproductive Health Hotline Professionals Solve Problems on Sex and Emotions, 2001, Terror in the Holy Land: Inside the Anguish of the Israelis and Palestinians, 2006, Beyond Bullets and Bombs: Grassroots Peace building between Israelis and Palestinians, 2007; columnist Family Circle mag., 1984—89, Whole Life Times, 1986—87, King Features Newspaper, 1984—86, N.Y. and L.I. Newsday, 1993—2000, Penthouse mag., 1995—, Soap Opera Update, 1995—96, Telluride Daily Planet, 1995—98, Cosmo Girl mag., 2001—03, Singapore Straits Times, 2002—, N.Y. Daily News website, 2004—; columnist: China Trends Health mag., 2004—; writer New Woman, Ad Age, Boardroom Reports, Am. Advt. Fedn. mag., Chgo. Tribune Woman News, South China Morning Post, 2001—; contbg. editor: Beauty Mag., 1989—90; guest editor Ladies Home Jour., 1993, AOL On-Line Show, Keyword: Dr. Judy, 1996—97, www.cameraplanet.com, 2001—02, www.matureamerica.com, 2002—03, mem. adv. bd. Single Living mag., 1997—99, adv. bd. Bottomline/Women's Health, 2007—. UN NGO rep. Internat. Assn. Applied Psychology and World Coun. for Psychotherapy, 2004—; bd. dirs. Scientists Com. for Pub. Info., 1977—79; mem. adv. bd. N.Y. City Self Help Orgn., 1983—85; mem. benefits com. Mental Health Svcs. for Deaf, 1980—82; bd. advisors Planned Parenthood, 1998—; exec. com. UN Com. on Mental Health, 2006—. Recipient Civilian Commendation, N.Y.C. Police Dept., 1984, Cert. for Unique Pub. Svc. AWRT, 1984, Star award for individual achievement in radio, 1997, Sabo Media Programming Visionary award, 1984, Maggie award Planned Parenthood, 1985, 93, Freedoms Found. award Children for a Better Soc., 1986, Olive award Coun. of Chs., 1986, Mercury award Larimi Comm., 1987, Lifetime Achievement in Sexology medal, AACS, 2004. Fellow APA (co-founder media divsn. 1985—, mem. internat. divsn. 2004—, exec. bd. peace divsn. 2007—); mem. Am. Women in Radio and TV (pres. N.Y. chpt. 1988-89, nat. found. vice chair 1988-90, nat. bd. treas. 1995-98, Internat. Outreach award 2003), Soc. Sex Therapy and Rsch. (charter), Am. Assn. Sex, Educators, Counselors and Therapists (exec. bd. 2004-05), TV Acad. of N.Y. (gov. 1987-91), Friars Club. Office Phone: 212-307-6771. Business E-Mail: drjudyaide@aol.com.

KURIN, RICHARD, museum program director; b. Bronx, NY, Nov. 27, 1950; m. Allyn Bland; children: Danielle, Jaclyn. BA, SUNY, 1972; MA in Anthropology, U. Chgo., 1974; cert. in Urdu lang., U. Calif., Berkeley, 1974; PhD in Anthropology, U. Chgo., 1981. Vis. asst. prof. dept. anthropology So. Ill. U., Carbondale, 1981-84, asst. prof., 1984-85; program coord., curator, cons. Festival of India, Aditi & Mela Exhbns., Smithsonian Instn., Washington, 1984-85; professorial lectr. Johns Hopkins U., Paul Nitze Sch. Adv. Internat. Studies, 1985-95; dep. dir. Ctr. for Folklife and Cultural Heritage Smithsonian Instn., Washington, 1985—87, acting dir., 1987-90, dir., 1990—, chair 150th Anniversary Program Com., 1993—, acting dir. Nat. Programs, 2004—, chair on demand com., 2006—, dir. nat. programs, 2006—. Collector Am. Mus. Natural History, Punjabi Indian village artifacts, 1970; vis. instr. cmty. devel. program So. Ill. U., Carbondale, 1979-81; program coord. Indian Puppetry Program, Smithsonian Instn., 1980; cons. anthropologist Harza Engring. Co., UNDP and World Bank, Indus Basin Master Planning Project, 1977; ethnic tours mgr. divsn. performing arts On-Tour India Program, Pakistan Program, Smithsonian Instn., 1976; adv. bd. Coun. Overseas Rsch. Ctrs., 1989; adj. prof. George Washington U., 1999; internat. jury UNESCO Masterpieces Intangible Cultural Heritage, 2000-04. Author: Aditi: The Living Arts of India, 1986, Reflections of a Culture Broker: A View From the Smithsonian, 1997, Smithsonian Folklife Festival: Culture Of, By, and For the People, 1998, Hope Diamond: The Legendary History of a Cursed Gem, 2006; (film) Aditi: The Living Arts of India, 1986; lead writer, organizer: Iowa Folklife: Our People, Traditions and Communities, 1996-97; advisor film: Jerusalem: Gateways to the City, 1995, Hosay: Muslim Transnationalism in Trinidad, 1994—, White House Overseers, 1994; edtl. advisor film Kathputli: An Indian Puppetry Tradition, 1986—; recs. Smithsonian Folkways Records, 1986—. Trustee Smithsonian Sec.'s Rep., Libr. of Congress, Am. Folklore Ctr., 1989—. Am. Pakistan Rsch. Orgn., 1989-92, U.S. Nat. Commn. for UNESCO, 2004—; mem. Fairfax County Citizen Assn. Edn. Com., 1991—; pres. Bailey's Elem. Sch. P.T.A., 1989-91. Fellow NDEA, Title VI, 1973, Fulbright-Hayes, HEW, 1976, Social Sci. Rsch. Coun., 1976, 83, Am. Inst. Pakistan Studies, 1983, Sec.'s Gold medal for exceptional svc. Smithsonian Instn., 1996; grantee Smithsonian Instn., 1979, 86, 89-90, 92, 95-96, NEH, 1982, 1991—, Nat. Endowment Arts, 1987; founders lecture, Harvard U. Peabody Mus., 2007. Fellow Soc. Applied Anthropology; mem. Am. Folklore Soc. (Benjamin Botkin lifetime achievement award 1999), Am. Ethnological Soc., Assn. Asian Studies, Am. Anthropol. Assn. Office: Ctr Folklife & Cultural Heritage Smithsonian Instn Washington DC 20560-0520 Business E-Mail: kurin@si.edu.

KURIT, NEIL, lawyer; b. Cleve., Aug. 31, 1940; s. Jay and Rose (Rainin) K.; m. Doris Tannenbaum, Aug. 9, 1964 (div.); m. Donna Chernin, Aug. 24, 1986. BS, Miami U., Oxford, Ohio, 1961; JD, Case Western Res. U., 1964. Bar: Ohio 1964. Prin. Kahn, Kleinman Co., L.P.A., Cleve., 1964—. Co-author Handbook for Attys. and Accts., Jewish Cmty. Fedn. Endowment Fund. Trustee, v.p. Montefiore Home, 1983-87; trustee Jewish Cmty. Fedn. Cleve., 1983-86, 90-95. Mem. ABA, Ohio State Bar Assn. Home: 2870 Courtland Blvd Cleveland OH 44122-2802 Office: Kahn Kleinman Co LPA 2600 Tower at Erieview Cleveland OH 44114 Office Phone: 216-736-3352. E-mail: nkurit@kahnkleinman.com.

KURITSYN, ALEXEY, physicist, researcher; s. Vladimir P. Kuritsyn and Klavdia V. Kuritsyna; m. Olga A. Tereshina, Aug. 29, 2003. BS, Nizhny Novgorod State U., Russia, 1993—97, MSc, 1997—2000; MA, Princeton U., NJ, 1998—2000, PhD, 1998—2005. Grad. rsch. asst. Princeton Plasma Physics Lab., 1998—2005; jr. rsch. scientist Inst. Applied Physics, Russian Acad. Scis., Nizhny Novgorod, 2000—01; rsch. assoc. U. Wis., Madison, 2005—. Mem.: Am. Phys. Soc. Achievements include research in magnetic reconnection reversed-field pinch, and advanced diagnostics in the field of plasma physics and fusion energy. Avocations: chess, travel, hiking, tennis.

KURITZKES, MICHAEL S., oil industry executive, lawyer; b. Tarrytown, NY, Oct. 30, 1960; BS in Indsl./Labor Rels., Cornell U., 1982; JD, U. Pa., 1985. Bar: NY 1987, Calif. 1994, Pa. 1998. Assoc. Kaye, Scholer, Fierman, Hays & Handler, NYC, 1985—87, Battle Fowler, NYC, 1987—91; corp. counsel Am. Ultramar Ltd., Greenwich, Conn., 1991—93; v.p., gen. counsel Ultramar, Long Beach, Calif., 1993—97; gen. atty. Sunoco, Inc., Phila., 1997—2000, v.p., gen. counsel, 2000—03, sr. v.p., gen. counsel, 2003—. Chmn. bd. overseers Annenberg Ctr., U. Pa. Office: Sunoco Inc 1735 Market St Ste LL Philadelphia PA 19103-7583*

KURLAENDER, MICHAL, education educator; d. Azriel and Ruth Kurlaender; m. Bryce Vinokurov, Sept. 6, 1998; 1 child, Noa Vinokurov. EdD, Harvard U., Cambridge, Mass., 2005. Rschr. Harvard U., 1997—2004; asst. prof. U. Calif., Davis, 2005—. Grantee Rsch. grant, NSF, 2004; Spencer Dissertation fellowship, Spencer Found., 2004. Mem.: Policy Analysis Calif. Edn. (assoc.), Warren Inst. (assoc.), New Vision (assoc.). Office: Univ Calif Sch Edn One Shields Ave Davis CA 95616 Office Fax: 530-752-5411. Personal E-mail: mkurlaender@gmail.com. Business E-Mail: mkurlaender@ucdavis.edu.

KURLAN, MARVIN ZEFT, retired surgeon; b. Wilkes-Barre, Pa., Feb. 20, 1934; s. Ephraigm Joseph and Fannye Lillian Kurlancheek; m. Eleanor Frank, June 21, 1964; 1 child, Todd. BA, Wilkes Coll., 1957; MS, U. Ill., 1958; MD, SUNY, Buffalo, 1964. Diplomate Nat. Bd. Med. Examiners, Am. Bd. Surgery. Intern then resident in surgery Millard Fillmore Hosp., Buffalo, 1964-69, dir. trauma svcs., 1974-82, sr. attending surgeon, 1984-95; surgeon emeritus, 1995—; plant surgeon Bethlehem Steel Corp., Pa., 1969-74; med. dir. Bros. of Mercy Health Facilities, Clarence, NY, 1974-82; clin. instr. surgery emeritus SUNY Sch. Medicine and Biomed. Scis., Buffalo, 1974—. Chmn. James Platt White Soc., 1992-94, dean's adv. coun., 1995-97; assoc. examiner Am. Bd. Surgery, Phila., 1987-95; cons. in surgery Walter Reed Army Med. Ctr., Washington. Contbr. articles to profl. jours. Vol. Empire State Games, Buffalo, 1986; mem. Jack Kemp Forum, Buffalo, 1985-91; bd. dirs. Jewish Fedn. Allentown, Pa., 1972-74. Served AUS (res.) to lt. col. Med. Corps, 1965-91, active duty operation Desert Shield and Desert Storm. Decorated Army Svc. medal with Oak Leaf Cluster, Army Achievement medal; named one of Top One Hundred Health Profls., Internat. Biographical Ctr., Cambridge, Eng., 2005, Am. Top Surgeons, Consumers Rsch. Coun. Am., 2007. Fellow Am. Coll. Gastroenterology, Am. Trauma Soc. (founder), NY Acad. Scis., James Gibson Anatomical Hon. Soc.; mem. ACS (life fellow leadership soc.), Assn. Mil. Surgeons US, Hastings on Hudson Bioethics Ctr., Buffalo Surg. Soc. (sec. 1986-88, v.p. 1988-89, pres. 1989-90), SUNY at Buffalo Found. (pres.'s assoc.), Grand Coun. World Parliament, Confedn. Chivalry, Knight of Humanity, Order White Cross Internat. (dist. comdr. NY, US), Res. Officers Assn. (life), Chevalier Grand Cross, Ordre Soverain et Militaire de Milice du St. Sepulchre, Am. Legion, Phi Lambda Kappa (nat. pres. 1993), Sci. Progress Rsch. Club (Buffalo, v.p. 1983-84), Equality Club (dir. 2006—), Masons, Shriners, James Gibson Anatomical Honor Soc., Nu Sigma Nu, Am. Legion. Republican. Jewish. Avocations: travel, genealogy. Home and Office: 413 Dan Troy Dr Buffalo NY 14221-3558 Business E-Mail: mkurlaw@roadrunner.com.

KURLAN, ROGER, neurologist, educator; m. Cathy Morris; children: Melissa, Matthew. BA, U. Rochester, 1974; MD, Wash. U., St. Louis, 1974—78. Cert. neurologist Am. Bd. Psychiatry and Neurology, 1984. Intern, resident in medicine Jewish Hosp., St. Louis, 1978—80; resident in neurology Sch. Medicine U. Rochester, NY, 1980—83, fellow in movement disorders and clin. neuropharmacology Sch. Medicine, 1983—84, 1984—88, assoc prof., neurology Sch. Medicine, 1988—92, prof., neurology Sch. Medicine, 1992—. Mem.: Movement Disorder Soc., Am. Acad. Neurology, Am. Neuropsychiatric Assn., Am. Neurol. Assn., Phi Beta Kappa. Office: Univ Rochester Med Ctr 1351 Mt Hope Ave Ste 100 Rochester NY 14620 Home Phone: 585-347-4555; Office Phone: 585-275-7937. Office Fax: 585-473-4678. Business E-Mail: roger_kurlan@urmc.rochester.edu.

KURLAND, HAROLD ARTHUR, lawyer; b. NYC, Jan. 20, 1952; s. Jordan Emil and Anita (Siegel) K.; m. Christine Rogers, June 28, 1975; children: Thomas Philip, Andrew Rogers. AB, Dartmouth Coll., 1973; JD, Cornell U., 1976. Bar: N.Y. 1977, D.C. 1977, U.S. Dist. Ct. (we. dist.) N.Y. 1977, U.S. Dist. Ct. (no. dist.) N.Y. 1983, U.S. Dist. Ct. (no. dist.) Tex. 1981, U.S. Ct. Appeals (2d cir.) 1980, U.S. Dist. Ct. (D.C. dist.) 1986, U.S. Ct. Appeals (D.C. cir.) 1986, U.S Ct. Appeals (3d cir.) 1988, U.S. Dist. Ct. (mid. dist.) Pa. 1988, U.S. Dist. Ct. (ea. and so. dists.) N.Y. 1991, U.S. Supreme Ct. 1980. Assoc. Nixon, Hargrave, Devans & Doyle LLP (now Nixon Peabody LLP), Rochester, NY, 1976-84, ptnr., 1985-2000; founding ptnr. Ward Norris Heller & Reidy LLP, Rochester, 2000—. Mediator, arbitrator Am. Arbitration Assn.; mem. adv. com. on civil practice N.Y. Office Ct. Adminstrn. Past chmn. bd. dirs. Rochester Philharm. Orch.; bd. dirs. Vol. Legal Svcs. Project. Fellow Am. Coll. Trial Lawyers; mem. ABA, Am. Bar Found., Am. Bd. Trial Advs. (assoc.), N.Y. State Bar Assn., D.C. Bar Assn., Monroe County Bar Assn. (co-chair litigation sect., trustee, past chair judicary com., cts. com., fed. ct. com.), Rochester Inn of Ct. (past. pres., master). Democrat. Home: 154 Council Rock Ave Rochester NY 14610-3335 Office: Ward Norris Heller & Reidy LLP 300 State St Rochester NY 14614 Office Phone: 585-454-0700. Business E-Mail: hak@wnhr.com.

KURLANDER, NEALE, accountant, law educator; b. Bklyn., Jan. 1, 1924; s. Sol and Eleanor Kurlander; m. Honey Wachtel, June 25, 1949; children: Harold M., Susan L. BS, Long Island U., 1948; JD, N.Y. Law Sch., NYC, 1951; MBA, Adelphi U., 1967. Bar: N.Y. 1952; CPA, N.Y. V.p., chief fin. officer Profit Motivation Svcs., Inc., Garden City, N.Y., 1967-71; cons.-reviewer Ernst & Ernst, Garden City, 1967-72; lectr. Practicing Law Inst., NYC, 1974; chmn. dept. acctng and law Adelphi U., Garden City, 1964-82; cons. Regent's External Degree, Albany, N.Y., 1974-87; pvt. practice law Old Westbury, N.Y., 1952—; pvt. practice acct., CPA, 1960—; prof. acctg. and law Adelphi U., Garden City, 1962—. Profl. developer Harris, Kerr, Forster & Co., N.Y.C., 1969-71; treas. Fin. Execs. Inst., Long Island, N.Y., 1974-76, chmn. acad. rels., 1975—, bd. dirs. 1975—; faculty Found. for Acctg. Edn., 1975—, bd. trustees, 1976-79. Author: Basic Accounting, 1962, Auditing, Vol. I and II, 1978; contbr. articles to profl. jours. Cmdr. post 6081 VFW, Bklyn., 1953-54; mem. Bd. Elections, Nassau County, N.Y., 1964-70, Citizens' Adv. Com. N.Y. State Dept. Taxation, Albany, 1975-87, Bd. Appeals, Old Westbury, 1988-93; legis. adv. coun. N.Y. State Assembly 15th Dist., 1991-93. Recipient cert. Delta Mu Delta, 1982, Dr. Emanuel Saxe Outstanding CPA in Edn. award N.Y. State Soc. Cert. Pub. Accts., 2000; named Outstanding Acctg. Educator, Found. for Acctg. Edn., N.Y., 1982, Acct. of Yr. Acctg. Soc., 1992. Mem. AICPA, N.Y. State Soc. CPA's (Dr. Emanuel Saxe Outstanding CPA in Edn. award 2000), Am. Acctg. Assn., Nassau County Bar Assn., N.Y. State Assembly 15th Dist. (legis. adv. coun.). Avocations: reading, woodworking, travel, walking, swimming. Home: 6185 Wooded Run Dr Columbia MD 21044 E-mail: nkurlander@aol.com.

KURLINSKI, JOHN PARKER, physician; b. Buchanon, W.Va., Jan. 17, 1948; s. John Peter and Jean (Holloway) K.; m. Claire Sawyer, June 12, 1971; children: Joshua John, Ryan Edward, Seth Parker. AB cum laude, Williams Coll., 1970; MD, Johns Hopkins Sch. Medicine, 1974. Intern, then resident Johns Hopkins Hosp., Balt., 1974-77; fellowship neonatal/perinatal medicine U. Calif., San Diego, 1977-79; chief resident pediatrician Johns Hopkins Hosp., 1979-80; pediatrician, co-dir. neonatology S.W. Regional Neonatal Ctr. at Sunrise Hosp. and Med. Ctr., Las Vegas, 1980-93; vice chief pediat. Sunrise Children's Hosp., Las Vegas, 1983-90, vice chief of staff, 1989-90, chief of staff, 1990-95, dir. NICU, 1994—2002; clin. assoc. prof. pediatrics U. Nev. Sch. Medicine, Reno, 1994—. Bd. dirs. S.W. Regional Neonatal Ctr. Edn. Found.; chmn. bd. dirs. Sunrise Children's Hosp. Found.; mem. Med.-Legal Screening Panel, Nev., 1986—; many hosp. coms., 1980—. Bd. dirs. So Nev. chpt. March of Dimes, Las. Vegas, 1984—. Mem. AMA, Am. Acad. Pediatrics (v.p. Nev. chpt. 1987-90, pres. 1990-93, coun. mem. dist. VIII sect. on perinatal pediatrics), Clark County Med. Soc., Las Vegas Pediatric Soc. (founding), Phi Beta Kappa. Avocations: rugby, skiing, hiking, camping. Home: 3322 Beam Dr Las Vegas NV 89139-5902 Office: Sunrise Childrens Hosp 3186 S Maryland Pky Las Vegas NV 89109-2317 Personal E-mail: kurli@cox.net.

KURMAN, JUTA, music educator; b. Wändra, Parnu, Estonia, Nov. 7, 1912; d. August and Maria (Reier) Tomberg; m. Alexander Pooman, Sept. 17, 1938 (dec. 1938); m. Hugo Kurman, Jan. 18, 1940 (dec. 1986); children: Jaan (dec. 1995), Juri-George (dec. 1994). Tchrs. Lic., Tchrs. Sem., Estonia, 1934; Artist Dipl., State Conservatory of Music (now Acad. Music), Estonia, 1940, NY Coll. of Music, 1952. Tchr. Tallinn (Estonia) Pub. Schs., 1934-38; performing artist concerts, state radio, and theater Estonia, 1932-40; TV voice soloist Maj. Bowes Original Amateur Hour,

Radio City, NY, 1949-50; with Claire Mann Show, Channel 5, NYC, 1952; pres. Estonian Music Ctr., NYC, 1973—. Club and ch. soloist; lectr in field; music critic Free Estonian Word, 1948—, Baltic Papers; lector Estonian Lang. Course, NYC, 1993—. Co-editor: Haapsalu Shawl, 1972, Kompiling Mart Saar VocalAlbum, 1965, Kompiling Kaljo Raid Estonian Volksongs Album, 1991; contbr. articles to profl. jurs. Sustaining mem. Rep. Nat. Com., 1990—; mem. Ronald Reagan Presdl. Found., 1987—; mem. Pres. Bush Task Force; presdl. coun. Rep. Party Decorated White Star V Orden, Estonian Republic; named Laureate of Estonian Letters and Scis. Found.; N.Y. Coll. Music grantee, 1948. Mem. Estonian Music Sorority (pres. 1951-63), Estonian Women's Club of N.Y. (pres.), Estonian Ednl. Soc. (hon. mem. elders coun.), Federated Estonian Women's Clubs Estonian Republic (hon.), World Fedn. Estonian Women's Clubs in Exile (West) (founding pres. 1966—), Baltic-Am. Women's Coun. (past pres.). Republican. Lutheran. Avocations: music, poetry, writing. Home: 68-50 Juno St Forest Hills NY 11375-5728 Office: Estonian Music Ctr 243 E 34th St New York NY 10016-4852

KURN, NEAL, lawyer; b. Springfield, Mass., July 19, 1934; s. Samuel and Jane Etta (Freeman) K.; m. Barbara Agron, June 9, 1957; children: Jeffrey Howard, Sharon Ilene Marcus-Kurn, Jennifer Rose Endsley. BSBA with high honors, U. Ariz., 1956, JD with honors, 1963. Bar: Ariz. 1963; cert. specialist tax and estate and trust law, Ariz.; CPA, Ariz. Staff mem. Price Waterhouse & Co., San Francisco, L.A. and Phoenix, 1956, 58-60; assoc., ptnr. Moore, Romley, Kaplan, Robbins & Green, Phoenix, 1963-71; ptnr. Powers, Ehrenreich, Boutell & Kurn, Phoenix, 1971-82; ptnr., also bd. dirs. Fennemore Craig, Phoenix, 1982—. Adj. prof. law Ariz. State U., 1980-82. Editor-in-chief Ariz. Law Rev., 1962-63. Past chmn. tax adv. commn. Ariz. State Bd. Legal Specialization; bd. dirs. Ariz. Cmty. Found., 1986—, chmn. 1994-96; bd. dirs. Ariz. Bar Found., 1983-89, chmn., 1988; bd. dirs. Jewish Fedn. Greater Phoenix, pres., 1977-79; bd. dirs. U. Ariz. Found., 1998-2004; v.p. coun. Jewish Fedn., 1988-90; chmn. Jewish Cmty. Found. Greater Phoenix, 1998-2001; bd. dirs. Trust for Jewish Philanthropy, 2000-2003; chmn. adv. bd. Leave a Legacy, State of Ariz., 2001-2004. With U.S. Army, 1956-58; bd. dirs. Vanbner Alzheimers Inst. Found. Fellow Am. Coll. Tax Counsel, Am. Bar Found., Am. Coll. Trust and Estate Counsel; mem. ABA, State Bar Ariz. (past chmn. taxation sect., bd. govs. 1991-93), Maricopa County Bar Assn., Phi Kappa Phi, Beta Gamma Sigma. Democrat. Jewish. Office: Fennemore Craig 3003 N Central Ave Ste 2600 Phoenix AZ 85012-2913 Office Phone: 602-916-5485. Business E-Mail: nkurn@fclaw.com.

KURNICK, NATHANIEL BERTRAND, retired oncologist, hematologist; b. Bklyn., Nov. 8, 1917; s. Jacob and Celia (Levine) K.; m. Dorothy Manheimer, Oct. 4, 1940 (dec. Dec. 1985); children: John E., Katherine(dec.) , James T.; m. Sally Ann Kreeger, June 23, 1989. BA, Harvard U., 1936, MD, 1940. Diplomate Am. Bd. Internal Medicine, Am. Bd. Med. Oncology, Am. Bd. Hematology, Am. Bd. Med. Examiners. Intern Mt. Sinai Hosp., NYC, 1941-42, chief resident internal medicine, 1946; asst. prof. medicine Tulane U. Med. Sch., New Orleans, 1949-54; chief hematology svc. VA Hosp., Long Beach, Calif., 1954-59, cons., 1959—; assoc. clin. prof. medicine U. Calif., LA, 1954-64, clin. prof. medicine Irvine, 1964-99; pvt. practice Long Beach, 1959-83; dir. Bixby Hematology-Oncology Lab. Long Beach Cmty. Med. Ctr., 1982—99. Chmn. cancer activities, 1968—90; chmn. dept. medicine, 1966—68; chmn. dept. med. oncology and hematology, 1982—87; pres. Long Beach Soc. Internal Medicine, 1971; chmn. Franklin Bank of Calif., Orange, Calif., 1988—2004. Contbr. over 150 articles to jours. in field. Trustee Garden Grove, Calif. Union High Sch.Dist., 1960-64. Capt. U.S. Army Med. Corps., 1942—46, Pacific Ocean area. Am. Cancer Soc./NRC fellow, 1946-47, Rockefeller Inst., 1946-47, Nobel Inst., 1947-49; NIH/Am. Cancer Soc. grantee, 1949-1972; Henry Hunter Workman rsch. fellow Harvard Med. Sch./Mass. Gen. Hosp., 1940-41. Fellow ACP; mem. Intern. Soc. Exptl. Hematology, Am. Soc. Hematology, Western Soc. Clin. Rsch., Cen. Soc. Clin. Rsch., Sigma Xi (fellow 1951). Democrat. Jewish. Avocations: sailing, skiing, travel. Business E-Mail: nbkurnick@post.harvard.edu.

KURNICK, ROBERT H., JR., automotive executive, lawyer; b. 1961; BA, Mich. State U.; JD, U. Notre Dame. Ptnr. Honigman Miller Schwartz and Cohn, Detroit, 1986—95; asst. gen. counsel Penske Corp., 1995—99; sr. v.p., gen. counsel Penske Auto Ctrs., Inc., 1995—2001, Penske Motorsports, Inc., 1996—99; exec. v.p., gen. counsel United Auto Group, Inc., 2000—; pres. Penske Corp., 2002—.*

KURNOW, ERNEST, statistician, educator; b. Bklyn., Oct. 21, 1912; s. Harry and Sarah Malka (Shagaloff) K.; m. Joyce Litzky, Oct. 6, 1938; children: Ruth (Mrs. Jeffrey Jarrett), Susan Carol (Mrs. Leonard Weistrop), Alice Rose (Mrs. Claude Morin). BS cum laude, CCNY, 1932, MS in Edn, 1933; PhD, NYU, 1951. Tchr. N.Y.C. Bd. Edn., 1935-40, statistician, 1941-48; mathematician ordnance div. War Dept., 1940-41; mem. faculty NYU, 1948—, prof. econs., 1960-63, prof. bus. stats., chmn. dept., 1963-86, prof. emeritus bus. stats., adj. prof. bus. stats., 1986—, chmn. dept., 1963-76; chmn. doctoral program N.Y. U., 1976-85, dir. Careers in Bus. program, 1979-88. Cons. N.Y. State Tax Structure Study Commn., 1959-64, Mayor N.Y.C. Com. Mgmt. Survey, 1950-51, Turkish Ministry Finance, 1955-56; cons. temporary commn. Revision N.Y. State Constn., 1958; temporary commn. fiscal affairs N.Y. State Govt., 1953-54; cons. Tri-State Transp. Commn., 1964-66, 73-75; participant Brazilian capital markets program, 1968; study dir. Govs.' Spl. Commn. on Financing Mass Transp., 1970-71; cons. Commn. on Charter Revision, City of N.Y., 1973-74, Temporary Commn. on City Finances, 1975-76 Author: The Turkish Budgetary Process, 1956, Statistics for Business Decisions, 1959, Theory and Measurement of Land Rent, 1961, also articles. Recipient Gt. Tchr. award NYU Alumni Assn., 1974; named Tchr. of Yr., 1999-2000; Fulbright grantee to Greece, 1966-67; Kurnow Classroom established in his honor, NYU, 1993; Ernest Kurnow doctoral fellowship established in his honor, 2003. Fellow Am. Statis. Assn.; mem. Internat. Statis. Inst. (elected), Am. Econ. Assn., Econometric Soc., Inst. Mgmt. Scis., Nat. Tax Assn., Am. Soc. Quality Control, Sphinx, Beta Gamma Sigma, Sigma Eta Phi, Delta Pi Sigma, Alpha Phi Sigma, Delta Sigma Pi. Jewish. Home: 3 Washington Square Vlg Apt 17I New York NY 10012-1810 Office: New York Univ Dept Stats Washington Sq N New York NY 10003-6635 Business E-Mail: ekurnow@stern.nyu.edu.

KUROCHKINA, NATALYA ALEXANDROVNA, biophysicist; b. Verkhny Ufaley, USSR, Dec. 6, 1957; came to US, 1991; d. Tatyana Ivanovna Lezhneva; m. Boris Konstantinovich Kurochkin; 1 child, Andrei Borisovich Kurochkin. MS in Computer Sci., Moscow Inst. Radio, 1984; PhD in Physics-Math., Russian Acad. Sci., Puschino, 1990. Leading engr. Inst. Protein Rsch. Russian Acad. Sci., Puschino, 1984-91; vis. fellow Nat. Cancer Inst./NIH, Bethesda, Md., 1991-96; rsch. scientist Applied Thermodynamics, Hunt Valley, Md., 1996-98; dir. Sch. Theoretical Modeling, Chevy Chase, Md., 1999—. Contbr. articles to profl. jours. Mem. AAAS, Biophysical Soc. Home and Office: PO Box 15676 Chevy Chase MD 20825-5676 E-mail: info@schtm.org.

KURODA, YASUMASA, political science professor, researcher; b. Tokyo, Apr. 28, 1931; arrived in U.S., 1951; s. Shohei and Take (Ishii) Kuroda; m. Alice Kassis, Mar. 21, 1961 (div. Mar. 1995); children: Kamilla, Kamil; m. Miyoko Otaguro, Aug. 14, 1998. Student, Waseda U., 1951; BA, U. Oreg., 1956, MA, 1958, PhD, 1962. From instr. to asst. prof. polit. sci. Mont. State U., Bozeman, 1960-64; asst. prof. polit. sci. U. So. Calif., LA, 1964-66; assoc. program officer advanced projects East-West Ctr., Honolulu, 1967-69; assoc. prof. U. Hawaii-Manoa, Honolulu, 1969—71, prof. polit. sci., 1971—2002, prof. emeritus, 2002—; lectr. Japan-Am. Inst. Mgmt. Sci., Honolulu, 1973-90; pres. Election Svcs. Hawaii, Inc., 1996—2001; exch. rschr. Waseda U., Tokyo, 2002—03; rsch. assoc. Inst. for Japanese Culture and Classics, Kokugakuin U., 2004—07. V.p. Minerva Rsch., Inc., Honolulu, 1981-96. Author: Reed Town, Japan, 1974, Chiho Toshi no Kenryokukozo, 1976, (with others) Palestinians Without Palestine, 1978; co-editor: Studies in Political Socialization in the Arab States, 1987, Japan in a New World Order: Contributing to the Arab-Israeli Peace Process, 1994, Japanese Culture in Comparative Perspective, 1997, The Core of Japanese Democracy: Latent Interparty Relations Politics, 2005. Bd. of govs. Japanese Cultural Ctr. Hawaii, Honolulu, 1988-2000, program com., 1988-2000. Recipient Disting. Vis. Lectr. award SUNY, 1994; Rockefeller Found. grantee, 1963-64, Social Sci. Rsch. Coun. grantee, 1966-67, Toyota Found. grantee, 1984-87, 87-90; vis. rsch. fellow Harry S. Truman Rsch. Inst. of the Advancement of Peace, Hebrew U., 1992, Inst. Legal Studies, Kansai U., 1994, Wadeda U. Inst. Asia-Pacific Studies, 2003-04, Kokugakuin U. Inst. for Japanese Culture and Classics, 2004—. Mem. Am. Polit. Sci. Assn., Internat. Polit. Sci. Assn., Internat. Assn. Mid. Ea. States (coll. of fellows 1986—). Democrat. Avocation: stamp collecting/philately. Business E-Mail: ykuroda@hawaii.edu.

KUROGHLIAN, GERALD E., English educator; b. Bridgeport, Conn., Apr. 15, 1945; s. Stephen and Eva Kuroghlian; m. Ellen Green Kuroghlian, Aug. 12, 1978. BA in English, U. Va., Charlottesville, 1967; MA in Am. Studies, Fairfield U., Conn., 1981; PhD in Curriculum, U. Ill., Urbana, 1987. Cert. tchr. secondary English Conn., 1967. Tchr. Staples HS, Westport, Conn., 1967—83, 1987—, U. Ill., Urbana, 1983—87. Cons. ACT, Iowa City, 1999—2001, 2007. Author: Course Taking in Secondary Schools, 1987. Treas. Westport Edn. Assn., 1995—2005; mem. HS Bldg. Com., Fairfield, 2005—. Finalist Tchr. of Yr., State of Conn., Hartford, 2005; named, Westport Bd. Edn., 2005, Citizen of Yr., Sportsmen of Westport, 2006; recipient Thomas Swain award, NE Coun. Tchrs. English, Nashua, NH, 2004. Mem.: Nat. Coun. Tchrs. English (New Eng. rep. SLATE bd. 2005—07, chair study com. on affiliates 1999—2003, chair resolutions com. 2000—04). Avocations: theater, music, art. Home: 246 Old Spring Rd Fairfield CT 06824 Office: Staples HS 70 North Ave Westport CT 06880

KUROGI, YASUHISA, chemist; b. Kawasaki, Japan, Oct. 8, 1964; s. Hisashi Kurogi, Junko Kurogi; m. Satoko Kurogi; children: Fumika, Takafumi. PhD, Hiroshima U., 1992. Med. chemist Otsuka Pharm. Factory, Inc., Naruto, Tokushima, Japan, 1992—2000, mgr., 2001—02, Otsuka Pharm. Co. Ltd., Tokushima, Japan, 2002—03; dir. Cambridge Isotope Labs. Inc., Andover, Mass., 2003—. Vis. lectr. Tohoku U., Sendai, Miyagi, Japan, 2000. Editor: SAR News, 2001—, Letters in Drug Design and Discovery, 2004—. Com. mem. Structure-Activity Relationship Soc. Japan, Tokyo, 2001—; chief sec. MSI Japan User Group, Urayasu, Chiba, Japan, 1999—2001; com. mem. EMIL project, Osaka, Japan, 1994—2002; co-organizer Third Australia-Japan Joint Symposium Drug Design, Naruto, Tokushima, Japan, 1998. Mem.: Pharm. Soc. Japan (organizer bioinformatics symposium 1999, Lecture award 1998). Avocation: travel. Office: Cambridge Isotope Laboratories Inc 50 Frontage Rd Andover MA 01810-5413 Personal E-mail: yasukisakurogi@yahoo.com. Business E-Mail: kurogi@isotope.com.

KURRASS, LISA, real estate company executive; Cert. Internat. Property Specialist. Pres. Briarglen Property Owner Assn., 2001—06. Mem.: Houston Assn. Realtors, Tex. Assn. Realtors (bd. dirs.), Nat. Assn. Realtors (internat. ops. com. 1996—98), Internat. Real Estate Fedn. (bd. dirs. 1995—2003, pres. leisure com. 1998—2004, pres. 2004). Office: Real Estate Connectiona International PO Box 58806 Houston TX 77258 Office Phone: 281-338-8088. Office Fax: 281-338-8086. E-mail: lkurrass@houston.rr.com.*

KURRILD-KLITGAARD, PETER, political science professor; b. Odense, Denmark, Oct. 11, 1966; s. Jørgen Klitgaard and Hanne Karla Elisabeth Kurrild; m. Camilla Cathrine Collet, 2000. BA, MSc, U. Copenhagen, 1991, PhD, 1997; MA, Columbia U., 1993. Sec. gen. Danish Young Conservatives, Copenhagen, 1985—86; journalist Finanstidende, Copenhagen, 1988—90, Børsinformation Telecom, Copenhagen, 1991—92; asst. rsch. prof., rsch. fellow U. Copenhagen, 1992—98; asst. prof. U. Aarhus, Denmark, 1998—2000; polit. commentator Berlingske Tidende, Copenhagen, 1999; prof. U. So. Denmark, Odense, 2000—06, U. Copenhagen, 2006—. Vis. rsch. fellow George Mason U., Fairfax, Va., 1993—94; vis. scholar Columbia U., NYC, 2001—02; bd. dirs. Ctr. for Polit. Studies, Copenhagen, 2004—05, Mont Pelerin Soc. Author: (books) Adam Smith, Rational Choice, Collective Action & The Paradox of Rebellion, 1997, Individ, Stat & Marked, 2005; editor: Jour. Pub. Choice, 2005. Chmn. Conservative Students, Copenhagen, 1986—88. Recipient Medal of Merit, Order of Malta, 2004; Hon. fellow, Young Conservatives, 1986, Fulbright scholar, Fulbright Commn., 1992, Rsch. grantee, Inst. Humane Studies, 1993, Danish Social Sci. Rsch. Coun., 2001, 2003. Fellow: Phila. Soc., Mont Pelerin Soc.; mem.: Nordic Polit. Sci. Assn. (sec. 2005), Danish Polit. Sci. Assn (pres. 2002—05), Columbia Club, City U. Club. Avocations: hunting, tennis, shooting, genealogy. Office: U Copenhagen Polit Sci Oster Farimagsgade 5 PO Box 2099 DK 1014 Copenhagen Denmark Office Phone: 45 2013 5606, 45 35 32 33 66. Personal E-mail: kurrild@ifs.ku.dk.

KURRUS, THOMAS WILLIAM, lawyer; b. Carmel, NY, May 13, 1947; s. Theo Hornsby and Jean Ellen (Cumming) K. BS magna cum laude, U. Fla., 1975, JD, 1979. Bar: Fla. 1980, U.S. Dist. Ct. (no. dist.) Fla. 1980, U.S. Ct. Appeals (5th cir.) 1980, U.S. Dist. Ct. (mid. dist.) Fla. 1981, U.S. Ct. Appeals (11th cir.) 1981, U.S. Ct. Appeals (4th cir.) 1984, U.S. Supreme Ct. 1984. Assoc. Law Firm Larry G. Turner, Gainesville, Fla., 1981-83; ptnr. Turner, Kurrus & Griscti, Gainesville, 1983-88; prin. Law Offices of Thomas W. Kurrus, Gainesville, 1988—. Mem. Fla. Supreme Ct. commn. on jury instructions, 1995. Contbr. articles to profl. jours. Mem. ACLU (Gainesville chpt. legal panel chmn. 1999), Nat. Assn. Criminal Defense Lawyers (Fla. chpt. bd. dirs., chmn. continuing legal edn. com., local legis. liaison, pres. award 1993, appreciation award 1998), Fla. Assn. Criminal Def. Lawyers (pres. 2004). Avocations: fishing, art, horses. Office: PO Box 838 Gainesville FL 32602-0838 Office Phone: 352-377-2332. Personal E-mail: tomkurrus@earthlink.net.

KURSH, GAIL, lawyer; b. NYC, Mar. 12, 1953; d. Harry and Marilyn Kursh; m. Zev Primor, June 12, 1983; children: Talia Sarah Primor, Maya Rachel Primor. JD, Am. U., Washington, 1979. Bar: Washington 1979, NY 1986. Trial atty., antitrust divsn US Dept. Justice Antitrust Divsn., Washington, 1979—88, asst. chief, professions and intellectual property sect., 1989—93, chief, health care task force, 1994—2002, dep. chief, legal policy sect., and spl. counsel fed.-state coop., 2002—. Sr. exec. svc. US Dept. Justice, Washington, 1994—. Recipient Distinction award, US Dept. Justice, 1991, Asst. Atty. Gen. and Spl. Achievement awards, 1986, 1990, 1992, 1994. Avocations: travel, walking, dance. Office: US Dept Justice 950 Pennsylvania Ave NW Washington DC 20530 Home Phone: 202-362-7693; Office Phone: 202-307-5799.

KURT, JOHNNY THOMAS, music educator; s. Thomas James Kurt and Sandra Sue Abel-Kurt. MusB, U. Nebr., Omaha, 1991; Med in Ednl. Adminstrn., U. Nebr., Lincoln, 1995; Endorsement in Gifted/Talented Edn., U. Iowa, 2002. Cert. tchr., adminstr. Iowa, Nebr., jazz edn. Internat. Assn. Jazz Educators, jazz pedogogy Baker U. and Internat. Assn. Jazz Educators, 2004. Grad. tchg. asst. Baylor U., Waco, Tex., 1991; substitute tchr. Omaha Pub. Sch. Dist., 1992—95; instrumental music instr. Lewis Ctrl. Pub. Sch. Dist., Council Bluffs, Iowa, 1995—; leadership team Lewis Ctrl. Mid. Sch., Council Bluffs, Iowa, 2006—. Music adjudicator Nebr. Sch. Activities Assn., 2000—; instr. in gifted/talented summer programs Creighton U., Omaha, 2001—; 2d oboe Orch. Omaha, 2005—. Performer saxophone and piccolo: jazz band Arturo Sandoval Concert at Lewis Ctrl. H.S., performer saxophone: Jazz Band featuring Maynard Ferguson; contbr. articles to profl. publs., procs. in field. (Publ., 1991). Vol. Nebr. Humane Soc., Omaha, 1998; mem. Lewis Ctrl. Mid. Sch. Leadership Team, 2006—. Nominee Disney Tchr. award, 2000, All Tchr. Team, USA Today, 2001, Tchr. of Yr. award, Lewis Ctrl. Mid. Sch.; named one of Outstanding Young Ams., 1992, 1996—98; recipient Above and Beyond Tchr. award, Lewis Ctrl. Mid. Sch., 2006, Ahno and Beyond Tchr. award, Lewis Ctrl. Mid. Sch., 2006; Belin-Blank Gifted/Talented Educator fellowship, U. Iowa, 2000—01. Mem.: NEA, Nebr. Sch. Activities Assn. Music (adjudicator 2000—), Iowa Bandmasters Assn. (R&D state bd. 1997—99), Iowa H.S. Music Assn. (adjudicator 1998—), Omicron Delta Kappa, Phi Delta Kappa. Office: Lewis Ctrl Sch Dist 1600 East South Omaha Bridge Rd Council Bluffs IA 51503 Business E-Mail: jkurt@lewiscentral.k12.ia.us.

KURTH, DONALD JAMES, JR., medical educator, mayor; b. Newport, RI, Apr. 26, 1949; s. Donald James and Isabelle Virginia (Statchen) Kurth; m. Dee Frances Matreyck-Kurth. BA, Columbia U., NYC, 1975, MD, 1979. Chief addiction medicine Loma Linda U., Behavioral Med. Ctr., Redlands, Calif., 1997—; assoc. prof. Loma Linda U., Calif., 1997—; mayor City of Rancho Cucamonga, Calif., 2006—. Recipient Brainard award, Columbia U., 1975. Fellow: Am. Soc. Addiction Medicine (treas. 2005—07).

KURTH, LIESELOTTE, foreign language educator; b. Wuppertal, Germany; came to U.S., 1951; s. Otto and Emmi (Klammer) Voigt. MA, Johns Hopkins U., 1960, PhD, 1963. Asst. prof. German Johns Hopkins U., Balt., 1964-68, assoc. prof., 1968-73, prof., 1973-89, chmn. dept., 1980-87, prof. emerita, 1989—. Author: Die Zweite Wirklichkeit, 1969, Perspectives and Points of View, 1974, Continued Existence, Reincarnation, and the Power of Sympathy in Classical Weimar, 1999; contbr. articles top profl. jours. and yearbooks; editor collections and edits. Gilman fellow, 1958-62; Gail fellow, 1962-63 Mem. MLA (hon.; mem. exec. com. South Atlantic br. 1982-84, pres. br. 1985-86), Lessing Soc., Goethe Soc. N.Am., Phi Beta Kappa. Home: 800 Southerly Rd Apt 914 Towson MD 21286-8409 Office: Johns Hopkins U Dept German 34th and Charles Sts Baltimore MD 21218 Personal E-mail: lkurth@verizon.net.

KURTH, RONALD JAMES, retired academic administrator, military officer; b. Madison, Wis., July 1, 1931; s. Peter James and Celia (Kuehn) K.; m. Esther Charlene Schaefer, Dec. 21, 1954; children: Steven, Audrey, John, Douglas. BS, U.S. Naval Acad., 1954; MPA, Harvard U., 1961, PhD, 1970. Commd. ensign U.S. Navy, 1954, advanced through grades to rear adm., 1981; U.S. naval attache Moscow, 1975-77; comdg. officer NAS, Memphis at Millington, Tenn., 1977-79; mil. fellow Council Fgn. Relations, NYC, 1979-80; exec. asst. to dep. chief naval ops. Dept. Navy, Washington, 1980-81, dir. Pol-Mil Policy and Current Plans, 1981-83, dir. Long Range Planning Group, 1983-84; U.S. def. attache Moscow, 1985-87; pres. U.S. Naval War Coll., Newport, RI, 1987-90, Murray (Ky.) State U., 1990-94; dean acad. affairs Air War Coll., Maxwell AFB, Ala., 1994-98; pres. St. John's Northwestern Mil. Acad., Delafield, Wis., 1998—2004, pres. emeritus, 2004—. Teaching fellow Harvard U., Cambridge, Mass., 1969-70. Author: The Politics of Technological Innovation in the Navy, 1970. Mem. nat. adv. bd. Boy Scouts Am. Decorated Def. D.S.M., Navy D.S.M., Legion of Merit with 2 gold stars, Meritorious Svc. medal with gold star. Mem. U.S. Naval Inst. (life), Naval War Coll. Found. (life), U.S. Naval Acad. Alumni, Harvard U. Alumni, Rotary. Episcopalian. Home: 8106 Ainsworth Ave Springfield VA 22152 Personal E-mail: randckurth@verizon.net. *Among those who know you, ponder whose respect you have and whose you do not. It will provide you with a measure of your worth.*

KURTZ, ALFRED BERNARD, radiologist; b. Albany, NY, May 1, 1944; s. Leonard and Esther Kurtz; m. Barbara Ellen, July 3, 1973; children: Dana, Liza, Amy. BA, NYU, 1966; MD, Stanford U., 1972. Diplomate Am. Bd. Radiology. Internal medicine intern Montefiore Hosp. and Med. Ctr., Bronx, N.Y., 1972-73, resident in internal medicine, 1973-74, resident in diagnostic radiology, 1974-77; from fellow in ultrasound and body CT to prof. Jefferson Med. Coll. Thomas Jefferson Univ. Hosp., Phila., 1977—85; prof. ob-gyn. Jefferson Med. Coll. Thomas Jefferson U. Hosp., Phila., 1985—, vice chmn. dept. radiology Jefferson Med. Coll., 1989—2002, dir. med. student edn. Dept. Radiology, 2004—. Examiner oral bds. in ultrasound category Am. Bd. Radiology, 1985—; med. advisor Blue Shield of Pa., Phila., 1983—; mem. adv. com. Ctr. of Excellence in Biomed. Imaging, Phila., 1987—. Author: Ultrasound: The Requisites, 1995, 2d edit., 2003, Obstetrical Measurements in Ultrasound: A Reference Manual, 1988; editor: Atlas of Ultrasound Measurements, 1990; assoc. editor Radiology; contbr. articles to profl. jours. Grantee Nat. Cancer Inst., NIH, 1993-96. Fellow Am. Inst. Ultrasound in Medicine (bd. govs. 1990-92, sec. 1993-97, pres.-elect 1999-2001, pres. 2001-03, immediate past pres., 2003-05), Am. Coll. Radiology (chmn. com. on edn. and tng. of commn. 1987-93, commn. on ultrasound 1987-93), Soc. Radiologists in Ultrasound (pres. 1991-93), Coll. Physicians Phila. Achievements include rsch. in ultrasound to establish an accurate fetal age; ultrasound patterns for analysis of diffuse liver disease; ultrasound in evaluation of obstetrical and gynecologic problems including intravaginal scanning and cross sectional imaging evaluation for ovarian cancer. Home: 1050 Indian Creek Rd Wynnewood PA 19096-3407 Office: Thomas Jefferson U Hosp 132 S 10th St 763C Main Bldg Philadelphia PA 19107-5084 Office Phone: 215-955-6343.

KURTZ, ANTHONY DAVID, physicist; b. NYC, May 3, 1929; s. Jacob Kurtz and Claire Juscow; m. Nora Morcos, May 27, 1985; 1 child, Sandria; m. Margery Geilich, Apr. 3, 1955 (div. May 1985); children: Jennifer Kurtz Unger, John. BS in Physics, MIT, 1951, MS in Physics, 1952, ScD in Phys. Metallurgy, 1955. Staff mem. semiconductor physics Lincoln Lab., 1952—55; project mgr. diffused device rsch. Clevite Transistor Products, 1955—56; dir. semiconductor applied rsch. Mpls.-Honeywell Regulatory Co., 1956—59; dir. R&D, sr. scientist, CEO Kulite Semiconductor Products, Inc., Leonia, NJ, 1959—. Adj. prof. dept. mech. engring. Columbia U., NYC, 2002—. Contbr. articles to profl. jours. Named to N.J. Inventors Congress and Hall of Fame, State N.J., 1991; recipient I R 100 for miniature semiconductor pressure transducer, Indsl. Rsch. Inc., 1968, Si Fluor Tech. award, Instrument Soc. Am., 1978. Achievements include patents in field; invention of MEMS technology. Home: 136 E Saddle River Rd Saddle River NJ 07458 Office: Kulite Semiconductor Products Inc 1 Willow Tree Rd Leonia NJ 07605 Home Phone: 201-825-6391; Office Phone: 201-461-0900. E-mail: drkurtz@kulite.com.

KURTZ, CHARLES JEWETT, III, lawyer; b. Columbus, Ohio, May 13, 1940; s. Charles Jewett, Jr. and Elizabeth Virginia (Gill) K.; m. Linda Rhoads, Mar. 18, 1983. BA, Williams Coll., 1962; JD, Ohio State U., 1965. Bar: Ohio 1965, D.C. 1967, U.S. Dist. Ct. (so. dist.) Ohio 1967, U.S. Dist. Ct. (no. dist.) Ohio 1976, U.S. Ct. Appeals (6th cir.) 1992. Law clk. to justice Ohio State Supreme Ct., Columbus, 1965-67; assoc. Porter, Wright, Morris & Arthur, Columbus, 1967-71, ptnr., 1972—2004, mng. ptnr. litigation dept., 1988-91, mem. directing ptnrs. com., 1988-89, of counsel, 2005—. Mem. faculty Ohio Legal Ctr. Inst. Trustee Ballet Met., Columbus, 1990-94; mem. vestry St. Albans Episcopal Ch., 1986-89. Mem. ABA, Am. Arbitration Assn. (mem. panel comml. arbitrators), Columbus Bar Assn. (common pleas ct. com.), Columbus Bar Found., Columbus Def. Assn.

(pres. 1976), Athletic Club, Columbus Country Club, Capital Club. Office: Porter Wright Morris & Arthur 41 S High St Ste 2900 Columbus OH 43215-6194 E-mail: Ckurtz@porterwright.com.

KURTZ, DAVID S., lawyer; b. Cleve., July 12, 1954; BA, Case Western Res. U., 1976, JD, 1979. Bar: Ohio 1979, Ill. 1980. Mem. Jones, Day, Reavis & Pogue, Chgo.; sr. ptnr. reorganization grp. Skadden, Arps, Slate, Meagher & Flom, Chgo.; mng. dir., co-head restructuring grp. Lazard, Chgo., 2002—. Recipient Bankruptcy Dealmaker of Yr., The Am. Lawyer mag., 2000. Office: Lazard Ste 2200 200 W Madison St Chicago IL 60606 Mailing: 1913 N Fremont St Chicago IL 60614-5016 Home Phone: 773-929-9112; Office Phone: 312-407-6600. Office Fax: 312-407-6620.*

KURTZ, ELLEN R., journalist; b. Bklyn., May 22, 1934; d. George and Gertrude (Troiansky) Rabinowitz; m. Raymond J. Kurtz, June 26, 1954 (dec. May 1988); children: Jill A., Michael S., Jack L.; m. Sol T. Horowitz. BA, Bklyn. Coll., 1955. Tchr. N.Y.C. Pub. Schs., 1955-56; lectr. Weight Watchers of N.J., Livingston, 1969-83; owner, dir. Livingston Coll. Bd. Rev., 1975-83; mng. editor On the Scene, Livingston, 1984-86; editor Regional Weekly News, East Hanover, NJ, 1986; writer spl. sects. Star-Ledger, Newark, 1987—2000. Cons. editor Hosp. News of N.J., Colonia, 1989—90; feature writer Drew U., Madison, NJ, 1996—2000; publicist Drew U. Ctr. for Holocaust Study, 1997—98; instr. The Adult Sch. of the Chathams, Madison and Florham Park, 1999; Holocaust coun. MetroWest, 2001—; lectr. Jewish Edn. Assn. MetroWest NJ, 2000—. Contbr. articles to newspapers, mags. Judge essay contest B'nai Brith/Albert Adler Meml. Scholarship Fund, Livingston, 1987—2002; active Vols. for Israel, 1989. Mem.: Livingston Writers' Group, N.J. Press Women (office holder, com. chairperson, Communicator of Achievement award 1997). Jewish. Avocations: travel, aerobics, reading, bowling. Home and Office: 1305 Bush Circle Rockaway NJ 07866

KURTZ, HAROLD PAUL, foundation executive; b. Milw., May 21, 1936; s. Henry John and Minnie Christina K.; m. Grace Jahn, June 16, 1963; children: Steven, David BA, Wartburg Coll., 1958; MS, U. Wis., 1961. Journalist Post-Crescent, Appleton, Wis., 1961-63; dir. pub. rels. Luth. Gen. Hosp., Park Ridge, Ill., 1963-73, Med. Coll. Wis., Milw., 1973-77; v.p. Children's Hosp., St. Paul, 1977-90; dir. devel. U. Minn., 1990-95; exec. dir. Lyngblomsten Found., 1995—2002; pres. Wright-Berglund Found., 2002—. Author: Public Relations for Hospitals, 1969; Public Relations and Fund Raising for Hospitals, 1981; (with M. Burrows) Effective Use of Volunteers, 1971; editor: Toward a Creative Chaplaincy, 1973, Fly the Banner High, 1991, Hardly a Silent Night, 2004. Bd. dirs. Bd. Edn., Dist. 621, Mounds View, 1985-95; bd. dirs. Spl. Intermediate Sch. Dist. 916, 1986-95; bd. dirs. Wright-Berglund Found., 1980—. Recipient Community Svc. citation Wartburg Coll., 1970; named Boss of Yr., Internat. Assn. Bus. Comms. Mem. Chgo. Hosp. Pub. Rels. Soc. (pres. 1971-72), Wartburg Coll. Alumni Assn. (bd. dirs. 1962-66). Lutheran. Home: 1465 17th Ave NW Saint Paul MN 55112-5524

KURTZ, HARVEY A., lawyer; BA, U. Wis., 1972; JD, U. Chgo., 1975. Bar: Wis. 1975, U.S. Dist. Ct. (ea. dist.) Wis. 1980. Ptnr. Foley & Lardner LLP, Milw., 1989—. Mem. ABA, State Bar of Wis. Assn., Milw. Bar Assn. (chmn. employee benefits sect. 1993-94), Greater Milw. Employee Benefit Coun., Wis. Retirement Plan Profls. (pres. 1987-88), Kiwanis, Phi Beta Kappa. Home: 3927 N Stowell Ave Milwaukee WI 53211-2461 Office: Foley & Lardner LLP Ste 3800 777 E Wisc Ave Milwaukee WI 53202-5306 Office Phone: 414-297-5819. Business E-Mail: hkurtz@foley.com.

KURTZ, HOWARD, journalist, author; b. Bklyn., Aug. 1, 1953; s. Leonard and Marcia (Turetzky) K.; m. Mary Tallmer, June 20, 1979; children: Judy, Bonnie. BA in English, SUNY at Buffalo, 1974; MJ, Columbia U., 1975. Reporter Bergen Record, Hackensack, NJ, 1975-76, Washington Star, 1978-81, Washington Post, 1981—90, media reporter, 1990—; and host, Reliable Sources CNN. Author: Media Circus: The Trouble with America's Newspapers, 1993, Hot Air: All Talk All the Time, 1996, Spin Cycle: How the White House and the Media Manipulate the News, 1998, The Fortune Tellers: Inside Wall Street's Game of Money, Media and Manipulation, 2000; contbr. to The New Republic, Columbia Journalism Rev., Am. Journalism Rev., NY Mag. Recipient Front Page award Washington-Balt. Newspaper Guild, 1982, 86, Mark Twain award AP, 1990, Best Media Critic in US award Am. Journalism Rev., 1994, Mongerson Prize, Northwestern U. Medill Sch. Journalism, 2004. Office: The Washington Post 1150 15th St NW Washington DC 20071-0002

KURTZ, JAMES P., retired judge; b. Highland Park, Mich., Dec. 5, 1932; s. A.T. and Virginia C. (Riley) K.; m. Barbara A. Gonczy, Feb. 2, 1957; children: Mary T., Christina M., Ann V., J. Peter, Karen M., Eileen M. AB, U. Detroit, 1955, JD, 1958. Bar: Mich. 1958, U.S. Dist. Ct. (ea. dist.) Mich. 1958, U.S. Ct. Appeals (6th cir.) 1964. Supervisory atty. 7th region NLRB, Detroit, 1958-67; ptnr. firm Brennan & Kurtz, Detroit, 1967-69; adminstrv. law judge Employment rels. commn. State of Mich. Dept. Labor, Detroit, 1969—2001; ret., 2001. Instr. labor and real estate Detroit Coll. Bus., Dearborn, 1968-73; adj. prof. adminstrv. law U. Detroit, 1969-72. Editor-in-chief U. Detroit Law jour., 1957-58; editor procs. Nat. Acad. Arbitrators, 1971-75. Mem. Mich. Bar Assn. (Labor Law sect.). Roman Catholic. Home: RR 1 Craig Beach 401 Erieview Harrow ON Canada N0R 1G0 E-mail: jpkurtz@sympatico.ca.

KURTZ, JEROME, lawyer, educator; b. Phila., May 19, 1931; s. Morris and Renee (Cooper) Kurtz; m. Elaine Kahn, July 28, 1956 (dec.); children: Madeleine, Nettie Kurtz Greenstein. BS with honors, Temple U., Phila., 1952; LLB magna cum laude, Harvard U., Cambridge, Mass., 1955. Bar: Pa. 1956, NY 1981, DC 1982; CPA, Pa. Assoc. Wolf, Block, Schorr & Solis-Cohen, Phila., 1955-56, 57-63, ptnr., 1963-66, 68-77; tax legis. counsel Dept. Treasury, Washington, 1966-68; commr. IRS, 1977-80; ptnr. Paul, Weiss, Rifkind, Wharton & Garrison, 1980-90; prof. law NYU, 1991-2001, dir. grad. tax program, 1995-98. Instr. Villanova Law Sch., 1964-65, U. Pa., 1969-74; vis. prof. law Harvard U., 1975-76; mem. adv. group to commr. IRS, 1976. Editor: Harvard Law Rev, 1953-55; contbr. numerous articles to profl. jours. Pres. Ctr. Inter-Am. Tax Adminstrn., 1980; bd. dirs. Common Cause, 1984-90, chmn. fin. com., 1985-88; bd. dirs. Nat. Capitol Area ACLU, 1990-91; mem. adv. bd. NYU Tax Inst., 1988-97, Little, Brown Tax Practice Series, 1994-96. Recipient Exceptional Service award Dept. Treasury, 1968, Alexander Hamilton award, 1980 Mem.: ABA (chmn. tax shelter com. 1982—84), Am. Coll. Tax Counsel, Am. Law Inst. (cons. fed. income tax project taxation of pass through entitites), Assn. Bar of City of NY (chmn. tax. coun. 1993—95), Phila. Bar Assn. (chmn. tax sect. 1975—76), Pa. Bar Assn., NY Bar Assn. (exec. com., tax sect. 1981—82), Internat. Sr. Lawyers Project (bd. dirs.), Beta Gamma Sigma. Home: 17 E 16th St New York NY 10003-3116 Office Phone: 212-727-7180. Personal E-mail: jeromekurtz2@aol.com.

KURTZ, JOEL BARRY, finance executive; b. Bklyn., Aug. 2, 1944; BBA, Pace U., 1970; MBA, C.W. Post Coll., 1981. Staff acct. Arthur Andersen & Co., Melville, NY, 1970-73; divsn. contr. Elec. Comp. divsn. Gould Inc., Farmingdale, 1973-78; contr. CBS-Holt, Rinehart & Winston, NYC, 1979-80, Siemans Data Switching Systems, formerly Databit Inc., Hauppage, 1981-87; v.p. fin. Linotype-Hell Co., 1987-93; CFO INS Devel. Inc., 1993-96; sr. dir. Nortel Networks Inc. (formerly Periphonics Corp.), Bohemia, 1996—2003; pvt. practice acctg., 2003—. Home and Office: 84 Vera Ln Commack NY 11725-1922 Home Phone: 631-499-8425; Office Phone: 631-838-9084. Personal E-mail: jbkurtz@aol.com. Business E-Mail: jbk@joelbkurtz-cpa.com.

KURTZ, MICHAEL JOSEPH, archivist, educator; b. Leesburg, Fla., May 8, 1949; s. Warren P. and Eleanor H. Kurtz. BA, Cath. U., Washington, DC, 1972; MA, Georgetown U., Washington, DC, 1974, PhD, 1982. Adj. prof. U. Md., College Park, Md., 1990—; staff archivist The Nat. Archives & Records Adminstrn., Washington, 1974—87, dep. asst. archivist, 1987—93, asst. archivist Office Records Svcs., 1993—. Author: John G. Morris: Man of God Man of Science, 1997, Managing Archival Repositories, 2004, America and the Return Nazi Contraband, 2006. Lay minister Magothy-Chelsea Cmty. Luth. Ch., Pasadena, Md., 1991—. Recipient Top 100 Execs., Fed. Computer Week, Falls Ch., Va., 2005. Mem.: Mid Atlantic Region Archivists Conf., Soc. Am. Archivists, Luth. Hist. Soc. (pres. 1990—2001). Lutheran. Avocations: travel, reading, gardening. Office: The Nat Archives & Records Adminstrn 8601 Adelphi Rd Ste 3400 College Park MD 20740 E-mail: michael.kurt@arch2.nara.gov.*

KURTZ, MYERS RICHARD, retired hospital administrator; b. Schaefferstown, Pa., June 18, 1924; m. Linda Bewan, Dec. 26, 1988; 1 child, Ronald Hayden; 1 stepchild, Erin B. Brown. BS, U. Md., 1958; MBA, Ind. U., 1963. Served as enlisted man U.S. Army, 1942-51, commd. 2d lt., 1951; advanced through grades to lt. col. Med. Svc. Corps, 1965; mem. staff Army Surgeon Gen., Washington, 1963-67; ret., 1967; affiliation adminstr. NYU Med. Ctr., NYC, 1967-69; exec. dir. Ephrata Community Hosp., Pa., 1969-76; supt. Longview State Hosp., Cin., 1976-79; asst. dir. Ohio Dept. Mental Health and Mental Retardation, Columbus, 1979-81, dir., 1981-82; sr. v.p. Cleve. Met. Gen. Hosp., 1982-83; supt., CEO Ctrl. State Hosp., Milledgeville, Ga., 1983-93; adminstr., CEO G. Pierce Wood Meml. Hosp., Arcadia, Fla., 1995-98, ret., 1998. Adj. asst. prof. dept. psychiatry U. Cin., 1977-83. V.p., bd. dirs. Coordinated Home Care Agy., Inc., Lancaster County; pres. Lancaster County Hosp. Coun.; bd. dirs. Pa. Hosp. Assn., Baldwin County United Way, 1986-91, Baldwin County Salvation Army; mem. adv. bd. Youth Devel. Ctr., 1984-91. Decorated Legion of Merit, Army Commendation medal with oak leaf cluster, Soldiers medal. Fellow Royal Soc. Health; mem. Am. Coll. Hosp. Adminstrs. (life fellow), Am. Acad. Med. Adminstrs., Am. Hosp. Assn., Milledgeville-Baldwin County C. of C. (bd. dirs. 1984-87, exec. com. 1986—, treas. 1987—), Nassau County Vol. Ctr. (bd. dirs. 1998-, pres. 2002-03), Sigma Iota Epsilon, Rotary Internat. Home: 95485 Captains Way Fernandina Beach FL 32034-4346 Personal E-mail: LmKurtz@bellsouth.net.

KURTZ, PAUL, philosopher, educator, writer, publisher; b. Newark, Dec. 21, 1925; s. Martin and Sara (Lasser) K.; m. Claudine C. Vial, Oct. 6, 1960; children: Valerie L., Patricia A., Jonathan, Anne. BA, NYU, 1948; MA, Columbia U., 1949, PhD, 1952. Instr. Queens Coll., 1950—52; instr. philosophy Trinity Coll., Hartford, Conn., 1952—55, asst. prof., 1955—58, assoc. prof., 1958—59, Vassar Coll., Poughkeepsie, NY, 1960—61; vis. prof. New Sch. Social Rsch., NYC, 1960—65; assoc. prof. Union Coll., Schenectady, 1961—64, prof., 1964—65; vis. prof. U. Besancon, France, 1965; prof. philosophy SUNY, Buffalo, 1965—91, prof. emeritus, 1992—. Moderator TV series Author (with Rollo Handy): A Current Appraisal of the Behavioral Sciences, 1964; author: Decision and the Condition of Man, 1965, The Fullness of Life, 1974, Exuberance, 1977, In Defense of Secular Humanism, 1983, A Skeptics Handbook of Parapsychology, 1985, The Transcendental Temptation, 1986, Forbidden Fruit, 1988, Eupraxophy, 1989, Philosphical Essays in Pragmatic Naturalism, 1990, The New Skepticism, 1992, Toward a New Enlightenment, 1994, The Courage to Become, 1997, Humanist Manifesto 2000, 1999, Embracing the Power of Humanism, 2000, Skepticism and Humanism: The New Paradigm, 2001, Affirmations, 2004; editor: The Humanist, 1967—78, American Thought Before 1900, 1966, American Philosophy in the Twentieth Century, 1966, Sidney Hook and the Contemporary World, 1968, Moral Problems in Contemporary Society, 1969; co-editor: International Directory of Philosophy and Philosophers, 4th edit., 1978—81, Tolerance and Revolution, 1970, Language and Human Nature, 1971, A Catholic/Humanist Dialogue, 1972, The Humanist Alternative, 1973, Idea of a Modern University, 1974, The Philosophy of the Curriculum, 1975, The Ethics of Teaching and Scientific Research, 1977, University and State, 1978, Sidney Hook: Philosopher of Democracy and Humanism, 1983, Building a World Community, 1989, Challenges to the Enlightenment, 1994, Skeptical Odysseys, 2001; author, co-editor Science and Religion, 2003; author, co-editor: Media-Graphy, 2004, Promethean Love: The Philosophy of Paul Kurtz, 2006, Science and Ethics, 2007; mem. editl. bd. The Humanist, 1964—78, Philosophers Index, 1969—85, Question, 1969—81, The Skeptical Inquirer, 1976—, chmn. Prometheus Books, 1970—, editor-in-chief Free Inquiry Mag., 1980—, pub. The Sci. Rev. of Alternative Medicine, 1998—; pub.: Sci. Rev. Mental Health Practice, 2002—. Chmn. Coun. for Secular Humanism, 1980—, Ctr. for Inquiry, 1995—; trustee Behavioral Rsch. Coun., Great Barrington, Mass.; bd. dirs. U.S. Bibliography of Philosophy, 1958-70, Univ. Ctrs. for Rational Alternatives, 1969-96, Internat. Humanist and Ethical Union, 1968-2000, co-chmn., 1986-94; chmn. Com. for Sci. Investigation Claims of Paranormal, 1976—. With AUS, 1944-46. Behavioral Rsch. Coun. fellow, 1962-63, French Govt. fellow, 1965, John Dewey fellow, 1986-87; recipient Bertrand Russell Soc. award, 1988, Internat. Humanist award, 1999, Chancellor Charles Norton award, 2001, hon. medal. San Marcos Univ., 2006. Fellow: AAAS; mem.: U.K. Rationalists Press Assn. (v.p. 1990—), Acad. Humanism (Laureate, pres. 1983—). Office: Prometheus Books Inc 59 John Glenn Dr Amherst NY 14228-2197 Personal E-mail: paulkurtz@aol.com. *Two passions have dominated my intellectual and professional life: (1) a commitment to critical intelligence-I am skeptical of the false beliefs and mythologies that have motivated other men and women; and (2) a belief in the importance of human courage, particularly in defending reason in society and in attempting to reconstruct ethical values so that they are more democratic and humane.*

KURTZ, PAUL MICHAEL, law educator; b. Bronx, NY, Sept. 22, 1946; s. Louis and Helen (Mechanic) K. m. Carol Porter, June 6, 1971; 1 child, Benjamin. BA, Vanderbilt U., 1968, JD, 1972; LLM, Harvard U., 1974. Bar: Tenn. 1972, U.S. Ct. Appeals (6th cir.) 1973, U.S. Ct. Appeals (5th cir.) 1977, U.S. Supreme Ct. 1978. Law clk. to chief judge U.S. Ct. Appeals (6th cir.), 1972-73; instr. Boston U. Law Sch., 1973-74, Boston Coll. Law Sch., 1974-75; asst. prof. law U. Ga., Athens, 1975-78, assoc. prof., 1978-83, prof., 1983-94, assoc. dean, 1991—, J. Alton Hosch prof., 1994—. Vis. prof. U. Mo. Law Sch., 1982, Mercer Law Sch., 1984, U. Tex., 1986, Vanderbilt U., 1987; commr. on Uniform State Laws, 2001—; reporter Nat. Conf. Commrs. on Uniform State Laws, Com. on Interstate Family Support Act, Com. on Status of Children of Aided Conception, Ga. Supreme Ct. Com. on Indigent Def. Reform, 2000-03; exec. comm. Ga. Pub. Defender Stds. Coun., 2003-07. Author: Criminal Offenses in Georgia, 1980, Family Law: Cases, Text, Problems, 1986, 4th edit., 2004; contbr. articles to profl. jours.; mem. editl. bd. Family Law Quar., 1983—. Mem. Am. Assn. Law Schs. (chmn. sect. family and juvenile law), ACLU, Am. Humane Assn. (bd. dirs. 1998-2004), Common Cause, Soc. Am. Law Tchrs., Am. Law Inst. (reporter 1995-96), Supreme Ct. Hist. Soc., Order of Coif, B'nai B'rith (Ga. state sec., pres. Athens lodge). Democrat. Avocations: reading, travel, bowling, politics. Home: 362 W Cloverhurst Ave Athens GA 30606-4212 Office: U Ga Law Sch Athens GA 30602 Business E-Mail: pmkurtz@uga.edu.

KURTZ, ROBERT ARTHUR, finance company executive; b. Holyoke, Mass., June 16, 1943; BS in Fin., Am. Internat. Coll., Springfield, Mass., 1967; MBA in Fin., U. Okla., 1969. Sr. fin. analyst corp. treas. office Gulf Oil Internat., Pitts., 1969-71; with corp. fin. staff Humble Oil div. Exxon, Houston, 1971-73; acct. mgr. Merrill Lynch, Atlanta, 1973-75; personal and corp. fin. advisor Atlanta, 1975-77; pres., founder Internat. Trade and Mktg. Corp., Atlanta, 1977-84; chmn. Kray Fin. Corp., Atlanta, 1984—86, pres., 1986—. Author: Diagnosing the Customer's Decision Strategy, 1994, Pick 'em Right the First Time, 1997. Mem. Soc. Neuro-Linguistic Programming (cert. trainer), Am. Assn. for Counseling and Devel. Lutheran. Home: 1630 Broadwell Oaks Dr Alpharetta GA 30004-1580 Business E-Mail: bobkurtz@kraymanagement.com.

KURTZ, SHELDON FRANCIS, lawyer, educator; b. Syracuse, NY, May 18, 1943; s. Abraham Kurtz and Rosalyn (Bronstein) Stern; m. Alice Kaufman, June 22, 1968; children: Andrea, Emily. AB, Syracuse U., 1964, JD, 1967. Bar: N.Y. 1967, Iowa 1973. Assoc. Nixon, Mudge, Guthrie, Alexander & Mitchell, NYC, 1967-69, Cleary, Gottlieb, Steen & Hamilton, NYC, 1970-73; prof. U. Iowa Coll. Law, Iowa City, 1973-89, U. Va. Sch. Law, Charlottesville, 1979-80; dean Coll. Law, Fla. State U., Tallahassee, 1989-91; prof. Coll. Law U. Iowa, Iowa City, 1991—, prof. Coll. Med. Author: Kurtz on Iowa Estates, 3 vols., 1981, 2d edit., 2 vols., 1989, Problems, Cases and Materials on Family Estate Planning, 1983; (with Hood and Shors) Estate Planning for Shareholders of a Closely Held Corporation, 2 vols. and supplement, 1986, (with Hovenkamp) American Property Law, 1987, 4th edit., 2003, The Law of Property, 2001; (with McGovern) Wills, Trusts and Estates, 3d edit., 2004, Introduction to the Law of Real Property, 4th edit., 2005; contbr. articles to profl. jours. Recipient Burlington No. tchg. award U. Iowa, 1987, Michael J. Brody Disting. Svc. award, 2001. Mem. Iowa Bar Assn. (commr. Uniform State Laws), Am. Law Inst. Avocations: cooking, hiking. Office: U Iowa Coll Law Rm 446 Iowa City IA 52242 Home Phone: 319-337-7185; Office Phone: 319-335-9069. Business E-Mail: sheldon-kurtz@uiowa.edu.

KURTZ, THOMAS EUGENE, retired mathematics professor; b. Oak Park, Ill., Feb. 22, 1928; s. Oscar Christ and Helen (Bell) K.; m. Patricia Anne Barr, June 13, 1953 (div. Aug. 1973); children— Daniel Barr, Timothy David, Beth Louise; m. Agnes Seelye Bixler, June 10, 1974. BA, Knox Coll., Galesburg, Ill., 1950; PhD, Princeton, 1956; DSc, Knox Coll., 1985. Mem. faculty Dartmouth Coll., 1956-93, prof. math. and computer sci., 1966-93, chmn. Program in Computer and Info. Sci., 1984—88, dir. Kiewit Computation Ctr., 1959-75; dir. Office Acad. Computing, 1975-78; ret., 1993. Author: Basic Statistics, 1963, (with J.G. Kemeny) Basic Programming, 1967, 2d edit., 1971, 3d edit., 1980, (with J.G. Kemeny) Structured Basic Programming, 1987. Trustee, chmn. coun. EDUCOM, 1974-78; chmn., bd. dirs. NERComp, Inc., 1970-78; trustee, vice chmn. Dartmouth Time Sharing Sys., Inc., 1972-78; chmn. X3J2 sub. com. Am. Nat. Standards Inst., 1974-84, convenor WG8 Internat. Standards Orgn. Basic Com., 1987-94; bd. dirs., vice chmn. True Basic, Inc., 1983-2003; mem. panel uses of computers in edn. Pres.'s Sci. Adv. Com., 1965-66. Democrat. Mem. United Ch. Christ. Achievements include co-designing BASIC computer lang. and Dartmouth time sharing system. Home: 3 Lakeview Dr Hanover NH 03755-3407

KURTZER, DANIEL CHARLES, former ambassador; b. Elizabeth, NJ, 1949; s. Nathan and Sylvia Kurtzer; m. Sheila D. Kurtzer; children: David, Yehuda, Jacob. BA, Yeshiva U., 1971; MA, MA, Columbia, PhD, 1976. Dean Yeshiva Coll., NYC, 1977—79; with Fgn. Svc. US Dept. State, Washington, 1976—77, 1979—; 2d sec. for polit. affairs Am. Embassy, Cairo, 1979-82, 1st sec. for polit. affairs Tel Aviv, 1982-86; dep. dir. Office Egyptian Affairs US Dept. State, Washington, 1986—87, speechwriter, mem. sec.'s policy planning staff, 1987—89, dep. asst. sec. for Nr. Ea. Affairs, 1989-94, prin. dep. asst. sec. for intelligence and rsch. Washington, 1994-97, acting asst. sec. for intelligence rsch., 1997, U.S. amb. to Egypt, Cairo, 1997—2001, U.S. amb. to Israel Tel Aviv, 2001—05. S. Daniel Abraham vis. prof. in Mid. East policy studies Princeton U., 2006—. Recipient Henrietta Szold award, 2005, Nat. Intelligence Community;s award for Achievement, Pres. Disting. Svc. award, Dir. Gen. of Fgn Svc. award for Polit. Reporting, Disting. Svc. award, US Dept State. Office: Princeton U Woodrow Wilson Sch 418 Robertson Hall Princeton NJ 08544 E-mail: dkurtzer@princeton.edu.

KURTZKE, JOHN FRANCIS, SR., neurologist, epidemiologist; b. Bklyn., Sept. 14, 1926; s. John Ambrose and Teresa Rose (Knipper) K.; m. Margaret Mary Nevin, June 30, 1950; children: John Francis Jr., Catherine Kurtzke Brown, Elizabeth Kurtzke Siebert, Joan Kurtzke Brennan, Robert, James, Christine Kurtzke Hughes. BS summa cum laude, St. John's U., 1948; MD, Cornell U., Ithaca, NY, 1952; MD (hon.), U. Ferrara, Italy, 2000. Diplomate in neurology Am. Bd. Psychiatry and Neurology, 1958 (asst. examiner, then examiner and sr. examiner in neurology 1964-96, cert. appreciation 1969, 90). Intern Kings County Hosp., Bklyn., 1952—53; resident in neurology VA Hosp., Bronx, NY, 1953-56, chief neurology svc. Coatesville, Pa., 1956—63, Washington, 1963—95; chief neuroepidemiology sect. VA Med. Ctr., Washington, 1995—2002, cons. in neurology, 1995—, cons. in neuroepidemiology, 2002—; cons. in neurology VA Multiple Sclerosis Ctr. Excellence East, Balt., 2004—. Mem. faculty Jefferson Med. Coll., Phila., 1958-63, asst. prof. clin. neurology, 1963; mem. faculty Georgetown Med. Sch., Washington, 1963—, prof. neurology, 1968-2000, prof. emeritus, 2000—, vice chmn. dept. neurology, 1976-95, prof. cmty. and family medicine, 1968-95; Disting. prof. neurology uniformed svcs. U. Health Scis., Bethesda, 1992—, USN med. student liaison officer, 1979-85; vis. prof. neurology and neuroepidemiology Temple U. Sch. Medicine, 1984-89; cons. neurology Nat. Naval Med. Ctr., Bethesda, 1966-2000, Surgeon Gen. Navy, 1970-97; mem. med. adv. bd. Nat. Multiple Sclerosis Soc., 1966-94, hon. mem., 1995—, mem. working group on design of clin. studies in multiple sclerosis, 1976-84, mem. exec. com., 1981-83, mem. task force on epidemiology, 2006—; mem. med. adv. bd. Internat. Fedn. Multiple Sclerosis Socs., 1972—, hon. mem., 1998—; mem. com. multiple sclerosis World Fedn. Neurology, 1967—, com. neuroepidemiology, 1977—; chmn. epidemiology sect. NIH Epilepsy Adv. Com., 1973-76; med. rsch. program specialist for neurology and neurobiology VA Rsch. Svc., 1977-80; chmn. work group epidemiology HEW Commn. Control of Huntington's Disease, 1976-78; mem. naval exam. bd. Naval Med. Command, 1980-83; mem. Residency Rev. Com. Neurology, 1983-88, vice chmn., 1985-86, chmn., 1987-88; chmn. US Naval Res. Med. Flag Coun., 1985-86; mem. instnl. rev. bd. Nat. Inst. Neurol. Diseases and Stroke, 1989-98; established investigator Nat. Multiple Sclerosis Soc., 1987—; mem. spl. panel Inst. Medicine, 1990; mem. oversight com. War-Related Illness and Injury Ctr., VAMC, Washington, 2002—; mem. oversight com. MS Ctrs. of Excellence, VA, 2003—; mem. Am. Com. Treatment and Rsch. in Multiple Sclerosis, L.Am. Com. on Treatment and Rsch. in Multiple Sclerosis, Consortium of Multiple Sclerosis Ctrs. Author, co-author: Epidemiology of Multiple Sclerosis, 1968, Epidemiology of Cerebrovascular Disease, 1969, Epidemiology of Neurologic and Sense Organ Disorders, 1973, Neuroepidemiology, 1998, Psychiatry/Neurology, 1998, Practice Questions. Book One, 1998, Psychiatry Neurology, 1998, Book Two, 1998, Encyclopedia of the Neurological Disorders (Neuroepidemiology), 2003; mem. editl. bd. Neuroepidemiology, 1980—, Neurology, 1984-92, Stroke, 1986-2000, Jour. Clin. Epidemiology, 1988-2005, Jour. Neurol. Sci., 1990-96, Acta Neurologica Scandinavica, 1990-97; contbr. some 500 articles to profl. jours., chpts. to books. Served with USN, 1944—46, rear adm. M.C. USNR, 1946—86, rear adm. USN ret., 1986—. Decorated Legion of Merit (2), Navy Commendation medal, Armed Forces Res. medal with gold hourglass, others; recipient cert. of merit, Surgeon Gen. Navy, 1969, Gold Bicennial medal, Georgetown U., 1982, Sec.'s Disting. Career award, Dept. Vets. Affairs, 1998, Charcot award, Internat. Fedn. MS Socs., 1999, Lifetime Achievement award, Consortium of MS Ctr., 2003, others. Fellow: ACP (life), AAAS (life), Pan Am. Med. Assn. (coun. neurology sect.), Am. Coll. Preventive Medicine, Am. Coll. Epidemiology, Am. Acad. Neurology (chmn. sect. on neuro-epidemiology 1971—75, chmn. com. nat. needs in neurology 1981—85, subcom. nat. needs in neurology 1985—86, mem. work force task force 1997, John Jay Dystel prize for mulitple sclerosis rsch. 1997), NY Acad. Sci., Am. Heart Assn. (stroke coun. 1991—2000); mem.: AMA, AAUP, Consortium

Multiple Sclerosis Ctrs. (Lifetime Achievement award 2003), Lat. Am. Com. Treatment and Rsch. in Multiple Sclerosis, Am. Com. Treatment and Rsch. in Multiple Sclerosis, Soc. Med. Cons. to Armed Forces (com. on res. affairs 1980—83, com. on manpower 1984—98, com. on med. edn. 2001—), Sr. Stroke Soc., Res. Officers Assn. (life), Naval Inst. (life), Fleet Res. Assn. (life), Naval Officers Assn. Am. (life), Am. Neurol. Assn. (hon.; chmn. bylaws ad hoc com. 1990—91), Danish Neurol. Soc. (hon.), French Soc. Neurology (hon.; fgn.), Assn. Nicoló Copernico (hon.), German Soc. Neurology (hon.), Assn. Mil. Surgeons (life), Naval Res. Assn. (life), Naval Order US (life), Internat. Stroke Soc., Am. Soc. Microbiology, Am. Epilepsy Soc., Assn. Rsch. in Nervous and Metal Disease, Internat. Epidemiol. Assn., Am. Epidemiol. Soc., So. Med. Assn., Navy League (life). Home: 7509 Salem Rd Falls Church VA 22043-3240 Office Phone: 703-560-6016. Office Fax: 703-560-6490. Business E-Mail: kurtzke2@aol.com. *To be a physician demands recognition of the intrinsic value and dignity of human life while pursuing the goal of relieving pain and impairment due to disease or injury.*

KURTZMAN, JOEL ALLAN, economist; b. LA, June 25, 1947; s. Samuel Michael and Roselle (Rosencranz) K.; m. Susan Leslie Kurtzman, Dec. 28, 1969; 1 child, Eli. AB, U. Calif., Berkeley, 1969; MS, U. Houston, 1976. Cons. United Nations, various locations worldwide, 1970; economist UN, NYC, 1978; editor devel. bus. World Bank, NYC, 1984; former exec. editor Harvard Business Review; former bus. columnist NY Times; founding editor-in-chief Strategy and Business mag.; former global lead ptnr., thought leadership and innovation PricewaterhouseCoopers; chmn. Kurtzman Group LLC, Concord, Mass., 1995—; also sr. fellow, pub., Milken Inst. Rev. Milken Inst., Santa Monica, Calif. Bd. dirs. Medtec Internat., Beverly Hills, Calif., Orbit Prodns., Washington, Soc. for Trial Peoples, Bombay. Author: Crown of Flowers, 1970 (Eisner Prize 1970), Sweet Bobby, 1976, No More Dying, 1976, Futurecasting, 1980, Decline and Crash of the American Economy, 1988, The Death of Money, 1993, Thought Leaders, 1997, How the Markets Really Work, 2002, Startups That Work, 2005; Co-author: Radical E: From GE to Enron Lessons on How to Rule the Web, 2001, MBA in a Box, 2004, co-editor New International Economic Order Library, 1978-82, editor: Thought Leaders, 1997; editl. bd Sloan Mgmt. Rev, MIT; lectr. in field. Grantee Moody Found., 1976, Govt. Italy, 1980, Govt. the Netherlands, 1982. Avocation: jogging. Office: Milken Inst Rev 1250 Fourth St Santa Monica CA 90401 also: Kurtzman Group LLC 904 Lowell Rd Concord MA 01742-5513 Office Phone: 310-570-4600, 978-369-6661. Office Fax: 310-570-4601. Business E-Mail: joel.kurtzman@kurtzmangroup.com.

KURTZMAN, RALPH HAROLD, JR., biochemist, researcher, consultant; b. Mpls., Feb. 21, 1933; s. Ralph Harold, Sr. and Susie Marie (Elwell) K.; m. Nancy Virginia (Leussler), Aug. 27, 1955; children: Steven Paul, Sue. BS, U. Minn., 1955; MS, U. Wis., 1958, PhD, 1959. Asst. prof. U. R.I., Kingston, 1959—62, U. Minn., Morris, 1962—65; biochemist USDA, Albany, Calif., 1965—97; ret., 1997. Instr. U. Calif., Berkeley, 1981-82; cons. Bliss Valley Farms, Twin Falls, Idaho, 1983-84, Kodik Farm, Lida, Belarus, 2003, Small Farms, Manazales, Colombia, 2004, VostokAgrabaza, Ust Kamenogorsk, Kazakhstan, 2004, Gusev Farm, Melenki, Russia 2005, Irzem Co. Batyrevo, Russia, 2005, CARE Farmers Assn., Upper Egypt, 2006-07, Assn. Mushroom Producers, Kiev, Ukraine, 2007, Technol. U. Tajikstan, Chkalovsk, 2007; pres. Santa Clara Valley Tex. Instrument PC Users' Group, 1991-92, editor, 1993-97; cons. and spkr. in field. Author: Oyster Mushroom Cultivation, 2004; editor Internat. Jour. Mushroom Sci., 1995-2000; co-editor Micologia Aplicada Internat., 2001—; editor, pub. Solliday/Sallade Family of Bucks County, Pa., 1999; mem. editl. bd. Pakistan Jour. Phytopathology, 2001—; inventor mushroom substrate (compost) preparation, decaffeination of beverages; contbr. articles to profl. jours. Chmn. Berkeley YMCA Camp Program Com., 1971-72; official Amateur Athletic Union (swimming), San Francisco, 1973-80; treas. Calif. Native Plant Soc., 1970; docent Oakland Mus. Calif., 2001—. Mem. Am. Mushroom Inst., Mycological Soc. Am. (organizer symposium mushroom cultivation in Am. tropics 1998), Mycological Soc. Japan, Sigma Xi. Avocations: computers, woodworking, photography, clock making. Home and Office: 445 Vassar Ave Berkeley CA 94708-1215 Home Phone: 510-526-2492. Personal E-mail: kurtzmanr@earthlink.net. Business E-Mail: rkurtzman@oystermushrooms.net.

KURY, BERNARD EDWARD, lawyer; b. Sunbury, Pa., Sept. 11, 1938; AB, Princeton U., 1960; LLB, U. Pa., 1963. Bar: NY 1964. Assoc. Dewey, Ballantine, Bushby, Palmer & Wood, NYC, 1963-71, ptnr., 1971—2004; v.p., gen. counsel Guidant Corp., Indpls., 2004—. Contbg. editor Ency. of Venture Capital. Editor: Pa. Law Sch. Review. Mem.: NY State Bar Assn., Assn. of the Bar of the City of NY, ABA. Office: Guidant Corp 111 Monument Cir #2900 Indianapolis IN 46204-5129 also: Guidant Corp PO Box 44906 Indianapolis IN 46244*

KURYK, DAVID NEAL, lawyer; b. Balt., Aug. 24, 1947; s. Leon and Bernice G. (Fox) K.; m. Alice T. Lehman, July 8, 1971; children: Richard M., Robert M., Benjamin A. BA, U. Md., 1969; JD, U. Balt., 1972. Bar: Md. 1972, US Dist. Ct. Md. 1973, US Ct. Mil. Appeals 1973, DC 1974, US Ct. Appeals (4th cir.) 1974, US Supreme Ct. 1976, US Ct. Appeals (Fed. cir.) 1982. Assoc. Harold Buchman, Esq., Balt., 1970—76; pvt. practice Balt., 1976—. Mem. editl. bd. Md. Bar Jour., 1973—76. Sgt. USAF, 1967—73. Mem. ABA (products gen. liability and consumer law com. 1976—, com. auto law 1977), Md. State Bar Assn., U. Balt. Alumni Assn., Zeta Beta Tau. Democrat. Jewish. Home: 11200 5 Springs Rd Lutherville MD 21093-3520 Office: Am Bldg 231 E Baltimore St Ste 702 Baltimore MD 21202-3446 Office Phone: 410-752-7125. Business E-Mail: david@kuryk.com.

KURZ, DAVID BRYAN, web site designer; s. Thomas Willard Kurz and Verna Carolyn Bryan; m. Helen Jean Gawthrop; m. Cheryl Lee Decker (div.); 1 child, Rosalee. BS in Botany, Ohio U., 1983, MS in Botany, 1990; MSLS, Case Western Res. U., 1984. Dir. Herbert Wescoat Meml. Libr., McArthur, Ohio, 1988—93, Wash. County Pub. Libr., Marietta, Ohio, 1993—95; sr. web developer Ohio U., Athens, Ohio, 1996—. Cons. Nat. Cancer Inst., Bethesda, Md., 1992—93. Prodr.(creator): (multimedia web site) Wired for Books, wiredforbooks.org (Streamers WebSage Award - Real Networks -San Francisco, 1999), (radio show) Talking about Science, A Christmas Carol (Hon. Mention - Arts - Ohio Pub. Radio, 2002). Co-founder, incorporator Athens Food Coop, Athens, Ohio, 1975—90; pres. Friends of the Athens Pub. Libr., Athens, Ohio, 1995—98, Friends of Ohio U. Libr., Athens, Ohio, 2001—02. Recipient Program of Year, Ohio Public Broadcasting awards, 2006. Mem.: Am. Soc. for Info. Sci. and Tech. Avocations: bicycling, boating, gardening. Office: Ohio U WOUB Ctr Public Media Athens OH 45701 Home Phone: 740-593-8505; Office Phone: 740-593-4789. E-mail: kurz@ohio.edu.

KURZ, KARL F., oil industry executive; BS magna cum laude in Petroleum Engring., Tex. A&M U., College Station, 1983. Lic. profl. engr., Tex. With ARCO Oil & Gas. Co., 1983, with crude oil mktg. dept., 1990; mgr. crude oil and NGL mktg. dept. Vastar Resources, Inc., 1995—98, gen. mgr. midstream and mktg., 1998—2000; mgr. energy mktg. Anadarko Petroleum Corp., The Woodlands, Tex., 2000—03, v.p. mktg., 2003—05, sr. v.p. mktg., gen. mgr. US Onshore, 2005—06, sr. v.p. N.Am. Ops., Midstream and Mktg., 2006, COO, 2006—. Mem. Kingsland Baptist Ch. Mem.: Soc. Petroleum Engrs. Office: Anadarko Petroleum Corp 1201 Lake Robbins Dr The Woodlands TX 77380-1046 Office Phone: 832-636-1000.*

KURZ, MITCHELL HOWARD, marketing communications executive; b. NYC, Nov. 5, 1951; s. Robert Sydney and Lorraine Ruth (Wolosky) K.; m. Sandy Mitchell, Aug. 25, 1979; children: Zachary, Maxwell. BA, Dartmouth Coll., 1973; MBA, Harvard U., 1975. Acct. exec. Young & Rubicam, NYC, 1976-77, v.p., account supr., 1978-80, sr. v.p., 1980-87, corp. sr. v.p., 1987-90; chmn. N.Am. Wunderman Worldwide, NYC, 1990-91; pres., CEO worldwide Wunderman Cato Johnson, NYC, 1992-97; pres., COO Young & Rubicam Advt., NYC, 1997-98, chair client svcs., 1998-99; chmn., CEO Kurz and Friends, Westport, Conn., 1998—. Bd. dirs. Young and Rubicam. Trustee Rheedlen Ctrs. for Children and Families, Town Sch., 1994—; bd. dirs. New Visions for Pub. Schs., 1994—, Teach for Am., 1996. Rufus Choate Scholar, Dartmouth Coll., 1971, 72, 73. Mem. Am. Mgmt. Assn., Pequot Runners, Phi Beta Kappa. Avocation: marathon running. Home: 95 Old Rd Westport CT 06880-4145 Office: Kurz and Friends 191 Post Rd W Westport CT 06880-4625

KURZ, MORDECAI, economics professor; b. Natanya, Israel, Nov. 29, 1934; came to U.S., 1957, naturalized, 1973; s. Moshe and Sarah (Kraus) K.; m. Lillian Rivlin, Aug. 4, 1963 (div. Mar. 1967); m 2d Linda Alice Cahn, Dec. 2, 1979. BA in Econs. and Polit. Sci., Hebrew U., Jerusalem, 1957; MA in Econs., Yale U., 1958, PhD in Econs., 1962; MS in Stats., Stanford U., 1960. Asst. prof. econs. Stanford U., 1962-63, assoc. prof., 1966-68, prof., 1969—, Joan Kenney prof. econs., 1997—, dir. econs. sect. Inst. for Math. Studies, 1971-89; sr. lectr. in econs. Hebrew U., 1963-66. Cons. econs. SRI Internat., Menlo Park, Calif., 1963-78; spl. econ. advisor Can. health and Welfare Ministry, Ottawa, Ont., 1976-78; spl. econ. advisor Pres.'s Commn. on Pension, Washington, 1979-81; rsch. assoc. Nat. Bur. Econ. Rsch., 1979-82; Lady Davis vis. prof. Hebrew U., Jerusalem, 1993; prin. investigator Smith Richardson Found., 2001—; mem. adv. bd. Annals of Fin., 2004—. Author: (with Kenneth J. Arrow) Public Investment, The Rate of Return and Optimal Fiscal Policy,1970, Endogenous Economic Fluctuations: Studies in the Theory of Rational Beliefs, 1997; co-editor Econ. Theory, 1997—. Bd. dirs. Ben-Gurion U. of the Negev, Israel, 1998—. Ford Found. faculty fellow Stanford U., 1973; Guggenheim Found. fellow Stanford U., Harvard U., Jerusalem, 1977-78; Inst. Advanced Studies fellow Hebrew U., Mt. Scopus, Jerusalem, 1979-80; prin. investigator NSF, 1969-93, Smith-Richardson Found., 2001—. Fellow Econometric Soc. (assoc. editor Jour. Econ. Theory 1976-90); mem. Am. Econ. Assn. Democrat. Jewish. Office: Stanford U Econs Dept Serra St at Galvez Stanford CA 94305-6702 Home Phone: 650-857-9085; Office Phone: 650-723-2220. Business E-Mail: mordecai@stanford.edu.

KURZ, WILLIAM CHARLES FREDERICK, lawyer; b. Baton Rouge, Aug. 26, 1942; s. William Charles Frederick Jr. and Helen Mae (Lafrantz) K. AB, Harvard U., 1964, LLB, 1967. Bar: N.Y. 1968, U.S. Dist. Ct. (so. dist.) N.Y. 1972, U.S. Supreme Ct. 1971. Assoc. Winthrop, Stimson, Putnam & Roberts, NYC, 1968-74, ptnr., 1975—2001; (Winthrop, Stimson, Putnam & Roberts merged with Pillsbury Madison & Sutro, 2001); ptnr., fin. & vice chair professional responsibility com. Pillsbury Winthrop LLP, NYC, 2001—05; (Pillsbury Winthrop LLP merged with Shaw Pittman LLP, 2005); ptnr., fin. Pillsbury Winthrop Shaw Pittman LLP, NYC, 2005—. Lectr. Sch. Law Columbia U., N.Y.C., 1987-92. Editorial advisor Internat. Fin. Law Rev., London, 1982-2002; contbr. articles to profl. jours. Mem. ABA, Assn. of Bar of City of NY, NY State Bar Assn., NY County Lawyers Assn., Down Town Assn., Harvard Club. Avocation: opera. Office: Pillsbury Winthrop Shaw Pittman LLP 1540 Broadway New York NY 10036 Office Phone: 212-858-1242. Business E-Mail: william.kurz@pillsburylaw.com.

KURZAWA, MARILYN TAYLOR, educational consultant; b. Buffalo, Aug. 15, 1942; d. Harry Newman and Dorothy Cannon Taylor; m. Richard Wade Gates, Aug. 5, 1967 (div. Dec. 0, 1988); children: Julie Gates, Matthew David Gates; m. David Frank Kurzawa, July 2, 1999. BA, Syracuse U., NY, 1964; MA, U. Iowa, Iowa City, 1969. Cert. French tchr. NY, 1965, elem. tchr. NY, 1981, sch. dist. adminstr. NY, 1984. Asst. supt. Pioneer Ctrl. Sch. Dist., Yorkshire, NY, 1989—92, Williamsville Ctrl. Sch. Dist., NY, 1992—94; dir. Erie 1 BOCES, West Seneca, NY, 1994—2001; cons. Learning Design Assocs., Inc, Silver Creek, NY, 2001—. Vol. ARC, Dunkirk, NY, 2005—; strategist, vol. WNY affiliate Susan G. Komen Found., Buffalo, 2004—; bd. dirs. Chautauqua County Habitat for Humanity, Silver Creek Satellite Cmty., 2007—, chair, 2006—. D-Liberal. Avocations: cooking, travel, walking, hiking. Office: Learning Design Assoc Inc 12765 Beach Ave Silver Creek NY 14136 Home Phone: 716-934-9543; Office Phone: 716-934-9543.

KURZBAN, IRA JAY, lawyer; b. Bklyn., May 9, 1949; s. Benjamin and Irene (Weiss) K.; m. Magda Montiel Davis, Apr. 15, 1989; children: Kathryn Montiel Davis, Paula Lindsay Davis, Magda Marie Marrache, Sadie Bethany Kurzban, Benjamin Kurzban. BA magna cum laude, Syracuse U., 1971; MA, U. Calif., Berkeley, 1973, JD, 1976; fellow (hon.), U. Pa. Law Sch., 1987. Bar: Calif. 1976, Fla. 1976, US Dist. Ct. (no. dist.) Calif., 1976, US Dist. Ct. (so. dist.) Fla., 1976, US Dist. Ct. (ctrl. dist.) Calif. 1999, US Ct. Appeals (5th cir.) 1978, US Ct. Appeals (11th cir.) 1981, US Ct. Appeals (4th cir.) 1994, US Ct. Appeals (6th cir.) 2002, US Ct. Appeals (2d cir.) 2003, US Supreme Ct. 1980. Ptnr. Kurzban, Kurzban, Weinger & Tetzeli P.A., Miami, Fla., 1977—. Adj. prof. immigration and nationality law U. Miami Sch. of Law, 1979—, Nova Southeastern Law Sch., 1982—; instr. polit. sci. U. Calif. Berkeley, 1973; mem. civil justice adv. com. US Dist. Ct. (so. dist.) Fla., 1993-94; mem. certification com. in immigration and nationality law Fla. Bar, 1994-96; gen. counsel Nat. Energy Civil Liberties Com., Fla., 1979-98; lectr. in field. Author: Kurzban's Immigration Law Sourcebook: A Comprehensive Outline and Reference Tool, 10th edit., 2006; contbr. articles to profl. jours. Founder Berkeley Law Found. Recipient Tobias Simon pro bono svc. award Fla. Supreme Ct., 1982, Trial Lawyer of Yr. award Trial Lawyers for Public Justice, Carol King award Nat. Lawyers Guild, 1996, Lawyer of the Ams. award U. Miami Sch. Law, 1992, Edith Lowenstein Meml. award for excellence in immigration scholarship, 2002; Polit. Sci. Dept. fellow U. Calif., Berkeley, 1971, Kent fellow Danforth Found., 1974-77, Law and Society fellow U. Calif., Berkeley, 1975-76, Wasserstein fellow Harvard Law Sch., 2003. Fellow Am. Immigration Law Found. (hon.); mem. ABA (chair refugee legal assistance com. 1983-84, mem. immigration coord. com. 1991-93), Am. Immigration Lawyers Assn. (pres. so. Fla. chpt. 1980-81, nat. pres. 1987, gen. counsel 1992-93, Jack Wasserman award for excellence in federal litigation 1983), Am. Inns of Ct., Phi Beta Kappa, Phi Kappa Phi. Office: Kurzban Kurzban Weinger & Tetzeli PA 2650 SW 27th Ave Miami FL 33133-3003 Office Phone: 305-444-0060. Business E-Mail: ira@kkwtlaw.com.

KURZMAN, ROBERT GRAHAM, lawyer, educator; b. NYC, July 3, 1932; s. Benjamin E. and Betty Kurzman; m. Carol Ellis, Aug. 26, 1956; children: Marc, Nancy, Amy. BA, Hofstra U., 1954; JD, Cornell U., 1957. Bar: N.Y. 1959, U.S. Dist. Ct. (no., so., ea. and we. dists.) N.Y. 1964, U.S. Supreme Ct. 1964. Assoc. Wynn, Blattmachr & Campbell, NYC, 1959-63; ptnr. Leaf, Kurzman, Deull & Drogin, NYC, 1963-79, Goldschmidt, Fredericks, Kurzman & Oshatz, 1979-83, Kurzman & Eisenberg and precedessor firms, White Plains, NY, 1982—. Adj. prof. law NYU; bd. dirs. Stratton Industries, Inc.; acting city. ct. judge City of New Rochelle, NY, 1981. Author (with Rita Gilbert): Paralegals and Successful Law Practice, 1981; contbr. articles to profl. jours. Pres. West Putnam coun. Boy Scouts Am., 1981; former chmn. New Rochelle Rep. Com.; trustee, pres. Temple Israel; mem. adv. bd. So. Meth. U. Sch. Law, Estate Planning Inst.; coord. estates and trusts paralegal program Manhattanville Coll., 1974—75. Capt. USAR, 1957—59. Named Man of the Yr., New Rochelle B'nai B'rith, 1977; recipient Silver Beaver award, Boy Scouts Am., Silver Antelope award. Fellow: Am. Coll. Probate Counsel; mem.: ABA, Assn. Bar City of N.Y., N.Y. State Bar Assn., Cornell Club (N.Y.C.) (pres.), Ridgeway Country Club (White Plains), Masons. Home: 166 Tewksbury Rd Scarsdale NY 10583-6036 Office: 1 N Broadway White Plains NY 10601-2310 Office Phone: 914-285-9800. Business E-Mail: rgk166@aol.com.

KURZWEG, ULRICH HERMANN, engineering science educator; b. Jena, Germany, Sept. 16, 1936; came to U.S., 1947, naturalized, 1952; s. Hermann Herbert and Erna Herta (Michaelis) K.; m. Sophia Speth, Dec. 21, 1963; 1 dau., Tina. BS, U. Md., 1958; MA (Woodrow Wilson fellow 1958-59), Princeton U., 1959, PhD in Physics, 1961. Sr. theoretical physicist United Tech. Rsch. Labs., East Hartford, Conn., 1962-68; adj. assoc. prof. math. Hartford (Conn.) Grad. Ctr., Rensselaer Poly. Inst., 1964-68; mem. faculty U. Fla., Gainesville, 1968—, prof. mech. and aerospace engring., 1968—2004, prof. emeritus, 2004—. Contbr. numerous articles to sci. and tech. publs. Fulbright grantee, 1961-62; recipient Cert. of Recognition, NASA, 1984, award for excellence in undergrad. teaching U. Fla., 1991. Mem. AAAS, Sigma Xi. Avocations: travel, woodworking. Home: 3742 SW 86th St Gainesville FL 32608-7900 Office: U Fla Dept Mech and Aerospace Engring Gainesville FL 32607 Office Phone: 352-392-6209. Business E-Mail: kurzweg@ufl.edu.

KURZWEIL, EDITH, social sciences educator, editor; b. Vienna; d. Ernest W. and Wilhelmine M. (Fischer) Weiss; widowed; 1 child, Allen J. BA, Queens Coll., CUNY, 1967; MA, New Sch. Social Rsch., 1969, PhD, 1973. Asst. prof. sociology Hunter Coll., NYC, 1972-75, Montclair State Coll., Upper Montclair, NJ, 1973-78; assoc. prof. Rutgers U., Newark, 1979-85, prof., chmn., 1985-92; Disting. Olin. Prof. Adelphi U., 1993, univ. prof., 1994—2001, prof. emeritus, 2001—. Vis. prof. Goethe U., 1984. Author: The Age of Structuralism, 1980, Italian Entrepreneurs, 1983, The Freudians: A Comparative Perspective, 1989, Freudians and Feminists, 1995, Briefe aus Wien: Nazi Laws & Jewish Lives, 1999, English lang. edit., 2005, The Partisan Century: 60 Years of Partisan Review, 1996, Full Circle: A Memoir, 2007; author: (with others) Literature and Psychoanalysis, 1983, Writers and Politics, 1983, Cultural Analysis, 1984; exec. editor: Partisan Rev., 1978—94; editor, 1994—2003; mem. editl. bd.: Psyche, 1990—, Psychoanalytic Books, 1990—2000, series editor: Psychiatry and Psychology Transaction, 1995—2004. Adv. bd. N.Y. Civil Rights Coalition, 2001—; bd. govs. New Sch. U., 1999—. Recipient Nat. Humanities medal, 2003; Rockefeller Humanities fellow, 1982—83, NEH fellow, 1987—88, NEH grantee, 1989—90, 1991—92, NYCH grantee, 1995. Mem.: PEN, Internat. Sociol. Assn., Internat. Assn. History Psychoanalysis, Tocqueville Soc., Am. Sociol. Assn., NY Civil Rights Coalition (bd. dirs. 2000—), Women's Freedom Network (bd. dirs. 1994—). Home: 1 Lincoln Plz New York NY 10023-7129

KURZWEIL, HARVEY, lawyer; b. Bklyn., Mar. 23, 1945; s. Martin E. Kurzweil and Muriel (Krause) Kanow; m. Barbara Kramer, Aug. 17, 1969; children: David, Paul (dec.), Emily, Elizabeth. AB, Columbia Coll., 1966, JD, 1969. Bar: N.Y. 1970, D.C. 1977, U.S. Dist. Ct. (ea. & so. dist. N.Y.), U.S. Ct. Appeals (2d, 3d, 5th, 7th, 8th, 9th, Fed. & D.C. cir.). Assoc. Dewey, Ballantine, Bushby, Palmer & Wood, NYC, 1969-77, ptnr., 1977-90, Dewey Ballantine LLP, NYC, 1990—, co-chmn. litig. dept. Contbr. chapters to books. Bd. dirs. Volunteer Lawyers for the Arts 1994-1999, Menningee Found., 1997-; trustee Menninger Found.1997-; bd. visitors Columbia Law Sch 2000-. Fellow Am. Bar Found., Internat. Acad. Trial Lawyers; mem. ABA, N.Y. State Bar Assn., D.C. Bar Assn., Assn. of Bar of City of N.Y. (trade regulation com. 1982-85), Fed. Bar Council, D.C. Bar Assn., Univ. Club. Jewish. Avocations: sports cars, reading, gardening, sports. Home: 1025 5th Ave New York NY 10028 Office: Dewey Ballantine LLP 1301 Avenue Of The Americas New York NY 10019-6092 also: PO Box 370 Saddle River NJ 07458-0389 Home Phone: 212-472-2225; Office Phone: 212-259-8300. Office Fax: 212-259-6333. Business E-Mail: hkurzweil@dbllp.com.

KURZWEIL, JEFFREY, lawyer; b. NYC, Feb. 4, 1950; AB cum laude, Duke Univ., 1972; JD, Vanderbilt Univ., 1975. Bar: NC 1975, DC 1980. Law clerk, Hon. Naomi E. Morris NC Ct. Appeals, 1975—76; spl. asst. to gen. counsel US Dept. Commerce, Washington, 1978—79; ptnr., legis., govt. affairs Venable LLP, Washington. Bd. dir., exec. com., treas. Best Friends Found. Office: Venable LLP 575 Seventh St NW Washington DC 20004 Office Phone: 202-344-4678. Office Fax: 202-344-8300. Business E-Mail: jkurzweil@venable.com.

KURZWEIL, RAYMOND C., computer scientist, entrepreneur; b. NYC, Feb. 12, 1948; s. Fredric and Hannah Kurzweil; m. Sonya Rosenwald, Aug. 3, 1975; 2 children. BS in Computer sci. and Lit., MIT, 1970; DHL (hon.), Hofstra U., 1982, Misericordia Coll., 1989; D of Music (hon.), Berklee Coll. Music, 1987; DSc (hon.), Renssalaer Polytech. Inst., 1988, Northeastern U., 1988, NJ Inst. Tech., 1990, Queens Coll., CUNY, 1991, Dominican Coll., 1993, Worcester Polytechnic Inst.; D of Engring. (hon.), Merrimack Coll., 1989; LHD (hon.), Misericordia Coll., 1989, Lnadmark Coll., 2002; D in Sci. and Humanities (hon.), Mich. State U., 2000. Founder, former CEO Kurzweil Computer Products, Inc. (now Xeroc Imaging Systems), Cambridge, Mass., 1974—80; chmn., former CEO (sold to Young Chang) Kurzweil Music Systems, Inc., Waltham, Mass., 1982—90; founder, former CEO Kurzweil Applied Intelligence, Inc. (acquired by Lernout & Hauspie), Waltham, Mass., 1982—97; founder, chmn., CEO Kurzweil Technologies Inc., 1995—; founder, former CEO Kurzweil Ednl. Systems Inc. (acquired by Lernout & Hauspie), 1996—98; founder, pres., CEO Med. Learning Co. Inc. and FamilyPractice.com, 1997—; founder, chmn., CEO FAT KAT Inc., 1999—, Kurzweil Cyber Art Technolgies, Inc., 2000; founder, CEO, and editor-in-chief KurzweilAI.net, 2001; co-founder, chmn., co-CEO Ray & Terry's Longevity Products, Inc., 2003. Chmn. exhbn. bd. Age of Intelligent Machines Exhbn. Mus. of Sci., Boston, 1985—; bd. dirs. Wang Labs., Med. Mgr. Corp., United Therapeutics, Inforte; lectr. in field. Author: The Age of Intelligent Machines, 1990 (Best Computer Sci. Book, 1990), The 10% Solution for a Healthy Life, 1993, The Age of Spiritual Machines, When Computers Exceed Human Intelligence, 1999 (Literary Lights prize, 1999), Fantastic Voyage: Live Long Enough to Live Forever, 2004, The Singularity Is Near: When Humans Transcend Biology, 2005, (collection of essays) The Ray Kurzweil Reader, (series of articles) "The Furturecast", Library Journal, 1991—93; contbr.; co-author (with Terry Grossman): Fantastic Voyage: The Science Behind Radical Life Extension, 2004; contbr. numerous articles to profl. jours., chapters to books; prodr.: (films) The Age of Intelligent Machines, 1987 (The Chris Plaque, 1987, Creative Excellence award, 1987, Gold Medal-Sci. Edu., 1987, CINE Golden Eagle award, 1987, Technology Culture award, 1988, Prize of the Pres. of the Festival, Internat. Film Festival of Czechoslovakia, 1988). Former mem. tech. adv. com. Nat. Ctr. Adult Literacy U. Pa.; chmn., founder The Kurzweil Found.; trustee Beth Israel Hosp.; overseer New. Eng. Conservatory of Music; incorporator Boston Mus. Sci.; mem. vis. com. MIT Sch. Music and MIT. Sch. Humanities; overseer, bd. overseers New England Conservatory Music; former dir. Boston Computer Soc.; chmn. Robots and Beyond: The Age of Intelligent Machines Exhbn. Named Hon. Chmn. for Innovation, White House Conf. on Small Bus., 1986, New Eng. Inventor of Yr., 1988; named to Computer Design Hall of Fame, Computer Design Mag., 1982, Nat. Inventors Hall of Fame, US Patent office, 2002; recipient First prize, Electronics and Comm., Internat. Sci. Fair, 1965, Gov.'s award, Mass. Gov. Michael Dukakis, 1977, Personal Computing to Aid the Handicapped Nat. award, Johns Hopkins U., 1981, Computer Sci. award, 1982, Francis Joseph Campbell award, Am. Libr. Assn., 1983, Best of the New Generation award, Esquire Mag., 1984, Disting. Inventor award, Intellectual Property Owners, 1986, Entrepreneurial Excellence award, White Ho. Conf. on Small Bus., 1986, Founders award, MIT, 1989, Engr. of Yr. award, Design News mag., 1990, Louis Braille award, Associated Svcs. for the Blind, 1991, Mass. Quincentennial award for innovation and discovery,

1992, Gordon Winston award, Can. Nat. Inst. Blind, 1994, Dickson prize, Carnegie Mellon U., 1994, Software Industry Achievement award, Mass. Software Coun., 1996, Access prize, Am. Found. Blind, 1995, Pres.'s award, Assn. Higher Edn. and Disability, 1997, Vision award, Stevie Wonder/SAP, 1998, Nat. Medal of Tech., 1999, Lemelson-MIT prize, 2000, Am. Composers Orchestra award, 2001, Migel Lay/Volunteer award, Am. Found. for the Blind, 2004. Fellow: Boston Computer Soc. (former bd. dirs.), Assn. Computing Machinery (Grace Murray Hopper Outstanding Young Computer Scientist of Yr. 1978). Achievements include patents in field; principal developer of the first omni-font Optical Character Recognition, the first print to speech reading machine for the blind, the first CCD flat-bed scanner, the first text-to-speech synthesizer; the first music synthesizer capable of recreating the grand piano and other orchestral instruments; the first commerically marketed large-vocabulary speech recognition; the first knowledge base system for creating medical reports; the first speech recognition dictation system for Windows; the first Continous Speech Natural Language Command and Control Software; the first print-to-speech reading system for persons with reading disabilities that reads from a displayed image of the page; the first virtual performing and recording artist (Ramona) to perform in front of a live audience with a live band; first host/hostess Avatar on the Web to combine a lifelike photo realistic, moving and speaking facial image with a conversational engine; developed a device, combining a personal digital assistant and a digital camera, called the Kurzweil-National Federation of the Blind Reader. Avocation: music. Office: Kurzweil Technologies Inc PMB 193 733 Turnpike St North Andover MA 01845 Office Phone: 781-263-0000. Office Fax: 781-263-9999. Business E-Mail: ray@kurzweiltech.com.

KUSAMA, YAYOI, sculptor, painter; b. Matsumoto-shi, Japan, Mar. 22, 1929; came to U.S., 1957, naturalized, 1963; Student, Kyoto Arts and Crafts Sch., Japan, 1948-49. Pres. Japan Edn. Co., 1977—. Author: Manhattan Suicide Addict, 1978, Christopher Homosexual Brothel, 1983, The Hustler's Grotto of Christopher Street (Tenth Lit. New Writers award 1983), 1983, Lost in Swapland, 1992, others; contbr. articles to mags. and newspapers; one-man shows include Aggregation One Thousand Boats, N.Y.C., 1963, Driving Image show, N.Y.C., 1964, Chrysler Mus., Provincetown, 1965, Castellane Gallery, N.Y.C., 1965, 66, Naviglio Gallery, Milan, Italy, 1966, 82 Thelen Gallery, Essen, Germany, 1966, Fillmore East Theatre Happening, 1968, Mus. Modern Art, N.Y.C., 1969, Fashion show Venice, Italy, 1971, The Haag, The Netherlands, 1971, Am. Ctr., Tokyo, 1980, Fuji Television Gallery, Tokyo, 1982, 84, 86, 88, 91, 94, Galerie Christian Cheaneau, Paris, 1986, Musée des Beaux-Art, Calais, 1986, Kitakyushu Mcpl. Mus., 1987, Musée Mcpl., Dôle, France, 1987, (retrospective) Ctr. Internat. Contemporary Arts, N.Y.C., 1989, Mus. Modern Art, Oxford, London, 1989, Sogetsu Mus. Art, Tokyo, 1992, Niigata City Art Mus., 1992, Japan Pavilion Venezia Biennale, 1993, Galleria Valentina Moncada, Rome, 1993, Naviglio Venezia, 1993, Paula Cooper Gallery, N.Y.C., 1996, Robert Miller Gallery, N.Y.C., 1996, Baumgertner Galleries, Inc., Washington, 1997; group shows include Bklyn. Mus., 1955, 58, De Cordova Mus., Boston, 1960, 65, Riverside Mus., N.Y.C., 1960, Städtisches Mus., Schloss Morsbroish, Leverkusen, Germany, 1960, 61, Whitney Mus. Am. Art, N.Y.C., 1961, 62, Pitts. Mus., 1961, City Mus., Städtisches Mus., Trier, Germany, 1961, Nul Stedelijk Mus., Amsterdam, 1962, Inst. Contemporary Art, 1964, 65, Modern Art Gallery, Washington, 1965, Chrysler Mus., Provincetown, Mass., 1965, Mus. Modern Art, Stockholm, Sweden, 1966, Met. Mus., Tokyo, 1965, Mus. Modern Art, N.Y.C., 1966, Woman's Work-Am. Art, Phila., 1974, Improbable Furniture, U. Pa., 1977, Neich und Plastisch-Soft Art, Zurich, 1979, Nat. Mus. Art, Osaka, 1980, Nat. Mus. Modern Art, Tokyo, 1981, Yokohama City Gallery, 1982, Landmark Tower, Yokohama, 1993, Guggenheim Mus., 1994, Scream Against the Sky, San Francisco Mus. Modern Art, 1995, Otis Gallery, L.A., 1995, Ars 95, Helsinki, 1995, Louisiana Mus., Denmark, 1995, L.A. County Mus. Art, Mus. Modern Art, N.Y., Walker Art Ctr., 1998, Taipei Biennale, Taipei Art Fair, 1998, Serpentine Gallery, 2000, Le consortium, Maison de culture Japan, Paris, Le Abattoirs, 2001, KUNSTHALLE, Wien, 2002, The Whitney Biennial, 2004, Kunstverein Braunschweig, Zacheta Nat. Gallery of Art, 2004, Nat. Mus. Modern Art, Tokyo, 2004, 05, Mori Art Mus., 2004, Nat. Mus. Modern Art, Kyoto, 2005, many others; represented in permanent collections Chrysler Mus., Stedelijk Mus., Amsterdam; prodr., star: Kusama's Self-Obliteration (Fourth Internat. Exptl. Film Competition prize, Ann Arbor Film Festival prize, Second Md. Film Festival prize 1968); organized, presented happenings worldwide. Decorated Officier; recipient Best Gallery Show prize Internat. Assn. Art Critics, 1995-96, 96-97, Edn. Minister's Art Encouragement prize, Fgn.-Min.'s commendations, 2000, Asahi prize, 2001, Dark Navy Blue Ribbon medal, 2002, Nagano Gov. prize contbn. in encouragement of art and culture, 2003, Praemium Imperiale (Painting), Japan Art Assn., 2006. Invented infinity mirror room. E-mail: love-forever@yayoi-kusama.jp.

KUSHAR, KENT, information technology executive; BS, Univ. Montana; postgrad. Advanced Bus. and Tech. Program, Harvard Bus. Sch., Kellogg Sch. at Northwestern, Chgo. Dir. IBM Consulting; gen. mgr. IBM-ROLM subs., Calif.; co-founder EDP Industries; tech. v.p. Citicorp; mng. prin. Unisys Cons.; v.p. & chief info. officer E&J Gallo Winery, Modesto, Calif. Nat. bd. advisors Univ. Ariz.; bus. advisory bd. Calif. State Univ., Stanislaus; bd. of advisors Info. Tech. Rsch. Ctr. Avocation: auto restoration. Office: VP & CIO E&J Gallo Winery PO Box 1130 Modesto CA 95353 Business E-Mail: kent.kushar@ejgallo.com.

KUSHEN, ALLAN STANFORD, retired lawyer, corporate executive; b. Chgo., Oct. 5, 1929; s. Barney and Ethel (Friedman) K.; m. Betty Cohen, Sept. 2, 1951 (dec. Jan. 2000); children: Annette Joyce, Robert Allan; m. Natalie Best, June 1, 2001. BBA cum laude, LLB cum laude, U. Miami, Fla., 1952; LLM, NYU, 1955. Bar: Fla. 1952, N.Y. 1956. Atty. Schering Corp., Bloomfield, NJ, 1955-67, atty. counsel labs. divsn., 1967-69, atty. domestic ops. divsn., 1969-73; v.p., gen. counsel Schering-Plough Corp., Kenilworth, NJ, 1973-80, sr. v.p. pub. affairs Madison, NJ, 1980-94; ret., 1994. Adv. com. Allendale Ins. Co., N.Y., 1986-94; lectr. in field. Trustee Food and Drug Law Inst., 1972-94, emeritus, 1994—, Arts Coun. Morris Area, 1983-93, 2005—, pres., 1989-93, Montclair Art Mus., 2000-05, Friends of Florham, 2005-, Harding Land Trust, 2006-. Food and Drug Law Inst. fellow NYU, 1955. Mem. Phi Delta Phi, Omicron Delta Kappa, Iron Arrow. Home: 58 Millbrook Rd New Vernon NJ 07976

KUSHLAN, JAMES ANTHONY, science administrator, educator, conservationist, writer; b. Cleve., Oct. 11, 1947; BS in Biology and Chemistry cum laude, U. Miami, 1969, MS in Biology, 1972, PhD in Biology, 1974; DSc (hon.), Thiel Coll., Greenville, Pa., John Cabot U., Rome, Italy. Rsch. biologist U.S. Dept. of Interior, 1975-84; assoc. prof. biology Tex. A&M U., Commerce, 1984—87, prof. biology, 1987-88, dir. ctr. water resources studies, 1986-88; prof. biology U. Miss., 1988-98, chmn. dept. biology, 1988—95; dir. Patuxent Wildlife Rsch. Ctr., 1995-2001; sr. sci. advisor U.S. Geol. Survey, 2001—02; sr. rsch. assoc. Smithsonian Inst., 2001—05. Author: The Herons Handbook, 1984, Freshwater Fishes of Southern Florida, 1987, Storks, Ibises and Spoonbills of the World, 1992, Heron Conservation, 2000, The Herons, 2005; contbr. to Dictionary of Birds, 1985, Encyclopedia of Birds, 1985, Ecosystems of Florida, 1990, The Rivers of Florida, 1991; editor Fla. Field Naturalist, 1981-86, Colonial Waterbirds, 1985-88; mem. editl. bd. Wetlands, 1982, assoc. editor, 1993-95; author 200 papers, revs., commentaries; contbr. articles to profl. jours. Mem. United Way Planning Coun., Oxford, Miss., 1991-92; bd. dirs. Miss. Nature Conservancy, 1991-95; bd. dirs. John Cabot U., Am. Bird Conservancy, N.Am. Bird Conservation Initiative, Waterbird Conservation for the Ams., Tropical Audubon Soc., Biscayne Nature Ctr., Hawk Mountain Sanctuary, Friends the Everglades; chair Bird Conservation Alliance, 2002-05; chair Herons Specialist Group, 1985-97, 2003—; mem. sci bd. Station Biology de la Tour du Valat. Recipient Citizen award WIOD Radio, Miami, 1980; Paul Harris fellow Rotary Internat., 1989. Fellow Am. Ornithologists' Union (life, mem. coun., v.p. 1998-99, pres. 2004-2006), mem. Soc. Wetland Scientist (life, assoc. editor), Waterbird Soc. (bd. dirs., pres. 1996-98, Lindahl award for internat. conservation 2003), Friends of the Everglades, Am. Rotary (chpt. pres. 1987-88), Sigma Xi (chpt. pres. 1983-84). Achievements include research in ornithology, wetland sciences, international wetland and biodiversity conservation, and waterbirds. Office Phone: 305-365-0306. Personal E-mail: jkushlan@earthlink.net.

KUSHLAN, SAMUEL DANIEL, internist, educator, hospital administrator; b. New Britain, Conn., Feb. 17, 1912; s. H. David and Bessie M. K.; m. Ethel Ross, June 24, 1934; children: Nancy Kushlan Wanger, David Ross. BS, Yale U., 1932, MD, 1935. Diplomate: Am. Bd. Internal Medicine with subsplty in gastroenterology. Intern New Haven Hosp., 1935-36, asst. resident, 1937; vol. research fellow Mass. Gen. Hosp., 1938; assoc. physician-in-chief Yale-New Haven Hosp., 1967-82, cons. to chief staff, 1982—; clin. prof. medicine Yale U., 1967—. Contbr. numerous articles to profl. jours. Mem. bequest and endowment program Yale Med. Sch. Alumni Fund, 1977—; cons. to office of alumni affairs Yale Med. Sch., 1990—. Named Physician of Yr. Conn. Digestive Disease Soc., 1975 Mem. AMA, Am. Gastroenterol. Assn., Am. Soc. Gastrointestinal Endoscopy, Conn. State Med. Soc., New Haven Med. Assn., Conn. Regional Soc. for Gastrointestinal Endoscopy, World Med. Assn., Assn. Yale Alumni in Medicine (pres. 1957-59), Yale Alumni Fund (bd. dirs. 1986-91), ACP (Lifetime Achievement award Conn. chpt. 2003), Sigma Xi, Alpha Omega Alpha. Office: Suite 1063 CB Yale-New Haven Hosp New Haven CT 06504 Office Phone: 203-688-2604. *Life must have Meaning.*

KUSHNER, BETH, lawyer; d. David and Patricia Kushner; m. Marc Rasansky, June 3, 1984. BA, U. Wis., Milw., 1975; JD, U. Va., 1979. Bar: Va. 1979, Wis. 1980, U.S. Dist. Ct. (ea. and we. dists.) Wis. 1987, lic.: U.S. Ct. Appeals (7th cir.) 1988, bar: U.S. Supreme Ct. 1992. Shareholder von Briesen & Roper, S.C., Milw., 1986—. Instr. U. Wis. Law Sch., Madison, 1995—. Bd. dirs. Meta Ho., Milw., 2003—06. Named a Wis. Super Lawyer, 2005—06; recipient Mentoring award, Assn. Women Lawyers, 2002, Pro Bono award, Gene and Ruth Posner Found., 1997. Office: von Briesen & Roper SC 411 E Wisconsin Ave Ste 700 Milwaukee WI 53202 Home Phone: 414-540-1602; Office Phone: 414-287-1373. Office Fax: 414-276-6281. Business E-Mail: bkushner@vonbriesen.com.

KUSHNER, EVA, academic administrator, educator, author; b. Prague, Czechoslovakia, June 18, 1929; d. Josef and Anna (Kafkova) Dubsky; m. Donn Jean Kushner, Sept. 15, 1949 (dec. 2001); children: Daniel Peter, Roland Joseph, Paul Joel. PhB, Coll. Marie de France, Montreal, 1946; BA, McGill U., 1948, MA, 1950, PhD in French Lit., 1956; D (hon.), Acadia U., 1988, United Theol. Coll., 1992, St Michael's U., 1993, U. Western Ont., 1996, U. Szeged, 1997, Victoria U., Toronto, Can., 2006. Lectr. French McGill U., Montreal, 1952-55, instr. French, 1956, 58, 61-62, 67-69, prof. French lang. and lit., 1976-87, chair dept. French, 1976-80; pres., vice chancellor Victoria U. U. Toronto, 1987-94, dir. ctr. comparative lit., 1994-95; vis. prof. Princeton U., 2000; Mary Rowell Jackman and Mary Coyne Rowell prof. Victoria Coll., 2001—. Sessional lectr. philosophy Sir George Williams U., 1952-53; lectr. U. Coll., London, 1958-59; lectr. Carleton U., 1961; asst. prof. French & comparative lit., 1963, assoc. prof., 1965, prof., 1969-76, chmn. comparative lit., 1965-69, 70-72, 75-76, adj. prof. lit., 1976-79; mem. exec. com. Can. Coun., 1975-81; v.p. Social Scis. & Humanities Rsch. Coun. Can., 1983-86; mem. adv. bd. Nat. Libr. Can.; pres. Humanities Rsch. Coun. Can. 1970-72; vice-chmn. George R. Gardiner Mus. Ceramic Arts, 1990-94. Author: Patrice de La Tour de Pin, 1961; Le Mythe d'Orphée dans la Littérature Française Contemporaine, 1961; Chants de Bohême, 1963; Rina Lasnier, Collection Ecrivains Canadiens d'Aujourd'hui, 1964; Poètes d'Aujourd'hui, 1969; Saint-Denys Garneau, 1967; François Mauriac, 1972, Japanese transl., 1976; co-author anthology Que. poetry, transl. into Hungarian, 1978, Polish, 1985, The Living Prism. Itineraries in Comparative Literature, 2001, Pontus de Tyard et son oeuvre poétique, 2001, Le dialogue à la Renaissance Histoire et poétique, 2004; editor Renewals in the Theory of Literary History; co-editor/co-author: L'Avènement de l'Esprit Nouveau (1400-80), 1988, Crises et essors nouveaux (1560-1610), 2000, Théorie Littéraire: Problèmes et Perspectives, 1989, Histoire des Poétiques, 1997; editor, co-author La Problématique du Sujet chez Montaigne, 1995; co-dir. rsch. Renaissance vols. Histoire Comparée des Littératures de Langues Européennes; dir. critical edit. Complete Works of Pontus de Tyard, Vol. 1, Oeuvres Poetiques, 2004, De la droite imposition des noms, vol. 7, 2007; mem. editl. com. Can. Comparative Lit. Rev., Dalhousie French Studies, Etudes Montaignistes; mem. internat. adv. bd. Synthesis, Lit. Rsch., 1990-95; contbr. articles to profl. publs. Named Officer Order of Can., 1997. Fellow Royal Soc. Can. (v.p. 1980-82); mem. MLA (del. assembly, chmn. 16th century French lit. divsn., mem. exec. coun. 1983-86, nominating com. 1986-88), Assn. Internat. des Études Françaises, Assn. Canadienne de Littérature Comparée (v.p. 1969-71), Académie Européenne des Lettres, des Sciences et des Arts, Am. Comparative Lit. Assn. (adv. bd.), Internat. Comparative Lit. Assn. (pres. 1979-82, co-editor proc. 7th and 9th ICLA Congress, 11th Congress, vols. IV-V, 1991, VI, 1992, VII-VIII, 1993, IX, 1994, X, 1995), Internat. Fedn. Modern Langs. and Lits. (v.p. 1987-93, pres. 1996-99), Internat. Coun. Philosophy and Humanistic Studies (v.p., 2006-), Internat. Assn. Neo-Latin Studies, Soc. Canadienne d'Études de la Renaissance, Assn. des Littératures Canadienne et Québecoise, Renaissance Soc. Am., Assn. des Professeurs de Français des Universités Canadiennes, Renaissance Soc. Am. (discipline rep. for French studies 1996-99), Can. Pensioners Concerned (mem. Ont. bd.), Ont. Coalition Sr. Citizens Orgns. (co-chair 2003-2004). Office: Victoria Coll 73 Queen's Park Toronto ON Canada M5S 1K7 Office Phone: 416-585-4592. Business E-Mail: eva.kushner@utoronto.ca.

KUSHNER, FREDERICK GARY, cardiologist, medical educator; b. NYC, May 20, 1948; s. Jack and Gloria Kushner; m. Ivy Erica Sommerstein, May 8, 1977; children: Adam Benjamin, Jared Scott. BA, Columbia U., 1970, MD, 1974. Med. intern, resident Harvard Beth Israel, Boston, 1974—76; cardiology fellow U. Pa., Phila., 1976—78, Mass. Gen. Hosp., Boston, 1978—79; clin. prof. medicine Tulane U. Sch. Medicine, New Orleans, 1993—; med. dir. Heart Clinic La., Marrero, 1995—. Chmn. credentials com. Leadership Com. of the Coun. on Clin. Cardiology of the Am. Heart Assn., Dallas, 1999—2001; com. mem. Guidelines Com. for mgmt. of ST Elevation MI of the Am. Heart Assn. and Am. Coll. of Cardiology, Washington, 2001—. Exhibitions include World Trade Ctr., New Orleans Acad. Fine Arts, others. Pres. The New Orleans Friends Music, 2000—03; bd. mem. Touro Synagogue, New Orleans, 2002—, Columbia Coll. Alumni Assn., NYC, 1996—; alumni coun. bd. mem. Columbia Coll. Physicians and Surgeons, NYC, 1996—. Fellow: ACP (licentiate), Am. Heart Assn., Soc. Cardiac Angiography and Interventions (licentiate), Soc. Nuc. Cardiology (licentiate), Am. Coll. Cardiology (licentiate; v.p. La. chpt. 1990); mem.: Alpha Omega Alpha (Vol. Clin. Faculty Tchg. award 1999). Achievements include research in nuclear cardiology and perfusion scanning. Avocations: painting, sailing, travel, reading, golf. Office: Heart Clinic La Suite 613 Physicians Center North Marrero LA 70072 Office Phone: 504-349-2010. Personal E-mail: fjakush@aol.com.

KUSHNER, GARY JAY, lawyer; b. Bronx, NY, Mar. 17, 1950; s. Israel Sol and Shyrle Renee (Mervish) K.; m. Gail Barbara Kline, June 27, 1981; children: Aaron, Jamie, Stuart. AB, U. Mich.; JD, Georgetown U. Bar: Md. 1975, D.C. 1976, U.S. Dist. Ct. D.C., 1976, U.S. Ct. Appeals (D.C. cir.) 1978, U.S. Ct. Appeals (fed. cir.) 1991, U.S. Ct. Appeals (5th cir.) 1992, U.S. Ct. Appeals (9th cir.) 1994, U.S. Ct. Appeals (11th cir.) 2004, U.S. Supreme Ct. 1984. Law clk. to judge Superior Ct., Washington, 1975-76; staff counsel Grocery Mfrs. Am., Washington, 1976-78; assoc. Leighton, Conklin & Lemov, Washington, 1978-80, Collier, Shannon, Rill & Scott, Washington, 1980-82, ptnr., 1985-89; v.p., gen. counsel Am. Meat Inst., Washington, 1982-85; ptnr. Hogan & Hartson LLP, Washington, 1989—, food drug & medical device practice group dir. Adv. bd. USDA Grad. Sch., 1989—; bd. dirs. Seed Programs, Inc.; adj. fellow Ctr. for Food and Nutrition and Agrl. Policy U. Md. Contbr. articles to profl. jours. Mem. adv. bd. Food Safety Letter, 1983-88, bd. govs., exec. com., nat. commn. nat. commn. Anti-Defamation League, Washington, 1995-; pro bono counsel Second Harvest, Chgo., 1989-95; bd. dirs. D.C. Hunger Action, 1995, 00, Advocates for Better Children's Diets, Washington, 1994-00. Mem. ABA, Fed. Bar Assn. (coun. chair 1975-95), Am. Agrl. Law Assn., Inst. Food Technologists, Am. Soc. Assn. Execs., City Club Washington (bd. dirs. 1995-), Disting. Order Zerocrats. Avocations: running, tennis, golf. Office: Hogan & Hartson LLP 555 13th St NW Ste 7W Washington DC 20004-1161 Office Phone: 202-637-5856. Office Fax: 202-637-5910. Business E-Mail: gjkushner@hhlaw.com.

KUSHNER, GORDON PETER, lawyer; b. Calgary, Alta., Can., Nov. 3, 1966; came to US, 1984; s. H. Peter and V. Marlene (Shatilla) K.; m. Patti A. Yakich, Aug. 10, 1991; children: Brantley Peter, Katerina Mari. BA summa cum laude, U. N.D., 1988; JD cum laude, U. Dayton, 1991. Bar: Ohio 1991, U.S. Dist. Ct. (so. dist.) Ohio 1991. Atty. Dinsmore & Shohl, Cin., 1991-94; atty. internat. ops. LensCrafters Internat., Inc., Cin., 1994-95; corp. atty. Structural Dynamics Rsch. Corp., Milford, Ohio, 1995-98—; v.p., chief tech. counsel Baan Co. N.V., Herndon, Va., Barneveld, Netherlands, 1998-2000; v.p., gen. counsel the Platform for Media, Herndon, 2000—. Dir. Rite Track Equipment Svcs., Inc., Cin., 1994-95; mem. Vision Coun. of Can., Toronto, Ont., 1994-95; spkr. U. Cin. Law Sch., 1993. Author: (newsletter) Cincinnati Small Business Newsletter, 1993; contbr. articles to profl. jours. Mem. Big Bros. and Big Sisters, Dayton, 1990-91; dir. Housing Network of Hamilton County, Cin., 1993-94; coach Lakota Sports Orgn., West Chester, Ohio, 1997-98; treas. Woodlea WaterMocs Swim Team, 2000—. Recipient Yale in Can. Outstanding Can. award Yale U. Can. Alumni Assn., 1990. Mem. ABA, Ohio Bar Assn., Cin. Bar Assn. (presenter NAFTA seminar 1992), Phi Alpha Delta, Phi Beta Kappa. Home: 1409 Moore Pl SW Leesburg VA 20175-5820 E-mail: gordonkushner@theplatform.com.

KUSHNER, HAROLD JOSEPH, mathematics professor; b. NYC, July 29, 1933; s. Hyman and Harriet Kushner; m. Linda Rosen, Sept. 20, 1960; children: Diana, Nina. BA, CCNY, 1955; MS, U. Wis., 1956, PhD, 1958. Mem. staff Lincoln Lab., Lexington, Mass., 1955-63, Rias, Balt., 1963-64; prof. applied math. Brown U., Providence, 1964—, dir. Lefschtez Ctr. Dynamical Systems, 1980-87, 95-99, chmn. divsn. applied math., 1988-91. Cons. numerous govt. agys. and cos., 1964—. Author: Stochastic Stability and Control, 1967, Introduction to Stochastic Control Theory, 1972, Probability Methods for Approximations in Stochastic Control, 1977, Stochastic Approximation, 1978, Weak Convergence Methods and Applications to Stochastic Systems, 1984, Weak Convergence Methods and Singularly Perturbed Stochastic Control and Filtering Problems, 1991, Numerical Methods for Stochastic Control Problems in Continuous Time, 1992, 2d edit. 2001, Stochastic Approximation Algorithms and Applications, 1997, 2d edit. 2003, Heavy Traffic Analysis of Controlled Queuing and Communication Networks, 2001. Recipient Louis E. Levy award, Franklin Inst., 1994, Bellman Heritage award, Am. Automatic Control Coun., 2004; grantee, U.S. govt. agys., 1964—. Fellow IEEE (life, Control Systems Field award 1992); mem. Inst. Math. Stats., Soc. Indsl. and Applied Math. (W.T. and Idalia Reid prize 2003), Ops. Rsch. Soc. Am., Inst. Mgmt. Sci. Home: 560 Lloyd Ave Providence RI 02906-5427 Office: Brown U Divsn Applied Math Providence RI 02912-0001 Business E-Mail: hjk@dam.brown.edu.

KUSHNER, HAROLD SAMUEL, rabbi; b. NYC, Apr. 3, 1935; s. Julius and Sarah (Hartman) K.; m. Suzette Estrada, Mar. 27, 1960; 1 child, Ariel. BA, Columbia U., 1955, MA, 1960; DHL, Jewish Theol. Sem., NYC, 1972; DLH, U. Mass. Med. Ctr., 1987. Ordained rabbi 1960. Assoc. rabbi Temple Israel, Great Neck, N.Y., 1962-66, Natick, Mass., 1966-90, rabbi laureate, 1991—. Author: When Bad Things Happen to Good People, 1981, When All You've Ever Wanted Isn't Enough, 1986, Who Needs God, 1990,To Life, 1993, How Good Do We Have To Be?, 1996. 1st lt. U.S. Army, 1960-62. Named on of The Top 50 Rabbis in America, Newsweek Mag., 2007. Office: 145 Hartford St Natick MA 01760-3125 also: care Curtis Brown Ltd 10 Astor Pl New York NY 10003-6935*

KUSHNER, HARVEY DAVID, management consultant; b. NYC, Dec. 28, 1930; s. Morris K. and Hilda Kushner; m. Rose Rehert, Jan. 14, 1951 (dec. 1990); children: Gantt A., Todd R., Lesley K.; m. Patricia E. Sacks, Jan. 1992. BS in Engring., Johns Hopkins U., 1951. Assoc. engr. U.S. Navy Bur. Ships, 1951-53; mem. tech. staff Melpar Inc., 1953-54; with ORI Inc., 1955-88, pres., 1969-83; chmn. bd., CEO ORI, Inc., 1977-88; chmn. bd., pres. The ORI Group, Inc., 1985-88; v.p. Reliance Group Inc. (parent co. of ORI, Inc.), 1970-77; pres. Disclosure Inc., 1972-77; group pres., sr. v.p. Atlantic Rsch. Corp. parent co. of ORI Group, Inc., 1987-88; pres. Kushner Mgmt. Planning Corp., Palos Verdes, Calif., 1988—; chmn. bd. trustees Maryland Venture Capital Trust, 1990-2001. Cons. in bus. and tech. devel., mgmt. and orgn.; bd. dirs. Computer Tech. Assocs., 1988-01, MRJ Tech., Inc., 1988-00, Naviant Tech., Inc., 1998-00, Stamet, Inc., 1994—, Hyperspace Comms., Inc., 2002—. Pub. Rose Kushner's If You've Thought About Breast Cancer. Chmn. Commn. Higher Edn. in Sci. and Tech., Montgomery County, Md., 1984-85, Md. Govs. High Tech. Roundtable, Annapolis, Md., 1983-86, United Way Campaign, Montgomery County, 1980, mem. exec. bd., 1981-85; bd. dirs. Montgomery County High Tech. Coun., 1986-96, chmn. 1986-1991; chmn. bd. dirs. Rose Kushner Breast Cancer Adv. Ctr., 1990—; mem. nat. subcom. on breast cancer detection and control Am. Cancer Soc., 1991-95; mem. bd. vis. Sch. Pub. Affairs, U. Md., 1988-93, chmn., 1991-92; mem. nat. adv. coun. Sch. Engring. Johns Hopkins U., 1987—, mem. adv. bd. Info. Security Inst., 2004—; mem. bd. visitors U. Md. Biotech. Inst., 1993—. Recipient Superior Pub. Svc. medal Dept. of Navy, 1988. Fellow AAAS, N.Y. Acad. Scis.; mem. ASME, IEEE (sr.), Nat. Security Indsl. Assn. (chmn. exec. com. 1987-88, chmn. anti-submarine warfare com. 1986-88, mem. bd. trustees 1982-97, vice-chmn. bd. trustees 1987-88, chmn. bd. 1988-89, Vice-Adm. Charles E. Weakley award 1991), Profl. Svcs. Coun. (bd. dirs. 1974-2002, v.p. 1983-88, chmn. bd. dirs. 1991-92), Inst. for Ops. Rsch. and the Mgmt. Scis., Am. Inst. Aerospace Sci., Nat. Def. Industry Assn. (trustee 1997-2001), (assoc.) Sigma Xi, Cosmos Club. E-mail: harveydk@aol.com.

KUSHNER, JACK, retired physician; b. Montgomery, Ala., Dec. 5, 1939; s. Louis Harry and Rose (Feldman) K.; m. Annetta Esther Horwitz, June 21, 1964; children: Reyna, Eve. Student, U. Sheffield, 1959—60; BA in History, Tulane, 1960; MD, U. Ala., 1964; M in Fin., U. Md., 1990. Diplomate Am. Bd. Neurosurgery, 1976, cert. in Neurosurgery. Intern George Washington U. Hosp., Washington, 1964-65; resident in surgery U. Mich., Ann Arbor, 1965-66; resident in neurosurgery Bowman Gray Sch. Medicine Wake Forest U., Winston-Salem, NC, 1968-72; pvt. practice neurosurgery, Annapolis, Md., 1972-95; clin. asst. prof. neurosurgery George Washington U., 1976—80; pres., CEO, Futuristic Instruments, Annapolis, 1995-98; chmn., bd. dirs. Telehealth, 1999; ret., 2000; cons. in field. Bd. mgrs. Anne Arundel Med. Ctr., Annapolis, Md., 1978-80; mem. Mil. Leadership Coun., U. Md., 2003—; bd. dirs. E-Global Telehealth, 1999—; chmn., CEO Am. Opportunity Portal, Annapolis, 2003—; cons. Artemis Strategy Fund.; lectr. UMUC-Graduate Sch. Bus Author: Preparing To Tack: When Physicians Change Careers, 1995; contbr. articles to profl. jours. With U.S Army, 1966-68, combat surgeon, Vietnam; founding mem. 1902 Soc. Decorated Bronze Star; recipient Most Disting. Alumnus award U. Md., 2001, laureate Marie Curie award for contbns. to neurosurgery and emerging med. tech. Oxford U., 2006, Lifetime Achievement award World Forum, Washington, 2007. Fellow ACS (emerging tech. and edn. com.), Internat. Coll. Surgeons; mem. Am. Assoc. Neurol. Surgeons, Congress of Neurol. Surgeons, So. Neurosurg. Soc., Pan Pacific Neurosurg. Soc., Tulane U. Alumni Assn. (bd. dirs., univ. coll. dir.-at-large), US Naval Acad. Golf Assn.(sr. men's tournament dir.). Republican. Jewish. Avocations: golf, yacht racing. Home: Ferry Farms 2030 Homewood Rd Annapolis MD 21409-5970 Office Phone: 410-757-3754. Personal E-mail: jkaoportal@comcast.net.

KUSHNER, JARED C., publishing executive, real estate developer; b. Jan. 10, 1981; s. Charles B. Kushner. BA, Harvard U., 2003; student, NYU Law Sch.; MBA student, NYU. Prin. Kushner Cos.; owner, pub. NY Observer, 2006—; owner PoliticsNJ.com, 2007—. Achievements include being involved in purchase or sale of more than 35 buildings since age 19; purchase of 666 Fifth Avenue, the largest single building transaction in the country. Office: NY Observer 9th Fl 915 Broadway New York NY 10010 Office Phone: 212-755-2400.*

KUSHNER, JEFFREY L., manufacturing executive; b. Wilmington, Del., Apr. 7, 1948; s. William and Selma (Kreger) K.; m. Carolyn Patricia Hypes, May 2, 1975; children: Tawnya Lynne. BBA summa cum laude, U. Hawaii, 1970; MBA, Columbia U., 1972. Sr. fin. analyst Black & Decker, Towson, Md., 1972-73, div. controller Solon, Ohio, 1973-74; asst. div. controller Rockwell Internat., Pitts., 1974-75; div. contr. Carborundum Corp., Niagara Falls, NY, 1975-77; mgr. fin. planning United Techs. Corp., Hartford, Conn., 1977-80, corp. v.p. fin. planning, 1986-88, corp. v.p. asset mgmt., 1989-92; asst. contr. Sikorsky Aircraft, Stratford, Conn., 1980-82, div. controller, 1982-83, v.p. fin., chief fin. officer, 1983-85; v.p. fin. and adminstrn. MasterBrand Industries Inc., Deerfield, Ill., 1993-98; sr. v.p. fin. and CFO Lorillard Tobacco Co., 1998; exec. v.p., CFO Cookson Electronics, 1999—2005; ret., 2005. Bd. dirs. ACR, Hartford. 1987-88. Recipient Bronfman Found. fellowship, 1970-71. Mem. Conf. Bd. (coun. 1987-88), Fin. Execs. Inst. Home: 195 Woodland Rd Westwood MA 02090-2631 Business E-Mail: jlk95@columbia.edu.

KUSHNER, LAWRENCE, rabbi; b. Detroit; m. Karen Kushner; 3 children. BA Phi Beta Kappa, U. Cincinnati. Cert. ordained Rabbi Hebrew Union Coll, 1969. Rabbi Congregation of Beth El, Sudbury, Mass.; rabbi-in-residence Hebrew Union College-Jewish Inst. Religion, NYC; vis. prof. Jewish Spirituality Grad. Theological U., Berkeley, Calif.; Emanu-El scholar in residence Emanu-El Congregation, San Francisco. Contbr. articles to numerous profl. jours.; author: (novels) Kabbalah: A Love Story. Named one of The Top 50 Rabbis in America, Newsweek Mag., 2007. Achievements include being first Rabbinic Chairman of Reform Judaism's Commission on Religious Living. Office: The Congregation Emanu-El 2 Lake St San Francisco CA 94118 Office Phone: 415-751-2541 148.*

KUSHNER, LAWRENCE MAURICE, physical chemist, consultant; b. NYC, Sept. 20, 1924; s. Hyman Tobias and Mary (Malkin) K.; children: Robb Adam, Leslie Meryl; m. Shirley Gayle Brown, June 24, 1972. BS, Queens Coll., 1945; A.M., Princeton U., 1947, PhD, 1949. Teaching asst. Princeton U., 1947-48; with Nat. Bur. Standards, 1948-73, chief, metal physics sect., 1956-61, chief, metallurgy div., 1961-66; dep. dir. Inst. Applied Tech., 1966-68, dir., 1968, dep. dir. bur., 1969-73, acting dir. bur., 1972-73; commr. Consumer Product Safety Commn., Washington, 1973-77; policy devel. Nat. Bur. Standards, 1977-80; mem. div. staff Mitre Corp., McLean, Va., 1980-85, cons. scientist, 1985-89; adj. prof. engring. and public policy Carnegie-Mellon U., 1981-91. Lectr. chemistry Am. U., 1952-60; spl. asst. for legis. to asst. sec. of commerce for sci. and tech., 1964-65; mem. ad hoc internat. group metal physics OECD, 1961 Recipient Superior Accomplishment award Dept. Commerce, 1954, gold medal, 1968; Meritorious Svc. award Am. Nat. Standards Inst., 1973. Mem. Am. Phys. Soc., AAAS, Fed. Profl. Assn., Am. Chem. Soc., Washington Acad. Scis., ASTM (hon.), Sigma Xi (nat. pres. 1976, bd. dirs.) Achievements include spl. rsch. crystal properties, surface phenomena in chemistry and metallurgy, materials sci., product safety and environ. regulation, sci. and tech. policy, technol. innovation. Home: 20506 Beaver Ridge Rd Montgomery Village MD 20886 E-mail: lskush@comcast.net.

KUSHNER, MARK JAY, engineering and physics educator; s. Leonard Harry and Muriel (Chelin) K. BA, BS, UCLA, 1976; MS, Calif. Inst. Tech., 1977, PhD, 1979. Postdoctoral Calif. Inst. Tech., Pasadena, 1979-80; physicist Sandia Nat. Labs, Albuquerque, 1980-81, Lawrence Livermore (Calif.) Nat. Labs, 1981-83; dir. electron, atomic and molecular physics Spectra Tech., Bellevue, Wash., 1983-86; prof., Founder prof. engring. U. Ill., Urbana, 1986—2004; dean, Coll. Engring. Iowa St. U., 2005—, Melsa Prof. Engring., 2005—. Chairperson Gaseous Electronics Conf., 1996-98, Gordon Rsch. Conf. Plasma Processing Sci., 2002-04; mem. plasma sci. com. NRC, 1998-2003. Assoc. editor Transactions Plasma Sci., 1989-; editl. bd. Plasma Sources Sci. and Tech., 1991-, Jour. Vacuum Sci. & Tech. A, 1998-2000, Jour. Phys. D, 2004—, Plasma Processes and Polymers, 2004—; Plasma Chemistry and Plasma Processing, 2006-; contbr. over 230 articles to tech. jours. Recipient Tech. Excellence award, Semiconductor Rsch. Corp., 1995. Fellow IEEE (Plasma Sci. and Applications award 2000), Am. Phys. Soc., Optical Soc. Am., Inst. Physics, Am. Vacuum Soc. (Plasma Sci. and Tech. award 1999), Japanese Soc. Advancement Sci.; mem. Materials Rsch. Soc., Am. Soc. Engring. Edn., Soc. Women Engrs. Office: Iowa St Univ Coll Engring 104 Marston Hall Ames IA 50011-2151 Office Phone: 515-294-9988. Business E-Mail: mjk@iastate.edu.

KUSHNER, MICHAEL JAMES, neurologist, consultant, educator; b. Hackensack, NJ, July 18, 1951; s. Samuel and Ruth Ellen (Paul) K.; m. Sarah Joan Warden, Aug. 14, 1976; children: Hunter Paul, Paul Macrae (dec.). BA in Physics, Yale U., 1973; MD, NYU, 1977. Diplomate Am. Bd. Psychiatry, Am. Bd. Neurology, Am. Bd. Med. Examiners; cert. Am. Bd. Electrodiagnostic Medicine, Am. Bd. Pain Medicine. Intern Parkland Meml. Hosp., U. Tex., Dallas, 1977-78; resident in neurology Neurol. Inst., Columbia-Presbyn. Med. Ctr., NYC, 1978-81; rsch. assoc. U. Pa., Phila., 1981-83, asst. prof. neurology, 1983-90; attending physician Hosp. of U. Pa., Phila., 1983-90; with Wilson (N.C.) Neurology Ctr., 1992—; clin. asst. prof. East. Carolina U. Sch. Medicine, 1997—. Dir. SPECT facility Hosp. of U. Pa., 1986-90, asst. dir. neurovascular lab., 1987-90; mem. sensory disorders and lang. study sect. NIH, Bethesda, Md., 1988-90; staff neurologist Wilson (N.C.) Orthop. Surgery Neurology Ctr.; legal medicine cons.; neurology physician advisor N.C. Blue Cross/Blue Shield; asst. prof. East Carolina U. Sch. Medicine; dir. Wilson Regional MRI Ctr. Contbr. numerous articles to profl. jours. Interviewer alumni schs. com. Yale U., Phila., 1984—. Fellow Am. Acad. Neurology, Am. Heart Assn. (stroke coun.); mem. AMA, Internat. Soc. for Blood Flow and Metabolism, N.C. Neurol. Soc. (pres. 1995-97), Yale of N.Y.C., Yale of Cen. N.C., Yale of N.C. Republican. Episcopalian. Avocations: oenology, travel, exercise, art. Home: 1110 Salem St NW Wilson NC 27893-2137 Office: Wilson Neurology Ctr PO Box 3148 Wilson NC 27895-3148 Office Phone: 252-243-9629.

KUSHNER, TODD ROGER, computer scientist, application developer; b. Bethesda, Md., June 18, 1956; s. Harvey David and Rose Molly (Rehert) Kushner; m. Lea Louise Friedman, Nov. 11, 1990; children: Joshua Philip, Daniel Stuart. BS in Life Scis., MIT, Cambridge, 1976; MS in Computer Sci., U. Md., 1980, PhD in Computer Sci., 1982. Rsch. technician NIH, Bethesda, 1976-77; programmer Tech. Mgmt. Inc., Washington, 1977-78, GTE-Telenet, McLean, Va., 1978-79; grad. rsch. asst. U. Md., College Park, 1980-82, mem. rsch. staff, 1985-88; computer scientist SRI Internat., Menlo Park, Calif., 1982-83; sr. software engr. Vicom Sys. Inc., San Jose, 1983-85; sr. engr. Stanford Telecoms., Reston, Va., 1988-89; adv. programmer IBM Corp., Gaithersburg, Md., 1989-93; sr. scientist CTA Inc., Rockville, 1993-96; mem. sr. software staff Lockheed Martin Fed. Systems, Denver, 1996-99; mem. tech. staff Lucent Techs., 1999—2002; sr. programmer CSG Systems, Inc., 2002—04; tech. lead Jeppesen Corp., Englewood, 2004—. Adj. lectr. U. Santa Clara, Calif., 1983, U. Md., Gaithersburg, 1989-90, Johns Hopkins U., Gaithersburg, 1989-93; participant Software Process Interchange Network, McLean, 1993. Contbr. articles to profl. publs. Fellow Grad. fellow, Air Force Office Sci. Rsch., 1980. Mem. IEEE Computer Soc., Assn. Computer Machinery. Democrat. Jewish. Avocations: swimming, racquetball, skiing, golf.

KUSHNER, TONY, playwright, scriptwriter; b. NYC, July 16, 1956; Student, Columbia U., NYU. Assoc. artistic dir. N.Y. Theatre Workshop, 1987; guest artist, grad. theater program Yale U., NYU & Princeton U., 1989—; dir. literary services Theatre Comm. Group, NYC, 1990—91; playwright-in-residence Juilliard Sch. of Drama, 1990—92. Author: (plays) A Bright Room Called Day, 1990, Angels in America: A Gay Fantasia on National Themes Part I "Millenium Approaches", 1992 (Pulitzer Prize for drama, 1993, Tony award best play, 1993), Part II "Perestroika", 1993 (Tony award best play, 1994), Slavs!, 1994, Thinking about the Longstanding Problems of Virtue and Happiness, 1995 (Lambda Literary award, 1996), Dybbuk and Other Tales of the Supernatural, 1997, Death and Taxes, 2000, Homebody/Kabul, 2001, Caroline, or Change, 2003 (Tony nom. best book of a musical, 2004, Obie award, 2004), Only We Who Guard the Mystery Shall Be Unhappy, 2004; adaptor The Illusion (Pierre Corneille), 1988, dir., author Yes Yes No No: The Solice of Solstice, Apogee/Perigee, Bestial/Celestial Holiday Show, 1985, In Great Eliza's Golden Time, 1986, writer (TV miniseries) Angels in America, 2003 (Emmy award, Outstanding Writing for a Miniseries, Movie or a Dramatic Series, 2004), (films) Munich, 2005. Recipient Princess Grace award, 1986, John Whiting award, Arts Council of Great Britain, 1990, Kesserling award, Nat. Arts Club, 1992, Will Glickman playwriting prize, 1992, London Evening Standard award, 1992, AAAL award, 1994; grantee NEA, 1985, 1987, 1993. Mem.: AAAL.

KUSHNIR, ANDREI, artist, consultant; b. Regensberg, Germany, Aug. 30, 1947; BA, U. Ill., Chgo., 1969; MA, Georgetown U., 1971; JD, Howard U., 1975. Bar: D.C., Ill. Atty. FAA, Washington, 1975—81; assoc. counsel Dept. Navy, Office Gen. Counsel, Washington, 1981—97; artist Taylor & Sons Fine Art, Washington, 1999—2001; owner Am. Painting, Washington, 2006—, Andrei Kushnir/Michele Taylor, LLC dba Am. Painting, NYC, 2004—. Guest instr. outdoor painting workshop South Fla. Coll., Sebring, 2002; ofcl. artist USCG. Book, My River, 1999, American Light, 2001, Painted History, 2004, exhibited in group shows at Holter Mus. Art, Helena, Mont., 1998, Art Inst. & Gallery, Salisbury, Md., 1998, Mus. Contemporary Art, Washington, 1999, Alexandria Art League, Va., 1991—98, Arts Coun., Md., 1995, Blue Ridge Arts Coun., Front Royal, Va., 1995—2002, Foundry Gallery, Washington, 1995, Touchstone Gallery, 1996, Capitol Hill Art League, 1997, Howard County Arts Coun., Ellicott City, 1998, Artists Atelier, Atlanta, 1996, Serendipity Gallery, Boca Grande, Fla., 1997—2007, Coun. for the Arts, Chambersburg, Pa., 1998, Nagano Olympics Ofcl. Art Exhbn., Japan, 1998, Spectrum Gallery, Washington, 1999, Hudson Valley Art Assn., NY, 1999, Period Gallery, Omaha, 2000, Nat. Oil and Acrylic Painters Soc., 2000—01, 2003, 2006, Crane Collection, Cape Ann, Mass., 2002—07, Schoharie County Arts Coun., Cobleskill, NY, 2001—02, Nat. Parks Acad. Arts, 2001—05, Howard County Arts Coun., Ellicott City, 2000, Alexander Gallery, NY, 2002, Mill Atelier, Santa Fe, 2003—06, Ratner Mus., Bethesda, Md., 2006, exhibitions include Mus. Fla. Art & Culture, Sebring, Fla., 1998, Capital Hill Art League, Washington, 1998, Univ. Club, 1999, Taylor & Sons Fine Art, 1999, 2001, Rehoboth Art League, Rehoboth Beach, Del., 2003, Va. Hist. Soc., 2004, Represented in permanent collections USCG, D.C. Commn. of Arts and Humanities, Univ. Club, Washington, Mus. of Fla. Art and Culture, Avon, Va. Hist. Soc., Richmond, paintings included in, Arcadia Pub., Rock Creek Park, Gail Silsbury, Johns Hopkins Press, Along the Potomac, Philip Ogilivie. Recipient First place oils, Casper Artist Guild, Wyo., 2002, Award of Excellence, Period Gallery, Omaha, 2000, Best in Show, Blueridge Arts Coun., Front Royal, Va., 2000. Mem.: Oil Painters of Am., Nat. Oil and Acrylic Painters Soc. (signature), Miniature Painters, Gravers and Sculptors Soc. (v.p. 1999—2001), Washington Soc. Landscape Painters, Salmagundi Club N.Y. Office: Am Painting 5118 MacArthur Blvd NW Washington DC 20016 Personal E-mail: artgallery@verizon.net, americanpaintingdc@verizon.net.

KUSMA, KYLLIKKI, retired lawyer; b. Tartu, Estonia, Dec. 8, 1943; came to US, 1951; d. August and Helju Kusma. BA, Ohio U., 1966; MA (VA Rehab. fellow), Ohio State U., 1967; JD, Ohio No. U., 1976; MLT, Georgetown U., 1980. Bar: Ohio 1977, DC 1978. Speech and hearing therapist Lima (Ohio) Meml. Hosp., 1967-70, Tipp City (Ohio) Schs., 1970-74; atty.-adv. Office Chief Counsel, IRS, Washington, 1977-81; v.p., assoc. tax counsel Security Pacific Nat. Bank., LA, 1981-83; ptnr. Brownstein Zeidman & Lore, Washington, 1983-95, Ernst & Young LLP, Columbus, Ohio, 1995—2002; ret., 2002. Instr. Wright State U., 1972-76. Author: (with others) Mortgage-Backed Securities Special Update: REMICs, 1988; contbr. articles to profl. jours. Vol. local civic and polit. activities. Mem. ABA, Ohio Bar Assn., Columbus Bar Assn., Columbus Women Execs. (v.p., sec.), Phi Kappa Phi. Personal E-mail: llikki2@wowway.com.

KUSPIT, DONALD BURTON, art historian, critic, educator; b. NYC, Mar. 26, 1935; s. Morris and Celia (Schmukler) Kuspit Sigmund; m. Judith Clements Price, Mar. 22, 1962. BA in Philosophy with distinction, Columbia U., 1955; MA in Philosophy, Yale U., 1957; DPhil magna cum laude, U. Frankfort, 1960; PhD in Art History, U. Mich., 1971; DFA (hon.), Davidson Coll., 1993; DFA, San Francisco Art Inst., 1996; LHD (hon.), U. Ill., 1998; DFA (hon.), NY Acad. Art. Asst. prof. Pa. State U., State College, 1960-66; assoc. prof. U. Windsor, Ont., Canada, 1966-70; prof. U. N.C., Chapel Hill, 1970-78; Univ. Disting. prof. Rutgers U., New Brunswick, NJ, 1982-83; prof. art, chmn. dept. art SUNY-Stony Brook, 1978-83; editorial cons. UMI Rsch. Press, Ann Arbor, Mich., 1980-90; Andrew Dixon White prof. at large Cornell U., Ithaca, NY, 1991-97. Editl. cons. Cambridge U. Press, 1991—. Ency. Brit. European Art 1900-1950, Art Criticism and Theory; mem. overview com. visual arts sect. NEA, Washington, 1983-85. Author: Clement Greenberg, ARt Critic, 1979, the Critiic as Artist: The Intentionality of Art, 1984, Leon Golub: Existentialist/Activist Painter, 1985, Idiosyncratic Indentities: Artists at the End of Avant-Garde, 1986, The New Subjectivism: Art of the 1980's, 1988, Eric Fischl, 1988, Louise Bourgeois, 1989, Alex Katz: Night Paintings, The Dialectic of Decandence, 1993, Alex Katz: Night Paintings, The Dialectic of Decadence, reprinted, 2000, The Cult of the Avant-Garde Artist, 1993, Signs of Psyche in Modern and Post-Modern Art, 1993, Albert Renger-Patzch, 1993, Primordial Prosences: The Sculpture of Karel Appel, 1994, Health and Happiness in Twentieth Century Avant-Garde Art, 1996, Dale Chihuly, 1997, Jamali, 1997, Joseph Raffael, 1998, The Rebirth of Painting in the Late 20th Century, 2000, Psychostrategies of Avant-Garde Art, 2000, Redeeming Art: Critical Reveries, 2000, Don Eddy, 2001, Steve Tobin, 2003, The End of Art, 2004, April Gornik, 2005, Albert Paley, 2006, A Critical History of Twentieth Century Art, 2006; editor: Art Criticism, 1984—; contbg. editor: Art in Am., 1978—92, Contemporanea, 1988—90, ArtForum, 1982—, Sculpture Mag., 1992—, New Art Examiner, 1993—2004. Recipient award for disting. contbn. to the visual arts Nat. Assn. Schs. Art and Design, 1997; Younger humanist fellow NEH, 1973, critic fellow Nat. Endowment for Arts, 1977, Guggenheim fellow, 1977; Robertson fellow U. Glasgow, 2005. Fellow Asian Cultural Coun.; mem. PEN, Coll. Art Assn. (Frank Jewett Mather award 1983), Am. Soc. Aesthetics, Internat. Assn. Art Critics (v.p. Am. sect. 1982-84), Am. Psychoanalytic Assn. Home: 38 W 26th St New York NY 10010-2012 Office: SUNY Dept Art Stony Brook NY 11794-5400 Office Phone: 631-632-7270.

KUSSEROW, JAMES, music educator; b. Susanville, Calif., July 18, 1958; s. Vernon James Teel and Maxine Eylner Baker; m. Kellie Munger, May 20, 1989; children: Kaylan, Michael, Christopher. AA, Porterville C.C., Calif., 1978; BA in Music with Distinction, San Jose State U., Calif., 1980; MA in Pub. Sch. Adminstrn., Calif. State U., Bakersfield, 1991. Tchg. credential Calif. Band dir. Mulcahy Mid. Sch., Tulare, Calif., 1981—88, Live Oak Mid. Sch., Tulare, 1989—90, Porterville H.S. and C.C., 1990—. Musician H.S. Band Dir. of Yr., 1991; musician, condr. concert J.F. Kennedy Ctr. for the Performing Arts, 1994; performed at White House, Carnegie Hall, Lincoln Ctr. for the Performing Arts, others. Pres. Tulare-Kings Music Educators Assn., 1984—85; prin. trumpet Tulare County Symphony, 1981—99; dir. Fabulous Studio Band. Named Nat. H.S. Band Dir. of Yr., Nat. Hall of Fame, 1990. Mem.: Internat. Trumpet Guild, Am. Sch. Band Dirs. Assn., Nat. Band Assn., Calif. Music Educators Assn., Music Educators Nat. Conf., Internat. Assn. Jazz Educators. Home: 3102 W Howard Ave Visalia CA 93277 Office: Porterville HS Panther Band 465 W Olive Ave Porterville CA 93257 Office Phone: 559-793-3436. Personal E-mail: jkusserow@comcast.net. E-mail: kussband@porterville.k12.ca.us.

KUSSEROW, RICHARD PHILLIP, federal agency administrator, corporate financial executive; b. San Jose, Calif., Dec. 9, 1940; s. Roger Berthold and Eve W. (Larson) K.; m. Rebecca Hatchell, Sept. 14, 1985; 1 child, Carrie Elizabeth. BA in Polit. Sci, UCLA, 1963; MA in Govt., Calif. State U., LA, 1964; postgrad., So. Meth. U., 1965, John Marshall Sch. Law, 1972, Harvard U., 1984. Cert. internal auditor, cert. govt. auditor; cert. govt. fin. mgr., cert. fraud examiner. Lectr. Calif. State U., LA, 1963, 64; case officer CIA, 1968-69; spl. agt. supr. in white collar and organized crime FBI, 1969-81; Insp. Gen., U.S. Dept. HHS, 1981-92; mem. Pres.'s Coun. on Integrity and Efficiency, 1981-92, vice chmn., 1986-89, chmn. legislation com., 1982-85, 89-92; mem. Pres.' Council on Mgmt. Improvement, 1986-89, 91-92; chair Nat. Task Force of Implementation of Chief Fin. Officers Act, 1990-91; chmn. Chief Fin. Officers Task Force, 1991; pres., CEO Strategic Mgmt. Sys., Inc., 1992—; ptnr. O.K. Real Estate, 1993—2005; pres. Govt. Mgmt. Sys., Inc., 1995—2002; pres., CEO, chmn. bd. Nat. Hotline Svcs., Inc., 1995—2006. Presdl. appointee to Nat. Adv. Commn. on Law Enforcement, 1989; mem. CFOs Coun., 1990-92, Def. Procurement Round Table, 1993-95; lectr. white collar crime, asset protection, health care, fraud and abuse, internal controls, corporate compliance programs, others; mem. Atty. Gen.'s Econ. Crime Coun., 1988-90; nat. chmn. Am. Compliance Inst., 1995. Author: Principles of Investigative Targeting, 1974, Management Principles for Asset Protection, 1995, Corporate Compliance Policies & Procedures: Guide to Assessment and Development, 2000, Compliance Training Manual, 2001, Sarbanes-Oxley: Best Practices for Private and Non Profit Health Care Entities, 2003, Compliance Programs for Universities, Grantees, and Non-Profits, 2004, Ultimate Hotline Manual, 2005, Forty-Nine Steps to Sarbonet-Oxley Compliance, 2006; contbr. articles to profl. jours. Pres. Nat. Honor Svc., 1996—. Capt. USMC, 1965-68. Recipient Sec.'s Bronze medal for good govt., 1983, Outstanding Leadership award Pres. Coun. on Mgmt. Improvement, 1988, Cert. of Svc. Appreciation, Pres. of U.S., 1989, Donald L. Scantlebury award for fin. mgmt. excellence Assn. Govt. Accts., 1992; H. Horton Rontree Disting. lectr. in health law, 1990. Mem. Assn. Fed. Investigators (nat. pres. 1984-85, chmn. awards com. 1986-87), Soc. Former FBI Agts., Assn. Govt. Accts. (nat. task force on fed. fin. mgmt. 1983-88, pres. Balt. chpt. 1987, chmn. nat. profl. devel. conf. 1989, nat. pres. 1990, nat. leadership awards Boston chpt. 1985, No. Va. chpt., Washington chpt., D.C. chpt. 1985, Nat. Assn. 1987), Am. Health Lawyers Assn., Nat. Health Care Anti-Fraud Assn. (pub. svc. award 1989), Inst. Internal Auditors (cert.), Am. Compliance Inst. (governing bd. 1996-2001), Army-Navy Club. Presbyterian. Avocations: reading, travel, tennis. also: 620 Kenmore Ave ste B Fredericksburg VA 22401-5759 Office Phone: 703-535-1411. Business E-Mail: rkusserow@strategicm.com.

KUSSMAN, MICHAEL JAMES, federal agency administrator; b. Troy, NY, May 22, 1944; MD, Boston U., 1968; MS, Salve Regina U., 1994; grad., Army War Coll.; grad. (hon.), Command Gen. Staff Coll. Cert. internal medicine. Joined US Army, 1970, advanced through ranks to brig. gen., 1996; med. resident Joslin Clinic, Boston, 1972—74; pvt. practice Pittsfield, Mass,, 1974—79; chief internal medicine Tripler Army Med. Ctr., Honolulu, 1979—84; chief, Dept. Medicine Brooke Army Med. Ctr., San Antonio, 1984—88, dep. comdr. clin. svcs.; chief cons. in internal medicine Army Surgeon Gen., 1988; gov. Army Region, ACP, 1988; comdr. Martin Army Comty. Hosp., Ft. Benning, Ga., 1993—95, Walter Reed Health Care Sys., Washington, Europe Regional Med. Command; command surgeon US Army Europe; TRICARE lead agt. for Europe; prin. dep. under sec. for health Veterans Health Adminstrn., US Dept. Veterans Affairs, Washington, 2005—06, acting under sec. for health, 2006—07, under sec. for health, 2007—. Mem. faculty Uniformed Svcs. U. Health Sciences. Decorated DSM, Legion of Merit with three oak leaf clusters, Defense Meritorious Svc. medal, Order of Military Medical Merit; recipient Laureate award, ACP/Am. Soc. Internal Medicine. Master: ACP. Office: US Dept Veterans Affairs 810 Vermont Ave rm 800 Washington DC 20420*

KUSSMAUL, DONALD, academic administrator; B, M, So. Ill. U.; Doctorate, Loyola U. Supt. East Dubuque (Ill.) Unit Sch. Dist. 119, 1983—. Mem. adv. com. to state supt. Ill.; dir. ext. svcs. East Dubuque campus Hillside C.C.; dir. Family T.I.E.S. Early Childhood At Risk Program. Co-author: (book) Preparing Schools and School Systems for the 21st Century. Active Greater Dubuque Area Red Cross, Jr. Achievement Orgn. Mem.: Ill. Assn. Sch. Adminstrs., Am. Assn. Sch. Adminstrs. (pres.-elect 2003—, exec. bd. 2000—, former chmn. rural/small schs. com.), Horace Mann League, Lions. Office: East Dubuque Sch Dist 119 200 Park Lane Dr East Dubuque IL 61025-9568

KUSSROW, NANCY ESTHER, educational association administrator; BA, Valparaiso U., 1952; MA, U. N.C., 1954. Exec. dir. Nat. Assn. prins. of Schs. for Girls; ret., 1996.

KUSTER, LARRY DONALD, lawyer; b. Kewanee, Ill., July 27, 1947; s. Donald Carl and Rosemary Ann (Riggins) Kuster; m. Mary Catherine Whitmore, July 11, 1970; children: David, Ryan. BA, Augustana Coll., 1969; JD with honors, U. Iowa, 1973. Bar: Ill. 1973, U.S. Dist. Ct. (cen. dist.): Ill. 1980, U.S. Dist. Ct. (so. dist.): Ill. 1996, U.S. Ct. Appeals (7th cir.): 1982, U.S. Tax Ct.: 1979. Assoc. Rammelkamp, Bradney PC, Jacksonville, Ill., 1973—75; shareholder Rammelkamp, Bradney PC, Jacksonville, Ill., 1976—. Moderator continuing legal edn. program Ill. Inst. Continuing Legal Edn., 1985—86; lectr. in field; master Lincoln-Douglas Inn of Ct., 1993—, pres., 2004—05; adj. faculty Lincolnland CC, 2006—. Contbr. articles to profl. jours. Mem. Am. Coun. on Germany, 1982—2005, City of Jacksonville Heritage Cultural Ctr. Bd., 1986—91; pres. West Central Ill. Council on World Affairs, 1982—83; bd. dirs. Sherwood Eddy Meml. YMCA, 1975—80, Jacksonville Area C. of C., 1981—84, pres., 1990; bd. dirs. Jacksonville Area Visitors and Tourism Bur., 1986—91; trustee MacMurray Coll., Jacksonville, 1991—2001; pres. Ill. Assn. Hist. Preservation Commns., 1982; vice-chmn. Jacksonville Hist. Preservation Commn., 1981—83, chmn., 1983—84. Mem.: Fedn. Def. and Corp. Counsel, Lincoln-Douglas Inn of Ct. (pres. 2004—05), Ill. Bar Assn. (civil practice and procedure coun. 1976—77, sec. workers' compensation sect. 1982—83, vice-chmn. 1983—84, chmn. 1984—85, civil practice and procedure coun. 1986—90), Morgan County Bar Assn. (pres. 1977—78), Am. Arbitration Assn. Lutheran. Home: RR 1 Box 19 Chapin IL 62628-9801 Office: Rammelkamp Bradney 232 W State St Jacksonville IL 62650-2002 Office Phone: 217-245-6177.

KUSTERER, THOMAS, program director; b. Balt., July 9, 1946; s. Edward Thomas and Anne Thelma (Ekas) K.; m. Janet Elizabeth Polunas, Sept. 16, 1972; children: David, Robert. BS, Loyola Coll., Balt., 1968, MBA, 1982; MS, Rutgers U., 1972. Instr. Balt. C.C., 1968-69; tchg. asst. Rutgers U., 1969—71; cons. Benedict Estuarine Lab., Md., 1971-72; planner Harford County Govt., Bel Air, Md., 1972-84; natural resources mgr. Md. Dept. of the Environment, Balt., 1984-89; program mgr. Montgomery County Govt., Rockville, Md., 1989—. Mem. Md. Coastal Resources Adv. Com., 1984-88, Govs. Solid Waste Mgmt. Task Force, 1987, Md. Acid Deposition Adv. Com., 1984-88, nat. round table on unit pricing for solid waste collection and disposal U.S. EPA, 1992, nat. round table on full cost acctg. for solid waste mgmt. systems, 1994. Contbg. author/advisor: Pay As You Throw: Lessons Learned about Unit Pricing, 1994; contbg. author Developing Agreements on the Siting of Waste Management Facilties, 1994, Innovative Approaches to Siting Solid Waste Management Facilities, 1992; editor (newsletter) Md. Environ., 1986, 87; contbr. articles to profl. jours. Mgr. youth sports teams Parks and Recreation Depts., Howard and Balt. Counties, 1983-97; officer Md. Save Our Streams, Annapolis, 1973-76. Mem. Baltimore Mus. Art, Cent. Pk. Conservancy, Guggenheim Mus., Hist. Ellicott City, Inc. (officer), Lower East Side Tenement Mus., Sierra Club, Nature Conservancy, Walters Art Mus., Whitney Mus. Am. Art.

KUSTIN, KENNETH, chemist; b. Bronx, NY, Jan. 6, 1934; s. Alex and Mae (Marvisch) K.; m. Myrna May Jacobson, June 24, 1956; children: Brenda Jayne, Franklin Daniel, Michael Thorpe. BSc, Queens Coll., Flushing, NY, 1955; PhD, U. Minn., 1959. Postdoctoral fellow Max Planck Inst. for Phys. Chemistry, Göttingen, Germany, 1959-61; asst. prof. chemistry Brandeis U., Waltham, Mass., 1961-66, assoc. prof., 1966-72, prof., 1972-97, prof. emeritus, 1997—, chmn. dept. chemistry, 1974-77. Vis. prof. pharmacology Harvard U. Med. Sch., 1977-78; Fulbright-Hays lectr., 1978; program dir. NSF, 1985-86; adj. rsch. scientist U.S. Army, Natick RD&E Ctr., 1991—. Editor: Fast Reactions, vol. 16 of Methods in Enzymology, 1969; bd. editors Internat. Jour. Chem. Kinetics, 1983-90, Inorganic Chemistry, 1993-95; co-editor: Vanadium: The Versatile Metal, 2007; rsch. and publs. in field. Mem. AAAS, Am. Chem. Soc. (councilor 1983-85), Phi Beta Kappa.

KUSTOFF, DAVID F., prosecutor; b. Memphis, Oct. 8, 1966; m. Roberta Kustoff; 1 child, Maggie. BBA, U. Memphis, 1989, JD, 1992. Bar: 1992. Ptnr. Kustoff & Strickland PLLC; US atty. (we. dist.) Tenn. US Dept. Justice, Memphis, 2006—. Head Bush-Cheney election effort, Tenn., 2000, 2004; chmn. Shelby County Rep. Party, Tenn. Office: US Attys Office 167 N Main St Ste 800 Memphis TN 38103 Office Phone: 901-544-4231. Office Fax: 901-544-4230.*

KUSTRA, ROBERT W. (BOB KUSTRA), former state official, academic administrator; b. St. Louis, Mar. 21, 1943; s. Walter and Loretto (Shaughnessy) K.; m. Kathleen Breidert, Sept. 10, 1989; children: Jennifer, Stephen; stepchild: Matthew Breidert. BA in Polit. Sci., St. Benedict's Coll., Atchison, Kans., 1965; MA in Pub. Adminstrn., So. Ill. U., 1968; PhD in Polit. Sci., U. Ill., 1975. Prof. Northwestern U., U. Ill. at Springfield (formerly Sangamon State U.), Roosevelt U., Chgo.; exec. asst. to U.S. Senator Charles Percy Chgo., 1978-80; state rep. Ill. Ho. of Reps., 1981-83; state senator Ill. State Senate, 1983-91; lt. gov. State of Ill., Springfield, 1991; chmn. Ill. Bd. Higher Edn., 1997; pres. Eastern Ky. U., Boise State U., 2003—. Prof. Roosevelt U., Loyola U., Lincoln Land. C.C., Springfield, bd. mem. Idaho Nature Conservancy, Western Interstate Commn. Higher Edn., Inland Northwest Rsch. Alliance, Sci. Technology Adv. Coun., State of Idaho. Host (radio program) New Horizons in Edn. Trustee Village of Glenview, Ill., 1978-80. Named Best Freshman Rep., Ill. Polit. Reporter, 1981, Best Freshman Senator, 1983; Outstanding Legislator, Ill. Assn. Sch. Bds., 1987-88, Friend of Edn., Ill. State Bd. Edn., 1987-88, Heritage award Ill. Divsn. of the Polish-Am. Congress., 1992. Republican. Roman Catholic. Office: Boise State University Business Bldg Rm B-307 1910 University Dr Boise ID 83725-1000 Office Phone: 208-426-1491. Office Fax: 208-426-3779.*

KUSUKAWA, AKIRA, demographer, educator; b. Fukuoka, Kyushu, Japan, May 13, 1925; s. Tokuzo Tanaka and Ko Kusukawa; m. Emiko Fujita, June 3, 1952. BS, Yamaguchi Coll., 1944; MPH, Johns Hopkins U., 1953; MD, Kyushu U., 1948, D of Med. Sci., 1956. Tech. advisor to Coun. of Mins. Govt. of Sudan, 1959—60; sec. UN Population Commn., NYC, 1964—74; spl. asst. UN Population Fund, NYC, 1974—77, dir., 1977—86; ret., 1986. Prof. Moscow State U., Russia, 1988, N.Y. Med. Coll., 1986—2004, L.I. U., NYC, 1986—, UN Demographic Centre, India, 1963—64. Author: Cardiovascular Epidemiology, 1956; co-author: Ageing Research, 1999; contbr. UN Documents on Population, 1973—86. Recipient Medal of Peace, State Coun. Bulgaria, 1986, Golden Order Labor, Presdl. Coun. Hungary, 1986. Mem.: APHA, Internat. Planned Parenthood Fedn., N.Y. Acad. Scis., Japanese Med. Soc. Am. (dir.), Population Assn. Am., Internat. Union Sci. Study Population. Avocations: music, painting, walking. Home: 214 Harriman Dr #2023 Goshen NY 10924-2425 Office: Long Island Univ Hoxie Hall 720 Northern Blvd Greenvale NY 11548-1300

KUSUNOSE, TARO, lawyer; b. Tokyo, July 27, 1973; married; 2 children. BA cum laude, UCSD, 1996; JD, U. Calif. Davis Sch. Law, 1999. Bar: Wash. 2000. Assoc. atty., bus. law., corp. law, real estate Lasher Holzapfel Sperry & Ebberson, PLLC, Seattle. Bd. mem., exec. com. mem. Nikkei Concerns; mem. Seattle Japanese Bus. Owner's Group. Contbr. articles to numerous profl. jours. Bd. mem. Transportation Club Seattle, Japan Am. Soc. State Wash. Mem.: ABA, King Co. Bar Assn., Wash. State Bar Assn. Office: Lasher Holzapfel Sperry Ebberson PLLC 2600 Two Union Square 601 Union St Seattle WA 98101-4000

KUTCHI, JUDITH ANN, elementary school educator; b. Hazelton, Pa., Oct. 20, 1942; d. Nicholas I. and Elizabeth Bachman; m. Robert John Kutchi, Aug. 10, 1963; children: Robert S., Steven N., Nicholas A., Elizabeth A.(dec.). BE, Bloomsburg State U., 1963, MEd, 1967. Tchr. Prince George County Bd. of Edn., Upper Marlboro, Md., 1963—67, resource tchr., 1967—69, tchr., 1969—92, St. Mary Star of the Sea, Indian Head, Md., 1992—2001; reading specialist, mentor, test coord. Prince George's County Bd. Edn., 2001—. Mem.: Internat. Reading Assn., Delta Kappa Gamma Soc. (past pres. Alpha Epsilon chpt.). Avocations: reading, quilting, sewing, travel. Home: 2951 Bannock Rd Bryans Road MD 20616 Office: Henry G Ferguson Elem Berry Rd Accokeek MD 20607

KUTEMEYER, PETER MARTIN, industrial engineering executive; b. Freiburg, Germany, Nov. 19, 1938; came to U.S., 1954, naturalized, 1956; s. Martin Henry and Gertrude Barbara (Buechel) K.; m. Fresquez, June 25, 1961 (div. Aug. 1986); children: Michael, Kristina. BME with distinction, Ariz. State U., Tempe, 1968, MS in Engrng. Mechanics, 1969; MBA, U. Utah, Salt Lake City, 1977. Enlisted USAF, 1958, commd. 2d lt., 1967, advanced through grades to capt., 1970, aero. engr., 1969-71, sys. devel. engr., 1971-74, tech. liaison officer to W. German Fed. Govt., 1974-78; indsl. mgr. Mining Progress, Inc., Highland Mills, NY, 1978-79, prodn. mgr., 1979-81; gen. mgr. Bischoff Environ. Sys. divsn. Intertech Inc., Highland Mills, NY, 1981-89, v.p., gen. mgr., 1989—92; pres. PMK Enterprises, Inc., Wilmington, Del., 1989—. Mem.: AIAA, ASME, Nat. Assn. Realtors. Home and Office: 5225 Pooks Hill Rd Apt 1020S Bethesda MD 20814-6718 Office Phone: 301-493-4149. Personal E-mail: p.kutemeyer@verizon.net.

KUTKA, J. JAMES, JR., metal products executive; Grad. in Acctg., U. Akron, Ohio, 1970. Prodn. worker Canton Roll and Machine Works US Steel, 1967, mem. acctg. staff Canton Works, 1970, acctg. position Lorain-Cuyahoga Works, acctg. position Haverhill Chems. plant, acctg. position Gary Works, acctg. position Pitts., gen. mgr. southern area purchasing Houston, mgr. bus. planning Geneva-Pittsburg Works Provo, Utah, dist. sales mgr. Detroit, gen. mgr. human resources Pitts., 1993, gen. mgr. bus. process reengineering, gen. mgr. mktg. & planning sheet products, gen. mgr. automotive Detroit, 1997—2001, v.p. comml. Pitts., 2001—05, pres. US Steel Internat., Inc., 2002—05, sr. v.p. comml., 2005—. Bd. dirs. Family House, Pitts. Mem.: Am. Iron and Steel Inst. (chmn. market devel. com.). Office: US Steel 600 Grant St Pittsburgh PA 15219-2800 Office Phone: 412-433-1121.*

KUTLAR, FERDANE, genetics educator, researcher; b. Turkey, Apr. 15, 1945; came to U.S., 1984; d. Mehmet and Sidika Tanrikulu; m. Abdullah Kutlar, Feb. 7, 1975. MD, Istanbul Med. Sch., Turkey, 1971. Bd. cert in internal medicine, Turkey, 1976. Resident in internal medicine Istanbul U. Sch. Medicine, 1972-76; chief resident dept. medicine Istanbul Hosp., 1977-81; rsch. fellow Med. Coll. Ga., Augusta, 1982; hematology fellow Istanbul U. Sch. Medicine, 1983; rsch. fellow Med. Coll. Ga., Augusta, 1984, asst. prof., 1985-99, assoc. prof. medicine, 1999—. Dir. DNA lab. Med. Coll. Ga., Augusta, 1994—; presenter in field. Contbr. articles to profl. jours. Mem. Am. Soc. Hematology, Am. Soc. Human Genetics, Med. Coll. Ga. Pres.'s Club. Avocations: painting, gardening, decorating, chess. Home: 623 Sawgrass Dr Martinez GA 30907-9137 Office: Med Coll Ga Dept Medicine 15th St AC-1000 Augusta GA 30912-2100 Office Phone: 706-721-9768. Business E-Mail: fkutlar@mail.mcg.edu.

KUTLER, ALISON L., lawyer; d. Stuart and Sandy Kutler. BA in Govt. cum laude, Georgetown U., 1993; JD, Stanford U., 1999. Bar: DC, Nebr. 1999. Mem. staff US Rep. Peter Hoagland, 1991—93; various positions with Clinton Adminstrn., 1993—96; asst. to US Sec. Commerce Ron Brown; Congl. affairs specialist US Dept. Commerce Bur Export Adminstrn., Small Bus. Adminstrn.; dep. chief of staff to Hadassah Lieberman Gore-Lieberman Presdl. Campaign, 2000; assoc. Arent Fox Kinter Plotkin & Kahn, Washington; assoc., pub. law & policy strategies group Sonnenschein Nath & Rosenthal LLP, Washington, 2002—. Office: Sonnenschein Nath & Rosenthal LLP Ste 600, E Tower 1301 K St NW Washington DC 20005 Office Phone: 202-408-9142. Office Fax: 202-408-6399. Business E-Mail: akutler@sonnenschein.com.

KUTLER, STANLEY IRA, historian, lawyer, educator; b. Cleve., Aug. 10, 1934; s. Robert P. and Zelda R. (Coffman) K.; m. Sandra J. Sachs, June 24, 1956; children: Jeffrey, David, Susan, Andrew. BA, Bowling Green State U., 1956; PhD, Ohio State U., 1960. Instr. history Pa. State U., State College, 1960-62; asst. prof. San Diego State U., 1962-64; from asst. prof. to prof. U. Wis., Madison, 1964-80, E. Gordon Fox prof. Am. instns., law and history, 1980—. Disting. exchange scholar to China Nat. Acad. Scis., 1982; Kenneth Keating lectr. Tel Aviv U., 1984; sr. Fulbright lectr. to Japan, 1977, to Israel, 1985, China, 1986; disting. vis. Fulbright scholar, Peru, 1987; Bicentennial prof. Tel Aviv U., 1985; cons. NEH, 1975—. The Constitution Project, 1985—; disting. chair Polit. Sci., U. Bologna, 1991; hist. cons. BBC/Discovery series Watergate, 1994. Author: Judicial Power and Reconstruction, 1968, Privilege and Creative Destruction, 1971, 2d edit., 1990, The American Inquisition, 1983, The Wars of Watergate: The Last Crisis of Richard Nixon, 1990, 92, Abuse of Power: The New Nixon Tapes, 1997; editor: Supreme Court and the Constitution, 1969, 3d edit., 1984, Looking for America, 1975, 80, The Encyclopedia of the Vietnam War, 1995, Encyclopedia of 20th Century America, 1995, American Perspectives: Historians on Historians, 1996, Watergate: The Fall of Richards Nixon, 1996, Dictionary of American History, 10 vols., 1996—; founding editor Rev. in Am. History, 1972-97; mem. adv. editor Greenwood Pub., 1968-73, Johns Hopkins U. Press, 1982—. Recipient Silver Gavel award ABA; fellow Sage Found., 1967-68, Emmy award, 1994, Peabody award, 1994, Best Reference Work award, Am. Assn. Pubs., 1996; fellow Guggenheim Found., 1971-72, Rockefeller Found., 1979-80. Jewish. Office: U Wis Dept History Madison WI 53706 Business E-Mail: sikutler@wisc.edu.

KUTNER, JANET, art critic, book reviewer; b. Dallas, Sept. 20, 1937; m. Jonathan D. Kutner, Jan. 15, 1961. Student, Stanford U., 1955-57; BA in English, So. Meth. U., 1959. Asst. dir. Dallas Mus. Contemporary Arts, 1959-61; art critic, book reviewer Dallas Morning News, 1970—; Dallas/Ft. Worth corr. ARTnews Mag., 1975—. Mem. arts adv. panel Dallas Mcpl. Libr., 1981-91; mem. adv. bd. Arts Magnet H.S. of Dallas, 1980-92; mem. adv. com. Sch. Architecture and Environ. Design, U. Tex., Arlington, 1985-87; mem. long range planning com. Dallas Mus. Art, 1985-86; mem. visual arts and architecture adv. panel Tex. Com. on Arts, 1980-82. Contbr. articles to profl. jours.; juror various art exhbns. Bd. trustees Greenhill Sch., Dallas, 1980-81. Art critics grantee Nat. Endowment for Arts, 1976-77, art critic's fellow Nat. Gallery Art, 1991-; recipient Legend award Dallas Ctr. Contemporary Art, 2005. Mem. Am. Assn. Museums, Dallas Mus. Art, Internat. Coun. Museums, ArtTable, Dallas Press Club (Critics award 1997). Office: Dallas Morning News PO Box 655237 Dallas TX 75265-5237

KUTOSH, SUE, artist; b. Elizabeth, NJ, Dec. 25, 1947; d. Stephen and Irene (Ribecky) K. BFA, Carnegie-Mellon U., 1971; MA, Kent State U., 1973. One-woman shows include Keane Mason Gallery, NYC, 1979, West Broadway Gallery, NYC, 1981, Kristen Richards Gallery, NYC, 1983, Mussavi Arts Gallery, NYC, 1987, NY Bot. Garden, Bronx, 1992, Montserrat Gallery, NYC, 1996, Pleiades Gallery, NYC, 1997; art included in books: The Films of Jane Fonda, 1981, Hispanic Hollywood, 1990, The Lavender Screen, 1993, Hollywood Babble On, 1994, New Art Internat., 1998-2000, Direct Art mag., 2005; scenic art contbns. Sesame Street. Recipient Daytime Emmy for Seseame Street, 1993-94. Mem. United Scenic Artists, Local 829, Catharine Lorillard Wolfe Art Club, N.Y. Artists Equity, Nat. Assn. Women Artists. Avocation: photography. Home: 200 E 16th St Apt 2-d New York NY 10003-3708

KUTRZEBA, JOSEPH S., theater producer, director; b. Lodz, Poland, Oct. 11, 1927; came to U.S., 1950; s. Israel and Malka (Hakman) Fajwiszys; m. Valerie M. Hageman, Sept. 1955 (div. 1959); 1 child, Karen Janina; m. Michaela Lacher, Jan. 14, 1979; children: Marcus, Claudia Nina. BA, U. Munich, 1950; MFA, Yale U., 1956; PhD, NYU, 1974. Rschr., prodn. coord., dir., stage mgr. CBS-TV, NYC, 1956-73; prodr., dir., writer, narrator UN Radio, NYC, 1959-69; dir., mem. Actors Studio, NYC, 1960-62; founder, prodr., artistic dir. Queens Playhouse, Flushing Meadows, NY, 1972-74, also mem. bd. dirs., pres.; mem. faculty New Sch. for Social Rsch., NYC, 1975-77. Interpreter, translator U.S. Cts.; tchr. English. Prodr., dir. documentary film Children in the Holocaust, 1980, (English and Polish versions) Helena: the Emigrant Queen, 1996 at La Mama and Kosciuszko Found.; dir. 7 stage plays, N.Y.C., 1995-2004; presented Shakespeare's Sonnets at St. Peter's Ch. with Sam Waterston and Jan Englert. Mem. citizens com. Study N.Y. Theater, 1971-72; aux. mounted officer N.Y.C. Police Dept., 1974-77; founder Warsaw Ghetto Resistance Orgn.; exec. sec., dep. presiding officer Hidden Child Found. Lt. U.S. Army, 1950-52, Korea. Recipient Tony award, Drama Desk award nominations for prodr. Best Broadway musical The Lieutenant, 1975; recipient bronze award Internat. Film and TV Festival N.Y. for Children in the Holocaust with Liv Ullman, 1980; MacDowell Colony fellow, 1973. Mem. Dirs. Guild Am., Chopin Soc. N.Y. (bd. dirs.), Yale U. Alumni Assn. Office Phone: 718-760-0863.

KUTSCHER, MARTIN L., pediatrician, neurologist; BA, Columbia Coll., 1977, MD, 1981. Diplomate Am. Bd. Pediats., 1986, cert. child neurologist Am. Bd. Pediats., 1986. Resident in pediats. St. Christopher Hosp. Children, Phila., 1981—84; fellow in child neurology Albert Einstein Coll. Medicine, Bronx, NY, 1984—87; physician Pediat. Neurol. Assocs., White Plains, NY, 1987—. Asst. prof. N.Y. Med. Coll., Valhalle, NY, 1987—. Contbr. articles to internet site; author: Adnobook: Living Right Now!, 2002, Special Nees Kids, 2003, Childhood Services, 2003. Bd. trustees Found. Thactology, NYC, 1988—, Jewish Family Congregation, South Salem, NY, 2000—, Soundview Prep. Sch., Mt. Kises, NY, 2002—. Named Top Doctor Child Neurology, N.y. Metro Area Connelly Guide, 2002—04, Westchester (N.Y.) Mag., 2002—04, N.Y. Mag., 2004. Fellow: Am. Acad. Neurology, Am. Acad. Pediatrics; mem.: Child Neurology Soc. Office: Pediatric Neurological Assoc 125 S Broadway White Plains NY 10605

KUTSCHER, RONALD EARL, retired federal agency administrator; b. Hebron, Nebr., Apr. 18, 1932; s. Earl Harvey and Doris Lillian (Zong) K.; m. Elizabeth Elin Granholm, Dec. 28, 1963; children: Laura Ingrid, Steven Ronald. BA, Doane Coll., 1955; postgrad., U. Ill., 1955-56. Economist Bur. Labor Stats., Washington, 1957-68, asst. chief for rsch. divsn. of econ. growth, 1968-76, asst. commr., 1976-82, assoc. commr., 1982-96. Contbr. articles to profl. jours. With US Army, 1952—54. Mem. Am. Statis. Assn. (chair com. on coms. 1989-91, chair program com. 1985, Prize Best Econ. Forecast 1973). Lutheran. Avocations: photography, golf. Personal E-mail: brekutsch@aol.com.

KUTTLER, JUDITH ESTHER, retired psychotherapist; b. Paterson, NJ, Feb. 26, 1938; d. Theodor Herzl and Roslyn Unterman; children: Hillel Moshe, David Eli, Nadine Eve. BA, Marymount Manhattan Coll., NYC, 1974; MSW, Hunter Coll. Sch. Social Work, NYC, 1978, post-masters cert. in adv. clin. social work in family therapy, 1982. RN Beth Israel Hosp. (now known as Beth Israel Med. Ctr.), NYC, 1960. Psychotherapist Creedmoor Psychiatric Ctr., Queens, NY, 1972—84, social worker, Manhattan Children's Psychiatric Ctr., Ward's Island, NY, 1986—88, Creedmoor Psychiatric Ctr., Queens, 1988—94; self-employed psychotherapist Adv. Ctr. for Psychotherapy, Jamaica Estates, 1994—2002. Docent Jewish Mus., NYC; com. mem. Penn South Housing Complex, NYC. Jewish. Avocations: reading, hiking, poetry, travel, writing. Home: 365 W 25th St Apt 20H New York NY 10001-5825

KUTTNER, BERNARD A., retired judge, lawyer; b. Berlin, Jan. 13, 1934; arrived in U.S., 1939; s. Frank B. and Vera (Knopfmacher) Kuttner; children: Karen M. Capato, Robert D., Stacey M. Gilby. AB cum laude, Dartmouth Coll., 1955; postgrad., U. Va. Law Sch., 1956; JD, Seton Hall U., 1959; postgrad., N.Y. U., 1960. Bar: N.J. 1960, U.S. Supreme Ct. 1964, U.S. Ct. Mil. Appeals 1967, N.Y. 1982, DC 1982, cert.: N.J. (civil trial lawyer). Assoc. Toner, Crowley, Woelper & Vanderbilt, 1959-62; pvt. practice Newark, 1962-75; corp. counsel Irvington, 1963-66; judge N.J. State Divsn. Tax Appeals, 1977-79; instr. civil litigation Montclair State Coll., 1979-82. Del. Jud. Conf. N.J. Supreme Ct., 1974—81; vice chmn. dist. ethics com. Supreme Ct. N.J., 1984—85, chmn., 1985—86, apptd. bd. trial atty. cert., NJ, 1986—90. Contbr. articles to profl. jours. Founding mem. Cesar E. Chavez Found.; commr. Essex County (N.J.) Pk. Commn., 1973—79. To lt. comdr. USNR, 1964—74. Mem.: ATLA (com. ethical conduct 2000—06), ABA (chmn. trial techniques com. 1988—89, co-editor trial techniques newsletter sect. tort and ins. practice, mem. sect. litig.), Am. Counsel Assn., Essex County Bar Assn. (trial and appellate litig., jud. com. 1972—75, chmn. 1973—75, treas. 1975—79, pres. 1980—81, products liability com. 1981—), Irvington Bar Assn. (pres. 1968—70), DC Bar Assn., Inst. Ethical Behavior (pres. 1985—). Jewish. Office: Kuttner Law Offices 24 Lackawanna Pl Millburn NJ 07041-1618 Office Phone: 973-467-9132. Personal E-mail: kuttnerbuck@aol.com.

KUTTNER, ROBERT LOUIS, editor, writer, columnist; b. NYC, Apr. 17, 1943; s. Arthur Paul Kuttner and Pauline M. Levy; m. Sharland Grace Trotter, Dec. 19, 1971 (dec. Nov. 1997); children: Gabriel A., Jessica A.; m. Joan Fitzgerald, May 7, 2000. AB, Oberlin Coll., 1965; MA, U. Calif., Berkeley, 1966; cert., London Sch. Econs., 1963-64; LLD (hon.), Swarthmore Coll., 1999. Asst. to I.F. Stone, Washington, 1966; legis. asst. to Congressman W.F. Ryan, 1967-68; corr. program dir. Pacifica Radio, NYC, 1968-71; editor Village Voice, Washington, 1971-73; staff writer Washington Post, 1974-75; chief investigator Senate Banking Com., Washington, 1975-78; editor Working Papers, Mass., 1980-83; econs. writer, editor New Republic, 1983-91; columnist Bus. Week, 1984—2006, Boston Globe and Washington Post Syndicate, 1985—; co-editor Am. Prospect, 1989—. Contbg. editor More Mag., Washington, 1973—78; lectr. Boston U., 1980—82, W. Colston Leigh Bur., NJ, 1987—; vis. prof. U. Mass., 1987—88, Brandeis U., Mass., 1991—92, Mass., 2003—05. Author: Revolt of the Haves, 1980, The Economic Illusion, 1984, The Life of the Party, 1987, The End of Laissez-Faire, 1991, Everything for Sale, 1997, Family Reunion, 2002; nat. policy corr.: New Eng. Jour. Medicine, 1996—2000. Exec. dir. Nat. Commn. Neighborhoods, Washington, 1978; bd. dirs. Econ. Policy Inst., Washington, 1986—, Families USA, Boston, 1989—96, Florence Fund, 1999—2004. Recipient Jack London award, United Steelworkers Assn. Am., 1982, John Hancock award, John Hancock Co., 1988, Paul Hoffman award, UN Devel. Program, 1996, Sidney Hillman award, Sidney Hillman Found., 1998; fellow, John Guggenheim Meml. Found., 1988, McCormack Inst., 1987—88, Radcliffe Pub. Policy Ctr., 1998—2000; Woodrow Wilson fellow, U. Calif., 1965—66, Kennedy fellow, Harvard U., 1979, Heller Sch. Brandeis U., 2004—, Disting. Sr. fellow, Demos, 2006—. Mem.: Nat. Acad. Social Ins. Avocations: tennis, photography, poetry. Office: Am Prospect 11 Beacon St Boston MA 02108 Home Phone: 617-227-9791; Office Phone: 617-570-8030.

KUTYNA, DONALD JOSEPH, air force officer; b. Chgo., Dec. 6, 1933; s. Frank A. and Isabel E. (Kmiec) K.; m. Lucille Mae Moellering, June 5, 1957; children: Dale J., Douglas J. Student, U. Iowa, 1951-53; BS, U.S. Mil. Acad., 1957; MS in Aero./Astronautics, MIT, 1965. Commd. 2d lt. USAF, 1957, advanced through grades to 4 star gen., 1990; pilot trainee Vance AFB, Enid, Okla., 1958; comdr. B-47 crew March AFB, Riverside, Calif., 1958; test pilot Edwards AFB, Calif., 1965-69; pilot 44th Tactical Fighter Squadron, Royal Takhli AFB, Thailand, 1969-70; planner R&D Pentagon, Washington, 1971-72; exec. officer Undersec. of Air Force, Washington, 1973-76; program mgr. Air Force Electronics Systems Div., Bedford, Mass., 1976-82; mgr. Dept. Def. Space Launch Program, LA, 1982-84; dir. space systems Pentagon, Washington, 1984-86; vice comdr. Space Div., LA, 1986-87; comdr. USAF Space Command, Peterson AFB, Colo., 1987-90; comdr.-in-chief N.Am. Aerospace Def. Command, U.S. Space Command, Peterson AFB, 1990-92; v.p. advanced space systems Lockheed Martin Corp. (formerly Loral Corp.), NYC, 1993-99; v.p. space tech. Loral Space & Comm. Corp., NYC, 1999—2004; ret., 2004. Recipient Space award Nat. Geog. Soc., 1987, James V. Hartinger award Nat. Security Indsl. Assn., 1990, Heritage award Polish Am. Congress, 1990. Mem. Air Force Assn. (Schriever award 1991). Avocations: skiing, surfing, fishing, hunting, antique cars. Office Phone: 719-550-1661.

KUTZ, ALEXANDRA ELLEN, prosecutor; b. Oceanside, NY, June 18, 1974; d. DiAnne Tiley and Allan Morris Kutz. BA in Polit. Sci., U. Rochester, NY, 1996, BA in Psychology, 1996, BA in Philosophy, 1996; JD, Am. U., Washington, DC, 1999. Bar: Md. 1999, DC 2000, Calif. 2004, Ohio 2006. Intern US Dist. Ct. for the DC, Washington, 1998; law clk. US

Atty.'s Office, Dist. of Md., So. Divsn., Greenbelt, Md., 1998—98; dean's fellow Am. U., Washington Coll. Law, 1997—98, 1998—99, student atty., criminal justice clinic, 1998—99; asst. atty. gen. appellate divsn. Office Atty. Gen. for DC, Washington, 1999—2000, asst. atty. gen., gen. crimes sect., 2000, asst. atty. gen. juvenile sect., 2000—06, asst. atty. gen. sex offense unit of the juvenile sect., 2003—06; asst. pros. atty., felony sect. Lake County Prosecutor's Office, Painesville, Ohio, 2006—. Xerox award scholar, U. Rochester, 1992—96. Mem.: ABA. Office: Lake County Prosecutor's Office 105 Main St PO Box 490 Painesville OH 44077 Office Phone: 440-350-2683.

KUTZBACH, JOHN E., climate scientist; PhD. Plaenert-Bascom prof. liberal arts U. Wisc., Madison, prof. emeritus atmospheric and oceanic scis. dept. Dir. Ctr. Climatic Rsch. U. Wisc. Ctr. Climatic Rsch., assoc. dir. Contbr. articles to sci. jours., chapters to books. Named Hon. Prof., Chinese Acad. Scis., Beijing, 1999; recipient Sr. Scientist award, Alexander von Humboldt Found., 1978, William Smith award, Geol. Scis., London, London, 1994, Milankovitch medal, European Geophys. Soc., France, 2001. Fellow: Am. Meteorol. Soc., NAS, Am. Geophys. Union (Roger Revelle medal 2006). Office: Ctr Climatic Rsch Gayloard Nelson Inst Environ Studies 1125 Atmospheric Oceanic and Space Sci 1225 W Dayton St Madison WI 53706-1695 E-mail: jek@wisc.edu.

KUWABARA, JAMES SHIGERU, research hydrologist; b. Honolulu, Apr. 26, 1953; s. Donald Shigeyuki and Setsue (Ogawa) K.; m. Rie Rita Kimura, June 6, 1982; children: Sara Mie, Annie Mako. BSCE, U. Hawaii, 1975; MS in Environ. Engring., Calif. Inst. Tech., 1976, PhD in Environ. Engring., 1980. Computer operator Computer Info. Svcs., Honolulu, 1971; engring. rschr. U. Hawaii, Honolulu, 1971-73; aquacultural rschr. Sea Grants Program, Honolulu, 1973-75; grad. rsch. fellow NSF, Pasadena, Calif., 1975-78; grad. rsch. asst. Calif. Inst. Tech., Pasadena, Calif., 1978-80; postdoctoral rsch. fellow Nat. Rsch. Coun., Menlo Park, Calif., 1980-82; rsch. hydrologist U.S. Geol. Survey, Menlo Park, Calif., 1982—. Conf. chmn. West Coast Water Chem. Workshop, Stanford, 1986; final rev. panel Water Res. Rsch. Grants, Reston, Va., 1988-89; session organizer Estuarine Rsch. Conf., San Francisco, 1991; session moderator Am. Chem. Soc., Washington, 1992; coord. San Francisco Bay Toxic Substances Hydrology Program, 1994-2005, rsch. adv. NRP, 2007-. Editor Estuaries, 1993; assoc. editor Water Resources Rsch., 2001, 2005, dep. editor, 2003; contbr. chpts. to books, numerous articles to Geochimica et Cosmochimica Acta, Limnology and Oceanography, Sci., other profl. jours. Mem. Eagle Scout rev. bd. Boy Scouts Am., Honolulu, 1974-75. Hawaii State Acad. scholar U. Hawaii, 1972; NSF Grad. fellow Calif. Inst. Tech., 1975; Nat. Rsch. Coun. postdoctoral rsch. assoc. U.S. Geol. Survey, 1980. Mem. ASCE, Am. Inst. Chemists, Estuarine Rsch. Fedn., Phycological Soc. Am. Achievements include development of a larval culturing system of State of Hawaii's prawn industry; optimization of gametophytic culturing of giant kelp for biomass conversion program; design of toxicant introduction device, process-interdependent solute transport modeling; modeling benthic flux of contaminants. Office: US Geol Survey Water Resources Discipline 345 Middlefield Rd # MS439 Menlo Park CA 94025-3591 Business E-Mail: kuwabara@usgs.gov.

KUWAYAMA, S. PAUL, physician, immunologist, allergist; b. Sapporo, Hokkaido, Japan, Nov. 8, 1932; s. Satoru and Chiyoko (Nishikawa) K.; m. Barbara Ann Dresback, June 29, 1974; children: David, Steven, Jason. BS, Hokkaido U., Sapporo, 1955, MD, 1959. Diplomate Am. Bd. Pediatrics, 1965, Am. Bd. Allergy & Immunology, 1972, Am. Bd. Pediatric Allergy, 1970; lic. Nat. Bd. Med. Examiners of Japan, 1960, Wis. State Bd. Med. Examiners, 1968, Ariz. State Bd. Med. Examiners, 1987, N.Mex. State Bd. Med. Examiners, 1987, Tenn. State Bd. Med. Examiners, 1992. Intern U.S. Naval Hosp., Yokosuka, 1959-60, St. Mary's Hosp., Milw., 1960-61; jr. resident in pediatrics Temple U. Sch. of Medicine, Phila., 1961-62; chief pediat. resident W.Va. U. Sch. of Medicine, Morgantown, 1962-63; postdoctoral fellow in immunology, jr. fellow in pediatric allergy The Children's Mercy Hosp.-U. Kans. Sch. of Medicine, Kansas City, 1964-65; staff pediatrician Atomic Bomb Casualty Commn. in Hiroshima, U.S. Nat. Acad. of Scis.-U.S. Atomic Energy Commn., 1966-67; sr. pediatric allergist, dept. immunobiology U. Kans. Sch. of Medicine, 1967-68. Asst. clin. prof. pediatric allergy and immunology Med. Coll. Wis., Milw., 1970—. Contbg. author texts and forward to books. Fulbright scholar, 1960-63. Fellow Am. Acad. Pediat. (sect. on allergy and immunology), Am. Coll. Allergy, Asthma and Immunology, Am. Assn. Cert. Allergists, Am. Acad. Allergy, Asthma and Immunology, Am. Assn. Clin. Immunology and Allergy; mem. AMA, Fulbright Scholarship Grantee Alumni Assn., Milw. Pediatric Soc. Office: 11035 W Forest Home Ave Hales Corners WI 53130-2541

KUYKENDALL, CRYSTAL ARLENE, educational consultant, lawyer; b. Chgo., Dec. 11, 1949; d. Cleophus Avant and Ellen (Campbell) Logan; m. Roosevelt Kuykendall, Apr. 10, 1969 (dec. Aug. 1972); children: Kahlil, Rasheki, Kashif. BA, Southern Ill. U., 1970; MA, Montclair State U., 1972; EdD, Atlanta U., 1975; JD, Georgetown U., 1982; LHD (hon.), Lewis and Clark Coll., Portland, 2002; MDiv, Va. Union U., 2005. Bar: D.C. 1988. Instr. Seton Hall U., South Orange, N.J., 1971-73; adminstrn. intern D.C. Pub. Schs., 1974-75; dir. citizens tng. inst. Nat. Com. for Citizens in Edn., Washington, 1975-77; dir. urban and minorities rels. dept. Nat. Sch. Bd. Assn., Washington, 1977-79; edn. dir. PSI Assocs., Inc., Washington, 1979-80; exec. dir. Nat. Alliance of Black Sch. Educators, Washington, 1980-81; dir. mktg. Roy Littlejohn Assoc., Inc., Washington, 1983—; pres., gen. counsel K.I.R.K., Inc. (Kreative and Innovative Resources for Kids), Washington, 1981—. Cons. to Ministry of Sport and Recreation, Western Australia Govt., 1990; chmn. U.S. Pres. Nat. Adv. Coun. on Continuing Edn., Washington, 1978-81; cons. U. Pitts. Race Desegregation Assistance Ctr., 1982-87, J.H. Lowry Assn., Chgo., 1982, U.S. Dept. of Edn. Transition Team, Washington, 1980. Author: Developing Leadership for Parent/Citizen Groups, 1975, You & Yours: Making the Most of this School Year, 1987, Improving Black Student Achievement by Enhancing Self Image, 1989, From Rage to Hope: Strategies for Reclaiming Black and Hispanic Students, 1992, 2d edit., 2004, Dreaming of a PHAT Century, 2000, 2nd edit., 2003, 2005 Mem. adv. bd. Inst. of the Black World, Atlanta, 1975-81; mem. steering com. Nat Conf. on Parental Involvement, Denver, 1977-78; mem. edn. task force Martin Luther King Jr. Ctr. for Social Change, Atlanta, 1978-80; mem. bd. dirs. Health Power, Inc., 1995-2001; chairperson, bd. dirs. Henry C. Gregory III Family Life Ctr. Found. of Shiloh Bapt. Ch. of Washington, 2003—, bd. mem., 1996—; mem. bd dirs. Md. Mentoring Partnership; assoc. min. Shiloh Bapt. Ch., Washington, 2005—. Named Honorary Citizen of New Orleans, Mayor's Office, 1976; Ford found. fellow, 1973-74; Honorary Ky Colonel award, 1993, 99, 2002; Cert. Congl. Recognition, 2001. Mem. Nat. Bar Assn., Nat. Alliance of Black Sch. Edn., Alpha Kappa Alpha. Democrat. Baptist. Avocations: poetry writing, card playing, swimming, jogging, skiing. Office: KIRK Inc PO Box 60115 Potomac MD 20859-0115 Office Phone: 301-299-4189. Personal E-mail: ckuykendal@aol.com.

KUYKENDALL, GREGORY JOHN, lawyer; b. Denver, Jan. 13, 1961; s. Louis George and Mary (Spragins) Kuykendall. BA, U. Colo., 1983; MA, Tulane U., 1985; JD, Northwestern U., 1988. Bar: Ariz. 1989, U.S. Dist. Ct. Ariz. 1989, U.S. Ct. Appeals (9th cir.) 1989, U.S. Dist. Ct. Mich. (Ea. Dist.) 1990, Colo. 1991, U.S. Dist. Ct. (Ctrl. Dist. Ill.) 1996, U.S. Supreme Ct. 2003, cert. specialist criminal law: Ariz. Bd. Legal Specialization. Atty. O'Connor, Cavanagh, Tucson, 1988-92, Butler & Stein, Tucson, 1992—94; pvt. practice Tucson, 1994—. Lectr. in field. Mem.: Ariz. Attys. Criminal Justice, State Bar Ariz., Fed. Bar Assn., Colo. Bar Assn., NACDL (life), Phi Beta Kappa. Democrat. Avocations: skiing, running, bicycling. Office: 145 S 6th Ave Tucson AZ 85701 Office Phone: 520-792-8033. Office Fax: 520-792-0113.*

KUYKENDALL, RICHARD G., music educator; s. F. G. and Mary Frances Kuykendall, Ruby Kuykendall (Stepmother); m. Susan M. Kuykendall, Aug. 22, 1993. BA, McNeese State U., Lake Charles, La., 1978, MusM, 1984. Band dir. Calcasieu Parish Sch. Board,J.I. Watson Mid. Sch., Iowa, La., 1995—; band dir., lagrange h.s. Calcasieu Parish Sch. Bd., Lake Charles, La., 1993—95. Band director,leesville h.s. Vernon Parish Sch. Bd., Leesville, La., 1985—93; band dir., carencro h.s. Lafayette Parish Sch. Bd., Lafayette, La., 1983—85; band dir., leesville h.s. Vernon Parish Sch. Bd., Leesville, La., 1979—82; band dir., hackberry h.s. Cameron Parish Sch. Bd., Hackberry, La., 1978—79; adj. instr. of low brass U. of La. at Lafayette, Lafayette, La., 1984—85; mem. of mcneese faculty brass quintet McNeese State U., Lake Charles, La., 1982—83; mem. u. of la. at lafayette faculty brass quintet U. of La. at Lafayette, Lafayette, La., 1984—85; mem. of so. assn. of colleges and schools com. (twice) S.A.C.S., La., 1981—82; teacher-computer music composition(summer) Calcasieu Parish Sch. Bd., Lake Charles, La., 2000—01. Performer for armed forces, civic groups and nursing homes, 1976—; bd. chmn., vice chmn., deacon First Christian Ch., Lake Charles, La., 2000—. Named J.I. Watson Mid. Sch. Tchr. of Yr., J.I. Watson Sch., 1998-99, J.I. Watson Tchr. of Yr., 2006, Calif. Parish Mid. Sch. Tchr. of Yr., 2006, La. Region V Tchr. of Yr., 2006; recipient Commendation for Achievements at Leesville H.S., Vernon Parish Sch. Bd., 1982, Commendation for Outstanding Civilian Support, US Army, Ft. Polk, La., 1982, Commendation for Ednl. Achievements at Leesville H.S., La. State Legislature, 1982, Sta. KPLC-TV Class Act award, Sta. KPLC-TV (Local Sta. NBC-TV affiliate), 1998, Mayoral Proclomation designating May 23, 2002 as Rick Kuykendall Day in the town of Iowa, La., Town of Iowa, 2002. Mem.: Dist. V Band Dirs. Assn. (pres. (twice) 1998—2000), Music Educators Nat. Conf., Am. Fedn. Tchrs. (state del. 2002, nat. del. 2003). Office: JI Watson Middle School 201 E First St Iowa LA 70647

KUZAK, DERRICK M., automotive executive; b. Detroit, Mich., 1951; BSEE, MSEE, Univ. Detroit, PhD sys. engring. Engring. & mgmt. positions Ford Motor Co., Dearborn, Mich., 1978—97, vehicle line dir., 1997—99; exec. dir. Ford Europe, 2000—02, v.p. product develop., 2002—05; v.p. N.Am. engring. Ford Motor Co., Dearborn, Mich., 2005—06, v.p. glob. product develop., 2006—. Office: Ford Motor Co 1 American Rd Dearborn MI 48126*

KUZMA, DEBORAH J., vice principal, music educator; d. Ethel C. and Walter Kuzma. MusB, Marywood U., 1974; MEd, William Paterson U., 1987; DEd, Seton Hall U., 2004. Lic. prin., supr. NJ, 1987, music tchr. NJ, 1974, math. tchr. NJ, 1987, elem. sch. tchr. NJ, 1987, nursery sch. tchr. NJ, 1987. Paramedic St. Clare, Denville, NJ; tchr. music Randolph Twp. Bd Edn., NJ, 1974—76, Mt. Olive Pub. Sch., Budd Lake, NJ, 1976—87; tchr. computers Mt. Olive Mid. Sch., 1987—99, tchr. math., 1987—90, dir. athletics and activities, 1993—2000, vice prin., 2000—06, Mt. Olive HS, 2006—. Various committees St. Jude Ch., Budd Lake, NJ, 1974—2006; membership dir. NJ. Mid. Sch. Assn., Ridgewood, NJ, 2004—06. Geraldine R. Dodge Found. grant, 1997. Office: Mt Olive HS Corey Rd Flanders NJ 07836 Home Phone: 973-770-3035. Personal E-mail: drdjkuzma@aol.com.

KUZMA, GEORGE MARTIN, retired bishop; b. Windber, Pa., July 24, 1925; s. Ambrose and Anne (Marton) K. Student, Benedictine Coll., Lisle, Ill.; BA, postgrad., Duquesne U., U. Mich.; grad., SS Cyril and Methodius Byzantine Cath. Sem. Ordained priest Byzantine Cath. Ch., 1955. Asst. pastor SS Peter and Paul Ch., Braddock, Pa., 1955—57; pastor Holy Ghost Ch., Charleroi, Pa., 1957—65, St. Michael Ch., Flint, Mich., 1965—70, St. Eugene Ch., Bedford, Ohio, 1970—72, Annunciation Ch., Anaheim, Calif., 1970—86; rev. monsignor Byzantine Cath. Ch., 1984, titular bishop, 1986, consecrated bishop, 1987; aux. bishop Byzantine Cath. Diocese of Passaic, NJ, 1987—90; bishop Van Nuys, Calif., 1991—2000; ret., 2000. Judge matrimonial tribunal, mem. religious edn. commn., mem. commn. orthodox rels. Diocese of Pitts., 1955—69; judge matrimonial tribunal, vicar for religious Diocese of Parma, 1969—82; treas., bd. dirs., chmn. liturgical commn., mem. clergy & seminarian rev. bd., liaison to ea. Cath. dirs. religious edn., bd. dirs. Diocese of Van Nuys, 1982—86, diocesan credit un, chmn. diocesan heritage bd., chmn. diocesan ecumenical commn., 1982—86; vicar gen. Diocese of Passaic; Episcopal vicar for Ea. Pa.; chmn. Diocesan Retirement Plan Bd.; pres. Father Walter Cizsek Prayer League; chaplain Byzantine Carmelite Monastery, Sugarloaf, Pa. Assoc. editor: Byzantine Cath. World; editor: The Apostle. With USN, 1943—46, PTO. Office: Byzantine Cath Eparchy of Van Nuys 8131 N 16th St Phoenix AZ 85020-3901

KUZMA, NORA LOUISE See LORDS, TRACI

KUZMANOVIC, JANE VIOLET, academic administrator; b. Akron, Ohio, Apr. 9, 1962; d. Ljubomir Emanuel and Viorika Violet Bodjanac; m. Dragan Kuzmanovic, May 1, 1983; children: Miriam Violeta Tomek, Lorraine Ljubica, Michael Miroslav, Daniel Branislav, Thomas Dragoslav, Stefanie Adela, Julianne Jovana, Melanie Dragana. BS in Bus. Mgmt., U. of Phoenix, 2004; MS in Human Rels. & Bus., Amberton U., 2006. Publications prodn. coord. Hughes Aircraft Co., El Segundo, Calif., 1984—93; dept. sec. Norstan Cabling Svcs., Van Nuys, Calif., 1995; exec. asst. AVEX, Inc., Camarillo, Calif., 1995—97; faculty and curriculum coord. Kennedy-Western U., Thousand Oaks, Calif., 1997—2000, sr. faculty and curriculum coord., 2000—02, faculty and curriculum mgr., 2002—04, sr. faculty and curriculum mgr., 2004—07; mgr. accreditation project Warren Nat. U., 2007—. Translator, office asst. Star Upholstering, Beverlywood, Calif., 1976—98; tchr., Sunday sch. Apostolic Christian Ch., Nazarean, Lawndale, Calif., 1989—. Dir.: (children's Sunday sch. choir) Apostolic Christian Ch., Nazarean. Grantee Pell, NAFSA, 2003. Avocations: gardening, travel, cooking, canning. Office: Warren Nat U 30301 Agoura Rd Agoura Hills CA 91301 E-mail: jkuzmanovic@wnuedu.com.

KUZNETSOVA, NATALIA P., music educator; b. Serov, Russia, Oct. 3, 1972; d. Petr Michailovich Kuznetsov and Tatiana Alexeevna Kuznetsova. MusB in Violin Performance, Krasnoturinskoye Music Coll., Russia, 1991; MusM in Violin Performance, Ural State Conservatory, Yekaterinburg, Russia, 1997; MusB in Edn. (hon.), Old Dominion U., Norfolk, Va., 2003, MusM in Edn., 2006. Violinist Moscow State Opera Theater Helikon Opera, 1997—99, Moscow State Chamber Orch. The Seasons, 1998—2000, Duetto Espressivo, Virginia Beach, Va., 2003—; dir. orch. Va. Beach City Pub. Schs., 2006—. Musician (concert violinist) solo, ensemble, orchestra performances. F. Ludwig Diehn scholar, Norfolk Found., 2002, 2004—06. Mem.: Music Educators Nat. Conf., Am. String Tchr. Assn. Avocations: swimming, travel, chess, crafts. Home Phone: 757-548-0918.

KUZNETSOVA, SVETLANA, professional tennis player; b. St. Petersburg, Russia, June 27, 1985; d. Alexandr Kuznetsov and Galina Tsareva. Profl. tennis player WTA Tour, 2001—. Named WTA Tour Newcomer of Yr., 2002. Achievements include winning 9 career singles titles, 13 doubles titles, WTA; winning 1 career singles title, ITF; mem. Russian Fed Cup Team, 2004, Russian Olympic Team, 2004. Office: c/o WTA Tour Corp Hdqs One Progess Plz Ste 1500 Saint Petersburg FL 33701*

KVALSETH, TARALD ODDVAR, mechanical engineer, educator; b. Brunkeberg, Telemark, Norway, Nov. 7, 1938; married; 3 children. BS, U. Durham, King's Coll., Eng., 1963; MS, U. Calif., Berkeley, 1966, PhD, 1971. Rsch. asst. engring. expt. sta. U. Colo., Boulder, 1963-64, tchg. asst. dept. mech. engring.; mech. engr. Williams & Lane Inc., Berkeley, Calif., 1964-65; rsch. asst. dept. indsl. engring. and ops. rsch. U. Calif., Berkeley, 1965-71, rsch. fellow, 1973; asst. prof. Sch. Indsl. and Systems Engring. Ga. Inst. Tech., Atlanta, 1971-74; sr. lectr. indsl. mgmt. div. Norwegian Inst. Tech. U. Trondheim, 1974-79, head indsl. mgmt. divsn., 1975-79; assoc. prof. dept. mech. engring. U. Minn., Mpls., 1979-82, prof., 1982—2005, prof. emeritus, 2005—. Guest worker NASA Ames Research Ctr., Calif., 1973; mem. organizing com. 1st Berkeley-Monterey Conf. Timespan, Pay and Discretionary Capacity, 1973; steering com. Internat. Conf. Human Factors in Design and Op. Ships, Gothenburg, Sweden, 1977; gen. session chmn. Conf. Work Place Design and Work Environ. Problems, Trondheim, 1978; presenter in field. Contbr. articles to profl. jours., chapters to books. Fellow AAAS; mem. IEEE, Inst. Indsl. Engrs. (sr.), Human Factors and Ergonomics Soc. (pres. upper Midwest chpt.), Nordic Ergonomics Soc. (coun. 1977-80), Internat. Ergonomics Assn. (gen. coun. 1977-80, v.p. 1982-85), Ergonomics Soc., Psychonomic Soc., Am. Psychol. Soc., Am. Statis. Assn., Math. Assn. Am., Sigma Xi. Lutheran. Achievements include patents in field. Home: 4980 Shady Island Cir Mound MN 55364 Office: U Minn Dept Mech Engring Minneapolis MN 55455 Office Phone: 612-625-5051. Business E-Mail: kvals001@umn.edu.

KVAMME, MARK D., marketing professional; BA in French, Econs. and Lit., U. Calif., Berkeley. Programmer Apple Computer; founding mem., then internat. product mgr. in U.S. Apple France; founder, pres., CEO Internat. Solutions, 1984-86; dir. internat. mktg. Wyse Tech., 1986-89; ptnr. CKS Group, Cupertino, Calif., 1989-91, chair, CEO, 1991-98; chair USWEB/CKS, Cupertino, Calif., 1998—99; ptnr. Sequoia Capital, Menlo Park, Calif., 1999—. Office: Sequoia Capital 3000 Sand Hill Rd Bldg 4 Menlo Park CA 94025-7113

KVANVIG, JONATHAN LEE, philosophy educator; b. Dickinson, ND, Dec. 7, 1954; s. Kenneth George and Alice Mae K., Edith Mae Kvanvig (Stepmother); m. Carol Dobbs Dobbs, June 9, 1958; children: Jared Daniel, Brittany Mae. BA, Evangel Coll., Springfield, Mo., 1977; MA, U. of Mo., Columbia, 1979; PhD, U. of Notre Dame, South Bend, Ind., 1982. Adj. asst. prof. U. Notre Dame, 1982—83; asst. prof. Tex. A&M U., College Station, Mo., 1983—88, assoc. prof., 1988—93, prof. philosophy, 1993—2001; philosophy prof. U. Mo., Columbia, Mo., 2001—06, chmn. Philosophy Dept., 2002—06; disting. prof. philosophy Baylor U., 2006—. Organizer Ann. Philosophy of Religion Conf., 2006—; bd. editl. consultants Faith and Philosophy; editor Oxford Studies in Philosophy of Religion, 2007—. Author: (books) The Possibility of an All-Knowing God, 1986, The Intellectual Virtues and the Life of the Mind: On the Place of the Virtues in Contemporary Epistemology, 1992, The Problem of Hell, 1993, Warrant in Contemporary Epistemology, 1996, The Value of Knowledge and the Pursuit of Understanding, 2003, The Knowability Paradox, 2006. Bd. govs. Clarendon Found., Washington, 1991—2003. Fellow, NEH, 1986, summer fellow, 1991. Mem.: Ctrl. States Philosophical Assn., Southwestern Philos. Soc. (sec.-treas. 1995—98), Soc. Christian Philosophers (exec. com. 1999—2001), Am. Philos. Assn. Avocations: bicycling, coaching, umpiring. Office: Dept Philosophy Baylor Univ MH 212 Waco TX 76704-7273 Office Phone: 573-882-2764, 254-710-6364. Office Fax: 254-710-3838. Business E-Mail: kvanvigj@missouri.edu. E-mail: Jonathan_Kvanvig@baylor.edu.*

KVETKO, COLLEEN M., bank executive; m. Kirk Kvetko. Undergraduate, Coll. Mt. St. Joseph. Mgmt. trainee Fifth Third Bank, Fla., Fla., from nat. comml. lender to pres., 1987—2002, pres., 2002—05. Bd. dir. NCH Found.; found. Exec. Women's Golf Assn.; mem. bd. Fla. Bankers Assn.; chmn. Econ. Devel. Coun. YMCA. Chmn. YMCA Collier County, Econ. Devel. Coun. Collier County; campaign chmn. United Way Collier County. Named 10th Most Powerful Woman in Banking, U.S. Bankers Mag., Vol. of Yr., YMCA Collier County, 1998, Businesswoman of Yr., Gulfshore Bus. Mag. Mem.: Fla. Bankers Assn. (bd. dir.), Naples C. of C. Office: Fifth Third Bank Fla Po Box 413021 Naples FL 34101-3021

KVETON, KYLE, lawyer; b. Huntington, NY, Jan. 7, 1959; s. Frank and Jean Kveton; m. Karen Renee Palmersheim, Apr. 3, 2004; children: Eric Matthew, Mark Bradley. BA, SUNY, Binghamton, 1980; JD, U. So. Calif., LA, 1983. Bar: Calif. 1983. Atty. Texaco Inc., LA, 1983—86; mem. Robie & Matthai, LA, 1987—. Mem. faculty Nat. Inst. Trial Advocacy, 2005—07; arbitrator, mediator in field; lectr. CLE. Contbr. chapters to books. Named Superlawyer, So. Calif., 2006—07. Mem.: ABA, Litigation Counsel Am. (assoc. fellow), Assn. So. Calif. Def. Counsel, Def. Rsch. Inst., LA County Bar Assn. Office: Robie & Matthai 500 S Grand Ave #1500 Los Angeles CA 90071 Office Phone: 213-706-8000. Office Fax: 213-624-2563. Business E-Mail: kkveton@romalaw.com.

KVINT, VLADIMIR LEV, economist, mining engineer, finance educator; b. Krasnoyarsk, Siberia, Russia, Feb. 21, 1949; arrived in US, 1990; s. Lev V. Kvint and Lidia E. Adamskaya; children: Liza, Valeria. MS in Mining Engring., Inst. Non-Ferrous Metals and Gold, Krasnoyarsk, 1972; PhD in Managerial Econs., Inst. Nat. Economy, Moscow, 1975; D of Econs., Inst. Econs., Acad. Scis., Moscow, 1988; HHD, U. Bridgeport, Conn., 1997; D (hon.), Acad. of Pub. Adminstrn. of Pres. of Russia, 2004, Vlora Tech. U., Albania, 2004, Donetsk Nat. Tech. U., 2007. Asst. prof. Inst. of Non-Ferrous Metals, Russia, 1972; chief dept. orgn. strategy Mining-Metallurgical Co., Norilsk, 1975—76; dep. chair, chief economist Automation of non-ferrous metals com., Russia, 1976—78; chief dept. sci.-tech. progress Siberian Br. Russian Acad. Scis., Novosibirsk, 1978—82; leading rschr., fellow Inst. Econs., Acad. Scis., Moscow, 1982—89; disting. prof. econ. Babson Coll. Bus., Wellesley, Mass., 1990; prof. Fordham U. Grad. Sch. Bus., NYC, 1990—2004; prof. internat. bus. Stern Grad. Sch. Bus. NYU, 1995—2000, Kogod Sch. Bus. Am. U., Washington, 2004—07, LaSalle U. Sch. Bus., Pa., 2005—. Part time prof. Russian univs., 1976—89; vis. prof. Vienna Econ. U., Austria, 1989—90; cons. GE, NYC, 1989—94, Cable & Wireless, London, 1989—97; mng. dir. emerging markets Arthur Andersen, 1992—97; econ. advisor King of Bulgaria, 1996—2001, Pres. UN, 1992—93, 1997—98; dir. govtl. affairs Metromedia Internat. Telecom. Inc., 1997—2000; econ. adviser Govt. Albania, 2001—05; chmn. expert econ. coun. Fed. Com. Sport and Tourism, Russia, 2002—; chmn. bd. dirs. St. Petersburg Sea Port Terminal, 2006—. Author: The Acceleration of Technological Development of Production, 1976, The Introduction and Use of Automation Systems, 1981, The Krasnoyarsk Experiment, 1982, Management of Scientific-Technical Progress, 1986, The Economic and Scientific-Technical Information, 1987, Development of Economy of Daghestan, 1988, The Barefoot Shoemaker: Capitalizing on the New Russia, 1993, A Different Perspective on Emerging Markets, 1995, Incorporating Global Risk Management in the Strategic Decision Making Process, 1997, The Global Emerging Market in Transition, 1999, 2d edit. 2004; co-author: Creating and Managing International Joint Ventures, 1996, International M&A, Joint Ventures and Beyond, 1998, 2d edit., 2002, Investing Under Fire: Winning Strategies, 2003; editor-in-chief: Emerging Market of Russia: Sourcebook for Investment and Trade, 1998; contbr. articles to CNN, Forbes, Harvard Bus. Rev., others. Bd. dirs. USSR Exporters Assn., Moscow, 1988-90; mem. internat. com. Muhlenberg Coll., Allentown, Pa., 1992-99; chmn. Summits Instl. Investors & Global Risk Management, World Econ. Devel. Congress, Washington, 1995-97. Recipient Silver medal for achievements in nat. economy, USSR Main Nat. Com., Moscow, 1986, GLOBE Ann. award, Fordham U., 2002, Gold medal Hon. Lawyer of Russia, 2003, Vernadskiy Silver medal, Russian Acad. Natural Scis., 2004, proclamation Outstanding Contbn. to City, State and Nation,

NYC City Coun., 2005, Peace medal, Caspian Region, Kazakhstan, 2006, Hon. Prof. Econs., St. Petersburg Acad. Mgmt. and Econs., 2006, Atyrau Inst. Oil and Gas, Kazakhstan, 2006, Order of the Friendship award, Pres. of Russia, 2006, Wassily Leontief medal, Russian Acad. Natural Scis., 2007; US Fulbright scholar, 2001. Fellow: Wexner Heritage Found., New Eng. Ctr. for Internat. and Regional Studies (hon.); mem.: Bus. Coun. Internat. Understanding (sr. advisor 2001—), Internat. Acad. Emerging Markets (pres.), Bretton Woods Com., Russian Acad. Scis. (life; fgn. mem.), Russian Acad. Natural Scis. (life), Internat. Acad. Regional Devel. (life), Internat. Informatization Acad. of UN (hon.), Am. Econ. Assn., Philos. Soc., NY Acad. Scis., World Jewish Acad. Scis. (pres.). Achievements include devel. of theory of regionalization of scientific tech. progress; evaluation of role of scientific-technical strategy in devel. of regional economy; devel. of regional programs, developed a theory of global emerging market, developed a system of optimization models of business strategies in new emerging markets, economic solutions to poverty. Office Phone: 212-585-2048. Personal E-mail: vlkvint@aol.com. *Terrorism is a social manifestation of evil and requires complete extermination. Terrorists interpret kindness as weakness—such methodologies will not solve their malevolence. Compromising with them only prolongs their ability to wage war against humanity and creates an ocean of grief and extended poverty as the existence of this plague diverts badly needed funds from the war on hunger. Just as barbarians destroyed Rome and plunged mankind into darkness, terrorists with modern weapons can bring a global catastrophe to civilization.*

KVITKO, ARKADY, mathematician, researcher; b. Slavyanka, Hasansky, Russia, June 6, 1949; arrived in U.S., 1989; s. Nikolay Zilberg and Leonora K.; m. Rachel Kravchenko, Apr. 30, 1974; children: Marina, Max. BS in Math. and Physics, City Coll., Odessa, Ukraine, 1970; MS in Ops. Rsch., Odessa State U., Odessa, Ukraine, 1974; PhD in Ops. Rsch., State U., Minsk, Russia, 1982. From asst. prof. to adj. prof. Odessa State U. City Coll., 1975-89; from SAS programmer, analyst to sr. statistician Merrill Lynch, NYC, 1990-97, sr. ops. rsch. analyst, 1997—. Cons., presenter in field. Co-author: (with M. Zholdak) Probabitlity Theory and Information Systems, 1989; contbr. articles to profl. jours. Poly. U. grant, 1982-89. Avocations: chess, reading. Home Phone: 718-373-0165; Office Phone: 212-647-2464. Personal E-mail: Alex_Kvitko@ml.com. Business E-Mail: alex_kvitko@yahoo.com.

KWAAN, JACK HAU MING, retired physician; b. Hong Kong, Apr. 9, 1928; came to U.S., 1953; s. Y.K. and Rose W. Kwaan; m. Min K. Ho, Feb. 11, 1973; children: Mary, Peter, Rebecca, Nicholas. MD, U. Hong Kong, 1952. Diplomate Am. Bd. Radiology, Am. Bd. Surgery, Am. Bd. Thoracic Surgery. Resident in radiology Roswell Park Meml. Inst., 1955-56; chief resident Peter Bent Brigham Hosp., 1956-57; rsch. fellow in radiology Harvard Med. Sch., Boston, 1956-57; sr. cancer rsch. radiol. therapist Roswell Park Meml. Inst., Buffalo, 1958-59; asst. prof. radiology U. Ky., Lexington, 1963-65; resident in surgery U. Calif., Irvine, 1965-68; rsch. fellow oncologic surgery M.D. Anderson Hosp., Houston, 1968-69; resident in thoracic U. Calif., Irvine, 1969-71, chief resident thoracic surgery, 1970, asst. prof. surgery, 1972-73; chief vascular surgery sect., co-dir. vascular surgery tng. program U. Calif. Irvine/Long Beach VA Med. Ctr., 1974-87; prof. surgery U. Calif., Irvine, 1983-87; sr. resident in thoracic surgery U. So. Calif./L.A. County Med. Ctr., 1971; staff thoracic cardiovasc. surgeon Long Beach VA Hosp., 1972-73; asst. chief dept. surgery Valley Med. Ctr., Fresno, Calif., 1973-74; prof. surgery U. Okla., Tulsa, 1987-93; ret., 1993. Chief dept. surgery Valley Med. Ctr., Fresno, Calif., 1973-74; chief vascular surgery sect. Long Beach VA Med. Ctr., 1974-87; surgical cons. Kaiser Permanente Hosp. Contbr. articles to profl. jours. Fellow Am. Coll. Surgeons; mem. Brit. Med. Assn., Gen. Med. Coun. London (registrant), Assn. Mil. Surgeons of U.S. (life), Assn. VA Surgeons, Internat. Cardiovascular Soc. Home: PO Box 50183 Long Beach CA 90815-6183

KWAK, SEUNG-KEON, research scientist; b. Seoul, Republic of Korea, Feb. 2, 1967; arrived in U.S., 1992; s. Sebom Kwak, Kyungja Lim; m. Jeong-Eun Rhee; 1 child, Bethia. BS, Hankook Aviation U., Kyunggi, Korea, 1989; MS, W.Va. U., 1994; PhD, Ohio State U., 1999. Postdoctoral rschr. Ohio State U., Columbus, 1999—2001; dir. rsch. and devel. Quality Rsch., Devel. and Cons., Inc., Chaska, Minn., 2001—04; CEO SenAnTech, Inc., 2004—06; engr., scientist Spirit Aerosys. Inc., 2006—. Tech. reviewer IEEE Trans. on Automatic Control, IEEE Conf. on Decision and Control, Am. Control Conf. Contbr. articles to profl. jours. Lt. Republic of Korea Air Force, 1989—92. Mem.: ASME (mem. organizing com. 2000 Conf. 1999—2000, tech. reviewer ASME Internat. Mech. Engring. Congress and Exposition). Home: 121 Radcliffe Ave Port Washington NY 11050 Office Phone: 316-523-0877. Business E-Mail: seung-keon.kwak@spiritaero.com.

KWAN, BENJAMIN CHING KEE, ophthalmologist; b. Hong Kong, July 12, 1940; came to U.S., 1959. s. Shun Ming and Lurk Ming (Lai) K.; m. Catherine Ning, Aug. 29, 1964; children: Susan San, David Daiwai. MD, Wash. U., St. Louis, 1967. Diplomate Am. Bd. Ophthalmology. Ptnr. So. Calif. Permanente Med. Ctr., Harbor City, 1976—2003, chief of svc. ophthalmology, 1976-88; clin. prof. dept. ophthalmology UCLA, 1995—. Chmn. winter blossom ball Chinese Am. Debutante's Guild, 1993; bd. dirs. Asian Am. Sr. Citizens Svc. Ctr., 1993-. Capt. U.S. Army, 1969-71. Recipient Svc. award Asian Am. Sr. Citizens Svc. Ctr., 1993, Proclamation award Calif. Sec. of State, 1993, Svc. award East L.A. Chinese Everspring Sr. Assn., 1994. Fellow Am. Acad. Ophthalmology; mem. Chinese Am. Ophthal. Soc. (pres. elect 1997-99, pres. 1999-00, Svc. award 1994, 2006), Chinese Physician's Soc. So. Calif. (bd. dirs., pres. 1983, Svc. award 1983, 89), Orgn. Chinese Ams. (pres. L.A. chpt. 1986-87). Roman Catholic. Avocations: ballroom dancing, singing, skiing. Home: 6327 Tarragon Rd Rancho Palos Verdes CA 90275-5834 Personal E-mail: benckwan@hotmail.com.

KWAN, DAVID CHUNG MAN, business executive; b. Hong Kong, June 6, 1966; s. Wai Kwong Kwan and Kam Hiu Wong. BS in Applied Math., UCLA, 1988. V.p. tech. DetectorMAIL, Las Vegas, Nev., 2004—. Mem.: The Magic Castle, Mensa Soc.

KWAN, MICHELLE WING, professional figure skater; b. Torrance, Calif., July 7, 1980; d. Danny and Estella Kwan. Student, UCLA, U. Denver, 2007—. Good-will amb. US Dept. State, 2006—. Spokesperson Walt Disney Co., 2006—. Published (book series) Michelle Kwan Presents Skating Dreams, guest appearances Disney and ABC Specials; performer: (TV special) based on the music of Disney's animated film, Mulan, 1998. Nat. spokesperson, Champions Across Am. Children's Miracle Network, 1996—, co-chair, ProKid's Program; founder Chevrolet/Michelle Kwan R.E.W.A.R.D.S. scholarship program. Recipient Skating Mag. Readers' Choice award for figure skater of yr., 1993-94, U.S. Figure Skating Skater of Yr. award, 1994-96, 98, 99, 2001-03, Dial award, 1997, Sullivan award for top amateur athlete in Am., 2001, Kids' Choice award, 2002, 03, Teen Choice award, 2002, Skating Mag. Reader's Choice award, 2003; named Female Athlete of Yr. U.S. Olympic Com., 1996, 98-2001, 2003, Women's Sports Found. Sportswoman of Yr., 2003, CosmoGirl of Yr., 2002. Achievements include being the youngest World Champion in US history; most decorated figure skater in US history; third youngest World Champion; received 50 perfect 6.0 marks in major competitions; victories include: World Junior Championships, 1994, 96, Nations cup, 1995, U.S. Postal Svc. Challenge, 1995, State Farm U.S. Championships, 1996, 1999, 2001, 2003, Champions Series Final, 1996, Japan Open, 1997, 1999, Skate Am., 1995, 1997, 1999, 2000, Skate Can., 1995, 1997, 1999, US Championships, 1996, 1998-2004, World Championships, 1998, 1999, 2000, 2001, 2003, Goodwill Games, 1998, 1998 Ultimate Four, 1998, Grand Slam Figure Skating, 1998, US Pro Classic, 1998, Masters of Figure Skating, 1998, 1999, 2000, Silver Medal, Olympics, 1998, Bronze Medal, 2002; Michelle Kwan Trophy named in her honor, 2004. Office: US Figure Skating Assn 20 1st St Colorado Springs CO 80906-3624

KWAN-RUBINEK, VERONIKA, broadcast executive; Pres. internat. distbn. Warner Bros. Pictures, 2001—. Named one of 100 Most Powerful Women in Entertainment, Hollywood Reporter, 2006. Office: Warner Bros Pictures International Distribution 4000 Warner Blvd Burbank CA 91522 Office Phone: 818-954-1663. Office Fax: 818-954-6112. E-mail: veronika.kwan-rubinek@warnerbros.com.*

KWARTLER, JED ARYEH, otolaryngologist; b. St. Louis, Feb. 4, 1958; s. Irwin E. and Shirley (Platt) K.; m. Carol L. Barash, Mar. 11, 1984; children: Zachary, Talia, Eliana. BS, Brown U., 1979; MD, U. Medicine Dentistry N.J., 1983. Diplomate Am. Bd. Otolaryngology, Nat. Bd. Med. Examiners. Intern dept. surgery U. Medicine Dentistry N.J., 1983-84, resident, 1984-85, 85-88, clin. asst. prof., 1990-95, clin. assoc. prof., 1995—; fellow in otology/neurotology House Ear Clinic and Inst., LA, 1989-90. Dir. neurotology, attending dept. otolaryngology, dir. temporal bone anatomy lab United Hosp., Newark; cons. otology/neurotology East Orange (N.J.) VA Hosp., attending otolaryngology Univ. Hosp., Newark, Overlook Hosp., Summit, N.J., St. Barnabas Med. Ctr., Livington, N.J.; cons. neurosurgery Morristown (N.J.) Meml. Hosp.; mem. numerous profl. coms.; lectr. in field; peer rev. Med. Interinsurance Exch., 1994; regional rep. ins. reimbursement task force Cochlear Implant Club Internat., 1992—. Contbr. articles to numerous profl. jours.; mem. editl. rev. bd. Archives in Otolaryngology, Head and Neck Surgery Jour., 1990—. Trustee Summit Speech Sch., 1990-96, chmn. ednl. policy com., 1992-93; mem. long range planning task force Oheb Shalom Congregation, South Orange, N.J., 1992. Recipient Ciba Geigy Cmty. Svc. award, 1980, Resident Travel award NIH-Assn. for Rsch. in Otolaryngology, 1988, Disting. Clin. Svc. award NJSHA, 1993. Mem. Am. Acad. Otolaryngology-Head and Neck Surgery (award of honor 1996), Am. Soc. Evoked Potential Monitoring, Am. Auditory Soc., Am. Neurotology Soc., N.Am. Skull Base Surgery Soc., William F. House Soc., Soc. Univ. Otolaryngologists, N.J. Hearing and Speech Assn., N.J. Acad. Otolaryngology (at-large mem. bd. govs. 1991-92, sec. 1992-93, v.p. 1993-94, pres. 1996), Sigma Xi. Avocations: sailing, tennis, skiing, woodworking. Office: Ear Splty Group 55 Morris Ave Ste 304 Springfield NJ 07081-1422

KWIATKOWSKI, TIMOTHY D., bank executive; b. Buffalo, Mar. 29, 1956; s. Daniel and Irene Theresa Kwiatkowski; m. Sheila M. Fisher, Aug. 14, 1982; 1 child, Rachel N. AS in Bus. Mgmt., Bryant & Stratton Bus. Inst., Buffalo, 1976; BS in Bus. Resource Devel., Medaille Coll., Buffalo, 1986. V.p. Empire Am., Buffalo, 1977—90; v.p. comml. workout officer Rochester Cmty. Savings Bank (now Citizen's Bank), NY, 1990—91; sr. v.p. Bank Am., Buffalo, 1991—2005; v.p. Five Star Bank, Warsaw, NY, 2005—. Adv. com. Orchard Pk. Performing Arts Ctr., NY, 2005—07; adv. bd. Bryant & Stratton Bus. Inst., Buffalo, 2007; mem. Orchard Pk. C. of C., NY, 2005—07; alumni bd. dirs. Medaille Coll., Buffalo, 2005—07. Recipient Entrepreneurial Spirit award, Fleet Bank, 1999. D-Conservative. Roman Catholic. Avocations: drums, sports. Home: 10 Glenmar Dr West Seneca NY 14224 Office: Five Star Bank 3233 Southwestern Blvd Orchard Park NY 14127 Office Fax: 716-677-9760; Home Fax: 716-677-9760. Personal E-mail: tdkwiat82@adelphia.net. Business E-Mail: tdkwiatkowski@five-starbank.com.

KWIK, CHRISTINE IRENE, physician, retired military officer, retired foreign service officer; b. Lvov, Poland, Sept. 12, 1939; d. Karol Stanislaus and Leonarda Fryderica (Seniuk) Kostek; widowed; children: Christine and Catherine. Grad. summa cum laude, Med. Acad. Cracow, Poland, 1956-62; grad. primary flight medicine, Brooks AFB, Tex., 1985; completed chief of profl. staff, Sheppard AFB, Tex., 1988. Diplomate Am. Bd. Emergency Medicine, Am. Bd. Internal Medicine, Poland; cert. Ednl. Coun. Fgn. Med. Grad.; re-cert. Extended Allergy Care Provider. Intern. Med. Acad., Cracow, Poland, 1962-63; residency internal medicine II Clinic Internal Diseases, Cracow, Poland, 1963-66; staff II Clinic of Internal Diseases, Cracow, Poland, 1966-69; gen. med. officer Gen. Hosp., Sokoto, Nigeria, 1969-72; intern. Frankford Hosp., Phila., 1972-73; house physician Holy Redeemer Hosp., Meadowbrook, Pa., 1973-74; emergency room physician John F. Kennedy Hosp., Phila., 1974-76, Emergency Rm. dir., 1976-78; commd. capt. USAF Med. Corp, 1978, advanced through grades to colonel, 1993; primary care physician USAF Clinic Emergency Rm., Ramstein, Germany, 1978-81; officer in charge Emergency Rm. and Gen. Practice Clinic, Peterson Field, Colo., 1981-84; primary care physician Malcolm Grow Med. Ctr., Andrews AFB, Md., 1984-88; chief clinic svc. 63d Med. Group/SGH, Norton AFB, Calif., 1988-93; staff physician 60h Med. Group, Travis AFB, Calif., 1993-96, Occupl. and Environ. Health and Safety Svc., Ft. George Meade, Md., 1996-99; ret. col. USAF, 1999; regional med. officer Dept. of State. Asst. tchr., sr. asst. tchr. Inst. Descriptive Anatomy, Cracow, Poland 1963-69; emergency physician on call First Aid Sta., Cracow, Poland 1966-69. Fellow: Am. Coll. Emergency Physicians; mem.: AMA, World Med. Assn. Avocations: photography, travel, gourmet cooking. Personal E-mail: kwikci@yahoo.com.

KWIRAM, ALVIN L., retired chemistry professor, academic administrator; b. Riverhills, Man., Can., Apr. 28, 1937; came to U.S., 1954; s. Rudolf and Wilhelmina A. (Bilske) K.; m. Verla Rae Michel, Aug. 9, 1964; children: Andrew Brandt, Sidney Marguerite. BS in Chemistry, Walla Walla Coll., Wash., 1958, BA in Physics, 1958; PhD in Chemistry, Calif. Inst. Tech., 1963; DS (hon.), Andrews U., 1995. Alfred A. Noyes instr. Calif. Inst. Tech., Pasadena, 1962-63; research asso. physics dept. Stanford (Calif.) U., 1963-64; instr. chemistry Harvard U., Cambridge, Mass., 1964-67, lectr., 1967-70; assoc. prof. chemistry U. Wash., Seattle, 1970-75, prof., 1975—2007, chmn. dept. chemistry, 1977-87, vice provost, 1987-88, sr. vice provost, 1988-90, vice provost for rsch., 1990—2002; ret., 2007. Bd. dirs. Seattle Biomed. Rsch. Inst.; environ. and health scis. divsn. rev. com. Pacific N.W. Nat. Lab., 1998—2001, adv. com., 2000—06; exec. dir. NSF Ctr. Materials and Devices Info. Tech. Rsch., 2002—07; vis. prof. dept. chemistry U. Berkeley, Calif., 1976—77; vis. prof. dept. physics U. Stuttgart, Germany, 1985—86; vis. scholar Wolfson Coll. Oxford U., England, 2006. Contbr. numerous articles to sci. jours. Bd. dirs. Seattle Econ. Devel. Commn., 1988-92, Wash. Rsch. Found., 1989-94, Seattle-King County Econ. Devel. Coun., 1989-98, Helen R. Whiteley Found., 1997-, Lumera Corp., 2001-03; mem. vis. com. divsn. chemistry and chem. engring. Calif. Inst. Tech., 1991-96; chmn. adv. bd. Sch. Engring., Walla Walla Coll., 1992-2005. Recipient Eastman-Kodak Sci. award, 1962, Univ.-Industry Rels/ award Coun. for Chem. Rsch., 1986; Woodrow Wilson fellow, 1958; Alfred P. Sloan fellow, 1968-70; Guggenheim Meml. Found. fellow, 1977-78. Fellow: AAAS (chmn.-elect, chmn., past chmn. sect. on chemistry 1991—94, program com. 1994—98), Am. Phys. Soc.; mem.: Nat. Acad. Sci. (com. on advanced rsch. instrumentation, com. sci. and pub. policy), Worldwide Univ. Network (acad. adv. bd. 2002—05, U.S. liaison 2003—, chmn. global acad. devel. adv. bd. 2007—), Coun. Chem. Rsch. (bd. dirs. 1980—84, chmn. 1982—83), Am. Chem. Soc. (sec.-treas. divsn. phys. chemistry 1976—86, divsn. councilor 1986—2005, com. on sci., chmn. subcom. on fed. funding for rsch. 1990—94, adv. bd. for grad. edn. 2000—, chair 2005—), Nat. Assn. State Univs. and Land Grant Colls. (chmn.-elect, chmn., past chmn. 2000—03, exec. com., coun. rsch. policy and grad. edn.), Sigma Xi. Office: Univ Wash Dept Chem Seattle WA 98195-1700 Office Phone: 206-543-4020. Business E-Mail: kwiram@u.washington.edu.

KWOH, STEWART, lawyer, cultural organization administrator; BA, JD, UCLA; PhD (hon.), Williams Coll., 1996. Pres., exec. dir. Asian Pacific Am. Legal Ctr. Bd. dirs., vice chair Nat. Asian Pacific Am. Legal Consortium; adjunct instructor UCLA. Mem. steering comm. Coalition for Humane Immigration Rights of Los Angeles; bd. mem. Los Angeles Charter Reform Commn., El Pueblo Historical Monument Authority Commn.; chair, bd. dirs. Calif. Endowment, 2000—02; trustee Methodist Urban Found., Calif. Consumer Protection Found., Calif. Wellness Found., Tang Family Found., Fannie Mae Found. Named MacArthur Found. fellow, 1998, Lawyer of the Yr., California Lawyer mag., 1998; recipient Professional award, L.A. County Human Relations Commn., 1992, Faith and Freedom award, UCLA U. Religious Conf., 1993, CORO Public Affairs award, 1993, Asian Pacific Heritage Month award, 1993, ACLU award, 1993, President's award, So. Christian Leadership Conf. & Martin Luther King Legacy Assn., 1994, Mayor's award, L.A. City Human Relations Commn., 1996. Mem.: So. Calif. Chinese Lawyers Assn. (former pres.). Office: Asian Pacific Am Legal Ctr 1145 Wilshire Blvd Los Angeles CA 90017

KWOK, WINGCHI EDMUND, physicist; b. Hong Kong, Feb. 6, 1962; arrived in US, 1984; s. Alice Lee. BS in Physics, Hong Kong Baptist U., 1984; PhD, Rensselaer Poly. Inst., 1990. Cert. radiologic physics diagnostician Am. Bd. Radiology. Assoc. prof. dept. radiology U. Rochester, NY, 1990—. Presenter in field. Contbr. articles to profl. jours.; rev.: various profl. jours. Fellow, Intermagnetics Gen. Corp., 1986—89; grantee, NIH, 2003—; scholar, Hong Kong Bapt. Coll., 1985. Mem.: Am. Phys. Soc., Internat. Soc. Magnetic Resonance in Medicine, Radiol. Soc. N.Am. (assoc. grantee 1995). Achievements include patents for magnetic resonance imaging. Office: U Rochester Dept Radiology 601 Elmwood Ave Rochester NY 14642 Home Phone: 585-359-8192; Office Phone: 585-275-6506. Office Fax: 585-273-1033. E-mail: edmund_kwok@urmc.rochester.edu.

KWOLEK, STEPHANIE LOUISE, chemist, researcher; b. New Kensington, Pa., July 31, 1923; d. John and Nellie (Zajdel) Kwolek. BS, Carnegie-Mellon U., 1946; DSc (hon.), Worcester Poly. Inst., 1981, Clarkson U., 1997, Carnegie Mellon U., 2001. Chemist E.I. duPont de Nemours & Co., Inc., Wilmington, Del., 1946—59, rsch. chemist, 1959—67, sr. rsch. chemist, 1967—74, rsch. assoc., 1974—86, cons. in polymer chemistry, 1986—. Contbr. articles to profl. jours.; prodr.: Named a Women in Tech. Internat., 1996; named to U. Akron Polymer Processing Hall of Fame, 1985, Dayton, Ohio Engring. and Sci. Hall of Fame, 1992, Nat. Inventors Hall of Fame, 1995; recipient award for contbns. to Kevlar, Am. Soc. Metals, 1978, Engring./Tech. award, Soc. Plastics Engrs., 1985, Harold deWitt Smith award, ASTM, 1988, George Lubin Meml. award, SAMPE, 1991, Medal of Excellence in composite materials, U. Del., 1992, Jack Kilby award, Kilby Awards Found., 1994, Am. Innovation award, Patent and Trademark Office, 1995, Achievement award, Indsl. Rsch. Inst., Inc., 1996, Nat. Medal of Tech. award, U.S. Dept. of Commerce Tech. Adminstrn., 1996, Perkin medal, Soc. Chem. Industry, 1997, Commonwealth award, Commonwealth Trust and PNC Bank, 1998, Lemelson-MIT Lifetime Achievement award, 1999, Henry E. Millson award, AATCC, 2001. Mem.: Phi Kappa Phi, Franklin Inst. Phila. (Howard N. Potts medal 1976), Nat. Acad. Engring., Am. Inst. Chemists (Chem. Pioneer award 1980), Am. Chem. Soc. (award for creative invention 1980), Carnegie Mellon U. Alumni Assn. (Merit award 1983, Disting. Achievement award 1998), DuPont Country Club, Phi Beta Kappa, Sigma Xi. discovery of the technology that led the development of Kevlar fiber, a bulletproof material five times stronger than steel; patents in field. Home and Office: 312 Spalding Rd Wilmington DE 19803-2422 Office Phone: 302-571-9971.

KWON, CHUL SOO, psychiatrist; b. Seoul, Korea, Sept. 10, 1948; m. Sung Hee Chung, Apr. 6, 1974; 1 child, Soon Jeong (Susan). MD, Seoul Nat. U., 1974. Diplomate in psychiatry and in psychosomatic medicine Am. Bd. Psychiatry and Neurology and Psychosomatic Medicine. Intern Washington Hosp. Ctr., 1975—76, resident in gen. surgery, 1976—77; resident in psychiatry Johns Hopkins Hosp., Balt., 1977—80; fellow in behavioral sci. Johns Hopkins U., Balt., 1977—80, asst. in psychiatry, 1980—86; dir. partial hospitalization program North Charles Genl. Hosp., Balt., 1981—88; med. dir. partial hospitalization program Homewood Hosp. Ctr., Balt., 1988—91; med. dir. psychiat. partial hospitalization program Union Meml. Hosp., Balt., 1991—; physician St. Joseph Med. Ctr., Towson, Md., 1991—, Church Hosp., Balt., 1991—99, Md. Gen. Hosp. (U. Md. Med. System), Balt., 1991—98, 2000—. Taylor Manor, Ellicott City, Md., 1987—98; mgmt. mem. EHP Group Practice, 1993—; physician JL Kernan Hosp., Balt., 1995—2000, Sheppard-Enoch Pratt Hosp., 1998—2001. Instr. psychiatry Johns Hopkins U., 1986—96; physician, sub-investigator Ctr. Behavioral Health, 1999—2004; psychiat. cons. U. Splty. Hosp. (U. Md. Med. System), 2001—; psychiatrist-in-charge, cons. Harbor Hosp. (Medstar Health Sys.), Balt., 2001—07. Mem.: AMA, Internat. Neuropsychiat. Assn., Korean Am. Med. Assn., Internat. Psychogeriatric Assn., Am. Soc. Clin. Psychopharmacology (cert.), Am. Acad. Clin. Psychiatrists, Md. Psychiat. Soc., Johns Hopkins Med. and Surg. Assn., Am. Neuropsychiat. Assn. Home: 2908 Chainita Ct Ellicott City MD 21042-7625 Office: Union Meml Hosp Dept Psychiat 201 E University Pkwy Baltimore MD 21218-2829 Business E-Mail: cskwon@jhu.edu.

KWON, IK HYUN, internist; b. Korea, Aug. 22, 1937; S. Soo Myong and Jin Joo (Rhim) K.; m. Sook Ja Kwon, 1986; children: Esther, James. MD, Seoul Nat. U., 1962; PhD, Rutgers U., 1974. Intern Martland Med. Ctr., Newark, 1966-67; resident in internal medicine Bklyn.-Cumberland Med. Ctr., 1967; pvt. practice specializing in internal medicine South Plainfield, N.J., 1976—. Mem. staff John F. Kennedy Med. Ctr., Edison, N.J., Muhlenberg Regional Med. Ctr., Plainfield, N.J. Served with Korean Army, 1963-66. Fellow: ACP. Home and Office: 1526 New Durham Rd South Plainfield NJ 07080-2317 Office Phone: 732-287-2273. E-mail: lhkwon@pol.net.

KWON, O-MUN, electrical engineer, researcher; b. Sept. 25, 1968; m. Euna Cho; children: Hannah, David Hyukju. BSEE, MSEE, Hanyang U., 1992; PhD, Rensselaer Poly. Inst., 2003. Rsch. engr. Hyosung Corp., Seoul, 1992—99; post doctoral fellow Rensselaer Poly. Inst., Troy, NY, 2003—06; sr. engr. Raser Tech., Orem, Utah, 2006—. Decan Shalom Korean Ch., Albany, 2002—04. Personal E-mail: omkwon@hotmail.com.

KWON, TAEK, Internet company executive; V.p., engring. & ops. Hotwire, San Francisco; exec. v.p. product & tech. Citysearch.com, LA, 2003—05; CEO Friendstar, Inc., Mountain View, Calif., 2005—. Office Phone: 650-618-2527.

KWON, YANG, neurosurgeon, medical educator; b. Seoul, Republic of Korea, Sept. 24, 1954; s. Seil Kwon and Suk Hee Kim; m. Seung Hee Suh, Oct. 1, 1983; 1 child, Jae Young. MD, Seoul Nat. U., 1980, MS, 1987, PhD, 1992. Resident Seoul Nat. U. Hosp., 1984—88; rsch. fellow U. Hsop. Zurich, Switzerland, 1988—89; fellow Asan Med. Ctr., Seoul, 1989—90, instr., 1990—92, asst. prof., 1992—96, assoc. prof., 1996—2001, prof., 2001—. With Korean Army, 1981—87. Avocations: reading, bicycling. Office: Asan Med Ctr Dept Neurol Surgery 388-1 Poongnap-dong Songpa-an Seoul 138-736 Republic of Korea Office Fax: 82-2-476-6778. Business E-Mail: ykwan@amc.seoul.kr.

KWON, YOUNG-NAM, environmental engineer; b. Busan, Republic of Korea, Dec. 16, 1972; s. Tae-Hwang Kwon and Han-Soo Choi. PhD, Stanford U., Calif., 2005. Rsch. asst. Stanford U., Calif., 1999—2005, postdoctoral scholar, 2006—. Contbr. articles to profl. jours. Office: Stanford U Terman B13 Civil and Environ Engring Stanford CA 94305-4020 Office Phone: 650-723-0315. E-mail: kwonyn@stanford.edu.

KWONG, EVA, artist, educator; b. Hong Kong, 1954; came to the U.S., 1967; d. Tony and Ivory Kwong; m. Kirk Mangus, 1976; children: Una, Jasper. BFA, RISD, 1975; MFA, Tyler Sch. Art/Temple U., Phila., 1977. Vis. artist, 1977—; vis. faculty Cleve. Inst. Art, 1982-83; part-time faculty U. Akron, Ohio, 1987, 89, 95, Kent (Ohio) State U., 1990—. Lectr. in field. Works in over 300 exhbns. Visual Arts Regional fellow Arts Midwest, Mpls., 1987, Visual Arts fellow Nat. Endowment for the Arts, Washington, 1988, Ohio Arts Coun., Columbus, 1988, 94, 99, 2004, Ohio Arts Coun. fellow in visual arts, 2004; recipient Internat. award China NCECA, 2003. Mem. Nat. Coun. on Edn. for the Ceramic Arts (dir.-at-large 1995-97).

KY, ALEX JENNY, surgeon, educator; b. Saigon, Vietnam, Jan. 22, 1968; BA, Brown U.; MD, SUNY, Stony Brook, 1994. Lic. NY, 1996, diplomate Am. Bd. Surgery, 2001. Intern Lenox Hill Hosp., NYC, 1994—95, resident dept. surgery, 1995—98, chief resident dept. surgery, 1998—99; resident colon and rectal surgery Mt. Sinai Hosp., NYC, 1999—2000; asst. prof. dept. surgery Mt. Sinai Sch. Medicine, NYC, 2000—. Presenter in field. Contbr. chapters to books, articles to profl. jours. Mem.: ACS, Japanese Med. Soc. Am., NY Soc. Colon and Rectal Surgeons, Chinese Am. Med. Soc., Am. Soc. Colon and Rectal Surgeons. Home: 124 East 79th St Apt 4B New York NY 10021 Office: Mt Sinai Sch Medicine 5 East 98th St 15th Fl New York NY 10029 Office Phone: 212-241-3547.

KYA-HILL, ROBERT, actor, educator; b. Whitaker, NC, Dec. 4, 1930; s. Herman and Fannie Hill; m. Sally V. Sherwin, Dec. 31, 1966; 1 child, Bouqui Ann Stautmeister. Student, CCNY, 1950—51, NY Coll. Music, 1953—57, Jarahal Sch. Music, NYC, 1953—57; MA, Goddard Coll., Plainfield, Vt., 1991. Cert. tchr. NY, 86. Pvt. tchr. guitar, vocal, 1956—57; tchr. Hunter Coll., NYC, 1973—74, Western Australian Inst. Tech., Perth, 1975—76, NYC Bd. Edn., 1983—97, YWCA, NYC, 1984—86; founder, pres. World's Winter Publ. Co., Inc., NYC, 1997—. Blue ribbon panelist Emmy awards NATAS, NYC, 1974; cons., lectr. in field. Actor: (plays) Porgy and Bess, 1959, Nat Turner, 1960, Abe Lincoln in Illinois, 1963, J.B., 1964, Othello, 1964, 1969, 1970, 1975, The One-Way Pendulum, 1964, Winterset, 1965—66, Lost in the Stars, 1966—67, Noah, 1966—67, King Lear, 1966—67, Purlie Victorious, 1967 (Obie nomination for best actor, 1967), The Merchant of Venice, 1967, Julius Caesar, 1967, The Trial, 1968, Young Martin Luther King, 1968—69, Irma La Douce, 1969, The Trial of A. Lincoln, 1970, Between Two Worlds, 1973, The Legacy, 1974, The Tempest, 1976, Of Mice and Men, 1981, The New Mount Olive Motel, 1981, F. Jasmine Addams, 1984, Boesman and Lena, 1985, Take Me Along, 1997, Standard of the Breed, 2002, Birdland, 2003, Sin Paradise, 2004, The Phoenician Women, 2004, Einstein's Secret Letters, 2005, The Medead, 2005, Medea in Aia, 2006, The Prostitute of Reverie Valley, 2006, Driving Miss Daisy, 2007; (TV series) Eight is Enough, 1977, Lou Grant, 1978, Good Times, 1979, Roots: The Next Generation, 1981; (films) Dark Valley, 1960—61 (Best Actor in a religious film, Nat. Evang. Film Found., 1962), Slaves, 1969, Shaft's Big Score, 1972, Death Wish, 1974, The Critical List, 1977, The Perfect Gentleman, 1979, Sue, 1997, The Shade, 1999, Beirut, 2000; musician (guitar): Carnegie Recital Hall, Town Hall, Judson Hall, Carl Fischer Hall, Hallmark Hall of Fame; dir., artistic dir. (plays) Guilt, the Touch of Death, Afro-Arts Permanent Summer Theatre, NYC, 1958, Nat Turner: Slave, Playwright's Creative Theatre, NYC, 1959, Ballad of Joe Smith, Theatre for Peace, NYC, 1968, Blackman vs. Blackman, Hunter Coll. Playhouse, NYC, 1974, Dream on Monkey Mountain, 1974—75, Revelation, for the Time is at Hand, 1975, J.B., 1975, A Streetcar Named Desire, 1976, The Trials of Brother Jero, 1976, Song of Esther, 1976, An Abortion Play, 1976, Gingerbread Lady, Ebony Theatre, LA, 1979, Finian's Rainbow, 1983, Riders to the Sea, 1983, Phoebe Fraunces, 1983; dir.: (plays) others; artistic dir.: Theatre-Go-Round, 1975—76; author: (plays) Guilt, the Touch of Death, 1958, Nat Turner: Slave, 1959, On the Turn of a Climax, 1962, The Trial of Secundus Generation Blackman vs. Hannah and William Blackman, 1973, The Legacy, 1974; composer: Nat Turner, 1960, Dark Valley, 1961, Moon on a Rainbow Shawl, 1962, Yerma, 1963, The Gospel According to John and., 1968, Purlie Victorious, 1969, Revelation, for the Time is at Hand, 1974, An Abortion Play, 1976. Judge Act-So Coalition NYC NAACP, 1992—97; mem. West Village Com. Bank/Bethune St. Block Assn., 1970—73; chmn. Westbeth Artists Meeting, 1970—72; choir Rutgers Presbyterian Ch., NYC, 1957—63, elder, 1957—63, Bible tchr., 1957—63, concert organizer, 1957—63. With US Army, 1951—53, Germany. Decorated medal US Army, Nat. Def. Svc. medal. Mem.: NATAS, AFTRA, SAG, NY State United Tchrs., United Fedn. Tchrs., Actors Equity Assn., Am. Music Ctr. Presbyterian. Avocations: chess, guitar. Office: Personal and World's Winter Publishing Co PO Box 747 New York NY 10014

KYDLAND, FINN E., economics professor; b. Norway, 1943; BS, Norwegian School of Economics and Business Admin., 1968; PhD, Carnegie Mellon U., 1973. Prof. econ. Carnegie Mellon, Tepper Sch. of Bus., U. Calif., Santa Barbara, 2006—. Lectr. in field. Contbr. articles to numerous profl. jours. Recipient Alexander Henderson award, Carnegie Mellon, 1973, John Stauffer National Fellowship Award, Hoover Institution, 1982—83, Nobel Prize in Econ., 2004. Fellow: Hoover Inst., Econometric Society. Office: Carnegie Mellon Unversity 5000 Forbes Avenue Pittsburgh PA 15213 E-mail: kydland@andrew.cmu.edu.*

KYESMU, PIUS MICHAEL, biology professor, researcher; b. Panyam, Plateau State, Nigeria, Sept. 4, 1960; arrived in US, 2004, permanent resident, 2004; s. Swapshak Michael and Chedugur Rahila Kyesmu; m. Paula Dooshima Semban, Sept. 27, 1992; children: Panquat, Peter, Poret. BS, U. Jos, Nigeria, 1984, MS, 1987; PhD, U. London, 1996. Lectr. U. Jos, 1986—2000; sr. rsch. fellow Sheda Sci. and Tech. Complex, Garki, Abuja, Nigeria, 2000—02; dep. dir. Nat. Biotech. Devel. Agy., Abuja, Nigeria, 2002—05. Adj. prof. biology and microbiology Fla. CC, Jacksonville, 2005—. Achievements include development of cryopreservation protocols and in vitro propagation techniques. Personal E-mail: pkyesmu@fccj.edu.

KYFF, KIMBERLY, elementary school educator; BA in Edn., Univ. Mich., Dearborn, 1979; M in Art of Tchg., Marygrove Coll., 1999. Cert. middle childhood generalist Nat. Bd. Tchg. Standards, 2003. Tchr., 1987—, Jamieson Elem. Sch., Detroit, 1996—. Facilitator, master's edn. program Univ. Phoenix, Southfield, Mich. Named Mich. Tchr. of Yr., 2007. Office: Jamieson Elem Sch 2900 W Philadelphia Detroit MI 48206 Personal E-mail: kimberyff@aol.com.*

KYHOS, THOMAS FLYNN, lawyer; b. Cheverly, Md., May 13, 1947. BA in Econs., DePauw U., 1969; JD, Cath. U., 1973. Bar: Md. 1974, DC 1974, US Tax Ct. 1974, US Supreme Ct. 1978. sole practice, Washington, 1974—; pres. First Oxford Corp., Washington, 1976—. Mem. ABA, Md. Bar Assn., DC Bar Assn. Home: 5714 Massachusetts Ave Bethesda MD 20816-1929 Office: 3528 K St NW Washington DC 20007-3503 Business E-Mail: tom.kyhos@firstoxford.com.

KYL, JON LLEWELLYN, senator; b. Oakland, Nebr., Apr. 25, 1942; s. John H. and Arlene (Griffith) K.; m. Caryll Louise Collins, June 5, 1964; children: Kristine Kyl Gavin, John Jeffry. BA in Polit. Sci., with honors, U. Ariz., 1964, LLB, 1966. Bar: Ariz. 1966, US Supreme Ct. 1971. Assoc. Jennings, Strouss & Salmon, Phoenix, 1966—70, ptnr., 1971—86; mem. US Ho. Reps. 100th-103rd Congresses from 4th Ariz. dist., 1987—95; US Senator from Ariz., 1995—. Chmn. Ariz. Young Rep., 1970; legal counsel Rep. Party, 1970—75; mem. com. fin. US Senate, com. judiciary, chmn. Rep. policy com. Founding dir. Ariz. Crime Victim Found, 1983; mem. Phoenix C. of C. Recipient Keeper of the Flame award, Ctr. Security Policy, 1994, Champion Small Bus. Cmty. award, Small Bus. Survival Com., 2000, Legis. of Yr. award, Am. Internat. Automobile Dealers, 2005, Medal of Honor award, US Oncology and Ariz Oncology Associates, 2005. Mem.: Ariz. State Bar Assn. Republican. Presbyn. Office: District Office Ste 120 2200 E Camelback Rd Phoenix AZ 85016-3455 also: US Senate 730 Hart Senate Bldg Washington DC 20510-0001 Office Phone: 602-840-1891, 202-224-4521. Office Fax: 202-224-2207, 602-957-6838.*

KYLE, CORINNE SILVERMAN, management consultant; b. NYC, Jan. 4, 1930; d. Nathan and Janno (Harra) Silverman; m. Alec Kyle, Aug. 29, 1959 (div. Feb. 1969); children: Joshua, Perry (dec.), Julia. BA, Bennington Coll., 1950; MA, Harvard U., 1953. Assoc. editor Inter-Univ. Case Program, NYC, 1956-60; co-founder, chief editor Financial Index, NYC, 1960-63; rsch. analyst McKinsey & Co., NYC, 1963-64; sr. rsch. assoc. Mktg. Sci. Inst., Phila., 1964-67; founding ptnr. Phila. Group, 1967-70; sr. assoc. Govt. Studies and Systems, Phila., 1970-72, cons. program planning and control, 1972-78; sr. assoc. Periodical Studies Svc., 1978-81; v.p., dir. rsch. Total Rsch. Corp., Princeton, NJ, 1981-82; mgr. social rsch. The Gallup Orgn., Princeton, 1982-86; v.p. Response Analysis Corp., 1986-91; dir. rsch. Gallup Internat. Inst., 1991-97; assoc. Krog & Ptnrs., Inc., 1997-99; survey rsch. cons., 1999—. Lectr. rsch. methods Temple U., 1981-82; vis. prof. Fairleigh Dickinson U., 1990-91, 93; dir. Verbena Corp., N.Y.C. Contbr. numerous articles to profl. publs. Mem. adv. coun. to 8th Dist. city councilman, Phila., 1971-79; mem. 22nd Ward Dem. Exec. Com., 1971-78, State Dem. Com., 1974-76; mem. Pa. Gov.'s Council on Nutrition, 1974-76; v.p. Miquon Upper Sch. Bd., Phila., 1977-78; trustee Princeton Regional Scholarship Found., 1982-85, pres., 1984-85; mem. bd. edn. Princeton Regional Sch. Dist., 1984-93, pres. 1987, 89; mem. exec. bd. Mercer County (N.J.) Sch. Bds. Assn., 1987-92, v.p., 1991-92; mem. exec. com. Princeton Community Dem. Orgn., 1992-97; mem. Princeton Regional Planning Bd., 1994-99, chair, 1997-99, Princeton Environ. Commn., 1994-97; chair Princeton Borough task force on consolidation, 1995; chair One Princeton, 1996-97; mem. West Orange Bd. Edn., 2002-, pres., 2004-05, v.p., 2007-08. Mem.: West Orange Advocates. Home: 32 Randolph Pl West Orange NJ 07052-4808 Personal E-mail: cskyle@earthlink.net.

KYLE, DAVID L., gas industry executive; b. Wichita, Kans. BS in Indsl. Engring. and Mgmt., Okla. State U., 1974; MBA, U. Tulsa, 1987; grad. advanced mgmt. program, Harvard U., 1992. Joined ONEOK, Inc., Tulsa, 1974, pres. ONG, 1995, pres., COO, 1997, chmn., CEO, 2000—06, chmn., 2007—. Office: ONEOK Inc 100 W Fifth St Tulsa OK 74103*

KYLE, GENE MAGERL, merchandise presentation artist; b. Phila., Oct. 11, 1919; d. Elmer Langham and Muriel Helen (Magerl) Kyle. Student, Ctr. for Creative Studies, Detroit, 1938—45. Mdse. presentation artist D.J. Healy Shops, Detroit, 1946—50, Saks Fifth Ave., Detroit, 1950—58, J.L. Hudson Co., Detroit, 1958—84, Grosse Pointe, Mich., 1989—95; freeland mdse. presentations for windows Grosse Point, 1989—. Papercraft Detroit Artists Mkt. Holiday Shows, 1997—2003; tchr. workshop classes. Exhibited in group shows at Mich. Watercolor Soc., 1944, 1953, 1974, Mich. Artists Exhbn., 1962, 1964, Scarab Club, 1948—49, 1952, Detroit Artist Mkt., 1946—97, Mich. Gallery, 1989—92, Coach House Gallery, 1980, 1990, Cmty. House, Birmingham, Mich., 1993—94, First Fed. Mich. Bank, 1994, 1995, Swann Gallery, 1996—97, Detroit Artists Mkt., 1997—2000. Vol. presentation work. Recipient various art awards. Mem.: Detroit Artists Market, Grosse Pointe Artists Assn., Windsor Art Gallery, Mich. Watercolor Soc., Detroit Inst. Arts Founders Soc.

KYLE, JAMES LEWIS, dean, physician; b. LA; BA in Religion, Loma Linda U., 1973; MDiv, Andrews Theological Seminary, Berrien Springs, Mich., 1977; MD, UCLA Sch. of Medicine, 1987. Internal medicine physician private practice, San Diego; pres., CEO Sharp Health Plan; chief med. officer, dir. clinical bus. develop., compliance officer and admin. dean coll. of medicine Charles R. Drew U. of Medicine and Sci., 1996—99; former v.p. Sharp Healthcare Community Care; former pres., CEO Genesis Healthcare Strategies; former v.p., Calif. market Schaller Anderson; chair, dept. of health admin. & dean, sch. of public health Loma Linda U., 2006—. Health presentations KUSI Television in San Diego, San Diego, 1992—96. Trustee Catholic Healthcare W., Shields for Families; bd. dirs. Calif. Endowment, 2004—. Captain, primary care physician USAR, 1995—2000. Decorated Army Commendation Medal. Office: Loma Linda U Dept of Health Administration Nichol Hall Rm 1321 Loma Linda CA 92350

KYLE, JOHN EMERY, retired religious organization administrator; b. San Diego, July 7, 1926; s. John E. and Agnes (McDaniel) Kyle; m. Lois Ellen Rowland, June 8, 1947; children: Arlette Marie, Jayson Duane, Marucs Justin, Darlene Patricia. BS in Agr., Oreg. State U., 1950; BDiv, Columbia Theol. Sem., 1961, MDiv, 1971; D in Ministry (hon.), Belhaven Coll., 1999. Ordained to ministry Presbyn Ch. U.S., 1961. Sr. buyer Eastwest Produce Co.-Safeway Stores Inc., San Francisco, 1951-57; pastor Presbyn. Ch. in U.S., Hazard, Ky., 1961-63; adminstr. Wycliffe Bible Translators, Manila, 1964-73, coord. internat. rels., 1976—77, exec. dir. Washington, 1977-79, Mission to the World, Presbyn. Ch. in Am., Decatur, Ga., 1974-77; missions dir., v.p. Intervarsity Christian Fellowship, Madison, Wis., 1979-88; exec. dir. mission to world Presbyn. Ch. Am., Atlanta, 1988-94; sr. v.p. Evang. Fellowship Mission Agencies., Norcross, Ga., 1994—2005; ret., 2005. Co-founder Townsend Inst. Internat. Rels., 1978; dir. Student Fgn. Missions Fellow, 1978—87, World Student Mission Conv., Urbana, Ill., 1979, Urbana, 81, Urbana, 84, Urbana, 87; trustee Columbia Bible Coll. and Sem., 1982—86, Overseas Missionary Fellowship, Robesonia, Pa., 1982—86, Crista Ministries Bd., 1984—88, Concerts Prayer Internat., 1988—99, Berkeley Heights, NJ, A.D. 2000 Movement, Colorado Springs, Colo., 1989—2000, Co mission, 1992—98, Christ's Coll., Taipei, Taiwan, 1992—98, World Relief Bd., 1997—2006, Culture Insights Bd., 1998—2001, Mid. East Media Bd., 1998—99; chmn. O.M. Logos Ship, 1988—91; pres. Sr. Leadership Xchange, 2006—. Editor: The Unfinished Task, 1982, Finishing the Task, 1987, Urban Missions, 1988; author: Now This Generation, 1990; co-author: Looking Forward - Voices from Church Leaders on Our Global Mission, 2002; contbr. chapters to books. With USNR, 1945—47, WWII, Iwo Jima. Recipient Presdl. Merit medal, Pres. of The Philiippines. Mem.: World Evang. Felloship, Assn. Ch. Missions Com., Nat. Assn. Evang., Evang. Fgn. Missions Assn. (trustee 1989—94), Concerts Prayer Internat. Presbyterian. Office: 2343A Granville Pl Monroe NC 28110 Office Phone: 704-291-7157. Business E-Mail: john-lois_kyle@wbt.org.

KYLE, RICHARD HOUSE, federal judge; b. St. Paul, Apr. 30, 1937; s. Richard E. and Geraldine (House) K.; m. Jane Foley, Dec. 22, 1959; children: Richard H. Jr., Michael F., D'Arcy, Patrick G., Kathleen. BA, U. Minn., 1959, LLB, 1962. Bar: Minn. 1962, U.S. Dist. Ct. Minn. 1992. Atty. Briggs and Morgan, St. Paul, 1963-68, 1970-92; solicitor gen. Minn. Atty. Gen. Office, St. Paul, 1968-70; judge U.S. Dist. Ct., St. Paul, 1992—. Pres. Minn. Law Rev., Mpls., 1962. Mem. Minn. State Bar Assn., Ramsey County Bar Assn. Office: Federal Courts Bldg 316 Robert St N Saint Paul MN 55101-1495

KYLE, ROBERT ARTHUR, medical educator, oncologist; b. Bottineau, ND, Mar. 17, 1928; s. Arthur Nichol and Mabel Caroline (Crandall) K.; m. Charlene Mae Showalter, Sept. 11, 1954; children: John, Mary, Barbara, Jean. AA, N.D Sch. Forestry, 1946; BS, U. N.D., 1948; MD, Northwestern U., 1952; MS, U. Minn., 1958. Diplomate Am. Bd. Internal Medicine; subsplty. Hematology. Fellow Mayo Grad. Sch., Rochester, Minn., 1953-59; clin. asst. Tufts U. Sch. Medicine, Boston, 1960-61; cons. internal medicine Mayo Clinic, Rochester, 1961—; prof. medicine and lab. medicine Mayo Med. Sch., Rochester, 1975—. Pres. med. subjects unit Am. Topical Assn., Johnstown, Pa., 1976-81; chmn. standards, ethics and peer rev. orgn. Cancer & Acute Leukemia Group B, Scarsdale, NY, 1978-82; Robert A. Hettig lectr. in hematology Baylor U. Coll. Medicine, Houston, 1984; Waldenström lectr., Stockholm, 1988; Redlich Meml. lectr Cedars-Sinai Med. Ctr., U. Calif., LA; vis. prof. St. Elizabeth's Med. Ctr., Tufts U. Sch. Medicine, Boston, 1998 Author: The Monoclonal Gammopathies, 1976, Medicine and Stamps, vols. 1 and 2, 1980, vol. 3, 2004; author, editor: Neoplastic Disease of the Blood, 4th edit., 2003, Myeloma: Biology and Management, 1995, 3rd edit. 2004 Chmn. bd. trustees First Presbyn. Ch., Rochester, Minn., 1967; chmn. Rochester Med. Ctr. Ministry, 1979-86; chmn. adv. bd. Internat. Waldenstrom's Macroglobulinemia Found. Capt. USAF, 1955-57. Named Disting. Topicl Philatelest, Am. Topical Soc., 1982; Recipient Waldenström award Internat. Workshop for Myeloma, Italy, 1991, Henry S. Plummer Distinguished Internist award Mayo Clin., 1995, Mayo Distinguished Clinician award 1996, Sioux award U. N.D., 1998, Robert A. Kyle Lifetime Achievement award IMF, 2003, Mayo Clinic Disting. Alumni award, 2005; Bruce Wiseman lectr. Ohio State U., 1991, Kauffman Meml. lectr. Meml. Sloan Kettering Med. Ctr., N.Y.C., 1997; Clement Finch prof. U. Wash., 1993. Master ACP; mem. Royal Coll. Pathologists (hon.), N.Y. Acad. Scis., Am. Soc. Hematology, Internat. Soc. Hematology (sec.-gen. Inter-Am. divsn. 1990-96), Am. Assn. Cancer Rsch., Internat. Myeloma Found. (chmn. sci. adv. bd. 1995), Internat. Soc. Amyloidosis (pres. 2001-), Phi Beta Kappa. Republican. Avocation: stamp collecting/philately. Home: 1207 6th St SW Rochester MN 55902-1918 Office: Mayo Clinic 200 1st St SW Rochester MN 55905-0002 also: 6-26 Stabile Rochester MN 55905-0001 Home Phone: 507-285-9138; Office Phone: 507-284-3039. Business E-Mail: kyle.robert@mayo.edu.

KYLE, ROBERT CAMPBELL, II, publishing executive; b. Cleve., Jan. 6, 1935; s. Charles Donald and Mary Alice (King) K.; children: Peter F., Kit C., Scott G. BS, U. Colo., 1956; MA, Case Western Res. U., 1958; MBA, Harvard U., 1963, DBA, 1966. Ptnr. McLagan & Co., Chgo., 1966-67; founder, pres. Devel. Sys. Corp. (subs. Longman Group USA), Chgo., 1967-82; pres. Longman Group USA, Chgo., 1982-89; chmn., CEO Dearborn Pub. Group, Inc. (formerly Longman Group USA), 1989-98. Chmn. CTS Fin. Pub., 1997-2000. Author: Property Management, 1979; co-author: Modern Real Estate Practice, 1967, How to Profit From Real Estate, 1988 (Chgo. Book Clinic Lifetime Achievement award 1998). Mem. dean's adv. coun. Coll. Bus. U. Colo., 1992-98, Ctr. for Entrepreneurship Adv. Bd., U. Colo., 1996-2002; trustee Mystic Seaport Mus., 1989—, exec. com., 1999—2004, vice chair, 2001—2004; dir. Chgo. Maritime Soc., pres. 1999-2000; trustee The Burnham Inst., 2002—, San Diego Maritime Mus., 2002—, exec. com., 2003—, chair audit com., 2003—. Mem. Real Estate Educators Assn. (pres. 1981), Internat. Assn. Fin. Planning, Chgo. Book Clinic (bd. dirs.), Harvard Club NY, Chgo. Econs. Club, San Diego Yacht Club (chair history com. 2004—, bd. dirs. 2006—), NY Yacht Club, Explorers Club, Rotary. Avocations: yacht racing, skiing. Home: 2910 Owens St San Diego CA 92106 E-mail: rckyle@aol.com.

KYLER, ARLENE, advertising executive; b. NYC, Apr. 21, 1944; d. Abraham S. and Evelyn Estrin Hoberman; m. Jerry Kyler, June 20, 1964; children: Elizabeth Amy, Alison Eve. BA, Bklyn. Coll., 1964. Cert. tchr. common branches subjects SUNY-State Edn. Dept. Elem. sch. tchr. Pub. Sch. 216K, Bklyn., 1964—67; pres. Parties Unlimited Entertainment, Inc., East Rockaway, NY, 1974—86, Take My Card, Inc., East Rockaway, 1985—. Founder PTA's 1st Pub. Pre-Sch. Program, Oceanside, NY, 1973—79; pre-sch. chairperson Nassau Dist. PTA, LI, NY, 1976—79; initiator PTA's Pre-Sch. Hearing Screening, LI, NY, 1976; legis. co-chairperson PTA Coun., Oceanside, 1978—79; trustee Temple Avodah Sisterhood, Oceanside, NY, 1976—80; co-founder Free Sons and Daughters Investment Club, LI, NY, 2000. Recipient Free Sons of Israel award, United Jewish Appeal Chai Lodge L.I., N.Y., 1994, People Who Love People award, Plantation, Fla., 2007. Mem.: Workmen's Benefit Fund of the U.S.A. (charter sec.-treas. br. #849 2002), N.Y. Soc. for Profl. Inventors (trustee 1995—99), Free Sons of Israel Inc. (dist. dep. 1984, founder Chai Singles' Lodge #230 1992, 2nd dep. grand master 1993—96, 1st dep. grand master 1996—99, U.S. Grand Master 1999—2002). Achievements include patents for card display stands; card display apparatus; display and dispensing apparatus. Avocations: theater, travel, watersports, medical studies, line dancing. Office: Take My Card Inc 3445 Park Ave Oceanside NY 11572

KYLES, CEDRIC ANTONIO (CEDRIC THE ENTERTAINER), comedian, actor; b. Jefferson City, Mo., Apr. 24, 1964; s. Rosetta Kyles; m. Lorna Wells, Sept. 3, 1999; children: Croix, Lucky Rose; 1 child from previous marriage, Tiara. Bachelor's in Mass Comm., S.E. Mo. State U., 1991. Actor: (films) Ride, 1998, Big Momma's House, 2000, The Smoker, 2000, Kingdom Come, 2001, Barbershop, 2002, Serving Sara, 2002, Intolerable Cruelty, 2003, Barbershop 2: Back in Bus., 2004, Lemony Snicket's A Series of Unfortunate Events, 2004, Man of the House, 2005, Be Cool, 2005, The Honeymooners, 2005, Talk to Me, 2007; voice actor: Ice Age, 2002; Dr. Dolittle 2, 2001; Madagascar, 2005; Charlotte's Web, 2006; actor: (TV series) The Steve Harvey Show, 1996—2002 (Image award for outstanding supporting actor comedy series, 1999, 2000, 2001, 2002); voice actor: The Proud Family, 2001 (Image award for outstanding supporting actor comedy series, 2003); host Black Entertainment TV's Comicview, 1993—94; creator, writer, prodr., actor, host Cedric the Entertainer Presents, 2002—03; exec. prodr. and comedian: (TV spl.) Cedric the Entertainer: Starting Lineup, 2002; prodr. and actor: (films) Johnson Family Vacation, 2004; performer: Kings of Comedy tour, 1997—2000; actor, exec. prodr.: (films) Code Name: The Cleaner, 2007. Co-founder CTE Charitable Found. Inc., 1995—. Named Richard Pryor Comic of Yr., Black Entertainment TV. Office: care of Marla Winston Entertainment Enterprises 401 Le Doux Rd Ste 401 Los Angeles CA 90048*

KYLSTRA, JOHANNES ARNOLD, physician; b. Manado, Indonesia, Nov. 30, 1925; s. Jan Arnold and Johanna Leonore (Van Praag) K.; m. Carol S. Rous (dec.); children: Jan Andrew, Kimberly; m. Yvonne C. Alden. MD, U. Leiden, 1952, PhD, 1958. Asst. prof. physiology U. Leiden, 1961-63; vis. asst. prof. physiology SUNY, Buffalo, 1963-65; asst. prof. medicine and physiology Duke U., Durham, NC, 1965-66, assoc. prof. medicine, 1966-72, prof. medicine, 1972-89, prof. emeritus medicine, 1989—, assoc. prof. physiology, 1972-89; TB control physician NC Dept. Environ., Health & Natural Resources, 1989-98. Contbr. numerous articles on respiratory physiology, liquid breathing and lung lavage to profl. jours. Served with Royal Netherlands Navy, 1955-58. Recipient Lockheed award Marine Technology Soc., 1970, Disting. Research award Sigma Xi, 1974, Stover-Link award Undersea Med. Soc., 1979

KYNCL, JOHN JAROSLAV, pharmacologist; b. Prague, Czechoslovakia, Aug. 16, 1936; arrived in US, 1971; s. Jan Petr and Marie (Mikesova) K.; m. Mila Marie Tomaides, Mar. 4, 1961; children: Marketa Kyncl Leisure, John Anthony. PhD, Komensky U., Bratislava, 1963; ScC, Czech. Acad. Sci., 1967. Pharmacologist Rsch. Inst. for Biochemistry & Pharmacy, Prague, 1963—68; A. von. Humboldt fellow U. Heidelberg, Germany, 1968—71; rsch. fellow Cleveland Clinic Found., 1971—72; E. Volwiler rsch. fellow Abbott Labs., North Chicago, Ill., 1972—. Contbr. over 100 articles to profl. jours. Fellow Coun. for High Blood Pressure Rsch. Am. Heart Assn., Am. Soc. Exptl. Biology; mem. Am. Hypertension Soc., Am. Endocrine Soc., Internat. Hypertension Soc. (Paris). Achievements include invention of terazosin (Hytrin) and terlipressin (Glypressin); patents in field. Home: 800 Green Bay Rd Lake Bluff IL 60044-1829 Personal E-mail: kynclj@comcast.net.

KYOFSKI, BONELYN LUGG, retired education educator; b. Nelson, Pa., Mar. 16, 1941; d. Robert Preston Lugg and Ila Hess Lugg Wiley; m. Joseph Theodore Kyofski, Nov. 22, 1979. BS, Mansfield U., 1962; MA in English, Pa. State U., 1966, PhD in English, 1976. Cert. secondary tchg. Pa. Dept. Edn. H.s. tchr. Otto Eldred Sch. Dist., Duke Center, Pa., 1962—63; tchg. asst. Pa. State U., University Park, 1963—64; asst. prof. English Harrisburg (Pa.) Area C.C., 1964—66; assoc. prof. English Lehigh County C.C., Allentown, Pa., 1967—73; dir. pub. rels. and alumni affairs Mansfield U., 1973—75; instr. English Pa. State U., University Park, 1976; coord. pub. rels., assoc. prof. Jefferson C.C., Louisville, 1977—80; h.s. tchr. No. Tioga Sch. Dist., Elkland, Pa., 1980—81, dir. fed. programs and curriculum svcs., 1981—84; prof. edn. Mansfield (Pa.) U., 1984—2003; ret.; assoc. Travel Places, Inc. Pres. Mansfield U. Senate, 1992—94; co-founder, bd. pres. No. Tier Cultural Alliance, Mansfield, 1995—; commonwealth spkr. Pa. Humanities Coun., Phila., 1999—; storyteller schs. in No. Pa., 1980—. Co-author, co-editor: cultural history Headwaters and Hardwoods: the folklore, cultural history and traditional arts of the Pennsylvania Northern Tier, editor, co-author: teachers' resource collection Northern Pennsylvania Freedom Trails: a k-12 guide to the Underground Railroad in the region. Pres. Domestic Violence Resource Ctr. Tioga County Women's Coalition, Wellsboro, Pa., 1990—92; bd. Pa. Humanities Council, 2006—; mem. Mansfield Univ. Alumni Bd., 2006—; candidate Pa. Gen. Assembly Dem. Party, 68th Assembly Dist., 1974; county committeewoman Dem. Party, Tioga County, 1980—; vice chair Tioga County Dem. Com., 2006—; elder, lay spkr. Beechers' Island Presbyn. Ch., Nelson, Pa., 1980—2005. Named Outstanding Vol. in Ky. for coll. program in women's prison, Gov. Julian Carroll, 1979; recipient founding and support grants for No. Tier Cultural Alliance, Pa. Coun. on Arts, 1995—2005, program grants for No. Tier Cultural Alliance, Dept. of Conservation and Natural Resources, 1999—2005, Pa. Gov.'s Office internship, Falk Found., 1960, grant for proposal of establishment of Displaced Homemaker Ctrs. in Ky. cmty. colls., Ky. Senate, 1980, founding and support grants for No. Tier Cultural Alliance, Ctr. for Rural Pa., 1996, 1997. Mem.: Friends of Laurel Health Sys. (hon. chair 2005), Mansfield U. Ret. Faculty (pres. 2005—), River City Bus. and Profl. Women (pres., bd. dirs. 1977—79), Hamilton Gibson Prodns. (endowment bd. trustees 2005), Coates Heritage Ho. (bd. trustees 1998—), Tioga County Hist. Soc. (publs. com. 2003—05), Lumber Heritage Region (adv. bd. 2005—), Endless Mountains Heritage Region (adv. bd. 1996—). Democrat. Presbyterian. Avocations: reading, travel, historical preservation, theater and the arts. Home: 1 Thornbottom Road Nelson PA 16940 Home Phone: 570-827-3231.

KYRIAKIDES, ELIAS, electrical engineer, educator; b. Nicosia, Cyprus, Aug. 20, 1975; s. Kyriacos and Chrysavgi Elia. BSc, Ill. Inst. Tech., Chgo., 2000; MS, Ariz. State U., Tempe, 2001, PhD, 2003. Rsch. assoc. Ariz. State U., 2000—03, faculty rsch. assoc., 2003—04; lectr. U. Cyprus, Nicosia, Cyprus, 2004—. Contbr. articles to profl. jours. Recipient Presdl. award, Higher Tech. Inst., 1996, Alumni Assn. award, Ill. Inst. Tech., 2000, Palais Outstanding Doctoral Student award, Elec. Engring. Dept., Ariz. State U., 2004, Appreciation cert., Grad. Coll., Ariz. State U., 2004. Mem.: IEEE (3d Pl. Poster award 2002), Internat. Network Engring. Edn. and Rsch., Tech. Chamber Cyprus (vice chmn. rsch. com. 2006), Internat. Coun. Large Electric Sys., Instn. Engring. and Tech., Tau Beta Pi. Achievements include patents pending for system and method of estimating synchronous generator parameters. Office Phone: +357-22892291.

KYRIAKIDES, STELIOS K., aerospace engineer, educator; b. Pentayia, Greece; m. Rebecca Kyriakides; 2 children. BSc with 1st class honors in Aero. Engring., U. Bristol, UK, 1975; MS in Aeronautics, Calif. Inst. Tech., 1976, PhD in Aeronautics, 1980. Registered profl. engr., Tex. Asst. prof. aerospace engring. & engring. mechanics U. Tex., Austin, 1980—85, assoc. prof., 1985—89, prof., 1989—, dir. Ctr. Rsch. in Mechanics of Solids, Structures and Materials, 1996—, Temple Found. Endowed prof. dept. aerospace engring. and engring. mechanics, 1999—. Vis. scholar aeronautics Calif. Inst. Tech., 1990; vis. scholar divsn. applied scis. Harvard U., 1996; mem. US Nat. Com. Theoretical and Applied Mechanics, 1998—. Contbr. articles to sci. jours., chapters to books; mem. editl. bd.: Internat. Jour. Plasticity, 1990—, Internat. Jour. Non-linear Mechanics, 1995—2005, Jour. Composite Materials, 2001—, assoc. editor: ASME Jour. Applied Mechanics, 1994—2000; editor: Internat. Jour. Solids and Structures, 2005—. Recipient Presdl. Young Investigator award, NSF, 1984—89. Fellow: ASME (chmn. exec. com. Applied Mechanics Divsn. 2002—03), Am. Acad. Mechanics; mem.: AIAA, NAE (pres. 2006), ASCE, Soc. Petroleum Engrs., Soc. Engring. Sci., Soc. Exptl. Mechanics. Office: Dept Aerospace Engring and Engring Mechanics U Tex Austin 1 University Sta C0600 Austin TX 78712 Office Phone: 512-471-5963. Office Fax: 512-471-5500. E-mail: skk@mail.utexas.edu.*

KYRIAKIDES, TASSOS CONSTANTINO, biostatistician; b. Nicosia, Cyprus, Mar. 2, 1969; s. Constantinos and Nina Kyriakides; m. Kristen Rachele Aversa, Oct. 9, 1999; children: Siena Christina children: Tassos Andreas. BSc, UCLA, 1993; MPhil, Yale U., New Haven, 1996; PhD, Yale U., 1999. Epidemiologist/biostatistician VACSPCC, West Haven, Conn., 1999—; assoc. rsch. scientist Yale AIDS Program, New Haven, Conn., 2002—. Cyprus del. UN, 2001; mem. clin. trials com. Can. Inst. Health Rsch., 2001—04. Fellow Berlex fellow, Berlex/Yale U. Sch. of Pub. Health, 1996; grantee John F. Enders Rsch. grantee, Yale U., 1997; scholar Fulbright scholar, AMIDEAST/AID, 1989—93. Office: VACSPCC West Haven 950 Campbell West Haven CT 06516 E-mail: tassos@aya.yale.edu.

KYRIAKOU, LINDA GRACE, communications executive; b. NYC; d. Frank T. and Dolores Helen Lagamma; m. Konstantinos G. Kyriakou, 1 child, Christina Elena. BA, Hunter Coll. Acct. exec., dir. rsch. Booke and Co., NYC, 1969-75; mgr. pub. rels. CIT Fin. Corp., NYC, 1975-79; dir. corp. comm. Sequa Corp., NYC, 1979-88, v.p. corp. comm., 1988—. Recipient Twin award, 1985. Mem. Pub. Rels. Soc. Am., Nat. Investor Rels. Inst. (bd. dirs. 1981-82, Sr. Roundtable), Women's Bond Club N.Y. (bd. govs. 1978-80). Office: Sequa Corp 200 Park Ave Rm 4401 New York NY 10166-4400 Business E-Mail: Linda_Kyriakou@sequa.com.

KYRIAZIS, ARTHUR JOHN (ATHANASIOS IOANNIS KYRIAZIS), lawyer, biotechnologist; b. Thessaloniki, Greece, Nov. 2, 1958; came to U.S., 1960; s. George A. and Elpis (Halkedis) K.; m. Maria M. Zissimos, Aug. 31, 1986; children: Cassandra Hope, Michael John, George Athanasios II. AB, Harvard U., 1981; postgrad., Pepperdine U., 1982—83; JD cum laude, Temple U., 1985; student in Biotechnology, U. Pa., 1998—. Bar: Pa. 1985, U.S. Dist. Ct. (ea. dist.) Pa. 1985, U.S. Bankruptcy Ct. (ea. dist.) Pa. 1985, U.S. Bankruptcy Ct. NJ, 1986, Calif. 1987, U.S. Dist. Ct. (ea. dist.) Calif. 1988, U.S. Ct. Appeals (3d cir.) 1991, U.S. Supreme Ct. 1994. Vol. Med. Coll. Hahneman U., Pa., 1974—76, lab. rsch. technician mouse mammers tumor virus project Coll. Medicine, 1977—78; assoc. Cardillo & Corbett, NYC, 1983; law clk. to Hon. Norma J. Shapiro U.S. Dist. Ct. (ea. dist.) Pa., 1984; assoc. Needleman Needleman Caney Stein & Kratzer, 1984—85; law clk. to Hon. James Gardner Colins Commonwealth Ct. Pa., Phila., Harrisburg, 1985—86; assoc. Rawle & Henderson, Phila. and Marlton, NJ, 1987—88, Lesser & Kaplin and predecessor firm, Phila., Blue Bell, Pa. and Marlton, 1988—89; prin. Kyriazis & Assocs., Springfield, 1989—92; intellectual property coord. ESI, 1992—93, React red, Inc., 1993—. Arbitrator Phila. Ct. Common Pleas, 1988—, Delaware County Ct. Common Pleas, 1993—; pro bono counsel Am. Assn. Univ. Students, 1989—; solicitor to Register of Wills, Montgomery County, Pa., 2000; law clk. Registrar Wills Del. County, 2002; rsch. assoc. U. Pa. Hosp., 1999—2000; tutor chemistry U. Pa., 1994—2000, clin. rsch. assoc. hosp. emergency rm., 2000—01; presenter in field. Contbr. articles to profl. jours. Pa. co-coord. Dukakis for Pres., 1987-88; del. Nat. Fin. Com., Dem. Conv., Atlanta, 1988; mem. Hellenic Am. for Dukakis, Pa., 1987-88; founder Am. Assn. Univ. Students, Cambridge, Mass. and Phila., 1978-79; v.p. Hercules-Spartan Phila. chpt. 26 Am. Hellenic Progressive Edn. Assn., 1989-90, pres., 1990-91, bd. govs., 1987-93; alumni assn. bd. trustees Haverford Sch., 1999—; mem. alumni bd. The Haverford Sch., 1998—, fin. com.; vol. rschr. Emergency Room Rsch. Project Clinical Trials U. Pa. Hosp., 2000-01. Mem. ATLA, ABA (young lawyers divsn., litig. and bus. law sect., bus., real estate sects.), Am. Hellenic Lawyers Assn. (founder, treas. 1992-94), Phila. Bar Assn. (exec. com. young lawyers sect. 1988-90, fin. sec. exec. com. 1990, sec. exec. com. 1989, co-chmn. law related edn. com. 1988—, bar edn. found. com. 1988—, mem. Bill Rights 200 coms., fed. cts. 200 com., chmn. debate com. and mock trial 1987—, debate dir. fed. cts. 200 nat. high sch. debate tournament 1990—), Pa. Bar Assn. (litig., young lawyers jud. adminstrn.), Pa. Trial Lawyers Assn., Am. Arbitration Assn. (comml. arbitrator 1988—), Pa. Bar Assn., State Bar Calif. (litig., intellectual property, entertainment), Am. Assn. Univ. Students (legal counsel 1989—), Coll. Admissions Inst. Am. (adv. bd. 1992—), Hellenic Univ. Club (bd. trustees 1996-98), Harvard Club, Penn Club, Maxwell Football Club, Nat. Press Club, Harvard-Radcliffe Club (schs. com., chmn. Del. county schs. com.), Penn Faculty Club. Republican. Greek Orthodox. Office: 336 Bay Ave Unit 503 Ocean City NJ also: Kyriazis & Associates 491 Baltimore Pike #217 Springfield PA 19064-3810 Office Phone: 610-543-6453. Personal E-mail: akbiotech@comcast.net.

KYSOR, DANIEL FRANCIS, psychologist; b. Corry, Pa., Aug. 3, 1956; s. Darrell Francis and Louise Mary (Col) K.; m. Kate Galbraith Morrison, Sept. 7, 1991; children: Kenneth Jon Kron, Samuel Morrison, Charles Col. BS, Edinboro U., 1980; MS in Ednl. Psychology, Edinboro U., Pa., 1988; MEd in Secondary Sch. Adminstrn., Edinboro U., 1994; postgrad., Miss. State U., 1991—. Cert. elem. edn., guidance, elem. and secondary adminstr., sch. psychologist; lic. psychologist, Pa. Tchr. Calhoun County Schs., Grantsville, W.Va., 1982; counselor, tchr. Bradford Children's Home, Pa., 1983; residential program counselor Assn. for Retarded Citizens, Meadville, 1984—86; resident hall dir. Edinboro U., 1984—86, counselor Edinboro Summer Acad. for the Gifted, 1985—96; guidance counselor Cranberry Sch. Dist., Seneca, 1986; dropout prevention counselor Erie Sch. Dist., 1988; sch. psychologist Seneca Highlands Intermediate Unit #9, Coudersport, 1989—. Pvt. practice Addis & Assocs., Bradford, Pa., 1994-97; CEO, dir. psychol. svc. Port Psychol. Svcs., Inc., 1996—. Pa. Rural Leadership Program scholar Pa. State U., 1989; Rsch. grantee St. Bonaventure U., N.Y.; recipient citations Pa. House of Reps., 1991, 93, 95. Mem. ACA (life), NASP, Am. Sch. Counselor Assn., Nat. Fedn. Interscholastic Ofcls. Assns., Pa. Interscholastic Athletic Assn., Pa. Sch. Bds. Assn., Ea. Wrestling League, Ea. Ind. Officials Wrestling Assn., Nat. Wrestling Officials Assn., Clowns of Am. Internat., Inc./POCO Clowns. Republican. Presbyterian. Avocations: wrestling officiating, reading, bicycling. Home: 109 Chestnut St Port Allegany PA 16743-1248 Office: Seneca Highlands IU #9 306 N Main St Coudersport PA 16915-1626 E-mail: kysor@zitomedia.net.

KYUNG, YUN SEUNG, biochemist, researcher; b. Inchon, Republic of Korea, Mar. 11, 1960; s. Ku-Hyun Kyung and Soonja Kim; m. Eun Kyung Lee; children: Sung Won, Erica. PhD, U. Minn., Mpls., 2000. Rsch. assoc. U. Minn., Mpls., 2000—03; sr. rsch. scientist Centocor R&D, Inc., Radnor, Pa., 2003—. Home: 7 Clayton Ct Exton PA 19341 Office: Centocor R&D Inc 145 King of Prussia Rd Wayne PA 19087 Office Phone: 610-240-8168. Personal E-mail: ykyung60@yahoo.com. E-mail: ykyung@cntus.jnj.com.

LAANE, JAAN, chemistry professor; b. Paide, Estonia, June 20, 1942; came to US, 1949. s. Robert Freidrich and Linda (Treufeldt) L.; m. Tiiu Virkhaus, Sept. 3, 1966; children: Christina J., Lisa A. BS in Chemistry, U. Ill., 1964; PhD in Chemistry, MIT, 1967; Doctorate (hon.), U. Tartu, Estonia, 2000. Asst. prof. of chemistry Tufts U., Medford, Mass., 1967-68; asst. prof. of chem. Tex. A&M U., Coll. Sta., 1968-72, assoc. prof. of chem., 1972-76, prof. of chemistry, 1976—, chmn. div. of phys. and nuc. chemistry, 1977-87, 93-94, dir. Inst. for Pacific Asia, 1987-90, assoc. dean sci., 1994-97; dep. exec. dir., sr. policy advisor Tex. A&M U./Koriyama, Coll. Sta., 1990-94; editor Jour. Molecular Structure, 1994—. Reviewer numerous profl. jour. and grant agys., 1968—; cons. indsl. and govt. orgn., 1970—; vis. prof. U. Bayreuth, Fed. Republic Germany, 1979-80; speaker Tex. A&M Faculty Senate, College Station, 1985-86; dir. NATO Advanced Rsch. Workshop, Ulm, Germany, 1992. Contbr. numerous articles to profl. jour.; lectr. numerous sci. presentations. Pres., founder College Station Assn. for Gifted and Talented, 1982-83. Recipient 13 rsch. grants Robert A. Welch Found., 1970—, 10 rsch. grants NSF, 1976-2007, US Sr. Sci. award Alex Von Humboldt Found., Fed. Republic Germany, 1979, Disting. Tchg. award Tex. A&M Assn. Former Students; elected to Estonian Acad. Sci., 1995, Lippincott award for molecular spectroscopy, 2005; Robert A. Welch Found. lectr., 1998-99. Fellow Am. Inst. Chemists, Am. Phys. Soc.; mem. Am. Chem. Soc. (sect. pres. 1977-78), Soc. for Applied Spectroscopy, Alexander von Humboldt Assn. Am. (bd. dirs. 2003-06, v.p. 2005—, pres. Tex. chpt. 2001-02, pres. 2007—), Coblentz Soc. (bd. dir., treas. 1986-89), Tex. A&M Faculty Club (pres. 1987-88), Phi Beta Delta (pres. 1990-91). Achievements include rsch. in molecular spectroscopy and vibrational potential energy functions of molecules, laser Raman spectroscopy, laser induced fluorescence spectroscopy, ft-infrared spectroscopy. Home: 1906 Comal Cir College Station TX 77840-4818 Office: Tex A&M U Chemistry Dept College Station TX 77843-3255 Home Phone: 979-693-5171; Office Phone: 979-845-3352. Office Fax: 979-845-3154. Business E-Mail: laane@mail.chem.tamu.edu.

LABA, MARVIN, management consultant; b. Newark, Mar. 17, 1928; s. Joseph Abraham and Jean Cecil (Saunders) L.; m. Sandra Seltzer, Apr. 16, 1961 (div. May 1974); children: Stuart Michael, Jonathan Todd; m. Elizabeth Luger, June 11, 1974 (div. 1979). BBA, Ind. U., 1951. Buyer Bamberger's (Macy's N.J.), Newark, 1951-67; v.p., mdse. adminstr. Macy's N.Y., 1967-73; v.p., gen. mdse. mgr. Howland/Steinback, White Plains, NY, 1973-75, Pomeroy's, Levittown, Pa., 1975-76; v.p., gen. mdse. mgr., sr. v.p., exec. v.p. May Co. Calif., North Hollywood, 1976-79; pres., chief exec. officer G. Fox & Co. (div. of the May dept. stores), Hartford, Conn., 1979-82; pres. Richard Theobald & Ascs., LA, 1983; pres., chief exec. officer Marvin Laba & Assocs., LA, 1983—. With U.S. Army, 1946-48. Avocations: coins, tennis, theater, travel. Office: Marvin Laba & Assoc 4336 Whitsett Ave Ste 5 Studio City CA 91604 Home Phone: 818-761-7555; Office Phone: 818-762-2122. Personal E-mail: marvin@marvinlaba.com.

LABADIE, BERNARD, performing company executive; b. Quebec, Can., 1963; Grad., Ecole de musique de l'Universite Laval. Founder Les Violons du Roy, 1984, La Chapelle de Quebec, 1985; condr. over 100 performances globally, 1988—; artistic dir. Opéra Que., 1994—2003, Opéra Montreal, 2002—. Named Personality of Yr., Que., 1997—98, Officer Order of Can., 2005; recipient Raymond Blais medal, Universite Laval, 1992, Rayonnement Internat. prize, Conseil de la Culture de Quebec, 1996. Office: L'Opera de Montreal 260 de Maisonneuve Blvd W Montreal PQ H2X 149 Canada Office Phone: 514-985-2222. Business E-Mail: mbarrette@operademontreal.com.

LABAN, MYRON MILES, physician, hospital administrator; b. Detroit, Mar. 9, 1936; s. Larry Max and Mary Marsha (Harris) LaBan; m. Rita Joyce Hochman, Aug. 17, 1958; children: Terry, Amy, Craig. BA, U. Mich., Ann Arbor, 1957, MD, 1967; M.Med. Sci., Ohio State U., Columbus, 1965. Diplomate Am. Bd. Phys. Medicine and Rehab. Intern Sinai Hosp., Detroit, 1961-62; resident Ohio State U. Hosp., 1962-65; assoc. dir. phys. medicine and rehab. Letterman Gen. Hosp., San Francisco, 1965-67; dir. phys. medicine and rehab. William Beaumont Hosp., Royal Oak, Mich., 1967—; Licht lectr. Ohio State U., 1986, clin. prof., 1993. Bd. dirs. Oakland County Med. Bd., Birmingham, Mich., 1982—87; clin. prof. Oakland U., Rochester, Mich., 1983, Wayne State U., Detroit, 1990, Ohio State U., Columbus, 1992; rep. to Commn. Phys. Medicine and Rehab. Mich. State Med. Soc. Contbr. chapters to books, articles to profl. jours. Med. dir. Oakland County March of Dimes, Mich., 1969—83; pres. Bloomfield Art Ctr., 2003—. Served to capt. US Army, 1965—67. Fellow: Am. Acad. Phys. Medicine and Rehab. (bd. dirs. 1980, pres. 1985—86, Bernard Baruch Rsch. award 1961, R. Rosenthal Rsch. award 1982, Zeiter lectureship, Disting. Clinician award 1991, Top Doc PM& R Detroit Monthly 1993, 1996, Frank H. Krusen award 1997); mem.: AMA, Mich. Acad. Phys. Med. and Rehab (pres. 1982—84, jud. commr. 1991—95, mem. editl. bd. Jour. Phys. Med. and Rehab.), Mich. State Med. Soc., Oakland County Med. Soc. (treas. 1983, pres.-elect 1987, pres. 1988—89), Am. Assn. Electromyography adn Electrodiagnosis (program dir. 1972), Am. Congress Rehab. Medicine. Republican. Jewish. Avocations: gardening, model building. Office: LMT Rehabilitation Assocs 3535 W 13 Mile Rd Rm 703 Royal Oak MI 48073-6710 Home Phone: 248-642-2547; Office Phone: 248-288-2210. Personal E-mail: myjoy@comcast.net.

LA BARBARA, JOAN, composer, musician, singer; b. Phila., June 8, 1947; d. John Jacob Lotz and Evelyn Lois Buckley; m. Morton Subotnick, Dec. 18, 1979; 1 child, Jacob Buckley-Lotz LB Subotnick. BS in Music Edn., NYU, 1970. Freelance composer, NYC, 1971—; faculty Calif. Inst. Arts, Valencia, Calif., 1981—86; artistic dir. When Morty Met John Series Carnegie Hall, NYC, 2001—04; curator, host Insights: Conversations with Composers Am. Music Ctr., NYC, 2003—05. Composer-in-residence DeutscherAkademischerAustauschdienstKuenstlerprogramm, Berlin, 1979—80; adj. prof. Coll. Santa Fe, 1996—2002; adj. faculty U. N.Mex., Albuquerque, 1999—2001; vis. Slee composer SUNY, Buffalo, 1976—77; lectr. dept. music Princeton U., 2006—07. Composer: (songs) 73 Poems, 2000, Landscape Over Zero, 2003, Messa di Voce, Dragons on the Wall (award Mary Flagler Cary Trust Commn., 2000), To Hear The Wind Roar (award Meet The Composer/Reader's Digest Commn., 1990), Prologue to The Book of Knowing (and) of Overthrowing (Interdisciplinary Arts award N.Mex Arts Coun., 1987), The Solar Wind (NEA award, 1981), Cyclone (Internat. Jury award Internat. Soc. Contemporary Music, 1977), Fleeting Thoughts, 2006, Desert Myths: Isle of Dunes, 2006, Live Music for Dance Commission, 2005—06; prodr.(host): KUNM-FM, 1987—2002. V.p. Electronic Music Found., NY, 2003—; dir., v.p. Am. Music Ctr., NYC, 1979—85; artistic dir., co-pres. New Music Am. Festival New Music Alliance, LA, 1984—86. Co-recipient First Collaboration award, Coalition of Profl. Women in the Arts and Media, 2006; recipient Creative Connections award, Meet The Composer, 2005—06, Akustische Kunst award, West Deutscher Rundfunk - Cologne, 1991, Music Composition Commn. award, St. Louis Symphony, 1989; fellow, DAAD Berlin, 1979, NEA, 1980, John Simon Guggenheim Meml. Found., 2004; grantee, N.Y. State Coun. Arts, 1976, 1979, NEA, 1981, 1983—87. Mem.: ASCAP (Composer award 1977—), SAG, Actors Equity Assn., Am. Fedn. TV and Radio Rec. Artists, Am. Music Ctr. (v.p. 1981—83). Achievements include development of unique vocabulary of extended vocal techniques. Home: 25 Minetta Lane 4B New York NY 10012 Home Phone: 212-477-0214; Office Phone: 646-220-6033.

LABARDI, MASSIMILIANO, research scientist; b. Capri, Italy, Mar. 1, 1967; s. Evaldo Labardi and Renata Maffia; m. Maria Luisa Chiofalo, June 18, 1995; 1 child, Anna. PhD, Scuola Normale Superiore, Pisa, 1997. Rschr. INFM, Pisa, Italy, 2003—04, CNR-INFM, Pisa, 2004—. Lt. Italian Army, 1993—94. Achievements include patents for measurement systems and methods for near-field optical microscopy. Office: polyLab-CNR Largo Pontecorvo 3 Pisa 56127 Italy Personal E-mail: labardi@df.unipi.it.

LABARGE, CHRISTOPHER W., priest; b. Pittsfield, Mass., May 9, 1953; s. Paul Willson LaB. and Nanette Marie Passier. BA in Sacred Theology, St. Francis de Sales Coll., Milw., 1979; BS in Theology, St. Mary's Sem. and U., Balt., 1985, MDiv, 1985; Lic. in Sacred Theology, St. Mary's Sem. and Univ., Balt., 1986. Ordained priest Roman Cath. Ch., 1985. Assoc. pastor Our Lady of Fatima, New Castle, Del., 1985—88, St. Elizabeth's, Wilmington, Del., 1988—92, Holy Cross, Dover, Del., 1992—95; adminstr. Immaculate Conception, Marydel, Md., 1995—96, pastor, 1996—. Chaplain Wilmington Fire Dept., 1989—92; leadership W.W. Marriage Encounter, Wilmington, 1992—95. Bd. dirs. Choptank Cmty. Health, Denton, Md., 2000—, Social Svcs. Adv. Bd., Denton, 1998—2005. Mem.: Mid Shore Regional Coun. (rep. 2003—), Gov.'s Commn. Hispanic Affairs (commr. 2003—), KC (friar 4th degree 1993—, Del. state chaplain 1998—2000, dean of the diocese 2002—). Home: 517 Main St PO Box 411 Marydel MD 21649 Office: Immaculate Conception PO Box 399 Marydel MD 21649 Business E-Mail: marydelfr@comcast.net.

LABARGE, MARGARET WADE, medieval history professor, historian, writer; b. NYC, July 18, 1916; arrived in Can., 1940; d. Alfred Byers and Helena (Mein) Wade; m. Raymond C. Labarge, June 20, 1940 (dec. May 1972); children: Claire Labarge Morris, Suzanne, Charles, Paul. BA, Radcliffe Coll., 1937; LittB, Oxford U., Eng., 1939; LittD (hon.), Carleton U., Ottawa, Ont., Can., 1976; LLD (hon.), U. Waterloo, Ont., Can., 1993; HHD (hon.), Mount St Vincent U., Halifax, NS, 2003. Lectr. history U. Ottawa, Carleton U., 1950-62; adj. prof. history Carleton U., Ottawa, 1983—2005. Author: Simon de Montfort, 1962, A Baronial Household, 1965, Gascony, 1980, A Small Sound of the Trumpet, 1987, A Medieval Miscellany, 1997, others; contbr. articles to profl. jours. Bd. dirs. St. Vincent's Hosp., Ottawa, 1969-81; chmn. 1977-79; pub. rep. bd. dirs. Can. Nurses Assn., 1980-83; bd. dirs. Carleton U., 1984-93, Coun. on Aging, 1986-93 (pres., 1989-91). Recipient Alumnae Recognition award Radcliffe Coll., 1987, Founders award, Carleton U., 2001 Fellow Royal Soc. Can.; mem. Medieval Acad., Soc. of Can. Medievalists (pres. 1993-94), Order of Can., Phi Beta Kappa. Roman Catholic. Avocations: travel, reading, walking. Home and Office: 402-555 Wilbrod St Ottawa ON Canada K1N 5R4 E-mail: mwlabarge@sympatico.ca.

LABARRE, CARL ANTHONY, retired federal agency administrator; b. Sherwood, ND, July 16, 1918; s. William Paul and Josephine K. LaB.; m. Persis Wester, Sept. 9, 1941; 1 son, William Paul, II. Student, U. Mont., 1936-40; postgrad., Naval Acad. Postgrad. Sch., 1945-46; grad., Naval War Coll., 1958-59, Advanced Mgmt. Program, Harvard U. Commd. ensign U.S. Navy, 1941, advanced through grades to capt., 1971; served in various fin., inventory control systems and purchasing assignments, to 1971; insp. gen. (Naval Supply Systems Command), to 1971; ret., 1971; dep. dir. materials mgmt. service GPO, Washington, 1971-75, dir. materials mgmt. service, 1975, asst. public printer, supt. documents, 1975-82. Decorated Navy Commendation medal with V, Joint Service commendation medal, Legion of Merit with gold star; recipient Public Printers Disting. Service award, 1977, 81 Mem.: Harvard Bus. Sch. (Washington).

LABARRE, DENNIS W., lawyer; b. Binghamton, NY, Dec. 27, 1942; BA, Northwestern U., 1965; LLB, U. Va., 1968. Bar: Ohio 1978. Ptnr. Jones, Day, Reavis & Pogue, NYC; now ptnr.-in-charge NYC office Jones Day. Office: Jones Day 222 E 41st St New York NY 10017-6702 Office Phone: 212-326-3600. Office Fax: 212-755-7306. Business E-Mail: dwlabarre@jonesday.com.

LABATON, STEPHEN, journalist, lawyer; b. Queens, NY, May 3, 1961; s. Edward and Laura (Wasserman) L. BA in Polit. Sci. and Philosophy (magna cum laude), Tufts U., 1983; MA in Philosophy, Duke U., 1986; JD, Duke U. Sch. Law, 1986. Bar: NY, Conn. Clerk NY Times, NYC, 1986, legal affairs corr., 1987-90, Washington corr., 1990—, regulatory agencies corr., Washington bur., 2002—. Recipient Gerald Loeb award, UCLA Anderson Sch. Mgmt., 2003. Mem.: Nat. Press Club (co-chair Freedom of Press com. 2000—, co-chair Freedom of Info. com. 2005—). Home: 3048 Davenport St NW Washington DC 20008-2115 Office: NY Times 7th Fl 1627 I St NW Washington DC 20006-4007

LABBETT, JOHN EDGAR, financial analyst; b. Chesham, Buckinghamshire, Eng., June 19, 1950; came to U.S., 1987; s. Gordon F. and Sylvia (Dalton) L.; m. Mary McGagh, Jan. 30, 1976; children: Jennifer F., Alexander T. Audit clk. White Withers and Co., Bexhill, England, 1966—71; auditor Peat Marwick Mitchell, London, 1971—73; chief acct. Guild S&V Ltd., London, 1973—74; from fin. analyst to contr. Roneo Vickers Ltd., London, 1974—81; fin. contr. Cambridge (Eng.) Instruments Ltd., 1981—82; fin. dir. Linfood C&C Ltd. subs. Dee Corp., Milton Keynes, England, 1982—85; fin. controller Dee Corp., Milton Keynes, 1985—87; exec. v.p., CFO Hermans Sporting Goods, Inc., Carteret, NJ, 1987—93; v.p., CFO The Petfood Giant, Inc., 1994—95; exec. v.p., CFO House of Fabrics, Inc., Sherman Oaks, Calif., 1995—98, Egghead.com, Inc., Menlo Park, Calif., 1998—2001; fin. cons. SoCal Ventures, Inc., La Canada, Calif., 2002—04; CFO, Oversee.net, L.A., 2004—06; CEO, First Street Food Group, San Fernando, Calif., 2006—. Fellow Inst. Chartered Accts. Eng. Anglican. Home: 80 Stagecoach Rd Bell Canyon CA 91307-1042 Office Phone: 818-332-5450. Personal E-mail: jlabbett@earthlink.net.

LABBIENTO, JULIANNE MARIE, mathematics professor; d. David Hurst and Carol Ann Landis; m. Michael L. Greenholt; 1 child, Jason Patrick. BS in math and actuarial sci., Clarion U., 1985—89; MS in math., Youngstown State U., 1992—94. Forecasting specialist Balt. Life Ins. Co., Balt., 1989—92; adj. prof., math. Youngstown State U., Youngstown, Ohio, 1992—95; adj. prof., math. and computer sci. Westminster Coll., New Wilmington, Pa., 1995—98; instr., math. Clarion U., Pa., 1998—2002; assoc. prof., math. Lehigh Carbon C.C., Schnecksville, Pa., 2002—. Mem.: Pa. State Math. Assn. Two-Yr. Colls. Office: Lehigh Carbon Community College 4525 Education Park Dr Schnecksville PA 18078 Home Phone: 610-798-0314; Office Phone: 610-799-1074. E-mail: jlabbiento@lccc.edu.

LABELLE, PATTI (PATRICIA LOUISE HOLTE), singer, entertainer; b. Phila., May 24, 1944; d. Henry and Bertha Holte; m. Armstead Edwards, 1969 (div. 2000); 5 children. PhD (hon.), Berkeley Sch. Music, 1996, Cambridge U., Drexel U. Singer Patti LaBelle and the BlueBelles, 1961—70; lead singer musical group LaBelle, 1970-76; solo performer, 1977—; entrepreneur Patti LaBelle's Fragrances & Cosmetics, 1995. Established clothing line Patti LaBelle Clothing, 2003—. Albums (with the BlueBelles) Sweethearts of the Apollo, 1963, Over the Rainbow, 1967, (with LaBelle) LaBelle, 1971, Moon Shadows, 1972, Pressure Cookin', 1973, Nightbirds, 1974, Phoenix, 1975, Chameleon, 1976, (solo) Patti LaBelle, 1977, Live at the Apollo, 1980, Gonna Take A Miracle-The Spirit's in It, 1981, I'm in Love Again, 1983, Winner in You, 1986, The Best of Patti LaBelle, 1987, Patti, 1985, Be Yourself, 1989, Burnin', 1991 (Grammy award best r&b vocalist, 1991), Live (Apollo Theater), 1992, Gems, 1994, Live! One Night Only, 1998 (Grammy award best trad. r&b vocal perf., 1998), Greatest Hits, 1996, Flame, 1997, When a Woman Loves, 2000, Timeless Journey, 2004, Patti Labelle: Classic Moment, 2005; actress (films) A Soldier's Story, 1984, Sing, 1989, On the One, 2005, Idlewild, 2006; (TV movies) For Colored Girls Who Have Considered Suicide, 1982, Working, 1982, Unnatural Causes, 1986, Fire and Rain, 1989, Parker Kane, 1990, Santa Baby! (voice), 2001, My Life in Idlewild, 2005; (TV series) A Different World, 1990-93, Out All Night, 1992; (guest appearances) Dolly, 1987, The Nanny, 1994, Cosby, 1997, All of Us, 2004; (TV specials) Live Aid, 1985, The Patti LaBelle Show, 1985, Sisters in the Name of Love, 1986 (CableACE award best perf. music special, 1987) Motown 30: What's Goin' On!, 1990, Sinatra Duets, 1994, The Remarkable Journey, 2000, Born to Diva, 2003, Nina Simone: A Tribute, 2003, VH1 Divas Live, 2004, (plays) Your Arms Too Short to Box with God (revival), 1980; author Don't Block the Blessings: Revelations of a Lifetime, 1997, LaBelle Cuisine: Recipes to Sing About, 1999, Patti's Pearls: Lessons in Living Genuinely, Joyfully & Generously, 2001, Patti LaBelle's Lite Cuisine; host (TV show) Living It Up with Patti LaBelle, 2004—. Spokesperson Am. Diabetic Assn., Nat. Minority AIDS Council, Nat. Cancer Inst., founder The Patti LaBelle Med. Ed. Scholarship Fund. Recipient award of Merit, Phila. Art Alliance, 1987, Soul Train Lifetime Achievement award, 1997, Walk of Fame honoree Black Entertainment TV, 2000; Entertainer of Yr. Image award NAACP, 1992. Office: Def Soul Classics 825 8th Ave 29th Fl New York NY 10019

LABELLE, THOMAS JEFFREY, research executive, academic administrator; b. Owen, Wis., Sept. 21, 1941; s. Wendell Allen and Katherine (Dolan) LaB.; m. Nancy Reik, June 16, 1966 (dec. 1981); children: Katherine Anne, Jeanette Marie AA, Pierce Coll., Woodland Hills, Calif., 1962; BA, Calif. State U., Northridge, 1964; MA, U. N.Mex., Albuquerque, 1967, PhD, 1969. Prof. UCLA, 1969-86, asst. dean edn., 1971-79, assoc. dean grad. div., 1980-86; prof. comparative and internat. edn. U. Pitts., 1986-90, dean Sch. Edn., 1986-90; v.p. acad. programs, provost Ga. State U., Atlanta, 1990-93; provost, v.p. acad. affairs and rsch. W.Va. U., Morgantown, 1993-96; provost v.p. acad. affairs San Francisco State U., 1996—2002; exec. dir. internat. and area studies U. Calif., Berkeley, 2002—05. Cons. InterAm. Found., US AID, Ford Found., CBS, Acad. Ednl. Devel., Juarez and Assocs.; disting. vis. prof. Obirin U., Tokyo, 2005—; adj. prof. Grad. Sch. Edn., U. Calif., Berkeley. Author: Education and Development in Latin America, 1972, Nonformal Education in Latin America and the Caribbean, 1986, Stability, Reform or Revolution, 1986, Education and Intergroup Relations, 1985, Multiculturalism and Education, 1994, Ethnic Studies and Multiculturalism, 1996. Vol. Peace Corps, Colombia, 1964-66. Grantee Fulbright Found., 1983, 96, InterAm. Found., Latin America, 1984; recipient Andres Bello award 1st Class, Venezuela, 1987. Fellow Soc. Applied Anthropology; mem. Comparative and Internat. Edn. Soc. (pres. 1981), Coun. on Anthropology and Edn. (bd. dirs. 1977), Inter-Am. Found. (chmn. learning fellowship on social change), Golden Key, Omicron Delta Kappa, Phi Kappa Phi. Democrat. Home: 601 Van Ness #52 San Francisco CA 94102 E-mail: thomas.labelle@sbcglobal.net.

LABENSKY, SARAH ROSS, culinary educator; b. Murray, Ky., Mar. 16, 1958; d. James Mason and Lucille Thomson Ross; m. Steven Jay Labensky, Oct. 14, 1983 (div. May 1995); m. Louis David Moline, Sept. 3, 1995 (dec. Aug. 2003) BS, Murray State U., Ky., 1980; JD, Vanderbilt U., 1983; cert., Scottsdale C.C., 1986. Atty. Hocker and Axford, Tempe, Ariz., 1983-85; cook/chef Phoenix, 1985-90; prof. Scottsdale C.C., Ariz., 1990-98; dir. Miss. U. for Women Culinary Arts Inst., Columbus, 1998—2005; editor Favorite Recipes Press, Nashville, 2005—06; restaurant owner Columbus, Miss., 2006—. Author: On Cooking, 1995, 4th edit., 2005, Webster's N.W. Dictionary of Culinary Arts, 1997, 2d edit., 2000, Applied Math for Food Service, 1998, Complete Idiot's Guide to Cooking Techniques and Science, 2002, On Baking, 2004. Mem.: Internat. Assn. Culinary Profls. (bd. dirs. 1999—2006, sec.-treas. 2002, v.p. 2003, pres. 2004, cert.), Am. Culinary Fedn. Office: 400 Main St Columbus MS 39701 Office Phone: 662-329-3693. Personal E-mail: frontdoor400@bellsouth.net.

LABENZ-HOUGH, MARLENE, mediator; b. St. Edward, Nebr., May 25, 1954; d. Ralph Labenz and Lorene (Laudenklos); m. Jeff Hough, Mar. 5, 1983. Assocs., Platte Coll., 1974; BS in Social Work magna cum laude, U. Nebr., 1976; MA in Clin. Psychology, Trinity U., 1980. Adminstrv. asst., mgmt. analyst II City of San Antonio Dept. Human Resources and Svcs., 1980, adminstrv. asst. II, 1980-82, casework supr., Victims of Crime Program, 1982-89, program coord., Children's Resources Divsn., 1989-90; asst. dir. Bexar County Dispute Resolution Ctr., San Antonio, 1990-92, dir., 1992—. Bd. dirs. KidShare, 1993-96, YWCA, 1990-93; mem. ADR sect. coun. State Bar Tex., 1996-99. Recipient Liberty Bell award, San Antonio Young Lawyers Assn., 2003, Recognition award, San Antonio Bar Found., 2004, Appreciation award, 2005, Recognition award for leadership. Mem.: ABA (chmn. conf. com. ADR sect. 2002), Tex. Bar Assn. (ADR sect.), Assn. Family and Conciliation Cts., Tex. Mediators Credentialing Assn., Alamo Area Mediators Assn., Tex. Dispute Resolution Ctrs. Dirs. Coun., Tex. Mediation Trainers' Roundtable, Assn. Conflict Resolution, Conflict Resolution and Peer Mediation Coun., Nat. Assn. Cmty. Mediation (founding dir.), Soc. Profls. in Dispute Resolution (co-chair S.W. region chpt. 1993, co-chair nat. conf. 1995, Profl. Dedication award 1994), Acad. Family Mediators, Tex. Assn. Mediators (chair conf. 1998, bd. dirs. 1998—2001, Heart of Tex. award 2007), Alpha Xi Delta. Home: 2518 Ashton Village Dr San Antonio TX 78248-2200

LABEOUF, SHIA, actor; b. LA, June 11, 1986; s. Jeffrey LaBeouf and Shayna Saide. Attended, Hamilton Acad. Music, LA. Co-founder Element record label, Grassy Slope prodn. co. Actor: (films) The Christmas Path, 1998, Monkey Business, 1998, Holes, 2003, Dumb and Dumber: When Harry Met Lloyd, 2003, Charlie's Angels: Full Throttle, 2003, The Battle of Shaker Heights, 2003, I, Robot, 2004, Constantine, 2005, The Greatest Game Ever Played, 2005, A Guide to Recognizing Your Saints, 2006 (Spl. Jury prize, Sundance Film Festival, 2006, Best actor, Gijón Internat. Film Festival, 2006), Bobby, 2006 (Hollywood Film award, Hollywood Film Festival, 2006), Disturbia, 2007 (Choice Movie Actor: Horror/Thriller, Teen Choice Awards, 2007), Transformers, 2007, (voice) Surf's Up, 2007,: (TV films) Breakfast with Einstein, 1998, Hounded, 2001, Tru Confessions, 2002, The Even Stevens Movie, 2003; (TV series) Even Stevens, 1999—2003 (Outstanding Performer in a Children's Series, Daytime Emmy awards, 2003); writer, dir. (films) Let's Love Hate, 2004 (Children's Audience award, Newport Internat. Film Festival, 2005, 2nd place, Children's Jury award, Chgo. Internat. Children's Film Festival, 2004). Named Male Star of Tomorrow, ShoWest Convention, 2007; recipient Choice Movie: Breakout Male, Teen Choice Awards, 2007.*

LABIOSA, WILLIAM BRUCE, civil engineer, researcher; s. Ralph Irvin and Eleanor (Cockerille) Labiosa; m. Rochelle Faye Grover, June 3, 2000. PhD in Environ. Engring., Stanford U., Calif., 2005. Regulation mgr. U.S. EPA, Washington, 1997—2001; decision sciences rschr. U.S. Geol. Survey, Menlo Park, Calif., 2001—. Vis. scholar dept. civil and environ. engring. Stanford U., Stanford, 2006—. Recipient Bronze medal, U.S. EPA, 1998, Spl. award, 2000; fellow, Dept. of Edn., 1991—93, Stanford U., 1993—94. Mem.: ASCE, Inst. Ops. Rsch. Mgmt. Sci. Avocations: hiking, travel. Office: US Geological Survey 345 Middlefield Rd MS-531 Menlo Park CA 94025-3561 Home Phone: 650-823-2743; Office Phone: 650-329-4279. Business E-Mail: blabiosa@usgs.gov.

LA BLANC, ROBERT EDMUND, information technology executive; b. NYC, Mar. 21, 1934; s. Charles Wesley and Anne R. (Dobson) La B.; m. Elizabeth Lammers, 1962; children: Elizabeth, Robert, Jeanne Marie, Paul, Michelle. BEE, Manhattan Coll., 1956; PhD honoris causa (hon.), Manhattan Coll., 1997; MBA, NYU, 1962. With Bell System, 1956-69; mem. tech. staff Bell Telephone Labs., 1961-62; seminar leader AT&T Long Lines, Cooperstown, NY, 1965-67; mktg. supr. AT&T Hdqrs., NYC, 1967-68; planning engr. N.Y. Telephone, 1968-69; mgr. Salomon Bros., NYC, 1969-73, v.p., 1973-75, gen. partner, 1975-79; vice chmn. Continental Telephone Corp., NYC, 1979-81; pres. Robert E. LaBlanc Assocs., Inc., 1981—. Bd. dirs. CA Inc., FiberNet Telecom. Group, Inc., 75 Prudential Mut. Funds. Vice chmn. bd. trustees Manhattan Coll., 1987—93, trustee, 1994—. Bklyn. Philharm. Scholarship Fund for Inner City Children, Acad. of the Holy Angels. Served to 1st lt. USAF, 1956—59. Named Wall St. Leading Analyst Instl. Investor Mag., 1973-78 Fellow: Fin. Analysts Fedn.; mem.: Assn. for Computing Machinery, NY Soc. Security Analysts (sr.), Econ. Club, Univ. Club, Equestrian Order Holy Sepulchre of Jerusalem (knight). Republican. Roman Catholic. Office Phone: 201-445-0195. Personal E-mail: rlablanc@aol.com.

LABODA, GERALD, oral and maxillofacial surgeon; b. Phila., Aug. 15, 1936; s. Lewis and Rose (Waldman) L.; m. Sheila Lois Plasky, Aug. 2, 1956; children: Amy, Michèle, Alane, Bruce. Student, Temple U., 1954-56, DMD, 1960; postgrad., U. Pa., 1960-61. Diplomate Am. Bd. Oral and Maxillofacial Surgery. Resident physician in oral and maxillofacial surgery Jefferson U. Hosp., Phila., 1961-63; pvt. practice oral and maxillofacial surgery S.W. Fla. Oral and Facial Surgery Assocs., Ft. Myers, 1965—. Bd. dirs S.W. Capital Bank; chmn. bd. trustees S.W. Fla. Regional Med. Ctr., Ft. Myers, 1989-94, sec. bd. trustees, 1974-89; med. dir. S.W. Fla. divsn. Columbia/HCA Healthcare Corp., 1994-99; trustee Gulf Coast Hosp., Ft. Myers; v.p. Flordeco, Inc. Contbr. articles to profl. jours. Pres. YMCA of Lee County, 1976; pres., bd. dirs. Found. for Lee County Pub. Schs., Ft. Myers, Fla., 1991, Fla. Gulf Coast Univ. Found.; vice chmn. Downtown Redevel. Agy., Ft. Myers, 1985—93; chmn., 1993—; bd. dirs. United Way of Lee County, 1981, Fla. Repertory Theater, 1999—, chmn., 2001—, Oral and Maxillofacial Surgery Found., 1990—2000; mem. bd. dentistry State of Fla., 1999—2003, chmn., 2002—. Fellow Am. Assn. Oral and Maxillofacial Surgeons (trustee Dist. III 1984-87, v.p. 1987-88, pres. 1989-90); mem. Fla. Soc. Oral and Maxillofacial Surgeons (pres. 1980-81), Fla. Dental Soc. of Anesthesiology (pres. 1978-79), S.W. Fla. Dental Soc. (pres. 1974), Southeastern Soc. Oral and Maxillofacial Surgery Found. (bd. dirs. 1993—, vice chmn. 1997, chmn. 1998-2000). Republican. Jewish. Avocations: flying, skiing, scuba diving, white water rafting. Office: SW Fla Oral Facial Surg Assocs Summerlin Med Park 5285 Summerlin Rd Fort Myers FL 33919-7602 Home: 9904 Bellagio Ct Fort Myers FL 33913-7041 Home Phone: 239-332-7571; Office Phone: 239-936-8151. Business E-Mail: Splaboda@comcast.net.

LABOON, LAWRENCE JOSEPH, human resources specialist, consultant; b. St. Louis, Aug. 4, 1938; s. Joseph Warren and Ruth (Aab) LaBoon; m. Glynys M. Brown, Sept. 16, 1989; children: Lawrence Bradley, Meredith Ashley;children from previous marriage: Lindsey Beth, Allison Ruth. BS magna cum laude, Tex. Wesleyan U., 1962. Cert. pers. cons., staffing profl. Oper. mgr. Firestone Tire & Rubber Co., Akron, Ohio, 1962—66; pres., CEO, Met. Pers., Inc., Phila., 1966—, chmn., 2000—; pres. Metro Tech, Valley Forge, Pa., 1977—, Metro Temps, Valley Forge, 1978—, Transport Tng. Corp., Valley Forge, 1993—, Metro Med., Valley Forge, 2001—; dir. Alpha-Indian Rock Savs. and Loan Assn., chmn. compensation com., 1986—90; chmn. pvt. employment agy. adv. coun. Pa. Dept. Labor and Industry, 1973—82. Guest lectr. Drexel U., 1976—91; human resources del. to USSR Citizen Amb. Program, 1991. Mem. People to People Internat. Mission to Vietnam and Asia, 1993; pres. Sunwood Farm Homeowners Assn., 2002—03; mem. exec. bd. Valley Forge Profl. Ctr., 2001—, pres., 2005—07. With USAF, 1954—60. Mem.: Am. Staffing Assn., Exec. Riders Ltd. (pres. 1986—88), Nat. Assn. Profl. Employers, TEMPNET (bd. dirs. 1986—88), Mid-Atlantic Assn. Temporary Svcs. (pres. 1983—84), Am. Soc. Pers. Adminstrn., Nat. Assn. Pers. Cons., Pa. Assn. Pers. Svcs. (pres. 1971—72, Blanchet Meml. award 1973), Nat. Employment Assn. (state certification bd. chmn. 1969—71, bd. dirs. 1972—74, chmn. bd. regents 1973, cert.), Glenhardie Condominium Assn. (non-resident exec. bd. 1989—91), Phoenixville Country Club, Alpha Chi. Republican. Home: 255 Country Ln Phoenixville PA 19460-1708 Office: 1260 Valley Forge Rd Valley Forge PA 19482-0641 Office Phone: 610-933-4000. Business E-Mail: ljl@metpersnl.com.

LABOR, EARLE GENE, literature and language professor; b. Tuskahoma, Okla., Mar. 3, 1928; s. Earle Labor and Sylvia Kirkpatrick Steger; m. Betty Garrett, Sept. 21, 1952 (dec. Aug. 1989); children: Royce, Kirk, Kyle, Isabel; m. Gayle Johnson, May 25, 1996; 1 child, Andrea. AB, So. Meth. U., Dallas, 1949, MA, 1952; PhD, U. Wis., Madison, 1961. Instr. English So. Meth. U., Dallas, 1950-52; asst. sales mgr. Haggar Co., Dallas, 1954-55; instr. English Centenary Coll., Shreveport, La., 1955-56, asst. prof. English, 1959-62, George A. Wilson prof. Am. Lit., 1966—; tchg. asst. U. Wis., Madison, 1956-59; head dept. English, chmn. dept. Humanities Adrian (Mich.) Coll., 1962-66. Adv. bd. Jack London Found., Glen Ellen, Calif., 1973—. Author: Jack London, 1974, 2d edit.,94; co-author: A Handbook of Critical Approaches to Literature, 1966, 5th edit., 2005; co-editor: The Letters of Jack London, 1988, The Complete Short Stories of Jack London, 1993; editor: Viking Portable Jack London, 1994. Fulbright prof., Denmark, 1973-74; named Jack London Man of Yr. Jack London Found., 1975, Humanist of Yr. La. Endowment for Humanities, 1991. Mem. MLA, Coll. English Assn. (editor 1967-75, pres. 1977-79, Disting. Svc. award 1983, Lifetime Membership award 1990), Internat. Assn. Univ. Profs. of English, Jack London Soc. (bd. dirs. 1990—), Nat. Assn. Scholars and Critics. Avocation: photography. Personal E-mail: elabor@centenary.edu.

LABORDE, ENRIQUE, retired communications engineer; b. Madrid, July 15, 1939; s. Francisco Laborde and Victoria Torrecilla; m. Clara Laborde; children: Enrique, Maria, Beatriz, Gonzalo, Ana. Ingenius Superior de Telecommunicacion, U. Madrid, Spain, 1966; MS in computer sys., U. Md., 1989. Tech. staff ITT Labs. of Spain, Madrid, 1966—72, asst. mgr. space divsn., 1972—74, mgr. transmission and space divsn., 1974—79, mgr. data comm. divsn., 1979—82; sr. sys. engr. Hughes Network Sys., Germantown, Md., 1982—88, adv. engr., 1988—95, chief scientist, 1995—2004; ret., 2004. Contbr. articles various profl. jours. Recipient Outstanding Achiev. award, Standards Com. Telecomm., 1997. Mem.: Inst. Electrical and Electronics Engrs. Democrat. Cath. E-mail: elaborde@comcast.net.

LABORE, BRIAN EDWARD, computer animator, artist; b. Nashua, NH, Sept. 20, 1975; s. Michael Raymond and Janet Labore; m. Heather Marie Parsons, Oct. 4, 2003. BA in Fine Art, Plymouth State Coll., NH, 1997; postgrad., Digipen Inst. Tech., Redmond, Wash., 1999—2000. Artist Nintendo Am., Redmond, EdMark Entertainment, Redmond; animation dir. Turbine Entertainment, Westwood, Mass., Blue Fang Entertainment, Waltham, Mass.; animation dir., lead artist Iron Lore Entertainment, Maynard, Mass.; sr. artist, animation dir. Green Monster Games, Maynard. The Special Frog, 1992, Snakes, Sharks and Dinos, 2006. Mem.: USA Triathlon, Mensa. Avocations: linguistics, sports, adventure racing, art, travel.

LABOW, THEODORE ALLAN, dermatologist, educator; b. New Haven, Conn., June 27, 1929; s. Rose Elaine and Aaron Labow; m. Joan Ruth Levy, June 20, 1954; children: Susan Bess Allen, Alaan Marc. BS, U. Miami, Coral Gables, 1951; MD, Tufts Med. Sch., Boston, 1955. Diplomate Am. Bd. Dermatology, 1961. Asst. clin. prof. dermatology Coll. Physicians & Surgeons, Columbia U., NYC, 1975—92. Surgeon US Pub. Health Svc., Staten Island, NY, 1955—61. Co-author: (text book) Common Skin Diseases, Diagnosis and Treatment. Fellow: Am. Acad. Dermatology (life). Home: 10 Jeanette Dr Massapequa NY 11758 Home Phone: 516-799-6160. Personal E-mail: smokeyiscat1@aol.com.

LABRECQUE, RICHARD JOSEPH, retired industrial executive; b. Lawrence, Mass., Dec. 19, 1938; s. Eugene N. and Ludivine M. (Roy) L.; m. Janet Marie Michaud, July 16, 1960; children: David R., Lisa M., Susan M. BSEE, Tufts U., 1962; MS in Indsl. Adminstrn., Union U., 1971. Mgr. mfg. engring. GE Aircraft Engine Group, Lynn, Mass., 1962-68; with Colt Industries, 1969-81; pres. FM Pump divsn., Kansas City, Kans., 1973-78, Quincy (Ill.) Compressor divsn., 1979-81; with ITT Industries, Inc., 1982-2000, pres. fluid handling divsn., 1982-95, sr. v.p., 1996-98; pres., CEO ITT Fluid Tech. Corp., Upper Saddle River, NJ, 1996-2000; exec. v.p. ITT Industries, 1998-2000, ret., 2000. Bd. dirs. Big Machines Inc., PeopleFlo Mfg. Inc. Campaign chmn. United Way Wyandotte County, Kansas City, 1979. Mem. Hydraulic Inst. (bd. dirs. 1976—, pres. 1979, 96, chmn. 1997), Oro Valley(Ariz.) Country Club (treas. 2002-03).

LABRUM, RONALD K., health facility administrator; Corp. v.p. Regional Cos./Health Systems Allegiance, 1987—2000; exec. v.p. Cardinal Health, Inc., 2000—04, group pres. med. products and svcs., 2000—04, chmn., CEO, 2004—. Office: Cardinal Health Inc 7000 Cardinal Pl Dublin OH 43017

LABRUYERE, THOMAS EDWARD, health facility administrator; b. St. Louis, Aug. 2, 1955; s. Thomas Edward and Daisy Lillian (Nussbaum) LaB.; m. Annette Sue Gusoskey, Oct. 27, 1979; children: Thomas Edward III, Christopher John, Sarah Elizabeth. AAS, Maryville Coll., 1979, BS in Mgmt. with honors, 1990; MBA, Maryville U., 1993. Registered respiratory therapist. Coord. insvc. edn. Normandy Hosp., St. Louis, 1977-79; mgr. dept. Lifemark Cardiopulmonary, Houston, 1979-81; from asst. supr. respiratory therapy to adminstrv. dir. St. Anthony's Med. Ctr., St. Louis, 1981-95, adminstrv. dir. Cardiopulmonary and Radiology, 1995—. Mem. respiratory care adv. com. Forest Park C.C., St. Louis, 1993—; bd. dirs. Nalco Credit Union, vice chmn., 1995—, mem. supervisory com., 1991-93. Asst. scoutmaster Boy Scouts Am., St. Louis, 1995-96, asst. cubmaster, 1993, 94, troop com. chmn., 1996—; coach CYC Baseball, St. Louis, 1993-96, CYC Soccer, 1993-97. Mem. Am. Coll. Healthcare Execs. (assoc.), Am. Coll. Cardiovascular Adminstrs., Am. Assn. Respiratory Care. Avocations: 2nd dan blackbelt tae kwon do (black belt), camping. Home: 3036 Armona Dr Saint Louis MO 63129-5202 Office: Saint Anthony's Med Ctr 10010 Kennerly Rd Saint Louis MO 63128-2106

LABUDDE, ROY CHRISTIAN, lawyer; b. Milw., July 21, 1921; s. Roy Lewis and Thea (Otteson) LaB.; m. Anne P. Held, June 7, 1952; children: Jack, Peter, Michael, Susan, Sarah. AB, Carleton Coll., 1943; JD, Harvard U., 1949. Bar: Wis. 1949, U.S. Dist. Ct. (ea. and we. dists.) Wis. 1950, U.S. Ct. Appeals (7th cir.) 1950, U.S. Supreme Ct. 1957. Assoc. Michael, Best & Friedrich, Milw., 1949-57, ptnr., 1958—. Dir. DEC-Inter, Inc., Milw. Western Bank, Western Bancshares, Inc., Superior Die Set Corp., Aunt Nellie's Farm Kitchens, Inc. Bd. dirs. Wis. Hist. Soc. Found.; chmn., bd. dirs. Milw. div. Am. Cancer Soc. Served to lt. j.g. USNR, 1943-46. Mem. Milw. Estate Planning Coun. (past pres.), Wis. Bar Assn., Wis. State Bar Attys. (chmn. tax sch., bd. dirs. taxation sect.), Univ. Club, Milw. Club, Milw. Country Club. Republican. Episcopalian. Home: 4201 W Stonefield Rd Mequon WI 53092-2771 Office: Michael Best & Friedrich 100 E Wisconsin Ave Ste 3300 Milwaukee WI 53202-4108

LABUNSKI, STEPHEN BRONISLAW, professional society administrator; b. Jordanow, Poland, Sept. 24, 1924; came to U.S., 1928, naturalized, 1943; s. Wiktor and Wanda (Mlynarski) L.; m. Betty E. Marley, Oct. 2, 1947 (div. June 1963); children: Linda, Richard, Roger; m. Jeralyn LeBrun, Aug. 28, 1967. Student, U. Kansas City, Mo., 1946-49, George Washington U., 1950. Adminstrv. asst. to U.S. Congressman Richard W. Bolling, 1949-51; with Storz Broadcasting Co., 1954-57; v.p. ABC radio network, 1957; head broadcast div. Crowell Collier Pub. Co., 1958; v.p., gen. mgr. WMCA Radio/Straus Broadcasting Group, NYC, 1958-65; pres. radio div.

NBC, 1965-69; mng. dir. WMCA Radio, 1969-71; v.p., partner Chuck Blore Creative Services, 1971-75; exec. v.p. Merv Griffin Group Radio, 1975-77; exec. dir. Internat. Radio and TV Soc., NYC, 1978-94, Circles Spl. Events, NYC, 1994-98; dir. spl. events Cahners Bus. Info., NYC, 1998—. Bd. dirs. Radio Advt. Bur., 1965-69, Nat. Assn. Broadcasters, 1965-67 Chmn. adv. com. Voice of Am., 1987-89; Democratic candidate for Mo. Legislature, 1948. With AUS and USAAF, 1943-46. Mem. Advt. Council. Home and Office: 30 E 37th St New York NY 10016-3019 Office Phone: 212-889-6716. Personal E-mail: sbl12a@aol.com.

LABUTTI, RONALD STEPHAN, orthopedist; b. Tacoma, Oct. 12, 1965; s. Ronald Justin and Judith Ann LaButti; m. Robin Michelle Ford, Sept. 2, 2001. BA in Psychology, Providence Coll., RI, 1987; DO, U. New England Coll. Osteopathic Medicine, Biddeford, Maine, 1994. Cert. Am. Osteo. Bd. of Orthop. Surgery. Intern, clin. instr., dept. internal medicine RI Hosp./Brown U., Providence, 1994—95; orthop. surgery resident Okla. State U. Coll. Osteo. Medicine, Tulsa, 1995—99, assoc. clin. prof., orthop. surgery, 2002—, asst. program dir. orthop. surgery residency program, 2003—; pediatric orthop. surgery rotation Shriners Hosp. for Children, Spokane, Wash., 1997—98; hip and knee reconstruction rotation U. Utah Med. Ctr., 1998; orthop. sports medicine rotation Detroit Med. Ctr./Hutzel Hosp., 1998; hand surgery rotation Detroit Med. Ctr./Harper Hosp., 1998; dept. orthop. surgery, lower extremity and joint reconstruction fellow Buffalo Gen. Hosp./SUNY, Buffalo, 1999—2000; pvt. practice Central States Orthop. Specialists, Inc, Tulsa, 2000—. Clin. instr. Okla. State U. Coll. Osteo. Medicine Western U. Health Scis., 1995—99; team physician Tulsa Pub. Schools, Tulsa, Okla., 1995—99, Internat. Profl. Rodeo Assn. Longhorn Rodeo, Tulsa, Okla., 1995—99, Cleve. Pub. Schools, Cleve., 1995—99, Tulsa Roughnecks Soccer Team, 1999; mem. orthop. peer review com. (rotating mem.) St. Francis Hosp., 2001—; mem. surgical morbidity and mortality com. Tulsa Regional Med. Ctr., 2000—; presenter in field. Contbr. articles various profl. jours. Physician for student history and phys. exams for athletic participation Cleve. Pub. Sch., Cleve., Okla., Holland,Hall Sch., Tulsa, Okla., Jenks Pub. Schools, Jenks, Okla.; lifetime mem. Osteo. Founders Found., Tulsa, 2003—04, chmn., Winterset Ball" Stepping Out 2004" Charity Ball, 2004; benefactor LaButti Scholarship for Academic Excellence, Okla. State U. Coll. Osteo. Medicine, 2001—; premier sponsor Tulsa Running Club, 2003—04. Named one of Am.'s Top Physicians, Consumers' Rsch. Coun. Am., 2004—05. Fellow: Am. Osteo. Acad. Orthop.; mem.: Tulsa Osteo. Med. Soc., Tulsa Orthop. Soc., Tulsa Orthop. Network, Tulsa County Med. Soc., Okla. Osteo. Assn., Am. Acad. Orthop. Surgeons, Am. Osteo. Acad. Orthop. Surgery (mem. newsletter com. 2003—), Am. Osteo. Assn. (Psi Sigma Alpha 1994), Psi Sigma Alpha. Achievements include being the first orthopedic surgeon in Tulsa to offer and perform ceramic-on-ceramic total hip replacement; the first orthopedic surgeon in Oklahoma to perform computer assisted total knee replacement. Avocations: fishing, hunting, playing the guitar. Office: Ctrl States Orthop Specialists Inc William Med Bldg 6585 S Yale Ste 200 Tulsa OK 74136 Office Phone: 918-481-2767. Office Fax: 918-481-7611. Personal E-mail: ronlabutti@cox.net.*

LABUZA, THEODORE PETER, food science educator; b. Perth Amboy, NJ, Nov. 10, 1940; s. Theodore and Catherine (Stycheck) L.; m. Mary K. Schmidl, Nov. 30, 1985; children: TJ, Peter, Katherine. BS, MIT, 1962, PhD, 1965. Asst. prof. MIT, Cambridge, 1965-69, assoc. prof., 1970-71, U. Minn., St. Paul, 1971-73, prof. food sci. and tech., 1973—, Morse Alumni disting. tchg. prof. food engring., 1983—, assoc. dean Grad. Sch. Mpls., 1993-96. Cons. to food industry; expert witness in field. Author: Shelf Life of Foods, 1983, Moisture Sorption, 1984, 2d edit., 2000, Food Science and Nutritional Health, 1985, Biotechnology of Food Processing, 1986; author: (with M. Schmidl) Functional Foods, 2000; author: others; contbr. more than 70 chpts. to books, more than 500 articles to trade and profl. jours.and another 100 tech. articles. Chmn. Com. on Interncollegiate Athletics, U. Minn., 1988-92. Named IFT Tanner lectr., 2007; named to Perth Amboy H.S. Hall of Fame, 1992; recipient DIFSA Food Engr. award, 1995, Acad. of Disting. Tchr., 1995, Coll. of Human Ecology Tchr. award, 2000, IFT Reister Davis award in food packaging, 2006, Harris award, Ohio State U., 2007, Fellow Internat. Union Food Sci. and Tech., Inst. Food Technologists (pres. 1988-90, Cruess award for tchg. 1970, S.C. Prescott Rsch. award 1973, Babcock Hart award 1988, Food Engr. award 1995, Nicholas Appert award 1998, Marcel Loncin Food Engr. Rsch. prize 1998; one of the most highly cited authors over the past 20 yrs. in agrl. and food sci.). Avocations: science fiction, computers, gardening. Home: 409 Vadnais Lake Dr Saint Paul MN 55127-7140 Office: Univ of Minn Dept Food Sci 1354 Eckles Ave Saint Paul MN 55108-1038 Office Phone: 612-624-9701. Business E-Mail: tplabuza@umn.edu.

LACAPRA, DOMINICK CHARLES, historian, educator; b. NYC, July 13, 1939; s. Joseph and Mildred Lacapra; m. Anne-Marie Hlasny, June 15, 1965 (div.); 1 dau., Veronique. BA, Cornell U., 1961; PhD, Harvard U., 1970. Tutor Harvard U., Cambridge, Mass., 1967-69; asst. prof. history Cornell U., Ithaca, NY, 1969-74, assoc. prof., 1974-79, prof. history, 1979—, Goldwin Smith prof. European intellectual history, 1985-92, Bryce and Edith M. Bowmar prof. humanistic studies, 1992—. Assoc. dir. Sch. of Criticism and Theory Cornell U., 1997-2000; dir. Sch. Criticism and Theory, 2000—. Author: Emile Durkheim, 1972, A Preface to Sartre, 1978, "Madame Bovary" on Trial, 1982, Rethinking Intellectual History, 1983, History and Criticism, 1985, History, Politics and the Novel, 1987, Soundings in Critical Theory, 1989, Representing the Holocaust, 1994, History and Memory after Auschwitz, 1998, History and Reading: Tocqueville, Foucault, French Studies, 2000, Writing History, Writing Trauma, 2001, History in Transit, 2004. Fulbright fellow France, 1961-62, Woodrow Wilson fellow Harvard U., 1962-63, sr. fellow NEH, 1979, Sch. Criticism and Theory; recipient Disting. Tchg. award Coll. Arts and Sci. Cornell U., 1979. Mem. MLA, Am. Hist. Assn., Internat. Assn. Philosophy and Lit., Soc. Phenomenological and Existential Philosophy, Am. Comparative Lit. Assn., Soc. for the Humanities (dir.1993-2003); fellow Am. Acad. Arts & Sciences Home: 624 Highland Rd Ithaca NY 14850 Office: Cornell U History Dept McGraw Hall Ithaca NY 14853 Business E-Mail: dominick.lacapra@cornell.edu.

LA CARNA, JOHN EDWARD, writer, social worker; b. Baton Rouge, May 5, 1936; s. James and Frances Jerome La Carna; m. Gustavia La Carna, Mar. 21, 1981. BA, La. State U., Baton Rouge, 1965, MSW, 1973. LCSW La. Probation officer EBR Family Ct., Baton Rouge, 1967—71; exec. dir. Capital Area Health Planning Coun., Baton Rouge, 1973—76; social worker Nicholls State U., Thiboreaux, La., 1976—79; clin. social worker State of La., 1979—88; pres. La Carna Health Care, Baton Rouge, 1988—2002; writer Baton Rouge, 2002—. Author: Build Your Vocabulary Skills, 2000. Mem.: Mensa. Avocation: chess. Home: 2100 College Dr Apt 142 Baton Rouge LA 70808-1809

LA CAVA, DONALD LEON, communications executive; b. Fair Lawn, NJ, July 11, 1928; s. Paul and Angela (Viviano) La C.; m. Mary A. Morrison (div. 1980); children: Anita, Mark, Brigid, Kevin, Christopher, Peter, David, Daniel. BA in English, UCLA, 1982. V.p. Batjac Prodns., Hollywood, Calif., 1956-69; pres. Markab Mgmt., Beverly Hills, Calif., 1969-73, Triton Prodns., Encino, Calif., 1973-86; v.p. Jet Charter Am., Inc., 1986-97; mng. dir. No. Global Fin. & Investment, Reno, Nev., 1997-98. V.p. Internat. Jet Airways, 1986—, LaCava Aviation, 1996—. Served to lt. USNR, 1951-63, Korea. Mem. Dirs. Guild Am. Avocation: aviation. Home: 4031 Coldwater Canyon Ave Studio City CA 91604

LACER, ALFRED ANTONIO, lawyer, educator; b. Hammonton, NJ, Feb. 14, 1952; s. Vincent and Carmen (Savall) Lacer; m. Kathleen Visser, June 15, 1974; children: Margaret, James, Matthew. BA in Polit. Sci., Gordon Coll., 1974; JD, Cath. U. Am., 1977. Law clk. to Honorable Joseph A. Mattingly, Sr. Cir. Ct. St. Mary's County, Leonardtown, Md., 1977-78; ptnr. Lacer, Sparling, Densford & Reynolds PA and predecessors, Lexington Park, Md., 1978-99; county atty. St. Mary's County, Md., 1999-2000, CEO, county adminstr. Md., 2000—03; atty. in pvt. practice, 2003—. Adj. prof. bus. law Fla. Inst. Tech., Patuxent, Md., 1989—92, 1995—99; vis. instr. St. Mary's Coll. Md., 1988, 91, 2004—; bd. dirs. Pro Bono Resource Ctr. Md., 2004—. Mem. inquiry panel Atty. Grievance Commn. Md., 1984—90; mem. bd. edn. St. Mary's County Pub. Schs., Md., 1989—94, pres. Md., 1991—92; bd. dirs. So. Md. Cmty. Action, Inc., Hughsville, 1982—84, St. Mary's County Tech. Coun., 1997—99, St. Mary's Hosp., Leonardtown, 1982—88, v.p., 1985—88. Excellence Local Governance fellow, U. Md., 2001. Fellow: Md. Bar Found.; mem.: ABA, St. Mary's County Bar Assn. (v.p. 1979—80, pres. 1980—81), Md. Bar Assn. (mem. com. jud. appointments 1982—85). Office Phone: 301-475-9600. Personal E-mail: al.lacer@alfredalacer.com.

LACEY, AARON MICHAEL, actor, director, film producer, scriptwriter; b. Washington, May 26, 1969; Advanced cert., Nat. Conservatory Drama Arts, 1993. CEO AML Productions, Washington, 1987—. Appearances include: (tv series) In Our Lives, 1987-94, (tv primetime spls.) Running Out of Time, 1989, Fatal Mix, 1990, (films) Major League II, 1993, Twelve Monkeys, 1995, Shadow Conspiracy, 1996; assoc. prodr., story writer, screenwriter, Edge, 1997; exec. prodr., story writer, screen writer, dir. Sync, 2000; screen plays include: (tv) (In Our Lives) Gangs, 1993, (films) Crimson Road, 1989, Cumulus Nine, 1990, Mind Walker, 1991. Supporter Anti Defamation League, People for Ethical Treatment of Animals, MADD, Wash. Regional Alcohol Program. Recipient Capital Region Emmy awards NATAS, 1991. Mem. Screen Actors Guild, Actors Equity Assn., Am. Fedn. TV Radio Artists. Avocation: karate (first-degree black belt). Home: 21034 Thoreau Ct Sterling VA 20164-2436 Personal E-mail: amlfilms@aol.com.

LACEY, CLOYD EUGENE, retired insurance company executive; b. New Lexington, Ohio, Mar. 12, 1918; s. Russell Anderson and Freda (Bahr) L.; m. Jane Linn Williams, Sept. 12, 1941; children: Thomas, Melinda Lacey Houfek, Janene Lacey Paulus. BS in Bus. Adminstrn., Ohio State U., 1941. Acct., asst. treas. Pioneer Mut. Causualty Co., Columbus, Ohio, 1945-51; various corp. fin. positions Nationwide Ins. Cos., Columbus, 1951-73, v.p., asst. controller, 1973-75, v.p., corp. controller, 1975-78, v.p. Office of Treas., controller, 1978-81, sr. v.p. fin., 1981-82, ret., 1982. Served with U.S. Army, 1943-45. Republican. Methodist. *I believe in God and put my trust in him. I believe in treating other people fairly and in giving them credit for accomplishments. I believe in maintaining a high degree of integrity. I believe in diligence and determination in performing a task. I believe in striving for excellence.*

LACEY, DAVID, biotechnology company executive; BS in Biology, U. Colo., Boulder, MD. Postgraduate rsch. assoc. dept. pathology U. Colo.; asst. prof. pathology Jewish Hosp., Washington U. Med. Ctr.; assoc. med. dir. dept. exptl. pathology Amgen, Inc., 1994, dir. pathology, sr. v.p., head rsch., 2007—, South San Francisco site leader. Mem.: Phi Beta Kappa. Office: Amgen Inc 1120 Veterans Blvd South San Francisco CA 94080 Office Phone: 650-244-2000. Office Fax: 650-837-9421.*

LACEY, PEELER GRAYSON, diagnostic radiologist; b. Kosciusko, Miss., June 16, 1954; s. Dick Grayson and Beatrice (Peeler) L.; m. Holley Anne Westbrook, July 8, 1978; children: Peeler Grayson Jr., Lauren Elizabeth. BA in Chemistry, Emory U., 1975; MD, U. Miss., 1979. Diplomate Am. Bd. Radiology. Intern U. Miss Med. Ctr., Jackson, 1979-80, resident in diagnostic radiology, 1980-83; diagnostic radiologist South Cen. Regional Med. Ctr., Laurel, Miss., 1983—, Jasper Gen. Hosp., Bay Springs, Miss., 1983—. V.p., ptnr. Radiology Assocs., Laurel, 1983— Past asst. scoutmaster Troop 32, exec. bd. mem. Pine Burr Area coun. Boy Scouts Am.; chmn. Chickasawhay dist. Boy Scouts Am.; Sun. sch. tchr., deacon. First Bapt. Ch., Laurel. Named one of Outstanding Young Men of Am., 1987; recipient Silver Beaver award Boy Scouts Am. Mem. AMA, NRA (life), Radiol. Soc. N.Am., So. Radiology Soc., Am. Coll. Radiology, Am. Heart Assn., Miss. State Med. Assn., Miss. Radiol. Soc., South Miss. Med. Soc. (pres. 1992), South Cen. Regional Med. Ctr. (pres. 1994), Roentgen Ray Soc., Miss. Bowhunters Assn. (life), Found. N.Am. Wild Sheep, Nat. Eagle Scout Assn. (life, past chmn. Pine Burr area coun.), Cum Laude Soc., Safari Club Internat. (life), Boone and Crockett Club (life assoc.), FND NA. Wild Sheep (life), Grand Slam club, Sigma Chi (life loyal Sig.). Avocations: hunting, fishing, reading. Home: 2432 Ridgewood Dr Laurel MS 39440-2147 Office: Radiology Assocs 235 S 12th Ave # 2427 Laurel MS 39440-4324

LACEY, TRUDI, professional athletics coach; Grad., N.C. State U., 1981. Asst. coach Manhattan Coll., 1981, James Madison Coll., 1982, N.C. State U., 1983—84; head coach Francis Marion Coll., SC, 1987—88, U. South Fla., 1989—96; asst. coach U. Md., 1996—97; asst. dir. women's program USA Basketball, 1997—2003; head coach, asst. gen. mgr. Charlotte Sting, NC, 2003—. Mem. women's player selection com. USA Basketball, 1993—96; asst. coach R. William Jones Cub team, 1995, Olympic Festival East team, 1994; participant USA Select Team, 1978, World U. Games team, 1981, USA Nat. eam, 1982, USA World U. Games Team, 1983; profl. player, Italy, 1985—87; founding pres. Life Coach Designs, LLC; analyst ESPN, FoxSportsNet. Named Sun Belt Conf. Coach of the Yr., 1989; recipient All-ACC honoree.

LACH, ALMA ELIZABETH, food and cooking writer, consultant; b. Petersburg, Ill. d. John H. and Clara E. Satorius; m. Donald F. Lach; 1 child, Sandra Judith. Diplome de Cordon Bleu, Paris, 1956. Feature writer Children's Activities mag., 1954-55; creator, performer childrens cooking TV show Let's Cook, 1955; food editor Chgo. Daily Sun-Times, 1957-65; hostess weekly food program on CBS, 1962-66; pres. Alma Lach Kitchens, Inc., Chgo., 1966—; performer TV show Over Easy, PBS, 1977-78. Dir. Alma Lach Cooking Sch., Chgo.; lectr. U. Chgo. Downtown Coll., Gourmet Inst., U. Md., 1963, Modesto (Calif.) Coll., 1978, U. Chgo., 1981; resident master Shoreland Hall, U. Chgo., 1978-81; food cons. Food Bus. Mag., 1964-66, Chgo.'s New Pump Room, Lettuce Entertain You, Bitter End Resort, Brit. V.I., Midway Airlines, Flying Food Fare, Inc., Berghoff Restaurant, Hans' Bavarian Lodge, Unocal '76, Univ. Club Chgo. Author: A Child's First Cookbook, 1950, The Campbell Kids at Home, 1953, Let's Cook, 1956, Candlelight Cookbook, 1959, Cooking a la Cordon Bleu, 1970, Alma's Almanac, 1972, Hows and Whys of French Cooking, 1974, reprint, 1998; contbr. to World Book Yearbook, 1961-75, Grolier Soc. Yearbook, 1962; columnist Modern Packaging, 1967-68, Travel & Camera, 1969, Venture, 1970, Chicago mag., 1978, Bon Appetit, 1980, Tribune Syndicate, 1982; inventor: Curly-Dog Cutting Bd., 1995, Alma's Walker Tray, 1996; one woman show: 50 pixellist art pictures, 1999, Tavern Club, Chgo., 2002-2004. Recipient Pillsbury award, 1958, Grocery Mfrs. Am. Trophy award, 1959, certificate of Honor, 1961, Chevalier du Tastevin, 1962, Commanderie de l'Ordre des Anysetiers du Roy, 1963, Confrerie de la Chaine des Rotisseurs, 1964, Les Dames D'Escoffier, 1982, Culinary Historians of Chgo., 1993, Lifetime Achievement award Les Dames D'Escoffier, 2007. Mem. Am. Assn. Food Editors (chmn. 1959), Tavern Club, Quadrangle Club (Chgo.). Home and Office: 5750 S Kenwood Ave Chicago IL 60637-1744 Office Phone: 773-684-4906. Fax: 773-363-2875. Personal E-mail: alma@almalach.com. *The art of cooking rests upon one's ability to taste, to reproduce taste, and to create taste. To achieve distinction the cook must taste everything, study cookbooks of all kinds, and experiment constantly in the kitchen. I stress in my writing and teaching the logic of food preparation, for the cook who possesses logic, knows how to create dishes rather than being content merely to duplicate the recipes of others.*

LACHANCE, JANICE RACHEL, professional association and federal agency administrator, lawyer; b. Biddeford, Maine, June 17, 1953; d. Ralph L. and Rachel A. (Desnoyers) L. BA, Manhattanville Coll., 1974; JD, Tulane U., 1978. Bar: Maine 1978, D.C. 1982, U.S. Supreme Ct. 1999. Staff dir. subcom. on antitrust Ho. of Reps., Washington, 1982-83; adminstrv. asst. Congresswoman Katie Hall, 1983-84; asst. pres. sec. Mondale-Ferraro Campaign, Washington, 1984; press sec. Congressman Tom Daschle, 1985; ptnr. Lachance and Assocs., Washington, 1985-87; dir. communications and polit. action Am. Fedn. Govt. Employees (AFL-CIO), Washington, 1987-93; dir. policy and communications U.S. Office Pers. Mgmt., Washington, 1993-96, chief of staff, 1996-97, dep. dir., 1997, dir., 1997—2001; mgmt. consultant Analytica Inc., Alexandria, Va., 2001; exec. dir. Spl. Librs. Assn. (SLA), Washington, 2003, now CEO. Vis. scholar Cornell U., 1972-73. Editor newsletter Govt. Standard, 1987-93. Mem. Delta Delta Delta, Phi Alpha Delta; fellow Nat. Acad. Pub. Admin. Democrat. Roman Catholic. Office: Spl Libraries Assn 331 South Patrick St Alexandria VA 22314 Office Phone: 703-647-4933. E-mail: janice@sla.org.

LACHANCE, PAUL ALBERT, food science educator, clergyman; b. St. Johnsbury, Vt., June 5, 1933; s. Raymond John and Lucienne (Landry) Lachance; m. Therese Cecile Cote; children: Michael P, Peter A, M-Andre, Susan A. BS, St. Michael's Coll., 1955; postgrad., U. Vt., 1955-57; PhD, U. Ottawa, 1960; cert. in pastoral counseling, N.Y. Theol. Sem., 1981; DSc (hon.), St. Michael's Coll., 1982. Diplomate Am. Assn. Integrative Medicine, 2005; ordained deacon Roman Cath. Ch., 1977. Assigned to St. Paul's Ch., Princeton, NJ; aerospace biologist Aeromed. Research Labs., Wright-Patterson AFB, Ohio, 1960-63; lectr. dept. biology U. Dayton, Ohio, 1963; flight food and nutrition coordinator NASA Manned Spacecraft Center, Houston, 1963-67; assoc. prof. dept. food sci. Rutgers U., New Brunswick, NJ, 1967-72, dir. Sch. Feeding effectiveness research project, 1969-72, prof., 1972—2004, prof. emeritus, 2005—, faculty rep. to bd. trustees, 1988-90, dir. grad. program food sci., 1988-91, chmn. food sci. dept., 1991-97, chmn. univ. senate, 1990-93, faculty rep. to bd. govs., 1990-94, dir. The Nutraceuticals Inst., 1989—2007. Mem. religious ministry com. Princeton Health Care Sys., 1968—, on-call chaplain, 1968—; mem nutrition adv comt Whitehall-Robins/Centrum Consumer div, 1989—2000; mem sci adv bd Roche chem div Hoffmann La Roche Co, 1976—88; mem nutrition policy comt Beatrice Food Co, 1979—86; trustee religious ministries com. Princeton Med Ctr; mem. Cert. Bd. Nutritional Scis.; bd dirs J R Short Milling Co; cons. Nutritional Aspects Food Processing, Nutraceuticals. Mem. editl. adv. bd.: Nutrition Reports Internat., 1963—83, Sch. Food Svc. Rsch. Rev., 1977—82, Profl. Nutritionist, 1977—80, mem. editl. adv bd.: Jour. Med. Consultation, 1985—2002, Jour. Medicinal Foods, 1998—, Food and Chem. Toxicology, 2000—07, Jour. Nutraceuticals Functional & Health Foods, 2000—05; contbr. articles to profl. jours. Served to capt USAF, 1960—63. Named to Academic Hall of Fame, St. Michael's Coll., 2002; recipient Endel Karmas award for excellence in tchg. food sci., 1988. Fellow: Am. Assn. Integrative Medicine, Am. Soc. Nutritional Sci., Am. Coll. Nutrition, Inst. Food Technologists (William Cruess award for excellence in tchg. 1991, Babcock-Hart award 2001); mem.: APHA, AAAS, Soc. Free Radical Biology and Medicine, Nat. Assn. Cath. Chaplains, Soc. Nutrition Edn., Am. Dietetic Assn., N.Y. Acad. Sci., Am. Soc. Clin. Nutrition, N.Y. Inst. Food Technologists (chmn 1977—78), Am. Assn. Cereal Chemists, Sigma Xi, Delta Epsilon Sigma. Home: 34 Taylor Rd Princeton NJ 08540-9521 Office: Rutgers U Food Sci 65 Dudley Rd New Brunswick NJ 08901-8520 Office Phone: 732-932-9611 ext. 243. Business E-Mail: lachance@aesop.rutgers.edu.

LACHANZE, (R. LACHANZE SAPP, RHONDA SAPP), actress; b. St. Augustine, Fla. m. Calvin Gooding (dec. Sept. 11, 2001); children: Celia, Zaya; m. Derek Fordjour, July 2005. BA in Theatre & Dance, U. Arts, Phila. Actress (Broadway plays) Uptown...It's Hot, 1986, Dreamgirls, 1987, Once on This Island, 1990—91 (Theatre World award, 1991, Tony award nominee, best featured actress in musical, 1991), Ragtime, 1999, Dessa Rosa, 2005, The Color Purple, 2005 (Tony award, best performance by leading actress in a musical, 2006), (plays) Playhouse, 1992, Hercules, Out of This World, Jesus Christ Superstar, 1991, Company, 1995, The Bubbly Black Girl Sheds Her Chameleon Skin, Funny Girl, 2002, Baby, 2004. Mailing: c/o Barbara Lawrence 19264 Pacific Coast Hwy Malibu CA 90265 Business E-Mail: lachanze@lachanze.com.

LACHAPELLE, CLEO EDWARD, retired social worker, real estate broker; s. Wilfrid M. and Alice (Michaud) L.; m. Ann Wilcox, July 17, 1954; children: Linda, Susan. BA in Sociology, St. Bonaventure U., NY, 1950. Real estate broker, R.I.; lic. clin. social worker, 1962-97. Probation officer R.I. Dept. Social Welfare, Cranston, 1951—53; prevention coord. R.I. Juvenile and Family Cts., Providence, 1953—63; asst. dir. Providence Youth Progress Bd., Inc., 1963—64, exec. dir., 1965—67, Progress for Providence, Inc., 1967—70; adminstr. Marathon House, Inc., Providence, 1970—77; dir. Washingtonian Hosp. and Ctr. for Addictions, Boston, 1977—80; state refugee coord. R.I. Office Refugee Resettlement, Cranston, 1980—85; broker, owner C.E. Lachapelle Real Estate Agy., Warwick, 1986—2004. Organizer, advisor Roger Williams Parent's Assn., 1954-62; organizer, chair So. Providence Youth Bd., 1961-64, supr. SPYB Brown U. Youth Guidance Student Mentors, 1961-64, Miami U. and Nat. Inst. Mental Health Southeast Drug Abuse Tng. Ctr., Coral Gables, Fla., 1972, ret. social svcs. cons. VA Hosp., 1971-72, Nat. Ctr. Urban Ethnic Affairs, Washington, 1974-76, City of Providence, 1976-77, HHS, 1985, NIMH, 1985, and others; part-time detached youth worker Providence Recreation Dept., 1953-63; mem. mayor's adv. bd. City of Providence Model Cities Program, 1968-70; mem. adv. panel Nat. Inst. Drug Abuse, Rockville, Md., 1978; mem. Harvard Sch. Public Health Cmty. Diagnostic Workshop, 1979-80; chair gov.'s study com. spl. needs population State of R.I., 1982-85; chair refugee policy Northea. Regional Consultations, Boston, 1983; active U.S. Refugee Coords. Policy Adv. Group, Washington, 1983, guest lectr. univs., profl. orgn. and cmty. interest groups 1954—, and others Sgt. USAF. Named to Athletic Hall of Fame, West Warwick HS, 1997. Mem. Audubon Soc. (life). Roman Catholic. Avocations: reading, golf.

LACHEY, NICK (NICHOLAS SCOTT LACHEY), singer, actor; b. Harian, Ky., Nov. 9, 1973; s. John and Cate (Fopma-Leimbach) Lachey; m. Jessica Simpson, Oct. 26, 2002 (div. July 2006). Attended, Creative and Performing Arts, Cin., Ohio; studied acting, U. So. Calif., LA, Calif.; studied sports medicine, Miami U., Oxford, Ohio. Co-owner Tacoma Rainier's AAA Baseball Affiliate, 2006—. Singer (with 98 Degrees): (albums) 98°, 1997, 98° and Rising, 1998, This Christmas, 1999, Revelation, 2000; singer: (solo albums) SoulO, 2003, What's Left of Me, 2006 (Music-Choice Love Song and Choice Red Carpet Fashion Icon (Male), Teen Choice Awards, 2006); actor: (TV series) Newlyweds: Nick and Jessica, 2003—05, (TV) Nick & Jessica's Variety Hour, 2004, Nick & Jessica's Family Christmas, 2004, Nick & Jessica's Tour of Duty, 2005, Bewitched, 2005; guest appearances City Guys, 1998, As The World Turns, 1999, Mad TV, 2000, 2004, Just Shoot Me!, 2000, The Apprentice, 2004, Charmed (6 episodes), 2004, Hope & Faith, 2004. Mem.: Sigma Alpha Epsilon Fraternity.*

LACHIEWICZ, PAUL FRANCIS, orthopedist, surgeon, educator; b. NYC, July 16, 1951; s. Frank and Helen L.; m. Ava Maria Staler, June 24, 1977; children: Jayne, Anne, Mark, John, Mary Claire. BS, Manhattan Coll., 1973; MD, Cornell Univ., 1977. Intern, then resident U. Minn.

Hosps., 1977-79; resident in orthopaedics Hosp. For Spl. Surgery, NYC, 1979-82; prof. orthopaedics U. N.C., Chapel Hill, 1983—. Recipient Phillip D. Wilson award Hosp. for Special Surgery, N.Y.C., 1983. Fellow Am. Acad. Orthopaedic Surgeons; mem. Hip Soc., Knee Soc., So. Orthopaedic Assn. Avocations: running, skiing. Office: Univ NC CB 7055 Dept Orthopaedics Chapel Hill NC 27599-7055

LACHMAN, LEIGH JAY, plastic surgeon, educator; b. 1953; BA, SUNY, Buffalo, NY, 1974, MD, 1978. Cert. Am. Bd. Otolaryngology, Am. Bd. Plastic and Reconstructive Surgery. Intern, surgery Georgetown Med. Ctr., 1978—79; resident, otolaryngology Bellevue Med. Ctr., 1979—82; resident, plastic and reconstructive surgery St. Luke's Roosevelt Hosp., 1982—84; clin. asst. prof., dept. otolaryngology NY Eye, Ear Infirmary, attending physician, dept otolaryngology; solo practice NJ. Treated many youth NJ Devils players. Mem.: Am. Soc. Plastic and Reconstructive Surgeons, Am. Acad. Otolaryngology, NY State Med. Soc. Office: NY Eye & Ear Infirmary 307 E 49th St New York NY 10017 also: 22 Old Short Hills Rd # 108 Livingston NJ 07039-5605 Office Phone: 212-752-7171.*

LACHMAN, MARGUERITE LEANNE, real estate investment advisor; b. Vancouver, BC, Can., Mar. 16, 1943; came to U.S., 1955; d. Wilfred Harry and Claire Elisha (Silverthorn) L. BA, U. So. Calif., 1964; MA, Claremont U., 1966. With Real Estate Rsch. Corp., 1965-87, sr. v.p., 1977-79, pres., CEO, 1979-87; mng. dir. Schroder Real Estate Assocs., 1987-99, Schroder Mortgage Assocs., 1992-98; prin. Lend Lease Real Estate Investments, 1999—2003; pres. Lachman Assoc., 2003—. Bd. dirs. Lincoln Nat. Corp., Liberty Property Trust; frequent lectr. seminars and profl. groups; exec.-in-residence Columbia Bus. Sch., 2000—. Author: (with Al Smith and Anthony Downs) Achieving Effective Desegregation, 1973, (with Susan Olson) Tax Delinquency in the Inner City, 1976, Emerging Trends in Real Estate, 1981, 82, 83, 84, 85, 86, 87, Decade to Decade, 1988, A Nation of Niches: Real Estate's Demand Demographics, 2002, Homeownership: Too Much of A Good Thing? 2003, The New Exports: Office Jobs, 2004, Global Demographics and Their Real Estate Investment Implicaitons, 2006; contbr. articles to profl. jours. Gov. Urban Land Found. Mem. Urban Land Inst., WX-N.Y. Office: Ste 19E 870 United Nations Plaza New York NY 10017 E-mail: lachmanassoc@aol.com.

LACHMANN, ELISABETH AMANDA, physician; b. Middletown, NY, Sept. 12, 1961; d. Erich Frederick and Christa Luise Lachmann; m. Kevin Charles Hunt, July 11, 1992; children: Lars Christian Hunt, Elisabeth Alexandra Hunt. AB, Bryn Mawr Coll., 1983; MD, Med. Coll. Pa., 1987. Intern internal medicine North Shore U. Hosp., Manhasset, NY, 1987—88; resident phys. medicine and rehab. N.Y. Hosp.-Cornell Med. Ctr., 1988—91; attending physiatrist N.Y. Presbyn. Hosp., 1991—, assoc. attending physiatrist, 1999—; assoc. prof. Weill Med. Coll. Cornell U., NYC, 1991—2001, clin. assoc. prof., 2001—; pvt. practice, 2001—. Program dir. Dept. Rehab. Medicine N.Y. Presbyn. Hosp., 1991-99, quality assurance rep., 1991-2001; advisor Weill Med. Coll. of Cornell U., 1995—. Author: (with others) Clinical Oncology, 1995, 00, Principles/Practice Supportive Oncology, 1998, 2001, Physical Medicine and Rehabiliation, The Complete Approach, 1999. Recipient Conrad Jobst Found award Am. Congress of Rehab. Medicine, 1990. Mem. AMA, Am. Acad. of Phys. Medicine and Rehab. (mem. spl. interest group cancer rehab.), Office of Women in Medicine (sr. advisor). Republican. Lutheran. Home: 17 Hungerford Rd Briarcliff Manor NY 10510-1308 Office: 115 E 64st St 1st Fl New York NY 10021 Office Phone: 212-535-3005.

LĀCIS, ARIS, health facility administrator, cardiac surgeon; b. Jelgava, Latvia, Aug. 1, 1936; s. Teodor and Zelma (Gedrovics) L.; m. Aija Ozolina, Sept. 8, 1958; children: Aigars, Andis. MD, Riga Med. Inst., Latvia, 1961. Resident gen. surgery Jelgava (Latvia) Gen. Hosp., 1961-62; resident thoracic surgery P. Stradina Clin. Hosp., Riga, Latvia, 1962-64; surgeon The Latvian Ctr. Pulmonary Surgery, Riga, 1964-69; asst. prof., chief surgeon Clinic Gen. and Cardiovascular Surgery, Riga Med. Inst., Riga, 1969-94; prof., head Latvian State Cardiology Ctr. Children, Riga, 1994—; head Clinic for Children's Cardiology, Latvian Med. Acad., Riga. Spl. editl. cons. Latvian Med. Acad., Riga, 1990—; dep. dirs. gen. JBC, 1997—. Contbr. articles to med. jours., chpts. to books; author 3 monographs; editl. bd. Latvian Pediat., Latvian Surgeon. Named Officier of the Three Star Order, 2001; recipient Bronze medal in Sci., Soviet Union Ctrl. Exhibn. for Scientific Achievement, 1977, Commemorative medal Man of the Yr., Am. Biographical Inst., 1995. Mem. The World Med. Assn. (assoc.), European Soc. Cardiology, Riga Hansa Rotary Club (pres. 1998-99), Internat. Soc. Cardiovascular Surgery, Assn. for European Paediatric Cardiology (nat. del.). Lutheran. Avocation: swimming. Home: Raunas str 45/3-108 1084 Riga Latvia Office: Cardiology Ctr for Children Juglas str 20 1079 Riga Latvia Home Phone: 371-7565227; Office Phone: 371-7536187. Business E-Mail: lacis@bsg.lv.

LACITIS, ERIK, journalist; b. Buenos Aires, Dec. 10, 1949; came to U.S., 1960, naturalized, 1965; s. Erik and Irene Z. L.; m. Malorie Nelson, Aug. 30, 1976. Student, Coll. Forest Resources, U. Wash., 1967-71. Editor U. Wash. Daily, 1970; pub. New Times Jour., 1970-71; reporter, pop-music cons. Seattle Post Intelligencer, 1972—; reporter, columnist Seattle Times, 1974—; v.p., treas. Malorie Nelson, Inc., 1980—; cons. editor Malheur Enterprise, 2006—. Bd. mem. Wash. News Coun., 2005. Recipient numerous awards from Wash. State chpt. Sigma Delta Chi; Nat. Headliners Club award, 1978; winner gen. interest competition Nat. Soc. Newspaper Columnists, 1987, 2003, Best of the West Journalism contest, 2000. Lutheran. Office: Fairview Ave N And John St PO Box 7070 Seattle WA 98133-2070 E-mail: lacitis@prodigy.net.

LACK, ANDREW R., music company executive; b. NYC, May 16, 1947; m. Betsy Kenny; children: Andrew, Sam. BFA, Boston U., 1968. Sr. exec. prodr. CBS Reports, 1978—85; exec. v.p. West 57th, 1985—89; pres. NBC News, 1993—2001; pres., COO NBC, Inc., 2001—03; chmn., CEO Sony Music Entertainment, 2003—04; CEO Sony BMG Music Entertainment, 2004—06, chmn., 2006—. Office: Sony BMG Music Entertainment 550 Madison Ave New York NY 10022

LACK, ROBERT JOEL, lawyer; b. Glen Ridge, NJ, Mar. 7, 1955; s. Walter and Carolyn Lack; m. Colleen Phyllis Kelly, June 9, 1979; children: Kelly Ann, Jonathan Andrew. AB, Princeton U., 1977, M in Pub. Affairs, 1978; JD, Harvard U., 1981. Bar: N.Y. 1982, N.J. 1990, U.S. Dist. Ct. (so. and ea. dist.) N.Y. 1982, U.S. Ct. Appeals (3d cir.) 1982, U.S. Ct. Appeals (1st cir.) 1984, U.S. Ct. Appeals (2d cir.) 1985, U.S. Supreme Ct. 1986, U.S. Ct. Appeals (7th cir.) 1987, U.S. Ct. Appeals (D.C. and 9th cirs.) 1988, U.S. Dist. Ct. (no. dist.) Calif. 1988, U.S. Dist. Ct. N.J. 1991. Law clk. to judge U.S. Ct. Appeals (3d cir.), Newark, 1981-82; assoc. Sullivan & Cromwell, NYC, 1982-90; ptnr. Friedman Kaplan Seiler & Adelman LLP, NYC, 1991—. Editor Harvard Law Rev. 1979-81. Recipient Whitney North Seymour medal Columbia U. Law Sch., 1981. Mem. ABA, N.Y. State Bar Assn. (mem. com. on civil rights 1984-90, mem. securities litigation com. 1998—), N.Y.C. Bar Assn. (sec. com. on lectures and continuing edn. 1984-86, mem. com. on antitrust and trade regulation 1991-94, mem. com. on fed. cts. 1998-2001), Fed. Bar Coun. Office: Friedman Kaplan Seiler & Adelman LLP 1633 Broadway New York NY 10019-6708 Office Phone: 212-833-1108.

LACKENMIER, JAMES RICHARD, academic administrator, priest; b. Lackawanna, NY, May 15, 1938; s. Harold and Margaret (Murphy) L. AB, Stonehill Coll., 1961; STL, Pontifical Gregorian U., Rome, 1965; AM, U.N.C., 1968; MA, U. Chgo., 1970. Ordained priest, Roman Catholic Ch. Tchr. English Notre Dame High Sch., Bridgeport, Conn., 1965-66, St. Peter's High Sch., Gloucester, Mass., 1966-68; chaplain St. Xavier Coll., Chgo., 1969-71; dir. collegiate formation Moreau Sem., Notre Dame, Ind., 1971-73; dir. campus ministry King's Coll., Wilkes-Barre, Pa., 1974-75, dir. devel., 1975-81, pres., 1981-99. Program dir. U. Portland Ctr., Salzburg, Austria, 1999-2001; treas. Congregaton of Holy Cross, Eastern Province, 2000—. Bd. regents U. Portland, 1993-99, 02—; bd. trustees Mercy Hosp., 1989-95; bd. dirs. Pa. Ednl. Telecom. Exch. Network, 1994-99, Com. on Econ. Growth, Earth Conservancy, 1992-99, Pa. Ind. Coll. and Univ. Rsch. Ctr., 1995-99, Ctr. Agile Pa. Edn., 1994-99, Greater Wilkes-Barre Partnership, Inc.; mem. United Way Campaign Cabinet, 1995-99; adv. bd. Pa. Mountains coun. Boy Scouts Am., Tuition Acct. Program, Office of Gov., Commonwealth Pa., 1992-96, 97-99; chmn. United Way Wyoming Valley, 1986; corp. mem. Holy Cross Family Ministries, bd. dirs., 2001—; bd. dirs. Pius XII Youth and Family Svcs., 2001-07. Mem. Rotary Internat. Lodges: Rotary Internat.; K.C. Democrat.

LACKER, JEFFREY MALCOLM, bank executive, economist; b. Lexington, Ky., Sept. 27, 1955; s. William Ralph and Marion (Spears) L.; m. Lisa Joy Halberstadt, June 7, 1981; children: Benjamin S.H., Daniel H. BA, Franklin and Marshall Coll., Lancaster, PA, 1977; PhD, U. Wis., Madison, 1984. Rsch. assoc. Wharton Econometric Forecasting Assocs., Phila., 1977-80; instr. Wardlaw-Hartridge Sch., Plainfield, NJ, 1978-79; asst. prof. Purdue U., Lafayette, Ind., 1984-89; rsch. economist Fed. Res. Bank Richmond, 1989-90, assoc. rsch. officer, 1991-93, rsch. officer, 1994-96, v.p., 1996-99, sr. v.p., dir. rsch., 1999—2004, pres., 2004—. Contbr. articles to profl. jours. Pres. Congregation Or Ami, Richmond, 1995-97; mem. adv. coun. Maggie L. Walker Gov. Sch.; mem. adv. bd. Jr. Achievement Ctrl. Va.; dir. World Affairs Coun. Gr. Richmond; bd. dirs. Richmond Jewish Found. Mem. Am. Econ. Assn., Richmond Assn. Bus. Economists. Avocation: backpacking. Office: Fed Res Bank 701 E Byrd St Richmond VA 23219 Office Phone: 804-697-8000.*

LACKEY, JOHN DERRAN, professional baseball player; b. Abilene, Tex., Oct. 23, 1978; Student, U. Tex., 1998, Grayson County Coll., Denison, Tex., 1999. Draft pick LA Angels of Anaheim (formerly Anaheim Angels), 1999, pitcher, 2002—. Named to Am. League All-Star Team, 2007. Achievements include leading the Am. League in shutouts (2), 2003, 06. Mailing: LA Angels of Anaheim 2000 Gene Autry Way Anaheim CA 92806*

LACKEY, KAYLE DIANN, elementary school educator; b. Willard, Ill., Oct. 22, 1937; d. Lon Edward and Eldora Grace (Pecord) Ogborn; m. Joseph Donald Lackey, Nov. 29, 1958 (dec. Feb. 10, 2006); 1 child, Dana Lyn Embree. BA in History, Asbury Coll., Wilmore, Ky., 1958; MA with honors, Webster U., 1975, cert. reading specialist, 1977; cert. gifted and talented educator, So. Ill. U., Edwardsville, 1990. Cert. elem. edn. Ill., pub. sch. tchr. Mo., reading specialist Mo., registered profl. real estate salesperson Mo. Tchr. kindergarten Dist. # 196, Dupo, Ill., 1959—63, reading specialist, 1973—79, tchr. 2d grade, 1979—84, tchr. 4th grade, 1985—93, tchr. gifted and talented, 1990—92; tchr. 1st grade Mehlville R-9 Dist., St. Louis, 1963—65, substitute tchr., 1965—72, 1993—. Clin. coop. tchr. So. Ill. U., Edwardsville, 1989; salesperson Coldwell Banker Real Estate, St. Louis, 1985—2000. Rep. for tchrs. Am. Fedn. Tchrs., Dupo, 1975—77, mem. negotiation com., 1981; tchr. U.S. divsn. Laubach Lit. Internat., St. Louis, 1987—89; author, tchr. gifted and talented enrichment summer program, 1991; participant travel seminary near eastern studies Asbury Coll., 1985; rep. ecumenical com. Cmty. Resource Svcs., 1986—89, trustee, 2000—02; active Ill. Tchrs. Retirement Sys., 1993—; vol. Am. Cancer Soc., 2000, 2004; active Gephardt for Congress, St. Louis, 1993—95; chmn. bd. edn. preschool Zion United Meth., St. Louis, 1987—88, 2000—02, trustee, 1986—90, adminstrv. bd. religion and race, ch. and soc., 1989—93, fin. sec., 1999, bd. dirs., 2000; active Met. Congregations United St. Louis, 2001—05. Named Senatorial Inner Cir. honoree, Mo., 2005, 2006; recipient Appreciation for Tchg. Excellence award, Bd. Edn. Dupo, 1993, award of Excellence, Ill. Math. and Sci. Acad., 1999. Mem.: St. Louis Art Mus., Mo. Bot. Soc., St. Louis Zoo Soc. Avocations: piano, travel, writing, reading, political campaign volunteerism. Home: 6511 Towne Woods Dr Saint Louis MO 63129-4521

LACKEY, MICHAEL E., JR., lawyer, educator; b. Hopkinsville, Ky., May 3, 1961; s. Michael E. Lackey, Sr. and Linda L. Sterling; m. Cynthia L. Sheppard, May 23, 1987; children: Michael E. III, Ashleigh L. BS in Aero. and Astronautical Engring., MIT, 1983; JD with high honors, George Washington U., 1993. Bar: Fla. 1993, DC 1994, U.S. Supreme Ct. 1999. Assoc. atty. Arnold & Porter, Washington, 1993—94, Mayer, Brown & Platt, Washington, 1995—97, 1998—2001; law clk. to Hon. Jacques L. Wiener U.S. Ct. Appeals, Shreveport, La., 1994—95; assoc. ind. counsel Office David Barrett Ind. Counsel, Washington, 1997—98; ptnr. Mayer, Brown, Rowe & Maw LLP, Washington, 2002—. Adj. prof. George Washington U. Law Sch., Washington, 1995—. Contbr. articles to profl. jours.; guest commentator (TV series) Supreme Court Watch with Fred Graham. Lt., naval aviator USN, 1983—90. Named Top Gun, USN, 1987; Nat. Merit scholar. Mem.: Fed. Bar Assn. (chmn. antitrust and trade regulation 2001—). Episcopalian. Avocations: golf, running, coaching children's sports teams. Office: Mayer Brown Rowe and Maw LLP 1909 K St NW Washington DC 20006 Office Phone: 202-263-3224. Business E-Mail: mlackey@mayerbrown.com.

LACKLAND, JOHN, lawyer, nurseryman; b. Parma, Idaho, Aug. 29, 1939; AB, Stanford U., 1962; JD, U. Wash., 1964; Master Gardener, Colo. State U., 1996. Bar: Wash. 1965, U.S. Dist. Ct. (we. dist.) Wash. 1965, (ea. dist.) Wash. 1973, U.S. Ct. Appeals (9th cir.) 1965, Conn. 1981, U.S. Dist. Ct. Conn. 1983, U.S. Supreme Ct. 1973, U.S. Dist. Ct. (so. dist.) N.Y. 1988; cert. profl. nurseryman, Idaho, 2005. Assoc. firm Lane Powell Moss & Miller, Seattle, 1965-69; asst. atty. gen. State of Wash., Seattle, 1969-72, asst. chief U. Wash. divsn., 1969-72; v.p., sec., gen. counsel Western Farmers Assn., Seattle, 1972-76, Fotomat Corp., Stamford, Conn., 1976-80; ptnr. Leepson & Lackland, 1981-88, Lackland and Nalewaik, 1988-92; pvt. practices Westport, Conn., 1992-94; prin. Lackland Assocs., Grand Junction, Colo., 1994—2002. Profl. nurseryman, 1995—; nursery mgr. Boutique Nursery, Twin Falls, Idaho, 2005; nurseryman Kimberly Nurseries, Twin Falls, 2004—07; mgr. Snake River Garden Ctr., Buhl, Idaho, 2007—. Bd. dirs. Mercer Island (Wash.) Congl. Ch., 1967-70, pres. bd. dirs., 1970; mem. land use plan steering com. City of Mercer Island, 1970-72; bd. dirs. Mercer Island Sch. Dist., 1970-73, v.p. bd. dirs., 1972, pres. 1973; trustee Mid-Fairfield Child Guidance Ctr., 1982-84, Norfield Congl. Ch., 1982-84; bd. dirs. Grand Junction Symphony Orch., 1995-99.

LACKLAND, THEODORE HOWARD, lawyer; b. Chgo., Dec. 4, 1943; s. Richard and Cora Lee (Sanders) L.; m. Dorothy Ann Gerald, Jan. 2, 1970; 1 child, Jennifer Noel. BS, Loyola U., Chgo., 1965; MA, Howard U., 1967; JD, Columbia U., 1975. Bar: N.J. 1975, U.S. Dist. Ct. N.J. 1975, Ga. 1982, U.S. Tax Ct. 1983, U.S. Supreme Ct. 1979, U.S. Dist. Ct. (no. dist.) Ga. 1982, U.S. Dist. Ct. (mid. dist.) Ga. 1985, U.S. Dist. Ct. (so. dist.) Ga. 2003. Assoc. Dewey, Ballantine, Bushby, Palmer & Wood, NYC, 1975-78; asst. U.S. atty. Dist. N.J., Newark, 1978-81; ptnr. Arnall Golden & Gregory, Atlanta, 1981-93, Lackland & Assoc., Atlanta, 1993-95, Lackland & Heyward, Atlanta, 1995-2000, Lackland & Assocs., LLC, Atlanta, 2000—. Adj. prof. law Ga. State U. Law Sch., 1989-99. Assoc. editor Columbia Human Rights Law Rev., 1974-75; contbr. articles to profl. jours. Adv. dir. Atlanta Bus. Devel. Ctr., Minority Bus. Devel. Coun., Atlanta, 1983-91; mem. exec. com. Leadership Atlanta, 1986, 1990-91; bd. dirs. APEX Mus., 2002—. Active duty US Army, 1967—71. Decorated Bronze Star with 1 oak leaf cluster, Purple Heart, Air medal. Mem.: AAJ, ABA, Atlanta Bar Assn., Ga. Bar Assn. Democrat. Roman Catholic. Home: 4400 Oak Ln Marietta GA 30062-6355 Office: Lackland & Assocs LLC 233 Peachtree St NE Atlanta GA 30303-1509 Office Phone: 404-522-8155. Business E-Mail: tlackland@e-lacklaw.com.

LACKNER, BERNARD, hotel executive; V.p., gen. mgr. Hôtel Plaza Athénée, NYC. Hon. trustee Am. Acad. Hospitality Scis. Mem.: Hotel Assn. NYC, Inc. (bd. mem.). Office: Plaza Athenee 37 E 64th St New York NY 10021-7023 Office Phone: 212-734-9100. Office Fax: 212-772-0958. E-mail: blackner@plaza-athenee.com.*

LACKNER, JAMES ROBERT, aerospace medicine educator; b. Virginia, Minn., Nov. 11, 1940; s. William and Lillian Mae (Galbraith) L.; m. Ann Martin Graybiel, Aug. 26, 1970. BSc, MIT, 1966, PhD, 1970. Asst. prof. psychology Brandeis U., Waltham, Mass., 1970-74, assoc. prof. psychology, 1974-79, Riklis prof. physiology dept. psychology, 1977—, chmn. dept. psychology, 1975-83, provost, dean faculty, 1986-89, dir. Ashton Graybiel Spatial Orientation Lab., 1982—. Research assoc. dept. psychology and clin. research ctr. MIT, Cambridge, 1970-80; sci. adv. bd. Space Biomed. Research Inst., Houston, 1982—, Aphasia Research Ctr. Boston U. Sch. Med., 1977-82, Eunice Kennedy Shriver Ctr. Harvard U. Med. Sch., Cambridge, 1980-90; sci. adv. panel astronaut longitudinal health program Johnson Space Ctr., NASA, 1983, exec. sec. space adaptation syndrome steering com., 1982-84, pre-adaption trainer working group, 1986—, artificial gravity working group, 1987—; fabricant com. life scis. experiments for a space sta., 1982; space scis. bd. sensory motor panel NAS, 1984-86; com. on hearing, bioacoustics and biomechanics NRC, 1985-89, com. on vision, 1987-92, com. on space, biology and medicine, 1991-99, mem. com. virtual reality rsch. and devel., 1992-95. Mem. editorial bd. Presence, 1992—, Jour. Vestibular Rsch., 1991-2001, Jour. Neurophysiology, 1995—, Exptl. Brain Rsch., 1997—, Jour. Exptl. Psychology, 2001—; contbr. more than 225 articles to sci. jours. Mem. Am. Soc. for Gravitational and Space Biology, Aerospace Med. Assn. (Arnold B. Tuttle award), Soc. for Neurosci., Psychonomics Soc., Internat. Brain Research Orgn., Barany Soc. (hon.), Internat. Acad. Astronautics (hon.). Achievements include research in human sensory-motor coordination and spatial orientation. Home: Boyce Farm Rd Lincoln MA 01773-4813 Office: Brandeis U Ashton Graybiel Lab 415 South St Waltham MA 02453-2728

LACKRITZ, MARC E., securities industry association executive; b. Columbus, Ohio, Sept. 29, 1946; m. Mary B. DeOreo, May 17, 1975; children: Anne, Katie, Sarah. AB in Pub. and Internat. Affairs, Princeton U., 1968; MPhil, Oxford U., 1971; JD cum laude, Harvard U., 1973. Asst. counsel U.S. Senate Watergate Com., Washington, 1973-74; dep. chief counsel U.S. Senate Budget Com., Washington, 1974-77; ptnr. Wald, Harkrader & Ross, Washington, 1977-84; staff dir., chief counsel U.S. Ho. Energy and Commerce subcom. telecommunications, consumer protection, fin., Washington, 1984-87; exec. v.p. Pub. Securities Assn., Washington, 1987-90, Securities Ind. Assn., Washington, 1990-92, pres., 1992—. Bd. dirs. Am. Coun. Capital Formation, Washington; mem. Fin. Acctg. Stds., Norwalk, Conn. Contbr. articles to profl. jours. Trustee Securities Industry Found. for Econ. Edn., Securities Industry Inst.; tutor Abram Simon Elem. Sch., Washington. Rhodes scholar 1968. Jewish. Avocations: running, tennis, golf. Office: Securities Industry Assn 120 Broadway 35th Fl New York NY 10271

LACLAIR, PATRICIA MARIE, physical education director, paramedic; b. East Liverpool, Ohio, Dec. 29, 1958; d. James Herbert and Irene Marie (Ruthledge) LaC. BS in Edn., Youngstown State U. Lic. paramedic Tex., cert. BLS instr., ACLS, sch. bus driver Tex. Dir. elem. phys. edn. Trinity Ind. Sch. Dist., Tex., 1985—2006; instr. CPR AHA, Bryan, Tex., 1985—, instr. phys. edn., 1989—; EMT Express Care EMS, 1999—2001; paramedic Prime Care EMS; with Med-Pro Emergency Med. Svc., 2004—; tchr. phys. edn. grades 5-6 Crockett Ind. Sch. Dist., Tex., 2006—. Emergency med. svcs. program instr., 1994—, emergency med. svcs. program examiner, 1994—, basic critical incident stress mgmt. trainer, 1994—; instr. Trinity Peninsula Ambulance Svc., 1994-95; sec. bd. dirs. Trinity Emergency Med. Svc., 1990-95, mgr. 1986-95; instr., trainer Primecare Emergency Med. Svc., 1996-99, Jacksonville Fire Dept. Emergency Med. Svcs., 1996—; instr.-examiner Tex. Emergency Med. Svc., 1992-99. Vol. EMT, 1985-95. Mem.: Tex. Assn. State Ofcls. Address: 206 Valley Ln Crockett TX 75835-1328 Office Phone: 936-594-5127.

LACOMBE, JACQUES, conductor; b. Cap-de-la-Madeleine, Québec; Student, Conservatoire de musique du Québec, Trois-Rivières, Montreal; grad. in Choral and Orchestral Conducting, Hochschule für Musik und darstellende Kunst, 1988; studied with Vaclav Neumann, Peter Eötvös, Karl Österreicher, Raffi Armenian. Assoc. condr. Amati Ensemble, 1987-94; prof. music theory and conducting Univ. Québec, Trois-Rivières, Can., 1989-94; music. dir. Philharm. de Lorraine, Metz, France; music dir., condr. Les Grands Ballets Canadiens, Montréal, 1992—; asst. condr., chorus master L'Opera de Montréal, Montréal, 1992—98; musical adv., condr. Laval Symphony Orch., Québec, 1993—95; asst. condr. L'Orchestre symphonique de Montreal, Montréal, 1994—98; music dir., prin. conductor Les Grands Ballets Canadiens de Montéal, Montréal, 2003—. Prin. guest condr. Montreal Symphony, 2002—. Condr. orchs. including Philharm. Orchs. of Slovakia and Savaria, Hungarian Radio TV Orch., Budapest Symphony Orch., L'orchestre métropolitan, CBC Vancouver Orch., L'Orchestre symphonique de Montréal, L'Orchestre symphonique de Québec; also numerous recs. Can. Arts Coun. grantee; recipient Joseph S. Stauffer award, 1988. Office: Montreal Symphony Orch 2d Fl 260 de Maisonneuve Blvd W Montreal PQ H2X1Y9 Canada*

LACOSTE, ALAN DANIEL, physician, educator, medical company executive; b. New Orleans, Aug. 25, 1943; s. Charles and Viola Lacoste; 1 child, Natasha. BA, Loyola U., New Orleans, 1971; MD, La. State U., New Orleans, 1975. Cert. Am. Bd. in Opthalmology. CEO The Eye Clinic, Lake Charles, La., 1979—; clin. prof. opthalmology La. State U. Sch. Medicine, 1997—. Physician, surgeon Benevolent Missions Internat., Africa, 1986—, 1986—, Belieze, El Salvador, Bolivia, Fiji. Office: The Eye Clinic 1717 Oak Park Blvd Ste 100 Lake Charles LA 70601 Office Phone: 337-478-3810. Office Fax: 337-478-6360.

LACOVARA, PHILIP ALLEN, lawyer; b. NYC, July 11, 1943; s. P. Philip and Elvira Lacovara; m. Madeline E. Papio, Oct. 14, 1961; children: Philip, Michael, Christopher, Elizabeth, Karen, Daniel, Andrew. AB magna cum laude, Georgetown U., 1963; JD summa cum laude, Columbia U., 1966. Bar: N.Y. 1967, DC 1974, U.S. Supreme Ct. 1970. Law clk. to presiding justice U.S. Ct. Appeals D.C. Cir., 1966-67; asst. to solicitor gen. U.S. Washington, 1967-69; assoc. Hughes Hubbard & Reed, NYC, 1969-71, ptnr. NYC and Washington, 1974-88; v.p., sr. counsel GE, Fairfield, Conn., 1988-90; mng. dir, gen. counsel Morgen Stanley & Co., NYC, 1990-93; sr. counsel Mayer, Brown & Platt, NYC and Washington, 1993—2003, Mayer Brown Rowe & Maw LLP, 2004—; counsellor, legal adviser Permanent Observer Mission Sovereign Mil. Order of Malta to UN, 2005—. Spl. counsel to N.Y.C. Police Commr., 1971—72; dep. solicitor gen. U.S. Dept. Justice, Washington, 1972—73; counsel to spl. prosecutor Watergate Spl. Prosecution Force, 1973—74; lectr. law Columbia U.; adj. prof. Georgetown U. Law Ctr.; vis. lectr. various colls., univs.; mem. Jud. Conf. DC Cir., 1973—; chmn. commn. admissions and grievances U.S. Ct. Appeals (DC cir.), 1980—86; spl. counsel com. stds. ofcl. conduct U.S. Ho. of Reps., 1976—77; chmn. bd. trustees Pub. Defender Svc. DC, 1976—81; sec. exec. com. bd. visitors Columbia U. Sch. Law; pres. Columbia U. Sch. Law Alumni Assn., 1986—88; bd. govs. DC Bar, 1981—84, gen. counsel, 1985—87, pres., 1988—89, mem. legal ethics com., 1976—81; panel arbitrator JAMS, Resolution Experts, 2004—. Contbr. articles to profl.

jours. Co-chair Washington Lawyers Com. Civil Rights Under Law, 1982—84; mem. DC Jud. Nomination Commn., 1981—86; bd. dirs. Legal Aid Soc. N.Y.C., NYC, 1992—. Fellow: Am. Coll. Trial Lawyers; mem.: ABA (ho. dels. 1978—89, vice-chmn. sect. individual rights and responsibilities 1985—87, 1989—91, chmn. 1991—92), London Ct. Internat. Arbitration, Practicing Law Inst. (trustee), Am. Law Inst., Human Rights First (trustee 1991—), Lotos Club, Knights of Malta. Roman Catholic. Home: 1137 Smith Ridge Rd New Canaan CT 06840-2333 Office: 1675 Broadway New York NY 10019-5820

LACRUE, ALEXIS NICHOLE, parasitologist; d. Wanda Jean Gamble-Hernandez; m. Joseph M. LaCrue, Jan. 3, 1972; 1 child, Tynan Samad Xanthos. BA in Biology, N.Mex State U., 2000, BS in Animal Sci., 2000; MS in Vet. Biomed. Sci., U. Mo., Columbia, 2003. Summer biol. asst. apprenticeship Fish and Wildlife Svc., Cheyenne, Wyo., 1996; study abroad Muresk Inst. of Agr., Northam, Western Australia, Australia, 1997; summer internship Ind. U., Bloomington, 1999, SC Dept. of Natural Resources, Charleston, 1998; rsch. asst. N.Mex State U., Las Cruces, N.Mex., 1998—2000; grad. rsch. asst. U. Mo., Columbia, 2000; internship Ctr. for Disease Control, Ft. Collins, Colo., 2000. Contbr. scientific papers, articles to profl. publs. Recipient Fourth Pl. award Phi Zeta poster competition, U. Mo. Vet. Coll., 2001, Third Pl. award grad. oral divsn. 1 competition, Minorities in Agr. Natural Resources and Related Scis. Conf., 2002, Top Ten Poster Design award, U. Mo., 2002; scholar, Air Force Aid Soc., 1995—97; Minority Biomed. Rsch. Tng. Initiative fellow, NIH, 2000—02, 2005—, Ford Predoctoral Honorable Mention fellow, 2002, Mo. Alliance Grad. Edn. and the Professoriate fellow, NSF, 2003—04, Grad. Student Rsch. grantee, Vet. Pathobiology Dept., 2005. Mem.: Am. Soc. Tropical Medicine and Hygiene, Golden Key. Home Phone: 573-356-5284; Office Phone: 573-884-1470. Office Fax: 573-884-5414. Business E-Mail: anebfb@missouri.edu.

LACY, ALEXANDER SHELTON, retired lawyer; b. South Boston, Va., Aug. 18, 1921; s. Cecil Baker and Lura Elizabeth (Byram) L.; m. Carol Jemison, Aug. 8, 1952; children: John Blakeway, Joan Elizabeth Chancey, Alexander Shelton. BS in Chemistry, U. Ala., 1943; LLB, U. Va., 1949. Bar: Ala. 1949, U.S. Ct. Appeals (5th, 11th and D.C. cirs.) 1981, U.S. Supreme Ct. 1979. Assoc. Bradley, Arant, Rose & White, Birmingham, Ala., 1949-54; with Ala. Gas Corp., Birmingham, 1954-86; v.p., asst. sec., atty. Ala. Gas Corp./Energen Corp., 1969-86; v.p., sec., atty. Ala. Gas Corp., 1974-86; with Patrick and Lacy, Birmingham, 1986-96, ret., 1996. Pres., chmn. bd. Birmingham Symphony Assn., 1964-67; chmn. Birmingham-Jefferson Civic Center Authority, 1965-71. Served with USN, 1943-46. Mem. ABA, Ala. Bar Assn. (chmn. energy law com. 1984-86), Birmingham Bar Assn., Am. Gas Assn. (chmn. legal sect. 1983-85), Fed. Energy Bar Assn., Fed. Bar Assn., Am. Judicature Soc., Mountain Brook Club, Phi Gamma Delta, Phi Delta Phi. Episcopalian. Home: 3730 Montrose Rd Birmingham AL 35213-3824

LACY, ANDRE BALZ, industrial executive; b. Indpls., Sept. 12, 1939; s. Howard J. Lacy II and Edna B. (Balz) Lacy; m. Julia Lello, Feb. 23, 1963; children: Mark William, Peter Lello, John Andre. BA Econs., Denison U.; DEng (hon.), Rose-Hulman Inst. Various mgmt. positions U.S. Corrugated, Indpls., 1961-69, exec. v.p., 1969-72; exec. v.p., chief ops. officer Lacy Diversified Industries, Indpls., 1972-78, chmn. bd. subs., 1973-78, pres., chief ops. officer, 1978-83; pres., chief exec. officer Lacy Diversified Industries, now LDI, Ltd., Indpls., 1983—, chmn., 1992. Bd. dirs. Herff Jones, Inc., Indpls., Patterson Dental Co., Mpls., Finish Master, Inc.; bd. dirs. Nat. Bank Indpls. Chmn. United Way Greater Indpls., 1989—91; Mem. bd. mgrs. Rose-Hulman Inst., Terre Haute, Ind.; pres. Indpls. Bd. Sch. Commn., Indpls., 1985—86; hon. mem. 500 Festival Assocs., Inc., Indpls.; bd. dirs. Indpls. Conv. and Visitors Assn., 1996; dir. Ctrl. Ind. Corp. Partnership, Indpls. Downtown, Inc.; mem. adv. com. on arts John F. Kennedy Ctr. for Performing Arts. Mem.: Nat. Assn. Wholesaler Distbrs. (dir.), Ind. Pres. Orgn., Kiwanis Club of Indpls., Young Pres. Orgn., Ind. C. of C. (bd. dirs. 1989), Columbia Club, Meridian Hills Golf and Country Club (Indpls.), Lost Tree Club. Republican. Episcopalian. Avocation: sailing. Home: 450 E Vermont St Indianapolis IN 46202-3680 Office: LDI Ltd 54 Monument Cir Ste 800 Indianapolis IN 46204-2928

LACY, BILL, former academic administrator, architect; b. Madill, Okla., Apr. 16, 1933; s. Leon and Eunice L.; m. Susan Cavert Butler, Dec. 27, 1992; children: Jan, Kate, Shawn, Ross, Jessica. BArch, Okla. State U., 1955, MArch, 1958; DFA (hon.), Miami U., Oxford, Ohio, 1985. Design architect Caudill, Rowlett, Scott, Houston, 1958-61; prof., assoc. chmn. dept. architecture Rice U., Houston, 1961-65; prof., dean sch. architecture U. Tenn., Knoxville, 1965-70; v.p. Omniplan, Dallas, 1970-71; dir. architecture and environ. arts Nat. Endowment Arts, Washington, 1971-77, dir. fed. design program, 1972-77; pres. Am. Acad. in Rome, NYC, 1977-80, The Cooper Union, NYC, 1980-88; pres. Purchase Coll. SUNY, 1993—2001. Archtl. cons. Fgn. Bldgs. Ops., Dept. State Author: 100 Contemporary Architects, 1991, Angels and Franciscans, 1992; contbr. articles, designs to profl. jours. Bd. dirs. Internat. Design Conf. Aspen, 1973-92; bd. dirs. Tiffany Found., Am. Archtl. Found.; cons. Rothschild Found., J. Paul Getty Trust; exec. dir. Pritzker Architecture Prize. With U.S. Army, 1955-57. Loeb fellow Harvard U., 1973; Getty scholar, 1991. Fellow AIA; mem. Univ. Club.*

LACY, ELIZABETH BERMINGHAM, state supreme court justice; b. 1945; BA cum laude, St. Mary's Coll., Notre Dame, Ind., 1966; JD, U. Tex., 1969; LLM, U. Va., 1992. Bar: Tex. 1969, Va. 1977. Staff atty. Tex. Legis. Coun., Austin, 1969-72; atty. Office of Atty. Gen., State of Tex., Austin, 1973-76; legis. aide Va. Del. Carrington Williams, Richmond, 1976-77; dep. atty. gen. jud. affairs div. Va. Office Atty. Gen., Richmond, 1982-85; mem. Va. State Corp. Commn., Richmond, 1985-89; justice va. Supreme Ct., Richmond, 1989—. Office: Va Supreme Ct PO Box 1315 Richmond VA 02321-1315*

LACY, JOHN FORD, retired lawyer; b. Dallas, Sept. 11, 1944; s. John Alexander and Glenda Arcenia (Ford) L.; m. Cece Smith, Apr. 22, 1978. BA, Baylor U., 1965; JD, Harvard U., 1968. Bar: Tex. 1968. Atty. Akin, Gump, Strauss, Hauer & Feld, Dallas, 1968—99; ret., 1999. Co-founder, chmn., pres. rsch. coun. U. Tex. Southwestern Med. Ctr., Dallas, 1985-91; bd. dirs. Vis. Nurse Assn. Tex., 1994-2001, 1st vice chmn., 2000-01. With USAR, 1968-74. Home: 3710 Shenandoah St Dallas TX 75205-2121 Home Phone: 214-522-0026. Personal E-mail: jofola@charter.net.

LACY, JOHN ROBERT, lawyer; b. Dallas, Dec. 15, 1942; BS, San Diego State U., 1966; MS, U. So. Calif., 1971; JD, U. Calif., 1973. Bar: Calif. 1973, Hawaii 1974. Atty. Goodsill Anderson Quinn & Stifel, Honolulu. Arbitrator Ct. Annexed Arbitration Program, 1986—, Nat. Assn. Security Dealers, 2006—. Comment editor Hastings Law Jour., 1972-73. Fellow: Am. Coll. Trial Lawyers; mem.: ABA, Maritime Law Assn. US, Am. Bd. Trial Advocates, State Bar Calif., Hawaii Bar Assn., Order of Coif, Thurston Soc. Office: Goodsill Anderson Quinn & Stifel PO Box 3196 1800 Alii Pl 1099 Alakea St Honolulu HI 96813-4511 Office Phone: 808-547-5600. Business E-Mail: jlacy@goodsill.com.

LACY, ROBINSON BURRELL, lawyer; b. Boston, May 7, 1952; s. Benjamin Hammett and Jane (Burrell) L. AB, U. Calif., Berkeley, 1974; JD, Harvard U., 1977. Bar: NY 1978, US Dist. Ct. (so. and ea. dists.) NY 1979, US Dist. Ct. (we. dist.) NY 1992, US Ct. Appeals (2d cir.) 1983, US Ct. Appeals (10th cir.) 1990, US Ct. Appeals (3d cir.) 2002, Ct. Appeals (4th cir.) 2007, US Supreme Ct. 1986. Law clk. to judge US Dist. Ct. (so. dist.) NY, NYC, 1977-78; law clk. to chief justice Warren Burger US Supreme Ct., Washington, 1978-79; assoc. Sullivan & Cromwell, NYC, 1979-85, ptnr., 1985—, and coord. reorganization/bankruptcy practice area. Mem.: ABA, NY State Bar Assn., Assn. of Bar of City of NY. Office: Sullivan & Cromwell 125 Broad St Fl 32 New York NY 10004-2489 Business E-Mail: lacyr@sullcrom.com.

LACY, STEPHEN M., publishing and broadcasting executive; m. Cathy Lacy; 2 children. B in acctg., Kans. State U., 1976, M in acctg., 1977. CPA. Sr. audit mgr. Deloitte & Touche, Des Moines, Kansas City, Mo.; v.p., CFO Commtron Corp., Des Moines, 1986—92; with Johnson & Higgins/Kirke-Van Orsdel Inc., Des Moines, 1992—98, v.p., CFO, exec. v.p., pres.; v.p., CFO Meredith Corp., Des Moines, 1998—2000, pres. mktg. group, 2000, COO, pres. publ. group, 2004—06, pres., CEO, 2006—. Bd. dirs. Advt. Coun. Chair bd. dirs. United Way Cent. Iowa; bd. dirs. Am. Red Cross, Jr. Achievement Cent. Iowa. Named Publ. Exec. Yr., Advt. Age, 2003. Mem.: Direct Mktg. Assn. (bd. dirs., exec. com., treas.). Office: Meredith Corp 1716 Locust St Des Moines IA 50309-3023*

LACY, TERRI, lawyer; b. Dillon, Mont., 1953; BA with highest honors, So. Meth. U., 1975, JD, 1978. Bar: Tex. 1978. Ptnr., Estates & Estates Planning Andrews & Kurth LLP, Houston. Mng. editor Southwestern Law Jour., 1977—78. Mem.: Houston Estate & Fin. Forum, Houston Bus. & Estate Planning Coun., Houston Bar Assn., State Bar Tex., ABA, Order of Coif. Office: Andrews Kurth LLP 600 Travis St Ste 4200 Houston TX 77002-3090 Office Phone: 713-220-4482. Office Fax: 713-238-7220. Business E-Mail: tlacy@andrewskurth.com.

LADANYI, BRANKO, civil engineer, educator; b. Zagreb, Croatia, Dec. 14, 1922; emigrated to Can., 1962, naturalized, 1967; m. Nevenka Zilic, Dec. 14, 1946; children: Branka, Thomas, Marc. BCE, U. Zagreb, 1947; PhD in Soil Mechanics, U. Louvain, Belgium, 1959. Design engr. Dept. Transp., Zagreb, 1947-52; teaching asst. U. Zagreb, 1952-58; research engr. Belgian Geotech. Inst., Ghent, 1958-62; asso. prof., then prof. civil engring. Laval U., Que., Canada, 1962-67; prof. civil engring. Ecole Poly., U. Montreal, 1967-94, prof. emeritus, 1994—, dir. North Engring. Centre, 1972—. Author papers in geotech. field, chpts. in books. Recipient Que. sci. award Que. Ministry Edn., 1974, De Beer Geotech. award Belgian Geotech. Soc., 1986, North Sci. award Govt. of Can., 1996. Fellow ASCE (Amity award 1995, Harold R. Peyton award 2003, Elbert F. Rice Meml. award 1991), Royal Soc. Can., Can. Acad. Engring., Engring. Inst. Can., Can. Soc. Civil Engring.; mem. ASTM, Order Engrs. Que., Can. Geotech. Soc. (R.F. Legget Geotech. award 1981, Roger J.E. Brown Meml. award 1993), Can. Inst. Mining and Metallurgy. Office: Ecole Polytech Box 6079 Succ Centre-Ville Montreal PQ Canada H3C3A7 E-mail: bladanyi@polymtl.ca. *There is no end to learning.*

LADD, CHARLES CUSHING, III, civil engineer, educator; b. Bklyn., Nov. 23, 1932; s. Charles Cushing and Elizabeth (Swan) Ladd; m. Carol Lee Ballou, June 11, 1954; children: Melissa, Charles IV, Ruth, Matthew. AB, Bowdoin Coll., 1955; SB, MIT, 1955, SM, 1957, ScD, 1961. Asst. prof. MIT, Cambridge, 1961-64, assoc. prof., 1964-70, prof., 1970-94, dir. Ctr. Sci. Excellence Offshore Engring., 1983-94, Edmund K. Turner prof., 1994-2001, Edmund K. Turner prof. emeritus, 2001—. Gen. reporter 9th Internat. Conf. Soil Mechanics and Found. Engring., Tokyo, 1977; co-gen. reporter 11th Internat. Conf. Soil Mechanics and Found. Engring., San Francisco, 1985; mem. geotech. bd. NRC, 1992—94; casagrande lectr. 12th Pan-Am. Conf. Soil Mechanics and Geotech. Engring., Cambridge, Mass., 2003. Contbr. articles to profl. jours. Commr. Concord Dept. Pub. Works, 1965—78, chmn., 1972—74; mem. Concord Rep. Town Com., 1968—82. Fellow: ASCE (hon.; Terzaghi lectr. 1986, mem. exec. com. geotechnical engring. divsn. 1989—96, chmn. 1993—94, Geo-Inst. bd. govs. 1996—98, Rsch. prize 1969, Croes medal 1973, Norman medal 1976, Middlebrooks award 1996, Karl Terzaghi award 1999, Middlebrooks award 2002); mem.: AAUP, NSPE, ASTM (Hogentogler award 1990), NAE, Can. Geotech. Soc., Brit. Geotech. Soc., Assn. Engring. Firms Practicing Geosci., Am. Soc. Engring. Edn., Internat. Soc. Soil Mechanics and Geotech. Engring., Transp. Rsch. Bd., Boston Soc. Civil Engr. (bd. govs. 1972—81, pres. 1977—78, Arthur Casagrande meml. lectr. 2000). Home: 7 Thornton Ln Concord MA 01742-4107 Office: MIT Dept Civil & Environ Engrng Cambridge MA 02139 Home Phone: 978-369-3886; Office Phone: 978-369-3886. Business E-Mail: ccladd@mit.edu.

LADD, CULVER SPROGLE, secondary school educator; b. Bismarck, ND, Nov. 15, 1929; s. Culver Sprogle and Eleanor (Pearson) Ladd. BS, U. Md., 1953; MA, Am. U., 1963, MA, 1978, PhD, 1984; postgrad., Harvard U., summer 1963, Oxford U., Eng., 1975-76; cert. by correspondence, Nat. Def. U., Thailand, 1972. Clk.-photographer Dept. Justice, FBI, Washington, 1946-54; intercept controller Dept. of Def., USAF, 1954-56; asst. office mgr. Covington & Burling, Lawyers, Washington, 1956-62; tchr. Internat. Sch. Bangkok, Thailand, 1964-66; lectr. U. Md., Thailand, 1966-67, 71-74; project dir. Bus. Rsch. Ltd., Thailand, 1966-67, 72-74; spl. lectr. Payap U., Chiang Mai, Thailand, 1974-75, 2000-2001; tchr. D.C. Pub. Schs., 1978-2000. Cons. USAID, Thailand, 1973—74; vis. scientist Brookhaven Nat. Labs., LI, 1988; master tchr. Woodrow Wilson Fellowship Found., 1989; bd. dirs. Chesapeake Water Assn., 2002—. Author: Pure Food Crusader, Edwin Fremont Ladd, Chemist, 1859-1925, 2006. Rep. candidate Md. Senate 29th Legis. Dist., 1998. Capt. USAFR, 1953—72. Recipient Appreciation award, Payap U., 1987. Mem.: Mid. States Coun. Social Studies, Nat. Coun. Tchrs. Math., Nat. Capital Area Polit. Sci. Assn., Mid-Atlantic Region Assn. Asian Studies, Exptl. Aviation Assn., Aircraft Owners and Pilots Assn., Pi Sigma Alpha, Omicron Delta Kappa. Republican. Presbyterian. Avocations: gardening, flying. Office: POACRE Airfield 845 Crystal Rock Rd PO Box 2084 Lusby MD 20657-1884

LADD, DAVID SCOTT, music educator; b. Milw., Wis., Feb. 7, 1962; s. Donald Alfie and Marilyn Bender Ladd; m. Katherine Lynne Condit-Ladd. MusB, U. Wis., 1985; MusM, Northeastern Ill. U., 1999. Cert. tchr. State of Ill. Music tchr. Waukesha Pub. Schs., Waukesha, Wis., 1986; choral music tchr. Deerfield HS, Deerfield, Ill., 1994—95, Mundelein HS, Mundelein, Ill., 1994—96, New Trier HS, Winnetka, Ill., 1996—2002, choral music tchr., music dept. chair, 2002—. Audition host Ill. Music Educators Assn., Winnetka, Ill., 2002, participating judge, 1994—2004. Author: Musical Theatre as Career Choice, 2004. Profl. actor, 1985—94; singing mem. Coriolis. Recipient Signature Sch. Gold, The Grammy Found., 2000, Grammy award, 2000. Mem.: Actor's Equity Assn., Am. Choral Dirs. Assn., Nat. Edn. Assn. Avocations: travel, golf, home renovation. Office: New Trier HS 385 Winnetka Ave Winnetka IL 60093 Office Phone: 847-784-6696. Office Fax: 847-784-6690. E-mail: laddd@newtrier.k12.il.us.

LADD, DIANE, actress, writer, film director, film producer; b. Laurel, Miss., Nov. 29, 1942; d. Mary Lanier; m. Bruce Dern, 1960 (div. 1969); 1 child, Laura; m. William Shea, Jr., 1969 (div. 1977); m. Robert C. Hunter, Feb. 14, 1999; stepchildren: Brandon Hunter, Amy Oleson, Emily Hunter. Grad., St. Aloysius Acad. Appearances include (films) The Wild Angels, 1966, The Reivers, 1969, Macho Callahan, 1970, Rebel Rousers, 1970, WUSA, 1970, White Lightning, 1973, Alice Doesn't Live Here Anymore, 1974, Chinatown, 1974, Embryo, 1976, The November Plan, 1976, All Night Long, 1981, Something Wicked This Way Comes, 1983, Black Widow, 1987, Plain Clothes, 1988, National Lampoon's Christmas Vacation, 1989, Wild at Heart, 1990, A Kiss Before Dying, 1991, Rambling Rose, 1991, Cemetery Club, 1992, Hold Me, Thrill Me, Kiss Me, 1992, Code Name: Chaos, 1992, Carnosaur, 1993, Father Hood, 1993, Spirit Realm, 1993, Obsession, 1994, Mrs. Munck (also dir., writer, co-prodr.), 1994, The Haunted Heart, 1995, Raging Angels, 1995, Ghosts of Mississippi, 1996, Mother (also exec. prodr.), 1996, Citizen Ruth, 1996, James Dean: Race With Destiny, 1997, Primary Colors, 1998, Daddy N Them, 1999, 28 Days, 2001, Rain, 2001, Law of Enclosures, 2001, Charlies War, 2002, World's Fastest Indian, 2005, Come Early Morning, 2005-06, When I Find the Ocean, 2006, Inland Empire, 2006, Woman Inside, 2007 (also dir., writer, co-prodr.); (TV series) Alice, 1980-81; (TV movies) The Devil's Daughter, 1973, Thaddeus Rose and Eddie, 1978, Black Beauty, 1978, Willa, 1979, Guyana Tragedy: The Story of Jim Jones, 1980, Desperate Lives, 1982, Grace Kelly, 1983, I Married a Centerfold, 1984, Crime of Innocence, 1985, Celebration Family, 1987, Bluegrass, 1988, The Lookalike, 1990, Rock Hudson, 1990, Shadow of a Doubt, 1991, Hush Little Baby, 1994, Ruby Ridge: An American Tragedy, 1996, Breach of Faith: Family of Cops II, 1997, The Waiting Game, 1997, The Staircase, 1998, Sharing the Secret, 2000, Christy: The Movie, 2001, Aftermath, 2001, Damaged Care, 2002, Gracie's Choice, 2004; (TV miniseries) Cold Lazarus, 1996, Kristy, James Van Praag Story, Christy, Choices of the Heart, Part I & II, 2001, Stephen King's Kingdom Hospital, ABC, 2004 (15 hour TV spl.), Montana Sky, Lifetime, 2006; author: (book) Spiraling Through the School of Life: A Mental, Physical & Spiritual Discovery, 2006. Pres. Art and Culture Taskforce; bd. advisors Nat. Found. for Alt. Medicine, Washington. Recipient award Brit. Acad., Spirit award, Golden Globe award, Tor Broadway award, 3 Acad. award nominations, 4 Golden Globe nominations, 3 Emmy nominations for Guest Actress in a Series (Grace Under Fire), 1994, Dr. Quinn, Medicine Woman, Touched by an Angel; named Woman of Yr. City of Hope, 1992; recipient Achievement award Women in Film, 1992, PATH Angel award, 1992, Disting. Artist award LA Music Ctr., 1994, Hollywood Legacy award, 1994, 1st Time Dir. award Dla. Film Festival, 1996, Tribuate award Newport Festival, 1996. Office Phone: 805-640-8920.

LADD, FLORENCE CAWTHORNE, writer; b. Washington, June 16, 1932; d. William and Eleanor Louise (Willis) Cawthorne; m. William Joseph Harris, May 21, 1984; m. John Ladd (dec.); 1 child, Michael Cawthorne. BS Psychology, Howard Univ., Wash., 1953; PhD Psychology, Univ. Rochester, NYC, 1958. Rsch. assoc. Age Ctr. of New Eng., Boston, 1958; assoc. prof. Robert Coll., Istanbul, Turkey, 1962—63; lectr., rsch. assoc. Harvard Grad. Sch. Edn., Cambridge, 1965—70; assoc. prof. Harvard Sch. of Design, 1972—77; assoc. dean MIT, 1977—79; cons. to South Africa edn. Inst. of Internat. Edn., NYC, 1984—85; edn. dir. assoc. Oxfau Am., Boston, 1985—89; assoc. dir. Bunting Inst. Radcliffe & Harvard, Cambridge, 1989—97; ret., 1997. Vice bd. trustees Hamshire Coll., Amherst, Mass., 1995—. Author: (novels) Sarah's Psalm, 1996 (Best Fiction, ALA's Black Caucus, 1997), Paris Reunion, 2007. Overseer Mus. Fine Arts, Boston, 1994—, Fine Arts Workshop, Providencetown, Mass., 2006—; advisory com. YCWA, Boston, 2003—, W.E.B. DuBois Inst., Harvard Univ., Cambridge, 2000—. Mem.: Black Women for Policy Action, Examiner Club, Sigma Zi, Phi Betta Kappa. Democrat. Avocation: art. Home: 82 Larch Rd Cambridge MA 02138 Personal E-mail: fladd1@earthlink.net.

LADD, JEFFREY RAYMOND, lawyer; b. Mpls., Apr. 10, 1941; s. Jasper Raymond and Florence Marguerite (DeMarce) L.; m. Kathleen Anne Crosby, Aug. 24, 1963; children: Jeffrey Raymond, John Henry, Mark Jasper, Matthew Crosby. Student, U. Vienna, Austria; BA, Loras Coll.; postgrad., U. Denver; JD, Ill. Inst. Tech. Bar: Ill. 1973, U.S. Dist. Ct. 1973. V.p. mktg. Ladd Enterprises, Des Plaines, Ill., 1963-66, v.p. mktg. and fin. Crystal Lake, Ill., 1966-70; ptnr. Ross & Hardies, Chgo., 1973-81, Boodell, Sears, et al., 1981-86, Bell, Boyd & Lloyd, Chgo., 1986—. Spl. asst. atty. gen. for condemnation State of Ill., 1977-82; chmn. Metra, 1984-2006. Mem., chmn. Ill. Bd. Govs. of State Colls. and Univs., 1972—75; mem. bd. regents Loras Coll., 2003—; del. 6th Ill. Constnl. Conv., 1969—70. Recipient W. Graham Claytor, Jr. award for disting. svc. to passenger transp., 1995, Disting. Svc. award IIT/Chgo.-Kent Law Sch., 1997; named Citizen of Yr., Chgo. City Club, 1995. Mem. ABA, Chgo. Bar Assn., Nat. Assn. Bond Lawyers, Ill. Assn. Hosp. Attys., Am. Acad. Hosp. Attys., Am. Health Lawyers Assn., Crystal Lake Jaycees (Disting. Svc. award), Crystal Lake C. of C. (past pres.), Econ. Club, Legal Club, Union League Club, Bull Valley Golf Club, Woodstock Country Club, Lambda Alpha. Roman Catholic. Avocations: golf, hunting, fishing, tennis, skiing. Office: Bell Boyd & Lloyd 3 First National Pla 70 W Madison St Ste 3100 Chicago IL 60602-4284

LADD, JOSEPH CARROLL, retired insurance company executive; b. Chgo., Jan. 26, 1927; s. Stephen C. and Laura (McBride) L.; m. Barbara Virginia Carter, June 5, 1965; children: Carroll, Joseph Carroll, Barbara, Virginia, William. BA, Ohio Wesleyan U., 1950; CLU, Am. Coll., Bryn Mawr; D in Bus. Adminstrn. (hon.), Spring Garden Coll., 1985. Agt. Conn. Gen. Life Ins. Co., Chgo., 1950-53, staff asst., 1953-54, mgr. Evanston (Ill.) br. office, 1954-60, dir. agys., 1960-62, mgr. Los Angeles br. office, 1963; v.p. sales Fidelity Mut. Life Ins. Co., Phila., 1964-67, sr. v.p. sales, 1968, exec. v.p., 1969-71, pres., chief exec. officer, dir., 1971-84, chmn., chief exec. officer, dir., 1984-89, chmn., dir., 1989-91; ret. Bd. dirs. Corestates Fin., Phila. Suburban Corp., Phila. Electric Co. Trustee Bryn Mawr Hosp.; trustee United Way of S.E. Pa.; trustee Phila. United Way, also gen. chmn. 1978 campaign; bd. dirs. Phila. YMCA. Served with USNR, 1945-46. Recipient Civic Achievement award Am. Jewish Com., 1978, Achiever's award WHEELS Med. and Specialized Transp., 1978, Ohio Wesleyan U. Life Achievement award Delta Tau Delta, 1982, William Penn award, Greater Phila. C. ofC. and PENJERDEL Coun., 1988, Robert Morris Citizenship award Valley Forge Coun. Boy Scouts Am., 1988; named YMCA Man of Yr., 1979, William Penn Found. Disting. Pennsylvanian, 1980. Mem. Greater Phila. C. of C. (dir., chmn. 1979, 83-84), Phila. Country Club, Union League Club (Phila.), Summer Beach (Fla.) Country Club.

LADD, MARCIA LEE, medical products executive; b. Bryn Mawr, Pa., July 22, 1950; d. Edward Wingate and Virginia Lee (McGinnes) Mullinix; m. Leroy D. Werley, III, Aug. 5, 2000; children from previous marriage: Joshua Wingate, McGinnes Lee. BA, U. Pa., 1972; MEd, U. Va., Charlottesville, 1973; MA, Emory U., Atlanta, 1979. Rsch. assoc. N.C. Tng. and Standards Coun., Raleigh, 1973-75; dir. counseling svc. N.C. State Youth Svcs. Agy., Raleigh, 1975-76; acad. dean Duke U., Durham, NC, 1976-77; prin. Ladd & Assocs. Mgmt. Cons., Chapel Hill, NC, 1979-88; v.p. adminstrn. CompuChem Corp., Research Triangle Park, NC, 1988-91; v.p. mktg. Prentke Romich Co., Wooster, Ohio, 1991-94; v.p. ops. Exec. Staffing Svcs., Inc., Cary, NC, 1994; pres., CEO, owner Triangle Aftercare, Durham, NC, 1994—. Bd. dirs. Home Med. Svcs., 1997—; mem. N.C. Bd. Pharmacy, 2004—, chair, 2006—. Bd. dirs. Oakwood Hist. Soc., Raleigh, 1981—84; mem. bd. vis. Carolina Friends Sch., Durham, 1986—89; bd. dirs. Orange Enterprises, 2000—07; Stephen min. Univ. Presbyn. Ch., Chapel Hill, 1994—97, 2003—06, youth group leader, 1995—97, 2000—02, trustee, 1998—2000; chair personnel com. Chapel in the Pines Presbyn., 2006—; bd. dirs. Wayne County Arts Coun., Wooster, 1992, Stoneridge/Sedgefield Swim/Racquet Club, Chapel Hill, 1985—88. Decorated Order of Long Leaf Pine Gov. of N.C.; named one of Impact 100 Most Influential People, Research Triangle, N.C., 1997. Office: Triangle Aftercare 105 W NC Hwy 54 Ste 267 Durham NC 27713

LADDAGA, LAWRENCE ALEXANDER, lawyer; b. New Hyde Park, NY, Aug. 12, 1957; s. Carmine Michael and Adeline (Lauricella) Laddaga; children: Amanda May, Rachel. BA cum laude, U. S.C., 1978, JD, 1981. Bar: S.C. 1981, U.S. Dist. Ct. S.C. 1981, U.S. Ct. Appeals (4th cir.) 1981, U.S. Tax Ct. 1982, U.S. Supreme Ct. 1989. Assoc. Wise & Cole, P.A., Charleston, SC, 1981—83; founding shareholder, sr. ptnr. Laddaga-Garrett PA, Charleston, 1983—. Adj. asst. prof. dept. health adminstrn. and policy Med. U. S.C., Charleston, 1999—. Bd. dirs., 1st v.p. Charleston chpt. Am. Cancer Soc., 1987-88 Fellow Healthcare Fin. Mgmt. Assn. (advanced, bd.

dirs. 1991-94, sec., v.p. 1991-95, pres. 1997-98, nat. principles and practices bd. 2002—), S.C. Bar Assn. (chairperson health care law com. 1995-97), Charleston County Bar Assn., Am. Health Lawyers Assn., S.C. Hosp. Assn., Order Ky. Cols., Kiwanis, Elks, Masons, Phi Beta Kappa Home: 1719 Villa Maison Mount Pleasant SC 29464 Office: 7301 River Ave Ste 230 PO Box 62498 North Charleston SC 29419 Home Phone: 843-856-9130; Office Phone: 843-325-4018. E-mail: LADDAGA@sehealthlaw.com.

LADENHEIM, JULES CALVIN, neurosurgeon; b. Union Hill, NJ, Apr. 21, 1923; s. Solomon and Miriam (Preminger) L.; m. Janet Bloom (dec.), Feb. 15, 1959; children: Eric, Fred (dec.), Karen. AB, Harvard U., 1944; MD, NY Med. Coll., 1947. Diplomate Am. Bd. Surgery, Am. Bd. Neurologic Surgery. Intern Queens Gen. Hosp., NYC, 1947-48; resident gen. surgery NY Med. Coll., 1948-50, Pitts. Med. Ctr., 1952-53, Mt. Sinai, Cleve., 1953-54; resident neurosurgery Serafimer Hosp., Stockholm, 1954-56, Med. Coll. Va., Richmond, 1956-57; resident in neurosurgery Neurology Inst. NY, 1957-58; resident neurosurgery Mary Hitchcock, Hanover, NH, 1958-60; pvt. practice Hackensack, NJ, 1960—. Staff neurosurgeon Hackensack U. Hosp., 1960—, Holy Name Hosp., Teaneck, NJ, 1960—, Meadowland Hosp., Secaucus, NJ, 1987—, St. Mary Hosp., Hoboken, 1987—. Co-author: Arteriovenous Aneurysm, 1956; author: Intraventric Meningiomas, 1961, Leonard Bertapaglia, 1991, Firearms and Ballistics, 1996, Alien Horseman, 2003, Custer's Thorn, 2007. Lt. USNR, 1950—52. Decorated Navy and Marine Corps medal. Mem. Am. Assn. Neurologic Surgeons, Congress of Neurosurgery, Nordiska Neurokirugiska Forening, Abraham Lincoln Soc. (pres. 1993-94), USS Columbus Vets. Assn., Harvard Club NY. Office: 664 River Rd Teaneck NJ 07666-1642 E-mail: julescalvin@aol.com.

LADENSON, SHARON, university librarian; Gender studies & comm. bibliographer, reference libr. Mich. State U. Librs. Mem.: ALA, Mich. Libr. Assn. (com. on orgn. sec. 2003—04), Assn. Coll. & Rsch. Librs. (Women's Studies sect., Edn. & Behavioral Sciences sect., WSS Significant Achievement award 2007). Office: Mich State U 100 Libr East Lansing MI 48824-1048 Office Phone: 517-432-6123 ext. 118. Office Fax: 517-432-8050. E-mail: ladenson@msu.edu.

LADER, MALCOLM HAROLD, pharmaceutical consultant; b. Liverpool, England, Feb. 27, 1936; s. Abe and Minnie (Sholl) L.; m. Susan Ruth Packer, Apr. 16, 1961; children: Deborah, Vicki, Charlotte. BSc, U. Liverpool, 1956, MB, ChB, 1959, MD, 1964; PhD, U. London, 1963, DSc, 1978; LLB, Coll. Law, 2006. Rsch. staff MRC, England, 1966—2001. Cons. Maudsley Hosp., 1970—2001; prof. clin. psychopharmacology U. London, 1978—2001, emeritus prof., 2001—; advisor WHO, 1995—2002; trustee Psychiatry Rsch. Trust. Author: Biological Treatments in Psychiatry, 1996; contbr. articles to profl. jours. Decorated Order of Brit. Empire. Fellow: Acad. Med. Scis., Royal Soc. Psychiatrists, Soc. for Study of Addiction (hon.), Am. Coll. Psychiatry (hon.), Brit. Assn. Psychopharmacology (hon.). Avocations: antiques, paintings. Home: 16 Kelsey Park Mansion 78 Wickham Rd Beckenham Kent BR3 6QH England Office Phone: 44-207-848-0372. Personal E-mail: m.lader@iop.kcl.ac.uk.

LADER, PHILIP, corporate financial executive, lawyer, academic administrator, diplomat; b. Jackson Heights, NY, Mar. 17, 1946; BA, Duke U., 1966; MA, U. Mich., 1967, Oxford U., Eng., 1968; JD, Harvard U., 1972. Bar: Fla. 1972, DC 1973, SC 1979. Atty. Sullivan & Cromwell, NYC, 1972; law clk. to U.S. cir. judge, 1973; pres. Sea Pines Co., Hilton Head Island, SC, 1979-83, Winthrop U., Rock Hill, SC, 1983-85; exec. v.p. Sir James Goldsmith's US Holding Co., 1986-88; pres. Bus. Execs. for Nat. Security, Washington, 1990—91; pres., vice chancellor Bond U., Queensland, Australia, 1991-93; adminstr. SBA, Washington, 1994-97; mem. President's Cabinet, Washington, 1994-97; U.S. amb. to Ct. of St. James, 1997-2001; chmn. WPP plc, 2001—; sr. advisor Morgan Stanley, 2001—; ptnr. Nelson Mullins Riley & Scarborough, 2001—. Dep. dir. for mgmt. Office Mgmt. and Budget, Exec. Office Pres., 1993; dep. chief of staff White House, asst. to Pres., 1993-94; chmn. Pres.'s Coun. on Integrity and Efficiency, 1993, chmn. Pres.'s Mgmt. Coun.; chmn. policy com. Nat. Performance Rev., 1993; candidate for gov. SC, 1986; bd. dirs Marathon Oil, AES Corp, RAND Corp., Songbird, Canary Wharf Plc. Rusal Corp.; trustee Smithsonian Am. Art Mus., mem. coun. Founder Renaissance Inst.; trustee Brit. Mus., 2001—06, Brit-Am. Bus. Coun., St. Paul's Cathedral Found., 2001—06, Windsor Leadership Trust, 2001—06, Found. for the 21st Century, Salzburg Global Seminar, 2001—06; chmn., Am. assoc. Royal Acad. Art., 2001—04; mem. vis. com. Harvard Law Sch., Harvard Divinity Sch., Yale Divinity Sch.; mem. internat. adv. com. Columbia U.; chmn. bd. visitors Duke U. Sanford Inst. Pub. Policy, 1999—2001; bd. dirs. ARC, 1996—97; mem. adv. bd. Prince of Wales Trust; mem. coun. Lloyd's of London, 2004—. Hon. fellow Pembroke Coll., Oxford U., London Bus. Sch., John Moores U.; hon. bencher Mid. Temple. Mem.: Chief Execs. Orgn., Coun. Fgn. Rels., Royal Soc. Arts, Mfrs. and Sci. (Benjamin Franklin medal 2001, Global Svc. Humanity award 2007), Soc. Internat. Bus. Fellows, Harvard Club N.Y.C., D.C. Met. Club, Rotary, Phi Beta Kappa. Episcopalian. Office: Liberty Ctr 151 Meeting St Ste 600 Charleston SC 29401

LADERMAN, GERALD, air transportation executive; Grad., Dartmouth Coll., Hanover, NH, U. Mich. Law Sch., Ann Arbor, 1982. With Hughes, Hubbard & Reed, NYC, 1982—88; v.p. corp. fin. Continental Airlines, Inc., 1988, staff v.p., sr. dir. corp. fin. and aircraft programs, v.p. corp. fin., sr. v.p. fin., treas., 1999—. Office: Continental Airlines Inc PO Box 4607 Houston TX 77210 Office Phone: 713-324-5000. Office Fax: 713-324-2637.*

LADEWIG, ANITA C., elementary school educator, researcher; d. William H. and Lillie Elizabeth Ladewig. BS in Elem. Edn., U. Tex., Austin, 1961. Elem. tchr. San Francisco Unified Sch. Dist., 1963—94; ret., 1994. Acting pres. San Francisco chpt. NOW, 1967. Mem.: AAUW, NEA, Marin Ret. Tchrs. Assn., Calif. Ret. Tchrs. Assn.

LADEWIG GOODMAN, JEANNE MARGARET, artist; b. Grand Rapids, Mich., June 26, 1923; d. Roland Adolph and Margaret Francis (Palmer) Ladewig; m. Larry Goodman, June 1963 (div. 1966). BEd, Concordia Coll., 1945; MS in Art Edn., Ill. Inst. Tech., 1970; postgrad., Chgo. Art Inst., 1959—68. Tchr. Luth. Schs., Chgo., 1952—62; tchr. art Park Ridge Pub. Sch. Dist. 64, Ill., 1962—74, coord. art, 1974—88. Workshop presenter NAEA-IAEA; guest lectr. U. Ill., 1971-72; mem. adv. bd. Contemporary Art Workshop, Chgo.; hiring cons. Evanston (Ill.) Schs., 1985; chair art bd. biannual art show Nat. Am. Pen Women, Denver, 2005-06. One-woman shows include Ariz. State U. down town, 1998, 2001, Artistic Expressions, Scottsdale, 2005, Meyers Gallery, 2005, Gallery Z, Providence, 2005, Meyers Art Gallery, 2006, Ariz. State U., 2007, exhibited in group shows at Ditmar Gallery Northwestern, 1972, Abney Galleries, 1973, Concordia U., 1996, Ariz. State U. Gammage Auditorium, 1998, World Fine Art, NY, 1997—2003, San Bernardino Ann. Ariz. Watercolor Art Show, 1999, 2001, 2003, Ariz. State down town, 2004, Meyers Gallery, Scottsdale; designer life-size horse for Scottsdale Parade Horses, 2001; contbr. articles to profl. jours. Vol. free meals Luth. Ch., Chgo., 1990-95; vol. Terra Mus. of Art, Chgo., 1989-95. Grantee Helene Wurlitzer Found., 1972; 1st prize water color show Artist Guild of Chgo., 1986; recipient Best of Show award, 1999, Vista Show Merit award, 2001, 2002. Mem.: AAUW, Scottsdale Artists League, Ariz. Artists League, Nat. League Am. Pen Women. (art bd. chair 2004—, pres. Scottsdale br.), Chgo. Artists Coalition, Chgo. Soc. of Artists. Lutheran. Avocations: travel, writing.

LADEWSKI, ROMAN SEBASTIAN, priest, educator; b. South Bend, Ind., June 5, 1914; s. Ladislaus John Ladewski and Martha Markowski. BA, U. Notre Dame, 1936; MA, Cath. U. Am., 1942; postgrad., Fresno State U., 1966—67, Ctr. for Person, 1967—75. Ordained priest Roman Catholic Church, 1940. Tchr., counselor U. Notre Dame, Ind., 1941—66; chaplain, counselor St. Mary's Coll. for Women, Notre Dame, 1966—70; chaplain, counselor, tchr. Ursuline Acad. and Motherhouse, Paola, Kans., 1970—79; chaplain St. Agnes Hosp., Fresno, 1980—82; asst. pastor, encounter group facilitator St. Francis Ch., Incline Village, Nev., 1982—86; tchr. Forever Learning Inst., South Bend, 1988—2006. Chaplain, cons. Holy Cross Sch. Nursing, South Bend, 1955—62; cnaplain Veteville married students' housing, Notre Dame, 1957—62, Univ. Village married students' housing, 1962—65. Contbr. articles to profl. publs. Chaplain Christian Family Movement, 1957—70. Recipient Bronze Pelican award, Boy Scouts Am., 1976, Development of Consciousness award, Internat. Meditation Soc., 1977; grantee svc. award, Univ. Village, 2002. Mem.: Chopin Fine Arts Club (scholarship chmn. 1955—70). Avocation: photography. Address: Holy Cross House Douglas Rd Notre Dame IN 46556-1048

LADIK, STEVEN M., lawyer; b. Chgo., Mar. 15, 1953; m. Robin Ridgeway, Nov. 3, 2001. BA, North Tex. State U., 1977; JD, So. Meth. U., 1983. Bar: Tex. 1983, US Dist. Ct. No. Dist. Tex. 1983, US Ct. Appeals 5th Cir. 1983. Shareholder Jenkens & Gilchrist, P.C., Dallas, 2000—, firm leader immigration practice group. Mem.: Am. Immigration Law Found. (pres. 2004—), Am. Immigration Lawyers Assn. (pres. 2001—02, past chair Tex. chpt.), State Bar Tex. Office: Jenkens & Gilchrist PC Ste 3700 1445 Ross Ave Dallas TX 75202-2799 Office Phone: 214-855-4117. Office Fax: 214-855-4300. Business E-Mail: sladik@jenkens.com.

LADISCH, MICHAEL R., engineering educator; b. Upper Darby, Pa., Jan. 15, 1950; s. Rolf Karl and Brigitte M. L.; m. Christine Schmitz, July 26, 1975; children: Sarah, Mark. BSChemE, Drexel U., Phila., 1973; MSChemE, Purdue U., 1974, PhD in Chem. Engring., 1977. Rsch. engr Lab. Renewable Resources Engring. and dept. chem. engring. Purdue U., West Lafayette, Ind., 1977-78, asst. prof. food and agrl. engring., 1978-81, assoc. prof., 1981-85, prof., 1985-2000, disting. prof., 2000—. Dir. Lab Renewable Resources, Eng., 1999—. Contbr. articles to profl. jours. Chmn. com. on bioprocess engring. Nat. Rsch. Coun., 1991—92. Recipient U.S. Presdl. Young Investigator award NSF, 1984, Johnson Rsch. award ACS, 2002. Mem. US Nat. Acad. Engring, AIChE (Food, Pharm., and Bioengring. Rsch. award 2001), Am. Chem. Soc. (librarian 1982-84, chmn.-elect 1985—86, program chmn. 1985-86, past chmn. 1986—87, coord. long range program 1990—94, Van Lanen award BIOT div. 1990, W.H. Peterson award Microbiol. div. 1977, Agrl. Rsch. award from Purdue U. 1985), Am. Soc. Agrl. Engrs. Achievements include patents in field. Office: Purdue U LORRE 500 Central Dr West Lafayette IN 47907 Office Phone: 765-494-7022. Business E-Mail: ladisch@purdue.edu.

LADJEVARDI, HABIB, historian; b. Tehran, Iran, May 28, 1938; came to U.S., 1950; s. Seyed Mahmoud and Tahereh (Kashani) L.; m. Mina Nassirzadeh, Aug. 3, 1962 (div. June 1979); children: Mahmoud, Mariam, Leila. BS, Yale U., 1961; MBA, Harvard U., 1963; DPhil, Oxford U., 1981. Personnel dir. Behshahr Ind. Group, Tehran, 1963-65, mktg. dir., 1966-69; pres. Paxan Corp., Tehran, 1969-70; chmn. bd. dirs. Container Corp. of Iran, 1969-79; founder, v.p. Iran Ctr. Mgmt. Studies, Tehran, 1970-79; sr. rsch. assoc. Harvard U. Bus. Sch., Cambridge, Mass., 1980-81; rsch. assoc. Harvard U. Ctr. for Middle Eastern Studies, 1981—, assoc. dir., 1987-90, dir. Iranian oral history project, 1981—. Mem. acceptance coms. Tehran Stock Exch., 1973-76; lectr. Iran Ctr. for Mgmt. Studies, 1975-79; vis. fellow Oxford (Eng.) Ctr. Mgmt. Studies, 1976-79; v.p. exec. coun. Harvard U. Bus. Sch., 1978-79; exec. sec. Soc. for Iranian Studies, Cambridge, 1982-87; chmn. Iranian Studies Harvard U. Ctr. for Middle Eastern Studies, 1990—, chmn. pubs. com., 1990—. Author: Labor Unions and Autocracy in Iran, 1985, Guide to the Iranian Oral History Collection, 1993, Memoirs of Ali Amini, 1995, Memoirs of Chapour Bakhtiar, 1996, Memoirs of Hamid Kadjar, 1996, Memoirs of M.E. Amirteymour, 1997, Memoirs of Abdolmajid Madjidi, 1998, Memoirs of Fatemeh Pakravan, 1998, Memoirs of Jafar Sharif-Emami, 1999, Memoirs of M.A. Modjtahedi, 2000, Memoirs of Mehdi Hairi-Yazdi, 2001, Memoirs of Mahmoud Foroughi, 2003; contbr. articles to profl. jours., chapters to books. Mem. coun. of state Adminstrv. and Employment Affairs of Iran, 1972-76; dir. devel. and investment Bank of Iran, 1972-79; mem. ctrl. coun. Pres. of Univs. and Colls. of Iran, 1971-78; pres. Tahereh Found., Cambridge, Mass., 1982—. NEH grantee, 1984-87. Mem. Am. Hist. Assn., Young Presidents Orgn., Acad. Polit. Sci., N.Y. Acad. Scis., Iranian Assn. of Boston (founder, pres. 1988-91), Yale U. Class Coun. Avocations: skiing, gardening.

LADJEVARDI, HAMID, portfolio manager; b. Tehran, Iran, June 11, 1948; arrived in U.S., 1948; s. Ahmad and Banoo (Barzin) Ladjevardi; children: Adella, Lilly. BA in Econs., BA in Polit. Sci., U. Calif., Berkeley, 1971; MBA, Harvard U., 1973. Dep. mng. dir. Behshahr Indsl. Group, Tehran, 1974-79; vice-chmn., fin. dir. Akam Group of Cos., Tehran, 1975-79; investment mgr., v.p. Morgan Stanley & Co., NYC, 1980-92; mgr. Baltic Fund 1 LLC, NY, 1994—2002, Am. Baltic Investments, 2002—. Instr. Fairleigh Dickinson U., Rutherford, NJ, 1984. Co-chmn. U.S. Baltic Found.; trustee Zimmerli Art Mus. Mem.: Carnegie Coun. Ethics and Internat. Affairs, Fgn. Policy Assn., Nat. Arts Club, Harvard Club, U.S. Senatorial Club. Home: 284 Lafayette St Apt #5D New York NY 10012 Office Phone: 0113717222275. E-mail: hamid@americanbaltic.com.

LADMER, WILLIAM EDWARD, food product engineering executive; s. Alfred and Lucille L.; children: Lisa Beth, David Aaron. BSME magna cum laude, U. Ctrl. Ariz., 1966, MSIE, 1969. Registered profl. engr.; cert. plant engr. Engr. mgr. Boeing Corp., Seattle, 1966-72; pres. Ladmer Engring., San Diego, 1972-80, Allentown, Pa., 1982-90; engr. mgr. Sohio Petroleum, San Francisco, 1980-82; plant engr. mfg. Kraft Foods, Champaign, Ill., 1990-93; corp. engring. group mgr. McKee Foods, Collegedale, Tenn., 1993-97, E2M, Atlanta, 1997-98; plant engring. mgr. Pontiac Foods, Columbia, SC, 1999—2000; ret., 2000. Author: Design Build-What Can You-What Should You Expect, 1996, Project Engineering-Food Plants, 1991, Food Plant Sanitation, 1984. Firefighter Tri Cmty. Vol. Fire Dept., Collegedale, 1993-97. With US Army, chief warrant officer US Army, 1961—63. Mem. Inst. of Indsl. Engrs. (sr. mem.), Inst. of Plant Engrs. (sr. mem.), Soc. of Mfg. Engrs. (sr. mem.). Achievements include 2 patents on the method of 2 sided welding, application of leaded glass on substrate. Home: 29 Founders Lake Ct Columbia SC 29229-7676 Personal E-mail: bladmer@earthlink.net.

LADNER, BENJAMIN, former academic administrator; b. Mobile, Ala. m. Nancy Bullard Ladner; 4 children. BA, Baylor U.; BD, Southern Seminary; PhD, Duke U.; D (hon.), Elizabethtown Coll., Pa., SookMyung Women's U., South Korea. Prof. dept. philosophy and religious studies U. N.C., Greensboro; pres. Nat. Faculty of Humanities, Arts & Scis., Atlanta, Am. U., Washington, 1994—2005. Bd. dir. chair Patriot League Coun. of Presidents; chair, bd. trustee Consortium of Universities of the Washington Met. Area; mem. Com. for Econ. Develop. Bd., Nat. Assn. for Independent Coll. and U., NCAA Divsn. I. Achievements include leading Am. U. team by providing leadership in the design, establishment, and operation of the Am. U. of Sharjah (AUS) in United Emirates since its inception in 1997.

LADNER, NORMA FOLEY, elementary school educator; d. Walter Thomas Foley and Emily Catherine Turan; m. Carvin John Ladner, Dec. 19, 1970; children: Michele Ladner Mills, Brian John. BS, U. So. Miss., Hattiesburg, 1970. Cert. tchr. secondary social studies La., 1978. Tchr. East Jr. H.S., Gulfport, Miss., 1970—71, West Jr. H.S., Gulfport, 1972—73, Our Lady of Perpetual Help, Corpus Christi, Tex., 1977—78, Holy Redeemer H.S., Lacombe, La., 1978—80, St. Margaret Mary Sch., Slidell, La., 1980—, chmn. dept. social studies, 1980—. Dir. plays St. Margaret Mary Sch., 1992—2004, dir. sch. talent show, 1991—, moderator student coun., 2005—. Named My Tchr. of Yr., East St. Tammany Elks Club, 1994, Tchr. of Yr., St. Margaret Mary Sch., 2006. Mem.: La. Coun. Social Studies, La. Mid. Sch. Assn., PTO (tchr. rep. 1996—2004). Roman Catholic. Office: St Margaret Mary Sch 1050 Robert Blvd Slidell LA 70458 Home Phone: 985-641-9429; Office Phone: 985-643-4612.

LADNER, RENEE, women's college basketball coach; m. Eddie Ladner; children: Allison, Jennifer. B in Health, Phys. Edn. and Recreation, U. Miss., Oxford, 1981. Instr. sci. and phys. edn. for 7th and 8th grades, coach North Gulfport, Miss., 1981—87; instr., coach Harrison Ctrl. Ninth Grade Sch., Gulfport, 1987—90; head coach St. John HS, Gulfport, 1990—2000; asst. coach U. Fla., Gaineville, 2000—02, U. Miss., 2003—07, head coach, 2007—. Named Girl's Basketball Coach of Yr., Miss. Assn. Coaches, 2000. Office: Ole Miss Womens Basketball Ole Miss Athletics All American Dr University MS 38677 Office Phone: 662-915-7500. Office Fax: 662-915-7871. E-mail: rladner@olemiss.edu.*

LADONNA, FRANK, psychologist; b. NYC, Apr. 19, 1952; s. Anthony and Maria Ladonna; 1 child, Francine Ladonna. BA, Iona Coll., New Rochelle, NY, 1974; MA, Fairfield U., Conn., 1976. Cert. advanced study Fairfield U., 1979, sch. psychologist NY State Edn. Dept., State Conn., Dept. Edn., Nat. Sch. Psychology Bd. Gen. office asst. Prentice Hall Inc., Englewood Cliffs, NJ, 1971—73; counselor, transportation facilitator New Rochelle Acad., NY, 1973—74; emotional health aid, child care worker St. Agnes Home and Sch. for Children, Sparkill, NY, 1974—77; sch. psychologist Bridgeport Bd. Edn., Conn., 1978—2003. Recipient Excellence in Tchg. award, Hall Sch. Parent Group, 1998. Mem.: NASP, Conn. Assn. Sch. Psychologists. Democrat. Roman Cath. Avocation: music. Home: 759 Judson Pl Unit RR Stratford CT 06615-5931

LADOW, C. STUART, financial consultant; b. Warren, Pa., Apr. 21, 1925; s. Clyde and Glendine (Bentley) LaD.; m. Donna Elizabeth Miller, Aug. 21, 1993; 1 child, Paul Stuart. BA, Cornell U., 1947. With Gen. Electric Co., 1947-50; mgr. N.Y. region Gen. Electric Credit Corp., NYC, 1950-80, v.p. Stamford, Conn., 1971-80; pres. GECC Fin. Services, 1975-78, Color Tyme TV Rental div. Curtis Mathes Corp., Athens, Tex., 1980; sr. v.p. Yegen Assocs., Inc., Paramus, NJ, 1981-85, exec. v.p., 1985-87; pres. Yegen Equity Loan Corp., Paramus, NJ, 1987; fin. svcs. cons. Allison Park, Pa., 1988-99; dir. Nat. Capital Holdings, Allison Park, Pa., 1997-98; ret., 1999. Bd. dirs. Puritan Life Ins. Co., Providence. V.p., bd. dirs. Jr. Achievement of Stamford, Inc., 1973-80; exec. budget com., chmn. budget panel United Way of Stamford, 1973-80; chmn. Stamford chpt. Am. Cancer Soc., 1977; pres. Spring Meadow Condominium Assn., Wyckoff, N.J., 1983, trustee, 1983-88; moderator Emmanuel Bapt. Ch., Ridgewood, N.J., 1985-86; trustee North Hills Community Baptist Ch., 1988-91; dir. Hampton Twsp. Mcpl. Authority, Allison Park, Pa., 1991-97, dir., treas. Baptist Homes of Western Pa., 1992-98, pres. Arbors Homeowners Assn., Allison Park, 1992-93; pres. Cornell U. Class of 1947, 1992-97. Recipient Cmty. Svc. award Gen. Electric Credit Corp., 1976. Mem. Nat. Second Mortgage Assn. (pres. 1987-88, Outstanding Service award, Meritorious Svc. award 1989), Nat. Consumer Finance Assn. (certificate of appreciation), Masons, Shriners, Cornell Club of Pitts. Republican. Baptist. Home and Office: 4211 Latour Ct Allison Park PA 15101-2968 *Ours is a great country that deserves the devotion and strong support of those who call it home. There can be few satisfactions in life greater than assisting in the moral, spiritual and career growth of those whom we have the opportunity to know and possibly influence.*

LADSON-BILLINGS, GLORIA J., education educator; BA, Stanford U., 1984. Prof. urban edn. Dept. Curriculum and Instrn. U. Wis., Madison, project dir. Wis. Ctr. Edn. Rsch.; vis. scholar Ctr. Advanced Study in Behavioral Sci., Stanford, Calif., 2003—04. Editor: Am. Edn. Rsch. Jour., sect. on teaching, learning & human devel.; author: The Dreamkeepers: Successful Teachers of African American Children, 1994; contbr. Fellow: Annenberg Inst. Sch. Reform, Brown U. (sr.); mem.: Nat. Acad. Edn. (mem. 2005—), Am. Ednl. Rsch. Assn. (mem. 1989—, pres. 2005, coun. mem. at large, mem. profl. devel. and tng. com., Palmer O. Johnson award, Early Career award). Office: U Wis Sch Edn 464c Teacher Edn 225 N Mills St Madison WI 53706 Office Phone: 202-223-9485, 608-263-1006. Office Fax: 202-775-1824. E-mail: gjladson@facstaff.wisc.edu.*

LADWIG, HAROLD ALLEN, neurologist; b. Manilla, Iowa, May 11, 1922; s. Ernest and Iva Marie (Allen) L.; m. Marjorie Lois Foster, June 26, 1946; children: Stephen H., Rosemary A. BA, U. Iowa, 1942, MD, 1947. Intern St. Joseph Hosp., Sioux City, Iowa, 1947-48; pvt. practice U. Minn., 1948-49, resident, 1949-50; pvt. practice Nebr., 1954-83, NC, 1983—; pres. Omaha Neurol. Clinic, 1972-83. Contbr. articles to profl. jours. Bd. dirs. Boys and Girls Club, Wilson, NC, 1995—, Salvation Army, Wilson, 1996-, Country Drs. Mus., Bailey, NC, 1995-2002, Mental Health Bd., Wilson, 1995-2007, Mental Health LM25, 2007-. Comdr. USNR, 1950-52. Fellow ACP, Am. Acad. Neurology; mem. AMA, Am. Assn. Electrodiagnostic Medicine, Am. Soc. Electroencephalography and Neurophysiology, Wilson County Med. Soc. (sec. 1993, v.p. 1994, pres. 1995), Wilson Meml. Hosp. Found. (pres. 1993-2006), Douglas County Med. Soc. (exec. bd. 1960-63), Kiwanis (pres. Wilson chpt. 1995, Kiwanian of Yr. award 1992-93), Phi Beta Kappa, Beta Beta Beta. Methodist. Avocation: computers. Home: PO Box 3164 Wilson NC 27895-3164 Personal E-mail: hal@usa.com.

LAEGER, THERESE ROACH, performing arts educator; b. Birmingham, Ala., Aug. 30, 1956; d. Robert Ernest and Jeanette Stephens Roach; m. Kenneth Edward Laeger, June 28, 1980; children: Brittany Anne, Colleen Jeanette. BA, Birmingham So. Coll., Ala., 1975—79. Soloist dancer Birmingham Ballet, 1974—76; dancer Cleve. Ballet, 1978—79; soloist/prin. dancer Ala. Ballet, Birmingham, 1980—87, ballet mistress/asst. to the artistic dir., 1980—96; dance instr. Ala. Sch. Fine Arts, Birmingham, 1980—96, dance chair, 1996—2007; artistic assoc. Arova Dance Co., Birmingham, 2007—. Chmn. regional dance competition Nat. Soc. Arts & Letters, Birmingham; scholarship chair Ala. Dance Coun., Birmingham, 2003—05. Dancer (ballet performance) Firebird (Obelisk award, 1978). Chmn. adminstrv. coun. Avondale United Meth. Ch., Birmingham, 2006—. Methodist. Home: 3114 Whitehall Rd Birmingham AL 35209 Office: Ala Sch Fine Arts 1800 8th Ave N Birmingham AL 35203 Home Phone: 205-871-8706. Home Fax: 205-251-9541.

LAESSIG, RONALD HAROLD, preventive medicine and pathology educator, state official; b. Marshfield, Wis., Apr. 4, 1940; s. Harold John and Ella Louise L.; m. Joan Margaret Spreda, Jan. 29, 1966; 1 child, Elizabeth Susan. BS, U. Wis., Stevens Point, 1962; PhD, U. Wis., 1965. Cert. chem. chemist Nat. Registry Cert. Chemists, 1968. Jr. faculty Princeton (N.J.) U., 1966; chief clin. chemistry Wis. State Lab. Hygiene, Madison, 1966-80, dir., 1980—; asst. prof. preventive medicine U. Wis., Madison, 1966-72, assoc. prof., 1972-76, prof., 1976—, prof. pathology, 1980—. Cons. Ctrs. Disease Control, Atlanta, bd. sci. counselors Nat. Ctr. Environ. Health Ga., 2004-; dir. Nat. Com. for Clin. Lab. Stds., Villanova, Pa., 1977-80; chmn. invitro diagnostic products adv. com. FDA, 1974-75; mem. rev. com. Nat. Bur. Stds., 1983-86; legis. coun., State of Wis., 2003-04; chair Pub. Health Adv. Com., Wis., 2003-05, mem. 1998-. Mem. editl. bd. Analytical Chemistry, 1970-76, Health Lab. Sci., 1970-76, Med. Electronics, 1970-80; contbr. articles to profl. jours. Mem. State of Wis.

Tech. Com. Alcohol and Traffic Safety, 1970-88; mem. adv. com. Newbon Screening, Wis. Recipient Excellence in Advocacy award, March of Dimes, 2004, Gold Std. for Pub. Health Excellence award, 2004; Sloan Found. grantee, 1966; recipient numerous grants. Mem. APHA (Difco award 1974), Am. Assn. Clin. Chemistry (chmn. safety com. 1984-86, bd. dirs. 1986-89, Natelson award 1989, Contbns. Svc. to Profession award 1990, Reiner award 1998, Eiler award 1999), Am. Soc. for Med. Tech., Nat. Com. Clin. Lab. Stds. (pres. 1980-82, bd. dirs. 1984-87), Assn. Pub. Health Labs. (chmn. environ. health com. 2001-04, Gold Std. Pub. Health Excellence award 2004), Nat. Ctr. Environ. Health/CDC (bd. counselors 2004-), Sigma Xi. Avocation: woodworking. Office: State Lab Hygiene 465 Henry Mall Madison WI 53706-1578 Office Phone: 608-262-3911. Business E-Mail: rhl@mail.slh.wisc.edu. *If you are doing something you really enjoy and it affords you the opportunity to really help your fellow man--you're really blessed (like I am).*

LAETTNER, CHRISTIAN DONALD, professional basketball player; b. Angola, NY, Aug. 17, 1969; Student, Duke U. Basketball player Minn. Timberwolves, 1992-1995, Atlanta Hawks, 1995-98, Detroit Pistons, 1998-99, Dallas Mavericks, 2000—01, Wash. Wizards, 2001—04, Dallas Mavericks, 2004—. Named Most Outstanding Player in NCAA Divsn. 1A Tournament, 1991, Sporting News Coll. Player of Yr., 1992, Naismith award, 1992, Wooden award, 1992; mem. Gold medal Winning Olympic Team, Barcelona, Spain, 1992. mem. NCAA Nat. I Championship Team, 1991, 1992. Office: c/o Dallas Mavericks The Pavillion 2909 Taylor St Dallas TX 75226

LAFANTANO, ELIZABETH, music educator; d. John Joseph and Joan Theresa Bestercy; m. Pascal Marc LaFantano, Apr. 11, 1992; 1 child, Mary Elizabeth. MusB in Music Edn., SUNY, Fredonia, 1978—82; MA in Liberal Studies in Music & Edn., SUNY at Stony Brook, Stony Brook, New York, 1985—87; Profl. Diploma in Sch. Adminstrn., SUNY, Stony Brook, 2004—06. Cert. in music edn. NY, 1987, sch. dist. adminstrn. NY, 2006. Music tchr. St. Anastasia's John Carroll HS, Fort Pierce, Fla., 1982—84, Kings Pk. Sch. Dist., NY, 1984—2005, supr. fine & applied arts, 2005—. Religious educator St. Joseph's Ch., Kings Park, 2002—06. Mem.: NY State Sch. Music Assn., Kings Pk. Classroom Tchrs. Assn. (assoc.; v.p. 2000—02, Saturn/ Am. Fedn. Tchrs. Partners in Leadership award 2002), Suffolk County Music Educators Assn. (assoc.), NY State Coun. Adminstrs. Music Edn. (assoc.), Music Educators Nat. Conf. (assoc.). Office: William T Rogers Mid Sch 97 Old Dock Rd Kings Park NY 11754 Home Phone: 631-255-4427; Office Phone: 631-269-3289. Business E-Mail: lafantanoe@mail.kpcsd.k12.ny.us.

LA FARGE, TIMOTHY, retired plant geneticist; b. NYC, Mar. 14, 1930; s. Louis Bancel and Hester Alida (Emmet) La F.; m. Anne Blackstone, Oct. 16, 1960 (div. Mar. 1964); m. Frances Madelyne Holst, Aug. 6, 1966 (dec. 1992); 1 child, Jason Emmet; m. Nkem R. Salako, Dec. 4, 1993 (div. Oct. 1998); m. Frances W. Stott, Sept. 5, 2002. BA in Dance, Black Mountain Coll., 1952; BSc in Forestry, U. Maine, 1964; M in Forestry, Yale U., New Haven, Conn., 1965; PhD, Mich. State U., East Lansing, 1971. Forestry aid Forest Svc., Orono, Maine, 1961—64; lab. technician geology dept. Yale U., New Haven, 1965; rsch. forester USDA Forest Svc., Macon, Ga., 1965-69, plant geneticist Southea. Sta., 1970-82, plant geneticist Nat. Forest Sys. Atlanta, 1982-2000; consulting assoc. Daniels and Assocs., Inc., Forest Genetics Cons., 2000. Contbr. articles to profl. jours, rsch. papers in field. Recipient Certs. of Merit, USDA Forest Svc., Atlanta, 1986, 88. Mem. AAAS, Soc. Am. Foresters (chair Bay area chpt. 2003-2004). Republican. Achievements include demonstration that backcrossing and hybridization between shortleaf pine and loblolly pine can effectively produce fast-growing back-cross hybrids that are resistant to fusiform rust; application of Best Linear Prediction to analysis of unbalanced or messy progeny test data. Home: 863 Foerster St San Francisco CA 94127-2307 Office Phone: 415-337-0304. Personal E-mail: timlaf@comcast.net.

LAFAVORE, MICHAEL J., editor-in-chief; b. Portland, Maine, Apr. 28, 1952; s. Joseph T. and Marion (Brown) L.; m. Trieste A. Kennedy; children: Nico, Alec. BA in English, U. Maine, 1975. Reporter Jour. Tribune, Biddeford, Maine, 1975-79; sr. editor Organic Gardening, Emmaus, Pa., 1979-84, Practical Homeowner, Emmaus, Pa., 1984-88; exec. editor Men's Health, Emmaus, Pa., 1988-96, editor-in-chief, 1996—2000, TV Guide, NYC, 2003—04; editl. dir. Meredith Mag., 2005—. Screening com. Nat. Mag. Awards, NYC, 1994; cons. in the field. Author: The Home Gym, 1978, Radon: The Invisible Threat, 1985; editor: Men's Health Advisor, 1992-93. Recipient Mont award Photo Design Mag., 1989, Mental Health Media award Nat. Mental Health Assn., 1991, Award for Excellence, Men's Fashion Assn., 1992, 95; named Editor of Yr., Advertising Age, 1995, Internat. Editor of Yr., Fgn. Press, 1998. Office: Meredith Mag 125 Park Ave New York NY 10017-5529

LAFEBER, WALTER FREDERICK, historian, educator, writer; b. Walkerton, Ind., Aug. 30, 1933; s. Ralph N. and Helen (Lidecker) LaF.; m. Sandra Gould, Sept. 11, 1955; children: Scott Nichols, Suzanne Margaret Kahl. BA, Hanover Coll., 1955; MA, Stanford, 1956; PhD, U. Wis., 1959. Asst. prof. history Cornell U., 1959-63, assoc. prof., 1963-67, prof., 1967—. Mem. adv. com. hist. div. State Dept., 1971-75; lectr. in field. Author: The New Empire...1860-1898, 1963, 2d edit., 1998, America, Russia and the Cold War, 1966, 10th edit., 2007, The Panama Canal, The Crisis in Historical Perspective, 1978, expanded edit., 1979, 2d edit., 1989, Inevitable Revolutions: The U.S. in Central America, 1983, 2d edit., 1992, The American Age...1750 to the Present, 1989, 2d edit., 1994, The American Search for Opportunity, 1865-1913, 1993, The Clash: U.S. Japanese Relations Throughout History, 1997, Michael Jordan and the New Global Capitalism, 1999, 2d edit., 2002, The Deadly Bet: LBJ, Vietnam, and the 1968 Election, 2005; co-author: The American Century, 5th edit., 1997, America in Vietnam, 1985; editor: John Quincy Adams and American Continental Empire, 1965, America in the Cold War, 1969, also others; co-editor: Behind the Throne, Essays in Honor of Fred Harvey Harrington, 1993; mem. editorial adv. bd.: Polit. Sci. Quar.; cons., appeared on PBS programs on Theodore Roosevelt, Harry Truman, 1900, War of 1898 and others. Recipient Gustavus Myers prize, 1985, Bancroft prize, 1998; Guggenheim fellow, 1990. Mem.: Soc. Historians of Am. Fgn. Rels. (pres. 1999—2000), Am. Acad. Arts and Scis., The Hist. Soc., Am. Hist. Assn. (Albert Beveridge prize 1962), Orgn. Am. Historians (Hawley prize 1998). Office: Cornell U Dept History McGraw Hall Ithaca NY 14853-4601 Business E-Mail: WFL3@cornell.edu.

LAFER, FRED SEYMOUR, data processing executive; b. Passaic, NJ, Mar. 17, 1929; s. Abraham David and Pauline (Braer) L.; m. Barbara Bernstein, Apr. 4, 1954; children: Deborah, Gordon, Diana. BIE, NYU, 1950, JD, 1961; LHD (hon.), William Paterson Coll., 1987. Bar: N.J. 1961. Sec. to Justice Hayden Proector, N.J. Supreme Ct., 1961-62; partner firm Hoffman Humphreys Lafer, Wayne, NJ, 1962-67; sec., gen. counsel Automatic Data Processing, Inc., Clifton, NJ, 1967-97, v.p., 1968-81, sr. v.p., 1981-96; pres. N.J. Nets Profl. Basketball Team, 1984. Pres. Taub Found., 1996—, Am. Friends Shalem Haryman Inst., 2007-. Chmn. United Jewish Appeal Fedn. North Jersey, 1973-74; pres. Jewish Fedn. North Jersey, 1976-77; v.p. N.J. Bd. Edn., 1967-68; bd. dirs. Chilton Meml. Hosp., Pompton Plains, N.J., 1970-72; trustee William Paterson Coll., 1974—, vice-chmn. bd., 1977, chmn. bd., 1978-80; pres. Am. Friends of Hebrew U., 1985-89; exec. com. Washington Inst. Near East Policy, sec.-treas., 1993-99, pres., 2000095, chmn., 2006—. Served to lt. USAF, 1951-52. Recipient honorary doctorate Hebrew U. Jerusalem, 1995. Mem. Computer Law Assn. (pres. 1972-74), Assn. Data Processing Service Orgns. (chmn. 1983), ABA Office: c/o Taub Found 300 Frank M Burr Blvd Teaneck NJ 07666

LAFEVER, HOWARD NELSON, botanist, educator, geneticist; b. Wayne County, Ind., May 13, 1938; s. Samuel L. and Flossie B. (Ellis) L.; m. Kay M. Schutz, Aug. 30, 1958; children: Julie, Jeff BS, Purdue U., 1959, MS, 1961, PhD, 1963. Instr. Wis. State U., LaCrosse, 1963; assoc. prof. Purdue U., West Lafayette, Ind., 1963; research geneticist USDA-Agrl. Research Service, Starkville, Miss., 1963-65; plant breeder, prof. agronomy Ohio State U., Ohio Agr. Research and Devel. Ctr., Wooster, 1965-91; owner Sunbeam Extract Co., 1991—2005; founder Sunbeam Ind., Inc., 2007—. Patentee Becker, Cardinal, Dynasty, Freedom Hopewell, Bravo and Daisy wheats and developer of 40 other small grain varieties; contbr. numerous articles to profl. jours. Fellow Am. Soc. Agronomy (bd. dirs. 1982-84, assoc. editor 1982-85); mem. Assn. Ofcl. Seed Certifying Agys., Ohio Seed Improvement Assn. (dir. 1968-83, grantee 1975-91). Presbyterian. Avocations: woodworking, golf. Office Phone: 330-465-0477. E-mail: hnlafever@aol.com.

LAFEVOR, KIMBERLY ANN, human resources specialist, educator; b. Detroit; d. Robert Lee and Mary Kathleen Calloway; m. Paul Earle Lafevor; children: Lauren, Meghan. BS in Psychology and Pers. Psychology, Athens State U.; MS in Human Resource Mgmt., Troy State U.; PhD in Bus. Adminstn. and Edn., U. Sarasota; cert. in human resources, Human Resource Cert. Inst. Human resources mgr. GM, Spring Hill, Tenn., leadership develop. advisor, tng. & develop. team leader; mem. faculty Athens State U., Ala., 2006—. Adj. faculty Columbia State Cmty. coll., Bethel Coll.; sr. human resources cons. Helton, Umberger & Assoc., Nashville. Contbr. articles to profl. jours. Leader Girl Scouts Am., Cumberland Valley Coun., Nashville. Mem.: Tenn. Employment Rels. Rsch. Assn. (first v.p.), Indsl. Rels. Rsch. Assn., Soc. Human Resources Mgmt., Rotary. Avocations: softball, travel. Office: Athens State U 300 N Beaty St Athens AL 35611 Office Phone: 256-233-8159. Business E-Mail: kim.lafevor@athens.edu.

LAFFER, ARTHUR BETZ, economist; b. Youngstown, Ohio, Aug. 14, 1940; s. William Gillespie Laffer; m. Traci Lynn Hickman; 6 children. BA, Yale U., 1963; MBA, Stanford U., 1965, Ph.D, 1971. Faculty mem. U. Chgo., 1967—76, assoc. prof. bus. economics, 1970—76; chief economist, Office Mgmt. & Budget Exec. Office of the Pres., Washington, 1970—72; prof. fin. & bus. economics U. So. Calif., LA, 1976-84, Charles B. Thornton prof. bus. economics, 1979-84; Disting. Univ. prof. Pepperdine U., 1984—87; founder, CEO Laffer Associates, 1979—. Cons. to sec. US Dept. Treasury, 1972—77; mem. Econ. Policy Adv. Bd. Exec. Office of the Pres., Washington, 1981—89; mem. exec. com. Reagan/Bush Fin. Com., 1984; co-chmn. Policy Coun. for the Free Enterprise Fund. Author: Supply Side Economics: Financial Decision -Making for the 80's. Bd. dirs. Com. Monetary Research and Edn.; hon. bd. dirs. Los Angeles County Mus. Natural History; mem. adv. bd. Taxpayers Found. Recipient Commerce Assocs. Dean's Facility award U. So. Calif., 1979, Teaching Excellence award U. So. Calif. Assocs., 1980, John J. Knezevich Americanism award, 1979, Daniel Webster award Internat. Platform Assn., 1979, Father of Yr. award West Coast Fathers' Day Com., 1983 Achievements include the invention of the Laffer Curve. E-mail: jax@laffer.com.

LAFFITTE, LARRY JAMES, industrial organizational psychologist, consultant; b. Tokyo, May 11, 1952; s. Leroy and Gennie Hiroko Laffitte; m. Mei Wen Laffitte, May 11, 2001; children: Jeffrey Wen, Lara Wen. BA with honors, So. Ill. U., 1985, MS, 1988; PhD, Ill. Inst. Tech., 1998. Cert. test adminstr. Wonderlic. Psychologist III Dept. Mental Health/Devel. Disabilities, Chester, 1989—98; cons., project mgr. Wonderlic Inc., Libertyville, Ill., 1998—2000; dir. performance consulting Psychol. Assocs., St. Louis, 2000—02; rsch. psychologist Army Rsch. Inst. - Leader Devel. Rsch. Unit, Leavenworth, Kans., 2002—06; authorized vendor program assessment mgr. Fifth Third Bank, Cin., 2006—. Cons., Leavenworth, 2000—05; presenter in field; equal employment opportunity/affirmative action officer Army Rsch. Inst. - LDRU, Leavenworth, 2002—06, safety officer, 2002—06, real property officer, 2006. Contbr. scientific papers to profl. confs. and publs. With US Army, 1969—73. Recipient Superior Unit award, Dept. of the Army, 2002. Mem.: APA, Soc. Indsl./Orgnl. Psychology (organizer symposium 2006, Consortium of Grad. Students award 1998, Rsch. in Army Rsch. and Orgn. award 2002). Achievements include research in advances in talent and performance management, selection, executive development and coaching; advances in measurement equivalence: new item parameter replication (IPR) approach for polytomous DIF; psychometric evaluation of 360 feedback; measurement equivalence of a 360 degree feedback assessment with confirmatory factor analysis and item response theory. Office: Fifth Third Bank MD 10GA51 38 Fountain Square Plz Cincinnati OH 45263 Office Phone: 513-534-0795. Office Fax: 513-534-0481. E-mail: larry.laffitte@53.com.

LAFLEUR, CHRISTOPHER J., ambassador; BA, Oberlin Coll. Diplomat U.S. Embassy, Paris, U.S. Mission to UN, NYC, Am. Inst., Taiwan, 1993—97; mission dep. chief U.S. Embassy, Tokyo, 1997—2001; dir. Indochina affairs US Dept. State, Washington, 1991—93, prin. dep. asst. sec. East Asia and Pacific affairs, 2001—03; Cyrus Vance fellow in diplomatic studies Coun. on Fgn. Rels., Washington, 2003—04; U.S. amb. to Malaysia US Dept. State, Kuala Lampur, 2004—. Office: 4210 Kuala Lumpur Pl Washington DC 20521

LAFLEUR, KENNETH CHARLES, ophthalmologist; b. Lawtell, La., Aug. 22, 1941; s. Alvin George and Mary Irene (Olivier) L.; m. Patricia Ione McNamara, Aug. 3, 1963; children: James Mathew, Suzanne Annette, Caroline Marie. BS, U. So. La., 1963; MD, Tulane U., 1966. Diplomate Am. Bd. Ophthalmology. Intern Hermann Hosp., Houston, 1966-67; ophthalmology resident U. Tex., 1967-70; practice medicine specializing in ophthalmology Opeloussas, La., 1972—. Clin. asst. prof. La. State U. Eye Ctr., New Orleans, 1983—. Trustee St. Landry Roman Cath. Ch., Opelousas, 1979-99. Maj. M.C., U.S. Army, 1970-72. Fellow Am. Acad. Ophthalmology, Soc. Mil. Ophthalmologists; mem. Am. Intraocular Implant Soc., Elks, K.C. (Knight of Yr. award 1984). Avocation: fishing. Office: 1110 Dr AC Terrence Blvd Opelousas LA 70570 Home Phone: 337-948-1246; Office Phone: 337-942-3613. Personal E-mail: klafleur@earthlink.net.

LAFLEY, ALAN G., consumer products company executive; b. Keene, NH, June 13, 1947; AB, Hamilton Coll., 1969; MBA, Harvard Bus. Sch., 1977. Brand asst. Joy The Procter & Gamble Co., 1977-78, sales tng. Denver Sales Dist., 1978-80, asst. brand mgr. Tide, 1978-80, brand mgr. Dawn & Ivory Snow, 1980-81, brand mgr. spl. assignment and Ivory Snow, 1981-82, brand mgr. Cheer, 1982-83, assoc. advt. mgr. PS&D Divsn. to advt. mgr., 1983-86, 86-88, gen. mgr. laundry products PS&D Divsn., 1988-91, v.p. laundry & cleaning products, 1991-92, group v.p., pres. laundry and cleaning products, 1992-94, group v.p., pres. Far East Divsn., 1994-95, exec. v.p., pres. Asia Divsn., 1995-98, exec. v.p., pres. N.Am. Divsn., 1998-99, pres. Global Beauty Care & North Am., 1999-2000, pres., CEO, 2000—, chmn., 2002—. Dir., Gen. Electric Co., 2000-, United Negro Coll. Fund; trustee Hamilton Coll., US Coun. Internat. Bus., Xavier U., Cin. Playhouse in the Park, Cin. Symphony Orchestra, Cin. Inst. of Fine Arts, The Seven Hills Sch.; past mem. Am. C. of C. in Japan, adv. coun. Schulich Sch. of Bus., York U., Toronto. With USN, 1970-75. Recipient Golden Plate award, Acad. Achievement, 2004. Mem. Hamilton Club of So. Ohio, Harvard Club of Cin., Met. Club, Commonwealth Club of Cin. Office: The Procter & Gamble Co 1 Procter & Gamble Plz Cincinnati OH 45202-3315 E-mail: lafley.ag@pg.com.*

LA FOLLETTE, DOUGLAS J., state official; b. Des Moines, June 6, 1940; s. Joseph Henry and Frances (Van der Wilt) La Follette. BS, Marietta Coll., 1963; MS, Stanford U., 1964; PhD, Columbia U., 1967. Asst. prof. chemistry and ecology U. Wis.-Parkside, 1969-72; mem. Wis. State Senate, 1973-75; sec. state State of Wis., Madison, 1975-79, 83—. Author: Wisconsin's Survival Handbook, 1971, The Survival Handbook, 1991. Mem. Coun. Econ. Priorities; mem. Lake Michigan Fed., Wis. Environ. Decade, 1971, S.E. Wis. Coalition for Clean Air, Dem. candidate for US Congress, 1970, for Wis. lt. gov., 1978, for US Senate, 1988. Recipient Environ. Quality EPA, 1976, Fulbright Disting. Am. scholar, 2003. Mem. Am. Fedn. Tchrs., Fedn. Am. Scientists, Phi Beta Kappa, Sierra Club (nat. bd. mem.). Democrat. Office: Office Sec of State PO Box 7848 Madison WI 53707-7848 Office Phone: 608-266-8888. Office Fax: 608-266-3159. E-mail: statesec@sos.state.wi.us.*

LAFOND, PETER B., lawyer; b. Quantico, Va., Oct. 3, 1951; s. Paul Decelle and Katharine (Boardman) LaF.; m. Michelle Jodoin; children: Elyse, Emily, Michael. BA, U. Maine, 1975; JD, Duke U., 1986. Bar: Maine 1987. Ptnr. litigation dept. Jensen Baird Gardner, Portland, Maine, 1987; atty. Office of Maine State Atty. Gen., Augusta, Maine. Bd. trustees Surety Breakwater Sch. Mem.: Maine Trial Attys. Assn., Maine State Bar Assn. (pres. 2006). Office: Office of Atty General 6 State House Station Augusta ME 04333-0006 Office Phone: 207-626-8873. E-mail: peter.lafond@maine.gov.

LA FORCE, HUDSON, III, federal agency administrator; BA summa cum laude, Baylor U.; MS, Northwestern U. Gen. mgr. Dell Inc., China; asst. sec. planning US Dept. Edn., Washington, 2005—06, sr. counselor to sec., 2006—. Founder Project on Govt. Leadership, 2002. Office: US Dept Edn 400 Maryland Ave SW Washington DC 20202*

LA FORCE, JAMES CLAYBURN, JR., economist, educator; b. San Diego, Dec. 28, 1928; s. James Clayburn and Beatrice Maureen (Boyd) La F.; m. Barbara Lea Latham, Sept. 23, 1952; children: Jessica, Allison, Joseph. BA, San Diego State Coll., 1951; MA, UCLA, 1958, PhD, 1962. Asst. prof. econs. UCLA, 1962-66, assoc. prof., 1967-70, prof., 1971-93, prof. emeritus, 1993—, chmn. dept. econs., 1969-78, dean Anderson Sch. Mgmt., 1978-93; acting dean Hong Kong U. Sci. & Tech., 1991-93. Bd. dirs. Arena Pharms., The Black Rock Funds, Payden & Rygel Investment Trust; adv. Series Trust, Cancavax; chmn. adv. com. Calif. Workmen's Compensation. Author: The Development of the Spanish Textile Industry 1750-1800, 1965, (with Warren C. Scoville) The Economic Development of Western Europe, vols. 1-5, 1969-70. Bd. dirs. Nat. Bur. Econ. Rsch., 1975-88, Found. Francisco Marroquin, Lynde and Harry Bradley Found., Pacific Legal Found., 1981-86; trustee Found. for Rsch. in Econs. and Edn., 1970—, chmn., 1977—; mem. bd. overseers Hoover Inst. on War, Revolution and Peace, 1979-85, 86-93; mem. nat. coun. on humanities NEH, 1981-88; chmn. Pres.'s Task Force on Food Assistance, 1983-84. Social Sci. Research Council research tng. fellow, 1958-60; Fulbright sr. research grantee, 1965-66; Am. Philos. Soc. grantee, 1965-66 Mem.: Mont Pelerin Soc., Econ. History Assn., Phi Beta Kappa. Office: UCLA Anderson Grad Sch Mgmt 405 Hilgard Ave Los Angeles CA 90095-9000

LA FORGIA, ROBERT M., hotel executive; BS summa cum laude, Providence Coll.; MBA, UCLA. With Hilton Hotels Corp., Beverly Hills, Calif., 1981—, v.p., corp. contr., 1994—96, sr. v.p. contr., 1996—2004, sr. v.p., CFO, 2004—06, exec. v.p., CFO, 2006—. Mem.: Nat Assn. Corp. Directors, Contr. Coun. Conf. Bd., Fin. Execs. Inst. Office: Hilton Hotels Corp 9336 Civic Center Dr Beverly Hills CA 90210*

LAFOUNTAIN, LLOYD P., III, state agency administrator; b. Portland, Maine, Apr. 23, 1962; m. Trisha; three children. BA, Coll. Holy Cross, 1984; JD, Suffolk U. Law Sch., 1987. Atty. pvt. practice, Maine, 1988—2005; mem. City of Biddeford Sch. Bd., Maine, 1994—96, Maine House Reps. from Dist. 19, 1994—96, Maine Senate from Dist. 32, Augusta, 1996—2004; chair ins. and fin. svcs. com. Maine Senate, 1996—2004; ptnr. LaFountain & LaFountain, Biddeford; bank supt. Maine Bur. Fin. Instns., 2005—. Flemming fellow Ctr. Policy Alternatives, Washington, 1997. Mem. York County Bar Assn., Conf. State Bank Suprs., Nat. Assn. State Credit Union Suprs. Democrat. Office: Dept Profl & Fin Regulation Bur Fin Instns 36 State House Sta Augusta ME 04333-0036 Office Phone: 207-624-8570. E-mail: lloyd.p.lafountain.III@maine.gov.

LAFRAMBOISE, JOAN CAROL, middle school educator; b. Bklyn., June 23, 1934; d. Anthony Peter and Nellie Eva (Zaleski) Ruggles; m. Albert George Laframboise, Aug. 5, 1961; children: Laura J., Brian A. BS in Edn., Springfield Coll., Mass., 1956. Cert. tchr. social sci., and mid. sch.; cert. tchr. support specialist; cert. tchr. gifted. Tchr. Meml. Jr. H.S., Wilbraham, Mass., 1956-61, Midland Park (N.J.) Jr./Sr. H.S., 1961-63, Luke Garrett Middle Sch., Austell, Ga., 1983-93; tchr. lang. arts Pine Mountain Middle Sch., Kennesaw, Ga., 1993-2001; ret., 2001. Coun. pres. Knights of Lithuania, Westfield, Mass., 1973-75, Holyoke, Mass., 1975-76, New Eng. dist. pres., 1976-77; mem. Wistariahurst Mus. Assocs., Holyoke, 1975-77. Jr. League mini-grantee, 1991. Mem. ASCD, NEA, Ga. Assn. Educators, Cobb County Assn. Educators, Nat. Coun. Tchrs. English, Nat. Coun. Social Studies. Home: 2891 Dara Dr Marietta GA 30066-4009

LAFRANCE, WILLIAM CURT PHILLIP, JR., neuropsychiatrist, educator, medical researcher; b. Monroe, La., Feb. 6, 1969; s. William C. and Emily F. LaFrance; m. Lori Anne Smith, Sept. 10, 1994; 1 child, William Curt Phillip III. BA, Wake Forest U., 1991; MD, Med. Coll. Ga., 1995; MPH, Brown U., Providence, 2007. Diplomate in neurology and in psychiatry Am. Bd. Psychiatry and Neurology. Intern internal medicine Brown U. Sch. Medicine, Providence, 1995—96, resident neurology and psychiatry, 1996—2001, fellow clin. rsch., 2001—03, asst. prof. psychiatry and neurology (rsch.), 2003—; chief resident neuropsychiatry Butler Hosp., Providence, 2000—01; chief resident neurology R.I. Hosp., Providence, 1998—99, dir. neuropsychiatry, 2003—. Asst. instr. clin. neuroscis. Brown U., Divsn. Biology and Medicine, Providence, 1998—99; lectr. in field. Contbr. articles to profl. jours. and books. Team leader Gainesville Aid Project, Ga., 1994, Summer Med. Inst., Phila., 1997; hosp. vol. Maua Meth. Hosp., Kenya, 1991. Recipient Instl. Nat. Rsch. Svc. award, NIH, 2001—03, Mentored Patient-oriented Rsch. Career Devel. award, Nat. Inst. Neurol. Disorders and Stroke, 2003—; Readers Digest Internat. fellow, Siriraj Hosp. Med. Assistance Program Internat., Bangkok, 1995. Mem.: Am Epilepsy Soc, Christian Med. and Dental Assns., Am. Acad. Neurology, Am. Psychiat. Assn., Am. Neuropsychiat. Assn. (rsch. com. 1997, Career Devel. award 2003). Independent. Achievements include research in treatments for nonepileptic seizures. Avocations: skiing, fishing, tennis. Office: RI Hosp Divsn Neuropsychiatry 593 Eddy St Potter 3 Providence RI 02903 Office Phone: 401-444-3534. Business E-Mail: william_lafrance_jr@brown.edu.

LAFRANCIS, NICOLE MARIE, secondary school educator; b. McHenry, Ill., Sept. 20, 1974; d. Raymond Robert and Jude Marie LaFrancis. BS in Corp. Fitness, Western Ill. U., Macomb, 1996; MS in Phys. Edn., No. Ill. U., DeKalb, 2006. Cert. Am. Coun. on Exercise, 2004. Fitness specialist The Meadow Club, Rolling Meadows, Ill., 1996—97; profl. dancer Milw. Bucks, 1997—98; grad. asst. No. Ill. U., DeKalb, 1998—2000; substitute tchr. Cook County Schs., Palatine, Ill., 2000—01; tchr. phys. edn., dance Palatine H.S., Ill., 2001—05, Wheaton Warrenville South H.S., Ill., 2005—. Coach dance team Palatine H.S. and Wheaton Warrenville South H.S., 2001—. Avocations: personal training, exercise, dance, travel, spending time with family and friends. Office: Wheaton Warrenville South HS 1993 Tiger Tr Wheaton IL 60187 Office Phone: 630-784-7005. E-mail: nlafrancis@yahoo.com.

LAFUZE, WILLIAM L., lawyer; b. Washington, Feb. 21, 1946; children: Molly, Betsy, William Jr. BS in Physics, U. Tex., Austin, 1969, JD, 1973; MS in Applied Sci., So. Meth. U., 1971; postgrad., U. London, 1973. Bar: Tex. 1973, US Patent and Trademark Office, US Supreme Ct., US Ct. Appeals Fed. Cir. Rsch. scientist Ctr. for Nuclear Studies, Austin, 1966-69; instr. computer sci. U. Tex., Austin, 1968-69, 71-73; assoc. Vinson & Elkins LLP, Houston, 1973-80, ptnr., 1980—, co-head Intellectual Property / Technical Litig. Sect. Mem. Bush Cheney Transition Team for Dept. Commerce, Patent and Trademark Office matters, 2000—01; mem. patent pub. adv. com. US Patent and Trademark Office, Dept. Commerce, 2002—04; mem. adv. bd. Houston Tech. Ctr. Contbr. articles to profl. jours. Fellow: Am. Intellectual Property Law Assn. (bd. dirs. 1983—94, chmn. amicus brief com. 1986—88, pres. 1992—93), Houston Bar Found., Greater Houston Partnership (life), ABA (life; intellectual property law sect. coun. 1998—, chair section of intellectual property 2004—05, chmn. 2004—), Texas Bar Found. (life); mem.: MIT Enterprise Forum of Tex. (past bd. dirs.), Licensing Executives Soc., Nat. Coun. Patent Law Associations (del. 1982—, bd. dirs. 1987—90, past pres.), US Trademark Assn. (bd. editors Trademark Reporter 1976—78), Houston Bar Assn., State Bar Tex. (intellectual property law sect. coun. 1979—83, consumer law sect. coun. 1981—88, chmn. 1984—85, computer sect. coun. 1990—97), Houston Intellectual Property Law Assn. (past pres.), Nat. Inventors Hall of Fame (bd. dirs. 1987—, pres. 1994—95). Office: Vinson & Elkins First City Tower 1001 Fannin St Ste 2300 Houston TX 77002-6760 Office Phone: 713-758-2595. Business E-Mail: blafuze@velaw.com.

LAGACE, PAUL ALFRED, aeronautical engineering educator; b. Lewiston, Maine, July 27, 1957; s. Lucien Alfred and Claire (Malo) L.; m. Robin Lea Pare, July 9, 1983. SB, MIT, 1978, SM, 1979, PhD, 1982. Rsch. fellow MIT, Cambridge, 1978-82, Draper asst. prof., 1982-86, assoc. prof. aeronautics and astronautics, 1986-91, prof., dir. Tech. Lab. for Advanced Materials and Structures, 1986—, exec. officer dept. aeronautics and astronautics, 1990-92, MacVicar faculty fellow, 1995—, assoc. dir. engring. sys. divsn., 1999-2001. Cons. Foster-Miller, Inc., Waltham, Mass., 1983-95, McClellan AFB, Sacramento, Calif., 1983-90, Raytheon, Mass., 1985—; co-dir. Leaders Mfg. Program and Sys. Design and Mgmt. Program, 1998-2003. Editor Jour. Composites Tech. and Rsch., 1990-91; contbr. articles to profl. jours. Hertz Found. fellow, 1978. Fellow AIAA (sr.) Am. Soc. for Composites; mem. ASTM (Wayne W. Stinchcomb award 2001, Merit award 2007), Internat. Com. on Composite Materials (pres. 1993-99; world fellow), Soc. for Advancement of Material and Process Engring., Am. Composite Tech. Assn. (chmn. sci. adv. bd. 1987-95), Sigma Xi, Tau Beta Pi, Sigma Gamma Tau. Avocations: football officiating, softball. Home: 10 Wilton Dr Wilmington MA 01887-2216 Office: 77 Massachusetts Ave Cambridge MA 02139-4301 Office Phone: 617-253-3628. Business E-Mail: pal@mit.edu.

LAGALLY, MAX GUNTER, physics professor; b. Darmstadt, Germany, May 23, 1942; came to U.S., 1953, naturalized, 1960; s. Paul and Herta (Rudow) L.; m. Shelley Meserow, Feb. 15, 1969; children: Eric, Douglas, Karsten BS in Physics, Pa. State U., 1963; MS in Physics, U. Wis.-Madison, 1965, PhD in Physics, 1968. Registered profl. engr., Wis. Instr. physics U. Wis., Madison, 1970-71, asst. prof. materials sci., 1971-74, assoc. prof., 1974-77, prof. materials sci. and physics, 1977—, dir. thin-film deposition and applications ctr., 1982-93, John Bascom Prof. materials sci., 1986—, E.W. Mueller Prof. materials sci. and physics, 1993—. Gordon Godfrey vis. prof. physics, U. New South Wales, Sydney, Australia, 1987; cons. in thin films, 1977—; vis. scientist Sandia Nat. Lab., Albuquerque, 1975; founder, pres. Piezomax Techs., Inc. (now nPoint, Inc.), 1997—, now chmn., chief sci. officer; founder, chmn., chief sci. officer Sonoplot, Inc., 2003—. Editor: Kinetics of Ordering and Growth at Surfaces, 1990, (with others) Methods of Experimental Physics, 1985, Evolution of Surface and Thin-Film Microstructure, 1993, Morphological Organization in Epitaxial Growth and Removal, 1998; mem. editl. bd., also editor spl. issue Jour. Vacuum Sci. and Tech., 1978-81; prin. editor Jour. Materials Rsch., 1990-93; mem. editl. bd. Surface Sci., 1994-2001, Revs. Sci. Instruments, 1997-2000, Diffusion and Defect Data, 1997-2002, Jour. Phys. D, 2004—, Nanotechnology Rsch. Letters, 2005-; contbr. articles to profl. jours.; patentee in field. Max Planck Gesellschaft fellow, 1968, Alfred P. Sloan Found. fellow, 1972, H.I. Romnes fellow, 1976, Humboldt Sr. Rsch. fellow, 1992, 93; grantee fed. agys. and industry; recipient Outstanding Sci. Alumnus award Pa. State U., 1996, Tibbetts award U.S. SBA, 2002. Fellow AAAS, Am. Phys. Soc. (D. Adler award 1994, Davisson-Germer prize 1995), Australian Inst. Physics, Am. Vacuum Soc. (M.W. Welch prize 1991, trustee 1995-97); mem. Materials Rsch. Soc. (medal 1994), Leopoldina-German Acad. Scis., Nat. Acad. Engring. Home: 5110 Juneau Rd Madison WI 53705-4744 Office: U Wis Materials Sci & Engring 1509 University Ave Madison WI 53706-1538 Office Phone: 608-263-2078. Personal E-mail: max.lagally@npoint.com. Business E-Mail: lagally@engr.wisc.edu. E-mail: lagally@sonoplot.com.

LAGANGA, DONNA BRANDEIS, dean; b. Bklyn., June 27, 1950; d. Sidney L. and Sylvia (Herman) Brandeis; m. Thomas LaGanga, Aug. 11, 1974. BS in Bus. Edn., Ctrl. Conn. State Coll., 1972, MS, 1975; EdD in Ednl. Adminstrn.-C.C. Leadership, U. Tex., 1999. Various secretarial positions, 1969-72; tchr. bus. Lewis S. Mills Regional H.S., Burlington, Conn., 1972-78; cons. nat. accounts Southwestern Pub. Co., Pelham Manor, N.Y., 1978-84, dist. sales mgr., 1984-89; pres. DBL Industries, Inc., Torrington, Conn., 1989—. Nat. accounts mgr. South-Western Pub. Co., Cin., 1989—93, from sr. sales and mktg. mgr. to nat. career sch. mgr., 1993—95; dir. admissions and records Tunxis C.C.-Bristol Career Ctr., Farmington, Conn., 1995—2000, dir. cmty. alliances, 2000—04, dir. continuing edn. and workforce devel., 2002—, dean workforce devel. and continuing edn., 2004—; v.p. adminstrv. svcs. Human Resource Devel. Assocs., 1996—; co-owner Colonial Welding Svc., seminar condr., 1980—; pres. DBL Industries, Inc.; mem. adv. bd. secretarial sci. dept. LaGuardia C.C., L.I. City, NY, 1982—95; mem. adv. bd. Krissler Bus. Inst. EDPA grantee, 1973; mem. non-partisan ednl. reform task force Pres. George Bush. Named Disting. Alumni, NY CC Bd. Trustees, 2006; recipient Visionary Leadership award, Criminal Justice Command Inst.: Supervisory Leadership Program, 2006. Mem. NAFE, Assn. Info./Sys. Profls., Am. Mgmt. Assn., Nat. Bus. Edn. Assn., Profls. Secs. Internat., Eastern Bus. Edn. Assn., Conn. Bus. Edn. Assn., New Eng. Bus. Edn. Assn., Profl. Secs. Assn., N.Y., Nat. Assn. Cert. Profls. Secs. (cert. profl. sec.), U.S. Golf Assn., Delta Pi Epsilon, Phi Kappa Phi. Avocations: reading, bicycling, golf. Home: 2929 Torringford St Torrington CT 06790-2332 Office: 430E N Main St Bristol CT 06010

LAGANI, DANIEL, publishing executive; married; 2 children. BA, SUNY, Oneonta, 1985. Pub. George mag.; assoc. pub. New Woman mag. Primedia, 1994—96; assoc. pub. Traveler mag. Condé Nast, 1997—99; ea. advt. mgr. & group advt. mgr. Better Homes and Gardens and Country Home mag. Meredith Corp., 1988—94, v.p., pub. Ladies Home Jour., 2001—02, v.p., pub. Better Homes & Gardens NYC, 2002—05; v.p., pub. Fairchild Bridal Group, NYC, 2002—05; pres. Fairchild Fashion Group, 2006—. Nominee Under 40 Hall of Fame, Am. Advt. Fedn., 2002—03. Office: Fairchild Fashion Group 750 Third Ave 8th Fl New York NY 10017

LAGANI, JOSEPH A., publishing executive; b. Yonkers, NY, Dec. 3, 1957; s. Salvatore Joseph and Joanne (D'Elia) L. BA in Psychology, SUNY, Albany, 1979. Media planner Nadler & Lariner, NYC, 1980-81; assoc. media dir. Benton & Bowles, NYC, 1981-85; acct. mgr. Woman's Day mag., NYC, 1985—88; eastern sales mgr. Ladies Home Jour. (Meredith Pub.), NYC, 1988—89, adv. dir.; pub. Country Home mag., NYC, 1992—95; pub. dir. Meredith Pub., NYC, 1995—99, v.p., pub. group, 1999—2004; v.p., pub. House & Garden mag. (Conde Nast Pub.), NYC, 2004—. Office: VP & Publisher House & Garden 8th Fl 4 Times Square New York NY 10036 Office Phone: 212-286-2191. Office Fax: 212-286-4549.

LAGANKE, ALLYSON ANN, psychologist; b. Cleve., Dec. 3, 1974; BA in English, Journalism, Miami U., 1997; MEd in Spl. Edn., U. Nev., Las Vegas, 2000, EdS in Sch. Psychology, 2001. Nationally Cert. Sch. Psychologist 2001. With mktg. dept. Cleve. Metroparks, Zoo, and Rainforest, 1995—96; editor Grad. Student Newsletter, 1996—97; editl. asst. Locomotive Engrs. Jour., 1997—99; grad. asst. U. Nev., Las Vegas, 2000—01; psychometrist Disability Resource Ctr., Las Vegas, 2000—01; sch. psychologist Clark County Sch. Dist., Las Vegas, 2001—. Mem.: NASP (assoc.), Nev. Assn. Sch. Psychologists (assoc.), Tri Delta (life). Avocations: travel, dance, swimming, hiking, horticulture. Home Phone: 702-838-2803.

LAGARDE, CHRISTINE, French government official, lawyer; b. Paris, Jan. 1, 1956; d. Lallouette Robert and Carre Nicole; m. Wilfrid Lagarde, June 17, 1982 (div. Apr. 1992); children: Pierre-Henri, Thomas. BA, U. Avignon, France, 1979; M of Law, U. Paris, 1979; M Polit. Scientist, Polit. Scis. Inst., 1977. Assoc. Baker McKenzie, Paris, 1981-87, ptnr., 1987-91, mng. ptnr., 1991-95, chmn. exec. com. Chgo., 1999—2004, chmn. policy com., 2004—05; min. trade Govt. of France, Paris, 2005—. Author: Breaking New Ground, 1991, Into France, 1993. Mem. French Prime Min. Adv. Bd. on Attractivity of France. Decorated chevalier de la Legion d'Honneur; named one of 100 Most Powerful Women in World, Forbes mag., 2005—06. Mem. Cercle Interallie (Paris), Athenaeum Club (London). Office: Min of Trade 139 rue de Bercy 75572 Paris France Office Phone: 3315384600.

LAGARDERE, ARNAUD, media company executive; b. Boulogne-Billancourt, France, Mar. 18, 1961; s. Jean-Luc Lagardere. B econ., Univ. Paris IX, Dauphiné; diploma econ., U. Paris IX, Dauphiné. Gen. mgr. Multimedia Beaujon, 1986—87; v.p. supervisory bd. Arjil Bank, 1987; CEO Grolier, Inc., Danbury, Conn., 1994—98; mng. ptnr. Lagardere Groupe, Paris, 1998—2003; CEO Lagardere Media, Lagardere Active, 1999—2003; pres., CEO Lagardere Active Broadcast, 2001—, Lagardere Active Broadband, 2003—; pres. Lagardere Capital & Mgmt., 2003—; gen. ptnr., CEO Lagardere Groupe, Paris, 2003—. Chmn. EADS; mem. supervisory bd. DaimlerChrysler. Office: Lagardere Groupe 4 Rue de Presbourg 75016 Paris France

LAGARES, PORTIA OCTAVIA, music educator; b. Bklyn., May 8, 1950; d. Henry Lee and Ellen Thomasina Smith; m. Peter Lagares, Dec. 19, 1976; children: Michael Andre, Matthew David. MusB, MusM, Manhattan Sch. Music, NY, 1973. Pvt. flute instr. Williamsburg Settlement Music Sch., Brooklyn, NY, 1966—71; music educator Pub. Sch. 156, Bronx, NY, 1972—, project arts liaison, 2000—. Choir dir. World Wide Ch. of God, Queens, Westchester, festival choir dir., Saratoga Springs, NY, 2000; vol. flutist piano acompanist Ruth Taylor Nursing Home, Westchester, 1999—2005, Hospice Meml. Services/ Caring Cir., Westchester, 2001—. Musician (flute, piccolo): Queens Symphony Orch., 1967—71; musician: NY Philharm., 1970. Office: Pub Sch 156 750 Concourse Village W Bronx NY 10451 Home Phone: 917-699-6093; Office Phone: 718-292-5070. Office Fax: 718-292-5071; Home Fax: 845-628-7161. Personal E-mail: plagare2@aol.com. Business E-Mail: plagare@schools.nyc.gov.

LAGASSE, EMERIL, chef, restaurant owner, television show host, writer; b. Fall River, Mass., Oct. 15, 1959; s. John and Hilda Lagasse; children: Jessica, Jillian. BS in Culinary Arts, Johnson & Wales U., Providence, RI, D (hon.); studied culinary arts, France. Exec. chef Commander's Palace, New Orleans, 1983—90; owner, chef Emeril's restaurant, New Orleans, 1990—, Nola restaurant, New Orleans, 1992—, Emeril's New Orleans Fish House restaurant, Las Vegas, 1995—, Delmonico Restaurant and Bar, New Orleans, 1998—, Emeril's Orlando, Orlando, Fla., 1999—, Delmonico Steakhouse restaurant, Las Vegas, 1999—, Tchoup Chop restaurant, Orlando, Fla., 2002—, Emeril's Atlanta, 2003—, Emeril's Miami Beach, 2003—; host cooking show Essence of Emeril (The Food Network), 1994—, Emeril Live (The Food Network), 1997—; food corr. Good Morning Am., ABC, 1998—. Ptnr. Emeril Profl. stoneware, 2005—. Author: (cookbook) New Orleans Cooking, 1993, Louisiana Real and Rustic, 1996, Emeril's Creole Christmas, 1997, Emeril's TV Dinners, 1998, Every Day's a Party, 1999, Prime Time Emeril: More TV Dinners from America's Favorite Chef, 2001, There's a Chef in My Soup, 2002, Emeril's Potluck: Comfort Food with a Kicked-Up Attitude, 2004, Emeril's Delmonico: A New Orleans Restaurant with a Past, 2005, There's a Chef in my World, 2006; actor: (TV series) Emeril, 2001. Established Emeril Lagasse Found., 2002. Named Best Southeast Regional Chef, James Beard Found., 1991, Chef of Yr., GQ Mag., 1998, Exec. of the Yr., Restaurants & Institutions mag., 2004; named one of America's Top Twenty-Five New Chefs, Food & Wine, 1991, Most Intriguing People of Yr., People Mag., 1998; named to Am. Express for Fine Dining Hall of Fame, 1994, MenuMasters Hall of Fame, 2006; recipient Esquire award for Restaurant of Yr., 1991, Food and Wine award for one of Am.'s Top 25 New Chefs, 1991, James Beard award for Best S.E. Chef, 1991, Best Esquire award for restaurant of yr., 1993, Ivy award for restaurants and instns., 1994, Cable ACE award for best informational Series, 1997, Salute to Excellence award, Nat. Restaurant Assn., 1998, Grand award, Wine Spectator Mag., 1999, Disting. Svc. award, Wine Spectator mag., 2005. Achievements include being first celebrity chef to have meals and recipes developed for NASA and served in Space, 2006. Office: Food Network 5757 Wilshire Blvd Los Angeles CA 90036*

LAGEMANN, ELLEN CONDLIFFE, history and education professor, dean; b. NYC, Dec. 20, 1945; d. John Charles and Jane Grace (Rosenthal); m. Jonathan Kord Lagemann, June 28, 1969; 1 child, Nicholas Kord. AB cum laude, Smith Coll., 1967; MA, Columbia U., 1968, PhD with distinction, 1978. Tchr. Roslyn H.S., Roslyn, NY, 1967-69; exec. dir. WMCA: Call for Action, NYC, 1969-71; asst. dir. Bank Street Sch. for Children, NYC, 1971-72; tching. and rsch. asst. Inst. Phil. and Politics of Edn., Tchrs. Coll. Columbia U., NYC, 1974-78; asst. prof., then assoc. prof. Tchrs. Coll. Columbia U. Dept. Hist., NYC, 1978-87, prof. history and edn., 1987-94, NYU, NYC, 1994—2000; pres. Spencer Found., 2000—02; dean Harvard Grad. Sch. Edn., Cambridge, Mass., 2002—05, Charles Warren prof. history of Am. edn., 2002—. Trustee Concord (Mass.) Acad.; bd. dirs. Jobs for the Future, Boston, Oasis Children's Svcs., NYC. Author: A Generation of Women: Education in the Lives of Progressive Reformers, 1979, Private Power for the Public Good (Outstanding Book award), 1983, The Politics of Knowledge, 1989, An Elusive Science: The Troubling History of Education Research, 2000; editor: Nursing History: New Perspectives, New Possibilities, 1983, Jane Addams on Education, 1985, Teachers College Record, 1990-95, Brown v. Bd. of Education: The Challenge for Today's Schools, 1996, Philanthropic Foundations: New Scholarship, New Possibilities, 1999, Issues in Educational Research, Problems and Possibilities, 1999; many articles and book chpts. Grantee Carnegie Corp., Spencer Found, Carnegie Found. for Advancement of Teaching, Kettering Found., Lilly Endowment, fellow Ctr. for Advanced Study in Behavioral Scis. Mem. Nat. Acad. Edn. (pres. 1998-2001), History of Edn. Soc. (pres. 1987-88), Am. Hist. Assn., Orgn. Am. Historians, Am. Ednl. Rsch. Assn., Century Assn., Cosmopolitan Club. Office: Harvard Grad Sch Edn Dean's Office Appian Way Cambridge MA 02138 Office Phone: 617-495-3401. E-mail: ellen_lagemann@harvard.edu.

LAGERFELD, KARL OTTO, fashion designer; b. Hamburg, Fed. Republic Germany, Sept. 10, 1938; arrived in Paris, 1952; s. Christian and Elizabeth L. Student, Lycee Montaigne, Paris. Owner Karl Lagerfeld Co., Biderman Industries, NYC, 1984—, Karl Lagerfeld Co., Paris, 1984—. Tchr. fashion U. Applied Art, Vienna, Austria. Fashion stylist (with Pierre Balmain), Paris, 1954-58, art mgr. (with Jean Patou), Paris, 1958-63, freelance designer (with fashion houses including), Fendi, Rome, 1964-, Chloe, Paris, 1964-83, dir. collections and ready-to-wear, Chanel, Paris, 1982—; designer Karl Lagerfeld Women's Wear, Inc., Karl Lagerfeld France, Inc., Paris, 1983—, H&M line, 2004; prodr. perfume fragrances including, Chloe, Lagerfeld for Men, K.L.; prodr. (portraits) Visionaire 33: The Emperor's New Clothes; Co-author (with Jean-Claude Houdret) The Karl Lagerfeld Diet, 2005 Decorated Bundesverdienst Kreuz (Fed. Republic Germany); recipient Golden Spinning Wheel Krefeld, 1980, Neiman-Marcus award, 1980, Munich Fashion Prize. Fluent in German, French, English and Italian. Office: Chanel 29-31 rue Cambon 75001 Paris France Office Phone: 33 (0)1 42 86 28 00.*

LAGIN, NEIL, landscape designer, consultant; b. Bronx, Jan. 10, 1942; s. Barney and Helen (Goldberg) L. Cert. Xeriscape instr. South Fla. Water Mgmt. Buyer Alexanders, NYC, 1961-69; sales mgr. Halldon, Ltd., NYC, 1969-79; mgr., ptnr. in concession Michele Craig, Westbury, N.Y., 1979-85; ptnr. ALW Trading, "9", NYC, 1985-87; owner, operator Accent Foliage, Delray Beach, Fla., 1987-89; pres. Neil Lagin Property Mgmt., Neil's Landscape Svc., Boca Raton, Fla., 1988—97; landscape dir. Am. Heritage Sch., Boca Raton; ptnr. All Star Landscaping, 1997-99; landscape mgmt. cons., 1999-2001; landscape dir. Every Bloomin' Thing Ltd., Cayman Islands, 2001—02; landscape cons. Vero Beach, Fla., 2002—05, Sebastian, Fla., 2005—. Cable TV host Five Minutes with Dr. Neil. Author numerous poems; exhibited in group shows at Ward Nasse Gallery-Salon, 1975-79, Timothy Blackburn Gallery, 1978, Washington Art Show, others. Nursery adv. bd. Habilitation Ctr. for the Handicapped, Boca Raton, 1991—; overall adv. com. Palm Beach County Ext., 1992—, sec., chair program rev. com.; bd. dirs. Greater Palm Beach Area Alzheimers Assn., 1993; mem. Environ. Resource Landscape Team; mem. Boca Raton Postal Customer Adv. Coun., 1994-96; bd. dirs. Pheasant Walk Homeowners Assoc., 1996-97; adv. coun. Plant the Planet TV series, 1997; mem. Sebastian Vol. Police; mem. Sebastian Tree and Landscape Adv. Bd. Named Fla. Master Gardener, Inst. Food and Agrl. Scis., U. Fla., 1989, Best Landscaper in Boca Raton, South Fla. Newspaper Network, 1991, Best Local Vol. in Boca Raton, 1994, Outstanding Master Gardener, State of Fla., 1995, Gold award Best Landscaping Indian River County, 2004. Mem. Internat. Palm Soc. (Palm Beach chpt.), Rare Fruit Coun. Internat. (Palm Beach chpt.), Boca Raton C. of C. (grad. leadership program 1991). Home and Office: c/o Neil's Landscape Svc 838 Wentworth St Sebastian FL 32958 Home Phone: 772-589-4312; Office Phone: 772-589-4312. Personal E-mail: doctorneil9@yahoo.com.

LAGLE, JOHN FRANKLIN, lawyer; b. Kansas City, Mo., Jan. 22, 1938; s. Ernest J. and Hilda B. Lagle; m. Nina E. Weston, Aug. 1, 1959; m. Diana G. Fogle, July 14, 1962 (dec. 1992); children: Robert, Gregory. BS, UCLA, 1961, JD, 1967. Bar: Calif. 1967, U.S. Dist. Ct. (no. dist.) Calif. 1967. Assoc. Hindin, McKittrick & Marsh, Beverly Hills, Calif., 1967-70, Macco Corp., Newport Beach, Calif., 1970, Rifkind & Sterling, Beverly Hills, 1971; mem. Fulop & Hardee, and predecessor firm, Beverly Hills, 1971-82; ptnr. Leff & Stephenson, Beverly Hills, 1983; pvt. practice LA, 1984; ptnr. Barash & Hill (formerly Wildman, Harrold, Allen, Dixon, Barash & Hill) L. A., 1985-91; of counsel Barbosa Garcia, 1998—2000, Hill, Farrer & Burrell, LLP, 2000—01; atty. pvt. practice, 1991—. Arbitrator NASD Regulation, Inc. Contbr. to Practice Under the California Corporate Securities Law of 1978. Served with U.S. Army, 1961-63. Mem.: LA County Bar Assn., Calif. Bar Assn. Republican. Mailing: 1451 E Goshen Ave Fresno CA 93702 Home Phone: 559-433-8922; Office Phone: 559-433-8922. Personal E-mail: johnlagle@comcast.net.

LAGNA, GIORGIO, molecular biologist, researcher; b. Galatina, Lecce, Italy, Jan. 6, 1966; s. Mario and Antonietta Lagna; m. Akiko Hata, June 11, 1998; children: Oscar Akira, Maia Elettra, Amelia Yoshi-e. PhD, U. Rome La Sapienza, 1997. Scientist, group leader Curis, Inc., Cambridge, Mass., 2000—02; scientist III Bionaut Pharmaceuticals, Inc., Cambridge, 2002—04; spl. and sci. staff Tufts-New Eng. Med. Ctr., Boston, 2005—; asst. prof. medicine Tufts U., Sch. Medicine, Boston, 2005—. Fellow, The Rockefeller U., NYC, 1997—2000; grantee, Am. Heart Assn., Nat. Ctr., 2006—.

LAGNADO, JENNIFER M., assistant principal; b. NYC, Oct. 9, 1974; d. Joseph and Mary A. Lagnado. BS, Cornell U., Ithaca, NY, 1996, MA Tchg., 1997; EdD, Columbia U., NYC, 2004. Sci. tchr. Lawrence H.S., Cedarhurst, NY, 1999—2005, asst. prin., 2005—. Mem.: NSTA, ASCD, NY State Assn. Women in Adminstrn., NY Jr. League. Office: Lawrence HS 2 Reilly Rd Cedarhurst NY 11516 Home Phone: 516-445-8960; Office Phone: 516-295-8012. Business E-Mail: jlagnado@lawrence.k12.ny.us.

LAGNADO, SILVIA, marketing executive; b. Brazil; m. Richard Lagnado; 2 children. Joined Unilever, Brazil, 1987, brand devel. dir. London and Buenos Aires, 1989, former global brand mgr., dir., Dove, 2001, former sr. v.p., Dove global; group v.p. Unilever USA, Englewood Cliffs, NJ, 2006—. Named one of Ad Age Women to Watch, 2003, 50 Women to Watch, Wall St. Jour., 2006. Office: Unilever 920 Sylvan Ave Englewood Cliffs NJ 07632 Office Phone: 201-894-7760.*

LAGO, RODRIGO M., internist; s. Gilberto P. and Silvia M. Lago; m. Larissa Q. Nobrega, Apr. 17, 2004. MD, U. Gama Filho, Brazil, 2002. Cert. Ednl. Commn. Fgn. Med. Grads., 2004. Internal medicine intern MetroWest Med. Ctr., Framingham Union Hosp., 2004—05, internal medicine resident, 2005—. Mem.: ACP (assoc.), Mass. Med. Soc. (assoc.). Achievements include research in cardiovascular disease. Home Phone: 617-697-0012.

LAGOMASINO, MARIA ELENA, investment company and retired bank executive; b. Havana, Cuba, Mar. 27, 1949; B in French Lit., Manhattanville Coll., 1970; MLS, Columbia U., 1975; MBA, Fordham U., 1982. Joined Citibank, 1976, v.p., 1977—83; mgr., divsn. exec. Chase Pvt. Banking Internat., 1983—89, mgr. Western Hemisphere ops., 1989—94, mktg. exec. Ams. region, 1994—97; sr. mng. dir. Chase Manhattan Pvt. Bank, 1997—2000; chmn., CEO J.P. Morgan Pvt. Bank, NYC, 2001—05; CEO, Asset Mgmt. Advisors, LLC, NYC, 2005—. Bd. dirs. Avon Products; trustee Synergos Inst.; adv. com. transformational diplomacy Sec. State, 2006—; fundraiser disaster victims Pres. Bush, 2005—, mem. commn. White Ho. fellowships, 2006—. Named Woman of Yr., Hispanic Bus. mag., 2007; named one of 25 Women to Watch, US Banker Mag., 2003; named to 2004 Hispanic Bus. Corp. Elite, Hispanic Bus. Mag., 2004. Mem.: Coun. on Fgn. Rels. Office Phone: 561-472-9245. Personal E-mail: mlagomasino@amagobal.com.

LAGON, MARK P., federal agency administrator; b. 1965; s. Zofia Lagon; m. Susan S. Lagon; 1 child. BA, Harvard U., 1986; PhD, Georgetown U., 1991. Prin. aide Dir. of Fgn. Policy Studies at the Am. Enterprise Inst., Amb. Jeane Kirkpatrick; sr. analyst Ho. Rep. Policy Com., 1995—98, dep. staff dir., 1997—98; fellow, specializing in China Coun. on Fgn. Rels. Internat. Affairs, Project for the New Am. Century, 1998—99; sr. staff mem. Rep. staff, Senate Fgn. Rels. Com., 1999—2002; mem. policy planning staff US Dept. State, 2002—04, dep. asst. sec. for internat. org. affairs, 2004—07, sr. adv. to sec., 2007—, dir. Office to Monitor & Combat Trafficking in Persons, 2007—. Adj. prof. Inst. of World Politics, Georgetown U. Author: (novels) The Reagan Doctrine: Sources of Am. Conduct in the Cold War's Last Chpt., 1994. Republican. Office: US Dept of State 2201 C Street NW Washington DC 20520*

LAGOO, ANAND SHREERAM, pathologist, educator; b. Pune, India, June 29, 1953; arrived in US, 1985; s. Shreeram Balkrishna and Malati Lagoo; m. Sandhya Anand Deenadayalan, July 16, 1982; children: Janaka, Tasmaya. MBBS, BJ Med. Coll., Pune, 1977, MD in Pathology, 1980; PhD, U. Tex., Houston, 1989. Lectr. in pathology BJ Med. Coll., Pune, 1978—84, reader in pathology, 1984—85; asst. prof. medicine U. Ala., Birmingham, 1992—93, U. Miss. Med. Ctr., Jackson, 1993—94, assoc. prof. pathology, 1999—2000; asst. prof. pathology Duke U. Med. Ctr., Durham, NC, 2000—06, assoc. prof. pathology, 2006—. Mem.: Am. Soc. Clin. Pathology, Coll. Am. Pathologists, Clin. Cytometry Soc., Indian Classical Music and Dance Soc. (bd. dirs. 2004—). Democrat. Avocations: acting, directing amateur theater, photography, swimming. Office: Duke U Med Ctr DUMC 3712 Durham NC 27710

LAGORIA, GEORGIANNA MARIE, curator, writer, editor, visual art consultant; b. Oakland, Calif., Nov. 3, 1953; d. Charles Wilson and Margaret Claire (Vella) L.; m. David Joseph de la Torre, May 15, 1982; 1 child, Mateo Joseph. BA in Philosophy, Santa Clara U., 1975; MA in Museology, U. San Francisco, 1978. Exhbn. coord. Allrich Gallery, San Francisco, 1977-78; asst. registrar Fine Arts Mus., San Francisco, 1978-79; gallery coord. de Saisset Mus., Santa Clara, Calif., 1979-80, asst. dir., 1980-83, dir., 1983-86, Palo Alto (Calif.) Cultural Ctr., 1986-91; ind. writer, editor and cons. mus. and visual arts orgns., Hawaii, 1991-95; dir. The Contemporary Mus., Honolulu, 1995—. V.p. Non-Profit Gallery Assn., San Francisco, 1980-82; bd. dirs. Fiberworks, Berkeley, Calif., 1981-85; field grant reviewer Inst. Mus. Svcs., Washington, 1984, 85, 97, 98; adv. bd. Hearst Art Gallery, Moraga, Calif., 1986-89, Womens Caucus for Art, San Francisco, 1987—; mem. adv. bd. Weigand Art Gallery, Notre Dame Coll., Belmont, Calif. Curator exhbns. The Candy Store Gallery, 1980, Fiber '81, 1981; curator, author exhbn. catalogue Contemporary Hand Colored Photographs, 1981, Northern Calif. Art of the Sixties, 1982, The Artist and the Machine: 1910-1940, 1986; author catalogue, guide Persis Collection of Contemporary Art at Honolulu Advertiser, 1993; co-author: The Little Hawaiian Cookbook, 1994; coord. exhbn. selections Laila and Thurston Twigg-Smith Collection and Toshiko Takaezu ceramics for Hui No'eau Visual Arts Ctr., Maui, 1993; editor Nuhou (newsletter Hawaii State Mus. Assn.), 1991-94; spl. exhbn. coord. Honolulu Acad. Arts, 1995; dir. The Contemporary Mus., Honolulu, 1995—. Mem. Arts Adv. Alliance, Santa Clara County, 1985-86; grant panelist Santa Clara County Arts Coun., 1987; mem. art adv. bd. Kapiolani C.C., 1994—. Exhbn. grantee Ahmanson Found., 1981, NEA, 1984, Calif. Arts Coun., 1985-89 Mem. Am. Assn. Mus., ArtTable, 1983—, Calif. Assn. Mus. (bd. dirs. 1987-89), Assn. Art Mus. Dirs., Hawaiian Craftsmen (bd. dirs. 1994-95), Honolulu Jr. League, Key Project (bd. dirs. 1993-94). Democrat. Roman Catholic. Avocations: dance, writing. Home and Office: 47-665 Mapele Rd Kaneohe HI 96744-4918

LAGOS, JAMES HARRY, lawyer, small business owner; b. Springfield, Ohio, Mar. 14, 1951; s. Harry Thomas and Eugenia (Papas) Lagos; m. Nike Daphne Pavlatos, July 3, 1976. BA cum laude, Wittenberg U., 1970; JD, Ohio State U., 1972. Bar: Ohio 1973, U.S. Dist. Ct. (so. dist.) Ohio 1973, U.S. Tax Ct. 1975, U.S. Supreme Ct. 1976, U.S. Ct. Appeals (6th cir.) 1979. Asst. pros. atty. Clark County, Ohio, 1972-75; with Lagos & Lagos, PLL, Springfield, 1975—. Mem. Springfield Small Bus. Coun., 1977—, past chmn.; mem. Ohio Small Bus. Coun., 1980—, past chmn., vice chmn.; past pres., v.p. Nat. Small Bus. United, 1982—; del., resource person regulatory and licensing reform com. Small Bus. Nat. Issues Conf., 1984. Chmn. Ohio del. White House Conf. Small Bus., 1985—86, del., 1995; past chmn. Clark County Child Protection Team, 1974—82; mem. Clark County WORKPLUS Bd., 1999—2004, v.p., pres.; bd. dirs. Center City Assn., 1999—2004; active Cmty. Improvement Corp. Springfield and Clark County, 2001—; chmn. bd. dirs. Cmty. Leadership Assn. Clark County, 2002; mem. Clark County Young Rep. Club, past pres., sec., treas., 1968—76; bd. dirs., past pres. Greek Orthodox Ch., 1974—; mem. coun. Greek Orthodox Diocese of Detroit, 1985—86. Staff sgt. Ohio Air N.G., 1970—76. Named Small Bus. Advocate of Yr., US SBA, 1991; named one of Outstanding Young Men of Am., 1978; recipient Disting. Svc. award, Springfield-Clark County, 1977, medal of St. Paul the Apostle, Greek Orthodox Archdiocese N.Am. and S.Am., 1985, Exec. Dirs. award, 2004, Leader of Yr. award. Mem.: West Ctrl. Ohio Hearing and Speech Assn. (bd. dirs., pres., v.p. 1973—84, Dr. Melvin Emanuel award 1983), Clark County Bar Assn. (mem. exec. com. 1973—, past sec.), Ohio State Bar Assn., Rsch. Inst. Small and Emerging Bus. (bd. dirs. 1993—2005), Am. Hellenic Ednl. Progressive Assn. (pres., past treas.), Jaycees (past chmn. several coms. 1973—89, Spoke award 1974), Am. Hellenic Inst. (pub. affairs com. 1979—, bd. dirs.), C. of C. (chmn., treas., bd. dirs., vice-chmn.), Pi Sigma Alpha, Tau Pi Phi, Phi Eta Sigma, Alpha Alpha Kappa. Home: 2023 Audubon Park Dr Springfield OH 45504-1113 Office: Lagos & Lagos PLL 1 S Limestone St Ste 1000 Springfield OH 45502-1294 Home Phone: 937-390-0023; Office Phone: 937-323-5555. Business E-Mail: jameshlagos@lagoscentral.com.

LAGOW, RICHARD JAMES, chemistry professor; b. Albuquerque, Aug. 16, 1945; BA, Rice U., 1967, PhD, 1969. Instr. dept. chemistry Rice U., Houston, 1967-69; from asst. to assoc. prof. dept. chemistry MIT, Cambridge, Mass., 1969-76; assoc. prof. dept. chemistry U. Tex., Austin, 1976-80, prof. dept. chemistry, 1980-94, L.N. Vauquelin Regents prof. chemistry dept. chemistry, 1994—. Recipient Alexander von Humboldt award, 1992, award for creative work in fluorine chemistry Am. Chem. Soc., 1997; Alfred P. Sloan fellow, 1974-75. Fellow AAAS.

LAGOWSKI, BARBARA JEAN, writer, editor; b. Adams, Mass., Nov. 9, 1955; d. Frank Louis and Jeanette (Wanat) L.; 1 child, Adam Dietrich. BA, U. South Fla., 1977; MA, Johns Hopkins U., 1978. Asst. editor Fred Jordan Books Grossett and Dunlap Pubs., NYC, 1978-80; mng. editor Methuen Inc., NYC, 1980-81; mng. assoc., sr. editor Bobb-Merrill Co Inc., NYC, 1981-84; editor New Am. Libr., NYC, 1984-85. Poet-in-the-schs. Hillsborough County Arts Council, Tampa., Fla., 1976-77; poet-in-residence Cloisters Children's Mus., Balt., 1977-78 Author: Silver Skates series, 1988—89; co-author: Good Spirits, 1986, Teen Terminators, 1989, How to Get the Best Public School Education for Your Child, 1991, The Sports Curmudgeon, 1993, How to Attract Anyone, Anytime, Anyplace, 1993, Daily Negotiations: A Malcontent's Book of Meditations for Every Interminable Day of the Year, 1996, 101 Ways to Flirt: How to Get More Dates and Meet Your Mate, 1997, Cyberflirt: How to Attract Anyone, Anywhere on the World Wide Web, 1999; singer: Angel Signs: A Celestial Guide to the Powers of Your Own Guardian Angel, 2002, Lucky in Love: 52 Fabulous Foolproof Flirting Strategies, 2006. Mem. Authors Guild, Phi Kappa Phi Home: 237 Lenox Ave Long Branch NJ 07740-5022 Office Phone: 732-610-1569. Personal E-mail: blagowski@aol.com.

LA GRASSE, CAROL WINTER, property rights activist, retired civil engineer; b. Flushing, NY, July 31, 1942; d. Henry Ernest and Caroline (Kunkel) Winter; m. Peter Jordan La Grasse, Apr. 25, 1965. B in Engring., CCNY, 1965. Registered profl. engr., N.Y. Structural engr. James Ruderman Co., NYC, 1965; civil engr. Am. Sugar Co., NYC, 1966-69; civil engr., dir. contracts Leonard S. Wegman, Inc., NYC, 1969-73, 74-80; corr. Adirondack Jour., Warrensburg, N.Y., 1987-92; councilman Stony Creek (N.Y.) Town Bd., 1985-93; organist Ch. of St. Cecelia, Warrensburg, N.Y., 1988-98; pres. Property Rights Found. Am., Inc., Stony Creek, N.Y., 1994—. Expert witness Ho. of Reps., Washington, 1994-97, U.S. Senate, Washington, 1999-2004, N.Y. State Senate and Assembly Eminent Domain hearings, 2005-06, Cato Inst., Washington, 2006; presenter, spkr. in field. Editor: The Moral High Ground, 1996, Prfamerica website, 2001—; editor, co-author: An Enduring Heritage: A Study of Prominent Buildings in Stony Creek Center, 1989; mem. editl. bd. Positions on Property, 1994—; editor newsletter NY Property Rights Clearinghouse, 1994-2006; contbr. articles to profl. jours. Councilman Stony Creek Town Bd., 1985-93; sec., treas. Adirondack chpt. Am. Lung Assn., Hudson Falls, N.Y., 1978-90. Recipient Patriot's award Adirondack Park Local Govt. Rev. Bd., 1997. Mem. ASCE (life), Tau Beta Pi, Chi Epsilon. Republican. Reformed Ch. Am. Achievements include research on environmental land designations, national heritage areas, conservation easements. Office: Property Rights Found Am Inc PO Box 123 Stony Creek NY 12878-0123 Office Phone: 518-696-5748. Business E-Mail: lagrasse@prfamerica.org.

LAGREW, DAVID CRUTCHER, obstetrician, gynecologist, medical association administrator, director; b. St. Augustine, Fla., Dec. 1953; m. Nancy Rose Greer; children: David, Jonathan. MD, U. Ky., Lexington, 1979. Lic. maternal fetal medicine Am. Bd. Ob-gyn., 1988. Med. dir. women's hosp. Saddleback Meml. Med. Ctr., Laguna Hills, Calif., 1988—; med. dir. informatics Meml. Care, Huntington Beach, Calif., 1996—. Bd. mem. Meml. Health Svcs., Hunington Beach, 2000—. Recipient Physician Yr., Saddleback Meml. Med. Ctr., 2003. Office: Meml Care 24411 Health Center Dr Ste 540 Laguna Hills CA 92653 Home Phone: 949-589-6128; Office Phone: 949-452-7161.

LAGROTTO, LOUISA, middle school educator; m. Tony LaGrotto. BA in Spanish, Ind. Univ., MA in Spanish Edn. Tchr., 1991—; Spanish tchr. Westlane Mid. Sch., Indianapolis. Named Spanish Tchr. of Yr. Grades K-8, Ind. Chpt. Am. Assn. Tchrs. Spanish and Portuguese, 2003, Fgn. Lang. Tchr. of Yr., Ind. Fgn. Lang. Tchr. Assn., 2003, Wash. Twp. Tchr. of Yr., 2005, Ind. Tchr. of Yr., 2006; recipient Excellence in Edn. award, Christel DeHaan Family Found., 2000. Office: Westlane Mid Sch 1301 W 73rd S Indianapolis IN 46260 Business E-Mail: llagrotto@msdwt.k12.in.us.*

LAGUARDIA, CHERYL M., school librarian, writer; b. Sidney, NY, July 07; d. Enrico Donato and Leta M. LaGuardia. MLS, SUNY Albany; BS in Lit., SUNY Oneonta. Public Library certification NY State. Head of interlibrary loan Schaffer Libr., Union Coll., Schenectady, NY, 1981—86; asst. head reference Davidson Libr., U. Calif., Santa Barbara, Calif., 1986—94; head of instrnl. svc. coll. libr. Harvard U., Cambridge, Mass., 1994—. Editor R. R. Bowker, Chanlon, NJ, 2000—; editor-in-chief Neal-Schuman Pub. Inc., New York, 1994—. Author: (book) Teaching the New Library, 1996; co-author: Becoming a Library Teacher, 2000; editor: Finding Common Ground: Creating the Library of the Future Without Diminishing the Library of the Past, 1998, Recreating the Academic Library: Breaking Virtual Ground, 1998; author: (reviewing) E-Views and Reviews (Libr. Jour. E-Media Reviewer Yr., 2000), (column) (RASD/Louis Shores Reviewer Yr. Award, 1996). Mem.: Reference Svc. Rev. Editl. Bd. Office: Widener Libr Harvard Coll Libr Harvard University Cambridge MA 02138 Home Phone: 617-686-1455; Office Phone: 617-496-4226. Business E-Mail: claguard@fas.harvard.edu.

LAGUEUX, RONALD RENE, federal judge; b. Lewiston, Maine, June 30, 1931; s. Arthur Charles and Laurette Irene (Turcotte) L.; m. Denise Rosemarie Boudreau, June 30, 1956; children: Michelle Simone, Gregory Charles, Barrett James. AB, Bowdoin Coll., 1953; LLB, Harvard U., 1956. Assoc. then ptnr. Edwards and Angell Law Firm, Providence, 1956-68; assoc. justice Superior Ct. State of R.I., Providence, 1968-86; judge U.S. Dist. Ct., Providence, 1986—; chief judge, 1992-99. Exec. counsel to Gov. Chafee, R.I., 1963-65. Rep. candidate for U.S. Senate, 1964; corporator R.I. Hosp., Providence, 1965-01; solicitor Southeastern New Eng. Province United Way, 1957-68. Mem. Bowdoin Coll. Alumni Council (past v.p., pres.), Am.-French Geneal. Soc. Home: 90 Greenwood Ave Rumford RI 02916-1934 Office: US Dist Ct 1 Exchange Ter Providence RI 02903-1744

LAGUZZI, CARINA, lawyer; d. Heraldo Olter Ricardo and Felinda Cristina Laguzzi. JD, Boston U., 2001. Bar: Pa. 2001. With dist. atty. office, Phila., 2001—03; assoc. Britt, Hankins, Schiable & Maughen, Phila., 2003—04; assoc., owner Laguzzi & Assocs., PC, Phila., 2004—. Mem.: ABA, Phila. Bar Assn., Hispanic Bar Assn., Pa. Bar Assn. Avocations: skiing, writing fictional works. Office: Laguzzi Law PC 1500 JFK Blvd Ste 200 Philadelphia PA 19102 Office Phone: 215-625-4547. Office Fax: 215-625-4541. Business E-Mail: cl@laguzzilaw.com.

LAHANN, JON CLIFFORD, retired music educator; s. Clifford and Arlene Rickert Lahann. BA, Luther Coll., 1971; Masters, U. Iowa, 1977; PhD, U. Minn., 1997. Music manuscript editor Concordia Pub. Ho., St. Louis, 1971—72; music tchr. Centennial Jr. H.S., Circle Pines, Minn., 1972—83; choir dir. Centennial H.S., Circle Pines, Minn., 1981—2006; ret. Singer Minn. Chorale, Mpls., 1972—; music dir./organist/pianist Messiah Luth. Ch., Mounds View, Minn., 1974—87; sect. leader Hennepin Ave United Meth. Ch. Sanctuary Choir, Mpls., 1991—; contracted singer Minn. Chorale, Mpls., 1992—; music student tchr. supr. Luther Coll., Decorah, Iowa, 2007—. Bd. mem. Minn. Chorale, Mpls., 1975—84. Mem.: NEA, Am. Choral Dirs. Assn., Minn. Music Educators Assn. (contest judge 2007—), Music Educators' Nat. Conf., Phi Kappa Phi. Avocations: reading, collecting, automobiles. Home: 4462 Arden View Ct Arden Hills MN 55112 Home Phone: 651-636-4240.

LAHAYE, BEVERLY, cultural organization administrator; b. Apr. 30, 1929; m. Tim LaHaye; 4 children. Founder, chmn. Concerned Women for Am., Washington, 1979—; founder, radio talk show host Beverly LaHaye Live (now Concerned Women Today). Author: The Spirit Controlled Woman, The Desires of A Woman's Heart, Who Will Save Our Children?; co-author (with Dr. Janice Crouse): The Strength of a Godly Woman, 2001; co-author: (with Terry Blackstock) (fiction series) Seasons Under Heaven; contbr. articles written routinely for USA Today, her editorials have been placed in other top papers across the country. Bd. dirs. Internat. Right to Life Fed., Liberty U., Childcare Internat. Named one of 25 Most Influential Evengelicals, Time Magazine, 2005; recipient Christian Woman of the Year, 1984, Church Woman of the Year, 1988, Religious Freedom Award, S. Baptist Convention, 1991, Thomas Jefferson award, 2001. Achievements include being featured on the CBS Evening News; NBC Nightly News; ABC's World News Tonight and Nightline, and Donahue. Office: Concerned Women For America 1015 15th St NW Ste 1100 Washington DC 20005-2619*

LAHAYE, TIMOTHY F., pastor, writer; b. 1926; m. Beverly LaHaye; 4 children. BA, Bob Jones U., 1950; PhD Ministry, Western Conservative Baptist Seminary; Phd Lit., Liberty U. Pastor Shadow Mountain Com. Church, 1958—83. Co-host, tv program The King is Coming, 2001; pres. Jerry Falwell's Liberty U., School of Prophecy. Co-author (with Jerry B. Jenkins): (novels) Left Behind: A Novel of the Earth's Last Days, 1995; co-author: Tribulation Force: The Continuing Drama of Those Left Behind, 1996, Nicolae: The Rise of Antichrist, 1997, Soul Harvest: The World Takes Sides, 1998, Apollyon: The Destroyer Is Unleashed, 1999, Assassins: Assignment: Jerusalem, Target: Antichrist, 1999, The Indwelling: The Beast Takes Possession, 2000, The Mark: The Beast Rules the World, 2000, Desecration: Antichrist Takes the Throne, 2001, The Remnant: On the Brink of Armageddon, 2002, Armageddon: The Cosmic Battle of the Ages, 2003, Glorious Appearing: The End of Days, 2004, The Rising: Before They Were Left Behind, 2005, The Regime: Before They Were Left Behind, 2005, The Rapture, 2006, Kingdom Come: The Final Victory, 2007; author Babylon Rising Series, four novels: Babylon Rising, The Secret on Ararat, The Europa Conspiracy, The Edge of Darkness, 2003—06, The Jesus Chronicles: John's Story, The Last Eyewitness; Mark's Story, The Gospel According to Peter, 2006—07, How to Study the Bible for Yourself, 1976, Revelation: Illustrated and Made Plain, 1973, No Fear of the Storm, 1977, The Power of the Cross, 1998, The Merciful God of Prophecy, 2002, The Battle for the Mind, 1980, The Act of Marriage, 1998, Spirit-Controlled Temperament, 1993. Coun. for Nat. Policy, 1981; American Coalition for Traditional Values; Coalition for Religious Freedom; founder San Diego Christian Coll., 1971. Christian. Office: The Pre-Trib Rsch Ctr Liberty University 1971 University Blvd Lynchburg VA 24502 Office Phone: 434-592-3773.*

LAHEY, JOHN H., lawyer; b. Cleve., June 25, 1946; BS in Econs., Miami U., 1968; JD, Ohio State U., 1971. Bar: Ohio 1972, DC 1998, NY 2002. Ptnr., mng. ptnr. Hong Kong office Jones, Day, Reavis & Pogue, Columbus, Ohio; ptnr. Ferrell Law, NYC. Adj. prof. law Capital U., 1980—83. Contbr. articles to profl. jours. Named one of Top 100 Attys., Worth mag., 2005, 2006. Mem.: Internat. Acad. Estate and Trust Law. Office: Ferrell Law 598 Madison Ave 2nd Fl New York NY 10022 Office Phone: 212-813-9500. Office Fax: 212-813-1155. E-mail: jlahey@ferrellworldwide.com.

LAHEY, RICHARD THOMAS, JR., nuclear and fluid mechanics engineer; b. St. Petersburg, Fla., Feb. 20, 1939; married, 1961; 3 children. BS, U.S. Mcht. Marine Acad., 1961; MS, Rensselaer Poly. Inst., Troy, NY, 1964; ME, Columbia U., NYC, 1966; PhD in Mech. Engring., Stanford U., Calif., 1971. Engr. Knolls Atomic Power Lab., 1961-64; rsch. assoc. Columbia U., NYC, 1964-66; mgr. core & safety devel. nuc. energy divsn. GE, 1966-75; chmn. dept. nuc. engring. Rensselaer Poly. Inst., Troy, NY, 1975-87, prof. nuc. engring. and engring. physics, 1987—, prof. dept. chem. engring., 1987—, Edward E. Hood, Jr. prof. engring., 1989—, dir. ctr. multiphase rsch., 1991-94, dean engring., 1994-98. Bd. mem. PJM Interconnect LLC, 1997-; mem. sci. adv. com. EG&G Idaho, Inc., 1976-83; mem. Advanced Code Rev. Group & LOFT Rev. Group U.S. Nuc. Regulatory Commn., 1976-84; commr. Engring. Manpower Commn., 1981-84; pres. R.T. Lahey, Inc., 1981-83; vis. prof. U. Pisa, Italy and Claude Bernard U., France, 1987; Alexander von Humboldt Sr. scientist fellow, 2005-2006. Editor: Jour. Nuc. Engring. & Design, 1983-94. Recipient Arthur Holly Compton award, 1989, Glenn T. Seaborg medal, 1992, E. O. Lawrence Meml. award U.S. Dept. Energy, 1988; Fulbright fellow Magdalen Coll., Oxford U., 1983-84. Fellow ASME (life), Am. Nuc. Soc. (Tech. Achievement award 1985), N.Y. Acad. Scis., Am. Soc. Engring. Edn. (Glen Murphy award 1985), Sigma Xi; mem. NAE, Russian Acad. Sci. (fgn. mem. Bashkorstan, Russia). Achievements include research in in two-phase flow and boiling heat transfer technology; nuc. reactor thermal-hydraulics and safety, sonofusion technology. Office: Rensselaer Poly Inst Jonsson Engring Ctr 110 8th St Troy NY 12180-3590 Home Phone: 518-371-9408; Office Phone: 518-276-6614. Business E-Mail: laheyr@rpi.edu.

LAHIRI, JHUMPA (NILANJANA SUDESHNA), writer; b. London, Eng., July 1967; m. Alberto Vourvoulias, 2001; 2 children. BA in English Lit., Barnard Coll., 1989; MA in English, Boston U., MA in Creative Writing, MA in Comparative Lit., PhD in Renaissance studies. Author: (short stories) The New Yorker, 1998, (collection of short stories) Interpreter of Maladies, 1999 (O. Henry award, Pulitzer prize for fiction, 2000, PEN/Hemingway award, New Yorker Debut of Yr. award, Am. Acad. Arts and Letters Addison Metcalf award), (photography collection) India Holy Song, 2000, The Namesake: A Novel, 2003, (short stories) The Third and Final Continent, 1999 (Nat. Mag. award for Fiction, 2000). Named one of Best Young Writers in Am., New Yorker Mag.; recipient M.F.K. Fisher Disting. Writing award, James Beard Found. Speaks Bengali. Office: c/o Houghton Mifflin 222 Berkeley St Boston MA 02116

LAHLOU, MOURAD, chef; BA in Econ., San Francisco U.; M in Econ. Chef, owner Kasbah, San Rafael, 1997—2001, Aziza, San Francisco, 2001—. Named a Rising Star Chef, San Francisco Chronicle, 1998; named one of San Francisco's Rising Stars, StarChefs.com, 2007. Office: Aziza 5800 Geary Blvd San Francisco CA 94121 Office Phone: 415-752-2222.*

LAHOOD, JULIE ANN, small business owner; b. Martins Ferry, Ohio, May 31; d. Joseph Noah LaHood and Thelma Marie Rafful LaHood. Student, Ray Coll. Design, Chgo., 1954—55; degree in theatre, fine arts and classics, Loyola U., Chgo., 1979. Jr. exec. Bonwit Teller, Chgo., 1959—62; asst. dept. mgr. Saks Fifth Ave., Chgo., 1962; owner Historic Properties, Monroe, Mich., Julie's Trading Post, Monroe, St. Charles, Ill. Author: numerous poems. Mem Monroe County Hist. Soc., Mich., Nat. ProLife Alliance, Washington, 2007; humane amb. Neglected Animals, St. Charles, 1999; mem. Rep. Senatorial Inner Cir. Commn., Washington, 2007. Recipient Best Poems and Poets award, Internat. Soc. Poets, 2002, 2003, 2005, Outstanding Achievement in Poetry award, 2006, award, Internat. Libr. Poetry, 2006, 2007, Spirit of Am. medal, Republican Senatorial Inner Cir., Washington, 2007. Mem.: Nat. Assn. Female Execs., USAF Assn., Navy League of USAF (Gt. Britain), Nat. Trust for Historic Preservation, Chgo. Hist. Soc. Republican. Roman Catholic. Avocations: gardening, cooking, poetry, music. Home: 707 Monroe Ave Saint Charles IL 60174

LAHOOD, MARVIN JOHN, retired language educator; b. Auburn, NY, Mar. 21, 1933; s. Salem and Anna (Mahfoud) L.; m. Marjorie Braun, Aug. 22, 1959; children: John, Melissa, Mark. BS, Boston Coll., 1954; MA in English, U. Notre Dame, 1958, PhD in English, 1962. Instr. Niagara U., 1960-61, assoc. prof., 1962-64, Buffalo State Coll., NY, 1964-67, prof., 1967-71, prof. ind. study, 1968-69, prof., assoc. for acad. devel., 1969-71, prof., 1978-95, Disting. tchg. prof., 1995—2005; prof., acad. dean Coll. Misericordia, 1971-72, Salem State Coll., 1972-75; prof., dean faculty D'Youville Coll., 1975-78; ret., 2005. Chair Burchfield Poets and Writers Com., 1985-2005; manuscript reviewer Prentice Hall, 1986-88, book reviewer Buffalo News, 2000-07; lectr. U. Dortmund, Germany, 1986, Lille U., France, Cath. U. Lille, 1991; chair senate ops. com. SUNY, 1994-97, chair undergrad com., 1999-2002, chair awards com., 2002-05; mem. SUNY Task Force on Distance Learning, 1994-95, Gen. Edn., 1998-99, Faculty Devel., 2002. Author: Conrad Richter's America, 1974, State University College at Buffalo, A History: 1946-1972, 1980; editor: Latvian Literature, 1964, Tender Is the Night: Essays in Criticism, 1969, Stories of Tragedy and Triumph, 1997; contbr. Grad. Degrees column Notre Dame Mag., 1996--; contbr. articles to prof. jours. Pres. Mt. St. Mary Acad. Bd. Trustees, 1990-94. Faculty Rsch. fellow SUNY, 1967-68, USOE fellow Inst. on Ednl. Media, 1967, SUNY fellow Inst. for Devel. Black Studies, 1969; SUNY Faculty Exch. scholar, 1969-2005; recipient Chancellor's award SUNY, 1985, Boston Coll. Alumni award, 1997, Tchr. of Yr. award Buffalo State Coll. United Student Govt., 1999. Mem. F. Scott Fitzgerald Soc. (bd. dir. 1999-2007). Home Phone: 716-691-4648.

LAHOOD, MARY ANNE, real estate investor; b. Grosse Pointe Farms, Mich., Aug. 23, 1947; d. Tom and Melinia (Simon) LaHood; children: Lila, Michael. BA, Wayne State U., 1972. Ptnr. LaHood Lanes, Inc., St. Clair Shores, Mich., 1972—, LaHood Properties, Grosse Pointe Shores, Mich., 1972—. Patron Detroit Inst. of Arts, Grosse Pointe Yacht Club; sec. environ. group NCLF, Detroit Hist. Soc. Avocations: fiction writing, art collecting, long distance walking, sailing, tennis. Home: 20 Stillmeadow Ln Grosse Pointe Shores MI 48236-1118 Personal E-mail: lahood@aol.com.

LAHOOD, RAY H., congressman; b. Peoria, Ill., Dec. 6, 1945; m. Kathleen (Kathy) Dunk LaHood; children: Darin, Amy, Sam, Sara. Student, Canton Jr. Coll., Ill.; BS in Edn. and Sociology, Bradley U., 1971. Tchr. Catholic and pub. jr. high schs., 1971-77; dist. administrv. asst. to congressman Tom Railsback, 1977; mem. Ill. Ho. of Reps., 1982—83; Chief of Staff to Congressman Bob Michels Ho. of Reps., 1993—94; mem. U.S. Congress from 18th Ill. dist., 1995—. Mem. appropriations com. US Congress, legis. br. subcom., intelligence task force. Mem. ITOO Soc., Downtown Rotary Club, Holy Family Ch. (Peoria), Peoria Area C. of C. Republican. Roman Catholic. Office: US Ho Reps 1424 Longworth Ho Office Bldg Washington DC 20515-1318 also: Peoria Dist Office Rm 100 100 NE Monroe St Peoria IL 61602-1003

LAHRECHE, HICHEM, chef; b. Algeria; Grad., L'Academie de Cuisine, Gaithersburg, Md., 1997, Internat. Sch. Culinary Arts. Cert. chocolate decoration and adv. artistic confections Notter Internat. Sch. Confectionery Arts. Pastry chef Citronelle Restaurant, Washington, The Willard Room, Intercontinental Hotel, Washington; asst. pastry chef Red Sage, Washington; exec. pastry chef, ptnr. Cafe Baba; exec. pastry chef Colvin Run Tavern, Vienna, Va., 2002, Kinkead's, Washington, 2006—. Named one of Washington DC's Rising Stars, StarChefs.com, 2006. Avocation: tennis. Office: Kinkeads 2000 Pennsylvania Ave NW Washington DC 20006 Office Phone: 202-296-7700.*

LAHTI, CHRISTINE, actress; b. Detroit, Apr. 4, 1950; d. Paul Theodore and Elizabeth Margaret (Tabar) L.; m. Thomas Schlamme, Sept. 4, 1983; children Wilson, Joseph, Emma. BA in Lang., Speech, Drama, U. Mich., 1972; MFA, Fla. State U., 1972-73; studies with William Esper, Uta Hagen, Herbert Berghof Studios. Actress: (stage prodns.) The Woods, 1978 (Theater World award 1979), Division Street, 1980, Loose Ends, 1981, Present Laughter, 1983, Landscape of the Body, 1984, The Country Girl, 1984, Cat on a Hot Tin Roof, 1985, Little Murders, 1987 (Obie award), The Heidi Chronicles, 1989, Three Hotels, 1993; regular mem. cast (TV series) Dr. Scorpion, 1978, The Harvey Korman Show, 1978, Chicago Hope, 1995-1999 (Golden Globe award, best actress in a leading role drama series, 1998, Emmy award, 1998), Jack & Bobby, 2004 (TV films) The Last Tenant, 1978, The Henderson Monster, 1980, The Executioner's Song, 1982, Single Bars, Single Women, 1984, Love Lives On, 1985, Amerika, 1987, No Place Like Home, 1989 (Golden Globe award, best actress in a leading role mini-series or TV movie, 1989), Crazy from the Heart, 1991, The Fear Inside, 1992, The Good Fight, 1985, The Four Diamonds, 1995, Subway Stories: Tales from the Underground, 1997, Hope, 1997, An American Daughter, 2000, The Pilot's Wife, 2002, Out of the Ashes, 2003 The Book of Ruth, 2004, Revenge of the Middle-Aged Woman, 2004 (feature films) ...And Justice For All, 1979, Whose Life Is It, Anyway?, 1981, Swing Shift, 1984 (N.Y. Film Critics Circle award for best supporting actress 1985, Acad. award nominee 1985, Golden Globe award nominee 1985), Ladies and Gentlemen: The Fabulous Stains, 1985, Just Between Friends, 1986, Housekeeping, 1987, Season of Dreams, 1987, Stacking, 1988, Running on Empty, 1988, Gross Anatomy, 1989, Miss Firecracker, 1989, Funny About Love, 1990, The Doctor, 1991, Leaving Normal, 1992, Hideaway, 1995, Pie in the Sky, 1995, A Weekend in the Country, 1996; prodr. short action film, actress: Lieberman in Love, 1995 (Oscar award, 1995, Acad. award nominee for best live action short film, 1996). Recipient Susan B. Anthony Failure is Impossible award, High Falls Film Festival, 2005. Office: ICM c/o Toni Howard 8942 Wilshire Blvd Beverly Hills CA 90211-1934

LAHTINEN, SILJA LIISA, artist; b. Lumivaara, Finland; arrived in U.S., 1978; d. Vaino Lambertinpoika and Katri Elisa (Tirri) Talikka; m. Pentti Kalervo Lahtinen; children: Karoliina, Katriina, Antti. BFA, MA, U. Helsinki, Finland, 1969; BFA, Atlanta Coll. Art, 1983; MFA, Md. Inst. Coll. Art, 1986. Tchr. Teknillinen Oppilaitos, Lahti, Finland, 1969-78; teaching asst. Md. Inst., Coll. of Art, Balt., 1986; artist, owner Siljas Fine Art Studio, Marietta, Ga., 1987—. V.p., creative advisor Pentec Internat. Inc., Marietta, 1994—; tchr. etching, painting Atlanta Coll. Art, 1997—. Solo exhbns. include Ariel Gallery, NYC, 1987, 350th Anniversary Swedish/Finnish Art, Atlanta, 1988, Callanwolde Arts Ctr., Atlanta, 1988, Morin-Miller Gallery, NYC, 1989, La Chapelle de la Sorbonne, Paris, 1990, TaideArt Gallery Helsinki, 1987, 88, 91, 92, Internat. Exhbn., Ward-Nasse Gallery, NYC, 1991, Pihagalleria, Lahti, Finland, 1995, Ars Arrakoski, Padasjoki, Finland, 1999, 2000, Nuutti Galleria, Virrat, Finland, 2002 Ward-Nasse-Chelsea, NYC, 2003; group exhbns. include Scandinavian Artists, Savannah Coll. Art & Design, 1989, La Chapelle de la Sorbonne, Paris, 1990, Ariel Gallery Group Exhbns., NYC, 1987, 89, 90, Med. Coll. Ga., Augusta, 1992, 93, 94, Abney Gallery, NYC, 1993, U. Alaska, Anchorage, 1993, Ward-Nasse Gallery, NYC, 1989-99, Ward-Nasse Gallery Yr. Round Salon, 1999-2002, New Visions Gallery, Atlanta, 1993, Seaside Art Gallery, Nags Head, NC, 1993, Spruill Ctr. Gallery, Atlanta, 1993, New Ams. Selected by Coca Cola Co., 1996, Telfair Mus. Art, Savannah, 1995, Albany Mus. Art, 1994, San Bernardino Art Mus., 1995, Orgn. of Ind. Artists, NYC, 1995, Rutgers Nat., 1994, Stedman Gallery, City of Atlanta Gallery, Chastain Pk., 1994, Rolling Stone Press Gallery, Printmakers Renaissance, 1996, Atlanta Coll. of Art Juried Alumni Exhbn., 1987, 96, Chattahoochee Valley Art Mus., La Grange, Ga., 1997, Barbara Archer Gallery, Atlanta, 2001, Fabulous Finishes, Inc. and Biasucci Co., 2002, Seminole Coll., Sanford, Fla., 2003 (Award of Merit 2003), Greenbelt (Md.) C.C., 2003, Kennesaw State U., Atlanta, 2003, other shows; selected collections include Barbara Archer Gallery, 2001, Trinity Sch., Dr. Weisman Ctr., Lahden Rautateollisuus, Rauma, Vuorineuvos Tauno Matomaki, Helsinki, Pentec Internat. Inc., Markku af Herlin, Helena Jaakonmaki Collection, Hugh and Sirkka Barbour, Boston and others; contbr. various articles to profl. jours. Recipient Internat. Art Competition, Cert. of Excellence in Printmaking, NYC, 1988, Award from FINNAIR to transport exhibit round trip Finland/USA, The State of Ga. award for achievement Ga. Women in the Visual Arts, 1997, Avery Gallery, 2 Painting awards, 1988. Mem.: Womens Caucus Art, Ward Nasse Gallery, Four Winds Soc., Roswell Fine Arts Alliance, Orgn. Ind. Artists, Am. Art Therapy Assn. Lutheran. Avocations: shamanism, trance dance, zen buddhism, haiku, yoga. Office: Siljas Fine Art Studio 5220 Sunset Trl Marietta GA 30068-4740 E-mail: pentec02@bellsouth.net.

LAI, FENG CHYUAN, engineering educator; b. Taipei, Taiwan, Aug. 6, 1956; came to the U.S., 1983; s. Chin-Mao and Matsuko (Suzuki) L.; m. Hongshing Cheng, July 26, 1986; children: Cathy B., Anthony C. BS, Nat. Tsinghua U., Hsinchu, Taiwan, 1978; MS, U. Del., 1985, PhD, 1988. Asst. engr. Energy Rsch. Lab., Hsinchu, 1980-82; rsch. assoc. Colo. State U., Fort Collins, 1986-92; asst. prof. U. Okla., Norman, 1992-98, assoc. prof., 1998—. Contbr. articles to Internat. Jour. Heat & Mass Transfer, Jour. Heat Transfer, Jour. Thermophysics & Heat Transfer. Recipient New Investigators award Okla. Ctr. for the Advancement Sci. and Tech., Oklahoma City, 1995. Fellow AIAA (assoc.), ASME; mem. IEEE, ASHRAE. Office: AME Univ Okla 865 Asp Ave Norman OK 73019-1050 Office Phone: 405-325-1748.

LAI, FENG-QI, instructional designer, educator; b. Shanghai, Mar. 25, 1948; arrived in U.S., 1992; d. Zheng-Zhong Lai and Yao-Zhang Zhu; m. Qun Zhang, Oct. 22, 1984. BA, Changsha (China) Railway Inst., 1982; MS, Purdue U., 1994, PhD, 1997. Asst. lectr. Shanghai Tiedao U., 1982-86, lectr., assoc. dir., 1986-91; instrnl. designer Nat. Edn. Tng. Group, Naperville, Ill., 1998; sr. instr., dir. tng. Advanced Tech. Support, Inc., Schaumburg, Ill., 1998-2000; sr. instrnl. designer, project mgr. Cognitive Concepts, Inc., Evanston, Ill., 2000—02; asst. prof. Ind. State U., Terre Haute, Ind., 2002—. Guest prof. Shanghai Normal U., 2006—. Transl.: Writing Scientific Papers in English, 1983; co-author: Applied Cryptography, 1999, Fundamental Computer Skills, 2004. Mem.: Soc. Internat. Chinese in Ednl. Tech. (pres. 2005—06), Phi Kappa Phi. Avocations: music, reading, Chinese poetry, photography, crafts. Business E-Mail: flai@indstate.edu.

LAI, MING-MING, finance educator; b. Aug. 1968; BBA with honors, Nat. U. Malaysia, 1993; MBA, Wichita State U., 1993; PhD, Multimedia U., Cyberjaya, Malaysia, 2002. Lectr. Tar Coll., Kuala Lumpur, Malaysia, 1995—97; lectr. mgmt. Multimedia U., Cyberjaya, 1997—. Contbr. articles to profl. jours. Recipient Book prize, U. Kebangsaan, Malaysia, 1993. Office: Multimeda Univ Faculty Mgmt Jalan Multimedia Cyberjaya 63100 Malaysia

LAI, ROBERT, urologist, surgeon; BSc, U. Toronto, Ont., Canada, 1987; MD, CM, McGill U., Montreal, Que., Canada, 1991. Diplomate Am. Bd. Urology, 2002. Asst. prof. urology SUNY, Syracuse, 2000—06; urol. surgeon Midwest Urology Associates, Ltd., Melrose Park, Ill., 2006—. Med. adv. bd. Nat. Kidney Found., Syracuse, 2000—06; adult literacy tchr. Toronto Bd. Edn., 1985—86. Contbr. articles to profl. jours. Advisor Nat. Kidney Found., Syracuse, 2000—06. Named one of America's Top Physicians, Consumer's Rsch. Coun. Am., 2003—06; recipient award, Natural Scis. and Engring. Rsch. Coun., 1986—87, Med. Rsch. Coun. Can., 1988—99, award in therapeutics, Merck Sharp and Dohme, 1988—89, Trainee award, Can. Soc. Clin. Investigation, 1989—90; grantee, Can. Spinal Rsch. Orgn., 1998—99; scholar, Ont. Neurotrauma Found., 1998—99; Ont. scholar, Ministry Edn., Can., 1983, faculty scholar, U. Toronto, 1984—87, fellow in neurology and female urology, LI Jewish Med. Ctr., 2000, Edwin Beer scholar, NY Acad. Medicine, 2001—02, Ferdinand Valentine scholar, 1998—99. Fellow: Royal Coll. Physicians and Surgeons Can. (licentiate; cert.); mem.: Can. Urol. Assn., Soc. Urodynamics and Female Urology, Am. Urol. Assn., Med. Coun. Can. (licentiate). Episcopalian. Achievements include first to sequence the genetic code of the 3' terminal region of Clover Yellow Mosiac Virus RNA. Avocation: photography. Office: Midwest Urology Associates Limited 675 West North Ave Ste 605 Melrose Park IL 60160 Home Phone: 708-450-5065; Office Phone: 708-450-5065. Office Fax: 708-338-2474.

LAI, SHU-FEN, language educator; b. Tainan, Taiwan, Oct. 12, 1964; arrived in US, 2004; m. Wen-Kuei Hsieh, Jan. 2, 1992; 1 child, I-Ting Hsieh. BA in English, Tamkang U., Tamsui, Taiwan, 1987; MA in TESOL, Oklahoma City U., 1990; PhD in English, Indiana U. Pa., 2007. Instr. Ta-Tung Inst. Commerce, Chiyi, Taiwan, 1990—92, De-Lin Inst. Tech., Taipei, Taiwan, 1992—2004, coord., 1994—2003, coord. internat. exchange program, 2003, coord. study abroad at U. Mont., 2006. Presenter in field. Mem.: Internat. TESOL, 3 River TESOL. Office: De-Lin Inst Tech No 1 Ln 380 Chin-Yan Rd Tu-Cheng Taipei 380 Taiwan

LAI, TZE LEUNG, mathematician, educator; b. Hong Kong, China, June 28, 1945; s. Chi Yau Lai and Wai Chun Cheng; m. Letitia Chow, June 23, 1975; children: Peter, David. PhD, Columbia U., 1971. Prof., chair of stats. Stanford U., Calif., 1987—; prof. math. stats. Columbia U., New York, 1977—87. Adv. bd. mem. Academia Sinica, Taipei, Taiwan, 1991—. Author books and jour. articles. Recipient Guggenheim Fellowship, Guggenheim Found., 1983—84. Fellow: Am. Statis. Assn. (COPSS Award 1983). Office: Stanford Univ Sequoia Hall Serra Mall Stanford CA 94305-4065 Office Phone: 650-423-2622. Business E-Mail: lait@stat.stanford.edu.

LAI, W(EI) MICHAEL, retired engineering educator; b. Amoy, Fukien, China, Nov. 29, 1930; naturalized U.S. citizen, 1967; m. Linda Yu-ling Chu, Dec. 21, 1963. BSCE, Nat. Taiwan U., 1953; MS in Engring. Mech., U. Mich., 1959, PhD, 1962. Asst. prof. mechanics Renssalaer Poly. Inst., Troy, NY, 1961—66, assoc. prof., 1967—77, prof., 1978—87, acting dept. chmn., 1986—87; prof. mech. engring. and orthopaedic bioengring. Columbia U., NYC, 1987—2004, prof. emeritus, 2004—, acting chmn. dept. mech. engring., 1995-96, chmn. dept. mech. engring., 1996—2002. Author: Elements of Elasticity, 1965, Introduction to Continuum Mechanics, 1974, 3rd edit., 1993, Fundamentals of Surface Mechanics, 2002. Recipient Disting. Faculty Tchg. award, Fu Found. Sch. Engring., COlumbia U. Fellow: ASME (Melville medal for best paper 1982, Best Paper award bioengring. divsn. 1991, Lissner medal for outstanding achievement in bioengring. 2001), Am. Inst. Med. and Biol. Engring. (founding mem.). Home: 215 W 95th St Apt 9H New York NY 10025-6355

LAICO, COLETTE, artist; d. Joseph Angelillo and Antonetta Leo; m. Frank D. Laico; children: Frank Jr., Annette. Student, Marymount Coll., Art Student League, NYC, Haystack Sch. Crafts, Deer Isle, Maine, Arrowmont, Tenn. Art tchr. Westchester Art Workshop, NY, 1967—71; workshop presenter Bd. Edn. Westchester County, 1968—75. One-woman shows include Silvermine Guild Art Gallery, Works Gallery, Art Place, Greenwich Arts Gallery, Pinnacle Gallery, Hammond Mus., 2006, exhibited in group shows at Brnachville So-Ho Gallery, Somerstown Gallery, Nat. Assn. Women Artists, Silvermine Guild Art Gallery, Hudson River Mus., Katonah Mus., Signature Gallery, Stamford Art Assn., Ridgefield Guild Artists, Elaine Horwitch Gallery, Monmouth Mus. Fine Arts, Univ. Gallery, Hammond Mus., NW Collage Soc., 2007, Nat. Collage Soc., Seattle Co-Arts, Represented in permanent collections Wood and Logan Assocs., Old Greenwich, Conn., Great No. Nekoosa Corp., Norwalk, Conn., Readers Digest, Pleasantville, NY, Apple Computer, Norwalk, Aetna Life Ins. Co., Hartford, Conn., GE Corp., NYC, Seidman & Seidman BDO, E.F. Hutton, White Plains, CBS Records, NYC, Burke Rehab. Ctr., White Plains, Am. Internat. Life Assurance Co., NYC. Mem. adv. bd. White Plains Recreation, NY, 1968—73, Katonah Mus., NY, 2003—06. Recipient Sara Winston Meml. award, Nat. Assn. Women Artist, 1998, Beaux Art award, Westchester County, 2004, Mixed Media award, Pen and Brush Soc., 2004. Address: 510 Forsyth Ln Apt 401 Edmonds WA 98020-4050

LAIDLAW, ANDREW R., lawyer; b. Durham, NC, Aug. 28, 1946; BA, Northwestern U., 1969; JD, U. NC, 1972. Bar: Ill. 1972. Ptnr. Seyfarth Shaw LLP, Chgo., mem. exec. com., head Contracts Practice Area, head Litig. Practice Area. Contbr. articles to profl. jour. Mem.: Barristers, ABA (securities law com. 1982—, antitrust com.). Office: Seyfarth Shaw LLP Mid Continental Plz 55 E Monroe St Ste 4200 Chicago IL 60603-5863 Office Phone: 312-269-8823. Office Fax: 312-269-8869. Business E-Mail: alaidlaw@seyfarth.com.

LAIDLAW, ROBERT RICHARD, retired publishing executive; b. Berwyn, Ill., Mar. 25, 1923; s. John and Mabel Josephine (Howard) Laidlaw; m. Evangeline Rene Harrelson, Aug. 12, 1944; m. Marilyn C. Carlson, Sept. 7, 1998; children: Andrew Robert, Kimberly, Lisa. Student, Dartmouth Coll., 1941-42; AB, U. N.C., 1947, JD, 1950. Sales rep. Laidlaw Bros. (textbook pubs.), River Forest, Ill., 1950-58, sales mgr., 1958-60, exec. v.p., 1960-68, pres., 1968-85; ret., 1985. With USNR, 1942—45. Congregationalist.

LAIDLER, DAVID ERNEST WILLIAM, economics professor; b. Tynemouth, Northumberland, Eng., Aug. 12, 1938; s. John Alphonse and Leonora (Gosman) L.; m. Antje Charlotte Breitwisch, Jan. 29, 1965; 1 dau., Nicole Joanna; m. Frances Joan Hutner, Aug. 1960 (div. 1964). B.Sc., London Sch. Econs., 1959; MA, U. Syracuse, 1960; PhD, U. Chgo., 1964; MA, U. Manchester, Eng., 1973. Temporary asst. lectr. London Sch. Econs., 1961-62; asst. prof. U. Calif.-Berkeley, 1963-66; lectr. econs. U. Essex, Colchester, Eng., 1966-69; prof. econs. U. Manchester, 1969-75; vis. prof. econs. Brown U., Providence, 1973; prof. econs. U. Western Ont., London, Canada, 1975—2004, prof. emeritus, 2004—. Chair Bank of Montreal, 2000-05; econ. adv. panel to Marc Lalonde, minister fin., Ottawa, Ont., 1982-84; rsch. coord. Macdonald Royal Commn., 1984-85; scholar in residence C.D. Howe Inst., 1990—; Canadian Bankers' Assn. scholar, 2000-03; mem. econs. com. Social Sci. Rsch. Coun., Gt. Britain, 1972-75; program adv. com. Carnegie-Rochester Pub. Policy Conf. Series, Rochester, Pitts., 1978-79; Lister lecter. Brit. Assn. Advancement Sci., 1972; spl. advisor Bank of Can., 1998-99. Author: The Demand for Money - Theories and Evidence, 1969, Introduction to Microeconomics, 1974, Essays on Money and Inflation, 1975, Monetarist Perspectives, 1982, Taking Money Seriously, 1990, The Golden Age of the Quantity Theory, 1991; (with W. Robson) The Great Canadian Disinflation, 1993, Money and Macroeconomics, Selected Essays, 1997, Fabricating the Keynesian Revolution, 1999, Two Percent Target, 2004, Macroeconomics in Retrospect: Selected Essays, 2004; mem. editl. bd. Rev. Econ. Studies, 1970-75, Am. Econ. Rev., 1976-78, Can. Jour. Econs., 1977-79, Jour. Econ. Lit., 1978-91; assoc. editor: Jour. Money, Credit and Banking, 1979—. Rsch. grantee NSF, 1964-66, Social Sci. Rsch. Coun., 1971-76, Social Scis. and Humanities Rsch. Coun. Can., 1977-81, 94-99, 94—, Bradley Found., 1991-96. Fellow Royal Soc. Can., mem. Am. Econ. Assn., Can. Econ. Assn. (exec. com. 1980-83, pres. 1987-88, Douglas Purvis Meml. prize 1994, Donner prize 2004). Office: U Western Ont Dept Econs London ON Canada N6A 5C2 Home: 45-124 N Centre Rd London ON Canada N5X 4R3 Business E-Mail: laidler@uwo.ca.

LAIKIN, ROBERT J., electronics executive; V.p. Centruy Cellular Network, 1986-87, pres., 1988—93; v.p., treas. Brightpoint, Inc., Indpls., 1989-92, pres., 1992—96, chmn., CEO, 1994—. Office: Brightpoint Inc 501 Airtech Pkwy Plainfield IN 46168-7408*

LAIMBEER, BILL, professional basketball coach, retired professional basketball player; b. Boston, May 19, 1957; s. William Laimbeer Sr.; m. Chris Laimbeer, 1979; children: Eric, Kerlann. Grad. in Econs., U. Notre Dame, 1979. Draft pick Cleve. Cavaliers, 1979, basketball player, 1980-82, Detroit Pistons, 1982-93; spl. cons. WNBA Detroit Shock, 2002, head coach, 2002—. Head coach WNBA Ea. Conf. All-Star Team, 2007. Named Coach of Yr., WNBA, 2003; named to NBA All-Star Team, 1983, 1984, 1985, 1987. Achievements include winning back-to-back NBA Championships as a member of the Pistons, 1989, 90; led Detroit to the WNBA Championship twice as head coach, 2003, 06. Office: Detroit Shock Palace Sports & Entertainment 5 Championship Dr Auburn Hills MI 48326*

LAIN, DAVID CORNELIUS, health scientist, researcher; b. Savannah, Ga., May 17, 1955; s. Marion Cornelius and Sandra (Weatherly) L.; m. Brenda Kay Gastin, May 24, 1980; children: Candace, Heather. BS, MS, Columbia Pacific U., 1985, PhD, 1987; JD, Newport U., 1996. Diplomate Am. Bd. Forensic Examiners, Am. Bd. Forensic Medicine; lic. respiratory care practitioner. Instr. dept. continuing edn. Ga. So. U., Statesboro, 1983; rsch. devel. coord. Meml. Med. Ctr. Inc., Savannah, Ga., 1983-87; rsch. coord., asst. prof. dept. allied health sci. Med. Coll. Ga., Augusta, 1987—; clin. mgr. Ohmeda Respiratory Care, Columba, Md., 1990—95; clin. mgr., v.p. clin. and program devel. Respironics, Inc., Murrysville, Pa., 1995-2001; pres. Lain Med. Consultants, Inc., Kennesaw, Ga., 1997-2000; pres., CEO Nationwide Sleep Cons., Inc., Murrysville, Cleve., 2001—04; sleep specialist S.W. Cleve. Sleep Ctr., 2002—04; v.p. clin. devel. Vapotherm, Stevensville, Md. Bd. dirs. Ga. Soc. Cardiopulmonary Tech., Atlanta, 1987; mem. Respiratory Therapy Adv. Com., Augusta, 1987-90; cons. Aero-Med. Internat., 1987; rsch. affiliate Siemen Elem., Schaumburg, Ill., 1986; manuscript reviewer Am. Assn. Respiration Therapy, Dallas, 1988, Am. Col. Chest Disease, 1990. Contbr. articles to profl. jours. Recipient Appreciation award Am. Heart Assn., 1985, Outstanding Achievement award Calif. Coll. Health Sci., 1986. Mem. AAAS, So. Med. Assn., N.Y. Acad. Sci., Am. Assn. Respiratory Care, Nat. Bd. Respiratory Care (registered respiratory therapist). Democrat. Achievements include 9 inventions; research on reduction of peak inspiratory pressure during acute lung injury to reduce Iatrogenic progression of lung pathology; diagnosis and treatment of newborn jaundice. Office: 198Log Canoe Cir Stevensville MD 21666 Office Phone: 410-604-3977 109.

LAINE, IRIS RUTH, minister, advertising executive, public relations executive; b. Aurora, Ill., Feb. 8, 1925; d. Herman Carl Butke and Ella Stallman; m. Steven Laine, Nov. 4, 1970; 1 child, Leah Reich; stepchildren: Karen McGivney, David, Mark. BA, Fla. Atlantic U., 1981; postgrad., Harvard Div. Sch., 1983, St. Vincent de Paul Sem., 1985-86; MDiv, Luth. Sem., 1988. Ordained to ministry Evangelical Luth. Ch., 1988. Advt. writer, prodr. Chgo. Advt. Agys. and Sears Roebuck & Co., Chgo., 1950—61; promotion copy chief Chgo. Sun-Times/Daily News, 1962—65; trade rels. dir. Smith, Bucklin & Assocs., Inc., Chgo., 1966—78; v.p., treas. Stirco, Inc., Boca Raton, 1979—82; pastor, preacher Evang. Luth. Ch. in Am., Fla., 1987—95. Author: Getting to Know God, 2001, Dancing Spirits, 2006; co-author: Promotion in Foodservice, 1972. Mem. Cmty. Interfaith Coalition, Boca Raton, 1992-94, Women in Ministry, Boca Raton, 1988-90, Tradewinds Conf. Mins., Palm Beach/Martin counties, Fla., 1987-92, Synodical Coun., Evang. Luth. Ch. in Am., Fla., 1989-90; dir. Coun. on Hotel, Restaurant and Instnl. Edn., 1969; dir., sec. Internat. Food Edit. Coun., Nat. Orgn., 1968; vol. Rep. Orgns., Palm Beach County, 1996—. Recipient Award Art Dirs. Club of Chgo., 1964; named Top Ten in TV Pharms. award Am. TV Commls. Festival, 1960. Mem. Rotary Internat., Phi Kappa Phi, Alpha Sigma Lambda. Avocations: writing, social service. Home: 500 S Ocean Blvd Apt 904 Boca Raton FL 33432 Fax: 561-392-4822. Personal E-mail: irislaine@aol.com.

LAING, JAMES THOMAS, retired not-for-profit developer; b. Charleston, W.Va., Jan. 2, 1934; s. James Tamplin and Claire (Lenila) Laing; m. Patricia Ann Boehmer, June 25, 1955 (div. Mar. 1976); children: Michael Thomas, Susan Kay; m. Barbara Jean Crossman, Apr. 11, 1981. AB, Kent State U., Ohio, 1955, MA, 1956. Navigator 1st lt. USAF, 1957—59; asst. exec. dir. United Cmty. Svcs., Lorain, Ohio, 1959-64; assoc. exec. sec. United Fund, Canton, Ohio, 1964-69, exec. dir. St. Joseph, Mo., 1969-73, United Way, South Bend, Ind., 1973-76, United Way Oakland County, Pontiac, Mich., 1976-97, pres., 1997-99; ret., 1999. Instr. sociology Kent State U., St. Mary's Coll., South Bend, Oakland U., Rochester, Mich., 1959—80; field cons. United Health Founds., NYC, 1967—71; mem. profl. adv. com. United Way Am., Alexandria, Va., 1979—84; mem. profl. adv. bd. United Way Internat., 1981—96. Bd. dirs. United Way Nat. Retiree Assn., 1998—2006, v.p., 2000—02; bd. dirs. Internat. Bluegrass Music Mus., Owensboro, Ky., 1994—2004, treas. bd., 1999—2001; bd. dirs. United Way Mich., 1999—2000. Mem.: Blue Key, Rotary (past pres.), Pi Gamma Mu, Alpha Kappa Delta, Phi Sigma Kappa. Methodist. Avocations: music, golf, photography. Home: 3254 Angelus Dr Waterford MI 48329-2512 Personal E-mail: frippster@sbcglobal.net.

LAING, KAREL ANN, publishing executive; b. Mpls., July 5, 1939; d. Edward Francis and Elizabeth Jane Karel (Templeton) Hannon; m. G. R. Cheesebrough, Dec. 19, 1959 (div. 1969); 1 child, Jennifer Read; m. Ronald Harris Laing, Jan. 6, 1973; 1 child, Christopher Harris. Grad., U. Minn., 1960. With Guthrie Symphony Opera Program, Mpls., 1969-71; account supr. Colle & McVoy Advt. Agy., Richfield, Minn., 1971-74; owner The Cottage, Edina, Minn., 1974-75; salespromotion rep. Robert Meyers & Assocs., St. Louis Park, Minn., 1975-76; cons. Webb Co., St. Paul, 1976-77, custom pub. dir., 1977-89; pres. K.L. Publs., Inc., Bloomington, Minn., 1989—. Contbr. articles to profl. jours. Cmty. vol. Am. Heart Assn., Am. Cancer Soc., Edina PTA; charter sponsor Walk Around Am., St. Paul, 1985. Mem.: Minn. Mag. Pub. Assn. (founder, bd. govs.), Direct Mail Mktg. Assn., Am. Bankers Assn., Advt. Fedn. Am., Fin. Instn.

Mktg. Assn., Bank Mktg. Assn., St. Andrews Soc. Republican. Presbyterian. Avocations: painting, gardening, reading, travel. Office: KL Publs 2001 Killebrew Dr Minneapolis MN 55425-1865

LAINGEN, LOWELL BRUCE, diplomat; b. Odin Twp., Minn., Aug. 6, 1922; s. Palmer K. and Ida Mabel (Eng) L.; m. Penelope Babcock, June 1, 1957; children: William Bruce, Charles Winslow, James Palmer. BA cum laude, St. Olaf Coll., 1947; MA in Internat. Relations, U. Minn., 1949, LLD honoris causa, 2005. Internat. rels. officer State Dept., 1949-50; joined U.S. Fgn. Svc., 1950; vice consul Hamburg, Germany, 1951-53; 3d sec. embassy Teheran, Iran, 1953-54; consul Meshed, Iran, 1954-55; asst., then officer chargé Greek affairs State Dept., 1956-60; 2d sec., then 1st sec. embassy Karachi, Pakistan, 1960-64; with Pakistan/Afghanistan affairs bur. State Dept., 1964-67; assigned Nat. War Coll., 1967-68; dep. chief mission to Afghanistan Kabul, 1968-71; country dir. Pakistan, Afghanistan and Bangladesh, State Dept., 1971-73, India, Nepal, Sri Lanka and the Maldives, 1973-74, acting dep. asst. sec. state for Near Eastern and South Asian affairs, 1974-75, dep. asst. sec. state for European affairs, 1975-76; ambassador to Malta, 1977-79; chargé d'affaires Am. Embassy, Teheran, Iran, 1979; held hostage by Iranian student militants, 1979-81; v.p. Nat. Def. U., Ft. McNair, Washington, 1981-86; exec. dir. Nat. Commn. Pub. Service, Washington, 1987-90. Lectr. Security Overseas Seminar, Fgn. Svc. Inst., 1995-2000; Sol Linowitz chair in internat. rels. Hamilton Coll., 1998; ex officio mem. Nat. Commn. Pub. Svc., 2002—. Recipient Fgn. Svc. cup, 1998, Alumnus Notable Achievement Coll. Liberal Arts U. Minn., 2007. Mem.: Am. Acad. Diplomacy (bd. dirs., ex officio 2006). Home: 5627 Old Chester Rd Bethesda MD 20814-1035 Personal E-mail: bplaingen@aol.com.

LAIOU, ANGELIKI EVANGELOS, history professor; b. Athens, Greece, Apr. 6, 1941; came to U.S., 1959; d. Evangelos K. and Virginia I. (Apostolides) Laios; m. Stavros B. Thomadakis, July 14, 1973; 1 son, Vassili N. BA, Brandeis U., 1961; MA, Harvard U., 1962, PhD, 1966. Asst. prof. history Harvard U., Cambridge, Mass., 1969-72, Dumbarton Oaks prof. Byzantine history, 1981—; assoc. prof. Brandeis U., Waltham, 1972-75; prof. Rutgers U., New Brunswick, NJ, 1975-79, disting. prof., 1979-81; chmn. Gennadeion com. (Am. Sch. Classical Studies), Athens, Greece, 1981-84; dir. Dumbarton Oaks, 1989-98; prof. history Harvard U., Cambridge, 1998—. Mem. Greek Parliament, 2000-2002; dep. min. fgn. affairs, Greece, 2000. Author: Constantinople and the Latins, 1972, Peasant Society in the Late Byzantine Empire, 1977, Mariage, amour et parenté à Byzance, XIe-XIIIe siècles, 1992, Gender, Society and Economic Life in Byzantium, 1992, The Economic History of Byzantium, 2002. Guggenheim Found. fellow, 1971-72, 79-80, Dumbarton Oaks sr. fellow, 1983—, Am. Coun. Learned Socs. fellow, 1988-89. Fellow: Acad. des Inscriptions et Belles Lettres, Am. Acad. Arts and Scis., Medieval Acad., Acad. Athens; mem.: Serbian Acad. Arts and Scis., Austrian Acad. Arts and Scis., Am. Hist. Assn., Medieval Acad. Am., Greek Com. Study of South Eastern Europe. Office: Harvard U Dept History Cambridge MA 02138 Home Phone: 617-547-9679; Office Phone: 617-495-5108. E-mail: laiou@fas.harvard.edu.

LAIR, VICKIE SUE, mathematics professor; b. Scotland, SD, Nov. 17, 1948; d. Lester and Veone Jennette Jucht; m. Alan Van Lair. BS summa cum laude, SD State U., Brookings, 1971; MAT, U. Nebr., Lincoln, 1973. Instr. U. SD, Vermillion, 1973—82, Wright State U., Dayton, Ohio, 1983—95, Sinclair C.C., Dayton, Ohio, 1987—96, 1996—2000, asst. prof., 2000—04, assoc. prof., 2004—. Mem. Concerned Women Am., Washington. Grantee, NSF, 2001—07. Mem.: Math. Assn. Am., Phi Kappa Phi, Alpha Lambda Delta. Republican. Baptist. Home: 1161 Sanctuary Dr Fairborn OH 45324 Office: Sinclair Cmty Coll 444 W 3rd St Dayton OH 45402

LAIRD, CHERYL F., mental health services professional, paralegal; d. Wallace F. Stalnaker, Sr. and Faith M. Stalnaker; children: Craig H., Christine Vickers, Tracy Wheeler, John T. BA in Psychology, U. Ctrl. Fla., Orlando, 1989; MA in Counseling ahd Human Devel., Liberty U., Lynchberg, Va., 1996; EdD in Human Sexuality, Inst. Advanced Study of Human Sexuality, San Francisco, 2001. Diplomate Am. Bd. Sexology; lic. mental health counselor Fla., cert. sex. therapist Fla., forensic addictions examiner, compulsive gambling treatment specialist, hypnotherpaist Fla., leader Active Parenting of Teens, substance abuse profl., comprehensive assessor, child and adolescent needs and strengths, juvenile assessor Health Svcs. Assn., juvenile sex offender evaluator. Intern. therapist Ctr. for Drug Free Living, 1995; mental health dir., therapist Altamonte Ctr. for Counseling, 1996—98; therapist Summit Counseling Group, 1998—. Fellow: Am. Bd. Forensic Sexologists; mem.: APA, Nat. Guild Hypnotists, Am. Assn. Christian Counselors, Fla. Assn. for Treatment of Sexual Abusers, Am. Profl. Soc. on Abuse of Children, Fla. Mental Health Counselor Assn. (bd. dirs., edn. chair), Mental Health Counselors of Ctrl. Fla. (pres.), Assn. of Family and Conciliation Cts., Am. Assn. Sex Educators, Counselors, and Therapists, Assn. for Treatment of Sexual Abusers (clin. mem., diplomat). Avocation: parrot foster care. Office Phone: 407-830-7903. Office Fax: 407-767-0812. E-mail: cslaird@cfl.rr.com.

LAIRD, DAVID, humanities educator emeritus; b. Marshfield, Wis., Oct. 17, 1927; s. Melvin Robert and Helen Melissa (Connor) L.; m. Helen Astrid Lauritzen, Sept. 10, 1955; 1 child, Vanessa Ann. PhB, U. Chgo., 1947; BA with highest honor, U. Wis., 1950, MA, 1951, PhD, 1955; postgrad., Courtauld Inst., 1953. Instr. to asst. prof. Oberlin Coll., 1955-58; mem. faculty Calif. State U., LA, 1958—, chmn. dept. English, 1969-73, chmn. dept. Am. studies, 1977-79. Nat. Humanities Inst. fellow U. Chgo., 1978-79; sr. Fulbright lectr. U. Tunis, Tunisia, 1979-80; fellow Folger Shakespeare Libr., 1982; Fulbright lectr. Odense U. (Denmark), 1983-84; vis. prof. U. Ottawa, 1984-85; cons. to Choice. Mem. editorial bd. Jour. Forest History; contbr. articles on Shakespeare, Am. lit. and cultural history to profl. jours. Mem. Western Shakespeare Seminar, Friends of Huntington Libr. Recipient Outstanding Prof. award Calif. State U., 1987, Nat. Endowment for the Humanities Summer Seminar award Northwestern U., 1989; Uhrig Found. grantee, 1964-65; Fulbright fellow, 1953-54. Mem. MLA, Malone Soc., Am. Studies Assn., Phi Beta Kappa. Home: 208 S Cherry Ave Marshfield WI 54449-3732 Office: Calif State U Humanities Dept Los Angeles CA 90032 Business E-Mail: laird208@wctc.net.

LAIRD, DORIS ANNE MARLEY, retired humanities educator, musician; b. Charlotte, NC, Jan. 15, 1931; d. Eugene Harris and Coleen (Bethea) Marley; m. William Everette Laird Jr., Mar. 13, 1964; children: William Everette III, Andrew Marley, Glen Howard. MusB, Converse Coll., Spartanburg, SC, 1951; opera cert., New Eng. Conservatory, Boston, 1956; MusM, Boston U., 1956; PhD, Fla. State U., 1980. Leading soprano roles S.C. Opera Co., Columbia, 1951-53, Plymouth Rock Ctr. of Music and Art, Duxbury, Mass., 1953-56; soprano Pro Musica, Boston, 1956, New Eng. Opera Co., Boston, 1956; instr. Stratford Coll., Danville, Va., 1956-58, Sch. Music Fla. State U., Tallahassee, 1958-60, dept. humanities, 1960-68; tchr. Fla. State U., 1973-79; asst. prof. Fla. A&M U., Tallahassee, 1979-89, assoc. prof., 1990—2002; ret., 2002. Vis. scholar Cornell U., 1988; participant So. Conf. on Afro-Am. Studies, Inc. Author: Colin Morris: Modern Missionary, 1980; contbr. articles to profl. jours. Soprano Washington St. Meth. Ch., Columbia, SC, 1951-53, Copley Meth. Ch., Boston, 1953-56; soloist Trinity United Meth. Ch., Tallahassee, 1983—; mem. Saint Andrews Soc., Tallahassee, 1986—; judge Brain Bowl, Tallahassee, 1981-84; alumnae bd. Converse Coll., 2004— Named subject of article, Glamour mag., 2001, Self mag., 2003; recipient NEH award, 1988, Disting. Alumna award, Converse Coll., 2001; scholar Phi Sigma Tau, 1960. Mem. AAUP, AAUW, Nat. Art Educators Assn., Tallahassee Music Tchrs. Assn., Tallahassee Music Guild, Am. Guild of Organists, DAR (mus. rep. 1984-85, registrar 2005-), Colonial Dames of 17th Century (music dir. 1984-85), Nat. Assn. Humanities Edn., U. Wyo. Women's Club, Woman's Club Tallahassee (v.p. 2004), Converse Coll. Alumni (bd. dirs. 2003—) Republican. Achievements include subject of article Self Magazine, 2004. Avocations: travel, dance, music. Home: 1125 Mercer Dr Tallahassee FL 32312-2833 Personal E-mail: dorismlaird@comcast.net.

LAIRD, EDWARD DEHART, JR., lawyer; b. Pitts., July 14, 1952; s. Edward D. Sr. and Miriam (Hellman) L.; m. Ellen Armstrong, July 30, 1977; children: Megan, Edward, Peter. BA, SUNY, Oswego, 1974; JD, Western New Eng. Sch. Law, 1977. Bar: N.Y. 1978, U.S. Dist. Ct. (no. dist.) N.Y. 1978, U.S. Dist Ct. (so. dist.) N.Y. 1989, U.S. Dist. Ct. Vt. 1995, U.S. Ct. Appeals (2d cir.) 1985, U.S. Supreme Ct. 1986. Shareholder Carter, Conboy, Case, Blackmore, Maloney and Laird, P.C., Albany, NY, 1977—. Instr. legal rsch. and writing Western New Eng. Sch. Law, Springfield, Mass., 1976-77. Master Am. Inns Ct. Albany Law Sch. chpt.; mem. ABA, N.Y. State Bar Assn., Albany County Bar Assn., Def. Rsch. Inst., Def. Rsch. Inst. of Northeastern N.Y. Office: Carter Conboy Case Blackmore Maloney and Laird PC 20 Corporate Woods Blvd Albany NY 12211-2350 Office Phone: 518-465-3484.

LAIRD, MARY See WOOD, LARRY

LAIRD, WILLIAM EVERETTE, JR., economics professor; b. Hattiesburg, Miss., Feb. 4, 1934; s. William Everette and Mildred Alvah (Howard) L.; m. Doris Anne Marley, Mar. 13, 1964; children: William Everette III, Andrew Marley, Glen Howard. BS, Stetson U., 1956; MA, George Washington U., 1958; PhD, U. Va., 1962. Asst. prof. Fla. State U., Tallahassee, 1960-66, assoc. prof., 1966-71, prof., 1971—, chmn. dept. econs., 1974-97, SERVICE prof., 1997—2002, prof. emeritus, 2002—. Contbr. articles to profl. jours. DuPont fellow, 1959-60; recipient awards Fla. State U. Grad. Research Council, 1965, 66, Faculty Devel. awards Fla. State U., 1971 Mem. Am. Econs. Assn., So. Econ. Assn., Plantagenet Soc. Magna Charta Barons, Jamestowne Soc., St. Andrew Soc., Order of First Families of Va., Econ. Club of Fla. Methodist. Home: 1125 Mercer Dr Tallahassee FL 32312-2833 Office Phone: 850-385-2705. Business E-Mail: wlaird@fsu.edu.

LAISKONIS, MICHAEL, chef; Attended, Wayne State U. Pastry chef, sous chef Emily's Restaurant, Northville, Mich.; cook Tribute, Farmington Hills, Mich., 1997—99, pastry chef, 1999—2004; exec. pastry chef Le Bernardin, NYC, 2004—. Named one of 10 Best Pastry Chefs in Am., Pastry Art and Design, 2002—03, NYC's Rising Stars, StarChefs.com, 2006; recipient Am. Food & Entertaining award, Bon Appétit Mag., 2004.

LAITIN, DAVID DENNIS, political science professor; b. Bklyn., June 4, 1945; s. Daniel and Frances (Blumenkranz) L.; m. Delia Fortune; children: Marc Oliver, Anna Elizabeth. BA, Swarthmore Coll., 1967; PhD, U. Calif., Berkeley, 1974. Instr. Nat. Tchr. Edn. Ctr., Afgoy, Somalia, 1969; master Grenada Boys' Secondary Sch., West Indies, 1970-71; asst. prof. dept. polit. sci. U. Calif.-San Diego, La Jolla, 1975-79, prof., 1984-87, chmn., 1986-87; reader dept. polit. sci. U. Ife, Nigeria, 1979-80; prof. polit. sci., dir. Wilder House Ctr. for Study Politics, History and Culture U. Chgo., 1987-99, William R. Kenan, Jr. prof., 1992—99; prof. polit. sci. Stanford U., Calif., 1999—, James T. Watkins IV and Elise V. Watkins prof. polit. sci. Calif., 2005—. Expert witness fgn. affairs subcom. U.S. Ho. Reps., 1981; resident Rockefeller Found., Bellagio Ctr., Sept. 1996. Author: Politics, Language and Thought: The Somali Experieince, 1977, Hegemony and Culture: Politics and Religious Change Among the Yoruba, 1986, Somalia: A Nation in Search of a State, 1987, Language Repertoires and State Construction in Africa, 1992, (with James Fearon) Explaining Ethnic Cooperation, 1996, Identity in Formation: The Russian-Speaking Populations of the Near Abroad, 1998, (with James Fearon) Ethnicity, Insurgency and Civil War, 2003, (with Alan B. Krueger) Misunderestimating Terrorism, 2004, Nations, States and Violence, 2007. Fellow NEH, 1979-80, Howard Found., 1984-85, German Marshall Fund, 1984-85, John Simon Guggenheim Found., 1995-96, Harry F. Guggenheim Found., 1997—, Ctr. for Advanced Study in Behavioral Scis., 1989-2000, Russell Sage Found., 2003-2004; co-prin. investigator award NSF, 1993-95, 2002—; recipient award Am. Assn. for the Advancement of Slavic Studies, Dogan award Soc. for Comparative Rsch.; co-prin. investigator award Carnegie Found., 2000-01. Mem. Am. Polit. Sci. Assn. (v.p. 2005-06, 2 awards), Am. Acad. Arts and Scis., Coun. Am. Polit. Sci. Assn., NAS. Office: Stanford U Dept Polit Sci Stanford CA 94305 Office Phone: 650-725-9556. Business E-Mail: dlaitin@stanford.edu.*

LAI-YUEN, SUSANA, engineering educator; b. Mexico; Asst. prof. U. South Fla., Tampa, Fla., 2005—. Fellow, NC State U.; scholar. Mem.: IEEE (Best Student Paper award 2006), ASME, Soc. Hispanic Profl. Engrs., Soc. Mfg. Engrs., Inst. Indsl. Engrs. (Pritsker Doctoral Dissertation award 2006, 2d Pl. Grad. Rsch. award 2002), Tau Beta Pi, Alpha Pi Mu, Phi Kappa Phi. Home Phone: 919-522-8553; Office Phone: 813-974-5547.

LAJOHN, LAWRENCE ANTHONY, research scientist; b. Jamestown, NY, Apr. 23, 1949; s. Anthony Raymond and Anne Theresa La John. BA, Ohio No. U., 1971; MS, George Washington U., 1976, Clarkson U., 1988, PhD, 1990. Chemist NIH, Bethesda, Md., 1972-76; rsch. asst. Miles Labs., Elkhart, Ind., 1976-77; U. Notre Dame, South Bend, Ind., 1977-78; So. Ill. U., Carbondale, 1978-82; Queen's U., Can., 1982-84; Clarkson U., 1985-90; postdoctoral fellow Dept. Applied Math., U. Western Ont., London, Ont., 1990-93; rsch. scientist dept. physics & astronomy U. Pitts., Pa., 1993—. Physics instr. U. Pitts., Carnegie Mellon U., Duquesne U. Contbr. articles to profl. jours. Mem. AAAS, Am. Chem. Soc., Am. Math. Soc., Am. Phys. Soc., Math. Assn. Am., N.Y. Acad. Sci., Sigma Xi. Avocations: weightlifting, baseball, bowling. Office: Dept Physics & Astronomy Univ Pitts Pittsburgh PA 15260 Office Phone: 412-624-9050. Business E-Mail: lajohn@stribor.phyast.pitt.edu. E-mail: lal18@pitt.edu.

LAJTHA, ABEL, biochemist; b. Budapest, Hungary, Sept. 22, 1922; naturalized; married; 2 children. PhD in Chemistry, Eotvos Lorand U., Budapest, 1945; MD (hon.), U. Padua. Asst. prof. biochemistry Eotvos Lorand U., 1945-47; asst. prof. Inst. Muscle Rsch. and Mass., 1949-50; sr. rsch. scientist N.Y. State Psychiat. Inst., 1950-57, assoc. rsch. scientist, 1957-62, prin. rsch. scientist, 1962-66; dir. N.Y. State Rsch. Inst. Neurochemistry, 1966—; prof. exptl. psychiatry Sch. Medicine NYU, 1971—; now dir. Ctr. for Neurochemistry Nathan S. Kline Inst., Orangeburg, NY. Asst. prof. Coll. Physicians & Surgeons, Columbia U., 1956-69. Zoology Station fellow Italy, 1947-48, Rsch. fellow Royal Inst. Great Britain, 1948-49. Mem. Armenian, Hungarian, Slovenian Acad. Sci., Internat. Brain Rsch. Orgn., Am. Soc. Biol. Chemists, Am. Acad. Neurology, Am. Coll. Neuropsychopharmacology, Internat. Soc. Neurochemistry (pres.), Am. Chem. Soc., Am. Soc. Neurochemistry (pres.). Achievements include rsch. in neurochemistry, amino acid and protein metabolism of the brain and the brain barrier system and drug addiction. Office: Nathan S Kline Inst 140 Old Orangeburg Rd Orangeburg NY 10962 Home Phone: 914-693-7988; Office Phone: 845-398-5530. Business E-Mail: lajtha@nki.rfmh.org.

LAKE, (W.) ANTHONY, former national security advisor; b. NYC, Apr. 2, 1939; married; 3 children. AB magna cum laude, Harvard U., 1961; PhD, Princeton U., 1974. Joined Fgn. Svc., US Dept. State, Washington, 1962, U.S. vice consul Saigon, Vietnam, 1963, Hue, Vietnam, 1964-65, spl. asst. to Pres. for nat. security affairs Washington, 1969-70; polit. coord. Muskie Election Campaign, 1971—72; exec. dir. Internat. Vol. Svcs., 1973—77; policy planning for US Dept. State, Washington, 1977-81; prof. Amherst Coll., 1981—84; Five Coll. Prof. Internat. Rels. Mount Holyoke Coll., 1984—92; sr. fgn. policy analyst Clinton-Gore Campaign, 1991—92; asst. to the Pres. for nat. security affairs NSC, Washington, 1993—97; dist. prof. diplomacy, Edmund A. Walsh Sch. Foreign Affairs Georgetown U., 1997—. Author: 'The Tar Baby Option': American Policy Toward Southern Rhodesia, 1976,Third World Radical Regimes: U.S. Policy Under Carter and Reagan, 1985 Somoza Falling: A Case Study of Washington at Work, 1989, 6 Nightmares, 2000; co-author: Our Own Worst Enemy: The Unmaking of American Foreign Policy, 1984; editor: After the Wars, 1990; contbg. editor: Legacy of Vietnam: The War, American Society, and the Future of U.S. Foreign Policy, 1976, After the Wars, 1990, Six Nightmares, 2000. Office: Georgetown U Bldg ICC Room 301 Washington DC 20057 Home Phone: 202-332-1317. Business E-Mail: lakea@georgetown.edu.

LAKE, BRUCE MENO, physicist; b. LA, Nov. 22, 1941; s. Meno Truman and Jean Ivy (Hancock)_ L. BS in Engring., Princeton U., 1963; MS, Calif. Inst. Tech., 1965, PhD, 1969. Mem. tech. staff advanced instrumentation dept. TRW Corp., Redondo Beach, Calif., 1969-73, head exptl. hydrodynamics sect., 1973-81, asst. mgr. dept. fluid mechanics, 1977-81, mgr. dept. fluid mechanics, 1981-96, mgr. computational physics bus. area, 1996-2000; pvt. cons., 2000—. Contbr. articles to profl. jours. and books. Ford Found. fellow, 1964-65, TRW tech. fellow. Mem. Am. Phys. Soc., Nat. Acad. Engring. Office: 41650 Calle Pino Murrieta CA 92562 Business E-Mail: blake@alumni.princeton.edu.

LAKE, CAROL LEE, anesthesiologist, physician, educator; b. Altoona, Pa., July 14, 1944; d. Samuel Lindsay and Edna Winifred (McMahan) L. BS, Juniata Coll., 1966; MD, Med. Coll. Pa., 1970; MBA, U. Calif., Irvine, 1997; MPH, U. Mich., 2000. Intern Mercy Hosp., Pitts., 1970-71, resident in anesthesiology, 1971-73; staff anesthesiologist Pitts. Anesthesia Assocs., 1973-75; asst. prof. anesthesiology U. Va., Charlottesville, 1975-80, assoc. prof., 1980-89, prof. anesthesiology, 1989-94; prof. anesthesiology, chair U. Calif., Davis, 1994-95, prof. clin. anesthesiology, 1996; chief of staff Roudebush VA Med. Ctr., 1997-99; asst. dean, prof. anesthesia Ind. U., Indpls., 1997-99; prof. anesthesiology, chair U. Louisville, 1999—2004, assoc. dean for continuing med. edn., 1999—2004, asst. v.p. for health affairs/continuing edn., 2002—04; CEO Verefi Techs., Inc., Elizabethtown, Pa., 2005—. Sr. assoc. examiner Am. Bd. Anesthesiology, 1981—2005. Author: Cardiovascular Anesthesia, 1985; editor: Pediatric Cardiac Anesthesia, 1988, 4th edit., 2004; Clinical Monitoring, 1990, 2d edit., 2000; editor Seminars in Cardiothoracic and Vascular Anesthesia, 1999—06; co-editor: Blood: Hemostasis, Transfusion and Alternatives in the Perioperative Period, 1995; editor Advances in Anesthesia, 1993—. Mem. Assn. Cardiac Anesthesiologists (pres. 1987-88), Soc. Cardiovascular Anesthesiologists (bd. dirs. 1988-92), Alpha Omega Alpha. Presbyterian. Avocations: music, entomology, gardening. Home Phone: 717-583-0842. E-mail: carol.lake@verefi.com.

LAKE, I. BEVERLY, JR., retired state supreme court justice; b. Raleigh, NC, 1934; s. I. Beverly, Sr. and Gertrude L.; m. Susan Deichmann Smith; children: Lynn Elizabeth, Guy, Laura Ann, I. Beverly III. Student, Mars Hill Coll., 1951; BS, Wake Forest U., 1955, JD, 1960. Bar: N.C. Pvt. practice, 1960-69, 76-85; asst. atty. gen. State of NC, 1969-74, dep. atty. gen., 1974-76; Gov.'s legis. liason, chief lobbyist, 1985; judge Superior Ct., 1985-91; assoc. justice NC Supreme Ct., 1992—2000, chief justice Raleigh, 2001—06. Chmn. bd. trustees Ridge Rd. Bapt. Ch., 1968-69; mem. N.C. Senate, 1976-80, chmn. Senate Judiciary Com.; Rep. nominee Gov. N.C., 1979-80; del. Rep. Nat. Convention, 1980; Rep. state fin. chmn., mem. ctr. com., mem. exec. com., 1980-82; N.C. eastern chmn. Reagan-Bush Campaign, 1984; bd. visitors Wake Forest U. Sch. Law, 1995—; bd. vis. Southeastern Bapt. Theol. Sem. Military intelligence staff officer USAR, 1958—68, captain USAR, 1958—68, colonel, state staff judge advocate NC State Militia, 1989—92. Mem. AMVETS, N.C. Bar Assn., Wake County Bar Assn., Assn. Interstate Commerce Commn. Practitioners, Navy League, Am. Legion, Masons, Shriners, Phi Alpha Delta.

LAKE, JANE BURFORD, special education educator, hypnotherapist, small business owner; b. Pitts., Oct. 9, 1937; d. Henry Isaac and Emily Louise (Castore) Burford; m. Howard Kenneth Lake, Jr., Aug. 20, 1960 (!div. 1983); children: Karen Lake Ray, Christopher Kenneth. BS in Elem. Edn., U. Del., 1960; Ryan specialist, U. Calif., Irvine, 1983; PhD, Am. Inst. Hypnotherapy, Santa Ana, Calif., 1986; MEd in Adminstrn., U.S. Internat. U., Irvine, Calif., 1991. Elem. tchr. Penn Delco Union Sch. Dist., West Chester, Pa., 1960-63, Sugartown Elem. Sch., Malvern, Pa., 1963-65; substitute tchr. Oceanview-Westminster Sch. Dist., Huntington Beach, Pa., 1979-83; mem. faculty Am. Inst. Hypnotherapist, 1986-90; tchr. spl. edn. Santa Ana Unified Sch. Dist., 1983—; owner, pres. For Heaven's Sake. Pvt. practice hypnotherapy, Tustin, Calif., 1986—; mem. staff for devel. stress mgmt. Century High Sch., Santa Ana, 1991-92; fellow Nat. B d. Hypnotherapy and Hypno Anesthesiology, 1986—, Am. Bd. Hypnotherapy, 1986—; symposium speaker Nat. Head Injury Found., 1986. Cons. vol. art edn. program Jr. League, Irvine, 1976. Recipient Outstanding Contbns. to Edn. in Hypnotherapy award Nat. Bd. Hypnotherapy and Hypno Anesthesiology, 1989. Mem. NEA, Santa Ana Edn. Assn. (grievance com. 1983—), Calif. Tchrs. Edn. Assn., Calif. Assn. Neurologically Handicapped, Assn. for Children and Adults with Learning Handicaps, Tchr. Advs. for Spl. Kids, So. Calif. Head Injury Found., AAUW (edn. advisor Tustin 1990-91), LWV. Avocations: gardening, writing journals, travel, singing, creating meditations. Home: 27945 Chiclana Mission Viejo CA 92692-1223 Personal E-mail: drjlake@cox.net.

LAKE, JOSEPH EDWARD, ambassador; b. Jacksonville, Tex., Oct. 18, 1941; s. Lloyd Euel and Marion Marie (Allen) L.; m. Sarah Ann Bryant (div.); children: Joseph Edward, Mary Elizabeth; m. Jo Ann Kessler, June 12, 1971; 1 child, Michael Allen. BA summa cum laude, Tex. Christian U., 1962, MA, 1967. 3rd sec. U.S. Embassy, Taipei, Taiwan, 1963-65, Bur. of European Affairs Dept. State, 1966-67; second sec. U.S. Embassy, Cotonou, Dahomey, 1967-69; with bur. intelligence and rsch. Dept. State, 1969-71; second sec. U.S. Embassy, Taipei, Taiwan, 1971-76; with office Philippine affairs Dept. State, 1976-77; second sec. U.S. Embassy, Lagos, Nigeria, 1977-78; prin. officer and consul U.S. Consulate, Kaduna, Nigeria, 1978-81; with Fgn. Svc. Inst., Washington, 1981-82; first sec. U.S. Embassy, Sofia, Bulgaria, 1982-84, charge d'affaires, 1984, counselor, dep. chief mission, 1984-85; dep. dir. regional affairs, bur. East Asian and Pacific Affairs Dept. State, 1985-86; advisor U.S. delegation 41st UN Gen. Assembly, 1986; dir. ops. ctr. Dept. State, Washington, 1987-90; amb. to Rep. of Mongolia, Ulaanbaatar, 1990-93, Rep. of Albania, Tirana, 1994-96; dep. asst. sec. of state for info. mgmt. Dept. State, Washington, 1996-97, chair com. on messaging and interagy. collaboration, 2002—05; dir. internat. affairs City of Dallas, 1997—2002; rsch. assoc. Tower Ctr. So. Meth. U. Mem. adv. bd. Asian studies program So. Meth. U. Contbr. articles to profl. jours. Mem. Dallas Com. on Fgn. Rels.; mem. exec. edn. adv. coun. U. Tex., Sch. Mgmt., Dallas. Mem.: Am. Fgn. Svc. Assn. Home: 6145 Highgate Ln Dallas TX 75214-2155

LAKE, KATHLEEN COOPER, lawyer; b. San Antonio, Jan. 11, 1955; d. Herschel Taliaferro and Virginia Mae (Hylton) Cooper; m. Randall Brent Lake, Apr. 9, 1977; 1 child, Ethan Taliaferro. AB in Polit. Sci. magna cum laude, Middlebury Coll., 1977; JD with high honors, U. Tex., 1980. Bar: Tex. 1980, U.S. Ct. Appeals (5th cir.) 1981, U.S. Ct. Appeals (D.C. and 3rd cirs.) 1984. Assoc. atty. Vinson & Elkins, Houston, 1980-88; ptnr. Vinson & Elkins, LLP, Houston, 1989—. Bd. advisors, columnist Utilities, Y2K Advisor, 1998-99. Adult leader, com. mem. Sam Houston Area Coun.-Golden Arrow dist. Boy Scouts Am., 1993—, chair troop com., 1998-2001. Recipient Unit Svc. award Sam Houston Area Coun.-Golden Arrow dist.

Boy Scouts Am., 1996, 98, 2005. Fellow Tex. Bar Found. (life), Houston Bar Found.; mem. ABA (vice-chair com. 1997-99), Energy Bar Assn., Electric Coop. Bar Assn., State Bar Tex., Tex. Law Rev. Assn. (life), Houston Bar Assn., Middlebury Coll. Alumni Assn. (com. mem. 1980-2000, Houston com. chair 2001—, class agent 2007-), Order of Coif, Phi Beta Kappa, Phi Kappa Phi. Office: Vinson & Elkins LLP 2500 First City Tower 1001 Fannin St Houston TX 77002-6760 Office Phone: 713-758-3826. E-mail: klake@velaw.com.

LAKE, KEVIN BRUCE, medical association administrator; b. Seattle, Jan. 25, 1937; s. Winston Richard and Vera Emma (Davis) L.; m. Suzanne Roto, Oct. 25, 1986; children from previous marriage: Laura, Kendrick, Wesley. BS, Portland State U., 1960; MD, U. Oreg., 1964. Intern Marion County Gen. Hosp. and Ind. Med. Ctr., Indpls., 1964-65; resident U. Oreg. Hosps. and Clinics, 1968-70, fellow in infectious and pulmonary diseases, 1970-71; fellow in pulmonary diseases U. So. Calif., 1971-72, instr. medicine, 1972-75, asst. clin. prof., 1975-79, assoc. clin. prof., 1979-84, clin. prof., 1986—. Dir. med. edn. and research La Vina Hosp., 1972-75; dir. respiratory therapy Methodist Hosp., Arcadia, Calif., 1975—; mem. staff Los Angeles County/U. So. Calif. Med. Center, Santa Teresita Hosp., Duarte, Calif., Huntington Meml. Hosp., Pasadena, Calif.; attending physician, mem. med. adv. bd. Foothill Free Clinic, Pasadena. Contbr. articles to profl. jours. Mem. exec. com. Profl. Staff Assn. U. So. Calif. Sch. Medicine; 2d v.p. bd. mgmt. Palm St. br. YMCA, Pasadena, 1974, 1st v.p., 1975, chmn., 1976-78, met. bd. dirs., 1976-84; bd. dirs. Mendenhall Ministries, La Vie Holistic Ministries, Hospice of Pasadena, Hastings Found. co-pres. PTA, Allendale Grade Sch., Pasadena, 1975-76. Served to lt. U.S. Navy, 1965-68. NIH grantee, 1971-72. Fellow ACP, Am. Coll. Chest Physicians; mem. Am. Thoracic Soc., Calif. Thoracic Soc. Home: 875 S Madison Ave Pasadena CA 91106-4404 Office: 444 N Altadena Dr Pasadena CA 91107-2501 Office Phone: 626-795-5118. Personal E-mail: kblmd@aol.com.

LAKE, PETER J., automotive executive; Grad. in Bus. With Lucas Industries, 1978, various sales and mktg. positions diesel and heavy-duty elec. divsn.; gen. mgr. Lucas Braking Parts and Svc.; mktg. dir. Lucas Aftermarket Divsn.; comml. dir. Lucas Varity Aftermarket Ops.; head Automotive mktg. LucasVarity Automotive, v.p. mktg.; v.p. bus. devel. & planning TRW Chassis Systems TRW Automotive Holdings Corp., Livonia, Mich., gen. mgr. parts & svc. divsn., v.p. sales & bus. devel., 2002—04, exec. v.p. sales & bus. devel., 2004—. Mem.: Original Equipment Mfrs. Assn., Soc. Automotive Engrs. Office: TRW Automotive Holdings Corp 12001 Tech Center Dr Livonia MI 48150 Office Phone: 734-855-2600.*

LAKE, RICKI (RICKI PAMELA LAKE), talk show host, actress; b. NYC, Sept. 21, 1968; m. Rob Sussman (separated); children Milo Sebastian, Owen Tyler Syndicated talk show host Ricki Lake, 1993—. Movie appearances include: Hairspray, 1988, Working Girl, 1988, Cookie, 1989, Cry-Baby, 11990, Last Exit to Brooklyn, 1989, Where the Day Takes You, 1992, Inside Monkey Zetterland, 1993, Serial Mom, 1994, Cabin Boy, 1994, Skinner, 1995, Mrs. Winterbourne, 1996, Cecil B. DeMented, 2000, Park, 2006; TV appearances include (series) China Beach, 1990, Kate and Allie, Fame, King of Queens, 2001, (spls.) A Family Again, 1988, Starting Now, 1989, Gravedale High, 1990, (movies) Babycakes, 1989, The Chase, 1991, Based on an Untrue Story, (pilot) Starting Now; stage actress: A Girl's Guide to Chaos, 1990, (off-Broadway) The Early Show, Youngsters, 1983; host Game Show Marathon, 2006. Recipient Gracie Allen award, Am. Women in Radio & TV, 2001, Angel award (2), Excellence in Media. also: WMA 151 S El Camino Dr Beverly Hills CA 90212-2704 also: 8530 Wilshire Blvd Beverly Hills CA 90211

LAKE, SUZANNE, singer, music educator; b. Palisade, NJ, June 26, 1929; d. Mayhew Lester and Suzanne Louise (Robin) Lake; m. George A. De Vos, Nov. 19, 1974. Pvt. tchr., Oakland, Calif., 1976-86, univ. extension U. Calif., Sacramento State U., 1981-84. Featured roles opera, NYC, 1948-51; appeared in Broadway plays The King and I, 1951-54, (TV) History of Musical Comedy with Leonard Bernstein, 1957 (Emmy award 1957), Flower Drum Song, 1960-61; featured singer with Guy Lombardo, 1964-65, Experiencing Music, Expressing Culture, Oxford U. Press; concert and supper club appearances in U.S., Can., Carribbean, Japan, Korea, Taiwan and Europe, 1955-91, recs. include the Soul of Chanson, Potpourri, others; also TV appearances. Mem. Actors Equity, AFTRA, Am. Guild Mus. Artists, Am. Guild Variety Artists. Home: 2835 Morley Dr Oakland CA 94611-2547

LAKE, VICTOR HUGO, former manufacturing company executive; b. Quincy, Mass., Nov. 11, 1919; s. Victor Hugo and Edna Beatrice (Blott) L.; m. Jeannette Elzena Stewart, Apr. 26, 1942; children: Victor Stewart, Valerie Jean; m. 2d, Jacqueline Rose Davis, July 4, 1975. Student, Lawrence Inst. Tech., 1939—42, U. Maine, 1943. Asst. supt. Taylor Winfield Corp., Detroit, 1938—43; mgr. prodn. control Fed. Machine & Welder Co., Warren, Ohio, 1944—49; with Am. Welding & Mfg. Co., Warren, 1949—82, mgr. materials, 1969—82; ret., 1982. Served with AUS, 1943-44. Mem. Am. Soc. Metals, Trumbull County Indsl. Mgmt. Assn. (pres. 1972-73). Republican. Methodist. Home: 9042 Tiara Ct New Port Richey FL 34655-1532 Personal E-mail: victorlake@verizon.net.

LAKE, WESLEY WAYNE, JR., internist, allergist, medical educator; b. New Orleans, Oct. 11, 1937; s. Wesley Wayne and Mary McGehee (Snowden) L.; m. Abby F. Arnold, Aug. 1959 (div. 1974); children: Courtenay B., Corinne A., Jane S.; m. Melissa Bowman, Mar. 1999. AB in Chemistry, Princeton U., 1959; MD, Tulane U., 1963. Diplomate Am. Bd. Internal Medicine, Am. Bd. Allergy and Immunology. Intern Charity Hosp. of La., New Orleans, 1963-64, resident internal medicine, 1966-69; NIH fellow allergy and immunology La. State U. Med. Ctr., 1969-70; instr. dept. medicine Tulane U., New Orleans, 1967-69; fellow dept. medicine La. State U., New Orleans, 1969-70, instr. dept. medicine, 1970-73, asst. clin. prof. medicine, 1973-77; chief allergy clinic La. State U. Svc. Charity Hosp. La., New Orleans, 1970-77; assoc. clin. prof. medicine Tulane U., 1978—93. Temp. staff positions various hosps., 1963-70, including Baton Rouge Gen. Hosp., Our Lady of the Lake Hosp., Glenwood Hosp., St. Francis Hosp., Monroe, La., Lallie Kemp Charity Hosp., Independence, La., Huey P. Long Hosp., Pineville, La.; gen. med. officer outpatient clinic Hunter AFB, Savannah, Ga., 1964-65, gen. med. officer internal medicine svc., 1965-66; cons. physician Seventh Ward Gen. Hosp., Hammond, La., 1971-77, Slidell (La.) Meml. Hosp., 1971-89, St. Tammany Parish Hosp., Covington, La., 1977-85; cons. physician East Jefferson Hosp., Metairie, La., 1971-77, staff physician, 1990—; asst. vis. physician Charity Hosp. New Orleans, 1970-75, staff physician, 1975-77, vis. phys. Tulane divsn., 1979-93; assoc. physician So. Bapt. Hosp., New Orleans, 1970-75, chmn. dept. medicine, chmn. internal medicine com., 1982-84, chmn. pharmacy and therapeutics, 1980-82, mem. investigative rev. com., 1984-85, mem. internal medicine quality assurance com., 1989-94; staff physician Kenner (La.) Regional Med. Ctr. (formerly St. Jude Med. Ctr.), 1985-99, chmn. quality assurance com., 1987-89; staff physician Drs. Hosp. of Jefferson, 1988—2005; mem. pharmacy and therapeutics com. and continuing med. edn. com. East Jefferson Gen. Hosp., 1997—. Author: (with others) Infiltrative Hypersensitivity Chest Diseases, 1975; contbr. articles to profl. jours. including Jour. Immunology, Internat. Archives Allergy and Applied Immunology, Jour. Allergy and Clin. Immunology; also chpts. in books concerning chest diseases. Fellow ACP, Am. Coll. Allergy, Sigma Xi; mem. New Orleans Acad. Internal Medicine, Musser-Burch Soc., S.E. Allergy Soc., La. Allergy Soc. (sec. 1975-76, v.p. 1976-77, pres. 1977-78). Republican. Episcopalian. Home: 4636 Perrier St New Orleans LA 70115-3920 Office: 4224 Houma Blvd Ste 250 Metairie LA 70006-2935 Office Phone: 504-456-5111. E-mail: lakejrmd@aol.com.

LAKE, WILLIAM ROBERT, school district administrator; b. Phila., Dec. 19, 1949; s. William Frederick and Veronica Victoria Lake; m. Joan Herrman Lake (div.); 1 child, Carolyn Claire; m. Patricia Ann Costa-Lake, Aug. 10, 2002. BS, Pa. State U., 1971; MEd, West Chester State Coll., Pa., 1976; MA, Glassboro State Coll., NJ, 1988; EdD, Nova Southea. U., 2001. Tchr. Phila. Sch. Dist., 1971—88; adminstr. Burlington County Coll., Pemberton, NJ, 1988—89, Lacey Twp. Sch. Dist., Lanoka Harbor, NJ, 1989—. Adj. faculty Rutgers U., Camden, NJ, 1987, Georgian Ct. Coll., Lakewood, NJ, 1987—89, Rowan U., Glassboro, 1987—92. Mem. World Affairs Coun., Phila.; cert. CPR/AFD for profl. rescuer ARC, NJ. Recipient commendation, Sch. Dist. Phila.-Bd. Edn., 1986, Burlington County Coll., 1989; grantee New Partnership for Work and Learning, NJ Gov.'s Office, 1988, Tech. Literacy Challenge, NJ Dept. Edn., 1997, Distance Learning Network Aid, 2000. Mem.: NJ Assn. for Edn. (charter, v.p. 1986—91), Internat. Soc. Tech. in Edn., Phi Delta Kappa. Avocation: tennis. Home: 192 S Lakeside Dr E Medford NJ 08055 Office: Lacey Twp Sch Dist 200 Western Blvd Lanoka Harbor NJ 08734 Office Phone: 609-971-5875. Office Fax: 609-971-5882. E-mail: lake@lacey.k12.nj.us.

LAKE, WILLIAM TRUMAN, lawyer; b. Henderson, Nev., Nov. 13, 1943; s. Meno Truman and Jean Ivy (Hancock) L.; m. Dorothy Ann Diehl, Nov. 26, 1965 (div. 1973); 1 child, Alison; m. Morgan Day Hodgson, Jan. 18, 1975; children: Devon, Spencer, Eve, Braden. BA, Yale U., 1965; LLB, Stanford U., 1968. Bar: Calif. 1969, DC 1972, US Dist. Ct. DC, 1972, US Ct. Appeals (DC cir.) 1973, US Ct. Appeals (2d cir.) 1975, US Ct. Appeals (5th cir.) 1979, US Ct. Appeals (11th cir.) 1981, US Ct. Appeals (9th cir.) 1987, US Ct. Appeals (8th cir.) 1996, US Ct. Appeals (10th cir.) 1997, US Ct. Appeals (6th cir.) 2005, US Ct. Fed. Claims 1996, US Supreme Ct. 1973. Law clk. to judge U.S. Ct. Appeals, NY, 1968-69; law clk. to Justice John M. Harlan U.S. Supreme Ct., Washington, 1969-70; counsel U.S. Coun. on Environ. Quality, Washington, 1970-73; assoc. Wilmer, Cutler & Pickering, Washington, 1973-76, ptnr., 1976-80; dep. legal adviser U.S. Dept. State, Washington, 1980-81; ptnr. Wilmer, Cutler & Pickering, Washington, 1981—2004; ptnr., Comm. dept., mem. mgmt. com. Wilmer Cutler Pickering Hale & Dorr, Washington, 2004—. Contbr. articles to profl. jours. Governing bd. Beauvoir Sch., Washington, 1987-93; bd. dirs. Little Folks Sch., Washington, 1981-89, Global Rights, Washington, 1982—, World Wildlife Fund, Washington, 1992— Mem. ABA, Calif. Bar Assn., DC Bar Assn., Fed. Communications Bar Assn., US Coun. Internat. Bus Episcopalian. Office: Wilmer Cutler Pickering Hale & Dorr 1801 Pennsylvania Ave Washington DC 20006 Mailing: Wilmer Cutler Pickering Hale & Dorr 1875 Pennsylvania Ave NW Washington DC 20005-3642 Office Phone: 202-663-6725. Office Fax: 202-663-6363. Business E-Mail: william.lake@wilmerhale.com.

LAKEFIELD, BRUCE R., air transportation executive; b. Jan. 29, 1944; m. Bernadine J. Lakefield; 2 children. BS, US Naval Acad., 1967. With Lehman Bros. Inc., 1974—99; chmn., CEO Lehman Bros. Internat., 1995—99; mng. dir. Lehman Bros. Inc., 1996—99, COO, 1999; non.-exec. dir. Constellation Corp., PLC, 2000—04; pres., CEO US Airways, Inc., 2004—07, US Airways Group, Inc., 2004—07, vice-chmn., 2007—. Sr. adv. investment policy com. HGK Asset Mgmt., 2000—04; mem. bd. dirs. US Airways Group, 2003—; non-exec. dir. Constellation Corp. PLC. With USN, 1968—71, with USNR, 1971—90, ret. as comdr., 1990. Office: US Airways Group Inc 2345 Crystal Dr Arlington VA 22227*

LAKES, RODERIC STEPHEN, biomedical engineering educator; b. NYC, Aug. 1948; m. Diana M. Vezzetti, Aug. 14, 1971. Student, Columbia U., NYC, 1964-65, U. Md., 1969-70; BS, Rensselaer Poly. Inst., Troy, NY, 1969, PhD, 1975. NIH predoctoral trainee HEW, 1972-75; rsch. assoc. dept. engring. and applied sci. Yale U., New Haven, 1975-77; asst. prof. physics Tuskegee Inst., Ala., 1977-78; asst. prof. biomed. and mech. engring. U. Iowa, Iowa City, 1978-82, assoc. prof., 1982-86, prof., 1986-98, prof. laser sci., 1987-98. Vis. prof. materials dept. Queen Mary Coll., London, 1984; vis. prof. engring. mechanics U. Wis., Madison, 1990, engring. physics, Wis. disting. prof., 1998-; vis. prof. theoretical and applied mechanics Cornell U., 1991; reviewer Allyn and Bacon, 1979-80; external reviewer Nat. Inst. Arthritis Metabolism and Digestive Diseases, NIH, 1979; ad hoc reviewer Pritzker Inst. Med. Engring., Ill. Inst. Tech., Chgo., 1981; workshop participant Am. Acad. Orthop. Surgeons, 1979. Author: (with J.B. Park) Biomaterials, 1992, 3d edit., 2007, Viscoelastic Solids, 1998; reviewer, contbr. numerous articles to profl. jours. Recipient Outstanding Faculty award Student Soc. Biomed. Engring., U. Iowa, 1985, 86, 88, 94, award for faculty achievement Burlington No. Found., 1987, Instrnl. Improvement award U. Iowa, 1989; Rensselaer scholar, 1965-69, Univ. Faculty scholar, 1990-93; Old Gold fellow, 1986. Fellow ASME (joint biomechanics com. 1984—), AAAS; mem. Am. Phys. Soc., Soc. Photo-Optical Instrument Engrs., Sigma Xi. Episcopalian. Achievements include patent on polyhedron cell structure foam which expands when stretched and method of making same; discovery of acoustic wave which can travel in wet bone, first evidence of cement line motion in bone, first experimental characterization of Cosserat elastic materials; invention of novel materials which expand laterally when stretched. Office: U Wis Dept Engring Physics 541 ERB 1500 Engring Dr Madison WI 53706-1687 Office Phone: 608-265-8697. Office Fax: 608-263-7451. Business E-Mail: lakes@engr.wisc.edu.

LAKEW, DEJENIE ALEMAYEHU, mathematician; b. Debre-Tabor, Gondar, Ethiopia, Dec. 12, 1963; arrived in U.S., 1996; s. Alemayehu Lakew and Chekolech Dessie; m. Melete Tesfamichael Gebrehiwot, Aug. 18, 1964; 1 child, Tewodros Dejenie Alemayehu. BSc, Addis Ababa U., 1984, MSc, 1988, U. Alberta, 1996; PhD, U. Ark., 2000. Asst. lectr. Asmara U., Ethiopia, 1984—86, math. lectr., 1988—90, Addis Ababa U., Ethiopia, 1990—92, sr. lectr., 1992—94; tchg. asst. U. Ark., Fayetteville, 1996—2000, asst. prof. Pine Bluff, 2000—. Adj. prof. dept. math., computer sci. Va. State U., Petersburg, Va. Contbr. articles pub. to profl. jour. Mem.: Math. Assn. Am., Am. Math. Soc. Office: Va State Univ Dept Math and Computer Sci Petersburg VA 23806 Office Phone: 804-524-5420. Business E-Mail: dlakew@vsu.edu.

LAKHANPAL, SHARAD, physician; b. Lucknow, India, Oct. 15, 1951; arrived in U.S., 1980; s. Rajendra Nath and Indra (Kalia) L.; m. Rashmi Sharma, Nov. 17, 1980; children: Akshai, Shuchi, Virad. Student, Colvin Coll., Lucknow, 1969; MB, BS, K.G. Med. Coll., Lucknow, 1974, Dr.med., 1977. Diplomate Am. Bd. Internal Medicine, Am. Bd. Rheumatology. Rotating intern Gandhi Meml. and Assocs. Hosps., King George's Med. Coll., 1974, resident in medicine, 1975-78; sr. house officer in internal medicine Sunderland Hosp., Hemlington Hosp., Poole Hosp., Eng., 1979-80; resident in internal medicine Meml. Hosp., U. Mass. Med. Sch., Worcester, 1980-82; fellow Mayo Clin., Rochester, Minn., 1983-86; attending physician St. Paul Med. Ctr., Dallas, 1987—; asst. prof. medicine U. Tex. Southwestern Med. Sch., Dallas, 1989-96, assoc. prof., 1996—2002, clin. prof., 2002—. Instr. Southwestern Med. Sch., Dallas, 1987-89; referee to numerous med. jours. Sr. editor Jour. Biol. and Chem. Rsch., 1987—; mem. editl. bd. Jour. Indian Rheumatism Assn., 1999—; contbr. chpt. to book and articles to profl. jours. Bd. dirs. North Tex. chpt. Arthritis Found., 1992-98; trustee DFW Hindu Temple, Dallas, 1994-99; bd. dirs. United Way of Met. Dallas, 1995-97, mem. exec com., 1995-96. Recipient Platinum Jubilee Gold medal King Georges Med. Coll., 1986; Am. Rheumatism Assn. fellow, 1984, 85, scholar, 1986; Philips Hench scholar, 1986. Fellow ACP, Am. Rheumatism Assn. (founding), Am. Coll. Rheumatology; mem. Indian Rheumatism Assn. (editl. bd.), Arthritis Found. (sci. com. and chmn. profl. edn. com. North Tex. chpt., also bd. dirs. 1992-98), Lupus Found. Am. (med. adv. bd.), Tex. Med. Assn., Dallas County Med. Soc., Tex. Indo-Am. Physicians Soc. (pres. 1994-95), King George Med. Coll. Alumni Assn. in Am. (sec.-treas. 1988-89, v.p. 1991-92, pres. 1993-94), Dallas-Ft. Worth Rheumatology Club (organizing sec.), Am. Assn. Physicians of Indian Origin (sec. 2000-01, v.p. 2001-02, pres.-elect 2002-03, pres., 2003-2004). Hindu. Avocations: running, travel, tennis. Office: Rheumatology Assocs 5939 Harry Hines Blvd Ste 400 Dallas TX 75235-5360

LAKHMNA, GAGAN(DEEP), real estate company executive, entrepreneur; MBA in Fin. and Mktg., Drexel U., 1995. Co-founder, ptnr. Creating Real Estate Innovations (CREI) (formerly Allied Devel. Group). Named one of 40 Under 40, Phila. Bus. Jour. Office: Creative Real Estate Innovations 626-636 N 5th St Philadelphia PA 19123 Office Phone: 800-960-2794.

LAKIN, JAMES DENNIS, allergist, immunologist, director; b. Harvey, Ill., Oct. 4, 1945; s. Ora Austin and Annie Pitranella (Johnson) L.; m. Sally A. Stuteville, July 22, 1972 (dec. July 27, 2002); children: Tracey A., Margaret K., Matthew A., Christian J., Anne E.; m. Debra J. Franz, May 29, 2004. PhD, Northwestern U., 1968, MD, 1969; MBA in Med. Group Mgmt., U. St. Thomas, 1996. Diplomate Am. Bd. Internal Medicine, Am. Bd. Allergy and Immunology; cert. comml. pilot FAA, cert. flight instr., aviation med. examiner. Dir. allergy rsch. Naval Med. Rsch. Inst., Bethesda, Md., 1974-76; clin. prof. U. Okla., Oklahoma City, 1976-89; dir. lab., chmn. allergy and immunology dept. Oxboro Clinics, Bloomington, Minn., 1989—2001; dir. Fairview Allergy and Asthma Svcs., Bloomington, 1995-2001; mng. ptnr. Minn. Allergy and Asthma Consultants, LLP, 2001—. Bd. dirs. Okla. Med. Rsch. Found., Oklahoma City, 1980-89; regional cons. Diver Alert Network, Duke U., Chapel Hill, N.C., 1987—; cert. diving med. officer NOAA, 1988. Co-author: Allergic Diseases, 1971, 3d edit., 1986; contbr. articles, revs. to profl. publs. Councilperson Our Lord's Luth. Ch., Oklahoma City, 1978-88, Faith Luth. Ch., Lakeville, Minn., 1990-91. Lt. comdr. USN, 1970—76, Vietnam, ret. Fellow ACP, Am. Acad. Allergy and Immunology, Am. Coll. Chest Physicians, Am. Coll. Med. Practice Execs. (E.B. Stevens Article of Yr. award 1998); mem. Am. Assn. Immunologists, Med. Group Mgmt. Assn. (bd. dirs. 2002-06, E.B. Stevens Article of Yr. award, 1998), Am. Coll. Physician Execs. Achievements include research in characterization of the immunoglobulin system of the rhesus monkey, alterations in allergic reactivity during immunosuppression. Office: 303 E Nicollet Ave # 362 Burnsville MN 55337-4559 Office Phone: 952-223-3040. Business E-Mail: jdlakin@minnesotaallergy.com.

LAKKIS, NASSER, cardiologist, educator; MD, Am. U., Beirut, 1989. Cardiovasc. and interventional cardiology program dir. Baylor Coll. Medicine, Houston; prof. medicine Baylor Coll. Cardiology, Houston, 2006—. Chief cardiology Ben Taub Gen. Hosp., Houston, 2004—. Vol. physcian create better methods to provide health care indigent patients Harris County Hosp. Dist., Houston, 2002. Recipient Fulbright and Jaworski Edn. award, 2006. Fellow: Amrican Coll. Cardiology. Home: 1709 Dryden BCM 620 Ste 990 Houston TX 77030 Office: Baylor Coll Medicine One Baylor Plz Houston TX 77030 Home Phone: 713-873-2083; Office Phone: 713-798-0284. Office Fax: 713-873-4903; Home Fax: 713-873-4903. Business E-Mail: nlakkis@bcm.tmc.edu.

LAKNER, GEORGE STEPHEN, military officer; b. Budapest, Hungary, Mar. 1, 1940; US, 1976; s. George A. Lakner and Lily I. Kun; m. Martha Gail Lakner, Nov. 8, 1977; 1 child, Veronica C. MD, Semmelweis U., Budapest, 1964; DSc, U. of Scis., Budapest, 1971; MPH, Johns Hopkins U., Balt., 1979; postgrad., Columbia U., NYC, 1982. Fellow Nat. Inst. Traumatology, Budapest, 1965—69, Inst. Med. Edn., Budapest, 1969—72; rsch. assoc. Inst. Medicine, Nat. Acad. Sci., Budapest, 1970—72; dept. head Nat. Inst. Health Edn., Budapest, 1972—74; rsch. fellow U. Toronto, Ont., Canada, 1974—75; cons. Ministry of Health, Toronto, 1975—77; chief resident Yale U., New Haven, 1977—78; fellow Johns Hopkins U., Balt., 1978—80, Columbia U./Einstein Coll., NYC, 1980—82. Clin. instr. Columbia U., NYC, 1982—83; clin. fellow Harvard U., Cambridge, 1983—84, instr., 1984—87; program adminstr. NIH, Washington, 1986—87; asst. prof. George Washington U., Washington, 1987—89; divsn. chief Nat. Naval Med. CTr., Bethesda, Md., 1988—90; svc. chief US Army Med. Ctr., Berlin, 1990—92; svc. chief US Dept. Justice, 1992—93; asst. prof. Yale U., 1993—96; faculty Menninger Clinic, Topeka, 1996; fellowship dir. assoc. SUNY, Bklyn., 1997—99; svc. chief US Army Hosp., Vicenza, Italy, 2002—03, Beaumont Army Med. Ctr., El Paso, Tex., 2003—04. Office: Ft McNair #70185 Washington DC 20319

LAKSHMI, PADMA, actress, television host, model; b. Madras, India, 1970; m. Salman Rushdie, Apr. 17, 2004 (separated). BA in Theater Arts, Clark U., Mass. Founder Lakshmi Films. Actor: (films) Glitter, 2001, Boom, 2003, The Darkness and the Light, Caribbeans, Mistress of Spices; (TV miniseries) The Ten Commandments, 2006, Sharpe's Challenge, 2006; host (TV series) Dominica In, Rai TV, Padma's Passport, Food Network, Top Chef, Bravo, 2006—, (documentaries) Planet Food; author: (cookbook) Easy Exotic, 2003 (Best First Book, World Cookbook Awards, Versailles, 1999); appeared in Vogue, Elle, In Style, modeled for Ralph Lauren, Alberta Ferretti, Herve Leger, La Perla, Roberto Cavalli. Named one of World's Most Successful Super Models, Max Mag., 1997. Office: Bravo c/o NBC Entertainment 3000 W Alameda Ave Burbank CA 91523*

LAKSHMIKANTHAM, VANGIPURAM, mathematics professor; b. Hyderabad, India, Aug. 8, 1926; arrived in US, 1960, naturalized, 1966; s. Soroja Bukkapatnam, Feb. 22, 1942; children: Sreekantham, Neerada, Nirupama. MA, Osmania U., Hyderabad, 1955, PhD, 1958. Mem. faculty UCLA, 1960-61, Math. Rsch. Ctr., U. Wis., Madison, 1961-62; mem. Rsch. Inst. Advanced Studies, Balt., 1962-63; assoc. prof. U. Alta., Calgary, Can., 1963-64; prof., chmn. dept. math. Marathwada U., Aurangabad, India, 1964-66, U. R.I., Kingston, 1966-73, U. Tex., Arlington, 1973-88; prof., head dept. math. scis. Fla. Inst. Tech., Melbourne, 1989—. Author 40 books; founder, editor: Jour. Nonlinear Analysis, A-Series, B-Series, C-Series, Nonlinear Studies, Stochastic Analysis and Applications, Mathematical Problems in Engring.; assoc. editor other jours.; contbr. over 400 rsch. articles to profl. publs. Mem. Am. Math. Soc., Indian Math. Soc., Soc. Indsl. and Aplied Math., Nat. Acad. Sci. India, Internat. Fedn. Nonlinear Analysts (founder). Office: Fla Inst Tech Dept Math Scis 150 W University Blvd Melbourne FL 32901-6975 Business E-Mail: lakshmik@fit.edu.

LAL, ANIL, health facility administrator; s. Sudhamo Lal and Kamla Devi; m. Mona Ahuja, May 26, 2000; 1 child, Arun. MBBS, U. of Karachi, 1992—97; M in healthcare adminstr., U. Minn., 2002, MBS, MBA, U. Minn., 2002. Adminstr. U. of Chgo., 2002—. State rep. Assn. of Otolaryngology Administrators, 2004—05. Office: Univ of Chgo 5841 S Maryland Ave Chicago IL 60637 Office Phone: 773-702-1862. Office Fax: 773-702-6809. E-mail: alal@uchicago.edu.

LAL, DEVENDRA, nuclear geophysics educator; b. Varanasi, India, Feb. 14, 1929; s. Radhe Krishna and Sita Devi L.; m. Aruna Damany, May 17, 1955 (dec. July 1993). BS, Banaras Hindu U., Varanasi, 1947, MS, 1949, DSc (hon. causa), 1984; PhD, Bombay U., 1960. Research student Tata Inst. of Fundamental Research, Bombay, 1949-60, research fellow, fellow, assoc. prof., 1960-63, prof., 1963-70, sr. prof., 1970-72; dir. Phys. Research Lab., Ahmedabad, India, 1972-83, sr. prof., 1983-89; vis. prof. UCLA, 1965-66, 83-84; prof. Scripps Instn. Oceanography, La Jolla, Calif., 1967—. Editor: Early Solar System Processes and the Present Solar

System, 1980, Biogeochemistry of the Arabian Sea, 1995. Recipient K.S. Krishnan Gold medal Indian Geophys. Union, 1965, Shanti Swarup Bhatnagar award for Phys. Sciences, Coun. Scientific and Indsl. Rsch., 1971, award for Excellence in Sci. and Tech., Gedn. of Indian Chamber Com., 1974, Pandit Jawaharlal Nehru award for Scis., 1986, Group Achievement award NASA, 1986, Raman Birth Centenary award, 1996, V.M. Goldschmidt medal, 1997. Fellow AAAS, Royal Soc. London, Indian Nat. Sci. Acad., Indian Acad. Scis., Geol. Soc. India (hon.), Phys. Rsch. Lab. Ahmedabad, Tata Inst. Fundamental Rsch., Geochem. Soc. USA, Am. Geophys. Union; mem. NAS U.S.A. (fgn. assoc.), Third World Acad. Scis. (founding mem.), Indian Geophys. Union, NAS India, Royal Astron. Soc. (assoc.), Internat. Acad. Aeronautics, Internat. Union of Geodesy and Geophysics (pres. 1984-87), Am. Acad. Arts and Scis. (fgn., hon.), Internat. Assn. Phys. Sci. of Ocean (hon., pres. 1979-83). Hindu. Avocations: chess, photography, painting, puzzles. Office: U Calif Scripps Inst Oceanography 9500 Gilman Dr GRD-0244 La Jolla CA 92093-0244 Home: No 20 Jayantilal Park Amli Bopal Rd Village Makarba Ahmedabad 380009 India Office Phone: 858-534-2134. Fax: 858-822-3310. Business E-Mail: dlal@ucsd.edu.

LAL, DHANANJAY, information technology executive, researcher; b. New Delhi, Delhi, India, July 6, 1977; s. Krishna B. and Bela Lal. BS, Indian Inst. Tech. Roorkee, 1999; PhD, U. Cin., 2004. Grad. rsch. asst. U. Cin., 1999—2004; postdoctoral fellow UCLA, 2004—05; wireless sys. engr. Rsch. and Tech. Ctr. N.Am. Robert Bosch Corp., Palo Alto, Calif., 2005—. Mem. rsch. staff WINMEC, LA, 2004—05. Author (innovative rsch.): (transactions) Performance Evaluation of Medium Access Control with Multiple Beam Smart Antennas in Wireless LANs. Pres. Grad. Students' Assn., Cincinnati, Ohio, 2004. Scholar Grad. Rsch. Assistantship, U. Cin., 1999—2004; Postdoctoral Fellowship, UCLA, 2004, Inst. Merit Scholarship, Indian Inst. Tech. Roorkee, 1995—99, Nat. Talent Scholarship, Govt. of India, 1994—95, Jr. Sci. Talent Scholarship, Govt. of Delhi, India, 1993. Mem.: IEEE. Achievements include patents pending for A Novel Scheme for Space Division Multiple Access in Wireless Ad Hoc Networks; A Scheme for Exploiting Spatial Parallelism at an Access Point with Multiple Beam Antennas. Avocations: drummer (percussion), travel, tennis, golf. Office: Robert Bosch Corp Rsch and Tech Ctr 4009 Miranda Ave Palo Alto CA 94304 Home Phone: 513-225-4948; Office Phone: 650-320-2970. Office Fax: 650-320-2999. E-mail: dhananjay.lal@rtc.bosch.com.

LALA, DOMINICK JOSEPH, manufacturing executive; b. NYC, June 2, 1928; s. Joseph and Mary Lala; m. Nancy Lala, Nov. 30, 1957; children: John, Steven, James, Thomas, Patrice. BS, NYU, 1951. Mem. staff BDO/Seidman (CPAs), NYC, 1951-62; v.p., contr. Universal Am. Corp., NYC, 1962-68; sr. v.p. fin. Paramount Pictures Corp., 1968-70; exec. v.p. Gould Paper Corp., NYC, 1970—2002. With AUS, 1946-47. Mem. AICPA, N.Y. State Soc. CPAs. Personal E-mail: dominick_lala@msn.com.

LALA, JAYNARAYAN HOTCHAND, computer engineer; b. Hyderabad, Sind, Pakistan, Jan. 12, 1951; came to U.S., 1971; s. Hotchand Menghraj and Jamuna (Gandhi) L.; m. Michele Simone Breton, Sept. 2, 1977. SB in Aero. Engring., Indian Inst. Tech., Bombay, 1971; SM in Aeros.-Astronautics, MIT, 1973, ScD in Instrumentation, 1976. Mem. tech. staff Charles Stark Draper Lab., Inc., Cambridge, Mass., 1976-83, chief systems architecture sect. NASA dept., 1983-85, div. leader fault tolerant systems div., 1985-91, leader advanced computer architectures group, 1991-93, prin. mem. tech. staff, 1993—99. Advisor USN Combat System Architecture Adv. Panel, 1985-86; session chmn. 8th Digital Avionics Systems Conf., San Jose, Calif., 1988, Workshop on Fault Tolerance in Parallel and Distributed Computing, 1987, Conf. on Dependable Computing for Critical Applications, 1989; mem. program com. 20th Internat. Symposium on Fault Tolerant Computing, 1990, 21st Internat. Symposium, 1991, tech. program chmn. 22nd Internat. Symposium, 1992; mem. program com. 2nd Conf. on Dependable Computing for Critical Applications, Tucson, 1991, program com. 3d Conf., Sicily, Italy, 1992, program com. Internat. Conf. on Recent Advances in Intrusion Detection, Zurich, Switzerland, 2002, program com. Internat. Conf. on Dependable Systems and Networks, San Francisco, 2003, Florence, Italy, 2004; mem. battle mgmt. panel Strategic Def. Initiative, 1992; tech. dir. Bosnia Command and Control Augmentation Program, 1996; chief architect NASA X-38 Crew Return Vehicle Avionics and Flight Critical Computers, 1998-99; program mgr. Intrusion Tolerant Sys. Def. Advanced Rsch. Projects Agy. U.S. Dept. Def., 1999-2003; engring. fellow Raytheon Co., 2003—, govt. advisor to 2000 Def. Sci. bd. on Defensive Info. Ops., gen. chair Internat. Conf. on Dependable Systems and Networks, Washington, 2002; del. on bilateral agreements countering cyber terrorism India, U.S. Govt., New Delhi, India, 2002; vice-chmn. IEEE Tech. Com. Fault Tolerant Computing, 2003-04, chmn. 2005-2006. Producer, dir., writer tech. documentary Advanced Information Processing System, 1989; contbr. articles to profl. jours., chpts. to books; patentee fault tolerant computer designs. Recipient Best Paper award C.S. Draper Lab., 1989, 94, Best Patent award, 1990; Draper fellow, 1972-76; scholar Indian Sci. Talent Bd., 1966, Indian Inst. Tech., 1967-71. Fellow AIAA (assoc., chmn. digital avionics tech. subcom. 1987-91), IEEE; mem. Internat. Fedn. Info. Processing (working group on dependable computing and fault tolerance 1988—), Indian Inst. Tech. Soc. New Eng. (v.p. 1995-97). Hindu. Avocations: flying, chess, tennis, piano. Home: 10103 Walker Lake Dr Great Falls VA 22066-3501 Office: Raytheon Co Crystal Ctr 2 2461 S Clark St Ste 1000 Arlington VA 22202 Home Phone: 703-757-7791; Office Phone: 703-419-1401. Business E-Mail: jay_lala@raytheon.com.

LALA, PEEYUSH KANTI, research scientist, educator; b. Chittagong, Bengal, India, Nov. 1, 1934; came to U.S., 1963, to Can., 1967; s. Sudhangshu Bimal and Nani Bala (Chaudhuri) L.; m. Arati Roy-Burman, July 7, 1962 (dec.); children: Probal, Prasun; m. Shipra Bhattachareya, Nov. 6, 1992. MB, BS, Calcutta U., India, 1957, PhD in Med. Biophysics, 1961, MD, 1962. Demonstrator, lectr. in pathology Calcutta Med. Coll., 1959-60, NRS Med. Coll., Calcutta, 1961-62; resident rsch. assoc. biol. and med. rsch. divsn. Argonne (Ill.) Nat. Lab., 1963-64; rsch. scientist, asst. prof. Lab. Radiobiology U. Calif. Med. Ctr., San Francisco, 1964-66; rsch. scientist Biol. and Health Physics divsn. Chalk River (Ont., Can.) Nuc. Lab., 1967-68; from asst. prof. to assoc. prof. to prof. dept. anatomy McGill U., Montreal, Quebec, Canada, 1968—83; prof. dept. anatomy and cell biology U. Western Ont., London, 1983-2000, chmn. dept. anatomy and cell biology, 1983-93, prof. dept. oncology, 1990-2000, prof. emeritus dept. anatomy and cell biology, dept. oncology, microbiology and immunology, 2000—. Mem. grants panel MRC Can., Can. Inst. Health Rsch., Ottawa, Ont., 1983-87, 93-96, NIH U.S.A., Bethesda, Md., 1977-01, Nat. Cancer Inst. Can., Toronto, 1987-90, Cancer Rsch. Soc., Montreal, 1987-90; mem. Cannaught Com., Toronto, 1990-91; vis. prof. Walter and Eliza Hall Inst. Med. Rsch., U. Melbourne, Australia, 1977-78. Mem. editl. bd.: Exptl. Hematology, 1974—77, Leukemia Rsch., 1977—86, Am. Jour. Reproductive Immunology, 1989—93, Early Pregnancy: Biology and Medicine, 1995—, Placenta, 1996—2001, Biology of Reproduction, 2001—04, assoc. editor: Am. Jour. Anatomy, 1987—90, guest editor: Cancer and Metastasis Revs., Vol. 17, 1998; contbr. 12 chapters to books, 200 articles to profl. jours. Chmn. Bengali Cultural Ctr., Montreal, 1978-83. Recipient Faculty of Medicine Rsch. award, U. Western Ont., 1996; fellow, Fulbright Found., 1962; grantee, MRC Can. (now CIHR), 1968—, NCI Can., 1968—, NIH, 1976—79, Cancer Rsch. Soc., 1978—96, U.S. Army Med. Rsch., 1996—2001, Breast Cancer Soc. Can., 1999—, Can. Breast Cancer Rsch. Alliance, 2001—05, Can. Breast Cancer Found., 2005—, Ontario Inst. Cancer Rsch., 2007—. Mem. Am. Assn. Cancer Rsch., Am. Assn. Anatomists, Can. Assn. Anatomists, Cell Biologists and Neurobiologists (chmn. awards com. 1987-89, v.p. and pres.-elect 1989-90, pres. 1991-93, J.C.B. Grant award 1990), Internat. Soc. Exptl. Hematology, Soc. Leukocyte Biology, Am. Assn. Immunologists, Can. Soc. Immunologists, Internat. Soc. Reproductive Immunology (councillor 1986-89), Am. Soc. Reproductive Immunology (v.p. 1985-86), Soc. Study Reproduction. Achievements include discovery of a new mode of cancer immunotherapy resulting in a successful phase two human trial; of mode of treatment of interleukin-2 therapy-induced side effects of capillary leakage; of mechanism responsible for prostaglandim and nitric oxide-mediated stimulation of breast cancer progression; research in production of normal, precancerous and cancerous trophoblast cell lines from first trimester human placentae; identification control mechanisms in the protection of the uterus from placental overinvasion of the uterus. Office: U Western Ont Dept Anatomy and Cell Biology London ON Canada N6A 5C1 Business E-Mail: pklala@uwo.ca.

LALAS, ALEXI (PANAYOTIS ALEXANDER LALAS), professional sports team executive, retired professional soccer player; b. Birmingham, Mich., June 1, 1970; BA in English, Rutgers U., 1991. Defender Padova Football Club, Italy, New England Revolution, 1996—97, N.Y./N.J. Metrostars, 1998, U.S. Nat. Team, 1992, 1996, Kans. City Wizards, 1999, LA Galaxy, 2001—03; ret., 2003; gen. mgr. San Jose Earthquakes, 2004—05; pres., gen. mgr. NY MetroStars, 2005—06, LA Galaxy, 2006—. Musician (with the Gypsies): (albums) Woodland, Jet Lag; musician: (solo albums) Ginger, 1998. Named U.S. Soccers Male Athlete of Yr., 1995, First Am.-born player in modern era to compete in Italy's Serie A, 1994; named to All-Copa Am. Team, 1995, Ea. Conf. All-Star Teams, 1996, 1997; recipient Gold medal, U.S. Olympic Festival, 1989, Pan Am. Games, 1991. Avocations: singing, guitar. Office: LA Galaxy The Home Depot Ctr 18400 Avalon Blvd Ste 200 Carson CA 90746

LALE, CISSY STEWART (LLOYD LALE), freelance writer; b. Port Arthur, Tex., Jan. 15, 1924; d. Lloyd M. and May (Cowart) Stewart; m. Max Sims Lale, Oct. 9, 1983 (dec. Apr. 2006). BJ, U. Tex., Austin, 1945. Reporter Record-News, Wichita Falls, Tex., 1945, News-Messenger, Marshall, Tex., 1945-47; editor Times-Rev., Cleburne, Tex., 1947-49; women's editor, columnist Star-Telegram, Ft. Worth, 1949-87; freelance writer Children's Promise mag., Health-Scope mag., Ft. Worth, 1987-89. Author: Sweetie Ladd's Historic Fort Worth, 1999. Bd. dirs. Trinity Ter. Retirement Cmty., 1991-94. Recipient Ballard Heritage award North Tex. Hist. Soc.; Cissy Stewart Day proclaimed by Ft. Worth City Coun., 1987, portrayed in outdoor mural City of Ft. Worth, 1987. Mem. Women in Comm., Inc. (nat. pres. 1968-71), Tex. State Hist. Assn. (pres. 1996-97), East Tex. Hist. Assn. (pres. 1994), Tex. Heritage, Inc. (bd. dirs. Ft. Worth chpt. 1990), Womans Club Ft. Worth, Ft. Worth Garden Club (v.p. 1995-96). Episcopalian. Home: # 101 3900 White Settlement Rd Fort Worth TX 76107-7822 Personal E-mail: cissymay@aol.com.

LALIBERTE, BRIAN J., prosecutor; b. Youngstown, Ohio, Mar. 8, 1974; s. Richard J. and Mary Jane Laliberte; m. Elizabeth Laliberte, July 24, 2004; 1 child, Parker John. BA in Polit. Sci. Commns., U. Mich., Ann Arbor, 1996; JD, Case Western Reserve U., Cleve., 1999. Cert.: Ohio Supreme Ct. 1999, bar: US Dist. Ct., North Dist., Ohio 2000, US Dist. Ct., South Dist., Ohio 2001, cert.: US Ct. Appeals, Sixth Circuit 2005. Jud. law clk. US Dist. Ct., North Dist., Youngstown, Ohio, 1999—2001; assoc. atty. Vorys, Sater, Seymour and Pease LLP, Columbus, 2001—06, Baker & Hostetler LLP, Columbus, 2006; dep. first asst., chief criminal divsn. Ohio Atty. Gen. Marc Dann, Columbus, 2007—. Mem. alumni bd. Case Western Reserve U., 2004—07. Co-chair Cystic Fibrosis Found. Halfway to St. Patrick's Day Fundraiser, 2003; elected mem. US Sentencing Commn. Practitioner's Advisory Group, 2006. Recipient Ohio Super Lawyer Rising Star, Law and Politics Mag. and Cin. Mag., 2006, 2007. Mem.: ABA, Ohio State Bar Assn., Columbus Bar Assn. (mem. jud. screening com. 2004—). Democrat. Avocation: reading. Office Phone: 614-728-5470.

LALLI, MICHAEL ANTHONY, lawyer; b. NYC, Sept. 14, 1955; s. Joseph and Maria (Magnacca) L.; m. Marigrace Ann Esposito, May 19, 1979; children: Elena Marie, Marissa Ann. BA, Fordham Coll., 1976, JD, 1979; LLM, NYU, 1984. Bar: N.Y. 1980, U.S. Dist. Ct. (so. dist.) N.Y. 1981. Assoc. counsel Equitable Life Assurance Soc, U.S., NYC, 1979—85; sr. tax atty. Chevron Texaco Corp., White Plains, NY, 1985—2002; dir., benefits counsel Pitney Bowes Inc., Stamford, Conn., 2002—. Mem. moot ct. bd. 1977-79. Mem. Fordham Urban Law Jour., 1977-79. Mem. ABA, N.Y. State Bar Assn., Phi Beta Kappa, Pi Sigma Alpha. Roman Catholic. Home: 16 Thomas St Scarsdale NY 10583-1031 Office: Pitney Bowes Inc 1 Elmcroft Rd Stamford CT 06926-0700 Personal E-mail: thomasst16@aol.com. Business E-Mail: michael.lalli@pb.com.

L'ALLIER, JAMES JOSEPH, training services executive, educator; b. St. Paul, June 24, 1945; s. Charlemagne Joseph and Mildred Marie (LeVasseur) L'A.; m. Susan Kay Margulies, Apr. 28, 1973. BS magna cum laude, U. Wis., River Falls, 1969, MS, 1973; PhD, U. Minn., 1980. Instr. English, multimedia specialist River Falls Sr. High Sch., 1969-71; instr. English Stillwater (Minn.) Sr. High Sch., 1971-80; mgr. computer assisted instrn. Wilson Learning Corp., Mpls., 1980-83, dir. R&D, 1983-86; v.p. R&D Wilson Learning Interactive Tech. Group, Santa Fe, 1986-89; v.p. product devel. Nippon Wilson Learning, Tokyo, 1989-90; v.p. instructional design Whole Systems International, Cambridge, Mass., 1990-93; v.p. product devel. NETg, A Thomson Learning Co., Naperville, 1993-98; v.p. R&D NETg, A Harcourt Brace Co., Naperville, Ill., 1998-2000; chief learning officer, v.p. R&D NETg, A Thomson Learning Co., 2000—05; pres., founding ptnr. LearnSure, Inc., Elburn, Ill., 2005—. Expert witness Universal Tng., Chgo., 1989-91; bd. dirs. Info. Tech. Tng. Assn., chair standards com. 2000—; chmn. CLO Acad., MediaTec Publs., Chgo., 2006—. Author: (video prodns.) Who Shot the Terminal?, 1984, The Tenth Woman, 1987, Working Toward the Future, 1991, America's Workforce: A Vision for the Future, 1992; mem. editorial bd. Learning Age, Mpls., 1987-89, CLO Mag., Chgo., 2002-; product reviewer Ednl. Tech., N.Y.C., 1981-83; assoc. editor Performance and Instrn., Washington, 1983-85; inventor Interactive Learning System-Skill Builder; holder 240 copyrights; inventor, patent for interactive learning sys. Skill Builder; inventor, patent holder Precision Skilling. Curriculum chair Total Info. Ednl. Systems, St. Paul, 1971-76; fund raiser U. Minn. Alliance, Mpls., 1983-89; contbr. Am. Cancer Soc., Washington, 1987—; mem. pub. svc. com. Instructional Systems Assn., Sunset Beach, Calif., 1988—; reviewer William H. Donner Found., Inc., N.Y.C., 1993—; mem. ednl. tech. adv. bd. Utah State U., Logan. U. Minn. Grad. Sch. Edn. sr. fellow, 1984; U.S. Dept. Labor grantee, 1991. Mem. U. Wis. Alumni Assn., Instructional Systems Assn. (conf. chair 1980, 84), U. Minn. Alumni Assn., Boston Computer Soc., Ednl. Tech. Adv. Bd., Utah Sate U., Pres.'s Club U. Minn., Heritage Soc. U. Wis. Avocations: reading, photography, music. Office: LearnSure Inc 41W700 Bowgren Dr Elburn IL 60119 Business E-Mail: jlallier@learnsure.com.

LALLY, JOHN PATRICK, investment company executive; b. Newark, Mar. 17, 1951; s. John James and Margaret Rita L.; m. Ann Bierbower, May 2, 1987; children: John B., Mark B. BS, Boston Coll., 1973; MBA, Columbia U., NYC, 1975. Staff acct. Coopers & Lybrand, Boston, 1975-78; v.p. Goldman, Sachs & Co., NYC, 1978-86; mng. dir. Bankers Trust Co., NYC, Atlanta, 1986-90; pres. Lally Percival & Co., Atlanta, 1991-95, Resurgens Capital Ptnrs., Atlanta, 1996—. Bd. dirs. Integrated Energy Svcs., Inc., Atlanta, EquipMD, Atlanta, Response Mktg. Group, LLC, Richmond, Va. Avocations: politics, outdoor activities, sports. Office Phone: 404-467-6504. Business E-Mail: jlally@criterionpartners.com.

LALLY, MICHAEL DAVID, writer, actor; b. Orange, NJ, May 25, 1942; s. James A. and Irene I. (Dempsey) L.; m. Lee Fischer, 1964 (dec. 1986); children: Caitlin Maeve, Miles Aaron; m. Jaina Flynn, 1997; 1 child, Flynn Albert James. BA, U. Iowa, 1968, MFA, 1969. Instr. Trinity Coll., Washington, 1969-74; book reviewer Washington Post, 1974-77; editor Franklin Library div. Franklin Mint, 1976-79; editor, pub. various newspapers and presses including Iowa Defender, Some of Us Press, The Washington Review of the Arts, 1966-80, Venice mag., 1988-91, The Hollywood Rev., 1991. Bd. dirs. The Print Center, Bklyn., 1972-75, Washington Film Classroom, 1970-72 Actor: (films) Last Rites, 1980, The Nesting, 1981, White Fang, 1991, Cool World, 1992, Basic Instinct, 1992, Not Again, 1996, The Technical Writer, 2003, Last Grave, 2005, (stage) The Heroes, 1981, Balm in Gilead, 1983, The Rhythm of Torn Stars, 1988-89, Short Eyes, 1994, (TV) Cagney and Lacey, 1984, Berrengers, 1985, Hardcastle and McCormick, 1986, L.A. Law, 1989, Father Dowling's Mysteries, 1991, Caught in the Act, 1993, Diagnosis Murder, 1994, NYPD Blue, 1995, 97, 99, Brooklyn South, 1997, JAG, 1997, 98, Law and Order, 2000, Ed, 2001, Deadwood, 2004; freelance writer, reviewer, actor, N.Y.C., 1975-82; screenwriter, actor, L.A., 1982-99, screenwriter, actor, N.Y.C., 1999—; author 20 books including Rocky Dies Yellow, 1974, German edit., 1982, Dues, 1974, Catch My Breath, 1976, 95, Just Let Me Do It, 1978, Attitude, 1982, Hollywood Magic, 1982, Cant Be Wrong, 1996, Of, 1999, It's Not Nostalgia, 1999, It Takes One to Know One, 2001, March 18, 2003, 3d edit., 2006; author, dir. (one-act play) Four Grown Men, N.Y.C., 1982, Hollywood Magic, L.A., 1983; co-author (play) The Rhythm of Torn Stars, 1988-89, (film) Fogbound, 2003; 3 short plays, 1995; recorded poems on CD, What You Find There, 1994; contbr. articles and poetry to profl. jours., newspapers, mags. Served with USAF, 1962-66. Nat. Endowment for Arts fellow, 1974, 81; recipient Discovery award N.Y. Poetry Ctr., 1972, award Poets Found., 1974, Lit. Prize award Pacificus Found., 1996, Am. Book award, 2000. Mem. SAG, AFTRA, Writers Guild Am., P.E.N. (Oakland Josephine Miles award for excellence in lit. 1997). Home: 8 Highland Pl Maplewood NJ 07040 Personal E-mail: lallyjmf@comcast.net.

LALLY, NORMA ROSS, retired federal agency administrator; b. Crawford, Nebr., Aug. 10, 1932; d. Roy Anderson and Alma Leona (Barber) Lively; m. Robert Edward Lally, Dec. 4, 1953 (div. Mar. 1986); children: Robyn Carol Murch, Jeffrey Alan, Gregory Roy. BA, Boise State U., Idaho, 1974, MA, 1976; postgrad., Columbia Pacific U., 1988—. With grad. admissions Boise State U., 1971-74; with officer programs USN Recruiting, Boise, 1974; pub. affairs officer IRS, Boise and Las Vegas, 1975-94; ret., 1994. Speaker in field, Boise and Las Vegas, 1977—. Contbr. articles to newspapers. Mem. task force Clark County Sch. Dist., Las Vegas, 1986-96, Las Vegas Art Mus. Staff sgt. USAF, 1950-54. Mem.: NAFE, Women in Mil. Svc. Am. (charter), Mensa, Marine's Meml. Club (life), Am. Legion (life). Avocations: writing, music, swimming, travel. Home: 3013 Hawksdale Dr Las Vegas NV 89134-8967 Personal E-mail: norlally@aol.com.

LALLY-GREEN, MAUREEN ELLEN, judge, educator; b. Sharpsville, Pa., July 5, 1949; d. Francis Leonard and Charlotte Marie (Frederick) Lally; m. Stephen Ross Green, Oct. 5, 1979; children: Katherine Lally, William Ross, Bridget Marie. BS, Duquesne U., 1971, JD, 1974. Bar: Pa. 1974, D.C., U.S. Dist. Ct. (we. dist.) Pa. 1974, U.S. Ct. Appeals (3d cir.) 1974, U.S. Supreme Ct. 1978. Atty. Houston Cooper, Pitts., 1974-75, Commodity Futures Trading Commn., Washington, 1975-78; counsel Westinghouse Electric Corp., Pitts., 1978-83; prof. law Duquesne U., Pitts., 1986-2000, adj. prof. law, 1983-86, 2000—; apptd. judge Superior Ct., 1998, elected judge, 2000—. Arbitrator U.S. Dist. Ct.; mem. criminal procedure rules com. Supreme Ct. Pa., 1994—97, mem. appellate rules com.; dir. European Union Law Conf., Dublin, 1995—97, Intellectual Law Conf., Italy, 1997; mem. Disciplinary Bd. Commonwealth of Pa. Chair Cranberry Twp. Zoning Hearing Bd., Pa., 1983-98; counsel Western Pa. Ptnrs. of Ams., 1987-90, pres. 1993-95, bd. dir., 1995-99; active Elimination of World Hunger Project, 1977-85, Bishop's Com. on Dialogue with Cath. Univs., 1999-2001; co-chair Millenium com. Duquesne U., 1997-2000; bd. regents St. Vincent Sem., Latrobe, Pa., 2002—; bd. trustees St. Francis U., Loretto, Pa., 2003—; bd. dir. Auberle House, 2004, Epilepsy Found. of Western Pa., 2005—; chair Gender Bias subcom. Supreme Ct., 2003-2004, mem. tri br. commn. pace and gender, 2004-, sec. race gender and ethnic fairness com., 2006; bd. dirs. Ireland Inst., Pitts., Pa., 2006. Fellow Kellogg Found. (for Ptnrs. of Ams.), 1990-92. Mem. Pa. Bar Assn. (ethics com. 1987-94, commn. on women in the profession 1994—, chair quality of work life com. 2002, mem. exec. com. of women in the profession), Allegheny County Bar Assn. (women in law com., professionalism com., ethics com., sec. bd. dir. 1992-2001), Duquesne U. Alumni Assn. (bd. dir. 1982-89, sec. 1988-89), Duquesne U. Law Alumni Assn. (bd. dir. 1987, treas. 1991, v.p. 1992), St. Thomas More Soc. (bd. dir. 2002—). Republican. Roman Catholic. Avocations: children's activities, sports. Office: 2420 Grant Bldg 330 Grant St Pittsburgh PA 15219-2202

LALONDE, BERNARD JOSEPH, finance educator; b. Detroit, June 3, 1933; s. John Bernard and Fannie (Napier) LaL.; m. Barbara Elaine Eggenberger, Sept. 6, 1958; children— Lisa Renee, Michell Ann, Christopher John. AB, U. Notre Dame, 1955; MBA, U. Detroit, 1957; PhD, Mich. State U., 1961. Asst. prof. mktg. U. Colo., Boulder, 1961-65; assoc. prof. Mich. State U., East Lansing, 1965-69; James R. Riley prof. mktg. and logistics Ohio State U., Columbus, 1969-85, Raymond E. Mason prof. transp. and logistics, 1985-95, prof. emeritus, 1995. Author: Physical Distribution Management, 2d edit, 1968, Customer Service: A Management Perspective, 1988; Editor: Jour. Bus. Logistics; Jour. book and monographs editor, Am. Mktg. Assn.; Contbr. articles to profl. jours. Pres. Transp. Research Found. Recipient John Drury Sheehan award, 1976; Formerly Ford scholar; Gen. Electric fellow. Mem. Am. Marketing Assn., Regional Sci. Assn., Council Logistic Mgmt., Soc. Logistics Engrs., Beta Gamma Sigma, Alpha Kappa Psi. Roman Catholic. Home: 8538 Pitlochry Ct Dublin OH 43017-9770 Office: Ohio State U Coll Bus Supply Chain Mgmt Rsch Grp 351 Fisher Hall 2100 Neil Ave Columbus OH 43210

LALONDE, MARC, lawyer, former Canadian government official; b. Ile Perrot, Que., Can., July 26, 1929; s. J. Albert and Nora (St-Aubin) L.; m. Claire Tetreau, Sept. 8, 1955; children: Marie, Luc, Paul, Catherine. BA, Coll. St. Laurent, Montreal, 1950; LLB, U. Montreal, 1964, LLM, 1955; MA in Econs. and Polit. Sci., Oxford U., Eng., 1957; LLD (hon.), Limburg U., The Netherlands, 1989, U. Western Ont., Can., 2005. Bar: Que. 1955, Queen's Coun. 1971, Order of Can, 1988. Prof. bus. law and econs. U. Montreal, 1957-59; spl. asst. to Minister of Justice, Ottawa, Ont., Canada, 1959-60; partner firm Gelinas, Bourque, Lalonde & Benoit, Montreal, 1960-68; policy adviser to Prime Minister Lester B. Pearson, Ottawa, 1967-68; prin. sec. to Prime Minister Pierre E. Trudeau, Ottawa, 1968-72; elected to House of Commons for Montreal-Outremont, 1972; minister of nat. health and welfare, 1972-77; minister of state for fed.-provincial relations, 1977-78; minister responsible for status of women, 1975-78; minister of justice and atty. gen. Can., 1978-79; minister of energy, mines and resources, 1980-82; minister of finance, 1982-84; sr. counsel Stikeman, Elliott, Montreal. Bd. dirs. Citibank Can., Sherritt Internat. Corp.; ad hoc judge Internat. Ct. Justice, 1995—. Decorated officer Order of Can.; Queen's Counsel; recipient Dana award APHA, 1978; named to Can. Med. Hall of Fame, 2004. Mem. Internat. Coun. on Comml. Arbitration, Am. Arbitration Assn., London Ct. Internat. Arbitration, Privy Coun. Can. Mem. Liberal Party. Home: 1477 boul Perrot Ile Perrot PQ Canada J7V 7P2 Office Phone: 514-397-3080. Personal E-mail: m_lalonde@rbs.rogers.com.

LALWANI, ANIL KUMAR, otolaryngologist; b. Sept. 17, 1960; MD, U. Mich., 1985. Diplomate Am. Bd. Otolaryngology. Intern Duke U., Durham, NC, 1985—86, resident in gen. & thoracic surgery, 1986—87; resident in otolaryngology & head & neck surgery U. Calif., San Francisco, 1987-91, fellow in otolaryngology skull base surgery, 1987—91; sr. staff fellow NIH, Bethesda, Md., 1992—94; staff U. Calif., San Francisco, 1994—2003; Mendik Found. prof. otolaryngology NYU Sch. Medicine, chmn. otolaryngology, prof. physiology and neurosci. Surgeon NYU Cochlear Implant Ctr. Mem.: ACS, Am. Acad. Otolaryngology and Head and Neck Surgery. Mailing: NYU Sch Medicine NBV5E5 550 First Ave New York NY 10016 Office Phone: 212-263-6344. E-mail: anil.lalwani@nyumc.org.

LALWANI, ASHOK K., marketing educator; b. Jaipur, Rajasthan, India, July 14, 1971; arrived in US, 2000; s. Mahendra Kumar and Lajwanti Lalwani; m. Leina Mary Joseph, Dec. 19, 2000; 1 child, Rohan A. B in Tech., Indian Inst. Tech., New Delhi, 1990—94; MS, Nat. U. Singapore, 1996—98, U. Fla., Gainesville, 2000—02; PhD, U. Ill., Urbana-Champaign, 2002—06. Mktg. officer Vardhman Spinning Mills, New Delhi, 1994—96; mktg. lectr. Temasek Poly., Singapore; asst. prof. mktg. U. Tex., San Antonio, 2006—. Editor monthly newsletter, postgrad. hall of residence Nat. U. Singapore, 1996—97; vice chmn. Ctr. Bus. Rsch., Temasek Poly., Singapore, 1997—98; co-organizer mktg. comm. symposium Temasek Poly., Singapore, 1998. Contbr. articles to profl. jours., chapters to books. Named to List of Excellent Instrs., U. Ill.; recipient Robert Ferber award excellence in rsch., 2002, 2005, Sheth-Sudman award for excellence in tchg., 2006, Raffles Hotel Rsch. award, Nat. U. Singapore. Mem.: Soc. Consumer Psychology, Assn. Consumer Rsch., Beta Gamma Sigma. Office: Univ Texas 6900 North Loop 1604 W San Antonio TX 78249-0632

LAM, CAROL CHIEN-HUA, communications executive, former prosecutor, lawyer; b. NY, 1959; BA in Philosophy, Yale U., 1981; JD, Stanford U., 1985. Law clk. to Hon. Irving R. Kaufman US Ct. Appeals (2nd cir.), 1985—86; asst. US atty. (so. dist.) Calif. US Dept Justice, 1986—97; chief, major fraud sect. US Dept. Justice, 1997—2000, US atty. (so. dist.) Calif., 2002—07; judge Calif. Superior Ct., San Diego, 2000—02; sr. v.p., gen. counsel QUALCOMM Inc., San Diego, 2007—. Recipient Spl. Achievement award, US Dept. Justice, 1990—94, 1997—99, Dir.'s award for Superior Performance as an Asst. US Atty., 1994, Health & Human Svc. Inspector Gen.'s Integrity award, 1995, Atty. Gen.'s award for Disting. Svc., 1997, Health & Human Svc. Inspector Gen.'s award for Exceptional Achievement, 1997. Mem.: Stanford Law Sch. bd. visitors, Stanford Alumni Assn. Office: QUALCOMM Inc 5775 Morehouse Dr San Diego CA 92121

LAM, DEREK, apparel designer; b. San Francisco, Calif. Grad., Parsons Sch. of Design, 1990. Designer Michael Kors, 1990—94; head designer KORS by Michael Kors, 1994—2002; launched collection Derek Lam Co., 2002—. Work featured in Women's Wear Daily, Vogue, Harper's Bazaar, Nylon Magazine, Fashion Wire Daily, Style.com, ELLE. Recipient Ecco Domani Fashion Found. award, 2004, Perry Ellis Swarovski award, Coun. Fashion Designers Am., 2005, Accessory Designer of Yr., 2007. Office: Derek Lam Company LLC 601 W 26th St # 1730 New York NY 10001-1103*

LAM, GALEN KA-RON, electrical engineer; b. Winnipeg, Man., Can., May 18, 1969; s. Peter Kuen-Yui and Sau-Yin (Ng) Lam; m. Mamiko Nishiguchi, Mar. 25, 1997. BSc in Elec. Engring., U. Calgary, Alta., Can., 1991. Sys. planning engr., overseas plant engring. dept. NEWJEC, Inc., Osaka, Japan, 1993-97; facilities planning, power sys. engr. TransAlta Utilities Corp., Calgary, 1997—98; transmission adminstr., tech. svcs. group ESB Internat., Calgary, 1998—2002; sys. planning engr. Transmission Adminstr. Alta. Ltd., Calgary, 2002—03; sr. tech. specialist, sys. planning Alta. Elec. Sys. Operator, Calgary, 2003—. Mem.: IEEE (sr.), Geologists and Geophysicists Alta., Assn. Profl. Engrs. Achievements include numerous pre-feasibility and feasibility studies on coal thermal, hydro and combined cycle plants, pumped storage, and nuclear power projects in numerous countries. Avocations: bicycling, music, reading, tennis, badminton. Home: 295 Applestone Park SE Calgary AB T2A 7W3 Canada Office: Alta Elec Sys Operator 2500 330 5th Ave SW Calgary AB Canada Office Phone: 403-539-2498. Personal E-mail: galen.lam@shaw.ca. Business E-Mail: galen.lam@aeso.ca.

LAM, PAULINE POHA, library director; b. Hong Kong, Oct. 21, 1950; came to U.S., 1971; d. Cheung and Kam-Chun (Mo) Li; m. Frank Sung-Lun Lam, Nov. 28, 1973; children: Candace See-Win Lam, Megan See-Kay Lam. BA, U. B.C., 1977; MLS, U. Tex., 1980; cert. City Mgmt. Acad., Austin C.C., 1994; grad., Cedar Park Leadership Class, 2004. Libr. dir. City of Cedar Park (Tex.). Bd. dirs. Cedar Park Pub. Libr. Found., 1994—. Mem. Work Force Literacy Com. Literacy Coun. of Williamson County, 1995, Cedar Park Leadership Class 2004, Williamson County Children's Advocacy Ctr. Bd., 2003; bd. dirs. ARC of Ctrl. Tex., Austin, 1995—97, Williamson County Children's Advocacy Ctr., 2003. Mem. ALA, Tex. Libr. Assn., Tex. Mcpl. League Libr. Dir. Assn. Avocations: reading, crocheting, painting. Office: Cedar Park Pub Libr 550 Discovery Blvd Cedar Park TX 78613-2200

LAM, SAU-HAI (HARVEY), aeronautical engineering educator; BS in Aero. Engring., Rensselaer Poly. Inst., 1954; MA, Princeton U., 1956, PhD (Guggenheim fellow), 1958. Asst. Princeton U., 1956-58, rsch. assoc., 1958-59, assoc. prof., 1963-68, prof. aerospace scis., 1968—, chmn. dept. mech. and aerospace engring., 1983-89, assoc. dean Sch. Engring. and Applied Sci., 1980-81, Edwin Wilsey '04 prof. emeritus mech. and aerospace engring. Asst. prof. aero. engring. Cornell U., 1959-60 Mem. AIAA, ASME, APS, NAE, Am. Soc. Engring. Edn., Soc. Indsl. and Applied Math., Sigma Xi Office: Princeton U D226 Engineering Quad Princeton NJ 08544-0001 Office Phone: 609-258-5133. Office Fax: 609-258-6109. Business E-Mail: lam@princeton.edu.

LAM, SIMON SHIN-SING, computer science educator; b. Macao, July 31, 1947; arrived in US, 1966; s. Chak Han and Kit Ying (Tang) Lam; m. Amy Leung, Mar. 29, 1971; 1 child, Eric. BSEE with distinction, Wash. State U., Pullman, 1969; MS in Engring., UCLA, 1970, PhD in Engring., 1974. Postgraduate rsch. engr. ARPA Network Measurement Ctr., UCLA, 1971-74, postdoctoral scholar, 1974; rsch. staff mem. IBM T.J. Watson Rsch. Ctr., Yorktown Heights, NY, 1974-77; asst. prof. U. Tex., Austin, 1977-79, assoc. prof., 1979-83, prof. computer sci., 1983—, David S. Bruton Centennial prof., 1985-88, anonymously endowed prof., 1988-2001, chmn. dept. computer sci., 1992-94, regents chair computer scis., 2001—. Editor-in-chief IEEE/ACM Transactions on Networking, 1995-99; editor: Principles of Communication and Networking Protocols; contbr. articles to profl. jours. Recipient William R. Bennett prize, 2001, Software Sys. award, 2004; grantee, NSF, 1978—; Chancellor's Tchg. fellow, UCLA, 1969—73. Fellow IEEE (Leonard G. Abraham prize 1975, William R. Bennett prize 2001, W. Wallace McDowell award 2004), Assn. Computing Machinery (prog. chmn. symposium 1983, SIGCOMM award 2004, Software Sys. award 2004); mem. NAE. Avocations: tennis, swimming, skiing, travel. Office: Dept Computer Scis U Tex 1 University Sta C0500 Austin TX 78712-0233 Office Phone: 512-471-9531. Office Fax: 512-471-8885. E-mail: lam@cs.utexas.edu.

LAM, SUM, medical educator; PharmD, U. Conn., Storrs. Cert. geriatric pharmacist ASCP, pharmacotherapy specialist ACCP. Asst. clin. prof. St. John's U., Jamaica, NY, 2003—. Office: St John's Univ 8000 Utopia Pky St Albert's H 114 Jamaica NY 11439 Business E-Mail: lams1@stjohns.edu.

LAMACH, BERNARD D., professional engineer, county commissioner; b. Big Timber, Mont., Oct. 10, 1934; m. Deborah Lamach; 6 children. BS, BA, Western Colo. U., 1975; ME, Internat. Corr. Sch., 1958. Owner retail store, Bradford, N.H.; cons. engr.; mem. N.H. Ho. of Reps., 1994-98; commr. Merrimack County, 1998—2003. Mem. Bradford budget com., solid waste com., bus. assn. Kearsarge regional sch. dist. budget com. N.H. Ho. of Reps., sci. tech. and energy com. Mem. Bradford Hist. Soc., Lake Massasecum Improvement Assn.; spl. projects coord. Estero Fire/Rescue, 2004-07. Republican. Address: 5309 Shalley CIR Fort Myers FL 33919-2211 Personal E-mail: blamach@yahoo.com.

LAMAGNA, CARLO M., art educator; BA in English, Coll. Holy Cross; MA in art history, U. Mass. Prof. & chmn. art dept. NYU. Office: New York U 82 Washington Sq East New York NY 10003 Office Phone: 212-998-5700. Office Fax: 212-995-4320. E-mail: carlo.lamagna@nyu.edu.

LAMANTIA, CHARLES ROBERT, management consulting company executive; b. NYC, June 12, 1939; s. Joseph Ferdinand and Catherine (Perniciaro) LaM.; m. Ann Christine Carmody, Sept. 16, 1961; children: Elise, Matthew. BA, Columbia U., 1960, BS, 1961, MS, 1962, ScD, 1965; grad. advanced mgmt. program, Harvard Bus. Sch., 1979. Cons. staff Arthur D. Little, Inc., Cambridge, Mass., 1967-77, v.p., 1977-81, pres., 1987—98, COO, 1987—88, CEO, 1988—99; pres. Koch Process Sys., Westboro, Mass., 1981-86, CEO, 1981—99, chmn., 1998—99. Mem. adv. coun. Sch. Engring. Columbia U., 1990-98; mem. adv. bd. Sch. Mgmt. Boston Coll., 1995—; bd. dirs. State St. Corp., 1994—, Marathon Techs., 2001-02, Neurometrics, Inc., 2004-; trustee Meml. Dr. Trust, 1988-99; bd. govs. New Eng. Med. Ctr., 1989-95; bd. advisors StoneGate Ptnrs., 2000-01, IntellectExchange.com, 2000—03. Mem. Corp. Woods Hole Oceanog. Inst., 1996-2004; mem. bd. overseers Mus. Sci., Boston, 1988-94, Sta. WGBH-TV, 1990-2004, mem. Conf. Bd., 1989-99; mem. Mass. Gov.'s Coun., Mass. Bus. Roundtable, 1992-99, bd. dirs. 1998-99; bd. dirs. Boston Pub. Libr. Found., 1997-2001. Lt. USN, 1965-67. Sloan Found. fellow, 1962, NSF fellow, 1965.

LAMAR, ANN HANNAFORD, state supreme court justice; d. Leon Hannaford; m. John T. Lamar, Jr.; children: John T. III, Vance. Student, NW Miss. Jr. Coll., 1970—71; BS in Edn., Delta State U., Cleve., Miss., 1974; law degree, U. Miss., 1982. Adminstrv. asst. Gov.'s Office of Edn. and Tng., 1974—77; ct. reporter Chancery Ct., Senatobia, Miss.; atty. Senatobia, 1982—87, 1993—95; asst. dist. atty. 17th Dist., 1987—93, 1996—99, dist. atty.; cir. judge 17th Cir. Ct., Miss., 2001—07; presiding judge 17th Cir. Drug Ct., 2007; justice Miss. Supreme Ct., 2007—. Vice chair Conf. Cir. Judges, 2005—06, chair, 2006—07. Baptist. Office: Miss Supreme Ct PO Box 249 Jackson MS 39205*

LAMAR, HOWARD ROBERTS, academic administrator, historian; b. Tuskegee, Ala., Nov. 18, 1923; s. John Howard and Elma (Roberts) L.; m. Doris Shirley White, Sept. 3, 1959; children: Susan Kent, Sarah Howard. BA, Emory U., 1944; MA, Yale U., 1945, PhD, 1951; LHD (hon.), Emory U., 1975; LLD (hon.), Yale U., 1993; LittD (hon.), U. Nebr., 1994. Instr. U. Mass., 1945-46, Wesleyan U., Middletown, Conn., 1948-49; mem. faculty Yale U., 1949-94, prof. Am. History and history Am. West, 1964-94, W.R. Coe prof. Am. history, 1979-87, Sterling prof. history, 1987—, chmn. history dept., 1962-63, 67-70, dir. history grad. studies, 1964-67, fellow Ezra Stiles Coll., 1961-94, dean, 1979-85, pres., 1992-93, Sterling prof. history emeritus, 1994—. Author: Dakota Territory, 1861-1889, 1956, 97, The Far Southwest, 1846-1912, A Territorial History, 1966, 2d edit., 2000, Charlie Siringo's West: An Interpretive Biography, 2005; also articles, reviews.; Editor: (Joseph Downey) Cruise of the Portsmouth, 1958, Western Americana Series, 1961—, New Encyclopedia of the American West, 1998, Gold Seeker: Adventures of A Belgian Argonaut in California, 1985, paperback, 1998, Voices of the New Republic: Connecticut Towns, 1800-1832, Vol. 2, 2003,; co-author, co-editor The Frontier in History: North America and Southern Africa Compared, 1981, History of the American Frontier Series, 1976—, Voices of the New Republic: Connecticut Towns, 1800-1832, Vol. 2, 2003. Alderman, New Haven, 1951-53. Mem. Orgn. Am. Historians, Western History Assn. (pres. 1971-72), Am. Antquarian Soc., Elihu Soc., Conn. Acad. of Arts and Scis., Phi Beta Kappa. Democrat. Home: 1747 Hartford Tpke North Haven CT 06473-1249 Office: Yale U Dept History New Haven CT 06520

LA MARCA, JEFFRY PETER, language educator, consultant; b. Long Beach, Calif., July 7, 1958; s. Raymond Thomas La Marca and Janet Marjorie Crowley; children: Stephen Jeffry, Samantha Rose, Antony Raymond. BA in Behavioral Sci., Calif. State Polytechic U., Pomona, 1982; MA in Edn., Calif. State U., San Bernardino, 1988. Cert. multiple subject tchg. credential, music Calif., 1987, Orff Schulwerk tchr. Levels I, II and III Chapman Coll., Calif., Orff-Schulwerk tchr. trainer Am. Orff-Schulwerk Assn., 1992. Bassoonist, contrabassoonist La Orquesta Filarmónica de la Ciudad de México, Mexico City, 1979—80; recreation therapy asst. Meth. Hosp. So. Calif., Arcadia, 1980—84; tchr. various schs., Calif., 1987—96; instr., child devel. dept. Victor Valley Coll., Victorville, Calif., 1993—99; music specialist Capistrano Unified Sch. Dist., San Juan Capistrano, Calif., 1996—2000; instr., Inst. for the Study of the Multiple Intelligences U. Calif., Riverside, 1992—, curriculum analyst ArtsBridge project Irvine, 2002—03; lang. lab adminstr. Soka U. Am., Aliso Viejo, 2002—. Author: Window to the Past - Door to the Future: A Glimpse at an American Genealogy, 1995; contbr. articles to profl. jours. Recipient WHO award, Victor Elem. Tchrs. Assn., 1995;, Orange County Music and Arts Adminstrn. Assn. grantee, 1999, Instrnl. Improvement grantee, Victor Elem. Sch. Dist., 1989—91, Sci. in Edn. grantee, Kiwanis Club of Victorville, 1990, Space and Tech. Program for Educators USAF Acad. scholars, Woodman of World, 1990. Mem.: Learning Disabilities Assn. Am., San Bernardino County Music Educators Assn. (bd. dirs. 1988—96, treas. 1992—94), Calif. Music Educators Assn. (bd. dirs. so. sect. 1991—93, first v.p. so. sect. 1993—95, pres. so. sect. 1995—97, bd. dir. 1995—97), Am. Orff-Schulwerk Assn. (nat. adv. bd. 1989—92, Inland Counties chpt. pres., mem. nat. bd. trustees 1992—96, founder Inland Counties chpt. 1989—92), Am. Kitefliers Assn. Avocations: music, travel, technology, photography, reading. Home: 50 Santa Loretta Rancho Santa Margarita CA 92688 Office: Soka U America 1 U Dr Aliso Viejo CA 92656 Home Phone: 949-888-1758; Office Phone: 949-480-4017. Business E-Mail: jlamarca@soka.edu.

LAMARRE, BERNARD, engineering executive; b. Chicoutimi, Que., Can., Aug. 6, 1931; s. Emile J. and Blanche M. (Gagnon) L.; m. Louise Lalonde, Aug. 30, 1952 (dec. Dec. 2002); children: Jean, Christine, Lucie, Monique, Michèle, Philippe, Mireille. BSc, Ecole Poly., Montreal, Que., Can., 1952; MSc, Imperial Coll., U. London, 1955; LLD, St. Francis Xavier U., NS, Can., 1980; DEng (hon.), U. Waterloo, Ont., 1984; LLD (hon.), U. Concordia, Montreal, 1985; DEng (hon.), U. Montreal, 1985; D in Applied Sci. (hon.), U. Sherbrooke, Que., 1986; D in Bus. Adminstrn. (hon.), U. Chicoutimi, Que., 1987; DSc (hon.), Queen's U., Kingston, Ont., 1987; DEng (hon.), U. Ottawa, Ont., 1988, Tech. U. N.S., 1989, Royal Mil. Coll., Kingston, 1990; PhD in Sci. (hon.), McGill U., 2001. Structural and founds. engr. Lalonde-Valois, Montreal, 1955-60, chief engr., 1960-62; ptnr., gen. mgr., pres. Lalonde, Valois, Lamarre, Valois, Montreal, 1962-72; chmn., CEO Lavalin Group, 1972-91; sr. advisor SNC-Lavalin Inc., 1991—99. Chmn. Soc. du Vieux Port de Montreal, 1993-2007, Bellechasse Santè, Ecole Polytechnique de Montreal. Chmn. Montreal Mus. Fine Arts. Decorated officer Ordre nat. du Quèbec, Order of Can.; Athlone fellow, 1952. Fellow Engring. Inst. Can., Can. Soc. Civil Engring.; mem. ASCE, Order Engrs. Que., Mont-Royal Club, St. Denis Club. Roman Catholic. Home: 4850 Cedar Crescent Montreal PQ Canada H3W 2H9 Personal E-mail: bernard.lamarre@bellnet.ca.

LAMARRE, MEAGHAN, internet communications specialist; b. Missoula, Mont., Nov. 17, 1980; d. Albert Leroy and Janet Elizabeth Lamarre. BA in Psychology, Lewis and Clark Coll., Portland, Oreg., 2002. Rsch. asst. Brown U., Providence, 2003—05; internet comm. coord. NOW, Washington, 2005—. Chair Alternatives to Marriage Project, Bklyn., 2003—07. Home Phone: 401-225-3543.

LAMATTINA, JOHN L., pharmaceutical executive; b. Jan. 1950; m. Mary B. LaMattina; 3 children. BS cum laude in Chemistry, Boston Coll., 1971; PhD in Organic Chemistry, U. NH, 1975. NIH postdoctoral fellow Princeton U., NJ; with Pfizer, Inc., 1977—, v.p. US discovery ops., 1993, sr. v.p. worldwide discovery ops., 1998, sr. v.p. worldwide devel., 1999—2003, pres. global R&D, sr. v.p., 2003—. Bd. dirs. Thermo Electron Corp. Contbr. articles to profl. jours. Bd. trustees Worcester Poly. Inst. Recipient Boston Coll. Alumni award of Excellence in Sci., 1998, Award for Leadership and Commitment in the Fight Against Diabetes, Am. Diabetes Assn., 2004. Achievements include patents in field. Office: Pfizer Inc 235 E 42nd St New York NY 10017*

LAMB, ASHLEY BROOKS, entomologist; b. Calgary, Alberta, Canada, Sept. 27, 1976; d. Freeman Clifford and Jo Ann Lamb. BS in Biology with distinction, U. Victoria, BC, Can., 2000; PhD in Entomology, Va. Poly. Inst. and State U., Blacksburg, 2005. Insectary technician Can. Forest Svc., Victoria, 1998—2000; tchg. asst. dept. entomology Va. Tech U., Blacksburg, 2001—03, rsch. assoc. dept. entomology, 2005—, instr. dept. entomology, 2005. Contbr. articles to profl. jours. Grantee, USDA Forest Svc., 2004—07; Gene A. and Ina Mae James scholar, Coll. Agr. and Life Scis., Va. Tech. U., 2003, J. M. Grayson scholar, Va. Tech. U., Dept. Entomology, 2005. Mem.: Entomol. Soc. Am. (assoc. Asa Fitch Meml. award 2002), Entomol. Soc. BC (assoc.), W.B. Alwood Soc. (assoc.; pres. 2002—04). Achievements include development of rearing procedures for a biological control agent for hemlock woolly adelgid; research in a new predator species that is potentially an excellent biological control agent. Avocations: softball, skiing, music, camping, hiking, travel. Office: Va Tech Dept Entomology 216 Price Hall Virginia Tech (MC 0319) Blacksburg VA 24061 Office Phone: 540-239-0893. Home Fax: 540-231-9131. Business E-Mail: aslamb@vt.edu.

LAMB, BRIAN PATRICK, broadcast executive; b. Lafayette, Ind., Oct. 9, 1941; married. BA, Purdue U., 1963. Asst. mgr. Sta. WLFI, Lafayette, Ind., 1968—69; press sec. to congressman Peter Dominich Ho. of Reps., Denver, 1969—71, asst. to dir. office telecomm. policy, 1971—74; pres. Media Rsch., Inc., Denver, 1974—76; Washington bur. chief Titsch Pub. Co., Denver, 1976—78; founder Cable Satellite Pub. Affairs Network (C-SPAN), Washington, 1977, chmn., CEO, 1979—. Served in USN, 1963—67. Office: C-Span 400 N Capitol St NW Ste 650 Washington DC 20001-1550

LAMB, CARL VERNON, writer, retired engineer; b. Jacksonville, Ark., Nov. 30, 1928; s. Fred Norman Lamb and Minnie Louise Anderson; m. Nancy J. Shields, July 30, 1950; children: Lisa, Mark, Carl II, Michael. Diploma in Mech. Engring., Internat. Corre Sch. ICS, Scranton, Pa., 1960. H.V.A.C. engr. Bechtel Inc., Ann Arbor, Mich., 1981, Gulf Chem. Co., Marietta, Ohio, 1981, Union Carbide, Charleston, W.Va., 1981—82; with Lambs Machine Shop, Boswell, Pa., 1982—83; facilities engr. IBM, Indicott, NY, 1983—84; project engr. MTI Corp., St. Albans, W.Va., 1984; facilities engr. Nissan Motors, Smyrna, Tenn., 1984—85; project engr. cons. Union Carbide, Charleston, W.Va., 1986—91; H.V.A.C. engr. Salem Tech. Svc., Coeur d' Alene, Idaho, 1991—92; self-employed land developer Scott Depot, W.Va., 1992—98; mech. engr. cons. Washington, 1993; self-employed writer Scott Depot, W.Va., 1998—. Author: (book) The Last Parade, 1999. Staff sgt. USMC, 1945—52. Republican. Avocation: poker. Office: Anderson Pub PO Box 611 Teays WV 25569 Office Phone: 304-743-3261.

LAMB, CHARLES F., retired minister, educator; b. Maryville, Tenn., Dec. 18, 1934; s. C. Fred and Sadie Ellen (Tedder) L.; children: Elizabeth Susan, Linda Louise, Jennifer Janet; m. Betty Jane Zimmerman, Dec. 29, 1979. BA, Maryville Coll., 1956; MDiv, Grad. Sem. of Phillips U., 1961; D in Ministry, N.Y. Theol. Sem., 1990. Ordained to ministry Christian Ch., 1961. Pastor East Aurora Christian Ch., NY, 1961-71; assoc. regional min. Christian Ch., Disciples of Christ, Northeastern Region, Buffalo, 1971-75, regional min., 1975-99; ret., 1999. Mem. orgns. clergy and coun. of chs. Trustee Village of East Aurora, 1968-73; active environ. groups Conf. Mayors and Village Ofcls. N.Y., 1968-73; adj. prof. Niagara U., 1998-2005; asst. to the minister First Presbyn. Ch., Youngstown, N.Y., 1999—; interim conf. regional minister N.Y. Conf. United Ch. of Christ, 2004; bd. dirs. Residents Responsible Govt., 2002—; bd. mem. Ctr. of Renewal Stellen Niagara Retreat Ctr., Beeman Found. Author: Doc's Diary, 1996, More Meanderings from Doc's Diary, 2000, web columnist. Pres. Coll. Regional Mins., 1997-99; mem. adminstrv. com. Gen. Bd. of Christian Ch., Disciples of Christ, 1997-99; mem. Town of Porter Dem. Com., 2006—. Mem. Conf. Regional Ministers and Moderators of the Disciples of Christ (pres. 1997-99), Sierra Club (mem. exec. com. Niagara group 2001-, co-editor Trailblazer, mem. adv. com. Sierra Atlantic). Democrat. Mem. Christian Ch. Home: 335 Walnut Ln Youngstown NY 14174-1348 E-mail: clamb9@roadrunner.com.

LAMB, CHARLES MOODY, political scientist, educator; b. Mar. 1, 1945; s. Edward Clay and Opal Irene Lamb. BS, Mid. Tenn. State U., 1967; MA, U. Ala., 1970, PhD, 1974. Adminstrv. specialist NASA, Washington, 1971; rsch. scientist George Washington U., Washington, 1973—75; equal opportunity specialist U.S. Commn. on Civil Rights, Washington, 1975—77; asst. prof. polit. sci. SUNY, 1977—84, assoc. prof., 1984—2006, prof., 2006—. Vis. assoc. prof. U. Wis., Madison, 1990—91; cons. U.S. Congress Office Tech. Assessment, Washington, 1974—75, Washington, 1984. Co-editor, contbg. author: Supreme Court Activism and Restraint, 1982 (Choice Outstanding Acad. Book award, 1983), Implementation of Civil Rights Policy, 1984, Judicial Conflict and Consensus, 1986, The Burger Court: Political and Judicial Profiles, 1991; author: Housing Segregation in Suburban America Since 1960: Presidential and Judicial Politics, 2005. 1st lt. US Army, 1972. Grantee, NSF, 1974—75, Office Tech. Assessment, 1974—75, SUNY Rsch. Found., 1982, Lyndon Baines Johnson Found., 1996, Gerald R. Ford Found., 1997, John F. Kennedy Found., 2007, Dwight D. Eisenhower Found., 2007, Harry S. Truman Libr. Inst., 2007. Mem.: Midwest Polit. Sci. Assn., Leadership Conf. on Civil Rights, Law and Soc. Assn., N.E. Polit. Sci. Assn., Am. Polit. Sci. Assn. (exec. com. sect. on law cts. and jud. process 1984—86, 1992—94), NY State Polit. Sci. Assn. (pres. 1985—86), Common Cause, Pi Sigma Beta, Pi Gamma Mu, Phi Sigma Alpha. Democrat. Presbyterian. Avocations: tennis, swimming. Office: SUNY Dept Polit Sci 520 Park Hall Buffalo NY 14221-5013 Home: 9640 The Maples Clarence NY 14031-1591 Office Phone: 716-645-2251 ext 503. Business E-Mail: clamb@buffalo.edu.

LAMB, CONNIE, retired elementary school educator; b. Collins, Miss., Oct. 3, 1951; d. Costee and Bernice Gamble; m. Douglas Eugene Lamb, July 9, 1973; children: Douglas Farrell, Candice Lakeisa, Deidre Raquel. BS, Jackson State U., Miss., 1973, MS in Edn., 1989. Spl. edn. tchr. Magnolia Elem. Sch., Miss., 1973—74; remedial tchr. Collins Elem. Sch., Miss., 1974—77, spl. edn. tchr., 1977—2003. Dir. after-sch. programs Collins Elem. Sch., 2001—03. Spkr. Head Start Parent Group, Collins, 1998, 1999; state youth dir. Miss. Ch. of God, 1998—; Sunday sch. tchr., pianist Zion Ch. of God, Oakvale, Miss. Named Tchr. of Yr., Collins Elem. Sch., 1989, 1999. Democrat. Home: 72 Faler Rd Collins MS 39428

LAMB, GORDON HOWARD, academic administrator; b. Eldora, Iowa, Nov. 6, 1934; s. Capp and Ethel (Hayden) L; m. Nancy Ann Painter; children: Kirk, Jon, Phillip. B in Music Edn., Simpson Coll., 1956; M of Music, U. Nebr., 1962; PhD, U. Iowa, 1973. Choral dir. Iowa Pub. Schs., Tama/Paullina, Sac City, 1957-68; asst. prof. music U. Wis., Stevens Point, 1969-70, U. Tex., Austin, 1970-74, prof., dir. divsn. music San Antonio, 1974-79, prof., v.p. acad. affairs, 1979-86; pres. Northeastern Ill. U., Chgo., 1986-95, pres. emeritus, 1996—; interim chancellor U. Wis., Parkside, 1997—98, U. Mo., Kansas City, 1999—2000; sr. v.p. EFL Assocs./TranSearch, Overland Park, Kans., 2000—07; interim pres. U. Mo. Sys., Columbia, 2007—. Vis. prof. music dept. Western Ill. U., 1996-97 Author: Choral Techniques, 1974, 3d edit. 1988; editor: Guide for the Beginning Choral Director; contbr. articles to scholarly and profl. jours.; composer numerous pieces choral music. Served with U.S. Army, 1957-58. Recipient Most Supportive Pres. or Chancellor award Am. Assn. Colls. for Tchr. Edn., 1992. Mem. Am. Assn. Higher Edn., Am. Assn. State Colls. and Univs., Am. Choral Dirs. Assn. (life, chmn. nat. com. 1970-72). Office: U Mo Office of Pres 321 University Hall Columbia MO 65211 Office Phone: 573-882-2011.

LAMB, IRENE HENDRICKS, medical researcher; b. Ky., May 9, 1940; d. Daily P. and Bertha (Hendricks) Lamb. Diploma in nursing, Ky. Bapt. Hosp.; student, Berea Coll., Ky., Calif. State U. L.A. RN, Ky. Charge nurse, head nurse acute medicine, med. ICU, surgical ICU, emergency room various med. ctrs., 1963—67; staff nurse rsch. CCU U. So. Calif./L.A. County Med. Ctr., 1968, nurse mgr. clin. rsch. ctr., 1969—74; sr. rsch. nurse cardiology Stanford U. Sch. Medicine, Calif., 1974—85, rsch. coord. pvt. clin., 1988; dir. clin. rsch. San Diego Cardiac Ctr., 1989—92; sr. cmty. health nurse Madison County Health Dept., Berea, Ky., 1993—97; sr. clin. rsch. mgr. stroke program U. Ky. Coll. Medicine, Lexington, 1997—2001. Contbr. articles to profl. jours., chapters to books. Bd. dirs. Ky. Stroke Assn., 1998—2000. Mem.: Am. Heart Assn. Home: 107 Lorraine Ct Berea KY 40403-1317 Personal E-mail: lambmeadows@msn.com.

LAMB, JAMIE PARKER, JR., retired mechanical engineer; b. Boligee, Ala., Sept. 21, 1933; s. Jamie Parker and Cletus (Hixson) Lamb; m. Nancy Catherine Flaherty, June 11, 1955; children: David Parker, Stephen Patrick. BS, Auburn U., 1954; MS, U. Ill., 1958, PhD, 1961. Asst. prof. engring. mechanics N.C. State U., Raleigh, 1961-63; mem. faculty dept. mech. engring. U. Tex., Austin, 1963-2001, prof., 1970-2001, prof. faculty aerospace engring., 1981-88, Ernest Cockrell Jr. Meml. prof., 1981-2001, prof. emeritus, 2001—, chmn. dept., 1970—76, 1981-88, 1996—2001, assoc. dean engring., 1976-81; dir. engring. program U. Tex.-Pan Am., 1993-94. Cons. LTV Aerospace Corp., Dallas, Marshall Space Flight Ctr., Huntsville, Ala., Tracor, Inc., Austin, Rocketdyne, McGregor, Tex., ARO, Inc., Tullahoma, Tenn., Tex. Gas Transport Co., Austin, Mobil Oil Corp., Dallas, Gilbarco, Inc., Greensboro, NC; spl. cons. U. São Paulo, Brazil, 1974; mem. rev. panel postdoctoral assoc. NRC, 1981—95; mem. U.S. nat. com. theoretical and applied mechanics, 1985—89; chmn. 10th U.S. Nat. Congress Applied Mechanics, 1986. Assoc. tech. editor: Jour. Fluids Engring., 1976—79; contbr. articles to profl. jours. Served to 1st lt. USAF, 1955—57. Recipient Joe J. King Profl. Engring. Achievement award, U. Tex., Austin, 1984, Disting. Alumnus award, U. Ill. Dept. Mech. and Indsl. Engring., 1986. Fellow: ASME (chmn. fluid mechanics tech. com. 1982—84, Founder's award Ctrl. Tex. sect. 1975, Leadership award 1976, 1981, Centennial award 1980), AIAA (assoc.); mem.: NSPE, Am. Soc. Engring. Edn. (chmn. summer faculty programs com. 1978—80, chmn. mech. engring. divsn. 1979—80, bd. dirs. profl. interest coun. I 1981—82), Sigma Xi, Sigma Gamma Tau, Tau Beta Pi, Pi Tau Sigma. Baptist. Home: 2605 Pinewood Ter Austin TX 78757-2136 Business E-Mail: jplamb@mail.utexas.edu.

LAMB, KEVIN THOMAS, lawyer; b. Quincy, Mass., Nov. 14, 1956; s. John Phillip and Kathleen Elaine (O'Brien) L. BA, Washington and Lee U., 1978, JD, 1982. Bar: Va. 1982, D.C. 1988, Mass. 1990, Fla., 2005. Law clk. to presiding justice U.S. Bankruptcy Ct. (we. dist.) Va., Lynchburg, 1982-84; atty. U.S. Dept. Justice, Los Angeles, 1984-85; assoc. Jones, Day, Reavis & Pogue, Los Angeles, 1985-86, Ballard, Spahr, Andrews & Ingersoll, Washington, 1986-89, Testa, Hurwitz & Thibeault, L.L.P., Boston, 1989-91, ptnr., 1992—2005, Gunster, Yoakley & Stewart PA, West Palm Beach, Fla., 2005—. Mem. ABA (com. on bus. bankruptcy), Am. Bankruptcy Inst. (com. on legis.), Comml. Law League Am. Office: Gunster Yoakley & Stewart PA Ste 500 East 777 S Flagler Dr West Palm Beach FL 33401 Office Phone: 561-650-0656. Business E-Mail: klamb@gunster.com.

LAMB, MICHAEL DONALD, secondary school educator; b. 1951; s. Donald and Louise Lamb; m. Miriam Jean Turner, Dec. 22, 1973; children: Brian, Catherine. BS, Oreg. State U., Corvallis, 1969—76; MEd, U. Ctrl. Ark., Conway, 1977—80. Cert. physics, chemistry, integrated sci. & advanced math. tchr. Oreg., 1977. Math & sci. tchr. N.Little Rock Sch. Dist., Ark., 1977—80, Sacred Heart Acad., Klamath Falls, Oreg., 1980—83, Butte Valley HS, Dorris, Calif., 1983—84, Mazama HS, Klamath Falls, 1984—; adj. chemistry instr. Oreg. Inst. Tech., Klamath Falls. Fight choreographer (11 plays plays). Cert. trainer US Jaycees, 1988—2006, pres. Klamath Falls, 1980—95, cmty. devel. v.p., 1988—89, regional dir., 1989—90, senator, 1992; co-chair 2d air quality com. Klamath County, 1993; ea. v.p. Oreg. JCI Senate, 1995—96; precinct committeeman Klamath County Repubs., 2004—06. Mem.: Oreg. Edn. Assn. (legis. adv. coun. 1996—99, oea-pie bd. 1999—2002), Klamath Falls Edn. Assn. (bldg. rep. 1990—, v.p. 2002—04), Am. Chem. Soc., S.Suburban Lions Club. Meth. Avocations: reading, travel, camping, fencing. Home Phone: 541-882-1635. Personal E-mail: mlamb1138@charter.net.

LAMB, PATRICK JOHN, retired financial consultant, state official; b. Charleston, W.Va., Oct. 22, 1938; s. Charles Bernard and Grace Frances (Jackson) L.; m. Kathleen Campbell, May 5, 1962; children: Christine M., Mary K., Charles P., Michael J., Karen P. BSBA, W.Va. State Coll., 1962; MBA, W.Va. Coll. Grad. Studies, 1984. Auditor W.Va. Tax Dept., Charleston, 1961-63; acct. The Diamond, Charleston, 1963-66, W.Va. Water Co., Charleston, 1966-69; sr. rsch. assoc., comptroller W.Va. Rsch. League, Charleston, 1969-97; assoc. dir., comptr. Putnam County Devel. Authority, Hurrican, W.Va., 1997-98; prin. Patrick Lamb, Fin. Cons., Charleston, W.Va., 1998—2005; ret., 2005. CFO W.Va. Solid Waste Mgmt. Bd., Charleston, 1999—2005. Author: The Economic Impact of the Arts in West Virginia. Mem. W.Va. Pub. Accts. Assn., KC (grand knight 1986-88, 94-96, Cath. layman 1981, dist. dep. 1988-93, state warden 1993-95, state advocate 1995-96, state treas. 1996-98, state sec. 1998-2000, state dep. 2000-02). Republican. Roman Catholic. Home and Office: 1403 Jackson St Charleston WV 25301-1909

LAMB, PETER JAMES, meteorology educator, researcher, consultant; b. Nelson, New Zealand, June 21, 1947; came to U.S., 1971; s. George Swan and Dorothy Elizabeth (Smith) L.; children: Karen Deborah Lockwood, Brett Timothy. BA, U. Canterbury, Christchurch, New Zealand, 1969, MA with honors, 1971; PhD, U. Wis., 1976; DSc, U. Canterbury, 2002. Asst. lectr. U. Canterbury, 1971; rsch. asst. U. Wis., Madison, 1971-76, rsch. assoc., 1976; lectr. U. Adelaide, Australia, 1976-79; sr. scientist Ill. Water Survey, Champaign, 1979-91, sect. head, 1984-90; prof. U. Okla., Norman, 1991—, George Lynn Cross rsch. prof., 2001—. Vis. rsch. assoc. U. Miami, Fla., 1978-79; adj. prof. U. Ill., Urbana, 1983-94; W. John and Gail M. Hussey Commemorative lectr. in meteorology Pa. State U., 2003; dir. Coop. Inst. Mesoscale Meteorol. Studies, Norman, 1991—; dir. Internat. Ctr. Disaster Rsch., 1994-99; assoc. dir. Weather Ctr. Programs, Norman, 1996—06; cons. Dept. State, Dept. Energy, Agy. Internat. Devel., NOAA, NSF, World Meteorol. Orgn., Kingdom of Morocco, U. Wis., U. Adelaide, U. Witwatersrand, Univs. Space Rsch. Assn., Stratus Cons., Inc., EPA, 1983—; site sci. atmospheric radiation measurement program Dept. Energy, 1992—. Contbr. articles to profl. jours. Coach Champaign Youth Soccer Orgn., 1983-91. Grantee NSF, EPA, Dept. Energy, NOAA, AID, World Meteorol. Orgn., MacArthur Found., Ins. Inst. Property Loss Reduction, Inst. Bus. and Home Safety, The Williams Cos., Japan Marine Sci. and Tech. Ctr., Ins. Australia Group. Fellow Am. Meteorol. Soc. (chief editor Jour. Climate 1989-95); mem. Am. Geophysical Union, Royal Meteorol. Soc. (Margary lectr. 1991), Sigma Xi. Achievements include research on heat transport by the Atlantic Ocean; investigations into the in causes of droughts in Sahelian Africa and Morocco; study of N.Am. precipitation patterns; assessment of economic value of weather and climate information. Home: 3616 Burlington Dr Norman OK 73072-3647 Office: Univ of Oklahoma CIMMS-Nat Weather Ctr Rm 2100 120 David L Boren Blvd Norman OK 73072-7304 Office Phone: 405-325-3041. Business E-Mail: plamb@ou.edu.

LAMB, PHILINA MAY ANN, dermatologist, educator; BS, Rensselaer Poly. Inst., Troy, NY, 1996; MD, Albany Med. Coll., NY, 1998. Diplomate Am. Bd. Dermatology, 2004. Asst. clin. prof. dermatology Davis med. ctr. U. Calif., Sacramento, 2004—. Office: UC Davis Med Ctr 3301 C St Ste 1400 Sacramento CA 95816 Home Phone: 916-690-3799; Office Phone: 916-734-6371. Personal E-mail: philinamlamb@gmail.com.

LAMB, RICHARD, cultural organization administrator; b. St. Petersburg, Fla., May 11, 1952; s. Richard Lamb Sr. and Joan Lamb. BA in Psychology, St. Edward's U., Austin, Texas, 1975. Lic. masters U.S. Coast Guard, 2001. Founder, dir. U.S. Maritime Lit. Awards, Annapolis, 2000—. Recipient award, Tex. Gov. George W. Bush, 1999, Tex. Gov. Rick Perry, 2007. Office: US Maritime Literature Awards PO Box 250 Fulton TX 78358 Home Phone: 361-463-1684; Office Phone: 361-463-1684. Personal E-mail: maritimeliterature@yahoo.com.

LAMB, ROBERT ANDREW, molecular biologist, virologist, educator; b. London, Sept. 26, 1950; came to U.S., 1974; s. Robert Gordon and Margarita Evelyn (Todd) L.; m. Reay Gilmour Paterson, Mar. 4, 1989; children: Alexander, Duncan, Gabriella. PhD, U. Cambridge, Eng., 1974; ScD, U. Cambridge, 1991. Rsch. assoc., asst. prof., then assoc. prof. Rockefeller U., NYC, 1974-82; assoc. prof. Northwestern U., Evanston, Ill., 1983-86, prof., 1986-90, John Evans prof., biochemistry, molecular biology, cell biology, 1990—; investigator Howard Hughes Med. Inst., Evanston, 1991—. Adv. bd. Seminars in Virology, Acad. Press., 1989. Editor Jour. Virology, 1987-93; editor-in-chief Virology, 1994—; contbr. sci. papers to profl. jours. Fulbright Hays award, 1974-77; recipient Irma T. Hirschl career scientist award Am. Heart Assn., 1979-83, Wallace P. Rowe award NIH, 1990, Merit awards, 1987, 97. Fellow Am. Acad. Arts & Sci.; mem. Am. Soc. Biochemistry and Molecular Biology, Am. soc. Cell Biology, Am. Soc. Virology, Am.Soc. Microbiology, Nat. Acad. Sci. Office: Northwestern U Dept Biochemistry 2153 Sheridan Rd Evanston IL 60208-3500 Business E-Mail: ralamb@northwestern.edu.

LAMB, ROBERT BOYDEN, finance and management educator; b. Washington, June 19, 1941; s. Robert Keen Lamb and Helen Elizabeth (Boyden) Lamb Lamont; m. Rosemarie Lamb (div.); m. Nancy Axelrod, June 31, 1975; children: Corinna, Robert, Roland, Helena. BA, U. Chgo., 1963; PhD, London Sch. Econs., 1970; MBA, Columbia U., 1976. Asst. prof. Columbia U., NYC, 1971-75; spl. lectr. Wharton Sch., U. Pa., Phila., 1976-78; prof. fin. and mgmt. Stern Sch. Bus., NYU, 1978—. Dir. Middleby Corp., bond holders Commn. Group, assoc. editor Fortune mag., N.Y.C., 1976-77; bd. dirs. Eagle Clothes Corp., N.Y.C. Author 18 books on mcpl. bonds and mgmt.; editor-in-chief Jour. Bus. Strategy, 1980—. Founding mem. Starndard and Poors' Academic Counsel. Mem.: Century, N.Y. Athletic (N.Y.C.); Waccabuc Country (N.Y.). Democrat. Mem. Soc. Of Friends. Office: NYU Stern Sch Business KMC 7-53 44 W Fourth St New York NY 10012 Home: Parsons Field 8 Cantitoe St Katonah NY 10536 E-mail: rlamb@stern.nyu.edu.

LAMB, ROBERT EDWARD, retired diplomat, professional society administrator; b. Atlanta, Nov. 17, 1936; s. T. E. and Lois (Harris) Lamb; m. Lucille Trujillo, Jan. 13, 1962; children: Robert Edward, Anne Gretchen, Michael David. BA in Internat. Rels., U. Pa., 1962. Joined Fgn. Svc. Dept. State, Washington, 1963, dir. fin. services, 1975-77, dir. passport office, 1977-79; adminstrv. counsellor U.S. Embassy, Bonn, Germany, 1979-83; asst. sec. of state for adminstrn. Dept. State, Washington, 1983-85; asst. sec. of state Diplomatic Security, Washington, 1985-89; U.S. Amb. to Cyprus Cyprus, 1990-93; spl. Cyprus coord., 1993-94; exec. dir Am. Philatelic Soc., State Coll., Pa., 1994—2006, ret., 2006. Pub.: Index of American Philatelic Literature, 1999—2001. With USMC, 1958—61. Mem.: Am. Fgn. Svc. Assn. (governing bd. 1999—2001), Bellefonte C. of C. (b. dirs.). Home: 1340 Oak Ridge Ave State College PA 16801 Personal E-mail: belpa383@msn.com.

LAMB, SYDNEY MACDONALD, linguistics educator; b. Denver, May 4, 1929; s. Sydney Bishop and Jean Louisa (MacDonald) L.; m. Sharon Reese Rowell, June 17, 1956 (div. 1971); children: Christina, Sarah, Nancy; m. Susan Ellen Jones, May 15, 1977. BA, Yale U., New Haven, Conn., 1951; PhD, U. Calif., Berkeley, 1958. From asst. to assoc. prof. linguistics U. Calif., Berkeley, 1958-64; from assoc. to prof. Yale U., New Haven, 1964-77; mng. ptnr. Semionics Assocs., Houston, 1977-93; prof. Rice U., Houston, 1980—. Fellow Ctr. for Advanced Study in Behavioral Scis., Stanford, Calif., 1973-74. Author: Outline of Stratificational Grammar, 1966, (with others) Sprung from Some Common Source, 1991, Pathways of the Brain: The Neurocognitive Basis of Language, 1999, Language and Reality, 2004; inventor associative computer memory, 1977, 80, 4 patents; contbr. articles to profl. jours. NSF grantee, 1959-64, 66-70; Am. Council of Learned Soc. grantee, 1973-74. Mem. Linguistic Soc. Am. (exec. com. 1966-68), Linguistics Assn. of Can. and U.S. (pres. 1983-84, chmn. bd. dirs. 1995—), Houston Philos. Soc. (pres. 1992-93). Avocation: music. Office: Rice U Dept Linguistics Houston TX 77251 Business E-Mail: lamb@rice.edu.

LAMB, WALLY, writer; b. Norwich, Conn., Oct. 17, 1950; BA in Edn., U. Conn., 1972, MA in Edn., 1977; MFA in Writing, Vt. Coll., 1984. English tchr. Norwich (Conn.) Free Acad., 1972—88, writing ctr. dir., 1988—97; dir. creative writing U. Conn., 1997—99. Writer-in-residence Union Inst. & Univ., 2006. Author: (poetry textbook) Always Begin Where You Are, 1979, Couldn't Keep It to Myself: Testimonies from Our Imprisoned Sisters, 2003, (novels) She's Come Undone, 1992, I Know This Much Is True, 1998. Recipient Govs. Arts award, Conn., 1998, William Peden award, Mo. Rev. Office: c/o Darhansoff Verrill Feldman Lit Agys 226 W 26th St New York NY 10001

LAMB, WILLIAM H., lawyer, former state supreme court justice; b. Bryn Mawr, Pa., 1940; m. Patricia Kelly Lamb; children: Amanda, Joshua, Kate. BA (hon.), Duke U., 1962; JD (hon.), U. Pa., 1965. Bar: Pa. 1965, US Dist. Ct. (3d cir.) Pa. 1966, Superior Ct. Pa. 1968, US Tax Ct. 1972, US Ct. Appeals (3d cir.) 1966, US Supreme Ct. 1974. Law clk. to chief justice Pa. Supreme Ct., 1965-66; asst. dist. atty. Chester County, 1967-72, dist. atty., 1972-80; ptnr. Lamb McErlane P.C., West Chester, Pa., 1967—2003, chmn., 2004—; justice Pa. Supreme Ct., Pa., 2003—04; pres. judge Pa. Ct. Jud. Discipline, 2007—. Mem. Supreme Ct. Fund for Client Security; bd. dirs. Jefferson Bank, Downingtown, Pa. Solicitor Rep. Party Chester County, campaign chmn. 1966, exec. com.; campaign mgr. congressman John H. Ware, 1968; chmn. Chester County Reps., 1983-94; del. Rep. Nat. Conv., 1984, 88, 92; former chmn. Upper Main Line Young Reps.; former vice chmn. Chester County Fedn. Young Reps.; pres. Little People's Nursery Sch., Paoli, Pa.; past bd. dirs. Chester Valley Little League, Upper Main Line Red Cross; bd. dirs. St. Davids Ch. Nursery Sch., Devon, Pa., lay server St. David's Episcopal Ch., Devon; vice chmn., trustee bd. Alumni mgrs. Episc. Acad.; presdl. adv. com. arts Kennedy Ctr., 2004-; chmn. med. malpractice task force Pa. Supreme Ct., 2003-. Recipient Citizen of the Yr., Chester County Chamber of Bus. & Industry, 2003. Fellow Am. Coll. Trial Lawyers; mem. ABA, Pa. Bar Assn., Chester County Bar Assn., Pa. Bar Inst. (lectr.), Pa. Trial Lawyers Assn. (lectr.). Lodges: Lions. Office: Box 565 24 E Market St West Chester PA 19381-0565 Home Phone: 610-687-3344; Office Phone: 610-430-8000. Business E-Mail: wlamb@chescolaw.com.

LAMB, WILLIS EUGENE, JR., physicist, researcher; b. LA, July 12, 1913; s. Willis Eugene and Marie Helen (Metcalf) Lamb; m. Ursula Schaefer, June 5, 1939 (dec. Aug. 1996); m. Bruria Kaufman, Nov. 29, 1996. BS, U. Calif., 1934, PhD, 1938; DSc (hon.), U. Pa., 1953, Gustavus Adolphus Coll., 1975, Columbia U., 1990; MA, Oxford U., Eng., 1956; MA (hon.), Yale U., 1961; LHD (hon.), Yeshiva U., 1965; Dr.rer.nat. (hon.), U. Ulm., Germany, 1997. Mem. faculty Columbia U., 1938—52, prof. physics, 1948—52, Stanford U., 1951—56; Wykeham prof. physics and fellow New Coll., Oxford U., 1956—62; Henry Ford 2d prof. physics Yale U., 1962—72, J. Willard Gibbs prof. physics, 1972—74; prof. physics and optical scis. U. Ariz., Tucson, 1974—, Regents prof., 1990—2003, Regents prof. emeritus, 2003—; prof. emeritus Ariz. Rsch. Lab., 2003—, Optical Sci. Ctr. and Dept. Physics, 2003—. Morris Loeb lectr. Harvard U., 1953—54; Gordon Shrum lectr. Simon Fraser U., 1972; cons. Philips Labs., Bell Telephone Labs., Perkin-Elmer, NASA; vis. com. Brookhaven Nat. Lab. Recipient Rumford premium, Am. Acad. Arts and Scis., 1953, award, Rsch. Corp., 1954, (with P. Kusch) Nobel prize in Physics, 1955, Yeshiva award, 1962, Einstein Medal, Soc. for Optical & Quantum Electronics, 1992, Nat. medal of Sci., 2000, Gian Carlo Wick Gold Medal, World Fedn. of Scientists, 2002; fellow Guggenheim, 1960—61, sr. Alexander von Humboldt, 1992—94. Fellow: Royal Sci. Edinburgh, N.Y. Acad. Scis., Optical Soc. Am., Am. Phys. Soc., Inst. Physics and Phys. Soc. (hon. Guthrie lectr. 1958); mem.: NAS, Sigma Xi, Phi Beta Kappa. Achievements include discoveries concerning the fine structure of the hydrogen spectrum. Office: U Ariz Optical Scis Ctr Meinel Bldg 1630 E University Blvd Tucson AZ 85721-0094 E-mail: willis@primus.opt-sci.arizona.edu.

LAMBACHER, KATHLEEN HARTWELL, retired education educator; b. Muskegon, Mich., Aug. 7, 1935; d. Shattuck Wellman and Kathleen Beatrice; m. Allen Lambacher, 1981; children: Philippe Pezet, Anne-Marie Pezet Dorfner. BA in Edn., Wheaton Coll., Norton, Mass., 1957. Tchr. history Lincoln Sch., Providence, 1957—59; sub. tchr. Forest Hills Jr. HS, 1968—70; legal asst. Rankin Thompson Hine, Cleve., 1977—83; cons. Mary Kay Cosmetics, 1984—92; with Squires Constrn. Co., 1997—99; tchr.-trainer Chinese tchrs. English Shanghai, 2003, Fouling, 2004, Harbin, China, 2005; with English Language Inst. China. Co-dir. Le Cercle Francais d'Amerique, 1964—75; ESL New Sch. Social Rsch., NYC, 1969; translator Berlitz Schs. of Lang. of Am., Inc., Cleve., 1983. ESL tchr. to wives of diplomates UN, NYC, 1970—72, hospitality com., 1970—72; trustee E. Cleve. Civil War Cemetery, 2006—; moderator Diaconite First Presbyn. Soc., Cleve. Mem.: Philanthropic Ednl. Orgn. (chaplain), Hudson League Svc., French Heritage Soc. (chpt. v.p. 2005—), Soc. Mayflower Descendants, Wheaton Coll. Alumni Assn. (R.I. state pres. 1963—65), Nat. Soc. Colonial Dames Am. Ohio (mem. town com. Cleve. chpt.). Avocations: travel, kayaking, gardening, bridge, French and German languages. Home: 70 S Hayden Pkwy Hudson OH 44236 Personal E-mail: klambacher@windstream.net.

LAMBE, JAMES PATRICK, lawyer; b. Washington, June 4, 1952; s. John Joseph and Patricia Ann (Job) Lambe; m. Marie Barbara Giardino, May 21, 1977; children: Katherine Mary, Joseph Patrick. AB with distinction, U. Mich., 1974; JD, U. Ill., 1977. Bar: Calif. 1977, DC 1985, US Dist. Ct. (ea. dist.) Calif. 1977, US Dist. Ct. (ctrl. dist.) Calif. 1983, US Ct. Appeals (9th cir.) 1978, US Supreme Ct. 1981, cert.: State Bar Calif. Bd. Legal Specialization (specialist in criminal law), Nat. Bd. Trial Advocacy (specialist in criminal trial advocacy). Assoc. Wagner & Wagner, Fresno, Calif., 1978-79, Parichan, Renberg & Crossman, Fresno, 1979; claims atty. CIGNA Corp., Fresno, 1979-85; dep. city atty. Fresno City Atty's Office, 1985-86; def. atty. Fresno County Pub. Defender's Office, 1986—2005, sr. def. atty., 2005—. Judge pro tem Fresno County Superior Ct., 2000—; instr. Summer Trial Skills Inst., San Diego, 2001—. Author: Continuing Education of the Bar, University of California/State Bar of California, Oakland, 1998—; co-author: California Criminal Law Procedure and Practice, 1998—. Named to Super Lawyers, Law and Politics, 2006—. Mem.: Nat. Assn. Criminal Def. Lawyers, State Bar Calif. (conf. of dels. 1996—99, criminal law sect. exec. com. 2001—), Calif. Pub. Defenders Assn., Calif. Attys. for Criminal Justice (bd. govs. 2002—), D.C. Bar, Fresno County Bar Assn. (bd. dirs. 1998—99), Am. Mensa, Phi Alpha Delta. Democrat. Avocation: running. Office: Fresno County Pub Defenders Office 2220 Tulare St Ste 300 Fresno CA 93721-2130

LAMBERG-KARLOVSKY, CLIFFORD CHARLES, anthropologist, archaeologist; b. Prague, Czechoslovakia, Oct. 2, 1937; came to U.S., 1939; s. Carl Othmar von Lamberg and Bellina Karlovsky; m. Martha Louise Veale, Sept. 12, 1959; children: Karl Emil Othmar, Christopher William. AB, Dartmouth Coll., 1959; MA (Wenner-Gren fellow), U. Pa., 1964, PhD, 1965; MA (hon.), Harvard U., 1970; DS (hon.), Russian Acad. Scis., 2002. Asst. prof. sociology and anthropology Franklin and Marshall Coll., 1964-65; asst. prof. anthropology Harvard U., 1965-69, prof., 1969-90, Stephen Phillips prof. archaeology, 1991—; curator Near Eastern archaeology Peabody Museum Archaeology and Ethnology, 1969—, mus. dir., 1977-90. Assoc. Columbia U., 1969—; trustee Am. Inst. Iranian Studies, 1968-98, Am. Inst. Yemeni Studies, 1976-77; dir. rsch. Am. Sch. Prehist. Rsch., 1974-79, 94—, Centro di Richerche Ligabue, 1984; Reckitt archaeol. surveys in Syria, 1965, excavation projects at Tepe Yahya, Iran, 1967-75, Sarazm, Tadjikistan, USSR, 1985, archaeol. surveys in Saudi Arabia, 1977-80, USSR, 1990-91; dir. survey and excavations Anau, Turkmenistan, 1992-97; corr. fellow Inst. Medio and Extremo Orient, Italy; mem. UNESCO com. for sci. study of mankind, 1989-97. Author: (with J. Sabloff) Ancient Civilizations: The Near East and Mesoamerica, 1979; editor: (with J. Sabloff) The Rise and Fall of Civilizations, 1973, Ancient Civilizations and Trade, 1975, Hunters, Farmers and Civilization, 1979, Archaeological Thought in America, 1988, Beyond the Tigris and Euphrates, 1996; author, gen. editor: Tepe Yahya: The Early Periods, 1986, Tepe Yahta: The Third Millenium, 2004, Tepe Yahya, The Iron Age, 2005. Recipient medal Iran-Am. Soc., 1972; NSF grantee, 1966-75, 78-80, 93, Nat. Endowment for Arts grantee, 1977—, NEH grantee, 1977—. Fellow AAAS (chmn. USA/USSR archaeol. exch. program), Am. Acad. Arts and Scis., Soc. Antiquaries Gt. Britain and Ireland (sec. N.Am. chpt. 1985-93), Am. Anthrop. Assn., N.Y. Acad. Sci., USSR Acad. Sci., Soc. Am. Archaeology, Archeol. Inst. Am.; mem. German Archaeol. Inst., Danish Archaeol. Inst., Brit. Archaeol. Inst., Tavern Club (Boston). Office: Peabody Mus Archaeology & Ethnology 11 Divinity Ave Cambridge MA 02138-2019 Home Phone: 781-662-6958; Office Phone: 617-496-8162. Business E-Mail: karlovsk@fas.harvard.edu.

LAMBERS, JAMES VINCENT, mathematician, researcher, petroleum engineer; b. Andover, Mass., Sept. 21, 1969; s. Vincent William and Mary Iglehart Lambers; m. Dianna Lynn Foster, Sept. 18, 2004. BS in Math. and Computer Sci., Purdue U., West Lafayette, Ind, 1991; MS in Sci. Computing and Computational Math., Stanford U., Calif., 1994; PhD in Sci. Computing and Computational Math., Stanford, Calif., 2003. Instr.

math. Iowa State U., Ames, 1994—96; software engr. Inlet, Cedar Rapids, Iowa, 1996—97; sr. software engr. Site Technologies, Scotts Valley, Calif., 1997—99, Starbase Corp., Santa Ana, Calif., 1999—2002; lectr., rschr., math. U. Calif., Irvine, 2003—04; rsch. assoc. petroleum engring. Stanford U., 2005—06, acting asst. prof., energy resource engring., 2006—. Sci.-4000 scholar, Purdue U. Sch. Sci., 1987—91, Grad. Rsch. fellow, NSF, 1991—94. Mem.: Math. Assn. Am., Soc. Petroleum Engrs., Am. Math. Soc., Soc. Indsl. and Applied Math. Achievements include research in first algorithm for computing integrals over general 2-D domains; high-order spectral method for solving time-dependent variable-coefficient PDE that are explicit but unconditionally stable. Office: Stanford U 367 Panama St Rm 094 Stanford CA 94305-2220 Home Phone: 408-280-5645; Office Phone: 650-725-2729. Office Fax: 650-725-2099. Personal E-mail: jlambers@doctorj.net. Business E-Mail: lambers@stanford.edu.

LAMBERSON, JOHN ROGER, insurance company executive; b. Aurora, Mo., Aug. 16, 1933; s. John Oral Lamberson and Golda May (Caldwell) Tidwell; m. Virginia Lee, Aug. 10, 1957; 1 child, John Clinton. BA, U. Calif., Berkeley, 1954. Coach, tchr. Thousand Palms (Calif.) Sch., 1954-55; underwriter trainee Fireman's Fund Ins. Co., San Francisco, 1955; surety mgr. Safeco Ins. Co. (formerly Gen. Ins. Co.), San Francisco and Sacramento, Calif., 1957-61; pres., COO Willis Corroon Corp., NYC, 1966-92, also bd. dirs., chmn. constrn. industry div., mem. exec. com., aquisition com.; pres., chmn., CEO Lamberson Consulting LLC, San Francisco, 1992—. Bd. dirs. Willis Cornoon Group PLC, London, Consumers Benefit Life Ins. Co., Constrn. Inst., FMI Corp., Griffith Co., Webcor, Rosendin Electric, Sheedy Drayage Co., Valentine Corp. Mem. ASCE (bd. dirs. Construction Institute), Nat. Assn. Heavy Engring. Constructors (bd. dirs. 1985—, Golden Beavers award for outstanding svc. to industry), Constrn. Fin. Mgmt. Assn. (bd. dirs. 1987-91, exec. com.), Assoc. Gen. Contractors Am. (membership devel. com., past chmn. bd. dirs. nat. assoc. mems. coun.), Assoc. Gen. Contractors Calif. (bd. dirs. 1976), Nat. Acad. Constrn., Consulting Contractors Coun. Am., Bldg. Futures Coun. (bd. dirs.), Nat. Assn. Surety Bond Prodrs. (past nat. dir., regional v.p.), Am. Inst. Contractors, Soc. Am. Mil. Engrs., The Moles-Heavy Engring. Constrn. Soc., Young Pres. Orgn. (sem. leader), Bankers Club, Sharon Heights Golf and Country Club, Bermuda Dunes Country Club, Villa Taverna Club. Home: 85 Greenoaks Dr Atherton CA 94027-2160 Office: Lamberson Consulting LLC 580 California St Ste 500 San Francisco CA 94104-1000 Home Phone: 650-322-9641; Office Phone: 415-439-4822. E-mail: jrlamberson@mindspring.com.

LAMBERT, BRUCE, journalist; Reporter New York Times. Author: (articles) NY Called Unprepared on AIDS, 1988, Big Science Revs up for A Big Bang, 2001 (D-7 Dailies Sci. and Tech. award, Press Club of Long Island, 2001). Mem.: New York Press Club. Office: The New York Times 3000 Hempstead Tpke Ste 200 Levittown NY 11756-1409

LAMBERT, DANIEL MICHAEL, retired academic administrator; b. Kansas City, Mo., Jan. 16, 1941; s. Paul McKinley and Della Mae Lambert; m. Carolyn Faye Bright, Dec. 27, 1969; children: Kristian Paige, Dennis McKinley. AB, William Jewell Coll., 1963; MA, Northwestern U., 1965; postgrad., Harvard U., 1965-66; PhD, U. Mo., Columbia, 1977. Dean student affairs William Jewell Coll., Liberty, Mo., 1970-77, exec. asst. to pres., 1977-80, v.p., 1980-85; pres. College Hill Investments Inc., Liberty, 1985-87; prof. edn. Baker U., Baldwin City, Kans., pres., 1987—2006. Bd. dirs. Ferrell Co., Liberty; dir. Kansas City Bd. of Trade, 1988-90; hon. trustee Dohto U., Japan. Bd. dirs. Nat. Assn. Intercollegiate Athletics, The Barstow Sch., Kans. Ind. Colls. Assn.; trustee Midwest Rsch. Inst., Bishop Seabury Acad., Kans., Douglas County Cmty. Found., Kans. Capt. U.S. Army, 1966-70, Vietnam. Recipient Civic Leadership award Mo. Mcpl. League, 1986. Mem. Nat. Assn. Ind. Colls. and Univs. (bd. dirs.), KC. E-mail: dmlambert@bakeru.edu.

LAMBERT, DAVID L., astronomer, educator; BA in Physics, Univ. Coll., Oxford, Eng.; PhD in Astrophysics, Balliol Coll., Oxford, Eng., 1965. Rsch. fellow Calif. Inst. Tech., Pasadena, 1967—69, Mt. Wilson Palomar Observatories; faculty assoc. dept. astronomy U. Tex., Austin, 1969—70, assoc. prof., 1970—74, prof. Austin, 1974—, Isabel McCutcheon Harte Centennial prof., 1983—87, Isabel McCutcheon Harte Centennial chair, 1987—, assoc. dir. McDonald Obs., 1989—90, dir. McDonald Obs., 1990—. Guggenheim fellow, vis. Erskine fellow U. Canterbury, New Zealand, 1985. Fellow Royal Astron. Soc.; mem. Am. Astron. Soc. (Dannie Heineman Prize for Astrophysics, 1987, Henry Norris Russell Lectureship, 2007), Internat. Astron. Union. Office: U Tex Austin Dept Astronomy Austin TX 78712-1083 Office Phone: 512-471-7438. Office Fax: 512-471-6016. E-mail: dll@astro.as.utexas.edu.*

LAMBERT, ETHEL GIBSON CLARK, secondary school educator; b. Atlanta, Apr. 18, 1943; d. Robert Harold and Ethel (Gibson) Clark; m. Hugh Felder Lambert, June 27, 1964 (div. Nov. 3, 1988); children: Courtney, Elizabeth, Hugh Jr. BA, Oglethorpe U., Atlanta, 1965; MEd, Kennesaw State U., Marietta, Ga., 1992; EdS, State U. West Ga., Carrollton, 1997. Lic. tchr. T-6 Ga. Tchr. Clayton County Bd. Edn., Jonesboro, Ga., 1965-66, tchr. remedial edn. program Riverdale HS, 1990—2004; tchr. English spkrs. of other langs. Babb Mid. Sch., 2004—05, Sequoyah Mid. Sch., Jonesboro, Ga., 2005—; tchr. English to spkrs. of other langs. McGarrah Elem. Sch. and Huie Elem. Sch., Forest Park, Ga., 2006—; tchr. Fulton County Bd. Edn., Atlanta, 1966—67; tchr. pre-sch. weekday program First Bapt. Ch., Gainesville, Ga., 1984-88. Author: The Impact of Geography on the Campaigns of the Civil War Fought in Georgia, 1993, The Utilization of Georgia Historical Sites as Teaching Methodology in Middle Grades Education, 1993, Obnoxious Bill, 1993, Research on Academic Motivation of Elementary, Middle and Secondary School Students in America, 1993, Reading Strategies that Address the Reluctant Reader in America's Public Middle and High Schools, 1995, Mathematics: Tying Together the World of School and the World of Work, 1996, A Martin Family History: An Interview of Aunt Clyde: "I Look Back...", 1999. Den leader Cub Scouts Am., Gainesville, 1980—83; mem. Christian Businessmen's Prayer Breakfast, Atlanta, 1990—95, 1996. Mem.: Ga. Assn. of Educators, College Park Hist. Soc., College Park Women's Club, Order Eastern Star, Pi Lambda Theta. Baptist. Avocations: swimming, water-skiing, reading, walking, genealogy. Home: 1881 Myrtle Dr SW Apt 711 Atlanta GA 30311-4919 Office: Huie Elem Sch 1260 Rock Cut Rd Forest Park GA 30297 Business E-Mail: elambert@clayton.k12.ga.us.

LAMBERT, FREDERICK WILLIAM, lawyer, educator; b. Millburn, NJ, Feb. 12, 1943; m. Barbara E. Fogell, Aug. 13, 1965; children: Elisabeth, Mark. BA, U. Mich., 1965, JD, 1969. Bar: Ohio 1969, Fla. 1973, Calif. 1973, U.S. Supreme Ct. 1975. Law clk. to Stanley N. Barnes, U.S. Cir. Judge U.S. Cir. Ct., LA, 1969-70; atty. advisor Office Legal Counsel U.S. Dept. Justice, Washington, 1970-71; law clk. to Justice William H. Rehnquist U.S. Supreme Ct., Washington, 1971-72; pvt. practice LA, 1973-90; acting gen. counsel Itel Corp., San Francisco, 1981-82; ptnr. Adams, Duque & Hazeltine, LA, 1985-90, chmn. bus. law dept., 1989-90; assoc. prof. Hastings Coll. Law, U. Calif., San Francisco, 1993-99, prof. law, 1999—. Vis. prof. U. Mich. Law Sch., Ann Arbor, 1990-91, Duke Law Sch., Durham, N.C., 1992-93, U. Leiden; bd. faculty advisors William H. Rehnquist Found., 2007—. Mem. Am. Law Inst., Am. Law and Econs. Assn., Econ. Round Table of LA, Calif. State Bar Assn Home: 1100 Pilarcitos Ave Half Moon Bay CA 94019-1459

LAMBERT, GEORGE H., physician, director; MD, U. Ill., 1972. Diplomate in pediats. and neonatal-perinatal medicine Am. Bd. Pediatrics. Intern Johns Hopkins Hosp., Balt., 1972—73, resident in pediats., 1973—74; rsch. assoc. molecular teratology NIH, Bethesda, 1974—76; fellow in neonatal pharmacology Children's Hosp. Phila., 1976—77; physician dept. pediats. Robert Wood Johnson Med. Sch., New Brunswick, NJ, 1987—; dir. divsn. pediat. pharmacology and toxicology EPA/NIH; dir. NIH Ctr. Childhood Neurotoxicology and Exposure Assessment Rutgers U., 2001—, Robert Wood Johnson Med. Sch., 2001—. Assoc. prof. pediatrics Robert Wood Johnson U. Hosp., New Brunswick, NJ, 1984—. Achievements include patents in field. Office Phone: 732-235-9710. E-mail: glambert@umdnj.edu.

LAMBERT, GEORGE ROBERT, lawyer, realtor; b. Muncie, Ind., Feb. 21, 1933; s. George Russell and Velma Lou (Jones) L.; m. Mary Virginia Alling, June 16, 1956; children: Robert Allen, Ann Holt, James William. BS, Ind. U., Bloomington, 1955; JD, Chgo.-Kent Coll. Law, 1962. Bar: Ill. 1962, U.S. Dist. Ct. (no. dist.) Ill. 1962, Iowa 1984, Pa. 1988, Ind. 1999. V.p., gen. counsel, sec. Washington Nat. Ins. Co., Evanston, Ill., 1970-82; v.p., gen. counsel Washington Nat. Corp., Evanston, 1979-82; sr. v.p., sec., gen. counsel Life Investors Inc., Cedar Rapids, Iowa, 1982-88; v.p., gen. counsel Provident Mut. Life Ins. Co., Phila., 1988-95; pres. Lambert Legal Consulting, Inc., Wilmington, Del., 1995—2002; realtor Coldwell Banker, North Palm Beach, Fla., 1996—2001, Cressy and Everett GMAC Real Estate, South Bend, Ind., 1999-2000; ind. real estate broker Granger, Ind., 2001—03; realtor Martinique II Realty Inc., Port St. Lucie, Fla., 2002—; ind. real estate broker Bloomington, Ind., 2004—. Alderman Evanston (Ill.) City Coun., 1980-82; mem. bd. edn. Lake Bluff (Ill.) Elementary Sch. Dist., 1970-71. Lt. USAF, 1955-57. Mem.: Assn. of Life Ins. Counsel (past pres.). Home: 7958 Poppy Hills Ln Port Saint Lucie FL 34986 Home (Summer): 9411 Harbour Pointe Dr Bloomington IN 47401 Personal E-mail: glamb10100@aol.com.

LAMBERT, JEFFREY SCOTT, secondary school educator; b. Albuquerque, Dec. 5, 1953; s. Richard Ellis and Barbara Anne Lambert; m. Anne L. Boulden, June 9, 1976; children: Megan Christine, Patrick Christopher. BS, US Naval Acad., Annapolis, Md., 1976. Lic. secondary tchr. N.Mex, 1996. Commd. ensign US Naval Acad., Annapolis, Md., 1976; with USS Mitscher DDG-35, USS John Rodgers DD-983, USS Nicholson DD-982, Surfaces Warfare Schs. Command, USS Sterett CG-17, Carrier Group Four, Mil. Liaison Group Caracas, 1976—96; ret.; tchr. chemistry, advanced placement chemistry. environ. sci. Rio Grande HS, 1997—2003; tchr. algebra and pre-algebra Truman Middle Sch., Albuquerque, 2003—. Author: (novels) Thief by Moonlight, 2001, Magic's Logic, 2002. Coach US Swimming Assn., Albuquerque, 1997—2002; commr. Albuquerque Mid. Sch. Soccer League, 2004—; owner therapy dog SW Canine Corp Vols., Albuquerque, 2004—06. Nominee Sandia Labs Sci. Tchr. of Yr., Sandia Nat. Labs., 2003; named Tchr. of Yr., Troops to Tchrs. SW Region, 2006. Mem.: N.Mex HS Coaches Assn., Nat. Coun. Tchrs. Math. Avocation: soccer. Home: 525 2nd St SW Rio Rancho NM 87124 Office: Albuquerque Public Schools 725 University Blvd SW Albuquerque NM 87106 Home Phone: 505-896-6607; Office Phone: 505-842-8211. Personal E-mail: jefflambert@cableone.net.

LAMBERT, JEREMIAH DANIEL, lawyer, educator; b. NYC, Sept. 11, 1934; s. Noah D. and Clara (Ravage) L.; m. Vicki Anne Asher, July 25, 1959 (div.); children: Nicole Stirling, Alix Stewart, Leigh Asher; m. Sanda Kayden, Dec. 3, 1983; children: Clare Kayden, Hilary Kayden. AB magna cum laude, Princeton U., 1955; LL.B., Yale U., 1959. Bar: N.Y. 1960, D.C. 1964, U.S. Ct. Appeals (5th cir.) 1964, U.S. Supreme Ct. 1964. Assoc. Cravath, Swaine & Moore, NYC, 1959-63; sr. ptnr. Peabody, Lambert & Meyers, Washington, 1969-84; ptnr. Shook, Hardy & Bacon, Washington, 1997—2002; co-chmn. bd. dirs. Global Crossing, Ltd., 2002—03, mem. exec. com., 2003—; chmn. bd. dirs. Asia Global Crossing, Ltd., 2002—03; founder, ptnr. Lambert & Ihm LLP, Washington, 2006—. Adj. prof. law Georgetown U., Washington, 1978-79; trustee Internat. Law Inst., Washington, 1983-88; mem. adv. com. on Electricity Futures Contracts, N.Y. Merc. Exch., 1994-95; mem. bd. editors Yale Law Jour., 1958-59. Author: Creating Competitive Markets: The PJM Model, 2001, Energy Companies and Market Reform: How Deregulation Went Wrong, 2006; author, editor (with Fereidun Fesharaki): Economic and Political Incentives to Petroleum Development, 1990; co-author (with Lawrence White): Handbook of Modern Construction Law, 1982; mem. editl. adv. bd., contbr. The Impact of Competition, 2000; contbr. articles to legal publs. 1st lt. USAR, 1963-66. Fulbright scholar U. Copenhagen, 1955-56. Mem. ABA, Am. Soc. Internat. Law, D.C Bar Assn., Assn. Bar City N.Y., Cosmos Club, Princeton Club, Yale Club, Chevy Chase Club, Nassau Club, Phi Beta Kappa. Office: Lambert & Ihm LLP 1350 I St NW Ste 510 Washington DC 20005 Home Phone: 202-332-3366; Office Phone: 202-747-0502. Business E-Mail: jlambert@lambertihm.com.

LAMBERT, JOHN BOYD, chemical engineer, consultant; b. Billings, Mont., July 5, 1929; s. Jean Arthur and Gail (Boyd) L.; m. Jean Wilson Bullard, June 20, 1953 (dec. 1958); children: William, Thomas, Patricia, Cathy, Karen; m. Ilse Crager, Sept. 20, 1980 (dec. 1995). BS in Engring., Princeton U., 1951; PhD, U. Wis., 1956. Rsch. engr. E.I. DuPont de Nemours Co., Wilmington, Del., 1956-69; sr. rsch. engr. Fansteel, Inc., Balt., 1969, mktg. mgr., plant mgr. North Chicago, Ill., 1970-73, mgr. mfg. engring. Waukegan, Ill., 1974-80, corp. tech. dir. North Chicago, 1980-86, gen. mgr. metals, 1987-90, v.p., corp. tech. dir., 1990-91. IESC vol., Brazil, 1995; ind. cons., Lake Forest, Ill., 1991—. Contbr. articles to profl. jours. Recipient Charles Hatchett medal Inst. Metals, London, 1986. Mem. AIChE, Am. Chem. Soc., Am. Soc. Metals, Sigma Xi. Episcopalian. Achievements include patents in field of dispersion-strengthened metals, refractory metals, chemical vapor deposition, both products and processes. Home and Office: 617 Greenbriar Ln Lake Forest IL 60045-3214 Home Phone: 847-234-7645; Office Phone: 847-234-7645. Office Fax: 847-234-7649. Personal E-mail: drjbl@aol.com.

LAMBERT, JOHN WALTON, music educator; s. James Alfred and Samaria Mercedes Lambert. B in Music Edn., Troy State U., Ala., 1973. Cert. tchr. Ala. Band dir. Dallas County HS, Plantersville, Ala., 1973—75, Escambia County Middle Sch., Atmore, 1976—77, Escambia County HS, Atmore, 1977—2000, Monroe Acad., Monroeville, 2001—05, Flomaton (Ala.) HS, 2005—. Freelance band dir., cons., 1993—; mem. Music Educators Nat. Conf., 1973—. Author: (textbook) Selection Committee, 2006. Mem. Atmore Fine Arts Coun., 1996—2000. Staff sgt. Nat. Guard US Army, 1975—2002. Recipient Army Achievement medal, Army Nat. Guard, 1990, 1992. Mem.: Phi Mu Alpha (pres. 1973). Avocations: nature, history.

LAMBERT, JOSEPH BUCKLEY, chemistry professor; b. Ft. Sheridan, Ill., July 4, 1940; s. Joseph Idus and Elizabeth Dorothy (Kirwan) L.; m. Mary Wakefield Pulliam, June 27, 1967; children: Laura Kirwan, Alice Pulliam, Joseph Cannon. BS, Yale U., 1962; PhD (Woodrow Wilson fellow 1962-63, NSF fellow 1962-65), Calif. Inst. Tech., 1965. Asst. prof. chemistry Northwestern U., Evanston, Ill., 1965-69, assoc. prof., 1969-74, prof. chemistry, 1974-91, Clare Hamilton Hall prof. chemistry, 1991—, Charles Deering McCormick prof., 1999—2002, chmn. dept., 1986-89, dir. integrated sci. program, 1982-85. Vis. assoc. Brit. Mus., 1973, Polish Acad. Scis., 1981, Chinese Acad. Scis., 1988. Author: Organic Structural Analysis, 1976, Physical Organic Chemistry through Solved Problems, 1978, The Multinuclear Approach to NMR Spectroscopy, 1983, Archaeological Chemistry III, 1984, Introduction to Organic Spectroscopy, 1987, Recent Advances in Organic NMR Spectroscopy, 1987, Acyclic Organonitrogen Stereodynamics, 1992, Cyclic Organonitrogen Stereodynamics, 1992, Prehistoric Human Bone, 1993, Traces of the Past, 1997, Organic Structural Spectroscopy, 1998, Nuclear Magnetic Resonance Spectroscopy, 2004; audio course Intermediate NMR Spectroscopy, 1973; editor in chief Journal of Physical Organic Chemistry; contbr. articles to sci. jours. Recipient Nat. Fresenius award, 1976, James Flack Norris award, 1987, Fryxell award, 1989, Nat. Catalyst award, 1993, Mosher award, 2003; Alfred P. Sloan fellow, 1968-70, Guggenheim fellow, 1973, Interacad. exch. fellow (U.S.-Poland), 1985, Air Force Office sci. rsch. fellow, 1990. Fellow AAAS, Japan Soc. for Promotion of Sci., Brit. Interplanetary Soc., Ill. Acad. Sci. (life); mem. Am. Chem. Soc. (chmn. history of chemistry divsn., 1996, F.S. Kipping award 1998, S.M. Edelstein award 2004), Royal Soc. Chemistry, Soc. Archaeol. Scis. (pres. 1986-87), Phi Beta Kappa, Sigma Xi (hon. lectr. 1997-98). Home: 1956 Linneman St Glenview IL 60025-4264 Office: Northwestern University Dept of Chemistry 2145 Sheridan Rd Evanston IL 60208-3113 Office Phone: 847-491-5437.

LAMBERT, JOSEPH EARL, state supreme court chief justice; b. Berea, Ky., May 23, 1948; s. James Wheeler and Ruth (Hilton) L.; m. Debra Hembree, June 25, 1983; children: Joseph Patrick, John Ryan. BS in Bus. and Econs., Georgetown Coll., 1970; JD, U. Louisville, 1974; PhD (hon.), Eastern Ky. U., 1999, Georgetown Coll., 1999, Northern Ky. U., 2002. Bar: Ky. 1974. Staff mem. to Sen. John Sherman Cooper U.S. Senate, Washington, 1970-71; law clk. to judge Rhodes Bratcher U.S. Dist. Ct., Louisville, 1974-75; ptnr. Lambert & Lambert, Mt. Vernon, Ky., 1975-87; justice Supreme Ct. Ky., Frankfort, 1987-98, chief justice, 1998—. Chmn. Appellate Rules Commn., 1989-91, Civil Rules Com., 1991-93, Criminal Rules Com., 1996-97, Jud. Form Retirement Commn., 1996-; mem. bd. directors Ctr. for Rural Devel., 1996-, Nat. Assn. Drug Ct. Professionals, 2001-, Conference of Chief Justices, 2001-03. Mem. Bd. Regents Eastern Ky. U., Richmond, 1988-92. Recipient Disting. Alumni award U. Louisville Sch. Law, 1988; named Outstanding Judge of Ky., 2000, Leadership award Nat. Assn. Drug Ct. Professionals, Ky. Public Advocate award, 2001. Fellow: Ky. Bar Foundation; mem.: ABA, Ky. Bar Assn. Republican. Baptist. Office: Ky Supreme Ct Rm 231 700 Capitol Ave Frankfort KY 40601 Business E-Mail: cjlambert@kycourts.net.*

LAMBERT, KIRSTEN SCHNOOR, public relations executive, writer; b. Chgo., Dec. 26, 1963; d. Walter Karl and Irmgard Schnoor; m. Christopher Jay Lambert, May 25, 1996; children: Evan, Noah. BA in Liberal Arts, DePaul U., 1995. Editl. and prodn. asst. Kraft Inc., Glenview, Ill., 1986-89; comm. assoc. Budget Rent A Car, Chgo., 1989-91; spl. events asst. Chgo. Sun-Times, 1992-94; editl. asst. Chgo. Reader, 1994-95; freelancer DonTech Corp., Chgo., 1995-96; comm. mgr. The Sherwood Group, Inc., Northbrook, Ill., 1996-00; mktg. and comm. mgr. Am. Orthopaedic Assn., Rosemont, Ill., 2000—02; pres. Watermark Comm., Chgo., 2002—. Author: Chicago '96 Democratic National Convention Visitors' Guide, 1996; editor newsletter Interactions, 1999 (Circle of Excellence award Am. Soc. Assn. Execs, 1999). Support mgr. Howard Brown Meml. Clinic, Chgo., 1987-91. Mem. Internat. Assn. Bus. Communicators (chpt. membership com. 1989-91). Avocations: writing, music, dance. Office Phone: 773-472-1969. Business E-Mail: kirsten@watermark-communications.com.

LAMBERT, LANNEAU WILLIAM, JR., lawyer; AB cum laude, Duke U., 1978; JD, U. SC, 1981. Bar: SC, US Dist. Ct. (Dist. SC), US Ct. Appeals (4th Cir.). Law clk. to Dan F. Laney Jr. SC Cir. Ct.; in-house counsel to real estate devel. and mortgage banking co.; atty. Turner Padget Graham & Laney PA, Columbia, SC, 1986—, mng. shareholder. Mem. Leadership Columbia, 1986; bd. dirs. Greater Columbia C. of C., exec. com., 1998—99. Recipient Compleat Lawyer award, U. SC Sch. Law Alumni Assn., 1992. Mem.: ABA (exec. coun. young lawyers divsn. 1990—92, chmn. house of delegates 2002—04, bd. gov. 1989—90, 1997—2000, 2002—, pres. young lawyers divsn. 1988—89), Richland County Bar Assn., Southeastern Adv. Bd. Mng. Partners Forum, SC Bar Assn. (sec. 2004—05, treas. 2005—06, peres.-elect 2006—07). Office: Turner Padget Graham & Laney PA PO Box 1473 Columbia SC 29202 Office Phone: 803-227-4248. Office Fax: 803-400-1503. E-mail: llambert@turnerpadget.com.

LAMBERT, LECLAIR GRIER, writer, lecturer, consultant, former state government public information administrator; b. Miami, Fla. s. George F. and Maggie (Grier) L. BS, Hampton Inst., Va., 1959; postgrad., Harvard U., Cambridge, Mass., 1959, U. Munich, 1965—66. Rschr., copy reader Time-Life Books, 1961-64; tchr. biology and Eng. lit., secondary level U.S. Dependent's Schs. Overseas, Tripoli, Libya, 1964-65; biology editor H.S. textbooks Holt, Rinehart & Winston, NYC, 1966-69; biology editor and writer Ency. Britannica, NYC, 1969; copy editor Russian sci. monographs The Faraday Press, NYC, 1970-71; writer Med. World News, NYC, 1971; pub. rels. writer Nat. Found./March of Dimes, White Plains, N.Y., 1972. Lectr. cmty. and human rels. Black Cultural heritage at local schs. and colls., 1977-87; guest lectr. Liberty Sq. (Fla.) 50th Anniversary, 1986, Black History Month Minn. Ho. of Reps., 1987-96, creator and coord. student spkr. Ho. of Reps. Youth Forum, 1992; radio commentator Sta. KEEY, 1975-80; reporter Twin Cities Courier, Mpls., 1976-86. Author: Reflections of Life--Poems, Prose and Essays, 1981, A Learning Journey Through Black History, 1982; editor, writer: Minnesota's Black Community, 1977; editor: Art in Development: A Nigerian Perspective, 1983; freelance writer, 1974—; contbr. articles to profl. jours. Dir. comm. St. Paul Urban League, 1972-80, asst. to exec. dir., 1985-86, bd. dirs., 1992—, sec. bd., 1999-2005, chair, 2006—, co-chair 75th and 80th Anniversary Celebrations; adv. bd. Archie Givens Found. for African Am. Lit. Rare Books Collection, U. Minn., 1988-2005, hon. bd., 2005-; exec. dir. African Am. Mus. Art and History, 1980-86; info. officer Mpls. Urban League, 1978-79; co-founder, bd. dirs. Summit-U. Free Press, 1974-79, U. Minn. Black Learning Resource Ctr., 1980-83; past mem. Roy Wilkins Meml. Com. Civic Ctr., St. Paul, 1985; state meml. com. Martin Luther King Celebration Com., 1987-96; mem. Ethiopian Famine Relief Com.; rev. com. Twin Cities Mayors' Pub. Art Awards, 1981; co-founder W. Suburban Annual Black History Month Celebration Com., 1983-86; mem. St. Paul Civic Ctr. Authority Bd., 1985-97, vice chair, 1991-97, bd. rep. pub. art, bldg. expansion com., bd. rep. Am.'s Smithsonian exhbn.; mem. St. Paul City Art Plan Com., 1987-88, Minn. Mus. Am. Art orgn. exhibits plan coms., 1989-91, trustee, 1991-96, v.p., 1992-93, pres., 1993-94, chair, 1994-95; adv. bd. YMCA Youth in Govt., 1997-2003; sgt-at-arms, officer Minn. Ho. of Reps., 1987-96, coord. ednl. programs, cultural diversity tng. task force, 1992-93, dir. pub. info., 1996-2003; pub. weekly column Reflections, Session Weekly; trustee Coll. Visual Arts, governance com., 1997-2006; mem. St. Paul-Mpls. com. on fgn. rels., 1998-2000; cons. ARD/USAID staff tng. Palestinian Legis. Coun., Curr. tng. plan for Birzeit U., West Bank, 1997; bd. dirs. Minn. Landmarks, 2001-2002; commr., St. Paul Human Rights Commn., 1999—2004; bd. dirs. St. Paul Visitors and Conv. Bur., 1990-93; sr. legis. cons., pub. info. and rels., Afghanistan Parliment, Kabul, 2007; internat. advisor leadership implementation workshop, New Delhi, 2007. 1st lt., Chem. Corps., U.S. Army, 1959-61. Recipient Cmty. Martin Luther King Comm. award, 1978, Spl. Recognition award Mpls. St. Acad., 1983, Spl. Achievement award Roosevelt H.S., 1985, Spl. Recognition award Twin Cities African Am. Mus., 1985, Liberty Sq. Tenants' Spl. Recognition award, 1986, Vol. Svc. award St. Paul Urban League, 1988, Spl. Recognition award Palestine Journalists Assn., 1997, Outstanding Achievement award Minn. Coun. Black Minnesotans, 2003, Info. Staff award Nat. Conf. State Legislatures, 2003, Hubert H. Humphrey Inst. Internat. Fellows award, 1998, 2000, Spl. Recognition award, Minn. Ho. of Reps., 2003; named Nat. Outstanding Info. and Media Staff Mem., Nat. Conf. State Legislatures, 2003; LeClair Lambert Day proclaimed by City of St. Paul, 1997. Mem. Pub. Rels. Soc. Am., African-Am. Mus. Assn. (mem. nat. legis. edn. com. 1983, exec. coun., Midwest region rep. 1984-89, Achievement award 1985). Home Phone: 651-647-9508; Office Phone: 651-647-9508.

LAMBERT, LLOYD LAVERNE, minister; b. Augusta, Ill., June 5, 1925; s. Charles N. Sr. and Lena (Johnson) L.; m. Dorothy Mae Spaar, June 22, 1946; children: Rebecca, Toby, Michael, Corey. Student, Millikin U., 1948-49, Anderson U., Ind., 1953-54, student, 1956-57. Ordained to ministry Ch. of God (Anderson, Ind.), 1955. Founder, exec. dir. The Christian Ctr., Anderson, 1956—. Chaplain Madison County Detention Ctr. Bd. dirs. Habitat for Humanity, Anderson, Recovery in Christ, Sowers of Seeds, Inc., Counselors for Alcohol and Other Drug Abuses; past chmn. Nursing Home Ministries; past pres. Madison County Svcs. Coun.; past dep. sheriff Madison County Sheriff's Dept.; mem. adv. bd. for drug abuse St. John's Hosp.; chmn. Human Rels. Commn., City of Anderson, 1981-84; founder Home for Alcoholics, Anderson. With F.A., U.S. Army, 1943-46; PTO. Recipient spl. recognition Exchange Club Anderson, 1971, recognition Ind. Dept. Corrections, 1972, Liberty Bell award ABA, 1973; Outstanding Citizenship award Ind. Elks, 1973-74, Svc. to Mankind award Sertoma Club, 1980, 98, 99, Chief Anderson award, 1986, Elmo A. Funk Ideal of Svc. award, 1990, Anderson/Madison County Homeless Task Force award, 2003; named as one of top people of the century Anderson Newspaper and Madison County, 1999, Sagamore of the Wabash Gov. State Ind. Frank O'Bannon; Rev. Lloyd Lambert Homeless Svc. award named in his honor. Mem. Anderson Ministerial Assn., Internat. Union Gospel Missions (past pres., sec.-treas. midwestern dist.), Rotary (past sargeant-at-arms and sec., pres. Anderson club 1975-76, Community Image award 1973, 80, Internat. Paul Harris fellow 1983). Home: 603 Main St Anderson IN 46016 Office: The Christian Ctr 625 Main St PO Box 743 Anderson IN 46015-0743

LAMBERT, LYN DEE, law librarian; b. Fitchburg, Mass., Jan. 5, 1954; m. Paul Frederick Lambert, Aug. 11, 1979; children: Gregory John, Emily Jayne, Nicholas James. BA in History, Fitchburg State Coll., 1976, MEd in History, 1979; JD, Franklin Pierce Law Ct., 1983; MLS, Simmons Coll., 1986. Law libr. Fitchburg Law Libr., Mass. Trial Ct., 1985-96; media specialist libr. Samoset Sch., Leominster, Mass., 1996—. Instr. paralegal studies courses Fisher Coll., Fitchburg, 1989-94, Anna Maria Coll., Paxton, Mass., 1995—, Atlantic Union Coll., Lancaster, Mass., 1995—, pre-law coll. courses Fitchburg State Coll., 1995—; tech. com. City of Leominster Shc., Net Day Participant and trainer/leader, Leominster H.S., Northwest, Johnny Appleseed, Fall Brook, Southeast and Samoset. Mem. Am. Legion Band, Fitchburg, 1959—, Westminster (Mass.) Town Band, 1965—, Townsend Town Band, 1999—; appt. to Mass. Strategic Plan Com. for delivery of libr. svcs. among multi-type librs. within the commonwealth; mem. Patrick S. Gilmore Cmty. Honor Band, Hatch Shell, Boston, 2000—02; mem. cmty. theatre Theatre at the Mount, Mount Wachusett Cmty. Coll., Gardner, Mass., 2002—; mem. cmty. theatre Theatre at the Mount Greater Gardner Cmty. Choir, 2004—. Recipient Community Leadership award Xi Psi chpt. Kappa Delta Pi-Fitchburg State Coll. chpt., 1993. Mem. ALA, Am. Assn. Law Librarians (copyright com. 1987-89, publs. rev. com. 1990-92, state, ct. and county law librs. spl. interest sect. publicity com. 1993—), Law Librarians New Eng. (conf. com. 1988), Mass. Libr. Assn. (edn. chair 1991-93, freedom of info. com., legislation com.), Mass. Computer Using Educators, Mass. Sch. Media Libr. Assn., New Eng. Libr. Assn., New Eng. Microcomputer Users Group (profl. assoc.), North Cen. Mass. Libr. Alliance (newsletter editor 1990—), Spl. Libr. Assn., Beta Phi Mu, Phi Alpha Delta, Phi Delta Kappa (newsletter editor Montachusett chpt. 1998-2000, pres. Montachusett chpt. 2000-02). Avocations: singing, guitar, clarinet, hiking, camping. Office: Samoset Libr Media Ctr 100 DeCicco Dr Leominster MA 01453-5161 Home Phone: 978-874-0359.

LAMBERT, MARIANNE T., retired elementary school educator; d. Roger and Ruth (Kustush) Lambert. BS in physical edn., So. Ill. U., 1980, MS in physical edn., motor learning and control, 1989. Cert. P.E. Elem. & Secondary, English as a Second Lang., first aid instr., HIV/AIDS instr. Advanced through grades to PN2 USN, 1969—80, ret., 2005; sales Fuller Brush, Berkeley, Ill., 1967; keypunch operator, verifier,teletype operator, receptionist Montgomery Ward, Berkeley, Ill., 1967; keypunch operator Jewell Food Co., Melrose Pk., Ill., 1968—69; pitter, sorter Libby and McNeil Food Co., Selma, Calif., 1969; machinist McCullough Chain Saws, Lake Havasu City, Ariz., 1969; seam, recruit transfers divsn. Bainbridge (Md.) Naval Tng. Ctr. USN, 1970, record's vault clerk Naval Tng. Ctr., 1971, chaplain's asst. Naval Tng. Ctr., 1971, master at arms, security clerk Naval Tng. Ctr., 1971—72, detailer Bur. of Naval Personnel Arlington, Va., 1972—74, various positions Bur. of Naval Personnel, 1972—76, congressional dept. HQ Navy Recruiting Commd., 1974—76; sec., receptionist J. Hugh Shelnutt, CPA, Carbondale, Ill., 1976—77; tchr. So. Ill. U., Carbondale, 1978, photographer Ctr. for Electron Microscopy, 1979, sec. Dept. Analytical Chemistry, 1979; basketball coach Unity Point Sch. Dist. #140, Carbondale, 1979—90, bus driver, 1979—2005, physical edn., health educator, track coach, 1980—99, physical edn., health educator, 2000—01, ESL tchr., 2001—02, health educator, 2002—03, physical edn. tchr., 2004—05, ret., 2005. Pres., southern dist. IAHPER, Ill., 1977—79; com. mem. Ill. Heart Assn., 1978—81; health and safety dir. Am. Red Cross, Carbondale, Ill., 1990—92; track and field athlete St. Domitilla's Sch., Hillside, Ill., 1963—64; tennis player Naval Tng. Ctr. USN, Bainbridge, 1971—72, umpire, judge, official various sports, 1971—72, 1977—85. Author: Bible Study Methods, 2007, Godliness with Contentment is a Great Gain, 1989. Missionary Erling Gospel Ctr., Taiwan, 2005—; tchr. Bread of Life Seminary, Kaohsiung, Taiwan, 2005—06; missionary pastor Erling Gospel Internat. Fellowship, 2006—. Mem.: Am. Red Cross. Avocations: chess, travel, cooking, ping pong/table tennis. Office: Erling Gospel Ctr 381 Hanmin Rd 10F Hsiaokang Dist Kaohsiung Taiwan Home: 84 KanJuang Rd 5F HsiaoKang Dist Kaohsiung Taiwan Personal E-mail: xiaoyangjer2911@yahoo.com.

LAMBERT, MIRANDA, vocalist; b. Lindale, Tex., Nov. 10, 1983; d. Rick Lambert and Bev. Mem. Tex. Pride Band; solo singer & performer, 2001—. Contestant (TV series) Nashville Star, 2003 (3rd-place winner); singer: (albums) Miranda Lambert, 2001, Kerosene, 2005, Crazy Ex-Girlfriend, 2007. Recipient Cover Girl Fresh Face of Country Music award, Acad. Country Music, 2005, Top New Female Vocalist award, 2007. Office: c/o Front Page Publicity 2827 Columbine Place Nashville TN 37204

LAMBERT, RICHARD BOWLES, JR., freelance writer; b. Clinton, Mass., Apr. 20, 1939; s. Richard Bowles and Dorothy Elisabeth (Peck) L.; m. Sherrill Faye Smith, July 4, 1964; 1 child, Lisa Beth Lauren. AB in Physics, Lehigh U., 1961; ScM in Physics, Brown U., 1964, PhD in Physics, 1966; postgrad., Goethe Inst., Germany, 1966, NATO Internat. Sch., 1966, Max Planck Inst. for Physics & Astrophysics, 1966. Fulbright fellow Inst. for Stromungsmechanik Tech. Hochschule, Munich, 1966-67; asst. prof. U. R.I. Grad. Sch. Oceanography, 1968-74, assoc. prof., 1974—75; program dir. physical oceanography program NSF, Washington, 1975-77; rsch. oceanographer Sci. Applications Internat. Corp., 1977-79, mgr. ocean physics divsn., 1979-83, asst. v.p., 1980-83, sr. rsch. oceanographer, 1983-84; assoc. program dir. physical oceanography program NSF, Washington, 1984-91, program dir. physical oceanography program, 1991-99; dir. ops. Master Works Festival, 1997—2003. Adv. com. NOAA; assoc. dir. U.S. TOGA Project Office 1985-91; delegate Intergovernmental TOGA Bd., 1985-91; delegation head Intergovernmental WOCE Pane, 1991-99; co-investigator, chief scientist on oceanographic rsch. cruises, 1971-74. Interim editor Jour. Geophys. Rsch.-Oceans, 1999-2000; contbr. articles to profl. jours. including Jour. Fluid Mech. Bd. dirs. Christian Performing Artist's Fellowship, Winona Lake, Ind., 1998-2007; adminstr. MW Festival, 1997-2003; elder 4th Presbyn. Ch., 2005—. Mem. Am. Geophys. Union (Ocean Scis. award 1999), The Oceanography Soc. (life), Am. Sci. Affiliation, Phi Beta Kappa, Sigma Xi. Independent. Presbyterian. Personal E-mail: rblambert@cavtel.net.

LAMBERT, ROBERT FRANK, electrical engineer, educator, consultant; b. Warroad, Minn., Mar. 14, 1924; s. Fred Joseph and Nutah (Gibson) L.; m. June Darlene Flatten, June 30, 1951; children: Cynthia Marie, Susan Ann, Katherine Cheryl. B.E.E., U. Minn., 1948, MS in Elec. Engring, 1949, PhD, 1953. Asst. prof. U. Minn. Inst. Tech., Mpls., 1953-54, assoc. prof., 1955-59, prof. elec. engring., 1959-94, prof. emeritus, 1994; dir. propagation research lab. U. Minn., 1968-87; assoc. dean U. Minn. (Inst. Tech.), 1967-68; asst. prof. Mass. Inst. Tech., 1954-55. Cons. elec. engr., also in acoustics, 1953—; guest scientist Third Phys. Inst., Göttingen, Fed. Republic Germany, 1964; vis. scientist NASA, Hampton, Va., 1979; dir. Inst. Noise Control Engring., Washington, 1972-75 Contbr. numerous articles to tech. jours. Served with USNR, 1943-46. Fellow IEEE, Acoustical Soc. Am. (assoc. editor jour. 1985-93); mem. Am. Soc. Engring. Edn., Am. Soc. Engring. Sci., AAAS, Inst. Noise Control Engring. (dir., John C. Johnson Meml. award), Sigma Xi, Tau Beta Pi, Eta Kappa Nu, Gamma Alpha. Lutheran. Achievements include rsch. in acoustics, communication tech. random vibrations. Home: 2503 Snelling Curv N Saint Paul MN 55113 Office: U Minn Inst Tech Dept Elec Engring Minneapolis MN 55455 Business E-Mail: lambe024@tcumn.edu.

LAMBERT, STEVEN CHARLES, lawyer; b. Kingsport, Tenn., Aug. 22, 1947; s. M. Charles and Janet (Sultner) L.; m. Barbara Marshall-Lambert; children: Shelley Elizabeth Carter, Charles Burnette. BA, Duke U., 1969; JD, Georgetown U., 1974. Bar: D.C. 1975, U.S. Ct. Fed. Claims, U.S. Ct. Appeals (fed. cir.), U.S. Tax Ct. Law clk. to Chief Judge Wilson Cowen U.S. Ct. Claims, Washington, 1974—75; assoc. Wilkinson, Cragun & Barker, Washington, 1975—80, ptnr., 1980—82, Hamel & Park, Washington, 1982—88, Hopkins & Sutter, Washington, 1988—2001, Foley & Lardner LLP, Washington, 2001—. Chmn. adv. coun. U.S. Ct. Claims, 1982-86, mem. adv. coun., 1986-2006, chmn. bicentennial commn., 1987-91. Co-author: Tax Ideas Desk Book, 1980; contbr. articles to profl. jours. Chmn. bd. trustees Ferrum Coll.; pres. bd. pensions United Meth. Ch.; chmn. bd. govs., Wesley Sem., 2006—. With U.S. Army, 1970-72. Fellow Am. Bar Found.; mem. ABA (sec. litig. and natural resources), Am. Arbitration Assn., Claims Ct. Bar Assn. (pres. 1990-91, bd. dirs.), Fed. Cir. Bar Assn. (bd. dirs. 1986-88, 2005-07, sec.), Bar Assn. D.C. (bd. dirs. 1981-83). Methodist. Avocations: boating, fishing, tennis. Office: Foley & Lardner 3000 K St NW Ste 500 Washington DC 20007-5143 Home: 7830 Brink Rd Laytonsville MD Home Phone: 301-926-2955; Office Phone: 202-295-4067. Business E-Mail: slambert@foley.com.

LAMBERT, VICKIE ANN, retired dean, nursing consultant; b. Hastings, Nebr., Oct. 28, 1943; d. Victor E. and Edna M. (Hein) Wagner; m. Clinton E. Lambert, Jr., June 30, 1974; 1 child, Alexandra. Diploma, Mary Lanning Sch. Nursing, 1964; BSN, U. Iowa, 1966; MSN, Case Western Res. U., 1973; DNSc, U. Calif., San Francisco, 1981. RN, Ga. Staff and head nurse U. Iowa Hosp., Iowa City, 1966—68; instr. Sch. Nursing U. Iowa, 1968—70; instr. Robert Packer Sch. Nursing, Sayre, Pa., 1970—71; instr. dept. nursing St. John's Coll., Cleve., 1973—74; asst. prof. Sch. Nursing U. Pa., Phila., 1974—78; assoc. prof., acting chair dept. nursing adminstrn. Med. Coll. Ga., Augusta, 1982-84, coord. doctoral program nursing, 1984-85, George Mason U., Fairfax, Va., 1986-88; assoc. dean Case Western Res. U., Cleve., 1989-90; dean Sch. Nursing Med. Coll. Ga., Augusta, 1990-2001, emeritus dean Sch. Nursing, 2001—; prof. Yamaguchi U., 2001—03, Wuhan U., China, 2003—. Internat. vis. prof. Lambert and Lambert Nursing Cons., Odenton, Md., 2001—. Contbr. articles to profl. jours. Fellow Am. Acad. Nursing (dean emerita 2001); mem. ANA, Sigma Theta Tau Methodist. Avocation: travel. Home: 8608 Wandering Fox Trail Unit 403 Odenton MD 21113 E-mail: Vlambert@mcg.edu.

LAMBERTH, JAMES A., lawyer; b. Coleman, Tex., 1961; BA, George Washington U., 1984, JD with honors, 1987. Bar: Ga. 1987, DC 1989. Assoc. Troutman Sanders LLP, 1987—92, 1993—94, ptnr., intellectual property, spl. investigations Atlanta, 1995—, and practice group leader, media and entertainment; atty. Howrey & Simon, Washington, 1992—93. Named a Super Lawyer, Atlanta Mag., 2004. Mem.: ABA, State Bar Ga. Office: Troutman Sanders LLP One Logan Sq Ste 5200 600 Peachtree St NE Atlanta GA 30308-2261 Office Phone: 404-885-3362. Office Fax: 404-962-6611. Business E-Mail: james.lamberth@troutmansanders.com.

LAMBERTI, MARJORIE, retired social studies educator; b. New Haven, Sept. 30, 1937; d. James and Anna (Vanacore) L. BA, Smith Coll., 1959; MA, Yale U., 1960, PhD, 1965. Prof. history Middlebury Coll., Vt., 1964—84, Charles A. Dana prof., 1984—2002, ret., 2002, full-time scholar, 2002—. Author: Jewish Activism in Imperial Germany, 1978, State, Society and the Elementary School in Imperial Germany, 1989, The Politics of Education: Teachers and School Reform in Weimar Germany, 2002; mem. editl. bd.: History of Edn. Quar., 1992—94; contbr. articles to profl. jours. Mem. exec. com. Friends of Smith Coll. Librs., 1995—2001. NEH fellow, 1968-69, 81-82, Inst. for Advanced Study, Princeton, 1992-93, The Woodrow Wilson Ctr., Washington, 1997-98; German Acad. Exch. Svc. rsch. grantee, 1988, Rockefeller Archive Ctr. rsch. grantee, 2003. Mem. Am. Hist. Assn., Conf. Group for Ctrl. European History, Leo Baeck Inst., Phi Beta Kappa. Home: 8 S Gorham Ln Middlebury VT 05753-1002 Office: Middlebury Coll Library Middlebury VT 05753 E-mail: Lamberti@middlebury.edu.

LAMBERTON, JACQUELYN EDMUNDS, retired psychotherapist; b. Dover, NH, July 15, 1924; d. Guy Ordway and Marjorie Gladys (Cheney) Edmunds; m. Bruce Alexander Lamberton, July 5, 1947 (dec. Mar. 9, 1988); children: Karen(dec.), Christopher J., Andrew B, Valerie A.; m. George Louis Frigie, Dec. 17, 1994. BS, Simmons Coll., Boston, 1947; Grad., Gestalt Inst., Cleve., 1991. Lic. ind. chem. dependency counselor. Therapist United Meth. Ch. Orgn., Berea, Ohio, 1980—85; therapist outpatient family program Glenbeigh Hosp., Cleve., 1985—87; dir. assessment, svcs. Glenbeigh Outpatient Family Program, 1987—89, dir., 1989—92; therapist chem. dependency Taylor, Dean, Masci, Inc., Broadview Heights, Ohio, 1992—95; addictions therapist Mosaics Integrated Health, Independence, Ohio, 1995—99; pvt. practice therapy Independence, Ohio, 1999—2006, Pepper Pike, 2003—06; ret., 2006. Instr. 4-week pub. edn. intervention program Glenbeigh of Rock Creek, Ohio, 2000. Author: Intervention - Why?...Why Not?... Alcohol is a Drug, and Drugs Kill...That's Why, 2004—05. Citizen advocate for C.D. prevention Ohio Citizen Advocates, Columbus, 2001—05; vestry woman St. Thomas Episcopal Ch., Berea, Ohio, 1997—2003; co-chair commn. on alcoholism Episcopal Diocese of Cleve., 1990—91. Mem.: Nat. Assn. Alcohol and Drug Abuse Counselors. Episcopalian. Avocations: music, pianist.

LAMBERT-SAUL, BETH, real estate company executive; Grad., La. Tech U. Portfolio mgr. to v.p., dir. loan investments Archon Grp., L.P. (subs. of Goldman Sachs), Irving, Tex., mem. investment, mgmt. and new bus. coms. Past bd. mem. Dallas Women's Found.; com. mem. Tejas Girl Scouts Coun., Girls, Inc., Dallas Court Appointed Spl. Advs., Habitat for Humanity. Mem.: Comml. Mortgage Securities Assn., Mortgage Bankers Assn., Real Estate Coun., Assn. Women Execs. (past pres.), Comml. Real Estate Women Network (pres. Dallas chpt. 2001, pres. 2006, Dallas Chpt. Outstanding Achievement award 2003). Office: Archon Grp LP 600 E Las Colinas Blvd Ste 400 Irving TX 75039*

LAMBERTSEN, CHRISTIAN JAMES, environmental physiologist, physician, educator; b. Westfield, NJ, May 15, 1917; s. Christian and Ellen (Stevens) Lambertsen; m. Naomi Helen Hill, Feb. 5, 1944; children: Christian James, David Lee, Richard Hill, Bradley Stevens. BS, Rutgers U., 1939; MD, U. Pa., 1943; DSc, Northwestern U., 1977. Prof. pharmacology and exptl. therapeutics, prof. medicine U. Pa. Sch. Medicine, 1946—87, Markle scholar in med. sci., 1948—53; founding dir. Inst. for Environ. Medicine, U. Pa. Med. Ctr., 1968—, disting. prof. environ. medicine, 1985—; mem. adv. panel on med. scis. Office of Asst. Sec. Defense, 1954—61; sec. basic scis. Nat. Bd. Med. Examiners, 1955—71; mem. Pres.'s Space Panel, 1967—70; mem. oceanographic adv. bd. Office of Asst. Sec. of Navy for R & D, 1968—77; mem. marine bd. Nat. Acad. Engring., 1973—77. Dir. Environ. Biomed. Stress Data Ctr., 1992—; adviser Office of Marine Resources, NOAA, 1972—76; med. adviser Ocean Sys. Inc., Houston, 1960—83; med. dir. SubSea Intern, 1984—; chmn. com. Man in Space; with Space Sci. Bd., NAS, 1960—62; chmn. life scis. adv. bd. McDonnell-Douglas Aircraft Corp., St. Louis, 1960—67; sr. life scis. adviser Union Carbide Corp., Buffalo, Westinghouse Elec. Corp., Annapolis, Md., 1972—74, Air Products and Chems. Corp., Allentown, Pa., 1983—87; pres. Ecosystems, Inc., Phila., 1972—. Editor: Underwater Physiology Symposium, II, III, IV, V, 1963—76; mem. editl. bd.: Marine Tech. Soc. Jour., 1977—85; contbr. articles to med. and sci. jours. Maj. AUS, OSS, 1944—46. Decorated Legion of Merit US Army; recipient Lindback award for disting. tchg., 1967, Tuttle award, Aerospace Med. Assn., 1970, Undersea Med. Behnke award, 1970, Dept. Def. Disting. Pub. Svc. medal, 1972, Marine Tech. Soc. award in Ocean Sci. and Engring., 1972, Dept. Navy Commendation Adv. Svc., 1972, award in environ. scis., NY Acad. Scis., 1974, Disting. Pub. Svc. award, USCG, 1976, Disting. Med. Grad. award, U. Pa., 1989, Lifetime Achievement award, UDT-Seal Assn., 1995, Spl. Forces Green Beret award, US Army, 1996, Pioneer award, Hist. Diving Soc., 2001, Socom medal, US Spl. Ops. Command, 2001, Lifetime Achievement award, Undersea and Hyperbaric Med. Soc., 2002; grantee, NIH, USN, USAF, NASA, NOAA. Fellow: Aerospace Med. Assn. (v.p. 1968); mem.: NAE, Phila. Maritime Mus., U.S. Army Spl. Forces Regiment One, Pa. Med. Soc., Phila. County Med. Soc., Undersea Med. Soc. (founding pres.), Peripatetic Med. Soc., Marine Tech. Soc., USN UDT/Seal Assn. (hon. life mem.), John Morgan Med. Rsch. Soc., Internat. Union Physiol. Scis., Internat. Astronautic Fedn., Internat. Acad. Astronautics, Phila. Coll. Physicians, Assn. Am. Med. Colls., Am. Soc. Clin. Investigation, Am. Physiol. Soc., Am. Soc. Pharmacology and Exptl. Therapeutics, Am. Coll. Clin. Pharmacology and Chemotherapy, Cosmos Club (Washington), Sigma Xi. Home: 3500 W Chester Pike 129 Newtown Square PA 19073-4101 Office: U PA Med Ctr Inst Envrion Medicine 1 John Morgan Bldg Philadelphia PA 19104-6068

LAMBETH, JUDY (E. JULIA LAMBETH), tobacco company executive, lawyer; b. Winston-Salem, 1951; m. Jerry L. McAfee. BA in English, Hollins U., 1973; JD, Wake Forest U., 1977. Atty. focused primarily on environmental issues DuPont, 1977—92, asst. gen. counsel Conoco Houston, 1992, lead atty. environmental, safety and health regulatory and litigation counsel, 1993—97, assoc. gen. counsel, mng. dir. Asia-Pacific region Hong Kong, 1997—2001; corp. sec., deputy gen. counsel Conoco Inc., 2001—02; corp. sec., deputy gen. counsel corp. services ConocoPhillips, 2002—06; exec. v.p., gen. counsel Reynolds American Inc., Winston-Salem, NC, 2006—, R.J. Reynolds Tobacco Co., Winston-Salem, NC, 2006—. Law bd. of vis. Wake Forest U., 2003—. Mem.: NC Bar Assn. Office: Reynolds American PO Box 2990 Winston Salem NC 27102-2990

LAMB-FAFFELBERGER, MARGARETE BARBARA, foreign language educator; b. Amstetten, Austria, Sept. 6, 1954; came to U.S., 1968; d. Othmar and Margarete Faffelberger; m. Walter James Lamb, Apr. 2, 1980; children: Thomas, Christina, Nikolas. BEd, Tchr's. Acad., Vienna, Austria, 1977, Tchr's. Acad., Baden, Austria, 1979; MA, Rice U., 1981, PhD in German, 1991. Tchr. secondary sch. Hauptschule, Ybbs, Austria, 1978-79; teaching asst. U. Ill., Urbana, 1979-81, Rice U., Houston, 1981-83, 87-91, postdoctoral fellow, 1991—92; prof. of German Lafayette Coll., Pa., 1992—, head, dept. fgn. langs. and lit. Pa. Editor: Austrian Culture Series, Peter Lang Pub., 2001—. Office: Lafayette Coll Pardee Hall 433 Easton PA 18042 also: Peter Long Publishing USA 275 Seventh AVe 28th Fl New York NY 10001 Office Phone: 610-330-5255. Business E-Mail: lambfafm@lafayette.edu.

LAMBIRTH, TIMOTHY A., mediator; s. Woodrow M. Lambirth and Evelyne L. Jenkins; m. Dena Hayden Lambirth, Nov. 15, 1987; children: Heather, Travis, Hayden, Jackson. BA in Polit. Sci., U. Calif., Riverside, 1974, BA in Urban Studies, 1974; JD, Whittier Law Sch., 1978. Bar: Calif. 1978, DC 1984, Md. 1985, bd. cert. civil trial adv.. Assoc. Strumwasser & Leichter, Beverly Hills, Calif., 1978—80, Monteleone & McCrory, LA, 1980—82, Ross & Ivanjack, LA, 1982—87; mng. ptnr. Ivanjack & Lambirth, LA, 1988—2004; ptnr. Aldrich & Bonnefin, Irvine, Calif., 2005—07; pvt. practice Valencia, Calif., 2007—. Governing bd. mem. Mng. Ptnrs. Roundtable, LA, 2002—05. Author: (column) Big Money, 2003—; founding editor: Whittier Law Schs. Law Rev., 1978. Founder Children's Rights Clinic Whittier Law Sch., 1999; bd. trustees Whittier Coll. Named Super Lawyer in Banking and Fin., LA Mag., 2005, 2006. Mem.: LA County Bar Assn. PPJR (exec. com. mem. 1995—2004), Italian Am. Lawyers (treas. 1989—91), Whittier Law Sch. Alumni (pres. 1997—99, 2001—). Office: 26910 The Old Rd Ste 135 Valencia CA 91381 Business E-Mail: TLambirth@lambirthlaw.com.

LAMBORN, DOUGLAS L., congressman; b. May 24, 1954; m. Jeanie Lamborn; children: Luke, Eve, Will, Nathan, Mark. Grad., U. Kans., 1978, JD, 1985. Atty., Colo. Springs, 1987—; mem. Colo. Ho. of Reps., 1994-96, Rep. whip, 1997; mem. Colo. Senate, Dist. 9, Denver, 1997—2006, US Congress from 5th Colo. dist., 2007—, mem. Natural Resources & Veterans' Affairs Coms. Mem. appropriations com., fin. com., state, veterans and mil. affairs com., 1999. Active mem. Antelope Trails Elem. Sch. Prins. Adv. Coun., former mem. Pike's Peak Area Coun. of Govs. Citizen's Adv. Com. Republican. also: 200 E Colfax Ave Ste 259 Denver CO 80203-1716 Office: 3730 Sinton Rd, Ste 150 Colorado Springs CO 80907 also: 437 Cannon House Office Bldg Washington DC 20515 Office Phone: 202-225-4422. Office Fax: 202-226-2638.*

LAMBORN, LEROY LESLIE, law educator; b. Marion, Ohio, May 12, 1937; s. LeRoy Leslie and Lola Fern (Grant) Lamborn. AB, Oberlin Coll., 1959; LLB, Western Res. U., 1962; LLM, Yale U., 1963; JSD, Columbia U., 1973. Bar: N.Y. 1965, Mich. 1974. Asst. prof. law U. Fla., 1965-69; prof. Wayne State U., Detroit, 1970-97, prof. emeritus, 1997—. Vis. prof. State U., Utrecht, 1981. Author: (book) Legal Ethics and Professional Responsibility, 1963; contbr. articles on victimology to profl. jours. Mem.: World Soc. Victimology (exec. com. 1982—94), Nat. Orgn. Victim Assistance (bd. dirs. 1979—88, 1990—91), Am. Law Inst.

LAMBOWITZ, ALAN MARC, biochemistry educator; b. Bklyn., Dec. 24, 1947; s. Michael Peter and Eva (Feldman) Lambowitz; m. Sheila Helene Mintz, Dec. 24, 1968. BS in Chemistry, Bklyn. Coll., 1968; MPhil, Yale U., 1970, PhD, 1972. Postdoctoral rschr. Dept. Biochemistry and Biophysics U. Pa., Phila., 1972—73; rsch. assoc. Rockefeller U., NYC, 1973—75; sr. staff fellow NIH, Bethesda, Md., 1975—76; asst. prof., assoc. prof. St. Louis U., 1976—82, prof. biochemistry, 1982; prof. Ohio State U.; prof. chemistry and biochemistry U. Tex., Austin, prof. molecular biology, Mr. and Mrs. A. Frank Smith Jr. and Nancy Lee and Perry R. Bass regents chair in molecular biology, dir. Inst. Cellular and Molecular Biology. Mem. molecular biology study sect. NIH, 1982; mem. policy com. Neurospora, 1982; cons. and sci. adv. bd. Panlabs Internat., Seattle, 1983. Contbr. articles to profl. jour. Recipient Merit award, NIH, 1993;

grantee NIH, NSF, March of Dimes. Mem.: AAAS, Am. Acad. Microbiology, Am. Acad. Arts and Sciences, NAS, Am. Soc. Cell Biology, Am. Soc. Microbiology, Sigma Xi. Achievements include patents in field. Office: Univ Tex Inst Cellular and Molecular Biology 1 University Station Austin TX 78712-0159

LAMBRIGHT, JAMES H., bank executive; b. St. Louis; BA, Stanford U., 1992; JD, Harvard U., 1996. V.p. pvt. equity Credit Suisse First Boston Corp.; with Export-Import Bank of U.S., 2001—, acting v.p. credit and risk mgmt. group, acting v.p. pub. affairs, sr. advisor to bd., exec. v.p., COO, 2003—05, acting pres., 2005—06, chmn., pres., 2006—. Mem. Coun. Fgn. Rels. Henry Crown Fellow, Aspen Inst. Office: Export-Import Bank of US 811 Vermont Ave NW Rm 1215 Washington DC 20571-0002 Office Phone: 202-565-3500. Office Fax: 202-565-3513. E-mail: jim.lambright@exim.gov.

LAMBRIGHT, STEPHEN KIRK, brewing company executive, lawyer; b. Kansas City, Mo., Dec. 3, 1942; s. Ray B. and Janet Lambright; m. Gail T. Tabler; children: Stephen K. Jr., James H., Sarah E., Catherine L. BS in Acctg., U. Mo., 1965; JD cum laude, St. Louis U., 1968, MBA in Fin., 1977, civil mediation tng., 2004; Transitional Tng., USA&M, 2005. Bar: Mo. 1968, Va. 1979, DC 1979, CPA Mo. 1969, U.S. Dist. Ct. (ea. dist.) of Mo., U.S. Ct. of Appeals (8th Cir.), U.S. Supreme Ct., Cir. Ct. of St. Louis County (21st Jud. Cir.), Cir. Ct. City of St. Louis (22nd Jud. Cir.). Tax acct. Arthur Andersen & Co., 1965-69; atty. Lashly, Caruthers, Thies, Rava & Hamel, 1970-77; asst. gen. counsel Anheuser-Busch Cos., St. Louis, 1977-78, exec. asst. chmn. bd., 1978-79, v.p., nat. affairs Washington, 1979-81, v.p., industry and govt. affairs St. Louis, 1981-83, mem. corp. policy com., 1981—, v.p. group exec., 1983—, group v.p., gen. counsel; of counsel Williams, Venker & Sanders LLC, St. Louis. Served USCGR, intelligence Officer(commander) USNR ret. 1983. Mem. Shriner's Hosp. for Crippled Children, Keep Am. Beautiful. Mem. C. of C. of U.S., Mo. Bar Assn., DC Bar Assn., Va. State Bar Presbyterian. Home: 7 Bonhomme Grove Ct Chesterfield MO 63017-6053 Office: Williams Venker & Sanders LLC Ste 1600 Equitable Bldg 10 S Broadway Saint Louis MO 63102 Office Phone: 314-345-5000, 314-345-5060. Office Fax: 314-345-5055. Business E-Mail: slambright@wvslaw.com.*

LAMBRO, DONALD JOSEPH, columnist; b. Wellesley, Mass., July 24, 1940; s. Pascal and Mary (Lapery) L.; m. Jacquelyn Mae Killmon, Oct. 6, 1968; 1 son, Jason Phillip. BS, Boston U., 1963. Reporter, Boston Herald-Traveler, 1963; freelance writer Washington, 1965-67; statehouse reporter UPI, Hartford, Conn., 1968-70, reporter Washington, 1970-80; columnist United Feature Syndicate, Washington, 1981—; commentator AP Radio Network, 1982-83, Nat. Pub. Radio, 1984-85. Writer, host TV documentary Star Spangled Spenders, 1982; host, co-writer PBS TV documentary Inside the Republican Revolution, 1995; nat. editor Washington Times, 1987-88; chief polit. corr. Washington Times, 1988—. Author: The Federal Rathole, 1975; The Conscience of a Young Conservative, 1976; Fat City: How Washington Wastes Your Taxes, 1980; Washington-City of Scandals, 1984; Land of Opportunity, 1986. Recipient Warren Brookes award for Excellence in Journalism, Am. Legis. Exch. Coun., 1995. Albanian Orthodox. Office: The Washington Times 3600 New York Ave NE Washington DC 20002-1996 also: United Media Syndicate 4th Fl 200 Madison Ave New York NY 10166 Business E-Mail: dlambro@washingtontimes.com.

LAMEAR, ARLINE JOAN, librarian, writer; b. Yuma, Ariz., June 19, 1939; d. Arnold Jesse and Agnes Jean Bauska; m. Charles Gordon Luton (div.); children: Todd Luton, Scott Luton; m. Clifford Galen LaMear, July 24, 1999. BA, Occidental Coll., LA, 1960; MEd, James Madison U., 1980. Tchr. Lighthouse Elem. Sch., Pacific Grove, Calif., 1960—62, Fayetteville NC Pub. Schs., 1962—63, Wattana Acad., Bangkok, 1969—70; sch. sec. Kings Pk. Elem. Sch., Springfield, Va., 1972—76, sch. libr., 1976—97; rsch. libr. Columbia River Maritime Mus., Astoria, Oreg., 1997—. Mem. steering com., no. coast dist. feasibility study Oreg. No. Coast Counties, 2004—. Author: (children's book) Lewis & Clark, The Astoria Cats, 2002. Ct. appt. spl. adv., 2001—; Va. del. White House Conf. Libraries and Info. Svcs., DC, 1991; pres. Va. Ednl. Media Assn., 1995—96; mem. Astoria Planning Commn., 2003—, chair, 2006—. Co-recipient Cmty. Ptnr. Yr., Clatsop County Commn. Children and Families, Oreg., 2002; recipient Meritorious Svc. award, Va.'s Ednl. Media Assn., 1997. Mem.: AAUW (pres. 2005—07, scholarship 2006), Friends of Columbia River Maritime Mus. (sec. 2003—), Clatsop County Commn. Children and Families. Democrat. Unitarian Universalist. Avocations: volkswalking, travel. Home: 288 Franklin Ave Astoria OR 97103 Office: Columbia River Maritime Mus 1792 Marine Dr Astoria OR 97103

LAMEL, LINDA HELEN, lawyer, arbitrator, professional society and retired insurance company executive, college president; b. NYC, Sept. 10, 1943; d. Maurice and Sylvia (Abrams) Treppel; 1 child, Diana Ruth Sands. BA magna cum laude, Queens Coll., 1964; MA, NYU, 1968; JD., Bklyn. Law Sch., 1976. Bar: N.Y. 1977, U.S. Dist. Ct. (3d dist.) N.Y. 1977. Secondary sch. tchr. Farmingdale Pub. Sch., NY, 1965-73; curriculum specialist Yonkers Bd. Edn., Yonkers, 1973-75; program dir. Office of Lt. Gov., Albany, 1975-77; dep. supt. N.Y. State Ins. Dept., NYC, 1977-83; pres. CEO Coll. of Ins., 1983-88; v.p. Tchr.'s Ins. and Annuity Assn., 1988-96; exec. dir. Risk and Ins. Mgmt. Soc., 1997-2000; CEO Claims on Line, Inc., 2000—02; adj. assoc. prof. Bklyn. Law Sch., 2005—. Bd. dirs. Universal Am. Fin. Corp. Contbr. articles to profl. jours. Campaign mgr. lt. gov.'s primary race, NY State, 1974; v.p. Ednl. Found., 1997-2000; bd. dirs. Greater NY coun. Boy Scouts Am., 2006—. Mem. ABA (tort and ins. sect. com. chmn. 1985-86), N.Y. State Bar Assn. (exec. com. ins. sect. 1984-88), Assn. of Bar of City of N.Y. (chmn. med. malpractice com. 1989-91, ins. law com. 1997-98), Am. Mgmt. Assn. (ins. and risk mgmt. coun.), Am. Soc. Workers Compensation Profls. (bd. dirs. 1999—), Assn. Profl. Ins. Women (bd. dirs. 2002—04, Woman of Yr. 1988), Bklyn. Law Sch. Alumni Assn. (pres.), Phi Beta Kappa Assocs. (bd. dirs. 1992—2002). Office Phone: 212-371-8257. Business E-Mail: lindalamel@msn.com.

LAMENDOLA, WALTER FRANKLIN, technology business executive, educator; b. Donora, Pa., Jan. 29, 1943; BA in English, St. Vincent Coll., 1964; MSW in Cmty. Orgn., U. Pitts., 1966; diploma in Sociology and Social Welfare, U. Stockholm, 1970; PhD in Social Work, U. Minn., 1976. Cmty. svcs. dir. Ariz. tng. programs State Dept. Mental Retardation, Tucson, 1970-73; assoc. prof. social welfare adminstrn. Fla. State U., 1976-77; pres., CEO Minn. Rsch. and Tech., Inc., 1977-81; assoc. prof., dir. Allied Health Computer Lab. East Carolina U., 1981-84; prof., dir. info. tech. ctr. Grad. Sch. Social Work U. Denver, 1984-87, 99—, cons. info. tech., rsch. human svcs., 1987-90; v.p. rsch. Colo. Trust, Denver, 1990-93, info. tech. and rsch. cons., 1993—. Cons. European Network Info. Tech. and Human Svcs.; mem. rebuilding cmtys. initiative PODER project Casey Found., 1996-97; adv. bd. ctr. Computers in Tchg. Initiative, U. Southampton, Brit. Rsch. Coun. Univs., Human Svc. Info. Tech. Applications, CREON Found., Netherlands; lectr. conf., symposia, univs. US, Europe; spkr. HUSITA conf., Hong Kong, 2004; nat. adv. bd. Native Elder Health Resource Ctr., 1994-96, Data Coord. Ctr., 1999—; co-founder Denver Free Net, 1993; adj. prof. U. Colo. Health Scis. Ctr., 1996—; dir. tech. GSSU, U. Denver, 1998—; info. tech. cons. Healthy Nations Program Robert Wood Johnson Found, 1993-96; evaluator Nat. Libr. Rsch. Program, Access Colo. grant, 1994, Nat. Info. Infrastructure grant Colo. State Libr.; cons. set up on the Internet for U.S. Cts.-Ct. for Mental Health Svcs., NIH, Frontier Mental Health Svcs. Network grant; collaborating investigator SBIR award Computerized Advance Directives, tech. plan San Mateo County and Seattle Dist. Cts.; keynote spkr. conf. Human Svc. Info. Tech. Applications, Finland, 1996; adj. prof. U. Colo., 1997-98; dir. tech., adj. prof. U. Denver, 1997-98; adj. prof. informatics U. Colo. Health Scis. Ctr., 1998, 03-; nat. adv. coun. Ctr. Substance Abuse Prevention Dept. HHS, 1998, co-chair prevention decision support sys. steering group, 1999; pres. ActiveGuide, LLC; nat. design team Decision Support Sys., U.S. Dept. HHS, 1998—; prin. investigator bridge project Cmty. Tech. Ctr., US Dept. Edn., 2000-03; prin. investigator Bridge Cmty. Tech. Ctr. Dept. Edn., 2000-03; mem. external steering com. Date Coord. Ctr., Ctr. Substance Abuse Prevention, 2003—. Co-author: Choices for Colorado's Future, 1993, The Integrity of Intelligence: A Bill of Rights for the Information Age, 1992, Choices for Colorado's Future: Executive Summary, 1991, Choices for Colorado's Future: Regional Summaries, 1991; co-editor: A Casebook of Computer Applications in Health and Social Services, 1989; contbr. numerous articles to profl. jours. Capt. U.S. Army, 1966-69. Recipient Innovative Computer Application award Internat. Fedn. Info. Processing Socs., 1979, Lacy Stevenson award U. Denver, 2006; Nat. Lib. Rsch. Evaluator grantee, Colo., 1994—, Nat. Info. Infrastructure grantee Dept. Edn., State Libr. and Adult Literacy, 1994-95, Rural Area Edn. Tech. Assessments Sliver grantee Colo. Dept. Edn., 2005-06; Funds & Couns. Tng. scholar United Way Am., 1964-66, Donaldson Fund scholar, 1965-66, NIMH scholar, 1964-66, 73-76, St. Vincent Coll. Benedictine Soc. scholar, 1963-64; vis. fellow U. Southampton, 1992-95. Office: GSSW Univ Denver 2148 South High St Denver CO 80208 also: ActiveGuide LLC PO Box 24994 Denver CO 80224-4994 Business E-Mail: wlamendo@du.edu. E-mail: walter.lamendola@du.edu.

LAMIA, THOMAS ROGER, lawyer; b. Santa Monica, Calif., May 31, 1938; s. Vincent Robert II and Maureen (Green) L.; m. Susan Elena Brown, Jan. 10, 1969; children: Nicholas, Katja, Jenna, Tatiana, Carlyn, Mignon. Student, U. So. Calif., 1956, BS, 1961; student, U. Miss., 1957—58; JD, Harvard U., 1964. Bar: Calif. 1965, D.C. 1980, N.Y. 1990, U.S. Dist. Ct. (ctrl. dist.) Calif. 1965, U.S. Dist. Ct. D.C. 1980, U.S. Dist. Ct. (so. and ea. dists.) N.Y. 2005, U.S. Tax Ct. 1982; cert. mediator, N.Y. Assoc. McCutchen, Black, Verleger & Shea, LA, 1964-66; lectr. in law U. Ife, Ile-Ife, Nigeria, 1966-67, U. Zambia, Lusaka, 1967-68; assoc. Paul, Hastings, Janofsky & Walker, 1968-72, ptnr., 1972-99, mem. exec. com., 1976-80, mng. ptnr. Washington office, 1980-83; pvt. practice NYC, 1999—. Chair, transp. com. NYC Bar Assn., 2003—06. Office: 54 Charles St New York NY 10014-2750 Home Phone: 212-255-2480; Office Phone: 212-206-9290. Business E-Mail: trlamia@lamialaw.com.

LAMID, SOFJAN, physician, educator; b. Pangkalan, West Sumatra, Indonesia, June 30, 1929; came to the U.S., 1969; naturalized, 1981. s. Datuk Besar and Zamrud (Muhamad) L.; m. Burlini Tamin, Feb. 4, 1962; children: Dicky Sofwandi, Rudy Sofriza. MD, U. Indonesia, Jakarta, 1960; MSc in Pharmacology, U. Calif., San Francisco, U.S.A., 1962. Diplomate Am. Bd. Phys. Medicine and Rehab. Chmn. dept. pharmacology U. Indonesia, Jakarta, Indonesia, 1960-68; residency in internal medicine, fellow in clin. pharmacology Southwestern Med. Sch., U. Tex., 1969-70; fellow in clin. pharmacology George Washington U., Washington, 1970-72; residency in anesthesiology Washington Hosp. Ctr., 1972-73; staff physician, clin. pharmacology Wood VA Med. Ctr., Milw., 1973-77, staff physican, spinal cord injury svc., 1977-84, acting chief, spinal cord injury svc., 1983-84; asst. adj. prof. pharmacology Med. Coll. Wis., Milw., 1975-77, asst. prof. physical medicine and rehab., 1978-84; residency in physical medicine and rehab. Medical Coll. Wis., Milw., 1978-91; assoc. prof. medicine and rehab. LSU Med. Ctr., New Orleans, 1984-87; assoc. dir. La. Rehab. Inst., New Orleans, 1984-87; pvt. practice New Orleans, 1987—; mem. staff Hotel Dieu Hosp., New Orleans, Jo Ellen Smith Med. Ctr., New Orleans, F. Edward Hebert Hosp., New Orleans. Vis. prof. pharmacology U. Tex., Dallas, 1969-70; pres. QRS Lamid Enterprises, Inc., Indonesian Am. Found., Inc. Mem. editorial bd. The Jour. Am. Paraplegia Soc., 1982—; manuscript reviewer Archives of Physical Medicine and Rehab., 1980—. Pres. Indonesian Am. Found., Inc.; past pres. Indonesian Am. Cmty. Assn. Grantee Travenol Labs., 1984; grantee (with Richard Crout) Vitamin Drug Co., 1969-70, (with Raymond Jenkins) Beecham Massengil Pharmacology, 1970-72. Fellow Am. Acad. Phys. Medicine and Rehab.; mem. Am. Soc. Clin. Pharmacology and Therapeutics, Am. Paraplegia Soc., Am. Congress Rehab. Medicine (program com. 1982-84, rehab. practice com. 1983—), Assn. Academic Physiatrists, Dutch New Am. Club. Home: 7243 Brookwood Dr Mandeville LA 70471-7443 Personal E-mail: slamid@aol.com.

LAMIS, LEROY, artist, retired art educator; b. Eddyville, Iowa, Sept. 27, 1925; s. Leo and Blanche (Bennett) L.; m. Esther Sackler, Aug. 13, 1954; children: Alexander, Jonas. BA, N.Mex. Highlands U., 1953; MA, Columbia U., 1956. Mem. faculty dept. art Ind. State U., 1961—, prof., 1972-89, retired 1989; artist-in-residence Dartmouth Coll., 1970; founder PC ART, 1983, milliondollarart.com, 2000. One-man sculpture exhbns. include Staempfli Gallery, N.Y.C., 1966, 69, 73, Gillman Gallery, Chgo., 1967, Tacoma Mus., 1970, Ft. Wayne Art Mus., 1968, Des Moines Art Ctr., 1970, La Jolla Mus., 1970, Ind. State U., 1976, Sheldon Swope Art Mus., Terre Haute, Ind., 1979; kinetic computer art exhbns. at Ben Shahn Gallery, William Patterson Coll., N.J., Ind. State U., 1985, Bronx Mus. Art, 1986, 55 Mercer Gallery, 1990, Indpls. Art Mus., 1992, Evansville Mus. Sci. and Art, 1994, Swope Art Mus., Terre Haute, 1996-97, Fifth Annual N.Y. Digital Salon Sch. Visual Arts, N.Y.C., 1997, Seventh Annual N.Y. Digital Salon Sch. Visual Arts, 99; represented in permanent collections Albright-Knox Mus., Des Moines Art Ctr., Mus. Fine Arts, Boston, Whitney Mus. Am. Art, Joseph H. Hirshorn Collection, Washington, Indpls. Mus., J.B. Speed Mus., Louisville; author: (computer program) Eighty 5, 1985; creator, prodr. various computer software. Served with AUS, 1943. Recipient Award Commn. N.Y. State Coun. of the Arts, 1970. Address: 12463 Los Indias Trail Apt 337 Austin TX 78729 E-mail: leroy@joink.com.

LAMKEN, JEFFREY A., lawyer; b. Mar. 26, 1964; BA in Polit. Sci., Haverford Coll., 1986; JD, Stanford Law Sch., 1990. Bar: Calif. 1990, DC 1995, US Supreme Ct. 1997. Clerk US Ct. of Appeals, Ninth Cir., 1990—91, US Supreme Ct., 1992—93; Bristow fellow, 1991—92; asst. to solicitor gen. US Dept. Justice; ptnr. Baker Botts LLP, Washington. Named an Litigation's Rising Stars, The Am. Lawyer, 2007; named one of America's Leading Bus. Lawyers, Chambers USA, 2005, 2006; named to Best Lawyers in Am., 2006, 2007. Office: Baker Botts LLP The Warner 1299 Pennsylvania Ave NW Washington DC 20004-2400 Office Phone: 202-639-7978. Office Fax: 202-585-4060.

LAMKIN, CELIA BELOCORA, physician; b. Dinalupihan, Bataan, Philippines, Mar. 10, 1957; d. Crispiniano Tumulac and Rufina Paule Belocora; m. Ronald Phillip Lamkin, Feb. 14, 1997; children: Jericho Belocora Santos, John Raymond Belocora Sablan. BS in Biol. Scis., U. Philippines, Manilla, 1978; MD, De La Salle U., Cavite, Philippines, 1984; post grad. in Occupl. Health and Safety, Coll. Pub. Health U. Philippines, Manila, 1989. Cert. physician Profl. Regulation Commn., Philippines, 1986, specialist in assistive tech. Calif. State U., Northridge, 2003. Intern U. Philippines, Philippines Gen. Hosp, Manila, 1984—85; physician Cainta Rural Health Ctr., Cainta Rizal, 1986; cons. and med. examiner Anthony Med. Clinic, Manila, 1987—88; med. examiner Insular Life Ins. Co., Makati City, 1988—93; co. physician M. Greenfield Garment Factory, Paranaque City, 1989, Drugmakers Laboratories, Inc., Paranaque City, Philippines, 1989; pvt. practice gen. practitioner Ermita, Manila and Cainta Rizal, 1986—93; HIV/ADS specialist and program coord. Pub. Sch. Sys., Saipan, Commonwealth No. Marianas Islands, 1995—96; human svcs. provider Philippine Consulate, Saipan, 1996—97; assistive tech. program coord. Coun. on Devel. Disabilities, 1997—2003; counselor and disability svcs. coord. No. Marianas Coll., 2003—05; temp. disability ret., 2005—. Workshop condr. disabilities and assistive tech.; vis. cons. Med. Ctr. Manila, 1988—91; translator U.S. Dist. Ct., 2002—05; spkr. in field. Vol. HIV instr. Am. Red Cross, first aid and CPR instr. Recipient cert. appreciation, No. Marianas Coll., 2005, Gov.'s Coun. Devel. Disabilities, Commonwealth No. Marianas Islands, 1998, 2003, Organizing Com. Internat. Biophilia Rehab. Acad., Philippines, 2004, Ho. Reps. Commonwealth No. Marianas Islands, 2004, Saipan and No. Islands Mcpl. Coun., 2004. Mem.: AMA, Internat. Biophilia Rehab. Acad. (cert. appreciation 2004), Biophilia Rehab. Acad. Japan, Am. Diabetes Assn., Pacific Disability Forum, U. Philippines Alumni Assn. Roman Catholic. Avocations: piano, organ, cooking. Home: PO Box 7497 Saipan MP 96950-7497 Personal E-mail: clamkinmd@yahoo.com.

LAMKIN, FLETCHER M., JR., academic administrator; b. Lakehurst, NJ, Apr. 2, 1942; married; 3 daus. BS, U.S. Mil. Acad., 1964; MS in Engring., U. Calif., Berkeley; DPhil, U. Wash.; grad., Army Command Gen. Staff Coll., Naval War Coll. Commd. 2d lt. U.S. Army, 1964; early assignments include battery exec. officer 7th bn., 11th field arty., Republic South Vietnam, bn. fire support officer, battery comdr., 1966-67; comdr. 1st spl. tng. co. Ft. Gordon, Ga., 1967-68; bn. ops. officer 1st bn., 38th field arty., Korea, 1975-76; bn. exec. officer, tng. officer, dep. ops. officer 9th infantry divsn., Ft. Lewis, Wash., 1976-80; inspections team chief, Office of Inspector Gen. U.S. Army Europe, Heidelberg, Germany, 1980—81; bn. comdr. 4th bn., 77th field arty., Babenhausen, FRG, Germany, 1981—83; instr., asst. prof. dep. mechs. U.S. Mil. Acad., West Pt., NY, 1971-74, assoc. prof. dept. engring., 1987-89, prof., dep. head dept. civil and mech. engring., 1989-92, vice dean acad. bd., 1993-94, prof., head dept. civil and mech. engirng., 1994-95, dean acad. bd., 1995—2000; pres. Westminster Coll., Fulton, Mo., 2000—. Office: Office of the President Westminster College 501 Westminster Ave Fulton MO 65251-1299

LAMKIN, MARTHA DAMPF, lawyer, foundation administrator; b. Talladega, Ala., May 20, 1942; d. Keith J. and Neva (Magness); m. E. Henry Lamkin Jr., Aug. 24, 1968; children: Melinda Lamkin Magaddino, Matthew Davidson. BA in English summa cum laude, Calif. Baptist U., 1964; MA in English and Am. Lit., Vanderbilt U., 1966; JD, Ind. U., 1970. Bar: Ind. 1970. Assoc. Joseph D. Geeslin, Indpls., 1971-72, Lowe, Gray, Steele & Hoffman, Indpls., 1976-82; field office mgr. U.S. Dept. Housing and Urban Devel., Indpls., 1982-87; exec. dir., corp. rep. responsibility and govtl. affairs Cummins Engine Co., Inc., Columbus, Ind., 1987-91; exec. v.p. corp. advancement USA Group, Inc., Indpls., 1991-2000; pres., CEO, bd. dirs. USA Group Found., Inc., 2000-2001; CEO, pres., bd. dirs. Lumina Foundation for Education Inc., 2001—. Pres., bd. dirs. Cummins Engine Found., 1989-91; bd. dirs. Meridian Mut. Ins. Co., Indpls., USA Group, Inc., USA Group Loan Svcs., Inc., United Student Aid Funds, 1994-2000, Citizens Gas & Coke Utility, Inc., vice chair, 1990-; bd. dirs. Coun. on Founds., 2005-, chair pub. policy com. Commr., sec., chmn. Indpls. Human Rights Commn., 1971-79; commr. Indpls. Housing Authority, 1979-82; chmn. exec. com. S.K. Lacy Exec. Leadership Alumni, Indpls., 1986-87; chmn. Ind. Leadership Celebration, Indpls., 1985-87; sec. Gov.'s Mansion Commn., Indpls., 1981-89; bd. dirs. Great Indpls. Progress Commn., 1986-87, Indpls. Symphony Orch., 1983-89, 98-99, Indpls. Project, 1986-91, Ind. Fiscal Policy Inst., 1998-2003, Ind. Colls. Ind., 1997-2000; bd. dirs., sec. COMMIT, Inc., COMMIT Found., 1990-97; chmn. bd. trustees Christian Theol. Sem., Indpls., 1983-93; hon. gov. Richard C. Lugar Excellence Pub. Svc. Series, 1990—; chair, 1997, 2003, trustee Indpls. Found., 1992-2003; mem. exec. com. Mayor's Task Force on Housing, 1987, exec. com., Ind. Sports Corp., 1997-2000; sec., bd. dirs. Indpls. Econ. Devel. Corp., 1997-2000; chair, dir. Ctrl. Ind. Cmty. Found., 1998-2003; mem. Hoosier Capitol Girl Scouts Adv. Bd., 1996-2002. Recipient Presdl. Rank award 1985, Mental Health Initiative Gov. Ind., 1986, Matrix award Women in Communication, 1987, Women in the Lead Indpls. Bus. Journ. 1999, Outstanding Alumni award, Ind. U. Sch. Law-Indlps., 2000; named Hon. Dr. Christian Theol. Sem. 1999. Mem. State Assembly Women (pres. 1977-79), Indpls. Jr. League, Indpls. C. of C. (bd. dirs. 1986-87). Mem.(Disciples Of Christ). Office: Lumina Found for Edn 30 S Meridian Ste 700 Indianapolis IN 46204

LAMLE, HUGH ROY, investment advisor, consultant; b. Yonkers, NY, July 20, 1945; s. Paul and Lee (Wolf) L.; m. Elizabeth Bowman, Jan. 12, 1969. BA in Polit. Sci. and Econs., Queens Coll., CUNY, 1968; MBA in Fin. and Investment, Baruch Coll., CUNY, 1970. Registered investment advisor. Owner, pres. Investment Rsch. Assocs., NYC, 1967-76; asst. to exec. v.p. Douglas T. Johnston, NYC, 1969-70; v.p. F.I. duPont/Lenox Capital Mgmt., NYC, 1970-74; prin., dir., pres. M.D. Sass Investors Svcs., NYC, 1974—, M.D. Sass Capital Mgmt. Corp., 1985-87; prin., dir., exec. v.p. Sass Elliot & Page, NYC, 1985-87; dir., pres. M.D. Sass Assocs., 1974—; v.p., former dir., prin. Corp. Capital Cons., NYC, 1975—2001; exec. v.p. Sass Southmark Mut. Funds, 1986-89; exec. v.p., dir. Corp. Renaissance Group Inc., 1994-2000; pres. Resurgence Asset Mgmt., 1998—. Pres., chief investment officer Chase & M.D. Sass Ptnrs., 1995—2001; dir. CCC Resources, NYC; bd. dirs. CCC Advs., NYC, FINEX; vice chmn. Coolsavings.com Inc., 1997—2005; bd. govs. NY Bd. Trade, 2000—; expert witness in securities and valuation litigation; lectr. in field. Contbr. articles to profl. jours., mags., newspapers, books. Trustee Citizen's Budget Commn. N.Y.C. Fellow Baruch Coll. fellow, CUNY. Fellow Fin. Analysts Fedn.; mem. N.Y. Soc. Security Analysts (Vol. of Yr. 1986), Nat. Instl. Options Soc., Investment Mgmt. Cons. Assn., Beta Gamma Sigma (hon.). Avocations: catamaran racing, windsurfing racing, pistol shooting, skiing. Home: 559 Dune Rd Westhampton Beach NY 11978-2946 also: LG Smith Blvd 494 Aruba Aruba also: 0220 Nottingham Rd #4 Avon CO 81620 Office: MD Sass Investors Svcs 18th Fl 1185 Ave of Americas New York NY 10036

LAMM, CAROLYN BETH, lawyer; b. Buffalo, Aug. 22, 1948; d. Daniel John and Helen Barbara Lamm; m. Peter Edward Halle, Aug. 12, 1972; children: Alexander P., Daniel E. BS, SUNY Coll. at Buffalo, 1970; JD, U. Miami, 1973. Bar: Fla., 1973, D.C., 1976, N.Y. 1983. Trial atty. frauds sect. civil div. U.S. Dept. Justice, Washington, 1973-78, asst. chief comml. litigation sect. civil div., 1978, asst. dir., 1978-80; assoc. White & Case, Washington, 1980-84, ptnr., 1984—. Mem. Sec. State's Adv. Com. Pvt. Internat. law, 1987—; arbitrator US Panel of Arbitrators, Internat. Ctr. Settlement Investment Disputes, 1994-02, Uzbekistan, 2003-; mem. com. on pvt. dispute resolution NAFTA Mem. editl. adv. bd. Inside Litigation; contbg. editor: Internat. Arbitration Law Rev., 1997—; contbr. articles to legal publs. Mem. Holy Trinity Parish Coun., 1998—2001. Named one of 100 Most Influential Lawyers, Nat. Law Jour., 2006, Top 20 Arbitration Specialists: In a Leagues of Their Own, PLC Cross-Border Quarterly, 2006, The 50 Most Influential Women Lawyers in Am., Nat. Law Jour., 2007; recipient Woman Lawyer of the Year Award, Best Lawyers in Am., 2002. Fellow: Am. Coll. Trial Lawyers, Am. Bar Found.; mem.: FBA (chmn. sec. antitrust and trade regulation), ABA (chmn. young lawyers divsn. 1982—83, bd. govs. 2002—05, chair ops. com., exec. com., rules and calendar com., chmn. ho. membership com., chmn. assembly resolution com., sec. 1984—85, chmn. internat. litig. com. coun. 1991—94, sect. litig., ho. dels. 1982—, nomination com. 1984—87, chair 1995—96, DC Cir. mem. 1992—95, standing com. fed. judiciary 1992—95, chmn. com. scope and correlation of work 1996—97, commn. on multidisciplinary practice, bd. govs. 2002—, steering com. 2005—, state del. DC, co-chair ABA Day Disaster Relief, state del. 2005—), Am. Uzbekistan C. of C. (bd. dirs., v.p., gen. counsel), Am. Indonesian C. of C. (bd. dirs.), Am. Soc. Internat. Law (co-chair Interest Group Dispute Resolution), Women's Bar Assn. DC (Woman Lawyer of Yr. 2002), Am. Law Inst. (coun.), DC Bar (pres. 1997—98, bd. govs. 1987—93, steering com., litig. sect., found. bd. 2001—), Bar Assn. DC (bd. dirs., sec., found. bd.), Am. Arbitration Assn. (bd., arbitrator, adv. com. internat. arbitration, exec. com.), Women's

Forum, Am. Turkish Friendship Coun. (bd. dirs.), Stratton Mountain Club, Manchester Country Club, Columbia Country Club. Democrat. Office: White and Case 701 13th St NW Washington DC 20005-3807 Business E-Mail: clamm@whitecase.com.

LAMM, DONALD STEPHEN, literary agent; b. NYC, May 31, 1931; s. Lawrence William and Aleen Antonia (Lassner) L.; m. Jean Stewart Nicol, Sept. 27, 1958; children: Douglas William, Robert Lawrence, Wendy Nicol. BA with honors, Yale, 1953; postgrad., Oxford U., Eng., 1956. With W.W. Norton & Co., Inc., NYC, 1956-2000, from v.p. to pres., 1968-94, chmn., 1984-2000, also dir. Also dir. New Directions Pub. Corp.; assoc. Fletcher & Parry, N.Y.C.; guest fellow Yale U., 1980, 85, Phi Beta Kappa lectr. 1994; Ida Beam disting. vis. prof. U. Iowa, 1987-88; guest fellow Woodrow Wilson Ctr., 1996; regents lectr. U. Calif., Berkeley, 1998-99; pres. Yale U. Press, 1985-2000; mem. bd. advisors Yale Rev., mem. bd. trustees U. Calif. Press; fellow Ctr. Advanced Study in the Behavioral Scis., 1998-99; trustee Sch. Advanced Rsch., Santa Fe. Author: (with others) The Spread of Economic Ideas, 1989, Beyond Literacy, 1990, Book Publishing in the United States Today, 1997, Perception, Cognition, and Language, 2000; mem. editl. bd. Am. Scholar. With Counter Intelligence Corps US Army, 1953—55. Fellow Branford Coll., Yale U. Fellow Am. Acad. Arts and Scis.; mem. Manuscript Soc., Century Assn., Elizabethan Club, Phi Beta Kappa (senator 1990—, exec. com. 1998—, v.p. 2003-06). Home: 741 Calle Picacho Santa Fe NM 87505 Office: Fletcher & Parry 78 Fifth Ave New York NY 10011

LAMM, FREDDIE RAY, research agricultural engineer; b. Boonville, Mo., Sept. 11, 1955; s. Henry Silas and Mildred Jean (Pfeiffer) L.; m. Donna Lee Gawith, Dec. 31, 1983; children: Elaine MaDonna, Henry Silas IV, Rachel Alison, Sarah Nicole. BS in Agrl. Engring., U. Mo., 1978, MS in Agrl. Engring., 1979; PhD in Engring., Kans. State U., 1990. Registered profl. engr., Kans. Instr. Kans. State U., Colby, 1979-90, asst. prof., 1990-94, assoc. prof. agrl. engring., 1994-2000, prof. agrl. engring., 2000—. Tri-editor Microirrigation for Crop Production; contbr. articles to profl. jours. Mem. Am. Soc. Agrl. Engrs. (chair SW-245 1993-94, Kans. sect. chair 1996-97, Young Mem. of Yr. 1993), Irrigation Assn. (chmn. agrl. irrigation com. 1995-97), Am. Soc. Agronomy, Kans. Acad. Sci., Am. Soc. Plasticulture, Sigma Xi, Alpha Epsilon, Gamma Sigma Delta. Democrat. Baptist. Achievements include research with use of microirrigation on field corn. Office: Kansas State Univ 105 Experiment Farm Dr Colby KS 67701-1697 Office Phone: 785-462-6281. Business E-Mail: flamm@ksu.edu.

LAMM, MICHAEL EMANUEL, pathologist, immunologist, educator; b. Bklyn., May 19, 1934; s. Stanley S. and Rose (Lieberman) L.; m. Ruth Audrey Kumin, Dec. 16, 1961; children: Jocelyn, Margaret. Student, Amherst Coll., 1951-54; MD, U. Rochester, 1959; MS in Chemistry, Western Res. U., 1962. Diplomate Am. Bd. Pathology. Intern, asst. resident in pathology Inst. Pathology Western Res. U. and Univ. Hosps. of Cleve., 1959-62; research assoc. NIMH, Bethesda, Md., 1962-64; asst. prof. pathology NYU Sch. Medicine, NYC, 1964-68, assoc. prof., 1968-73, prof., 1973-81; prof. dept. pathology Case We. Res. U. Sch. Medicine, 1981—; chmn. dept. Case Western Res. U. Sch. Medicine, 1981-2001. Vis. sci. dept. biochemistry U. Oxford, 1968; vis. prof. dept. pathology U. Geneva, 1976-77; mem. cancer spl. program adv. com. Nat. Cancer Inst., Bethesda, 1976-79, mem. bd. sci. counselors divsn. cancer biology, diagnosis and ctrs., 1993-95; mem. sci. adv. com. Damon Runyon-Walter Winchell Cancer Fund, N.Y.C., 1978-82; mem. immunol. sci. study sect. NIH, Bethesda, 1988-92; mem. immunotoxicology subcom. NRC, 1989-90; mem. toxin peer rev. panel Am. Inst. Biol. Sci., 1990—; bd. dirs. Univ. Associated for Rsch. and Edn. Pathology. Mem. editl. bd. Procs. Soc. Exptl. Biology and Medicine, 1973-82, Molecular Immunology, 1979-83, Jour. Immunol. Methods, 1980—, Jour. Immunology, 1981-85, Am. Jour. Pathology, 1982-92, Regional Immunology, 1988-95, Modern Pathology, 1989-96; contbr. articles to profl. jours. Recipient Excellence in Tchg. award NYU Sch. Medicine, 1974, Gold-Headed Cane award Am. Soc. for Investigative Pathology, 2004; named Career Scientist Health Rsch. Coun., City of NY, 1966-75; NIH grantee 1965—. Fellow AAAS, N.Y. Acad. Scis.; mem. Am. Assn. Pathologists (councilor 1986-88, sec. treas. 1988-90, v.p. 1990-91, pres. 1991-92), Am. Assn. Immunologists, Am. Soc. Biochemistry and Molecular Biology, Coll. Am. Pathologists, U.S. and Can. Acad. Pathology, Soc. for Exptl. Biol. Medicine, Clin. Immunology Soc., Soc. Mucosal Immunology, Am. Soc. Clin. Pathologists, Harvey Soc., Sigma Xi, Alpha Omega Alpha. Home: Apt 6B 13515 Shaker Blvd Cleveland OH 44120-5602 Home Phone: 216-561-6470. Business E-Mail: mel6@case.edu.

LAMM, NORMAN, academic administrator, rabbi; b. Bklyn., Dec. 19, 1927; s. Samuel and Pearl (Baumol) L.; m. Mindella Mehler, Feb. 23, 1954; children: Chaye Lamm Warburg, Joshua B., Shalom E., Sara Rebecca Lamm Dratch. BA summa cum laude, Yeshiva Coll., 1949; PhD, Bernard Revel Grad. Sch., 1966; Dr. of Hebrew Letters (hon.), Hebrew Theol. Coll., 1977, Gratz Coll., 1999. Ordained rabbi, 1951; asst. rabbi Congregation Kehilath Jeshurun, NYC, 1952—53; rabbi Congregation Kodimoh, Springfield, Mass., 1954—58, Jewish Center, NYC, 1958—76; Erna and Jakob Michael prof. Jewish philosophy Yeshiva U., NYC, 1966—, pres., 1976—2002, chancellor, 2002—; pres. Rabbi Isaac Elchanan Theol. Sem., NYC, 1976—. Vis. prof. Judaic studies Bklyn. Coll., 1974-75; dir. Union Orthodox Jewish Congregations Am. Author: A Hedge of Roses, 1966, The Royal Reach, 1970, Faith and Doubt, 1971, Torah Lishmah, 1972 (rev. English edition 1989), The Good Society, 1974, Halakot ve'Halikhot: Essays on Jewish Law, 1990, Torah Umadda: The Encounter of Religious Learning and Worldly Knowledge in the Jewish Tradition, 1990, The Shema: Spirituality and Law in Judaism, 1998, The Religious Thought of Hasidism: Text and Commentary, 1999 (Nat. Jewish Book awrd); editor: Library of Jewish Law and Ethics, 1975—; co-editor: The Leo Jung Jubilee Volume, 1962, A Treasury of Tradition, 1967, The Joseph B. Soloveitchik Jubilee Vol., 1984, Halakhot ve'Halikhot (Heb.): Essays on Jewish Law, 1990, Saving Faces: Articles of Faith, 2002. Trustee-at-large Fedn. Jewish Philanthropies, N.Y.; mem. exec. com. Assn. for a Better N.Y.; bd. dirs. Am. Friends-Alliance Israelite Universelle; mem. Pres.'s Commn. on the Holocaust, 1978-89; chmn. N.Y. Conf. on Soviet Jewry, 1970; mem. Halakhah Commn., Rabbinical Council Am. Recipient Abramowitz Zeitlin award, 1972 Mem. Assn. Orthodox Jewish Scientists (charter; bd. govs.) Office: Yeshiva U Office of Chancellor 500 W 185th St New York NY 10033-3201 also: Rabbi Isaac Eichanan Theol Sem 2540 Amsterdam Ave New York NY 10033-2807 E-mail: nlamm@yu.edu.*

LAMMIE, JAMES LOUIS, engineering executive, retired military officer; b. 1931; BS, U.S. Mil. Acad., 1953; MSE, Purdue U., 1957; MSBA, George Washington U., 1969. Commd. lt. U.S. Army Corps of Engrs., 1953; advanced through grades to col. U.S. Army, 1972, ret., 1974; with Atlanta Transit Sys. Parsons Brinckerhoff, Inc., NYC, 1975—82, COO, 1982—90, CEO, 1990—96, dir. Endowed chair civil engr. U.S. Mil. Acad., 2005. Office: Parsons Brinckerhoff Inc One Penn Plz New York NY 10119-0061 Office Phone: 212-465-5006. Business E-Mail: lammie@pbworld.com.

LAMON, HARRY VINCENT, JR., lawyer; b. Macon, Ga., Sept. 29, 1932; s. Harry Vincent and Helen (Bewley) Lamon; m. Ada Healey Morris, June 17, 1954; children: Hollis Morris, Kathryn Gurley. BS cum laude, Davidson Coll., 1954; JD with distinction, Emory U., 1958. Bar: Ga. 1958, DC 1965. Of counsel Troutman Sanders LLP, Atlanta, 1995—. Adj. prof. law Emory U., 1960—79. Contbr. articles to profl. jours. Pension and benefits reporter adv. bd. Bur. Nat. Affairs, 1972—2003; adv. coun. employee welfare and pension benefit plans U.S. Dept. Labor, 1975—79; nat. adv. bd. Salvation Army, 1976—, chmn., 1991—93, life mem. chmns. cir., 2005—; founding trustee, pres. So. Fed. Tax Inst., Inc., 1965—, emeritus, 2000—; trustee Am. Tax Policy Inst., Inc., 1989—96, Embry-Riddle Aero. U., 1989—2001, emeritus mem., 2001—; trustee Cathedral St. Philip Endowment Fund, Atlanta, 1989—. 1st lt. US Army, 1954—56. Named Atlanta Centennial honoree, Salvation Army, 1990. Fellow: Am. Coll. Employee Benefits Counsel (emeritus), Internat. Acad. Estate and Trust Law, Am. Coll. Trust and Estate Counsel (emeritus), Atlanta Bar Found. (life), Am. Bar Found. (life), Ga. Bar Found. (life), Am. Coll. Tax Counsel; mem.: ABA, Practicing Law Inst., Am. Law Inst. (life), Atlanta Bar Assn. (life), So. Employee Benefits Conf. (hon. Hazelhurst Lamon outstanding achievement award named in his honor), Atlanta Tax Forum, Am. Judicature Soc., State Bar Ga. (chmn. sect. taxation 1969—70, vice chmn. comm. continuing lawyer competency 1982—89), Group, Inc. (hon. life), Nat. Emory U. Law Sch. Alumni Assn. (pres. 1967), Am. Bar Retirement Assn. (bd. dirs. 1989—96, pres. 1994—95), Inquiry Club, Lawyers Club of Atlanta (life), Capital City Club (life), Cosmos Club (Washington), Atlanta Coffee House Club, Peachtree Racket Club (pres. 1986), Kiwanis (hon.; pres. Atlanta 1974), Phi Beta Kappa (fellow), Phi Delta Theta (chmn. nat. cmty. svc. day 1969—72, legal commr. 1973—76, province pres. 1976—79, Golden Legion 2001), Phi Delta Phi, Omicron Delta Kappa. Episcopalian. Home: 4415 Paces Battle NW Atlanta GA 30327-3023 Office: Lamon & Sherman Consulting LLC 1950 N Park Pl Ste 125 Atlanta GA 30339 Office Phone: 770-933-0060. E-mail: harry.lamon@Lamonsherman.com.

LAMONT, BRIDGET LATER, librarian, consultant; b. Nov. 13, 1948; d. George Philip and Margaret (Behrens) Later; m. Thomas R. Lamont, Mar. 8, 1947; children: Michael Thomas, Jeffrey Stephen. BA, Clarke Coll., Dubuque, Iowa, 1970; MLS, U. Ill. Grad. Sch. Libr. Info. Sci., 1972. Asst. dir. Children's Champaign Pub. Libr., 1971—72; cons. Ill. State Pub. Libr., Springfield, 1972—78, assoc. dir. libr. devel., 1978—81, dep. dir., 1981—83, dir., 1983—99; dir. policy devel. State of Ill., 1999—. Appointed mem. Nat. Presidential Comm. Libr. Info. Sci., 2004. Mem.: ALA, Ill. Libr. Assn. Office: US Nat Comm Libr and Info Sci Ste 350 No Tower 1800 M Street NW Washington DC 20036 E-mail: blamont@nclis.gov.

LAMONT, EDWARD MINER, JR., telecommunications industry executive; b. Washingyton, Jan. 3, 1954; s. Edward M. and Camille (Buzby) L.; m. Ann Greenlee Huntress, 1983; children: Emily, Lindsay, Teddy BA, Harvard U., 1976; MPPM, Yale U., 1980. Project dir. Cablevision, 1980—84; founder, pres., chmn. Lamont Digital Systems, Greenwich, Conn., 1984—. Selectman Town of Greenwich, Conn., 1987-95. Mem. Coun. Fgn. Rels., Harvard Club, Round Hill club. Democrat. Episcopalian.*

LAMONT, GENE, professional baseball coach and former team manager; b. Rockford, Ill., Dec. 25, 1946; m. Melody; children: Melissa, Wade. Student, No. Ill. U., Western Ill. U. Player various minor league teams Detroit Tigers, 1965-73, 75-77; mgr. minor league team Kansas City Royals, Fort Myers, Fla., 1977-79, Jacksonville, Fla., 1979-84; coach Pitts. Pirates, 1986-91; mgr. Chgo. White Sox, 1991-95, Pittsburgh Pirates, 1995—2001; coach Houston Astros, 2001—. Named Southern League Mgr. of Yr., 1982. Office: Houston Astros PO Box 288 Houston TX 77001

LAMONT, JOHN THOMAS, gastroenterologist, educator; b. Lockport, NY, Oct. 2, 1938; s. Duane George and Marjorie Elizabeth (Heary) L.; m. Emily Marie Lamont, June 24, 1964; children: Ian Thomas, Maura Kathryn, Margaret O'Neil. BS, Canisius Coll., Buffalo, 1960; MD, U. Rochester, NYC, 1965. Diplomate Am. Bd. Internal Medicine. Intern and resident in medicine UCLA Med. Ctr., Los Angeles, Calif., 1965—67; fellow in gastroenterology Mass. Gen. Hosp., Boston, 1971—73; asst prof. medicine Harvard Med. Sch., Boston, 1975—80, prof., 1996—; assoc prof. Boston U. Sch. Medicine, 1980—85, prof., 1986—96; chief gastroenterology Beth Israel Deaconess Med. Ctr., Boston. Chief gastroenterology Boston U. Sch. Medicine, 1980-95, Beth Israel Deaconess Med. Ctr., Boston, 1996—. Editor: (book) Gastrointestinal Infections, 1997; sr. assoc. editor: Gastroenterology, 1995-00. Maj. U.S. Army, 1967-70. Maj. US Army, 1967—70. Recipient Clin. Investigator award NIH, 1975-77, Career Devel. award, 1978-83, Merit award, 1997-02. Mem. Am. Gastroenterology Assn. (mem. governing bd. 1999-02). Achievements include research in GI infections and inflammation. Avocations: fiction, photography, music, art, travel. Home: 390 Waltham St West Newton MA 02465 Office: Beth Israel Deaconess Med Ctr 330 Brookline Ave Boston MA 02215 Home Phone: 617-969-5693; Office Phone: 617-667-8377. Office Fax: 617-667-2767. Business E-Mail: jlamont@caregroup.harvard.edu.

LAMONT, LANSING, journalist, writer, public affairs and trust executive; b. NYC, Mar. 13, 1930; s. Thomas Stilwell and Elinor (Miner) L.; m. Ada Jung, Sept. 18, 1954; children: Douglas Ranlet, Elisabeth Jung Lamont Wolcott, Virginia Alden Lamont Cazedessus, Thomas Stilwell II. AB, Harvard U., 1952; MS in Journalism with honors, Columbia U., 1958. Reporter Washington Star, 1958-59; Washington corr. Worcester (Mass.) Gazette, also other New Eng. papers, 1959-60; sci. reporter Washington bur. Time mag., 1961-63, polit. reporter, 1964-68, corr., dep. chief London bur., 1969-71, chief Can. corr., chief Ottawa bur., 1971-73; chief corr. UN bur. Time mag., NYC, 1973-74; v.p., mng. dir. Can. Affairs The Americas Soc., 1981-91, sr. fellow, 1991-94. Author: Day of Trinity (alt. selection Lit. Guild Am.), 1965, Campus Shock, 1979, Journey to the Last Empire: The Soviet Union in Transition, 1991, Breakup: The Coming End of Canada and the Stakes for America, 1994 (Notable Books of Yr., N.Y. Times), Sand and Glitter: Exploring the Ancient Middle East, 1994-95, In the Land of Sangria and Sorrows: Spain, 1997, No Twilight About Me: A Life in Letters, 1999; co-editor Private Letters of John Masefield, 1979, Friends So Different: Essays on Canada and U.S. in the 1980's, 1989. Mem. alumni bd. dirs. Harvard U., also chmn. nominating com. for overseers; trustee Milton Acad., 1976-88, Am. Mus. Natural History, N.Y.C., Nat. Inst. for Music Theatre; pres. Am. Trust for the Brit. Libr., 2000—; pres. Century Assn. Archives Found., 1998-2004; mem. Can.-Am. Com., 1984-94, Coun. Fgn. Rels. 1985—, Carnegie Coun. on Ethics and Internat. affairs. Served to 1st lt., inf. U.S. Army, 1954-57. William Cullen Bryant fellow Met. Mus. Art, 1984-. Mem. Century Assn. (N.Y.C.), Harvard Club (N.Y.C.). Episcopalian. Office: 133 E 80th St New York NY 10021-0317 Office Phone: 212-772-6581.

LAMONT, LEE, music company and communications executive; b. Queens, NY; m. August Tagliamonte, Apr. 30, 1951; 1 child, Leslie Lamont. With Nat. Concerts & Artists Corp., NYC, 1955-58; asst. Sol Hurok Concerts, NYC, 1958-67; person rep. for concerts, rec. and TV Isaac Stern, NYC, 1968-76; v.p. ICM Artists Ltd., NYC, 1976-85; pres. ICM Artists Ltd. and ICM Artists (London) Ltd., NYC, 1985-95, chmn. bd. dirs., 1995—2002, chmn. emeritus, 2002—. Former mem. adv. com. Hannover (Germany) Internat. Violin Competition. Former mem. bd. overseers Curtis Inst. Music. Mem. Ams. for the Arts, Japan Soc., Asia Soc., Am. Symphony Orch. League (bd. dirs.), Bohemian Club. Avocations: painting, sculpture. E-mail: llamont@opus3artists.com.

LAMONT-GORDON, MELISSA LYNNE, orchestra director, music educator; b. Elmhurst, Ill., Aug. 1, 1965; d. Lawrence Michael and Lynne Laughlin Lamont; m. Steven Howard Gordon, July 19, 1992. Attended, Carnegie-Mellon U., 1983—85; MusB, U. Pitts., 1986; post grad., Va. Commonwealth U., 1992—93, Ohio State U., Columbus, 1997, Ind. U., Bloomington, 2004. Cert. in Music Edn. Va. Commonwealth U., Advanced Placement Music Theory Instr. Ind. U. Orch. dir. Henrico County Schs., 1992—94, Hanover County Schs., 1994—98; dir. orchs., chamber ensembles Clover Hill HS, Chesterfield County Schs., 1998—, advisor student coun. assn., 2000—02. Dir. all county orchs. Chesterfield County Schs., 1997; dir. youth concert orch. Richmond Symphony Young Performers Program, 2003—05; Celtic and pedal harpist; music festival judge; guest condr., composer, arranger. Named Gov.'s Sch. Outstanding Educator, 2005. Mem.: Music Educator's Nat. Conf., Va. Band and Orch. Dir. Assn. Home: 8535 Chester Forest Ln Richmond VA 23237 Office: Clover HS 13900 Hull St Rd Midlothian VA 23112 Office Phone: 804-739-6230. E-mail: Melissa_Gordon@ccpsnet.net.

LAMONT-HAVERS, RONALD WILLIAM, retired physician, medical association administrator; b. Wymondham, Norfolk, Eng., Mar. 6, 1920; came to U.S., 1955, naturalized, 1964; m. Gabrielson, Oct. 16, 1965; children: Wendy, Melinda, Ian. BA, U. B.C., 1942; MD, U. Toronto, 1946; diploma in internal medicine, McGill U., 1953. Intern Vancouver (B.C., Can.) Gen. Hosp., 1946-48; resident in internal medicine Queen Mary Vets. Hosp., Montreal, Que., Canada, 1949-51; Can. Arthritis and Rheumatism Soc. fellow Columbia Presbyterian Hosp., Coll. Physicians and Surgeons, Columbia U., NYC, 1951-53; med. dir. Can. Arthritis and Rheumatism Soc., B.C. divsn., Vancouver, 1953-55, Arthritis and Rheumatism Found., NYC, 1955-64; instr. in medicine Coll. Physicians and Surgeons, Columbia U., 1955-64; assoc. dir. extramural programs NIAMD, Bethesda, Md., 1964-68, dep. dir., 1972-74; assoc. dir. extramural programs NIH, Bethesda, 1968-72, acting dir., dep. dir., 1974-76, acting dir., 1975, dep. dir., 1974-76; dep. to gen. dir. for rsch. policy and adminstrn. Mass. Gen. Hosp., Boston, 1976-87, v.p. rsch. and tech. affairs, 1987-90, sr. cons. for rsch., 1990-99; dep. dir. Cutaneous Biology Rsch. Ctr. Mass. Gen. Hosp. and Harvard U., 1990—99, sr. advisor, 1999—2005; ret., 2005. Del. USSR-Arthritis Exch. Program, 1964; U.S. coord. U.S.-USSR Coop. Program in Arthritis, 1973-75. Served with M.C. Royal Can. Army, 1944-46. Recipient Superior Svc. award HEW, 1973; Spl. citation Sec. HEW, 1975. Fellow Royal Coll. Physicians (Can.); mem. Am. Coll. Rheumatology (dir. Met. Washington sect. 1964-66), N.Y. Rheumatism Assn. (pres. 1960), Arthritis Found. (dir., governing mem. 1966-80, pres. Mass. chpt. 1987-89), Alpha Omega Alpha. Address: 173 Morse Rd Sudbury MA 01776 Personal E-mail: rwlh@att.net.

LAMOREAUX, PHILIP ELMER, geologist, hydrologist, consultant; b. Chardon, Ohio, May 12, 1920; s. Elmer I. and Gladys (Rhodes) L.; m. Ura Mae Munro, Nov. 11, 1943; children: Philip E Jr., James W., Karen L. BA, Denison U., 1943, PhD (hon.), 1972; MS, U. Ala., 1949. Registered profl. geologist, Ga., Tenn., Ind., Ariz., Fla., Pa., Ala. Geologist U.S. Geol. Survey, Tuscaloosa, Ala., 1943-45, dist. geologist Groundwater Office, 1945-57, divsn. hydrologist water resources programs, 1957-59, chief ground water br. Washington, 1959-61; state geologist, oil and gas supr. Ala. Geol. Survey, Tuscaloosa, 1961-76; pres. P.E. LaMoreaux & Assocs. Inc., Tuscaloosa, 1976-87, chmn. bd. dirs., 1987-90, sr. hydrologist, 1990—. Lectr. Am. Geol. Inst. Coll. Program, 1969-71, Am. Geophys. Union Coll. Program, 1961—, NSF, Ala. Acad. Sci. H.S. Program, 1961—, No. Engring. and Testing, Salt Lake City, 1985, Ga. State U., Fla. State U., Vanderbilt U., Denison U., Auburn U., U. of Montpellier, France, U. Christ Church, New Zealand, U. Praetoria, South Africa; hydrogeology cons. to 30 fgn. countries. Editor in chief Jour. Environ. Geology, 1982—; editor in chief: Annotated Bibliography Carbonate Rocks, vols. 1-5; contbr. articles to profl. jours. Active Nat. Drinking Water Adv. Coun. EPA, 1984-88; tech. rev. group Oak Ridge Nat. Lab., 1984-88; trustee Denison U.; adv. Boy Scouts Am. Black Warrior Coun., 1993—. Recipient Comdrs. medal C.E., 1990. Mem.: AAAS, NAS (nat. rsch. coun. geotech. bd. 1990—92, water sci. and tech. bd. 1990—97, bd. earth scis. and resources 1992—97, earth resources com. 1995—97, nat. landslide hazard mitigation strategy com. 2001—02), AIME, ASTM, NAE, Ala. C. of C. (Pres.'s adv. com., Rep. of Energy 1980), Southeastern Geol. Soc., Soil Conservation Soc. Am., Soc. Econ. Paleontologists and Mineralogists, Soc. Econ. Geologists, Nat. Ground Water Assn. (group 2020 2001—), Nat. Water Well Assn., Nat. Water Resources Assn., Nat. Speleological Soc., Nat. Rivers and Harbors Congress, Nat. Assn. Geology Tchrs., Miss. Geol. Soc., Interstate Oil Compact Commn. (vice chmn. 1963, chmn. rsch. com.), Internat. Water Resources Assn. (Karst Commn. 1961—), Internat. Assn. Hydrogeologists (v.p. 1973—77, pres. 1977—80, com. on water rsch. 1978—80, chmn. hydrology hazardous waste commn. 1983—91, mem. com. thermal and mineral waters 1994—, adv. to pres. 1995—), Geol. Soc. London, Geol. Soc. Am. (1st. chmn. hydrogeology group 1963, chmn. O.E. Meinzer award com. 1965, cons. membership S.E. sect. 1967—68, chmn. nominating com., bd. dirs., bd. trustees, publs. com., chmn.), Assn. Am. State Geologists (statistician 1966—69, trustee), Am. Inst. Profl. Geologists (chmn. com. on rels. with govtl. agencies 1967—70, chmn. liaison com. fed. agencies 1968—70, bd. dirs. 1969—70, pres.), Am. Inst. Hydrology, Am. Geophys. Union, Am. Geol. Inst. (chmn. com. on publs. 1968—70, pres. 1971—72, chmn. environ. geosci. adv. com. 1994—, found. bd. trustees, chmn. environ. awareness com., trustee, Ian Campbell award 1990, William B. Heroy award 1995), Am. Assn. Petroleum Geologists (acad. liaison com., Ho. of Dels. 1970—72, com. preservation samples and cores 1998—, chmn. divsn. geosci. hydrogeology com., mem. pubs. com. 1998—), Ala. Geol. Soc., Ala. Acad. Sci. Republican. Presbyterian. Avocations: photography, stamp collecting/philately, coin collecting/numismatics, gardening. Office: PE LaMoreaux PO Box 2310 Tuscaloosa AL 35403 Office Phone: 205-391-3535. Business E-Mail: pel@dbtech.net.

LAMORIELLO, LOU (LOUIS ANTHONY LAMORIELLO), professional sports team executive; b. Providence, Oct. 21, 1942; s. Nicholas Schiano and Rose (Ventura) Lamoriello; m. Patricia A. Renaldo, Aug. 9, 1970; children: Christopher, Heidi, Timothy. BA in Math. and Econs., Providence Coll., 1963. Hockey coach Providence Coll., 1968—82, athletic dir., 1982—87; CEO, pres., gen. mgr. NJ Devils, 1987—, interim head coach, 2005—06, 2007; CEO NJ Nets, 2002—04. Commr. Hockey East Assn., Providence, 1984—87; mem. hockey com. U.S. Olympics, 1984, 88; pres. Am. Hockey Coaches Assn., 1982—83. Named to Hall of Fame, Providence Coll. Athletic Dept., 1982, I.T.L.U.-Am. Hall of Fame, 1986, R.I. Hall of Fame, 1987. Mem.: Nat. Collegiate Athletic Assn. (profl. devel. com. 1984—87). Achievements include being the general manager of Stanley Cup Champion NJ Devils, 1995, 2000, 2003. Office: c/o NJ Devils Nat Newark Bldg 744 Broad St, 33rd Fl Newark NJ 07102*

LAMORTE, JOYCE E., music educator; b. Buffalo, June 8, 1962; d. Wayne A. and Eva M. Dodge; m. David S. LaMorte, Aug. 12, 1995. BFA in Music Edn., SUNY, Amherst, NY, 1985; MA in Music Edn., Penn. Sate U., State Coll., 1989. Cert. music edn. NY, piano adjudicator. Choral/music tchr. Belfast Ctrl. Sch., NY, 1985—87; grad. assistantship music edn. Penn. State U., 1987—89; choral music tchr. Tangier Smith Elem. Sch., Mastic Beach, NY, 1989—99, The Michael J. Petrides Sch., SI, NY, 1999—. Coop. tchr. for music student tchrs. The Michael J. Petrides Sch., SI, 1999—2005; music edn. elem. edn. Wagner Coll., SI, 2001—; music edn. facilitator NYC Dept. Edn., 2002—; elem. edn. adj. lectr. Coll. SI, 2002—; NYSSMA piano adjudicator NY State Sch. Music Assn., LI, 2003—; music edn. cons. Arts Connection, NYC, 2005—06; choir dir. vocal instrn. SI Ballet Summer Inst, 2006. Asst. minister Trinity Luth. Ch., SI, 2002—, flower deliverer to shut-ins, 2003—. Mem.: Music Educator's Assn. NYC, LI Am. Orff schalwerk Assn., NYS Sch. Music Assn. Avocations: horseback riding, reading, exercise, bowling.

LAMOTTE, JANET ALLISON, retired management consultant; b. Norfolk, Va., Mar. 3, 1942; d. Charles Nelson Jr. and Geneva Elizabeth (Baird) Johnson; m. Larry LaMotte, Aug. 30, 1964 (div. Aug. 1979); children: Lisa Renee LaMotte Buchholz, Lori Louise. AA, Rose State Coll., 1982; BA, U. Ctrl. Okla., 1984; MA in Human Rels., U. Okla., 1986.

Clk./typist U.S. Army, Washington, 1960, Fort Belvoir, Va., 1961, Dallas, 1961, IRS, Dallas, 1962, Richmond, Va., 1962—63, sec., 1963—64; pers. asst. State Bd. Control, Austin, Tex., 1964—65; procurement clk. FAA, Oklahoma City, 1965—66; clk./typist DLA, Alexandria, Va., 1978, IRS, Oklahoma City, 1978—79, Tinker AFB, 1979; acctg. clk., 1980—81; clk./stenographer, 1980—81; sec., 1981—82; supply specialist, 1982—87; worldwide inventory mgmt. specialist, 1987—98. Safety chmn. Kensler Elem. Sch. PTA, Wichita, 1974-75; vol. CONTACT Crisis Helpline, 1986-89. Federally Employed Women scholar, 1984. Mem.: AARP, AAUW, Tinker Mgmt. Assn. (membership, ticket monitor 1994—98, scholar 1981—85), Okla. Air Force Assn. (v.p. comm. 1995—97, exec. sec. 1996—97, Okla. Mem. of Yr. 1996, Nat. Exceptional Svc. award 1996), Air Force Assn. (v.p. pub. rels. Gerrity chpt. 1994, v.p. comm. 1995—98, Nat. medal of Merit 1995, Nat. Exceptional Svc. award 1996, Chpt. Exceptional Svc. award 1998), Nat. Assn. Ret. Fed. Employees, Am. Bus. Women's Assn. (v.p. membership downtown reflections chpt. 1992—93), Nat. Geol. Soc., Nat. Geneal. Soc., Nat. Women's History Mus. (charter mem.), Nat. Air Force Meml. (charter), Wythe County Hist. and Gen. Assn., Okla. Geneal. Soc., Nat. WWII Meml. (charter), Okla. Hist. Soc., Toastmasters (edn. v.p. 1988, pres. Tinker chpt. 1989, area gov. 1991—92, area editor K-3 Newsletter 1992—93, awards), Morrow County Geneal. Soc., Pulaski County Hist. Soc., Nat. Trust for Hist. Preservation. Methodist. Avocations: history, writing, genealogy, computers, reading. Home: 9525 Ridgeview Dr Oklahoma City OK 73120-3419 Personal E-mail: jlamott99@msn.com.

LAMOUR, KENOL, artist, educator; s. Kis Lamour and Anne Adrienne Petion Lamour. AA, Coll. S.I., NYC, 1979; BFA, Fashion Inst. Tech., NYC, 1988; MEd, Cambridge Coll., Mass., 2005. Cert. pattern design 2000 Gerber Tech., N.Y., 2002, basic AccuMark grading and marking Gerber Tech., N.Y., 2002; profl. program development and grant comm. The Grant Inst., L.A., 2005. Instr. Wood Tobe Coburn, NYC, 1997—99; asst. prof. Centenary Coll., Hackettstown, NJ, 1999—. Cons, writer Kingsboro Temple Seventh Day Adventists, Bklyn., 2005—06. Recipient Design First prize, PPF Internat., 1985, Sportswear Design award, Cotton Inc., 1986, Fashion award, I Love N.Y. Campaign, 1986, Fashion & Jazz award, Beefeater's Gin, 1987; scholar, Dorot Found., 2005. Mem.: Artist Cultural Soc. (co-chmn. 1996—2002). Achievements include design of pattern accordian sleeves to apparel. Office: Centenary College 400 Jefferson Street Hackettstown NJ 07840 Home Phone: 718-638-6114; Office Phone: 908-852-1400 2258. Personal E-mail: omnipotent2@verizon.net. Business E-Mail: lamourk@centenarycollege.edu.

LAMP, BENSON J., tractor company executive; b. Cardington, Ohio, Oct. 7, 1925; m. Martha Jane Motz, Aug. 21, 1948; children: Elaine, Marlene, Linda, David. BS in Agr. and B in Agrl. Engring., Ohio State U., Columbus, 1949, MS in Agrl. Engring., 1952; PhD in Agrl. Engring., Mich. State U., East Lansing, 1960. Registered profl. engr., Ohio. Prof. agrl. engring. Ohio State U., Columbus, 1949-61, 87-91, prof. emeritus, 1991—; product mgr. Massey Ferguson Ltd., Toronto, Can., 1961-66; product planning mgr. Ford Tractor Ops. div. Ford Motor Co., Troy, Mich., 1966-71, mktg. mgr., 1971-76, bus. planning mgr., 1978-87; v.p. mktg. and devel. Ford Aerospace div. Ford Motor Co., Dearborn, Mich., 1976-78. Author: Corn Harvesting, 1962. Served to 2d lt. USAF, 1943-45. Fellow Am. Soc. Agrl. Engrs. (pres. 1985-86, Gold medal 1993); mem. Nat. Acad. Engring., Country Club at Muirfield Village (Dublin, Ohio). Avocations: golf, tennis, bridge. Office: BJM Company Inc 6128 Inverurie Dr E Dublin OH 43017-9472 Office Phone: 614-761-9745. Personal E-mail: blamp2@aol.com.

LAMPASONA, EYDI M., art educator; b. Neward, NJ, Jan. 9, 1955; d. Dominick and Edith Ferullo. BFA, Fla. Atlantic U., Boca Raton, 2001; MFA, Vt. Coll., Montpelier, 2007. Art tchr. Boca Raton Mus. Art, 1999—. Contbr. chapters to books. Mem.: Nat. Watercolor Soc., Soc. Layerists in Multi Media, Internat. Soc. Experimental Artists, Nat. Coll. Soc., Nat. Assn. Women Artists. Home: 11035 Baybreeze Way Boca Raton FL 33428 Office Phone: 561-477-9977. Personal E-mail: pydi@bellsouth.net.

LAMPEN, RICHARD JAY, lawyer, investment banker; b. New Brunswick, NJ, Nov. 12, 1953; s. J. Oliver and Miriam (Walsh) L.; m. Susan Matson, June 8, 1975; children: Katharine, Caroline. BA, Johns Hopkins U., 1975; JD, Columbia U., 1978. Bar: Fla. 1978, U.S. Dist. Ct. (so. dist.) Fla. 1978. From assoc. to ptnr. Steel Hector & Davis, Miami, Fla., 1978-86, co-chmn. corp. dept., 1992-95; mng. dir. Salomon Bros. Inc., NYC, 1986-92; exec. v.p., gen. counsel New Valley Corp., Miami, Fla., 1995—2005; exec. v.p. Vector Group Ltd., Miami, 1996—; pres., CEO Ladenburg Thalmann Fin. Svcs. Inc., Miami, 2006—. Bd. dirs. CDSI Holdings Inc., Ladenburg Thalmann Fin. Svcs. Inc., Douglas Elliman Realty, LLC. Pres. Miami Children's Mus., 2000—05; chmn. Ransom-Everglades Sch., 2004—06. Mem. Fla. Bar Assn. (chmn. securities law com. 1985-86), City Club, Riviera Club. Office: Vector Group Ltd 100 SE 2nd St Fl 32 Miami FL 33131-2158 Home Phone: 305-663-9016; Office Phone: 305-579-8000. Business E-Mail: rlampen@vectorgroupltd.com.

LAMPERT, EDWARD S. (EDDIE LAMPERT), investment company executive; b. Roslyn, NY, July 19, 1962; s. Floyd and Dolores Lampert; m. Kinga Lampert; 3 children. BS in Econs., Yale U., New Haven, 1984. With Goldman Sachs Grp. Inc., 1984—88; founder, chmn. ESL Investments, Inc., Greenwich, Conn., 1988—. Bd. mem. AutoNation, Inc., AutoZone, Inc., 1999—2006; chmn. bd. Kmart Holding Corp., Troy, Mich., 2003—05; corp. chmn. Sears Holdings Corp., 2005—. Named one of World's Richest People, Forbes mag., 2004—, Forbes' Richest Ams., 2004—, 100 Most Influential People, Time mag., 2006. Mem.: Skull and Bones, Phi Beta Kappa. Office: ESL Investments Inc 200 Greenwich Ave Greenwich CT 06830 Office Phone: 203-861-4600.*

LAMPERT, ELEANOR VERNA, retired human resources specialist; b. Porterville, Calif., Mar. 23; d. Ernest Samuel and Violet Edna (Watkins) Wilson; m. Robert Mathew Lampert, Aug. 23, 1935; children: Sally Lu Winton, Lary Lampert, Carol R. John. Student in bus. fin., Porterville Jr. Coll., 1977-78; grad., Anthony Real Estate Sch., 1971; student, Laguna Sch. of Art., 1972, U. Calif., Santa Cruz, 1981. Bookkeeper Porterville (Calif.) Hos., 1956-71; real estate sales staff Ray Realty, Porterville, 1973; sec. Employment Devel. Dept. State of Calif., Porterville, 1973-83; orientation and tng specialist CETA employees, 1976-80; ret. Sec. Employer Adv. Group, 1973-80, 81—. Author: Black Bloomers and Han-Ga-Ber, 1986. Mem. U.S. Senatorial Business Adv. Bd., 1981-84, Rep. Nat. congl. Com., 1982-88, Sierra View Hosp. Vol. League, 1988-89 (pres.); charter mem. Presdl. Republican Task Force, 1981—, Republican National Committee; vol. Calif Hosp. Assn., 1983-89, Calif. Spl. Olympics Spirit Team, Sonora Cmty. Hospital Oak Plus League, Special Olympics Northern Calif. partner. Recipient Merit Cert., Gov. Pat Brown, State of Calif., 1968. Mem. Lindsay Olive Growers, Sunkist Orange Growers, Am. Kennel Club, Internat. Assn. Personnel in Employment Security, Calif. State Employes Assn. (emeritus Nat. Wildlife Fedn., NRA, Friends of Porterville Library, Heritage Found., DAR (Kaweah chpt. rec. sec. 1988—), Internat. Platform Assn., Dist. Fedn. Women's Clubs (recording sec. Calif. chpt. 1988—), Ky. Hist. Soc., Women's Club of Calif. (pres. Porterville chpt. 1988-89, dist. rec. sec. 1987-89), Mo. Rep. Women of Taney County, Internat. Sporting and Leisure Club, Ladies Aux, VFW (No. 5168 Forsyth,Mo.), Ozark Walkers League, Women of the Moose Lodge, Humane Soc. U.S., History Channel Club, Srs. Club Sonora. Republican.

LAMPERT, JAMES B., lawyer; b. Montpelier, Vt., June 26, 1938; s. James Benjamin Lampert and Margery Frances (Mitchell) Lampert-Dudley; m. Mary Elizabeth Shugrue; children: Nicholas, Michael, Stephen. BSME, MIT, 1961; JD magna cum laude, Harvard U., 1964. Bar: Mass. 1964, U.S. Dist. Ct. Mass., U.S. Ct. Appeals (1st cir.) 1967, U.S. Patent and Trademark Office 1967, U.S. Ct. Appeals (fed. cir.) 1985. Sr. ptnr. Fish & Richardson, Boston, 1964-85; adj. prof. law Boston U., 1972-87; sr. ptnr. Hale and Dorr, Boston, 1985—2004; ptnr., chmn. Intellectual Property dept., mem. Litigation dept. & Corp. dept. Wilmer Cutler Pickering Hale & Dorr, Boston, 2004—. Capt. U.S. Army Corps of Engineers, 1964-66. Named a Mass. Super Lawyer, Boston Mag., 2004. Mem. Mass Bar Assn., Boston Patent Law Assn., Tau Beta Pi, Pi Tau Sigma, Sigma Xi. Avocations: sailing, skiing, swimming. Home: 148 Washington St Duxbury MA 02332-4523 Office: Wilmer Cutler Pickering Hale & Dorr 60 State St Boston MA 02109-1816 Office Phone: 617-526-6456. Office Fax: 617-526-5000. Business E-Mail: james.lampert@wilmerhale.com.

LAMPERT, LYNN DENISE, librarian, educator; b. LA, Jan. 10, 1972; d. Howard Victor and Frances Sandra Lampert; m. Andrew Tony Diekmann, Mar. 24, 2002. BA in History, U. Calif., Santa Barbara, 1994; M Libr. and Info. Sci., M History, UCLA, 1998. Info. specialist Calif. Luth. U., Thousand Oaks, 1998—2001; chmn. reference and instrnl. svcs. Calif. State U., Northridge, 2001—. Cons., writer in field, 1998—. Contbr. articles to profl. publs. Regents scholar, U. Calif., Santa Barbara, 1990—94. Mem.: Assn. Coll. and Rsch. Librs. (assoc.; com. chmn. 2005). Democrat. Jewish. Achievements include research in information literacy, student plagiarism. Avocations: movies, reading, travel. Office: California State U 18111 Nordhoff St Northridge CA 91330-8327 Home Phone: 818-981-3465; Office Phone: 818-677-7104. Business E-Mail: lynn.lampert@csun.edu.

LAMPERT, MICHAEL ALLEN, lawyer; b. Phila., May 6, 1958; s. Arnold Leonard and Marilyn Lampert; 1 child, David Max. AB in Econs. cum laude, U. Miami, Coral Gables, Fla., 1979, postgrad., 1980; JD, Duke U., 1983; LLM in Taxation, NYU, 1984. Bar: Fla. 1983, DC 1984, Pa. 1984, US Tax Ct. 1984, US Ct. of Appeals for the Armed Forces 1995; U.S. Dist. Ct. (S. Dist. Fla.), 2000, bd. cert. tax lawyer, Fla. Bar; cert. Bd. Legal Specialization and Edn., Fla. Assoc. Cohen, Scherer, Cohn & Silverman, P.A., North Palm Beach, Fla., 1984-88; instr. divsn. continuing edn. Fla. Atlantic U., Boca Raton, Fla., 1988—98; prin. Jacobson & Lampert, P.A., Boca Raton, 1988—91; pvt. practice West Palm Beach, 1991—. Bd. dir. Nat. Holocaust and War Tracing Ctr., 2003—. Mem. editl. bd. Southeastern Tax Alert, 1993-97, Sales and Use Tax Alert, 1997—. Instr., trainer, past chpt. vice-chair, sect. bd. dirs. ARC, Palm Beach County, Fla., 2006—; bd. dirs. Jewish Fedn. Palm Beach County, 1989-91, 97-99, Jewish Family and Children's Svc. Palm Beach County, 1988—, treas., 1991-94, pres., 1997-99; pres. Jewish Residential and Family Svc., Inc., 1997-2003, T & M Ranch Cmty., Inc., 2000-03; mem. Commn. for Jewish Edn.-Palm Beach, 1997-99; past nat. planned giving com. Weismann Inst., Israel; exec. bd., past v.p. planned giving Am. Soc. for Tech., Palm Beach. Recipient Young Leadership award, 1988, Safety award ARC, 1989, Cert. of Merit, Am. Radio Relay League, West Palm Beach Club, 1988, Cert. of Appreciation for Leadership, ARC Disaster Svc., Palm Beach County, 1989, Disaster Svc. award, 1994, Human Resources award, 1993, Tax Law award Legal Aid Soc. Palm Beach County and Palm Beach County Bar Assn., 1993, Young Leadership award Jewish Fedn. Palm Beach County, 1998, Thelma Starks Disting. Svc. award, 2005. Mem. Palm Beach Tax Inst. (pres., bd. dir. 1993-94), Fla. Bar (exec. coun., mem. dir. com. tax sect., mem. taxation cert. com., past vice-chair taxation com., bd. legal specialization and certification), Palm Beach County Bar Assn. (chair bus. and corp. continuing legal edn. com. 1989-90, chair legal asst. com. 1988-91, Tax Law award 1993), Legal Aid Soc. of Palm Beach County, Inc. Avocations: aquatics, amateur radio, running. Office: Ste 900 1655 Palm Beach Lakes Blvd West Palm Beach FL 33401-2211 Office Phone: 561-689-9407. E-mail: lamperttaxlaw@att.net.

LAMPERT, S. HENRY, retired dentist; b. Bklyn., Mar. 10, 1929; s. Joseph and Sadie (Bass) L.; m. Jacqueline Adler, Mar. 27, 1955; children: Karen Ann, Beth Robin, Judith Ellen. BA, U. Ill., 1950; DDS, NYU, 1954. Intern in dentistry Mt. Sinai Hosp., NYC, 1954-55; gen. practice dentistry Essex Junction, Vt., 1957-95; ret., 1995. Dir. Temporo Mandibular Joint Program, Med. Ctr. Hosp. Vt., Burlington, 1970-76, attending staff 1957-92, peer rev. com., 1978-92; mem. staff Fanny Allen Hosp., Winooski, Vt., 1961-89; assoc. prof. Sch. Allied Health Scis., U. Vt., Burlington, 1963-73, clin. instr. Coll. Medicine, 1974-75, clin. instr. dept. oral surgery, 1986-96. Sec., Vt. Bd. Dental Examiners, 1973-76, pres., 1976-77; instr. photography Church St. Ctr. for Cmty. Edn., U. Vt., until 1998; mem. N.E. Regional Bd. Dental Examiners, 1973-84, 96-98, cons. and examiner; CPR instr. Vt. Heart Assn., 1977-2000; photographer Essex (Vt.) Reporter, 1997—02; instr. photography Essex Town Parks and Recreation Dept., 1999—; lectr. in field Contbr. articles to profl. jours., photographs pub. in numerous mags. and jours. Capt. AUS, 1955-57, USAR, 1957-60; col. Vt. State Guard, 2005. Fellow Internat. Coll. Dentists; mem. ADA (standard setting com. of coun. on nat. bd. exams. 1978-81), Champlain Valley Dental Soc. (pres. 1961-62), Acad. Operative Dentistry, Vt. Dental Soc., Masons, Rotary, Alpha Omega. Jewish (bd. govs. synagogue 1967-70, 72-73, chmn. bd. edn.). Home: 13 Hopkins St Voorhees NJ 08043 Personal E-mail: jackieejvt@mac.com.

LAMPERTI, JOHN WILLIAMS, mathematician, educator; b. Montclair, NJ, Dec. 20, 1932; s. Frank A. and Louise (Williams) L.; m. Claudia Jane McKay, Aug. 17, 1957; children— Matthew, Steven, Aaron, Noelle. BS, Haverford Coll., 1953; PhD, Calif. Inst. Tech., 1957. Instr., then asst. prof. math. Stanford (Calif.) U., 1957-62; rsch. assoc. Rockefeller Inst., 1962-63; faculty Dartmouth Coll., Hanover, NH, 1963-98, prof. math., 1968-98, prof. emeritus, 1998—. Sci. exch. visitor to USSR, 1970; vis. prof. U. Aarhus, Denmark, 1972-73, Nicaraguan Nat. U., 1990; cons. Am. Friends Svc. Com., 1980, 85, 91. Author: Probability: A Survey of the Mathematical Theory, 1966, 2d edit., 1996, Stochastic Processes: A survey of the Mathematical Theory, 1977, What Are We Afraid Of? An Assessment of the "Communist Threat" in Central America, 1988, Enrique Alvarez Cordova: Life of a Salvadoran Revolutionary and Gentleman, 2006. Fellow Inst. Math. Stats.; mem. ACLU, War Resisters League, Peace Action, Amnesty Internat., Union Concerned Scientists. Home: Upper Loveland Rd Norwich VT 05055 Office: Dartmouth Coll Dept Math Hanover NH 03755 Office Phone: 802-649-1359. Business E-Mail: j.lamperti@dartmouth.edu.

LAMPERT-SHEPEL, ELINA, education educator; b. Mar. 21, 1961; BA in Linguistics, English and French, Kharkov State U., Ukraine, 1983; MEd, Columbia U., NYC, 1998, EdD, 2006. English tchr. Kharkov pub. schs., 1983—90; adj. instr. Regional Tchrs.' Ctr., Kharkov, 1983—90; head curriculum dept. Ednl. Ctr. Socio-Pedagogical Design and Innovation, Moscow, 1988—90; acad. dean, prof., coord. univ. internat. programs Eureka U. Sch. Edn., Moscow, 1990—94; assoc. prof., chmn. dept. Globe Inst. Tech., NYC, 1994—2003; instr., rschr. dept. curriculum and tchg. Columbia U. Tchrs. Coll., 2001—03; asst. prof. Mercy Coll., 2004—. Presenter in field. Contbr. articles to profl. publs. Mem.: ISCAR, AERA.

LAMPINEN, JOHN A., newspaper editor; b. Waukegan, Ill., Nov. 26, 1951; s. Walter Valentine and Patricia Mae Irene (Pruess) L.; m. Belinda Walter, Oct. 20, 1973; children: Amanda Michelle, Heidi Elizabeth. BS in Comm., U. Ill., 1973. Staff writer Paddock Cir. Newspapers, Libertyville, Ill., 1973-75; regional editor The Jour., New Ulm, Minn., 1975-76; various positions Daily Herald, Arlington Heights, Ill., 1976-90, asst. v.p., mng. editor, 1990—97, asst. v.p., exec. editor, 1997—99, v.p., exec. editor, 1999—2001, sr. v.p., editor, 2001—. Adj. prof. Medill Sch. Journalism, Northwestern U., Evanston, Ill., 1995-98. Mem. Assoc. Press Mng. Editors, Soc. Profl. Journalists, Am. Soc. Newspaper Editors. Avocations: baseball, long-distance running, coaching girls softball, sports memorabilia. Office: Daily Herald 155 E Algonquin Rd Arlington Heights IL 60005-4617

LAMPING, KATHRYN G., medical educator, medical researcher; BS in Biology, U. Ill., 1976; MS in Pharmacology, Med. Coll. Wis., 1982, PhD in Pharmacology, 1983. Postdoctoral rsch. fellow Dept. Internal Medicine, U. Iowa, Iowa City, 1983-86, asst. rsch. scientist, 1986-89, adj. asst. prof., 1989-95, asst. prof., 1995—. Contbr. articles to profl. jours. Mem. Am. Heart Assn. (Established Investigator award 1995), Am. Physiol. Soc., Microcirculatory Soc. Office: U Iowa Ctr on Agin 2159 Westlawn S Iowa City IA 52242-1100

LAMPKIN, TONI K., elementary school educator; b. Spokane, May 9, 1951; s. Anthony and Shirley Zielinski; m. Michael Lampkin, Mar. 18, 1982; 1 child, Heather Michelle Tunno. BS, Portland State U., Oreg., 1973. Cert. tchr. Nat. Bd. Certification, 2002. Tchr. Portland Sch. Dist., Hermiston Sch. Dist., Oreg. Mem. Stanfield City Coun., Stanfield, Oreg., 1982—84; mem. Relay for Life, Am. Cancer Soc., Hermiston, 1996—; bd. dirs. Habitat for Humanity, Hermiston, 1997—2000. Named Tchr. of Yr., Hermiston Sch. Dist., 1987; recipient Fulbright Seminar award, Fulbright Assn., New Delhi, 2004, award, Japan Fulbright Meml., Tokyo, 2006. Mem.: Nat. Coun. Social Studies, Oreg. Edn. Assn. (mem. PAC bd. 1993—96). Avocations: travel, reading. Home: PO Box 66 Stanfield OR 97875 Office: Sandstone Mid Sch 400 NE 10th Hermiston OR 97838

LAMPL, PEGGY ANN, public information officer; b. NYC, Dec. 12, 1930; d. Joseph and Alice L. BA, Bennington Coll., 1952. Dir. program devel. dept. mental health AMA, Chgo., 1962-66; spl. asst. NIMH, HEW, Washington, 1967-69; public relations dir. LWV, Washington, 1969—73, exec. dir., 1973—78; dep. asst. Sec. of State for congressional relations Dept. State, Washington, 1978-81; dep. dir. Iris Systems Devel., 1982-83; exec. dir. Children's Def. Fund, Washington, 1984-89, LWV, Washington, 1989—90; project mgr. Crimes of War, W.W. Norton, 1999; founder Project Vote Smart, Washington, 1993—; bd. dirs. Crimes of War Project, Washington, 1998—. Home: 2500 Q St NW Washington DC 20007-4373

LAMPMAN, RICHARD H. (DICK LAMPMAN), former computer company executive; b. 1945; BSEE, MSEE, Carnegie Mellon U. With Hewlett-Packard, 1971—2007, with HP labs., 1981—86, dir. measurement sys. lab., 1986—88, dir. computer systems lab., 1988—92, dir. worldwide Computer Rsch. Ctr., 1992—99, dir. HP Labs. Palo Alto, Calif., 1999—2007, sr. v.p. rsch., 2001—07. Bd. govs. EPCglobal. Mem. adv. bd. Carnegie Inst. Tech., Ga. Inst. Tech., Internet Soc. Adv. Coun., Corp. Exec. bd.; rep. HP on the adv. bd. Bay Area Sci. Infrastructure Consortium, Computer Systems Policy Project CTO. Mem.: IEEE (sr.), Assn. Computing Machinery, Computing Rsch. Assn., Silicon Valley Computer Sci. Rsch. Dirs., Math. Scis. Rsch. Inst. (mem. adv. bd.), Internet Soc. (mem. adv. coun.).*

LAMPORT, ANTHONY MATTHEW, venture capitalist; b. NYC, Dec. 8, 1935; s. Harold and Golden (Siwek) L.; m. Cynthia Hullinger, 1961; children: Sarah, Aaron. BA, Harvard U., 1957, MBA, 1959. With Drexel Burnham Lambert, NYC, 1959-90; pres. Lambda Fund Mgmt., Inc., NYC, 1990—. Bd. dirs. Prophesy Software, Sr. Bridge Family Cos., Paladin, Inc. Trustee Found. for Investor Edn., N.Y.C., 1976—. Office: Lambda Fund Mgmt Inc 1041 Third Ave New York NY 10021-8110 Home Phone: 212-288-7267; Office Phone: 212-308-7782.

LAMPRECHT, ELIZABETH ANN, mathematics professor; b. Buffalo, Sept. 7, 1966; d. James Alois and Christine Ann Lamprecht; m. James Joseph Carson, Aug. 13, 1988; children: Christopher Michael Lamprecht-Carson, Alexandra Maria Lamprecht-Carson, Gregory James Lamprecht-Carson, Daniel Peter Lamprecht-Carson, Andrew Stephen Lamprecht-Carson, Philip Anthony Lamprecht-Carson. BS magna cum laude, SUNY, Buffalo, 1988; MA, SUNY, Binghamton, 1990, PhD, 1994. Rsch. project asst. GE, Johnson City, NY, 1991—92; prof., chair math. dept. Adrian Coll., Mich., 1995—. Vis. asst. prof. SUNY, Oswego, 1993—95. Contbr. text reviews Stats. Tchr. Network. Recipient Tchg. award, Mortar Bd. Soc., 1999. Mem.: Nat. Coun. Tchrs. Math., Am. Statis. Assn., Assn. Women Math., Math. Assn. Am. Avocations: piano, reading, cooking. Office: Adrian Coll 110 South Madison St Adrian MI 49221 Office Phone: 517-264-3936. Personal E-mail: lampcar@aol.com. Business E-Mail: elamprecht@adrian.edu.

LAMPSON, BUTLER WRIGHT, computer scientist; b. Washington, Dec. 23, 1943; s. Edward Tudor and Mary Caroline (Wright) L.; m. Lois Helen Alterman, Sept. 23, 1967; children: Michael Alterman, David Wright AB, Harvard U., 1964; PhD, U. Calif.-Berkeley, 1967; D.Sc. (hon.), Eidgenossiche Technische Hochschule, Zurich, 1986; D in Info. (hon.), U. Bologna, 1996. Asst. prof. U. Calif.-Berkeley, 1967-70, assoc. prof., 1970-71; dir. system devel. Berkeley Computer Corp., 1969-71; prin. scientist Xerox Research Ctr., Palo Alto, Calif., 1971-75, sr. research fellow, 1975-84; sr. cons. engr. Digital Equipment Corp., Palo Alto, 1984-86, corp. cons. engr., 1986-93, sr. corp. cons. engr., 1993-95; arch. Microsoft Corp., Cambridge, Mass., 1995—2000, disting. engr., 2000—05, tech. fellow, 2005—. Adj. prof. elec. engring. and computer sci. MIT, 1987—. Contbr. articles to profl. jours. Patentee in field Recipient IEEE Computer Pioneer award, 1996, Nat. Computer Sys. Security award NIST/NSA, 1998, von Neumann medal IEEE, 2001, Charles Stark Draper prize NAE 2004. Fellow AAAS, Assn. Computing Machinery (Software System award 1984, A.M. Turing award 1992); mem. NAE, NAS. Office Phone: 425-703-5925. Business E-Mail: blampson@microsoft.com.

LAMPSON, NICK (NICHOLAS VALENTINO LAMPSON), congressman; b. Beaumont, Tex., Feb. 14, 1945; s. Nancy Jebbia Lampson; m. Susan Floyd Lampson; children: Hillary, Stephanie. BA, Lamar U., 1968, MA in Edn., 1974. Biology tchr. South Pk. Ind. Sch. Dist., 1968—71; prof. Lamar U., 1971—76; tax assessor-collector Jefferson County, 1977—95; mem. US Congress from 9th Tex. dist., 1997—2005, US Congress from 22nd Tex. dist., 2007—, mem. agrl. com., sci. & tech. com., transp. & infrastructure com. Founder Congl. Caucus on Missing & Exploited Children. Del. White Ho. Conf. Aging, 1995; dir. Area Agy. Aging; active Am. Heart Assn., Land Manor, Young Men's Bus. Assn.; chair Bishop's Faith Appeal St. Jude Cath. Ch., 1995. Named Outstanding Young Man of Beaumont Tex. Jaycees, 1978. Democrat. Roman Catholic. Office: 436 Cannon House Office Bldg Washington DC 20515 also: 10701 Corp Dr Ste 118 Stafford TX 77477*

LAMPTON, DUNN O., prosecutor; b. Oskya, Miss. married; 2 children. AA, SW Miss. Jr. Coll.; BE, U. Miss., JD, 1975. Bar: Miss. 1975. Ptnr. Phillips, Regan & Lampton, 1976—80; dist. atty. 14th Cir. Ct. Dist., 1976—2001; US atty. (so. dist.) Miss. US Dept. Justice, Jackson, 2001—. Staff judge adv. to col. USNG, 1980—. Office: US Attys Office So Dist Miss 188 E Capital St Ste 500 Jackson MS 39201*

LAMPTON, LESLIE B., SR., oil industry executive; b. 1926; married. Grad., U. Miss., 1947. With Joe T. Dehmer Distbr., Jackson, Miss., 1949-51, 53-54, Lampton Oil Co., Jackson, Miss., 1954-70; prin. Ergon Inc., Jackson, Miss., 1970—, chmn., pres., CFO. With USN, 1947—49, with USN, 1951—53. Office: Ergon Inc PO Box 1639 Jackson MS 39215

LAMSON, ROBERT WOODROW, retired school system administrator; b. LA, Dec. 28, 1917; s. Ernest K. and Mabel (Mahoney) L.; m. Jeannette Juett, July 22, 1949; children: Robert Woodrow Jr., Nancy Virginia,

Kathleen Patricia. BA, Occidental Coll., LA, 1940; MA, U. So. Calif., 1955. Cert. tchr., prin., supt., Calif. Tchr. El Monte (Calif.) Sch. Dist., 1940-43, L.A. City Sch. Dist., 1945—78, prin., 1949-55, supr., 1955-57, adminstrv. asst., 1957-59, area supt., 1959-78; ret., 1978; agt. Keilholtz Realtors, La Canada, Calif. Instr. colls. and univs. so. Calif.; founding mem., v.p. US Acad. Decathlon, Cerritos, Calif., 1981-86. Bd. dir. 10th Dist. PTA, LA, 1965-70; chmn. Scout-O-Rama, Gt. Western coun. Boy Scouts Am., 1980. Lt. comdr. USNR, 1943-46, mem. Res. ret. Mem. Am. Assn. Sch. Adminstrs., Assn. Adminstrs. LA, Occidental Coll. Alumni in Edn. Assn. (co-founder, past pres., bd. dirs.), Town Hall, Nat. PTA (hon. life), Calif. PTA (hon. life, bd. dir. 1978-80), 31st Dist. PTA (hon. life, bd. dir. 1965-78, auditorium named in his honor 1978), Phi Beta Kappa, Alpha Tau Omega Republican. Avocations: gardening, reading. Home: 4911 Vineta Ave La Canada Flintridge CA 91011-2624 Office: Richard Keilholtz Realtors 727 Foothill Blvd La Canada Flintridge CA 91011-3405

LAMSTER, IRA BARRY, dean, academic administrator; b. NYC, Mar. 6, 1950; s. Nathan and Mollie (Garber) L.; m. Gail Maxine Marcovitz, Aug. 28, 1971; children: Rachel Amy, Stephanie Anne. BA, CUNY, 1971; SM, U. Chgo., 1972; DDS, SUNY, Stony Brook, 1977; M.M.Sc., Harvard U., 1980; grad. splty. training in periodontology and oral medicine, Harvard U. Sch. Dental Medicine. Diplomate Am. Bd. Periodontology, Am. Bd. Oral Medicine. Assoc. prof., dir. rsch. ctr. Coll. Dental Medicine Fairleigh Dickinson U., Hackensack, NJ, 1980-88; dir. divsn. periodontics Columbia U. Sch. Dental and Oral Surgery, NYC, 1988—98, vice dean, 1998—2001, dean, 2001—. Cons. VA, various oral health care companies. Inventor in field; contbr. chpts. to books and articles to profl. jours. Recipient Young Investigator Rsch. award Pub. Health Svc., 1982-85, Individual Rsch. award 1985-89, 2002-, prin. Investigator Program Project 1991-97. Fellow: Am. Coll. Dentists. Mem.: AAAS, ADA, Am. Acad. Periodontology (editorial bd.), Am. Assn. Dental Rsch., Am. Acad. Oral Medicine, N.Y. Acad. Scis., Northeastern Soc. Periodontists (contbg. editor). Avocations: golf, tennis, reading. Office: Columbia U Sch Dental and Oral Surgery Dean's Office Box 20 630 W 168th St New York NY 10032 Office Phone: 212-305-4511. Business E-Mail: ibl1@columbia.edu.

LAMY, M. REBECCA (MARY REBECCA LAMY), consultant, land developer, government official; b. Ft. Bragg, NC, Nov. 21, 1929; d. Charles Joseph and Sarah Esther (Koonce) Lamy. BA, U. N.C., Greensboro, 1952. Procurement analyst Air Force Mil. Interdept. Purchase Request Mgmt. Office, Washington, 1958-60, procurement and fiscal officer, 1960-68; budget analyst Naval Air Sys. Command, Washington, 1968-69, indsl. specialist, 1969-71, Armament Devel. and Test Ctr., Eglin AFB, Fla., 1971-74, Def. Logistics Agy., Alexandria, Va., 1974-81; logistics mgmt. specialist Strategic Sys. Project Office, Dept. Navy, Washington, 1981-82; procurement analyst Hdqrs. Dept. Army, Washington, 1982-85. Emeritus mem. Onslow Mus. Found. Bd., Richlands, NC, Onslow Meml. Hosp. Aux., Jacksonville, NC, 1985—91. Recipient Outstanding Performance awards USAF, 1956, 65, 72, 73, Quality award Def. Logistics Agy., 1979, Outstanding Performance award, 1978, 79, Exceptional Svc. award, 1983, 84, 85, Comdr.'s award Hdqrs. Dept. Army, 1985, others. Mem. U. N.C. at Greensboro Alumni Assn. Harriet Elliott Soc., Unbroken Band.

LAN, CHUAN-TAU EDWARD, aerospace engineering educator; b. Kangshan, China, Apr. 21, 1935; arrived in US, 1961, naturalized, 1972; s. Tu-sen and Tsai-mei Lan; m. Sumy Chen, Feb. 12, 1961; children: Susan, Justin, Austin. BS, Nat. Taiwan U., 1958; MS, U. Minn., 1963; PhD, NYU, 1968. Asst. engr. NYC Bd. Water Supply, 1963-65; asst. prof. dept. aerospace engrng. U. Kans., Lawrence, 1968-74, assoc. prof., 1974-78, prof., 1978-92, Warren S. Bellows disting. prof., 1992-98, J.L. Constant disting. prof., 1998—2007, prof. emeritus, 2007. Prin. investigator Ctr. Rsch., Inc., Lawrence, 1972. Author: Applied Airfoil and Wing Theory, 1988, Airplane Aerodynamics and Performance, 2003; contbr. articles to profl. jours. NASA grantee, 1972—2005. Fellow: AIAA (assoc.); mem.: Tau Beta Pi, Sigma Gamma Tau. Avocation: classical music. Office: U Kans Dept Aerospace Engring 1530 W 15th St Lawrence KS 66045-0001 Home: 18229 28th Dr SE Bothell WA 98012 Business E-Mail: vortex@ku.edu.

LAN, DONALD PAUL, JR., lawyer; b. Orange, NJ, July 19, 1952; s. Donald Paul and Hannah Paula (Resnik) L.; m. Deborah Sue Rothenberg, Aug. 20, 1978; children: Jennifer Robyn, Adam Christopher, Eric Jacob. BS in Acctg., U. R.I., 1974; JD, Rutger U., 1977; LLM in Taxation, Georgetown U., 1982. Bar: D.C. 1978, Tex. 1983, U.S. Dist. Ct. (no., so., we. and ea. dists.) Tex. 1983, U.S. Ct. Claims 1978, U.S. Tax Ct. 1977, U.S. Ct. Appeals (fed. cir.) 1978, U.S. Ct. Appeals (5th cir.) 1984, U.S. Ct. Appeals (8th cir.) 1997. Clk. to spl. trial judge U.S. Tax Ct., Washington, 1977-78; trial atty. tax div. U.S. Dept. Justice, Washington, 1978-82; assoc., ptnr. Shank, Irwin & Conant, Dallas, 1982-87; ptnr. Finley, Kumble Wagner et al, Dallas, 1987, Strasburger & Price, Dallas, 1988-96; shareholder Kroney, Mincey, Inc., Dallas, 1996—2005, Kroney Morse Lan, PC, Dallas, 2005—. Adj. prof. law So. Meth. U., 1990-2005; lectr. tax controversy and litigation, 1983—. Named Outstanding Atty. tax div. U.S. Dept. Justice, 1980. Fellow: Am. Coll. Tax Counsel, Am. Coll. Trust and Estate Counsel; mem.: ABA (ct. procedures com. tax sect. 1987—, stds. in tax practice com. tax sect. 1992—, chmn. 2001—03), D.C. Bar Assn., Dallas Bar Assn., State Bar Tex. (chmn. ct. procedures com. tax sect. 1995—97, coun. mem. 1997—2000), Beta Gamma Sigma, Beta Alpha Psi, Phi Kappa Phi. Jewish. Avocation: all sports. Office: Kroney Morse Lan PC 12221 Merit Dr Ste 1210 Dallas TX 75251-2244 Office Phone: 972-386-8500. Business E-Mail: dlan@kmllaw.com.

LANAHAN, DANIEL JOSEPH, lawyer; b. Bklyn., Jan. 13, 1940; Attended, L.I. U., Temple U.; JD, San Francisco Law Sch., 1969. Bar: Calif. 1970. Dir. Ropers, Majeski, Kohn & Bentley, P.C., Santa Rosa, Calif., 1970-96; mng. ptnr. Lanahan & Reilley L.L.P., Santa Rosa, 1997—. Mem. State Bar Calif., Sonoma County Bar Assn., Internat. Assn. Def. Counsel, Assn. Def. Counsel. Home Phone: 707-575-5726; Office Phone: 707-524-4200. Business E-Mail: dlanahan@lanahan.com.

LANARO, CLARA MARRAMA, music educator, writer; b. Aquila, Abruzzi, Italy, Oct. 26, 1920; arrived in US, 1946; d. Daniele Marrama and Giovanna Galli; children: Severo, Francesco, Augusto, Goffredo, Ginerva, Manlio, Oberto, Clara. BA in organ, Liceo Musicale Luisa D'Annunzio, Pescara, Italy, 1939; diploma in Piano, Scuola Statale di Musica Luisa D' Annunzio, Pescara, Italy, 1942. Tchr. undergrads. Scuola Statale Di Musica & D'Annunzio Pescara, 1942—43; tchr. piano Liceo Musicale Luisa D'Annunzio, Pescara, Italy, 1943, San Francisco, 1948-51, U.S., Northwest Africa, 1954-61. Author: Time Signature in Super Games, The Grand Staff XL, The Staff XL, The Grand Staff XL Book I, Book II (Private/Class), The Staff XL Book I, Book II (Private/Class), Music for Piano Volume I-II, Rhythms and Insufficient Rhythms, From Games to Songs, Amplified, 2003; patentee Musical Toy Teaching Device, Directly on the Keyboard, 1972, 2000. Achievements include patents for Super Learning; a music-teaching device which shows a student of piano exactly the keys to reproduce each note on the grand staff and where notes written on the grand staff belong on the keyboard. Avocations: languages, reading. Home: Apt A 1183 Ayala Dr Sunnyvale CA 94086-5734

LANCARTE, LANNY P., II, chef; Grad., Culinary Inst. Am., NYC. Mgr. Joe T. Garcia's, Fort Worth, Tex.; chef Topolobampo, Chgo., Frontera Grill, Chgo.; owner, exec. chef Lanny's Alta Cocina Mexicana, Fort Worth, Tex., 2004—. Named Forth Worth's most exciting new culinary personality, Tex. Highways; named one of Dallas' Rising Stars, StarChefs.com, 2007. Office: Lanny's Alta Conina Mexicana 3405 W 7th St Fort Worth TX 76107*

LANCASTER, BARBARA MAE, management consulting company executive; b. Stafford Springs, Conn., Feb. 18, 1930; d. Harold D. and Ruth (Bristol) Stebbins; m. Colin T. Lancaster, June 5, 1948 (div. July 1979); children: Wayne, Sharon, Kevin, Karen, Kim. BS in Commerce, Rider Coll., 1981, MBA, 1984; PhD in Bus. Adminstrn., Kennedy Western U., 2006. CPA, N.J.; cert. fin. planner, life underwriter; chartered fin. cons. Acct. Electro Mech. Research, Princeton Junction, N.J., 1963-70; treas. Raritan Valley Ceilings, Inc., Monmouth Junction, N.J., 1970-78; adminstrv. asst. Total Enterprises, Princeton, N.J., 1979-81; pres. Lancaster Mgmt., Inc., Monmouth Junction, 1981—. Tchr. Adult Sch., South Brunswick, N.J., 1986-94; adj. prof. Rutgers U., 1989, also vis. prof.; speaker in field. Author: Entrepreneurial Training Institute Course I-Business Plan, 1994, Guide to Living Styles for Retirees-Professional Education, 1995. Mem. small bus. adv. com. Princeton C. of C., 1984-90; mem. adv. bd. Small Bus. Devel.Ctr., Newark, 1986-96, Nat. Coun. Aging, 1995—; chair N.J. Devel. Authority for Small Bus., Minorities and Women's Enterprises, 1991-94. Named Advocate of Yr., U.S. SBA, N.J., 1987. Mem. Nat. Assn. Women Bus. Owners (treas. N.J. chpt. 1987—), N.J. Assn. Women Bus. Owners (pres. 1986-88), Women Life Underwriters Conf. (pres. 1987-88, nat. pres. 1991-92), Bus. and Profl. Women, Mid-Atlantic Venture Capital (v.p. 1988). Democrat. Avocations: dance, playing piano. Home and Office: 112 Appletree Ct Monmouth Junction NJ 08852-2102 Office Phone: 732-329-4540. Personal E-mail: barblancaster@comcast.net.

LANCASTER, CARROLL TOWNES, JR., health services executive; b. Waco, Tex., Mar. 14, 1929; s. Carroll T. and Beatrice L.; m. Catherine Virginia Frommel, May 29, 1954; children: Loren Thomas, Barbara, Beverly, John Tracy. Student, U. Tex., 1948-51, 52-53. Sales coord. Union Tank div. Butler Mfg. Co., Houston, 1954-56, sales rep. New Orleans, 1956-57, br. mgr., 1957-60; asst. to exec. v.p. Maloney-Crawford Mfg. Co., Tulsa, 1960-62; mktg. cons., sr. assoc. Market/Product Facts, Tulsa, 1962-63; market devel. asst. Norriseal Controls divsn. Dover Corp., Houston, 1963-66; area dir. Arthritis Found., Houston, 1966-69, regional dir., 1969-71; exec. dir. United Cerebral Palsy, Tex. Gulf Coast, 1971-74, Leukemia Soc. Am., Gulf Coast, 1974-76, Lancaster & Assocs., 1976—. Christian edn. tchr., 1970, supr. 1971, asst. youth football coach, Bellaire, 1967-68, 70-71; mem. Houston-Galveston Area Health Commn. Study Group, 1972-76, co-chmn. 1976; dir. essayist Tex. Low Vision Coun., 1976-79, sec.-treas., 1978-81, pres. 1981-85; pres. Bellaire Civic Action Club, 1987-88, del. Houston Interfaith Sponsoring Com., 1979-81; bd. dirs. Coun. Chs. Greater Houston, 1966-68, v.p. 1968. With USNR, 1946-48, 51-52. Recipient award for securing free blood for indigent Harris County Hosp. Dist., 1968. Mem. Am. Mktg. Assn., Huguenot Soc., Military Order of Stars and Bars, San Marcos Acad., Ex-Students Assn. (pres. 1982-84), SAR, Delta Sigma Phi. Episcopalian (vestryman 1975-78). Home: 6900 County Road 261 Zephyr TX 76890-3779

LANCASTER, H(AROLD) MARTIN, congressman, academic administrator; b. Patetown Community, NC, Mar. 24, 1943; s. Harold Wright and Eva (Pate) L.; m. Alice Matheny; children: Ashley Elizabeth, Mary Martin. AB, U. N.C., 1965, JD, 1967; DUniv (hon.), U. Ulster, 2005. Asst. staff judge adv. 12th Naval Dist., San Francisco, 1968; staff judge adv. USN, USS Hancock, 1968-70; ptnr. Baddour, Lancaster, Parker, Hine & Keller P.A., Goldsboro, N.C., 1970-86; rep. N.C. Gen. Assembly, Raleigh, 1978-86; mem. 100th-103rd Congresses from 3d N.C. dist., Washington, D.C., 1987-94; spl. advisor to the President on chem. weapons, 1995; asst. sec. of the Army, 1996-97; pres. N.C. Cmty. Coll. Sys., 1997—. Mem. armed svcs. com., readiness subcom., mil. pers. subcom.; chmn. morale, welfare and recreation panel; small bus. com. Mcht. Marine and Fisheries com.; chmn. judiciary com. N.C. Ho. of Reps., 1983-86; chmn. hwy. safety com., 1981-83; chmn. congrl. study group on Germany, 1994, North Atlantic Assembly, 1989-94; former mem. numerous other coms.; bd. dirs. Nat. Ctr. Family Literacy, 1998—, Global Transpark Auth., 1997—, N.C. Global Ctr., N.C. Pub. Sch. Forum, 1997—. Chmn. N.C. Arts Coun., 1977-81, Goldsboro Wayne Bicentennial Commn., 1975-76; pres. Community Arts Coun., 1973-74, Wayne Community Concert Assn., 1972-73; chmn. bd. trustees Wayne County Pub. Libr., 1979-80; chmn. Wayne chpt. ARC, 1978-79; mem. adv. bd. Z. Smith Reynolds Found.; deacon First Presbyn. Ch., 1972-75, elder, 1980-86; elder White Meml. Presbyn. Ch., 2002—, chmn. worship com., 2002—. Recipient Disting. Svc. award Goldsboro Jaycees, 1977, N.C. Crime and Justice award Gov.'s Crime Commn., 1984, Spl. award Gov.'s Adv. Coun. for Persons with Disabilities, 1985, Valand award Mental Health Assn. N.C., 1985, Outstanding Legislators awards Neuse River Coun. Govts., N.C. Assn. Sch. Counselors, Nat. Security Leadership award, 1987, 89, 90, 91, 92, Sound Dollar award, 1988, 89, 90, Spirit of Enterprise award U.S. C. of C., 1989, 92, 93, Doer of Deeds award House Leadership, 1989, Pub. Health Svc. award N.C. Primary Care Assn., 1991, Charles Dick Medal of Merit, U.S. Nat. Guard Assn., 1992, Tad Davis Meml. award, U.S. Mil. Sports Assn., 1992, Lifetime Achievement award Y-H, 2004; named N.C. and U.S. Alumnus of Yr., 4-H, 1987, Knight Comdr. of the Ct. of Honor, 1994, 33 degree Mason Scottish Rite, 1997, Silver Order of the de Fleuriers (Corps of Engrs.), 1997, Tar Heel of the Week, Raleigh News and Observer, 2000, Outstanding Alumnus U. NC Sch. of Law, 2002. Mem. ABA, Assn. Trial Lawyers Am., N.C. Bar Assn. (bd. govs.), Eighth Jud. Dist. Bar Assn., N.C. Acad. Trial Lawyers (Outstanding Legislator award), Wayne County Hist. Soc. Lodges: Masons (33d degree), Shriners, Elks. Office: NC Cmty Coll Sys 200 W Jones St Raleigh NC 27603-1378 Office Phone: 919-807-6950. Personal E-mail: martinl@nccs.cc.nc.us.

LANCASTER, JEANETTE (BARBARA LANCASTER), dean, nursing educator; BSN, U. Tenn.; MSN, Case Western Res. U.; PhD, U. Okla. Staff nurse U. Tenn.; nurse clinician Univ. Hosps. of Cleve.; assoc. prof. psychiat. nursing Tex. Christian U.; coord. cmty. health nursing U. Ala., Birmingham, chair master's degree program Sch. Nursing; dean, prof. Sch. Nursing Wright State U., Dayton, Ohio; now dean, prof. nursing U. Va., Charlottesville; assoc. dir. patient care svcs. U. Va. Health Scis. Ctr., Charlottesville. Former chmn. bd. dirs. Va. Statewide Area Health Edn. Ctr.; former pres. Charlottesville and Albemarle divsn. Am. Heart Assn.; presenter in field. Author: Community and Public Health Nursing: Nursing Issues in Leading and Managing Change; editor: Family and Cmty. Health; contbr. Bd. dirs. U. Va. Women's Ctr., Hospice of the Piedmont. Recipient Disting. Alumni award Frances Payne Bolton Sch. Nursing, Case We. Res. U., 1984, Outstanding Alumni award, U. Tenn. Coll. Nursing, 1985, honored with establishment of Jeanette Lancaster Professorship in Nursing, 1999. Fellow: Am. Acad. Nursing; mem.: Am. Assn. Colls. Nursing (pres. elect). E-mail: lancaster@virginia.edu.

LANCASTER, JOAN ERICKSEN, judge; b. 1954; BA magna cum laude, St. Olaf Coll., Northfield, Minn., 1977; spl. diploma in social studies, Oxford U., 1976; JD cum laude, U. Minn., 1981. Atty. LeFevere, Lefler, Kennedy, O'Brien & Drawz, Mpls., 1981-83; asst. U.S. atty. Dist. Minn., Mpls., 1983-93; shareholder Leonard, Street and Deinard, Mpls., 1993-95; dist. ct. judge 4th Jud. Dist., Mpls., 1995-98; assoc. justice Minn. Supreme Ct., 1998—2002; judge U.S. Dist. Ct., St. Paul, 2002—. Office: US District Court 316 N Robert St Saint Paul MN 55101

LANCASTER, KENNETH G., lawyer; b. Stafford Springs, Conn., Dec. 6, 1949; s. Talbot Augustin and Helen Collier (McRae) Lancaster; m. Margaret Jane Royer, Aug. 25, 1973; children: Kimberly Jane, John Talbot, Christopher Andrew. BA, U. Miami, 1971, JD, 1974. Bar: Fla. 1974, U.S. Dist. Ct. (so. dist.) Fla. 1975, U.S. Dist. Ct. (mid. dist.) Fla. 1976. Adminstr. Met. Dade County, Miami, Fla., 1971-73; assoc. Robert A. Spiegel, Coral Gables, Fla., 1973-78; pvt. practice South Miami, Fla., 1978-80; ptnr. Clark, Dick & Lancaster, South Miami, 1980-87, King & Lancaster PA, South Miami, 1987—. Mem. endowment com. U. Miami, 1982—; cons. 1st City Bank Dade County, Miami, 1983—84; dir. U. Miami Bus. Sch.; pres. U. Miami Sports Hall of Fame, Coral Gables, 1984—2006, bd. dirs., 1984—. V.p., trustee South Fla. coun. Boy Scouts Am. Mem.: Dade County Attys. Real Property Coun., Fla. Acad. Elder Law Attys., Nat. Acad. Elder Law Attys., Dade County Bar Assn. (Disting. Svc. award 1984), Fla. Bar Assn., Hurrican Club/U. Miami (bd. dirs. 1984—, pres. 1996—97). Home: 10241 SW 141st St Miami FL 33176-7005 Office: King & Lancaster PA 5975 Sunset Dr Ste 703 Miami FL 33143-5198 Home Phone: 305-232-3942; Office Phone: 305-666-6000.

LANCASTER, KIRSTEN KEZAR, psychologist; b. Lincoln, Nebr., May 22, 1964; d. Edward Fraze and Lois Paulson Kezar; m. John Talmadge Lancaster, June 20, 1987. BSBA, High Point U., NC, 1985; MBA, Am. U., Washington, 1987; MA, Pepperdine U., Malibu, Calif., 1991; MS, Nova Southeastern U., Ft. Lauderdale, Fla., 1995; PsyD, Nova Southeastern U., Ft. Lauderdale, 1999. Lic. psychologist N.C. Asst. coord., rsch. asst. child trauma program Nova Southeastern U. Cmty. Mental Health Ctr., Ft. Lauderdale, 1995—96, psychology resident, 1998—99; evening counselor The Renfrew Ctr., Coconut Creek, Fla., 1996—98, postdoctoral psychology resident, 1999—2000; psychologist pvt. practice Raleigh, NC, 2003—04; psychologist Holly Hill Hosp. Crisis and Assessment, Raleigh, 2003—05; sr. psychologist Wake County Human Svcs., Raleigh, 2000—05; psychologist Harbin & Assocs., 2005—. Grants com. mem. Susan G. Komen Breast Cancer Found., 2003—05; planning com. mem. WCHS Pink Ribbon Campaign, Wake County, NC, 2004—05; rschr., editor Breast Cancer Resource Directory N.C., 2004—; contbr. domestic violence legis. NC, 2004—05. Mem.: APA, N.C. Psychol. Assn. Methodist. Avocations: walking, reading, travel. Office Phone: 910-609-1990. Business E-Mail: klancaster@harbinandassociates.com.

LANCASTER, PETER MCCREERY, lawyer; b. 1954; AB, Princeton U., 1976; JD, Yale U., 1980. Bar: Minn. 1984. Ptnr., co-chair intellectual property litig. group Dorsey & Whitney LLP, Mpls. Mem.: Minn. Intellectual Property Law Assn., Am. Intellectual Property Law Assn. Office: Dorsey & Whitney LLP Ste 1500 50 S Sixth St Minneapolis MN 55402-1498 Office Phone: 612-340-7811. Office Fax: 612-340-2868. Business E-Mail: lancaster.peter@dorsey.com.

LANCASTER, RALPH IVAN, JR., lawyer; b. Bangor, Maine, May 9, 1930; s. Ralph I. and Mary Bridget (Kelleher) L.; m. Mary Lou Pooler, Aug. 21, 1954; children: Mary Lancaster Miller, Anne, Elizabeth Peoples, Christopher, John, Martin. AB, Coll. Holy Cross, 1952; LLB, Harvard U., 1955; LLD (hon.), St. Joseph's Coll., 1991. Bar: Maine 1955, Mass. 1955. Law clk. U.S. Dist. Ct. Dist. Maine, 1957-59; ptnr. firm Pierce Atwood, Portland, Maine, 1961—, mng. ptnr., 1993-96; ind. counsel In Re Herman apptd. by spl. divsn. D.C. Ct. Appeals, 1998—2001. Condr. trial advocacy seminar Harvard U.; lectr. U. Maine; chmn. merit selection panel U.S. Magistrate for Dist. of Maine, 1982, 88; bd. visitors U. Maine Sch. Law, 1991-96, chair, 1991-93; spl. master by appointment U.S. Supreme Ct. in State of N.J. vs. State of Nev. et al, 1987-88, spl. master NJ vs. Del., 2006-; mem. 1st Ctr. Adv. Com. on Rules, 1991-96, legal adv. bd. Martindale Hubbell, Lexis Nexis, 1990—; represented U.S. in Gulf of Maine in World Ct. at The Hague, 1984; U.S. Supreme Ct. apptd. spl. master Commonwealth of Va. vs. State of Md., 2000-03, chmn. bd. trustees Davis Family Found., 2000-; chmn. Maine Lawyers Assistance Program, 2002-03; nat. membership chair, Supreme Ct. Hist. Soc., 2002-03. Former mem. Diocese of Portland Bur. Edn., mem. Cath. Found. of Maine (chair governance com., 2003). With U.S. Army, 1955-57. Mem. Maine Jud. Coun., Am Coll. Trial Lawyers (chmn. Maine 1974-79, bd. regents 1982-87, treas. 1985-87, pres. 1989-90), Maine Bar Assn. (pres. 1982), Cumberland County Bar Assn., Canadian Bar Assn. (hon.). Republican. Roman Catholic. Home: 162 Woodville Rd Falmouth ME 04105-1120 Office: 1 Monument Sq Portland ME 04101-4033 Office Phone: 207-791-1260. Business E-Mail: RLancaster@PierceAtwood.com.

LANCASTER, ROBERT CARL, secondary school educator; b. Nyssa, Oreg., Jan. 22, 1946; s. Benjamin and Dorothy Lancaster; m. Bessie Bea Millholin, Feb. 6, 1964; children: Lynette Faircloth, Robby, Tabitha Cardin, Adam, Kelly, Mark, Patti Medina, Bessie Carrillo, Scott. AAS, C.C. Air Force, Maxwell AFB, Ala., 1980; BS in Biology, U. So. Colo., Pueblo, Colo., 1988; MA in Secondary Edn., Adams State Coll., Alamosa Colo., 1993. Commd. lt. USAF, 1964, advanced through grades to master sgt., 1978, ret., 1984; tchr. Walsh Pub. Schs., Colo., 1993—. Home: 49681 County Road X Walsh CO 81090 Office: Walsh Pub Schs 301 N Calif Walsh CO 81090 Home Phone: 719-324-5717; Office Phone: 719-324-5221. Personal E-mail: rlancast@hotmail.com.

LANCASTER, ROGERS, retired minister; b. Woodland, Ala., Dec. 4, 1933; s. McKinley and Mary Etta Lancaster; m. Jessie G. Holley, Aug. 1989; children: Xavier, Janine, Juan, Rana, Charles. ThD, Candler Sch. Theology, Atlanta, 1989. Clin. technician pharmacy US Army, Republic of Korea, Germany, Greenland; sr. pastor United Meth. Ch., Hampten, Va., 1963—79, Woodland, Ala., 1979—82, Huntsville, Ala., 1982—88, Lafayette, Ala., 1988—93. Bd. dirs. East Ala. Regional Planning Commn. Democrat. Methodist. Avocation: auto racing.

LANCASTER, SARAH, research scientist; b. Mexico, Mo., Jan. 3, 1980; d. Roger and Linda Hans; m. Phillip Lancaster, July 31, 2004. BS, BS, U. Mo., Columbia, 2002; MS, NC State U., Raleigh, 2004. Rsch. asst. NC State U., Raleigh, 2002—04, Tex. A&M U., College Station, 2004—. Mentor Save Our Sts. Ministries, Bryan, Tex., 2006—. Tom Slick Grad. fellow, Tex. A&M U., 2007. Mem.: Am. Chem. Soc. (Agrochem. Edn. award 2006), Am. Soc. Agronomy, Weed Sci. Soc. Am., Gamma Sigma Delta. Office: Texas A&M Univ 360 Olsen Blvd College Station TX 77843 Home Phone: 979-822-9464; Office Phone: 979-845-4629.

LANCE, ALAN GEORGE, federal judge, former state attorney general; b. McComb, Ohio, Apr. 27, 1949; s. Cloyce Lowell and Clara Rose (Wilhelm) Lance; m. Sheryl C. Holden, May 31, 1969; children: Lisa, Alan Jr., Luke. BA, S.D. State U., 1971; JD, U. Toledo, 1973. Bar: Ohio 1974, U.S. Dist. Ct. (no. dist.) Ohio 1974, U.S. Ct. Mil. Appeals 1974, Idaho 1978, U.S. Supreme Ct. 1996. Asst. pros. atty. Fulton County, Wauseon, Ohio, 1973—74; ptnr. Foley and Lance, Chartered, Meridian, Idaho, 1978—90; prin. Alan G. Lance, Meridian, 1990—94; mem. Idaho Ho. of Reps., Boise, 1990—94, majority caucus chmn., 1992—94; atty. gen. State of ID, Boise, 1995—2003; prin. Lance, Elia & Assocs. PLLC, Boise, 2004; judge US Ct. Appeals Vets. Claims, Washington, 2004—. Capt. US Army, 1974—78. Mem.: Idaho Trial Lawyers Assn., Idaho Bar Assn., Ohio Bar Assn., Nat. Assn. Attys. Gen. (vice-chmn. conf. western attys. gen. 1998, chmn. 1999), Meridian C. of C. (pres. 1983), Elks, Am. Legion (judge adv. 1981—90, state comdr. 1988—89, alt. nat. exec. com. 1992—94, nat. exec. com. 1994—96, chmn. nat. fgn. rels. commn. 1996—97, ex-officio mem. nat. POW/MIA com. 1996—99, nat. comdr. 1999—2000, chmn. nat. adv. com. 2000—01). Avocation: fishing. Office: US Ct Appeals Vets Claims 625 Indiana Ave Ste 900 Washington DC 20004 Office Phone: 202-501-5887.

LANCE, HOWARD L., communications executive, industrial engineer; BS in Indsl. Engring., Bradley U.; MS in Mgmt., Purdue U. With Sales and Mktg. Dept. Scott-Fetzer Co., Caterpillar Inc.; from mem. staff to exec. v.p. Emerson Electric Co., 1984—2000, exec. v.p. Electronics and Telecom., 2000—01; co-pres., COO Retail and Fin. Group NCR Corp., 2001—02; chmn., pres., CEO Harris Corp., 2003—. Bd. govs. Aerospace Industries

Assn.; exec. com. bd. trustees Mfrs. Alliance; bd. trustees Fla. Inst. Tech. Bd. dirs. United Way Brevard County. Mem.: Fla. Coun. 100. Office: Harris Corp 1025 W NASA Blvd Melbourne FL 32919*

LANCE, LEONARD, state legislator; b. Easton, Pa., June 25, 1952; s. Wesley L. and Anne (Anderson) L.; m. Heidi A. Rohrbach. BA, Lehigh U., 1974; JD, Vanderbilt U., 1977; MPA, Princeton U., 1982. Law clk. to judges Warren County Ct., Belvidere, NJ, 1977-78; asst. counsel Office of Gov., State of N.J., Trenton, NJ, 1983-90; mem. N.J. Gen. Assembly, Trenton, 1991—2002, N.J. State Senate, 2002—, minority leader, 2004—. Mem. Grandin Libr. Bd., Clinton, N.J., 1990-2000, N.J. Coun. for Humanities, Trenton, 1994—; trustee Newark Mus., 1995—, Centenary Coll., Hackettstown, N.J., 1998—, McCarter Theatre, 1998-2007. Mem. Princeton Club N.Y., Phi Beta Kappa. Republican. Home: PO Box 5240 Clinton NJ 08809-0240 Office: NJ State Senate 119 Main St Flemington NJ 08822-1615

LANCHNER, BERTRAND MARTIN, lawyer, advertising executive; b. Boston, Oct. 3, 1929; s. Abraham Joseph and Mina (Grossman) L.; m. Nancy Nelson, Apr. 26, 1979; 1 son by previous marriage, David; 1 stepdau., Renate. BA, Stanford U., 1951; postgrad., Columbia U. Grad. Sch. Bus., 1951-52, U. Vienna, Austria, summer 1955; JD, Harvard U., 1955. Bar: N.Y. bar 1956. Asso. firm Sage, Gray, Todd & Sims, NYC, 1955-57; atty. Warner Bros. Pictures, NYC, 1957-59; asst. gen. counsel Dancer-Fitzgerald-Sample, NYC, 1959-62; gen. counsel Lawrence C. Gumbinner Advt. Agy., NYC, 1962-63; dir. bus. affairs and sports contract negotiations CBS-TV, NYC, 1963-69; gen. counsel, exec. v.p. Videorecord Corp. Am., Westport, Conn., 1969-73; sr. v.p., sec., gen. counsel N.W. Ayer, Inc., NYC, 1973-97, bd. dirs., 1973—97; with Lanchner Law Firm, NYC, 1997—. Bd. dirs. 170 E. 79th St. Corp., Advt. Info. Services Inc., N.Y.C.; guest lectr. Yale U. Law Sch. Mem. adv. bd.: Communications and the Law. Mem. ABA, N.Y. State Bar Assn., Assn. of Bar of City of N.Y. (chmn. subcom. advt. agy. 1981-83), Copyright Soc. U.S., Am. Assn. Advt. Agys. (chmn. legal com. 1986-89, 95-97), Am. Corp. Counsel Assn. (chair advt. com. 1996-2002), Am. Advt. Fedn. (mem. legal com.), Harvard Club N.Y.C., East Hampton Tennis Club (bd. dirs. 2004-, pres. 2006-), Tennisport Club. Office: Lanchner Law Firm 170 E 79th St New York NY 10021-0436 Office Phone: 917-885-7974. E-mail: nelly3940@aol.com.

LANCIONE, BERNARD GABE, lawyer; b. Bellaire, Ohio, Feb. 3, 1939; s. Americus Gabe and June (Morford) L.; m. Rosemary C., Nov. 27, 1976; children: Amy, Caitin, Gillian, Bernard Gabe II, Elizabetta Marie. BS, Ohio U., 1960; JD, Capitol U., 1965. Bar: Ohio 1965, U.S. Dist. Ct. (so. dist.) Ohio 1967, U.S. Supreme Ct. 1969, U.S. Ct. Appeals (4th cir.) 1982, U.S. Dist. Ct. (no. dist.) Ohio 1989. Pres. Lancione Law Office, Co., L.P.A., Bellaire, Ohio, 1965-87; mng. atty. Cichon Lancione Co., L.P.A., St. Clairsville, Ohio, 1982-85; of counsel Ward, Kaps, Bainbridge, Maurer, Bloomfield & Melvin, Columbus, Ohio, 1987-88; Ohio Asst. Atty. Gen. Columbus, 1988-91; pvt. practice, 1991—2002; assoc. Mills & Mills Law Office, Westerville, Ohio, 2003—; of counsel McGuire & Schneider, LLP, Columbus, 2003—04; pvt. practice Westerville, 2005—. Spl. counsel Ohio Atty. Gen.'s Office, 1991-95; solicitor Bellaire City (Ohio), 1968-72; asst. prosecutor County of Belmont (Ohio), 1972-76. Pres. Young Dems. Ohio, 1970-72; pack com. chmn. Pack 961, Westerville, Ohio Cub Scouts Am., 1992-93. Mem. ABA, Assn. Trial Lawyers Am., Ohio State Bar Assn., Columbus Bar Assn., Ohio Acad. Trial Lawyers (award of merit 1972). Democrat. Roman Catholic. Office: 3212 N High St Columbus OH 43202 Office Phone: 614-447-3110. Personal E-mail: blancione@sbcglobal.net.

LAND, GEORGE AINSWORTH, philosopher, consultant, writer; b. Hot Springs, Ark., Feb. 27, 1933; s. George Thomas Lock and Mary Elizabeth Land; m. Jo A. Gunn, 1957 (dec. 1969); children— Robert E., Thomas G., Patrick A.; m. Beth Smith Jarman, 1987. Student, Millsaps Coll., 1952-54, U. Veracruz, Mexico, 1957-59; numerous hon. degrees U.S. and abroad. Program dir. Woodall TV Stas. of Ga., Columbus, 1951-52; ops. mgr. Lamar Broadcasting, Jackson, Miss., 1952-54; anthrop. research Cora, Huichole and Yaqui tribes, Latin Am. Mexico, 1955-60; dir. gen. Television del Norte (NBC), Mexico, 1960-62; v.p. Roman Corp., St. Louis, 1962-64; chmn. Transolve Inc., Cambridge, Mass., and St. Petersburg, Fla., 1964-68; chief exec., chmn. Innotek Corp., NYC; also pres. Hal Roach Studios, Los Angeles and NYC, 1969-71; chmn. emeritus Turtle Bay Inst., NYC, 1971-80, Farsight Group, NYC, 1971—80; vice chmn. Wilson Learning Corp., Mpls., 1980-86; chmn., CEO Leadership 2000 The Farsight Group, Phoenix, 1986—; prof. Mankato State U., 1973-74; sr. fellow U. Minn., 1982—; chmn. Global Alliance for Creative Peace; chmn., adv. bd. Advanced Integrated Tech. Inc., 2006—. Cons.-in-residence Synplex Inc., NYC, AT&T, Forest Hosp., Des Plaines, Social Systems Inc., Chapel Hill, NC, Children's Hosp., Nat. Med. Ctr., Washington, Herman Miller Inc., Arthur Anderson & Co., strategy cons. Intermedics Orthopedics; mem. Nat. Action Com. on Drug Edn., 1974-75, sr. exec. svc. U.S. Govt. 2001-2002, Assn. Non-profit mgmt., 1999, The Congerence Bd. 1999, 2000, Ctr. for Disease Control, 2002, The Concours Group, 2002, Global Fourm Ctr., 2002, CEO, 2002; co-chmn. Syncon Conf., So. Ill. U., 1972-74; keynoter Emerging Trends in Edn. Conf., Minn., 1974, 75, Bicentennial Conf. on Limits to Growth, So. Ill. U., 1976, No. States Power Conf., 1975, U.S. Office Edn., Nat. Conf. Improvements in Edn., 1979, World Conf. on Gifted, 1977, S.W. Conf. on Arts, 1977, World Symposium on Humanity, 1979, Internat. Conf. Internal Auditors, 1977, Four Corners Conf. on Arts, 1977, Chautaugua Inst., 1977, 78, Conf. Am. Art Tchrs. Assn., 1979, Internat. Conf. on Gifted, 1982, Japan Mgmt. Assn., Nat. Conf. Art Curators, Chgo., 1985, others; keynoter, Nat. Conf. on Econ. Devel., Mex., 1988, Credit Union Roundtable, Tampa, Fla., 1988, Internat. Bihai Conf., Princeton, NJ, 1982, co-chmn. com. on society World Conf. Peace and Poverty, St. Joseph's U., Phila., 1968, Internat. Bahai Conf. Princeton U., 1987, Gov.'s Trade Corridor Conf., Phoenix, 1994, Cath. Hosp. Assn., Phila, 1994, Am. Assn. Adminstrs., 1994, Inst. Pub. Execs., 1994, Fed. Conf. Quality, Washington, 1994, MAC IS Nat. Conf., Ont., 1994, Innovative Thinking Conf., 1994, Ventana Groupware Conf., 1994, Assn. Non-Profit Orgs., 1998, The Conf. Bd., 1999-2000, Strategic Innovation Conf., 1999, Tng. Dirs. Forum, 1999, Young Pres.' Orgn., Cannes, 1993, Assn. Convn. and Visitors Bur., Phoenix, 1993, Profession Conv. Mgmt. Assn., Atlanta, Internat. Assn. Law Enforcement, 1995, Cath. Health Assn., 1995, Excellence in Govt. Fellows, 1996, U.S. Govt. Sr. Exec. Svc., 2000-01, Chautauqua Instn., 2001, PEMEX, 2002, Coca-Cola, 2002, US Fish and Wildlife Svc., 2003, Innovation Convergence, Mpls., 2003, Internat. Conference Energy, Geneva, 2003, Am. Med. Systems, France, 2003, Adv. Innovation, Zurich, Switzerland, 2003, Mex. Petroleum Inst., Mexico City, 2004, Ctr. for Competitiveness, Belfast, No. Ireland, 2004, Creative Edn. Found., Buffalo, 2004, Congress Innovation and Quality Pub. Adminstrn., Mex. DF, 2005, Internat. Petroleum Conf., Venacruz, Mex., 2005, Delphi, Xerox, Groupo, Bal (Mex.), Petroles (Mex.), others; mem. Nat. Security Sem., U.S. Dept. Def., 1975; faculty Edison Electric Grad. Mgmt. Inst., 1972-78; lectr., seminarian in transformation theory, strategic planning and interdisciplinary rsch. Menninger Found., U. Ga., Emory U., Waterloo, Can., Office of Sec. HEW, Jamestown Coll., NY, Hofstra U., U.S. Office Edn., Calif. Dept. Edn., St. Louis U., Coll. William and Mary, Webster Coll., St. Louis, Wash. State Dept. Edn., U. Ky., So. Ill. U., St. John's U., Harvard U., U. South Fla., MIT, U. Veracruz, Children's Hosp. D.C., Gov.'s Sch. NC, Scottsdale Ctr. Arts, Ariz., Humbolt U., East Berlin, AAAS, others; advanced faculty Creative Problem SolvingInst., SUNY, 1965—, S. Conn. Coll.; disting. lectr. Northwestern State U., La., SUNY, Coll. of the Lakes, Ill.; chmn. adv. bd. Advanced Integrated Tech., Inc., 2006—; cons. in field. Author: Innovation Systems, 1967, Innovation Technology, 1968, Four Faces of Poverty, 1968, (as George T.L. Land) Grow or Die: The Unifying Principle of Transformation, 1973, Creative Alternatives and Decision Making, 1974, The Opportunity Book, 1980, (with Vaune E. Ainsworth), Breakpoint and Beyond, 1994, (with Beth Jarman) New Paradigm in Business, 1994, Community Building in Business, 1995, Forward to Basics; contbr. to profl. jours. and gen. mags. Sr. fellow U. Mich. Fellow: World Bus. Acad., NY Acad. Scis.; mem.: Authors League Am., Authors Guild, Com. for Future (colleague), World Future Soc., Am. Soc. Value Engrs. (past dir.), Creative Edn. Found. (trustee, Lifetime Achievement award 1993, named to Hall of Fame 2006), Am. Soc. Cybernetics (past v.p.), Soc. Gen. Sys. Rsch. Achievements include research on interdisciplinary unification, orginated transformation theory; invention of computer-assisted group creative thinking processes, The Innovator, CoNexus, TeamWare, Synnovas, FarSightPro, others. Home: 7470 E San Miguel Ave Scottsdale AZ 85250-6446 Office: Leadership 2000 The Farsight Group 6619 N Scottsdale Rd Scottsdale AZ 85250 *I was fortunate enough in my youth to experience and learn what has been the most important idea and principle in my life, the natural law of enrichment through diversity. This concept means that change and growth come about more by combining differentnesses than by adding likenesses. As in the biological world, where such behavior produces the vitality of hybrids, and as in chemistry, where the co-valent bonds of carbon make life possible, in human life we can also benefit immeasurably from using our differences as a creative way to grow anew. Thus, we can evolve beyond polarizations such as nationalism, racism, sexism, institutionalism and other obstacles that separate us and stunt our ability to realize the full community of Man.*

LAND, H. BRUCE, III, electronics engineer, aerospace engineer; s. H. B. Land, Jr and Evelyn J. Land; m. Sharon Lee Land; children: Cynthia D. Nickel, Janette E. Lovell, Joel B. BEE, Johns Hopkins U., Balt., 1984. Data contr. Goddard Space Flight Ctr., Greenbelt, Md., 1967—67; sr. electronics technician JHU/APL, Laurel, Md., 1967—73, engring. asst., 1973—76, engring. staff assoc., 1976—87, sect. supr., 1987—97; program mgr. Johns Hopkins U. Applied Physics Lab., Laurel, Md., 1991—, systems engr., 1991—2003. Assoc. dir. Instrument Soc. of Am., Research Triangle Park, NC, 1988—; chmn. of com. on symposiums Internat. Instrumentation Symposium, Instrument Soc. of Am., Research Triangle Park, NC, 1999—, registration chmn., 2000—; newsletter editor Aerospace Industries Divsn., ISA, Research Triangle Park, NC, 2003—; expert witness Before the Nat. Transp. Safety Bd., Washington, 2000. Contbr. articles to profl. jours. Chmn., vice chair, sec. 1st Bapt. Ch. of Laurel, Md., 1980—; pres., treas. Northgate Woods Cmty. Assn., Laurel, Md., 1997—. Recipient Letter of Commendation, Rear Adm. R. B. Horne, Jr, 1990, Inventor of Yr., Johns Hopkins U., 2007. Fellow: Instrumentation Systems and Automation Soc. (assoc. dir. aerospace industries divsn. 1988—). Southern Baptist. Achievements include patents for Thermal Ionization Detector; patents pending for Pulsed Plasma Thruster; development of Arc Fault Detector System for Switchboards; Continuous Thermal Monitoring for Switchboards; System to protect nuclear power plants from electrical fires. Home: 9426 Northgate Rd Laurel MD 20723 Office: Johns Hopkins Univ Applied Physics 11100 Johns Hopkins Rd Laurel MD 20723 Home Phone: 443-832-4284; Office Phone: 240-228-6083. Business E-Mail: bruce.land@jhuapl.edu.

LAND, HENRY BRUCE, III, electronics engineer, researcher; s. Henry Bruce Land, Jr. and Evelyn Janette Land; m. Sharon Lee Headley, June 5, 1971; children: Cynthia Land Nickel, Janette Elizabeth Lovell, Joel Bruce. AAEE, Catonsville C.C., Catonsville, Md., 1979; BEE, Johns Hopkins U., Balt., 1984. Electronics technician Sperry Piedmont divsn. Sperry Rand, Charlottesville, Va., 1965—67; launch data contr. Goddard Space Flight Ctr., Greenbelt, Md., 1967; sr. electro-chem. technician Johns Hopkins U. Applied Physics Lab, Laurel, Md., 1967—73, engring. asst., 1973—76, engring. staff, 1976—87, sect. supr., 1987—97, systems engr., 1988—, program mgr., 1991—. Chmn. Com. on Symposiums ISA, Research Triangle Park, NC, 1999—; chmn. of com. on symposiums Internat. Instrumentation Symposium, Research Triangle Park, NC, 1999—, registration chmn., 1999—; expert witness arcing faults Nat. Transp. Safety Bd., Washington, 2000. Contbr. articles to profl. jours. Chmn., vice chair, sec., of trustees First Bapt. Ch. of Laurel, Laurel, Md., 1980—2005; treas., pres. Northgate Woods Cmty. Assoc, Laurel, Md., 1997—2005. Recipient Letter of Commendation, Rear Adm. R. B. Horne, Jr, 1990, Commendation, Asst. Dep. Under Sec., Dept. of the Navy, 1993, Inventor of Yr., Johns Hopkins U., 2007. Fellow: ISA (assoc. dir. 1988—2005, newsletter editor Aerospace Industries divsn. 2003—); mem.: AIAA. Baptist. Achievements include patents for Detector for prediction of electrical fires; development of System to protect electrical switchboards from fires; System to protect nuclear power plants from electrical fires; System for Continuous Thermal Monitoring of electrical switchboards; invention of Means of locating impacts on a surface; development of Arc Fault Detector System to protect Switchboards; patents pending for Pulsed Plasma Thrusters; Unattended spaces monitoring system; development of System to protect nuclear power plants from electrical fires; patents pending for Enhanced sampling device for SPME Sampling; Micro Pulsed Plasma Thrusters; High temperature fiber optic connector. Avocations: teaching sunday school, handyman. Home: 9426 Northgate Rd Laurel MD 20723 Office: Johns Hopkins Univ Applied Physics Lab 11100 Johns Hopkins Rd Building 10 Laurel MD 20723 Home Phone: 443-832-4284; Office Phone: 240-228-6083. Personal E-mail: hbland3@verizon.net. E-mail: bruce.land@jhuapl.edu.

LAND, JENNIFER REBEKAH, mathematics educator, science educator; b. Mar. 8, 1974; BS, Union U., Jackson, Tenn., 1996. State tchrs. lic. Tenn., 1996. English tchr. Milam Intermediate Sch., Tupelo, Miss., 1997—2000; math. tchr. St. Paul Christian Acad., Nashville, 2000—05; math. and sci. tchr. St. Bernard Acad., Nashville, 2005—. Mem.: Nat. Coun. Tchrs. Math.

LAND, JOHN CALHOUN, III, lawyer, state senator; b. Manning, S.C., Jan. 25, 1941; s. John Calhoun, Jr. and Anna Abbott (Weisiger) L.; m. Marie Mercogliano, Oct. 23, 1965; children— John Calhoun IV, Frances Ricci, William Ceth. Student vocat. forestry U. Fla., 1960-62; B.S., U. S.C., 1965, J.D., 1968. Bar: S.C. 1968. Mem. Land, Parker and Welch, P.A., Manning, 1968—; mem. S.C. Ho. of Reps., 1975-76, mem. S.C. Senate, 1977—. Sec. Clarendon County Democratic Com., 1968-70; commr. S.C. Hwys. and Pub. Transp., 1971-74. Mem. ABA, Clarendon County Bar Assn., S.C. Bar Assn., S.C. Trial Lawyers Assn. Avocations: hunting; fishing. Office: 504 Gressette Bldg Columbia SC 29202 Home Phone: 803-435-2314; Office Phone: 803-435-8894.

LAND, KARL-HEINZ, corporate communications specialist; b. 1964; Gen. mgr., v.p. Sales, Ctr. and Eastern Europe, MicroStrategy; mng. dir. Voice Bus. (Angel.com today), Germany; co-founder, CEO VoiceObjects, 2001—05, chief strategy officer, 2005—. Recipient VoiceObjects wins "Product of the Year", Comm. Solutions Magazine, 2004. Office: VoiceObjects Inc 1875 South Grant St Ste 720 San Mateo CA 94402 Office Phone: 650-288-0299. Office Fax: 650-525-9414.

LAND, KENNETH CARL, sociologist, educator, demographer; b. Llano, Tex., Aug. 19, 1942; s. Otto Carl and Tillie (Lindemann) L.; m. Jacqueline Yvette Apere, Mar. 22, 1969; 1 child, Kristoffer Carl. BA, Tex. Luth. Coll., 1964; MA, U. Tex., 1966, PhD, 1969. Staff assoc. Russell Sage Found., NYC, 1969-73; lectr. Columbia U., NYC, 1970-73; assoc. prof. U. Ill., Urbana, 1973-76, prof., 1976-81; prof. sociology U. Tex., Austin, 1981-86; prof., chmn. dept. sociology Duke U., Durham, NC, 1986-97, John Franklin Crowell prof. sociology, 1990—. Editor: Social Indicator Models, 1975, Social Accounting Systems, 1981, Multidimensional Mathematical Demography, 1982, Forecasting in the Social and Natural Sciences, 1987; contbr. articles to profl. jours.; co-author: Criminal Circumstance, 2003. Fellow AAAS, Am. Statis. Assn., Am. Soc. Criminology, Internat. Soc. Quality Life Studies; mem. Sociol. Rsch. Assn., Am. Sociol. Assn. (Paul F. Lazersfeld award methodology sect. 1997), Population Assn. Am. Lutheran. Office: Duke U Dept Sociology Durham NC 27708-0088 Office Phone: 919-660-5615. Business E-Mail: kland@soc.duke.edu.

LAND, REGINALD BRIAN, library administrator; b. Niagara Falls, Ont., Can., July 29, 1927; s. Allan Reginald and Beatrice Beryl (Boyle) L.; m. Edith Wyndham Eddis, Aug. 29, 1953; children— Mary Beatrice, John Robert Eddis. BA, U. Toronto, Ont., Can., 1949, BLS, 1953, MLS, 1956, MA, 1963. Catalogue copy editor T. Eaton Co. Ltd., Toronto, 1950-51; reference librarian Toronto Pub. Library, 1953-55; cataloguer U. Toronto Library, 1955-56, asst. librarian, 1959-63, assoc. librarian, 1963; head div. bus. and industry Windsor Pub. Library, Ont., Canada, 1956-57; asst. editor Canadian Bus. Mag., Montreal, Que., Canada, 1957-58, assoc. editor, 1958-59; exec. asst. to Minister Fin. of Can., Ottawa, Ont., 1963-64; prof. library sci. U. Toronto, 1964-78, part-time prof., 1978-93, prof. emeritus, 1993—, dean Faculty Library Sci., 1964-72; exec. dir. Ont. Legis. Library, Toronto, 1978-93. Author: Sources of Information for Canadian Business, 1962, 4th rev. edit., 1985, Eglinton: The Election Study of a Federal Constituency, 1965; founder, gen. editor: Directory of Associations in Canada, 1974, 18th rev. edit., 1997. Mem. Canadian Radio-TV and Telecommunications Commn., 1973-78, Ont. Hist. Soc. Decorated Knight Hospitaller Order of St. John of Jerusalem; recipient Kenneth R. Wilson Meml. award Bus. Newspapers Assn. Can., 1959, Disting. Achievement award Ont. Library Trustees Assn., 1968, Queen Elizabeth IIs Silver Jubilee medal, 1977, Spl. Librarianship award Can. Assn. for Spl. Librs. and Info. Svcs., 1991, 125th Anniversary Confederation Can. medal, 1992, Alumni Jubilee award U. Toronto Libr. & Info. Sci. Alumni Assn., 1994. Mem. ALA (chmn. com. on accreditation 1973-74), Assn. Parliamentary Librs. in Can. (pres. 1982-84), Can. Libr. Assn. (pres. 1975-76), Ont. Libr. Assn. (1st v.p. 1962-63), Ont. Govt. Librs. Coun. (chmn. 1984-85), Assn. for Libr. and Info. Sci. Edn. (pres. 1973-74), Can. Assn. for Grad. Edn. in Libr. Archival and Info. Studies (pres. 1966-67), Can. Coun. Libr. Schs. (chmn. 1971-72), Ex Libris Assn. (bd. dirs. 1994-99, pres. 1998), Inst. Profl. Librs. Ont. (pres. 1961-62), Ont. Coun. Libr. Schs. (chmn. 1968-72), Spl. Librs. Assn. (Mem. of Yr. award Toronto chpt. 1986), Ont. Geneal. Soc., Ont. Coll. and Univ. Librs. Assn. (merit award 1992), Ont. Hist. Soc., United Empire Loyalists' Assn. Can. Mem. Anglican Ch. Home: 9 Wild Rose Court Guelph ON Canada N1G 4X7 E-mail: brian-edith.land@sympatico.ca.

LAND, RICHARD DALE, minister, religious organization administrator; b. Houston, Nov. 6, 1946; s. Leggette Sloan and Marilee (Welch) L.; m. Rebekah Ruth Van Hooser, May 29, 1971; children: Jennifer, Richard Jr., Rachel. BA, Princeton U., 1969; ThM, New Orleans Bapt. Theol. Sem., 1972; D.Phil., U. Oxford, Eng., 1980. Ordained to ministry So. Bapt. Conv., 1969. Pastor S. Oxford Bapt. Ch., Oxford, Eng., 1972-75; prof. theology and ch. history Criswell Coll., Dallas, 1975-76, acad. dean, 1976-80, v.p. for acad. affairs, 1980-88; pres. ethics and religious liberty commn. So. Bapt. Conv., Nashville, 1988—. Mem. exec. com. Nat. Coalition against Pornography, Cin., 1989—; bd. dirs. Bapt. Joint Com. Pub. Affairs, Washington, 1987-91, Nat. Pro-Life Religious Coun., Washington; host nationally syndicated daily radio program For Faith & Family, 1998—, daily radio commentary 1999—; host weekly call-in talk show Richard Land Live, 2002—; apptd. mem. US Commn. on Internat. Religious Freedom, 2001-04, 05—. Cons. editor Criswell Study Bible, 1979. Mem. Gov.'s Task Force on Welfare Reform, Austin, Tex., 1988, Pres.'s Campaign for a Drug-Free Soc., Washington, 1991—; bd. dirs. Nat. Law Ctr., Arlington, Va., 1991—. Recipient Disting. Alumnus award New Orleans Bapt. Theol. Sem., 1997. Mem. Bapt. World Alliance (spl. com. on racism 1992, gen. bd. 1993, v. chmn. christian ethics com. 1995—). Office: Ethics & Religious Liberty Commn 901 Commerce St Ste 550 Nashville TN 37203-3600*

LAND, SUSAN KATHLEEN, application developer; b. Memphis, Nov. 5, 1963; d. Benjamin Fulton and Linda Patricia Pike (Stepmother); m. Jay Ellis Land, May 3, 1961; children: Kimberly Kay, Benjamin Ellia. BS, U. Ga., Athens, 1984. Computer specialist Info. Mgmt. Resources Office, Pacific Missile Test Ctr., Point Mugu, Calif., 1985—91; lead software engr. Tybrin Corp., Shalimar, Fla., 1992—95, BTG/Titan Engring., Niceville, Fla., 1995—99; database developer and principle arch. Andersen Cons., Fort Walton Beach, Fla., 1999—2000; principle mem. tech. staff Northrop Grumman Info. Tech., Fort Walton Beach, 2000—03, tech. dir., program mgr. Huntsville, Ala., 2003—. Author: (novel) Practical ISO 9001 Software Process Documentation- Using IEEE Software Engineering Standards; editor: The IEEE Computer Society's Software Engineering Workbook, Real World Examples for Today's Software Professional; author:, Practical CMMI Software Process Documentation- Using IEEE Software Engineering Standards, Jumpstart CMM/CMMI Software Process Improvement - Using IEEE Software Engineering Standards. Mem. Gulf Coast C.C. Dept. Computer Sci., Gulfport, Miss., 2002. Recipient Internal R & D award, Northrop Grumman IT/TASC, 2003, Mgmt. Spl. Performance award, 2004, 2005, Pres. Coin award, 2005; fellow, 2006—; grantee, 2004, 2005. Mem.: DAR, IEEE (computer soc. disting. vis. program 2006—, computer soc. software and sys. engring. stds. exec. com. 2001—, computer soc. internat. design competition judge 2003—06, computer soc. v.p. stds., chair stds. adv. bd. 2004—06, computer soc. v.p. confs. and tutorials 2007—, computer soc. 2d v.p. 2006—07, computer soc. 1st v.p. 2007—, computer soc. bd. govs. 2005—06, computer soc. software and sys. engring. stds. mgmt. bd. 2001—05, Computer Soc. Outstanding Contbn. award 2006), Colonial Dames Am. Achievements include development of database of all IEEE CS Software Engineering Terminology (3000+ terms) in support. Home Phone: 256-534-0975.

LAND, SUZANNE PRIEUR, lawyer; b. Youngstown, Ohio, Oct. 26, 1964; AB in Acctg. and Econs. summa cum laude, Youngstown State U., Ohio, 1987; JD summa cum laude, Case Western Res. Sch. Law, Cleve., 1990. Bar: Ohio 1990, Ky. 2005. Atty. Greenebaum, Doll & McDonald, Covington, Ky. Adj. prof. law U. Cin. Law Sch., 1998—; bd. advs. No. Ky. C. of C. Bd. visitors Salmon P. Chase Coll. Law; bd. trustees St. Luke Cmty. Found., Redwood Rehab. Ctr., Boys & Girls Clubs Greater Cin.; corp. guild mem., steering com. mem. Dressed for Success Cin. Named one of Top 100 Attys., Worth mag., 2005—06. Mem.: ABA, Ky. State Bar Assn., Ohio State Bar Assn., Cin. Bar Assn. Office: Greenebaum Doll & McDonald 1800 RiverCenter I 50 E RiverCenter Blvd Covington KY 41011-1660 Office Phone: 513-455-7619. Office Fax: 513-762-7919. E-mail: spl@gdm.com.*

LAND, TERRI LYNN, state official; b. Grand Rapids, Mich., June 30, 1958; m. Dan Hibma; children: Jessica Hibma, Nicholas Hibma. BA in Polit. Sci., Hope Coll., Holland, Mich. County clk. Kent County, Mich., 1992—2000; sec. state State of Mich., 2003—. Atty. Grievance Commn., 1999—2002; sec. Atty. Grievance Commn., 2001—02; mem. Secchia Millennium Commn., 2000, Cmty. Archives & Rsch. Ctr., 1997—, 54 Jefferson Study Com., 1997—. Mem. Grandville Rotary, 1990—99; bd. dirs. Am. Heart Assn., 1995—99, Jr. Achievement Alumni Bd., 1997—99, Project Rehab Found., 1997—98. Mem.: Mich. Supreme Ct. Hist. Soc., US Supreme Ct. Hist. Soc., Women's Resource Ctr. (v.p., bd. of dirs. 2001—02), Grand Rapids Pub. Mus. Found. Bd., Grand Rapids Rotary, Grand Rapids Early Morning Riser's Club, Friends of John Ball Zool. Pk., Byron Ctr. Fine Arts Found. (pres. 1999—), Friends of Van Andel Mus., Frederick Meijer Gardens, Grand Rapids C. of C., Byron Ctr. Hist. Soc. (pres. 1990—92), Byron Ctr. Cmty. Fine Arts Coun., Potters House Found. (mem., bd. dirs. 1997—). Republican. Office: Office Sec of State Treasury Bldg First Floor 430 West Allegan St Lansing MI 48918 Office Phone: 517-373-2510. Office Fax: 517-373-0727.*

LANDA, HOWARD MARTIN, lawyer, management consultant; b. Bklyn., Oct. 12, 1943; s. George and Lilli (Skolnik) L.; m. Nori Neinstein, Mar. 14, 1971; children— Alyson, David. BA (N.Y. State Regents scholar), Bklyn. Coll., 1964; JD (tuition scholar), U. Chgo., 1967. Bar: N.Y. 1968. Pvt. practice, NYC, 1968-69; assoc. Garfield, Solomon & Mainzer, NYC, 1969-70, Szold, Brandwen, Meyers & Altman, NYC, 1970-74; v.p., sec., gen. counsel IPCO Corp., White Plains, NY, 1974-90, also bd. dirs.; pres., mng. dir. Martin Hand Assocs., Inc., Greenwich, Conn., 1990-92, also bd. dirs.; owner Law Offices of Howard M. Landa, NYC, 1990-94; counsel Rand Rosenzweig Radley & Gordon LLP, White Plains, NY, 1994—. Lectr. Dental Lab. Conf., 1977. Contbr. articles to profl. jours. Mem. Mayor N.Y.C. Panel to Study Dept. Gen. Services' Div. Mcpl. Supplies, 1978-79; vice-chmn. So. N.Y. chpt. Nat. Multiple Sclerosis Soc., 1984-86, bd. dirs., 1984-2003. Mem.: ABA, Bus. Network Internat. (chpt. pres. 1998—2000, 2003—04). Office: Rand Rosenzweig Radley & Gordon LLP 50 Main St 12th Fl White Plains NY 10606 Home Phone: 845-634-8218; Office Phone: 914-406-7000 x 203. E-mail: hlanda@randrose.com.

LANDAN, HENRY SINCLAIR, financial and business consultant; b. Chgo., Aug. 4, 1943; BS, DePaul U., 1965, JD, 1969; LLM in Taxation, NYU, 1970. Bar: Ill. 1969-97, N.Y. 1971-97, U.S. Supreme Ct. 1976-97. Assoc. Altman, Kurlander & Weiss, Chgo., 1969-70, Roberts & Holland, NYC, 1970-72; sr. ptnr. Kamensky & Landan and predecessor, Chgo., 1972—85, Law Offices of Henry S. Landan, Chgo., 1985—88; of counsel Keck, Mahin & Cate, Chgo., 1988-90, ptnr., 1990—96, HSL Consulting, Louisville, 1996—, pres. Chgo. and Louisville, 2002—; dir. atty. placement Legal Solutions, Inc., Chgo., 2005—07. Counsel Caribbean Hotel Assn., Santurce, P.R., 1975-83. Contbg. author: Tax Planning for Professionals; contbr. articles to profl. jours. Exec. com., bd. dirs. Jewish Coun. for Youth Svcs., 1972-77, predecessor Young Men's Jewish Counsel; exec. com., bd. dirs. Men's Coun., Mus. Contemporary Art Chgo., 1977-84, pres., 1980-82; bd. dirs. Little City, Chgo., 1977-82, Mus. Contemporary Art, Chgo., 1980-82; bd. dirs., exec. com. Renaissance Soc. U. Chgo., 1984-96, v.p., 1988-95; mem. Soc. Contemporary Art, Art Inst. Chgo., 1982-95; mem. Contemporary Arts Coun., Chgo., 1994-96; bd. mgrs. Henry Horner Boys and Girls Club, 1992-95, James Jordan Boys and Girls Club, 1995-96; bd. dirs., exec. com. Randolph St. Gallery, Chgo., 1983-88, adv. bd., 1988-96. Named Life Dir., Jewish Coun. Youth Svcs., 1980, Man of Yr., 1985. Office: HSL Consulting 8500 Atrium Dr Ste 201 Louisville KY 40220 E-mail: hsl@insightbb.com.

LANDAU, DAVID H., lawyer; b. NYC, July 26, 1962; BS cum laude, U. Pa., 1984; JD, NYU, 1987. Bar: NY 1988. Ptnr. Katten Muchin Zavis Rosenman, NYC. Mem.: ABA. Office: Katten Muchin Zavis Rosenman 575 Madison Ave New York NY 10022 Office Phone: 212-940-6608. Office Fax: 212-940-8776. E-mail: david.landau@kmzr.com.

LANDAU, EMILY FISHER, art collector, foundation administrator; b. Glen Falls, NY, Aug. 23; d. Samuel and Cecelia (Greene) Lanzner; m. Martin A. Fisher (dec.); children: Richard L. Fisher, M. Anthony Fisher (dec.), Candia Fisher; m. Sheldon Landau. Ptnr. Fisher Bros., NYC; prs. Fisher Landau Found., NYC, 1984—; founder Fisher Landau Ctr. Art, Long Island City, 1991; PhD (hon.) Yeshiva U., 1998—. Trustee Whitney Mus. Am. Art, N.Y.C., 1987—, co-chmn. contemporary com., 1994—; mem. chmn.'s coun. Mus. Modern Art, N.Y.C., 1992—, mem. com. on painting and sculpture, 1997—, mem. com. on prints and illustrated books, 1985—; bd. dirs. The Georgia O'Keeffe Mus., Santa Fe, 1996; adv. dir. Met. Opera Assn., N.Y.C., 1986-88, mng. dir., 1988—; sponsor Emily Fisher Landau professorship of neurology Harvard Med. Sch., Cambridge, Mass., 1995—; founder Fisher Landau Ctr. for Treatment of Learning Disabilities, Albert Einstein Coll. Medicine/Yeshiva U., N.Y.C., 1997—; founding mem. Nat. Mus. Women in the Arts, 1987; charter mem. U.S. Holocaust Meml. Mus., 1992; bd. dirs. Site Santa Fe, 1994. Pub. exhbn. catalog Jasper Johns: The Screenprints, 1996; Mishoo Cosmopolitan Cat (children's storybook), 2000. Vice chmn. Anti-Defamation League of B'nai B'rith, N.Y.C.; sec. Anti-Defamation Found., N.Y.C.; sponsor Music Outreach, West End Symphony Pub. Sch. Project, N.Y.C. Decorated Chevalier Order Arts and Letters (France); named one of Top 200 Collectors, ARTnews mag., 2004. Mem. Met. Club, Doubles, Palm Beach Country Club. Avocation: collector of contemporary Am. art.

LANDAU, FELIX, lawyer; b. Hof, Germany, June 29, 1947; came to U.S., 1950; s. Fiszel and Ursula Landau; children: Erik Lloyd, Kelly Anne, Kristine Marie. BS, U. Colo., 1969; MA, U. No. Colo., 1972; JD cum laude, Gonzaga U., 1982. Bar: Wash. 1983, Wis. 1988. Assoc. Liebman, Conway, Olejniczak and Jerry, S.C., Green Bay, Wis., 1987-90; pvt. practice, Bellevue, Wash., 1990—. Assoc. editor Gonzaga U. Law Rev., 1981-82; author: Accident Investigation - Documenting the Facts, WSTLA Automobile Accident Litigation Deskbook, 2000. Founder, head coach Bellevue Eagles Track and Cross Country Team. Capt. USAF, 1983-87. Mem. ABA, Wash. Bar Assn., Wash. State Trial Lawyers Assn. (Eagle mem., chmn. Eastside roundtable 1995-98), East King County Trial Lawyers Assn., Wis. Bar Assn., Phi Delta Phi. Avocations: sports, golf, basketball, tennis, jogging, coaching usa track and field and cross country running. Office: 110 110th Ave NE Ste 670 Bellevue WA 98004 Office Phone: 425-641-5507. Business E-Mail: landaulawoffice@aol.com.

LANDAU, JOEL, health services administrator; b. Goshen, NY, Aug. 22, 1980; s. Joseph Landau; m. Rachel Stein; children: Judah, Rebecca. Master's, UTA, 2000. Rabbi diplomat 1999. CEO E-ZBILL, LLC, Bklyn., 2002—. Advisor Yetev Lev, Bklyn., 2001—03. Mem.: Bus. Advisory Coun. Office: E-ZBILL, LLC 199 Lee Ave #182 Brooklyn NY 11211 Home Phone: 718-930-7443; Office Phone: 718-858-4944. Office Fax: 718-504-5339. Business E-Mail: joe@e-zbill.com.

LANDAU, JON, music producer, manager; m. Barbara Landau. Grad., Brandeis U., 1968. Rock critic Crawdaddy!, Boston Phoenix, Rolling Stone, The Real Paper; founder, co-owner Jon Landau Mgmt.; former mgr. for Shania Twain, Natalie Merchant; mgr. for Bruce Springsteen, Train, Patti Scialfa; has produced albums for MC5, Livingston Taylor, Jackson Brown, Bruce Springsteen. Author: It's Too Late to Stop Now: A Rock and Roll Jour., 1972. Named one of Top 200 Collectors, ARTnews mag., 2004. Achievements include Famous for line "I saw rock and roll future and its name is Bruce Springsteen", which appeared in his article for The Real Paper on May 22, 1974. Avocation: Collector Old Masters painting and sculpture, 19th-century French painting, Am. modernist art. Office: Jon Landau Mgmt 80 Mason St Greenwich CT 06830

LANDAU, LAURI BETH, accountant, consultant; b. Bklyn., July 21, 1952; d. Jack and Audrey Carolyn (Zuckernick) L. BA, Skidmore Coll., 1973; postgrad., Pace U., 1977-79. CPA, N.Y. Mem. staff Audrey Z. Landau, CPA, Suffern, N.Y., 1976-78, Ernst & Whinney, NYC, 1979-80, mem. sr. staff, 1980-82, supr., 1982-84; mgr. Arthur Young & Co., NYC, 1984-87, prin., 1987-89; sr. mgr. Ernst & Young, NYC, 1989-92; ptnr. Landau & Landau, Pomona, N.Y., 1992—. Ptnr. Audrey Z. Landau & Co., Wilmington, Vt., 1995—; spkr. World Trade Inst., N.Y.C., 1987—, Nat. Fgn. Trade Coun., N.Y.C., 1989—. Composer songs. Career counselor Skidmore Coll., Saratoga Springs, N.Y., 1977—; mem. leadership com. Class of 1973, 83-85, pres., 1985-93, fund chmn., 1987-88, mem. planned gift com., 1989—. N.Y. State Regents scholar, 1970. Mem. Nat. Conf. CPA Practitioners, N.Y. State Soc. CPAs, Rockland Bus. Assn., Skidmore Coll. Alumni Assn. (mem. nominating com. 1989-92). Skidmore Alumni Club. Democrat. Avocations: music, ballet, photography, sports. Office: 26 Firemans Memorial Dr Pomona NY 10970-3553 Business E-Mail: LBinfo@aol.com.

LANDAU, MARTIN, actor; b. Bklyn., June 20, 1931; m. Barbara Bain Jan. 31, 1957 (div. 1993); children: Susie, Juliet. Student, Art Students League, Actors Studio. Staff artist, cartoonist N.Y. Daily News. Star TV series Mission: Impossible, 1966-69 (Golden Globe award 1967), Space 1999, 1974-77, Corsairs, 2002, The Evidence, 2006-, others; TV appearances include Omnibus, Playhouse 90, G.E. Theatre, Gunsmoke, Twilight Zone; also TV movies Welcome Home, Johnny Bristol, 1972, Savage, 1973, The Death of Ocean View Park, 1979, The Harlem Globetrotters on Gilligan's Island, 1981, The Fall of the House of Usher, 1982, The Neon Empire, 1989, By Dawn's Early Light, 1990, Something to Live For: The Alison Gertz Story, 1992, Legacy of Lies, 1992 (Ace award), 12:01, 1993, miniseries Joseph, 1995, Merry Christmas, George Bailey, 1997, Bonanno: A Godfather's Story, 1999, In the Beginning, 2000; films include Pork Chop Hill, North by Northwest, 1959, Stagecoach to Dancer's Rock, 1961, Cleopatra, 1962, Hallelujah Trail, 1964, The Greatest Story Ever Told, 1965, Nevada Smith, 1966, They Call Me Mr. Tibbs, 1970, Operation SNAFU, 1970, A Town Called Hell, 1971, Johnny Bristol, 1971, Black Gunn, 1972, Strange Shadows in an Empty Room, 1977, Meteor, 1979, The Last Word, 1979, Without Warning, 1980, Operation Moonbase Alpha, 1980, Earthright, 1980, Beauty and the Beast, 1981, Alone in the Dark, 1982, Trail by Terror, 1983, Tucker: The Man and His Dreams, 1988 (Acad. Award nominee 1988), Crimes and Misdeameanors, 1989 (Golden Globe award 1989, Acad. award nominee 1989), Paint It Black, 1990, Real Bullets, 1990, Firehead, 1991, Eye of the Widow, 1991, Mistress, 1992, Silver, 1993, Intersection, 1994, Ed Wood, 1994 (Best Supporting Actor Acad. award 1994, Golden Globe award 1994, SAG award 1994, Am. Comedy award 1994, N.Y. Film Critics award 1994, L.A. Film Critics award 1994, Chgo. Film Critics award 1994, Nat. Soc. Film Critics award 1994, Boston Film Critics award 1994, Tex. Film Critics award 1994, Lifetime Achivement award Houston Film Festival 1994, Lifetime Achivement award Charleston Film Festival 1994), The Elevator, 1996, City Hall, 1996, The Adventures of Pinocchio, 1996, Legend of the Spirit Dog (voice), 1997, Animals, 1997, B*A*P*S, 1997, The Long Way Home (voice), Winter, 1998, The Joyrides, 1998, The X Files: Fight the Future, 1998, Rounders, 1998, ED-TV, 1999, Carlo's Wake, 1999, The Joyriders, 1999, The Commission, 1999, (mini-series) The Life and Times of Joe Bonnano, 1999, The New Adventures of Pinocchio, 1999, In the Beginning, 2000, Haven, 2000, Very Mean Men, 2000, The Majestic, 2001, Wake, 2002, An Existential Affair (also prodr.), 2002, Hollywood Homicide, 2003, The Commission, 2003, Wake, 2003, The Aryan Couple, 2004, An Existential Affair, 2005; stage appearances include Middle of the Night, Uncle Vanya, Stalag 17, Wedding Breakfast, First Love, The Goat Song, Dracula, Sixteen Wounded. Emmy nominee; recipient Lifetime Achievement award San Diego Film Festival, 1998. Mem. Acad. Motion Picture Arts and Scis., Actors Studio (W. Coast dir.) Home: 3300 Irvine Ave Ste 105 Newport Beach CA 92660-3115

LANDAU, MICHAEL B., law educator; b. Wilkes-Barre, Pa., July 3, 1953; s. Jack Landau and Florence (Rabitz) Simon. BA, Pa. State U., 1975; JD, U. Pa., 1988. Vis. prof. law Dickinson Sch. Law, Pa. State U., Carlisle; assoc. Cravath, Swaine and Moore, NYC, 1988-90, Skadden, Arps, NYC, 1990-92; assoc. prof. Coll. Law Ga. State U., Atlanta, 1992-99, prof. law, 1999—, dir. intellectual property, tech. and media law program. Vis. prof. law U. Ga. Law Sch., 1998; guest lectr. Johannes Kepler U., Linz, Austria, summer 1994, 95, 96; vis. scholar Univ. Amsterdam, 2000, U. Helsinki, Finland, 2005 Contbr. articles to law jours. on copyright, art, patent, entertainment law. Scholar, Fulbright Found., 2005. Mem. ABA, N.Y. State Bar Assn., Internat. Bar Assn., Vol. Lawyers for Arts, Am. Fedn. Musicians, Am. Intellectual Property Law Assn., Copyright Soc. U.S. Am., Phi Kappa Phi, Omicron Delta Epsilon. Democrat. Avocations: photography, jazz guitar, jazz piano. Office: Ga State U Coll Law University Pla Atlanta GA 30303 Office Phone: 404-651-2084. Business E-Mail: mlandau@gsu.edu.

LANDAU, PETER EDWARD, editor; b. NYC, July 16, 1933; s. Edward and Charlotte (Schmidt) L. AB, Duke U., 1955; MS in Econs., Columbia U., 1959. Editl. asst. Newsweek mag., NYC, 1955-57, asst. editor, 1958-61, assoc. editor, 1962-67; v.p. Tiderock Corp., 1967; sr. editor Instl. Investor, NYC, 1968, mng. editor, 1968-70, editor, 1971-91, editor-at-large, 1991-97; historian St. Andrew's Golf Club, 1993—. Author: St. Andrew's in the Gilded Age, 2006; co-author: Presidential Lies: The Illustrated History of White House Golf, 1996. Home: 10 Old Jackson Ave Unit 11 Hastings On Hudson NY 10706

LANDAU, SIDNEY IVAN, lexicographer; b. NYC, Apr. 11, 1933; s. Emanuel and Sadie Mildred (Halpern) L.; m. Sarah Gaston Bradford, June 19, 1959; children: Paul, Amy. BA in English, Queens Coll., 1954; MFA in Creative Writing, U. Iowa, 1959. Instr. English Miami U., Oxford, Ohio, 1959-61; editor, then editor-in-chief dictionaries Funk & Wagnalls, NYC, 1961-70; editor-in-chief Doubleday Dictionary, Doubleday Roget's Thesaurus Doubleday & Co., NYC, 1975-77; editor-in-chief Internat. Dictionary of Medicine and Biology, John Wiley & Sons, NYC, 1977-88, mgr. med. jours., 1982-84, exec. editor medicine, 1985-87, pub. chemistry and life scis. sci.-tech. div., 1987-88; editl. dir. N.Am. br. Cambridge U. Press, NYC, 1988-93; editor-in-chief Cambridge Dictionary of Am. English, 2000. Author: Dictionaries: The Art and Craft of Lexicography, 1984, 2d edit., 2001; contbr. numerous articles to profl. jours. With U.S. Army, 1954-56. Fellow: Dictionary Soc. N.Am. (pres. 1993—95). Home: 50 W 96th St Apt 2A New York NY 10025-6527

LANDAU, YAIR, film company executive; m. Susan Purcell; children: Erin, Maya. Grad. summa cum laude, U. Chgo., 1985; MBA, Stanford U., 1989. Assoc. Kidder, Peabody & Co., Chgo., Wasserstein, Perella & Co.; dir. fin. planning and analysis Sony Pictures Entertainment, 1991, v.p. bus. planning motion picture operations, 1992, sr. v.p. fin. and corp. develop., 1994, exec. v.p. corp. develop. and strategic planning, 1997—99, founder, pres. Sony Pictures Digital, 1999—, vice chmn., 2002—. Mem.: Phi Beta Kappa. Office: Sony Pictures 10202 W Washington Blvd Culver City CA 90232

LANDAW, STEPHEN ARTHUR, physician, educator; b. Paterson, NJ, June 20, 1936; s. Louis and Ida (Machowsky) L.; children: Jared Lawrence, Nicole Renee. BS, U. Wis., 1955; MD, George Washington U., 1959; PhD, U. Calif., Berkeley, 1969. Intern Mt. Sinai Hosp., NYC, 1959-60, resident in internal medicine, 1960-61; fellow in hematology Med. Coll. Va., 1962-63; fellow in nuclear medicine Donner Lab., U. Calif., 1963-69, asst. physician, 1970-73; chief isotope lab. Highland-Alameda County Hosp., Oakland, Calif., 1970-73; asso. prof. SUNY, Syracuse, 1973-78, prof., 1978-99; assoc. chief staff research and devel. VA Med. Center, Syracuse, 1973-94; chief, hematology VA Med. Ctr., Syracuse, 1997-99; vis. prof. Rockefeller U., NYC, 1988; vis. physician Rockefeller U. Hosp., NYC, 1988; dep. editor, hematology Uptodate, Inc., Waltham, Mass., 1999—; attending physician hematology-oncology Beth Israel Deaconess Med. Ctr., Boston, 2003—. Pres. Ctrl. NY Rsch. Corp., 1989—94; clin. instr. medicine Harvard Med. Sch., Boston, 2003—; weekend guide Mus. Fine Art, Boston, 2005—. Contbr. in field. Weekend guide Mus. Fine Arts, Boston, 2005—. With US Army, 1961—62. VA grantee, 1973-93; NASA grantee, 1976-82; recipient NASA Kosmos Achievement awards, 1975, 77 Fellow ACP; mem. Am. Soc. Hematology, Am. Fedn. Clin. Rsch., Soc. Pediat. Rsch., Soc. Exptl. Biology and Medicine, N.Y. Acad. Sci., Sigma Xi, Alpha Omega Alpha. Jewish. Home: 241 Perkins St Apt C105 Jamaica Plain MA 02130-4058 Office: Uptodate Inc 95 Sawyer Rd Waltham MA 02453-3471 Office Phone: 781-392-2021. Personal E-mail: slandaw@uptodate.com.

LANDECK, CARL, corporate financial executive; CPA. V.p. fin., chief acctg. and fin. officer Herman's Sporting Goods, Inc.; CFO Nobody Beats the Wiz, Carteret, NJ; exec. v.p. Cablevision Electronics Investments Inc., Edison, NJ, 1998; CFO, chief adminstrv. officer Levitz Home Furnishings Inc.; CFO Bally's Total Fitness, Chgo., 2005—06.

LANDEFELD, STEWART M., lawyer; b. Cleve., Mar. 13, 1954; BA, Yale U., 1976; JD, U. Chgo., 1980. Bar: Wash. 1980, US Ct. Appeals (9th Cir.). Firmwide chair nat. bus. practice group Perkins Coie LLP, Seattle. Co-author: Washington Business Entities, 1991—. Chmn. bd. trustees Seattle Found.; past chmn. bd. trustees Henry Art Gallery. Named a Wash. Super Lawyer, Wash. Law & Polit. Office: Perkins Coie LLP 1201 3rd Ave Ste 4800 Seattle WA 98101-3029 Office Phone: 206-359-8430. Office Fax: 206-359-9430. Business E-Mail: slandefeld@perkinscoie.com.

LANDEL, MICHEL, food service and management company executive; b. 1952; MBA, European Bus. Sch., Paris; student, France, UK, Germany, With acctg. and control dept. for Europe, Chase Manhattan Bank, France, founder, country ops. mgr. Ivory Coast; gen. mgr. Poliet Group, mfrs. and distbrs. bldg. materials, France, 1980-84; chief operating mgr. for Ea. Africa, Libya and Algeria, Sodexho, 1984-86, pres. remote site ops. in Africa, 1986-89; pres., CEO, Sodexho N.Am. (merger with Marriott Mgmt. Svcs.), 1989-98; exec. v.p., pres. corp. svcs. divsn. Sodexho Marriott Svcs., Inc., Gaithersburg, Md., 1998-99, pres., CEO, 1999—, group pres., COO, 2003—, also chmn. bd. dirs. Gaithersburg, Md. Recipient Golden Chain award Multi-Unit Food Svc. Operators, 1997, Ivy award Restaurant & Instns., 1998. Office: Sodexho Marriott Svcs Inc 9801 Washington Blvd Gaithersburg MD 20878

LANDEN, ASHLEY RENEE, mechanical engineer; b. Marietta, Ga., Mar. 4, 1980; d. Radford Barton and Teresa Kay Landen. Degree in Mech. Engring., Clemson U., SC, 2005. Cert. engr. in tng. Ga. Design engr. Newcomb & Boyd, Atlanta, 2005—. Mem.: Ashrae. Office: Newcomb and Boyd 303 Peachtree Ctr Ave Atlanta GA 30303 Business E-Mail: alanden@newcomb-boyd.com.

LANDEN, ROBERT GERAN, retired historian, academic administrator; b. Boston, July 13, 1930; s. Harry James and Evelyn Gertrude (Geran) L.; m. Patricia Kizzia, July 19, 1958; children— Michael Geran, Robert Kizzia, Jill Arnett, Amy Patricia. AB, Coll. of William and Mary, 1952; MA, U. Mich., 1953; A.M., Princeton U., 1958, PhD (Ford Found. fellow), 1961. Asst. prof. social sci. Ball State U., Muncie, Ind., 1959-60; asst. prof. near eastern studies U. Mich., Ann Arbor, 1960-61; asst. prof. history Dartmouth, Hanover, NH, 1961-66, asst. dean of freshmen, 1963-64, asso. prof. history, 1966-67; prof., head dept. history Va. Poly. Inst. and State U., Blacksburg, 1967-69; prof. history U. S.C., Columbia, 1969-75, asso. vice provost, 1971-72, asso. provost, 1972-73; dean U. S.C. (Coll. of Social and Behavioral Scis.), 1972-75; prof. history U. Tex. at Arlington, 1975-77, dean Coll. Liberal Arts, 1975-77; prof. history U. Tenn., Knoxville, 1977-86; dean Coll. Arts and Scis., 1977-85; prof. history, v.p. acad. affairs, provost U. Montevallo, 1986-88; prof. history and humanities, dir. programs in the humanities Va. Poly Inst. and State U., Blacksburg, 1988-95, prof. emeritus history and humanities, 1995—. Author: Oman Since 1856, 1967, The Emergence of the Modern Middle East, 1970, (with Abid Al-Marayati) The Middle East, Its Governments and Politics, 1972; contbr. articles to profl. jours. and book revs. to hist. publs. Served with AUS, 1953-55. Am. Coun. Learned Socs. fellow, 1965-66, Comparative Studies Ctr. Faculty fellow, 1965-66, Malone fellow, 1988. Fellow Middle East Studies Assn. of N. Am.; mem. Theta Delta Chi, Phi Kappa Phi. Roman Catholic. Home: 108 Edgewood Ln Williamsburg VA 23185-3213

LANDER, ERIC STEVEN, geneticist, molecular biologist, mathematician; b. Bklyn., Feb. 3, 1957; BA in Math. with hons., Princeton U., 1978; DPhil in Math., Oxford U., Eng., 1981. Asst. prof. Grad. Sch. Bus., Harvard U., 1981-86, assoc. prof., 1987-90; Whitehead fellow MIT, Cambridge, 1986, vis. scientist, 1984-89, assoc. prof., 1989-93, prof. dept. biology, 1993—, mem. Whitehead Inst. Biomed. Rsch., 1989—, founder, dir. Whitehead Ctr. Genome Rsch., 1990—, founding dir., Broad Inst., 1990—. Med. geneticist Mass. Genl. Hosp., Boston, 1993—; Ralph R. Braund disting. vis. prod. U. Tenn., 1994; mem. U.S. Presdl. Commn. Nat. Medal Sci., 1995-97; mem. genetics working group NIMH, 1997—; Christian A. Herter disting. lectr. NYU, 1993; Gladstone disting. lectr. Gladstone Inst., 1994; Herbert Boyer lectr. genetics U. Calif., San Francisco, 1995. Contbr. articles to profl. jours. Named Millennium Lectr., The White House, 1999, Scientist of Year, Nat. Disease Rsch. Interchange, 2003, R&D Mag., 2003; recipient Beckman prize for lab automation, Chiron prize in biotechnology, Woodrow Wilson prize for pub. svc., Princeton U., Dickson prize in cancer, Rhodes prize in cancer, Gairdner award, Gairdner Found., 2002, Pub. Understanding of Sci. and Tech. award, AAAS, 2004; fellow MacArthur fellow, 1987; scholar Rhodes scholar, 1978. Fellow AAAS; mem. NAS (mem. math. and molecular biology com. 1989-90), Human Genome Orgn., Genetics Soc. Am., Am. Soc. Human Genetics, Math. Assn. Am., Am. Acad. Forensic Sci., Am. Assn. Cancer Rsch., Inst. Medicine. Achievements include founding the center which is the leading contributor to the Human Genome Project. Address: MIT 77 Massachusetts Ave Cambridge MA 02139-4307 Office: Whitehead Inst/MIT 9 Cambridge Center Cambridge MA 02142-1479 Office Phone: 617-252-1906. Office Fax: 617-258-0903.

LANDER, ERNEST MCPHERSON, JR., history and economics professor; b. Calhoun Falls, SC, Dec. 16, 1915; s. Ernest McPherson and Kizzie Jones Lander; m. Sarah Ray Shirley; children: Elizabeth, Caroline. AB, Wofford Coll., 1937; MA, U. N.C., 1939, PhD, 1950; DLitt (hon.), Lander U., 1986. Tchr. New Prospect H.S., Inman, SC, 1937—38; tchr., coach Dillon H.S., SC, 1939—40; prof., coach Reinhart Coll, Waleska, Ga., 1940—41; prof. Clemson Coll., SC, 1941—42, Clemson U., SC, 1946—83. Spkr. in field. Author or co-editor: 16 books; contbr. over 60 articles to profl. jours. Staff sgt. US Army, 1942—46. Mem.: S.C. Hist. Soc., So. Hist. Assn., Phi Beta Kappa. Democrat. Home: 217 Riggs Dr Clemson SC 29631

LANDER, HOWARD, entertainment newspaper publisher; b. NYC, Oct. 25, 1950; s. Leo T. and Doris (Davis) L.; m. Gail Melanie Ravitz, Sept. 6, 1976; children: Aimee, Jared. BA, Rutgers U., Newark, 1972. Sportswriter Buffalo Courier-Express, 1973; reporter Amusement Bus., NYC, 1973-76, sales rep., 1976-79, pub. Nashville, 1981-88; advt. mgr. Residential Interiors mag., NYC, 1980; v.p., group pub. BPI Comm., 1988-90; pub. Billboard Mag., NYC, 1990-91; sr. v.p. BPI Comm., 1991-92, exec. v.p., 1993—; pres., pub. Billboard Music Group, 1994—, Billboard Literary Group, 1994—; COO, VNU Bus. Media, 2004—. Recipient Spirit of Life award City of Hope, 1998. Avocations: sports, literature, music.

LANDER, JAMES ALBERT, retired military officer, controller; b. Abbeville, SC, Apr. 9, 1930; s. William Jones and Annie (Cheatham) L.; m. Jolene Patricia Smith, June 8, 1952; children: Theresa (dec.), Britt, Leslie, Victoria (dec.), Gail, Jean, David. BS, Lander Coll., 1986; LLD (hon.), Lander U., 2000. Technician S.C. Nat. Guard, Abbeville, 1952-53; life ins. salesman Gulf Life Pilot, Met., Anderson, SC, 1953-66; maj. U.S. Army, 1966-71; plans and ops. officer, chief of staff S.C. Army N.G., Columbia, 1971-85, maj. gen. mil., 1988-91; mem. S.C. Senate, Columbia, 1993-99; elected state comptr. State of S.C., Columbia, 1999—2003. Chmn. RSVP Adv. Com., 1991—, Newberry County Literacy Assn., 1991-93; deacon Newberry 1st Bapt. Ch.; past chmn. Boy Scouts Am., Newberry. Decorated Bronze Star, Legion of Merit; recipient Arc Legis. award, 1999, Order of Palmetto State of S.C., 1985, Palmetto Cross, 1991, Silver Beaver award

Boy Scouts Am., 1990; named Legislator of Yr. S.C. Assn. Counties and S.C. Assn. Deaf, 1994. Mem.: AARP (pres.), VFW, Mil. Officers Assn. Am., C. of C. Newberry, Assn. U.S. Army, Mil. Order World Wars, Vietnam Vets. Assn., Exch. Club (pres.), Rotary, Masons, Shriners, Am. Legion. Democrat. Baptist. Avocations: reading, gardening. Home: 2029 Main St Newberry SC 29108-3521 Personal E-mail: jalander@bellsouth.net.

LANDER, JOYCE ANN, retired nursing educator, retired medical/surgical nurse; b. Benton Harbor, Mich., July 27, 1942; d. James E. and Anna Mae Remus LPN, Kalamazoo Practical Nursing, Ctr., 1967; AAS, Kalamazoo Valley C.C., 1981, Grad. Massage Therapy Program, 1995. LPN-RN Bronson Meth. Hosp., Kalamazoo, 1972-82; RN med./surg. unit Borgess Med. Ctr., Kalamazoo, 1982-84; RN pediat. Upjohn Home Health Care, Kalamazoo, 1984-88; supr. nursing lab Kalamazoo Valley Comm. Coll., 1982—2005, ret., 2005. Therapeutic massage therapist in client homes with Business Kneading Peace Therapeutic Massage, Kalamazoo, 1995—; nursing asst., instr. State of Mich. Observer, 1990-96. Author: What Is A Nurse, 1980. Address: 3300 Woodstone Dr E Apt 108 Kalamazoo MI 49008-2548

LANDER, RUTH A., medical association administrator; b. Fitchburg, Mass., Dec. 13, 1948; d. H. Allison and Violet K. (Erickson) Linné; m. C. Stephen Lander, June 28, 1968; children: Timothy, Mary. BA, Ohio State U., 1978. Cert. med. practice exec. 1994. Dir. fin. Luth. Svc. Assn. New England, Natick, Mass., 1973—76; gen. mgr. Logos, Columbus, Ohio, 1976—87; practice adminstr. Columbus Oncology Assocs., Inc., 1987—. Sec., treas. Adminstrs. Oncology Hematology Assembly, Englewood, Colo., 1994-95, legis. liaison, 1994-95, pres.-elect, 1995-96, pres., 1996-97; spkr. med. group mgmt. issues. Editor Administrs. in Oncology Hematology Assembly News, 1994-95; mem. editl. bd. Oncology Issues Mag., 1998-2000; mem. editl. adv. bd. for coding and reimbursement Oncology & Hematology, 2001; contbr. articles to profl. jours. Mem. task force Cmty. Oncology Alliance, 2004-05. Fellow Med. Group Mgmt. Assn., Am. Coll. Med. Practice Execs. (nat. chair membership devel. com. 1999, nat. bd. dir. 2004-06, exam. com., 2006—); mem. Am. Soc. Clin. Oncology (assoc.), Nat. Oncology Soc. Network, Ctrl.-Ohio Med. Group Mgmt. Assn. (pres. 1993-94, sec. 1992-93, program dir. 1991-92, exec. com. 1990-97), Assn. Cmty. Cancer Ctr. (editl. bd. mag. 1998-2000), Ohio Med. Group Mgmt. Assn. (exec. com. 1994-2001, sec. 1995-96, pres. 1998, rep. to Medicare POE adv. group 2003—, grass roots legis. group 1994—), Ohio Oncology Med. Group Mgmt. Assn. (pres. 1997), Ohio State Med. Assn. (assoc.; group practice task force 2000—), Columbus Med. Assn. (group practice mgrs. task force 2002—). Republican. Avocations: reading, computers, crafts, knitting, bible study. Office: Columbus Oncology Assocs 810 Jasonway Ave Ste A Columbus OH 43214-2329

LANDERHOLM, ELIZABETH JANE, early childhood education educator; b. Oak Park, Ill. d. Daniel R. and Dorothy E. LaBar; m. Wayne A. Landerholm, June 6, 1964; 1 child, Arthur Scott. BA in Sociology, DePauw U., 1963; MS in Tchg., U. Chgo., 1966; EdD in Curriculum and Instrn., No. Ill. U., DeKalb, 1980. Cert. early childhood and elem. edn., Ill. Tchr. Chgo. Bd. Edn., 1966-69; student tchg. supr. Nat. Coll. Edn., Chgo., 1970-79; asst. prof. Roosevelt U., Chgo., 1980-83; project dir. Children's Devel. Ctr., Rockford, Ill., 1984-86; assoc. prof. Northeastern Ill. U., Chgo., 1986-92, prof., 1993—. Therapist Theraplay Inst., Chgo., 1980—84; project dir. McCosh Even Start, 1994—2003; project coord. Early Childhood Cohort/Ill. Profl. Learning Ptnrships. (TQE grant), 1999—2004; prin. investigator Early Reading First Grant, Dept. Edn., 2004—. Contbr. articles to profl. jours. McCosh Even Start grant Ill. State Bd. Edn., Chgo., 1994—, Ill. Profls. Learning Partnerships grant, 1999—. Home: 325 N Humphrey Ave Oak Park IL 60302-2516 Office: Northeastern Ill Univ 5500 N Saint Louis Ave Chicago IL 60625-4699 Home Phone: 708-848-1265; Office Phone: 773-442-5383. Personal E-mail: eland325@aol.com. Business E-Mail: e-landerholm@neiu.edu.

LANDERS, AUDREY, actress, singer; b. Phila., July 18, 1959; d. Ruth Landers; m. Donald Berkowitz, May 1988; 2 children. BA, Barnard Coll. Records singles and albums with sister Judy Landers. Actress (films) 1941, 1979, Underground Aces, 1981, Tennessee Stallion, 1982, Deadly Twins, 1985, A Chorus Line, 1985, Getting Even, 1986, Johann Strauss: The King Without a Crown, 1987, California Casanova, 1991, Last Chance Love, 1997, Island Forever, 2005, (TV films) Our Voices Ourselves, 1982, Popeye Doyle, 1986, Ghost Writer, 1989, Dallas: J.R. Returns, 1996, (TV series) The Secret Storm, 1972—73, Somerset, 1974—76, Highcliffe Manor, 1979, Dallas, 1981—84, 1989, Lucky/Chances, 1990, One Life to Live, 1990—91, The Huggabug Club, 1995. Office: care Jo-Ann Geffen & Assocs 3151 Cahuenga Blvd W Ste 235 Los Angeles CA 90068-1749

LANDERS, MARY DEAN J., music educator; b. Toombs County, Ga. d. Ted Curtis Jarriel Sr. and Mildred Everest Mayo; m. John Rodney Landers, Oct. 13, 1962; 1 child, Gretchen Elizabeth Landers Brand. B in Music Edn., Fla. State U., Tallahassee, 1961; post. grad., Wagner Coll., SI, NY, 1963; student, Ruth Pinkerton, NYC, 1963—69, Ruth Pinnell Syracuse U., NY, 1980—82; post grad., Oberlin Coll., Ohio, 1991, Columbia U. Tchrs. Coll., NYC, 1992, SUNY Upstate Med. Ctr., Syracuse, 1995; post grad. in piano, Eastman Sch. Music, 1983, post grad. in piano, 1988, post grad. in piano, 1992, post grad. in piano, 1994. Cert. elem. tchr. NY, 1963. Tchr. music elem. sch. Atlanta Pub. Schs., 1961—62, SI Pub. Schs., NY, 1962—66; tchr. music Ashdun Hall Montessori Sch., Atlanta, 1966—68; substitute tchr. Liverpool Ctrl. Schs., Liverpool, NY, 1969—76; tchr. elem. music, dir. girl's vocal ensemble Faith Heritage Sch., Syracuse, 1977—82; pvt. practice Liverpool, 1969—2007. Soloist Richmond County Chorus, SI, NY, 1963; mem. Atlanta Symphony Chamber Chorus, 1967—68; performer Talent Co. Empire State Theater, Syracuse, NY, 1995—98. Soloist Meml. Day Observances, Liverpool, NY, 1970—2007, Am. Legion Meml. Svcs., Liverpool, NY, 1970—2007; chmn. Onondaga County Hist. Cemetery program, 1994; mem. Onondaga WWII Commemorative Com., 1995—97; participant NY State Mus. Hist. Markers project, 1996—98; chmn. NYS Fair Constitution and Revolutionary War Exhibit, 1996—2001; soloist Presbyn. Ch., SI, NY, 1962—65, Chamblee, Ga., 1966—68, First United Meth. Ch., Liverpool, NY, 1970—81, co-founder, co-dir. bell chior, dir. angel choir; soloist Redeemer Evang. Covenant Ch., Liverpool, NY, 1982—2000, First Presbyn. Ch., Liverpool, 2000—07; vis. soloist First Bapt. Ch., Vidalia, Ga.; competitions chmn. Salt City Figure Skaters, 1980—85, bd. mem., 1980—85, treas., 1984—85; bd. mem. Fedn. Women's Clubs, 1997—98. Mem.: DAR (vice regent Gen. Asa Danforth chpt. 1989—95, dir. Empire State Chorus 1991—97, regent Gen. Asa Danforth chpt. 1995—97; NY State Outstanding Chpt. Regent 1997), Performing Arts Med. Assn., Suzuki Assoc. Tchrs. Young Children, Nat. Fedn. Music Tchrs., Nat. Assn. Piano Tchrs., Nat. Assn. Tchrs. Singing, Ctrl. NY Assn. Music Tchrs. (gen. chair competitions 1983—94, treas. 1987—92, v.p. 1992—94, pres. 1994—97, competitions co-chair 1994—97), Colonial Daus. 17th Century (state registrar 1997—), Dau. Am. Colonists (state rec. sec. 1994—97, state 2d vice regent 1997—2000, regent Gov. John Cranston chpt. 1997—2000, state first vice regent 2000—03, NY state regent 2003—, nat. v.p. Appalachian region 2006—07), Colonial Dames Am., Colonial Order of Crown, Nat. Soc. Magna Charta Dames, Plantagenet Soc. Home: 111 Hiawatha Trail Liverpool NY 13088-4432

LANDERS, PATRICIA GLOVER, language educator; b. Pine Bluff, Ark., Nov. 15, 1945; d. Maurice Alexander Glover and Ruth Wells-Glover Wimberly; 1 child, Wendolynn. BS in Edn., Ark. State U., 1967; MS in Edn., OBU, 1976; postgrad., U. Ark., 1980—81, U. Ariz., 1980—81, Ariz. State U., 1983—88, U. Phoenix, 1988—89. Cert. tchr. English, reading specialist K-12 Ariz., C.C., English, lang. arts, composition Ariz. Elem. music supr. Greene County Tech. Schs., Paragould, Ark., 1967—68; band and choir dir. Naylor (Mo.) Schs., 1968—70; elem. tchr. Poughkeepsie (Ark.) Schs., 1970—72; reading specialist Sheridan (Ariz.) Schs., 1975—82, Casa Grande Union High Sch., Casa Grande, Ariz., 1982—; assoc. prof. Pima C.C., Tucson, 1982—94, Centra Ariz. Coll., Coolidge, Ariz., 1983—93; English tchr. Casa Granda Regional Med. Ctr. Alternative, Casa Grande, 1994—2001; lang. arts tchr. Toltec Jr. H.S.; owner Landers' Tutoring Svc., Casa Grande, 2001—. Test supr. SAT, ACT Testing Svcs., Casa Grande, 1997—. Author: Making English Make Sense, 1996. Invited rep. U.S. to China People to People Amb. Program, 2000; French hornist CAC Cmty. Concert Band, Coolidge, Ariz., 1984—2000; organist North Trekell Bapt. Ch., Casa Grande, 1996—, founder instrumental music founds. group, 2001; chair babysitting com. Casa Grand Regionl Med. Ctr., Casa Grande, 1995—98. Mem.: NEA, Ark. Reading Coun., Ctrl. Ariz. Reading Coun., Ariz. Reading Coun., Ariz. Edn. Assn., Casa Grande Edn. Assn. (pres. 1985—86, Outstanding Svc. award 1985—86), Sheridan Ednl. Assoc. (pres. 1978—79), Internat. Reading Assoc., CGRMC Aux. (com. chairperson 1995—98, Vol. of Month 1995). Democrat. Baptist. Avocations: reading, jogging, musical instruments. Home: PO Box 589 Arizona City AZ 85223 Office: CGUHS 2730 N Trekell Rd Casa Grande AZ 85222 Office Phone: 520-466-5747, 520-836-8500 4179. Business E-Mail: planders@cguhs.org. E-mail: landers@egmailbox.com.

LANDERS, THOMAS LEE, dean, educator; b. Dumas, Tex., May 7, 1950; s. Sidney Wayne and Murriel K. Landers; m. Patti Sue Stone, Aug. 19, 1972; children: Stephen Thomas, David Wayne, Andrew Stone. BS in Indsl. Engring., Tex. Tech. U., 1972, MS in Indsl. Engring., 1973, PhD, 1985. Registered profl. engr., Okla., Ark. Rsch. asst. dept. indsl. engring. Tex. Tech. U., Lubbock, 1972—73, lectr., rsch. asst. dept. indsl. engring., 1984—85; reliability and maintainability engr. divsn. aero. sys. Wright-Patterson AFB, Dayton, Ohio, 1973—77; devel. engr. Tex. Instruments Inc., Lubbock, 1978; mgr. Arthur Young and Company, Dallas, 1979—83; engr., cons. project engr., warranty mgr. Lone Star Mfg. Co., Ft. Worth, 1983; from asst. prof. to prof. dept. indsl. engring. U. Ark., Fayetteville, 1985—98; dir. U. Okla. Sch. Indsl. Engring., Norman, 1998—2001; assoc. dean for rsch. and grad. programs U. Okla. Coll. Engring., Norman, 2001—05, dean, 2005. Rsch. program leader Material Handling Rsch. Ctr., 1992—95; dir. Logistics Inst., 1995—98, Inst. for Okla. Tech. Applications, Norman, 2004—06; co-dir. Ctr. for Aircraft and Sys. Support Infrastructure, Okla., 1999—2001, dir., 2001—03; co-dir. Okla. Transp. Ctr., 2001—05, exec. dir., 2003—04; co-dir. Ctr. for Engring. Logistics and Distbn., 2001—05; presenter, cons. in field. Co-author (with W. Brown, E. Fant, E. Malstrom, N. Schmitt): Electronics Manufacturing Processes, 1994; contbr. articles to profl. jours. Capt. USAF, 1970—77. Named Outstanding Tchr., Halliburton, 1986—87, 1992—93, Outstanding Rschr., 1988—90, Tex. Instruments, 1995—97, Outstanding Prof., Phillips Petroleum Co., 1992; recipient Outstanding Svc. award, ASME, 2000; grantee, NSF, 1994, Global Concepts, 1999, Trane Co., 1999—2000, USAF, 2000—02, FAA, 2000—05, Okla. Dept. Transp., 2001—02, US Dept. Transp., 2002, Fed. Transit Adminstrn., 2004, others. Mem.: AAAS, Acad. Indsl. Engrs. at Tex. Tech. U., Soc. Am. Mil. Engrs., Am. Soc. Engring. Edn., Coun. Logistics Mgmt., Inst. Indsl. Engrs. (Fellows award 2005), Coll. Industry Coun. on Material Handling Edn., Phi Kappa Phi, Alpha Pi Mu, Tau Beta Pi, Sigma Xi. Office: Univ Okla 202 W Boyd CEC 107 Norman OK 73019 Home: 4401 Shoreline Dr Norman OK 73026-1310 Fax: 405-325-7805. Business E-Mail: landers@ou.edu.

LANDES, GEORGE MILLER, biblical studies educator; b. Kansas City, Mo., Aug. 2, 1928; s. George Y. and Margaret B. (Fizzell) L.; m. Carol Marie Dee, Aug. 30, 1953; children: George Miller Jr., Margaret Dee, John Christopher. AB, U. Mo., 1949; M.Div., McCormick Theol. Sem., 1952; PhD, Johns Hopkins U., 1956. Minister to youth Second Presbyn. Ch., Balt., 1952-53, Govans Presbyn. Ch., Balt., 1953-56; instr. Old Testament Union Theol. Sem., NYC, 1956-58, asst. prof. Old Testament, 1958-62, assoc. prof., 1962-70, prof., 1970-95, prof. emeritus, 1995—. Ann. prof. Am. Sch. Oriental Rsch., Jerusalem, Israel, 1967-68 Author: Building Your Biblical Hebrew Vocabulary, 2001; author, editor: Report on Archaeological Work, 1975. Nettie F. McCormick fellow, 1952-54; Am. Council Learned Socs. fellow, 1967-68 Mem. Soc. Bibl. Lit., Amman Ctr. Archaeol. Rsch. (v.p. 1969-79), Am. Schs. Oriental Rsch. (sec. 1972-94), Phi Beta Kappa. Personal E-mail: g.m.landes@att.net.

LANDES, WILLIAM M., law educator; b. 1939; AB, Columbia U., 1960, PhD in Econs., 1966. Asst. prof. economics Stanford U., 1965—66, U. Chgo., 1966—69; assoc. prof. Columbia U., 1969—72, CUNY Grad. Ctr., 1972—74; prof. economics U. Chgo. Law Sch., 1974—80, Clifton R. Musser prof. economics, 1980—92, Clifton R. Musser prof. law & economics, 1992—; founder, chmn. Lexecon, Inc., 1977—98, chmn. emeritus, 1998—; mem. bd. examiners GRE in Econs., ETS, 1967—74. Author (with Richard Posner): The Economic Structure of Tort Law, 1987; editor (with Gary Becker): Essays in the Economics of Crime and Punishment, 1974; editor: Jour. Law and Econs., 1975—91, Jour. Legal Studies, 1991—. Mem.: Am. Law and Econ. Assn. (v.p. 1991—92, pres. 1992—93), Am. Econ. Assn., Mont Pelerin Soc. Office: U Chgo Sch Law 1111 E 60th St Chicago IL 60637-2776 also: Lexecon Inc 332 S Michigan Ave Ste 1300 Chicago IL 60604-4406

LANDES, WILLIAM-ALAN, film company executive; b. Bronx, NY, Apr. 27, 1945; s. Sidney H. and June Dorothy (Heal-Gordon) L.; m. Sharon, Dec. 14, 1991 (div. Apr. 1995); children: William, Paula, Wendy. BA, BS, Hunter Lehman Coll., 1968; MS, NYU, 1969; MA, Calif. State U., 1972; PhD, UCLA, 1976. Mgr. Jay's, NYC, 1967-69; assoc. producer New World Prodns., Hollywood, Calif., 1971-72; entertainment editor Showcase Mag., Hollywood, Calif., 1972-75; artistic dir., dir. theatre Players U.S.A., San Gabriel, Calif., 1975-78; artistic dir. Merrick Studios, Hollywood, 1978-79; producer, dir. Empire Entertainment, Studio City, Calif., 1979—; chmn. Players Press, Inc., Studio City, Calif., 1980—97; mng. dir. Empire Publishing Svc., England, 1998—2005; pres. Empire Entertainment, England, 2005—. Capt. USAF, 1962-67. Mem. SAG, AFTRA, AEA, DGA, SSDC, Writers Guild. Avocations: writing, painting.

LANDESBERG, STEVE, actor; b. NYC, Nov. 23, 1945; Mem. The New York Stickball Team comedy group; actor: (TV series) Bobby Darin Amusement Company, 1972-73, Paul Sand in Friends and Lovers, 1974-75, Barney Miller, 1976-82, (TV films) Black Bart, 1975, Final Notice, 1989, Mission of the Shark: The Saga of the U.S.S. Indianapolis, 1991, Sodbusters, 1994, Best Defense, 1995, (films) You've Got to Walk It Like You Talk It or You'll Lose That Beat, 1971, Blade, 1973, Leader of the Band, 1987, Ladybugs, 1992, Little Miss Millions, 1993, The Crazysitter, 1995, Puppet, 1999, A Lousy Ten Grand, 2004, Wild Hogs, 2007; guest appearances on TV shows including The Rockford Files, 1977, Fish, 1977, Dinosaurs, 1991, The Golden Girls, 1991, Pearl, 1996, Tracey Takes On, 1997, Dave's World, 1997, Law & Order, 1997, Cosby, 1998, Two Guys, a Girl and a Pizza Place, 1999, Twice in a Lifetime, 2000, Harvey Birdman, Attorney at Law, 2002, Ghost Whisperer, 2005, That 70s Show, 2006.*

LANDESMAN, HOWARD M., retired academic administrator; b. Bklyn., 1938; m. Lynne Landesman; 1 child, Lori. BS, UCLA, 1958; DDS, U. So. Calif., 1962, MS in Edn., 1971. Named co-dir., grad. prosthodontics program U. So. Calif. Sch. Dentistry, 1973, chair, dept. restorative dentistry, assoc. dean academic and faculty affairs, exec. assoc. dean, dean, 1991—99; dean. Sch. Dentistry U. Colo., 1999—2004; v.p. devel. U. Colo. Denver & Health Sciences Ctr. Mem.: Acad. Prosthodontics. Mailing: Colo Univ Foundation 4740 Walnut St Boulder CO 80301

LANDESS, FRED STONE, retired lawyer; b. Memphis, Jan. 27, 1933; s. Sterling Stone and Beulah Elizabeth (Melton) L.; m. Catherine Sue Lee, Dec. 27, 1953; children— Susan Elinor, Charles Barton, Catherine Elizabeth Student, Wake Forest Coll., 1951-53; AB, George Washington U., 1955; LL.B., U. Va., 1958. Bar: Va. 1958. Enforcement atty. NLRB, Washington, 1958-60; assoc., then ptnr. McGuire, Woods, Battle & Boothe LLP, Charlottesville, Va., 1960-99, ret., 1999. Sec. Bd. Zoning Appeals, City of Charlottesville, Va., 1967-69; bd. dirs. YMCA, Charlottesville, 1975, Westminister Child Care Ctr., Charlottesville, 1978 Fellow Am. Coll. Real Estate Lawyers; mem. Charlottesville-Albemarle Bar Assn. (pres. 1983-84), Va. Bar Assn. (real estate com.), Va. State Bar (7th dist. disciplinary com. 1986-88, sec. 1987, chmn. 1987-88), Charlottesville-Albemarle Bd. Realtors (assoc.), Blue Ridge Homebuilders Assn. (assoc.). Clubs: Boar's Head Sports (Charlottesville). Democrat. Presbyterian. Avocations: tennis, sailing, gardening. Home: 515 Wiley Dr Charlottesville VA 22903-4650

LANDESS, MIKE (MALCOLM LEE LANDESS III), newscaster; b. Houston, June 20, 1946; s. Malcolm Lee Jr. Landess and Joyce Ardis (Halley) Quitter; children: Kristen and Jennifer. Grad., Robert E. Lee H.S., Tyler, Tex. Radio reporter WFAA-AM, Dallas, 1969-70; TV reporter WFAA-TV, Dallas, 70-72, KTRK-TV, Houston, 1972-73; noon anchor, reporter KYW-TV, Phila., 1973-74; NBC news anchor WKYC-TV, Cleve., 1974-77; news anchor KUSA-TV, Denver, 1977-93; Gannett anchor WXIA-TV, Atlanta, 1993—2002; news anchor KMGH-TV, Denver, 2002—. Anchor, reporter, producer: (TV documentary) Wednesday's Child, 1978, Fight of His Life, 1982; anchor, reporter (TV spl.) Say "NO" to Strangers, 1979. Bd. dirs. Am. Cancer Soc., Denver, 1982-86, Colo. Head Injury Assn., Denver, 1990-93, Brain Injury Assn Ga., Atlanta, 1994—. Recipient numerous Emmy awards: Outstanding Achievement Anchor, 1988, 91, Outstanding Achievement Children's Programming, 1983, TV Programming Excellence, 1995, Outstanding Achievement award Luth. Social Svcs., Am. Cancer Soc. Mem. NATAS, Radio & TV News Dir. Assn., Atlanta Press Club, Sigma Delta Chi. Baptist. Avocations: vintage guitars, motorsports. Office: KMGH-TV 123 Speer Blvd Denver CO 80203-3417 E-mail: mike_landess@thedenverchannel.com.

LANDGRAF, KURT M., educational association administrator; b. Oct. 12, 1946; m. Barbara Landraf. B in Econs. and Bus. Adminstrn., Wagner Coll.; M in Econs., Pa. State U.; M in Adminstrn., Rutgers U.; M in Sociology, Western Mich. U.; grad. advanced mgmt. prog., Harvard U., 1992. Mergers and acquisitions intern Kidder Peabody, Inc., NYC; sales rep., brand mgr. Johnson & Johnson, Inc., New Brunswick, NJ; assoc. dir. Ednl. Testing Svc., Princeton, NJ, chmn., CEO, 2000—; with The Upjohn Co., 1974—80; mgr. worldwide mktg. svcs. DuPont, 1980—83, mktg. dir. pharms. for Europe, Mid. East and Africa Frankfurt, Germany, 1983—85, dir. pharms. for Europe, Mid. East and Africa, 1985—86, planning mgr. corp. plans dept. Wilmington, Del., 1986—87, dir. bus. devel. and internat. divsn. pharms. divsn. dir., 1987—88, dir. pharms. divsn., 1988—89, dir. pharms. and imaging agts. divsn., 1989, CFO, 1996, exec. v.p., 1997; with DuPont Merck, 1991—95; chmn., CEO DuPont Pharms., 2000. Co-chair bd. dirs. DuPont Merck Pharm. Co.; bd. dirs. DuPont Can., DuPont Dow Elastomers, Nat. Pharm. Coun.; instr. econs., sociology and labor rels. various colls. Bd. dirs. United Way Del., Del. Assn. for Rights of Citizens with Mental Retardation, Wilmington Med. Ctr. Found., Biotech. Industry Orgn., Nat. Alliance Bus., U. Del. Rsh. Found., Wilmington Grand Opera House; trustee Goldey-Beacom Coll., Wagner Coll. Mem. Pharm. Rsch. and Mfrs. Am. Mem. Del. State C. of C. (vice chmn. Mfg. Assn.). Office: Ednl Testing Svc Rosedale Rd Princeton NJ 08541 Office Phone: 609-921-9000.*

LANDGREBE, DAVID ALLEN, electrical engineer; b. Huntingburg, Ind., Apr. 12, 1934; s. Albert E. and Sarah A. L.; m. Margaret Ann Swank, June 7, 1959; children: James David, Carole Ann, Mary Jane. BSEE, Purdue U., 1956, MSEE, 1958, PhD, 1962. Mem. tech. staff Bell Telephone Labs., Murray Hill, NJ, 1956; electronics engr. Interstate Electronics Corp., Anaheim, Calif., 1958, 59, 62; mem. faculty Purdue U., West Lafayette, Ind., 1962—, dir. lab. for applications of remote sensing, 1969-81, prof. elec. engring., 1970—2002, assoc. dean engring., 1981-84, acting head sch. elec. and computer engring. West Lafayette, 1995-96, prof. emeritus of elec. and computer engring., 2002—. Rsch. scientist Douglas Aircraft Co., Newport Beach, Calif., 1964; dir. Univ. Space Rsch. Assn., 1975-78. Author: Signal Theory Methods in Multispectral Remote Sensing, 2003, (with others) Remote Sensing: The Quantitative Approach, 1978. Recipient medal for exceptional sci. achievement NASA, 1973, William T. Pecora award NASA/U.S. Dept. Interior, 1990. Fellow IEEE (pres. Geosci. and Remote Sensing Soc. 1986-87, Exceptional Svc. award 1988, Sci. Achievement award 1992, Edn. award 2003), AAAS, Am. Soc. Photogrammetry and Remote Sensing; mem. NAE, Am. Soc. for Engring. Edn., Sigma Xi, Tau Beta Pi, Eta Kappa Nu. Office: Purdue U Dept Elec Engring West Lafayette IN 47907-1285 Business E-Mail: landgreb@ecn.purdue.edu.

LANDGREBE, JOHN ALLAN, chemistry professor; b. San Francisco, May 6, 1937; s. Herbert Frederick and Janet Miller (Allan) L.; m. Carolyn Jean Thomson, Dec. 23, 1961; children— Carolyn Janet, John Frederick BS, U. Calif.-Berkeley, 1959; PhD, U. Ill., 1962. Asst. prof. U. Kans., Lawrence, 1962—67, assoc. prof., 1967—71, prof., 1971—2002, prof. emeritus, 2002—, dept. chmn., 1970—80. Vis. prof. U. Calif.-Berkeley, 1974 Author: Theory and Practice in the Organic Laboratory, 1973, 5th edit., 2005. NSF fellow, 1960-62; E. Watkins Faculty fellow U. Kans., 1963; recipient Career Tchg. award Chancellors Club, 1999. Mem. Am. Chem. Soc., Royal Soc. of Chemistry, Phi Lambda Upsilon. Republican. Lutheran. Avocations: gardening, camping, hiking. Home: 1125 Highland Dr Lawrence KS 66044-4523 Office: U Kansas Dept Chemistry Lawrence KS 66045-0001

LANDIN, DAVID CRAIG, lawyer; b. Jamestown, NY, Aug. 1, 1946; s. David Carl and Rita L.; m. Susan Ann Gregory, July 11, 1970; children: Mary Stuart, Alexander Craig, David Reed. BA, U. Va., 1968, JD, 1972. Bar: Va. 1972, Pa. 1991, Tex. 1992, U.S. Supreme Ct. 1979. Ptnr. McGuire, Woods & Battle, Richmond, Va., 1972-95, mgr. of product liability and litigation mgmt. group, 1987-95; gen. counsel Va. Assn. Ind. Schs., 1989—, Coun. for Religion in Ind. Schs., 1990—95; ptnr., litig., intellectual property, antitrust Hunton & Williams LLP, Richmond, Va., 1995—, and co-chair recruitment com., 2001—05. Pres. The Landin Cos., 1994—. Chmn. ctrl. Va. chpt. Nat. Multiple Sclerosis Soc., 1995-96; chair standing com. on fed. jud. improvements ABA, 2003-. With USAR, 1968-74. Fellow: Va. Law Found. (pres. 1987—88, DRI Exceptional Performance award 1988); mem.: ABA (chair standing com. on fed. jud. improvements 2004—05), Greater Richmond C. of C. (bd. dirs. 1998—2000), Va. Assn. Def. Attys. (pres. 1987—88), Va. Bar Assn. (chmn. young lawyers sect. 1979—80, pres. 1999—2000). Roman Catholic. Avocations: squash, tennis, golf. Home: 310 Oak Ln Richmond VA 23226-1639 Office: Hunton & Williams Riverfront Plaza East Tower PO Box 1535 Richmond VA 23218-1535 Office Phone: 804-788-8387.

LANDIS, DONNA MARIE, nursing administrator, women's health nurse; b. Lebanon, Pa., Sept. 5, 1944; d. James O.A. and Helen Joan (Fritz) Muench; m. David J. Landis, Feb. 4, 1967 (div. Jan. 1985); children: Danielle M. Landis Barry, David J., Derek J.; m. John C. Broderick, May 8, 1990 (div. Jan. 1995). RN Pa., 1993, cert. densitometry technologist. DXA technologist and clin. dir. Osteoporosis Diagnostic and Monitoring Ctr., Laurel, Md., 1985-95, owner, 1995—; clin. dir., clin. rsch. coord. Osteoporosis Assessment Ctr., Wheaton, Md., 1985-95; owner, clin. dir., clin. rsch. coord. Women's Health Rsch. Ctr., Laurel, Md., 1996—; pvt. practice as cons. in osteoporosis, bone densitometry and women's health

Donna M. Landis, LLC, 2004—. Mem. nurses adv. bd. NPS Pharms., 2005—06; cons. applied physics lab. Johns Hopkins U., 2007. Mem. task force on osteoporosis State of Md., 1996—2006. Named one of Md.'s Top 100 Women in Bus., 2002. Mem.: Nat. Osteoporosis Risk Assessment Project (specialist practice and lead technologist trainer 1997—98), Allied Health Profls./Arthritis Found. (pub. policy contact), Nat. Osteoporosis Found. (pub. policy contact), Internat. Soc. Clin. Densitometry (steering com. 1993—94, contbg. editor SCAN newsletter 1994—2002, cert. com. technologists and physicians 1995—2000, sci. adv. com. 1996—2007, trustee 1999—2002, technologist edn. subcom. 2000—03, facility accreditation coun. 2004—), St. Joseph's Hosp. Alumni Assn., Balt. Bone Club, Washington Met. Bone Club (steering com. 1996, bd. dirs. 1999—2001, sec. 1999—2001, bd. dirs. 2007—), Kiwanis Internat. (bd. dirs. Prince Georges County 1997—2002, pres. Prince Georges County 2000—01, Capital Dist. lt. gov. 2003—04, key leader chmn. Mason-Dixon region). Personal E-mail: dmlandis@verizon.net.

LANDIS, EDGAR DAVID, business consultant; b. Myerstown, Pa., Jan. 7, 1932; s. Edgar Michael and Anna Irene (Dubble) L.; m. Patricia Ann Leininger, June 13, 1953; children: Susan, Jean. BS, Lebanon Valley Coll., 1953; MBA, U. Pa., 1957. CPA. Acct., audit supr. Peat, Marwick, Mitchell & Co. (now KPMG), Phila., 1957-64; corp. contr., divsn. exec. v.p. Carlisle Corp., Pa., 1964-73; v.p., sr. v.p., exec. v.p. CDI Corp., Phila., 1973-97, also dir.; dir. affiliates in U.S. and Europe; dir., vice chmn., co-chmn., chmn. Allegiance Bank N.A., Bala Cynwyd, Pa., 1998—. Cons. to CDI Corp., Phila., 1998-2001; dir. Sabal Palm Bank, Sarasota, Fla. Bd. dirs. Carlisle Sch. Dist., 1967-71, YMCA, Ardmore, Pa., 1981-87, chmn., 1984-86, YMCA, Phila., 1988-97, vice chmn. 1991-97, YMCA, Sarasota, Fla., 1998—, Capital U. Integrative Medicine, Washington, 2002-06. With U.S. Army, 1954-56, Japan. Mem. Lebanon Valley Coll. Alumni Assocs. (regional chmn. 1977-82). Republican. Methodist. Home: 988 Blvd Of The Arts 511 Sarasota FL 34236-4872

LANDIS, ERIC N., civil engineer, educator; BS in Civil and Environ. Engring., U. Wis., Madison, 1985; PhD in Civil Engring., Northwestern U., 1993. Lic. profl. engr., Maine. Postdoctoral rsch. fellow Ctr. Advanced Cement-Based Materials Northwestern U., Evanston, Ill., 1993—94; asst. prof. civil engring. U. Maine, Orono, 1994—2000, assoc. prof., 2000, prof., interim dept. chair, cooperating assoc. prof. constrn. mgmt. Vis. prof. École Polytechnique Fédéral de Lausanne, Switzerland, 1998. Contbr. articles to sci. jours.; assoc. editor: Jour. Engring. Mechanics; co-author: Fracture and Fatigue of Wood, 2003. Recipient CAREER award, NSF, 1998, US Prof. of Yr. award, Carnegie Found. for Advancement of Tchg. and Coun. for Advancement and Support of Edn., 2006. Mem.: Soc. Exptl. Mechanics, Forest Products Soc., Internat. Union of Labs. and Experts in Constrn. Materials Systems and Structures, Am. Soc. Engring. Edn., ASCE, Chi Epsilon. Office: Dept Civil and Environ Engring U Maine 5711 Boardman Hall Orono ME 04469-5711 E-mail: landis@maine.maine.edu.*

LANDIS, FLOYD, professional cyclist; b. Lancaster County, Pa., Oct. 14, 1975; m. Amber Basile; 1 child, Ryan. Profl. cyclist Mercury team, 1999—2001, US Postal Svc. team, 2002—04, Phonak Hearing Systems team, 2005—. Achievements include winning first overall in the Tour du Poitou-Charentes, 2000, Boulevard Road Race, 2001, Volta ao Algarve, 2004, Tour of California, 2006, Paris Nice, Tour of Georgia; finished first in team time trial in the Vuelta Espana, 2004, Tour de France, Volta a Catalunya, 2005; finished first in individual time trial in the Tour of Georgia, 2005, 06, Tour of California, 2006; winner, Tour de France, 2006; third American to win the Tour de France. Mailing: Phonak Cycling Team Eichtal 8634 Hombrechtikon Switzerland

LANDIS, JOHN WILLIAM, retired engineering executive, consultant, government advisor; b. Kutztown, Pa., Oct. 10, 1917; s. Edwin Charles and Estella Juliabelle (Barto) L.; m. Muriel Trayes Souders, July 5, 1941; children: Maureen Lucille, Marcia Millicent BS in Engring. Physics summa cum laude, Lafayette Coll., Easton, Pa., 1939, ScD (hon.), 1960. Registered profl. engr., Calif. Research engr. Eastman Kodak Co., Rochester, NY, 1939-43; cons. Navy Dept., Washington, 1946-50; head sci. and engring. dept. Ednl. Testing Service, Princeton, NJ, 1948-50; reactor engr. AEC, Washington, 1950-53; dir. customer relations atomic energy div. Babcock & Wilcox Co., NYC, 1953-55, asst. mgr. atomic energy div. Lynchburg, Va., 1955-62, mgr. atomic energy div., 1962-65, gen. mgr. Washington ops., 1965-68; regional v.p. Gulf Gen. Atomic Co., Washington, 1968-69, group v.p. LaJolla, Calif., 1969-70, pres., dir. subs., 1970-74; pres. Power Systems Co., Gen. Atomic Partnership, LaJolla, Calif., 1974-75; sr. v.p., dir., pres. subs. Stone & Webster Engring. Corp., Boston, 1975-92, pvt. cons., 1992—. Founding dir. Ctrl. Fidelity Banks, Inc., Richmond, Va.; founding gov. Nat. Materials Property Data Network, Inc., Phila.; chmn. adv. com. isotopes and radiation devel. and four other adv. coms. AEC, Washington, 1957—70; chmn. coms., co rep. Atomic Indsl. Forum (now US Nuc. Energy Inst.), Washington, 1953—95; mem. NY State Adv. Com. on Atomic Energy, 1956—59, Va. State Adv. Com. on Nuc. Energy, 1959—68; vice chmn. mgmt. com. Nat. Environ. Studies Project, Washington, 1974—89; dir., v.p., pres., chmn. bds. and coms., trustee Internat. Fund, Am. Nat. Stds. Inst., NYC, 1957—; vice chmn. ISO-9000 Registration Com.; dir., chmn. Fusion Power Assocs., Gaithersburg, Md., 1981—98; chmn. US Fusion Industry Coun., Internat. Thermonuc. Exptl. Reactor Industry Coun., 1994—98; chmn. com. on energy-related atmospheric pollution World Energy Conf., London, 1984—90, N.Am. coord. global energy study, 1989—93; dir., chmn. com. on protection of environment US Energy Assn., Washington, 1981—98; fusion adv. panel US Ho. Reps., Washington, 1979—87; charter mem. magnetic fusion adv. com. US Dept. Energy, Washington, 1982—84, chmn. internat. R&D panel, chmn. civilian nuc. power panel, vice chmn., chmn. energy rsch. adv. bd., 1984—90; mem. adv. bd. Sec. of Energy, 1990—93, fusion energy adv. com., 1994—99; advisor Carnegie-Mellon U., Pitts., 1971—73, Pa. State U., State College, 1980—83, U. Calif., San Diego, 1974—82, U. Fla., Gainesville, 1984—95; vis. and sustaining fellow MIT, Cambridge, Mass., 1971—90; chmn. bus. adminstrn., adv. bd. U. San Diego, 1972—75; mem. engring. adv. com. Lafayette Coll., 1988—98. Co-author: six books; contbr. articles to profl. and trade jours. Trustee, chmn. Randolph Coll., Lynchburg, Va., 1963-92; trustee Lafayette Coll., Easton, Pa., 1962—, Va. Poly. Inst. and State U., Blacksburg, 1966-70; bd. dirs. Va. Poly. Inst. Ednl. Found., Blacksburg, 1968-80; mem. U. Calif. Pres.'s Coun. on the Nat. Labs., 1993-99; chmn. MIT Reactor Com., 1995—; mem. Sr. Rev. Group, Amarillo Nat. Resource Ctr. for Plutonium, 1994-99; mem. Va. Adv. Bd. on Indsl. Devel. and Planning, Richmond, 1962-72; bd. dirs. Va. Engring. Found., Charlottesville, 1962-65; trustee Seven Hills Sch., Lynchburg, Va., 1960-65; dir. Harvard U. Ctr. for Blood Rsch., 1992-99; mem. Mayor's Com. on Energy, San Diego, 1973-75; chmn., mem. six coms. Nat. Rsch. Coun., 1976-96. Served to lt. USN, 1943-46, ETO. Decorated Letter of Commendation, two battle stars; recipient Gen. of Industry award State of Okla., 1971, George Washington Kidd award, Joseph E. Bell award, Lafayette medal, Lafayette Coll., Lehigh Valley Favorite Son award State of Pa., 1976, Dwight D. Eisenhower Award of Honor, 1990, Winston Churchill Medal of Wisdom, 1988, Disting. Career award Fusion Power Assocs., 1991, Howard Coonley medal Am. Nat. Standards Inst., 1991, Exceptional Pub. Svc. award U.S. Dept. Energy, 1992, Henry DeWolf Smyth Nuclear Statesman award Am. Nuclear Soc. and Nuclear Energy Inst., 1996; named Hon. Citizen City of Dallas, 1973, Alumni fellow Lafayette Coll., 1984, Internat. Scientist of Yr., 2004; elected to Soc. d'Honneur Lafayette Coll., 1989; named to Wisdom Hall of Fame, 1987 Fellow ASME, Am. Nuclear Soc. (pres. 1971-72, v.p. 1970-71, treas. 1964-68, chmn. coms. 1956—, bd. dirs. 1956-74, Disting. Svc. award 2006, Leadership award, 2007), Am. Soc. Macro-Engring. (pres. 1985-88, chancellor 1988—, charter bd. dirs. 1983—); mem. NAE, Internat. Assn. Macro-Engring. Socs. (founding dir. 1987—, treas. 1989—, pres. 1999-2006), San Diego Hall Sci. (life), Phi Beta Kappa, Sigma Xi, Tau Beta Pi, Pi Delta Epsilon, Omicron Delta Kappa. Avocations: photography, landscaping, book-collecting, hiking. Home: 2131 Chestnut Oak Ct SW Roanoke VA 24018-2118 Office Phone: 540-774-0987. Personal E-mail: jwlandis@cox.net.

LANDIS, KEVIN, diversified financial services company executive; BSEE, U. Calif., Berkeley; MBA, Santa Clara U., Calif. With S-MOS Sys., Dataquest; co-founder Firsthand Capital Mgmt., San Jose, Calif., 1993—, CIO, 1993—. Office: Firsthand Capital Management 125 S Market St Ste 1200 San Jose CA 95113-2206

LANDIS, STORY CLELAND, federal agency administrator, neurobiologist; m. Dennis Landis; 1 child, Michael. BA in biology, Wellesley Coll., 1967; MA, Harvard U., 1970, PhD, 1973. Mem. faculty Dept. Neurobiology Harvard Med. Sch.; mem. faculty Dept. Pharmacology Case Western Res. U. Sch. of Medicine, Cleve., 1985—95, chair Dept. Neurosciences, 1990—95; sci. dir. Nat. Inst. Neurol. Disorders and Stroke, NIH, 1995—2003, dir., 2003—. Contbr. articles to profl. jours. Fellow: Am. Neurol. Assn., AAAS, Am. Acad. Arts and Sciences; mem.: Soc. Neuroscience (pres.-elect 2002). Achievements include research in the study of the developmental interactions required for the formation of functional synapses. Office: Nat Inst Neurol Disorders and Stroke Bldg 31 Rm 8A52 31 Center Dr MSC 2540 Bethesda MD 20892 Office Phone: 301-496-9746. Office Fax: 301-496-0296. E-mail: landiss@ninds.nih.gov.

LANDMAN, JONATHAN, editor; b. NYC, 1952; m. Bonnie Van Gilder; 2 children. BA history, Amherst College, 1974; MS journalism, Coumbia U., 1978. Deputy city editor Daily News; asst. nat. editor NY Times, 1989—90, asst. metropolitan editor, 1990—91, asst. editor Washington, 1991—92, deputy editor, 1992—94, Week in Review editor, 1994—99, metropolitan editor, 1999—2003, enterprise editor, 2003—04, The New York Times, 2004—05, dep. mng. editor, digital journalism, 2005—. Recipient Alfred I. duPont-Columbia U. award, 2007. Mem.: bd. trustees, Amherst College. Office: c/o NY Times 229 W 43rd St New York NY 10036*

LANDO, JEROME BURTON, macromolecular science educator; b. Bklyn., May 23, 1932; s. Irving and Ruth (Schwartz) L.; m. Geula Ahroni, Dec. 2, 1962; children: Jeffrey, Daniel, Avital. AB, Cornell U., 1953; PhD, Poly. Inst. Bklyn., 1963. Chemist Camille Dreyfus Lab., Research Triangle Inst., Durham, NC, 1963-65; asst. prof. macromolecular sci. Case Western Res. U., Cleve., 1965—68, assoc. prof., 1968—74, prof., 1974—2005, prof. emeritus, 2005—; pres., CEO Edison Polymer Inovation Corp., 2000—. Dept. chmn. Case Western Res. U., Cleve., 1978—85; Erna and Jakob Michael vis. prof. Weizmann Inst. Sci., Rehovot, Israel, 1987; Lady Davis vis. prof. Technion, Haifa, Israel, 1992—93. Author: (with S. Maron) Fundamentals of Physical Chemistry, 1974; mem. editl. adv. bd. Polymers for Advanced Techs. Served to lt. U.S. Army, 1953-55. Named Alexander Von Humboldt Sr. Am. Scientist U. Mainz, Germany, 1974, disting. alumnus Poly. U., 1990. Fellow Am. Phys. Soc.; mem. Am. Chem. Soc., Am. Crystallographic Assn., Soc. Plastics Engrs. (rsch. award 1994, edn. award 1999), Sigma Xi. Jewish. Home: 21925 Byron Rd Cleveland OH 44122-2942 Office: Case Western Res U Dept Macromolecular Sci Kent Hale Smith Bldg 321 Cleveland OH 44106 Office Phone: 216-368-6366. Business E-Mail: jblr@case.edu.

LANDON, DAIN CHARLES, lawyer; b. Indiana, Pa., Jan. 30, 1974; s. Dale Ellwood and Evelyn Deigert Landon. BA, MA, U. Pa., Phila., 1997; JD, Columbia U., NYC, 2001. Assoc. Proskauer Rose LLP, NYC, 2000—06; sr. counsel New Line Cinema, 2006—. Exec. editor: Columbia Bus. Law Rev., 2000. Fulbright scholar, Fulbright Assn., 1997—98. Mem.: NY State Bar, 2001. Office: New Line Cinema 888 7th Ave New York NY 10019 Home Phone: 917-499-4999; Office Phone: 212-649-4925. Business E-Mail: dain.landon@newline.com.

LANDON, JAMES HENRY, lawyer; b. Atlanta, Oct. 24, 1945; s. Ralph Henry and Gertrude Leola (Rew) L. BA, Vanderbilt U., 1967; JD, Harvard U., 1970. Bar: Ga. 1971, U.S. Dist. Ct. (no. dist.) Ga. 1971, U.S. Ct. Claims 1972, U.S. Supreme Ct. 1976, U.S. Tax Ct. 1980. Assoc. Hansell & Post, Atlanta, 1971-76, ptnr., 1976-89, Jones Day, Atlanta, 1989—. Adj. prof. Emory Law Sch., Atlanta, 1983—84; dir. TRC Staffing Svc., Inc., Atlanta, 1987—; mem. steering com. So. Pension Conf., Atlanta, 1985—88; mem. Ga. adv. coun. Asset Mgmt. Assocs., 2004—. Co-author: Transportation Politics in Atlanta, 1970; contbr. article to profl. jour. Dir. Atlanta Symphony Orch., 1981-87, 89-92; trustee Atlanta Hist. Soc., 1983-98, 99-2006, Ctr. for Puppetry Arts, Inc., 1995-2001, Atlanta Bot. Garden, 1998-2004, 2006—; mem. cmty. adv. bd. Jr. League of Atlanta, 1987-90; gen. counsel Woodruff Arts Ctr., Inc., 1993—; trustee Atlanta Med. Heritage, Inc., 1993—, pres., 1996-97; trustee The Hambidge Ctr., 1994-99, chmn. 1998-99; trustee Cherokee Garden Libr., 2000-03, 04—. Mem. ABA, Ga. Bar Assoc., Atlanta Bar Assoc., Explorers Club of N.Y.C., Phi Beta Kappa. Presbyterian. Avocations: mountain climbing, hiking. Home: 1327 Peachtree St NE Apt 503 Atlanta GA 30309-3254 Home Phone: 404-885-9976; Office Phone: 404-581-8907.

LANDON, JOHN CAMPBELL, research and development company executive; b. Hornell, NY, Jan. 3, 1937; s. Earl Shephard and Eleanor (Crane) Landon; m. Nancy Ann Bachenheimer, Aug. 24, 1958; children: David Bachenheimer, Martha Susan, Katherine Ellen, Peter Crane. BA in Biology, Alfred U., NY, 1959; MS in Biology, George Washington U., Washington, 1962, PhD in Biology, 1967. Biologist Nat. Cancer Inst., NIH, Bethesda, Md., 1960-65; from virologist to dir. sci. Frederick Cancer Rsch. Ctr., Litton Bionetics, Kensington, Md., 1965-75; pres., dir. EG&G Mason Rsch. Inst., Worcester, Mass., 1975-82; pres., CEO Bioqual, Inc., Rockville, Md., 1982—; founder, v.p., co-owner Brewster (Mass.) Book Store, Inc., Brewster, Mass., 1982—; pres., CEO Sema, Inc., Rockville, 1986-91; pres. BIOQUAL Inc. (formerly Diagnon Corp.), Rockville, 1986—, also chmn. bd. dirs.; founder, pres., CEO Enhanced Therapeutics, Inc., Rockville, 1994—. Cons. EG&G, Worcester, Mass., 1982—85; reviewer ad hoc com. NIH, Bethesda, Md., 1981—; mem. nat. coun. arts and scis. George Washington U., 1996—2005; mem. credit com. Potomac Cmty. Fed. Credit Union, 1982—85. Contbr. articles to profl. jours. Bd. dirs. Found. Comparative and Conservation Biology, 1999—, Peirce Warwick Adoption Svc., Washington, 1970—79, pres., 1972—75; bd. dirs. Venture Expeditionary, Washington, 1979—83, pres., 1981—83. Mem.: AAAS, N.Y. Acad. Scis., Am. Soc. Microbiology, Am. Soc. Cell Biology, NIH Alumni Assn. (bd. dirs. 2002—), Sigma Xi. Office: Bioqual Inc 9600 Medical Center Dr Rockville MD 20850-3336 also: Brewster Bookstore 2648 Main St Brewster MA 02631-1958 E-mail: jlandon@bioqual.com.

LANDON, JOHN R., real estate developer; With Ernst & Whinney; various positions sales and land devel. Trammel Crow Residential Group; mgr. land acquistion, devel. ops. Dallas; founder, pres. Legacy Homes, 1987-97; COO, Co-CEO, Meritage Corp. (merger with Legacy Homes), Plano, Tex., 1997-98; co-chmn., co-CEO Meritage Corp., Plano, Tex., 1998—2006; pres. Landon Develop. Co., Plano, Tex., 2006—. Mem. Nat. Assn. Homebuilders, Dallas Home and Apt. Builders' Assn. Office: Landon Development Co Ste 860 5800 Granite Pkwy Plano TX 75024*

LANDON, JOHN WILLIAM, retired minister, social worker, educator; b. Marlette, Mich., Mar. 24, 1937; s. Norman A. and Merle Irene (Lawrason) L. BA, Taylor U., 1959; MDiv, Northwestern U., Christian Theol. Sem., 1962; MSW, Ind. U., 1966; PhD in Social Sci., Ball State U., 1972. Regional supr. Iowa Dept. Social Welfare, Des Moines, 1965-67; acting chmn. dept. sociology Ind. Wesleyan U., Marion, 1967—69; asst. prof. sociology and social work Ball State U., Muncie, Ind., 1969-71; asst. prof. social work, coord. base courses Coll. Social Work U. Ky., Lexington, 1971-73, assoc. prof., coord. Undergrad. Program in Social Work, 1974-85, prof., assoc. dean, 1985—98, prof. emeritus, 1998—. Dir. social work edn. Taylor U., Upland, Ind., 1973-74. Author: From These Men, 1966, Jesse Crawford, Poet of the Organ, Wizard of the Mighty Wurlitzer, 1974, Behold the Mighty Wurlitzer, The History of the Theatre Pipe Organ, 1983, The Development of Social Welfare, 1986. Mem. AAUP, Coun. on Social Work Edn., Nat. Assn. Social Workers, Am. Guild Organists. Home Phone: 859-276-3424. Personal E-mail: landon.jw@verizon.net.

LANDON, MICHAEL DE LAVAL, retired history professor; b. St. John, NB, Can., Oct. 8, 1935; arrived in U.S., 1960; s. Arthur Henry Whittington and Elizabeth Worthington (Fair) Landon; m. Doris Lee Clay, Dec. 31, 1959 (div. May 1980); children: Clay de Laval, Letitia Elizabeth; m. Carole Marie Prather, Feb. 28, 1981. BA, Oxford U., Eng., 1958, MA, 1961, U. Wis., 1962, PhD, 1966. Asst. master Manor House Sch., Horsham, England, 1957, Dalhousie Sch., Ladybank, Scotland, 1958, Lakefield Coll. Sch., Ont., Canada, 1958—60; asst. prof. history U. Miss., Oxford, 1964—67, assoc. prof., 1967—72, prof., 1972—2000; prof. emeritus, 2000—; acting dir. librs. U. Miss., 1986—87, acting chair modern langs., 1996—99. Author: The Triumph of the Lawyers, 1970, The Honor and Dignity of the Profession, 1979, Erin and Britannia, 1980, The Challenge of Service, 1995, The University of Mississippi Law School--A Sesquicentennial History, 2006. Commr. City Housing Authority, Oxford, 1983—, chmn., 1993—; lay Eucharistic min. Episcopal Ch. Am. Am. Philos. Soc. Rsch. grantee, 1967, 1974. Fellow: Royal Hist. Soc. (Eng.); mem.: Am. Soc. Legal History (sec.-treas. 1988—97), Pi Delta Phi, Phi Alpha Theta, Eta Sigma Phi, Phi Kappa Phi. Avocation: bird feeding. Home: 219 Bramlett Blvd Oxford MS 38655-3434 Home Phone: 662-236-2373; Office Phone: 662-915-7148. Business E-Mail: hslandon@olemiss.edu.

LANDON, ROBERT GRAY, retired manufacturing company executive; b. Portsmouth, Ohio, Dec. 22, 1928; s. Herman Robert and Hazel Ruth Landon; m. Carole A. Beaumont, Aug. 30, 2001; children: Geoffrey, Suzanne. Student, Cornell U., 1947-49; BA in Econs., U. Pa., 1955; grad. advanced mgmt. program, Harvard Sch. Bus., 1978. Loan officer Nat. City Bank, Cleve., 1955-60; SEC adminstr. Smith Kline Corp., 1960-64; controller, treas. Grumman Allied Industries, Inc., Garden City, N.Y., 1964-76, v.p., 1977-82; v.p. investment mgmt. Grumman Corp., Bethpage, N.Y., 1978-79; pres. Grumman Ohio Corp., Worthington, Ohio, 1979-88. Served with AC, USN, 1949-53. Mem. The Oaks Club.

LANDON, ROBERT KIRKWOOD, volunteer; b. NYC, Apr. 27, 1929; s. Kirk A. and Edith (Ungar) L.; children: Chris, Kathleen Landon Staley, Kellyann Landon Spears. Student, U. Va., 1946-48; BS, Ga. Inst. Tech., 1950. With Am. Bankers Life Assurance Co., Miami, Fla., 1952-99, pres., 1960-74, 95, chmn., chief exec. officer, 1974-99; chmn. bd., CEO Am. Bankers Ins. Group Inc., Miami, 1980-95, chmn. bd., 1980-99; pres. Landon Corp., Dover, Del., 1971-99; charter mem. advisory bd. Fla. Internat. U., 1972-74. Trustee Kirk A. and Dorothy P. Landon Found., 1969—, Fla. Internat. U., 2005—. Lt. (j.g.) USNR, 1950-53. Mem. World Bus. Coun., Scabbard and Blade, Phi Gamma Delta. Republican. Congregationalist. Home: 10 Edgewater Dr Apt 16E Coral Gables FL 33133-6969 Office: The Kirk Found 255 Alhambra Cir Ste 820 Coral Gables FL 33134-7412 Office Phone: 305-442-1118. Business E-Mail: kirk.landon@assurant.com.

LANDON, SUSAN MELINDA, petroleum geologist; b. Mattoon, Ill., July 2, 1950; d. Albert Leroy and Nancy (Wallace) L.; m. Richard D. Dietz, Jan. 24, 1993. BA, Knox Coll., 1972; MA, SUNY, Binghamton, 1975. Cert. profl. geologist; cert. petroleum geologist. Petroleum geologist Amoco Prodn. Co., Denver, 1974—87; mgr. exploration tng. Amoco, Houston, 1987—89; ind. petroleum geologist Denver, 1990—. Editor: Interior Rift Basins, 1993. Mem., chmn. Colo. Geol. Survey Adv. Com., Denver, 1991-98; mem. Bd. on Earth Sci. and Resources-NRC, 1992-97, chair com. on earth resources, 1998-2003; mem. Nat. Coop. Geologic Mapping Program Fed. Adv. Com., 1997—. Recipient Disting. Alumni award Knox Coll., 1986. Mem. Am. Assn. Petroleum Geologists (hon., treas., Disting. Svc. award 1995), Am. Inst. Profl. Geologists (pres. 1990, Martin Van Couvering award 1991, Ben H. Parker medal 2001), Am. Geol. Inst. (pres. 1998), Rocky Mountain Assn. Geologists (pres. 2000, Disting. Svc. award 1986, Disting. Pub. Svc. to Earth Sci. award 1995). Achievements include frontier exploration for hydrocarbons in U.S. Home: 780 Ballantine Rd Golden CO 80401-9503 Office: Thomasson Ptnr Assocs 1410 High St Denver CO 80218-2609 Home Phone: 303-526-7723; Office Phone: 303-436-1930. Personal E-mail: susanlandon@att.net.

LANDON, SUSAN N., humanitarian, arts and environmental advocate, poet; b. Pitts., Feb. 20, 1946; d. Kenneth L. and Nina H. Landon. BA cum laude, Tufts U., 1967; MA in Counseling Psychology, Lesley U., 1988. Assoc. staff software engring. MIT Lincoln Lab., Cambridge, Mass., 1967—78; tech. staff software engr. Adaptive Optics, Cambridge, 1978—81; program office mgr. software engring. Intermetrics, Inc., Cambridge, 1981—85; compiler group mgr. software engring. Boston Systems Office, Waltham, Mass., 1985—86; pvt. practice Cambridge, 1989—92; freelance journalist focusing on environment and edn., 1991—95; sr. mem. of tech. staff (software engring.) Draper Lab., Cambridge, Mass., 1995—98. Vol. bus. advisor Mother Earth Natural Foods, Lexington, Mass., 1973—75; self-image subgroup leader MIT Lincoln Lab. Women's Forum, Lexington, Mass., 1973—78; founder & pres. Data Acquisition & Lab. Control SIG of Data Gen. Users Group, 1979—82; founder Intermetrics Women's Network, Cambridge, Mass., 1984—85; counseling intern Horizons Transitional Housing Program, 1985—86. Author: numerous poems. Del. People to People Internat. Mission Understanding to South Africa, 2004; vol. Somerville Environ. and Recycling Vol., 1995—96; vol. tutor Somerville Cmty. Adult Learning Experiences, Somerville, Mass., 1998—2001; com. mem. Hoyt-Sullivan Com., Somerville, 1999—2001; writer for cmty. newspaper funded to stabilize the neighborhood after subway expansion disrupted it. North Cambridge News, Cambridge, Mass., 1991—92; Boston coord. Found. for Shamanic Studies, 1986—91; internat. friendship del. Global Peace Initiative to Egypt, 2003; clk. First Congl. Ch. of Somerville, 1996—97; writer Nat. Orgn. for Women (Boston chpt.), Cambridge, 1982—85; internat. friendship del. to Egypt: Women in Soc. trip People to People Internat., Kansas City, Mo., 2000, internat. friendship del., a Mission in Understanding to Cuba, 2002; Transcendental Meditation tchr. Students Internat. Meditation Soc., Cambridge, Mass., 1971—75; vol. computer aide Somerville Cmty. Computing Ctr., 1998—2004; activist Mass. Choice, Cambridge, Mass., 1979—81; vol. computer cons. Cambridge Multicultural Arts Ctr., Cambridge, 1999—2004; vol. Ten Thousand Villages, Cambridge, 1999—2004. Named to Wall of Tolerance, So. Law Poverty Ctr., 2002; recipient Poetry prize, Spare Change News, 2001, Peace Medal, So. Sinai Governorate/Egypt, 2003, Cambridge Poetry award Best Modern Poem, Cambridge Ctr. Adult Edn., 2003, Cambridge Poetry award Best Traditional Poem, 2004. Mem.: Nat. Mus. Women Arts, New Eng. Poetry Club. Avocations: reading, languages, travel, yoga. Personal E-mail: landon_susan@hotmail.com.

LANDON, WILLIAM J., retired intelligence officer; b. Menno, SD, June 23, 1939; s. Helmuth Samuel and Violet A. (McPherson) Neuharth. LLB, Blackstone Sch. Law, 1962, JD, 1968; AA in Bus. Mgmt., Coastline C.C., 1984; postgrad., Am. Mil. U., 2001—; degree in criminal justice, Ashworth Coll., 2003. Criminal investigator Internat. Acad. Police Sci., Oklahoma

City, Southwestern Inst. Criminology, Lawton, Okla.; criminal investigator, intelligence officer ASI divsn. Internat. Investigators and Police, St. John, N.B., Canada, 1964-94; intelligence officer, analyst Internat. Investigators & Police, Rapid City, SD, 1990—2001, ret., 2001. Sponsor Robin Anne Syperda Benedict meml. scholarship Calif. State U., Fullerton, 1990—. With USMC, 1957-65. Mem.: Internat. Assn. for Study of Organized Crime, Marine Corps Intelligence Assn., Nat. Mil. Intelligence Assn., Assn. Former Intelligence Officers, Internat. Investigators Police Assn. Avocations: martial arts, classical music, fencing. Home Phone: 605-343-4591. Personal E-mail: nmiaafio@aol.com.

LANDOW-ESSER, JANINE MARISE, lawyer; b. Omaha, Sept. 23, 1951; d. Erwin Landow and Beatrice (Hart) Appel; m. Jeffrey L. Esser, June 2, 1974; children: Erica, Caroline. BA, U. Wis., 1973; JD with honors, George Washington U., 1976. Bar: Va. 1976, DC 1977, Ill. 1985. Atty. U.S. Dept. Energy, Washington, 1976-83, Bell, Boyd & Lloyd, Chgo., 1985-86, Seyfarth, Shaw, Fairweather & Geraldson, Chgo., 1986-88, Holleb & Coff, Chgo., 1988-2000, Quarles & Brady, Chgo., 2000—. Contbr. articles to profl. jours. Bd. dirs. Bernard Zell Anshe Emet Day Sch. Parent-Tchr. Orgn., 1991-95. Mem. ABA, Chgo. Bar Assn. (vice chmn. environ. law com. 1990-91, chmn. 1991-92), Nat. Brownfield Assn. (Ill. chpt. chmn. legis. and policy com. 2005—), Am. Jewish Congress (bd. dirs., pres. Midwest Region 2001-04). Office: Quarles & Brady 500 W Madison St Ste 3700 Chicago IL 60661-2592 Home Phone: 773-528-1034; Office Phone: 312-715-5055. Business E-Mail: je3@quarles.com.

LANDRAM, CHRISTINA LOUELLA, librarian; b. Dec. 10, 1922; d. James Ralph and Bertie Louella (Jordan) Oliver; m. Robert Ellis Landram, Aug. 7, 1948; 1 child, Mark Owen. BA, Tex. Woman's U., 1945, BLS, 1946, MLS, 1951. Preliminary cataloger Libr. of Congress, Washington, 1946—48; cataloger U.S. Info. Ctr., Tokyo, 1948—50, U.S. Dept. Agr., Washington, 1953—54; libr. Yokota AFB, Japan, 1954—55, St. Mary's Hosp., West Palm Beach, Fla., 1957—59, Jacksonville H.S., Ark., 1959—61; coord. Shelby County Librs., Memphis, 1961—63; head catalog dept. Ga. State U. Libr., 1963—86, libr., assoc. prof. emeritus, 1986—. Contbr. articles to libr. jours. Mem. ALA (chmn. cataloging norms 1979-80, nominating com. 1977-78), Ga. Libr. Assn. (chmn. resources and tech. svcs. sect. 1969-71), Metro-Atlanta Libr. Assn. (pres. 1967-68), Southeastern Libr. Assn. (govtl. rels. com. 1975-78, intellectual freedom com. 1984-86, Rothrock awards com. 1987-90). Presbyterian. Home: 15201 Olive Blvd Apt 495 Chesterfield MO 63017-1819 Personal E-mail: bobland2@juno.com.

LANDRIEU, MARY LORRETTA, senator; b. Arlington, Virginia, Nov. 23, 1955; m. E. Frank Snellings. BA, La. State U., 1977. Real estate agt.; La. state rep. from dist. 90, 1980—88; La. state treas., 1988—96; US Senator from La., 1997—; mem. small business com.; mem. energy and natural resources com.; mem. appropriations com. Del., Dem. Nat. Conv., 1980 Author: (novels) Nine and Counting: The Women of the Senate, 2000. Mem. LWV, Women Execs. in State Govt., Fedn. Dem. Women, Delta Gamma. Democrat. Roman Catholic. Office: 724 Hart Senate Off Bldg Washington DC 20510-0001

LANDRIEU, MITCHELL JOSEPH, lieutenant governor; b. Aug. 16, 1960; m. Cheryl P. Quirk; children: Grace, Emily, Matthew, Benjamin, William. BA, Catholic U.; JD, Loyola U., New Orleans. Mem. La. State Ho. of Reps., Baton Rouge, 1988—2003; lt. gov. State of La., Baton Rouge, 2004—. Adj. prof. Loyola U. Law Sch., New Orleans; pres. Internat. Mediation and Arbitration, Ltd. Recipient Friends of the Parishes award, La. Police Jury Assn., 1988, Bus. Champion award, C. of C., 2001, 2002, Legislator of Yr. award, Alliance for Good Govt., 2002, Orleans Parish Med. Soc., 2002, Outstanding Legislator award, Victims and Citizens Against Crime, 2002. Democrat. Mailing: Office of Lt Gov PO Box 44243 Baton Rouge LA 70804-4243

LANDRIGAN, PHILIP JOHN, epidemiologist; b. Boston, June 14, 1942; s. John Joseph and Frances Joan (Conlin) Landrigan; m. Mary Florence Magee, Aug. 27, 1966; children: Mary Frances, Christopher Paul, Elizabeth Marie. AB, Boston Coll., 1963; MD, Harvard U., 1967; MS, DIH, London Sch. Hygiene and Tropical Medicine, 1977. Diplomate Am. Bd. Pediat., Am. Bd. Preventive Medicine, Am. Bd. Occupl. Medicine, Am. Coll. Epidemiology. Intern Cleve. Met. Gen. Hosp., 1967—68; resident in pediatrics Children's Hosp. Med. Ctr., Boston, 1968—70; fellow in pediatrics Harvard U. Med. Sch., Boston, 1969—70; clin. instr. pediatrics Emory U. Sch. Medicine, Atlanta, 1970—71; epidemic intelligence service officer Ctrs. for Disease Control, Atlanta, 1970—73, dir. research and devel. smallpox erradication program, 1973—74, chief environ. hazards activity, 1974—79; dir. div. Surveillance, Hazard Evaluations and Field Studies Nat. Inst. for Occupational Safety and Health, Cin., 1979—85; prof. community medicine and pediatrics Mt. Sinai Sch. Medicine, NYC, 1985—, dir. div. environ. and occupational medicine, 1985—90; prof., chmn. dept. community and preventative medicine, 1990—. Mem. bd. on toxicology and environ. health hazards NAS, Washington, vice chmn., 1981—86, chmn. com. on pesticides in the diets of infants and children, 1988—93; sr. advisor to adminstr. on children's health and environment U.S. EPA, Washington, 1997—98; clin. prof. environ. health Sch. Pub. Health U. Wash., Seattle, 1983—. Contbr. numerous articles to prlfl. jours.; cons. editor: Archives of Environ. Health, 1982—, Am. Jour. Indsl. Medicine, 1979—, editor-in-chief: Environ. Rsch., 1987—. Recipient Vol. award, Dept. HEW, 1973, Pub. Health Svc. Career Devel. award, 1975, group citation as mem. of Ctr. for Disease Control beryllium rev. panel, 1978, Meritorious Svc. medal, USPHS, 1985. Fellow: Royal Soc. Medicine; mem.: AAAS, APHA, Soc. for Epidemiologic Rsch., Am. Epidemiol. Soc., Inst. of Medicine Internat. Commn. on Occupl. Health. Home: 915 Stuart Ave Mamaroneck NY 10543-4124 Office: Mt Sinai Sch Medicine Dept Community Medicine 1 Gustave L Levy Pl # 1057 New York NY 10029-6500 E-mail: phil.landrigan@nasa.gov.

LANDRÓN, ANA, school psychologist; d. Sidney Kruset and Carlina Figueroa; m. Jose R. Landron, June 29, 1974; children: Rafael A. Landron, Miguel O. Landron. BS in Psychology, Queens Coll. CUNY, 1969; MS in Sch. Psychology, St. John's U., 1995, postgrad., 1999—. Cert. in sch. psychology U. State NY, 1996, lic. bilingual sch. psychologist NYC Dept. Edn., 1996, primary and advanced practicum in rational emotive behavior therapy Albert Ellis Inst. Family counselor Children's Aid Soc., Sloane Head Start, NYC; sch. psychologist NYC Dept Edn., Forest Hills; bilingual sch. psychologist Oyster Bay-East Norwich Sch. Dist., NY, 1995—. Mem. Sen. Marcellino's Mental Health Adv. Com., Nassau County, NY, 2001; bd. advisor Centro Cultural Hispano de Oyster Bay-East Norwich y Vecinidades; mem. majority task force on children's health and safety NY State Senate. Recipient cert. acad. excellence, St. John's U., 1995, Woman of Distinction, Humanitarian award, Town of Oyster Bay, 2001. Mem.: APA, Soc. for Study of Peace, Conflict, and Violence, Soc. for Psychol. Study of Ethnic Minority Issues, Nat. Assn. Sch. Psychologists. Avocations: reading, hiking, gardening. Office: Roosevelt Elem Sch 150 W Main St Oyster Bay NY 11771 Home Phone: 718-739-8673.

LANDRUM, BRIAN, energy executive; b. Feb. 17, 1962; B in Indsl. Engring., Stanford U., 1984; MBA in Fin. and Internat. Bus., U. Chgo., 1991. Gen. mgmt. and info. tech. consulting McKinsey and Accenture; gen. mgr. worldwide comml. displays bus. unit Compaq Computer Corp., bus. unit mgr. large comml. customer segment Internet and eCommerce divsn.; v.p. internet & eBusiness Reliant Energy, Inc., Houston, 1999—2001, sr. v.p. eBusiness, pres. retail ops., 2001—03, pres. retail services, 2003—04, sr. v.p. customer ops & info. tech., 2004—05, sr. v.p. comml. & real estate ops., 2005—06, exec. v.p. ops., 2006—07, exec. v.p., COO, 2007—. Bd. dirs. N.Am. Energy Stds. Bd., Grande Comm. Mem. edn. com. Ctr. for Houston's Future. Office: Reliant Energy Inc PO Box 3765 Houston TX 77253-2286*

LANDRY, BROCK R., lawyer; b. Detroit, Sept. 15, 1947; BA cum laude, Yale U., 1970; JD, U. Mich., 1974. Bar: Ill. 1974, DC 1982. Ptnr., trade assn. law, mgr., govt., regulatory affairs divsn. Venable LLP, Washington. Exec. com., dir., treas. Cancer Rsch. Found. Mem.: ABA, DC Bar Assn. Office: Venable LLP 575 Seventh St NW Washington DC 20004 Office Phone: 202-344-4877. Office Fax: 202-344-8300. Business E-Mail: brlandry@venable.com.

LANDRY, DONALD WILLIAM, physician, educator, director, scientist; b. Jersey City, May 19, 1954; s. Donald O. and Gloria A. Landry; m. Maureen O'Reilly, Sept. 3, 1978; children: Christopher D., Michael J. BS in Chemistry summa cum laude, Lafayette Coll., 1975; PhD in Organic Chemistry, Harvard U., 1979; MD, Columbia U. Coll. Physicians & Surgeons, 1983. Diplomate Nat. Bd. Med. Examiners, Am. Bd. Internal Medicine, Am. Bd. Nephrology; Lic. NY. Intern, resident in medicine Mass. Gen. Hosp., Boston; attending physician NY Presbyn. Hosp., NYC, dir. divsn. clin. pharmacology and exptl. therapeutics, 1998—, dir. divsn. nephrology, 2003—; attending physician NY Presbyn. Hosp./Columbia U., NYC, 2004—; prof. medicine with tenure Columbia U. Physicians and Surgeons, NYC, 2004—. Contbr. articles to profl. jours., chapters to books; mem. editl. bd. Regenerative Medicine, 2005. Mem. Am. Soc. Clin. Investigation, Am. Assn. Physicians, NY Acad. Scis., Alpha Omega Alpha, Phi Beta Kappa. Roman Catholic. Achievements include patents in field of ten. Avocation: running. Home: 29 Claremont Ave #2-S New York NY 10027-6802 Office: Columbia U Coll Physicians & Surgeons Rm 10-445 630 W 168th St New York NY 10032 Office Phone: 212-305-2436. Business E-Mail: dwl1@columbia.edu.

LANDRY, JANE LORENZ, architect; b. San Antonio, Feb. 12, 1936; d. John Henry and Lulie Amanda (Sample) L.; m. Duane Eugene Landry, Sept. 8, 1956; children: Rachel, Claire, Ellyn, Jean. Student, U. Tex., 1952-55, Yale U., 1955-56; BArch, U. Pa., 1957. Registered arch., Tex. Project arch. O'Neil Ford & Assoc., San Antonio, 1959-65; prin. Duane Landry, Arch., San Antonio, 1965-68, Dallas, 1968-76; ptnr. Landry & Landry, Archs. & Planners, Dallas, 1976—, Meyer, Landry & Landry, Archs. & Planners, Dallas, 1977-80. Instr. San Antonio Coll., 1965. Dir. at large Interfaith Forum on Religion, Art and Architecture, 1991—; mem. Liturgical Commn. Diocese of Dallas, 1978-90. Recipient design awards Interfaith Forum on Religion, Art and Architecture, 1985, 89, 90, 97, 98, 2000, 2003. Fellow AIA (mem. hist. resources com., design awards Dallas chpt. 1970, 75, 76, 77, 80); mem. Tex. Soc. Architects (design award 1969, 81), The Liturgical Design Consultancy. Roman Catholic. Office: Landry & Landry Archs & Planners 6319 Meadow Rd Dallas TX 75230-5140 Office Phone: 214-265-8398.

LANDRY, JOSEPH L., JR., retired affirmative action specialist; b. Woodlawn, La., Dec. 23, 1940; s. Joseph L. Landry and Clara Desmairs; widowed; children: Alan Joseph, Kevin Dale. Student, Northwestern State U. La., 1959-61, McNeese State U., 1961-62, Hosp. Corps. Sch., Great Lakes, Ill., 1962, Cardiopulmonary Technique Sch., Bethesda, Md., 1964, Instr. Tng. Sch., Norfolk, Va., 1968, Pers. Adminstrn. & Career Counseling Sch., San Diego, 1973, Disease Vector Ecology Control Ctr. Sch., Jacksonville, Fla., 1974; AA, Prince George's C.C., Largo, Md., 1975. Gas meter reader Tex. La. Gas Co., Alexandria, La., 1959; hosp. orderly Lake Charles (La.) Meml. Hosp., 1961-62; staff hosp. corpsman Charleston (S.C.) Naval Hosp., 1962-63; staff instr. Cardiopulmonary Technique Sch., U.S. Naval Hosp., Bethesda, Md., 1964-66, chief respiratory therapy dept., 1967-70; staff pulmonary technologist VA Hosp., Washington, 1966-67, staff cardiopulmonary technologist, 1970-74; clin. instr. Respiratory Therapy Sch., Washington Technical Inst., D.C. U., 1970-74; cardiopulmonary technologist divsn. coal mine workers' compensation U.S. Dept. Labor, Washington, 1974-82; program analyst Office Fed. Contract Compliance Programs, 1982-84, equal opportunity specialist, 1984-96; ret., 1996. Co-writer guidelines for Freedom of Info. Act and Privacy Act; cons. Peopleclick, New Orleans, 1996—; lectr. in field. Acting chair citizens adv. com. Reston Police Dist., 1986; past pres., bd. dirs. Deepwood Homeowners' Assn.; bd. dirs., "F" lic. coach Reston Soccer Assn.; mem. PTA and Booster Club of South Lakes High Sch.; bd. dirs., past v.p. amateur divsn. La. Soccer Assn.; past asst. dist. dir., past dist. dir. Boy Scouts Am., St. Tammany Parish.; cert. referee USSF Region III; Region III state select teams coord. With USN, 1962-66, USNR, 1966-89, ret. 1989. Mem. Nat. Active and Ret. Fed. Employees (past pres. chpt. 1428, past v.p. dist. IV, LA fedn. chpts., 1st v.p. La. fedn. chpts.), Am. Legion (adj. post 415 Mandeville), Mil. Officers Assn. Am. (past pres. Ozone chpt.), Am. Heart Assn. Democrat. Roman Catholic. Home: PO Box 8823 Mandeville LA 70470-8823 Office Phone: 985-630-9573. Personal E-mail: josephllj@yahoo.com.

LANDRY, MARK EDWARD, podiatrist, researcher; b. Washington, May 24, 1950; s. John Edward and Daphne (Fay) L.; m. Mary Ann Kotey, Sept. 7, 1974; children: John Ryan, Christopher John, Jessica Marie. D in Podiatry, Ohio Coll. Podiatric Medicine, 1975; MS in Edn., U. Kans., Lawrence, 1982. Diplomate Am. Bd. Podiatric Surgery, Am. Bd. Podiatric Orthopedics and Primary Podiatric Medicine; cert. NAUI, 2000, RADI scuba diver, 2004. Gen. practice podiatry, Kansas City, Mo., 1977—, Overland Park, Kans., 1980—; clin. asst. prof. U. Health Scis., Kansas City, 1985-98; clin. assoc. prof. Coll. Podiatric Medicine and Surgery U. Osteo. Medicine and Health Scis., Des Moines, 1985-92; clin. instr. Sch. Medicine U. Mo., Kansas City, 1987-95. Founder, bd. dirs. Kansas City Podiatric Residency Program, Kansas City, 1982-91; adv. bd. Rockport Shoe Co., 1988-89; chmn. podiatry dept. Park Lane Med. Ctr., Kansas City, Mo., 1995-97; dir. continuing edn. Kans. Podiatric Med. Assn., 1997—. Contbr. articles to profl. jours. Cons. Mid-Am. Track and Field Assn., Lenexa, Kans., 1978-88; com. chmn. Boy Scouts Am., Overland Park, Kans., 1986; coach Johnson County Soccer League, 1987-90; head coach 6th and 7th grade girls' Cath. Youth Orgn. Basketball, 1995-96, 97; sponsor 8 & 11 Baseball League, 1987-90. 1st lt. USAF, 1975-77. Recipient Pres.'s award Ohio Sch. Podiatric Medicine, 1975; USAF scholar Armed Forces Health Professions, 1973-75. Fellow Am. Coll. Foot and Ankle Surgeons, Acad. Podiatric Sports Medicine; mem. Kans. Podiatric Med Assn. (bd. dirs. 1997—), Brit. Podiatry Assn. (hon.), Am. Bd. Primary Podiatric Medicine (founding dir., bd. examiner 1994-2000), Holy Cross Social Club (pres. 1983-84), Prairie Life Club, Leukemia Assn. of Am. (team in tng. 1997-2000, 2005, team capt. 1999, K.C. corp. challenge participant 1997-99), K.C. (4th degree 1995—, chancellor 1998, 99), KC Ski Club (trip capt. 1999), Fifty States Marathon Club, 50 State Marathon Group, D.C. Marathon Group. Republican. Roman Catholic. Avocations: triathlon, skiing. Office: 10550 Quivira Rd Ste 260 Overland Park KS 66215-2375 Office Phone: 913-438-9898. E-mail: mlandry4@kc.rr.com.

LANDRY, PAUL LEONARD, lawyer; b. Mpls., Nov. 23, 1950; s. LeRoy Robert Landry and Alice Ruth (Swain) Stephens; m. Lisa Yvonne Yeo, Dec. 13, 1984; children: Marc, Lauren, Matthew. BA, Macalester Coll., 1974; postgrad., Georgetown U., 1976-77; JD, Boston U., 1977. Bar: Va. 1977, D.C. 1978, Minn. 1984, U.S. Dist. Ct. D.C., U.S. Dsit. Ct. Va., U.S. Dist. Ct. Minn., U.S. Ct. Appeals (D.C., 2d, 4th and 8th cirs.). Dancer Dance Theater Harlem, NYC, 1971-72; prin. dancer Dance Theatre Boston, 1972-75; atty. EPA, Washington, 1976-77; assoc. Reed, Smith, Shaw & McClay, Washington, 1977-83; officer, shareholder Fredrikson & Byron, P.A., Mpls., 1984—. Adj. prof. law William Mitchell Coll. Law, St. Paul, 1985-89. Bd. dirs. Ind. Sch. Dist. 284, Wayzata, Minn., 1989-96, 2002-, chmn., 1992-93; bd. dirs. Walker Art Ctr., Mpls., 1992—; bd. dirs., vice chair Greater Twin Cities Youth Symphonies, 1999-2001; advisor Kevin McCary Scholarship Fund. Mem. ABA (conf. of minority ptnrs. adv. com.), Nat. Bar Assn., Minn. State Bar Assn. (art and entertainment sect., labor and employment sect.), D.C. Bar, Hennepin Conty Bar Assn., Black Entertainment and Sports Lawyers Assn., Barristers. Avocations: golf, music, basketball. E-mail: plandry@fredlaw.com.

LANDRY, RICHARD, architect; BArch, U. Montreal; diploma in Architecture and Urban Design, U. Copenhagen. Lic. arch., Calif., Conn., Fla., Ill., Idaho, NJ, NY, NC, Wash., cert. Nat. Coun. Archtl. Registration Bds. Prin. Landry Design Group, Inc., LA, 1987. Prin. works include Glaser Residence (Merit award for best renovated or restored single house, Golden Nugget Awards, 2007), Zeiden Residence (Merit award for custom home from 5,000 to 10,000 sq. ft., Golden Nugget Awards, 2007), Haselton Residence (Merit award for custom home from 5,000 to 10,000 sq. ft., Golden Nugget Awards, 2007), Gores Residence (Merit award for custom home over 10,000 sq. ft., Golden Nugget Awards, 2007), Gretzky Residence (Grand award for custom home over 10,000 sq. ft., Golden Nugget Awards, 2007). Recipient Stars of Design award for Architecture, Pacific Design Ctr., 2004. Mem.: AIA. Office: Landry Design Group 11333 Iowa Ave Los Angeles CA 90025 Office Phone: 310-444-1404. Office Fax: 310-444-1405.*

LANDRY, SHERRY S., lawyer; BA, U. New Orleans; JD summa cum laude, Loyola U., New Orleans. Bar: La. 1996. Atty. Locke Liddell & Sapp; sr. chief dep. Law Dept., New Orleans, 2002—03, city atty., 2003—05; atty. Elkins, P.L.C., New Orleans, 2006—. Mem.: United Way for Greater New Orleans Area. Office: Elkins PLC Ste 4400 201 St Charles Ave New Orleans LA 70170 Office Phone: 504-658-9800. Office Fax: 504-565-7691.

LANDSBERG, DAVID, publishing executive; b. Fla., 1962; m. Anoly Landsberg; children: Jessica, Natasha, Daniela. Grad., U. Fla.; MBA, U. Miami. With Miami Herald Media Co., 1984—, gen. mgr., 2005—06, pres., 2006—; pub. Miami Herald & El Nuevo Herald, 2006—. Office: Miami Herald 1 Herald Plz Miami FL 33132 Office Phone: 800-437-2535. E-mail: dlandsberg@miamiherald.com.*

LANDSBERG, LEWIS, dean, endocrinologist, medical researcher; b. NYC, Nov. 23, 1938; AB, Williams Coll., 1960; MD, Yale U., 1964. Intern Yale-New Haven Hosp., 1964—65, resident in internal medicine, 1965—66, 1968—69; fellow in endocrinology NIH, 1966—68; from instr. to asst. prof. medicine Sch. Medicine Yale U., 1969-72; from asst. prof. to assoc. prof. Harvard Med. Sch., 1972-77, from assoc. prof. to prof., 1977-86; Irving S. Cutter prof., chmn. dept. medicine Northwestern U. Feinberg Sch. Medicine, Chgo., 1990—2000, dir. Ctr. Endocrinology, Metabolism & Nutrition, 1990-93, dean, v.p. for medical affairs, 2000—. Assoc. physician Yale-New Haven Hosp., 1969-71, attending physician, 1971-72, Beth Israel Hosp., 1974-79, physician, 1979-88, sr. physician, 1988-90; attending physician West Haven VA Hosp., 1970-72; assisting physician Boston City Hosp., 1972-73, assoc. vis. physician, 1973-74; physician-in-chief dept. medicine Northwestern Meml. Hosp., 1990—. Fellow ACP, AAAS; mem. Am. Fedn. Clin. Rsch., Endocrine Soc., N.Y. Acad. Scis., AHA, Am. Soc. Pharmacology and Exptl. Therapeutics, Am. Physiology Soc., Am. Soc. Clin. Investigators, Am. Clin. and Climatological Assn., Assn. Am. Physicians. Achievements include rsch. in catecholamines and the sympathoadrendal system, nutrition and the sympathetic nervous system, obesity and hypertension. Office: Northwestern Univ Med Sch Morton 4-656 310 East Superior St Chicago IL 60611-2958

LANDSMAN, RICHARD, investment company executive, finance educator; b. NYC, Oct. 31, 1949; s. Irving and Shirley (Siegel) L.; m. Wendy Benfield, Apr. 18, 1988; 1 child, Nerys. BS, Queens Coll., 1970, MS, 1971; MSW, Hunter Coll., 1977; MBA, Pace U., 1982. Exec. dir. CoPay Inc., Great Neck, N.Y., 1972-84; sr. v.p. Smith Barney Inc., NYC, 1984-89, 92-96, Shearson Lehman Inc., NYC, 1989—92, Prudential Securities, Garden City, N.Y., 1996; pres. Nottinghill Capital Mgmt. Inc., Roslyn, NY, 1997—. Prof. Grad. Sch. Bus. Columbia U., N.Y.C., 1996—; disting. prof. St. Johns U. Grad. Sch. Bus., N.Y.C., 1999—. Contbr. articles to profl. jours. Office: 2 Main St Ste 1 Roslyn NY 11576 Home Phone: 516-946-2509; Office Phone: 516-621-6080. E-mail: nhillcap@aol.com.

LANDSMAN, STEPHEN N., lawyer; BA, U. Ill., Urbana, 1981, JD, 1984. Sr. atty. Nalco Holding Co., Naperville, Ill., now v.p., gen. counsel, corp. sec. Office: Nalco Holding Co 1601 W Diehl Rd Naperville IL 60563 Office Phone: 630-305-1000. Fax: 630-305-2922.*

LANDSMARK, TED (THEODORE C. LANDSMARK), academic administrator; b. Kansas City, Mo., May 17, 1946; BS in Polit. Sci., Yale U., 1969, JD; PhD in Am. Studies, Boston U. Asst. prof. MIT, U. Mass., Boston; adminstr. Harvard U.; dean Grad. and Continuing Edn. Mass. Coll. Art; pres., CEO Boston Archtl. Coll. (formerly Boston Archtl. Ctr.), 1997—. Spl. asst. Mayor of Boston; dir. Office of Cmty. Partnerships. Contbr. Maine Antique Digest, editl. bd. mem. Architecture Boston, Jour. Early So. Decorative Arts. Subject of Pulitzer Prize winning photograph, 1977; trustee Mus. Fine Arts, Boston, New England Found. for Arts, Boston Fund for Arts. Recipient Whitney M. Young Jr. award, 2006; fellow Winterthur Mus., Mus. of Early So. Decorative Arts, Winston-Salem, NSF. Office: Boston Architectural Ctr 320 Newbury St Boston MA 02115 Office Phone: 617-262-5000.*

LANDSTROM, ELSIE HAYES, retired editor; b. Kuling, Kiangsi, China, June 22, 1923; came to the U.S., 1935; d. Paul Goodman and Helen Mae (Wolf) Hayes; m. Victor Norman Landstrom, Jan. 21, 1953 (dec. Oct. 1989); children: Peter S., Ruth H. BA magna cum laude, Hamline U., 1945. Writer, editor adminstrv. staff Am. Friends Svc. Com., Phila., 1946-52, MIT, Cambridge, Mass., 1952-53; mem. editl. bd. Approach Mag., Phila. and Needham, 1947-67; sr. editor Word Guild, 1976-82; freelance writer and editor Conway, Mass., 1976-98; ret., 1998. Author: Closing the Circle-An American Family in China, 1998; (poetry) Lions Walk Around My Bed, 2007; editor: Propaganda and Aesthetics, 1979, Taoism and Chinese Religion, 1981, Hyla Doc in China 1924-1949, 1991, Hyla Doc in Africa 1950-1961, 1994; exhibits include Greenfield, Mass., 1996, Book Mill, Montague, Mass., 1997. Newsletter editor, draft resisters support com. Wellesley (Mass.) Friends Meeting; chair Fair Housing Com., Needham. Avocations: birding, reading, painting. Home and Office: 86 Kendal Dr Kennett Square PA 19348-2327

LAND-WEBER, ELLEN, photography professor; b. Rochester, NY, Mar. 16, 1943; d. David and Florence Epstein; 1 child, Julia. BA, U. Iowa, 1965, MFA, 1968. Faculty mem. UCLA Extension, 1970-74, Orange Coast Coll., Costa Mesa, Calif., 1973, U. Nebr., Lincoln, 1974; asst. prof. photography Humboldt State U., Arcata, Calif., 1974-79, assoc. prof., 1979-83, prof., 1983—. Photographer Seagram's Bicentennial Courthouse Project, 1976-77, Nat. Trust for Hist. Preservation/Soc. Photographic Edn., 1987. Author: The Passionate Collector, 1980, To Save a Life: Stories of Holocaust Rescue, 2000; contbr. sects. to books; photographs pub. in numerous books and jours. Named Humboldt State U. Scholar of Yr., 2004-2005; Nat. Endowment for Arts fellow, 1974, 79, 82; Artist's support grantee Unicolor Corp., 1982, Polaroid 20X24 Artist's support grantee, 1990, 91, 93, 94; Fulbright sr. fellow, 1993-94. Mem. Soc. for Photog. Edn. (exec. bd. 1979-82, treas. 1979-81, sec. 1981-83) Avocation: weaving. Office: Humboldt State U Art Dept Arcata CA 95521

LANDY, BURTON AARON, lawyer; b. Chgo., Aug. 16, 1929; s. Louis J. and Clara (Ernstein) L.; m. Eleonora M. Simmel, Aug. 4, 1957; children: Michael Simmel, Alisa Anne. Student, Nat. U. Mex., 1948; BS, Northwestern U., 1950; postgrad. scholar, U. Havana, 1951; JD, U. Miami, 1952; postgrad. fellow, Inter-Am. Acad. Comparative Law, Havana, Cuba, 1955-56. Bar: Fla. 1952. Practice law in internat. field, Miami, 1955—; ptnr. firm Ammerman & Landy, 1957-63, Paul, Landy, Beiley & Harper, P.A. and predecessor firm, 1964-94, Steel Hector & Davis, 1994-97; ptnr. firm, chmn. emeritus Internat. Practice Group Akerman, Senterfitt & Eidson, P.A., 1997—. Lectr. Latin Am. bus. law U. Miami Sch. Law, 1972-75; also internat. law confs. in U.S. and abroad; mem. Nat. Conf. on Fgn. Aspects of U.S. Nat. Security, Washington, 1958; mem. organizing com. Miami regional conf. Com. for Internat. Econ. Growth, 1958; mem. U.S. Dept. Commerce Regional Export Expansion Council, 1969-74, mem. Dist. Export Council, 1978—; mem. U.S. Sec. State Adv. Com. on Pvt. Internat. Law; dir. Fla. Council Internat. Devel., 1977—, chmn. 1986-87, 99; mem. U. Miami Citizens Bd., 1977—; chmn. Fla. del. S.E. U.S.-Japan Assn., 1980-82; mem. adv. com. 1st Miami Trade Fair of Ams., 1978; dir., v.p. Greater Miami Fgn. Trade Zone, Inc., 1978—; mem. organizing com., lectr. 4 Inter-Am. Aviation Law Confs.; bd. dirs. Inter-Am. Bar Legal Found., VIII FTAA Ministerial, Am. Bus. Forum; participant Aquaculture Symposium Sci. and Man in the Ams., Mexico City, Fla. Gov's Econ. Mission to Japan and Hong Kong, 1978; mem. bd. exec. advisors Law and Econs. Ctr.; mem. vis. com., internat. adv. bd. U. Miami Sch. Bus.; mem. internat. fin. council Office Comptroller of Fla.; founding chmn. Fla.-Korea Econ. Coop. Com., 1982—, Southeast U.S.-Korea Econ. Com., 1985—; chmn. Expo 500 Fla.-Columbus Soc., 1985-87; founding co-chmn. So. Fla. Roundtable-Georgetown U. Ctr. for Strategic and Internat. Studies, 1982-85; chmn. Fla. Gov.'s Conf. on World Trade, 1984—; founding gen. counsel Fla. Internat. Bankers Assn.; dir., former gen. counsel Fla. Internat. Ins. and Reins. Assn., chmn. Latin Am. Carribbean Bus. Promotion Adv. Counc. to U.S. Sec. of Commerce and Aid Adminstr; appointee Fla. Internat. Trade and Investment Coun.; mem. steering com. Summit of Ams., 1994—, co-chair post summit planning com.; strategic planning com. Mayor Miami Dade County Internat. Trade Commn. Contbg. editor Econs. Devel. Lawyers of the Ams., 1969-74; contbr. numerous articles to legal jours. in U.S. and fgn. countries. Chmn. City of Miami Internat. Trade and Devel. Com., 1984-86; chmn. internat. task force Beacon Coun. of Dade County, Fla., 1985, dir., chmn., 1991—; bd. dirs., exec. com. Internat. Comml. Dispute Resolution Ctr., Miami Internat. Arbitration and Mediation Inst.; chmn. Comml. Dispute Resolution Ctr. Ams., Miami, 1995—; apptd. by Gov. of Fla. to Internat. Currency and Barter Commn., 1986; lectr. U. Miami Inter-Ban course L.Am. bankers; steering com. Summit of the Americas, Miami, 1994, co-chair post Summit Planning Com., 1994; co-chair mayor Miami-Dade County Strategic Planning for Internat. Trade, 1998—; co-chair strategic planning com. Mayor of Miami Dade County Internat. Trade Commn.; bd. dirs. Trade Mission Ctr. Am., 2000—, Internat. Trade Coun. Miami-Dade County, Fla., Fla. Free Trade Area Agreement, Inc.; mem. internat. adv. com. Enterprise Fla., 2000—; bd. trustee Fla. Free Trade Area of the Americas; bd. dirs. Fla. Free Trade Agreement Ams., Inc., chmn., 2006—; chmn. World Svcs. Group, 2006-07, chmn., 2006-07. With JACGC, USAF, 1952-54, Korea; to maj. Res. Recipient Pan Am. Informatica Comunicaciones Expo award, 1983, Lawyer of Americas award U. Miami, 1984, Heung-in medal (Order of Diplomatic Service), 1986, Ministerial Citation, Min. of Fgn. Affairs, 1988, Richard L. McLaughlin award Fla. Econ. Devel. Coun., 1993, Order of the Rising Sun Golden Rays with Garnet medal, Emperor of Japan, 2004; named Internat. Trader of Yr., Fla. Council Internat. Devel., 1980, Bus. Person of Yr., 1986, hon. consul gen. Republic of Korea, Miami, 1983-88, State of Fla., 99—; apptd. Hon. consul Ft. Lauderdale, Fla., 1991-98; apptd. Hon. consul gen. State of Fla., 1999—. Fellow ABA Found. (chmn. com. arrangements internat. and comparative law sect. 1964-65, com. on Inter-Am. affairs of ABA 1985-87); mem. Inter-Am. Bar Assn. (asst. sec.-gen. 1957-59, treas. 11th conf. 1959, co-chmn. jr. bar sect. 1963-65, mem council 1969—, exec. com. 1975—, pres. 1982-84, Diploma de Honor 1987, William Roy Vallance award 1989), Spanish Am. Bar Assn., Fla. Bar Assn. (vice chmn. adminstrv. law com. 1965, vice chmn. internat. and comparative law com. 1967-68, chmn. aero. law com. 1968-69), Dade County Bar Assn. (chmn. fgn. laws and lang. com. 1964-65), Internat. Ctr. Fla. (World Trade Ctr., pres. 1981-82), World Peace Through Law Ctr., Miami Com. Fgn. Rels., Inst. Ibero Am. Derecho Aero., Am. Soc. Internat. Law, Coun. Internat. Visitors, Am. Fgn. Law Assn. (pres. Miami 1958), appointed to Nat. and Internat. panels of Arbitrators of the Am. Arbitration Assn., 2003-, Bar of South Korea (hon. mem.), Greater Miami C. of C. (bd. gov. 1986—), Colombian-Am. C. of C. (bd. dirs. 1986—), Peruvian-Am. C. of C. (bd. dir.), Norwegian Am. C. of C. (bd. dir.), Phi Alpha Delta. Home: 605 Almeria Ave Coral Gables FL 33134-5602 Office: One SE Third Ave 28th Flr Miami FL 33131 Business E-Mail: burton.landy@akerman.com.

LANDY, LISA ANNE, lawyer; b. Miami, Fla., Apr. 20, 1963; d. Burton Aaron and Eleonora Maria (Simmel) L. BA, Brown U., 1985; JD cum laude, U. Miami, 1988. Bar: Fla. 1988, U.S. Dist. Ct. (so. dist.) Fla. 1988. Atty. Paul, Landy, Beiley & Harper, P.A., Miami, Fla., 1988-94, Steel Hector & Davis, Miami, 1994-97, ptnr., 1996-97; shareholder Akerman Senterfitt & Eidson P.A., Miami, 1997—. Bd. dirs. Miami City Ballet, 1992-97, pres., 1996, Women in Internat. Trade, Miami, 1992—, pres., 1995, Orgn. Women in Internat. Trade, 1994—, v.p., 1997, 98, pres. 1998-2000; bd. dirs. Women in Tech. Internat. South Fla.; bd. dirs., pres. Commonwealth Inst. So. Fla.; chmn. The Next Step Youth Cmty. Ctr., Inc., 2000-02, IT Women, Inc., 2002—, Women Lawyers of Interlaw Ams., 2004—; mem. children and families impact coun. United Way. Mem. ABA, Inter-Am. Bar Assn. (asst. sec. 1997-2000). Avocations: sports, arts, languages.

LANDZBERG, JOEL SERGE, cardiologist; b. NYC, Dec. 20, 1958; s. Sol and Marilyn Joy (Aboff) L.; m. Barbare Eugene Ross, May 1, 1983; children: Rebecca, Elizabeth. BA summa cum laude, Columbia Coll., 1979; MD, Columbia U., 1983. Resident medicine Vanderbilt U., Nashville, 1983-86, chief resident medicine, 1987-88; rsch. fellow cardiology U. Calif. San Francisco, Cardiovascular Rsch. Inst., 1986-87; cardiology fellow Brigham & Woman's Hosp., Boston, 1988-90; instr. medicine Harvard U., Boston, 1990-91; pvt. practice cardiology Westwood, N.J., 1991—. Fellow Am. Coll. Cardiology; mem. AMA, Am. Med. Athletic Assn., Phi Beta Kappa. Office: Westwood Cardiology 333 Old Hook Rd Ste 200 Westwood NJ 07675-3267

LANE, ANDREW, oil industry executive; B in Mech. Engring., So. Meth. U., Dallas. Field engr. Gulf Oil, prodn. engr. Pipeline Design and Permits Group; design engr. Halliburton, 1984, global v.p. prodn. enhancement Energy Svcs. Group, pres., CEO Landmark, 2002, v.p. Energy Svcs. Group regional orgn., 2004, various mgmt., dir. and vice presdl. positions Energy Svcs. Group, pres., CEO KBR, exec. v.p., COO. Mem. exec. bd. So. Meth. U. Sch. Engring. Mem.: Soc. Petroleum Engrs. Office: Halliburton 5 Houston Ctr 1401 McKinney Ste 2400 Houston TX 77010-4008 Office Phone: 713-759-2600.*

LANE, ANN JUDITH, history and women's studies educator, director; b. NYC, July 27, 1931; d. Harry A. and Elizabeth (Brown) Lane; children: Leslie Patricia, Joni Alexandra. BA, Bklyn. Coll., 1952; MA, NYU, 1958; PhD, Columbia U., 1968. Mng. editor Challenge Mag., NYU, 1953-56; asst. prof. Douglass Coll., Rutgers U., New Brunswick, N.J., 1968-71; prof. John Jay Coll., SUNY, 1971-83; vis. prof. Wheaton Coll., Norton, Mass., 1981-82; prof. history, dir. women's studies Colgate U., Hamilton, N.Y., 1983-90, U. Va., Charlottesville, 1990—. Author: To Herland and Beyond, 1990, Mary Ritter Beard: A Sourcebook, 1977, 2d edit., 1988, The Brownsville Affair, 1971, Gender, Power and Sexuality: First, Do No Harm, 2006; editor: Charlotte Perkins Gilman Reader, 1980, Herland: A Lost Utopian Novel, 1979. Chair Com. on Status of Women in the Profession, Orgn. of Am. Historians, 1992-95; dir. History Tchr. Inst., N.Y. Coun. for Humanities, summer 1985; mem. historians adv. com. Nat. Women's Hall of Fame, 1986—; bd. dirs. Louis M. Rabinowitz Found., 1972-76. Recipient Va. Soc. Sci. Outstanding History scholar, 2005; fellow, Berkshire Conf. Women Historians, 1988, Ford Found., 1981—82, Nat. Endowment for Humanities, 1980—81, Lilly Endowment, Inc., 1977—79, AAUW, 1959—60. Mem. AAUP (mem. com. on women 1987—), Orgn. Am. Historians (mem. Frederick Jackson Turner prize com. 1979), Women in Hist. Profession (exec. bd., coordinating com. 1971-74). Home: 2603 Jefferson Park Cir Charlottesville VA 22903-4133 Office Phone: 434-982-2961. Business E-Mail: annlane@virginia.edu.

LANE, ARTHUR ALAN, lawyer; b. NYC, Dec. 2, 1945; s. George and Delys L.; m. Jane Ficocella, Dec. 30, 1972; 1 child, Eva B. BA, Yale U., 1967; JD, Columbia U., 1970, MBA, 1971. Bar: N.Y. 1971. Assoc. Webster, Sheffield, Fleischmann, Hitchcock & Brookfield, NYC, 1971-72; asst. to divsn. counsel Liggett & Myers, Inc., NYC, 1973; assoc. Wickes, Riddell, Bloomer, Jacobi & McGuire, NYC, 1974-78, Morgan, Lewis & Bockius, NYC, 1979; ptnr. Eaton & Van Winkle, NYC, 1980—94, DeForest & Duer, NYC, 1994-99, Lamb & Barnosky, Melville, 1999—. Mem. ABA, Assn. of Bar of City of N.Y. Avocation: gardening. Home: 103 Brooksite Dr Smithtown NY 11787-4456 Office: Lamb & Barnosky 534 Broadhollow Rd Melville NY 11747 Office Phone: 631-694-2300. Business E-Mail: aal@lambbarnosky.com.

LANE, BARBARA MILLER (BARBARA MILLER-LANE), humanities educator; b. NYC, Nov. 1, 1934; d. George Ross Rede and Gertrude Miller; m. Jonathan Lane, Jan. 28, 1956; children: Steven Gregory, Eleanor. BA, U. Chgo., 1953, Barnard Coll., NYC, 1956; MA, Radcliffe Coll., Cambridge, Mass., 1957; PhD, Harvard U., Cambridge, 1962. Tutor history and lit. Harvard U., Cambridge, Mass., 1960-61; lectr. to prof. history Bryn Mawr Coll., Pa., 1962-75, dir. Growth and Structure of Cities Program, 1971-89, Andrew W. Mellon prof. humanities, 1981-99, Katherine McBride prof., 1999—2005, dir. grad. group in archaeology, classics and history of art, 2004. Vis. prof. architecture Columbia U., 1989; cons. NEH sr. fellowships, Washington, 1971-73, Time-Life Books, NYC, 1975; advisor Macmillan Ency. of Architects, NYC, 1979-82; vis. examiner U. Helsinki, 1991; vis. lectr. Technische Universität, Berlin, 1991, Royal Inst. Tech., Stockholm, 2002. Author: (books) Architecture and Politics in Germany, 1968, 1985, National Romanticism and Modern Architecture in Germany and the Scandinavian Countries, 2000, Housing and Dwelling, 2006; co-author: Nazi Ideology Before 1933, 1978; contbg. author: books Growth and Transformation of the Modern City, 1979; author (contbg.): Macmillan Encyclopedia of Architects, 1982, Urbanisierung im 19. und 20. Jahrhundert, 1983, Perspectives in American History, 1984, The Evidence of Art: Images and Meaning in History, 1986, Art and History, 1988, Nationalism in the Visual Arts, 1991, Moderne Architektur in Deutschland: Expressionismus und Neue Sachlichkeit, 1994, Ultra terminum vagari: Scritti in onore di Carl Nylander, 1997, Oxford Companion to Architecture, 2006; contbg. editor: Urbanism Past and Present, 1980—85; mem. editl. bd. Archtl. History Found., 1988—, Ctrl. European History, 1992—97; contbr. articles to profl. jours. Co-founder, dir., chmn. bd. dirs. New Gulph Child Care Ctr., Bryn Mawr, 1971-75; mem. Mid. Atlantic Regional Com., Mellon Fellowships in the Humanities, 1985-87; mem. vis. com. Harvard U. Dept. History, 1986-92, Berlin Stadtforum (adv. coun. to Senator for Urban Devel. and Environment), 1991-96; mem. nat. screening com. Inst. Internat. Edn., 1999-2004; mem. com. NEH sr. fellowships, 2002. Recipient Lindback award for excellence in tchg., 1988, medal of honor U. Helsinki, 1996; fellow AAUW, 1959-60, Fels Found., 1961-62, Am. Coun. Learned Socs., 1967-68, Guggenheim Found., 1977-78, Sr. fellow Ctr. for Advanced Study in Visual Arts, Nat. Gallery Art, Washington, 1983; Am. Scandinavian Found. fellow, 1989, Wissenschaftskolleg zu Berlin fellow, 1990-91; NEH grantee, 1989; NEH sr. fellow, 1998; emeritus fellow Mellon Found., 2005-07. Mem. Soc. Archtl. Historians (bd. dirs. 1977-80, Alice Davis Hitchcock award 1968, chmn. awards coms. 1976, 82, chmn. jour. com. 1982-83), Conf. Group on Ctrl. European History (bd. dirs. 1977-79, chmn. awards com. 1987), Am. Hist. Assn. (mem. coun. 1979-82, chmn. com. on Popular Mag. of History 1982), Coll. Art Assn., Phi Beta Kappa. Office: Bryn Mawr Coll Bryn Mawr PA 19010

LANE, BRUCE STUART, lawyer; b. New London, Conn., May 15, 1932; s. Stanley S. and Frances M. (Antis) L.; m. Ann Elizabeth Steinberg, Aug. 10, 1958; children: Sue Ellen, Charles M., Richard I. Student, Boston U., 1948-49; AB magna cum laude, Harvard U., 1952, JD, 1955. Bar: Ohio 1955, D.C. 1966, U.S. Ct. Claims 1960, U.S. Tax Ct. 1961, U.S. Supreme Ct. 1961. Assoc. Squire, Sanders & Dempsey, Cleve., 1955-59; sr. trial atty. tax div. Dept. Justice, Washington, 1959-61; tax atty. Dinsmore, Shohl, Barrett, Coates & Deupree, Cin., 1961-65; sec., asst. gen. counsel corp. and tax matters Communications Satellite Corp., Washington, 1965-69; v.p., gen. counsel Nat. Corp. Housing Partnerships, Washington, 1969-70; pres. Lane and Edson P.C., Washington, 1970-89; ptnr. Kelley Drye & Warren, Washington, 1989-93, Peabody & Brown, Washington, 1993-99, Nixon Peabody LLP, Washington, 1999-2000, sr. counsel, 2001—. Co-editor-in-chief Housing and Devel. Reporter; author publs. and articles on tax, partnership and real estate. Prin., All About Wine, LLC 2000-; incorporator, bd. dirs., past pres. D.C. Inst. Mental Health; past chmn. citizens Com. sect. 5 Chevy Chase, Md.; past mem. Montgomery County Hist. Preservation Commn., Md.; mem. nat. coun. Smithsonian Nat. Mus. of the Am. Indian; trustee The Round House Theatre, Bethesda, Md.; mem. chmn. coun. Crow Canyon Archaeol. Ctr., Cortez, Colo. Maj. JAG, USAR, 1952-68. Mem.: ABA, Anglo-Am. Real Property Inst., Am. Coll. Real Estate Lawyers (pres. 1986—87), Am. Law Inst., Phi Beta Kappa. Office: Nixon Peabody LLP 401 9th St NW Ste 900 Washington DC 20004-2134 Office Phone: 202-585-8777. Business E-Mail: blane@nixonpeabody.com.

LANE, CARRIE BELLE (HAIRSTON), retired music educator; b. Columbus, Ohio, Nov. 12, 1936; d. Samuel Arthur and Carrie Belle Hairston; m. LeRoy Elsworth Lane, June 27, 1964; children: Peter Kevin, Samuel Elsworth, Todd Lucien. BS in Edn., Ohio State U., 1960. Cert. music tchr. Ohio, Wash., N.J., 1960. Music tchr. Ctrl. Local Schs., Farmer, Ohio, 1961—64, Cleve. Pub. Schs., 1964—66, Clover Pk. Pub. Schs., Tacoma, 1969, Columbus Pub. Schs., 1968—69, Mt. Laurel Pub. Schs., NJ, 1967, Pemberton Twp. Schs., NJ, 1974—77, Willingboro Pub. Schs., NJ. Pvt. voice and piano tchr., Willingboro, 1977—2002, Delanco, NJ, 2004—; presenter in field. Dir.: Messiah, 2005. Charter mem. and sec., v.pres. Willingboro Chpt. NAACP, 1977—88; mem. adv. bd. for Burlington County mentally ill and their families Cath. Charities, 2005—; mem. Arthritis Found. Walk, Alpha Kappa Alpha, 2007; v.p. Willingboro Dem. Com., 1982; pres. Willingboro Zoning Bd. of Adjust., 1978—94; committeewoman dist. 26 Willingboro Dem. Club, 1992—94; sr. choir soloist and dir. Willingboro Presbyn. Ch., 1977—90; soloist and asst. dir. Christ Bapt. Ch. Sr. Choir, Burlington, NJ, 1991—; dir. Messiah Christ Bapt. Ch., Burlington, NJ, 2006. Recipient Cmty. and Edn. award, Willingboro NAACP, 1982, Ft. Dix Mil. Wife of the Yr., Ft. Dix Post Comdr. and Cmty., 1974, Edn. award, Nat. Orgn. Black Law Enforcement, Camden, NJ, 1992, Edn. plaque, Camden/Phila. chpt. The Hairston Clan, Inc., 2002, Edn. and Cmty. award, Nothing But the Word Deliverance Ch., Florence, NJ, 2002, Retirement cert., NJ Senate and Assembly, WEA, Willingboro Bd. Edn., 2002. Mem.: Nat. Alliance for the Mentally Ill-Family and Consumer Exch., N.J. Ret. Edn. Assn., NEA Ret. Tchrs. (assoc.), N.J. Edn. Assn. (assoc.; union rep. jr. hs 2001—02), Alpha Kappa Alpha (assoc.; charter mem. treas. 1978—, philactor 2006—, corres. sec., asst. sec., parliamentarian, mem. Pearls Ensemble Theta Pi Omega chpt. 2006). Democrat-Npl. Baptist. Avocations: reading, travel, singing, teaching, directing. Home: 11 Shipps Way Delanco NJ 08075 Office Phone: 856-764-0428. Personal E-mail: chlane29@comcast.net.

LANE, CHARLOTTE R., federal official, lawyer; b. 1948; 1 child, Hatton Lane. AB, Marshall U., 1966—69; JD, W.Va. U., 1969—72. Bar: W.Va. 1972. Mem. W.Va. House of Delegates, 1978—80, 1984, 1990—92; interim US atty. (So. dist.) W. Va. US Dept. State, 1987; commr. W.Va. Pub. Svc. Commn., 1985—89, 1997—2003, chmn., 1997—2001; commr. US Internat. Trade Comm., Washington, 2004—. Mem. W.Va. Bar Assn. (pres.-elect), Charleston Chamber of Commerce (bd. dirs.), Charleston Rotary (bd. dirs.), former mem. W. Va. Ho. Del., 1978-80, chmn. Public Svc. Commn. 1997-2001 Office: US Internat Trade Comm 500 E St SW Washington DC 20436 Office Phone: 202-205-2000.

LANE, CORNELL D., psychology professor, director; s. William S. and Thelma Lane; m. Hattie R. Boleyjack, Dec. 27, 1963; children: Monique Lane Brasfield, Angela. BS, Tenn. State U., Nashville, 1962, MS, 1965; EdD, U.Tenn., Knoxville, 1976. Lic. sch. psychologist Tenn., 1964, psychol. examiner Tenn., cert. secondary tchr. Tenn., spl. edn. tchr. grades K-12 Tenn., crisis prevention intervention instr. Sch. psychologist Metro Nashville Pub. Sch. Bd., 1965—76, coord. PPS teams, 1976—77, coord. of pschology services, 1977—81; assoc. prof. Tenn. State U., Nashville, 1992—. Adj. prof. George Peabody Coll., Nashville, 1977—78; hearing officer Tenn. State Edn., Nashville, 1980—84; adv. bd. Genesis Learning Ctr., Nashville, Inst. Learning Rsch. Inc., Nashville, bd. dirs., Genesis Learning Ctr., Nashville; bd. mem. Bill Wilkerson Speech & Hearing Clinic, Nashville; tchg. asst. ednl. psychology U. Tenn., Knoxville; book reviewer Jour. Psycholoeducational Assessement, Knoxville, Tenn.; improvement planning com. Metro Schools Pupil Pers., Nashville; critique Tennessean Newspaper, Nashville. Prodr.: (film documentary sch. psychology) Role and Function of the School Psychologist (Program Designer and Pub. award, 1972); contbr. alumni. Recipient Founders Day Alumni award, Tenn. State U. Alumni, 1972, Changing Lives award, George Peabody Coll., Vanderbilt U., 2003; grantee, US Dept. Edn., 1999—2002, Inst. on Spl. Edn., Tenn. State Dept. Edn., 1996—2007, 1996—2006. Mem.: APA, NASP (charter mem. 1969, nat. cert. sch. psychologist, southeastern dist. dir., chairperson planning and devel. com., mem. con. com., mem. adv. bd., com. mme. std. rev., folio reviewer), NEA (life), Alpha Phi Alpha. Home: 3951 Kings Ln Nashville TN 33721-146 Office: Tennessee State University 3500 John Merritt Blvd AWC 134 Nashville TN 37209 Home Phone: 615-876-3033; Office Phone: 615-963-7290.

LANE, DIANE, actress; b. NYC, Jan. 22, 1965; d. Burt Lane and Colleen Farrington; m. Christopher Lambert, Oct. 1988 (div. Mar. 1994); 1 child, Eleanor; m. Josh Brolin, Aug. 14, 2004. Actress: (stage prodns.) Medea, 1972, Agamemnon, 1977, The Cherry Orchard, 1977, Runaways, 1978, Electra, The Trojan Woman, As You Like it, The Good Woman of Setzuan, (films) A Little Romance, 1979 (Young Artist Award for best juvenile actress motion picture, 1980), Cattle Annie and Little Britches, 1981, National Lampoon Goes to the Movies, 1981, Six Pack, 1982, Ladies and Gentlemen, The Fabulous Stains, 1982, The Outsiders, 1983, Rumble Fish, 1983, The Cotton Club, 1984, Streets of Fire, 1984, Lady Beware, 1987, The Big Town, 1987, Vital Signs, 1990, Chaplin, 1992, Knight Moves, 1992, Indian Summer, 1993, Wild Bill, 1995, Judge Dredd, 1995, Jack, 1996, Mad Dog Time, 1996, The Only Thrill, 1997, Murder at 1600, 1997, Over the Moon, 1998, GunShy, 1998, A Walk on the Moon, 1999, The Setting Sun, 1999, My Dog Skip, 1999, The Perfect Storm, 2000, Hard Ball, 2001, The Glass House, 2001, Unfaithful, 2002 (Acad. Award nomination for best actress, 2003, Golden Satellite award for best actress, 2003, Nat. Soc. of Film Critics award for best actress, 2003, NY Film Critics Circle award for best actress, 2003), Under the Tuscan Sun, 2003, Fierce People, 2005, Must Love Dogs, 2005, Hollywoodland, 2006; (TV movies) Child Bride of Short Creek, 1981, Miss All-America Beauty, 1982; (TV miniseries) Lonesome Dove, 1989, The World's Oldest Living Confederate Widow Tells All, 1994, A Streetcar Named Desire, 1995, Grace and Glorie, 1998. Named Actress of Yr., Hollywood Film Festival, 2003. Mem. Actors' Equity Assn., AFTRA. Office: The Endeavor Agy 9601 Wilshire Blvd Beverly Hills CA 90212

LANE, DOROTHY SPIEGEL, preventive medicine physician; b. Bklyn., Feb. 17, 1940; d. Milton Barton and Rosalie (Jacobson) Spiegel; m. Bernard Paul Lane, Aug. 5, 1962; children: Erika, Andrew, Matthew. BA, Vassar Coll., 1961; MD, Columbia U., 1965, MPH, 1968. Diplomate Am. Bd. Preventive Medicine, Am. Bd. Family Practice. Resident in preventive medicine NYC Dept. Health Dist., 1966-68, project dir. children and youth project Title V, HHS Rockaway, 1968-69; med. cons. Maternal and Child Health Svc. HHS, Rockville, Md., 1970-71; asst. prof. preventive medicine Sch. Medicine SUNY, Stony Brook, 1971-76, assoc. prof., 1976-92, prof., 1992—2002, Disting. Svc. prof., 2002—, assoc. dean, 1986—; chair dept. cmty. medicine, dir. med. edn. Brookhaven Meml. Hosp. Med. Ctr., Patchogue, NY, 1972-86. Contbr. articles to profl. jours. Exec. com. LI divsn. Am. Cancer Soc., 1975—96, pres. LI divsn., 1982, mem. nat. assembly, 1996—2001, nat. bd. dir., 1994—96; corp. mem. Nassau Suffolk Health Sys. Agy, 1977—97; bd. dir. Cmty. Health Plan Suffolk, Hauppauge, NY, 1986—91. Grantee, HHS-USPHS, 1977—2002, 2004—, Nat. Cancer Inst., 1987—, Nat. Heart, Lung and Blood Inst., 1994—, Ctrs. for Disease Control, 2005—. Fellow: APHA, Am. Bd. Preventive Medicine (trustee 1991—2000, chair 1998—2000), NY Acad. Medicine, Am. Acad. Family Physicians, Am. Coll. Preventive Medicine (regent 1988—96, sec.-treas. 1994—96, pres.-elect 1998—2001, pres. 2001—03, immediate past pres. 2003—05, past pres. 2005—07), Assn. Tchrs. Preventive Medicine (pres. 1996—98); mem.: Accreditation Coun. for Continuing Med. Edn. (bd. dirs. 2002—06, exec. commn. 2005—06). Office: SUNY at Stony Brook Sch Medicine Health Scis Ctr L2 Rm 142 Stony Brook NY 11794-8222 Home Phone: 631-751-9471; Office Phone: 631-444-2094. Business E-Mail: dorothy.lane@stonybrook.edu.

LANE, ELIZABETH ANN, genealogist, researcher; b. Horton, Kans., Mar. 9, 1957; d. Dale D. Sheets and Marlene E. Kletchka; m. Rex L. Lane; children: Laura, Catherine. BSW, U. Kans., 1983. Dir. CASA, Atchison, Kans., 1997—98; asst. dir. Juvenile Intake and Assessment, Oskaloosa, Kans., 1998—2001. Mem.: AAUW, Atchison Preservation Alliance (bd. dirs. 1999—2001, treas., bd. dirs. 2004—05), Friends Atchison Libr. (pres. 2001—03), Atchison County Hist. Soc. (bd. dirs. 1998—2002, pres. 2001—02). Avocations: gardening, reading, music, travel. Home: EA Lane Rsch Svcs 841 S Fourth St Atchison KS 66002-2904 Office Phone: 913-426-1981. Personal E-mail: ealane39@allegiarce.tv.

LANE, FIELDING H., lawyer; b. Kansas City, Mo., May 6, 1926; s. Ralph Fielding and Nancy Lee (Greene) L.; m. Patricia Cecil Parkhurst, Jan. 25, 1980 BS in Bus. Adminstrn., U. Mo.-Columbia, 1948; LL.B. cum laude, Harvard U., 1951. Bar: Mo. 1951, Calif. 1956. Assoc. Watson Ess Marshall & Enggas, Kansas City, Mo., 1951-55; assoc. Thelen Marrin Johnson & Bridges, San Francisco, 1955-66, ptnr., 1967—95. Served with USN, 1944-46; PTO; lt. comdr. Res. (ret.) Home: PO Box 1495 Aptos CA 95001-1495 Office: Thelen Reid Brown Raysman & Steiner LLP 101 2d St Ste 1800 San Francisco CA 94105 Office Phone: 415-371-1200. Business E-Mail: fhlane@thelenreid.com.

LANE, GLORIA JULIAN, foundation administrator; b. Chgo., Oct. 6, 1932; d. Coy Berry and Katherine (McDowell) Julian; m. William Gordon Lane (div. Oct. 1958); 1 child, Julie Kay Rosewood. BS in Edn., Cen. Mo. State U., 1958; MA, Bowling Green State U., 1959; PhD, No. Ill. U., 1972. Cert. tchr. Assoc. prof. William Jewell Coll., Liberty, Mo., 1959-60; chair forensic div. Coral Gables (Fla.) High Sch., 1960-64; assoc. prof. No. Ill. U., DeKalb, 1964-70; prof. Elgin (Ill.) Community Coll., 1970-72; owner, pub. Lane and Assocs, Inc., San Diego, 1972-78; prof. Nat. U., San Diego, 1978-90; pres., chief exec. officer Women's Internat. Ctr., San Diego, 1982—. Founder, dir. Living Legacy Awards, San Diego, 1984—. Author: Project Text for Effective Communications, 1972, Project Text for Executive Communication, 1980, Positive Concepts for Success, 1983; editor Who's Who Among San Diego Women, 1984, 85, 86, 90—, Systems and Structure, 1984. Named Woman of Accomplishment, Soroptimist Internat., 1985, Pres.'s Coun. San Diego, 1986, Center City Assn., 1986, Bus. and Profl. Women, San Diego, 1991, Woman of Yr., Girls' Clubs San Diego, 1986, Woman of Vision, Women's Internat. Ctr., 1990, Wonderwoman 2000 Women's Times Newspaper, 1991; recipient Angel in Action award, 1999, Independence award Ctr. for Disabled, 1986, Founder's award Children's Hosp. Internat., Washington, 1986, Making Difference for Women award, Soroptimist Internat., 1998, Women Who Mean Business Courage Award San Diego Bus. Jour., 1998. Avocations: computers, painting, writing. Home and Office: 6202 Friars Rd Unit 311 San Diego CA 92108-5000 E-mail: gloria311@aol.com.

LANE, H. CLIFFORD, internist; b. Detroit, June 15, 1950; s. Henry Talbot Lane, Jr. and Clara Elizabeth Lane; m. Linda Susan Scott, May 16, 1998; children: Rebecca Triantis, Chelsea Edwards, Emily Judith, Claire Elizabeth. BS, U. Mich., Ann Arbor, 1972; MD, U. Mich., 1976. Diplomate Am. Bd. Internal Medicine with subspecialties in allery and immunology and infectious diseases. Resident in internal medicine U. Mich., Ann Arbor, 1976—79; clin. assoc. NIAID/NIH, Bethesda, Md., 1979—82, sr. investigator lab. immuno-regulation, 1982—, clin. dir., 1991—. Contbr. over 233 articles to profl. jours. Recipient DSM, USPHS. Fellow: Infectious Diseases Soc. Am.; mem.: ACP, Internat. Assn. Physicians AIDS Care, Inst. Scientific Info., Inst. Medicine Nat. Acad. Scis., Assn. Am. Physicians. Achievements include invention of co-inventor use of IL-2 in HIV infection. Office: National Institutes of Health Bldg 10/Rm 4-1479 Bethesda MD 20892 Office Phone: 301-496-7196.

LANE, HANA UMLAUF, editor; b. Stockholm, Mar. 14, 1946; came to U.S., 1951, naturalized, 1957; d. Karel Hugo Antonin and Anatolia (Spitel) Umlauf; m. John Richard Lane, Feb. 16, 1980; 1 stepchild, Matthew John AB magna cum laude, Vassar Coll., 1968; AM in Russian and East European Studies, Yale U., 1970. Asst. to exec. editor Newspaper Enterprise Assn., NYC, 1970-72, sr. asst., asst. editor World Almanac divsn., 1972-75, assoc. editor World Almanac, 1975-80, spl. project editor, 1977-80; editor World Almanac and World Almanac Publs., NYC, 1980-85; editor in chief Pharos Books, NYC, 1984-91, sr. editor, 1991-93, John Wiley & Sons, 1993—. Editor: World Almanac Book of Who, 1980, World Almanac and Book of Facts, 1981-85; editor: (with others) The Woman's Almanac, 1977. Democrat. Home: 140 Fairview Ave Stamford CT 06902-8040 Business E-Mail: hlane@wiley.com.

LANE, HOLLY DIANA, artist; b. Cleve., Sept. 13, 1954; d. Edwin Joseph and Ursula Anna (Neustadt) Selyem; m. L.A. Lane, Apr. 20, 1975. AA in 2-Dimensional Art, Cuesta Coll., San Luis Obispo, Calif., 1982; BFA with great distinction, San Jose State U., 1986, MFA in Pictorial Art, 1988. One-woman shows include Ivory/Kimpton Gallery, San Francisco, 1989, Rutgers Barclay Gallery, Santa Fe, 1990, Bingham Kurts Gallery, Memphis, 1992, (solo survey show with catalog) Art Mus. S.E. Tex., Beaumont, 1995, Natalie & James Thompson Gallery, San Jose State U., 2001, Yellowstone Art Museum, 2001, Lyman Allyn Mus. Art, 2001, Schmidt Bingham Gallery, NYC, 1991, 93, 95, 97, 99, 2001, Forum Gallery, NYC, 2003, 06(with catalog); exhibited in group shows at Eiteljorg Mus., Indpls., 1995, 00, Yerba Buena Ctr. for the Arts, San Francisco, 1994, Knoxville (Tenn.) Mus. Art, 1993-94, Fine Arts Ctr. U. RI, Kingston, 1992, Contemporary Mus., Honolulu, 1993, 02, Boise (Idaho) Art Mus., 1994, Castle Gallery-Coll. New Rochelle, NY, 1996, Kennedy Mus. Am. Art, Athens, Ohio, 1996, Calif. Ctr. for the Arts Escondido Mus., 1996, Samuel P. Harn Mus., U. Fla., Gainesville, 1996, Whitney Mus. Am. Art, Champion, Conn., 1997-98, Arnot Art Mus., Elmira, NY, 1997-98, Susan H. Arnold Art Gallery Lebanon Valley Coll., Anneville, Pa., 1997-98, Pelham (NY) Art Ctr, 1998, Art Mus. Western Va., 1999-00, San Jose Mus. Art, 1999-2000, Santa Cruz Art Mus., 2000, Brevard Mus. Art and Sci., Melbourne, Fla., 2000, Gallery of Contemporary Art, Sacred Heart U., Fairfield, Conn., 2002, NJ Ctr. For Visual Arts, Summit, 2002, Javitz Ctr., NYC, 2002, Forum Gallery, NYC, 2002, 04, 05, 06, 07, Internat. Art and Design Fair, NYC, 2004, San Francisco Internat. Art Exposition, 2005, N.Y. 7th Regiment Armory, 2005, 07, Palm Beach, Palm Beach County Conv. Ctr., Fla., 2006, Forum Gallery, LA, 2006, Art 20, The Pk. Armory, NYC, 2006, 07, others; represented in permanent collections Art Mus. S.E. Tex., Contemporary Mus., Honolulu, A.R.A. Svcs., Phila., Dow Jones & Co., NYC, Detroit Zool. Gardens, Prin. Fin. Group, Des Moines, IDS, Mpls., Memphis Cancer Ctr., Seven Bridges Found., Greenwich, Conn.; works reproduced in books, mags., calendars, jours., including ARTNews, Art in America, NY Times, NY Sun, 2003, 06, NY Press, Notre Dame Rev., 2007, Where NY, Art Papers, Art & Antiques, New Yorker Mag., Artweek, Christian Sci. Monitor, Pvt. Arts, Forensic Examiner, NYarts Mag., The Wilson Quar., Review Mag., NYC, 1999, Women Artists calendar 1996-98, San Raphael, Calif., The Sciences, NY Acad. Scis., 1992-93, (textbook) Artist and Audience, (London) 1996, Dreams 1900-00, CAA News, 2003: Sci., Art and the Unconscious Mind (book), 1999, Wilson Quar., 1998, Rev. Mag., 1999, Dreamworks: Twentieth-Century Artistic and Psychological Perspectives, 1999; works presented in TV documentaries including Welcome to Nocturnia, 1993, Women in Art, Time-Warner, Manhattan Cable, NYC, 1993-94; in books accompanying TV show Bill Moyers Genesis, A Living Tradition, PBS, 1996, Healing and the Mind, 1993. Named Alumna of Yr., Cuesta Coll., 1992; pres.'s scholar San Jose State U., 1986, Johanna Rietz scholar Art Assn. of Morro Bay, Calif., 1981. Mem. Coll. Art Assn. Avocations: nature walks, reading. Studio: 182 Brian Ln Santa Clara CA 95051 Office Phone: 212-355-4545. Personal E-mail: hlane42@earthlink.net.

LANE, JAMES MCCONKEY, retired investment banker; b. Pitts., July 9, 1929; s. Mortimer Bliss and Mary (Knapp) L.; m. Arlyne Ruth Nelson, Dec. 16, 1950; children: James, Theodore, Thomas, Karen, David. BA, Wheaton Coll., 1952; MBA, U. Chgo., 1953; postgrad., NYU, 1956, U. Buffalo, 1960. Credit corr. John Plain & Co., Chgo., 1951; trainee Chase Manhattan Bank, NYC, 1953-55, account mgr. investment adv. divsn., 1955-59, investment officer, 1959-62, 2d v.p., 1962-64, v.p., mgr. corp. pension trust investments, 1964-66, v.p. divsn. exec. pension trust investment divsn., 1966-68, chmn. investment policy com., 1968-78, sr. v.p., investment group exec., 1968-70, exec. v.p. fiduciary investment dept., 1970-78; pres., dir. Chase Investors Mgmt. Corp., NYC, 1972-78; mng. dir. Cyrus J. Lawrence Inc., NYC, 1978-82; sr. v.p., chief investment officer, head trust investment divsn. NBD Bank N.A., Detroit, 1982-94, sr. mgmt., 1984-94; ret., 1994. Bd. dirs. NAIC Growth Fund, Inc., Christian Camps Inc., 1978-, Baseball Chapel Inc., 1994-. Trustee Wheaton Coll., 1971—; chmn. Wheaton Coll. Trust Co., 2000—. Mem. Stone Harbor Golf Club, Boca Raton Resort and Club, Premier Club. Home and Office: 3700 S Ocean Blvd Unit 1006 Highland Beach FL 33487 also: 2 86th St Stone Harbor NJ 08247-1607

LANE, JEFFREY BRUCE, diversified financial services company executive; b. Bklyn., June 25, 1942; s. Murray and Arlene (Avram) L.; m. Nancy Stern, June 24, 1982. BA, NYU, 1964; MBA, Columbia U., 1970. With Shearson Lehman Hutton, NYC, CFO, vice chmn., 1983-84, COO, 1984-87, pres., 1987-90, Primerica Holdings, NYC, 1990-94; vice chmn. Smith Barney Harris Upham & Co. Inc., NYC, 1991—, Smith Barney, Shearson Inc., NYC, Smith Barney, Shearson, Inc., NYC, Travelers Group, Inc.; chief adminstrv. officer Neuberger Berman, NYC, pres. CEO; vice chmn. Lehman Bros.; chmn., CEO Bear Stearns Asset Mgmt. Inc., NYC, 2007—. Former vice chmn. Am. Stock Exchange, chmn. welath and asset divsn., Lehman Bros. Bd. dirs. Woodmere Acad., N.Y., L.I. Jewish Hosp. Served to 1st lt. U.S. Army, 1966-68 Republican. Jewish. Office: Bear Stearns Asset Mgmt Inc 383 Madison Ave New York NY 10179*

LANE, JEFFREY H., lawyer; b. NYC, Apr. 14, 1949; AB, Columbia U., 1970; JD cum laude, Boston U., 1975. Bar: Wis. 1975. With Foley & Lardner, Milw., 1975—96, ptnr.; sr. v.p., gen. counsel, sec. MGIC Investment Corp., 1996—. Mem. ABA, State Bar Wis. Office: MGIC Investment Corp MGIC Plz 250 E Kilbourn Ave PO Box 488 Milwaukee WI 53201-0488 Office Phone: 414-347-6406. Office Fax: 414-347-6696.

LANE, JOAN FLETCHER, academic administrator; b. San Francisco, May 7, 1928; d. Howard French and Kathryn Elizabeth (Kraft) Fletcher; m. Melvin Bell Lane, Feb. 15, 1953; children: Whitney Lane-Miller, Julie Lane-Gay. AB, Smith Coll., 1949. Staff World Affairs Coun. No. Calif., San Francisco, 1949-51, Inst. Internat. Edn., Stanford, Calif., 1952; spl. asst., dean Sch. H&S Stanford U., 1982-93, spl. asst. bd. trustees, 1993—. Bd. dirs. McClatchy Newspapers, Sacramento; dir. The James Irvine Found., San Francisco, 1990-02. Trustee San Francisco Found., 1984-92; trustee Smith Coll., Northampton, Mass., 1978-85, chmn. bd. trustees, 1982-85, v.p. alumnae assn., 1975-78; bd. dirs. Internat. House, U. Calif., Berkeley, 1971-80; pres., assoc. coun. Mills Coll., Oakland, Calif., 1974-78. Recipient John M. Greene award, Smith Coll., 1988, Gold Spike award, Stanford U., 2005. Avocations: hiking, gardening. Home: 99 Tallwood Ct Atherton CA 94027-6431

LANE, JOHN DENNIS, lawyer; b. Norwalk, Conn. s. John J. and Theresa A. (Donnelly) L.; m. Elizabeth J. Galliher, Apr. 28, 1949; children: Elizabeth J., John Dennis, Margaret A., Robert E., Paul G. BS, Georgetown U., 1943, JD, 1948. Bar: D.C. 1948, Conn. 1950. Atty. Office Chief Counsel, Bur. Internal Revenue, Washington, 1948-49; exec. sec. to U.S. Senator Brien McMahon, 1949-50; adminstrv. asst., 1950-52; pvt. practice Washington and Norwalk, 1953-2001; ptnr. Hedrick & Lane, 1954— 82, Wilkes, Artis, Hedrick & Lane, 1982-2000, Wilkes Artis, 2000-2001. Mem. coun. Adminstrv. Conf. U.S., 1961; bd. regents Georgetown U., 1979—. Served to capt. USMCR, 1943-45. Recipient Citation of Merit. Fellow Am. Bar Found.; mem. ABA (chmn. standing com. unauthorized practice of law 1971-73, chmn. standing com. nat. conf. groups 1973-75, D.C. cir. mem. standing com. on fed. judiciary 1984-86, Fed. cir. mem. 1987-90), Fed. Commn. Bar Assn. (pres.-elect 1990, pres. 1991-92, alt. rep. to UN 1997-99), Am. Law Inst., Met. Club, Columbia Country Club (Chevy Chase, Md.). Home: 5045 Van Ness St NW Washington DC 20016-1960

LANE, JOHN RODGER, museum director; b. Evanston, Ill., Feb. 28, 1944; s. John Crandall Lane and Jeanne Marie (Rodger) L. Moritz; m. Inge-Lise Eckmann, 1992. BA, Williams Coll., 1966; MBA, U. Chgo., 1971; AM, Harvard U., 1973, PhD, 1976; DFA (hon.), San Francisco Art Inst., 1995. Asst. dir. Fogg Art Mus., Cambridge, Mass., 1974; exec. asst. to dir., adminstr. curatorial affairs, asst. dir. curatorial affairs Bklyn. Mus., NYC, 1975-80; dir. Carnegie Mus. Art, Pitts., 1980-86, San Francisco Mus. Modern Art, 1987-97; Eugene McDermott dir. Dallas Mus. Art, 1999—. Author: Stuart Davis: Art and Art Theory, 1978; co-editor: Abstract Painting and Sculpture in America, 1927-1944, 1983, Carnegie International, 1985, Dallas Mus. Art 100 Years, 2003, Sigmar Polke: The History of Everything, Paintings, and Drawings, 1998-2003, Gerhard Richert Edits., 1965-2004, Lothar Baumgartern: Carbon, 2004; exec. editor: The Making of a Modern Museum/SFMOMA, 1995. Trustee Fountain Valley Sch., Colorado Springs, 1999—2005. Served to lt. USNR, 1966-69. Nat. Endowment Arts Mus. fellow, 1974-75 Mem. Assn. Art Mus. Dirs. (trustee 2000—02), Am. Assn. Museums. Office: Dallas Mus Art 1717 N Harwood St Dallas TX 75201-2398 Office Phone: 214-922-1304. Business E-Mail: jlane@DallasMuseumofArt.org.

LANE, KATHY S., information technology executive, consumer products company executive; Dir. tech. svcs. Pepsi Cola Internat., 1997—98; mgr. corp. initiatives group Gen. Electric Co., 1998—99, sr. v.p. and chief info. officer, vendor fin. svcs., 1999—2000; gen. mgr. e- bus. and info. tech. Gen. Electric Oil & Gas, 2000—02; sr. v.p. corp. info. tech. and applications Gillette Co., Boston, 2002—, chief info. officer, 2002—. Named one of Premier 100 IT Leaders, Computerworld, 2006. Office: The Gillette Co Prudential Tower Boston MA 02199-8004

LANE, KENNETH JAY, jewelry designer; b. Detroit, Apr. 22, 1932; s. Mack and Beatrice (Holinstat) L. Student, U. Mich., 1951-52; B.F.A., R.I. Sch. Design, 1954. Mem. mdse. art staff Vogue, 1954-55; asst. designer Delman Shoes, NYC, 1956-58; assoc. designer Christian Dior Shoes, NYC, 1958-63; owner Kenneth Jay Lane, Inc., NYC, 1963—. Recipient Coty award, 1967, Harpers Bazaar Internat. award, 1967, Maramodo di Capri Tiberio D'oro award, 1967, Tobe Coburn Award-Spl. Swarowski award, 1967, Neiman Marcus award, 1968 Office: Kenneth Jay Lane Inc 20 W 37th St New York NY 10018-7479

LANE, KENNETH ROBERT, producer, distributor; b. NYC, Dec. 3, 1942; s. Carl Lane and Freda Rosalind; m. Marjory Horowitz, Dec. 1965 (div. 1967); m. Nicole Sloan Helguero (div.); m. Yolanda Natalia Bianco, Mar. 1990; 1 child, Jonathan. BA, CUNY, 1965. Cert. engr. Prodn. mgr. Saul Bass & Assocs., Los Angeles, 1968-70; cameraman, prodn. mgr. Nat. Film Bd. Can., Vancouver, 1970-71; producer, distbr. Troma Inc., NYC, 1976-77; prin. Ken Lane Films, NYC, 1976—; producer, prodn. mgr. Platinum Prodns./Platinum Pictures, NYC, 1977-78, Ganymede Prodns., NYC, 1978-80; cameraman, audio mixer Madison Sq. Garden Network, NYC, 1981-82; tech. dir. Sta. WNET Channel 13 (PBS), NYC, 1983; cameraman Fox Broadcasting Co., Sta. WNYW, NYC, 1981—; audio mixer, engr. ABC, NYC, 1982—, CBS, NYC, 1988—, NBC, NYC, 1991—. Producer/distbr.: (motion pictures) Delora, 1977, Legacy of Horror, 1981, The Navy vs. the Night Monsters, 1981, Women of the Prehistoric Planet, 1981. Treas. Washington Market Community Park, N.Y.C., 1985-86. Mem.: Nat. Ct. Reporters Assn. (cert. legal video specialist), Internat. Brotherhood Elec. Workers, Internat. Brotherhood Elec. Workers, Nat. Assn. Broadcast Engrs. Technicians, Internat. Alliance Theatrical and Stage Employees. Jewish. Avocations: tennis, baseball, golf, art collecting. Office: 80 N Moore St Apt 26G New York NY 10013-2734 Home Phone: 212-732-6004; Office Phone: 917-833-7977. Business E-Mail: kenlaneproductions@earthlink.net.

LANE, LAURA ALICE, retired librarian; b. NYC; d. Cedric R. and Alice J. (Lay) Lane; m. David R. DeVoe; 1 child, Charles. AB, Lake Erie Coll., Painesville, Ohio, 1963; MLS, U. Calif., Berkeley, 1964. Fine arts libr. acquisitions dept. Fogg Art Mus./Harvard U., Cambridge, Mass., 1964-67; humanities cataloger U. Minn., Mpls., 1967-69; head libr. Am. Heritage Pub. Co., NYC, 1969-82; ref. libr. Mt. Sinai Sch. Medicine, NYC, 1983-87; bibliographer Temple U., Phila., 1991—2000, sci. libr., 2000—07; ret., 2007. Mem. ALA.

LANE, LAURENCE WILLIAM, JR., retired ambassador, publisher; b. Des Moines, Nov. 7, 1919; s. Laurence William and Ruth (Bell) L.; m. Donna Jean Gimbel, Apr. 16, 1955; children: Sharon Louise, Robert Laurence, Brenda Ruth. Student, Pomona Coll., 1938-40, LLD (hon.), 1976; BJ, Stanford U., 1942; DHL (hon.), Hawaii Loa Coll., 1991. Chmn. bd. Lane Pub. Co.; pub. Sunset Mag., Sunset Books and Sunset Films; U.S. amb. to Australia and Nauru, 1985-89; ret., 1990. Bd. dirs. Calif. Water Svc. Co., Crown Zellerbach Corp., Pacific Gas and Electric Co.; bd. dirs. Time Inc.; bd. dirs. Oreg. Coast Aquarium, Internat. Bd. Advice, ANZ Bank; U.S. amb. and commr. Gen. Worlds Fair, Japan, 1975-76; hon. fellow Coll. Notre Dame, 1974. Former mem. adv. bd. Sec. Interior's Bd. Nat. Parks; mem. adv. coun. Grad. Sch. Bus., Stanford U., SRI; mem. Pres.'s Nat. Productivity Adv. Com.; mem. Pacific Basin Econ. Coun.; former bd. dirs. Pacific Forum, CSI, Nat. Parks Found.; vol. The Nat. Ctr.; mem. bd. overseers Hoover Instn. War, Revolution and Peace; mem. exec. com. Ctr. for Australian Studies, U. Tex., Austin. Lt. USNR, World War II, PTO. Decorated officer Order of Australia; recipient Conservation Svc. award Sec. Interior; Theodore and Conrad Wirth award NPF, 1994; Wiliam Penn Mott Jr. Conservationist of Yr. award NPCA, 1995; named hon. prof. journalism Stanford U. Mem. Newcomen Soc. N.Am., Pacific Asia Travel Assn. (life mem., chmn. 1980-81), Coun. of Am. Ambs., Los Rancheros Vistadores, Advt. Club San Francisco, No. Calif. Alumni Assn., Bohemian Club, Pacific Union, Men's Garden Club L.A., Alpha Delta Sigma. Republican. Presbyterian. Office: 3000 Sand Hill Rd Bldg 215 Menlo Park CA 94025-7113

LANE, LAWRENCE JUBIN, retired electrical engineer, consultant; b. Morganton, NC, Feb. 19, 1927; s. Lawrence and Sarah Virginia (Jubin) Lane; m. Gladys Verna Lee Hock, Dec. 25, 1947 (dec. 1975); children: Priscilla Gayle, Richard Jubin; m. Helen Elizabeth Sollazzo, Dec. 19, 1975. B.E.E., N.C. State Coll., 1950; MSE.E., U. Va., 1972. Lic. profl. engr., Va. Engr. GE, Schenectady, NY, 1950-54, class supr. Phila., 1954-55, devel. engr. Waynesboro, Va., 1955-63, sr. devel. engr., 1963-78, sr. systems design engr. Roanoke, Va., 1978-83, cons. engr., 1983-95; ret., 1995. Patentee in field. Pres. Stuarts Draft PTA, Va., 1960, 61. Served as petty officer USN, 1944-46, 50-51. Recipient Managerial award Gen. Electric Co., 1965 Fellow IEEE (chpt. chmn. 1982-83); mem. Eta Kappa Nu, Tau Beta Pi, Phi Eta Sigma, Phi Kappa Phi. Methodist. Home and Office: 1601 Chatham Rd Waynesboro VA 22980-3203 Office Phone: 540-943-7502. Personal E-mail: juhelane@comcast.net. *Since my occupational accomplishments have been judged to be noteworthy, I am indeed fortunate. I thank God and Jesus Christ for my abilities and for the opportunities for such accomplishments.*

LANE, MARGARET ANNA SMITH, property manager, real estate developer; b. Aspinwall, Pa., Nov. 26, 1918; d. Max Charles and Mary Ann (Jones) Smith; m. Frank A. Lane, Jr., Feb. 7, 1954; 1 child, Alan Michael. AB, UCLA, 1940; MS, U. So. Calif., 1949. Cert. secondary tchr. Calif. Demonstration and tng. tchr. UCLA, U. Calif., Northridge, 1948—74; pvt. practice Cottonwood, Ariz., 1975—. Tchr., dept. chmn. LA City Schs., 1948—74; sec.-treas. Silver Hoof, Inc., Sedona, Ariz., Stone Pine Gallery, Ltd., Sedona. Mem.: Pi Gamma Mu. Avocations: Native American cultures, art. Home: PO Box 4289 West Sedona AZ 86340-4289

LANE, MARK, lawyer, educator, writer; b. NYC, Feb. 24, 1927; s. Harry Arnold and Elizabeth Lane; m. Patricia Ruth Erdner, 1987; children: Anne-Marie, Christina. LLB, Bklyn. Law Sch., 1951. Bar: N.Y. 1951, D.C. 1995. Mng. mem. The Lane Law Firm; pvt. practice, 1952—; founder Mid-Harlem Community Parish Narcotics Clinic, 1953, East Harlem Reform Dem. Club, 1959; prof. law Cath. U., Washington, 1975—76. Founder and dir. Citizens Commn. Inquiry; founder Wounded Knee Legal Def.-Offense Com., 1973, The Covered Wagon, Mountain Home, Idaho, 1971. Author: (books) Rush to Judgment, 1966, A Citizen's Dissent, 1968, Chicago Eye-Witness, 1969, Arcadia, 1970, Conversations with Americans, 1970, Executive Action, 1973, (with Dick Gregory) Code Name Zorro, 1977, The Strongest Poison, 1980, Plausible Denial, 1991, Murder in Memphis, 1993; prodr. films Rush to Judgment, 1967, Two Men in Dallas, 1987, 92; writer, prodr. plays Trial of James Earl Ray, 1978, Plausible Denial, 1992, Winds of Doctrine, 1994; writer, prodr. screenplays, Arcadia, 1992, Slay the Dreamer, 1992, Plausible Denial, 1993; founder publs. Citizens Quar., 1975, Helping Hand, 1971. Mem. N.Y. State Assembly, 1960-62. With AUS, 1945-47. Office: 4 Old Farm Rd Charlottesville VA 22903 Office Phone: 434-293-2349. *I do not believe that our fate is pre-ordained. I do believe that women and men, working together, can determine their own destiny and that the people write their own history. What moves me most directly into action is the fact that I hate bullies. What concerns me the most in contemporary America is the influence of the police and spy organizations with the national news media. Together these are bullies to contemplate and oppose.*

LANE, MARY WINSTON, retired secondary school educator; b. Middlesboro, Ky., Oct. 10, 1923; d. Shelton and Rena (Ward) Evans; m. Richard Alan Lane, Aug. 15, 1965 (dec.); children: Barbara Ann Lane Partin, John Brian BS, Ea. Ky. U., Richmond, 1944; MS in Chemistry, U. Mo., Rolla, 1966; postgrad., Ohio State U., Columbus, 1971—73. Cert. secondary chemistry, math. and physics tchr., Ohio, Ky., gifted and talented tchr., Ky. Chemist med. physics rsch. Donner Lab. U. Calif., Berkeley, 1944—59; tchr., head dept. Bell County H.S., Pineville, Ky., 1959—66; tchr. Ottiville Schs., Ohio, 1969—71, Bath H.S., Lima, Ohio, 1974—79, Middlesboro H.S., Ky., 1979—99; ret., 1999. Prof. Lincoln Meml. U., summers 1988-89, 91; organizer, dir. Southeastern Regional Sci. Fair, 1962-66; organizer Southeastern Alliance Sci. Tchrs., 1991; workshop presenter Chem 93; presenter Woodrow Wilson Workshop, 1993 Recipient Award of Excellence in Tchg. Chemistry for Ky., Am. Chem. Soc., 1995, award for rsch. and tng. Brazilian rschrs. Brazilian Sociol. Soc., 2005; named Tandy tchr., 1992, 93 Mem. NEA, NSTA, Middlesboro Edn. Assn., Ky. Sci. Tchrs. Assn. (state bd. dirs., Disting. Svc. award 1994), Alliance 5th Dist. Sci. and Math. Tchrs. (co-dir. 1989—), Delta Kappa Gamma Democrat. Baptist. Avocations: gardening, designing and building geo solar homes. Home: RR 1 Box 519A Rose Hill VA 24281-9720

LANE, MATTHEW JAY, lawyer; b. Cin., Mar. 6, 1955; s. Joseph Alan and Adele L.; m. Susan Carol. BA, Emory U., 1977; JD, Northwestern U., 1980. Bar: Ohio 1981, U.S. Dist. Ct. (so. dist.) Ohio 1981, U.S. Ct. Appeals (6th cir.) 1981, Fla. 1982, U.S. Ct. Appeals (11th cir.) 1982. Law clk. to chief judge U.S. Dist. Ct. (so. dist.) Ohio, Cin., 1980-82; prin. Matthew Lane & Assocs., P.A., West Palm Beach, Fla. Legal counsel Juvenile Diabetes Found., Cin., 1984-92; legal counsel MADD, 1986-92, pres. S.W. Ohio chpt., 1988-91, pres. Palm Beach County chpt., 1993-95; active Big Bros./Big Sisters Devel. Com., 1985-88. Mem.: South Palm Beach County Bar Assn. (family law com.), Fla. Bar Assn. (family law com.), Palm Beach County Bar Assn. (marital and family law com.), Phi Beta Kappa. Office: 777 S Flagler Dr Ste 800 West West Palm Beach FL 33401 Office Phone: 561-651-7273. Business E-Mail: m.lane@laneandassociates.biz.

LANE, MICHELE JEANNE, special education educator; b. Portland, Oreg., Apr. 25, 1953; d. Robert William and Ann Emeline (Austin) L.; m. Edward Brien McDonough, May 14, 1983; children: Tim, Megan, Justin. AA in Pre-Sch. Edn., College of Marin, 1975; BA in Liberal Studies, Calif. State Coll., 1977; MS in Spl. Edn., Dominican Coll., 1980. Cert. multi-subject tchr., Calif., learning-handicapped specialist, Calif., severely-handicapped specialist, Calif.; bd. cert. ednl. therapist. Pres-sch. tchr. Corte Madera (Calif.) Larkspur Co-op., 1973, Beginning Sch., Marin City, Calif., 1974, Tamalpais Nursery Sch., Mill Valley, Calif., 1975-76; teacher's aide 1st grade Forestville (Calif.) Sch., 1976-77; student tchr. 2d, 3rd and 6th grades Hamilton Sch., Novato, Calif., 1978; tutor Dominican Coll. Learning Ctr., 1978-80; learning disabilities specialist, music and movement instr. Arena Learning Ctr., 1979-82; dir., learning disabilities specialist Lane's Learning Ctr., Novato, 1981—. Intern Magnolia Park Sch., St. Vincent Boys Sch., Casa Allegra; intern speech pathologist Sonoma (Calif.) State Hosp.; developer "Music in Motion" programs Recreation for the Gifted; coord. Red Ribbon Week, Novato, 1992-93. Speaker Morning Star Farm, Novato, 1992. Spl. edn. del. to People's Republic of China with Citizens Ambassador Program Internat., 1994. Mem. Assn. Ednl. Therapists (profl.), Educators in Pvt. Practice (profl.). Avocations: equestrian, gardening, hiking, cross country skiing, dance. Home and Office: Lane's Learning Ctr 1 Gustafson Ct Novato CA 94947-2882 Office Phone: 415-892-7706. Personal E-mail: michlane@aol.com.

LANE, NATHAN (JOSEPH LANE), actor; b. Jersey City, Feb. 3, 1956; Appeared in plays (off-Broadway) A Midsummer Night's Dream, Dedication or the Stuff of Dreams, 2005; Present Laughter, Merlin, The Wind in the Willows, Some Americans Abroad, On Borrowed Time, Guys and Dolls (Tony nomination, Drama Desk and Outer Critics Circle awards), Laughter on the 23rd Floor, A Funny Thing Happened... (Tony, Drama Desk and Outer Critics Circle awards), Love, Valour, Compassion (Drama Desk and Outer Critics Circle awards, Obie award), Love, N.Y.C., 1984, Raving, N.Y.C., 1984, She Stoops to Conquer, N.Y.C., 1984, The Common Pursuit, 1984-85, A Backer's Audition, N.Y.C., 1985, Wind in the Willows, 1985, The Common Pursuit, 1986-87, Claptrap, N.Y.C., 1987, Uncounted Blessings, 1988, The Film Society, 1988, The Lisbon Traviata, 1989 (Drama Desk award best actor 1989), A Pig's Valise, 1989, Some Americans Abroad, 1990, Bad Habits, 1990, Lips Together, Teeth Apart, 1991, On Borrowed Time, 1991, Guys and Dolls, 1992, Laughter on the 23rd Floor, 1993-94, Love! Valor! Compassion!, 1995, A Funny Thing Happened On The Way To The Forum, 1996 (Tony award best actor in a musical, 1996), The Man Who Came to Dinner, The Producers, 2001-02, 2003 (Tony award best actor in a musical, 2001), Trumbo Red White and Blacklisted, 2003, The Frogs, 2004; (TV series) Teacher's Pet, 2000-02 (Daytime Emmy award for Outstanding Performer in an Animated Program 2001); (TV miniseries) Valley of the Dolls, 1981, One of the Boys, 1982, host the 50th anniversary Tony awards show, 1996, Encore!Encore!, 1998-99, Charlie Lawrence, 2003; (films) Ironweed, 1987, The Lemon Sisters, 1990, Joe Versus the Volcano, 1990, He Said, She Said, 1991, Frankie and Johnny, 1991, Life With Mikey, 1993, Addams Family Values, 1993, The Lion King (voice), 1994, The Birdcage, 1996 (SAG and Am. Comedy awards, Golden Globe nomination), The Boys Next Door, 1996, Mouse Hunt, 1997, Merry Christmas, George Bailey, 1997, At First Sight, 1999, Isn't She Great?, 2000, Love's Labour's Lost, 1999, Trixie, 2000,(voice) Stuart Little, 1999, (voice) Titan A.E., 2000, Man Who Came to Dinner, 2000, Laughter on the 23rd Floor, 2001, Nicholas Nickelby, 2002, Stuart Little 2, 2002, Austin Powers in Goldmember, 2002, Teacher's Pet (voice), 2004, Win a Date with Tad Hamilton!, 2004, The Producers, 2005; actor, exec. prodr.: (TV series) Charlie Lawrence, 2003. Named to Hollywood Walk of Fame, 2006. Office: Creative Artists Agy 9830 Wilshire Blvd Beverly Hills CA 90212-1825

LANE, NATHAN, III, lawyer; b. Phila., 1946; AB, Duke U., 1968; JD cum laude, U. Pa., 1971. Bar: Calif. 1972, registered: US Dist. Ct. (No. Dist.) Calif. 1972, US Ct. Appeals (9th cir.) 1972, US Dist. Ct. (So. Dist.) Calif. 1976, US Dist. Ct. (Ctrl. Dist.) Calif. 1980, US Ct. Appeals (10th cir.) 1985, US Dist. Ct. (Ea. Dist.) Calif. 1987, US Ct. Appeals (8th cir.) 1991, US Tax Ct. 1992, US Ct. Appeals (Fed. Cir.) 1997, US Patent & Trademark Office 1999. Ptnr. Graham & James, San Francisco, Squire, Sanders & Dempsey LLP, San Francisco, chmn., Intellectual Property Practice Group. Editl. bd. U. Pa. Law Rev., 1969—71; author: Discovery in Other Nations, 1988. Bd. dir. Legal Aid Soc., San Francisco, 1986—91. Mem.: Bar Assn. San Francisco (chmn. Antitrust Sect. 1988), ABA (Antitrust Sect., Intellectual Property Sect., Internat. Law Sect., Litig. Sect.), Order of Coif. Office: Squire Sanders & Dempsey LLP One Maritime Plaza Ste 300 San Francisco CA 94111-3492 Office Phone: 415-954-0249. Office Fax: 415-393-9887. Business E-Mail: nlane@ssd.com.

LANE, NEAL FRANCIS, physics professor, retired federal agency administrator; b. Oklahoma City, Aug. 22, 1938; s. Walter Patrick and Harietta (Hattie) Charlotte (Hollander) Lane; m. Joni Sue Williams, June 11, 1960; children: Christy Lynn Lane Saydjari, John Patrick. BS, U. Okla., 1960, MS, 1962, PhD, 1964, DHL (hon.), 1995; DSc (hon.), U. Ala., 1994, Mich. State U., 1995; DHL (hon.), Marymount U., Arlington, Va., 1995; DSc (hon.), Ohio State U., 1996, Washington Coll., 1998, Mt. Sinai Sch. Medicine, 1999, U. Colo., 1999, Queen's U., Belfast, No. Ireland, 2000, N.C. State U., 2001, SUNY, 2002; DHL and Sc (hon.), Ill. Inst. Tech., 2000. NSF postdoctoral fellow Queen's U., Belfast, Northern Ireland, 1964—65, Rice U., Houston, asst. prof. physics, 1966—69, assoc. prof., 1969—72, prof. physics and space physics and astronomy, 1972—84, chmn. dept. physics, 1977—82, provost, 1986—93, Malcolm Gillis prof., 2005—; dir. divsn. physics NSF, Washington, 1979—80, dir., 1993—98; chancellor U. Colo., Colorado Springs, 1984—86; asst. to pres. for sci. and tech., dir. Office Sci. and Tech. Policy, Washington, 1998—2001; prof., Dept. Physics and Astronomy, sr. fellow James A. Baker III Inst. Pub. Policy, Rice U., 2001—. Adj. fellow Joint Inst. for Lab. Astrophysics, U. Colo., Boulder, 2001—, vis. fellow, 1965—66, 1975—76; mem. commn. on phys. sci., math. and applications NRC, 1989—93; bd. overseers Superconducting Super Collider (SSC) Univs. Rsch. Assn., 1985—93; disting. Karcher lectr. U. Okla., Norman, 1983; disting. vis. scientist U. Ky., Lexington, 1980; mem. adv. com. math. and phys. sci. NSF, 1992—93; mem. adv. bd. Kavli Inst. Theoretical Physics, U. Calif., Santa Barbara; mem. adv. com. Sci. and Tech. Adv. Group, Taiwan; mem. com. on pub. and govt. affairs Nat. Acads., mem. com. on elementary particle physics. Co-author: Quantum States of Atoms, Molecules and Solids, Understanding More Quantum Physics; contbr. articles to profl. jours. Active Cath. Commn. Intellectual and Cultural Affairs, 1991; trustee U. Corp. Atmospheric Rsch.; Houston Mus. Sci. Recipient George Brown prize for superior teaching, Rice U., 1973—74, 1976—77, Brown Coll. Tchg. award, 1972—73, Disting. Svc. award, Nat. Assn. Biology Tchrs., 1997, Pres.'s award, ASME, 1999, Support Sci. award, Coun. Sci. Soc. Pres., 2000, Pub. Svc. award, Am. Math. Soc., Am. Astron. Soc. and Am. Phys. Soc., 2001; fellow Alfred P. Sloan Found., 1967—71. Fellow: AAAS (Philip Hauge Abelson award 2000, William D. Carey award 2001), Am. Acad. Arts and Sci. (mem. coun.), Am. Phys. Soc. (chmn. divsn. electron and atomic physics 1977—78, exec. com. 1981—83, councilor-at-large 1983); mem.: Am. Assn. Physics Tchrs., Am. Inst. Physics (governing bd. 1984—87), Am. Chem. Soc. (Pub. Svc. award 1999), Sigma Xi (pres.-elect 1992, pres. 1993), Phi Beta Kappa. Roman Catholic. Avocations: tennis, squash. Office: Baker Inst for Pub Policy MS-40 PO Box 1892 Houston TX 77251 Office Phone: 713-348-2925. Office Fax: 713-348-5143. E-mail: neal@rice.edu.

LANE, PENELOPE DIANE, special education educator; d. Frank Owen and June Hagler Adams; m. Edward Robert Lane, July 25, 1987; children: Curtis, Aaron, Samantha. BBA, U. Mary Hardin Baylor, Belton, Tex., 1997; MS, Tarleton State U., Killeen, Tex., 2005. Tchr. Belton Ind. Sch. Dist., 2002—04, spl. edn. counselor, LSSP, 2004—06; LSSP Killeen Ind. Sch. Dist., 2006—. Mem.: Nat. Assn. Sch. Psychologists. Avocations: exercise, reading. Office: Kileen Ind Sch Dist 9 10th St Killeen TX 76541

LANE, RICHARD ALLAN, preventive medicine physician, educator; b. Camp LeJuene, NC, Feb. 5, 1956; s. Howard Allan and Elizabeth Jane (Fischer) L.; m. Cynthia Diane Gastineau, Jan. 7, 1978; children: Tiffany Marie, Laurel Christina. BS, U. Md., 1978, MD, 1982; MPH in Tropical Medicine, Tulane U., 1986. Diplomate Am. Bd. Preventive Medicine. Intern Md. Gen. Hosp., Balt., 1982-83; squadron flight surgeon, 363rd Tactical Fighter Wing USAF, Shaw AFB, 1983-85, resident in aerospace medicine Brooks AFB, 1986-87, advanced through grades to maj., 1983-87; chief aeromed. svcs. Warner Robins Air Logistics Ctr., Robins AFB, 1987-89; staff physician, microbiology instr. Liberty U., Lynchburg, Va., 1989-91, assoc. prof. health scis., 1991—. Cons., spkr. Liberty Godparent Home, Lynchburg, 1989—; mem. residency adv. bd. Meharry Med. Coll., Nashville, Tenn., 1987-89; adj. faculty health sci. Internat. Health Honduras project James Madison U., Harrisonburg, Va., 1993-2000; adj. clin. prof. nurse practitioner program Old Dominion U., 1997-2000; sentinel provider U.S. Influenza Surveillance Network, 2004—; mem. AstaZeneca Spkrs. Bur., 2006—. Contbr. articles to profl. jours. Bd. dirs. Network for Women in Crisis, Lynchburg, 1990-91; exec. bd. Lynchburg chpt. ARC, 1991-93; founder Emmanuel Bapt. Ch., chpt. AWANA, Warner Robins, Ga., 1987-89; trainer Youth at the Crossraods Internat. AIDS Prevention Program, 1996—; med. cons. World Help. Fellow Am. Coll. Preventive Medicine; mem. APHA, Gideons Internat. (camp treas. 1988-89). Republican. Evangelical. Business E-Mail: rlane@liberty.edu.

LANE, ROBERT W., farm equipment manufacturing executive; b. Washington, Nov. 14, 1949; m. Patricia Lane; 3 children. BA with high honors, Wheaton Coll., Ill., 1972; MBA, U. Chgo. Grad. Sch. Bus., 1974. First Nat. Bank Chgo., Europe; various positions Deere & Co., Moline, Ill., 1982—, CFO, sr. v.p. fin./tax/acctg., 1996—98, sr. v.p., mng. dir. mfg. mktg. Europe, Africa, Middle East, 1998—99, pres. worldwide agrl. equip. divn., 1999, pres., COO, 2000, chmn., CEO, 2000—. Bd. dirs. Deere & Co., 2000—, Verizon Communications Inc., 2004—, GE Co., 2005—; trustee Com. for Econ. Devel.; mem. Bus. Roundtable, Bus. Coun. Mem. Nat. Adv. Coun. Figge Art Mus., Iowa. Mem.: Lyric Opera bd. in Chgo. Office: Deere & Co 1 John Deere Rd Moline IL 61265-8098*

LANE, ROBIN R., lawyer; b. Kerrville, Tex., Nov. 28, 1947; d. Rowland and Gloria (Benson) Richards; m. Stanley Lane, Aug. 22, 1971 (div.); 1 child, Joshua; m. Anthony W. Cunningham, Nov. 22, 1980 (div.); 1 child, Alexandra Cunningham. BA in Econs. with honors, U. Fla., Gainesville, 1969; MA, George Wash. U., Washington, DC, 1971; JD, Stetson U., DeLand, Fla., 1978. Bar: Fla. 1979, NY 2001, DC 2002, US Ct. Appeals (11th cir.) 1981, US Supreme Ct. 1986, US Ct. Appeals (DC cir.) 1992, US Ct. Appeals (3d cir.) 1993. Mgmt. trainee internat. banking Gulf Western Industries, NYC; internat. rsch. specialist Ryder Systems, Inc., Miami, 1973, project mgr., 1974; assoc. Wagner, Cunningham, Vaughan & McLaughlin, Tampa, Fla., 1979—85; pvt. practice law, 1985—. Guest lectr. med. jurisprudence Stetson U. Coll. Law, 1982—91, also mem. exec. coun. law alumni bd. Contbr. articles to various revs. Recipient Am. Jurisprudence award-torts, Lawyers Co-op. Fla., 1979; Scottish Rite fellow, 1968—69. Mem.: ATLA, ABA, DC Bar Assn., NY Bar Assn., Fla. Bar Assn., Acad. Fla. Trial Lawyers (mem. com. 1983—84), Fla. Women's Alliance, Omicron Delta Epsilon. Office: 345 Bayshore Blvd #1813 Tampa FL 33606-2388 also: 880 5th Ave 15C New York NY 10021 Office Phone: 917-312-6773, 813-254-4447, 212-794-7270. Personal E-mail: RRL1128@aol.com.

LANE, SHAWN LANARD, journalist, motivational speaker; b. Ennis, Tex., Sept. 11, 1972; s. Edward Charles Lane Sr. and Linda Diane (Giddings) Dorrough. AS, U. Md., 1995; BA in Journalism, U. North Tex., 2000. Salesperson Sears, Dallas, 1989-91; security guard Pinkerton Security, Dallas, 1992-93; credit officer J.C. Penney's, Dallas, 1996-97; news reporter Dallas Examiner, 1996-98, The Writer's Consortium, Dallas, 1998-2001; mktg. specialist Am. Airlines, Dallas, 2001—. Founder Words from Within. With U.S. Army, 1993-96. Recipient Best Sports Feature award Tex. Publ. Assn., 1997, Best Ednl. Feature award, 1997. Mem. NAACP, Nat. Assn. Black Journalists (parliamentarian 1996), Soc. Profl. Journalists, Phi Beta Sigma (historian 1997—, parliamentarian). Democrat. Baptist. Avocations: socializing, reading, writing. E-mail: shawnlanard@hotmail.com.

LANE, SYLVIA, economist, educator; b. NYC; m. Benjamin Lane, Sept. 2, 1939; children: Leonard, Reese, Nancy. AB, U. Calif., Berkeley, 1934, MA, 1936; postgrad., Columbia U., 1937; PhD, U. So. Calif., 1957. Lectr., asst. prof. U. So. Calif., 1947—60; assoc. prof. econs. San Diego State U., 1961-65; assoc. prof. finance, assoc. dir. Ctr. for Econ. Edn. Calif. State U., Fullerton, 1965-69, chmn. dept. fin., 1967-69; prof. agrl. econs. U. Calif., Davis, 1969-82, prof. emerita, 1982—; prof. emerita and economist Giannini Found., U. Calif.-Berkeley, 1982—; vis. scholar Stanford U., 1975-76. Cons. Calif. Adv. Commn. Tax Reform, 1963, Adv. Office Consumer Affairs, Exec. Office of Pres., 1972-77, FAO, UN, 1983, Consumer food Subsidiaries Project, 1993. Author: (with E. Bryant Phillips) Personal Finance, 1963, rev. edit., 1979, The Insurance Tax, 1965, California's Income Tax Conformity and Withholding, 1968, (with Irma Adelman) The Balance Between Industry and Agriculture in Economic Development, 1989; author video: Women in Agriculture - Africa, 1994; editl. bd. Agrl. Econs., 1986-92; also articles, reports in field. Project economist Los Angeles County Welfare Planning Coun., 1956-59; del. White House Conf. on Food and Nutrition, 1969, Pres.'s Summit Con. on Inflation, 1974; mem. adv. com. Ctr. for Bldg. Tech., Nat. Bur. Stds., 1975-79; bd. dirs. Am. Coun. Consumer Interests, 1972-74; exec. bd. Am. Agr. Econ. Assn. 1976-79. Ford Found. fellow UCLA, 1963; Ford Found. fellow U. Chgo., 1965; fellow U. Chgo., 1968; fellow Am. Agrl. Econ. Assn., 1984; fellow Sylvia Lane Fellowship Fund, 1993. Mem. Am. Econ. Assn., Am. Coun. Consumer Interests, Omicron Delta Epsilon (pres. 1973-75, trustee 1975-83, chmn. bd. trustees 1982-84). Home and Office: Pacific Regent - La Jolla 3890 Nobel Dr #1508 San Diego CA 92122 Personal E-mail: blane5@san.rr.com. *Select goals carefully.*

LANE, TED A., music educator, musician; s. Clifford A. and Evelyne Lane. MusB, The Juilliard Sch., 1975, MusM, 1977. Cert. music edn. tchr. Tex., 1998. Prof. music Fla. State U., Tallahassee, 1979—81, U. Nebr., Omaha, 1982—84, Calif. State U., Sacramento, 1984—92, U. Tex., Brownsville, 2000—; music tchr. Alamo Ind. Sch. Dist., San Juan, Tex., 1987—; prof. clarinet Wichita State U., Kans., 1994—95; head testing & quality control The Leblanc Corp., Kenosha, Wis.; prin. clarinetist South Tex. Symphony, Edinburg, Am. Sinfonietta, Bellingham, Wash. Prin. clarinetist La Bienalle, Venice, 1975—76; clarinetist NY Philharm., NYC, 1975—77; bd. mem. Sacramento Chamber Music Soc., Sacramento, 1986—91; owner Alvin Ltd., Mission, Tex., 2000—; founder Kansa Winds, Mission. Recipient First Prize award, Naftzger Competition, 1976, First Place award, Internat. Clarinet Competition, 1983, Most Meritorious Tchg. award, 1985; scholar Full Music Scholarship to study at Juilliard, Naumberg, 1975-1977. Mem.: Internat. Clarinet Congress (assoc.). Achievements include clarinet mouthpiece design. Home Phone: 956-793-3305. E-mail: tlane@rgv.rr.com.

LANE, WILLA JOAN MANES, retired psychologist; b. Oklahoma City, May 25, 1930; d. Marvin Talmadge and Ethel May (Southern) Manes; m. Lynn Roland Lane (div.); 1 child, Lee Nathan. BA, U. Ariz., Tucson, 1951; MA, Ariz. State U., Tempe, 1967; PhD, Walden U., Mpls., 1981. Lic. tchr. Ariz., 1951, cert. counselor Ariz., 1967, lic. sch. psychologist Ariz., 1971, cert. counselor Tex., 1989, lic. psychologist Tex., 1995. Tchr. Williams AFB, Chandler, Ariz., 1951—53; dancer Hormel Girls Caravan, Hormel Foods, Austin, Minn., 1953—54; tchr. Madison Sch. Dist., Phoenix, 1961—71; counselor, psychologist Creighton Sch. Dist., Phoenix, 1971—88; counselor Joshua Ind. Sch. Dist., Tex., 1990—97, Roswell Ind. Sch. Dist., N.Mex., 1998—2003. Sunday sch. adult class tchr. 1st United Meth. Ch., Glen Rose, Tex., 2006. Mem.: NEA, Am. Psychol. Assn., Am. Sch. Counselor Assn., Nat. Assn. Sch. Psychologists, Ariz. Sch. Psychologists, Ariz. Elem. Sch. Counselors. Republican. Avocations: reading, theater, meditation, travel, self-help workshops. Home: 408 Grace St Glen Rose TX 76043

LANE, WILLIAM H., education educator; s. Dorothy M. Lane; 1 child, Kristen Jill. EdD, Widener U., Chester, Pa., 1995. Cert. in spl. edn. Del., 2000, in edn. administn. K-12 Del., 2001. Tchr. students with exceptionalities Smyrna Sch. Dist., Del., 1985—89; asst. prin. Delmar Sch. Dist., Del., 1989—97, Cape Henlopen Sch. Dist., Lewes, Del., 1997—2000, Seaford Sch. Dist., Del., 2001—04; asst. prof. Wilmington Coll., Georgetown, Del., 2006—. Adj. prof. U. Md. Ea. Shore, Princess Anne, Del., 1999—. Jr. bd. mem. Bayhealth Ctr., Dover, Del., 1984. With USN, Yokosuka, Japan. Office: Wilmington Coll Seashore Hwy Georgetown DE 19947 Home Phone: 302-644-1216; Office Phone: 302-856-5780. Home Fax: 302-856-5787. Business E-Mail: william.h.lane@wilmcoll.edu.

LANE, WILLIAM W., electronics executive; b. Roanoke, Va., Feb. 25, 1934; s. Melvin V. and Cecile (Lane); m. Ronnie G Lane, Sept. 14, 1978; children: Jonathan D., Drew H., Craig M. BA, Bklyn. Coll., 1956; MBA, Cornell U., 1958. V.p. Major Electronics Corp., 1959-70, chmn., dir., 1970; v.p., dir. Internat. Transistor Corp., Burbank, Calif., 1971-73; vice chmn., dir. Internat. Chia Hsin, Taipai, Taiwan, 1973-76; chmn., dir. Emerson (H.K. Ltd.), Hong Kong, from 1976; chmn., CEO, dir. Emerson Radio Corp., North Bergen, NJ, 1974-91; officer, bd. dirs. Star Light Electronics, Ridgefield, NJ; mng. dir. yo4 Ocean Road LLC, 2000—. Pres. Majorette Enterprises, from 1961; chmn. MAJ EXCO Imports Inc., 1977-85, Emerson Computer Corp., 1989-91, H.H. Scott, Inc. Cardiac Resuscitator Corp., Portland, Oreg., Emerson Italy, Emerson Spain, Atlantic Shore 400 Cons. Corp., Emerson Investment Corp., Major Realty Corp., Emteck Tech. (U.K.) Ltd.; pres. W. Lane & Assocs. Inc., 1992—. Served with AUS, 1958-59. Mem. bus. adv. bd. U.S. Senate.

LANER, RICHARD WARREN, lawyer; b. Chgo., July 12, 1933; s. Jack E. and Esther G. (Cohon) L.; m. Barbara Lee Shless, Aug. 15, 1954 (dec. Oct. 1997); children: Lynn, Kenneth; m. Daryl Lynn Homer, Sept. 17, 1998. Student, U. Ill., 1951-54; BS, Northwestern U., 1955, LLB, 1956. Bar: Ill. 1956. Assoc. Laner, Muchin, Dombrow, Becker, Levin & Tominberg, Ltd., Chgo., 1956-62, ptnr., 1962-99, of counsel, 1999. Editor Northwestern Law Rev., 1954-56; contbr. articles to profl. jours. Mem. Chgo. Bar Assn. (chmn. com. labor law 1972-73), Chgo. Assn. Commerce and Industry, Order of Coif. Home: 161 E Chicago Ave Unit 41de Chicago IL 60611-2601 Office: Laner Muchin Dombrow Becker Levin & Tominberg Ltd 515 N State St Fl 28 Chicago IL 60610-4325 Office Phone: 312-467-9800. Business E-Mail: rlaner@lanermuchin.com.

LANESE, HERBERT J., multi-industry executive; b. 1945; V.p. fin. Tenneco Chems.; v.p., CFO Newport News Shipbuilding & Drydock Co., 1983-86; v.p. Tenneco Inc., 1986-89; sr. v.p. McDonnell Douglas Corp., 1989-92, exec. v.p., CFO, 1992; chmn. bd. McDonnell Douglas Fin. Corp., Long Beach, Calif., 1993, pres.; pres., CEO DynCorp Internat. Inc., Falls Church, Va., 2006—. Office: DynCorp Internat Inc 3190 Fairview Park Dr Ste 700 Falls Church VA 22042 Office Phone: 571-722-0210.*

LANE-TRENT, PATRICIA JEAN, social worker; b. Belleville, Ill., Apr. 3, 1970; d. Lawrence R. and Nola Jean (Bosick) L.; m. Jerry J. Trent Jr. (div.); 1 child, Corey Andrew. AA, AS, Belleville Area Coll., 1992; BS, So. Ill. U., 1994; student, Women's Campaign Sch., 1995. Cert. info. rsch. specialist. Co-owner Jerry's Lawncare and Landscaping, Trent's Quality Constrn., Belleville, Ill., 1993—; youth specialist Mo. Dept. Social Svcs., St. Louis, 1994-95; owner Tracks & Traces Infosource, Belleville, 1997—98; social worker Royal Hts. Nursing and Rehab., 1999—2001. Mem. NOW, NAFE. Democrat. Avocations: fishing, softball, music, singing, writing. Office: 907 Martin Luther King East Saint Louis IL 62205 Office Phone: 618-482-7376.

LANEVE, MARK R., automotive executive; b. Beaver Falls, Pa., Mar. 8, 1959; m. Paula LaNeve; children: Jake, Drew. Bachelor in bus. comm., Univ. Va. Sales & mktg. positions GM, 1981—95, brand mgr., Pontiac Bonneville, 1995—97, gen. mgr. Cadillac, 2001—04, v.p. mktg. & advt., GM No. Am., 2004—05, v.p. vehicle sales, svc. & mktg., GM N Am., 2005—; v.p. mktg. Volvo Cars No. Am., 1997—2000, pres. & CEO, 2000—01. Trustee Judson Ctr. Named Grand Marketer of the Year, Brandweek mag., 2003. Office: General Motors Corp 300 Renaissance Ctr Detroit MI 48265-3000

LANEY, DAVID M., railroad industry executive, lawyer; b. Dallas, Jan. 19, 1949; s. James J. and Jean M. L.; m. Eleanor Watkins; children: Margaret W., Virginia M. BA, Stanford U., 1971; JD, So. Meth. U., 1977. Ptnr. Jackson Walker L.L.P., Dallas; chmn. Nat. RR Passenger Corp. (AMTRAK), 2003—. Bd. dirs. Tex. Fin. Commn., 1989-95, N. Tex. Tpke. Authority, 1995-97, Coastal Coordinating Coun., 1995-97, Tex. Tpke. Authority, 1998-99, Nat. RR Passenger Corp. (AMTRAK), 2002-; chmn. Tex. Transp. Commn., 1995-2001 Bd. govs. Symphony Assn. Dallas, 1982-87; mem. Com. Fgn. Rels., Dallas, 1988—, Dallas Citizens Coun., 1995-2001; advisory coun., Tex. Transp. Inst., 2001-; bd. trustees St. Mark's Sch. Tex., 1985-90 Found. for Collier and Com., Dallas, 1984-88, Hockaday Sch., 1993-95, Stanford U., 1998-2003, Southwestern Med. Found., 2001-, mem. exec. bd., Dedman Sch. Law, 2001- Named a Tex. Superlawyer, Tex. monthly mag., 2003, 2004. Mem. Tex. Bar Found., ABA, Dallas Bar Assn., Tex. Bar Found., Dallas Bar Found. Office: Jenkens & Gilchrist 1445 Ross Ave Ste 3200 Dallas TX 75202-2785

LANEY, JAMES THOMAS, former ambassador, educator; b. Wilson, Ark., Dec. 24, 1927; s. Thomas Mann and Mary (Hughey) L.; m. Berta Joan Radford, Dec. 20, 1949; children: Berta Joan Vaughan, James T., Arthur Radford, Mary Ruth Laney Reilly, Susan Elizabeth Castle. BA, Yale U., 1950, BD, 1954, PhD, 1966; DD (hon.), Fla. So. Coll., 1977, Wofford Coll., 1986, Emory U., 1994, Yonsei U., Korea, 1997, Kwansei Gakuin U., Japan, 2000; DD (hon.), Africa U., Zimbabwe, 2004; LHD (hon.), Rhodes Coll., 1979, Millsaps Coll., 1988, Austin Coll., 1990, W.Va. Wesleyan Coll., 1990, Yale U., 1993, U. S.C., 1997, Queens Coll., 1998, LaGrange Coll., 2000; LHD (hon.), Nebr. Wesleyan U., 2004; LHD (hon.), U. Richmond, 2001; HHD (hon.), Mercer U., 1980; LLD (hon.), DePauw U., 1985, U. St. Andrews, Scotland, 1994, Alaska Pacific U., 1994; LLD (hon.), Piedmont Coll., 1999; D in Internat. Affairs, Am. U., 1998. Chaplain Choate Sch., Wallingford, Conn., 1953-55; ordained to ministry Meth. Ch., 1955; asst. lectr. Yale Div. Sch., 1954-55; pastor St. Paul Meth. Ch., Cin., 1955-58; sec. student Christian movement, prof. Yonsei U., Seoul, Korea, 1959-64; asst. prof. Christian ethics Vanderbilt U. Div. Sch., 1966-69; dean Candler Sch. Theology, Emory U., 1969-77, pres. univ., 1977-93, pres. emeritus, 1993—; US amb. to Republic of Korea, 1993-97; spl. presdl. envoy, 1997—99. Vis. prof. Harvard Div. Sch., 1974. Author: The Education of the Heart, 1994; (with J.M. Gustafson) On Being Responsible, 1968; contbr. columns NY Times, Washington Post, LA Times. Fgn. Affairs pres. Nashville Cmty. Rels. Coun., 1968-69; mem. Yale Coun. Com., 1972-77; bd. dir. Fund Theol. Edn.; chmn. United Bd. Christian Higher Edn. in Asia, 1990-93, 97-2002; bd. dir. Atlanta Symphony, 1979-91; chmn. bd. overseers com. to visit Harvard Div. Sch., 1980-85; mem. Yale U. Coun. Exec. Com., 1990-93; mem. Carnegie Endowment Nat. Commn. on Am. and the New World; mem. adv. com. Atlanta Project; chmn. so. dist. Rhodes Scholarship Com., 1980-90; bd. dir. Atlantic Coun., 1987-93. Henry Luce Found., 1990—; mem. tercentenary steering com. Yale U., 1998-01; co-chmn. Faith & City, Atlanta, Ga.; trustee Carter Ctr., 1997—. With AUS, 1946-48. Selected for Leadership Atlanta, 1970-71; recipient Disting. Alumnus award Yale U. Div. Sch., 1979, 93, Kellogg award for leadership in higher edn., 1983, Wilbur Cross medal Yale Grad. Sch., 1996, James Van Fleet award, Korean Soc., 1996, Kangwa medal for disting. diplomatic svc., Rep. Korea, 1997, Dept. Defense medal for disting. pub. svc., U.S. Govt., 1997, 1st Internat. Human Rights award Inst. Human Rights, Korea, 1998; D.C. Macintosh fellow Yale U., 1965-66. Mem. Soc. Values Higher Edn. (pres. 1987-91), Coun. on Fgn. Rels. (co-chair task force on Korean Peninsula 1997-2002), Pilgrim Soc., Atlanta C. of C., Commerce Club, Atlanta Rotary Club, Phi Beta Kappa, Omicron Delta Kappa, Elihu Soc. (hon). Home: 2015 Grand Prix Dr NE Atlanta GA 30345-3931 Personal E-mail: jtlaney@emory.edu.

LANEY, JOHN THOMAS, III, federal judge; b. Columbus, Ga., Mar. 27, 1942; s. John Thomas Jr. and Leila (Davis) L.; m. Louise Pierce, Nov. 23, 1974; children: Thomas Whitfield, Elizabeth Davis. AB, Mercer U., 1964, JD magna cum laude, 1966. Bar: Ga. 1965, U.S. Dist. Ct. (mid. dist.) Ga. 1966, U.S. Ct. Appeals (5th cir.) 1966, U.S. Ct. Mil. Appeals 1967, U.S. Ct. Appeals (11th cir.) 1981. Assoc. Swift, Pease, Davidson & Chapman, Columbus, 1970-73; ptnr. Page, Scrantom, Harris & Chapman, Columbus, 1973-86; judge mid. dist. Ga. U.S. Bankruptcy Ct., Columbus, 1986—. Co-editor-in-chief Mercer Law Rev., 1965—66; contbr. articles to profl. jours. Former pres., dir. Metro. Boys Club of Columbus. Capt. U.S. Army, 1966-70. Mem. ABA (judge adminstrv. divsn. Nat. Conf. Fed. Trial Judges), State Bar Ga. (chmn. gen. practice and trial sect. 1983-84, chmn. state disciplinary bd. 1984-85), Am. Judicature Soc., Nat. Conf. Bankruptcy Judges, Columbus Bar Assn., Inc. (pres. 1985-86), Rotary. Presbyterian. Office: US Bankruptcy Ct 1 Arsenal Pl 901 Front Ave Ste 309 Columbus GA 31901-2797 Home Phone: 706-561-7391; Office Phone: 706-649-7840. E-mail: k4bai@worldnet.att.net.

LANEY, LEROY OLAN, economist, banker, educator; b. Atlanta, Mar. 20, 1943; s. Lee Edwin and Paula Izlar (Bishop) L.; m. Sandra Elaine Prescott, Sept. 3, 1966; children: Prescott Edwin, Lee Olan III. B Indsl. Engring., Ga. Inst. Tech., 1965; MBA in Fin., Emory U., 1967; MA in Econs., U. Colo., 1974, PhD in Econs., 1976. Budget analyst Martin-Marietta Corp., Denver, 1971—72; economist Coun. Econ. Advisers, Washington, 1974—75; internat. economist U.S. Treasury Dept., Washington, 1975—78; sr. economist Fed. Res. Bank Dallas, 1978—88; prof. econs., chmn. dept. Butler U., Indpls., 1989—90; sr. v.p. lst Hawaiian Bank, Honolulu, 1990—98; prof. econs. and fin. Hawaii Pacific U., Honolulu, 1998—. Chmn. Fed. Res. Com. on Internat. Rsch., Washington, 1981-83; vis. prof. U. Tex., Arlington and Dallas, 1978-85; adj. prof. So. Meth. U., Dallas, 1982-85. Editor bank periodicals, 1975-88; contbr. articles to profl. jours. Mem. Internat. Fin. Symposium, Dallas, 1982-85; Hawaii Coun. on Revenues. Lt. USN, 1967-71. Scholar Ga. Inst. Tech., 1961; rsch. fellow Emory U., 1965-67, teaching fellow U. Colo., 1972-73; rsch. grantee Butler U., 1989-90. Mem. Am. Econ. Assn., Western Econ. Assn., Indpls. Econ. Forum, Plaza Club, Honolulu Rotary, Omicron Delta Epsilon, Lambda Alpha, Kappa Sigma. Avocations: sailing, reading, fly fishing. Office: Sch Bus Adminstrn Hawaii Pacific Univ Honolulu HI 96813 Office Phone: 808-544-0233. Personal E-mail: lO9_laney@hotmail.com.

LANEY, MARTI OLSEN, psychoanalyst, researcher; b. Valparaiso, Ind., May 16, 1945; d. Howard Albert and Julano H. (Oleson) Miller; m. Michael L. Laney, Dec. 31, 1964; children: Tynna Elise DeMillier, Kristen Beth Parks. BA, Calif. State U., Northridge, 1972; MLS, U. So. Calif., LA, 1977; MA, Azusa Pacific U., Calif., 1980; D of Psychoanalysis, Inst. of Contemporary Psychoanalysis, LA, 2001. Lic. marriage, family and child therapist Calif., 1982. Children's libr. and head of circulation dept. Inglewood Pub. Libr., 1973—78; therapist Ctr. Individual and Family Counseling, 1978—83; tng. rep. Rockwell Internat., LA, 1978—83; tng. specialist and mgr. First Interstate Svcs. Co., LA, 1986—88; faculty mem. Inst. of Contemporary Psychoanalysis, LA, 1997—, Newport Psychoanalytic Inst., Newport, Calif., 2003—. Exec. dir. Inst. Study of Introverted Temperaments. Author: The Introvert Advantage, 2002 (Books for Better Life award, 2002), How to Thrive in an Extrovert World, 2002, The Hidden Gifts of the Introverted Child: Helping Your Child Thrive in an Extroverted World, 2005, The Introver and Extrovert in Love: Maing It Work When Opposites Attract, 2006; contbr. articles to profl. jours. Mem.: Assn. Psychol. Type, Am. Counseling Assn., Internat. Fedn. Psychoanalytic Edn., Am. Assn. Marriage and Family Therapy. Avocations: reading, travel, singing, reflecting.

LANEY, MICHAEL L., manufacturing executive; b. LA, Sept. 10, 1945; s. Roy and Wanda Laney; m. Marti Miller, Dec. 31, 1964; children: Tynna, Kristen. BS with honors, Calif. State U., Northridge, 1967; MBA, UCLA, 1969. CPA, Calif. Sr. tax acct. Haskins-Sells, Los Angeles, 1967-69; asst. prof. acctg. Calif. State U., Northridge, 1969-72; tax prin. M. Klaiman Acctg. Corp., Beverly Hills, Calif., 1972-75; pvt. practice Beverly Hills, 1975-80; v.p., controller Ducommun, Inc., Los Angeles, 1980-87; sr. v.p., fin. and adminstrn. Monarch Mirror Door Co. Inc., Chatsworth, Calif., 1987-92; v.p. ops. feature animation Walt Disney Pictures and TV (part of The Walt Disney Co.), Glendale, Calif., 1992-93; sr. v.p. ops. Warner Bros., Glendale, Calif., 1994-96; pres. Children's Wonderland, Agoura, Calif., 1996-97; CFO Dacor, Pasadena, Calif., 1997-2001; pres., CEO Cool Roof of Calif., Inc., Calabasas, 2001—; pres. M. Laney & Assocs., Portland, 2002—; CFO Energy Trust Oreg., Inc., 2004—05. Mem. Fin. Execs. Inst. (pres. Portland chpt.), Am. Inst. CPA's, Calif. Soc. CPA's; Assn. Corp. Growth., Am. Sch. Counselors Assn., Soc. Human Resources (practioner), Assn. Psychol. Type. Office Phone: 503-946-8798. Personal E-mail: mlaneyassoc@yahoo.com.

LANEY, PATRICIA ANN, elementary school educator; married. BS in Elem. Edn., SUNY; MEd, Fayetteville (NC) State Univ. Dept. Def. sch. tchr., Bad Kreuznach, Germany, Terrance Hills Elem. Sch., El Paso, Tex., Irwin Middle Sch., Fort Bragg, NC, Murray Elem. Sch., Fort Bragg, NC. Named Dept. Def. Edn. Activity Tchr. of Yr., 2007. Office: Murray Elem Sch PO Box 70089 Fort Bragg NC 28307 Business E-Mail: pat.laney@am.dodea.edu.*

LANEY, SANDRA EILEEN, information technology executive; b. Cin., Sept. 17, 1943; d. Raymond Oliver and Henrietta Rose (Huber) H.; m. Dennis Michael Laney, Sept. 30, 1968; children: Geoffrey Michael, Melissa Ann. AS in Bus. Adminstrn., Thomas More Coll., 1988, BA in Bus. Adminstrn., 1993. Adminstrv. asst. to chief exec. officer Chemed Corp., Cin., 1982, asst. v.p., 1982-84, v.p., 1984-91, v.p., chief adminstrv. officer, 1991-93, sr. v.p., chief adminstrv. officer, 1993-2001, bd. dirs., 1986—, exec. v.p. chief adminstrn. officer, 2001—02; CEO, chmn. Cadre Computer Resources Co., 2001—. Bd. dirs. Omnicare Inc., Covington, Ky., Ind. U. Found., Chem. Corp. 1986—; bd. visitors Ind. U. Sch. Public and Environ. Affairs. Mem. bd. advisors Sch. Nursing U. Cin., 1992—; bd. overseers Cin. Symphony Orch., 1998; trustee Lower Price Hill Cmty. Sch., Cmty. Land Coop. of Cin. Mem. AAUW, NOW, Internat. Platform Assn., Amnesty Internat., World Affairs Coun., Women's Action Coun. Roman Catholic. Office: Cadre Computer Resources Co 1200 Chemed Ctr 255 E 5th St Cincinnati OH 45202-4700 Office Phone: 513-762-6912. Business E-Mail: sandra.laney@cadre.net.

LANFORD, LUKE DEAN, retired electronics company executive; b. Greer, SC, Aug. 4, 1922; s. John D. and Ethel W. (Ballenger) L.; m. Donna Marie Cellar, Dec. 20, 1945 (dec. Apr. 29, 1984); 1 dau., Cynthia Lea Lanford Brown; m. Jacquelyn Sue Carr Bussell, Feb. 14, 1986 BSE.E., Va. Poly. Inst., 1943. With Western Electric Co., Inc., 1946-78, asst. mgr. tng. NYC, 1957-60, mgr. engring. Kansas City, 1960-63, asst. works mgr. Allentown, Pa., 1963-65; plant mgr. Reading, Pa., 1965-69; gen. mgr. Indpls., 1969-78. Dir. Met. Indpls. Television Assn., Inc., Sta. WFYI-TV, 1970—. pres., 1975-79 Served with U.S. Army, 1943-46. Mem. IEEE, Telephone Pioneers Am., Jacaranda West Country Club, Eta Kappa Nu, Tau Beta Pi, Phi Kappa Phi. Republican. Roman Catholic. Home: 1935 Pebble Beach Ct Venice FL 34293-3830

LANG, CHRISTINE JOANN, elementary school educator; b. Monmouth Beach, NJ, Oct. 27, 1979; d. Peter James and JoAnn Elizabeth Lang. BA in Psychology, Marist Coll., 2002; postgrad., Monmouth U., 2002—03, Western Conn. State U., 2003—. 1st grade tchr. Margaret Vetter Elem. Sch., Eatontown, NY, 2002—03, 2d grade tchr. aide, 2002; head tchr. infants and toddlers Merryhill Child Care, Newtown, Conn., 2004; spl. edn. tchr. grades 6-8 North End Mid. Sch., Waterbury, Conn., 2004—. Mem.: Pi Lambda Theta. Avocations: reading, movies. Office: North End Mid Sch 534 Bucks Hill Rd Waterbury CT 06704 E-mail: CJLang2003@aol.com.

LANG, DANNY ROBERT, planning consultant; b. St. Louis, June 4, 1955; s. George Robert and V. Arlene (Underwood) L.; m. Diane Marie Martin, Aug. 14, 1976; children: Douglas Gerald, Derek Robert, Darin Kenneth. BS, U. Mo., 1977. Dir. lakes and pks. Lake Saint Louis (Mo.) Cmty. Assn., 1977-80; environ. planner Harland Bartholomew & Assoc., St. Louis, 1980-81, Booker Assocs., St. Louis, 1981—87; dir. cmty. devel. City of St. Peters, Mo., 1987-95; dir. city devel. City of St. Charles, Mo., 1995—2001; sr. planner Horner & Shifrin, St. Louis, 2001—05; pres. The Lang Gang, Inc., 2005—. Dir. deanery planning St. Charles Deanery-St. Louis Archdiocese. Recipient Eagle Scout Boy Scouts Am., 1972, Disting. Leadership award, APA Mo. Chapt., 2002. Mem. Am. Planning Assn. (past pres. Mo. chpt. 1992-97, Excellence in Planning award 1985, 87, 91, 96, 2002), Mo. Tax Increment Fin. Assn. (bd. dirs. 1995-97). Roman Catholic. Avocations: coaching little league baseball, stamp collecting/philately. Office: The Lang Gang Inc 15 Fox Valley Dr Lake Saint Louis MO 63367 Office Phone: 636-625-2465. Personal E-mail: thelangang@charter.net.

LANG, DOUGLAS STEWART, judge; b. St. Louis, July 25, 1947; s. Ervin Jacob and Jacqueline Helen (Kratky) L.; m. Martha Kay Taylor, Aug. 25, 1973; children: Brian Chester and Christopher John (twins), Stewart Taylor. BSBA, Drake U., 1969; JD, U. Mo., Columbia, 1972. Bar: Mo. 1972, Tex. 1973, U.S. Dist. Ct. (no. dist.) Tex. 1973, U.S. Ct. Appeals (5th cir.) 1977, U.S. Dist. Ct. (ea. dist.) Tex. 1992, U.S. Dist. Ct. (we. dist.) Tex. 1993. Law clk. to Hon. Fred L. Henley Mo. Supreme Ct., St. Louis, 1972—73; assoc. Weber, Baker & Allums, Dallas, 1973—78; ptnr. Gardere, Porter & DeHay, Dallas, 1978-79, Gardere Wynne Sewell LLP, Dallas, 1979—2002; justice Ct. Appeals 5th Dist., Dallas, 2002—. Bd. dirs. Legal Svcs. of North Tex., Inc., 1997—2000, vice chair, 1998, chair, 1999-2000. Chalice bearer and lay reader Ch. of Incarnation, Dallas, 1984—, vestry mem. 1990-95; bldg. campaign chmn.; troop com. Boy Scout Troop 72, Dallas, 1989-97, asst. scoutmaster, 1992-97; v.p. Park Cities Ctrl. Dads' Club, Dallas, 1990-91; pres. Univ. Park Grade Sch. Dad's Club, 1990-91; trustee Drake U., 2002—; bd. councillors U. Dallas, 1991-93; bd. dirs. Com. for Qualified Judiciary, 1999-2002; trustee, vice chmn. chair long range planning com., exec. com. Anglican Sch. Theology, 2000-05; exec. coun. Episcopal Diocese of Dallas, 2002-05, 06-. Recipient Outstanding Svc. award Legal Svcs. North Tex., Dallas, 1991, Alumni Achievement award Drake U., Des Moines, 1992, Double D award Drake U., 1993. Fellow Tex. Bar Found. (life, trustee 1997-00), Am. Bar Found., Dallas Bar Found (trustee 1991—, sec.-treas. 1994-96, vice chair 1996-98, chair 1998-01); mem. ABA (exec. coun. Nat. Conf. of Bar Pres. 1995-98, pres., 2004-05, exec. com. Met. Bar Caucus 1991-97, sec.-treas. 1992-93, pres.-elect 1993-94, pres. 1994-95, house of dels. 1996-00), State Bar Tex. (bd. dirs. 1992-95, exec. com. 1994-95, Outstanding Third Yr. Dir. award 1995, Presdl. Citation 1999), Dallas Bar Assn. (bd. dirs. 1976-78, 80-00, pres. 1991), Dallas Assn. Young Lawyers (bd. dirs. 1975, v.p. 1976, treas. 1975, pres. 1977, Outstanding Young Lawyer in Dallas 1981), Tex. Young Lawyers Assn. (bd. dirs. 1976-78), Am. Law Inst., Tex. Assn. Bank Coun. (bd. dirs. 1990-93, v.p. 1994-95, pres. 1996-97), MacTaylor Inn of Ct. (membership chmn. 1991-95, exec. com. 1991-99, counselor 1995-96, pres. 1997-99), Am. Inns of Ct. Found. (trustee 2005-), Salesmanship Club of Dallas, Tex. Ctr. for Ethics and Professionalism (chair 1999-02), Drake U. Nat. Alumni Assn. (bd. dirs. 1998—, v.p. programming 2000-02, v.p. 2000-02, pres. 2002-04). Republican. Avocations: golf, hiking, rafting, camping. Office: Tex Ct Appeals 5th Dist 2d Fl 600 Commerce St Dallas TX 75202

LANG, EVERETT FRANCIS, JR., brokerage house executive; b. Providence, Sept. 27, 1942; s. Everett Francis and Catherine Mary (Cuddigan) L.; m. Margaret Letitia McKenna; 1 child, Joseph; m. Frances Marie Biasi. BS, Boston U., 1965; MEd, U. Va., Charlottesville, 1972, EdD, 1976. Lic. security broker. Elem. sch. tchr. Henrico County Sch. Systems, Highland Springs, Va., 1970-71, middle sch. tchr., 1971-72; asst. regional dir. Sch. Continuing Edn. U. Va., Charlottesville, 1972-76; assoc. dir. human resources Met Property & Liability Ins. Co., Warwick, RI, 1976-79; human resources cons. Colonial Penn Group, Phila., 1979-81; v.p. Bankers Trust Co., NYC, 1981-86; v.p. sales BT Brokerage Corp., NYC, 1986-90; chmn., pres., chief exec. officer Bankers Trust Brokerage Corp., NYC, 1990-92; pres. Nat. Discount Brokers, NYC, 1993-95, pres., CEO, 1995-98; pres. of Digital Trading facility Soundview Tech., NYC, 1999-2000; exec. v.p. Fleet Securities, 2001—04; sr. mng. dir. Bank of Am., 2004—05; chief bus. devel. officer ITP Corp., 2006—; sr. mng. dir. strategic bus. devel. Patrina Corp., 2007—. Capt. USAF, 1965-69, Vietnam. Decorated with Bronze Star, Army Commendation medal. Mem. Phi Delta Kappa, Kappa Delta Pi, Sigma Alpha Epsilon. Avocation: golf. Home: 5 Michele Ct Allendale NJ 07401-1013 Office: Patrina Corp 2 Wall St New York NY 10005 Personal E-mail: everett_lang@yahoo.com.

LANG, GEORGE, restaurateur; b. Székesfehérvár, Hungary, July 13, 1924; arrived in U.S., 1946, naturalized, 1950; s. Simon and Ilona Lang; m. Jenifer Lang; children: Andrea, Brian, Simon John, Georgina Kathlyn. Attended, U. Szeged, Hungary, 1945, Mozarteum, Salzburg, Austria, 1945-46, U. Stranieri, Perugia, Italy, 1950-51; LHD (hon.), Ind. U., 1994, U. Johnson and Wales, 2004. Asst. banquet mgr. Waldorf-Astoria, 1953-58; v.p. sales and mktg. Brass Rail Orgn., 1958-60; v.p. Restaurant Assocs., 1960-71; pres. George Lang Corp., NYC, 1971-83; co-owner Gundel Restaurant, Budapest, Hungary, 1990—2004, Café des Artistes Restaurant, NYC, 1975—. Author: The Cuisine of Hungary, 1971, Lang's Compendium of Culinary Nonsense and Trivia, 1980, The Café des Artistes Cookbook, 1984, Nobody Knows the Truffles I've Seen, A Memoir, 1998; co-author: Gundel Album, 1993; cons. editor Time-Life Book div. Foods of the World series, 1966-70; contbg. editor Town and Country mag.; contbr. to Ency. Brit., 1974, also various columnist mag. Pub. mem. Am. Revolution Bicentennial Commn., 1969-, mem. exec. com., chmn. Festival U.S.A. coordinating art, internat. exchange and spl. events for Bicentennial celebrations. Recipient James Beard Lifetime Achievement Award, 2002. Address: 33 W 67th St New York NY 10023-6224 Home Phone: 212-873-1436; Office Phone: 212-721-3100. E-mail: glang@cafenyc.com. *In the great recipe of life, salt is the passion and the spice is enthusiasm.*

LANG, GORDON, JR., retired lawyer; b. Evanston, Ill., July 27, 1933; s. Gordon and Harriet Kendig Lang; m. Clara Bates Van Derzee, Sept. 26, 1970; children: Elizabeth K., Gordon III, Harriet B. BA, Yale U., 1954; MA History, U. Ariz., 1958; LLB, Harvard U., 1960. Bar: Ill. 1960. Assoc. Gardner Carton & Douglas, Chgo., 1960—67, ptnr., 1967—98; ret., 1998. Cons. in field. Dir. North Side Boys' Clubs, Chgo., 1961-67, Yale Scholarship Trust Ill., 1966-69, pres., 1967; mem. Assocs. Rush-Presbyn.-St. Luke's Med. Ctr., Chgo., 1962-2003, Assocs. Northwestern U., Evanston, 1970—; dir. Chgo. Youth Ctrs., 1967—, pres., 1982-84; trustee Chgo. Latin Sch. Found., 1978—, pres., 1995-2003; trustee Groton (Mass.) Sch., 1982-93; dir. United Way Chgo., 1984-90, United Way/Crusade Mercy (Met. Chgo.), 1989-95; apptd. Bush/Cheney elector 2000 presdl. election. 1st lt. USAF, 1955-57. Mem. ABA (sect. bus. law), Ill. State Bar Assn., Chgo. Bar Assn. (Corp. Law Com. 1975-98, Fin. Instns. Com. 1985-98), Chgo. Club (former dir. and sec.), Econ. Club Chgo. (former dir. and sec.), Onwentsia Club, Racquet Club Chgo., Chgo. Commonwealth Club, Yale Club Chgo. (former dir., past pres.). Republican. Episcopalian. Avocations: golf, skiing, hiking. Home: 1520 N Astor St Chicago IL 60610-1610 Office: DrinkerBiddleGardnerCarton 191 N Wacker Dr Ste 3700 Chicago IL 60606-1698 Office Phone: 312-569-1084. Business E-Mail: gordon.lang@dbr.com.

LANG, GREGORY P., music educator; b. Nekoosa, Wis. s. Kenneth Joseph and Lucille May Lang; m. Tina Sailor Lang, June 21, 1980; children: Jamie, Amanda. B of Music Edn., U. Wis., Eau Claire, 1978; M of Music Edn., U. Wis., Stevens Point, 1991. Dir. band Baraboo Sch. Dist., Wis., 1979—. Named Walmart Tchr. of Yr., 2001. Methodist. Home: 55593 Glacier Dr Baraboo WI 53913 Office: Baraboo High Sch 1201 Draper St Baraboo WI 53913

LANG, HOWARD LAWRENCE, electrical engineer; b. St. Louis, Nov. 16, 1958; s. William and Hermine L.; m. Karen Friedman, June 26, 1988; children: Arielle Ilyssa, Emily Danielle. BS in Biophysics with high distinction, U. Ill., 1981; MSEE, Cert. Biomed. Engring., Washington U., St. Louis, 1984; MSE in Computer and Info. Sci., U. Pa., 1990. Registered profl. engr., Pa., NJ, NY. Biomed. engr. Midwest Rsch. Inst., Kansas City, Mo., 1983; sr. engr. AT&T Bell Labs., Holmdel, NJ, 1984—. Contbr. articles to profl. jours. Chmn. AT&T Magic Club, Holmdel, 1985-88, Illini Emergency Med. Svcs., Urbana, 1979-81. Mem. IEEE (sr., sec. Computer Soc. NJ coast sect. 1998-99, Svc. award 1984), NSPE, NJ Soc. Profl. Engrs., Tau Beta Pi, Phi Eta Sigma. Achievements include patents for method determining concurrent voice over IP calls; design of fiber optic comm. sys; patents for voice over-IP. Avocations: magic, bicycling. Home: PO Box 200 Holmdel NJ 07733-0200

LANG, JAMES DEVORE, JR., ministry executive; b. Ft. Lewis, Wash., Apr. 29, 1941; s. James Devore and Margaret Lang; m. Barbara Jo Drury, July 3, 1965; children: Kathrena, Teresa, Christina, Angela. BS, USAF Acad., 1963; postgrad., Pepperdine U., 1977-79. Commd. 2d lt. USAF, 1963, advanced through grades to capt., resigned, 1969; regional dir., v.p. Lorraine L. Blair, Inc., San Francisco, 1969-71; v.p. Capital Planning Assn., San Rafael, Calif., 1971-73; pres. Delger Corp., Novato, Calif., 1973-76; chmn., CEO Delger Fin. Corp., Novato, 1976-83; pres., chmn., CEO Alternate Energy Corp., Novato, 1978-81; pres., CEO Shiloh Resources, Novato, 1980-83; sales rep., engr., v.p. Aztec Bldg., Inc., Norman, Okla., 1985-90; pres., CEO Amerex Corp., Norman, 1990-93; v.p., exec. dir. Bill Glass Prison Ministries, Inc., Dallas, 1994-99, exec. v.p., 1996—98, pres., 1999-2001; exec. v.p. Bill Glass/Champions for Life, 2001—04, Performance Consulting Group LLC, 2004—. Elder, pastor Trinity Bapt. Ch., Norman, 1990-93. Author: Real Estate Investment Trusts in Financial Planning, 1973; contbr. numerous articles to profl. publs. Regent Coll. for Fin. Planning, 1974-76; exec. dir. Christian Fellowship Enrichment. Decorated Air medal with 7 oak leaf clusters, Air Force Commendation medal; Paul Harris fellow Rotary Internat., 1978; recipient Golden Bull award Bank of Marin, 1977. Mem. Internat. Assn. Fin. Planning (nat. pres. 1973-74, chmn. 1974-75). Avocations: ministry, sports, flying. Office: Christian Fellowship Enrichment PO Box 382732 Duncanville TX 75138 Home Phone: 972-298-9084; Office Phone: 972-283-7871. E-mail: jimlang41@aol.com.

LANG, JAMES RICHARD, software designer, magician; b. Cleve., Feb. 7, 1945; s. Francis H. and Rachel L. (Boyce) L.; m. Marilyn F. Hosken, July 1, 1967; children: Christopher Charles, James Walter. Salesman Stas. WOHI-AM/WRTS-FM, East Liverpool, Ohio, 1967-68; gen. mgr. Sta. WEIR-AM, Weirton, W.Va., 1969-76; v.p. sales Paperwork Systems, Inc., Bellingham, Wash., 1976-78; v.p. market devel. Sta. Bus. Systems div. Control Date Corp., Greenwich, Conn., 1978-85; mgr. Eaglestone div. Siber Hegner N.Am., Inc., Milford, Conn., 1986-89; dir. mktg. MacMillan/McGraw-Hill, Avon, Conn., 1990-93; pres. Imagination Works, Trumbull, 1993—. Com. mem. Town of Trumbull CableTV, 2002—; adv. com. Charter Cable TV, 2002. With USN, 1968—69. Recipient Outstanding Service to Cmty. award Italian Sons and Dads Am., 1970. Mem. Instrument Soc. Am., Direct Mtkg. Assn., Jaycees (Cmty. Svc. award 1975), Internat. Brotherhood of Magicians (IBM Ring 1959, Wizard award 2003), Rotary (pres. 1996-97, area rep. 1997-98, asst. gov. dist. 7980, 1999-2001, dist. gov. 2002-2003, bequest soc. mem., Man of Yr. 1975, Paul Harris fellow dist. 1980, Norm Parsells award 2000, Rotary Found. Cert. Meritorious Svc. 2005), Fellowship of Rotary Magicians, Paul Harris Soc. Methodist. Office: Imagination Works 24 Primrose Dr Trumbull CT 06611-5043 Office Phone: 203-377-1747. Business E-Mail: jimlang@imaginationworks.net.

LANG, JANELLE J., accountant; b. Oelwein, Iowa, May 11, 1948; d. Arthur and Esther Louise (Moeller) Andrew; m. Robert Martin Lang, Sept. 4, 1971; children: Sybil, Jacqueline. BA in Bus. and Music Edn., Upper Iowa Coll., Fayette, 1970; BA in Acctg., Buena Vista Coll., Storm Lake, Iowa, 1993. Tchr. Davenport Cmty. Schs., Iowa, 1971-72, Bennett Cmty. Schs., Iowa, 1972-73, Madison Cmty. Schs., Wis., 1973-74; acct. Robert M. Lang, M.D., P.C., Ottumwa, Iowa, 1976—. Mem. governing bd. S.E. Iowa Symphony Orch., 1995—; bd. dirs. Ottumwa Civic Music, 1996; violist S.E. Iowa Symphony, 1996—, Ottumwa Symphony Orch., 1996—; pianist 1st Luth. Ch., Ottumwa, 1995, bell choir dir., 2005-. Mem. NAFE, Am. Mgmt. Assn., Nat. Soc. Accts. Lutheran. Avocation: gardening. Home and Office: 818 E Highland Ave Ottumwa IA 52501-2134 Personal E-mail: janellejlang@pcsia.net.

LANG, JOSEPH HAGEDORN, lawyer; b. Cleve., Sept. 30, 1937; s. Carl Frederick and Martha Clotilda (Hagedorn) L.; m. Elsie A. O'Berry, Aug. 8, 1965; children: Joseph H. Jr., Robert Warren, James O'Berry. AA, St. Petersburg Jr. Coll., Fla., 1959; BA, Duke U., Durham, NC, 1961; JD, U. Fla., Gainesville, 1963. Bar: Fla. 1964, US Dist. Ct. (mid. dist.) Fla. 1965, US Ct. Appeals (5th cir.) 1965, US Supreme Ct. 1975. Assoc. Baynard McLeod & Overton, St. Petersburg, Fla., 1964-69; ptnr. Baynard McLeod & Lang, St. Petersburg, 1969-80; pres. Baynard McLeod & Lang, P.C., St. Petersburg, 1980—. Charter mem., chmn. Police Cmty. Coun., Cmty. Alliance; chmn. bd. dirs. St. Petersburg Jr. Coll., Pinellas County, 1983-97, trustee, 1977-97, chmn., 1982-89, 92-96, chmn. emeritus, 1997—; mem. State Bd. C.C.'s, 1997-2001, vice chmn. 1998-99, chmn., 1999-2000. Named Sch. Adv. Com. Mem. of Yr.; recipient Trustee of Yr. award Fla. Assn. Cmty. Coll., 1993, Bob Graham C.C. Disting. Svc. award, 1994, Trustee Leadership award So. Region, ACCT, 1994, Alumni award St. Petersburg Jr. Coll., 1990, Disting. Alumni award LeRoy Collins C.C., 2002, Leadership Cmty. Svc. award, 2002. Mem. Fla. Bar Assn., St. Petersburg Bar Assn., St. Petersburg C. of C. (Outstanding Mem. award 1990), Suncoasters Club, Dragon Club, Phi Theta Kappa (Disting. Alumni award 1978). Democrat. Roman Catholic. Office: Baynard McLeod & Lang 669 1st Ave N Saint Petersburg FL 33701-3696 Office Phone: 727-894-0676.

LANG, K. D. (KATHERINE DAWN LANG), country music singer, composer; b. Consort, Alta., Can., Feb. 11, 1961; d. Adam and Audrey L. Lang. Mem. Tex. swing fiddle band, 1982—; formed band The Reclines. Albums include A Truly Western Experience, 1984, Angel with a Lariat, 1986, Shadowland, 1988, Absolute Torch and Twang, 1990 (Can. Country Music Awards album of the yr.), Ingenue, 1992, Even Cowgirls Get the Blues (soundtrack), 1993, Drag, 1997, Australian Tour, 1997, Invincible Summer, 2000, Live By Request, 2001; (with others) All You Can Eat, 1995; actress (film) Salmonberries, 1991; Teresa's Tattoo, 1994, The Last Don, 1997, TV guest appearance Ellen, 1997, Eye of The Beholder, 1999. Recipient Can. Country Music awards, including Entertainer of Yr., 1989, Grammy award, 1990, 1993, Best Pop Female Vocal for Constant Craving, Grammy nomination Best Pop Female Vocal for Miss Chatelaine, 1994, William Harold Moon award Soc. of Composers, Authors and Music Publishers of Can., 1994. Office: Warner Bros Records Inc 3300 Warner Blvd Burbank CA 91505-4694

LANG, LAURA SMITH, lawyer; m. John Lang. BA in Speech Lang. Pathology and Music cum laude, Butler U., Indpls., 1997; JD, So. Meth. U.

Dedman Sch. Law, 2000. Assoc. Brewer, Anthony & Middlebrook, P.C., Irving, Tex. Vol. Dallas Mus. Natural Hist., Habitat for Humanity, Dallas. Named a Rising Star, Tex. Super Lawyers mag., 2006. Mem.: Dallas Assn. Young Lawyers, Tex. Young Lawyers Assn., Dallas Bar Assn., Jr. League Dallas. Office: Brewer Anthony & Middlebrook 5201 N O'Connor Blvd 5th Fl Irving TX 75039-3768 Office Phone: 972-870-9898. E-mail: llang@bamlawyers.net.*

LANG, LAURA W., marketing executive; b. Oct. 20, 1955; Grad. summa cum laude, Tufts U., 1977; MBA, U. Pa. Brand mgmt. Quaker Oats Co., 1980; dir. internal consulting Pfizer Pharms., 1983—85; product dir. Bristol Myers, 1986—89; sr. v.p., group mgr. Yankelovich Clancy Shulman, 1989—95; ptnr. Mktg. Corp. Am., 1995—96, pres., 1996—99; exec. v.p. mktg. Digitas LLC, 1999—2003, pres. NY & Chgo. office, 2003—04, pres., 2004—; CEO Digitas USA. Bd. dirs. Benchmark Electronics, Inc., 2005—. Named a Women to Watch, Advt. Age, 2007. Office: Digitas 33 Arch St Boston MA 02110*

LANG, LINDA A., food service executive; B in Fin., U. Calif., Berkeley; MBA, San Diego State U. Joined Jack in the Box Inc., 1985, divsn. v.p. new products and promotions, 1994—96, v.p. products, promotions and consumer rsch., 1996—99, v.p. mktg., 1999—2001, sr. v.p. mktg., 2001—02, exec. v.p. mktg. and ops., human resources, restaurant devel., quality assurance and logistics, 2002—03, pres., COO San Diego, 2003—05, chmn., CEO, 2005—. Bd. dir. WD-40 Co. Office: Jack in the Box Inc 9330 Balboa Ave San Diego CA 92123*

LANG, MABEL LOUISE, classics educator; b. Utica, NY, Nov. 12, 1917; d. Louis Bernard and Katherine (Werdge) L. BA, Cornell U., 1939; MA, Bryn Mawr Coll., 1940, PhD, 1943; Litt.D., Coll. Holy Cross, 1975, Colgate U., 1978; L.H.D., Hamilton Coll. Mem. faculty Bryn Mawr Coll., 1943-91, successively instr., asst. prof., 1943-50, assoc. prof., 1950-59, prof. Greek, 1959-88, chmn. dept., 1960-88, acting dean coll. 2d semester, 1958-59, 60-61; chmn. mng. com. Am. Sch. Classical Studies, Athens, 1975-80, chmn. admissions and fellowship com., 1966-72; Blegen disting. rsch. prof. semester I Vassar Coll., 1976-77; Martin classical lectr. Oberlin Coll., 1982. Co-author: Athenian Agora Measures and Tokens; author: Palace of Nestor Frescoes, 1969, Athenian Agora Graffiti and Dipinti, 1976; Herodotean Narrative and Discourse, 1984, Athenian Agor Ostraka, 1990; contbr. articles profl. jours. Guggenheim fellow, 1953-54; Fulbright fellow Greece, 1959-60 Mem. Am. Philos. Soc., Am. Acad. Arts and Scis., German Archaeol. Inst., Am. Philol. Assn., Soc. Promotion Hellenic Studies (Eng.), Classical Assn. (Eng.). Office: Dept Greek Bryn Mawr Coll Bryn Mawr PA 19010 Home: 138 Montrose Ave #36 Bryn Mawr PA 19010

LANG, MICHAEL, mathematics professor; s. Stuart and Lynn Lang. BS, St. Norbert Coll., De Pere; PhD, U. Wis., Madison, 2001. Asst. prof. U. Wis., La Crosse, 2001—03, Bradley U., Peoria, Ill.

LANG, NICHOLAS PAUL, surgeon; b. Jonesboro, Ark., Apr. 11, 1947; s. Paul Alexandra and Lula (Cornish) L.; m. Carol Ann Holl, Aug. 1968 (div. May 1978); 1 child, Christopher; m. Helen Felecia Haley, July 25, 1979; children: Patrick, Courtney. Student, U. Ark., 1969; MD, U. Ark. Med. Scis., 1973. Diplomate Am. Bd. Surgery. Resident in surgery U. Ark. Med. Scis., Little Rock, 1973-77, assoc. prof. surgery, 1977-84, 1984-90, prof. surgery, 1990—; rsch. fellow Nat. Cancer Inst., Bethesda, Md., 1977-79; staff surgeon Little Rock VA Hosp. (now Ctrl. Ark. Vets. Healthcare Sys.), 1979-95, chief of surgery, 1995—2002, chief of staff, 2001—, acting medical ctr. dir., 2004—. Contbr. articles to profl. publs. Mem. nat. bd. Am. Cancer Soc., Atlanta, 1989-96; bd. dirs. CARTI, Little Rock, 1994—. Grantee Nat. Cancer Inst., 1995-2000, EPA, 1996-99, NIA, 1997-2003. Fellow ACS, Southwestern Surg. Congress (councillor 1989-95, pres. 2000-2001); mem. AMA, So. Surg. Assn., Assn. for Surg. Edn. (pres. 2000-2001), Am. Assn. Cancer Rsch. Baptist. Avocations: woodworking, gardening. Home: 1323 White Rd Little Rock AR 72211-4019 Office: Ctrl Ark Vets Healthcare Sys # 11-LR 4300 W 7th St Little Rock AR 72205-5446 Office Phone: 501-257-5300. Business E-Mail: nick.lang@med.va.gov.

LANG, NORTON DAVID, physicist; b. Chgo., July 5, 1940; s. Charles and Sadelle Lang; m. Enid Asher, June 8, 1969; children: Eugenie, Aaron. AB summa cum laude, Harvard U., 1962, A.M., 1965, PhD, 1968; postgrad. (Knox fellow), London Sch. Economics, 1962-63. Asst. research physicist, lectr. U. Calif., San Diego, 1967—69; mem. staff IBM Rsch. Ctr., Yorktown Heights, NY, 1969—. Erwin W. Mueller meml. lectr., Pa. State U., 1992; adj. prof. elec. engring. Columbia U., 2005. Contbr. articles on theoretical physics to profl. jours.; asso. editor: Phys. Rev. Letters, 1980-83. Fellow: Am. Phys. Soc. (chmn. fellowship com. divsn. condensed matter physics 1985—87, chmn. Davisson-Germer prize com. 1990, Davisson-Germer prize 1977), N.Y. Acad. Scis.; mem.: IEEE (sr.), Am. Chem. Soc., Phi Beta Kappa. Office: IBM Rsch Ctr Yorktown Heights NY 10598 Business E-Mail: LangN@us.ibm.com.

LANG, PEARL, dancer, choreographer; b. Chgo., May 1922; d. Jacob and Frieda (Feder) Lack; m. Joseph Wiseman, Nov. 22, 1963. Student, Wright Jr. Coll., U. Chgo.; DFA (hon.), Juilliard Sch. Music, 1995; PhD (hon.), Juilliard Sch., 1995, DFA, 1995. Formed own co., 1953; faculty Yale, 1954-68; tchr., lectr. Juilliard, 1953-69, Jacobs Pillow, Conn. Coll., Neighborhood Playhouse, 1963-68, Israel, Sweden, Netherlands. Founder Pearl Lang Dance Found.; mem. Boston Symphony, Tanglewood Fest. Soloist, Martha Graham Dance Co., 1944-54; featured roles on Broadway include Carousel, 1945-47, Finian's Rainbow, 1947-48, Danced Martha Graham's roles in Appalachian Spring, 1974-76, El Pentitente, 1954, Primitive Mysteries, 1978-79, Diversion of Angels, 1948-70, Herodiade, 1977-79; role of Solvieg opposite John Garfield Broadway include, ANTA Peer Gynt; choreographer: TV shows CBC Folio; co-dir. T.S. Eliot's Murder in the Cathedral, Stratford, Conn., Direction, 1964-66, 67, Lamp Unto Your Feet, 158, Look Up and Live TV, 1957; co-dir., choreographer: full length prodn. Dybbuk for CBC; dir. numerous Israel Bond programs; assumed roles Emily Dickinson: Letter to the World, 1970; Clytemnestra, 1973; Jocasta in: Night Journey, 1974, for Martha Graham Dance Co.; choreographer: dance works Song of Deborah, 1952, Moonsung and Windsung, 1952, Legend, 1953, Rites, 1953, And Joy Is My Witness, 1954, Nightflight, 1954, Sky Chant, 1957, Persephone, 1958, Black Marigolds, 1959, Shirah, 1960, Apasionada, 1961, Broken Dialogues, 1962, Shore Bourne, 1964, Dismembered Fable, 1965, Pray for Dark Birds, 1966, Tongues of Fire, 1967, Piece for Brass, 1969, Moonways and Dark Tides, 1970, Sharjuhm, 1971, At That Point in Place and Time, 1973, The Possessed, 1995, Prairie Steps, 1975, Bach Rondelays, 1977, I Never Saw Another Butterfly, 1977, A Seder Night, 1977, Kaddish, 1977, Icarus, 1978, Cantigas Ladino, (10 sephardic songs), 1978, Notturno, 1980, Gypsy Ballad, 1981, Hanele The Orphan, 1981, The Tailor's Megilleh, 1981, Bridal Veil, 1982, Stravinsky's opera Oedipus Rex, 1982, Song of Songs, 1983, Shiru L'adonay, 1983, Tehillim, 1983, Sephardic Romance and Tfila, 1989, Koros, 1990, Eyn Keloheynu, 1991, Schubert Quartetsatz No. 12, 1993, Schubert Quartet 15 1st Mov., 1994, And Again a Begining, 1994, Dream Voyages, 1996, Memories and Dreams of Isaac the Blind, 1997, A Bouquet of Love Song Waltzes, 1998, Song of Azerbaijan, 1999, Icarus, 1999, The Time Is Out of Joint, 2000, Dance Panel #7, 2000, Cityscape, 2000. Recipient 2 Guggenheim fellowships; recipient Goldfadden award Congress for Jewish Culture, Achievement award Artists and Writers for Peace in the Middle East, Cultural award Workmen's Circle, Queens Coll. award, 1991, Jewish Cultural achievement award Nat. Found. for Jewish Culture, 1992; named to Hall of Fame, Internat. Com. for the Dance Libr. of Israel, 1997. Mem. Am. Guild Mus. Artists. Home and Office: Dance Foundation Inc 382 Central Park W New York NY 10025-6054 Office Phone: 212-866-2680.

LANG, PHILIP DAVID, retired state legislator, insurance company executive; b. Portland, Oreg., Dec. 16, 1929; s. Henry W. and Vera (Kern) L.; m. Marcia Jean Smith, May 29, 1952 (div. Oct. 1979); 1 son, Philip David, III; m. Virginia Ann Wolf, Feb. 16, 1980. Student, Lewis and Clark Coll., 1951-53, Northwestern Coll. Law, 1956. Police officer Oreg. Dept. State Police, Salem, 1953-55; claims adjuster Glenns Falls Ins. Co., Portland, 1955-57, Oreg. Automobile Ins. Co., Portland, 1959-61; adminstrv. asst. to mayor City of Portland, 1957-58; spl. agt., underwriter North Pacific Ins. Co., Portland, 1961-63, mgr., 1963-65, asst. v.p., 1965-80, v.p., 1980-95; ret., 1995; asst. v.p. Oreg. Automobile Ins. Co., 1965-80, v.p., 1980-95; ret., 1995; appt. chmn. Oreg. Liquor Control Commn., 1998—. Mem. Oreg. Ho. of Reps., 1960-79, speaker, 1975-79; Div. leader Multnomah County (Oreg.) Democratic Com., 1956-60, precinct com., 1956—. With USAF, 1947-50. Mem. Oreg. Ins. Underwriters Assn., Nat. Alcoholic Beverage Control Assn. (mem. bd. 2001, pres. elect 2005), VFW, Masons, DeMolay (Legion Honor), Theta Chi. Roman Catholic. Home: 5769 SW Huddleson St Portland OR 97219-6645 Fax: 503-245-2452. E-mail: pdavidlang@msn.com. *Success is achieved through commitment to, and perserverance in, all that is undertaken; balanced with tolerance and understanding of all persons.*

LANG, RICHARD GORDON, physician; s. Richard Gordon and Charlotte Gifford (Fuller) Lang. BA, U. Mass., Amherst, 1966; MD, Temple U., Phila., 1970. Fellow Am. Acad. Family Physician, diplomate Am. Bd. Family Practice, fellow Am. Bd. Chem. Deficiency. Intern to resident family practice US Naval Hsp., Camp Pendleton, Calif., 1970—97; family physician Long Beach Naval Hosp., Calif., 1977—79; assoc. med. dir. Care Unit Hosp., Orange, Calif.; staff family physician Friendly Hius Med. Group, Whittier, Calif.; geriatric physican Dr. Herman Mathias, Hemet, Calif., 1997—99; ret., 1999. Comdr. USN. Recipient plaque, Pomona Valley Med. Ctr., 1981. Mem.: AA, Am. Legion. Democrat. Avocations: stamp collecting/philately, scuba diving, photography, plate collecting. Personal E-mail: drdiklng@aol.com.

LANG, ROBERT MAYS, JR., manufacturing and not-for-profit executive; s. Robert Mays Lang and Mary Elizabeth Davis Lang Mannweiler, Gordon Banatynne Mannweiler (Stepfather); m. Janice Ruth Mooney, Sept. 23, 1978; m. Sarah N. McIntyre, Aug. 21, 1965 (div. Nov. 15, 1974). AB in Econs., Miami U., Oxford, Ohio, 1965. Rep. Creative Packaging Inc., 1965—68, Arkay Packaging Inc., 1968—72; pvt. practice, 1972—82; pres. Reach for the Stars Inc., Cross River, NY, 1982—94, Imagination Grp., Ltd., Cross River, 1990—; CEO Fabrique Cosmetique, Inc., Cross River, 1992—; ptnr. Symphonic Teamwork, LLC, Cross River; CEO Mary Elizabeth & Gordon B. Mannweiler Found., Inc., Cross River, 2005—. Bd. dirs. Naumburg Orchestral Concerts, Inc.; cons. and advisor to non-profit orgn. Contbr. articles to profl. jours. and trade mags., to mags. and newspapers. Treas. Pound Ridge (NY) Cmty. Ch., Pound Ridge, 1984—87; fin. com. Katonah (NY) Meth. Ch., 1997—99; bd. mem. Alliance Charitable Reform. Recipient Cosmetic Innovator Yr. award, Ind. Cosmetic Mfr. and Distbr. Assn., 2004. Mem.: Nat. Assn. Watch Clock Collectors (pres. chpt. 84 2003—), Various Sq. Dance Clubs (pres. 1998—99). Independent. Methodist. Achievements include development of custom blended cosmetic system, cosmetic filling equipment and unique forumlations; L3C, a unique hybrid organizational form creating a for profit organization which performs social and beneficial services. Avocations: book collecting, clock collecting & repair, gardening, woodworking, square dancing. Home: PO Box 362 Cross River NY 10518 Office: Fabrique Cosmetique Inc PO Box 361 Cross River NY 10518

LANG, ROBERTA LYNN, food products company executive, lawyer; b. South Bend, Ind., Oct. 16, 1958; d. Robert Aschielle and Charlene Theresa (Leffert) Plasschaert; m. Richard Alan Lang, Dec. 2, 1991; 1 child, Daniel Marek; 1 stepchild, Cole. BA, Ind. U., South Bend, 1987; JD, Valparaiso U., 1990. Bar: Ind. 1990, U.S. Dist. Ct. (no. and so. dists.) Ind. 1990, Ill. 1992, U.S. Dist. Ct. (no. dist.) Ill. 1992. Assoc. Krisor & Nussbaum, South Bend, 1990-91, Momkus, Ozog & McCluskey, Downers Grove, Ill., 1992-94; pvt. practice, 1994—98; v.p., gen. counsel Whole Foods Market Inc., 1998—. Bd. dirs. Animal Compassion Found., 2005—, Whole Planet Found. Vol. Legal Svcs. Program No. Ind., Inc., South Bend, 1985-87. Mem. DuPage County Assn. Women Lawyers. Office: Whole Foods Market Inc 550 Bowie St Austin TX 78703

LANG, SHELDON, pathologist; b. NY, Jan. 31, 1932; s. Emil and Anna Lang; m. Marie Christabel Hoyos; children: Melissa Ellen, Maximilian Edward. BA, NYU, 1953; MD, SUNY, Bklyn., 1957. Lic. doctor NJ, 1958, Calif., 1958, Nev., 1958. Pvt. practice pathogist, Henderson, Nev., 1964—. Dir. lab. Beth Israel Hosp., Passaic, NJ, 1975—89. Author: A FLAWED VISION: A History of Battlecruisers. Lt. med. corps. USN, 1959—61. Fellow: Coll. Am. Pathologists. Independent. Avocations: history, painting. Home: 1981 Moyer Dr Henderson NV 89074 Home Phone: 702-837-8732. Home Fax: 702-837-8732. E-mail: sheldonlang@cox.net.

LANG, STEPHEN, actor; b. NYC, July 11, 1952; s. Eugene M. and Theresa (Volmer) L.; m. Kristina Watson, June 1, 1980; children: Lucy Jane, Daniel. BA, Swarthmore Coll., 1975. Actor: (Broadway) Saint Joan, Circle in the Square, 1977, Defiance, 2006;(stage prodns.) Othello, 1969, Hamlet, 1975, The Barbarians, 1980, Wild Oats, or the Strolling Gentleman, 1980, Rip Van Winkle, or The Works, 1981, The Clownmaker, 1982, Henry IV, Part I, 1982, Hannah, 1983, Death of a Salesman, 1984 (Drama Desk award 1984), Rosencrantz and Guildenstern Are Dead, 1987, A Few Good Men, The Speed of Darkness, Gods and Generals, 2003 (Grace award 2003), Beyond Glory, 2007; (feature films) Twice in a Lifetime, 1985, Manhunter, 1986, Band of the Hand, 1986, Project X, 1987; (TV series) We're Fighting Back, 1980, Crime Story, 1986; (TV movies) Stone Pillow, 1985, Death of a Salesman, 1985. Mem. SAG, Actors' Equity Assn. Clubs: Players. Office: care David Williams Internat Creative Mgmt 40 W 57th St New York NY 10019-4001

LANG, THOMPSON HUGHES, publishing executive; b. Albuquerque, Dec. 12, 1946; s. Cornelius Thompson and Margaret Miller (Hughes) L. Student, U. N.Mex., 1965-68, U. Americas, Mexico City, 1968-69. Advt. salesman Albuquerque Pub. Co., 1969-70, pres., 1971—; pub., pres., treas., dir. Jour. Pub. Co., 1971—; pres., dir. Masthead, Internat., 1971—; pres. Magnum Systems, Inc., 1973—; pres., treas., dir. Jour. Ctr. Corp., 1979—; chmn. bd., dir. Starline Printing, Inc., 1985—. Chmn. bd. dirs. Corp. Security and Investigation, Inc., 1986—; pres., bd. dirs. Eagle Systems, Inc., 1986—. Mem. HOW Orgn., Sigma Delta Chi. Home: 8643 Rio Grande Blvd NW Albuquerque NM 87114-1301 Office: Albuquerque Pub Co PO Drawer JT 87103 7777 Jefferson St NE Albuquerque NM 87109-4343

LANG, WILLIAM CHARLES, retail executive; b. Bronx, NY, Jan. 29, 1944; s. Harold C. and Katherine L. (Pratt) L.; m. Marilyn Warshow, June 27, 1965 (dec.); children: Kenneth William, Pamela Sue. BS magna cum laude, Lehigh U., 1965. C.P.A. Accounting supr. Peat, Marwick, Mitchell & Co., 1965-69; contr. Pueblo Internat., Inc., NYC, 1970-72, v.p. fin., 1972-77; exec. v.p. adminstrn. and fin. Kenyon & Eckhardt, Inc., 1977-85; exec. mng. dir. Finley, Kumble, Wagner, Heine, Underberg, Manley, Myerson & Casey, 1985-88; pres., CO, Furr's Inc., Lubbock, Tex., 1989-92; exec. v.p. fin. and adminstrn., chief fin. officer Duane Reade, NYC, 1993-96, chief adminstrv. officer, 1993-96; exec. v.p. fin, CFO, CAO GAF Materials Corp., Wayne, NJ, 1997-2001; prof. acctg., law and taxation Montclair (N.J.) State U., 2001—03. Mem. AICPA, Fin. Execs. Inst., Am. Acctg. Assn., N.Y. State Soc. CPAs, Beta Gamma Sigma, Sigma Phi. E-mail: wlang9@optonline.net.

LANG, WILLIAM WARNER, physicist; b. Boston, Aug. 9, 1926; s. William Warner and Lilla Gertrude (Wheeler) Lang; m. Asta Ingard, Aug. 31, 1954; 1 child, Robert. BS, Iowa State U., 1946, PhD, 1958; MS, MIT, 1949. Acoustical engr. Bolt Beranek and Newman, Inc., Cambridge, Mass., 1949-51; instr. in physics US Naval Postgrad. Sch., Monterey, Calif., 1951-55; cons. engr. E.I. du Pont de Nemours & Co., Wilmington, Del., 1955-57; mem. research staff MIT, 1958; physicist IBM, Poughkeepsie, NY, 1958-92, program mgr. acoustics tech., 1976-90, mem. sr. tech. staff, 1990-92; pres. Internat. Inst. Noise Control Engring., Leuven, Belgium, 1988—99. Editor: Designing for Noise Control, 1978. Pres. Noise Control Found., Poughkeepsie, 1975-92, 1994—; adj. prof. physics Vassar Coll., 1979-96; chmn. working group Internat. Orgn. Standardization, 1969—; chmn. tech. com. 29 Internat. Electrotech. Commn., 1975-84. With USN, 1944-47, 52. Decorated Meritorious Svc. medal; recipient Pro Silentio medal, Hungarian Optical, Acoustical and Film Tech. Soc., 1989, Clarissima award, Brazilian Acoustical Soc., 2005. Fellow AAAS, IEEE (Audio and Electroacoustics Achievement award 1970, dir. 1970-71, Centennial medal 1984), Audio Engring. Soc., Acoustical Soc. Am. (Silver medal 1984, treas. 1994-98), Inst. Acoustics (U.K.) (hon. fellow); mem. Nat. Acad. Engring., Inst. Noise Control Engring./U.S.A. (pres. 1978, chair study team on nat. noise policy 2000—, Disting. Noise Control Engr. award 2002), Rotary (pres. local club 1975-76). Episcopalian. Home and Office: 29 Hornbeck Rdg Poughkeepsie NY 12603-4205 Home Phone: 845-471-5537; Office Phone: 845-471-5493. Business E-Mail: langww@noisecontrolfoundation.org.

LANGA, BRIAN D., lawyer; b. Marietta, Ga., Mar. 1, 1973; BS, Rice Univ., 1995; JD, Univ. Washington, 1998. Bar: Calif. 1998, US Dist. Ct. Ctrl. & No. Calif. Ptnr., environ. & real estate law Demetriou, Del Guerico, Springer & Francis LLP, LA. Contbr. articles to profl. jours. Named a Rising Star, So. Calif. Super Lawyers, 2006. Mem.: Fed. Bar Assn., LA County Bar Assn., Internat. Right of Way Assn., Calif. Waste Assn. (past chmn. steering com., LA county chapter), Harbor Assn. Ind. & Comm. Office: Demetriou Del Guerico Springer & Francis LLP 10th Fl 801 S Grand Ave Los Angeles CA 90017-4613 Office Phone: 213-624-8407. Office Fax: 213-624-0174. Business E-Mail: blanga@ddsffirm.com.

LANGACKER, RONALD WAYNE, linguistics educator; b. Fond du Lac, Wis., Dec. 27, 1942; s. George Rollo and Florence (Hinesley) L.; m. Margaret G. Fullick, June 5, 1966 (dec.); m. Sheila M. Pickwell, Mar. 28, 1998. AB in French, U. Ill., 1963, A.M. in Linguistics, 1964, PhD, 1966. Asst. prof. U. Calif. at San Diego, La Jolla, 1966-70, asso. prof., 1970-75, prof. linguistics, 1975—2003; ret. Author: Language and its Structure, 1968, Fundamentals of Linguistic Analysis, 1972, Non-Distinct Arguments in Uto-Aztecan, 1976, An Overview of Uto-Aztecan Grammar, 1977, Foundations of Cognitive Grammar I, 1987, Concept, Image and Symbol, 1990, Foundations of Cognitive Grammar II, 1991, Grammar and Conceptualization, 1999; assoc. editor: Lang, 1971-77, Cognitive Linguistics, 1989—; contbr. articles in field to profl. jours. Guggenheim fellow, 1978 Mem. Linguistic Soc. Am., Cognitive Sci. Soc., Soc. for Study Indigenous Langs. of Ams., Internat. Cognitive Linguistics Assn. (pres. 1997-99), ACLU. Home: 7381 Rue Michael La Jolla CA 92037-3915 Office: U Calif San Diego Dept Linguistics 0108 La Jolla CA 92093 E-mail: rlangacker@ucsd.edu.

LANGAN, KENNETH J., lawyer; b. Sept. 14, 1955; BSFS cum laude, Georgetown U., 1977; JD, Columbia U., 1980. Bar: N.Y. 1981, Calif. 1993, England & Wales (solicitor) 1998. Ptnr., Project Fin. Practice Group Arnold & Porter, LA. Mem.: Phi Beta Kappa. Office: Arnold & Porter 777 S Figueroa St Los Angeles CA 90017-2513 Office Phone: 213-243-4114. Office Fax: 213-243-4199. Business E-Mail: kenneth.langan@aporter.com.

LANGAN, RICHARD F., JR., lawyer; b. Darby, Pa., 1955; BA magna cum laude, Fordham U., 1977; JD, George Washington U., 1980. Ptnr., chair bus. and fin. dept. Nixon Peabody LLP, NYC. Dir. Minetta Brook. Mem.: ABA, Assn. Bar of City NY (mem. securities regulations com. 2001—05, fin. reporting com. 2005—), Phi Beta Kappa. Office: Nixon Peabody LLP 437 Madison Ave New York NY 10022-7001 Office Phone: 212-940-3140. Office Fax: 866-947-2436. Business E-Mail: rlangan@nixonpeabody.com.

LANGBAUM, ROBERT WOODROW, language educator; s. Murray and Nettie (Moskowitz) L.; m. Francesca Levi Vidale, Nov. 5, 1950; 1 child, Donata Emily. AB, Cornell U., 1947; MA, Columbia U., 1949, PhD, 1954. Instr. English Cornell U., 1950-55, asst. prof., 1955-60; assoc. prof. U. Va., Charlottesville, 1960-63, prof. English, 1963—67, James Branch Cabell prof. English and Am. lit., 1967—99, prof. emeritus, 1999—. Vis. prof. Columbia U., summer 1960, 65-66, Harvard U., summer 1965; mem. supervising com. English Inst., 1970-71, chmn., 1972; mem. Christian Gauss Book Award Com., 1984-86; U.S. Info. Svc. lectr. Japan, Taiwan, Hong Kong, 1988. Author: The Poetry of Experience: The Dramatic Monologue in Modern Literary Tradition, 1957 (Spanish trans. 1996), The Gayety of Vision: A Study of Isak Dinesen's Art (Danish trans. 1964), 1964, The Modern Spirit: Essays on the Continuity of Nineteenth and Twentieth Century Literature, 1970, The Mysteries of Identity: A Theme in Modern Literature, 1977, The Word From Below: Essays on Modern Literature and Culture, 1987, Thomas Hardy in Our Time, 1995; editor: The Tempest (Shakespeare), 1964; anthology The Victorian Age: Essays in History and in Social and Literary Criticism, 1967; mem. edit. bd. Victorian Poetry, 1963—, New Lit. History, 1969—, Bull. Rsch. in Humanities, 1977—, Studies in English Lit., 1978—, So. Humanities Rev., 1979—, Studies in Browning and His Circle, 1987—, Victorian Lit. and Culture, 1991—, Symbiosis, 1995—. Served to 1st lt. M.I. AUS, 1942-46. Ford Found. fellow Center for Advanced Study, Stanford, Calif., 1961-62; Guggenheim fellow, 1969-70, Sr. fellow Nat. Endowment for Humanities, 1972-73; Am. Council Learned Socs. grantee, 1961, 75-76; fellow Clare Hall, Cambridge U., Eng., 1978; U. Va. Ctr. Advanced Study fellow, 1982; resident scholar Bellagio Study and Conf. Ctr. Rockefeller Found., Italy, 1987. Mem. MLA (del. assembly 1979-81), AAUP, PEN, Assn. Lit. Scholars and Critics, Phi Beta Kappa. Home: 223 Montvue Dr Charlottesville VA 22901-2022 Home Phone: 434-296-6781. Business E-Mail: rwl8v@virginia.edu.

LANGBEIN, JOHN HARRISS, lawyer, educator; b. Washington, Nov. 17, 1941; s. I. L. and M. V. (Harriss) L.; m. Kirsti M. Hiekka, June 24, 1973; children: Christopher, Julia, Anne. AB, Columbia U., 1964; LLB, Harvard U., 1968, Cambridge U., 1969, PhD, 1971; MA (hon.), Yale U., 1990. Bar: D.C. 1969, Fla. 1970; barrister-at-law Inner Temple, Eng., 1970. Asst. prof. law U. Chgo., 1971-73, assoc. prof., 1973-74, prof., 1974-80, Max Pam prof. Am. and fgn. law, 1980-90; Goodhart Prof. Legal Sci. Cambridge Univ., 1997-98, Chancellor Kent prof., 1990—2001; Sterling prof. law and legal history Yale U., New Haven, 2001—. Commr. Nat. Conf. Commrs. on Uniform State Laws, 1984—; reporter Uniform Prudent Investor Act; assoc. reporter Am. Law Inst., Restatement of Property (3d): Wills and Other Donative Transfers, 1990—. Author: Prosecuting Crime in the Renaissance, 1974, Torture and the Law of Proof: Europe and England in the Ancient Regime, 1977, 2006, Comparative Criminal Procedure, 1977, The Origins of Adversary Criminal Trial, 2003 (Coif Book award, 2006); author: (with L. Waggoner) Uniform Trusts and Estate Statutes, rev. edit., 2007—; author: (with R. Helmholz et al.) The Privilege Against

Self-Incrimination, 1997; author: (with B. Wolk and S. Stabile) Pension and Employee Benefit Law, 1990, 2006; contbr. articles to profl. jours. Recipient Biennial Coif award for the oustanding Am. work of legal scholarship, 2006. Fellow Trinity Hall Cambridge U. (hon.); mem. ABA, Am. Acad. Arts. and Scis., Am. Coll. Trust and Estate Counsel, Am. Law Inst., Am. Soc. Legal History, Am. Hist. Assn., Selden Soc., Gesellschaft fuer Rechtsvergleichung, Internat. Acad. Estate and Trust Law, Internat. Acad. Comparative Law. Republican. Episcopalian. Office: Yale Univ Sch Law PO Box 208215 127 Wall St New Haven CT 06520-8215 Office Phone: 203-432-7299. Business E-Mail: john.langbein@yale.edu.

LANGBERG, BARRY BENSON, lawyer; b. Balt., Nov. 24, 1942; s. Nathan and Marion (Cohen) L.; m. Vickie Williams, Mar. 27, 1978 (div. 1987); children: Mitchell, Marie, Elena. BA, U. San Francisco, 1964, JD, 1968. Bar: Calif. 1971, U.S. Dist. Ct. (cen. dist.) Calif. 1971, U.S. Supreme Ct. 1974, U.S. Tax Ct. 1976. Dep. pub. defender Los Angeles County, 1971-72; assoc. Trope & Trope, LA, 1972-74, Hayes & Hume, Beverly Hills, Calif., 1974-85; pres. David Jamison Carlyle Corp., LA, 1979-84; ptnr. Hayes, Hume, Petas & Langberg, LA, 1985-89; atty. Barry B. Langberg & Assocs., LA, 1989-97; ptnr. Bronson, Bronson & McKinnon, LA, 1997—2000; mng. ptnr., LA office, entertainment law practice area Stroock & Stroock & Lavan LLP, LA, 2000—. Prof. Mid-Valley Coll. Law, L.A., 1972-82; lectr. U. So. Calif., 1980. Mem. ABA. Democrat. Avocations: sailing, baseball. Office: Stroock & Strook & Lavan LLP 2029 Century Pk E Los Angeles CA 90067-3086 Office Phone: 310-556-5861. Office Fax: 310-556-5959. Business E-Mail: blangberg@stroock.com.

LANGBO, ARNOLD GORDON, former food company executive; b. Richmond, BC, Can., Apr. 13, 1937; s. Osbjourn and Laura Marie (Hagen) Langbo; m. Martha Marie Miller, May 30, 1959; children: Sharon Anne, Maureen Bernice, Susan Colleen, Roderick Arnold, Robert Wayne, Gary Thomas, Craig Peter, Keith Edward. Student, U. B.C. Retail salesman Kellogg Co., Vancouver, 1956-57, dist. mgr. Prince George, B.C., 1957-60, supermarket salesman Vancouver, 1960, dist mgr. Winnipeg, Man., 1964-65; acct. mgr. Kellog Co. of Can., Ltd., Toronto, 1965-67; sales staff asst. Kellogg Co., Battle Creek, Mich., 1967-69, adminstrv. asst. to pres., 1969; exec. v.p. Kellogg Co. of Can. Ltd., London, Ont., 1970; v.p. sales and mktg. Kellogg Salada Can. Ltd., Toronto, 1971-74, sr. v.p. sales and mktg., 1974-76, pres., CEO, 1976-78; pres. food products divsn. Kellogg U.S., Battle Creek, 1978-81; group exec. v.p. Kellogg Co., Battle Creek, 1983-86, exec. v.p., 1986—; pres. Mrs. Smith's Frozen Foods Co. subs. Kellogg Co., Battle Creek, 1983-85, chmn., CEO, 1985—86; pres. Kellogg Internat., 1986—90, pres., COO, internat. bd. dirs., 1990-99; chmn., CEO, pres. Kellogg Co., Battle Creek, 1992-99, also bd. dirs., retired, 1999. Bd. dirs. Johnson & Johnson, 1991—, Whirlpool Corp., 1994—, Weyerhaeuser Co., 1999—, Atlantic Richfield Co.; chmn. Grocery Mfrs. Am. Co-trustee W.K. Kellogg Found. Trust; chmn. trustees Albion Coll. Bd.; bd. dirs. Internat. Youth Found., America's Promise; mem. adv. bd. J.K. Kellogg Grad. Sch. of Mgmt., Northwestern U. Mem.: Bus. Roundtable.

LANGBORT, POLLY, retired advertising executive; b. NYC; d. Julius and Nettie (Berman) L. BA, Adelphi U. Sec. Young & Rubicam, Inc., NYC, media buyer, media planner, 1960-65, planning supr., 1965-70, v.p. group supr., 1970-75, v.p. dir. planning devel., 1975-80, sr. v.p., dir. comm. planning, 1980-85, sr. v.p. direct mktg. and media services Wunderman, Worldwide div., 1985-86, exec. v.p. dir. mktg. & media services, 1986-90; assoc. pub. Lear's Mag., NYC, 1990-91; ret., 1991. Author: DMA Factbook, 1986; contbr. articles to profl. jours. Spl. gifts chairperson Am. Cancer Soc., N.Y.C., 1985-90. Mem. Boca Raton Resort and Club, Boca Pointe Country Club. Avocations: classical music, outdoor activities, bridge. Home: 7614 La Corniche Cir Boca Raton FL 33433-6055 Personal E-mail: pollylang@aol.com.

LANGDALE, MARK, ambassador, former hotel executive; b. Houston, May 4, 1954; m. Patty Langdale; children: Paul, Olivia. BBA in Fin. with honors, U. Tex.; JD, U. Houston. Former v.p. Thompson Realty Co.; mng. gen. ptnr., mng. dir. CapRock Comms. Corp.; pres. Posadas USA, Inc., Mexico City, 1989—2005; US amb. to Costa Rica US Dept. State, San Jose, 2005—. Chmn. governing bd. Tex. Dept. of Econ. Devel., 1997-2005. Chmn. Lone Star Dallas chpt. Young Pres. Orgn.; chmn. Tex.-Mexico Authority; advisor to gov. legis. issues Tex. rels. with Mex. Office: Am Embassy 3440 San Jose Pl Washington DC 20521

LANGDALE, NOAH NOEL, JR., retired education educator, academic administrator; b. Valdosta, Ga., Mar. 29, 1920; s. Noah N. and Jessie Katharine (Catledge) Langdale; m. Alice Elizabeth Cabaniss, Jan. 8, 1944; 1 child, Noah Michael. AB, U. Ala., 1941, LLD, 1959; LLB, Harvard U., 1948, MBA, 1950. Bar: Ga. 1951. Asst. football coach U. Ala., 1942; pvt. practice law Valdosta, 1951-57; from instr. to asst. prof. econs. and social studies, chmn. dept. acctg., econs., bus. adminstrn. Valdosta State Coll., 1954-57; pres. Ga. State U., Atlanta, 1957-88, Disting. univ. rsch. prof., 1988-89, pres. emeritus, disting. rsch. prof. emeritus, 1989—; ret., 1989. Past mem. U.S. Adv. Commn. Ednl. Exch.; former mem. Pres.'s Commn. NCAA. Served to lt. (s.g.) USNR, 1942—46. Recipient 1st Georgian of the Yr. award, Ga. Assn. Broadcasters, 1962, Silver Anniversary All-Am. award, Sports Illustrated, 1966, Myrtle Wreath award, Hadassah, 1970, Salesman of the Yr. award, Sales and Mktg. Execs. Atlanta, 1975, Silver Knight of Mgmt. award, Lockheed-Ga. chpt. Nat. Mgmt. Assn., 1978, Humanitarian award, Nat. Jewish Hosp. and Rsch. Ctr./Nat. Asthma Ctr., 1980, Robert T. Jones award, Boy Scouts Am. Mem.: SAR (past v.p. Ga.), ABA, Ga. Assn. Colls. (pres. 1962—63), Ga. Bar Assn., Ga. Bar Found. (life), Rotary, Gridiron Soc., Phi Beta Kappa, Phi Kappa Phi, Delta Chi, Omicron Delta Kappa. Methodist.

LANGDON, JAMES CALHOUN, JR., lawyer; b. LA, Sept. 20, 1945; BBA, U. Tex., 1967, JD, 1970. Bar: Tex. 1970, D.C. 1976. Assoc. adminstr. Fed. Energy Office, Washington, 1972-73, Fed. Energy Adminstrn., Washington, 1973-74; dir. Office Comml. Affairs US Dept. Treasury, Washington, 1974-75; mem. Akin Gump Strauss Hauer & Feld LLP, Washington, 1975—, now sr. exec. ptnr. energy-related issues and mem. mgmt. com. Washington, Texas, Moscow; prin. AG Global Solutions (joint venture of Akin Gump and First Internat. Resources). Mem. Pres. Fgn. Intelligence Advisory Bd., 2002—. Mem. ABA, State Bar Tex., DC Bar. Office: Akin Gump Strauss Hauer & Feld LLP Ste 400 1333 New Hampshire Ave NW Washington DC 20036-1564 Office Phone: 202-887-4044. Office Fax: 202-955-7758. Business E-Mail: jlangdon@akingump.com.

LANGE, ANDREW E., astrophysicist; BA, Princeton U., 1980; PhD, U. Calif., Berkeley, 1987. Vis. assoc. Calif. Inst. Tech., 1993—94, prof., 1994—2001, Marvin L. Goldberger prof. physics, Observational Cosmology Group, 2001—. Named Calif. Scientist Yr., Calif. Sci. Ctr., 2003. Mem.: NAS. Achievements include expert in structure and geometry of very early universe and in measurement of irregularities in cosmic microwave background radiation. Office: Calif Inst Tech Mailcode 59-33 Pasadena CA 91125 Office Phone: 626-395-6887. Office Fax: 626-584-9929. Business E-Mail: ael@astro.caltech.edu.

LANGE, CARL JAMES, retired psychology professor; b. Seneca, Pa., June 1, 1925; s. Otto Carl and Rose Marie (Jetter) L.; m. Veronica Szelypecz, Jan. 14, 1950; children: David Carl, Veronica Jean. BS, Duke U., 1945; MS, U. Pitts., 1948, PhD, 1951. Lic. psychologist, Va. Project dir. Human Resources Research Office, George Washington U., 1953-60, dir. research, planning, 1960-69; asst. v.p. research George Washington U., 1969-75, v.p. adminstrn., research, prof. psychology, 1975-88, v.p. rsch., prof. psychology, 1988-89, prof. emeritus, 1989—. Cons. NSF, Ford Found.; bd. dirs. Sch. for Contemporary Edn., Nat. Lab. Higher Edn., Eric Clearinghouse for Higher Edn., Southeastern Univs. Rsch. Assn. Contbr. articles in field to profl. jours.; bd. editors: Research in Higher Education. Served with USN, 1943-45. Fellow Am. Psychol. Assn.; mem. AAAS, Sigma Xi. Home: 7 Clarendon Ct Williamsburg VA 23188-1513

LANGE, CLIFFORD ELMER, retired librarian; b. Fond du Lac, Wis., Dec. 29, 1935; s. Elmer H. and Dorothy Brick (Smithers) L.; m. Janet M. LeMieux, June 6, 1959; children: Paul, Laura, Ruth. Student, St. Norbert Coll., 1954-57; BS, Wis. State U., 1959; MSL.S. (Library Services Act scholar), U. Wis., 1960, PhD (Higher Edn. Act fellow), 1972. Head extension dept. Oshkosh (Wis.) Pub. Libr., 1960-62, head reference dept., 1962-63; asst. dir. Jervis Libr., Rome, 1962; dir. Eau Claire (Wis.) Pub. Libr., 1963-66; asst. dir. Lake County Pub. Libr., Griffith, Ind., 1966-68; asst. prof. Sch. Libr. Sci., U. Iowa, 1971-73; dir. Wauwatosa (Wis.) Pub. Libr., 1973-75; asst. prof. U. So. Calif., 1975-78; state libr. N.Mex. State Libr., Santa Fe, 1978-82; dir. Carlsbad City Libr., Calif., 1982—2005; ret., 2005. Served with U.S. Army, 1958. Mem. ALA, Calif. Libr. Assn. Home: 3575 Ridge Rd Oceanside CA 92056-4952 Personal E-mail: clifflange@cox.net.

LANGE, DALE LOWELL, language educator, researcher; b. Granite Falls, Minn., Nov. 4, 1934; m. Estella Marie Gahala, Apr. 18, 1998; m. Sylvia Ann Martinsen, Apr. 30, 1957 (div. Apr. 23, 1981); m. Linda Marie Crawford, July 11, 1981 (div. Mar. 20, 1992); children: Bryan Andre, Stefan Peter, Erik David, Kevin Mark, Kristofer Brent, Sara Stephanie, Heather Ann. BS, U. Minn., 1958, MA, 1963, PhD, 1966. Tchg. asst. German dept., NDEA Inst. Stanford (Calif.) U., 1960, instr. German dept., NDEA Inst., 1961; instr. U. H.S., Coll. Edn., U. Minn., Mpls., 1958—65, lectr., 1965—66; asst. prof. dept. secondary edn. Coll. Edn. U. Minn.-Twin Cities, Mpls., 1966—69, assoc. prof. dept. secondary edn. Coll. Edn., 1969—72, prof. dept. curriculum and instrn. Coll. Edn., 1972—99, assoc. dean for academic affairs Coll. Edn., 1989—94, dir. Ctr. for Advanced Rsch. on Lang. Acquistion, 1994—95, prof. emeritus Coll. Edn. and Human Devel., 1999—. Presenter in field. Co-editor: Foreign Language Learning Today and Tomorrow: Essays in Honor of Emma M. Birkmaier, 1979, Culture as the Core: Perspectives on Culture in Second Language Learning, 2003; contbr. articles to profl. publs. Docent Albuquerque Mus. Art and History, 1996—2000; bd. dirs., v.p., sec./treas. Art in the Sch., Inc, Albuquerque, 2001—05; chair fin. team First United Meth. Ch., Albuquerque, 2007—. Recipient Emma Birkmaier award for Svc. to Fgn. Lang. in the State of Minn., Minn. Coun. on the Tchg. Fgn. Langs. and Cultures, 1981; scholar NDEA Inst., U. Texas,Austin, 1959, Stanford U., 1960. Mem.: MLA, Am. Assn. Tchrs. French, Am. Assn. Tchrs. German, Am. Edn. Rsch. Assn., Am. Coun. on the Tchg. Fgn. Langs. (bibliographer 1969—73, pres. 1980—80). Dfl. Avocations: genealogy, art collecting, gardening, music. Home: 2315 Madre Drive NE Albuquerque NM 87112-2503 Home Phone: 505-298-9138; Office Phone: 505-298-9138. Office Fax: 505-298-0307; Home Fax: 505-298-0307. Personal E-mail: dalelange@aol.com.

LANGE, FREDERICK EDWARD, JR., computer information systems architect; b. Johnstown, Pa., Oct. 21, 1946; s. Frederick Edward and Jean Louise (Huebner) L.; m. Karen Ann Mawson, Mar. 15, 1975; 1 child, Sharon Ann. BA in Social Scis., Cleve. State U., 1969, MA in Econs., 1978. Cert. secondary tchr., Ohio; cert. master data architect, 2006. Vol. Peace Corps, Liberia and Micronesia, 1969-73; tchr. Cleve. Pub. Schs., 1973-74; dir. Westside Inst. Tech., Cleve., 1974-81; systems analyst Case Western Res. U., Cleve., 1982-83; systems engr. Profl. Support, Inc., Brecksville, Ohio, 1983-91; analyst Setpoint, Brecksville, 1991-93; prin. cons. Cap Gemini Am., Beechwood, Ohio, 1994-96; sr. prin. cons. Oracle Corp., Cleve., 1996—2001; info. arch. Nat. City Corp., Highland Hills, Ohio, 2001—03; enterprise data arch. Key Bank, Cleve., 2005—; cons., 2003—04; ind. cons. in field. Bd. dirs. Zoe, Inc., Cleve., Fast Refund Svc. Editor: Fuel Efficiency and Safety, 1979; contbr. Data Mgmt. Rev. Active Richmond Heights Civic League, Ohio, 1986, Northeast Ohio Returned Vol. Assn. (Beyond War award 1987), Cleve., 1978—, Nat. Peace Corps Assn.; judge Internat. Sci. and Engring. Fair Grand Awards, 2003-07. Mem. Am. Econs. Assn., Data Processing Mgmt. Assn., Assn. Computing Machinery, Instument Soc. Am. (Dedicated Svc. award 1980), Javelin Class Assn. (fleet capt. 1982-83, sec. 1987-88, commodore 1989-91), Forest City Yacht Club. Avocations: sailing, gardening, genealogy. E-mail: frederickklange@lsp.com, fred_lange@keybank.com.

LANGE, HARRY W., investment company executive; BS in Mech. Engring., Gen. Motors Inst.; MBA, Harvard Univ. Sr. rsch. engr., engring. mgr. Chevrolet Motors Divsn. Gen. Motors, 1970—83; assoc. Idanta Ptnrs., 1983—84; with Fidelity Investments, 1987—, dir rsch. Far East, 1988—92, mgr. select computers portfolio, 1992—96, mgr. Capital Appreciation Fund, 1996—2005, adv. Small Cap Fund, 1998—2001, mgr. Growth Am. Fund, 2001—05, mgr. Fidelity Magellan Fund, 2005—. Office: Fidelity Investments 82 Devonshire St Boston MA 02109 Office Fax: 617-476-6152. Business E-Mail: harry.lange@fmr.com.

LANGE, JESSICA PHYLLIS, actress; b. Cloquet, Minn., Apr. 20, 1949; d. Al and Dorothy Lange; m. Paco Grande, 1971 (div. 1981); 1 child with Mikhail Baryshnikov, Alexandra; children with Sam Shepard: Hannah Jane, Samuel Walker Student, U. Minn.; student mime, with Etienne DeCroux, Paris. Dancer Opera Comique, Paris; model Wilhelmina Agy., NYC. Film appearances include King Kong, 1976, All That Jazz, 1979, How to Beat the High Cost of Living, 1980, The Postman Always Rings Twice, 1981, Frances, 1982 (Acad. award nominee 1982), Tootsie, 1982 (Acad. award 1983), Country, 1984, Sweet Dreams, 1985, Crimes of the Heart, 1986 (Acad. award nominee 1987), Everybody's All American, 1988, Far North, 1988, Music Box, 1989 (Acad. award nominee 1990), Men Don't Leave, 1990, Cape Fear, 1991, Night and the City, 1992, Blue Sky, 1994 (Golden Globe award Best Actress in a Drama 1995, Acad. award for Best Actress 1995), Losing Isaiah, 1995, Rob Roy, 1995, A Thousand Acres, 1997, Hush, 1998, Cousin Bette, 1998, Titus, 1999, Big Fish, 2003, Broken Flowers, 2005, Don't Come Knocking, 2005, Neverwas, 2005; TV movies: Cat on a Hot Tin Roof, 1984, O' Pioneers!, 1992, A Streetcar Named Desire, 1995 (Golden Globe award 1996), Prozac Nation, 2001, Normal, 2003; in summer stock prodn. Angel on My Shoulder, N.C., 1980, A Streetcar Named Desire, 1992; prodr. Country, 1984; TV guest appearance Inside the Actors Studio, 1994; theatre: The Glass Menagerie, 2005, in London, 2007.*

LANGE, LESTER HENRY, mathematics professor; b. Concordia, Mo., Jan. 2, 1924; s. Harry William Christopher and Ella Martha (Alewel) L.; m. Anne Marie Pelikan, Aug. 17, 1947 (div. Oct. 1960); children: Christopher, Nicholas, Philip, Alexander; m. Beverly Jane Brown, Feb. 4, 1962; 1 son, Andrew. Student, U. Calif., Berkeley, 1943-44; BA in Math, Valparaiso U., 1948; MS in Math, Stanford, 1950; PhD in Math, U. Notre Dame, 1960. Instr., then asst. prof. math. Valparaiso U., 1950-56; instr. math. U. Notre Dame, 1956-57, 59-60. Mem. faculty San Jose State U., Calif., 1960—, prof. math., head dept., 1961-70, dean Sch. Natural Scis. and Math., 1970—, dean Sch. Sci., 1972-88, emeritus prof. math., emeritus dean, 1988—; founder Soc. Archimedes at San Jose State U., 1982; now spl. asst. to dir. Moss Landing (Calif.) Marine Labs.; founding bd. dirs. Friends of MLML, Inc. Author text on linear algebra; sr. editor Calif. Math, 1981-84; contbr. to profl. jours. Served with inf. AUS, 1943-46, ETO. Decorated Combat Infantryman's Badge and Bronze Star; Danforth fellow, 1957-58; NSF faculty fellow, 1958-59. Fellow Calif. Acad. Scis.; mem. Math. Assn. Am. (bd. govs., L.R. Ford Sr. award 1972, George Polya award 1993, Meritorious Svc. award 2003), Calif. Math. Coun., London Math. Soc., Fibonacci Assn. (bd. dirs. 1987-97). Home: 308 Escalona Dr Capitola CA 95010-3419 Office: Moss Landing Marine Labs Moss Landing CA 95039 Business E-Mail: lange@cruzio.com.

LANGE, LIZ, apparel designer, director; b. NY; m. Jeffrey Lange; 2 children. BA in Comparative Lit., Brown U., 1988. Asst. editor Vogue; fashion designer Stephen DiGeronimo; founder Liz Lange Maternity Clothing Line, NYC, 1997—. Named one of 40 Under 40, Crain's NY Bus. Jour., 2006. Office: Liz Lange Maternity Corp Office 2nd Fl 347 W 36th St New York NY 10018

LANGE, MARVIN ROBERT, lawyer; b. Bronx, Mar. 25, 1948; s. Arthur A. and Beatrice L. Lange; m. Ellen Metzger, Apr. 20, 1986; 1 child, Rebecca Hillary. BA cum laude, Queens Coll., 1968; JD magna cum laude, Harvard U., 1971. Bar: NY 1972, US Dist. Ct. (ea. & so. dists.) NY 1975, US Ct. Appeals (2d cir.) 1975, US Supreme Ct. 1980, US Ct. Appeals (6th cir.) 1986, DC Bar, US Dist. Ct. Ill. (no. dist.). Law clk. U.S. Dist. Ct., Phila., 1971-72; atty. FTC, Washington, 1972-75; assoc. Rosenman & Colin, NYC, 1975-81, ptnr., 1981-93; pvt. practice law, 1993-98; counsel Shaw Pittman, 1998—; ptnr. Bracewell & Giuliani, NYC. Editor Harvard Law Rev., 1969-71. Mem. ABA, Assn. Bar NYC. Jewish. Office: Bracewell & Giuliani 1177 Ave of Americas 19th Fl New York NY 10036-2714 Office Phone: 212-508-6108. Office Fax: 212-938-3808. Business E-Mail: marvin.lange@bgllp.com.

LANGE, PETER, academic administrator; BA, Oberlin Coll., 1967; PhD in Polit. Sci., MIT, 1975. Assoc. prof. Duke U., Durham, NC, 1982—89, prof., 1989—, spl. asst. to the provost for internat. affairs, 1993—94, vice provost for acad. and internat. affairs, 1994—96, chair dept. polit. sci., 1996—99, provost, 1999—. Woodrow Wilson fellow, 1967, Fulbright Rsch. scholar, Milan, 1986. Office: Duke Univ Office of the Provost Box 90005 Durham NC 27708

LANGE, PHIL C., retired education educator; b. North Freedom, Wis., Feb. 26, 1914; s. Richard Samuel and Martha (Grosinske) L.; m. Irene Oyen, June 8, 1940; children— Dena Rae, Richard (dec.). BA, U. Wis., 1934, MA, 1936, PhD, 1941. Tchr. Reeseville (Wis.) Pub. Sch., 1935-37; chmn. English dept. Wayland Jr. Coll. and Acad., Beaver Dam, Wis., 1937-39; instr. English, student teaching supr. Beloit (Wis.) High Sch., 1939-40; asst. instr. U. Wis., Madison, 1940-41, summers 1938, 39; chmn. psychology dept., dean men. Ariz. State Coll., Flagstaff, 1941-42; chmn. edn. dept. SUNY, Fredonia, 1942-50; prof. edn., coordinator student teaching Tchrs. Coll., Columbia U., 1950—. Cons., expert for Dept. State, UNESCO, AID, 1948, Korea, 1958-59, Chile, 1970, India, Pakistan, 1972-73, Afghanistan. Author, editor curriculum materials. Coord. Issues and Ideas program Cmty. Ch. Coll. Served with USNR, 1943-46. Recipient Filmstrip award Graphic Arts, 1966; Comm. award Nat. Soc. Programmed Instrn., 1968; award Ednl. Press Assn. Am., 1969 Office: Tchrs Coll Columbia Univ New York NY 10027 Home: 727 Foxhills Dr Sun City Center FL 33573

LANGELL, JOHN THOMAS, surgeon, researcher; s. Thomas Langell and Ellen Ludington; m. Sara Ann Whittingham, June 5, 2005; children: Micheal, Ashley, Christian, Kira. BS, UCLA, 1991; MD, PhD, Drexel U., Phila., 1999; MPH, U. Tex. Med. Br., Galveston, 2006. Diplomate Am. Bd. Surgery. Flight surgeon/OIC aerospace medicine 731st ALS, Peterson AFB, Colo.; surgery resident Stanford U., Calif., 1999—2006; aerospace medicine resident NASA/U. Tex. Med. Br., 2002—04; clin. specialist critical care medicine MD Anderson Cancer Ctr., Houston, 2002—05; asst. prof. surgery U. Utah, Salt Lake City, 2006—, dir. acute care surgery, 2006—. Dir. surg. intensive care Salt Lake City VA Hosp., 2006—. Contbr. articles to profl. jours., chpts. to books. Decorated 445th Mil. Airlift Wing Chief's Award USAF, 7th Air Force Disting. Airman, 445th Mil. Airlift Wing Airman of the Yr.; recipient Donald R. Cooper, MD award for excellence in surgery, Drexel U. Sch. Medicine, 1999, Merck Manual award for excellence in clin. medicine, 1999; grantee, Lifeline Found., 1998, Sigma Xi, 1996, Am. Heart Assn., 1995; scholar, Drexel U., 1992—99; William K. Douglas scholar, 2003. Fellow: ACS (assoc.); mem.: Aerospace Medicall Assn., Alpha Omega Alpha. Achievements include patents for utilization of mesenchymal stem cells to facilitate bone marrow transplantation. Avocations: flying, triathlons, scuba diving.

LANGELLA, FRANK, actor; b. Bayonne, NJ, Jan. 1, 1940; m. Ruth Weil, June 14, 1977 (div. 1996); 2 children. Student, Syracuse U.; studies with Seymour Falk. Apprenticed Pocono Playhouse, Mountain Home, Pa., appeared Erie (Pa.) Playhouse, 1960, mem. original, Lincoln Center repertory tng. co., 1963; actor (Broadway shows) Yerma, 1966, Seascape, 1974-75 (Tony award best featured actor, 1975, Drama Desk award, 1975), A Cry of Players, 1968 (Drama Desk award, 1968), Dracula, 1977-80 (Drama League award, 1978, Tony nom. best actor in a play, 1978), Passion, 1983, Design for Living, 1984, Hurlyburly, 1985, Sherlock's Last Case, 1987, The Father, 1996, Present Laughter, 1996-97, Fortune's Fool, 2002, Match, 2004 (Tony nom. best actor in a play, 2004); other stage appearances include: The Immoralist, 1963, Benito Cereno, 1964, The Old Glory, 1964-65 (Obie award, 1965), Good Day, 1965-66 (Obie award, 1966), The White Devil, 1965-66 (Obie award, 1966), Long Day's Journey Into Night, The Skin of Our Teeth, The Cretan Woman, all 1966, The Devils, Iphigenia at Aulis, all 1967, Cyrano de Bergerac, 1971, A Midsummer Night's Dream, 1972, The Relapse, The Tooth of Crime, 1972, The Taming of the Shrew, 1973, The Seagull, 1974, Ring Round the Moon, 1975, After the Fall, 1984, Booth, 1994, The Prince of Hamburg, Cleve. Playhouse Co., 1967-68, L.I. Festival repertory, 1968, Les Liaisons Dangereuses, Frost/Nixon, 2006 (Drama Desk award outstanding actor in a play 2007, Outer Critics Cir. award outstanding actor in a play, 2007, Tony award best performance by a leading actor in a play, 2007); stage directing debut in John and Abigail, 1969; (films) Diary of a Mad Housewife, 1970 (Nat. Soc. Film Critics award, 1970), The Twelve Chairs, 1970, The Deadly Trap, 1972, The Wrath of God, 1972, Dracula, 1979, Those Lips Those Eyes, 1980, Sphinx, 1981, The Men's Club, 1986, Masters of the Universe, 1987, And God Created Woman, 1988, True Identity, 1991, 1492: Conquest of Paradise, 1992, Dave, 1993, Body of Evidence, 1993, Brainscan, 1994, Junior, 1994, Bad Company, 1995, Cutthroat Island, 1995, Eddie, 1996, Lolita, 1997, I'm Losing You, 1998, Alegría, 1998, Small Soldiers, 1998, The Ninth Gate, 1999, Stardom, 2000, Sweet November, 2001, House of D, 2004, The Novice, 2004, Breaking the Fifth, 2004, How You Look to Me, 2005, Return to Rajapur, 2005, Good Night, and Good Luck, 2005, Superman Returns, 2006; (TV movies) Benito Cereno, 1965, Good Day, 1967, The Mark of Zorro, 1974, The Ambassador, 1974, The Seagull, 1975, The American Woman: Portraits of Courage, 1976, Eccentricities of a Nightingale, 1976, Sherlock Holmes, 1981, I, Leonardo: A Journey of the Mind, 1983 (Emmy nom. best actor, 1983), Liberty, 1986, The Doomsday Gun, 1994, Moses, 1996, Kilroy, 1999, Jason and the Argonauts, 2000, Cry Baby Lane, 2000, 111 Gramercy Park, 2003, Now You See It..., 2005, The Water is Wide, 2006, 10.5: Apocalypse, 2006. Bd. dirs. Berkshire Festival. Mem. Actors Equity, Screen Actors Guild. Office: Special Artists Agency 9465 Wilshire Blvd Ste 880 Beverly Hills CA 90212-2607*

LANGENBERG, BRET JAMES, surgeon; s. Stephen L. and Virginia G. Langenberg; m. Alexandra Hiler Perryman, July 15, 1995; children: Carson Hiler, Parker Gault. BS, Citadel, Charleston, SC, 1992. Cert. dr. osteo. medicine Midwestern U., Chgo., 1998, diplomate American Bd. Surgery, 2006. Gen. surgeon USN Med. Corps, San Diego, 1993—; gen. surgery resident Naval Med. Ctr., San Diego, 2005. Lt. comdr. USN, 1998—2006, San Diego. Office: Naval Med Ctr Dept Surgery San Diego CA 92134-5000 Home Phone: 858-271-9065; Office Phone: 619-532-7579. Personal E-mail: langenberg@medscape.com.

LANGENBERG, DONALD NEWTON, retired academic administrator, physicist; b. Devils Lake, ND, Mar. 17, 1932; s. Ernest George and Fern (Newton) L.; m. Patricia Ann Warrington, June 20, 1953; children: Karen Kaye, Julia Ann, John Newton, Amy Paris. BS, Iowa State U., 1953; MS, UCLA, 1955; PhD (NSF fellow), U. Calif., Berkeley, 1959; DSc (hon.), U. Pa., 1985, MA (hon.), 1971; DSc (hon.), SUNY, 1998. Electronics engr. Hughes Research Labs., Culver City, Calif., 1953-55; acting instr. U. Calif. at Berkeley, 1958-59; mem. faculty U. Pa., Phila., 1960-83, prof., 1967-83; dir. Lab. for Research on Structure of Matter, 1972-74; vice provost for grad. studies and research, 1974-79; chancellor U. Ill.-Chgo., 1983-90, U. Sys. Md., Adelphi, 1990—2002. Maitre de conference associe Ecole Normale Superieure, Paris, France, 1966-67; vis. prof. Calif. Inst. Tech., Pasadena, 1971; guest researcher Zentralinstitut für Tieftemperaturforschung der Bayerische Akademie der Wissenschaften and Technische Universität München, 1974; dep. dir. Nat. Sci. Found., 1980-82 Rschr., contbr. to publs. on solid state and low temperature physics including electronic band structure in metals and semiconductors, quantum phase coherence and nonequilibrium effects in superconductors, sci. and edn. policy and rsch. adminstrn. Recipient John Price Wetherill medal Franklin Inst., 1975, Disting. Contribution to Research Adminstrn. award Soc. Research Adminstrs., 1983, Disting. Achievement Citation, Iowa State Alumni Assn., 1984, Significant Sig award Sigma Chi, 1985; fellow NSF, 1959-60, Alfred P. Sloan Found., 1962-64; Guggenheim Found., 1966-67 Fellow AAAS (pres. 1990), Am. Phys. Soc. (pres. 1993), Sigma Xi. Address: 130 Chancellor Ln Queenstown MD 21658-1347 Office: Univ Md Dept Physics College Park MD 20742-4111 Home Phone: 410-827-8422; Office Phone: 301-405-9983. E-mail: dnl@usmd.edu.

LANGENBERG, FREDERICK CHARLES, manufacturing executive; b. NYC, July 1, 1927; s. Frederick C. and Margaret (McLaughlin) L.; m. Jane Anderson Bartholomew, May 16, 1953; children: Frederick C., Susan Jane; m. Marguerite Cardone, Apr. 13, 1996. BS, Lehigh U., 1950, MS, 1951; PhD, Pa. State U., 1955; postgrad. execs. program, Carnegie-Mellon U., 1962. With U.S. Steel Corp., 1951-53; vis. fellow MIT, 1955-56; with Crucible Steel Corp., Pitts., 1956-68, v.p. research and engring., 1966-68; pres. Trent Tube div. Colt Industries, Milw., 1968-70; exec. v.p. Jessop Steel Co., Washington, Pa., 1970, pres., 1970-75; pres., bd. dirs. Am. Iron and Steel Inst., Washington, 1975-78; pres. Interlake Corp., Oak Brook, Ill., 1979-81, pres., chmn, chief exec. officer, 1981-91, also bd. dirs.; chmn. Langand Corp., Pitts., 1991—. Contbr. articles to tech. jours.; patentee in field. With USNR, 1944—45. Named Oak Brook Bus. Leader of the Yr., 1986, Disting. Bus. Leader, DuPage County, 1988; Alumni fellow Pa. State U., 1977; recipient Disting. Alumni award, Pa. State U., 1989, Lehigh U., 1990. Fellow Am. Soc. Metals (disting. life mem. 1982, trustee, Pitts. Nite lectr. 1970, Andrew Carnegie lectr. 1976; David Ford McFarland award Penn State chpt. 1973); mem. AIME, Am. Soc. Metals, Metals Powder Industry Fedn., Phi Beta Kappa, Sigma Xi, Tau Beta Pi. Clubs: Duquesne, St. Clair Country (Pitts.), Congl., Burning Tree, Chgo. Golf, Chgo., Laurel Valley, Rolling Rock (Ligonier, Pa.), Belleair County Club (Fla.). Office: Langand Corp PO Box 1286 Mc Murray PA 15317 Home Phone: 412-835-3969; Office Phone: 724-941-1914. E-mail: peggycl15241@yahoo.com.

LANGENBRUNNER, JAMIE, professional hockey player; b. Duluth, Minn., July 24, 1975; m. Elizabeth Langenbrunner; 3 children. Left wing Dallas Stars, 1994—2002, NJ Devils, 2002—. Mem. U.S. Olympic Hockey Team, Nagano, Japan, 1998, Team U.S.A, World Cup of Hockey, 2004. Achievements include being a member of Stanley Cup Champion Dallas Stars, 1999, NJ Devils, 2003. Office: c/o NJ Devils Nat Newark Bldg 744 Broad St, 33rd Fl Newark NJ 07102

LANGENFELD, MARK E., healthcare educator; BA, Miami U., Oxford, Ohio, 1976; MA, Ohio State U., 1978, PhD, 1980; BA, SE Mo. State U., 2004. Asst. prof. U. Maine, Orono, 1980—81, Miami U., 1981—87; prof. SE Mo. State U., Cape Girardeau, 1987—, chmn. dept. health, human performance and recreation, 1998—2003. Contbr. articles to profl. publs. Congregation pres. St. Mark Luth. Ch., Cape Girardeau, Mo., 1990—92, 1998—2000. Recipient Faculty Merit award, SE Mo. State U., 1990, 125th Anniversary Creative Writing award, 1999, Outstanding Undergrad. program award, Assn. Worksite Health Promotion, 1995. Fellow: Am. Coll. Sports Medicine (mem. adminstrv. coun. ctrl. states 1995—98, bd. dirs. Midwest 1983—87). Avocations: bicycling, travel, outdoor activities. Office: SE Mo State U 1 University Plz MS7650 Cape Girardeau MO 63701

LANGENHEIM, JEAN HARMON, biologist, educator; b. Homer, La., Sept. 5, 1925; d. Vergil Wilson and Jeanette (Smith) Harmon; m. Ralph Louis Langenheim, Dec. 1946 (div. Mar. 1962). BS, U. Tulsa, 1946; MS, U. Minn., 1949, PhD, 1953. Rsch. assoc. botany U. Calif., Berkeley, 1954-59, U. Ill., Urbana, 1959-61; rsch. fellow biology Harvard U., Cambridge, Mass., 1962-66; asst. prof. biology U. Calif., Santa Cruz, 1966-68, assoc. prof. biology, 1968-73, prof. biology, 1973-93, prof. biology emerita, 1993—, rsch. prof. ecol. and evolution biology, 2001—. Acad. v.p. Orgn. Tropical Studies, San Jose, Costa Rica, 1975—78; chmn. com. humid tropics US Nat. Acad. Nat. Rsch. Coun., 1975—77; mem. com. floral inventory Amazon NSF, Washington, 1975—87; mem. sci. adv. bd. EPA, Washington, 1977—81. Author: (Book) Botany-Plant-Biology in Relation to Human Affairs, 1988, Plant Resins: Chemistry, Evolution, Ecology and Ethnobotany, 2003 (Klinger Best Ethnobotany Book award, Soc. Economic Botany, 2004); contbr. articles to profl. jours. Recipient Disting. Alumni award, U. Tulsa, 1979, Dedication of Madrono, Calif. Bot. Soc., 2004, Fellow's Medal, Calif. Academy Scis., 2006; grantee, NSF, 1966—88. Fellow: AAUW, AAAS, Bunting Inst., Calif. Acad. Scis.; mem.: Soc. Econ. Botany (pres. 1993—94), Assn. Tropical Biology (pres. 1985—86), Internat. Soc. Chem. Ecology (pres. 1986—87), Ecol. Soc. Am. (pres. 1986—87), Bot. Soc. Am. (Centennial award 2006). Home: 191 Palo Verde Ter Santa Cruz CA 95060-3214 Office: Univ California Dept Ecol and Evolutionary Biology Earth and Marine Scis Bldg Santa Cruz CA 95064 Home Phone: 831-426-3058; Office Phone: 831-459-2918. Business E-Mail: lang@darwin.ucsc.edu.

LANGENKAMP, MARY ALICE (M.A. LANGENKAMP), artist, educator; b. NYC, Feb. 19, 1939; d. Horace Ralph and Pattie Lera (Turner) Myers; m. Robert Dobie Langenkamp; children: Heather, Matthew, Daniel, Lucinda. BA, George Washington U., 1962, MFA, 1985. Prof. art George Washington U., Washington, 1992-96. Exhbn. juror Arts Club Washington, 1996, George Washington U. Gallery, 2002; lectr. art law seminar Harvard Law Sch., 2002; vis. prof. art Tulsa U.; rsch. archivist Smithsonian Mus. Hist. and Tech.; instr. Philbrook Mus. Exhibited paintings and prints at U.S. Capitol, State Capitol of Okla., U.S. Embassy to Vatican, Galerie Schneider, Rome, Grand Palais, Paris, Hotel de Ville of Malaucene, France, Citibank, Washington; pvt. collections. in U.S. and Europe; work pub. in Nimrod Mag., Joyce Quar., Tulsa Tribune, Washington Post, others. Founding mem. Friends Brady Gallery, George Washington U.; mem. Tulsa County Libr. Book Review Bd., Martin Luther King's March on Washington, 1963; staff U.S. Congress; chmn. Dem. Precinct. Recipient Alfandre prize George Washington U., 1982, Gov.'s award Gov. of Okla., 1989, Air France prize, 1981; donor M.A. Langenkamp prize in Design, George Washington U. Mem. ACLU, LWV, Coll. Art Assn., F St. Hist. Soc., U.S. Capital Hist. Soc., Tulsa Shakespeare Soc., Friends Historic Village Malaucene, First Families of Va., Am. REvolution Descs. Democrat. Roman Catholic. Avocations: travel, films, theater, history, politics. Office: Fontalys Malaucene Vaucluse 84340 France

LANGENKAMP, R. DOBIE, lawyer, educator; b. Tulsa, Aug. 14, 1936; BA, Stanford U., 1958; JD, Harvard U., 1961. Bar: D.C. 1962, Okla. 1964, U.S. Supreme Ct. 1968. Assoc. Steadman Collier & Shannon, Washington, 1962—64; ptnr. Doerner Stuart Saunders Daniel & Langenkamp, Tulsa, 1964—77; dep. asst. sec. U.S. Dept. Energy, Washington, 1977—81; pres. & owner Cherokee Operating Co., Okla., 1981—96; adj. prof. U. Tulsa Law Sch., 1981—89, Chapman disting. vis. prof., 1989—91, prof., 2000—, dep. dir. Nat. Energy-Environ. Law & Policy Inst., 1989—91, dir., 2000—06; dep. asst. sec. US Dept. Energy, Washington, 1996—97; cons. in Kazakhstan & Georgia USAID, 1997—2000; owner Petroleum Assocs. Internat., 1997—2000. Trustee Okla. Sch. Sci. & Math., 1994—99; regent Rogers Univ., 1996—98; trustee & regent Univ. Ctr. Tulsa, 1992—96, chmn., 1992—93; trustee Okla. Ordnance Works Authority, 1998—2002, chmn., 2002—; trustee Okla. Nature Conservancy, 2001—. Recipient Patriotism in Energy award, Internat. Soc. Energy Adv., 1998. Mem.: Phi Beta Kappa.*

LANGENKAMP, SANDRA CARROLL, retired human services administrator; b. St. Joseph, Mo., Feb. 10, 1939; d. William Harry Minger and Beverly (Carroll) Lee; m. R. Hayden Downie, June 1, 1963 (div. Feb. 1979); children: Whitney Downie, Timothy Downie, Allyson Downie; m. R. Dobie Langenkamp, Aug. 1993. BS, Tex. Women's U., 1960. Adjunctive therapist Menninger Meml. Hosp., Topeka, 1960-66; asst. adminstr. Hillcrest Med. Ctr., Tulsa, 1977-82; dir. Vol. Action Agy., Tulsa, 1982-83; exec. dir. Tulsa Bus. Health Group, 1983-95; v.p. Met. Tulsa C. of C., 1985-95; exec. dir. Tulsa Program Affordable Health Care, 1986-96; ret., 1996. Cons. mem. Okla. Employment Security Commn., Oklahoma City, 1988—; exec. dir. Tulsa Cmty. Found. Indigient Health Care, 1986—96, Long-Term Car Authority, 1999—; officer State of Okla. Basic Health Benefits Bd., 1985—96, chmn., 1992—93; mem. health benefit com. Okla. Ins. Commn., 1994—; mem. Gov.'s Com. Health Care, 1993; bd. dirs. Exec. Svc. Corps Tulsa, Associated Ctrs. Therapy. Editl. columnist: Point of View, 1985—, Tulsa Mag., 1985—. Count commn. appointee Tulsa Met. Area Planning Commn., 1973—81; mayor's appointee Tulsa Housing Authority, 1985—88; vol. Police Svc. Homicide Divsn., Police Svc. Detective Divsn., 1999—; exec. dir. Tulsa Met. Literacy Coalition, 1998—; apptd. mem. Okla. Health Care Auth., 2005—; pres. Tulsa Met. Ministry, 1980—83; bd. dirs. ARC, Tulsa, 1971—73, 1984—85, Okla. Arts Inst., 1995—, Simon Estes Found., 2000—, Tylsa Philharm., Inc., 2000—, City of Tulsa Arts Commn., 2003—; mem. City of Tulsa Comprehensive Steering Com., 2007—. Mem.: Met. Tulsa C. of C. (v.p. 1983—95), Am. C. of C. (exec. dir. Okla. chpt.), Tulsa Tennis Club. Democrat. Roman Catholic. Avocations: reading, gardening, knitting, drawing, pottery, painting.

LANGER, ALOIS, biomedical engineer; b. Pitts. BSEE, MIT, 1967; PhDEE, Carnegie Mellon U., 1973. Project engr., chief engr. Medrad/Intec, 1973—91; founder, past pres. Cardiac Telecom Corp., Pitts., 1991—. Named to National Inventors Hall of Fame, 2002. Achievements include invention of Telemetry @ Home; design of of automatic implantable cardioverter defibrillator. Office: Cardiac Telecom Ste 1 212 Outlet Way Greensburg PA 15601 Personal E-mail: a.a.la@gmx.net.

LANGER, BERNHARD, professional golfer; b. Anhausen, Germany, Aug. 27, 1957; m. Vikki Langer; children: Jackie Carol, Stefan Bernhard, Christina Joy, Jason D. Winner Masters, 1985, 1993, 58 internat. tournament victories, 12 German Open Championships, 1974—92. Mem. European Ryder Cup team, 2004; rep. Germany Hennesy Cognac Cup, Nissan Cup, Asahi Glass Four Tours, Dunhill Cup. Winner 7 German Nat. Opens and 2 German Nat. PGAs, over 65 internat. tournaments including Dunlop Masters, 1980, Colombian Open, 1980, German Open, 1981, 82, 85, 86, Bob Hope Brit. Classic, 1981, Italian Open, 1983, Glasgow Classic, 1983, Johnnie Walker Tournament, 1983, Caslo World, 1983, Irish Open, 1984, 87, Dutch Open, 1984, French Open, 1984, Spanish Open, 1984, Australian Masters, 1985, European Open, 1985, Sun City Challenge, 1985, PGA Championship Eng., 1987, Belgian Classic, 1987, European Epson Match Play, 1988, Peugeot Spanish Open, 1989, German Masters, 1989, Madrid Open, 1990, Benson & Hedges Open, 1991, Heineken Dutch Open, 1992, Honda Open, 1992, Volvo PGA Championship, 1993, European Open, Volvo PGA, 1995, Dunhill Asian Masters, 1996, Italian Open, Benson & Hedges Internat. Czech Open, Linde German Masters, Argentine Masters, 1997; winner Lancome Trophy, 1986, TNT Dutch Open, 2001, Linde German Masters, 2001, Volvo Masters, 2002, Father/Son Challenge (with Stefan), 2005, 06, World Cup (with Marcel Siem), 2006; leader European Order of Merit, 1981, 84; tour victories include Masters, 1985, 93, Sea Pines Heritage Classic, 1985. Achievements include finishing 2003 with a career high ranking of No. 4. Avocations: skiing, football, tennis, cycling. Office: c/o PGA Tour 112 PGA Tour Blvd Ponte Vedra Beach FL 32082*

LANGER, BRUCE ALDEN, lawyer; b. NYC, Mar. 17, 1953; s. Samuel S. and Yvette Langer. BA summa cum laude with distinction, Boston U., 1975, JD cum laude, 1978. Bar: N.Y. 1979, U.S. Dist. Ct. (so. and ea. dists.) N.Y. 1979, U.S. Tax Ct. 1979, U.S. Ct. Appeals (2d cir.) 1983, U.S. Supreme Ct. 1985. Law clk. to presiding chief justice U.S. Bankruptcy Ct. (ea. dist.) N.Y., summers 1976-77; with Breed Abbott & Morgan, NYC, 1978-81, White & Case, NYC, 1981-84, Fishman Forman & Landau, NYC, 1984-85, Fishman Forman & Langer, NYC, 1985-86, Paradise & Alberts, NYC, 1986-89; pvt. practice NYC, 1989—. Editor Boston U. Law Rev., 1977-78; contbg. author: Pensions and Investments, 1979; contbr. articles to profl. jours. Harold C. Case Presdl. scholar, 1974-75. Mem. Phi Beta Kappa, Phi Alpha Theta. Office: McLaughlin & Stern LLP 260 Madison Ave 18th Fl New York NY 10016

LANGER, DAVID J., neurological surgeon; b. June 18, 1963; BA (cum laude) in Psychology, U. Pa., 1985; MD, U. Pa. Sch. Medicine, 1991. Cert. Neurological Surgery, lic. NY. Intern, gen. surgery Hosp., U. Pa., 1991—92, resident, neurological surgery, 1992—98; neurovascular fellow, Inst. Neurology and Neurosurgery Beth Israel North Med. Ctr., 1998—99; attending neurosurgeon, Inst. Neurology and Neurosurgery Beth Israel Singer Med. Ctr., 1999—2004; attending neurosurgeon, dir. cerebrovascular neurosurgery St. Luke's /Roosevelt Hosp. Med. Ctr., 2004; asst. adj. surgeon, dept. otolaryngology NY Eye and Ear Infirmary, 2005; attending neurosurgeon LI Coll. Hosp., 2005; asst. prof., neurological surgery Albert Einstein Coll. Medicine, NYC, 1999; private practice NYC. Rsch. with Woods Hole Marine Biol. Lab., Mass., 1984—85, Cambridge U., England, 1985—86; rsch. with dept. medicine U. Pa. Sch. Medicine, 1989—90; visiting surgeon Neurovascular Surgery Academisch Ziekenhuis Utrecht, Holland, 1999; mem. med. adv. bd. Vycor Med., LLC, VasSol, Inc., Elana bv; mem. scientific adv. bd. Vassol, Inc., Clearant, Inc.; frequent lectr. in field; course co-dir. St. Louis U. Cerebral Revascularization Mtg., 2006. Contbr. chapters to books, articles to profl. jours.; interviewed by NY Times about AVM and Senator Tim Johnson's Surgery, 2006, NY Times about Supreme Court Justice John Robert Jr. recent seizure attack, 2007, appeared on CBS News Health segment called Why Do Teens Make Wrong Decisions?, 2006. Mem. com. admissions Albert Einstein Coll. Medicine; mem. alumni giving com. U. Pa. Sch. Medicine. Recipient Four Schs. Physician Scientist award, 1989, I.S. Ravdin Meml. prize, 1991, Morris Ginsberg Meml. prize, 1991, George Householder Meml. award, 1991. Mem.: Congress Neurosurgery, Am. Assn. Neurological Surgeons (Upjohn Cerebrovascular Resident Rsch. award 1995). Achievements include performing a groundbreaking surgery on a giant aneurysm, utilizing the ELANA Technique, featured story in NY Times in 2006; uses the latest state-of-the-art technology, including NOVA (Non-Invasive Optimal Vessel Analysis), featured in a story on FOX News in 2006; only surgeon in the NYC area to use the Vycor ViewSite System; first in US to use Vyvor's Brain Access System. in 2006. Office: 1000 Tenth Ave Ste 5G-49 New York NY 10019 Office Phone: 212-636-3204. Office Fax: 212-636-3201.*

LANGER, DENNIS HENRY, pharmaceutical company executive; b. NYC, Sept. 8, 1951; s. Nathan and Mira (Kenig) L.; m. Susan D. Follett, Jan. 21, 1980; children: William, Thomas. BA, Columbia U., 1971; MD, Georgetown U., 1975; JD cum laude, Harvard U., 1983. Diplomate Am. Bd. Psychiatry. Intern, resident, chief resident Yale U. Sch. Medicine, New Haven, 1975-78; clin. assoc. Nat. Inst. Mental Health, Bethesda, Md., 1978-80; clin. fellow Harvard Med. Sch., Boston, 1980-82, instr., 1982-83; assoc. clin. investigator Eli Lilly and Co., Indpls., 1983-84; assoc. med. dir. Abbott Lab., North Chicago, 1984-86; product mgr. Abbott Lab, North Chicago, 1986-87, sr. product mgr., 1987-88; sr. group product dir. G.D. Searle and Co., Skokie, Ill., 1988-89, sr. dir. mktg., 1989-91; pres., CEO, dir. Neose Technols. Inc., Horsham, Pa., 1991-94; v.p. bus. strategy-U.S. SmithKline Beecham Pharm., Phila., 1994-96, v.p. health mgmt. svcs., 1996-98; sr. v.p. rsch. and devel. SmithKline Beecham Healthcare Svcs., Phila., 1998-99; sr. v.p. product devel. strategy, rsch. and devel. SmithKline Beecham Pharmaceuticals, 1999-2000; sr. v.p. project mgmt. and rsch. and devel. strategy Glaxo SmithKline, King of Prussia, Pa., 2000—04; pres. N.Am. Dr. Reddy's Labs., 2004—05; mng. ptnr. Phoenix IP Ventures, Phila., 2005—. Cons. Food and Drug Adminstrn., Rockville 1980-82, clin. assoc. prof. Ind. U. Sch. Medicine, Indpls. 1983-84, U. Health Scis. Chgo. Med. Sch., 1984-91; clin. prof. Georgetown U., Sch. Medicine, 2003-. Contbr. articles to profl. jour. Bd. dirs. Epilepsy Svcs. Northeast Ill., 1985-91, v.p., 1986-89, SmithKline Beecham Found., 1996-2000; bd. vis. Georgetwon U. Sch. medicine, 1998—; bd. regents Georgetown U., 2000—; dir. Myriad Genetics, Inc., 2004—, Cytogen, 2005—, Transkaryotic Therapies, Inc., 2003-05. Mem. Am. Acad. Child and Adolescent Psychiatry (Com. On Rights and Legal Matters), Am. Psychiatric Assn., Am. Soc. Law and Medicine. Home Phone: 609-683-5090; Office Phone: 267-765-3223. Personal E-mail: dennislanger@dennislanger.com. Business E-Mail: dennis@phoenixipv.com.

LANGER, ELLEN JANE, psychologist, educator, writer, artist; b. NYC, Mar. 25, 1947; d. Norman and Sylvia (Tobias) L. BA, NYU, 1970; PhD, Yale U., 1974. Cert. clin. psychologist. Asst. prof. psychology The Grad. Ctr. CUNY, 1974-77; assoc. prof. psychology Harvard U., Cambridge, Mass., 1977-81, prof., 1981—. Cons. NAS, 1979-81, NASA; mem. div. on aging Harvard U. Med. Sch., 1979—, mem. psychiat. epidemiology steering com., 1982-90; chair social psychology program Harvard U., 1982-94, chair Faculty Arts and Scis. Com. of Women, 1984-88. Author: Personal Politics, 1973, Psychology of Control, 1983, Mindfulness, 1989, The Power of Mindful Learning, 1997, On Becoming an Artist: Reinventing Yourself Through Mindful Creativity, 2005; editor: (with Charles Alexander) Higher Stages of Human Development, 1990, (with Roger Schank) Beliefs, Reasoning and Decision-Making, 1994; contbr. articles to profl. and scholarly jours.; exhibits at Julie Hellery Gallery, Provincetown, Mass., J&W Gallery, New Hope, Pa. Guggenheim fellow; grantee NIMH, NSF, Soc. for Psychol. Study of Social Issues, Milton Fund, Sloan Found., 1982; recipient Disting. Contbn. of Basic to Applied Psychology award APS, 1995. Fellow Computers and Soc. Inst., Am. Psychol. Assn. (Disting. Contributions to Psychology in Public Interest award 1988, Disting. Contributions of Basic Sci. to Applied Psychology 1995); mem. Soc. Exptl. Social Psychology, Phi Beta Kappa, Sigma Xi. Democrat. Jewish. Avocations: tennis, horseback riding. Office: Harvard U Dept Psychology 33 Kirkland St Cambridge MA 02138-2044 Business E-Mail: langer@wjh.harvard.edu.

LANGER, GLENN ARTHUR, cellular physiologist, educator; b. Nyack, NY, May 5, 1928; s. Adolph Arthur and Marie Catherine (Doscher) L.; m. Beverly Joyce Brawley, June 5, 1954 (dec. Nov. 1976); 1 child, Andrea; m. Marianne Phister, Oct. 12, 1977. BA, Colgate U., 1950; MD, Columbia U., NYC, 1954. Diplomate Am. Bd. Internal Medicine. Asst. prof. medicine Columbia U. Coll. Physicians and Surgeons, NYC, 1963-66; assoc. prof. medicine and physiology UCLA Sch. Medicine, 1966-69, prof., 1969-97, Castera prof. cardiology, 1978-97, assoc. dean rsch., 1986-91, dir. cardiovascular rsch. lab., 1987-97, emeritus prof., 1997—. Griffith vis. prof. Am. Heart Assn., L.A., 1979; cons. Acad. Press, N.Y.C., 1989-97; founder, dir. Partnership Scholars Program, 1996—. Author: Understanding Disease, 1999; editor: The Mammalian Myocardium, 1974, 2d edit., 1997, Calcium and the Heart, 1990; mem. editl. bd. Circulation Rsch., 1971-76, Am. Jour. Physiology, 1971-76, Jour. Molecular Cell Cardiology, 1974-97; contbr. more than 200 articles to profl. jours. Co-pres., dir., founder Partnership Scholars Program for disadvantaged youth, 1996—. Capt. U.S. Army, 1955-57. Recipient Disting. Achievement award Am. Heart Assn. Sci. Coun., 1982, Heart of Gold award, 1984, Cybulski medal Polish Physiol. Soc., Krakow, 1990, Pasarow Found. award for Cardiovascular Sci., 1993, Outstanding Acad. Title citation Choice mag., 2001, Spl. award LA County, 2006; Macy scholar Josiah Macy Found., 1979-80. Fellow AAAS, Am. Coll. Cardiology, Internat. Soc. for Heart Rsch.; mem. Am. Soc. Clin. Investigation, Am. Assn. Physicians. Achievements include research on control of cardiac contraction. Personal E-mail: glang@mcn.org.

LANGER, JUDITH ANN, psychologist; b. NYC; BA, CUNY, 1962, MSEd, 1965; PhD, Hofstra U., Hempstead, NY, 1978; PhD (hon.), U. Uppsala, Sweden, 2005. Asst. prof. LI U., 1973-78; asst. prof. dept. ednl. psychology NYU, 1978-80; sr. rschr. lang. behavior rsch. lab. U. Calif., Berkeley, 1980-84; assoc. prof. sch. of edn. Stanford U., 1984-87; prof. SUNY, Albany, 1987—, disting. prof., 2001—. Dir. Albany Inst. for Rsch. in Edn., Nat. Rsch. Ctr. on English Learning & Achievement; co-dir. Nat. Rsch. Ctr. Lit. Tchg. and Learning; trustee Rsch. Found.; task force mem. Nat. Commn. on Edn. Stds. and Testing; adv. com. New Stds. in Edn. Project, Literacy Unit, LRDC and Nat. Ctr. on Edn. and the Economy; adv. bd. Nat. Coun. of Chief State Sch. Officers, Nat. Objective in Reading, Nat. Assessment of Ednl. Progress, Reading and Writing Assessments, 1980—; cons. Calif. Assessment Program, NC English Lang. Arts Standards, Calif. State Dept. Edn., Ctr. for Lang. Edn. and Rsch., Ctr. for the Study of Writing, Rev. of Rsch. on Reading and Writing Relationships, Mich. State Edn. Dept. Author: Reader Meets Author/Bridging the Gap, 1982, Understanding Reading and Writing Research, 1985, Children Reading and Writing: Structures and Strategies, 1986, Language, Literacy, and Culture, 1987, Issues of Society and Schooling, How Writing Shapes Thinking: Studies of Teaching and Learning, 1987, Literature Instruction: A Focus on Student Response, 1992, Literature Instruction: Practice & Policy, 1994, Envisioning Literature, 1995, Effective Literacy Instruction: Building Successful Reading and Writing Programs, 2002, Getting To Excellent: How to Create Better Schools, 2004; contbr. articles to profl. jours.; editor: Research in the Teaching of English, 1984-92; editl. bd. English Internat., Discourse Processes, Jour. of Reading Behavior, Newsletter, Lab. of Comparative Human Cognition, Jour. of Reading and Writing, Internat. Jour. of Reading and Writing; reviewer in field. Recipient numerous grants, Presdl. award for lifetime achievement, Hofstra U., 1992, Chancellor's award for Exemplary Contbns. to Rsch., 2001, Albert J. Harris award, 2003; fellow, Rockefeller Found., Internat. Reading Hall of Fame; Benton fellow, U. Chgo., 1997. Fellow Am. Psychol. Assn., Nat. Conf. on Rsch. in English; mem. MLA, Am. Ednl. Rsch. Assn., Am. Psychol. Soc., Conf. on Coll. Composition and Comm., Internat. Reading Assn., Nat. Reading Conf., Nat. Coun. of Tchrs. of English (trustee), Soc. for Rsch. in Child Devel., Soc. for Text and Discourse, Kappa Delta Pi. Office: Univ at Albany 1400 Washington Ave Albany NY 12222-0100

LANGER, RALPH ERNEST, journalist, retired editor; b. Benton Harbor, Mich., July 30, 1937; s. Ralph L. and Mary (Skuda) L.; m. Katherine B. McGuire, June 25, 1960; children: Terri B., Tammi L. Student, Central Mich. U., 1955-57; BA in Journalism, U. Mich., 1957-59. Telegraph editor, reporter Grand Haven (Mich.) Daily Tribune, 1959-60; mng. editor Port Angeles (Wash.) Evening News, 1962-66; copy desk Detroit Free Press, 1966-68; asst. mng. editor Dayton Jour. Herald, 1968, mng. editor, 1968-75; editor Everett (Wash.) Herald, 1975-81; mng. editor Dallas Morning News, 1981-83, exec. editor, 1983-86, v.p., 1986-91, sr. v.p., exec. editor, 1991-96, exec. v.p., editor, 1997-98; ret., 1999; exec.-in-residence So. Meth. U., 1999—2002. Pres. Freedom of Info. Found. Tex., 1985-89; founding pres. Nat. Freedom of Info. Coalition, 1989-93, Coun. of Presidents, 1991-92. 1st lt. U.S. Army, 1960-62. Named to Journalism Hall of Fame, Ctrl. Mich. U., 2003. Mem. Am. Soc. Newspaper Editors (bd. dirs. 1997—99), Press Club Dallas (pres. 1985-86), A.P. Mng. Editors Assn. (bd. dirs. 1980—, sec. 1989, v.p. 1990, pres. 1990-91), Coun. of Pres.'s (founding pres. 1992-93), AP Mng. Editors Assn. Found. (pres. 1991-92), Scabbard and Blade, Alpha Phi Gamma, Sigma Phi Epsilon. Personal E-mail: ralphlanger@sbcglobal.net.

LANGER, RAY FRITZ, retired insurance executive; b. Manchester, NH, Apr. 29, 1921; s. Fritz Bruno and Clara (Lindh) L.; m. Myrtle Elaine Sargent, May 23, 1942; 1 child, Barry Frederick. Cert., U. N.H., 1940. Chief statistician N.H. Ins. Co., Manchester, 1942-71; chief statistician, asst. sec. N.H. & Am. Internat. Group, Manchester, 1972-84, asst. sec., 1984-91; cons. N.H. Group, Manchester. Dir. Suncook Bank, 1979—83. Selectman Town of Hooksett, N.H., 1970-78, councilor, 1988-91, state rep., 1993-05; pres. Hooksett-ites Sr. Citizens, 1993-97; vol. VA Hosp., 2005-. Capt. USAF, 1943-46, PTO, 1955-57, Korea, ret. 1981. Mem. Soc. Ins. Accts. (past pres.), Am. Legion. Republican. Methodist. Avocations: hunting, fly fishing, painting.

LANGER, RICHARD J., lawyer; b. Rockford, Ill., June 10, 1944; s. John W. and Dorothy E. (Brunn) Langehr; m. Audrey A. Russo, Jan. 28, 1967; children: Kathleen M., Michael R. BS, U. Ill., 1967; JD, U. Wis., 1974. Bar: Wis. 1974, U.S. Dist. Ct. (we. dist.) Wis. 1974. Assoc. Ela, Esch, Hart & Clark, Madison, Wis., 1974-76; ptnr. Stolper, Koritzinsky, Brewster & Neider, Madison, 1976-91, Michael, Best & Friedrich, Madison, 1991—. Pres. Hospice Care Found., Inc. Author: The Marital Property Classification Handbook, 1986, 2d edit., 1998, Workbook For Wisconsin Estate Planners, 1997, Family Estate Planning in Wisconsin, 1996, Conservation Easements: An Important Estate Planning Tool, 2002; contbr. articles to profl. jours. Named Outstanding Vol. Fund Raiser, Hospice Care Found., Inc., 2002. Fellow Am. Coll. Trust and Estate Coun.; mem. ABA, State Bar Wis., Madison Estate Coun. Avocations: scuba diving, travel, bicycling. Home: 1502 Windfield Way Madison WI 53562-3808 Office: Michael Best & Friedrich 1 S Pinckney St Madison WI 53703-2892 Office Phone: 608-283-2248. Business E-Mail: rjlanger@michaelbest.com.

LANGER, ROBERT MARTIN, retired chemical engineering company executive, consultant; b. Boston, May 29, 1925; s. Samuel Morton and Ethel (Shlivek) L. B.Engring., Yale U., 1945, D.Engring., 1952; S.M., MIT, 1948. Sales mgr. The Badger Co., Inc., Cambridge, Mass., 1968-70; dep. mng. dir. Badger B.V., The Hague, The Netherlands, 1970-74, mng. dir., 1974-78; v.p., project adminstrn. The Badger Co., Inc., Cambridge, 1978-80; sr. v.p. Badger Am., Inc., Cambridge, 1981-83; v.p., treas. The Badger Co., Inc., Cambridge, 1983-87. Served to lt. j.g. USNR, 1945-46 Mem. AIChE. Home: 280 Commonwealth Ave Boston MA 02116-2422

LANGER, ROBERT SAMUEL, JR., chemical and biomedical engineering educator; b. Albany, NY, Aug. 29, 1948; s. Robert Samuel Sr. and Mary (Swartz) L.; m. Laura Feigenbaum, July 31, 1988; children: Michael David, Susan Katherine, Samuel Alexander. BS in Chemical Engring., Cornell U., 1970; ScD in Chemical Engring., MIT, 1974; PhD (hon.), ETH, Switzerland, 1996, Technion U., Israel, 1997, U. Catholique Louvain, Brussels, 1999, Hebrew U., 2002, U. Liverpool, 2003, U. Uppsala, 2005, Pa. State U., 2005, U. Nottingham, 2005, Albany Med. Coll., 2006, Northwestern U., 2006, Yale U., 2007. Rsch. assoc. Children's Hosp. Med. Ctr., Boston, 1974—; asst. prof. chem. and biomed. engring. MIT, Cambridge, Mass., 1978-81, assoc. prof., 1981-85, prof., 1985-89, Germeshausen prof., 1989—2004, inst. prof., 2005—. Bd. dirs. Alkermes, Cambridge, Acusphere, Cambridge, Wyeth, NJ, Boston Life Scis.; tchr. Group Sch., Lexington, 1971—73; endowed lectr. U. P.R., 1983, Case Western Res. U., 1986, U. Mich., 1987, U. Wash., 1988, U. Kans., 1989, U. Calif., San Francisco, 1991, U. Wis., 1991, Ga. Inst. Tech., 1991, Ohio State U., 1991, U. Pitts., 1992, Purdue U., 1992, U. Del., 1993, Pa. State U., 1993, Beth Israel Hosp., 1994, Cornell U., 1994, Calif. Inst. Tech., 1995, Ill. Inst. Tech., 1995, Ohio State Med. Sch., 1995, U. Calif., 1996, U. Tenn., 1996, U. N.C., 1997, 97, U. Pa., 1998, Wash. U., 1998, U. Tex., San Antonio, 1998, U. MIch., 1998, U. Calif., Berkeley, 1999, U. Notre Dame, 1999, U. Liverpool, 2000, Brown U., 2001, Stanford U., 2001, Cornell U., 2001, U. Pa., 2002, U. Louisville, 2002; cons. Genentech, San Francisco, 1981—, Merck Sharpe and Dohme, 1981—85; others; sci. advisor Cygnus, Redwood City, Calif., 1987—97, Opta Foods, Bedford, Mass., 1991—; mem. FDA Sci. Bd., 1995—2002, chmn., 1999—2002. Author: (with D. Cincotta and K. Cole) Group School Chemistry Curriculum, 1972, (with W. Thilly) Laboratory in Applied Biology, 1978, Analaytical Practices in Biochemistry, 1979, (with W. Hrusheysky and F. Theeuwes) Temporal Control of Drug Delivery, 1991; editor: (with M. Chasin) Biodegradable Polymers in Drug Deliveryy, 1990, (with D. Wise) Medical Applications on Control Release, Vols. I and II, 1984, (with R. Steiner and P. Weisz) Angiogenesis, 1992; contbr. articles to sci. jours.; patentee in field. Recipient John W. Hyatt Svc. to Mankind award Soc. Plastics Engrs., 1995, Internat. award, 1996, Ebert Prize, Am. Pharm. Assn., 1995, 96, 99, Rsch. award Am. Diabetes Assn., 1996, Internat. award Gairdner Found., 1996, Wiley medal FDA, 1997, Killian award MIT, 1997, Lemelson-MIT prize for invention, 1998, Nagai Found. Internat. award, 1998, Dickson prize for Sci., 2002, Heinz award for Tech., Economy and Employment, 2003, Harvey prize, 2003, John Fritz award, 2003, Gen. Motors Kettering award for Cancer Rsch., 2004, Albany Med. Ctr. prize in Medicine and Biomedical Rsch., 2005, Dan David prize, 2005; Union Oil fellow, 1970-71, Chevron fellow, 1971-72; cited for Outstanding Patent in Mass., Intellectual Property Owners Inc., 1989; named one of the 25 most important individuals in biotech. in the world by Bio World mag, 1990 and Forbes mag., 1999, 100 Most Important People in Am. and 18 Top People in Sci. or Medicine in Am., Time mag. and CNN, 2001, 20 Most Important People in the Area, Discovery mag, 2002, 15 innovators worldwide who will reinvent the future, 2002, six heroes whose rsch. may save your life, Parade mag., 2004, 2006 Nat. Medal Sci. Laureate, NSF, 2007; named to Nat. Inventors Hall of Fame, 2006. Fellow: World Tech. Network (World Tech. Network award (Health and Medicine) 2005), Am. Inst. Med. and Biol. Engrs. (founding fellow), Am. Assn. Pharm. Scis. (Disting. Pharm Sci. award 1993), Soc. Biomaterials (Clemson award 1990); mem.: NAE (Charles Stark Draper prize 2002), AIChE (Food, Pharm. and Bioengring. award 1986, Profl. Progress award 1990, Charles M. Stine Materials Sci. and Engring. award 1991, William Walker award 1996), NAS, Controlled Release Soc. (bd. govs. 1981—85, chmn. regulatory affairs com. 1985—89, pres. 1991—92, Founders award 1989, Outstanding Pharm. Paper award 1990, 1992, Millerial Pharm. award 2000, Glaxo Wellcome award 2000), Internat. Soc. Artificial Internal Organs, Am. Soc. Artificial Internal Organs (mem. program com. 1984—87), Biomed. Engring. Soc. (bd. dirs. 1991—94, Whitaker lectr. 1994), Internat. Soc. Artificial Internal Organs (Organon-Teknika award 1991), Am. Chem. Soc. (Creative Polymer award 1989, Phillips Applied Polymer Sci. award 1992, Pearlman Meml. Lectr. award 1992, Polymer Chemistry award 1999, Materials award 2007, award in the chemistry of materials 2007), Am. Acad. Arts and Scis., Inst. Medicine of NAS. Achievements include patents in field; patents pending in field. Avocations: magic, jogging. Office: MIT Dept Chem Engring Bldg #E25 Rm 342 77 Mass Ave Cambridge MA 02139-4307 Office Phone: 617-253-3123.*

LANGER, STEVEN, human resources specialist, consultant, psychologist; b. NYC, June 4, 1926; s. Israel and Anna (Glaisner) L.; m. Jacqueline White, Oct. 11, 1954 (dec. Dec. 1969); children: Bruce, Diana, Geoffrey; m. Elaine Catherine Brewer, Dec. 29, 1979 (dec. Feb. 1992). BA in Psychology, Calif. State U., Sacramento, 1950; MS in Pers. Svcs., U. Colo., 1958; PhD, Walden U., 1972. Lic. psychologist, Ill. Asst. to pers. dir. City and County of Denver, 1956-59; pers. dir. City of Pueblo, Colo., 1959-60; pers. cons. J.L. JAcobs & Co., Chgo., 1961-64, adminstrv. mgr., 1966-67; sales selection mgr. Reuben H. Donnelly Corp., Chgo., 1964-66; pres. Abbott, Langer & Assocs., Crete, Ill., 1967—2007, Langer Assocs., Inc., Park Forest, Ill., 2007—. Vis. prof. mgmt. Loyola U., Chgo., 1969-71; community prof. behavioral scis. Purdue U., Calumet campus, Hammond, Ind., 1973-75. Contbr. articles to profl. jours. Mem. Ill. Psychol. Assn. (chmn. sect. indsl. psychologists 1971-72), Chgo. Psychol. Assn. (pres. 1974-75, 94-95), Chgo. Indsl./Orgnl. Psychologists, Soc. Human Resources Mgmt. (accredited, chmn. rsch. award com. 1966-69), World at Work, Chgo. Compensation Assn. (sec. 1976-77), Mensa (pres. Chgo. chpt. 1972-74). Unitarian Universalist. Home: 309 Herndon St Park Forest IL 60466-1132 Office: Abbott Langer & Assoc 548 1st St Crete IL 60417-2199 Office Phone: 708-748-6983. Personal E-mail: abblan@sbcglobal.net.

LANGEVIN, JAMES R. (JIM LANGEVIN), congressman, former state official; b. Providence, Apr. 22, 1964; s. Richard Raymond and June Katherine (Barrett) Langevin B, RI Coll., 1990; MPA, Harvard U. John F. Kennedy Sch. Govt., 1994. Mem. RI State Ho. Reps., 1988-94; sec. state, 1995-2001; mem. US Congress from 2nd RI dist., 2001—, mem. armed svcs. com., 2001—07, mem. homeland security com., 2003—, chmn. subcommittee on emerging threats, cybersecurity and sci. and tech., 2007—, mem. permanent select com. on intelligence, 2007—. Bd. mem. ARC, Pawtucket, RI, 1993—, Tech Access, Providence, 1995, RI State Ho. Restoration Com., 1995, March of Dimes, Warwick Shelter, Naval War Coll. Found., Pari Ind. Living. Mem. Save the Bay RI, KC, Lions Democrat. Roman Catholic. Avocations: reading, public speaking, community involvement. Office: US House Reps 109 Cannon House Office Bldg Washington DC 20515 Office Phone: 202-225-2735. Office Fax: 202-225-5976.*

LANGEVIN, THOMAS HARVEY, retired educational association administrator, consultant; b. St. Paul, Mar. 20, 1922; s. Thomas E. and Myrtle (Damsgard) L.; m. Pearl E. Mattfeld, Aug. 29, 1942; children: Dennis, Timothy. BS, Concordia Tchrs. Coll., Seward, Neb., 1947; MA, U. Neb., 1949, PhD, 1951. Quarantine insp. USPHS, 1943-45; grad. asst., asst. instr. U. Neb., 1947-51; prof. Concordia Tchrs. Coll., 1951-63, dean coll., 1961-63, acting pres., 1961-63; dir. long-range planning project Luth. Ch.-Mo. Synod, 1964-65; also cons. Bd. Higher Edn.; acad. v.p. Pacific Luth. U., 1965-69; pres. Capital U., Columbus, Ohio, 1969-79, pres. emeritus, 1979—; pres. Thomas H. Langevin Assoc., LadyLake, Fla., 1979—2007; ret., 2007. Prin. Registry for Coll. and Univ. Pres., 1992—; chmn. Luth. Edn. Conf. N.Am., 1980-87; cons. Battelle Inst., 1979-87; cons., vis. fellow Battelle Seattle Rsch. Ctr., 1976. Co-chmn. Tacoma Area Urban Coalition Edn. Task Force, 1967-69; mem., past chmn. Ohio Com. Pub. Programs in Humanities; former exec. com. Fedn. Pub. Programs in Humanities; former mem. Ohio Higher Edn. Facilities Commn.; former mem. Commn. on Future Lutheran Edn., Luth Edn. Conf. N.Am., pres., 1977-78; bd. dirs. Nat. Urban League, 1979-83; mem. Columbus Urban League; former mem. Met. Columbus Sch. Com.; bd. dirs. Tacoma Citizens Com. Pub. TV, 1967-69, Design for Progress Tacoma, 1969, Tacoma Area Urban Coalition, 1967-69; bd. rev. Air U.; former adv. com. Center Sci. and Industry, Columbus; assoc. in urban affairs Nat. Inst. Pub. Affairs; bd. control Concordia Coll., Portland, Oreg., 1965-69; bd. overseers Acad. Contemporary Problems, Columbus, 1972-75; trustee Columbus Symphony Orch., pres., 1979-81; past trustee Columbus Sch. Girls, Columbus Met. Area Community Action; hon. trustee Internat. Council of Mid-Ohio; past bd. govs. Goodwill Industries Central Ohio, Salesian Inner City Boys' Club; past bd. dirs., pres. Blue Cross Central Ohio; bd. dirs. Options, Learning Connections, Franklin County Heart Br., Columbus Area Mental Health Center; bd. dirs. Battelle Meml. Inst. Found., chmn., 1977-78; mem. bd. dirs. Nationwide Corp. Served with USCGR, 1943-45. Recipient Carnegie grant, postdoctoral fellow Center for Study Higher Edn., U. Mich., 1963-64 Mem. Assn. Ind. Colls. and Univs. Ohio (chmn. 1971-74), Orgn. Am. Historians, Nebr., Ohio hist. socs., Am. Assn. Higher Edn., Newcomen Soc. N.Am., Navy League U.S. (past dir. Columbus council), Columbus Area C. of C. (dir. 1971-74) Clubs: Columbus Rotary (dir.). Lutheran. Home: 441 San Pedro Dr Lady Lake FL 32159-8664 Office Phone: 352-753-1488. E-mail: thlangevin@aol.com.

LANGFEDLT, ANDREW, engineer; b. Northridge, Calif., July 26, 1957; s. Paul Julian and Joan Elizabeth Langfeldt; m. Jeanne Luciue Smith (div.); 1 child, Vivienne Langfeldt. BA in Psychology, U. Calif., Irving, 2002; MBA, Keller Grad. Sch. Mgmt., Oakbrook Terrace, Ill., 2006. Jr. engr. Rockwell Internat., Anaheim, Calif., 1980—85; sr. engr., scientist McDonnell Douglas, Long Beach, Calif., 1985—91; sr. sys. engr. Sci. Applications Internat. Corp., San Diego, 1996—97. Nat. Merit scholar, 1975. Mem.: Mensa, Golden Key, Phi Beta Kappa. Avocations: music, harmonica. Home: 3048 Whitbeck Blvd Eugene OR 97405

LANGFELD, PATRICIA ANN, trade association administrator; b. Washington, Nov. 4, 1942; d. Charles Edwards and Kathryn Marie (Griffin) Junkin; m. Stanley Chaitt Langfeld, May 1, 1981. Cert. in orgn. mgmt. U.S. C. of C. Mgr. adminstrv. svcs. Nat Stone Assn., Washington, 1966-76; dir. comm. Nat. Ice Assn., Bethesda, Md., 1976-77; dir. mem. svcs. Optical Labs. Assn., Bethesda, 1977-82; v.p. confs. and edn. Internat. Franchise Asn., Washington, 1982-94; dir. profl. edn. svc. Congl. Quar. Inc., Washington, 1994-98; dir. meetings and exhibits Nat. Assn. Life Underwriters, Washington, 1998-2000; v.p. mktg. and devel. Competitive Telecom. Assn., Washington, 2000—02; dir. mktg. and bus. devel. Nat. Parking Assn., Washington, 2002—. Mem. coun. advisors Walt Disney World, Orlando, Fla., 1992-94; mem. bd. advisors Greenbrier Resort, White Sulphur Springs, W.Va., 2001—. Editor, contbr. monthly newsletters Stone News, 1974-76, Ice News, 1976-77, OLA News, 1977-82; contbr. writer Franchising World, 1982-94. Mem. ball exec. com. Nat. Symphony Orch., Washington, 1995—, com. chmn., 1997—, mem. com. for wine tasting and silent auction benefit, 1993-96; mem. campaign leadership bd. Salvation Army Turning Point Ctr. for Homeless Women and Children, Washington, 1996—; mem. fall benefit com. Woodrow Wilson House Armistice Day Event, Washington, 1998—; mem. benefit com. Woodrow Wilson Princeton Centennial Celebration, 2002. Mem. Am. Soc. Assn. Execs., Profl. Conv. Mgmt. Assn., Greater Washington Soc. Assn. Execs. (innovate adv. coun. 1997-98, Springtime in Park adv. coun. 1998-2000, profl. women's forum 1998-2000). Republican. Jewish. Avocations: collecting oriental art, classical music, deep sea fishing, travel adventures, interior decorating. Home: 5300 Camberley Ave Bethesda MD 20814 Office: Nat Parking Assn 1112 16th St NW Washington DC 20036 Office Phone: 202-296-4336. E-mail: plangfeld@npapark.org.

LANGFELD, STANLEY CHAITT, government executive; b. Harrisburg, Pa., Jan. 10, 1945; s. Millard Ash Jr. and Bessie Chaitt; m. Patricia Ann Junkin, May 1, 1981. BA in History, U. Md., 1968; MS in Real Estate and Urban Devel. Planning, Am. U., 1971. Market analyst The Rouse Co., Columbia, Md., 1971-72; dir. residential and recreational devel. couns. Urban Land Inst., Washington, 1972-74; realty specialist U.S. Gen. Svcs. Adminstrn., Washington, 1975-78, sr. realty specialist, 1978-81, program control officer, 1981-83, dep. dir. Office of Program Control, 1983-85, spl. asst. to asst. commr. Office Real Property Mgmt./Safety, 1985-88, spl. asst. to asst. commr. for real property devel., 1988-90, dep. dir. Office Real Estate Pub. Bldgs. Svc., 1990-91, dir. real estate policy divsn. Office Real Estate, 1991-95, dir. real property policy div. Office Government-wide Policy, 1995—. Mem. bd. editors: Pub. Mgr. Quart. Mag., 1998—; author: (publs.) The Balanced and Orderly Development of a Site in Close Proximity to a Metro Station as a Contributor to a More Viable Urban Environment in the Washington Metropolitan Area, 1971, Federal Real Property Asset Management Principles, 1996, Project Reference Files, Urban Land Institute, 1973, Real Property Policies Update, Federal Management Regulation Final Rule Amendment, 2005, Real Property Asset Management Guiding Principles, 2006, others. Mem. com. for wine tasting and silent auction benefit Nat. Symphony Orch., Washington, 1993—96; mem. exec. com. Nat. Symphony Orch. Ball, 2000—01; advisor to bd. Salvation Army's Turning Point Ctr. for Homeless Women and Children, Washington, 1996—; mem. benefit com. Woodrow Wilson Princeton Centennial Celebration, 2002; mem. fall benefit com. Woodrow Wilson House Armistice Day Event, 1998—. Recipient Morris Cafritz Meml. scholar, Am. U., 1970, Dean's scholar, 1970, Hammer award, Nat. Partnership for Reinventing Govt., 1999, Disting. Svc. award, U.S. Govt., 2001, Meritorious Svc. award, US Archtl. and Transp. Compliance Bd., 2005;, Urban Transp. Ctr., Urban Mass Transit Adminstrn., U.S. Dept. Transp. fellow, 1971. Mem.: Fed. Exec. Inst. Alumni Assn. (bd. dirs., exec. sec., treas., chair 2000—02), Cosmos Club (new mem. orientation com. 2000—02, mem. house com. 2002—04, mem. fin. com. 2005—). Republican. Jewish. Avocations: reading, travel, walking, collecting fine arts and Oriental carpets. Home: 5300 Camberley Ave Bethesda MD 20814 Office: US Gen Svcs Adminstrn 1800 F St NW Washington DC 20405 Office Fax: 202 219 0104. E-mail: stanley.langfeld@gsa.gov.

LANGFIELD, RAYMOND LEE, real estate developer; b. Houtzdale, Pa., Jan. 31, 1921; s. Arthur H. and Sadie L. (Morris) L.; m. Helen Deborah Elion, Oct. 15, 1952; 1 child, Joanna Langfield Rose. BS in Indsl. Engring., Pa. State U., 1942. Registered profl. engr., Conn. Chief mgmt. engr. CIT Fin. Corp., NYC, 1947-50; v.p. Mosler Safe Co., NYC, 1950-60; pres. Spicer Fuel Co., Groton, Conn., 1960-86, United Fuel Corp., Groton, 1962-86, Spicer Gas Co., Groton, 1982-86, Conn. Hotel Corp., New London, 1986-94; real estate developer, 1980—. Bd. dirs. New London Fed. Savings and Loan, 1982—86; founder, bd. dirs. Bank of Mystic, 1987—90. Mem. Conn. Energy Adv. Bd., Hartford, 1985-87; pres. Grade Arts Ctr., New London, 1985-87. Lt. comdr. USNR, 1941-47. Mem. Southeast Conn. C. of C. (bd. dirs., chmn. bd. 1978-80), Ind. Conn. Petroleum Assn. (chmn. bd. 1973-74, Oil Man of Yr., 1975), New Eng. Fuel Inst. (bd. dirs. 1972-84), Navy League Conn. (bd. dirs. 1985-87). Jewish. Avocations: fresh-water fishing, electronics. Home: 23362 Torre Cir Boca Raton FL 33433-7026 Personal E-mail: rlangfield@msn.com.

LANGFORD, GEORGE MALCOLM, cell biology educator; b. Halifax, NC, Aug. 26, 1944; s. Maynard and Lillie Virginia (Grant) L.; m. Sylvia Audrey Tyler, June 8, 1968; children: George II, Joy, Grant. BS in Biology, Fayetteville State U., 1966; MS, Ill. Inst. Tech., Chgo., 1969; PhD, Ill. Inst. Tech., 1971. Postdoctoral fellow U. Pa., Phila., 1971-73; asst. prof. U. Mass., Boston, 1973-77, Howard U., Washington, 1977-79; from assoc. prof. to full prof. physiology U. N.C., Chapel Hill, 1979—91; program dir. cell biology program NSF, 1988—89; Ernest Everett Just prof. biol. scis. and physiology Dartmouth Coll. and Dartmouth Med. Sch., Hanover, NH, 1991—. Dir. cell biology program NSF, Washington, 1988-89. Editorial bd. Biol. Bulls., 1987-91; contbr. articles to profl. jours. Trustee Marine Biol. Lab., Woods Hole, Mass., 1984-92. Fellow NIH, 1971-73, Marine Biol. Lab, 1972-78; grantee NIH, 1978-86, NSF, 1986-91, NATO, 1986-90. Mem. Am. Soc. Cell Biology (chair minorities affairs com. 1986-90), Sigma Xi. Achievements include research in dynamic instability of native microtubules from squid axous, gliding and vesicle transport. Office: Dartmouth Coll Dept Biol Scis Rm 416 6044 Gilman Lab Hanover NH 03755

LANGFORD, JAMES JERRY, lawyer; b. Birmingham, Ala., May 19, 1933; S. N.B. and Margaret Elizabeth (Fuller) L.; m. Mary Elizabeth Fryant, Mar. 21, 1958; children: Jan Carol Langford Hammett, Joel Fryant L. BS, U. So. Miss., 1955; JD, U. Miss., 1970. Bar: Miss. 1970, U.S. Dist. Ct. (no. and so. dists.) Miss. 1970, U.S. Ct. Appeals (5th cir.) 1971, U.S. Ct. Appeals (11th cir.). Agt. Met. Life Ins. Co., Jackson, Miss., 1957—58; sales rep. Employers Mut. of Wausau, Jackson, 1958—64; v.p. Reid-McGee Ins. Co., Jackson, 1964—67; from assoc. to sr. ptnr., mng. ptnr. Wells Marble & Hurst, Jackson, 1970—97, sr. ptnr., 1997—2006, of counsel, 2006—. Editor-in-chief Miss. Law Jour., 1969-70. 1st lt. U.S. Army, 1955-57. Fellow Miss. Bar Found.; mem. ABA, Fed. Bar Assn. (pres. Miss. chpt. 1981-82), Fedn. Def. and Corp. Counsel, Nat. Assn. RR Trial Counsel, Miss. Bar Assn. (mem. ethics com. 1998-2004), Miss. Def. Lawyers Assn. (pres. 1992-93), Country Club Jackson, Phi Delta Phi, Omicron Delta Kappa, Pi Kappa Alpha. Presbyterian. Avocations: military history, baseball. Home: 12 Plum Tree Ln Madison MS 39110-9620 Office: Wells Marble & Hurst PO Box 131 Jackson MS 39205-0131 Personal E-mail: jlangfordesq@aol.com. *People respect honesty, trustworthiness, hard work and sincerity. Do what you truly want to do for your vocation, for that is the secret of happiness in a business career.*

LANGFORD, LAURA SUE, corporate financial executive; b. Evansville, Ind., Sept. 28, 1961; d. Lee Denmar Miller and Susan E. (Morton) Reitz; m. John E. Langford, May 15, 1992; 1 child, Rowan Diane. BFA in Drama, U. So. Calif., LA, 1983; MBA in Fin. & Pub./Non-Profit, Columbia U., 1992. Credit mgr. Super-Freeze Co., Inc., Burbank, Calif., 1984-86; asst. Salomon Bros. Inc., LA, 1986-87; rsch. analyst Bank of Calif., N.A., LA, 1987, pub. fin. officer, 1988-90; intern Citizens Budget Commn., NYC, 1991; analyst Standard & Poor's Ratings Group, NYC, 1992-93, assoc., 1993-94, assoc. dir., 1994-95, dir., 1996-98; v.p. Duff & Phelps Credit Rating Co., NYC, 1998—2000; dir. HypoVereinsbank, NYC, 2000—; CFO HVB Global Assests Co., 2003—. Contbr. to periodical Standard & Poor's Credit Week, 1993—98, Duff & Phelps Credit Rating Co. Issues Update, 1998—2000; founder, editor: GAA Gazette, 1985—. Fellow Divsn. Rsch. Assn. Student Officer fellow, Columbia U., 1991—92; scholar Pres.'s scholar, U. Evansville, 1979—81. Avocations: skiing, rollercoaster riding, science fiction. Office: HVB Group 150 E 42nd St New York NY 10017 Home Phone: 212-499-0985; Office Phone: 212-672-5614. Business E-Mail: Laura_Langford@HVBAMERICAS.com.

LANGGUTH, MARGARET WITTY, health facility administrator; b. Evanston, Ill., June 21, 1950; d. LeRoy and Catherine Ann (Conrad) Witty; m. Gregory Bryce Bukar, June 5, 1971 (dec. 1989); children: Michael Bryce, Caroline Nicole; m. Franklin James Langguth, Feb. 2, 2002. BS, DePaul U., 1972, MBA, 1981; MS, Rosalind Franklin U. Medicine and Sci., 1996. Staff med. technologist The Evanston Hosp., 1972-75, immunopathology lab. supr., 1975-77, lab. mgr., 1977-84, dir. lab. adminstrn., 1984-85; bookkeeper Ronald Knox Montessori Sch., Wilmette, Ill., 1986-87; beauty cons. Mary Kay Cosmetics, 1990-96; sec. Northwestern U., Evanston, 1991-94; physician asst. Women's Med. Group, P.C., Skokie, Evanston, Ill., 1996-98; ind. sales assoc. Mannatech, Inc., 1998—2001; adminstrv. dir. clin. lab. Rush North Shore Med. Ctr., Skokie, Ill., 1999—, six sigma facilitator, 2004—. Den leader Cub Scouts, Boy Scouts Am., Wilmette, 1985—87, den leader coach, 1987—88; active PTA of St. Francis Xavier Sch., 1985—94, chair rummage sale, 1987—88, scouting coord., 1991—92, sch. bd., 1986—90, sec., 1988—89, vice chmn., 1989—90; troop co-leader, song leader Girl Scouts Am., 1992—98;

campaign 2001 com. mem. United Way of Skokie Valley-Rush North Shore, co-chair for campaign 2002; exec. bd. mem. Rush North Shore Med. Ctr., 2004—, co-chair edn. com., 2005—06; eucharistic min. sick St. Francis Xavier Ch., 1990—93, liturgical song leader, 1993—2002. Recipient Emily Withrow Stebbins award, Evanston Hosp., 1985, Team Yr. award, Rush North Shore Med. Ctr., 2006. Mem.: Am. Assn. Clin. Chemistry, Clin. Lab. Mgmt. Assn., Am. Soc. Clin. Pathologists, Wilmette Hist. Soc. Avocations: knitting, interior design, reading. Office: Rush North Shore Med Ctr Clin Labs 9600 Gross Point Rd Skokie IL 60076 Office Phone: 847-933-6611. Business E-Mail: mlangguth@rsh.net.

LANGHAMMER, FRED H., cosmetics company executive; b. Germany, Jan. 13, 1944; Gen. mgr. Dodwell Japan subs. Inchcape, Brit. trading com.; pres. Estee Lauder Japan, Tokyo, 1975-82; mng. dir. Estee Lauder Germany, 1982-85; exec. v.p.; COO, Estee Lauder Cos., Inc., NYC, 1985, in-charge rsch. and quality control, 1991-95, pres.; COO, 1995—99, CEO, 1999—2004, chmn. global affairs, 2004—. Bd. dirs. Gillette Co., 2003—05, Shinsei Bank, 2005—, Am. Internat. Group Inc., 2006—; ind. dir. The Walt Disney Co., 2004—. Bd. dirs. Johns Hopkins U. Am. Inst. for Contemporary German Studies. Mem.: Mem. Cosmetic, Toiletry and Fragrance Assn. (bd. dirs.). Office: Estee Lauder Cos Inc 767 5th Ave New York NY 10153-0003

LANGHANS, EDWARD ALLEN, drama and theater educator; b. Warren, Pa., Mar. 11, 1923; s. Allen Milton and Frances Allen L. BA, U. Rochester, 1948, MA in English, 1949; MA in Theatre, U. Hawaii, 1951; PhD in Theatre, Yale U., 1955. Asst. prof. drama U. Tex., Austin, 1955-57; asst. prof. drama and theatre U. Hawaii, Honolulu, 1957-64, assoc., 1964-71, prof., chmn. dept., 1971-85, assoc. dean arts and humanities, 1987, prof. emeritus, 1988—. Vis. prof. Tufts U., 1967-68; rsch. prof. George Washington U., 1975-76. Author: (with Philip Highfill and Kalman Burnim) A Biographical Dictionary of Actors, Actresses, Musicians, Dancers, Managers and Other Stage Personnel in London 1660-1800, 16 vols., 1973-93, Five Restoration Theatrical Adaptations, 1980, Restoration Promptbooks, 1981, Eighteenth-Century British and Irish Promptbooks, 1987; co-author: An International Dictionary of Theater Language, 1985; contbr. chpts. to books and articles to The New Grove Dictionary of Opera, 4 vols., 1992, International Dictionary of Theatre: Actors, Directors and Designers, 1996, Cambridge and Blackwell Companions to Restoration Drama, 2000, 01, Brief Lives, 2003; dir., designer numerous plays. Bd. dirs. Honolulu Theatre for Youth, 1958-63, Hawaii Theatre Council, 1965-70, Hawaii Theatre Festival, 1978-82. Served with USAAF, 1942-47. Decorated Air medal, D.F.C.; Nat. Endowment for Humanities grantee, 1975-76, 85-86; Folger Shakespeare Library fellow, 1970-73 Mem. Soc. Theatre Rsch., Am. Soc. Theatre Rsch. Home: 1212 Punahou St Apt 3402 Honolulu HI 96826-1026

LANGHINRICHS, RUTH IMLER, playwright, writer; b. Chgo., Oct. 30, 1922; d. Roy Franklin Imler and Susan Martha Smith; m. Richard Alan Langhinrichs, May 31, 1958 (dec. July 31, 1990); children: Julia Marie Lewis-Langhinrichs, Jennifer Florence Langhinrichsen-Rohling. BS cum laude, Northwestern U., Evanston, IL, 1944. Rsch. asst. LOOK Mag., NYC, 1944—46; asst. editor Sci. Illus., NYC, 1946—49; asst. feature editor Scholastic Mag., NYC, 1949—51; assoc. editor Ladies Home Jour., Phila., 1951—58; faculty Purdue U., Fort Wayne, Ind., 1966—76; instr. Channing Sch. for Girls, London, 1974—75; writer Fort Wayne Fine Arts Found., Ind., 1977—79; pub. rels. Pk. Ctr., Fort Wayne, Ind., 1979—84; writing cons. Ind.-Purdue U. a, Fort Wayne, Ind., 1998—. Facilitator: memoir writing workshops Friends of the Libr., Fort Wayne, Ind., 1998—. Playwright (play) Feathers, The Heart of the Limberlost: Gene Stratton-Porter, Mermaids in the Basement; author: (book) Boy Dates Girl, You're Asking Me?, (novel) The Maiden and the Crone; playwright (play) A Night on Walden Pond. Charter mem. Fort Wayne Civic Youtheatre, Ind., 1973—77; bd. mem. Martin Luther King Montessori Sch., Fort Wayne, Ind., 1975—78; founding mem. Cinema Ctr., Fort Wayne, Ind., 1976—80; bd. mem. Citizen's Cable, Fort Wayne, Ind., 1981—84; pres. Aging and In Home Svcs. of N.E. Ind., Fort Wayne, Ind., 1976—2001; bd. mem. Ft. Wayne Women's Bur., Ind., 1991—97, N.E. Ind. Coun. of Tchrs. of English, Fort Wayne, Ind., 1969—73. Recipient Four-year scholarship, Chgo. Women's Ideal Club, 1940, Woman of the Yr. award, Ft. Wayne Women's Bur., 2001, Summit award, Zonta Club Internat., 2003. Mem.: Internat. Assn. of Bus. Communicators (charter mem. 1978—79), Zonta Club Internat. (v.p. 2003), Fortnightly Club, Delta Delta Delta (life). Unitarian Universalist. Avocations: gardener, artist, commissioned clown. Home: 4422 S Wayne Ave Fort Wayne IN 46807 Personal E-mail: ruthlangx@aol.com.

LANGHOUT, REGINA D., psychology professor; b. Calif. BA in Psychology, U. Calif., Santa Cruz, 1994; PhD in Psychology, U. Ill., Urbana-Champaign, 2001. Asst. prof. psychology Wesleyan U., Middletown, Conn., 2001—06, U. Calif., Santa Cruz, Calif., 2006—. Mem. North End Action Team, Middletown, Conn., 2001—06. Served with USNR, 1988—94. Recipient Michele Alexander Early Career award, Herman Eisen Memorial award. Mem.: Soc. Cmty. Rsch. and Action. Green Party. Office: University of California at Santa Cruz Psychology Dept 1156 High Street Santa Cruz CA 95064 Office Phone: 831-459-2535. Business E-Mail: langhout@ucsc.edu.

LANGLAND, OLAF ELMER, retired dental educator; b. Madrid, Iowa, May 30, 1925; s. Raymond F. and Minnie Margaret (Kinsey) L.; m. Carolyn Anderson, Oct. 1955 (div. 1973); children: Sara Mindell, Beth Langland (dec. Feb. 2002); m. Ruth Klabunde, July 1, 1975 (dec. Jan. 1985); children: Julie Van Delden, Gary Kablunde; m. Gwen E. Stokes, Apr. 25, 1991; children: Renée Schatz, Richard Stokes, Deborah Fato, D. Scott Stokes. DDS, U. Iowa, 1951, MS, 1961. Prof., head dept. oral diagnosis U. Iowa Sch. Dentistry, Iowa City, 1963-68; prof., head dept. oral diagnosis, medicine and radiology La. State U. Med. Ctr. and Dental Sch., New Orleans, 1968-74; prof., head div. oral and maxillofacial radiology U. Tex. Health Sci. Ctr., San Antonio, 1975-99, prof. emeritus, 1999—. Rotator U.S. Hope Ship, Maceio, Brazil, 1973. Author: Textbook of Dental Radiology, 1984, Radiology for Dental Assistants and Dental Hygienists, 1987, Principles and Practice of Panoramic Radiology, 1989, Diagnostic Imaging of the Jaws, 1994, Principles of Dental Imaging, 1997, 2nd edit. 2001. With inf. AUS, 1943-45, ETO. Decorated Purple Heart, Combat Infantry badge with star, Bronze Star; recipient Outstanding Tchr. award U. Tex. Health Sci. Ctr., 1992. Fellow Am. Coll. Dentists, Internat. Assn. of Dental Maxillofacial Radiology (hon.); mem. Am. Acad. Oral and Maxillofacial Radiology (diplomate, pres. 1984-85), Am. Acad. Dental Schs. (pres. sect. oral radiology 1974-75), Orgn. Tchrs. Diagnosis (pres. 1975-76), Masons, Shriners, Mil. Order of Purple Heart, Am. Legion. Avocation: civil war medical history. Home: 1819 Babcock Rd Apt 207 San Antonio TX 78229-4630 Personal E-mail: olangland@msn.com.

LANGLANDS, ROBERT PHELAN, mathematician, educator; b. New Westminster, Can., Oct. 6, 1936; arrived in US, 1960; s. Robert and Kathleen (Phelan) L.; m. Charlotte Lorraine Cheverie, Aug. 13, 1956; children: William, Sarah, Robert, Thomasin. BA, U. BC, 1957, MSc, 1958, DS honoris causa, 1985; PhD, Yale U., 1960; DSc (hon.), McMaster U., 1985, CUNY, 1985; D in Math. (hon.), U. Waterloo, 1988; DSc (hon.), U. Paris, 1989, McGill U., 1991, Toronto U., 1993, U. Montréal, 1997, U. Laval, 2002, U. Madras, India, 2005. From instr. to assoc. prof. Princeton U., NJ, 1960-67; prof. math. Yale U., New Haven, 1968-72, Inst. Advanced Study, Princeton, NJ, 1972—, Hermann Weyl prof. math. Author: Euler Products, 1971, (with H. Jacquet) Automorphic Forms on GL (2), 1970, On the Functional Equations Satisfied by Eisenstein Series, 1976, Base Change for GL (2), 1980, Les Débuts d'une Formule des Traces Stable, 1983. Recipient Wilbur Lucius Cross medal Yale U., 1975, Common Wealth award Sigma Xi, 1984, Mathematics award Nat. Acad. Sci., 1988, Wolf prize in math. Wolf Found., Israel, 1995-96, la Grande Médaille d'Or de l'Académie des Scis., 2000; co-recipient Shaw prize, Math. Scis., Shaw Prize Found., Hong Kong, 2007 Fellow Royal Soc. London, Royal Soc. Can.; mem. NAS, Am. Math Soc. (Cole prize in Number Theory, 1982, Steele prize 2005, Frederic Esser Nemmers prize in Math., 2006), Can. Math. Soc. Office: Inst Advanced Study Sch Math Olden Ln Princeton NJ 08540*

LANGLEY, CHARLES HUNT, geneticist, educator; BA in Zoology, Univ. Tex., 1968, PhD, 1971. Disting. prof., genetics, evolution biology Univ. Calif., Davis. Fellow: Am. Acad. Arts & Scis.; mem.: Genetics Soc. Am. (Genetics Soc. Am. Medal 1999). Office: 3342B Storer Hall Univ Calif One Shields Ave Davis CA 95616 Office Phone: 530-752-4085. Business E-Mail: chlangley@ucdavis.edu.*

LANGLEY, DONNA, film company executive; Sr. v.p. prodn. New Line Cinema, 1994—2001, Universal Pictures, 2001—03, exec. v.p. prodn., 2003—05, pres. prodn., 2005—. Exec. prodr.: (films) Austin Powers: The Spy Who Shagged Me, 1999, Drop Dead Gorgeous, 1999, The Astronaut's Wife, 1999, The Bachelor, 1999, The Cell, 2000, Lost Souls, 2000, Highway, 2002. Named one of 100 Most Powerful Women in Entertainment, Hollywood Reporter, 2996. Office: Universal Pictures 100 Universal City Plz Universal City CA 91608*

LANGLEY, GEORGE ROSS, medical educator; b. Sydney, NS, Can., Oct. 6, 1931; s. John Goerge Elmer and Freda Catherine (Ross) L.; m. Jean Marie Ballantyne, June 22, 1957; children: Joanne Marie, Mark Ross, Richard Graham. BA, Mt. Allison U., 1952; MD, Dalhousie U., 1957. Intern Victoria Gen. Hosp., Halifax, N.S., 1957, resident, 1958, Toronto Gen. Hosp., 1960, U. Melbourne, Australia, 1961, U. Rochester, NY, 1962; John and Mary Markle scholar in acad. medicine Dalhousie U., Halifax, 1963-68, from lectr. to prof. medicine, 1963-69, prof., chmn. dept. medicine, 1974-82; chief of service medicine Camp Hill Hosp., Halifax, 1969-74; head dept. medicine Victoria Gen. Hosp., 1974-82; prof. medicine Dalhousie U., Queen Elizabeth II Health. Sci. Ctr., 1982—2002; exec. dir. Strategic Hlth. Svcs. Dept. Hlth. Provinces, Nova Scotia, Canada, 1998-2000, prof. emeritus, 2002—, Dalhousie U., 2002—. Chmn. clin. investigation grants com. Med. Rsch. Coun., 1976-78; chmn. clin. and epidemiol. research adv. com., bd. dirs. Nat. Cancer Inst. Can., 1978-86 Contbr. articles to profl. jours. Recipient Queen's Silver Jubilee medal, 1977, Queen's Golden Jubilee medal, 2002, Dalhousie Med. Alumnus of Yr., 2003. Master ACP (bd. govs. 1973-78, laureate Atlantic region 1996, Mastership 2007); fellow Internat. Soc. Hematology, Royal Coll. Physicians and Surgeons (v.p., coun., Wightman vis. prof. 1990, Drs. Nova Scotia Disting. Svc. award 2007), Royal Coll. Physicians (Edinburgh); mem. Can. Hematology Soc. (pres. 1976-78), Can. Soc. Clin. Investigation, Am. Soc. Hematology, Can. Soc. Oncology, Alpha Omega Alpha. Mem. United Ch. Can. Home: 6025 Oakland Rd Halifax NS Canada B3H 1N9 Office: Victoria Gen Hosp Ste 8-024 Halifax NS Canada B3H 2Y9 Business E-Mail: ross.langley@dal.ca.

LANGLEY, GRANT F., municipal lawyer; b. Worcester, Mass., July 20, 1945; BA, U. Wis., 1967; JD, Marquette U. Bar: State of Wis. Asst. city atty. City of Milw., 1971-84, city atty., 1984—. Mem. Supreme Ct. Selection Com., 2001—. Mem. Internat. Mcpl. Lawyers Assn. Office: Office of City Atty City Hall Rm 800 200 E Wells St Milwaukee WI 53202-3515

LANGLEY, HAROLD DAVID, historian, educator; b. Amsterdam, NY, Feb. 15, 1925; s. Walter Benedict Langley and Anna McCaffrey; m. Patricia Ann Piccola, June 12, 1965; children: Erika, David. BA, Cath. U. Am., Washington, 1950; MA, U. Pa., Phila., 1951; PhD, U. Pa., 1960. Manuscript asst. and specialist Libr. of Congress, Washington, 1951—52, 1954—55; instr., asst. prof. Marywood Coll., Scranton, Pa., 1955—57; diplomatic historian U.S. Dept. State, Washington, 1957—64; assoc. prof./prof. Cath. U. Am., Washington, 1964—70, adj. prof., 1971—2001; assoc. curator, curator Smithsonian Instn., Washington, 1970—96; ret. Hist. cons. Versar Corp., Arlington, Va., 1998—99. Author: Social Reform in the U.S. Navy, 1798-1862, 1967; co-editor: Roosevelt and Churchill: Their Secret Wartime Correspondence, 1975; editor: So Proudly We Hail: A History of the U.S. Flag, 1980; author: Medicine in the Early U.S. Navy, 1996 (K. Jack Bauer award, 1996). Founding mem. Lorcom Lane Def. Com., Arlington, 1988—89; parish historian St. Stephen Martyr Ch., Washington, 1966—; adv. bd. Cath. Hist. Soc. of Washington, 1996—. Cpl. AUS, 1943—46. Recipient Alumni Achievement award, Cath. U. Am., 2000, Samuel Eliot Morison award, USS Constitution Mus., Boston, 2002, Gondos award, Soc. for Mil. History, 1978. Mem.: N.Am. Soc. for Oceanic History, Orgn. Am. Historians, Cosmos Club (history com.). Avocation: travel. Home: 2515 N Utah St Arlington VA 22207-4031

LANGLEY, JAMES T., imaging company executive; BS in Mech. Engring., U. Calif., Berkeley; MS in Mech. Engring. and Computer Sci., Stanford U., Calif.; grad. Exec. MBA Program, U. Mich., Ann Arbor. With Hewlett-Packard Co., 1972—2002, gen. mgr. Vancouver Printer Divsn., 1993—97; v.p. Inkjet Worldwide Office Printers, 1997—2000, v.p. comml. printing, 2000—02; pres. Graphic Comm. Group (formerly Comml. Printing Group) Eastman Kodak Co., Rochester, NY, 2003—, sr. v.p., 2003—, COO, 2007—. Office: Eastman Kodak Co 343 State St Rochester NY 14650 Office Phone: 585-724-4000.*

LANGLEY, RICKY LEE, occupational medicine physician; b. Fountain, NC, Aug. 31, 1957; s. Ernest Lee and Janie Ruth (Fulford) L.; m. Sandra Jane Ward, June 7, 1980; children: Patrick, Nicholas, Megan. BS magna cum laude, NC State U., Raleigh, 1979; MD, Bowman Grey Sch. Medicine, 1983; MPH, U. NC, 1988. Diplomate Am. Bd. Internal Medicine, Am. Bd. Preventive Medicine. Intern East Carolina Sch. Medicine, Greenville, NC, 1983-84, resident, 1984-86; asst. prof. dept. preventive medicine and health policy East Carolina U., Greenville, 1989-91, adj. asst. prof. dept. family medicine, 1989-91, adj. asst. prof. dept. environ. health, 1989-98, asst. prof. dept. internal medicine, 1991; fellow Sch. Medicine Duke U., Durham, NC, 1986-88, asst. cons. prof. in occupl. medicine, 1989-90, asst. clin. prof. dept. cmty. and family medicine, 1991-96; pvt. practice occupl. medicine Health and Hygiene, Inc., Greensboro, NC, 1988-89; med. dir. Mebane (NC) Med. Ctr., 1996-98, Kernodle Clinic, Inc., 1998; pub. health physician Occupl. and Environ. Epidemiology, Dept. Health & Human Svc., Raleigh, NC, 1998—. Adj. asst. prof. dept. biol. and agrl. engring. NC State U., 1996—99; cons. in field; mem. planning com. on agrl. safety NC State Fair, 1991; mem. task force Agri-Bus. for Gov.'s Commn. on Reduction of Infant Morality, 1992; mem. NC State Task Force on Blood-Borne Pathogens NC Occupl. Health and Safety Adminstrn., 1991—92; presenter in field.; mem. Nat. Pork Procedures Coun. Task Force on Worker Health and Safety, 1995; occupl. medicine residency program evaluator for NIOSH, 1992—96, mem. spl. emphasis panel, 1996—; mem. agrl. safety and health coun. NC Dept. Labor, 1996—; mem. NC Pesticide Bd., 1998—; occupl. medicine residency adv. com. Duke U., 1998—; mem. bd. collaborators NC Inst. Health and Safety in Agr., Forestry & Fisheries, 2001—. Author: Sex and Gender Differences in Health and Disease, 2003; editor: Safety and Health in Agriculture, Forestry and Fisheries, 1997, (textbook) Animal Handlers; guest editor NC Med. Jour., 1992-93, 95, mem. editl. bd., 1999—; mem. editl. bd. Jour. Agromedicine, 2004-05; co-editor Environmental Health Secrets, 2001; reviewer, contbr. articles to profl. jours. Vol. Greenville Cmty. Shelter, 1990, Health Hotline, WITN, 1990, 91, State Employee Wellness Day 1989, Adopt-A-Hwy. Project, 1989; Dr. of the Day, NC State Legislature, 1991; doctor on call blood drive ARC, Greensboro, 1989; vol. Freemont Peoples Clinic, 1993, Open Door Clinic, Burlington, 2006-07; pub. affairs officer, mem. USCG Aux., 1996-99, flotilla 18-11, 1995-98; hunting safety educator, NC, 1996—; mem. Alamance County (NC) Bd. Adjustment, 1997-99. Lloyd T. Weeks scholar, 1978, Benjamin Elloit Ibie and Benjamin Elliot Ibie Jr. Meml. scholar, 1976. Fellow ACP, Am. Coll. Occupl. and Environ. Medicine (del. 1995-98), Am. Coll. Preventive Medicine; mem. AMA, NC Med. Soc. (environ. health subcom. 1991—, vice chair 1999-2000, chair 2000-01), Am. Occupl. Med. Assn. (med. ctr. occupl. health com. 1990-97), Carolinas Occupl. Med. Assn. (sec.-treas. 1991-92, pres-elect 1992-93, pres. 1993-94, del. 1995-98), NC Archeol. Soc. (exec. bd. 1998-2000), Tarheel Archaeology Soc. (edn. chair 1996-2000), Found. for Advanced Lithics Studies (sec.-treas. 2000—), Alamance County Astronomy Club (founding mem.), Sigma Xi, Phi Kappa Phi, Phi Eta Sigma, Gamma Sigma Delta, Alpha Epsilon Delta. Avocations: astronomy, archaeology. Home: 1506 Miles Chapel Rd Mebane NC 27302-9008 Office: Mebane Med Clinic Mebane NC 27302 Office Phone: 919-707-5920. Personal E-mail: rick.langley@ncmail.net.

LANGLEY, ROLLAND AMENT, JR., engineering and management consultant; b. San Francisco, Aug. 22, 1931; s. Rolland Ament and Kathryn Lee (Beals) L.; m. Pamela Winston, May, 15, 1954 (div. 1978); children: Owen C., Cynthia, James R.; m. Chiara Bini-Sexton, Apr. 12, 1978. BS in Engring. and Physics, U. Calif., Berkeley, 1953; MME, U. Pitts., 1961; MBA, Golden Gate U., 1973. Engr. Bettis Atomic Power Lab. of Westinghouse Electric Corp., Pitts., 1957-62; with Bechtel Corp., San Francisco, 1962-71; mgr. refinery and chem. nuclear fuel ops. Bechtel Inc., San Francisco, 1977-78; mgr. projects nuclear fuel ops. Bechtel Nat. Inc., San Francisco, 1979-80, mgr. decontamination and restoration nuclear fuel ops., 1980-81, v.p., mgr. nuclear fuels ops. Oak Ridge, Tenn., 1981-84, sr. v.p., mgr. div. ops., R & D ops. San Francisco, 1985-89; dep. mgr. Uranium Enrichment Assocs., San Francisco, 1972-76; v.p. Uranium Enrichment Tech. Inc., San Francisco, 1976-77; pres., dir. Bechtel Systems Mgmt. Inc., 1988-90; pres., CEO BNFL Inc., 1990-97, 98-99, also bd. dirs., 1994-2000; exec. v.p. Project Time & Cost, Inc., 2005—. Bd. dirs. 21st Century Coatings, Plato Sys., GmbH; trustee, pres. World Mem. Fund-U.S.A., 1993-98; chmn., Pajarito Sci. Corp., 1995-97, bd. dirs.; pres. Pacific Nuclear Coun., 1998-2000; mem. Nat. Acad. Sci. panel on nuclear separation and transmutation, 1992-95; counsellor Atlantic Coun. U.S., 2003—; adv. dir. European Inst., 2000—. Contbr. articles to profl. jours. Trustee Environ. Sci. and Tech. Inst., 1995-98. Capt. USNR. Recipient Bausch and Lomb Sci. award, 1948. Mem. Naval Res Assn. (past pres. Golden Gate chpt.), Brit.-Am. Bus. Assn. (bd. dirs. 1996—). Achievements include patents in nuclear fuel and reactor systems design; research on uranium enrichment, nuclear waste disposal, fast breeder reactors, and engineering management. Home: PO Box 208 Middleburg VA 20118-0208 Office Phone: 540-687-4137. E-mail: ralangley@earthlink.net.

LANGLEY, WILLIAM M., educator; b. Dayton, Jan. 22, 1943; s. Milford and Catherine Rose Langley; m. Lisa Christine Skerbetz, Feb. 21, 1990; children: Amber, Adam, Abbey. BA, Earlham Coll., Richmond, Ind., 1965; MS, Mich. State U., East Lansing, 1968; PhD, Ariz. State U., Tempe, 1978. Asst. prof. Whichita State U., Kans., 1975—82; lead instr. Butler CC, El Dorado, 1982—. Office: Butler CC 9018 Haverhill Rd El Dorado KS 67042

LANGLOIS, MICHAEL A., financial consultant; b. Springfield, Mass., July 4, 1956; s. Arthur Edward and Maria (Duchesneau) Langlois; children: Michelle, Jeffrey. BBA, Bryant Coll., Smithfield, RI, 1978, MBA, 1982. Registered investment adviser. Prin., owner Strategic Fin. Group, Cranston, 1993—; devel. mgr. Monarch Fin. Group, Providence, 1988-91. Pres. Langlois & Assocs., Cranston, 1986; instr. Bryant Coll. Co-author: Living and Learning Retirement Planning, 2005; contbr. articles to profl. jours. Nominee bus. adv. co-chmn., R.I., 2003. Mem.: Nat. Assn. Estate Planners, Internat. Bd. Cert. Fin. Planners, Internat. Assn. Registered Fin. Planners, Fin. Planning Assn., Internat. Assn. Fin. Planning, Am. Assn. Individual Investors, Am. Arbitration Assn. (arbitrator), Nat. Assn. Life Underwriters, Nat. Assn. Securities Dealers. Roman Catholic. Home: 45 Mollie Dr Cranston RI 02921-1415 Office: Langlois & Assocs 55 Old Bald Hill Rd Cranston RI 02920 Office Phone: 401-463-3150.

LANGMAN, LAUREN, sociology educator; b. Chgo., June 16, 1940; s. Henry and Anne (Moorvitz) L.; married, 1 child, Anais Richman. BA, U. Ill., 1961; PhD, U. Chgo., 1969. Sociologist Loyola U., Chgo., 1968—. Contbr. chpts. to books and articles to revs. Mem. Am. Sociol. Assn., Midwest Sociol. Assn., Soc. Study Social Problems, Internat. Sociology Assn. (sec.-tres. 1991—, treas. 1990—). Avocations: sailing, travel, scuba, classical music. Home: 2012 N Howe St Chicago IL 60614-4414 Office: Loyola U 6525 N Sheridan Rd Chicago IL 60626-5385

LANGMAN, PETER FABBRI, psychologist, poet, playwright; b. Honolulu; BA in Psychology and Geography, Clark U., Worcester, Mass., 1984; MA in Counseling Psychology, Lesley Coll., Cambridge, Mass., 1989; PhD in Counseling Psychology, Lehigh U., Bethlehem, Pa., 2000. Lic. psychologist Pa., 2002. Dir. psychology KidsPeace, Orefield, Pa., 2004—. Lectr./spkr. in field. Author: Jewish Issues in Multiculturalism, 1999; contbr. articles to profl. jours., chapters to books. Mem.: APA, Lehigh Valley Writers Acad. (pres.), Pa. Psychol. Assn., Dramatist Guild Am. (assoc.). Achievements include research in school shootings. Office: KidsPeace 5300 Kids Peace Dr Orefield PA 18069 Home Phone: 610-740-9449; Office Phone: 610-799-7777. Office Fax: 610-799-8801. Personal E-mail: peterlangman@yahoo.com. Business E-Mail: plangman@kidspeace.org.

LANGMEAD, JOSEPH MICHAEL, accountant, consultant, educator; b. Balt., Nov. 5, 1944; s. Richard James and Dorothy Kathleen (DeCarlo) L.; m. Judy Kay Kearney, June 26, 1969; children: Maureen Langmead Cochran, Gregory, Benjamin. BSBA, Loyola Coll., 1968, MBA, 1973; MA in Sacred Theology, St. Mary's Sem. and Univ., Balt., 2006. CPA Md.; licentiate in sacred theology St. Mary's Sem., U., 2006. Acct. Kushnick & Waldman, Balt., 1965—68; auditor KPMG, Balt., 1968—76, ptnr. NYC, 1976—2000. SEC reviewing ptnr. KPMG, London, 1994—2000; exec. in residence, adj. prof. acctg. and fin. Sellinger Sch. Bus. and Mgmt., Loyola Coll., 2002—; cons. in field. Pres. bd. trustees Ctr. Stage, Balt., 1981-88, chmn. capital campaign, 1988-91; chmn. bd. trustees Loyola H.S., Towson, Md., 1983-87; bd. fin. City of Balt., 1988-92; trustee Roland Pk. Country Sch., Balt., 1990-93, Md. State Arts Coun., Balt., 1991-94; chmn. Balt. Arts Stabilization Project Com., 1991-94; bd. dirs. Nat. Arts Stabilization, Balt., 1991-2001, chmn., 2000-01; bd. dirs. Md. chpt. Nat. Multiple Sclerosis Soc., 2002-04, vice chmn., 2003-04; bd. dirs. Inst. for Christian and Jewish Studies, 2006—. With U.S. Army, 1968-70 Mem. AICPA, Md. Assn. CPA (bd. dirs. 1990-93), Mensa. Democrat. Roman Catholic. Avocations: opera, music, theology, history. Home and Office: 102 Witherspoon Rd Baltimore MD 21212 Office Phone: 410-435-8333. Personal E-mail: joseph.langmead@verizon.net.

LANGMUIR, CHARLES HERBERT, geology educator; b. Chalk River, Ont., Can., Nov. 24, 1950; came to U.S., 1954; s. David Bulkeley and Marianna (Lawrence) L.; m. Diane Marie Langmuir, Sept. 22, 1973 (div. 1999); 1 child, Molly Kathryn. BA, Harvard U., 1973; MS, SUNY, Stony Brook, 1978, PhD, 1980. From asst. to assoc. prof. Lamont-Doherty Geol. Observatory Columbia U., Palisades, NY, 1981-88, prof., 1988—92, Arthur D. Storke Meml. prof., 1989—2002; prof. Harvard U., Cambridge, Mass., 2002—. Vis. scientist Inst. de Physique du Globe, Paris, 1989-90, 2002-2003; mem. adv. com. on ocean scis. NSF, 1990-93; mem. lithosphere panel Joint Oceanographic Instns. for Deep Earth Sampling, 1984-87; chmn. Conf. on Sci. Ocean Drilling II, Work Group on Mantle-Crust Interactions, 1986-87; mem. steering com. Ridge Interdisciplinary Global Experiments, 1990-93; chmn. coord. com. Project French-Am.-Ridge Atlantic, 1989-97; mem. steering com. Inter Ridge, 1992-96. Editor: Earth and Planetary Sci. Letters, 1989—; mem. editorial bd. Chem. Geology, 1985-96; contbr. over 100 articles to profl. jours. Alfred Sloan Rsch. fellow, 1983-85, Henry Shaw fellow Harvard U., 1974. Fellow Geochem. Soc., Am. Geophys. Union (fellows com. 1995—, Bowen award 1996), European Unidei Geoscis. (Holmes medal), Am. Acad. Arts & Scis.; mem. Geol. Soc. Am., NAS. Office: Dept Earth & Planetary Scis Harvard U 20 Oxford St Cambridge MA 02138 Office Phone: 617-384-9948, 617-384-9948. Office Fax: 617-495-6958. E-mail: langmuir@eps.harvard.edu.

LANGONE, KENNETH G., investment company executive; b. Roslyn Heights, NY, Sept. 16, 1935; m. Elaine Langone; 3 children. BA, Bucknell U., 1957; MBA, NYU Stern Sch. of Bus. Exec. v.p. R.W. Pressprich & Co.; founder, chmn., CEO Invemed Assocs. LLC, NYC, 1974—, dir., 1999; co-founder, dir., mem. exec. com. Home Depot Inc., 1978. Bd. dirs. Home Depot, 1978—, Yum Brands, Inc., 1997—, GE, 1999—, Unifi, Inc., TRICON Global Restaurants, AutoFinance, Inc., InterWorld Corp., DBT Online, Inc., US Satellite Broadcasting of Minn., Choicepoint, Inc.; former mem. NY Stock Exch. Vice-chmn. bd. overseers Stern Sch. Bus.; chmn. bd. trustees NYU Med. Sch.; trustee, chmn. nominating com., chmn. endowment com., mem. exec. com. Bucknell U.; contbr., adv., transformation team Mayor Rudolph Giuliani, 1993; chmn. NY State Sen. Bob Dole, presdl. election, 1996; trustee, chmn. nominating com., chmn. endowment com., mem. exec. com. NY Philharm., Children's Oncology Soc. (Ronald McDonald House), Robin Hood Found.; trustee, mem. exec. com. NYU; bd. dirs., vice-chmn. bd. develop. Damon Runyon-Walter Winchell Found.; trustee Ctr. for Strategic & Internat. Studies (CSIS). Named one of 400 Richest Ams., Forbes mag., 2006. Office: Invemed Assocs 375 Park Ave Ste 2205 New York NY 10152-2201

LANGRAN, ROBERT WILLIAMS, political scientist, educator; b. NYC, Feb. 15, 1935; s. Robert Joseph and Leona Gertrude (Williams) L.; m. Eleanor Victoria Groh, Dec. 26, 1959; children: Irene, Elizabeth, Thomas. BS with honors, Loyola U., Chgo., 1956; MA, Fordham U., 1959; PhD, Bryn Mawr Coll., 1965. Prof. polit. sci. Villanova U., Pa., 1959—. Author: The United States Supreme Court: An Historical and Political Analysis, 1989, 6th edit. 2007, The Supreme Court: A Concise History, 2004; co-author: Government, Business, and the American Economy, 2001, 2d edit., 2007, You Decide! Controversial Cases in American Politics, 2007; contbr. articles to profl. jours. Served to 1st lt. U.S. Army, 1956-58. Mem. Am. Polit. Sci. Assn., Supreme Ct. Hist. Soc. Office: Villanova Univ Political Sci Dept Villanova PA 19085 Office Phone: 610-519-4734. Business E-Mail: robert.langran@villanova.edu.

LANGRANA, ANITA, financial analyst, personal trainer; b. Ithaca, NY, July 13, 1975; d. Noshir A. and Dinaz Langrana. BS, Rutgers U., New Brunswick, NJ, 1998; MBA, Pace U., NYC, 2004. Cert. athletic trainer NJ. Human resources coord. Sports Phys. Therapy Inst., Princeton, NJ, 1998—2002, cert. athletic trainer, 2000—02; procurement divsn. intern UN, NYC, 2003; ad sales and stewardship intern Universal TV Group, NYC, 2003; fin. analyst Bristol-Myers Squibb, Princeton, 2004—05, Wyndham Worldwide, Parsippany, NJ, 2005—. Athletic Tng. scholar, Rutgers Sports Medicine Club, 1997—98. Mem.: Nat. Athletic Trainers Soc. (assoc.), Lubin Grad. Soc. (v.p. 2003—04), Lubin Bus. Sch. Alumni Assn. (bd. dirs., award 2004), Omicron Delta Epsilon, Sigma Iota Epsilon, Beta Gamma Sigma (hon.). Zoroastrian. Avocations: sports, exercise, travel, reading. Office: Wyndham Worldwide 7 Sylvan Way Parsippany NJ 07054 Home Phone: 646-265-8394. Personal E-mail: anita.langrana@gmail.com. Business E-Mail: anita.langrana@rci.com.

LANGRIDGE, ROBERT, biophysicist, educator, computational biologist; b. Essex, Eng., Oct. 26, 1933; came to U.S., 1957; naturalized, 1987. s. Charles and Winifred (Lister) L.; m. Ruth Gottlieb, June 26, 1960; children: Elizabeth, Catherine, Suzanne. BSc in Physics (1st class honours), U. London, Eng., 1954, PhD in Crystallography, 1957. Vis. research fellow biophysics Yale, 1957-59; research assoc. biophysics M.I.T., 1959-61; research assoc. pathology Children's Cancer Research Found., Boston; research assoc. biophysics, lectr. biophysics, also tutor biochem. scis. Harvard, 1961-66; research assoc. Project MAC, Lab. for Computer Sci., M.I.T., 1964-66; prof. biophysics and info. scis. U. Chgo., 1966-68; prof. chemistry and biochem. scis. Princeton, 1968-76; prof. pharm. chemistry, biochemistry and biophysics, dir. Computer Graphics Lab. U. Calif., San Francisco, 1976-94, prof. emeritus, 1994—, mem. adv. com. resource for biocomputing visualization and informatics, 1998—2004. Vis. prof. computer sci. Stanford U., 1983-84; vis. prof. biochem., biophys. Oreg. State U., 1995-97; mem. computer and biomath. rsch. study sect. NIH, USPHS, 1968-72, chmn., 1975-77, mem. nat. adv. rsch. resources coun., 1992-96, mem. adv. com. to dir., 1993-95, mem. biomed. informatics expert panel, 2004—; mem. vis. com. biology dept. Brookhaven Nat. Lab., 1977-80, mem. adv. com. neutron diffraction, biology dept., 1980-83; mem. sci. and ednl. adv. com. Lawrence Berkeley Labs., 1988-92; chair U. Calif. Berkeley/U. Calif. San Francisco Grad. Group in Bioengring., 1991-93; mem. computer sci. and telecomm. bd. NRC, NAS, 1988-91. Guggenheim fellow, 1983-84 Fellow AAAS; mem. NAS, Inst. of Medicine. Home: 60 The Crescent Berkeley CA 94708-1702

LANGROCK, KARL FREDERICK, writer, retired academic administrator; b. Toeterville, Iowa, Jan. 26, 1927; s. Lee Henry and Alice Dora (Grube) L.; m. Rose Marie Meyer, June 4, 1950; children: Laura Sue, Charles Alan. BA, U. No. Iowa, 1949; MA, U. Iowa, 1951; MDiv, Luth. Sch. Theology, Chgo., 1955; LittD (hon.), Grand View Coll., 1989. Pastor Lake Park Luth. Ch., Milw., 1955-57, Resurrection Luth. Ch., Franklin Park, Ill., 1957-62, Luth. Ch. of the Holy Spirit, Deerfield, Ill., 1962-69; asst. to pres. Berea (Ky.) Coll., 1969-72; pres. Grand View Coll., Des Moines, 1972-88. Mem. Iowa Coll. Aid Commn., Des Moines, 1980-84, Luth. Social Services of Ill., Chgo., 1962-70, pres., 1968-70. Served in USN, 1945-46. Mem. Iowa Assn. Independent Colls. and Univs. (bd. dirs. 1972-87, chmn. 1986-87), Council of Luth. Ch. in Am. Colls. (pres. 1978), Phi Eta Sigma. Lutheran. Home: 32200 SW French Prairie Dr Apt B328 Wilsonville OR 97070-5473 E-mail: klangrock@centurytel.net.

LANGSLEY, PAULINE ROYAL, psychiatrist; b. Lincoln, Nebr., July 2, 1927; d. Paul Ambrose and Dorothy (Sibley) Royal; m. Donald G. Langsley, Sept. 9, 1955; children: Karen Jean, Dorothy Ruth Langsley Runman, Susan Louise. BA, Mills Coll., 1949; MD, U. Nebr., 1953. Cert. psychiatrist, Am. Bd. Psychiatry and Neurology. Intern Mt. Zion Hosp., San Francisco, 1954; resident U. Calif., San Francisco, 1954-57, student health psychiatrist Berkeley, 1957-61, U. Colo., Boulder, 1961-68; assoc. clin. prof. psychiatry U. Calif. Med. Sch., Davis, 1968-76; student health psychiatrist U. Calif., Davis, 1968-76; assoc. clin. prof. psychiatry U. Cin., 1976-82; pvt. practice psychiatry Cin., 1976-82; cons. psychiatrist Federated States of Micronesia, Pohnpei, 1984-87; fellow in geriatric psychiatry Rush-Presbyn./St. Luke Hosp., Chgo., 1989-91. Mem. accreditation rev. com. Accreditation Coun. for Continuing Med. Edn., 1996-98. Trustee Mills Coll., Oakland, 1974-78, 2001—; bd. dirs. Evanston Women's Club. Fellow Am. Psychiat. Assn. (chair continuing med. edn. 1990-96); mem. AMA, Am. Med. Womens Assn., Ohio State Med. Assn., Ill. Psychiat. Soc. (sec. 1993-95, pres.-elect 1995-96, pres. 1996-97, accreditation coun. 1996-98). Home and Office: 1111 Race St 10A Denver CO 80206 Home Phone: 303-321-4193; Office Phone: 303-321-4193.

LANGSNER, ALAN MICHAEL, pediatric cardiologist; b. NYC, Dec. 21, 1948; s. Herman and Celeste (Prince) L.; m. Hilary Schmidt, Dec. 19, 1971. BA in Psychology, Fairleigh Dickinson U., 1970; MD, U. Autonomia Guadalajara, Jalisco, Mex., 1977; postgrad., NYU, 1977-78. Cert. Am. Bd. Pediat. and Pediat. Cardiology. Resident in pediatrics N.Y. Med. Coll./Met. Hosp. Ctr., NYC, 1978-79, resident in pediatrics-primary care tng. program, 1979-80, chief resident in pediatrics-primary care tng. program, 1980-81; pvt. practice pediatric cardiology NYC, 1983—; attending pediatrics, sr. cons. pediatric cardiology St. Barnabas Med. Ctr., Livingston, NJ, 1983—; assoc. cons. pediatric cardiology St. Vincent's Med. Ctr., SI, NY, 1983—; chief dept. pediatric cardiology Children's Hosp. of N.J. at Newark Beth Israel Hosp., 1999—2004. Cons. pediatric cardiology, asst. prof. pediat. NYU Sch. Medicine,1983—, SI U. Hosp., 1985-2003; perinatal rev. com., med. bd. St. Barnabas Med. Ctr.; presenter in field Contbr. articles to profl. jours. Fellow: Am. Acad. Pediatrics, Am. Coll. Cardiology (councilor NJ chpt. 2006—); mem.: AMA, Essex County Med. Soc. Office: 405 Northfield Ave West Orange NJ 07052-3023 Office Phone: 973-736-9997.

LANGSTON, EDWARD LEE, physician, pharmacist; b. Logansport, Ind., Sept. 28, 1944; m. Linda Langston; 2 children. BS in pharmacy, Purdue U. Sch. Pharmacy; MD, Ind. U. Sch. Medicine. Bd. cert. in family practice. Resident in family practice St. Mary's Grad. Med. Ctr., Evansville, Ill.; chair Commn. on Legis.; dir. family practice program, assoc. prof. Tex. Med. Ctr., 1993—96; v.p. med. affairs and med. edn. Trinity Regional Health Sys., Rock Island, Ill., 1996—2000; pvt. practice family physician Lafayette, Ind., 2000—. Affiliate asst. prof. Purdue U., Sch. Pharmacy, West Lafayette, Ind.; mem. adv. com. State Medicaid Prescription Drug; coord., sec. Lafayette Med. Edn. Found., 2001—; vol. faculty Cmty. Hosp. Family Practice Residency Program, dir., 1988—92; mem. bd. trustees US Pharmacopeia, 1995—2000; bd. dir. Accreditation Coun. on Grad. Med. Edn., 1998—2003; bd. commr. Joint Commn. on Accreditation of Healthcare Orgn., 2005—. Mem.: Ind. State Med. Assn., Am. Acad. Family Physicians (bd. dir. 1991—93, v.p. 1994, chair delegation 1999—2002), AMA (house del. 1987—, mem., coun. on med. edn. 1997—2003, bd. trustees 2003—, chair-elect bd. trustees 2006—07, chmn. bd. trustees 2007—, mem., chair, specialty and svc. soc.), Ind. Acad. Family Physicians (pres. 1982—83), Alpha Omega Alpha. Avocations: jogging, reading, furniture refinishing. Office: 2323 Ferry St Ste 101 Lafayette IN 47904 Office Phone: 765-448-4511.*

LANGSTON, JAMES LELAND, electronics engineer; b. Atlanta, Tex., July 26, 1942; s. Paul T. and Vernie D. (Bridges) Langston; m. Alice Jean Evans, 1985; 1 child, Brent Leland. BSEE, So. Meth. U., 1966, postgrad., 1966-67. Registered profl. engr., Tex. Technician Collins Radio, Richardson, Tex., 1961-65, design engr., 1965-67, lead engr., 1967-70, sr. engr., 1970-71, Tex. Instruments, Dallas, 1971-73, project engr., 1973-75, sys. engr., 1975-78, mem. tech. staff, 1978-82, sr. mem. tech. staff, 1982-98, disting. mem. tech. staff, 1998-99, engring. fellow, 1999—, program mgr. com. and signal processing, 1986-92, chief engr. comm. and electronic sys., 1992-96; chief tech. officer Crosspan divsn. Raytheon, 1998-2000, mgr. sys. engring. Colorado Springs, Colo., 2000—05, chief engr. civil comms., 2005—. Contbr. articles pub. to profl. jours. Recipient Group Achievement award, NASA, 1976, Pub. Svc. Award medal, 1981. Mem.: AIAA, ASCE, AAS, IEEE (sr.), Nat. Soc. Profl. Engr. Achievements include patents in field. Personal E-mail: leland_langston@msn.com. Business E-Mail: j-langston2@raytheon.com.

LANGSTON, MALINDA L., lawyer; b. Lexington, Ky., May 10, 1971; BS, Ga. Southern U., 1993; JD, U. Dayton, 1997. Bar: Ohio 1997, Ky. 1999. Asst. pros. atty. Montgomery County, Ohio; assoc. Kohnen & Patton LLP, Cin. Named one of Ohio's Rising Stars, Super Lawyers, 2006. Mem.: Northern Ky. Bar Assn., Ky. Bar Assn., Ohio State Bar Assn., Cin. Bar Assn. Office: Kohnen & Patton LLP PNC Ctr Ste 800 E Fifth St Cincinnati OH 45202 Office Phone: 513-381-0656. Office Fax: 513-381-5823.

LANGSTON, PAUL T., dean, composer, music educator; b. Marianna, Fla., Sept. 15, 1928; s. Howard McGhee and Rosa (Jeffries) L.; m. Esther Howard, Aug. 12, 1950; children: Claire Beth, Erin, Howard. Pvt. study with, Nadia Boulanger, 1962-63; diploma, Conservatoire Americaine, France; BA, U. Fla., 1950; MS in Music, So. Bapt. Theol. Sem., 1953; SMD, Union Theol. Sem., 1963; DMus (hon.), Stetson U., 1985. Organist-choirmaster St. John's Bapt. Ch., Charlotte, NC, 1953-60; instr. music theory Davidson Coll., 1959-60; mem. faculty Stetson U., De Land, Fla., 1960-93, dean Sch. Music, 1963-85, William Kenan Jr. prof. music, 1985-93, prof. and dean music emeritus, 1993—; assoc. condr. Charlotte Oratorio Singers, 1954-60. Dir. Fla. Internat. Music Festival, Fla. Internat. Music Festival Inst.; research fellow Inst. Sacred Music, Yale U., 1985 Composer organ, choral works.; oratorio Petros (premier Nov. 1983). Recipient Hand award for outstanding rsch., 1993; NEH fellow, U. N.C., Chapel Hill, 1978. Mem.: Assn. Anglican Musicians, Am. Guild Organists (McEniry award for tchg. excellence 1991), Delta Tau Delta, Pi Kappa Lambda, Omicron Delta Kappa. Home: 313 N Salisbury Ave Deland FL 32720-4054 E-mail: plangsto@dnet.net.

LANGSTON, THOMAS SAMUEL, political science professor; b. Louisville, Nov. 25, 1960; s. John Harold and Patricia Marie Langston; m. Mary Anne Sprague, May 15, 1982; children: Jessica, Taylor. Student, Duke U., 1980; BA cum laude, U. Tex., 1982; PhD, MIT, 1989. Tchr. Keystone Sch., San Antonio, 1982—83; vis. instr. SUNY, Geneseo, 1988—89; asst. prof. dept. polit. sci. Tulane U., New Orleans, 1989—95, assoc. prof., 1995—2002, prof., 2003—, dept. chmn., 1999—2002, 2005—. Author: Ideologues and Presidents, 1992, With Reverence and Contempt, 1995, Lyndon Baines Johnson, 2002, Uneasy Balance, 2003, George Washington, 2003, The Cold War Presidency, 2007. Vestry mem. St. George's Episcopal Ch., New Orleans, 1995-98, 2001-03. Moody grantee Lyndon Johnson Presdl. Libr. Found., 1987, O'Donnell grantee George Bush Presdl. Libr. Found., 2000; John M. Olin fellow Boston U. Inst. for Study of Econ. Culture, 1990-91. Mem. Am. Polit. Sci. Assn. (bd. dirs. Presidency Rsch. Group 2000-05, editor Presidency Rsch. Group Report 2000-05). Thackeray Soc. Episcopalian. Avocations: triathlon, marathons, photography. Office: Dept Polit Sci Tulane U New Orleans LA 70118 E-mail: langston@tulane.edu.

LANGTON, CLEVE SWANSON, advertising executive; b. NYC, Sept. 1, 1950; s. Raymond Benedict and Viola (Swanson) L.; m. Patricia Scott, July 16, 1976; children: Elizabeth Renwick, Cleve., Jr. BA, NYU, 1972; MBA, Columbia U., 1974. Product mgr. Gen. Foods Corp., White Plains, NY, 1974-76; account supr. Dancer Fitzgerald Sample, NYC, 1976-79; v.p. account dir. D'Arcy MacManus Masius, NYC, 1979-83; corp. v.p. bus. devel. worldwide DMB&B, 1983-89; corp. sr. v.p. DDB Needham Worldwide, 1990-92, corp. exec., v.p., dir. bus. devel. worldwide, 1993—. Bd. dirs. Weissman Ctr. Internat. Bus. CUNY. Mem. Met. Club. Office: DDB Worldwide Inc 437 Madison Ave New York NY 10022-7001

LANGTON (TOMASIEWICZ), DAWN THERESA, literature and language educator; d. John Donald and Pam Theresa Tomasiewicz; m. Kevin John Langton, June 7, 2003. BA in English, Elmhurst Coll., Ill., 1997; MA in Tchr. Leadership, Roosevelt U., Chgo., 2000; M, Aurora U., Ill., 2003, St. Xavier U., Chgo., 2006. Tchr. English Barking Abbey Sch., Essex, England, 1997—97, Driscoll Cath. H.S., Addison, Ill., 1997—2000, Prospect H.S., Mount Prospect, 2000—. Coord. Saturday acad. Prospect H.S., 2001—04; coach volleyball Driscoll Cath. H.S., Addison, 1998—2000, dir. theater tech., 1997—98; advisor student coun. Prospect H.S., 2002—04, world lit. and composition team facilitator, 2005—, mgr. theater ho., 2000—02. Author: (literary criticism) Exam on the Victorian Age, (plays) So In Love. Avocations: travel, reading, exercise, theater, photography. Office Phone: 847-718-5553.

LANGTON, JACKSON MAURICE, mining executive, geologist; b. Corpus Christi, Tex., Nov. 21, 1939; s. Claude Maurice Langton and Irma Reid Pettus; 1 child from previous marriage, Jennifer Brooke. MS in Geol. Engring., Okla. U., Norman, 1963; postgrad, Stanford U., Palo Alto, Calif., 1966. Cons. Pick Enterprises, Saratoga, Calif., 1964—66; chief mine geologist Phelps Dodge Corp., Morenci, Ariz., 1966—76; gen. mgr. minerals Superior Oil Co., Tucson, 1976—81, v.p., gen. mgr. minerals, 1981—82, pres. Superior Mining Co., 1982—84. Bd. dirs. Office Con. Planning & Devel. State of Ariz., Morenci, 1970—75. Author: All Trappers Don't Wear Fur Hats!, 2005. Home: 2700 NE 98th St Oklahoma City OK 73131

LANGTON, JEFFREY H., judge; b. Hamilton, Mont., Apr. 22, 1953; s. Richard L. and N. Louise (Mittower) L.; m. Patricia L. Stanbery, June 17, 1978 (div. Feb. 1999); children: Melanie, Matthew, Stephen, Thomas. BA in history with high honors, U. Mont., 1975, JD, 1978. Bar: Mont. 1978, U.S. Dist. Ct. Mont. 1978. Assoc. Schultz Law Firm, Hamilton, 1978-82; pvt. practice Hamilton, 1982-92; dist. judge 21st Dist. Ct., Hamilton, 1993—. Bd. clin. visitors Law Sch., U. Mont., Missoula, 1993-99; Mont. Sentence Review Divsn., 1998-2001, chmn., 2000-01; chmn. self represented litigants Mont. Supr. Ct. Commn., 2000-04. Author: The Victor Story, 1985. Bd. dirs. Victor Heritage Mus., 1990-95. Mem. ABA (Mont. del. 1994—), Am. Jud. Soc., Mont. Bar Assn., Mont. Judges Assn. Presbyterian. Avocations: Montana history, environmental issues, forestry. Home: 2975 Mittower Rd Victor MT 59875-9542 Office: 21st Jud Dist 205 Bedford St Hamilton MT 59840-2853 Home Phone: 406-642-3846; Office Phone: 406-375-6780.

LANGUM, DAVID JOHN, law educator, historian; b. Oakland, Calif., Oct. 24, 1940; s. John Kenneth and Virginia Anne (deMattos) Langum; m. Frances M. Short, 1996; children: Virginia Eileen, John David, David John Jr., Audrey Leora Kari, Anna Louisa Kari. AB, Dartmouth Coll., 1962; JD, Stanford U., 1965; MA in History, San Jose State U., 1976; LLM in Legal History, U. Mich., 1981, SJD in Legal History, 1985. Bar: Calif. 1966, Mich. 1981, Ala. 2003, U.S. Supreme Ct. 1972. Rsch. clk. Calif. Ct. Appeals, San Francisco, 1965-66; assoc. Dunne, Phelps & Mills, San Francisco, 1966-68; ptnr. Christenson, Hedemark, Langum & O'Keefe, San Jose, Calif., 1968-78; adj. prof. Lincoln U. Sch. Law, 1968-78; prof. law Detroit Coll. Law, 1978-83; prof. Old Coll. Sch. Law, Reno, Nev., 1983-85, dean, 1983-84; prof. Cumberland Sch. Law Samford U., Birmingham, 1985—. Editor: Law in the West, 1985; author: Law and Community on the Mexican California Frontier, 1987 (Hurst prize, 1988); author: (with Harlan Hague) Thomas O. Larkin: A Life of Patriotism and Profit in Old California, 1990 (Caroline Bancroft prize, 1991), Crossing Over the Line: Legislating Morality and the Mann Act, 1994; author: (with Howard Walthall) From Maverick to Mainstream: Cumberland School of Law, 1847-1997, 1997, William M. Kunstler: The Most Hated Lawyer in America, 1999; author: Antonio de Mattos and the Protestant Portuguese Community in Antebellum Illinois, 2006; contbr. articles to profl. jours. Mem. House of Flag, pro bono litig., San Francisco, 1973-76; past pres. Victorian Preservation Assn., Santa Clara County, Calif.; bd. dirs. ACLU of Ala., 1999—, pres., 2000-02; founder, dir. Langum Charitable Trust; pres. Friends of Birmingham Pub. Libr., 2000-06. Mem.: Western History Assn. (Bolton award 1978), Am. History Assn., Am. Soc. for Legal History (bd. dirs. 1992—95). Office: Samford U Cumberland Sch Law 800 Lakeshore Dr Birmingham AL 35229-0002 Office Phone: 205-726-2424. Business E-Mail: djlangum@samford.edu.

LANGWELL, DENNIS J., insurance company executive; Sr. v.p., CFO Liberty Mutual Ins. Co., Boston. Mem. bd. overseers Mus. Fine Arts, Boston. Office: Liberty Mutual Ins Co 175 Berkeley St Boston MA 02117*

LANGWORTHY, EVERETT WALTER, professional society administrator, natural gas exploration company executive; b. West Springfield, Mass., Aug. 17, 1918; s. Walter Carr and Lucy Anne (Laurent) L.; m. Mary Jane Mateer, Nov. 30, 1946 (dec. Oct. 1966); children: John Alan, Jo Ann Langworthy Sears, Robert Carr; m. Joan E. Scott, Feb. 27, 1982; stepchildren: Russell, Michael, Gregory BA, U. Mass., 1940, MA, George Washington U., 1964; grad., Nat. War Coll., 1964. Commd. 2d lt. U.S. Army, 1943; commd. capt. U.S. Air Force, 1947; advanced through grades to col., 1963; ret., 1972; v.p. ops. Meteor Aero Inc., Gaithersburg, Md., 1972-76; sec. contest and record bd. Nat. Aero. Assn., Washington, 1976-80, exec. v.p., 1980—. V.p. LABCO Inc., Martinsburg, W.Va., 1974—; gen. ptnr. M&E Assocs., Gaithersburg, 1976—; dir. Acad. Model Aeronautics, Reston, Va.; cons. FBI, 1992—; cons. FBI; cons., expert witness, 1995—. Contbr. articles and columns on aerospace activities to profl. publs. U.S. rep. Fedn. Aeronautique Internat., Paris, 1980—. Decorated DFC, Air medal African Campaign award, Berlin Air Life medal; recipient Paul Tissandier diploma Fedn. Aeronautique Internationale, 1987. Mem. Nat. Aviation Club (elder statesman aviation 1990), Aero Club Washington, Air Force Assn., Ret. Officers Assn., Soaring Soc. Am. (bd. dirs. 1980—), U.S. Hang Gliding Assn. (bd. dirs. 1980—), VFW. Clubs: Lakewood Country (Rockville, Md.). Republican. Avocations: golf, writing. Home: 610 Gunston Ln Wilmington NC 28405-5317 Office: Nat Aeronautic Assn 1815 Ft Myer Dr Arlington VA 22209-1805 Office Fax: 910-256-0480. Personal E-mail: ewlang@earthlink.net.

LANGWORTHY, ROBERT BURTON, lawyer; b. Kansas City, Mo., Dec. 24, 1918; s. Herman Moore and Minnie (Leach) L.; m. Elizabeth Ann Miles, Jan. 2, 1942 (dec. Dec. 2006); children: David Robert, Joan Elizabeth Langworthy Tomek, Mark Burton. AB, Princeton U., 1940; JD magna cum laude, Harvard U., 1943. Bar: Mo. 1943, U.S. Supreme Ct. 1960, Kans. 2006. Pvt. practice, Kansas City, 1943—; assoc., then mem. and v.p. Linde, Thomson, Langworthy, Kohn & Van Dyke, P.C., 1943—91; pres., mng. shareholder Blackwood, Langworthy & Schmelzer, P.C., Kansas City, 1991—96; mng. mem. Blackwood, Langworthy & Tyson, L.C., and predecessor, Kansas City, 1996—. Lectr. on probate, law sch. CLE courses U. Mo., Kansas City. Mem. bd. editors Harvard Law Rev., 1941-43; contbr. chpts. to Guardian and Trust, Powers, Conservatorships and Nonprobate Desk Books of Mo. Bar. Mem. edn. appeal bd. U.S. Dept. Edn., 1982-86; commr. Housing Authority Kansas City, 1963-71, chmn., 1969-71; chmn. Bd. Election Commrs. Kansas City, 1973-77; chmn. bd. West Ctrl. area YMCA, 1969-95; bd. dirs. Mid-Am. region YMCA, 1970-83, vice chmn., 1970-73, chmn., 1973-78; pres. Met. Bd. Kansas City (Mo.) YMCA (now YMCA Greater Kansas City), 1965, bd. dirs., 1965-2004, nat. bd. 1971-78, 79-83; bd. dirs. YMCA of Rockies, 1974-2003, bd. sec., 1994-99, adv. dir., 2004—; bd. dirs. YMCA Found. Kansas City, 2005-; trustee Sioux Indian YMCAs, 1983-2002, chmn. bd. trustees, 1983-2002, chmn. hon. trustees, 2003—; bd. dirs. Armed Svcs. YMCA, 1984-85; pres. Met. Area Citizens Edn., 1969-72; chmn. Citizens Assn. Kansas City (Mo.), 1967, bd. dirs., 1995-96; bd. dirs. Project Equality Kans.-Mo., 1967-80, pres., 1970-72, treas., 1972-73, sec., 1973-76; 1st v.p. Human Resources Corp. Kansas City, 1969-73, bd. dirs., 1965-73; hon. v.p. Am. Sunday Sch. Union (now Am. Missionary Fellowship), 1965—; vice chmn. bd. trustees Kemper Mil. Sch., 1966-73; U.S. del. YMCA World Coun., Buenos Aires, 1977, Estes Park, Colo., 1981, Nyborg, Denmark, 1985; bd. dirs. Mo. Rep. Club, 1960-2001; del., platform com. Rep. Nat. Conv., 1960; Rep. nominee U.S. Congress, 1964; mem. gen. assembly Com. on Representation Presbyn., 1991-97, moderator, 1993-94; commr. to gen. assembly Presbyn. Ch., 1984, gen. assembly com. on location of hdqrs. 1984-87; moderator Heartland Presbytery, 1984. Lt. (j.g.) USNR, 1943-46, capt. Res. ret. Mem.: ABA, Kans. Bar Assn., Harvard Law Sch. Assn. Mo. (v.p. 1973—74, pres. 1974—75, 1985—87), Lawyers Assn.

Kansas City, Mo. State Bar (chmn. probate and trust com. 1983—85, chmn. sr. lawyers com. 1991—93), Kansas City Met. Bar Assn. (chmn. probate law com. 1988—90, 1999—2000, living will com. 1989—91), Kansas City Club. Presbyterian. Home: Claridge Ct Apt 305 8101 Mission Rd Prairie Village KS 66208-5238 Office: 1220 Washington St Ste 300 Kansas City MO 64105-1439 Home Phone: 913-381-2787; Office Phone: 816-474-6200. Business E-Mail: robert.langworthy@blackwoodlaw.com.

LANGWORTHY, ROBERT H., law educator; MS, SUNY Albany, PhD, 1983. Prof. U. Cin., 1987—97, U. Alaska, Anchorage, 1997—. Mem. Cmty. Oriented Policing Project Nat Inst. Justice, 1995—96; dir. Justice Ctr. U. Alaska, Anchorage. Author: The Structure of Police Organizations, Policing in America; contbr. articles to prof. jour. Office: U Alaska Justice Ctr 3211 Providence Dr Anchorage AK 99508 Office Phone: 907-786-1810. Business E-Mail: afrhl@uaa.alaska.edu.*

LANGWORTHY, WILLIAM CLAYTON, retired college official; b. Watertown, NY, Sept. 3, 1936; s. Harold Greene and Carolyn (Peach) L.; m. Margaret Joan Amos, Sept. 6, 1958; children: Kenneth, Geneva. BS magna cum laude, Tufts U., 1958; PhD, U. Calif.-Berkeley, 1962. Asst. prof. Alaska Meth. U., Anchorage, 1962-65; asst. prof. chemistry Calif. State U.-Fullerton, 1965-67, assoc. prof., 1967-72, prof., 1972-73, assoc. dean Sch. Letters Arts and Scis., 1970-73; prof. chemistry Calif. Poly. State U., San Luis Obispo, 1973-76, head dept. chemistry, 1973-76; dean Sch. Sci. and Math Calif. Poly State U., San Luis Obispo, 1976-83; v.p. acad. affairs Ft. Lewis Coll., Durango, Colo., 1983-95, prof., 1995-2000. Author: monograph Environmental Education, 1971; contbr. articles to profl. jours. Treas. Coun. Concerned Citizens, Inc., Arroyo Grande, Calif., 1976—83; mem. Clean Air Coalition, San Luis Obispo, 1978—83, Jacksonville Boosters, 2001—, treas., 2002—04, pres., 2004—05; active Mozart Festival, 1981—82; mem. Rogue Valley Harmonizers, 2001—05; mem. forestry com. City of Jacksonville, Oreg., 2002—05; mem. Stoneybrook arch. com. Corvallis, 2006; bd. dirs. Durango Choral Soc., 1984—93, San Juan Symphony League, pres, 1997—2000; bd. dirs. Durango Repertory Theatre Co., 1990—96, pres., 1992—94; bd. dirs. Skagit Symphony, 2007—. Mem. AAAS, AAHE, Am. Chem. Soc., Coun. Colls. Arts and Scis. (bd. dirs. 1982), Sierra Club, Phi Beta Kappa, Sigma Xi, Kappa Mu Epsilon, Phi Kappa Phi. Home: 3825 Carpenter St Mount Vernon WA 98274 Personal E-mail: hillsidebill@aol.com.

LANHAM, RICHARD J., oncologist, educator; b. St. Louis, June 7, 1935; s. Richard Horatio and Helen Edwards Lanham; children: Richard Edwards, Richard Renault, Winifred Brook. BA, CCNY, 1956; MD, Albert Einstein Coll. Medicine, 1962. Cert. internal medicine Am. Bd. Internal Medicine, hematology Am. Bd. Internal Medicine, med. oncology Am. Bd. Internal Medicine, med. rev. officer Am. Soc. Med. Rev. Officers. Med. intern Balt. City Hosps., Johns Hopkins Sch. Medicine, 1972—73; med. resident Montefiore Hosp. and Med. Ctr., Albert Einstein Coll. Medicine, NYC, 1973—74, hematology resident, 1973—74; hematology fellow Cabrini Health Care Ctr., NYU Sch. Medicine, NYC, 1975—76; med. oncology fellow Bronx Mcpl. Hosp. Ctr., Albert Einstein Coll. Medicine, NYC, 1982—83; clin. instr. medicine Albert Einstein Coll. Medicine, NYC, 1978—83, asst. clin. prof. medicine, 1983—88, Wright State U. Coll. Medicine, Dayton, Ohio, 1985—88, Sch. Medicine and Biomed. Scis. of SUNY, Buffalo, 1990—96; pvt. practice NY and Ohio, 1977—. Adj. prof. Empire State Coll., 2007—; presenter and lectr. in field. Contbr. articles to profl. jours. and chpts. to books. Mem.: Pure Knowledge US (founder), Am. Assn. for Chronic Fatigue Syndrome (mem. clin. affairs com.), Johns Hopkins Med. and Surg. Assn., Albert Einstein Coll. Medicine Alumni Assn., Nat. Assn. Scholars, Math. Assn. Am., Assn. Literary Scholars and Critics, Am. Coll. Occupl. and Environ. Medicine, Am. Soc. Med. Rev. Officers, Hist. Soc. Avocations: rollerblading, wilderness hiking, camping, canoeing, sailing, collecting Inuit artifacts and carvings. E-mail: richardjlanham@gmail.com.

LANIER, ANITA SUZANNE, musician, educator; b. Talladega, Ala., May 21, 1946; d. Luther Dwight and Elva (Hornsby) L. BS in Music Edn., Jacksonville State U., Ala., 1969. Elem. music tchr. Talladega City Schs., 1969-81; librarian, elem. music tchr. Talladega Acad., 1981-84; tchr. piano and organ Talladega, 1981—. Organist Trinity United Meth. Ch., Talladega, 1981—. Recipient Commemorative Honor medallion, 1990, World Decoration of Excellence medallion, 1990; named Woman of the Yr., 1990, Rsch. Adv. of Yr., 1990, ABI, 1990. Mem. Delta Omicron. Home: 601 North St E Talladega AL 35160-2525

LANIER, CATHY L., police chief; B in Mgmt., M in Mgmt., Johns Hopkins U.; M in Nat. Security Studies, Naval Postgrad. Sch., Montgomery, Calif.; grad., FBI Nat. Acad., Drug Enforcement Adminstrn. Drug Unit Commanders Acad. With Metropolitan Police Dept., 1990—, foot patrolman, sergeant, lieutenant, patrol supr., comdr. fourth dist., comdg. officer major narcotics br. unit, vehicular homicide unit, comdr. spl. ops. divisn., comdg. officer office homeland security and counter-terrorism, 2006, acting chief of police, 2006—07, chief of police, 2007—. Office: Metropolitan Police Dept John A Wilson Bldg 1350 Pennsylvania Ave NW Washington DC 20004*

LANIER, ROBERT LEWIS, oncologist; b. St. Louis, Mo., Sept. 10, 1944; s. Raymond and Virginia Lanier; m. Elizabeth Lanier, Sept. 3, 1998; children: Paul, Leslie. BA, U. Colo., Boulder, 1966; MD, U. Colo., Denver, 1970. Owner Internal Med. Group, Cheyene, Wyo., 1977—2001, Cheyenne Hematology Oncology Svcs., 2001—. Maj. USAF, 1972—74. Fellow: Am. Coll. Physicians; mem.: Am. Soc. Hematology. Home: 2500 Klipstein Rd Cheyenne WY 82009 Office: Cheyenne Hematology Oncology Svcs 421 E 17th Cheyenne WY 82009 Office Phone: 307-634-0233.

LANIER, TROY, lawyer; b. Lincolnton, Ga., 1966; m. Gentry Shannon Lanier; 1 child. BA, U. Ga., 1988, JD, 1992. Bar: Ga. 1992. Civil litig., trial atty. Tucker, Everitt, Long, Brewton, Lanier, Augusta, Ga. Spkr. in field. Contbr. articles to numerous profl. jours. Named Ga. Rising Star, Super-Lawyer Mag., 2006. Mem.: ABA, Young Lawyers Club Augusta, State Bar Assn. Ga. Office: Tucker Law 453 Greene St Augusta GA 30901

LANIER, W. MARK, lawyer; b. Dallas, Oct. 20, 1960; m. Becky Lanier; 5 children. BA, David Lipscomb Coll., 1981; JD, Tex. Tech. U., 1984. Bar: Tex. 1985, US Dist. Ct. (all dists. Tex.) 1985, U.S. Ct. Appeals (5th cir.) 1985, US Supreme Ct. 1985, NY 2005, cert.: Tex. Bd. Legal Specialization (personal injury trial law). With Fulbright & Jaworski, Houston, 1983—89; founder The Lanier Law Firm, P.C., Houston, 1990—. Named a Tex. Super Lawyer, Tex. Monthly Mag., 2003, 2004, 2005, 2006; named one of Top 40 Attys. Under the Age of 40 in US, Nat. Law Jour., 1995, Top 10 Trial Lawyers in Am., 1998, 2006, 100 Most Influential Lawyers, 2006, Top 5 Personal Injury Lawyers, Tex. Lawyer Go-To-Guide, 2002, Top 45 Lawyers Under the Age of 45, Am. Lawyer, 2003. Mem.: ABA, Christian Trial Lawyers Assn. (founder), Am. Bd. Trial Advs., Tex. Trial Lawyers Assn., Houston Bar Assn., Com. Econ. Devel. (bd. trustees), Order of Barristers.*

LANIGAN, JOHN, radio personality; b. Pgallala, Nebr., 1942; With WGAR, 1971—85; radio host WMJI, Cleve., 1985—. Co-host (radio shows) The Lanigan & Malone Show. Co-recipient (with Jimmy Malone) Large Market Personality of Yr., NAB Marconi Radio Awards, 2005; named Cleveland's Favorite Radio Performer (twice), WJW Cleve. Office: WMJI 105.7 6200 Oak Tree Blvd 4th Fl Independence OH 44131 also: WMJI 105.7 FM Fl 6 310 W Lakeside Ave Cleveland OH 44113 E-mail: lanigan@wmji.com.

LANIGAN, JOHN P., JR., rail transportation executive; BS in Mgmt. Sci., USCG Acad., 1977; MBA, Baldwin-Wallace Coll., Berea, Ohio, 1989. With Schneider Nat., 1984—95, pres. transp. sector, 1995—99, COO, 1999—2000; mng. dir., COO Logistics.com, 2000—02; exec. v.p., chief mktg. officer Burlington No. Santa Fe Corp., Fort Worth, Tex., 2002—. Comdr. USCG. Office: Burlington No Santa Fe Corp PO Box 961056 Fort Worth TX 76161-0056 Office Phone: 817-867-6100.*

LANIGAN, RICHARD LEO, JR., humanities educator, writer, editor; b. Santa Fe, Dec. 31, 1943; s. Richard Leo Lanigan, Sr. and Margaret Alcy Kendall; m. Rui-hong Guo, Sept. 14, 1990 (div. Jan. 1, 2001); children: James Guo, Robert Guo. BA, U. N.Mex, 1967, MA, 1968; PhD in Communicology, So. Ill. U., 1969. Cert. English lang. examiner Sichuan U., China, 1996. Rsch. assoc. Dundee (Scotland) U. and St. Andrews U., Joint Postgraduate Program in Philosophy, 1970—72; founding chair philosophy comm. divsn. Internat. Comm. Assn., Berlin, 1977; rsch. assoc. East-West Ctr., Honolulu, 1980—81; Andrew Mellon fellow in linguistics Vanderbilt U., Nashville, 1981—82, Andrew Mellon fellow in philosophy, 1984—85; rsch. assoc. U. Calif., Berkeley, 1982—83; pres. Semiotic Soc. Am., Houston, 1994—95, editor Am. Jour. Semiotics, 1996—; fellow Internat. Acad. for Intercultural Rsch., University, Miss., 1998—; dir. and fellow Internat. Communicology Inst., Carbondale, Ill., 2000—. Author: (book) The Human Science of Communicology, Phenomenology of Communication (Transl. into Korean, 1997), Semiotic Phenomenology of Rhetoric, Speech Act Phenomenology, Speaking and Semiology (2nd edit., 1991); mem. editl. bd.: Critical Studies in Mass Comm., 1986—89, Signifying Behavior, 1993—98, TEXT: An Interdisciplinary Jour. for the Study of Discourse, 1997—, guest editor: Semiotica Vol. 41, 1982. Chpt. pres. So. Ill. U. AAUP, Carbondale, 1984—87. Scholar, Nat. Comm. Assn., 1995. Mem.: NEA, Internat. Assn. Semiotic Studies (v.p. 2004—), Ill. Edn. Assn., Am. Philos. Assn., Tau Kappa Alpha, Phi Sigma Tau. Democrat. Roman Catholic. Avocations: writing, reading, travel, swimming. Home: 335 May Apple Ln Carbondale IL 62903-7695 Office: Southern Illinois Univesity Spcm 6605 Carbondale IL 62901-6605 Office Phone: 618-453-1894. Business E-Mail: rlanigan@siu.edu.

LANIGAN, SUSAN S., lawyer; b. May 1962; BA, JD, U. Ga. Assoc. gen. counsel Zale Corp., Irving, Tex., 1996—97, sr. v.p., gen. counsel, sec., 1997—2002; v.p., gen. counsel, corp. sec. Dollar Gen. Corp., Goodlettsville, Tenn., 2002—03, gen. counsel, corp sec., 2003—, sr. v.p., 2003—06, exec. v.p., 2006—. Office: Dollar General Corp 100 Mission Ridge Goodlettsville TN 37072*

LANING, ROBERT COMEGYS, retired physician, retired military officer; b. Haiti, Sept. 20, 1922; s. Richard Henry and Marguerite C. (Boyer) L.; m. Alice Teresa Lech, Sept. 9, 1961; 1 dau., Maria Laning LeBerre. MD, Jefferson Med. Coll., 1948; BA, U. Va., 1986; MA, Ohio State U., 1988; PhD in Edn., George Mason U., 1997. Diplomate: Nat. Bd. Med. Examiners, Am. Bd. Surgery. Intern Jefferson Hosp., Phila., 1948-50; enlisted USN, 1950, advanced through grades to rear adm., 1973, mem. astronaut recovery teams, 1960-66; chief of surgery Naval Hosp., San Diego, 1967-71, Portsmouth, NH, 1963—66, Chelsea, Mass., 1966—67, med. dir. Yokosuka, Japan, 1972-73; med. officer Pacific Fleet, 1973-75; asst. chief Bur. Medicine and Surgery for Operational Med. Support, Washington, 1975-77; dep. dir. surg. service Cen. Office, VA, Washington, 1977-79, dir. surg. service, 1979-87. Fellow ACS (gov. 1984-87); mem. AMA, KC (4th degree), Am. Assn. Mil. Surgeons, Soc. Med. Cons. to Armed Forces (pres. 1988-89, bd. dirs.), Ret. Officers Assn. Roman Catholic. Home: 6532 Sunny Hill Ct Mc Lean VA 22101-1639 Personal E-mail: laning@verizon.net.

LANK, EDITH HANDLEMAN, journalist, educator; b. Boston, Feb. 27, 1926; m. Norman Lank; children: Avrum, David, Anna. BA magna cum laude, Syracuse U. Columnist L.A. Times Syndicate, 1976—2000; TV host Sta. WOKR-TV, Rochester, NY, 1983-84; radio host Sta. WBBF-AM, Rochester, 1984-85; columnist Tribune Media Svcs., 2000—02, Creators Syndicate, 2003—. Lectr. St. John Fisher Coll., Rochester, 1977-89; commentator Sta. WXXI-FM, Rochester, 1977—; guest Pub. Radio Internat., St. Paul, 1987—; speaker in field. Author: Home Buying, 1981, Selling Your Home, 1982, Modern Real Estate Practice in New York, 1983, rev. 9th edit., 2006, The Home Seller's Kit, 1988, rev. 4th edit. 1997, The Complete Home Buyer's Kit, 1989, rev. 4th edit., 1997, Dear Edith, 1990, Essentials of New Jersey Real Estate, rev. 9th edit., 2006, 201 Questions Every Homebuyer and Seller Must Ask, 1996, Jane Austen Speaks to Women, 2000, I've Heard It All, 2006; co-author: Your Home as a Tax Shelter, 1993; contbr. articles to Time, New Yorker, McCall's, Real Estate Today, Persuasions, Modern Maturity, others. Recipient media award Bar Assn. Monroe County, 1982, Matrix award Women in Comm., 1984; named Woman of Distinction Gov. of NY, Communicator of Yr. SUNY, Brockport, 1986. Mem. Real Estate Educators Assn. (bd. dirs., Consumer Edn. award 1982, 83, 86, 96, Real Estate Educator of Yr. 1984), Nat. Assn. Real Estate Editors (bd. dirs), Jane Austen Soc. N.Am. (dir.), Phi Beta Kappa. Avocation: scuba diving. Home and Office: 240 Hemingway Dr Rochester NY 14620-3316 E-mail: edithlank@aol.com.

LANKOWSKY, ZENON P., lawyer, retail executive; BA, U. Syracuse, 1976; JD, Western New England Coll. Sch. Law, 1980. V.p., gen. counsel, sec. CVS Corp., Woonsocket, R.I. Mem.: ABA, Ctr. Bus. Ethics, Am. Soc. Corp. Secs., Am. Corp. Counsel Assn. Office: CVS Corp One CVS Dr Woonsocket RI 02895 Office Phone: 401-770-3550.

LANNAMANN, RICHARD STUART, executive search consultant; b. Cin., Sept. 4, 1947; s. Frank E. and Grace I. (Tomlinson) Lannamann; m. Katharine Tinkham Scheffler, Sept. 5, 1998; children from previous marriage: Thomas Cleveland, Edward Payne, John Stewart. AB in Econs., Yale U., 1969; MBA, Harvard U., 1973. Chartered fin. analyst, CPA. Investment analyst US Trust Co. NY, NYC, 1969-71; rsch. analyst Smith, Barney & Co., NYC, 1973-75, 2d v.p., 1975-77; v.p. successor firm Smith Barney, Harris Upham & Co., NYC, 1977-78, Russell Reynolds Assocs., Inc., NYC, 1978-83, mng. dir., 1983—86, 1987—2002; sr.v.p. Mgmt. Asset Corp., Westport, Conn., 1986-87; vice chmn. Spencer Stuart & Assocs., NYC, 2002—. Chmn. bd. Orpheus Chamber Orch.; trustee Jackson Lab., Bar Harbor, Maine, Fgn. Policy Assn. Mem.: Chartered Fin. Analyst Inst., NY Soc. Security Analysts, Oaks Club (Osprey, Fla.), Links Club NY, Yale Club NY, Riverside Yacht Club (Conn.). Home: 21 Willowmere Cir Riverside CT 06878-2503 Office: 277 Park Ave New York NY 10172-2998 Personal E-mail: rlannamann@spencerstuart.com.

LANNAN, MAURA ANNE KELLY, reporter; b. Bridgeport, Conn., Apr. 2, 1971; d. Richard Francis and Margaret Mary Kelly; m. Robert Lannan; 1 child, Margaret Mary. BA, Boston Coll., Mass., 1993; MS in Journalism, Northwestern U., Evanston, Ill., 1994. Intern The Patriot Ledger, Quincy, Mass., 1993; corr. Conn. Post, Bridgeport, 1993; reporter Naugatuck bur. Waterbury Rep.-Am., Conn., 1994—95, edn. reporter, 1995, city hall reporter, 1995—96, state capitol reporter, 1996-99; reporter Chgo. Tribune, 2000—01, AP, 2001—05; freelance reporter, 2005—. Mem. reporters' roundtable discussion Conn. Jour. on Conn. Pub. TV, Hartford, 1998-99 and WFSB's CT '97, CT '98, Ct '99 in Hartford. Co-recipient Explanatory Reporting-Team Coverage, Pulitzer Prize, 2001. Mem. Soc. Profl. Journalists (Reporting awards Conn. chpt. 1998, 99, 2000, co-recipient Peter Lisagor award for deadline reporting, Headline Club chpt. 2003, co-recipient Peter Lisagor award for business reporting, Headline Club chpt. 2005), Investigative Reporters and Editors, Boston Coll. Alumni Assn., Northwestern U. Alumni Club Conn. Roman Catholic. Avocations: photography, travel, skiing, tennis, swimming. Home: 8904 Saddle Ln Potomac MD 20854 Personal E-mail: makelly42@hotmail.com.

LANNERT, ROBERT CORNELIUS, manufacturing executive; b. Chgo., Mar. 14, 1940; s. Robert Carl and Anna Martha (Cornelius) L.; children: Jacqueline, Krista, Kevin, Meredith. BS in Indsl. Mgmt., Purdue U., 1963; MBA, Northwestern U., 1967; grad. Advanced Mgmt. Program, Harvard U., 1978. With Navistar Internat. Corp. (formerly Internat. Harvester), Chgo., 1963—; staff asst. overseas fin. Navistar Internat. Transp. Corp. (formerly Internat. Harvester), Chgo., 1967-70; asst. mgr., treas. and contr. IH Finanz AG, Zurich, Switzerland, 1970-72; mgr. overseas fin. corp. hdqrs. Internat. Truck & Engine Co., Chgo., 1972—76, asst. treas., 1976—79, v.p., treas., 1979—90; exec. v.p., chief fin. officer Navistar Internat. Corp., Chgo., 1990—2002, vice chmn., CFO, 2002—, also bd. dirs. Bd. dirs. Internat. Truck and Engine Co., Harbour Assurance Co., Bermuda, Navistar Fin. Corp., Chgo. Home: 904 Kenmare Dr Burr Ridge IL 60527 Office: Navistar Internat Corp 4201 Winfield Rd PO Box 1488 Warrenville IL 60555

LANNES, WILLIAM JOSEPH, III, electrical engineer; b. New Orleans, Oct. 12, 1937; s. William Joseph, Jr. and Rhea Helen (Simon) Lannes; m. Patricia Ann Didier, Jan. 17, 1961; children: David Mark, Kenneth John, Jennifer Anne. BEE, Tulane U., New Orleans, 1959; MEE, US Naval Postgrad. Sch., 1966. Registered profl. engr., La. Commd. 2d lt. US Marine Corps, 1959, advanced through grades to maj., 1967, served as electronics officer, ops. officer, 1967-70; substation engr. La. Power & Light, New Orleans, 1970-71, utility engr., 1971-76, systems relay engr., 1976-77, systems substation engr., 1977-79, engring. supr. for substation, 1979-83, substation engring. mgr., 1983-86, dir. systems engring., 1986—, v.p. systems engring., 1986-88, with ctrl. engring., 1988-89; sr. v.p. Energy Supply Fossil, 1989-91; v.p. svc. and support Entergy Corp., 1991-92; assoc. dean rsch. and grad. studies Coll. Engring. U., New Orleans, 1992-97. Dir. U. New Orleans EPRI Cmty. Initiative Ctr., 1993-95; assoc. dir. Ctr. Energy Resources Mgmt., 1993-96, dir. Ctr. Energy Resources Mgmt., 1996-2002; dir. Engring. Mgmt. Program, 1995-2002, chmn. engring. mgmt. dept., 2002-06, prof. emeritus, 2006-; instr. Delgado Jr. Coll., 1973-74; instr. elec. engring. U. New Orleans, 1979-80; lead dir. 5th Dist. Savs. Bank, 1982—; spkr. profl. confs. Contbr. articles to profl. jours. Committeeman New Orleans Area Coun., Boy Scouts Am., 1972-76; vol. United Way 1975, 76, 81; treas. PTA, 1971; vol. tchr. Confraternity of Christian Doctrine, 1972; mem. bus. adv. coun. Our Lady of Holy Cross Coll., 1981-86; chmn. engring. adv. coun. U. New Orleans; bd. dirs. New Life in La.; vol. coach New Orleans Recreation Dept., 1973; mem. La. Employees Com. on Polit. Action, Tulane Univ. Engring. Coun., New Orleans Archdiocesan Pastoral Coun., 1988-91; mem. adv. bd. Bridge House, 1992-95. Decorated Bronze Star; Cross of Gallantry Republic S. Vietnam; recipient Cert. of Merit Mayor New Orleans, 1964, Disting. Svc. to Coll. of Engring. U. New Orleans, 2006. Fellow IEEE (profl. mem. 1996, chmn. New Orleans sect. 1981-82, Outstanding Svc. award 1976, Edward Freitag award 1988, Region 3 Outstanding Engr. award 1991, Outstanding Svc. to Coll. Engring. award 2006); mem. Electric Power Rsch. Inst. (industry advisor), Edison Electric Inst. (systems and equipment com.), Soc. Power Rsch. and Implementation (chmn. 1987-94), Southeastern Electric Exch. (substation com. 1977-85), Power Engring. Soc. (Prize Paper award 1988), Sigma Xi, Eta Kappa Nu. Republican. Roman Catholic. Office: Coll Engring U New Orleans New Orleans LA 70148-0001 Office Phone: 504-280-7122. Business E-Mail: wlannes@uno.edu.

LANNI, TERRY (JOSEPH TERRENCE LANNI), hotel corporation executive; b. LA, Mar. 14, 1943; s. Anthony Warren and Mary Lucille (Leahy) L. BS, U. So. Calif., 1965, MBA, 1967. Vice pres. Intervest, Inc., Los Angeles, 1967-69; treas. Republic Corp., LA, 1969-76; treas., CFO Caesars World Inc., LA, 1977-78, sr. v.p., 1978-79, exec. v.p., 1979-81, pres., COO, 1981—95, Caesars N.J., Inc., 1981—95; pres. MGM Mirage, 1995, chmn., 1995—, CEO, 1995—99, 2001—. Author: Anthology of Poetry, 1965. Trustee St. John's Hosp. and Med. Ctr., Archdiocese of L.A. Edn. Found., Loyola Marymount U.; bd. councillors U. So. Calif. Sch. Bus. Adminstrn. Mem. Calif. C. of C. (bd. dirs.), Commerce Assocs., Regency Club, Rep. Senatorial Inner Circle, Clermont Club (London), Annabel's (London. Clubs: Bachelors; Crockfords (London), Beach (London). Office: MGM Mirage 3600 Las Vegas Blvd Las Vegas NV 89109*

LANNIE, PAUL ANTHONY, lawyer, energy executive; b. Hayti, Mo., Feb. 21, 1954; m. Donna Dean; children: Heather, Anthony. BA magna cum laude, Vanderbilt U., 1974, JD, 1978. Bar: Tex. 1978. Assoc. Johnson & Swanson, Dallas, 1978-83; exec. v.p. BusLease Inc., Dallas, 1983-87, GLI Holding Co., Dallas, 1987—91, Greyhound Lines Inc., Dallas, 1987-91; v.p., gen. counsel, sec. Baroid Corp., Houston, 1991-94; sr. v.p., gen. counsel Tejas Gas Corp., Houston, 1994—98, Coral Energy, Houston, 1995—99; pres. Coral Energy Can., 1999, Kinder Morgan Power Co., Houston, 2000—03; v.p., gen. counsel Apache Corp., Houston, 2003—04, sr. v.p., gen. counsel, 2004—. Bd. dirs. Dallas Indsl. Devel. Corp., 1985-87; exec. mem. Ctrl. Dallas Assn., 1990. Mem. Order Coif, Phi Beta Kappa. Office: Apache Corp 2000 Post Oak Blvd Ste 100 Houston TX 77056-4400

LANNING, CHRISTOPHER GLENN, lawyer; b. Va. Beach, Aug. 26, 1969; s. Eugene Perry and Anne Walker Lanning. BA, U. Va., 1991, JD, 1995. Bar: Va., N.Y. Atty. Paul Weiss Richard Warrin & Gamson, NYC, 1995—98, Hunter & Wittemer, Richmond, Va., 1998—2000; sr. v.p. gen. contracts Gen. Atlantic, Greenwich, Conn., 2000—. Mem.: Union League Club, Buglers Club. Republican. Episcopalian. Office: General Atlantic 3 Pickwick Plaza Ste 200 Greenwich CT 06830

LANNING, JAMES WILFORD, sales executive, retired music educator; b. Washington, Oct. 3, 1948; s. Ralph Bertrand and Willette Harmon Lanning; m. Jean Elizabeth Carver, Dec. 13, 1969; children: Jessica E., Justin Warren. BA in Music Edn., Evangel U., Mo., 1971; M in Edn. and Adminstrn., Drury U., Mo., 1980. Dir. bands and choir Bunker Reorganized I Schs., Mo., 1971—72, Lockwood Region I Schs., Mo., 1972—75, Pierce City Region VI Sch., Mo., 1975—89, East Newton HS, Granby, Mo., 1989—92; dir. bands and orch. Ctrl. HS, Springfield, 1992—95; asst. dir. bands Monett (Mo.) Region I Sch., 1995—2000; sr. sales mgr. S&K Menswear, Branson, Mo., 2000—06, gen. mgr., 2006—07; sales rep. Thousand Hills Golf Resort, 2007—. Treas. Southwest Mo. Music Assn., 1977—84, Cert. Tchrs. Assn., Monett, Mo., 1996—98, pres., 1998—2000. Composer: (percussion music) Drum Cadences and Ensembles, 1997—2000. Pres. bd. Ozark Festival Orch., Monett, Mo., 1981—85; pres. Home Owners Assn., Kirbyville, Mo., 2002—; bd. mem. C. of C. Small Bus. Advisory Com., Branson, Mo., 2001—; assignment sec. Gideons Internat., Monett, Mo., 1980—87. Mem.: Music Educators Nat. Conf., Mo. Band Masters Assn., North Am. Hunting Club. Republican. Mem. Assemblies Of God. Avocations: hunting, fishing, boating, tennis. Office: S&K Menswear Branson Landing Ste 209 Branson MO 65616 Home: 351 Ventura Branson MO 65616

LANNON, PAUL G., lawyer; b. Needham, Mass. BA, Harvard Coll., Cambridge, Mass., 1988; JD, U. Va. Sch. Law, Charlottesville, 1992. Bar: Mass. 1993. Ptnr. Holland & Knight, LLP, Boston, 1996—. Capt. USAR, 1988—96.

L'ANNUNZIATA, MICHAEL FRANK, chemist, nuclear scientist, consultant; s. Michael Peter and Irene M. L'Annunziata; m. Maria del Carmen; children: Michael O., Helen, Frank E. BS, St. Edward's U., Austin, Tex., 1965, MS, U. Ariz., 1967, PhD, 1970. Rsch. chemist Amchem Products, Inc., Ambler, Pa., 1971—72; rsch. assoc. U. Ariz., Tucson, 1972—73; prof., sect. head U. Chapingo, Mexico, 1973—75; rsch. scientist Nat. Inst. Nuc. Rsch., Mexico City, 1975—77; assoc. officer IAEA, Vienna, 1977—80, 2d officer, 1980—83, 1st officer, head sci. visits program, 1983—86, sr. officer, head fellowships and tng. sect., 1986—91; mng. dir.

LMS Internat. Tech. Svcs., Ltd., Coronado, Calif., 1992—95; dir. WorldTech Internat. Tech. Svcs., Oceanside, Calif., 1995—99; pres. Montague Group, 1999—. Bd. dirs. internat. sci. programs Uppsala (Sweden) U.; internat. IAEA cons.; cons., lectr. Forestry Rsch. Inst., Ibadan, Nigeria, 1994-95, Ministry Edn., Jakarta, Indonesia, 1995, Internat. Sales, Mktg., Tng., Packard BioScis. Co., Meriden, Conn., 1995-2002, PerkinElmer Life and Analytical Scis., Downers Grove, Ill., 2003—, Canberra Industries, Inc., Meriden, Conn., 2003, Egypt Atomic Energy Authority, Cairo, 1995-96, Gezira Rsch. Sta., Wad Medani, Sudan, 1995, Ethopian Sci. and Tech. Commn., Addis Ababa, 1996, Nat. Radiation Commn., Arusha, Tanzania, 1996; vis. lectr. Advanced Sch. Tropical Agriculture, Cardenas, Mexico, 1973, Atomic Energy Commn. of Ecuador, Quito, 1978, Timiryazev Agrl. Acad., Moscow, 1980-81, Nuc. Rsch. Inst. in Vet. Medicine, Lalahan, Turkey, 1981, IAEA Seilbersdorf Labs., Seibersdorf, Austria, 1978-82, U. Guanajuato, Mex., 1981, Coll. Montecillo, Chapingo, Mex., 1989, Korea Atomic Energy Rsch. Inst., Seoul, 1991, Nat. Atomic Energy Agy., Jakarta, 1991-94, Zhejiang U., Hangzhou, China, 1992, Ctrl. Nuc. La Reina, Santiago, Chile, 1992, Internat. Atomic Energy Agy., Vienna, 1993-2006, Mt. Makulu Ctrl. Rsch. Sta., Lusaka, Zambia, 1994, Office Atomic Energy Peace, Bangkok, 1995, Swedish Radiation Protection Inst., Stockholm, 1996, CIEMAT, Madrid, 1996, Laguna Verde Nuc. Power Plant, Vera Cruz, Mex., 1996, Oak Ridge (Tenn.) Nat. Labs., 1998, Min. Water and Irrigation, Amman, Jordan, 1998, Wyeth-Ayerst, Pearl River, NY, 1998, Chem. Industry Inst. Toxicology, Rsch. Triangle Park, NC, 1998, Los Alamos Nat. Labs., N.Mex., 2000, U.S. Dept. Energy Idaho Nat. Engrng. and Environ. Labs., Idaho Falls, 2000, China Atomic Energy Auth, Beijing, 2004, King Abdul Aziz City for Sci. and Tech., Riyadh, 2007. Author: (textbooks) Radiotracers in Agricultural Chemistry, 1979, Radionuclide Tracers, Their Detection and Measurement, 1987, Radioactivity: Introduction and History, 2007; author, editor (with J.O. Legg) Isotopes and Radiation in Agricultural Sciences, Vol. 1, 1984, Vol. 2, 1984, Handbook of Radioactivity Analysis, 1998, 2d edit., 2003, Radioactivity: Introduction and History, 2007; contbr. articles to profl. jours. Recipient hon. tchg. diploma, silver plaque Ctrl. U., Ecuador, Quito, 1978; hon. prof. Zhejiang U., 1992. Mem. AAAS, N.Y. Acad. Scis., Am. Nuc. Soc., Sigma Xi, Phi Lambda Upsilon, Gamma Sigma Delta. Achievements include discovery of molecular D-chiro-inositol phosphate in soil/plant systems; determination of a biochemical pathway involved in the formation of soil chiro-inositol phosphate; discovered microbial epimerization as origin of inosital phosphate isomers in soil; elucidated mechanisms of soil organic phosphorus fixation; separation of the radioactive nuclides Sr-90 from soil surfaces after nuclear fallout; first separation of radioactive nuclides Sr-90 and Y-90 by electrophoresis; execution of over 80 fact-finding, planning, and implementation missions to over 50 countries of Asia, Africa, Europe, Latin America, North America, and the Middle East for United Nations, International Atomic Energy Agy. from 1978 to the present; development of several chemical and instrumental techniques for the analysis of radioactive nuclides. Mailing: The Montague Group PO Box 5033 Oceanside CA 92052-5033 Office: The Montague Group Barrister Exec Stes 11622 El Camino Real Ste 100 San Diego CA 92130

LANO, CHARLES JACK, retired financial executive; b. Port Clinton, Ohio, Apr. 17, 1922; s. Charles Herbin and Antoinette (Schmitt) L.; m. Beatrice Irene Spees, June 16, 1946 (dec. 1995); children: Douglas Cloyd, Charles Lewis. BS in Bus. Adminstrn. summa cum laude, Ohio State U., 1949. C.P.A., Okla. With U.S. Gypsum Co., 1941-46, Ottawa Paper Stock Co., 1946-47; accountant Arthur Young & Co. (C.P.A.'s), Tulsa, 1949-51; controller Lima div. Ex-Cell-O Corp., 1951-59, electronics div. AVCO Corp., 1959-61, Servomation Corp., 1961; asst. comptroller Scovill Mfg. Co., Waterbury, Conn., 1961-62, comptroller, 1962-67; controller CF&I Steel Corp., Denver, 1967-69, v.p., controller, 1969-70; controller Pacific Lighting Corp., 1970-76; exec. v.p. Arts-Way Mfg. Co., Armstrong, Iowa, 1976-85; mgmt. auditor City of Anaheim, Calif., 1985-96; ret., 1996. Served with USMCR, 1942-45. Mem. Am. Inst. C.P.A.'s, Calif. Soc. C.P.A.'s, Inst. Internal Auditors. Home: 6274 E Calle Jaime Anaheim CA 92807-4005

LANOU, ROBERT EUGENE, JR., physicist, researcher; b. Colchester, Vt., Feb. 13, 1928; s. Robert E. and Flora G. (Goyette) L.; m. Cornelia Rockwell Wheeler, May 14, 1960; children: Katharine, Gregory, Elizabeth, Steven. BS, Worcester Poly. Inst., 1952; PhD, Yale U., 1957. Physicist Lawrence Berkeley (Calif.) Lab., 1956-59; asst. prof. physicist Brown U., Providence, 1960-63, assoc. prof., 1963-67, prof., 1967—, chair dept. physics, 1986-92, prof. rsch., 2001—, prof. emeritus, 2001—. Cons. Brookhaven Nat. Lab., Upton, N.Y., Los Alamos (N.Mex.) Nat. Lab.; sci. advisor Gov. State of R.I., Providence, 1986-88. Contbr. articles to profl. jours. With USN, 1946-48, ETO. Grantee Dept. Energy, 1960—, NSF, 1995—2000. Fellow AAAS, Am. Phys. Soc.; mem. Sigma Xi, Tau Beta Pi. Achievements include research in experimental particle physics and astrophysics. Home: 90 Keene St Providence RI 02906-1508 Office: Brown U Dept Physics Providence RI 02906

LANOUE, DAVID J., political science professor, department chairman; b. Central Falls, RI, June 25, 1958; s. Raymond A. and Rosalys R. Lanoue; m. Suzanne M. McGlone, July 30, 1982. BA, U. Calif., La Jolla, 1982; MA, Stony Brook U., NY, 1983, PhD, 1986. Asst. prof. Ill. State U., Normal, 1987—89; assoc. prof. U. Calif., Riverside, 1989—97; prof. Tex. Tech U., Lubbock, 1997—2001; prof., dept. chair U. Ala., Tuscaloosa, 2001—. Author: (books) From Camelot to the Teflon President, 1988; co-author: The Joint Press Conference: The History, Impact, and Prospects of American Presidential Debates, 1991. Mem.: Southwestern Polit. Sci. Assn. (v.p. 2005—06), Am. Polit. Sci. Assn. Home Phone: 205-554-7393.

LANOUE, ELAINE ROSE, visual artist, painter; d. Thomas and Olga Ann Graiko; m. Guiteau Lanoue, Oct. 26, 1984; children: Tamara Eatwell, Nicole Twine. Student, El Camino Jr. Coll., 1963, U. Tenn., 1974. Artist, Houston, 1976—; gallery owner E. Rose Studio, Houston, 1976—86. Writer Sunshine Artist Mag., Winterpark, Fla., 2004—; staff writer for Tex. Nat. Assn. Ind. Artists, 2004—. Painting, Red Roofs (Poster Artist for State St. Area Art Festival in Ann Arborn, MI, 2006), Meet Me Downtown (Poster Artist for Leesburg FL Art Assn., 2006), Crooked Houses (Art Pin Designer for OKC Festival of Arts, 2005). Mem. Braeswood Assembly of God, Houston, 1984—2006. Recipient 12 Purchase awards, OKC Arts Coun., 1998—2000, McCarthy award for Mixed Media, Friends of Modern Art, 2001, First Pl. Painting, ESAC Art Ctr., 2002, 2003 Best of Painting award, Tulsa Internat. Mayfest, 2003, Finalist award, Metris Uptown Art Festival, 2003, Excellence award, Ea. Shore C. of C., 2004, 2005 Hon. Mention, Grand Festival by the Bay ESAC, 2005, 11 Purchase awards, OKC, 2005—06, Hon. Mention, Carmel Internat. Art Festival, 2006. Mem.: Ea. Shore Art Assn. Conservative. Home and Office: Rose-Lanoue Art Studio 8800 Bissonnet St Suite G Houston TX 77074 Home Phone: 832-541-5058; Office Phone: 713-789-8385. Personal E-mail: artfuldesign@earthlink.net.

LA NOUE, TERENCE DAVID, artist, educator; b. Hammond, Ind., Dec. 4, 1941; s. George David and Lois (Lish) L.; children: Daniel, Alexandra. BFA, Ohio Wesleyan U., 1964; Fulbright meister student, Hochschule fur Bildenden Kunste, West Berlin, 1964-65; MFA, Cornell U., 1967; DFA, Ohio Wesleyan U., 1994. Prof. Trinity Coll., Hartford, Conn., 1967-72, CUNY, NYC, 1972-85, NYU, 1987. Works represented in various museums, including Whitney Mus., Guggenheim Mus., Bklyn. Mus., Albright-Knox Mus., Corcoran Gallery Art, Carnegie Inst., Power Inst. Fine Arts, Sydney, Australia, Musé d'Art et Archeologie, Toulon, France, Musée de Strasbourg, France, Mus. Contemporary Art, Teheran, Iran, Mus. Modern Art, NYC, Tate Mus., London, (retrospective) Tucson Mus. Art, 2003, Metropolitan Mus. of Art, NY, Singapore Mus. Art; monograph, Terence La Noue, Ashton Dore, 1992. Grantee Fulbright Found., Berlin, 1964-65, NEA, 1972-73, 83-84, Guggenheim Found., 1982-83. Address: PO Box 22 Patagonia AZ 85624 Home Phone: 520-287-3066. E-mail: terencedlanoue@aol.com.

LANPHER, BEN EVERT, psychologist, researcher; b. Cape Girardeau, Mo., July 15, 1958; s. Paul Gene and Mildred Wanda Lanpher; m. Kerri Lynn Seabaugh, Oct. 20, 1984; children: Lindsey Michelle (Lanpher) McClelland, Levi Lemual, Harry D. BS, S.E. Mo. State U., 1988, MA, 1992; PhD, U. Akron, 1999. Lic. psychologist Mo., social worker Mo., cert. health svc. provider Mo. Cottage supr. Cottonwood Residential Treatment Ctr., Cape Girardeau, Mo., 1988—89; cmty. support worker Beetheel Counseling Svc., Dexter, Mo., 1989—92, psychotherapist, 1992—93; rsch. asst. U. Akron, Ohio, 1993—96; intern in psychology The Guidance Ctr., Murfreesboro, Tenn., 1996—97, Cmty. Counsing Ctr., Cape Girardeau, Mo., 1997—99; pvt. practice psychologist Advance, Mo., 1999—. Rschr. People of the Trail Rsch. Project, Advance, Mo., 2003—. Sec. sch. bd. Advance R-IV Sch. Dist., Mo., 2002—; pk. bd. dir. City of Advance, Mo., 2000—; bd. dir. Stoddard County Mental Health, Bloomfield, Mo., 2003—. Mem.: APA. Democrat. Avocations: backpacking, tennis, fishing, camping, golf. Home: 19103 State Hwy C Advance MO 63730 Office Phone: 573-895-2145. E-mail: benlanpher@hotmail.com.

LANPHER, KATHERINE, radio personality, columnist; b. May 27, 1959; BA, Northwestern U.; MA in Am. Cultural History, U. Chgo. Columnist St. Paul Pioneer-Press, Minn.; host Weeknights with Katherine Lanpher, KSTP-AM 1500, Mpls., 1995—96, Midmorning, Minn. Pub. Radio, 1988—2004, Talking Volumes; co-host The Al Franken Show, Air Am. Radio, NYC, 2004—05. Guest host Talk of the Nation, Nat. Pub. Radio, 1999; commentator CNN, MSNBC, CNBC. Author: (memoir) Leap Days: Chronicles of a Midlife Move, 2006.

LANS, DEBORAH EISNER, lawyer; b. NYC, Oct. 26, 1949; d. Asher Bob and Barbara (Eisner) L. AB magna cum laude, Smith Coll., 1971; JD cum laude, Boston U., 1974. Bar: NY 1975, U.S. Dist. Ct. (so. and ea. dists.) NY 1975, U.S. Ct. Appeals (2d cir.) 1975, U.S. Supreme Ct. 1983. Assoc. Lans, Feinberg & Cohen, NYC, 1975-80, ptnr., 1980-84, Morrison Cohen Singer & Weinstein, NYC, 1984-2000; counsel Morrison Cohen Singer & Weinstein LLP, NYC, 2000—01, Wasserman Grubin & Rogers LLP, 2001—03; mng. ptnr. Cohen Lans LLP, NYC, 2003—. Exec. dir. Mentoring USA, 2000-02; mem. Supreme Ct. appellate divsn. first dept. disciplinary com., 2000-04; bd. dirs. Literacy Inc., Mark and Helene Eisner Found. Mem. ABA (bd. editors comml. banking litig. sects. 1998-2000), Nat. Arbitration Forum (comml. panel arbitrators), Assn. Bar City of NY (chmn. young lawyers com. 1981-83, joint com. fee disputes, 1982, judiciary com. 1984-85, exec. com. 1985-89, spl. com. bioethical issues, 1992-94, coun. on jud. adminstrn. 1996—), NY State Bar Assn. (ho. of dels. 1984-87, comml. and fed. litig. sect. com. on judiciary, alternative dispute resolution 1992—, environ. law sect. 1995—, family law sect., co-chair women in cts. com. 1994—), NY Bar Found. Office: Cohen Lans LLP 885 Third Ave New York NY 10022 Home Phone: 212-439-9890; Office Phone: 212-326-1704. Business E-Mail: dlans@cohenlans.com.

LANSBURY, ANGELA BRIGID, actress; b. London, Oct. 16, 1925; came to U.S., 1940; d. Edgar and Moyna (Macgill) L.; m. Richard Cromwell, Sept. 27, 1945 (div. Aug. 1946); m. Peter Shaw, Aug. 12, 1949 (dec. Jan. 29, 2003); children: Anthony, Deirdre. Student, Webber-Douglas Sch. Drama, London, 1939-40, Feagin Sch. Drama, NYC, 1940-42; LHD (hon.), Boston U., 1990. Host 41st-43d Ann. Tony Awards, 45th Ann. Emmy Awards. Actress with Metro-Goldwyn-Mayer, 1943-50; films include: Gaslight, 1944 (Acad. award nomination), National Velvet, 1944, The Picture of Dorian Gray, 1944 (Golden Globe award, Acad. award nomination), The Harvey Girls, 1946, The Hoodlum Saint, 1946, Till the Clouds Roll By, 1946, The Private Affairs of Bel Ami, 1947, If Winter Comes, 1948, Tenth Avenue Angel, 1948, State of the Union, 1948, The Three Musketeers, 1948, The Red Danube, 1949, Samson and Delilah, 1949, Kind Lady, 1951, Mutiny, 1952, Remains to be Seen, 1953, A Life at Stake, 1955, The Purple Mask, 1956, A Lawless Street, 1956, Please Murder Me, 1956, The Court Jester, 1956, The Long Hot Summer, 1958, Reluctant Debutante, 1958, A Breath of Scandal, 1960, Dark at the Top of the Stairs, 1960, Season of Passion, 1961, Blue Hawaii, 1961, All Fall Down, 1962, Manchurian Candidate, 1962 (Golden Globe award, Acad. award nomination), In the Cool of the Day, 1963, Dear Heart, 1964, The World of Henry Orient, 1964, The Greatest Story Ever Told, 1965, Harlow, 1965, The Amorous Adventures of Moll Flanders, 1965, Mister Buddwing, 1966, Something for Everyone, 1970, Bedknobs and Broomsticks, 1971, Death on the Nile, 1978, The Lady Vanishes, 1980, The Mirror Crack'd, 1980, The Pirates of Penzance, 1982, The Company of Wolves, 1983, Beauty and the Beast, 1991, Your Studio and You, 1995, Beauty & the Beast: Enchanted Christmas (vioce), 1997, Anastasia (voice), 1997, Nanny McPhee, 2005; star TV series Murder, She Wrote, 1984-96 (Golden Globe awards 1984, 86, 91, 92, 12 Emmy nominations, Lead Actress - Drama), Murder, She Wrote: A Story to Die For, 2000, Murder, She Wrote: The Last Free Man, 2001, Murder, She Wrote: The Celtic Riddle, 2003; appeared in TV mini-series Little Gloria, Happy at Last, 1982, Lace, 1984, Rage of Angels, part II, 1986; other TV movies include: The First Olympics-Athens 1896, A Talent for Murder, Gift of Love, 1982, Shootdown, 1988, The Shell Seekers, 1989, The Love She Sought, 1990, Mrs. 'Arris Goes to Paris, 1992, (musical) Mrs. Santa Claus, 1996; appeared in plays Hotel Paradiso, 1957, A Taste of Honey, 1960, Anyone Can Whistle, 1964, Mame (on Broadway), 1966, 83 (Tony award for Best Mus. Actress 1966), Dear World, 1968 (Tony award for Best Mus. Actress 1969), All Over (London Royal Shakespeare Co.), 1971, Prettybelle, 1971, Gypsy, 1974 (Tony award for Best Mus. Actress 1975, Sarah Siddons award), The King and I, 1978, Sweeney Todd, 1979 (Tony award for Best Mus. Actress 1979, Sarah Siddons award), Hamlet, Nat. Theatre, London, 1976, A Little Family Business, 1983, Deuce, 2007; TV appearances Law & Order: SVU, 2005. Named Woman of Yr., Harvard Hasty Pudding Theatricals, 1968, Comdr. of British Empire by Queen Elizabeth II, 1994; named to Theatre Hall of Fame, 1982, TV Hall of Fame, 1996; recipient British Acad. award, 1991, Silver Mask Lifetime Ach. Award, British Acad. Film and TV Arts, 1992, Lifetime Achievement award, Screen Actors' Guild, Hollywood, 1997, 16 Emmy Award Nominations, 8 Golden Globe Nominations; Won 6 Golden Glode Awards; received Nat. medal of the Arts from President Clinton, 1997. Office: c/o William Morris Agy 151 El Camino Dr Beverly Hills CA 90212*

LANSBURY, EDGAR GEORGE, theatrical producer; b. London, Jan. 12, 1930; came to U.S., 1941, naturalized, 1953; s. Edgar Isaac and Charlotte Lillian (McIldowie) L.; m. Rose Anthony Kean, Aug. 12, 1955; children: James, Michael, David, George, Brian, Kate. Student, UCLA. Designer stock and off-Broadway prodns., 1953-55; art dir. ABC-TV, 1955, CBS-TV, 1955-62, Channel 13, NYC, 1962-63; motion picture art dir., 1963-64; formed Edgar Lansbury Prodns. Inc., for ind. prodn. in theatre and films, 1964—; chmn. The Acting Co. Bd. dirs. drama dept. Story Line Press; chair Russian Mus. Arts Soc. Am. Producer Broadway plays: First One Asleep Whistle, 1966, The Subject Was Roses, (Critics Circle award, Antoinette Perry award, Pulitzer Prize) 1964, That Summer-That Fall, 1967, The Only Game in Town, 1968, Promenade, 1970, Look to the Lilies, 1970, Engagement Baby, 1971, Godspell, 1971, Elizabeth I, 1972, The Night That Made America Famous, 1974, The Magic Show, 1974, Gypsy, 1975, American Buffalo, 1977, Broadway Follies, 1981, O, Pioneer!, 1989, Club XII, 1990, Amphigorey, 1992, Any Given Day, 1993, Curtains, Grace and Glorie, 1996, In Circles, 1997, As Bees in Honey Drown, 1997, June Moon, 1998, Lennon, 2005; films The Subject was Roses, 1968, Godspell, 1973, The Wild Party, 1974, Squirm, 1976, Blue Sunshine, 1978, He Knows You're Alone, 1980, The Clairvoyant, 1982, Summer Girl, 1983, A Stranger Waits, 1986, Advice from a Caterpillar, 1999, Gypsy "83", 2001; dir. Without Apologies, 1989, All the Queen's Men, 1989, Advice from a Caterpillar, 1990, The Country Club, 1992. Pres. Agni Yoga Soc., Nicholas Roerich Mus., NYC; bd. govs. League N.Y. Theatres and Prodrs.; chmn. Russian Chamber Chorus, NYC, The Acting Co., NYC. With US Army, 1951—53. Recipient N.Y. Art Dirs. award for best comml. film, 1963; N.Y. Outer Critics Circle award, 1965; N.Y. Critics Circle award, 1965; Antoinette Perry award for best produced play, 1965; nomination for Antoinette Perry award for best mus. play, 1977; N.Y. Critics Circle award for best drama, 1977 Office: Edgar Lansbury Prodns 630 9th Ave Ste 214 New York NY 10036-3708 Home: 15 W 81st St #8c New York NY 10024-6022

LANSDOWNE, WILLIAM M., police chief; b. May 10, 1944; s. Leonard M. and Grace (Dabuque) L.; m. Sharon L. Young, June 12, 1994; children: Greg, Erik. BS in Law Enforcement, San Jose State U., 1971. Asst. chief San Jose (Calif.) Police Dept., 1966-94; chief Richmond (Calif.) Police Dept., 1994—98; chief of police San Jose Police Dept., Calif., 1998—2003, San Diego Police Dept., Calif., 2003—. Mem. Internat. Assn. Chiefs of Police, Calif. Police Chiefs Assn., Police Exec. Rsch. Forum, Calif. Homeland Security Pub. Safety Adv. Com., Maj. Cities Chiefs Assn. Office: San Diego Police Dept 1401 Broadway San Diego CA 92101-5729 Office Phone: 619-531-2777.

LANSFORD, EDWIN GAINES, accountant; b. Chattanooga, Aug. 20, 1924; s. Frederick Duke Lansford and Edwina (Gaines) Lansford Stone; m. Sue Ann Kemmer, May 29, 1954; children: Virginia Nan, Sue Ann, Edwin Gaines, Jr., James Robert, Frederick Scott. BBA, U. Chattanooga, 1948; LLB, McKenzie Coll., 1958. Bar: Tenn. Cost acct. Cavalier Corp., Chattanooga, 1948-52; staff acct. O.T. Draewell and H.L. Oakes, Chattanooga, 1952-54; pvt. practice Crossville & Chattanooga, 1954-98; v.p. Lansford Kawasaki, Inc., Crossville, 1978—; of counsel Lansford & Stephens, CPAs, Pikeville and Crossville, Tenn., 1999—. Bd. dirs. Rotary Found. of Cumberland County, 2001—, sec.-treas., 2003—; scoutmaster Cherokee Area coun. Boy Scouts Am., 1947-52. With U.S. Army, 1943-46, ETO. Mem.: NRA, AICPA (hon.), Tenn. Bar Assn., Cumberland County C. of C. (bd. dirs. 1976—79), Tenn. Shooting Sports Assn. (H.P. Rifle Team 1963—64, pres. 1969—71), Nat. Assn. Tax Profls. (bd. dirs. Tenn. chpt. 1996—, treas. 1998—2001), Tenn. Soc. CPAs (life; pres. Chattanooga chpt. 1962—63, 1st pres., co-founder Upper Cumberland chpt. 1978—79, sec., various coms.), Elks, Rotary (all offices and bd. dirs. Crossville noon chpt. 1983—, Paul Harris fellow), Lions (treas. Signal Mountain club 1974—75). Methodist. Avocations: hunting, hiking. Office: 92 Rockwood Ave Crossville TN 38555-4610 E-mail: cpa@multipro.com.

LANSFORD, JAMES LOWELL, technologist; b. Huntland, Tenn., June 9, 1957; BS, Auburn U., Ala., 1980; MS, Ga. Tech, 1982; PhD, Okla. State U., Stillwater, 1988. Sr. mem. tech staff Ga. Tech Rsch. Inst., Atlanta, 1987—90; asst. prof. U. of Colo., Colorado Springs, 1990—95; chief tech. officer Momentum Microsys., Colorado Springs, 1994—96; sr. staff Intel Corp., Hillsboro, Oreg., 1996—2000; chief tech. officer, vp bus. devel. Mobilian, Portland, Oreg., 2000—03; chief tech. officer Alereon, Inc., Austin, Tex., 2003—. Pres. Mobile Data Sys., Colorado Springs, 1993—96. Bd. dirs., pres.-elect Unitarian-Universalist Ch., Stillwater, 2000—04. Mem.: IEEE. Unitarian. Achievements include patents in field; patents pending for. Avocation: travel. Office: Alereon Inc 7600C N Capital of Texas Hwy Austin TX 78731 Office Phone: +1 512 345 4200 x2166. Office Fax: +1 206 337 1703. E-mail: jim.lansford@ieee.org.

LANSFORD, RAYMOND WILLIAM, retired finance educator; b. Linn, Mo. s. August Franklin and Annie Louise (Miller) L.; m. Beuna Alma Ridenhour, May 25, 1945. BS, S.W. Mo. State U., 1947; MBA, Northwestern U., 1948; PhD, NYU, 1954. Prof. Ctrl. Mo. State U., Warrensburg, 1949—57, U. Mo., Columbia, 1957—85, asst. dean Coll. Bus., 1961—75, ednl. dir., 1975—85, prof. emeritus, 1985—, disting. prof., 1992; CEO Analytical Biochemistry Corp., Columbia, 1993—94. Author: Real Estate Contracts, 1967, Real Estate Closing Guide, 1968, (booklet) Renting Property, 1971, Appraisal Primer, 1973. Ch. county com. Boone County Reorgn., Columbia, 1967-68; v.p. U. Children's Hosp., 1987-88. Decorated Air medal with five oak leaf clusters; named Realtor of Yr., Mo. Assn. Realtors, 1976. Mem. Kiwanis (gov. 1974-75, trustee 1977-84, v.p. 1982-83, bd. dirs. 1992-93, internat. pres. 1984-85, Disting. Leader award, Tablet of Honor, Hixson Fellow), Heritage Soc. Avocation: antique tool collecting. Home: 2 Springer Dr Columbia MO 65201-5425

LANSING, SHERRY LEE, foundation administrator, former film company executive; b. Chgo., July 31, 1944; d. Norton and Margo L.; m. William Friedkin, July 6, 1991. BS summa cum laude in Theatre, Northwestern U., 1966; DFA (hon.), Am. Film Inst. High sch. tchr. math., LA, 1966-69; model TV commls. Max Factor Co., 1969-70, Alberto-Culver Co., 1969-70; story editor Wagner Internat. Prodn. Co., 1972-74, dir. west coast devel., 1974-75; story editor MGM, 1975-77, v.p. creative affairs, 1977; senior v.p. prodn. Columbia Pictures, 1977-80; pres. studio 20th Century Fox Prodns., Hollywood, 1980-82; founder Jaffee-Lansing Prodns., 1983—92; pres. Paramount Communications, 1990—2005; chmn. Paramount Motion Pictures Group, LA, 1992—2005; CEO The Sherry Lansing Found., 2005—. Bd. dirs. QUALCOMM Inc., 2006—. Actress (films) Loving, 1970, Rio Lobo, 1970; (TV appearances) Ironside, 1971, Frasier, 1996; exec. prodr. (films) Racing With the Moon, 1984, Firstborn, 1984; prodr. (films) Fatal Attraction, 1987, The Accused, 1988, Black Rain, 1989, School Ties, 1992, Indecent Proposal, 1993; exec. prodr. (TV movies) When the Time Comes, 1987, Mistress, 1992. Bd. dirs. ARC; bd. regents U. Chgo., U. Calif., 1991—; bd. trustees The Carter Center, 2005—, Am. Assn. Cancer Rsch. Named Pioneer of Yr., Found. of the Motion Picture Pioneers, 1996; named one of 100 Most Powerful Women in Entertainment, Hollywood Reporter, 2003, 2004; recipient Producers Guild of Am. Milestone award, 2000, Horatio Alger Humanitarian award, 2004, Exemplary Leadership in Mgmt. award, UCLA Anderson Sch. Mgmt., 2005, Jean H. Hersholt Humanitarian award, Acad. of Motion Picture Arts & Sciences, 2007, Woodrow Wilson award for Corp. Citizenship, Alfred P. Sloan, Jr. Meml. award, Disting. Community Svc. award, Brandeis U. Achievements include being the first woman to head a major film studio when she was named president of 20th Century Fox, 1980.*

LANSKY, LEWIS, history professor; b. Buffalo, Apr. 8, 1938; s. Jacob and Lillian Lansky; 1 child, Joshua Michael. BA in History, U. Rochester, 1960; MS in Social Scis., SUNY, Buffalo, 1962; PhD in History, Case Western Res. U., 1976. Permanent cert. in social studies Bd. Regents, NY. Asst. prof. history and polit. sci. Monroe C.C., Rochester, NY, 1962—67, 1971—75, assoc. prof., 1975—84, prof., 1984—2004, prof. emeritus, 2004—. Mem. edn. com. Friends of F.I.G.H.T., Rochester, 1965—66; commr. City Planning Commn., Rochester, 1984—89, Rochester Environ. Commn., 1989—95; mem. Rochester-Rehovoth Sister City Com., 1984—, Mayor's Vision 2000 Adv. Com., Rochester, 1989—92; chair Jonathan Michael Lansky Fund for Disabled Students/Monroe C.C. Found.; mem. Monroe County Dem. Com., Rochester, 1976—. Served with US Army, 1962—68. Mem.: Orgn. Am. Historians, Am. Hist. Assn. Jewish. Avocations: jazz, model trains, travel. Home: 1057 Monroe Ave Rochester NY 14620

LANSNER, GABRIELLE, choreographer, dancer, performing company executive, actress; Attended, Juilliard, SUNY, Purchase, NYU Exptl. Theatre Wing. Assoc. mem. and performer Wooster Group; founder Gabrielle Lansner and Dancers, 1980—87; founder, artistic dir. Gabrielle

Lansner and Co. Mem. Lincoln Ctr. Directors Lab., NYC, 1998—; tchr. movement for actors Am. Acad. Dramatic Arts, Mint Theatre Co. Performer: (plays) Three Places in Rhode Island, Query, 1978, Holocaust Stories, 2003, The Jewish Wife, 2003; dancer Black and White in Color, 1987; dir. and choreographer (plays) The Boy With the Glasses, 2001; choreographer (plays) Him & Her, NY Internat. Fringe Festival, 2002; dir., choreographer, book adaptation (musical) River Deep: A Tribute to Tina Turner, 2006—. Office: Artistic Director Gabrielle Lansner and Co 32 West 38th St #2 New York NY 10018 Office Phone: 212-768-0644. E-mail: gabrielle_lansner_company@yahoo.com.

LANSNER, RUTH L., lawyer; b. NYC, June 29, 1950; BA cum laude, Yale U., 1971; JD, NYU Sch. Law, 1974. Bar: NY 1975. Practiced Gilbert, Segall and Young LLP (joined Holland & Knight), 1974—2001; ptnr. Holland & Knight LLP, NY, 2001—, mem. dir. com., dep. sect. leader bus. law sect. NY. Mem. def. adv. com. on women in the svcs. (DACOWITS) US Dept. Def., 1998—2000; lectr. in field. Mem. bd. editors Leader's Equipment Leasing Newsletter, 1986, newsletter editor Aeronautical Law Com.; contbr. articles to profl. jours. Nat. commr. Anti-Defamation League, chmn., Nat. Legal Affairs Com., 1990—98; mem. Nat. Exec. Com.; vice-chair Nat. Religious Freedom Task Force. Fellow: ABA (vice-chair women's interest network sect. on internat. law & practice 1999—, rep. to UN econ. and social coun. for NY 2000—01, mem. sect. internat. law and practice, reg. coord. for NY women's interest network's); mem.: Inst. of Trade Mark Attys. (UK), Internat. Trademark Assn., Am. Fgn. Law Assn. (v.p. 1997—2000), Am. Fgn. Lawyers Assn. (dir. 2001—03), NY County Lawyers Assn. (dir. 1997—2000), Internat. Bar Assn. (co-chair of a panel "Sale of a Bus. Using an Auction Process" 2002, vice-chair 2002—, former chmn. subcommitte on the sale contract, former chmn. com. on internat. sales & related comml. transactions), Assn. Bar City NY (mem. com. on aeronautics 1978—81, sec. 1981—83, chair 1983—86, mem. com. on aeronautics 1983—86). Office: Holland & Knight LLP 195 Broadway 24th Fl New York NY 10007 Office Phone: 212-513-3440. Business E-Mail: rlansner@hklaw.com.

LANTER, LANORE, writer, educator; b. Argenta, Ill., Apr. 30, 1928; d. Floyd Depin Lanter and Goldie May Elkins; m. Andrew Kasparian, Oct. 17, 1948 (div. July 1976); children: Andra Kay, Dana Lee, Mark Scott, David Andrew. BA in English, Fresno State Coll., 1969. Cert. std. elem. tchr., 1972, early childhood, 1972, registered Calif., 1972. Tutor lang. skills Fresno County, Calif., 1972; co-dir. curriculum N.W. Ch. Day Care, Fresno, 1972—73; writer curriculum, head tchr. First Presbyn. Ch., Fresno, 1973—74; owner, tchr., writer curriculum Children's Corner Presch., Fresno, 1977—83; educator (older adults writing) Clovis Adult Edn./Clovis Unified Sch. Dist., Calif., 1995—; columnist Wryte Rite Tips Win Win Writing Orgn., Fresno, 2001—05. Editor, cons. San Joaquin Valley Sr. Writers, Fresno, 1994—. Author: (textbook) You Can Wryte Rite Series, 1994, (columns) Wryte Rite Tips, 2005; editor: (6 book anthologies) Inklings, 1994, 1995, 1996, We Remember When, 1997, Flights of Fantasy, 2000, Poemscapes, 2005. Vol. tchr., writing educator (55 yrs. and older) St. Agnes Hosp. Club 55 Plus, Herndon, Fresno, 1994—; mem. task force Muscular Dystrophy Assn., Shaw, Fresno, 1994; vol. Win Win Writers Orgn., 2002—05. Named Highest Achiever with muscle disease, Muscular Dystrophy, Shaw, Fresno, 1995; recipient Best Tchr. plaque, San Joaquin Valley Sr. Writers, 1997, Tolerance award, So. Poverty Law Ctr., Mont., Ala., 2003, First Pl. Srs. of William Saroyan Writing Contest, 1992, Cert. of Recognition for Outstanding Contbn., Muscular Dystrophy Assn., Calif. Legis. Assembly, 1995. Independent. Protestant. Avocations: reading, flower arranging, painting, poetry writing. Home: 2934 E Ashlan Ave Fresno CA 93726-3304 Office Phone: 559-243-1156. Personal E-mail: lanorewriter@comcast.net.

LANTERMAN, JENNIFER L., researcher, educator; d. Margaret E.S. and Thomas M. Lanterman. BS, Rutgers Coll., New Brunswick, NJ, 2001; MA, Rutgers U., Newark, 2002, PhD, 2007. Lectr. Rutgers U., Newark, 2002—; rsch. assoc. Police Inst., Newark, 2003—. Contbr. McGraw-Hill Cos., NYC, 2003. Mem.: US Naval Inst., Soc. for the Study Social Problems, Law and Soc. Assn., Am. Soc. Criminology, Am. Mensa. Avocations: marathons, triathlons, travel, puzzles, reading. Business E-Mail: jlantern@andromeda.rutgers.edu.

LANTHIER, RONALD ROSS, retired manufacturing executive; b. Montreal, Que., Can., May 2, 1926; s. Emile Edgar and Edith (Martin) L.; m. Jacqueline Barbara Dyment; children: April Carolyn, Bonnie Alice, Ronald Dyment, Andrea Elizabeth, John Elliott. Chartered Accountant, McGill U., 1952. Pub. accountant, 1944-51; chief accountant St. Lawrence Flour Co., 1951-52; controller Canadian Underwriters Assn., 1952-54; div. controller Canadian Aviation Electronics Co., 1954-56; treas. Webb & Knapp, Can., 1956-62; dir. adminstrn., mem. exec. com. Greenshields, Inc. (investment dealers), 1962-67; v.p. finance, treas., mem. exec. com. Canadian Marconi Co., 1967-72; v.p. finance, dir., mem. exec. com. Macdonald Tobacco, Inc., 1972-75; pres. Lanco Mgmt. Ltd., 1975-98; v.p. finance MacDonald Stewart Textiles, 1976-77; v.p. fin., mem. exec. com. Electrolux Can., 1978-79; pres. Robert R. Bramhall & Assos. (Can.) Ltd., 1980-81; sr. v.p. Camflo Mines Ltd., 1981-84; v.p. fin. Starnav Corp., 1984-86; v.p. VR Fin. Svcs., 1987-95. Mem. Inst. Chartered Accts. Que. and Ont., Phi Kappa Pi. Anglican. Home: 100 Westview Dr Aurora ON Canada L4G 7C9 Home Phone: 905-727-6786. E-mail: jarba@interhop.net.

LANTOS, THOMAS PETER, congressman; b. Budapest, Hungary, Feb. 1, 1928; m. Annette Tillemann; children: Annette, Katrina. BA, U. Wash., 1949, MA, 1950; PhD, U. Calif., Berkeley, 1953. Faculty U. Wash., San Francisco State U., 1950-83; TV news analyst, commentator; sr. econ. and fgn. policy adviser to several US senators; mem. Presdl. Task Force on Def. and Fgn. Policy, US Congress from 12th Calif. dist., 1981—; ranking minority mem., internat. rels. com., mem. govt. reform com. Founder study abroad program Calif. State U. and Coll. Sys. Mem. Millbrae Bd. Edn., 1950-66; co-founder, co-chair Congl. Human Rights Caucus. Democrat. Office: US Ho Reps 2413 Rayburn Ho Office Bldg Washington DC 20515-0512*

LANTZ, JOANNE BALDWIN, retired academic administrator; b. Defiance, Ohio, Jan. 26, 1932; d. Hiram J. and Ethel A. (Smith) Baldwin; m. Wayne E. Lantz. BS in Physics and Math., U. Indpls., 1953; MS in Counseling and Guidance, Ind. U., 1957; PhD in Counseling and Psychology, Mich. State U., 1969; LittD (hon.), U. Indpls., 1985; LHD (hon.), Purdue U., 1994; LLD (hon.), Manchester Coll., 1994. Tchr. physics and math. Arcola (Ind.) High Sch., 1953-57; guidance dir. New Haven (Ind.) Sr. High Sch., 1957-65; with Ind. U.-Purdue U., Fort Wayne, 1965—, interim chancellor, 1988-89, chancellor, 1989-94, chancellor emeritus, 1994—. Bd. dirs., hon. dir. Ft. Wayne Nat. Corp.; bd. dirs. Foellinger Found., 1992-2007. Contbr. articles to profl. jours. Mem. Ft. Wayne Econ. Devel. Adv. Bd. and Task Force, 1988-91, Corp. Coun., 1988-94; bd. advisors Leadership Ft. Wayne, 1988-94; mem. adv. bd. Ind. Sml. Bus. Devel. Ctr., 1988-90; trustee Ancilla System, Inc., 1984-89, chmn. human resources com., 1985-89, exec. com., 1985-89; trustee St. Joseph's Med. Ctr., 1983-84, pers. adv. com. to bd. dirs., 1978-84, chmn., 1980-84; bd. dirs. United Way Allen County, sec., 1979-80; bd. dirs. Anthony Wayne Vocat. Rehab. Ctr., 1969-75. Mem.: AAUW (Am. women fellowship com. 1978—83, program com. 1981—83, chmn. 1981—83, internat. fellowship com. 1986—88, trust rsch. grantee 1980), APA, Southeastern Psychol. Assn. (referee conv. papers 1987—88), Ft. Wayne Ind.-Purdue Alumni Soc. (hon.), Ind. Sch. Women's Club (v.p. program chair 1979—81), Delta Kappa Gamma (leadership devel. com. 1978—82, dir. N.E. region 1982—84, exec. bd. 1982—84, adminstrv. bd. 1982—84, gen. chair conv. 1985—86, editl. bd. 1986—88, bd. trustees ednl. found. 1996—2002, nominating com. 2002—06), Sigma Xi, Pi Lambda Theta. Avocations: swimming, reading, knitting, boating. Personal E-mail: joalantz@aol.com.

LANTZ, PHILLIP EDWARD, security firm executive, consultant; b. Laramie, Wyo., Sept. 21, 1938; s. Everett Delmer and Elizabeth Mary (Stratton) L.; m. Paula Bogel, June 16, 1962; children: Kirk Edward, Eric William. BA in Math., U. Colo., 1960; MA in Math., U. Wyo., 1966; MS in Ops. Rsch., Johns Hopkins U., 1972. Grad. teaching asst. U. Wyo., Laramie, 1964-65; sr. engr. Applied Physics Lab. Johns Hopkins U., Silver Spring, Md., 1965-70; v.p. Ops. Rsch. Inc., Silver Spring, Md., 1970-72; dir. Tetra Tech. Inc., Arlington, Va., 1972-74; pres., chief exec. officer Systems Planning and Analysis, Inc., Alexandria, Va., 1974—, also bd. dirs. Lt. USN, 1960-64. Home: 2911 Eddington Ter Alexandria VA 22302-3503 Office: Systems Planning and Analysis Inc 2001 N Beauregard St Alexandria VA 22311-1739 Home Phone: 703-836-0866; Office Phone: 703-931-3500. Business E-Mail: plantz@spa.com.

LANYON, ELLEN, artist, educator; b. Chgo., Dec. 21, 1926; d. Howard Wesley and Ellen (Aspinwall) L.; m. Roland Ginzel, Sept. 4, 1948; children: Andrew, Lisa. BFA, Art Inst. Chgo., 1948; MFA, U. Iowa, Iowa City, 1950; Fulbright fellow, Courtauld Inst., U. London, 1950-51; D (hon.), Art Inst. Chgo., 2007. Tchr. jr. sch. Art Inst. Chgo., 1952-54; past tchr. day sch., tchr. Rockford Coll., summer 1953, Oxbow Summer Sch. Painting, Saugatuck, Mich., 1961-62, 67-70, 71-72, 78, 88, 94, U. Ill., Chgo., 1970, U. Wis. Extension, 1971-72, Pa. State U., 1974, U. Calif., 1974, Sacramento State U., 1974, Stanford U., 1974, Boston U., 1975, Kans. State U., 1976, U. Mo., 1976, U. Houston, 1977; assoc. prof. Cooper Union, NYC, 1980-93; ret., 1993. Founder, sec.-treas. Chgo. Graphic Workshop, 1952-55; participant Yaddo, 1973, 75, 76, Ossobow Island Project, 1976; adj. vis. prof. So. Ill. U., 1978, No. Ill. U., 1978, SUNY, Purchase, 1978, Cooper Union, N.Y.C., 1978-79, Parsons Sch. Design, N.Y.C., 1979; disting. vis. prof. U. S.D., 1980, U. Calif. Davis, 1980, Sch. Visual Arts, N.Y.C., 1980-83; vis. artist U. N.Mex., 1981, So. Ill. U., 1984, Sch. Art Inst., Chgo., 1985, U. Tenn., Md. Inst., Northwestern Grad. Sch., 1988, U. Pa., U. Iowa, 1991, 92; instr. workshops Anderson Ranch Workshop, Snow Mass, Colo., 1994, 96, Aspen Design Conf., 1994; vis. prof. U. Iowa, 1991-92; bd. dirs. Oxbow Summer Sch. Painting, 1972-82, emeritus, 1982—, instr., 1960, 72-82, 88, 94,2005; vis. artist, instr. workshops Vt. Studio Sch., 1996, 97, 2001, 2005, Oxbow, 2005, Vt. Studio, 2005, U. Costa Rica, San Pedro and San Ramon, 1995; instr. Interlaken Sch. of Art, 1996; tchr. master class Nat. Acad. Design, 1999, Nat. Acad. Abbey Mural Workshops, 2001-2005. One woman shows, Superior St. Gallery, Chgo., 1960, Stewart Richart Gallery, San Antonio, 1962, 65, Fairweather Hardin Gallery, Chgo., 1962, Zabriskie Gallery, N.Y.C., 1962, 64, 69, 72, B.C. Holland Gallery, Chgo., 1965, 68, Ft. Wayne Art Mus., 1967, Richard Gray Gallery, Chgo., 1970, 73, 76, 79, 82, 85, Madison Art Center, 1972, Nat. Collection at Smithsonian Instn., 1972, Odyssia Gallery, Rome, 1975, Krannert Performing Arts Center, 1976, Oshkosh Pub. Mus., 1976, U. Mo., 1976, Harcus Krakow, Boston, 1977—, Fendrick Gallery, Washington, 1978, Ky. State U., 1979, Ill. Wesleyan U., 1979, U. Calif., Davis, 1980, Odyssia Gallery, NY, 1980, Landfall Press, 1980, Alverno Coll., Milw., 1981, Susan Caldwell, Inc., NYC, 1983, N.A.M.E. Gallery, Chgo., 1983, Printworks, Ltd., Chgo., 1989, 93, 99, 02-03, 07, Pretto Berland Hall, NYC, 1989, Struve Gallery, Chgo., 1990, 93, Berland Hall Gallery, N.Y.C., 1992, Sioux City Art Mus., Iowa, 1992, U. Iowa Mus. Art, 1994, Andre Zarre Gallery, NYC, 1994-97, TBA, Chgo., 1996, Centrocultural Costarricense Norteamericano, San Jose, Costa Rica, 1997, Jean Albano Gallery, 1997, 99, 2001, Jan Abrams Fine Arts, NYC, 2005, Valerie Carberry Gallery, Chgo., 2005; retrospective exhbns. include Krannert Art Mus., McNay Art Mus., Chgo. Cultural Ctr., Stamford Mus., U. Tenn., Nat. Mus. Women in Arts, 1999, Brauer Mus., Valparaiso, Ind., 2007; exhibited in group shows at Am. Fedn. Arts, 1946-48, 50, 53, 57, 65-66, 69; Art Inst. Chgo., 1946-47, 51-53, 55, 57-58, 60-62, 64, 66-69, 71, 73, Corcoran Gallery Art, 1961, 76, Denver Art Mus., 1950, 52, Exhbn. Momentum, Chgo., 1948, 50, 52, 54, 56, Libr. Congress, 1950, 52, Met. Mus. Art, 1952, Mus. Modern Art, 1953, 62, Phila. Mus. Art, 1946, 47, 50, 54, San Francisco Mus. Art, 1946, 50, U. Ill., 1953, 54, 57, Drawing Soc., 1965-66, Mus. Contemporary Art, Chgo., 1969, Graham Gallery, NYC, 1969-71, Ill. Arts Coun., 1968-71, HMH Publs. Europe, 1971, Chgo. Imagists, 1972, Chgo. Sch, 1972, Am. Women, 1972, Artists Books, 1973; Downtown Whitney, NYC, 1978—, Queens Mus., 1978, Dayton Art Inst., 1978, Odyssia Gallery, NYC, 1979, Chgo. Cultural Center, 1979, Aldrich Mus. Contemporary Art, 1980, Bklyn. Mus., 1980, Walker Art Ctr., 1981, also Lisbon, Venice biennales, Voorhees Mus. Rutgers U., Mus. Contemporary Art, Chgo., Milw. Art. Mus., Berkeley Art Mus., 1987, Cooper Union, 1989, Randall Gallery, St. Louis, 1991, Printworks Ltd., Chgo., 1989-99, 03, 05, 07, Berland Hall, NYC, 1991, Cultural Ctr., Chgo., 1992, Matnan Locks Gallery, Phila., 1992, Art Inst. Chgo., 1992, Nat. Mus. Women in Arts, Washington, 1994-97, 2006, Wadsworth Atheneum, Hartford, Conn., 1996, Mus. Contemporary Art, 1996, Block Gallery, Northwestern U., 1996, 07, Rockford Art Mus., Ill. State Mus., 1997, Nat. Acad. Design, 1999, 01, 03, 05, CUNY, Neuberger Mus. Art, 1999, Nat. Acad. Biannuals, NY, Am. Acad. Arts and Letters, NY, 2004 Racine Art Mus., Wis., 2001-03, 05, 07, Valerie Carberry Gallery, 2005-07, Pa. Acad., 2006, David Findlay Fine Arts, NYC, 2006, Adam Baumgold Gallery, NYC, 2005-07; represented in permanent collections Art Inst. Chgo., Denver Art Mus., Libr. Congress, Inst. Internat. Edn., London, Finch Coll., NY, Krannert Mus., U. Ill., U. Mass., NJ State Mus., Ill. State Mus., Bklyn. Mus., Mus. Contemporary Art, Chgo., Nat. Coll. Fine Arts, Walker Art Ctr., Mpls., Boston Pub. Libr., Des Moines Art Ctr., Albion Coll., Met. Mus., McNay Art Inst., Albion Coll., Kans. State U., U. Dallas, U. Houston, Cornell U., Racine Art Mus., Grand Rapids Mus. Art, Mich., U. Iowa Mus. Art, Nat. Mus. Women in Arts, Washington, Williams Coll. Mus., Mass., Pa. Acad. Fin. Arts; also numerous pvt. collections.; mural paintings: Working Men's Coop. Bank Boston, 1979, Boston Pub. Libr., 2000, State of Ill. Bldg., Chgo., 1985, State Capitol, Springfield, Ill., 1989, City of Miami Beach, Art in Public Places project, Police and Court Facility, 1993; also commns.: City Of Chicago, 1999, Riverwalk Gateway Project, 1999,St. Patrick's Ch., Chgo, 1999, Hiawatha-LRT, Mpls., 2004; published: Wonder Production Vol. I, 1971, Jataka Tales, 1975, Transformations, 1976, Transformations II (Endangered), 1983, Index, 2003; editorial bd.: Coll. Art Jour., 1982-92; illustrator: The Wandering Tattler, 1975, Perishible Press, 1976—, Red Ozier Press, 1980—. Recipient Armstrong prize Art Inst. Chgo., 1946, 55, 77, Town and Country purchase prize, 1947, Purchase prize Denver Art Mus., 1950, Purchase prize Libr. of Congress, 1950, Blair prize, 1958, Chan prize, 1961, Palmer prize, 1962, 64, Vielehr prize, 1967, Cassandra Found. award, 1970, Logan prize, 1981; grantee NEA, 1974, 87, Herewood Lester Cook Found., 1981, Florsheim Found., 1999, Purchase prize Am. Acad. Arts and Letters, 2004; named to Nat. Acad., 1997. Mem. Nat. Acad. (mem. coun. 2002-07, chair exhbn. com. 2004-2005, elected treas. 2005), Coll. Art Assn. (bd. dirs., exec. com. 1977-80), Century Assn. (elected), Delta Phi Delta. Address: 138 Prince St New York NY 10012-3135 Office Phone: 212-966-9758. Personal E-mail: ellenlanyon@verizon.net.

LANZA, DONALD CHARLES, otolaryngologist, rhinologist; b. Yonkers, NY, Jan. 16, 1959; s. Donald Charles and Lenore Angela (Boccia) L.; m. Suzanne Terse Moons, Jan. 7, 1989; children: Douglas Reid, Andrew Joseph. BS in Biology, Fordham U., 1979; MS in Physiology, Georgetown U., 1980, rsch. toward PhD in Physiology, 1980—81; MD, SUNY, Bklyn., 1985. Diplomate Am. Bd. Otolaryngology, Med. Examiners; lic. Pa., Md., N.Y. General surgery intern Albany Med. Ctr. Hosp., NY, 1985—86, gen. surgery resident NY, 1986-87, otolaryngology resident NY, 1987-90; fellow rhinology and endoscopic sinus surgery Johns Hopkins Med. Instns., Balt., 1990-91, U. Pa., Phila., 1991; tchg. asst., physiology Georgetown U., 1980—81; instr. surgery Albany Med. Coll., 1989-90; instr. otolaryngology Johns Hopkins Med. Instns., Balt., 1990-91; lectr., otorhinolaryngology: head & neck surgery U. Pa., Phila., 1991, asst. prof. otolaryngology: head & neck surgery, 1991-96, assoc. prof. otolaryngology: head & neck surgery, 1996—99, dir., divsn. otolaryngology, dept. otorhinolaryngology, head & Neck Surgery, 1991—99; sect. head of nasal and sinus disorders, dept. otolaryngology & Communicative disorders Cleve. Clinic Found., Ohio, 1999—2004; dir., sect. head Sinus & Nasal Inst. Fla., P.A., St. Petersburg, 2004—. Mem. numerous coms. U. Pa., 1992, dept. otorhinolaryngology Hops. U. Pa., 1991; guest faculty Shadyside Hosp., Pitts., 1993, Health Comms., Inc., Princeton, N.J., 1993, Albany Med. Ctr., 1990-91; course dir. U. Pa., 1991-92; instr. Med. Coll. Ga., Boca Raton, Fla., 1991, Lahey Clinic, Boston, 1990, Tulane U., New Orleans, 1990, U. Mich., Ann Arbor, 1990; advanced pediatric life support Children's Hops. Albany Med. Ctr., 1990; mem. otolaryngology panel, U.S. Pharmacopeia, Silver Spring, Md., 1996-98; lectr. in field 1989-. Peer reviewer: Jour. Allergy and Clin. Immunology, 1992—, Am. Jour. Rhinology, 1991—; contbr. articles to profl. jours., chpts. to books. Mem. adv. bd., steering com., Sinus & Allergy Health Partnership. 2001-04. Recipient Otolaryngology Resident Rsch. award Albany Med. Ctr., 1988, 89. Fellow Am. Rhinology Soc. (mem. membership com., 1993-2000, cons. to bd. dirs. 1993-95, mem. rhinology think tank, 1994, bd. dir. 1995-98, mem. Cottle internat. rhinology centennial symposium, 1995-97, chair mem. com., 1996-2001, 2nd v.p., 1999, chair, com. on committees, 2000-01, chair nominating com., 2000-01, mem. long range planning com., 2000-02, first v.p., 2000-01, pres.-elect, 2001-02, pres. 2002-03, immediate past pres. 2003-04, Golden Head Mirror award), Am. Coll. Surgeons, Am. Acad. Otolaryngology-Head Neck Surgery (mem. rhinology & paranasal sinus com., 1997-99, mem. ethics com., 1997-99, mem. steering com. sinus & allergy health partnership, 2001-); mem. AMA, Internat. Soc. Otorhinolaryngolical Allergy and Immunology (founding mem. 1996), Am. Acad. Otolaryngic Allergy (assoc.), Am. Sleep Disorders Assn., Assn. Chemoreception Scis., Pa. Med. Soc., Pa. Acad. Otolaryngology, Phila. County Med. Soc., Ohio State Med. Soc., Northeast Ohio Otolaryngology-Head & Neck Soc., Soc. Univ. Otolaryngologists-Head & Neck Surgeons, Pan American Assn. Otorhinolaryngology-Head and Neck Surgery. Office: Sinus & Nasal Inst Fla PA Carillon Outpatient Ctr 900 Carillon Pkwy Ste 200 Saint Petersburg FL 33716

LANZA, ROBERT PAUL, medical scientist; b. Boston, Feb. 11, 1956; s. Samuel and Barbara (Corbett) L. BA, U. Pa., 1978, MD, 1983. Sr. scientist Biohybrid Techs., Shrewsbury, Mass., 1990-93, dir. transplantation biology, 1993-98; clin. assoc. prof. surgery Tufts U., 1994-95; sr. dir. tissue engring. and transplant medicine Advanced Cell Tech., Inc., Worcester, Mass., 1999-2000; med. dir., v.p. rsch. and sci. devel. Advanced Cell Tech. Group Inc., Worcester, Mass., 1999—. Rschr. Lab. of Richard Hynes, 1975, Gerald Edelman, 1976, Jonas Salk, 1978, B.F. Skinner, 1979-81, Christiaan Barnard, 1981-84; assoc. surgery Harvard Med. Sch., 1991-93; adj. prof. Inst. Regenerative Medicine, Wake Forest U. Sch. Medicine, 2004-. Author: Xeno, 2000; editor: Heart Transplantation, 1984, Medical Science and the Advancement of World Health, 1985, Procurement of Pancreatic Islets I, 1994, Immunomodulation of Pancreatic Islets II, 1994, Immunoisolation of Pancreatic Islets III, 1994, One World, 1996, Tissue Engineering/Cellular Medicine Series, 1995—, Yearbook of Cell and Tissue Transplantation, 1996—, Principles of Tissue Engineering, 1997, 3d edit., 2007, Encapsulated Cell Technology and Therapeutics, 1999, Methods of Tissue Engineering, 2001, Principles of Cloning, 2002, Handbook of Embryonic Stem Cells, 2004, Handbook of Adult and Fetal Stem Cells, 2004, Essentials of Stem Cell Biology, 2005, Methods in Enzymology: Embryonic Stem Cells, 2006, Methods in Enzymology: Adult Stem Cells, 2006, Principles of Regenerative Medicine, 2007; contbr. articles to profl. and lit. jours. Active Conservation Commn., Town of Clinton, 1998—, open space com., 1996-98; founder, dir. South Meadow Pond and Wildlife Assn., 1998—; bd. dirs. Clinton Greenway Conservation Trust, 2001-07. Prof. Howe Buck scholar, 1974-75, Benjamin Franklin scholar, 1975-78, Univ. scholar, 1976-83, Fulbright scholar, 1978-79; Hon. Christiaan Barnard fellow, 1981-84, Mary K. Iacocca Transplantation fellow, 1988-90; recipient Rave award in Medicine, WIRED, 2005. Achievements include cloned first endangered species; first to reverse aging using nuclear transfer; was part of team that cloned first human embryo for medical purposes; first to demonstrate "proof-of-principle" for therapeutic cloning; patents in field. Home: South Meadow Pond Island 35 S Meadow Rd Clinton MA 01510-4327 Address: Advanced Cell Tech 381 Plantation St Biotech V Worcester MA 01605 Office Phone: 508-756-1212 ext. 655. Fax: 508-756-4468. Business E-Mail: rlanza@advancedcell.com.

LANZEROTTI, LOUIS JOHN, physicist; b. Carlinville, Ill., Apr. 16, 1938; s. Emanuel Louis and Mary Pauline (Orienti) L.; m. Mary Yvonne DeWolf, June 19, 1965; children: Mary Yvonne, Louis DeWolf. BS, U. Ill., 1960; MA, Harvard U., 1963, PhD, 1965. Postdoctoral fellow Lucent Techs. Bell Labs., Murray Hill, NJ, 1965-67; mem. tech. staff AT&T Bell Labs., Murray Hill, NJ, 1967-82, Disting. mem. tech. staff, 1982—2002; Disting. rsch. prof. N.J. Inst. Tech., Newark, 2002—; physics cons. Lucent Techs., 2002—. Adj. prof. U. Fla., Gainesville, 1978-97; mem. polar rsch. bd. NRC, Washington, 1982-91, mem. space sci. bd., 1980-84, chmn. space studies bd., 1988-94, mem. ocean studies bd., 1995-99, chmn. bd. rev. Army Rsch. Lab., 1996-2000, report rev. com., 2000—, chmn. survey com. solar space physics rsch., 2001—; mem. phys. sci. com. NASA, Washington, 1975-79, chmn. space and earth adv. commn., 1984-88, mem. adv. coun., 1984-94; mem. adv. com. on future U.S. space program, 1990, mem. v.p.'s space policy adv. bd., 1992-93, v.p. blue ribbon adv. com. on redesign of space sta., 1993-94; mem. corp. Woods Hole Oceanographic Instn., 1993-2001; mem. governing bd. Am. Inst. Physics, 1997—, mem. exec. com. of governing bd., 2002-06; mem. Nat. Sci. Bd., NSF, 2004-. Co-author: Particle Diffusion in Rad. Belts, 1974; co-editor 3 books related to space physics, 1977, 79, 2004; contbr. more than 500 tech. papers to profl. jours. V.p. Harding Twp. Sch. Bd., NJ, 1982-90, com., 1993—, dep. mayor, 1999-2005, mayor, 2007. Recipient Antarctic Svc. medal U.S., 1979, Disting. Pub. Svc. award NASA, 1988, 94, Disting. Sci. medal NASA, 1998, Achievement award Blackburn Coll. Alumni Assn., 1993, COSPAR William Nordberg medal, 2004; mountain named in his honor in Antarctica; minor planet 5504 named in his honor. Fellow AIAA, IEEE, Am. Phys. Soc., Am. Geophys. Union, AAAS; mem. NAE, Internat. Acad. Astronautics. Office: Dept Physics NJ Inst Tech Newark NJ 07102

LANZEROTTI, MARY YVONNE, physicist, researcher; AB in Physics, Harvard-Radcliffe Colls., Cambridge, Mass., 1989; MPhil in Physics, U. Cambridge, England, 1990; MS, Cornell U., Ithaca, NY, 1996, PhD in Physics, 1996. Rsch. staff mem. T. J. Watson Rsch. Ctr. IBM, Yorktown Heights, NY, 1996—. Contbr. articles to profl. jours. Recipient Detur prize, Harvard-Radcliffe Colls., 1986, Jr. Sci. prize, 1988, IBM Rsch. Divsn. Outstanding Contbn. award, 1998, Outstanding Contbn. award, IBM Rsch. Divsn., 1998, 1st Plateau Patent Achievement award, IBM, 2003, Engr. of Yr. (NY sect.), IEEE Women in Engring. Soc., 2007, Recognition award (NY sect.), 2007; fellow, NSF, 1990—93; grantee, AT&T, 1990—96; scholar, Fed. Employee Edn. and Assistance, Wash., 1988, The Winston Churchill Found. U.S., 1989—90; John Harvard scholarship, Harvard Coll., 1986—88, Elizabeth Cary Agassiz scholarship, Radcliffe Coll., 1987—88, Andrew Dickson White fellow, Cornell U., 1990—91, Spencer T. and Ann W. Olin Found. Grad. fellow, 1991—95. Mem.: IEEE (sr.; assoc. editor Lasers and Electro-Optics Soc. Newsletter 1995—2000, exec. editor Lasers and Electro-Optics Soc. Newsletter 2001—06, bd. govs. Laser and Electro-Optics Soc. 2003—05, co-editor Solid State Cirs. Soc. Newsletter 2005—, apptd. spectrum adv. bd. 2006—, spectrum rep. pub. svcs. and products bd., Women in Engring. award 2007, NY chpt. Engr. of Yr. award 2007, Lazers and Electro-optics Disting. Svc. award 2007,

Disting. Svc. award 2007), IEEE Computer Soc. (award of merit NY State chpt. 2006), Am. Phys. Soc. (com. careers and profl. devel. 2005—), Soc. Mayflower Descs. in State of NJ (life), Harvard Club of NYC, Phi Beta Kappa. Achievements include patent for digital instant camera with printer. Office: IBM T J Watson Rsch Ctr Route 134 1101 Kitchawan Rd Yorktown Heights NY 10598 Office Phone: 914-945-1347. Personal E-mail: marylanzerotti@yahoo.com.

LANZINGER, JUDITH ANN, state supreme court justice; b. Toledo, Apr. 2, 1946; m. Robert C. Lanzinger, Jr., 1967; 2 children. BA in Edn., U. Toledo, 1968, JD, 1977; MS in Jud. Studies, Nat. Jud. Coll., U. Nev., Reno, 1992. Bar: Ohio, U.S. Supreme Ct., U.S. Dist. Ct. for Northern Dist. of Ohio, U.S. Dist. Ct. for Eastern Dist. of Mich., Sixth Circuit Ct. of Appeals. Atty. environmental law Toledo Edison Co., 1978—81; atty. employment law and litigation Shumaker, Loop and Kendrick, 1981—85; judge Toledo Municipal Ct., 1985—88, Lucas County Common Pleas Ct., 1989—2003, Ohio Sixth Dist. Ct. of Appeals, 2003—04; justice Ohio Supreme Ct., 2005—. Adjunct prof. U. Toledo Coll. of Law, 1988—; prof. Nat. Jud. Coll., 1990—; mem. Ohio Criminal Sentencing Commn., 1991—97; co-chair Public Ed. and Awareness Task Force Ohio Cts. Futures Commn., 1996—2000; chair Ohio Jud. Coll., 2000—01; former mem. Ohio Supreme Ct. Bd. of Grievances and Discipline; chair Commn. Rules of Superintendence, Ohio Cts., 2006—. Recipient Superior Jud. Service award, Ohio Supreme Ct., 1985, Arabella Babb Mansfield award, Toledo Women's Bar Assn., 1995, Service to Judicial Ed. award, Ohio Jud. Coll., 2002, Golden Gavel award, Ohio Common Pleas Judges' Assn., 2002. Fellow: Ohio Bar Found.; mem.: Thurgood Marshall Assn., Am. Judicature Soc., Nat. Assn. of Women Judges, Am. Judges Assn., Ohio Bar Assn., Morrison R. Waite Am. Inn of Ct. (pres. 2000—02). Office: Ohio Supreme Ct 65 S Front St Columbus OH 43215-3431 Office Phone: 614-387-9090.

LANZINGER, KLAUS, language educator; b. Woergl, Tyrol, Austria, Feb. 16, 1928; arrived in U.S., 1971, naturalized, 1979; m. Aida Schuessl, June, 1954; children: Franz, Christine. BA, Bowdoin Coll., 1951; PhD, U. Innsbruck, Austria, 1952. Rsch. asst. U. Innsbruck, 1957-67; assoc. prof. modern langs. U. Notre Dame, Ind., 1967-77, prof., 1977-97, prof. emeritus, 1997—. Resident dir. fgn. study program, Innsbruck, 1969-71, 76-78, 82-85; acting chmn. dept. Modern and Classical Langs., U. Notre Dame, fall 1987, chmn. dept. German and Russian, 1989-96. Author: Epik im amerikanischen Roman, 1965, Jason's Voyage: The Search for the Old World in Am. Lit., 1989; editor: Americana-Austriaca, 5 vols., 1966-83; contbr. articles to profl. jours. Fgn. Student scholar Bowdoin Coll., 1950-51; Fulbright Rsch. grantee U. Pa., 1961; U. Notre Dame Summer Rsch. grant Houghton Libr., Harvard U., 1975, 81; named to Internat. Order of Merit, 2001; recipient Lifetime Achievement award Internat. Biographical Ctr., Cambridge, Eng., 2007. Mem. MLA, Deutsche Gesellschaft für Amerikastudien, Thomas Wolfe Soc. (Zelda Gitlin Lit. prize 1993). Home: 52703 Helvie Dr South Bend IN 46635-1215 Office: Dept German Russian Langs & Lits U Notre Dame Notre Dame IN 46556

LANZINO, GIUSEPPE, physician; b. Cosenza, Italy, Jan. 6, 1965; arrived in US, 1992; MD, U. Bologna, Italy, 1989. Rsch. fellow dept. neurosurgery U. Pitts., 1990—91, U. Va., Charlottesville, 1992—94, resident dept. neurosurgery, 1994—97; endovascular fellow dept. neurosurgery U. Buffalo, 1997—99; sr. registrar dept. neurosurgery Plymouth (Eng.) Hosp., 1999—2000; chief resident dept. neurosurgery U. Va., Charlottesville, 2000—01; cerebrovascular fellow Barrow Neurol. Inst., 2001—02; assoc. prof. dept. neurosurgery U. Ill. Coll. Medicine, Peoria, 2002—. Fellow Am. Coll. Angiology; mem. Soc. Critical Care, Am. Heart Assn., N.Y. Acad. Scis. Avocations: history of medicine, history of neurosurgery, soccer. Home: 1324 Independence Ct Metamora IL 61548 Office: Ill Neurol Inst Dept Neurosurgery 530 NE Glen Oak Ave Peoria IL 61637-0001 Office Phone: 309-676-0766. Business E-Mail: lanzino@uic.edu.

LANZKRON, ROLF WOLFGANG, manufacturing executive; b. Hamburg, Germany, Dec. 9, 1929; arrived in US, 1951, naturalized, 1961; s. Aron Artur and Hanna (Farbstein) Lanzkron; m. Amy Virginia Yarri, Mar. 5, 1961; children: Paul Joshua, Sophie Miriam, Lisa Rachel. BS, Milw. Sch. Engring., 1953; MS, U. Wis., 1955, PhD, 1956. Registered profl. engr., Calif. Computer designer Univac Sperry Rand, St. Paul, 1956-58; guidance and control systems integrations staff Martin Marietta, Orlando, Fla., 1958-61, sys. engr. Balt., 1961-68; advanced chief command svc. module flight project divsn. NASA Manned Spacecraft Ctr., Apollo Program, Houston, 1963; graphic ops. mgr. Raytheon Co., Marlborough, Mass., 1968-82, dep. dir. air traffic control, 1982-92, dir. air traffic control, 1992-95; pres. RWL Assocs. Cons., Gloucester, Mass., 1995—. With Israeli Army, 1948—51. Recipient Outstanding Achievement award, NASA, 1964, Spl. Svc. award, 1966, Clifford Eurto Medallion award, 1995. Mem.: IEEE, AIAA, Am. Mgmt. Assn., Am. Math. Soc., Sigma Xi. Home and Office: RWL Assocs Cons 11 Island Ave 1811 Miami Beach FL 33139 Office Phone: 410-484-3209.

LANZNAR, HOWARD S., lawyer; b. Champaign, Ill., Aug. 15, 1955; BA, Amherst Coll., 1977; JD, U. Chgo., 1983. Bar: Ill. 1983. Ptnr. Katten Muchin Zavis Rosenman, Chgo. Mem.: ABA, Chgo. Bar Assn., Lincoln Park Zoological Soc. Office: Katten Muchin Zavis Rosenman 525 W Monroe St Chicago IL 60661 Office Phone: 312-902-5696, 312-577-8798. E-mail: howard.lanznar@kmzr.com.

LANZONE, JIM, Internet company executive; BA, UCLA; JD/MBA, Emory U., Atlanta. Product mktg. position KnowX.com (divsn. of Thomson Corp.); co-founder, pres. eTour (acquired by Ask.com), 1997—2001; v.p. product mgmt. to sr. v.p., gen. mgr. US IAC Search & Media (Ask.com), Oakland, Calif., 2001—06, CEO, 2006—. Office: IAC Search & Media 555 12th St Ste 500 Oakland CA 94607

LAO, DEBANG, electrical engineer, researcher; s. Huixing Lao; m. Zhiyu Han; 1 child, Yi. B, U. Sci. and Tech., Hefei, China, 1988, M, 1993; PhD, N.J. Inst. Tech., Newark, 2003. Asst. elec. engr. Beijing New-Product Co., Beijing, 1988—90; elec. engr. Beijing Astron. Obs., Beijing, 1993—98; rsch. engr. Intelligent Automation, Inc., Rockville, Md., 2004—07; electrical engr. Sci. & Engring. Svcs., Inc., Columbia, Md., 2007—. Engr. Zhongshan Station of China, 1994—96. Contbr. articles to profl. jours. Mem.: Alpha Epsilon Lambda. Achievements include patents for an illustrator for playing music.

LAO, JOSEPH R., humanities educator, researcher; b. Bay Shore, NY, Sept. 29, 1955; s. Mary and Israel Lao; m. Deborah E Bynoe-Lao, Feb. 19, 2000; 1 child, Asa K. BA, LI U., 1973—78; MA, Columbia Univeristy, 1979—85; PhD, Columbia U., 1992—99. Adj. assoc. prof. of psychology and edn. Teachers Coll., Columbia U., NYC, 2003—; adj. asst. prof. Hunter Coll., NYC, 2002—. Pres. Internat. Ctr. Accelerated Devel., 2004—06, Accelerated Devel. Ctr. Internat., 2006—. Membership reviewer United Way of NY, 1999—2002; bd. mem. Lincoln Sq. Neighborhood Ctr., Inc., 2004—, Bronx Cmty. Health Network, 2006—. Mem.: APA (internat. divsn.), Am. Ednl. Rsch. Assn., N.Y. Acad. Scis. (life). Buddhist. Avocations: horseback riding, chess. Office: Tchrs Coll Human Devel Dept 525 West 120th St New York NY 10027 Office Phone: 212-678-3861. E-mail: jrl19@columbia.edu.

LAO, KENNY, restaurant manager; b. Pasadena, Calif., 1977; MBA, NYU Stern Sch. Bus., 2004. Worked at Nobu, Tribeca Grill, Montrachet; spl. projects dir. Myriad Restaurant Group, NYC; founder Rickshaw Dumping Bar, NYC, 2005—. Named one of 30 Under 30, NY Daily News, 2006, 40 Under 40, Crain's NY Bus., 2007; winner, Maximum Exposure Bus. Plan Competition, NYU Stern Sch. Bus., 2004. Office: Rickshaw Dumpling Bar 61 W 23rd St New York NY 10010 Office Phone: 212-924-9220. Office Fax: 212-924-9229. E-mail: info@rickshawdumplings.com.*

LAO, LANG LI, nuclear scientist, physicist; b. Hai Duong, Vietnam, Jan. 28, 1954; came to US, 1972; s. Thich Cuong and Boi Phan (Loi) L.; m. Ngan Hua, Dec. 22, 1979; children: Bert J., Brian J. BS, MS, Calif. Inst. Tech., Pasadena, 1976; MS, U. Wis., 1977, PhD, 1979. Staff scientist Oak Ridge Nat. Lab., Tenn., 1979-81, TRW, Redondo Beach, Calif., 1981-82; mgr. integrated modeling br. Gen. Atomics, San Diego, 1982—. Contbr. articles to sci. jours. Recipient award for Excellence in Plasma Physics Rsch. Am. Physical Society, 1994 Fellow Am. Phys. Soc. (co-recipient excellence in plasma physics rsch. award 1994). Achievements include rsch. in equilibrium analysis of magnetic fusion plasma physics experiments; developed computer code essential for successful operation and interpretation of tokamak fusion experiments. Office: General Atomics 3550 General Atomics Ct San Diego CA 92121-1122

LAPAGLIA, ANTHONY, actor; b. Adelaide, Australia, Jan. 31, 1959; m. Gia Carides, Sept. 1998; 1 child, Bridget. Actor: (films) Cold Steel, 1987, God's Payroll (Phone Calls), 1988, Slaves of New York, 1989, Mortal Sins, 1990, Betsy's Wedding, 1990, Criminal Justice, 1990, He Said, She Said, 1991, One Good Cop, 1991, 29th Street, 1991, Keeper of the City, 1992, Whispers in the Dark, 1992, Innocent Blood, 1992, The Custodian, 1993, So I Married an Axe Murderer, 1993, Killer, 1994, Lucky Break, 1994, The Client, 1994, Mixed Nuts, 1994, Empire Records, 1995, Chameleon, 1995, Commandments, 1996, Brilliant Lies, 1996, Trees Lounge, 1996, Phoenix, 1998, The Repair Shop, 1998, Summer of Sam, 1999, Sweet and Lowdown, 1999, Company Man, 2000, Looking for Alibrandi, 2000, The House of Mirth, 2000, Autumn in New York, 2000, Jack the Dog, 2001, Lantana, 2001, The Bank, 2001, The Salton Sea, 2002, Dead Heat, 2002, I'm With Lucy, 2002, The Guys, 2002, Manhood, 2003, Happy Hour, 2003, Spinning Boris, 2003, The Architect, 2006, Played, 2006, (voice) Happy Feet, 2006,: (plays) A View From the Bridge (Tony award for Best Performance Male in a Drama, 1998); (TV miniseries) Murder One: Diary of a Serial Killer, 1997; (TV films) Police Story: Gladiator School, 1988, Frank Nitti: The Enforcer, 1988, The Brotherhood, 1991, Black Magic, 1992, Past Tense, 1994, Never Give Up: The Jimmy V. Story, 1996, Garden of Redemption, 1997, Black and Blue, 1999, Lansky, 1999, The Other Side, 2001; (TV series) Normal, Ohio, 2000, Frasier, 2000, 2002—04, Without a Trace, 2002—06 (Gloden Globe award for best actor in a dramatic series, 2004); exec. prodr., actor: (films) Winter Solstice, 2006; exec. prodr.: (TV films) The Away Game, 2004.*

LAPALOMBARA, JOSEPH, political science educator, industrial management educator; b. Chgo., May 18, 1925; s. Louis and Helen (Teutonico) LaP.; m. Lyda Mae Ecke, June 22, 1947 (div.); children— Richard, David, Susan; m. Constance Ada Bezer, June, 1971. AB, U. Ill., 1947, AM, 1950; AM (Charlotte Elizabeth Proctor fellow), Princeton U., 1952, PhD, 1954; student, U. Rome, 1952-53; MA (hon.), Yale U., 1964. Instr., then asst. prof. polit. sci. Oreg. State Coll., 1947-50; instr. politics Princeton U., 1952; mem. faculty Mich. State U., 1953-64, prof. polit. sci., 1958-64, head dept., 1958-63; prof. polit. sci. Yale U., 1964-96, prof. polit. sci. and mgmt., 1996—2001, Arnold Wolfers prof., 1969—2001, Arnold Wolfers prof. polit. sci. and mgmt. emeritus, 2001—, chmn. dept. polit. sci., 1974-78, 82-85, prof. Sch. Orgn. and Mgmt., 1979—84, 1997—2001; sr. rsch. scholar Yale Ctr. for Comparative Rsch., 2001—; dir. Instn. for Social and Policy Studies, 1987-92; chmn. Coun. Comparative and European Studies, 1966-71; cultural attache, first sec. U.S. embassy, Rome, 1980-81. Vis. prof. U. Florence, Italy, 1957-58, U. Calif.-Berkeley, 1962, Columbia U., 1966-67, U. Turin, 1974, U. Catania, 1974, John Cabot U., 2003, LUISS, Rome, 2003; cons. FCDA, 1956, Carnegie Corp., 1959, Brookings Instn., 1962, Ford Found., 1965-76, Twentieth Century Fund, 1965-69, AID, 1967-68, Fgn. Svc. Inst., 1968-72, 74-76, Ednl. Testing Svc., 1970-75, Rohm & Haas, 1975-76, GE, 1978-80, Alcoa, 1978-80, Union Carbide, 1981-92, Ente Nazionale Idrocarburi, 1983-93, Montedison, 1984-85, Guardian Industries, 1990-93, Praxair, 1992—, Swiss Bank Corp., 1994-99, Athena, 1994-95, Richard Medley Advisors, 1995-2001, Telecom Italia, 1996-99, S.I.A.D., 1999—, Open Soc. Inst., 2004—; sr. rsch. assoc. Conf. Bd. N.Y., 1976-81; pres. Italian-Am. Multimedia Corp. N.Y., 1988—; bd. dirs. Transparency Internat.-U.S.A., 1994—. Author: The Initiative and Referendum in Oregon, 1950, The Italian Labor Movement: Problems and Prospects, 1957, Guide to Michigan Politics, rev. edit, 1960, (with Alberto Spreafico) Elezioni e Comportamento Politico in Italia, 1963, Bureaucracy and Political Development, 1963, Interest Groups in Italian Politics, 1964, Italy: The Politics of Planning, 1966, (with Myron Weiner) Political Parties and Political Development, 1966, Clientela e Parentela, 1967, Burocracia y desarrolo politico, 1970, Crises and Sequences of Political Development, (with others), 1972, Politics Within Nations, 1974, Multinational Corporations and National Elites: A Study in Tensions, 1975, (with Stephen Blank) Multinational Corporations in Comparative Perspective, 1976, Multinational Corporations and Developing Countries, 1979, A Politica nos Interior das Nações, 1982, Democracy, Italian Style, 1987, Democrazia all'italiana, 1988, Die Italiener: oder Demokratie als Lebenskunst, 1988, Democratie à l'italienne, 1990, SIAD at Seventy Five, 2002; bd. editors Midwest Jour. Polit. Sci, 1956-57, Yale U. Press, 1965-72, 73-76, ABC-CL10, 1976—, Global Perspectives, 1983-2000; mem. editorial bd. Comparative Politics, 1968—, Jour. Comparative and European Studies, 1969—, Am. Jour. Polit. Sci, 1976-80, Italian Jour., 1988, Yale Rev., 1993—; editor series comparative politics Prentice-Hall Co., 1971-85; editor Jour. Internat. Bus. Edn., 2001-; mem. editorial adv. bd. Jour. Comparative Adminstrn, 1970-74, Adminstrn. and Soc, 1974—; adv. bd. ABC Polit. Sci; N.Am. editor: Mediterranean Observer, 1981-86; editor in chief Italy, Italy, 1988—; contbr. articles to profl. jours. Mem. exec. com. Inter Univ. Consortium Polit. Rsch., 1966-70; mem. staff Social Sci. Rsch. Coun., 1966-73; chmn. West European fgn. area fellowship program Social Sci. Rsch. Coun.-Am. Coun. Learned Socs., 1972-74; bd. dirs. Mich. Citizenship Clearing House, 1955; mem. internat. coun. Ctr. for Strategic and Internat. Studies, 1990—; mem. Coun. on Fgn. Rels.; U.S. com. Am. Fgn. Policy, 1996—2005. Decorated knight comdr. Order of Merit, Republic of Italy; Fulbright scholar, 1952-53, 57-58, Penfield scholar U. Pa., 1953; fellow Social Sci. Rsch. Coun., 1952-53, Ctr. Advanced Study Behavioral Scis., 1961-62, Rockefeller Found., 1963-64, Ford Found., 1969, Guggenheim Found., 1971-72, European U. Inst., 1996, Wissenschaftszentrum Berlin, 1996; recipient Guido Dorso prize, Italy, 1984, Medal of Honor, Italian Constitutional Ct., 1993, Presidency of Italian Republic, 1993, Disting. Alumni Achievement award U. Ill., 2003. Mem. Am. Acad. Arts and Scis., Conn. Acad. Arts and Scis., Am. Acad. in Rome (trustee 1984-90), Social Sci. Rsch. Coun. (com. comparative politics 1958-72), Am. Polit. Sci. Assn. (exec. coun. 1963-65, exec. com. 1967-68, v.p. 1979-80, mem. conf. group on Italian politics and soc. 1978, conf. pres. 1984-85, Career Achievement award 2005), Am. Acad. Polit. and Social Sci., Soc. for Italian Hist. Studies, Società Italiana di Studi Elettorali, Consiglio Italiano di Scienze Sociali, Phi Beta Kappa, Phi Kappa Phi, Phi Eta Sigma, Yale Club of N.Y., Elizabethan Club. Home: 50 Huntington St New Haven CT 06511-1333 Office Phone: 203-432-5580. Business E-Mail: joseph.lapalombara@yale.edu.

LAPE, ROBERT CABLE, broadcast journalist; b. Akron, Ohio; s. C. Robert and Mary Elizabeth (Cable) L.; m. Marcia Giesy, 1954 (div. 1969); children: Debra, Robert S., Alida, Douglas; m. Eve Bergman, Feb. 14, 1982 (dec. 2002); m. Joanna Pruess, Sept. 19, 2004. BS in Journalism and Radio Speech, Kent State U., 1955. Reporter, asst. news dir. WCUE Radio, Akron, 1954-56; news dir. WICE Radio, Providence, 1956-61; corr., news dir. WBZ Radio, Boston, 1961-68, WABC-TV, NYC, 1968-82; critic, writer on food and travel, lectr. WABC, WCBS, Crain's N.Y. Bus., N.Y. Law Jour., Agenda N.Y., NYC, 1983—2002, LaCucina Italiana, N.Y. Pocket Guide, The Record (N.J.), Foodwinetravel.com, 1999—. Bd. dirs. Internat. Food Media Conf., N.Am., 1986—; anchor The CPA Report, 1999-2000. Author: Epicurean Rendezvous, 1990-96, Bob Lape's Restaurant Index, 1987-91; co-author: (with Joanna Pruess) Seduced by Bacon, 2006. Nat. judge food March of Dimes, 1991—; spkr., M.C. Crohn's and Colitis Found., N.Y., Nat. Cancer Soc.; judge James Beard Found. Awards. Decorated chevalier d'honneur Swiss Ordre du Channe, 2004; Recipient Emmy award for TV News Coverage, 1980, 1st Ann. Lifetime Achievement award N.Y. State Restaurant Assn., 1998. Mem. SAG, AFTRA, N.Y. Press. Club, Broadcasters' Found., Broadcasters' Hall of Fame, Assn. Italian Sommeliers, Commanderie de Cordon Bleu de France, Compagnons de Beaujolais, Friars Club, Lambs Club. Avocations: travel, reading. Office Phone: 718-694-2050. E-mail: foodbob@aol.com.

LA PENTA, ROBERT VINCENT, venture capitalist; b. Yonkers, NY, Aug. 20, 1945; s. John Peter and Nancy Ann (Delanni) La P.; 1 child, Robert Vincent Jr. BBA, Iona Coll., 1967, LHD (hon.), 2000. CPA, Tex. Sr. acct. Deloitte Haskins & Sells, NYC, 1967-72; corp. v.p., controller Loral Corp., NYC, 1972—96; corp. v.p., CFO C4ISR Group Lockheed Martin, 1996—97; pres., CFO, bd. mem. L-3 Communications, 1997—2005; founder, chmn., CEO L-1 Investment Partners, Stamford, Conn., 2005—. Bd. dirs. Travel Video Systems, Inc., NYC, 1984; chmn. Viisage, 2005-. Trustee Iona Coll. Mem. Am. Inst. CPA's, Fin. Execs. Inst., Assn. Govt. Fin. Execs. Office: L-1 Investment Partners 177 Broad St Stamford CT 06901

LAPERRIERE, JACQUES (JOSEPH HUGHES LAPERRIERE), professional hockey coach, retired professional hockey player; b. Rouyn-Noranda, Que., Can., Nov. 22, 1941; m. Elaine Laperriere; children: Martin, Daniel, Michele. Defenseman Montreal Canadiens, 1963—74, asst. coach, 1981—97, Boston Bruins, 1997—2001, NY Islanders, 2001—03, NJ Devils, 2003—07, spl. assignment coach, 2007—. Recipient Calder Meml. Trophy, 1964, James Norris Meml. Trophy, 1966, NHL All-Star Team, 1964—66. Achievements include being a member of 6 Stanley Cup Championship teams; being inducted into the Hockey Hall of Fame, 1987. Office: NJ Devils 33 Fl 744 Broad St Newark NJ 07102*

LAPHAM, LEWIS HENRY, editor, television personality, writer; b. San Francisco, Jan. 8, 1935; s. Lewis Abbot and Jane (Foster) L.; m. Joan Brooke Reeves, Aug. 10, 1972; children: Lewis Andrew, Elizabeth Delphina, Winston Peale. Grad., Hotchkiss Sch., 1952; BA, Yale U., 1956; postgrad., Cambridge U., 1956—57; LLD, Hampden-Sydney Coll., Va. Reporter San Francisco Examiner, 1957-60, N.Y. Herald Tribune, 1960-62; author, editor USA-1, NYC, 1962, Saturday Evening Post, NYC, 1963-67; writer Life mag., Harper's, NYC, 1968-70; mng. editor Harper's, NYC, 1971-75, editor, 1975—81, 1983—2006, Lapham's Quar., NYC, 2006—. Host (TV weekly series) Bookmark, Sta. PBS-TV; host, author (documentary series) America's Century; (documentary film) The American Ruling Class; author: (essays) Fortune's Child, 1980, Money and Class in America, 1988, Imperial Masquerade, 1989, The Wish for Kings, 1993, Hotel America, 1995, Waiting for the Barbarians, 1997, The Agony of Mammon, 1999, Lapham's Rules of Influence, 1999, Lights, Camera, Democracy!, 2001, Theater of War, 2002, 30 Satires, 2003, Gag Rule: On the Stifling of Dissent and the Suppression of Democracy, 2004 With the Beatles, 2005, Pretensions to Empire: Notes on the Criminal Folly of the Bush Administration, 2006. Bd. dirs. Americans for Libraries Coun., The Harry Frank Guggenheim Found. Mem. Coun. on Fgn. Rels., Century Assn., The Blind Book Club, Inc. Office: Lapham's Quarterly 33 Irving Pl 8th Fl New York NY 10003 Office Phone: 212-590-6871. Business E-Mail: lhl@laphamsquarterly.org.

LAPHEN, MICHAEL W., computer services company executive; b. 1950; BS in Acctg., Pa. State U., 1972; MBA, U. Pa., Phila.; postgraduate student, Temple U., Phila. With Computer Scis. Corp., El Segundo, Calif., 1977—, pres. systems group Integrated Systems Divsn., 1992—98, pres. fed. sector Civil Group, 1998—2000, pres. European group, 2000—03, v.p. El Segundo, Calif., 2001, pres., COO, 2003—07, pres., CEO, 2007—, chmn., 2007—. With USAF. Mem.: Nat. Def. Indsl. Assn., Armed Forces Comm. and Electronics Assn., Info. Tech. Assn. Am. Office: Computer Scis Corp 2100 E Grand Ave El Segundo CA 90245 Office Phone: 310-615-0311.*

LAPIDUS, ARNOLD, mathematician, educator; b. Bklyn., Nov. 6, 1933; s. Morris and Mollie L. m. Nancy Beatrice Latner, Aug. 9, 1952 BS, Bklyn. Coll., 1956; MS, PhD, NYU, 1967. Rsch. scientist Courant Inst., NYC, 1956—68; math. analyst computer application Goddard Inst. for Space Studies, NYC, 1968—70, math. analyst programming methods, 1970—71, sr. mem. tech. staff computer scis., 1971—73; assoc. prof. quantitative analysis Fairleigh Dickinson U., Teaneck, NJ, 1973—83, prof., chair dept. computer and decision sys., 1983—85; sr. engr. Singer Electronic Sys. Corp., Little Falls, NJ, 1986—87; pvt. practice Englewood, 1987—. Vol. mathematician U. Medicine Dentistry N.J., Newark, 1998-2001; owner Advanced Math. Co., Englewood, 1987-2000. Contbr. articles to profl. publs. Mem. AAAS, AAUP, Math. Assn. Am., Am. Math. Soc., Soc. Indsl. and Applied Math Home and Office: 401 Fergus Way Tobyhanna PA 18466-4068 Personal E-mail: alapidus@aol.com.

LAPIDUS, JULES BENJAMIN, educational association administrator; b. Chgo., May 1, 1931; s. Leo R. and Lillian D. LaPidus; m. Anne Marie Liebman, June 8, 1970; children: Steven, Amy, Mark, Marilyn. BS, U. Ill., 1954; MS, U. Wis., 1957, PhD, 1958. Prof. medicinal and pharm. chemistry Ohio State U., 1958-84; assoc. dean Grad. Sch., 1972-74; dean Grad. Sch., 1974-84; vice provost for research, 1974-82; pres. Council Grad. Schs., 1984-2000. Mem. pharmacology and toxicology tng. com. NIH, 1965-67, pharmacology program com., 1971-74; mem. Grad. Record Exam. Bd., 1982-2000.

LAPIDUS, MITCHELL, lawyer; b. Miami, Fla., July 7, 1962; s. Robert and Mabel (Roth) L.; m. Laura B. Shapiro, June 9, 1992. BA cum laude, NYU, 1983, JD, 1986, LLM in Taxation, 1989. Bar: NY 1987. Assoc. Tanner, Propp, Fersko & Sterner, NYC, 1986-91; ptnr. Tanner, Propp & Fersko, NYC, 1992, Propp, Lubell & Lapidus, LLP, NYC. Pres. NY Tax Study Grp., Inc., 2000—06. Named one of Top 100 Attys., Worth mag., 2005. Mem. ABA, Phi Beta Kappa, Pi Sigma Alpha, Omicron Delta Epsilon. Democrat. Jewish. Avocations: sports, general reading, swimming. Office: Propp Lubell & Lapidus LLP Times Sq Plz 1500 Broadway 21st Fl New York NY 10036 Office Phone: 212-986-7714. Office Fax: 212-687-0056.*

LAPIERRE, DOMINIQUE, writer, historian, philanthropist; b. Chatelaillon, France, July 30, 1931; s. Jean and Luce (Andreota) L.; m. Dominique Conchon, Apr. 5, 1980. Student (Fulbright Exchange scholar), U. Polit. Sci., Paris, 1950-51; BA, Lafayette Coll., Easton, Pa., 1952, LittD (hon.), 1982. Sr. editor Paris Match News mag., 1955—67. Author: The City of Joy, 1985, Beyond Love, 1990, A Thousand Suns, 1999, Five Past Midnight in Bhopal, 2002; co-author: Is Paris Burning?, 1964, ...Or I'll Dress You In Mourning, 1967, O Jerusalem, 1971, Freedom at Midnight, 1975, The Fifth Horseman, 1980, Is New York Burning?, 2004. Founder, pres. Action Aid for Lepers' Children of Calcutta. Decorated comdr. Order of Tastevin, grand cross Civil Order of Social Solidarity (Spain), chevalier Legion of Honor (France); recipient Christopher award, US, 1986, 02, Gold medal City of Calcutta for humanitarian action, 1987, Rainbow

Internat. award UN, 1999, Internat. Peace prize Vatican, 1999, Gold medal humanitarian action City of Milan, 2006. Home: 37 rue Charles-Laffitte 92200 Neuilly-sur-Seine France Office: care Morton Janklow Lit Agy 445 Park Ave New York NY 10022-2606 Office Phone: 33 4 94971731. Business E-Mail: d.lapierre@wanadoo.fr.

LAPIERRE, WAYNE R., JR., lobbyist; b. Schenectady, NY, Nov. 8, 1949; BA, Siena Coll.; MA, Boston Coll., in Govt. & Politics. State liaison NRA, Fairfax, Va., 1978—79, dir. state & local affairs, 1979—80, exec. dir. Inst. for Legis. Action, 1986—91, exec. v.p., CEO, 1991—. Mem. bd. dirs. Am. Assn. of Political Consultants. Author: Guns, Crime, and Freedom, 1994, Guns, Freedom, and Terrorism, 2003, Corporate Fascism: How America's Companies Are Butting into the Private Lives of Their Employees, 2005, The Global War on Your Guns: Inside the UN Plan To Destroy the Bill of Rights, 2006; co-author (with James Jay Baker): Shooting Straight: Telling the Truth About Guns in America, 2002. Roman Catholic. Office: NRA 11250 Waples Mill Rd Fairfax VA 22030

LAPIN, DANIEL, rabbi; b. 1950; Studied Math., Econ., Philosophy and Theology, Jerusalem and London. Cert. ordained Rabbi. Founding Rabbi Pacific Jewish Ctr., Venice, Calif.; syndicated radio host Toward Tradition, Seattle; co-chmn. Conservative Alliance of Jews and Christians. Vis. lectr. Christian Coalition, US Army, Harvard Law Sch., Family Rsch. Coun. Contbr. articles to numerous profl. jours, mags. and newspapers incl. Wall Street Jour., National Review, Commentary, the American Enterprise, and the Washington Times; author: (nonfiction) America's Real War, Thou Shall Prosper, Buried Treasure. Named one of The Top 50 Rabbis in America, Newsweek Mag., 2007. Republican. Jewish.*

LAPIN, HARVEY I., lawyer; b. St. Louis, Nov. 23, 1937; s. Lazarus L. and Lillie L. Lapin; m. Cheryl A. Lapin; children: Jeffrey, Gregg. BS, Northwestern U., 1960, JD, 1963; LLM in Tax Law, Georgetown Law Ctr., Washington, 1967. CPA Ill.; bar: Ill. 1963, Fla. 1980, Wis. 1985, cert.: Fla. (tax lawyer). Atty. Office Chief Counsel, IRS, Washington, 1963-65; trial atty. Office Regional Counsel, IRS, Washington, 1965-68; from assoc. to ptnr. Fiffer & D'Angelo, Chgo., 1968-75; pres. Harvey I. Lapin, P.C., Chgo., 1975-83; mng. ptnr. Lapin, Hoff, Spangler & Greenberg, Chgo., 1983-88, Lapin, Hoff, Slaw & Laffey, Chgo., 1989-91; ptnr. Gottlieb and Schwartz, Chgo., 1992-93; prin. Harvey I. Lapin & Assocs., P.C., Northbrook, Ill., 1993—2003, Harvey I. Lapin, P.C. (formerly Harvey I. Lapin & Assocs., P.C.), Northbrook, 2004—. Instr. John Marshall Law Sch., 1969—; facility adv. lawyers asst. program Roosevelt U., Chgo.; mem. cemetery adv. bd. Ill. Comptr., 1974—96, 1999—; mem. IRS Gt. Lakes TE/EO Coun., 2001—. Asst. editor: Fed. Bar Jour., 1965—67; contbg. editor: (book) Cemetery and Funeral Service Business and Legal Guide; contbr. articles to profl. jours. Bd. mem. Cotswold Homeowners Assn., 1994—, pres., 1994—97, treas., 1997—; bd. mem. Art Alliance Contemporary Glass, 2006—, Midwest Contemporary Glass Arts Group, 2003—, pres., 2007—. Mem.: ABA, Chgo. Bar Assn., Ill. Bar Assn., Wis. Bar Assn., Fla. Bar Assn. Jewish. Office: Harvey I Lapin PC PO Box 1327 Northbrook IL 60065-1327 Business E-Mail: harv4law@sbcglobal.net.

LAPINE, JAMES ELLIOT, playwright, director; b. Mansfield, Ohio, Jan. 10, 1949; s. David Sanford and Lillian (Feld) L.; m. Sarah Marshall Kernochan, Feb. 24, 1985; 1 child, Phoebe BA, Franklin and Marshall Coll., Lancaster, Pa.; degree (hon.), Franklin and Marshall Coll., 1994; MFA, Calif. Inst. of Arts, Valencia. Author, dir.: (plays) Photograph, 1977 (Obie award 1977), Table Settings, 1980 (George Oppenheimer/Newsday award), Twelve Dreams, 1983, Sunday in the Park with George, 1984 (N.Y. Drama Critics' Circle award 1984, Pulitzer prize for drama 1984), Into the Woods, 1987 (Tony award 1988, N.Y. Drama Critics' Circle award 1988, Drama Desk award 1988), Falsettoland, 1990 (2 Tony awards 1992), Luck, Pluck and Virtue (La Jolla Playhouse), 1993, Passion, 1994 (Tony award 1994); dir.: March of the Falsettos, 1982, Merrily We Roll Along (La Jolla Playhouse), A Midsummer Night's Dream, A Winter's Tale, 1988, Golden Child, (Broadway revival) The Diary of Anne Frank, Earthly Possessions, 1999, (films) Impromptu, Passion, 1990, Life with Mikey, 1993, The 25th Annual Putnam County Spelling Bee, 2005 (Drama Desk award, ouststanding director of a musical, 2005). Recipient 4 Drama Desk awards, Outer Critics Circle award, Evening Standard award, Olivier award; Guggenheim fellow Mem. Dramatists Guild.

LAPINSKY, JOSEPH F., manufacturing executive; married; 2 daughters. MS in Indsl. Rels., W.Va. U., 1973; MBA in Mgmt., Youngstown State U., 1984. Early career positions include conditioning foreman Copperweld Steel Co., then ops., mgr. human resources, v.p. human resources, 1974-91, also exec. v.p.; ind. industry cons., 1991-95; gen. mgr. hot rolled bar ops. Republic Techs. Internat., Akron, Ohio, 1995-97, pres. Hot Rolled Bar divsn., 1997-98; pres., COO Republic Engineered Steels and Bar Techs., Akron, 1998—99; COO Republic Techs. Internat., Akron, 1999—2002; CEO, pres. Republic Engineered Products (formerly Republic Techs. Internat.), 2002—.

LAPIZ-BLUHM, MARIA DANET SANCHEZ, neuroscientist, medical/surgical nurse; d. Victor Infiesto and Flora Sanchez Lapiz. BSN, Cebu State Coll., Cebu City, Philippines, 1993; BS, U. Queensland, St. Lucia, Queensland, Australia, 1992, BS cum laude, 1994; PhD in Biomed. Scis., U. Nottingham, England, 2001. RN Philippine Regulatory Commn., Philippines, 1994, U.K. Coordinating Coun. for Nursing, Midwifery and Health Visitors, 2000. Rsch. asst. Cerebral and Sensory Functions Unit U. Queensland, Brisbane, 1993—94; asst. adminstrv. officer Asian Inst. Tech., Pathumthani, Thailand, 1995—97; rsch. trainee dept. pharmacology Karolinska Inst., Stockholm, 1997—97; tchg. asst. Sch. Biomed. Scis. U. Nottingham, 1997—2000, sr. tutor Sherwood Hall, 1998—2000; nurse Sherwood Nursing Home, Nottingham, 1998—2000; rsch. scientist H. Lundbeck A/S, Copenhagen, 2001—04; fellow U. Tex. Health Sci. Ctr., San Antonio, 2004—06, asst. prof. rsch., 2006—. Guest lectr. Cebu State Coll., Cebu City, 1995; lang. transl., cons. clin. trials ClinPhone (formerly the Allo Lang. Svcs.), Nottingham, 2000; guest lectr. Copenhagen U., 2003. Dir.(leader, organizer): (exhibition) Singles for Christ Discovery Weekend; leader, coord. (dance exhibition) ASEAN-European Summit in Copenhagen; contbr. articles to profl. jours. Leader Singles for Christ, Copenhagen, 2002—03. Recipient First Pl. Poster award, Biomedical Neurosci. Symposium, 2005, Young Investigator award, Mental Health Assn., 2006, 1st place, Ctr. Neuroscience Symposium, 2006, Young Scientist Travel award, Am. Soc. Pharm. and Exptl. Therapeutics, 2006; grantee, Brit. Assn. for Psychopharmacology, 1999, 2001, Australian Neuroscience Soc. and Cochlear Ltd., Australia, 1999, Sch. Biomed. Scis., U. Nottingham, 1999, 2000, Grad. Sch. Conf. Funds, U. Nottingham, 2000, Brit. Neuroscience Assn., 2000, Brit. Pharmacological Soc., 2001; scholar, U. Queensland, 1997—2001, Chancellors and Vice Principals of the U.K., 1997—2001, Neurology for Neuroscientists, 1999, 2000; Equity and Merit scholar, Australian Internat. Devel. Assistance Bur., Australia, 1990—94. Mem.: Philippine Nurses Assn., Brit. Pharmacol. Soc., Brit. Assn. for Psychopharmacology, Brit. Neurosci. Assn., Soc. for Neurosci. Roman Catholic. Avocations: travel, languages, dance, badminton/tennis, yoga. Personal E-mail: brains_md@hotmail.com.

LAPLANTE, KERRY L., pharmacist, educator; b. Buffalo, Dec. 3, 1973; BS in Biology, Canisius Coll., Buffalo, 1996; BS in Pharm. Scis., Wayne State U., Detroit, 2000, PharmD, 2002. Lic. pharmacist Mich., RI. Instr. Canisius Coll., Buffalo, 1997; postdoctoral fellow in infectious diseases, pharmacotherapy, clin. instr. Wayne State U., Detroit, 2002—04; clin. pharmacy specialist Detroit Receiving Hosp., 2002, Vets. Affairs Med. Ctr., Providence, 2004—; asst. prof. pharmacy U. RI, Kingston, 2004—. Presenter in field. Co-author: Antimicrobial Therapy and Vaccines Vol. II, 2d edit.; contbr. articles to profl. jours. Organizer Nat. Pharmacy Week Henry Ford Hosp., Detroit, 2001; vol. Roswell Pk. Cancer Inst., Buffalo, 1996—97; vol. Operation Immunization Walgreen, Dearborn, 2000; vol. Ask the Pharmacist St. Johns Riverview Hosp. Sr. Ctr., Detroit, 2000—01; vol. Get Smart About Your Heart, Bellville, 2001. Recipient Disting. Young Pharmacist award, Mich. Pharmacist Assn., 2004, Roland T. Lakey award, Wayne County Pharmacist Assn., 2005, Presdl. Svc. award, 2005; grantee, U RI, 2005, Am. Assn. Colls. Pharmacy, 2005—06, Cubist Pharms., 2005, 2006—07, RI-INBRE, 2005, 2006, Pfizer, 2006—07, VA Health Svcs. R&D Svc., 2006—; scholar, Wayne State U., 2002—04; George McCracken Infectious Diseases fellow, 2003. Mem.: Am. Coll. Clin. Pharmacy (mem. rels. com. 2005), Soc. Infectious Diseases Pharmacists (chairperson elections com. 2006—07), Am. Soc. Microbiology, RI Soc. Health Sys. Pharmacists. Home: 14 Cedar Pond Dr Apt 11 Warwick RI 02886 Office: U RI Dept Pharmacy Practice 144 Fogerty Hall Kingston RI 02881 Mailing: Vets Affairs Med Ctr Rsch Bldg # 35 830 Chalkstone Ave Providence RI 02908

LAPOINTE, LUCIE, research institute executive; b. Valleyfield, Que., Can., Dec. 23, 1954; d. Paul and Jeannette (Gagne) LaPointe; 1 child, Lauren LaPointe-Shaw. BSc in Biol. Scis., McGill U., Montreal, Can., 1977; MBA, U. Ottawa, Can., 1982. Tech. officer divsn. biol. scis. NRC, Ottawa, 1977—80, officer program svcs. secretariat, 1982—84, exec. mgr. pub. rels. and info. svcs., 1984—87, dir. mgmt. svcs. br., 1987—89, sec. gen., 1989—2001; v.p. adminstrn., sec.-treas. Pulp and Paper Rsch. Inst. Can., Pointe-Claire, Que., 2001—; exec. mem. Internat. Coun. for Sci. Contbr. articles to profl. jours. Avocations: reading, skiing. Office: PAPRICAN 570 boul St-Jean Pointe-Claire PQ Canada H9R 3J9 Home Phone: 514-693-5062; Office Phone: 514-630-4103. Business E-Mail: llapointe@videotron.ca.

LAPONCE, JEAN A., political scientist, educator; b. Decize, France, Nov. 1925; s. Fernand and Fernande (Ramond) L.; m. Joyce Price, July, 1950; children: Jean-Antoine, Marc, Patrice; m. Iza Fiszhaut, Apr. 10, 1972; 1 child, Danielle. Diploma, Inst. d'études politiques, Paris, 1947; PhD, UCLA, 1955; LLD (hon.), U. B.C., Can., 2003. Instr. U. Santa Clara, 1956; asst. prof. polit. sci. U. B.C., Can., Vancouver, 1956-61, assoc. prof., 1961-66, prof., 1966—; dir. Inst. Interethnic Rels. U. Ottawa, 1993-2001. Mem. grad. faculty Aichi Shukutoku U., 1994-97. Author: The Protection of Minorities, 1961, The government of France under the Fifth Republic, 1962, People vs Politics, 1970, Left and Right, 1981, Langue et territoire, 1984, Languages and Their Territories, 1987, Loi de Babel et autres régularités des rapports entre langue et politique, 2006. Fellow Royal Soc. Can. (pres. Acad. Humanities and Social Scis. 1988-91); mem. Can. Polit. Sci. Assn. (pres. 1972-73), Am. Polit. Sci. Assn., French Polit. Sci. Assn., Internat. Polit. Sci. Assn. (pres. 1973-76) Office: U BC Dept Polit Sci Vancouver BC Canada V6T 1Z1 Home Phone: 604-731-0823; Office Phone: 604-822-2832. Office Fax: 604-822-5540. Business E-Mail: jlaponce@interchange.ubc.ca.

LAPORTE, CLOYD, JR., retired lawyer, manufacturing executive; b. NYC, June 8, 1925; s. Cloyd and Marguerite (Raeder) L.; m. Caroline E. Berry, Jan. 22, 1949; children— Elizabeth, Marguerite, Cloyd III. AB, Harvard U., 1946, JD, 1949. Bar: N.Y. 1949. Assoc. mem. firm Cravath, Swaine & Moore, NYC, 1949-56; dir. adminstrn. Metals div. Olin Corp., NYC, 1957-66; legal counsel Dover Corp., NYC, 1966-93, sec., 1971-93. Dir. Putnam Hosp. Ctr., 2000—. 2d lt. A.C. AUS, WWII. Mem. Harvard Club (N.Y.C.). Home: Gipsy Trail Club Carmel NY 10512

LAPORTE, GERALD JOSEPH SYLVESTRE, lawyer; b. Windsor, Ont., Can., Oct. 16, 1946; came to U.S., 1948, naturalized, 1954; s. Rosaire Joseph and Catherine Rose (Sylvestre) L. BA, Sacred Heart Sem. Coll., 1968; STB, St. Paul U., Ottawa, Ont., 1971; BTh, U. Ottawa, 1971; MA, Georgetown U., 1974; JD, George Washington U., 1976. Bar: Mich. 1976, D.C. 1977. Legis. asst. to U.S. Congressman William J. Randall, Washington, 1971-75; law clk. to Judge U.S. Dist. Ct., Washington, 1976-77; assoc. Wilmer, Cutler & Pickering, Washington, 1977-82; spl. counsel Office Gen. Counsel, SEC, Washington, 1982—84, sr. spl. counsel, 1984—85, counsel to commr., 1985-87; assoc. Nutter, McClennen & Fish, Washington, 1987—88; assoc., then ptnr. Patton Boggs, LLP, Washington, 1988-96; counsel Hogan & Hartson LLP, Washington, 1996—2002; chief Office of Small Bus. Policy, SEC, Washington, 2002—. Chmn. steering com. sect. corp., fin. and securities law D.C. Bar, 1997-98; vice chmn. securities law & disclosure com., Nat. Assn. Bond lawyers, 1994-96. Mng. editor George Washington Law Rev., 1975-76. Mem. Arlington County Hist. Affairs and Landmark Rev. Bd., 2001—. Mem. ABA (sect. on bus. law, fed. regulation of securities com.), Arlington Hist. Soc. Inc. (bd. dirs. 1997—, pres. 2001-03, 05—06). Democrat. Roman Catholic. Home: 3154 Key Blvd Arlington VA 22201-5037 Office: SEC 100 F St NE Washington DC 20549-3628 Home Phone: 703-527-6783. Personal E-mail; g.laporte@verizon.net. Business E-Mail: LaporteG@SEC.gov.

LAPORTE, LEO, writer, blogger, radio personality; Radio talk show host, disc jockey KGO, KSFO, KNBR, KLOK, KMBY, San Francisco, Monterey, 1977—98; tech. mng. editor, chief corr., The Site MSNBC, 1996—97; mng. editor Ziff Davis TV, 1994—99; host, mng. editor TechTV, 1998—2004; radio talk show host Premiere Radio Networks, 2004—; host, mng. editor Call for Help tech. TV show, 2004—; blog host Leoville.com. Co-author (with Gina Smith): 101 Computer Answers You Need to Know, 1995; author: Technology Almanac. Named one of Top 25 Web Celebs, Forbes mag., 2007; recipient Best Newscast award, Computer Press Assn., 1996, Emmy award for The Site, 1997. Mailing: Box 1018 Petaluma CA 94953-1018 Business E-Mail: leo@leoville.com.*

LAPORTE, LEO FREDERIC, geologist, educator, paleontologist; b. Englewood, NJ, July 30, 1933; s. Leo Frederic and Edea (Giacobbe) L.; married, 1956 (div. 1983); children: Leo G., Eva R.; m. Margaret Liniecki, 1985; 1 child, Noel A. Student, Fordham Coll., 1951-53; AB, Columbia U., 1956, PhD, 1960. From instr. to prof. dept. geol. scis. Brown U., Providence, 1959-71; prof. dept. earth scis. U. Calif.-Santa Cruz, 1971-94, prof. emeritus, 1994, chmn., 1972-75, dean div. natural scis., 1975-76, provost Crown Coll., 1993-98, assoc. vice chancellor for undergrad. edn., 1994-98. Vis. prof. Yale U., 1964; geologist N.Y. State Geol. Survey, 1962-64; petroleum rsch. cons.; mem. com. geol. scis. Nat. Acad. Sci.-NRC, 1970-72; sec. U.S. Nat. Commn. on the History of Geology, 1991-93, chair, 1994-96; mem. Internat. Commn. on the History of Geology, 1994—; docent Jasper Ridge Biol. Preserve, Stanford U., 2004—. Author: Ancient Environments, 1968, 79, 89, Encounter with the Earth, 1975, George Gaylord Simpson-Paleontologist and Evolutionist, 2000; prin. author: The Earth and Human Affairs, 1972; editor: Reefs in Time and Space, 1974, Evolution and the Fossil Record, 1978, Simple Curiosity: Family Letters of George G. Simpson, 1987, Establishment of a Geologic Framework for Paleoanthropology, 1990; contbr. articles to profl. jours. Recipient President's award Am. Assn. Petroleum Geologists, 1969; U. Calif. Santa Cruz Alumni Disting. Tchg. award, 1980. Fellow: AAAS, Calif. Acad. Sci., Geol. Soc. Am.; mem.: Soc. Econ. Mineralogists and Paleontologists (chmn. rsch. com., paleontology councilor, editor PALAIOS 1984—89, pres. 1995—96, Hon. Mem. award 1999), History of Earth Scis. Soc. (pres. 1994). E-mail: laporte@ucsc.edu.

LAPORTE, LEON JOSEPH, retired military officer; b. Providence, 1946; Grad., U. R.I., 1968; MS in Adminstrn., U. Calif., 1975; grad., Command and Gen. Staff Coll. Commd. 2d lt. US Army, 1968, advanced through grades to gen., 2002, platoon leader, motor officer, Alpha Co. 3rd Bn., 64th Armor, 1969—70, platoon comdr., co. exec. officer 238th Aerial Weapons Co., 1971, G3 Ops. Officer 4th Infantry Divsn. (Mechanized), 1971—73, comdr. Bravo Co., 6th Bn., 32nd Armor Ft. Carson, Colo., 1973—75; instr., then asst. prof. US Mil. Acad., West Point, NY, 1977—80; exec. officer 2nd Squadron, 9th Cavalry, 24th Infantry Divsn. (Mechanized) US Army, Ft. Stewart, Ga., 1980—83, S3, 2nd Brigade, 24th Infantry Divsn. (Mechanized), 1983—84, armor Colonel's assignment officer, Mil. Pers. Ctr. Alexandria, Va., 1984—86, comdr. 3rd. Bn., 64th Armor, 3rd Infantry Divsn. Schweinfurt, Germany, 1986—88, G3, 1st Cavalry Divsn. Ft. Hood, Tex., 1989—90, chief of staff 1st Cavalry Divsn., 1990—91, comdr. 3rd (Greywolf) Brigade, 1st Cavalry Divsn., 1991—93, chief of staff, III Corps & Ft. Hood Ft. Hood, Tex., 1993-94, comdr. Nat. Tng. Ctr. Ft. Irwin, Calif., 1994-95, comdr. 1st Cavalry Divsn. Ft. Hood, Tex., 1995-97, asst. dep. chief of staff ops. and plans, US Army Hdqs. Washington, 1997—98, commdr., III Corps & Ft. Hood Ft. Hood, Tex., 1998—2001; dep. commdg. gen., chief of staff US Army Forces Command (FORSCOM), Ft. McPherson, Ga., 2001—02; comdr. UN Command, Republic of Korea / US Combined Forces Command, US Forces Korea, Osan, Republic of Korea, 2002—06. Decorated Disting. Svc. medal, Legion of Merit with 3 oak leaf clusters, Disting. Flying Cross, Bronze Star medal, Meritorious Svc. medal with 2 oak leaf clusters, Air medal, Army Commendation medal, Vietnamese Cross of Gallantry (with Palm), Kuwait Liberation medal Achievements include serving in Operations DESERT SHIELD & DESERT STORM, 1990-1991.

LAPOSATA, JOSEPH SAMUEL, army officer; b. Johnstown, Pa., Oct. 3, 1938; s. Joseph Thomas and Mary Marie (Coco) L.; m. Anita Louise Sabo, Aug. 12, 1961; children: Joseph S. Jr., David G., Matthew M. BS, Indiana U. Pa., 1960; MS, Cornell U., 1968; grad., Command and Gen. Staff Coll., Leavenworth, Kans., 1971, Indsl. Coll. Armed Forces, Washington, 1980. Commd. 2d lt. US Army, 1960, advanced through grades to lt. gen., 1991; asst. chief of staff for logistics 5th Inf. Div., Ft. Polk, La., 1978-79; chief war res. div. Office Dep. Chief of Staff for Logistics, Hdqrs. Dept. Army, Washington, 1980-81; comdr. 8th Support Group, US Army So. European Task Force, Livorno, Italy, 1981-84, dep. comdr., chief of staff Vicenza, Italy, 1984; exec. to dep. chief of staff for logistics Hdqrs. Dept. Army, Washington, 1984-86, dir. plans and ops., dep. chief of staff for logistics, 1986-88; comdg. gen. US Army Material Command-Europe, Heidelberg, Germany, 1988-89; dep. chief of staff for logistics US Army Europe and 7th Army, Heidelberg, 1989-91; chief of staff Allied Forces So. Europe, Naples, Italy, 1991-93; Presdl. appointee as sec. Am. Battle Monuments Commn., Washington, 1994-95; ret. Apptd. diplomatic post as dep. gen. mgr. and dir. logistics ops. and programs NATO Maintenance and Supply Agy., Luxembourg; ret.; lectr. in field. Established Joseph S. and Anita L. Laposata scholarship Ind. U., Pa.; disting. mem. Quartermaster Found., sponsor. Decorated Def. DDSM, DSM (2), Legion of Merit (3), Bronze Star (2); knight comdr. Republic of Italy; recipient Man of Yr. award Interclub Coun., Johnstown, Pa., 1990, Disting. Alumnus award Ind. U. of Pa., 1992, medal for meritorious svc. Am. Battle Monuments Commn., medal for disting. svc., NATO Maint. and Supply Agy., 1999; inducted into Quartermaster Hall of Fame, 1994, Order of St. Martin; named Col. Emeritus, US Army Q.M. Rgt. Mem. Assn. US Army (pres. European dept. 1989-91), Rotary, Phi Kappa Phi, Tau Kappa Epsilon, Mil. Officers Assoc. Am. Roman Catholic. Avocation: golf. Address: 1823 Freedom Dr Melbourne FL 32940-6875 Home Phone: 321-751-9586; Office Phone: 321-751-9586. Personal E-mail: jlaposata@cs.com.

LAPP, CAROL ANNE, oral biology educator; b. Phila. d. Joseph Henry and Ellen Veronica Schellman; m. David Frank Lapp, June 26, 1965; children: Jennifer Lynn, David Joseph. BS, Bucknell U., 1963; MS, U. RI, 1968; PhD, Med. Coll. Ga., 1985. Rsch. scientist dept. pathology M.D. Anderson Hosp. and Tumor Inst., Houston, 1965-70; tchg. asst. dept. endocrinology Med. Coll. Ga., Augusta, 1980-85, asst. rsch. scientist dept. medicine, 1985-88, postdoctoral fellow dept. pharmacology and toxicology, 1988-90, asst. prof. dept. oral biology Sch. Dentistry, 1990-96, assoc. prof. oral biology Sch. Dentistry, 1996—. Contbr. numerous articles to sci. jours. Violinist Augusta Symphony Orch., 1972-2002; tchr. Suzuki method violin instrn., Augusta, 1974-1985; elder Presbyn. Ch. U.S.A., Augusta, 1993-96, 2005—. Named one of Outstanding Young Women of Am., 1967, 73. Mem. Am. Physiol. Soc., Endocrine Soc., Internat. Cytokine Soc., Med. Coll. Ga. Grad. Studies Alumni Assn. (pres.-elect 1994-95, pres. 1995-1996), Phi Beta Kappa, Sigma Xi, Phi Kappa Phi. Avocations: violin, sailing, genealogy. Office: Med Coll Ga Dept Oral Biol & Maxillofacial Pathology AD 1434 Augusta GA 30912

LAPPAS, SPERO THOMAS, lawyer; b. Danbury, Conn., Oct. 20, 1952; s. Tom John and Alexandria (Manolakes) L.; m. Josephine Wahrendorf, Nov. 8, 1981 (div. 1986); 1 child, Thom Spero; m. Julie Marie Waugh, July 12, 1986 (div. 1995); 1 child, Alexandria Julia. BA cum laude, Allegheny Coll., Meadville, Pa., 1974; JD cum laude, Dickinson Sch. Law, Carlisle, Pa., 1977. Bar: Pa. 1977, U.S. Dist. Ct. (mid. dist.) Pa. 1977, U.S. Ct. Appeals (3rd cir.) 1980, U.S. Supreme Ct. 1991, U.S. Dist. Ct. (we. dist.) Pa., 2002. Assoc. Law Office of Arthur Kusic, Harrisburg, Pa., 1977-79; atty. Kusic & Lappas, P.C., Harrisburg, 1979-84; pvt. practice Harrisburg, 1984-85; ptnr. Stefanon & Lappas, Harrisburg, 1985-88; prin. Law Offices Spero T. Lappas, Harrisburg, 1988—2002; mem. Serratelli, Schiffman, Brown & Calhoon P.C., Harrisburg, 2002—. Mem. Pa. Bar Assn., Dauphin County Bar Assn., Nat. Assn. Criminal Def. Lawyers, Pa. Assn. Criminal Def. Lawyers, Mensa, U.S. Fencing Assn. Office: 2080 Linglestown Rd Ste 201 Harrisburg PA 17110 Office Phone: 717-238-4286. Business E-Mail: slappas@ssbc-law.com.

LAPPEN, CHESTER I., lawyer; b. Des Moines, May 4, 1919; s. Robert C. and Anna (Sideman) L.; m. Jon Tyroler Irmas, June 29, 1941; children: Jonathan Bailey, Timothy, Andrea L., Sally Morris. AB with highest honors in Econs, U. Calif., 1940; LL.B. magna cum laude (Faye diploma), Harvard, 1943. Bar: Calif. bar 1943. Practice in, Los Angeles, 1946—; sr. partner firm Mitchell, Silberberg & Knupp, 1949—; advisory bd. Bank Am., 1962-65; chmn. bd., dir. Zenith Nat. Ins. Corp., 1975-77. Bd. dirs. Arden Group, Inc. (chmn. exec. com. 1978), 1963-91, Data Products Corp. (chmn. fin. com.), 1965-93, City Nat. Bank Corp., 1967-92; trustee, pres. Citinat, Devel. Trust; bd. dirs., chmn. bd. Pacific Rim Holding Corp., 1987-94. Editor-in-chief: Harvard Law Rev, 1942-43. Chmn. bd. trustees Immaculate Heart Coll., 1981-88; trustee UCLA Found.; v.p., dir. Ctr. for Childhood. Spl. agt., counter intelligence US Army, 1943—46. Named to Artus Econs. Honor Soc., U. Calif., 1939. Mem. ABA, Los Angeles Bar Assn. (dir. 1953), Los Angeles Jr. Bar Assn. (pres. 1953), Beverly Hills (Calif.) Bar Assn., Harvard Law Sch. Alumni Assn. So. Calif. (pres. 1973-82). Republican. Office: Mitchell Silberberg & Knupp 11377 W Olympic Blvd Los Angeles CA 90064-1625

LAPPIN, HARLEY G., federal agency administrator; b. 1956; BA in Forensic Studies, Ind. U., 1978; MA in Criminal Justice and Correctional Adminstrn., Kent State U., 1985. Case mgr. to ctrl. inmate monitoring adminstr. Fed. Correctional Instn. Fed. Bur. Prisons, Texarkana, Tex., 1985—89, camp adminstr. Fed. Correctional Instn. Jesup, Ga., 1989—91, assoc. warden Fed. Med. Ctr. Carville, La., 1991, br. adminstr. program rev. divisn. Wash., 1993—96, warden, dir. habilitation program Fed. Correctional Instn. Butner, NC, 1996—98, warden, founder spl. confinement unit U.S. Penitentiary Terre Haute, Ind., 1998—2001, regional dir. Mid-Atlantic Region, 2001—03, dir., 2003—. Chmn. Mgmt. Reengineering Team Fed. Bur. Prisons, chmn. Forward Thinking Workgroup; mem. Am. Correctional Assn. Standards Com. Recipient Assoc. Warden of the Year award, Fed. Bur. Prisons, 1992, Excellence in Prison Mgmt. award, 2000, Atty. Gen.'s award for Excellence in Mgmt., US Dept. Justice, 2001, Presdl. Rank award for Meritorious Exec., 2004. Office: Fed Bur Prisons 320 First St NW Washington DC 20534*

LAPPIN, MICHAEL BRUCE, ophthalmologist, surgeon, medical educator; b. Poplar Bluff, Mo., Dec. 11, 1941; s. Morris and Nettie Lappin; m. Cyli Teitelbaum, Apr. 20, 1968; children: Lauri, Steven, Sarah. BS, U. Fla., Gainesville, 1963; MD, U. Tenn., Memphis, 1967. Diplomate Am. Bd. Ophthalmology. Med.-surg. intern LA County and U. So. Calif. Med. Ctr., LA, 1967—68; resident in orthopedic surgery LA County Harbor, UCLA Med. Ctr., Torrance, Calif., 1968—69; resident in ophthalmology Baylor Coll. Medicine, Houston, 1971—74; assoc. clin. prof. ophthalmology U. Calif. Coll. Medicine, Irvine, 1977—; chmn. dept. ophthalmology Western Med. Ctr., Santa Ana, Calif., 1981, 1987—88. Commr. oral exams. med. licensure Calif. Bd. Med. Quality Assurance, 1976—90. Ophthal. assoc. Rsch. to Prevent Blindness, LA, 1975—; qualified med. evaluator State of Calif. Maj. Med. Corps USAF, 1969—71. Fellow: ACS, Am. Acad. Ophthalmology; mem.: AMA, Orange County Med. Assn., Calif. Med. Assn., Am. Soc. Cataract and Refractive Surgery, Orange County Soc. Ophthalmology (pres. 1979—80), Alpha Omega Alpha. Avocations: classical and contemporary music, literature, racket sports. Office: 801 N Tustin Ave # 700 Santa Ana CA 92705

LAPSLEY, ANDREA RICARDS, marketing and development professional, librarian; b. Newark, Nov. 20, 1950; d. Harold Andrew and Eleanor M. (Connor) Ricards; m. Robert E. Lapsley, May 14, 1977. BA in History, Tulane U., 1972. Cons. M. David Lowe Personnel, Houston, 1972-81; mgr. customer svcs. Fannin BK, Houston, 1975-81; membership dir. Houston C. of C., 1981-83; campaign dir. United Way, Houston, 1983-87; dir. mktg. and devel. Houston Pub. Libr., 1987—. Author: (periodicals) LA&M, 1993-95, Bottom Line, 1995-98. Pres. Old Braeswood Civic Club, Houston, 1992-94. Recipient Bravo award. Mem. ALA, Libr. Adminstrn. Mgmt. Assn. (bd. dirs. libr. adminstrn. and mgmt. divsn. 1995-97, chair fundraising and fin. devel. sect. 1996-97, pres. 2006-07), Tex. Libr. Assn. (co-chair ann. conf. 1995-96), Nat. Soc. Fundraising Execs. (v.p., bd. dirs. 1992—), Houston C. of C. (life). Republican. Congregationalist. Avocations: travel, collecting antiques, gardening. Office: Houston Pub Libr 500 Mckinney St Houston TX 77002-2534

LAPSLEY, JAMES NORVELL, JR., minister, educator; b. Clarksville, Tenn., Mar. 16, 1930; s. James Norvell and Evangeline (Winn) L.; m. Brenda Ann Weakley, June 4, 1953 (dec. May 1989); children: Joseph William, Jacqueline Evangeline; m. Helen Joan Winter, Feb. 24, 1990. BA, Rhodes Coll., 1952; BD, Union Theol. Sem., 1955; PhD (Div. Sch. fellow, Rockefeller fellow), U. Chgo., 1961. Ordained to ministry Presbyn. Ch., 1955; asst. min. Gentilly Presbyn. Ch., New Orleans, 1955-57; instr. Princeton (N.J.) Theol. Sem., 1961-63, asst. prof., 1963-67, assoc. prof., 1967-76, prof. pastoral theology, 1976-80, Carl and Helen Egner prof. pastoral theology, 1980-92, acad. dean, 1984-89, prof. emeritus, 1992—. V.p. N.W. Maricopa UN Assn., 1995-96, pres., 1997-98; pres. Critical Issues Coun. of Sun Cities, 1996-97; sec. Sun City Orch., 1999-2001, pres. 2001-2003. Editor: The Concept of Willing, 1967, Salvation and Health, 1972, Renewal in Late Life Through Pastoral Counseling, 1992, (with B.H. Childs, D.W. Waanders), Festschrift: The Treasure of Earthen Vessels, 1994; chmn. editl. bd. Pastoral Psychology Jour., 1975-84; mem. editl. bd. Jour. Pastoral Care, 1966-69, 91—. Bd. dirs. Westminster Found., Princeton U., 1970-76. Danforth fellow Menninger Found., 1960-61 Mem.: Soc. for Pastoral Theology (co-founder 1985), Phi Beta Kappa. Presbyterian. Home: 6024 Mountain Oaks Dr Flagstaff AZ 86004 Personal E-mail: jlapsley@infomagic.com.

LAPUZ-DE LA PENA, ERLINDA LARON, retired pathology professor; b. Nov. 26, 1933; d. Eriberto Mallari and Teodora Quiero (Laron) Lapuz; m. Cordell De La Pena, Apr. 1, 1957; children: Leslie, Nina, Cordell. MD, U. Santo Tomas, 1957. Diplomate Am. Bd. Pathology. Intern St. John's Hosp., Lowell, Mass., 1959—60; attending physician Tewksbury (Mass.) Hosp., 1960—63; resident in pathology Mercy Hosp., Pitts., 1967—71; instr. pathology U. Pitts. Med. Sch., Pitts., 1967—71; chief lab. svc. VA Hosp., Clarksburg, W.Va., 1971—, chief of staff, 1983—99; courtesy staff United Hosp. Ctr.; prof. pathology W.Va. U. Sch. Medicine, 1994—; asst. prof. Coll. Nursing Salem (W.Va.) Coll., 1978; asst. prof. Coll. Nursing and Physician Assts. Alderson Broadus Coll., Phillipi, W.Va. Contbr. articles to med. jours. Fellow: Am. Soc. Clin. Pathology, Am. Coll. Pathologists; mem.: W.Va. Assn. Pathologists (bd. dirs. 1983—, pres. 1987—89, 1997—98), W.Va. Med. Assn., AMA, Clarksburg Country Club. Roman Catholic.

LAQUAGLIA, MICHAEL PATRICK, pediatric surgeon, neuroblastoma researcher; b. Newark, Aug. 6, 1950; s. Michael and Dorothy Theresa (Livsey) LaQ.; m. Joanne Drako, June 26, 1982; children: Michael Joseph, Catherine Elizabeth. BS, N.J. Inst., 1972, MD, 1976. Diplomate Am. Bd. Surgery; Cert. Spl. Competence Pediatric Surgery. From intern to chief resident in gen. surgery Mass. Gen. Hosp., Boston, 1976-83, clin. fellow in transplantation, 1980-81, clin. fellow in vascular surgery, 1984; hon. sr. registrar in surgery Broadgreen Regional Chest Ctr., Liverpool, Eng., U.K., 1982; assoc. chief resident in pediatric surgery Children's Hosp. Med. Ctr., Boston, 1985-86, chief resident in pediatric surgery, 1986-87; assoc. surgeon and mem., assoc. attending pediatrician Meml. Sloan-Kettering Cancer Ctr., NYC, 1987—, chief pediatric surgery, 1994—; assoc. attending Cornell U. Med. Ctr., NYC, 1989—, assoc. prof. surgery Med. Sch., 1989—. Fellow: Am. Surg. Assn.; mem.: AAAS, Soc. Surg. Oncology, Am. Pediatric Surg. Assn., Am. Assn. Cancer Rsch. Office: Meml Sloan Kettering Cancer Ctr Box 325 1275 York Ave New York NY 10021-6094

LAQUATRA, JOSEPH, humanities educator; b. Pitts., Apr. 28, 1952; s. Joseph Laquatra and Carmela Zito; life ptnr. Gregory Lee Potter, Feb. 17, 1998. BS in Hotel Adminstrn., Cornell U., Ithaca, NY, 1974, MS in Consumer Econs. and Housing, 1981, PhD in Consumer Econs. and Housing, 1984. Vista vol. Weber-Davis Housing Corp., Layton, Utah, 1974—75, Project REACH, Wayland, NY, 1975—76; gen. contractor self-employed, Wayland, 1976—77; housing dir. Project REACH, Wayland, 1977—79; vis. staff mem. Los Alamos Nat. Lab., N.Mex., 1981; ext. assoc. Cornell U., 1984—86, asst. prof., 1986—92, assoc. prof., 1992—2003, prof., 2003—04, Hazel E. Reed human ecology prof. family policy, 2004—; scholar-in-residence American-Polish Home Builders Inst., Gdansk, Poland, 1994; dir. advanced edn. Home Builders Inst., DC, 1996—97, dir. for advanced edn., 1996—97. Cons. in field, 1986—. Author: (books) An Economic Analysis of a Passive Solar Multiple Family Dwelling for Upstate New York, 1982, Builders, Remodelers, and Indoor Air Quality, 1998 (Cert. Appreciation, US EPA, 1999), Energy Efficient Construction, 1999; editor: (book) Indoor Air Quality in Homes: Synthesizing the Issues and Educating Consumers, 1991; prodr.: (video tape) Talking Trash: On-Site Residential Construction Waste Management, 1997, (DVD) Healthy Homes: Assessing Your Indoor Environment, 2006; contbr. articles to profl. jours., chapter to book. Com. chair Ithaca Energy Commn., 1984—86; mem. NY State Bldg. Industry Adv. Com., Albany, 1989—92, NY State Rural Devel. Coun., Albany, 1998—2001, Town Planning Bd., Dryden, NY, 2002—, Dryden Dem. Com., NY, 1985—87. Recipient Blue Ribbon award, Am. Soc. Agrl. Engrs., 1992, Hands That Work award, Home Builders Inst., 1994, Outstanding Ext. Health Programming award, Jeanne M. Priester Ann. Ext. Health Conf., 2005, Cert. of Recognition award, US Dept. Agr., 2005, US EPA, 2005, Outstanding Engagement award, Nat. Assn. State Univs. & Land Grant Colls., 2006; grantee Rsch. grant, Cornell U. Agrl. Expt. Sta., 1986—92, NY State Energy Office, 1988—90, US Dept. Energy, 1990—92, NY State Energy Rsch. & Devel. Authority, 1991—92, Cornell U., 1996—2007, US EPA, 1996—2006, Consumer Fedn. Am. Found., 1997—2002, US Dept. Agr., 1998—2007, NY State Targeted Academic Rsch., 2001—06, NY State Energy Rsch. & Devel. Authority, 2003—07, Cornell U. Agrl. Expt. Sta., 2004—, NY State Indoor Environ. Quality Ctr., 2004—06. Mem.: Faculty Senate, Cornell U. (senator 1988—2006), Com. Oversight and Assessment Partnership for Advancing Tech. Housing, Nat. Consortium Housing Rsch. Ctrs. (chair 2004—06), Housing Edn. and Rsch. Assn. (pres. 2001—02), Gamma Sigma Delta (chpt. pres. 1996—97). Democrat-Npl. Achievements include research in indoor air quality and energy efficiency; design of passive solar dollhouse; building energy awareness models. Avocations: swimming, cooking, hiking, woodworking. Home: 393 Groton Rd Freeville NY 13068 Office: Cornell Univ E-208 MVR Hall Ithaca NY 14853 Office Phone: 607-255-2145. Office Fax: 607-255-0305; Home Fax: 607-255-0305. Business E-Mail: jl27@cornell.edu.

LAQUEUR, WALTER, history professor, writer; b. Breslau, Germany, May 26, 1921; s. Fritz and Else (Berliner) L.; m. Barbara Koch, May 29, 1941 (dec.); children: Sylvia, Shlomit; m. Christa Susi Wichmann, 1996. Grad., Johannesgymnasium, Breslau, 1938; student, Hebrew U., Jerusalem, 1938-39; HHD (hon.), Hebrew Union Coll., 1988, Adelphi U., 1993, Brandeis U., 1994. Agrl. worker, Palestine, 1940-44; newspaper corr., free-lance author, 1944-55; founder, editor Survey, London, 1955-67; vis. prof. Johns Hopkins, 1957, U. Chgo., 1958, Harvard, 1977; dir. Inst. Contemporary History, Wiener Library, London, 1964-92; prof. history ideas and politics Brandeis U., Waltham, Mass., 1967-72; prof. history U. Tel Aviv, 1970-80; chmn. internat. rsch. coun. Ctr. Strategic and Internat. Studies, Washington, 1973—2001; univ. prof. govt. Ctr. Strategic and Internat. Studies Georgetown U., Washington, 1977-91. Author: Communism and Nationalism in the Middle East, 1956, The Soviet Union and the Middle East, 1959, Young Germany, 1962, Russia and Germany, 1966, The Fate of the Revolution, 1967, The Road to War, 1967, The Struggle for the Middle East, 1969, Europe Since Hitler, 1970, Out of the Ruins of Europe, 1971, Confrontation: The Middle East and World Politics, 1974, A History of Zionism, 1972, Weimar, 1975, Guerrilla, 1976, Terrorism, 1977, Guerrilla Reader, 1977, Terrorism Reader, 1978, A Continent Astray, 1979, The Missing Years, 1980, Political Psychology of Appeasement, 1980, Farewell to Europe, 1981, The Terrible Secret, 1981, America, Europe, and the Soviet Union, 1983, Germany Today, 1985, A World of Secrets, 1985, The Age of Terrorism, 1987, The Long Road to Freedom: Russia and Glasnost, 1989, Stalin, 1991, Thursday's Child Has Far to Go, 1992, Black Hundred, 1993, The Dream That Failed, 1994, Generation Exodus, 2001, Antisemitism, 2006, The Last Days of Europe, 2007; editor: The Holocaust Encyclopedia, 2001; co-editor, founder: Jour. Contemporary History, 1966-05; founder Washington Papers, 1972—. Recipient 1st Distinguished Writer's award Center Strategic and Internat. Studies, 1969, Inter Nationes award, 1985-05, Grand Cross of Merit German Fed. Republic, 1987. Personal E-mail: walter@laqueur.net.

LARAGH, JOHN HENRY, cardiologist, surgeon, educator; b. Yonkers, NY, Nov. 18, 1924; s. Harry Joseph and Grace Catherine (Coyne) L.; m. Adonia Kennedy, Apr. 28, 1949; children: John Coyne, Peter Christian, Robert Sealey; m. Jean E. Sealey, Sept. 22, 1974. MD, Cornell U., 1948. Intern Presbyn. Hosp., NYC, 1948-49, asst. resident, 1949-50; cardiology trainee Nat. Heart Inst., 1950-51; rsch. fellow N.Y. Heart Assn., 1951-52; asst. physician Presbyn. Hosp., 1950-55, asst. attending, 1954-61, assoc. attending, 1961-69, attending physician, 1969-75, pres. elect med. bd., 1972-74; faculty Coll. Physicians and Surgeons Columbia U., 1950-75, prof. clin. medicine, 1967-75, spokesman exec. com. faculty coun., 1971-73; vice-chmn. bd. trustees for profl. and sci. affairs Presbyn. Hosp., 1974-75; dir. Hypertension Ctr., chief nephrology divsn. Columbia-Presbyn. Med. Ctr., 1971—76; Master prof. medicine, dir. Hypertension and Cardiovascular Ctr., N.Y. Hosp.-Cornell Med. Ctr., 1975—96, chief cardiology divsn., 1975—96. Cons. USPHS, 1964—. Editor-in-chief Am. Jour. Hypertension, 1985—, Cardiovascular Reviews and Reports, 1980—; Editor: Hypertension Manual, 1974, Topics in Hypertension, 1980, Frontiers in Hypertension Rsch., 1981; editor Hypertension: Pathophysiology, Diagnosis, and Management, 1990, 1995; editorial bd.: Am. Jour. Medicine, Am. Jour. Cardiology, Kidney Internat., Jour. Clin. Endocrinology and Metabolism, Hypertension, Jour. Hypertension, Circulation, Am. Heart Jour., Procs. of Soc. Exptl. Biology and Medicine. Mem. policy adv. bd. hypertension detection and follow-up program Nat. Heart and Lung Inst., 1971, bd. sci. counselor, 1974-79; chmn. U.S.A.-USSR Joint Program in Hypertension, 1977-93. With U.S. Army, 1943-46. Recipient Stouffer prize Med. Rsch., 1969, J.K. Lattimer award Am. Urol. Assn., 1989, Robert Tigerstedt award Am. Soc. Hypertension, 1990, John P. Peters award Am. Soc. Nephrology, 1990, Lifetime Achievement in Medicine award N.Y. Acad. Medicine, 1993, Disting. Alumnus award Cornell U. Med. Coll., 1993, Bristol Myers Squibb award for disting. achievement cardiovalcular rsch., 1996, Disting. Achievement award Coun. for High Blood Pressure Rsch., Am. Heart Assn., 1999, Stevo Julius awrd for edn. in hypertension Internat. Soc. Hypertension, 2002, Lewis and Jack Rudin NY prize medicine and health, 2005; subject of Time Mag. cover story, 1975; Most Frequently Cited Scientist: Top Ten Advances in Cardiopulmonary Medicine, 1946-75. Fellow Am. Coll. Cardiology; mem. ACP (Master), Am. Heart Assn. (chmn. med. adv. bd. coun. high blood pressure rsch. 1968-72), Am. Soc. Clin. Investigation, Assn. Am. Physicians, Assn. Univ. Cardiologists, Endocrine Soc., Am. Soc. Nephrology, Am. Soc. Hypertension (founder, 1st pres. 1986-88), Internat. Soc. Hypertension (pres. 1986-88), Harvey Soc., Kappa Sigma, Nu Sigma Nu, Alpha Omega Alpha, Country Club of Fla., Shinnecock Hills Golf Club (Southampton, N.Y.). Achievements include discovery of renin-angiotensin-aldosterone hormonal control system and the causal roles of its overactivity in malignant and in most essential hypertension. Home: 5 Sandpiper Dr Village Of Golf FL 33436-5621 Office: NY Hosp-Cornell Med Ctr 525 E 68th St New York NY 10021-4885 Office Phone: 212-746-2206. Business E-Mail: jhl2001@med.cornell.edu. *In my research, a key resource has been the ability to perceive everyday clinical phenomena differently, to recognize and develop new ideas and experiments about human physiology and the causes of hypertension and major cardiovascular diseases. These perceptions enable hypotheses and experiments for creation and synthesis of new knowledge that redirects medical thinking.*

LARAYA-CUASAY, LOURDES REDUBLO, pediatrician, pulmonologist, educator; b. Baguio, Philippines, Dec. 8, 1941; came to U.S., 1966; d. Jose Marquez and Lolita (Redublo) Laraya; m. Ramon Serrano Cuasay, Aug. 7, 1965; children: Raymond Peter, Catherine Anne, Margaret Rose, Joseph Paul. AA, U. Santo Tomas, Manila, Philippines, 1958, MD cum laude, 1963. Diplomate Am. Bd. Pediatrics. Resident in pediatrics U. Santo Tomas Hosp., 1963-65, Children's Hosp. Louisville, 1966-67, Charity Hosp. New Orleans-Tulane U., 1967-68; fellow child growth and devel. Children's Hosp. Phila., 1968-69; fellow pediatric pulmonary and cystic fibrosis programs St. Christopher's Hosp. for Children, Phila., 1969-71, rsch. assoc., 1971-72; clin. instr. Tulane U., New Orleans, 1967-68; asst. prof. pediatrics Temple Health Scis. Ctr., Phila., 1972-77; assoc. prof. pediatrics Thomas Jefferson Med. Sch., Phila., 1977-79, U. Medicine & Dentistry N. J., Robert Wood Johnson Med. Sch., New Brunswick, 1980-85, prof. clin. pediatrics, 1985-98, prof. pediat., 1998—2005; med. dir. pediat. asthma ctr. K. Hovnanian Children's Hosp., Jersey Shore U. Med. Ctr., Neptune, NJ, 2006—. Dir. pediatric pulmonary medicine and cystic fibrosis ctr. U. Medicine and Dentistry, Robert Wood Johnson Med. Sch., New Brunswick, 1981-2004 Co-editor: Interstitial Lung Diseases in Children, 1988. Recipient Pediatric Rsch. award Mead Johnson Pharm. Co., Manila, 1965. Fellow Am. Coll. Chest Physicians (steering com., chmn. cardiopulmonary diseases in children 1976—), Airways Network, Am. Acad. Pediatrics (tobacco free generation rep. 1986-92); mem. Am. Ambulatory Pediatric Soc., Am. Thoracic Soc., Am. Sleep Disorder Assn., N.J. Thoracic Soc. (chmn. pediatric pulmonary com. 1986-91, governing coun. mem. 1981-94), European Respiratory Soc. Avocation: piano. Home: 100 Mercer Ave Spring Lake NJ 07762-1208 Office: Med Arts Bldg Ste 204 1944 State Hwy East 33 Neptune NJ 07754 Office Phone: 732-776-4860. Business E-Mail: llarayacuasay@meridianhealth.com.

LARBERG, JOHN FREDERICK, retired social welfare executive; wine consultant, educator; b. Kansas City, Mo., Jan. 21, 1930; s. Herman Alvin and Ann (Sabrowsky) L. AA, Kansas City Jr. Coll., 1948; AB cum laude, U. Mo., 1950, postgrad., 1955-56; MSW, Bryn Mawr Coll., 1961. Cert. social worker. With Westinghouse Electric Corp., 1953-56; dir. House of Industry Settlement House, Phila., 1957-61; asst. to exec. dir. Health and Welfare Coun., Inc., Phila., 1961-66; sr. staff cons., 1966-73, dir. Washington office, 1971-72, Nat. Assembly for Social Policy and Devel., Inc., NYC; nat. dir. community and patient services Nat. Multiple Sclerosis Soc., NYC, 1974-81, nat. dir. spl. projects, 1981-82; adminstrv. v.p. Fedn. Protestant Welfare Agys. NY, 1982-86; sr. advisor, 1986-87; exec. dir. Am. Assn. State Social Work Bds., 1987-89; cons. The Wine Aficionado, NY, 1990—. Cons. exec. com. Commn. on Vol. Svc. and Action, 1967-76, cons. Met. NY Project Equality, 1968-73, Encampment for Citizenship, 1973-74, Symphony for UN, 1974-77, Lower Eastside Fam. Union, 1984-89, Wielenga Psych. Svc., 1993—, Malignant Hyperthermia Assn. US, 1994—, Internat. Fedn. Multiple Sclerosis Socs., 1995—, Nat. Multiple Sclerosis Soc., 1997-2002; bd. dirs. Health Systems Agy. of NY, 1984-86, NE Region Ch. of Christ, Disciples of Christ, 1997-; trustee The Riverside Ch., NYC, 1985-89, worship commn., 1992-94, ordination com., 1993-2000, chmn., 1996-2000, layman, vol., mem. Ecumenical and Denominational Com., 1998—; bd. dirs., mem. exec. com. Metro Assn. United Ch. of Christ, NY, 1993-2004, dir. NY state exec. coun., 1995—, nat. del. Gen. Synod United Ch. of Christ, 1997-99; mem. Disciples of Christ/United Ch. of Christ NY State Joint Task Force, 1996—, co-chair, 1999—; ecumenical officer Met. Assn. of United Ch. of Christ, NYC, 1999-; co-chair planning com. Biennial Joint Assembly for Disciples of Christ, United Ch. of Christ, 2000; nat. dir. Coun. Soc. Wk. Edn., 1985-86. Served with AUS, 1951-53. Achievements include attending seven general synods of the United Ch. of Christ; having an active role in the 1998 approval of the Formula of Agreement for Full Communion, allowing the four major Protestant denominations to take Holy Communion together for the first time in 400 years; engaging in efforts to promote Churches Uniting in Christ. Mem. Acad. Cert. Social Workers (charter), Nat. Assn. Social Workers (chpt. legis. com. 1968-70, nat. publs. com. 1968-71, nat. legal regulation com. 1987-89), Internat. Coun. Social Welfare (internat. com. of reps. 1980-84, US com. for Internat. Coun. Social Welfare, bd. dirs. 1983-90, exec. com. 1983-90), Internat. Fedn. Multiple Sclerosis Socs. (vice chmn. patient services com. 1976-81, chmn. 1981-84, mem. individual and family services com. 1984-97, non-govtl. rep. to UN, 1990-96, rep. to Rehab. Internat. Med. Commn. 1976-81), Nat. Conf. Social Welfare (program com. 1966-73, chmn. combined assoc. groups 1969-70, nat. dir. 1971-73, 83-87), NY State UCC Commn. for Ecumenical and Interfaith Dialogue, Fedn. of Assns. Regulatory Bds. (nat. dir. 1988-89), Malignant Hyperthermia Assn. US (nat. dir. 1984-93, nat. pres. 1985-89, rep. 10th Quad. World Congr. Anesth. Hague 1992), Am. Acad. Polit. and Social Sci., Nat. Urban League (nat. trustee-at-large 1968), Hawk Mountain Sanctuary Assn., Bryn Mawr Social Work Alumni Assn. (pres. 1963-65), Am. Mus. Natural History, NYC Citizens Union, NY Mcpl. Art Soc., Phi Beta Kappa Assn. NY (pres. 1980-82), Omicron Delta Kappa, QEBH, Alpha Phi Omega, Alpha Pi Zeta, Pi Sigma Alpha, Alpha Kappa Psi. Home and Office: 400 E 58th St Apt 2F New York NY 10022-2333 Personal E-mail: jfl149@aol.com.

LARCH, SARA MARGARET, healthcare executive; b. Des Moines, Iowa, Feb. 14, 1956; d. William Arthur and Beverly Frances (Klanjac) L. BA in Pub. Adminstrn., Miami U., Oxford, Ohio, 1978; MSHA, VCU, Richmond, 1992. Personnel clk. City Nat. Bank, Detroit, 1978-79; econ. anlyst asst. Cargill, Inc., Mpls., 1979-81; ob-gyn. adminstr. Ind. U. Med. Ctr., Indpls., 1981-88; adminstr. Georgetown U. Med. Ctr., Washington, 1988-94, dir. quality and capitation sys., 1995; COO Univ. Physicians, Inc. Univ. Md., Balt., 1995—. Author: The Physician Billing Process: Avoiding Potholes in the Road to Getting Paid, 2004. Mem. Assn. Mgrs. Gynecology and Obstetricians (pres. 1986-87), Med. Group Mgmt. Assn. (bd. dirs. 1995-96, 98—, chmn. 2001-02), Acad. Practice Assembly (pres. 1994-95), Am. Coll. Med. Prac. Exec. (fell., 1995), Women Bus. Leaders of the U.S. Health Care Industry Found. Avocations: piano, reading, travel, public speaking. Office: Univ Physicians Inc 419 W Redwood St Ste 220 Baltimore MD 21201-7004 Office Phone: 410-328-1722. E-mail: slarch@upi.umaryland.edu.

LARDENT, ESTHER FERSTER, lawyer, consultant; b. Linz, Austria, Apr. 23, 1947; arrived in US, 1951; d. William and Rose (Seidweber) Ferster; m. Dennis Robert Lardent, July 27, 1969 (div. Dec. 1981). BA, Brown U., 1968; JD, U. Chgo., 1971. Bar: Ill. 1972, Mass. 1975, admitted to practice: US Dist. Ct. (Ill.) 1972, US Dist. Ct. (Mass.) 1975. Civil rights specialist Office of Civil Rights U.S. HEW, Chgo., 1971-72; staff dir. individual rights ABA, Chgo., 1972-74; staff atty., supr. Cambridge (Mass.) Problem Ctr., 1975-76; exec. dir. Vol. Lawyers Project Boston Bar Assn., 1977-85; legal and policy cons. Santa Fe and Washington, 1985—; ind. legal and policy cons. Ford Found., Washington, 1990—96; pres. and CEO Pro Bono Inst., 1996—. Vis. prof. U. N.Mex. Sch. Law, Albuquerque, 1985; cons. Nat. Vets. Legal Svcs. Program, Washington, 1991—; vis. scholar ethics program Boston U. Sch. Law, 1991—92; reporter ABA/Tulane Law Sch., New Orleans, 1988—90; adj. prof. law Georgetown U., Washington. Contbr. Vis. com. U. Chgo. Law Sch., 1992—. Recipient Founder Award, Phila. Bar Assn., 1991, Outstanding Pub. Interest Adv. Award, Nat. Assn. Pub. Interest Law, 1992, Exemplar Award, Nat. Legal Aid and Defender Assn., William Reece Smith Jr. Award, Nat. Assn. Pro Bono Coordinators. Mem.: DC Bar (spl. adv. pub. svc. activities rev. com. 1990—), Nat. Legal Aid and Defenders Assn. (bd. dirs. 1990—), ABA (Ho. of Dels. 1991—, cons. 1974—76, legal cons. postconviction death penalty 1987—96, legal cons. law firm pro bono project 1989—96, bd. gov. 1996—99). Office: Pro Bono Institute at Georgetown Univ Law Ctr 600 New Jersey Ave NW Washington DC 20001

LARDNER, GEORGE, JR., journalist, writer; b. NYC, Aug. 10, 1934; s. George Edmund and Rosetta (Russo) Lardner; m. Rosemary Schalk, July 6, 1957; children: Helen, Edmund, Richard, Charles, Kristin(dec.). AB in Journalism summa cum laude, Marquette U., 1956, MA, 1962. Reporter The Worcester (Mass.) Telegram, 1957—59, The Miami (Fla.) Herald, 1959—63, The Washington Post, 1963—64, 1966—2004, columnist, 1964—65; pub. policy fellow Woodrow Wilson Internat. Ctr. for Scholars, 2005; assoc. Ctr. for Study of the Presidency, 2005—. Bd. Fund for Investigative Journalism, Washington, 1992—, chmn., 1997—2004. Author: The Stalking of Kristin, 1995; contbg. author Deadlock: The Inside Story of America's Closest Election, 2001. Recipient Byline award, Marquette U., 1967, Front-page Nat. News award, Washington-Balt. Newspaper Guild, 1984, 1986, Pulitzer Prize for feature writing, 1993. Roman Catholic. Home: 5604 32nd St NW Washington DC 20015-1623 Personal E-mail: lardnerg@yahoo.com.

LARDNER, HENRY PETERSEN (PETER LARDNER), insurance company executive; b. Davenport, Iowa, Apr. 5, 1932; s. James Francis and Mary Catharine (Decker) L.; m. Marion Cleaveland White, Dec. 28, 1954; children: Elisabeth, Emily, David, Peter, Sarah (dec.). BSE. (Indsl. Engring.), U. Mich., 1954; MA, Augustana Coll., 1982. C.P.C.U. Indsl. engr. Cutler-Hammer, Milw., 1954; Agt. H.H. Cleaveland Agy., Rock Island, Ill., 1956-60; with Bituminous Ins. Cos., Rock Island, 1960—2001, exec. v.p., 1968-72, pres., 1972-95, chmn. and CEO, 1984-2000, chmn., 2000—01; pres. Bitco Corp., Rock Island, 1973-95, chmn. bd. dirs., 1973—2001. Bd. dirs. Old Republic Internat., 1985—; trustee Underwriters Lab., Inc.,

1997-2004. Bd. govs. State Colls. and Univs., 1971-80; trustee Black Hawk Coll., 1964-72; mem. Ill. Bd. Higher Edn., 1976-77; chmn. Ill. State Scholarship, 1982-85. Served with AUS, 1954-56. Home: 3227 29th Ave Rock Island IL 61201-5568 E-mail: peter.lardner@verizon.net.

LARDY, HENRY A(RNOLD), biochemistry professor; b. Roslyn, SD, Aug. 19, 1917; s. Nicholas and Elizabeth (Gebetsreiter) L.; m. Annrita Dresselhuys, Jan. 21, 1943; children: Nicholas, Diana, Jeffrey, Michael. BS, S.D. State U., 1939, DSc (hon.), 1979; MS, U. Wis., 1941, PhD, 1943. Asst. prof. U. Wis., Madison, 1945-47, assoc. prof., 1947-50, prof., 1950-88, Vilas prof. biol. sci., 1966-88, prof. emeritus, 1988—. Henry Lardy annual lectr. S.D. State U., Brookings, 1985. Mem. editl. bd. Archives Biochemistry and Biophysics, 1957-60, Jour. Biol. Chemistry, 1958-64, 80-85, Biochem. Preparations, Methods of Biochem. Analysis, Biochemistry, 1962-73, 75-81; contbr. over 470 articles to profl. jours. Pres. Citizens vs McCarthy, Wis., 1950. Recipient Neuberg medal Am. Soc. European Chemists, 1956, Wolf prize in agr., Wolf Found., Israel, 1981, Nat. award Agrl. Excellence, 1982. Fellow Wis. Acad. Arts and Scis.; mem. Am. Chem. Soc. (chmn. biol. divsn. 1958, Paul-Lewis Labs. award 1949), Am. Soc. Biol. Chemists (pres. 1964, William Rose award 1988), Am. Acad. Arts and Scis. (Amory prize 1984), Am. Philos. Soc., Am. Diabetes Assn., Nat. Acad. Scis., Biochem. Soc. Great Britain, Harvey Soc., Soc. for Study of Reprodn. (Carl Hartman award 1984), The Endocrine Soc., Japanese Biochem. Soc. (hon.), Golden Retriever Club Am. (pres. 1964). Democrat. Achievements include patents for steroid compounds and lab. apparatus. Home: 1829 Thorstrand Rd Madison WI 53705-1052 Office: U Wis 1710 University Ave Madison WI 53726-4087 Home Phone: 608-233-1584; Office Phone: 608-262-3372. Business E-Mail: halardy@wisc.edu.

LARDY, NICHOLAS RICHARD, economist, educator; b. Madison, Wis., Apr. 8, 1946; s. Henry Arnold and Annrita (Dresselhuys) Lardy; m. Barbara Jean Dawe, Aug. 29, 1970; children: Elizabeth Brooke, Lillian Henry. BA, U. Wis., 1968; MA, U. Mich., 1972, PhD, 1975. Asst. prof. Yale U., New Haven, 1975-79, assoc. prof., 1979-83, asst. dir. econ. growth ctr., 1979-82, Frederick Frank adj. prof. in internat. trade and fin. Sch. Mgmt., 1997-2000; assoc. prof. U. Wash., Seattle, 1983-85, chair China program, 1984-89, prof., 1985-95, dir. The Henry M. Jackson Sch. Internat. Studies, 1991-95; sr. fellow Brookings Instn., Washington, 1995—2003, Inst. Internat. Econs., Washington, 2003—. Bd. dirs. Nat. Com. U.S.-China Rels., NYC, 1986—, Comm. Internat. Rels. Studies with China, 1989—92, Program Internat. Studies in Asia, 1993—95; chmn. Com. Advanced Study in China; vice chmn. com. scholarly comm. China NAS, Washington, 1991—95; bd. mgrs. Blakemore Found., 1993—95; founding mem. Pacific Coun. Internat. Policy, 1995—; mem. Coun. Fgn. Rels. Author: Economic Growth and Distribution in China, 1978, Agriculture in China's Modern Economic Development, 1983, Foreign Trade and Economic Reform in China, 1978-1990, 1992, China in the World Economy, 1994, China's Unfinished Economic Revolution, 1998, Integrating China into the Global Economy, 2002, Economic Policy Toward China in the Post-Reagan Era, 1989; co-author: Prospects for a US-Taiwan Free Trade Agreement, 2004, China: The Balance Sheet, 2006; mem. editl. bd.: The China Quar., China Econ. Rev., Jour. Contemporary China. Rsch. fellow, Am. Coun. Learned Socs., 1976, 1978—79, 1989—90, Henry Luce Found., Inc., 1980—82, Faculty Rsch. grantee, Yale U., 1976, 1978. Mem.: Assn. Comparative Econ. Studies (mem. exec. com. 1986—88), Assn. Asian Studies (mem. nominating com. 1986—87), Am. Econ. Assn. Avocations: skiing, squash, tennis, sailing. Home: 2811 Albemarle St NW Washington DC 20008-1037 Office: Peterson Inst for Internat Econs 1750 Massachusetts Ave NW Washington DC 20036-1903 Office Phone: 202-328-9000. Business E-Mail: nlardy@iie.com.

LARET, MARK R., health facility executive; BS in Polit. sci., UCLA; M in Polit. sci., U. So. Calif. Asst. dir. UCLA Med. Ctr., 1985, assoc. dir. marketing and planning, 1990, dep. dir., 1994; CEO UCLA Med. Group, 1994, Univ. Calif. Irvine Med. Ctr., Orange, Calif., 1995—2000, exec. dir., 1995; CEO Univ. Calif. San Francisco (UCSF) Med. Ctr., 2000—, Univ. Calif. San Francisco (UCSF) Children's Hosp., 2000—. Exec. com. bd. Univ. Healthcare Consortium; bd. dir. CaloPTIMA, 1997, AAMC Coun of Teaching Hosp. and Health Systems (COTH), 2003—04. Named Orange County Manager of Year, Soc. for Advancement of Mgmt., 1999. Office: Med Ctr Adminstrn Univ Calif San Francisco Box 0296 500 Parnassus Ave MU 509E San Francisco CA 94143-0296 Office Phone: 415-353-2733. Office Fax: 415-353-2765. Business E-Mail: mark.laret@ussfmedctr.org.

LARGE, JOHN ANDREW, library and information service professor; b. Mexborough, Yorkshire, Eng., Mar. 27, 1947; arrived in Can., 1989; s. Gordon and Winifred Mary L.; m. Valerie Merle Wilson, Aug. 30, 1972; children: Amanda Fiona, Kirsty Jane. BSc in Econs., London U., 1968, diploma in libr., 1973; PhD, Glasgow U., Scotland, 1973. Asst. libr. Glasgow U. Libr., 1973-74; libr. Inst. Soviet and East European Studies, Glasgow U., 1974-78; prin. lectr. Coll. Librarianship Wales, Aberystwyth, 1978-89; prof., dir. Grad. Sch. Libr. and Info. Studies McGill U., Montreal, Que., Can., 1989-98, CN-Pratt-Grinstad prof. of info. studies, 1998—. Vice chmn. U.K. Online User Group, London, 1987-89; chmn. Can. Coun. Libr. Schs., 1991-93, 97-98; external examiner U. W.I., 1991-99, U. Ibadan, Nigeria, 1992-95; bd.d irs. Atwater Libr. and Computer Ctr., 1999-2002. Author: The Foreign-Language Barrier, 1983, The Artificial Language Movement, 1985, Japanese edit., 1995, A Modular Curriculum for Information Studies, 1987; co-author: Online Searching: Principles and Practice, 1990, Information Seeking in the Online Age, 1999, Digital Libraries, 2005; editor: Manual of Online Search Strategies, 1988, 3d edit., 2001, CD-ROM Information Products: An Evaluative Guide vol. 1, 1990, vol. 2, 1991, vol. 3, 1992, World Info. Report, 1997, ICT for Library and Information Professionals: A Training Package-Modules 1-6, 2001-02; mem. editl. bd. Jour. Librarianship and Info. Sci., 1992—, Jour. Universal Lang., 2000—, South African Jour. Librs. and Info. Sci., 2002—, Can. Jour. Info. and Libr. Sci., 2003—; editor jour. Edn. for Info., 1983—, Treasures of Islam, 1999, CD-ROM Info. Products, 1993. Rsch. grantee Brit. Libr. R&D Dept., 1981-82, 85-86, European Space Agy., 1983-85, Nat. Libr. Can., 2002; IBM Acad. Info. Exch. fellow, 1991-92, Social Sci. and Humanities Rsch. Coun. fellow, 1991-94, 96-99, 2002-05, 2006—, Heritage Can., 2005-06; recipient Commemorative medal for 125th Anniversary Confedn. Can., 1992. Avocation: music listening and playing. Office: McGill U Grad Sch Libr and Info Studies 3459 McTavish Montreal PQ Canada H3A 1Y1 E-mail: andrew.large@mcgill.ca.

LARGE, LARRY DENTON, academic administrator; b. Lewiston, Idaho, Aug. 8, 1940; s. Clifford Denton and Cleo Elva (Pixley) L.; m. Jeanne M. Large, Mar. 22, 1964 (div. 1978); children: Elizabeth, Timothy; m. Marsha Lee Lancaster, 1990. BS in Psychology, Portland State U., 1964; MA in History, U. Oreg., 1970, PhD in Edn., 1974. Dir. fin. aid U. Oreg., Eugene, 1971-72; v.p. Willamette U., Salem, Oreg., 1972-82; v.p. devel. & coll. rels. Reed Coll., Portland, Oreg., 1982-87; v.p. pub. affairs & devel. U. Oreg., 1987-89; vice chancellor pub. affairs Oreg. State System Higher Edn., Portland, 1989—; pres. Oglethorpe U., Atlanta, 1999—2005; exec. cons. Sierra Nev. Coll., Incline Village, Nev., 2005—, interim pres., 2006—. Spl. asst. to deputy commr. for postsecondary edn., U.S. Office Edn., Washington, 1980-81; adj. prof. U. Oreg. Coll. Edn., 1987; cons. in field; lectr. in field. Contbr. articles to profl. jours. Gov. appointed mem. Bicentennial commn., 1988-90; bd. dirs. Magna Carta Am., 1985—; vol. cons. Oreg. State Coun. Alcoholism and Drug Abuse, 1983, trustee, 1984-85; independent coll. rep. Oreg. Ednl. Coord. Comms, State Wide Planning Com., 1985-86. With U.S. Army Res., 1958-59. Mem. Coun. Advancement Support Edn. (nat. ednl. fund raising com. 1985-87. trustee), Oreg. Assn. Student Fin. Aid Officers (v.p. 1971), Assn. Independent Colls. and Univs. (trustee). Office: Sierra Nevada College Office of President 999 Tahoe Blvd Incline Village NV 89451-9500 Office Phone: 775-831-1314.*

LARGEN, JOSEPH, retail executive, purchasing agent; b. Union, NJ, June 13, 1940; s. Fred and Wilma Largen; children: Lori, Lisa. BS in Econs, U. Mo., 1963. Mgmt. trainee R.R. Donnelly Corp., Chgo., 1964-67; distbn. mgr., material control and distbn. Warwick Electronic Co., Niles, Ill., 1967-69; with Brodart, Inc., 1969—, v.p. prodn. Williamsport, Pa., 1973-75, exec. v.p., 1975-78, pres., 1978—. Served with USCG, 1963-64. Office: Brodart Co 500 Arch St Williamsport PA 17701-7809 Home: 500 Arch St Williamsport PA 17701-7809

LARIMER, PHYLLIS MILLER, artist, art gallery director; d. Fred Henry Miller and Vesta Mae Weaver; m. Gray Welty Larimer, Aug. 28, 1948; 1 child, Fred Kenneth. Student, W.Va. State Coll., 1995—2000. Pres. Gallery 11, Charleston, W.Va., 1997—. Exhibited in group shows at Season of Colors, 1997 (1st Pl., 97), French Art Colony, 1999 (Best of Show), Va. Juried Exhbn., 2003, W.Va. Divsn. Culture and History, Charleston, 2003. Mem.: Nat. League Am. Pen Women (sec. 1997—98, treas. 1999—2000), Allied Artists W.Va. (asst. treas. 1991—94, treas. 1995—97). Lutheran. Home: 534 Sheridan Cir Charleston WV 25314 Office Phone: 304-342-0083. E-mail: plarimer@citynet.net.

LARIMORE, TOM L., lawyer; b. Ft. Worth, Sept. 21, 1937; s. T.R. and Mildred Elizabeth (Angell) L.; m. Bobbie Jeanne Wingo, Dec. 20, 1999; children: Thomas Lee, Robert Karl, Susan Lynne, Natalie Jeanne. BA, Wash. and Lee U., Lexington, Va., 1959; LLB, So. Meth. U., Dallas, 1962. Bar: Tex. 1962, US Dist. Ct. (no. dist.) Tex. 1965, US Dist. Ct. (so. dist.) Tex. 1975, US Ct. Appeals (5th cir.) 1977. Assoc. Walker & Bishop, Ft. Worth, 1962-66; ptnr. Walker, Bishop & Larimore, Ft. Worth, 1966-73, Bishop, Larimore, Lamsens & Brown, Ft. Worth, 1973-79; v.p., gen. counsel, sec. Western Co. of N.Am., Ft. Worth, 1979-80, v.p. law and adminstrn., sec., 1980-86; ptnr. Whitaker, Chalk, Swindle & Sawyer, LLP, Ft. Worth. Pres., bd. dirs. YMCA (West), Ft. Worth, 1966-68; sr. warden, vestryman All Saints Episcopal Ch., Ft. Worth, 1973-74, named Churchman of Yr., 1969; pres., bd. dirs. Sr. Citizens Ctrs., Ft. Worth, 1974-78. Fellow Tex. Bar Found.; mem. ABA, Tarrant County Bar Assn. (bd. dirs. 1978-80), Am. Corp. Counsel Ass.n, Ft. Worth Bar Assn. (chmn. dist. admissions com. 1975-77), Ft. Worth C. of C. (bd. dirs. 1985—, chmn. West Area Coun. 1985-86), Tex. Rsch. League (bd. dirs. 1980-86), Shady Oaks Country Club (Ft. Worth), Rotary (past pres. Western club Ft. Worth 1974-75, bd. dirs., Paul Harris fellow 1982). Home: 11 Lombardy Terr Fort Worth TX 76132 Office: Sparks & Larimore LLP 4800 Overton Plz Ste 310 Fort Worth TX 76109 Office Phone: 817-738-6723. Business E-Mail: tlarimore@sparks-larimore.com.

LARIN, KIRILL V., biomedical engineer, educator; b. Shikhani, Russia, Mar. 16, 1973; m. Irina V. Ashitkova, Mar. 7, 1992; children: Katherine Larina, Maria Larina. PhD, U. Tex., Galveston, 2002. Asst. prof. U. Houston, 2004—. Recipient Presdl. award, Russian Pres., 1997. Office: U Houston 4800 Calhoun Rd N207 Engring Bldg1 Houston TX 77204-4006 Home Phone: 713-743-4623; Office Phone: 713-743-4623. E-mail: klarin@uh.edu.

LARIVIERE, RICHARD WILFRED, academic administrator, educator; b. Chgo., Jan. 27, 1950; s. Wilfred Francis and Esther Irene Lariviere; m. Janis Anne Worcester, June 5, 1971; 1 child, Anne Elizabeth. BA, U. Iowa, Iowa City, 1972; PhD, U. Pa., Phila., 1978. Lectr. U. Pa., Phila., 1978-79; asst. prof. U. Iowa, Iowa City, 1980-82; prof. U. Tex., Austin, 1982—, Ralph B. Thomas Regents prof. Asian studies, 1993—, assoc. v.p., 1995-99, dean Coll. Liberal Arts, 1999—2006; exec. vice chancellor, provost U. Kans., 2006—. Dir. Sinha & Lariviere Ltd., Austin; founder Doing Bus. in India seminar; cons. Perot Sys. Corp., Dallas, 1993—; bd. dirs. eMR Tech. Ventures, Coun. Am. Overseas Rsch. Ctrs., Washington; Mossiker chair in humanities, 2003-06; mem. Kans. Univ. Hosp. Authority, Kans. Tech. Enterprise Corp. Author: Ordeals in Hindu Law, 1981, Narada Smrti, 2003; gen. editor Studies in South Asia. Fellow NEH, 1979-83. Fellow Royal Asiatic Soc.; mem. Am. Oriental Soc., Am. Inst. Indian Studies (sr.fellow 1989, 95, v.p. 1990), Assn. Asian Studies, Coun. on Fgn. Rels. Home: 1006 Avalon Rd Lawrence KS 66044 Office Phone: 785-864-4904.

LARKAM, BEVERLEY MCCOSHAM, social worker, marriage and family therapist; b. Vancouver, Can., Mar. 3, 1928; arrived in U.S., 1951; d. William Howard and Marjorie Isobel (Jerome) McCosham; children: Elizabeth, Charles, Daphne, Peter, John. A Royal Conservatory of Mus., U. Toronto, Toronto, 1948; BA, U. B.C., Can., 1949; BSW, U. B.C., 1950, MSW, 1951. Bd. cert. diplomate in clin. social work; LCSW; lic. marriage and family therapist, Tex., diplomate Internat. Conf. Advancement Profl. Practice of Clin. Social Work. Psychiat. social worker Brackenridge Hosp., 1952-54; chmn. dept. sr. high. sch. Univ. Presbyn. Ch., Austin, Tex., 1952-55, mem. Christian edn. com., 1961-67, bd. dirs. developing and organizing nursery sch., 1967-70; social worker Counseling-Psychol. Svcs. Ctr., U. Tex., 1971-72; psychiat. social worker, chief supr. Adult, Children's Mental Health Human-Devel. Ctr.-South, Austin, Tex., 1972-79; pvt. practice marriage and family therapy, sex therapy and individual and group psychotherapy Austin, Tex., 1975—. Field supr. Sch. Social Work U. Tex.; cons. in field. Mem. cmty. orgn. to establish classes for mentally retarded children, 1966-68; active City of Austin Commn. for Women, 1978—, chmn., 1982-84, emeritus, 1985—; organizer Austin Assn. for Marriage and Family Therapy, 1980-82, bd. dirs. Tex. Assn. for Marriage and Family Therapy, 1980-82, Nat. Assn. Commns. for Women, 1985-88; vol. usher Austin Symphony Orch. Soc., 1972—; mem. Heritage Soc. Austin, Georgetown Heritage Soc., Women's Symphony League of Austin, Austin Art Mus., Williamson County Hist. Mus.; mem. Dean Sch. Social Work, profl. linkage com., 1993—; vol. family therapist Child Inc./Headstart Ranch Weekends, 1995-96. Mem. NASW, Am. Assn. Marriage and Family Therapy (approved supr., com. on racial, ethnic and cultural diversity 1992-95), Am. Group Psychotherapy Assn. (cert. group psychotherapist), Southwestern Group Psychotherapy Soc. (sr. faculty), Austin Group Psychotherapy Soc., Am. Assn. Sexuality Educators, Counselors and Therapists (cert. therapist, supr.), Acad. Cert. Social Workers, Register Clin. Social Workers, Tex. Soc. for Clin. Social Work (bd. dirs. 1990—, pres. 1997-99, chmn. Austin study groups 2006—), Clin. Social Work Fedn. (fin. chmn. 1998-2000), PEO Sisterhood, Austin Woman's Forum (pres. 1994-95, 2002-03). Presbyterian (elder, session of Univ. Presbyterian Ch. 1997—). Home and Office: 2102 Raleigh Ave Austin TX 78703-2128 also: 207 E 9th St Georgetown TX 78626-5908 Personal E-mail: blarkam@earthlink.net.

LARKIN, DENIS M., geneticist, researcher; b. Novosibirsk, Russia, Feb. 8, 1975; arrived in U.S., 2001; PhD, Novosibirsk State U., 1997. Cert. geneticist Russia. Postdoctoral rsch. assoc. U. Ill., Urbana, 2001—04, vis. asst. prof., 2004—. Office: U Ill 210 ERML 1201 W Gregory Dr Urbana IL 61801 Home Phone: 217-417-5312; Office Phone: 217-333-3623. Personal E-mail: dmlarkin@gmail.com.

LARKIN, EUGENE DAVID, artist, educator; b. Mpls., June 27, 1921; s. John Peter and Martha Lavinia (Vandevere) L.; m. Audrey Jean Krueger, Jan. 29, 1947; children: Andrew, Alan. BA, U. Minn., Mpls., 1946, MA, 1949. Mem. faculty dept. art Kans. State Coll., Pittsburg, 1949-54; head printmaking dept., chmn. divsn. fine arts Mpls. Sch. Art, 1954-69; prof. design dept. U. Minn., St. Paul, 1969—, prof. emeritus design, housing and apparel, 1991—. One man shows include, Mpls. Inst. Arts, 1957, 60, 68, Syracuse U., 1962, Walker Art Center, Mpls., 1967, New Forms Gallery, Athens, Greece, 1967, U. Kans., 1972, Macalester Coll., 1974, U. Minn., St. Paul, 1973, 78, 87, 91; exhibited in groups shows at Phila. Printmakers Club, 1966, 20 American Artists, Geneva, Switzerland, 1964, Big Prints, NYU, 1968, Midwestern Printmakers, Walker Art Center, 1973, Cabo Frio Internat. Print Biennial, Brazil, 1983, Nat. Works on Paper, Minot State Coll., 1986, 17th Annual Works on Paper SW State U., San Marcos, Tex., 4th Annual North Coast Coll. Soc. Exhbn., Hiram Coll., Hudson, Ohio, 1988, 20th Annual Works on Paper Dulin Nat. Knoxville, Knoxville Mus. Art, 1988, Paepcke Meml. Bldg. Gallery, 1993, Aspen Inst. and Music Assoc. of Aspen, 1993, U. St. Thomas, Mpls./St. Paul, 1999, Weisman Gallery, U. Minn., 2005; represented in permanent collections, Mus. Modern Art, NYC, Nat. Mus. S.Africa, Capetown, Library Congress, Chgo. Art Inst., Mpls. Inst. Arts, U. Minn. Gallery, Des Moines Art Center, U. Tenn., Kans. State Coll., Minn. Mus. Art, Nat. Collection Fine Arts, Smithsonian Instn; author: Design: The Search for Unity, 1988. Recipient juror's award Rockford Internat. Print and Drawing Biennale, 1983 Mem.: Coll. Art Assn. Am. Home: 1010 W Washington South Bend IN 46601

LARKIN, JOAN, poet, literature and language educator; b. Boston, Apr. 16, 1939; d. George Joseph and Celia Gertrude (Rosenberg) Moffitt; m. James A. Larkin, Dec. 23, 1966 (div. 1969); 1 child, Kate. BA, Swarthmore Coll., 1960; MA, U. Ariz., 1969; MFA, Bklyn. Coll., 2005. Asst. prof. English CUNY-Bklyn. Coll., 1969—94, ret., 1994, adj. faculty MFA program, 1997—98; assoc. faculty MFA program Goddard Coll., 1994—96, 2002. Mem. guest faculty poetry writing Sarah Lawrence Coll., Bronxville, NY, 1984—86, 1988, 1997—2006; mem. core faculty MFA program New Eng. Coll., 2002—; disting. vis. poet Columbia Coll., Chgo., 2006, 07. Author: (poems) Housework, 1975, A Long Sound, 1986, Cold River, 1997, My Body: New and Selected Poems, 2007, (rec. poetry reading) A Sign I Was Not Alone, 1980, (prose) If You Want What We Have, 1998, Glad Day, 1998; co-editor: Gay and Lesbian Poetry in Our Time: An Anthology, 1988 (Lambda Lit. award 1988), Amazon Poetry, 1975, Lesbian Poetry, 1981; editor: A Woman Like That, 1999; co-translator: Sor Juana's Love Poems, 1997; contbr. poems to periodicals including Am. Poetry Rev., Conditions, Ms., Paris Rev., Sinister Wisdom, The Village Voice, Aphra, Endymion, The Lamp in the Spine, Global City Rev., Am. Rev., Genesis West, Sojourner, Margie, Hanging Loose. NEA fellow in poetry, 1987-88, 96, N.Y. Found. for Arts fellow in poetry, 1987-88; Creative Artists Pub. Svc. Program grantee N.Y. State Coun. Arts, 1976, 80; Mass. Cultural Coun. grantee in playwriting, 1995. Personal E-mail: larkin7@earthlink.net.

LARKIN, JOHN EDWARD, JR., orthopedic surgeon; b. St. Paul, Nov. 8, 1930; s. John E. and Ann G. (Wedebrand) L.; m. Colles Baxter, June 16, 1981. BS, U. Minn., 1953, MD, 1960. Intern Detroit Receiving Hosp., 1960-61; resident Harvard Surgery Svc./Boston City Hosp., 1961-62, Children's Hosp., Boston, 1963-66, Mass. Gen. Hosp., Boston, 1963-66; pvt. practice St. Paul, 1966-98; emeritus asst. prof. orthopedic surgery U. Minn., 1998—. Pres. Orthop. Surgery, P.A., St. Paul, 1966-98. Bd. dirs. Minn. Coun. for Quality Edn., 1970-79, Minn. Opera, 1974-79, Minn. Mus. Art, St. Paul, 1971-86, 94-95, Irish Am. Cultural Inst., 1974—2005, U. Minn. Arboretum, 1998-2007, James Ford Bell Libr., 2000-07; trustee Mpls. Inst. Art, 1980-89, mm. accessions com., 1979—. With U.S. Army, 1953-55. Fellow Am. Bd. Orthop. Surgery; mem. AMA, N.Am. Spine Soc., Minn. State Med. Assn., Minn. Orthop. Soc., Ramsey County Med. Soc., Min-Da-Mann Orthop. Soc., Irish Am. Orthop. Soc., Twin City Orthop. Soc., New Eng. Orthop. Soc. (hon.), Irish Orthop. Soc. (hon.).

LARKIN, LEE ROY, retired lawyer; b. Oklahoma City, Aug. 11, 1928; s. William Patrick and Agnes (Matthis) L.; m. Mary Jane Langston, Apr. 17, 1965; children— James William, John Patrick (dec.). BS, Oklahoma A&M U., Stillwater, 1950; MA, Vanderbilt U., 1952; LLB, William Mitchell U., St. Paul, 1959. Bar: Minn. 1959, Tex. 1963, D.C. 1963. Economist U.S. Dept. Agr., Washington, 1953; economist, lawyer Pillsbury, Mpls., 1953-62; ptnr. Harris & Larkin, Houston, 1963-65; sr. ptnr. Andrews & Kurth, Houston, 1966-93; retired, 1994. Speaker Continuing Legal Edn. Officer Sharpstown Civic Assn., Houston, 1966-94; elder St. Philip Presbyn. Ch., Houston; moderator Presbytery of New Covenant, Houston, 1980. Served to capt. USAR, 1951-58. Fellow Tex. Bar Found., Houston Bar Found.; mem. ABA, State Bar Tex., Houston Bar Assn., Riverbend Country Club, Rotary (pres. 1978-79), Delta Theta Phi. Avocations: golf, tennis, travel. Home: 3725 Wickersham Ln Houston TX 77027-4013

LARKIN, MICHAEL JOHN, editor, journalist; b. Boston, Sept. 27, 1950; s. Alfred Sinnott and Lillian Louise L.; m. Sarah Jane Wood, July 6, 1970 (div. 1985); children— Jonathan Michael, Joshua Stuart; m. Alison Rose Biggs, June 1, 1986. BA in English, U. Mass., 1973. News copy editor Boston Globe, 1974-76, sports copy editor, 1976-80, asst. bus. editor, 1980-82, Sunday editor, 1982, mag. editor, 1982-85, living/arts editor, 1985-89, sr. asst. met. editor zoned editions, 1989-92, Sunday editor, 1992-95, asst. mng. editor, 1995-2000, dep. mng. editor/news ops., 2001—. Contbr. BBC, 1997-99. Mem., editl. com., New England Newspaper Assn., 1998—. Office: The Boston Globe PO Box 55819 Boston MA 02205-5819

LARKIN, THOMAS ERNEST, JR., investment management company executive; b. Wilkes-Barre, Pa., Sept. 29, 1939; s. Thomas Ernest and Margaret (Gorman) L.; m. Margaret Givan, Nov. 2, 1979; 1 child, Thomas Ernest III. BA in Econs., U. Notre Dame, 1961; postgrad., Grad. Sch. Bus., NYU, 1962-66. New bus. rep. Mfrs. Hanover Trust Co., 1963-66; mgr. pension dept. Eastman Dillon, Union Securities, 1966-69; v.p. Shearson Hayden Stone, Inc., NYC, 1969-75; sr. v.p. Bernstein Macaulay Inc., NYC, 1969-75, Crocker Investment Mgmt. Corp., San Francisco, 1975-77, Trust Co. of the West, LA, 1977, mng. dir., 1982—, pres., COO, 1989-2000; vice chmn. The TCW Group, Inc., 2000—. Trustee U. Notre Dame, Loyola Marymount U., Mt. St. Mary's Coll., Childrens Hosp. LA, Amateur Athletic Found. LA, Heart and Lung Surgery Found., Orange County Performing Arts Ctr. With US Army, 1961-63. Mem.: Investment Counsel Assn. Am., Assn. Investment Mgmt. Sales Execs., LA Country Club, Westchester Country Club, Regency Club, Wilshire Country Club, Jonathan Club, Calif. Club. Republican. Roman Catholic. Office: TCW Group 865 S Figueroa St Ste 1800 Los Angeles CA 90017-2593

LARKIN, WILLIAM VINCENT, JR., corporate financial executive; b. NYC, July 19, 1953; s. William Vincent and Gloria Ann (Stone) L.; m. Margaret Catherine Gunn, Nov. 12, 1988; children: William Vincent III, Jeremy Stone. AB cum laude, Harvard U., 1976; MBA, Yale U., 1980. Intern White House, 1975; staff acct. Price Waterhouse & Co., NYC, 1976-78; mktg. asst. AMF Ben Hogan Co., Ft. Worth, 1980-81; asst. to pres. AMF Biol. & Diagnostic Co., Seguin, Tex., 1981-82; mktg. mgr. AMF Tuboscope, Houston, 1982-83, mgr. mill divsn., 1983-84; v.p. Tuboscope Inc., Houston, 1984-91; pres., COO Tuboscope Vetco Internat., Houston, 1991-93, pres., CEO, 1993-96; pres., COO Galtney Group, Inc., Houston, 1996-98; pres., CEO Travis Internat., Inc., Houston, 1999—2002; pres. The Six Stars Club, Houston, 2003—06; pres., CEO Corrpro Cos., Inc., 2006—. Chmn. The Six Stars Club, 2006—. Trustee Groton Sch., 2000-02. Young Pres. Orgn., 1992-2004. Mem. World Pres.' Orgn., Yale Sch. Mgmt. Alumni Assn. (chmn. nominating com. 1980-82), A.D. Club (Cambridge, Mass.), Harvard Club (NYC), Yale Club (NYC), River Oaks Country Club. Republican. Episcopalian. Avocations: woodworking, golf, tennis, crossword puzzles. Home: 369 Piney Point Rd Houston TX 77024 Office Phone: 713-460-6049. Personal E-mail: wvlarkin@corrpro.com. E-mail: wvlarkin@sixstarsclub.com.

LARO, DAVID, federal judge; b. Flint, Mich., Mar. 3, 1942; s. Samuel and Florence (Chereton) L.; m. Nancy Lynn Wolf, June 18, 1967; children:

Rachel Lynn, Marlene Ellen. BA, U. Mich., 1964; JD, U. Ill., 1967; LLM, NYU, 1970. Bar: Mich. 1968, US Dist. Ct. (ea. dist. Mich.) 1968, US Tax Ct. 1971. Ptnr. Winegarden Booth Shedd and Laro, Flint, Mich., 1970-75; sr. ptnr. Laro and Borgerson, Flint, 1975-86; prin. David Laro, P.C., Flint, 1986-92; judge US Tax Ct., Washington, 1992—. Of counsel Dykema Gossett, Ann Arbor, Mich., 1989-90; pres., CEO, Durakon Industries, Inc., Ann Arbor, 1989-91, chmn., Lapeer, Mich., 1991—; chmn. Republic Bank, 1986—, vice chmn. Republic Bancorp, Inc., Flint, 1986—; instr. Nat. Inst. Trial Advocacy, vis. prof. U. San Diego Law Sch., 1994—; cons. lectr. on tax reform and litig. in Moscow Harvard U., 1997, Ga. State U., 1998. Regent U. Mich., Ann Arbor, 1975-81; mem. Mich. State Bd. Edn., 1982-83; chmn. Mich. State Tenure Commn., 1972-75; commr. Civil Svc. Commn., Flint, 1984—. Mem. Am. Coll. Tax Counsel, State Bar Mich., Phi Delta Phi. Republican. Office: US Tax Ct 400 2nd St NW Rm 217 Washington DC 20217-0002

LAROBARDIER, GENEVIEVE KRAUSE, lawyer; d. Allan Joseph and Genevieve Ferington Krause; m. Lamont Marcell LaRobardier; children: Lamont Jr., Allan Lamont, Suzanne, Marie Bernadette, Genevieve. BA, Barnard Coll., NYC; MAT summa cum laude, Fairleigh Dickenson U., Teaneck, NJ, 1966; JD, Rutgers U, NJ, 1983. Bar: N.J. 1983, N.Y. 1985, U.S. Dist. Ct. N.J. 1983, U.S. Ct. Appeals (3d cir.) 1985, U.S. Ct. Appeals (2d cir.) 1987, U.S. Dist. Ct. (ea. dist.) N.Y. 1987, U.S. Dist. Ct. (so. dist.) N.Y. 1987, U.S. Supreme Ct. 1989. Asst. to dir. Latin Am. affairs Nat. Fgn. Trade Coun., NYC; legal intern, assoc. Margolis Law Firm, Verona, NJ, 1983—90; spl. counsel Hannoch Weisman Law Firm, Roseland, NJ, 1990—93; assoc. to ptnr. Bressler, Amery & Ross, P.C., Florham Park, NJ, 1993—. Editor and mem. jud. bd. Rutgers Law Rev., Newark; adj. faculty lang. Fairleigh Dickenson U., Teaneck, NJ. Contbg. author: N.J. Federal Civil Practice Handbook, N.J. Federal Civil Procedure Handbook; contbr. articles to profl. jours. Mem.: ABA, N.Y. State Bar Assn., N.J. State Bar Assn. (first vice chair internat. litigation and arbitration com., mem. internat. law orgns. sect., chair 2006—, Disting. Legis. Svc. award 1997).

LA ROCCA, ISABELLA, artist, educator; b. El Paso, Apr. 14, 1960; d. Remo and Alicia Estela (Gonzalez) La Rocca. BA, U. Pa., 1984; MFA, Ind. U., 1993. Freelance photographer, NYC, 1986—90; assoc. instr. Ind. U., Bloomington, 1991—93; instr. Herron Sch. Art, Indpls., 1992; vis. asst. prof. Ind. U., 1994—; asst. prof. DePauw U., Greencastle, Ind., 1994—95; vis. asst. prof. Bloomsburg (Pa.) U., 1995—96; freelance photographer, designer, animator San Francisco, 1996—. Instr. art Vista C.C. (now Berkeley City Coll.), 1998—, Coll. of Marin, 1999—2000, Calif. State U., Hayward, 1999—2001, City Coll. San Francisco, 2000—. One-woman shows include Haas Gallery, Bloomsburg, 1996, Ctr. Photography Woodstock, N.Y., Moore Coll., Pa., 1994, Emison Art Ctr., Greencastle, 1996, exhibited in group shows at 494 Gallery, N.Y.C., 1993, Kala Art Inst., Berkeley, Calif., 2000; prodr., dir.: (films) Mariana of the Universe, 2004. Ind. U. CIC Minority fellow, 1990-91; Jewish Found. Edn. Women scholar, 1990; recipient Friends of Photography Ferguson award, 1993, Serpent Source Grant for Women Artists, 1998. Office Phone: 510-981-2963. Personal E-mail: ilr@isabellalarocca.com.

LAROCCA, SALVATORE, sports association executive; m. Pam LaRocca; children: Phoebe, Samantha. Ea. regional sales mgr. NBA, 1990, dir. licensing, adult apparel, 1992—95, dir. grp. mgr. apparel, v.p. apparel, consumer products grp., 1996, v.p. e-commerce, exec. v.p. global merchandising grp. Office: NBA Olympic Tower 645 5th Ave Fl 10 New York NY 10022-5986*

LA ROCCO, ANTHONY P., lawyer; BA magna cum laude, Rutgers U., 1979; JD, Seton Hall U., 1982. Bar: N.J. 1982, N.Y. 1983, US Dist. Ct. (N.J., so. & ea. N.Y.), US Ct. Appeals (3d cir.). Adminstrv. ptnr. & mem. mgmt. com. Kirkpatrick & Lockhart Nicholson Graham LLP, Newark. Mem.: ABA, Def. Rsch. Inst., N.J. State Bar Assn., Nat. Diocesan Attorneys Assn., Essex County Bar Assn., Assn. Knights & Ladies of Equestrian Order of Holy Sepulchre of Jerusalem, Phi Beta Kappa, Phi Alpha Theta. Office: Kirkpatrick & Lockhart Nicholson Graham LLP 10th Fl One Newark Ctr Newark NJ 07102-5252 Office Phone: 973-848-4014. Office Fax: 973-848-4001. Business E-Mail: alarocco@klng.com.

LAROCCO, LARRY, former congressman; b. Van Nuys, Calif., Aug. 25, 1946; m. Christine Bideganeta, 1967; children: Anna, Matthew BA, U. Portland, 1967; MA, Boston U., 1969; student, Johns Hopkins Sch. Advanced Internat. Studies, 1968—69. N Idaho field rep. for Seantor Frank Church US Senate, 1976—81; asst. v.p., dir. mktg. Twin Falls Bank and Trust; v.p. Piper, Jaffray & Hopwood, 1989—90; mem. US Congresses from 1st Idaho Dist., 1991—95, mem. interior & insular affairs com., banking, fin. & urban affairs com.; v.p. First Idaho Corp.; fin. services cons. Shearson Lehman Hutton, Inc.; sr. lobbyist Fleishman-Hillard, Inc., 2002—04; gen. mgr. Fleishman-Hillard Govt. Rels., Washington, 2004—. Capt. U.S. Army, 1969-72. Democrat. Roman Catholic. Office: PO Box 1068 Boise ID 83701

LAROCHE, ROGER RENAN, psychiatrist; b. St. Paul, July 12, 1960; s. Gerard Auguste and Carolyn Mae (Seese) L.; m. Elizabeth Ann Tollerud, June 25, 1988; children: Austin, Hope, Cordon, Nathan. BA, Bethel Coll., St. Paul, 1982; MD, U. Minn., 1987. Diplomate Nat. Bd. Med. Examiners, Am. Bd. Psychiatry and Neurology, Am. Soc. Addiction Medicine, Geriatric Psychiatry, Addiction Psychiatry. Med. intern Hennepin County Med. Ctr., Mpls., 1987-88; resident dept. psychiatry Mayo Clinic Grad. Sch. Medicine, Rochester, Minn., 1988-91, fellowship addiction medicine dept. psychiatry, 1991-92; med. dir. dept. psychiatry Bradford (Pa.) Regional Med. Ctr., 1992—; med. dir. Cattaraugus County Coun. on Alcoholism and Substance Abuse, 1995—, Maple Manor Residential Rehab. Treatment Ctr., 2002—. Psychiat. cons. Beacon Light Behavioral Health Sys. for Children and Adolescents, 1998—; forensic psychiatrist cons. McKean County Fed. Corrections Inst., 1993-98; rotating med. student educator Mayo Med. Sch., 1987-92; contract forensic psychiatrist U.S. Bur. Prisons, Fed. Med. Ctr., Rochester, 1990-91; prin. investigator for carbamazepine in smoking cessation Mayo Clinic, Rochester, 1991-92, psychiat. rsch. com. cons., 1991-92; pvt. and cons. psychiatrist, Bradford, Pa., 1992—; staff sec.-treas. Bradford Regional Med. Ctr., 1995—96, pres. med. staff, 1997-98, chmn. credentials com., 2001—04; chmn. Bradford Nursing Pavillion's Utilization Rev. Com., 1999-, vice chair bd. Twin Tiers Pregnancy Care Ctr., 2002-04; chmn. bd. Twin Tiers Pregnancy Care Ctr., 2005—; med. dir. Maple Manor Rehab. Ctr., 2002—. Contbr. articles to profl. jours. County del. Rep. Party Conv., Rochester, 1990. Recipient Medtronic Corp.'s Med. Fellow scholarship of excellence in leadership and acads., 1983, Acad. Writing Excellence award Mayo Clinic, 1991; Mayo Clinic Grad. Sch. Medicine grantee, 1991-92. Mem. AMA (resident physician sect. nat. del. 1990, 91), Am. Psychiat. Assn., Am. Soc. Addiction Medicine, Minn. Med. Assn. (del. ho. of dels. 1990, 91, resident physician sect. state governing officer 1990, 91), Pa. Med. Assn., Pa. Psychiat. Soc., Pa. Soc. Addiction Medicine, McKean County Med. Soc. Avocations: violist, vocal soloist, painting, weight training, distance biking. Home: 80 Stone Ave Bradford PA 16701-1050 Office Phone: 814-362-2287.

LA ROCQUE, EUGENE PHILIPPE, retired bishop; b. Windsor, Ont., Can., Mar. 27, 1927; s. Eugene Joseph and Angeline Marie (Monforton) LaR. BA, U. Western Ont., 1948; MA, Laval U., 1956. Ordained priest Roman Cath. Ch., 1952, consecrated bishop 1974. Asst. parish priest Ste. Therese Ch., Windsor, 1952-54; registrar, then dean men, lectr. Christ The King Coll., U. Western Ont., 1956-64; asst. spiritual dir. St. Peter's Sem., 1964-65; prin., dean King's Coll., 1965-68; pastor St. Joseph's Ch., Rivière-aux-Canards, Ont., Canada, 1968-70, Ste. Anne's Ch., Tecumseh, 1970-74; bishop of Alexandria-Cornwall, Ont., Canada, 1974—2002; bishop emeritus, 2002—. Dean Essex County, 1970-73; trustee Essex County Roman Cath. Separate Sch. Bd., 1972-74; 1st chmn. liaison com. Can. Jewish Congress Can. Coun. Chs. and Can. Cath. Conf. Bishops, 1977-84, mem. pro-life com., 1992-94; pres. Ont. Conf. Cath. Bishops, 1992-96; pres. Fedn. Couns. Priests of Can., 1973-74. Mem. KC (3d degree, chaplain Ont. 1977-87). Roman Catholic. Address: St Joseph Parish 9399 Townline Rd Windsor ON Canada N9J 2W6 E-mail: stjosephrc@rcec.london.on.ca. *Belief in God, who creates my unique human life and has a loving plan and concern for each of his children, sustains me amidst the strains, challenges and turmoils of life.*

LAROCQUE, LINDA LOU, interior designer, educator, playwright; b. Lake Odessa, Mich., May 10, 1944; d. Emory Eugene and Lillian Martha Blakslee; m. Robert Bonte, Feb. 29, 1980 (div. May 15, 1989); 1 child, Timothy; m. Raymond John LaRocque, 1960 (div. 1977). Interior design educator Kalamazoo Valley Coll., Kalamazoo, Mich., 1973—77; interior designer Jacobson Store Home, Kalamazoo, Mich., 1974—76; owner, operator Linda LaRocque Interiors, Kalamazoo, Mich., 1976—99; interior design educator Civic and Art Groups throughout Mich. and Fla., 1973—. Author: (play) Aint Tina Turner Classical Music (Second Pl., 1998), Revival at Possum Kingdom Cmty. Ch. (Second Pl., 1999, First Pl., Mich. Cmty. Theatre Assn. Play Festival, 2007, 1st pl. award, 2007), Joyce's Choices (First Pl., 2000), Revival at Possum Kingdom Community Church (First Pl., 2007); contbr. short stories to various publs. including Guideposts, Signs of the Times, Chicken Soup for the Soul and others. Active Ministry Cmty., Kalamazoo, Mich., 1991—97, Mich. Maritime Mus., South Haven, Mich., 1994—99. Recipient Writer of the Yr., Am. Christian Writers Assn., 1997, Second Pl. Prodn., Mich. Play Festival, 1997, Third Pl. Prodn., 2001, 1st pl. playwriting award, Nat. League Am. Pen Women Ark. Writers Conf., 2005. Mem.: South Haven Ctr. Arts, Douglas Writers Club, Cmty. Theatre Assn. Mich., Am. Pen Women, Scott Club Writers Group. R-Conservative. Roman Catholic. Avocations: rehabilitating distressed real estate, gardening, cooking, music, theater. Home: 118 Superior Street South Haven MI 49090 Address: 3610 S Ocean Blvd Palm Beach FL 33480 Office Phone: 269-637-3416, 561-202-9919.

LAROIA, RAJIV, communications executive; B in EE, Indian Inst. Tech., 1985; MS, U. Md., College Park, 1989, PhD, 1992. With Mathematical Scis. Rsch. Ctr. Lucent Technologies Bell Laboratories, 1992, head Bell Labs' Digital Comm. Rsch. Dept., Wireless Rsch. Ctr., 1997; founder, CTO Flarion Technologies, Inc., Bedminster, NJ, 2000—. Lectr. in the field. Assoc. editor: IEEE Transactions on Information Theory; contbr. to numerous publs. Recipient NY Ten Awards, Exec. Coun., 2005. Fellow: IEEE. Generated over 35 patents (granted and applied); Flarion's FLASH-OFDM® technology which originated in Bell Labs under his leadership and his wireless team in early 1998. Flarion was created to commercialize that technology. Office: Flarion Technologies Inc Bedminster One 135 Rt 202/206 S Bedminster NJ 07921

LAROSE, KATHERINE STENCEL, music educator; b. Croswell, Mich., Oct. 3, 1945; d. Jacob Stanley and Catherine Marie Stencel; m. Alan Roger LaRose; children: Renee Catherine, Alan Gregory. MusB, We. Mich. U., 1969; MusM, U. Mass., 1971. Tchg. asst. U. Mass., Amherst, Mass., 1969—71, lectr. piano, 1972—80; pvt. piano tchr. San Lorenzo, Calif., 1981—87, Fremont, Calif., 1987—. Dir., organist St. Christopher's Episc. Ch., San Lorenzo, 1993—2000; dir. music St. Barnabas Ch., Alameda, Calif., 2000—. Musician: numerous recitals, 1963—, Isabella Stewart Gardner Mus., 1974—. Mem.: Music Tchrs. Assn. Calif. (coord. theory site, bd. dirs. 1984—2004), Am. Guild Organists. Home: 4265 Jacinto Dr Fremont CA 94536 Office: St Barnabas Church 1427 Sixth St Alameda CA 94501

LAROSE, LAWRENCE ALFRED, lawyer; b. Lowell, Mass., Oct. 26, 1958; s. Alfred M. and Rita B. (Plunkett) L.; m. Janet G. Yedwab, Aug. 12, 1984. BA summa cum laude, Tufts U., 1980; JD magna cum laude, Georgetown U., 1983. Bar: N.Y. 1984. Assoc. Sullivan & Cromwell, NYC, 1983-85, 87-90, Melbourne, Australia, 1985-87, Cadwalader, Wickersham & Taft, NYC, 1990-92, ptnr., 1993-2001; ptnr., co-head fin. restructuring group King & Spalding, NYC, 2001—06; ptnr., head corp. restructuring LeBoeuf, Lamb, Greene & MacRae, NYC, 2006—. Vis. fellow Faculty of Law, U. Melbourne, 1986-87; mem. adv. bd. Nat. Acad. Design Coun. Co-author: Public Companies, 2002; contbr. articles to profl. publs. Mem. adv. bd. and coun. Nat. Acad. Design, NYC. Mem. ABA, N.Y. State Bar Assn., N.Y. County Lawyers Assn., Assn. Bar City N.Y., Am. Soc. Internat. Law, Down Town Assn. in City of N.Y., Union League Club, Phi Beta Kappa. Avocations: art collecting, art history. Office: LeBoeuf Lamb Greene & MacRae 125 W 55th St New York NY 10019

LAROSSA, RALPH, utilities executive; B in Indsl. Engring., Stevens Inst. Tech., Hoboken, NJ; grad. Mgmt. Devel. Program, Harvard Bus. Sch. Assoc. engr. Pub. Svc. Electric & Gas Co., 1985, dist. mgr., field engr. gas distbn., asst. divsn. mgr., project mgr. automated work mgmt. sys., mgr. gas distbn., dir. distbn. ops., divsn. mgr. Met. electric divsn., v.p. delivery ops. support, pres., COO, 2006—. Mem. PJM Designated Officers Com., PJM Transmission Owners Agreement adminstrv. com. Bd. trustees Montclair State U., NJ; bd. dirs. Bergen County United Way. Recipient Outstanding Mgr. of Yr. award, Gas Industry Mag., 1998. Mem.: Electric Power Reliability Inst. (mem. rsch. adv. com.), Assn. Edison Illuminating Cos. (mem. com. on power delivery). Office: Pub Svc Electric & Gas Co PO Box 570 Newark NJ 07101 Office Phone: 973-430-7000.*

LAROUNIS, GEORGE PHILIP, manufacturing executive, director; b. Bklyn., Mar. 19, 1928; s. Philip John and Helen (Cormentelou) L.; m. Mary G. Efthymiatou, Jan. 13, 1958; 1 child, Daphne H. B.E.E., U. Mich., 1950, postgrad. in Law; JD, N.Y. U., 1954. Electronics engr. in research and devel. Columbia U. Electronics Research Lab., 1952-54; assoc. firm Pennie, Edmonds, Morton, Barrows & Taylor, NYC, 1954-58; fgn. patent atty. Western Electric Co., NYC, 1958-60; asst. dir. Bendix Internat., Paris, 1960, dir. licensing and indsl. property rights, to 1974; v.p. staff ops. Bendix Europe, 1974-77; v.p. Bendix Internat. Fin. Corp.; v.p. Europe, Middle East and Africa Bendix Corp., Paris, 1977-82; pres. Bendix Internat. Cons. Corp., 1974-86; v.p., group exec. Allied Automotive, 1982-85; pres. Allied-Signal Fibers Europe S.A.; v.p. Allied-Signal Internat., 1985-93. Bd. dirs. Hellenic Link, Inc., CopyTele, Inc., Delphi Soc., Am. Farm Sch., Greece. With U.S. Army, 1946-47. Decorated chevalier Legion of Honor (France). Mem. NY Patent Bar Assn., Fed. Patent Bar Assn., Licensing Execs. Soc., Am. C. of C. in France and Greece (dir., pres., exec. com. European Coun.), PanHellenic Sci.-Culture Union, Polo Club de Paris, Papagou Tennis Club (Athens), EU Club (Athens), Tau Beta Pi, Eta Kappa Nu. Home: 15-17 A Tsoha St Athens 11521 Greece Personal E-mail: mglar@otenet.gr.

LAROWE, MILES, academic administrator; m. Betsy LaRowe; children: Meighan, Margaux. BBA, MA, EdD. Instr., adminstr. Laramie County Cmty. Coll.; instr. Ea. Wyo. Coll., Chatman Coll.; dean Dodge City Coll., 1993—96; pres. Ea. Idaho Tech. Coll., 1996—2003, Northwest Coll., Powell, Wyo., 2003—. Bd. dir. Cody County C. of C. Office: Northwest Coll President's Office 231 W 6th St Powell WY 82435*

LAROWE, RICHARD PHILIP, systems engineer; b. Norwich, Conn., Apr. 21, 1964; s. Richard Philip and Pauline Pinette LaRowe; m. Tracey Elizabeth Kirchner, Aug. 19, 1989; children: Lisa Renee, Timothy Philip, Brian Richard. BS, Northeastern U., Boston, 1987; PhD, Duke U., Durham, NC, 1991. Tech. cons. Encore Computer, Marlboro, Mass., 1991—91; sr. scientist Worcester Poly. Inst., Mass., 1991—94, Enterprise Computing Inst., Hopkinton, Mass., 1994—96; sr. sys. engr. BBN Technologies, Cambridge, Mass., 1996—98; product arch. GTE CyberTrust, Needham, Mass., 1998—2000; v.p. engring. Balt. Techs., Needham, Mass., 2000—02; fellow engring. Raytheon Co., Portsmouth, RI, 2002—. Contbr. articles to profl. jours. Mem.: IEEE, Assn. Computing Machinery. Achievements include patents in field. Home: 16 Hunters Run Franklin MA 02038 Home Phone: 508-541-8267.

LARPENTEUR, JAMES ALBERT, JR., retired lawyer; b. Seattle, Aug. 6, 1935; s. James Albert and Mary Louise (Coffey) L.; m. Hazel Marie Arntson, Apr. 23, 1965 (div. 1983); children: Eric James, Jason Clifford; 1 adopted child, Brenda Mon Fong; m. Katherine Annette Bingham, Nov. 8, 1986. BS in Bus., U. Oreg., 1957, LLB, 1961. Bar: Oreg. 1961, U.S. Dist. Ct. Oreg. 1961, U.S. Tax Ct. 1962, U.S. Ct. Appeals (9th cir.) 1962, U.S. Supreme Ct. 1965. Assoc. Schwabe Williamson & Wyatt, Portland, Oreg., 1961-69, ptnr., 1969-82, sr. ptnr., 1982—2002, mem. exec. com., 1989—93, ret., 2003. Dir. exec. com. Portland Rose Festival Assn., 1975—2004, pres., 1987; ex-officio dir. Portland Visitors Assn., 1981—2005; bd. dirs., mem. exec. com. Providence Child Ctr. Found., 1983—94, chmn. exec. com., 1986—87; bd. dirs. Willamette Light Brigade, 1987—, Cath. Charities Portland, 1989—92, Albertina Kerr Ctrs., 1996—2003, Japanese Garden Soc., 2000—07. Mem.: Oreg. Bar Assn. (chmn. bus. law sect. 1986—87, editor, writer, spkr. numerous continuing legal edn. programs, real estate, alternate dispute resolution, securities regulation sects), Thunderbird Country Club of Rancho Mirage, City Club of Portland, Waverley Country Club, Univ. Club of Portland, Multnomah Athletic Club (pres. 1984). Avocation: golf. Office: Schwabe Williamson & Wyatt 1211 SW 5th Ave Ste 1800 Portland OR 97204-3713 Office Phone: 503-796-2920.

LARR, PETER, retired bank executive; b. Indpls., Jan. 17, 1939; s. David and Marjorie Kathleen (Hearne) L.; m. Rosamond Holmes Woodfield, July 7, 1962; children— Alexia Aisha, Diana Kirsten, David Hearne BA, Princeton U., 1960. Asst. mgr. London and Beirut brs. Chase Manhattan Bank, 1961-67, v.p., div. exec. land transp., 1976-78, v.p., group exec. credit tng. and devel., 1978-80, v.p., div. exec. commodity fin., 1980-83; sr. v.p., bus. exec. nat. corr. banking Chase Manhattan Bank, NYC, 1983-85, sr. v.p., exec. domestic instl. banking, 1985-90, sr. v.p., risk asset rev. exec., 1990-97, sr. v.p. sr. credit and porfolio mgmt. exec. Asia Hong Kong, 1997—; mgr. dir. group credit officer Global Bank, 1997-2000; ret., 2000—. Assoc. vestry Christ Ch., Rye, N.Y., 1983-85; planning commr., City of Rye, 1992-94, 97—, human rights commr., 2001—. Mem. Assn. Res. City Bankers (assoc., bank pay sys. com. 1984-90), Am. Bankers Assn. (chmn. corp. banking divsn. 1988-94), Robert Morris Assn. N.Y. (pres. 1994), Am. Yacht Club, Apawamis Club. Avocations: tennis, golf, genealogy.

LARRABEE, BARBARA PRINCELAU, retired intelligence officer; b. Oakland, Calif., Sept. 21, 1923; d. Paul and Mary Emilie (Rueger) Princelau; m. John Joseph Boyle, Oct. 21, 1950 (dec.); m. Donald Richard Larrabee, Nov. 2, 1996. BA, U. Calif., Berkeley, 1948. Intelligence officer CIA, Langley, Va., 1954-82. Bd. dirs. The Thrift Shop, Washington, 1988-92; mem. Women's Bd. Columbia Hosp. for Women, Washington, 1986-2001, mem. exec. com., 1989-91, 96-98; mem. com. Washington Antiques Show, 1989-2004; active Rep. Womens Fed. Forum, Washington, League of Rep. Women of D.C., Inc. Recipient Cert. of Distinction CIA, 1982. Mem.: Assn. Former Intelligence Officers (bd. dirs. 1993—99, v.p. 1997—99, exec. com. 1997—99), Ctrl. Intelligence Retiree Assn., Evergreen Garden Club (v.p. 2001—02), Sulgrave Club, Nat. Press Club, U. Calif. Berkeley Alumni Club of Washington (rec. sec. 1976—77, v.p. 1984—86), Sigma Kappa (v.p. No. Va. alumnae 1992—95, devel. com. Sigma Kappa Found., Inc. 1993—95). Episcopalian. Avocations: aerobics, needlecrafts, travel. Home: 4956 Sentinel Dr Apt 304 Bethesda MD 20816-3562

LARRABEE, DONALD RICHARD, publishing executive; b. Portland, Maine, Aug. 8, 1923; s. Henry Carpenter and Marion (Clapp) L.; m. Mary Elizabeth Rolfs, Oct. 9, 1948 (dec. Feb. 1996); children: Donna Louise (Mrs. John Palmer), Robert Rolfs; m. Barbara Princelau Boyle, Nov. 2, 1996. Student, Syracuse U., 1941-43. Reporter Portland Press Herald, 1941-43, Syracuse Post Standard, 1943; reporter Griffin-Larrabee News Bur., Washington, 1946-54, mng. editor, 1954-67, bur. chief, 1967-69, owner, 1969-78; dir. Washington office, State of Maine, 1978-89. Dir. Nat. Press Bldg. Corp., 1973-85 Bd. dirs. Nat. Press Found., 1978—. Served with USAAF, 1943-45. Mem.: Assn. Former Intelligence Officers (bd. dirs. 1999—2002), Corrs. for Congl. Press Galleries, Maine Soc. Washington (pres. 1950—53), Chevy Chase Club, Nat. Press Club (Washington) (sec. 1953—54, treas. 1966—67, chmn. bd. 1969, pres. 1973), Gridiron Club (Washington). Episcopalian. Home and Office: 4956 Sentinel Dr #304 Bethesda MD 20816-3562

LARRABEE, MATTHEW L., lawyer; b. Palo Alto, Calif., July 7, 1955; AB, U. Calif., Davis, 1977; JD, U. Calif., San Francisco, 1980. Bar: Calif. 1980. Atty. Heller, Ehrman, White & McAuliffe, San Francisco, 1990—, Co-Chair, San Francisco Litigation Dept., 1995—97, San Francisco Managing Ptnr., 1997—99, Firmwide Practice Chair, Litigation, 1999—2005, chmn., 2005—. Mem. ABA, Am. Law Inst., Order of Coif. Office: Heller Ehrman White & McAuliffe 333 Bush St San Francisco CA 94104-2806 Office Phone: 415-772-6000. Business E-Mail: matt.larrabee@hellerehrman.com.

LARRABEE, WAYNE FOX, JR., facial plastic surgeon; b. Ft. Benning, Ga., May 10, 1945; s. Wayne Fox and Ruth (Truex) L.; m. Tane; children: Shane, Sascha, Kai, Spencer, Gregory. BS in Math., Midland Coll., 1967; postgrad., U. Edinburgh, 1965-66; MD, MPH in Epidemiology, Tulan U., 1971. Diplomate Am. Bd. Otolaryngology; lic. MD, Wash. Intern Letterman Gen. Hosp., San Francisco, 1971-72; resident in surgery Tulane U. Svc. Charity Hosp., New Orleans, 1975-76, resident in otolaryngology and maxillofacial surgery, 1976-79; head sect. reconstructive and aesthetic plastic surgery Va. Mason Med. Ctr., Seattle, 1986-88, head sect. otolaryngology, 1985-88. Instr. dept. surgery Tulane Med. Sch., 1975-79, instr. dept. otolaryngology, 1976-79; clin. assoc. prof. U. Wash., 1979-88; clin. prof., U. Wash., 1988-2001; pres. med. bd. Virginia Mason Rsch. Ctr., 1985-88; observations fellowship Moorfields Eye Hosp., London, 1988; presenter in field; pres. Am. Bd. Facial Plastic Surgery, 2000-03. Author: Surgical Anatomy of the Face, 1993, Principles of Facial Reconstruction, 1995, Roslyn A Town's Portrait, 2d edit., 1999; mem. editl. bd. JAMA, 1999—; editor Archives of Facial Plastic Surgery, 1999—. Maj. U.S. Army Med. Corps, 1972-75, Panama Canal Zone. Fellow ACS, Am. Acad. Facial Plastic and Reconstructive Surgery (pres. 1996), Am. Soc. Head and Neck Surgery, Triological Soc., Am. Bd. Otolaryngology (bd. dirs., pres. 2002—); mem. King County Med. Soc., Am. Acad. Otolaryngology-Head and Neck Surgery. Avocations: photography, poetry. Office: Ctr for Facial Plastic Surgery 600 Broadway # 280 Seattle WA 98122 Home Phone: 206-232-8868; Office Phone: 206-386-3550. Business E-Mail: info@larrabeecenter.com.

LARRANAGA, JIM, men's college basketball coach; b. Bronx, NY, Oct. 2, 1949; m. Liz Larranaga; children: Jay, Jon. BA in Economics, Providence Coll., 1971. Coll. basketball player Providence Coll., 1967—71; basketball player Geronemo Basketball Club, Belgium, 1976—77, coach, 1977; asst. coach Davidson Coll., 1971—76; head coach Am. Internat. Coll., 1977—79; asst. coach U. Va., 1979—86; head coach Bowling Green State U., 1986—97, George Mason U., 1997—. Named to Providence Coll. Hall of Fame, 1991. Achievements include coaching first unranked final four team, 2006. Office: George Mason U Office PC 1090 Mail Stop 1D4

4400 University Dr Fairfax VA 22030 Office Phone: 703-993-3240. Office Fax: 703-993-3025. Business E-Mail: jlarrana@gmu.edu.

LARROCA, RAYMOND G., lawyer; b. Jan. 5, 1930; s. Raymond Gil and Elsa Maria (Morales) L.; m. Barbara Jean Strand, June 21, 1952 (div. 1974); children: Denise Ann Sheehan, Gail Ellen, Raymond Gil, Mark Talbot, Jeffrey William. BSS, Georgetown U., 1952; JD, 1957. Bar: DC 1957, U.S. Supreme Ct. 1960. Assoc. Kirkland, Fleming, Green, Martin & Ellis, Washington, 1957-64; ptnr. Kirkland, Ellis, Hodson, Chaffetz & Masters, Washington, 1964-67, Miller, Cassidy, Larroca & Lewin, Washington, 1967-2000, Baker Botts, Washington, 2000—. Served with arty. U.S. Army, 1948-49, to 1st lt., inf., 1952-54. Mem. ABA, D.C. Bar, Bar Assn. D.C., The Barristers. Republican. Roman Catholic. Club: Congl. Country (Potomac, Md.). Office: Baker Botts LLP 1299 Pennsylvania Ave NW Washington DC 20004-2400 E-mail: ray.larroca@bakerbotts.com.

LARRY, R. HEATH, lawyer, director; b. Huntingdon, Pa., Feb. 24, 1914; s. Ralph E. and Mabel (Heath) L.; m. Eleanor Ketler, Sept. 10, 1938; children: David Heath, Dennis Ketler, Thomas Richard. AB, Grove City Coll., 1934, LL.D., 1964; JD, U. Pitts., 1937. Bar: Pa. 1937, D.C. 1937. Pvt. practice, 1937-38; atty. Nat. Tube Co., 1938-44, sec., dir., 1944-48; gen. atty. U.S. Steel Corp., Pitts., 1948-52, asst. gen. solicitor, 1952-58, adminstrv. v.p. labor relations, 1958-66, exec. v.p., asst. to chmn., 1966—76, vice chmn. bd., 1976—77; pres. N.A.M., 1977-80; of counsel Reed Smith Shaw & McClay, Washington, 1980—. Dir. emeritus Textron, Inc. Trustee emeritus Grove City Coll.; former trustee Conf. Bd. Mem. Am. Iron and Steel Inst. Clubs: Met. (Washington); Economic (N.Y.C.); Gulf Stream Golf, Gulf Stream Bath and Tennis, Little. Presbyterian. Home: 4333 N Ocean Blvd Apt A53 Delray Beach FL 33483-7559 Personal E-mail: heathlarry@aol.com.

LARRY THE CABLE GUY, (DANIEL LAWRENCE WHITNEY), comedian, radio personality; b. Pawnee City, Neb., Feb. 17, 1963; Student, Baptist U. Am. Radio commentator, 1992—; comedian Blue Collar Comedy Tour, 2000—03. Comedian (albums) Lord, I Apologize, 2001, A Very Larry Christmas, 2004, The Right to Bear Arms, 2005, (DVD special) Git-R-Done, 2004, (films) Blue Collar Comedy Tour: The Movie, 2003, Blue Collar Comedy Tour Rides Again, 2004; actor: (films) Larry the Cable Guy: Health Inspector, 2006; (TV series) Blue Comedy TV, 2004—. Office: c/o Parallel Entertainment Ste 1040 9255 Sunset Blvd Los Angeles CA 90069

LARSDOTTER, ANNA-LISA, retired translator, artist; b. Uddevalla, Bohus Län, Sweden, May 12, 1932; d. Lars Helge Svensson and Signe Ingeborg Jacobsson-Svensson; m. Erich S. Weibel, Aug. 17, 1956 (div. 1962). Student, Tchrs. Coll. for Women, Stockholm, 1951—52, Art Student's League, NYC, 1953—55, New Sch. for Social Rsch., 1963—66, Summit Art Ctr., NJ, 1964—68, Academie des Beaux-Arts, Lausanne, Switzerland, 1960—62. Sec., translator internat. program Mus. Modern Art, NYC, 1956; archivist Lawrence-Myden Collection, NYC, 1963—64; archivist, translator Frederick Kiesler Catalogue, NYC, 1979; freelance translator Data Profls. Inc., Ft. Lauderdale, Fla., 1986—97. Mem. exec. com. Summit Art Ctr., 1967—69. Contbr. articles to profl. jours.; performer: (dances) Byrd Hoffman Sch., 1969—75; appeared in: (films) Strong Medicine, 1984; (plays) Life and Times of Sigmund Freud, 1969—74; Life and Times of Joseph Stalin, 1973; Attic Clouds, 1973; A Letter for Queen Victoria, 1974; Festival d'Automne, 1974; Overture in N.Y.C., 1972; actor: (tour) Theatre des Nations, 1973; organizer: (exhbns.) with Summit Art Ctr. and Bell Tel. Labs., 1964—69; preparer: catalogue pvt. collection of composer Jack Lawrence and Walter Myden, 1963. Lutheran. Avocations: art, music, history, genealogy. Personal E-mail: allarsdotter@yahoo.com.

LARSEN, CLARK SPENCER, anthropology educator; b. Omaha, Apr. 10, 1952; s. Leon Reuben and Patricia Ann (Loper) L.; m. Christine E. Najjar, May 16, 1987. BA, Kans. State U., Manhattan, 1974; MA, U. Mich., 1975, PhD, 1980. Asst. prof. anthropology U. Mass., Dartmouth, 1979-83, No. Ill. U., DeKalb, 1983-85, assoc. prof. anthropology, 1985-87, chmn., assoc. prof. anthropology, 1987-89; assoc. prof. biol. anthropology Purdue U., West Lafayette, Ind., 1989-91, prof. biol. anthropology, 1991-93; assoc. prof. biol. anthropology U. N.C., Chapel Hill, 1993-95, prof. biol. anthropology, 1995—2001; disting. prof., chair anthropology Ohio State U., Columbus, Ohio, 2001—. Rsch. assoc. Am. Mus. Natural History, N.Y.C., 1980—. Author: (monograph) Anthropology of St. Catherines 3, 1982, (book) Human Origins, 1985, 2d edit., 1991, Bioarchaeology: Interpreting Behavior from the Human Skeleton, 1997; editor: Antiquity and Origin of Native North Americans, 1985, (monograph) Archaeology of Mission Santa Catalina 2, 1990, American Jour. Physical Anthropology, 2001- NSF grantee, 1984-89, 1993-96, 2002-, L.S.B. Leakey Found. grantee, 1990. Fellow AAAS; mem. Am. Assn. Phys. Anthropologists, Am. Anthropol. Assn., Soc. for Am. Archaeology, Paleopathology Assn., Sigma Xi (Disting. Lectr. 2006-). Avocations: film, music, camping, hiking, genealogy. Office: Ohio State U Dept Anthropology Columbus OH 43210-1364 Home Phone: 614-451-8573; Office Phone: 614-292-4117. Business E-Mail: larsen.53@osu.edu.

LARSEN, DAVID ALLEN, educational consultant; BS in Edn., English, Northern Ill. U., DeKalb, 1969, MS in Edn., Reading, 1978. Cert. sch. adminstrn. Ill., 1985. Tchr., clinician, dean students Dempster Jr. HS, Mt. Prospect, Ill., 1969—82; asst. prin., dept. chmn. Grove Jr. HS, Elk Grove Village, Ill., 1982—90; asst. prin. Holmes Jr. HS, Mt. Prospect, 1990—93, Rupley Elem. Sch., Elk Grove Village, 1993—94; prin. John Jay Elem. Sch., Mt. Prospect, Ill., 1994—2002; sch. advisor, substitute prin. Cmty. Consolidated Sch. Dist 59, Arlington Heights, Ill., 2002—; sch. reform cons. North Cook Intermediate Svc. Ctr., Des Plaines, Ill., 2005—. Educational grant writer. Named a Mt. Prospect Shining Star, Village of Mt. Prospect, 2000; recipient Mayor's Unity award, 2002, Svc. Above Self award, Rotary, 2002. Mem.: Phi Delta Kappa (svc. key 1996). Home: 83 Dunham Pl Saint Charles IL 60174

LARSEN, DONALD E., education educator; s. Haakon Amandus and Charlotte Larsen; m. Janice M. Erickson, July 29, 1972; children: Karl A., Jon A. BA in English, Seattle Pacific U., 1965—69; MA in Humanities, Pacific Luth. U., Tacoma, Wash., 1971—78; MA in Ednl. Adminstrn., Pacific Luth. U., Tacoma, 1984—88; PhD in Ednl. Adminstrn., Wash. State U., Pullman, 1999—2002. Tchr. Clover Pk. Sch. Dist., Lakewood, Wash., 1969—83, adminstr., 1983—2000; post-doctoral appointment Wash. State U., Pullman, Wash., 2002—03; asst. prof. ednl. adminstrn. U. Pacific, Stockton, Calif., 2003—05, We. Wash. U., Bellingham, 2005—. Mem. profl. edn. adv. com. Office Supt. Pub. Instrn., chair, 1997—98. Grantee David L. Clark fellowship, U. Coun. Ednl. Adminstrn., 2002; Faculty Resource grant, U. Pacific, 2004—05. Mem.: Coun. Secondary Schs. (chair 1997—98), Nat. Mid. Sch. Assn., Am. Ednl. Rsch. Assn., Wash. Coun. Ednl. Adminstrn. Programs, Phi Kappa Phi. Home Phone: 253-376-5926.

LARSEN, GARY LOY, physician, researcher; b. Wahoo, Nebr., Jan. 10, 1945; s. Allan Edward and Dorothy Mae (Hengen) L.; m. Letitia Leah Hoyt, Dec. 22, 1967; children: Kari Lyn, Amy Marie. BS, U. Nebr., 1967; MD, Columbia U., 1971. Diplomate Am. Bd. Pediat., Am. Bd. Pediatric Pulmonology (chmn. 1990-92). Pediatric pulmonologist Nat. Jewish Med. and Rsch. Ctr., Denver, 1978—, head divsn. pediatric pulmonary medicine, 1989—; mem. faculty U. Colo. Sch. Medicine, Denver, 1978—, dir. sect. pediatric pulmonary medicine, 1987—2003, prof. pediat., 1990—; head dept. respiratory medicine The Children's Hosp., Denver, 2002—03. Editl. councillor Pediat. Pulmonology; editl. adv. bd. Child Mag., 2007—. Assoc. editor: Jour. Allergy and Clin. Immunology; contbr. articles to prof. jours. Mem. sci. adv. panel Nat. Urban Air Toxics Rsch. Ctr., 1998-2005. Maj. M.C., U.S. Army, 1974-76. Med. rsch. grantee NIH, 1981—. Mem. Am. Thoracic Soc. (chmn. pediatric assembly 1987-88), Soc. Pediatric Rsch., N.Y. Acad. Scis., Chilean Respiratory Soc. (hon.), Western Soc. Pediat. Rsch., Phi Beta Kappa, Alpha Omega Alpha. Lutheran. Office: Nat Jewish Med & Rsch Ctr 1400 Jackson St Denver CO 80206-2761 Business E-Mail: larseng@njc.org.

LARSEN, JONATHAN ZERBE, journalist; b. NYC, Jan. 6, 1940; s. Roy Edward and Margaret (Zerbe) L.; m. Katharine Wilder, May 28, 1966; m. Jane Amsterdam, Aug. 31, 1985 (div. 2000); 1 child, Edward Roy. BA, Harvard U., 1961, MAT, 1963; DHL, Cambridge Coll., 1997. Contbg. editor Time mag., NYC, 1965-66, corr. Chgo., 1966-68, Los Angeles, 1968-70, bur. chief Saigon, Vietnam, 1970-71, asso. editor, 1972-73; editor New Times mag., NYC, 1974-79; Nieman fellow Harvard U., 1979-80; news editor Life mag., 1980-81, sr. editor, 1981-82; editor-in-chief The Village Voice, NYC, 1989-94; free-lance writer, 1982—. Chmn. editl. bd. OnEarth Mag. Trustee Natural Resources De. Coun., 1982—2005, hon. trustee, 2005—; bd. dirs. Larsen Fund, mem. panel of judges John B. Oakes award; chmn. bd. Cambridge Coll. Recipient Clarion award, 1986. Home: 565 West End Ave New York NY 10024 E-mail: JLarsen186@aol.com.

LARSEN, KIMBERT E., journalist; b. Boulder, Colo., June 14, 1941; s. Junius and Dorothy May (Cavanaugh) Larsen. AA, Idaho State U., 1963. Bur. reporter Deseret News, Salt Lake City, 1959-60, Salt Lake Tribune, Salt Lake City, 1960-63; assoc. editor Register Sys. of Newspapers, Denver, 1963—64, 1966-69; city hall reporter Ind.-Record, Helena, Mont., 1964; editor Western Mont. Register, 1965-66; nat. affairs staff writer Nat. Cath. News Svc., Washington, 1969-70; reporter, editor Billings (Mont.) Gazette, Billings, 1970-90; freelance writer Billings, 1990—; news editor The Harvest, 1999—. Author: The Case for Rimrocks National Monument, 1970, From Age to Age: A History of the Catholic Church in Eastern Montana, 2004; contbr. Ecotage!, 1972; mem. editl. bd. The Billings Gazette, 1983-85. Pres. Idaho Young Dems., Pocatello, Idaho, 1963; chmn. Diocesan Pastoral Coun., diocese of Great Falls-Billings, 1995-99, Parish Pastoral Coun. of Holy Rosary Ch., Billings, 1994-97, 2000-03, 06-; bd. dirs. Mont. Cath. Conf., 1999-2005, sec.-treas., 1999-2001, v.p., 2001-05; del. Mont. Assn. Chs., 2004-; mem. Mont. Human Rights Network, Oblates St. Benedict. Travel grant, Norwegian Royal Ministry of Fgn. Affairs, Oslo, 1980. Mem. Yellowstone Valley Audubon Soc., Sierra Club. Independent. Roman Catholic. Avocations: books, classical music, travel, hiking. Home: 2451 Cascade Ave Billings MT 59102-0535 E-mail: harvestnews@bresnan.net.

LARSEN, LAUREN, school system administrator; Dir. curriculum and assessment Dept. Edn. VI, dep. commr. edn., acting commr. edn., 2006—. Co-author (with George F. Tyson and Arnold Highfield): Emancipation in the US Virgin Islands: 150 Years of Freedom 1948-1998, 1999. Office: VI Dept Edn No 44-46 Kongens Gade St Thomas VI 00802

LARSEN, MARSHALL O., manufacturing executive; b. ND; BS, U.S. Mil. Acad., West Point, 1970; MS, Purdue Univ. Op. analyst and fin. mgr. Goodrich Corp., Charlotte, NC, 1977—81, dir. of planning and analysis, dir. of product mktg., 1981—86, asst. to the pres., gen. mgr., 1986—94, v.p., 1994—95, exec. v.p., 1995—2002, pres., COO, 2002—03, pres., CEO, 2003—, chmn., 2004—. Lt. US Army, 1970—76. Office: Goodrich Corp Four Coliseum Ctr 2730 W Tyvola Rd Charlotte NC 28217-4578*

LARSEN, POUL STEEN, retired information science educator; b. Copenhagen, Jan. 30, 1940; s. Kaj Poul and Inger Elise (Seligmann) L.; m. Marianne Pugdahl, July 27, 1963; children: Mara, Anne. Exam.Phil., U. Copenhagen, 1961. Lectr. Copenhagen Coll. Engring., 1961-73, Royal Sch. Library/Info. Sci., Denmark, 1971-73, libr., 1972, asst. dept. head, assoc. prof., 1973-76, head dept. info. media, prof., 1976—2006, chmn. faculty, 1992-99, prof. emeritus, 2006—. Chmn. Danish Best Books of Yr. Com., 1982-89, Danish Standards Com. Phys. Characteristics of Media, 1988-2001; vice-chmn. ISO com. Terminology of Info. and Documentation, 1993-2001; convenor ISO Expert Group Standardization of Graphic Materials, 1991-2001; vis. prof. UCLA, 1983. Author: Contemporary Danish Book Art, 1986, 2nd edit., 1989; co-author: Informationsordbogen (Danish Standards Dictionary of Information Terms), 1991, 3d edit., 2002; contbg. author: Danish Dictionary of National Biography, 1978-85, Danish Handbook of Cultural History, 1991, Danish National Ency., 1993-00, ISO 5127 Information and Documentation-Vocabulary, 2001; contbr. articles to profl. jours.; editor, book designer, designer typefaces for digital typesetting: LIBER, 1993, MEGA, 1996, COLONNA, 1996; mem. editl. bd. The Libr. Quar., U. Chgo., 1999-04; mem. editl. adv. bd. Ency. Libr. and Info. Scis., 2005-. Recipient Prize of Distinction, Soc. for Bookcrafts, 2003; Yale U. fellow, 1984. Home: Paltholm Ter 8 F DK-3520 Farum Denmark Home (Summer): Byledsgade 5 Bornholm DK 3790 Hasle Denmark Business E-Mail: psl@psl.dk.

LARSEN, RALPH IRVING, retired environmental engineer; b. Corvallis, Oreg., Nov. 26, 1928; s. Walter Winfred and Nellie Lyle (Gellatly) L.; m. Betty Lois Garner, Oct. 14, 1950 (dec. Feb. 1989); children: Karen Larsen Cleeton, Eric, Kristine Larsen Burns, Jan Alan; m. Annie Harmon King, Aug. 3, 1991; children: Vikki King Ball, Terri King Blankenship, Cindi King King (dec.). BSCE, Oreg. State U., 1950; MS, Harvard U., 1955, PhD in Air Pollution and Indsl. Hygiene, 1957. San. engr. divsn. water pollution control USPHS, Washington, 1950-54; chief tech. svc. state and cmty. svc. sect. Nat. Air Pollution Control Adminstrn., Cin., 1957-61; with EPA and Nat. Air Pollution Control Adminstrn., 1961—2006; environ. rsch. engr. Nat. Exposure Rsch. Lab., Rsch. Triangle Park, NC, 1971—2006. Air pollution cons. to Poland, 1973, 75, Brazil, 1978; condr. seminars for air pollution researchers, Paris, Vienna and Milan, 1975; adj. lectr. Inst. Air Pollution Tng., 1969-1980. Contbr. more than 55 articles to profl. jours. Elder Christian and Missionary Alliance Ch. Recipient Commendation medal USPHS, 1979; named to Engring. Hall of Fame at Oreg. State U., 2001. Mem. Air and Waste Mgmt. Assn. (mem. editl. bd. jour. 1971-88), Conf. Fed. Environ. Engrs., USPHS Commd. Officers Assn. (past br. pres.), Sigma Xi. Republican. Home: 4012 Colby Dr Raleigh NC 27609-6045 *God issued me a 1928-model body. It works best, for others and me, as I read a chapter of the Owner's Manual (The Holy Bible) first thing each morning.*

LARSEN, RALPH S(TANLEY), retired pharmaceutical executive; b. Bklyn., Nov. 19, 1938; s. Andrew and Gurine (Henningsen) L.; m. Dorothy M. Zeitfuss, Aug. 19, 1961; children: Karen, Kristen, Garret. BBA, Hofstra U., 1962. Mfg. trainee, then supr. prodn. and dir. mfg. Johnson & Johnson, New Brunswick, NJ, 1962—77; v.p. ops., v.p. mktg. McNeil Consumer Products Co. div. Johnson & Johnson, Ft. Washington, Pa., 1977—81; pres. Becton Dickenson Consumer Products, Paramus, NJ, 1981—83; pres. Chicopee divsn. Johnson & Johnson, New Brunswick, NJ, 1983—85, co. group chmn., 1985—86, vice chmn., exec. com., bd. dirs., 1986—89, chmn. bd., pres., CEO, 1989—2002, bd. dirs., mem. exec. com. Bd. dirs. Xerox Corp., GE. Trustee Robert Wood Johnson Found. Republican. Avocations: skiing, boating, art. Office: 100 Albany St Ste 200 New Brunswick NJ 08901

LARSEN, RICHARD GARY, finance company executive; b. Tampa, Fla., Nov. 28, 1948; s. Dagfinn T. Larsen and Elizabeth M. Thompson; m. Harriet Taylor Jones, Dec. 19, 1970; children: Daniel, Alice Taylor. BBA in Acctg., George Washington U., 1971, JD, 1974; postgrad., Columbia U., 1985. Bar: Va. 1974; CPA, D.C., Va. Mem. staff U.S. Senate, Washington, 1967-73; ptnr. Ernst & Young, Washington, 1973—; adj. prof. U. Md., College Park, 1976-78, Am. U., Washington, 1977-78. Mem. ABA, Va. Bar Assn., AICPAs, Md. Soc. CPAs, Met. Club (Washington), Coral Beach and Tennis Club (Bermuda), Chatham Beach and Tennis Club, Eastward Ho Country Club (Chatham), Belle Haven Country Club. Home: 319 S St Asaph St Alexandria VA 22314-3745 Office: Ernst & Young 1225 Connecticut Ave NW Washington DC 20036-2621 E-mail: richard.larsen@ey.com.

LARSEN, RICHARD LEE, city manager, consultant, retired mayor, arbitrator; b. Jackson, Miss., Apr. 16, 1934; s. Homer Thorsten and Mae Cordelia (Amidon) L.; m. Virginia Fay Alley, June 25, 1955; children: Karla, Daniel, Thomas (dec.), Krista, Lisa. BS in Econs. and Bus. Adminstrn, Westminster Coll., Fulton, Mo., 1959; postgrad., U. Kans., Lawrence, 1959-61. Fin. dir. Village of Northbrook, Ill., 1961-63; city mgr. Munising, Mich., 1963-66, Sault Ste. Marie, Mich., 1966-72, Ogden, Utah, 1972-77, Billings, Mont., 1977-79; mcpl. cons., 1979—2003; pub./pvt. sector labor rels. cons., arbitrator, 1979—2003; semi-ret., 2003. Mayor City of Billings, Mont., 1990-95; dep. gen. chmn. Greater Mich. Found., 1968. Bd. dir. Ctrl. Weber Sewer Dist., 1972-77; chmn. labor com. Utah League Cities and Towns, 1973-77, Mont. League Cities and Towns, 1977-79; bd. dir., coach Ogden Hockey Assn., 1972-77, Weber Sheltered Workshop, 1974-77, Billings YMCA, 1980-86, Rimrock Found., 1980-86; chmn. cmty. rels. coun. Weber Basin Job Corps Ctr., 1973-77; bishop LDS Ch.; missionary LDS Ch., Portland, Oreg., 2003-05. With USCG, 1953-57. Recipient Cmty. Devel. Disting. Achievement awards Munising, 1964, Cmty. Devel. Disting. Achievement awards Sault Ste. Marie, 1966-70, Citizen award Dept. of Interior, 1977, Alumni Achievement award Westminster Coll., 1990, Dist. award of merit Boy Scouts Am., 1993, Silver Beaver award Boy Scouts Am., 1994; named Utah Adminstr. of Yr., 1976. Mem. Utah City Mgrs. Assn. (pres. 1972-74), Greater Ogden C. of C. (dir.), Rotary (pres. Billings 1997-98), Phi Gamma Delta. Home and Office: 1733 Parkhill Dr Billings MT 59102-2358 Office Phone: 406-248-4252. Business E-Mail: rllarsen@bresnan.net.

LARSEN, RICHARD RAY (RICK LARSEN), congressman; b. Arlington, Wash., June 15, 1965; m. Tiia Larsen; children: Robert, Per. BA, Pacific Luth. U., Tacoma; M in Pub. Affairs, U. Minn. Dir. pub. affairs Wash. State Dental Assn.; econ. devel. ofcl. Port of Everett; councilman Snohomish County, Wash., County Coun. chair Wash., 1999; mem. US Congress from 2nd Wash. dist., 2001—, mem. armed svcs. com., mem. transp. and infrastructure com., mem. agr. com., co-chair Congl. Caucus to Fight and Control Methamphetamine, mem. No. Border Caucus. Named Friend of the Nat. Pks., Nat. Pks. Conservation Assn. Democrat. Office: US Ho Reps 107 Cannon Ho Office Bldg Washington DC 20515 Office Phone: 202-225-2605.*

LARSEN, ROBERT LEROY, artistic director; b. Walnut, Iowa, Nov. 28, 1934; s. George Dewey and Maine M. (Mickel) L. MusB, Simpson Coll., Indianola, Iowa, 1956; MusM, U. Mich., 1958; MusD, Ind. U., 1972. Music prof. Simpson Coll., 1957—, chmn. music dept., 1965-99. Founder, artistic dir. Des Moines Met. Opera, 1973—, mus. and stage dir. over 100 prodns., 1973—. Mus. coach Tanglewood, Lenox, Mass., 1963, Oglebay Pk. (W.Va.) Opera, 1965, Chgo., N.Y. studios; condr., stage dir. Simpson Coll., Des Moines Met. Opera, Miss. Opera, U. Ariz.; solo pianist, song recital coach and accompanist; adjudicator Met. auditions and competitions, Mpls., Chgo., Kansas City, Mo., Tulsa, San Antonio; stage dir., condr. operas, Simpson Coll., Des Moines Met. Opera, 1973—; editor Opera Anthologies by G. Schirmer; piano rec. artist for G. Schirmer Libr. Recipient Gov's. award State of Iowa, 1974, Iowa Arts award for long term commitment to excellence in the arts, 1998. Mem. Am. Choral Dir. Assn., Nat. Opera Assn., Music Tchrs. Nat. Assn., Pi Kappa Lambda, Phi Kappa Phi, Phi Mu Alpha Sinfonia (faculty advisor). Presbyterian. Avocations: reading, theater, coaching students. Office: Des Moines Metro Opera 106 W Boston Ave Indianola IA 50125-1836 Home Phone: 515-961-4036; Office Phone: 515-961-1571.

LARSEN, RONALD L., dean, information scientist, educator; BS, Purdue U., 1968; MS in Applied Physics, Cath. U. Am., 1971; PhD in Computer Sci., U. Md., College Park, 1981. Math., aerospace technologist Network Computing & Analysis Div. NASA Goddard Space Flight Ctr., 1968—73, math., aerospace technologist Ops. Support Computing Div., 1973—81; program mgr. computer sci. and automation Office Aeronautics and Space Tech., NASA Hdqs., Washington, 1980—85; asst. vice chancellor computing U. Md. Sys. Adminstrn., 1985—88; affiliate assoc. prof. Computer Sci. Dept. U. Md., College Park, 1985—; assoc. dir. info. tech. U. Md. Librs., 1988—96; asst. dir. Info. Tech. Office Defense Advanced Rsch. Projects Agency, 1996—99; dep. dir. Md. Info. and Network Dynamics (MIND) Lab U. Md. Inst. Advanced Computer Studies (UMIACS), 2001—02; exec. dir. Md. Applied Info. Tech. Initiative, 1999—2002; dean, prof. Sch. Info. Scis., U. Pitts., 2002—. Office: U Pitts Sch Info Scis 512 IS Bldg 135 N Bellefield Ave Pittsburgh PA 15260 Office Phone: 412-624-5139. Office Fax: 412-624-5231. E-mail: rlarsen@mail.sis.pitt.edu.*

LARSEN, SYLVIA B., state legislator; b. Troy, Ohio, July 1949; m. Robert M. Larsen; 2 children. Student, Briarcliff Coll., 1968-69; BA, U. Wis., 1972. Bd. dirs. NH Healthy Kids, Child Trust Fund, Land and Com. Heritage, Ctrl. Sr. Ctr., Concord, 1994—2000; chmn. NH Unique Coll. Savs. Program; cons. pub. rels. Concord; mem. Concord City Coun., 1989-98; mem. Dist. 15 NH Senate, Concord, 1994—, mem. fin., joint fiscal coms., internal affairs com., Dem. leader, 2002—05, pres., 2006—. Named Servant of Yr. Pineconia Grange, 1992, Legislator of Yr., NH Grange, 2001, Woman of Yr. Bus. and Profl. Women, Concord, Athena award Concord Chamber. Democrat. Address: 23 Kensington Rd Concord NH 03301-2528 Office: State House Rm 302 107 N Main St Concord NH 03301-4951

LARSEN, WALLACE LAWRENCE, retired transportation engineer, county official; b. Union County, SD, Mar. 15, 1931; s. Peder and Iva Fern (Beeler) Larsen; m. Gladys Marie Erickson, Aug. 28, 1952; children: Cynthia Marie, Janet Sue, Linda Kay(dec.). BS in Mining Engring., SD Sch. Mines and Tech., Rapid City, 1953. Mining engr. Anaconda Co., Butte, Mont., 1953—59; civil engr. III Ill. State Hwy. Dept., Dixon, 1959—60; project engr. SD Dept. Hwys., Beresford, 1960—63, resident engr. Watertown, 1963—66, right of way engr., planning engr. Pierre, 1966—78; dep. sec. SD Dept. Transp., Pierre, 1978—89, dir. divsn. engring. state hwy. engring., 1989—93; ret., 1993. Mem. bd. tech. professions State SD, Pierre, 1993—2005; mem. Pierre Planning and Zoning Commn., 1993—2003, Pierre Transit Bd., 2002—04. County commr. Hughes County, Pierrre, 1994—2002; chmn. Hughes County Rail Authority, Pierrre, 1996—; Expo Bldg. bd. mem. various counties, SD, 1998—; bd. mem. SD Employees Investment Trust, Pierrre, 1993—. Named to, SD Hall of Fame, 1993, SD Transp. Hall of Honor, 1995; recipient Excellence in Mgmt. award, Gov. SD, 1990. Mem.: NSPE (regional v.p. 1979—83), SD Profl. Land Surveyors, SD Engring. Soc. (state rep. 1974—78). Republican. Lutheran. Avocations: birdwatching, photography, fishing, gardening, genealogy. Home: 104 W 7th St Pierre SD 57501

LARSEN, WILLIAM LAWRENCE, engineering educator; b. Crookston, Minn., July 16, 1926; s. Clarence M. and Luverne (Carlisle) L.; m. Gracie Lee Richey, June 19, 1954; children— Eric W., Thomas R. BME, Marquette U., Milw., 1948; MS, Ohio State U., 1950, PhD, 1956; postgrad., U. Chgo., 1950—51. Registered profl. engr., Iowa. Research assoc. Ohio State U., Columbus, 1951-56; research metallurgist E. I.

duPont de Nemours & Co., Wilmington, Del., 1956-58; metallurgist Ames Lab., AEC, Iowa, 1958-73; assoc. prof. Iowa State U., Ames, 1958-73, prof. materials sci. and engring., 1973-93; prof. emeritus, 1993—. Cons. metallurgical engring., 1960— Contbr. articles to profl. jours. Served with USNR, 1944-46 Mem.: NSPE, NACE Internat., ASTM, ASM Internat. (life). Home and Office: 2332 Hamilton Dr Ames IA 50014-8201

LARSEN-BASSE, JORN, mechanical and materials engineering educator, researcher, consultant; b. Maribo, Denmark, Oct. 14, 1934; came to U.S., 1962; s. Asger Bernhard Bjerregaard and Ragnhild Sofie (Jorgensen) Larsen Badse; m. Margarita Simpson, Mar. 31, 1959; 1 child, Kai Erik. MSME, Royal Danish Tech. U., Copenhagen, 1958, PhD in Metallurgy, 1961. Registered mech. engr., Denmark; cert. corrosion specialist, U.S. Rsch. metallurgist Soderfors Bruk, Soderfors, Sweden, 1961-62; rsch. assoc. Stanford (Calif.) U., 1963-64; prof. mech. engring. U. Hawaii, Honolulu, 1964-86, chmn. dept., 1976-81, 82-85; prof. mech. engring. Ga. Inst. Tech., Atlanta, 1986-91; program dir. NSF, Washington, 1988—2005. Cons. Honolulu, 1964-86, Washington, 1992—; vis. prof. U. NSW, Sydney, Australia, 1978, Tsinghua U., Beijing, 1983; vis. researcher in tribophysics Commonwealth Sci. and Indsl. Rsch. Orgn., Melbourne, Australia, 1979; guest rschr. Nat. Inst. Standards and Tech., Gaithersburg, Md., 2003-04; embassy sci. fellow NSF, Reykjavik, 2002, Zagreb, 2005. Assoc. editor Jour. Tribology, 1989-91; contbr. numerous articles to profl. jours. Fellow ASME, Am. Soc. for Metals, Soc. Tribologists and Lubrication Engrs.; mem. Materials Rsch. Soc. Home: 6200 Perthshire Ct Bethesda MD 20817-3348 Office Phone: 301-530-3274. E-mail: jornlb@verizon.net.

LARSGAARD, MARY LYNETTE, librarian, writer; b. Dickinson, ND, Aug. 4, 1946; d. Martin Vilhelm and Helen Maud (Brooks) L. BA in Geology, Macalester Coll., 1968; MALS, U. Minn., 1969; MA in Geography, U. Oreg., 1978. Asst. documents/maps libr. Ctlr. Wash. State Coll., Ellensburg, 1969-76; map libr. Colo. Sch. Mines, Golden, 1978-86, asst. head spl. collections, 1986-88; asst. head map & imagery lab. U. Calif., Santa Barbara, 1988—. Author: Map LIbrarianship: an Introduction, 3d edit., 1998, Topographic Mapping of the Americas, Australia and New Zealand, 1984, Topographic Mapping of Africa, Australia & Eurasia, 1992. Recipient SLAG&M Honors award, 1995, ALCTS Presdl. Citation, 2002. Mem.: ALA (Magert Honors award 1983, MAGERT Honors award 1983), We. Assn. Map Librs. (pres. 1975—76, SLAG & M Honors award 1995, ALCTS Presdl. citation 2002), Beta Phi Mu., Phi Beta Kappa. Avocations: walking, reading, dance. Office: U Calif Santa Barbara Davidson Libr Map and Imagery Lab Santa Barbara CA 93106 Home Phone: 805-687-6945; Office Phone: 805-893-4049. Business E-Mail: mary@library.ucsb.edu.

LARSON, ALAN PHILIP, former federal agency administrator; b. Osage, Iowa, July 19, 1949; s. Philip Harold and Marilyn (Lack) L.; m. Nancy Ruth Naden, June 3, 1972; children: Nathan Christopher, Lara Marie, Philip Gardner. BA, U. Iowa, 1971, MA, 1978, PhD, 1982. Econ. officer U.S. Embassy US Dept. State, Kinshasa, 1975-77, dep. dir. Washington, 1978-82, counselor for econ. and comml. affairs U.S. Embassy Kingston, Jamaica, 1982-84, exec. asst. to under sec. Washington, 1984-86, dep. asst. sec. for internat. energy, 1986-87, prin. dep. asst. sec. for econs. and bus., 1987-90, US amb. to OECD Paris, 1990-94, dep. asst. sec. for internat. fin. & devel. Washington, 1994-96, asst. sec. for econ. & bus. affairs, 1996-99, under sec. econ. for bus. & agrl. affairs, 1999—2005; sr. internat. policy adv. Covington & Burling LLP, Washington, 2005—. Chmn. Transparency Internat./USA; bd. mem. Bread for the World; mem. bd. counselors Kissinger McLarty Associates; Disting. Fellow Coun. on Competitiveness. Named a Career Amb., US Dept. State, 2004; recipient Disting. Alumnus award, U. Iowa, 2003, Sec. State's Disting. Svc. award, US Dept. State, 2005. Office: Covington & Burling LLP 1201 Pennsylvania Ave NW Washington DC 20004 E-mail: alarson@cov.com.*

LARSON, ALLAN LOUIS, political scientist, educator, lay worker; b. Chetek, Wis., Mar. 31, 1932; s. Leonard Andrew and Mabel (Marek) L. BA magna cum laude, U. Wis., Eau Claire, 1954; PhD, Northwestern U., 1964. Instr. Evanston Twp. (Ill.) High Sch., 1958-61; asst. prof. polit. sci. U. Wis., 1963-64; asst. prof. Loyola U., Chgo., 1964-68, assoc. prof., 1968-74, prof., 1974—. Author: Comparative Political Analysis, 1980, Soviet Society in Historical Perspective: Polity, Ideology and Economy, 2000, (essay) The Human Triad: An Introductory Essay on Politics, Society, and Culture, 1988; (with others) Progress and the Crisis of Man, 1976; contbr. articles to profl. jours. Assoc. mem. Paul Galvin Chapel, Evanston, Ill. Norman Wait Harris fellow in polit. sci. Northwestern U., 1954-56 Mem. AAAS, ASPCA, AAUP, Humane Soc. U.S., Northwestern U. Alumni Assn., Am. Polit. Sci. Assn., Am. Acad. Polit. and Social Sci., Acad. Polit. Sci., Midwest Polit. Sci. Assn., Nat. Assn. Scholars, Spiritual Life Inst., Anti-Cruelty Soc., Nat. Wildlife Fedn., N.Am. Butterfly Assn., Acad. of Am. Poets (assoc.), Policy Studies Orgn., Noetic Scis. Inst., Nat. Assn. Scholars, Humane Soc. U.S., Kappa Delta Pi, Pi Sigma Epsilon, Pi Sigma Alpha. Roman Catholic. Home: 11152 43d Ave Chippewa Falls WI 54729-6626 Office: Loyola U 6525 N Sheridan Rd Damen Hall Rm 915 Chicago IL 60626 *We are each of us mysteries to ourselves. We are on a life-long search for meaning: questions about where we have come from, what we are doing and where we are going. The deepest desires of a person embody the spiritual quest. The Kingdom of God tells us where to place our priorities. Life is short. No one is untouched by tragedy. We are reminded every day of our finiteness. We care because it is our nature to care. Christianity teaches a reverence for life that urges us to transcend narcissism and selfishness.*

LARSON, ARVID GUNNAR, electrical engineer; b. July 26, 1937; s. Arvid G. and Marion Edith (Parker) L.; m. Gladys Lorraine Anderson, June 6, 1959 (dec. 1987); 1 child, Gregory Monte; m. Nicole Sours, Aug. 26, 1989. BSEE, Ill. Inst. Tech., Chgo., 1959; MSEE, Stanford U., Calif., 1966, PhD in Elec. Engring., 1973. Registered profl. engr., Calif., Va. Rsch. engr. Stanford Rsch. Inst., Menlo Park, Calif., 1964-74; mgr. advanced rsch. Planning Rsch. Corp., McLean, Va., 1974-78; project mgr. Sys. Planning Corp., Arlington, Va., 1978-80; mgr. Washington divsn. Advanced Rsch. and Applications Corp., Vienna, Va., 1980-85; v.p. Analytical Disciplines Inc., Vienna, 1985-86; prin. Booz, Allen and Hamilton, Inc., 1986-90; sr. v.p. JJH Inc., Arlington, 1990-91; chmn. Nicole Larson Assocs., San Diego, 1991—. Rsch. prof. George Mason U., Fairfax, Va., 1991-93; chmn. bd. dirs. Electronics and Aerospace Sys. Conf., 1982-84; bd. dirs. Rsch. Inst. in Info. Scis. and Engring., 1978-99; chmn. 3d NATO Advanced Study Inst. in Info. Scis., 1978. Author: Information Science in Action: System Design, 1983; contbr. articles to profl. jours. Trustee Cabrillo Nat. Monument Found., 2005—, treas., 2006—. Lt. USN, 1959—63. Fellow IEEE (chmn. def. R&D com. 1985-86, chmn. No. Va. sect. 1986-87, vice-chmn. tech. activities com. 1986-87, chmn. new tech. issues com. 1987-89, chmn. fed. govt. activities 1989-90, gen. chmn. U.S. Tech. Policy Conf., 1988, 89, inst. editl. bd. 1986-88, editl. bd. jour. Spectrum 1988-91, Centennial medal 1984, Profl. Achievement award 1987, chmn. U.S. activities 1992, v.p. 1992, bd. dir. 1992, chmn. govt. fellow com. 1997-98); mem. Am. Assn. Engring. Socs. (chmn. R&D task force 1996-99), Armed Forces Comms. and Electronics Assn., U.S. Naval Inst., Sigma Xi, Cosmos Club (chmn. fin. com. 1993-96, treas. 1997-00, mem. bd. mgmt. 1997-00), Shady Oaks Yacht Club (commodore 1991-93). Home and Office: PO Box 83130 San Diego CA 92138-3130 Office Phone: 858-274-6160. Personal E-mail: larsons@n2.net.

LARSON, BARBARA JEAN, art history professor; d. Chester Albert and Delores Vivian Larson; m. John Andrew Johnson, Feb. 14, 1999 (div. Nov. 8, 2001); 1 child, Vivian Johnson. BA, Northwestern U., Evanston, Ill., 1978; MA, NYU, NYC, 1989, PhD, 1996. Nat. Heritage Trust fellow Bklyn. Mus., 1984—85; editor Abaris Books, NYC, 1985—87; NEA Sr. Rsch. fellow Guggenheim Mus., NYC, 1987—89; sr. mus. educator Mus. Modern Art, NYC, 1989—93; vis. asst. prof. U. No. Mich., Marquette, 1996—97; asst. prof. Syracuse U., NY, 1997—2005; assoc. prof. U. West Fla., 1996—2006. Author: The Dark Side of Nature: Science, Society and the Fantastic in the Work of Odilon Redon, 2005; contbr. articles to profl. jours. Grantee, Cantor Found., 2004, NEH, 2006; Rsch. fellowship, Nat. Endowment for Arts, 1987—88. Mem.: Assn. of Historians of 19th Century Art, Soc. for Art, Lit. and Sci., Coll. Art Assn. Achievements include illuminating connections between the history of science and trends in art and literature; the way in which transformations in science effect culture, society and art imagery. Avocations: hiking, movies. Home: 1602 Governors Dr # 2217 Pensacola FL 32514 Office: Univ West Fla 11000 University Pky Pensacola FL 32514 Office Phone: 850-474-2482. Fax: 850-474-2043. E-mail: blarson@uwf.edu.

LARSON, BENNETT CHARLES, solid state physicist, researcher; b. Buffalo, ND, Oct. 9, 1941; s. Floyd Everet and Gladys May (Hogen) L.; m. Piola Anne Taliaferro, June 6, 1969; children: Christopher Charles, Andrea Kay BA in Physics, Concordia Coll., Moorhead, Minn., 1963; MS in Physics, U. N.D., 1965; PhD in Physics, U. Mo., 1970. Rsch. physicist, x-ray diffraction Oak Ridge Nat. Lab., Tenn., 1969—, corp. fellow materials sci. and tech. divsn. Tenn., 1969—. Contbr. numerous articles to profl. jours. Recipient Sidhu award Pitts. Diffraction Soc., 1974 Fellow Am. Phys. Soc.; mem. Am. Crystallographic Assn. (Bertram E. Warren Diffraction Physics award 1985), Materials Research Soc. Office: Oak Ridge Nat Lab Condensed Matter Scis PO Box 2008 Oak Ridge TN 37831-2008 Business E-Mail: larsonbc@ornl.gov.

LARSON, BRIAN A., lawyer; Acct. Coopers and Lybrand, Ernst and Young; ptnr. Snell and Wilmer, Phoenix; v.p. devel. Boyd Gaming Corp., Las Vegas, 1993, assoc. gen. counsel, 1993—98, sr. v.p., gen. counsel, 1998—, sec., 2001—. Office: Boyd Gaming Corp 2950 Industrial Rd Las Vegas NV 89109*

LARSON, BRYAN ALAN, lawyer; s. Byron Ancedus and Betty Marilyn Larson; m. Kathy Stevenett; children: Aaron, Adam, Conor, Kaden, Sara, Aubrey. BA, Brigham Young U., 1980, JD, 1983. Bar: Utah 1983. Assoc. Christensen, Jensen & Powell, Salt Lake City, 1983-86, McKay, Burton & Thurman, Salt Lake City, 1986-91; ptnr. Larson, Jenkins & Halliday, Salt Lake City, 1991-95, Larson, Kirkham & Turner, Salt Lake City, 1995-99, Larson, Turner & Etherington, Salt Lake City, 1999—2004, Larson, Turner, Dalby & Etherinton, 2004—. Seminar lectr. in field. Editor: Backtalk Newsletter, 1995—, Utah Auto Body Watch Dawg, 2002—; contbr. articles to mags. in field. Mem. ATLA (mem. polit. action com. 1991—), Utah Bar Assn. (com. chmn. 1990-92), Utah Trial Lawyers Assn. (exec. bd., pres.-elect, bd. govs.), Spkrs. Bur., Order of Barristers. Mem. Lds Ch. Avocations: boating, skiing. Office: Larson Turner Dalby & Ethington 1218 W South Jordan Pkwy Ste B South Jordan UT 84095 Office Phone: 801-446-6464. E-mail: larson@bestattorneys.com.

LARSON, CAROL S., foundation administrator, lawyer; BA, Stanford U.; JD, Yale Law Sch. Law clerk to Judge Warren J. Ferguson U.S. Dist. Crt., Central Dist. of Calif.; former atty., civil litigation O'Donnell and Gordon; dir. rsch., grants, law and public policy, Ctr. for Future of Children David and Lucile Packard Found., 1989—94, dir. prog., 1995—2003, v.p., 2000—03, pres., CEO, 2004—. Special asst. and speechwriter for pres. Am. Bar Assn., 1998; lecturer Stanford Law Sch., 1994—96; coordinator of advocacy Exceptional Children's Found., Los Angeles, 1980—81. Former bd. mem. Grantmakers for Children, Youth and Families; bd. mem. No. Calif. Grantmakers, Am. Leadership Forum, Silicon Valley. Office: David and Lucile Packard Found 300 Second St Los Altos CA 94022

LARSON, CHARLES FRED, management consultant; b. Gary, Ind., Nov. 27, 1936; s. Charles F. and Margaret J. (Taylor) Larson; m. Joan Ruth Grupe, Aug. 22, 1959; children: Gregory Paul, Laura Ann. BSME, Purdue U., 1958; MBA summa cum laude, Fairleigh Dickinson U., Teaneck, NJ, 1973. Registered profl. engr., NJ. Project engr. Combustion Engring., Inc., East Chicago, Ind., 1958-60; sec. Welding Rsch. Council, NYC, 1960-70, asst. dir., 1970-75; exec. dir. Indsl. Rsch. Inst., Inc., Washington, 1975-99, pres., 1999—2001, Innovation Rsch. Internat., Washington, 2001—. Mem. mech. engring. adv. bd. Purdue U.; mem. selection com. Nat. Inventors Hall of Fame, 2000—05. Assoc. editor: Jour. Pressure Vessel Tech., 1973—75, mem. bd. advisors: Who's Who in Am. Mem. Wyckoff (N.J.) Bd. Edn., 1973—78, pres., 1976—77; reader In Touch Networks, Inc., NYC, 1979—89; chmn. 43d Nat. Conf. Advancement Rsch. Fellow: ASME, AAAS; mem.: Burning Tree Club, Kenwood Club, Univ. Club. Republican. Methodist.

LARSON, DAVID LEE, surgeon; b. Kansas City, Mo., Dec. 9, 1943; s. Leonard Nathaniel and Mary Elizabeth (Stuck) L.; m. Sherrill Ankli, Apr. 16, 1977; children: Jeffrey David, Dawn Elizabeth, Bradley Jesse. BS, Bowling Green State U., 1965; MD, La. State U., 1969. Diplomate Am. Bd. Plastic Surgery (bd. dirs. 1996—, sec.-treas. 1998—). Intern Charity Hosp. of La., New Orleans, 1969-70; resident otolaryngology Baylor Coll. Medicine, Houston, 1972-76; plastic surgery resident Ind. U., Indpls., 1976-78; surgeon M.D. Anderson Cancer Ctr., Houston, 1978-85; prof., chmn. dept. plastic and reconstructive surgery Med. Coll Wis., Milw., 1986—, George S. Korkos prof. plastic surgery, 2007. Alano J. Ballantyne prof. in head and neck surgery M.D. Anderson Cancer Ctr., Houston, 1985; sec.-treas. Am. Bd. Plastic Surgery, 1996-2002. Editor: Cancer in the Neck, 1987, Essentials of Head and Neck Oncology, 1998. Capt. USNR, 1991—. Mem. Am. Assn. Plastic Surgeons, Nat. Inst. Healthcare Rsch. (chmn. bd. dirs. 1995-2000), Plastic Surgery Ednl. Found. (pres. 2001—02). Avocations: reading, exercise. Home: 13510 Braemar Dr Elm Grove WI 53122-2509 Office: Med Coll Wis 8700 Watertown Plank Rd Milwaukee WI 53226-3522 E-mail: dlarson@mcw.edu.

LARSON, DONALD CLAYTON, physics professor, consultant; b. Wadena, Minn., Jan. 29, 1934; s. Clyde Melvin and Selma (Wilson) L.; m. Susan Dunnet, July 17, 1960; children: Tor Frederick, Jun Dunnet (dec.), Erika Rose. BS, U. Wash., 1956; SM, Harvard U., 1957, PhD, 1962. Asst. prof. U. Va., Charlottesville, 1962-67; assoc. prof. Drexel U., Phila., 1967-83, full prof., 1983—. Vis. prof. Univ. Chile, Santiago, 1969, 73, Tel-Aviv (Israel) U., 1984, 92; vis. scientist Naval Air Devel., Warminster, Pa., summers 1981-91; cons. NIST, Gaithersburg, Md., 1984-95. Author: Physics of Thin Films, vol. VI, 1971, Experimental Methods in Preparation and Measurement of Thin Films, vol. II, 1974. Mem. Optical Soc. Am., Phi Beta Kappa, Tau Beta Pi, Sigma Xi. Home: 409 Drew Ave Swarthmore PA 19081-2407 Office: Drexel U Physics Philadelphia PA 19104 Home Phone: 610-543-8007; Office Phone: 215-895-2724. Business E-Mail: donlarson@drexel.edu.

LARSON, EDWARD JOHN, history and law professor; b. Mansfield, Ohio, Sept. 21, 1953; s. Rex and Jean (Uncapher) Larson; m. Lucy Marie Kaiser, July 28, 1990; children: Sarah Marie, Luke Anders. BA, Williams, 1974; MA, U. Wis., 1976, PhD, 1985; JD, Harvard U., 1979; DHL (hon.), Ohio State U., 2004. Bar: Wash. 1979, U.S. Dist. Ct. (we. dist.) Wash. 1979, U.S. Ct. Appeals (9th cir.) 1979, U.S. Tax Ct. 1981, U.S. Supreme Ct. 1984. Atty. Davis, Wright & Tremaine, Seattle, 1979—82; assoc. counsel U.S. House Com. on Edn. and Labor, Washington, 1983—86; counsel U.S. Office Edn. Rsch. and Improvement, Washington, 1986—87; Richard B. Russell prof. history and Talmadge prof. law Univ. Ga., Athens, 1987—, chair history dept., 2001—04; Darling chair law and history Pepperdine U., Malibu, Calif., 2006—, prof., 2006—. Adv. US Dept. Edn., Washington, 1987—93; vis. prof. U. Jean Moulin, Lyon, France, 1996; John Adams chair Fulbright program U. Leiden, The Netherlands, 2000—01; participant Antarctic Artists and Writers Program, NSF, 2003—04; Straus disting. vis. prof. Pepperdine Law Sch., 2005; panelist human genome project NIH, Washington, 2006—. Author: Trial & Error, 1985, Sex, Race & Science, 1995, Summer for the Gods, 1997, A Different Death, 1998, Evolution's Workshop, 2001, Evolution, 2004, Constitutional Convention, 2005, The Creation-Evolution Debate, 2007, A Magnificent Catastrophe, 2007. Counsel Wash. State House Reps., Olympia, 1981—82; analyst Wis. State Senate, Madison, 1974—76. Recipient Pulitzer prize for history, 1998, Templeton Found. Article prize, 1997, George Sarton Lectr. award, AAAS, 2000, James Livingood award, Conf. on So. Lit., 2003; scholar, Rockefeller Found., 1996. Mem.: Forum History Sci. Am. (exec. com. chair 1992—94), History Sci. Soc. (com. chair 1994—97), Wash. State Bar Assn. Avocations: travel, hiking, bicycling, birdwatching. Home: 253 Cobb St Athens GA 30601-2407 Office: Pepperdine U Sch Law Malibu CA 90263 Office Phone: 706-542-2660, 310-506-7593. Business E-Mail: edlarson@uga.edu, elarson@pepperdine.edu.

LARSON, ERIC B., medical educator, director, internist; BA in History (with great distinction), Stanford Univ., Stanford, Calif, 1969; MD, Harvard Med. Sch., 1973; MPH, U. Wash. Sch. Pub. Health, Seattle, Wash., 1977. Cert. Nat. Bd. Med. Examiners (Parts I, II, III), 1974, diplomate Am. Bd. Internal Medicine, 1977, lic. Wash., 1975. Assoc. diener, dept. pathology Children's Hosp., Boston, 1969—71; intern, medicine Beth Israel Hosp., Harvard Med. Sch., Boston, 1973—74, asst. resident, medicine, 1974—75; internist, outpatient dept. Harborview Med. Ctr., Seattle, 1975—77; rsch. assoc. Va. Mason Hosp./Rsch. Found., Seattle, 1975—77; chief resident, medicine U. Hosp., Seattle, 1977—78, attending physician, 1977—; Robert Wood Johnson Clin. scholar, sr. fellow, dept. medicine U. Wash., Seattle, 1975—77, assoc. dean clin. affairs; med dir. U. Wash. Med. Ctr., 1989—2002; sr. investigator, dir., Group Health Coop. Ctr. for Health Studies, Seattle, 2002—06, exec. dir., Group Health Coop., 2006—. Instructor, medicine Harvard Med. Sch., Boston, 1973—75; acting instructor, medicine U. Wash. Sch. Medicine, Seattle, 1977—78, assoc. dean for clin. affairs, 1989—2002; asst. prof., medicine U. Wash., Seattle, 1978—82, assoc. prof., medicine, 1982—88, prof. medicine, 1988—; adj. asst. prof., cmty. medicine Sch. Pub. Health, Seattle, 1979—82; adj. assoc. prof., health services & cmty. medicine U. Wash. Sch. Pub. Health, Seattle, 1982—88, adj. prof., health services & cmty. medicine, 1988—; sect. head, gen. internal medicine U. Hosp., Seattle, 1988—89; sr. investigator and dir. Ctr. for Health Studies, Group Health Coop., 2002; commr. Joint Commn. for Accreditation Health Care Orgns., 1999—. Contbr. articles to profl. jours.; assoc. editor: Jour. of Gen. Internal Medicine, 1989—94, editl. bd.: Annals of Internal Medicine, 1992—95, Health Services Rsch., 1994—, Am. Jour. Medicine, 1997—, Primary Care Case Reviews, 1988—, editl. adv. bd.: Rsch. and Practice, 1998—. Nat. reviewer, abstract selection Soc. of Gen. Internal Medicine (SGIM), 1984, co-chmn., NW regional mtg., 1983, chmn., NW regional mtg., 1986, regional rep., 1986—87, coun., 1986—89, pres., 1994—95; commr. Joint Commn. on Accreditation of Healthcare Orgns., 2003; nat. reviewer Am. Fedn. for Clin. Rsch.-Clin. Epidemiology-Health Care Rsch., 1983—88, western regional reviewer, 1985, chmn., abstract selection, 1990 Nat. Mtg., 1989—90; DHHS Adv. Panel on Alzheimer's Disease Office of Tech. Assessment, 1987—89, chmn., 1993—98. Henry J. Kaiser Family Found. Faculty Scholar in Gen. Internal Medicine, 1981. Fellow: ACP (regent 1998—2006, chmn. publications comm. 2000—03, chair-elect, bd. regents 2003, chair, bd. regents 2004, master 2006, George Morris Piersol Tchg. and Rsch. Scholar 1978, Laureate award, Wash. Chpt. 2006); mem.: ACP Jour. Club (editl. adv. bd. 1990—), Wash. State Medical Soc., King County Med. Soc. (editl. adv. bd. 1987—90), Am. Fedn. for Med. Rsch. (clin. epidemiology-Health Care Rsch., Nat. reviewer 1983—88, clin. epidemiology-Health Care Rsch., Western Regional Reviewer 1985, chmn., abstract selection 1990 Nat. Mtg. 1989—90), Seattle Acad. of Medicine, Soc. Gen. Internal Medicine (co-chmn., northwest regional mtg. 1983, nat. reviewer, abstract selection 1984, chmn., Northwest Regional Mtg. 1986, regional rep. 1986—87, councilor 1986—89, pres. 1994—95, Robert J. Glaser award 2004), AMA, Am. Clin. and Climatological Assn., Am. Soc. Clin. Investigation, Am. Geriatrics Soc. (editl. bd. 1988—91, Service award 1992), Assn. Am. Physicians, Phi Beta Kappa. Office: Ctr for Health Studies Ste 1600 1730 Minor Ave Seattle WA 98101-1448 Office Phone: 206-287-2988. Business E-Mail: larson.e@ghc.org. E-mail: ebl@u.washington.edu.*

LARSON, ERIK, writer; b. Bklyn., Jan. 1, 1954; m. Christine Gleason; children: Kristin, Lauren, Erin. BA in Russian history summa cum laude, U. Pa., 1976; MA, Columbia Grad. Sch. of Journalism, 1978. Features writer The Wall St. Jour., TIME mag. Author: The Naked Consumer: How Our Private Lives Become Public Commodities, 1992, Lethal Passage: How the Travels of a Single Handgun Expose the Roots of America's Gun Crisis, 1994, Isaac's Storm: A Man, a Time and the Deadliest Hurricane in History, 1999 (Pacific Northwest booksellers award), The Devil in the White City: Murder Magic and Madness at the Fair that Changed America, 2003 (Nat. Book award nominee, Edgar award in Best Fact Crime category, 2004), Thunderstruck, 2006.

LARSON, GARY ARTHUR, farmer, financial consultant; b. Madison, Minn., Dec. 16, 1959; s. Alvin J. and Leona L.; m. Ingrid Carol Bellows, Aug. 9, 1986; children: Brent, Sonja. BS in Agrl. Bus., S.D. State U., 1982. Farmer Gary A. Larson Farm, Canby, Minn., 1981—; loan officer, computer programmer Farm Credit Svcs., Canby and Madison, Minn., 1983-85, credit analyst, computer programmer Wilmar and Marshall, Minn., 1986-91, computer sys. coord. Wilmar, 1992-93. Fin., computer cons. Larson Cons., Canby, 1993—; cons. Small Bus. Adminstr., Brookings, S.D., 1982. Inventor windpower model/report, 1978; patent for planting toolbar. Chmn. parish coun. St. James Ch., Dawson, Minn., 1995-99; mem., worker PTA, Dawson, 1997-2002; mem., telethon worker Pioneer Pub. TV, Appleton, Minn., 1988-2001. Finalist Top 100 Best Managed Farms, Farm Futures Mag., 2002; named one of, 1993—2002; recipient 1st place for wheat yield, Nat. Assn. Wheat Growers, 1990. Mem. Corn Growers Assn., Wheat Growers Assn., Soybean Growers Assn., Lac Qui Parle County Soybean Growers Bd., Mortar Bd., Alpha Zeta (vice chmn. 1981-82). Avocations: restoring classic cars and tractors, hunting, reading. Home and Office: Gary A Larson Farm 2282 130th St N Canby MN 56220

LARSON, GLORIA ANN CORDES, academic administrator, lawyer; b. Rosewell, N.Mex., Apr. 15, 1950; d. Harry N. and Rogene (Corn) Cordes; m. Macklin Daniel W., Nov. 8, 1975 (div. 1982); m. Larson Allen R., Dec. 20, 1987. BA with honors, Vassar Coll., 1972; JD, U. Va., 1977; LLD (hon.), Northeastern U., 2005, Mt. Wachusett CC, 2003. Bar: Va. 1978, Mass. 1989, US Supreme Ct. Dir. statewide legal svcs. for elderly Legal Svcs. Corp., Richmond, Va., 1977-79; program advisor funeral rule FTC, Washington, 1979-81, legal counsel to commr., 1981-88; ptnr. Larson, Curry & Larson, Hyannis, Mass., 1988-98, Foley, Hoag & Eliot LLP, Boston, 1999—2007, co-chair Govt. Strategies Group; pres. Bentley Coll., Waltham, Mass., 2007—. Sec. consumer affairs and bus. regulation Commonwealth of Mass., Boston, 1991—93, sec. econ. affairs, 1993—96; bd. dirs. KeySpan Corp., UnumProvident Corp., Blue Cross and Blue Shield of Mass. Contbr. articles to profl. jours. Bd. mem. New England Coun., United Way Mass. Bay, Boston Ctr. Arts, Mass. Women's Forum, Harbor Island Alliance, Rosie's Place, Dimock Cmty. Health Ctr.; chair bd. dirs. Mass. Conv. Ctr. Authority; co-chair bd. MassINC; co-chair Great Schs. Campaign; mem. Boston Host Com. for Dem. Nat. Conv., 2004, Rose Fitzgerald Kennedy Greenway Conservancy Bd., 2005—. Named one of Outstanding Young Women in Am., 1979; recipient Outstanding Svc. award, FTC, 1991, Wonder Woman award, Mass. Women's Polit. Caucus,

Outstanding Women Bus. Leaders, New Eng. Coun., 1995, Pinnacle award Greater Boston C. of C., 1999. Mem.: ABA, Boston Bar Assn., Mass. Bar Assn., Va. Bar Assn. (chmn. Com. on Legal Needs of Elderly 1978—82), U. Va. Law Women Club (pres. 1976—77). Republican. Home: 30 Main St Yarmouth Port MA 02675-1618 Office: Bentley Coll 175 Forest St Waltham MA 02452 E-mail: glarson@bentley.edu.*

LARSON, JANICE TALLEY, application developer; b. Houston, Sept. 29, 1948; d. Hiram Peak Talley and Jennie Edna Donahoo; m. Harold Vernon Larson Jr., Apr. 8, 1977; children: Randall Neil, Christopher Lee. AA in Computers, San Jacinto Coll., 1981; BA in Computer Info. Systems, U. Houston, Clear Lake, 1984, MA in Computer Info. Systems, 1988; EdD in Instrnl. Tech., U. Houston, 1999. Programmer Control Applications, Houston, 1985-86, Tex. Eastern Pipeline, Houston, 1988-90; instr. computer sci. San Jacinto Coll., Houston, 1990-94; computer sci. reader Ednl. Testing Svc., Houston, 1996—2000; programmer for shuttle cockpit avionics upgrade United Space Alliance, 2000—02; programmer Creative Process Cons., League City, Tex., 2003—06. Adj. instr. U. Houston, Clear Lake, Tex., 1996, 99, 2003-05; sponsor Computer Sci. Club, Houston, 1992-94. Mem.: AIAA, IEEE (assoc.), U. Houston Clear Lake Alumni Assn., U. Houston Alumni Assn., Kappa Delta Pi, Phi Delta Kappa. Personal E-mail: burnwuffie@aol.com.

LARSON, JERRY LEROY, state supreme court justice; b. Harlan, Iowa, May 17, 1936; s. Gerald L. and Mary Eleanor (Patterson) L.; m. Debra L. Christensen; children: Rebecca, Jeffrey, Susan, David. BA, State U. Iowa, 1958, JD, 1960. Bar: Iowa. Partner firm Larson & Larson, 1961-75; dist. judge 4th Jud. Dist. Ct. of Iowa, 1975-78; justice Iowa Supreme Ct., 1978—. Office: Supreme Ct Iowa PO Box 109 Des Moines IA 50319-0001*

LARSON, JOAN ISBELL, musician, educator; b. Seattle, Wash., May 14, 1934; d. Robert Lyle and Lillian Darnall (Soward) Isbell; m. Carl Frithiof Larson, May 31, 1956; children: Dale James, Linda Darleen, Brian Carlyle, Mark Edward. BA magna cum laude Edn with music major, U. Ariz., Tucson, 1956, postgrad. studies, 1965—69; master counseling courses, Liberty U., Lynchburg, Va. Cafeteria food server Yellowstone Nat. Park, Wyo., 1955; tchr. 3d grade Lineweaver Sch., Tucson, 1956—57; substitute tchr. Owego-Appalachian Schs., 1966—69; saleswoman Worldbook-Childcraft, Field Entrprises, Owego, NY. Accompanist, performer religious services Chs. of Many Christian Denominations and charity events, 1985—; ch. pianist and singer Nichols United Meth. Ch., NY, 1978—; private music tchr. self-employed, Owego, NY, 1959—. Contbr. poetry to Poetic Voices of Am. Trainee to be mediator Broome and Tioga Counties, NY, 2005—; peformer with comty. groups and local bands, 1995—; spiritual dir. and guide Candlehouse Teen Challenge, Owego, NY, 1996—, edn. dir., 1995—2003. Recipient Gold Ring award, Sherwood Music Sch., Chgo., 1952; scholar summer session, 1951. Mem.: Am. Coll. Musicians (Internat. Piano Recording Competition, 6th place Tchr. Divsn. 1986, Paderewski medal 1996), Nat. Guild of Piano Tchrs. (adjudicator), Am. Assn. Christian Counselors., Phi Kappa Phi, Pi Lambda Theta, Sigma Alpha Iota (past pres. Alpha Beta chpt., Province Leadership award, Ruby Sword of Honor). Avocations: art, gardening, dance.

LARSON, JOANNE CAROLINE, education educator; b. Kelowna, BC, Can., Sept. 30, 1956; arrived in U.S., 1963; d. John Arthur Horn and Margaret Ann Little; m. Cameron Allen Larson (div.); m. Morris Edward Smith, June 8, 1995; children: Anna Caroline, Eric Joseph, Marcus Edward Smith. Cert. in French lang. and culture, U. Paul Valery, Montpellier, France, 1977; BA in Fine Arts, UCLA, 1981, PhD in Curriculum, 1995. Asst. art dir., ceramics tchr. Exceptional Children's Found., 1981—85; substitute elem. tchr. L.A. Unified Sch. Dist., 1989—90; tchr., dir. La Playa Cooperative Nursery Sch., 1990—93; rsch. asst. UCLA, 1992—95; asst. prof. Warner Grad. Sch. Edn. and Human Devel. U. Rochester, NY, 1995—2000, assoc. prof., 2000—06, chair tchg. and curriculum, 2000—, Michael W. Scandling prof. of edn., 2006—. Editor: Literacy as Snake Oil: Beyond the Quick Fix, 2001; co-editor: Handbook of Early Childhood Literacy, 2003; co-author: Making Literacy Real: Theories and Practices in Teaching and Learning, 2005; contbr. chapters to books, articles to profl. jours. Recipient Betty Pool award, Warner Grad. Sch. Edn. and Human Devel., U. Rochester, 1999; grantee in field; Deptl. Merit Based fellow, UCLA, 1993—95. Mem.: Nat. Coun. Tchrs. English (com. chair 1998—2005), Am. Ednl. Rsch. Assn. Office: Warner School Box 270425 Dewey Hall Rochester NY 14627

LARSON, JOHN BARRY, congressman, insurance executive; b. Hartford, Conn., July 22, 1948; s. Raymond and Pauline (Nolan) L.; m. Leslie Best, Sept. 20, 1981; children: Carolyn, Laura, Raymond. BS, Cen. Ct. State U., 1971. HS teacher, 1972—77; ptnr. Larson & Lysik Ins., 1977—90; mem. Conn. Senate, 1983—94, pres. Pro Tempore, 1987—94; mem. U.S. Congress from 1st Conn. dist., 1998—; mem. ways and means com. Mem. East Hartford Town Coun., 1979—83, East Hartford Bd. of Edn., 1978—79. Recipient Outstanding Alumni award East Hartford High Sch. Nat. Honor Soc., 1985, Legis. Leadership award Conn. Assn. Human Svcs., 1987, Disting. Alumni award Cen. Conn. State U., 1987; Legislator of Yr. award Jr. League Conn., 1988, Conn. Valley Girl Scouts, 1989, Cath. Charities/Cath. Family Svcs., 1989; Man of Yr. award United Irish Socs., 1990, Champion for Children award Conn. Commn. on Children, 1990, recognition award Alzheimer's Assn. Greater Hartford, 1991, appreciation award Conn. AIDS Consortium/United Way Conn., 1991, Child Advocacy Legis. Leadership award Conn. Coalition for Children, 1991, sr. fellow, Yale Bush Ctr. for Child Devel., others. Mem. Hartford Club. Democrat. Roman Catholic. Achievements include creator/chmn. ConneCT96 Project, 1996. Office: US Ho Reps 1005 Longworth Ho Office Bldg Washington DC 20515-0701 also: Dist Office 2nd Fl 221 Main Street Hartford CT 06106-1890*

LARSON, JOHN DAVID, insurance company executive, lawyer; b. Madison, Wis., July 6, 1941; s. Lawrence John and Anna Mathilda (Furseth) Larson; m. Evelyn Vie Smith, Jan. 22, 1966 (div. Apr. 1980); children: Eric John, Karen Annette; m. Nancy With Jay, Nov. 29, 1980 (div. Dec. 1998); stepchildren: Andrew Zachary Jay, Anne Elizabeth Jay, Christopher Allen Jay; m. Sherri Ann Sturtz Kliczak, July 12, 2002; 1 stepchild, Christopher Howard Kliczak. BBA, U. Wis., 1964, JD, 1965, MBA, 1966. CPA Wis.; CLU; bar: Wis. 1965, U.S. Ct. Mil. Appeals 1966; chartered fin. cons. With Nat. Guardian Life Ins. Co., Madison, 1969—, exec. v.p., treas., 1973, pres., dir., 1974—, pres., CEO, 1989—2004, chmn., pres., CEO, 2004—. Bd. advisors U.S. Bank, Madison; bd. dirs. TV Wis., Inc., KELAB, Inc. Chmn. Madison chpt. ARC, 1974—75; pres. United Way Dane County, Wis., 1975, Wis. N.G. Assn., 1992—96; trustee Village of Maple Bluff, Wis., 1997—2003, pres., 2003—07. With US Army, 1966—69, brig. gen. Wis. Army N.G., 1998. Named Disting. Bus. Alumnus, U. Wis.-Madison, 1996; recipient Know Your Madisonian award, Wis. State Jour., 1973. Mem.: ABA, Am. Soc. Fin. Svc. Profls., State Bar Wis., U. Wis. Bus. Alumni (bd. dirs. 1986—90), Madison C. of C. (dir. 1976—80), Maple Bluff Club (bd. dirs. 1974—80), Rotary. Lutheran. Home: 401 New Castle Way Madison WI 53704-6070 Office: PO Box 1191 Madison WI 53701-1191 Business E-Mail: jdlarson@nglic.com.

LARSON, JOHN HYDE, retired utilities executive; b. Phila., Sept. 15, 1930; s. Roy Frank and Olive (Alden) L.; m. Priscilla Hibbs Beane; children: Michael Alden, Christopher Hibbs, Cynthia Ann. BA, Trinity Coll., 1953; M City Planning, MIT, 1955. Vice-pres. The Potomac Edison Co., Hagerstown, Md., 1969-72; treas. Allegheny Power System, Inc., NYC, 1973-79; v.p. fin. Conn. Energy Corp., Bridgeport, Conn., 1980-85, pres., chief exec. officer, 1985-89; exec. v.p., chief operating officer So. Conn. Gas. Co., Bridgeport, Conn., 1981-85, pres., CEO, 1985—89; acting dir. fin. City of Bridgeport, 1989-90, chmn. mgmt. adv. com., 1990—93; chmn. selectman's com. on ops. improvement Westport, Conn., 1991; chmn. oversight and audit com., pres. trustees Epis Diocese, Vt., 1998—2005. Mem. Internat. Exec. Svc. Corps., Vladimir, Russia, 1996. Vice chmn. Bridgeport Hosp., 1991-93; chmn. Nova Med. Corp., 1991-95; hon. chmn. capital funds drive Family Svcs. Woodfield, 1988; treas. Christ Episcopal Ch., Bethel, Vt., 1995-98, 2003; trustee Clara Martin Ctr.; pres. Barnard Edn. Fund, Inc., 2000-07. Lt. (SC) USNR. Recipient Corp. Leadership award MIT, 1987, Century Svc. award Bridgeport Boys and Girls Club, 1991, Richard P. Bodine Community Leadership award, 1993. Mem. New Eng. Gas Assn. (chmn. 1988-89). Home: PO Box 185 Barnard VT 05031 Personal E-mail: vtlars@aol.com.

LARSON, JOHN WILLIAM, lawyer; b. Detroit, June 24, 1935; s. William and Sara Eleanor (Yeatman) L.; m. Pamela Jane Wren, Sept. 16, 1959; 1 dau., Jennifer Wren. BA with distinction, honors in Economics, Stanford, 1957; LLB, Stanford U., 1962. Bar: Calif. 1962. Assoc. Brobeck, Phleger & Harrison, San Francisco, 1962-68, ptnr., 1968—71, 1973—2003, CEO, 1988—96; asst. sec. Dept. Interior, Washington, 1971-73; exec. dir. Natural Resources Com., Washington, 1973; counsellor to chmn. Cost of Living Coun., Washington, 1973; ptnr. Morgan, Lewis & Backius LLP, 2003—. Faculty Practising Law Inst.; bd. dirs. Sangamo Bio Scis., Inc. Mem. 1st U.S.-USSR Joint Com. on Environment; mem. bd. visitors Stanford U. Law Sch., 1974-77, 85-87, 95-96; pres. bd. trustees The Katherine Branson Sch., 1980-83. With AUS, 1957-59. Mem. ABA, Calif. Bar Assn., San Francisco C. of C. (bd. dirs., chmn. 1996), Bay Area Coun., Calif. Acad. Sci., Order of Coif, Pacific Union Club, Burlingame Country Club, Bohemian Club, Lagunitas Country Club. Home: PO Box 349 Ross CA 94957-0349 Office: Morgan Lewis & Bockius LLP Spear St Tower 1 Market Plz San Francisco CA 94105-1420 Office Phone: 415-442-1000. Business E-Mail: jlarson@morganlewis.com.

LARSON, JON M., physiatrist; s. Milton and Sadie Larson; 1 child, Ethan. BS magna cum laude, Ariz. State U., Tempe, 1971; MD, U. Ariz., Tucson, 1975. Bd. cert. family practice, bd. cert. geriatric medicine, Am. Bd. Family Practice, bd. cert. Am. Bd. Electrodiagnostic Medicine; bd. cert. phys. medicine and rehab. Family practice intern Ariz. Health Scis. Ctr., Tucson, 1975—76, family practice resident, 1976—78; resident phys. medicine and rehab. U. Calif., Irvine Med. Ctr., Orange, 1978—80; ptnr. Rehab. Medicine, Tucson, 1980—86, Physiatry Assocs. Ltd., Tucson, 1986—. Assoc. dept. family and cmty. medicine Ariz. Health Scis. Ctr., Tucson, 1980—86; nat. surveyor Commn. for the Accreditation of Rehab. Facilities, 1981—82; mem. Pima County Home Health Adv. Com., 1982—95; cons. Polio Epic So. Ariz. Post Polio Support Group, 1985—; med. dir. rehab. unit Carondelet St. Joseph's Hosp. and Health Ctr., Tucson, 1985—86, med. dir. Bridges Day Treatment Program for Head Injury, 1985—86, chmn. divsn. phys. medicine and rehab., 1985—86, med. dir. transitional care unit, 1994—96; med. dir. HealthSouth Rehab. Inst. Tucson, 1996—; assoc. dept. internal medicine Ariz. Health Scis. Ctr., Tucson, 1996—; team physician Sunnyside H.S., Ariz. Orgn. for Disabled Athletics, Tucson Gila Monsters Profl. Hockey Team. Contbr. articles to profl. jours. Recipient Pres. award for outstanding med. dir., Western Region HealthSouth, 2002. Mem.: Pima County Med. Soc. (bd. mem. 1996—98), Ariz. Med. Soc., Ariz. Acad. Family Physicians, Am. Acad. Family Physicians, Ariz. Geriatrics Soc., Ariz. Soc. Phys. Medicine and Rehab., Arm. Paraplegia Soc., Am. Acad. Phys. Medicine and Rehab., Am. Acad. for Cerebral Palsy and Developmental Medicine, Am. Assn. Electromyography and Electrodiagnosis. Office: Physiatry Assocs Ltd 2102 N Country Club Bldg B Tucson AZ

LARSON, JOSEPH STANLEY, environmentalist, educator; b. Stoneham, Mass., June 23, 1933; s. Gustave Adolph and Marian (Kelly) Larson; m. Wendy Nichols, Nov. 23, 1958; children: Marion Elizabeth, Sandra Frances. BS, U. Mass., 1956, MS, 1958; PhD, Va. Poly. Inst., 1966. Exec. sec. Wildlife Conservation, Inc., Boston, 1958-59; state ornithologist Mass. Divsn. Fisheries and Wildlife, Boston, 1959-60; head conservation edn. divsn. Natural Resources Inst., U. Md., Annapolis, 1960-62; rsch. asst. prof. LaVale, 1965-67; wildlife rsch. biologist U.S. Fish and Wildlife Svc., Amherst, Mass., 1967-69; prof., dir. The Environ. Inst., U. Mass., Amherst, 1969-2000, prof. emeritus natural resources conservation, 2000—. Cons. in field. Contbr. articles to profl. jours. Apptd. by gov. Mass. Fisheries and Wildlife Bd., 2000—; mem. adv. com. Mass. Natural Heritage, 2000—. Named Conservationalist of the Yr., Mass. Wildlife Fedn., 1997; recipient Chevron Conservation award, 1990, Dir.'s award, N.E. Sci. Ctr., Nat. Marine Fisheries Svc., 2000; grantee, in field. Mem.: AAAS, AAUP (pres. Mass. chpt. 1976—77), Internat. Union Conservation Nature and Natural Resources (commn. ecosystem mgmt. Switzerland), Soc. Wetland Scientists (profl. wetland scientist), Am. Assn. Mammalogists, Ecol. Soc. Am. (cert. sr. ecologist), Wildlife Soc. (cert. wildlife biologist), Cosmos Club, Faculty Univ. Club, Xi Sigma Pi, Phi Sigma, Sigma Xi. Congregationalist. Home: 27 Arnold Rd Pelham MA 01002-9757 Office: U Mass Environ Inst Blaisdell House Amherst MA 01003-0820 Office Phone: 413-545-2842. E-mail: larson@tei.umass.edu.

LARSON, JUDY L., museum director, curator; b. Glendale, Calif., Mar. 9, 1952; d. John Arthur and Lorraine V. Larson. BA, UCLA, 1974, MA, 1978; PhD, Emory U., 1998. Acting asst. curator Los Angeles County Mus. Art, LA, 1978; sr. cataloguer Am. Antiquarian Soc., Worcester, Mass., 1978-85; curator High Mus. Art, Atlanta, 1985—98; exec. dir. Art Museum of W. Va., W.Va., 1998—2002; dir. Nat. Museum of Women in the Arts, Washington, 2002—. Author: (catalogue) Am. Illustration 1890-1925, 1986; co-author: (catalogue) Am. Paintings at High Mus. Art, 1994; editor: Graphic Arts and the South, 1993. Office: Nat Museum of Women in the Arts 1250 New York Ave NW Washington DC 20005

LARSON, KERMIT DEAN, finance educator; b. Algona, Iowa, Apr. 7, 1939; s. Loren L. and Hansena Laurena (Andersen) L.; m. Nancy Lynne Weber, June 17, 1961; children: Julie Renee, Timothy Dean, Cynthia Lynne. AA, Ft. Dodge Jr. Coll., 1960; BBA, U. Iowa, 1962, MBA, 1963; PhD, U. Colo., 1966. CPA Tex. Faculty U. Tex., Austin, 1966-94, Arthur Andersen & Co. Alumni prof. emeritus, 1994—, chmn. dept. acctg., 1971-75. Vis. assoc. prof. Tulane U., New Orleans, 1970-71; cons. sales tax audit litig., pvt. anti-trust litig., expropriation ins. arbitration. Author: (with John Wild and Barbara Chiappetta) Fundamental Accounting Principles, 1978, 17th edit., 2005, Financial Accounting, 7th edit., 1997, (with Charlene Spoede and Paul Miller) Fundamentals of Financial and Managerial Accounting, 1994; contbr. articles to profl. jours. Mem.: Beta Alpha Psi, Beta Gamma Sigma. Home: 1310 Falcon Ledge Dr Austin TX 78746-5120

LARSON, LARRY, retired librarian; b. El Dorado, Ark., July 18, 1940; s. Willie Lee and Myrtle Elizabeth (McMaster) L.; m. Dorothy Ann Bing, Apr 23, 1966; 1 child, Larisa Ann. BS, Ouachita Baptist U., 1962; MLS, George Peabody Coll., 1967. Asst. librarian, media specialist Hall High Sch., Little Rock, 1962—65; asst. librarian, circulation Ark. Tech. U., Russellville, 1965—67; asst librarian reference Hendrix Coll., Conway, Ark., 1967—73; head librarian U. Ark., Monticello, 1973—75; librarian, dir. N. Ark. Regional Library, Harrison, 1975—85, Ft. Smith (Ark.) Pub. Library, 1985—2004. Mem. adv. bd. Sparks Regional Med. Ctr., 1998—2001. Bd. dirs. Ft. Smith Hist. Soc., 1986—90, Info. Network Ark., 1997—2001; treas. bd. dirs. Pub. Awareness Com., Ft. Smith, Ark., 1986—2004. Mem.: ALA, Ark. Adminstrs. Pub. Librs. (chair 1988—89, del. Ark. govs. conf. on librs. 1990), Ark. Libr. Devel. Dist. (chair 1985—87), Ark. Libr. Assn. (vice chair membership com. 1968, chair pub. libr. divsn. 1993, Disting. Svc. award 1985, Frances P. Neal Leadership award 2005), Info. Network Ark. (bd. dirs. 1997—2001). Democrat. Baptist. Avocations: gardening, woodworking.

LARSON, LYNN WOOD, artist, musician; b. Twin Falls, Idaho, Mar. 22, 1935; d. Harvey Edgar and Carrie Lane (Meiden-Powel) Wood; m. Donald Keith Larson; children: Angela Lynne, Gregory Donald. Student, U. Idaho, Moscow, 1954. Artist, 1967—. One-woman shows include, Bozeman, Mont., 1967, Gooding Libr., 1967, War Meml. Hall, Montana, Md., Idaho, 2000. Recipient Best of Fair, Oil painting, 1993, 1995, 1999, 2002, 2005. Mem.: Sage Brush Art Guild (pres. 1992—93), Am. Legion Aux. Avocations: music, piano, auto harp, organ. Home and Office: 1105 Calif St Gooding ID 83330-1726 Business E-Mail: lynnanddkl@onewest.net.

LARSON, MARK DEVIN, communications executive; b. Rockford, Ill., Aug. 6, 1955; s. Burdette D. Larson and Inga Mae Sandberg; m. Marcia L. Sutton, Feb. 14, 1976; children: Jeffrey, Brandon, Kristin. Grad. high sch., Rockford, 1973. Announcer WRWC Radio, Rockton, Ill., 1971-72; announcer, asst. prodn. dir. WRRR-AM, Rockford, 1972-73; prodn. dir., afternoon host WROK-AM, Rockford, 1973-76; announcer KFMB-AM, San Diego, 1976-77, asst. program dir., 1977-78, program and ops. mgr., afternoon personality, 1978-94; gen. mgr. KPRZ-AM Radio, San Diego, 1994—2002, Sta. KPRZ-AM and Sta. KCBQ-AM Radio, San Diego, 1999—2002; talk show host Sta. KCBQ and KPRZ, 1995—2004, mgr., program cons., 2002—04; guest host for Michael Medved, Dennis Prager and Hugh Hewitt Network Radio Talk Shows, 2000—04; talk show host KOGO-AM, San Diego, 2004—07, talkshow host, 2004—; founder ML Spkrs. Group, 2003—; dir. program, host talk show San Diego 1700-AM Broadcast Co. Ams., 2007—. Co-founder The Program Group, San Diego, 1984-94; co-owner, cons. KISN AM/FM, Salt Lake City, 1985-95; founder, pres. Mark Larson Media Svcs. Inc., El Cajon, Calif., 1985—; nat. program dir./radio Midwest TV, 1988-93; morning talk show host Sta. KRLA-AM, L.A., 2002-03, Sta. KCBQ-AM, San Diego, 2000-04. Creator (audio seminar series) Personal Program Power, 1985-93; host (TV show) KTTY-TV, 1993-94 (Emmy award 1993); columnist Daily Californian, 1995-2000. Chmn., co-founder Family Heritage Found., 1988—, FHF chmn., 1994—, Prison Fellowship, San Diego, 1990-96; vice chair Arts Ctr. Found., 2003—; comm. chmn. San Diego County Rep., 1995; active San Diego Youth for Christ, 1987-97; nat. bd. dirs., mem. global leadership coun. Heart to Heart Internat., 2002—; charter mem. Salem Comm. Polit. Action Com. Named Citizen of Yr., San Diego City Club and Jaycees, 1995, Best Talk Show Host, Achievement in Radio awards, 2002, Hon. Plank Owner USS Ronald Reagan, 2003; named to Local Legends List, Radio and Records, 2006, 07. Mem. Media Fellowship Internat. (chmn. 1998—2003), San Diego Radio Broadcasters Assn. (pres. 1998—2004), San Diego Aerospace Mus. (bd. dirs.), City Club San Diego, Navy League US (life), Coun. Nat. Policy. Avocations: collecting rare books, collecting political autographs and memorabilia. Office: Mark Larson Media Svc Inc 4025 Camino del Rio S Ste 300 San Diego CA 92108 Office Phone: 619-542-7735. Business E-Mail: mark@marklarson.com.

LARSON, MARK EDWARD, JR., lawyer, educator, financial planner; b. Oak Park, Ill., Dec. 16, 1947; s. Mark Edward and Lois Vivian (Benson) L.; m. Patricia Jo Jekerle, Apr. 14, 1973; children: Adam Douglas, Peter Joseph, Alex Edward, Gretchen Elizabeth. BS in Acctg., U. Ill., 1969; JD, Northwestern U., 1972; LLM in Taxation, NYU, 1977. Bar: Ill. 1973, N.Y. 1975, D.C. 1976, Minn, 1982, Tex. 1984, U.S. Dist. Ct. (no. dist.) Ill. 1973, U.S. Dist. Ct. (so. dist.) N.Y. 1975, U.S. Ct. Appeals (2d cir.) 1975, U.S. Ct. Appeals (7th cir.) 1976, U.S. Dist. Ct. D.C. 1977, U.S. Ct. Appeals (D.C. cir.) 1977, U.S. Dist. Ct. Minn. 1982, U.S. Ct. Appeals (8th cir.) 1982, U.S. Tax Ct. 1976, U.S. Supreme Ct. 1976; CPA, Ill. Acct. Deloitte & Touche (formerly Haskins & Sells), NYC, 1973—76, Chgo., 1978—81; atty., ptnr. Larson, Perry & Ward, P.C. and former firms, Chgo., 1983—; prin. Winfield Fin. Svcs. and affiliates, Houston, Austin and Chgo., 1986—. Adj. faculty U. Minn., Mpls., 1981—83, Aurora U., Ill., 1990—98, St. Xavier U., Chgo., 2000—04; bd. dirs. Rush-Wood Imaging Ptnrs., Ltd., 1994—; exec. dir. CFP bd. registered edn. program Marquette U., Milw., 1996—. Contbr. articles to profl. jours. Mem.: AICPA, ABA, Acad. Fin. Svcs., Acad. Molecular Imaging, Am. Assn. Atty.-CPAs, Am. Hosp. Lawyers Assn. Office: 1212 S Naper Blvd Ste 119-131 Naperville IL 60540-7349 Business E-Mail: larsgen@attorney-cpa.com.

LARSON, MICHAEL LEN, newspaper editor, hospital administrator, publishing executive; b. St. James, Minn., Feb. 3, 1944; s. Leonard O. and Lois O. (Holte) L.; m. Kay M. Monahan, June 18, 1966; children: Christopher, David, Molly. BA, U. Minn., 1966; MBA, Mankato State U., 1986. Mng. editor Paddock Circle Inc., Libertyville, Ill., 1972-74, New Ulm (Minn.) Journal, 1974-76, Republican-Eagle, Red Wing, Minn., 1976-79, Mankato (Minn.) Free Press, 1979-84, editor, 1984-95, editor of editl. page, 1995-97; editor Minot (N.D.) Daily News, 1997-2000; bus. editor St. Cloud (Minn.) Times, 2000—01; asst. adminstr. Melrose Area Hosp. Complex, 2001—03; pres., pub. Red Hat Enterprises, Bloomington, Minn., 2003—. Bd. dirs. Minot Area Devel. Corp. Bd. dirs. Valley Indsl. Devel. Corp., Mankato, 1985-95, treas.; adv. bd. Mankato State U. Bus. Sch.; bd. dirs. Sartell Planning Commn., 2003—. With U.S. Army, 1966-68, Vietnam. Recipient First Place award for investigative reporting Minn. Newspaper Assn., 1969, 71, 72, 76, 78, First Place award for feature writing, Suburban Newspapers Am., 1974. Mem. Minn. AP (pres. 1988—), Kiwanis. Roman Catholic. Avocation: bicycling. Home: 1808 N Eighth St Sartell MN 56377-1697 Office: Red Hat Enterprises 11025 Irwin Ave S Bloomington MN 55437

LARSON, NANCY CELESTE, information technology manager; b. Chgo., July 17, 1951; d. Melvin Ellsworth and Ruth Margaret (Carlson) L. BS in Music Ed., U. Ill., 1973, MS in Music Edn., 1976; postgrad., Purdue U., 1982—86. Vocal music educator Consol. Sch. Dist., Gilman, Ill., 1975-77; elem. vocal music tchr. Sch. Dist. 161, Flossmoor, 1977-87; instr. Vander Cook Coll., Chgo., 1980-88; systems programmer analyst Sears, Roebuck & Co., 1987-92, tech. instr., 1989-90, project leader, 1990-91, sr. systems analyst, 1991-92, Trans Union LLC, 1992-94, mgr., 1994—2005, sr. mgr., 2006—. Tchr. adult computer edn. Homewood-Flossmoor HS, 1986—90. Chmn. Faith Luth. Ch., 1982-87, pres. bd., 1988-91, vocal soloist and voice-over performer. Mem. Ill. Music Educators Assn., Music Educators Nat. Conf., Ill. Educators Assn., Nat. Educators Assn., Am. ORFF Schulwerk Assn., Flossmoor Edn. Assn. (negotiator 1983-86). Republican. Lutheran. Avocations: swimming, reading, antiques. Office: Trans Union LLC 555 W Adams St Fl 4 Chicago IL 60661-3696

LARSON, PAUL MARTIN, lawyer; b. Tacoma, June 8, 1949; s. Charles Philip and Margaret (Kobervig) L.; m. Kristina Simonson, June 19, 1971; children: Kristin Ilene, Paul Philip, Erika Louise. AB, Stanford U., 1971; JD, Gonzaga U., 1974. Bar: Wash. 1975, U.S. Dist. Ct. (we. dist.) Wash. 1975, U.S. Dist. Ct. (ea. dist.) Wash. 1978, U.S. Ct. Appeals (9th cir.) 1981. Assoc. Hoff & Cross, Tacoma, 1975-76; ptnr., prin. Brooks & Larson, P.S., Yakima, Wash., 1976-87; ptnr. Bogle & Gates, Yakima, 1987-93, Larson & Perkins, 1994—2006, Larson Berg & Perkins PLLC, 2006—. Author: (with others) Commercial Law Deskbook, 1981 Pres. Cardio & Pulmonary Inst., Yakima, 1981; bd. dirs. Yakima YMCA, 1981-98, pres.-elect bd. dirs. 2000, pres., 2001-2003; bd. dirs. Yakima Youth Commn., 1989-93, Yakima Valley chpt. ARC, 1990-93; bd. dirs. Sisters of Providence Med. Ctr.-Yakima Found., 1986-96, pres., 1992-93, Area Svc. bd. mem., 2000—; bd. dirs. Yakima Schs. Found., 1993-2000, pres., 2000; bd. dirs. EPIC, 2003-. Fellow ABA (standing com. lawyer's responsibility for client protection 1984-89); mem. Wash. State Bar Assn. (spl. dist. counsel, 1985-96, pres. corp. bus. and banking sect. 1987-88, chmn. unauthorized practice of law task force 1995-96), Yakima Estate Planning Coun. (pres. 1981), Rotary (pres. 2005-06). Avocations: tennis, fishing. Office: Larson Berg & Perkins PLLC PO Box 550 Yakima WA 98907-0550 Office Phone: 509-457-1515. Business E-Mail: paul@lbplaw.com.

LARSON, PAUL WILLIAM, public relations executive; b. Wilmington, NC, May 28, 1956; s. Robert WIlliam and Helen Joyce (Hillen) L. BA, U. Calif., Berkeley, 1981; MS in Journalism Medill Sch. of Journalism, Northwestern U., Evanston, Ill., 1991. Reporter Turlock (Calif.) Daily Jour., 1982-84; writer, editor Paul Larson Commns., Modesto, Calif., 1984-90, Evanston, Ill., 2002—; dir. external affairs and publs. Medill Sch. Journalism, Northwestern U., Evanston, 1991-96; mgr. strategic com. AMA, Chgo., 1996-98, dir. membership com., 1998-2000, v.p. mem. and bus. comms., 2000—02; prin. Paul Larson Comms., 2002—. Bd. dirs. Housing Options for Mentally Ill, Evanston, 1993-2000, chmn. comm. com. 1995-2000; docent Evanston Hist. Soc., 1992-95. Recipient Rotary Group Study Exchg. award Rotary Internat., 1986, Rotary Found. Dist. Svc. award, 1995, Leadership Evanston Evanston Cmty. Rels., 1995-96, Vol. of the Yr. award Evanston McGaw YMCA, 1995. Mem. Rotary (bd. dirs. Evanston 1991-95). Home: 1017 Greenleaf St Evanston IL 60202-1235

LARSON, PETER N., manufacturing executive; b. 1939; BS, Oreg. State U.; JD, Seton Hall U. With Johnson & Johnson, N.J., 1967-78, 91-95, Kimberly Clark; chmn. bd., CEO Brunswick Corp., Lake Forest, Ill., 1995—. Office: Brunswick Corp One Northfield Ct Lake Forest IL 60045

LARSON, PHILIP C., lawyer; b. Clarinda, Iowa, June 14, 1946; BS, Iowa State U., 1968; JD with honors, Duke U., 1971. Bar: D.C. 1971, U.S. Supreme Ct. 1975. Ptnr. Hogan & Hartson LLP, Washington, chmn. antitrust practice group. Article editor Duke Law Jour., 1970-71; contbr. articles to profl. jours. Mem. ABA (antitrust law sect.), DC Bar, Order of Coif. Office: Hogan & Hartson LLP Columbia Square 555 13th St NW Ste 800E Washington DC 20004-1109 Office Phone: 202-637-5738. Office Fax: 202-637-5910. Business E-Mail: pclarson@hhlaw.com.

LARSON, RANDALL J., energy executive; BBA, MBA, Univ. Wis. Ptnr. KPMG, Denver & NYC, 1981—96, San Jose, Calif., 1996—2002; exec. v.p., chief acctg. officer TransMontaigne Inc., Denver, 2002—03; exec. v.p., CFO TransMointaigne Inc., Denver, 2003—06; pres., CEO, CFO TransMontaigne Partners LP, Denver, 2006—. Profl. acctg. fellow Office of Chief Acct., SEC, 1992—94. Office: TransMontaigne Inc Ste 3100 1670 Broadway Denver CO 80202 also: TransMontaigne Partners LP Ste 3100 1670 Broadway Denver CO 80202*

LARSON, REED EUGENE, foundation administrator; b. Smith County, Kans., Sept. 27, 1922; s. George Christian and Edith Hazel (Whitney) L.; m. Marjorie Jeanne Hess, Aug. 31, 1947; children: Patricia Kay Larson Sween, Barbara Ann Larson Finnegan, Marcia Lynn Larson Craig. Student, Kans. Wesleyan U., 1940-41, Ohio State U., 1943-44; BS in E.E, Kans. State U., 1947. Design engr. Stein Labs., Atchison, Kans., 1947-48; processing engr. Coleman Co., Wichita, Kans., 1948-54; exec. v.p. Kansans for the Right to Work, Wichita, 1954-58; from exec. v.p. to chmn. exec. com. Nat. Right-to-Work Com., Washington, 1959—, Nat. Right-to-Work Legal Def. Found., 1968—. Chmn. Hallmark Bank & Trust, 1984-96; vice chmn. F&M Bank-No. Va., 1996-99. Served with AUS, 1943-46. Recipient Seldon Waldo award U.S. Jaycees, 1956; Silver Anvil award Pub. Rels. Soc. Am., 1966; James J. Kilpatrick award Internat. Platform Assn., 1980; Awarded Doctor of Laws Campbell U., 1988. Mem. Mont Pelerin Soc., Phila. Soc., Eta Kappa Nu, Tau Beta Pi. Clubs: Kansas Jaycees (pres. 1953-54), Rotary, Am. Legion. Baptist. Office: 8001 Braddock Rd Springfield VA 22160-0001 Home: 3013 Downing St Williamsburg VA 23185 Office Phone: 703-321-9820. Business E-Mail: larson@nrtw.org.

LARSON, RICHARD SMITH, pathologist, researcher; b. Ithaca, NY, Aug. 27, 1962; s. Richard Ingwald and Judith Ann (Larsen) Larson; m. Blaire Martin, June 4, 1989. AB in Chemistry summa cum laude, U. N.C., 1984; MD, PhD, Harvard U., 1990. Diplomate Am. Bd. Pathology. Resident Barnes Hosp., St. Louis, 1990-93; hematopathology fellow Vanderbilt U., Nashville, 1993-96; from asst. prof., divsn. chief to prof., sr. assoc. dean, v.p. rsch. U. N.Mex., 1996—. Co-founder Cancer Svcs. N.Mex.; bd. dirs., chmn. Tricore Corp.; bd. dirs. Lit. Coun., N.Mex. Biotech. Bus. Assn.; pres. CSNM Found. Contbr. over 100 articles and abstracts to profl. jours., chapters to books. Named designated investigator, Am. Cancer Soc. Coaches Against Cancer, Hoops for Lymphoma; recipient Lansky award, UNM Regents' Lectureship, Chief Scientist Excellence award, Def. Intelligence Agy.; grantee, Am. Cancer Soc., Am. Heart Assn., NIH, NSF. Mem.: Pediat. Oncology Group, Am. Soc. Hematology, Coll. Am. Pathologists, Phi Beta Kappa. Achievements include patents in field. Office Phone: 505-272-6950.

LARSON, ROBERT CRAIG, real estate company officer; b. Mpls., June 15, 1934; s. Eugene and Frances (Wescott) L.; m. Lucy Ann Ballinger, June 20, 1957 (div. 1981), m. Karen Chase, Sept. 5, 1981; children: Elizabeth, Eric, Kathryn. BA, Carleton Coll., Northfield, Minn., 1956. Various staff positions Inland Steel Co., Chgo., 1956-67; gen. mgr. Inland Steel Container Co., Cleve., 1967-70; v.p. Inland Steel Devel. Co., Washington, 1970-74; gen. mgr. Georgetown Inland Corps., Washington, 1970-74; sr. v.p. Taubman Co., Washington, 1974-78, pres. and chief exec. officer Bloomfield Hills, Mich., 1978-90, vice chmn., 1990—, dir. Bloomfield Hills, Mich., 1978—; now principal, non-exec. chmn. Larson Realty Group; mng. dir., chmn. Lazard Freres Real Estate Investors, LLC. Bd. dirs. Intercontinental Hotels Group PLC, Brandywine Realty Trust; chmn. United Dominion Realty Trust, Inc.; bd. dirs. Atria Senior Living Group, Inc., Destination Europe Limited, Commonwealth Atlantic Properties, Inc., ARV Assisted Living, Inc. Chmn. Nat. Urban League, N.Y.C.; bd. govs. Cranbrook Acad. Art, Bloomfield Hills, Mich.; trustee, vice chmn. Children's Hosp. of Mich., Cranbrook Ednl. Community, Detroit, Citizens Rsch. Coun. of Mich., Detroit, Detroit Med. Ctr., Detroit Symphony Orch., Inc.; dir. Detroit Econ. Growth Corp.; trustee Kresge Found. Mem. Nat. Realty Com. (chmn. 1986—), Urban Land Inst., Internat. Coun. Shopping Ctrs., Bloomfield Open Hunt (Bloomfield Hills), City Tavern (Washington), World Trade (San Francisco).

LARSON, ROBERT WILLIAM, education educator, consultant; b. Iowa City, Feb. 8, 1935; s. Robert William and Mary Alice (Scannell) Larson; m. Linda Louise Carolan, Nov. 30, 2002. BS, U. Wyo., Laramie; MA, EdD, U. N. Colo., Greeley. Pres. Media, Inc., 1967—72; dir. Title 1 and fed. programs Greeley Sch., Colo., 1972—74; advt., pub. rels. dir. Blue Cross/Blue Shield, Cheyenne, Wyo., 1976—83; mktg. cons. Stress Mgmt. Inst., Cheyenne, Wyo., 1983—86; asst. prof. Minn. State U., Moorhead, 1987—90; mktg. cons. Ad Pro, Duluth, Ga., 1990—92; assoc. prof. Breneau U., Gainesville, Ga., 1990—92; asst. prof. Pitts. State U., 1992—98, Northwestern Okla. State U., 1998—2002; adj. assoc. prof. Washburn U., Topeka, 2002—06, Kansas City (Kans.) C.C., 2003—, Avila U., 2005—. Contbr. Wild Horses, 1963; contbg. editor: Wyo. Wildlife Mag., 1963-66. Dir. Joplin (Mo.) AdFedn., 1996-98; county coord. Sally Thompson Senate, Pittsburg, Kans., 1996; states coord., Kathy Karpan Sec. of State, Cheyenne, Wyo., 1986. Maj. USMC, 1958-62, USMCR, 1963-85. Mem. Pittsburg C. of C., Moorhead C. of C., Lions Club (bd. dirs., pub. rels. dir. Overland Park chpt.). Democrat. Methodist. Avocations: triathlons, waterskiing, basketball, tennis, woodworking. Personal E-mail: blarson83@aol.com.

LARSON, ROGER KEITH, physician, writer; b. Cadillac, Mich., Apr. 27, 1924; s. William E. and Ethel Lydia (Rose) Larson; m. Frances Ann Appel, July 1, 1949; children: Ronald Allen, John William, Joan Elizabeth, Sharon Ruth. BS, Wheaton Coll., 1944; MD, U. Ill., Chgo., 1947. Diplomate in internal medicine and pulmonary disease Am. Bd. Internal Medicine. Intern Cook County Hosp., Chgo., 1947—49; resident Kern Gen. Hosp., 1949—52; pvt. practice, 1957—61; chief of medicine Univ. Med. Ctr., Fresno, Calif., 1961—90; dir. HRSA and NIMH AIDS Profl. Edn. and Trng. Grant, Calif., Oregon, Nevada, Ariz., 1990—93. Instr. UCLA Sch. Medicine, 1955—76; clin. prof. U. Calif., San Francisco, 1976—93, prof. emeritus, 1993—. Contbr. chapters to books, articles to profl. jours. Capt. US Army, 1952—54, Korea, Japan. Recipient Disting. Svc. award, Am. Heart Asasn., 1969, Henry E. Randel award, Ctrl. Calif. Lung Assn., 1980, Kasier award, USCF, 1981, Award for Outstanding Cmty. Svc, Fresno Med. Soc., 1991, Laureate award Calif. chpt. ACP, 1992. Achievements include first to link smoking to chronic lung disease; research in pulmonary alveolar proteinosis; first to devel. major acad. med. program in Calif. San Joaquin Valley. Faculty grew from one time person to approx. fifty and from non-Univ. affiliated to full UCSF affiliation. Avocations: music, history.

LARSON, ROLAND ELMER, health facility administrator; b. Chgo., Jan. 21, 1939; s. Elmer Gustav and Anna (Alphida) L.; children: Eric R., Jennifer L., Melissa K. BA, Augustana Coll., 1961; MHA, U. Iowa, 1963; postgrad., Harvard U., 1978. Adminstrv. asst. U. Vt. Med. Ctr., Burlington, 1962-64; assoc. adminstr. Roger Williams Hosp., Providence, 1964-73; v.p. adminstrn. Norwalk (Conn.) Hosp., 1973-81; pres., chief exec. officer Nashoba Community Hosp., Ayer, Mass., 1981-88; v.p. Charles River Assn., Boston, 1988-90; cons. Charles River Assocs., Boston, 1990-93; ind. healthcare cons. Harvard, Mass., 1990—. Chmn. Harvard (Mass.) Coalition Against Drugs and Alcohol, Opportunities, Inc., Providence, 1966-68, Greater Norwalk Community Coun., 1980; bd. dirs. Nat. Arthritis Found., N.Y.C., 1967-71, Am. Cancer Soc., Stamford, Conn., 1978-81 Fellow Am. Coll. Healthcare Execs.; mem. Cen. Mass. Hosp. Coun. (chmn. 1987-88), Rotary. Avocations: sailing, bicycling, golf, squash, woodworking. Home and Office: Larson & Assocs PO Box 602 Boylston MA 01505-0602

LARSON, ROY, journalist, publishing executive; b. Moline, Ill., July 27, 1929; s. Roy W. and Jane (Beall) L.; m. Dorothy Jennisch, June 7, 1950; children: Mark, Bruce, Jodie, Bradley. AB, Augustana Coll., Rock Island, Ill., 1951; M.Div., Garrett Theol. Sem., 1955. Ordained to ministry Methodist Ch., 1956; min. Covenant United Meth. Ch., Evanston, Ill., 1963-68, First United Meth. Ch., Elmhurst, Ill., 1968-69; religion editor Chgo. Sun-Times, 1969-85; pub. The Chgo. Reporter, 1985-94; exec. dir. Garrett-Medill Ctr. for Religion and News Media, Evanston, Ill., 1995—2002; dir. comm. Chgo. Temple, 2003—. Home: 1508 Hinman Ave Evanston IL 60201-4664 Office: Chgo Temple 77 W Washington Chicago IL 60602 Office Phone: 312-236-4548. E-mail: drlarson29@comcast.net.

LARSON, SHERYL ANN, social worker, researcher, writer; b. Mpls., Nov. 26, 1963; d. Donald and Marian Larson. BA, Bethel U., 1985; MA, U. Minn., 1993, PhD, 1997. LISW Minn. Bd. Social Work, 1993; cert. tchr. Minn., 1985, tchr. severe disabilities Minn., 1990. Behavior analyst Merrick Companies Inc, White Bear Lake, Minn., 1985—88; social worker Dakota County, West St. Paul, Minn., 1988; sr. rsch. dir., rsch. assoc., rsch. fellow, rsch. asst. U. Minn., Mpls., 1987—. Cons. Luth. Social Svc. Minn., St. Paul, 1997—, Ctrs. Disease Control; cons. Us dept, edn. Nat. Inst. Disability and Rehabilitation Rsch.; chmn. devel. disabilities com., citizens adv. com. Ramsey County, St. Paul, 1992—95; mem. Minn. Gov.'s Coun. Devel. Disabilities, St. Paul, 2004—; mem. adv. com. Dept. Human Svcs., Managed Care Options for People with Disabilities State of Minn., St. Paul, 2005—. Author, editor Staff recruitment, retention and training in community human services organizations, (books) Crisis: Prevention and response in the community, Challenges for a Service System in Transition: Ensuring Quality Community Experiences for Persons with Developmental Disabilities, Health promotion for persons with intellectual/developmental disabilities: The state of scientific evidence; author: (books) Embarking on a New Century; co-editor: Disability research within the NHIS-D: The results of a user's conference. Research in Social Sciences and Disability, (Vol. 3); author: (book chapter) Destructive Behavior in Developmental Disabilities: Diagnosis and Treatment, National goals and research for persons with intellectual and developmental disabilities, Costs and outcomes of community services for people with intellectual disabilities, Clinical Services, Social Adjustment, and Work Life in Community Living; editl. cons.: Jour. Intellctual and Developmental Disability, 2002—; author: (book chapter) Mental Retardation in the Year 2000; contbr. articles to profl. jours. Bd. sec. Ctrl. Evang. Free Ch., Mpls., 2000—01; dir. No Pl. Like Home, Robbinsdale, Minn., 2004—06; bd. dirs. Arc Minn., 2007—. Fellow: Am. Assn. Intellectual and Devel. Disabilities (pres. cmty. svcs. divsn. 2004—06, consulting editor jour. 1993—, Presdl. award 2001); mem.: Internat. Assn. Sci. Study Intellectual Disabilities). Avocations: travel, swimming. Office: Institute on Community Integration UMN 214B Pattee Hall 150 Pillsbury Drive SE Minneapolis MN 55455 Home Phone: 763-717-9882; Office Phone: 612-624-6024. Office Fax: 612-625-6619. Business E-Mail: larso072@umn.edu.

LARSON, STEPHEN G., federal judge; b. Fontana, Calif., 1964; BS, Georgetown U., 1986; JD, U. So. Calif. Law Sch., 1989. Bar: Calif. 1989. Assoc. O'Melveny & Myers, 1989—91; asst. US atty. US Atty.'s Office (Ctrl. dist.) Calif., 1991—2000; US magistrate judge US Dist. Ct. (Ctrl. dist.) Calif., 2000—06, dist. judge, 2006—. Adj. asst. prof. Glendale Coll. Law, 1997—2001; instr. Calif. So. Law Sch., 2001—05; adj. prof. U. LaVerne Coll. Law, 2002—. Office: US Dist Ct Rm 1 3470 12th St Riverside CA 92501 Office Phone: 951-328-4464, 950-274-0844. E-mail: James_Holmes@cacd.uscourts.gov.*

LARSON, STEVEN MARK, physician; b. Tacoma, Wash., Nov. 30, 1941; s. Louis Edward and Evelyn Agusta (Peterson) L.; married; children: Nathan, Justine. BA in Zoology, Univ. Wash., 1963, MD, 1968. Diplomate Am. Bd. Nuclear Medicine, Am. Bd. Internal Medicine. Various positions in field to chief, dept. nuclear medicine NIH, Bethesda, Md., 1983-88; prof. dept. radiology Uniformed Svcs./Univ. Health Scis., Bethesda, 1983-88; attending physician Meml. Hosp./Meml. Sloan-Kettering Cancer Ctr., 1988—; prof. radiology Cornell Med. Coll., NYC, 1988—; chief, Nuclear Medicine Svc., Dept. Radiology Meml. Sloan-Kettering Cancer Ctr., 1988—, dir. radiology rsch. Dept. Radiology, 1988—, attending physician Div. Hematologic Oncology, 1990—. Vis. clinician Brookhaven Nat. Lab., 1990—; cons. FDA, 1973, Nat. Libr. Medicine, 1972—, NIH, 1972-74, Bur. of Drugs/FDA, 1973-82, others; mem. BERAC Com. Dept. Energy. Editorial bd. Jour. Nat. Cancer Inst., 1986—, Hybridoma, 1986—, Jour.: Antibody, Immunoconjugates and Radiopharmaceuticals, 1987—; assoc. editor The Jour. of Nuclear Medicine, 1989—, others; editor-in-chief: Clin. Positron Imaging. Capt. USPHS, 1972-90. Named Outstanding Zoology Undergrad., Univ. Wash., Seattle, 1963, Rockwell Meml. Lectr., U. Iowa Coll. of Medicine, 1985, Disting. AMA Lectr. in Med. Scis., 1986; recipient Smith-Kline Instrumentation prize, 1968, Zetein award in Nuclear Medicine, 1968, Disting. Alumnus award Div. Nuclear Medicine, Johns Hopkins Med. Instns., 1985, Eugene Pendergrass award New Horizons Lectr./Radiol. Soc. North Am., 1986, award from Louise and Lionel Berman Found., Inc., 1990, G.V. Hevesy Lectr. Medal, Hungary, Elis Berven Lecture medal Swedish Soc. Oncology, 1999. Mem. Soc. Nuclear Medicine (chmn. coms. 1973-78, pres. Pacific Northwest chpt. 1982-84), Am. Coll. Nuclear Physicians (regent 1973-75, coms., Ralph Robinson lectureship 1997), Am. Coll. Radiology, Am. Soc. Clin. Oncology, Radiol. Soc. N. Am., Inst. Medicine. Independent. Presbyterian. Achievements include development of positron emission tomagraphy for oncology, first "kit" methods for nuclear medicine; discovery of action of gallium-67 citrate, a radiopharmaceutical that binds to the transferrin receptor; research in immunokinetics of radiolabeled anti-tumor antibodies, and application of anti-tumor antibodies to diagnosis and treatment. Office: Meml Sloan-Kettering Cancer Ctr 1275 York Ave New York NY 10021-6094 Home Phone: 212-675-3601; Office Phone: 212-639-7373. Business E-Mail: larsons@mskcc.org.

LARSON, THOMAS D., energy and food products executive; B in Agr. Edn., SD State U., Brookings. Vo-ag tchr.; agronomy sales position Cenex, mgr. local coop. Hoffman, Minn., mktg. and planning positions regional coop., 1978, agronomy position, 1987, dir. agronomy svcs. Cenex/Land O'Lakes Agronomy Co., 1988, v.p. agronomy svcs., v.p. Supply and Mktg., 1996; exec. v.p. bus. solutions CHS Inc. (merger of Cenex and Harvest States), 2005—. Bd. dirs. Cofina Fin., LLC. Office: CHS Inc PO Box 64089 Saint Paul MN 55164-0089 Office Phone: 651-355-6974. E-mail: tom.larson@chsinc.com.*

LARSON, VERN L., state official; b. Pierre, SD, Oct. 25, 1948; BS in Polit. Sci. and English, No. State U., 1970. Aide to Rep. Jim Abdnor, SD, 1974—78; state auditor State of S.D., Pierre, 1979—2002, state treas., 2003—. Republican. Achievements include being the longest serving constitutional officer in South Dakota history. Office: Office of State Treasurer Capitol Bldg 2d Fl 500 E Capitol Pierre SD 57501-5070

LARSON, VICKI LORD, academic administrator, communication disorders educator; b. Prentice, Wis., Sept. 21, 1944; d. Edward A. and Stella Mae (Hilton) Lord; m. James Roy Larson, Sept. 3, 1966. BSEd, U. Wis., Madison, 1966, MS, 1968, PhD, 1974. Speech-lang. pathologist Coop. Ednl. Svc. Agy. 2, Minoqua, Wis., 1967—69; instr. U. Wis., Whitewater, 1969—71, rsch. asst. Madison, 1971—73, asst. prof. Eau Claire, 1973-77, assoc. prof., 1977—81, prof. communication disorders, 1981—91, dept. chair, 1978—83, asst. dean grad. studies and univ. rsch., 1984—89, assoc. dean grad. studies and univ. rsch., 1989—91, interim chancellor, 2005—06, prof. comm. Oshkosh, 1991—2000, dean Grad. Sch. Rsch., 1991—94, provost, vice chancellor acad. affairs, 1994—2000. Acquistions editor Thinking Publs., Eau Claire, 2001—04, acquistions mgr., 2004—06. Author: Adolescents: Communication Development and Disorder, 1983, Communication Assessment and Intervention Strategies for Adolescents, 1987; contbr. Handbook of Speech-Language Pathology and Audiology, 1988, Language Disorders in Older Students, 1995, Working Out With Listening, 2002, Communication Solutions for Older Students, 2003, S-MAPs curriculum-based assessment, 2004, Aspergers Syndrome: Strategies for Solving the Social Puzzle, 2005; contbr.: Working Out With Writing, 2005. Fellow: Am. Speech, Lang., Hearing Assn. (councilor); mem.: Wis. Speech, Lang., Hearing Assn. (pres. 1976, honors 1991, pres. found. 2000—04, v.p. 2005—07, treas. 2005—07), Golden Key, Phi Kappa Phi, Omicron Delta Kappa. Avocations: traveling, quilting, reading. E-mail: larsonvl@uwec.edu.

LARSON, WANDA Z., writer, poet; b. Cle Elum, Wash., Aug. 26, 1926; d. Stanley Aloysius and Anele (Valenta) Zackovich; m. Glen B. Larson, Nov. 18, 1950 (div. Mar. 1967); children: Karen Holk, Margot Huffman, Lisa Larson Landrey (dec. 1998). BA, U. Wash., 1949. Columnist North Bend Herald, Snoqualmie, Wash., 1955-61, Goldendale (Wash.) Sentinel, 1962-67; news editor West Seattle Herald, 1950-51; editor employee newsletter Alaska Steamship Co., Seattle, 1951; editl. asst. Associated Publs., Portland, Oreg., 1970-72, staff writer, 1974-78; pub. Blue Unicorn Press Inc., Portland, 1990—; poet Sta. KOPB, Portland, 1991—. Author: Portlandia, 1991, Miracle at Blowing Rock, 1992, Elisabeth: A Biography, 1997, 2nd edit., 2002, Our Flag - Born Through Valor, 1999, Bird Woman/Mojave (Sacajawea), 2001, numerous poems. Co-recipient 2nd pl. award Poetry Forum Quar., 1990; hon. mention Still Water Press, 1990. Avocations: humanitarian interests, history. Home and Office: PO Box 40300 Portland OR 97240-0300 Office Phone: 503-234-7781.

LA RUE, CARL FORMAN, lawyer; b. Ann Arbor, Mich., Aug. 4, 1929; s. Carl D. and Evelina F. La R.; children: Steven, Edward; m. Ann Williams Lindbloom, June 28, 1971; stepchildren: Eric, Sarah Relyea. AB, Harvard U., 1952; LL.B., U. Mich., 1957. Bar: Ohio 1957, Ill. 1964, Calif. 1969. Assoc. firm Fuller & Henry, Toledo, 1957-59; asst. U.S. atty. for Northwestern Ohio, Dept. Justice, 1959-61; staff atty. Aeroquip-Vickers, Inc. (then Libbey-Owens-Ford Co., now part of Eaton Corp.), Toledo, 1961-64; sr. atty. Armour and Co., Chgo., 1964-68; asst. gen. counsel Rockwell Internat., LA, 1968-78; v.p., gen. counsel, sec. Aeroquip-Vickers, Inc. (then Trinova Corp.), Toledo, 1978-87; of counsel Marshall & Melhorn, Toledo, 1988-96. With U.S. Army, 1952-54. Mem.: Toledo Tennis Club, Toledo Club. Home: 3553 Brookside Rd Toledo OH 43606-2610

LARUE, LILLIAN JAYNE, electrical engineer, educator; d. William A. and Johanna U. Craft; 1 child, Sean William. AA in Phys. Edn., Miami Dade CC, Fla., 1975; BS in Phys. Edn., Fla. Internat. U., 1980; postgrad., U. Wis., 1994—. Cert. master electrician Wis. Phys. edn. tchr., coach Broward County Sch. Bd., Ft. Lauderdale, Fla., 1980—83; electrician Internat. Brotherhood Elect. Workers, Ft. Lauderdale, 1983—91; elec. instr. Northeast Wis. Tech. Coll., Green Bay, 1991—; lighting specialist, tech. support Badger Electric Supply Corp., Green Bay, 1995—96. Instr. nat. electrical code Chippewa Valley Tech. Coll., Eau Claire, Wis., 1988—91. Avocation: flying. Office: Northeast Wis Tech Coll 2740 W Mason St Green Bay WI 54307 Office Phone: 920-498-5741.

LARUE, PAUL HUBERT, retired lawyer; b. Somerville, Mass., Nov. 16, 1922; s. Lucien H. and Germaine (Choquet) LaR.; m. Helen Finnegan, July 20, 1946; children: Paul Hubert, Patricia Fell, Mary Hogan. PhB, U. Wis., 1947, JD, 1949. Bar: Ill. 1955, Wis. 1949, U.S. Supreme Ct. 1972. Grad. asst. instr. polit. sci. dept. U. Wis., 1947-48; mem. staff Wis. Atty. Gen., 1949-50; trial atty., legal advisor to commr. FTC, 1950-55; pvt. practice Chgo.; mem. Chadwell & Kayser, Ltd., 1958-90; ptnr. Vedder, Price, Kaufman & Kammholz, 1990-93; of counsel, 1993-99; ret., 1999. Spkr. profl. meetings; mem. Com. Modern Cts. in Ill., 1964; mem. Com. for Constl. Conv. Ill., 1968, Better Govt. Assn., 1966-70 Contbr. articles to profl. jours. Mem. lawyers com. Met. Crusade of Mercy, 1967-68, United Settlement Appeal, 1966-68; apptd. pub. mem. Ill. Conflict of Interest Laws Commn., 1965-67. With AUS, 1943-45, ETO; capt. JAGC, USAFR, 1950-55. Fellow Ill. Bar Found. (charter mem.); mem. ABA (mem. coun. sect. antitrust law 1980-83, chmn. Robinson-Patman Act com. 1975-78), Ill. State Bar Assn., Chgo. Bar Assn. (chmn. antitrust com. 1970-71), Wis. State Bar (emeritus mem.), Rotary. Roman Catholic. Home: 250 Cuttriss St Park Ridge IL 60068 Personal E-mail: paullarue@sbcglobal.net.

LA RUSSA, TONY, JR., (ANTHONY LA RUSSA JR.), professional baseball manager; b. Tampa, Fla., Oct. 4, 1944; m. Elaine Coker, Dec. 31, 1973; children: Bianca, Devon. Student, U. Tampa; BA, U. So. Fla., 1969; LLB, Fla. State U., 1978. Bar: Fla., 1979. Player numerous major league and minor league baseball teams, 1962-77; coach St. Louis Cardinals orgn., 1977; mgr. minor league team Knoxville, 1978, Iowa, 1979; coach Chgo. White Sox, 1978, mgr., 1979-86, Oakland A's, 1986-95, St. Louis Cardinals, 1996—. Mgr. Am. League All-Star Team, 1988, Nat. League All-Star Team, 2005 Co-founder Tony LaRussa's Animal Rescue Found., 1991—. Mgr., Am. League Champions, 1988-90; Nat. League Champions, 2004, 2006; World Series Champions, 1989, 2006; Named Am. League Mgr. Yr. Major League Baseball Writers' Assn., 1983, 88, 92; Nat. League Mgr. Yr., 2002; named to Mo. Sports Hall of Fame, 2006; recipient C.I. Taylor award Negro League Hall of Fame, 2004 Achievements include becoming the secong manager in major league baseball history to win the World Series in both leagues, 1989, 2006. Office: St Louis Cardinals Busch Stadium 250 Stadium Plz Saint Louis MO 63102-1722*

LARUSSO, ANTHONY CARL, company executive, lecturer, consultant; b. May 5, 1949; s. Nicholas and Rose (Ruspini) LaR.; m. Marianne Elizabeth Baviello, Apr. 4, 1971; children: Anne, Tony. BA, Fordham U., 1971; MBA, NYU, 1972. Cert. mgmt. acct. Sr. project mgr. Office Mgmt. and Control NYC Dept. Human Resources, 1972-73; mgr. econ. planning Trans World Airlines, NYC, 1973-76; mgr. planning and analysis AMAX, Inc., Greenwich, Conn., 1976-81, mgr. corp. devel., 1981-84, v.p. planning and mktg. metals, 1984-86, from v.p. to pres. metal refining ops., 1986—89, pres. climax performance materials corp., 1990-93; gen. mgr. CRI-MET, White Plains, N.Y., 1994-95; pres. Elkem Metals Co., Pitts., 1996—2003; instr. Ctr. for Profl. Edn., Inc., Pa., 2003—06, AICPA, Tex., 2003—. Adj. prof. mgmt. Pace U., 1975—95. Author: Management: Ready Aim Fire, 2005; author workbooks/classes in fin. and mgmt. AICPA, 2006—; contbr. articles to profl. jours. Officer local homeowners assn., Pa., 1997-2003; former chmn. local homeowners assn., Mahopac, N.Y.; asst. to chmn. ann. cookie sale Girl Scouts USA, Shrub Oak, N.Y.; coach/safety dir. Am. Youth Soccer Orgn., Yorktown, N.Y. Mem. Acad. Mgmt., Am. Mgmt. Assn., Chief Exec. Network, Inst. Mgmt. Acctg., Orgn. Devel. Inst., Strategic Mgmt. Soc., Ferroalloys Assn. (officer 1996-2003), Soc. for Advancement of Mgmt., Inc. Republican. Roman Catholic. Avocations: racquetball, swimming, fishing. Home: PO Box 7548 Naples FL 34101 E-mail: tonyclarusso@hotmail.com.

LARUSSO, NICHOLAS F., gastroenterologist, educator, scientist; Dir. Ctr. Basic Rsch. Digestive Disorders Mayo Clinic Coll Medicine, Rochester, Minn., 1977—2002, prof., chmn. dept. internal medicine, 1977—, Charles H. Weinman endowed prof. medicine, 2006—. Office: Mayo Clinic Ctr Basic Rsch Digestive Disease Guggenheim 17 Rochester MN 55905-0001 Home Phone: 507-292-1877; Office Phone: 507-284-3725. Business E-Mail: larusso.nicholas@mayo.edu.

LARWOOD, LAURIE, psychologist; b. NY, 1941; PhD, Tulane U., 1974. Pres. Davis Instruments Corp., San Leandro, Calif., 1966—71; cons., 1969—; asst. prof. orgnl. behavior SUNY, Binghamton, 1974—76; assoc. prof., chair dept. psychology Claremont (Calif.) McKenna Coll., 1976—83, assoc. prof. bus. adminstrn., 1976—83, Claremont Grad. Sch., 1976—85; prof., head dept. mgmt. U. Ill., Chgo., 1983—87; dean sch. bus. SUNY, Albany, 1987—90; dean Coll. Bus. Adminstrn. U. Nev., Reno, 1990—92, prof., 1990—2003, prof. emerita, 2003—; dir. Inst. Strategic Bus. Issues, 1992—2003; mng. ptnr. Quail Lane Studios, Reno, 2003—. Western regional adv. coun. SBA, 1976-81; dir. Mgmt. Team; pres. Mystic Games, Inc.; mng. ptnr. Quail Lane Studios, 2003-. Author: (with M.M. Wood) Women in Management, 1977, Organizational Behavior and Management, 1984, Women's Career Development, 1987, Strategies-Successes-Senior Executives Speak Out, 1988, Women's Careers, 1988, Managing Technological Development, 1988, Impact Analysis, 1999; mem. editl. bd. Sex Roles, 1979-2003, Consultation, 1986-91, Jour. Orgnl. Behavior, 1987-2003, Jour. Vocat. Behavior, 1999-, Group and Orgn. Mgmt., 1982-84, editor, 1986-91; founding editor Women and Work, 1983, Jour. Mgmt. Case Studies, 1983-87; contbr. articles to profl. jours. Mem. Acad. Mgmt. (editl. rev. bd. Rev. 1977-82, past chmn. women in mgmt. divsn., managerial consultation divsn., tech. and innovation mgmt. divsn.), Am. Psychol. Assn., Assn. Women in Psychology. Office: Quail Ln Studios 10225 N Quail Ln Tucson AZ 85742 Mailing: Box 89789 Tucson AZ 85752 Personal E-mail: larwood@earthlink.net.

LARY, BANNING KENT, film producer, writer; b. Chgo., Aug. 27, 1949; s. Banning Gray and Katherine Lee (Tedrow) L.; m. Janice Ann, Dec. 22, 1974 (div. Aug. 1977); 1 child, Venus Ayn Katherine; m. Valerie Maria Dalli, Dec. 28, 1987; children: Alexandra Lee, Kristin Gray. BJ, U. Tex., 1970. Editor-in-chief Beach & Town, Miami, Fla., 1976-77; gen. contractor Larydome Inc., Miami, 1977-80; exec. dir. Legal Devel. Resources, Austin, 1989—; pres. Promedion, Inc., Austin, 1990—, Am. Multimedia Pubs., Austin, 1996—. Dir., 1985—; freelance writer, 1970—; creative troubleshooter, writer, editor various orgns.; video pub., 1987—. Author: Twist of Faith, 1996; writer, prodr., dir. Robbery! The Aftermath, 1988, Ten Commandments of Avoiding Legal Malpractice, 1989, Ten. Procedures for Avoiding Medical Malpractice, 1990, The Belli Tapes: Winning at Trial, 10 vols., 1991, Childproof: Home Safety Checklist, 1991, Webmaster Secret Internet Marketing Strategies, 1999; video prodr. Bad Paper, 1987, Extortion Set, 1988; prodr. The Sexual Harassment Prevention Kit, 1992, Teens-At-Risk Series, 8 vols., 1998, numerous TV comml.s, and many others; contbr. articles to mags.; editor: How to Win Your Case in Court, 1996; pub. Do What You Want to Do, 1996, Gold Medal Performance Without Dangerous Steroids, 1997; editor, prodr.: Living Well Past 50, 1998; prodr., dir.: Heroin Story, Please Remember Suzi, 1998 (silver award), Teen Drinking, 1998 (gold award), Human Communications Theory, 1998 (bronze award), Teen Finances (bronze apple), 1999, Psychology of Criminal Behavior, 2001, Teens, Sex and the Law, 2003 (Communicator Crystal award of excellence, 2003), Terrorism: Weapon of Fear, 2003, Chekhov's the Seagull with Edward Albee, Culture, Identity and Behavior, 2003, The History of Sociology, Interpreting Nonverbal Communications, American Law: How It Works, Theories in Social Work Practice, China Welcomes Austin, AB Negative, 2006, History of Academic Education in America, 2006, History of Psychology, 2006; inventor roller washer II, golf swing muscle articulator. Bd. dirs. Alpha Nu House Corp., Austin. Recipient Gold award for video prodn., 1987, silver award, 1988, 91, Prize Stories Anthology award, 1989, O'Henry awards, Best of Austin award Internat. Assn. Bus. Communicators, 1986, 93, Disting. Achievement award Am. Soc. Ind. Security-Video, 1987, 1st pl. U.S.A. Hometown Video Festival, 1991, award of excellence ACTV, 1992, Bronze award Charleston Internat. Film Festival, 1993, Bronze award Worldfest, 1995, Gold award Flagstaff Internat. Film Festival, 1998, Pegasus award, 1998, Crystal award of Excellence, 1999, Telly award, 2004; named to Top 100 Multimedia Prodrs. Am. Mem. Am. Acad. Poets, Tex. Writers League, Austin Writers League, Amnesty Internat., Sigma Chi. Avocations: photography, painting, philosophy, securities analysis, films. Office: Am Visionary Artists PO Box 3551 Austin TX 78764-3551 Office Phone: 512-282-9006. Personal E-mail: banning@austin.rr.com.

LASA-FERRER, ARMANDO, lawyer; b. 1937; BA, U. Miami, 1962; JD, Interamerican U., 1966. Bar: P.R. Sr. ptnr. Lasa Monroig & Veve, Guaynabo, PR. Mem. sub-com. on universal svc. com. Assn. Competitive Providers Telecom.; mem. task force in charge of drafing the P.R. telecom. act of 1996 P.R. Ho. Reps.; prof. Interamerican U. Sch. Law, PR; mem. Gov. P.R. Task Force on Health Care Reform; gen. counsel Rep. Nat. Hispanic Assembly. Nat. advisor New Majority Coun., Rep. Nat. Com. Mem.: ABA (bd. govs. 18th dist. 2001—, sec.-elect 2002—05, chair and mem. numerous coms., sec. 2005—). Office: Lasa Monroig & Veve Buchanan Office Ctr 40 Road 165 Ste 304 Guaynabo PR 00968 Business E-Mail: alasa@lmvpr.com.

LASALA, STEPHEN R., lawyer, oil industry executive; b. NYC; B, LLD, Fordham U., NY; LLM in Taxation, NYU. Tax counsel Mobil Oil Corp., NYC, 1974, various tax positions, 1974—92; asst. treas. exploration and prodn. divsn. Mobil Corp., Fairfax, Va., 1992—96, gen. tax counsel, asst. contr., 1996—2000; assoc. gen. tax counsel Exxon Mobil Corp., 2000—07, v.p., gen. tax counsel, 2007—. Office: Exxon Mobil Corp 5959 Las Colinas Blvd Irving TX 75039-2298*

LA SALLE, ARTHUR EDWARD, historic foundation executive; b. Aug. 9, 1930; s. Rene Charles and Jeanne Matilda (Senac) La Salle; children: Carl Alan, Adam David, Jeanne Ambre Victoria. Student, Jesus Holy Name of Jesus Coll., New Orleans. Founder, pres. R.R. Equipment Assn., Asheville, NC, 1960—; founder Trains of Yesterday Mus., Hilliard, Fla., 1964—73; owner, restorer Brush Hill mansion, Irwin, Pa., 1973—77; lessee, restorer Springfield mansion, Fayette, Miss., 1977—; founder, pres. Hist. Springfield Found., Fayette, 1977—. Cons. Smithsonian Instn., 1959, 75, Japanese Nat. Rys., Tokyo, 1968, Henry Ford Mus., 1975, City of Natchez, Miss., 1985, Old South Soc., Church Hill, Miss., 1985—; cons., lectr. in field. Author: The Marriage of Andrew Jackson at Springfield Plantation, 1987; contbr. articles to profl. jours. Mem.: U.S. Naval Inst., Natchez Hist. Soc., Nat. Trust for Hist. Preservation, Ry. and Locomotive Hist. Soc. Avocations: historic preservation and study, writing, painting. Home and Office: Springfield Plantation 8733 River Rd 553 South Fayette MS 39069-9527 Office Phone: 601-786-3802.

LASANSKY, LEONARDO, artist, educator; b. Iowa City, Mar. 29, 1946; s. Maurcio Lasansky and Emilia Barragan; 1 child, Amadeo Galgo. B of Gen. Studies, U. Iowa, 1971, MA, MFA, U. Iowa, 1972. Prof. art Hamline U., St. Paul, 1972—, chair fine arts divsn., 1981—85; artist-in-resident Dartmouth Coll., Hanover, NH, 1982—82; dir. exhbns. Hamline U., St. Paul, 1995—, chair dept. studio arts and art history, 1995—; artist-in-resident Hamline U. Coll. of Liberal Arts, St. Paul, 2004—. Mem. adv. panel Minn. State Arts Bd., St. Paul, 1988—90; academician Nat. Acad., NYC, 1994—. Curator (exhibitions) España: The Legacy of War: Works by Francisco Goya (Best Curated Exhbn. in the Twin Cities, Mpls. Star Tribune, 1998), Africa: A Legacy in Memory, Hamline U., loan from Mus. African Art, NYC, 2004, Star Tribune, Mary Abbe, Icons of Perfection: Figurative Scuplture from Africa, 2005—06; exhibitions include Norfolk Mus. of Arts and Scis., Va., 1969, Figura 3, IBA, Leipzig, Germany, 1982, Bklyn. Mus., 1983, Internat. Triennial of Coloured Graphic Prints, Grenchen, Switzerland, 1985, Internat. Print Triennial, Krakow, Poland, 1986, 1988, 1994, Am. Printmaking, Belgrade, Yugoslavia, 1989, Premio Internazional, Biella, Italy, 1987, Grabado Latinoamericano, San Juan, Puerto Rico, 1988, 1998, Jane Haslem Gallery, Washington, 1990, Prefectural Mus. of Art, Fukuoka, Japan, 1990, Mus. Modern Art, Wakayoma, Japan, 1991, Heard Mus., Phoenix, 1993, Nat. Acad. and Mus., NYC, 1995, 1998, Ball State Univ. Mus. of Art, 1996, AAAL, NYC (Spl. Purchase Award, 1979), Intergrafic '80, Berlin, Germany, Intergrafia '94, Prague, Czechoslovakia, Augsburg, Germany, Krakow and Torun, Poland, rep. in numerous permanent collections, included in publ., Icons of Perfection: Figurative Sculpture from Africa, 2006. Grantee, Regis Found., 2007—. Mem.: Nat. Acad. Office: Hamline Univ Dept Studio Arts and Art History 1536 Hewitt Ave Saint Paul MN 55104 Office Phone: 651-523-2386. Office Fax: 651-523-3057.

LASATER, W(ILLIAM) ROBERT, JR., lawyer; b. El Dorado, Kans., Oct. 31, 1944; s. W. Robert and Marguerite Lasater; m. Janet Lynn Lasater; children: W. Robert III, Alisa Linn. BA, Kans. U., 1966, JD, 1969. Bar: Kans. 1969, U.S. Ct. Mil. Appeals 1972, N.Mex. 1974, U.S. Supreme Ct. 1976. Legal aid Wyandotte Co., Kansas City, Kans., 1969; forensic medicine cons. USAF, 1971-74; assoc. Rodey, Dickason, Sloan, Akin & Robb, Albuquerque, 1974-78, ptnr., 1978—. Bd. dirs. Bernalillo County (N.Mex.) chpt. Am. Cancer Soc., 1984. Capt. JAG, USAF, 1969-71. Named one of best lawyers in Am., 2005—06. Fellow Am. Acad. Health Care Attys.; mem. ABA, N.Mex. State Bar Assn.(chmn. Dental-Legal Panel 1981-1990, chmn. Health Law Sect. 1988-1989, Med. Legal Liaison Com. 1991-, Med. Rev. Com. 1989-), Am. Bd. Trial Advs., Am. Coll. Trial Lawyers, Kans. Bar Assn., Albuquerque Bar Assn., N. Mex Health Lawyers Assn., Am. Arbitration Assn. (panel neutrals), Phi Delta Phi. Republican. Methodist. Office: Rodey Dickason Sloan Akin & Robb PO Box 1888 Albuquerque NM 87103-1888 Office Phone: 505-768-7287. Business E-Mail: rlasater@rodey.com.

LASCH, CHRISTOPHER, architect; BArch, U. Ill., Urbana; MArch, Columbia U., NYC. Co-founder Aranda/Lasch, NYC, 2003—. Non-Linear Systems Orgn. fellow U. Pa. Sch. Design, 2005—06. Prin. works include Grotto, Baskets; co-author (with Benjamin Aranda): Tooling, 2006. Named Co-winner of Young Archs. Forum, Archtl. League NY, 2007. Office: Aranda/Lasch 212 Forsyth St New York NY 10002 Office Phone: 917-534-9767. Office Fax: 707-281-1543. E-mail: chris@arandalasch.com.*

LASCH, PAT, artist, educator; b. NYC, Nov. 20, 1944; d. Fred and Helen Lasch; 1 child, Melinda. BA, Queens Coll., 1970; FAAR, Am. Acad. in Rome, 1983; MFA, Ga. State U., Atlanta, 1990. Mem. found. faculty Parsons Sch. of Design, NYC, 1979-88; asst. prof. R.I. Sch. of Design, Providence, 1988-89; assoc. prof. U. Mass., Amherst, 1990-97, prof., 1997—. Artist: solo exhibits include A.I.R. Gallery, N.Y.C., 1973, 77, 79, 80, 94, Zabrskie Gallery, N.Y.C., 1975, Galleriet, Lund, Sweden, 1980, Galerie Ahlner, Stockholm, 1980, Kathryn Markel Gallery, N.Y.C., 1981, 84, 85, Albright Knox Gallery, Members' Gallery, Buffalo, 1977-84, Thomas Segal Gallery, Boston, 1988, Sculpture Ctr., N.Y.C., 1993, Herter Gallery, U. Mass., Amherst, 1993; group shows inclde Inst. Contemporary Art, Phila., Street Scenes, 1981, Malmo (Sweden) Konsthall, Food, 1984, San Francisco Internat. Airport, The Right Foot Show, 1987, Thomas Segal Gallery, The Raw and the Cooked, Boston, The New Mus., N.Y.C., Bad Girls, 1994; spl. exhibition The Mus. of Modern Art (50th Anniversary), Homage 1929-79; represented in permanent collections Met. Mus. Art, N.Y.C., Mus. Modern Art, N.Y.C., Nat. Acad. Design, N.Y.C., Woman's Mus., Washington, Oberlin Mus., Queen's Coll. Recipient Yaddo, 1978, 80, 94, 98, Rome prize, 1982-83, Lilly fellowship, 1993-94, NEA-MCC fellowship, 1995-96; grantee: C.A.P.S., 1980, NEA, 1980-81, N.Y. State Coun. for the Arts, 1984-85, Ariana Found., 1987-88, Pollock-Krasner, 1987-88. Fellow Soc. of Fellows Am. Acad. in Rome; mem. Nat. Acad. Design (life). Democrat. Roman Catholic. Home: 463 West St Apt 228 G New York NY 10014-2030 Office: Univ Mass Fine Arts Ctr Amherst MA 01002

LASER, CHARLES, JR., oil company executive; b. Redford Twp., Mich., July 8, 1933; s. J.C. and Gertrude L.; m. Glenda Johnson, Sept. 27, 1972; 1 child, Susan Faye. Student, Mich. Tech. U., 1952-54, Ctrl. Mich. U., 1959-60; DD (hon.), Palm Beach Theol. Sem. Coll., 1991; LLD (hon.), Northwood U., 2000. With Retail Credit Co., 1958-60; exec. dir. Saginaw County Rep. Com., 1960-65, Rep. Com. D.C., 1967; fin. dir. San Joaquin Rep. Party, Stockton, Calif., 1968; owner Laser Advt., Bay City, Mich., 1969-75; exec. v.p. Vindell Petroleum, Inc., Midland, Mich., 1972-75, Geo Spectra Corp., Ann Arbor, Mich., 1977-86; pres. Laser Exploration Inc., Deerfield Beach, Fla. Task force Domestic Violence Gov. Jeb Bush, 1999—; adv. bd. Union Bank, Boca Raton, Fla.; sr. cons. Peking U. Resource Coll., China, 2004. Chmn. Genesee County Rep. Com., 1981-82, mem. Broward County Rep. Exec. Com., 1987-88, indsl. bond screening com. Deerfield Beach, 1992; chmn. U.S. Senator Connie Mack Palm Beach County Round Table; bd. dirs. Palm Beach County Libr. Found., Shepherd Care Ministries, Hollywood, Foa., 1991—; adv. com. Tall Pines coun. Boy Scouts Am., mem. adv. bd. Gulf Stream Coun., 1980; mem. gov. prevention adv. com. Juvenile Justice Deliquency, Fla., 1988-96; mem. adv. bd. Humanitarian Soc., 1989—; bd. dirs., life mem. Large Freedoms Found., Valley Forge Broward County, Fla. chpt., 1995—; bd. govs. Northwood U., West Palm Beach, Fla., 1997; chmn. emeritus Fla. Symphonic Pops Orch., 1998; apptd. mem. Task Froce on Domestic Violence. With U.S. Army, 1954-58. Decorated Knight Order of St. John of Jerusalem Knights Hospitallier. Mem. Deerfield Beach C. of C. (v.p.), World Trade Coun. (Palm Beach, Fla. chpt.), Detroit Econ. Club, Bankers Club (Boca Raton), Humanitarian Soc. (adv. bd.), Rep. Men's Club (past pres., v.p. Boca Raton chpt.), Gold Coast Venture Capital Club (Delray Beach chpt.), Palm Beach Roundtable (bd. dirs., chmn. exec. com., sec. 1994-2002), Hillsboro Cove Condominium Assn. (pres. 1994), Rotary, Elks. Home: PO Box 8604 1523 E Hillsboro Blvd Apt 131 Deerfield Beach FL 33441-4301

LASH, STEPHEN SYCLE, auction company executive; b. Boston, Feb. 10, 1940; s. Samuel George and Carolyn Virginia (Sycle) L.; m. Wendy Lehman, Oct. 29, 1967; children: Abigail Sycle, William Lehman. BA, Yale U., 1962; MBA, Columbia U., 1966. V.p. Bali Footwear, Inc., Marlborough, Mass., 1962-64, 66-68, S.G. Warburg and Co., London, NYC, 1968-76, Christies, NYC, 1976-80, sr. v.p., 1980-84, exec. v.p., 1984-93, vice chmn., 1993-2000, chmn., 2000—; also bd. dirs. Christies Internat. PLC & Christies Fine Art Ltd. Vis. prof. residential coll. seminar Yale U., 2004. Co-author: A Vision of Paradise: Robertson Ward and the Mill Reef Club. Founder, pres. Ocean Liner Mus., 1983—88, co-chmn., 1988—96; commr. NYC Landmarks Preservation Commn., 1973—76; pres. Am. Friends of Israel Mus., 2005—; mem. coun. Nat. Trust for Historic Preservation, 2002—; bd. dirs. NY Landmarks Conservancy, NYC, 1975—, chmn., 1992—95; bd. dirs. Nat. Bldg. Mus., Washington, 2001—06, Mus. City N.Y., 2003—, Avon Old Farms Sch., 2004—; bd. overseers Peabody-Essex Mus., Salem, Mass., 2000—, co-chmn. maritime visiting com.; bd. dirs. 7th Regiment Armory Conservancy, Found. Internat. Cultural Diplomacy, 2007—. Pan Am. Union fellow, 1965. Mem. Yale U. Alumni Assn. Metro N.Y. (pres. 1987-90), River Club, Mill Reef Club, Century Assn., Wadawanuck Club (Stonington, Conn.), The Pilgrims, French Heritage Soc. (bd. dirs. 2007—). Home: 151 E 79th St New York NY 10021-0417 Office: Christies 20 Rockefeller Plz New York NY 10020-1902 Home Phone: 212-744-7935; Office Phone: 212-636-2905. Business E-Mail: slash@christies.com.

LASHBROOKE, ELVIN CARROLL, JR., law educator, consultant; b. Dec. 14, 1939; s. Elvin Carroll Sr. and Lois Lenora (Weger) L.; m. Margaret Ann Jones, Dec. 19, 1964; children: Michelle Ann, David C. BA, U. Tex., 1967, MA, 1968, JD, 1972, LLM, 1977; PhD, Mich. State U., 1993. Bar: Tex. 1972, Fla. 1973. Legis. counsel Tex. Legis. Coun., Austin, 1972-75; pvt. practice law, 1975-77; asst. prof. coll. of law DePaul U., Chgo., 1977-79, Stetson U., St. Petersburg, Fla., 1979-80; assoc. prof. sch. law Notre Dame, South Bend, Ind., 1981-85; prof., chmn. bus. law dept. Mich. State U., East Lansing, 1985-95; assoc. dean adminstrn. Eli Broad Coll. Bus., East Lansing, 1993-97; pvt. practice cons., 1986-97; dean Coll. Bus. U. Nev., Las Vegas, 1997-99; assoc. dean Broad Grad. Sch. of Mgmt. Mich. State U., East Lansing, 1999—2001, dir. study abroad and e-learning initiatives, 2001—03, dir. edn., 2003—04, assoc. dean emeritus, 2004—; exec. mem. Lashbrooke of Barrowfield, LLC, 2004—. Instr. St. Edward's U., Austin, 1975-76. Author: Tax Exempt Organizations, 1985, The Legal Handbook of Business Transactions, 1987; contbr. articles to profl. jours. Mem. Tex. Bar Assn., Fla. Bar Assn. Avocation: computers. Home: 6204 E Golfridge Dr East Lansing MI 48823 Office: Mich State Univ Broad Grad Sch of Mgmt East Lansing MI 48824-1122 Home Phone: 517-337-1847; Office Phone: 517-353-4336. Business E-Mail: lashbrooke@bus.msu.edu.

LASHER, ESTHER LU, minister; b. Denver, June 1, 1923; d. Lindley Aubrey and Irma Jane (Rust) Pim; m. Donald T. Lasher, Apr. 9, 1950 (dec. Mar. 1982); children: Patricia Sue Becker, Donald T., Keith Alan, Jennifer Luanne Oliver. A of Fine Arts, Colo. Women's Coll., 1943; BA, Denver U., 1945, MA, 1967; MA in Religious Edn., Ea. Bapt. Sem., 1948; grad., Jerusalem Ctr. for Bibl. Studies, 1995. Ordained to ministry Bapt. Ch., 1988. Christian edn. dir. 1st Bapt. Ch., Evansville, Ind., 1948-52; min. Perrysburg Bapt. Ch., Macy, Ind., 1988-95; min.-at-large Am. Baptist Conv./USA, 1996—; interim pastor United Bapt. Ch., Lewiston, Maine, 1997-98. Libr. Peru (Ind.) Pub. Schs., 1990—91; sec. Ind. Ministerial Coun., Indpls., 1990—92; chairperson Women in Ministry, Indpls., 1988—93; min. Kairos Ministry to Women in Prison, 2002; chmn. Fellowship Mission Circle, Rochester, Ind., 1988—93; mem. Partnership in Ministry, Indpls., 1990—94; bd. mgrs. Am. Bapts./Ind., 1991—93; asst. dir. Greenwood Pub. Libr., 1978—84; dir. Fulton County Pub. Libr., 1984—90; ch. & cmty. chair Am. Bapt. Conv. of Maine, 2002—06; caregiver Edge Nursing Home, Damariscotta, Maine, 2002—, chaplain, 2004—; mem. Seacoast Cmty. String Orch., 1997—. Mem. Evansville Symphonic Orch., 1948—55, Denver Civic Orch., 1955—65, Augusta Symphony Orch., 1998—, Midcoast Cmty. Orch., 1999—; founder Fulton County Literacy Coalition, Rochester, 1989—90; tutor/trainer Peru Literacy Coalition of Peru Pub. Libr., 1994—95; active CASA Lincoln Co., Maine, 1996—; vol. libr. Rutherford Libr., South Bristol, Maine, 1996—, So. Bristol Libr., Lincoln Retirement Home; mem. Sea Coast Cmty. Orch., 1999—; chair for ch. and cmty. ABC of Maine, 2002—; chmn. diaconate bd. Damariscotta Bapt. Ch., 2004—; tutor Literacy of Lincoln County, 2005—, Lincoln County Literacy Damariscotta, 2005—; chaplain Coves Edge Nursing Home, Damariscotta; sec.-treas. North Miami County Mins. Fellowship, 1993—95; chmn. Christian Edn. Bd. and ch. planter, Denver, 1953—59, Colorado Springs, 1959—68; chaplain vol. Miles Hosp., 1997—; prayer advisor Christian Women's Club Damariscotta Bapt. Ch., 1997—2002, hostess, 1995—97, exec. bd., 1995—, chair missions com., 1997—, small group, 2003—, Sunday sch. tchr., 2006—; pres. Women's Mission Cir., Damariscotta Bapt. Assn., 1997—; chaplain-on-call Miles Meml. Hosp.; sec. Lincoln County Clergy, 1998—; ch. planter Indpls. and Zionsville, 1970—82; bd. dirs. Manitau Tng. Ctr., Rochester, 1988—90, Peru Civic Ctr., 1995; pres. Toastmasters, Rochester, 1984—90, 1995, edn. v.p., 1992—93; v.p. Mental Health Ctr., Rochester, 1987—90; sec. Northwest Area ABC/IN, 1994—95. Named Outstanding Libr., Biog. Inst., 1989, Profl. Woman of Year, 2005. Mem. Leadership Acad. (bd. dirs., sec.), Bus. and Profl. Women (pres. Greenwood, Ind. chpt. 1984-86), Rochester Women's Club (pres. 1989-92), Fulton County Mins. Assn. (treas. 1993-95), Logansport Assn. Bapt. Women, Peru Lit. Club (v.p.-elect 1995), CASA Miami County, Rotary, Sigma Alpha Iota (adv.), Christian Edn. (chmn. 1996-98), Damariscotta Assn. Women (pres. 1998—, mem. small ch. com. 1998-2003, chmn. diaconate bd. 2001—), Christian Women's Club (prayer group 1999—); Success 6 Reader Program, 2004-, Tutoring to Read Literacy Program. Republican. Home and Office: 2063 State Route 129 South Bristol ME 04568-4317 Personal E-mail: revlulasher@yahoo.com. *Wisdom is a powerful tool, without knowledge, it can entice or terrify an individual, all depending on how it is used with much forethought.*

LASHER, HIRAM NELSON, entrepreneur, consultant; b. Catskill, NY, Feb. 8, 1920; s. Nelson Frederick and Elizabeth Esther (Palmer) L.; m. Bertha Mae Van Vlierden, Dec. 12, 1948; children: Steven Hiram (dec.), Douglas Nelson, Sandra Elizabeth, Hiram Dennis, Denise Helen, Michael Clark, Michele Betty. Studied, Hougton Coll., 1938; DVM, Cornell U., 1942; AAS, Del. Tech. C.C., 1978. Hon. diplomate Am. Coll. Poultry Vets.; lic. vet., Del., N.Y. Pvt. practice, Catskill, 1942-48; poultry pathologist State Bd. Agr., Millsboro and Frankford, Del., 1948-50; founder, pres. Del. Poultry Labs./Sterwin Labs., 1950-79, Inter-Continental Biologics, Inc. (Intervet Am.), Millsboro, 1979-82, Lasher Assocs., Inc., Millsboro, 1982—. Founder, life mem. Assn. Vet. Biol. Cos., 2005—. With Del. State Bd. Edn., 1962, v.p., 1963—70; found. founder Del. Tech. and Cmty. Coll., 1965—98. Lasher Dining Hall named in his honor Boy Scouts Am., Wilmington, 2000, Lasher Lab., U. Del. named in his honor, 1997; recipient Disting. Citizen award Delmarva Poultry Industry, Inc., 2000, Svc. to Agr. award U. Del., 1999, Order of 1st State, Del. Gov. Tom Carper, 1994, Disting. Leadership award U. Del., 1993, Medal of Achievement, Delmarva Poultry Industry, Inc., 1998, Health Care award Beebe Med. Ctr., 1989, Spl. Svc. award U. Ga., 2001; founder Caswell S. Eidson chair U. Ga. Coll. Vet. Medicine, 2001. Mem.: Assn. Vet. Biologies Cos. (co-founder 1995, Lifetime award 2006), NY Acad. Scis., Poultry Sci. Assn., Am. Assn. Avian Pathologists (charter mem.) (life Lasher-Bottorff award 1994, Spl. Svc. award 2001, Am. Poultry Hall of Fame 2004). Republican.

United Methodist. Avocations: philanthropic activities, capital campaigns and scholarships. Office: Lasher Assocs Inc DuPont Hwy PO Box 1727 Millsboro DE 19966 Office Phone: 302-934-8710. Office Fax: 302-934-8745. Business E-Mail: lasherinc@mchsi.com.

LASHER, LARA ELAINE, epidemiologist, researcher; d. Lawrence and Natalia Lasher. BS in Microbiology with honors, U. Calif., Santa Barbara, 1995; MPH in Epidemiology, UCLA, 2003. Instr. yoga and fitness Hawaii Athletic Club and Honolulu Club, Honolulu, 1989—; rsch. writer Hawaii State Dept. Health, Honolulu, 2002—06, epidemiologist, 2004—06, influenza surveillance coord., 2005—06. Tchg. asst. med. microbiology U. Hawaii, Honolulu, 2000—01; rsch. asst. lung cancer study UCLA, LA, 2001—03. Contbr. articles to profl. jours. Pres. Golden Key Nat. Honor Soc., Santa Barbara, 1994—95. Mem.: Golden Key Nat. Honor Soc. (life; pres. 1994—95, Grad. award 1995). Avocations: mountain hiking, ocean swimming, marathon running, yoga, skydiving. Home Phone: 808-375-9925. Personal E-mail: laralasher@netscape.net.

LASHER, LORI L., lawyer; b. June 16, 1960; BA in Polit. Sci. magna cum laude, Westminster Coll., 1981; JD cum laude, Dickinson Sch. Law, 1984. With Reed Smith LLP, Phila., 1994—, mem. exec. com., head mergers & acquisitions/gen. corp. practice group. Mem. exec. bd. Homeless Advocacy Project. Mem.: Phila. Bar Assn., Pa. Bar Assn., ABA. Office: Reed Smith LLP 2500 One Liberty Pl 1650 Market St Philadelphia PA 19103-7301 Office Phone: 215-851-8136. Office Fax: 215-851-1420. Business E-Mail: llasher@reedsmith.com.

LASHLEY, CURTIS DALE, lawyer; b. Urbana, Ill., Nov. 3, 1956; s. Jack Dale and Janice Elaine (Holman) L.; m. Tamara Dawn Yahnig, June 14, 1986. BA, U. Mo., Kansas City, 1978, JD, 1981. Bar: Mo. 1981, U.S. Dist. Ct. (we. dist.) Mo. 1981, U.S. Tax Ct. 1982, U.S. Ct. Appeals (8th cir.) 1992. Assoc. Melvin Heller, Inc., Creve Coeur, Mo., 1982; ptnr. Domjan & Lashley, Harrisonville, Mo., 1983—86; asst. gen. counsel Mo. Dept. Revenue, Independence, 1986—89, assoc. gen. counsel, 1989—92, sr. counsel Kansas City, 1992—, adminstrv. hearing officer, 1995—; spl asst. atty. gen., 1986—; spl. asst. prosecutor Jackson County, Mo., 1990—. City atty., Adrian and Strasburg, Mo., 1985-86. V.p. Cass County Young Reps., Harrisonville, 1985. Recipient honor Senate Resolution 830 and Mo. Ho. Resolution 2314, 2001, Cert. of Appreciation, Kansas City Bd. Police Commrs., 2001, Legis. Resolution honor, Jackson County Mo., 2001. Mem. ABA, NRA, Federalist Soc., Kiwanis (treas. Harrisonville chpt. 1985-86, Harrisonville Disting. Svc. award 1985), Phi Alpha Delta. Republican. Presbyterian. Office: Mo Dept Revenue Daniels State Office Bldg 615 E 13th St Ste 504 Kansas City MO 64106 E-mail: curtisl752@excite.com.

LASHLEY, FELISSA ROSE, dean, nursing educator, researcher; b. NYC, Apr. 6, 1941; d. Jack and Ruth (Dorbin) Lashley; divorced; children: Peter, Heather, Neal. BS, Adelphi Coll., 1961; MA, NYU, 1965; PhD, Ill. State U., 1973. Cert. Am. Bd. Med. Genetics., Am. Coll. Med. Genetics. Dean Coll. Nursing, Rutgers U., Newark, 2002—. Author: Clinical Genetics in Nursing Practice, 1998 (book of yr. award); editor: The Person with AIDS: Nursing Perspectives, 1987 (Book of Yr. award), Tuberculosis: A Sourcebook for Nursing Practice and Women, Children and HIV/AIDS (Book of Yr. award, 1993), Emerging Infectious Diseases: Trends and Issues, 2002, The Person with HIV/AIDS: Nursing Perspectives, 2000. Mem.: AAAS, ANA (coun. nurse researchers), Am. Coll. Med. Genetics, Ill. Nurses Assn., Midwest Nursing Rsch. Soc., Nat. League Nursing, Am. Acad. Nursing, Am. Soc. Human Genetics. Office Phone: 973-353-5293 ext. 647. Business E-Mail: flashley@rutgers.edu.

LASHLEY, LENORE CLARISSE, lawyer; b. NYC, June 3, 1934; d. Leonard Livingston and Una Ophelia (Laurie) L.; children: Donna Bee-Gates, Michele Bee, Maria Bee. BA, CUNY, 1956; MSW, U. Calif., Berkeley, 1970, MPH, 1975; JD, U. Calif., San Francisco, 1981. Bar: Calif. 1981. Atty. W.O.M.A.N., Inc., San Francisco, 1982-84; pvt. practice San Francisco, 1984-87; dep. dist. atty. Monterey Dist. Atty., Salinas, Calif., 1987-89; trial atty. State Bar of Calif., LA, 1989; dep. dist. atty. L.A. Dist. Atty., 1989; dep. city atty. Office of City Atty., LA, 1989—2002; pvt. practice Glendale, Calif., 2003—; pvt. practice victimology, 2006—. Chair, bd. dirs. St. Anthony's Dining Room, San Francisco, 1986-87; sec., bd. dirs. NAACP, Monterey, 1987-88; bd. dirs. Childrens Home Soc., Oakland, Calif., 1966-68. Active Pet Rescue City Mutts. Recipient Cert. of Merit, Nat. Assn. Naval Officers, 1987. Mem. L.A. County Bar Assn. (del. to state bar 1992, 93). Roman Catholic. Avocations: running, reading, writing. Office: 23 W Alexander Ave # 55 Merced CA 95348 Office Phone: 888-832-5108. Personal E-mail: justice@sonic.net.

LASHLEY, VIRGINIA STEPHENSON HUGHES, retired computer science educator; b. Wichita, Kans., Nov. 12, 1924; d. Herman H. and Edith M. (Wayland) Stephenson; m. Kenneth W. Hughes, June 4, 1946 (dec.); children: Kenneth W. Jr., Linda Kihlowicz; m. Richard H. Lashley, Aug. 19, 1954; children: Robert H., Lisa Lashley Van Amberg, Diane Lashley Tan. BA, U. Kans., Lawrence, 1945; MA, Occidental Coll., LA, 1966; PhD, U. So. Calif., 1983. Cert. info. processor, tchr. secondary and community coll., Calif. Tchr. math. La Canada (Calif.) High Sch., 1966-69; from instr. to prof. Glendale (Calif.) Coll., 1970-92, chmn. bus. div., 1977-81, coord. instructional computing, 1974-92, prof. emeritus, 1992—; sec., treas., dir. Victory Montessori Schs., Inc., Pasadena, Calif., 1980—; pres. The Computer Sch., Pasadena, 1983-92, ret., 1992—. Real estate investor, 1992—; pres. San Gabriel Valley Data Processing Mgmt. Assn., 1977-79, San Gabriel Valley Assn. for Systems Mgmt., 1979-80; chair Western Ednl. Computing Conf., 1980, 84. Editor Jour. Calif. Ednl. Computing, 1980. Grantee NSF, 1967-69, EDUCARE scholar U. So. Calif., 1980-82; John Randolph and Dora Haynes fellow, Occidental Coll., 1964-66; named student computer ctr. in her honor Dr. Virginia S. Lashley Ctr., 1992. Mem. AAUP, AAUW, DAR (scholarship chair, 1994-2002, vice regent 2002—), Calif. Edn. Computing Consortium (bd. dirs. 1979—, v.p. 1983-84, pres. 1985-87), Orgn. Am. Historians, San Marino Women's Club, Colonial Dames, XVII Century (scholarship chair, 1997-99), Nat. Geneal. Soc., New Eng. Hist. Geneal. Soc. (life mem.), Town Hall, World Affairs Coun., Trojan Guild, Phi Beta Kappa, Pi Mu Epsilon, Phi Alpha Theta, Phi Delta Kappa, Delta Phi Upsilon, Gamma Phi Beta. Republican. Congregationalist. Home: 1240 S San Marino Ave San Marino CA 91108-1227 Personal E-mail: vslash@aol.com.

LASHLEY, WILLIAM BARTHOLOMEW, county official; b. Dayton, Ohio, Jan. 2, 1952; s. William Bartholomew and Reta Carolyn (Reicken) L.; m. Loukia Simopoulos, June 30, 1973; children: Nichole E., Felicite D. BA in Econs., Wright State U., 1976; opthomol. sci. degree, Regis U., 1982. Asst. mgr. First Nat. Bank, Dayton, Ohio, 1973-77; mgr. store Kroger Co., Dayton, 1977-80; cashier Frontier Bank, Denver, 1980-82; asst. v.p. Empire Savs., Denver, 1982-85; mgr. investor acctg. Security Pacific Mortgage Corp., Denver, 1985-88; corp. acct. investors Crossland Mortgage Corp., Salt Lake City, 1988-89; dir. fin. and adminstrv. svcs. Montgomery County Cts., Dayton, 1989—. Mem. Montgomery County Fiscal Task Force, Dayton, 1990—. Mem. ABA (assoc.), Am. Bankers Assn., Govt. Fin. Officers Assn. (mem. select review com.), Mortgage Bankers Assn., Ohio State Bar Assn. (assoc.). Home: 3307 Waltham Ave Kettering OH 45429-3529 Office: Montgomery County Cts 41 N Perry St Dayton OH 45402-1431

LASHMAN, L. EDWARD, arbitrator, mediator, consultant; b. New Orleans, June 6, 1924; s. L. Edward and Edith Ruth (Deutsch) L.; m. Elizabeth Gitt Fichman, June 6, 1948 (dec. Aug. 1984); children: Deborah, Rebekah, David W. (dec. Feb. 1993), Judith; m. Joyce Blicher Schwartz, July 25, 1987. Student, U. N.C., 1940-42, Tulane U., New Orleans, 1951—52. Ptnr. Caire Assocs., New Orleans, 1946-51; with CIO and AFL-CIO, 1951-67; asst. to sec., dir. cong. liason HUD, Washington, 1967-69; mng. ptnr. Urban Housing Assocs., Denver, 1969-70; v.p. U. Mass., 1970-75; dir. external affairs, sr. planning counselor Harvard U., Cambridge, Mass., 1975-89; sec. adminstrn. and fin. Commonwealth of Mass., Boston, 1989-91, chmn. Mass. bd. regents pub. higher edn., 1986-88; chmn. Commonwealth Land Bank, Boston, 1975-77, Mass. Housing Fin. Agy., Boston, 1977-79; ret., 1991. Acting exec. dir. (pro bono) Mass. State Lotterty, 1999; contract mediator U.S. Equal Employment Opportunity Commn.; contract arbitrator U.S. Postal Svc. Exec. com. Denver County Dem. Party, 1952-64; chmn. Colo. Urban League, Denver, 1961-63; acting COO (pro bono) Judge Baker Children's Ctr., Boston, 1993-94; dir. Nat. Housing Conf., Washington, 1969-75; v.p. Handel & Haydn Soc., Boston, 1982-84; chmn. Housing Needs Com., Town of Weston, Mass., 2001-06. With U.S. Army, 1943-46, ETO. Mem. Am. Arbitration Assn., Mass. Assn. Mediation Programs, Norfolk and Suffolk County Superior Ct. Mediation Panels, Joint Labor Mgmt. Com. Mediation Panel. Avocations: fly fishing, cooking, photography. Home and Office: 236 Conant Rd Weston MA 02493-1654 Business E-Mail: elashman@comcast.net.

LASHMAN, SHELLEY BORTIN, retired judge; b. Camden, NJ, Aug. 18, 1917; s. William Mitchell and Anna (Bortin) L.; m. Ruth Horn, Jan. 3, 1959; children: Karen E. Lashman Hall, Gail A. McBride, Mitchell A., Christopher R. BS, William and Mary Coll., 1938; postgrad., Columbia U., 1938, postgrad., 1939; JD, U. Mich., 1946. Bar: N.Y. 1947, N.J. 1968. Judge N.J. Workers Compensation, 1981—2001; ret., 2001. With USNR, 1940—70. Mem. Atlantic County Bar Assn., Am. Judges Assn., US Navy League, Mil. Officers Assn. Am., USS Yorktown CV-5 Club, NJ Workers' Compensation Inns of Ct. Republican. Home: 1209 Old Zion Rd Egg Harbor Township NJ 08234-7667 Home Fax: 608-653-6686.

LASHOF, JOYCE COHEN, public health service officer, educator; b. Phila. d. Harry and Rose (Brodsky) Cohen; m. Richard K. Lashof, June 11, 1950; children: Judith, Carol, Dan. AB, Duke U., 1946; MD, Women's Med. Coll., 1950; DSc (hon.), Med. Coll. Pa., 1983. Dir. Ill. State Dept. Pub. Health, 1973—77; dep. asst. sec. for health programs and population affairs Dept. Health, Edn., and Welfare, Washington, 1977—78; sr. scholar in residence IOM, Washington, 1978; asst. dir. office of tech. assessment U.S. Congress, Washington, 1978—81; dean sch. pub. health U. Calif., Berkeley, 1981—91; prof. pub. health U. Calif. Sch. Pub. Health, Berkeley, 1981—94, prof. emeritus, 1994—. Co-chair Commn. on Am. after Roe vs. Wade, 1991—92; mem. Sec.'s Coun. Health Promotion and Disease Prevention, 1988—91; chair Pres.'s Adv. Com. on Gulf War Vets. Illnesses, 1995—97. Mem. editl. bd.: Wellness Letter, 1993—, Ann. Rev. of Pub. Health, 1987—90. Recipient Alumni Achievement award, Med. Coll. Pa., 1975, Sedgewick Meml. medal, APHA, 1995. Avocation: hiking. Home: 601 Euclid Ave Berkeley CA 94708-1331 Office: U Calif Sch Pub Health 140 Earl Warren Hl Berkeley CA 94720-7360 Office Phone: 510-642-2493. Business E-Mail: jlashof@berkeley.edu.

LASHUTKA, GREGORY S., mayor, lawyer; b. NYC, 1944; m. Catherine (Adams); children: Nicholas, Lara, Stephanie, Michael. BS, Ohio State U., 1967; JD, Capital U., 1974. Bar: Ohio, 1974, Fla. and D.C., 1975. Ptnr. Squire, Sanders, and Dempsey, Columbus, Ohio; elected mayor City of Columbus, Ohio, 1991—99; former Columbus City Atty., Ohio; sr. v.p. corp. rels. Nationwide, Columbus, Ohio, 2000—. Past chmn. Columbus Area Sports Devel. Corp.; pres. Nat. League of Cities; comentator of the Ohio State U. Football Color, 1983-90; active civic and charitable orgn.; bd. dir. Simon Kenton, coun. Boy Scouts Am.; bd. dir. Cath. Social Svc., lt., USN. Named Mcpl. Leader of the Yr., Am. City and County mag., 1993. Mem. Nat. Acad. Pub. Adminstr. Office: Nationwide One Nationwide Plz Columbus OH 43215-2220

LASICH, VIVIAN ESTHER LAYNE, secondary school educator; b. Hopewell Twp., Pa., Dec. 17, 1935; d. Charles McClung and Harriette Law (George) Layne; m. William G. Lasich, Apr. 10, 1958; children: C. Laurence, Celeste M., Michelle R. AB, Geneva Coll., Beaver Falls, Pa., 1956; MA in Edn., No. Mich. U., Marquette, 1970; postgrad., No. Mich. U. Secondary tchr. Freedom (Pa.) High Sch., 1956-57; elem. educator Gilbert Elem. Sch., Gwinn, Mich., 1967-69; lang. arts educator Gwinn Mid. Sch., 1970-99; ret., 1999. Adv. bd. panel Mich. Dept. Edn./Arts, 1976-79; mem. sch. improvement team, 1988-91, 93-94, co-chair, 1995-98; mid sch. concept team, 1992-98, mid sch. at-risk coord. dist. curriculum coord. coun., 1995-96; dist. curriculum strategy action team, 1993-94; dist. profl. devel. strategy action team, 1993-94; mem. sounding bd. Mid. Sch., 1994-98, dist. sch. improvement team, 1994-98; lang. arts curriculum design com., 1997-98; rep. Gwinn Edn. Assn. Mid. Sch., 1995-98. Author: Prophets Without Honor: Teachers, Students, & Trust, 1991. V.p. Marquette (Mich.) Community Theatre, 1962-63 bd. dirs. 1963-74, mem. 1961-92; pres. Marquette Arts Coun. 1973-74, v.p. 1972-73, bd. dirs. 1970-78, mem. 1970-84; pres. Upper Peninsula Arts Coordinating Bd. 1976-78, v.p. 1974-76, bd. dirs. 1978-84; bd. dirs. Mich. Community Theatre Assn. 1972-73; bd. dirs. Mich Community Arts Agys., 1976-79. Recipient Committment to Excellence award Marquette Community Theatre, 1965. Devotion to Arts Development award Upper Peninsula (Mich.) Arts Coord. Bd. 1979. Mem. ASCD, NEA, AAUW, Mich. Edn. Assn., Phi Delta Kappa. Presbyterian. Avocations: writing, theater, music. Home: 508 Pine St Marquette MI 49855-3838 Office: Gwinn Area Community Schs Gwinn MI 49841

LASKARIS, E(VANGELOS) TRIFON, technologist, researcher; PhD, Rensselaer Polytechnic Inst., 1974. Chief technologist Imaging Technologies GE Global Rsch., Niskayuna, NY. Recipient Coolidge Fellowship Award, 1998, Dushman Award, 2002. Mem.: NAE. Office: GE Global Rsch Ctr 1 Research Cir Niskayuna NY 12309

LASKARIS, MARIA, dean; Grad., Dartmouth Coll., 1984. From asst. dir. to sr. assoc. dir. admissions Dartmouth Coll., Hanover, NH, 1987—96, dir. admissions, 1996—2007, dean admissions and fin. aid, 2007—. Office: Dartmouth Coll Dead Admissions Campus Mail Box 6016 Hanover NH 03755 Office Phone: 603-646-2875. E-mail: Maria.Laskaris@Dartmouth.EDU.*

LASKARZEWSKI, DEBRA SUE, language educator; b. Bklyn., Apr. 26, 1968; d. Barry Charles and Frances Marilynn Blumen; m. James John Laskarzewski, July 13, 1996; children: Daniel John, Amy Rose. BA in French summa cum laude, U. N.H., 1990, MA in Tchg. summa cum laude, 1991. Level II profl. educator's lic. in French Vt. State Bd. Edn., level II profl. educator's lic. in Spanish Vt. State Bd. Edn., level I profl. educator's lic. in phys. edn. Vt. State Bd. Edn. Summer field hockey camp coach U. N.H., Durham, 1987—95; tchr. English as 2d lang. Lycee Professionnel Robert Garnier, La Ferte Bernard, France, 1991—92; world lang. tchr. French and Spanish Missisquoi Valley Union Jr./Sr. H.S., Swanton, Vt., 1993—95; summer field hockey camp coach U. Vt., Burlington; head field hockey coach U.S. Field Hockey Assn. Future's Program (Olympic Devel.), Hanover, N.H., and Burlington, Vt., 1991—98; asst. field hockey coach U. Vt., Burlington, 1993—2000; world lang. and cultural comm. tchr. Union 32 Jr. /Sr. H.S., Montpelier, Vt., 1995—97; world lang. tchr. French and Spanish Williston (Vt.) Cen. Sch., 1997—; asst. field hockey coach U.S. Field Hockey Assn. Future's Program, Burlington, Vt., 1999—2001. Transl. computer installation manual Hallam Assocs., South Burlington, Vt. Team coord. Nat. Multiple Sclerosis Soc. and Williston Cen. Sch., 2001—05; vol. walker, fund raiser Nat. Multiple Sclerosis Soc., Burlington, 1999—2005; vol. mailer, fundraiser Am. Heart Assn., Essex Junction, Vt. Named one of 50 Greatest Sports Figures of Century (1900 - 2000) from Vt., Sports Illus., 1999; recipient athletic scholarship, U. N.H., 1986—91, 1989—91. Mem.: NEA, Vt. Assn. Health, Phys. Edn., Recreation and Dance, Vt. Fgn. Language Assn., Phi Beta Kappa, Phi Kappa Phi (life). Avocations: field hockey, travel, running. Home: 1 Mohawk Ave Essex Junction VT 05452 Office: Williston Cen Sch 195 Central School Dr Williston VT 05495 Home Phone: 802-878-9307; Office Phone: 802-878-2762. Personal E-mail: skimail1@verizon.net. Business E-Mail: laskarzewsd@wsdvt.org.

LASKAWY, PHILIP ALAN, retired accounting and management consulting firm executive; b. Mar. 1941; m. Patricia Laskawy; 2 children. Grad, U. Penn., Wharton Sch., 1961. Ptnr. Ernst & Whinney (acquired S.D. Leidesdorf 1978), 1978-81, dir. personnel, N.Y region, 1979—80, mng. ptnr., 1981-85; vice chmn., regional mng. ptnr. merger Ernst & Whinney and Arthur Young, 1985-93, dep. chmn., 1993, chmn., CEO, 1994—2001; also bd. dirs. Ernst & Young (merger of Ernst & Whinney and Arthur Young 1993). Mem., bd. directors Goodyear Tire & Rubber Co., 2001—02, General Motors Corp., 2002—.

LASKER, JONATHAN LEWIS, artist; b. Jersey City, July 30, 1948; s. Lester and Henrietta Selma (Gross) L. Student, Sch. Visual Arts, NYC, 1975-77, Calif. Inst. Arts, 1977. One-man shows include Landmark Gallery, NY, Gunnar Kaldeway, Dusseldorf, Fed. Republic Germany, 1981, Annette Gmeiner, Kirchzarten, Fed. Republic Germany, 1984, Tibor de Nagy, NYC, 1984, 1986, Michael Werner, Cologne, Fed. Republic Germany, 1986, 1987, 1990, Massimo Audiello, NYC, 1986, 1988, 1989, Anders Tornberg, Lund, Sweden, 1987, 1990, Gian Enzo Sperone, Rome, 1988, 1991, Sperone Westwater Gallery, NYC, 1991, 1993, 1996, 1999, 2002, 2003, Lars Bohman, Stockholm, 1991, 1994, 2001, Inst. Contemporary Art U. Pa., Phila., 1992, Thaddaeus Ropac Gallery, Paris, 1992, 1997, 2000, Witte de With Ctr. Contemporary Art, Rotterdam, 1993, Rhona Hoffman Gallery, Chgo., 1993, Soledad Lorenzo, Madrid, 1995, 1998, L.A. Louver Gallery, 1995, Kunsthalle Bielefeld, Germany, 1997, Stedelijk Mus., Amsterdam, Holland, 1998, Kunstverein St. Gallen, Switzerland, 1998, Timothy Taylor, London, England, 1998, 2004, Forum for Contemporary Art, St. Louis, Mo., The Power Plant Contemporary Art Gallery, Toronto, Canada, 1999, Rose Art Mus. Brandeis U., Waltham, Mass., 2000, Thomas Schulte, Berlin, 2002, 2003, K-20 Kunstsammlung Nord-Rhein-Westfalen, Düsseldorf, Germany, 2003, Museo Nacional Centro de Arte Reina Sofia, Madrid, 2003, Kunstallen Brandts Klaedefabrik, Odense, Denmark, 2005, Galleria Cardi & Co., Milan, 2005, numerous others, exhibited in group shows at Mus. Ludwig, Cologne, Wacoal Art Ctr., Tokyo, 1985, Rose Art Mus. Brandeis U., Waltham, Mass., 1986, 1999, Corcoran Gallery Art, Washington, 1987, Roos Mus., Malmo, Sweden, U. N. Tex., Denton, J.B. Speed Mus., Louisville, Alta. Coll. Art, Edmonton, Can., Contemporary Arts Ctr., Cin., Santa Fe Community Coll., Gainesville, Fla., Met. Mus. Art, NYC, 1988, Stedelijk Mus., Amsterdam, The Netherlands, 1989, Marc Richards Gallery, LA, Thaddaeus Ropac, Salzburg, Austria, 1989, 2001, 2003, 2004, Paris, 1992, 1999, Scott Hansen Gallery, N.Y.C., 1990, Pace Gallery, 1990, Sperone Westwater Gallery, 1991, 1994, 1995, 1996, 1997, 1998, 2001, Gallery Modern Art, Bologna, Italy, 1991, Hirshhorn Mus. and Sculpture Garden, Washington, 1991, 2004, Mus. Contemporary Art of Dayton Art Inst., 1992, Documenta IX, Kassel, Germany, Gallerie Nächst Sankt Stephan, Vienna, 1992, Ruth Bloom Gallery, L.A., 1993, Hayward Gallery, London, 1994, Ctr. for the Fine Arts, Miami, 1994, Va. Mus. Fine Arts, Richmond, 1995, Mus. Contemporary Art, Helsinki, Folkwang Mus., Essen, Germany, 1995, Mus. Reina Sofia, Madrid, 1996, Kunsthalle Zurich, Switzerland, 1996, Musée D'Art Modern Centre, St. Etienne France, 1997, Mus. Am. Art of Pa. Acad. Fine Arts, Phila., 1998, Malmø Konsthall, Sweden, 1998, Menil Collection, Houston, 1999, Aargauer Kunsthaus, Aarau, Switzerland, 2000, Palazzo Cavour, Turin, Italy, 2000, Michael Hue-Williams, London, England, 2000, Rudolfinum Ctr for Contemporary Art, Prague, Czech Republic, 2001, Kunstverein St. Gallen in Kunstmuseum, Switzerland, 2001, Yale U. Art Gallery, New Haven, Conn., 2002, Mus. Morsbroich, Leverkusen, Germany, 2003, Orlando Mus. Art, Fla., 2004, Samuel Dorsky Mus. Art, New Platz, N.Y., 2005, Chelsea Mus. Art, NYC, 2005, BA-CA Kunstforum, Vienna, Austria, 2005, Nat. Acad. Mus., NYC, 2006, numerous others, Represented in permanent collections Corcoran Gallery, Hirshhorn Mus. and Sculpture Garden, Washington, Mus. Ludwig, Cologne, Wacoal Art Ctr., Tokyo, Whitney Mus. Am. Art, NYC, Moderna Museet, Stockholm, Fond. Nat. d'Art Contemporain, Paris, High Mus., Atlanta, Museo de Arte Contemporaneo, Seville, Spain, La Fundacion Caja De Pensiones, Barcelona, Albright Knox Art Gallery, Buffalo, NY, Los Angeles County Mus. Art, Calif., Museo Nacional Centro de Arte Reina Sofia, Madrid, Musée Nat. D'Art Modern Centre Pompidov, Paris, Birmingham Mus. Art, Ala.; critic (numerous art books, catalogs, mags. including) Beyond Boundaries: New York's New Art (Jerry Saltz), N.Y. Art Now, The Saatchi Collection (Dan Cameron), The Silent Baroque (Christian Leigh editor), Interpreting Contemporary Art (Rainer Crone and David Moos), Art at the End of the Social (Collins and Milazzo), Art Since Mid-Century: 1945 to the Present (Daniel Wheeler), Jonathan Lasker, Telling the Tales of Painting (Rainer Crone and David Moos), The 20th Century Art Book (Tony Godfrey, Melissa Larner, et al), Hist. Modern Art (H.H. Arnason and Marla Prather) 4th edit., Hist. Modern Art (H.H. Arnason and Peter Kalb) 5th edit., Art of the 20th Century (Ingo Walther, editor) Taschen Verlag, Modern Art (Sam Hunter, John Jacobus, Daniel Wheeler) 3d rev. edit., Caravaggio on the Beach: Essays on Art in the 1990's (Richard Milazzo), Art News (Feb. 1990, Apr. 1992, Feb. 2004), Le Monde (June 1992), Art in America, (Apr. 1995), Contemporary Visual Arts (Apr.-May 2000), Frankfurter Allgemeine Zeitung (Oct. 2003), New Yorker, Peter Schjeldahl (Dec. 2003). NEA fellow, 1987, 89. Office: care Cheim & Read Gallery 547 W 25th St New York NY 10001

LASKER, JOSEPH L., artist, illustrator; b. NYC, June 26, 1919; s. Isidore and Rachel (Strollowitz) L.; m. Mildred Jaspen, Nov. 28, 1948; children: David Raymond, Laura, Evan. Student, Cooper Union Art Sch., evenings 1936-39, Escuela Universitaria de Bellas Artes, Mexico, 1948. Tchr. Coll. City N.Y., 1947; vis. assoc. prof. art U. Ill., 1953-54. Exhibited one-man shows Kraushaar Galleries, N.Y.C., most recently 2003; works represented in permanent collections Whitney Mus., Cal. Palace Legion of Honor, Phila., Springfield Mus., Mass., Joseph Hirschorn Collection, Balt. Mus., Munson-Williams Proctor Inst., Phila. Mus. Art; murals in Calumet (Mich.) P.O., Millbury, Mass., Henry Street Settlement Play House, N.Y.C.; author, illustrator juvenile books: Mothers Can Do Anything, 1972, He's My Brother, 1974, Tales of a Seadog Family, 1974, Merry Ever After (best illustrated children's book, N.Y. Times, 1976, Notable Bk. of Yr. Am. Library Assn. 1977), 1976, The Strange Voyage of Neptune's Car, 1977, Lentil Soup, 1977, Nick Joins In, 1980, The Do-Something Day, 1982, The Great Alexander the Great, 1983, Tournament of Knights, 1986; illustrator numerous other children's Books. Served with U.S. Army, 1941-45. Abbey Meml. scholar, 1946, 47; Prix de Rome fellow, 1950, 51; Guggenheim fellow, 1954; Benjamin Altman prize (figure) Nat. Acad. Design, 1958, 80; grantee Nat. Inst. Arts and Letters, 1968 Mem. NAD (academician, 1965-) Office: care Kraushaar Galleries 724 5th Ave New York NY 10019-4106

LASKER, MORRIS E., judge; b. Hartsdale, NY, July 17, 1917; m. Helen M. Schubach; 4 children. BA magna cum laude, Harvard U., 1938; LLB, JD, Yale U., 1941. Bar: N.Y. 1941. Atty. Nat. Def. Com., U.S. Senate, 1941-42, Battle, Fowler, Jaffin & Kheel, 1946-68; fed. judge U.S. Dist. Ct. (so. dist.) N.Y., 1968-94, U.S. Dist. Ct., Boston, 1994—. Contbr. articles to profl. jours. Hon. trustee, bd. dirs. Vera Inst. Justice. Maj. U.S. Army, 1942-46. Recipient Learned Hand medal Fed. Bar Coun., Edward Weinfeld award N.Y. County Lawyers Assn. Mem. ABA, Assn. of Bar of City of

N.Y. (exec. com. 1985-89). Avocations: gardening, reading, history, english and american literature. Office: US Dist Ct US Courthouse 1 Courthouse Way Boston MA 02210-3002 Business E-Mail: honorable_morris_lasker@mad.uscourts.gov.

LASKI, JOHN N., finance educator; b. Passaic, NJ, Jan. 14, 1954; m. Priscilla Laski; children: Alicia, Michelle, Veronica, Michael, Jonathan. AS in Criminal Justice, Salve Regina U.; BS in Orgn. Mgmt., Nyack Coll.; MBA in Fin., St. Thomas Aquinas Coll.; PhD in Fin., Nova Southeastern U. Nat. sales mgr. UVA Machine Co., Bromma, Sweden; fin. cons. Merrill Lynch, Wayne, NJ; investment mgr. Citicorp, LI, NY; asst. v.p. Jaron Equities, Hicksville, NY; asst. v.p. investments N.E. Securities, NYC; assoc. prof. fin., dir. MBA program Nyack (N.Y.) Coll., NYC; prof. fin. and internat. bus. Coll. Profl. Studies, N.J. City U., Jersey City; assoc. prof. fin. and internat. bus. New Jersey City U. Commr. Passaic County Planning Bd., Paterson, NJ; bn. chief UGL Vol. Fire Co., Hewitt, NJ; asst. arson investigator Tiverton (R.I.) Fire Dept. With USN, 1973—80. Recipient medal of honor, Passaic County Bd. Freeholders, Paterson, N.J. Mem.: Masons. Avocations: boating, golf, target shooting, photography. Office: NJ City U Coll Profl Bus 2039 Kennedy Blvd Ste P-419 Jersey City NJ 07305-1597 Office Phone: 201-200-3353. Business E-Mail: jlaski@njcu.edu.

LASKIN, DANIEL M., oral and maxillofacial surgeon, educator; b. Ellenville, NY, Sept. 3, 1924; s. Nathan and Flora (Kaplan) L.; m. Eve Pauline Mohel, Aug. 25, 1945; children: Jeffrey, Gary, Marla. Student, NYU, 1941—42; BS, Ind. U., 1947; MS, U. Ill., 1951; DSc (hon.), Ind. U., 2001. Diplomate Am. Bd. Oral and Maxillofacial Surgery, Am. Dental Bd. Anesthesiology. Faculty U. Ill., Chgo., 1949-84, prof. dept. oral and maxillofacial surgery, 1960-84, head dept., 1973-84, clin. prof. surgery, 1961-84, dir. temporomandibular joint and facial pain research center, 1963-84; prof., chmn. dept. oral and maxillofacial surgery Med. Coll. Va., Richmond, 1984—2002, chmn. emeritus, 2003, dir. temporomandibular joint and facial pain rsch. ctr., 1984—2002; affiliate clin. prof., dept. psychology Va. Commonwealth U.; head dept. dentistry MCV Hosp., Richmond, 1986—2002; former attending oral surgeon Edgewater, Swedish Covenant, Ill. Masonic, Skokie Valley Cmty. hosps., Chgo.; former chmn. dept. oral surgery Cook County Hosp., Chgo. Cons. oral surgery to Surgeon Gen. Navy, 1977-83; dental products panel FDA, 1988-92, cons., 1993-95; Francis J. Reichmann Lectr., 1971, Cordwainer lectr., London, 1980, Donald B. Osborn Meml. lectr., 1999. Author: Oral and Maxillofacial Surgery, Vol. I, 1980, Vol. II, 1985; contbr. articles to profl. jours.; editor-in-chief: Jour. Oral and Maxillofacial Surgery, 1972-2002; mem. editl. bd. Internat. Jour. Oral and Maxillofacial Surgery, 1978-88, Topics in Pain Mgmt., Densat, Internat. Jour. Oral and Maxillofacial Implants, Quintessence Internat., Revista Latino America Cirugia Traumatologia Maxilofacial, Va. Dental Jour., Jour. Dental Rsch.; mem. internat. editl. bd. Headache Quar.; mem. editl. bd. Greek Jour. Oral and Maxillofacial Surgery, Electronic Jour. Dentistry; assoc. editor Odontology; mem. internat. adv. bd. Asian Jour. Oral and Maxillofacial Surgery; OMFS editor Jewish Med. Jour. Nat. hon. chmn. peer campaign A.A.O.M.S. Edn. and Rsch. Found., 1990; bd. dirs. Internat. Assn. Oral and Maxillofacial Surgeons Found.; chmn. Nat. Acad. Dentistry, 1997-99; pres.-elect Nat. Acad. of Practice, 1999, pres., 2002—04. Recipient Disting. Alumni Svc. award, Ind. U., 1975, William J. Gies editl. award 1st prize, 1978—79, 1984, 1987, 1989, 1992, 1996, 2001, Simon P. Hullihen Meml. award, 1976, Arnold K. Maislen Meml. award, 1977, Thomas P. Hinman medallion, 1980, W. Harry Archer Achievement award for rsch., 1981, Heidbrink award, 1983, Disting. Alumnus award, Ind. U. Sch. Dentistry, 1984, U. Ill. Coll. Dentistry, 2003, Rene Lefort medal, 1985, Semmelweis medallion, Semmelweis Med. U., 1985, Golden Scroll award, Internat. Coll. Dentists, 1986, Internat. award, Friends Sch. Dental Med., U. Conn. Health Ctr., Donald B. Osbon award, 1991, Achievement medal, Alpha Omega, 1992, Norton M. Ross Excellence in Clin. Rsch. award, 1993, Va. Commonwealth U. Faculty award of excellence, 1994, named Zendium Lectr., 1989, Edward C. Hinds Lectr., 1990, Disting. Practitioner Nat. Acads. Practice, 1992, Hon. Diplomate Am. Soc. Osseointegration, 1992, Silver Scroll award, Internat. Coll. Dentists, 2004, Distinction medal, U. Seville, 2005, Alumni Achievement award, U. Ill., 2006; fellow in dental surgery, Royal Coll. Surgeons Eng.; grantee, Glasgow Royal Coll. Physicians and Surgeons (hon.). Fellow: AAAS, Am. Acad. Implant Prosthodontists (academia), Internat. Coll. Dentists (Spl. Editl. citation 1999, Silver Scroll award 2004), Am. Coll. Dentists, Acad. Internat. Dental Studies (hon.), Internat. Assn. Oral and Maxillofacial Surgeons (hon.; exec. com. 1980—95, pres. 1983—86, sec. gen. 1989—95, exec. dir. 1995—99, gen. chmn. 14th Internat. Conf. on Oral and Maxillofacial Surg. 1999, found. cons.); mem.: ADA (adv. com. advanced edn. in oral surgery 1968—75, cons. Coun. on Dental Edn. 1968—82, mem. Commn. on Accreditation 1975—76), Hungarian Assn. Oral and Maxillofacial Surgeons, Odontographic Soc., William F. Harrigan Soc., Nat. Chronic Pain Outreach Assn. (adv. bd.), Am. Dental Bd. Anesthesiology (pres. 1983—92), Turkish Assn. Oral and Maxillofacial Surgeons (hon.), Sadi Fontaine Acad. (hon.), Internat. Congress Oral Implantologists (hon.), Soc. Maxillofacial and Oral Surgeons South Africa (hon.), Japanese Soc. for Temporomandibular Joint (hon.), Am. Soc. Laser in Dentistry (hon.), Internat. Study Group for Advancement of TMJ Arthroscopy (hon.), Can. Assn. Oral and Maxillofacial Surgeons (hon.), Japanese Soc. Oral and Maxillofacial Surgeons (hon.), Scandinavian Assn. Oral and Maxillofacial Surgeons (hon.), Brazilian Coll. Oral and Maxillofacial Surgery and Traumatology (hon.), Chilean Soc. Oral and Maxillofacial Surgery (hon.), Hellenic Assn. Oral Surgery (hon.), Royal Soc. Medicine, Am. Assn. Dental Editors, Am. Soc. Exptl. Pathology, Am. Dental Soc. Anesthesiology (pres. 1976—78), Internat. Assn. Dental Rsch., Am. Assn. Oral and Maxillofacial Surgeons (editor Forum 1965—96, pres. 1976—77, editor AAOMS Today 1996—, Disting. Svc. award 1972, rsch. recognition award 1978, William J. Gies award 1979, dedication 73d ann. meeting and sci. sessions 1991), Ill. Splty. Bd. Oral Surgery, Sigma Xi, Omicron Kappa Upsilon. Rsch. and publs. on connective tissue physiology and pathology, particularly cartilage and bone metabolism, craniofacial growth, oral maxillofacial surgery, and pathology of temporomandibular joint. Office: Va Commonwealth U Dept Oral/Maxillofac Surg PO Box 980566 Richmond VA 23298-0566 Office Phone: 804-828-3547. Business E-Mail: dmlaskin@vcu.edu.

LASKIN, LEE B., judge, state senator; b. Atlantic City, June 30, 1936; m. Andrea Solomon; 1 dau., Shari. Student, Am. U., Temple U., Rutgers U., 1960. Bar: NJ. Asst. U.S. atty., NJ, 1964-68; mem. NJ Gen. Assembly, NJ, 1968-70, Camden County Bd. Chosen Freeholders, NJ, 1970-73, NJ Senate, NJ, 1977-92; judge NJ Superior Ct., NJ, 1994—. Mcpl. atty. Audubon, Berlin Borough, Berlin Twp., Clementon, Laurel Springs, Mt. Ephraim and Waterford, NJ, and Winslow Twp.; counsel Bellmawr Bd. Edn., Berlin Zoning Bd., Camden County Welfare Bd., Non-Resident Taxpayers Assn., Animal Welfare Assn., Brith Sholom Fed. Credit Union, Camden Hebrew Fed. Credit Union, Union Fed. Savs. and Loan Assn., Div. 880 Amalgamated Transit Union, Local 18 of Am. Fed. Tech. Engrs., Camden Fire Officers Assn., Am. Postal Workers Union, Fuel Mchts. Assn., Shamong Twp. Bd. Edn., Cherry Hill Zoning Bd.; field counsel Fed. Nat. Mortgage Assn.; founder, 1st chmn. Glendale Nat. Bank. Del. Rep. Nat. Conv., 1984. With USMC, 1957-64, USMCR. Office: Camden County Hall Justice 5th and Mickle Blvd Camden NJ 08103-4001 Home Phone: 856-596-3339; Office Phone: 856-379-2314. E-mail: gerrymander3010@aol.com.

LASKIN, RICHARD SHELDON, orthopedic surgeon; b. Bklyn., July 13, 1940; s. Herman Myron and Gertrude (Klein) L.; m. Joyce Sparrow, Mar. 3, 1991; children: Joanthan, Andrew. AB, Hofstra U., 1960; MD, NYU, 1964. Diplomate Am. Bd. Orthopedic Surgery. Intern, resident Albert Einstein Coll. Medicine Affiliated Hosps., NYC, 1964-66, resident, 1968-70, Nassau County Med. Ctr., 1970-71; chmn. dept. orthopedic surgery L.I. Jewish Med. Ctr., 1980-91; prof. SUNY, Stony Brook, 1984-89, Albert Einstein Coll. Medicine, 1989-91, Cornell U., 1991—. Mem. NY Hosp.; chief knee svc. Hosp. for Spl. Surgery. Author: Replacement of Knee Joint, Total Knee Replacement, Controversies in Total Knee Replacement; editor: Hospital in Special Surgery Jour.; dep. editor: Clinical Orthopaedics and Related Research; contbr. clin. rsch. articles to orthopedic surgery to profl. jours., also papers in Amsterdam, Milan, Jerusalem, Athens, Copenhagen, Oslo, Paris, London, Mex., US, Madrid, Barcelina, Sweden, Australia, Japan, China, Berlin. With MS, AUS, 1966-68, col. MC USAR, 1989-91. Decorated Bronze Star, Combat Med. Badge, Air medal. Mem. ACS, Am. Acad. Orthopedic Surgeons, Am. Orthopaedic Assn., Internat. Arthroscopy Assn., NY Acad. Medicine, Knee Soc., Ea. Orthopedic Soc., NY State Orthopedic Surgeons, NY Stqte Med. Soc., Internat. Knee Soc., Orthopedic Rsch. Soc., Norwegian Orthopedic Assn., Spanish Orthopedic Soc., Soc. Mil. Orthopedic Surgery, SICOT, SIROT, Assn. Bone & Joint Surgeons. Office: The Hosp for Spl Surgery 535 E 70th St New York NY 10021-4898 Office Phone: 212-606-1041. Business E-Mail: laskinr@hss.edu.*

LASKO, ALLEN HOWARD, pharmacist; b. Chgo., Oct. 27, 1941; s. Sidney P. and Sara (Hoffman) L.; m. Janice Marilynn Chess, Dec. 24, 1968 (div. Aug. 1993); children: Stephanie Paige, Michael Benjamin. BS, U. Ill., 1964. Staff pharmacist Michael Reese Hosp. and Med. Ctr., Chgo., 1964-68; clin. pharmacist City of Hope Med Ctr., Duarte, Calif., 1968-73; chief pharmacist Monrovia (Calif.) Cmty. Hosp, 1973-74, Santa Fe Meml. Hosp., LA, 1974-77; pvt. investor, 1977-93; clin. pharmacist Foothill Presbyn. Hosp., Glendora, Calif., 1993—. Author: Diabetes Study Guide, 1972, A Clinical Approach to Lipid Abnormalities Study Guide, 1973, Jet Injection Tested As an Aid in Physiologic Delivery of Insulin, 1973. Mem. Magic Castle. Recipient Roche-Hosp. Pharmacy rsch. award, 1972-73; James scholar U. Ill. Mem. Mensa (life), Rho Pi Phi. Jewish. Home: 376 Hill St Monrovia CA 91016-2340 Office: Foothill Presbyn Hosp 250 S Grand Ave Glendora CA 91741-4218 E-mail: allenlasko@aol.com.

LASKO, JOEL, marketing executive; b. NYC, Nov. 1, 1932; s. Max Lasko and Charlotte Parker; m. Mary Anne Thune, Dec. 19, 1973; children: Elizabeth, Andrew. BS in Mktg., Syracuse U., 1955; MBA in Mktg. Mgmt., CCNY, 1957. Br. mgr. Olivetti Corp., Washington, 1958—70; pres. Washington Photocopy, Washington, 1970—. Recipient Mktg. medal Am. Mktg. Assn., 1957. Avocations: tennis, skiing. Office: Washington Photocopy 4380 Macarthur Blvd NW Washington DC 20007-2594 Office Phone: 202-333-4585.

LASKOWSKI, LEONARD FRANCIS, JR., microbiologist; b. Milw., Nov. 16, 1919; s. Leonard Francis and Frances (Cyborowski) L.; m. Frances Bielinski, June 1, 1946; children— Leonard Francis III, James, Thomas. BS, Marquette U., 1941, MS, 1948; PhD, St. Louis U., 1951. Diplomate: Am. Bd. Microbiology. Instr. bacteriology Marquette U., 1946-48; mem. faculty St. Louis U., 1951—, prof. pathology and internal medicine, Div. Infectious Diseases, 1969-90, prof. emeritus, 1990—, assoc. prof. internal medicine, 1977-90—. Dir. clin. microbiology sect. St. Louis U. Hosps. Labs., 1965—; cons. clin microbiology Firmin Desloge Hosp., St. Louis U. Group Hosps., St. Marys Group Hosps.; cons. bacteriology VA Hosp.; asst. dept. chief Pub. Health Lab., St. Louis Civil Def., 1958—; cons. St. Elizabeths Hosp., St. Louis County Hosp., St. Francis Hosp., Alexian Bros. Hosp., St. Clements Hosp., St. Mary's Hosp., East St. Louis. Contbr. articles to profl. jours. Health and tech. tng. coordinator for Latin Am. projects Peace Corps, 1962-66. Served with M.C. AUS, 1942-46. Fellow Am. Acad. Microbiology; mem. Soc. Am. Bacteriologists, N.Y. Acad. Scis., Am., Mo. pub. health assns., AAUP, Med. Mycol. Soc. Am., Alpha Omega Alpha. Home: 505 Cedar Summit Ln Villa Ridge MO 63089

LASKY, DAVID, lawyer; b. NYC, Nov. 12, 1932; s. Benjamin and Rebecca (Malumed) L.; m. Phyllis Beryl Sumper, Apr. 14, 1957; children— Jennifer Lee, Robert Barry. BA, Bklyn. Coll., 1954; LLB, Columbia U., 1957. Bar: N.Y. 1957. Atty. N.Y.C. R.R. Co., 1957-62; with Curtiss-Wright Corp., NYC, 1962—, corp. counsel, 1966-67, gen. counsel, 1967-93, v.p., 1972-80, sr. v.p., 1980-93, sec., 1989-93, pres., 1993-99, chmn., 1995-2000, bd. dirs., 1993—. Bd. dirs. Primex Technologies, Inc. Chmn. zoning bd. appeals, Ramapo, N.Y., 1968-72; dir., v.p. Oak Trail Homeowners Assn., 1987-90. Mem. ABA (chmn. com. corp. gen. counsel 1992-93), Phi Beta Kappa.

LASKY, RICHARD DONALD, psychoanalyst, educator; b. NYC, Jan. 22, 1943; s. Sidney Lasky and Alice Presser; m. Judith Faye Sherman. PhD in Psychology, NYU, 1970, postdoctoral cert., 1974. Lic. psychologist, N.Y.; diplomate Am. Bd. Profl. Psychology. Jr. rsch. scientist Rsch. Found. State N.Y., Downstate Med. Ctr., SUNY, Bklyn., 1964-68; asst. prof. L.I. Univ., Greenvale, N.Y., 1969-74; clin. assoc., supr. psychologist doctoral program psychology CUNY, NYC, 1975—; chmn. of faculty Inst. for Psychoanalytic Tng. and Rsch., NYC, 1985-2000; clin. prof. psychology postdoctoral program NYU, 1990—. Author: Multiple Personality and the Related Dissociative Disorders, 1984, Dynamics of Development and the Therapeutic Process, 1993; editor: Symbolization and Desymbolization: Essays in Honor of Norbert Freedman, 2002. Rsch. fellow VA, 1968, NIMH fellow, 1969-71. Fellow Acad. of Psychoanalysis; mem. APA, Internat. Psycho-Analytical Assn., Am. Psychoanalytic Assn., Nat. Register of Health Care Providers in Psychology. Office Phone: 212-595-0442. E-mail: richardlasky@nyc.rr.com.

LASKY, WILLIAM M., manufacturing executive; BBA, Norwich Univ. Mgmt. positions through v.p. Spicer clutch div. Dana Corp., 1978—95, v.p., gen. mgr. No. Am. filtration group, 1995—97, pres. filtration products group, 1979—99; pres., COO JLG Industries, Hagerstown, Md., 1999—2000, pres., CEO, 2000—01, chmn., pres., CEO, 2001—06. Served to capt. US Army, Korea.

LASLETT, LAWRENCE J., physician, educator; b. Boston, Apr. 17, 1942; BS, Iowa State U., Ames, 1964; MD, U. Iowa, Iowa City, 1969. Diplomate in internal medicine, cardiology and interventional cardiology Am. Bd. Internal Medicine. Intern Hennepin County Gen. Hosp., Mpls., 1969-70; resident in internal medicine U. Calif., Davis, 1973-76, fellow in cardiology, 1976-78, asst. prof. clin. medicine, 1978-85, assoc. prof. clin medicine, 1985-96, dir. fellowship tng. in cardiology, 1994—2002, prof. clin. medicine, 1996—2004, prof. emeritus, 2005—; dir. cardiac catheterization lab. U. Calif. Davis Med. Ctr., Sacramento, 1984-94. Contbr. articles to med. jours. Mem. tech. adv. com. on free-standing catheterization labs. Calif. Dept. Health Svcs., Sacramento, 1990-94. Served to lt. comdr. USPHS, 1969-71. Fellow Am. Coll. Cardiology (past chair Calif. chpt. and nat. govt. rels. coms., No. Calif. gov. 2003-06). Office: U Calif Davis Divsn Cardiology 4860 Y St Ste 2800 Sacramento CA 95817-2307 Office Phone: 916-734-3764. Business E-Mail: ljlaslett@ucdavis.edu.*

LASLEY, THOMAS J., II, education educator; b. Delaware, Ohio, July 23, 1947; s. Thomas J. and Anna F. (Cooper) L.; m. Janet L. Olney, Apr. 21, 1973; children: Julianne Marie, Elizabeth Ann. BS, Ohio State U., 1969, MA, 1972, PhD, 1978. Cert. tchr. and adminstr. Ohio. Tchr. Upper Arlington, Ohio, 1969-75; rsch. assoc. Ohio State U., 1975-77. Cons. Ohio Dept. Edn., 1977-80, asst. dir. tchr. edn. and cert., 1980-83; prof. U. Dayton (Ohio), 1983—, chmn. dept., 1983-92, dean Sch. Edn., 1998—; cons. on sch. research and disruptive student behavior. Author: Issues in Teacher Education, 1986, Dynamics of Change in Teacher Education, 1986, Teaching Peace, 1994, Strategies for Teaching in a Diverse Society: Instructional Models, 2002, Strategies for Effective Teaching, 2004, Secondary and Middle School Methods, 2005; contbr. articles to profl. jours. Mem. Am. Ednl. Rsch. Assn., Phi Delta Kappa. Office: U Dayton Chaminade Hall Dayton OH 45469 Office Phone: 937-229-3327. Business E-Mail: thomas.lasley@notes.udayton.edu.

LASORDA, THOMAS W., automotive company executive; b. Windsor, Ont., Can., July 24, 1954; s. Frank and Bea LaSorda; m. Doreen LaSorda; 2 children. BA, U. Windsor, 1977, B of Commerce, 1977, MBA, 1980. Various labor rels., mfg. and quality-related positions in Can., the U.S. and Europe General Motors Corp., 1977—2000; sr. v.p. powertrain mfg. Chrysler Group, 2000—02, sr. v.p. production, 2002—04, dep. mem. bd. mgmt., COO, 2004—05, CEO, pres., 2005—07, mem. bd. mgmt., 2005—07; vice-chmn., pres. Chrysler LLC, Auburn Hills, Mich., 2007—. Achievements include being President of Opel-Eisenach GmbH from 1991-93, the first auto assembly plant in eastern Germany after the fall of the Berlin Wall. Office: Chrysler LLC 1000 Chrysler Dr Auburn Hills MI 48326*

LASORDA, TOMMY (THOMAS CHARLES LASORDA), professional baseball team manager; b. Norristown, Pa., Sept. 22, 1927; s. Sam and Carmella (Covatto) Lasorda; m. Joan Miller Lasorda, Apr. 14, 1950; children: Laura, Tom Charles. Student pub. schs., Norristown. Pitcher Bklyn. Dodgers, 1954—55, Kansas City A's, 1956; with L.A. Dodgers, 1956—, mgr. minor league clubs Pocatello, Idaho, Ogden, Utah, Spokane, Albuquerque, 1965—73, coach, 1973—76, mgr., 1976—96, v.p. fin., 1996—98, gen. mgr., 1998—, sr. v.p., 1998—. Author (with David Fisher): autobiography The Artful Dodger, 1985. With US Army, 1945—47. Named Pitcher of Yr., Internat. League, 1958, L.A. Dodgers winner, Nat. League pennant, 1977, 1978, 1981, 1988, 2d Nat. League mgr. to win pennant first two yrs. as mgr., Nat. League Mgr. Yr., UPI, 1977, AP, 1977, Baseball Writers' Assn. Am., 1988, Sporting News, 1988, Baseball Writers Assn. Am., 1983, 1988, coach, Nat. League All-Star team, 1977, 1983—84, 1986, 1993; named to Baseball Hall of Fame, 1997; recipient World Championship, 1981, 1988, Milton Richman Meml. award, Assn. Profl. Baseball Players Am. Mem.: Profl. Baseball Players Am., Variety Club of Calif. (v.p.). Roman Catholic. Office: c/o Los Angeles Dodgers 1000 Elysian Park Ave Los Angeles CA 90012-1112

LASPADA, CARMELLA, government agency administrator; BS in Psychology and TV Comm., Pa. State U., 1960. Founder No Greater Love, 1971; White House liaison and exec. dir. White House Commn. on Remembrance, 2001—. Initiator Nat. Moment of Remembrance, 2000. Named Washingtonian of Yr., Unsung Heroine, VFW Women's Aux.; recipient U.S. Spl. Ops. Command medal, Ellis Island Medal of Honor, Dickey Chapelle award, USMC League, Spirit of Enterprise award, U.S. C. of C., Rotary Club Humanitarian award, Outstanding Alumni award, Pa. State U., Woman of Yr. award, Christopher Columbus Assn. Office: White House Commn on Remembrance 1750 New York Ave NW Washington DC 20006

LA SPATA, MICHELLE GAYLE, school psychologist; b. Naperville, Ill., Feb. 1, 1978; d. Michael Joseph Madach and Bonnie Lynn Owens; m. Adam La Spata. BS in Psychology and Music, Bradley U., Peoria, Ill., 2000; Specialist in Sch. Psychology, Western Ill. U., 2003. Cert. type 73 sch. svc. pers., sch. psychologist. Grad. asst. Western Ill. U., Macomb, Ill., 2000—02; sch. psychology intern Peoria Pub. Sch. Dist. 150, 2002—03; sch. psychologist Round Lake Area Sch. Dist. 116, Round Lake, Ill., 2003—07, presenter in svc., 2005; sch. psychologist Cmty. Consol. Sch. Dist. 158, Lake in the Hills, Ill., 2007—. Musician, webmaster Arlington Hts. Cmty. Concert Band, 2003—. Mem.: Ill. Sch. Psychologists Assn., Nat. Assn. for Sch. Psychologists, Sigma Alpha Iota (v.p. membership 1998—99, Sword of Honor Scholastic award 2000). Avocations: music, photography, puzzles, exercise.

LASPINA, PETER JOSEPH, computer resource educator; b. Bay Shore, NY, June 28, 1951; s. Peter Celestine and Barbara Elizabeth (Rodee) L.; 1 child; Joseph Peter. BMus with high honors, N.Y. State Coll., Potsdam, 1973, Performer's Cert. on Piano, 1973; MS in Music Edn., L.I. U., 1978; MS in Tech. Sys. Mgmt., SUNY, Stony Brook, 1987; postgrad., Nova Southeastern U., 1995-97. Tchr. music E. Meadow (N.Y.) pub. schs., 1974-75, Northport-East Northport Pub. Schs., 1975-86, computer resource tchr., 1986—. Adj. faculty SUNY, Stony Brook, 1991—; writer master trainer N.Y. State Edn. Dept., Albany, 1987-88; cons. ednl. tech., Smithtown, N.Y., 1987—; invited del. U.S./China Joint Conf. on Edn., Beijing, 1992, 95-96, and conf. presenter. Contbr. articles to profl. jours. Mem. Am. Fedn. Tchrs., N.Y. State United Tchrs., Suffolk County Music Educators Assn., Nat. Assn. Sci., Tech. and Soc., N.Y. State Assn. Computers and Techs. (mem. conf. com. 1994), Internat. Soc. for Tech. in Edn., Assn. Ednl. Comm. and Tech., Assn. for Advancement of Computers in Edn. Presbyterian. Avocations: reading, oenology, home repair, travel. Home: 21 Knolltop Dr Nesconset NY 11767-2221 Office: SUNY Tech And Soc Program Stony Brook NY 11794-0001 Personal E-mail: plaspina@optonline.net.

LASS, DIANE, marriage and family therapist; b. Vermillion, SD, June 26, 1957; d. Donald and Eunice Purvis; m. Steve Lass, Oct. 15, 1994; children: Steve, Chris, Jon Williams, Brandon Williams, Dustin Williams, Jonathan. BA in Psychology (hon.), Point Loma Nazarene U., 2000; MA in Clin. Psychology, Calif. Sch. Profl. Psychology, 2002; PhD in Clin. Psychology, Alliant Internat. U., San Diego, 2007. Real estate sales and property mgmt. Purvis Realty, San Diego, 1983—97; crisis intervention counselor Halcyon Crisis Ho., El Cajon, Calif., 2001—02; therapist and sex offender group facilitator Calif. Dept. Corrections, San Diego, 2002—03; domestic violence therapist San Diego Family Justice Ctr., 2004—, cmty. ptnr. with integrated mental health svcs. Scholar, Alliant Internat. U., 2000—05; Presidents scholar, Point Loma Nazarene U., 1998—2000. Mem.: APA (assoc.). Avocations: weightlifting, basketball, football, cooking, writing. Home Phone: 619-223-9543; Office Phone: 619-533-6089. Personal E-mail: lassoct1015@aol.com.

LASSEN, JOHN KAI, development company executive; b. Youngstown, Ohio, Mar. 28, 1942; s. Kai Kierulff and Helen Susanne (Elsaesser) L.; m. Marion duPont McConnell, Sept. 26, 1987; children: Christian K., Laura Wick, William duPont, James Tyler. BA, Yale U., 1964; JD, U. Pa., 1967. Bar: Del. 1971, U.S. Dist. Ct. Del. 1972. Ptnr. Morris, Nichols, Arsht & Tunnell, Wilmington, Del., 1977-83, Lassen, Smith Katzenstein & Furlow, Wilmington, 1984-91; pres. Chesapeake Industries, Inc., Wilmington, 1992—2001; vice-chmn., COO Krapfcandoit Co., Wilmington, 1995-2000; pres. So. Sr. Devel. Svcs., Inc., Wilmington, 2000—02; gen. counsel Pettinaro Enterprises, Wilmington, 2002—05. Lt. UNSR, 1967-70. Mem.: SAR, ABA, Nat. Soc. Huguenot Descs. (v.p. Del. chpt.), Del. Bar Assn. (chmn. decedents, estate and trusts 1979—81), Soc. Descs. of War of 1812, Friends of Winterthur, Soc. Mayflower Descs. (sec. 2006—, dep. gov. 1990—93, capt. 2002—06, sec. 2006—), Soc. Colonial Wars, Yale Club N.Y.C., Lincoln Club, Ocean Reef Club, Vicmead Hunt Club, Wilmington Country Club, Wilmington Club, Rotary. Episcopalian. Home: Crooked Billet PO Box 3712 3510 Kennett Pike Wilmington DE 19807-3019 Personal E-mail: kl328@aol.com.

LASSER, GAIL MARIA, psychologist, educator; b. Saddle River, NJ, Feb. 29, 1960; d. Dominick A. and Genevieve M. Sanzo; children: Michael, Jason, Jonathan. BA, Seton Hall U., 1971; postgrad., Seton HaLL u., 1975—77; tchg. cert., William Paterson Coll., 1973; MA, Montclair State Coll., 1975. Cert. staff clin. psychologist N.J., 1977; lic. real estate agt. N.J., 1977, notary pub. Pub. rel. rep. European Health Spa, 1970—71; med. asst. Sci. Prevention and Rehab. Assn., 1973; grad. tchg. and rsch. asst. Montclair State Coll., 1973—74; clin. asst. Dr. Brower, 1974; instr. psychology Essex County Coll., 1976—77; clin. psychologist intern Cmty. Mental Health Ctr., Mt. Carmel Guild, Newark, 1976—77; lectr. St. Michaels Med. Ctr.-N.J. Coll. Medicine, 1977—80; instr. psychology Bergen Cmty. Coll., Paramus, NJ, 1977—. Asst. to ct. adminstr. Bergen County Cts., 1977—78; cons. telecom., 1994. Vol. Am. Heart Assn. Mem.: Am. Soc. Phy. Rsch., Am. Psychol. Assn., Psi Chi, Pi Lambda Theta. Home: 234 E Saddle River Rd Saddle River NJ 07458-2614

LASSER, HOWARD GILBERT, chemical engineer, consultant; b. NYC, Nov. 24, 1926; s. Milton and Tessie Lasser; m. Barbara Ann Katz, Aug. 24, 1950; children: Cathy, Ellen Lasser-LeVee, Alan. BSChemE, Lehigh U., 1950; postgrad., Columbia U., 1951; DEng, Darmstadt Tech. Inst., Germany, 1956. Registered profl. engr., DC, Va., Calif. Chem. engr. Belvoir Rsch. Engring. & Devel. Ctr., Ft. Belvoir, Va., 1951-55, 58-72, Naval Sea Sys. Command, Washington, 1955-56, Naval Facilities Engring. Command, Alexandria, Va., 1972-82, Materials Rsch. Cons., Alexandria, Springfield, Va., 1982—; materials engr. GSA, Washington, 1956-57. Author: Electroplating Facilities, 1991, Chemical Engineering: Electroplating Processes, 1992, Design of Electroplating Facilities, 1992, Lasser's List. The Hamilton Watch Co. American Production, 2004; co-author: Painting of Buildings, 1990, Petroleum Distribution Facilities, 1992; contbr. articles to profl. jours. Fellow: AAAS, Am. Inst. Chemists, Oil and Colour Chemists Assn.; mem.: AIChE, Am. Watch Makers Soc., SSPC Coatings Soc., ASM Internat., NACE Internat., Am. Electroplaters and Surface Finishers Soc., Nat. Watch and Clock Collectors Assn., Sigma Xi, Pi Delta Epsilon, Alpha Chi Sigma, Tau Beta Pi. Achievements include patents for electroplating and metal finishing with medical applications; description of thermodynamic properties of carbon dioxide; development of thermotropic dyes for aluminum oxides; dyes to match laser wavelengths to enhance etching of substrates used in the electronics industry and medicine. Home: 5912 Camberly Ave Springfield VA 22150-2438 Office: Materials Rsch Cons 1121 King St Alexandria VA 22314-2973 Home Phone: 703-451-8737; Office Phone: 703-683-4288. Personal E-mail: hlasser@cox.net.

LASSER, JOSEPH ROBERT, investment company executive; b. NYC, Sept. 25, 1923; s. Milton and Tessie (Rosenthal) L.; m. Ruth Jean Pollak, May 4, 1925; children: James, Carol Lasser Kornblith, Jean. BS, Lehigh U., 1946; MBA, NYU, 1951. Sr. analyst Lewisohn and Co., NYC, 1946-51; dir. research Walston and Co., NYC, 1951-55, Wertheim and Co., NYC, 1956-67; ptnr. Shufro, Rose, Ehrman, and Stanley Marks, Lasser & Co., NYC, 1967-75; sr. portfolio mgr. C.J. Lawrence, NYC, 1975-76; prin., sr. portfolio mgr. Neuberger & Berman, NYC, 1977—2002. Treas. Bronx House, N.Y., 1978-95; past trustee United Jewish Appeal/Fedn. Jewish Philanthropies, mem. bd. overseers. 1st lt. USAF, 1943-45. Decorated Air medal with three bronze oak leaf clusters, one silver oak leaf cluster; recipient 1st Lit. award Soc. Paper Money, 1976. Mem. Am. Numismatic Soc. (councillor 1990-93), N.Y. Soc. Security Analysts, Chartered Fin. Analysts Assn., Phi Beta Kappa, Princeton Club (N.Y.C.), Quaker Ridge (Scarsdale N.Y.). Office: 605 3rd Ave 43d Fl New York NY 10158-3698 Home: 22 Glenbrooke Dr White Plains NY 10605-5008 Business E-Mail: jlasser@nb.com.

LASSER, LAWRENCE J., former investment company executive; b. 1942; BA, Antioch Coll.; MBA, Harvard U., 1967. With Putnam Investments, Boston, 1969—2003, v.p., asst. dir. rsch., 1973-75, sr. v.p., dir. rsch. to exec. v.p., chief investment officer, 1975-80, 81-85, CEO, pres., 1985—2003. Bd. govs., exec. com. Investment Co. Inst.; dir. Marsh and McLennan Cos., Inc.; trustee The Putnam Mut. Funds, Vineyard Open Land Found.; pres. Putnam Investment Mgmt.; v.p. The Putnam Funds; chmn. operating, mgmt. and exec. coms. Putnam Investments; bd. govs., exec. com. Investment Co. Inst.; mem. CareGroup Bd. Mgrs. Investment Com., Coun. on Fgn. Rels. Trustee Mus. of Fine Arts, Boston; bd. dirs. United Way of Mass. Bay; trustee, fin. com., exec. com. Beth Israel/Deaconess Med. Ctr., Boston.

LASSETER, JOHN A., film company executive, computer animator; b. Hollywood, Calif., Jan. 12, 1957; m. Nancy Lasseter; 5 children. BFA in Film, Calif. Inst. Arts, 1979; degree (hon.), Am. Film Inst. Animator The Walt Disney Co., Burbank, Calif., 1979—84; with animation divsn. Lucasfilm Industrial Light & Magic, 1984—86; founding mem. Pixar Animation Studios, Richmond, Calif., 1986, exec. v.p. creative, chief creative officer, 2006—; prin. creative advisor Walt Disney Imagineering, 2006—. Dir., writer, prodr.: (films) Luxo Jr., 1986 (Silver Berlin Bear award Berlin Internat. Film Festival, 1986, nominated Oscar for Best Short Films, Animated Films, 1986); dir., writer: Red's Dream, 1987, Tin Toy, 1988 (Acad. award for Best Achievement in Short Films, 1988), Knick Knack, 1989 (Best Short Film award Seattle Internat. Film Festival 1989), Toy Story, 1995 (Academy award for Spl. Achievement 1995), A Bug's Life, 1998, Toy Story 2, 1999, Cars, 2006 (runner-up LA Film Critics Circle awards, 2006); exec. prodr.: Geri's Game, 1997, For the Birds, 2000, Spirited Away, 2001, Monsters Inc., 2001, Finding Nemo, 2003, Boundin', 2003, Howl's Moving Castle, 2004, The Incredibles, 2004, One Man Band, 2005, Meet the Robinsons, 2007; actor: Computer Illusions, 1998. Recipient Humanitarian award ShoWest Conv., 1997, Outstanding Contribution to Cinematic Imagery award Art Directors Guild, 2004; named one of 50 Most Powerful People in Hollywood, Premiere mag., 2002-06. Fellow: Am. Acad. Arts & Scis. Office: Pixar Animation Studios 1200 Park Ave Emeryville CA 94608 Office Phone: 510-752-3000.*

LASSETER, KENNETH CARLYLE, pharmacologist; b. Jacksonville, Fla., Aug. 12, 1942; s. James and Retta (Shad) L.; m. Kathy G. Marks, Aug. 6, 1977; children: Kenneth C. III, Susan, Frank L. BS, Stetson U., 1963; MD, U. Fla., 1967. Diplomate Am. Bd. Clin. Pharmacology. Intern, resident in medicine U. Ky. Med. Ctr., 1967—71; asst. prof., assoc. prof. pharmacology and medicine U. Miami Med. Sch., Fla., 1971—81, clin. assoc. prof., 1981—. Adj. assoc. prof. pharmacology, Barry U., 1986—; v.p., dir. Clin. Pharmacology Assos., Inc., Miami, 1981-2003; v.p., med. dir. SFBC Internat. Inc., 2003—. Contbr. articles to profl. jours. With USAR, 1971-76. Recipient William B. Peck Sci. Rsch. award Interstate Postgrad. Med. Assn., 1976, Rsch. award Alpha Omega Alpha, 1967. Fellow Am. Coll. Clin. Pharmacology; mem. ACP, Am. Soc. Pharmacology and Exptl. Therapeutics, Am. Soc. Clin. Pharmacology and Therapeutics, Sigma Xi. Republican. Presbyterian. Office: SFBC Internat Inc 11190 Biscayne Blvd Miami FL 33181 Home Phone: 305-945-2252; Office Phone: 305-895-0304 2344. Business E-Mail: klasseter@sfbci.com.

LASSETER, ROBERT HAYGOOD, electrical engineering educator, consultant; b. Miami, Fla., Apr. 4, 1938; s. J. Haygood and Elsiemae (Davis) L.; m. Lucy Taylor, Sept. 2, 1979; children: Courtney M., Malahn P., Robert M., Lauren L. BS in Physics, N.C. State U., 1963, MS in Physics, 1967; PhD in Physics, U. Pa., 1971; postgrad., U. Pa., Phila., 1971—73. Cons. engr. GE Co., Phila., 1973—80; asst. prof U. Wis., Madison, 1980—82, assoc. prof., 1982—85, prof., 1985—. Dir. power sys. Engring. Rsch. Ctr.- Wis., 1994—; cons. engr. Siemens AG, Germany, 1985-86. Contbr. articles to profl. jours. Fellow IEEE. Achievements include pioneering work in application of digital methods to the design of high voltage direct current power systems; basic development of analytical methods for design and study of power electronic controllers in power systems; creating a concept of Microgrids as applied to distributed resources in power systems. Office: Univ Wisconsin Electrical & Computer Engineering 1415 Engineering Dr Madison WI 53706-1607

LASSETER, TOM, journalist; b. Atlanta, 1978; BA, U. Ga. Intern Anniston Star, Ala., NY Times, Atlanta bur.; reporter Lexington (Ky.) Herald-Leader, 1999—2003, Knight Ridder, Iraq, 2003—04; Iraq corr. Knight Ridder Washington bur., 2004—. Co-recipient Hal Boyle award, Overseas Press Club, 2006; recipient John E. Drewry award, U. Ga., 2005, Excellence award, Knight Ridder, 2005. Office: Knight Ridder Washington Bur Ste 1000 700 12th St NW Washington DC 20005-3994 Office Phone: 202-383-6000. E-mail: tlasseter@krwashington.com.

LASSETTER, SCOTT D., lawyer; b. Dallas, Dec. 25, 1958; BA magna cum laude, Tex. Tech U., 1980; JD, U. Tex. Sch. Law, 1983. Bar: Tex. 1983, US Dist. Ct. (So., Ea. and No. Districts Tex.), US Ct. Appeals, 5th Cir., US Supreme Ct. Mng. ptnr. Weil, Gotshal & Manges, LLP, Houston. Lectr. in field. Mem.: State Bar Tex., Houston Bar Assn., Tex. Bar Found. (bd. certified, personal injury trial law & civil trial law, Tex. bd. legal specialization). Office: 708 Main St Ste 200 Houston TX 77002 Office Phone: 713-546-5101. Office Fax: 713-224-9511. Business E-Mail: scott.lassetter@weil.com.

LASSNER, ANDY, television producer; b. Bogota, Colombia, Dec. 30, 1966; Supervising prodr. The Rosie O'Donnell Show, 1996—99; exec. prodr. The List, 1999—2000, The Test, 2001; supervising prodr. The Ellen Degeneres Show, 2003, co-exec. prodr., 2004, exec. prodr., 2005—. Recipient Emmy award for Best Talk Show, 2003, 2004, 2005, Best Television Series or Special (Variety), The Producers Guild Am., 2006. Office: The Ellen Degeneres Show 3000 W Alameda Ave Burbank CA 91523

LASSONDE, PIERRE, mining executive; BA, U. Montreal; BSEE, Polytech. Sch. Montreal; MBA, U. Utah, 1973. Registered profl. engr., Assn. Profl. Engrs. Ontario, 1976. Pres. Franco-Nev., 1982—2002; pres., CEO Euro-Nev. Mining Corp., 1985—99; pres., co-CEO Franco-Nev., 1999—2002; pres. Newmont Mining Corp., Denver, 2002—06, vice chmn., 2007—. Author: Gold Book, The Complete Investment Guide to Precious Metals. Office: Newmont Mining Corp 1700 Lincoln St Denver CO 80203*

LASSWELL, MARCIA LEE, psychologist, educator; b. Oklahoma City, July 13, 1927; d. Lee and Stella (Blackard) Eck; m. Thomas Lasswell, May 29, 1950 (div. July 1990); children: Marcia Jane, Thomas Ely, Julia Lee. BA, U. Calif., Berkeley, 1949; MA, U. So. Calif., 1952; postgrad., U. Calif., Riverside, U. So. Calif., U. N.C. Individual practice psychotherapy, marriage/family therapy, Claremont, Calif.; asst. prof. Pepperdine Coll. LA, 1959—60; asst. prof. psychology behavioral sci. dept. Calif. State U., Pomona, 1960—64, assoc. prof., 1965—69, prof., 1970—, chmn. dept., 1964—69, emeritus, 2005—; assoc. clin. dir. Human Rels. Ctr. U. So. Calif., 1975—98. Vis. assoc. prof. Scripps Coll., 1968-69, U. So. Calif., 1969-70, Occidental Coll., 1971-72; lectr. various Calif. univs.; mem. staff spl. project alcoholics and narcotics offenders Calif. Prison System, 1970-73; mem. Calif. Accreditation Com. Secondary Schs. and Colls., 1965—1990; mem. commn. accreditation for marriage and family tng. US Dept. Edn., 1981-87. Author: College Teaching of General Psychology, 1967, Love, Marriage and Family, 1973, No-Fault Marriage, 1976, Styles of Loving, 1980, Marriage and Family, 1982, rev. edit., 1987, 91, Equal Time, 1983. Recipient Outstanding Tchrs. award Calif. State U., 1971, Outstanding Contbn. to Marriage and Family Therapy, 1991, Disting. Clin. Mem. award Calif. Assn. Marriage and Family Therapists, 1995, award Outstanding Marriage and Family Therapy Orgn., 1999. Fellow Am. Assn. Marital and Family Therapy (bd. dirs. 1970-72, 87-91, pres. elect 1993-95, pres. 1995-97, past pres. 1997-98); mem. AAAS, Nat. Coun. Family Rels. (exec. com. 1978-80), Am. Acad. Family Therapy, So. Calif. Assn. Marital and Family Therapy (pres. 1972-73), Groves Family Conf. Acad., Groves Family Conf. (sec. 2001-2004), Alpha Kappa Delta, Phi Delta Gamma, Pi Gamma Mu. Home: 800 W 1st St Apt 2908 Los Angeles CA 90012-2444 Office: 250 W First St # 352 Claremont CA 91711 Office Phone: 909-624-4641. Personal E-mail: mlass@aol.com.

LAST, MICHAEL P., lawyer; b. Chgo., July 31, 1946; s. Jules Hilbert and Muriel Esther (Ruekberg) L.; m. Yong-Hee Chyun, Dec. 1970 (div.); m. Jane Antoinette Nooy Bunnell, May 29, 1983. BA magna cum laude, Lawrence U., 1968; JD cum laude, Harvard U., 1971. Bar: Mass. 1971. Ptnr., head real estate, environ. law dept. Warner & Stackpole, Boston, 1972-84; ptnr., head environ. law dept. Gaston & Snow, Boston, 1984-91; ptnr., co-chair environ. law sect. Mintz, Levin, Cohn, Ferris, Glovsky and Popeo P.C., Boston, 1991-99; mng. dir. ML Strategies, Inc., Boston, 1991-99, v.p., 1999; co-counsel Rackemann, Sawyer & Brewster, Boston, 1999—; prin. Nexus Environ. Ptnrs., Boston, 1999—2003; founding mem., prin. Creative Resolutions, LLC, Boston, 2003—. Bd. dirs. Newell Enterprises Inc., 1983-87; co-chair Am. Law Inst./ABA Ann. Course Study Minimizing Liability for Hazardous Waste Mgmt.; lectr. in field. Contbr. articles to profl. jours. Chair wetlands regulation rev. bd. Mass. Dept. Environ. Quality Engring., 1983-85, Town Wellesley Wetlands Protection Com., 1980-82; mem. Town Wellesley Planning Bd., 1983-88; rep. Town Meeting, Wellesley; mem. rev. bd. Mass. Dept. Environ. Protection, 1991-92; mem. bd. environ. mgmt. Mass. Dept. Environ. Mgmt., 1991-03, chmn., 1994-97, 00-03; founder, pres. Santa Fe Coun. Environ. Excellence, 1991—; founder, pres. Berkshire Inst., Inc.; mem. corp. gifts com. Boston Mus. Fine Arts Capital Fund Dr., 1979; vice chair open space plan implementation com. Town Wellesley, 1978-79; trustee, bd. govs. New Eng. Aquarium, 1995-2002, overseer, 2002—, chmn. David B. Stone award com.; trustee Mass. Eye and Ear Infirmary, 1990-98, Mt. Kearsarge Indian Mus., 1997-2002; trustee, bd. govs., exec. com. Newton-Wellesley Hosp., 1987-94, hon. trustee and overseer, 1994—, chmn. joint trustee staff com., 1992-93; mem. corp. Ptnrs. Healthcare Sys., Inc., 1999—; bd. dirs. Environ. Bus. Coun. New Eng., Inc., 1997—, chmn. Brownfields Com., chmn. ann. retreat, mem. exec. com., 2001-, vice chmn., 2005—. 1st lt. USAF, 1971-72 Warren Hurst Stevens scholar Lawrence U., 1964. Mem. ABA (standing com. environ. law 1989-91, natural resources sect., corp., banking, bus. law sect., real property, probate, trust law sect.), Boston Bar Assn. (bd. dirs. 1984-87, chair environment com. 1979-81, chair urban affairs sect. 1983-87, co-chair mcpl. planning process com. 1983-87), Greater Boston C. of C. (real estate devel. com. 1979-80, co-chair Boston 2000 project review com. 1982-90, Boston 2000 steering com. 1983-90, co-chair adv. com. Devel. Design Guideline Study Downtown Boston 1983-92), Phi Beta Kappa. Avocations: canoeing, cross country skiing, camping. Office: One Financial Center 29th Fl Boston MA 02111 Office Phone: 617-951-1192. Business E-Mail: mlast@lastlaw.com.

LASTER, LEONARD, internist, gastroenterologist, academic administrator, educator, writer, researcher; b. NYC, Aug. 24, 1928; s. Isaac and Mary (Ehrenreich) L.; m. Ruth Ann Leventhal, Dec. 16, 1956; children: Judith Eve, Susan Beth, Stephen Jay. AB, Harvard U., Cambridge, Mass., 1949, MD, 1950. Diplomate Nat. Bd. Med. Examiners, Am. Bd. Internal Medicine (gastroenterology). From intern to resident medicine Mass. Gen. Hosp., Boston, 1950—53; vis. investigator Pub. Health Rsch. Inst., NYC, 1953—54; commd. lt. USPHS, 1954, advanced through grades to asst. surgeon gen. (rear adm.), 1971, ret., 1973; exec. dir. Assembly Life Scis., also divsn. med. scis. NAS-NRC, 1973—74; v.p. acad. and clin. affairs Med. Ctr., also dean Coll. Medicine, prof. medicine SUNY Downstate Med. Ctr., Bklyn., 1974—78; pres., prof. medicine Oreg. Health Scis. U., Portland, 1978—87; chancellor U. Mass. Med. Ctr., Worcester, 1987—90, chancellor emeritus, 1990—, Disting. prof. medicine and health policy, 1990—2002, emeritus, 2002—; adj. scientist Marine Biol. Lab., Woods Hole, Mass., 2002—. Bd. dirs. TEI Biosci., Boston; lab. investigator Marine Biol. Lab., Woods Hole, 1962—69, chmn. organizer symposia on nat. policy and biomed. scis., 1971—72, libr. reader, 1973—76; chmn. steering com. Falmouth Forum, 1994—2002, mem. coun. visitors, 2003—; cons. in field; mem. staff Nat. Inst. Arthritis, Metabolic and Digestive Diseases NIH, Bethesda, Md., 1954—73, chief digestive and hereditary diseases br., 1969—73; from spl. asst. to asst. dir. human resources Pres.'s Office Sci. and Tech., 1969—73. Author: Life After Medical School, 32 Doctors Describe How They Shaped Their Medical Careers, 1996; contbr. articles on gastrointestinal disease, inborn errors of metabolism, devel. biology to profl. jours.; contbr. op-ed column and other pieces to Washington Post, essays to Hosp. Practice and MD Mag. columnist Cape Cod Times, 2002-07. Active Found. Advanced Edn. Scis., Bethesda, 1965-69, Bedford Stuyvesant Family Health Ctr., Bklyn., 1975-78, Med. Rsch. Found., Oreg., 1979-87, Oreg. Symphony, 1979-85, Oreg. Contemporary Theatre, 1981-83; pres. Burning Tree Elem. Sch. PTA, Bethesda, 1972-73; bd. dirs. Internat. Artists Series, Worcester, 1988-91, Mass. Biotech. Ctrs. for Excellence, Boston, 1988-96, Mass. Biotech. Rsch. Inst., Worcester, 1988-90, Worcester Bus. Devel. Corp., 1988-91; co-chmn. United Way Ctrl. Mass., COMEC Campaign, 1989; mem. exec. com. Worcester Econ. Club, 1988-91; mem. citizen gov. bd. Worcester Fights Back, 1990-95; chmn. corp. liaison com. Marine Biol. Lab., 1991-92; mem. Worcester Com. Fgn. Rels. (affiliated with Coun. Fgn. Rels.), 1992-96. Fellow gastro-enterology, Mass. Meml. Hosp., 1958—59. Fellow ACP; mem. Am. Fedn. Clin. Rsch., Am. Gastroenterol. Assn., Am. Soc. Biol. Chemists, Am. Soc. Clin. Investigation (emeritus), Marine Biol. Lab. Corp., Portland C. of C. (dir. 1980-84), Mass. Med. Soc., Harvard Inst. for Learning in Retirement, Cosmos Club, Harvard Club NYC, Harvard Club, Harvard Faculty Club, Phi Beta Kappa, Alpha Omega Alpha. Home and Office: 8 Lawrence Farm Rd Woods Hole MA 02543-1416 Personal E-mail: lencolumn@aol.com. *Education is nurturing excellence in others and facilitating its spread as an infectious disease.*

LASTER, RICHARD, biotechnologist, consultant; b. Vienna, Nov. 10, 1923; arrived in U.S., 1940, naturalized, 1944; s. Alan and Caroline (Harband) L.; m. Liselotte (Schneider), Oct. 17, 1948; children: Susan Laster Rubenstein, Thomas. Student, U. Wash., 1941-42; BChE cum laude, Poly. Inst. Bklyn., 1943; postgrad., Stevens Inst. Tech., 1945-47. With Gen. Foods Corp., 1944-82, corp. R & D Hoboken, NJ, 1944-58, ops. mgr. Franklin Baker divsn., 1958-64, ops. mgr. Atlantic gelatin divsn. Woburn, Mass., 1958-64, mgr. R & D Jell-O divsn. White Plains, NY, 1967-68, exec. v.p. Maxwell House divsn., 1968-69, pres. Maxwell House divsn., 1969-71, corp. v.p., 1971-73, exec. v.p., 1974-82, also dir. R & D and food-away-from-home, 1975-82. Bd. dirs., DNA Plant Tech. Corp., 1982-94, chmn., 1988-94, CEO, 1982-92, pres., 1982-91; mgmt. cons., 1994—; bd. dirs., Rice Tec; bd. dirs., chmn. Well Gen, Inc. Contbg. articles to profl. pub.; patentee in field. Mem. Sch. Bd., Chappaqua, NY, 1971—74, pres., 1973—74; chmn., bd. dirs., 1st v.p. United Way of Westchester, 1978; chmn. adv. com. Poly. Inst. Westchester, 1977; trustee Poly. Inst. N.Y., 1978—; mem. coll. coun. SUNY Purchase, Purchase Coll. Found., 1986—2007; mem. corp. N.Y. Bot. Garden; mem. subcom. export adminstrn. Pres.'s Export Coun., 1995; chmn. Westchester Edn. Coalition, 1992—2001, Holocaust & Human Rights Edn. Ctr., 1994—, Am. Soc. Plant Physiologists Edn. Found., 1995—2000; mem. New Castle Town Bd., 1996—2001; dir. Weizmann Inst., 2007—. Recipient Disting. Alumnus award, 1996, Disting. Svc. award,NCCJ, Poly Inst. N.Y. fellow. Mem. AAAS, AIChE (Food and Bioengring. award 1972), N.Y. Acad. Sci., Am. Chem. Soc., Am. Inst. Chemists, Tau Beta Pi, Phi Lambda Upsilon. Home: 23 Round Hill Rd Chappaqua NY 10514-1622 Office: 103 S Bedford Rd Mount Kisco NY 10549-3440 Home Phone: 914-238-8892; Office Phone: 914-241-4959. E-mail: rilaster@aol.com.

LASTOWKA, JAMES ANTHONY, former federal agency administrator, lawyer; b. Chester, Pa., Oct. 1, 1951; s. Joseph Edward and Mary A. (O'Malley) L.; m. Sandra L. Pugh, Apr. 28, 1979; children: Conor David, Carey Anna, Austin Tucker. BA in Econs. cum laude, Syracuse U., 1973; JD, Georgetown U., 1976. Bar: Pa. 1976, D.C. 1990, U.S. Ct. Appeals (4th, 5th, 9th, 10th, 11th, D.C. cirs.) 1981. Staff atty. U.S. Occupational Safety and Health Rev. Commn., Washington, 1976-78, asst. gen. counsel, 1979-80; supervisory atty. Fed. Mine Safety and Health Rev. Commn., Washington, 1978-79, dep. gen. counsel, 1980-81, gen. counsel, 1981-84, commr., 1984-90; with Jones, Day, Reavis & Pogue, Washington, 1990-92, McDermott, Will & Emery, Washington, 1992—. Contbr. editor Occupational Hazards Mag. Mem. ABA (mem. labor law sect., com. occupational safety and health law). Office: McDermott Will & Emery 600 13th St NW Fl 12 Washington DC 20005-3096 Office Phone: 202-756-8245. Business E-Mail: jlastowka@mwe.com.

LASYS, JOAN, medical/surgical nurse, educator; b. Siauliai, Lithuania, Sept. 1, 1924; arrived in Can., 1948; came to U.S., 1960; d. Joseph-Apolinarius and Elena (Šlapokaite) Barcevičius; m. Bill Lasys, July 31, 1949. RN degree, Lithuanian Red Cross Sch. Nursing, 1945; student, Ariz. State U., Tempe, 1981—86, Ea. Ariz. Coll., Thatcher, 1981—86. RN, Can., Nebr.; cert. nursing tchr., Ariz.; C.C., occupl. tchg. cert. Ariz. Staff RN St. Mary's Hosp., Montreal, Canada, 1949—51, Montreal Gen. Hosp., 1951—53, 1959—60; pvt. duty Nurses Registry, Montreal, 1953—56; Can. civil svc. RN R.H.O. Ctr. Dept. Vets. Affairs, Ottawa, 1956—57, Queen Mary Vets. Hosp., Montreal, 1957-58; staff RN St. Joseph's Hosp., Omaha, 1968—69, Meryvale Hosp., Phoenix, 1969—71, Valley View Hosp., Youngtown, Ariz., 1971—72, Boswell Hosp., Sun City, Ariz., 1972—76; RN Kivel Care Ctr., Phoenix, 1986—93, 2000—02. Past v.p. and officer Pine-Strawberry Health Svcs., Ariz.; columnist/reporter Payson Roundup, Ariz. Pub. (mag.) Small Town U.S.A.; prodr. audio tapes: Time Management, Nursing Communications; author numerous poems Mem. Payson Regional Med. Ctr. Aux.; mem Rep. Presdl. Task Force. Named Poet of Yr., Nat. Soc. Poetry, 2007; recipient Bronze Poet of Merit medal, Poetry Conv. and Symposium Intl. Soc. Poets, 2005, Silver bowl Outstanding Achievement in Poetry, 2005, Crystal tower, 2006, Poetry Gold Medal of Excellence, Famous Poets, 2007. Mem.: AAUW, Libr. Congress, Nat. Mus. Women in the Arts, Payson Libr., County Attys. and Sheriffs Assn. (hon.), Kivel Geriatric Ctr. Aux. (life), Arbor Day Found., Nature Conservancy, Cooking Club of Am. (charter). Republican. Roman Catholic. Avocations: cooking, poetry, public speaking, arts and crafts. Home: 506 N William Tell Cir Payson AZ 85541-4050

LASZEWSKI, BOLESLAW TADEUSZ, civic volunteer; b. Gora Ropczycka, Poland, Nov. 22, 1912; s. Jozef and Katarzyna (Toton) L.; m. Sophie Kinel, Sept. 26, 1947 (div. 1968); children: Barbara, Marzena, Dorothy; m. Christine Gaszynski. BSBA, CUNY, 1957; MS, Columbia U., 1956; MA, Jagiellonian U., 1937. Co-founder, hon. pres. Polish Assistance, NYC, 1952—. Co-founder, pres., Polish Combatants Assn., London, 1945-50; v.p. Worldwide Orgn. Poles Abroad, London, 1947-80; mem. Kostiuszko Found., N.Y.C., 1952—; co-founder, pres. Polish Daily News, N.Y.C., 1970—; pres. Polish Am. Army Veterans Assn., 1985—; exec. dir. Polish Inst. Arts & Scis., N.Y.C., 1986-90; v.p., dir. Polish Am. Congress, 1986-88; pres. Polish Fed. Credit Union, Bklyn., 1985-90. Author: From Army to Civilian Life, 1984, Krakow, 1985, East West Russia—USSR—USA—Poland, 1986, Diary of a Soldier, 2000.

LAT, DAVID B., former assistant US attorney, online-journalist, editor, blogger; b. June 19, 1975; BA in English magna cum laude, Harvard Coll., 1996; JD, Yale Law Sch., 1999. Clerk for Judge Diarmuid F. O'Scannlain US Ct. Appeals, 9th Cir.; with Wachtell, Lipton, Rosen & Katz, NYC, US Attorney, Dist. NJ, 3rd Cir. Appeals; writer, creator Underneaththeirrobes-.com, Washington, 2004—06; co-editor Wonkette.com, Washington, 2006; editor-in-chief Abovethelaw.com, NYC, 2006—. Mem.: Phi Beta Kappa. Avocation: blogging. Office: Above the Law 262 Mott St Ste 102A New York NY 10012 Business E-Mail: dlat@abovethelaw.com.*

LATAIF, LOUIS EDWARD, dean; b. Fall River, Mass., Jan. 24, 1939; s. Louis and Linda Adele (Salwan) Lataif; m. Najia Ann Koury, June 8, 1963; children: Louis Edward Jr., Nina Walters, Nancy Ruiz, Stephanie Stiker. BS in Bus. Adminstrn., Boston U., 1961, LLD (hon.), 1990; MBA, Harvard U., 1964; DBA (hon.), U. Mass., 1986; LLD Lycoming Coll. (hon.), 1993. Sales and mktg. mgmt. trainee Ford Motor Co., Dearborn, Mich., 1964-66, Calif. mktg. mgr. LA, 1975-76, dist. sales mgr., regional sales mgr. Chgo., 1976-78, gen. mktg. mgr. Ford divsn. Dearborn, Mich., 1978-81, v.p., gen. mgr. Ford divsn., 1981-84, N.Am. sales ops. v.p., 1984-88, pres. Ford of Europe Brentwood, Eng., 1988-91, v.p. worldwide quality & mktg. Dearborn, Mich., 1991; dean Sch. Mgmt. Boston U., 1991—. Bd. dirs. Abiomed. Inc., Interaudi Bank, Group 1 Automotive, 2002-, Magna Entertainment Corp. Mem. editl. bd. European Bus. Jour., London, 1992—. Bd. dirs. Lahey-Hitchcock Clinic, Burlington, Mass., 1991—97, Iacocca Found. Mem. Brae Burn Country Club, Boston, Bonita Bay Country Club, Fla. Roman Catholic. Avocations: skiing, piano, golf. Office: Boston U Sch Mgmt 595 Commonwealth Ave Office 508B Boston MA 02215-1704

LATAILLE, RONALD H., telecommunications industry executive; married; 3 children. BS in Acctg., Providence Coll.; MBA in Fin., U. RI. CPA. With NJ Bell, 1979; v.p. fin. Bell Atlantic; pres. Verizon Media Ventures Verizon Comm., exec. dir. performance assurance, dir. switched and spl. access svcs., dir. carrier bus. planning, v.p. fin. planning and analysis Domestic Telecom Grp., 2000, sr. v.p. investor rels., 2005—. Mem. adv. bd. BPM Forum. Office: Verizon Comm 140 West St New York NY 10007

LATANÉ, BIBB, social psychologist; b. NYC, July 19, 1937; s. Henry Allen and Felicité Gillman (Bibb) L.; children: Julia Gillman, Claire Augusta, Henry Arbiter. BA, Yale U., 1958; PhD, U. Minn., 1963. Mem. faculty dept. social psychology Columbia U., NYC, 1962-68; prof. psychology, dir. behavioral scis. lab. Ohio State U., Columbus, 1968-82; prof. psychology, dir. Inst. Research Social Sci. U.N.C.-Chapel Hill, 1982-90; prof. psychology Fla. Atlantic U., Boca Raton, 1990—2000. Pres. Social Sci. Confs., Inc.; founder Nags Head Confs., Sea Frolic Conf. Ctr., Ctr. Human Sci. Contbr. articles to profl. jours. Guggenheim fellow, 1974-75; James McKeen Cattell fellow, 1981-82; NSF, Office of Naval Research grantee. Mem. APA (coun. rep. 1971-75), Soc. Personality and Social Psychology (pres. 1976-79, Campbell award 1986), Midwestern Psychol. Assn. (pres. 1981-84), Acad. Mgmt., AAAS (Socio-Psychol. prize 1968, 80), Soc. Exptl. Soc. Psychology (Disting. Scientist award 1998), Am. Sociol. Assn., Animal Behavior Soc. Home: 212 Vance St Chapel Hill NC 27516 E-mail: latane@humanscience.org. *We know so much, yet understand so little about human beings and the social realities they create.*

LATANISION, RONALD MICHAEL, materials science and engineering consultant; b. Richmondale, Pa., July 2, 1942; s. Stephen and Mary (Kopach) Latanision; m. Carolyn Marie Domenig, 1964; children: Ivan, Sara. BS, Pa. State U., 1964; PhD in Metall. Engring., Ohio State U., 1968. Postdoctoral fellow Nat. Bur. Stds., Washington, 1968-69; research scientist Martin Marietta, Balt., 1969-73, acting head materials sci., 1973-74; dir. H.H. Uhlig Corrosion Lab. MIT, Cambridge, 1974—2003, Shell Disting. prof. materials sci. and engring., 1983-88, dir. Materials Processing Ctr., 1984-91; co-founder ALTRAN Materials Engring. Corp., Boston, 1992—; corp. v.p., prin., dir. mechanics and materials practice Exponent Inc., 2003—. Mem. tech. adv. bd. Modell Devel. Corp., Framingham, Mass., 1987—94; mem. sci. advisor com. sci. and tech. U.S. Ho. Reps., 1982—83; chmn. ad hoc com. Mass. Advanced Materials Ctr., Boston, 1985—; mem. adv. bd. Mass. Office Sci. and Tech.; co-PI NSF/SSI project PALMS; chmn. MIT Coun. Primary and Secondary Edn. Editor: Surface Effects in Crystal Plasticity, 1977, Advances in Mechanics and Physics of Fracture, 1981, 1983, 1986, Atomistics of Fracture, 1983, Chemistry and Physics of Fracture, 1987; contbr. articles to profl. jours. Named Henry Krumb lectr., AIME, 1984, Disting. Alumnus, Ohio State U. Coll. Engring., 1991, Hon. Alumnus, MIT, 1992; recipient Sr. Scientist award, Humboldt Found., 1974—75, David Ford McFarland award, Pa. State U., 1986, T. P. Hoar award, Inst. Corrosion, U.K., 2001, Henry B. Linford award, Electrochem. Soc., 2004; Centennial fellow, Coll. Earth and Mineral Scis., Pa. State U., 1996. Fellow: Nat. Assn. Corrosion Engrs. (A.B. Campbell award 1971, Willis R. Whitney award 1994), Am. Soc. Metals Internat. (mem. govt. and pub. affairs com. 1984); mem.: Nat. Materials Adv. Bd., Am. Acad. Arts and Scis., Nat. Acad. Engring., New Eng. Sci. Tchrs. (founder, co-chmn.), Masons. Roman Catholic. Office: Exponent 21 Strathmore Rd Natick MA 01760 Home Phone: 781-729-0691; Office Phone: 508-652-8560. Business E-Mail: rlatanision@exponent.com.

LATHAM, AMY MOORE, academic administrator; d. Lawrence and Nannie Lou Moore; m. William Todd Latham, Dec. 12, 1992; children: Will, Ashley. B of Bus. Adminstrn., Delta State U., Miss., 1986. Computer programmer N.W. Miss. CC, Senatobia, Miss., 1986—89, mgr. computer ctr., 1989—96. Dir. of MIS N.W. Miss. CC, Senatobia, Miss., 1996—. Crafts fair chmn. Arkabutla Vol. Fire Dept., Miss., 2003—05. Mem.: COMMON. Baptist. Achievements include development of a preregistration system for the college. Most of our administrative software is written and maintained in-house, while keeping pace with what other colleges are offering. Avocations: gardening, travel. Office: NW Miss C C 4975 Highway 51 North Senatobia MS 38668 Home Phone: 662-562-4617; Office Phone: 662-562-3201. E-mail: a_latham@northwestms.edu.

LATHAM, BENJAMIN ERWIN, music educator; b. Belle Fourche, SD, Apr. 7, 1971; s. Erwin and Shirley Latham. BA in Music Edn., Black Hills State U., 1996, BS in Speech and Theater, 1994; M Conducting, Calif. State U., Fresno, 2001. Actor Black Hills Passion Play, Spearfish, SD, 1990—97; prodr., dir. Why Knot Theatre Co., Spearfish, SD, 1992—, Pacificia, Calif., 1992—; dir. music and speech Riverdale (Calif.) H.S., 1997—99; dir. music Corcoran (Calif.) H.S., 1999—2001; carddealer Old Style Saloon No. 10, Deadwood, SD, 2001—02; dir. bands Cabrillo and Vallemar Schs., Pacifica, 2002—. Asst. condr. Fresno Wind Ensemble, Calif. State U., Fresno, 1999—2001. Contbr. articles to Pacific Tribune; composer: (symphonic overture) Civic Overture, 2003. Co-founder, co-dir. Ctrl. Valley United Marching Band, Fresno, 1999—2001; mem., prin. trumpet San Francisco Civic Symphony, 2001—; pres. Civic Symphony Assn., San Francisco, 2003—; mem. Skyline Coll. Concert Band, 2001—; SD Boys State auditor Am. Legion, Aberdeen, SD, 1987. Named Am. Mus. Amb., West Lafayette, Ind., 1988—98. Mem.: ASCAP, Calif. Music Educators Assn., Calif. Band Dirs. Assn. (auditioner 1997—), Lions Club (tail twister 1997—99). Roman Catholic. Home: 1537 Terra Nova Blvd Pacifica CA 94044 Office: Pacifica Sch Dist 375 Reina Del Mar Pacifica CA 94044 Office Phone: 650-738-6660 102. E-mail: lathbe@yahoo.com.

LATHAM, JOHN L., lawyer; b. Dallas, Tex., July 12, 1954; BA, U. Toledo, 1976; JD, Emory U., Atlanta, 1979. Bar: Ga. 1979. Ptnr., securities, litig., capital mkts. group Alston & Bird LLP, Atlanta. Office: Alston & Bird LLP One Atlantic Ctr 1201 W Peachtree St NW Atlanta GA 30309-3424 Office Phone: 404-881-7000. Office Fax: 404-881-7913. Business E-Mail: jlatham@alston.com.

LATHAM, PATRICIA HORAN, lawyer; b. Hoboken, NJ, Sept. 5, 1941; d. Patrick John and Rosemary (Moller) Horan; m. Peter Samuel Latham, June 12, 1965; children: John Horan, Kerry Patricia. BA, Swarthmore Coll., 1963; JD, U. Chgo., 1966. Bar: D.C. 1967, U.S. Dist. Ct. D.C. 1967, U.S. Ct. Appeals 1967, U.S. Supreme Ct. 1970, Va. 1989, U.S. Dist. Ct. (ea. dist.) Va. 1989, U.S. Dist. Ct. Md. 1991. Assoc. Fried, Frank, Harris, Shriver & Kampelman, Washington, 1966-69; atty. Office of Gen. Counsel, SEC, Washington, 1969-71; assoc. Martin & Smith, Washington, 1971—, ptnr., 1974-85, Latham & Latham, Washington, 1986—. Lectr. Columbus Sch. Law, Cath. U. Am., Washington, 1978-92; mem. panel of arbitrators N.Y. Stock Exch., 1985—; co-founder, co-dir. Nat. Ctr. Law and Learning Disabilities, 1992—; mem. disability adv. com. GED Testing Svc., 1999-2005. Co-author: Attention Deficit Disorder and the Law, 1992, 2d edit., 1997, Learning Disabilities and the Law, 1993, 2d edit., 2000, Succeeding in the Workplace, 1994, Higher Education Services for Students with Learning Disabilities and Attention Deficit Disorder: A Legal Guide, 1994, Documentation and the Law, 1996, Tales from the Workplace, 1997, Terrorism and the Law: Bringing Terrorists to Justice, 2002, Learning Disabilities/ADHD and the Law in Higher Education and Employment, 2007, Special Education Law, 2007; contbr. chapters to books. Co-founder, trustee Beacon Coll., 1989-93, chmn. bd. trustees, 1990-92; mem. adv. bd. Disability Law Reporter Svc., 1996-2001; bd. dirs., pres. Watergate West, 2006—. Mem.: ABA, Learning Disabilities Assn. Am. (nat. adv. bd. 1996—2000, nat. bd. dirs. 2000—, treas. 2005—07), Nat. Attention Deficit Disorders Assn. (bd. dirs. 1993—98, nat. adv. bd. 1998—), Am. Arbitration Assn. (panel arbitrators and mediators 1982—), Va. Bar Assn., DC Bar Assn., Ft. Myer and Ft. McNair Club. Roman Catholic. Home: The Watergate 2700 Virginia Ave NW # 707 Washington DC 20037 Office: Latham & Latham The Watergate 2700 Virginia Ave NW Washington DC 20037 Office Phone: 202-333-1713. Business E-Mail: lathamlaw@earthlink.net.

LATHAM, PATRICIA S., physician; b. Annapolis, Md., Aug. 22, 1946; BS, Simmons Coll., 1968; MD, U. So. Calif., 1972. Intern Yale-New Haven Hosp., 1972-73, resident, 1973-75, fellow in hepatology, 1975-78; resident in anatomic pathology U. Toronto (Can.) Hosp., 1978-80; asst. prof. pathology and medicine U. Md., 1981-88, Nat. Cancer Inst., 1988-90, George Washington U., 1990-92, assoc. prof. pathology and medicine, 1992—. Office: George Wash U 2300 I St NW Washington DC 20037-2336 Office Phone: 202-994-3391.

LATHAM, PETER SAMUEL, lawyer; b. Boston, July 23, 1940; s. Earl Gansen and Margaret (Perrier) L.; m. Patricia Ann Horan, June 12, 1965; children: John Horan, Kerry Patricia. BA with honors, Swarthmore Coll., 1962; LLB, U. Pa., 1965. Bar: D.C. 1966, U.S. Ct. Appeals (D.C. cir.) 1982, U.S. Dist. Ct. Md. 1991. Atty. SEC, Washington, 1965—68; assoc. Vom Baur, Coburn, Simmons & Turtle, Washington, 1969—71; mem. Wachtel, Ross and Matzkin, Washington, 1971—80; ptnr. Latham & Latham and predecessor firms, Washington, 1980—. Arbitrator Am. Arbitration Assn., 1978-2001. Author: Government Contract Disputes, 1981, 86; co-author: Attention Deficit Disorder and the Law: A Guide for Advocates, 1992, Learning Disabilities and the Law, 1993, Succeeding in the Workplace, 1994, Higher Education Services for Students with Learning Disabilities and Attention Deficit Disorder: A Legal Guide, 1994, Documentation and the Law, 1996, Tales from the Workplace, 1997, Attention Deficit Disorder and the Law, 2d edit., 1997, Learning Disabilities and the Law, 2d edit., 2000, Terrorism and the Law-Bringing Terrorists to Justice, 2002, Learning Disabilities/ADHD and the Law in Higher Education and Employment, 2007, Special Education Law, 2007; contbg. author ADD and the College Student, 1993, A Comprehensive Guide to ADD in Adults, 1995, Managing Attention and Learning Disorders in Late Adolescence and Adulthood, 1996, Textbook of Pediatric Neuropsychiatry, 1998, Learning Disabilities and Employment, 1997, ADD in Children and Adults, 1999, Pediatric Neuropsychiatry, 2006; prodr., dir. The ABC's of ADD, other videos on legal topics. Co-founder, trustee Beacon Coll., 1989-93; co-founder Nat. Ctr. for Law and Learning Disabilities. Lt. USN, 1966-69. Decorated Navy Achievement medal with combat V. Mem.: ABA, D.C. Procurement Reform Taskforce (mem. Alternate Dispute Resolution subcom. 1995—), Nat. Attention Deficit Disorders Assn. (bd. dirs. 1993—97), Ft. Myer and Ft. McNair Club. Republican. Roman Catholic. Avocations: tennis, swimming. Home: The Watergate 2700 Virginia Ave NW # 707 Washington DC 20037 Office: Latham and Latham The Watergate 2700 Virginia Ave NW Washington DC 20037 Office Phone: 202-333-1713. Business E-Mail: lathamlaw@gmail.com.

LATHAM, ROBERT RICHARD, JR., retired emergency services administrator; b. Memphis, Mar. 31, 1951; s. Robert Richard Sr. and Maxine Waldrop Latham; m. Charlotte Anne Eoff; children: Robert Richard III, Steven Edward. Fire chief Senatobia Fire Dept., 1982—2000; dir. Tate County Emergency Mgmt. Agy., Senatobia, 1995—2000; exec. dir. Miss. Emergency Mgmt. Agy., Jackson, 2000—06; ret., 2006. Gov.'s homeland security advisor State of Miss., Jackson, 2002—04; bd. dirs. Ctrl. US Earthquake Consortium, Memphis, 2000—06, chmn. bd. dirs., 2004—05; fire coord. Tate County, Senatobia, Miss., 1988—2000; pres. Tate County E911 Bd., Senatobia, 1993—2000. Sgt. maj. USNG, 1969—95. Decorated Miss. Magnolia Cross Miss. Army N.G.; named Outstanding Citizen of Yr., Woodmen of the World, 1994, Citizen of Yr., Civitan Internat., 1992, Emergency Mgr. of Yr., Miss. Civil Def./Emergency Mgmt. Assn., 2000; named one of Outstanding Young Men of the Yr., US Jaycees, 1982. Mem.: Nat. Emergency Mgmt. Assn. (assoc.; chmn.legislative com. 2005). Baptist. Home and Office: 104 Wildberry Way Pearl MS 39208 Office Phone: 601-420-0211. Personal E-mail: rlathamjr@comcast.net.

LATHAM, TOM, congressman; b. Hampton, Iowa, July 14, 1948; s. Willard and Evelyn L.; m. Kathy Swinson, 1975; children: Justin, Jennifer, Jill. Student, Watrburg Coll., Iowa State U. Bank teller, bookkeeper, Brush, Colo., 1970-72; ind. ins. agent Fort Lupton, Colo., 1972-74; mktg. rep. Hartford Ins. Co., Des Moines, 1974-76; with Latham Seed Co., Alexander, Iowa, 1976—, now v.p., co-owner; mem. US Congress from 4th Iowa dist. (formerly 5th), 1994—, Ho. Appropriations Com. Sec. Republican Party of Iowa; rep. 5th dist. Republican State Ctrl. com.; co-chair Francklin County Republican Ctrl. com.; whip Iowa del. Republican Nat. Conv., 1992. Past chair Franklin County Extension Coun.; mem. Nazareth Lutheran Ch., past pres.; citizens adv. coun. Iowa State U. Mem. Am. Soybean Assn., Am. Seed Trade Assn., Iowa Farm Bur. Fedn., Iowa Soybean Assn., Iowa Corn Growers Assn., Iowa Seed Assn., Agribusiness Assn. of Iowa. Republican. Lutheran. Office: US Ho Reps 440 Cannon Ho Office Bldg Washington DC 20515-1504 Office Phone: 202-225-5476. Office Fax: 202-225-3301. E-mail: tom.latham@mail.house.gov.

LATHAM, WELDON HURD, lawyer; b. Bklyn., Jan. 2, 1947; s. Aubrey Geddes and Avril (Hurd) L.; m. Constantia Beecher, Aug. 8, 1948; children: Nicole Marie, Brett Weldon. BA, Howard U., 1968; JD, Georgetown U., 1971; postgrad., George Washington U., 1975-76. Bar: D.C. 1972, U.S. Ct. Appeals (D.C. cir.) 1972, U.S. Ct. Mil. Appeals 1974, U.S. Ct. Claims 1975, U.S. Supreme Ct. 1975, Va. 1981, U.S. Ct. Appeals (fed. cir.) 1988. Mgmt. cons. Checchi & Co., Washington, 1968-71; atty. Covington & Burling, Washington, 1971-73; sr. atty. Fed. Energy Adminstrn., Washington, 1974; asst. gen. counsel Exec. Office Pres. Office Mgmt. and Budget The White House, Washington, 1974-76; atty. Hogan & Hartson, Washington, 1976-79; gen. dep. asst. sec. HUD, Washington, 1979-81; v.p., gen. counsel Sterling Sys., Inc. (subs. PRC.); exec. asst., counsel to chmn., CEO and assoc. gen. counsel Planning Rsch. Corp., McLean, Va., 1981-86; mng. ptnr. Va. office Reed, Smith, Shaw & McClay, McLean, Va., 1986-91; sr. ptnr. Shaw Pittman, Washington, 1992-2000; sr. ptnr., practice area leader corp. diversity counseling Holland & Knight, Washington, 2000—04; sr. ptnr. and chmn. Corp. Diversity Counseling Group Davis Wright Tremaine LLP, 2004—. Chmn. diversity adv. bd. Deloitte & Touche, 2002—; bd. visitors Georgetown U. Law Ctr., 2002—05; mem. adv. coun. Coca-Cola Procurement, 2000-03; adj. prof. Howard U. Law Sch., Washington, 1972-82; guest prof. U. Va., Charlottesville, 1976-90; mem. Va. Govs. Bus. and Industry Adv. Com. on Crime Prevention, 1983-85, Va. Govs. Regulatory Reform Adv. Bd., 1982-84; chmn. task force SBA, 1982; legal counsel Md. Mondale for Pres. Campaign, 1984; gen. counsel Nat. Coalition Minority Bus., 1993-03; trustee The Am. Univ., 1999-2002; bd. dirs., chmn. legal com. Metro Washington Airports Authority, 1997-; bd. dirs. Telecomms. Sys., Inc., 1999-; bd. govs. Joint Ctr. Polit. and Econ. Studies, 1998-2004; adj. prof. Georgetown U. Law Ctr., 2004-; mem. Deloitte & Touche Women's Initiative Coun., 2005-, Diversity Best Practices Coun., Am. Employment Law Coun. Columnist Minority Bus. Entrepreneur Mag., 1991-2004, Diversity Jour., 2002--; mem. editl. adv. bd. Washington Bus. Jour., 1985-87. Washington steering com. NAACP Legal Def. Fund, 1975-95, Fairfax County Airports Adv. Com., 1987-88; bd. dirs., gen. counsel Northern Va. Minority Bus. and Profl. Assn., 1985-92; trustee Va. Commonwealth U., Richmond, 1986-90, George Mason U., Fairfax, Va., 1990-94; bd. dirs. Washington Urban League, 1986-90, U. D.C. Found., 1982-87, Washington Coun. Lawyers, 1973, Profl. Svcs. Coun., 1983-88, Minority Bus. Enterprise Legal Def. and Edn. Fund, 1989-91, Wash. Hosp. Ctr. Found., 1996-98; appointee Greater Washington Bd. Trade, Blue Ribbon Task Force on Home Rule, 1985-86, bd. dirs., exec. com., chmn. regional affairs com., corp. sec. Greater Washington Bd. Trade, 1990-95; adv. bd. First Union Nat. Bank, 1995-99; civilian aide to Sec. of Army, 1995-2000; mem. nat. adv. coun. SBA, 1993-2003, Burger King Corp. Diversity Action Coun., 1996-98, Diversity Best Practices Coun., 2001--, Md. Econ. Devel. Commn., 1996-98, Gov. Bd. Transition Team, 1995, Dem. Nat. Com., 1996, Platform Drafting Com., 1996; prin. coun. for Excellence in Govt., 1989-95; at-large mem. Dem. Nat. Com., 2001--; mayor D.C. Internat. Ins. Adv. Commn., 1994-95; chmn. D.C. Mayors Bus. Adv. Coun., 1994-96; vice-chmn. Dem. Bus. Coun. DNC, 1994-98; co-chmn. UNCF Sportsfest Fundraiser, 1994; hon. vice-chmn. Clinton-Gore Campaign, 1996; mem. corp. adv. coun. Congrl. Black Caucus Found., 1999-2005; gen. counsels Honors Program Office Sec. Capt. USAF, 1973-74. Recipient SES Effective Mgr. award HUD, 1980, Nat. Assn. for Equal Achievement Opportunity in Higher Edn. award, 1987, A. Philip Randolph award Amtrak, 2001, Ron Brown Legacy award Nat. Black MBA Assn., 2002. Mem. NAACP (life), ABA (vice-chmn. subcom. pub. contract law sect. 1988-93), Fed. Bar Assn., Nat. Bar Assn., D.C. C. of C. (gen. counsel 1979), State Va. Bar Assn., Washington Bar Assn.(elected to Hall of Fame, 2001), Bar Assn. D.C., Nat. Contract Mgmt. Assn., Econ. Club Washington. Democrat. Home: 7004 Natelli Woods Ln Bethesda MD 20817-3924 Office: Davis Wright Tremaine LLP 1919 Pennsylvania Avenue NW Ste 200 Washington DC 20006 Office Phone: 202-508-6664. Business E-Mail: weldonlatham@dwt.com.

LATHAN, CORINNA ELISABETH, aerospace engineer; b. Nov. 7, 1967; m. David Kubalak. BA in Biopsychology and Math., Swarthmore Coll., 1988; PhD in Neurosci., MIT, 1994, SM in Aeronautics and Astronautics, 1995. Asst. prof. biomed. engring. Cath. U., Washington, 1995—99, assoc. prof. biomed. engring., 1999—2000, assoc. adj. prof.; adj. prof. aerospace engring. U. Md., 2002—; founder, pres., CEO AnthroTronix, College Park, Md., 1999—; CEO AT KidSystems, 2005—. Mem. adv. bd. Cath. U. Am. Mem. editl. bd.: Jour. Human Performance in Extreme Environs., 1998—. Founder Keys to Empowering Youth; spl. projects advisor FIRST, Inc. Named Top Innovator of Yr., Md. Daily Record, 2002, Tech. Pioneer, World Econ. Forum, 2004; named one of Top 100 World Innovators Under the Age of 35, Tech. Review-MIT's Mag. of Innovation, Top 100 Women, Md. Daily Record, 2003, Young Global Leaders, Forum of Young Global Leaders, 2006; recipient Creating a Future of Opportunity award, Dept. Aeronautics and Astronautics, MIT, 2000, Women in Tech. Leadership award for entrepreneurship, 2002. Mem.: Assn. for Advancement of Med. Instrumentation (mem. human engring. stds. com. 1997—). Office: AnthroTronix Inc 387 Technology Dr Ste 1101 College Park MD 20742*

LATHE, TIMOTHY J., bank executive; B in Econs., Tulane U., New Orleans; grad. student in Bus. Adminstrn., U. New Orleans. Mgmt. trainee Corp. Banking Nat. City Corp., 1981, dir. Corp. Automation Sys. Project, mgr. Multinational Dept. Corp. Banking, 1995, chmn., CEO Bank of the Midwest, 2000, chmn. NatCity Investments, Inc., exec. v.p. pvt. client group, 2004—. Bd. trustees Arch Devel. Ptnrs., Mich. Bus. Roundtable, SW Mich. First. Pres., bd. trustees Achievement Ctrs. Children; bd. trustees, mem. exec. com. Leadership Cleve. Office: Nat City Corp Nat City Ctr 1900 E Ninth St Cleveland OH 44114-3484 Office Phone: 216-222-2000.*

LATHEROW, ROBERT L., retired music educator; b. La Harpe, Ill., Oct. 24, 1928; s. Robert Ivan and Genevieve Wright Latherow. BS in Edn., Western Ill. U., Macomb, 1949; MusM Butler U., Indpls., 54; EdD in Music, Columbia U., NYC, 1962. Assoc. prof. singing Newark State Coll., Union, NJ, 1962—64; pvt. voice tchr. Wayne, 1962—2000; prof. singing William Paterson U., Wayne, NJ, 1962—88. Condr. workshops and seminars in singing in French; adjudicator numerous singing contests, Met. Opera auditions. Pres. Allison Tallman Scholarship Com., Cresskill, NJ, 1980—86; fundraiser YMCA, San Diego, 1994—2000. Staff sgt. US Army, 1951—53, Korea. Mem.: NY Singing Tchrs. Assn. (pres. 1972—74), Nat. Assn. Tchrs. Singing (gov. 1970—74). Avocations: travel, cooking, exercise. Home: 2727 De Anza Rd Space 32 San Diego CA 92109

LATHI, BHAGAWANDAS PANNALAL, retired electrical engineering educator; b. Bhokar, Maharashtr, India, Dec. 3, 1933; came to U.S., 1956; s. Pannalal Rupchand and Tapi Pannalal (Indani) L.; m. Rajani Damodardas Mundada, July 27, 1962; children: Anjali, Shishir. BEEE, Poona U., 1955; MSEE, U. Ill., 1957; PhD in Elec. Engring., Stanford U., 1961. Rsch. asst. U. Ill., Urbana, 1956-57, Stanford (Calif.) U., 1957-60; rsch. engr. Gen. Electric Co., Syracuse, NY, 1960-61; cons. to semicondr. industry India, 1961-62; assoc. prof. elec. engring. Bradley U., Peoria, Ill., 1962-69, U.S. Naval Acad., Annapolis, Md., 1969-72; prof. elec. engring. Campinas (Brazil) State U., 1972-78, Calif. State U., Sacramento, 1979—2001, prof. emeritus, 2002—. Vis. prof. U. Iowa, Owa City, 1979. Author: Signals, Systems and Communication, 1965, Communication Systems, 1968 (transl. into Japanese 1977), Random Signals and Communication Theory, 1968, Teoria Sygnalow I Ukladow Telekomunikacyjnych, 1970, Sistemy Telekomunikacyjne, 1972, Signals, Systems and Controls, 1974, Sistemas de Comunicacion, 1974, 86, Sistemas de Comunicacao, 1978, Modern Digital and Analog Communication Systems, 1983, 89 (transl. into Japanese 1986, 90, Korean, 2001), Signals and Systems, 1987, Linear Systems and Signals, 1992, 2d rev. edit., 2005, Signal Processing and Linear Systems, 1998; contbr. articles to profl. jours. Fellow IEEE. Office: Calif State U 6000 J St Sacramento CA 95819-2605 Address: 3021 Scenic Height Way Carmichael CA 95608 Personal E-mail: bercamb@yahoo.com.

LATHROP, IRVIN TUNIS, retired dean; b. Platteville, Wis., Sept. 23, 1927; s. Irvin J. and Marian (Johnson) Lathrop; m. Eleanor M. Kolar, Aug. 18, 1951; 1 child, James I. BS, Stout State Coll., 1950; MS, Iowa State U., 1954, PhD, 1958. Tchr. Ottumwa (Iowa) H.S., 1950-55; mem. faculty Iowa State U., 1957-58, Western Mich. U., 1958-59, Calif. State Coll., 1959-88, prof. indsl. arts, 1966-88, chmn. dept. indsl. edn., 1969-88, assoc. dean extended edn., 1978-88, prof. emeritus, 1988—. Cons. Naval Ordnance Lab., Corona, Calif., 1961—63. Author (with Marshall La Cour): Photo Technology, 1966; author: (with John LIndbeck) General Industry, 1969, with John LIndbeck: rev. edit., 1977;; author: Laboratory Manual for Photo Technology, 1973, Photography, 1979, rev. edit., 1992, The Basic Book of Photography, 1979; author: (with Robert Kunst) Photo-Offset, 1979; editl. cons. Am. Tech. Soc.; contbr. articles to profl. jours. Mem. Orange County Grand Jury, 1989—90, Orange County Juvenile Justice Commn., 1991—2002; mem. adv. com. El Camino and Orange Coast Coll. Mem.: Am. Ednl. Rsch. Assn., Internat. Tech. Assn., Nat. Assn. Indsl. and Tech. Tchrs., Am. Vocat. Assn., Am. Coun. Indsl. Arts Tchr. Edn., Nat. Soc. Study Edn., Phi Kappa Phi, Phi Delta Kappa, Psi Chi, Epsilon Pi Tau. Home: PO Box 3430 Laguna Woods CA 92654-3430 Office: 1250 N Bellflower Blvd Long Beach CA 90840-0006 Personal E-mail: ilathrop@sbcglobal.net.

LATHROP, KAYE DON, nuclear scientist, educator; b. Bryan, Ohio, Oct. 8, 1932; s. Arthur Quay and Helen Venita (Hoos) L.; m. Judith Marie Green, June 11, 1957; children: Braxton Landess, Scottfield Michael. BS, U.S. Mil. Acad., 1955; MS, Calif. Inst. Tech., 1959, PhD, 1962. Staff mem. Los Alamos Sci. Lab., 1962-67; group leader methods devel. Gen. Atomic Co., San Diego, 1967-68; mem. staff Los Alamos Sci. Lab., 1968—72, group leader transport theory, 1972—75, asst. divsn. leader theoretical divsn., 1973—75, assoc. div. leader reactor safeguards and reactor safety and tech. div., 1975-77, alt. div. leader energy div., 1977-78, div. leader computer sci. and svcs. div., 1978-79, assoc. dir. for engring. scis., 1979-84; assoc. lab dir., prof. applied rsch. Stanford Linear Accelerator Ctr. Stanford U., 1984-94, prof. emeritus, 1994—; adminstrv. law judge Atomic Safety and Licensing Bd. Panel, US Nuc. Regulatory Commn., 2006—. Vis. prof. U. N.Mex., 1964-65, adj. prof., 1966-67; guest lectr. IAEA, 1969; adv. com. reactor physics ERDA, 1973-77; reactor physics vis. com. Argonne Nat. Lab., 1978-83; mgmt. adv. com. y-12 divsn. Union Carbide Corp., 1979-82; mem. engring. nat. adv. com. U. Mich., 1983-92; steering com. Joint MIT-Idaho Nat. Engring. Lab. Rsch. Program, 1985-89; external adv. com. Nuc. Tech. and Engring. divsn. Los Alamos Sci. Lab., 1988-93; com. on material control and acctg. for spl. nuc. materials NRC, 1988-89; energy rsch. adv. bd. panel on new prodn. reactor tech. assessment Dept. of Energy, 1988; electric power/energy sys. engring. peer com. NAE, 1992-94, chair, 1994, com. on membership, 1994-97, presdl. nominating com., 1996-97, membership policy com., 1997-99; chair divsn. rev. com. tech. and safety assessment divsn. Los Alamos Nat. Lab., 1994-97, divsn. rev. com. tech. and safety assessment, 1997-99, divsn. rev. com. applied physics divsn., 1997-2005, weapons program rev. com., 2002-04; burn code rev. panel Dept. Energy, 2000-04; mem. U. Calif. Pres.'s Coun. on Nat. Labs., 1995-99, sci. and tech. panel, 1993-99, nat. sec. panel, 1996-99; tech. judge Atomic Safety and Licensing Bd., US NRC, 2006—. Author reports, papers, chpts. to books; mem. editorial adv. bd. Progress in Nuclear Energy, 1983-85 Served to 1st lt. C.E. U.S. Army, 1955-58. Spl. fellow AEC, 1958-61; R.C. Baker Found. fellow, 1961-62; recipient E.O. Lawrence Meml. award ERDA, 1976; Disting. Svc. award Los Alamos Nat. Lab., 1984 Fellow Am. Nuclear Soc. (chmn. math. and computation div. 1970-71, nat. dir. 1973-76, 79-82, treas. 1977-79, Outstanding Performance award 1980); mem. Am. Phys. Soc., Nat. Acad. Engring. Republican. Episcopalian. Home: 190 Cedar Ln E Ridgway CO 81432 E-mail: klathrop@independence.net.

LATHROP, MITCHELL LEE, lawyer; b. LA, Dec. 15, 1937; s. Alfred Lee and Barbara (Mitchell) L.; m. Lynn Mara Dalton; children: Christin Lorraine Newlon, Alexander Mitchell BSc, US Naval Acad., 1959; JD, U. So. Calif., 1966. Bar: DC 1966, Calif. 1966, U.S. Supreme Ct. 1969, NY 1981; cert. arbitrator Nat. Arbitration Forum, ARIAS-US, Chartered Inst. Arbitrators, London; cert. civil trial specialist Nat. Bd. Trial Advocacy; London Ct. Internat. Arbitration. Dep. counsel LA County, Calif., 1966-68; with Brill, Hunt, DeBuys and Burby, LA, 1968-71; ptnr. Macdonald, Halsted & Laybourne, LA and San Diego, 1971-80; sr. ptnr. Rogers & Wells, NYC, San Diego, 1980-86; sr. ptnr., exec. com. Adams, Duque & Hazeltine, LA, San Francisco, NYC, San Diego, 1986-94, firm chmn., 1992-94; sr. ptnr. Luce, Forward, Hamilton & Scripps, San Diego and NYC, 1994—2003; ptnr. Duane Morris LLP, NYC, of counsel San Diego, 2003—. Presiding referee Calif. Bar Ct., 1984-86, mem. exec. com., 1981-88; lectr. law Calif. Judges Assn., Practicing Law Inst. NY, Continuing Edn. of Bar, State Bar Calif., ABA, others. Author: State Hazardous Waste Regulation, 1991, Environmental Insurance Coverage, 1991, Insurance Coverage for Environmental Claims, 1992; mem. editl. bd. Def. Counsel Jour., 1997—, Jour. Ins. Coverage. Western Regional chmn. Met. Opera Nat. Coun., 1971—81, v.p., mem. exec. com., 1971—, now chmn; trustee Honnold Libr. at Claremont Colls., 1972—80; sec. Music Ctr. Opera Assn., 1974—80; v.p. San Diego Opera Assn., 1985—89, pres.-elect, 1993, pres., 1994—96; bd. dirs. Music Ctr. Opera Assn., LA, 1973—80, San Diego Opera Assn., 1980—2003, Met. Opera Assn., NYC, 1971—; mem. adv. bd. Internat. Dominican Found., Rome. Mem.: ABA, Internat. Assn. Def. Counsel, Judge Advocates Assn. (dir. LA chpt. 1974—80, pres. So. Calif. chpt. 1977—78), Am. Bd. Trial Advocates, Assn. So. Calif. Def. Counsel, Am. Intellectual Property Law Assn., Assn. Bus. Trial Lawyers, San Diego County Bar Assn. (chmn. ethics com. 1980—82, bd. dirs. 1982—85, v.p. 1985), DC Bar Assn., Calif. Bar Assn., Fed. Bar Coun., Fed. Bar Assn., NY Bar Assn., S.R. (pres. 1977—79), Calif. Soc., Mensa Internat., Friends Claremont Coll. (dir. 1975—81, pres. 1978—79), Soc. Colonial Wars in Calif. (gov. 1970—72), LA Opera Assocs. (pres. 1970—72), Order St. Lazarus of Jerusalem, Brit. United Svcs. Club (dir. LA 1973—75), Univ. Club, Calif. Club (LA), The Naval Club (London), Met. Club (NYC), Phi Delta Phi. Republican. Office: Duane Morris LLP 101 W Broadway 9th Fl San Diego CA 92101-8285 also: 1540 Broadway New York NY 10036-4086 Office Phone: 212-692-1022. Business E-Mail: mllathrop@duanemorris.com.

LATHROP, THOMAS ALBERT, language educator, publisher; b. LA, Apr. 18, 1941; s. Donald C. and Ethel M. (Challacombe) L.; m. Constance Ellen Cook, Aug. 30, 1969; 1 child, Aline. BA, UCLA, 1964, MA, 1965, PhD, 1970. Mem. faculty Spanish & Portuguese UCLA, 1964-66, U. Wyo., 1966-68, Transylvania U., 1973-76, Lafayette Coll., 1976-80; prof. Romance langs. U. Del., Newark, 1980—. Founding editor Juan de la Cuesta Hispanic Monographs, 1978—; co-editor The Cabrilho Press, 1974-89; pres. Linguatext, Ltd., 1989—; asst. editor Cervantes Bull. of the Cervantes Soc. Am., 1980-90. Author: The Legend of the Siete Infantes de Lara, 1972; (with F. Jensen) The Syntax of the Old Spanish Subjunctive, 1973, La Vie Saint Eustace, 2000; Espanol--Lengua y cultura de hoy, 1974; The Evolution of Spanish, 1980; De Acuerdo! and Tanto Mejor, 1986; (with E Dias) Portugal, Lingua e Cultura, 1978, 2d edit., 1995, Curso de gramatica historica espanola, 1984, 89, (with E. Dias) Brasil: Lingua e Cultura, 2002, student edit. Don Quixote, 1997, Don Quixote translation, 2005, Zola's Therese Raquin (student edition), 2007, Marcel Pagnol's La Gloire de mon pere (student edition) 2007, others; editor: European Classics, 2001-. AID grantee, 1968; Nat. Endowment for Humanities grantee, 1976, 81; Gulbenkian Found. grantee, 1973; Del Amo Found. grantee, 1972. Decorated Order of Don Quijote by Nat. Spanish Honorary, 2006, Orden de Isabel la Catolica by the Casa Real de Espana, 2007. Mem. MLA, Cervantes Soc. Am., Internat. Assn. Hispanists, Am. Coun. on Tchg. of Fgn. Lag., Am. Assn. Tchrs. Spanish and Portuguese. Home: 270 Indian Rd Newark DE 19711-5204 Office Phone: 302-453-8695. Business E-Mail: lathrop@udel.edu.

LATHROPE, DANIEL JOHN, law educator; BSBA, U. Denver, 1973; JD, Northwestern U., Evanston, Ill., 1977; LLM, NYU, 1979. Bar: Ariz. 1977, Calif. 1978. Assoc. Evans, Kitchel & Jenckes, Phoenix, 1977-78; instr. law NYU, 1979-80; assoc. prof. U. Calif. Hastings Coll. Law, San Francisco, 1980-86, prof., 1986—. Assoc. acad. dean U. Calif. Hastings Coll. Law, San Francisco, 1986-87, acting dean, 1987-88, acad. dean, 1988-90, dir. LLM program US legal studies, 2004-07; prof., assoc. dean, dir. grad. tax program U. Fla. Coll. Law, Gainesville, 1995-96. Co-author: (with Lind, Schwarz and Rosenberg) Fundamentals of Corporate Taxation, 6th edit., 2005, Fundamentals of Business Enterprise Taxation, 3d edit., 2005, Fundamentals of Partnership Taxation, 7th edit., 2005; (with Schwarz) Black Letter on Federal Taxation of Corporations and Partnerships, 5th edit., 2005; (with Freeland, Lind and Stephens) Fundamentals of Federal Income Taxation, 14th edit., 2006; (with McNulty) Federal Income Taxation of Individual in a Nutshell, 7th edit., 2004; author: The Alternative Minimum Tax-Compliance and Planning with Analysis, 1994 Mem. Order of Coif, Beta Gamma Sigma. Office Phone: 415-565-4636.

LATIES, VICTOR GREGORY, psychologist, educator; b. Racine, Wis., Feb. 2, 1926; s. Simon Gregory and Rima (Kapnik) L.; m. Martha Ann Fisher, July 29, 1956; children: Nancy, Andrew, Claire. AB, Tufts U., 1949; PhD, U. Rochester, NYC, 1954. Ford Found. teaching intern Brown U., 1954-55; instr., asst. prof. dept. pharmacology Johns Hopkins U. Sch. Medicine, 1955-65; assoc. prof. U. Rochester Sch. Medicine and Dentistry, 1965-71, prof., 1971—, dir. toxicology tng. program, 1978-91, 95-96. Mem. preclinical psychopharmacology research rev. com. NIMH, 1967-71; mem. bd. on toxicology and environ. health hazards Nat. Acad. Sci.-NRC, 1977-80, mem. toxicology info. program com., 1981-85; mem. sci. rev. com. for health research EPA, 1981-89. Editor: Jour. Exptl. Analysis of Behavior, 1972-76, exec. editor, 1966-72, 76—; editor: (with B. Weiss) Behavioral Toxicology, 1975, Behavioral Pharmacology, 1976; mem. editorial bd.: Jour. Pharmacology and Exptl. Therapeutics, 1965-71, Psychopharmacology, 1968-78, 81-89, The Behavior Analyst, 1980-82, Experimental and Clinical Psychopharmacology, 1993-99; contbr. articles to profl. jours. Served with USN, 1944-46. Fellow Am. Psychol. Assn. (pres. div. psychopharmacology 1968-69, div. exptl. analysis of behavior 1979-82, bd. sci. affairs 1983-85), Behavioral Pharmacology Soc. (pres. 1966-68), Am. Soc. Pharmacology and Exptl. Therapeutics, Assn. for Behavior Analysis, Soc. Toxicology, Am. Psychol. Soc., Soc. for Exptl. Analysis of Behavior (sec.-treas. 1966—). Home: 55 Dale Rd E Rochester NY 14625-2137 Office: U Rochester Medical Ctr Dept Environ Medicine Box EHSC Rochester NY 14642

LATIFUR RAHAMAN, RASUL BOAKSH, legal association administrator; b. Kushita, Bangladesh, Jan. 1, 1945; arrived in India, Jan. 3, 1945; s. Fazlur Rahman and Rabya Khatun Ruby Rabia Khatun; married; children: Rassel, Boaksel Diploma, Kushtia Coll., 1963, LLB, 1966; M Commerce, Dhaka U., 1967. Headmaster Talberia HS, Kushtia Dist., 1961; head asst. Indsl. Promo Svcs., Dacca, 1966-67; income tax cons. Bangladesh Bar Assn., Segun Bagicha/Dacca, 1967-69; pres. Kushtia Income Tax Bar Assn., 1970-90, Padma Devel., Kushtia, 1980—. Chmn. Bangladesh Cons., Padma, Kushtia, 1971—; chmn. Cen. Capital, Padma; leader of party/chmn., Bangladesh Internat. Moisen Order Internat. Command Party, Padma, 1980—; chmn. Ctrl. Capital of Bangladesh, Padma, 299100; trade consulate Bangladesh Trade, Padma, 1980—; chmn. Bazar com., Padma. Mem. Pub. Libr., Kushtia, 1965-66. Office: The Income Tax Bar Assn B06000 Kushtia Padma Bangladesh

LATIF-ZADE, ALISHER, composer; b. Dushanbe, Tadjikistan, June 2, 1962; m. Sabrie Belyalova Latif-Zade, Feb. 26, 1988; children: Daler, Tamila. MusM, Moscow State Conservatory, 1985. Admitted to Union of Composers of the USSR, 1985; tchr. composition, orchestra, score reading and theoretical disciplines Kazahk Nat. Kurmangazy Conservatory, Almaty, Tajikistan, 1986—2004, with, 2003—. Organizer, permanent participant Internat. Musical Festivals, 1998, 2003, 04; participant Internat. Silk Road Project, Inc., 2000; initiated by internat. acclaimed cellist Yo-Yo Mama, 2000. Compositions include Al Zikr, Tolerance; compositions include: Dervish's Book; compositions include 1000 and One Seconds in notes, TOJ, Alvidoh, Liber Scriptus, Zimchurud, Cross & Crescent, Oriental minatures, Heaven's Voice, Apocalypse. Mem.: NACUSA, ASCAP, Union Russian Composers, Union Composers Uzbekistan, Tajik-Slavonic U. Cathedra Culturology (hon.). Home: Apt C10 2530 Ocean Ave Brooklyn NY 11229 Personal E-mail: latif-zadeh@hotmail.com.

LATIMER, ALLIE B., retired lawyer; b. Coraopolis, Pa. d. Lawnye S. and Bennie Latimer BS, Hampton Inst.; JD, MDiv, DMin, Howard U.; LLM, Cath. U.; postgrad., Am. U., 1960—61. Bar: N.C. bar 1955, D.C. bar 1960. Vol. in projects Am. Friends Svc. Com., N.J, and Europe, 1948—49; correctional officer Fed. Reformatory for Women, Alderson, W.Va., 1949—51; pers. clk. NIH, Bethesda, 1953—55; realty officer Mitchell AFB, NY, 1955—56; with Office Gen. Counsel, GSA, Washington, 1957—76, chief counsel, 1966—71, asst. gen. counsel, 1971—76, gen. counsel, 1977—87; asst. gen. counsel NASA, 1976—77; spl. counsel Gen. Svcs. Adminstrn., Washington, 1987—96. Past chmn. central office com. Fed. Women's Program, GSA; mem. membership and budget com. Health and Welfare Council, 1967-72 Bd. dirs. D.C. Mental Health Assn., pres., 1977-79; bd. dirs. Friendship House, Washington; elder Presbyn. Ch.; mem. com. on office of Gen. Assembly, Presbyn. Ch. USA; pres. Interacial Council, 1964-75; chmn. Presbyn. Econ. Devel. Corp., 1975-81; mem. governing bd. Nat. Council Chs. of Christ in U.S.A.; bd. trustees Johnson C. Smith Theol. Sem. Recipient GSA Sustained Superior Service award, 1959, Meritorious Svc. award, 1964, Commendable Svc. award, 1964, Pub. Svc. award, 1971, Outstanding Performance award, 1971, Presdl. Rank awards, 1983, 95, Disting. Svc. award, 1984. Mem. ABA, Nat. Bar Assn. (sec. 1962-74, Hall of Fame award 1999), Fed. Bar Assn., Washington Bar Assn. (Ollie M. Cooper award 1998, Hall of Fame award 2004, pres.'s vol. award 2007, Hall of Fame Legacy award for Law 2007), N.C. Bar Assn., Nat. Bar Found. (dir. 1970-71, pres. 1974-75), Hampton Alumni Assn. (pres. Washington chpt. 1970-71), Howard Law Alumni Assn. (v.p. alumni assns. 1962-63), Links (pres. Washington chpt. 1971-74, nat. v.p. 1976-80, gen. counsel 1970-80), Federally Employed Women (co-founder, 1st pres.). Home: 3050 Military Rd NW #520 Washington DC 20015-1364

LATIMER, JAMES HAROLD, musician, conductor, composer, music educator; b. Tulsa, June 27, 1934; s. Major Sylvester and Maria Louise (Wilson) L. MusB, Ind. U., 1956; MusM, Boston U., 1964; postgrad., Harvard U., 1968. Instr., asst. dir. bands Fla. A&M U., Tallahassee, 1957-62; freelance performer Boston, 1963-68; prof. music-percussion U. Wis., Madison, 1968-99; music dir. Wis. Youth Symphony Orchs., Madison, 1972-78. Timpanist Madison Symphony Orch., 1968-99; clinician Ludwig Industries, Chgo., 1971-99; condr. Capitol City Band, Madison, 1981—; marimbist Madison Marimba Quartet, 1982-; Fulbright lectr. Cairo Conservatoire, 1984-85; Commonwealth vis. prof. Radford (Va.) U., 1985-87. Percussionist Boston Pops Orch., 1968-74; contbr. Inquiring About Communities, 1971; composer, arranger various titles for percussion and bands. Mem. ASCAP, Percussive Arts Soc., Am. Fedn. Musicians, Wis. Federated Music Club (hon. life mem.), Rotary (Madison chpt.), Phi Mu Alpha, Kappa Kappa Psi, Phi Beta (hon.). Mem. Soc. Of Friends. Avocations: amateur radio, electronics, woodworking, collecting. Business E-Mail: jhlatime@wisc.edu.

LATIMER, KATHARINE RUTH, lawyer; b. Lafayette, La., Apr. 5, 1961; d. Ewing Craig and Beverly Elise (Dalferes) L. BA magna cum laude, U. Tenn., 1983; JD cum laude, Georgetown U., 1986. Bar: DC 1986, US Dist. Ct., Md., DC, US Ct. Appeals, Third Cir., Fourth Cir., Sixth Cir., Seventh Cir., Eighth Cir., Ninth Cir., Tenth Cir., Eleventh Cir. Jud. clk. 19th Jud. Cir. Va., Fairfax, 1986-87; assoc. then ptnr. Spriggs & Hollingsworth, Washington, 1987—. Consulting editor, adv. mem. Expert Evidence Reporter; mem. Toxic Tort Adv. Coun. Recipient Nat. Law Jour. Top Defense Verdict, 1998, 2000, 2001. Mem. ABA (litig. sect.), DRI, Bar Assn. DC Office: Spriggs & Hollingsworth 1350 I St NW Washington DC 20005-3399 Office Phone: 202-898-5800. Office Fax: 202-682-1639. Business E-Mail: klatimer@spriggs.com.

LATIMER, KENNETH ALAN, lawyer; b. Chgo., Oct. 26, 1943; s. Edward and Mary (Schiller) L.; m. Carole Ross, June 23, 1968; children: Cary, Darren, Wendy. BS, U. Wis., 1966; JD with honors, George Washington U., 1969. Bar: D.C. 1969, Ill. 1970. Atty. U.S. Office of Comptroller, Washington, 1969-70; assoc. Berger, Newmark & Fenchel, Chgo., 1970-74, ptnr., 1975-86, Holleb & Coff, Chgo., 1986-99, Duane, Morris LLP, Chgo., 1999—. Guest speaker Ill. Inst. for Continuing Legal Edn., Chgo., 1975-87; lectr. Banking Law Inst., 1996—. Pres. North Suburban Jewish Cmty. Ctr., Highland Park, Ill., 1985; bd. dirs. Jewish Cmty. Ctrs. Chgo., 1985-95. Mem. ABA Fellows, Ill. Bar Assn. (chmn. sect. coun. on comml. banking and bankruptcy 1990-91), ABA (com. on banking and comml. finance), Chgo. Bar Assn. (com. on fin. instns.), Comml. Fin. Assn. Edn. Found. (founders coun.), Assn. Comml. Fin. Attys., Am Coll. Comml. Fin Attys.(bd. regents), Standard Club. Avocations: jogging, travel. Office: Duane Morris LLP 227 W Monroe St Ste 3400 Chicago IL 60606-5098 Home Phone: 847-433-8116; Office Phone: 312-499-6730. E-mail: kalatimer@duanemorris.com.

LATIMER, STEPHEN MARK, lawyer; b. Bklyn., July 15, 1939; s. Ted and Martha (Goldberg) L.; m. Judith R. Shulman, June 3, 1964 (dec. Mar. 29, 1984); 1 child, Gary. BA, Tufts U., 1961; JD, NYU, 1968. Bar: N.Y. 1968, N.J. 1979, U.S. Dist. Ct. (so. dist.) N.Y. 1970, U.S. Dist. Ct. (ea. dist.) N.Y. 1972, U.S. Dist. Ct. N.J. 1979, U.S. Dist. Ct. (we. dist.) N.Y. 1984, U.S. Dist. Ct. (no. dist.) Tex. 1992, U.S. Ct. Appeals (2d cir.) 1974, U.S. Ct. Appeals (3rd cir.) 1981, U.S. Ct. Appeals (5th cir.) 1986, U.S. Supreme Ct. 1975, U.S. Dist. Ct. (we. dist.) Tex. 2002. Clk. Burke & Parsons, NYC, 1966-67; mng. clk. Otterbourg, Steindler, Houston & Rosen, NYC, 1967-68, assoc., 1968-69, Halpern, Schivitz, Scholer and Steingut, NYC, 1969-71; dir. supervised pre-trial release project N.Y. Lawyers Com. for Civil Rights Under Law, NYC, 1972-73; dir. cmty. devel. and law reform Bronx Legal Svcs., NYC, 1973-79, acting mng. atty., 1974; dir. litigation Camden (N.J.) Regional Legal Svcs., Inc., 1979-81, acting dir., 1981-82; statewide litigation coord. Legal Svcs. of N.J., New Brunswick, 1982-84; sr. litigation atty. Prisoners' Legal Svcs. of N.Y., NYC, 1984-94; asst. dep. pub. defender N.J. Pub. Defender, Newark, 1994-95; ptnr. Loughlin & Latimer, Hackensack, N.J., 1995—. Lectr. Rutgers U. Law Sch., 1975-90. Contbr. articles to profl. jours. Trustee ACLU of N.J., 1982-2001, exec. com. 1984-99, N.J. Assn. Correction, 1986—, Planned Parenthood of Middlesex County, 1981-85. Lt. USN, 1961-66, USNR, 1966-68. Instr. U.S. Marine Acad., Kings Point, N.Y., 1964-66. Mem. N.J. Bar Assn. (vice chmn. individual rights 1998-99, chmn. individual rights, 1999-2001), UN Assn. USA (bd. dirs. NJ divsn. 2005—, co-chair human rights and humanitarian assistance com. 2005—, Roger Baldwin award, 2006). Home: 120 Floyd Ave Bloomfield NJ 07003-5610 Office: Loughlin & Latimer 131 Main St Hackensack NJ 07601-7140 Office Phone: 201-487-9797. Personal E-mail: slatimer@mindspring.com.

LATIOLAIS, MINNIE FITZGERALD, retired nurse, health facility administrator; b. Dec. 26, 1921; d. Thomas Ambrose and Mildred Surita (Nagle) Fitzgerald; m. Joseph C. Latiolais Jr., July 19, 1947; children: Felisa, Diana, Sylvia, Mary, Amelia, Joseph Clifton III. RN La. Asst. night supr. Touro Infirmary, New Orleans, 1943; orthopaedic surg. nurse Ochsner Clinic, New Orleans, 1943-47; asst. DON Ochsner Found. Hosp., 1947; supr. Lafayette (La.) Gen. Hosp., 1960-64; adminstrv. asst., supr. oper. rm. Abbeville (La.) Gen. Hosp., 1964-68; gen. mgr., neurol. surg. nurse J. Robert Rivet, neurol. surgeon, Lafayette, 1968-78; hosp. cons. assoc. B.J. Landry & Assocs.; hosps. cons. Lafayette, 1979-90; DON Acadia St. Landry Hosp., Church Point, 1981-82; supr. supplies, processing and distbn. Univ. Med. Ctr., Lafayette, 1982-90, ret. 1990. Pres. SW La. Rehab. Assn., 1979-80; mem. Mid-La. Health Systems Agy., 1977-82, project rev. chmn., 1978-80; vice chmn. Acadica Regional Clearing House, 1984-86; mem. crafts and practical nurse com. Lafayette Regional Vocat.-Tech. Inst., 1980-84, chmn. 1983-84. Roman Catholic.

LA TORRE, CARISSA DANITZA, counselor; d. Luis Francisco and Elia Danitza La Torre. AA in Spanish, Saddleback C.C., Mission Viejo, Calif., 1995, AA in Psychology, 1995, AA in Bus. Adminstrn., 2002; BA in Spanish, Calif. State U., Fullerton, 1998, BA in Psychology, 1998, MS in Edn., 2000. Lic. Behavior Modification Case Mgr./Specialist Calif., 1999, cert. Specialist Mild/Moderate/Severe Disabilities Calif., 1999, Multiple Subject Calif., 1999, Single Subject Calif., 1999. Educator Capistrano Unified Sch. Dist., San Juan Capistrano, Calif., 1997—99; bilingual grad. rschr. UCLA/Calif. State U., 1998—2003; office/human resource mgr. GlobalStar Electronics, Inc., Aliso Viejo, Calif., 2002—03; birth mother counselor Adoption Network Law Ctr., Inc., Lake Forest, Calif., 2003—. Presenter in field of infant devel. Rep. and spkr. MADD, Tustin, Calif., 1996—; youth group ministry leader Mission San Juan Capistrano, 2001—. Recipient Dedication and Svc. in Counseling award, Outreach Concern, Inc., 1997, 1998. Mem.: Coun. Children with Behavioral Disorders (assoc. presenter internat. conf. 2001), Divsn. Early Childhood (assoc. presenter internat. confs. 2000—01), Harley Owners' Group (life), Phi Kappa Phi (life), Zeta Tau Alpha (life; pres. and v.p. 1995—97). Office Phone: 800-455-6055, 800-455-6055. Personal E-mail: xclatorre@collegeclub.com. Business E-Mail: carissal@adoptionnetwork.com.

LATOURETTE, AUDREY WOLFSON, law educator; d. Benjamin and Ann Wolfson; m. John Latourette, May 26, 1974; 1 child, Joshua W. BA magna cum laude, Rutgers U., 1968; MA, Rowan U., 1971; JD cum laude, Temple U., 1975. Bar: N.J. 1975, Pa. 1975, Supreme Ct. of NJ. 1975, U.S. Dist. Ct. (ea. dist.) Pa. 1975. Tchr. elem. sch. Pennsauken (N.J.) Pub. Schs., 1968—72; atty. Wolf, Block, Schorr & Solis-Cohen, Phila., 1975—77, Audrey Wolfson Latourette, Esq., sole practitioner, Woodbury, NJ, 1977—83; prof. bus. law Richard Stockton Coll. N.J., Pomona, NJ, 1977—. Mem. dean's external adv. coun. Rutgers U., 1999—2003; presenter in field. Editor: Temple Law Quar., 1974—75; contbr. chapters to books, articles to profl. jours. Judge Nat. Mock Trial Competition, Phila., 2005; mem. Pa. parents vol. program U. Pa., Phila., 2004—07; mem. adv. panel affordable housing Mayor, Cherry Hill, NJ, 1988—94; mem. Sch. Age Child Care Com., Cherry Hill, 1986—87; bd. dirs. Italian Lang. Preservation Found., Phila., 2000—05. Named one of Five Notable Faculty, Richard Stockton Coll. N.J., 2005; named to Hall Finest Alumni, Rutgers U., 2006; recipient Sadie and Nathan Kessler award, Temple U. Sch. Law, 1973, Barenkopf award, 1973, Am. Jurisprudence Criminal Law, Adminstrv. Law and Constl. Law award, 1975, Merit award, Richard Stockton Coll. N.J., 1986, Outstanding Svc. award, Rutgers U., Camden, 2003, Best Paper award, McGraw Hill, 2006; fellow, Richard Stockton Found., 1989, 1992, 1996; grantee, Richard Stockton Coll. N.J., 1979, 1981, 1987, 1986, 1988, 1993—94, 1996, 2004, 2006, NJ Dept. Higher Edn., 1985; scholar, Faculty Resource Network, NYU, 2004—05, 2007; Provost Faculty grant, 2006. Mem.: N.E. Acad. Legal Studies in Bus. (pres. 1989—90, co-editor Jour. Legal Studies 1992—95, u. assoc. 2007—, Best Paper award 1994, 2005, 2007). Office: Richard Stockton College of New Jersey PO Box 195 Pomona NJ 08240-0195 Office Phone: 609-652-4426. Business E-Mail: audrey.latourette@stockton.edu.

LATOURETTE, STEVEN C., congressman; b. Cleve., July 22, 1954; 5 children. BA in Hist., U. Mich., 1976; JD, Cleve. State U. Marshall Coll. Law, 1979. Asst. pub. defender Lake County, Ohio, 1980-83, prosecutor Ohio, 1987—94; assoc. Cannon, Stern, Aveni & Krivok, Painesville, 1983-86; with Baker, Hackenberg & Collins, Painesville, 1986-88; mem. US Congress from 14th Ohio dist., 1994—, mem. US Holocaust Meml. Coun., 1995—, mem. transp. and infrastructure com., ranking mem. subcommittee on Coast Guard and maritime transp., mem. fin. svcs. com. Bd. dirs. Regional Forensic Lab.; bd. trustees Cleve. Police Hist. Soc. Recipient Anchor award, Nat. Credit Union Found., 1998, Consumers Choice award, Credit Union Nat. Assn., 1998, Leading Light of Long-Term Care award, Am. Health Care Assn., 2005. Mem.: Ohio Prosecuting Attys. Assn., Nat. Dist. Attys. Assn. Republican. Methodist. Office: 1 Victoria Pl Rm 320 Painesville OH 44077 Office Phone: 202-225-5731, 440-352-3939.*

LATOURRETTE, JAMES THOMAS, retired electrophysics, electrical engineering and computer science educator; b. Miami, Ariz., Dec. 26, 1931; s. Emery Everest and Carrie D. (Hoffman) LaT.; m. Muriel Ashe,

Aug. 28, 1955; children: Mary Beth, John Emery, James Thomas, Joanne. BS, Calif. Inst. Tech., 1953; MA (Gen. Communication Co. fellow), Harvard U., 1954, PhD (NSF fellow), 1958. Rsch. assoc., lectr. physics Harvard U., 1957-59; physicist Gen. Electric Research Lab., Schenectady, 1960-62; sr. supervisory scientist TRG, Inc., Melville, NY, 1962-66; sect. head TRG div. Control Data Corp., Melville, 1966-67; prof. electrophysics, elec. engring. and computer sci. Poly. U. (formerly Poly. Inst. Bklyn. and Poly. Inst. N.Y.), Farmingdale, NY, 1967—93, prof. emeritus, 1993. Assoc. dir. Weber Rsch. Inst., Poly. U., 1987-90. Contbr. articles to profl. jours. NSF postdoctoral fellow Physikalisches Institut der U. Bonn, Germany, 1959-60 Mem. IEEE, Sigma Xi, Tau Beta Pi. Home: 2 Candlewood Ct Huntington NY 11743-1827 Personal E-mail: j.latourrette@ieee.org.

LATSON, RICHARD CHARLES, retired audio-visual specialist; b. Nov. 13, 1947; s. Robert Lee and Ruby (Kent) Latson; m. Sherilyn Day (div.). BA in Radio and TV Comm., Tex. Tech U., 1970. Radio-TV broadcaster, 1967-70; TV prodn. specialist Naval Acad., Annapolis, Md., 1974-79; mgr. TV prodn. Walter Reed Army Med. Ctr., Washington, 1979-87; audio visual mgmt. officer Dept. Army, Washington, 1987-90; mgr. audio visual prodn. and distbn. program Dept. Def., Alexandria, Va., 1990—2002. Mem. fed. audiovisual com. Office Mgmt. and Budget, Washington, 1990—96; U.S. judge Internat. Mil. Film Festival, Argentina, 1998, Bracciano, Italy, 2001, Bracciano, 03, U.S. del., Rome, 1998; mgr. DoD Audiovisual Prodn. Awards Program, 1998—2002; judge Clarion Awards-Assn. Women in Comm., 2002, 03. Mem. NATO Mil. Audiovisual Working Group, Joint Svcs. Adv. Group Advanced Distributed Learning, 1995—2002; judge U.S. Army Audiovisual Prodn. Competition, 2000, 2001, 2002, USN Audiovisual Prodn. Competition, 2001. 1st lt. USAF, 1970—74. Decorated Air Force commendation medal; recipient medal for exceptional civilian svc., Office of Sec. of Def. Mem.: English-Speaking Union, Brit. & Commonwealth Soc. N.Am. (past pres.), Internat. Imaging Industry Assn. (stds. mgmt. bd. 1992—2002), Am. Nat. Stds. Inst. (image tech. stds. bd. 1990—98, info. sys. stds. bd. 1990—2002). Avocations: old time radio programs, big band music, collecting art. Home: 3364 Gleneagles Dr Apt 1E Silver Spring MD 20906

LATTA, DIANA LENNOX, retired interior designer; b. Lahaina, Maui, Hawaii, Aug. 5, 1936; d. D. Stewart and Jean Marjorie (Anderson) Lennox; m. Arthur McKee Latta, Jan. 26, 1957 (dec.); children: Mary-Stewart, Marion McKee Davidson. Grad., The Bishop's Sch., La Jolla, Calif., 1954; student, U. Wash., Seattle, 1954—56. Dir. Vero Beach (Fla.) br. of Wellington Hall Ltd., Thomasville, NC, 1970—72; asst. to chief designer Rablen-West Interiors, Vero Beach, 1972—75; design and adminstrv. asst. to pres. Design Studio Archtl. & Interior Design Concepts, Inc., Vero Beach, 1975—82; owner, designer The Designery, Vero Beach, 1983—87; designer's asst. Frank J. Lincoln Interiors, Inc., Vero Beach, Locust Valley, NY, 1987—90; sr. staff designer Chancellor's Inc., Bellingham, Wash., 1992—93. Leading actress (Vero Beach Theatre Guild prodns) The Laughmaker, 1964, Oklahoma, 1966, model Holly Fashion Show, Vero Beach, 1962—69. Mem. Indian River Meml. Hosp. Women's Aux., Vero Beach, 1957—70, chmn. charity ball and gift shop, 1960, v.p., 1962—64; advisor to steering com. The Malt Shoppe After-Sch. Program, Mill Creek, 1995—97; mem. coun. Snohomish County Federated Health and Safety Network, 1999—2003; founding mem. Indian River Land Trust, Vero Beach, 1989—90; chmn. Mill Creek for Youth Com., 1994; bd. dir. and chmn. hospitality com. Vero Beach Mut. Concert Assn., 1973—76; mem. adv. bd. Indian River 4-H Horsemaster's Club, 1973—76; founding mem. McKee Jungle Gardens Preservation Soc., Inc., 1988—89, treas. bd. dir., chmn. fundraising com., pub. rels. com., 1988; bd. dir. Vero Beach Theatre Guild, 1964; mem. adv. com. Safe and Drug Free Schs. Edmonds Sch. Dist., Wash., 1996—2002; mem. key leaders bd. Cmtys. That Care Project Edmonds Sch. Dist., 2001—. Mem.: Internat. Platform Assn., Riomar Bay Yacht Club (chmn. tennis com. 1964—66, club tennis champion 1964, 1966), Kappa Kappa Gamma (founding mem. Indian River Alumnae Club 1968—90, mem. adv. bd. U. Wash., Seattle chpt. 1997—2000, founding mem. N. Sound Alumnae Assn. 2002—). Republican. Episcopalian. Home: 16018 Village Green Dr # B Mill Creek WA 98012-5874

LATTA, GEORGE HAWORTH, III, neonatal/perinatal nurse practitioner; b. Chattanooga, Sept. 4, 1960; s. George Haworth Jr. and Charlotte (Major) L. BS in Physics, Ga. Inst. Tech., 1982; MD, East Tenn. State U., 1986. Cert. in pediat., neonatology. Intern, resident in pediat. Dartmouth (N.H.) U., 1986-88; resident in pediat. Stanford (Calif.) U., 1988-89; fellow in neonatology Vanderbilt U., Nashville, 1989-90, U. Tenn., Memphis, 1990-92; attending neonatologist Rose Med. Ctr., Denver, 1992-94, Forrest Gen. Hosp., Hattiesburg, Miss., 1994-95, Meth. Hosps., Memphis, 1995-99; neontalogist Intermountain Healthcare, Provo, Utah, 2000—05, Children's Hosp. Ctrl. Calif., Madera, 2006—, Kaweah Delta Hosp., 2007—. NIH pulmonary trainee grantee Vanderbilt U., 1989; March of Dimes scholar East Tenn. State U., 1984, Johnny J. Jones scholar, 1981. Fellow: Am. Acad. Pediat.; mem.: Wildnerness Med. Soc., Phi Eta Sigma. Roman Catholic. Avocations: skiing, camping, jazz, aquariums, scuba diving. Personal E-mail: ghlatta3@comcast.net. Business E-Mail: uvglatta@ihc.com.

LATTA, THOMAS ALBERT, lawyer; b. Tulsa, Nov. 3, 1931; s. Albert Lloyd and Myrtle Irene (Lay) L.; m. Shirley Elaine Glauser, June 20, 1965 (div. 1985); children: Thomas Albert, John Montgomery, Shannon Elaine. Student, Carnegie Mellon U., 1949-52; BA, U. Tex., 1955; JD, U. Tulsa, 1959. Bar: Okla. 1959, Ariz. 1964, D.C. 1965, Calif. 1974. Atty. U.S. Dept. Justice, 1960, Securities and Exchange Commn., 1961—64; pvt. practice San Francisco, 1974, Phoenix, 1975; dir., shareholder Wentworth & Lundin, P.A., Phoenix, 1975-86, San Francisco, 1980-84; of counsel Whitehead & Porter LLP, San Francisco, 1997—2006; pvt. practice Sausalito, 2006—. Mem. Ariz. Bd. Accountancy, Phoenix, 1979-83. Capt. JAGC, US Army, 1959-60. Avocations: sailing, flying. Home Phone: 415-887-9268. Personal E-mail: tomlatta@earthlink.net.

LATTANZI, GREGORY DENIS, archaeologist; b. Freeport, NY, Feb. 26, 1969; s. Denis Stephan Lattanzi and Geraldine Paradiso; m. Haviva M. Goldman, Oct. 13, 1996; 1 child, Denis Ethan. BA, SUNY, Binghamton, 1991; Masters, CUNY, 1995. Registered profl. archaeologist. Registrar N.J. State Mus., Trenton, 2001—. Recipient Appreciation award, Archaeological Soc. for N.J., 2004. Mem.: Soc. Am. Archaeology (assoc.), Mid. Atlantic Archaeol. Conf. (assoc.), Ea. State Archaeology Fedn. (assoc.; webmaster 2005—06), Archaeol. Soc. N.J. (life; v.p. 1999—2005). Liberal. Jewish. Home: 135 W Gravers Ln Philadelphia PA 19118 Office: NJ State Mus PO Box 530 Trenton NJ 08625 Home Phone: 215-242-5622; Office Phone: 609-984-9327. Business E-Mail: gregory.lattanzi@sos.state.nj.us.

LATTANZIO, STEPHEN PAUL, astronomy educator; b. Yonkers, NY, June 29, 1949; s. Anthony Raymond and Anella Lattanzio; children: Gregory Paul, Timothy Paul. BA in Astronomy, U. Calif., Berkeley, 1971; MA in Astronomy, UCLA, 1973, postgrad., 1973-75. Planetarium lectr. Griffith Obs., Los Angeles, 1973-75; instr. astronomy El Camino Coll., Torrance, Calif., 1974-75; planetarium lectr. Valley Coll., Los Angeles, 1975; prof. astronomy Orange Coast Coll., Costa Mesa, Calif., 1975—, planetarium dir., 1975—. Mem. adv. commn. Natural History Mus. Orange County, Calif., 2006—; scientific advisor instructional TV series Astronomy: Observations & Theories, 2004—. Contbr. articles to profl. jours. Mem. Astron. Soc. Pacific, The Planetary Soc., Sigma Xi (assoc.), Phi Beta Kappa. Avocation: astronautics. Office: Orange Coast Coll 2701 Fairview Rd Costa Mesa CA 92626-5563 E-mail: slattanzio@cccd.edu.

LATTIMER, GARY LEE, physician; b. Nanticoke, Pa., Dec. 4, 1939; s. Paul Floyd and Gene Elizabeth L.; m. Patricia Sara Weise, June 14, 1958; children: Toni Jo, Gregory Weise. MD, Temple U., 1966; postgrad., Jefferson Med. Coll., 1970-72. Intern Allentown (Pa.) Hosp.; resident Presbyn.-Univ. Hosp., Phila., 1969-70, Jefferson Med. Coll. Hosp., Phila., 1970-71, chief med. resident, 1971-72; chief infectious diseases Allentown-Sacred Heart Hosp. Center, 1972-80; assoc. prof. medicine U. N.D., 1980-81, chief infectious diseases, 1980-81, New Britain (Conn.) Gen. Hosp., 1981—; assoc. prof. medicine U. Conn., 1981-83; dir. infectious diseases Williamsport Hosp., Divine Providence Hosp., 1983—. Author: Legionnaires' Disease, 1981; contbr. articles to profl. jours. Served with M.C. U.S. Army, 1967-69. Decorated Bronze Star; recipient Disting. Service award Pa. chpt. Am. Legion. Fellow ACP; mem. Am. Soc. Microbiology, AAAS, Nat. Found. Infectious Diseases, Am. Legion. Office: 17 Durban Pl Hilton Head Island SC 29926-2217 Personal E-mail: garylatt@roadrunner.com.

LATTIMORE, STEVEN, classicist, educator; b. Bryn Mawr, Pa., May 25, 1938; s. Richmond and Alice Bockstahler Lattimore; m. Deborah Lee Nourse, July 14, 1976 (div. July 1994); children: Judith, Nicholas, Isabel. BA, Dartmouth Coll., 1960; MA, Princeton U., 1964, PhD, 1968. Instr. Dartmouth Coll., Hanover, NH, 1964, Haverford Coll., Pa., 1965—66; asst. prof. Intercollegiate Ctr. Classical Studies, Rome, 1966—67, U. Calif., LA, 1967—74, assoc. prof., 1974—98, prof., 1998—2006, prof. emeritus, 2006—. Author: Marine Thiasos in Greek Sculpture, 1976, Isthmia Marble Sculpture 1967-1980, 1996; translator: Thucydides, Peloponnesian War, 1998. Fellow, John Simon Guggenheim Meml. Found., 1975—76. Mem.: German Archaeol. Inst. (elected), Am. Philogical Assn., Archaeol. Inst. Am. Avocations: travel, hiking. Address: 1146 Say Rd Santa Paula CA 93060

LATTMAN, LAURENCE HAROLD, retired academic administrator; b. NYC, Nov. 30, 1923; s. Jacob and Yetta (Schwartz) L.; m. Hanna Renate Cohn, Apr. 12, 1946; children— Martin Jacob, Barbara Diane. BSChemE, Coll. City N.Y., 1948; MS in Geology, U. Cin., 1951, PhD, 1953. Instr. U. Mich., 1952-53; asst. head photogeology sect. Gulf Oil Corp., Pitts., 1953-57; asst. prof. to prof. geomorphology Pa. State U., 1957-70; prof., head dept. geology U. Cin., 1970-75; dean Coll. of Mines U. Utah, 1975-83, dean Coll. Engring., 1978-83; pres. N.Mex. Tech., Socorro, 1983-93, pres. emeritus, 1993—. Bd. dirs. Pub. Svc. Co. of N.Mex.; cons. U.S. Army Engrs., Vicksburg, Miss., 1965-69, also major oil cos. Author: (with R.G. Ray) Aerial Photographs in Field Geology, 1965, (with D. Zillman) Energy Law; Contbr. articles to profl. jours. Mem. N.Mex. Environ. Improvement Bd., 1995-2002. With AUS, 1943-46. Fenneman fellow, U. Cin., 1953. Fellow Geol. Soc. Am.; mem. Am. Assn. Petroleum Geologists, Am. Soc. Photogrammetry (Ford Bartlett award 1968), Soc. Econ. Paleontologists and Mineralogists, AIME (Disting. mem. 1981, Mineral Industries Edn., award 1986—), Assn. Western Univs. (chmn. bd. dirs. 1986-87), Sigma Xi. Home: 11509 Penfield Ln NE Albuquerque NM 87111-6526 Personal E-mail: lhlattman@comcast.net.

LATTO, LEWIS M., broadcast executive; b. Duluth, Minn., Jan. 21, 1940; s. Lewis M. and Ethel S. L.; divorced; children: Aaron, Caroline. BA, U. Minn., 1963. Owner, mgr. Sta. KXTP, Duluth, 1965-94, Sta. WAKX-FM, 1974-94; owner Sta. KRBT-AM, WEVE-FM, Eveleth, Minn., 1978—, Sta. KGPZ-FM, Grand Rapids, Minn., 1995—. Mem. Duluth City Council, 1969-75, pres., 1974. Mem. Nat. Radio Broadcasters Assn. (dir.), Minn. Broadcasters Assn. (pres. 1992-93). Republican. Methodist. Office: Northland Radio Stas 5732 Eagle View Dr Duluth MN 55803-9498 E-mail: lewlatto@aol.com.

LATZA, WILLIAM D., lawyer; b. Neb., May 28, 1955; BS with distinction, U. Neb., Lincoln, 1977; JD, Georgetown U., 1981. Grad. fellow London Sch. Econ. and Polit. Sci; adminstrv. ptnr, insurance practice area Stroock & Stroock & Lavan LLP, NYC. Frequent writer, lectr. in field. Mem.: ABA, Internat. Assn. Insurance Receivers (legal counsel), Insurance Regulatory Examiners Soc., Soc. Fin. Examiners (gen. counsel), NY County Lawyers Assn., Internat. Bar Assn. (sec. on bus. law, com. on insurance), NY State Bar Assn. (insurance, negligence, compensation law sect.), Assn. Bar City NY (com. on insurance law 1998—2001), Omicron Delta Epsilon, Beta Gamma Sigma. Office: Stroock & Stroock & Lavan LLP 180 Maiden Ln New York NY 10038-4982 Office Phone: 212-806-5807. Office Fax: 212-806-6006. Business E-Mail: wlatza@strooc.com.

LAU, BOBBY WAI-MAN, marketing professional, investment advisor; b. Hong Kong, Dec. 24, 1944; s. Nelson and Ruby (Choy) L.; m. Sharon Tsai. BS in Math., U. Calif., Davis, 1969, MA in Math., 1971; postgrad. in math., Calif. Inst. Tech.; postgrad. in math and computers, UCLA, 1972-75. Ins. agt. Equitable Life Assurance Soc. of U.S., LA, 1975-80, sr. dist. mgr., 1980-90; pres. Bobby Lau Seminars for Profls., 1979—. Chmn. bd. dirs. Success Mortgage & Ins. Svcs. Corp., 1990—; dir. Fin. Depot Inc. Contbr. articles to mags. and newspapers. Office: 9110 Las Tunas Dr Temple City CA 91780 Home Phone: 626-215-8721; Office Phone: 626-292-7777. Personal E-mail: bobbylauusa@hotmail.com.

LAU, CONSTANCE H. (CONNIE LAU), electric power industry executive; b. Honolulu; 3 children. BS, Yale Univ.; JD, Univ. Calif. Hastings Coll. Law; MBA, Stanford Univ. With Hawaiian Elec. Industries, Honolulu, 1984—99; treas. Hawaiian Elec. Industries, Hawaiian Elec. Co., 1989—99; fin. v.p., CFO HEI Power Corp.; sr. exec. vice-pres., COO Am. Savings Bank, 1999—2001, pres., CEO, 2001—, Hawaiian Elec. Industries, Honolulu, 2006—. Mem. bd. Punahou Sch., Kamehameha Sch., Charles Reed Bishop Trust, Alexander & Baldwin Inc. Named one of 25 Most Powerful Women in Banking, US Banker, 2006. Mem.: Maunalani Found., Hawaii Bus. Roundtable, Hawaiian Bankers Assn. Office: Hawaiian Elec Industries Bldg 1 900 Richards St Honolulu HI 96813 Office Phone: 800-272-2566.*

LAU, EUGENE WING IU, lawyer; b. Canton, China, Sept. 23, 1931; came to US, 1939; s. Eugene K. F. and Ann (Leung) L.; m. Dierdre Florence, July 20, 1962; children: Elyse M., Jennifer M. AB, U. Mich., 1953; LLB, Yale U., 1960. Bar: Hawaii 1960, U.S. Supreme Ct. 1965. Dep. Pros. Attys. Office, Honolulu, 1960-63; pvt. practice Honolulu, 1963-67, 73—; v.p. Hawaii Corp., Honolulu, 1967-73. Del. People to People Legal Del. to China, 1987; mem. Commn. on Manpower and Full Employment, Honolulu, 1965-67. With U.S. Army, 1954-55. Mem. ABA, Hawaii Bar Assn., Punahou Tennis Club (Honolulu). Home: 3079 La Pietra Cir Honolulu HI 96815-4736 Home Phone: 808-923-9760; Office Phone: 808-545-3622. E-mail: EL923@aol.com.

LAU, H. LORRIN, obstetrician, gynecologist; b. Honolulu, Apr. 21, 1932; s. Henry S. and Helen (Lee) L.; m. Maureen Lau; children: David, Marianne, Mike, Mark, Linda. AB cum laude, Harvard U., 1950-54; MD, Johns Hopkins U., 1954-58, MPH, 1970-71. Asst. prof. Sch. Med. Johns Hopkins U. (Balt.), 1964-82; assoc. prof. U. Hawaii, 1982-84; chief ob-gyn. St. Francis West Hosp., Honolulu, 1990-92, Kuakini Hosp., Honolulu, 1994-95. Fellow AMA; mem. ACOG, Internat. Soc. Biology and Medicine. Inventor pregnancy tests, helped introduce alpha-fetoprotein tests into obstetrics in USA, 1971. Home: 1121 Wilder Ave 1700B Honolulu HI 96822 Office: 1010 S King St Honolulu HI 96814-1701 Office Phone: 808-596-0164. Personal E-mail: drhllau@yahoo.com.

LAU, JENNY KWOK WAH, theater educator, consultant, film educator, consultant; arrived in U.S.A., 1979; d. Wai-Wing and Yau-Ying L.; children: Daniel, Esther. BSc in Physics, U. Hong Kong, 1976; MA in Mass Comm., Bowling Green State U., Ohio, 1981; PhD in Cinema Studies, Northwestern U., 1989. Lectr. dept. T.V. and film Hong Kong Bapt. Coll., 1983-85, asst. prof., 1990-91; vis. prof. dept. radio, T.V., film Northwestern U., 1991-92; asst. prof. Ohio U., 1992-96, assoc. prof. sch. film, 1997; assoc. prof. cinema dept. San Francisco State U., 2005—. Radio culture critic Radio Hong Kong, 1983-86; prodr., dir. Sta. 32, Chgo., 1988-89; spkr. in field; presenter numerous confs. Contbr. articles to books and profl. jours.; creator numerous exptl. films. Recipient Best Short Film Award PBS, Chgo., Boston, 1990, Baker Award, 1995; grantee for Libr. Acquisition, 1992-93, Hong Kong Office Econ. Trade, 1995, for Devel. of Web Based Courses in Film, 1997, Coll. Fine Arts, 1997, David C. Lam Inst. for East West Studies, 1998. Mem. Hong Kong Film Scholar Assn., Soc. Cinema Studies (co-chair Asian-Asian Pacific caucus, exec. coun. mem.). Achievements include being the first Chinese national (men or women) to receive a PhD degree in Cinema Studies. Avocations: singing, piano, photography, films, debates with friends. Office: San Francisco State U Cinema Dept San Francisco CA 94132

LAU, JOHN HON SHING, electronics scientist; b. China, June 17, 1946; arrived in U.S., 1973; s. Shui Hong and Mary Au L.; m. Teresa Yu, Sept. 2, 1972; 1 child, Judy M. BS in Civil Engring., Nat. Taiwan U., 1970; MASc in Structural Engring., U. B.C., 1973; MS in Engring. Mechanics, U. Wis., 1974; PhD in Theoretical and Applied Mechanics, U. Ill., 1977; MS in Mgmt., Fairleigh Dickinson U., 1981. Registered profl. engr., N.Y., Calif. Rsch. engr. Exxon Prodn. and Rsch. Co., Houston, 1977; structural specialist Control Data Corp., Sunnyvale, Calif., 1977-78; rsch. assoc. Internat. Paper Co., Tuxedo Park, N.Y., 1978-79; sr. engr. Ebasco Svcs. Inc., NYC, 1979-81, Bechtel Power Corp., San Francisco, 1981-83; MTS Sandia Nat. Lab., N.Mex., 1983-84, Hewlett-Packard Labs., Palo Alto, Calif., 1984-95; pres. Express Packaging Sys., Inc., Palo Alto, Calif., 1995-2000; sr. scientist Agilent Techs., Inc., San Jose, Calif., 2000—06; head microsystems Modules and Components Lab. Inst. Microelectronics, Singapore, 2007—. Contbr. articles to profl. jours. and 14 tech. books; assoc. editor: ASME Transaction Jour. Elec. Packaging. Fellow ASME, IEEE; mem. ASM Internat., AAAS, N.Y. Acad. Scis., Sigma Xi. Roman Catholic. Office: Inst Microelectronics 11 Science Park Rd Singapore 117685 Singapore Office Phone: 65-6779-5424. Business E-Mail: lauhs@ime.a-star.edu.sg.

LAU, LAWRENCE JUEN-YEE, academic administrator, economics professor, consultant; b. Guizhou, China, Dec. 12, 1944; arrived in U.S., 1961, naturalized, 1974; s. Shai-Tat and Chi-Hing (Yu) Liu. BS with great distinction, Stanford U., 1964; MA, U. Calif., Berkeley, 1966, PhD, 1969; D.Social Sci. honoris causa, Hong Kong U. Sci. and Tech. From acting asst. prof. econs. to assoc. prof. Stanford U., Palo Alto, Calif., 1966-76, prof., 1976—, Kwoh-Ting Li prof. econ. devel., 1992—; dir. Stanford Inst. Econ. Policy Rsch., 1997—99; vice chancellor The Chinese U. Hong Kong, 2004—. Co-dir. Asia/Pacific Rsch. Ctr., Stanford U., 1992-96; cons. The World Bank, Wash., 1976-; vice chmn. Bank of Canton of Calif. Bldg. Corp., San Francisco, 1981-85; mem. acad. adv. bd. Ctr. for Employment Policy, Hudson Inst., Washington, 2005—; bd. dirs. Taiwan Fund, Inc. Co-author (with D.T. Jamison): Farmer Education and Farm Efficiency, 1982, Models of Development: A Comparative Study of Economic Growth in South Korea and Taiwan, 1986, rev. edit., 1990, Econometrics and the Cost of Capital: Essays in Honor of Dale W. Jorgenson, 2000; co-author: (with C.H. Yoon) North Korea in Transition: Prospects for Economic and Social Reform, 2001; co-author: (with K.C. Fung and J.S. Lee) U.S. Direct Investment in China, 2005; contbr. articles to profl. jours. Adv. bd. Self-Help for Elderly, San Francisco, 1982—; bd. dirs. Chiang Ching-Kuo Found. for Internat. Scholarly Exch., 1989—; govs. coun. econ. policy advisors State of Calif., 1993-99; mem. Asian Art Commn., San Francisco, 1998-2001; mem. adv. coun. Innovation and Tech., Hong Kong, 2000-02. John Simon Guggenheim Meml. fellow, 1973, fellow Ctr. for Advanced Study in Behavioral Scis., 1982, Overseas fellow Churchill Coll., Cambridge U., Eng., 1984 Fellow Econometric Soc.; mem. Academia Sinica Taipei (academician), Conf. Rsch. in Income and Wealth, Chinese Acad. Social Scis. (hon.), Internat. Eurasian Acad. Scis. (academician). Episcopalian. Office: Chinese Univ Hong Kong Shatin New Territories Hong Kong Office Phone: (852) 2609 8600. Business E-Mail: lawrencelau@cuhk.edu.hk.

LAU, MARY APPLEGATE, lawyer, arbitrator, mediator; b. Washington, Dec. 17, 1952; d. Robert Lee and Barbara Edith (Pressler) Applegate; m. James Victor Lau, Apr. 1, 1982; 1 child, Chelsea Nicole. BA magna cum laude, Mich. State U., 1974; JD with honors, Fla. State U., 1976. Bar: Fla. 1977, U.S. Dist. Ct. (mid. dist.) Fla. 1977, U.S. Ct. Appeals (11th cir.) 1977. Assoc. atty. Holland and Knight, Tampa, Fla., 1977-82, ptnr., 1982-86; shareholder Lau, Lane, Pieper, Conley & McCreadie, P.A., Tampa, 1986—. Mem. Fed. Bar Assn., (treas. Tampa Bay chpt. 1993), Hillsborough County Bar Assn. Republican. Roman Catholic. Office: Lau Lane Pieper Conley & McCreadie PA 100 S Ashley Dr Tampa FL 33602-5360 Office Phone: 813-229-2121. Business E-Mail: mlau@laulane.com.

LAU, PAULINE YOUNG, chemist; b. Harbin, China, June 18, 1943; d. Ching-ju and Chuan-erh (Fu) Young; m. Roland Lau, Sept. 16, 1967 (div. 1990); 1 child, Joan Mann. BS in Med. Tech., Nat. Taiwan U., 1964; MS in Chemistry, Wayne State U., Detroit, 1967; PhD in Chemistry, 1984. Med. technologist Detroit Gen. Hosp., 1967-68; adminstrv. asst. in rsch. Purdue U., W. Lafayette, Ind., 1970-72; supr. chemistry dept. Raritan Valley Hosp., Greenbrook, N.J., 1973-75; head chemistry dept. Princeton (N.J.) Med. Ctr., 1975-80; mgr. S.E. region RIA Ctr., Columbia, S.C., 1980-82; rsch. chemist Med. Product dept. DuPont Co., Wilmington, Del., 1984-88; mgr. rsch./devel. Boehringer Mannheim Diagnostics, Indpls., 1988—. Com. mem. Nat. Com. on Clin. Lab. Stds., 1989—. Author: Clinical Chemistry Laboratory Procedures, 1977. Recipient Outstanding Product Devel. award, Boehringer Mannheim Co., 1990. Mem. Chinese Acad. and Profl. Assn. in Mid-Am. (bd. dirs. 1990—), Ind. Assn. Chinese Ams. (pres. 1993), Mt. Jade Assn. (chmn. biomed. div. 1990—), Ctrl. Ind. Clin. Biochemistry Forum (pres. 1993—), Am. Assn. Clin. Chemistry (chpt. treas. 1989-92, divsn. sec. 1992-93), Am. Chem. Soc. (chpt. bd. dirs. 1990-91), Ind. Chinese Profl. Assn. (v.p. 1990-91, pres. 1992-93), N.Am. Chinese Clin. Chemists Assn. (bd. dirs. 1988-91, pres. 1992—). Office: Roche Diagnostic Corp 9115 Hague Rd Indianapolis IN 46256-1025 Home: 4238 Suzanne Dr Palo Alto CA 94306-4335

LAU, VINCENT W., lawyer; BA, Yale U., 1993; MA in Higher Edn. Adminstrn., Boston Coll., 1997, JD, 1997. Bar: Mass. 1997, Fed. Dist. Ct., MA 1999. Assoc. Fletcher, Tilton & Whipple, P.C., Worcester, Mass., 1998—99, Flynn & Clark, P.C., Cambridge, 1999—. Assoc. editor (conference handbook) Advanced Immigration Solutions for Small Businesses and Entrepreneurs. Mem.: Asian Am. Lawyers Assn. Mass. (bd. dirs. 2006—), Am. Immigration Lawyers Assn. (co-chmn. New Eng. chpt. young lawyers divsn. com. 2002—03). Office: Flynn & Clark PC 1 Main St Cambridge MA 02142 Office Phone: 617-354-1550. Office Fax: 617-661-2576. Business E-Mail: vlau@flynnclark.com.

LAUB, SANDRA, secondary school educator; b. New Rochelle, NY, Dec. 15, 1956; d. Murray and Diana Laub; m. Shelby Michael Chodos, Nov. 30, 1991; 1 child, Emma Chodos. BA, Northwestern U., Evanston, Ill., 1978; profl. cert., Am. Conservatory Theater, San Francisco, 1981. Adj. prof. theater U. RI, Kingston, 1999—2002, Brown U., Providence, 2000—02; English tchr., drama advisor Chariho Regional H.S., Wood River Junction, RI, 2002—. Adapter: (plays) Wild Desires The Story of Madame Bovary, 1993; adapter: plays Mrs. Campbell! Mr. Shaw, 2003, This Is Our Youth - Songs, Scenes and Dreams, 2006 (Outstanding Creative Work award RI Theater Edn. Assn.). Mem.: RI Theater Edn. Assn. (sec. 2006—). Jewish. Home: 239 Woodville Alton Rd Hope Valley RI 02832

LAUB, WILLIAM MURRAY, SR., retired utilities executive; b. Ft. Mills, Corregidor, Philippines, July 20, 1924; s. Harold Goodspeed and Marjorie M. (Murray) L.; m. Mary McDonald, July 26, 1947; children: William, Andrew, Mary, David, John. BSBA, U. Calif., Berkeley, 1947, LLB, 1950. Bar: Calif. 1951. Practice law, Los Angeles, 1951-55; with Southwest Gas Corp., Las Vegas, Nev., 1948-88, v.p., gen. counsel, 1958-60, exec. v.p., 1960-64, pres., chief exec. officer, 1964-82, chmn., chief exec. officer, 1982-88. Pres. Boulder Dam Area council Boy Scouts Am., 1967-69, So. Nev. Indsl. Found., 1967-68, So. Nev. Meth. Found., 1967-74; chmn. Nev. Equal Rights Commn., 1966-68; Chmn. Clark County Republican Central Com., 1964-66; nat. committeeman Nev. Rep. Com., 1968-80; trustee Sch. Theology at Claremont, Calif., 1977-2004, emeritus; trustee Inst. Gas Tech., 1983-89; nat. bd. advisors, coll. bus. and pub. adminstrn. The U. Ariz., 1985-89; bd. dirs. Alliance for Acid Rain Control, 1985-89; vice chmn., bd. trustees KNPR Pub. Radio Sta., 1996-2003, emeritus; dir. First Nat. Bank Nev., 1964-88; mem. Defense Orientation Conf. Assn., 1955-. Served to lt. USNR, 1941—45. Mem. ABA, Am. Gas Assn. (bd. dirs., chmn. 1986-87), Pacific Coast Gas Assn. (chmn. 1983), Calif. Bar Assn., Nat. Coal Coun., Def. Orientation Conf. Assn., Jonathan Club, Pauma Valley Country Club, Spanish Trail Golf and Country Club, Las Vegas Country Club. Office: 2810 W Charleston Blvd Ste 53 Las Vegas NV 89102-1906 Office Phone: 702-259-5241.

LAUBACH, STEPHEN ERNEST, research scientist; s. Gerald and Winifred Laubach; m. Ann Marie Lantleme; children: Eva, Isabel. BS in Geology, Tufts U., Medford, Mass., 1978; PhD, U. Ill., Urbana, 1986. Jackson rsch. fellow Jackson Sch. Geosciences, Austin, Tex.; sr. rsch. scientist Bur. Econ. Geology, Austin, 1996—, sr. tech. advisor, 2006—. Dir. GDL Found., Conn.; panel on energy and mineral resources Geol. Soc. Am., 2007. Author numerous tech. papers and monographs. Named Disting. Lectr., Soc. Petroleum Engrs., 2003—04. Mem.: Am. Assn. Petroleum Geologists (chair various coms., acad. liaison, Jules Braunstein Meml. award 1999). Achievements include patents for method for determining optimal horizontal drilling direction and drilling horizon. Office: Bureau of Economic Geology 10100 Burnet Rd Austin TX 78713 Home Phone: 512-452-5898; Office Phone: 512-636-1026. Office Fax: 512-471-0140. Business E-Mail: steve.laubach@beg.utexas.edu.

LAUBE, ROGER GUSTAV, retired banker; b. Chgo., Aug. 11, 1921; s. William C. and Elsie (Drews) L.; m. Irene Mary Chadbourne, Mar. 30, 1946; children: David Roger, Philip Russell, Steven Richard. BA, Roosevelt U., 1942; postgrad., John Marshall Law Sch., 1942, 48-50; LLB, Northwestern U., 1960; postgrad., U. Wash., 1962-64. Cert. fin. cons. With Chgo. Title & Trust Co., Chgo., 1938-42, 48-50, Nat. Bank Alaska, Anchorage, 1950-72, mgr. mortgage dept., 1950-56, v.p., trust officer, mgr. trust dept., 1956-72; v.p., trust officer, mktg. dir., mgr. estate and fin. planning div. Bishop Trust Co., Ltd., Honolulu, 1972-82; instr. estate planning U. Hawaii, Honolulu, 1978-82; exec. v.p. Design Capital Planning Group, Inc., Tucson, 1982-83; pres., sr. trust officer, registered investment adviser Advanced Capital Advisory, Inc. of Ariz., Tucson, 1983-89; registered rep., pres. Advanced Capital Investments, Inc. of Ariz., Prescott, 1983-89; pres., chief exec. officer Advanced Capital Devel., Inc. of Ariz., Prescott, 1983-89; mng. exec. Integrated Resources Equity Corp., Prescott, 1983-89. Pres. Anchorage Estate Planning Coun., 1960-62, Charter mem., 1960-72, Hawaii Estate Planning Coun., 1972-82, v.p., 1979, pres., 1980, bd. dirs., 1981-82; charter mem. Prescott Estate Planning Coun., 1986-90, pres. 1988. Charter mem. Anchorage Community Chorus, 1946, pres., 1950-53, bd. dirs., 1953-72, Alaska Festival of Music, 1960-72; mem. Anchorage camp Gideons Internat., 1947-72, Honolulu camp, 1972-82, mem. Cen. camp, Tucson, 1982-85, Prescott, 1985-90, Port Angeles-Sequim Camp, 1990—; mem. adv. bd. Faith Hosp., Glenallen, Alaska, 1960—, Cen. Alaska Mission of Far Ea. Gospel Crusade, 1960—; sec., treas. Alaska Bapt. Found., 1955-72; bd. dirs. Anchorage Symphony, 1965-72; bd. dirs. Bapt. Found. of Ariz., 1985-90; bd. dirs., mem. investment com. N.W. Bapt. Found., 1991-97; mem. mainland adv. coun. Hawaii Bapt. Acad., Honolulu, 1982—; pres. Sabinovista Townhouse Assn., 1983-85; bd. advisers Salvation Army, Alaska, 1961-72, chmn., Anchorage, 1969-72, bd. advisers, Honolulu, 1972-82, chmn. bd. advisers, 1976-78; asst. staff judge adv. Alaskan Command, 1946-48; exec. com. Alaska Conv., 1959-61, dir. music Chgo., 1938-42, 48-50, Alaska, 1950-72, Hawaii, 1972-82, Tucson, 1982-85, 1st So. Bapt. Ch., Prescott Valley, Ariz., 1985-90; 1st Bapt. of Sequim, Wash., 1990-98; chmn. bd. trustees Hawaii, 1972-81, Prescott Valley, 1986-89, Sequim, Wash., 1991—; worship leader Waikiki Ch., 1979-82. 1st lt., JAGD, U.S. Army, 1942-48. Recipient Others award Salvation Army, 1972 Mem. Am. Inst. Banking (instr. trust div. 1961-72), Am. Bankers Assn. (legis. com., trust div. 1960-72), Nat. Assn. Life Underwriters (nat. com. for Ariz.), Yavapai County-Prescott Life Underwriters Assn. (charter), Anchorage C. of C. (awards com. 1969-71), Internat. Assn. Fin. Planners (treas. Anchorage chpt. 1969-72, exec. com. Honolulu chpt. 1972-82, Ariz. chpt. 1982-90, del. to World Congress Australia and New Zealand 1987), Am. Assn. Handbell Ringers. Baptist. Home: Sunland Country Club 212 Sunset Pl Sequim WA 98382-8515

LAUBSCHER, ROBERT JAMES, consumer products company executive; b. Tucson, Mar. 20, 1961; s. James Albert and Geri Lee (Bird) L.; m. Deborah Elaine Fuggles, Apr. 14, 1984; children: Stephanie Claire, Samuel Robert, Jonathan Daniel. BA in Econs., Calif. State U., Northridge, 1985; AS in Fire Tech., Oxnard Coll., 1986; cert. in ind. tax prep., Coll. for Fin. Planning, Denver, 1989. Acctg. mgr. Morning Star Labs., Inc., Moorpark, Calif., 1985-89; acctg., credit mgr. Am. Tombow, Inc., Westlake Village, Calif., 1989-92, pres., COO Suwanee, Ga., 1992—. Owner Gold Coast Acctg. Svcs., Camarillo, Calif., 1989-92. With USMCR, 1981-87. Mem. Writing Instruments Mfg. Assn. (bd. dirs.), Bus. Products Credit Assn. (bd. dirs., Timothy J. Teal Credit Exec. of Yr. 2005), Nat. Eagle Scout Assn. Republican. Avocations: running, guitar. Home: 10739 Bell Rd Duluth GA 30097-1801 Business E-Mail: rlaubscher@tombowusa.com.

LAUCHENGCO, JOSE YUJUICO, JR., lawyer; b. Manila, Philippines, Dec. 6, 1936; came to US, 1962; s. José Celis Sr. Lauchengco and Angeles (Yujuico) Sapota; m. Elisabeth Schindler, Feb. 22, 1968; children: Birthe, Martina, Duane, Lance. AB, U. Philippines, Quezon City, 1959; MBA, U. So. Calif., 1964; JD, Loyola U., LA, 1971. Bar: Calif. 1972, US Dist. Ct. (ctrl. dist.) Calif. 1972, US Ct. Appeals (9th cir.) 1972, US Supreme Ct. 1975. Banker First Western Bank/United Calif. Bank, LA, 1964-71; assoc. Demler, Perona, Langer & Bergkvist, Long Beach, Calif., 1972-73; ptnr. Demler, Perona, Langer, Bergkvist, Lauchengco & Manzella, Long Beach, 1973-77; sole practice Long Beach and L.A., 1977-83; ptnr. Lauchengco & Mendoza, LA, 1983-92; pvt. practice LA, 1993—. Mem. commn. on jud. procedures County of LA, 1979; tchr. Confraternity of Christian Doctrine, 1972-79; counsel Philippine Presdl. Commn. on Good Govt., LA, 1986. Chmn. Filipino-Am. Bi-Partisan Polit. Action Group, LA, 1978. Recipient Degree of Distinction, Nat. Forensic League, 1955. Mem. Philippine-Am. Bar Assn. (life), Calif. Pub. Defenders Assn., U. Philippines Vanguard Assn. (life), KC, Beta Sigma. Roman Catholic. Avocations: classical music, opera, romantic paintings and sculpture, camping, shooting. Office: PO Box 767 Los Angeles CA 90078-0767 Office Phone: 323-462-1555.

LAUCKS, RICHARD CONRAD, otolaryngologist; b. Reading, Pa., Nov. 27, 1949; married; 3 children. BA in Psychology, Villanova U., 1976; postgrad., U Pa., 1976—77; MD, Temple U., Phila., 1983. Diplomate Am. Bd. Otolaryngology. Rsch. asst. gastroenterology Temple U. Hosp., Phila., 1978—79, intern gen. surgery, 1983—84, resident gen. surgery, 1984, resident otolaryngology, head and neck surgery, 1984—88; fellow pediat. otolarynology St. Christopher's Hosp. for Children, Phila., 1988—89, chmn. dept. pediat. otolaryngology, 1989—91, attending surgeon, 1989—95; pvt. practice otolaryngology Haddonfield, NJ, 1990—95; pres., mng. ptnr. group practice North Fla. Otolaryngology Assocs., Jacksonville, 1997—; chief pediat. otolaryngology Wolfson's Children's Hosp., 1999—2001; chief divsn. otolaryngology St. Vincent's Med. Ctr., 2001—04. Clin. asst. prof. pediat. and adult otolaryngology Temple U. Sch. Medicine, Phila., 1988—95; clin. asst. prof. otolaryngology U. Medicine and Dentistry NJ, 1990—95, Cooper Hosp., U. Med. Ctr., Camden, NJ, 1990—95; sr. profl. cons. otolaryngology/head and neck surgery Medicare NJ Region, 1989—95; mem. exec. bd. Our Lady of Lourdes Med. Ctr., 1995; profl. cons. quality assurance, surg. utilization, claims rev. Aetna US Healthcare, 1998—; regional adv. bd. ProAssurance Malpractice Ins. Co., 2003—. Contbr. articles to profl. jours. Robert Wood Johnson scholar, 1980—81, Bernard J. scholar, 1983. Fellow: ACS; mem.: Duval County Med. Soc., Am. Acad. Facial Plastic and Reconstructive Surgery, Am. Acad. Otolaryngology/Head and Neck Surgery. Achievements include research in gastroesophageal reflux; head and neck trauma; sudden hearing loss; sleep apnea; newborn hearing screening; sleep apnea surgery; laryngeal papillomas. Address: 4314 McGirts Blvd Jacksonville FL

LAUDA, DONALD PAUL, retired dean; b. Leigh, Nebr., Aug. 7, 1937; s. Joe and Libbie L.; m. Sheila H. Henderson, Dec. 28, 1966; children: Daren M., Tanya R. BS, Wayne State Coll., 1963, MS, 1964; PhD, Iowa State U., 1966. Assoc. dir. Communications Center U. Hawaii, 1966-67; assoc. prof. indsl. arts St. Cloud (Minn.) State Coll., 1967-69; asst. dean Ind. State U., 1970-73; chmn. tech. edn. W.Va. U., 1973-75; dean Sch. Tech., Eastern Ill. U., Charleston, 1975-83; dean Coll. Health and Human Svcs. Calif. State U., Long Beach, 1983—2002, dean emeritus, 2002—. Cons. traditional Chinese medicine edn. Author: Advancing Technology: Its Impact on Society, 1971, Technology, Change and Society, 1978, 2d edit., 1985; contbr. articles to profl. jours. Pres. Council on Tech. Tchr. Edn.; dir. Charleston 2000 Futures Project, 1978-81. Served with USAR, 1957-59. EPDA research fellow, 1969-70; Eastern Ill. U. faculty research grantee, 1971 Mem. Future Soc. Internat. Tech. Edn. Assn., Coun. Tech. Tchr. Educators (pres., Tchr. of Yr. award 1978), World Future Soc., Internat. Tech. Edn. Assn. (pres. 1990), World Coun. Assn. Tech. Edn., Am. Vocat. Assn., Phi Kappa Phi (pres. 1993), Epsilon Pi Tau (Laureate citation 1982), Long Beach C. of C. (bd. dirs. 1995—), Japan Am. Soc. (adv. bd.). Office: Calif State U Coll Health & Human Svcs Long Beach CA 90840-0001 Office Phone: 949-916-2735. Personal E-mail: dlauda@aol.com. *Jobs and careers come through a great deal of effort, education, but, most importantly, through the help of others. It is this input that helps one clarify goals, gain new insights, and synthesize information. The process is reciprocal in that one helps others grow. Reflecting on the past always brings to mind people rather than degrees, positions, salaries, etc. When one loses sight of this, he/she is missing the greatest achievement of life.*

LAUDER, AERIN, cosmetics executive; d. Ronald and Jo Carole Lauder; 2 children. Degree, U. Pa. From dir. mktg. Prescriptives to v.p. global adv. Estée Lauder Inc., NYC, 1992—2001, v.p. global adv., 2001—04, sr. v.p. global creative directions, 2004—. Jr. assoc. Mus. Modern Art, NYC; bd. trustees Thirteen WNET, NYC; costume inst. visiting com. Met. Mus. Art, NYC; bd. trustees Animal Med Ctr.; advisory bd. NY Botanical Garden. Named one of America 's Top Women in Bus.-Game Changers, Pink mag. & Forté Found., 2007. Office: Estée Lauder Inc Corp HQ 767 Fifth Ave New York NY 10153*

LAUDER, EVELYN H., cosmetics executive; b. Vienna; arrived in U.S., 1940; m. Leonard A. Lauder, 1959; children: William, Gary. BA, Hunter Coll.; degree (hon.), Muhlenberg Coll., 1996. Joined as edn. dir. Estée Lauder Cos., NYC, 1959, v.p., sr. corp. v.p., 1989—. Photographer: (book) The Seasons Observed, 1994, An Eye For Beauty, 2002. Founder, chmn. Breast Cancer Rsch. Found., 1993—; mem. bd. overseers Meml. Sloan-Kettering Cancer Ctr.; trustee Ctrl. Pk. Conservancy Inc.; trustee emirata The Trinity Sch., NYC; bd. dirs. New Yorkers for Parks. Named Disting. Fgn. Born Citizen, Internat. Ctr., 1987; named one of 75 Most Influential Bus. Women, Crain's Newspaper, 1996, Women of Yr., Glamour mag., 1999, Top 200 Collectors, ARTnews Mag., 2004, New York's Influentials, New York Mag., 2006; recipient Spirit Achievement award, Albert Einstein Coll. Medicine, 1991, Mary Waterman award, Breast Cancer Alliance, 1998, Humanitarian award, Coun. Fashion Designers Am., 2001, award for excellence in philanthropy, Soc. Meml. Sloan-Kettering, 2001, Ellis Island Medal of Honor, Nat. Ethnic Coalition Orgns., 2001. Achievements include founder of The Breast Cancer Research Foundation, the largest national organization dedicated solely to breast cancer research; implementing breast cancer awareness programs from Pink Ribbon campaigns to illuminating world landmarks in a pink glow for Breast Cancer Awareness Month. Avocation: Collector of Modern art especially Cubism. Office: Estée Lauder Cos 767 5th Ave New York NY 10153-0023*

LAUDER, GEORGE V., marine biologist; AB in Biology, Harvard U., 1976, MA in Biology, 1978, PhD in Biology, 1979. Asst. to assoc. prof. anatomy U. Chgo., 1981—86; assoc. dean grad. studies, Sch. Biol. Scis. U. Calif., Irvine, 1987—96, prof. ecology and evolutionary biology, 1990—99; prof. organismic and evolutionary biology Harvard U., 1999—. Mem. editl. bd. Physiological and Biochemical Zoology, Jour. Morphology, Jour. Exptl. Biology. Contbr. articles to profl. jour. Fellow, Andrew W. Mellon Found., 1981. Fellow: AAAS, Zoological Soc. London, Linnean Soc. London; mem.: Internat. Soc. Neuroethology, Soc. Vertebrate Paleontology, Am. Soc. Zoologists, Soc. Exptl. Biology, Soc. Study Evolution, Soc. Systemic Biology, Soc. Neuroscience, Phi Beta Kappa, Sigma Xi. Office: Harvard U Mus Comparative Zoology 26 Oxford St Cambridge MA 02138 Business E-Mail: glauder@oeb.harvard.edu.

LAUDER, JO CAROLE, art association administrator; m. Ronald S. Lauder, July 1967; children: Aerin, Jane. Mem. bd. dirs. The Ronald S. Lauder Found.; pres. internat. coun. Mus. of Modern Art; mem. bd. trustees Ind. Curators Internat., Mt. Sinai Medical Ctr.; chmn. bd. dirs. Friends of Art & Preservation in Embasies. Named one of Top 200 Collectors, ARTnews Mag, 2004. Avocation: Collector of Old Masters; 19th and 20th century art, especially German. Office: Mus Modern Art 11 W 53rd St New York NY 10019

LAUDER, LEONARD ALAN, cosmetic and fragrance company executive; b. NYC, Mar. 19, 1933; s. Joseph H. and Estée (Mentzer) Lauder; m. Evelyn Hausner Lauder, July 5, 1959; children: William Phillip, Gary Mark. BS, Wharton Sch., U. Pa., 1954. With Estée Lauder, Inc., NYC, 1958—, exec. v.p., 1962-72, pres., 1972—95, CEO, 1982—99, chmn., 1995—. Vice chmn. bd. CFTA, NYC, 1976—79. Bd dirs. Adv. Commn. on Trade Negotiations, Washington, 1983—87; trustee Aspen Inst. for Humanistic Studies, 1978; bd. govs. Joseph H. Lauder Inst. Mgmt. and Internat. Studies, 1983; co-founder Inst. for Study of Aging, 1998; trustee Whitney Mus. Art, NYC, 1977—90, past pres., 1990—94, chmn., 1994—. Lt. USNR, 1955. Named an Officer of French Order of Arts and Letters, 1994, Officier de la Légion d'Honneur, France, 2002; named one of Top 200 Collectors, ARTnews Mag., 2004, Forbes' Richest Americans, 1999—, World's Richest People, Forbes mag., 1999—; recipient Nat. Order of Merit, French Govt., 1986, (with Evelyn Lauder) Philanthropists of Yr., Greater NY Chapter of Nat. Soc. of Fund Raising Execs., 1993, American Art award, Whitney Mus. of Am. Art, 1996, Am. Spirit award, Nat. Retail Fedn., 1998, Ellis Island Medal of Honor, 2000, Disting. Alumni Award, USN Supply Corps Found., 2002. Mem.: Chief Execs. Orgn., French-Am. C. of C. in U.S. (coun. fgn. relations). Avocation: collector of modern art, especially Cubism. Office: Estée Lauder Cos Inc 767 5th Ave New York NY 10153-0023 Address: Whitney Mus Am Art 945 Madison Ave New York NY 10021*

LAUDER, RONALD STEPHEN, investor; b. NYC, Feb. 26, 1944; s. Joseph H. and Estee (Josephine) (Mentzer) L.; m. Jo Carole Knopf, July 8, 1967; children: Aerin Rebecca, Jane Alexandra. Degree in French Lit., U. Paris, 1964; BS in Internat. Bus., U. Pa., 1965. With Estee Lauder, Inc., Brussels, Paris, NYC, 1965-83; chmn. Estee Lauder Internat., Inc. & Clinique Laboratories Inc.; dep. asst. Sec. of Def., Washington, 1983-85; ambassador to Austria Vienna, 1986-87; chmn., pres. Lauder Investments, Inc.; pvt. investor Ea. and Cen. Europe. Founder, chmn. Cen. European Devel. Corp; chmn. Ctrl. European Media Enterprises Ltd. Author: Fighting Violent Crime in America, 1985 Mem. N.Y. State Econ. Devel. Bd., 1972-78; fin. chmn. N.Y. State Republican Com., 1979-82; chmn. 500 Club of N.Y. Rep. Com., 1979-83; founder Ronald S. Lauder Found., 1983; trustee Mus. Modern Art, N.Y.C., 1975—. chmn. 1995-; pres. Neue Galerie, N.Y.C., 2001-, Jewish Nat. Fund; trustee, Mt. Sinai Med. Ctr., 1981—; Rep. candidate, Conservative nominee for Mayor of N.Y.C., 1989. Recipient Ordre De Merit, France, 1985, Disting. Pub. Svc. medal award Dept. Def., 1986; decorated Great Cross of the Order of Aeronautical Merit with White Ribbon, Spain, 1985; Ronald S. Lauder Drawing Gallery at Mus. Modern Art named in his honor, 1984; Named One of the Forbes' Richest Americans, 1999—, World's Richest People, Forbes mag., 1999—; named one of the Top 200 Collectors, ARTnews mag., 2004-2006 Avocation: Old Masters; 19th and 20th century art, especially German. Office: Estee Lauder Inc 767 5th Ave Ste 4200 New York NY 10153-0023*

LAUDER, VALARIE ANNE, editor, educator; b. Detroit, Mar. 01; d. William J. and Murza Valerie (Mann) L. AA, Stephens Coll., Columbia, Mo., 1944; postgrad., Northwestern U. With Chgo. Daily News, 1944-52, columnist, 1946-52; lectr. Sch. Assembly Svc., also Redpath lectr., 1952-55; freelance writer for mags. and newspapers including New York Times, Yankee, Ford Times, Travel & Leisure, Am. Heritage, 1955—; editor-in-chief Scholastic Roto, 1962; editor U. N.C., 1975-80, lectr. Sch. Journalism, 1980—. Gen. sec. World Assn. for Pub. Opinion Rsch., 1988-95; nat. chmn. student writing project Ford Times, 1981-86; pub. rels. dir. Am. Dance Festival Duke U., 1982-83, lectr., instr. continuing edn. program, 1984. Editor Sustainable Resource Mgmt.: REality of Illusion, 2007; contbg. editor So. Accents mag., 1982-86. Mem. nat. fundraising bd. Kennedy Ctr., 1962-63; bd. dirs. Chapel Hill Mus., Inc., 1996-98. Recipient 1st place award Nat. Fedn. Press Women, 1981, 1st place awards Ill. Women's Press Assn., 1950, 51. Mem. Pub. Rels. Soc. Am. (treas. NC chpt. 1982, sec. 1983, v.p. 1984, pres.-elect 1985, pres. 1986, chmn. coun. past pres., chmn. 25th Ann. event 1987, del. Nat. Assembly 1988-94, S.E. dist. officer, nat. nominating com. 1991, 1st pres.'s award 1993), Women in Comms. (v.p. matrix N.C. Triangle chpt. 1984-85), NC Pub. Rels. (mem. Hall Fame com. 1988-2006), DAR, Soc. Mayflower Desc. (bd. dirs. Ill. Soc. 1946-52), Chapel Hill Hist. Soc. (bd. dirs. 1981-85, 94-2001, chmn. pub. com. 1980-85, pres. 1996-2001), Chapel Hill Preservation Soc. (bd. trustees 1993-96, nominating com. 1994), NC Press Club (3d v.p. 1981-83, 2d v.p. 1983-85, pres. 1985, 1st pl. awards 1981, 82, 83, 84), Univ. Women's Club (2nd v.p. 1988), The Carolina Club, The Nat. Press Club. Office: U NC Sch Journalism and Mass Comm CB 3365 Chapel Hill NC 27599-0001 Home Phone: 919-929-1019; Office Phone: 919-843-8297.

LAUDER, WILLIAM P., cosmetics executive; married; 2 children. Degree, U. Pa.; student, U. Grenoble, France. Assoc. merchandising mgr. NY Divsn./Dallas Store Macy's, 1985—86; from regional mktg. dir. Clinique USA to COO Estée Lauder Inc., NYC, 1986—2003, COO, 2003—04, pres., CEO, 2004—. Avocations: golf, skiing, tennis, hiking. Office: Estée Lauder Inc Corp HQ 767 Fifth Ave New York NY 10153*

LAUDERDALE, KATHERINE SUE, lawyer; b. Wright-Patterson AFB, Ohio, May 30, 1954; d. Azo and Helen Ceola (Davis) L. BS in Polit. Sci., Ohio State U., 1975; JD, NYU, 1978. Bar: Ill. 1978, U.S. Dist. Ct. (no. dist.) Ill. 1978, Calif. 1987. Assoc. Schiff, Hardin & Waite, Chgo., 1978-82; from dir. bus. and legal affairs to sr. v.p. Sta. WTTW-TV, Chgo., 1982—2000, sr. v.p. strategic partnerships and gen. counsel, 2000—02; sr. v.p., gen. counsel PBS, Alexandria, Va., 2002—, corp. sec., 2006—. Mem. Lawyers Com. for Harold Washington, Chgo. 1983; bd. dirs. Midwest Women's Ctr., Chgo., 1985-94; active Chgo. Coun. Fgn. Rels., 1981-99, mem. fgn. affairs com., 1985-99; mem. adv. bd. Malcolm X Coll. Sch. Bus., 1996-99 Mem. ABA, Chgo. Bar Assn. (bd. dirs. TV Prodns., Inc. 1986-2002), Lawyers for Creative Arts (bd. dir. 1984-2002, v.p. 1998-2002), ACLU (bd. dirs. 1987-94), Nat. Acad. TV Arts and Scis., NYU Law Alumni Assn. Midwest (mem. exec. bd. 1982-86), The Ohio State U. Pres.'s Nat. Adv. Coun. on Pub. Affairs (Chgo. com., 1994-98), The History Makers (nat. adv. bd. 2003—), Hands on Network (nat. bd., 2005—, sec. exec. com. 2006) Democrat. Office: PBS 2100 Crystal Dr Arlington VA 22202 Office Phone: 703-739-5063.

LAUDERDALE, VANCE, JR., anesthesiologist; b. NYC, Sept. 11, 1923; MD, Columbia U., 1947. Diplomate Am. Bd. Anesthesiologists. Intern Kings County Hosp., NYC, 1947-49; resident anesthesiology Presbyn. Hosp., NYC, 1949-51; cons. emeritus anesthesiology Columbia-Presbyn. Med. Ctr., NYC, 1985—; spl. lectr. anesthesiology Columbia U., 1985—. Fellow Am. Coll. Anesthesiologists; mem. AMA, Am. Soc. Anesthesiologists, N.Y. County Med. Soc. (mem. peer review com. bd. censors 1975-85).

LAUDNER, KEVIN, athletic trainer, educator; b. Chula Vista, Calif., July 22, 1973; s. Larry and Mary Laudner; m. Jenny LaBelle, July 8, 2000; children: Samantha, Jack. PhD, U. Pitts., 2004. Asst. athletic trainer U. Chgo., 1999—2001; rsch. grad. asst. U. Pitts., 2001—04; prof. Ill. State U., Normal, 2004—. Cons. Cross Country Edn., Nashville, 2006—. Contbr. articles to profl. jours. Mem.: Nat. Athletic Trainers' Assn. (cert.), Am. Coll. Sports Medicine, Am. Soc. Shoulder and Elbow Therapists. Office: Illinois State University Campus Box 5120 Normal IL 61790

LAUDONE, ANITA HELENE, lawyer, business executive; b. 1948; m. Colin E. Harley; children: Clayton T. Harley, Victoria Harley. B.A., Conn. Coll., 1970; J.D., Columbia U., 1973. Admitted to N.Y. State bar, 1974, practiced in N.Y.C., 1973-79; asst. sec. Phelps Dodge Corp., N.Y.C., 1979-80, sec., 1980-84, v.p., sec., 1984-85. Editor Columbia Law Rev., 1973. Mem. Phi Beta Kappa.

LAUE, BRUCE ANTONIO, financial consultant, writer; b. NYC, July 21, 1953; s. William Rollini and Yolande Violette (Dodelin) Laue; m. Sherry Lynn Locher, May 18, 1996. BA, Fairleigh Dickinson U., 1975. Mng. dir. Geneva Capital Resources, Inc., NYC, 1992—. Chmn. scholarship com. Youth Found., NYC, 1996—2001; mem. French Am. Friendship Found.; mem. adv. bd. Soldier's, Sailor's, Marines' and Airmen's Club, NYC, 1988—; mem. St. George's Soc., NYC, 1989—; steward New Eng. Soc., NYC, 1983—; spl. legate to Principality of Seborga Internat. Federative Alliance of Sovereign Mil. Order of Temple of Jerusalem, 1998. Lt. col. intelligence officer Vets. Corps Arty., 1981—. Recipient Civic Commendation, Coun. City of N.Y., 1989, N.Y. State Hist. Mil. Command commendation, N.Y. Soc. Mil. and Naval Officers, 1998, N.Y. State Mil. Commendation medal, N.Y. State Dept. Mil. and Naval Affairs, 1993, Def. of Liberty medal, 2004. Mem.: Army and Navy Union, Masons, Order of Lafayette (pres.-gen. 1996—), Sovereign Order of Orthodox Knights Hospitaller of St. John of Jerusalem (knight of grace), Old Guard City of N.Y., Nat. Gavel Soc. Roman Catholic. Home and Office: 243 W 70th St New York NY 10023-4318

LAUENSTEIN, ANN GAIL, librarian; b. Milw., Nov. 8, 1949; d. Elmer Lester Herbert and Elizabeth Renatta (Bovee) Zaeske; m. Mark Lauenstein, Aug. 16, 1986; 1 child, Maria. MA, U. Wis., 1972. Asst. libr. U. Wis.,

Wausau, 1972—73; cataloger, libr. MacMurray Coll., Jacksonville, Ill., 1973—76; corp. libr. Anheuser-Busch Cos. Inc., St. Louis, 1976—. Facilitator Anheuser-Busch Quality Circle, St. Louis, 1984—. Treas. Friends of Kirkwood Libr., 1986-98; mem. adv. coun. Sch. Info. Sci. U. Mo., 1987-95. Mem. AAUW (editor jour. 1981-84, publicity chmn. 1985-87, scholar 1984), Spl. Librs. Assn. (network liaison 1981-83, chmn. employment com. 1983-84, chmn. hospitality com. 1984-85, membership chmn. 1988-89, newsletter editor 1992-94, advt. editor 1995-97, bus. mgr. 1999—), St. Louis Regional Libr. Network (coun. 1981-83), St. Louis Online Users Group, Women in Bus. Network (adv. panel 1980-82, 86-87, programs planner 1987-88, asst. coord. 1988-89), Ohio Coll. Libr. Consortium Acquisitions Users Coun. Avocations: stamp collecting/philately, cooking, cookbook collecting. Office: Anheuser-Busch Co Inc 1 Busch Pl Saint Louis MO 63118-1852

LAUER, ELIOT, lawyer; b. NYC, Aug. 17, 1949; s. George and Doris (Trenk) L.; m. Marilyn Steinberg, June 5, 1977; children: Tamar Rachel, Ilana Jennifer, Michael Jonathan, Samuel Geoffrey. BA, Yeshiva U., 1971; JD cum laude, Fordham U., 1974. Bar: D.C. 1975, N.Y. 1975, U.S. Dist. Ct. (so. and ea. dists.) N.Y. 1975, U.S. Ct. Appeals (2d cir.) 1975, U.S. Supreme Ct. 1984. Assoc. Curtis, Mallet-Prevost, Colt & Mosle, NYC, 1974-82, ptnr., 1982—. Counsel Keren-Or Inc., NYC, 1985—; bd. dirs. Ctr. for Mid. East Peace and Econ. Cooperation, 1991—, Rep. Jewish Coalition, 2002—, Hebrew Acad. Long Beach, NY, 1985—. Mem.: ABA, N.Y. State Bar Assn., Fed. Bar Coun., Assn. of Bar of City of N.Y. Republican. Office: Curtis Mallet-Prevost Colt & Mosle 101 Park Ave Fl 34 New York NY 10178-0061 Home Phone: 516-569-5103; Office Phone: 212-696-6192. Business E-Mail: elauer@cm-p.com.

LAUER, JAMES LOTHAR, physicist, researcher; b. Vienna, Aug. 2, 1920; came to U.S., 1938, naturalized, 1943; s. Max and Friederike (Rapaport) L.; m. Stefanie Dorothea Blank, Sept. 4, 1955; children: Michael, Ruth. AB, Temple U., 1942, MA, 1944; PhD, U. Pa., 1948; postgrad., U. Calif., San Diego, 1964-65. Scientist Sun Oil Co., Marcus Hook, Pa., 1944-52, spectroscopist, 1952-64, sr. scientist, 1965-77; asst. prof. U. Pa., 1952-55; lectr. U. Del., 1952-58; rsch. fellow mech. engring. U. Calif., San Diego, 1964-65; rsch. prof. mech. engring. Rensselaer Poly. Inst., Troy, NY, 1978-85, prof. mech. engring., 1985-93, prof. mech. engring. emeritus, 1993—; rsch. sci. Ctr. Magnetic Recording Rsch. U. Calif., San Diego, 1993-95, vis. scholar applied mechanics and engring. sci., 1995—. Sr. faculty summer rsch. fellow NASA-Lewis Rsch. Ctr., 1986-87; vis. prof. Ctr. for Magnetic Rec. Rsch., U. Calif., San Diego, 1991; cons. Digital Equipment Corp., 1992-94, NASA-Lewis Rsch. Ctr., 1993-95. Author: Infrared Fourier Spectroscopy--Chemical Applications, 1978; co-author: Handbook of Raman Spectroscopy, 2001; mem. editl. bd. Tribology Letters, 1995—; contbr. articles to profl. jours. Active Penn Wynne Civic Assn., 1959—77, Country Knolls Civic Assn., 1978—93. Sun Oil Co. fellow, 1964-65, Air Force Office Sci. Rsch. grantee, 1974-86, NASA Lewis Rsch. Ctr. grantee, 1974-86, Office Naval Rsch. grantee, 1979-82, Army Rsch. Office grantee, 1985-89, NSF grantee, 1987-95, Innovative Rsch. award Soc. Mech. Engrs., 1991, Discovery awards NASA, 1993, 96. Fellow: Inst. Physics (U.K.); mem.: AAAS (life), Optical Soc. Am. (emeritus), Soc. Applied Spectroscopy, Am. Phys. Soc. (emeritus), Am. Chem. Soc. (emeritus), Materials Rsch. Soc., Sigma Chi. Jewish. Achievements include patents in field. Home: 7622 Palmilla Dr Apt 78 San Diego CA 92122-4710 Office: U Calif San Diego La Jolla CA 92037 *My advice to those contemplating a career in experimental research is to give much thought to these points: (1) interest, enthusiasm, willingness to work are only basics, (2) a loving and understanding wife is essential, and (3) the knowledge that one can create one's own success at any time is the driving force.*

LAUER, JEANETTE CAROL, dean, history educator, writer; b. St. Louis, July 14, 1935; d. Clinton Jones and Blanche Aldine (Gideon) Pentecost; m. Robert Harold Lauer, July 2, 1954; children: Jon, Julie, Jeffrey. BS, U. Mo., St. Louis, 1970; MA, Washington U., St. Louis, 1973, PhD, 1975. Assoc. prof. history St. Louis C.C., 1974-82, U.S. Internat. U., San Diego, 1982-90, prof., 1990-94, dean Coll. Arts and Scis., 1990-94, rsch. prof., 1997—. Author: Fashion Power, 1981, The Spirit and the Flesh, 1983, Til Death Do Us Part, 1986, Watersheds, 1988, The Quest for Intimacy, 5th edit., 2002, 6th edit. 2006, No Secrets, 1993, The Joy Ride, 1993, For Better of Better, 1995, True Intimacy, 1996, Intimacy on the Run, 1996, How to Build a Happy Marriage, 1996, Sociology: Contours of Society, 1997, Windows on Society, 1999, 7th edit., 2005; Becoming Family: How to Build a Stepfamily that Works, 1999, How to Survive and Thrive in an Empty Nest, 1999, Troubled Times: Readings in Social Problems, 1999, Love Never Ends, 2002, The Play Solution: How to Put the Fun Back into your Relationship, 2002, Social Problems and the Quality of Life, 10th edit., 2005, Marriage and the Family: The Quest for Intimacy, 6th edit., 2005. Woodrow Wilson fellow, 1970, Washington U. fellow, 1971-75. Mem.: Am. Hist. Assn., Orgn. Am. Historians. Democrat. Presbyterian.

LAUER, LEN J., former telecommunications executive; b. 1956; BS in Managerial Econ., U. Calif., San Diego. With IBM, 1979—92, Bell Atlantic Corp., 1992—98, pres., CEO NJ, 1995—98; joined Sprint Corp., 1998, pres. consumer svcs. group, global mkts. group Overland Park, Kans., 1999, pres., Sprint Bus., 1999, pres. global markets group Overland Park, Kans., 2000—03; pres., COO Sprint Corp. (now Sprint Nextel Corp.), Overland Park, Kans., 2003—05; COO Sprint Nextel Corp., Reston, Va., 2005—06. Bd. dirs. Children's Mercy Hosp., Maplewood Ptnrs., Nat. Orgn. on Disability, Virgin Mobile USA, VeriSign, Inc. Bus. coun. steering com., bd. trustee Nelson-Atkins Mus. Art; bd. dirs. C. of C., Kansas City.

LAUER, MATT, television personality; b. Dec. 30, 1957; s. Jay Robert and Marilyn L.; m. Annette Roque, Oct. 3, 1998; children: Jack Matthew, Romy, Thijs. BA in Comm., U. Ohio, Athens, 1997. Prodr. WOWK-TV, Huntington, W.Va., 1979—80; program host various locations, 1980—88; substitute host Day's End, ABC-TV, 1989, Esquire Show, King Prodns./Lifetime, 1988—89, 9 Broadcast Plaza, WWOR-TV, NYC, 1989—91; with WNBC, NYC, 1992—96; co-anchor News 4/Live at Five, NYC, 1993—96; news anchor NBC News' Today Show, NYC, 1994—96, co-anchor, 1997—. Office: NBC News Today Show 30 Rockefeller Plz Fl 3D New York NY 10112-0002

LAUER, RICHARD T., lawyer; b. Cin., Feb. 26, 1969; BA, U. Mass. Amherst, 1991. Bar: Ohio 1994, US Dist. Ct. Southern Dist. Ohio 1995, US Ct. of Appeals Sixth Cir. 2000, Ky. 2001, US Dist. Ct. Eastern Dist. Ky. 2002. Ptnr. Robbins, Kelly, Patterson & Tucker, Cin. Named one of Ohio's Rising Stars, Super Lawyers, 2006. Office: Robbins Kelly Patterson & Tucker Federated Bldg Ste 1400 7 W 7th St Cincinnati OH 45202-2417 Office Phone: 513-721-3330. Office Fax: 513-721-5001.

LAUER, RONALD MARTIN, pediatric cardiologist, researcher; b. Winnipeg, Man., Can., Feb. 18, 1930; m. Eileen Pearson, Jan. 12, 1959; children: Geoffrey, Judith Lauer. BS, U. Man., 1953, MD, 1954. Diplomate Am. Bd. Pediatrics. Asst. prof. pediatrics U. Pitts., 1960-61; asst. prof. pediatrics U. Kans., 1961-67, assoc. prof. pediatrics, 1967-68; prof. pediatrics, dir. pediatrics cardiology U. Iowa, 1968-95, vice chmn. pediatrics, 1974-82, prof. pediatrics and preventive medicine 1980—. Recipient Sci. Couns. Disting. Achievement award Am. Heart Assn., 1991, award of meritorious achievement, 1998, Eugene Braunwald Mentorship award, 2002, named Disting. Scientist, 2004; Founder's award Am. Acad. Pediatrics, 1997. Office: U Iowa Coll Medicine Divsn Pediat Cardiology 200 Hawkins Dr Iowa City IA 52242-1009 Office Phone: 319-356-2839. Business E-Mail: ronald-lauer@uiowa.edu.

LAUER, WARREN A., lawyer; b. Lusk, Wyo., Dec. 3, 1951; BS in Agr., U. Wyo., 1976, JD, 1980. Bar: Wyo. 1981. Pvt. practice Lauer Law Offices, Laramie, Wyo. Bd. dirs. U. Wyo. Coll. Law Alumni Assn., pres., 2002—03; bd. dirs., treas. Laramie Regional Airport. Contbr. articles to profl. jours. Mem. pres. coun. U. Wyo.; mem. state small bus. air quality adv. panel, 1994—97; mem. bd. adjustment Laramie Zoning Bd., 1983—89; mem. Albany County Planning and Zoning Commn., 1998—2000. Mem.: ABA, Wyo. Trial Lawyers Assn., Wyo. State Bar (commr. 1998—2001, sec.-treas. 2002—03, v.p. 2003—04, pres.-elect 2004, pres. 2005), Albany County Bar Assn. (sec., treas. 1995, v.p. 1996, pres. 1997). Office: Lauer Law Offices 208 Garfield St Ste 200 A Laramie WY 82070 Office Phone: 307-742-7288. Office Fax: 307-745-5502. E-mail: warrenlauer@lauerlegal.com.*

LAUERHASS, LUDWIG, JR., history professor; b. Asheville, NC, Jan. 6, 1935; s. Ludwig and Betty Bronson Lauerhass; m. Frances Horne Lauerhass, Sept. 5, 1957; 1 child, Theresa Lauerhass Wiegmann. BA in Polit. Sci. with honors, U. NC, Chapel Hill, 1957; MA in L.Am. Studies, UCLA, LA, 1959, PhD in History, 1972, MLS, 1976. Lectr., asst. prof. U. Calif., Riverside, 1964—67; bibliographer L.Am. UCLA Libr., LA, 1968—93; asst., assoc. and dir. L.Am. Ctr. UCLA, 1975—84, lectr. history, 1976—93, chair Brazil program, 1989—94, lectr. emeritus, 1993—. Vis. prof., Washington, 1997—. Co-author: Brazil in the Making, 2006. Sgt. USN, 1952—57. Recipient Hubert Herring Meml. prize, Pacific Coast Coun. L.Am. Studies, 1975; fellow, Fulbright Found., Brazil, Mex., 1984—85, Inst. L.Am. Studies, U. Tex., Austin, 1986; grantee, NEH, 1988—89. Mem.: Am. Hist. Assn., Cosmos Club. Avocation: book collecting. Home: 319 Dalkeith Ave Los Angeles CA 90049 Office: UCLA Dept History Los Angeles CA 90095

LAUERMAN, WILLIAM, medical educator; b. NYC, Dec. 27, 1954; s. Sidney and Veronica Lauerman; m. Cynthia Tull, Sept. 24, 1983; children: Katie, Kevin. BA in Natural History, Johns Hopkins U., Balt., 1978; MD, Georgetown U., DC, 1982. Lic. orthopaedic surgeon Am. Bd. Orthopaedic Surgeons, 1990. Intern surgery Georgetown U. Med. Ctr., 1982—83, resident orthop. surgery, 1983—87; fellow spine surgery U. Minn., 1987—88; maj., orthop. surgeon USAF Med. Ctr., 1988—92; asst. prof. U. Pitts. Med. Ctr., 1992—95; assoc. prof. Georgetown U. Med. Ctr., DC, 1995—2000, prof. orthopaedic surgery, 2000—. Maj. USAF, 1988—92, Lackland AFB, Tex. Fellow: Am. Acad. Orthopaedic Surgeons (chair subcom. on spine evaluation 2004—07), Scoliosis Rsch. Soc. Avocations: skiing, golf, travel. Office: Georgetown Univ Hosp 3800 Reservoir Rd NW Washington DC 22066*

LAUFER, HANS, developmental biologist, educator; b. Germany, Oct. 18, 1929; s. Sol and Margarete (Freundlich) L.; m. Evelyn Green, Oct. 31, 1953 (dec. May 2001); children: Jessica, Marc, Leonard. BS, CCNY, 1952; MA, Bklyn. Coll., 1953; PhD (James fellow), Cornell U., 1958. Rsch. and tchg. asst. Cornell U., Ithaca, NY, 1953-57; NRC fellow Carnegie Instn. of Washington, 1957-59; asst. prof. biology Johns Hopkins U., 1959-65; assoc. prof. U. Conn., Storrs, 1965-72, prof., 1972—98, rsch. prof., 1998—. Vis. prof. Karolinska Inst., Stockholm, 1972, Charles U., Prague, 1974, Yale U., 1980, Hebrew U., Jerusalem, 1988, Harvard U., 1989-90, Ben-Gurion U., Beer-Sheva, 1997; Rosenstiel vis. scholar Brandeis U., 1974; participant Nat. Acad. Scis.-Czechoslovak Acad. exchange program, 1974, 77; ad hoc mem. study sect. tropical medicine NIH, 1981, mem., 1982-85; Conklin Meml. fellow Marine Biology Lab., Woods Hole, Mass., 1956, Lalor fellow, 1962, 63, mem. staff, embryology course, 1968-72, mem. corp., 1962, corp. trustee, 1978-82, mem. exec. com., 1979-80; vis. scholar Case Western Res. U., 1962; mem. NSF-NATO Fellowship Rev. Panel, 1974, 76 Contbg. author numerous books; assoc. editor Jour. Exptl. Zoology, 1969-73, 90-93, Archives Insect Physiology and Biochemistry, 1983-95, Invertebrate Reprodn. and Devel., 1984-86, mng. editor, 1991—; contbr. numerous articles to profl. jours. Recipient Rsch. Svc. award NIH, 1989, Marcus Singer medal for rsch., 1986, 95; NATO sr. fellow, 1973, fellow Lady Davis Trust, Hebrew U., 1988; Japan Soc. Promotion of Sci. Fell., 1980; Rosenstiel scholar Brandeis U., 1973; Dozor vis. prof., Ben Gurion U., 1997. Fellow AAAS (chmn. sect. biology 1975), Royal Entomology Soc. London (fgn. fellow); mem. Internat. Soc. Devel. Biology, Internat. Soc. Invertebrate Reprodn. and Devel. (mem. exec. coun. and v.p. 1995—), Rsch. Couns. (nat. bd. on grad. edn. of conf. bd. 1971-75), Am. Soc. Zoology (chmn. divsn. developmental biology 1981-82), Soc. Devel. Biology, Am. Soc. Cell Biology, European Soc. Comparative Endocrinology, Am. Assn. Advancement Aging Rsch., Internat. Soc. Differentiation, Tissue Culture Assn. (coun. 1979-82), World Aquaculture Soc., Conn. Acad. Sci. and Engring. Home: 57 Davis Rd Storrs Mansfield CT 06268-2525 Office: U Conn Dept Molecular & Cell Biology U-3125 91 N Eagleville Rd Storrs Mansfield CT 06269-3125 Home Phone: 860-429-2120; Office Phone: 860-486-4117. E-mail: laufer@uconn.edu.

LAUFER, JACOB, lawyer; b. Munich, Feb. 28, 1949; came to the US, 1951; s. Moritz and Felicja (Pruszanowska) L.; m. Clara G. Schwabe, Jan. 27, 1983; children: Samara, Aviva, Mia. BS, CUNY, 1971; JD cum laude, Fordham U., 1974. Bar: NY 1975, DC 1975, US Ct. Appeals (2d cir.) 1975, US Dist. Ct. (so. and ea. dists.) NY 1976, US Ct. Appeals (5th cir.) 1979, US Supreme Ct. 1980, US Ct. Appeals (3d cir.) 1985, US Ct. Appeals (DC cir.) 1994. Spl. atty. U.S. Dept. Justice Organized Crime and Racketeering Sect., 1974-77; asst. U.S. atty. So. Dist. NY, NYC, 1977-79; of counsel Bartels, Pykett & Aronwald, White Plains, NY, 1979-81; ptnr. Bornstein & Laufer, NYC, 1981-85, Laufer & Farkash LLP, NYC, 1986—96; with Laufer & Halberstam LLP, NYC, 1996; pvt. practice NYC, 2006—. Mem., contbr. Fordham Law Rev., 1973-74. Mem. DC Bar Assn., Bklyn. Bar Assn., Assn. Bar City of NY (com. criminal advocacy 1998—). Democrat. Jewish. Notable cases include: Pavelic & LeFlore vs. Marvel Entertainment Group; and Allen vs. National Video, Inc. Office: Ste 1005 65 Broadway New York NY 10006 Office Phone: 212-422-8500. Business E-Mail: jlaufer@lauferlaw.com.

LAUFER, LEONARD JUSTIN, management consultant; b. Hartford, Conn., Sept. 30, 1965; s. Hans and Evelyn Alice (Green) L.; m. Terry Gushner; children; Arianna Olivia, Eli Tyler. AB, Harvard U., 1987; MBA, U. Pa., 1992. Assoc. The MAC Group Gemini Cons., NYC, 1992-93; cons. First Manhattan Cons. Group, NYC, 1994; prin. KLH Assocs., White Plains, NY, 1994—. Prin. Argus Info. and Adv. Svcs., LLC, White Plains, NY, 1995—. Mem.: Sunningdale Country Club. Home: 2 Richbell Rd Scarsdale NY 10583-4422 E-mail: llaufer@argusinformation.com.

LAUFER, MARC R., gynecologist; s. Hans and Evelyn G. Laufer; m. Susan F. Rosenfeld, Sept. 28, 1997; children: Isabella O., Alexandra B. BA, U. Pa., Phila., 1982, MD, 1986. Diplomate Am. Bd. Ob-gyn., 1993. Staff gyn. Brigham and Women's Hosp., Boston, 1986—; chief gyn. Children's Hosp. Boston, 1991—; staff gyn. Dana Farber Cancer Inst., 1993—; co-dir. Ctr. Young Women's Health, 1998—; assoc. prof. ob-gyn. and reproductive biology Harvard Med. Sch., 2005—. Author: (medical text book) Pediatric and Adolescent Gynecology, 5th edit. Bd. mem. Candies Found., NYC, 2004. Scholar, U. Pa., 1979; Benjamin Franklin scholar, 1979, AC Barnes scholar, U. Pa., Sch. Medicine, 1982. Mem.: Internat. Endometriosis Assn. (med. adv. bd. 1996—), Am. Coll. Ob-gyn. (chair com. adolescent health 2002—06, com. immunization 2005—). Achievements include design of Operations for care of girls and young women; research in Adolescent Endometriosis; Congenital anomalies of the reproductive tract; Preservation of fertility in cancer patients. Office: Childrens Hosp 300 Longwood Ave Boston MA 02115 Office Phone: 617-355-5785. Office Fax: 617-730-0186. Business E-Mail: marc.laufer@childrens.harvard.edu.

LAUFER, MARK VLADIMIR, retired engineering educator; b. Kiev, Ukraine, Sept. 30, 1910; arrived in U.S., 1994; s. Vladimir Ieseevich and Ida (Naumovna) Laufer; m. Raisa Lvovna Bespalko, Oct. 21, 1977 (dec.); 1 child, Tatyana; m. Vera Mikhaylovna Vaks, Sept. 25, 1993 (dec. Nov. 2003). Diploma in engring., Kiev Poly. Inst., 1936; M, Tashkent Poly. Inst., Uzbekistan, 1943. Prof. Motion Picture Engr. Inst., Kiev, 1936—41, chief chair, 1944—53; chief engr. Motion Picture Studio, Tashkent, 1942—43; prof. Poly. Inst., Kiev, 1954—78, ret., 2004—. Cons. Acad. Scis. Ukraine, Kiev, 1937—41, Sci. Rsch. Inst., Kiev, 1961—77; pres. Assoc. Magnetic Rec., Kiev, 1937—77. Author: Theory of Magnetic Recording, 1980, Bases on Record Magnetical Carrier, 2004; editor: Questions Radioelectronics, 1962—77. Capt. USSR Air Force, 1941—45. Recipient Hon. medal, Acad. Scis. USSR, 1959, Hon. emblem, Ministry of Comm., 1961. Mem.: N.Y. Acad. Scis. Achievements include 30 inventions. Avocations: swimming, gardening. Home: 174 Ave A Apt 6F New York NY 10009 Office Phone: 212-674-1382. Personal E-mail: marklauf95@verizon.net.

LAUFER, NATHAN, cardiologist; b. Montreal, Mar. 12, 1953; came to US, 1981; s. Jack and Pearl (Brachfeld) Laufer; m. Judy Franceska Egett, Sept. 2, 1986; 1 child, Andrew. DCS, McGill U., Montreal, Quebec, 1972, MD, 1977. Diplomate Nat. Bd. Med. Examiners, Am. Bd. Internal Medicine; cert. Profl. Corp. Physicians Que. Intern, resident U. Toronto, Can., 1977-81; fellow cardiology U. Mich., Ann Arbor, 1981-83, faculty dept. cardiology, 1983-84; cardiologist Affiliated Cardiologists, Phoenix, 1984-2001, mng. cardiologist, 1996-2001; med. dir. Heart & Vascular Ctr. Ariz., 2001—; chief cardiovascular svcs. Banner Estrella Med. Ctr., 2004—. Dir. coronary care Good Samaritan Hosp., Phoenix, 1986—92, dir. interventional cardiology, 1987—; vis. prof. Chigasaki Tokushi-kai Med. Ctr., Kanagawa-ken, Japan, 1988, Leningrad Postgrad. Med. Inst., St. Petersburg, Russia, 1991; bd. dirs. Integrated Cardiovascular Group, Maricopa Med. Ctr., 2002—04. Contbr. articles to profl. jours. Fellow ACP, Am. Coll. Cardiology, Am. Coll. Chest Physicians, Royal Coll. Physicians and Surgeons Can.; mem. AMA, N.Am. Soc. Pacing and Electrophysiology, Soc. Cardiac Angiography and Intervention, Am. Assn. Nuclear Cardiology, Ariz. Med. Assn., Can. Cardiovascular Soc., Maricopa County Med. Assn., Cardiovascular Soc. Ariz. (founder, pres.). Avocations: skiing, tennis, computers, music, films. Home: 9100 N 55th St Paradise Valley AZ 85253-1632 Office: Heart & Vascular Ctr Ariz 1331 N 7th St Ste 375 Phoenix AZ 85006-2712 Home Phone: 480-443-1722; Office Phone: 602-307-0070.

LAUFF, GEORGE HOWARD, biologist; b. Milan, Mich., Mar. 23, 1927; s. George John and Mary Anna (Klein) L. BS, Mich. State U., 1949, MS, 1951; postgrad., U. Mont., 1951, U. Wash., 1952; PhD, Cornell U., 1953. Fisheries research technician Mich. Dept. Conservation, 1950; teaching asst. Cornell U., 1952-53; instr. U. Mich., 1953-57, asst. prof., 1957-61, asso. prof., 1961-62; research asso. Gt. Lakes Research Inst., U. Mich., 1954-59; dir. U. Ga. Marine Inst., 1960-62; asso. prof. U. Ga., 1960-62; research coord. Sapelo Island Research Found., 1962-64; dir. Kellogg Biol. Sta., 1964-90; prof. dept. fisheries and wildlife and zoology Mich. State U., East Lansing, 1964-91, prof. emeritus, 1991—. Mem. cons. and rev. panels for Smithsonian Inst., Nat. Water Commn., NSF, Nat. Acad. Sci., Am. Inst. Biol. Sci., U.S. AEC, Inst. Ecology, others. Editor: Estuaries, 1967, Experimental Ecological Reserves, 1977. Served with inf. U.S. Army, 1944-46. Office of Naval Research grantee; U.S. Dept. Interior grantee; NSF grantee; others. Fellow AAAS; mem. Am. Inst. Biol. Sci., Am. Soc. Limnology and Oceanography (pres. 1972-73), Ecol. Soc. Am., Freshwater Biology Assn., INTECOL, Societas Internationalis Limnologiae, Orgn. Biol. Field Stas., Sigma Xi, Phi Kappa Phi. Home: PO Box 53185 Kalamazoo MI 49005-3185 Office: 3700 E Gull Lake Dr Hickory Corners MI 49060-9505 Business E-Mail: lauff@msu.edu.

LAUFMAN, HAROLD, surgeon, consultant; b. Milw., Jan. 6, 1912; s. Jacob and Sophia (Peters) L.; m. Marilyn Joselit, 1940 (dec. 1963); children: Dionne Joselit Laufman Weigert, Laurien Laufman Kogut; m. June Friend Moses, 1980 (dec. 1999). BS, U. Chgo., 1932; MD, Rush Med. Coll., Chgo., 1937; MS in Surgery, Northwestern U., Chgo., 1946, PhD, 1948. Diplomate Am. Bd. Surgery. Intern Michael Reese Hosp., Chgo., 1936-39; fellow in gen. surgery St. Marks Hosp., London, Northwestern U. Med. Sch., Cook County Hosp., Hines VA Hosp., 1939-46; attending surgeon Michael Reese Hosp., 1940-53; mem. faculty Northwestern U., 1941-65; from clin. asst. to prof., attending surgeon Passavant Meml. Hosp., Chgo., 1953-65; prof. surgery, history of medicine Albert Einstein Coll. Medicine, NYC, 1965-81, prof. emeritus, 1982—; dir. Inst. Surg. Studies, Montefiore Hosp. and Med. Ctr., Bronx, NY, 1965-81; pvt. practice gen. and vascular surgery Chgo., 1941-65, NYC, 1965-82; ret. professorial lectr. surgery Mt. Sinai Sch. Medicine, NYC, 1979-83, emeritus, 1983—; attending surgeon Mt. Sinai Hosp., NYC, 1979-83. Cons., lectr. in field; chmn. FDA Classification Panel Gen. and Plastic Surgery Devices, 1975-78; pres. Harold Laufman Assocs., Inc., 1977-2003, sr. ptnr., 1988-2004. Author: (with S.W. Banks) Surgical Exposures of the Extremities, 1953, 2d edit., 1986, (with R.B. Erichson) Hematologic Problems in Surgery, 1970, Hospital Special Care Facilities, 1981, The Veins, 1986, (with P Ped, Brush, Fidric and Segal) Ones Man's Century, 2007; editor Chgo. Medicine, 1959-63; contbg. editor Modern Medicine, 1965-70; chmn. editl. bd. Diagnostica, 1974-79; mem. editl. bd. Med. Devices, 1969-80, Tech. for Surgery, 1976-86, Surgery, Gynecology and Obstetrics, 1974-92, Infection Control, 1980-88, Med. Instrumentation, 1972-83, Med. Rsch. Engring., 1972-79; contbr. articles to sci. publs. Chmn. bd. dirs. NY Chamber Soloists, 1974-80, Chamber Music Conf. and Composers Forum of the East, 1975-91, pres., 1987-90. Maj. head of surg. team, 5th army USMC, 1942—46, North Africa, Sicily, Italy. Recipient James IV Traveling Professorship in Surgery, Israel, Vienna and Moscow, 1963, Disting. Alumnus award, Rush Med. Coll., 1993, U. Chgo. divsn. Biol. Svcs., 1999. Fellow: ACS, Am. Surg. Assn.; mem.: Surg. Infection Soc. (councillor 1980—84, founding mem.), Soc. Surgery Alimentary Tract (founding mem.), Internat. Cardiovasc. Soc., Soc. Vascular Surgery, NY Surg. Soc., Ctrl. Surg. Assn., Western Surg. Assn., Societe Internationale de Chirurgie, Am. Med. Writers Assn. (pres. 1968—69, award 1969), Am. Assn. Healthcare Cons., Assn. Advancement Med. Instrumentation (pres. 1974—75, chmn. bd. 1976—77), Harmonie Club (NYC), Sigma Xi, Alpha Omega Alpha, Zeta Beta Tau. Home and Office: 31 E 72nd St New York NY 10021-4131 Personal E-mail: halauf@aol.com.

LAUGA, ERIC, physical mathematician, educator; BS, École Polytechnique, France, 1998; MA, Ecole des Mines de Paris, 2001; MS in Fluid Mechanics, U. Paris VI - Pierre and Marie Curie, 2001; PhD in Applied Math., Harvard U., Cambridge, Mass., 2005. Lectr. divsn. engring. and applied scis. Harvard U., Cambridge, Mass., 2005; postdoctoral assoc. dept. mech. engring. MIT, Cambridge, 2005—06, asst. prof. dept. math., 2006—. Contbr. articles to sci. jours. Mem.: Biophysical Soc., Am. Phys. Soc. (Andreas Acrivos Dissertation award, Fluid Dynamics 2007). Office: MIT Dept Math Rm 2-363C 77 Mass Ave Cambridge MA 02139 Office Phone: 617-324-2809. Office Fax: 617-253-8911. E-mail: lauga@mit.edu.*

LAUGHLIN, CHRISTEL RENATE, translator, consultant; b. Berlin, Dec. 18, 1940; came to U.S., 1966; d. Werner Wilhelm and Rosa Ida (Conrad) Friedrich; m. Phillip Edward Laughlin, July 1, 1966; 1 child, Christina Rosa. Cambridge proficiency diploma, Davies's Sch., London, 1960; French lang. diploma, U. Paris, 1961; Italian lang. diploma, Centri Europei Lingua, Florence, Italy, 1961; BA in Translating, U. Geneva, 1964; accredited travel agt., N.Am. Sch. Travel, Newport, Calif., 1976. Mem. touring svc. Swiss Touring Club, Geneva, 1962-63; hostess, interpreter

Intercontinental Hotel, Geneva, 1964, Swiss Nat. Exhbn., Lausanne, 1964; exec. sec. Intercom S.A., Geneva, 1964-65, Soc. Luchard, Paris, 1965-66; outside saleswoman Hunnicutt Travel, Ft. Worth, 1974-76; pres. Simon Stevens Laughlin Travel, Ft. Worth, 1976-81; cons., translator K.T. Lendt & Co., NYC, 1969-96; tax acct. Tarrant Operators, Inc., Ft. Worth, 1996-98. Market rsch. analyst Power Base, Denver, 1997; cons. Schwartzkopf Cosmetics, Duesseldorf, Germany, 1997; traffic cons. ADAC-Automobil Club Germany, Munich, 1997. Pres. Symphony League Ft. Worth, 1972-74; juror host family, interpreter Van Cliburn Internat. Piano Competition, Ft. Worth, 1973-97; host family interpreter XX World Gymnastics Championships, Ft. Worth, 1979, U.S. Gymnastics Internat., Ft. Worth, 1982. Mem. AAUW, Nat. Assn. Market Rsch. Analysts, Bot. Rsch. Inst. Tex. (sponsor), Arts Coun. Ft. Worth, Modern Art Mus. Fort Worth. Avocations: tennis, skiing, classical music, opera, travel. Home: 6212 Indian Creek Dr Fort Worth TX 76107-3526 E-mail: texasmanlaughlin@hotmail.com.

LAUGHLIN, DAVID EUGENE, materials scientist, educator, metallurgist, consultant; b. Phila., July 15, 1947; s. Eugene L. and Myrtle M. (Kramer) L.; m. Diane Rae Seamans, June 13, 1970; children: Jonathan, Elizabeth, Andrew, Daniel BSc, Drexel U., 1969; PhD, MIT, 1973. Asst. prof. materials sci. Carnegie-Mellon U., Pitts., 1974-78, assoc. prof., 1978-82, prof., 1982—, Alcoa prof. phys. metallurgy, 2001—. Rsch. scientist Oxford (Eng.) U., 1985; vis. scientist Alcoa Tech. Ctr., Pa., 1996. Editor: Solid-Solid Phase Transformations, 1982; category editor of copper: Am. Soc. Metals-Nat. Bur. Stds. Phase Diagram Program, 1981-94; assoc. editor: Metall. Trans., 1982-87, editor, 1987—; contbr. more than 350 articles to profl. jours.; holder 8 patents Mem. sch. bd. Trinity Christian Sch., Pitts., 1976-85, 87-95, pres., 1978-83, sec., 1988-91, pres., 1991-94; ruling elder Covenant Presbyn. Ch., Pitts., 1982-96; foster parent Children's Home of Pitts., 1984-90; bd. dirs. Christian Schs. Internat., 1991-98; vestry mem. Ch. of the Ascension, 1998—, clk., 1999—2000, warden, 2001—. Recipient Ladd Tchg. award Carnegie-Mellon U., 1975, B.R. Teare award for excellence in engring. edn., 1999, Outstanding Rsch. award Carnegie-Mellon U.; postdoctoral fellow Nat. Acad. Scis., 1974. Fellow Am. Soc. Metals; mem. Metall. Soc. AIME, Am. Sci. Affiliation, Materials Rsch. Soc., IEEE Magnetics Soc. Avocations: sports, books. Home: 2357 Mcnary Blvd Pittsburgh PA 15235-2779 Office: Carnegie-Mellon U Dept Materials Sci Eng Pittsburgh PA 15213 Office Phone: 412-268-2706. Business E-Mail: Laughlin@cmu.edu.

LAUGHLIN, EDWARD HUMES, surgeon, educator; b. Huntsville, Ala., July 22, 1932; s. James Burnett and Mary Cleophas (Mahoney) Laughlin; children: Page Lewis, Leedy Stockton. BA, U. Va., Charlottesville, 1954; MD, Duke U., 1958. Diplomate Am. Bd. Surgeons. Intern Johns Hopkins Hosp., Balt., 1958—59; resident in surgery U. Va. Hosp., Charlottesville, 1959—64; surgical fellow Lahey Clinic, Boston, 1962; chmn. surg. programs U. Ala. Sch. Primary Med. Care, Huntsville, 1975—79; prof. surgery U. Ala. Sch. Medicine, Huntsville, 1998—. Author: Coming to Terms with Cancer, 2001. Lt. col. USAR, 1986—88. Fellow: ACS; mem.: Am. Soc. Clinical Oncologists, Soc. Surgical Oncology. Avocations: fishing, hunting, weight training. Home: 1901 Asbury Rd Huntsville AL 35801

LAUGHLIN, FELIX B., lawyer; b. New Orleans, Dec. 4, 1942; m. Betty Gayle Laughlin. BS with honors, JD with honors, U. Tenn., 1967; LLM, Georgetown U., 1971. Bar: Tenn. 1967, D.C. 1972, U.S. Ct. Claims 1969, U.S. Tax Ct. 1968, U.S. Dist. Ct. D.C. 1972, U.S. Ct. Appeals (D.C. cir.) 1988, U.S. Ct. Appeals (fed. cir.) 1992, U.S. Supreme Ct. 1970. With interpretation divsn. Office Chief Counsel IRS, 1967-71; assoc. Dewey Ballantine LLP, Washington, 1972-74, ptnr. & chmn. tax dept., 1975—. Dir. Friends of U.S. Nat. Arboretum, Nat. Bonsai Found. (pres.). Fellow ABA (tax sect.); mem. Fed. Bar Assn. (chmn. tax sect. 1989), Met. Club (Washington), George Town Club (Washington), Order of Coif, Sigma Alpha Epsilon, Phi Eta Sigma, Phi Kappa Phi, Phi Delta Phi. Office: Dewey Ballantine LLP 1775 Pennsylvania Ave NW Washington DC 20006-4605 Office Phone: 202-862-1040. Office Fax: 202-862-1093. Business E-Mail: flaughlin@deweyballantine.com.

LAUGHLIN, GREGORY H. (GREG LAUGHLIN), lawyer, former congressman; b. Bay City, Tex., Jan. 21, 1942; m. Linda Winterrowd; children: Mary, Brad. BA, Tex. A&M U.; LLB, U. Tex. Asst. dist. atty. Harris County, Tex., 1970-74; pvt. practice Tex.; mem. US Congresses from 14th Tex. dist., Washington, 1989-97; of counsel, Legis. Affairs, Public Policy, Energy Policy practices Patton Boggs, LLP, Washington, 1997—2006; sr. counsel Pillsbury Winthrop Shaw Pittman LLP, Washington, 2006—. Founder & co-chmn. U.S. / Former Soviet Union Energy Caucus. Col. USAR, active Persian Gulf, Oper. Desert Storm, 1991. Office: Pillsbury Winthrop Shaw & Pittman LLP 2300 N St NW Washington DC 20037 E-mail: greg.laughlin@pillsburylaw.com.

LAUGHLIN, JAMES HAROLD, JR., lawyer; b. Charleston, W.Va., July 18, 1941; s. James Harold and Pearl Ruby L; m. Eleanor Blackford Watson, II, Aug. 3, 1968; children: C. Michelle, Jeanette C., Cheryl Adele. BS in Chem. Engring., W.Va. U., 1964; JD, Am. U., 1968. Bar: D.C. 1968, Va. 1969. Atty. Am. Cyanamid Co., Wayne, NJ, 1968-70, Xerox Corp., Rochester, NY, 1971-77; ptnr. Benoit, Smith & Laughlin, Arlington, Va., 1977-93, Lane & Mittendorf, LLP, Washington, 1993-97, Shook, Hardy & Bacon, LLP, Washington, 1997-99, Arter & Hadden, LLP, Washington, 2000-01, Swidler Berlin Shereff Friedman, LLP, 2001—05, Holland & Knight, LLP, 2005—. Mem. ABA, Am. Intellectual Property Law Assn. (bd. dirs. 1976-79, treas. 1982-85, councilman 1993-94), Va. State Bar (chmn. PTC sect. 1982-83), Nat. Coun. Patent Law Assns. (Va. del. 1983-2002), Nat. Inventors Hall of Fame Found. (bd. dirs. 1988-93, pres. 1991-92). Office: 2099 Pennsylvania Ave NW Washington DC 20006 Office Phone: 202-828-1866. E-mail: jim.laughlin@jlaughlin.com.

LAUGHLIN, LOUIS GENE, economic analyst, consultant; b. Sept. 20, 1937; s. Eston A. and Cornelia Helen Laughlin Student, Pomona Coll., 1955-58; BA, U. Calif., Santa Barbara, 1960; postgrad., Claremont Grad. Sch., 1966-70, 85-86, Sch. Bank Mktg., U. Colo., 1974-75, Grad. Sch. Mgmt., U. Calif., Irvine, 1983. Mgr. Wheeldex-L.A. Co., 1961—62; v.p. Warner/Walker Assocs., Inc., LA, 1964—65; rep. A.C. Neilsen Co., Chgo., 1962—64; rsch. analyst Security Pacific Nat. Bank, LA, 1964—67, asst. rsch. mgr., 1967—68, asst. v.p., 1968—72, v.p., mgr. market info. and rsch. divsn., 1972—76, v.p. rsch. adminstrn., pub. affairs/rsch. dept., 1976—82, v.p. govt. rels. dept., 1982—85; dir. R & D Applied Mgmt. Sys., South Pasadena, Calif., 1986; pres. L.G. Laughlin & Assocs., Houston, 1987—. Prin. Courtyard Holdings, Houston, 1988—; pres. CEO, Mastodon Capital Corp., Houston, 1988-89, 94-98; corp. sec. Kestco Co. Inc., Laguna Beach, Calif., 1996-98; mem. Nat. Conf. on Fin. Svcs., 1982-84, mem. policy coun., 1983-84; mem. policy coun. Nat. Conf. on Competition in Banking, 1978-79, 81. Sec. econs. Town Hall of Calif., 1966. Mem. Am. Econs. Assn., Western Econs. Assn., Nat. Assn. Bus. Economists, L.A. C. of C. (food and agr. adv. com. 1981). E-mail: lougl77@cs.com.

LAUGHLIN, MONIQUE MYRTLE WEANT, mental health counselor; b. Paton, Iowa, Aug. 30, 1924; d. Irving Leroy Weant and Ella Florence (Bauer) Blaylock; m. Gerald Dean Laughlin, July 15, 1944 (div. July 1975); children: Roy Melvin, Owen Willard, James Byron. BA, William Penn Coll., Oskaloosa, Iowa, 1949; MS, So. Ill. U., 1975; PhD, U. Okla., 1980. Lic. profl. counselor Okla. State Dept. Health, marital and family therapist; cert. alcohol and drug counselor Okla. State Bd. Alcohol and Drug Counselors, Okla. State Bd. Mental Health; nat. cert. counselor Nat. Bd. Cert. Counselors; nat. cert. alcohol and drug counselor Drug and Alcohol Profl. Counselor Cert. Bd., internat. alcohol and drug counselor Internat Cert. and Reciprocity Consortium, Alchohol and Drug Abuse Inc., biofeedback therapist Neurotherapy and Biofeedback Cert. Bd., clin. hypnotherapist, Am. Coun. Hypnotist Examiners. Asst. v.p. 1st Nat. Bank, Higgins, Tex., 1962-74; alcohol and drug counselor Mercy Health Ctr., Oklahoma City, 1975-76; pub. rels./counselor Cmty. Counseling Ctr., Oklahoma City, 1977-79; tng. cons. and counselor in pvt. practice Oklahoma City, 1979-80; petroleum landman Johnco Inc., Oklahoma City, 1981; tng. officer, staff devel. Dept. Human Svcs., Oklahoma City, 1981-85; developer counseling svcs., exec. dir. Break-Through, Oklahoma City, 1985—; owner, dir. Pathfinders, Inc., Oklahoma City, 1990—. With Citizen's Amb. program People to People, Spain and Portugal, 1991. Mem. Am. Assn. Marriage and Family Therapy (clin.), Okla. Psychol. Assn., Okla. Drug and Alcohol Profl. Counselor Assn., Nat. Assn. Adult Children of Dysfunctional Families. Avocation: travel. Home: 14126 Springhill Rd Edmond OK 73013-4734

LAUGHLIN, ROBERT B., academic administrator, physics professor; b. Visalia, Calif., Nov. 1, 1950; m. Anita Rhona Perry, Apr. 22, 1979; children: Nathaniel David, Todd William. AB in Math, U. Calif., Berkeley, 1972; PhD in Physics, MIT, 1979. Postdoctoral fellow Bell Tel. Labs., 1979—81, Lawrence Livermore Nat. Lab., 1981—82; research scientist Lawrence Livermore Nat Lab, 1982—; assoc. prof. physics Stanford U., Calif., 1985—89, prof. physics Calif., 1989—2004, Anne T. and Robert M. Bass prof. Sch. Humanities and Scis. Calif., 1992, prof. applied physics Calif., 1993—; pres. Korea Advanced Inst. Sci. & Tech. (KAIST), Daejeon, Republic of Korea, 2004—. Lectr. in field. Author: A Different Universe: Reinventing Physics from the Bottom Down, 2005; contbr. articles to profl. jours. With US Army, 1972—74. Named Eastman Kodak lectr., 1989, Van Vleck lectr., 1994; recipient E.O. Lawrence award for Physics, 1985, Franklin Inst. medal, 1998, Nobel Prize in Physics, 1998; fellow, IBM, 1976—78. Fellow: Am. Phys. Soc. (Oliver E. Buckley prize 1986); mem.: NAS, AAAS (fellow), Aspen Ctr. Physics, Am. Acad. Arts and Scis. (fellow, 1990). Office: Stanford U Dept Physics LAM Rm 342 McCullough Bldg 476 Lomita Mall Stanford CA 94305

LAUGHLIN, STEVEN L., advertising executive; b. 1948; Copy writer Fuller Biety Connell Agy., Milw., 1968-74, Cramer Krusselt Co., Milw., 1974-75; with Laughlin/Constable Inc., Milw., 1976—, pres., ptnr., creative dir., writer, ptnr. Office: Laughlin/Constable Inc 207 E Michigan St Milwaukee WI 53202-4996

LAUGHLIN, WILLIAM EUGENE, retired electric power industry executive; b. Sheffield, Ala., May 4, 1936; s. Rawlie Wayne and Nina Louise (Campbell) L.; m. Donna Lynn Blackburn, Jan. 3, 1958; children: Kevin McGregor, Christopher Scott, Laura Shannon, Alison Paige. BS, Auburn U., 1961. Registered profl. and electrical engr., Ala., Tenn., Miss. Elec. engr. Dept. Power, Water and Gas, City of Sheffield, 1961-66; chief engr., asst. mgr. Electric Plant Bd., Bowling Green, Ky., 1966-76; systems mgr. Bowling Green Mcpl. Utilities, 1975-77; gen. mgr. Fayetteville (Tenn.) Electric Systems, 1977-81, Talquin Electric Coop. Inc., Quincy, Fla., 1981—2002. Bd. dirs., v.p. Seminole Electric Coop., Inc., Tampa, Fla.; pres. Fla. Rural Electric Coop. Assn., Tallahassee. Pres. Boys Club, Bowling Green, 1972; v.p. Bowling Green C. of C., 1975, Fayetteville C. of C., 1979; dist. chmn. Boy Scouts Am., Bowling Green, 1972, Fayetteville, 1978; pres. Fayetteville United Way, 1980. Mem. Nat. Rural Elec. Coop. Assn. (mem. regional com., nat. water task force 1995), Am. Water Works Assn., Rotary (bd. dirs. 1986-87, pres. Quincy club 1996-97), Fayetteville 1978-79, Paul Harris fellow), Kiwanis (dir. Bowling Green club 1973-74). Democrat. Mem. Ch. of Christ. Home: 2110 Ellicott Dr Tallahassee FL 32308-0818

LAUGHREY, NANETTE KAY, federal judge; b. Cheyenne, Wyo., Feb. 11, 1946; m. Christopher Sexton Kelly; children: Hugh, Jessica Katherine. BA, UCLA, 1967; JD, U. Mo. Columbia, 1975. Bar: Mo. 1975, U.S. Dist. Ct. (we. dist.) Mo. 1975, U.S. Ct. Appeals (8th cir.) 1976, U.S. Supreme Ct. 1978. Asst. atty. gen. Mo. Atty. Gen.'s Office, Kansas City, 1975-79; assoc. Craig Van Matre, P.C., Columbia, 1980-83; assoc. prof. law U. Mo. Columbia, 1983-87, prof. law, 1987-89, William H. Pittman prof. law, 1989-96; judge U.S. Dist. Ct. (we. dist.) Mo., Kansas City, 1996—. Mcpl. judge City of Columbia, 1979-83; vis. prof. law U. Iowa, 1990; dep. atty. gen. Mo. Atty. Gen.'s Office, 1992-93. Contbr. articles to profl. jours. Bd. dirs. Columbia Housing Authority. Mem.: ABA, Mo. Bar Assn., Am. Law Inst., U. Mo. Alumni Assn., Am. Whitewater Assn., Mo. Whitewater Assn. Office: US Dist Ct 400 E 9th St Ste 7452 Kansas City MO 64106-2670

LAULICHT, MURRAY JACK, lawyer; b. Bklyn., May 12, 1940; s. Philip and Ernestine (Greenfield) L.; m. Linda Kushner, Apr. 4, 1965; children: Laurie Hasten, Pamela Hirt, Shellie Davis, Abigail Herschmann. BA, Yeshiva U., 1961; LLB summa cum laude, Columbia U. Sch. Law, 1964. Bar: N.Y. 1965, N.J. 1968, U.S. Supreme Ct. 1976. Legal staff Warren Commn., Washington, 1964; law clk. Hon. Harold R. Medina U.S. Ct. Appeals, 1964-65; assoc. Kaye, Scholer, Fierman, Hays & Handler, NYC, 1965-68; ptnr. Lowenstein, Sandler, Brochin, Kohl & Fisher, Newark, 1968-79, now Day Pitney (formerly Pitney, Hardin, Kipp & Szuch), Florham Park, NJ, 1979—. Mem. N.J. Consumer Affairs Adv. Com., 1991-93; mem. N.J. Commn. on Holocaust Edn., 1991—, chmn. 1992-95; mem. N.J. Commn. on Character Edn., 2002; pres. Jewish Edn. Assn., 1981-84, Jewish Fedn. Metro West, 1996-99, Edah, 2001-02, chmn. Cmty. Rels. Com., 1988-91, chmn. com. on religious pluralism, 1999-2002; exec. comm. Coun. of Jewish Fedn., 1996-99; trustee United Jewish Cmtys., 1999-2003; bd. govs. Jewish Agy. Israel, 2004—. Recipient Julius Cohn Young Leadership award Jewish Fedn. Metrowest, 1976. Mem. ABA, N.J. State Bar Assn. (dist. X ethics com. 1986-89, bd. editors N.J. Law Jour. 1986-93), N.J. Lawyer Mag. (chmn. 1993-95). Democrat. Avocations: jewish studies, communal activities. Home: 59 Cummings Cir West Orange NJ 07052-2268 Office: Pitney Hardin Kipp & Szuch now Day Pitney PO Box 1945 200 Campus Dr Florham Park NJ 07932-1007 Office Phone: 973-966-8030. Business E-Mail: mlaulicht@daypitney.com.

LAUMANN, EDWARD OTTO, sociology educator; b. Youngstown, Ohio, Aug. 31, 1938; m. Anne Elizabeth Solomon, June 21, 1980; children: Christopher, Timothy; children by previous marriage: Eric, Lisa. AB summa cum laude, Oberlin Coll., 1960; MA, Harvard U., 1962, PhD, 1964. Asst. prof. sociology U. Mich., Ann Arbor, 1964-69, assoc. prof., 1969-72; prof. sociology U. Chgo., 1973—, George Herbert Mead Disting. Service prof., 1985—, dean divsn. of social scis., 1984—92, provost, 1992—93, chmn. dept., 1981—84, 1997—99, 2002—03. Bd. govs. Argonne Nat. Lab., 1992-93. Author: Prestige and Associations in an Urban Community, 1966, Bonds of Pluralism, 1973, (with Franz U. Pappi) Networks of Collective Action, 1976, (with John P. Heinz) Chicago Lawyers, 1982, (with David Knoke) The Organizational State, 1987, (with John P. Heinz, Robert Nelson and Robert Salisbury) The Hollow Core, 1993, (with John Gagnon, Robert Michael, Stuart Michaels) The Social Organization of Sexuality, 1994, (with Robert Michael, John Gagnon, Gina Kolata) Sex in America, 1994, (with Robert T. Michael) Sex, Love and Health, 2001, (with Stephen Ellison, Jenna Mahay, Anthony Pain, Yoosik Youm), The Sexual Organization of the City, 2004, (with John Heinz, Robert Nelson, Rebecca Sandefur) Urban Lawyers, 2005; editor Am. Jour. Sociology, 1978-84, 95-97. Mem. sociology panel NSF, Washington, 1972-74; commr. CBASSE, NRC, 1986-91; chair bd. trustees NORC, 2001—; trustee U. Chgo. Hosps., 1992-93; mem. Panel on Elder Mistreatment, 2000-02; bd. dirs. Family Inst., 2004—. Fellow AAAS (chmn. sect. K 2001-04), Soc. Sci. Study Sexuality, Internat. Acad. Sex Rsch.; mem. Sociol. Rsch. Assn., Am. Sociol. Assn., Population Assn. Am.; Chgo. Coun. Fgn. Rels. (pres.'s cir.). Office: U Chgo 1126 E 59th St Chicago IL 60637 Home Phone: 312-587-0097; Office Phone: 773-702-8691. Business E-Mail: e-laumann@uchicago.edu.

LAUMONT, PHILIPPE EMILE, communications executive; b. Liege, Belgium, June 17, 1944; came to U.S., 1957; s. Gustave J. and Germaine (Cattet-Thellier de Poncheville) L.; m. Anne Colton Adams, July 19, 1978; children: Anne Sophie, Julia Adams, Laura Philippa. BA, U. Louvain, Belgium, 1964, MA, 1965; MBA, Columbia U., 1978. Film producer CBS Inc., NYC, 1969-78; pres. Laumont Labs Inc., NYC, 1979—, Laumont Photographics, 1993—, Laumont Editions, 1998—. Mem. Coffee House Club, Ausable Club. Office: Laumont Editions 333 W 52nd St New York NY 10019-6238 E-mail: pl@laumont.com.

LAUN, LOUIS FREDERICK, government official; b. Battle Creek, Mich., May 19, 1920; s. Louis Frederick and Roena (Graves) L.; m. Margaret West, Jan. 25, 1947; children: Nancy, Kathryn Webb, Margaret. BA, Yale U., 1942. Asst. advt. mgr. Bates Fabrics, Inc., NYC, 1946-48; asst. to pres., indsl. and public relations Bates Mfg. Co., Lewiston, Maine, 1948-55; advt. dir. Burlington Industries, NYC, 1955-57; gen. merchandising mgr. Celanese Fibers Co., NYC, 1957-60, v.p., dir. mktg., 1960-63, exec. v.p. mktg., 1963-64; pres. Celanese Fibers Mktg. Co. div. Celanese Corp., 1964-71, also v.p. corp., 1964-71; assoc. adminstr. ops. SBA, Washington, 1973, dep. adminstr., 1973-77; pres. Am. Paper Inst., NYC, 1977-86; asst. Sec. Commerce for Internat. Econ. Policy Dept. of Commerce, Washington, 1986-89, exec. br. commr., H elsinki Commn. on Security and Cooperation in Europe, 1988-89; cons. Nat. Exec. Svc. Corp, 1989—2001. U.S. pulp and paper rep. food and agrl. orgns. UN; bd. dirs. Overseas Pvt. Investment Corp., Noranda Aluminum, Inc.; exec. br. mem. Commn. on Security and Cooperation in Europe (Helsinki Commn.); vol. cons. Nat. Exec. Svc. Corps, 1989-2001. Bd. dirs. N.Y. Bd. Trade, Better Bus. Bur. N.Y., Alliance to Save Energy, Bus. Adv. Com. on Fed. Reports; bd. dirs., mem. exec. com. The Grace Commn. on Govt. Waste; indsl. asst. to chmn. Opportunities Industrialization Ctrs. Am.; nat. adv. coun. SBA; chmn. Rep. Industry Workshop program; field dir. Com. for Re-election of Pres., 1972; trustee Taft Sch.; mem. exec. com. President's Pvt. Sector Survey on Cost Control; chmn. Kids to Kids Internat., 1999; bd. dirs. New Castle Hist. Soc., 1999-2001, Edwin Gould Svcs. for Families and Children, 1997-2001, United Way of No. Westchester, 1998-2001. Lt. col. USMC, 1942-46. Decorated Bronze Star; recipient Human Rights award Anti-Defamation League, 1968; Achievement award Textile Vets. Assn., 1970; named Young Man of Yr. Lewiston-Auburn C. of C., 1953, Man of Yr. Textile Salesman Assn., 1970, Man of Yr. Fabric Salesmen's Guild, 1971; Gold medal for disting. service SBA, Citation Merit Taft Sch., 1988. Mem. Color Assn. U.S. (sec.), Man-Made Fiber Producers Assn. (chmn. 1967-69), Yale Club (N.Y.C.), Sleepy Hollow Country Club (Scarborough, N.Y.), Met. Club (Washington), Mid-Ocean Club (Bermuda). Home and Office: 25 Spring Ln Chappaqua NY 10514-2607 Personal E-mail: lflcl@aol.com.

LAUNER, LELAND C., JR., insurance company executive; BS in Chemistry, U. Redlands, 1977; MBA in Acctg. and Fin., U. So. Calif., 1979. With investments dept. MetLife, Inc., Calif., 1979, treas., exec. v.p., chief investment officer, 2003—05, pres. instl. bus., 2005—. Chmn. bd. dirs. Reinsurance Grp. Am., Inc.; bd. dirs. MetLife Bank, Met. Tower Realty Co., Inc., CRB Co., Inc., CRH Co., Inc., GA Holding Corpn., N.L. Holding Corpn., Met. Asset Mgmt. Corpn. Office: MetLife Inc 200 Park Ave New York NY 10166

LAUR, WILLIAM EDWARD, retired dermatologist; b. Saginaw, Mich., Nov. 17, 1919; s. Vertner Linton and Ruth Gae (Eyre) L.; m. Mary Elizabeth Kirby, Dec. 31, 1943; children: Eric, Edward, John, J. Michael. BS, Mercer U., Macon, Ga., 1941; MD, U. Mich., 1943; MS in Medicine, Wayne State U., Detroit, 1949. Diplomate Am. Bd. Dermatology. Intern John Sealy Hosp., Galveston, Tex., 1943; resident Wayne State U., 1946-49; pvt. practice Amarillo, Tex., 1949-70; pres. High Plains Dermatology Ctr., P.A., Amarillo, 1975—90; ret., 1990. Cons. VA, USAF, 1952-90; assoc. prof. Tex. Tech. Health Sci. Ctr., Amarillo, 1965-90. Contbr. articles to profl. jours. including Archives of Dermatology, Internat. Jour. Dermatology, Cutis, So. Med. Jour., Jour. Am. Acad. Dermatology, Panhandle Med. Soc. Bull., Urologic and Cutaneous Rev. Dir. Moon Watch, NASA, Amarillo, 1956. Capt. U.S. Army, 1944-46, ETO. Fellow Am. Acad. Dermatology; mem. AMA, Tex. Med. Assn., Noah Worcester Dermatol. Soc., Potter Randall County Med. Soc. (pres. 1964), Alpha Tau Omega. Avocations: cooking, bridge, computers. Home: 1607 S Fannin St Amarillo TX 79102-2412

LAUREANO, MARI, government agency administrator, writer; b. NYC, Nov. 6, 1970; d. Jose Antonio Miranda and Blanca Iris Velez- Miranda; m. Pedro Antonio Laureano, Sept. 16, 1991; children: Laura, Nia. BA, Hunter Coll. CUNY, 1987—91. Immigration officer US Immigration & Naturalization Svc., NYC, 1991—2000; tax examiner US IRS, Holtsville, NY, 2002—04; dist. adjudications officer US Citizenship and Immigration Svc. Dept. Homeland Security, Garden City, NY, 2004—. In-house expert on Nicaraguan adjustment and ctrl. am. relief act US Immigration Svc., NYC, 1998—98. Author: (poetry books) Maelstrom Rising, 2001, By What Light I Shed, 2002, Riverborne, 2003, Into the Quicksilver Mirror, 2004, The Fairytale Journals, 2005. Rudin fellow, The Am. Mus. of Natural History, 1989-1991. Avocations: poetry writing, drawing, spoken word artist. Office: US Citizenship and Immigration Svc Dept Homeland Security 711 Stewart Ave Garden City NY 11530 Personal E-mail: babygirlpress@optonline.net, mlaureanol@optonline.net.

LAUREN, RALPH, fashion designer; b. Bronx, NY, Oct. 14, 1939; s. Frank and Frieda Lifshitz; m. Ricky Low Beer, Dec. 30, 1964; children: Andrew, David, Dylan. Student, CCNY; DFA (hon.), Pratt U., 1988; HDL (hon.), Brandeis U., 1996. Salesperson Brooks Bros., NYC; asst. buyer Allied Stores, NYC; rep. Rivetz Necktie Mfrs., NYC; neckwear designer Polo divsn. Beau Brummel, NYC, 1967-69; founder, chmn. Polo Fashions, Inc. (now Polo Ralph Lauren Corp.), NYC, 1967—; established Polo Men's Wear Co., NYC, 1968—, Ralph Lauren Womenswear, NYC, 1971—, Polo Leathergoods, 1978—, Polo/Ralph Lauren for Boys, 1978—, Polo/Ralph Lauren Luggage, 1982—, Ralph Lauren Home Collection, 1983—; launched fragrances Polo for Men, Lauren for Women, 1979—; opened RL Restaurant, Chgo., 1999. Chmn. Polo Ralph Lauren Corp. (flagship store NYC, 65 other stores in US and 140 stores worldwide); launched fragrances Lauren, Lauren Style, Purple Label, Ralph Lauren Blue, Silver, Polo Blue, Romance for men and women, Polo, Polo Sport, Ralph, Safari for men and women, and Glamourous. Served in US Army. Recipient Coty Am. Fashion awards, 1970, 73, 74, 76, 77, 81, 84, also Coty Hall of Fame award for Menswear and Womenswear, Tommy award Am. Printed Fabrics Coun., 1971, Neiman Marcus Disting. Svc. award, 1973, Am. Fashion award, 1975, award Coun. Fashion Designers Am., 1981, Lifetime Achievement award, 1992, Menswear Designer of Yr. award, 1996, 2007, Womenswear Design of Yr. award, 1996, Humanitarian Leadership award, 1998, Am. Fashion Legend award, 2007, Humanitarian award Breast Cancer Rsch. Found., 1998, VH1/Vogue Lifetime Achievement award, 2002, Man of Yr. award GQ, 2002; named one of Forbes' Richest Americans, 1999—, World's Richest People, Forbes mag., 2001—, 100 Most Influential People, Time mag., 2006. Achievements include established the American Heroes Fund following Sept. 11, 2001; established the Pink Poney Campaign to address the significant lack of access to cancer screening, education, outreach and quality cancer care for people in these communities, 2000; opened the Ralph Lauren Center for Cancer Care and Prevention to provide individuals, many of who are medically underserved, with access to the highest quality cancer screening and treatment services. Office: Polo Ralph Lauren Corp 650 Madison Ave New York NY 10022-1029*

LAURENCE, JEFFREY CONRAD, immunologist, educator; b. NYC, Oct. 21, 1952; s. Harry and Stephanie (Maderic) L.; m. Susan Paley, Mar. 2003; children: Auden, Galen, Luca. BA summa cum laude, Columbia U., 1972; MD, U. Chgo., 1976. Diplomate Am. Bd. Internal Medicine. Rsch. assoc. Inst. for Cancer Rsch., Osaka, Japan, 1974-75; intern, resident, then hematology fellow N.Y.C. Hosp.-Cornell, 1976-82; assoc. physician The Rockefeller U., NYC, 1980-84; asst. prof. Cornell U. Med. Coll., NYC, 1982-87, assoc. prof., 1988-2000, prof., 2001—; dir. Lab. AIDS Rsch. Cornell Med. Coll., NYC, 1986—; attending physician N.Y. Presbyn. Hosp., NYC, 2001—. Sr. dir. Immune Tech., Inc., N.Y.C., 1986-95; sr. scientist Am. Found. AIDS Rsch., N.Y.C. and Beverly Hills, Calif., 1986—. Author: (play) Many Happy Returns, 1982; editor-in-chief The AIDS Reader, 1991—; editor AIDS Targeted Info. Newsletter, 1987-92; assoc. editor AIDS Rsch. and Human Retroviruses, AIDS, 1987-95; editor-in-chief AIDS Patient Care and STDs, 1996—, Translational Rsch., 2006—; cons. editor Infections in Medicine, 1987—; patentee in field Recipient Clinician-Scientist award Am. Heart Assn., 1980-85; William S. Paley Found. fellow, 1982-84; Henry Luce Found. scholar, 1974, Rhodes scholar-elect, 1973. Mem. NIH (mem. study sect.), AMA, Fedn. Am. Soc. Exptl. Biology-Medicine, Am. Soc. Microbiology, Am. Soc. Clin. Investigation, Phi Beta Kappa. Presbyterian. Avocations: collecting ancient med. books and sci. instruments, contemporary art, sports, yoga. Home: 86 Brookside Dr Greenwich CT 06831-5345 Office: NY Presbyn Hosp-Cornell Med Ctr Dept Medicine Lab AIDS Rsch 411 E 69th St New York NY 10021-5608 Business E-Mail: jlaurenc@med.cornell.edu.

LAURENCE, MICHAEL MARSHALL, foundation administrator; b. NYC, May 22, 1940; s. Frank Marshall and Edna Ann (Roeder) L.; m. Patricia Ann McDonald, Mar. 1, 1969; children: Elizabeth Sarah, John Marshall. AB cum laude, Harvard U., 1963. From sr. editor to asst. pub. Playboy mag., Chgo., 1967—77, asst. pub., 1977—82; mng. editor Oui mag., Chgo., 1973-77; editor, pub. Linn's Stamp News, Sidney, Ohio, 1982—2002, also columnist Editor's Choice; sr. v.p., editl. dir. Amos Hobby Pub., Sidney, 2002—05; exec. dir. Philatelic Found., NYC, 2006—. Co-founder, dir. U.S. 1869 Pictorial Rsch. Assocs., 1975-82. Author: Playboy's Investment Guide, 1971; editor-in-chief The Chronicle of the U.S. Philatelic Classics Society, 2005—; editor: U.S. Mail and Post Office Assistant, 1975; author articles. Recipient G.M. Loeb award for disting. mag. writing U. Conn., 1968; named to Writers Hall of Fame, Am. Philatelic Soc., 1994. Mem. U.S. Philat. Classics Soc. (life, Elliott Perry award 1975, bd. dirs. 1975-81, Disting. Philatelist award 2003), Harvard Club (N.Y.C.), Collectors Club Chgo. (bd. dirs. 1978-82), Collectors Club N.Y.C. Avocations: stamp collecting/philately, gardening. Office: The Philatelic Found 70 West 40th St 15th Fl New York NY 10018 Office Phone: 212-221-6555.

LAURENCE, ROBERT LIONEL, chemical engineering professor; b. West Warwick, RI, July 13, 1936; s. Lionel Gerard and Gertrude Sara (Lefebvre) L.; m. Carol Leah Jolicoeur, Sept. 7, 1959; children: Jonathan, Lisa, Andrew. BSChemE, MIT, 1957; MSChemE, U. R.I., 1960; PhD-ChemE, Northwestern U., 1966; DSc (honoris causa), Inst. Nat. Poly., Toulouse, France, 1989. Rsch. engr. Gen. Dynamics, Groton, Conn., 1957-59, E. I. du Pont de Nemours, Wilmington, Del., 1960-61, field svc. engr. Beaumont, Tex., 1961-63; asst. prof. chem. engring. Johns Hopkins U., Balt., 1965-68; rsch. engr. Monsanto Co., Springfield, Mass., 1968; assoc. prof. U. Mass., Amherst, 1968-73, head dept. chem. engring., 1982-89, prof., 1973-2001, prof. emeritus, 2001—. Vis. prof. Imperial Coll., London, 1974-75, Coll. de France, Paris, 1982-83, Rijks U. Gent, 1996; invited prof. ENSIGC, Toulouse, France, 1990; vis. rsch. fellow GE, Schenectady, 1989; cons. UN Devel. Program, Argentina, 1978, 80, Beijing, 1982; mem. Conseil Technologique Groupe Rhone-Poulenc, Paris, 1988-96; MIT practice sch. sta. dir. Badische Analin und Soda Fabrik, Ludwigstafen, Germany, 2007. Fellow Am. Inst. Chem. Engrs., Am. Inst. Chemists; mem. Am. Chem. Soc., Tau Beta Pi. Roman Catholic. Avocation: rugby. Home: 5 Ashley Terr Waterville ME 04901 Home Phone: 207-872-0133; Office Phone: 413-545-0470. E-mail: rlaurence@ecs.umass.edu.

LAURENCIN, CATO THOMAS, biomedical engineer, orthopaedic surgeon; b. Phila., Jan. 15; s. Cyril Alexander and Helen Isabella (Moorehead) L. BS in Engring., Princeton U., 1980; PhD, MIT, 1987; MD, Harvard U., Boston, 1987. Diplomate Nat. Bd. Med. Examiners. Instr. biochem. engring. MIT, Cambridge, 1987—92; clin. fellow in orthopaedic surgery Mass. Gen. Hosp.-Harvard Med. Sch., 1988—89; rsch. scientist div. of health sciences & tech. MIT, Cambridge, 1992—97; adjunct prof. biomedical engring. Drexel U., Phila., 1994, rsch. prof. materials engring., 1994, rsch. prof. chemical engring., 1994—98, vice chmn. orthopaedic surgery & Helen I. Moorehead prof. chemical engring., 1998—2002; assoc. prof. orthopaedic surgery Hahnemann U. Sch. Medicine, Phila., 1994—98, clinical assoc. prof. orthopaedic surgery, 1998—2002, rsch. prof. pharmacology & physiology, 2000; prof. biomedical & chemical engring., Lillian T. Pratt disting. prof. & chair orthopaedic surgery U. Va., Charlottesville, Va., 2003—. Asst. dir., clin. coord. Harvard Health Professions Program, 1983-85; Lowell Inst. lectr. Suffolk U., Boston, 1991. Recipient resident rsch. award Am. Orthopaedic Assn., 1991, William Grimes award, Am. Inst. Chemical Engineers, Leadership in Tech. award, New Millennium Found.; named one of Top 100 Black Physicians in Am., Black Enterprise Mag., 2001. Mem. Inst. Medicine, Nat. Med. Assn. (chmn. resident planning com. 1990-91), Nat. Soc. Black Engrs. (mem., chmn. acads. com. 1976-80); fellow Am. Inst. for Med. & Biological Engring.; internat. fellow in Biomaterials Sci. & Engring. Office: Dept Orthopaedic Surgery Univ Va PO Box 800159 Charlottesville VA 22908

LAURENSON, ROBERT MARK, mechanical engineer; b. Pitts., Oct. 25, 1938; s. Robert Mark and Mildred Othelia (Frandsen) L.; m. Alice Ann Scroggins, Aug. 26, 1961; children: Susan Elizabeth Laurenson Matchael, Shari Lynn Laurenson Lawson. Student, Drury Coll., 1956-58; BS in Mech. Engring., Mo. Sch. Mines, 1961; MS in Mech. Engring., U. Mich., 1962; PhD in Mech. Engring. (NASA tng. grantee), Ga. Inst. Tech., 1968. Registered profl. engr., Mo. Dynamics engr. McDonnell Douglas Corp., St. Louis, 1962-64, sr. dynamics engr., 1968-71, group engr., 1971-74, staff engr., 1974-75, tech. specialist, 1975-78, sr. tech. specialist, 1978-81, sect. chief, 1981-85, prin. tech. specialist, 1985-87, br. chief, 1987-89, prin. mgr. engring., 1989-92; prin. tech. specialist, systems engring. mgr. The Boeing Co., Seabrook, Md., 1992-93, sr. mgr., 1993-95, asst. dir. engring., 1995-97, gen. mgr., 1998-99; ret.; pvt. cons. Crofton, Md., 1999—. Participant 14th Midwestern Mechanics Conf., 1975; lectr. engring. mechanics St. Louis U., part-time 1969-71; adj. assoc. prof. U. Mo.-Rolla Grad. Engring. Ctr., St. Louis, 1980-88; lectr. mech. engring. Johns Hopkins U., 1996-99; participant Symposium on Dynamics and Control of Large Flexible Spacecraft, Blackburg, Va., 1977, In-Space Tech. Experiments Workshop NASA, 1988, Damping, '89 Conf., 1989; mem. panel Am. Astronautical Soc. Symposium on Dynamics and Control of Nonridig Spacecraft, UCLA, 1974; mem. accreditation bd. engr. and tech. Engring. Accredidation Commn., 1998-2003, mem. exec. com., 2000-03, vice chair ops., 2003-04, chair, 2005-06, past chair, 2006-, mem. accredidation coun., 2004—, Vol. Participation Project steering com., 2005—; bd. dirs., mem. exec. com. ABET, 2005-06; project coord. ASME/NSF Project Grant, 2000-01. Author: How to Write Winning Proposals, 2003, Systems Engineering, 2003; contbr. articles to profl. jour.; reviewer profl. jour.; author tech. papers Jour. Engring. for Industry, 1972, Jour. Spacecraft and Rockets, 1973, AIAA Jour., 1976, 78, 80, 85; numerous papers presented at tech. conf. Vestryman Episcopal Ch., 1972-76, sr. warden, 1976, uscher chmn., 1978-80, Sunday sch. tchr., 1980-84, chmn. every mem. canvas, 1983, mem. steering com., 1983-88, chmn. steering com., 1987-88, mem. search com., 1984-85, mem. exec. com., 1991-92, warden, 1991-92; mem. Commn. on Ministry, Diocese of Mo., 1985-91, chmn., 1989-91; mem. standing com. Diocese of Mo., 1990-92; trustee Corp. of Episcopal Diocese of Mo., 1990-92; mem. seminarian com., 1993-98, 2001-03, chair, 1994-97, engring. mentor Holy Trinity Episcopal Day Sch., chmn. Parish Commn. on Ministry, 1999-2000, chair parish strategic planning com., 2001-03, chair comms. ministry area, 2005—; pres. Crabtown Square Dance Club, 1998-2000. Fellow ASME (structures materials com. aerospace divsn. 1975-84, com. chmn. 1979-81, session organizer, chmn. ann. meeting 1975, participant ann. meeting 1986, 89, mem. exec. com. aerospace divsn. 1980-85, sec.-treas. 1981-82, vice-chmn. 1982-83, chmn. 1983-84, Flag award aerospace divsn. 1990, mem. Guggenheim medal bd. 1989-92, mem. conf. organizing com., session chmn. Structures, Structural Dynamics and Materials Conf., 1977, chmn. tech. program 1978, gen. co-chmn. 1979, gen. chmn. 1981, mem. SDM planning com. 1978-82, chmn. 1981-82, session chmn. 1985, 88, adv. com. 1978-82, participant 1979, 83, 86, 90, mech. engring. evaluator Accreditation Bd. Engring. and Tech. 1985-91, 94-98, organizer symposium on microgravity fluid mechanics 1986, mem. planning com. edn. conf. 1986, editor Advances in Aerospace Structures 1982, Procs. of 1986 Edn. Conf. The Decade Ahead, bd. engring. edn. K thru 12 task force 1992-93, bd. pre-coll. edn. 1992-95, 1st alt. nat. nominating com. 1993-94, bd. on engring. edn. 1998-2003, engring. accreditation com. 1998-2003, exec. com. 1993-2003, sec. 1995-96, vice chair 1996-97, rep. on Am. Assn. Engring. Soc.'s Precoll. Edn. Coun. 1993-95, exec. com. 1993-95, Dedicated Svc. award 1995); mem. AIAA (sr., gen. chmn. dynamics specialist conf. 1981, session chmn. 1987), Edison Electric Inst. (adv. com. power engring. edn. forgivable loan program 1993-94), Sigma Xi, Pi Tau Sigma, Tau Beta Pi, Phi Kappa Phi, Sigma Phi Epsilon. Home: 1104 Jasper Ct Crofton MD 21114-1658

LAURENT, JERRY SUZANNA, communications executive; b. Oklahoma City, Dec. 28, 1942; d. Harry Austin and M. LaVerne (Barker) Minick; m. Leroy E. Laurent, July 2, 1960; children: Steven, Sandra, David, Debra. AS in Engr. Tech., Okla. State U., 1986. Owner, CEO Technically Write, Mustang, Okla., 1989-95; sr. tech. comm. specialist Applied Intelligence Group, Edmond, Okla., 1995-98, DCA Svcs., Oklahoma City, 1998—2003; owner, CEO Comm. Design Group, 2003—, pres. Oklahoma City, 2003—. Fellow: Soc. Tech. Comm. (assoc.; Superscript editor 1985, v.p. 1985, feature editor 1986, student chpt. pres. 1986, program coord. Okla. chpt. 1992—93, sec. 1993—94, v.p. 1994—95, state pres. 1995—96, state treas. Okla. chpt. 1998—99, dir./sponsor region 5 1999—2002, bylaws com. mgr. 2001—02, Region 5 conf. mgr. 2002, 2nd v.p. 2003—04, 1st v.p. 2004—05, internat. pres. 2005—06, internat. immediate past pres. 2006—07, mgr. nominating com. 2007—, Disting. Chpt. Svc. award 1997, Outstanding Achievement award 2001, Vol. of Yr. award 2006); mem.: Internat. Coun. Tech. Comm. (v.p. 2006—07), Am. Bus. Women's Assn. (area coun. pres. 1987—89, v.p. dist. III 1988—89, sec. 1990—91, conf. gen. chair 1992, chmn. bd. dirs. Help Us Grow Spiritually 1993—95, editor Smoke Signals, Bull. award 1977, Woman of Yr. 1978, Bull. award 1981, 1983, Bus. Assoc. of Yr. 1983—84, Bull. award 1984, 1993, 1995, Woman of Yr. 1996, 1997, named One of Top Ten Bus. Women in Nation 1997, Bull. award 1997—99, Nat. Newsletter award 1999, Bull. award 2003—04, 2006, 2007, named Al-Lu-We Boss of Yr. 2007). Democrat. Baptist. Avocations: reading, public speaking, motivating people, volunteer activities. Home and Office: Comm Design Group 347 W Forest Dr Mustang OK 73064-3430

LAURENT, LAWRENCE BELL, communications executive, retired journalist; b. Monroe, La., Mar. 09; s. Lewis Emeal and John Ethel (Dawkins) L.; m. Margaret F. Goodwillie, Nov. 1, 1949 (dec. May 7, 2006); children: Richard Sandford, Arthur Halliday, Margaret Funsten, Elizabeth MacLean Student, U. Colo., 1943—44, U. Va., 1946—49; pvt. study with, Dr. W.Y. Elliott, 1954—56, Dr. Franklin Dunham, 1957—58. With Bluefield Daily Telegraph, W.Va., 1949—50, Charlottesville Daily Progress, Va., 1950—51, Washington Post, 1951—82, radio-TV editor, 1953—82, radio-TV editor emeritus, 1982—; cons. Assn. Ind. TV Stas., 1982—85, dir. comm., 1985—86, v.p. comm., 1986—91; congl. cons., 1991—; editor-in-residence Broadcast Pioneers Libr., 1985—96; adj. prof. comm. Am. U., Washington, 1963—85; chmn. editl. bd. TV Quar., 1963—74, bd. dirs. Guest prof. Syracuse U., 1965; vis. prof. U. Detroit, 1967, George Washington U., 1982-95, professorial lectr., 1996—; former judge Alfred I. duPont awards, Saturday Rev. Lit. TV awards, Sigma Delt Chi pub. svc. TV awards, Humanitas awards Editor, author: (with Newton N. Minow) Equal Time, 1964; Contbr. to books, mags Trustee Human Family Edn. and Cultural Inst.; bd. dirs. Pioneers Edn. Fund, Inc., 1984-94, trustee, 1995-2002. With USNR, 1943-46 Recipient Front Page award Am. Newspaper Guild, 1964, Disting. Tchr. award Am. U., 1978, TV Acad.'s Silver Cir. award, 1988, Pres.'s medal George Washington U., 1999; named to Broadcast Pioneers' Hall of Fame, 1984; du Pont Journalism scholar U. Va., 1947-49 Mem. AAUP, NATAS (life), VFW (life), DAV (life), 55rd Joint Assault Signal Co. Assn., USS Belle Grove Historic Assn., Nat. Press Club, White House Corrs. Assn., Washington Post E-Streeters, Am. Legion (life), Thomas Jefferson Soc. Alumni (U. Va.), Sigma Delta Chi, Pi Delta Epsilon, Theta Chi Episcopalian. Home: Goodwin House Apt 558 4800 Fillmore Ave Alexandria VA 22311

LAURENT, PIERRE-HENRI, retired history professor; b. Fall River, Mass., May 15, 1933; s. Henri and Harriet (Moriarty) L.; m. Virginia Brayton, 1958; children: Paul-Henri, Bradford Webb, Nicole, Alexa. AB, Colgate U., 1956; AM, Boston U., 1960, PhD, 1964. Instr. polit. economy Boston U., 1961-64; asst. prof. history Sweet Briar Coll., 1964-66; vis. asst. prof. history U. Wis., Madison, 1966-67; asst. prof. history Tulane U., New Orleans, 1967-68, assoc. prof., 1968-70; assoc. prof. history Tufts U., Medford, Mass., 1970—75, prof., 1975—2003, chmn. dept., 1987—89, chmn. Exptl. Coll., 1973-75, adj. prof. diplomatic history/Fletcher Sch. Law and Diplomacy, 1977, 1984, acting dir. internat. rels. program, 1979, dir. internat. relations program, 1984—88, co-dir. internat. relations program France, 1979—80; acad. dir. Tufts European Ctr., 1996; prof. emeritus Tufts U., Medford, Mass., 2003—. Mem. history devel. bd. Ednl. Testing Svc. of Princeton, 1979-82; instr. JFK Inst. Polit., Harvard U., Cambridge, 1989; mem. nat. screening com. Fulbright-Hays program Inst. Internat. Edn., 1988-91; rsch. assoc. Ctr. for Internat. Affairs, Harvard U. Mem. editorial bd. Jour. Social History, 1966-74; sect. editor Am. Hist. Rev., 1967-77; co-editor: The State of the European Union: Deepening and Widening, 1998, NATO and the European Union: Confronting the Challenges of European Security and Enlargement, 1999; contbr. chpts. to books, articles to profl. jours., mags., encys. Mem. Town of Wellesley Hist. Commn., 2003—06. With USAF, 1956—58. NATO fellow, 1967, NEH fellow, 1969, Paul-Henri Spaak Found. fellow, 1976-77; Sweet Briar Faculty rsch. grantee, 1965, Tufts Faculty rsch. grantee, 1972, 1994, Inst. European Studies-Exxon Ednl. Fund grantee, 1983; Fulbright Rsch. scholar, 1992-93; Fulbright chair Coll. of Europe, Bruges, 1998. Fellow Inst. des Rels. Internationales, Acad. Assoc. Atlantic Coun.; mem. AAUP (exec. com. Mass. State Conf. 1974-76, pres. Tufts U. chpt. 1982-84, 2000-2002), European Union Studies Assn. (exec. com. 1988-92, 95-99, chmn. 1991-92, vice-chmn. 1997-99). Personal E-mail: ginnypierre@msn.com.

LAURENTI, JOSEPH LUCIANO, language educator, writer; b. Hespérange, Luxembourg, Dec. 10, 1931; arrived in U.S., 1949; s. Ernesto Carlo and Angelina Teresa (Dal Canton) Laurenti; m. Luellen W. Watson, June 10, 1967 (dec. June 2000). BA in Spanish, French, Italian, U. Ill., Urbana, 1958; MA in Spanish, French, Italian, U. Ill., 1959; PhD in Spanish, French, U. Mo., 1962. Instr. Spanish U. Ill., Urbana, 1959, U. Mo., Columbia, 1959—62; prof. Spanish, Italian and German Ill. State U., Normal, 1962—2001; ret., 2001. U.S. corres. Quaderni Ibero-Am., Torino, Italy, 1974—93, AZB Revista de Cultura Internacional. Author: Lazarillo de Tormes: A Critical Study of the Second Part of Juan de Luna, 1965, A Bibliographic Essay of the Spanish Picaresque Novel, 1968, Studies in the Spanish Picaresque Novel, 1970, Critical Prefaces in the Spanish Picaresque Novel, 1971, A Critical Bibliography of Picaresque Literature, 1973, The Spanish Golden Age (1472-1700), 1979, A Catalog of Rare Books in the Library of the University of Illinois and in Selected North American Libraries, 1979, A Catalog of Spanish Rare Books (1701-1974) in the Library of the University of Illinois and in Selected North American Libraries, 1984, Hispanic Rare Books of the Golden Age (1470-1699) in the Newberry Library of Chicago and in Selected North American Libraries, 1989, Catálogo bibliográfico de la literatura Picaresca (Siglos XVI-XX), 1991, Bibliografia de la Literatura Picaresca, 1991 (Nicolá Antonio prize, 1994), Nuevos estudios bibliograficos sobre la Edad de Oro: Fondos raros y colecciones en la Biblioteca de la Universidad de Illinois, 1994, Estudios Bibliográficos Sobre La Edad de Oro (1474-1699), 1997, Estudios Bibliográficos sobre le Edno de Oro y el Siglo de Las Luces (1472-1799), 2000, Catálogo bibliográfico de la literatura Picaresca, 2000; co-author (with Alberto Porqueras Mayo): A Bibliographic Essay of the Prologue in Literature, 1971; co-author: (with Joseph Siracusa) Literary Relations Between Spain and Italy, 1972, The World of Federico Garl Lorca, 1974; co-author: (with A Porqueras Mayo) Estudios bibliográficos sobre la Edad de Oro, 1984; co-editor (with Mayo): Antonio de Guevara en la biblioteca de la universidad de Illinois, 1974; co-editor: (with Vern Williamsen) Varia hispanica. Estudios en los siglos de oro y literatura moderna: Homenaje a Alberto Porqueras Mayo, 1989; reviewer: Modern Lang. Jour., 1978—; mem. editl. bd. (jour.) Edit. Reichenberger, Kassel, Germany, 1983—; contbr. over 230 articles, revs. to profl. publs. Cpl. US Army, 1952—54. Recipient Antonio Nicolas prize, Syracuse U., 1992, Disting. Svc. award, Ill. State U., 1962—2001; fellow, Newberry Libr., Chgo., 1986, Gutenberg Gesellschaft, Mainz, Germany, 1992; grantee Dip. Prov. grantee, Diputacion Provincial, Seville, Spain, 1991—94, Intercambios Culturales Hispano-Americanos, Barcelona, Spain, 1984, Program for Cultural Coop. between Spain's Min. of Culture and U.S. Govt., 1989, 1994. Mem.: AAUP, MLA (nominated prize for disting. bibliography 2002), Ill. Assn. Tchrs. of Modern Langs., Midwest Modern Lang. Assn., Am. Assn. Tchrs. of Spanish and Portuguese, Am. Assn. Profs. of Italian, Internat. Assn. Philogists, Internat. Assn. of Hispanists, Assn. de Cervantistas (life), Assn. de Bibliografia Española (life), Sigma Delta Pi (chpt. pres. 1958—59, Medal of Order of Don Quixote). Independent. Roman Catholic. Home: 2703 Wedgewood Bloomington IL 61704

LAURIE, HUGH, actor; b. Oxford, Oxfordshire, Eng., June 11, 1959; s. George Ranald and Patricia Mundell; m. Jo Green, June 16, 1989; children: Charlie, Bill, Rebecca. Actor, writer: (TV series) Alfresco, 1983—84; A Bit of Fry and Laurie, 1986—95; actor, dir. Fortysomething, 2003; actor: Blackadder the Third, 1987, Les Girls, 1988, Blackadder Goes Forth, 1989, (voice) Treasure Island, 1993, Tracey Takes On..., 1996, (voice) Preson Pig, 2000, Little Grey Rabbit, 2000, Stuart Little, 2003, House, M.D., 2004— (Best Performance by an Actor in a TV Series-Drama, Hollywood Fgn. Press Assn. Golden Globe award, 2006, Best Performance by an Actor in a TV Series-Drama, Golden Globe award, Hollywood Fgn. Press Assn., 2007, Outstanding Performance by a Male Actor in a Drama Series, SAG, 2007, Choice TV Actor: Drama, Teen Choice Awards, 2007); (TV films) Cambridge Footlights Revue, 1982, The Crystal Cube, 1983, Mrs. Capper's Birthday, 1985, The Laughing Prisoner, 1987, Hysteria 2!, 1989, All or Nothing at All, 1993, The Adventures of Mole, 1995, The Place of Lions, 1997, The Nearly Complete Utter History of Everything, 1999, Life with Judy Garland: Me and My Shadows, 2001, The Young Visitors, 2003; (films) Plenty, 1985, Peter's Friends, 1992, A Pin for the Butterfly, 1994, Sense and Sensibility, 1995, 101 Dalmatians, 1996, The Borrowers, 1997, The Man in the Iron Mask, 1998, Cousin Bette, 1998, Stuart Little, 1999, Blackadder Back and Forth, 1999, Carnivale, 2000, The Piano Tuner, 2001, Stuart Little 2, 2002, Flight of the Phoenix, 2004, The Big Empty, 2005, Valiant, 2005. Named an Honorary Knight Comdr. of the Most Excellent Order of the British Empire, Queen Elizabeth II, 2007. Office: The Gersh Agy 232 N Canon Dr Beverly Hills CA 90210*

LAURIE, JAMES ANDREW, broadcast executive, consultant, director, television executive producer, journalist; b. Eustis, Fla., June 16, 1947; s. Andrew Louis and Geneva Lavina (Pryor) L. BA in History, Am. U., Washington, 1970; postgrad., George Washington U. Free-lance writer Far Eastern Econ. Review, Washington, 1969, 73-74, Phnom Penh, Cambodia and Saigon, Vietnam, 1970-71; reporter NBC News, Saigon, 1971-73, 75, Tokyo, 1976-78; with ABC News, 1978-99, corr., bur. chief, Hong Kong, 1978-81, opened 1st Am. radio-TV bur. in Peking, 1981, bur. chief, Peking, 1981-82, chief Asia corr., Tokyo, 1983-88, corr., bur. chief Moscow, 1989-91, sr. corr. London, 1991-96, Hong Kong, bur. chief, 1996-99; vice pres. Network News and Current Affairs, Newscorps/Satellite Television, Asia region, 1999—2005; sr. advisor broadcasting U. Hong Kong, 2005—; pres., exec. prodr. Focus Asia Prodns., 2005—; dir. broadcast program U. Hong Kong, 2005—. Writer, narrator: (ABC Closeup documentaries) Japan: Myths behind the Miracle, 1981, The Unruly Dragon: China's Yellow River, 1988, Soviet segment ABC Spl. "Beyond the Cold War", 1989; covered Mikhail Gorbachev in Cuba, East Germany, Rome, Malta, 1989, Tien An Men Crushing of Democrats Movement, 1989, Gorbachev summit in U.S., 1990, Bush-Gorbachev summit, Moscow, 1991, coup d'etat Moscow, 1991, Somalia Famine, 1992, Iraq Crisis, 1993, Bosnia Crises, 1993, Israeli-Palestinian Negotiations, 1993, Russian Crisis October, 1993, South African elections, 1994, U.S. operation in Haiti, 1994, Crisis in Rwanda, 1995, Human Right Coverage China, 1996, Hong Kong Handover, 1997, Reporting from Tibet, 1997, coup d'etat in Cambodia, 1997, Afganistan, 2001; interviewed Pakistan Pres. Musharaf, 2001, Russian Pres. Putin, 2003. Recipient George Foster Peabody Broadcasting award for reporting fall of Saigon, 1976; Columbia-Dupont award for ABC Closeup documentary Cambodia: This Shattered Land, 1981; award for radio news coverage of assassination of Philippine leader Benigno Aquino, Overseas Press Club, 1983; Emmy award, 1987, N.Y. Festivals award. Office: Eliot Hall Journalism Media Studies Ctr U Hong Kong Pokfulam Rd Hong Kong Hong Kong also: U Hong Kong Parkview Tower 3 Ste 2127 Hong Kong Hong Kong Home Phone: 852 9096 3416; Office Phone: 852 2219 4013. Personal E-mail: jlaurie@pacific.net.hk. E-mail: jlaurie@hku.hk.

LAURIE, NANCY WALTON, retail executive; b. 1952; d. James Walton; m. Bill Laurie. BA, BA, U. Memphis. Founder, pres. NYC Cedar Lake Ensemble, Columbia Performing Arts Ctr., Mo. Co-owner St. Louis Blues Hockey Team; stake holder Wal-Mart, 1995—. Named one of Forbes' Richest Americans, 1995, 1998, 2001, 2004, 2006. Office: Cedar Lake Ensemble 547 W 26th St New York NY 10001*

LAURIE, ROBIN GARRETT, lawyer; b. Mobile, Ala., June 10, 1956; s. George and Margaret Eloise (Garrett) L.; m. Deborah Dockery; children: Elizabeth Anne, Robin Garrett. AA, Marion Mil. Inst., Ala., 1976; BS in Bus., U. Ala., Tuscaloosa, 1978; JD, U.Ala., Tuscaloosa, 1988. Bar: Ala. 1988, U.S. Dist. Ct. (no., mid. and so. dists.) Ala. 1988, U.S. Ct. Appeals (11th cir.) 1988. Ptnr. Balch & Bingham LLP, Montgomery, Ala., 1988—. Lead articles editor Ala. Law Rev., 1986-88. Recipient Outstanding Svc. award Ala. Law Rev., 1988. Mem. ABA, Ala. State Bar, Montgomery County Bar Assn., Montgomery Rotary Club, Order of the Coif. Methodist. Avocations: flying small airplanes, fishing, hunting. Office: Balch & Bingham LLP PO Box 78 Montgomery AL 36101-0078 Office Phone: 334-834-6500. Business E-Mail: rlaurie@balch.com.

LAURIER, MAURICE JOSEF, marine architect, engineer, consultant; b. Faulkton, SD, Oct. 11, 1926; s. William and Alice Wing Laurier; m. Margaret Lee Shriver (dec.); children: David Bruce, Brian Douglas(dec.), Karen Lee Laurier Morisato; m. Nancy Liang, Nov. 14, 1998 (dec. 2004). BS in Naval Architecture, Webb Inst., Glen Cove, NY, 1950; MS in Indsl. Mfmt., MIT, Cambridge, Mass., 1961. Engr. electric boat divsn. Gen. Dynamics, Groton, Conn., 1950—58, mgr. shipyard tests, 1958—60, mgr. prodn. engring., 1961—66, mgr. prodn. control Quincy divsn. Mass., 1966—69, asst. dir. ops., 1969—71; pres., chmn. bd. dirs. Glass Marine, Inc., Gloucester, Va., 1972—88; pvt. practice marine surveyor, cons. Yorktown, Va., 1989—. Mem. collections and exhibits, supr. boat shop Watermen's Mus., Yorktown, 1995—. Lt. (j.g.) USNR, 1950—55. Sloan fellow, MIT, 1960. Mem.: Am. Boat and Yacht Coun., US Naval Inst., Webb Inst. Alumni Assn. Episcopalian. Home and Office: 230 Nelson St PO Box 265 Yorktown VA 23690

LAURIN, PIERRE, finance company executive; b. Charlemagne, Que., Can., Aug. 11, 1939; MBA, U. Montreal, 1963; D in Bus. Adminstrn., Harvard U., 1969; PhD (hon.), Concordia U., Montreal, 1983. Dean bus. sch. U. Montreal, 1975-82; v.p. planning and adminstrn. Alcan Co. of Can., 1982-87; vice chmn., pres., Que. Merrill Lynch Can. Inc., Montreal, 1987—99. Exec. in residence, HEC Montréal, 1999. Author mgmt. textbook. Named officer Order Can. Office: HEC Montréal Montreal PQ Canada H3T 2A7 Home Phone: 514-762-1278; Office Phone: 514-340-7186.

LAURSEN, FINN, political science professor; b. Romlund, Denmark, June 17, 1944; s. Laurits and Hedvig (Kristensen) L.; m. Berenice Lara, May 10, 1962; children: Jannik, Itzel. Grad., Aarhus U., Denmark, 1974; PhD, U. Pa., 1980. Rschr. European U. Inst., Florence, Italy, 1977-80; vis. fellow Princeton U., NJ, 1980-81; asst. prof. Odense U., Denmark, 1981-82, assoc. prof., 1982-84; vis. fellow Woods Hole Oceanographic Inst., Mass., 1984-85; lectr. London Sch. Econs., 1985-88; assoc. prof. European Inst. Pub. Adminstrn., Maastricht, The Netherlands, 1988-90, prof. internat. politics, 1990-95; prof., dir. Thorkil Kristensen Inst., South Jutland U. Ctr., Esbjerg, Denmark, 1995-98. Vis. prof. U. Tsukuba, Japan, 1998-99, Schuman prof. Fudan U., China, 1998-99; prof. internat. politics dept. polit. sci. U. So. Denmark, Odense, 1999—2006, dir. Ctr. for European Studies, 2002—06, pres. Danish Soc. for European Studies, 2002—04, Jean Monnet chair European polit. economy, 2003—06; Can. rsch. chair in European Union studies Dalhousie U., Halifax, Can., 2006—; dir. European Union Ctr. of Excellence, 2006—. Author: Superpower at Sea, 1983, L'Europe Bleue, 1987, Danmark og Havretten, 1988, Small Powers at Sea, 1993; editor: Toward a New International Marine Order, 1982, Efta and the EC: Implications of 1992, 1990, Europe, 1992, World Partner?, 1991, The Intergovernmental Conference on Political Union, 1992, The Ratification of the Maastricht Treaty, 1994, The Political Economy of European Integration, 1995, The EU and Central Europe: Status and Prospects, 1996, The Amsterdam Treaty, 2002, Comparative Regional Integration, 2003, The Treaty of Nice, 2006. Recipient Am. Studies award, Fulbright Commn., Copenhagen, 1975, Penfield scholar U. Pa., Phila., 1977, J.P. Compton fellow Princeton U., 1980. Office: Dalhousie Univ Dept Polit Sci Halifax NS B3H 4H6 Canada Office Phone: 902-494-6611. E-mail: finn.laursen@dal.ca.

LAURSEN, LIN L., women's college basketball coach, educator; b. Sioux Rapids, Iowa, Dec. 12, 1943; d. Marius Nissen and Gerda (Miller) L. BS, Iowa State U., Ames, 1965; MS, Ariz. State U., Tempe, 1971. Tchr. Rich East HS, Park Forest, Ill., 1965-69; tchr. phys. edn. Ctrl. Ariz. Coll., Coolidge, 1971—, head coach women's basketball, 1974—. Mem. Kodak All-Am. Selection Com., 1983-90. Named Converse Coach of Yr., 1983, Russell Athletic Women's Basketball Coaches Assn. Coach of Yr., 2005; recipient Coach of Yr. award Nat. Jr. Coll. Athletic Assn., 1989, 98, 2005, Win #400 award Nat. Jr. Coll. Athletic Assn. Basketball Com., 1990, Alberta Lee Cox Sportsmanship award, 1994; named to Women's Basketball Hall of Fame, 2007. Mem. Women's Basketball Coaches Assn. Avocations: golf, bicycle riding, tennis, reading. Office: Womens Basketball Ctrl Ariz Coll 8470 Overfield Rd Coolidge AZ 85228 E-mail: lin.laursen@centralaz.edu.*

LAURSEN, THOMAS E., lawyer; BA, MA, U. Ariz.; JD, Columbia U. Atty. Sullivan & Cromwell, NYC, 1984, O'Conner Cavanagh, Tucson, Phoenix; ptnr. Holme, Roberts & Owen LLC, Denver, London, 1999—2004; exec. v.p., gen. counsel, sec. Zions Bancorp., Salt Lake City, 2004—. Office: Zions Bancorp One S Main 15th Fl Salt Lake City UT 84111

LAUSE, MICHAEL FRANCIS, lawyer; b. Washington, Mo., Aug. 3, 1948; s. Walter Francis and Junilla Rose (Marquart) L.; m. Ann G. Hellman, Aug. 29, 1981; children: Andrew Edward, Scott Michael. BA, St. Benedict's Coll., 1970; JD, U. Ill., 1973. Bar: Mo. 1973. Ptnr. Thompson Coburn LLP, St. Louis, 1973—, mem. exec. com., 2002—. Chmn. corp. dept. Thompson Coburn LLP, St. Louis, 2002-, exec. com. Gen. counsel Mo. Health and Ednl. Facilities Authority, 1986—, St. Louis Zoo, 1992—. Mem. ABA, Mo. Bar Assn., St. Louis Bar Assn., Nat. Assn. Bond Lawyers, Bellerive Country Club. Roman Catholic. Home: 9822 Old Warson Rd Saint Louis MO 63124-1066 Office: Thompson Coburn LLP One US Bank Plz Saint Louis MO 63101 Office Phone: 314-552-6000. Business E-Mail: mlause@thompsoncoburn.com.

LAUTENBACHER, CONRAD CHARLES, JR., federal agency administrator, retired naval officer; b. Phila., June 26, 1942; s. Conrad Charles and Dorthea Henrietta (Jensen) L.; m. Susan Elizabeth Scheihing, June 20, 1964; children: Elizabeth Lautenbacher Katz, Conrad John. BS, U.S. Naval Acad., 1964; MS, Harvard U., 1965, PhD, 1968. Commd. ensign USN, 1964, advanced through grades to vice adm., 1974, aide to Vice Chief Naval Ops., Chief Naval Ops. Washington, 1974-75, exec. officer USS Benjamin Stoddert Pearl Harbor, Hawaii, 1975-77, program analyst Chief Naval Ops. Washington, 1977-80, comdg. officer USS Hewitt San Diego, 1980-82, dir. program planning Chief Naval Ops. Washington, 1982-86, comdg. officer Naval Sta., Norfolk Va., 1986-88, insp. gen. U.S. Pacific Fleet Hdqrs. Pearl Harbor, 1988-90; comdr. Cruiser-Destroyer Group 5 San Diego, 1990-91; dir. force structure, resources and assessment J-8, Joint Staff, Washington, 1991-94; spl. asst. to asst. sec. navy USN, 1994; commdr. U.S. Third Fleet, 1994-96; dir. office of program appraisal, 1996-97; dep. chief of naval ops. N-8, 1997-2000; ret., 2000; mgmt. cons. Tech., Stategies, and Alliances, Inc., 2000-01; pres., CEO Consortium for Oceanographic Rsch. and Edn., 2001—02; under sec. of commerce, adminstr. NOAA US Dept. Commerce, 2002—. Decorated D.S.M. (4), Legion of Merit with 3 gold stars, Meritorious Svc. medal with 2 gold stars, Navy Commendation medal, Navy Achievement medal. Mem. U.S. Naval Inst. Lutheran. Office: NOAA 1401 Constitution Ave NW Washington DC 20230 Office Phone: 202-482-3436. Business E-Mail: conrad.c.lautenbacher@noaa.gov. *Life is about people and relationships. True happiness begins with sensitivity and responsiveness to the needs of others.*

LAUTENBERG, FRANK RALEIGH, senator; b. Paterson, NJ, Jan. 23, 1924; s. Samuel and Mollie L. Lautenberg; m. Lois Levenson (div.); children: Ellen, Nan, Lisa, Joshua; m. Bonnie S. Englebardt, 2004. BS in Economics, Columbia U., 1949; DHL, Hebrew Union Coll., Cin. and NYC, 1977; PhD (hon.), Hebrew U., Jerusalem, 1978; LHD (hon.), NJ Inst. Tech., 2000. Salesman Prudential Ins. Co., Newark, 1949—52; met Joe and Henry Taub and became salesman (fifth employee hired) Automatic Data Processing, Inc., Clifton, NJ, 1952-55, exec. v.p. adminstrn., 1955-69, pres., 1969—77, CEO, chmn., 1977—82; owner FRL Enterprises, Rochelle Park, NJ, 2001—; US Senator from NJ, 1982—2001, 2003—; mem. commerce, sci. and transp. com. US Senate, environment and public works com., budget com., appropriations com. Commr. Port Authority NY and NJ, 1978-82, NJ econ. devel. coun.; former disting. vis. prof. Univ. of Medicine & Dentistry, New Brunswick, NJ. Trustee Sch. Bus., Columbia U.; nat. pres. Am. Friends Hebrew U., 1973-74; former hon. gen. chmn., pres. Nat. United Jewish Appeal, 1975-77; mem. bd. overseers NJ Symphony Orch.; founder Lautenberg Ctr. General and Tumor Immunology, Med. Sch. Hebrew U., Jerusalem, 1971; bd. mem. Montclair Art Mus. Served with US Army, 1942—46, Britain, France, Belgium and the Netherlands. Recipient Torch of Learning award Am. Friends Hebrew U., 1971, Scopus award, 1975, James Madison award, ALA, 1991, Congressional Leadership award Airports Coun. International-North America Commissioners Roundtable, 1993, George Falcon Golden Spike award, Nat. Assn. Railroad Passengers, 1988, 2000, Albert D. Chemin award, Jewish Coun. for Public Affairs, 2007; honoree Military Officers Assn. Am., 2007. Mem. Nat. Assn. Data Processing Service Orgns. (pres. 1968-69, dir. from 1974). Democrat. Jewish. Office: District Office 23rd Floor One Gateway Ctr Newark NJ 07102 also: US Senate 324 Hart Senate Office Bldg Washington DC 20510 Office Phone: 973-645-8700, 202-224-3224. Office Fax: 973-639-8723, 202-228-4054.*

LAUTENSCHLAGER, PEGGY A., former state attorney general; b. Fond du Lac, Wis., Nov. 22, 1955; d. Milton A. and Patsy R. (Oleson) L.; m. Rajiv M. Kaul, Dec. 29, 1979 (div. Dec. 1986); children: Joshua Lautenschlager Kaul, Ryan Lautenschlager Kaul; m. William P. Rippl, May 26, 1989; 1 child, Rebecca Lautenschlager Rippl. BA, Lake Forest Coll., 1977; JD, U. Wis., 1980. Bar: Wis., U.S. Dist. Ct. (we. dist.). Pvt. practice atty., Oshkosh, Wis., 1981-85; dist. atty. Winnebago County Wis., Oshkosh, 1985-88; mem. Wis. State Assembly, Fond du Lac, 1988-92; U.S. atty. (we. dist.) Wis. US Dept. Justice, Madison, Wis., 1992—2000, 2006; atty. gen. State of Wis., Madison, 2003—07; atty. Lawton & Cates, SC, Madison. Apptd. mem. Govs. Coun. on Domestic Violence, Madison, State Elections Bd., Madison; bd. dirs. Blandine House, Inc. Active Dem. Nat. Com., Washington, 1992-93; com. Wis., 1989-92. Named Legislator of Yr., Wis. Sch. Counselors, 1992, Legislator of Yr., Wis. Corrections Coalition, 1992. Mem. Wis. Bar Assn., Dane County Bar Assn., Fond du Lac County Bar Assn., Phi Beta Kappa. Democrat. Avocations: gardening, house renovation, sports, cooking. Office: Lawton & Cates SC 10 E Doty St Ste 400 Madison WI 53703 Business E-Mail: peglautenschlager@lawtoncates.com.

LAUTER, JAMES DONALD, retired stockbroker; b. LA, Sept. 3, 1931; s. Richard Leo and Helen M. (Stern) L.; m. Neima Zwieli, Feb. 24, 1973; children: Walter James (dec.), Gary. BS, UCLA, 1956. Market rsch. mgr. Germain's Inc., LA, 1961; sr. v.p. investments, former br. mgr. Dean Witter Reynolds, Inc., Pasadena, Calif., 1961-96, ret., 1996. With Armed Forces, 1954-56. Recipient Sammy award L.A. Sales Execs. Club, 1961. Mem. AARP, UCLA Alumni Assn., UCLA Chancellors Assocs., Pasadena Bond Club (pres. 1995-96), Bruin Athletic Club, Bruin UCLA Varsity Club (formerly UCLA Athletics Life Pass Club), El Caballero Country Club. Home: 3717 Marfield Ave Tarzana CA 91356 Personal E-mail: jlauter@flash.net.

LAUTERBACH, EDWARD CHARLES, psychiatric educator; b. Chgo., Mar. 21, 1955; s. Edward G. and Virginia C. (Pochelski) L. AB cum laude, Augustana Coll., Rock Island, Ill., 1977; MD, Wake Forest U., 1982. Lic. psychiatrist, Mo., Pa., N.J., N.C., Ga.; diplomate Nat. Bd. Med. Examiners, Am. Bd. Psychiatry and Neurology with qualifications in geriat. psychiatry. Intern Washington U. Sch. Medicine/Barnes Hosp., St. Louis, 1982-83, resident in psychiatry, 1983-86, clin. asst., 1982-86; instr. neurology movement disorder fellow U. Medicine and Dentistry of N.J., New Brunswick, 1986-87; asst. prof. Mercer U. Sch. Medicine, Macon, Ga., 1988-92, chief div. adult and geriatric psychiatry, dept. psychiatry and behavioral scis., 1988-98, coord. grand rounds dept. psychiatry and behavioral scis., 1989-98, assoc. prof., 1992-96, prof., 1996—, prof. internal medicine/neurology, 1996—, prof. radiology, 1996—; pvt. practice Charlotte, NC, 1987-88. Chair free comm. IVth World Congress Biol. Psychiatry, Phila., 1985; mem. neurology staff Lyons VA Hosp., 1986; med. staff privileges in neurology Mercy Hosp., Charlotte, 1987, cons., 1987; privileges in psychiatry Med. Ctr. Ctrl. Ga., 1994—, Coliseum Psychiat. Hosp., 1994—, dir. med. staff continuing edn., 1994-96, Middle Ga. Hosp., 1997-2002; med. dir. geropsychiatry program The Sr. Ctr., Middle Ga. Hosp., 1997-2002. Guest editor Psychiatric Annals, 2002; editor: Psychiatric Management in Neurological Disease, 2000, Psychiatric Management in Neurological Disease, Spanish and Italian edits., 2002; editl. reviewer Neuropsychiatry, Neuropsychology and Behavioral Neurology, Biological Psychiatry, Movement Disorders, assoc. editor Jour. Neuropsychiatry and Clin. Neuroscis., 1999—; contbr. articles to profl. jours. Recipient Med. Dir. of Yr. award S.E. region, Horizon Mental Health Mgmt., Inc., 1999—2001; scholar Rock Sleyster scholar, Wake Forest U., 1981. Fellow: Am. Psychiat. Assn. (course dir. 1990—92, 1994—95, symposium chmn. 1995—97, co-dir. 1998—2001, symposium chmn. 2001, Disting.), Am. Neuropsychiat. Assn. (rsch. com. 1992—, vice-chair 1998—99, chmn. 1999—); mem.: Charlotte Psychiat. Soc., Movement Disorder Soc., Med. Assn. Ga., Mecklenburg County Med. Soc., N.C. Psychiat. Assn., Bibb County Med. Soc., Ga. Psychiat. Physicians Assn. (state com. on contg. med. edn.), Am. Acad. Neurology, AMA.

LAUTERBACH, MICHAEL ALAN, artist; b. Blue Island, Ill., Sept. 6, 1954; s. Harry Lewis and Donna Rae (Jones) L. AA in Art, U. Wis. Ctr., Rice Lake, 1976; BS in Mid. Eastern & S.W. Asian Studies, U. Minn., 1986, BA in Art, 1988; postgrad. in Fine Arts, U. Tex., San Antonio, 1989—90; MFA in Visual Arts, U. Ariz., 1992. Material coord. Bell Helicopter Internat., Isfahan, Iran, 1976-78; expediter, material coord. Raymond Internat., Ju'Aymah, Saudi Arabia, 1978-79; storekeeper Air Base Constructors, Ramat-Matred, Negev, Israel, 1980; artist, 1986—. Exhibited in group shows at U. Tex., San Antonio, 1989, U. Ariz. Mus. Art, Tucson, 1992, Park Ave. Armory, NY, 1996, Pro Arts, Oakland, Calif., 10th Internat. Biennial Print & Drawing Exhbn., Republic of China, 2001, Taipeii Biennia, 2003. Vol. Bethany Luth. Ch., Mpls., 1997-98. Fellow, Bush Found., 1996. Avocations: travel, music, cooking, meditation, world cultures. Home: 565 Fell St San Francisco CA 94102 Personal E-mail: zenvoodooshaman@yahoo.com.

LAUTERSTEIN, JOSEPH, cardiologist; b. Vienna, Dec. 1, 1934; came to US, 1940; s. Bernard and Hajnalka (Stern) L.; m. Erika Stein, Jan. 24, 1964 (dec. Aug. 1990); children: Deborah Ann Ehret, Brenda Rose Horton; m. Elisabeth Spiegl Lazaroff, Nov. 27, 1994. BA, Syracuse U., 1955; MD, U. Vienna, 1964. Lic. physician, NY. Intern, then resident in internal medicine The Bklyn. Cumberland Med. Ctr., 1964-66, 68-69, fellow in cardiology, 1969-70; attending physician, cons. internal medicine and cardiology Hamilton Ave. Hosp., Monticello, NY, 1970-78, Catskill Regional Med. Ctr., Harris, NY, 1970—2005, chief cardiology, 1971—2005, chief of staff, 1981—82; mem. courtesy staff dept. internal medicine and cardiology The Bklyn. Hosp. Ctr., 1971-95; clin. asst. dept. internal medicine and cardiology St. Vincent's Hosp. and Med. Ctr. N.Y., 1974-80, asst. attending physician, 1981-86, assoc. attending physician, 1987-94, attending physician, 1995—2005; with Sullivan Internal Medicine Group, P.C., Monticello, 1970—2005; ret., 2005. Dir. ICU Catskill Regional Med. Ctr., Harris, 1971—79, dir. CCU, 1978—2005, dir. spl. diagnostics, 1984—2005, pres. med. bd., 1981—82; mem. pacemaker task force Empire State Med. Sci. and Ednl. Found., 1985—89; med. dir. Sullivan County EMT-D Program, 1989—2005; police surgeon Village of Monticello, 1972—, Sullivan County, 1972—2005; med. advisor Monticello Vol. Ambulance Corps, 1970—80, 1989—2004; mem. Sullivan County Emergency Svcs. Coun., 1990, 91; instr. outdoor emergency care, 1991—. Co-contbr. articles to Jour. Cardiovascular Surgery, Annals of Thoracic Surgery, Angiology, Chest. Trustee Catskill Regional Med. Ctr., 1981-82, Catskill Regional Med. Ctr. Found., 1990-2004, 2007—, hon. trustee, 2004—; mem. Nat. Ski Patrol, 1979—, med. advisor So. NY region, 1989-94, 97—, med. advisor So. Catskill sect., 1994-97; patroller Holiday Mountain Ski Patrol, 1979—; bd. dir. Hospice of Orange and Sullivan Counties, 2005-, mem. fin. exec. com., 2006-, mem. profl. adv. com., 2007—. Capt. med. corps USAF, 1966—68. Named Citizen of Yr., SYDA Found. Sullivan County, 1991. Fellow Am. Coll. Cardiology (emeritus; NY state chpt. councilor 1991—, com. mem. 1990—), Am. Coll. Chest Physicians (assoc.), Am. Coll. Angiology, Internat. Coll. Angiology, NY Cardiol. Soc. (exec. bd. dirs. 1982—, mem. various coms.), NY Acad. Medicine; mem. AMA, Am. Geriatrics Soc., ACP/Am. Soc. Internal Medicine, Soc. for Critical Care Medicine, NY Acad. Scis., N.Am. Soc. for Pacing and Electrophysiology, Med. Soc. State of NY (cardiology del. to interspecialty com., cardiology del. to ho. of dels.), others. Home Phone: 845-794-1737. Personal E-mail: joe_lauterstein@yahoo.com.

LAUTNER, JANE E., development associate; b. Glen Cove, NY, Aug. 24, 1948; d. Clifford F. Buttermark and Hilda M. Coombes-Buttermark; m. Vern Russell Lautner, Nov. 4, 2000; children: Lisa Jane Ross, Tere, Jodi Lubrant. Student, C. W. Post Coll., Greenvale, NY, 1971; student in choral conducting, Westminster Choir Coll., 1986—87. Intake counselor Women's Resource Ctr., Sarasota, Fla., 1993—96; fin. assoc. A. G. Edwards & Sons, Sarasota, 1996—2000, Raymond James and Assocs., Sarasota, 2000—04, Gary Moore and Co., Sarasota, 2004; devel. assoc. Pines of Sarasota Found., 2006—. Author: (dramatic monologue) Mary's Road to the Cross. Founder, organizer Annual Choir Festival, 1996—; organizer, founder ann. choir festival, 1994—; dir. music St. Armands Key Luth. Ch., Sarasota, 2001—; grants chmn. St. Armands Key Luth. Ch. Found., Sarasota, 2003—. Mem.: Am. Guild Organists. Home: 4536 Glebe Farm Rd Sarasota FL 34235 Office: Pines of Sarasota Found 1501 N Orange Ave Sarasota FL 34236 Home Phone: 941-379-9040; Office Phone: 941-955-6293. Business E-Mail: jlautner@pinesofsarasota.org.

LAUTTENBACH, CAROL, artist; b. New Haven, Nov. 26, 1934; d. Gustav Fredrick and Wanda M. (Eshner) Stolze; m. Francis John Lauttenbach; children: Daniel M., William J. Grad. in oils and watercolors with honors, Wash. Sch. Art, Port Wash., NY, Chgo., 1967. One-woman shows include Greene Art Gallery, Guilford, Conn., Carriage House Gallery Ltd., Guilford, Gallery 53, Meriden, Conn., John Slade Ely House Gallery, New Haven, exhibited in group shows at Conn. Classic Arts, Fairfield, 1984 (Gabriel D. Luchetti award), 1986—87 (Gabriel D. Luchetti award, 1986), 1993—95 (1st prize, 1993, 3d prize, 1994, Rosemary Landina Meml. award, 1995), 1997—98 (Westport Framing & Art Gallery award, 1997, 2d prize acrylic and oils, 1998), Mt. Carmel Art Assn., Inc., 1986—88 (Best in Show, 1986, Elizabeth Greeley Meml. award, 1987, Donald L. Perlroth, Inc. award, 1988), 1990 (Marc D. Rosenberg Meml. award), 1998 (New Haven Savings Bank award), 2002 (Mayor Carl Amento award), Arts and Crafts Assn. Meriden, Inc., 1986—88 (Jerry's Artarama award, 1988), 1990, 1993, 1995, 1997—98, 2001, 2004—05 (Best Theme award, 2005), exhibitions include Mary Lou Fischer Gallery, Guilford, 2005, Hamden Art League, 2004—05 (Utrech art Supplies award, 2004, Dusa Chiropractic Ctr. award, 2005). Recipient Prix de Paris award, Mus. Duncan, France, 1976, 1980, Grand Salon des Superintendents, Paris, 1981, numerous awards including First prize, Conn. Classic Arts, Fairfield, 1987, Jean Cowles award, Shoreline Alliance Arts, Guilford., 1987, Koenig Art Emporium prize, New Haven Brush and Palette Club, 1990, Henry T and Stella King Meml. award, Arts and Crafts Assn. Meriden, Inc., 1990, Merriam Motors award Jubilee 325, 1995, Grumbacher Gold Medal award, 1995, Stella King Meml. award, 1997, Harvey Fuller award, 2001, Artist's Alternative award, 2004, Best Theme award, Arts and Crafts Assn. Meriden, 2005, Robert Pison Meml. award, 2005, First prize, Conn. Classic Arts, Fairfield, 1993, Beazley Realtors award, Mt. Carmel Art Assn., Hamden, 2000, Group Show award, New Haven Paint and Clay Club Group, 2005. Mem.: Arts and Crafts Assn. Meriden (1st prize 1976, Best in Show award 1982, Grumbacher Silver medal 1983—84, Hon. mention 1986, 1987, Henry T. & Stella King Meml. award 1990, Jerry's Artarama Cert. award 1990, Gold medal 1993, Grumbacher Gold medal 1993, Merriam Motors award Jubilee 325 Wallingford Theme 1995, Stella King Meml. award 1997, Harvey Fuller award 2001, Artist's Alternative award 2004, Best Theme award 2005, Jerry's Artarama Cert. award 1998), Conn. Classic Arts, Inc. (3d prize 1981, 1st prize 1982, 3d prize 1983, Gabriel D. Luchetti award 1984, 1986, 1st prize 1987, 1993, 3d prize 1994, Rosemary Landino Meml. award 1995, Westport Framing and Art Gallery Award 1997, 2d prize in acrylic and oils 1998), Internat. Soc. Artists, Provincetown Art Assn., New Haven Paint & Clay Club (Members' Show award 1978, Hon. mention 1996, Grp. Show award 2005), Wadsworth Athenium (life), Conn. Acad. Fine Arts (life), Wallingford Hist. Soc. (life). Home: 39 Ridgewood Rd Wallingford CT 06492-2116

LAUTZENHEISER, BARBARA JEAN, insurance company executive; b. LaFeria, Tex., Nov. 15, 1938; d. Fred E. and Verna V. L. BA with high distinction, Nebr. Wesleyan U., 1960. Actuarial trainee Bankers Life Ins. Co. Nebr., Lincoln, 1960-64, programmer and systems analyst, 1964-65, asst. actuary, 1965-69, assoc. actuary, 1969-70, 2d v.p., actuary, 1970-72, v.p., actuary, 1972-80; sr. v.p. Phoenix Mut. Life Ins. Co., Hartford, Conn., 1980-84; pres. Montgomery Ward Life Ins. Co., Montgomery Ward Ins. Co., Forum Ins. Co., Schaumberg, Ill., 1984-85; prin., CEO Lautzenheiser & Assocs., East Hartford, Conn., 1986—. Spokesperson for ins. industry, witness U.S. Senate and Ho. of Reps. coms., commns. and state legislatures; featured on TV, nat. mags. and newspaper articles; mem. Interim Actuarial Std. Bd., 1986-88, Actuarial Std. Bd., 1989-90; chmn. Com. for Fair Ins. Rates, 1983-86; mem. adv. com. Nat. Assn. Ins. Commrs. Life Disclosure (A) Com. working group, 1993; bd. dirs. LifeUSA Holding Co. Contbr. articles to profl. jours. Mem. Lincoln Electric Sys. Adminstrv. Bd., 1977-79; bd. dirs. Nebr. Wesleyan U., 1977-82, 89-93, Am. Coll., 1987-97. Recipient Young Alumni svc. award Nebr. Wesleyan U., 1971, Corp. Woman award Women Bus. Owners of N.Y., 1983, C.H. Poindexter award for disting. achievement and exceptional svc. to the assn. and ins. industry Nat. Assn. Life Cos., 1989. Fellow: Conf. Cons. Actuaries (dir. 1997—98, bd. dirs. 2006—), Soc. Actuaries (dir. 1975—80, exec. com. 1978—80, chmn. adminstrn. and fin. com. 1981—82, exec. com. 1981—84, dir. 1981—85, pres. 1982—83, assoc. editor The Actuary 1992—93, life nonforfeiture task force 1995—96); mem.: Am. Coun. Life Ins. (risk classification com. 1973—81), Life Office Mgmt. Assn. (corp. fin. planning com. 1974—81, chmn. 1976—78), Nat. Alliance Life Companies (bd. dirs. 1992—95), Soc. of Actuaries Found. (founding trustee 1994—98, trustee emeritus Actuarial Found. 1998—), Am. Acad. Actuaries (dir. 1974—77, chmn. com. on publs. 1980—81, disclosure working group 1994—2001, nonforfeiture working group 1994—, com. on life ins. 1995—98, life practice coun. vice chair 1998, co-chair 1998—99, v.p. life 1999—2001, pres.-elect 2002—03, editl. adv. bd. mem. Contingencies mag. 2002—, pres. 2003—04, immediate past pres. 2004—05, task force revise ASOP no.12 2004—, past pres. 2005—), Greater Hartford C. of C. (actl. policies panel 1980—84), Nebr. Actuaries Club (dir. 1969—70, sec.-treas. 1971—72, dir. 1971—74, pres. 1972—73, chmn. 1973—74, dir. 1992—94). Home: 17 Huntingridge Dr South Glastonbury CT 06073-3614 Office: Lautzenheiser & Assocs 235 East River Dr #306 East Hartford CT 06108-5018 Office Phone: 860-246-0893. Personal E-mail: lautzenheiser@aol.com.

LAVALLEE, DAVID KENNETH, chemistry professor, academic administrator; b. Malone, NY, Oct. 1, 1945; s. Bernard Martin and Eleanor June (Magoon) Lavallee; m. Eileen Marie (Gilmartin); children: Jeffrey

Michael, Gregory James, Jocelyn Marie. BS, St. Bonaventure U., 1967; MS, U. Ill., Chgo., 1968, PhD, 1971. Asst. prof. Colo. State U., Ft. Collins, 1972—78; assoc. prof. Hunter Coll., CUNY, NYC, 1978—82, prof. chemistry, 1983—94, assoc. provost, 1990—94; provost, v.p. acad. affairs CCNY, NYC, 1994—99, State Univ. of N.Y., New Paltz, 1999—. Edn. adv. bd. Chemtech, Washington, 1978—84. Author: The Chemistry and Biochemistry of N-substituted Porphyrins, 1987; author: (with others) Chemistry, 1978. Mem. NY State Regents Adv. Bd. Accreditation, 2003—. Recipient NATO Rsch. award, Ecole Normale Superieure, Paris, 1983—85, Catalyst award, Chem. Mfrs. Assn., 1986; USPHS fellow, U. Ill., Chgo., 1971—72, Fulbright rsch. scholar, U. Rene Descartes, Paris, 1985—86. Mem.: AAAS, Soc. Nuclear Medicine, Am. Chem. Soc. (chair Internat. Chemistry Olympiad 1986—93, soc. com. chem. edn. 1990—96, bd. publs. divsn. chem. edn. 1986—99, chair 1993—97). Democrat. Achievements include patents for N-substituted metalloporphyrins as anti-tumor agents; synthesis of radiolabelled metalloporphyrins via N-substituted precursors. Office: State Univ NY 75 S Manheim Blvd Ste 1 New Paltz NY 12561-2499 Home: 944 Rte 308 Rhinebeck NY 12572-3447 Office Phone: 845-257-3275. E-mail: lavallee@newpaltz.edu.

LAVANDEIRA, MARIO ARMANDO See **HILTON, PEREZ**

LAVANI, ROMEEN M., physician; b. Mumbai (Bombay), India, Feb. 25, 1970; s. Mohmed R. and Mumtaz M. Pathan; m. Vaishali R. Mody, June 16, 1998. MBBS, T.N. Med. Coll., Mumbai(Bombay), India, 1993; DCH, L.T.M Med. Coll. and Sion Hosp., Mumbai(Bombay), India, 1995, MD, 1996, U. Ill. at Chgo., Chicago, Ill., 2001, U. Chgo. Hosp., 2004. Lic. Physicians (pediatrics) Ill., 1998, Physicians(pediatrics) Wis., 2003, Ind., 2003. Physician-pediat. residency Sion Hosp., Mumbai, India, 1993—96; physician-pediat. pvt. practice Pvt. practice, Mumbai, India, 1996—98; physician-pediatrics residency U. Ill. at Chgo. Hosp., Chgo., 1998—2001; physician-pediat.c critical care fellowship U. Chgo., Chgo., 2001—04; physician-primary care/critical care St. Anthony Hosp., Chgo., 2004—. Primary care(outpatient) pediatrician, inpatient dir., dir. of residency rotation St.Anthony Hosp., Chicago, Ill., 2004—. Recipient Gold Medal in Pediat., Bombay U., 1996, Sir James Flett Award-second prize, Indian acad. of Pediat., 1997, APA Internat. Health Award, 1997; grantee Travel Grant - APA meeting, Wash., DC, Ambulatory pediat. Assn., 1997, Travel Grant - Am. Heart Assn. Meeting, Orlando, Fla., U. Chgo.-Emergency Resuscitation Ctr., 2003, Travel Grant - Soc. for Pediatric Rsch. Meeting, San Fransisco, Calif., U. Chgo., Emergency Resuscitation Ctr., 2004. Mem.: AHA, AAP, Soc. for Critical Care medicine(SCCM). Achievements include research in the role of amylase rich foods in nutritional rehabilitation of severely malnourished children with diarrhea; the effect of pH/CO2 on global cardiomyocyte ischemia-reperfusion injury. Avocation: cricket. Home: 724 S Oakley # 1 Chicago IL 60612 Office: St Anthony Hosp 2875 West 19th St Chicago IL 60612 Home Phone: 312-388-0698. Office Fax: 773-521-4587; Home Fax: 773-521-4587. Personal E-mail: yomeen@gmail.com.

LAVE, CHARLES ARTHUR, economics professor; b. Phila., May 18, 1938; s. Israel and Esther Lave; 1 child, Rebecca. BA, Reed Coll., 1960; PhD, Stanford U., 1968. Mem. faculty U. Calif., Irvine, 1966—, prof. econs., chmn. econs. dept., 1978—85, 1989—92. Vis. prof., vis. scholar Hampshire Coll., 1972, Stanford U., 1974, MIT, 1982, Harvard U., 1982, U. Calif., Berkeley, 1988, 94. Author: (with James March) An Introduction to Models in the Social Sciences, 1975, Energy and Auto Type Choice, 1981, Urban Transit, 1985, others. Trustee Reed Coll., Portland, Oreg., 1978-82; bd. dirs. Nat. Bur. Econ. Rsch., Cambridge, 1991-97; chmn. bd. Irvine Campus Housing Authority, Inc., 1982-96, asst. to chancellor, 1996-97. With USAF, 1957. Recipient Extraordinarius award U. Calif., 1993. Fellow Soc. Applied Anthropology; mem. Am. Econ. Assn., AAAS, Transp. Rsch. Bd. (Pyke Johnson award 1987) Office: U Calif Dept Econs Irvine CA 92697-5100 Office Phone: 949-824-6502. Business E-Mail: calave@uci.edu.

LAVE, JUDITH RICE, economics professor; b. Campbellton, May 18, 1939; d. J.H. Melville and G.A. Pauline (Lister) Rice; m. Lester Bernard Lave, June 21, 1965; children: Tamara Rice, Jonathan Melville. BA in Econs., Queen's U., Kingston, Ont., Can., 1957-61; MA in Econs., Harvard U., 1964, PhD, 1967; LLD, Queen's U., 1994. Lectr., asst. prof. econ. Carnegie Mellon U., Pitts., 1966-73, assoc. prof., 1973-78; dir. econ. analysis Office of Sec., Dep. of Asst. Sec. Planning and Evaluation, Washington, 1978-79; dir. office of rsch. Health Care Fin. Adminstrn., Washington, 1980-82; prof. health econ. U. Pitts., 1982—, co-dir. Ctr. for Rsch. on Health Care, 1996—, chair dept. health policy and mgmt., 2003—. Cons. Nat. Study Internal Medicine Manpower, Chgo., 1976, Wash. State Hosp. Assn., 1984, Horty, Springer & Mattern, Pitts., 1984, Hogan and Hartson, Washington, 1989, Ont. Hosp. Assn., Conn. Hosp. Assn., 1991; cons. various agys. U.S. HHS (formerly U.S. HEW), 1971-89; mem. adv. panel Robert Wood Johnson Found., Princeton, N.J., 1983-84, 96—, Leonard Davis Inst., Phila., 1984, U.S. Congress, 1977, 82, 83—; com. mem. Inst. Medicine Coms., Washington, 1975-, Project 2000 Commn. on Future of Podiatry, Washington, 1985-86. Editl. bd. Wiley Series in Health Svcs., 1989-90, Health Svcs. Rsch., 1970-74, Inquiry, 1979-82, AUPHA Press, 1986, Jour. of Health Policy Politics and Law, Health Affairs, 1998—; co-author: Hospital Construction Act - An Evaluation of the Hill Burton Program, 1948-73, 74, Health Status, Medical Care Utilization and Outcome: A Bibliography of Empirical Studies (4 vols.) 1989, Providing Hospital Services, 1989; contbr. numerous articles to profl. jours. Mem. Prospective Payment Assessment Commn., 1993—97, Medicare Payment Adv. Commn., 1997—2000; mem. planning com. ARC, Pitts., 1986—; mem. rev. com. United Way, Pitts., 1988—90. Bd. Health Svcs., Inst. Medicine; bd. dirs. Craig House, Pitts., 1976—77, Presbyn. Sr. Care, Pitts., Jewish Health Care Found., 2002—. Woodrow Wilson fellow, 1961—62. Disting. fellow Acad. Health (pres. 1977-88, bd. dirs. 1983-93); mem. Found. for Health Svcs. Rsch. (pres. 1988-89, bd. dirs. 1983—), Am. Pub. Health Soc., Am. Econ. Soc. (com. mem.), Inst. Medicine (bd. health svcs. 2000-), Nat. Acad. Social Ins., Robert Wood Johnson Found. (com. on econ. impact of health sys. change 1996—), Internat. Health Eco Assn. Democrat. Home: 1008 Devonshire Rd Pittsburgh PA 15213-2914 Office: U Pitts A620 Pub Health Pittsburgh PA 15213 Office Phone: 412-624-0898. Business E-Mail: lave@pitt.edu.

LAVECCHIA, JAYNEE, state supreme court justice; b. Paterson, NJ, Oct. 9, 1954; m. Michael R. Cole. Grad., Douglass Coll., 1976, Rutgers U., 1979. Bar: N.J. 1980. Pvt. law practice; dep. atty. gen. divsn. of law State of NJ; asst. counsel to Gov. Thomas H. Kean Office of Counsel, dep. chief counsel to Gov. Thomas H. Kean; dir. divsn. of law dept. law anf pub. safety State of NJ, 1984-98; dir., chief adminstrv. law judge Office of Adminstrv. Law, 1989-94; commr. banking and ins. State of NJ, 1998-99; assoc. justice NJ Supreme Ct., Trenton, 2000—. Chair various N.J. Supreme Ct. Coms. Fellow ABA. Office: Supreme Ct PO Box 970 25 Market St Trenton NJ 08625*

LAVELLE, BRIAN FRANCIS DAVID, lawyer; b. Cleve., Aug. 16, 1941; s. Gerald John and Mary Josephine (O'Callaghan) L.; m. Sara Hill, Sept. 10, 1966; children: S. Elizabeth, B. Francis D. Jr., Catherine H. BA, U. Va., 1963; JD, Vanderbilt U., 1966; LLM in Taxation, NYU, 1969. Bar: NC 1966, Ohio 1968, US Tax Ct. 1969, US Ct. Appeals (4th cir.) 1998. Assoc. VanWinkle Buck, Wall, Starnes & Davis, Asheville, N.C., 1968-74, ptnr., 1974—. Lectr. continuing edn. NC Bar Found., Wake Forest U. Estate Planning Inst., Am. Coll. Trust and Estate Counsel, San Diego, Hartford Tax Inst., Duke U. Estate Planning Inst. Contbr. articles on law to profl. jours. Trustee Carolina Day Sch., 1981-92, sec., 1982-85; bd. dirs. The Salvation Army, 1986—, Western NC Cmty. Found., 1986-2001, sec., 1987-90; bd. advs. U. NC Ann. Tax Inst., 1981—. Capt. JAG USAF, 1966-67. Mem. ABA, Am. Coll. Trust and Estate Counsel (state chmn. 1982-85, regent 1984-90, lectr. continuing edn.), NC Bar Assn. (bd. govs. 1979-82, v.p. 1997-2000, councillor tax sect. 1979-83, councillor estate planning law sect. 1982-85, 2002-05), NC State Bar (splty. exam. com. on estate planning and probate law 1984-90, chmn. 1990-91, cert. 1987), Rotary, Biltmore Forest Country, Royal Brigade of Guards. Anglican. Home: 45 Brookside Rd Asheville NC 28803-3015 Office: 11 N Market St PO Box 7376 Asheville NC 28802-8506 Business E-Mail: blavelle@vwlawfirm.com.

LAVELLE, JOHN PAUL, urologist; b. Dublin, Oct. 9, 1960; s. Ruaire Stephen and Ena Rose Lavelle; m. Ursula Mary Barry, Aug. 26, 1989; children: Ruaire John, Kevin William, Maeve Ursula. MB, BChir, Royal Coll. Surgeons in Ireland, Dublin, 1984; BSc with honors, Nat. U. Ireland, Dublin, 1986. Diplomate Am. Bd. Urology. Fellow U. Pitts., 1998—2000; asst. prof. urology U. NC, Chapel Hill, 2000—. Recipient Sylvia Sorkin Greenfield award; fellow, Am. Found. Urol. Disease, 1998—2000. Mem.: Am. Urol. Soc., Internat. Continence Soc., Soc. Urodynamics and Female Urology, Soc. Basic Urol. Rsch. (life). Office: U NC CB 7235 2140 Bioinformatics Bldg Chapel Hill NC 27599-7235 Home Phone: 919-967-4203; Office Phone: 919-966-2571. Office Fax: 919-966-0098. E-mail: lavelle@med.unc.edu.

LAVELLE, JOSEPH P., lawyer; b. Scranton, Pa., Sept. 7, 1957; s. Patrick Leo and Anne M. (Antal) L.; m. Kathy A. Mlodzienski, Aug. 14, 1982; children: Remy, Joseph, Taylor. BS in Physics, Wilkes Coll., 1979; JD summa cum laude, U. Pitts., 1982. Bar: D.C. 1982, U.S. Ct. Appeals (Fed. cir.) 1982, U.S. Patent and Trademark Office 1982, U.S. Ct. Appeals (3d, 2d and 6th cir.). Assoc. Howrey & Simon, Washington, 1982-90, ptnr., 1991—. Adj. prof. Georgetown U. Law Ctr., 1995—. Editl. bd. ABA Antitrust Law Developments, III, 1992; contbr. articles to profl. jours.; mng. editor U. Pitts. Law Rev., 1981-82. Mem. ABA, AAAS, Am. Phys. Soc., Order of the Coif. Republican. Office: Howrey LLP 1299 Pennsylvania Ave Washington DC 20004 Office Phone: 202-383-6888. Business E-Mail: lavellej@howrey.com.

LAVELLE, WILLIAM AMBROSE, lawyer, judge; b. Athens, Ohio, Jan. 18, 1925; s. Francis Anthony and Belle Elizabeth (Schloss) L.; m. Marion Helen Yanity, Aug. 7, 1954 (dec. Feb. 2002); children: Frank A., John P., Lydia E., Amy M.; m. Ann Chanell Olsen, Oct. 12, 2002. BBA, Ohio U., 1949; JD, Ohio State U., 1952. Bar: Ohio 1952, U.S. Dist. Ct. (so. dist.) Ohio 1952. Sr. ptnr. Lavelle Law Offices, Athens, Ohio, 1952-91; judge probate/juvenile divsn. Athens County Common Pleas Ct., 1991-94; assigned judge Supreme Ct. of Ohio, 1994; pvt. practice estate planning, trusts, probate, 1994—. Former solicitor City of Nelsonville, Villages of Albany, Chauncey, Coolville, Glouster, Trimble and Zaleski; counsel Margaret Creek Conservancy Dist., L-Ax Water Distbn. Co., Sunday Creek and Hollister Water Assns.; instr. wills, trusts, estate planning Ohio U., Athens, 1991—; mem. commn. on cert. as atty. specialists Supreme Ct. Ohio, 1994. Former chmn. Athens County and Ohio Dem. Party; former mem. Dem. Nat. Com.; chmn. Athens County Bd. Elections, 1967-80, 2005—; chmn. pers. rev. bd. State of Ohio, 1983-91; trustee, chmn. trustees Ohio U., 1975-81; mem. parish fin. com., parish coun., sch. bd., diocesan bd. lay consultors St. Paul's Cath. Ch., Athens. Served with inf. U.S. Army, 1943-46, ETO, PTO. Mem. ABA, Ohio State Bar Assn. (bd. govs. 1989-92, probate and trust law sect. 1993—, coun. of dels. 1986-89), Athens County Bar Assn. (past pres.), Nat. Acad. Elder Law Attys., Ohio Horse Coun., Tenn. Walking Horse Breeders and Exhibitors Assn., Walking Horse Owners Assn., Athens Symposiarch Club (past pres., Symposiarch of Yr. 1996), Athens Cotillion Club, Athens Country Club, Athens Rotary Club, VFW, Am. Legion, Am. Vets, Sons of Union Vols., Ohio U. Green and White Club, KC (3d and 4th deg.), St. Francis Soc. Avocations: breeding, raising, riding and driving tennessee walking horses. Home: 20 McGuffey Ln Athens OH 45701-1828 Office: 207 Columbus Rd Ste B Athens OH 45701 Fax: 740-594-3343. E-mail: walavelle@eurekanet.com.

LAVENDER, CHERYL ANN, music educator, composer, writer; b. Lincoln Park, Mich., June 18, 1951; d. Thomas Joseph and Gwendolyn Ann Umlauf; m. Charles Paul Lavender, June 1, 1974; children: Charles Eric, Brandon Thomas, Krista Leigh. BS in Edn., Ctrl. Mich. U., 1973. Cert. tchr. Wis. Music educator, choral dir. Beal City (Mich.) Pub. Schs., 1974—76, St. Joseph Sch., Beal City, 1974—76, Flushing (Mich.) Cmty. Schools, 1977—81, Warwick Pointe Acad., Grand Blanc, Mich., 1981—82, Fox Point (Wis.)-Bayside Sch. Dist., 1982—86, Brookfield (Wis.) Acad., 1982—84, Sch. Dist. Elmbrook, Brookfield, 1986—. Clinician Oakland U., Rochester, Mich., 1980—81, Mich. Schs. Vocal Music Assn., Lansing, U. Mich., Flint, 1983, Stanton's Music, Columbus, Ohio, 1991—, Oreg. Music Educators Assn., Eugene, 1992, Karnes Music, Chgo., 1992—2004, Pender's Music, Dallas, 1992—2002, JW Pepper, Billings, Mont., 1992—2000, Fargo, ND, 1992—2000, Moorhead, Minn., 1995—2000, Indpls., 1999, Mpls., 2001, Ward-Brodt Music, Madison, Wis., 1992—2003, JW Pepper / Wingert-Jones Music, Kansas City, Mo., 1992—2004, Schmitt Music, Mpls., 1994—2004, Fargo, ND, 2002, NW Music Svcs., Vancouver, British Columbia, Canada, 1994—2001, Ill. Music Educators Assn., Peoria, 1996—2001, SD Am. Choral Directors Assn., Sioux Falls, SD, 1996, Marquette U., Milw., 1996—2001, Tex. Music Educators Assn., San Antonio, 1997—2003, Onandoga Music Svcs., Washington, 1997, VanderCook Coll. Music, Chgo., 1997—98, Onandoga Music Svcs., NYC, 1997, Ohio Music Educators Assn., Columbus, Ohio, 1998, SD Music Educators Assn., Brookings, SD, 1998, Orff Chpt. of Iowa, Cedar Falls, Iowa, 1998, Tri-City Music, Bay City, Mich., 1999, Hal Leonard Corp., Milw., 2002—04, Iowa Music Educators Assn., Mason City, Iowa, 2002, Shattinger's Music, St. Louis, 2003, Popplers Music, Grand Forks, ND, 2005; composer, author Jensen Publications, New Berlin, Wis., 1986—89, Hal Leonard Corp., Milw., 1989—; keynote spkr. Ctrl. Mich. U., Mount Pleasant, Mich., 2003. Author: Skills Evaluation Kit, 1986, Elementary Form Pack, 1986, The Song-Writing Kit, 1986, Help! I'm a Substitute Music Teacher!, 1987, Staging a Children's Musical, 1987, See, Sing, and Play, 1987, Making Each Minute Count, 1991, The Ultimate Music Assessment and Evaluation Kit, 2000; composer: (CD) Rhythm Bingo Level 1 and Level 2, 1986, Instrument Bingo, 1987, It's Your Turn!, 1988, Composer Bingo, 1988, Music Round Robin, 1989, Music Symbol Bingo, 1989, Melody Bingo, 1990, Moans, Groans, and Skeleton Bones, 1991, Music Listening Bingo, 1992, A Spring Song Sing-Along, 1993, Come Dance a Jig, 1994, Melody Flashcard Kit Vol. I, 1994, Melody Flashcard Kit Vol. II, 2005, Rhythm Flashcard Kit Vol. I, 1994, Rhythm Flashcard Kit Vol. II, 2005, Lines and Spaces Bingo, 1996, Rockin' Rhythm Raps, 1996, It's Your Turn...Again!, 1997, Songs of the Rainbow Children, 1998, Rock 'n Raps Rhythm Tracks Vol. 1, 1999, Rock 'n Raps Rhythm Tracks Vol. II, 2005, World Instrument Bingo, 1999, Americans All, 2000, Music Styles Bingo, 2002, John Jacobson's Music Express, 2002, Solfege Bingo, 2003, Friendship Family, 2005. Del. US-South Africa Edn. Conf. Citizens Ambassador Program, Johannesburg, 1996; co-founder Swanson Sch., Loehmann's Plz. Ednl., Corp. Partnership, Brookfield, Wis., 1995—99. Recipient Disting. Alumni award, Ctrl. Mich. U., 2005; grantee, NEA Found. for Improvement of Edn., 2004. Mem.: NEA (assoc.), ASCAP (life), Elmbrook Edn. Assn., Music Educators Nat. Conf. (assoc.), Alpha Lambda Delta. Home: 20230 Liberty Ct Brookfield WI 53045 Home Phone: 262-786-9199. Personal E-mail: clavender@wi.rr.com.

LAVENDER, MARYANN MICHELLE, history educator; d. Mirl Chatman and Lula Mae Sharpley; m. Kevin James Lavender, Sr., Aug. 2, 1980; children: Kevin James Jr., Jeffrey Aaron, Jennifer Renee, Kandace Rochelle. BA, Spring Arbor U., Jackson, Mich., 1999, MA, 2002; postgrad., Western Mich. U., Kalamazoo, 2003—. Asst. v.p. Nat. City Corp., Kalamazoo, 1994—2006; part time tchg. faculty Western Mich. U., Kalamazoo, 2006—. Nat. conf. planner Fundamental Bapt. Fellowship Assn., Portsmouth, Va., 2006; missionary, ch. planter Bapt. Mission N.Am., Elyria, Ohio, 1984—93. Recipient Five Yr. Svc. award, Nat. City Corp., 1999, Ten Yr. Svc. award, 2004; fellow, Western Mich. U., 2006; scholar, Soc. Orgnl. Learning, 2004. Mem.: Phi Theta Alpha. Home: 4127 Londonderry Ave Kalamazoo MI 49006 Home Phone: 269-341-3195. Personal E-mail: mamlavender@yahoo.com.

LAVENDER, ROBERT EUGENE, state supreme court justice; b. Muskogee, Okla., July 19, 1926; s. Harold James and Vergene Irene (Martin) L.; m. Maxine Knight, Dec. 22, 1945; children— Linda (Mrs. Dean Courter), Robert K., Debra (Mrs. Thomas Merrill), William J. LL.B., U. Tulsa, 1953; grad., Appellate Judges Seminar, 1967, Nat. Coll. State Trial Judges, 1970. Bar: Okla. bar 1953. With Mass. Bonding & Ins. Co., Tulsa, 1951-53, U.S. Fidelity & Guaranty Co., Tulsa, 1953-54; asst. city atty. Tulsa, 1954-55; practice, 1955-60, Claremore, Okla., 1960-65; justice Okla. Supreme Ct., 1965—, chief justice, 1979-80. Guest lectr. Okla. U., Oklahoma City U., Tulsa U. law schs. Republican committeeman, Rogers County, 1961-62. Served with USNR, 1944-46. Recipient Disting. Alumnus award U. Tulsa, 1993. Mem. ABA, Okla. Bar Assn., Rogers County Bar Assn., Am. Judicature Soc., Okla. Jud. Conf., Phi Alpha Delta (hon.) Methodist (adminstrv. bd.). Club: Mason (32 deg.). Home: 2910 Kerry Ln Oklahoma City OK 73120-2507 Office: US Supreme Ct Okla State Capitol Room 208 Oklahoma City OK 73105

LAVENSON, SUSAN BARKER, hotel corporate executive, consultant; b. L.A., July 26, 1936; d. Percy Morton and Rosalie Laura (Donner) Barker; m. James H. Lavenson, Apr. 22, 1973 (dec. Sept. 1998); 1 child, Ellen Ruth Stanclift. BA, Stanford U., 1958, MA, 1959; PhD (hon.), Thomas Coll., 1994. Cert. gen. secondary credential tchr., Calif. Tchr. Benjamin Franklin Jr. H.S., San Francisco, 1960; tchr. French dept. Lowell H.S., San Francisco, 1960-61; v.p. Monogram Co., San Francisco, 1961-62, creative dir. NYC, 1973-86; pres. SYR Corp., Santa Barbara, Calif., 1976-89; mng. ptnr. Lavenson Ptnrs., Camden, Maine and Scottsdale, Ariz., 1989—; founding mem. The Piper Group, 2006—. Mem. commn. on co-edn. Wheaton Coll., Norton, Mass., 1985-87; mem. Relais et Chateaux, Paris, 1978-89; cons. World Bank Recruit Divsn., 1993. Author: Greening of San Ysidro, 1977 (Conf. award 1977). Trustee Camden Pub. Libr., 1989—95, v.p., 1991—93; vice chair bd. trustees Thomas Coll., Waterville, Maine, 1990—2001, trustee emerita, 2001—; trustee Atlantic Ave. Trust, 1989—91; founding pres. Maine chpt. Internat. Women's Forum, 1991—; mem. Coun. of Advisors Coll. of the Atlantic, Bar Harbor, Maine, 1996—2001, Ariz. Women's Forum; chair dean's adv. coun. Ariz. State U., 2002—04, chair coun. advisors Virginia Piper Creative Writing Ctr., 2004—05; mem. com. fgn. rels. City Phoenix, 2006—. Recipient Piper award for entrepreneurial excellence, 2002. Mem. Advice Inc., Stanford Alumni Assn., Com. of 200 (treas. 1985-86), Women's Entrepreneur Corps, Phi Delta Kappa (Stanford U. chpt., founding mem.). Home and Office: 7841 E Shooting Star Way Scottsdale AZ 85266 Office Phone: 480-575-7722. E-mail: sbl1@cox.net. *Three rules to remember: 1) Never take anything personally. 2) Never lose your sense of humor. 3) Keep your eye on the objective - I also like the Apocryphal words: "I am not made or unmade by things that happen to me, but by my reactions to them".*

LAVERDIERE, CLAUDETTE MARIE, nun, head of religious order; BS in Edn., Mary Rogers Coll., Maryknoll, NY, 1967; M Theol. Studies, Cath. Theol. Union, Chgo., 1986; licentiate in Sacred Theology, Weston Jesuit Sch. Theology, 2000. Joined Maryknoll Sisters Congregation, 1956. Tchr. Nganza Secondary Sch. for Girls, Mwanza, Tanzania, 1967-71; with devel. dept. Maryknoll Sisters Congregation, 1972-74; tchr. religious edn. dept. secondary schs. Nakuru, Kenya, 1974-76; catechetical dir. Nakuru Diocese, Kenya, 1976-79; team mem. devel. edn. program Mombasa Diocese, Kenya, 1980-84; registrar, tchr. Theol. Centre Religious, Nairobi, Kenya, 1987-90; pres. Maryknoll Sisters Congregation, 1991-97, student, 1997-2000; tchr. Theological Ctr. Religious, Nairobi, Kenya, 2000-01; tchr. sacred scripture Religious Sisters Inst., Kenya, 2001—03; family ministry Winslow, Maine, 2003—.

LAVERNIA, ENRIQUE JOSE, materials science and engineering educator; b. Havana, Cuba, July 30, 1960; arrived in US, 1965; s. Carlos Manuel and Ana Margot (Borrego) L.; m. Julie M. Schoenung, Oct. 4, 1986. BS in solid mechanics, Brown U., 1982; MS in metallurgy, MIT, 1984, PhD in materials engring., 1986. Rsch. asst. MIT, Cambridge, 1982-86, postdoctoral assoc., 1986, rsch. assoc., 1986-87; asst. prof. dept. chem. and aerospace engring. U. Calif., Irvine, 1987-91, assoc. prof. dept. chem. engring. and materials sci., 1991—95, prof., 1995—2002, dept. head, 1998—2002, dean Coll. Engring. Davis, 2002—, prof. dept. chem. engring. and materials sci., 2002—; vis. prof. Max Planck Inst., Stuttgart, Germany, 1997. Adv. bd. Advanced Composites Newsletter, 1994—, Key Engring. Materials, Trans Tech, 1996—; bd. review Jour. Applied Composite Materials, 1994—, Metallurgical and Materials Transactions, 1994—. Internat. Jour. Non-Equilibrium Processing, 1996—; co-editor Jour. Materials Synthesis and Processing, 1996—; editl. bd. Electronic Jour., Ciencia Abierta, U. of Chile, 1999—, Jour. Materials Processing Tech., 1999—; assoc. editor Jour. Metastable and Nanostructured Materials, 2000—; adv. bd. NSF-Ctr. for Advanced Materials & Smart Structures, NC State U., 1998—; mem. Nat. Materials Adv. Bd., 2002—. Co-recipient Best Paper Award, Jour. Thermal Spray Tech., 1995, Marion Howe Medal for Best Paper, Metallurgical and Materials Transaction, 1998, Marcus A. Grossmann Award for Best Paper, 1999; named Chancellor's Prof., U. Calif. Irvine, 2002, Outstanding Asst. Prof., U. Calif. Irvine Sch. Engring., 1989—90, Presdl. Young Investigator, NSF, 1989—94; recipient Faculty Career Devel. Award, U. Calif. Irvine, 1989, Chem. and Biochem. Engring. and Materials Sci. Tchr. of Yr., 1998, Young Investigator Award, Office Naval Rsch., 1990—93; Rockwell Internat. Fellowship, 1982—84, Aluminum Co. Am. Fellowship, 1990—92, Iketani Sci. and Tech. Found. Fellowship, Japan, 1993, Alexander Von Humboldt Fellowship, Germany, 1995, Ford Found. Fellowship, 1995. Fellow: AAAS; mem.: Am. Metal Powder Industries Fedn., Minerals, Metals and Materials Soc., Materials Rsch. Soc., ASM Internat. (Bradley Stoughton Award for Young Teachers 1993, Materials Sci. Divsn. Silver Medal 1995), Phi Beta Delta, Sigma Xi. Avocations: tennis, jogging, handball, scuba diving. Office: U Calif Coll Engring 1021A Kemper Hall 1 Shields Ave Davis CA 95616-5294 Home Phone: 530-758-4485; Office Phone: 530-752-0554. Business E-Mail: lavernia@ucdavis.edu.

LAVERTY, MARILYN T., public relations executive, media consultant; b. Phila., July 3, 1954; d. John Martin and Teresa (O'Neil) L.; m. Alan B. Betrock BA in Philosophy cum laude, Cornell U., 1976. Editorial asst. Ithaca Jour., N.Y., 1976-77; publicity mgr. RCA Records, NYC, 1978-79, Columbia Records, NYC, 1978-82, publicity dir., 1983-87, v.p. press & pub. info., 1987—90; pres. Shore Fire Media, Bklyn., 1990—. Active Amnesty Internat., NYC., 1987; Mus. Am. Folk Art, NYC, 1984—. Recipient Entertainment Marketer of Yr. award, Advt. Age, 2003. Mem. Nat. Assn. Female Execs. Avocations: reading, gardening, collecting antiques. Office: Shore Fire Media Ste 1600 32 Court St Brooklyn NY 11201 Office Phone: 718-522-7171. Office Fax: 718-522-7242. E-mail: info@shorefire.com.*

LAVERY, DANIEL P., management consultant; b. NYC, June 28, 1932; m. Doris E. Guenther, Oct. 23, 1954; children: Daniel, Brian, Kevin, Michael. BS with honors, Manhattan Coll., 1954; MBA, Rutgers U., 1963. Mem. prodn. mgmt. staff, photo products dept. E.I. DuPont de Nemours & Co., Inc., 1954-65; divsn. mgr. Anken Industries, Williamstown, Mass., 1965-71; gen. mgr. Dymo Industries, NYC, 1971-73; dir. cons. studies

Quantum Sci. Corps., NYC, 1973-79; mgr. strategic mktg. ITT, NYC, 1979-80; sr. dir. market rsch. Western Union, 1980-82; v.p. Pactel, Inc., mgmt. cons., NYC, 1982-83; ptnr. Palo Alto Mgmt. Group, Wyckoff, NJ, 1983-98, Matterhorn Group, Wyckoff, NJ, 1998—. Served as capt. USAF, 1955-57. Mem. Inst. Mgmt. Cons. (cert. mgmt. cons.), Am. Arbitration Assn. (panel mem. 1985—). Office: Matterhorn Group 458 Sicomac Ave Wyckoff NJ 07481-1120 Office Phone: 201-891-6162. Business E-Mail: danlavery@matterhorngroup.com.

LAVERY, ROBERT MICHAEL, internist, cardiologist; b. Pitts., Feb. 7, 1951; BS magna cum laude, Univ. Notre Dame, 1972; MD, Johns Hopkins U., 1976. Diplomate Am. Bd. Internal Medicine, Am. Bd. Cardiology. Intern Boston U. Hosp., 1976-77, resident in internal medicine, 1977-78; fellow in cardiology Boston U. Med. Ctr., 1978-80; pvt. practice Cardiology Assoc. of Manchester, NH, 1980—86, NH Cardiology Cons., Manchester, NH, 1986—, chief of cardiology, 2002—. Mem. staff Elliot Hosp., Manchester, Cath. Med. Ctr., Manchester. Named one of Top Cardiologists in NH, NH Mag., 2000, 2001, 2005. Fellow Am. Coll. Cardiology (coun. on clin. cardiology, NH affiliate pres. 1987-88, bd. dir. 1981-2000, gov. NH 2000-03, tri-state No. New Eng. chpt. pres. 2001-02); mem. Am. Heart Assn., Hillsborough County Med. Soc. Office: NH Cardiology Cons Ste 100 1 Elliot Way Manchester NH 03103-3547*

LAVET, ROBERT, lawyer; b. Phila., 1954; BA cum laude, U. Pa., Phila., 1976; JD cum laude, Georgetown U. Law Ctr., Washington, 1979. Bar: DC 1979, US Ct. Appeals (DC cir.) 1980. Assoc. Howrey & Simon, Washington, 1979—82, Cole, Corette & Abrutyn, Washington, 1985—89, ptnr., 1989—92; trial atty. US Dept. Justice, 1982—85; various legal positions SLM Corp., Reston, Va., 1992—98, v.p., dep. gen. counsel, 1998—2001, sr. v.p., dep. gen. counsel, 2001—05, sr. v.p., gen. counsel, 2005—. Pres. Washington Met. Assn. Corp. Counsel, 2001; mem. law alumni bd. Georgetown U. Law Ctr.; mem. adv. bd. Georgetown U. Law Ctr. Corp. Counsel Inst.; bd. dirs. Mentors, Inc., Appleseed. Mem.: Bar Assn. DC. Office: SLM Corp 12061 Bluemont Way Reston VA 20190 Office Phone: 703-810-5016. Office Fax: 513-469-1468.*

LAVEY, STEWART EVAN, lawyer; b. Newark, July 24, 1945; m. Suzanne Laurence, July 9, 1972. AB, Syracuse U., 1967; JD, Fordham U., 1970. Bar: N.Y. 1971, N.J. 1987, Pa. 1988, D.C. 1988. Assoc. Kelley Drye & Warren, NYC, 1970-71, Zimet Haines Moss & Goodkind, NYC, 1972-75; asst. sec., asst. gen. counsel Norlin Corp., NYC, 1975-78, sec., asst. gen. counsel, 1978-85; of counsel Shanley & Fisher, P.C., Morristown, NJ, 1985-87, ptnr., 1987—99; ptnr. corp. and securities group Drinker Biddle & Reath LLP, Florham Park, NJ, 1999—, assoc. head corp. and securities practice group, 1999—2007, mng. ptnr., 2006—. Adj. assoc. prof. law Fordham U., N.Y.C., 1976-79, adj. prof., 1980-2004, lectr. Fordham U. Continuing Legal Edn., 1991-93. Mem. Fordham Law Rev., 1968-70. Trustee Pingry Sch., Martinsville, N.J., 1996-2000. Recipient Bene Merenti medal Fordham U. Mem. Am. Bar Assn., N.Y. State Bar Assn., Assn. of Bar of City of N.Y., N.J. Bar Assn. (securities law com.), Pa. Bar Assn., D.C. Bar Assn., Pingry Sch. Alumni Assn. (pres. 1996-2000). Office: Drinker Biddle & Reath LLP 500 Campus Dr Florham Park NJ 07932-1047 Office Phone: 973-360-1100. Office Fax: 973-360-9831. Business E-Mail: stewart.lavey@dbr.com.

LAVEZZI, JOHN CHARLES, retired art history educator, archaeologist; b. Chgo., July 7, 1940; s. Francis M. and Dorothy M. (Kopal) L. AB magna cum laude, Cath. U. Am., 1962; MA, U. Cin., 1965; postgrad., Am. Sch. Classical Studies, Athens, Greece, 1967-70; PhD, U. Chgo., 1973. Sec. of the sch. Am. Sch. Classical Studies at Athens, 1968-70; asst. prof. Sch. Art Bowling Green (Ohio) State U., 1973-80, assoc. prof., 1980—2005, head divsn. art history, 1998—2001, acting head, 2003—04, assoc. prof. emeritus, 2005—. Sr. assoc. mem. Am. Sch. Classical Studies at Athens, 1972—, rsch. assoc. Corinth Excavations, 1972—. Author: (book chapter) Corinth XX, 2003; contbr. articles to profl. jours. and symposia. Mem. Toledo Mus. Art. Recipient CUA Statemeier award, 1962, Medici Circle teaching awards, 1986, 94; grantee Am. Philos. Soc., 1973. Mem. Archeol. Inst. Am., Midwest Art History Soc., Soc. for Preservation of Greek Heritage, Nat. Geog. Soc., Smithsonian Instn. Friends, Cyprus Am. Archeol. Rsch. Inst., Cath. Assn. Scientists and Engrs., Blue Key, Phi Beta Kappa (pres. chpt. 1992), Phi Alpha Theta, Delta Epsilon Sigma, Phi Eta Sigma. Roman Catholic. Home Phone: 708-453-5929. E-mail: lavezzi@bgnet.bgsu.edu.

LAVIDGE, ROBERT JAMES, marketing research executive; b. Chgo., Dec. 27, 1921; s. Arthur Wills and Mary Beatrice (James) L.; m. Margaret Mary Zwigard, June 8, 1946 (dec., Aug. 28, 2006); children: Margaret, Kathleen, William, Lynn Elizabeth. AB, DePauw U., 1943; MBA, U. Chgo., 1947. Analyst Pepsodent divsn. Lever Bros., Chgo., 1947-48, new products mktg. rsch. mgr. Pepsodent divsn., 1948-49; asst. dir. mktg. Am. Meat Inst., Chgo., 1950-51; ptnr. Elrick, Lavidge and Co., Chgo., 1951-56; pres. Elrick and Lavidge, Inc., Chgo., 1956-86; pres. emeritus Elrick and Lavidge, Scottsdale, Ariz., 1997—2002; ret. Lectr. mktg. rsch., sales adminstrn. Northwestern U., 1950-80; mem. Nat. Mktg. Adv. Com., 1967-71, exec. com.; bd. govs. Brand Names Edn. Found., 2000-02. Trustee Village Western Springs, Ill., 1957-61, pres., 1973-77; trustee McCormick Theol. Sem., 1981-90, 92-96; mem. coun. U. Chgo. Grad. Sch. Bus.; bd. dirs. Ariz. Faith Counseling Ctr.; mem. coun. Ctr. Svcs. Leadership. Mem. Am. Mktg. Assn. (v.p. 1963-64, pres. 1966-67, trustee found. 1992—, chmn. 1992-99), Internat. Rels. Soc. (chmn. 1961-65), DePauw U. Alumni Assn. (pres. 1967-68), Klinger Lake Club (Mich.), Paradise Valley Country Club, Phi Beta Kappa, Beta Gamma Sigma, Sigma Delta Chi. Presbyterian. Personal E-mail: rlavidge@lavidge.com.

LAVIGNE, AVRIL, singer; b. Napanee, Ont., Can., Sept. 27, 1984; d. John and Judy Lavigne; m. Deryck Whibley, July 15, 2006. Singer: (albums) Let Go, 2002 (nominee Grammy award Best New Artist, 2002, nominee Grammy award Best Pop Vocal Album, 2002, nominee Grammy award for Song of Year for Complicated, 2002, nominee Grammy award for Best Female Pop Vocal Performance for song Complicated, 2002, nominee Grammy award for Best Female Rock Vocal Performance for song Sk8er Boi, 2002), Under My Skin, 2004, The Best Damn Thing, 2007; voice actor: (films) Over the Hedge, 2006. Achievements include signed with L.A. Reid of Arista Records at age 16. Avocations: hockey, basketball, skateboarding. Office: Network Mgmt 1650 W 2nd Ave Vancouver BC Canada V6J 4R3*

LAVIGNE, PETER MARSHALL, conservationist, lawyer, educator; b. Laconia, NH, Mar. 25, 1957; s. Richard Byrd and D. Jacquiline (Cobleigh) L.; m. Nancy Gaile Parent, Sept. 20, 1979; 1 child, Rhiannon Genevra Lavigne Parent. BA, Oberlin Coll., 1980; MSEL cum laude, Vt. Law Sch., 1983, JD, 1985. Bar: Mass. 1987. History tchr. Cushing Acad., Ashburnham, Mass., 1983-84; rsch. writer Environ. Law Ctr., Vt., 1985; lobbyist Vt. Natural Resources Coun., Montpelier, 1985; exec. dir. Westport (Mass.) River Watershed Alliance, 1986-88, Merrimack River Watershed Coun., West Newbury, 1988-89; environ. cons. Mass., N.H., Vt., and Oreg., 1990—2001; N.E. coord. Am. Rivers, Washington, 1990-92; dir. river leadership program River Network, Portland, Oreg., 1992-95, dir. spl. programs, 1995-96; dep. dir. For the Sake of the Salmon, Portland, 1996-97; pres. Watershed Cons., Portland, 1997-2001; pres., CEO Rivers Found. Ams., Portland, Oreg., 2001—05, bd. dirs., 2001—; prof. environ. studies Fullbright Commn., Brazil, 2007. Adj. prof. Antioch New Eng. Grad. Sch., Keene, NH, 1991-92; mem. Portland Willamette River Task Force, 1997-99; chair adv. bd. Cascadia Times, Portland, 1995-99; adv. bd. Amigos Bravos, Taos, N.Mex., 1993-98; trustee Rivers Coun. Washington, Seattle, 1993-98; bd. dirs. Alaska Clean Water Alliance, 1995-98, acting pres. 1997-98; adv. bd. Glen Canyon Inst., 2000-01, 05—, bd. dirs., 2002-04; Watershed adv. group Natural Resources Law Ctr. U. Colo., 1995-96; coastal resources adv. bd. Commonwealth of Mass., Boston, 1987-91; adj. assoc. prof. Portland State U., 1997—; Watershed Mgmt. Profl. program dir., Portland State U., 1999-01, sr. fellow exec. leadership inst., 2001—; pres. Cascadia Times Rsch. Fund, 1998-99; dir. Colo. water workshop, prof. environ. studies Western State Coll., Gunnison, Colo., 2006—. Co-author: Vermont Townscape, 1987; contbr. articles to profl. jours. Dir. Mass. League of Environ. Voters, Boston, 1988-92; mem. steering com. N.H. Rivers Campaign, 1988-92; co-founder, co-chair New England Coastal Campaign, 1988-92; EMT South Royalton (Vt.) Vol. Rescue Squad, 1982-86; dir., chair Vt. Emergency Med. Svcs. Dist. 8, Randolph, 1984-86; co-founder, v.p. Coalition for Buzzards Bay, Bourne, Mass., 1987; housing renewal commn. City of Oberlin, Ohio, 1980-81 Recipient Environ. Achievement award Coalition for Buzzards Bay, 1988; land use rsch. fellow Environ. Law Ctr., Vt. Law Sch., 1984-85; Mellon found. rsch. grantee Oberlin Coll., 1980. Mem. Natural Resources Def. Coun., River Alliance Wis., Aldo Leopold Found., NH Rivers Coun., No. Forest Ctr., Sitka Conservation Soc., League Conservation Voters, Glen Canyon Inst., Island Inst. Democrat. Unitarian-Universalist. Avocations: sea kayaking, mountain climbing, woodwork, reading, photography. Home and Office: River Found Ams 451 Candlelight Ln Gunnison CO 81230 Office Phone: 970-943-3162. Business E-Mail: pete@riversfoundation.org, plavigne@western.edu.

LAVIK, BRICKER L., lawyer; b. 1950; BA magna cum laude, U. Minn., 1974; JD cum laude, Hamline U., 1977. Bar: Minn. 1977. Atty. Legal Aid Soc., Mpls., 1977—86; atty., trial dept. Dorsey & Whitney LLP, Mpls., 1986—93, ptnr., sr. counsel, trial group, dir., pro bono program, 1994—, dir., pro bono dept., 1996—. Adj. prof. Hamline Univ. Sch. Law., 1986—92, 1995, William Mitchell Coll. Law., 1989—92. Lectr. in field. Named a Super Lawyer, Minn. Law & Politics, 2002; recipient Outstanding Svc. award, Minn. Justice Found., 1992, Pro Bono Publico award, Hennepin County Bar Assn., 1994, Disting. Alumni award, Hamline Univ. Law Sch., 2000, Pro Bono Atty. award, Minn. Legal Services Coalition, 2001. Mem.: Minn. State Bar Assn. (construction Law sect. 1998—, gov. coun.), Hennepin County Bar Assn. (co-chair, delivery legal svcs. com. 2001—). Office: Dorsey & Whitney LLP Ste 1500 50 S Sixth St Minneapolis MN 55402-1498 Office Phone: 612-340-5645. Office Fax: 612-340-2868. Business E-Mail: lavik.bricker@dorsey.com.

LAVIN, BERNICE E., cosmetics executive; b. 1925; m. Leonard H. Lavin, Oct. 30, 1947; children: Scott Jay (dec.), Carol Marie, Karen Sue. Student, Northwestern U. Vice chairperson of bd., sec.- treas. Alberto-Culver Co.; dir., v.p., sec.- treas. Alberto-Culver U.S.A., Inc. Sec.-treas., dir. Alberto-Culver Internat., Inc.; sec.-treas. Sally Beauty Co., Inc.

LAVIN, FRANKLIN LEO, federal agency administrator, former ambassador; b. Canton, Ohio, Nov. 26, 1957; married; 3 children. BSc in Fgn. Svc., Georgetown U., 1980, MSc in Chinese Lang. and History, 1985; MA in Internat. Econ./Internat. Rels., Johns Hopkins U., 1990; MBA, U. Pa., 1996. Asst. to dep. dir. personnel The White House, Washington, 1981, asst. dir. Pres. Commn. on Exec. Exch., 1982—83, assoc. dir. Office of Pub. Liaison, 1984—85, dir. Office of Polit. Affairs, 1987—89; dir. pvt. & voluntary programs, Asia Bur. US Agy. for Internat. Devel., 1981—82, spl. asst., asst. adminstr. for African Affairs, 1983—84; dep. exec. sec. for coord NSC, Washington, 1986—87; dep. asst. sec. for East Asia and Pacific US Dept. Commerce, Washington, 1991-93; trade economist, exec. dir. Asia Pacific Policy Ctr., Washington, 1994—96; v.p. emerging markets Citibank; regional mgr. Bank of Am.; US amb. to Singapore US Dept. State, 2001—05; under sec. for internat. trade US Dept. Commerce, Washington, 2005—. Adj. fellow Ctr. Strategic and Internat. Studies; mem. US Com. on Security and Cooperation in the Asia Pacific; mem. Nat. Policy Forum; mem. steering com. Am. Coun. on Germany's Young Leaders' Program. Contbr. chpts. to book, articles to NY Times, Wall St. Jour., Fgn. Affairs, others. Officer USNR. Office: US Dept Commerce 14th St & Constitution Ave NW Rm 3850 Washington DC 20230

LAVIN, HOWARD S., lawyer; b. NYC, June 28, 1957; BS in Indsl. and Labor Rels., Cornell U., 1979; JD, Emory U., Atlanta, 1982. Bar: NY 1983. Adminstrv. ptnr., labor & employment practice area Stroock & Stroock & Lavan LLP, NYC. Frequent lectr. in field. Mem.: NY State Bar Assn., NY C of C. Office: Stroock & Stroock & Lavan LLP 180 Maiden Ln New York NY 10038-4982 Office Phone: 212-806-6046. Office Fax: 212-806-9046. Business E-Mail: hlavin@stroock.com.

LAVIN, PHILIP TODD, medical executive; b. Rochester, NY, Nov. 21, 1946; s. Albert A. and Mary (Rapkin) Lavin; m. Mary Ellen Saunders, Aug. 23, 1970; children: Andrew, Abby. AB, U. Rochester, 1968; PhD, Brown U., Providence, 1972. Rsch. asst. prof. Brown U., Providence, 1972-74, SUNY Buffalo, Amherst, 1974-77; asst. prof. Sch. Pub. Health Harvard U., Boston, 1977-83, assoc. prof. surgery, 1983—. Trainee NSF, 1968—72; pres., founder Averion Internat. (formerly Boston Biostatistics, Inc.), 1983—; dir., founder Boston Biostat Rsch. Found., Framingham, 1988—; cons. FDA, 1983—86, spl. govt. employee, 1992—; co-chmn. clin. trial com. Mass. Biotech. Coun., 2003—. Contbr. articles to scholarly jours. Bd. dirs. William Graves Fund, Boston, 1989—2001. Grantee, Nat. Cancer Inst., 1976—80, Nat. Heart Lung Blood Inst., 1985—89. Mem.: Regulatory Affairs Profl. Soc., Soc. Clin. Trials, Am. Statis. Assn., Biometric Soc., Phi Beta Kappa. Achievements include development of statistical methods for the analysis of serial biomarker data applicable to the detection of biomarker shifts and trends over time; natural history models for neonatology, cancer, transplantion, dermatology, obesity, peridontology, renal failure and device implants; founding an international contract research organization and not for profit research foundation; support for 51 FDA approvals for drugs, devices and biologics; research in chronic disease models. Home: 3 Cahill Park Dr Framingham MA 01702-6105 Office: Averion International 225 Turnpike Rd Southborough MA 01772 Business E-Mail: plavin@averionintl.com.

LAVIN, STEPHEN MICHAEL, university basketball coach; b. San Francisco, Sept. 4, 1964; s. Cap and Mary Lavin. BS, Chapman U., 1987. Grad. asst. basketball coach, staff mem. Purdue U., 1988-91; staff mem. UCLA, 1991-95, asst. coach, 1995-97, recruiting coord., 1996-97, head coach, 1997—. Dir., founder Lavin Basketball Camps, 1984—; summer camp and coaches clinic spkr., 1989—; cons./advisor Korean Nat. Profl. Team, Samsung Profl. Team, 1992-96. Named Nat. Rookie Coach of Yr. Basketball Times mag., 1997; recipient Internat. Inspiration award Hugh O'Brien Youth Found., 1997. Office: UCLA 325 Westwood Plz Los Angeles CA 90095-8356

LAVINE, ALAN, columnist, writer; b. Sharon, Pa., Feb. 17, 1948; s. Milton and Doris (Helfman) L.; m. Gail Jeanne Liberman, Dec. 20, 1991. BA, Kent State U., 1970; MA, U. Akron, 1973; MBA, Clark U., 1981. Dir. of rsch. Donoghue Orgn., Holliston, Mass., 1981-83; nat. syndicated fin. columnist North Palm Beach, Fla., 1983—; columnist Dow Jones Market Watch and other newspapers. Presenter papers in field ann. meeting AAAS, 1972, ann. meeting Mass. Psychol. Assn., Wellesley, 1978, ann. meeting APA, 1979, Nat. Symposium on Rsch. in Art, U. Ill., 1980; guest lectr. Cornell U., 1990, 91, 92, 93. Author: Diversify: Investor's Guide to Asset Allocation Strategies, 1990 (alt. selection Fortune Book Club), Your Life Insurance Options, 1993 (endorsed Inst. CFPs), Improving Your Credit and Reducing Your Debt, 1994 (endorsed Inst. CFPs), Getting Started in Mutual Funds, 1994, Diversify Your Way to Wealth, 1994 (alt. selection Fortune Book Club), 50 Ways to Mutual Fund Profits, 1995, The Complete Idiot's Guide to Making Money with Mutual Funds, 1996, Love, Marriage and Money, 1998, Rags To Riches: Motivationing Stories of Ordinary People Who Achieved Extraordinary Wealth, 2000, Short and Simple Guide to Life Insurance, 2000, More Rags to Riches: All New Stories of Ordinary People Who Achieved Extraordinary Wealth, 2002, Short and Simple Guide to Smart Investing, 2002, Rags to Retirement, 2002, Quick Step to Financial Stability, 2006; contbr. articles to profl. jours. Mem. Nat. Writers Union, Soc. Am. Bus. Editors and Writers, Inc., Authors' Guild. Office: Alan Lavine Inc PO Box 14697 North Palm Beach FL 33408 Home: PO Box 14697 North Palm Beach FL 33408-0697 Office Phone: 561-630-7112. Personal E-mail: mwliblav@aol.com.

LAVINE, HENRY WOLFE, lawyer; b. Phila., Apr. 21, 1936; s. Samuel Phillips and Sarah Pamela (Leese) Lavine; m. Meta Landreth Doak, Feb. 20, 1960 (div. Feb. 1980); children: Lisa, Lindsay; m. Martha Putnam Cathcart (div. Feb. 1995); children: Samuel Putnam, Gwenn Cathcart; m. Ronda S. McCrea, June 12, 2004. BA, U. Pa., 1957, JD, 1961. Assoc. Squire, Sanders & Dempsey L.L.P., Cleve., 1961-70, ptnr. Washington, 1970-85, mng. ptnr. Washington office, 1985-91, sr. mng. ptnr., 1991—2002, sr. counsel, 2003—. Pres. Sawyer & Co. LLC. Mem. The Bretton Woods Com. Mem. Metropolitian Club Office: Squire Sanders & Dempsey 1201 Pennsylvania Ave NW PO Box 407 Washington DC 20044-0407 Office Phone: 202-626-6689.

LAVINE, STEVEN DAVID, academic administrator; b. Sparta, Wis., June 7, 1947; s. Israel Harry and Harriet Hauda (Rosen) L.; m. Janet M. Sternburg, May 29, 1988. BA, Stanford U., 1969; MA, Harvard U., 1970, PhD, 1976. Asst. prof.-English Lit. U. Mich., Ann Arbor, 1974-81; asst. dir. arts and humanities Rockefeller Found., NYC, 1983-86, assoc. dir. arts and humanities, 1986-88; pres. Calif. Inst. Arts, Valencia, 1988—. Cons. Wexner Found., Columbus, Ohio, 1986-87; selection panelist Input TV Screening Conf., Montreal, Can., and Granada, Spain, 1985-86; faculty chair Salzburg Seminar on Mus., 1989; co-dir. Arts and Govt. Program, The Am. Assembly, 1991; mem. arch. selection jury L.A. Cathedral, 1996, Arch. L.A., 1998-2001; adv. com. The Asia Soc., So. Calif. Ctr., 1998-; co-chair The Arts Coalition for Acad. Progress, L.A. Unified Sch. Dist., 1997-; vis. com. J. Paul Getty Mus., 1990-1997; cons. in field. Editor: The Hopwood Anthology, 1981, Exhibiting Cultures, 1991, Museums and Communities, 1992. Bd. dirs. Sta. KCRW-FM (NPR), 1989—, Endowments, Inc., 1994—, Cotsen Family Found., 2000—, Villa Aurora, 2003—, Am. Coun. Edn., 2004—; trustee Idyllwild Arts Found., 2003—. Recipient Class of 1923 award, 1979, Faculty Recognition award, U. Mich., 1980, Highlight award, W.O.M.E.N., Inc., LA, 2005; Ford fellow, 1969—74, Charles Dexter traveling fellow, Harvard U., 1972. Jewish. Office: Calif Inst Arts Office Pres 24700 McBean Pkwy Santa Clarita CA 91355-2397 Home Phone: 818-995-7613. Business E-Mail: slavine@calarts.edu.

LAVINE, THELMA ZENO, philosophy educator; b. Boston; d. Samuel Alexander and Augusta Ann (Pearlman) L.; m. Jerome J. Sachs, Mar. 31, 1944; 1 child, Margaret Vera. AB, Radcliffe Coll., 1936; A.M., Harvard U., 1937, PhD, 1939. Instr. Wells Coll., 1941-43, asst. prof., 1945-46; asst. prof. philosophy Bklyn. Coll., 1946-51; asst. prof. U. Md., 1955-57, assoc. prof., 1957-62, prof., 1962-65; Elton prof. George Washington U., 1965-85, chmn. dept., 1969-77; Clarence J.Robinson Univ. prof. George Mason U., Fairfax, Va., 1985—. Lectr., seminar cons. Inter-Am. Def. Coll., 1975—; exec. bd. Jour. of Speculative Philosophy, 2000—. Author: From Socrates to Sartre, 1980; co-author: introduction to Collected Works of John Dewey, Vol. 16, 1990, contbg. author: Reading Dewey, 1998, contbg. editor: Free Inquiry, 1980—, exec. bd.: Jour. of Speculative Philosophy, 2000—; contbr. articles to profl. jours., chpts. to books; author: (TV course) From Socrates to Sartre: The Philosophic Quest, 1984; co-author: History and Anti-History Philosophy, 1989, contbg. author: Philosophy of Paul Ricoeur, 1995, Rorty and Pragmatism, 1996, contbg. author: Perspectives on Habermas, 2000, contbg. author: Philosophy of Paul Ricoeur, 1995, mem. exec. bd.: Jour. Speculative Philosophy, 2000—; contbr. articles to profl. jours., revs., chpts. to books; series editor Transaction, 2003. Recipient Outstanding Faculty award U. Md., 1965, Outstanding Faculty award George Washington U., 1968, Alumnae Achievement award Radcliffe Coll., 1991; NEH sr. rsch fellow, 1980; Am. Enterprise Inst. Public Policy Research fellow, 1980-81, Va. Found. Humanities fellow, 1990; Herbert W. Schneider award contbns. to Am. Philosophy, 2000. Mem. Am. Philos. Assn. (5th Ann. Romanell lectr. 1991), Soc. Advancement Am. Philosophy (exec. com. 1979-82, pres. 1992-94), Internat. Soc. Sociology Knowledge, Internat. Soc. Polit. Psychology, Metaphys. Soc. Am., Washington Philosophy Club (pres. 1967-68), Washington Sch. Psychiatry, Forum Psychiatry and Humanities (exec. bd.), Cosmos Club, Harvard Club, SOPHIA, Phi Beta Kappa (pres. chpt. 1978-80). Home: 1625 35th St NW Washington DC 20007-2316 Office: George Mason U Robinsons Profs E 207 Fairfax VA 22030 Office Phone: 703-993-2171. E-mail: tzlavine@awol.com.

LAVIOLETTE, PAUL A., medical products executive; BA, Fairfield U.; MBA, Boston Coll. With Hosp. Products Div. Kendall Co.; v.p. USCI div. C. R. Bard, 1990—91, v.p., gen. mgr. USCI angioplasty div., 1991—93, pres. USCI angioplasty div., 1993, pres. USCI div., 1993; pres. Boston Sci. Internat., Natick, Mass., 1994—95, 1998; sr. v.p., group pres. nonvascular bus. Boston Sci., 1995—98, sr. v.p., group pres. Scimed, EP Technologies and Target divs., 2000, pres. Scimed, 2001, sr. v.p., group pres. interventional cardiology, peripheral interventions, vascular surgery, electrophysiology and neurovascular bus., COO, 2004—. Bd. dirs. Advanced Med. Tech. Assn., New England Heath Care Inst. Office: Boston Sci One Boston Scientific Pl Natick MA 01760-1537 Office Phone: 508-650-8000.

LAVIOLETTE, PETER, professional hockey coach; b. Franklin, Mass., Dec. 7, 1964; m. Kristen Laviolette; children: Peter, Jack, Elizabeth Rose. Coach Wheeling Thunderbirds, 1997—98, Providence Bruins, 1998—2000; head coach NY Islanders, 2000—03, Carolina Hurricanes, 2003—. Coach USA Hockey Team, Olympic Games, Torino, Italy, 2006. Recipient Louis A.R. Pieri Meml. Award, Am. Hockey League, 1999. Achievements include being the head coach of Stanley Cup Champion Carolina Hurricanes, 2006. Office: c/o Carolina Hurricanes RBC Ctr 1400 Edwards Mill Rd Raleigh NC 27607

LAVIZZO-MOUREY, RISA JUANITA, medical foundation and academic administrator; b. 1954; MD, Harvard U., 1979; MBA, U. Pa., 1986. Dep. adminstr. Agy. Healthcare Policy and Rsch., U.S. Dept. Health and Human Svcs., 1992—94; Sylvan Eismann prof. of medicine U. Penn, Phila., 1995—2001, dir. Inst. of Aging, 1995—2001, chief, div. geriatric med., assoc. exec. v.p., health policy, 1995—2001; associate chief of staff for geriatrics and extended care Phila. Veterans Admin. Med. Ctr.; sr. v.p., dir., Health Care Group Robert Wood Johnson Found., Princeton, NJ, 2001—03, pres., CEO, 2003—, also mem. bd. trustees. Mem. Pres.'s Commn. on Consumer Rights and Quality in the Healthcare Industry, 1997-98; mem. advisory com. Task Force on Aging Rsch., Office of Tech. Assessment Panel on Preventive Services for Medicare Beneficiaries, Inst. of Medicine's Panel on Disease and Disability Prevention Among Older Adults, Nat. Com. for Vital and Health Statistics. Mem., IOM, Nat. Acad. Sciences, Amer. Geriatrics Soc., The Assn. of Acad. Minority Physicians, Nat. Med. Assn., Acad. for Health Services Rsch. & Health Policy, Gerontological Soc. Amer. Office: The Robert Wood Johnson Foundation PO Box 2316 College Road East and Route 1 Princeton NJ 08543-2316

LAVOIE, DANIEL JOSEPH, II, archivist, historian; s. Daniel Joseph and Mary Ellen Lavoie. BA in History, St. Anselm Coll., 2001; MA in History, Duquesne U., 2003. Archivist/historian History Assocs. Inc., Rockville, Md., 2003—. Collections com. Peerless Rockville Historic Preservation Ltd., 2005—. Bd. dir. Peerless Rockville Hist. Preservation Ltd., 2007—.

Mem.: Nat. Coun. on Pub. History, Mid-Atlantic Regional Archives Conf. (outreach com. 2005—07), Soc. Am. Archivists, US Naval Inst., Phi Alpha Theta. Avocations: travel, archaeology, mountain biking. Office: History Associates Inc 300 N Stonestreet Ave Rockville MD 20850 Home Phone: 240-461-0223; Office Phone: 301-279-9697. Office Fax: 301-279-9224. Business E-Mail: dlavoie@historyassociates.com.

LAVOIE, JAMES A., lawyer; b. Pawtucket, RI, Mar. 24, 1948; s. Albert J. and Ellen M. Lavoie; children: Benjamin A., Joseph L. BA magna cum laude, U. Minn., Minneapolis, 1972; JD cum laude, U. Minn. Law Sch., Minneapolis, 1977. Bar: Minn. Supreme Ct. 1977, Minn. (US Dist. Ct.) 1983, Wis. (Supreme Ct.) 2001, 8th Circuit (US Ct. Appeals) 2006. County atty. Mille Lacs County, Milaca, Minn., 1979—85; lawyer Hall and Lavoie, P.A., St. Cloud, Minn., 1985—91, Meshbesher, Birrell, and Dunlap, Ltd, Minneapolis, Minn., 1991—97; law ptnr. Lindell & Lavoie, LLP, Minneapolis, Minn., 1997—. Qualified neutral mediator/arbitrator Equitable Dispute Resolution, Minneapolis, 2001. Mock trial instr. Milaca HS, Milaca, Minn., 1997—2007. Chief warrant officer 2 US Army, Aviation, 1968—71, USA, Viet Nam. Mem.: Acad. Cert. Trial Lawyers, Minn. Trial Lawyers Assn., Am. Assn. For Justice, Viet Nam Helicopter Pilots' Assn. Dfl. Achievements include Certified civil trial specialist, MSBA; Designated Super Lawyer, Law & Politics Mag., 1997. Avocations: shooting, hunting, fishing, hiking, camping. Home: 12345 165th Street Milaca MN 56353 Office: Lindell & Lavoie LLP 431 South 7th St Ste 2420 Minneapolis MN 55415-1897 Home Phone: 320-983-3518; Office Phone: 612-339-8811. Office Fax: 612-349-6806; Home Fax: 320-983-3339. Business E-Mail: lavoie@lindellandlavoie.com.

LAVOIE, LIONEL A., physician, health science association administrator; b. St. Brieux, Sask., Can., Aug. 24, 1937; s. Athanase T. and Ella Marie (Mevel) L.; m. Mary Tina Luchenski, Oct. 12, 1964; children: Robert, Michelle, Nicole, Andrea. BA, Ottawa U., Ont., Can., 1958, MD, 1964. Intern, then resident Univ. Hosp., Sask.; clin. prof. family medicine U. Sask., 1978—; chief of staff Melfort Union Hosp., Sask., 1985-90. Commr. Med. Care Ins. Commn., 1984-88. Chmn. Melfort Dist. Minor Sports, 1978-80, Melfort Pks. and Recreation, 1983-86, Sask. Summer Games 1988, 1986-88. Recipient Ramstead award, Jaycees of Province Sask., 1975, Dedication award, Sask. Parks, Recreation and Culture, 1988, Cmty. Recreation award, Melford C. of C., 1989, Commemorative medal, 125th Anniversary Can. Confedn., 1993, Recognition award, Coll. Medicine, U. Sask., 1999, award of merit, Faculty of Medicine U. Ottawa Alumni Assn., 2001, Rural Long Service award, Soc. Rural Physicians Can., 2002, Queen's Jubilee medal Can., 2002, Award of Merit, Can. Paraplegic Assn., 2005, Sask. Centennial medal, 2005. Fellow Coll. Family Physicians (Can., cert.),; mem. Can. Med. Assn. (sr., bd. dirs. 1978-83, pres. elect 1989-90, pres. 1990-91, life), Sask. Med. Assn. (bd. dirs. 1971-76, v.p. 1974, pres. 1975, life), Can. Acad. Sports Medicine, Am. Geriatric Soc., Coll. Family Physicians Can. (sec. Sask. province 1967-70), Sask. Acad. Sports Medicine (pres. 1986-88, Cert. of Merit 2004), Coun. Med. Assn. (chmn. 1985-89), Sask. Paraplegic Assn. (bd. dirs. 1978—), Can. Cancer Soc. (adv. com. Sask. div. 1986—), Nat. Aerospace Med. Assn., KC (grand knight 1980-81), Rotary (pres. Melfort club 1987-88). Avocations: golf, curling, horticulture. Home: 402 Stovel E Melfort SK Canada S0E 1A0 Office: Can Med Assn 1867 Alta Vista Dr Ottawa ON Canada K1G 0G8 Office Phone: 306-752-2876. Personal E-mail: lionelmarylavoie@hotmail.com.

LAVORATO, LOUIS A., retired state supreme court justice; s. Charles Lavorato; m. Janis M. Lavorato; children: Cindy, Natalie, Anthony, Dominic. BS in Bus. Adminstrn., Drake U., 1959, JD, 1962. Sole practice, Des Moines, 1962-79; judge Iowa Dist. Ct., Des Moines, 1979-86; justice Iowa Supreme Ct., Des Moines, 1986—2000, chief justice, 2000—06, sr. judge, 2006—. Mem. Iowa Supreme Ct. Administrative Subcom.; former chair Iowa Supreme Ct. Equality in the Courts Task Force Subcom. Recipient Judicial Achievement award, Iowa Assn. of Trial Lawyers, 1985, Merit award, Iowa Judges Assn., 1996. Home: 1123 SW Rose Ave Des Moines IA 50315

LAVORGNA, GREGORY JOSEPH, lawyer; b. Phila., Apr. 30, 1950; BEE, Drexel U., 1972, MEE, 1975; JD cum laude, Temple U., 1981. Bar: Pa. 1981, US Dist. Ct. (ea. dist.) Pa. 1981, US Patent Office 1981, US Ct. Appeals (Fed. cir.) 1982, DC 1986, US Supreme Ct. 1988. Electronics engr. RCA Corp., Camden, NJ, 1972-75, Gen. Electric Co., Phila., 1975-79; assoc. Seidel, Gonda, Goldhammer & Abbott, P.C., Phila., 1981-87; ptnr. Seidel, Gonda, Lavorgna & Monaco, P.C., Phila., 1988—2001; ptnr., head, intellectual property practice group Drinker Biddle & Reath LLP, Phila., 2001—. Editor in chief Drexel U. Tech. Jour., 1971-72; contbr. articles to profl. jours. Trustee 1st Bapt. Ch., Phila., 1978-88, Lower Merion Bapt. Ch., Bryn Mawr, Pa., 1989-92, moderator, 1995—. Mem. ABA, Pa. Bar Assn., Phila. Bar Assn., Am. Intellectual Property Law Assn., Justinian Soc., Am. Law Inst. Office: Drinker Biddle & Reath LLP One Logan Sq 18th & Cherry Sts Philadelphia PA 19103-6996 Office Phone: 215-988-3309. Office Fax: 218-988-2757. Business E-Mail: gregory.lavorgna@dbr.com.

LAW, CLARENE ALTA, small business owner, retired state legislator; b. Thornton, Idaho, July 22, 1933; d. Clarence Riley and Alta (Simmons) Webb; m. Franklin Kelso Meadows, Dec. 2, 1953 (div.); children: Teresa Lin Meadows, Charisse Meadows Haws, Steven Riley; m. Creed Law, 1973. Student, Idaho State Coll., 1953. Sec., sub. tchr. Grand County Schs., Cedar City, Utah, 1954-57; UPI rep. newspaper agy. Moab, Utah Regional Papers, Salt Lake City and Denver; auditor Wort Hotel, Jackson, Wyo., 1960-62; innkeeper, CEO Elk Country Motels, Inc., Jackson, Wyo., 1962—; rep. Wyo. Ho. of Reps., Cheyenne, 1991—2004. Bd. dirs. Jackson State Bank, Snow King Resort; mem. bank bd. Wyo. State Ho. Reps., 1991-98, chmn. travel com., 1993-2000, chmn. minerals and econ. devel. com., 2001-04. Chmn. sch. bd. dirs. Teton County Schs., Jackson, 1983-86; bd. dirs. Wyo. Taxpayers Assn., Bus. Coun., 1998—2004. Named Citizen of Yr. Jackson C. of C., 1976, 99, Bus. Person of Yr. Jackson Hole Realtors, 1987, Wyo. Small Bus. Person SBA, 1977. Mem. Wyo. Lodging and Restaurant Assn. (pres., chmn. bd. dirs. 1988-89, Big Wyo. award 1987), Soroptimists (charter), Bus. Profl. Womens Orgn. (Woman of Yr. 1975, mem. Heritage steering com. 1996—), Gov.'s 15-Mem. Bus. Coun. Republican. Avocations: travel, study. Address: PO Box 575 Jackson WY 83001-0575 Office: Elk County Motels Inc Box 575 43 W Pearl Jackson WY 83001 Home Phone: 307-733-4158. E-mail: antlerjh@aol.com.

LAW, DAVID HILLIS, physician; b. Milw., July 24, 1927; s. David Hillis Law III and Hazel Janice (May) Young; m. Patricia Bicking Thornton, Sept. 14, 1949 (dec. 2005); children: Linda Clark, Wendy, David, Kimberly Rankin, Cassandra. BA, Cornell U., 1950, MD, 1954. Resident in internal medicine Cornell U. Med. Coll., NYC, 1954-57, fellow in gastroenterology, 1957-59; dir. personnel health svcs. N.Y. Hosp., Cornell Med. Ctr., NYC, 1959-60; asst. prof. medicine, chief gastroenterology Vanderbilt U. Med. Coll., Nashville, 1960-69; prof., vice chmn. dept. medicine U. New Mex. Sch. Med., Albuquerque, 1969-85; chief med. svcs. Vets. Adminstrn. Med. Ctr., 1969-85; dir. med. svcs. Vets. Adminstrn. Ctrl. Office, Washington, 1985-86, dep. asst. chief med. dir. for clin. svcs., 1986-89, asst. chief med. dir. clin. affairs, 1989-91, acting dep. assoc. chief med. dir. for hosp.-based svcs., 1991-95, assoc. dep. chief med. dir. for clin. program, 1993-95, acting chief patient care officer, 1995-96; assoc. chief of staff for edn. Bay Pines Med. Ctr., Fla., 1996—2002; prof. internal medicine U. South Fla., 1998—; cons. Health Care Exec. Devel., 2003—. Human rsch. com. Los Alamos (N.Mex.) Sci. Lab., 1972-80; sabbatical dept. clin. physiology Karolinska Inst., Stockholm, 1980; officer N.Mex. Nutrition Improvement Program, 1970-75; sub-com. chmn. U.S. Pharmacopeia Commn. on Revision, 1975-80. Editor, Parenteral Nutrition; mem. editorial bd., Am. Jour. Digestive Diseases, 1968-74; rev. numerous med. jours.; contbr. articles to numeous profl. jours. Bd. dirs., officer Albuquerque Friends of Music, 1975-85; active Nat. Digestive Disease Adv. Bd., 1989-95, Interdepartmental Digestive Disease Coordinating Com.; pres. Bay Pines Edn. Found., Inc., 2001, bd. dirs., 2003-05. With U.S. Army, 1945-46. Named Tchr. and Attending Physician of Yr. Dept. Medicine House Staff, 1985. Fellow ACP (gov. 1989-96); mem. AMA (lectr.), Western Assn. Physicians, Western Soc. Clin. Rsch., Am. Gastroenterol. Assn., Am. Inst. Nutrition, Alpha Omega Alpha. Republican. Presbyterian. Avocation: hot air ballooning. Office: Vets Adminstrn Med Ctr 11-B Bay Pines FL 33744 Home Phone: 727-319-0358. Personal E-mail: clawoakhur@aol.com. Business E-Mail: david.law@med.va.gov.

LAW, JAN, artist; b. Newton, Mass., May 24, 1946; d. Charles McCallum and Phyllis Law. AA, Pine Manor Coll., Chestnut Hill, Mass., 1966, BA in Art History, 1982. Tchr. painting, drawing Children's Art Studio, Wellesley, Mass., 1993—94. One-woman shows include South Shore Bank, Wellesley, 1983, exhibited in group shows at Wellesley Soc. Artists, 1982, 1983, exhibitions include Artique, Inc., Framingham, Mass., 1983, Framery, 1984, Picture It Frames, Sudbury, Mass., 1986, So This Is Art, Wellesley, Mass., 1995. Mem. Mass. Rep. State Com., Boston, 1974—77; fundraiser Mass. Rep. Club, Boston, 1974—78; vol. Sen. Edward Brooke, Boston, 1978. Avocations: writing, dance, gardening, drawing. Home and Studio: 1 Lanteen Ln Natick MA 01760

LAW, JERRIANN MARCELLA, artist, poet, writer; b. Franklin, Ky., Mar. 22, 1958; d. Charles Utah and Sylvia Martine (Cassetty) Law. Exhibitions include Medical Ctr. Gallery, Bowling Green, Ky., 2003; author: (anthology) Noble House Labours of Love, 2005, Goose River Press, 2005, co-author songs with Ramsey Kearney. Mem. Civil War Preservation Trust, 2002—05; mem., Tchrs. Against Hate So. Poverty Law Ctr., Birmingham, Ala., 2004—05; mem. Nat. Com. to Preserve Social Security & Medicare, 2004—05; founding mem. Nat. Mus. US Army, Washington, 2005—06, Nat. Mus. of the Am. Indian, America's Nat. WWII D-Day mus., New Orleans, 2005—06. Recipient 5th Place for Children's Fiction, Writers Digest Writing Competition, 2001. Mem.: ACLU, Acad. Am. Poets, Internat. Libr. Poetry, Cherokee Wolf Clan, Sierra Club. Avocations: scrapbooks, doll collecting. Home: PO Box 755 Franklin KY 42135

LAW, JOHN HAROLD, biochemistry educator; b. Cleve., Feb. 27, 1931; s. John and Katherine (Frampton) L.; m. Jeannette Ward Belcher, Nov. 9, 2000. BS, Case Inst. Tech., Cleve., 1953; PhD, U. Ill., 1957; D (hon.), U. Sofia, 1995, U. South Bohemia, 2004. Fellow Harvard U., Cambridge, Mass., 1957—59; instr. Northwestern U., Evanston, Ill., 1959—60; from instr. to asst. prof. biochemistry Harvard U., Cambridge, Mass., 1960—65; prof. U. Chgo., 1965—81, U. Ariz., Tucson, 1981—91, Regents prof., 1991—2001, Regents prof. emeritus, 2001—; prof. entomology U. Ga., Athens, 2007—. Gov. bd. Internat. Ctr. Insects, Nairobi, Kenya, 1980—87; chmn. dept. biochemistry U. Ariz., Tucson, 1981—86, dir. biotech. program, 1986—92, assoc. dean Coll. Agr., 1988—90; mem. bd. trustees Gordon Rsch. Conf., 1992—98, chmn., 1996; dir. Ctr. Insect Sci. U. Ariz., Tucson, 1993—98. Recipient Gregor Mendel medal Czech Acad. Sci., 1992, J.E. Purkinje medal Czech Acad. Sci., 1994, Alumni Achievement award U. Ill., 2002. Fellow AAAS, ESA (Recognition award 1999); mem. NAS, Am. Soc. Biochem. Molecular Biology (mem. coun. 1993-96), Am. Chem. Soc., Entomol. Soc. Am. Home: 201-8 Hamilton Rd Athens GA 30606-6619 Office: U Ga Dept Entomology Bio Sci 518 Athens GA 30602-2603 E-mail: jhlaw@u.arizona.edu.

LAW, JUDE (DAVID JUDE LAW), actor; b. London, Eng., Dec. 29, 1972; s. Peter and Maggie Law; m. Sadie Frost, Sept. 2, 1977 (div. Oct. 29, 2003); children: Rafferty, Iris, Rudy Indiana Otis 1 stepchild, Finlay Munro. Ptnr. production comp. Natural Nylon. Actor: (TV series) The Tailor of Gloucester, 1989, Families, 1990, The Marshal, 1993; (films) Shopping, 1994, The Crane, 1994, I Love You, I Love You Not, 1996, Bent, 1997, Wilde, 1997, Gattaca, 1997, Midnight in the Garden of Good and Evil, 1997, Music from Another Room, 1998, Final Cut, 1998, The Wisdom of Crocodiles, 1998, eXistenZ, 1999, Presence of Mind, 1999, The Talented Mr. Ripley, 1999 (BAFTA award for best supp. actor, 2000, Santa Fe Film Critics Circle award for best supp. actor, 2000), Love, Honour and Obey, 2000, Enemy at the Gates, 2001, Artificial Intelligence: AI, 2001, Road to Perdition, 2002, Cold Mountain, 2003 (Acad. Award nomination for best actor, 2004, Golden Globe nomination for best actor in a drama, 2004), I Heart Huckabees, 2004, Alfie, 2004, Closer, 2004, The Aviator, 2004, (voice) Lemony Sniket's A Series of Unfortunate Events, 2004, All the King's Men, 2006, Breaking and Entering, 2006, The Holiday, 2006; dir.: (TV) Tube Tales (segment "A Bird in the Hand"), 1999; actor, prodr. (films) Sky Captain and the World of Tomorrow, 2004. Named Sexiest Man Alive, People Mag., 2004; named to 50 Most Beautiful List, 2000, 2004. Office: Endeavor Agy 10th Fl 9601 Wilshire Blvd Beverly Hills CA 90212*

LAW, MARCIA ELIZABETH, rehabilitation services professional; b. Spokane, Wash., Oct. 9, 1950; d. John Glen and Jean Carolyn (Lines) L.; 1 child, Michael Sean. AA, Spokane C.C., 1973. Notary public. Data entry operator, controller CyCare Sys., Spokane, Wash., 1974-78, tape libr., 1978-79; data entry operator Wash. state Dept. Employment Security, Spokane, 1986-87, Cath. Charities, Spokane, 1987, Cath. Diocese Spokane, 1987-90, Divsn. Vocat. Rehab. Dept. Health & Social Svcs., Seattle, 1990-95, sec. sr., 1994-99, counselor aide, 1999—2003, rehab. tech., 2003—. Mem. adv. com. Divsn. Vocat. Rehab. Dept. Health & Social Svcs., Seattle; state internal adv. com. Stakeholders Commn. Avocations: reading, movies, cross stitch, crafts, travel.

LAW, MARK EDWARD, electrical engineer, educator; b. St. Paul, July 19, 1959; s. Paul Rock and Bernice Edna (Brookshaw) L.; m. Alison Leigh Retz, May 30, 1981; children: Christopher, Heather. BS CprE, Iowa State U., 1981; MSEE, Stanford U., 1982, PhD in Elec. Engring., 1988. Engr. Hewlett Packard, 1982-84; rsch. asst. Stanford (Calif.) U., 1984-87, rsch. assoc., 1988; asst. prof. elec. engring. U. Fla., Gainesville, 1988-93, assoc. prof. elec. engring., 1993-97, prof. elec. engring., 1997—, prof., chair, elec. engring., 2003—. Presenter, spkr. in field; session chmn. various tech. meetings in field. Author: Floods/Floops User's Manual, 1993; contbr. articles to profl. jours., chpts. to books. Recipient Young Faculty Devel. award IBM, 1988, Tech. Excellence award Semicondr. Rsch. Corp., 1993, Outstanding Young Alumnus award Iowa State U., 1994, Profl. Progress award Iowa State U., 1994; Nat. Merit scholar, 1977-81; grantee NSF, 1992—, SRC, 1989—, 93—, IBM, 1991-93; NSF Presdl. fellow, 1992. Fellow IEEE (guest editor publ. 1991, assoc. editor IEEE Transactions on Semicondr. Mfg. 1996-97, editor Jour. on Tech. Computer Aided Design 1996-02, editor Circuits and Devices Mag. 1996-98), Am. Soc. Engring. Edn., Am. Phys. Soc., Electrochem. Soc., Sigma Xi, Phi Beta Pi, Phi Kappa Phi. Avocations: soccer, golf. Office: U Fla 216 Larsen Gainesville FL 32611-6200 Business E-Mail: law@tec.ufl.edu.

LAW, MICHAEL R., lawyer; b. Rochester, NY, Nov. 30, 1947; s. George Robert and Elizabeth (Stoddart) L.; m. Cheryl Heller. BS, St. John Fisher Coll., 1969; JD, U. Louisville, 1975. Bar: N.Y. 1976, U.S. Supreme Ct. 1982. Assoc. Wood, P.C., Rochester, NY, 1976-77; pvt. practice Rochester, 1977-78; assoc. Sullivan, Peters, et al, Rochester, 1978-80; ptnr., 1980-81, Phillips, Lytle, Hitchcock, Blaine & Huber, Rochester, 1982—. With USAR, 1968—74. Mem.: ABA (alternate dispute resolution com. 1995—, trial law sect., trial techniques com., editor 1986 Trial Techniques), N.Y. State Acad. Trial Lawyers, Genesee Valley Trial Lawyers Assn. (treas. 1992—93, pres.-elect 1993—95, pres. 1995—98), Monroe County Bar Assn. (judiciary com. 1981—88, personal injury com. 1988—, profl. responsibility com. 1996—, bd. dirs. 2003), N.Y. State Trial Lawyers (bd. dirs. 1990—2004), N.Y. State Bar Assn. (trial sec., ins. negligence com.), Am. Bd. Trial Advs. Republican. Roman Catholic. Home: 3373 Elmwood Ave Rochester NY 14610-3425 Office: Phillips Lytle Et Al 1400 1st Federal Plz Rochester NY 14614-1981 Office Phone: 585-238-2000. Business E-Mail: mlaw@phillipslytle.com.

LAW, STEVEN J., business association and former federal agency administrator; b. Oakland, Calif. married; 2 children. BA cum laude in Music, U. Calif., Davis, Calif., 1983; JD, Columbia U., 1986. Bar: D.C., N.Y., U.S. Supreme Ct. Chief of staff to Senator Mitch McConnell US Senate, Washington; dir. polit. strategy media advt. & fundraising devel. Nat. Rep. Senatorial Com.; chief of staff US Dept. Labor, Washington, 2001—04, dep. sec., 2004—07; chief legal officer, gen. counsel US C. of C., Washington, 2007—. Mem.: Federalist Soc. Office: US Chamber of Commerce 1615 H St Washington DC 20062*

LAW, STUART A., JR., lawyer; b. Broomall, Pa., 1957; BA, Ind. U. Pa., 1979; JD, Pa. State U., 1982. Bar: Pa. 1982, NJ 1989. Law clerk, Hon. John B. Hannum US Dist. Ct. (ea. dist.) Pa.; ptnr., construction litig. Drinker Biddle & Reath LLP, Princeton, NJ, and co-chair, construction law practice group. Nat. panel arbitrators Am. Arbitration Assn. Editor: (newsletter) The Construction Lawyer. Office: Drinker Biddle & Reath LLP Ste 300 105 College Rd E Princeton NJ 08540-6622 Office Phone: 609-716-6548. Office Fax: 609-799-7000. Business E-Mail: stuart.law@dbr.com.

LAW, THOMAS MELVIN, academic administrator; b. Bristol, Va., Sept. 23, 1925; s. Thomas Keen and Rebecca Ellen (Davis) L; m. Katherine Iris Tillar, Oct. 14, 1954; 1 child, Thomas Fenimore. BS summa cum laude, St. Paul's Coll., 1950, LHD (hon.), 1982; MA, NYU, 1953; EdD, Cornell U., 1962; LHD (hon.), Cuttington U., Liberia, 2001, SS Va. CC, 2001. Dean., prof. St. Paul's Coll., Lawrenceville, Va., 1967-69, pres., trustee, 1989—; v.p. acad. affairs Washington Tech. Inst., 1969-71; pres. Penn Valley Community Coll., Kansas City, Mo., 1971-76, Va. State U., Petersburg, 1976-82; dep. to chancellor spl. programs SUNY, Albany, 1982-86, dep. to chancellor for CC, 1986, assoc. vice chancellor contracts/purchasing, 1986-89, pres., 1989—2001; pres. emeritus St. Paul's Coll. Bd. dirs. Nat. Alumni Assn, Sch. of Human Ecology, Cornell U.; mem. Cornell U. Coun (life). Bd. dirs. Brunswick County C. of C., Lawrenceville, 1990—, Va. C. of C., Brunswick County Indsl. Devel. Authority, 1994-2002, A.L. Philpott Mfg. Extension Partnership1994-2002; life mem. NAACP; mem. commn. black mins. Union Black Episcs., Inc., by-laws com. United Negro Coll. Fund, Inc. Sgt. U.S. Army, 1942-46. Mem. Am. Assn. Higher Edn., Nat. Assn. Ind. Colls. and Univs. (com. campus concerns), Coun. Ind. Colleges in Va. (exec. com., pres.), Assn. Va. Colls. and Univs. (exec com., pres.), Am. Coun. on Edn. (com. leadership), Rotary, Phi Delta Kappa, Alpha Phi Alpha (life), Sigma Pi Phi. Address: 117 Scrimshaw Dr Chester VA 23836-1200 Personal E-mail: tlaw@saintpauls.edu.

LAWAL, TAIWO MUNIR, civil engineer; b. Lagos State, Nigeria, Apr. 14, 1955; arrived in U.S., 1978; s. Alhaji Raji Akangbe and Alhaja Nusirat Asakun Lawal; m. Foluso Temitope Marinho, Dec. 6, 1992; children: Fatima Omolola, Folashade Adejumoke. AS, Roger Williams U., 1983, BSc, 1985; MPA, City U., 2001; PhD, Pacific We. U., 2004. Registered profl. engr., Coun. Register Engr. Nigeria, 1998, cert. Am. Soc. Engrs., 1984. Sr. exec. officer Fed. Ministry Def., Lagos, Nigeria, 1974—78; asst. mgr. planning ITT Grinnell Corp., Providence, 1979—82; mgr. Harwood Mfg. Co., Providence, 1982—85; grad. asst. City U., Washington, 1997—2001; sr. civil engr. Ridot, Providence; dir. engring. Meml. Hosp. RI, Pawtucket, RI, 2001—. Author: In Search of Creative Excellence, 1992, The Role of Foreign Aid and Investment in Economic Development: A Case Study of Nigeria, 2003-2005; contbr. articles to profl. jours. Recipient Govt. Scholarship award, Govt. of Nigeria, 1977—78, Svc. award, Meml. Hosp. RI, 1995—99. Mem.: ASCE, Nigerian Inst. Mgmt., Inst. Transp. Engrs. (assoc.), Alliance Democracy, Nigerian Assn. Am. (mem. com. 1984—), Roger Williams U. Alumni Assn., Island Club (Lagos). Democrat. Achievements include research in areas of science and engineering education, public administration and management, infreasturcture and transportation planning, economics growth and development. Avocations: reading, sports, travel, walking, writing. Home: 24 Inkerman St Providence RI 02908 Office: Meml Hosp RI PO Box 28194 Providence RI 02908 Address: No 19 Muyibi St Olodi Apapa Lagos Nigeria Office Phone: 401-831-1235. Personal E-mail: taiwo50@hotmail.com.

LAWER, BETSY, banker, small business owner, vintner, director; b. Anchorage, July 27, 1949; d. Daniel H. and Betti Jane Cuddy; m. David A. Lawer, June 9, 1972; 1 child. Vice chair bd., COO 1st Nat. Bank Alaska, 1974—; pres. Lawer Family Winery Inc., 2005—, Lawer Family Vineyard Properties, Inc., 2005—. Bd. dirs., mem. audit com. Fed. Res. Bank San Francisco, Seattle, 1997—2003; emeritus bd. dirs. Providence Health Care Found., 2001; bd. dirs. Commonwealth North. Named Jr. Achievement Hall of Fame Laureate, 2007; named one of the Top 25 Most Powerful Alaskans, Alaska Jour. Commerce, 1999—2003, 25 Women to Watch, US Banker, 2003. Mem.: Anchorage Athena Soc. (Athena award 2001).

LAWHEAD, VICTOR BERNARD, education educator; b. Vincennes, Ind., Feb. 26, 1919; s. William Augustus Lawhead and Rilla Belle Wood; m. Doris Jean Barber, July 11, 1953. *The Lawheads have engaged jointly in special projects in international education and in supporting the enhancement of culture in the city of Muncie, Indiana.* AB, De Pauw U., 1940; MA, Ohio State U., 1947, PhD, 1950. Hist. tchr. Kokomo Ind. Pub. Schools, Ind., 1940—48; prof. of edn. Ball State U., Ind., 1950—84; vis. lectr. Mich. State U., 1952; vis. prof. U. Md., 1957; asst. dean, undergraduate programs Ball State U., 1958—63, dean, undergraduate programs, 1964—84, prof. higher edn., 1984—. Cons. examiner No. Ctrl. Assn. for Colleges and Schools, Chgo., 1962—84; participant/observer United Nations Unesco Offices, Paris, 1967—81; cons., tchg. adv. duties Ball State U., 1984—. *Ball State University presents annually The Lawhead Teaching award to a faculty member who makes an outstanding contribution to the general and liberal arts component of its undergraduate curriculum.* Contbr. articles to jours.; co-author: (book) Meanings, Values and Commitment, 1962—66; contbr. author (book) Teachers and Mentors, 1996. Mem., sponsor of programs So. Poverty Law Ctr., 1995—, People for the American Way, 1982—; founding assoc. Minnetrista Ctr. Natural and Cultural Heritage, 1990—. Lt. USN, 1943—46, Pacific Theater, Japan. Recipient Disting. Svc. award, Acad. Affairs Conf. Midwest Univ., 1976; Rector scholar, DePauw U., 1936—40, Univ. fellow, Ohio State U., 1948—50. Mem.: Assn. for Integrative Studies, Assn. for Gen. and Liberal Studies, Kiwanis Club. Avocations: sailing, poetry, fishing. Home: 801 N Briar Rd Muncie IN 47304 Office: Ball State Univ Bracken Libr 304 2000 W Univ Ave Muncie IN 47306 Business E-Mail: vblawhead@bsu.edu.

LAWHON, CHARLA, editor; Grad., Drake U. With Apt. Life Mag., Des Moines; dir. editl. svcs. Meredith Design Group, 1990; exec. editor Met. Home, 1992; dep. editor InStyle Mag., NYC, 1994—98, exec. editor, 1998—2002, mng. editor, 2002, editor-in-chief. Office: InStyle Mag 1271 Ave of the Ams New York NY 10020*

LAWHON, JOHN, III, lawyer, retired county official; b. Denton, Tex., Dec. 14, 1934; s. John E. and Gladys (Barns) L.; m. Tommie Collins, Aug. 27, 1967; 1 son, David Collins. Student, U. N.Tex., 1951-53; BBA, JD, U. Houston, 1958. Bar: Tex. 1958; cert. specialist in estate and probate law; bd. cert. in family law. Asst. dist. and county atty., Denton County, Tex., 1958-61; dist. and county atty., 1961-77; dir. Southridge, Inc., Denton, 1962-72, Lawyers Title Agy. Denton, 1965-74; Legal adviser Denton

City-County Day Nursery, 1972-80; tchr. bus. law U. North Tex. (formerly North Tex. State U.), Denton, 1969-71; mem. adv. bd. Tex. Criminal Justice Council, 1973-79; univ. atty. Tex. Woman's U., 1977-83, gen. counsel, 1983—, sec. bd. regents, 1987—. Bd. dirs. Denton County Welfare Coun., 1970-78, Denton Community Coun., 1978-79, 80-82; mem. Denton Forum; chmn. Denton County ARC, 1985-87, Denton County Probation Adv. Bd., 1985-92; mem. City of Denton Land Use Com., 1986-88. Mem. Tex. Bar Assn., Denton Bar Assn. (pres. 1968-69, bd. dirs. 1978-81), Tex. Dist. and County Attys. Assn. (bd. dirs. 1964-66), Denton Jaycees (sec. 1961), Denton C. of C., Tex. Assn. State Univ. Attys. (pres. 1983-84, Denton County crim. justice task force 1992-93, state bar coll. fellow 1995—), K.P., Kiwanis (bd dirs 1981-86, pres 1984-85). Baptist (deacon 1968—2005). Home: 2810 Carmel St Denton TX 76205-8310 Office: Tex Woman's U Adminstrn Tower Bldg PO Box 44 Denton TX 76202-0044 Office Phone: 940-387-4401.

LAWHON, PATRICIA PATTON, literature and language professor, writer educator; b. Edgewood Arsenal, Md., Jan. 10, 1924; d. Jack Murray Patton and Elizabeth Cotter; m. Zim E. Lawhon, Dec. 23, 1944; children: Elizabeth Cotter, Mary Jane, Zim Edan, John Patton, Margaret Arnold, Bridget Jamieson, Martha Kone, Mary Benedict, Patricia Titus, Catherine Chad, Rebecca Anne, Rachel Julia, James Newton. BA, U. N.C., 1944; MA, U. Scranton, 1976. Instr. Keystone Coll., La Plume, Pa., 1974—76; adj. faculty U. Scranton, Pa., 1976—; instr. Marywood U., Scranton, 1977—82. Former mem. bd. Women's Resource Ctr. Mem.: Lackawanna River Corridor Assn., Archtl. Heritage Assn. (bd. dirs.), Friends of Libr., Lackawanna Hist. Soc., Alpha Sigma Nu. Address: 1527 N Washington Ave Scranton PA 18509-2361 Personal E-mail: lawhonp1@aol.com. Business E-Mail: lawhonp1@scranton.edu.

LAWHON, TOMMIE COLLINS MONTGOMERY, humanities educator; b. Shelby County, Tex., Mar. 15; d. Marland Walker and Lillian (Tinsley) Collins; m. David Baldwin Montgomery, Mar. 31, 1962 (dec. Aug. 1964); m. John Lawhon, Aug. 27, 1967; 1 child, David Collins. BS, Baylor U., 1954; M in Home Econs. Edn., Tex. Woman's U., 1964, PhD in Child Devel. and Family Studies, 1966. Cert. tchr., Tex.; cert. family and consumer scis.; cert. family life educator. Tchr. Victoria Pub. Schs., Tex., 1954-55; stewardess, supr. Am. Airlines, Dallas/Ft. Worth, 1955-62; assoc. prof. home econs. Ea. Ky. U., Richmond, 1966-67, U. North Tex., Denton, 1968—, head divsn. child devel. and family studies, dept. counseling, devel. and higher edn., 1974—77, univ. tenure com., 1978—84, head program devel. and family studies, 1993-94, mem. faculty senate, 1984-90, chmn. com. on coms., 1987-88, mem. com. status on women, 1984-87, mem. faculty salary com., 1989-95, chmn., 1989-91, mem. tradition com., 1989-95, recorder, 1989-91. Bd. dirs. U. North Tex., Univ. Union, 1985-88, mem. student mentor com., 1990-00, mem. benefits com., 1994-00, vice chair, 1994-95, chair, 1997-98, mem. faculty sen. Faculty Handbook com., 1998-2004, mem. faculty sen. mentor com., 1990-, mem. coll. edn. greivance com., 2003—, chair, 2003-07; presenter in field. Co-author: Children are Artists, 1971, Hidden Hazards for Children and Families, 1982; editor: What to Do with Children, 1974, Field Trips for Children, 1984; contbr. articles to profl. jours. Chmn. United Way North Tex. State U., 1980-81; chmn. crusade Am. Cancer Soc., Denton County, 1982-83; chmn. nominating com. First Bapt. Ch., Denton, 1983-84, 84-85; mem. career action adv. com. Girls Inc. of Met. Dallas, 1999, chmn., 2000-01; advisor North Tex. Student Coun. on Family Rels., 1993—. Recipient Presdl. award Tex. Coun. on Family Rels., 1979, Fessor Graham award North Tex. State U., 1980, Svc. award Am. Cancer Soc., 1983, Outstanding Home Economists Alumni award Baylor U., 1985, Outstanding Event award, 12th Ann. State Conf., U. North Tex., 2006; named Hon. Prof. North Tex. State U., 1975, Meritorious award Nat. Coun. on Family Rels. Assn. of Couns., 2004; Disting. Svc. award Outstanding Orgn. Advisor, U. North Tex., 2005, SGA Exemplary Orgnl. award U. North Tex., 2007. Mem. Tex. Coun. on Family Rels. (pres. 1977-79, chmn. policy advisor com. 1986-88, nominating com. 1986-88, 94-96, chair 1994-96, family life edn. com. 1994-97, Moore-Bowman award 1994), Denton Assn. for Edn. Young Children (pres. 1970-72, 84-85, 85-86, v.p. 1986-87), Tex. Assn. Coll. Tchrs. (nominating com. 1988-89, 89-90, v.p. 1990-92, v.p. U. North Tex. chpt. 1987-88, pres. 1988-89, 89-90), Tex. Home Econs. Assn. (chmn. family living and child devel. nominating com. 1983-84, chmn. child devel. and family rels. sect. 1988-90, sec. rep. bd. 1989-90), Nat. Coun. Family Rels. (com. 1982-83, cert. family life's continuing edn. com. 1996-99, chair elect cert. family life continuing edn. com. 1996, chair 1997-98, cert. family life edn. focus group and regional-state coord., chair 1996-97, coord. of all student asst. annual conf., 2001-02), Nat. Assn. Early Childhood Tchr. Educators (membership com. 1995-97), North Tex. Home Econs. Inter-orgnl. Coun. (adviser 1983-85), Phi Delta Kappa (pres. local chpt. 1991-92), Alpha Iota/Phi Upsilon Omicron (advisor 1970-82, chmn. nat. com. 1984-87, nat. bd. dirs. edn. found. 1990-94, com. pubs. 1991-92, vice chair ednl. found. 1992-94), Tri D Club (v.p. Baylor U. chpt. 1953-54), Univ. Grad. Club (pres. Tex. Woman's U. chpt. 1965-66). Democrat. Office: U North Tex Coll Edn Denton TX 76203

LAWHORN, CARON A., gas industry executive; BS, Univ. Tulsa, 1983. CPA. Sr. mgr. KPMG LLP; CFO Emergency Med. Services Authority, Tulsa, Okla.; mgr. audit services ONEOK Inc., Tulsa, Okla., 1998—2003, v.p. audit & risk control, 2003—04, v.p., controller, 2004—05, sr. v.p. fin. services., treas., 2005—07, sr. v.p., chief acctg. officer, 2007—. Chair adv. bd. Ronald McDonald House Charities Tulsa; treas. St. Simeon's Episcopal Home. Mem.: Am. Inst. CPAs, Inst. Internal Auditors, Okla. Bus. Ethics Consortium. Office: ONEOK Inc 100 W Fifth St Tulsa OK 74103*

LAWI, DAVID STEVEN, utilities executive, merchant banker; b. Baghdad, Iraq, Aug. 3, 1935; came to U.S., 1946, naturalized, 1952; s. Steven David and Marcelle (Masry) L.; m. Anne Shamash, June 9, 1968; children— Nicole, Neil. AA in Sci, N.Y. State Coll., 1955. Registered rep. domestic and fgn. arbitrage Bear, Stearns & Co., NYC, 1956—62; dir. Adobe Brick & Supply, West Palm Beach, Fla., 1962—64; v.p. Molly Corp., Reading, Pa., 1962—64; gen. mgr. United Shoe Machinery Corp., Reading, 1964—65; co-founder, sec., treas., mem. exec. com., dir. Unimax Group Inc. (formerly Riker-Maxson Corp. ASE), NYC, 1966—80; also dir. all subs., v.p., treas. Telepictures Corp. ASE, NYC, 1980—81; chmn. fin. com., sec. Telepictures Corp., NYC, 1980—86; exec. v.p., sec. Helm Capital Group, Inc. (ASE), Greenwich, Conn., 1980—; founder, chmn. exec. com., also bd. dirs. Helm Capital Group, Inc., Greenwich, Conn. Founder, bd. dir., sec. Teletrak Advanced Tech. Sys., Inc., 1983—, Continuing Care Assocs., 1982—; sec., bd. dir., founder, chmn. exec. com. Seitel Inc. (NYSE; formerly Seismic Enterprises, Inc.), 1982-84, now bd. dir.; advisor Lorimar-Telepictures (acquired by Warner Comm., Inc. 1989/NYSE), 1986, now Time-Warner/NYSE, 1990—; founder, bd. dir., chmn. exec. com. Intersys., Inc. (ASE; formerly Bamberger Polymers, Inc.), Unipix Entertainment, Inc. (EquiFin, Inc., formerly ASE; formerly Majestic Entertainment, Inc.), Cliff Engle Ltd., Unapix Entertainment Inc. Served with AUS, 1968. Home: 120 Polly Park Rd Rye NY 10580 also: 13 Sloans Curve Dr Palm Beach FL 33480

LAWIT, JOHN WALTER, lawyer; B in U. Studies, U. N.Mex., 1972; JD, Franklin Pierce Law Ctr., Concord, NH, 1977. Bar: Pa. 1978, N.Mex. 1980, Tex. 1992, U.S. Dist. Ct. (ea. dist.) Pa. 1978, US Dist. Ct. N.Mex. 1980, US Ct. Appeals (5th cir.) 2006. Sole practitioner, NYC, 1978-79, Albuquerque, 1980—. Adj. prof. immigration law U. N.Mex. Sch. Law, 1983, 84, 88; spl. immigration counsel U. N.Mex., Albuquerque, 1987—; U.S. immigration judge US. Dept. Justice, 1985; apptd. mem. N.Mex. Internat. Trade/Investment Coun., 1984-87, N.Mex. Border Commn., 1982-86; hon. cons. atty. Ministry Fgn. Affairs Republic of Mex., 1983; lobbyist, author, drafter N.Mex. Immigration & Nationality Law Practice Act. Presenter in field. Founder, profl. cons. Jewish Family Svcs. of Albuquerque, 1988—; bd. dirs., pres. Rainbow House Internat. Adoption, Belen, N.Mex., 1987-2000; v.p. N.Mex. Refugee Assn., Albuquerque, 1979-84; bd. dirs. N.Mex. Civil Liberties Union, 1988-90; mem. adv. bd. Healing the Children, Albuquerque, 1989—; bd. dirs. Inst. for Spanish Arts, 1994-96. Recipient Disting. Svcs. award, Cath. Social Svcs., 1988. Mem. N.Mex. State Bar (chair internat. and immigration lawyers sect. 1990-91, bd. dirs. 1988-90), Albuquerque Bar Assn., Am. Immigration Lawyers Assn., El Paso Assn. Immigration and Nationality Lawyers. Avocations: biking, travel, whitewater rafting, hiking. Office: 2305 Renard Pl SE Ste 210 Albuquerque NM 87106 Office Phone: 505-243-0733. Fax: 505-244-1834. Business E-Mail: jlawit@jlawit.com.

LAWLER, GARY M., academic administrator; MA in Math., SUNY, Albany; PhD in Curriculum and Instruction, U. Albany. Prof. math. Adirondack CC, Queensbury, NY, asst. to v.p. academic affairs; dean Coll. St. Joseph, Rutland, Vt., 2001—04, v.p. academic and student affairs, 2004—07; chancellor Pa. State U., Hazleton, 2007—. Office: Pa State U Office of Chancellor 76 University Dr Hazleton PA 18202 Office Phone: 570-450-3032.

LAWLER, GREGORY FRANCIS, mathematics professor; b. Alexandria, Va., July 14, 1955; s. Thomas Comerford and Patricia Ann (Fullerton) L.; m. Marcia Fenker Curtis, May 5, 1990. BA, U. Va., 1976; PhD in Math., Princeton U., 1979. Asst. prof. math. Duke U., Durham, NC, 1979-85, assoc. prof. math., 1985-91, prof. math., 1991—2001, A. Hollis Edens prof. math., 2001—03; prof. math. Cornell U., Ithaca, NY, 2001—06; prof. math. & statistics U. Chgo., 2006—. Vis. assoc. prof. Cornell U., 1989; vis. rsch. scientist U. BC, 1994—95. Author: Intersections of Random Walks, 1991, Introduction to Stochastic Processes, 1995, Conformally Invariant Processes in the Plane, 2005. Sloan Found. rsch. fellow, 1986-90; recipient: George Polya prize, 2006 Fellow Inst. Math. Stats. Office: U Chgo Dept Math 5734 S University Ave Chicago IL 60637 E-mail: lawler@math.uchicago.edu.

LAWLER, JAMES EDWARD, physics professor; b. St. Louis, June 29, 1951; s. James Austin and Dolores Catherine Lawler; m. Katherine Ann Moffatt, July 21, 1973; children: Emily Christine, Katie Marie. BS in Physics summa cum laude, U. Mo., Rolla, 1973; MS in Physics, U. Wis., 1974, PhD in Physics, 1978. Rsch. assoc. Stanford (Calif.) U., 1978-80; asst. prof. U. Wis., Madison, 1980-85, assoc. prof., 1985-89, prof., 1989—, Arthur & Aurelia Schawlow prof., 1999—. Product devel. cons. Nat. Rsch. Group, Inc., Madison, 1977-78; cons. GE, Schenectady, N.Y., 1985-96, Teltech, Inc., 1990—; exec. com. Gaseous Electronics Conf., 1987-89, treas., 1992-94, DAMOP program com., 1993-95. Editor: (with R.S. Stewart) Optogalvanic Spectroscopy, 1991; contbr. articles to profl. jours. Recipient Penning award Internat. Conf. on Phenomena in Ionized Gases, 1995; Schumberger scholar U. Mo., 1971-72; grad. fellow U. Wis. Alumni Rsch. Found., 1973-74, NSF, 1974-76, H.I. Romnes faculty fellow U. Wis., 1987. Fellow Am. Phys. Soc. (Will Allis prize 1992), Optical Soc. Am.; mem. Sigma Xi. Achievements laser and lighting patents; development of laser diagnostics for glow discharge plasmas, of methods for measuring accurate atomic transition probabilities and radiative lifetimes. Office: U Wis Dept Physics 1150 University Ave Madison WI 53706-1302 Home Phone: 608-231-1473. Business E-Mail: jelawler@wisc.edu.

LAWLER, JAMES RONALD, French language educator; b. Melbourne, Australia, Aug. 15, 1929; married, 1954; 2 children. BA, U. Melbourne, 1950, MA, 1952; DUniv., U. Paris, 1954. Lectr. French U. Queensland, Australia, 1955-56; sr. lectr. U. Melbourne, 1957-62; prof., head dept. U. Western Australia, 1963-71; prof., chmn. dept. UCLA, 1971-74; McCulloch prof. Dalhousie U., Halifax, N.S., Canada, 1974-79; prof. French U. Chgo., 1979—, Edward Carson Waller Disting. Svc. prof., 1983-97, prof. emeritus, 1998. Vis. prof. Coll. de France, 1985, Tokyo, 1996, 98-99; chmn. vis. com. Romance Langs. and Lits. Harvard U., 1991-94, Soc. Amis U. Paris coun. Author: Form and Meaning in Valery's Le Cimetiere Marin, 1959, Lecture de Valery: Une Etude de Charmes, 1963, The Language of French Symbolism, 1969, The Poet as Analyst, 1974, Rene Char: The Myth and the Poem, 1978, Edgar Poe et les Poetes Francais, 1989, Rimbaud's Theatre of the Self, 1992, Poetry and Moral Dialectic: Baudelaire's Secret Architecture, 1997; co-author: Paul Valery; Poems, 1971, Paul Valery: Leonardo, Poe, Mallarme, 1972, Paul Claudel: Knowing the East, 2004, Edgar Allan Poe: Histoires, Essais, Poèmes, 2007; editor: An Anthology of French Poetry, 1960, Paul Valery: An Anthology, 1977, Paul Valery, 1991, Rimbaud Vivant; founding editor Essays in French Literature, 1964, Dalhousie French Studies, 1980. Decorated officier Palmes Academiques; recipient Prix Internat. Amities Françaises, Prix du rayonnement de la langue francaise Acad. Francaise, 1999; Brit. Coun. interchange scholar, 1967; Australian Acad. Humanities fellow, 1970, Guggenheim Found. fellow, 1974, NEH fellow, 1985; Grad. Students Tchg. award U. Chgo., 1998. Mem. MLA (coun. 1978-82), Internat. Assn. French Studies (pres. 1998-2001), Australian Acad. the Humanities, Soc. Amis de Rimbaud (pres. 2006—). Achievements include rsch. in modern French poetry, poetics, 20th century novel. Office: U Chgo Dept Romance Langs & Lit 1050 E 59th St Chicago IL 60637-1559

LAWLER, JEAN MARIE, lawyer; b. San Francisco, Aug. 7, 1954; d. Jack Wofford and Evelyn Mary (Matkovich) Suggs; m. Timothy Lawler, May 20, 1978; children: Kathleen, Megan, Colleen, Timothy. AA, Riverside City Coll., 1974; BBA, Loyola Marymount U., LA, 1976; JD, Loyola U. Law Sch., LA, 1979. Bar: Calif. Supreme Ct. 1979, Oreg. Supreme Ct. 1981. Assoc. law firm David L. Rosner, LA, 1979-80; instr. Lane CC, Eugene, Oreg., 1981-82; sole practice law, Eugene, 1981-82, and Beaverton, Oreg., 1982-84, with Murchison & Cumming, LA, 1985-, sr. ptnr., chair ins. law practice group. Editor: Copyright Law, 1979-80; Business Associates Review, 1974; contbr. poetry to Coll. Poetry Rev., 1974, 76. Chmn. legal asst. adv. com. Lane CC, 1981-82. Recipient Riverside County Bar Assn. scholarship, 1977; Loyola U. Jesuit Cmty. scholarship, 1978; Named Calif. Super Lawyer, 2005, 06. Mem. State Bar of Calif., Oreg. State Bar Assn., ABA, Washington County Bar Assn., Fedn. Def. & Corp. Counsel (bd. dir. 1996-2006, pres. 2004-05), Assn. So. Calif. Def. Counsel (bd. dirs. 1994-2000), Def. Rsch. Inst. (bd. dirs. 2003-06), Lawyers for Civil Justice (bd. dirs. 2003-06). Democrat. Roman Catholic. Club: Jonathon Club. Office: Murchison & Cumming 9th Fl 801 S Grand Ave Los Angeles CA 90017 Office Phone: 213-630-1019. Office Fax: 210-623-6336. Business E-Mail: jlawler@murchisonlaw.com.

LAWLER, JOHN A., publishing executive; BA, Williams Coll.; MBA, U. Va. With Dun and Bradstreet, London, 1992—93, head, European mktg. and sales Tokyo, 1994—95, vice-pres. global product devel.; CEO Reed Elsevier New Providence (RENP), which includes Martindale-Hubbell, New Providence, NJ, 2001—, also pres.*

LAWLER, WILLIAM E., III, lawyer; b. Washington, May 21, 1960; BA cum laude, U. Notre Dame, 1982; JD cum laude, Georgetown U., 1985. Bar: Md. 1985, D.C. 1986. Asst. U.S. atty. US Atty.'s Office, Washington, 1989—96; ptnr. Vinson & Elkins LLP, Washington. Lectr. FBI Tng. Acad.; Quanticio, Va. Contbr. articles to profl. jours. Named Young Lawyer of Yr., D.C., 1992. Mem.: ABA (Ho. of Dels. 1992—93, 2001—03), Bar Assn. D.C. (bd. dirs. 1993—2004, chair Young Lawyers sect. 1994—95, pres.-elect 2000—01, pres. 2001—02). Office: Vinson and Elkins LLP Willard Office Bldg 1455 Pennsylvania Ave NW Washington DC 20004-1008

LAWLESS, LUCY (LUCILLE FRANCIS RYAN), actress; b. Auckland, New Zealand, Mar. 28, 1968; m. Garth Lawless 1991 (div. 1995); 1 child, Daisy; m. Robert G. Tapert Mar. 28, 1998; children Julius Robert Bay Tapert, Judah Miro Tapert. Student, Auckland U., William Davis Ctr. Actor Study, Vancouver, Can.; trained with martial arts master, Douglas Wong. Previous jobs include TV comml. actress, gold miner, Kalgoorlie, Australia. Actress (films) A Bitter Song, 1990, Within the Law, 1990, The End of the Golden Weather, 1991, The Black Stallion, 1992, The Rainbow Warrior, 1992, Peach, 1995, Spider-Man, 2002, EuroTrip, 2004, Boogeyman, 2005, The Darkroom, 2006, (TV) Funny Business, 1987, Typhon's People, 1993, Hercules and the Amazon Women, 1994, Women from Down Under, 1995, Xena: Princess Warrior, 1995-2005, (TV Films) Locusts, 2005, Vampire Bats, 2005; co-host Air New Zealand Holiday, 1992-93, (film, voice of Xena) Hercules and Xena-The Animated Movie: The Battle for Mount Olympus, 1998; guest appearances Shark in the Park, 1990, For the Love of Mike, 1991, High Tide, 1994, 95, Hercules: The Legendary Journeys, 1995, 97, 98, Just Shoot Me!, 2001, The X-Files, 2001, Tarzan, 2004, Less Than Perfect, 2004, Veronica Mars, 2006, Battlestar Galactica, 2005, 2006, Two and Half Men, 2005, Celebrity Duets, 2006

LAWLESS, MICHAEL RHODES, pediatrics educator; b. Baytown, Tex., Oct. 13, 1942; s. Wallace Ervin and Amy Ruth (Broussard) L.; m. E. Sandra Johnson, Aug. 27, 1967; children: Melanie Lawless York, Stephanie Lawless Setzer. BA in Zoology, U. Tex., 1964, MD, 1968. Diplomate Am. Bd. Pediat. Intern City Memphis Hosp., 1968-69; resident in pediat. U. Tex. Med. Br., Galveston, 1969-71; instr. U. Rochester (N.Y.) Sch. Medicine, 1971-72; staff pediatrician Portsmouth (Va.) Naval Hosp., 1972-74; asst. prof. pediat. Wake Forest U. Sch. Medicine, Winston-Salem, NC, 1974-80, assoc. prof. pediat., 1980-2001, prof. pediat., 2001—, dep. assoc. dean student affairs, 1988-96, chief gen. pediat. and adolescent medicine, 1997—2005. Lt. comdr. USNR, 1972-74. Fellow U. Rochester, 1971-72. Fellow Am. Acad. Pediat. (legis. liaison 1980—); mem. Am. Profl. Soc. on Abuse of Children, N.C. Pediatric Soc. (child adv. 1974—), Coun. Med. Student Edn. in Pediat. (pres. 1998-00), Ambulatory Pediatric Assn., Am. Bd. Pediat. (bd. dirs. 2003—). Avocation: outdoor activities.

LAWLESS, ROBERT J., food products executive; b. Dec. 4, 1946; m. Catherine McKenna; 1 child. Grad., St. Clair Coll., Windsor Ont. Mgmt. positions through v.p. sales Club House Foods Inc. (Canadian subs. McCormick), 1977—89, pres., CEO, 1989—91, chmn., 1991—97; v.p., dep. gen. mgr. internat. group McCormick & Co., Sparks, Md., 1991—93, group v.p. Europe, 1993—94, sr. v.p. Americas zone & McCormick Schilling div. head, 1994—95, exec. v.p., COO, 1995-96, pres., COO, 1996—97, pres., CEO, 1997—99, chmn., pres., CEO, 1999—2006, chmn., CEO, 2006—. Bd. dir. Constellation Energy Group, Balt. Life Ins. Co., Grocery Mfr. Am. Bd. dir. Believe in Tomorrow Nat. Children's Found.; chmn. Kennedy Krieger Inst.; bd. dir. Md. Bus. Roundtable for Edn., Jr. Achievement Ctrl. Md.; mem. Md. Gov. Workforce Investment Bd. Named Bus. Leader of the Yr., Loyola Coll., 2001; named to Bus. Hall of Fame, Md. C. of C.; recipient Henry A. Rosenberg Sr. Disting. Citizen award, Balt. Area Council, Boy Scouts Am., 2004, Gov. Leadership award, Gov. Md., 2004. Mem.: Caves Valley Golf Club (bd. dir.). Office: McCormick 18 Loveton Cir Sparks MD 21152-6000*

LAWLESS, ROBERT WILLIAM, retired academic administrator; b. Baytown, Tex., Feb. 13, 1937; s. James Milton and Belva Ambaline (Mode) Lawless; m. Marcella Jane Emmert; children: Christopher, Cheryl, Diana. BS, U. Houston, 1964; PhD, Tex. A&M U., 1968. Instr., asst. prof. Tex. A&M U., College Station, 1967—69; prof., sr. vice chancellor U. Houston, 1969—82; v.p., CFO S.W. Airlines, Dallas, 1982—85, exec. v.p., COO, 1985—89; cons. Tex. Hosp. Assn., 1966—82, banks, savs. and loans, 1970—72, NASA, 1970; pres. Tex. Tech U. and Tex. Tech. U. Health Scis. Ctr., Lubbock, 1989—96, U. Tulsa, Okla., 1996—2004. Ind. dir. Salomon Bros. Asset Mgmt Co., 1991—2001, Central and SW Corp., 1991—2000, Williams Comms. Group Inc., 2000—02; chmn. Coun. Pub. Univ. Pres. and Chancellors, Tex. Higher Edn. Sys., 1993—95; mem. pres.'s commn. NCAA, 1994—97, mem. exec. com., 1998—2003, chmn., exec. com., 2001—03, bd. dirs. Divsn. 1; bd. dirs. Nat. Assn. Ind. Colls. and Univs., Assn. Presbyn. Coll. and Univs. Contbr. articles to profl jours. Mem formula adv comt Tex State Coordinating Bd, Austin, 1977—89; chmn bd dirs Col Football Asn, 1990—92. Recipient Teaching Excellence Award, Univ Houston, 1972, Disting Alumni Award, 1990, Disting Faculty Award, Col Bus Alumni, 1971, Disting Alumni Award, Lee Col, 1984. E-mail: robert-lawless@utulsa.edu.

LAWLESS, THOMAS WILLIAM, lawyer; b. West Palm Beach, Fla., Mar. 14, 1954; s. Joseph Francis and Ethel Joan (Sliney) L.; m. Sandra Mae Bryant, June 18, 1989; children: S. Joseph, Erin E. BS, Middle Tenn. State U., 1976; JD, Nashville Sch. Law, 1980. BAr: U.S. Ct. Internat. Trade 1981, U.S. Dist. Ct. (ctrl. dist.) Tenn. 1981, U.S. Dist. Ct. (ea. and we. dists.) Tenn. 1984, U.S. Ct. Appeals (D.C. cir.) 1982, U.S. Ct. Appeals (6th cir.), 1982, U.S. Supreme Ct. 1985; bd. cert. Creditors' Rights Specialist, Am. Bd. Cert. Rule 31 Mediator Commn. on ADR. Ptnr. Webb & Lawless, Nashville, 1981-83; v.p., counsel First Am. Corp., Nashville, 1983-85; ptnr., sec., treas. Combos & Lawless, P.C., Nashville, 1985—89; pres. Lawless & Assocs., P.C., 1989—2000, mng. dir., 2004—; of counsel Gsrrish & McCreary, 2000; ptnr. Wilson & Assocs., 2001—04. Mem. Cheatham County Rep. Exec. Com., Ashland City, Tenn., 1979-80. Fellow: Nashville Bar Assn. (chmn. ethics and professionalism com., Best of Bar 2004, 2005); mem.: ABA, Federalist Soc. Nashville (chpt. pres.), Internat. Bar Assn., Nat. Assn. Chapt. 13 Trustees, Am. Bankruptcy Inst., Davidson County Republic Party (exec. com., party coun., vice-chmn.), Assn. Trial Lawyers Am., Tenn. Trial Lawyers Assn., Tenn. Bar Assn. Roman Catholic. Office Phone: 615-351-7839. E-mail: tomlawless@comcast.net.

LAWLEY, ALAN, materials engineer, educator; b. Birmingham, Eng., Aug. 29, 1933; s. Archibald and Millicent A. (Olorenshaw) L.; m. Nancy A. Kressler, Mar. 26, 1960; children: Carolyn Ann, Elizabeth Ann, Jennifer Ann. BSc, U. Birmingham, 1955, PhD, 1958. Rsch. assoc. U. Pa., 1958—61; mgr. rsch. labs. Franklin Inst. Labs., 1961—66; A.W. Grosvenor prof. materials engrng. Drexel U., Phila., 1993—2003, head dept., 1969—79, 1992—98, prof. emeritus, 2003—. Cons. to govt., industry. Editor-in-chief Internat. Jour. Powder Metallurgy; contbr. chpts. to books, articles to profl. jours. Recipient Disting. Svc. award Metal Powder Industries Fedn., 1991. Fellow APMI Internat., ASM Internat. (life mem., Gold Medal award); mem. NAE, Inst. Metals, Mining and Materials, Minerals, Metals and Materials Soc. (pres. 1982, Educator award 2002), Am. Inst. Mining, Metall. and Petroleum Engrs. (hon.; pres. 1987), Sigma Xi, Phi Kappa Phi, Tau Beta Pi, Alpha Sigma Mu. Home: 336 Hathaway Ln Wynnewood PA 19096-1925 Office: Drexel Univ Dept Materials Sci Engrng Philadelphia PA 19104

LAWLEY, THOMAS JOSEPH, dean, medical educator; b. Buffalo, 1947; m. Christine Lawley, 1969; children: Thomas Jr., John, Megan. Grad., Canisius Coll., 1968; MD, SUNY Sch. Medicine, Buffalo, 1972. Intern SUNY Sch. Medicine, Buffalo, 1973—74; resident Yale U. Affiliated Hosps., 1974—75; sr. investigator dermatology br. Nat. Cancer Inst. NIH; prof. and chair. dept. dermatology Emory U. Sch. Medicine, Atlanta, 1988—96, William Patterson Timmie Prof. Dermatology, 1993—, exec. assoc. dean, 1995—96, dean, 1996—; vice chair Emory U. Sys. Health Care, Atlanta, 1996—; core dir. Emory Skin Disease Rsch. Ctr., Atlanta. Pres. Emory Med. Care Found., Emory Children's Ctr.; adminstrv. coun. Assn. Am. Med. Colls. Mem.: Am. Profs. Dermatology, Soc. Investigative

Dermatology, Am. Acad. Dermatology (Marion Sulzberger Award 1995), Assn. Am. Physicians, Am. Soc. Clin. Investigators. Office: Emory U Sch Medicine Woodruff Health Scis Ctr Adminstrv Bldg 1440 Clifton Rd NE Atlanta GA 30322-1053

LAWLOR, LYNNANN JENNIFER, reading educator; b. NYC, Jan. 10, 1961; d. William and Elizabeth Fallon; m. Thomas Lawlor, Sept. 28, 1996; children: Sean, Shannon. Bachelor, Jersey City State Coll., 1983, Masters, 1991. Reading tchr. Assumption Sch., Wood Ridge, NJ, 1983—2001. Recipient Disting. Tchg. award, Archdiocese of Newark, 2001. Mem.: Internat. Reading Assn.

LAWNICZAK, JAMES MICHAEL, lawyer; b. Toledo, Sept. 11, 1951; m. Christine Nielsen, Dec. 31, 1979; children: Mara Katharine, Rachel Anne, Amy Elizabeth. BA, U. Mich., 1974, JD, 1977. Bar: Mich. 1977, Ill. 1979, Ohio 1989. Law clk. to the Honorable Robert E. DeMascio U.S. Dist. Ct. (ea. dist.) Mich., Detroit, 1977-79; assoc. Levy and Erens, Chgo., 1979-83; assoc. then ptnr. Mayer, Brown & Platt, Chgo., 1983-88; ptnr. Calfee, Halter & Griswold, LLP, Cleve., 1988—. Contbg. author: Collier on Bankruptcy, 15th edit. rev., 1997—. Mem. Chgo. Bar Assn. (subcom. on bankruptcy 1983-88), Cleve. Bar Assn. (trustee 2005—). Home: 14039 Fox Hollow Dr Novelty OH 44072-9773 Office: Calfee Halter & Griswold LLP 800 Superior Ave E Ste 1400 Cleveland OH 44114-2601 E-mail: jlawniczak@calfee.com.

LAWRANCE, CHARLES HOLWAY, retired civil and sanitary engineer; b. Augusta, Maine, Dec. 25, 1920; s. Charles William and Lois Lyford (Holway) L.; m. Mary Jane Hungerford, Nov. 22, 1947; children: Kenneth A., Lois R., Robert J. BS in Pub. Health Engring., MIT, 1942; MPH, Yale U., 1952. Registered profl. engr., Calif. Sr. san. engr. Conn. State Dept. Health, Hartford, 1946-53; assoc. san. engr. Calif. Dept. Pub. Health, LA, 1953-55; chief san. engr. Koebig & Koebig, Inc., Cons. Engrs., LA, 1955-75; engr., mgr. Santa Barbara County Water Agy., Santa Barbara, Calif., 1975-79; prin. engr. James M. Montgomery Cons. Engrs., Pasadena, Calif., 1979-83; v.p. Lawrance, Fisk & McFarland, Inc., Santa Barbara, 1983-96; cons. engr., retired Santa Barbara, 1996-99. Author: The Death of the Dam, 1972; co-author: Ocean Outfall Design, 1958; contbr. articles to profl. jours. Bd. dirs. Pacific Unitarian Ch., Palos Verdes Peninsula, Calif., 1956-60, chmn. bd. 1st lt. USMCR, 1942-46, PTO. Fellow ASCE (life, Norman medal 1966); mem. Am. Water Works Assn. (life), Am. Acad. Environ. Engrs. (life diplomate), Water Environment Fedn. (life). Republican. Unitarian Universalist. Home and Office: 1340 Kenwood Rd Santa Barbara CA 93109-1224 E-mail: charleslawrance@earthlink.net.

LAWRENCE, ANNETTE, artist; b. NYC, 1965; BFA, U. Hartford, 1986; MFA, Md. Inst., 1990. Mem. artist com. Lawndale Art and Performance Ctr., 1991—95; mem. cmty. arts panel Tex. Commn. on Arts, 1995—96; artist-in-residence Cmty. Artist's Collective, Houston, 1990—91, Housing Authority City of Houston, 1992—93, Glassell Sch. Art, Houston, 1993; guest artist Tex. So. U., Houston, 1992; cons. HSPVA, Houston, 1993—94; affiliate artist U. Houston, 1995; adj. faculty U. Houston-Downtown, 1993—96, U. North Tex., Denton, 1996—. One-woman shows include ArtPace, San Antonio, 1995, Art League of Houston, 1996, Gerald Peters Gallery, Dallas, 1996, one-man shows include, 1998, one-woman shows include Women and Their Work, Austin, 1996, African Am. Mus., Dallas, 1998, exhibited in group shows at Minor Injury Gallery, Bklyn., 1986, Bronx River Art Gallery, N.Y., 1987, Manhattan Cable, N.Y.C., 1988, Meyerhoff Gallery, Balt., 1990, Laguna Gloria Mus. Art, Austin, Tex., 1992, Inman Gallery, Houston, 1993, Tex. Gallery, 1994, Gerald Peters Gallery, Dallas, 1995, 1996, 1997—98, U. Houston, Clearlake, Tex., 1998, numerous others, Represented in permanent collections Dallas Mus. Art, ArtPace, San Antonio, Mus. Fine Arts, exhibited in group shows at Texas Trialogues, 2003, Artists and their Mentors, 2003, Flip, 2003, Dunn and Brown Contemporary, 2004, Perspectives at 25, 2004, For Nothing, 2004, Double Consciousness: Black Conception Art Since 1970, 2005, performances include, Sangoma, 1990, Square One, 1990, Amazon Papers, 1991, Parachute Project, 1995; actor;. Recipient Artist award, Cultural Arts Coun., Houston, 1994, Arch and Anne Giles Kimbrough award, Dallas Mus. Art, 1994; fellow W.E.B. Dubois fellow, W.Va. U., 1987—88, Patricia Robert Harris fellow, Md. Inst., 1988—90, Skowhegan Camille Hanks Cosby fellow, African-Am. Artists, 1996; Art Matters grantee, 1994. Office: care Gerald Peters Gallery 2913 Fairmount St Dallas TX 75201-1455

LAWRENCE, BRYAN HUNT, investment company executive; b. NYC, July 26, 1942; s. Bryan and Suzanne (Walbridge) L.; m. Elizabeth D. Lawrence, Sept. 25, 1965; children: Bryan R., E. Corey. BA, Hamilton Coll., 1964; MBA, Columbia U., 1966. Assoc. Dillon, Read & Co. Inc., NYC, 1966-70, v.p., 1971-74, sr. v.p., 1975-81, mng. dir., 1982-97; mem. Yorktown Ptnrs. LLC, NYC, 1997—. Bd. dirs. PetroSantander Inc., Houston, Hallador Petroleum, Denver, Savoy Energy LP, Traverse City, Mich., Camden Resources, Dallas, Crosstex Energy, Dallas, ESI Energy Svcs. Inc., Calgary, Ellora Energy Inc., Boulder, Colo., Dernick Resources, Inc., Houston, Cinco Natural Resources, Dallas, Peak Energy Resources, Durango, Colo., Approach Resources, Ft. Worth, Compass Energy, Calgary, Nytis Exploration, Denver, Windstar, Calgary, Kestrel Energy, NY, Armstrong Land, St. Louis, Star Gas, NY. Trustee Hamilton Coll., Clinton, N.Y., 1991-94. Republican. Home: 580 Park Ave New York NY 10021-7325 Office: Yorktown Ptnrs LLC 410 Park Ave New York NY 10022-4407

LAWRENCE, CHRISTOPHER RUECKERT, investment banker; b. NYC, May 24, 1953; s. Gerard R. and Nancy Lee (Rueckert) L.; m. Cathy Sogg, Apr. 7, 1979; children: Alexander Edward, Zoe Elizabeth, Charles Joseph. AB, Vassar Coll., 1976; MBA, Harvard U., 1981. With mktg. dept. IBM, NYC, 1976-79; investment banker, mng. dir. to vice chmn. Salomon Bros., Inc. (acquired by Citigroup), NYC, 1981—2000; vice chmn. investment banking, global head telecom group Credit Suisse First Boston, 2000, chief strategic officer, 2003—05; vice chmn. Rothschild, 2005—. Bd. dirs. Playwrights Horizons. Office: Rothschild 1251 Sixth Ave 51st Fl New York NY 10020

LAWRENCE, CORDELL G., state agency administrator; BA in Liberal Studies, Spalding U.; grad., U. Wis. Sch. Bank Adminstrn. Cert. corp. trust specialist Cannon Fin. Inst. and Inst. Cert. Bankers. Sr. v.p., mgr. Liberty Nat. Bank and Trust Co., Louisville; v.p., regional mgr. charitable and endowment svcs. divsn. Nat. City Bank Ky.; dep. commr. Gov.'s Office Local Devel.; exec. dir. Ky. Office Fin. Instns., Frankfort, 2005—. Trustee Spalding U. Office: Ky Office Fin Instns 1025 Capital Center Dr Ste 200 Frankfort KY 40601 Office Phone: 502-573-3390. Office Fax: 502-573-8787. E-mail: cordell.lawrence@ky.gov.

LAWRENCE, DAVID, JR., journalist, early childhood advocate; b. NYC, Mar. 5, 1942; s. David Sr. and Nancy Wemple (Bissell) Lawrence; m. Roberta Phyllis Fleischman, Dec. 21, 1963; children: David III, Jennifer Beth, Amanda Katherine, John Benjamin, Dana Victoria. BS, U. Fla., 1963; postgrad. advanced mgmt. program, Harvard U., 1983; LHD (hon.), Siena Heights Coll., Adrian, Mich., 1985; HHD (hon.), Lawrence Inst. Tech., Detroit, 1986; LHD (hon.), No. Mich. U., 1987; LD (hon.), Barry U., 1991, Fla. Meml. U., 1992, Northwood U., 1993, U. Fla., 1993, Nova Southeastern U., 1997, Colgate U., 1998, Fla. Internat. U., 2005, St. Thomas U., 2006. Reporter, news editor St. Petersburg (Fla.) Times, 1963—67; news editor Style/Washington Post, 1967—69; mng. editor Palm Beach (Fla.) Post, 1969—71, Phila. Daily News, 1971—75; exec. editor Charlotte (N.C.) Observer, 1975—76, editor, 1976—78; exec. editor Detroit Free Press, 1978—85, pub., chmn., 1985—89, The Miami Herald, 1989—99. Univ. scholar for early childhood devel. and readiness U. Fla. Chair The Children's Trust, Miami-Dade Early Learning Coalition. Named Disting. Alumnus, U. Fla., 1982; recipient Nat. Human Rights award, Am. Jewish Com., 1986, First Amendment Freedoms award, Anti-Defamation League, 1988, Ida Wells Nat. award for advancement of minorities, Nat. Assn. Black Journalists and Nat. Conf. of Editl. Writers, 1988, John S. Knight Gold medal, Knight-Ridder, 1988, Silver Medallion award, NCCJ, 1992, Disting. Svc. award, Nat. Assn. Schs. Journalism and Mass Comm., 1992, Scripps Howard First Amendment award, 1993, Lifetime Achievement award, Nat. Assn. Minority Media Execs., 2002, Award of Excellence, Am. Pub. Health Assn., 2002, Lewis Hine award for Children and Youth, 2002. Mem.: Early Childhood Initiative Found. (pres.), Inter-Am. Press Assn. (pres. 1995—96), Am. Soc. Newspaper Editors (pres. 1991—92). Office: 3250 SW 3rd Ave 5th Fl Miami FL 33129 Home Phone: 305-444-8875; Office Phone: 305-646-7229. Business E-Mail: dlawrence@childreadiness.org.

LAWRENCE, DAVID LONG, radiologist; b. Jamestown, Ky. s. Marshall Marvin Lawrence and Opal Hilden Long; m. Jeanette Wesley, Jan. 30, 1954 (div. 1990); children: Julia L., David W.; m. Sandra B. Hubbard, Feb. 14, 1992. AB, Centre Coll., Danville, Ky., 1955; MS, U. Ky., 1958; MD, U. Louisville, 1962. Diplomate Am. Bd. Radiology, Nat. Bd. Med. Examiners. Intern Baroness Erlanger Hosp., Chattanooga, 1967—68; resident in gen. radiology U. Louisville, 1968—71; radiologist, v.p. Springfield (Ohio) Radiology, 1971-96; locum tenens cons. Global Med. Staffing, Salt Lake City, 1995—, Vista Med. Staffing, Salt Lake City, 1997—. Med. staff Mercy Med. Ctr.; chmn. bd. Missionary Health Svc., 1991. Lt. comdr., USNR, 1966-68. Mem. Am. Coll. Radiology, Clark County Med. Soc. (pres. 1983), Ohio State Med. Assn. (alternate del.). Episcopalian. Avocations: fly fishing, cosmology, mind/brain interface, etymology. E-mail: sandavidl@hotmail.com.

LAWRENCE, DAVID MICHAEL, lawyer, educator; b. Portland, Oreg., Dec. 26, 1943; s. Robert A. and Maude (Davis) L.; m. Alice Oviatt, June 18, 1966 AB, Princeton U., 1965; JD, Harvard U., 1968. Asst. prof. Inst. Govt., U. N.C., Chapel Hill, 1968-71, assoc. prof., 1971-76, prof. pub. law and govt., 1976-94; Kenan prof. pub. law and govt. U. N.C., Chapel Hill, 1994—. Counsel N.C. Local Govt. Study Commn., 1972-73, N.C. Open Meetings Study Commn., 1978-79 Author: Local Government Finance in North Carolina, 2d edit., 1991 (award for excellence Rsch. and Publs. Govt. Fin. Officers Assn. U.S. and Can. 1991), numerous other books on local govt. law and fin.; contbr. law articles to profl. jours. Chmn. Durham (N.C.) Hist. Dist. Commn., 1985-89. Recipient Herald prize Princeton U., 1965 Mem. N.C. State Bar, Princeton U. Campus Club, Harvard Club of N.Y. Democrat. Office: University of NC Knapp Bldg Clb # 3330 Chapel Hill NC 27599-0001 Office Phone: 919-966-4214. Business E-Mail: lawrence@sog.unc.edu.

LAWRENCE, GERALD GRAHAM, management consultant; b. U.K., June 21, 1947; came to U.S., 1962, naturalized, 1967; s. Raymond Joseph and Barbara Virginia Lawrence; 1 child, Ian Andrew; m. Julie Ann Quiram. BA in Math., Northeastern U., 1970, MA in Econs., 1973; MBA, U. Pa., 1975. Optics rsch. technologist Polaroid Corp., Cambridge, Mass., 1968-70; intern Corning Glass Works, Inc., NYC, 1974; asst. brand mgr. Procter and Gamble, Cin., 1975-76; assoc. Theodore Barry & Assocs., NYC, 1976-79; dir. performance improvement systems Stone & Webster Mgmt. Cons., NYC, 1979-84; mgr. utility MAS Deloitte Haskins & Sells, NYC, 1984-86; pres. PMC Mgmt. Cons., Inc., Three Bridges, N.J., 1986—. Advisor Commerce & Econ. Devel. Dept. State of N.J.; speaker in field. Designer: auditor system nuclear power plant constrn; innovator; quality assurance for profl. cons. svcs; contbr. articles to profl. jours. Econs. fellow Northeastern U., 1973, adminstrv. fellow Wharton Sch. U. Pa., 1975. Office: PMC Mgmt Cons PO Box 332 Three Bridges NJ 08887-0332 Home: 43304 Hill Head Pl Leesburg VA 20176 E-mail: pmc@pmc-management.com.

LAWRENCE, GLENN ROBERT, arbitrator, mediator, lawyer; b. NYC, Nov. 8, 1930; m. Nina M. Scaturro; children: David P., Eric A. JD, Bklyn. Law Sch., 1954; BA, U. Louisville, 1968; MA in Psychology, Cath. U., 1977; PhD, Am. U., 1980. Bar: N.Y. 1955, D.C. 1973, U.S. Supreme Ct. 1976, Va. 1997; cert. family mediator, Va., 2002-04. Atty. N.Y.C. Legal Aid, 1955-57; ptnr. Lawrence & Lawrence, NYC, 1957-64; agt. N.Y. State, Babylon, NY, 1964-66; atty. U.S. Army Engrs., 1966-69; assoc. chief trial atty. U.S. Dept. Navy, Washington, 1969-78; judge adminstrv. law HEW, Camden, NJ, 1978-79, U.S. Dept. Labor, Washington, 1979-93, SEC, Washington, 1993-96; mem. bd. contract appeals U.S. Dept. Labor, Washington, 1981-93; arbitrator Nat. Assn. Securities Dealers, Inc., Washington, 1996—, Superior Ct., Washington, 1996—; mediator Women's Ctr., Vienna, Va., 1996—2001. Adj. prof. law George Mason U., Fairfax, Va., 1980-83, Ctrl. Mich. U., Washington, 1981-95, Nat. Jud. Coll. U. Nev., Reno, 1985-88; lectr. Banares Hindu U., Varanasi, India, 1988, Law Coll., Ernakulum, Cochin, India, 1989, Washington Lee U., Lexington, Va., 1990; mem. adv. com. Georgetown U. State Cts. and Toxic Torts, 1991; advisor Judiciary Leadership Devel. Coun. Inc., 1990-99; v.p. Fed. Bar Found., 1996-99, chair profl. ethics com., 1999-2001, chair sr. lawyers divsn., 1999-2000. Author: Condemnation Law, 1969. Bd. dirs. Democracy Devel. Initiative, Parkinson Found., 2004—. Mem. ABA (chmn. nat. conf. adminstrv. law judges edn. com. 1985-90, chmn. internat. conf. jud. edn. London 1985, pres. fed. adminstrv. law judge conf. 1984-85, chmn. edn. jud. adminstrn. divsn. 1987-91, chmn. confs., chmn. jud. edn. standards program 1991-95, vice chmn. govt. lawyers com. sr. lawyers divsn. 1991-95), Fed Bar Assn. (chmn. adminstrv. judiciary com. 1984-88, continuing edn. bd. 1988-91, chmn. judiciary sect. 1989-91, sect. coord. exec. com. 1992-94, editor Fed. Jurist 1991-96, chair pub. rels. com. 1995-96, chair profl. ethics com. 1996-98), Adminstrv. Trial Lawyers Assn. (pres. 1979-80, chmn. sr. lawyers divsn. 1999—).

LAWRENCE, JAMES A., food products executive; m. Mary G. Lawrence; 3 children. BA, Yale U., 1974; MBA with distinction, Harvard U., 1976. With Fidelity Funds, Boston Cons. Group; ptnr. Bain & Co.; co-founder, ptnr. The LEK Partnership, 1983—92; pres., CEO Asia, Africa & Mid. E. bus. units The Pepsi-Cola Co., 1992—96; exec. v.p., CFO Northwest Airlines, St. Paul, 1996—98, General Mills, Inc., Mpls., 1998—2006, exec. v.p. internat. ops., 2000—06, vice-chmn., CFO, 2006—07; CFO Unilever, Englewood Cliffs, NJ, 2007—. Bd. dirs. Avnet Inc. Mem. bd. overseers Carlson Sch. Bus. Univ. Minn.; bd. mem. Univ. Minn. Found. Office: Unilever 800 Sylvan Ave Englewood Cliffs NJ 07632*

LAWRENCE, JAMES KAUFMAN LEBENSBURGER, lawyer; b. New Rochelle, NY, Oct. 8, 1940; s. Michael Monet and Edna (Billings) L.; m. George-Ann Adams, Apr. 5, 1969; children: David Michael, Catherine Robin. AB, Ohio State U., 1962, JD, 1965. Bar: Ohio 1965, U.S. Dist. Ct. (so. dist.) Ohio 1971, U.S. Ct. Appeals (6th cir.) 1971, U.S. Ct. Appeals (4th cir.) 1978. Field atty. NLRB, Cin., 1965-70; ptnr. Frost Brown Todd LLC, Cin., 1970—. Adj. prof. econs. dept. and Coll. Law U. Cin., 1975—; treas. Potter Stewart Inn of Ct., Cin., 1988—90; tchg. fellow Harvard Negotiation Project, 1991; chmn. adv. panel on appointment of magistrate judges US Dist. Ct. for So. Dist. Ohio, 1993—97; adj. prof. McGregor Sch., Antioch U., 1993—98; adj. prof. Moritz Coll. Law Ohio State U., 1995—; adj. prof. Xavier U., 1995; adj. prof. MBA program Otterbein Coll., 2002—05; adj. prof. Pepperdine U., 2007—. Contbr. articles to profl. jours.; editor: (newsletter) Pass the Gavel, 2002—03. Mem. nat. coun. Ohio State U. Coll. Law, 1974—; steering com. Leadership Cin., 1985-89; mem. Seven Hills Neighborhood Houses, Cin., 1973-95, pres., 1992-94; bd. dirs. Beechwood Home, Cin., 1973-85; adv. bd. Emerson Behavioral Health Svcs., 1990-95, chmn., 1995; chmn. Labor Dept., 1978-89, Franciscan Hosp. Devel. Coun., 1995-99, chmn., 1996-97; trustee Ctr. for Resolution of Disputes, Inc., 1988-91, treas., 1990-91; mem. Ohio Gov.'s Ops. Improvement Task Force, 1991. Recipient Outstanding Adj. Faculty award, U. Cin., 1998. Fellow Coll. Labor and Employment Lawyers; mem. ABA, Cin. Bar Assn. (chmn. labor law com. 1979-82, comm. adv. com. 1994-96, alternative dispute resolution com. 1996—), Ohio Bar Assn. (cert. specialist in labor and employment law, vice chmn. labor and employment law sect. 1987-90, chmn. 1990-92, Ohio's Friend of Legal Edn. award 2003), Indsl. Rels. Rsch. Assn. (bd. govs. 1977-80), Alumni Assn. Coll. Law Ohio State U. (pres. 1984-85), Assn. for Conflict Resolution, Cincinnatus Assn. (pres. 1985-86), Collaborative Law Ctr. (steering com. 1996—2004), Univ. Club; master Potter Stewart Inn of Ct. Avocations: collecting movie posters, Lionel trains. Home: 3300 Columbia Pkwy Cincinnati OH 45226-1044 Office: Frost Brown Todd LLC 2200 PNC Ctr 201 E 5th St Cincinnati OH 45202-4182 Home Phone: 513-871-2220; Office Phone: 513-651-6822. Business E-Mail: jlawrence@fbtlaw.com.

LAWRENCE, JENNIFER L., lawyer; b. Cin., May 30, 1971; BA, Ohio State U., 1993; JD, Salmon P. Chase Coll. Law, 1996. Bar: Ohio 1996, Ky. 1997, US Dist. Ct. Southern Dist. Ohio. Assoc. The Lawrence Firm L.P.A., Cin. Bd. mem. Birth Trauma Litig. Grp., Commn. CLE, Ohio. Co-author: Medical Malpractice: Understanding the Evolution, Rebuking the Revolution. Named one of Ohio's Rising Stars, Super Lawyers, 2006. Mem.: Salmon P. Chase Am. Inn of Ct., Assn. Trial Lawyers of Am., Ohio Acad. Trial Lawyers, Ky. Acad. Trial Lawyers, Northern Ky. Bar Assn., Cin. Bar Assn. Office: The Lawrence Firm LPA 8804 Montgomery Rd Ste 700 Cincinnati OH 45202 Office Phone: 513-651-4130. Office Fax: 513-651-0525.

LAWRENCE, JOHN KIDDER, lawyer; b. Detroit, Nov. 18, 1949; s. Luther Ernest and Mary Anna (Kidder) L.; m. Jeanine Ann DeLay, June 20, 1981. AB, U. Mich., 1971; JD, Harvard U., 1974. Bar: Mich. 1974, U.S. Supreme Ct. 1977, D.C. 1978. Assoc. Dickinson, Wright, McKean & Cudlip, Detroit, 1973-74; staff atty. Office of Judge Adv. Gen., Washington, 1975-78; assoc. Dickinson, Wright, McKean, Cudlip & Moon, Detroit, 1978-81; ptnr. Dickinson, Wright, Moon, VanDusen & Freeman, Detroit, 1981-98, Dickinson Wright PLLC, Detroit, 1998—. Exec. sec. Detroit Com. on Fgn. Rels., 1988—; trustee Ann Arbor (Mich.) Summer Festival, Inc., 1990—; patron Founders Soc. Detroit Inst. Arts, 1979—; dir. Mich. C. of C., 2002—. With USN, 1975-78. Mem. AAAS, ABA, Am. Law Inst., State Bar Mich., D.C. Bar Assn., Am. Judicature Soc., Internat. Bar Assn., Am. Hist. Assn., Mich. C. of C. (bd. dirs. 2002—), Detroit Athletic Club, Econ. Club Detroit, Phi Eta Sigma, Phi Beta Kappa. Democrat. Episcopalian. Office: Dickinson Wright PLLC 500 Woodward Ave Ste 4000 Detroit MI 48226-3416 Office Phone: 313-223-3500.

LAWRENCE, JOHN R., academic administrator; B, M, N.E. M, EdS, N.E. Mo. State U.; EdD, U. Mo., Columbia. Supt. Troy (Mo.) R-3 Schs., Mo., 1984—, Schuyler County R-I Pub. Schs., Lancaster, Mo. Mem.: Mo. Assn. Sch. Adminstrs. (pres.), Assn. Sch. Adminstrs. (mem. exec. com. 1999—, pres.-elect 2002, pres. 2003). Office: Lincoln County R-III Sch Dist 951 W College St Troy MO 63379

LAWRENCE, KAREN R., academic administrator, literature and language professor; BA magna cum laude, Yale U., 1971; MA in English, Tufts U., 1973; PhD in English, Columbia U., 1978. Prof. English U. Utah, 1978—97; prof. English and comparative lit. U. Calif., Irvine, dean Sch. Humanities, 1998—2007; pres. Sarah Lawrence Coll., Bronxville, NY, 2007—. Vis. lectr. Internat. Yeats Summer School, Sligo, Ireland. Author: The Odyssey of Style in Ulysses, Penelope Voyages: Women and Travel in the British Literary Tradition, he McGraw-Hill Guide to English Literature, Decolonizing Tradition: New Views of Twentieth-Century British Literary Canons, Transcultural Joyce. Mem. English Lit. Bd., Graduate Record Examination; co-chair U. Calif. Humanities Commn. Recipient Ramona Cannon Award, Rosenblatt Prize; grantee John Simon Guggenheim Found. Fellowship. Mem.: Internat. Soc. for Study of Narrative Lit., Internat. James Joyce Found. (past pres.). Office: Sarah Lawrence Coll Office of Pres One Mead Way Bronxville NY 10708 Office Phone: 914-395-2201.*

LAWRENCE, LAUREN, psychotherapist, writer; b. NYC, June 26, 1950; d. Jack and Elaine (Gaumont) Soefer; m. David Lawrence, June 24, 1972; 1 child, Graham. BA, Hunter Coll., NYC, 1970; MA in Psychology, New Sch. for Social Rsch., NYC, 1993. Psychoanalyst, NYC, 1992—. Author: Dream Keys: Unlocking the Power of Your Unconscious Mind, 1999, Dream Keys for Love, 1999, Dream Keys for the Future: Unlocking the Secrets of Your Destiny, 2000, La Llave De Los Suenos, 2001, A Quoi Revent Les Stars, 2002, Private Dreams of Public People, 2002; contbr. scientific papers to profl. jours. and mags., articles to local newspapers and popular mags.; performer: (TV series) The Dream Zone, RISE TV, BBC; appeared on numerous TV and radio shows. Friend N.Y. Psychoanalytic Soc. Achievements include founding of a third person analysis, a new method of analysis in clinical practice, which provides the analysand a narrational objectivity; the covert seduction theory, which expounds the dangers of a non-physical parental seduction, the Actualized Dream, a conscious behavioral manifestation of symbolic material-unconscious desires that manifest themselves during consciousness through extreme behavioral acts, the undisclosed visual cliche, as an attribute or assessment drawn from a visual that leads to a cliche, and the externalized dream as a manifestation of a vision. Home and Office: 31 E 72d St New York NY 10021-4146 Office Phone: 212-737-3911. E-mail: laurenlawrence@aol.com.

LAWRENCE, MARGERY H. (MARGERY HULINGS LAWRENCE), marketing consultant; b. Harmarville, Pa., June 17, 1934; d. Richard Nuttall and Alva (Burns) Hulings. Student, Bethany Coll., 1951-52; BS in Mktg., Carnegie-Mellon U., 1955. Asst. mdse. buyer Joseph Horne Co., Pitts., 1955-57; home econs. editor Pitts. Group Cos. Columbia Gas Sys., Pitts., 1957-64, dir. home econs., 1968-72, dist. mktg. mgr. Jeannette, 1972-87, divsn. mgr., 1987-91; dir. mktg. Columbia Gas Pa. and Columbia Gas Md., 1991-96; mktg. and bus. cons. M.H. Lawrence Ltd., Beaver Falls, Pa., 1996—. Bd. dirs., sec. Ohio Valley Gen. Hosp.; chmn. Ohio Valley Gen. Hosp. Found Mem.: DAR (chmn. state conf. 2005, past regent Fort McIntosh chpt.).

LAWRENCE, MARTIN, actor, comedian; b. Frankfurt, Germany, Apr. 16, 1965; s. John and Chlora L.; m. Patricia Southall Jan. 7, 1995 (div. Sept. 17, 1996); 1 child. Actor: (TV series) What's Happening Now, 1985, HBO One Night Stand, 1989, Kid 'N' Play, 1990 (voice), Russell Simmons' Def Comedy Jam, 1991-93 (host); (films) Do the Right Thing, 1989, House Party, 1990, House Party 2, 1991, Talkin' Dirty after Dark, 1991, Boomerang, 1992, You So Crazy, 1994 (concert film, also exec. prodr.), Bad Boys, 1995, Nothing to Lose, 1997, Life, 1997, Blue Streak, 1999, Bad Boys II, 2003, Open Season (voice), 2006, Wild Hogs, 2007; actor, exec. prodr., writer, dir. A Thin Line Between Love and Hate, 1997; actor, exec. prodr.: Big Momma's House, 2000, What's the Worst That Could Happen, 2001, Black Knight, 2001, National Security, 2003, Rebound, 2005, Big Momma's House 2, 2006, (TV series) Martin, 1992-97. Office: United Talent Agy 9560 Wilshire Blvd Ste 500 Beverly Hills CA 90212*

LAWRENCE, MARY JOSEPHINE (JOSIE LAWRENCE), artist, retired library official; b. Carbondale, Pa., Mar. 9, 1932; d. Domenick Anthony and Teresa Rose (Zaccone) Gentile; m. John Paul Lawrence, Apr. 25, 1953 (dec. June 1977); children: Mary Josephine, Jane Therese, Susan Michele. BFA, Mass. Coll. Art, 1989; postgrad., Chelsea (Eng.) Sch. Art, 1989, San Pancrazio Art Sch., Tuscany, Italy, 1990, 91, 92; cert. in grad.

studies, Guangzhou Acad. Fine Arts, China, 1993; postgrad., Md. Inst. Fine Art, Sorrento, Italy, 1994, Ctrl. Acad. Arts and Design, Beijing, 1997, Skopelos, Greece, 1998, N.Y. Sch. Visual Arts, Barcelona, Spain, 1999, Internat. Sch. Art, Umbria, Italy, 2000. Sales clk. Gorins, 5&10, Jordan Marsh, Boston, 1946-49; clk.-typist, sec. John Hancock Ins. Co., Boston, 1950-53; machine operator, quality control supr. Rust Craft Greeting Cards, Dedham, Mass., 1961-69; restaurant hostess Tony's Villa, Waltham, Mass., 1972-73; mus. sales clk., artist John F. Kennedy Libr., Boston, 1979-87, mgr. mus. store, supr., 1988-2000; freelance artist, 2000—. Tchr.'s asst. San Pancrazio Art Sch., 1992; guest appearance TAKE TWO cable TV, Channel 11, 1996, Walpole Cmty. TV, 2001, WEZE Family 590 Talk Show, 2001. One woman shows include de Havilland Fine Art Gallery, Boston, 1997, Dr. James McDermott Gallery, Boston, 1996, Cranberry Cafe, Boston, 1997, Belmont Gallery Art, 2007; exhibited in group shows at South Shore Arts Ctr., Cohasset, Mass., 1991, North River Arts Soc., Marshfield Hills, Mass., 1994 (Best of Show), de Havilland Fine Art Gallery, Boston, 1997, United South End Open Studios, 1998, Artana Gallery, Framingham, Mass., 2000, Logan Airport, 2006. Juror Quincy Art Assn., 1996, 98, 2002, 2005, Weymouth Art Assn., 1995, 97, Arts Affair, 1999. Recipient Outstanding Achievement award, Nat. Archives and Rsch. Adminstrn., 1989, 1994, 1996—97, Svc. award, 1990, Blue Ribbon Mems. award, 2003, Best of show award, De Havilland Fine Arts Gallery, 1992, honorium, Weymouth Art Assn., 1995, 1997, Quincy Art Assn. award, 1996, 1998, 2002, 2005; grantee Vt. Studio Ctr., 2002, 2004. Mem. de Havilland Fine Art Gallery, South Shore Art Ctr., North River Arts Soc., Nat. Mus. Women in Arts (charter), Milton Art Mus., United S. End Artists, Fuller Mus. Art., South Boston Arts Assn., Portland Mus. Art, Farnsworth Art Mus. Democrat. Roman Catholic. Personal E-mail: josielawrence@comcast.net.

LAWRENCE, MELL, architect; BArch, U. Tex., Austin, 1981. Project arch. Black Atkinson Vernooy Archs., Austin, 1983—85, Charles W. Moore, Arch., Austin, 1985—90; ptnr. Lamb and Lawrence Archs., Austin, 1987—92; founder, prin. Mell Lawrence Archs., Austin, 1992—. Prin. works include Walls Residence, Hays County, Tex., 2001 (Austin AIA Design award, 2004), Foshee Residence, Fayette County, Tex., 2002 (Austin AIA Design award, 2004), Bridle Path Addition, Austin, 2003, Travis Heights Addition, 2003, Graves Residence, 2003, Cuernvaca Pool House, 2004, Breakwater Residence, Jonestown, Tex., 2004, Red Hawk Residence, Wimberley, Tex., 2004, Boonville Hotel + Winery, Boonville, Calif., 2004, Tuttle Garage Apt., Austin, 2004, Sugar Creek Studio/Garage, West Lake Hills, 2005, Big Ranch Rd. Residence, Napa, Calif., 2005. Fellow: AIA. Office: Mell Lawrence Archs 913 W Gibson Austin TX 78704 Office Phone: 512-441-4669. Office Fax: 512-441-9125.*

LAWRENCE, MERLOYD LUDINGTON, editor; b. Pasadena, Calif., Aug. 1, 1932; d. Nicholas Saltus and Mary Lloyd (Macy) Ludington; m. Seymour Lawrence, June 21, 1952 (div. 1984); children: Macy, Nicholas; m. John M. Myers, 1985 AB, Radcliffe Coll., 1954, MA, 1957. With Houghton Mifflin Co., 1955-57; freelance translator, 1957-65; editor, treas., v.p. Seymour Lawrence Inc., Boston, 1965-83; pres. Merloyd Lawrence, Inc., Boston, 1983—. Translator works of Flaubert and Balzac, modern French fiction, German and Swedish children's books. Treas., v.p. Milford Ho. Properties, Ltd., NS, Canada, 1975—80; trustee Milton Acad., Mass., 1974—82; mem. com. clin. investigations Beth Israel/Deaconess Hosp., 1986—2007; mem. adv. bd. World Land Trust, 2006—; bd. dirs. NE Wilderness Trust, 2002—, Woods Hole Rsch. Ctr., 2004—, Island Press, 2005—. Mem. Am. Translators Assn., New Eng. Forestry Found. (exec. bd. officer 1989—), Mass. Audubon Soc. (dir. 1974-2001, exec. com. 1992-2001, hon. dir. 2001—), Tavern Club, Phi Beta Kappa. Home: 102 Chestnut St Boston MA 02108-1120 Office: 102A Chestnut St Boston MA 02108-1120

LAWRENCE, NINA, publishing executive; married; 2 children. B cum laude, Middlebury Coll., 1982. Media planner Benton & Bowles, Inc., 1983—85; with Mag. Sales Develop. Program Time Inc., 1985—86, with advt. sales dept., 1986—87; advt. sales dir. Diversion mag. Hearst Publishing, 1987—89, pub. Hearst Profl. Magazines, 1989—90; pres. Family Publishing Concepts, 1991—92; advt. dir. Discover mag., 1992—93; pub. Disney Adventures mag., 1993—94; assoc. pub. Mademoiselle mag. Conde Nast Pubs., NYC, 1994-96; pub. Modern Bride mag. Primedia Inc., NYC, 1996-98; pub. Bride's mag. Conde Nast Pubs., NYC, 1999—2005; v.p. & pres. W mag., NYC, 2005—. Office: W Mag 7 West 34th St New York NY 10001*

LAWRENCE, PAUL ROGER, retired psychology professor; b. Rochelle, Ill., Apr. 26, 1922; s. Howard Cyrus and Clara (Luther) L.; m. Martha G. Stiles, Dec. 14, 1948; children: Anne Talcott, William Stiles. Student, Grand Rapids Jr. Coll., 1939-41; AB, Albion Coll., 1943; MBA, Harvard U., 1947, DCS, 1950. Mem. faculty Harvard U. Bus. Sch., Boston, 1947-91, asst. prof., 1951-56, assoc. prof., 1956-61, prof. organizational behavior, 1961-68, Donham prof. organizational behavior, 1968; retired, 1991. Author (with others): Renewing American Industry, 1983, HRM, Trends and Challenges, 1985; author: Behind the Factory Walls, 1990, Driven, How Human Nature Shapes Our Choices, 2002. Served to lt. USNR, 1943-46. Fellow Acad. Mgmt.; mem. Am. Sociol. Assn. Office: Cumnock Hall Soldiers Field Boston MA 02163 Home: 206 Wintrop Terr Bedford MA 01730 E-mail: plawrence@hbs.edu.

LAWRENCE, ROBERT SWAN, physician, educator; b. Phila., Feb. 6, 1938; s. Thomas George and Catherine (Swan) Lawrence; m. Cynthia Starr Cole, July 1, 1960; children: Job Scott, Matthew Swan, Hannah Starr, Jin Sook, Sang Bo. AB magna cum laude, Harvard U., Cambridge, Mass., 1960, MD, 1964. Intern, resident in internal medicine Mass. Gen. Hosp., 1964—66; surgeon USPHS, 1966—69; resident in internal medicine Mass. Gen. Hosp., 1969—70; asst. prof., then assoc. prof. medicine, chief divsn. cmty. medicine Med. Sch. U. NC, 1970—74; dir. divsn. primary care Harvard U. Med. Sch., 1974—91, assoc. prof. medicine, 1980—81, Charles S. Davidson assoc. prof. medicine, 1981—91; prof. environ. health sci., health policy Johns Hopkins Bloomberg Sch. Pub. Health, Balt., 1995—; prof. medicine Johns Hopkins Sch. Medicine, Balt., 1996—. Chmn. dept. medicine Cambridge Hosp., Mass., 1980—91; adj. prof. NYU Sch. of Medicine, 1992—95; assoc. dean profl. edn. Johns Hopkins Bloomberg Sch. Pub. Health, 1995—2006, Edyth Schoenrich prof. preventive medicine, 2000—06; mem. com. human rights NAS, 1986—97; chmn. bd. health promotion and disease prevention IOM, 1981—86, chmn. com. health and human rights, 1990—94; chmn. U.S. Preventive Svc. Task Force HHS, 1984—89, active mem., 1990—96; fellow Ctr. Advanced Study in Behavioral Scis., 1988—89; dir. health scis. Rockefeller Found., 1991—95; found. dir. Ctr. Livable Future, John Hopkins U., 1996—; mem. global health advisory com. Open Soc. Inst., 2005—; bd. trustees Albert Schweitzer Fellowships, 2003. Editor Am. Jour. Preventive Medicine, 1990—92; contbr. articles to profl. jours., chapters to books. Bd. trustees Columbia U. Tchrs. Coll., 1992—98; bd. dir. Physicians for Human Rights, 1986—91, 1997—2003, 2007—, pres., 1999—2003, 2007—, chair, bd. dirs., 2007—. Recipient Maimonides prize, 1964, John Atkinson Ferrell prize, 1997, Albert Schweitzer Humanitarian prize, 2002. Master: ACP; fellow: Am. Coll. Preventive Medicine (Spl. Recognition award 1988); mem.: APHA, Soc. Tchrs. Preventive Medicine (Spl. Recognition award 1993), Soc. Gen. Internal Medicine (pres. 1978—79, Leadership award 1997), Inst. Medicine NAS, Phi Beta Kappa, Delta Omega. Home: Highfield House 1112 4000 N Charles St Baltimore MD 21218-1760 Office Phone: 410-614-4590. Business E-Mail: rlawrenc@jhsph.edu.

LAWRENCE, SALLY CLARK, retired academic administrator; b. San Francisco, Dec. 29, 1930; d. George Dickson and Martha Marie Alice (Smith) Clark; m. Henry Clay Judd Jr., July 1, 1950 (div. Dec. 1972); children: Rebecca, David, Nancy; m. John I. Lawrence, Aug. 12, 1976; stepchildren: Maia, Dylan. Grad., Castilleja Sch. Girls, 1948; attended, House in the Pines Jr. Coll., Norton, Mass., 1948—49, Stanford U., 1949—50. Docent Portland Art Mus., Portland, Oreg., 1958-68; gallery owner, dir. Sally Judd Gallery, Portland, Oreg., 1968-75; art ins. appraiser, cons. Portland, Oreg., 1975-81; from interim dir. Mus. Art Sch. to pres. Pacific NW Coll. Art, Portland, Oreg., 1981—2003, pres. emerita, 2003—. Bd. dirs. Contemporary Crafts Gallery, Portland, 1970—73, Art Coll. Exch., 1982—91, Portland Arts Alliance, Portland, Oreg., 1987—2003, Portland Inst. Contemporary Art, 2005—, sec., 2006. Fellow: Nat. Assn. Sch. Art and Design (life; bd. dirs. 1984—91, 1994—2002, pres. 1996—99); mem.: Assn. Ind. Coll. of Art and Design (pres. 1995—96, sec. 1996—2001), Oreg. Ind. Coll. Assn. (bd. dirs. 1981—2003, exec. com. 1989—94, pres. 1992—93, v.p. 2001—03), Pearl Arts Found. (chair bd. dirs. 2000—03). Personal E-mail: sallyl@carrollsweb.com.

LAWRENCE, SANFORD HULL, physician, immunochemist, author; b. Kokomo, Ind., July 10, 1919; s. Walter Scott and Florence Elizabeth (Hull) L. AB, Ind. U., 1941, MD, 1944. Fellow in biochemistry George Washington U., 1941; intern Rochester (N.Y.) Gen. Hosp., 1944-45; resident Halloran Hosp., Staten Island, NY, 1946-49; chief med. svce. Ft. Ord Regl. Hosp., 1945-46; dir. biochemistry rsch. lab. San Fernando (Calif.) VA Hosp.; asst. prof. UCLA, 1950—. Cons. internal medicine and cardiology U.S. Govt., Los Angeles County; lectr. Faculte de Medicine, Paris, various colls. Eng., France, Belgium, Sweden, USSR, India, Japan; chief med. svc. Ft. Ord Regional Hosp.; chmn. Titus, Inc., 1982—. Author: Zymogram in Clinical Medicine, 1965, Gyert, 2000, Whitley Heights, 2002; contbr. articles to sci. jours.; author: Threshold of Valhalla, Another Way to Fly, My Last Satyr, and other short stories; traveling editor: Relax Mag. Mem. Whitley Heights Civic Assn., 1952—; pres. Halloran Hosp. Employees Assn., 1947-48. Served to maj. U.S. Army, 1945-46. Recipient Rsch. award TB and Health Assn., 1955-58, Los Angeles County Heart Assn., 1957-59, Pres. award, Queen's Blue Book award, Am. Men of Sci. award; named one of 2000 Men of Achievement, Leaders of Am. Sci., Ky. Col., named Hon. Mayor of West Point, Ky. Mem. AAAS, AMA, N.Y. Acad. Scis., Am. Fedn. Clin. Research, Am. Assn. Clin. Investigation, Am. Assn. Clin. Pathology, Am. Assn. Clin. Chemistry, Los Angeles County Med. Assn. Republican. Methodist. Avocations: bridge, comml. pilot, piano, organist. Home: Whitley Heights 2014 Whitley Ave Los Angeles CA 90068-3235 also: 160 rue St Martin 75003 Paris France

LAWRENCE, VICTOR B., computer and systems engineer; b. Accra, Ghana, May 10, 1945; BSc, U. London, 1968, PhD, 1972. Tech. staff mem. through v.p. advanced comm. tech. Bell Labs., 1974—2005; Batchelor Chair prof. elec. engring., assoc. dean spl. progs. Stevens Inst. Tech., Hoboken, NJ, 2006. Bd. dir. mPhase Technologies Inc., 2006—; instr. Kumasi U. Sci. & Tech., Ghana; lectr. U. Pa., Rutgers U., Princeton U., U. Calif. Berkeley, US Indsl. Coll. Armed Forces; adv. to US Senate sub-committee on sci. & tech. & US Senator Bill Frist. Author: Introduction to Digital Filters, Tutorials on Modem Communications, Intelligent Broadband Multimedia Networks, Design & Engineering of Intelligent Communications Systems, The Art of Scientific Innovation; contbr. articles to profl. jours. Fellow IEEE (assoc. editor IEEE Comm. Mag. 1978-81, assoc. editor IEEE Transactions on Cirs. and Sys. 1981-83, tech. prog. chmn. first internat. workshop on VLSI in comm. 1981, gen. chmn. fourth internat. workshop on VLSI in comm. 1986, tech. prog. chmn. first internat. workshop on met. area networks 1986, chmn. tech. com. on signal processing and comm. electronics, mem. AdCom., Cirs. and Sys. Soc. 1986-89, mem. awards policy planning com. 1989-91, mem. bd. govs. Comm. Soc. 1990-92, vice-chmn. 1992-93, chmn. 1994—, Guillemin Cauer prize paper award 1981, Simon Ramo Medal 2007); Bell Labs. Fellow; mem. NAE. Office: Stevens Inst Tech Castle Point on Hudson Hoboken NJ 07030*

LAWRENCE, WALTER, JR., surgeon, educator; b. Chgo., May 31, 1925; s. Walter and Violette May (Matthews) L.; m. Susan Grayson Shryock, June 20, 1947; children: Walter Thomas, Elizabeth, William Amos, Edward Gene. Student, Dartmouth Coll., 1943-44; PhB, U. Chgo., 1944, SB, 1945, MD with honors, 1948. Diplomate Am. Bd. Surgery (examiner 1974-78, sr. mem. 1978—). Intern Johns Hopkins, 1948-49, asst. resident, 1949-51; fellow Meml. Sloan-Kettering Cancer Ctr., 1951-52, 54-56, rsch. fellow, 1956, asst. mem., asst. attending surgeon, 1957-60, assoc. mem., assoc. attending surgeon, 1960-66; practice medicine specializing in surgery NYC, 1956-66, Richmond, Va., 1966—. Instr. surgery Cornell U., 1957-58, asst. profl. clin. surgery, 1958-63, clin. assoc. prof., 1963-66; vis. investigator Queen Victoria Hosp., East Grinstead, Eng., 1964-65; prof. surgery Med. Coll. Va., Richmond, 1966-90, prof. emeritus, 1990--, chmn. divsn. surg. oncology, 1966-90, exec. vice chmn. dept. surgery, 1966-73, acting chmn., 1973-74, Am. Cancer Soc. prof. clin. oncology, 1972-77; dir. Massey Cancer Ctr., 1974-88, dir. emeritus, 1988—; chmn. surgery test com. Nat. Bd. Med. Examiners, 1973-77; med. dir.-at-large Va. divsn. Am. Cancer Soc., 1967—, med. v.p. Am. Cancer Soc., 1975-77, pres., 1977-79, nat. del., 1972-76, mem. nat. coun. for rsch. and clin. investigation, 1974-78, mem. profl. edn. com., 1982-96, bd. dir., 1985-98, vice chmn., chmn. M&S com., 1986-88, chmn. M&S exec. com., 1989-90, pres. elect, 1990-91, nat. pres., 1991-92, past office dir., 1993-99, hon. life mem., 1999—; bd. sci. counsellors Nat. Cancer Inst., 1978-82, chmn. surg. oncology rsch. devel. com.; mem. Nat. Cancer Adv. Bd., 1988-94; governing coun. Internat. Union Against Cancer, 1994-2002. Author: (with J.J. Terz) Cancer Management, 1977, (with J.J. Terz, J.P. Neifeld) Manual of Soft Tissue Surgery, 1983; mem. editl. bd. Va. Med., 1977-93, Jour. Surg. Oncology, 1978—, assoc. editor, 1991—, dep. editor, 005—; editl. bd. Jour. Cancer Edn., 1986; asst. editor Cancer, 1962-65, assoc. editor, 1991-2000, mem. editl. bd., 2000--; contbr. articles to med. jour. Served with USNR, 1942-46, with US Army, 1952-54. Recipient Cancer Rsch. award Alfred P. Sloan Found., 1964; J. Shelton Horsley award Am. Cancer Soc., 1973; Disting. Svc. award U. Chgo., 1976; Va. Commonwealth U. Univ. Award for Excellence, 1988, Disting. Faculty award Med. Coll. Va. Alumni Assn., 1988, Va. Cultural Laureate award, 1992, OBICI award, 1992, Dean's award for Disting. Svc., 1992; named to Humera Soc. (hon.), 1992, Beckstrand Cancer Found. Cancer Fighter of Yr., 1999, Presdl. medallion Va. Commonwealth U., 2000, Lifetime Sci. Achievement award Sci. Mus. Va., 2002; Disting. Svc. Award of Richmond Acad. Medicine, 2003. Fellow ACS (commn. on cancer 1973-85, chmn. 1979-81), NY Acad. Sci., Royal Soc. Medicine, Soc. Black Acad. Surgeons (hon.), So. Surg. Assn.; mem. AAAS, AMA, Am. Assn. Cancer Edn., Am. Assn. Cancer Rsch., Am. Gastroenterol. Assn. (coun. on cancer 1972-76), Am. Surg. Assn., Halsted Soc. (pres. 1975), James Ewing Soc., Soc. Head and Neck Surgeons, Am. Soc. Clin. Oncology, Am. Radium Soc. (exec. coun. 1985-87), Soc. Surgery Alimentary Tract (founder), Soc. Surg. Oncology (exec. com. 1976-77, v.p. 1977-78, pres. 1979-80, chmn. exec. coun. 1980-81, Heritage honoree 2002), Soc. Univ. Surgeons, Surg. Biol. Club III (founding mem.), Transplantation Soc., Collegium Internat. Chirurgiae Digestive, Southeastern Surg. Congress, Pan Am. Med. Assn., Sociètè Internationale de Chirurgie, Va. Surg. Soc. (v.p. 1973-74), Richmond Surg. Soc. (pres. 1986-87), Richmond Acad. Medicine (trustee 1986-87, 1st v.p. 1988, Disting. Svc. award 2003), So. Surg. Assn. (1st v.p. 1999-2000, hon. fellow, 2004), Argentine Surg. Assn. (hon.), Sigma Xi, Alpha Omega Alpha. Home: 6501 Three Chopt Rd Richmond VA 23226-3118 Office: Med Coll Va Hosps 1200 E Broad St PO Box 980011 Richmond VA 23298-0011 Business E-Mail: wlawrence@mcvh-vcu.edu.

LAWRENCE, WALTER THOMAS, plastic surgeon; b. Balt., Sept. 5, 1950; s. Walter Jr. and Susan (Shryock) L.; m. Marsha Blake, May 30, 1987. BS, Yale U., 1972; MPH, Harvard U., 1976; MD, U. Va., 1976. Diplomate Am. Bd. Surgery, Am. Bd. Plastic Surgery. Intern and resident in gen. surgery U. NC, Chapel Hill, 1976-78; resident gen. surgery Med. Coll. Va., Richmond, 1978-81; resident plastic surgery U. Chgo., 1981-83; expert NIH, Bethesda, Md., 1983-85; asst. prof. U. NC, Chapel Hill, 1985-92, assoc. prof., div. chmn., 1992-95; prof., divsn. chmn. U. Mass. Med. Ctr., 1995-99, U. Kans. Med. Ctr., Kansas City, 1999—. Treas. Plastic Surgery Rsch. Coun., 1991—94, Plastic Surgery Ednl. Found., 2005—06; mem. Residency Rev. Com. for Plastic Surgery, 2000—06; pres. Assn. Academic Chmn. in Plastic Surgery, 2006—07. Fellow ACS; mem. Am. Assn. Plastic Surgeons, Am. Soc. Plastic and Reconstructive Surgeons, Assn. Academic Chmn. Plastic Surgery, Plastic Surgery Rsch. Coun., Humera Soc., Womack Soc., Wound Healing Soc. Avocations: skiing, sailing, tennis. Office: U Kans Med Ctr Sutherland Inst/Pl Surgery 3901 Rainbow Blvd Kansas City KS 66160-0001 Office Phone: 913-588-2000. Business E-Mail: tlawrence@kumc.edu.

LAWRENCE, WENDY B., astronaut; b. Jacksonville, Fla., July 2, 1959; d. William P. Lawrence and Anne Haynes. BS in Ocean Engring., U.S. Naval Acad., 1981; MS in Ocean Engring., MIT and Woods Hole Oceanographic Institution, 1988. Naval aviator USN, 1982; with Helicopter Combat Support Squadron SIX (HC-6); officer in charge of detachment ALFA Helicopter Anti-Submarine Squadron Light THIRTY HSL-30; physics instr., novice women's crew coach U.S. Naval Acad., 1990-92; mission specialist, astronaut NASA, 1992—, flight software verifier Shuttle Avionics Integration Lab., astronaut office asst. tng. officer, ascent/entry flight engr., blue shift orbit pilot on STS-67, 1995, dir. ops. Gagarin Cosmonaut Tng. Ctr. Star City, Russia, with crew on STS-86 on space shuttle Atlantis, 1997, with crew on STS-91 on space shuttle Discovery, 1998, mission specialist 4 (MS-4) for STS-114 (Discovery) Return to Flight mission, 2005. Recipient Defense Superior Svc. medal, Defense Meritorious Svc. medal, NASA Space Flight medal, Navy Commendation medal, Navy Achievement medal, Capt. Winifred Collins award for inspirational leadership Nat. Navy League, 1986. Mem. Assn. Naval Aviation, Women Mil. Aviators, Naval Helicopter Assn., Phi Kappa Phi. Avocations: running, rowing, triathlons. Office: NASA Lyndon B Johnson Space Ctr Houston TX 77058

LAWRENCE, WILLIAM, JR., retired elementary school educator; b. LA, Mar. 2, 1930; s. Willie and Nellie (January) L.; m. Elizabeth Johnson, Jan. 13, 1951; children: William III, Timothy Dwight, Walter Fitzgerald, Dane Timothy, Christy Anne Lawrence. BA in Psychology, Columbia Coll., Mo., 1981; LLB, LaSalle U., 1982; MA in Edn., Claremont Coll., 1992. Enlisted US Army, 1947, advanced through grades to capt., 1957, commd. sgt. maj., 1965, served Vietnam, 1965-70, with Berlin Brigade Berlin, 1973-76; instr. US Mil. Acad., West Point, NY, 1970-73; dep. sheriff LA, 1958-65; probation officer San Berdnardino County, Calif., 1985-89; own recognizance investigator LA County, 1989; tchr. Pomona Unified Sch. Dist., Pomona, Calif., 1989—2005, ret., 2004. Sch. site technician, 1996. Ret. US Army, 1982. Decorated U.S. Army D.S.C. for Extraordinary Heroism in Combat, 2 Silver Stars, Purple Hearts (7). Mem. Legion of Valor (nat. bd. dirs., comdr. Calif. chpt.), 555th Parachute Bn. (past pres.). Democrat. Roman Catholic. Avocations: photography, free fall parachuting, writing memoir. Home: PO Box 294 Bloomington CA 92316-0294

LAWRENCE, WILLIAM CLARENCE, lawyer, mediator; b. Tuskegee, Ala., Dec. 15, 1945; s. James Clarence and Nellie Mae James Lawrence; m. Audrey Rochelle Diggs Rackley, Dec. 30, 1973 (div. Sept. 1979); 1 child, Kimberly Ann; m. Grace Louise McDonald, June 23, 1984; children: Antoinette, Robert David. BS in Polit. Sci., Tuskegee U., 1968; M in Pub. Adminstrn., St. Mary's U., 1976; JD, Ind. U., 1979; M in Mgmt., U. Dallas, 1993. Tax atty. audit divsn. U.S. Treasury Dept., Indpls., 1979-80; commodities mgr. Cummins Engine Co., Columbus, Ind., 1980-82; staff mgr. GTE Network Svcs. Planning, Stamford, Conn., 1982-86; product mgr.-consumer GTE Product Mgmt., Irving, Tex., 1986-89, group product mgr.-wireless, 1989-92, group product mgr.-devel., 1992-96; group mktg. mgr.-systems GTE Bus. Sales Ops., Irving, 1996-99; pres., CEO Dakiman Co., Highland Village, Tex., 1999—. Chmn., bd. dirs. GTE Hdqrs. PAC, Irving, 1995-98. Pres., bd. dirs. Boston Home Childrens Found., Dallas, 1988-93; commr. Planning and Zoning Commn., Highland Village, 1996-99; chmn. Irving Sch. Dist. Improvement Com., 1998—; mem. Tex. State Textbook Rev. Adv. Panel, 2000; city coun. and mayor pro tem Highland Village, 1999-2000; mayor City of Highland Village, 2000-06; rep. candidate Tex. Ho. Reps., 2006. Col. USAF Res., 1976-2001. Mem. ABA (assoc., alternate disputes resolution sect.), New Product Devel. Assn., Project Mgmt. Inst., Tex. St. Bd. Prfl. Engrg., 2002-05, Nat. Council Examiners for Engrg. Surveying, 2002-05, Alpha Phi Alpha, Phi Alpha Delta. Republican. Baptist. Avocations: golf, racquetball, volleyball. Home: 2800 Woodlake Ct Highland Village TX 75077-6496

LAWRENCE-WATER, BETTE ANN, community health leader; m. George Water, Sept. 9, 1999; 1 child, Kimberly Gailes. MS in Managerial Leadership, Nat. Louis U., Wheaton, Ill., 2001. Account exec. CSX Intermodal, Oakbrook, Ill., 1991—98; v.p. Exec. Preference Limousines, Inc., Naperville, Ill., 1999—; dir. initiatives Healthy DuPage, Carol Stream, Ill., 2000—04; exec. dir. The CareLink Found., West Chicago, Ill., 2005—06; program mgr. cmty. health svcs. DuPage County Health Dept., Wheaton, Ill., 2007—. Vice chair DEECA bd. LWV of Naperville, 1999—2001; instr. Coll. DuPage, Glen Ellyn, Ill., 2001—06, steering com. Acad. for Nonprofit Excellence, 2003—06; vice chair Lupus Found. Am. - Ill. Chpt., Chgo., 2005—06; adj. faculty, lectr. Benedictine U., Lisle, Ill., 2006. Local arrangements chair LWV of the US, Washington, 1982—84; diversity taskforce Am. Heart Assn., Chgo., 2005—06; health initiatives taskforce Am. Cancer Soc. - DuPage Region, Oakbrook Terrace, Ill. Recipient Regional Dirs. award, CSX Intermodal, 1992, Sistas - Leadership Excellence award, WJLB/WMXD Radio, Detroit, 1997, RampArts award, Naperville City Coun., 2004, Heart Health Hero award, Am. Heart Assn., 2006. Mem.: AAUW, African Am. Leadership Roundtable. Avocations: writing, painting. Office: DuPage County Health Department 111 North County Farm Rd Wheaton IL 60187 Home Phone: 630-718-1990; Office Phone: 630-682-7979 7095. Personal E-mail: blawrencewater@email.com.

LAWS, EDWARD RAYMOND, JR., neurological surgery educator; b. NYC, Apr. 29, 1938; s. Edward Raymond and Jessie (Mancini) L.; m. Margaret Patricia Anderson, Sept. 15, 1962; children: Elizabeth, Margaret, Victoria, Eleanor. AB, Princeton U., 1959; MD, Johns Hopkins U., 1963. Diplomate Am. Bd. Neurol. Surgery (bd. dirs. 1989—). Intern Johns Hopkins, Balt., 1963-64, residency, 1966-71, asst. prof. neurosurgery, 1971-72; prof. neurosurgery Mayo Clinic, Rochester, Minn., 1972-87, George Washington U., Washington, 1987-92; prof. neurosurgery & prof. medicine U. Va., Charlottesville, 1992—. Pres. Congress Neurol. Surgeons, 1984-85. Author: Pituitary Adenomas, 1976, Orbital Tumors, 1988, Glioma, 1992; editor: Neurosurgery, 1987-92; contbr. over 250 papers to profl. jours. Bd. dirs. Nat. Found., Balt., 1968-72, Nat. Found. for Brain Rsch., Washington, 1988—. NIH grantee. Mem. Am. Acad. Neurol. Surgery, Am. Assn. Neurol. Surgeons (former pres., bd. dirs. 1988—), Am. Coll. Surgeons (past pres.), Congress Neurological Surgeons (former pres.), Inst. Medicine, Soc. Neurol. Surgeons, So. Neurosurg. Soc., Internat. Soc. Pituitary Surgeons, World Fedn. Neurol. Socs. (former pres.), Sigma Xi, Alpha Omega Alpha. Roman Catholic. Home: 555 Rodes Dr

Charlottesville VA 22903-9244 Office: U Va Health Scis Ctr Dept Neurosurgery PO Box 800212 Charlottesville VA 22908 Office Phone: 434-924-2650, 434-982-3752. Office Fax: 434-924-5894. E-mail: elg@virginia.edu.

LAWS, KENNETH L., physics professor; b. Pasadena, Calif., May 30, 1935; s. Allen L. and Florence (Windsor) L.; m. Priscilla Watson, June 3, 1965; children: Kevin Allen, Virginia. BS, Calif. Inst. Tech., 1956; MS, U. Pa., 1959; PhD, Bryn Mawr Coll., 1962. Instr. physics Hobart and William Smith Colls., Geneva, NY, 1958-59; from asst. prof. to prof. physics Dickinson Coll., Carlisle, Pa., 1962-2000, assoc. dean, dir. summer sch., 1971-77, prof. emeritus, 2000—; adminstrv. dir. summer ballet program Ctrl. Pa. Youth Ballet, Carlisle, 1977-87, pres. bd. dirs., 1988-93. Guest faculty Scientific Aspect of the Art of Dance, U. Washington Med. Sch. and Dance Dept., 1982; bd. reviewers Dance: Current Selected Research, 1985—. Author: The Physics of Dance, 1984; (with Cynthia Harvey) Physics, Dance and the Pas de Deux, 1994, Physics and the Art of Dance, 2002; contbr. articles on dance, physics to profl. jours. Office: Dickinson Coll Dept Physics Carlisle PA 17013 Business E-Mail: laws@dickinson.edu.

LAWS, MAURICE WESLEY, set decorator, museum exhibit designer; b. Ferndale, Mich., Sept. 27, 1925; s. George Winslow Laws and Marion Jane Greenleaf; m. Betty Elaine Stein, June 1955 (div. Sept. 1957). Attended, N.Y. Sch. Interior Design, 1948—50. Set decorator CBS TV, NYC, 1950—88. Designer mus. exhibits Edward Dean Mus. Decorative Arts, Cherry Valley, Calif., 1995—. Set decorator: (films) A View from the Bridge, 1962. Chmn.svc. coun. Palm Springs Art Mus., 2006; mem. Palm Springs Desert Mus. Svc. Coun., Calif., 1990—; bd. mem. Friends of Edward Dean Mus., 1996—, Cabots Mus. Commn., Desert Hot Springs, 1998—2001; pres. Cabots Mus. Found., Desert Hot Springs, 2001—05. SM2/C USN, 1943—46. Nominee Emmy award six times, Acad. TV Arts & Sci.; recipient 4 Emmy awards. Mem.: Friends Edward Dean Mus. (treas. 2006), Internat. Wedgwood Soc., Wedgwood Soc. So. Calif. Achievements include member of CBS team covering first moon landing of Apollo XI (TV Acad. nomination). Avocations: travel, archaeology. Home: 12075 Highland Ave Desert Hot Springs CA 92240

LAWSON, A. PETER, lawyer; AB, Dartmouth Coll., 1968; JD, Columbia U., 1971. Bar: NY 1971, Ill. 1979. Assoc. Sullivan & Cromwell, 1971-78; sr. counsel Baxter Internat., 1978-79; assoc. gen. attorney Motorola Inc., 1980—84, v.p., gen. attorney, 1985—87, corp. v.p., asst. gen. counsel, 1987—94, sr. v.p., asst. gen. counsel, 1994—96, sr. v.p., sec., gen. counsel, 1996-98, exec. v.p., gen. counsel, sec., 1998—. Mem.: Am. Soc. Corporate Sec., North Shore Gen. Counsel Assn., CLO Roundtable, American Corporate Counsel Assoc., ABA, Association of Gen. Counsel. Office: Motorola Inc 1303 E Algonquin Rd Schaumburg IL 60196-1079 Office Phone: 602-732-3188.*

LAWSON, BARBARA SLADE, elementary school educator, artist; b. Kobe, Japan, Dec. 16, 1930; arrived in US, 1940; d. Ewell William and Michaela Carpenter Slade; m. Alvin H. Lawson, Jan. 31, 1953; children: Lawrence(dec.), Leslie, Leigh(dec.), Katherine(dec.). BA, San Francisco State Coll., 1952. Tchr. Calif. Pub. Elem. Sch. Dist., 1953, Hayward Pub. Elem. Sch. Dist., Calif., 1954, So. San Francisco Sch. Dist., 1956, Los Lamites Sch. Dist., Calif., 1957—58, Los Altos Sch. Dist., 1960—61, Cypress Sch. Dist., 1964—86. Mem.: Watercolor West (sec. bd. dirs. 1998—2004), San Diego Watercolor Soc., Eastern Wash. Watercolor Soc., Northwestern Watercolor Soc., Pa. Watercolor Soc. Democrat. Avocation: swimming. Home: 5861 Huntley Ave Garden Grove CA 92845-2041 Office: Showcase Gallery 3851 South Bear St Ste B15 Santa Ana CA 92707 Office Phone: 714-540-6430.

LAWSON, CAROLE JEAN, religious educator, author, poet; b. San Antonio, June 18, 1944; d. Albert Joseph and Pearl Nettie (Garner) Fuller; m. James Ray Lawson, Sept. 7, 1962; children: Regina Anne (Lawson) Kacho, Clinton Ray. Founder Love Makes the World Go Around in Peace, Ft. Worth, 1988—; founder, dir. Healing Thru Love Seminars, Ft. Worth, 1988—; founder Sunshine 'n Rainbows Stress Overcomers, Ft. Worth, 1985-87; founder, head Omni-Vision Pub. and Prodns., Ft. Worth, 1990—93, 2002—. Life mgmt. cons., 2003—. Pub. editor Omni Vision newsletter, 1985-93, 2002-; author: To God Be the Glory, poetry collection, 1988-90, My Rocky Mountain High, 1989, The Reflection of God's Smile, 1991. Sec. Lightly Speaking Forum, Ft. Worth, 1987—89; supporter publicity Campaign for the Earth, 1990—91; mem. North Greenbriar Neighborhood Revitalizing Bd., 2004—; founder Omni Vision Ministries, 1993—99, 2002—; dir. Chapel of Light Conf. Ctr., Lake Whitney, 2001—02; founder Universal World Investments, Chi Energy Wholeness Ctr., Lake Whitney, Tex., 2001—02, life mgmt. cons., 2003; Chi technician Fort Worth, 2005. Named Honorary Mayan Centurian. Mem. Internat. Platform Assn. Home and Office: 1112 Edney St Fort Worth TX 76115-4317 Home Phone: 817-924-2920; Office Phone: 817-924-2920. Personal E-mail: enchantedlanes@yahoo.com. E-mail: omni_vision@peoplepc.com. *With the energy shifting at excelerated speed to usher in the new, we must also excelerate our consciousness into the reality of our oneness with God and all creation. We must not live in the past, nor in future daydreams. We must live in the present moment...The Now! If you don't want a part in the play...don't become part of the production! Just watch the performance. If it doesn't serve you don't get involved in it...create your chosen reality with inward harmony and peace. Unconditional love is a must. God is Love!.*

LAWSON, CAROLINA DONADIO, language educator, translator; b. Naples, Italy, Mar. 11, 1920; arrived in U.S., 1947; d. Joseph and Concetta (Bartolomeo) Donadio; m. Allan Leroy Lawson, Sept. 15, 1945; 1 child, John. Laurea in European langs., lit., instns., We. Group Instituto Universitario Orientale, Naples, 1946; PhD in French and Italian, Tulane U., 1971. Lectr. overseas divsn. U. Md., Leghorn, Italy, 1952; tchr. Warren Easton H.S., New Orleans, 1958—61; tchg. asst. Newcomb Coll. Tulane U., New Orleans, 1961—64; instr. Tex. Christian U., Ft. Worth, 1964—65; lectr. Downtown Ctr. U.Chgo., 1967—73; lectr. U. Akron, Ohio, 1975—76; pvt. practice lectr., translator, ind. scholar, freelance writer Moncks Corner, SC, 1985—. Vis. prof. Kent (Ohio) State U., 1977-84; mem., lectr. S.C. Humanities Coun., 1989-93. Author: (textbook) Nuove Letture di Cultura Italiana, 1975; fgn. lang. editl. reviewer Ency. Brit. Chgo., 1971; rev. editor: Italian Culture, 1981-84; contbr. many articles and revs. in lit. criticism, art history, textbooks of fables, fairy tales and biographies to profiles of famous Italians. Recipient cert. of proficiency in Japanese lang. and culture Tokyo Coll., 1958. Mem. MLA, Am. Assn. Tchrs. of Italian, Am. Assn. Italian Studies, Am. Assn. Tchrs. of French, Nat. Italian-Am. Found. Republican. Roman Catholic. Avocations: classical music, painting, sports, travel.

LAWSON, DONNA YVETTE, special education educator; b. Bklyn., Mar. 2, 1960; d. Richard James and Dorothy Lawson; children: Dionna Y. Shinn, Brionna A. Edmundson. BA, Pace U., NYC, 1983; MA, Norfolk State U., Va., 2001. Postgrad. lic., cert. adminstr. supervision k-12, emotional disturbance K-12, specific learning disabilities K-12. Dir. instr. Va. Sch., Hampton, dir. student life, spl. edn. prin., IEP coord.; spl. edn. tchr. Hampton City Schs. Dir. Advanced Devel. Learning Ctr., Hampton, Both Worlds Inc., Hampton; treas. Soleria Christian Resource Ctr., 2004. Advocate Va. Sch., Hampton. Mem.: CEC, Assn. Christian Schs. Avocation: reading. Home: 101 Montrose dr Hampton VA 23666

LAWSON, EDWARD EARLE, neonatal/perinatal nurse practitioner; b. Winston-Salem, NC, Aug. 6, 1946; s. Robert Barrett and Elsie Chatterton (Earle) L.; m. Rebecca Newhall Fitts, June 21, 1969; children: Katherine Tabor, Robert Barrett II. BA magna cum laude, Harvard U., 1968; MD, Northwestern U., 1972. Diplomate Am. Bd. Pediat. and Neonatal/Perinatal Medicine. Intern then resident pediat. Children's Hosp., Boston, 1972-75, fellow neonatology, 1975-78; from asst. prof. pediat. to prof. pediat. U. N.C., Chapel Hill, 1978-99, chief divsn. neonatal medicine, 1987-95, interim chmn. dept. pediat., 1993-95; vice chmn., dept. pediat., 1995-99; prof. pediat., vice chair dept. pediat. Johns Hopkins U., Balt., 1999—; chief divsn. neonatology, dept. pediat. Johns Hopkins U. Hosp., Balt., 1999—. Editor-in-chief Jour. Perinatology, 2001—; assoc. editor Jour. of Pediat., 1985-95; contbr. numerous articles to profl. jours. Recipient Sidney Farber Meml. Rsch. award United Cerbral Palsy, 1982, Rsch. Career Devel. award NIH, 1982-87; E.L. Trudeau fellow, 1978-81, Alexander Von Humboldt fellow, 1985-86; NIH grantee, 1979—. Fellow Am. Acad. Pediat.; mem. Am. Lung Assn. (sci. adv. com. 1989-91), Am. Thoracic Soc. (bd. dirs. 1988-90), Am. Pediat. Soc., Perinatal Rsch. Soc. Achievements include research on developmental aspects of respiratory control, particularly physiology and neurobiology. Office: Johns Hopkins Hosp Dept Pediatrics 600 N Wolfe St NH2-133 Baltimore MD 21287-0001 Office Phone: 410-955-5259. Business E-Mail: elawson@jhmi.edu.

LAWSON, EVE KENNEDY, dancer; b. Washington, Mar. 28, 1964; d. John and Elizabeth Lawson. Student, Sch. Am. Ballet, NYC, 1972-83. Prin. dancer State Ballet Mo., Kansas City, 1983-87; dancer Miami City Ballet, Miami Beach, Fla., 1988-94, coord. edn., 1993-94, ballet mistress, 1994—. Created prin. roles in ballet Voyager (Bolender), 1984, Miniatures (Gamonet), 1990, Tango Tonto (Gamonet), 1991. Office: Miami City Ballet 2200 Liberty Ave Miami Beach FL 33139-1641

LAWSON, FRED RAULSTON, banker; b. Sevierville, Tenn., Mar. 26, 1936; s. Arville Raulston and Ila Mary (Lowe) L.; m. Sharon Sheets, Jan. 1, 1982; children: Terry Lawson Akins, Laura Lawson Rathbone, Kristi Watson Newvine. Student, U. Tenn., 1953—59, La. State U. Sch. Banking of South, 1965—68, Harvard Inst. Fin. Mgmt., 1968; D (hon.), Maryville Coll. From br. mgr. to exec. v.p. Blount Nat. Bank, Maryville, Tenn., 1958-68, pres., 1968-86, also bd. dirs.; pres. Tenn. Nat. Bancshares, Inc., Maryville, 1971-86, Bank of East Tenn., Knoxville, 1986-92; pres., CEO BankFirst, Knoxville, 1993-2001; commr. dept. fin. instns. State of Tenn., 2001—03; chmn. BankEast, 2004—. Mem. Covenant Health Fin./Investment Com., 2000-2001, also bd. dirs. Mem. Blount County Indsl. Devel. bd., 1969—; chancellors assoc. U. Tenn., Knoxville, 1971-78; trustee Carson-Newman Coll., Jefferson City, 1984-94, Harrison-Chilhowee Bapt. Acad., Seymour, Tenn., 1972-85, Pellissippi State Found., 1989-96; adv. bd. U. Tenn. Med. Rsch. Ctr. and Hosp.; bd. regents Mid-South Sch. banking, Memphis, 1982-90; bd. dirs. Thompson Cancer Survival Ctr., Knoxville, 1987-2000, The Downtown Orgn., Tenn. Resource Valley, East Tenn. Hist. Soc., Maryville Coll., 1995-07; bd. dirs., exec. com. BancInsure, 1991-01. Recipient Tenn. Indsl. Devel. Vol. award, 1977. Mem. Assn. Bank Holding Cos. (bd. dirs. 1978-82), Tenn. Bankers Assn. (chmn. state legis. com. 1980, banking practice com. 1983, bd. dirs. 1990—, pres. 1994-95). Republican. Baptist. Home: 2101 Cochran Rd Maryville TN 37803 Office: Bank East PO Box 24 607 Market St Knoxville TN 37901 Office Phone: 865-540-5830.

LAWSON, H(ERBERT) BLAINE, JR., mathematician, educator; b. Norristown, Pa., Jan. 4, 1942; s. Herbert Blaine and Mary Louise (Corson) L.; m. Carolyn Elaine Pieroni, June 6, 1964 (div. Sept. 1977); children: Christina Corson, Heather Brooke. AB, ScB in Applied Mat. and Russian Lit., Brown U., 1964; MS in Math., Stanford U., 1966, PhD in Math., 1968. Lectr. math. U. Calif., Berkeley, 1968-70, assoc. prof., 1971-74, prof., 1974-80, asst. dean, 1975-77; Disting. prof., chmn. SUNY, Stony Brook, 1978—. Vis. asst. prof. IMPA, Rio de Janeiro, 1970-71; vis. prof. Inst. des Hautes Etudes Scientifiques, Bures-sur-Yvette, France, 1977-78, Ecole Poly., Palaiseau, France, 1983-84; bd. dirs. U.S.-Brazilian Math. Exch., Stony Brook and Rio de Janeiro; trustee Math. Scis. Rsch. Inst., Berkeley; chmn. Nat. Com. Math. NAS, Washington, 1989-91; mem. Inst. Advanced Study, Princeton U., 1973-74; lectr. in minimal submanifolds, 1971. Author: The Theory of Gauge Fields in 4 Dimensions, 1985, Spin Geometry, 1989; editor Jour. Differential Geometry, Topology, The Princeton Mat. Series; contbr. articles to profl. jours. Sloan Found. fellow, 1971, Guggenheim Found. fellow, 1983, Japan Soc. Promotion Sci. fellow, 1985. Mem. Nat. Acad. of Sci., Am. Math. Soc. (coun. 1988-91, v.p. 1997-2000,, editor jour., Steele prize 1975), Brazilian Acad. of Scis. Achievements include construction of minimal surfaces in the 3-dimensional sphere, construction of foliations on higher dimensional spheres; characterization of boundaries of analytic varieties; co-creation of Calibrated Geometries; basic results on manifolds of non-positive curvature, on spaces of positive scalar curvature, on stability of Yang-Mills fields, on relations between algebraic cycles and topology, and on structure of Chow Varieties. Home: 29 North Rd Stony Brook NY 11790-1009 Business E-Mail: blaine@math.sunysb.edu.

LAWSON, JACK WAYNE, lawyer; b. Decatur, Ind., Sept. 23, 1935; s. Alva W. and Florence C. (Smitley) L.; m. Sarah J. Hibbard, Dec. 28, 1961; children: Mark, Jeff. BA in Polit. Sci., Valparaiso U., 1958, JD, 1961. Bar: Ind. 1961, U.S. Dist. Ct. (no. and so. dists.) Ind. 1991, U.S. Ct. Appeals (7th cir.) 1991, U.S. Supreme Ct. 1970. Ptnr. Beckman, Lawson LLP, Ft. Wayne, Ind., 1961-84, sr. ptnr., 1984—. Seminar presenter and writer Ind. CLE Forum, Indpls., 1970—, Nat. Health Lawyers Assn., Washington, 1986. Editor-in-chief Indiana Real Estate Transactions; contbr. articles to profl. jours. Mem. Ft. Wayne C. of C., 1975—; small claims ct. judge, Allen County, Ind., 1963-67. Recipient Sagamore Wabash award, Gov. State of Ind., 2001. Mem. Am. Coll. Real Estate Lawyers. Republican. Lutheran. Avocations: sailing, teaching religious seminars, antique consulting. Office: Beckman Lawson LLP 800 Standard Federal Plaza PO Box 800 Fort Wayne IN 46801-0800 Office Phone: 260-422-0800. Business E-Mail: jwl@beckmanlawson.com.

LAWSON, JANE ELIZABETH, retired bank executive; b. Cornwall, Ont., Can. d. Leonard J. and Margaret Lawson. BA, U. N.B., Can., LLB, 1971. With law dept. Royal Bank Can., Montreal, Que., 1974-78, sr. counsel, 1978-84, v.p., corp. sec., 1988-92, sr. v.p., sec., 1992—, ret., 2005—. Mem.: Am. Soc. Corp. Secs., Inst. Corp. Dirs., Inst. Chartered Secs. and Adminstrs., N.B. Bar Assn., Can. Bar Assn., Royal Can. Yacht Club, Mt. Royal Tennis Club. Office: Royal Bank Plz PO Box 1 Toronto ON Canada M5J 2J5

LAWSON, JENNIFER, broadcast executive; b. Birmingham, Ala., June 8, 1946; d. Willie DeLeon and Velma Theresa (Foster) L.; m. Elbert Sampson, June 1, 1979 (div. Sept. 1980); m. Anthony Gittens, May 29, 1982; children: Kai, Zachary. Student, Tuskegee U., 1963—65; MFA, Columbia U., 1974; LHD (hon.), Teikyo Post U., Hartford, Conn., 1991. Assoc. producer William Greaves Prodns., NYC, 1974-75; asst. prof. film studies Bklyn. Coll., 1975-77; exec. dir. The Film Fund, NYC, 1977-80; TV coord. Program Fund Corp. for Pub. Broadcasting, Washington, 1980-83, assoc. dir. TV Program Fund, 1983-89, dir. TV Program Fund, 1989; exec. v.p. programming PBS, Alexandria, Va., 1989-95; broadcast cons. Md. Pub. TV, 1995—98, exec. cons., 1996—, exec. prodr. Africa, 1998-2001; pres. Magic Box Mediaworks, 1996—; gen. mgr. WHUT-TV32, 2004—; exec. prodr. Security v. Liberty, 2007. V.p. Internat. Pub. TV, Washington, 1984-88; panelist Fulbright Fellowships, Washington, 1988-90. Author, illustrator: Children of Africa, 1970; illustrator: Our Folktales, 1968, African Folktales: A Calabash of Wisdom, 1973. Coord. Nat. Coun. Negro Women, Washington, 1969. Avocations: painting, reading. Office: 1838 Ontario Pl NW Washington DC 20009-2109 Office Phone: 202-806-3010. Business E-Mail: j_lawson@howard.edu.

LAWSON, JOHN JOSEPH, vocational educator, consultant; s. William and Jean Lawson. AAS, Ferris State U., 1976, BE, 1981. Registered social worker Mich., 1990; cert. architectural design Lawrence Inst. Tech., 1974, vocational drafting instr. 1981. Draftsman Penn-Dixie Steel Corp., Grand Rapids, Mich., 1976—78; property mgr. Altman/Allstate Mgmt., Mich., 1979—80; owner Lawson Mgmt. & Constrn., 1980—; life skills instr. Ackco Svcs., Mich., 1985—88; supervising shop foreman Meml. Ctr. Work Reconditioning Svcs., Owosso, Mich., 1988—89; instr. Baker Coll., Owosso, 1989—97; constrn. instr. United Auto Workers, Flint, Mich., 1997—98; drafting tchr. Linden HS, Mich., 2001—; CAD drafting instr. So. Lakes Career Ctr., Flint, 2002—. Cons. Rehab. Svcs., Owosso, 1989—. Mem.: Linden Edn. Assn., Mich. Edn. Assn. Avocation: golf.

LAWSON, JOHN QUINN, architect; b. Tucumcari, N.Mex., Apr. 11, 1940; s. Tom L. and Mable Marie (Hagglund) L.; m. Elizabeth Jo Waddel, June 4, 1961 (div. 1980); children: Bevan Eugene, Cary Augusta; m. Lorna Miriam Katz, Feb. 20, 1981. BA, Rice U., 1961, BSArch, 1962; MFA in Architecture, Princeton U., 1964. Registered architect, Pa., N.J., N.Y. Staff architect Doxiadis Assocs., Phila., 1961, Collins, Uhl, Hoisington, Princeton, NJ, 1963, Frank Schlesinger, Doylestown, Pa., 1964, Kneedler Mirick & Zantzinger, Phila., 1964, Mitchell/Giurgola Architects, Phila., 1965-71, assoc., 1972-73, ptnr., 1974-85, John Lawson Architects, Phila., 1986—. Mem. adj. faculty Grad. Sch. Fine Arts U. Pa., 1972-87, Sch. Arch. Phila. U., 2004-; chmn. archtl. adv. bd. Spring Garden Coll., Phila., 1986-92. Prin. works include United Way hdqrs. bldg., Phila., 1971, Lang Music Bldg. Swarthmore (Pa.) Coll., 1973, Ind. Nat. Hist. Park maintenance bldg., Phila., 1981, Columbia Ave. Sta. improvements, Phila., 1983, all recipients Pa. Soc. Architects awards, Benjamin Franklin Bridge Lighting Competition, Phila., 1986 (1st runner-up), Diamond Park Competition, Phila., 1987 (winner with Chuck Fahlen), Evancich residence, Phila., 1990 (1st prize Best Residential Renovation), Ctr. Animal Health and Productivity, Sch. Vet. Medicine, U. Pa., 1990, Surg. Edn. Ctr., Hosp. Univ. Pa., 1996, Comparative Orthop. Rsch. Lab., Sch. Vet. Medicine, U. Pa., 1998, The Vistas at Lake Worth Apts., Ft. Worth, 1998, Coll. Hall Interior Renovations South Central Ground Floor, East Wing, U. Pa., 1999-00, Smart Classroom, Delaware Valley Coll., Doylestown, Pa., 2001, Surgery Theatre Rm., Hosp. U. Pa., 2003, Kahn Residence, Hillsdale, NY, 2004, Arden Theatre Artists House, Phila., 2005, Langer/Jaffe Renovations, Phila., 2006, Winston Lofts Renovations, Phila., 2007, Bridge Addition and Interior Renovations, Gladwyne, Pa., 2007. V.p. Logan Sq. Neighborhood Assn., Phila., 1971-72; mem. Cmty.y Leadership Seminar Alumni, Phila., 1982-85; cons. Friends of Starr Garden, Inc., Phila., 1989; vol. exec., Internat. Exec. Svc. Corps, Cairo, 1998. Lowell M. Palmer fellow Princeton U., 1964, NEA Mid-Career fellow Am. Acad. in Rome, 1980. Fellow AIA (mem. architecture for edn. com. 1976-85, chmn. urban design com. Phila. chpt. 1986-98, Fellows steering com. Phila chpt. 1988—); mem. Pa. Soc. Architects, Soc. Hill Civic Assn., City Pks. Assn. (bd. dirs. 1988-2002), Awbury Arboretum Assn. (bd. dirs. 1989-99), Soc. Hill Towers (coun. 1994-2002). Democrat. Office: John Lawson Architects 812 Chestnut St Apt 2 Philadelphia PA 19107-5115 Office Phone: 215-351-0560. Business E-Mail: jlawson@johnlawsonarchitects.com.

LAWSON, JONATHAN NEVIN, academic administrator, educator; b. Latrobe, Pa., Mar. 27, 1941; s. Lawrence Winters and Mary Eleanor (Rhea) L.; m. Leigh Farley (div.); children: Paul, Joshua, Jacob; m. Pamela (Cross)L. AA, York Coll., Penn., 1962; BFA, Tex. Christian U., Tex., 1964, MA, 1966, PhD, 1970. Dir. composition U. Minn., St. Cloud, Minn., 1971—77, assoc. dean, 1977-81; asst. vice chancellor Minn. State U. Sys., St. Paul, 1980-81; dean liberal arts U. Minn., Winona, Minn., 1981-84; dean arts and sci. U. Hartford, West Hartford, Conn., 1984-86, sr. v.p., dean of faculty, 1986-95; v.p. acad. affairs Idaho State U., Pocatello, 1995—2005, prof. higher edn., 2005—, chair ednl. leadership and tech., 2007—. Mem. S.E. Idaho Works Bd., 2000—05. Author: Robert Bloomfield, 1980; editor: Collected Works: Robert Bloomfield, 1971; contbr. articles and papers to scholarly pub.; assoc. editor Rhetoric Soc. Quar., St. Cloud,Minn., 1974-79. Mem. regional adv. bd. Greater Hartford C.C., 1992-94; trustee Hartford Coll. for Women, 1992-94; mem. acad. affairs com. Idaho Bd. Edn., 1995-2005; bd. dir. Bannock County Devel. Corp., 1998—, sec., treas., 2001—; bd. govs. The Rennaisance Group, 2003-05. Mem. Am. Coun. Edn., Coun. Fellows Alumni, Coun. Liberal Learning, Assn. Gen. and Liberal Studies, Assn. Am. Colls., N.E. Assn. Schs. and Colls. (chmn. commn. on instns. higher edn. 1992-95), Asian Studies Consortium (chmn. bd. 1991-94), Pocatello C. of C. (bd. dirs., v.p.), Lambda Iota Tau (hon.), Alpha Chi (hon.). Episcopalian. Avocations: fishing, camping, writing, walking. Home: 1401 Juniper Hill Rd Pocatello ID 83204-4921 Office: Idaho State U PO Box 8063 Pocatello ID 83209-0001 Office Phone: 208-282-1036. Business E-Mail: lawsjona@isu.edu.

LAWSON, KELLI, communications executive; b. 1967; m. Keith Lawson; 2 children. B in Econ., Howard U., 1989. Brand mgr. Procter & Gamble; v.p., publisher, BET Books Black Entertainment TV, 1998, exec. v.p., Corp. Mktg., 1999—; owner 9 Maternity, Rockland, Md. Named one of 40 Executives Under 40, Multichannel News, 2006. Mem.: Women in Cable & Telecom. (Betsy Magness fellow 1999—2000), Nat. Black MBA Assn., Nat. Assn. Minorities in Cable, Jr. League of Wash., Delta Sigma Theta. Office: BET Holdings 1200 W Pl NE Washington DC 20018

LAWSON, NIGELLA, cookbook writer, celebrity chef; b. London, Eng., Jan. 6, 1960; d. Nigel Lawson; m. John Diamond, 1992 (dec. 2001); children: Cosima, Bruno; m. Charles Saatchi, Sept. 3, 2003. Student, Oxford Univ. Dep. literary editor Sunday Times; book reviewer, columnist The Spectator, London; food columnist Vogue; columnist, Dining In/Dining Out sect. NY Times, 2002—, syndicated columnist, At My Table, 2002—. Freelance writer The Guardian, Daily Telegraph, Times Mag. (UK), Gourmet, Bon Appetit. Author: (cookbooks) How to be a Domestic Goddess, 2001 (British Book award, Cookery Book of Yr., Guild of Food Writers, 2001, shortlisted for Lifestyle Book of Yr., WH Smith Book award, 2001), Nigella Bites: From Family Meals to Elegant Dinners, 2002 (Lifestyle Book of Yr., WH Smith Book award, 2002), How to Eat: The Pleasures and Principles of Good Food, 2002, Forever Summer, 2003, Feast: Food to Celebrate Life, 2004; host (TV series) Nigella Bites, 2000, 2001 (Gold Ladle for best TV food Show, World Food Media award, 2001), Forever Summer with Nigella, 2002, Nigella Bites Christmas Special, 2001. Named Author of Yr., British Book Awards, 2000. Address: c/o Hyperion Edit Dept 77 West 66th St New York NY 10023

LAWSON, PETER RODERICK, physicist, researcher; b. Montreal, Quebec, Can., July 3, 1963; s. Ray Newton and Anne Burns (Richardson) L.; m. Laurence Cador, Apr. 29, 1996. BSc in Physics, Acadia U., Wolfville, Can., 1984; MASc in Elec. Engring., U. Toronto, Can., 1987; PhD in Physics, U. Sydney, Australia, 1994. Vis. scientist Cornell U., Ithaca, N.Y., 1987-88; Henri Poincaré fellow Observatoire de La Côte d'Azur, Nice, France, 1993-95; postdoctoral rsch. assoc. Cavendish lab. Cambridge U., England, 1995—. Contbr. articles to profl. jours. Massey Coll. jr. fellow, 1985-87, Commonwealth fellow, Australia, 1990-93. Mem. IEEE, Optical Soc. Am., Astron. Soc. Australia, Soc. Photo-Optical and Instrumentation Engrs. Avocations: bushwalking, amateur radio, abseiling, juggling. Office: Cavendish Lab Madingley Rd Cambridge CB3 OHE England

LAWSON, RANDALL CLAYTON, II, finance company executive; b. Wabash, Ind., June 20, 1948; s. Randall Clayton and Evelyn Beatrice

(Wright) L.; m. Julie Ann Severin, June 30, 1973; children: Randall Clayton III, Erin Elizabeth. BS, Butler U., 1970. CPA, Ind., Ohio. Jr. acct. Price Waterhouse, Indpls., 1970-73, sr. acct. Indpls. and Cin., 1973-76, audit mgr. Cin., 1976-79; unit devel. contr. Ponderosa, Inc., Dayton, Ohio, 1979-81, asst. corp. contr., 1981-82, corp. contr., 1982-84, v.p., corp. contr., 1984-85, sr. v.p., chief acctg. officer, 1985-87, sr. v.p., CFO, 1987; v.p., CFO Tad Tech. Svcs. Corp., Cambridge, Mass., 1988-89; v.p. fin. Hydro-Logic, Inc., Asheville, NC, 1993; dir. mgmt. acctg. Rust Indsl. Cleaning Inc., Ashland, Ky., 1994-95; East region contr. Rust Indsl. Svcs., Inc., LaPorte, Tex., 1995, divsn. v.p., contr., 1996-97, v.p., contr., 1997—; group dir. fin. and adminstrn. waste mgmt. indsl. svcs. In Plant Svcs. Group, LaPorte, Tex., 1998—. V.p., CFO Onyx Indsl. Svcs., La Porte, 1999—, Veoliaes Indsl. Svcs., Baytown, Tex., 2006-, Veolia ES Spl. Svcs., Appleton, Wis., 2007; adj. prof. Wilmington Coll., 1991; bus. cons., 1987—. Mem. agy. audit com. United Way Greater Cin., 1975; mem. fin. and resource allocation com. United Way Greater Dayton, 1985, mem. com. on agy. fins., 1986-87. Mem. AICPA, Ohio Soc. CPAs, Fin. Execs. Internat., Queen City Assn. Club (bd. dirs. 1978), Dayton Racquet Club, Elks, Phi Kappa Psi. Independent. Presbyterian. Avocations: golf, tennis, reading, antiques, crafts. Home: 2810 Countrylake Dr Cincinnati OH 45233-1735 Office Phone: 513-353-2250. Business E-Mail: jslawson@fuse.net.

LAWSON, RHEA BROWN, library director; b. SC; 1 child, Ebony. BA in Polit. Sci., Morgan State U., Balt.; M in Libr. and Info. Sci., U. Md., College Park; PhD in Libr. and Info. Studies, U. Wis., Madison. Chief Ctrl. Libr. Bklyn. Pub. Libr., NY, 1999—2003; dep. dir. Detroit Pub. Libr., Mich., 2003—05; dir. Houston Pub. Libr., Tex., 2005—. Bd. dirs. Pub. Libr. Assn.; exec. bd. mem. Black Caucus of ALA; mem. Money Smart adv. bd. Fed. Res. Bank; adv. bd. mem. Medgar Evers Coll. Ctr. Black Lit. Office: Houston Pub Libr 500 McKinney St Houston TX 77002 Office Phone: 832-393-1313. E-mail: library.director@cityofhouston.net.*

LAWSON, ROBERT BERNARD, psychology professor; b. NYC, June 20, 1940; s. Robert Bernard Sr. and Isabella Theresa (McPeake) L.; children: Christina Megan, Steven Robert, Jennifer Erin. BA in Psychology, Monmouth U., 1961; MA in Psychology, U. Del., 1963, PhD in Psychology, 1965. Mem. faculty U. Vt., Burlington, 1966—, asst. prof. psychology, 1966-69, assoc. prof., 1969-74, prof., 1974—, assoc. v.p. acad. affairs, 1978, assoc. v.p. rsch., dean Grad. Coll., 1978-86, dir. gen. exptl. psychology, 1988-90, chmn. dept. pub. adminstrn., 1990-95, acting dir. MPA program, 1998-99, dir. MPA program, 1999—2002, chmn. dept. psychology, 2002—06. Presenter, worker in China, Russia, and Italy; cons. Mgmt. Sys., 1986—; vis. scholar Stanford U., 1986-87; pres. Alliance Mgmt. Cons. Group, Burlington, 1987—, N.E. Assn. Grad. Schs., Princeton, N.J., 1983-86; bd. dirs. Grad. Record Exams-ETS, Princeton, 1984-88. Author: (with S.G. Goldstein and R.E. Musty) Principles and Methods of Psychology, 1975; (with W.L. Gulick) Human Stereopsis: A Psychophysical Approach, 1976; (with Zheng Shen) Organizational Psychology: Foundations and Applications, 1998; (with Jean E. Graham and Kristin M. Baker) A History of Psychology: Globalization, Ideas, and Applications, 2007. Mem. bd. govs. Univ. Press New England, 1978-86, bd. dirs., 1979-80. Recipient George V. Kidder Disting. Faculty award U. Vt., 2003; numerous grants NIH, NSF, USDA, numerous awards from Nat. Eye Inst. Mem. AAAS, APA, Psychonomic Soc., Coun. Grad. Schs., N.Y. Acad. Scis., Ea. Psychol. Assn. Office: U Vt Dept Psychology John Dewey Hl Burlington VT 05405-0001 Business E-Mail: robert.lawson@uvm.edu.

LAWSON, ROBERT DAVIS, theoretical nuclear physicist; b. Sydney, July 14, 1926; came to U.S., 1949; s. Carl Herman and Angeline Elizabeth (Davis) L.; m. Mary Grace Lunn, Dec. 16, 1950 (div. 1976); children: Dorothy, Katherine, Victoria; m. Sarah Virginia Roney, Mar. 13, 1976 (dec. 1994). BS, U. B.C., Can., 1948; MS, U. B.C., 1949; PhD, Stanford U., 1953. Research assoc. U. Calif., Berkeley, 1953-57; research assoc. Fermi Inst. U. Chgo., 1957-59; assoc. physicist Argonne (Ill.) Nat. Lab., 1959-65; sr. physicist Argonne Nat. Lab., 1965—. Vis. scientist U.K. Atomic Energy Authority, Harwell, Eng., 1962-63, Oxford U., Eng., 1970, 85; vis. prof. SUNY, Stony Brook, 1972-73; vis. fellow Australian Nat. U., Canberra, 1982; vis. prof. U. Groningen, 1973, U. Utrecht, 1974, Technische Hochschule, Darmstadt, 1975, 78, Free U., Amsterdam, 1976, 81, others; TRIUMF, U. B.C., Vancouver, Can., 1984. Author: Theory of the Nuclear Shell Model, 1980; contbr. articles to profl. jours. Fellow Weizmann Inst. Sci., 1967-68, Niels Bohr Inst., 1976-77; Sir Thomas Lyle fellow U. Melbourne, Australia, 1987. Fellow Am. Phys. Soc. Office: Argonne Nat Lab Bldg 203 Argonne IL 60439 Home: 35 N Main #25 Glen Ellyn IL 60137 Office Phone: 630-972-4092.

LAWSON, RODGER A., diversified financial services company executive; Pres., CEO Dreyfus Svc. Corp., 1982—85; mng. dir., CEO Fidelity Investments-Retail, 1985—91; pres., CEO Global Pvt. Banking and Mutual Funds, Bankers Trust Co., 1992—94, VanEck Global, 1994—96; exec. v.p., mktg. and planning Prudential Ins., Newark, 1996—98, exec. v.p., internat. investments and global mktg. comm., 1998—2001; exec. v.p. Prudential Fin., Newark, 2001—02, vice chmn. internat. div., 2002—07; pres. FMR Corp. (Fidelity Investments), Boston, 2007—. Office: FMR Corp 82 Devonshire St Boston MA 02109*

LAWSON, SCOTT D., oral surgeon; b. Rochester, NY, Jan. 28, 1971; s. Charles D. and Jane M. Lawson; m. Jacqueline M. Thibodeaux, Aug. 1, 1998; children: Matthew C., Corey D., Matthew C., Corey D., Zoe E. BS, Buffalo State Coll., NY, 1989—93. Lic. dental surgeon U. Buffalo, 1997, medical dr. U. Miami, 2001, oral & maxillofacial surgeon Jackson Meml. Hosp., Fla., 2002. Anesthesiology fellow Jackson Meml. Hosp., 2003; oral & maxillofacial surgeon Fla. Oral & Facial Surg. Assocs., Daytona Beach, 2003—. Fellow: Am. Acad. Cosmetic Surgery, Am. Dental Soc. Anesthesiology, Am. Bd. Oral & Maxillofacial Surgeons; mem.: Am. Assn. Oral & Maxillofacial Surgeons. Office: Florida Oral & Facial Surgical Assocs 549 Health Blvd Daytona Beach FL 32114 Home Phone: 386-852-9391. Office Fax: 386-258-1989. Personal E-mail: facialcrunch@yahoo.com.

LAWSON, THOMAS CHENEY, fraud examiner; b. Pasadena, Calif., Sept. 21, 1955; s. William McDonald and Joan Bell (Jaffe) Lawson; m. Susan Sullivan; children: Christopher, Brittany, Courtney, Madison. Student, Calif. State U., Sacramento, 1973-77. Cert. internat. investigator, fraud examiner. Pres. Tomatron Co., Pasadena, 1970-88, Tom's Tune Up & Detail, Pasadena, 1971-88, Tom's Pool Svc., Sacramento, 1975-78, Tomsupply Co., 1975—; mgmt. trainee Permoid Process Co., LA, 1970-75; prof. automechanics Calif. State U., Sacramento, 1973-75; regional sales cons. Hoover Co., Burlingame, 1974-76; mktg. exec. River City Prodns., Sacramento, 1977-78; territorial rep. Globe div. Burlington House Furniture Co., 1978; So. Calif. territorial rep. Marge Carson Furniture, Inc., 1978-80; pres. Ted L. Gunderson & Assos., Inc., Westwood, Calif., 1980-81; pres., CEO Apscreen, Newport Beach, Calif., 1980—. Founder Creditbase Co., Newport Beach, Calif., 1980-89, Worldata Corp., Newport Beach, 1980-89, Trademark Enforcement Corp., L.A., 1985-86; pres. Carecheck, Inc., Newport Beach, 1990—, CEO Badchex, Inc., Newport Beach, 1992-2006, Corp. Security Inc., Nev., 2006-; expert witness Calif. Superior Ct. Mem. editl. rev. bd. Fraud Mag. Calif. Rehab. scholar, 1974—77. Mem.: Nat. Assn. Profl. Background Screeners (founding mem.), Pub. Record Retrievers Network, Forensic Expert Witness Assn., World Investigators Network, Soc. Human Resource Mgmt., World Assn. Detectives, Profls. in Human Resources Assn., Nat. Pub. Records Rsch. Assn., Am. Soc. Indsl. Security (cert., chmn. Orange County chpt. 1990), Coun. Internat. Investigators, Christian Businessmen's Com. Internat., Assn. Cert. Fraud Examiners (life; editl. rev. bd. 1995—), Nat. Hot Rod Assn. Mus., 1320 Club. Office: PO Box 80639 Rancho Santa Margarita CA 92688

LAWSON, THOMAS SEAY, JR., lawyer, actor; b. Montgomery, Ala., Oct. 30, 1935; s. Thomas Seay and Rose Darrington (Gunter) L.; m. Sarah Hunter Clayton, May 27, 1961 (dec. Oct. 2004); children: Rose Gunter, Gladys Robinson, Thomas Seay III. AB, U. Ala., 1957, JD, 1963. Bar: Ala. 1963, U.S. Supreme Ct. 1969. Law clk. to chief judge U.S. Dist. Ct. (no. dist.) Ala., 1963-64; assoc. Steiner, Crum & Baker, Montgomery, 1964-68; ptnr. Capell, Howard, Knabe & Cobbs P.A., Montgomery, 1968-98; asst. dist. atty. 15th jud. cir. of Ala., 1969-70; ptnr. Capell & Howard, P.C., Montgomery, 1999—2005, of counsel, 2005—. Lawyers adv. com. U.S. Ct. Appeals, 5th cir. 1978, 11th cir. 1979-82. Actor: So. Appalachian Repertory Co., 2001, Ala. Shakespeare Festival, 2000, 2006, The Lost Nation Theatre, 2004, 2005, The Springer Opera House, 2003, The Broadway Palm Dinner Theatre, 2006, others. Pres. The Lighthouse, 1978-79. Lt. USNR, 1957-60. Fellow: Ala. Law Found.; mem.: ABA, Actors Equity Assn., Fed Bar Assn., Ala. Law Sch. Found. (trustee 1985—2001), Ala. Law Inst. (bd. dirs. 1986—), Montgomery Inn of Ct. (master bencher, bd. dirs. 1989—92, chancellor 1991, pres. 1992—93, emeritus 1994—), Farrah Law Soc. (pres. 1986—88, Outstanding Alumnus award U. Ala. student chpt. 1989), Lawyers Adv. Com. U.S. Dist. Ct. (mid. dist.) Ala. (chmn. 2000—), 11th Cir. Hist. Soc. (pres. 1999—2001), Am. Judicature Soc., Montgomery County Bar Assn. (pres. 1980), Ala. State Bar (pres. young lawyers' sect. 1970—71), Montgomery Country Club, Soc. Pioneers of Montgomery (pres. 1983). Independent. Episcopalian. Home: 1262 Glen Grattan Montgomery AL 36111-1402 Office: Capell & Howard PC PO Box 2069 Montgomery AL 36102-2069 Studio: The Continental 321 East 48th St Apt 8E New York NY 10017 Home Phone: 334-546-0071; Office Phone: 334-241-8042, 334-546-0071, 646-413-8551. Personal E-mail: ogieboat@aol.com. Business E-Mail: tsl@chlaw.com.

LAWSON, TRENT, artist; b. Oklahoma City, Apr. 30, 1980; BFA in Studio Art, Oklahoma City U., 2002. Vol. Arts Coun. Okla. City, 2004—07. Mem.: Okla. Visual Arts Coalition, Individual Artists Okla. (bd. dirs. 2005—07, chmn. visual arts com. 2005—), Leadership Okla. City Alumni Assn. Home Phone: 405-682-1166. Personal E-mail: trent@trentlawson.net.

LAWSON, WILLIAM, otolaryngologist, educator; b. NYC, Nov. 23, 1934; s. Alexander and Sophia (Elkind) L.; m. Miriam Patkin, Nov. 7, 1965; 1 child, Vanessa Ann. BA, NYU, 1956, DDS, 1961, MD, 1965. Diplomate Am. Bd. Otolaryngology, Am. Bd. Cosmetic Surgery, Am. Bd. Facial Plastic Surgery. Intern Mt. Sinai Hosp., NYC, 1965-66, rsch. fellow in otolaryngology, 1969-70, resident in otolaryngology, 1970-73; resident in gen. surgery Bronx (N.Y.) VA Hosp., 1966-67, chief otolaryngology, head and neck surgery, 1974—2003, cons., 2003—; prof. Mt. Sinai Sch. Medicine, NYC, 1980—; vice chmn., 1996—. Co-dir. Paranasal Sinus Rsch. Lab.; dir. facial plastic surgery clini Mt. Sinai Hosp., N.Y.C.; cons. Nat. Space Biomed. Rsch. Consortium, cons. in physical anthropology, Am. Mus. Natural History. Author: Paraganglionic Chemoreceptor Systems, 1982, Surgery of the Paranasal Sinuses, 1988, 2nd edit., 1992, External Ear, 1995; contbr. over 250 articles to med. jours., chpts. to books. Capt. Med. Corps. US Army, 1967—69. Fellow ACS, Am. Acad. Facial Plastic and Reconstructive Surgery (svc. awrd), Am. Soc. Head and Neck Surgery, Am. Soc. Maxillofacial Surgeons, Am. Rhinologic Soc., Otologic and Laryngologic Soc., Am. Laryngol. Soc.; mem. Am. Acad. Otolaryngology (svc. award), Am. Bronchoesophagologic Soc. (included in Best Drs. Am., Best Drs. in N.Y.). Avocations: photography, art history, horology. Office: Mt Sinai Med Ctr Box 1191 1 Gustave L Levy Pl New York NY 10029-6500

LAWSON, WILLIAM DAVID, III, retired cotton company executive; b. Jackson, Miss., Oct. 30, 1924; s. William David Jr. and Elizabeth Vaiden (Barksdale) L.; m. Elizabeth Coppridge Smith, June 9, 1948; children: Margaret Monroe, William David IV, Susan Barksdale, Thomas Nelson. Student, Woodberry Forest Sch., 1940-42; BS, Davidson Coll., 1948; MBA, U. Pa., 1949. Trainee T.J. White and Co., Memphis, 1949-52; v.p. W.D. Lawson and Co., Gastonia, NC, 1952-70, pres., 1971-81, Lawson, Lewis & Peat, Gastonia, 1981-85, Lawson Cotton Co., Gastonia, 1985-95; v.p. Hohenberg Bros. Co. div. Cargill Inc., Memphis, 1988-95; ret., 1995; pres. Lawson-Harris Cotton, Inc., 1997—. Pres. Covenant Village, 1979-81; hon. dir. 1st Union Nat. Bank, Gastonia. Mem. adv. coun. aging Gov., 1998—2000; del. Sr. Tar Heel Legislature, 1998—2004; elder Presbyn. Ch.; pres. Sister Cities Com., Gastonia, 1990—94, Gaston Cmty. Found., 2002—05; bd. advisors Davidson Coll., 1976—80; bd. mgrs. N.Y. Cotton Exch., 1974—80. 1st lt. inf. US Army, 1943—46, WWII. Named Cotton Man of Yr. Cotton Digest, 1969, 76; recipient Duke Kimbrell Lifetime Civic Achievement award, 1999, Harry S. Baker Disting. Svc. award Nat. Cotton Coun., 2002. Mem.: Svc. Corps. Ret. Execs., Gaston County C. of C. (pres. 1972—73), Am. Cotton Exporters Assn. (pres. 1979—80), Cotton Coun. Internat. (pres. 1972—73), Atlantic Cotton Assn. (pres. 1957—58), Am. Cotton Shippers Assn. (pres. 1968—69), Nat. Cotton Coun. (pres. 1975—76, advisor 1976—), Rotary Internat., Am. Legion, Newcomen Soc., The Point Lake and Golf Club, Gaston Country Club, Benefactor Bequest Soc. (pres. 1964—65, dist. gov. 1995—96, pres.' rep. 2000, Major Donor award 1999, citation for Meritorious Svc. 2001, Disting. Rotarian award 2004), Kappa Sigma. Avocations: scuba diving, tennis, golf. Home: 1341 Covenant Dr Gastonia NC 28054-3861 Home Fax: 704-868-3173.

LAWSON-JOHNSTON, PETER, II, investment company executive; BA, Trinity Coll.; MS in Real Estate Devel., Columbia U. Mng. ptnr. Jack Primus Partners LP, Harper Partners; dir. & v.p. Elgerbar Corp. Trustee Solomon R. Guggenheim Found., chmn. investment com.; sr. ptnr. Guggenheim Brothers; dir. Harry Frank Guggenheim Found., chmn. investment com.; dir. emeritus Charles A. & Anne Morrow Lindberg Found. Mailing: c/o Solomon R Guggenheim Found 1071 Fifth Ave New York NY 10128-0173 Fax: 212-423-3650.

LAWSON-JOHNSTON, PETER ORMAN, foundation executive; b. NYC, Feb. 8, 1927; s. John R. and Barbara (Guggenheim) L.; m. Dorothy Stevenson Hammond, Sept. 30, 1950; children: Wendy, Tania, Peter, Mary. Grad. with honors, U. Va., 1951. Reporter, yachting editor Balt. Sun Papers, 1951-53; exec. dir. Md. Classified Employees Assn., Balt., 1953-54; pub. info. dir. Md. Civil Def. Agy., Pikesville, 1954-56; dir. Zemex Corp., NYC, 1960—, v.p., 1966—72, vice chmn., 1972—75, pres., 1975—76, chmn., 1975—2003, also bd. dirs.; dir. Feldspar Corp., subsidiary of Zemex Corp. (formerly Pacific Tin Consolidated Corp.), 1959—2003, sales mgr., 1956—60, v.p. sales, 1961—66, v.p., 1966—72, chmn., 1972—81. Trustee Solomon R. Guggenheim Found., 1964, v.p. bus. adminstrn., 1965-69, pres., 1969-95, chmn., 1995-98, hon. chmn., 1998—; pres. adv. bd. Peggy Guggenheim Collection; dir. Harry Frank Guggenheim Found., 1968—, chmn., 1971—; ptnr. Guggenheim Bros., 1962-70, sr. ptnr., 1971—; chmn. Anglo Energy, Inc., 1973-86; pres., bd. dirs. Elgerbar Corp.; bd. dirs. Nat. Rev. Inc. Author: Growing Up Guggenheim: A Personal History of a Family Enterprise, 2005. Trustee The Lawrenceville Sch., 1977-99, trustee emeritus, 1999—, pres., 1990-97; trustee St. Elmo Found., 1996-05, trustee emeritus, 2005—; mem. adv. bd. U. Va. Art Mus., 1997—, chmn., 1997-05, chmn. emeritus, 2005-. With AUS, 1945-47 Recipient Gertrude Vanderbilt Whitney award Skowhegan Sch. Painting and Sculpture, 1986, Ellis Island Medal of Honor, Nat. Ethnic Coalition Orgns., 1993, Lawrenceville medal Lawrenceville Sch., 1997. Mem. Pilgrims of U.S., Carolina Plantation Soc., US Srs. Golf Assn., Edgartown Yacht Club, Edgartown Reading Room Club, Century Assn., Links, Bedens Brook Club, Pretty Book Tennis Club, Seminole Golf Club, Jupiter Island Club, Brook Club (NYC), Yeamans Hall Club. Republican. Episcopalian. Office: 25 W 53rd St 16 New York NY 10019-5401 Office Phone: 212-644-4901.

LAWSON-JOWETT, MARY JULIET, lawyer; b. Mobile, Ala., May 26, 1959; d. William Max Lawson and Perina Juliet (Barich) Franc; m. Adam Geoffrey Jowett; 1 child, Caitlin Victoria Jowett. BA, U. Miss., 1981, JD, 1987. Bar: Miss. 1988, U.S. Dist. Ct. (no. and so. dists.) Miss. 1988. Tchr. Ocean Springs (Miss.) Sch. System, 1981-85; atty. Ronald W. Lewis & Assocs., Oxford, Miss., 1988-89; ptnr. occupl. hearing loss and hand-arm vibration syndrome Scruggs, Millette, Lawson, Bozeman & Dent, P.A., Pascagoula, Miss., 1989—; gen. practice, civil rights and employment law Juliet Jowett, P.A., 1997—. Cons. Occupational Hearing Loss, P.A., 1989-96. Contbr. articles to profl. jours. Mem. Walter Anderson Players, Ocean Springs, 1973-96. Mem. ABA, ATLA (chmn. occupational hearing loss litigation group 1990-94), Miss. Trial Lawyers Assn. (editor 1990-92), Magnolia Bar Assn. Democrat. Roman Catholic. Avocations: reading, golf, horseback riding, gardening, acting. Home: 5728 Shore Dr Ocean Springs MS 39564-2214

LAWSON-NDU, OVUNDA A., emergency physician, surgeon; b. Elelenwo, Nigeria, 1951; s. Lawson Ngbachi and Esther Adanma (Nwogbe) N.; m. Elsie Nnenne Jenewari, Dec. 13, 1977 (div. Jan. 1980); children: Jennifer Mboma, Sandra Njimole; m. Donna Marie Grimes, June 27, 1986; 1 child, Anuugo Michelle. BS in Chemistry with highest honors, U. Wis., 1977; DO, U. Health Sci., 1980. Diplomate Am. Bd. Emergency Medicine. Intern Metro Health Ctr., Erie, Pa., 1981-82; resident in gen. surgery Howard U. Hosp., Washington; mem. staff Lower Bucks Hosp., Bristol, Pa. Mem. hypertension and diabetes screening program Rivers State, Nigeria, 1992—; vice chmn. dept. emergency medicine Temple U. Hosp., Bristol, Pa., 1997—, asst. dir., 1997-2000, assoc. dir., 2000—. Active Nat. Exch. Club, Amnesty Internat. Fellow Am. Coll. Emergency Physicians, Am. Acad. Emergency Medicine. Address: PO Box 640 Medford NJ 08055-0640

LAWTON, BARBARA, lieutenant governor; b. Milw., Wis., July 5, 1951; m. Cal Lawton; children: Joseph, Amanda Krupp. BA summa cum laude, Lawrence U., 1987; MA, U. Wis., 1991. Lt. gov. State of Wis., Madison, 2003—. Founding mem. Ednl. Resource Found.; founding trustee Cmty. Found.; founding mem. Latinos Unidos; mem. adv. bd. Green Bay Multicultural Ctr., Women's Polit. Voice; mem. bus. planning and resource team Entrepreneurs of Color; bd. mem. Planned Parenthood Advs. Wis., Northeastern Wis. Tech. Coll. Edn. Found. Named Feminist of the Yr., Wis. Chpt. NOW, 1999; recipient Ft. Howard Founds. Humanitarian award. Mem.: AAUW, LWV, Nat. Women's Polit. Caucus. Democrat. Office: Office of Lt Governor 19 East State Capitol PO Box 2043 Madison WI 53702 Office Phone: 608-266-3516. Office Fax: 608-267-3571. E-mail: ltgov@ltgov.state.wi.us.

LAWTON, FLORIAN KENNETH, artist, educator; b. Cleve., June 20, 1921; m. Lois Mari Ondrey, June 19, 1948; children: Kenneth R., David F., Dawn M., Patricia A. Student, Cleve. Sch. Art, 1941-43, Cleve. Inst. Art, 1948-51, John Huntington Polytech. Inst., 1946-50. Instr. Cooper Sch. Art, Cleve., 1976-80, Cleve. Sch. Art, 1980-82. Cons., instr. Orange Art Ctr., Pepper Pike, Ohio, 1978—; cons. in field, juror, 1968—. Exhbns. include Am. Watercolor Soc., N.Y., Cleve. Mus. Art, Butler Mus., Youngstown, Ohio, Canton (Ohio) Mus., Massillon (Ohio) Mus., Nat. Arts Club, N.Y.C., Pitts. Watercolor Soc., Audubon Artists, N.Y.C., Salmagundi Club, N.Y.C., Parkersburg (W.Va.) Art Ctr., Boston Mills Arts Festival, Peninsula, Ohio, Marietta (Ohio) Coll., Nat. Pks. Assn. Exhbn., 1996, 97, 2000, many others; 25 yrs. retrospective exhbn. Amish paintings, Butler Inst. Am. Art, 1989; represented in collections including Am. Soc. Metals, Ctrl. Nat. Bank, Diamond-Shamrock, Diocese Cleve., Kaiser Found., Ohio Conservation Found., Nat. City Bank Ohio, TRW, Standard Oil Co., Huntington Bank, Nat. Mennonite Mus., Lancaster, Pa., Ohio Bell Telephone Co., Day-Glo Corp., Soc. Bank Corp., The White House Collection, Washington, numerous others U.S. and internat., also pvt. collections; featured mags., calendars; Mill Pond Press; cons., artist (documentary) Amish Romance, 1979; official Coast Guard artist; artist Amish Documentary-PBS, 1996. Cons. Aurora (Ohio) Community Libr., 1990—. Cpl. USAF, 1943-46, PTO. Recipient Disting. Alumni award Garfield Hgts. (Ohio) High Sch., 1990, 1st place award Grand Invitational Exhbn., Akron, Ohio, 1996, numerous others. Mem. Ohio Watercolor Soc. (signature, charter, Grand Buckeye award 1983), Am. Watercolor Soc. (signature, Strathmore award 1977), Nat. Watercolor Soc. (signature), Akron Soc. Artists, Assoc. Audubon Artists, Artists Fellowships Inc. (N.Y.), Ky. Watercolor Soc. (signature), Midwest Watercolor Soc., Pa. Watercolor Soc. (signature), Ga. Watercolor Soc., Whiskey Painters Am., Rotary Club Chagrin Valley (Paul Harris fellow 1989). Office: 410-29 Willow Cir Aurora OH 44202-9131 Fax: 330-562-4102.

LAWTON, JACQUELINE AGNES, retired communications executive, management consultant; b. Bklyn., June 9, 1933; d. Thomas J. and Agnes R. (McLaughlin) Maguire; m. George W. Lawton, Feb. 14, 1954; children: George, Victoria, Thomas. With N.Y. Telephone, 1954-82, mktg. mgr. govt., edn. and med. Mid State, 1978-81, mktg. mgr. health care N.Y.C., 1982-82, dist. field market mgr. health care and lodging; with N.E. and Mid Atlantic region AT&T-Am. Bell, NYC, 1982-83; ea. region mgr. pers., mktg. and sales AT&T Info. Sys., Parsippany, N.J., 1983-86; pvt. practice mgmt. and travel cons., Cornish Flat, N.H., 1986-96; diocesan dir. Medjugirje in Am., Manchester, NH, 1992—2000. Republican. Roman Catholic. Home: 27 Fountain Way West Lebanon NH 03784 Personal E-mail: jamjal1@msn.com.

LAWTON, KELLY MARIE LEE, secondary school educator, performing arts director; b. Pitts., Sept. 17, 1970; d. Francis Xavier and Helen Louise Lawton. BS Music Edn., Clarion U. Pa., 1993; MEd, Shenandoah U., 2000. Cert. PreK-12 music tchr., adminstr., supr. Va. Dir. performing arts Page County Pub. Schs., Shenandoah, Va., 1996—. Named Tchr. of Month, Sylvan Learning Ctr. and WHSV-3, 2004; named to Nat. Honor Roll Outstanding Am. Tchrs., 2006; recipient Tchr. Achievement award, McDonald's Ray A. Kroc, 2004, award, Nat. Soc. H.S. Scholars, 2004, Outstanding Educator award, Regional Gov.'s Sch., 2005. Mem.: NEA (assoc.), Music Educators Nat. Conf. (assoc.), Va. Choral Dirs. Assn. (assoc.), Va. Band and Orch. Dirs. Assn. (assoc.), Va. Music Edn. Assn. (assoc.), Page County Edn. Assn. (assoc.), Women's Nat. Bandmaster's Assn. (life), Tau Beta Sigma (hon.), Beta Sigma Phi (hon.). Office Phone: 540-652-8712.

LAWTON, LORILEE ANN, small business owner, accountant; b. Morrisville, Vt., July 17, 1947; d. Philip Wyman Sr. and Margaret Elaine (Ather) Noyes; m. Lee Henry Lawton, Dec. 6, 1969 (dec. Nov. 2004); children: Deborah Ann, Jeffrey Lee. BBA, U. Vt., 1969. Sr. acct., staff asst. IBM, Essex Junction, Vt., 1969-72; owner, pres., chmn. bd. Red-Hed Supply Inc., Colchester, 1972-2001; owner, pres. Firetech Sprinkler Corp., Colchester, 1992—. Bd. dirs. Mchts. Bank, Burlington, Mchts. Bankshares. Mem. Am. Fire Sprinkler Assn., Nat. Fire Protection Assn., Vt. Subcontractors Assn. Republican. Avocations: reading, gardening. Home: 571 Middle Rd Colchester VT 05446-7310 Office: Firetech Sprinkler Corp 340 Hegeman Ave Colchester VT 05446-3173 Office Phone: 802-655-1800.

LAX, PETER DAVID, mathematician, educator; b. Budapest, Hungary, May 1, 1926; arrived in U.S., 1941, naturalized, 1944; s. Henry and Klara (Kornfeld) Lax; m. Anneli Cahn, 1948; 1 child, John; 1 child, James D.

BA, NYU, 1947, PhD, 1949; DSc (hon.), Kent State U., 1976, Brown U., 1993; DHC (hon.), U. Paris, 1979; D. Natural Scis. (hon.), Technische Hochschule Aachen, Germany, 1988; DSc (hon.), Herriot Walt U., 1990; D. (hon.), Leningrad State U., 1991; D. (hon.), U. Md. Baltimore County, 1993; PhD (hon.), Tel Aviv U., 1992, Beijing U., 1993. Asst. prof. NYU, 1949—57, prof., 1957—99, dir. Courant Inst. Math. Scis., 1972—80. Author (with Ralph Phillips): Scattering Theory, 1967; author: Hyperbolic Systems of Conservation Laws and the Mathematical Theory of Shock Waves, 1973, Scattering Theory for Automorphic Functions, 1976; author: (with A. Lax and S.Z. Burstein) Calculus with Applications and Computing, 1976; author: Linear Algebra, 1997, Functional Analysis, 2002. Mem. Pres.'s Com. on Nat. Medal of Sci., 1976; Nat. Sci. Bd., 1980—86. With US Army, 1944—46. Recipient Semmelweis medal, Semmelweis Med. Soc., 1975, Nat. medal Sci., 1986, Wolf prize in math., Wolf Found., Israel, 1987, Abel prize, Norway, 2005. Mem.: NAS (applied math. and numerical analysis award 1983), AAAS, Russian Acad. Sci. (fgn. assoc.), Acad. des Scis. (fgn. assoc.), Soc. Indsl. and Applied Math., Am. Philos. Soc., Am. Acad. Arts and Scis., Math. Assn. Am. (bd. govs., Chauvenet prize 1974), Am. Math. Soc. (pres. 1979—80, Norbert Wiener prize 1973, Leroy P. Steele prize 1993), London Math. Soc. (hon.), Moscow Math. Soc. (hon.), Hungarian Acad. Sci. (hon.), Acad. Sinica (hon.). Office: Courant Inst Math Scis NYU 251 Mercer St Rm 910 New York NY 10012-1185 Home Phone: 212-362-9006; Office Phone: 212-998-3232. Office Fax: 212-995-4121. Business E-Mail: lax@cims.nyu.edu.

LAX, PHILIP, land developer, space planner; b. Newark, Apr. 22, 1920; s. Nathan and Beckie (Hirschhorn) L; m. Madeline Blondman, June 13, 2004; children from previous marriage: Corinne, Barbara. BS, NYU, 1940, postgrad., 1941-42. With Lax & Co., Newark, 1942-77, v.p., 1950-77; pres. Chathill Mgmt., Inc., 1977—. Cons. World Book of Am. Heritage, 1992. Pres. B'nai Brith Ctr., Rochester, Minn., 1965-70, now hon. pres.; trustee Rutgers U. Hillel; pres. B'nai Brith Rutgers U. Hillel Found. Bldg. Corp., 1969—; chmn. United Jewish Appeal, Maplewood, N.J., 1966, 76; mem. N.J. region exec. bd. Anti-Defamation League, mem. nat. community rels. bd.; mem. Gov.'s Conf. on Edn., N.J., 1966, mem. bd. trustees Soc. Friends of Touro Synagogue, Newport, R.I., 1996; v.p. Touro Synagogue, 2000—; bd. dirs. Hebrew Immigration Soc. (HIAS); hon. chair B'nai B'rith Ctr. for Pub. Policy. 1999; mem. Mayor's Budget Com., Maplewood, 1958-59; co-chmn. N.J. Opera Ball, 1977; trustee B'nai Brith Found., Washington, 1967— (Philip Lax Gallery of B'nai Brith History and Archives named for him in Philip Klutznick Mus., Room named in his honor Stern Sch. Econs., NYU); co-chmn. B'nai Brith Internat. Coun., 1979-84, chmn., 1982-94; voting del. to Jewish Agy., Jerusalem; represented ICBB in UN as NGO, ECOSOC mem. UN, representing coordinated Bd. Jewish Orgns.; attended UNESCO Conf. in Mex., 1982, with Internat. Coun. B'nai Brith and U.S.; trustee, mem. exec. com. N.J. sect. NCCJ, 1981; trustee Henry Monsky Found., Washington, 1968—; trustee Leo N. Levi Hosp., Hot Springs, Ark., 1968-71, B'nai Brith World Jewish Ctr., Jerusalem, 1982, Nat. Arthritis Hosp., 1976—, N.Y. Statue of Liberty Centennial Found., Touro Synagogue, Newport, R.I., 1996—,; hon. trustee Arts Coun. of Suburban Essex, N.J., 1980, Soc. Friends Touro Synagoague, Newport, 1996; mem. Econ. Devel. Commn., Twp. of Maplewood, 1979—; mem. steering com. to Restore Ellis Island, 1977—; nat. pres. Ellis Island Restoration Commn., 1978—, responsible for planning, funding and operating Family History Ctr. on Ellis Island; apptd. to planning team of Statue of Liberty and Ellis Island by Pres. Carter, Dept. of Interior; mem. Statue of Liberty/Ellis Island Centennial Commn., chmn. bd. Com. of Architecture and Restoration of Statue of Liberty-Ellis Island, past chmn.; bd. dirs. Hebrew Immigration Aid Soc. Decorated Cavaliere Ufficiale (Knighted) Order of Merit of the Republic of Italy; recipient Found. award B'nai Brith, 1968, Humanitarian award, 1969, Pres.'s Gold medal, 1975; Pro Mundi Beneficio medal Brazilian Acad. Humanities, 1976; Philip Lax chapel at Rutgers U. Hillel named in his honor; named One of 100 Most Influential New Jersey Jews in the 20th Century, Eminent Wisdom fellow Wisdom Hall of Fame, 2000; honored by N.J. State Senate. Mem. Am. Soc. Interior Designers, Nat. Soc. Interior Designers (trustee 1970-73), Am. Arbitration Assn., Am. Jewish Hist. Com. (v.p.), Am. Jewish Hist. Soc. (trustee 1984), Am. Soc. Israel Philatelists, Masons (32 deg.), Shriners, B'nai Brith (v.p. Supreme Lodge 1968-71, internat. bd. govs. 1971—, mem. exec. com. of internat. coun.), NYU Club (founding mem. 1956), Nat. Press Club. Office Phone: 973-635-7700.

LAXMINARAYANA, DAMA, geneticist, researcher, educator; b. Hyderabad, India, Apr. 20, 1953; came to U.S., 1990; s. Kishtaiah and Sathyamma; m. Dara Jayalakshmi; children: Dama Bhargavi, Dama Sriharsha, Dama Vishnupriya. BSc, Osmania U., Hyderabad, 1974, MSc, 1976, PhD, 1982. Jr. sci. asst. dept. genetics Osmania U., 1977-78, lectr. dept. zoology, 1985-90; jr. rsch. fellow Indian Dept. Atomic Energy, 1978-81, postdoctoral fellow, 1982-83, rsch. assoc., 1983-85; postdoctoral fellow dept. medicine Case Western Res. U. Sch. Medicine, Cleve., 1990-91; rsch. assoc. dept. internal medicine Wake Forest U. Sch. Medicine, Winston-Salem, N.C., 1991-94, rsch. instr., 1994-98, rsch. asst. prof., 1998—. Conf. presenter in field. Contbr. articles to sci. jours., chpts. to books. Mem. AAAS, Am. Assn. Immunologists, Am. Coll. Rheumatology, Environ. Mutagen Soc. India, India Soc. Cell Biology, Soc. Geneticists and Cytologists India, N.Y. Acad. Scis. Home: 444 Lynn Ave Winston Salem NC 27104 Office: Wake Forest U Sch Medicine Dept Internal Medicine Medical Center Blvd Winston Salem NC 27157 Office Phone: 336-716-0616. Personal E-mail: laxmina@triad.rr.com. Business E-Mail: dlaxmina@wfubmc.edu.

LAY, MARION, sports association executive; M of Sociology, Calif. State U., Hayward. Mem. exec. com. Can. Olympic Assn.; founder, chair Nat. Sport Ctr., Greater Vancouver; chair PacificSport Group; co-chair BC Games com.; mem. WomenSport Internat. Former Can. Olympic swimmer; founding mem. Can. Assn. for Advancement of Women in Sport & Phys. Activity; pres. 2010 LegaciesNow Society (Vancouver Olympic bid), 1998—. Recipient Women of Distinction award Recreation and Sport, YWCA, 1991, Herstorical award, CAAWS, 1994, Bryce Taylor Meml. award Outstanding Contbn. Amateur Sport, 1995, Can. Citizenship award, 1996, Bobbie Steen award Excellence Leadership Sport Cmty., 1998, Bronze medal 4x100 metre relay, Olympics, Mexico City, 1968, Internat. Olympic Com.'s Women and Sport Trophy, 2001, Leadership in Sports award, Can., 2001, Carole Anne Letheren Internat Sport Leadership award, COC & CAAWS, 2002, History Breakthrough award award, CAAWS, 2002. Office: Can Assn Adv Women & Sport & Phys Act N202 801 King Edward Ave Ottawa ON K1N 6N5 Canada

LAY, NORVIE LEE, law educator; b. Cardwell, Ky., Apr. 17, 1940; s. Arlie H. and Opha (Burns) L.; 1 dau., Lea Anne. BS, U. Ky., 1960; JD, U. Louisville, 1963; LLM, U. Mich., 1964, SJD, 1967. Bar: Ky. 1963. Asst. prof. law U. Louisville, 1964-67, assoc. prof., 1967-70, prof., 1970—; asst. dean U. Louisville (Sch. Law), 1971-73, assoc. dean, 1973-84, acting dean, 1981-82. Vis. prof. Southwestern U. Sch. Law, summer 1983, N.Y. Law Sch., 1983-84, Coll. of Law U. Iowa, summer 1989. Author: Tax and Estate Planning for Community Property and the Migrant Client, 1970; contbr. articles to profl. jours. Trustee St. Joseph's Infirmary, 1974-78, S.W. Jefferson Community Hosp., 1979-80, Suburban Hosp., 1981-84, Humana-Audubon Hosp., 1985-88, U. Louisville Law Sch. Alumni Found., from 1982-85; bd. dirs. Louisville Ballet, from 1982-88, Louisville Theatrical Assn., 1985-88, Louisville Art Gallery, 1984-87, Watertower Art Assn., 1986-89, Chamber Mus. Soc. of Louisville, 1985-88, Louisville Chorus, 1985-88, Ky. Contemporary Theatre, 1984, Ky. Country Day Sch., 1985-88, Ky. Arts Coun., 1991—; mem. Nat. Conf. Commrs. Uniform State Laws. Recipient Scholarship Key Delta Theta Phi, 1963, Outstanding Graduating Sr. award Omicron Delta Kappa, 1963 Fellow Am. Coll. of Trust and Estate Counsel (acad.), Am. Coll. Tax Counsel; mem. ABA, Ky. Bar Assn., Louiville Bar Assn., Am. Judicature Soc. Republican. Baptist. Office: U Louisville Sch Law Belknap Campus Louisville KY 40292-0001 Office Phone: 502-852-6374.

LAY, THORNE, geosciences educator; b. Casper, Wyo., Apr. 20, 1956; s. Johnny Gordon and Virginia Florence (Lee) L. BS, U. Rochester, 1978; MS, Calif. Inst. Tech., 1980. Rsch. assoc. Calif. Inst. Tech., Pasadena, 1983; asst. prof. geosciences U. Mich., Ann Arbor, 1984-88, assoc. prof., 1988-89; prof. U. Calif., Santa Cruz, 1989—. Cons. Woodward Clyde Cons., Pasadena, 1982—84; dir. Inst. Tectonics, 1990—94, chmn. earth sci. dept., 1994—2000; dir. Inst. Geophysics and Planetary Physics, 2002—05, assoc. dean math., 2003—05; chmn. bd. dirs. Incorp. Rsch. Instns. Seismology, 2005—07; dir. Ctr. for Study of Imaging and Dynamics of the Earth, 2007—. Author: Structure and Fate of Subducting Slabs, 1997; co-author: (with T.C. Wallace) Modern Global Seismology, 1995; contbr. numerous articles to profl. jours. NSF fellow, 1978-81, Guttenberg fellow Calif. Inst. Tech., 1978, Lilly fellow Eli Lilly Found., 1984, Sloan fellow, 1985-87, Presidential Young Investigator, 1985-90. Fellow Royal Astron. Soc., Am. Geophys. Union (Macelwane medal 1991), Soc. Exploration Geophysicist, Seismol. Soc. Am., AAAS; mem. Nat. Acad. Sci. (life assoc.). Home: 2114 Harborview Ct Santa Cruz CA 95062-1678 Office: Univ California Santa Cruz Earth Planetary Sciences Dept 1156 High St Earth Marine Sciences Bldg Santa Cruz CA 95064 Home Phone: 831-454-8246; Office Phone: 831-459-3164. Business E-Mail: thorne@pmc.ucsc.edu.

LAYBOURNE, GERALDINE B., broadcast executive; b. Plainfield, NJ, 1947; m. Kit Laybourne; children: Emily, Sam. BA art history, Vassar Coll., 1969; MS elem. ed., U. Pa., 1971. Former high sch. tchr.; joined Nickelodeon as program manager, 1980; created Nick at Nite, 1985; exec. v.p./gen. mgr. Nickelodeon/Nick at Nite, 1986—89, pres., 1989—96; vice chmn. MTV Networks, 1993—96; pres. Disney/ABC Cable Networks, NYC, 1996—98; co-founder, CEO Oxygen Media, NYC, 1998—. Bd. dirs. Insight Comm. Co., The YES Network, Nat. Coun. Families and TV, Move, Inc. Bd. dirs. Nat. Coun. Families and TV, Children Affected by AIDS Found., Nat. Ctr. Children's TV, The Nat. Cable TV Assn., Vassar Coll. Named one of 25 Most Influential People in Am., Time mag., 1996, 100 Most Powerful Women in Entertainment, Hollywood Reporter, 2006; named to, Broadcasting Hall of Fame, 1995, Broadcasting and Cable Hall of Fame, 1995; recipient Idell Kaitz award, Nat. Cable and Telecom. Assn. Vanguard Awards, 1990, Film Muse award, NY Women, 1991, Entrepreneur of Yr. award, U. Mo., Kans. City, 1991, Women in Cable award, 1992, Genii award, Am. Women in Radio and TV, 1992, Govs. award, Nat. Acad. Cable Programming, 1993, Grand Tam award, Cable TV Adminstrn. and Mktg. Com., 1994, Spotlight award, Creative Coalition, 1995, Matrix award for broadcasting, NY Women in Comm., 1996, award for disting. lifetime contbn. to children and TV, Annenberg Pub. Policy Ctr., 1997, Crystal Apple award, Mayor Rudy Giuliani, 2001, award for disting. lifetime contbn. to children and TV, Annenberg Pub. Policy Ctr., Matrix award for broadcasting, NY Women in Comm., Spotlight award, Creative Coalition. Mem.: Nat. Cable TV Assn. (bd. dirs.), Cable Positive (hon. chair), NY Women in Film and TV (adv. bd.). Office: Oxygen Media 75 9th Ave Fl 7 New York NY 10011-7006*

LAYBOURNE, STANLEY, computer technology company executive; CPA. With Touche, Ross & Co. (now Deloitte & Touche), 1972—85, audit ptnr., 1983—85; pres., CEO Scottscom Group, 1985—89; exec. v.p. Ovation Broadcasting Co., 1989—90; CFO, treas. Insight Enterprises, Inc., 1991—, sec., 1994—, exec. v.p. Tempe, Ariz., 2002—. Office: Insight Enterprises Inc 1305 W Auto Drive Tempe AZ 85284

LAYCOCK, ANITA SIMON, psychotherapist; b. Cheyenne, Wyo., Dec. 17, 1940; d. James Robert and Dorothy (Dearmin) Simon; m. Maurice Percy Laycock, June 18, 1965(dec. 1976); 1 child, (dec.). BA, U. Wyo., 1962, MA, 1971. Lic. counselor, Wyo., nationally cert. addiction specialist. Grad. student counselor, psychometrist Wyo. State Prison, Rawlins, 1971-73; counselor, trainer Dept. of Insts. State of Colo., Denver, 1973-75; counselor, tchr. supr. Jefferson County Evaluation-Diagnostic Ctr., Rawlins, 1975-78; psychometrist Wyo. State Penitentiary, Rawlins, 1978-79; counselor, therapist Rocky Mountain Arts and Scis., Cheyenne, 1979-81; counselor, therapist supr., dir. SWARA, Rock Springs, Wyo., 1981-85; therapy dir. St. Joseph Residential Treatment, Torrington, Wyo., 1985-88; dir. psychiatric unit Nat. Med. Enterprises Hill-Haven-Pk. Manor, Rawlins, 1988-89; chief exec. officer Simon-Laycock & Assocs., Rawlins, 1989—. Cons. Kids in Distressed Situations, Rawlins, 1990-91, Child Devel. Ctr., Rawlins, 1991—; dir. Pub. Offender and Forensic Mental Health Program, Rawlins, 1988-91. Author: (programs) related to sex offenders. Pres. Cheyenne City Panhellenic, 1965-68. Named Miss Wyo.-Miss Universe, 1960; named Miss Wool of Wyo., 1965. Mem. ACA, Nat. Sex Offenders Counselors, Nat. Assn. Drug and Alcohol Counselors, Pub. Offenders Counselors Assn., Western Corrections Assn., Wyo. Assn. Addiction Specialists (pres. 1988—). Avocations: professional animal trainer, art. Office: Simon Laycock & Assocs 1716 Old Yellowstone Rd # 124 Cheyenne WY 82009-9183

LAYCOCK, HAROLD DOUGLAS, law educator, writer; b. Alton, Ill., Apr. 15, 1948; s. Harold Francis and Claudia Anita (Garrette) L.; m. Teresa A. Sullivan, June 14, 1971; children: Joseph Peter, John Patrick. BA, Mich. State U., 1970; JD, U. Chgo., 1973. Bar: Ill. 1973, US Dist. Ct. (no. dist.) Ill. 1973, Tex. 1974, US Dist. Ct. (we. dist.) Tex. 1975, US Ct. Appeals (5th and 11th cirs.) 1975, US Supreme Ct. 1976, US Ct. Appeals (6th cir.) 1987, US Ct. Appeals (8th cir.) 1994, US Ct. Appeals (10th cir.) 1997, US Ct. Appeals (3rd cir.) 2003, Mich. 2007. Law clk. to judge U.S. Ct. Appeals (7th cir.), Chgo., 1973-74; pvt. practice Austin, Tex., 1974-76; asst. prof. U. Chgo., 1976-80, prof., 1980-81, U. Tex., Austin, 1981—, endowed professorships, 1983-88, assoc. dean for acad. affairs, 1985-86, endowed chair, 1988—2006, assoc. dean for rsch., 1991—2006, emeritus endowed chair, 2006—; endowed chair U. Mich., Ann Arbor, 2006—. Vis. prof. U. Mich., 1990; reporter com. on motion practice Ill. Jud. Conf., 1977-78. Author: Modern American Remedies, 1985, 3d edit., 2002, The Death of the Irreparable Injury Rule, 1991; mem. bd. advisors Religious Freedom Reporter, 1990-2001; contbr. articles to profl. jours. Adv. bd. Consumer Svcs. Orgn., Chgo., 1979-80; exec. bd. Ctr. for Ch./State Studies, DePaul U., Chgo., 1982-87; adv. com. on religious liberty Presbyn. Ch. U.S.A., 1983-88, advisor restatement of restitution, 1984-85, 97—; v.p. St. Francis Sch., 1990-92, bd. dirs., 1990—, pres. 1992-2001; bd. adv. J.M. Dawson Inst. Ch./State Studies, Baylor U., 1990—; judicial speech adv. com., Supreme Ct. of Tex., 2002; adv. com. jud. ethics Supreme Ct. Tex., 2004. Recipient Scribes Book award, ABA, 1991, Civil Libertarian of Yr., ACLU of Tex., 2000, Civitatis award for disting. lifetime svc., U. Tex., 2005. Fellow AAAS, Internat. Acad. for Freedom of Religion and Belief; mem. AAUP (mem. com. on status of women in acad. profession 1982-85), Am. Law Inst. (mem. coun. 2001—), Chgo. Coun. Lawyers (v.p. 1977-78), Assn. Am. Law Schs. (chmn., sec. on remedies 1983, 94), chmn., sec. on constitutional law, 2000). Office: Univ Mich Law Sch 625 S State St Ann Arbor MI 48109 Home: 2197 Gray Fox Ct Ann Arbor MI 48103 Business E-Mail: laycockd@umich.edu.

LAYDEN, CHARLES MAX, lawyer; b. Lafayette, Ind., Nov. 10, 1941; s. Charles E. and Elnora M. (Parvis) L.; m. Lynn D. McVey, Jan. 28, 1967; children: David Charles, Kathleen Ann, John Michael, Daniel Joseph. BA in Indsl. Mgmt., Purdue U., 1964; JD, Ind. U., 1967. Bar: Ind. 1967, U.S. Dist. Ct. (no. and so. dists.) Ind. 1967, U.S. Ct. Appeals (7th cir.) 1970, U.S. Tax Ct. 1986. Assoc. Vaughan & Vaughan, Lafayette, 1967-70; ptnr. Vaughan, Vaughan & Layden, Lafayette, 1970-86, Layden & Layden, Lafayette, 1986—. Chmn. profl. div. United Way Lafayette, 1986. Mem. ABA, Ind. Bar Assn., Tippecanoe County Bar Assn. (pres. 1994-95), Am. Bd. Trial Advs. (charter mem. Ind. chpt. 1984—), Ind. Trial Lawyers Assn. (bd. dirs. 1983—). Republican. Roman Catholic. Avocations: photography, classic cars, flying. Home: 2826 Ashland St West Lafayette IN 47906-1510 Office: Layden & Layden PO Box 909 Lafayette IN 47902-0909 Office Phone: 765-742-7646. Personal E-mail: cmlayden@iquest.net.

LAYMAN, DALE PIERRE, retired medical educator, researcher, writer; b. Niles, Mich., July 3, 1948; s. Pierre Andre and Delphine Lucille (Lenke) L.; m. Kathleen Ann Jackowiak, Aug. 8, 1970; children: Andrew Michael, Alexis Kathryn, Allison Victoria, Amanda Elizabeth. AS in Life Sci., Lake Mich. Coll., Benton Harbor, 1968; BS in Anthropology and Zoology with distinction, U. Mich., Ann Arbor, 1971, MS in Physiology, 1974; EdS in Physiology and Health Sci., Ball State U., Muncie, Ind., 1979; PhD in Health and Safety Studies, U. Ill., Champaign-Urbana, 1986; Grand PhD in Medicine, World Info. Distributed U., Belgium, 2003. Histological technician in neuropathology U. Mich. Med. Sch., Ann Arbor, 1971-72, tchg. fellow human physiology, 1972-74; instr. human anatomy, physiology, and histology Lake Superior State U., Sault Ste. Marie, Mich., 1974-75; prof. med. terminology, human anatomy and physiology Joliet Jr. Coll., Ill., 1975—2007; ret., 2007. Author: The Terminology of Anatomy and Physiology, 1983, The Medical Language: A Programmed Body-Systems Approach, 1995, Biology Demystified, 2003, Anatomy Demystified, 2004, Physiology Demystified, 2004, Medical Terminology Demystified, 2005; contbr. articles to profl. jours. Founder Robowatch. Mem. Ill. C.C. Faculty Assn. (campus coord.), London Diplomatic Acad. (mem. acad. coun.), European Acad. Informatization (cavalier-knight, prof.), Internat. Assn. Bus. Leaders (life), Phi Kappa Phi, Kappa Delta Pi. Avocations: running, swimming, reading. Home: 509 Westridge Ln Joliet IL 60431-4883 Business E-Mail: drdlayman@sbcglobal.net.

LAYMAN, LAWRENCE, naval officer; b. Laclede County, Mo., Oct. 28, 1930; s. Archibald A. and Zoe Ellen (Hoke) L.; m. Carmen Elizabeth Meyer, Oct. 5, 1953; children: Linda Carmen, Lawrence, Harry Arthur, John Robert. BS, U.S. Naval Acad., 1952; MS in Internat. Affairs, George Washington U., 1972. Commd. ensign U.S. Navy, 1952, advanced through grades to rear adm., 1979; service to Korea and Vietnam; dep. comdr. Naval Telecommunications Command, 1978-79; dir. command, control and communications systems U.S. European Command, 1979-81; vice dir. Def. Communications Agy., Washington, 1981-83; dir. Naval Communications, Washington, 1983-86; dir. space command and control Office Chief Naval Ops., Washington, 1986-89, ret., 1989. Decorated D.S.M., Def. Superior Svc. medal with oak leaf cluster, Legion of Merit with Gold Star, Bronze Star with combat V, Meritorious Svc. medal. Home: 6800 Fleetwood Rd Unit 202 Mc Lean VA 22101 E-mail: llayman@cox.net.

LAYMON, JOE W., human resources specialist, automotive executive; married; 3 children. BA, Jackson State U.; MA, U. Wis. Various sr. human resouces positions including chief labor negotiator Xerox Corp., 1979—96; dir., v.p. human resources Kodak; with agency for internat. devel. U.S. State Dept.; exec. dir., human resources ops. Ford Motor Co., 2000—01, v.p. corp. human resources, 2001—03, group v.p., corp. human resources and labor affairs, 2003—. Bd. dirs. Am. Soc. Employers, Nat. Action Coun. Minorities in Engring., Douglas A. Fraser Ctr. Workplace Issues, Molex Inc., Nat. Tech. Inst. Deaf Rochester Inst. Tech., U. Wis., Human Resources Policy Assn., Am. Soc. Employers, Volvo Cars. Avocations: golf, cooking. Office: Ford Motor Co 1 American Rd Dearborn MI 48126-2798 Office Phone: 313-322-3000. Office Fax: 313-845-6073.*

LAYNE, JAMES NATHANIEL, retired vertebrate biologist; b. Chgo., May 16, 1926; s. Leslie Joy and Harriet (Hausmann) L.; m. Lois Virginia Linderoth, Aug. 26, 1950; children: Linda Carrie, Kimberly, Jamie Linderoth, Susan Nell, Rachel Pratt. BA, Cornell U., Ithaca, NY, 1950, PhD, 1954. Grad. teaching asst. Cornell U., Ithaca, NY, 1950-54, assoc. prof. zoology, 1963-67; asst. prof. zoology So. Ill. U., Carbondale, 1954-55; asst. prof., then assoc. prof. biology U. Fla., 1955-63; asst. curator, then assoc. curator mammals Fla. State Mus., Gainesville, 1955-63, research assoc., 1963-65; dir. research, then exec. dir. Archbold Biol. Sta.; Archbold curator mammals Am. Mus. Natural History, 1967-85; sr. rsch. biologist Archbold Biol. Sta., 1985-94, sr. rsch. biologist emeritus, 1994—. Rsch. assoc. Fla. State Collection of Arthropods, Am. Mus. Natural History; vis. scientist primate ecology sect. Nat. Inst. Neurol. Diseases and Blindness, summers 1961-62; adj. prof. biology U. South Fla., 1968-89; adj. prof. biol. scis. Fla. Atlantic U., 1980-84; cons. ecology sect. WHO, 1969; mem. Fla. com. Rare and Endangered Plants and Animals; mem. Fla. Panther Recovery team US Dept. Interior; mem. rodent specialist group Species Survival Commn.; mem. reclamation rsch. com. Fla. Ins. Phosphate Rsch.; mem. resource planning and mgmt. com.Kissimee River. Contbr. articles and chpts. to profl. jours. and books. Hon. trustee Fla. Defenders of Environment; bd. dirs. Fla. Audubon Soc.; mem. Fla. Nongame Wildlife Adv. Council, Peace River Basin Bd., Fla. Panther Tech. Adv. Council. Served with USAAF, 1944-46. bd., Inst. of Environ. Studies U. of South Fla. Fellow AAAS; mem. Am. Soc. Zoologists, Am. Soc. Mammalogists (pres. 1970-72, hon. mem. 1993, C. Hart Merriam award 1976), Ecol. Soc. Am., Soc. for Study of Evolution, Am. Soc. Naturalists, Wildlife Soc., Wildlife Disease Assn., Nature Conservancy (trustee Fla. chpt.), Fla. Acad. Scis. (pres. 1984-85, medalist 1995), Orgn. Biol. Field Stas. (pres. 1986-87), Phi Beta Kappa, Sigma Xi, Phi Kappa Phi, Phi Sigma. Home Phone: 863-465-4240. Personal E-mail: jlayne@strato.net.

LAYNE, JEFFREY TODD, urologist; b. Bklyn., Nov. 23, 1964; s. Alan Norman and Naomi Shirley Layne; m. Sandra Deborah Rafiy; children: Sabrina, Rebecca, Jessica. AB, Cornell U., Ithaca, NY, 1985; MD, SUNY, Stony Brook, 1989. Diplomate Am. Bd. Urology. Resident gen. surgery Tufts NEMC, Boston, 1989—91, resident urology, 1991—95; attending physician, ptnr. All Am. Urology, Plainview, NY, 1995—2006, Integrated Med. Profls., Nassau, NY, 2006—. Sec., bd. mem. Integrated Med. Profls., Nassau, NY, 2006. Mem.: Nassau Surg. Soc., Am. Urological Assn. Office: 1181 Old Country Rd Plainview NY 11803

LAYNE, JONATHAN K., lawyer; b. July 16, 1953; BA in Econs., Coll. William and Mary, 1975; MBA, Emory U., Atlanta, 1979, JD with distinction, 1979. Bar: Ga. 1979, Calif. 1979. Joined Gibson Dunn & Crutcher LLP, LA, 1979—, now ptnr. and co-chair corp. transactions and securities practice group. Mem. exec. com, Gibson Dunn & Crutcher. Mng. editor Emory Law Jour., 1978—79. Bd. dir. Calif. C. of C.; past chmn. and pres. John Thomas Dye Sch. Mem.: ABA, LA County Bar Assn., State Bar of Calif., Order of Coif. Office: Gibson Dunn & Crutcher LLP 2029 Century Pk E Los Angeles CA 90067-3026 Office Phone: 310-552-8641. Office Fax: 310-552-7053. Business E-Mail: jlayne@gibsondunn.com.

LAYTON, DONALD HARVEY, retired banker; b. May 9, 1950; s. Irving and Charlotte (Bell) L.; m. Sandra Lynn Lazo, June 1, 1974; children: Todd Samuel, Ross Charles. SB in Econs., SM in Econs., MIT, 1972; MBA, Harvard U., 1974. Rsch. asst. Harvard Bus. Sch., Boston, 1974-75; various positions through sr. mng. dir. Mfrs. Hanover Trust Co., NYC, 1975-91; sr. exec. v.p. Chemical Bank, NYC, 1992—95, vice-chmn., 1995, Chase Manhattan Bank, NYC, 1995-2001, J.P. Morgan Chase & Co., NYC, 2001—04; sr. advisor Securities and Fin. Markets Assn., NYC, 2006—. Mem. internat. capital markets adv. coun. Fed. Res. Bank N.Y., 1999—; mem. vis. com. for econs. MIT, 1999—; bd. dirs. Internat. Exec. Svc. Corps, 2004—, Partnership for the Homeless, 2004—, chmn. bd., 2007—; bd. dirs. Assured Guaranty Ltd., 2005—. Gov. Fgn. Policy Assn., 1998-

2006. Baker scholar Harvard U., 1974. Office: Securities and Fin Markets Assn 360 Madison Ave New York NY 10017 Office Phone: 646-637-9271. Personal E-mail: dhlaytonny@aol.com.

LAYTON, HARRY CHRISTOPHER, art director; b. Safford, Ariz., Nov. 17, 1938; s. Christopher E. and Eurilda (Welker) L.; m. Karol Barbara Kendall, July 11, 1964 (div. Jan. 1989); children: Deborah, Christopher, Joseph, Elisabeth, Faith, Aaron, Gretchen, Benjamin, Justin, Matthew, Peter. LHD, Sussex Coll., Eng., 1969; PhD, DRE, St. Matthew U., Ohio, 1970; DFA (hon.), London Inst. Applied Rsch., Ohio, 1972; DSC (hon.), London Inst. Applied Sci., 1972. Cert. clin. hypnotherapist. Pres., mgr. Poems, Art & Myths; pres., CEO Layton Studio Graphic Design, LA. Lectr. ancient art Serra Cath. H.S., Gardena, Calif., 1963-64, L.A. Dept. Parks and Recreation, summers 1962-64; interior decorator Cities of Hawthorne, Lawndale, Compton, Gardena, and Torrance, Calif., 1960-68. One-man shows Nahas Dept. Stores, 1962, 64; group shows include Gt. Western Savs. & Loan, Lawndale, 1962, Gardena Adult Sch., 1965, Serra Cath. H.S., 1963, Salon de Nations, Paris, 1983; represented in permanent collections Sussex Coll., Culver City-Foshey Masonic Lodge, Gt. Western Savs. & Loan; paintings inlcude The Fairy Princess, 1975, Nocturnal Covenant, 1963, Blindas Name, 1962, Creation, 1962; author numerous poems. Elder LDS Ch., Santa Monica, Calif., 1963—. Mem. Am. Hypnotherapy Assn., Internat. Soc. Artists, Internat. Platform Assn., Am. Security Coun., Soc. for Early Hist. Archaeology, Am. Councilor's Soc. Psychol. Counselors, Salon des Nation Paris Geneva, Ctr. Internat. Art Contemporain, Internat. Soc. Poets (disting.), Internat. Masonic Poetry Soc., Am. Legion, Masons (32d degree), Shriners, KT, Alpha Psi Omega. Republican. Home and Office: Layton Studio Graphic Design Inc 3654 Centinela Ave Apt 10 Los Angeles CA 90066-3147 Office Phone: 310-390-0543. Personal E-mail: poetlayton@hotmail.com. Business E-Mail: lsgd@ca.rr.com.

LAYTON, KENNITH F., neuroradiologist; BS, Okla. State U., Stillwater, 1996; MD, U. Okla., 1999. Diplomate Am. Bd. Radiology, 2004. Resident Baylor U. Med. Ctr., Dallas, 2000—04, attending physician, 2006—; postgrad. fellow Mayo Clinic, Rochester, Minn., 2004—06. Contbr. articles to profl. jours. Mem.: Am. Soc. Interventional and Theapeutic Neuroradiology. Office: Baylor U Med Ctr 3500 Gaston Ave Dallas TX 75246 Office Phone: 214-820-3219.

LAYTON, ROBERT E., JR., retired aeronautical engineer; b. Corsicana, Tex., Jan. 22, 1925; m. Margaret Marshall, June 7, 1947; children: Marsha Layton Anderson, Robert E. III. Grad., US Naval Air Tech. Tng. Ctr., Norman, Okla., 1945; BS in Aero. Engring., Tex. A&M Coll., College Station, 1947. Registered profl. engr., Tex., 1951. Sales engr. Layton Supply Co., Tyler, Tex., 1947—50; owner, CEO Layton Engring. Co., Tyler, 1950—86; regional adminstr. US EPA Region 6, Dallas, 1987—92; dir. pilot program in environ. edn. U. Tex., Tyler, 1992—93; ret., 1993. Apptd. Tex. State Bd. Registration for Profl. Engrs., 1975—83, chmn. bd., 1983—85; mem. Nat. Coun. Engring. Examiners, 1976—83, Nat. Law Enforcement Com., 1976—83, chmn., 1981. Co-author: Manual for Law Enforcement P.E.'s, 1988. Chmn. emeritus Hist. Aviation Meml. Mus., Tyler, Tex.; adv. com. vocat. tng. program Tyler Ind. Sch. Dist., 1975—80; adv. com. tech. tng. Tyler Jr. Coll., 1975—80; adv. coun., devel. coun. Sch. Medicine Tex. A&M U., adv. coun. Sch. Engring., R&D, 1996—2004, adv. coun. fellowt, 2004; charter bd. dirs., former chmn. Good Will Industries East Tex.; past adv. bd. Leadership Tyler, Mother Frances Hosp.; past pres. Tyler Hosp. Authority; past chmn. bldg. com. Med. Ctr. Hosp., past bd. dirs.; past chmn. airport adv. bd. City of Tyler, past chmn. appeals bd. bldg. codes, mem. city coun., 1974—76, mayor, 1975—76; mem. ch. orch. Green Acres Bapt. Ch., Tyler; past bd. dirs. East Tex. Hosp. Found., Med. Ctr. Hosp. With USN, 1944—46, PTO. Master: USAF Meml. Found.; mem.: DAV (life), VFW (life), NRA (life), ASHRAE (life; pres. 1989, charter mem. East Tex. chpt., chpt. pres.), NSPE (life), Am. WW II Mus. Gt. Britain, Nat. Soc. Environ. Cons., Soc. Mil. Engrs. (life; amb. avication assn.), Tex. Soc. Profl. Engrs. (life Outstanding Engr. of Yr. 1977), Tailhook Assn., Tex. Rifle Assn. (life), Am. Legion (life), Air Force Assn. (life), Am. Def. Preparedness (life), Shriners (life), Masons (life), Rotary (life; pres. 1973, dist. gov. 1975—76). Home: 1811 Rickety Ln Tyler TX 75703-1633

LAYTON, ROBERT GLENN, radiologist; b. Bklyn., Oct. 14, 1946; s. Irving and Charlotte (Bell) L.; m. Judith Helene Bohrer, May 31, 1969; children: Andrew, Julia. BS, Union Coll., 1968; MD, Boston U., 1972. Diplomate Am. Bd. Radiology. Resident in radiology Boston City Hosp., 1972-75; jr. attending radiologist L.I. Jewish Hosp., Hillside, NY, 1975-76; staff radiologist Cedars Med. Ctr., Miami, Fla., 1978-98, chief of radiology, 1999—2003; assoc. med. dir. MedSolutions Inc., Franklin, Tenn., 2004—. Radiologist Highland Park Gen. Hosp., Miami, 1978-84; clin. asst. prof. U. Miami Sch. Med., 1985-87. Pres. Michael-Ann Russell Jewish Cmty. Ctr., Miami, 1980-82; bd. dirs. Jewish Cmty. Ctrs. South Fla., 1982-86; trustee Temple Sinai of North Dade, North Miami Beach, 1982-01, v.p., 1985-92, pres., 1992-94; nat. bd. dirs. Union Am. Hebrew Congregations, trustee, 1999-2004. Served to maj. USAF, 1976-78. Mem. AMA, Am. Coll. Radiology, Colo. Radiol. Soc., Begg Soc., Alpha Omega Alpha. Avocations: contemporary art, skiing, golf. Office Phone: 615-468-4181. Personal E-mail: rglmd1@yahoo.com.

LAYTON, WILLIAM GEORGE, consultant, retired human resources and import/export company executive; b. Missouri Valley, Iowa, Sept. 11, 1931; s. George Holbert and Margaret (Wilson) L.; m. Caroline R. Tiffany, June 27, 1953; children: Kathleen Layton Medl, Sara Layton Howe, Thomas William. BA, Coe Coll., 1953; MA, U. Ill., 1955. Indsl. rels. trainee Procter & Gamble Co., Cin., 1955-57, pers. specialist, 1957-62, indsl. rels. mgr. France, 1962-66, pers. mgr. European Tech. Ctr., 1966-69, pers. mgr. internat., 1969-72; v.p. human resources Food Svc. div. Heublein, Inc., Louisville, 1972-77; sr. v.p. human resources Holiday Inns, Inc., Memphis, 1977-83; pres. Layton Group, St. Petersburg, Fla., 1983—2001; sr. ptnr. Johnson-Layton Co. Mgmt. Cons., L.A. and St. Petersburg, 1985-95; pres. CompCom, Inc., 1994-97; chmn., CEO Appliances Internat., Inc., 1997—2002; cons. Transylvania County NC Econ. Devel. Dept., 2004—. Bd. dirs., pres. Jr. Achievement of Memphis, 1981-83; mem. Tenn. Jobs Tng. Coordinating Coun., 1982-88; mem. Pvt. Industry Coun. of Memphis and Shelby County, 1982-88; mem. Pres.'s Coun., Rhodes Coll., Memphis, 1983-90. Served with USAF, 1953-55. Mem.: Coun. Mgmt. Cons. (Sr. Examiner Sterling Quality award Fla. 1994), Inst. Mgmt. Cons. (cert. mgmt. cons.), Am. Mgmt. Assn. (human resources coun. 1981—83), Rotary, Phi Beta Kappa. Independent. Presbyterian. E-mail: wglayton@citcom.net.

LAZANSKY, EDWARD, artist, art educator; b. Bklyn., Oct. 31, 1930; s. Charles and Jeannette Lazansky; 1 child, Nadja Carol. BFA, Syracuse U., NY, 1948—52; MA, Oberlin Coll., Ohio, 1953—54. Instr. art Swain Sch. Design (now U. Mass.), New Bedford, 1964—66, Queens Coll., NY, 1967—68, SI CC, NY, 1967—68; assoc. prof. Pratt Inst., Bklyn., 1967—, prof. art & design, 1967—. Theatrical designer/artist United Scenic Artists, NYC, 1980—90. Artwork for films, The Verdict, 1980, Rollover, 1981, Cotton Club, 1982, set designer, The Making of Americans, Judson Poets Theater, 1972, designer, Play by H. Busch, La Mama Theater Group, 1973, Listen to Me, Judson Poets Theater, 1973, The Coop, Theater for the New City, 1972, extensive work in theatrical design, theater prodns. for numerous groups, paintings, Factory, Syracuse Mus. (First Prize award, 1952), paintings at art students' league, 1963, exhibitions include, Everson Mus., Syracuse, 1953, March, James, and Phoenix Galleries, NYC, 1959—60, exhibitions include prints, Butler Art Inst., Ohio, 1953, Bklyn. Mus., 1953, Allen Art Mus., Oberlin Art Gallery, 1953, exhibitions include paintings, Bertha Schaefer Gallery, 1968, Rubelle and Norman Schaefer Gallery, 2002, Woodstock Mus. Art, 2006, Represented in permanent collections, Dr. Lore Perls Estate, David K. Gordon, Ira and Sally Freedman, Ura Mohr, Lawrence Kornfeld, Estelle Horowitz, Louise McAllen, S. and G. Bierhorst, Marjorie Jarecki, and numerous others; stage designer LaMama Theater Grp., The Judson Poets Theater, The Theater for the New City, scenic artist NBC TV, Paramount Pictures, NY City Ballet. Pvt. first class US Army, 1954—56, Germany. Decorated Army of Occupation US Army; grantee Harriet Hale Woolley scholarship, 1960. Avocations: fossil hunting and collecting, painting, travel, hiking, music. Home: PO Box 96 Woodstock NY 12498 Office: Pratt Inst 200 Willoughby Ave Brooklyn NY 12498 Home Phone: 845-679-8594. Personal E-mail: edlazan@yahoo.com.

LAZAR, CHARNA L., education educator, retired CIA officer, security consultant; BA in Polit. Sci., CCNY, 1968; Cert. in French Lang. & Civilization, U. Paris, 1973; MS in Pub. Adminstrn., George Wash. U., 1979. Lic. pvt. investigator Fla., 2006. Polit. coord. Robert F. Kennedy Presdl. Campaign, Garden City, NY, 1968; clandestine svc. officer US CIA, Washington, 1969—94; pvt. investigator, security cons. Wonder Woman Investigations, Boca Raton, Fla., 2003—06; regional coord. Safe Cmty. Initiative (Am. Jewish Com. & local police agencies), Boca Raton, 2003—06; adj. prof. Fla. Atlantic U., Boca Raton, 2005—. Guest lectr. Boca Raton Resort and Club, 2006—. Mem. fundraising com. Boca Helping Hands, 2003; cert. mem. Cmty. Emergency Response Team, Boca Raton, 2003—; v.p. Boca Raton Dog Club, 1999—2001; elected mem. Palm Beach County Dem. Exec. Com., Boca Raton, 2000—04; dem. candidate Fla. Ho. Reps., Boca Raton, 2001—02; exec. vice-chair Va. Women's Polit. Caucus, 1979—81; candidate Palm Beach County Commn., 2004; mem. ambassadorial com. Am. Jewish Com., Palm Beach, Fla., 2001—05; life mem. Ctrl. Intelligence Retirees Assn., McLean, Va., 1994; chpt. v.p. Assn. Former Intelligence Officers, Palm Beach County, 2000. Mem.: Assn. Former Intelligence Officers (life; Palm Beach County chpt. v.p. 2000), Ctrl. Intelligence Retirees Assn. (life), Boca Raton Dog Club (v.p. 1999—2001), Boca Raton Martin Luther King Meml. Found. (assoc.; fund-raising com. 1997—2003), Am. Mensa, Weimaraner Club of South Fla. Democrat. Avocations: pure-bred dogs (weimaraners), public speaking (homeland security issues), political activism & consulting. Office: PO Box 272482 Boca Raton FL 33427-2482

LAZAR, ERIC LOREN, pediatric surgeon, director; m. Lorraine May Spano; children: Paige Sara, Kimberly Grace, Olivia Renee. BA, U. Pa., Phila., 1985; MD, Coll. Physicians and Surgeons, NY, 1989; MS, Columbia U., NY, 2004. Lic. Surgery Am. Bd. Surgery, 1997, Pediat. Surgery Am. Bd. Surgery, 2000. Asst. prof. surgery Columbia U., 1998—2004; surgery tng. program dir. Morristown Meml. Hosp., NJ, 2004—; attending surgeon Goryeb Children's Hosp., 2004—. Cons. Island Peer Rev., NYC, 1998—; faculty mem., clin. trials course ACS, Chgo. Fellow: Am. Acad. Pediat., ACS; mem.: Am. Pediatric Surgery Assn. (trauma com. 2003—06), Soc. for Clin. Trials. Avocations: skiing, sports. Office: Morristown Meml Hosp 100 Madison Ave Morristown NJ 07962 Home Phone: 973-895-2399; Office Phone: 973-971-5684. Office Fax: 973-290-7350. Personal E-mail: ericlazar@hotmail.com. Business E-Mail: eric.lazar@atlantichealth.org.

LAZAR, HAROLD LEE, cardiothoracic surgeon; AB, Boston U., 1970, MD, 1974. Diplomate Am. Bd. Surgery, Am. Bd. Thoracic Surgery. Resident in gen. surgery U. Mich. Med. Ctr., Ann Arbor, 1974-81; rsch. fellow in cardiac surgery UCLA Med. Ctr., 1977-79; fellow in cardiothoracic surgery Columbia-Presbyn. Med. Ctr., NYC, 1981-83; attending surgeon Univ. Hosp., Boston, 1984—, Boston City Hosp., 1984—, VA Med. Ctr., Boston, 1990—. Asst. dir. thoracic surgery Boston City Hosp., 1990—; chmn. Mass. Consortium Lung Transplantation, Boston, 1992; from asst. prof. to prof. cardiothoracic surgery Med. Sch., Boston (Mass.) U., 1984-98, prof., 1998—. Editor: Current Therapy for Acute Coronary Ischemin, 1993; mem. editl. bd. Jour. Thoracic and Cardiovascular Surgery, 2002-. Fellow ACS, Am. Coll. Cardiology, Mass. Med. Soc.; mem. Am. Coll. Chest Physicians (sec. sect. cardiac surgery 1993—), Am. Assn. Thoracic Surgery, Soc. Thoracic Surgery, Soc. Univ. Surgeons. Office: Boston U Med Ctr 88 E Newton St Boston MA 02118-2308 Office Phone: 617-638-7350. E-mail: harold.lazar@bmc.org.

LAZAR, IRVING, psychologist; b. NYC, Feb. 20, 1926; s. Charles and Sylvia L.; m. Jules M. Marquart, Dec. 24, 1981; children: Kathryn S., James Bradford, Richard Alan. BS, CCNY, 1948; MA, Columbia U., 1950, PhD, 1954. Intern Menninger Clinic, Topeka, 1946—47; instr. clin. psychology U. Rochester, NY, 1948—49; instr. psychology Bard Coll., Amandale-on-Hudson, NY, 1949—50; instr. child devel. U. Ill. Coll. Edn., Urbana, 1950—54; assoc. chief mental health sect. Nev. State Dept. Health, Las Vegas, 1954—60; dir. Peterson-Guedel Family Ctr., Beverly Hills, Calif., 1960—64; exec. dir Neumeyer Found., Beverly Hills, 1963—68; western mgr. Kirschner Assoc., LA, 1968—70; assoc. dir. Appalachian Regional Commn., Washington, 1969—72; prof. dept. human svc. studies Cornell U., 1972—91, prof. emeritus, 1991—; external faculty Santa Fe Inst., 1994—99; rsch. prof. Peabody Coll. Vanderbilt U., Nashville, 1991—98, resident scholar Kennedy Ctr. Rsch. Human Devel. Peabody Coll., 1991—. Cons. in field. Contbr. articles to profl. jour. Trustee Coalition for Quality Children's Media, Santa Fe, 1994—. Rsch. Fellow Population Inst., East-West Ctr., Honolulu, 1987. Home: 313 Cana Cir Nashville TN 37205 Home Phone: 615-354-1505; Office Phone: 615-354-1505. Business E-Mail: irving@santafe.edu.

LAZAR, JILL SUE, home healthcare company executive; b. Oak Park, Ill., June 15, 1954; d. Norton David and Carol Ellen (Kaufmann) Freyer; m. Bruce Horwich, Aug. 21, 1976 (div. Sept. 1982); 1 child, Mathew Freyer Horwich; m. Neil Lazar, Nov. 23, 1986. BS in Mktg., No. Ill. U., 1975. Mktg. rsch. assoc. McDonald's Corp., Oak Brook, Ill., 1976-80; renewal coord. Time, Inc., Chgo., 1984-87; product mgr. Macmillan Directory Div., Wilmette, Ill., 1987-92; with DependiCare, Broadview, Ill., 1992—. Mem. provider adv. panels Chad Therapeutics, Aradigm Corp., others. Mem. Chgo. Health Execs. Forum. Avocations: swimming, reading. Office: DependiCare 1815 Gardner Rd Broadview IL 60155-4401

LAZAR, JOHN EDWARD, social services administrator, not-for-profit developer; b. Bklyn., Mar. 24, 1950; s. John and Elizabeth (Titch) Lazar. BA, St. John's U., Bklyn., 1971; postgrad., Bklyn. Coll., 1972-73; MDiv, Sem. of Immaculate Conception, 1980. Ordained Roman Cath. Ch., 1980; cert. tchr. N.Y. English tchr. N.Y.C. Bd. Edn., Bklyn., 1973-79; clergyman Roman Cath. Diocese of Bklyn., 1980-93; pres. POMOC, Inc., NYC, 1981-84; dir. housing Argus Cmty., Inc., Bronx, NY, 1993-96; devel. cons. Met. Cmty. Ch., LA, 1997—; exec. dir. San Fernando Valley Am. Cancer Soc., Sherman Oaks, Calif., 1998—2001, sr. v.p. So. Atlantic divsn., 2007—; regional v.p. Greater Bay Area Redwood Empire region Am. Cancer Soc., 2001—07. Exec. dir. Peregrinatio Ad Petri Sedem-U.S. Office of Pilgrimages, Vatican City, 1985—86. Author: Outpouring the Spirit: Gay and Lesbian Spirituality in the Judeo Christian Tradition, 1996; TV show host Polish Profiles, 1989—93, prodr., host City of West Hollywood Town Hall-Gay Spirituality, 1999, 2000, prodr., moderator, 2001. Commr. City of West Hollywood Lesbian and Gay Adv. Bd., Calif., 1998—2001, co-chair; bd. dirs. City Vol. Corps, NYC, 1990—96; v.p. Polish Am. Congress, NYC, 1989—93; co-prodr. civic celebration Bklyn. Outdoor Mus. Art, 1993; mem. com. Mayor's Planning Com. L.A. Vol. Festival, 1998, 1999; chmn. N.Y.C. Compter.'s Polish Adv. Com., 1982—89, 1994—96; panelist City of West Hollywood Town Hall Election, 2000; co.-chmn. polit. action com. Alice B. Toklas GLBT Dem. Club, 2002—05; co-chmn. PAC Alice B. Toklas GLBT Dem. Club, 2005—; moderator LGBT World AIDS Day Program, 2005; bd. dirs. Stonewall Dem. Club, LA. Named Hon. Alumnus, Our Lady of the Lake Sem., 1982, Citizen of Yr., Polish Am. World, 1982; recipient Pres.'s award, Stonewall Dem. Club, 1998, Commendation award, N.Y.C. Comptr., 1995. Mem.: Polish Inst. Arts and Scis. in Am., Inc., So. Calif. Assn. Non Profit Housing, Inc., Commonwealth Club (moderator LGBT Spirituality Panel 2004, moderator Get to Know Your LGBT customer 2005, chmn. GLBT forums 2005—, moderator World AIDS Day program 2005, moderator, discussion with Craig Newmark and Betty Sullivan 2006). Democrat. Avocations: bicycling, reading, prestidigitation, downhill skiing. Office: Am Cancer Soc 1700 Webster St Oakland CA 94612 Home: 1220 N St NW Apt 2B Washington DC 20005 Office Phone: 510-452-5229. Personal E-mail: jelazer324@aol.com.

LAZAR, LUDMILA, concert pianist, music educator; b. Celje, Slovenia; married; two children. MusB, Roosevelt U., 1963, MusM, 1964; D of Musical Arts, Northwestern U., 1987. Faculty Roosevelt U., Chgo., 1967—, prof. piano Chgo. Musical Coll., 1988—, prof. emerita, 2003—, chmn. keyboard dept., 1983—2003. Lectr., demonstrator in field. Rsch. grant Roosevelt U., 1988, 96; recipient Goethe Inst. award, 1987, Outstanding Coll. Tchr. award Roosevelt U., 1981; named to All Star Profs. Team Chgo. Tribune, 1993. Mem. AAUP, Music Tchrs. Nat. Assn. (master tchr. cert. 1991), European Piano Tchrs. Assn., Ill. State Music Tchrs. Assn., Soc. Am. Musicians (pres., v.p.), Coll. Music Soc., Musicians Club of Women (v.p.), Mu Phi Epsilon (pres., v.p.). Office: Roosevelt U 430 S Michigan Ave Chicago IL 60605-1394 Office Phone: 312-341-3779.

LAZAR, MARIOARA, psychiatrist; b. Traian, Romania, Nov. 4, 1957; arrived in U.S., 1991; d. Constantin and Cristina Conda; m. Stefan Lazar, Feb. 19, 1994 (div.); 1 child, Emanuel. MD with honors, U. Medicine, Timisoara, Romania, 1994. Resident Harlem Hosp., NYC, 1989—2001, fellow child and adolescent psychiatry, 2001—03; psychiatrist Fla. Med. Ctr., Ft. Lauderdale, Fla., 2003—04, Broward Gen. Hosp., Ft. Lauderdale, 2003—04, Parkway Hosp., Miami, 2003—04, Aventura Hosp., Fla., 2003—04; pvt. practice psychiatrist Weston, Fla., 2004—; psychiatrist South Fla. Reception Ctr., Miami, 2004—; med. dir. child psychiatry Meml. Regional Hosp., Hollywood, Fla., 2006—. Contbr. articles to profl. jours. Mem.: Am. Acad. Child and Adolescent Psychiatry, Am. Psychiat. Assn. Avocations: classical music, history, travel. Office: 1040 Weston Rd 210 Weston FL 33326

LAZAR, MAX SEYMOUR, retired pharmaceutical company executive; b. Bklyn., Dec. 6, 1943; s. Harry and Bessie L.; m. Sherry Dorf, Sept. 5, 1965; children: Lawrence Jay, Lisa Jill. BA in Chemistry, CUNY, 1966. Lab. analyst, supr. Hoffmann-LaRoche Inc., Nutley, NJ, 1966—69; dir. quality control Roche Vitamins & Fine Chems., Belvidere, NJ, 1969—86, dir. tech. svcs., 1986—88, divsnl. dir. quality assurance Nutley, NJ, 1988—89; asst. v.p., dir. corp. quality assurance Hoffmann-LaRoche Inc., Nutley, NJ, 1989—93, v.p. quality assurance, 1993—94, v.p. FDA and drug enforcement adminstrn. (DEA) compliance, 1994—2001; ret., 2001; pres. FDA Regulatory Compliance Cons., Surprise, Ariz., 2001—. Vice-chair pharm. waters expert com. USP Pharm. Waters, 2000-05, mem. expert com. 2005—. Mem. editl. bd. Jour. Current Good Mfg. Practices, 1997—; contbr. articles to profl. jours., including Pharm. Tech. Bd. dirs. Parkette Nat. Gymnastics Tng. Ctr., Allentown, Pa., 1980-2001. Recipient Spl. citation for ICH Q7A work, USA FDA Commr., 2004. Mem. Am. Chem. Soc., Pharm. Rsch. & Mfrs. Assn. (group leader internat. conf. on hamonization Q7A), Am. Soc. Quality. Avocations: amateur radio operator, photography. Home and Office: 15359 W Sierra Vista Dr Surprise AZ 85374 Office Phone: 623-556-0556. E-mail: maxslazar@aol.com.

LAZAR, RANDE HARRIS, otolaryngologist; b. NYC, Feb. 27, 1951; s. Irving and Dorothy (Tartasky) L.; m. Linda Zishuk, Aug. 11, 1974; 1 child, Lauren K. BA, Bklyn. Coll., 1973; MD, U. Autonoma de Guadalajara, Mexico, 1978; postgrad., N.Y. Med. Coll., 1978-79. Diplomate Am. Bd. Otolaryngology-Head and Neck Surgery; lic. physician, N.Y., Ohio, Tenn. Gen. surgery resident Cornell-North Shore Community Hosp., Manhasset, NY, 1979-80, Cleve. Clinic Found., 1980-81, otolaryngology-head and neck surgery resident, 1980-84, chief resident dept. otolaryngology & communicative disorder, 1983-84; physician Otolaryngology Cons. Memphis, 1984—. Fellow pathology head and neck dept. otolaryngologic pathology Armed Forces Inst. Pathology, Washington, 1983; pediatric otolaryngology fellow Le Bonheur Children's Med. Ctr., Memphis, 1984-85, dir. pediatric otolaryngology fellowship tng., 1989—, chief surgery, 1989, chief staff East Surgery Ctr.; chmn. dept. otolaryngology head and neck surgery Meth. Health Systems, 1990-91; courtesy staff Bapt. Meml. Hosp., Bapt. Meml. Hosp.-East, Eastwood Med. Ctr., Meth. Hosp., Germantown, Tenn.; chief dept. otolaryngology Les Passees Rehab. Ctr., 1988—. Contbr. articles to profl. jours. Bd. dirs. Bklyn. Tech. Found. Recipient award of honor Am. Acad. Otolaryngology-Head and Neck Surgery, 1991. Fellow Internat. Coll. Surgeons; mem. AMA, Am. Acad. Otolaryngology-Head and Neck Surgery, Am. Acad. Facial Plastic and Reconstructive Surgery, Am. Acad. Otolaryngic Allergy, Centurions Deafness Rsch. Found., Am. Auditory Soc., Nat. Hearing Assn., Soc. Ear, Nose Throat Advances in Children, Am. Soc. Laser Medicine and Surgery, So. Med. Assn., N.Y. Acad. Scis., Tenn. Med. Soc., Tenn. Acad. Otolaryngology-Head and Neck Surgery, Memphis and Shelby County Med. Soc., Memphis/Mid South Soc. Pediatrics Office: Otolaryngology Cons Memphis 791 Estate Pl Memphis TN 38120 E-mail: Lazarent@aol.com.

LAZAR, RAYMOND MICHAEL, lawyer, educator; b. Mpls., July 16, 1939; s. Simon and Hessie (Teplin) L; children: Mark, Deborah; m. Judith Mares Lazar. BBA, U. Minn., 1961, JD, 1964. Bar: Minn. 1964, U.S. Dist. Ct. Minn. 1964. Spl. asst. atty. gen. State of Minn., St. Paul, 1964-66; pvt. practice Mpls., 1966-72; ptnr. Lapp, Lazar, Laurie & Smith, Mpls., 1972-86; ptnr., officer Fredrikson & Byron P.A., Mpls., 1986—. Lectr. various continuing edn. programs, 1972—; adj. prof. law U. Minn., Mpls., 1983-99. Fellow Am. Acad. Matrimonial Lawyers; mem. ABA (chair divorce laws and procedures com. family law sect. 1993-94), Minn. Bar Assn., Hennepin County Bar Assn. (chair family law sect. 1978-79). Home: 400 River St Minneapolis MN 55401 Office: Fredrikson & Byron PA 200 S 6th St Ste 4000 Minneapolis MN 55402-3314 Office Phone: 612-492-7121. E-mail: rlazar@fredlaw.com.

LAZAR, THEODORE AARON, retired manufacturing executive, lawyer; b. Chgo, July 16, 1920; s. Philip and Rena (Goodman) L.; m. Betty Jean Papermaster, July 6, 1952; children: Mark D., Paul A., Nancy Paula. JD, John Marshall Law Sch., Chgo., 1951. Bar: Ill. 1951, Wis. 1962, Ohio 1966. Sole practice, Chgo., 1951-62; asst. corp. counsel City of Chgo., 1956-59; atty. NLRB, Chgo., 1962—64, LA, 1964—65; corp. counsel Lancaster Colony Corp., Columbus, Ohio, 1965-83, v.p. law, 1983-88, ret., 1988. Sgt. Air Corps US Army, 1942—46. Mem.: Columbus Bar Assn. Home: 270 Bryant Ave Columbus OH 43085-3009

LAZAR, ZOE L., psychologist; b. NYC, June 27, 1948; d. Ira Gerald and Charlotte (Silverstein) Levy; m. Ira Lazar, Apr. 5, 1970; children: Alexander David, Samantha Chloe, Damien Jacob. BA, Brandeis U., 1969; MEd, Boston U., 1972, EdD, 1974; cert. in psychoanalysis, William Alanson White Inst., NYC, 1984. Lic. psychologist, N.Y. Intern in clin. psychology McLean Hosp./Harvard U. Med. Sch., Belmont, Mass., 1973-74; staff psychologist out-patient clinic Coney Island Hosp., Bklyn., 1974-75; pvt. practice psychology and psychoanalysis Scarsdale, N.Y., 1976—; instr. psychology in psychiatry Cornell U. Med. Coll., NY, 1978—82, clin. asst. prof. psychology in psychiatry NY, 1982—; profl. assoc. in psychology N.Y. Hosp., 1978-82, asst. attending psychologist, 1982—. Pub. BaBoom Press, 2002. Contbr. articles to profl. jours. Cornell U. fellow, 1975-77. Mem. APA, N.Y. State Psychol. Assn., Westchester

Psychol. Assn., William Alanson White Soc. Avocations: theater, dance, hiking, gardening, bicycling. Home Phone: 914-723-9180; Office Phone: 914-723-4893. Personal E-mail: zoelazer@yahoo.com.

LAZARAN, FRANK, former retail executive; b. 1957; BS, Calif. State U., Long Beach; Masters, Calif. State U. Group v.p. sales, advt. and merchandising Ralphs Grocery Co., Compton, Calif.; sr. v.p. sales & merchandising Randalls Food Markets Inc., Houston, 1997—99, pres., 1999—2002; exec. v.p., COO Winn-Dixie Stores, Inc., Jacksonville, Fla., 2002—03, pres., CEO, 2003—04, Marsh Supermarkets, Indpls., 2006—. Mem. bd. dirs. Winn-Dixie Stores, Inc., 2003—04. Office: Marsh Supermarkets 9800 Crosspoint Blvd Indianapolis IN 46256*

LAZARCHICK, JOHN, hematologist, educator; b. Pottsville, Pa., Nov. 1, 1942; s. John and Ann (Peshock) L.; m. Lynda Lazarchick; 1 child, John Jeffery. BA, Lafayette Coll., Easton, Pa., 1964; MD, Jefferson Med. U., 1968. Asst. prof. U. Conn. Health Sci. Ctr., Farmington, Conn., 1977-79; from asst. prof. to prof. Med. U. S.C., Charleston, 1979—. Author: Clinical Hematology and Fundamentals of Hemostasis, 1988; contbr. over 100 articles to profl. jours. Lt. comdr. USN, 1972-75. Rsch. grantee NIH, 1980-83, Ames, Miles Laboratories, 1985-90, Wyeth-Ayerst Corp., 1989-91. Fellow ACP; mem. Assn. Clin. Scientists (chmn. immunohematology, 1988—), Am. Soc. Hematology, Hematopathology Soc. Office: 171 Ashley Ave Charleston SC 29425-0001 Office Phone: 843-792-3424. Business E-Mail: lazarj@musc.edu.

LAZARCIK, GREGOR, economist, educator, financial research company executive; b. Horna Streda, Slovakia, Mar. 10, 1923; came to U.S., 1953, naturalized, 1958; s. Gaspar and Maria (Rehak) L.; m. Theresa M. Good, Aug. 14, 1971. BS, State Coll., Slovakia, 1945; MS, Coll. Agr., Brno, Czechoslovakia, 1948; cert., Swiss Inst. Tech., Zurich, 1949; AM, U. Strasbourg, France, 1952; LLM, LLD (fellow), U. Paris, 1953; PhD (fellow), Columbia, 1960. Asst. to mgr. Ctrl. Cutter Dairy, Lucerne, Switzerland, 1948-49; controller dairy products Agrl. Syndicate, Hazebruck, France, 1949-50; with Rsch. Project on Nat. Income Columbia U., NYC, 1956-00, sr. rsch. economist, 1961-70, seminar assoc., 1970—; pres., chmn. bd. L.W. Internat. Financial Rsch., Inc., NYC, 1961-00. Lectr. econs. Hunter Coll., CUNY, 1963-64, Columbia U., 1964-68; prof. econs. SUNY, 1968-85, CUNY, 1984—. Author: Le Commerce en Matiere Agricole Entre l'Europe de l'Ouest et l'Europe del'Est, 1959; co-author: Czechoslovak National Income and Product, 1947-56, 1962, The Performance of Socialist Agriculture, 1963, Scientific Research and its Relation to Earnings and Stock Prices, 1965, Comparison of Agricultural and Nonagricultural Income, 1937, 48-65, 1968, Defense, Education and Health Expenditures and Their Relation to GNP in Eastern Europe, 1978, Economic Growth in Eastern Europe, 1965-82, 1983, Agricultural Output and Productivity in Eastern Europe and Some Comparisons with the USSR and USA, 1985; contbr. to East European Economics Post-Helsinki, 1977, Pressure for Reform in the East European Economics, Joint Econ. Com., U.S. Congress, 1989, The Development of the Private Sector in East Central Europe, 1993, Overview of Transportation Infrastructure in East Central Europe, 1994, The Status of and Prospects for Agriculture in East Central Europe, 1996, Energy in Eastern Europe: Production, Consumption, and Trade, 1970-1987, 1999. Mem. Am. Econ. Assn., Am. Regional Sci. Assn., Assn. Comparative Economic Studies, Am. Assn. Advancement Slavic Studies. Roman Catholic. Address: 100 La Salle St Apt 17-b New York NY 10027-4730 E-mail: gregorlazarcik@aol.com.

LAZARE, AARON, dean, psychiatrist; b. Newark, Feb. 14, 1936; s. H. Benjamin and Anne (Storfer) L.; m. Louise Cannon; children: Robert, Jacqueline, David, Sam, Sarah, Hien, Thomas, Naomi. AB, Oberlin Coll., 1957; MD, Case Western Reserve U., 1961. Intern in medicine Bronx Mcpl. Hosp. Ctr., NY, 1961-62; resident in psychiatry Mass. Mental Health Ctr., 1962-65; asst. in psychiatry Mass. Gen. Hosp., Boston, 1967-68; chief day hosp. inpatient unit Yale-New Haven Hosp., 1967-68; assoc. dir. adult outpatient psychiatry Mass. Gen. Hosp., Boston, 1968-70, dir. adult outpatient psychiatry, 1970-75, acting dir. residency tng., 1972, dir. outpatient psychiatry, 1975-82, dep. chief psychiatry, 1976-82, clin. dir. psychiatry, 1978-82; prof. Harvard U., 1982; prof., chmn. dept. psychiatry U. Mass. Med. Ctr., Worcester, 1982—90, interim dean, 1989-90, dean, 1990—, chancellor, 1991—. Editor: Outpatient Psychiatry, 1979, 1989, 2nd edit.; contbr. articles to profl. jours.; co-author of books in field. Capt. US Army, 1965—67. Named for Disting. Pub. Svc. Commonwealth of Mass., honorable mention U. Mass., 1987, Commonwealth of Mass., U. Mass., Boston, 1988, Brotherhood award NCCJ, 1992, Maimonides award for outstanding commitment as a physician and educator Anti-Defamation League New Eng., 1993, Friend and Leader award Mass. Assn. Mental Health Inc., 2001. Mem. AAAS, AMA, Am. Psychiat. Assn. (Benjamin Rush award 1992), Mass. Psychiat. Soc. Office: U Mass Med Ctr Off Chancellor 55 Lake Ave N Worcester MA 01655-0002

LAZAREFF, JORGE ANTONIO, neurosurgeon, researcher; b. Buenos Aires, Jan. 11, 1953; s. Nicolas and Vera (Budinska) L.; m. Ines Garcia Lloret, May 28, 1982; children: Nicolás, Ana Maria. MD, Nat. Univ. Buenos Aires, 1977. cert. neurosurgeon Edu. Comm. for Foreign Med. Grads., 1980, Mexican Coun. Neurosurgeons, 1991, Medical Bd. of Calif., 1993, Colegio Argentino de Neurocirujanos, 1996. Resident in neurosurgery Hosp. de Niños, Buenos Aires, 1979-83; chief resident in neurosurgery Hosp. Fernandez, Buenos Aires, 1983-84; registrar in neurosurgery Groote Schuur Hosp., Red Cross Meml. Children Hosp., Cape Town, 1984-86; rsch. fellow dept. surgery U. Alberta, Edmonton, Can., 1986-88; head dept. exptl. surgery Hosp. Infantil de Mexico, 1988-91, head dept. neurosurgery, 1991—93; assist. prof. dept. neurosurgery UCLA Med. Ctr., Los Angeles, Calif., 1993—99, dir. pediatric neurosurgery, 1997—, assoc. prof. dept. neurosurgery, 1999—; co. dir., Cerebral Palsy Clinic, co. dir., Pediatric Brain Tumor Prog. Mem. rsch. com. Hosp. Infantil de Mexico, 1991. Inventor biopsy probe for sterotactic brain surgery; separated conjoined twins, 2002; author papers on neurosurgery and neurophistology. Recipient Rsch. award for spasticity Aaron Saenz Found., 1991, Ulrich Batzdorf, M.D. Faculty Teaching award, 2001. Mem. Soc. for Neurosci., 1991, Sociedad Mexicana de Cirugia Neurologica, 1992, Research Soc. of Neurological Surgeons, 1993, Internat. Soc. for Pediatric Neurosurgery, 1993, Academic Senate, UCLA, 1994, Johnson Comprehensive Cancer Ctr. 1994. Roman Catholic. Office: UCLA Med Ctr Divsn Neurosurgery PO Box 957039 Los Angeles CA 90095-7039

LAZARIDIS, MIKE, information technology executive, entrepreneur; b. Istanbul, Mar. 14, 1961; s. Nick and Dorothy Lazaridis; m. Ophelia Lazaridis; 2 children. DEng (hon.), U. Waterloo, 2000; Doctorate (hon.), McMaster U., 2005. Founder, pres., co-CEO Rsch. in Motion, 1984—; founder Perimeter Inst., 2000—. Chancellor U. Waterloo, 2003—, also bd. gov.; mem. Natural Sciences Engring. Rsch. Coun., Ont. Rsch. and Innovation Coun. Co-recipient Ernest C. Manning Prin. award, 2002; named Officer to the Order of Can., 2006, Canada's Nation Builder of Yr., Ontario's Entrepreneur of Yr.; named one of 26 Most Fascinating Entrepreneurs, Inc.com, Top 10 Technology Innovators, InfoWorld, 2002, World's 100 Most Influential People, Time Mag., 2005; recipient technical Emmy award, 1994, Oscar award for a film bar-code reader, 1999, Kitchener Waterloo C. of C. Cmty. Leader of the Yr. award, 2002, Golden Plate award, Acad. Achievement, 2004. Mem.: Info. Tech. Assn. Can. (gov.). Achievements include over 30 patents in field; development of BlackBerry; contributed funds for the development of the Institute for Quantum Computing at the University of Waterloo and for the establishment of the Perimeter Institute for Theoretical Physics. Office: Rsch in Motion Ltd 295 Phillip St N2L 3W8 Waterloo ON Canada Office Phone: 519-888-7465. Office Fax: 519-888-7884.*

LAZARIN, MELISSA Y., director; d. Arturo and Irma S. Lazarin. AB, Stanford U., Calif., 1996; M Pub. Affairs, U. Tex., Austin, 2001. Policy analyst Sr. Policy Rsch. Assocs., Oakland, Calif., 1997—99; assoc. dir. edn. policy Nat. Coun. La Raza, Washington, 2001—. Home: 1613 Harvard St NW Washington DC 20009 Home Phone: 202-232-0687.

LAZARIS, PAMELA ADRIANE, community planning and development consultant; b. Dixon, Ill., Oct. 13, 1956; d. Michael Christ and Ellen Euridice (Eftax) L.; m. Eugene Dale Monson, Oct. 17, 1987; children: Anthony Edward, Anna Adriane. BFA in Fine Arts, U. Wis., Milw., 1978; MS in Urban and Regional Planning, U. Wis., Madison, 1982; MBA, U. St. Thomas, St. Paul, 1992. Analyst planning Wis. Dept. Natural Resources, Madison, 1979-82; asst. city planner City of Albert Lea, Minn., 1982-83; specialist community devel. City of Winona, Minn., 1983-85; dir. community devel. City of Waseca, Minn., 1985-98; assoc. Real Estate Dynamics, Inc., Madison, Wis., 1998-99; prin. Planning Svc. and Solutions, Lake Mills, Wis., 1999—. Vol. spl. events Farmam-Minn. Agrl. Interpretive Ctr., Waseca, 1985—86; mem. Waseca County Econ. Devel. Commn., 1989—98; com. dir. Waseca Area Found., 1989—98; mem. dist. 2 city coun. City of Lake Mills, 1999—, city plan commn., 1999—, city coun. v.p., 2003—; troop 148 advancement coord. Boy Scouts Am., 2002—. Named one of Oustanding Young Women of Am., 1986. Mem. Am. Inst. Cert. Planners (cert.), Am. Planning Assn. (chpt. bd. dirs. 1986-89), Minn. Planning Assn. (v.p. 1989-90, dist. bd. dirs. 1985-89), Toastmasters (chpt. sgt.-at-arms 1987, ednl. v.p. 1988, 91-98), Lake Mills Area C. of C. Avocations: public speaking, travel, art. Home: PO Box 17 Lake Mills WI 53551-0017 Office: 110 E Madison St Lake Mills WI 53551-1644 Home Phone: 920-648-6617. Business E-Mail: pal@gdinet.com.

LAZAROV, RAICHO DIMITROV, mathematician, educator; b. Kardjaly, Bulgaria, Jan. 23, 1943; s. Dimitar and Theodora (Djerahova) L.; m. Donka Dimitrova (Mutafchieva) Lazarova, Aug. 3, 1969; children: Dora, Trina. MS, U. Wroclaw, Poland, 1966; PhD, U. Moskow, 1972; DSc, U. Sofia, Bulgaria, 1982. Mathematician Inst. Math., Bulgarian Acad. Sci., Sofia, 1966-68, sci. officer, 1972-76, sr. sci. officer, 1978-86, head dept. high performance computer architecture and algorithms, 1985—, prof. math., 1986—; research assoc. Rutherford Lab. SRC, Chilton, Eng., 1976-77. Vis. prof. math. U. Wyoming, Laramie, 1987—; research assoc. Joint Inst. Nuclear Research, Dubna, USSR, 1980. Author: Finite Difference Schemes for Differential Equations with Generalized Solutions, 1987; contbr. articles to sci. jours. Mem. Am. Math. Soc., Union Bulgarian Mathematicians, Gesellschaft Awgewante Math and Mecharnik. Mem. Christian Orthodox Ch. Home: Mladost 1 Block 9 vA Apt 51 Sofia Bulgaria Office: Bulgarian Acad Scis Inst Math Acad G Boncevstrasse Bl 8 1113 Sofia Bulgaria

LAZARSFELD, ROBERT KENDALL, mathematician, educator; B, Harvard U.; PhD, Brown U., 1980. Prof. UCLA, U. Mich., 1997—. Editor Jour. of Am. Math. Soc. Author: (monograph) Positivity in Algebraic Geometry. Fellow: Am. Acad. Arts and Sciences. Office: Dept Math Univ Michigan 3858 East Hall Ann Arbor MI 48109 Office Phone: 734-763-1472. Office Fax: 734-763-0937. E-mail: rlaz@umich.edu.

LAZARUS, ADRIENNE, retail executive; Asst. merchant Ann Taylor Stores, 1991, various merchandising positions, 1991—97; merchandising mgr. Ann Taylor Loft, 1997—2001, sr. v.p., gen. merchandising mgr., 2001—04, Ann Taylor Stores, 2004—05, exec. v.p. merchandising and design, 2005, pres., 2006—. Named one of 40 Under 40, Crain's NY Bus., 2007. Office: Ann Taylor Stores Corp 7 Times Square 15th Fl New York NY 10036*

LAZARUS, ALLAN MATTHEW, retired newspaper editor; b. New Orleans, Nov. 21, 1927; s. Harry Adolph and Edna Mary (Wodiker) L.; m. Martha Elizabeth Ellis, July 26, 1946; children— Kenneth Wayne, Virginia Lynn BA in History, Centenary Coll., 1951. Copy boy The Times, Shreveport, La., 1944-45, reporter, 1945-46, telegraph editor, 1947-58, news editor, 1958-69, mng. editor, 1969-90. Pulitzer Prize Juror, 1978; pres. La.-Miss. AP Assn., 1977-78. Pres. Ark.-La.-Tex. chpt. Soc. Profl. Journalists, 1971—72; bd. dirs. AP Mng. Editor's Assn., 1975—80. Cpl. USAF, 1946—47. Roman Catholic. Home: 7713 Tampa Way Shreveport LA 71105-5701

LAZARUS, ARNOLD ALLAN, psychologist, educator; b. Johannesburg, Republic of South Africa, Jan. 27, 1932; came to U.S., 1963; s. Benjamin and Rachel Leah (Mosselson) L.; m. Daphne Ann Kessel, June 10, 1956; children: Linda Sue, Clifford Neil. BA with honors, U. Witwatersrand, Johannesburg, 1956, MA, 1957, PhD, 1960. Diplomate: Am. Bd. Profl. Psychology, Am. Bd. Med. Psychotherapists (fellow), Internat. Acad. Behavioral Medicine, Counseling and Psychotherapy. Pvt. practice clin. psychology, Johannesburg, 1959-63, 64-66; vis. asst. prof. dept. psychology Stanford (Calif.) U., 1963-64; prof. psychology Temple U. Med. Sch., Phila., 1967-70; dir. clin. tng. Yale U., New Haven, 1970-72; disting. prof. Rutgers U., New Brunswick, NJ, 1972-98; pres. Ctr. for Multimodal Psychol. Svcs., Princeton, NJ, 1998—2005; exec. dir. Lazarus Inst., Skillman, NJ, 2005—. Mem. adv. bd. Psychologists for Social Responsibility, 1984—; cons. in field. Author: (18 books including) Behavior Therapy and Beyond, 1971, Multimodal Therapy, 1981, rev. edit., 1989, In the Mind's Eye, 1984, Martial Myths, 1985, Mind Power: Getting What You Want Through Mental Training, 1987, The Essential Arnold Lazarus, 1991, A Dialogue with Arnold Lazarus, 1991, Don't Believe It For A Minute!, 1993, Abnormal Psychology, 1995, Brief But Comprehensive Psychotherapy, 1997, The 60 Second Shrink, 1997, I Can If I Want To, 2000, Marital Myths Revisited, 2001, Dual Relationships and Psychotherapy, 2002; editl. bd.: sci. jours.; contbr. articles to profl. jours. Recipient Disting. Svc. award Am. Bd. Profl. Psychology, Disting. Career Achievement award Am. Bd. Med. Psychotherapists, Outstanding Contbns. to Mental Health award Psychiat. Outpatient Ctrs. of the Americas, 1991, Presdl. award ACA, 2003, NJ Psychol. Assn., 2003. Fellow APA (Disting. Psychologist award divsn. of psychotherapy 1992, 1st Ann. Cummings Psyche award 1996, Disting. Profl. Contbns. award Divsn. Clin. Psychology 1997), Am. Bd. Profl. Psychology (diplomate), Internat. Acad. Eclectic Psychotherapists, Acad. Clin. Psychology, Am. Psychotherapy Assn. (mem. exec. adv. bd. 2001—); mem. Internat. Assn. Marriage and Family Counselors (Disting. Presenter Series award 2000), Am. Acad. Psychotherapy, Assn. for Advancement Psychotherapy, Nat. Acads. Practice in Psychology (disting.), Soc. for Exploration of Psychotherapy Integration, Calif. Psychol. Assn. (Lifetime Achievement award 1999), Assn. Advancement Behavior Therapy (Lifetime Achievement award 1999), Internat. Assn. Marriage and Family Counselors (Disting. Presenter award 2000), Am. Counseling Assn. (presdl. award 2003), N.J. Psychol. Assn. (presdl. award 2003). Home: 56 Herrontown Cir Princeton NJ 08540-2924 Office Phone: 609-240-3612. E-mail: aalaz@aol.com. *To respect others for their exceptional capacities, but never to deify them, enables one to learn from others instead of envying them and denigrating oneself. This egalitarian view transforms acquisitiveness, power, and aggression into love, intimacy, and productive activity.*

LAZARUS, ARTHUR, JR., lawyer; b. Bklyn., Aug. 30, 1926; s. Arthur and Frieda (Langer) L.; m. Gertrude Chiger, Jan. 8, 1956; children: Andrew Joseph, Edward Peter, Diana Ruth. BA with honors, Columbia U., 1946; JD, Yale U., 1949. Bar: N.Y. 1951, D.C. 1952, U.S. Supreme Ct. 1954. Assoc. Fried, Frank, Harris, Shriver & Jacobson, Washington, 1950-57, ptnr., 1957-91, mng. ptnr. Washington office, 1974-86; of counsel Sonosky, Chambers, Sachse, Endreson & Perry, LLP, Washington, 1994—. Vis. lectr. Yale Law Sch., 1973-81. Trustee Arena Stage, 1987-98, Georgetown Day Sch., 1963-71. Home: 3201 Fessenden St NW Washington DC 20008-2032 Office Phone: 202-682-0240. Business E-Mail: ALazarus@Sonosky.com.

LAZARUS, BRUCE I., restaurant and hotel management educator; b. Pitts. s. Arnold H. and Belle Lazarus. BS, Pa. State U., 1975; JD, U. Pitts., 1980. Bar: Pa. 1980. Ops. analyst ARA Services, Phila., 1976-77; legal intern Pa. Human Relations Commn., Pitts., 1978-79; food service dir. Martin's Run Life Care, ARA Services, Phila., 1980-81; asst. dir. dept. nutrition Bryn Mawr (Pa.) Hosp., ARA Services, 1981-84; prof. restaurant and hotel mgmt. Purdue U., West Lafayette, Ind., 1984—96, prof. emeritus, 1996—. Mem. membership com. Coun. Hotel, Restaurant and Instnl. Edn., 1984—, mem. paper rev. com. 1988—. Contbr. articles to profl. pubs. Nat. Inst. Food Service Industry grantee, 1986, Internat. Franchise Assn., 1987; recipient Mary Mathew award for Outstanding Undergraduate teaching Consumer anf Family Svcs., 1993, Purdue Univ. award Outstanding Undergraduate Teaching, 1993. Mem. ABA, Ind. Bar Assn., Pa. Bar Assn., Nat. Restaurant Assn., Phi Kappa Phi.

LAZARUS, DAVID, physicist, researcher; b. Buffalo, Sept. 8, 1921; s. Barney B. and Lillian (Markel) L.; m. Betty Jane Ross, Aug. 15, 1943; children: Barbara, William, Mary Ann, Richard. BS, U. Chgo., 1942, MS, 1947, PhD, 1949. Instr. electronics U. Chgo., 1942-43, electronics engr., 1946-49, instr. physics, 1949; research assoc. radio research lab. Harvard, 1943-45; mem. physics faculty U. Ill., Urbana, 1949—, prof., 1959—. Vis. prof. U. Paris, 1968-69, M.I.T., 1978-79, Harvard U., 1978-79; vis. scientist Am. Inst. Physics, N.Y.C., 1962-69; cons. Phys. Sci. Study Com., 1957-59, Hallicrafters Co., Chgo., 1957-69, Gen. Electric Co., Cin., 1960-68, Gen. Atomic, La Jolla, Calif., 1962-63, Lawrence Radiation Lab., 1967-68, Sandia Lab., 1970-72, Addison-Wesley Pub. Co., Reading, Mass., 1964-80; dir. Council on Materials Sci., U.S. Dept. Energy, 1981-85 Author: (with H. de Waard) Modern Electronics, 1966, (with R.I. Hulsizer) The World of Physics, 1972, (with M. Raether) Practical Physics: How Things Work, 1979; also articles. Guggenheim fellow, 1968-69 Fellow AAAS, Am. Phys. Soc. (coun. 1974-78, 80-91, exec. com. 1980-91, editor-in-chief 1980-91, publs. com. 1980-91, exec. com. div. contensed matter physics 1968-70, 74-78, chmn. New Materials prize com. 1976, chmn. Buckley prize com. 1979); mem. Am. Inst. Physics (governing bd. 1981-92, exec. com. 1981-89, publs. policy com. 1981-92). Home (Summer): PO Box 484 Chilmark MA 02535-0484 Home: 502 W Vermont Ave Urbana IL 61801 Personal E-mail: d-lazars@uiuc.edu.

LAZARUS, DAVID, journalist; Crime reporter Daily (Californian) at Berkeley; columnist Japan Times; with San Francisco Chronicle, 1999—. Contbg. writer: Fortune, Wired, Salon.com, Nat. Geographic; author: two books. Recipient Journalist of Yr. award, Consumer Fedn. Calif., 2004, C. Everett Coop award, 2003, Nat. Headliner award, 2002, Calif. Journalism award, Ctr. Calif. Studies Calif. State U., 2002, John Jacobs award, 2001, Journalist of Yr. award, Soc. Profl. Journalists, 2001. Office: San Francisco Chronicle 901 Mission St San Francisco CA 94103-2988 Office Phone: 415-777-8827. Business E-Mail: dlazarus@sfchronicle.com.

LAZARUS, FRED, IV, academic administrator; b. NYC, Jan. 1, 1942; s. Fred and Irma (Mendelson) L.; m. Jonna Gane, Nov. 27, 1970; children: Anna Mendelson, Fred Lazarus V. BA, Claremont McKenna Coll., 1964; MBA, Harvard U., 1966; PhD (hon.), Osaka U. Arts. Staff assoc. Nat. Council for Equal Bus. Opportunity, Washington, 1969-71; pres. Washington Council for Equal Bus. Opportunity, 1971-74; exec. asst. to chmn. Nat. Endowment for Arts, Washington, 1975-78; pres. Md. Inst. Coll. Art, Balt., 1978—. Trustee Alliance Ind. Colls. Art, 1978-91, chmn., 1984-86, 89-91, Assn. Ind. Colls. Art and Design, 1992-, vice chair, 1992-96; founding chmn. Nat. Coalition Edn. in Arts, 1988-90; bd. dirs. Midtown Devel. Corp. Trustee St. Paul's Sch., 1988—96, Am. Coun. for Arts, 1980—97, sec., 1991—94; trustee Visionary Art Mus., 1993—2005, Ams. for the Arts, 1998—, chmn., 1998—2001; trustee Md. Art Place, 1988—96, Baltic Ptnrs. Enhanced Learning, 2006—; trustee emeritus Ptnrs. for Livable Places; bd. dirs. Afro-Am. Newspapers, 1990—2003, Balt. Artists Housing Corp.; chmn. Balt. Coun. for Equal Bus. Opportunity, 1978—2002; trustee Md. Ind. Coll. and Univ. Assn., 1978—, vice chmn., 1995—99, 2006—, chmn., 1999—2003; mem. Thurgood Marshall Meml. Statue Commn., 1996—98; bd. dirs. Greater Balt. Cultural Alliance, 2001—, chmn., 2001—04; mem. Md. Artistic Properties Commn., 2000—; bd. dirs. Balt. Ptnrs. for Enriched Learning, 2006—. Recipient mayor's art award, City of Balt., 1988. Mem. Harvard Club (N.Y.C.) Office: Md Inst Coll Art 1300 W Mount Royal Ave Baltimore MD 21217-4134 Business E-Mail: flazarus@mich.edu.

LAZARUS, GERALD SYLVAN, dermatologist, educator, dean; b. NYC, Feb. 16, 1939; s. Joseph W. and Marion (Goldstein) Lazarus; m. Sandra Jacob, Sept. 3, 1961 (dec. 1985); children: Mark, Elyse, Lynne, Laura; m. Audrey Fedyszyn Jakubowski, Apr. 7, 1990. BA, Colby Coll., 1959; MD, George Washington U., 1963. Intern, then resident U. Mich., Ann Arbor, 1963—64, resident in medicine, 1964—65; rsch. asso. NIH, Bethesda, Md., 1965—68; resident in dermatology Harvard U., Cambridge, Mass., 1968—70; rsch. fellow Strangeways Labs., Cambridge, England, 1970—72; assoc. prof. medicine, co-dir. dermatology tng. program Albert Einstein Med. Coll., NYC, 1972—75; J. Lamar Callaway prof. Duke U., Durham, NC, 1977—82, chief dermatology, 1975—82; Milton B. Hartzell prof. U. Pa. Sch. Medicine, Phila., 1982—, chmn. dept. dermatology, 1982—93; dean Sch. Medicine U. Calif., Davis, 1993—97; vis. scholar U. Calif., Inst. Health Policy Rsch., San Francisco, 1997—98; prof. dermatology, biol. chemistry U. Calif. Scholar Inst. for Health Policy, 1998—99; dean, prof. emeritus U. Calif. Davis Sch. Medicine, 1999—; prof. dermatology Johns Hopkins Med. Inst., Balt., 2002—; dir. Johns Hopkins Medicine Wound Healing Ctr. Sr. investigator Arthritis Found., 1972—77; mem. study sect. NIH, 1976—80; prof. dermatology U. Calif., San Francisco; faculty Inst. of Health Policy; advisor to univ. pres. and hosp. dir. advisor Ministry of Health; vis. prof. Peking Union Med. Coll., Beijing, 1999—2002; advisor to pres. Peking Union Med. Coll. Hosp.; co-dir. China Med. Be. Mgmt. Program. Author (with L. Goldsmith): Diagnosis of Skin Disease, 1980; author: (with Herman Beerman) Tradition of Excellance: History of Dermatology at Univ. Pa. Sch. of Medicine; assoc. editor Jour. Investigative Dermatology, 1977—82; contbr. numerous articles to profl. jours. Trustees George Washington U., Washington, 2005—. With USPHS, 1965—68. Fellow John Simon Guggenheim, U. Geneva, 1986; grantee, NIH. Fellow: ACP, Am. Soc. Clin. Investigation, Assn. Am. Physicians; mem.: Am. Acad. Dermatology (Sultzberger award 1986), Biochem. Soc., Soc. Investigative Dermatology (pres. 1996—97, dir., Disting. Alumnus award George Washington U. 1996), Am. Dermatol. Assn. (Carl Herzog fellow 1970—72). Republican. Jewish. Home: 2010 Bennett Point Rd Queenstown MD 21658 Office: Johns Hopkins Bayview Med Ctr 4940 Eastern Ave Baltimore MD 21224 Office Phone: 410-550-4724. Business E-Mail: lazaruspumc@hotmail.com.

LAZARUS, HAROLD, management educator; b. NYC, Jan. 16, 1927; s. Louis and Anna (Fritz) L.; m. Carol Nunes, June 22, 1952 (dec. Aug. 9, 1987); children: Mark Leander, Eric Lewis. BA in Econs. and Philosophy cum laude, NYU, 1949; MS in Mktg., Columbia U., 1952, PhD in Mgmt., 1963. Asst. prof. mgmt. Hofstra U., Hempstead, NY, 1952-63, dean Sch. Bus., 1973-80, also mem. Pres.'s and Provost's Adv. Couns, Mel Weitz Disting. prof. bus., 1980—; prof. mgmt. Grad. Sch. Bus. Adminstrn., NYU, NYC, 1963-73; fellow Internat. Acad. Mgmt., 1989. Research dir. manpower lab. AT&T, N.Y.C., 1970-71; adj. prof. Columbia U. Grad. Sch. Bus. and Tchrs. Coll., N.Y.C., 1969-70; lectr. Harvard U. Grad. Sch. Bus. Adminstrn., Cornell U. Sch. Indsl. and Labor Relations, NBC-TV, UN Office Tech. Cooperation, Advanced Mgmt. Sch. IBM, Fgn. Svc. Inst. U.S.

Dept. State, Athens Sch. of Piraeus, Greece, SUNY Stony Brook; mgmt. cons. to govt. agys. and industry; bd. dirs. N.Am. Mgmt. Coun., World Mgmr. Coun.; bd. dirs. Paragon Fin. Corp., MyTurn.com, The Sweet Life, Inc., CompuDawn, Inc., Graham-Field Health Products, Inc., Stage II Apparel Corp., Ideal Toy Corp., Labtron Sci. Corp., Patient Tech., Inc., Diamond Med., Inc., Bristoline, Inc., Ventilator Corp., Medisco, Inc., ExNewt, Inc., M.E. Team, Inc., Graham-Field Temco, Inc., Diplomat Electronics Corp., Aquatherm Corp., Health and Med. Techniques, Inc., Graham Field Distbn., Inc., Graham Field Bandage, Inc., Graham Field Health Care Products Corp., Graham Field European Distbn. Corp., Health Team, Inc., Continental Plastics Corp., Ideal Internat. Ind., Interstate Molding & Hobbing Co., Crown Recreation Inc., Superior Surg. Mfg. Co., Rust Warehousing Corp., Alabe Products Inc., BINY Inc., Superior Surg. Mfg. Co.; mem. planning com. 21st World Mgmt. Coun., 1989; chmn. bd. The Sweet Life, Inc.; lectr. numerous bus. orgns., govt. agys., hosps., univs.; cons. to deans, presidents, chairs and faculty numerous univs. Author: The American Business Dictionary, 1957,, (with E. Tomeski) People-Oriented Computer Systems, The Computer in Transition, 1975, rev. edit., 1983,; mem. editorial bd. Acad. Mgmt. Jour., 1969-70; editor: Human Values in Management, 1968; editor: (with others) The Progress of Management: Process and Behavior in a Changing Environment, 2d edit., 1972, 3d edit., 1977; mem. editorial rev. bd. Acad. Mgmt. Rev., 1986-87; mem. editorial adv. bd. The Jour. Mgmt. Devel., 1988—, editor spl. issues, 1993-94; sr. editorial advisor Ency. Mgmt., 1978-2005; contbr. chpts. and intros. to books, articles to bus. jours. With USN, 1945-46 Recipient award for teaching excellence NYU, 1972; recipient award for teaching excellence Hofstra U., 1985; Tchr. of Yr. award Hofstra U., 1987; Met. Life Ins. Co. fellow, 1965; War Service scholar, 1946-49; Columbia U. fellow, 1949-50; Bronfman Found. fellow, 1960-62; Ford Motor Co. fellow, 1964 Fellow Internat. Acad. Mgmt.; mem. Middle Atlantic Assn. Colls. Bus. Adminstrn. (past pres.), Eastern Acad. Mgmt. (past pres.), N.Am. Mgmt. Coun. (past pres.), Soc. for Advancement Mgmt. (past v.p.), Acad. Mgmt. (past dir.), AAUP (past pres. Hofstra U. chpt.), LWV, NOW, Phi Beta Kappa (pres. alumna and alumni of L.I., chmn. 1980-2001), Beta Gamma Sigma, Beta Alpha Psi, Mu Gamma Tau, Omicron Chi Epsilon, Pi Delta Epsilon Home: TH8 20191 E Country Club Dr Aventura FL 33180-3015 Office: Hofstra U Dept Mgmt Weller Hall Hempstead NY 11550 Home Phone: 305-935-5046; Office Phone: 516-463-5734. Personal E-mail: hallaz@bellsouth.net.

LAZARUS, KENNETH ANTHONY, lawyer; b. Passaic, NJ, Mar. 10, 1942; s. John Joseph and Margaret (Di Cenzo) L.; m. Marylyn Jane Flemming, Aug. 13, 1966; children: Maggi Ann, John, Joseph. BA, U. Dayton, 1964; JD, U. Notre Dame, 1967; LLM in Taxation, George Washington U., 1971. Bar: N.J. 1967, U.S. Tax Ct. 1970, U.S. Ct. Claims 1970, U.S. Supreme Ct. 1971, D.C. 1976. Trial atty. U.S. Dept. Justice, 1967-71; assoc. counsel and chief counsel to Minority Com. on Judiciary, U.S. Senate, 1971-74; assoc. counsel to Pres. U.S., 1974-77; ptnr. Bierbower & Rockefeller, 1977—81, Ward, Lazarus & Grow, Washington, 1981—91; of counsel Dixon & Jessup, Washington, 1991-97, Krooth & Atlman, 1997—. Mem. adv. bd. Sch. Law Dayton U., 1975-85; adj. prof. Sch. Law Georgetown U., 1979—; mem. U.S. Adv. Com. on Trade Negotiations, 1983-87; chmn. Sailors and Mchts. Bank and Trust Co., Vienna, Va., 1987-89. Mem. adv. bd. Houston Jour. Internat. Law, 1983-90; contbr. numerous articles to profl. publs. U.S. reporter to UN, 1975-77; mem. adv. coun. Rep. Nat. Com., 1977-80; mem. Presdl. transition team Office of Pres.-Elect, 1980-81; caucus mgr. George Bush, Rep. Conv., 1988; trustee Internat. Law Inst., pres., 1990-92. Mem.: ABA, Am. Judicature Soc., N.J. Bar Assn., Fed. Bar Assn., Bar Assn. D.C., D.C. Bar Assn., Am. Law Inst. (life). Home: 4501 Connecticut Ave NW Apt 716 Washington DC 20008-3712 Office: Lazarus & Assocs 1850 M St NW Ste 400 Washington DC 20036-5815 Office Phone: 202-457-0380.

LAZARUS, MARK, broadcast executive; married; 3 children. BA, Vanderbilt U. Network buyer & planner Backer, Spielvogel & Bates, Inc.; account exec. NBC Cable, Turner Broadcasting Sales, 1990—98; exec. v.p. Turner Sports Sales, 1998—99; pres. Turner Sports, 1999—2002, Turner Entertainment Sales & Mktg., 2002—03, Turner Entertainment Group, 2003—. Nat. trustee Boys & Girls Clubs Am. Named one of Media Mavens, Ad Age, 2000, 40 Under 40 Top Sports Execs., Sports Bus. Jour., 2000, 2001, 100 Most Powerful People in Sports, Sporting News, 2000. Mem.: Sigma Chi. Office: TBS Inc 1 CNN Ctr Atlanta GA 30303 Office Phone: 404-827-1700.*

LAZARUS, MELL, cartoonist; b. NYC, May 3, 1927; s. Sidney and Frances (Mushkin) L.; m. Eileen Hortense Israel, June 19, 1949; children: Marjorie, Suesan, Catherine; m. Sally Elizabeth Mitchell, May 13, 1995. Cartoonist-writer Miss Peach, 1957—, Momma, 1970—; author anthologies Miss Peach, Miss Peach, Are These Your Children?, Momma, We're Grownups Now!; novels The Boss is Crazy, Too, 1964, The Neighborhood Watch, 1986; plays Everybody into the Lake, Elliman's Fly, Lifetime Eggcreams, 1969-70; juvenile Francine, Your Face Would Stop a Clock, 1975; co-author Miss Peach TV spl. programs Turkey Day Pageant and Annual Heart Throb Ball. With USNR, 1945, USAFR, 1951-54. Mem. Nat. Cartoonists Soc. (pres. 1989-93, chmn. membership com. 1965, nat. rep., Humor Strip Cartoonist of Yr. 1973, 79, Reuben award 1981, Silver T-Square award 2000), Nat. Press Club, The Century Assn., Am. Mensa. Office: Creators Syndicate Inc 5777 W Century Blvd Los Angeles CA 90045-5600 Personal E-mail: kpop3@aol.com.

LAZARUS, SHELLY (ROCHELLE BRAFF LAZARUS), advertising executive; b. NYC, Sept. 1, 1947; d. Lewis L. and Sylvia Ruth (Eisenberg) Braff; m. George M. Lazarus, Mar. 22, 1970; children: Theodore, Samantha, Benjamin. AB, Smith Coll., 1968; MBA, Columbia U., 1970. Product mgr. Clairol, NYC, 1970-71; account exec. Ogilvy & Mather, NYC, 1971-73, account supr., 1973-77, mgmt. supr., 1977-84, sr. v.p., 1981—, account group dir., 1984-87; gen. mgr. Ogilvy & Mather Direct, NYC, 1987-88, mng. dir., 1988-89, pres., 1989-91, Ogilvy & Mather, NYC, 1991-94, pres. N. Am., 1991-94; pres., COO Ogilvy & Mather Worldwide, NYC, 1995-96, CEO, 1996—, chmn., 1997—. Bd. dirs. GE, 2000—, Merck & Co., Inc., 2004—, Com. to Encourage Corp., Philanthropy, NY Presbyn. Hosp., Advt. Edn. Found., Am. Mus. Nat. History, World Wildlife Fund; mem. bd. overseers Columbia Bus. Sch. Mem. adv. bd. Judge Inst. Mgmt. Studies Cambridge U., England, Women's Forum, Yale Pres.'s Coun. Internat. Activities, Bus. Coun., 4A's Adv. Coun., Com. Fgn. Rels., Advt. Women NY, Com. 200. Recipient YWCA Women Achievers award, 1985, Matrix award, 1995; named Businesswoman of Yr. NYC Partnership and C. of C., 1996; named one of 100 Most Powerful Women in World, Forbes mag., 2005, 50 Most Powerful Women in Bus., Fortune mag., 2006. Mem.: Am. Assn. Advt. Agys. (vice chmn. 1998—99, chmn. 1999—2000, bd. dirs.), Advt. Women N.Y. (coun. fgn. rels., com. to encourage corp. philanthropy, Woman of Yr 1994). Home: 106 E 78th St New York NY 10021-0302 Office: Ogilvy & Mather Worldwide 309 W 49th St New York NY 10019-7316

LAZARUS, STEVEN, technology company executive; b. NYC, May 31, 1931; s. Jesse and Dorothy (Gold) L.; m. Arlene Doris Travin, June 18, 1953; children: Paul M., Scott R., Jeffrey T. AB, Dartmouth Coll., 1952; MBA, Harvard U., 1965. Commd. ensign USN, 1953, advanced through grades to capt., 1973, ret., 1969; asst. maritime adminstr. U.S. Dept. Commerce, Washington, 1969-72, dept. asst. sec. commerce for east-west trade, 1972-74; various positions to group v.p. for health care systems Baxter Travenol Labs. Inc., Chgo., 1974-86; assoc. dean grad. sch. of bus. U. Chgo., 1986—94; founder, mng. dir. Arch Venture Partners, 1986—; chief exec. officer, pres. Arch Devel. Corp., Chgo., 1986—94. Bd. dirs. Amgen Corp., Thousand Oaks, Calif., Primark Corp., McLean, Va, First Consulting Group, R2 Tech., Inc. Trustee Highland Park (Ill.) Hosp., 1985—. Office: Arch Venture Partners 8725 W Higgins Rd Ste 290 Chicago IL 60631

LAZARUS, STEVEN S., management and marketing consultant; b. Rochester, NY, June 16, 1943; s. Alfred and Ceal H. Lazarus; m. Elissa C. Lazarus, June 19, 1966; children: Michael, Stuart, Jean. BS, Cornell U., 1966; MS, Poly. U. N.Y., 1967; PhD, U. Rochester, 1974. Pres. Mgmt. Systems Analysis Corp., Denver, 1977—; dir. Sci. Application Intern Corp., Englewood, Colo., 1979-84; assoc. prof. Metro State Coll., Denver, 1983-84; sr. v.p. Pal Assocs. Inc., Denver, 1984-85; with strategic planning and mktg. McDonnell Douglas, Denver, 1985-86; mktg. cons. Clin. Reference Systems, Denver, 1986; pres. Mgmt. Sys. Analysis Corp., 1986-89, 95—; assoc. exec. dir. Ctr. Rsch. Ambulatory Health Care Adminstrn., Englewood, 1990-94. Spl. cons. State of Colo., Denver, 1976-81; mktg. cons. IMX, Louisville, 1986-87; speaker Am. Hosp. Assn., Chgo., 1983; asst. sec. Work Group for Elec. Data Interchange, 1995-96, bd. dirs., 1997—, chmn. bd. dirs., 2001-02; trustee WEDI Found., 2003—, sec., 2004-05, chmn. bd. trustees, 2006-; pres. Boundary Info. Group, 1995—; founder, bd. dirs. Train for Compliance, Inc., 2003-, vice chmn., 2003—; co-founder Health IT Cert., LLC, 2004—. Co-author: Handbook for HIPAA Security Implementation, 2003, Complete Guide to HIPAA Security Risk Analysis: A Step-by-Step Approach, 2004, Electronic Health Records: Transforming Your Medical Practice, 2005; contbr. chapters to books. NDEA fellow U. Rochester, 1968-71; recipient Book of Yr. award Healthcare Info. and Mgmt. Sys. Soc., 2006. Fellow Healthcare Info. and Mgmt. Sys. Soc.; mem. Med. Group Mgmt. Assn., Optimists (program chmn. Denver club 1976-78). Achievements include patents for med. quality assurance. Home: 7023 E Eastman Ave Denver CO 80224-2845 Office: MSA Corp 4401 S Quebec St Ste 100 Denver CO 80237-2644 Home Phone: 303-757-7562; Office Phone: 303-488-9911.

LAZEAR, EDWARD PAUL, federal official, economics professor; b. NYC, Aug. 17, 1948; s. Abe and Rose (Karp) L.; m. Victoria Ann Allen, July 2, 1977; 1 child, Julia Ann AB, A.M., UCLA, 1971; PhD, Harvard U., 1974; LLD (hon.), Albertson Coll., 1997. Asst. prof. econs. U. Chgo., 1974-78, assoc. prof. indsl. relations, 1978-81, prof. indsl. relations, 1981-85, Isidore and Gladys Brown prof. urban and labor econs., 1985-92; sr. fellow Hoover Instn. Stanford U., Calif., 1985—2002, coord. domestic studies Hoover Instn., 1987-90, prof. econs. and human resource mgmt. Grad. Sch. Bus., 1992-95, Jack Steele Parker prof. econs. and human resource mgmt., 1995—2006, mem. steering com. Stanford Inst. for Econ. Policy Rsch., 1996—2006; chmn., Coun. Econ. Advisers Exec. Office of the Pres., Washington, 2006—. Econ. advisor to Romania, Czechoslovakia, Russia, Ukraine, Georgia; rsch. assoc. Nat. Bur. Econ. Rsch., Econs. Rsch. Ctr. of Nat. Opinion Rsch. Ctr.; chmn. rsch. adv. bd. World at Work; fellow Inst. Advanced Study, Hebrew U., Jerusalem, 1977-8; lectr. Inst. Advanced Study, Vienna, 1983-84, Nat. Productivity Bd., Singapore, 1982, 85, Adam Smith lctr., Seville, Spain, 2003; vis. prof. Inst. des Etudes Politiques, Paris, 1987; Wicksell lectr., Stockholm, 1993; chmn. Am. Compensation Assoc. Adv. Bd., 1999—; mem. Pres.'s Panel on Tax Reform, 2005. Author: (with R. Michael) Allocation of Income Within the Household, 1988; (with J.P. Gould) Microeconomic Theory, 1989, Personnel Economics, 1995, Personnel Economics for Managers, 1998; editor: Economic Transition in Eastern Europe and Russia, 1995; founding editor Jour. Labor Econs., 1982-2001; assoc. editor Jour. Econ. Perspectives, 1986-89, German Econ. Rev., 2000—; co-editor: Jour. Labor Abstracts, 1996—; contbr. articles to profl. jours. Recipient Leo Melamed prize for outstanding scholarship, 1998; NSF grad. fellow, 1971-74, Morris Arnold Cox sr. fellow Hoover Instn., 2002. Fellow Am. Acad. Arts and Scis., Econometric Soc., Soc. Labor Economists (1st v.p. 1995-96, pres. 1997-98), Ctr. Corp. Performance Denmark; mem. Am. Econs. Assn., Inst. Study Labor (prize for outstanding contbns. in labor econs. 2004), Nat. Acad. Scis. (bd. testing and assessment), Bd. Tng. Assessment. Office: Coun Econ Advisors 725 17th St NW Washington DC 20502*

LAZENBY, JUSTIN WYATT, forensic scientist; b. Feb. 14, 1975; BA in Chemistry, Carleton Coll., Northfield, Minn., 1997; MS in Criminalistics, Calif. State U., LA, 2004. Freelance theater technician, Minn., 1998—99; casting dir. Kids! Mgmt., Burbank, Calif., 1999—2004; forensic scientist Oreg. State Police, Clackamas, 2004—. Mem.: Internat. Assn. Chem. Testing, Mensa. Home: 260 SE Liberty Ct Gresham OR 97080 Personal E-mail: justin.lazenby@gmail.com.

LAZERSON, EARL EDWIN, retired academic administrator; b. Detroit, Dec. 10, 1930; s. Nathan and Ceil (Stashefsky) L.; m. Ann May Harper, June 11, 1966; children from previous marriage: Joshua, Paul. BS, Wayne State U., Detroit, 1953; postgrad., U. Leiden, Netherlands, 1957-58; MA, U. Mich., 1954, PhD, 1982. Mathematician Inst. Def. Analyses, Princeton, NJ, 1960-62; asst. prof. math. Washington U., St. Louis, 1962-65, 66-69; vis. asso. prof. Brandeis U., 1965-66; mem. faculty So. Ill. U., Edwardsville, 1969—, prof. math., 1973—, chmn. dept. math. studies, 1972-73, dean Sch. Sci. and Tech., 1973-76, univ. v.p., provost, 1977-79, pres., 1980-93; pres. emeritus, 1994—. Chmn. Southwestern Ill. Devel. Authority, City of East St. Louis Fin. Adv. Authority; active Leadership Coun. Southwestern Ill., Gateway Ctr. Met. St. Louis, Inc., St. Louis Symphony Soc.; trustee Jefferson Nat. Expansion Meml. Assn., Ill. Econ. Devel. Bd. Recipient Sr. Teaching Excellence award Standard Oil Found., 1970-71 Mem. Am. Math. Soc., Math. Assn. Am., European Math. Soc., London Math. Soc., Soc. Mathematique France, Fulbright Alumni Assn., Sigma Xi. Home: 122 Forest Grove Dr Glen Carbon IL 62034 E-mail: elazerson@sbcglobal.net.

LAZIO, RICK ANTHONY (ENRICO ANTHONY LAZIO), bank executive, former congressman; b. Amityville, NY, Mar. 13, 1958; s. Anthony and Olive E. (Christensen) L. m. Patrica Moriarity, 1990, children: Molly Ann, Kelsey. AB in Polit. Sci., Vassar Coll., 1980; JD, Am. U., 1983. Bar: N.Y. 1984, U.S. Dist. Ct. (ea. and so. dists.) N.Y., 1985. Asst. dist. atty. Suffolk County Rackets Bureau, Hauppauge, N.Y., 1983-88; exec. asst. dist. atty. Suffolk County, N.Y., 1987-88; village atty. Village of Lindenhurst, N.Y., 1988-93; mng. ptnr. Glass, Lazio and Glass, Esqs., Babylon, N.Y., 1988-93; mem. Suffolk County Legislature from 11th Dist., N.Y., 1989-93, 103rd-106th Congresses from 2nd N.Y. dist., Washington, 1993-2001; dep. majority whip 103d-106th Congresses from 2nd N.Y. dist., Washington; asst. majority leader 106th Congress from 2nd N.Y. dist., Washington; pres., CEO Fin. Services Forum, NYC and Washington, 2001—04; exec. v.p. global govt. relations & pub. policy J.P. Morgan Chase & Co., NYC, 2004—. Mem. commerce com., banking com., subcom. on health and environ., subcom. on fin. and hazardous materials, chmn. subcom. on housing and cmty. opportunity. Republican. Roman Catholic. Avocations: coin collecting/numismatics, guitar. Office: JP Morgan Chase Co 270 Park Ave New York NY 10017-2070

LAZO, JOHN STEPHEN, science educator, director; b. Phila., Dec. 15, 1948; s. John and Mildred Doris Lazo; m. Jacqui Lynne Fiske; 1 child, Jacquelyn Kristina. AB, Johns Hopkins U., Balt., 1967—71; PhD, U. Mich., Ann Arbor, 1971—75. Postdoctoral fellow Yale U., New Haven, 1976—78, asst. prof., 1978—83, assoc. prof., 1983—87; allegheny found. prof., chmn. U. Pitts., 1987—2004, inst. dir., 2004—. Mem. Am. Assn. Cancer Rsch., Phila., 1991—94, Carniege Mus. Natural History, Pitts., 2001—06; chmn. Coun. Extramural Grants Am. Cancer Soc., Altanta, 2003—04. Recipient Disting. Rsch. Achievement in Cancer Rsch. award, Am. Cancer Soc., 2004; grantee Postdoctoral fellowship, 1977, Postdoctoral fellowship, NIH, 1978. Achievements include patents for phosphatase inhibitors and methods of use thereof. Office: U Pitts 3501 Fifth Ave Pittsburgh PA 15260 Home Phone: 412-648-9580. Office Fax: 412-648-9009. Business E-Mail: lazo@pitt.edu.

LAZOVSKY, LORNA DEANE, minister; b. Harrisburg, Ill., Nov. 24, 1936; d. Curtis James Williams and Lillian May Rigsby; m. Daniel Lazovsky; children: David Eli, Michael Lyndon; m. Fred Plyler (div.); children: Scott Gregory Plyler, James Kevin Plyler, Susan Jane Plyler, Leslie Lorriane Plyler, Lily Ann Plyler. Founder Youth for Jesus, Desert Hot Springs, Calif.; minister state prisons; internat. pres. Women's Agape. Sr. pastor Desert Christian Fellowship Ch., Desert Hot Springs, Calif. Avocation: singing. Office Phone: 760-288-3739. Personal E-mail: lorna@macmail.com.

LAZOWSKA, EDWARD DELANO, computer science educator; b. Washington, Aug. 3, 1950; AB, Brown U., 1972; MSc, U. Toronto, Can., 1974, PhD, 1977. Asst. prof. U. Wash., Seattle, 1977-82, assoc. prof., 1982-86, prof. dept. computer sci. & engring., 1986—, chair dept. computer sci. and engring., 1993—2001, Bill and Melinda Gates chair, 2000—. Vis. scholar computer sci. Stanford U., 1984—85; vis. scientist Digital Equipment Corp., 1984—85; vis. scholar computer sci. U. Calif., San Diego, 2001—02; tech. adv. bd. mem. Microsoft Rsch., Voyager Capital, Ignition, Madrona Venture Group, Impinj; bd. dirs. Washington Software Alliance, Tech. Alliance of Washington, Data I/O Corp.; co-chair Pres.'s Info. Tech. Adv. Com., 2003—05. Chair Computing Cmty. Consortium. Fellow: AAAS, IEEE, Am. Acad. Arts and Sci., Assn. Computing Machinery (chmn. spl. interest group on measurement and evaluation 1985—89); mem.: Nat. Acad. Engring. Office: U Wash Dept Computer Sci & Engring PO Box 352350 Seattle WA 98195-2350 Home Phone: 206-789-0477. Business E-Mail: lazowska@cs.washington.edu.

LAZUKA, ROBERT, artist, art educator; BFA in painting, Art Inst. Chgo.; MFA, Ariz. State U. Prof. Sch. Art, Ohio. U., 1984—, interim dir. Represented in permanent collections, Whitney Mus. Art, N.Y., Smithsonian Nat. Mus. Am. Art, Washington, DC, Nelson-Atkins Mus. Art, Kans. City, MO, Clemson U., S.C., Chattahoochee Valley Art Mus., Ga., Baseball Hall Fame Mus. Mem.: Coll. Bd. Advanced Placement Program (mem. 1988—, chief faculty consultant, studio art 1996—2000, devel. com.). Office: Ohio University School of Art 417 Seigfred Hall Athens OH 45701 Office Phone: 740-593-1676. Office Fax: 740-593-0457. E-mail: lazuka@ohiou.edu.

LAZZARA, BERNADETTE See PETERS, BERNADETTE

LAZZARA, MARGO VALENTINE, counselor, writer; b. NY, Jan. 23, 1958; d. Francisco Santos Valentine and Maria Guzman; m. Sebastian Lazzara, Feb. 7, 1998. Student in Gestalt Therapy, Ziegler Inst., 1990; student in Human Behavior, Psychology, NYU; degree, Am. Inst. Hypnotherapy, 1993; degree in Aromatherapy, Sch. Essentials, 1995. Cert.; hypnotherapist Johnson Inst. Hypnotherapy, 1994. Med. technician Diagnostic Ctr. Preventive Medicine, NYC; assoc. prodr. WOR Radio, NYC; sex therapist Am. Assn. Sex Educators, Counselors and Therapists, NYC, hypnotherapist. Rape crisis counselor St. Vincents Hosp., NYC; couselor HEAL Orgn., NYC; cons. in field. Author: The Healing Aromatherapy Bath, 1999 (Best Book award, 2000), Blissful Bathtimes, 2000 (Best Book award, 2001); contbr. articles to mags. Vol. Salvation Army, NYC, 1997. Named Miss Puerto Rico, 1976. Mem.: Am. Assn. Sex Educators, Counselors and Therapists, Internat. Assn. Counselors and Therapists, Nat. Guild Hypnotherapists. Democrat. Roman Cath. Avocations: painting, decoupage. Home and Office: Aromatica 1075 Father Capodanno Blvd Staten Island NY 10306 E-mail: margolazzara@aol.com.

LAZZARO, ANTHONY DEREK, academic administrator; b. Utica, NY, Jan. 31, 1921; s. Angelo Michael and Philomena (Vanilla) L.; m. Shirley Margaret Jones, Dec. 20, 1941; 1 child, Nancy. BS in Indsl. and Sys. Engring., U. So. Calif., 1948; LL.D. with honors, Pepperdine U., 1974. Registered profl. engr., Calif. Asst. bus. mgr. U. So. Calif., LA, 1948-60, asst. bus. mgr., dir. campus devel., 1960-65, asst. bus. mgr., dir. campus devel., 1965-71, asso. v.p. bus. affairs, 1971-72, v.p. bus. affairs, 1972-86, sr. v.p. bus. affairs, 1986-88, univ. v.p., 1988-91, v.p. emeritus, 1991—. Cons. HEW. Editorial cons. College and University Business, 1955-58. Mem. nat. adv. coun. United Student Aid Funds, N.Y.C., 1974-77, chmn., 1976-77; spl. studies cons. div. higher edn. Office Edn. HEW, 1956-59; mem. citizens com. Palos Verdes Bd. Edn., 1955-57; mem. Hoover urban renewal adv. com. Cmty. Redevel. Agy. City of L.A., 1960-88. Lt. USNR, 1941-46, PTO. Recipient Pres.'s Outstanding Svc. award U. Redlands, 2000. Mem. Nat. Assn. Coll. and Univ. Bus. Officers (pres. 1978-79, dir. 1972-80, chmn. goals and programs com. 1978, chmn. large inst. com. 1986-87, Disting. Bus. Officer award 1986), Western Assn. Coll. and Univ. Bus. Officers (pres. 1971-72), Soc. Coll. and Univ. Planning, Blue Key, Golden Key, Phi Kappa Phi, Tau Beta Pi, Jonathan Club. Home: 4012 Via Larga Vis Palos Verdes Estates CA 90274 Office Phone: 213-740-2131. Business E-Mail: lazzaro@usc.edu.

LE, ANH-THU, physicist, researcher; b. Quang Ninh, Vietnam, May 20, 1967; s. Tran-Ba Le and Thi-Ly Ngo; m. Thanh-Huong Pham; children: Tracy, Alice, Hannah. B in Physics, Belarussian State U., 1990, PhD in Physics, 1994. Rsch. fellow Inst. of Physics, Hanoi, Vietnam, 1995—2000; guest scientist Max Planck Inst., Dresden, Germany, 1998—99; postdoctoral rsch. fellow physics Meml. U. of Nfld., St. John's, Canada, 2000—01; rsch. assoc. physics Kans. State U., Manhattan, Kans., 2001—06, rsch. asst. prof. physics, 2006—. Contbr. articles to profl. jours. Mem.: Am. Phys. Soc. Achievements include development of a quantum-mechanical ion-atom collision theory, known as the hyperspherical close-coupling method; first to Found The Quantum Signatures Of Chaos In Doubly-Excited States Of Atoms. Office: Dept of Physics Kans State U 116 Cardwell Hall Manhattan KS 66506 Home Phone: 785-587-4131; Office Phone: 785-532-1635.

LÊ, AN-MY, photographer, educator; BA in Biology and French with honors, Stanford U., 1982, MS in Biology, 1985; MFA in Photography, Yale U., 1993. Rsch. asst. in immunology Blood Ctr., Med. Ch. Stanford (Calif.) U., 1981—86, lectr. photography art dept., 1996—97, lectr. photography continuing studies dept., 1997; tchg. asst. photography dept. Yale U. Sch. Art, New Haven, 1992; lectr. photography Fordham U., NYU, Bard Coll., NYC, 1998; free-lance photographer, 1993—; asst. prof. photography Bard Coll. Staff photographer Compagnons du Devoir, France, 1986—91; vis. asst. prof. Bard Coll., 1999. Author: Small Wars, 2005; Exhibited in group shows at Canton (China) Cultural Ctr., 1993, Lowinski Gallery, N.Y., 1994, Houston Ctr. for Photography (traveled to Webster U., St. Louis and Silver Eye Ctr. for Photography, Pitts.), 1994—96, 1997, Mus. Modern Art, N.Y.C., 1997, Fotofest, Houston, 1998, Scott Nicols Gallery, San Francisco, 1999, Represented in permanent collections Mus. Fine Arts, Houston, Mus. Modern Art, N.Y.C., San Francisco, Met. Mus., N.Y.C., Bibliotéque Nationale, Paris. Fellow Photography fellow, N.Y. Found. for Arts, 1996; CameraWorks Inc. grantee, 1995, Guggenheim fellow, 1997, 1998—. Office: Dept Photography Bard Coll PO Box 5000 Annandale On Hudson NY 12504-5000

LE, DUY-LOAN, electrical engineer; b. Vietnam; arrived in U.S., 1975; married; 2 children. BSEE magna cum laude, U. Tex., 1982; MBA, U. Houston. With Tex. Instruments, 1982—, now sr. fellow. Contbr. articles to profl. publs. Named One of Houston's Women on the Move, Tex. Exec. Women, Nat. Technologist of Yr., Women of Color, Asian Am. Engr. of Yr., WITI; named one of America 's Top Women in Bus.-Game Changers, Pink mag. & Forté Found., 2007; named to Internat. Hall of Fame, WITI. Achievements include 22 patents in field. Office: Texas Instruments MS 722 12203 SW Freeway Stafford TX 77477 Office Phone: 281-274-3714. E-mail: zlon@Ti.com.*

LE, THUY TRONG, nuclear engineer, educator; b. Vietnam, Jan. 20, 1958; came to US, 1980; s. Thich Trong and Le-Phi Thi (Vuong) V.; m. Nhan Thi Le, Aug. 20, 1985; children: Thuy-Nhu Thi, Thi Trong. BS in Nuclear Engring., U. Calif., 1985, MS in Nuclear Engring., 1987, PhD in Engring., 1990. Nuclear reactor operator, health physicist asst. Nuc. Engring. Dept. U. Calif., Berkeley, 1985-88, grad. student instr. Nuc. Engring. and Physics Dept., 1987-90; rsch. asst. physics divsn. Lawrence Berkeley Nat. Lab., 1988-89; physics instr. Calif. Coll. of Alameda, 1989-90; rsch. engr. sci. computation divsn. applied physics group Westinghouse Savannah River Lab., 1990-93; sr. rschr. high performance computing group Fujitsu Am. Incorporation, Calif., 1993-2000. Cons. engr. Sierra Nuclear Corp., Scotts Valley, Calif., 1989—; adj. prof. U. S.C., Aiken, 1991-93; prof. San Jose State U., 1996—; cons. Fujitsu America Inc. 2001—. Contbr. numerous articles to profl. jours. Mem. IEEE, Am. Nuclear Soc. (math. and computation divsn.). Achievements include authoring GRIMH3 computer code: multi dimensional reactor analysis code, WINDEX System: detailed energy residence treatment code, research in computer architectures, real-time embedded systems, networking, numerical methods, parallel computing and algorithms, computational physics and engineering, criticality and radiation shielding, nuclear reactor analysis and design. Address: 44291 Pomace St Fremont CA 94539-6537 Home Phone: 510-659-0419. Business E-Mail: thuytle@email.sjsu.edu.

LEA, LORENZO BATES, lawyer; b. St. Louis, Apr. 12, 1925; s. Lorenzo Bates and Ursula Agnes (Gibson) L.; m. Marcia Gwendolyn Wood, Mar. 21, 1953; children— Victoria, Jennifer, Christopher. BS, MIT, 1946; JD, U. Mich., 1949; grad. Advanced Mgmt. Program, Harvard U., 1964. Bar: Ill. 1950. With Amoco Corp. (formerly Standard Oil Co. Ind.), Chgo., 1949—89, asst. gen. counsel, 1963-71, assoc. gen. counsel, 1971-72, gen. counsel, 1972-78, v.p., gen. counsel, 1978-89. Trustee Village of Glenview, Ill., 1963-64, mem. Zoning Bd., 1961-63; bd. dirs. Chgo. Crime Commn., 1978—, Midwest Coun. for Internat. Econ. Policy, 1973—, Chgo. Bar Found., 1981—, Chgo. Area Found. for Legal Svcs., 1981—; bd. dirs. United Charities of Chgo., 1973—, chmn., 1985—; bd. dirs. Cmty. Found. Collier County, 1997—, Naples Bot. Garden, 2000—. Served with USNR, 1943-46. Mem. ABA, Am. Petroleum Inst., Am. Arbitration Assn. (dir. 1980—), Ill. Bar Assn., Chgo. Bar Assn., Assn. Gen. Counsel (bd. dirs. 1983-89), Order of Coif, Law Club, Econs. Club, Legal, Mid-Am. (Chgo.), Glen View, Wyndemere, Hole-In-The-Wall, Sigma Xi. Republican. Mem. United Ch. of Christ.

LEA, ROBERT LEE, III, social sciences educator; b. Norfolk, Va., June 25, 1952; s. Robert Lee Lea Jr. and Charley Cooper Lea; m. Helen Simmons Lea, Sept. 4; children: John, Jeremy, Crystal Henley, Jason, Ashley Purnell, Jodi. Student, Danville C.C., Va., 1984—85; BA in Social Sci. and History summa cum laude, Averett Coll., Danville, 1988; MEd in Curriculum and Instrn., Averett U., Danville, 2003; postgrad., Lynchburg Coll., U. Va., Longwood Coll., Radford U. Lic. secondary social scis. and history tchr. Va., mid. sch. social studies, history, and lang. arts tchr. Va. Founder, owner, operator PTL Contractors, Ringgold, Va., 1975—81; pastor, sch. prin. Ringgold Christian Fellowship, 1981—88; dist. dir. Network 2000 Comm. Corp./U.S. Sprint, 1989—90; tchr. social studies Danville Pub. Schs., Va., 1990—. Staff writer Danville Register & Bee Spl. Publs., 2006—. Avocations: music, cooking, fishing, gardening. Home: 2332 Ridge Rd Danville VA 24540 Office: Galileo Magnet HS 231 S Ridge St Danville VA 24541

LEA, SCOTT CARTER, retired packaging company executive; b. New Orleans, Nov. 14, 1931; s. Leonard G. and Helen (Stoughton) L.; m. Marilyn Ruth Blair, Oct. 25, 1957; children: Scott, Nancy B., Mark S. BA, Amherst Coll., 1954; MBA, U. Pa., 1959. Sales and mktg. positions Riegel Paper, 1959-66, sales mgr. folding carton dept. southeastern div., 1966-67, gen. sales mgr., 1967-69, v.p. folding carton dept., 1969-71; v.p. bd. conversion div. Rexham Corp., Charlotte, NC, 1971-73, v.p. packaging group, 1973-74, pres., 1974-90; chmn. bd. Rexham Industries, Inc., 1990-92; chmn. bd. dirs. Lance Inc., Charlotte, 1996-99; ret., 1999. Trustee Johnson C. Smith U., Charlotte, N.C., 1977-2003, vice chmn. bd. trustees, 1998-2003; bd. dirs. Ctrl. Piedmont C.C. Found., Charlotte. With U.S. Army, 1954-57. Mem.: N.C. Zool. Soc. (bd. dirs. 1996—2002), Charlotte C. of C. (bd. dirs. 1977—78), Wild Dunes Club (Isle of Palms, S.C.), Quail Hollow Country Club, Carmel Country Club. Home: 3704 Stone Ct Charlotte NC 28226-7343 Office: 6135 Park South Dr Ste 510 Charlotte NC 28210

LEA, STANLEY E., artist, educator; b. Joplin, Mo., Apr. 5, 1930; s. Everett G. and Edna F. L.; m. Ruth Lowe, Aug. 19, 1951; children: Kristy Ruth, Kraig, Kelly B. B.F.A., Pitts. State U., 1953; M.F.A., U. Ark., 1961. Prof. art Sam Houston State U., Huntsville, 1961-93, Mexican Field Sch., Puebla, Mexico, 1963-65; vis. artist prof. Mus. Fine Arts, Houston, 1968, 69, 70; prof. art study abroad program London, 1977-78. Juror various art exhibits, 1970-81; workshop demonstrator, E. Tex. State U., Commerce, 1977, 10th ann. color print symposium, Tex. Tech. U., Lubbock, 1983, City of Huntsville mural, 1980; one-man shows paintings and/or prints, Valley House Gallery, Dallas, 1963, Inst. Mex. N. Am. de Rels., Mexico City, 1967, Main Place Gallery, Dallas, 1970-71, U. Tex. Med. Ctr., San Antonio, 1970, Moody Gallery, Houston, 1976, Sol Del Rio, San Antonio, 1978, 89, Adelle M. Fine Arts, Dallas, 1978, Dubose Gallery, Houston, 1980, Cultural Activities Ctr., Temple, Tex., 1982, Tex. A&M U., College Station, 1986, Mus. at E. Tex., Lufkin, 1989Cultural Ctr., Bryan, Tex., 1993; numerous group shows, latest being Moody Gallery, Houston, 1975, 77, Pecan Square Gallery, Austin, Tex., 1977, Am. Painters In Paris, 1975-76, Waco Art Center, Waco, Tex., 1977, East Tex. State U., Commerce, 1977, Galveston (Tex.) Art Center, 1978, Twenty Five Nat. Printmaker, Lubbock, Tex., 1978, Beaumont (Tex.) Art Mus., 1978, Art League of Houston, 1978, Gates Gallery, Port Arthur, Tex., 1979, Ars Longa, Houston, 1974, Laguna Gloria Mus., Austin, 1979; represented in permanent collections, Library of Congress, Washington, Smithsonian Mus. Am. Art, Washington, Calif. Palace of Legion of Honor, San Francisco, Brit. Mus., London, Mus. Fine Arts, Houston, USIA, N.Y.C., N.Y. Public Library, N.Y.C., Mpls. Inst. Art, Kalamazoo Inst. Art, Boise (Idaho) Gallery of Art, Madison (Wis.) Art Center, Spiva Art Center, Joplin, Mo., Ft. Worth Art Mus., Convention Ctr., The Woodlands, Tex., Cleve. Mus., Inst. Mexicano Norteamericana de Relationes, Mexico City, also corp. and pvt. collections. (Recipient numerous awards, latest being, Southwest Graphics Invitational award 1971, Dimensions IX Exhbn. award 1974, 68th Nat. Tex. Fine Arts Exhbn. 1979). Sam Houston State U. grantee, 1970, 74, Lakeside (Mich.) Studio grantee 1972, Casa Argentina grantee, Buenos Aires, 1973, Europe, 1982. Home: 3324 Winter Way Huntsville TX 77340-8919 Office Phone: 936-295-2853.

LEAB, DANIEL JOSEPH, history professor; b. Berlin, Aug. 29, 1936; s. Leo and Herta (Marcus) L.; m. Katharine Kyes, Aug. 16, 1964; children: Abigail Elizabeth, Constance Martha, Marcus Rogers. BA, Columbia U., 1957, MA, 1961, PhD, 1969. With Columbia U., NYC, 1966-73, Seton Hall U., 1974—. Co-editor Am. Book Prices Current. Author: A Union of Individuals: The Formation of the American Newspaper Guild, 1970, I Was a Communist for the FBI: the unhappy life and times of Matt Cvetic, 2000, Orwell Subverted: The CIA and the Filming of Animal Farm, 2007; mng. editor: Labor History, 1974—2002, Am. Communist History, 2002—. Mem. Bd. of Edn. Region 12 (Washington, Roxbury, Bridgewater), 1997-2002, 03—05; justice of the peace, 2001—. Recipient Commerford award. N.Y. State Labor History Assn., 1997. Fellow Met. Mus. Art; mem. Historians of Am. Communism (gen. sec.), Century Assn., Grolier Club. Home: PO Box 1216 Washington CT 06793-0216 Personal E-mail: danleab@earthlink.net.

LEACH, ANTHONY RAYMOND, financial executive; b. Gerrards Cross, Eng., Nov. 11, 1939; came to U.S., 1969; s. John Raymond Geoffrey and Edith Eileen (Blackburn) L.; m. Shirley Ann Kidd, Apr. 17, 1965; children: Mark Irwin, Amanda Jane, Christopher John. Supr. Ernst & Whinney, London, 1957-63, San Francisco, 1967—, mgr. Paris, 1963-69; mgr. fin. acctg. Occidental Petroleum Corp., LA, 1965-74, asst. controller, 1974-81, v.p. acctg., 1981-91, v.p., contr., exec. v.p., CFO, 1991, now v.p. fin. Fellow Inst. Chartered Accts.; mem. Fin. Execs. Inst. Clubs: Palos Verdes Breakfast. Office: Occidental Petroleum Corp 10889 Wilshire Blvd Los Angeles CA 90024-4201

LEACH, BERTON JOE, medical educator; b. Tuscola, Ill., Mar. 30, 1932; s. William Howard Leach and Frances Margaret De Haven; m. Barbara English, June 5, 1955; children: Laura Anne, Berton Franklin. AB, Washington U., 1957; MA, U. Mo., 1960, PhD, 1963. Assoc. prof. George Washington U., Washington, 1963—66; scientist adminstr. NSF, Washington, 1966—69; chmn., prof. Ctrl. Meth. Coll., Fayette, Mo., 1969—74; exec. sec. NIH, Bethesda, Md., 1974—76; sr. scientist pvt. industry, Rockville, Md., 1976—89; scientist Omni Rsch., Capital Sys. Group, 1976—89; admissions team leader Shady Grove Adventist Hosp., Rockville, 1988—; adj. prof. neurosci. Georgetown U., Washington, 1989—2003. Vis. scholar Harvard U., Cambridge, Mass., 1969; gen. reader Marine Biol. Lab., Woods Hole, Mass., 1985—87; guest rschr. NIH/Brain Behavior Lab., Poolesville, Md., 1991—92. Author: Structure and Development of Vertebrates, 1973, Vertebrate Biology Courseware, 1979, Human Neuroanatomy, 1999. Program chmn. Rotary Internat., Bethesda, 1975; vol. swimming instr. Rockville Swim Ctr., 2001; pres. Meth. Men's Club, Columbia, Mo., 1960. Decorated Am. Spirit Honor medal U.S. Army; named F. H. Dearing endowed prof., Ctrl. Meth. Coll., Fayette, 1970—74; fellow USPH rsch. fellow, NIH, Bethesda, 1962—63; grantee, NSF, Washington, 1973—74. Mem.: Am. Soc. Mammalogists (life), Sigma Xi. Republican. Methodist. Achievements include first scientist to ovulate polyovular follicles using exogenous hormones. Avocations: gardening, landscaping. Home: 12707 Weiss St Rockville MD 20853 Office: Shady Grove Adventist Hosp Admissions 9901 Medical Center Dr Rockville MD 20850

LEACH, BERTRAM GEORGE, retired military officer, securities dealer; b. Detroit Lakes, Minn., Nov. 18, 1929; s. Bertram George and Mabel Eliza (Wilkins) Leach; m. Norma Elizabeth Neprud (dec.); children: Bertram G. III, Mark A. BS, U. Minn., Mpls., 1952. Registered pharmacist. 2nd lt. U.S. Army, 1952, advanced through grades to lt. col., 1967, ret., 1972; surveyor Minn. State Bd. Pharmacy, St. Paul, 1972—73; middle level mgr. Advance Machine Co., Spring Park, Minn., 1973—75; mgr. Air Emergency, Mpls., 1975—76; bond broker MH Novick & Co., Mpls., 1976—90, Miller, Johnson & Levhn, 1990—2001, Smith Barno, 2001—02. Mgr. bldg. project Minnetonka Luth. Ch., Minn., 1992—2000. Decorated 11 Air medals US Army, Bronze Star US Army, Vietnam, Disting. Flying Cross US Army, Legion of Merit. Mem.: Beta Theta Pi. Republican. Avocations: golf, sailing, swimming, walking, bicycling. Home: 6710 Vernon Ave #318 Edina MN 55436

LEACH, BRENDA LEE, special education educator; d. Dayton Larue Leach and Rose Marie Clements Leach Garrison. BS in Elem., Spl. Edn., Moorhead State U., Minn., 1987; MA in Curriculum, Instrn., U. St. Thomas, St. Paul, 1996; MEd in Tchr. Leadership, U. Minn., Mpls., 1999. Classroom tchr. Cleve. Pub. Schs., 1987—90; spl. edn. tchr. St. Paul Pub. Schs., 1990—. Sgt. USAF, 1978—82. Avocations: reading, gardening, walking, bicycling, running.

LEACH, BRYAN, music company executive; b. Harlem, NY; Mem. rap group Smooth and Easy; dir. artist devel. TVT Records, 1995—98; v.p. A&R TVT Records, 1998—2006; sr. v.p. urban music RCA Music Group Sony/BMG, 2006—; pres. Polo Grounds Music, 2006—. Judge Uplifting Minds II Conf., 2004. CEO FanMale Inc., NYC. Named one of 40 Under 40, Crain's NY Bus., 2007. Office: RCA Music Group 745 5th Ave New York NY 10151*

LEACH, HOWARD H., former ambassador, former health care products company executive; b. Salinas, Calif., June 19, 1930; m. Gretchen Cooper, 1977; 5 children. BS, Yale U., 1952; studied at Stanford Grad Sch. of Bus., 1953, studied at Stanford Mgmt. Coll., 1968. Chmn. Sybron Corp., Saddle Brook, NJ, 1995—2000; U.S. amb. to France U.S. Dept. State, 2001—05.

LEACH, JAMES GLOVER, lawyer; b. Panama City, Fla., Jan. 26, 1948; s. Milledge Glover and Thelma Louise (Hamilton) L.; m. Judith A. Leach, Feb. 26, 1972 (div. 1987); children: Allison, Arica; m. January Parker, Dec. 1997. AS, Gulf Coast Coll., 1968; BA, Duke U., 1970; MBA, Ga. State U., 1974, MI, 1976; JD, Drake U., 1989. Bar: Iowa 1990; CPCU, CLU. Bank officer Bank South, Atlanta, 1972-75; asst. v.p. Johnson & Higgins, Atlanta, 1975-78; pres. Nat. Gen. Ins. Co., St. Louis, 1978-85, AOPA Svc. Corp., St. Louis, 1985-87, Kirke-Van Orsdel Specialty, Des Moines, 1987-89, Gallagher Specialty, St. Louis, 1990-92; prin., dir., counsel Pauli & Co. Inc., St. Louis, 1992-93; sr. v.p., gen. counsel Am. Safety Ins., Atlanta, 1993-98; pres., CEO, gen. counsel, dir. Unistar Fin. Svc. Corp., Dallas, 1998—2001; exec.-in-residence U. Hartford, 2001; sr. v.p., gen. counsel Bldrs. Ins. Group, Atlanta, 2001—. Cons. McDonnell Douglas, St. Louis, 1987; dir. Gateway Ins. Co., St. Louis, 1992; corp. assembly Blue Cross/Blue Shield, St. Louis, 1991-92. Contbr. articles to profl. jours. 1st lt. USAF, 1970-72, Korea. Avocations: pilot, golf. Office: Builders Insurance Group PO Box 723099 Atlanta GA 31139-0099 E-mail: jleach@buildersinsurancegroup.com.

LEACH, JIM (JAMES ALBERT SMITH LEACH), former congressman; b. Davenport, Iowa, Oct. 15, 1942; s. James Albert and Lois (Hill) L.; m. Elisabeth Debra Foxley, Dec. 6, 1975; 1 child, Gallagher BA, Princeton U., 1964; MA, Johns Hopkins U., 1966; postgrad., London Sch. Econs., 1966-68. Mem. staff Congressman Donald Rumsfeld, 1965-66; U.S. fgn. svc. officer, 1968-69, 70-73; spl. asst. to dir. Office Econ. Opportunity, 1969-70; pres. Flamegas Companies Inc., Bettendorf, Iowa, 1973-76; chmn. bd. Adel Wholesalers, Inc., Bettendorf, Iowa, 1973-76; mem. US Congress from 2nd Iowa dist. (formerly 1st), Washington, 1977—2007; vis. prof. Princeton U., 2007—. Chmn. banking and fin. svcs. com. Ho. Reps., chmn. subcom. Asia and Pacific, mem. com. internat. rels., co-chmn. US commn. improving effectiveness of UN; trustee Princeton U.; bd. dirs. Century Incidation. Chmn. Iowa Rep. Directions '76 Com. Republican. Episcopalian.

LEACH, JOHN F., editor, director, journalist, educator; b. Montrose, Colo., Aug. 6, 1952; s. Darrell Willis and Marian (Hester) L.; m. Deborah C. Ross, Jan. 2, 1982; children: Allison, Jason. BS in Journalism, U. Colo., 1974, MA in Journalism, 1979; MA in Am. Studies, U. Sussex, Brighton, Eng., 1983. News reporter Boulder (Colo.) Daily Camera, 1974-79, The Ariz. Republic, Phoenix, 1979-85, asst. city editor, 1985-93; news editor The Phoenix Gazette, 1993-94; asst. mng. editor Phoenix Gazette, 1994-95, The Ariz. Republic and The Phoenix Gazette, 1995-97; sr. editor The Ariz. Republic, Phoenix, 1997-99, sr. editor for online news, 1999—2002, sr. editor digital media, 2002—06, sr. mgr. online news, 2006—07; sr. editor for online news azcentral.com, 1999—2002, sr. editor digital media, 2002—06, editor, 2006—07; mng. editor news and digital media The Arizona Republic and azcentral.com, 2007—. Faculty assoc. Ariz. State U., Tempe, 1990—; pres., dir. Best of the West, Phoenix, 1987—; adv. bd. sch. journalism and mass comm. U. Colo., Boulder. Bd. Regents scholar U. Colo., 1970-74, Rotary Found. scholar, 1982-83. Mem. Ariz. Press Club (treas. 1984-86, pres. 1986-87), Soc. Profl. Journalists, Online News Assn., Newspaper Assn. Am. New Media Fedn. Office: The Ariz Republic 200 E Van Buren St Phoenix AZ 85004-2238 Home Phone: 602-840-7402. Personal E-mail: jfleach@hotmail.com. Business E-Mail: jleach@azcentral.com.

LEACH, MAURICE DERBY, JR., librarian, educator; b. Lexington, Ky., June 23, 1923; s. Maurice Derby and Sallie Eleanor (Woods) L.; m. Virginia Stuart Baskett, Mar. 16, 1953; 1 dau., Sarah Stuart. AB, U. Ky., 1945; B.L.S., U. Chgo., 1946. Bibliographer Dept. State, 1947-50; fgn. service officer Dept. State (USIS), vice consul, attache Cairo and Alexandria, Beirut, 1950-59; chmn. dept. library sci. U. Ky., 1959-66; regional program officer Ford Found., Beirut, 1967-68; univ. librarian, prof. Washington and Lee U., Lexington, Va., 1968-85, prof., asst. to pres., 1985-88; library adviser Nat. Library, Egypt, Lebanon and acad. libraries in Middle East. Contbr. articles to profl. jours. Served with AUS, 1948-49. Mem. English Speaking Union (pres. Lexington br. 1970-75), Va. Libr. Assn. (pres. 1976), Assn. Preservation of Va. Activities (dir. Lexington br. 1989-91), Rockbridge Hist. Soc., SAR (v.p. 1990-93). Episcopalian. Home: 1 Courtland Cir Lexington VA 24450-1813

LEACH, MIKE, college football coach; b. Mar. 9, 1961; m. Sharon Leach; children: Janeen, Kim, Kiersten, Cody. BS in Am. Studies, Brigham Young Univ., 1983; JD, Pepperdine Univ., 1986; MS in Sports Sci., Coaching, US Sports Acad., 1988. Asst. coach, offensive line coach Cal-Poly., 1987; asst. coach Coll. of the Desert, 1988; asst. offensive coord. Iowa Wesleyan, 1989—91, Valdosta St, 1992—96, Kentucky Univ., 1997—98; asst. coach, offensive coord. Okla. Univ., 1999—2000; head coach Tex. Tech., 2000—04. Office: Tex Tech Univ 2500 Broadway Lubbock TX

LEACH, RALPH F., banker; b. Elgin, Ill., June 24, 1917; s. Harry A. and Edith (Sanders) L.; m. Harriet C. Scheuerman, Nov. 18, 1944; children: C. David, H. Randall, Barbara E. AB, U. Chgo., 1938. Investment analyst Harris Trust & Savs. Bank, Chgo., 1940-48, Valley Nat. Bank, Phoenix, 1948-50; chief govt. finance sect. Fed. Res. Bd., Washington, 1950-53; treas. Guaranty Trust Co., NYC, 1953-59, v.p., 1958-59; v.p., treas. Morgan Guaranty Trust Co., NYC, 1959-62, sr. v.p., treas., 1962-64, exec. v.p., treas., 1964-68, vice chmn. bd. dirs., 1968-71, chmn. exec. com., 1971-77; dir. Merrill Lynch and Co., NYC, 1978—89. Chmn. emeritus Energy Conversion Devices Inc. Bd. trustees The Juilliard Sch., 1963—87, vice chmn., 1968—87. Capt. USMC, 1940—45. Mem.: Phi Kappa Psi. Home: Apt 446 2855 W Commercial Blvd Fort Lauderdale FL 33309-2973 Office Phone: 954-777-3188.

LEACH, RICHARD MAXWELL, JR., (MAX LEACH JR.), corporate professional, consultant; b. Chillicothe, Tex., June 14, 1934; s. Richard Maxwell and Lelia Booth (Page) L.; m. Wanda Gail Groves, Feb. 4, 1956; children: Richard Clifton, John Christopher, Sandra Gail, Kathy Lynn. BS in Acctg. magna cum laude, Abilene Christian U., 1955. Registered fin. cons., CLU. Asst. dir. agys. Am. Founders Ins. Co., Austin, Tex., 1960—62; owner A.F. Ins. Planning Assocs., Temple, Tex., 1962—65; v.p. sales Christian Fidelity Life Ins. Co., Waxahachie, Tex., 1966—67; exec. v.p. Acad. Computer Tech., Inc., Dallas, 1968—69; pres., chief exec. officer Insta-Search Internat., Inc., Dallas, 1969—71; prin., chief exec. officer, fin. cons. Leach and Assocs., Albuquerque, 1971—; pres. The Wright Edge, Inc., 1988—90; pres., CEO Action Mktg. Programs, Inc., 1989—92; CEO Vacation Premiums Internat., Inc., 1990—92; pres., CEO ITM Corp., Albuquerque, 1993—98; founder, chmn., CEO Health Maximization Rsch. Studies Inst. Internat., Albuquerque, 1999—. Chmn. bd. United Quest Inc., Albuquerque, Hosanna Inc., Albuquerque; real estate broker; commodity futures broker; exec. dir., bd. dirs. New Heart, Inc., Albuquerque, 1975-85; owner Insta-Copy, Albuquerque, 1973-76, Radio Sta. KYLE-FM, Temple, 1963-64. Editor, author Hosanna newspaper, 1973-74. Gen. dir. Here's Life, New Mexico, Albuquerque, 1976; exec. dir. Christians for Cambodia, Albuquerque, 1979-80. With U.S. Army, 1955-57. Home: 3308 June St NE Albuquerque NM 87111-5029 Office: 10308 Candelaria NE # 345 Albuquerque NM 87112-1505 *Personal philosophy: Success is doing what God wants you to do when and where He would have you do it.*

LEACH, ROBERT ELLIS, orthopedist, surgeon, educator; b. Sanford, Maine, Nov. 25, 1931; s. Ellis and Estella (Tucker) L.; m. Laurine Seber, Aug. 20, 1955; children: Cathy, Brian, Michael, Craig, Karen, Diane. AB, Princeton U., 1953; MD, Columbia U., 1957. Diplomate Am. Bd. Orthopedic Surgery (treas. 1986-93). Resident orthopedic surgery U. Minn., 1957-62; orthopedic surgeon Lahey Clinic, Boston, 1964-68, chmn. dept., 1968-70; prof., chmn. dept. Boston U. Med. Sch., 1970—. Head physician U.S. Olympic Team, 1984; chmn. sports medicine coun. U.S. Olympic Com., 1984-93; vice chmn. sports medicine coun. U.S. Tennis Assn., 1988-2002. Editor-in-chief Am. J. Sports Med.; editor emeritus Am. Jour. Sports Medicine, 2002; contbr. articles to profl. jours. Served to lt. comdr. USNR, 1962-64. Named Sports Medicine Man of Yr., 1988; named to Sports Medicine Hall of Fame, 2003; recipient Rovere Career Tchg. award, 1995, Ernst Jokl Sports Medicine award, 2000; Am., Brit., Can. Orthop. Travelling fellow, 1971. Mem. Am. Acad. Orthopedic Surgeons, Continental Orthopedic Soc. (sec. 1966), Am. Orthopedic Assn. (pres. 1994), Am. Orthopedic Soc. Sports Medicine (pres. 1983), Longwood Cricket Club. Home: 40 Rockport Rd Weston MA 02493-1428 Office: 230 Calvary St Waltham MA 02453-8366 Office Phone: 617-638-5633. Personal E-mail: releachrock@aol.com.

LEACH, RONALD GEORGE, education educator, librarian; b. Monroe, Mich., Feb. 22, 1938; s. Garnet William and Erma (Erbadine) L.; m. Joy Adeline Moore, Dec. 21, 1956; children— Ronald George, Debra Mabel, Catherine Louise, Shane John. BS in Secondary Edn, Central Mich. U., 1966; MA in L.S. (U.S. Office Edn. fellow 1968-69), U. Mich., 1969; PhD in Higher Edn. Adminstrn, Mich. State U., 1980. Head libr. Ohio State U., Mansfield, 1969-70; asst. dir., then acting dir. libr. Lake Superior State Coll., Sault Ste. Marie, Mich., 1970-76; assoc. dir. librs. Central Mich. U., 1976-80; dean libr. svcs. Ind. State U., Terre Haute, 1980-93, assoc. v.p. info. svcs., dean of librs., 1994-97, prof. higher ednl. adminstrn., 1997—. Prof. edn., mem. accreditation teams North Ctrl. Assn. Author articles in field. Served with N.G., 1955-61. Mem. ALA, INFORMA (steering com. 1990—), Assn. Coll. and Rsch. Librs., Libr. Info. and Tech. Assn., Ind. Libr. Assn., Am. Soc. Info. Sci., Libr. Adminstrn. and Mgmt. Assn. (pres. 1985-86), Online Computer Libr. Ctr. User Council (exec. com. 1986, 88). Office: Ind State U Dept Leadership Admin Found Terre Haute IN 47809-0001

LEACHMAN, RUSSELL DEWITT, lawyer; b. Amarillo, Tex., Aug. 8, 1965; s. William D. and Alexia (Hall) L.; m. Margaret Feuille, July 8, 1989; children: William Benton, Richard Boone. BA in Polit. Sci., Tex. Tech. U., 1986, JD, 1990. Bar: Tex. 1990, U.S. Dist. Ct. (we. dist.) Tex. 1992, U.S. Dist. Ct. (no. dist.) Tex. 1994, U.S. Dist. Ct. (ea. dist.) Tex. 1998, U.S. Ct. Appeals (5th cir.) 1994; Bd. cert. criminal law, 1996. Asst. dist. atty. 34th Judicial Dist. Tex., El Paso, 1990-92; atty. Leachman & Escobar LLP, El Paso, 1992-94, Diamond Rash Gordon & Jackson, El Paso, 1994—2001, Mounce, Green, Myers, Safi & Galatzan, P.C., El Paso, 2001—04, US Attys. Office, El Paso, 2004—. Dir. El Paso Young Lawyers Assn. Mock Trial Competition, El Paso, 1990-95; mem. Ducks Unltd. Area Com., El

Paso, 1991—, area chmn., 1999-2000, dist. chmn., 2001—. Mem. Lodge 130 (mason), Phi Gamma Delta, Delta Theta Phi, Delta Phi Epsilon, Phi Rho Pi, Pi Sigma Alpha. Baptist. Office Phone: 915-534-6884. E-mail: russell.leachman@usdoj.gov.

LEADBETTER, TIFFANY, hotel executive; b. Tex., 1976; BA, Cornell U., 1998; MBA, U. Chgo. Grad. Sch. Bus. Sales mgmt. trainee Hyatt Regency McCormick Place, Chgo., 1998; from intern to dir. devel. Global Hyatt Corp., Chgo., 1999—2006, asst. v.p. N.Am. acquisitions & devel., 2006—. Named one of 40 Under 40, Crain's Chgo. Bus., 2006. Office: Global Hyatt Corp 71 S Wacker Dr Chicago IL 60606

LEADER, BRUCE ROBERT, secondary school educator; b. Buffalo, Mar. 9, 1967; s. Bennett and Fay (Broder) L. BA in History and Philosophy, SUNY, Binghamton, 1989; MA in History, SUNY, Buffalo, 1991. Programming asst. Sta.-WBFO Radio, NY, 1989-90; supr. computer lab. Williamsville Ctrl. Schs., NY, 1991; tchr. social studies Starpoint Ctrl. Schs., Lockport, NY, 1991—; head of history Anglican Internat. Sch., Jerusalem, 2000—02. Head coach soccer Starpoint Ctrl. Schs., 1992—; tchr. Bridges for Edn., Poland, summer 1995; mem. U.S. Bicycling Tour, summer 1991; English lang. tchr. Yew Wah Lang. Sch., Shanghai, China, summer 1999. Head coach Amherst Soccer Assn., 1989-92. Recipient Nat. Sallie Mae award outstanding first yr. tchr. Democrat. Jewish. Avocations: reading, bicycling, travel, camping. Home: 650 Auburn Ave Buffalo NY 14222-1415 Office: Starpoint Ctrl Schs 4363 Mapleton Rd Lockport NY 14094-9652

LEADER, JONATHAN M, archaeologist, researcher; b. Rochester, Ny, May 3, 1955; m. Bonnie Hill, Apr. 27, 1975. BA, Western Mich. U., Kalamazoo, 1979; MA, U. Fla., Gainesville, 1985, PhD, 1988. State archaeologist U. SC., Columbia, 2000—; interim dir. Inst. of Archaeolgy & Anthropology, 2003—05. Com. mem. Govs. Ad Hoc Com. on Native Am. Affairs. SC. Commn. for Minority Affairs., Columbia, 2001—03; adv. bd. mem. Palmetto Trust for Hist. Preservation., 1998—2006; bd. mem. Hist. Camden, SC, 2000—06; statutory mem. SCDNR Heritage Trust, Columbia, 2000—, Native Am. Adv. Com. for the Commn. of Minority Affairs, 2004—06; nat. rsch. and tech. studies chair Am. Inst. for Conservation, Washington, 1999—2000, nat. wooden artifacts group chair, 1994—95. Recipient Outstanding Svc. award, Archaeol. Soc. SC., 2006, Edisto Tribal Camp Program award, Four Holes Reservation Indian Orgn., 1994, SOS Program award, SC. Fedn. of Mus., 1994, Hansinger Spl. Paleoanthropology award, Fla. Acad. Scis., 1985, Disting. Alumni Anthropology award, Western Mich. U., 2005, Nat. Preservation award, Nat. Trust Adv. Coun., 2002, Partnership award, Dept. of the Interior, Nat. Pk. Svc., 2001, Native Am. Com. award, SC. United Meth. Ch., 1998, Native Am. Program award, US Army Chaplain Ctr. and Sch. Ft. Jackson, SC, 2000, Chester Cannons Project award, Chester Hist. Soc., 1998, Dirs. award, Inst. of Archaeology and Anthropology, 1996. Fellow: Royal Geog. Soc., Explorer's Club (Nat. fellow 2005); mem.: Sigma Xi, Phi Kappa Phi. Office: Inst Archaeology & Anthropology 1321 Pendleton St Columbia SC 29208 Office Phone: 803-777-8170.

LEADER, LEONARD, lawyer; b. NYC, 1950; BA cum laude, CUNY City Coll., 1970; JD cum laude, Fordham U., 1973; LLM in Taxation, NYU Grad. Sch. Law, 1982. Bar: NY 1974, US Ct. Appeals (2nd cir.) 1975, US Dist. Ct. (so. dist. NY) 1975, Conn. 1983. Assoc. Parker, Chapin, Flattau & Klimpl, LLP, NYC, 1973—81; atty. Kleban & Samon, P.C., Southport, Conn., 1981—96; ptnr., chair trusts and estates dept. Wiggin & Dana, LLP, Stamford, Conn. Contbr. articles to profl. publs. Sec., bd. dirs. Jewish Home for the Elderly of Fairfield Men's Club; bd. dirs. Ctr. Family Bus. U. New Haven. Named one of Top 100 Attys., Worth mag., 2006. Mem.: Bridgeport Bar Assn. (probate sect.), Conn. Bar Assn. (probate sect.), NY State Bar Assn. (trusts and estates sect.), ABA (taxation sect., mem. generation skipping trusts com.), Phi Beta Kappa. Office: Wiggin & Dana LLP PO Box 110325 400 Atlantic St Stamford CT 06911-0325 Office Phone: 203-363-7602. Office Fax: 203-363-7676. E-mail: lleader@wiggin.com.*

LEADER, ROBERT JOHN, lawyer; b. Syracuse, NY, Oct. 14, 1933; s. Henry John and Dorothy Alberta (Schad) Leader; m. Nancy Bruce, Sept. 23, 1960 (dec.); children: Henry, William, Catherine, Thomas, Edward. AB, Cornell U., 1956; JD, Syracuse U., 1962. Bar: N.Y. 1963. Assoc. Ferris, Hughes, Dorrance & Groben, Utica, N.Y., 1962-64; ptnr. Cole Leader & Ehmer, Gouverneur, N.Y., 1964-66, Case & Leader, Gouverneur, 1966—; corp. counsel Village of Edwards, 2005—. Sec. North Country Hosps. Inc., 1972—; atty. Town of Gouverneur, 1967-94, Town of Pitcairn, NY, 1974—, Town of Edwards, 1974—, Town of Rossie, 1985—, Town of Fowler, 1978—; corp. counsel Village of Gouverneur, 1973—2004; counsel Gouverneur Ctrl. Sch. Dist., 1980—; bd. dirs. Gouverneur Savs. and Loan Trustee Edward John Noble Hosp., Gouverneur, 1972—, Gouverneur Libr., 1973-83, Governeur Nursing Home Co., Inc., 1972—; past pres., 1979-81, past chmn. bd. trustees, 1979-81; Republican chmn. Town and Village of Gouverneur, 1969-72; del. N.Y. State Jud. conv., 1981—. Capt. USAF, 1956-59. Mem. Rotary (pres. 1988-89). Roman Catholic. Office: 107 E Main St Gouverneur NY 13642-1408 Home: 157 St Croix Ave Cocoa Beach FL 32931 Office Phone: 315-287-2000.

LEAF, ALEXANDER, preventive medicine physician, epidemiologist; b. Yokohama, Japan, Apr. 10, 1920; arrived in U.S., 1922, naturalized, 1936; s. Aaron L. and Dora (Hural) Leaf; m. Barbara Louise Kincaid, Oct. 1943; children: Caroline Joan, Rebecca Louise, Tamara Jean. BS, U. Wash., 1940; MD, U. Mich., 1943; MA, Harvard, 1961. Intern Mass. Gen. Hosp., Boston, 1943—44, mem. staff, 1949—, physician-in-chief, 1966—81; resident Mayo Found., Rochester, Minn., 1944—45; rsch. fellow U. Mich., 1947—49; practice internal medicine Boston, 1949—90; faculty Med. Sch., Harvard, 1949—66, Jackson prof. clin. medicine, 1966—81, Ridley Watts prof. preventive medicine, 1980—90, chmn. dept. preventive medicine and clin. epidemiology, 1980—90, Jackson prof. clin. medicine emeritus, 1990—; Disting. physician VA Medical Ctr. Brockton/W. Roxbury Hosps., Boston, 1992—97. Capt. M.C. US Army, 1945—46. Recipient Outstanding Achievement award, U. Minn., 1964; fellow Vis. fellow, Balliol Coll., Eng., 1971—72, Guggenheim, 1971—72. Master: ACP; fellow: Am. Acad. Arts and Scis.; mem.: NAS, Internat. Soc. Nephrology (A.M. Richards award 1997), Assn. Am. Physicians (Kober medal 1995), Biophys. Soc., Am. Physiol. Soc., Am. Soc. Clin. Investigation (past pres.), Inst. Medicine. Home: 5 Sussex Rd Winchester MA 01890-3846 Office: Mass Gen Hosp Bldg 149 13th St Charlestown MA 02129 Office Phone: 617-726-5908. Business E-Mail: aleaf@partners.org.

LEAF, HOWARD WESTLEY, retired military officer; b. Menominee, Mich., Sept. 22, 1923; s. Joseph Conrad and Hilda Eugene (Lavoy) L.; m. Madonna Anne; children: Mary Elizabeth, Timothy M., Barbara Anne, Anne Marie Moore, Thomas M., James D. BS, Colo. Sch. Mines, 1950; MS, St. Louis U., 1955; grad., Command and Staff Coll., 1961, Indsl. Coll. Armed Forces, 1969. Commd. 2d lt. U.S. Air Force, 1951, advanced through grades to lt. gen., 1980, ret., 1985; aviation cadet, 1950-51; jet pilot Korea, 1952-53; test pilot, 1955-60; geophysicist, 1961-64; ops. officer (49th Tactical Fighter Wing), Europe, 1965; squadron comdr. S.E. Asia, 1966; staff officer (Hdqrs. USAF), 1966-68, 69-71; wing comdr. 1st and 366th Tactical Fighter Wings, 1971-74; dep. chief staff for requirements Tactical Air Command, 1974-76; comdr. Air Force Test and Evaluation Ctr., Kirtland AFB, N.Mex., 1976-80; insp. gen. U.S. Air Force, Washington, 1980-83, asst. vice chief of staff, 1983-85; sr. v.p. BDM Internat. Corp., McLean, Va., 1984-91; dir. test and evaluation Hdqrs. USAF The Pentagon, Washington, 1992—. Mem. Air Force Sci. Adv. Bd. Decorated D.S.M., Silver Star with one oak leaf cluster, Legion of Merit, D.F.C.; recipient Eugene M. Zuckert Mgmt. Award, 1978, Disting. Achievement award Colo. Sch. Mines, 1982, Exceptional Svc. award USAF, 1997. Mem. Internat. Test and Evaluation Assn. (sr. adv. bd., Allen R. Mattews Award, 1994). Presbyterian. Home: 16002 Dr Bowen Rd Brandywine MD 20613 Office: Hdqs USAF TE 4E-995 The Pentagon Washington DC 20330-0001 Personal E-mail: leafhq@aol.com.

LEAF, PAUL, film producer, writer; b. NYC, May 2, 1929; s. Manuel and Anna (Dardick) L.; m. Nydia Ellis, Oct. 22, 1955 (div. 1990); children: Jonathan, Alexandra, Ellen; m. Christine Hardy, Dec. 15, 1999. BA in Drama with honors, CCNY, 1952. Pres. Sea Gate Co. Dir., prodr.: 17 Broadway prodns., including The Subject Was Roses, 1964 (Pulitzer prize, 1964), films include: The Anatomy of Cindy Fink, 1967, The Last Mohican, 1967, Bach to Bach, 1968, Sunday Father, 1968, I Never Promised You a Long Run, 1970, The Reason Why, 1970, Nightside, 1972, Desperate Characters, 1972, Hail to the Chief, 1973, Judge Horton and the Scottsboro Boys, 1976 (Peabody award), Sister Aimee, 1977, Every Man a King, 1977, Top Secret, 1979, God, Sex and Apple Pie, 1998, TV prodns. include Sgt. Matlovich vs. the U.S. Air Force, 1978 (Best Feature Austin Film Fesival, Audience Favorite Ariz. Internat. Film Festival, Best Comedy Marco Island Film Festival, Best Dir. Ariz. Film Festival); author: Comrades, 1987, Red, Right, Returning, 1989. Founder, chmn. Santa Monica Arts Commn., Santa Monica Arts Found.; founder, cons., bd. dirs. Santa Monica Coll. Art, Design and Architecture, 1990—; mem. grants panel Nat. Endowment for the Arts, 1993, Nat. Endowment for the Humanities, 1994. With U.S. Army, 1952-54. Decorated Meritorious Service medal; recipient 20 internat. festival and profl. awards, including Venice, 1967, London, 1967, 68, 69, 98-99, N.Y., 1967, 68, 69, Berlin, 1972, Austin, Tucson, N.Y., San Diego film festivals. Mem. Dirs. Guild Am., Writers Guild Am.

LEAF, ROBERT JAY, dental insurance consultant; b. Mt. Vernon, NY, July 27, 1944; s. Jules William and Evelyn (Schneider) L.; m. Jeanette Ann Benjamin, June 17, 1973; children: Jeremy Robert, David Evan. DMD, Harvard U., 1969. 100T captain's lic. USCG. Pres. Universal Profl. Ctrs., NYC, 1971-74; dentist in pvt. practice NYC, 1973-80; pres. Am. Dental Examiners, Inc., NYC, 1978—; chmn. Better Benefits, Inc., NYC, 1990—. Pres., founder LeafRe Reins. Co., Ariz., 1993—, Dental Profl. Rev. Sys., 2006; founder Dental Health Alliance, 1994, pres. 1994-96; cons. Guardian Life Ins. Co., N.Y.C., 1979, Prin. Life Ins. Co., Iowa, 1981, 93, Mass. Mut. Life Ins. Co., 1983, 94, Equitable, N.Y., 1985, Empire Blue Cross, 1986, Prudential, N.J., 1987, Gen. Mills, Minn., 1988, Aetna, Conn., 1989, Am. Airlines, Tex., 1990, Protective Life Ins. Co., Alabama, 1991, 96, 99, Gen. Am. Life Ins. Co., 1992, 94, Blue Cross/Blue Shield, R.I., 1993, Fortis Benefits Ins. Co., Mo., 1988, 93, Chubb Life Ins. Co. Am., N.H., 1993, Jefferson Pilot Life, 1994, Trustmark Life, 1994, Delta Dental Minn., 1994, Healthsource Provident Life Inst. Co., 1996, Delta Dental California, 1997, Shenandoah Life Ins. Co., 1997, WalMart, 1999, 2004, Protective Life, 1999, Boston Mut., 2000, Hannover Life Reins., 2000, TransAm. and Delta Dental, 2001, 02, 05,06, Am. Pioneer Life, 2003; thcr. Columbia U. Dental Sch., 1994-, Harvard Sch. Dental Medicine dental econs., 3d party programs, 2004-; lectr. at nat. confs. on dental ins., vol. dental ins., and managed dental care, group officers round table, 1985. Author: The Dental Logic System, 1984, The Dental Learning System, 1987, Dental Professional Review Systems Software, 2006; also articles; devel. vol. dental ins. plan. Bd. dirs. Jewish Community Ctr., Harrison, N.Y., 1992. Mem. ADA, Dental Soc. State of N.Y., First Dist. Dental Soc., Acad. Gen. Dentistry, Am. Assn. Dental Cons., Am. Soc. for Preventive Dentistry, Beach Point Yacht Club (rear commodore). Avocations: sailing, skiing, reading. Office: Am Dental Examiners Inc 277 North Ave 2d Fl New Rochelle NY 10801 Home Phone: 914-777-1313; Office Phone: 914-712-0100. Personal E-mail: robert@betterbenefits.com. Business E-Mail: rjleaf13@gmail.com.

LEAF, ROBERT STEPHEN, public relations executive; b. NYC, Aug. 9, 1931; s. Nathan and Anne (Feinman) L.; m. Adele Ornstein, June 8, 1958; 1 child, Stuart Nathan. BJ, U. Mo., Columbia, 1952; MA, U. Mo, Columbia, 1954. Account exec. Herbert Kaufman, NYC, 1956-57; various positions Marsteller Orgn., NYC, 1957-65; v.p., gen. mgr. Marsteller Internat., Brussels, 1965-68, v.p. Europe, 1968-70; pres. Burson-Marsteller Internat. and Marsteller Internat., London, 1970—97; chmn. Burson-Marsteller Internat., London, 1985-97, Robert S. Leaf Cons., England, 1997—2005. Contbr. articles to profl. jours. Mem. Inst. Pub. Relations Eng., Pub. Relations Consultancy Assn. (London), Fgn. Press Assn., Pub. Relations Soc. Am., Hurlingham Club, Alpha Pi Zeta, Kappa Tau Alpha Clubs: Hurlingham (London). Home: 3 Fursecroft George St London W1H 5LF England Office: Robert S Leaf Cons Ltd 24 Bloomsbury Way London WC14 2PX England Home Phone: 0207 262 4686; Office Phone: 0207 43 9787. Business E-Mail: bob.leaf@bm.com.

LEAHEY, LYNN, editor-in-chief; married; 1 child, Jack. BA in English, Colgate U., 1981. From asst. editor, to mng. ed then editor-in-chief Soap Opera Digest, NYC, 1984—91, editor-in-chief, 1991—; editl. dir. Soap Opera Weekly, NYC, 2001—. Office: Soap Opera Digest 261 Madison Ave Fl 10 New York NY 10016-2303 Office Phone: 212-716-2700. Office Fax: 212-645-0683. E-mail: SODeditor@aol.com.*

LEAHEY, MILES CARY, economist; b. Washington, Sept. 14, 1952; s. Thomas Francis and Eva Smith (Hardy) L.; m. Patricia C. Mosser, Aug. 1, 1987. AB with honors, Clark U., 1974; MA, U. Pa., 1977, PhD, 1978. Fiscal economist Office of Mgmt. and Budget, Washington, 1978-80; sr. economist DRI, Lexington, Mass., 1980-83; sr. v.p., sr. economist Shearson Lehman Bros., NYC, 1983-88; dir. econ. staff GM, NYC, 1988-91; chief U.S. fin. markets economist Lehman Bros., NYC, 1991-97; chief U.S. economist High Frequency Econ., Valhalla, N.Y., 1997-98; mng. dir., sr. U.S. economist Primark Decision Econs., NYC, 1998—2000; dir., sr. US economist Deutsche Bank, NYC, 2000—04; sr. mng. dir. Decision Econ., NYC, 2005—. Lectr. U. Pa., 1977, Swarthmore (Pa.) Coll., 1978, Boston U., 1983. Author: Government and Capital Formation, 1979; contbr. articles to profl. jours. Mem. Am. Econs. Assn., Nat. Assn. Bus. Economists, Columbia Golf Club, Blue Hill Troupe (N.Y.C.). Democrat. Avocations: theater, opera, golf. Home: 340 Riverside Dr Apt 7C New York NY 10025-3436 Office: Decision Econ 530 Fifth Ave 7th Fl New York NY 10036 Office Phone: 212-884-9449. Business E-Mail: cary.leahey@decisioneconomicsinc.com.

LEAHY, CHRISTINE A., lawyer, information technology executive; b. Providence, June 1964; m. Adam Weinberg; children: Annika, Sammantha. BA, Brown U., 1986; JD, Boston Coll., 1991. Ptnr. Sidley, Austin, Brown & Wood, Chgo., 1991—2001; sr. v.p., gen. counsel, corp. sec. CDW Corp, Vernon Hills, Ill., 2002—. Mem. YWCA Cir. Friends, Chgo. Women in Tech. Grp. Mem.: DC Bar Assn., Chgo. Bar Assn., ABA. Office: CDW Corp 200 N Milwaukee Ave Vernon Hills IL 60061*

LEAHY, JEANNETTE (JEANNETTE OLIVER LEAHY TINEN KAEHLER), actress; b. Sept. 9, 1927; d. Kenneth A. and Berthe Hortence (Borie) Oliver; m. Thomas J. Leahy (dec.); children: Denyse Leahy Karsten Feeney, Thomas J.; m. Wallace W. Kaehler, Jan. 13, 1980. Student, various acting workshops. TV personality Jeannette Lee Sta. WFBM-TV, Indpls., 1950-53; actress Peninsula Players Summer Stock Theatre, Door County, Wis., 1960—. Numerous radio, TV, stage, film, commls. appearances. V.p. Evanston Drama Club, 1961-62; dir. Wilmette Children's Theatre, 1960-65; bd. dirs. Easter Seal Soc., 1070-75. With U.S. Army, WWII. Mem. AFTRA, SAG, Equity Union, Mich. Shores Club, Wilmette-Kenilworth Club (pres. 1956-57, 1999-2001), North Shore Assocs. Club (pres. 1982-83, 94-95, 2002-2003). Republican. Roman Catholic.

LEAHY, JOHN L., software development company executive; B in Fin., Merrimack Coll.; MBA, Boston Coll. With PepsiCo, 1982—99; exec. v.p. Keane, Inc., Mass., CFO, interim pres., CEO, 2006—, member, office of pres. Mem. Financial Exec. Inst. Office: Keane Inc 100 City Square Boston MA 02129

LEAHY, MICHAEL JOSEPH, retired newspaper editor; b. Chgo., Feb. 24, 1939; s. Joseph Michael and Elizabeth Catherine (Keefe) L.; m. Harriet Smith Friday, Sept. 18, 1971; children: Christine Elizabeth, Thomas Joseph, Christopher Michael. AB, Georgetown U., 1961; MS in Journalism, Columbia U., 1966. From copy boy, news clk., copy editor to editor L.I. Weekly N.Y. Times, NYC, 1961-77, editor Conn. Weekly, 1977-81, travel editor, 1982-86, editor arts and leisure sect., 1986-90, dep. editor The Week in Review, 1990-92, real estate editor, 1992—2004, spl. projects editor, 2004—05, cons., 2005—. Editor: If You're Thinking of Living All About 115 Great Neighborhoods In & Around New York, (with A.M. Rosenthal, A. Gelb and N. Kerr) The Sophisticated Traveler series. Bd. advisors Georgetown U., 1990-96; mem. edn. com. St. David's Sch., 1991-93. 1st lt. U.S. Army, 1961-64. Pulitzer Traveling fellow Columbia U., 1967 Mem. Georgetown Libr. Assocs. (trustee 1981-94, 97—), Columbia Journalism Alumni (pres. 1981-83), Century Assn. Roman Catholic. Office: NY Times Co 229 W 43rd St New York NY 10036-3959

LEAHY, PAT (P. PATRICK LEAHY), geologist, former federal official; b. Troy, NY, Feb. 9, 1947; s. William P. and Shirley A. (Breen) L.; m. Catherine McGuane, July 8, 1972; children: Sarah J., W. Dennis, M. Brendan. BS, Boston Coll., 1968, MS, 1970; PhD, Rensselaer Poly. Inst., 1979. Registered profl. hydrogeologist. Hydrologist US Geol. Survey, US Dept. Interior, Dover, Del., 1974-79, asst. dist. chief Trenton, NJ, 1979-88, staff scientist Reston, Va., 1988-91, dep. asst. chief hydrologist, 1991-95, chief geologist, 1995—2006, assoc. dir. for geology, geologic discipline, 2005—06, dir., 2005—06; exec. dir. Am Geological Inst, Alexandria, Va., 2007—. Mem. U.S. nat. com. on geology NRC, 1999. Author: U.S. Geological Survey Professional Paper. Recipient Meritorious Svc. award US Dept. Interior, 1996, Award of Excellence in Sci., Boston Coll. Alumni Assn., 1996; Rensselaer Poly. Inst. Alumni Assn. Sci. fellow, 1995. Fellow Geol. Soc. Am.; mem. Am. Geophys. Union, Am. Water Resources Assn., Am. Inst. Hydrology, Internat. Assn. Hydrologists (pres. 1999). Office: Am Geological Inst 4220 King St Alexandria VA 22302

LEAHY, PATRICK JOSEPH, senator; b. Montpelier, Vt., Mar. 31, 1940; s. Howard and Alba (Zambon) L.; m. Marcelle Pomerleau, Aug. 25, 1962; children: Kevin, Alicia, Mark. BA in Polit. Sci., St. Michael's Coll., Vt., 1961; JD, Georgetown U., 1964. Bar: Vt. 1964, D.C. 1979, U.S. Ct. Appeals (2d cir.) 1966, Vt. Fed. Dist. Ct. 1965, U.S. Supreme Ct. 1968. State's atty., Chittenden County, Vt., 1966-75; US rep. to UN gen. assembly, 2004; US Senator from Vt., 1975—. Mem. com. agr., nutrition and forestry US Senate, com. appropriations, com. judiciary. Bd. regents Smithsonian Inst., Washington; bd. vis. US Military Acad., West Point, NY, Gallaudet U., DC, Nat. Coll. Deaf, DC, Nat. Dist. Atty. Assn., 1971—74. Recipient 1st Amendment award Soc. Profl. Journalists, John Peter and Anna Catherine Zenger award for outstanding contributions in support of press freedom & the people's right to know, 1999, Award Disting. Public Svc. Med. Library Assn., 2003, Champion for Real and Lasting Change award Save the Children, 2005. Mem. Nat. Dist. Attys. Assn. (v.p. 1971-74) Democrat. Roman Catholic. Office: US Senate 433 Russell Senate Ofc Washington DC 20510-0001 also: District Office Courthouse Plz 199 Main St Burlington VT 05401-8309 Office Phone: 202-224-4242, 802-863-2525. Office Fax: 202-224-3479.*

LEAHY, ROBERT LOUIS, psychologist; b. Alexandria, Va., Mar. 8, 1946; s. James J. and Lillian (DeVita) L.; m. Helen Butleroff, Aug. 8, 1987. BA, Yale U., 1967, MS, MPhil, Yale U., 1972, PhD, 1974. Lic. psychologist, NY, Pa. Postdoctoral fellow dept. psychiatry U. Pa. Med. Sch., Phila., 1982-83; assoc. prof. New Sch. for Social Rsch., NYC, 1976-81; vis. assoc. prof. U. B.C., Vancouver, 1981-82; assoc. prof. Hofstra U., Hempstead, NY, 1984-86; clin. prof. dept. psychiatry NY Hosp.-Cornell Med., NYC, 1991—; dir. Am. Inst. for Cognitive Therapy, NYC, 1985—. Editor: Development of the Self, 1985, Child's Construction of Social Inequality, 1983; author: Cognitive Therapy Techniques, 2003, The Worry Cure: Seven Steps to Stop Worry from Stopping You, 2005; contbr. articles to profl. jours. NIMH grantee, 1976-79. Mem. Am. Psychol. Assn., Assn. for Advancement of Behavior Therapy, Internat. Assn. Cognitive Therapy (pres.), Acad. Cognitive Therapy (pres.), Assn. for Behavioral and Cognitive Therapies (pres.-elect). Avocations: windsurfing, hiking, biking, sailing. Office: Am Inst for Cognitive Therapy Ste 1101 136 E 57th St New York NY 10022

LEAHY, T. LIAM, business development and technology investor; s. Thomas James and Margaret May L.; m. Shannon Kelly Brooks, Apr. 21, 1990. BS, St. Louis U., 1974, MA, 1975. V.p. sales Cablecom Inc., Chgo., 1976-80, Kaye Advt., NYC, 1980-82; group pub. Jour. Graphics Pub., NYC, 1983-85; pres., gen. mgr. Generation Dynamics, NYC, 1985-86; pres., dir. Leahy & Assocs., NYC, 1982—99, LA, 1982—2001; v.p., gen. mgr., dir. RBAC, Inc., 1999—; pres. Global Area Network, 2001—. Chmn. Global Area Network; bd. dirs. RBAC, Inc. Contbr. articles to profl. jours. Mem. Turnaround Mgmt. Assn., L.A. C. of C. Avocations: jazz, woodwinds, films, music. Business E-Mail: lleahy@globalareanet.com.

LEAHY, SIR TERRY, food products executive, marketing professional; b. Liverpool, Eng., Feb. 28, 1956; m. Alison Leahy; children: Kate, Tom, David. Attended, St. Edwards Coll.; BSc in mgmt. sci. with honors, UMIST, 1977. Joined Tesco, 1979; comml. dir. fresh foods Tesco PLC, 1986, mktg. dir., 1992—, dep. mng. dir., 1995, CEO, 1997—. Vis. prof. mktg. UMIST, 1984—; co-chancellor Manchester U.; European bus. leader Wall St. Jour., 2005. Dir. Liverpool Vision. Named European Businessman Yr., Fortune mag., 2004, Most Admired Leader in UK, Mgmt. Today, 2005; recipient Alumnus Yr. award, UMIST, 1996, Freedom of the City of Liverpool, 2001, knighthood for svcs. to food retailing, 2002. Avocations: football, theater. Office: Tesco PLC Tesco House Delamare Rd Cheshunt Hertfordshire EN8 9SL England

LEAHY, WILLIAM PATRICK, academic administrator, historian, educator; b. Omaha, July 16, 1948; s. Edward and Alice (McGinnis) Leahy. Student, Creighton U., 1966—67, Jesuit Coll., 1967—70; BA in Philosophy, St. Louis U., 1972, MA in U.S. History, 1975; MDiv in Theology, Jesuit Sch. Theology, Berkeley, Calif., 1978, STM in Hist. Theology, 1980; PhD in U.S. History, Stanford U., 1986. Ordained to ministry Cath. Ch., 1978. Tchr. Campion Jesuit H.S., Prairie du Chien, Wis., 1973—75; tchg. asst. Stanford U., 1981; instr. history Marquette U., Milw., 1985—86, asst. prof., 1986—91, acting asst. chmn., 1988—90, assoc. prof. history, exec. v.p., 1991—96; pres. Boston Coll., Chestnut Hill, Mass., 1996—. Author: Adapting to America: Catholics, Jesuits and Higher Education in the Twentieth Century, 1991; contbr. articles to profl. jours. Trustee Boston Coll., St. Joseph's U., Phila.; bd. dirs. Weston Jesuit Sch. Theology, Assn. Cath. Colls. and Univs., Nat. ASsn. Ind. Colls. and Univs; mem. pres. com. Bishops and Cath. Coll. and Univs. Mem.: Assn. Jesuit Colls. and Univs. (mem. bd.), History Edn. Soc. Office: Boston Coll Office of the Pres 18 Old Colony Rd Chestnut Hill MA 02467-3934 Office Phone: 617-552-3250. E-mail: leahy@bc.edu.*

LEAK, ROBERT EDWARDS, economic development consultant; b. Charlotte, NC, Sept. 15, 1934; s. James Pickett and Cornelia (Edwards) L.; m. Martha Councill, Aug. 25, 1956; children: Robert E., James Councill. BS, Duke U., 1956; MS, U. Tenn., 1957. With Pan Am. Petroleum Co.,

Lafayette, La., 1957-59, Allied Securities Corp., Raleigh, NC, 1961-62, Cameron Brown Mortgage Co., Raleigh and Charlotte, 1962-64, N.C. Dept. Natural and Econ. Resources, Raleigh, 1959-61, 64-76, dir. divsn. econ. devel., until 1976; dir. S.C. State Devel. Bd., Columbia, 1976-84; pres. Rsch. Triangle Park Found., NC, 1984-88; prin. Leak-Goforth Co., LLC, Raleigh, 1988—. Mem. U.S. Dept. Commerce Small Bus. Adv. Coun., vice-chmn. Dist. Export Coun.; leader industry organized govt. approved trade and indsl. devel. missions to Can., Europe, S.Am., Australia, Far East. Bd. dirs. Raleigh YMCA, S.C. Tech. and Comprehensive Edn., N.C. Symphony Fedn., Duke Alumni Assn., Carolina Ballet; chmn. bd. dirs. Wake Tech. C.C. Found.; adv. bd. Duke Hosp.; sr. warden vestry Christ Episcopal Ch.; past pres. Internat. Econ. Devel. Coun. Mem. Nat. Assn. State Devel. Agys. (past pres.), Raleigh Rotary Club (bd. dirs., Paul Harris fellow). Episcopalian. Home: 3301 Landor Rd Raleigh NC 27609-7012 Office: 4601 Six Forks Rd Ste 500 Raleigh NC 27609 Office Phone: 919-786-2502. E-mail: bobbleak@aol.com.

LEAKEY, RICHARD ERSKINE, paleoanthropologist, museum director; b. Nairobi, Kenya, Dec. 19, 1944; s. Louis Seymour and Mary Douglas (Nicol) L.; m. Meave Epps, 1970; children: Anna, Louise, Samira. Student, Lenana Sch., Nairobi; DSc (hon.), Wooster Coll., 1978, Rockford Coll., 1983; LittD, U. Kent, 1987; LHD, Ohio U., 1990; DSc, U. Aberdeen, 1994, St. Louis, 1994. Dir. tour co., Kenya, 1965-66; asst. dir. Center for Prehistory and Palaeontology, 1966-67; adminstrv. dir. Nat. Museums of Kenya, Nairobi, 1968-74, dir., chief exec., 1974-89; dir. Kenya Wildlife Svc., Nairobi, 1989-94; chmn. East African Wildlife Soc., 1985-89; head Wildlife Conservation Dept., 1989-90; vis. prof. of Anthropology State Univ of NY at Stony Brook, 2002—. Leader expdn. to West Lake Baringo, Kenya, 1966, Internat. Omo River Expdn. in So. Ethiopia, 1967, East Rudolf Expdn., 1968; leader, coordinator Koobi Fora Research Project, Lake Turkana, 1969—; mem. Kenya del. UNESCO, 1972, 76; chmn. Found. Research into Origins of Man; trustee, vice chmn. Found. Social Habilitation; vice-chmn. Environ. Prep. Group, Kenya, 1972-74; mem. Nakali/Suguta Valley Expdn., 1978, West Turkana Research Project, 1982, 84, 85, 86, Buluk-Early Miocene Project, 1982, advisor TV series The Making of Mankind; numerous pub. and scholarly lectures, U.S., Can., U.K., Scandinavia, New Zealand, Kenya, China, 1968—. Author: (with R. Lewin) Origins, 1977, Koobi Fora Research Project: a Catalogue of Hominid Fossils, Vol. I, 1978, People of the Lake, 1978, Making of Mankind, 1981, One Life An Autobiography, 1984; films include The Ape that Stood Up, 1977; lecture films on prehistory; various sci. programs, talk shows and news interviews since 1968; contbr. (with R. Lewin) chpts. to books, articles to profl. jours. Trustee Nat. Fund for the Disabled in Kenya, trustee Rockford Coll., Nat. Kidney Found. Kenya, Agrl. Research Found., Kenya, Gallmann Meml. Found., Kenya. Recipient Franklin Burr prize, 1965, 73, Centennial award Nat. Geographic Soc., 1988, Explorers Club medal, 1985, James Smithson medal Smithsonian Instn., 1990, Gold medal Royal Geographic Soc. London, 1990, Medal Portugese Archaeol. Soc., 1990, Hubbard medal Nat. Geographic Soc., 1994, others; decorated Chevalier de l'ordre de Leopold II, 1990. Fellow Royal Anthrop. Inst., AAAS, Kenya Acad. Scis. (founding fellow), Inst. Cultural Research UK, Royal Soc. UK; mem. Explorers Club, Wildlife Clubs of Kenya (trustee, hon. chmn. 1969-85), Kenya Exploration Soc. (chmn. 1969-72), East African Wildlife Soc. (hon. chmn. 1984—), Pan African Assn. Prehistoric Studies (sec.), Sigma Xi. Office: State Univ of NY at Stony Brook Social and Behavioral Sciences Stony Brook NY 11794

LEALE, OLIVIA MASON, small business owner, import marketing executive; b. Boston, May 5, 1944; d. William Mason and Jane Chapin (Prouty) Smith; m. Euan Harvie-Watt, Mar. 11, 1967 (div. Aug. 1979); children: Katrina, Jennifer; m. Douglas Marshall Leale, Aug. 29, 1980. BA, Vassar Coll., 1966. Cert. paralegal, beginning yoga instr. Sec. to dir. Met. Opera Guild, NYC, 1966; sec. to pres. Friesons Printers, London, 1974—75; guide, trainer Autoguide, London, 1977—79; ptnr. Inmark Internat. Mktg. Inc., Seattle, 1980—. Owner and mgr. Argus Ranch Facility for Dogs, Seattle, 2001—. Social case worker Inner London Ednl. Authority, 1975-76. Democrat. Presbyterian. Avocations: reading, making doll house furniture, painting, knitting, dog agility. Home and Office: 1233 Shenandoah Dr E Seattle WA 98112-3727 Office Phone: 253-333-2347. Personal E-mail: oleale@comcast.net.

LEALI, BRADFORD CHARLES, musician, educator; b. Denver, June 15, 1965; s. Charles and Beverly Leali; m. Megumi Mori, Nov. 12, 2002. B in Music Edn., U. North Tex.; MusM, Rutgers U., NJ, 2005. Lead alto saxophone Harry Connick, Jr. Orch., NYC, 1992—92, musical dir., 1992—95; solo alto saxophone Count Basie Orch., NYC, 1995—2000; lead alto saxophone Duke Ellington Orch., 2000—04; dir. jazz studies Tex. Tech U. Sch. Music, Lubbock, 2005—. Leader Brad Leali Quartet, NYC, 1998—; endorser Keilwerth Saxophone, LA, Rico Reeds; clinician Internat. Assn. Jazz Educators; mem. Kennedy Ctr. Honor Band, Washington. Musician: (rec.) Stars Crossed Lovers (nominee Solo Grammy award, 1999); composer, band leader, soloist (rec.) Maria Juanez, featured artist (recs.) Brad Leali Quartet-Live in Europe, Brooklyn Soul Organization-Cookin' Good, Priority Soul!; composer: DA's Time, Puddin' Time, Pimple Juice, Priority Soul, T-Strut, Little Dre, Dos Angelitos, Soul Interlude. Exec. dir. Lubbock Jazz Festival, 2006—. Named Hon. Trustee, Dirs. Choice Found. Music Edn., 2005—; recipient Jazz Big Band Grammy award, 1999, Bradford C. Leali Scholarship named in his honor, Dirs. Choice Found. Music Edn., 2005—, Black History Month cert. appreciation, Tex. Tech U., 2006; Ralph Bunch fellow, Rutgers U., 2003—05, Jazz scholar, Tex. Tech U. Parents Assn., 2006—. Mem.: ASCAP (assoc.), Tex. Music Educators Assn., Internat. Assn. Jazz Educators (assoc. award for outstanding svc. to jazz edn. 2000, 2002, 2005, 2006), Phi Mu Alpha (hon.). Home Phone: 806-783-9197; Office Phone: 806-742-2270 ext 260.

LEAMAN, J. RICHARD, JR., paper company executive; b. Lancaster, Pa., Sept. 22, 1934; s. J. Richard and Margaret B. (Leaman); m. Helen Brown, June 15, 1957; children: Lynda B., J. Richard, III. BA, Dartmouth Coll., 1956, MBA, 1957; PhD (hon.), Widener U., 1988. With Scott Paper Co., Phila., 1960-95, v.p. comml. products, 1975-78, exec. v.p. mktg. and sales, 1978—, pres. Packaged Products div., 1983-86, vice chmn., 1991-94, dir., 1986; pres. Scott Worldwide, 1986-91; pres., CEO, S.D. Warren Co., Boston, 1991-95. Bd. dirs. Church & Dwight Co., Inc., Elwyn Inc., Stonebridge Fin. Corp. Recipient Disting. Performance in Mgmt. award Widener U. Mem. Conf. Bd.'s Coun. on Global Bus. Mgmt., Dartmouth Club (Phila.). Republican. Episcopalian. Home: 317 Boot Rd Malvern PA 19355-3317 Office: 225 Franklin St Boston MA 02110-2804 Office Phone: 610-296-0241. E-mail: jrl2assoc@aol.com.

LEAMER, LAURENCE ALLEN, writer; b. Chgo., Oct. 30, 1941; s. Laurence Eugene and Helen Mae (Burkey) L.; m. Eliana Robitschek, Sept. 12, 1968 (div. Sept. 1980); 1 child, Daniela; m. Vesna Obradovic, Dec. 16, 1984. Diploma, U. Besancon, France, 1962; BA, Antioch Coll., 1964; M.Internat. Affairs, U. Oreg., 1968; M.J., Columbia U., 1969. Vol., tchr. Peace Corps, Nepal, 1964-66; assoc. editor Newsweek, NYC, 1969-70; dir. study on underground press 20th Century Fund, NYC, 1970-71. Author: The Paper Revolutionaries, 1972, Playing for Keeps in Washington, 1977 (Notable Book of Yr., NY Times Book Rev. 1977), Assignment, 1981, Ascent: The Spiritual and Physical Quest of Willi Unsoeld, 1982, Make-Believe: The Story of Nancy and Ronald Reagan, 1983, As Time Goes By: The Life of Ingrid Bergman, 1986, King of the Night: The Life of Johnny Carson, 1989 (N.Y. Times Bestseller list), The Kennedy Women: The Saga of an American Family, 1996 (NY Times Bestseller list), Three Chords and the Truth: Hope, Heartbreak, and Changing Fortunes in Nashville, 1997, The Kennedy Men: 1901-1963, 2001 (N.Y. Times Bestseller list), Sons of Camelot: The Fate of an American Dynasty, 2004 (N.Y. Times Bestseller list), Fantastic: The Life of Arnold Schwarzenegger, 2005; contbr. articles to Harper's mag., NY Times mag., New Republic, Playboy, others. Internat. fellow Columbia U., 1968-69; Pulitzer travel fellow, 1969; recipient citation Overseas Press Club, 1973. Mailing: 2501 M St NW 712 Washington DC 20037-7002 Address: Joy Harris Agy 156 Fifth Ave New York NY 10010

LEAMER, ROBERT ELDON, lawyer, hospital administrator; b. Chgo., Jan. 4, 1950; s. Laurence Eugene and Helen Mae (Burkey) L.; m. Mary Frances Leamer; children: Stephen, Christina. AB, Colgate U., 1972; JD, Albany U., 1976. Bar: N.Y. 1977, U.S. Dist. Ct. (no. dist.) N.Y. 1977. Asst. counsel N.Y. State Assembly, Albany, 1976-79; counsel N.Y. State Assembly Com. on Health, Albany, 1979-86; pvt. practice law Binghamton, N.Y., 1979-88; gen. counsel United Health Svcs., Binghamton, 1988—98; sr. v.p., gen. counsel Met. Jewish Health Sys., Bklyn., 1998—. Adj. prof. New Sch. for Social Rsch., Sch. Mgmt. Binghamton U. Mem. N.Y.-Pa. Health Sys. Agy., 1980-88; bd. dirs. Broome Legal Assistance Corp., 1985-93, Good Shepard Fairview Home, Inc., 1989-96, Broome County Coun. on the Arts, 1988-94, Ctr. for Adolescent Svcs., 1993-98, Partnership 2000. Mem. ABA, N.Y. State Bar Assn., Broome County Bar Assn., Assn. Bar City N.Y., Am. Health Lawyers Assn., Am. Coll. Healthcare Execs. (diplomate). Democrat. Episcopalian. Home: 207 Noe Ave Chatham NJ 07928-1507 Office: MJHS 6323 7th Ave Brooklyn NY 11220-4711 Home Phone: 973-410-9181; Office Phone: 718-491-7169. E-mail: rleamer@mjhs.org.

LEANSE, THOMAS J., lawyer; b. LA, Feb. 21, 1954; BA, U. Calif., San Diego, 1975; JD, U. San Diego, 1978. Bar: Calif. 1978, Ill. 1979, US Supreme Ct. 1982. Asst. state atty. Cook County, Ill., 1979—81; gen. counsel US Ski Assn. and US Ski Team, 1985—94; ptnr. Katten Muchin Rosenman LLP, LA. Mem.: ABA, LA County Bar Assn., Internat. Coun. of Shopping Ctrs., Calif. Bus. Properties Assn., Anti-Defamation League, Cedars-Sinai Med. Ctr. Office: Katten Muchin Rosenman LLP Ste 2600 2029 Century Park E Los Angeles CA 90067 Office Phone: 310-788-4475. Office Fax: 310-712-8426. Business E-Mail: thomas.leanse@kattenlaw.com.

LEAPE, JAMES P., science foundation director; b. 1956; Environ. atty., advisor UN Environ. Program; exec. v.p. WWF Internat., Switzerland, 1989—99, dir. gen., 2005—, dir. conservation and sci. initiatives David and Lucile Packard Found., 1999—2005. Co-author: (textbook) Eviron. Regulation: Law Science and Policy, 2006. Office: WWF Internat Gland CH Av du Mont Blanc 1196 1196 Gland Switzerland*

LEAPHART, W. WILLIAM, state supreme court justice; b. Butte, Mont., Dec. 3, 1946; s. Charles William and Cornelia (Murphy) L.; m. Barbara Berg, Dec. 30, 1977; children: Rebecca, Retta, Ada. Student, Whitman Coll., 1965—66; BA, U. Mont., 1969, JD, 1972. Bar: Mont. 1972, U.S. Dist. Ct., U.S. Ct. Appeals (9th cir.) 1975, U.S. Supreme Ct. 1975. Law clk. to Hon. W.D. Murray U.S. Dist. Ct., Butte, 1972—74; ptnr. Leaphart Law Firm, Helena, Mont., 1974—94; justice Mont. Supreme Ct., Helena, 1995—. Former assoc. ed. Mont. Law Review. Mem.: Am. Law Inst., Am. Acad. of Appellate Lawyers. Office: Mont Supreme Ct Justice Bldg 215 N Sanders St Rm 315 Helena MT 59601-4522 also: PO Box 203001 Helena MT 59620-3001*

LEAR, ERWIN, anesthesiologist, educator; b. Bridgeport, Conn., Jan. 1, 1924; s. Samuel Joseph and Ida (Ruth) L.; m. Arlene Joyce Alexander, Feb. 15, 1953; children: Stephanie, Samuel MD, SUNY, 1952. Diplomate Am. Bd. Anesthesiology, Nat. Bd. Med. Examiners. Intern L.I. Coll. Hosp., Bklyn., 1952-53; asst. resident anesthesiology Jewish Hosp., Bklyn., 1953-54, sr. resident, 1955, asst., 1955-56, adj., 1956-58, assoc. anesthesiologist, 1958-64; attending anesthesiologist Bklyn. VA Hosp., 1958-64, cons., 1977—; assoc. vis. anesthesiologist Kings County Hosp. Ctr., Bklyn., 1957-80, staff anesthesiologist, 1980-81; vis. anesthesiologist Queens Gen. Hosp. Ctr., 1955-67; dir. anesthesiology Queens Hosp. Ctr. Jamaica, 1964-67; chmn. dept. anesthesiology Catholic Med. Ctr., Queens and Bklyn., 1968-80; dir. anesthesiology Beth Israel Med. Ctr., NYC, 1981-98; clin. instr. SUNY Coll. Medicine, Bklyn., 1955-58, from clin. asst. prof. to clin. prof., 1958-80, prof., vice-chmn. clin. anesthesiology, 1980-81; prof. anesthesiology Mt. Sinai Sch. Medicine, 1981-94, Albert Einstein Coll. of Medicine, 1994—. Cons. in field. Author: Chemistry Applied Pharmacology of Tranquilizers; contbr. articles to profl. jours. Served with USNR, 1942-45 Fellow: N.Y. Acad. Medicine (sec. sect. anesthesiology 1985—86, chmn. sect. anesthesiology 1986—87), Am. Coll. Anesthesiologists; mem.: AMA, SUNY Coll. Medicine Alumni Assn. (pres. 1983; trustee alumni fund 1980), N.Y. County Med. Soc., N.Y. State Med. Soc. (chmn. sect. anesthesiology 1966—67, sec. sect. 1977—81), N.Y. State Soc. Anesthesiologists (chmn. pub. rels. 1963—73, assoc. editor Bulletin 1963—77, chmn. com. local arrangements 1968—73, dist. dir. 1972—73, bd. dirs. 1972—94, v.p. 1974—75, pres. 1976, chmn. jud. com. 1977—81, editor Sphere 1978—87, Disting. Svc. award 1996), Am. Soc. Anesthesiologists (ho. of dels. 1973—94, dir. 1981—97, chmn. com. on by-laws 1982—83, editor newsletter 1984—98, chmn. adminstrv. affairs com. 1987—94), Alpha Omega Alpha. Address: 1 Harriman Dr Sands Point NY 11050-1246 Office Phone: 516-944-9061.

LEAR, M. KATHLEEN, artist, music educator, small business owner; d. Charles Cecil and Margaret Ruth (Burnside) Lear; children: Kamee Lynn, Merry Rose, Jasmine Capri, Skye Benjiman. MusB, Seton Hill U., Greensburg, Pa., 1988; MA in Music Edn., Duquesne U., Pitts., 1991. Music libr. Seton Hill U., Greensburg, Pa., 1983—87, piano tchr., 1987—92; asst. to dir. Sch. Music, Duquesne U., Pitts., 1989—91; piano/voice tchr. Broken Arrow Sch. Fine Arts, Pa., 1992—95; pvt. piano/voice/guitar tchr. Tulsa, 1995—96, Ligonier, Pa., 1997—99; owner Kit's Music, Art, Gifts, Ligonier, Pa., 1999—. Mem.: Kindermusik Internat., Music Tchrs. Nat. Assn., Phi Beta Theta. Avocations: art, painting, poetry. Office Phone: 724-516-6892. Personal E-mail: kitsmusic@hotmail.com.

LEAR, NORMAN MILTON, producer, writer, director; b. New Haven, July 27, 1922; s. Herman and Jeanette (Seicol) Lear; m. Lyn Davis; children: Benjamin Davis, Brianna, Madeline; children: Ellen, Kate B. Lear LaPook, Maggie B. Student, Emerson Coll., 1940-42, HHD, 1968. Engaged in pub. relations, 1945-49; founder Act III Comms., 1987—. Comedy writer for TV, 1950—54; dir.(writer): (films, and TV), 1954—59; prodr.: (films) Never Too Late, 1965, Start the Revolution Without Me, 1970; (TV series) Sanford and Son, Maude, 1972, Good Times, 1974, Hot L Baltimore, 1975, All That Glitters, A Year at the Top, 1977, The Baxters, 1979, Sunday Dinner, 1991; exec. prodr.: (films) Fried Green Tomatoes, 1991, Way Past Cool, 2000, Stand By Me, 1986, Princess Bride, 1987; (TV series) The Andy Williams Show, 1962, One Day at a Time, 1975, The Nancy Walker Show, 1976, Heartsounds, 1984, a.k.a. Pablo, 1984, 704 Hauser, 1994, Channel Umptee-3, 1997; prodr.(dir., creator): All in the Family, 1971 (4 Emmy awards 1970-73, Peabody award, 1977), The Powers That Be, 1992, (screenwriter): (films) Come Blow Your Horn, 1963, Divorce American Style, 1967, The Night They Raided Minsky's, 1968, (dir., screenwriter): Cold Turkey, 1971; screenwriter Scared Stiff, 1953, creator The Jeffersons, 1975, Fernwood 2-Night, 1977. Pres. Am. Civil Liberties Found. So., Calif., 1973—; trustee Mus. Broadcasting; founder Bus. Enterprise Trust; bd. dirs People for the American Way. With USAF, 1942—45. Decorated Air medal with 4 oak leaf clusters; named One of Top Ten Motion Picture Producers, Motion Picture Exhibitors, 1963, 1967, 1968, Showman of Yr., Publicists Guild, 1971—77, Assn. Bus. Mgrs., 1972, Broadcaster of Yr., Internat. Radio and TV Soc., 1973, Man of Yr. Hollywood chpt., Nat. Acad. Television Arts and Scis., 1973; named to TV Acad. Hall of Fame, 1984; recipient Humanitarian award, NCCJ, 1976, Mark Twain award, Internat. Platform Assn., 1977, William O. Douglas award Pub. Counsel, 1981, 1st Amendment Lectr. Ford Hall Forum, 1981, Gold medal Internat. Radio and TV Soc., 1981, Disting. Am. award, 1984, Mass Media award, Am. Jewish Com. Inst. of Human Relations, 1986, Internat. award of Yr., Nat. Assn. TV Program Execs., 1987, Nat. Arts Medal, 1992, Achievement award in TV, Producers Guild Am., 2006. Mem.: AFTRA, Writers, and Dirs., Caucus Producers, Dirs. Guild Am., Writers Guild Am. (Valentine Davies award 1977). Office: Act III Comm 100 N Crescent Dr, Ste 250 Beverly Hills CA 90210

LEARD, DAVID CARL, lawyer; b. Hartford, Conn., 1958; BA, Bucknell U., 1981; JD, U. Conn., 1984. Bar: Conn. 1984, U.S. Dist. Ct. Conn. 1985; cert. specialist in workers' compensation law. Assoc. Podorowsky and Wladimer, Hartford, 1985, Manasse, Slaiby & Leard, Torrington, Conn., 1985-88, ptnr., 1989—. Contbr. articles to profl. jours. Dir., past pres. Winchester (Conn.) Land Trust, 1988-93; mem. allocations com. United Way Torrington, 1989—. Mem.: Nat. Orgn. Social Security Claimants Reps., Conn. Bar Assn. (workers compensation sect., cert. specialist in worker's compensation). Office: Manasse Slaiby & Leard PO Box 1104 Torrington CT 06790 Office Phone: 860-482-3503.

LEARISH, JOHN, retail executive; Mktg. positions Giant Eagle Foodstores and Phar-Mor Drugstores; various positions Rite Aid Corp., Camp Hills, Pa., 1994—, v.p. mktg., sr. v.p. mktg., 2002—. Office: Rite Aid Corp 30 Hunter Lane Camp Hill PA 17011 Office Phone: 717-761-2633.*

LEARNARD, JAMES MICHAEL, special education educator, retired collections and bad debt manager; b. Worcester, Mass., June 13, 1947; s. James Felix and Katherine M. (Slater) L.; m. Mary Kathryn Douglas, Mar. 16, 1972 (div. June 1974); 1 child, Sean Patrick; m. Joyce Stanek Hogan, June 10, 1989 (div. Nov. 1991); m. Donna Cecile Courtney, Aug. 12, 1993 (div. Aug. 1995). AA, Fla. Jr. Coll., Jacksonville, 1968; BSBA, Century U., Beverly Hills, Calif., 1987, MBA, 1988; PhD (hon.), Century U., 2001, MA in Edn., 2002; BA, Augusta Coll., Ga., 1991. Cert. paralegal, Ga.; cert. nursing asst. Epidemiologist L.A. Dept. Health, 1972-73; credit collector supr. Levy-Wolf, Inc., Jacksonville, 1973-75; correctional officer S.C. Dept. Corrections, Aiken, 1975-76; v.p., office mgr. Nat. Auto Fin. Corp., Aiken, 1976-81; ins. agt. Security Life Ins. Co. of Ga., Augusta, 1981-82, United Ins. Co. of Am., Aiken, 1982-86, Life Ins. Co. of Ga., Atlanta, 1986-87, The Keller Agy., Aiken, 1992-94; collector ARC, Inc., Augusta, Ga., 1994; owner, collector CSRA Recovery Svcs., Inc., Aiken, 1994-99; collection mgr. Service Loan Co., Augusta, 1999—; tchr. Richmond County Bd. Edn., Ga., 2001—. Collector Apex Fin. Co., Inc., Augusta, 1999; telemarketer So. Ind., Augusta, 1999, Hospitality Mktg. Concepts, Inc., Augusta, 1999, DialAm. Mktg., North Augusta, S.C., 1999; nursing asst. Anna Maria Nursing and Rehab. Ctr., North Augusta, 1999. Author: Words of Love, 1985, Thoughts of Love and Inspiration, 1988, Student Protests at Harvard College, 1766-1780, 1986, Catholic Hospitals in the American Healthcare System, 1988, I Praise Your Name, A Collection of Love Poems, 1998, Recipes from the Heart: Cooking for the One You Love, 1999, How Do I Love Thee? A Collection of Love Poems, 2000, Love Lasts Eternal--Love Poems to a Lovely Lady, 2000, The Not So Famous Quotations and Other Writings of James M. Learnard, 20 vols., 2000; composer: Tonight (soul ballad), 1982, (pop rock ballad), 1982, Friends (pop rock ballad), 1983, Do You Remember (soul ballad), 1983, Eastern Morn (hymn), 1983, Christmas Day, 1982, Sunset on Tampa Bay (soul ballad), 1982, 83, My Angel (soul ballad), 1983, What Will She Say? (pop rock ballad), 1983, Easter Morn, 1983; prodr. album: Michael Hicks/Love Songs, 1983. Past chmn. Animal Control Adv. Bd., Aiken. Recipient Golden Poet award World of Poetry, 1986, 87, Silver Poet award, 1988, Recognition by the S.C. House of Reps. for accomplishment as an author, poet and lycricist, 1986, Internat. Peace prize, 2002; commd. admiral S.C. Navy, 1986; recipient Medal of Honor commemorating disting. lifelong achievement Am. Biog. Assn., 1990; Eagle Scout with Bronze Palm, Boy Scouts Am., 1963. Mem. Assn. of MBA Execs., Healthcare Fin. Mgmt. Assn., Fedn. of Am. Health Svcs., Am. Hosp. Assn., Soc. for Hosp. Healthcare and Mktg., K.C. (4th degree). Roman Catholic. Home: 117 Green St Graniteville SC 29829-3026

LEARNER, HOWARD ALAN, lawyer; b. Chgo., June 1, 1955; s. Donald and Patricia Learner; m. Lauren S. Rosenthal, Oct. 22, 1988; children: Daniel J., Samuel D., David N. AB, U. Mich., 1976; JD, Harvard Law Sch., 1980. Bar: Ill 1980, U.S. Dist. Ct. (no. dist.) Ill. 1980, U.S. Ct. Appeals (7th cir.) 1981, U.S. Supreme Ct. 1993. Gen. counsel Bus. and Profl. People for Pub. Interest, Chgo., 1980-93; pres., exec. dir. Environ. Law and Policy Ctr. Midwest, Chgo., 1993, now exec. dir. Chmn., pres., dir. Citizens Utility bd., Chgo., 1984-93; bd. govs. Chgo. Coun. Lawyers, 1986-90; dir. Environ. Law Inst., Washington, 1998—. Treas., dir. Ill. Environ., Springfield, 1982-88; legal counsel Ill. chpt. Sierra Club, Chgo., 1984—; dir. Jewish Coun. Urban Affairs, Chgo., 1984-92, Jewish Fund Justice, N.Y.C., 1990—, Leadership Greater Chgo. Fellows' Assn., 1995—, Pub. Interest Law Initiative, 1983-99. Environ. fellowship German Marshall Fund U.S. Fellow Leadership Greater Chgo., Royal Soc. Arts, Mfg. and Commerce. Office: Environ Law & Policy Ctr Midwest 35 E Wacker Dr Ste 1300 Chicago IL 60601-2110

LEARSY, RAYMOND J., private investor; b. Luxembourg; m. Melva Bucksbaum. Author: Over a Barrel: Breaking the Middle East Oil Cartel; contbr. Huffington Post. Mem. Nat. Coun. on Arts, 1982—88; trustee Whitney Mus. Am. Art. Named one of top 200 collectors, ARTnews Mag., 2004; recipient Gertrude Vanderbilt Whitney Award for outstanding arts patronage & philanthropy (with Melva Bucksbaum), 2004. Mem.: Whitney Mus. Am. Art, Tate Gallery. Avocation: collector of contemporary art. Mailing: 253 Amenia Union Rd Sharon CT 06069

LEARY, CAROL ANN, academic administrator; b. Niagara Falls, NY, Mar. 29, 1947; d. Angelo Andrew and Mary Josephine (Pullano) Gigliotti; m. Noel Robert Leary, Dec. 30, 1972. BA, Boston U., 1969; MS, SUNY, Albany, 1970; PhD, Am. Univ., 1988. Asst. to v.p. for student affairs, dir. women's programs Siena Coll., Loudonville, NY, 1970-72; asst. dir. housing Boston U., 1972-78; dir. residence Simmons Coll., Boston, 1978-84, assoc. dean, 1984-85; assoc. dir. The Washington Campus, Washington, 1985-86; adminstrv. v.p., asst. to pres. Simmons Coll., Boston, 1988-94; pres. Bay Path Coll., Longmeadow, Mass. Bd. dirs. Mass. Mut. Fin. Group, United Bank. Past pres., bd. govs. Colony Club; past pres. Cooperating Colls. of Greater Springfield; exec. com. Cmty. Found.; treas. Women's Coll. Coalition; past pres. WGBY; bd. dirs. Frank Stanley Beveridge Found., Go Fit Found. Mem.: Assn. Ind. Colls. and Univs. Mass. (past chair). Avocations: art, traveling overseas, hiking. Office: Bay Path Coll Office of the President 588 Longmeadow St Longmeadow MA 01106-2212 Office Phone: 413-565-1241. Business E-Mail: cleary@baypath.edu.

LEARY, DANIEL, artist; b. Glens Falls, NY, July 20, 1955; s. John Andrew and Maud Houston (Parkhurst) L. BFA, Antioch Coll., 1977; MFA, Syracuse U., 1996. One person exhbns. include Breedlove Gallery, Westark Cmty. Coll., Fort Smith, Ark., 1984, 85, Comart Gallery, Syracuse U., 1985, 87, The Printspace, U. Ark., Fayetteville, 1985, The Fort Smith Art Ctr., 1986, Printworks Gallery, 1991, 99, 2000, Chgo., 1988, 95, The Hyde Collection, Glens Falls, N.Y., 1990, The Blanden Meml. Art Mus., Fort Dodge, Iowa, 1992, The Bobbit Visual Art Ctr., Albion Coll., Mich., 1993, Sharon Campbell Gallery, Greenville, S.C., 1994, We. Mich. State U., Kalamazoo, 1994, Greenville County Fine Arts Ctr., 2002; group exhbns. include East Tenn. State U., Johnson City, 1985, Gallery Sixty-

Eight, Belfast, Maine, 1985, The Fort Smith Arts Ctr., 1985, Syracuse U., 1985, The Ark. Arts Ctr. and the Decorative Arts Mus., Little Rock, 1985, The Soc. Am. Graphic Artists, 1986, Westminster Coll., New Wilmington, Pa., 1986, Joe Fawbush Editions, N.Y., 1986, Cazenovia (N.Y.) Coll., 1987, Jan Turner Gallery, L.A., 1987, The Greenville County Mus. Art, 1988, The Mpls. Inst. Arts., 1988, The Munson-Williams-Proctor Inst. Mus. Art, Utica, N.Y., 1989, The Statesville Arts and Scis. Mus., 1989, The Nat. Exhbn. Ctr. Can., Alma, Quebec, 1989, The Pyramid Arts Ctr., Rochester, N.Y., 1989, The Vero Beach Ctr. For the Arts, Fla., 1989, The Jane Voorhees Zimmerli Art Mus., Rutgers U., New Brunswick, N.J., 1990, Bradford Art Galleries and Mus., England, 1990, The Contemporary Arts Ctr., Cin., 1991, Northwest Art Gallery, Ind. U. Northwest, Gary, 1993, Printworks Gallery, Chgo., 1996, 97, Bibliotèque Nat. Quèbec, Montréal, Can., 1998, 2003, Adirondack C.C., Queensbury, N.Y., 1998, 2003, Parkland Coll., Champaign, Ill., 1998, Wayne State U., Detroit, 1999, S.C.'s Gov's. Sch. Arts and Humanities, Greenville, S.C., 1999, 2000, Jean Albano Gallery, Chgo., 2003, Mary and Leigh Block Mus. Art, Northewestern U., Evanston, Ill., 2007; public collections include Adirondack Comty. Coll., Queensbury, Albion (Mich.) Coll., The Ark. Arts Ctr., The Boston Pub. Library, The Blanden Meml. Art Mus., The Carnegie Mus. Art, Pitts., East Tenn. State U., Greenville (S.C.) County Arts Ctr., Greenville County Mus. Art, The Hyde Collection, Glens Falls, The Library of Congress, Washington, D.C., The Metropolitan Mus. Art., N.Y., The Milw. Art Mus., The Mpls. Inst. Arts, The Munson-Williams-Proctor Inst. Mus. Art, The N.Y. Pub. Library, The Spencer Mus. Art, U. Kans., Syracuse U., The Toledo Mus. Art, U. Ariz. Mus. Art, U. Indpls., The Walker Art Ctr., Mpls., We. Mich. U., The Williams Coll. Mus. Art, Williamstown, Mass., Wright State U., Dayton, Ohio, Yale U. Art Gallery, The Jane Voorhees Zimmerli Art Mus., Rutgers U., New Brunswick, N.J. Visual Artists Fellow NEA, 1989, N.Y. Found. for the Arts fellow, 1988. Home: PO Box 384 Hudson Falls NY 12839 Home Phone: 518-932-9854; Office Phone: 518-932-9854. Business E-Mail: dan@danielleary.com.

LEARY, FRANCES ELIZABETH COOPER, secondary school educator; b. Tampa, Fla., Apr. 23, 1972; d. Richard Randolph and Susan Tuthill Cooper; m. Del Michael Leary. BS in Interdisciplinary Studies, U. Houston, 1995; MA, Meml. U. of Nfld., St. John's, Newfoundland, Canada, 2004. K-8 general teacher Tex., Miss., 1995, 7-12 English teacher Miss., 2003, 7-12 Social Studies teacher Miss., 2004, K-12 music teacher Miss., 2002, Gifted and Talented Teacher Tex., 1996, STAI mentor Miss., 2003, cert. early Early Adolescence English Nat. Bd. Profl. Tchg. Stds., 2006. Tchr. Durkee Elem., Houston, 1995—97; tchr. English Macario Garcia Mid. Sch., Sugar Land, 1997—2000; grad. tchg. asst., rschr. Folklore Dept. Meml. U. Nfld., St. John's, Canada, 2000—02; tchr. Crenshaw Elem., Miss., 2002—03; tchr. English Oxford U. Sch., 2003—06; tchr. English and history Ctr. Hill Mid. and H.S., Olive Branch, 2006—. Piano tchr., Oxford, Miss., 2003—; mid. sch. team leader, curriculum coord. Oxford U. Sch., Miss., 2004—06. Author: (book) Lord, Help Me... I'm Single. Cmty. svc., Oxford, Miss., 2003—06; mus. guide Nfld. Mus., St. John's, Canada, 2001; mission work Towel Ministries, Boone, NC, 1995—97; ch. youth leader Episcopal Ch., Houston, 1993—2000. Recipient Fellow of the Sch. of Grad. Studies, Meml. U. of Nfld., 2003; State Farm Nat. Bd. scholarship, State Farm, 2005, Grad. fellowship, Meml. U. of Nfld. Dept. of Folklore, 2000—02. Mem.: ASCD, Coll. Bd., Nat. Coun. for the Social Studies, Nat. Coun. of Teachers of English, Chi Omega Frat. Christian. Avocations: writing, reading, music. Office: Ctr Hill Mid and HS 13250 Kirk Rd Olive Branch MS 38654 Home Phone: 601-914-5705; Office Phone: 662-890-2491. Personal E-mail: frances.leary@hotmail.com.

LEARY, G. EDWARD, state agency administrator; m. Betty Chamberlain; 5 children. BS in Polit. Sci., U. Utah, 1971, MBA, 1981. Cert. Internat. Rels. With collections and lending dept. Draper Bank and Trust, 1974—77; examiner Utah Dept. Fin. Instns., Salt Lake City, 1977—82, industry supr., 1982—87, chief examiner, 1987—92, commr., 1992—. Chmn. Bd. Fin. Instns.; mem. Utah Housing Fin. Agy. Bd., Utah Appraiser Registration and Cert. Bd. Served in USN, 1971—73, ret. capt. USNR, 1995. Mem. Conf. State Bank Suprs. (frmr. chmn.). Office: Utah Dept Fin Instns Box 146800 Salt Lake City UT 84114-6800 Office Phone: 801-538-8830. Office Fax: 801-538-8894. E-mail: eleary@utah.gov.*

LEARY, JAMES FRANCIS, biomedical research scientist, educator; b. Portsmouth, NH, Apr. 12, 1948; s. Frank Joseph and Etta Myrtle (Ford) L.; m. Rosemary Conrad, May 27, 1978; children: Charles, Elaine, Selena, Michael. SB in Aeros. and Astronautics, MIT, 1970, SB in Philosophy, 1970; MS in Physics, U. N.H., 1974; PhD in Biophysics, Pa. State U., 1977. Postdoctoral fellow Los Alamos (N.Mex.) Nat. Lab., 1977-78; asst. prof. pathology U. Rochester, N.Y., 1978-83, assoc. prof. pathology and pediatrics N.Y., 1983-94; prof. internal medicine, pathology, microbiology/immunology Med. br. U. Tex., Galveston, 1994—. Sr. scientist Sealy Ctr. for Hematology and Oncology, Sealy Ctr. for Molecular Studies; dir. cell analysis and sorting facility dept. pathology U. Rochester, 1983-94. Contbr. articles to profl. jours.; patentee in field. Mem. sch. bd. Our Sch., Rochester, 1990-95. Mem. Internat. Soc. for Analytical Cytology, N.Y. Acad. Scis. Democrat. Unitarian Universalist. Avocations: downhill skiing, running, youth athletics coach, computers. Office: Univ Tex Med Br Rt 0835 Molecular Cytometry Unit Galveston TX 77555-0835 Home: 2711 Manchester St West Lafayette IN 47906-1393

LEARY, MARGARET A., law library director; b. 1942; BA, Cornell U., 1964; MLS, U. Minn., 1966; JD, William Mitchell Coll. Law, St. Paul, 1973. Bar: Minn. 1973, Mich. 1974. Chpt. cataloger U. Minn. Law Libr., 1968—69; cataloger William Mitchell Coll. Law, 1970—72; atty. Legal Aid Soc., Mpls., 1972—73; lectr. U. Mich. Sch. Info. and Libr. Studies, 1974—88; asst. dir. U. Mich. Law Sch. Libr., 1973—81, assoc. dir. Ann Arbor, 1982—84, dir., 1984—. Exec. com. mem. Inst. for Continuing Legal Edn., 2004, Am. Assn. Law Libraries, 1983—86, pres., 1988—89. Contbr. articles to profl. jours. Trustee William Mitchell Coll. Law, 1993—2002; vice chmn. Planning Commn. City of Ann Arbor, 1994—2002, mem. Planning Commn., 1994—2002. Named Volunteer of Yr., Habitat for Humanity, Huron Valley, 2002. Achievements include being first woman to head a library at one of the top 5 US law schools. Office Phone: 734-764-4468. Fax: 734-615-0178. Business E-Mail: mleary@umich.edu.*

LEARY, THOMAS BARRETT, lawyer, former federal agency administrator; b. Orange, NJ, July 15, 1931; s. Daniel and Margaret (Barrett) L.; m. Stephanie Lynn Abbott, Dec. 18, 1954, June 3, 1991; children: Thomas A., David A., Alison Leary Estep. AB, Princeton U., 1952; JD magna cum laude, Harvard U., 1958. Bar: N.Y. 1959, Mich. 1972, D.C. 1983. Assoc. White & Case, NYC, 1958-68, ptnr., 1968-71; atty.-in-charge antitrust Gen. Motors Corp., Detroit, 1971-77, asst. gen. counsel, 1977-82; ptnr. Hogan & Hartson, Washington, 1983-99, of counsel, 2006—; commr. FTC, Washington, 1999—2005. Served to lt. USNR, 1952-55 Mem. ABA (antitrust sect., coun. mem. 1979-83, mem. antitrust adv. bd., BNA antitrust & trade reg. rep., 1981-99, 2006-). Republican. Business E-Mail: tbleary@hhlaw.com.

LEARY, WILLIAM JAMES, educational association administrator; b. Boston, Oct. 1, 1938; s. John Gilbert and Josephine Marie (Kelley) L.; m. Joann Linda Parodi, June 25, 1960; children: Lorraine, Lisa, Linda. S.B., Boston Coll.; M.Ed., Boston State Coll.; postgrad. (Fulbright fellow), Sophia U., Tokyo, 1967; cert. advanced study, Harvard U., 1972, Ed.D., 1973, Boston U., 1971. Tchr. pub. schs., Boston, 1960—67; chmn. dept. social studies Dorchester High Sch., Boston, 1967—68; dir. curriculum Boston Dist. Pub. Schs., 1969—72, supt. schs., 1972—75; exec. dir. Met. Planning Project, Newton, Mass., 1975—77; supt. schs. Rockville Centre, NY, 1977—82, North Babylon, NY, 1982—84, Broward County, Ft. Lauderdale, Fla., 1984—88; supt. Gloucester (Mass.) Pub. Schs., 1989—93; assoc. prof. dept. ednl. leadership, dept. chair U. Miss., Oxford, 1993—98, dir. PhD Program; prof. coll. edn. Lynn U., Boca Raton, Fla., 1998—2000. Assoc. prof. dept. continuing studies Boston State Coll., 1970-72; assoc. in edn. Harvard U. Grad. Sch. Edn., 1972-75; adj. prof. edn. Boston U., 1973-75, C.W. Post Ctr., L.I. U., 1979-84, Fla. Internat. U., 1984-88, Salem (Mass.) State Coll., 1990-93; prof. Suffolk U., 1977-82; TV commentator Channel 5, Boston, 1975-76; prodr. edn. programs New Eng. Cablevision, 1989-93; keynote spkr. Harvard U. Grad. Sch. Edn., 1976, NYU, 1980; faculty senate U. Miss., 1994-96, chair subcom. on athletics, 1994-95. Columnist Boston Herald, 1975-78, L.I. News, 1982-84, Gloucester Times; edn. commentator New Eng. Cablevision, 1989-93; contbr. articles to profl. jours. Edn. coord. Boston chpt. United Way, 1974, Rockville Centre United Fund, 1979-80, Broward County chpt., 1985-87; trustee Mus. Fin. Arts, Boston, 1972-77; bd. dirs. Boston Youth Symphony, 1972-77, Edn. Devel. Ctr., 1972-77, Broward Com. of 100, Boys Club Broward County, 1985-88; nat. alumni bd. Boston U., 1975—; vis. com. Suffolk U., 1978-80; adv. bd. Harvard N.Y. Alumni Forums, 1980-84; mem. L.I. Regional Planning Bd., 1983-84, Gov.'s Task Force on Alt. Edn., Fla., 1986-88; lector, Eucharistic min. Ascension Cath. Ch., Boca Raton; bd. dirs., v.p., Mill Pond Homeowners Assn., Boca Raton, 2002—. With 2d armored divsn U.S. Army. Recipient Friend of Youth award Hayden Goodwill Boys' Home, 1973, Ida M. Johnston Outstanding Alumni award Boston U. Sch. Edn., 1976, Man of Yr. award Pope's Hill Assn., 1976, Jenkins Meml. award for ednl. leadership N.Y. State Coun., PTA, 1980, Ednl. Leadership award L.I. chpt. NCCJ, 1980, Broward County Med. Aux., 1984, Lifetime Achievement award Matignon H.S. Alumni, 1995, Civil Rights award NAACP Layfayette County, MS, 1996; selected as mem. Exec. Educator 100, Nat. Sch. Bd. Assn., 1987; named to Matignon H.S. Hall of Fame, 1995. Mem. ASCD (nat. commn. on supervision 1984-85), Am. Assn. Sch. Adminstrs. (del. assembly 1991-93, resolutions com. 1988-89, 93-96), Am. Hist. Assn., Horace Mann League, Assn. for Asian Studies, Nat. Coun. Social Studies (nat. urban affairs com. 1977-80), Large City Sch. Supts., Harvard Club N.Y.C., Boston Coll. Alumni Club, Varsity Club, KC, Rotary, Harvard Club of Boston and N.Y., Harvard Club of Palm Beach, Am. Legion, DAV, Comdrs. Club, Phi Delta Kappa. Roman Catholic. Office: Lynn U Grad Sch Edn Boca Raton FL 33431 Personal E-mail: bjleary@comcast.net. Business E-Mail: wleary@lynn.edu. *A person's ability for creative and imaginative thinking is limited only by his/her fear to dream.*

LEASE, JOHN G., plastic surgeon; b. Western Springs, Ill., Oct. 26, 1957; s. William David and Carolyn Sellars Lease. BA, NC State U., Raleigh, 1979; MD, Duke U., Durham, NC, 1983. Plastic and reconstructive surgeon U. Chgo. Hosps., 1990—92; pvt. practice plastic and reconstructive surgeon Chgo., 1992—. Governing mem. Chgo. Symphony Orch. Office: 3000 N Halsted Ste 707 Chicago IL 60657

LEASE, MARY MUNDY, literature and language professor; b. St. Louis, Jan. 13, 1946; d. Charles Bernard and Frances Mundy; m. Cecil E. Lease, Aug. 2, 1968; children: Amber Renee, Charles Royal. BE, Truman U., Kirksville, Md., 1967; MA in Curriculum and Instrn. and English Edn., U. South Fla., Tampa, 1982. Cert. tchr. Nat. Bd. Prof. Tchg. Stds., 1999. Tchr. Burlington Sch. Dist., 1967—68, North Kirkwood Sch. Dist., Kirksville, Mo., 1968—70, Lee County Schs., Ft. Myers, Fla., 1970—2003; tchr. in residence Nat. Bd. Profl. Tchg. Stds., Arlington, Va., 2000—03, exec. assoc., 2003—07. Presenter Health Edn. Conf., San Diego, 2002, NCTE, Ill., 2003—06; host com. chair Nat. Bd. Profl. Tchg. Stds. Nat. Conf., Washington, 2004, Washington, 07. Mem.: Alpha Delta Kappa (pres. 1977—79), Phi Delta Kappa. Avocations: sewing, camping, reading. Office: Nat Bd Profl Tchg Stds 1525 Wilson Blvd Arlington VA 22209 Office Phone: 703-465-8878.

LEASE, ROBERT K., lawyer; b. Cleve., 1948; AB magna cum laude, Dartmouth Coll., 1970; JD cum laude, U. Conn., 1976. Bar: Ohio. Ptnr. Baker & Hostetler LLP, Cleve. Mem. Phi Beta Kappa. Office: Baker & Hostetler LLP 3200 Nat City Ctr 1900 E 9th St Ste 3200 Cleveland OH 44114-3485 Office Phone: 216-621-0200. E-mail: rlease@bakerlaw.com.

LEATH, CHERYL LYNN, retired pre-school educator, poet, painter; b. Chgo., Apr. 10, 1961; d. Wayne Lee Cutliff and Judith Louise Edwards, Sharron Cutliff (Stepmother); m. Thomas Richard Leath, Dec. 6, 1980 (div. Nov. 4, 1987); children: Cristin Lynnette McCoy, Dustin Scott, Allison Rene German. AA in applied sci., Carl Sandburg Coll., 1987—90. Practicum/internship Creative Childhood Ctr., Galesburg, Ill., 1990; preschool tchr./child care provider Children's Sch., Galesburg, Ill., 1991; child care provider Teddy Bear Day Care Ctr., Monmouth, Ill.; preschool tchr./child care provider Cameron Christian Care Ctr., Cameron, Ill., 1994—94; lead early childhood preschool tchr./child care provider Spires Child Care Ctr., Galesburg, Ill., 2003; ret. Painting in acrylics, Back Upon A Time; author: (poetry) A Veteran's Day Poem, Our World's Rainbow (editor's choice award cert., 2004), Pain, A Day Spent With Depression (editor's choice award cert., 2004), From the Heart Poetry, 2005, Creative Expressions, 2005, Thoughts and Design, 2006, Uniquely Created Poetry, 2006. Vol. Relay for Life. Mem.: Coalition of Citizens with Disabilities in Ill. Conservative-R. Avocations: writing, painting, reading, volunteering, walking. Home Phone: 309-335-6654. Personal E-mail: cherieskids@yahoo.com.

LEATH, KENNETH THOMAS, plant pathologist, educator, agriculturist, consultant; b. Providence, Apr. 29, 1931; s. Thomas and Elizabeth (Wootten) L.; m. Marie Andreozzi, Aug. 1955; children: Kenneth, Steven, Kevin, Maria Beth. BS, U. R.I., 1959; MS, PhD, U. Minn., 1966. Rsch. plant pathologist U.S. Regional Pasture Rsch. Lab. USDA-ARS, 1966-94; prof. Pa. State U., 1966-94; pvt. agrl. cons. Boalsburg, Pa., 1994—. Advisor numerous state and nat. orgns. Contbr. numerous articles to profl. jours. and chpts. to books. With USN, 1951-55. Recipient state and nat. recognition for contbns. to improvements in grassland agr. Mem. Elks. Achievements include research on root diseases and systemic wilts of forage species.

LEATH, PAUL LARRY, physicist, educator, former university official; b. Moberly, Mo., Jan. 9, 1941; s. James Lewis and Naomia (Burton) L.; m. Rosemary Rippel, June 2, 1962; children: Steven, Kimberly. Grad., Moberly Jr. Coll., 1960; BS, U. Mo., 1961, MS, 1963, PhD, 1966. Rsch. officer Oxford U., Eng., 1966-67; asst. prof. physics Rutgers U., New Brunswick, 1967-71, assoc. prof., 1971-78, prof., 1978—, assoc. provost for acad. affairs, 1978-87, provost, 1987-92, chair dept. physics and astronomy, 1995—2005. Sr. vis. fellow Oxford U., 1972-73, 93-94; vis. prof. Mich. State U., 1992-93. Co-author: The Theory and Properties of Randomly Disordered Crystals and Related Physical Systems, 1974. Active Millstone Borough Coun., NJ, 1979-84, pres., 1984; bd. dirs. New Brunswick Tomorrow, 1989-92, R&D Coun. NJ, 1980-83; bd. trustees Rutgers Preparatory Sch., 2002-. Mem. Am. Phys. Soc., Inst. Physics, AAAS, NY Acad. Sci., Sigma Xi. Achievements include research in theoretical physics, properties of alloys and disordered materials, percolation processes, breakdown phenomena, and vibrational and electronic properties. Office: Rutgers U Dept Physics and Astro 136 Frelinghuysen Rd Piscataway NJ 08854-8019 Office Phone: 732-445-2521. Business E-Mail: leath@physics.rutgers.edu.

LEATHER, VICTORIA POTTS, college librarian; b. Chattanooga, June 12, 1947; d. James Elmer Potts and Ruby Lea (Bettis) Potts Wilmoth; m. Jack Edward Leather; children: Stephen, Sean. BA cum laude, U. Chattanooga, 1968; MSLS, U. Tenn., 1978. Libr. asst. East New Orleans Regional Libr., 1969-71; libr. Erlanger Nursing Sch., Chattanooga, 1971-75; chief libr. Erlanger Hosp., Chattanooga, 1975-77; dir. Eastgate Br. Libr., Chattanooga, 1977-81; dir. libr. svcs. Chattanooga State Tech. C.C., 1981-95, dean libr. svcs., 1996—. Mem. ALA, Southeastern Libr. Assn., Tenn. Libr. Assn. (past chair legis. com.), Chattanooga Area Libr. Assn. (pres. 1978-79), Tenn. Bd. Regents Media Consortium (chair 1994-95), Phi Delta Kappa. Episcopalian. Avocations: reading, needlecrafts, travel. Home Phone: 423-622-4588; Office Phone: 423-697-2576. Business E-Mail: vicky.leather@chattanoogastate.edu.

LEATHERBURY, THOMAS SHAWN, lawyer; b. Ft. Worth, Dec. 7, 1955; s. John Raymond and Hester Louise (Hoffecker) L.; m. Patricia Villareal, Nov. 27, 1982; children: Sean, Colin. BA, Yale U., 1976, JD, 1979. Bar: Tex. 1979, U.S. Dist. Ct. (no. dist.) Tex. 1979, U.S. Ct. Appeals (5th cir.) 1982, U.S. Dist. Ct. (we. dist.) Tex. 1984. Law clk. to presiding justice U.S. Dist. Ct. (no. dist.) Tex., Dallas, 1979-80; assoc. Locke, Purnell, Boren, Laney & Neely P.C., Dallas, 1980-86, ptnr., 1987—92; ptnr., co-head appellate sect. Vinson & Elkins LLP, Dallas, 1992—. Mem. Tex. Bar Assn., Dallas Bar Assn., Dallas Assn. Young Lawyers. Home: 4430 Woodfin St Dallas TX 75220-6420 Office: Vinson & Elkins LLP Trammell Crow Ctr 2001 Ross Ave, Ste 3700 Dallas TX 75201 Office Phone: 214-220-7792. E-mail: tleatherbury@velaw.com.

LEATHERBY, DENNIS, food products executive; b. Overland Park, Kans., 1960; BS in Acctg. and Fin., Kans. State U. Asst. treas. Tyson Foods Inc., 1990, treas., 1994, v.p., treas., 1997, sr. v.p. fin., treas. Springdale, Ark., 1998—, interim CFO, 2004—. Office: Tyson Foods Inc 2210 W Oaklawn Dr Springdale AR 72762-6999

LEATHERDALE, DOUGLAS WEST, insurance company executive; b. Morden, Man., Can., Dec. 6, 1936; came to U.S., 1968; s. Walter West and Lena Elizabeth (Gilligan) L.; children: Mary Jo, Christopher BA, United Coll., Winnipeg, Man., 1957. Investment analyst, officer Gt. West Life Assurance Co., Winnipeg, 1957-68; assoc. exec. sec. Bd. Pensions, Luth. Ch., Mpls., 1968-72; exec. v.p., then v.p. St. Paul Investment Mgmt. Co., subs. St. Paul Cos., Inc., 1972-77; v.p.-fin. St. Paul Cos., Inc., 1974-81, sr. v.p.-fin., 1981-82, exec. v.p., 1982-89, also dir., pres., chief oper. officer, 1989-90, chmn.,ceo and pres., 1990—. Bd. dirs. St. Paul Fire and Marine Ins. Co., St. Paul Land Resources, Inc., St. Paul Real Estate of Ill., Inc., John Nuveen & Co. Inc., St. Paul Properties, Inc., St. Paul Oil and Gas Corp., St. Paul Fire & Marine Ins. Co, (U.K.) Ltd., St. Paul Mercury Ins. Co., St. Paul Guardian Ins. Co., St. Paul Surplus Lines Ins. Co., Nat. Ins. Wholesalers, Atwater McMillian, 77 Water St., Inc., Ramsey Ins. Co., St. Paul Risk Services, Inc., St. Paul Plymouth Ctr., Inc. Athena Assurance Co., St. Paul Fin. Group, Inc., Graham Resources, Inc., Carlyle Capital, L.P., United HealthCare Corp. Mem. Twin Cities Soc. Security Analysts, Fin. Execs. Inst. Clubs: Minnesota (St. Paul).

LEATHERMAN, HUGH KENNETH, SR., state legislator, engineering executive; b. Lincoln County, NC, Apr. 14, 1931; s. John Bingham and Ada Annis (Gantt) L.; m. Jean Helms, Nov. 11, 1978; children: Sheila Dianne, Hugh Kenneth, Karen Ann, Joyce Lynn, Amy Jean, Sarah Ada. BS in Civil Engring., N.C. State U., 1953. Engr. then sec. Florence (S.C.) Concrete Products Inc., 1955-72, pres., 1972-93. Mem. S.C. Senate, 1980—; commr. S.C. Dept. Consumer Affairs. Mem. S.C. State Budget & Control Bd Home: 1817 Pineland Ave Florence SC 29501-5419 Office: 111 Gressette Bldg Columbia SC 29201

LEATHERMAN, STEPHEN PARKER, geologist, educator, writer; b. Charlotte, NC, Nov. 6, 1947; s. John F. and Evelyn M. (Parker) Leatherman. BS with honors, NC State U., 1970; PhD, U. Va., 1976. Petroleum geologist Texaco, Houston, 1970—72; asst. prof. Boston U., 1975—77; dir. rsch. unit U. Mass., Amherst, 1976—81; environ. scientist Barrier Island Task Force, Dept. Interior, Washington, 1977—78, US Geol. Survey, Reston, Va., 1980—81; asst. prof. U. Md., College Park, 1981—83, assoc. prof., 1983; prof., dir. Internat. Hurricane Rsch. Ctr., Fla. Internat. U., Miami, co-dir. Lab. for Coastal Rsch. Author: Barrier Islands from the Gulf of St. Lawrence to the Gulf of Mexico, 1979, Barrier Island Migration: An Annotated Bibliography, 1985, America's Best Beaches, 1998, Dr. Beach's Survival Guide: What You Need to Know About Sharks, Rip Currents, and More Before Going in the Water, 2003; co-editor: Sea Level Rise: History and Consequences, 2000; contbr. articles to profl. jours. Served US Army, 1970—72. Mem.: AAAS, Geol. Soc. Am., Soc. Econ. Paleontologists and Mineralogists, Sigma Xi. Office: Fla Internat U Internat Hurricane Rsch Ctr University Park, MARC 360 11200 SW 8th St Miami FL 33199 Office Phone: 305-348-1607. Office Fax: 305-348-1761. E-mail: Stephen.Leatherman@fiu.edu.*

LEAVELL, ELIZABETH BOYKIN, retired pediatrician; b. Sumter, SC, 1924; d. William de Saussure and Elizabeth (Hood) Boykin; m. Seth Eugene Latham (dec.); children: Seth Eugene Latham Jr., Margaret Elizabeth Latham Davis, Richard Boykin Latham, William deSaussure Latham; m. Lewis Edward Leavell, Jr., Aug. 16, 1985 (dec.). BS in Biology, Winthrop U., Rock Hill, SC, 1946; MD, Med. U. SC, Charleston, 1950. Diplomate Am. Bd. Pediat., 1956. Rotating intern Roper Hosp., Charleston, 1950—51, resident Pediat., 1951—53, chief resident, 1953—54; pediatrician Civil Svc. Tripler Army Hosp., Honolulu, 1954—55; pediatrician Aiken, SC, 1955—61, Atlanta, 1962—86; ret., 1986. Chief pediat. Holy Family Hosp., Atlanta, 1967, South Fulton Hosp., Atlanta, 1970; clinic pediatrician Crippled Children's Clinic, Atlanta, 1980—85; dir. med. edn. Pediat. St. Joseph Hosp., Atlanta, 1962—68; med. dir. Ctrl. Presbyn. Baby Clinic, Atlanta, 1962—68. Pres. Sumter County Hist. Soc., 2007. Recipient Mary Mildred Sullivan Outstanding Alumna award, Winthrop U., 1970; tchg. fellow dept. pediat., Med. U. SC, 1953—54. Fellow: Am. Acad. Pediat. (chmn. Fetus and Newborn com. Ga. chpt.). Home: 623 Antlers Dr Sumter SC 29150

LEAVER, BETTY LOU, educational administrator, writer; b. Rochester, NH, Feb. 16, 1950; d. Herman Nathan and Mary Elizabeth (Germon) Ham; m. Carl Don Leaver, Mar. 20, 1970; children: Echo Elizabeth, Fawn Noelle, Shawn Thomas, Shenan Carl. BA, Pa. State U., 1971, MA, 1978; PhD, Pushkin Inst., 1998. Officer U.S. Army, 1974-82; tchg. fellow U. Pitts., 1978-82; instr. Allegheny County (Pa.) C.C., Monroeville, 1982-83; lang. tng. supr. Fgn. Svc. Inst. U.S. Dept. State, Arlington, Va., 1983-89; dean Sch. Ctrl. European Langs. Def. Lang. Inst., 1992-93, dean Sch. Slavic Langs. Monterey, Calif., 1989-92; pres. Am. Global Studies Inst., Salinas, Calif., 1993—. Vis. prof. Middlebury (Vt.) Coll., 1994, Bryn Mawr (Pa.) Coll., 1995, 96, Monterey Inst. Internat. Studies, 1996, U. Helsinki, 1989; cons. Portland (Oreg.) Pub. Schs., Accels and Uzbekistan Ministry of Justice, 1995-97, ACCELS programs in Moldova, 1997, Ctr. for Advancement of Lang. Learning, Washington, 1994, 95, pub. schs., Krasnoyarsk, Siberia, 1993—, joint U.S./Russian Space Agy. projects, 1996, Soros Founds., Belarus, 1993, Russia, 1993-94, USIA (Embassy Tashkent Uzbekistan) 1997, Ukraine, 1994, Ohio State U., 1988-91, 93, lang. tng. for astronauts and cosmonauts NASA, 1998, numerous others; external evaluator Hot Line & White House Communicators, 1984-89; interpreter in U.S. and Russia; mem. fgn. lang. adv. com. Arlington County (Va.) Pub. Schs., 1985-88, chmn. 1988; founder consortia CIFLI Georgetown U., Am. Global Studies Inst., Columbia U., UCLA, Harvard U., Middlebury Coll., Bryn Mawr Coll., U. Md., 1994-95, U.S. Nval Acad., West Point, N.Y., CIA, NSA, Def. Lang. Inst., Fgn. Svc. Inst., U.S. Air Force Acad., others. 1st lt. U.S. Army, 1974-78. Mem. Am. Assn. for

Advancement of Slavic Studies (coord. open house 1985 World Congress), Am. Coun. Tchrs. of Russian (bd. dirs. 1988—, editor newsletter 1987-92), Am. Coun. Tchg. Fgn. Langs., Prunedale Grange, Profl. Women's Network.

LEAVITT, DAVID LIVINGSTONE, architect; b. Omaha, Aug. 26, 1918; s. Frederick William and Mattie Louise (Knapp) Bennett. BArch, U. Nebr., 1940; M in Architecture, Princeton U., 1942. Assoc. prof. Princeton (N.J.) U., 1941-42; chief designer Raymond and Rado, NYC, Tokyo, 1946—53, 1960—66; with Firm Leavitt & Henshell, NYC, 1953-60; instr. in design Columbia U., NYC, 1956, Pratt Inst., Bklyn., 1957-59; dir. architecture and interior design Hilton Internat., NYC, 1968-76; archtl. designer Bailey Assocs., Athens, 1977-80; hotel design cons. NYC, 1982—. Prin. works include U.S. Embassy Housing, Tokyo, 1953, residencies Russel Wright, 1956, Reader's Digest Bldg., Tokyo, 1964, Nanzan U., 1966. Lt. Aerial Navigator USN, 1942—46, PTO. Recipient Princeton prize, 1940, Rome prize, 1950; Regents scholar, U. Nebr., 1936. Mem.: AIA, Far E. Assn. Archs. and Engrs., Nat. Archs. Registration (bd. dirs. 1946—99). Avocations: painting, piano, reading, swimming, tennis. Home: 118 W 72nd St Apt 903 New York NY 10023-3321 Office: c/o ADA 170 E 61st St New York NY 10021-8551 Office Phone: 212-751-3420.

LEAVITT, JEFFREY STUART, lawyer; b. Cleve., July 13, 1946; s. Sol and Esther (Dolinsky) L.; m. Ellen Fern Sugerman, Dec. 21, 1968; children: Matthew Adam, Joshua Aaron. AB, Cornell U., 1968; JD, Case Western Res. U., 1973. Bar: Ohio 1973. Assoc. Jones Day, Cleve., 1973—80, ptnr., 1981—. Contbr. articles to profl. jours. Trustee Bur. Jewish Edn., Cleve., 1981-93, v.p., 1985-87; trustee Fairmount Temple, Cleve., 1982-2002, v.p., 1985-90, pres., 1990-93; trustee Citizens League Greater Cleve., 1982-89, 92-94, pres., 1987-89; trustee Citizens League Rsch. Inst., Cleve., 1989-98, Great Lakes Region of Union Am. Hebrew Congregations, 1990-93; mem. bd. govs. Case Western Res. Law Sch. Alumni Assn., 1989-92; sec. Kulas Found., 1986-88, 93-99, asst. treas., 1989-92. Named Ohio Super Lawyer, Cin. Mag. and Law and Politics, 2004, 2005, Leading Lawyer, Chanmbers USA Guide, 2006. Mem.: ABA (employee benefits coms. 1976—). Jewish. Home: 7935 Sunrise Ln Novelty OH 44072-9404 Office: Jones Day N Point 901 Lakeside Ave E Cleveland OH 44114-1190 Home Phone: 440-338-4485; Office Phone: 216-586-7188. Business E-Mail: jleavitt@jonesday.com.

LEAVITT, LYNDA, school system administrator, educator; d. Herbert and JoAnn Dollus; m. Dan Leavitt, Aug. 22, 1981; children: Shelby, Kelly, Andrew. BS in Polit. Sci., Ctrl. Mo. State U., Warrensburg, 1980; BS in Elem. and Spl. Edn., U. Mo., St. Louis, 1994; MEd, Nat. Louis U., Chgo., 1998; D in Edni. Leadership, St. Louis U., Mo., 2003. Cert.: (paralegal) 1983; sch. adminstr. Mo., human and orgnl. devel. Fielding Univ., 2006. Elem. tchr. Ft. Zumwalt Sch. Dist., Saint Peters, Mo., 1994—99; asst. prin. Parkway Sch. Dist., Saint Louis, 1999—2003; adj. prof. Lindenwood U., St. Charles, Mo., 2003—; area coord. Spl. Sch. Dist., St. Louis, 2003—; adj. prof. Fontbonne U., St. Louis, 2004—. Mem.: ASCD, Coun. Adminstrs. of Spl. Edn., Coun. Exceptional Children, Phi Delta Kappa, Sigma Sigma Sigma. Achievements include research in Leadership Initiatives in School Reform; U.S. Delegate to the China and U.S. Conf. on educating students with special needs Beijing, China. Office: Special Sch Dist 12110 Clayton Rd Saint Louis MO 63131 Home Phone: 636-443-9236; Office Phone: 314-989-8324 2766. Business E-Mail: lleavitt@ssd.k12.mo.us.

LEAVITT, MARTIN JACK, lawyer; b. Detroit, Mar. 30, 1940; s. Benjamin and Annette (Cohen) L.; m. Janice C. McCreary; children: Michael J., Paul J., David A., Keleigh R. LLB, Wayne State U., 1964. Bar: Mich. 1965, Fla. 1967. Assoc. Robert A. Sullivan, Detroit, 1968-70; officer, bd. dirs. Law Office Sullivan & Leavitt, Northville, Mich., 1970—, pres., 1979—. Bd. dirs. Tyrone Hills of Mich. Lt. comdr. USNR, 1965—68. Detroit Edison upper class scholar, 1958—64. Mem. ABA, Mich. Bar Assn., Fla. Bar Assn., Assn. Transp. Law, Logistics and Policy, ICC Practitioners, Meadowbrook Country Club, Huron River Hunting and Fishing Club (past pres.), Rolls Royce Owners Club (bd. dirs.). Jewish. Office: Sullivan and Leavitt PC 22375 Haggerty Rd PO Box 5490 Northville MI 48167-5490 Office Phone: 248-349-3980. Business E-Mail: mjl@sullivanleavitt.com.

LEAVITT, MICHAEL OKERLUND, secretary of health and human services; b. Cedar City, Utah, Feb. 11, 1951; s. Dixie and Anne (Okerlund) L.; m. Jacalyn Smith; children: Michael Smith, Taylor Smith, Anne Marie Smith, Chase Smith, Weston Smith. BA, So. Utah U., 1978. CPCU. Sales rep. Leavitt Group, Cedar City, 1972-74, account exec., 1974-76, mgr. underwriting Salt Lake City, 1976-82, COO, 1982-84, pres., CEO, 1984-92; gov. State of Utah, 1993—2003; adminstr. EPA, Washington, 2003—05; sec. US Dept. Health & Human Services, Washington, 2005—. Bd. dirs. Pacificorp, Portland, Oreg., Utah Power and Light Co., Salt Lake City, Great Western Thrift and Loan, Salt Lake City; vice-chmn. Grand Canyon Visability Transport Commn.; co-chair Western Regional Air Partnership. Chmn. instl. coun. So. UT St. U., Cedar City, 1985-89, chmn. UT St. Bd. Regents, 1989-92, campaign chmn. U.S. Sen. Orrin Hatch, 1982, 88, U.S. Sen. Jake Garn, 1980, 86; cons. campaign Gov. Norman Angerter, 1984; mem. staff Reagan-Bush '84. 2d lt. USNG, 1969-77. Named Disting. Alumni So. Utah State Coll. Sch. Bus., 1986. Mem. CPCU. Republican. Mem. Lds Ch. Avocation: golf. Office: US Dept Health & Human Services Hubert Humphrey Bldg 200 Independence Ave SW Rm 615 F Washington DC 20201*

LEAVITT, PAUL DAVID, director music arts, pianist, composer; b. Fitchburg, Mass., Sept. 18, 1963; s. David Bernard and Anne Theresa Leavitt. MusM, The Juilliard Sch., NYC, 1987. Tchr. piano, artist Ecole Nat. Sup. des Telecom., Paris, 1995—2000; artistic dir. Assn. Internationale Musique Ensemble, Paris, 1995—2000; dir. music, arts Ch. Reformation, Washington, 2002—. Composer: (choral work) Chanukah Benedictions- Al hanissim (Commn. from Congl. Chorus, 2004), Oseh Shalom (Commn. from GMCW, 2003). Office: Church of the Reformation 212 East Capitol St NE Washington DC 20003 Office Fax: 202-543-4201; Home Fax: 703 476-0884. Personal E-mail: pdleavitt3@comcast.net. E-mail: leavitt@reformationdc.org.

LEAVITT, THOMAS WHITTLESEY, retired museum director, educator; b. Boston, Jan. 8, 1930; s. Richard C. and Helen M. (Pratt) L.; m. Jane O. Ayer, June 23, 1951 (div. 1969); children: Katherine, Nancy, Hugh; m. Lloyd B. Carter, Sept. 14, 1978 (div. 1985); m. Michele C. McDonald, Apr. 20, 1991; children: Zachary Leavitt, Collin McDonald. AB, Middlebury Coll., Vt., 1951; MA, Boston U., 1952; PhD, Harvard, 1958. Asst. to dir. Fogg Mus., Harvard, 1954-56; exec. dir. fine arts com. People to People Program, 1957; dir. Pasadena (Calif.) Art Mus., 1957-63, dir. Santa Barbara (Calif.) Mus. Art, 1963-68; dir. Andrew Dickson White Mus. Art, Cornell U., Ithaca, NY, 1968—73, Herbert F. Johnson Mus. Art, 1973-91; univ. prof. history art Cornell U., 1968-91, prof. emeritus, 1991—; interim dir. RISD Mus. Art, 1993-94, Newport Art Mus., 1994-95, The Menil Collection, Houston, 1999-2000. Dir. mus. program Nat. Endowment for Arts, 1971-72, mem. museum panel, 1972-75; vice chmn. Council on Museums and Edn. in Visual Arts, 1972-76; trustee Gallery Assn. N.Y. State, 1972-78; mem. mus. panel N.Y. State Council Arts, 1975-78, 1980-82; chmn. art adv. com. Nat. Air and Space Mus., 1988—. Author exhbn. catalogs, articles. Trustee Am. Fedn. Arts, 1972-91, Newport Art Mus., 1995-2001; bd. dirs. Am. Arts Alliance, 1976-82, Ind. Sector, 1980-84; bd. govs. N.E. Mus. Conf., 1973-76; trustee Williamstown Regional Art Conservation Lab., 1979-91, pres., 1984-87. Named to Centennial Honor Roll, Am. Assn. Museums, 2006. Mem. Assn. Art Mus. Dirs. (pres. 1977-78, trustee 1978-80), Am. Assn. Museums (council 1976-79, v.p. 1980-82, pres. 1982-85, Disting. Svc. to Museums award 1997). Home: 25 Waterway Rd Saunderstown RI 02874-3906 Office Phone: 401-419-9076. E-mail: leavitt25@cox.net.

LEAVY, EDWARD, federal judge; b. Oreg., Aug. 14, 1929; m. Eileen Leavy; children: Thomas, Patrick, Mary Kay, Paul. AB, U. Portland, 1950; LLB, U. Notre Dame, 1953. Dist. judge Lane County, Eugene, Oreg., 1957—61, cir. judge, 1961—76; magistrate US Dist. Ct. Oreg., Portland, Oreg., 1976—84, judge, 1984—87, US Ct. Appeals (9th cir.), Portland, Oreg., 1987—97, sr. judge, 1997—; judge Fgn. Intelligence Surveillance Ct., 2001—. Recipient Sid Lezak award, 2003. Office: US Ct Appeals Pioneer Courthouse 700 SW Sixth Ave Ste 226 Portland OR 97204-1323*

LEAVY, HERBERT THEODORE, publisher; b. Detroit, July 10, 1927; s. Morris and Thelma (Davidson) L.; m. Patricia J. Moran, June 20, 1953; children: Karen, Kathryn, Jill, Jacqueline. BS in Journalism, Ohio U., 1951. Supervisory editor Fawcett Books, NYC, 1951-60; v.p., editorial dir. Davis Publs., NYC, 1960-69; founder, pres. Internat. Evaluations, Hauppage, NY, 1969-70; pub. dir. Countrywide Publs. Inc., NYC, 1970-75; pres. Communications Devel. Co., NYC, 1975-79; editorial dir. Watson-Guptil Publs., NYC, 1979-80; pres. Books from Mags., Inc., Smithtown, NY, 1980—, Resumes Unltd., Smithtown, 1984—. Author: 101 Fast Track Resumes, The Pleasure, Executive Handbook, Vegetarian Times Cookbook, McCall's Houseplant and Indoor Landscaping Guide, Working Mother Cookbook, Carpentry, Shoe and Leather Repair at Home, The Complete Book of Beards and Moustaches, Air Conditioning-Repair and Maintenance, Designing and Building Beds, Lofts and Sleeping Areas, Wallcovering, Floor Stripping and Refinishing, Packing and Moving, Recreational Vehicles, Appliance Repair, Plumbing Handbook, Successful Small Farms; numerous others; editor-in-chief: The Ohioan Mag. Ohio U., 1950-51. Acting 1st sgt. USAF, 1946—47. Mem. Sales Exec. Club, Am. Soc. Mag. Editors, Nat. Sporting Goods Assn., Am. Mgmt. Assn., Mag. Advts. Sales Club, Electronics Press Club, U.S. Tennis Ct. and Track Builders Assn., Am. Motorcycle Assn., Am. Horse Council, Authors Guild, Motorcycle Industry Council, Nat. Indoor Tennis Assn., Bus./Profl. Advt. Assn., Sigma Delta Chi.

LEAZER, WILLIAM, retired biomedical consultant; BA, Concordia Coll., Moorhead, Minn., 1951; MA, Western Res. U., Cleve., 1955; postgrad., Akademie Musik, Vienna, Austria, 1956—59. Promotion mgr. Springer Verlag, NYC, 1963—71; v.p. Majors Sci. Subscriptions, Dallas, 1972—93; coord. spl. projects Ebsco Subscriptions, Birmingham, 1993—95, biomed. cons., 1995—2002. Photography exhbns. include, Taos, N.Mex., Dallas, Nuevo Laredo, Mex. Asst. mgr. Quaker Relief, Vienna, 1956. Staff sgt. USMC, 1951—53. Mem.: Am. Guild Organists. Independent. Episcopalian. Avocations: travel, music, photography.

LEBANO, EDOARDO ANTONIO, foreign language educator; b. Palmanova, Italy, Jan. 17, 1934; came to U.S., 1957, naturalized, 1961; s. Nicola and Flora (Puccioni) L.; m. Mary Vangell, 1957; children: Tito Nicola, Mario Antonio. Student, U. Florence, Italy, 1955; MA, Cath. U. Am., 1961, PhD, 1966. Tchr. high sch., Florence, 1955-57; Italian lang. specialist Bur. Programs and Stds., CSC, Washington, 1958; lang. instr. Sch. Langs., Fgn. Svcs. Inst., Dept. State, Washington, 1959-61; lectr. Italian, U. Va., Charlottesville, 1961-66; asst. prof. Italian, U. Wis., Milw., 1966-69, assoc. prof., assoc. chmn. dept. French and Italian, 1969-71; assoc. prof. dept. French and Italian, Ind. U., Bloomington, 1971-83, prof., 1983—2000, prof. emeritus, 2000—. Dir. Sch. Italian, Middlebury Coll., Vt., 1987-95. Author: A Look at Italy, 1976, Buon giorno a tutti, 1983, L'Insegnamento dell'italiano nei college e nelle universita del nordamerica, 1983; author introduction and notes to Morgante by Luigi Pulci, 1998; contbr. articles to profl. jours. Decorated cavaliere Ordine al Merito della Repubblica Italiana; recipient Uhrig award U. Wis.-Milw. faculty, 1968. Mem. MLA, AAUP, Am. Assn. Tchrs. Italian (sec.-treas. 1980-84, pres. 1984-87, exec. dir. 2006-, Disting. Svc. award 1994), Dante Soc. Am., Renaissance Soc. Am., Boccaccio Soc. Am., Nat. Italian Am. Found., Am. Italian Hist. Assn., Am. Assn. Italian Studies, Midwest MLA. Home: 4323 Falcon Dr Bloomington IN 47403-9044 Office: Ind U Ctr for Italian Studies Bloomington IN 47405 Home Phone: 812-824-6145; Office Phone: 812-855-2508. Business E-Mail: lebano@indiana.edu.

LEBDA, DOUGLAS R., Internet company executive; BBA, Bucknell U., 1992; attended, U. Va., Darden Sch. Bus., 1998. Auditor, cons. PriceWaterhouse Coopers; founder LeadingTree, LLC (acquired by IAC.InterActiveCorp in 2003), 1998; CEO, LeadingTree, LLC, GetSmart.com, Real-Estate.com, INest & Domania IAC Fin. Services and Real Estate, 1998; pres., COO IAC/InterActiveCorp, 2005—; CEO IAC Search & Media, Oakland, Calif., 2006—. Bd. dir. Bucknell U. Alumni Assn.; bd. trustee Darden Sch. Found., 2002—05; mem. Charlotte C. of C. Recipient Ernst & Young Entrepreneur of Yr. award, Coun. for Entrepreneurial Development's Trailblazer award, Inman Innovator of Yr. award; vis. scholar Shermet Scholar. Achievements include patents in field. Office: IAC Search & Media 555 12th St Ste 500 Oakland CA 94607*

LEBEAU, DICK, professional football coach and retired player; b. Ohio, Sept. 9, 1937; m. Nancy LeBeau; 1 child, Brandon Grant. Attended, Ohio State Univ., 1955—58. Player, cornerback Detroit Lions, 1959—72; asst. coach Green Bay Packers, 1976—79, Phila. Eagles, 1976—79; defensive coord. Cin. Bengals, 1984—91, asst. head coach & defensive coord., 1997—2000, head coach, 2000—02; asst. head coach Buffalo Bills, 2003; asst. coach Pitts. Steelers, 1992—94, defensive coord., 1995—96, 2004—. Office: c/o Pitts Steelers 3400 S Water St Pittsburgh PA 15203-2349

LEBEAU, MARY DELLE, dancer, educator, writer; b. El Paso, Tex., Oct. 24, 1951; d. George Louis LeBeau, Jr. and Rachel Elaine (McGibboney) LeBeau. BA in Russian and French cum laude, U. Tex., 1974; diploma in Eurythmy, Sch. Eurythmy, Spring Valley, NY, 1982—87; MA in Russian, SUNY, Albany, 2001; postgrad. in Russian, U. So. Calif., LS. Cert. tchr., secondary Edn. in French, Russian, Eng. U. Tex., 1978. Tchr. of English Kashmere Sr. High, Houston, 1980—82; tchr. of eurythmy, Russian, French Hawthorne Valley Sch., Ghent, NY, 1987—93; founding tchr. Acad. of Art of Eurythmy, Moscow, 1993—97; grad. asst. in Russian SUNY, 1999—2001; tchg. asst. U. of So. Calif., 2003—. Guest artist in eurythmy at confs., NY, 1990—97; guest spkr. on Russia at confs., NY, 1993—97; performer Acad. of the Art of Eurythmy, Moscow, 1993—97. Dir., performer, creator of program (performance: eurythmy, poetry, jazz) And Still I Rise: African Am. poetry & music (N.Y. State Grant, 1993); translator: (transl. of poems) The Russian poet, Ol'ga Sedakova. Recipient Phi Beta Kappa, U. of Tex., 1974; grantee Decentralization Grant, N.Y. State, 1993, Spl. Opportunity Grant, 1992; Admunson fellow, U. So. Calif., 2001—03. Mem.: MLA, Am. Coun. of Teachers of Russian, Assn. for Women in Slavic Studies, Am. Assn. of Slavic and East European Languages, Eurythmy Assn. Am. Avocations: gardening, observing and reading about nature, weather; reading poetry, raising exotic finches, collecting Russian folk toys & crafts, birdwatching. Office: U of So Calif SLL 2nd Fl Taper Hall Los Angeles CA 90089 Business E-Mail: mlebeau@usc.edu.

LEBEDEV, KONSTANTIN VLADIMIROVICH, oceanographer, researcher; s. Vladimir Lvovich Lebedev and Natalia Konstantinovna Lebedeva, Erik Rudolfovich Kolman (Stepfather); m. Marina Sergeevna Lobanova, Oct. 13, 1981 (div. Aug. 9, 1985); 1 child, Julia Lebedeva; m. Alla Pavlovna Pikina, Sept. 7, 2001; children: Georgiy, Anna. MS in Aerodynamics and Thermodynamics, Moscow Inst. Physics and Tech., 1978—85; PhD in Phys. Oceanography, P. Shirshov Inst. Oceanology, Moscow, 1995. Sr. rsch. scientist P.Shirshov Inst. Oceanology, Moscow, 1985—98; vis. asst. rschr., data assimilation specialist Internat. Pacific Rsch. Ctr., SOEST, U. Hawaii, Honolulu, 1998—. Tchr. Moscow Inst. Physics and Tech., 1996—98. Contbr. articles to profl. jours. Grantee, Russian Acad. Scis. Mem.: Nat. Geographic Soc., Am. Geophys. Union. Achievements include research in numerical modeling and data assimilation in oceanography. Office: IPRC-SOEST Univ Hawaii 1680 E West Rd Post #401 Honolulu HI 96822 Office Phone: 808-956-9710. Office Fax: 808-956-9425. Business E-Mail: klebedev@soest.hawaii.edu.

LEBEDOFF, DAVID MILLER, lawyer, writer; b. Mpls., Apr. 29, 1938; s. Martin David and Mary Louise (Galanter) Lebedoff; m. Randy Louise Miller, Feb. 7, 1981; children: Caroline, Jonathan, Nicholas. BA magna cum laude, U. Minn., 1960; JD, Harvard U., 1963. Bar: Minn. 1963. Spl. asst. atty. gen. Atty. Gen. of Minn., St. Paul, 1963-65; pvt. practice law Mpls., 1967-81; ptnr. Lindquist & Vennum, Mpls., 1981-91, Briggs & Morgan, Mpls., 1991-95; of counsel Gray, Plant, Mooty, Mooty & Bennett, Mpls., 1995—. Spl. master U.S. Dist. Ct., Mpls., 1974—75. Bd. dirs. Coun. Crime and Justice, 1999—; past bd. dirs. Guthrie Theatre, 1980—85, U. Minn. Found., 1997—99, Blake Sch., 1988—94, Ctr. Am. Experiment; bd. dirs. Mpls. Inst. Art, 1975—, chmn., 1989—91, life trustee, 1997—; bd. regents U. Minn., Mpls., St. Paul, 1977—89, chmn. bd. regents, 1987—89. Recipient Outstanding Achievement award, U. Minn., 1991, Minn. Book award, 1998. Mem.: Minikahda Club, Mpls. Club (former bd. dirs.), Phi Beta Kappa. Home: 1738 Oliver Ave S Minneapolis MN 55405-2222 Office Phone: 612-632-3214.

LEBEDOFF, JONATHAN GALANTER, retired judge, mediator; b. Mpls., Apr. 29, 1938; s. Martin David and Mary (Galanter) L.; m. Sarah Sargent Mitchell, June 10, 1979; children: David Shevlin, Ann McNair. BA, U. Minn., 1960, LLB, 1963. Bar: Minn. 1963, U.S. Dist. Ct. Minn. 1964, U.S. Ct. Appeals (8th cir.) 1968. Pvt. practice, Mpls., 1963-71; judge Hennepin County Mcpl. Ct., State Minn., Mpls., 1971-74; dist. ct. judge State of Minn., Mpls., 1974-91; U.S. magistrate judge U.S. Dist. Ct., Mpls., 1991—2002, chief U.S. magistrate judge, 2002—05; pvt. mediator and arbitrator Mpls., 2005—. Mem. Gov.'s Commn. on Crime Prevention, 1971-75; mem. State Bd. Continuing Legal Edn.; mem. Minn. Supreme Ct. Task Force for Gender Fairness in Cts., mem. implementation com. of gender fairness in cts. Jewish. Avocation: bridge. Office: 4900 IDS Ctr 80 S 8th St Minneapolis MN 55402 Home Phone: 952-473-1414; Office Phone: 612-338-0505. E-mail: jglebedoff@yahoo.com.

LEBEDOFF, RANDY MILLER, lawyer; b. Washington, Oct. 16, 1949; m. David Lebedoff; children: Caroline, Jonathan, Nicholas. BA, Smith Coll., 1971; JD magna cum laude, Ind. U., 1975. Assoc. Faegre & Benson, Mpls., 1975-82, ptnr., 1983-86; v.p., gen. counsel Star Tribune, Mpls., 1989—2001; asst. sec. Star Tribune Cowles Media Co., Mpls., 1990—98; pvt. practice Mpls., 2001—02; v.p., gen. counsel Twin Cities Public Television, 2002—. Bd. dirs. Milkweed Editions, 1989-96. Bd. dirs. Minn. Opera, 1986-90, YWCA, 1984-90, Planned Parenthood Minn., 1985-90, Fund for Legal Aid Soc., 1988-96, Abbott-Northwestern Hosp., 1990-94. Mem. Newspaper Assn. Am. (legal affairs com. 1991-2002), Minn. Newspapers Assn. (bd. dirs. 1995-2002, pres. 2002). Home: 1738 Oliver Ave S Minneapolis MN 55405-2222 Office: 172 E Fourth St Saint Paul MN 55101

LEBEDOW, AARON LOUIS, consulting company executive; b. Chgo., Aug. 19, 1935; s. Isidor and Fannie (Perchikoff) L.; m. Madeleine Hellman; children: Ellen, Francine, Sheri, Tracey. BS in Indsl. Engring, Ill. Inst. Tech., 1957; MBA, U. Mich., 1958. Cert. mgmt. cons. Asst. marketing mgr. Imperial-Eastman, Chgo., 1960-61; mgr. Corplan Assos., Chgo., 1961-66; chmn. bd. Technomic, Inc., Chgo., 1966-87, Technomic Consultants Internat., Deerfield, Ill., 1987-93, Global Devel. Network, Inc., 1993—, Sheldon Good Auctioneers, 2004—. Bd. dirs. Coun. for Jewish Elderly. Served to 1st lt. USAF, 1958-60. Mem. Am. Mgmt. Assn., Am. Mktg. Assn., Tau Epsilon Phi. Office: Global Devel Network Inc 6540 N Kilbourn Ste A100 Lincolnwood IL 60712-3437 Office Phone: 847-674-7300. Personal E-mail: lebedowa@aol.com.

LEBEL, ROBERT, retired bishop; b. Trois Pistoles, Que., Can., Aug. 11, 1924; s. Wilfrid and Alexina (Belanger) L. L.Theol., St. Paul U., Ottawa, 1950; D.Theol., Athenee Angelicum, Rome, 1951. Ordained priest Roman Cath. Ch., 1950, consecrated bishop, 1974; tchr. theology Major Sem., Rimouski, Que., 1951-65, rector, 1963-65, Minor Sem., 1965-68; tchr. domatic theology U. Rimouski, 1970-74; aux. bishop St. Jean, Que., 1974-76; bishop Valleyfield, Que., 1976-2000; bishop emeritus, 2000—. Contbr. ch. publs. Mem. Roman Synod on the Christian Family, 1980. Mem. Conf. Can. Cath. Bishops, Soc. Canadienne de Theologie, KC. Roman Catholic. Address: 183 chemin St Louis Beauharnois PQ Canada J6N 2H8 E-mail: robert.lebel@sympatico.ca.

LEBENTHAL, ALEXANDRA, investment firm executive; d. James and Jacqueline Beymer Lebenthal; m. Jeremy Diamond, 1991; children: Benjamin, Charlotte. AB history, Princeton U., 1986. Municipal bond dept. Kidder Peabody & Co., 1986—88; joined sales department Lebenthal & Co., NYC, 1988, bd. dirs., 1992—2005, v.p., dir. mut. fund dept., 1993—94, v.p., dir. sales, 1994—95, pres., CEO, 1995—2005; chmn. Lebenthal Funds Inc., NYC; bd. dirs. Advest Inc., NYC; CEO broker dealer unit Alexandra & James Israel Discount Bank of New York, NYC, 2006—. Mem. adv. bd. Barbara K. Enterprises. Trustee Nightingale Bamford Sch., Citizen's Budget Commn.; co-founder, bd. dirs. The Women's Exec. Cir.; bd. dirs. United Jewish Appeal Fedn. N.Y. Named one of New York's 100 most influential women, Crain's N.Y. Bus., 1999. Mem.: Bond Market Assn. (bd. dirs. 2004), The Com. of 200, The Young Pres. Orgn. Office: IDB Bank 511 Fifth Ave New York NY 10017

LEBLANC, DANIEL G., state official; b. Sept. 1944; m. Mary LeBlanc; 3 children. Pres. Va. State Coun. of Machinists; sec., treas. State Fedn. Labor, 1984—90; pres. Va. State AFL-CIO, Richmond, 1990—2006; sec. of commonwealth Commonwealth of Va., 2006—. Mem. Dem. Nat. Com. Mem.: Internat. Assn. Machinists and Aerospace Workers Union. Office Phone: 804-786-2441.

LEBLANC, HUGH LINUS, political science professor, consultant; b. Alexandria, La., Oct. 30, 1927; s. Moreland Paul and Carmen Marie (Haydel) LeB.; m. Shirley Jean Smith, Feb. 28, 1953; children: Leslie Ann, Alexander Hugh. BA, La. State U., 1948; MA, U. Tenn., 1950; PhD, U. Chgo., 1958. Asst. prof. George Washington U., Washington, 1955-58, assoc. prof., 1959-63, prof., 1964-90, prof. emeritus dept. polit. sci., 1991—, chmn. dept., 1963-65, 70-76, 82-88; v.p. Area Inc., Arlington, Va., 1961-63. Author: American Political Parties, 1982, (with D. Trudeau Allensworth) The Politics of States and Urban Communities, 1971; contbr. articles to polit. sci. jours. Served to lt. (j.g.) USNR, 1944-45, 52-55. Named Outstanding Prof. Interfraternity Council, George Washington U., 1963 Mem. Amelia Island Plantation Club (Fla.). Personal E-mail: hllssl@aol.com, hllssl@comsat.net.

LEBLANC, JANET M., addictions and relationship counselor; b. Altamonte Springs, Fla., Oct. 8, 1947; BA, U. Fla., 1969; MA, Rollins Coll., 1989. Lic. mental health counselor, Fla.; cert. addictions profl.; cert. drug counselor level II; cert. master addictions counselor; cert. alcohol and drug counselor; cert. employee assistance profl.; cert. clin. criminal justice specialist. Dir. Mgmt. Consulting Svcs., Altamonte Springs; dir. outpatient adult alcohol and drug treatment program, substance abuse evaluations, and EAP work; substance abuse provider DOT. Mem.: Fla. Alcohol and

Drug Assn. for Counselors, Mental Health Counselors Ctrl. Fla. (chair cmty. rels. 1999—2002, pres. 2002—04, past pres. 2004, spl. events chair 2005—06, legis. chairperson 2006—07), Employee Assistance Program Assn. (treas. 1996—99, v.p. 2000—04, pres. 2004—07), Nat. Alcohol and Drug Assn. for Counselors. Office: Mgmt Cons Svcs PO Box 450 Altamonte Springs FL 32715-0450 Office Phone: 407-260-8533.

LEBLANC, JENNIFER DAWN, lawyer; JD, U. Houston, 1997. Bar: Tex. 1997. Assoc. Macdonald Devin, PC, Dallas, 2000—06, shareholder, 2006—. Named Rising Star, Tex. Monthly, 2006. Mem.: Dallas Bar Assn. Office: Macdonald Devin PC 1201 Renaissance Tower Ste 3800 Dallas TX 75270 Office Phone: 214-744-3300. Office Fax: 214-747-0942. Business E-Mail: jleblanc@macdonalddevin.com.

LEBLANC, JONATHAN M., lawyer; b. New Orleans, Sept. 3, 1969; m. Jennifer D. LeBlanc; 1 child. BA magna cum laude, U. SC, 1991; JD cum laude, Tulane Law Sch., 1995. Bar: Tex. 1995, US Dist. Ct. (all dists. Tex.), US Ct. Appeals (5th cir.). Assoc. Chamblee & Ryan PC, Dallas. Bd. dirs. Plano Homeowner's Coun., HOA for Cambridge Pl. at Russell Creek. Named a Rising Star, Tex. Super Lawyers mag., 2006. Mem.: Greater Dallas C. of C., Plano C. of C., Tex. Assn. Def. Counsel, Dallas Bar Assn. (mem. judiciary, continuing legal edn. and cmty. involvement coms.).*

LEBLANC, LEONARD JOSEPH, retired electronics company executive; b. Amherst, NS, Can., Feb. 4, 1941; came to U.S., 1952 naturalized 1959; s. Edgar Marcel and Mary Catherine (Bourgeois) LeB.; m. Janice May Dittrich, Sept. 11, 1965; children: Bryan, Jeffrey, Steven. BS, Coll. of Holy Cross, 1962, MS, 1963, George Washington U., 1966. Fin. analyst to mgr. Philco-Ford Corp., Blue Bell, Pa., 1966-72; asst. corp. controller Centainteed Corp., Valley Forge, Pa., 1972-73; sr. v.p. fin. Data Tech. Corp., Costa Mesa, Calif., 1973-76; v.p., controller Memorex Corp., Santa Clara, Calif., 1976-82; v.p. fin., treas. Saga Corp., Menlo Park, Calif., 1982-87; exec. v.p. fin. and adminstrn. Cadence Design Systems Inc., San Jose, Calif., 1987-92; sr. v.p. fin. and adminstrn., CFO GTech Corp., West Greenwich, RI, 1993-94; exec. v.p., CFO, COO Infoseek Corp., Santa Clara, Calif., 1996-97; exec. v.p., CFO Vantive Corp., Santa Clara, Calif., 1998-2000, ret., 2000. Bd. dirs. OpLink Comms., Inc., EBest Inc., AXT Inc. Mem. Monte Sereno Archtl. Com., Calif., 1981-93; bd. dirs. Eastfield Children's Ctr., Campbell, Calif., 1984-87. Served to lt.(j.g.) USN, 1963-66. Recipient commendation U.S. Navy Med. Sch., Bethesda, Md., 1966; fellow Coll. of Holy Cross, 1962 Mem. Fin. Execs. Inst. (pres. Santa Clara chpt. 1986-87).

LEBLANC, MARIANNE CAMILLE, lawyer; b. Boston, June 19, 1968; d. Norman Roger and Barbara Ann (Camille) L.; m. John Joseph Cummings III, Sept. 18, 1993. BA with honors, Wellesley Coll., 1990; JD with honors, Boston Coll., 1993. Bar: Mass. 1993, U.S. Dist. Ct. Mass. 1994. Assoc. Sugarman and Sugarman, P.C., Boston, 1993—2000, ptnr., 2000. Co-editor Jour. Mass. Acad. Trial Attys., 1998-2001. Bd. dirs. Support Com. for Battered Women, 1993-98, pres. 1994-96; bd. trustees Ursuline Acad., 2003—. Named one of Lawyers Yr., Mass. Lawyers Weekly, 1999, Top Boston Lawyers, Boston Mag., 2004, Mass. Super Lawyers, Law & Politics, 2004, Top 100 Mass. Super Lawyers, 2005, Top 50 Female Mass. Super Lawyers, 2004, 2005; recipient 40 Under 40 award, Boston Bus. Jour., 2002. Mem. ATLA (new lawyers divsn. gov., 1996-98), New. Eng. Bar Assn. (bd. dirs. 2002—), Mass. Acad. Trial Attys. (co-editor jour., bd. govs. 1999—, exec. com. 2006—, New Lawyers award, 1996), Mass. Bar Assn. (civil litig. sect. coun. 2000-02, ho. dels. 2001-02, chair civil litig. sect. coun. 2001-02), Women's Bar Assn. Mass. (bd. dirs. 1999—, co-chair legis. policy com. 2001-02, ann. gala chair 2003, v.p. 2002-03, pres-elect 2003-04, pres. 2004-05), Women's Bar Found. Mass. (bd. trustees 2001—, pres.-elect 2006, pres. 2007), New Eng. Bar Assn. (bd. dirs. 2002-05), Ursuline Acad. (bd. trustees 2003—), Children's Law Ctr. Mass. (pro bono atty. program). Democrat. Roman Catholic. Avocation: running. Office: Sugarman and Sugarman PC 1 Beacon St Boston MA 02108-3107 Office Phone: 617-542-1000. Business E-Mail: mleblanc@sugarman.com.

LEBLANC, MATT (MATTHEW STEVEN LEBLANC), actor; b. Newton, Mass., July 25, 1967; m. Melissa McKnight, May 3, 2003 (div. Oct. 6, 2006); 1 child, Marina Pearl stepchildren: Tyler, Jacquelyne. Actor (films) The Killing Box, 1993, Lookin Italian, 1994, Ed, 1996, Lost in Space, 1998, Charlie's Angels: The Movie, 2000, All the Queens Men, 2001, Charlie's Angels: Full Throttle, 2003; (TV movies) Reform School Girl, 1994; (TV series) TV 101, 1988, Anything to Survive, 1990, Top of the Heap, 1991, Vinnie and Bobby, 1992, Friends, 1994-2004, Joey, 2004-2006; (TV appearances) Just the Ten of Us, 1989, Monsters, 1988, Married...With Children, 1991, Red Shoe Diaries, 1992-1994. Named one of 50 Most Beautiful People, People Mag., 2000.

LEBLANC, RICHARD PHILIP, lawyer; b. Nashua, NH, Aug. 5, 1946; s. Ronald Arthur and Jeanette G. (Chomard) LeB.; m. Doris Julie Lavoie, May 25, 1968; children: Justin D., Renée M., Anne-Marie. AB summa cum laude, Coll. of the Holy Cross, 1968; JD cum laude, Harvard U., 1972. Bar: Maine 1972, U.S. Dist. Ct. Maine 1972. Assoc. Bernstein, Shur, Sawyer & Nelson, Portland, Maine, 1972-75, shareholder, 1976-95, LeBlanc & Young, Portland, 1995—. Pres. United Way Greater Portland, 1982-84; trustee Cleverus H.S., Portland, 1982-88; bd. dirs. Habitat for Humanity, Portland, 1984-92, Cumberland County Affordable Housing Venture, Portland, 1987-94, Maine Spl. Olympics, 1988-94, United Way Found. of Greater Portland, 1997-2004, Cath. Found. Maine, 2003—. Fellow: Am. Coll. Trust and Estate Counsel; mem.: ABA, Maine Estate Planning Coun., Maine Bar Assn., ABA. Democrat. Roman Catholic. Office: LeBlanc & Young PO Box 7950 Portland ME 04112-7950 Home: 10 Glenhaven Cir Saco ME 04072 Office Phone: 207-772-2800. Business E-Mail: rleblanc@leblancyoung.com.

LEBLANC, ROGER MAURICE, chemistry professor; b. Trois Rivières, Que., Can., Jan. 5, 1942; s. Henri and Rita (Moreau) L.; m. Micheline D. Veillette, June 26, 1965; children: Daniel, Hughes, Marie-Jose, Nancy. BSc, U. Laval, 1964, PhD, 1968. NRC postdoctoral fellow Davy Faraday Rsch. Lab. Royal Inst. Great Britain, London, 1968-70; prof. phys. chemistry U. Que., Trois-Rivières, 1970-93, chmn. dept., 1971-75, dir. Biophysics Rsch. Group, 1978-81, chmn. Photobiophysics Rsch. Ctr., 1981-91; prof., chmn. dept. chemistry U. Miami, Coral Gables, Fla., 1994—2002. Hon. prof. Jilin U., Changchun, China, 1992. Recipient Barringer award Spectroscopy Soc. Can., 1983, Medaille du Merite U. Que. a Trois-Rivieres, 1987, Commemorative medal for 125th Anniversary of Confedn. Can., 1993, Rsch. award Soc. Cosmetic Chemists Fla. chpt., 1999, Provost's award, 2002. Fellow Chem. Inst. Can. (Noranda award 1982, John Labatt Ltd. award 1992); mem. Am. Chem. Soc. (Fla. award 2006), Assn. Canadienne Francaise pour l'Avancement des Sciences (Prix Vincent 1978), Am. Soc. Photobiology, Biophys. Soc., European Photochem. Assn., Soc. Phys. Chemistry of Serbia (hon.), Royal Sci. Sc. Belgium (corr.). Roman Catholic. Home: 713 Crandon Blvd Apt 203 Key Biscayne FL 33149-2530 Office: U Miami Dept Chemistry Cox Sci Bldg Rm 315 1301 Memorial Dr Coral Gables FL 33124-0431 Office Phone: 305-284-2194. Business E-Mail: rml@miami.edu.

LEBLANC, TINA, dancer; b. Erie, Pa. m. Marco Jerkunica, May 1988; children: Marinko James, Sasha Johan. Trained, Carlisle, Pa. Dancer Joffrey II Dancers, NYC, 1982-83, The Joffrey Ballet, NYC, 1984-92; prin. dancer San Francisco Ballet, 1992—. Guest tchr. Ctrl. Pa. Youth Ballet, 1992, 94—. Work includes roles in (with San Francisco Ballet) Con Brio, Bizet Pas de Deux, Swan Lake, Nanna's Lied, Handel--A Celebration, La fille mal gardée, Rubies, Tchaikovsky Pas de Deux, Wanderer Fantasy, Seeing Stars, The Nutcracker, La Pavane Rouge, Company B, Romeo and Juliet, Sleeping Beauty, The Dance House, Terra Firma, Lambarena, Fly by Night, In the Night, Ballo della Regina, The Lesson, The Tuning Game, Quartette, Etudes, Western Symphony, Maelstrom, Pacific, Criss-Cross, Giselle, Theme and Variations, Gala Performance, The Vertiginous Thrill of Exactitude, Taiko, Sandpaper Ballet, La Bayadere, Night, Serenade, Celts, Stars & Stripes, Tarantella, Symphony in C, Dances at a Gathering, Don Quixote (full length), Square Dance, Apollo, Rush, Paquita, Who Cares, Study in Motion, 7 for Eight, Symphonic Variations, Two Bits, Valses Poeticos, Sea Pictures, Elite Syncopations, Smile with Your Heart, Falling, Harlequinade, Rodeo, Other Dances, Blue Rose, Quaternary, Chaconne, Artifact Suite, The Death of a Moth, Divertimento #15, On Common Ground; (with other companies) The Green Table, Les Presages, Le sacre du printemps, Les Noces, Light Rain, Romeo and Juliet, Runaway Train, Empyrean Dances, La Vivandière, L'air D'esprit, Corsaire Pas de deux, Don Quixote pas de deux, Lacrymosa, Confetti, Kettentanz Le Beau Danube, Offenbach in the Underworld, Suite Saint Saens, Forgotten Land, Dream Dances, Postcards, Coppelia, Remembrances, Reflections, Cotillon, Forcefield Petrouchka Cabochon. Recipient Princess Grace Found. award, 1988, Princess Grace Statuette award, 1995, Isadora Duncan award, 1998-99, 2000-01. Office: San Francisco Ballet Assn 455 Franklin St San Francisco CA 94102-4471 Home Phone: 650-375-8905; Office Phone: 415-861-5600.

LEBLANG, SKIP ALAN, lawyer; b. Phila., Jan. 14, 1953; s. Morton and Leah LeB.; m. Beth Siegel, Nov. 27, 1977; children: Kaitlyn Alexa, Chelsey Jenna. BA magna cum laude, U. Pitts., 1974; JD, U. San Diego, 1977. Bar: Pa. 1977, U.S. Dist. Ct. (we. dist.) Pa. 1977, D.C. 1980, N.Y. 1980, U.S. Dist. Ct. (so. and ea. dists.) N.Y. 1980. Jud. clk. Pa. Ct. Common Pleas, Pitts., 1977-78; atty. FTC, NYC, 1978-81; asst. corp. counsel law dept. City of N.Y., 1981-84; assoc. Kramer, Dillof, NYC, 1984-87; pvt. practice law NYC, 1987—, 1987—. Mem. faculty N.E. regional seat Nat. Inst. Trial Advocacy, Hofstra U., Uniondale, NY, 1984—; mem. faculty advanced trial program Law Sch., Hofstra U., 1984-93, 2007, adj. instr. law ctr., 2007, ABA/USTA Trademark Trial Advocacy Inst., 1993; spkr. in field. Author: Police Misconduct, 1981, Emergency Vehicle Liability, 1981, Sidewalks and Roadways, 1981. Co-dir. Coalition to Save Hempstead Harbor, Sea Cliff, N.Y., 1987-00, pres., 1998-00; mem. Environ. Leaders Network, Hicksville, N.Y., 1988; mem. adv. com. Internat. Environ. Conf., Hofstra U., 1990; pres., North Country Reform Temple, 2002-04. Recipient award of merit N.Y. State Gov., 1990. Mem. ATLA, NY State Trial Lawyers Assn., Pa. Bar Assn., Assn. Bar City of NY, Million Dollar Advs. Forum (life mem.). Avocations: marathon running, basketball, skiing, fly fishing. Office: Ste 402 325 Broadway New York NY 10007-1112 Office Phone: 212-271-0215. Business E-Mail: s.leblanglaw@covad.net.

LEBLANG, THEODORE RAYMOND, law educator, lawyer; s. Morton and Leah L.; m. Pamela Kay; children: Danielle Rosalyn, Yale Phillip. BA, Pa. State U., 1970; JD, U. Ill., 1974. Bar: Ill. 1974, U.S. Supreme Ct. 1977. Legal counsel So. Ill. U. Sch. of Medicine, Springfield, 1975-92; prof. med. jurisprudence So. Ill. U. Sch. Law, Carbondale, 1991—2006; prof., chair dept. med. humanities So. Ill. U. Sch. Medicine, Springfield, 1993—2006, prof. emeritus, 2006—. Adj. prof. Sangamon State U., Springfield, 1984-89; co-annotator AMA Code Med. Ethics with Annotations, 1994-2006. Co-author: The Law of Medical Practice in Illinois, 1986, 2d edit., 1996; author column Legalities in Am. Druggist mag., 1988-99; editor: Jour. Legal Medicine, 1981-2003, editor emeritus, 2004—; editor: Series in Med. Humanities, So. Ill. U Press, 1993-99, Ill. Bar. Jourl., 2000-02; mem. editl. bd. Law, Medicine and Health Care, 1981-2006, Ill. Bar Jour., 1987—, Jour. Law and Medicine, 1998-2003, Ill. Child Welfare, 2003—, Medicine and Law, 2005—; assoc. editor Health Care Lawyer, 1992—; contbg. editor Am. Druggist Mag., 1996-99; mem. Textbook Com. Legal Medicine, 7th edit., 2007. Adv. com. Children Family Stress Cons. Team, Springfield, 1976-99; co-host Children's Miracle Network, 1987-2000; bd. dirs. Mid-Am. Playwrights Theatre, 1990-92; pres. Springfield Jewish Fedn., 1997-99; chair UJA/Fedn. Campaign, 1992-93; chmn. Endowment Fund Bd., 2001-; fin. com. Jewish Fedn. Metro. Chgo. Pooled Endowment, 2004—. Lt. comdr. ret. JAGC, USNR. Fellow Am. Coll. Legal Medicine (past pres. 2004-05, Gold Medal award 2007); mem. ABA (past chair TIPS medicine and law com. 1986-87), Med. Malpractice Nat. Inst. (co-chair 1986-90), Ill. State Bar Assn. (Bd. Govs. award 1995, founding chair, bar publs. bd. 1992-95, past chair interprofl. cooperation com. 1985-86, past chair health care sect. coun. 1990-91, past chair CLE com. 1994-95, past chair tellers of election 1998, vice chair spl. com. comm. for next century 1998-2000, rep. assembly 1986-88, interdisciplinary panel life support sys., inst. pub. affairs 1986-87), U.S. Agy. Healthcare Rsch. and Policy (task force liability determination 1991), Nat. Bd. Med. Examiners (task force on law and ethics in medicine 1980-84, ethics task force 1990-91), So. Ill. U. Sch. Law Alumni Assn. (Hon.), World Assn. Med. Law (coun. pres. 2004, Maccabi award Outstanding paper, 1994) Naval Res. Assn. (life). Avocations: skiing, scuba diving, softball, films. Office: So Ill U Sch Medicine PO Box 19603 913 N Rutledge St Springfield IL 62794-9603

LEBLOND, ANTOINE, computer company executive; m. Lucie Leblond; 2 children. BS in Math., McGill U., Montreal. With Microsoft Corp., Redmond, Wash., 1989—, software design engr., 1989—98, dir., office develop., 1998—2002, disting. engr., 2000, corp. v.p., office program mgmt., 2002—06, corp. v.p., office productivity applications, 2006—. Office: Microsoft Corp One Microsoft Way Redmond WA 98052-7329

LEBLOND, PAUL HENRI, oceanographer, educator; b. Que., Can., Dec. 30, 1938; s. Sylvio and Jeanne (Lacerte) LeB.; m. Josee Michaud (div. 1985); children: Michel, Philippe, Anne. BA, Laval U., Quebec, 1957; BS, McGill U., Montreal, Que., 1961; PhD, U. B.C., Vancouver, Can., 1964; DSc (hon.), Meml. U., Newfoundland, 1992. Prof. depts. oceanography and physics U. B.C., Vancouver, 1965, assoc. dean faculty of sci., 1982-85, head dept. oceanography, 1987-92, dir. program earth and ocean scis., 1992-96, prof. emeritus, 1996—. Chmn. Can. nat. com. World Ocean Circulation Expt., 1987-92; program leader Ocean Prodn. Enhancement Network, Can., 1991-93; pres. Can. Open Frontiers Rsch. Found., 1996-98. Co-author: Waves in the Oceans, 1978, Cadborosaurus, 1995; contbr. articles to profl. jours. Mem. Fisheries Resource Conservation Coun., 1993-98; mem. Pacific Fisheries Resource Conservation Coun., 1998—, chair, 2005—; chair sci. and industry bd. Inst. Pacific, Ocean Sci. and Tech., 1998-2002; trustee Can. Found. Climate Atmosphere, 2000—07; mem. Galiano Parks and Recreation Commn., 2005—. Recipient Wooster award, North Pacific Marine Sci. Orgn., 2005. Fellow Royal Soc. Can., Can. Meteorol. and Oceanographic Soc. (Pres.'s prize 1981, Tully medal 1991); mem. Am. Geophys. Union, Galiano Conservancy Assn. (bd. dirs. 1996—2004), Can. Parks & Wilderness Soc. (B.C. chpt. bd. dirs. 2000-05), Galiano Mus. Soc. (pres. 2003—07). Avocations: hiking, history, science fiction. Business E-Mail: leblond@gulfislands.com.

LEBLOND, RICHARD KNIGHT, II, banker; b. Cin., Nov. 16, 1920; s. Harold R. and Elizabeth (Conroy) LeB.,; m. Sara Cordial Chapman, Dec. 11, 1948; children— Mary, Richard, E. Chapman, Elizabeth, David, Virginia, William, Thomas, Sara, Joseph BA, Princeton U.; DCS (hon.), St. John's U., Jamaica, NY, 1978. Exec. v.p. Chem. Bank, NYC, 1968-73, vice-chmn. bd., 1973-85, sr. advisor, 1985—. Sr. advisor JP Morgan Chase, Bedford Stuyvestant D&S Corp., Bklyn. Pres. Robert T. Jones Jr. Scholarship Fund. 1st lt. US Army, 1943—46, PTO. Mem. N.Y. State Bankers Assn. (pres. 1979-80), Harvard Bus. Sch. Assn. (pres. 1975-76) Republican. Roman Catholic. Office: JP Morgan Chase & Co 11 W 51st St Fl 2 New York NY 10019-6901 Office Phone: 212-307-8710.

LEBMAN, ROBERT RICHARD, social services administrator; b. Amsterdam, NY, Sept. 20, 1945; s. Harry and Catherine (Spitzkopf) L. BA cum laude, Harpur Coll., Binghamton, NY, 1967; MA, Pa. State U., 1968. With Peace Corps, 1968-72; project dir. AID mission, Afghanistan, 1972-73; cons. Rochester Sch. Dist., NY, 1973; rsch. assoc. Applied Behavioral Rsch. Assocs., Rochester, 1973-74; from caseworker to clin. dir. Delphi House, Rochester, 1974-78; dir. N.W. Youth Ctr. of Charles Settlement House, Rochester, 1978-80; exec. dir. Livingston County Youth Bur., Rochester, 1981-83, Monroe County Youth Advocacy, Rochester, 1983-86; dir. in-patient svcs. DayBreak Alcoholism Treatment Facility, Rochester, 1986-89; exec. dir., pres. Huther-Doyle Meml. Inst., Rochester, 1989—, CEO. Author: English Language Teaching in Afghanistan, 1972. Past pres. Helping People with AIDS, Region II Consortium on Alcoholism and Substance Abuse Svcs.; pres. Jewish Family Svcs.; mem. profl. adv. HRC, Inc.; mem. behavioral health adv. Excellus Inc.; mem. Monroe County Task Force on Youth and Alcohol, 1976—86, Monroe County Cmty. Svcs. Bd.; mem. 4-H adv. com. Monroe County Coop. Extension, 1978—80; mem. Black Seeds Scholarship Com., 1981—86, Jewish Chm. Dependency Task Force Com. on Youth and Alcohol; mem. budget adv. com. Rochester City Schs., 1983—85; chmn. Regional Youth Workers Tng. Network; mem. harm reduction adv. bd. AIDS Rochester; past pres. Recovery Net; treas. Coun. Agy. Execs.; mem. steering com. Rochester Drug Summit; bd. dirs. Finger Lakes Health Sys. Agy., Operation U-Turn, Inc.; past vice chair bd. dirs. Rochester Area Task Force on AIDS; bd. dirs. NY State Assn. Alcoholism and Substance Abuse Providers; v.p., bd. dirs. Jewish Family Svcs. NDEA fellow, 1967. Mem.: Arts and Scis. Acad. Rochester (bd. dirs.), Nat. Coun. Crime and Delinquency, Am. Judicature Soc., Acad. Polit. and Social Sci., Am. Polit. Sci. Assn., Acad. Polit. Sci. Democrat. Jewish. Home: 29 Old Winding Ln Fairport NY 14450-1108 Office: 360 East Ave Rochester NY 14604-2612 Home Phone: 585-388-5177; Office Phone: 585-325-5100. E-mail: rlebman@hutherdoyle.com.

LEBOEUF, EDMOND ARTHUR, human resources specialist; s. Arthur and Betty Leboeuf. BS in Psychology, Kans. State U., Manhattan, 1995, M in Pub. Adminstrn., 1995; AA, Washburn U., Topeka, 1998, BA in Mass Media magna cum laude, 2004, B in Legal Studies magna cum laude, 2006. Cert. Regional and Cmty. Planning Kans. State U., 1994. Spl. investigator Kans. Dept. Transp., Topeka, 2000—06, human resource profl., 2006—. Musician: (CD) Faith. Pres. Abilene Jr. C. of C., Kans., 1987—88. Home Phone: 785-234-2762; Office Phone: 785-296-0431.

LE BON, DOUGLAS KENT, investment manager; b. Rapid City, SD, Oct. 27, 1953; s. Stanley and Elodis (Holm) Le B. BSBA, Calif. State U., Dominguez Hills, 1976, MBA, 1979. Valuation cons. Houlihan, Lokey, Howard & Zukin, LA, 1979-83; v.p., prin. Wilshire Assocs., Inc., Santa Monica, Calif., 1983-90; co-founder, mng. dir. Pathway Capital Mgmt., LA, 1990—. Office: Pathway Capital Mgmt 5 Park Plz Irvine CA 92614-5995

LEBON, RACHEL L., musician, educator; d. Raymond Joseph and Georgette Lebon. BS, North Tex. State U., 1977, MS, 1979; PhD, U. of Miami, 1986. Asst. prof. Belmont Coll., Nashville, 1979—83; performer Air Force Tops in Blue, Randolph A.F.B., Tex., 1973; acad. instr. USAF, Sheppard A.F.B., Tex.; prof., coord. of jazz voice U. of Miami, Coral Gables, Fla., 1986—. Voice specialist Profl. Voice Inst., Hallandale Beach, Fla., 1985. Author: The Professional Vocalist: A Handbook for Commerical Singers and Teachers, 1999, The Versatile Vocalist: Singing Authentically in Contrasting Styles and Idioms, 2006; singer: (CD) Voicings. Child adv. Guardian Ad Litem, Miami, Fla., 1990—2006. Staff sgt USAF, 1973. Recipient Vol. of Year, Buddies on Nashville, 1983. Mem.: Internat. Assn. for Jazz Edn., Nat. Assn. Tchrs. Singing, Pi Kappa Lambda. Personal E-mail: rllebon@aol.com.

LEBOUITZ, MARTIN FREDERICK, diversified financial services company executive, consultant; b. Phila., May 16, 1946; s. William and Sylvia (Magen) L.; m. Helene A. Pepper, Oct. 15, 1977; children: Clarke S., Jacqueline B. BS, U.S. Air Force Acad., 1971, MA, 1972; MA Fletcher Sch. Law and Diplomacy, Tufts U., 1972. Asst. v.p. Bankers Trust Co., NYC, 1976—82; v.p. mgr. of planning Barclays Bank of N.Am., NYC, 1982—85; v.p. corp. devel. Chase Manhattan Bank, NYC, 1985—88; v.p. planning and devel. Paine Webber Group Inc., NYC, 1988—90; prin. DRI/McGraw-Hill, NYC, 1990—91; mng. dir. Fin. Svcs. Cons., NYC, 1991—95; v.p. global payments project exec. and industry issues exec. JP Morgan Chase, NYC, 1995—99; v.p. planning and devel. JP Morgan, Fin. Markets Solutions, 1999—; pres. Global Payments Strategies, Tampa, Fla., 2004—. Dir. Mag-Lev Energy, Inc. Capt. USAF, 1971-76. Mem. Strategic Leadership Forum (dir., chmn. program com. NY chpt.), Assn. for Corp. Growth, Am. Mgmt. Assn. (pres.), USAF Acad. Assn. of Grad. (Tampa chpt.), Harvard Club, Fletcher Sch. Club NY (chmn. sch. rels. com.), Ctr. Club, Champion Hills Country Club, Feather Sound Country Club. Office: 2202 West Shore Blvd Ste 200 Tampa FL 33607 E-mail: martin.lebouitz@paymentstrategies.org.

LEBOW, IRWIN LEON, communications engineering consultant; b. Boston, Apr. 27, 1926; s. Samuel and Ruth (Tobey) L.; m. Grace H. Hackel, July 8, 1951; children: Judith, William, David. SB, MIT, 1948, PhD, 1951. Staff mem. MIT Lincoln Lab., 1951-60, assoc. leader satellite communications surface techniques group, 1960-65, leader, 1965-70, assoc. head communications divsn., 1970-72, assoc. head data systems divsn., 1972-75, mem. steering com., 1970-75; chief scientist, assoc. dir. tech. Def. Communications Agy., Washington, Dept. Def., Washington, 1975-81; v.p. engring. Am. Satellite Co., Rockville, Md., 1981-84; v.p. Systems Research and Applications Corp., Arlington, Va., 1984-87; ind. cons. Washington, 1987—. Adj. prof. U. Md., Univ. Coll., 1998—. Author: (with others) Theory and Design of Digital Machines, 1962, The Digital Connection, 1991, Information Highways and Byways, 1995, Understanding Digital Transmission and Recording, 1997, (with others) Coping with Your Difficult Older Parent, 1999. Bd. dirs. Osher Lifelong Learning Inst., Am. U.; with USNR, 1944-46. Awarded rank of Meritorious Sr. Exec., 1980; recipient Meritorious Civilian Service medal Dept. Def., 1981. Fellow Am. Phys. Soc., IEEE; mem. Sigma Xi. Avocations: cooking, bread baking. Home and Office: Apt 909 5600 Wisconsin Ave Chevy Chase MD 20815-4411 Office Phone: 301-652-4026. Personal E-mail: irwinle@cs.net.

LEBOW, MARK DENIS, lawyer; b. Harrisburg, Pa., Apr. 2, 1940; s. Sylvan and Ruth M. (Lebowitz) L.; m. Catherine Maugee, Nov. 22, 1972 (div. 1982); m. Patricia Edith Harris, Jan. 30, 1988; children: Michael, Jeffrey, Alexandra. AB, Yale U., 1961; JD, Harvard U., 1964. Bar: N.Y. 1965, U.S. Ct. Appeals (2d cir.) 1965, U.S. Dist. Ct. (so. and ea. dists.) N.Y. 1966, U.S. Supreme Ct., 1972. Assoc. Coudert Bros., NYC, 1965-71, ptnr., 1972-98; mng. ptnr. Sokolow Carreras LLP, NYC, 1999—. Chmn. N.Y.C. CSC, 1979-92; bd. dirs. Met. Transp. Authority of N.Y. State, 1992—. Chmn. St. Francis Friends of the Poor, Inc., 1991—; trustee St. Bona Venture U., 1997—; pres. Am. Red Magen David for Israel, 2001—. Home: 1067 5th Ave New York NY 10128-0101 Office: Sokolow Carreras LLP 770 Lexington Ave 6th Flr New York NY 10021-8165 Home Phone: 212-534-4748; Office Phone: 212-935-6000. Personal E-mail: Mark@Lebow.net. Business E-Mail: mlebow@scassocies.net.

LEBOWITZ, ALBERT, lawyer, writer; b. St. Louis, June 18, 1922; s. Jacob and Lena (Zemmel) L.; m. Naomi Gordon, Nov. 26, 1953; children: Joel Aaron, Judith Leah. AB, Washington U., St. Louis, 1945; LL.B., Harvard U., 1948. Bar: Mo. bar 1948. Assoc. Frank E. Morris, St. Louis, 1948-55; partner firm Morris, Schneider & Lebowitz, St. Louis, 1955-58, Crowe, Schneider, Shanahan & Lebowitz, St. Louis, 1958-66; counsel firm Murphy & Roche, St. Louis, 1966-67, Murphy & Schlapprizzi, St. Louis,

1967-81; partner firm Murphy, Schlapprizzi & Lebowitz, 1981-86; editor lit. quar. Perspective, 1961-80; of counsel Donald L. Schlapprizzi, P.C., 1986—, John T. Murphy, Jr., 1986-88. Author: novel Laban's Will, 1966, The Man Who Wouldn't Say No, 1969, A Matter of Days, 1989; also short stories. Served as combat navigator USAAF, 1943-45, ETO. Decorated Air medal with 3 oak leaf clusters. Mem. Mo. Bar Assn., Phi Beta Kappa. Home: 743 Yale Ave Saint Louis MO 63130-3120

LEBOWITZ, CATHARINE KOCH, state legislator; b. Winchester, Mass., June 30, 1915; d. William John and Carolyn Sophia (Kistinger) Koch; m. Murray Lebowitz, Sept. 21, 1971 (dec. Oct. 1978). Student, Northwestern U., 1948-49, Boston Coll., 1949-52; degree (hon.), Ea. Main Tech. Coll., 2003. Sec. ERA, Bangor, Augusta, Maine, 1935-38, WPA, Portland, Maine, 1938-42; pers. officer, exec. sec. USN, Portland, 1942-47; exec. sec. Clark Babbitt, Boston, 1947-48; adminstrv. asst. Moore Bus. Forms, Boston, 1948-52; apt. mgr., wholesale appliance divsn. Coffin-Wimple Inc., 1952-62; clk. U.S. Dist. Ct. Bangor (no. dist.), 1962-79; sec. Portland Credit Bur., 1980-86; mem. Bangor City Coun., 1985-87, Maine State Legislature, 1982-92. Bd. dirs. Eastern Transp., 1989—94; mem. Bus. Adv. Coun., 1991—; active Program Rev. Subcom., 1991—; mem. adv. coun. Ea. Maine Tech. Coll., 1992—; bd. dirs. Rural Health Ctrs. Maine, Inc., 1992—99; chair, adv. bd., Gala decorating com. Maine Ctr. for Arts, U. Maine, 1992—2003. Sec. Symphony Women, Bangor, 1964—84; bd. dirs. Opera House Com., 1978—94; legis. com. United Way of Penobscot Valley, 1988—93, bd. dirs., 1993—99; adv. com. Maine Devel. Found., 1988—90; adv. bd. Aftercare, Cmty. Health & Counseling Svc., 1992; planning bd. St. Joseph Hosp., 1987—92; dir., v.p. St. Joseph Hosp. Aux., 1994—99, Maine Ctr. Arts Adv. Bd., 1994—2002; apptr. by gov. Maine Commn. Cmty. Svc., 1996—2002; mem. Bangor City Hosp. Aux., 1988—99; bd. dirs. Penobscot Theater, 1990; accredited Beauty Pageant judge, 1986—; mem. Eastern Main Commn. Cmty Svc., 1996; del. Rep. Nat. Conv., 1984, 1988. Recipient Civilian Meritorious Svc. award USN, Portland, Maine, 1946, Paul Bunyan award, C. of C., 1997, Cmty. Spirit award Sr. Star recognition Merrill Merchants Bank Bangor, 1999; named Hon. Alumnus Secretarial Sci., Husson Coll., 1980, Ea. Main Tech. Coll. Champion award, 2002. Mem.: Ea. Maine Med. Ctr. Aux., Ret. Fed. Employees (v.p. 1994—, pres. 1996), Newcomb Soc., Penobscot County Reps., Bangor C. of C. (mem. comsumer rels. coun., 1981-90, gov. affairs com. 1996—, coord. 150th ann. prodn. Music Man 1984), Bangor Dist. Nursing Assn. (corp. mem. at large), Credit Women Bangor (sec. 1965—67), Nat. Assn. Ret. Fed. Employees (v.p. bd. dirs. 1993—, sec. 1994), Credit Profls. Bangor Cmty. Theater (treas. 1973—98), Credit Women Internat. (treas. 1975—77), Penobscot County Ext. Svc. (hon.; bd. dirs. 1995—), Main Art N.G. (hon.), Maine N.G. Assn. (hon.), Bangor Hist. Soc. (bd. dirs. 1993—, exec. bd. sec. 1994—99, pres. 1999—2002), U. Maine Maine Masque Theater (judge 1983—90), Mgmt. Club, Bangor City Rep. Club (bd. dirs., treas. 1993—97), Penobscot County Rep. Women's Club (sec. 1979), Zonta Club (pres. Bangor 1962—64, 1980—82, v.p. 1994, adv. bd. Maine migrant health program 2001—, cooperator cmty. health and counseling svcs. 2001—, Outstanding Leader 1991).

LEBOWITZ, JOEL LOUIS, mathematical physicist, educator; b. May 10, 1930; arrived in US, 1946, naturalized, 1951; m. Estelle Mandelbaum, June 21, 1953 (dec. Dec. 1996); m. Ann Keay Beneduce, June 3, 1999. BS, Bklyn. Coll., 1952; MS, Syracuse U., 1955, PhD, 1956; doctorate (hon.), Ecole Poly. Federale, Lausanne, Switzerland, 1977, Clark U., 1999. NSF postdoctoral fellow Yale U., New Haven, 1956-57; mem. faculty Stevens Inst. Tech., Hoboken, NJ, 1957-59, Yeshiva U., NYC, 1959-77, prof. physics, 1965-77, acting chmn. Belfer Grad. Sch. Sci., 1964-67, chmn. dept., 1967-76; George William Hill prof math. and physics, dir. Ctr. for Math. Scis., Rutgers U., New Brunswick, NJ, 1977—. Co-editor: Phase Transitions and Critical Phenomena, 1980, editor Jour. Statis. Physics, 1975—, Studies in Statis. Mechanics, 1973—, Com. Math. Physics, 1973—; contbr. articles to profl. jours. Recipient Boltzmann medal Internat. Union Pure and Applied Physics, 1992, Max Planck Rsch. award, 1993, Delmar S. Fahrney medal Franklin Inst., 1995, Henri Poincare prize Internat. Assn. of Math. Physics/Daniel Iagolnitzer Found., 2000, Vito Volterra medal Academia Nazionale dei Lincei, 2001, Max Planck medal German Phys. Soc., 2007; Guggenheim fellow, 1976-77. Fellow AAAS (Sci. Freedom and Responsibility award 1998), Am. Phys. Soc. (Nicholson medal for humanitarian svc. 2004), NY Acad. Scis. (pres. 1979, A. Cressy Morrison award 1986, Heinz R. Pagels Human Rights of Scientists award 1996); mem. NAS, AAUP, Am. Math. Soc., Phi Beta Kappa, Sigma Xi. Office: Rutgers U Ctr Math Sci Rsch 110 Frelinghuysen Rd Piscataway NJ 08854-8019 Business E-Mail: lebowitz@math.rutgers.edu.

LEBRAS, PAUL J., retired career military officer; b. NYC, Oct. 27, 1949; BA in Edn., Manhattan Coll., 1971; MA in African Area Studies, UCLA, 1979; Grad., Army Command & Gen. Staff Coll., Ft. Leavenworth, 1984; Grad. Air War Coll., Maxwell AFB, 1990. Commd. 2d lt. USAF, 1971, advanced through grades to maj. gen., 2002; target analyst Nakhon Phanom Royal, Thai AFB, Thailand, 1972; operational intelligence officer 8th Tactical Fighter Wing, Ubon Thai Royal AFB, 1972-73; staff officer Hdqrs. Pacific Air Forces, Hickam AFB, Hawaii, 1973-77; air staff tng. program officer Hdqrs. USAF, The Pentagon, Washington, 1977-78, chief Middle East and African br. regional estimates divsn., 1984-87; analyst Def. Intelligence Agy., Washington, 1980-83; dir. White Ho. Situation Rm., Washington, 1987-89; commdr. 12th Tactical Intelligence Squadron, Bergstrom AFB, Tex., 1990-91; dir. intelligence Hdqrs. 4th Air Force, Yokota AB, Japan, 1991-94; dir. of intelligence Hdqrs. Pacific Air Forces, Hickman AFB, 1994-96; dir. intelligence Hdqrs. Air Combat Command, Langley AFB, Va., 1996-97, various assignments, 1997-98; vice comdr. Air Intelligence Agy., Kelly AFB, 1998-99; vice dir. intelligence, Joint Staff (J-2) Def. Intelligence Agy., Washington, 1999—2001; dep. comdr. info. ops. 8th Air Force, Barkdale AFB, La., 2002—05; comdr. Air Intelligence Agy. & Joint Info. Ops. Ctr., Lackland AFB, Tex., 2002—05; ret., 2005. Decorated Def. Superior Svc. medal with two oak leaf clusters, Legion of Merit, Def. Meritorious Svc. medal, Meritorious Svc. medal with four oak leaf clusters, Joint. Svc. Commendation medal, Air Force Commendation medal; Recipient Presdl. Svc. Badge.

LEBRECHT, THELMA JANE MOSSMAN, retired reporter; b. Indpls., Feb. 21, 1946; d. Elmore Somerville and Lois Thelma (Johnson) Mossman; m. Roger Dublon LeBrecht, May 4, 1968. BS in Journalism, U. Fla., 1968. Pub. affairs reporter WBT and WBTV, Charlotte, NC, 1967-72; freelance reporter Toronto and NYC, 1972-76; reporter KYW Newsradio, Phila., 1976-80; editor ABC Radio Network, NYC, 1980-81; reporter AP Broadcast, Washington, 1981—2004, ret., 2004. Bd. dirs. Washington Press Club Found., 1995-2004. Mem. Radio and TV Corrs. Assn. in U.S. Capitol (chmn. 1991, AP Oliver S. Gramling Disting. Reporter award 1996).

LEBRETON, MARIETTA M., history professor; d. Guy Joseph and Marietta Schneidau LeBreton. BS, La. State U., 1958, MA, 1961, PhD, 1969. Instr. social sci. Northwestern State U., Natchitoches, La., 1963—65, asst. prof. history, 1965—70, assoc. prof. history, 1970—73, prof. history, 1973—, head dept. history, 1980—83. Vis. asst. prof. history Tulane U., New Orleans, 1968—70. Author: Northwestern State University: A History, 1985; contbr. chapters to books, articles to profl. jours. Mem. pastoral coun. Holy Cross Ch., Natchitoches, 2003—. Recipient Frank Gipson trophy, DAR, 1976, Outstanding Tchr. award, Northwestern State U., 1990; fellow, Nat. Trust for Hist. Preservation, 1960. Mem.: La. Preservative Alliance, Assn. for Preservation Hist. Natchitoches, No. La. Hist. Assn. (bd. dirs. 1970—73), La. Hist. Assn. (bd. dirs. 1970—72, 1977—80, 1983). Avocations: travel, gardening. Home: 515 Marion Pl Natchitoches LA 71457 Office: Northwestern State Univ University Pkwy Natchitoches LA 71457 Office Phone: 318-357-5503.

LEBRYK, DAVID A., federal agency administrator; b. 1964; AB in Economics, Harvard Coll.; MA in Pub. Adminstrn., Harvard U. With US Dept. Treasury, Washington, 1989—2002, presdl. mgmt. intern, acting dep. asst. sec. human resources, 1997, dep. asst. sec. fiscal ops. and policy, dep. dir., US Mint, 2002—, acting dir., 2005—06. Recipient Presdl. Rank award, 2005. Office: US Mint 801 9th St NW 8th Fl Washington DC 20220

LECAPITAINE, JOHN EDWARD, counseling psychology educator, researcher, writer; b. Nov. 21, 1950; s. Vincent Bernard and Evelyn Lucille LeCapitaine; m. Jessica Dale; 1 child, Katherine Briee. BS in Math. and Psychology, U. Wis., 1973, MS in Sch. Psychology, 1975; D in Counseling Psychology, Boston U., 1980, D in Metaphysics, 2000. Diplomate forensic psychologist, psychotherapist. Counseling and sch. psychologist Martin Luther King Jr. Ctr., Boston, 1976-78; prof. counseling psychology Boston U., 1980-90; rsch. cons. Dept. Mental Health, 1985-90; prof. counseling psychology U. Wis., River Falls, 1990—. Contbr. chpts. to books; contbr. poetry, fiction, and acad. articles to profl. jours. Recipient Disting. award, Ed. Jour., 1999, Disting. Author award, Schools As Devel. Clinics. Mem. APA, ACA, Inst. Noetic Scis., Nat. Assn. Sch. Psychologists, Internat. Coun. Psychologists, Assn. Play Therapy, Assn. Multicultural Counseling and Devel., Assn. Humanistic Devel. and Edn., Internat. Soc. Poets, Phi Delta Kappa. Avocations: fiction writing, poetry, painting. Home: 731 Lumphrey Ct River Falls WI 54022-3426 Office: U Wis Grad Dept Counseling/Sch Psychology WEB 232 410 S 3d St River Falls WI 54022-5013

LECAT, ROBERT J., retired aeronautical engineer; s. Paul and Suzanne Vigne Lecat; m. Veronica Joan Miller (dec.); children: Nicole, Daphne, Gabrielle(dec.), Paul. BS in Aerospace, Cath. U., 1949, MS in Aerospace, 1953, D in Aerospace Engring., 1964. Engr. Washington Gas Light Co., 1948—50, McDonnel, St. Louis, 1950—52, Kellex/Vitro, Silver Spring, Md., 1953—54, Applied Physics Lab., John Hopkins U., Silver Spring, 1954—55; head preliminary design Fairchild Guided Mass, Wyandanch, NY, 1956—57; head aerospace/design specialist Grumman, Bethpage, NY, 1957—90. Cons., 1990—; adj. asst. prof. SUNY, Stony Brook, 1988—93; engr. Pluf Ultra Tech., Stony Brook, 2000—02; project engr. Soc. A/C Restoration, Commack, NY, 1988—2004. Author: In Dynamics Reentry Scala, 1963, Goniometric Aerodynamics, 1969; contbr. scientific papers pub. to profl. jour. With French 12th Royal Marine/Militia Brigade, 1976—, Milford, Conn., ensign French Aeronavale, 1944—46. Recipient Indsl. Svc. award, Engrs. Joint Com. LI, 2006. Fellow: Am. Inst. Aero Astro Coun. (assoc.); mem.: Assn. Naval Aviation, Soc. Flight Test Engr. Achievements include patents in field; design of Gruman reentry vehicles; wind tunnel & flight test for a supersonic towed decoy; research in jovian atmosphere using a nuclear ramjet flyer. Avocations: model building, aviation, history.

LECAVALIER, VINCENT, professional hockey player; b. Ile Bizard, Que., Can., Apr. 21, 1980; Center Rimouski Oceanic, 1996—98, Tampa Bay Lightning, Fla., 1998—. Mem. Team Can., World Cup of Hockey, 2004. Named Tournament MVP, World Cup of Hockey, 2004; named to NHL All-Star Game, 2003, 2007, Second All-Star Team, NHL, 2007; recipient Maurice Richard Trophy, 2007, Mark Messier Leadership Award, 2007. Achievements include being a member of Stanley Cup Champion Tampa Bay Lightning, 2004; being a member of World Cup Champion Team Canada, 2004. Office: Tampa Bay Lightning St Pete Times Forum 401 Channelside Dr Tampa FL 33602*

LECHEVALIER, HUBERT ARTHUR, microbiology educator; b. Tours, Indre et Loire, France, May 12, 1926; came to US, 1948; s. Jean Gaston and Marie Emilie L.; m. Mary Pfeil, Apr. 10, 1950; children: Marc, Paul. L ès Sci., Laval U., 1947, MS, 1948, DSc (hon.), 1983; PhD, Rutgers U., 1951. Asst. prof. Rutgers U., New Brunswick, NJ, 1951-56, assoc. prof., 1956-66, prof. microbiology, 1966-91, assoc. dir. Waksman Inst., 1980-88; prof. emeritus, 1991—. Vis. scientist Acad. of Scis. USSR, Moscow, 1958-59, Pasteur Inst., Paris, 1961-62 Author: (with others) A Guide to the Actinomycetes and Their Antibiotics, 1953, Neomycin--Its Nature and Practical Application, 1958, Antibiotics of Actinomycetes, 1962, Three Centuries of Microbiology, 1965, Hungarian transl., 1971, The Microbes, 1971, The Development of Applied Microbiology at Rutgers, 1982; co-editor: CRC Critical Reviews in Microbiology (1970-78), CRC Handbook of Microbiology (1970-89); contbr. numerous articles to profl. jours.; 4 patents. Trustee Am. Type Culture Collection, Rockville, Md., 1973-79. Recipient Lindback award 1976, Bergey award 1989; inducted into NJ Inventors Hall of Fame, 1990. Mem. Soc. Française de Microbiologie (hon.), Soc. for Indsl. Microbiology (emeritus); Charles Thom award 1982, Soc. for Actinomycetes Japan (hon.) Home: 131 Goddard-Nisbet Rd Morrisville VT 05661-8041 Personal E-mail: mheques@together.net.

LECHEVALIER, MARY PFEIL, retired microbiologist, educator; b. Cleve., Jan. 27, 1928; d. Alfred Leslie Pfeil and Mary Edith Martin; m. Hubert Arthur Lechevalier, Apr. 7, 1950; children: Marc E.M., Paul R. BA in Physiology-Biochemistry, Mt. Holyoke Coll., 1949; MS in Microbiology, Rutgers U., 1951. Rsch. fellow Rutgers U., New Brunswick, NJ, 1949-51, rsch. assoc. inst. microbiology, 1962-74, from asst. to assoc. rsch. prof., 1974-85, rsch. prof. Waksman inst. microbiology, 1985-91, prof. emerita, 1991—; ind. rschr., 1955-59; microbiologist steroid preparative lab. E.R. Squibb and Sons, New Brunswick, 1960-61; vis. investigator Inst. Biology Czechoslovak Acad. Scis., Svc. de Mycologie Pasteur Inst., Prague, Paris, 1961-62. Cons. in field. Contbr. over 100 chpts. to books and articles to rsch. jours.; mem. adv. com. actinomycetes Bergey's Manual of Determinative Bacteriology, 8th edit.; chair adv. com. muriform actinomycetes Bergey's Manual, 9th edit. Assoc. mem. Bergey's Trust, 1989—92. Recipient Charles Thom award, Soc. Indsl. Microbiology, 1982, Waksman award, Theobald Smith Soc., 1991. Mem. AAAS, US Fedn. Culture Collections (exec. com. 1982-85, J. Roger Porter award nominating com. 1983-84, 87-88, chair 1989-90, J. Roger Porter award 1992), Soc. for Actinomycetes Japan, Sigma Xi (pres. Rutgers U. chpt. 1977-78). Achievements include patents in field. Home: 131 Goddard-Nisbet Rd Morrisville VT 05661-8041

LECHLEITER, JOHN C., pharmaceutical executive; BS in Chemistry summa cum laude, Xavier U., Cin., 1975; MS in Organic Chemistry, Harvard U., 1980, PhD, 1980; D in Bus. Adminstrn. (hon.), Marian Coll., Indpls., 2006. Sr. organic chemist process R & D Eli Lilly & Co., 1979, head process R & D, 1982, dir. pharm. devel. Lilly Rsch. Ctr. Ltd. Windlesham, England, 1983—86, mgr. rsch. devel. projects Europe Indpls., 1986—88, dir. devel. projects mgmt., pharm. regulatory affairs, 1988, dir. chemistry, mfg. and control, 1989, exec. dir. pharm. product devel., 1991—93, v.p. pharm. prodn. and devel., 1993, v.p. regulatory affairs, 1994, v.p. Lilly Rsch. Labs., 1996, sr. v.p. pharm. products, 1998, exec. v.p. pharm. products and corp. devel., 2001, exec. v.p. pharm. ops., 2004—05, pres., COO, 2005—. Vis. com. Harvard Bus. Sch., 2004—; health policy and mgmt. coun. Harvard Sch. Pub. Health, 2004—; bd. trustees Xavier U., Cin.; disting. advisor Children's Mus. Indpls.; Dean's adv. bd. Ind. U. Sch. Med. Mem.: Am. Chem. Soc. Office: Eli Lilly and Co Lilly Corp Ctr Indianapolis IN 46285 Office Phone: 317-276-2000.*

LECHLEITER, RICHARD A., medical products executive; CPA. V.p., contr. Humana Inc., 1990—93, Galen Health Care, Inc., 1993, Columbia/HCA Healthcare Corp., 1993—95; dir. fin. Vencor, 1995, v.p. fin. corp. contr., 1995—98; v.p., fin. corp. contr., treas. Kindred Healthcare, Louisville, 1998—2002, sr. v.p., CFO, treas., 2002—. Office: Kindred Healthcare 680 S Fourth St Louisville KY 40202

LECHNER, ALFRED JAMES, JR., (JIM LECHNER), lawyer, former federal judge; b. Elizabeth, NJ, Jan. 7, 1948; s. Alfred J. and Marie G. (McCormack) L.; m. Gayle K. Peterson, Apr. 3, 1976; children: Brendan Patrick, Coleman Thomas, Mary Kathleen. BS, Xavier U., Cin., 1969; JD, U. Notre Dame, 1972. Bar: NJ 1972, US Dist. Ct. NJ 1972, NY 1973, US Dist. Ct. (so. and ea. dists.) NY 1974, US Ct. Appeals (2d cir.) 1974, US Supreme Ct. 1975, US Ct. Appeals (3d cir.) 1980. Assoc. Cadwalader, Wickersham & Taft, NYC, 1972-75, MacKenzie, Welt & Duane, Elizabeth, 1975-76, MacKenzie, Welt, Duane & Lechner, Elizabeth, 1976-84; judge NJ Superior Ct., 1984-86, US Dist. Ct. NJ, 1986—2001; ptnr. Morgan, Lewis & Bockius LLP, 2001—05; v.p., chief counsel for litig. Tyco Internat. Ltd., 2005—06; ptnr. Lerner David Littenberg Krumholz & Mentlik LLP, Westfield, NJ, 2006—. Note and comment editor Notre Dame Law Rev., 1972; contbr. articles to profl. jours. Mem. Union County Adv. Bd. Cath. Cmty. Svcs., NJ, 1981-83, chmn., 1982. Lt. col. USMCR. Fellow Am. Bar Found.; mem. ABA, Assn. Fed. Bar of State NJ, Friendly Sons of St. Patrick (pres. 1982), Union County Club. Office: Lerner David Littenberg Krumholz & Mentlik LLP 600 South Ave West Westfield NJ 07090 Office Phone: 908-654-5000.

LECHNER, BERNARD JOSEPH, consulting electrical engineer; b. NYC, Jan. 25, 1932; s. Barnard Joseph and Lillian L.; m. Joan Camp Mathewson, Nov. 21, 1953. BSEE, Columbia U., 1957; postgrad., Princeton U., 1957-60. Mem. tech. staff RCA Labs., Princeton, NJ, 1957-62, project leader, 1962-67, group head, 1967-77, lab. dir., 1977-83, staff v.p., 1983-87; cons., Princeton, 1987—. Cons. expert on TV matters including high definition TV and flat-panel displays; bd. dirs. Palisades Inst., N.Y.C.; chmn. adv. commn. Mercer County Coll., Trenton, N.J., 1968-85. Contbr. articles to profl. jours. Reader Recording for the Blind, Princeton, 1967-72. Served to cpl. U.S. Army, 1953-55. Recipient David Sarnoff Gold medal RCA Corp., 1962, Outstanding Contributor award Advanced TV Sys. Com., 2000, TV Engring. Achievement award NAB, 2002. Fellow: IEEE (chpt. chmn. 1964—66, Best Paper award Solid State Cirs. Conf. 1966), Soc. Motion Picture and TV Engrs. (David Sarnoff Gold Medal award 1996, Progress Medal award 2001), Soc. for Info. Display (pres. 1978—80, Frances Rice Darne award 1971, Beatrice Winner award 1983); mem.: Am. Relay Radio League, Princeton Sqs. (pres. 1981-87), Eta Kappa Nu, Tau Beta Pi, Sigma Xi. Episcopalian. Achievements include 10 patents; development of home video tape recorders in the late 1950s; flat-panel matrix displays in the 1960s including pioneering work on active-matrix liquid crystal displays; advanced two-way cable TV systems and pay-TV systems in the early 1970s; electronic tuning systems and CCD comb-filters for TV receivers in the mid-1970s and early 1980s; contributed to the early development of HDTV in the mid-1980s; led the development of many of the standards for HDTV during the 1990s. Avocations: amateur radio, square dancing, stamp collecting/philately, sailing, swimming. Address: 59 Carson Rd Princeton NJ 08540-2207 Office Phone: 609-924-7545. Business E-Mail: tvbernie@ieee.org.

LECHNER, ROGER A., priest; b. Brawley, Calif., July 2, 1940; s. George A. and Anna Catherine Lechner. BS, U. San Diego, Calif., 1964; Degree, St. Francis Seminary, San Diego, 1958—62, Immaculate Heart Seminary, 1966, North Am. Coll., 1980. Assoc. pastor St. Joseph Cathedral, San Diego, 1966—68; vice chancellor San Diego Diocese, 1968—76, sec. to Bishop, 1968—73, preseminary dir., 1973—76; assoc. pastor St. Francis, Vista, Calif., 1976—81; founding pastor St. Stephen's Cath. Ch., Valley Ctr., Calif., 1981—87; pastor Resurrection Ch., Escondido, Calif., 1981—92, Holy Spirit Ch., San Diego, 1992—. Lay advisor bd. Barnes - Hinds Corp., San Diego, 1987—90; lectr. St. Antony Coll., Oxford, England, St. Joseph Seminary, Ho Chi Hinh City, Vietnam. Founder Sparksplugs Youth Group, San Diego, 1967, Higher Values for Youth, San Diego, 1998. Cath. Avocations: reading, travel, art, photography. Home: 2725 55th St San Diego CA 92105 Office: Holy Spirit Ch 2725 55th St San Diego CA 92105 Business E-Mail: pinjag1@aol.com.

LECHTENBERG, VICTOR L., agricultural studies educator; b. Butte, Nebr., Apr. 14, 1945; m. Grayce Lechtenberg; 4 children. BS, U. Nebr., 1967; PhD in Agronomy, Purdue U., 1971. Prof. agronomy Purdue U., West Lafayette, Ind., 1971—, assoc. dir. Agrl. Experiment Sta., 1982-89, exec. assoc. dean agr., 1989-93, dean agr., 1994—2004, vice provost engagement, 2004—07, interim provost, 2007—. Contbr. articles to profl. jours., chpts. to books. Scoutmaster Boy Scouts Am., 1983-85. Recipient Nebr. 4-H Dist. Alumni award, 1981. Fellow Am. Soc. Agronomy (Ciba-Geigy award), Crop Sci. Soc. Am. (past pres.); mem. Crop Sci. Soc. Agrnomy, Coun. Agrl. Sci. and Tech. (past pres., bd. dirs.), USDA (past chmn. nat. agrl. rsch., extension, edn. and econs. adv. bd.). Sigma Xi, Alpha Zeta, Gamma Sigma Delta. Roman Catholic. Avocation: woodworking. Office: Purdue Univ Hovde Hall 610 Purdue Mall West Lafayette IN 47907 Office Phone: 765-494-9095. Business E-Mail: vll@purdue.edu.

LECKEY, DOLORES R., religious organization administrator, writer; b. NYC, Apr. 12, 1933; d. Joseph Francis and Florence Marie Conklin; m. Thomas Philip Leckey, June 22, 1957 (dec.); children: Mary Kate Marcellus, Celia E., Thomas Joseph, Colum. BA, St. John's U., Bklyn., 1954; MA, George Washington U., 1971. English tchr. Delahanty H.S., NYC, 1954-56; elem. tchr. Oliver Sch., South Bend, Ind., 1957-58; sem. prof., adminstr DeSales Sch. Theology, Washington, 1971-77; TV prodr. Pub. TV/WNVT, Annandale, Va., 1971—76; ch. exec. Nat. Conf. Cath. Bishops, Washington, 1977-97; sr. fellow WTC, Georgetown U., Washington, 1998—. Author: The Ordinary Way, 1982, Laity Stirring the Church, 1987, Practical Spirituality, 1987, Women and Creativity, 1991, Winter Music, 1992, 7 Essentials for the Spiritual Journey, 1999, Blessings All Around, 1999; co-author: Facing Fear with Faith, 2002, Spiritual Exercises for Church Leaders, 2003; gen. editor: Just War, Lasting Peace, 2006, The Laity and Christian Education; exec. prodr. videos. Founder Arlington Partnership for Affordable Housing, 1989—; mem. Arlington Com. of 100, 1976—; mem. adv. bd. Arlington Street People Assistance, 1998—; trustee U. Dayton, 1991-2001, St. Mary's U. and Sem., Balt., 1989-95 Recipient Disting. Svc. award, Washington Theol. Union, 1988, Recognition award, Nat. Assn. Cath. Family Life Mins., 1998, Cardinal Bernardin award for promoting Cath. common ground., 2004; grantee, Louisville Inst., 1998. Mem. Assn. for Religion and Intellectual Life. Democrat. Roman Catholic. Achievements include 12 honorary degrees. Avocations: piano, theater and opera, hiking, reading. Office: Georgetown U Woodstock Theol Ctr Washington DC 20052-0001 Home: Apt 601W 3835 9th St N Arlington VA 22203-4083 Office Phone: 202-687-6531.

LECKIE, JAMES OLIVER, engineering educator; b. Denver, May 9, 1939; s. Edward and Maria Anna (Valdez) L.; m. Malinda Ann Mahrt, Feb. 11, 1962; children: Carmela, Raúl, Rafael. BS, San Jose State U., 1964; SM, Harvard U., 1965, PhD, 1970. Asst. prof. engring. San Jose State U., Calif., 1969-70, Stanford U., 1970-74, assoc. prof., 1974-81, prof., 1991—, C L Peck Class of 1906 prof. environ. engring. and applied earth scis., dir. Environ. Engring. Lab., co-dir. Singapore Stanford Partnership. Prin. investigator Clean Water Programme. Author: Other Homes and Garbage, 1975, More Other Homes and Garbage, 1981, Water chemistry Laboratory Manual, 1980; editor Particulates in Water, 1980. Recipient Engring. award of Distinction San Jose State U., 1983; Fulbright-Hays fellow Internat. Communications Agy., 1979; Mellon Found. fellow, 1974; Stanford U. fellow, 1982. Mem. NAE, Geochem. Soc., Am. Chem. Soc., ASCE (Rudolf Hering medal 1981), Am. Soc. Limnology and Oceanography. Office: Stanford U Dept Civil and Environ Engring Terman Bldg, Rm M-25 Stanford CA 94305 Office Phone: 415-723-2524. E-mail: leckie@stanford.edu.

LECKMAN, JAMES FREDERICK, psychiatry and pediatrics educator; b. Albuquerque, Dec. 3, 1947; s. Frederick Arnold and Alberta Beatrice (Lane) L.; m. Hannah Jean Hone, Dec. 27, 1971; children: Emily Beth, Peter Edwin. BA, Coll. Wooster, 1969; MD, U. N.Mex., 1973; MA (hon.), Yale U., 1990. Diplomate Am. Bd. Psychiatry, Am. Bd. Child Psychiatry. Intern USPHS Marine Hosp., San Francisco, 1973-74; clin. assoc. NIMH, Bethesda, Md., 1974-76; adult and child psychiatric resident Yale U., New Haven, 1976-80, from asst. prof. to assoc. prof., 1980-90, Neison Harris prof. child psychiatry and pediat., 1990—. Mem. psychopathology and clin. biology initial rsch. rev. com. NIMH, 1985-90; Milton M. & Harriet H. Parker lectr. psychiatry and human genetics Ohio State U., 1985; cons. U.S. Army, Heidelberg, 1986, Nat. Adv. Mental Health Coun., 1989-90; chmn. steering com. study of rsch. on child and adolescent mental disorders Inst. Medicine, 1988-89, child psychology and treatment initial rsch. rev. com. NIMH, 1992—; sci. adv. bd. Sophia Found. Med. Rsch., Rotterdam, The Netherlands, 1989-94. Co-author: Tourette's Syndrome and Tic Disorders, 1988, Fragile X Syndrome, 1993; mem. editl. bd. Devel. and Psychopathology, 1988-94. Acta Paedopsychiatrica, 1992—; N. Am. corr. editor Jour. Child Psychology and Psychiatry, 1995—, Neuropsychopharmacol., 1995—; contbr. over 250 articles to profl. jours. Recipient Seymour L. Lustman Rsch. award, 1978, 79; fellow USPHS-AAMC, 1972; William T. Grant Found. Rsch. scholar, 1980-83, Merck Faculty scholar, 1982-91; grantee NIH, 1972-93, 92-95, Nat. Inst. Child Health and Human Devel., 1970-95, Nat. Inst. Neurol. Disease and Stroke, 1980-96, NIMH, 1980-83, 89-93, 92-96. Fellow APA (Blanche Ittelson award 1995, Am. Coll. Neuropsychology, Am.Acad. Child and Adolescent Psychiatry (editl. bd. jour. 1982-88, guest co-editor spl. sect. Tourette's syndrome 1984, sci. program com. 1983-87, Outstanding Mentor 1990,92, 95); mem. ACP (H.P. Laughlin fellow 1981), Tourette Syndrome Assn. (sci. adv. bd. 1991-95), Conn. Coun. Child and Adolescent Psychiatrists (pres. 1991-93), Phi Beta Kappa, Alpha Omega Alpha, Sigma Xi. Home: 125 Spring Glen Ter Hamden CT 06517-1538 Office: Yale U Child Study Ctr 230 S Frontage Rd New Haven CT 06519-1124

LECLAIR, DON (DONAT R. LECLAIR JR.), automotive executive; b. 1952; B in Econs., U. Mich., MBA. Fin. analyst Lorain Assembly Plant Ford Motor Co., 1976, various leadership positions in product devel., mfg. and fin., contr. Ford Australia, contr. Global Product Devel. and Mfg., contr. N.Am., 2001—03, group v.p., CFO, 2003—05, exec. v.p., CFO, 2005—. Office: Ford Motor Co One American Rd Dearborn MI 48126-1899 Office Phone: 313-322-3000. Office Fax: 313-845-0570.*

LECLAIR, JOHN CLARK, professional hockey player; b. St. Albans, Vt., July 5, 1969; Left wing Montreal Canadiens, 1987—94, Phila. Flyers, 1995—2005, Pitts. Penguins, 2005—06. Named to ECAC All-Star 2d Team, 1990—91, Sporting News All-Star 1st Team, 1994—95, NHL All-Star 1st Team, 1994—95. Achievements include being a member of Stanley Cup Champion Montreal Canadiens, 1993.

LECLERC, PAUL, library director; b. Lebanon, NH, May 28, 1941; s. Louis and M. Juliette (Trottier) LeC; m. Judith Ginsberg, Oct. 26, 1980; 1 child, Adam Louis. BS, Coll. Holy Cross, 1963; student, U. Paris, 1963—64; MA, Columbia U., 1966, PhD with distinction, 1969; LHD (hon.), LI U., 1994, Coll. Holy Cross, 1994, Hamilton Coll., 1995, Union Coll., 1997, Hunter Coll., 1997, Fordham U., 1997, U. Paris, 2000, NY Med. Coll., 2002. Assoc. prof. French Union Coll., Schenectady, NY, 1969—79, chmn. dept. modern langs. and lit., 1972—77, chmn. humanities divsn., 1975—77; univ. dean for acad. affairs CUNY, 1979—84; provost and acad. v.p. Baruch Coll., CUNY, 1984—88; pres. Hunter Coll., CUNY, 1988—93; pres., CEO NY Pub. Libr., NYC, 1994—. Bd. dirs. NY Alliance Pub. Schs., NYC, 1981-84, El Museo del Barrio, The Feminist Press; pres. NY Tchr. Edn. Conf. Bd., Albany, 1983-84; mem. adv. bd. The Papers of Benjamin Franklin, Yale U. Author: Voltaire and Crebillon Pere, 1972, Voltaire's Rome Sauvée, 1992; co-editor: Lettres d'André Moreliet, vol. I, 1991, vol. II, 1994, vol. III, 1996; contbr. articles to profl. jours. Former mem. Pres.'s Com. Arts and Humanities; trustee Andrew W. Mellon Found., J. Paul Getty Trust, 2007—; bd. dirs. Nat. Book Found., The Andrew W. Mellon Found., Am. Acad. in Rome. Decorated officier Palmes Académiques, chevalier Legion of Honor, France; grantee NEH, 1971, 79, Am. Coun. Learned Socs., 1973, Ford Found., 1979. Fellow Am. Acad. Arts and Scis.; mem. MLA, Am. Soc. 18th Century Studies. Office: NY Pub Libr Fifth Ave & 42nd St New York NY 10018 Office Phone: 212-930-0736.*

LECOMPTE, ANDREW C., freelance/self-employed interpreter; b. Hartford, Conn., Nov. 21, 1943; s. Stuart Burnette LeCompte and Eleanor Clare; m. Svetlana F. Novikova, June 21, 1999. BA, Princeton U., NJ, 1966; MA, Ohio State U., Columbus, 1971. Freelance interpreter US State Dept., Washington, 1970—. Fed. ct. interpreter, 1995—. Named Interpreter of Yr., Nat. Assn. Internat. Visitors' Couns., Washington, 1978. Avocations: shortwave radio, gardening, mineral collecting. Home: 802 Elmcroft Blvd Apt K201 Rockville MD 20850 Office Phone: 202-431-5114. Home Fax: 301-869-7255. Personal E-mail: andyleco@cs.com.

LECOUNTE, LOLA HOUSTON, literature and language professor, educational consultant; d. Simpson and Lillian Edna Houston; widowed; children: Ernest Jerome, Karen Yvette, Mark Houston. BA, U. Md. Eastern Shore, 1956; MA, Trinity U., 1974; EdD, George Washington U., 1982. Tchr. English and French Accomack (Va.) County Pub. Schs., Va., 1957—59; tchr. English and history Fairfax (Va.) County Pub. Schs., 1959—67; tchr. English D.C. Pub. Schs., Washington, 1967—76, supr. English, 1976—81, asst. dir. English, 1981—92; asst. prof. Bowie (Md.) State U., 1996—, chair dept. tchg., 2001—04. Ednl. cons. E & L Consultants, Washington, 1976—88, Scholastic Book Co., NYC, 1991—96, D.C. Pub. Schs., Washington, 1992—97; presenter papers at confs. Co-author: (hist./ednl. kit) Black Women in America Contribute to Our Heritage, 1983, Black Women for Social Change, 1984. Named Disting. Alumnus, Nat. Assn. Equal Opportunity in Higher Edn., 1987; named to Hall of Fame for Disting. Alumni, U. Md. Eastern Shore; recipient Outstanding Svc. award, Alpha Kappa Alpha, 1994, Oustanding Svc. in Edn. award, U. Md. Eastern Shore alumni chpt., 1992; grantee, NSF, 2004—05. Mem.: Nat. Coun. Tchrs. English, Assn. Supervision and Curriculum Devel., Assn. Tchr. Educators. Avocations: reading, poetry, singing, theater. Office: Bowie State U 14000 Jericho Park Rd Bowie MD 20715

LEDBETTER, CALVIN REVILLE, JR., (CAL LEDBETTER), political science professor, legislator; b. Little Rock; s. Calvin Reville Sr. and Virginia Mae (Campbell) L.; m. Mary Brown Williams, July 26, 1953; children: Grainger, Jeffrey (dec.), Snow. BA, Princeton U., 1951; LLB, U. Ark., 1954; PhD, Northwestern U., 1960. Bar: Ark., 1954. Pvt. practice, Little Rock, 1954; faculty dept. polit. sci. U. Ark., Little Rock, 1960-97, prof., 1960-97, prof. emeritus, 1997—, dean, 1978-88; cons. law enforcement program, advisor pre-law program; mem. Ark. Ho. of Reps., 1967-76; chmn. spl. legis. com., com. on legis. orgn.; vice chmn. legis. com. state agys. and govt. affairs; cons. pub. schs.; mem. Nat. Adv. Com. on Criminal Justice Goals and Standards; mem. adv. com. Nat. Inst. Law Enforcement and Criminal Justice. Dept. head. U. Ark., Little Rock, 1968-78; election night analyst for Ark. congl. and Presdl. elections ABC, 1964-84 Co-author: Politics in Arkansas: The Constitutional Experience, 1972, The Arkansas Plan: A Case Study in Public Policy, 1979, Arkansas Becomes a State, 1985, Carpenter from Conway: George W. Donaghey as Governor of Arkansas 1909-1913, 1993; contbr. articles, book reviews to profl. jours. Mem. Ark. Adv. Coun. on Pub., Elem. and Secondary Edn.; Gov.'s rep. So. Regional Growth Policies Bd.; mem. Ark. Legis. Coun.; del. Ark. Constl. Conv., 1979, v.p., 1979-80; chmn. law enforcement and criminal justice task force Nat. Legis. Conf. Former chmn. coll. and univ. sect. United Fund; del. Dem. Nat. Conv., 1968, 84; mem. exec. com. Ark. Young Dems.; bd. dirs. Health and Welfare Coun. Pulaski County; trustee Philander Smith Coll., chmn. council community advisers; sec. bd. dirs. St. Vincent's Infirmary; bd. dirs. Ark. Humanities Coun., 1989-93, v.p., 1991-93, pres. 1993-94; bd. trustees Ark. Mus. Sci. and History. Served with JAGC AUS, 1955-57. Scholarships U. Ark., Little Rock, 2002; recipient award outstanding contbn. to humanities Little Rock Arts and Humanities Commn., 1993; named Educator of Yr., Greater Little Rock Fedn. Women's Clubs, 1968. Mem. ABA, Ark. Bar Assn. (Writing Excellence award 1985-86), Pulaski County Bar Assn., Nat. Conf. State Legislators (exec. com.), Nat. Conf. Acad. Deans (pres. 1987-88), Am. Polit. Sci. Assn., So. Polit. Sci. Assn., Ark. Polit. Sci. Assn. (pres. 1980-81), Ark. Acad. Sci., Am. Acad. Polit. and Social Sci., Ark. Hist. Assn., Ark. Edn. Assn., Pulaski County Hist. Soc. (bd. dirs. 1988-90), Ark. Hist. Commn. (v.p. 1989—, pres. 1990—), Rotary (pres. West Little Rock chpt. 1987-88). Presbyterian. Achievements include endowment of a monograph press and non-traditional scholarships at the U. Arkansas at Little Rock. Home: Unit 11 3901 Cedar Hill Rd Little Rock AR 72202 Office: Univ Ark Little Rock Polit Sci Dept Little Rock AR 72204

LEDBETTER, DAVID OSCAR, lawyer; b. Santa Rosa, Calif., Mar. 16, 1950; s. Oscar Smith Ledbetter and Nova Nell (Huckaby) Kramer; m. Judith Louise Fischer, Dec. 14, 1976; children: Hannah J., Jordan B. BA, U. Redlands, 1972; JD, Hastings Coll. Law, 1977. Bar: Calif. 1977, Va. 1987. Assoc. Moran, Urich & Evans, San Francisco, 1977-79; trial atty. land and natural resource divsn. U.S. Dept. Justice, Washington, 1979-85; assoc., counsel, ptnr. Hunton & Williams, Richmond, Va., 1985—. Bd. adv. Chem. Waste Litigation Reporter, Washington, 1983—. Co-editor: Outline RCRA/CERCLA Enforcement Issues and Holdings, 2005; contbr. articles to profl. jours. Bd. dirs. John Tyler C.C. Found., Chester, Va., 1992—; ednl. adv. coun. Charles City (Va.) County Vocat., 1990—. Mem. ABA, Va. State Bar Assn., Calif. Bar Assn., Environ. Law Inst., Charles City Ruritan Club. Democrat. Methodist. Avocations: gardening, fishing, hunting. Home: 16530 The Glebe Ln Charles City VA 23030-3837 Office: Hunton & Williams 951 E Byrd St Ste 200 Richmond VA 23219-4074 Office Phone: 804-788-8364. Business E-Mail: dledbetter@hunton.com.

LEDBETTER, JENNIFER LYNN, anthropologist, educator; b. Hamlin, Te., Nov. 4, 1975; d. Gary Lynn and Norma Taness Ledbetter; 1 child, Corbyn Rylynn. BA in Sci., U. N. Tex., Denton, 1999, MS, 2005. Tchg. asst. Tex. Tech. U., Lubbock, 2002—04; grad. asst. U. N. Tex., Denton, 2005; adj. prof. Cyfan C.C., Cyress Spring, Tex., 2005—.

LEDBETTER, KENNETH W., federal agency administrator; b. Calif., Sept. 1946; MS in Aerospace Engrng., U. Colo., 1969. Mem. Viking Mars landing team NASA, Pasadena, 1976, dep. payload ops mgr. Space Shuttle flight of Space Sextant, 1982, spacecraft ops. mgr. launch and flight of Magellan mission to Venus, 1989—92, Hubble Space Telescope program mgr., 1992—94, flight programs br. chief OSS astrophysics divsn., 1994—95, dir. mission and payload devel. divsn., 1996—2001, dep. assoc. adminstr. for programs Office Space Sci., 2001—04; dir. mission and systems mgmt. divsn. Sci. Mission Directorate, 2005—06, chief engr., 2006—. Co-author: Design of Mission Operations Systems for Scientific Remote Sensing, 1991; contbr. articles to profl. pubs. Office: NASA Hdqs Mail SMD 300 E St SW Washington DC 20546 Business E-Mail: kenneth.w.ledbetter@nasa.gov.

LEDBETTER, PAUL MARK, lawyer, writer; b. San Francisco, Oct. 14, 1947; s. John Paul and Joyce (Mayo) L.; m. Jerald Ann Broyles, Sept. 18, 1971; children: Paul Mark, Sarah Broyles. BA in English, Ouachita Bapt. U., 1970; JD, U. Ark., 1973. Bar: Ark. 1974, Tenn. 1995, U.S. Dist. Ct. (ea. dist.) Ark. 1974, U.S. Ct. Appeals (8th cir.) 1974, U.S. Ct. Appeals (6th cir.) 1991, U.S. Dist. Ct. (mid. dist.) Tenn. 1995. From assoc. to ptnr. Frierson, Walker, Snellgrove & Laser, Jonesboro, Ark., 1974-82; city atty. Monette, Ark., 1979—80; regional def. counsel Sq. D. Co., 1980-82; pres. Mark Ledbetter, P.A., Jonesboro, 1982-86; ptnr. Gerber, Gerber & Agee, Memphis, 1986-89, Taylor, Halliburton, Ledbetter & Caldwell, Memphis, 1989—2002, Taylor, Halliburton & Ledbetter, Memphis, 2003—. Product safety cons., sch. bus safety cons. CNN, 1997—; lectr. dept. mech. engrng. U. Memphis, 1997—; lectr. dept. rehab. engrng. U. Tenn., 1994—95. Author: The Hearing, 1994, The Thayer Class, 1998, The Wait, 2000; contbr. chpts. to books. Tutor Memphis Literacy Coun., 2003—; mem. forum commn. City of Jonesboro, 1978—80; co-founder St. Mark's Episcopal Day Sch., Jonesboro, Ark., 1978; mem. vestry St. Mark's Episcopal Ch., 1979. Conservation Found. grantee, 1976; Rotary Internat. grantee, Japan, 1979. Mem. ATLA, Am. Bd. Trial Advs. (assoc.), Tenn. Bar Assn., Ark. Bar Assn. (mem. tort reform com. 1980, ho. of dels. 1979-80), Ark. Trial Lawyers Assn. (chmn. amicus curiae com. 1980-81, gov. 1980—), Tenn. Trial Lawyers Assn., Jonesboro C. of C. (bd. dirs. 1978-80), Human Factors and Ergonomics Soc., Rotary. Office: Taylor Halliburton Ledbetter 254 Court Ave 3d Fl Memphis TN 38103 Office Phone: 901-523-8153. E-mail: mark794@aol.com.

LEDEBOER, NANCY, library director; b. Mont. Student, Diablo Valley Coll., Pleasant Hill, Calif., 1974—77; BA in Hist., U. Calif., 1979; MLS, U. Calif., Berkeley, 1980. Libr. Contra Costa Times, 1980—81; children's/young adult libr. Contra Costa County Libr. Sys., Calif., 1983—84, children's libr. Calif., 1989—91, El Sobrante br. mgr. Calif., 1991—92; head libr. Heritage Coll. Libr., 1985—87; info. specialist St. Mary's Coll., 1987—89; youth svcs. coord. Spokane Pub. Libr., Wash., 1992—96, dep. dir. pub. svcs. Wash., 1996—98; assoc. dir. pub. svcs. King County Libr. Sys., Wash., 1998—99; dep. dir., COO Las Vegas-Clark County Libr. Dist., Nev., 1999—2005; dir. Pima County Pub. Libr., Tucson, 2005—. Bd. dirs. Wash. Libr. Assn., 1993—95. Bd. dirs. Literacy Vols. Tucson. Named Libr. of Yr., Nev. Libr. Assn., 2004; recipient Spl. Citation award, 2004. Mem.: ALA, Ariz. Libr. Assn., Pub. Libr. Assn. (mem. Gordon M. Conable Award jury), REFORMA (pres. Nev. chpt. 2001—02). Office: Pima County Pub Libr 101 N Stone Ave Tucson AZ 85701-1501 Office Phone: 520-791-4391. Office Fax: 520-791-3213. E-mail: Nancy.Ledeboer@pima.gov.

LEDEEN, ROBERT WAGNER, neuroscientist, educator; b. Denver, Aug. 19, 1928; s. Hyman and Olga (Wagner) L.; m. Lydia Rosen Hailparn, July 2, 1982. BS, U. Calif., Berkeley, 1949; PhD, Oreg. State U., 1953. Postdoctoral fellow in chemistry U. Chgo., 1953-54; rsch. assoc. in chemistry Mt. Sinai Hosp., NYC, 1956-59; rsch. fellow Albert Einstein Coll. Medicine, Bronx, NY, 1959, asst. prof., 1963-69, assoc. prof., 1969-75, prof., 1975-91; prof., dir. div. neurochemistry U. Medicine and Dentistry N.J., Newark, 1991—. Contbr. articles to profl. jours.; dep. chief editor Jour. Neurochemistry. Mem. neurol. scis. study sect. NIH; mem. study sect. Nat. Multiple Sclerosis Soc. With US Army, 1954—56. NIH grantee, 1963—; Nat. Multiple Sclerosis Soc. grantee, 1967-74, 97—; recipient Humboldt prize, Javits Neurosci. Investigator award. Mem. Internat. Soc. Neurochemistry, Am. Soc. Neurochemistry, Am. Chem. Soc., Am. Soc. Biol. Chemists, N.Y. Acad. Sci. Jewish. Achievements include discoveries in the biochemistry of brain glycolipids and myelin. Home: 8 Donald Ct Wayne NJ 07470-4608 Office: U Medicine and Dentistry NJ Dept Neuroscis 185 S Orange Ave Newark NJ 07103-2757

LEDER, MIMI, television and film director, producer; b. NYC, Jan. 26, 1952; d. Paul and Etyl Leder; m. Gary Werntz, Feb. 6, 1986; 1 child, Hannah. Student, Los Angeles City College, Am. Film Inst. Dir. (TV films) A Little Piece of Heaven (also known as Honor Bright), 1991, Woman with a Past, 1992, Rio Shannon, 1992, Marked for Murder, 1992, There Was a Little Boy, 1993, House of Secrets, 1993, The Sandman, 1993, The Innocent, 1994, John Doe, 2002; dir. (TV series) L.A. Law, 1986, Midnight Caller, 1988, A Year in the Life, 1988, Buck James, 1988, Just in Time, 1988, Crime Story, 1988, ER, 1994-95 (Emmy award 1995, 96), John Doe, 2002, China Beach (also prodr.), The Beast (also exec. prodr.), 2001, Jonny Zero (also prodr.), 2005, Vanished, (also exec. prodr.), 2006, (films) The Peacemaker, 1997, Deep Impact, 1998, Sentimental Journey, 1999, Pay it Forward, 2000; supervising prodr. China Beach, 1988-91 (Emmy nominations for outstanding drama series 1989, 90, and outstanding directing in drama series 1990, 91), Nightingales, 1989. Mem. Dirs. Guild Am. Office: c/o Creative Artists Agy 9830 Wilshire Blvd Beverly Hills CA 90212-1804 also: United Talent Agy 9560 Wilshire Blvd Beverly Hills CA 90212

LEDERBERG, JOSHUA, geneticist, educator; b. Montclair, NJ, May 23, 1925; s. Zwi Hirsch and Esther Lederberg; m. Marguerite S. Kirsch, Apr. 5, 1968; children: David Kirsch, Anne. BA, Columbia U., 1944; PhD, Yale U., 1947. With U. Wis., 1947-58; founder, genetics dept., prof. biology and computer sci. Stanford U. Sch. Medicine, Calif., 1959-78; pres. Rockefeller U., NYC, 1978-90, univ. prof., Raymond and Beverly Sackler Found. scholar, 1990—, head, molecular genetics and informatics, 1990—. Mem. adv. com. WHO, 1971; chmn. adv. bd. Ellison Med. Found., 1997—; mem. bd. sci. advisors Antigenics, NYC, Quark Biotech, Fremont, Calif., Paladin Homeland Security Adv. Fund; past co-chmn. Carnegie Commn. on Sci., Tech. and Govt.; chmn. Congl. Tech. Assessment Adv. Coun.; mem. US Def. Sci. Bd.; scientific counselor to world leaders on an array of issues from cancer & emerging infectious diseases to space exploration & biol. weapons disarmament; cons. in field. Mem. editl. bd.: The Scientist. Trustee Camille and Henry Dreyfus Found. With USN, 1943—45. Named Sr. Scholar, Stanford U. Ctr. Internat. Security and Arms Control, 1998; recipient Nobel prize in physiology and medicine for rsch. in genetics of bacteria, 1958, U.S. Nat. Medal of Sci., 1989, Alan Newell award, Assn. Computing Machinery, 1996, John Stearns award, N.Y. Acad. Medicine, 1996, Maxwell Finland award, NCIH, 1997, Morris Collen award, Am. Med. Info. Assn., 1999, Most Admirable Order of Direkgunabhorn Thailand, Knight Grand Cross, 1st Class, 2005, Freedom medal, US Pres., 2006. Fellow: AAAS, Am. Acad. Arts and Scis., Am. Philos. Soc. (Benjamin Franklin medal 2002); mem.: NAS, N.Y. Acad. Scis. (hon. life gov.) (chmn.), Royal Soc. London (fgn.), Inst. Medicine (David Rall medal), Coun. Fgn. Rels. (dir.). Office: Rockefeller U Stop 174 1230 York Ave New York NY 10021-6399 Office Phone: 212-327-7809. Business E-Mail: lederberg@rockefeller.edu.

LEDERER, EDITH MADELON, journalist; b. NYC, Mar. 27, 1943; d. Samuel B. Weiner and Frieda (Rich) Weiner Lederer; adopted d. Irving A. Lederer. BS with distinction, Cornell U., 1963; MA, Stanford, 1964. With Sci. Service, Washington, 1964-65; free-lance writer, 1965-66; mem. staff AP, 1966—, South Vietnam, 1972-73, chief bur. Lima, Peru, 1975; chief Caribbean services, San Juan, P.R., 1975-78; corr. Hong Kong, 1978-81, Nairobi, 1981-82, London, 1982—90, 1991—98, Gulf War, Saudi Arabia, 1990-91; chief corr. UN, 1998—. Participant World Econ. Forum. Co-author: War Torn, 2002. Mem. pres.'s coun. Internat. Women's Media Found. Recipient resolution Calif. Assembly, 1974, Nat. Press Club award, 1993, Nat. Headliner award, 1994, Journalism Honor medal for disting. svc. in journalism U. Mo. Sch. Journalism, 1996, Silver medal, UN Correspondents Assn., 2001, Voices Unabridged award for excellence in journalism, 2006. Mem. Cornell Women (pres.'s coun.), Journalist and Women's Symposium, Mortar Bd., Internat. Women's Media Found., Overseas Press Club, Phi Kappa Phi, Omicron Nu, Sigma Delta Chi. *Women should take more risks to live their dreams, which otherwise turn to nightmares of frustration as empty years pass. It is better to fail and touch the essence of life than to stand forever on the threshold as a gutless spectator.*

LEDERER, JOHN MARTIN, retired aeronautical engineer; b. Solomon, Kans., May 12, 1930; s. George Martin and Angie Belle (Faubion) L.; m. Joan Elizabeth Patrick, June 15, 1963; children: Jeffrey Mark, Carol Elizabeth. BS in Aero. Engrng., Kans. State U., 1953; MSEE, Air Force Inst. Tech., 1955; postgrad., U. N.Mex., 1962-65. Registered profl. aero. engr., Ohio. Project engr. Air Force Spl. Weapons Ctr., Albuquerque, 1955-63, chief project engrng. div., 1963-67, chief electromagnetics div., 1967-70; tech. adviser Air Force Weapons Lab., Albuquerque, 1970-73, 76-87, chief nuclear systems surety div., 1988-91; dir. nuclear systems engrng. Nuclear Systems Engrng. Directorate/USAF Systems Command, Albuquerque, 1991-92; dir. nuclear systems engrng. aero. systems ctr. Air Force Materiel Command, Albuquerque, 1992-93; tech. dir. 4900th test group, Albuquerque, 1973-76, ret. Chmn. Dept. of Def. Design Rev. and Acceptance Group, Albuquerque, 1979-91; flying instr. airplanes, instruments. Co-inventor digital distance measuring instrument. Founder One of Ten Young Am. Football League, Albuquerque, 1964. Served to 1st lt. USAF, 1953-58. Recipient Outstanding Performance award Dept. Air Force, Albuquerque, 1965, 66, 68, 73, 74, 79, Sustained Superior Performance award, 1961, 81, 83-86, 88-93, Air Force Disting. Civilian Svc. award, 1993. Mem. NSPE, FAA (cert. flight instr.), Inst. Aerospace Scis. Republican. Episcopalian. Avocations: archery, flying. Home: PO Box 653 200 Northern Dr Elephant Butte NM 87935-0653 Personal E-mail: fishhooks@windstream.net.

LEDERER, MARION IRVINE, cultural administrator; b. Brampton, Ont., Can., Feb. 10, 1920; d. Oliver Bateman and Eva Jane (MacMurdo) L.; m. Francis Lederer, July 10, 1941. Student, U. Toronto, 1938, UCLA, 1942-45. Owner Canoga Mission Gallery, Canoga Park, Calif., 1967—, cultural heritage monument, 1974—. V.p. Screen Smart Set women's aux. Motion Picture and TV Fund, 1973, pres., 2002—03; founder sister city program Canoga Park-Taxco, Mex., 1963. Mem. Mayor's Cultural Task Force San Fernando Valley, 1973—, LA Cultural Affairs Commn., 1980—85; pres. Women's Aux. of Motion Pictures, TV Fund. Recipient Pub. Svc. award, mayor, city council, C. of C. Mem. Canoga Park C. of C. (cultural chmn. 1973-75, dir. 1973-75) Presbyterian. Home: PO Box 32 Canoga Park CA 91305-0032 Office: Canoga Mission Gallery 23130 Sherman Way Canoga Park CA 91307-1402

LEDERER, MAX DONALD, JR., lawyer; b. Plattsburgh, NY, June 21, 1960; s. Max Donald and Mary Lilian (Adie) L. BA magna cum laude, Marshall U., Huntington, W.Va., 1982; JD, U. Richmond, 1985, Bar: Pa. 1986, U.S. Army Ct. Mil. Rev. 1986. Commd. 2d lt. U.S. Army, 1982-86, advanced through grades to capt., 1987—; def. counsel Ft. Sill, Okla., 1986-87; command judge advocate CP Red Cloud, Korea, 1987-88; sr. trial counsel Combined Field Army, 1989; chief adminstrv. law div. Combined Field Army- 2d armored div. (forward), 1989-90; command judge adv. Op. Desert Storm 2d armored div. (forward), 1991; officer-in-charge Bremerhaven Legal Ctr., Fed. Republic of Germany, 1991-92; gen. counsel European Stars and Stripes, 1992-96, gen. mgr., 1996-2000; gen. mgr., gen. counsel European and Pacific Stars and Stripes, 2000—, COO, gen. counsel, 2003—. Fellow ABA, Pa. Bar Assn. Avocation: running. Home: 2427 Pondside Ter Silver Spring MD 20906-5752 Office: 529 14th St NW Ste 350 Washington DC 20045 E-mail: ledererm@stripes.usd.mil.

LEDERER, PETER DAVID, lawyer; b. Frankfurt, Germany, May 2, 1930; came to US, 1938; s. Leo and Alice Lederer. BA, U. Chgo., 1949, JD, 1957, M in Comparative Law, 1958. Bar: Ill. 1959, U.S. Supreme Ct. 1966, N.Y. 1967. Law and behavioral sci. rsch. fellow U. Chgo. Law Sch., 1958-59; ptnr. Baker & McKenzie, Zurich, Switzerland, 1960-66, NYC, 1966-94, of counsel, 1994—2002. Chmn. bd. dirs. Coverage Connect, Inc., 1999-2002; mem. adv. bd. TeslaLab LLC, 2002-, CareSpeak Comms., Inc., 2006—; pres. Japanese Am. Social Svcs., Inc., N.Y.C., 2003-06. Dir. Asian-Am. Legal Def. and Edn. Fund, NYC, Asian-Am. Fed. of N.Y.; chmn. emeritus bd. dirs. The Midori Found.; pres. bd. trustees The Calhoun

Sch., NYC, 1980—83; mem. vis. com. U. Miami Law Sch., Coral Gables, Fla., 1974—, U. Chgo. Law Sch., 1988—91, 2000—06. With AUS, 1951—53. Fellow Am. Bar Found.; mem. ABA, Assn. of Bar of City of N.Y., Internat. Nuc. Law Assn. Personal E-mail: peterdlederer@gmail.com.

LEDERER, RICHARD HENRY, writer, educator, columnist; b. Phila., May 26, 1938; s. Howard Jules and Leah (Perry) L.; m. Rhoda Anne Spangenberg, Aug. 25, 1962 (div. 1986); m. Simone Johanna van Egeren, Nov. 29, 1991; children: Howard Henry, Anne Labarr, Katherine Lee. BA, Haverford Coll., 1959; student, Harvard U., 1959—60, M of Arts and Tchg., 1962; PhD, U. N.H., 1980. Tchr., coach St. Paul's Sch., Concord, NH, 1962-89. Lectr. in field. Author: Anguished English, 1987, Get Thee to a Punnery, 1988, Crazy English, 1989, The Play of Words, 1990, The Miracle of Language, 1991, More Anguished English, 1993, Building Bridge, 1994, Adventures of a Verbivore, 1994, The Cunning Linguist, 1995, The Write Way, 1995, Pun and Games, 1996, Fractured English, 1996, The Word Circus, 1998, Sleeping Dogs Don't Lay, 1999, The Bride of Anguished English, 2000, The Circus of Words, 2001, Word Play Crosswords, 2000, A Man of My Words, 2003, The Cunning Linguist, 2003, The Revenge of Anguished English, 2005, Comma Sense, 2005, The Giant Book of Animal Jokes, 2005, Word Wizard, 2006, Puns Spoken Here, 2006, Have a Punny Christmas, 2006 Literary Trivia, 2007, Classic Literary Trivia, 2007, The Ants aRe My Friends, 2007, Presidential Trivia, 2007; weekly columnist Looking at Lang.; contbr. over 3000 articles to mags. and jours.; broadcaster various radio stas.; numerous TV appearances; host A Way With Words KPBS, San Diego. Recipient Chmns. award, Am. Mensa, Ltd., 2000, Toastmasters Internat. Golden Gavel, 2002, Lifetime Achievement award Columbia Scholastic Press Assn., N.Y.C., 1989, Leadership in Comms. award San Diego Toastmasters, Odin award San Diego Writers and Editors, 2004; named Internat. Punster of Yr. Internat. Save the Pun Found., Toronto, 1990, Celebrity in Action, San Diego Found. for Ednl. Achievement, 2002; Paul Harris Rotary fellow. Mem. Am. Mensa, Phi Beta Kappa, Phi Delta Kappa. Avocations: tennis, cards, films. Office: Ste 201 9974 Scripps Ranch Blvd San Diego CA 92131-1825 Home Phone: 858-549-6788; Office Phone: 858-549-6788. E-mail: richard.lederer@pobox.com. *Whatever you hear about the closing of the American mind and cultural illiteracy, there has never been a more passionate moment in the history of the American love affair with language than right now. I'm exceedingly fortunate to have written books that embrace that passion.*

LEDERMAN, BRUCE RANDOLPH, investment company executive, retired lawyer; b. NYC, Oct. 12, 1942; s. Morris David and Frances Lederman; m. Ellen Kline, Aug. 4, 1979; children: Eric, Jeffrey, Joshua. Cert., U. London, 1963; BS Econs. cum laude, U. Pa., 1964; LLB cum laude, Harvard U., 1967. Bar: U.S. Dist. Ct. (cen. dist.) Calif. 1967. Law clk. to Hon. Irving Hill U.S. Dist. Ct. Cen. Dist., LA, 1967-68; sr. ptnr. Latham & Watkins, LA, 1968—2000; co-founder Investment Equity Capital, LLC, LA. Avocations: bicycle riding, real estate investments. Office: Investment Equity Capital, LLC Ste 320 2601 Ocean Park Blvd Santa Monica CA 90405 Office Phone: 310-452-8300 ext. 11. Office Fax: 310-452-8305. E-mail: bruce@iecap.com.

LEDERMAN, GARY, dentist; Grad. rsch. in Periodontics and Oral Microbiology, U. Rochester, 1973—77; attended, U. Pa. Sch. Dental Medicine, 1977—81; MS, USAF Regional Med. Ctr. Keesler AFB, 1981—82. Dentist Where Dreams Become Smiles, NY. Mem.: Integrated Dental Study Club, Suffolk County Dental Assn., Nassau County Dental Soc., First Dist. Dental Soc. NY, NYS Dental Assn., ADA, Acad. Gen. Dentistry, Dental Orgn. Conscious Sedation, Am. Acad. Cosmetic Dentistry. Avocations: windsurfing, sailing, reading, theater. Mailing: 100 Centre Ave Bellmore NY 11710 Office Phone: 516-785-0032. Office Fax: 516-785-0066.

LEDERMAN, IRA SETH, insurance company executive, lawyer; b. NYC, Apr. 25, 1953; m. Carol Susan Jupiter; children: Rachael, Aaron. BA, Queens Coll., NYC, 1975; MPA, NYU, 1977; JD, Hofstra Univ., 1979. Bar: N.Y. 1980. Assoc. Rein Mound and Cotton, NYC, 1979-83; assoc. counsel W.R. Berkley Corp., Greenwich, Conn., 1983-86, v.p., ins. counsel, 1986-89, v.p., asst. gen. counsel, 1989—2001, sr. v.p., gen. counsel, 2001—. Mem. ABA, N.Y. County Lawyers Assn., The Corp. Bar Assn., Am. Soc. Corp. Secs. Office: W R Berkley Corp 475 Steamboat Rd Greenwich CT 06830 Office Phone: 203-629-3000. Office Fax: 203-769-4097.*

LEDERMAN, LAWRENCE, lawyer, writer, educator; b. NYC, Sept. 8, 1935; s. Herman Jack and Lillian (Rosenfeld) Lederman; m. Kitty Hawks; children: Leandra, Evin. BA, Bklyn. Coll., 1957; LLB, NYU, 1966. Bar: NY 1968. Law clk. chief justice Calif. Supreme Ct., 1966—67; assoc. Cravath, Swaine & Moore, NYC, 1968—74; ptnr. Wachtell, Lipton, Rosen & Katz, NYC, 1975—91; ptnr., chmn. corp. practice Milbank, Tweed, Hadley & McCloy, 1991—2004, of counsel, 2005—. Adj. prof. law NYU Law Sch., 1974—, N.Y. Law Sch., 2005—. Author: Tombstones: A Lawyer's Tales from the Takeover Decades, 1992; contbr. articles to profl. jours.; calendar, Trees in Their Seasons at the N.Y. Bot. Garden, 2003, 2005, 2006. Chmn. bd. Phoenix House Devel. Corp.; mem. Phoenix House Found.; bd. dirs. The Nat. Mentoring Partnership, Tails in Need. With US Army, 1957—59. Mem.: ABA, NY State Bar Assn., Order of Coif. Office: Milbank Tweed Hadley & McCloy 1 Chase Manhattan Plz Fl 47 New York NY 10005-1413 Office Phone: 212-530-5000. Business E-Mail: ledlaw@milbank.com.

LEDERMAN, LEON MAX, physicist, researcher; b. NYC, July 15, 1922; s. Morris and Minna (Rosenberg) Lederman; m. Florence Gordon, Sept. 19, 1945; children: Rena S., Jesse A., Heidi R.; m. Ellen Carr, Sept. 17, 1981. BS, CCNY, 1943, DSc (hon.), 1980; AM, Columbia U., 1948, PhD, 1951; DSc (hon.), No. Ill. U., 1984, U. Chgo., 1985, Ill. Inst. Tech., 1987; 35 additional hon. degrees. Assoc. in physics Columbia U., NYC, 1951, asst. prof., 1952—54, assoc. prof., 1954—58, prof., 1958—89, Eugene Higgins prof. physics, 1972—79; Frank L. Sulzberger prof. physics U. Chgo., 1989—92; dir. Fermi Nat. Accelerator Lab., Batavia, Ill., 1979—89, dir. emeritus, 1989—; Pritzker prof. sci. Ill. Inst. Tech., Chgo., 1992—; resident scholar Ill. Math. and Sci. Acad., 1998—. Dir. Nevis Labs., Irvington, NY, 1962—79; guest scientist Brookhaven Nat. Labs., 1955; cons. Nat. Accelerator Lab., European Orgn. for Nuc. Rsch. (CERN), 1970—; mem. high energy physics adv. panel AEC, 1966—70; mem. adv. com. to divsn. math. and phys. scis. NSF, 1970—72; sci. advisor to gov. State of Ill., 1989—93; chmn. XXIV Internat. Physics Olympiad, 1991—93; co-chair com. on capacity bldg. in sci. Internat. Sci. Unions, 1994—2001; pres. bd. sponsors Bull. Atomic Scientists, 2000—; mem. adv. com. to dean U. Chgo., 2000—; pres.'s coun. The Cooper Union, 2002—. Author: Quarks to the Cosmos, 1989, The God Particle, 1993, Symmetry and the Beautiful Universe, 2005; editor, contbr.: Portraits of Great American Scientists, 2001; editor: Science Education (NATO Sci. series), 2002; contbr. articles over 200 to profl. jours. including. Commr. White House Fellows Program, 1997—2000; Univ. Rsch. Assocs., 1967—71, 1992—; founder sci. edn. program ARISE, 1995; mem. sci. adv. bd. Sec. of Energy, 1991—2001; bd. dirs. Mus. Sci. and Industry, Chgo., 1989—, Weizmann Inst. Sci., Israel, 1988—. Named Hon. Prof., Beijing Normal U., The Lederman Sci. Edn. Ctr. in his name, Fermi Nat. Accelerator Lab., 1997; recipient Nat. medal of Sci., 1965, Townsend Harris medal, CUNY, 1973, Elliot Cresson medal, Franklin Inst., 1976, Wolf prize in physics, Wolf Found., Israel, 1982, Nobel prize in Physics, 1988, Enrico Fermi prize, 1992, Rosenblith lectr. in Sci. and Tech., NAS, Joseph Priestly award, Dickinson Coll., 1996, Pres.'s medal, CCNY, 1993, Heald prize, Ill. Inst. Tech., 2000, Pupin Med. award, Columbia U., 2000, Faraday award, NSTA, Discover, 2002, Dedication of Science Literacy in the 21st Century, to him and including one of his articles; fellow Guggenheim, 1958—59, Ford Found., European Ctr. for Nuc. Rsch., Geneva, 1958—59, NSF, 1967, Presdl., World Bank, 1996—99; scholar Great Minds program, Ill. Math. Sci. Acad. Fellow: AAAS (pres. 1990—91, chmn. 1991—92, Abelson award 2001), Am. Phys. Soc. (mem. coun., Compton medal 2005); mem.: IEEE, NAS (U.S., Argentina, Finland, Mex., Russia), World Assn. Young Scientists (hon. pres. 2004—), Russian Acad. Scis. (fgn. mem.), Coun. Advancement of Sci. Writing, Italian Phys. Soc. (hon.), Tchrs. Acad. for Math. and Sci. in Chgo. (co-chmn. 1990—2001), Ill. Math. Sci. Acad. (founding vice chmn. 1985—98), Aspen Inst. Physics (pres. 1990—92). Home Phone: 630-840-4780; Office Phone: 630-907-5911. Business E-Mail: Lederman@fnal.gov. E-mail: lederman@imsa.edu.

LEDERMAN, SUSAN STURC, public administration professor; b. Bratislava, Slovakia, May 28, 1937; came to US, 1948; d. Ludovit and Helen Sturc; m. Peter Bernd Lederman, Aug. 25, 1957; children: Stuart, Ellen. AB in Polit. Sci., U. Mich., 1958; MA in Polit. Sci., Rutgers U., 1970, PhD in Polit. Sci., 1978. Vis. instr. Fairleigh Dickinson U., Madison, NJ, 1973-74, Drew U., Madison, 1975-76; from asst. prof. to assoc. prof. pub. adminstrn. Kean U., Union, NJ, 1977-89, prof., dir. MPA program, 1989-97; exec. dir. Gateway Inst. Regional Devel. Kean U., Union, NJ, 1997-2000; prof. Kean U., Union, NJ, 1990—. Vis. fellow Woodrow Wilson Sch., Princeton U., NJ, 1988-89. Co-author: (book) Elections in America—Control and Influence in Democratic Politics, 1980, (monograph) Campaign Watch: A Report on the 1992 Campaign Watch Project, 1993; editor: (book) The SLERP Reforms and Their Impact, 1989; contbr. articles to profl. jours. Mem. nat. gov. bd. Common Cause, Washington, 1994-2000; bd. dirs., sec.-treas. The Jefferson Ctr., Mpls., 1992-2002; dir. Regional Plan Assn., NYC, 1991—; pres. LWV of NJ, 1985-89, program v.p., 1983-85, sec., fiscal policy dir., 1981-83, fiscal policy dir., 1979-81, adminstrn. of justice dir., 1976-79; pres. LWV of US, 1990-92, chair edn. fund., 1990-92; mem. bd. trustees exec. com., sec. NJ Future, 1993—; pub. mem. Supreme Ct. of NJ Disciplinary Oversight Com., 1994-98, Coun. of Engring. and Sci. Splty. Bds., 1996-2002; mem. Property Tax Commn., 1998; mem. NJ Legis. Coun. of Acad. Advisors; commr. NJ State and Local Expenditure Revenue Policy Commn., 1985-88, NJ Election Law Enforcement Commn., 2000-04; pres. Northeastern Polit. Sci. Assn., 1984-85; bd. dirs., sec. NJ Appleseed, 2002-07; mem. Gov. Corzine's Adv. Panel on Judicial Appointments, 2007-. Recipient Disting. Svc. award NJ Polit. Sci. Assn., 1984, Pub. Svc. award ASPA, 1993, Eric Neisser Pub. Svc. award Pub. Interest Law Ctr., 2001; rsch. grantee Fund for NJ, 1981, Florence and John Schumann Found., 1988-89. Mem. Internat. Women's Forum (NJ Forum bd. dirs. 1998—, bd. trustees 2002-,v.p. 2005-), Phi Kappa Phi, Pi Sigma Alpha, Pi Alpha Alpha. Office: Kean U 1000 Morris Ave Union NJ 07083-7131 Office Phone: 908-737-4311. Business E-Mail: slederma@kean.edu.

LEDFORD, JANET MARIE SMALLEY, real estate appraiser, consultant; b. Willimantic, Conn., June 1, 1951; d. Harold Eugene and Elizabeth Louise (Loehr) Smalley; m. Timothy Eugene Ledford, Jan. 23, 1988. AA, Young Harris (Coll., 1971; BS, W. Ga. Coll., 1973; MEd, U. Ga., 1978. Tchr. math. secondary schs., Atlanta and V.I., 1973—82; assoc. appraiser Childers Assoc., Atlanta, 1985—87, Am. Realty Concepts, Atlanta, 1987—88; owner, appraiser, cons. Ledford & Assoc., Atlanta, 1988—. Avocations: travel, gardening, tennis, dogs, boating.

LEDFORD, SHIRLEY LOUISE, practical nurse; b. Jasper, Ga., July 25, 1952; d. Laymon James and Edna Louise (Buchanan) Pendley; m. Kenneth Weldon Ledford, Nov. 20, 1976; 1 child, Letisha Lynn. LPN, Pickens Tech. Inst., 1977. cert. integrated computer applications; cert. CNA tchr., Ga.; cert. IV, Tex., restorative nursing, Tex. Practical nurse, asst. dir. nursing Grandview Healthcare, Jasper, 1979-93; practical nurse, infection control nurse, nurse, employee health nurse performance improvement coord., med. records coord. Mountain Side Nursing Home, Jasper, 1993—. Home: 249 Sunset Ln Ellijay GA 30536-7645 Office: Mountain Health Care PO Box 490 Jasper GA 30143-0490

LEDGER, HEATH, actor; b. Perth, Australia, Apr. 4, 1979; s. Kim and Sally Ledger; 1 child, Matilda Rose. Actor: (films) Clowning Around, 1992, Blackrock, 1997, Paws, 1997, 10 Things I Hate About You, 1999, The Patriot, 2000, A Knight's Tale, 2001, Monster's Ball, 2001, Four Feathers, 2002, The Sin Eater, 2002, Ned Kelly, 2002, The Order, 2003, Lords of Dogtown, 2005, The Brothers Grimm, 2005, Brokeback Mountain, 2005 (Best Actor, NY Film Critics Circle, 2005), Casanova, 2005, Candy, 2006; (TV series) Ship to Shore, 1993, Sweat, 1996, Home and Away, 1997. Mailing: 2222 N Beachwood Dr Apt 408 Los Angeles CA 90068 also: c/o Shanahans Mgmt PO Box 478 Kings Cross NSW 1340 Australia*

LEDGER, WILLIAM JOE, obstetrician, educator; b. Turtle Creek, Pa., 1932; BA, Princeton U., 1954; MD, U. Pa., 1958; MS, Temple U., 1964. Diplomate Am. Bd. Ob-Gyn. Intern Hamot Hosp. Assn., Erie, NY, 1958-59; resident Temple U. Hosp., Phila., 1961-64; attending physician Women's Hosp.-Mich. Med. Ctr., 1964-72; assoc. prof. U. Mich., Ann Arbor; prof. U. So. Calif., LA, 1972-79; Given Found. prof., chmn. ob-gyn. Cornell U. Med. Coll., NYC, 1979—99, chmn. emeritus, 1999—. Served to capt. USMC, 1959-61 Fellow ACS, Am. Coll. Ob-Gyn. Office: NY Presbyn Hosp Weill Med Coll Cornell U 525 E 68th St Ste J-130 New York NY 10021-4870 Home Phone: 609-924-7569. Business E-Mail: wjledger@med.cornell.edu.

LEDLEY, ROBERT STEVEN, biophysicist; b. NYC, June 28, 1928; DDS, NYU, 1948; MA in Theoretical Physics, Columbia U., 1949. Rsch. physicist Columbia U. Radiation Labs., Columbia, 1948—50; instr. physics Columbia U., 1949—50; vis. scientist Nat. Bur. Standards, 1951—52; physicist, 1953—54; ops. rsch. analyst Johns Hopkins U., 1954—56; assoc. prof. elec. engring George Washington U., 1957—60; instr. pediat. Johns Hopkins U., Sch. Medicine, 1960—63; prof. elec. engring. George Washington U., 1968—70; prof. physiology, biophysics & radiology Georgetown U., 1970—; pres., rsch. dir. Nat. Biomed. Rsch. Found., 1960—; pres. Digital Info. Sci. Corp., 1970—75. Contbr. articles to profl. jours. and author of several books; editor-in-chief Pattern Recognition, Elsevier Science, Oxford, Eng., Computers in Biology and Medicine, Computerized Medical Imaging and Graphics, Computer Languages. Named to Nat. Inventor Hall of Fame, 1990; recipient Nat. medal of Tech., U.S. Dept. Commerce, 1997, Morris E. Collen, MD award, Am. Coll. of Medical Informatics, 1998, Goldhaber award, Harvard Sch. Dental Medicine, 1998, Cert. of Appreciation, Nat. Inst. Dental Rsch., NIH, 1998, Disting. Alumni NYU, 1999. Mem.: NIH, IEEE, NAS (mem. Inst. Medicine), Pattern Recognition Soc., N.Y. Acad. Scis., Biophys. Soc., Soc. Math. Biophysics. Achievements include invention of CT Scanner. Office: Nat Biomed Rsch Found Georgetown U Med Ctr 3900 Reservoir Rd NW Washington DC 20007 Address: Georgetown U Med Ctr LR-3 Preclinical Science 4000 Reservoir Rd NW Washington DC 20057 Office Phone: 202-687-2121. Office Fax: 202-687-1662. Business E-Mail: ledley@georgetown.edu.

LEDNICKY, JOHN A., virologist, microbiologist; s. John A. and Mercedes B. Lednicky; m. Julia A. Nelson. PhD, U. Tex., Austin, 1991. Cert. technologist microbiology Am. Soc. Clin. Pathology, Ill., 1980, registered microbiologist Am. Acad. Microbiology, Wash., 1980. Asst. prof. dept. pathology Loyola U., Maywood, Ill., 2001—05; prin. scientist Midwest Rsch. Inst., Kans. City, Mo., 2005—. Contbr. articles to profl. jours. Mem.: ACS, AAAS, Am. Soc. Virology, Am. Soc. Clin. Pathology, Am. Soc. Microbiology. Roman Catholic. Achievements include discovery of SV40-K661 and SV40-CAL, two slowest growing natural isolates of SV40 to be described. Avocations: scuba diving, soccer. Office: Midwest Research Inst 425 Volker Blvd Kansas City MO 64110 Home Phone: 913-832-2723; Office Phone: 913-753-7600 1980. Personal E-mail: johnadledn@yahoo.com. Business E-Mail: jlednicky@mriresearch.org.

LEDOGAR, STEPHEN J., retired diplomat; b. NYC, Sept. 14, 1929; m. Marcia Hubert, Sept. 16, 1967; children: Lucy, Charles. BS, Fordham U., 1954, LLB, 1958. Bar: N.Y. 1959. Surety claims atty. Chubb & Son, NYC, 1954-59; with Fgn. Svc., 1959-97, ret., 1997; press spokesman, U.S. del. Vietnam Peace Talks, Paris, 1967-72; with U.S. Mission to NATO, 1973-76; spl. asst. to undersec. of state, 1976-77; dir. Office of NATO Affairs, 1977-80; mem. State Dept. Senior Seminar, 1980-81; dep. chief of mission U.S. Mission to NATO, Brussels, 1981-87; amb., U.S. rep. European Conventional Stability Negotiations and Mutual and Balanced Force Reductions Talks, 1987-89; amb. and head U.S. Del. to Negotiations on Conventional Armed Forces in Europe, 1989; amb. and U.S. rep. Conference on Disarmament, 1989-97; prin. U.S. negotiator of chem. weapons conv., 1993; prin. U.S. negotiator Comprehensive Nuclear Test Ban Treaty, 1996. Lt. USN, 1949-52, USNR, 1954-60 (Naval Aviator). E-mail: hubert.ledogar@verizon.net.

LEDOUX, ELLEN G., music educator; b. Lake Charles, La., July 2, 1963; d. Charles Allen and Diane Elizabeth Gay; children: Roberto William Rodriguez, Suzanne Kathleen Rodriguez, Eduardo Christopher Rodriguez. MusB, U. So. Miss., Hattiesburg, 1996; M in Secondary Edn., William Carey Coll., Gulfport, Miss., 2001; post grad., Walden U., 2005—; post grad. in K-12 specialization, Capella U., 2007—. Cert. music tchr. Tex., 2004. Asst. band dir. Ocean Springs H.S., Miss., 1997—2002, North Garland H.S., Tex., 2002—. Named Most Influential Tchr., 2005; named an Outstanding Instrumentalist, Dept. Music, Coll. of Ozarks, 1990—91, Outstanding Instrumentalist, U. So. Miss., 1995—96, All Star Tchr., Ocean Springs H.S., 2001—02; recipient Semper Fidelis award, 1981, John Philip Sousa award, Coll. of Ozarks, 1991—92; Jean Cantwell scholar, 1991—93. Home: PO Box 496178 Garland TX 75049-6178 Office: North Garland High School 2109 W Buckingham Rd Garland TX 75042 Office Phone: 972-675-3136. Personal E-mail: percussiondr@yahoo.com. Business E-Mail: egledoux@garlandisd.net.

LEDOUX, JOHN LANCE, military officer; b. Sarasota, Fla., Oct. 12, 1954; s. John Walter and Gerry Collins Ledoux; m. Marilyn Kay Vice, Sept. 6, 1975; children: Nick Andrew, Meridith Kelly, Kathryn Collins, Michael Claude. BA, U. Ctrl. Fla., Orlando, 1977; Masters, Naval War Coll., Newport, 2000. Commdg. officer 3d bn., 2d marines US Marines, Jacksonville, NC, 1997—99, commdg. officer 23d marine rgt. San Bruno, Calif., 2000—02, asst. chief of staff G-3 (ops.) and G-7 (tng.) Jacksonville, NC, 2002—04, chief staff multinational force- west II marine expeditionary force Al Anbar, Iraq, 2004—06. Col. US Marines, 1974—2007, Global. Decorated Legion of Merit US Marines; recipient Warren Medallion, Director of CIA. Mem.: Marine Meml. Club (assoc.; mil. advisor 2000—02). Avocations: boating, travel. Office Phone: 910-937-0237.

LEDOUX, JOSEPH E., neuroscientist, educator; PhD in Psychology, SUNY, Stony Brook, 1977. Postdoctoral fellow dept. neurology Cornell U. Med. Coll., asst. prof.; mem. faculty to Henry and Lucy Moses prof. sci. dept. psych. and Ctr. Neural Sci. NYU, 1989—. Contbr. articles to profl. jours.; author: Emotional Brain: The Mysterious Underpinnings of Emotional Life, 1996, Synaptic Self: How Our Brains Become Who We Are, 2002. Recipient Fyssen Internat. prize, 2005. Fellow: NY Acad. Scis., Am. Acad. Arts & Scis., AAAS. Office: Ctr Neural Sci NYU 4 Washington Pl Rm 809 New York NY 10003-6621 E-mail: ledoux@cns.nyu.edu.

LEDUC, JOHN ANDRE, lawyer; b. Oberlin, Ohio, Apr. 13, 1954; son Mr. & Mrs. Thomas Harold LeDuc; m. Laura Jean Hagen. AB summa cum laude, Princeton U., 1975; JD cum laude, Harvard U., 1978. Bar: Ohio 1978, Ill. 1984. Counsel (com. on fin.) US Senate, 1981—83; ptnr. Winston & Strawn, Chgo., Skadden Arps & Slate, Chgo., 1992, Skadden, Arps, Slate, Meagher & Flom LLP, Chgo. Adj. prof. law U. Chgo., 1985-91, U. Miami 1993-1995, active Fed. Income Tax Project Tax Adv. Grp. Contbr. articles to profl. jours. Mem. ABA (mem. corp. tax com. tax sect. 1985-), Ill. Bar Assn., Chgo. Bar Assn., Am. Law Inst., Phi Beta Kappa. Office: Skadden Arps Slate Meagher & Flom LLP 333 W Wacker Dr Chicago IL 60606 Office Phone: 312-407-0770. Office Fax: 312-407-8516. E-mail: aleduc@skadden.com.

LEDWELL, JAMES R., oceanographer; BS in Physics, Boston Coll., 1970; MS in Physics, U. Mass., Amherst, 1974; MS in Applied Physics, Harvard U., 1979, PhD in Applied Physics, 1982. Assoc. rsch. scientist Columbia U. Lamont-Doherty Geol. Obs., 1982—83, 1985—88, rsch. scientist, adj. assoc. prof., 1988—90; NCR-NASA resident rsch. assoc. Goddard Inst. Space Studies, 1983—85; assoc. scientist Woods Hole Oceanog. Instn., Mass., 1990, sr. scientist dept. applied ocean physics and engring. Contbr. articles to sci. jours. Recipient Alexander Agassiz medal, NAS, 2007. Mem.: Oceanography Soc., Am. Meteorol. Soc., Am. Geophys. Union. Office: Woods Hole Oceanog Instn Bigelow 111 MS 12 Woods Hole MA 02543 Office Phone: 508-289-3305. Office Fax: 508-457-2194. E-mail: jledwell@whoi.edu.

LEDWIDGE, PATRICK JOSEPH, lawyer; b. Detroit, Mar. 17, 1928; s. Patrick Liam and Mary Josephine (Hooley) L.; m. Rosemary Lahey Mervenne, Aug. 3, 1974; stepchildren: Anne Marie, Mary Clare, John, David, Sara Edleman. AB, Coll. Holy Cross, 1949; JD, U. Mich., 1952. Bar: Mich. 1952. Assoc. firm Dickinson, Wright, Moon, Van Dusen & Freeman, Detroit, 1956-63; mem. Dickinson Wright PLLC, Bloomfield Hills, Mich., 1964—. Served to lt. j.g. U.S. Navy, 1952-55. Mem. Mich. Bar Assn., Detroit Bar Assn., Am. Law Inst. Clubs: Detroit Athletic, Detroit Golf. Roman Catholic. Office: Dickinson Wright PLLC 38525 Woodward Ave Ste 2000 Bloomfield Hills MI 48304-5092

LEDWIG, DONALD EUGENE, association executive, consultant, retired broadcast executive, military officer; s. Paul Lawrence and Rose Ledwig; m. Gail Wilcox, Jan. 30, 1965; children: Donald Eugene Jr., David W. BS, Tex. Tech U, 1959; MBA, George Washington U., 1973; disting. grad., Naval War Coll., 1977. Commd. ensign USN, 1959, advanced through grades to capt., 1980; ship's officer U.S. Pacific Fleet, 1959-65, 77-79; mem. staff Adm. H.G. Rickover, Nuclear Propulsion Program, 1966-72; dir. contract policy Naval Materiel Command, Washington, 1979-81; dep. comdr. Naval Electronic Sys. Command, Washington, 1981-84; ret., 1984; v.p., treas. Corp. for Pub. Broadcasting, Washington, 1984-86, pres., CEO, 1987-92; exec. dir. Am. Prodn. and Inventory Control Soc., Falls Church, Va., 1992-95; pres. Am. Logistics Assn., Washington, 1995-96; COO Anchor Health Assn., 1997-98; cons. Assn. Mgmt., 1998—. Chair Alexandria (Va.) Electoral Bd., 2000—. Decorated Legion of Merit; recipient Barrow Meml. award Hastings Coll. Law, 1989, award Nat. Captioning Inst., 1990, Disting. Alumnus award Tex. Tech U., 1992. Mem.: Va. Electoral Bd. Assn., Nat. Press Club, Alexandria Assn., Army-Navy Country Club, Am. Legion.

LEDWITH, JOHN FRANCIS, lawyer; b. Phila., Oct. 3, 1938; s. Francis Joseph and Jane Agnes (White) L.; m. Mary Evans, Aug. 28, 1965; children: Deirdre A., John E. AB, U. Pa., 1960, JD, 1963. Bar: Pa. 1965, N.Y. 1984, U.S. Dist. Ct. (ea. dist.) Pa. 1965, U.S. Ct. Appeals (3d cir.) 1965, U.S. Supreme Ct. 1970. Assoc. Joseph R. Thompson, Phila., 1965-71; mem. Schubert, Mallon, Wallheim & deCindis, Phila., 1971-81,

LaBrum & Doak, Phila., 1981-95, Marshall, Denchey, Warner, Coleman & Goggins, Phila., 1995—. Author: (with others) Philadelphia CP Trial Manual, 1982. Bd. dirs. Chestnut Hill Cmty. Assn., Pa., 1975-76. With USCG, 1963-71. Mem. ABA, Pa. Bar Assn., Phila. Bar Assn., Def. Rsch. Inst., Fedn. Ins. Corp. Coun., Racquet Club (Phila.), Phila. Cricket Club, Avalon Yacht Club (commodore 1982). Republican. Roman Catholic. Office: Marshall Dennehey Warner Coleman & Goggins 1845 Walnut St Philadelphia PA 19103-4708 Home Phone: 215-248-5080; Office Phone: 215-575-2604. Business E-Mail: jfledwith@mdwcg.com.

LEDYARD, JOHN ODELL, economics professor, consultant; b. Detroit, Apr. 4, 1940; s. William Hendrie and Florence (Odell) L.; m. Bonnie Higginbottom, May 23, 1970 (div. July 2004); children: Stephen, J. Henry, Meg; m. Elaine Fleming, Dec. 12, 2006. BA, Wabash Coll., 1963; PhD, Purdue U., 1967; PhD (hon.), Purdue U./Ind. U., 1993. Asst. prof. Carnegie-Mellon U., Pitts., 1967-70; prof. Northwestern U., Evanston, Ill., 1970-85, Calif. Inst. Tech., Pasadena, 1985—, exec. officer for social sci., 1989-92, chmn. div. humanities and social scis., 1992—2002. Contbr. articles to profl. jours. Fellow Am. Acad. Arts and Scis., Econometric Soc., Pub. Choice Soc. (pres. 1980-82); mem. Econ. Sci. Assn. (exec. com. 1986-88). Office: Calif Inst Tech Dept HHS Pasadena CA 91125-0001

LEDYARD, ROBINS HEARD, lawyer; b. Nashville, Oct. 14, 1939; s. Quitman Robins and Alma Elizabeth (Stevenson) L.; m. Julia Bordeaux Gambill, Dec. 19, 1962; children: Stevenson Gambill, Quitman Robins II, Margaret Dabney. BA, Vanderbilt U., 1965, JD, 1966. Bar: Tenn. 1966, U.S. Supreme Ct. 1975. Atty. Nat. Life & Accident Ins. Co., Nashville, 1966-68, asst. counsel, 1968-69, assoc. counsel, 1969-70, counsel, 1970-72, assoc. gen. counsel, 1972-75, gen. counsel, 1975-80; partner Bass, Berry & Sims, 1980—. Tchr. C.L.U.s, 1967-75 Asst. editor: Vanderbilt Law Rev., 1965-66; contbr. articles to profl. jours. Active United Way, Nashville, 1967—, Heart Fund, 1970—73; vice chmn. United Diocesan Givers, 1975; bd. dirs. St. Thomas Hosp., 1990—. With USMC, 1958—61. Named one of Best Lawyers in Am., Global Leaders for the South; recipient Bennett Douglas Bell Meml. prize, 1986; Marr scholar, 1965—66. Mem. ABA, Am. Coun. Life Ins. (chmn. tax com. 1978-80), Assn. Life Ins. Counsel (chmn. tax com. 1979-80), Tenn. Bar Assn., Nashville Bar Assn., Internat. Assn. Ins. Counsel, Global Leaders for the South, Order of Coif, Phi Delta Phi, Alpha Tau Omega. Clubs: Belle Meade Country, Capitol of Nashville, KC. Democrat. Roman Catholic. Home: 1215 Chickering Rd Nashville TN 37215-4519 Office: Amsouth Ctr Ste 2700 315 Deaderick St Nashville TN 37238-3001 Office Phone: 615-742-6259. Business E-Mail: rledyard@bassberry.com.

LEE, ADRIAN ISELIN, JR., journalist; b. Miami, Fla, Nov. 6, 1920; s. Adrian Iselin and Adriana Lanier (Owen) L.; m. Marie Lainé Santa Maria, Oct. 14, 1950; children: Adrian Iselin III, Catherine Taney, Thomas Sim, William Owen, Anne Marie, Louisa Carrell. BA, Spring Hill Coll., Mobile, Ala., 1943. With The Bulletin, Phila., 1948—; gen. assignment reporter The Bull., 1960-82, edit. writer, 1967-72, columnist op-ed page, 1972-82; with Phila. Daily News, 1982-88; speech and op-ed writer US Atty. Gen. Edwin Meese III, 1988-89; writer CBS Radio News, 1989-90. Tchr. editorial writing, dept. journalism Temple U. Active Chestnut Hill Community Assn. Lt. (j.g.) USNR, 1943-46, PTO. Decorated Navy Unit Commendation medal. Mem. Nat. Press Club, Pen and Pencil Club, Phila. Press Assn. (prize for coverage John F. Kennedy assassination 1963), Vietnam War, 1966; Sigma Delta Chi (prize for column writing 1978) Republican. Roman Catholic. Home and Office: 20 Haws Ln Flourtown PA 19031-2048

LEE, ALVIN A., literary educator, scholar, author; b. Woodville, Ont., Can., Sept. 30, 1930; s. Norman Osborne and Susanna Elizabeth (Found) L.; m. Hope Arnott, Dec. 21, 1957 (dec.); children: Joanna, Monika, Fiona, Alison, Margaret. BA, U. Toronto, 1953, MA in English, 1958, PhD, 1961; MDiv, Victoria U., Toronto, 1957. Tchg. fellow in English U. Toronto, 1957-59; asst. prof. English McMaster U., Hamilton, Ont., 1960-65, assoc. prof., 1966-70, prof., 1970-92, prof. emeritus, 1990—, asst. dean Sch. Grad. Studies, 1968-71, dean Sch. Grad. Studies, 1971-73, acad. v.p., 1974-79, pres., vice-chancellor, 1980-90, pres. emeritus, 1994—; Northrop Frye prof. literary theory U. Toronto, 1992, rsch. assoc. Victoria Coll., 1997—. Mem. Western Ont. coun. Conf. Bd. Can., 1983-90; mem. adv. bd. Medieval and Renaissance History, 1991—. Author: James Reaney, Twayne's World Authors Series, 49, 1968, The Guest-Hall of Eden: Four Essays on the Design of Old English Poetry, 1972, Gold-Hall and Earth-Dragon: 'Beowulf' as Metaphor, 1999; editor: Northrop Frye, The Great Code, 2006, (with Hope Arnott Lee) Wish and Nightmare, 1972, Circle of Stories: One, 1972, Two, 1972, The Garden and the Wilderness, 1973, The Temple and the Ruin, 1973, The Peaceable Kingdom, 1974; (with Robert D. Denham) The Legacy of Northrop Frye, 1994; gen. editor: McMaster Old English Studies and Texts, 1982-92, Collected Works of Northrop Frye, 1995—; editl. bd. English Studies in Canada, 1982-88; contbr. articles to profl. jours. Trustee, mem. exec. com. Chedoke-McMaster Hosps., 1980-90; mem. Community Edn. Coordinating Com., 1981-90; mem. Council Ont. Univs., 1980-90, vice chmn., 1981-83, chmn., 1983-85, mem. exec. com., 1981-87; mem. Health Scis. Liaison Com., 1980-90; dir. Council Ont. Univ. Holdings Ltd., 1981-90; mem. chancellors coun. Victoria U., U. Toronto, 1983—; hon. bd. dirs. Operation Lifeline, Hamilton, 1980-90; hon. Patron Opera Hamilton, 1982-90; vice chmn. bd., mem. exec. com. Royal Bot. Gardens, Hamilton, 1980-90, chmn. provincial and fed. relations com., 1981-90, vice chmn. sci. and ednl. com., 1981-90, mem. nominating com., 1981-90; vice chmn. bus. adv. conf. Regional Municipality of Hamilton-Wentworth, 1983-90; chmn. fund-raising liaison com. McMaster Hosps. Found/McMaster U., 1983-90; hon. patron Edn. Found. of Fedn. Chinese Can. Profls., Ont., 1984-90; mem., vice chair Can. Merit Scholarship Found., 1990-93; bd. dirs. Art Gallery Hamilton, 1991-94; mem. adminstrn. bd. McMaster Mus. Art. Mem. MLA, Mediaeval Acad. Am., Assn. Univs. and Colls. Can. (coun. univ. pres. 1980-90), Hamilton Assn. Advancement Lit., Sci. and Art (hon. pres. 1980-88), Can. Inst. Advanced Rsch., Internat. Assn. Anglo-Saxonists, Corporate-Higher Edn. Forum, McMaster U. Alumni Coun. (hon. pres. 1980-90), McMaster U. Letterman's Assn. (hon.), Hamilton and Dist. C. of C. (dir., mem. program com. 1982-87, Hamilton Gallery of Distinction 1996—). Office: Stormont Box 72, West Flamborough ON L0R 2K0 Canada Office Phone: 905-627-3085. E-mail: alvinlee@mcmaster.ca.

LEE, AMY, singer; b. Riverside, Calif., Dec. 13, 1981; d. John and Sara (Cargill) Lee. Co-founder & lead singer Evanescence, 1998—. Singer: (albums) Origin, 2002, Fallen, 2003 (album went Double Platinum, Grammy award best new artist, 2003), Anywhere But Home, 2004, The Open Door, 2006, (songs) Breathe, 2000, Broken, by Seether, 2002, Bring Me To Life, 2003 (Grammy award best hard rock performance, 2003), Call Me When You're Sober, 2006. Office: Wind-Up Records 72 Madison Ave New York NY 10016 Office Phone: 212-895-3100.

LEE, ANDREA JANE, academic administrator, nun; 1 adopted child, Lahens. AA in Italian, Villa Walsh Coll.; BA in music and elem. edn., Northeastern Ill. U.; MEd, Pa. State U., PhD in edn. adminstrn. Instr. tchr. edn. Pa. State U.; dean continuing edn. and comty. svcs. Marygrove Coll., 1981—84, exec. v.p. and COO, 1984—97, interim pres., 1998; pres. Coll. of St. Catherine, St. Paul, 1999—. Office: Coll of St Catherine 2004 Randolph Ave Saint Paul MN 55105

LEE, ANG, film director; b. Pingtung, Taiwan, Oct. 23, 1954; m. Jane Lin, 1983; children: Haan, Mason. Grad., Nat. Taiwan Coll. Arts, 1975; BFA in Theater, U. Ill., 1980; MFA in Film, NYU, 1984. Arts & culture cons. 2008 Summer Olympics, 2006—. Dir. (films) Fine Line, 1985, Sense and Sensibility, 1996 (N.Y. Film Critics Circle award, Boston Film Critics award, Nat. Bd. Rev. award, Golden Bear award, Berlin Film Festival award, nominee Brit. Acad. Film and TV Arts award, nominee Dirs. Guild award, nominee Golden Globe award, all as best dir.), Chosen, 2001, The Hulk, 2003, Brokeback Mountain, 2005 (Best Dir., NY Film Critics Circle, 2005, Boston Soc. Film Critics award, 2005, Nat. Bd. Review, 2005, Broadcast Film Critics Assn., 2006), Outstanding Directorial Achievement in Feature Film, Director's Guild Am. 2005, Best Picture, 2005, Best Dir., Hollywood Fgn. Press Assn. (Golden Globe award), 2006, David Lean award for Achievement in Direction, British Acad. Film and TV Arts, 2006, Best Director, Spirit Independent award, 2006, Achievement in Directing, Acad. Motion Picture Arts & Sciences, 2006); dir., prodr. (films) Pushing Hands, 1991 (several Golden Horse award nominations, Taiwan, Spl. Jury prize for Direction, Best Film honors Asian Pacific Film Festival 1992), The Wedding Banquet, 1993 (Asian Am. Media award 16th Asian Am. internat. Film Festival, Golden Bear award Berlin Film Festival, nominee Acad. award for Best Fgn. Lang. Film, nominee Golden Globe award for Best Fgn. Lang. Film, several Ind. Spirit award nominations, Golden Horse awards for Best Film and Best Dir.), The Ice Storm, 1997, Crouching Tiger, Hidden Dragon, 2000; screenwriter (with Hui Ling Wang and James Schamus), Eat Drink Man Woman, 1994 (Best Fgn. Lang. Film award Nat. Bd. Rev., nominee Acad. award for Best Fgn. Lang. Film, nominee Golden Globe award for Best Fgn. Lang. Film, honored for Best Film and as Best Dir. Asian Pacific Film Festival, various Ind. Spirit award nominations), Ride With the Devil, 1999; exec. prodr. (films) One Last Ride, 2003; The Wedding Banquet and Eat Drink Man Woman included in book: Two Films by Ang Lee, 1994. Named one of 100 Most Influential People, Time Mag., 2006, 50 Most Powerful People in Hollywood, Premiere mag., 2006. Address: Creative Artists Agy 9830 Wilshire Blvd Beverly Hills CA 90212-1804

LEE, ANN L., biotechnology company executive; BSChemE, Cornell U.; MSChemE, Yale U., New Haven, D in Engring. and Applied Scis. Sr. leadership positions up to v.p. chem. tech. and engring. in mfg. divsn. Merck & Co.; v.p. process devel. Genentech Inc., South San Francisco, 2005—. Contbr. articles to profl. publs.; assoc. editor: Biotechnology and Applied Biochemistry. Sr. adv. com. Yale U. Faculty of Engring. Fellow: Am. Inst. Med. and Biol. Engring.; mem.: NAE. Achievements include patents in field. Office: Genentech Inc 1 DNA Way South San Francisco CA 94080-4990 Office Phone: 650-225-1000. Office Fax: 650-225-6000.*

LEE, BAO-SHIANG BOB, biochemist, researcher; b. Fon-Shang, Taiwan, Apr. 18, 1957; arrived in U.S., 1984; s. Sheng-Hang Lee and Fon Su; m. Jun Quan, June 17, 1991; 1 child, Jenny. BS, Chinese Culture U., 1980; MS, Nat. Taiwan U., 1982; PhD, The Ohio State U., 1988. Postdoctoral fellow chemistry and biochemistry Ga. Inst. Tech., Atlanta, 1989—91; vis. rsch. assoc. Inst. Biomedical Scis. Academia Sinica, Taipei, Taiwan, 1991—93; postdoctoral fellow chemistry U. Ill., Urbana-Champaign, Ill., 1993—96, rsch. asst. prof. biochemistry Chgo., 1996—98, dir. Protein Rsch. Lab. Rsch. Resources Ctr., 1996—. Grantee, NIH. Mem.: Am. Peptide Soc., Am. Protein Soc., Assn. Biomolecular Resource Facilities. Achievements include development of many new biochemical techniques such as countercurrent affinity electrophoresis, antibody affinity electrophoresis, functional affinity electrophoresis; avidin functional affinity electrophoresis, 3-D SDS PAGE, and microwave-assisted partial acid hydrolysis of glycoprotein; first to use of mathematic and statistic methods ininterpreting mass spectra of peptides and proteins. Office: E-102 Msb M/C 937 Rrc Uic 835 S Wolcott Avenue Chicago IL 60612 Home Phone: 630-922-4679; Office Phone: 312-996-1411. Business E-Mail: boblee@uic.edu.

LEE, BARBARA, congresswoman; b. El Paso, Tex., July 16, 1946; m. Michael Millben (div.); children: Tony, Craig. BA, Mills Coll., 1973; M in Social Welfare, U. Calif. Berkeley, 1976. Chief of staff U.S. Rep. Ron Dellums, 1975—87; rep. Calif. State Assembly, 1990-96; mem. Calif. State Sen., 1996-98, U.S. Congress from 9th Calif. dist., Washington, 1999—; mem. fin. svcs. com., internat. rels. com. Co-chmn. Progressive Caucus; chmn. Congl. Black Caucus Task Force HIV/AIDS; whip Congl. Black Caucus, mem. Minority Bus. Task Force; mem. adv. bd. Alameda Boys Club; bd. dirs. Bay Area Black United Fund; with Black Women Organized Polit. Action; founder Calif. Commn. Status African Am. Male; mem. Calif. Commn. Status Women; mem. bd. Calif. Coastal Conservancy/Dist. Export Coun. Recipient Most Influential Black Americans, Ebony mag., 2006. Democrat. Office: US Ho Reps 1724 Longworth Ho Office Bldg Washington DC 20515-0509 also: Dist Office Ste 1000 N 1301 Clay Oakland CA 94612 Office Phone: 202-225-2661, 510-763-0370. Fax: 202-225-9817; Office Fax: 510-763-6538.*

LEE, BARBARA, political activist, foundation administrator; b. July 1945; d. Sidney and Ruth Fish; m. Thomas Lee, 1968 (div. 1996); children: Zach, Robbie. BA, Simmons Coll., 1967; MSW, Boston U.; degree (hon.), Pine Manor Coll., 2004. Pres., treas., dir. Barbara Lee Family Found., Cambridge, Mass.; vice chair bd. dirs. Inst. Contemporary Art, Boston; pres., treas. Revolutionary Women, Cambridge. Founding chair contemporary arts program Isabella Stewart Gardner Mus., Boston; co-founder The White House Project, 1997. Named one of Top 200 Collectors, ARTnews Mag., 2004, 21 Leaders for the 21st Century, Women's E News, 2005; named to The 100 Women Who Run this Town, Boston Mag., The 100 People Who Run this Town, 2004; recipient Opening Doors award, Women's Inst. for Housing and Econ. Devel., 2003, George Alden Dean Leadership award, Women's Campaign Sch., Yale U., 2003. Democrat. Avocation: Collector of Modern and contemporary art by women. Office: 131 Mt Auburn St, Ste 2 Cambridge MA 02138 Office Phone: 617-234-0355. Office Fax: 617-234-0357.

LEE, BARBARA ANNE, law educator; b. Newton, NJ, Apr. 9, 1949; d. Robert Hanna and Keren (Dalrymple) L.; m. James Paul Begin, Aug. 14, 1982; 1 child, Robert James. BA, U. Vt., 1971; MA, Ohio State U., 1972; JD, Georgetown U., 1982; PhD, Ohio State U., 1977. Bar: NJ 1983, US Dist. Ct. NJ 1983. Instr. Franklin U., Columbus, Ohio, 1974—75; rsch. asst. Ohio State U., Columbus, 1975—77; policy analyst US Dept. Edn., Washington, 1978—80; dir. data trands Carnegie Found., Washington, 1980—82; asst. prof. Grad. Sch. Edn. Rutgers U., Brunswick, NJ, 1982—84, asst. prof. Sch. Mgmt. and Labor Rels., 1984—88, assoc. prof., 1988—94, prof., 1994—, assoc. provost, 1995—96, dean, 2000—06. Mem. Study Group on Excellence in Higher Edn., Nat. Inst. Edn., 1983-84; project dir. Carnegie Corp., NYC, 1982-84. Author: Academics in Court, 1987; co-author: The Law of Higher Education, 4th edit., 2006; contbr. numerous articles to profl. jours. Corse fellow U. Vt., 1971; recipient John F. Kennedy Labor Law award Georgetown U., 1982; grantee Bur. Labor-Mgmt. Rels. and Coop. Programs, 1985-86. Mem. ABA, NJ Bar Assn. (mem. exec. com. labor and employment law sect. 1987—, women's rights sect.), Am. Ednl. Rsch. Assn., Indsl. Rels. Rsch. Assn., Acad. Mgmt., Assn. Study Higher Edn. (legal counsel 1982-88), Nat. Assn. Coll. and Univ. Attys. (vice chair editl. bd. 1986-89, chair 1995-96, chair publs. com. 1988-91, bd. dirs. 1990-93). Office: Rutgers U Sch Mgmt and Labor Rels 94 Rockafeller Rd Piscataway NJ 08854-8054 Office Phone: 732-445-1350. Business E-Mail: lee@smlr.rutgers.edu.

LEE, BARBARA S., special education educator; b. Long Beach, Calif., Oct. 25, 1942; d. George Hubert Staley and Doris Emma Geer/Staley; m. Stanley Yau Ning Lee, Sept. 7, 1963; children: Tracey Golden, Linda Samuels, Tanya Prucher. BS in Phys. Sci., U. N.D., 1964; tchg. cert., Nat. U., Irvine, Calif., 1988; M in Spl. Edn., U. Phoenix, 2005. Cert. tchr. Ariz., ELL cert. 1997. Tchrs. aide Fountain Valley Sch. Dist., Calif., 1979—89; tchr. Pk. Pvt. Day Sch., Costa Mesa, Calif., 1990—96, Laveen Sch. Dist., Ariz., 1997—2000, Ariz. Dept. Juvenile Corrections, Phoenix, 2000—. Mem. curriculum com. Adobe Mountain Sch., Phoenix. Life mem. PTO-Moiola Sch., Fountain Valley, 1985. Recipient Svc. Recognition award, Ariz. Dept. Juvenile Corrections, 2006. Mem.: ASCD, Ariz. Pub. Employees Assn., Assn. for Rsch. and Enlightment. Avocations: dance, hiking, camping, reading, quilting. Home: 10251 W Snead Cir N Sun City AZ 85351 Office: Adobe Mountain Sch 2800 W Pinnacle Peak Phoenix AZ 85027 E-mail: thebobbiwobbi@msn.com.

LEE, BOBBY, actor, comedian; b. San Diego, Calif., Sept. 17, 1972; Actor: (films) The Underground Comedy Store, 1999, Harold & Kumar Go To White Castle, 2004, Accidentally on Purpose, 2005, Undoing, 2006, Kickin It Old Skool, 2007, (video) American Misfits, 2003; actor, contbg. writer (TV series) Mad TV, 2001—; performer: (TV series) Asian Street Comedy, 2004; guest appearances Minding the Store, 2005, Mind of Mencia, 2005, Curb Your Enthusiasm, 2005, stand-up comedian Tonight Show with Jay Leno, regular performer Comedy Store, West Hollywood.*

LEE, BOVEY, artist, educator; BA, Chinese U., Hong Kong, 1991; MFA, U. Calif., Berkeley, 1995, Pratt Inst., NY, 2000. Asst. prof. Lock Haven U., Pa., 1999—2000; owner Bovey Lee Studio, Pitts., 2000—; asst. prof. U. Pitts., 2000—. Vis. lectr. U. Calif., Santa Barbara, 1995; panelist, stream segment Asian Am. Arts Ctr., NYC, 1997, critic, commentator Artslam, 2006; co-chair exhibition com. Sloan Fine Arts Gallery, Lock Haven U., 1999; panelist, artist and software symposium Taipei Gallery, NYC, 2001; editl. adv. The Original U. Pitts., 2006—; presenter in field. Exhibitions include Asian Am. Arts Ctr., NYC, 2007, Urban Coun. Fine Arts, Hong Kong (award, 1992). Recipient Innovation in Tchg. award, U. Pitts., 2001, Ctrl. Rsch. Devel. Fund award, 2001; Jack K. and Gertrude Murphy Fine Arts fellow, San Francisco Found., 1994, Artist Opportunity grant, Greater Pitts. Arts Coun., 2007. Home Phone: 412-335-5404. Personal E-mail: boveylee@yahoo.com.

LEE, BRANDI GREMILLION, elementary school educator; b. Lake; A in Gen. Studies, BA in Elem. Ed., McNeese State U., Lake Charles, La., 2002. Tchr. Calcasieu Parish Sch. Bd., Lake Charles, La., 2002—. Tap mentor Calcasieu Parish Sch. Bd., Lake Charles, La., 2005—. Tchr. advancement program mentor Calcasieu Parish Sch. Bd., Lake Charles, La., 2005—06. Mem.: La. Fedn. of Tchrs. (assoc.). Avocations: reading, travel. Office: Oak Park Mid Sch 2200 Oak Park Blvd Lake Charles LA 70601 Home Phone: 337-439-9576; Office Phone: 337-478-3310.

LEE, BRANT THOMAS, lawyer, educator, federal official; b. San Francisco, Feb. 17, 1962; s. Ford and Patricia (Leong) L.; m. Marie Bernadette Curry, Sept. 20, 1991. BA in Philosophy, U. Calif., Berkeley, 1985; JD, Harvard U., 1990, M in Pub. Policy, 1994. Bar: Calif. 1992. Counsel subcom. on Constitution, U.S. Senate Judiciary Com., Washington, 1990-92; assoc. Breon, O'Donnell, Miller, Brown & Dannis, San Francisco, 1992-96; dep. staff sec., spl. asst. to Pres. (acting) The White House, Washington, 1993; vis. asst. prof. Syracuse (N.Y.) U. Coll. Law, 1996-97; asst. prof. U. Akron (Ohio) Sch. Law, 1997-2001, assoc. prof., 2001—. Commr. San Francisco Ethics Commn., 1995-96. Bd. dirs., Asian Svcs. in Action, Inc., Akron, 1998—; trustee Chinese for Affirmative Action, San Francisco, 1992-96; bd. dirs. Conf. Asian Pacific Am. Leadership, Washington, 1990-92; staff mem. Dukakis for Pres., Boston, 1988. Mem. ABA, Nat. Asian Pacific Am. Bar Assn. Office: U Akron Sch Law Akron OH 44325-0001 Office Phone: 330-972-6616. Business E-Mail: btlee@uakron.edu.

LEE, BRIAN EDWARD, lawyer; b. Oceanside, NY, Feb. 29, 1952; s. Lewis H., Jr. and Jean Elinor (Andrews) Lee; m. Eleanor L. Barker, June 5, 1982; children: Christopher Martin, Alison Ruth, Danielle Andrea. AB, Colgate U., 1974; JD, Valparaiso U., 1976. Bar: N.Y. 1977, U.S. Dist. Ct. (so. and ea. dists.) N.Y. 1978, U.S. Ct. Appeals (2d cir.) 1992. Assoc. Marshall, Bellofatto & Callahan, Lynbrook, NY, 1977-80, Morris, Duffy, Ivone & Jensen, NYC, 1980-84; sr. assoc. Ivone, Devine & Jensen, Lake Success, NY, 1984-85, ptnr., 1985—. Pres., trustee Trinity Christian Sch. Montville, Inc., NJ, 1985—, track coach NJ. Mem.: ABA, N.Y. County Lawyers Assn., N.Y. State Bar Assn., Christian Legal Soc. Republican. Baptist. Home: 292 Jacksonville Rd Pompton Plains NJ 07444-1511 Office: Ivone Devine & Jensen LLP 2001 Marcus Ave New Hyde Park NY 11042-1024 Office Phone: 516-326-2400. Personal E-mail: brianelee@verizon.net. Business E-Mail: blee@idjlaw.com.

LEE, BRYAN, information technology executive; m. Lisa Lee; 4 children. BA in Acctg., U. Miss. With Arthur Andersen & Co., Houston, Sony Pictures Entertainment, Inc., 1987—2000, former exec. v.p. bus. affairs; gen. mgr. bus. devel. home and entertainment group Microsoft, Redmond, Wash., 2000—02, corp. v.p., CFO worldwide mktg. and pub. home and entertainment group, 2002—07, v.p., entertainment bus. group, 2005—07.*

LEE, BURTON HOYT, aerospace engineer; s. Margaret Gallaher and Ruth Balch Lee (Stepmother), Frank Freeman Lee and adopted s. Alma Lehtinen Lerum. AB in Econs. and Physics, Brown U., Providence, RI, 1978; Cert. in Space Studies, Internat. Space U., Strasbourg, France, 1988; PhD in Mech. & Elec. Engring., Stanford U., Palo Alto, Calif., 2002; MBA in Fin. and Strategy Johnson Grad. Sch. Mgmt., Cornell U., Ithaca, NY, 2004—04. Cert. PMP, Project Mgmt. Inst., 2005. Legislative analyst; corp. and industry analyst Am. Fedn. of Labor (AFL-CIO), Washington, 1978—80; sr. econ. advisor Office of Prime Min. of Jamaica, Kingston, 1983—86; sr. venture devel. cons. NASA Ames Rsch. Ctr., Mountain View, Calif., 1988—96; sr. rschr., bus. devel. mgr. Hewlett Packard Corp., Santa Clara, Calif., 1997—99; sr. rschr. DaimlerChrysler AG R&D Labs., Esslingen, Schwaben, Germany, 1998—2001; sr. corp. strategy and devel. mgr. GE Global Rsch., Niskayuna, NY, 2003—04; sr. strategy cons. Futron Corp., Bethesda, Md., 2005—06; sr. tech. and legis. advisor Personal Spaceflight Fedn., Washington, 2006—; invited conf. spkr. Harvard Bus. Sch., Cyberposium, Cambridge, Mass., 2006—; mng. ptnr. Innovarium Ventures, Washington, 2006—. Author: various jour. articles and conf. proceedings. Mentor and coach, Washington, 1997—; math. tutor Palo Alto, Calif., 1998—2002. Recipient Lope de Vega Prize in Spanish, Brown U., 1975; fellow, NASA Johnson Space Ctr., 1989—92, U.S. Dept. Energy, 1997-2001, The Space Found., 1988, Nat. Acad. Sci., 2006. Mem.: ASME, AIAA. Achievements include founder Spaceport America, New Mexico, 1990; founding webmaster Japanese National Parliament, Tokyo; co-founder Aerospace States Association. Avocations: scuba diving, flying, languages, yoga. Home Phone: 703-282-4513. Personal E-mail: burton.lee@gmail.com.

LEE, BYOUNG-KUK, engineering educator; b. Seoul, Republic Of Korea, Dec. 25, 1968; s. Won-Bock Lee and Myung-Ja Kim; m. Jin-Sun Lee, May 16, 1998; children: Yasmine, Caleb J. BS in Elec. Engring., Hanyang U., Seoul, 1994, MS in Elec. Engring., 1996; PhD in Engring., Tex. A&M U., College Station, 2001. Sr. rschr. Korea Electrotech. Rsch. Inst., Changwon, Gyungnam, Republic of Korea, 2002—05; editor Jour. Elec. Engring. and Tech., Korean Inst. Elec. Engring., 2006—. Contbr. chapter to book. Named one of Outstanding Scientists of 21st Century, IBC, 2007; recipient Best Rschr. award, KERI, 2004. Mem.: IEEE (sr.; assoc. editor 2007—, reviewer transaction papers, session conf. chair 2005), ICEMS (gen. sec. 2007), Korean Inst. Elec. Engring. Achievements include patents for simulation program for brushless DC motor drives. Office: Sungkyunkwan Univ 300 Cheoncheon-dong Gyeonggi-do Suwon 440-746 Republic of Korea Office Fax: 82 31 299 4612. Business E-Mail: bkleeskku@skku.edu.

LEE, CARL B., lawyer; b. San Antonio, Tex., Feb. 27, 1947; AB cum laude, Harvard Coll., 1968; JD, Univ. Chgo., 1971. Bar: Tex. 1971. Assoc. Akin Gump Strauss Hauer & Feld LLP, 1974, ptnr. Dallas, 1978—, now ptnr., co-chair firmwide real estate and fin. practice group. Former group leader, Konrad Adenauer Found/Am. Jewish Com. German-Jewish Exchange Program.; past pres. Dallas Chpt. Am. Jewish Com.; trustee and officer Temple Emanu-El; bd. dir. SW Region, Union of Am. Hebrew Congregations; mem. steering com. Hillcrest/Forest Neighborhood Assn. Capt. Quartermaster Corps USAR. Named one of World's Leading Real Estate Attorneys, Euromoney, World's Leading Real Estate Adv., Mondaq's Guide; recipient Excellence in Devel. Highest Honor award for effective citizen planning, No. Ctrl. Tex. sect., Am. Planning Assn. Mem.: ABA (real property sect.), Real Estate Fin. Execs. Assn., Real Estate Coun., Tex. Acad. of Real Estate, Probate and Trust Lawyers, Dallas Bar Assn. (past pres., real property sect., past chair, legal aid and legal svcs. com., past vice chair, lawyer referral com.), State Bar of Tex. (real property sect.), Order of Coif. Office: Akin Gump Strauss Hauer & Feld LLP Ste 4100 1700 Pacific Ave Dallas TX 75201-4675 Office Phone: 214-969-2726. Office Fax: 214-969-4343. Business E-Mail: clee@akingump.com.

LEE, CARLOS NORIEL, professional baseball player; b. Aguadulce, Panama, June 20, 1976; m. Mary Lee; children: Cassandra, Karla, Karlos. Outfielder Chgo. White Sox, 1999—2004, Milw. Brewers, 2004—06, Tex. Rangers, 2006, Houston Astros, 2006—. Named to Nat. League All-Star Team, Maj. League Baseball, 2005—07; recipient Silver Slugger award, 2005. Mailing: Houston Astros PO Box 288 Houston TX 77001-0288*

LEE, CATHERINE, sculptor, painter; b. Pampa, Tex., Apr. 11, 1950; d. Paul Albert and Alice (Fleming) Porter; m. B. R. Mangham, 1967 (div. 1976); 1 child, Monk Parker; m. Sean Scully, 1977 (div. 2004). BA, San Jose State U., 1975. Asst. prof. sculpture U. Tex., San Antonio, 2000. Artist-in-residence Mpls. Coll. Art and Design, Minn. Inst. Art, 1982; vis. asst. prof. painting U. Tex., San Antonio, 1983, vis. asst. prof. sculpture, 2001; adj. asst. prof. Columbia U., N.Y.C., 1986-87. Group exhbns. include Albright-Knox Mus., Buffalo, 1987, Mus. Art, Carnegie Inst., Pitts., 1988, Am. Acad. and Inst. Arts and Letters, N.Y.C., 1988, Mus. Folkwang, Essen, Germany, 1992, Stadtische Galerie im Lenbachhaus, Munich, 1992, Neue Galerie Der Stadt Linz, Austria, 1992, Cleve. Mus. Art, 1993, Galleria Nazionale d'Arte Moderna, San Marino, Italy, 1996, The Tate Gallery, 1994, U. R.I. Art Gallery, 1996, Sonoma State U. Art Gallery, 1997, Bemis Ctr. for Contemporary Art, 1998, Städtische Gallery, Lenbachhaus, Munich, 1999, Lafayette Coll. Art Ctr., Easton, Pa., 1999, San Diego State U. Art Gallery, San Diego, 1999, Lyman-Allen Art Mus., New London, Conn., 2000, Grounds for Sculpture, The Johnson Atelier, 2002, S.W. Sch. Arts and Crafts Gallery, 2004, Irish Mus. Modern Art, Dublin, 2005, Hotel des Arts Musee, Toulon, France, 2006, Musee d'Art Moderne, St. Etienne, France, 2006. Creative Artists Pub. Svc. fellow, 1978, NEA grantee, 1989. also: Galerie Karsten Greve Drususgasse 1-5 5000 Koln Germany also: Galerie Lelong 528 W 26th St New York NY 10001 E-mail: catherlee@aol.com.

LEE, CATHY, emergency physician; b. Jan. 6, 1973; BA, U. Calif., Berkeley, 1996; MD, NY Med. Coll., Valhalla, 2000. Chief resident Met. Hosp., NYC, 2006, asst. prof. clin. emergency medicine, 2006—. Contbr. articles to profl. jours. Mem.: AMA, Am. Coll. Emergency Physicians, Alpha Omega Alpha.

LEE, CHAN-YUN, physicist, process engineer, educator; b. Hwa-Liang, Taiwan, July 19, 1952; came to U.S., 1988; s. Hsiao-Feng and Shu-Yun (Huang) L.; m. Chia-Li Yang, Jan. 13, 1983; children: Yifan E., Ethel Y., Elias Y. BS in Physics, Soochow U., Taipei, Taiwan, 1974; MS, U. So. Calif., 1980; PhD, U. Notre Dame, 1988. Cert. assoc. prof., lectr. Dept. Edn. Asst. prof. physics Tatung Inst. Tech., Taipei, 1982-86, assoc. prof., 1986-88, chmn. physics sect., 1986-88; cons. Tatung Semiconductor Divsn., Taipei, 1985-88; dir. Tatung Natural Sci. Mus., Taipei, 1986-88; lab. instr. U. Notre Dame, Notre Dame, Ind., 1988-94; process engr. Lam Rsch. Co., Fremont, Calif., 1994-96, sr. process engr., 1996-99, mgr. metal etch key accounts, 1998-99; assoc. prof. physics San Jose City Coll., Calif., 1998-99; regional chief process technologist Silicon Valley Group, 1999-2000; West Coast process coord., tech. staff Tokyo Electron Am., Santa Clara, Calif., 2000—. Rsch. asst. U. So. Calif., L.A., 1977-79. Contbr. numerous articles to profl. jours. 2d lt. Chinese Artillery, 1974-76. Recipient Excellent Rschrs. prize Chinese Nat. Sci. Coun., Taipei, 1986-88, Outstanding Acad. Pub. prize Hsieh-Tze Indsl. Revival Com., Taipei, 1987, 88, Sci. & Tech. Pers. Rsch. & Study award Chinese Nat. Sci. Coun., 1989. Mem. Chinese Physics Assn. Achievements include development of model of relativistic corrections to semiconducting properties of selected materials, simulated and calculated the dynamical susceptibility of square lattice antiferromagnets; successfully developed the first large size SAC process in the world on high density plasma TCP etcher with satisfactory yields; designed and developed the single chamber dry clean process with a MW downstream and RF plate chamber for metal via applications; designed and constructed a spectrophotometer to measure the absolute photoabsorption cross section of atomic potassium in VUV region. Home: 471 Via Vera Cruz Fremont CA 94539-5325 Office: Tokyo Electron Am Inc 2953 Bunker Hill Ln Santa Clara CA 95054 Home Phone: 810-490-8746. Personal E-mail: cylee9334@yahoo.com.

LEE, CHARLES, cytologist; PhD in Med. Svcs., U. Alberta, 1996. Cert. in clin. cytogenetics Am. Bd. Med. Genetics, 2002. Fellow in clin. cytogenetics Harvard Med. Sch., 1999—2001, asst. prof. pathology; NSERC rsch. fellow, dept. pathology Cambridge U., 1996—98; assoc. cytogeneticist Brigham and Women's Hosp.; asst. dir. Dana Farber/Harvard Cancer Ctr. Cytogenetics Core. Contbr. articles to profl. jour. Office: Brigham and Womens Hosp Dept Pathology 20 Shattuck St Thorn 628 Boston MA 02115

LEE, CHARLES SUNG CHULL, otolaryngologist; b. Korea, Mar. 29, 1963; MD, Washington U., St. Louis, 1989. Cert. in otolaryngology. Intern Loma Linda U., 1989, resident in otolaryngology, 1994; fellow in plastic surgery U. Miami Sch. Medicine, 1996, fellow in microsurgery, 1997; craniofacial surgery fellow Paik-Inje Hosp., Seoul, 1997.

LEE, CHAVA CHERTA, psychotherapist, consultant; arrived in Thailand, 1980, arrived in U.S., 1980; s. Khoua Pao Lee and True Thao; m. Chaeng Moua, Dec. 5, 1963; children: Linda, David L., Elvis, Yen, Tumuakong. AA, Fresno City Coll., 1986, ASc, 1987; BS, MS, Nat. U., 1992; postgrad., Family Therapy Tng. Inst., Milw., 1996—98; PhD, U. Devonshire, 2000. Cert. marriage and family therapist Wis. Psychotherapist Aurora Health Care, Milw., 2001—, Chava Counseling Practice, LLC, Milw., 1996—. Cons. Sebatian Family Psychology Practice, Milw. Mem.: Am. Mental Health Counselor Assn., Am. Assn. Marriage and Family Therapy.

LEE, CHEEGWAN, environmental engineer, consultant; b. Ulleong, Kyungpook, Republic of Korea, Aug. 23, 1967; s. Youngbaik Lee and Youngza Cho; m. Heejeong Son, Dec. 28, 1996; children: Daniel Seunghoon, Samuel Jihoon. PhD, U. Wis., 2002. Post doctoral rschr. NOAA Gt. Lakes Environ. Rsch. Lab U. Mich., Ann Arbor, Mich., 2002—04; rsch. scientist Pacific Northwest Nat. Lab., Battelle Meml. Inst., Seattle, 2004—. Contbr. articles to profl. jours. First lt. Korean Air Force Operation Command, 1991—94, Osan, South Korea. Recipient award, NRC, 2002. Achievements include research in sediment transport and hydrodynamic modeling. Avocations: travel, scuba diving. Office: Battelle Memorial Institute 1100 Dexter Ave North Suite 400 Seattle WA 98109 Home Phone: 425-486-3822; Office Phone: 206-528-3556. Office Fax: 206-528-3556; Home Fax: 206-528-3556. Personal E-mail: cheegwan@hotmail.com. Business E-Mail: cheegwan.lee@pnl.gov.

LEE, CHRISTOPHER, chef; b. Long Island, NY, 1976; Grad., Calif. Culinary Acad. Chef Fifth Floor, San Francisco, Daniel, NYC, Jean Georges, NYC; sous-chef Oceana, NYC, 2003; chef de cuisine Striped Bass, Philadelphia, 2004—06; exec. chef Gilt, NYC, 2006—. Named Best Chef 2005, Philadelphia Mag.; named one of NYC's Rising Stars, StarChefs.com, 2007; recipient Rising Star Chef of the Yr. award, James Beard Found., 2005, Best New Chef award, Food and Wine Mag., 2006. Achievements include receiving Four Bell review from the Philadelphia Inquirer. Office: Gilt 455 Madison Ave New York NY 10022 Office Phone: 212-891-8100.*

LEE, CLAUDIA S., retired elementary school educator; b. Yonkers, NY, May 29, 1944; d. Cornell and Corrine B. Lee. BA, Morgan State U., 1966; MS, CUNY, 1971, Manhattan Coll., 1983; postgrad., L.I. U., 1988. Cert. history tchr., spl. edn. tchr., adminstr., supr. NY. Spl. edn. tchr. Union Free Dist., Dobbs Ferry, NY, 1966—71, City Sch. Dist. New Rochelle, NY, 1971—2000; ret., 2000. Adj. instr. adults Westchester C.C. Edn. Opportunity Ctr., Yonkers, NY, 1970—2001; adj. instr. Manhattan Coll., Riverdale, NY, 1972, 75; ret.; mem. adv. bd. Ann. Multicultural Bus. Youth Embarkment, Danbury, Conn., 1983—2003. Mem. allocation com. United Way of Westchester, White Plains, NY; bd. dirs. YWCA of Yonkers, 2000—01. Recipient Sojourner Truth Meritorious Svc. award, Nat. Assn. Negro Bus. and Profl. Women, Inc., 2002, Dr. Martin Luther King Svc. award, Nepperhan Cmty. Ctr., Yonkers, 2004, Franore award, Franore Svc. Orgn., White Plains, 2004. Mem.: NAACP, Nat. Assn. Negro Bus. and Profl. Women, Westchester Alliance Black Sch. Educators, Nat. Coun. Negro Women (life), Wesley and Friends (treas. 1992—2004), Westchester County Club (life). Avocations: travel, decorating, reading, museums. Home: 1116 Warburton Ave Yonkers NY 10701

LEE, CLEMENT WILLIAM KHAN, trade association administrator; b. NYC, Feb. 7, 1938; s. William P. and Helen M. BTh, Concordia Coll., 1958; MDiv, Concordia Theol. Sem., 1962; MA, New Sch. for Social Research, 1976. Asst. exec. dir. Greater Detroit Luth. Ctr., 1962; editor Detroit and Suburban Luth. Newspaper, 1963; assoc. comm. dir. Met. Detroit Council of Chs., 1964; dir. media ops. Am. Bible Soc., NYC, 1967; dir. media relations Luth. Council U.S.A., NYC, 1971-82, asst. exec. dir. comm. and interpretation, 1977-82; dir. dept. telecomm. Luth. Ch. in Am., NYC, 1983-87; dir. electronic media Episcopal Ch., NYC, 1987-93, program dep. for comm., 1989-93, Episcopal telecomm. dir., 1993-97; dir. telecomm. Lambeth Conf. Bishops, 1998; dir. Ecusa Media Svc., NYC, 1997—2003; dir. telecomm. Anglican Communion Office, London, 2003—05, web publishing cons., 2005—. Media cons. Luth. Ch.-Mo. Synod, Spaulding for Children, Metro News of Metro NY, Synod of Luth. Ch. Am., archtl. newsletter Window, Luth. Deaconess Assn., Concordia Coll., Bronxville, Physicians for Social Responsibility, Wheatridge Found., Luth. Sch. Theology, Chgo.; chmn. broadcast ops. com. Nat. Council Chs. of Christ USA, 1976-80; vice chmn. bd. mgrs. Communications Commn., 1977-80; chmn. inter-faith Media Data System, 1981; mem. TV awards com. NY Council Chs.; mgr. Lutherans-in-Media Conf. I and II, 1980, Luth. Audio-Visual Conf., 1981; project dir. Lambeth Conf. Inter-Anglican Telecommunication Network, 1988; internat. computer network resource leader Religious Communications Congress 90, 1990; bd. dirs. FACTA TV News, Inc.; pres. NY chpt. Religious Pub. Rels. Coun.; telecommunication cons. World Coun. of Chs., Canberra Assembly, 1990-91, Episc. Bd. Theol. Edn., 1993—; priest assoc. Trinity St. Paul Episcopal Ch., 2002-; diocesan canon for comm., Episcoal Diocese LI, 2007-. Editor: Media Alert newsletter, 1980-86, Luth. Comm. newsletter, 1983-87, Episcopal Media Adv. newsletter, 1989—; creator children's TV series Storyline; producer multi-image sequences, Augustana Jubilee, 1980, multi-image program Proclaim, 1984, multi-image effects, Milw. Conv., 1986, (films) Mission on Six Continents, 1975, Room for a Stranger, 1978, Winter Wheat, 1982; exec. producer, One in Mission, 1985, Gathering of the Family, 1988, Doers of the Word, 1988, The Tully-Freeman Report, 1988, Outpourings of Love, 1989, Faith on a Tightrope, 1989, Fresh Winds Blowing, 1989, Prophecy Fulfilled in Me, 1990, President Carter Center Health Video, 1990, To Walk in Beauty, 1990, Pathways for Peace, 1990, Word in the World, 1991, Executive Council Presents, 1991, Cantenbury in North Carolina, 1992. Mem. Metro NY Synod Evangelical Luth. Ch. in Am. Comm. Commn., Religious Pub. Rels. Coun.; mem. communication dept. nat. adv. com. Evang. Luth. Ch. in Am.; chair Telecomm. Task Force Lambeth Anglican Bishops Confs., 1988, Bldg. Restoration com. St. John's Episc. Ch., NYC, 1993-95; gov. Inter-Anglican Info. Network Quest Internat. Mgmt. team convener, 1988-98; mem. bd. dir. Episcopal Social Svcs. NY, 2005-. Recipient award Detroit Press Club Found., 1963, silver medal Internat. Film and TV Festival, 1975, 79, Creative Excellence award U.S. Indsl. Film Festival, 1986, Brit. Telecomm. award, 1988, Polly Bond award, 1989, 90, 91, 92, N.Y. TV Festival finalist, 1990. Mem. Assn. Edn. Comm. Tech., Internat. Assn. Bus. Communicators, Internat. TV Assn., World Assn. Christian Comm. (chmn. N.Am. broadcast sect. 1975), Nat. Interfaith Cable Coalition VISN (members' com.), Satellite TV Network (bd. dirs.), Episcopal Cathedral Teleconferencing Network (steering com.), NY Athletic Club. Office: ACO Telecom 29 Gramatan Ct Bronxville NY 10708

LEE, CONRAD S., councilman; b. China; m. Winnie Lee; children: Christopher, Jennifer. BS in Engring., U. Mich., 1962; MBA, U. Wash., 1980. Various positions including engnr., mktg. sls. mgr. and energy analyst Boeing Co., 1962—78; project mgr. City of Seattle Solid Waste Utility, 1979—96; regional administrator US Small Bus. Administration, 2002—. Former pres. Am. Pacific Am. Municipal Officials; mem. Bellevue City Council, 1994—, Econ. Develop. Council of Seattle & King County, King County Solid Waste Adv. Com.

LEE, COREY, chef; b. Korea; Prep cook, dishwasher Blue Ribbon, NYC; chef Pied a Terre, London, Le Meridian, London, La Tante Claire, London, Lespinasse, NYC, DB, NYC; sous chef Per Se, NYC; chef de partie French Laundry, Yountville, Calif., 2000—02, sous chef, 2002, chef de cuisine, 2005—. Named one of Bay Area's Rising Star Chefs, San Francisco Chronicle Mag., 2006; recipient Rising Star Chef award, James Beard Found., 2006. Office: French Laundry 6640 Washington St Yountville CA 94599 Office Phone: 707-944-2380.*

LEE, DALE W., lawyer; b. Spokane, Wash., Sept. 16, 1948; AB in Am. Civilization, Brown U., 1970; JD, So. Meth. U., 1974. Bar: Hawaii 1974. Investigator, dep. prosecuting atty., felony prosecutor; ptnr. Kobayashi, Sugita & Goda, Honolulu. Arbitrator Ct. Annexed Arbitration Program, Hawaii; mem. hearing com., Office Disciplinary Counsel Supreme Ct. State Hawaii; pvt. arbitrator, mediator and discovery master; adj. prof. law William S. Richardson Sch. Law. Dir. Hawaii Justice Found., Vol. Legal Services of Hawaii; bd. adv. Korean Am. Found., Hawaii. Named one of Best Lawyers in Am. Mem.: ABA (bd. gov. 2006), Am. Judicature Soc., Korean Am. Bar Assn. Hawaii, Hawaii State Bar Assn. (treas. Young Lawyers sect. 1979—80, pres. 2004), Delta Theta Phi. Office: Kobayashi, Sugita & Goda 26th Floor 999 Bishop St Honolulu HI 96813 Office Phone: 808-539-8700. Office Fax: 808-539-8799. Business E-Mail: dwl@ksglaw.com.*

LEE, DAN M., retired state supreme court chief justice; b. Petal, Miss., Apr. 19, 1926; s. Buford Aaron and Pherbia Ann (Camp) L.; m. Peggy Jo Daniel, Nov. 27, 1947 (dec. 1952); 1 child, Sheron Lee Anderson; m. Mary Alice Gray, Sept. 30, 1956; 1 child, Dan Jr. Attended, U. So. Miss., 1946; LLB, Jackson Sch. Law, 1949; JD, Miss. Coll., 1970. Bar: Miss. 1948. Ptnr. Franklin & Lee, Jackson, Miss., 1948-54, Lee, Moore and Countiss, Jackson, Miss., 1954-71; county judge Hinds County, 1971-77; cir. judge Hinds-Yazoo Counties, 1977-82; assoc. justice Miss. Supreme Ct., Jackson, 1982-87, presiding justice, 1987-95, chief justice, 1995-98; ret., 1998; of counsel Dogan & Wilkinson, PLLC, Jackson, 1999. With U.S. Naval Aviation, 1944-46. Mem. ABA, Hinds County Bar Assn., Miss. State Bar Assn., Aircraft Owners and Pilots Assn., Am. Legion, VFW, Kiwanis Internat. Baptist. Office Phone: 601-351-3200. E-mail: judgeanddr@aol.com.

LEE, DANIEL, retired physician, public health service officer; b. Pinehurst, Ga., Apr. 28, 1918; s. Amos and Leila (Fowlkes) L.; m. Thelma Modestine, Dec. 26, 1944 (dec. Jan. 1986); children: Daniel Jr., Kenneth Amos, Sharon Diane. BA, Lincoln U., 1940; MD, Howard U., 1945. Diplomate Nat. Bd. Med. Examiners. Intern Harlem (N.Y.) Hosp., 1946; asst. prof. Coll. Hygiene Lincoln (Pa.) U., 1946-48; mem. med. staff Pottstown (Pa.) Meml. Hosp., 1948-55; mem. staff Coatesville (Pa.) and Brandywine Hosps., 1955—. Sch. physician Pine Forge Acad. Seventh Day Adventists; past mem. staff Atkinson Meml. Hosp.; sch. physician Coatesville Area Schs., 1965—; hon. mem. med. staff Brandywine Hosp., Caotesville, 1992—. Bd. dirs. Western Chester Coun., Ctr. and Western Chester County Indsl. Devel. Authority and Corp., United Cerebral Palsy Assn. Chester County; mem. Pa. State bd. dirs. United Cerebral Palsy Assn.; mem. adv. bd. Sr. Citizens Coatesville, Southeastern Pa. High Blood Pressure; trustee Second Bapt. Ch., Pottstown; mem. health and safety com. 15th Continental Dist. Boy Scouts Am.; past pres., founder Pottstown Civic League; past pres. Pottstown Com. on Human Rels.; former mem. aloocations com. United Way, Pottstown; past mem. Chester County Health Dept.; adv. bd. Chester County Boy Scouts Am., Senoir Citizens, Coatesville, Pa.; sustaining mem. Coatesville YMCA; corp. bd. dirs. Coatesville and So. Chester County YMCA, 1995—; past trustee Embreeville State Hosp.; past mem. Coatesville Day Care Com.; past bd. dirs. Brandywine Red Cross, Chester County Hosp. Authority; adv. bd. Vis. Nurses of Coatesville. Maj. U.S. Army, 1955-57. Recipient Man of Yr. award So. Chester County Bus. and profl. Women, Scott Jr. High Sch. award for Community Svc., 1992, Cert. of Appreciation Coatesville Jaycees for Concern of Mankind and the Nation, 1973, Cert. of Appreciation for Vol. Svcs. Pub. Welfare Com. Southeastern Region, 1973; named to Coatesville Hall of Fame, 1977, Legion of Honor, Chapel of Four Chaplains, 1968, Laura S. Greenwood scholarship fund, 1970, 73, Black Heritage award for Bricklayers Mt. Tabor AME Ch., Avondale Pa., 1992, Be A Hero award YMCA, 1992; Gundaker Fellow Rotary Club of Coatesville, 1992; honoree Zeta Phi Beta. Fellow Am. Acad. Family Physicians, Am. Geriatrics Soc.; mem. AMA, NAACP (life, past trustee), Pa. Med. Soc., Nat. Med. Assn., Chester County Med. Soc., Howard U. Med. Alumni Assn., Rotary (pres. Coatesville chpt. 1976-77, Paul Harris fellow 1978, Gundake fellow 1992), Western Chester County C. of C. (pres. 1978-79, Joe Filoromo Cmty. Svcs. award 1983, awards com. 1992), Pottstown C. of C., Elks (health dir., Mount Vernon lodge, supr. high blood pressure clinic and annual bloodmobile), Men of Malvern (St. Joseph;s retreat), Chester County Pan Hellenic Assembly (past pres.), Club XV (chaplain), Elks (Man of Yr. 1991, Diamond Ebony award 1991), Kappa Alpha Psi (Outstanding Alumni Brother award Epsilon chpt., honoree 75th yr. celebration). Republican. Avocations: fishing, hunting, writing. Home: 1289 Lone Eagle Rd Coatesville PA 19320-4766 Office: 723 Merchant St Coatesville PA 19320-3300

LEE, DAVID A.H., pharmaceutical executive; MD, PhD, U. of London. Specialized in internal medicine and gastroenterology before joining pharmaceutical industry; various positions from head global clinical devel. programs to v.p. R&D Solvay Duphar, Brussels, 1980—92; exec. v.p. R&D ConCensys, Irvine, Calif., 1992—97; sr. v.p. R&D and regulatory affairs Endo Pharmaceuticals, Chadds Ford, Pa., 1997—2004, exec. v.p. R&D, chief scientific officer, 2004—. Scientific advisory com. Abeille Pharmaceuticals, Inc. Mem.: Royal Coll. of Physicians of London. Office: Endo Pharmaceuticals 100 Endo Blvd Chadds Ford PA 19317*

LEE, DAVID AMES, lawyer; b. Syracuse, NY, Jan. 15, 1930; s. George and Alicia (Ames) L.; m. Brenda A. Amerman, Dec. 15, 1962; children: David, Geoffrey, Elizabeth. BA, Yale U., 1952; JD, Cornell U., 1957. Bar: NY 1957. Assoc. Hiscock & Barclay, Syracuse, 1957-62, ptnr., 1962—, chmn. real estate dept., 1972-94; atty. Syracuse Savs. Bank, 1968-87, trustee, 1968—87; dir. exec. com. Monroe Title Corp. Editor NY Real Property Svc., The Lawyers Co-op Pub. Co. Bd. dirs., exec. com. Elmcrest Children's Ctr., 1966—, pres. 1984—88; mem. Yale U. Alumni Bd., 1967-70; sec., v.p. Syracuse Symphony, 1969-75. Lt. (j.g.) USN, 1952-54; Korea. Child at Heart award Elmcrest Children's Ctr., 2005. Mem. NY State Savs. Bank Assn. (past chmn., legis. com.), ABA, NY State Bar Assn. (assoc. exec. com. real property law sect.), Onondaga County Bar Assn., Century Club (Syracuse). Home: 116 Cherry Hl Syracuse NY 13214-2304 Office Phone: 315-422-2131.

LEE, DAVID HEE-DON, trade association administrator, educator; b. Seoul, Republic of Korea, Mar. 28, 1959; arrived in US, 1985; s. Dong Pyo Lee and Boo Nam Han; m. Sun Song Yi, Dec. 18, 1956; children: Grace Eun-Hae, Jonathan Eun-June. BA in Spanish, Hankuk U. of Fgn. Studies, Seoul, 1978—82, MA in Internat. Rels., 1982—84; PhD, Madrid Nat. U., 1984—89; JD, Western State U., Sch. Law, Fullerton, Calif., 1991—92; studied, U. Calif., La Jolla, 1993—95. V.p. for regional devel. and edn. World Trade Ctrs. Assn., NYC, 1997—2002, vice chmn., 2002—. Sr. fellow, coord. Ctr. for U.S.-Mexican Studies, U. Calif. San Diego, La Jolla, 1995—97; disting. fellow Harris Manchester Coll., Oxford (Eng.) U., 1997—2002; pres., CEO World Trade Ctr. U., Palm Springs, Calif., 1998—; coun. mem. BTM Inst., NY, 2005—; mem. bd. regents U. Oxford, England, 2006—, founder fellow, 2006—. Author: Korea-Mexico Cooperation and its Role in the Pcific Economic Community, 1990, The Pacific Economic Cooperation and Strategy for Collective Security, 1997; co-author (with Van Whiting, Jr.): The Triangle and the Star: A New Approach to Comparative Regional Development, 2001; co-author: (with Mark Minevich, Frank-Jürgen Richter and Faisal Hoque) Six Billion Minds-Managing Outsourcing in the Global Knowledge Economy, 2006. Pres. Christopia Found., Washington, 2005; pres., CEO WTC Corps, Washington, 2000; chmn. bd. dirs. WTC Found., LA, 2001. Recipient Hon. Citizenship of Mex., Mexican Govt., 1992, Honor Plaque, Nat. Assembly of Republic of Korea, 1998. Mem.: AAUP (assoc.), Norway, Noble Performance Theater (World Bus. Forum), Oxford and Cambridge Club, Am. Polit. Sci. Assn. (assoc.). Republican. Evangelical. Achievements include development of online trade one-stop svc. in the fields financing, edn. and bus. tourism; World Trade Ctrs. in disputed countries such as North Korea; trade specialized IPTV/Cable networks worldwide; establishing and mng. pvt. equity funds for World Trade Ctr. devel. worldwide. Avocation: golf. Office: World Trade Ctrs Assn Ste 1901 60 E 42nd St New York NY 10165 also: Ste 700 1300 Pennsylvania Ave Washington DC 20004 Office Phone: 202-789-1998. Personal E-mail: dlee@wtcu.com. Business E-Mail: dlee@wtca.org.

LEE, DAVID INKOO, urologist; b. Wayne, Mich., Mar. 14, 1968; s. Jung Pil and Kyungja Irene Lee; m. Tessi Yunkyong Kwon; children: Alexandra, David. BA, U. Pa., 1990; MD, Loma Linda U., 1995. Resident in surgery Thomas Jefferson U. Hosp., Phila., 1995—97, resident in urology, 1997—2001; fellow minimally invasive urology Washington U. Sch. Medicine, St. Louis, 2001—02; clin. instr. Dept. Urology UCI Med. Ctr., Orange, Calif., 2002—; dir. robotic and laparoscopic surgery Urology Assocs. North Tex., 2003—05; chief urology Pa. Presbyn. Med. Ctr.; asst. prof. urology U. Pa. Sch. Medicine, 2005—. Author: (book) 5 Minute

Urology Consult, 2000; contbr. articles to profl. jours. Recipient Resident Achievement award, TAP Pharms., 1998, 2001, Resident's Night Competition First prize, Phila. Urol. Soc., 1999, Pfizer Scholars in Urology award, Pfizer, 2000—02; scholar, Am. Found. Urol. Disease, 2001. Mem.: Endourology Soc. (First Prize Essay Contest award 2003), Am. Urol. Assn. (Resident's Essay Contest Second prize Mid-Atlantic divsn. 1998), Alpha Omega Alpha. Republican. Seventh Day Adventist. Avocations: computers, golf. Home: 221 Trianon Ln Villanova PA 19085-1443 Office: Pa Presbyn Med Ctr 51 N 39th St Philadelphia PA 19104 Office Phone: 215-662-8699. Personal E-mail: Davidleegumd@yahoo.com.

LEE, DAVID MALLIN, physicist; b. Bklyn., Jan. 18, 1944; s. George Francis Lee and Winifred Rita (Jones) Wyatt; m. Judith Carol Silliman, Aug. 20, 1966; children: David, Timothy, Karen, Jeffrey, Rebecca. BS, Mannhattan Coll., 1966; PhD, U. Va., 1971. Vis. mem. staff Los Alamos (N.Mex) Nat. Lab., 1971-74, mem. staff, 1974-80, 81—; U.S. tech. expert IAEA, Vienna, Austria, 1980-81. Patentee in field. Mem. Am. Phys. Soc., AAAS, Sigma Xi. Democrat. Roman Catholic. Home: 48 Wildflower Way Santa Fe NM 87506-2116 E-mail: dLee@lanl.gov.

LEE, DAVID MORRIS, physics professor; b. Rye, NY, Jan. 20, 1931; s. Marvin and Annette (Franks) Lee; m. Dana Thorangkul, Sept. 7, 1960; children: Eric Bertel, James Marvin. AB, Harvard U., 1952; MS, U. Conn., 1955; PhD, Yale U., 1959. Instr. of physics Cornell U., Ithaca, NY, 1959—60, asst. prof. physics, 1960—63, assoc. prof. physics, 1963—69, prof. physics, 1969—99, James Gilbert White disting. prof. phys. scis., 1999—. Vis. scientist Brookhaven Nat. Lab., Upton, NY, 1966—67; vis. prof. U. Fla., Gainesville, 1974—75, Gainesville, 1994, U. Calif., San Diego, 1988, La Jolla, 88; vis. lectr. Peking U., Beijing, 1981; chair mcpl. Joseph Fourier U., Grenoble, France, 1994. Contbr. articles Phys. Rev. Letters, Phys. Rev., Physica and Nature. With US Army, 1952—54. Co-recipient Nobel prize for physics, 1996; recipient Sir Francis Simon Meml. prize, Brit. Inst. Physics, 1976, Wilber Cross medal, Yale U., 1998; fellow John Simon Guggenheim, Guggenheim Found., 1966—67, 1974—75, Japan Soc. Promotion of Scis., 1977. Fellow: AAAS, Am. Acad. Arts and Scis., Brit. Inst. Physics, Am. Phys. Soc. (Oliver Buckley prize 1981); mem.: Russian Acad. Sci. (fgn. mem.), Nat. Acad. Scis. Achievements include co-discovery of superfluid 3He, of the tricritical point of 3He-4He mixtures; co-observation of spin waves in spin polarized hydrogen gas. Office: Cornell U Physics Dept 610 Clark Hall Ithaca NY 14853-2501 E-mail: dml20@cornell.edu.

LEE, DAVID STODDART, retired investment company executive; b. Boston, Jan. 12, 1934; s. George Cabot and Kathleen Bowring (Stoddart) L.; m. Lucinda Hopkins, Apr. 29, 1972; children: Alexander Putnam, Madeline Jackson, Alice Ingalls. AB, Harvard U., 1956, MBA, 1960. V.p., dir. Lee Higginson Corp., NYC, 1960-65; mng. dir., Scudder, Stevens and Clark, Boston, 1965-97; ret., 1997. Trustee Cotting Sch., Boston, 1974—, New Eng. Med. Ctr., 1974; bd. dirs. Rogerson Cmtys., 1978—; corporator Mass. Gen. Hosp., 1975—. Lt. (j.g.) USN, 1956—58. Mem.: Soc. Chartered Fin. Analysts (chartered investment counsellor), Country Club, Somerset Club (Boston), The Boulders, Bald Peak Colony Club. Republican. Episcopalian. Office: Ten Post Office Sq Ste 600 Boston MA 02109 Office Phone: 617-426-6050.

LEE, DEBRA LOUISE, cable television company executive; b. Columbia, SC, Aug. 8, 1954; d. Richard M. and Delma L. Lee; children: Quinn Spencer, Ava. BA in Polit. Sci., Brown U., 1976; MPP, JD, Harvard U., 1980. Law clk. to Hon. Barrington Parker U.S. Dist. Ct. D.C., 1980—81; atty. Steptoe & Johnson, Washington, 1981—86; v.p., gen. counsel BET (Black Entertainment TV), 1986—92, exec. v.p. legal affairs dept., gen. counsel, 1992—96, corp. sec., pres., pub. pub. divsn., 1992—96; pres., COO BET Holdings, Inc., 1996—2005, pres., CEO, 2005—, chmn., 2006—. Bd. dirs. Revoln, Inc., 2005—, BET Holdings, Inc., Eastman Kodak Co., Marriott Internat., Wash. Gas & Light Co.; nat. bd. dirs. Nat. Cable & Telecom. Assn., Cable & Telecom. Assn. for Mktg., Alvin Ailey Dance Theater, Nat. Symphony Orch., Ctr. for Comm., Kennedy Ctr. Community & Friends Bd.; trustee Brown U. Bd. dirs. Kennedy Ctrs. Comty. Bd., Women in Cable, Nat. Symphony Orch. Bd. Named Woman of Yr., Women in Cable and Telecom., 2001; named one of Hundred Heavy Hitters, Cable Fax Mag., 100 Most Powerful Women in Washington, Washingtonian Mag., 50 Women to Watch, Wall St. Jour., 2006, 100 Most Powerful Women in Entertainment, Hollywood Reporter, 2006; recipient Eva A. Mooar award, Brown U., 1976, Nat. Achievement award, Area Chapter of the Nat. Alumnus Assn., 1992, Tower of Power Trumpet award, Turner Broadcasting Sys., 2000, Vanguard award, Nat. Cable & Telecom. Assn., 2003, Quasar award, Nat. Assn. Minorities in Communication, 2003, Silver Star award, Am. Women in Radio and TV, Par Excellence award, Dollars and $ense Mag., Wonder Woman award, Cablevision Mag. Office: BET Holdings Inc One BET Plaza 1235 W St NE Washington DC 20018-1211*

LEE, DENNIS PATRICK, lawyer, judge; b. Omaha, Feb. 12, 1955; s. Donald Warren and Betty Jean (O'Leary) L.; children: Patrick Michael, Katherine Marie, Megan Elizabeth. BA, Creighton U., 1977, JD, 1980. Bar: Nebr. 1980, U.S. Dist. Ct. Nebr. 1980, U.S. Ct. Appeals (8th cir.) 1980, Iowa 1990. Assoc. Thompson Crounse & Pieper, Omaha, 1980-84; ptnr. Lee Law Offices, Omaha, 1984-87, Silverman, Lee & Crounse Law Offices, 1987-94, Lee & Jones Law Offices, P.C., L.L.O., 1994—2003; pvt. practice Lee Law Offices, PC, LLO, 2003—. Atty. Nebr. State Racing Commn., Lincoln, 1984-87, commr. 1988—, chmn., 1991—; adminstrv. law judge, State of Nebr., 1985-87; lectr. Creighton U., Omaha, 1982-85. Author: Law of Conservatorships, 1981: Legal Aspects of Equine Veterinary Practice, 1984, Planning Opportunities with Living Trusts in Nebraska, 1995; others. Trustee Holy Name Cath. Ch., Omaha, 1980-84; chmn. nat. enforcement officers com. Nat. Assn. State Racing Commrs., Lexington, Ky., 1984-87; commr. Nebr. State Racing Commn., 1988—. Mem. ABA, Nat. Assn. Trial Attys., Comml. Law League Am., Nebr. State Racing Commn. (chmn. 1991), Assn. Racing Commrs. Internat. (treas. 1996-97, v.p. 1997-2000, chmn. and CEO 2000——), Nebr. Bar Assn, Omaha Bar Assn. (chmn. conservatorship com. 1981—), Nebr.-Iowa Referees Assn. (v.p. 1981-88), Omaha C. of C. (Outstanding Young Omahan 1993). Home: 608 S 123d St Omaha NE 68154-1944 Office Phone: 402-334-8055. Business E-Mail: denny@leelawoffice.com.

LEE, DERREK LEON, professional baseball player; b. Sacramento, Sept. 6, 1975; m. Christina Lee, 2001. Draft pick San Diego Padres, 1993, first baseman, 1997, Fla. Marlins, 1997—2004, Chgo. Cubs, 2004—. Mem. US Team World Baseball Classic, 2006. Supporter Cornerstones for Kids programs including Youth Baseball Clinics, World of Baseball; co-chmn. Cornerstones for Kids programs. Named to Nat. League All-Star Team, Maj. League Baseball, 2005, 2007; recipient Gold Glove award, 2003, 2005, Silver Slugger award, 2005. Achievements include winning the Nat. League batting title (.335 average), 2005; led the Nat. League in hits (199), 2005, and doubles (50), 2005. Office: Chicago Cubs 1660 W Addison Chicago IL 60613-4397*

LEE, DON YOON, publishing executive, academic administrator, writer; b. Seoul, Korea, Apr. 7, 1936; came to U.S., 1957; s. Yoo-ehn and Ch'i-ho (Kim) L. BA, U. Wash., 1963; MA, St. John's U., Jamaica, NY, 1967; MS, Georgetown U., 1971; MA, Ind. U., 1975-90; PhD, World Info. Distributed U., 2003. Founder, pub. Eastern Press, Inc., Bloomington, Ind., 1981—. Author: History of Early Relation Between China and Tibet, 1981, An Introduction to East Asian and Tibetan Linguistics and Culture, 1981, Learning Standard Arabic, 1988, An Annotated Bibliography of Selected Works on China, 1981, Light Literature and Philosophy of East Asia, 1982, An Annotated Bibliography on Inner Asia, 1983, An Annotated Archaeological Bibliography of Selected Works on Norther and Central Asia, 1983, Traditional Chinese Thoughts: The Four Schools, 1990, others. Office: Eastern Press Inc PO Box 881 Bloomington IN 47402-0881 E-mail: dongyoonlee2002@yahoo.com.

LEE, DONALD HAN, surgeon, orthopedist; b. Huntington, W.Va., Oct. 28, 1955; s. Kwan Ho and Kay Hee Lee; m. Dawn Thomas Thomas, May 13, 1989; children: David Thomas, Dana Elizabeth, Diane Louise, Daniel Thomas, Dustin Thomas. BS, Georgetown U., 1977; MD, W.Va. Sch. Medicine, 1982. Diplomate Nat. Bd. Med. Examiners, 1983, Am. Bd. Orthop. Surgeons, 1991. Intern surgery W. Va. U. Sch. Medicine, 1982—83, George Washington U. Sch. Medicine, 1983—84, resident orthop. surgery, 1984—88; Hand fellowship Columbia Presbyn. Med. Ctr., 1988—89; assoc. prof. orthop. surgery U. Ala., Birmingham, 1989—2005; prof. orthop. surgery Vanderbilt U., Nashville, 2005—, dir. hand fellowship, 2005—. Dir. hand fellowship U. Ala., Birmingham, 1993—2005; dir. hand and upper extremity fellowship Vanderbilt U., Nashville, 2005—; bd. examiner Am. Bd. Orthop. Surgery; joint com. surgery of hand Am. Bd. Orthop. Surgeons; reviewer Jour. Bone and Joint Surgery, Clinical Orthopedics and Related Rsch., Jour. Shoulder and Elbow Surgery. Pres. parish coun., 2000—01. Rsch. grantee, Merck and Co., Biomet, Inc. Mem.: Am. Soc. Reconstructive Microsurgery, Am. Soc. Surgery of Hand, Am. Acad. Orthop. Surgeons, Assn. Bone and Joint Surgeons, Am. Orthop. Assn. Office: Vanderbilt Orthop Inst Med Ctr East South Tower Ste 3200 Nashville TN 37232-8829 Office Phone: 615-322-4683. E-mail: donald.h.lee@vanderbilt.edu.

LEE, DONALD YOUNG (DON LEE), publishing executive; b. Tokyo, Dec. 11, 1959; s. Victor Young and Jean Ann (Kim) L. BA in English, UCLA, 0982; MFA in Creative Writing, Emerson Coll., 1986. Writing instr. Emerson Coll., Boston, 1985-89; mng. editor Ploughshares, Boston, 1988-92, dir., 1992—. Cons. AGNI, Boston, 1993, Asian Pacific Am. Jour., 1994, New Eng. Rev., 1995, Columbia, 1998, Ga. Rev., 1999, CLMP, 1999, Salamander, 1999, Lannan Found., 2000. Author: Yellow: Stories, 2001, Country of Origin, 2004; contbr. short stories, articles to jours. Recipient Sue Kaufman prize for 1st fiction, 2002, Am. Book award, 2005, Edgar award for best first novel, 2005; fellow, St. Botolph Club Found., 1990, 1991; Mass. Cultural Coun. Fiction fellow, 1998. Mem.: PEN. Democrat. Office: Ploughshares Emerson Coll 120 Boylston St Boston MA 02116-4624

LEE, DONG HWAN, business administration educator; b. Seoul, Nov. 8, 1952; s. Hee Kwon and Yong Boon (Kim) L.; m. Young Ja Lee, Apr. 16, 1981; 2 children; Hyon Jae and Joan. B of Agr. summa cum laude, Kon-Kuk U., 1977; MBA, Okla. State U., 1984; PhD in Bus., Ind. U., 1989. Cert. internat. trade specialist, Ministry of Commerce and Industry/Seoul; cert. tchr. Ministry of Edn., Seoul. Sr. staff mem. overseas bus. Divsn. Gold Star Telecomm. Co., Inc., Seoul, 1976—80; advisor to comml. counsellor Brit. Embassy in Seoul, 1980—82; lectr. mktg. Sch. of Bus. Ind. U., Bloomington, 1989—90; asst. prof. mktg. SUNY, Albany, 1990—97; assoc. prof. mktg. Manhattan Coll., NYC, 1997—. Mem. editl. rev. bd. Jour. Bus. Rsch., 1997—, Jour. Consumer Satisfaction, Dissatisfaction and Complaining Behavior, 1997—. Elder Stony Point Presbyn. Ch. Recipient Faculty Rsch. awards SUNY, Albany, 1990, 92, 94, 95; Faculty Devel. award, N.Y. State/United U. Profls., 1991, 93, 94; rsch. grantee Manhattan Coll., 1999, 2003; Garbriel Hauge Faculty fellow Manhattan Coll., 1999-2000. Mem. Am. Mktg. Assn. (Outstanding Doctoral Dissertation award 1990), Acad. Mktg. Sci., Assn. Consumer Rsch., Soc. Consumer Psychology, Beta Gamma Sigma. Presbyterian. Home: 9 Old Clave Ct Congers NY 10920-1101 Office: Manhattan College Sch of Business DLS 517 Bronx NY 10471 Office Phone: 718-862-7195. Business E-Mail: dongh.lee@manhattan.edu.

LEE, DONGHYUNG, psychologist; b. Hongsung, Republic of Korea, Apr. 5, 1972; arrived in US, 1997; s. Sangsoon and Kibun Lee; m. Kyunghee Shin, Jan. 2, 1999; children: Jedidiah Jaywoo, Joyanne Jungin. BA in Psychology, Chungnam Nat. U., Republic of Korea, 1994; PhD, Tex. A&M U., Coll. Sta., 2004. Lic. sch. psychologist Tex. State Bd. Examiners Psychologists, 2004. Rschr. Korean Inst. Stress and Stress Mgmt. Ctr., Taegu, 1996—97; grad. rsch. asst. Tex. A&M U., 1999—2003; intern psychology Houston Ind. Sch. Dist., 2003—04, spl. edn. psychologist, 2004—. Contbr. chapters to books, articles. Lay pastor Vision Mission Ch., 2001—03; ho. ch. leader Seoul Bapt. Ch. Houston, 2004—. Recipient Sch. Psychology Rsch. Excellence award, Dept. Ednl. Psychology, Tex. A&M U., 2003, Outstanding Dissertation of Yr. award, Coll. Edn., Tex. A&M U., 2004; scholar, Tex. A&M U., 1998, Chungnam Nat. U., Republic of Korea, 1989, 1990, 1992, 1993, 1994, 1995, 1997, Dept. Ednl. Psychology, Tex. A&M U., 2003. Mem.: NASP (Outstanding Student Poster award Tex. chpt. 2001). Office: HISD Office Spl Edn Svc 4400 West 18th St Houston TX 77092-8501 Office Phone: 713-556-7025. Business E-Mail: donhlee@hotmail.com.

LEE, DONNA JEAN, retired nurse; b. Huntington Park, Calif., Nov. 12, 1931; d. Louis Frederick and Lena Adelaide (Hinson) Munyon; m. Frank Bernard Lee, July 16, 1949 (dec. Jan. 2006); children: Frank (dec.), Robert, John. AA in Nursing, Fullerton Jr. Coll., Calif., 1966; student, U. Calif., Irvine, 1966—74, U. N.Mex., 1982. RN, Calif.; cert. Intraventous Therapy Assn. U.S.A. Staff nurse Orange (Calif.) County Med. Ctr., 1966-71, staff and charge nurse relief ICU, CCU, Burn Unit, ER, Communicable Disease, Neo-Natal Care Unit, 1969-71, charge nurse communicable disease unit, 1969-70; staff and charge nurse ICU, emergency rm., CCU, med./surg. units Anaheim (Calif.) Meml. Hosp., 1971-74; charge and staff nurse, relief Staff Builders, Orange, 1974-82; agy. nurse Nursing Svcs. Internat., 1978-89; asst. DON Chapman Convalescent SNF, Orange, 1982; geriat. and pediat. nurse VNASS, 1985-93; hospice/respite nurse VIA Upjohn Home Healthcare Svcs and VNA Support Svcs. of Orange, 1985-93; ret. Staff relief nurse ICU/CCU various hosps. and labs, including plasmapheresis nurse Med. Lab. of Orange, 1978. Life mem. in honor of spouse Republican Presdl. Task Force, 1982—, Nat. Rep. Senatorial Com., Nat. Rep. Com. Ocean Conservancy, Natl. Park Trust, Wildlife Land Trust, Rep. Nat. Com., Nat. Rep. Congl. Com., Ronald Reagan Presdl. Libr. Found., Young Americas Found. Named 25th Anniversary honoree, Calif. Rep. Presdl. Task Force, 2006. Mem. AACN, Harvard Med. Sch. Nurses, Am. Lung Assn., Am. Heart Assn., Arthritis Found., Life Extension Found., Sierra Club (life), Audubon Soc. (life), Environ. Def. Fund (life), Defenders of Wildlife (life), World Wildlife Found. Baptist. Home: 924 S Hampstead St Anaheim CA 92802-1740

LEE, DOUGLAS A., musicologist; b. Carmel, Ind., Nov. 3, 1932; s. Ralph Henley and Flossie Ellen (Chandler) Lee; m. Beverly Ruth Haskell, Sept. 2, 1961. MusB with High Distinction, DePauw U., 1954; MusM, U. Mich., 1958, PhD, 1968; postgrad., U. Md., 1985. Instr. Nat. Mus. Camp, Interlochen, Mich., 1959-62, Mt. Union Coll., Alliance, Ohio, 1959-61, chmn. keyboard instrn., 1959-61; asst. prof. music Wichita (Kans.) State U., 1964-68, assoc. prof., 1968-74, coord. Music History and Lit., 1968-71, coord. grad. studies in Music, 1969-70, chmn. dept. Musicology, 1971-74, prof. Music, 1974-86, administrv. intern, v.p. bus. affairs, 1983, spl. events coord., 1974—85; prof. musicology Vanderbilt U., Nashville, 1986—, chmn. music history and lit., advisor, 1987—98, 1998. Radio commentator Sta. KMUW-FM, 1969-76; judge various competitions, Mu Phi Epsilon, 1980, Kans. Music Tchrs. Assn., 1975-83, Baldwin Found. awards, 1979, 80; program annotator Nashville Symphony Orch., 1988-2001; cons. U.S. Dept. Edn. Jacob Javits fellowship program, 1988, 89, United Meth. Publishing Ho., 1988, Mayfield Pub. Co., 1990, Prentice-Hall, Inc., 1993, 97. Author: The Instrumental Works of Christoph Nichelmann: The Thematic Index, 1971, Franz Benda: A Thematic Catalogue of His Works, 1984, Franz Benda: A Musician at Court, 1998, Masterworks of 20th-Century Music, 2002; editor: Christoph Nichelmann: Clavier Concertos in E Major and A Minor, 1977, Six Sonatas for Violin and Bass by Franz Benda, with Embellishments, 1981, The Sonneck Soc. Bull., 1988-90; contbg. editor: Carl Phillip Emanuel Bach: Collected Works, 2003—; contbr. articles to The New Grove Dictionary of Music and Musicians, 1980, The New Grove Dictionary of Music in the United States, 1986, America in the Fifties, 2004; contbr. articles to profl. jours., chpts. to books. With U.S. Army, 1955-57, Japan. Rector Scholar Found., 1950-54; Rackham fellow U. Mich., 1961-63, fellow NEH, 1980, 85, Am. Philos. Soc., 1980, Kans. Arts Coun., 1985, Tenn. Arts Coun., 1988, 89, Packard Humanities Inst., Cambridge, Mass., 2002, 04 Mem. Am. Musicological Soc. (program chmn. Midwest chpt. 1984, South-Ctrl. chpt. 1989, nat. coun. 1986, pres. South-Ctrl. chpt. 1990-91), Music Tchrs. Nat. Assn. (editor 1971-90), Am. Soc. Eighteenth Century Studies, Coll. Music Soc., Soc. for Am. Music (program coord. 1987-88). Roman Catholic. Avocation: photography. Office: 6517 Cornwall Dr Nashville TN 37205-3041 Business E-Mail: douglas.lee@vanderbilt.edu.

LEE, EARL WAYNE, library science educator; b. Rockford, Ill., Nov. 8, 1954; s. Earl Ray and Opal (Sharp) L.; m. Kathleen R. DeGrave, Mar. 10, 1978; children: Nathan, Cambria, Erin. BA, Lyon Coll., 1975; MA, U. Ark., Fayetteville, 1978, U. Wis., 1985. Instr. English No. Ill. U., DeKalb, 1979-80; lectr. English U. Wis., Green Bay, 1983-84; info. specialist Dept. of Transp., Madison, Wis., 1985-86; libr. Phillips U., Enid, Okla., 1986-87, Pittsburg (Kans.) State U., 1987—. Author: Drakulya, 1994, Libraries in the Age of Mediocrity, 1998, Drakulya: The Vampire Play, 2001; contbr. articles to profl. jours. Shrenk scholar U. Wis., 1985, McCain scholar Lyon Coll. Mem. ALA, Kans. Libr. Assn. Unitarian Universalist. Office: Axe Bldg Pittsburg State U Pittsburg KS 66762

LEE, EDMOND, internist, cardiologist; b. Oakland, Calif., 1954; Intern U. Calif. Davis Med. Ctr., Sacramento, 1981-82, resident internal medicine, 1982-85; fellow cardiology Wadsworth VA Hosp., LA, 1985-87; fellow echocardiography U. Calif. San Francisco Moffit Hosp., 1987-88; internist, cardiologist No. Calif. Cardiology Assocs., Sacramento. Mem. ACP, Am. Coll. Cardiology, Am. Heart Assn. Office: No Calif Cardiology Assocs 5301 F St Ste 117 Sacramento CA 95819-3220 also: Divsn Cardiology Sutter Meml Hosp 5271 F St Sacramento CA 95814 Office Phone: 916-733-1788.*

LEE, EDWARD, lawyer; b. Phila., Oct. 29, 1965; s. Y. and M. Lee; m. C. Lee, May 23, 2004; 1 child, Ethan Y. BA, Cornell U., Ithaca, NY, 1989; JD, Fordham U., NYC, 1996. Bar: D.C. 2001. Spl. counsel judge adv. gen. USAR, Washington, 2003—. Office: Ste 550 1920 L St Washington DC 20036

LEE, ELLA LOUISE, librarian, educator; b. Pitts., Aug. 15, 1929; d. Louis C. and Ida Lily (Ward) Lee; 1 child, Lily I. Lee-Braithwaite. BA in French Lang., History & Culture, San Francisco Coll. for Women, 1971; MA in History, U. San Francisco Jesuit U., 1978; MLS, San Jose State U., 1993. Cert. tchg. K-12 Calif., tchg. 13-14 Calif. Clk. U.S. Fgn. Svc., Japan, Denmark, Germany, Paris, 1951—61; adult ednl. profl. UN - UNESCO, Paris, 1961—67; tchr. French and history San Francisco Unified Sch., 1972—80; instr. San Francisco C.C., 1994—96; assoc. libr. Richmond Calif. Pub. Libr., 1997—99, U. San Francisco Jesuit U., 2000—05. Mem.: Commonwealth Club (San Francisco). Home and Office: 415 MacArthur Blvd #3 Oakland CA 94610 Office Phone: 510-832-8267. Personal E-mail: ella.lee@sbcglobal.net.

LEE, ERIC MCCAULEY, museum director, art historian; b. Clinton, NC, Feb. 23, 1966; s. Harry McCauley and Mary Thompson Lee; m. Rima Canaan, June 12, 1994; children: Edward Marshall, Graham William. BA, Yale U., 1988, MA, 1991, PhD, 1997. Rsch. asst. U.S. Senate Select Com. on Intelligence, Washington, 1989—90; acting asst. curator paintings Yale Ctr. for Brit. Art, New Haven, 1995—96; acting dir. Fred Jones Jr. Mus. Art, U. Okla., Norman, 1997—98, Wylodean and Bill Saxon dir., 1998—2006; dir. Taft Mus. Art, Cin., 2006—. Co-author: (book) The Fred Jones Jr. Museum of Art at the University of Oklahoma: Selected Works; author: (exhibition catalogue) Translations: Turner and Printmaking. A. Bartlett Giamatti fellow, Yale U., 1990—91, Theodore Rousseau fellow, Met. Mus. of Art, N.Y., 1994. Mem.: Coll. Art Assn., Accreditation Vis. Com., Am. Assn. Mus. Office: Taft Mus Art 316 Pike St Cincinnati OH 45202 Business E-Mail: elee@taftmuseum.org.

LEE, EUGENE, theatrical set designer; b. Beloit, Wis., Mar. 9, 1939; m. Franne Newman; m. Brooke Lee. BFA, Art Inst. Chgo., Carnegie-Mellon U.; MFA, Yale Drama Sch.; PhD (hon.), DePaul U., RI Coll. Resident designer Trinity Repertory Co., Providence, 1967—; adj. prof. Brown U., RI. Scenic design (Broadway plays) Wilson in the Promised Land, 1970, Dude, 1972, Candide, 1974 (Drama Desk award outstanding set design, 1974, Tony award best scenic design, 1974), The Skin of Our Teeth, 1975, Some of My Best Friends, 1977, Sweeney Todd, 1979 (Tony award best scenic design, 1979), Gilda Radner - Live From NY, 1979, Merrily We Roll Along, 1981, The Hothouse, 1982, Show Boat, 1994 (Drama Desk award outstanding set design, 1995), On the Waterfront, 1995, Ragtime, 1998, Colin Quinn - An Irish Wake, 1998, A Moon for the Misbegotten, 2000, Seussical, 2000, Wicked, 2003 (Drama Desk award outstanding set design of musical, 2004, Tony award best scenic design, 2004), The Pirate Queen, 2007, (plays) End Game, 1965, Slave Ship, 1969, Alice in Wonderland, The Normal Heart, Agnes of God, 1982, Grandchild of Kings, Uncle Vanya, Son of Man and the Family, 1970, The Ballad of Soapy Smith, 1983, The Ruby Sunrise, 2005 (Lucille Lortel award outstanding scenic design, 2006), (films) Easy Money, 1983, Hammett, 1982, Mr. North, 1988, Vanya on 42nd Street, 1994, Bounce, Kennedy Ctr., Washington, DC, prodn. designer Saturday Night Live, 1974—. Named to Theatre Hall of Fame, 2007. Office: Trinity Repertory Co 201 Washington St Providence RI 02903*

LEE, E(UGENE) STANLEY, engineering educator; b. Hopeh, China, Sept. 7, 1930; arrived in US, 1955; s. Ing Yah and Lindy (Hsieng) L.; m. Mayanne Lee, Dec. 21, 1957 (dec. June 1980); children: Linda J., Margaret H.; m. Yuan Lee, Mar. 8, 1983; children— Lynn Hua Lee, Jin Hua Lee, Ming Hua Lee. BS, Chung Cheng Inst. Tech., Taiwan, Republic of China, 1953; MS, N.C. State U., 1957; PhDChemE, Princeton U., 1962. Rsch. engr. Phillips Petroleum Co., Bartlesville, Okla., 1960-66; asst. prof. chem. engring. Kans. State U., Manhattan, 1966-67, assoc. prof. indsl. engring., 1967-69, prof. indsl. engring., 1969—; prof. chem. and elec. engring. U. So. Calif., 1972-76. Hon. prof. Chinese Acad. Sci., 1987—; chaired prof. Yuan-ze Inst. Tech., Taiwan, Republic of China, 1993—; cons. govt. and industry. Author: Quasilinearization and Invariant Imbedding, 1968, Coal Conversion Technnology, 1979, Operations Research, 1981, Fuzzy and Evidence Reasoning, 1996, Fuzzy and Multi-level Decision Making, 2000; editor: Energy Sci. and Tech., 1975; assoc. editor: Jour. Math. Analysis and Applications, 1974—, Computers and Mathematics with Applications, 1974—; mem. editl. bd. Jour. Engring. Chemistry and Metallurgy, 1989—, Jour. of Nonlinear Differential Equations, 1992—, Jour. Chinese Fuzzy Sys. Assn., 1995—, Internat. Jour. Applied Fuzzy Sets Theory, 1995—, Fuzzy Optimization and Decision Making, 2000—, Internat. Jour. Modeling and Optimization, 2001—, Internat. Jour. Ops. Rsch., 2005, Jour. Uncertain Sys., 2006—; contbr. articles to profl. jours. Grantee Dept. Def., 1967-72, Office Water Resources, 1968-75, EPA, 1969-71, NSF, 1971—, USDA, 1978-90, Dept. Energy, 1979-84, USAF, 1984-88. Mem. Soc. Indsl. and Applied Math., Ops. Rsch. Soc. Am., N. Am. Fuzzy Info. Processing Soc., Internat. Neural Network Soc., Sigma Xi, Tau Beta Pi, Phi

Kappa Phi. Office: Kans State U Dept Indsl Engring Manhattan KS 66506 Business E-Mail: eslee@ksu.edu. *Nothing can replace hard work and persistence.*

LEE, EUNICE, music educator; b. Yong San, Seoul, Republic of Korea, Mar. 16, 1967; d. Jung In and Byung Joo Lee; m. Steve Rhee, July 5, 2000. MusB, San Francisco Conservatory of Music, 1991; MusM, U. So. Calif., 2000; grad., Am. Coll. Musicians, Calif., 2005. Accompanist San Jose Korean Bapt., San Jose, 1985—92; keyboard collaborator various univs., LA, San Francisco, NY, Aspen, Ohio, 1987—2000; accompanist Foothill Coll., Palo Alto, Calif., 1988—89; dir. San Jose Piano Studio, Santa Clara, Calif., 1991—95; condr. Ch. of Love, San Jose, Calif., 1993—94; faculty De Anza Coll., Cupertino, Calif., 1993—94; tchg. asst. U. So. Calif., LA, 1995—2000, Aspen Summer Music Festival, Colo., 1998—98; accompanist Santa Monica First Christian Ch., Santa Monica, Calif., 1999—2002; pvt. piano tchr. Bakersfield, Calif., 2004—. Adjudicator Nat. Guild Piano Audition, Am. Christian Sch. Instn. Piano Festival, 2004—05. Music dir., organist, LA, 1994—2002. Recipient Grand prize, Concerto Competitions, 1989, Leo Poldofsky award, 1996—99, Keyboard Ensemble, 1996-2000; scholar, San Francisco Conservatory of Music, 1986—91, U. of So. Calif., 1995—2000. Mem.: Nat. Guild Piano Tchrs. (assoc.), Music Tchrs. Assn. Calif. (assoc.; first v.p. 2004—). Mem. Citizens Party. Avocations: breeder, cooking, interior decorating. Home Phone: 661-654-0398; Office Phone: 661-205-9300. Home Fax: 661-654-0398. Personal E-mail: e.rhee04@yahoo.com.

LEE, FRANCES HELEN, editor; d. Murray and Rose (Rothman) Lee. BA, Queens Coll., 1957; MA, NYU, 1962. Editl. asst. Christian Herald Family Bookshelf, NYC, 1957-62; with Gordon and Breach Sci. Pubs., Inc., NYC, 1964-66, Am. Electric Power Svc. Corp. AEP Operating Ideas, NYC, 1966-69, Indsl. Water Engring. Mag., NYC, 1969-71; directory editor photographic divsn. United Bus. Publs., NYC, 1971-80; editor Am. Druggist Blue Book Hearst Books/Bus. Publs. Group, 1980-81; spl. projects coord. motor manuals Hearst Book Divsn., 1981-82; editor New Price Report, 1982-84, Am. Druggist Blue Book, 1982-88; freelance editor, cons., 1988—. Supr. Bronx divsn. NY State Civil Defense, 1953-59; com. on NYC charter revision Citizens Union, 1975, com. on city mgmt., 1977-92, bd. dirs., co-chmn. com. on NYC cultural concerns, 1979-97, chmn., 1997-98; vol. NYC Opera, 1988—, info. project mgr., 2001—. Recipient cert. of honor NYU Alumni Fedn., 1985, Meritorious Svc. award, 1986. Mem. N.Y. Bus. Press Editors (bd. dirs. 1988-90, sec. 1990-91), Women's Equity Action League (chmn. rsch. com.), NYU Alumnae Club (dir. 1976-78, rec. sec. 1978-80, v.p. 1980-82, pres. 1982-84, rep. to bd. dirs. fedn. 1984-86), NYU Alumni Fedn. (dir. emerita 2007—), Villa-Lobos Music Soc. (sec. 1989-91, treas. 1992-95), NYU Club (bd. govs. 1987-89). Republican. Jewish. Home: 170 2nd Ave New York NY 10003-5754 Personal E-mail: franceslee397@hotmail.com.

LEE, FRED C., electrical engineering educator; b. China, 1946; naturalized Am. citizen; BS, Nat. Cheng Kung U., Taiwan, 1968; MSA, Duke U., 1972, PhD, 1974. Tchg. asst. Duke U., Durham, NC, 1970-72; rsch. asst. Spacecraft Sys. Rsch. Lab., 1972-74; mem. tech. staff TRW Systems, 1974-77; from asst. prof. to prof. Va. Poly. Inst. and State U., Blacksburg, 1977-83, James S. Tucker prof., 1986-94, Lewis A. Hester engring. chair, 1994-99, univ. disting. prof., 1999—, dir. Va. Power Electronics Ctr., 1985-98; bd. dirs. Zytec, 1986-97; dir. NSFERC Ctr. for Power Electronics Sys., 1998—. Bd. dirs. Artesyn Techs., 1997—2004, Delta Electronics, 2003-, Delta Environ. and Ednl. Found., 2002-; mem. adv. bd. Power Integrations Inc., 1988-94; chmn., CEO Va. Power Techs., Inc., 1994—, Primarion Inc., 2004-. Recipient PCIM award for Outstanding Power Electronics Edn., 1990, Arthur Fury award for Outstanding Powere Electronics Innovation, 1998, IEEE Millennium medal, 2000, Ernst Blickle award for Sci. Achievement, SEW Eurodkive Found. 2005. Fellow IEEE William E. Newell Power Electronics award 1989, IEEE Power Electronics Soc. (chmn. meeting com., mem. advt. com., mem. fellow evaluation com., chmn. power electronics specialists conf. 1987, v.p. 1988, pres. 1993-94), IEEE Engrs. Indsl. Applications Soc., Brit. Inst. Engrs. Office: NSFERC Ctr for Power Electronics Sys 655 Whitemore Blacksburg VA 24061-0111 Business E-Mail: fclee@vt.edu.

LEE, GAVIN, actor, choreographer; b. Woodbridge, Suffolk, Eng., Oct. 15, 1971; m. Emily Harvey. Choreographer (plays) Cabaret, The Wonderful West End, 1990, Du Barry Was a Lady, 2001, Horse and Carriage, 2001, Into the Woods, 2001; choreographer and dir. (plays) Smile, Snoopy, choreographer and actor Crazy for You, 1997, Jubilee!, Whenever, 2000; actor: (plays) Government Inspector, Half a Sixpence, Immaculate Deception, Sondheim's Saturday Night, Snoopy, 1982, Bugsy Malone, 1983, Me and My Girl, Saturday Night, 1998, Oklahoma!, 1998, Singin' in the Rain, Of Thee I Sing, A Saint She Ain't, 1999, Peggy Sue Got Married, 2001, Let's Kick Arts, Masterpieces, Contact, Over My Shoulder, Mary Poppins, 2004 (Drama Desk award outstanding featured actor in a musical, 2007, Theatre World award Outstanding Broadway Debut, 2007); (Broadway plays), 2006; (films) Beyond the Sea, 2004, The Phantom of the Opera, 2004.*

LEE, GEORGE TERRY, JR., lawyer; b. Dallas, Oct. 28, 1935; s. George Terry and Isabel (Breckenridge) T.; m. Natalie Blythe Henderson, Aug. 17, 1957; children: George Terry III, Blythe, Rebecca, Hamilton. BA, Yale U., 1957; LLB, Stanford U., 1960. Assoc. Goldberg, Fonville, Gump & Strauss, Dallas, 1960-65; gen. counsel George A. Fuller Co. and OKC Corp., Dallas, 1965-73; ptnr. Akin, Gump, Strauss, Hauer & Feld, LLP, Dallas, 1973—, hiring ptnr., 1983—88, 1993—95, mem. Dallas office & firmwide mgmt. coms., 1982—95. Trustee Found. for Arts, Dallas, 1963—, St. Mark's Sch. of Tex., Dallas, 1966-72; bd. dirs. Dallas Mus. Fine Arts; pres. Brit.-Am. Commerce Assn., Dallas, 1986. Fellow (life) Tex. Bar Found.; mem. ABA, University Club (NYC)., Brook Hollow Golf Club (Dallas), Koon Kreek Klub (Athens, Tex.), Crescent Club (Dallas). Office: Akin Gump Strauss Hauer & Feld LLP Ste 4100 1700 Pacific Ave Dallas TX 75201-4675 Home: 3101 Greenbrier Dr Dallas TX 75225-4603 Office Phone: 214-969-2727. Office Fax: 214-969-4343. E-mail: glee@akingump.com.

LEE, GLENN RICHARD, medical association administrator, educator; b. Ogden, Utah, May 18, 1932; s. Glenn Edwin and Thelma (Jensen) L.; m. Pamela Marjorie Ridd, July 18, 1969; children— Jennifer, Cynthia. BS, U. Utah, 1953, MD, 1956. Intern Boston City Hosp.-Harvard U., 1956-57, resident, 1957-58; clin. asso. Nat. Cancer Inst., NIH, 1958-60; postdoctoral fellow U. Utah, 1960-63; instr. U. Utah Coll. Medicine, 1963-64, asst. prof. internal medicine, 1964-68, assoc. prof., 1968-73, prof., 1973-96, assoc. dean for acad. affairs, 1973-76, dean, 1978-83, prof. emeritus, 1996—; chief of staff Salt Lake VA Med. Ctr., 1985-95. Author: (with others) Clinical Hematology, 10th edit, 1998; Contbr. (with others) numerous articles to profl. jours.; editorial bd.: (with others) Am. Jour. Hematology, 1976-79. Served with USPHS, 1958-60. Markle Found. scholar, 1965-70; Nat. Inst. Arthritis, Metabolic and Digestive Disease grantee, 1977-82. Mem. A.C.P., Am. Soc. Hematology, Am. Soc. Clin. Investigation, Western Assn. Physicians, Am. Inst. Nutrition. Mem. Lds Ch. Home and Office: 194 Harvest Run Idaho Falls ID 83404 Personal E-mail: grichardl@cableone.net.

LEE, GORDON KAY, humanities educator; b. St. Ignatius, Mont., Oct. 12, 1946; s. J. Ernest and A. Bertha Maughan Lee; 1 child, Hannah. BA in English, U. Mont., Missoula, 1973; MA in English, Ariz. State U., Tempe, 1980; PhD in English, U. Tenn., Knoxville, 1987. Instr. English U. Tenn., Knoxville, 1987—94; instr. Lee Coll., Baytown, Tex., 1994—, chmn. english humanities divsn., 2006—. With US Army, 1969—71. Mem.: Nat. Coun. Tchrs. English. Avocations: bicycling, gardening, reading. Office: Lee College 511 S Whiting St Baytown TX 77522 Home Phone: 281-460-5442; Office Phone: 281-425-6417. Office Fax: 281-425-6228. Business E-Mail: glee@lee.edu.

LEE, GREGORY A., human resources specialist; BS in Mktg., Southern Ill. U. V.p. human resources PepsiCo, 1983—92; sr. v.p. human resources St. Paul Companies, 1992—98, Whirpool, 1998—2000, Sears, Roebuck and Co., 2001—. Bd. dirs. Boys and Girls Club of Chgo. Mem.: Human Resources Policy Assn. (bd. dirs.). Avocations: photography, woodworking, golf, history. Office: Sears Roebuck and Co 3333 Beverly Rd Hoffman Estates IL 60179 Office Phone: 847-286-2500. Office Fax: 847-286-7829.

LEE, GREGORY PRICE, neuropsychology educator; b. Orange, NJ, July 3, 1952; s. John Landon and Olga (Squeo) Lee; m. Susan L. Haverstock, Oct. 3, 1988; children Stuart Haverstock Lee. BA in Psychology, U. No. Colo., 1975; MA in Clin. Psychology, Lone Mountain Coll., 1975; PhD in Clin. Psychology, Fla. Inst. Tech., 1980. Diplomate Am. Bd. Clin. Neuropsychology, Am. Bd. Profl. Psychology; lic. psychologist, Ga. Predoctoral intern Harlem Valley Psychiat. Ctr., White Plains, NY, 1977—79; instr. dept. psychology Coll. V.I., St. Thomas, 1981—82; rsch. assoc. Tex. Rsch. Inst. Mental Sci., Tex. Med. Ctr., Houston, 1983—84; postdoctoral fellow dept. psychology, sect. neuropsychology U. Houston, Baylor Coll. Medicine, 1983—84; postdoctoral fellow dept. neurology U. Wis. Med. Sch., Milw., 1984—86; dir. neuropsychology svc. neurosurgery and psychiatry Med. Coll. Ga., Augusta, 1986—2002, med. student ednl. enrichment program, 1987—2003, asst./assoc. prof. dept. neurosurgery, 1986—2001, prof. dept. neurology, 2001—. Dir. adult neuropsychology svc. Med. Coll. Ga.; oral examiner Am. Bd. Clin. Neuropsychology, 1989—, bd. dirs., 2004—; cons. editor Jour. Internat. Neuropsychol. Soc., 1994-97, Archives of Clin. Neuropsychology, 2002—; mem. Med. Student Promotions Com. Med. Coll. Ga., 1989-2001, Med. Student Admissions Com., 1998-2001, course dir. Applied Pathophysiology, 2002—05, clin. rsch. I and II, Neurosci., 2001-05, Brain & Behavior, others; bd. trustees Am. Bd. Profl. Psychology, 2005—. Co-author: Amobarbital Effects and Lateralized Brain Function: The Wada Test; contbr. numerous articles to profl. jours.; contbr. chpts. to books. Mem. med. adv. com. Alzheimer's Disease and Related Disorders Assn., 1986-97; bd. dirs. Red Devil, Inc., 1985-92. Grantee, Med. Coll. Ga. Found./Smith Kline Glaxo, 2003—07, Med. Coll. of Ga. Rsch. Inst., 2002—07, NIH/NINDS, 2003—, Berlex Labs., 2002—03. Fellow APA (divsn.40, membership program com. 2000-05, chair awards com., 2000-06), Nat. Acad. Neuropsychology (chair publs. com., mem. investment com. 2001-04, program com. 2000-05); mem. Internat. Neuropsychol. Soc., Am. Acad. Neurology, Am. Epilepsy Soc., Am. Bd. Profl. Psychology (bd. trustees), Sigma Xi. Office: Med Coll Ga Dept Neurology (BA-3278) 1120 15th St Augusta GA 30912-3275 Office Phone: 706-721-3851. Business E-Mail: glee@mcg.edu.

LEE, GYUNGHO, engineering educator; b. Seoul, Republic Of Korea, July 5, 1954; arrived in US, 1982; BS, Sogang U., Seoul, 1977; PhD, U. Ill., Urbana-Champaign, 1986. Asst. prof. U. Minn., Mpls., 1992—96; dir. Samsung Austin Design Ctr., Austin, Tex., 1997—98; assoc. prof. Iowa State U., Ames, 1999—2001; prof. U. Ill., Chgo., 2002—. Grantee Computer Sys. Architecture, NSF, 2000, Info. Tech. Rsch., 2001, Cyber Trust, 2006. Fellow: AAAS; mem.: IEEE (assoc. editor IEEE Transactiona on Parallel and Distributed Sys. 2003—06, Outstanding Paper award Internat Conf. on Parallel Processing 1986, Best Paper award Internat. Conf. on Comm. and Computer Network 2003). Achievements include patents for invalidation method for reducing coherence overheads in a bus-based shared-memory multiprocessor apparatus; Non-Inclusive Memory Access Mechanism; design of Samsung SSM7000 multiprocessor computer system. Office: Univ Illinois at Chicago 851 S Morgan St (MC 154) Chicago IL 60607 Office Phone: 312-413-9657. Office Fax: 312-996-6465. Business E-Mail: ghlee@ece.uic.edu.

LEE, HARRISON HON, librarian, consultant; b. Stockton, Calif., Sept. 20, 1943; s. Hon Bo and Lulu Joyce Lee; m. Estelle Toby Wlosko, May 11, 1980. AA, Stockton Coll., 1967; BA, Stanislaus State Coll., Turlock, Calif., 1969; MA, Sonoma State U., Cotati, Calif., 1973; MLS, Simmons Coll., 1978. Lectr. Ecole d'Humanite, Reuti, Switzerland, 1973-75; libr. M. Rosenblatt & Son, Inc., NYC, 1978-89; libr. cons. SELF, Stockton, 1989—. Mem.: Soc. Naval Archs. and Marine Engrs., Spl. Libr. Assn. Unitarian Universalist. Personal E-mail: lejosun@sbcglobal.net.

LEE, HEESOO, engineering educator; b. Seoul, Republic of Korea, Jan. 1, 1966; s. Hyungoo and Youngyeon Lee; m. Yeonsun Hwang, June 20, 1990; children: Youjun, Jungwoo. PhD, Hanyang U., Seoul, 1998. Team leader, prin. rschr. Material Testing Team Korea Testing Lab., 2005; prof. Sch. Material Sci. and Engring. Pusan Nat. U., Republic of Korea, 2007—. Contbr. articles to profl. jours. Achievements include development of standardization for ISO TC 206 fine ceramics working group 35 powder characterization. Office: Pusan Nat U San 30 Jangjeon-Dong Gumgeong-Gu Busan 609-735 Republic of Korea Office Phone: 82-51-510-2388. Business E-Mail: heesoo@pusan.ac.kr.

LEE, HELIE, writer; b. Seoul, S. Korea, Aug. 29, 1964; arrived in US, 1970; BS in Polit. Sci., UCLA, 1986. Mem. Asian Am. Writers Workshop. Writer (TV series) In Living Color, Saved By The Bell, Martin Lawrence Show; author: (novels) Still Life With Rice, 1996, In The Absence of Sun, 2002, (articles) Mademoiselle, Essence, KoreAm Journal. Office: c/o Harmony Books 1745 Broadway New York NY 10019

LEE, HENRY C., forensic scientist; b. China, Nov. 22, 1938; came to U.S., 1965; s. An-Fu and Ho-Ming Lee; m. Margaret Song, 1962; children: Sherry, Stanley. Degree in Police Sci., Ctrl. Police Coll., Taiwan, Republic of China, 1960; BS in Forensic Sci., John Jay Coll. Criminal Justice, NYC, 1972; MS in Sci., NYU, 1974, PhD in Biochemistry, 1975; DSc (hon.), U. New Haven, West Haven, Conn., 1990; LHD (hon.), St. Joseph's Coll., West Hartford, Conn., 1996; LLD (hon.), Roger Williams U., RI, 1997; LHD (hon.), U. Bridgeport, Conn., 1999; DSc (hon.), Am. Internat. Coll., Springfield, Mass., 2002; LLD (hon.), Mitchell Coll., New London, Conn., 2003; DSc (hon.), U. Conn., Storrs, Conn., 2003; LHD (hon.), Gateway Cmty. Coll., New Haven, Conn., 2006; attended several special tng. courses offered by the FBI Acad., ATF, post grad. schs., post med. schs. and profl. orgns. cert. Am. Bd. Criminalists, 1992. From police lt. to capt. Taipei Police Hdqs., Taiwan, 1960—63; newspaper reporter, asst. editor, chief editor Haw Lain Daily News, Sarawak, Malaysia, 1964—65; rsch. tech., biochemistry dept. NYU Med. Ctr., 1968—74, rsch. scientist, biochemistry dept., 1974—75; asst. prof. criminal justice U. New Haven, West Haven, Conn., 1975—77, assoc. prof. & dir., forensic sci., 1977—78, prof. forensic sci., program chmn., 1978—2000, dir. forensic sci. lab., 1975—79, dir., Ctr. of Applied Rsch., 1977—80, disting. chair prof., 2000—; dir., founder Henry C. Lee Inst. Forensic Sci., 1996; chief criminologist Conn. State Police Forensic Lab., Meriden, 1978—2000, lab. dir., 1978—2000; commr. Dept. Pub. Safety & Conn. State Police, 1998—2000; chief emeritus, divsn. scientific svcs. Dept. Pub. Safety, 2000—; dir., bd. chmn. Forensic Rsch. & Tng. Ctr., 2000—. DNA analysis expert in cases including Helle Crafts, William Kennedy Smith, O.J. Simpson, among others; assisted prosecutors across the country and the world with difficult forensic investigations including mass grave identification in Bosnia and Herzegovina, Branch Davidian (Waco, Tex.) cult; cons. in cases including reivestigation of Sacco-Vanzetti affair, JonBenet Ramsey murder, John F. Kennedy assassination, and Vincent Foster's death; served as expert witness, testified and investigated several criminal and civil cases; cons. to NJ Burlington County Forensic Sci. Lab., Conn. State Pub. Defender's Office, Tech. Adv. Svcs. for Attys., Pa., PRC Pub. Mgmt. Svcs., Vir. U. Ala., John Jay Coll. of Criminal Justice, NYC, U. SC, Elmira Coll., NYC, Nat. Inst. Justice, Maine State Police, Del. Dept. Justice, Allegheny County Dept. Lab., Pa., Rothman Arch. Inc., Mass., County of Prince William, Va., Pub. Defender's Office, Sullivan County, NY, NJ, Del., Dist. Atty's office, Cambridge, Mass., Anchorage, State Atty's Office, Va. Beach, Miami, Taiwan Nat. Police Criminal Investigation Bur., Bur. Investigation, Dept. Pub. Safety State Miss., Jackson, Miss., Crown Atty's office, Ottawa, Can., and Hawaii Police Dept., Hilo, Hawaii, Taiwan Nat. Police, 1986-, Singapore Nat. Police, 2005 and others; forensic chief advisor Min. Justice, Bur. Investigation, Taiwan, 1996-, Pub. Safety Dept., Lian Yei Chit, China, 2004; guest lectr. several prominent univs. and acads.; instr. Nat. Coll. Dist. Atty's., 1986, Mcpl. Police Tng. Acad., Meriden, Conn., 1980, Conn. State Police Acad., 1980; vis. prof., Bilingual Edn., Seton Hall U., 1976, Sch. Law, People's U., Peking, China, 1985, Guangxi U., China, 2004, Johnson & Wales, 2005, Shandong Police Coll., China, 2006, Guandong Police Coll., China, 2006, Anhui Police Coll., China, 2006; adj. prof., Forensic Sci. Program, Inst. Chemical Analysis, Northeastern U., Mass., 1977-79, forensic sci. program, sch. criminal justice, Northeastern U., 1983, dept. adminstrn. justice, Western Conn. State U., 1984, biology dept., biology program, grad. program, Bridgeport U., Conn., forensic sci. program, John Jay Coll. Criminal Justice, CUNY, 1987, U. Conn. Sch. Law, 1992 & 2000, dept. sociology, Ctrl. Conn. State U., 1993, Tze An Med. Sch., China, 1998, Quinnipiac U. Law Sch., Hamden, Conn., 1998-, U. Conn. Law Sch., West Hartford, Conn., 2000, Lin Yei U., Shan Tung, China, 2004; vis. faculty, biochemistry dept., Yale U., New Haven, Conn., 1978; Disting. prof., criminology, Ctrl. Conn. U., 2000, rsch. prof., U. Conn., 2000; prof., Pub. Safety U. & Criminal Police Coll., People's Republic of China; hon. prof., Zhejian Coll. Pub. Security, Zhejian, China, 2003, Guangxi U., China, 2004; disting. prof., Ctrl. Police Univ., Taiwan, 2006, Hubei Police Coll., 2006; hon. dean, vis. prof., Sch. Criminal Justice, East China U. Politics and Law, 2006; instructed/conducted several courses, workshops, and seminars. Author and co-author of several books, chpts. reports and monographs on forensic sci.; contbr. several articles to profl. jours.; editor for the following jours.: Hwa-Lian Daily News, Forensic Serology News, Jour. of Forensic Sci., Crime Lab. Digest, Advances in Forensic Scis., Jour. Forensic Identification, Great Crime Cases, Forensic Sci. Review, Crime Lab. Digest, FBI, Am. Jour. Forensic Pathology, Ency. Forensic Scis.; featured in Trace Evidence: The Case Files of Dr. Henry Lee, Court TV, 2005. Docent scholarship fund U. New Haven, Conn. Dept. Pub. Safety; mem., Forensic Serology Cert. Com. Nat. Inst. Justice/Acad. Forensic Sci, 1978, Conn. State Rape Com., Dept. Health/ Dept. Public Safety, 1980, Forensic Scis. Svcs. Comt, Conn. Justice Com., 1981, Nat. Steering Com. Arson Evidence, ATF/NBS, 1982, Ad Hoc Com. on the Reliability of Genetic Marker Typing in Blood and Body Fluid Stains, AAFS, 1984; chmn., Forensic Science Operation and Program Com., FBI/ ASCLD, 1985, Capitol Region Investigative Support Team, 1991; accreditation inspector, Am. Crime Lab. Accreditation, 1983; assoc. referee. forensic sci., Assn. Official Analytical Chemists, 1981; Chief Del., Chinese-Am. Police Conf., Taipei, Taiwan, 1986; bd. dir., University of New Haven, 1987; com. mem., Nat. Orgn. Against Liquor in Candy for Children, 1987, Conn. State Rape Com., 1987; Oral Boards, Mass. State Police, Framingham, MA, 1997. Recipient Disting. Svc. award. for distinguished svc. in criminal investigation., Taipei Police Hdqs., 1962, Commendation award, Greenburgh Police Dept. for assistance in solving homicide case, 1976, Alumni Achievement award, John Jay College of Criminal Justice for achievement, contribution and svcs. in forensic science, 1979, 1990, Disting. Mgr. Award, Gov. Connecticut, 1982, State Conn. General Assembly Citation received in recognition of disting.managerial svcs., 1982, Recognition Citation, Conn. State General Assembly for distinguished svc. to the State of Connecticut in solving difficult crimes, 1983, Special award, Conn. Divsn. Criminal Justice in recognition of the svc. to the criminal justice system, 1984, Lewis Memorial Lecture award, St. Joseph's College Chemistry Club, 1984, Special award. Connecticut Law Foundation for innovation and dedication to the advancement of professionalism in law enforcement, 1984, Recognition award, The People's University of China in recognition of outstanding svc. to forensic science and training, 1985, Lecture award, Am. Chemical Soc., Hartford State Technical Coll., 1986, Disting. Svc. award, Acad. of Forensic Scis. for outstanding contribution to criminalistics and forensic science, 1986, Commendation award, Criminal Investigation Bur., Taiwan Nat. Police for outstanding contribution in criminal investigation and training, Police medal, The Ministry of Interior, Republic of China, distinguished svcs. in police work, 1986, Alumni award, The Central Police Coll., Taiwan, Republic of China for outstanding achievements and svcs. to the community, 1989, J. Donero award, Internat. Assn. for Identification, 1989, Svc. Award, Am. Bd. Criminalistics, 1990, Svc. award, ATF, 1990, Svc. award, Taiwan Criminal Investigation Bur., 1991, Disting. Svc. award, Police Commr. Assn. Conn., Inc., Norwalk, 1992, Appreciation award, NH State Police, Concord, 1993, Svc. award, Drug Enforcement Agency, 1995, VIDOCQ Medal of Honor, VIDOCQ Soc., Phila., 1996, Alfred C. Fones award, Conn. State Dental Assn.,1996, NESCAN award, New England Coll. Sexual Assault Network, Storrs, CT, 1996, State Ethics award, presented by State Ethics Comm., Hartford, 1996, Presdl. Sci. Initiative award, Sacred Heart U., Bridgeport, Conn., 1997, Lifetime Leadership award, Boy Scouts of Am., Milford, Conn., 2002, President's medal, Ctrl. Conn. State U., Cmty. Leaders of Am. Outstanding Scientific Achievement, 50th Years Edn. award, Internat. Assn. Identification, Conn. Divsn., 2003, Spl. award, Abu Dhabi Police Directorate, 2003, Paul Harris Fellow award, The Rotary Found. Rotary Internat., 2003, Diversity Leadership award, 2003, Lifetime Achievement award, Chinese Am. Assn. Colo., 2003, Appreciation award, Kittering Police Found., 2004, Honoree of Yr., Outstanding Contribution to Law and Sci., Chinese-Am. Planning Coun., NY, 2004, Outstanding Achievement award, Chinese Am. Profl. Soc., LA, Calif., 2004, Forensic Sci. award, Va. Commonwealth U., Coll. Humanities and Sciences, 2005, Medal of Honor, Ellis Island Found., 2004, Medal of Pub. Svc., State Conn., 2005, Presdl. Medal Honor, Croatia Govt., 2005, Disting. Pub. Svc. award, Conn. Bar Assn., 2005, Official Citation, Gen. Assembly, State Conn., 2005, Hon. Citizen award, Govt. Peng-hu County, Taiwan, ROC, 2006 and several others; named Hon. Deputy Sheriff. Middlesex County Sheriff's Assn., Hon. Deputy Sheriff. Bergen County Sheriff's Office, NJ, Hon. Captain. Maine State Police, Maine, Hon. Lt. Colonel, State Ga., Hon. Tex. Lawman, State Tex., Hon. Fire Marshal, State RI. Fellow Am. Acad. Forensic Sci., Disting. Fellow, 1990, chmn. nomination com., 1983, 1984, chmn., Ad Hoc Com. on DNA Typing, 1989, 1990, 1991), Northeastern Assn. Forensic Scientists (reg. dir., 1977-80, chmn., Ethics Com., 1978, 1980), Forensic Sci. Soc., England, Am. Acad. Criminal Justice, Northeastern Criminal Justice Educator's Assn., Internat. Assn. Identification (Cert. Latent Fingerprint Examiner, com. chmn. 1985, disting. mem., 1988, mem., lab. safety com., 1985, mem. Scholarship Com., 1985, publication com., 1986, advisor, crime scene cert. com., 1987, chmn., forensic lab. analysis com., 1988), NY Acad. Sci., AAAS, Am. Soc. for Testing and Materials, Am. Soc. Crime Laboratory (dir., bd. dir., chmn., edn. and tng. com., 1980, 1982, 1986, 1990), Internat. Assn. Forensic Sci., Assn. Official Analytical Chemists, (Referee, 1980), Conn. Chromatography Coun., Fingerprint Society, England (Fellow, 1984), Internat. Assn. Bloodpattern Analysis (reg. v.p., 1987), PR Forensic Scis. Assn. (hon. mem.), Fla. Homicide Investigators Assn. (hon. mem.), Conn. Arson Investigator Assn. (hon. mem.), Internat. Homicide Detective's Assn, (Advisor, 1990), Internat. Assn. Bloodstain Analysts (v.p., 1990), Am. Bd. Criminalists (cert. bd. mem., 1992), Internat. Chief of Police, 1998, Com. 100, Aca. Sci. and Engr. (bd. dir. 2003), Nat. Assn. Asian-Am. Law Enforcement Commanders, Indo-Pacific Assn. Medicine, Law and Forensic Sci. (invited mem. 2004), Nat. Assn. Med. Examiner and Coroner (invited mem., 2004), Internat. Assn. Private Investigator (cert. bd. advisor, 2005). Avocations: cooking, gardening, chinese calligraphy, fossils. Office: Dept Pub Safety 278 Colony St Meriden CT 06451 Address: U New Haven Forensic Science Program

300 Orange Ave West Haven CT 06516 also: Forensic Rsch and Tng Ctr 82 Limewood Ave Branford CT 06405 Office Phone: 203-639-6400, 203-932-6119, 203-488-1475. Office Fax: 203-639-6485, 203-931-6073.*

LEE, HI YOUNG, physician, acupuncturist; b. Seoul, Republic of Korea, Oct. 18, 1941; arrived in U.S., 1965, naturalized, 1976; s. Jung S. and Hwa J. (Kim) Lee; m. Sun M. Lee, June 4, 1965; children: Sandra, Grace, David. MD, Yon Sei U., Seoul, 1965. Diplomate Am. Bd. Family Practice. Intern Grasslands Hosp., Valhalla, NY, 1965-66; resident VA Hosp., Dayton, Ohio, 1966-70; mem. staff Eastern State Hosp., Medical Lake, Wash., 1970-74; practice family medicine, acupuncturist Empire Med. Office, Spokane, Wash., 1974—. Active staff St. Lukes Meml. Hosp., Spokane, 1974—; courtesy staff Deaconess Med. Ctr., Spokane, 1974—, Sacred Heart Med. Ctr., Spokane, 1974—; sr. disability analyst, diplomate Am. Bd. Disability Analysts, 2000. Author: Von Recklinghousen's Disease, 1970; columnist: Rainier Forum Korea Post Weekly News, 1996—. Trustee St. Georges Prep Sch., Wash., 1986—; elder First Presbyn. Ch., Spokane, 1975. Fellow: Am. Acad. Family Practice; mem.: Christian Med. Soc., Ctr. Chinese Medicine, Nat. Acupuncture Rsch. Soc., Spokane County Med. Soc. Home: 2006 W Liberty Ave Spokane WA 99205-2570 Office: Empire Med Office 17 E Empire Ave Spokane WA 99207-1707 Personal E-mail: drhileemd@yahoo.com.

LEE, HON-CHI, medical educator; m. Gina Lee; 1 child, Kristin T. BS, MIT, Cambridge, Mass., 1973; MD, PhD, Harvard U., Boston, 1981. Diplomate Am. Bd. Internal Medicine, 1984, cert. subspecialty bd. cardiovasc. diseases Am. Bd. Internal Medicine, 1987, subspecialty bd. clin. cardiac electrophysiology Am. Bd. Internal Medicine, 1992, Am. Bd. Internal Medicine, 2002. Asst. prof. medicine U. Iowa, Iowa City, 1989—94, assoc. prof. medicine, 1994—2001, prof. medicine, 2001, Mayo Clinic, Rochester, Minn., 2001—. Cons. Mayo Clinic, Rochester, 2001—. Vol. Habitat for Humanity, Rochester, 2004. Grantee, NIH, 2000—, VA, 1989—94, 1996—2003. Fellow: ACP, Am. Coll. Cardiology, Am. Heart Assn., Am. Heart Assn.; mem.: Ctrl. Soc. for Clin. Rsch., Soc. for Gen. Physiologists, Biophysical Soc., Heart Rhythm Soc., Phi Lambda Upsilon. Office: Mayo Clinic 200 First St SW Rochester MN 55905 Office Phone: 507-255-8353. Office Fax: 507-255-7070. Business E-Mail: lee.honchi@mayo.edu.

LEE, HOWARD N., educational association administrator; b. Lithonia, Ga., July 28, 1934; m. Lillian Lee; 3 children. BA, Ft. Valley State Coll., 1959; MSW, U. N.C., 1966. Mem. faculty U. N.C., Chapel Hill; mem. N.C. Senate, Raleigh, 1990—94, 1997—2003; chmn. N.C. State Bd. of Edn., Raleigh, 2003—. Chmn. appropriations on edn. and higher edn. com., edn. and higher edn. com., mem. appropriations/base budget com., fin. com., inf. tech. com., judiciary II com., vice chmn. commerce com., transp. com. Mayor, Chapel Hill, NC, 1969—75; sec. N.C. Dept. Environment and Natural Resources, 1977—81. With US Army, 1959—61, with USAR, 1961—63. Democrat. also: 109 Glenview Pl Chapel Hill NC 27514-1948 Office: NC State Bd of Edn 301 N Wilmington St 6302 Mail Svc Ctr Raleigh NC 27699-6302 also: Dobbs Bldg Raleigh NC 27699-6302 Personal E-mail: hlee@nc.rr.com.

LEE, HWAN-SOO, materials scientist, researcher; s. Tae-Sik Lee and Myung-Sook Wie; m. Jaehee Kim, Jan. 20, 1995; children: Chang-Yub, Julie. BS in Engring., Seoul Nat. U., 2002, MS in Engring., 1994, Carnegie Mellon U., Pitts., 2001, PhD, 2004. Sr. rsch. engr. Samsung Corning, Suwon, Kyounggi-do, Republic of Korea, 1994—2000; vis. rschr. Sony (Sendai Tech. Ctr.), Miyagi-ken, Japan, 2003, Samsung Info. Sys. Am., San Jose, Calif., 2004; postdoctoral rsch. assoc. Carnegie Mellon U., Pitts., 2004—06; rschr. Seagate Rsch./Carnegie Mellon U., Pitts., 2007—. Session chmn. Intermag, San Diego, 2006; mem. com. 17th Magnetic Rec. Conf., Pitts., 2006; referee J. Appl. Phys., 2005—, IEEE Trans. Mag., 2005—. Contbr. articles to profl. publs. Named Outstanding Employee, Samsung Corning, 1997; recipient Best Presentation award, 2000; fellow, Info. Storage Industry Consortium, 2000—04; scholar, Seoul Nat. U., 1990; postdoctoral fellow, Intel, 2004—. Mem.: Materials Rsch. Soc. (assoc.), IEEE Magnetics Soc. (assoc.). Achievements include research in role of defects in resistive memories to gain a better picture of the underlying switching mechanism; new area of sputtered tape media for tape storage applications; patents pending for new barrier-rib forming method for plasma display back panel. Avocations: basketball, football, golf, skiing, guitar. Home Phone: 1-412-781-6742; Office Phone: 1-412-268-4034. Office Fax: 1-412-268-6978. Business E-Mail: hwansoo@ece.cmu.edu.

LEE, HWA-WEI, librarian, educator, consultant; b. Guangdong, China, Dec. 7, 1933; came to U.S., 1957, naturalized, 1962; s. Luther Kan-Chun and Mary Hsiao-Hsei (Wang) L.; m. Mary F. Kratochvil, Mar. 14, 1959; children: Shirley, James, Pamela, Edward, Charles, Robert. BEd, Nat. Taiwan Normal U., 1954; MEd, U. Pitts., 1959, PhD, 1964; MLS, Carnegie Mellon U., 1961. Asst. libr. U. Pitts. Librs., 1959-62; head tech. svcs. Duquesne U. Libr., Pitts., 1962-65; head libr. U. Pa., Edinboro, 1965-68; dir. libr. and info. ctr. Asian Inst. Tech., Bangkok, 1968-75; assoc. dir. librs., prof. libr. adminstrn. Colo. State U., Fort Collins, 1975-78; dean librs., prof. Ohio U., Athens, 1978-99, dean emeritus, librs., 1999—; disting. vis. scholar OCLC, 2000—02; chief Asian divsn. Libr. of Congress, 2003—. Fulbright sr. specialist, 2001; cons. FAO, UNESCO, U.S. AID, World Bank, Internat. Devel. Rsch. Ctr., Asia Found., OCLC; del.-at-large White House Conf. Libr. and Info. Svcs., 1991. Author: Librarianship in World Perspectives, 1991, Fundraising for the 1990s: The Challenge Ahead, 1992, Modern Library Management, 1996, Knowledge Management: Theory and Practice, 2002; exec. editor Jour. Ednl. Media and Libr. Sci., 1982—; mem. editl. bd. Internat. Comm. in Libr. Automation, 1975-76, Jour. Libr. and Info. Sci., 1975-78, Libr. Acquisition: Practice and Theory, 1976-83; adv. bd. Jour. Info., Comm. and Libr. Sci., 1994—; contbr. articles to profl. jours. Recipient Disting. Svc. award Libr. Assn. of China (Taiwan), 1989; new bldg. on Ohio U. campus named in his honor: Hwa-wei Lee Libr. Annex, and 1st flr. of the main libr.: Hwa-wei Lee Ctr. for Internat. Collections, 1999. Mem. ALA (councilor 1988-92, 93-97, John Ames Humphry/Forest Press award 1991), Acad. Libr. Assn. Ohio, Am. Soc. Info. Sci., Asian-Pacific Am. Librs. Assn. (Disting. Svc. award 1991), Internat. Fedn. Libr. Assns. and Instns. (standing com. univ. librs. and other gen. rsch. librs. 1989-93), Assn. Coll. and Rsch. Librs. Chinese-Am. Librs. Assn. (Disting. Svc. award 1983), Internat. Assn. Orientalist Librs., Ohio Libr. Coun. (bd. dirs. 1991-92, Libr. of the Yr. 1987, Hall of Fame Libr. 1999), Online Computer Libr. Ctr. (users coun. 1987-91), Ohio Chinese Acad. and Profl. Assn. (founding pres. 1988-90), China Soc. Libr. Sci (hon. life). Home: 2800 Clarendon Blvd W608 Arlington VA 22201 Office: Libr of Congress Asian Divsn Washington DC 20540 Home Phone: 703-919-9005; Office Phone: 202-707-5919. Business E-Mail: hlee@loc.gov.

LEE, IL-OK, anesthesiologist, education educator; b. Seoul, Republic of Korea, Nov. 10, 1958; d. Byoung-Cheol Lee and Soon-Rye Shin; m. Jae-Ryong Lee, May 11, 1991; children: Ji-Hyun, Tae-Sun. Bachelor's degree, Korea U., Seoul, 1984, M in Medicine, 1988, PhD, 1992. Cert. bd. anesthesia and pain medicine Korea Med. Assn., 1989. Assoc. prof. Korea U., Seoul, Republic of Korea, 1998—2002, prof., 2003—. Rsch. fellow Harvard Med. Sch., Boston, 1995—96; vis. prof., rsch. assoc. Dept. Anesthesiology, Pharmacology and Therapeutics Med. Sch. U. BC, Vancouver, Canada, 2006—07. Author: (articles) Corresponding author, (article) Corressponding author; contbr. articles pub. to profl. jour. (Abott academic award, 2000, Korea U. Alumni Award, 2002). Mem. com. Cert. Bd Examination Of Anesthesia. Grantee, Korea U. Med. Rsch. Found., 2005, Korea Academic Rsch. Found., 1997, Korea Sci. Found., 1999. Mem.: Korea Assn. of Pain Rsch., Korea Assn. of Pediatric Anesthesia, Korea Assn. of Neuroanesthesia, Korea Assn. of Intravenous Anesthesia, Korea Assn. of Anesthesiology (assoc.; korea 1989—2005). Roman Catholic. Achievements include research in C-Fos In Spinal Preemption. Avocation: travel. Home: Shinjung dong 1279 MokHyundai Apt106-906 Seoul 158-072 Republic of Korea Office: Korea Univ Guro Hosp Gurodong 80 Guro ku Seoul 152-703 Republic of Korea Home Phone: 82-2-2645-5004; Office Phone: 82-2-818-6789. Office Fax: 82-2-851-9897. Business E-Mail: iloklee@korea.ac.kr.

LEE, INAH, psychology professor; b. Seoul, Republic of Korea, Oct. 17, 1970; s. Taeheang Lee and Sukyung Baek; m. Sujeong Lee; children: Serin, Sejune. BA in Psychology, Seoul Nat. U., 1996; PhD, U. Utah, Salt Lake City, 2002. Rsch. fellow U. Tex. Med. Ctr., Houston, 2002—04; rsch. fellow Ctr. for Memory and Brain, Boston U., 2004—05; asst. prof. dept. psychology U. Iowa, Iowa City, 2006—. Contbr. articles to profl. jours. Recipient James W. Prahl Meml. award, U. Utah, 2002; Pickwick Postdoctoral Rsch. fellow, Nat. Sleep Found., 2004—05, Old Gold Summer Rsch. fellow, U. Iowa, 2006, rsch. grantee, NIH, 2007. Office: U Iowa E11 SSH Dept Psychology Iowa City IA 52242 Office Phone: 319-335-3659. Office Fax: 319-335-0191. Business E-Mail: inah-lee@uiowa.edu.

LEE, IN-YOUNG, lawyer; b. In-Cheon, Kyonggi-do, Korea, Dec. 5, 1952; arrived in US, 1978; s. In-Seok and H.B. Lee; m. Young-Lae Hong, July 1, 1978; children: Casey K., Brian K. LLB, Seoul Nat. U., Korea, 1975; LLM, Harvard U., 1980; JD, UCLA, 1983. Bar: Ill. 1983, N.Y. 1987, D.C. 1989, U.S. Ct. Internat. Trade. Assoc. Baker & McKenzie, Chgo., 1983—86, Marks & Murase, NYC, 1986—87, Baker & McKenzie, NYC, 1987—91; ptnr. Marks & Murase, NYC, 1991—96, McDermott, Will & Emery, NYC, 1996—. Gen. counsel Korean C. of C. and Industry in USA, Inc., 1993—, Assn. Korean Fin. Instns. Am., Inc. Articles editor Pacific Basin Law Jour. Presbyterian. Avocations: fishing, golf. Office: 340 Madison Ave New York NY 10017 E-mail: ilee@mwe.com.

LEE, JACK (JIM SANDERS BEASLEY), broadcast executive; b. Buffalo Valley, Tenn., Apr. 14, 1936; s. Jesse McDonald and Nelle Viola (Sanders) Beasley; m. Barbara Sue Looper, Sept. 1, 1961; children: Laura Ann, Elizabeth Jane, Sarah Kathleen. Student, Wayne State U., Detroit, 1955-57; BA, Albion Coll., Mich., 1959. Announcer Sta. WHUB-AM, Cookeville, Tenn., 1956; news dir., program dir. Sta. WALM-AM, Albion, Mich., 1957-59; radio-TV personality WKZO-Radio-TV, Kalamazoo, 1960-62; prodn. dir. Stas. WKMH-WKNR, Detroit, 1962-63; gen. mgr. Sta. WAUK-AM-FM, Waukesha, Wis., 1963-65; asst. program mgr. Sta. WOKY, Milw., 1965-70; program mgr. Sta. WTMJ-WKTI, Milw., 1970-76; gen. mgr. Sta. WEMP-WMYX, Milw., 1976-88; pres. Jack Lee Enterprises Ltd., Milw., 1977—; pres., CEO, Milw. Area Radio Stas., 1989—2006; dir. integrated media Lake Front Comm. LLC, Milw., 2006—. Instr. dept. mass comm. U. Wis.-Milw., 1972-81. With US Army, 1959, 61-62; maj. CAP, 1964-01, ret. Decorated Army Commendation medal; cert. radio mktg. cons., Broadcasters Hall of Fame, 1999; Milw. Air awards Lifetime Achievement, 2003 Mem. AFTRA, Actors Equity, Omicron Delta Kappa, Alpha Epsilon Rho. Office: Milw Radio Group 5407 W McKinley Ave Milwaukee WI 53208 Office Phone: 414-978-9470. Office Fax: 414-978-4001. *It is a constant struggle to balance my greatest gift—the ability to express myself—with my biggest failing—the inability to keep my mouth shut.*

LEE, JAEKYUNG, education educator, researcher; b. Seoul, Republic of Korea, Jan. 28, 1967; US, 1992; s. Gapsoo Lee and Sookja Baek; children: Jin, Jane. BA, Yonsei U., 1989, MA, 1991; PhD, U. Chgo., 1997. Asst. prof. U. Maine, Orono, 1997—2002, SUNY, Buffalo, 2002—, 2006—. Adv. com. mem. State Maine Dept. Edn., 2000—02; cons. Ohio Columbus Bd. Edn., 2001—02; expert panelist Smart Libr. on Closing the Achievement Gap, 2002—; academic adv. bd. mem. Harvard U. Civil Rights Project, Cambridge, Mass., 2003—; senator SUNY Buffalo Faculty Senate, 2005—. Guest editor: special issue KEDI Jour. Edn. Policy, mem. editl. bd.: Edn. Policy Analysis Archive, 2007—; contbr. articles to profl. jours. Recipient New Scholars award, Am. Ednl. Fin. Assn., 1996; grantee, U.S. Dept. Edn., 1998, 2004, 2005, NSF, 1999; doctoral fellow, Korea Found. for Advanced Studies, 1992—97, postdoctoral fellow, Nat. Acad. Edn., 1999—2001. Mem.: Am. Ednl. Rsch. Assn. (grantee 1995, 1997, Early Career award 2007). Achievements include discovery of closing the achievement gap and the impact of No Child Left Behind Act on the gap trend. Office: SUNY Buffalo 409 Baldy Hall Buffalo NY 14260-1000 Office Phone: 716-645-2484 1257. Business E-Mail: jl224@buffalo.edu.

LEE, JAMES A., health facility finance executive; b. Red Level, Ala., Dec. 19, 1939; s. H. Alton Lee; m. Charlotte Phillips, Dec. 19, 1963 (div. July 1971); children: Phillip, Michele, Jenifer; m. Melanie Cooper, Dec. 14, 1973; children: Christopher, Amanda. BBA in Acctg., Jacksonville State U., 1964; MS in Hosp. and Health Adminstrn., U. Ala., 1980. CPA, Ala. Sr. acct. Macke, Eldredge, McIntosh, Birmingham, Ala., 1964-67, Touche, Ross, Bailey & Smart, Birmingham, 1967-68; bus. functions mgr. Druid City Hosp., Tuscaloosa, Ala., 1968-71; sr. assoc. adminstr., fin. Univ. Ala. Hosp., Birmingham, 1971-94; CFO Montgomery Cardiovasc. Assocs., PC, 1994—. Asst. prof. health services adminstrn. Univ. Ala. Birmingham, 1980—; asst. prof. Dept. Pub. Health, Univ. Ala. Birmingham, 1984—. Mem. AICPA, Health Care Fin. Mgmt. Assn., Ala. Soc. CPAs. Republican. Baptist. Home: 109 Pemberton Pl Pelham AL 35124-2817 E-mail: jleecpa@aol.com.

LEE, JAMES BAINBRIDGE, JR., bank executive; b. NYC, Oct. 30, 1952; s. James Bainbridge and Marylou (Orteig) L.; m. Elizabeth B. Lee, Feb. 8, 1981; children: Alexandria, James B., Elizabeth G. BA in Economics & Art History, Williams Coll., Williamstown, Mass., 1975. With Chem. Bank, NYC, 1975-79, calling officer ASEAN, 1977-79, dep. rep. Sydney, 1979, rep., 1979-81; mng. dir. Merchant Bank, Melbourne, Australia, 1982-83; chief of staff Chem. Bank, NYC, 1983-85, v.p. syndications, 1985-87, mng. dir. structured fin., syndications and pvt. placements, 1987—94; vice chmn. JP Morgan Chase & Co., NYC, 1994—, chmn., investment banking N. Am., 2002—. Pres. Berkshire Broadcasting Corp., Danbury, Conn. Pres. Norton Bay Property Owners Assn., Darien, Conn., 1987-89. Recipient Harvard Book award, 1971. Mem. Royal Prince Edward Yacht Club, Athanaeum Club, Woodbury Country Club. Office: JP Morgan Chase & Co 270 Park Ave New York NY 10017*

LEE, JAMES EDWARD, JR., educational consultant; b. Pitts., Mar. 9, 1939; s. Willard and Gladys Hilda (Jenkins) L.; children: Stephen Michael, Monica Michelle, Brian Patrick, Priscilla Demone. BS, Wayne State U., 1962, EdS, 1969; MA, U. Mich., 1964; postgrad., Mich. State U., Wayne State U., U. Minn., U. Colo., 1964—65, Ctrl. Mich. U. Cert. tchr., adminstr., Mich. Tchr. Miller, Durfee and Michael Jr. High Schs., Detroit, 1962—67; team leader Nat. Tchr. Corps, Detroit, 1967—69; dept. head Noble Jr. HS, Detroit, 1969—74; asst. prin. MacKenzie HS, Detroit, 1974—80, Drew Mid. Sch., Detroit, 1980, prin., 1980—97, Chandler Park Acad., Detroit, 1997—98; ops. supr. Detroit Mfg. Partnership, 1999—2000; exec. dir. Detroit Pub. Schs., 2000—01; prin. Rivers Mid. Sch., Charleston, SC, 2001—02, ednl. cons., 2002—; prin. mentor, coach Detroit Pub. Schs., 2004—; prin. coach Wayne County Regional Ednl. Svc. Agy., 2006—. Instr. Wayne State U., Detroit, 1967-69, edn. cons., 1970-71; instr. Wayne CC, 1967-81; prin. adult evening sch., 1974-80, summer gifted program, Detroit, 1986-92; profl. stds. commn. for sch. adminstrs. Mich. Dept. Edn., 1992-96, adminstrv. waiver com., 1992-94; mem. sch. improvement team Wayne County Regional Ednl. Svc. Agy., 1996-97. Contbg. author: The Development of Micro Teaching as an Evaluative Instrument in Teacher Training, 1969, (manual) The Principalship, 1990. Co-chair ednl. audit com. Oak Park (Mich.) Sch., 1988-90; bd. dirs. Scott Cmty. Ctr., Detroit, 1988-97; adv. bd. Adrian/Scott Program To Inspire Readiness for Ednl. Success, Detroit, 1990-97; adv. coun. Christ Child House, Detroit, 1990-92. With USMC, 1956-58. Recipient Prins. and Educators award Booker T. Washington Bus. Assn., Detroit, 1986, 90, Citation for Outstanding Leadership Detroit Bd. Edn., 1986; named finalist Boss of Yr., Detroit chpt. Am. Bus. Women's Assn., 1987. Mem. Nat. Assn. Secondary Sch. Prins., Nat. Mid. Sch. Assn., Mich. Assn. Supervision and Curriculum Devel., Mich. Assn. Secondary Sch. Prins. (exec. bd. 1986-88, Outstanding Mid. Level Prin. of Yr. 1991), Mich. Assn. Mid. Sch. Educators (bd. dirs. 1988-91). Avocation: tennis. Home: 16500 North Park Dr Apt 1117 Southfield MI 48075 E-mail: leejam777@aol.com.

LEE, JAMES HAROLD, investment company executive; b. Wilmington, Del., Nov. 11, 1969; s. Jerald D. and Virginia D. Lee; m. Stephanie A. Fuller, Aug. 10, 2006. BA in Econs., Coll. William and Mary, Williamsburg, Va., 1991; postgrad., U. Houston, 2002—. Chartered fin. analyst Assn. Investment Rsch. and Mgmt., 2000, chartered market tech. Market Techs. Assn., 2006, cert. fin. planner CFP Bd. Stds., 1995. Fin. planner Am. Express Fin. Advisors, Wilmington, Del., 1991—97, Lau & Assocs. Ltd., Wilmington, 1998—2000; investment mgr. Lau Associates LLC, Wilmington, 2000—. Mem.: Assn. Profl. Futurists, Mensa. Office: Lau Associates LLC 300 Bellevue Pky Ste 200 Wilmington DE 19809 Office Phone: 302-792-5955. Personal E-mail: lee-advisor@operamail.com.

LEE, JANET, professional tennis player; b. Lafayatte, Ind., Oct. 22, 1976; d. Shun-Yi and Vanni. Profl. tennis player WTA, 1995—. Named Jr. Player of Yr., Tennis Mag., 1993. Achievements include winner 3 career doubles titles, WTA; winner 2 career singles titles, 9 career doubles titles, ITF; mem. Taipei Fed Cup Team, 2000, Chinese Taipei Olympic Team, 2000; winner (juniors) USTA Girls 14s Nationals, 1991, Easter Bowl, 1991, USTA 18s Nationals, 1993, Easter Bowl, 1993. Avocations: Scrabble, photography, emailing, internet, reading, arts and crafts, karaoke. Office: WTA Tour Inc Bank Ln Roehampton London SW15 5XZ England Office Phone: 44 20 8392 4760. Office Fax: 44 20 8392 4765.*

LEE, JANIE C., curator; b. Shreveport, La., Apr. 22, 1937; d. Birch Lee and Joanna (Glassell) Wood; m. David B. Warren, Jan. 2, 1980. Student, Nat. Cathedral Sch., 1951-55; BA, Sarah Lawrence Coll., 1959. Asst. to Cheryl Crawford, Actors Studi o, NYC, 1962-63; co-prodr. Off Broadway Theatre Co., NYC, 1963-65; owner, pres. Janie C. Lee Gallery, Dallas, 1967-74, Houston, 1973-96, Janie C. Lee Master Drawings, NYC, 1983-96; curator of drawings Whitney Mus. Am. Art, 1997—2004. Mem. art appraisal panel IRS, Washington, 1987-94; trustee Menil Found., Inc., 2000—. Prodr. ann. catalogue on 20th Century drawings, 1979-93. Mem. Alumnae Bd. Sarah Lawrence Coll. (1972-74); pres. Nancy Graves Found., 1996—. Mem. Art Dealers Assn. Am. (bd. dirs. 1980-88, 92-94, v.p. 1984-88). Office: 3711 San Felipe St # 4E Houston TX 77027 Office Phone: 713-355-5300. E-mail: janieclee@aol.com.

LEE, JASON, actor; b. Huntington Beach, Ca., Apr. 25, 1970; m. Carmen Llywelyn, July 1995 (div. July 2001); 1 child, Pilot Inspektor Riesgraf Lee. Pro skateboarder, 1989—96; owner Stereo Manufacturing Corp. (skateboarding), 2003—. Actor: (films) Video Days, 1991, My Crazy Life, 1993, Mallrats, 1995, Drawing Flies, 1996, Chasing Amy, 1997, A Better Place, 1997, Kissing a Fool, 1998, American Cuisine, 1998, Enemy of the State, 1998, Dogma, 1999, Mumford, 1999, Almost Famous, 2000, Heartbreakers, 2001, Jay and Silent Bob Strike Back, 2001, Vanilla Sky, 2001, Big Trouble, 2002, Stealing Harvard, 2002, A Guy Thing, 2003, Dreamcatcher, 2003, I Love Your Work, 2003, Jersey Girl, 2004, (voice only) The Incredibles, 2004, The Ballad of Jack and Rose, 2005, Drop Dead Sexy, 2005, (voice only) Jack-Jack Attack, 2005, Clerks II, 2006, Monster House, 2006, (voice only) Underdog, 2007,: (TV films) Weapons of Mass Distraction, 1997, Sonic Youth Video Dose, 2004; actor, prodr. (TV series) My Name is Earl, 2005—. Office: c/o United Talent Agency 9560 Wilshire Blvd Beverly Hills CA 90212*

LEE, JASON SCOTT, actor; b. LA, Nov. 19, 1966; s. Robert and Sylvia Lee. Student, Fullerton Coll. Actor, mem. Friends and Artists Theater Ensemble. Appeared in films Born in East L.A., 1987, Back to the Future, Part II, 1989, Map of the Human Heart, 1993, Dragon: The Bruce Lee Story, 1993, Rudyard Kipling's The Jungle Book, 1994, Rapa Nui, 1994, Murder in Mind, 1997, Tales of the Mummy, 1998, Soldier, 1998, Balls of Fury, 2007; TV appearances include Vestige of Honor, 1990, The Lookalike, 1990, CBS Schoolbreak Spl., 1990, Hunger Series, 1997. Office: United Talent Agy c/o Cynthia Shelton-Droke 9560 Wilshire Blvd Ste 500 Beverly Hills CA 90212-2427*

LEE, JEANETTE, professional billiards player; b. Bklyn., July 9, 1971; m. George Breedlove; 1 child, Cheyeene Lee. Profl. billiards player, 1993—; nat. spokeswoman The Scoliosis Assn., Inc. Founder The Jeanette Lee Found. Appearances: (on several television shows including) Arli$$; David Letterman; HBO Real Sports; Regis and Kelly; co-author (with Adam Gershenson): The Black Widow's Guide to Killer Pool, 2000. Mem. Women's Sports Found. Bd. Trustees, 2001—. Named Player of Yr., Billiards Digest, 1994, Billiard mag., 1994, Sportsperson of the Yr. award, Women's Profl. Billiards Assn., 1998; recipient Gold medal, Akita World Games, 2001. Mem.: Women's Sports Found., Scoliosis Assn., Inc. winner: Balt. Billiards Classic, 1994, Kasson Twin Cities Classic, 1994, BCA San Francisco Classic, 1994, US Open 9-Ball Championship, 1994, Olhausen Los Angeles Classic, 1995, 1997, Brunswick New York Classic, 1995, BCA Charlotte Classic, 1996, Huebler Cues Nashville Classic, 1997, Olhausen San Diego Classic, 1997, ESPN Ultimate 9-Ball Challenge, 1998, Penn Ray Recreational Ariz. Classic, 1998, Cuetec Cues Hawaii Classic, 1999, Gentleman Jack Great Dallas Shootout, 1999, Ladies Tournament of Champions, 1999, BCA Open 9-Ball Championship Women's Divsn., 2001, Ladies Tuornament of Champions, 2003, BCA Open 9-Ball Champion, 2004, Cuetec Cues Fla. Classic, 2004, Trick Shot Magic, 2004, Atlanta Women's Open, 2004. Office: c/o Octagon 7th Fl 8687 Melrose Ave Los Angeles CA 90069*

LEE, JENNIFER, journalist; b. NYC, Mar. 15, 1976; BA, Harvard Univ., 1999. V.p. Harvard Crimson Newspaper, 1999; tech., bus. reporter New York Times, 2001, circuits sect. reporter, 2002, DC corr., 2003—04, met. reporter, 2005—. Intern Boston Globe, 1996, Washington Post, 1998, Wall St. Jour., 1999. Office: NY Times 620 8th Ave New York NY 10018

LEE, JEONG-KYU, education educator, researcher, academic administrator; b. Choongmoo, Republic of Korea, July 15, 1950; arrived in Can., 2003; s. Jong-Rak Lee and Sang-Eun Bae; m. Ok-Hee Yang, May 10, 1980; 1 child, Kirim. BA, Korean Union Coll., Seoul, Republic of Korea, 1981; MEd, U. Mont., Missoula, 1994; PhD, U. Tex., Austin, 1997; postgrad., U. Trier, 1990—91. Rsch. fellow Korean Ednl. Devel. Inst., Seoul, 1998—2004; joint prof. Hongik U., Seoul, 2000—03; vis. scholar U. B.C., Vancouver, Canada, 2003—. Chmn. UNESCO Follow-up World Conf., Tashkent, Uzbekistan, 2000; tchr., counselor Unbong and Sunhwa Vocat. Sr. H.S., Incheon, Republic of Korea, 1981—85; rschr. U. Tex. Austin, 1996; instr. Korean Hongik U., Seoul, 2000, Yonsei U., Seoul, 2000—01, Dongkuk U., Seoul, 2001; pres. Ctrl. Coll., Burnaby, BC, Canada, 2003—04; planner, supr., site visitor Ministry Edn., Korean Ednl. Devel. Inst., 2001; dir. Nat. Stats. Korean Higher Edn. Ministry Edn., Seoul, 1998—99; owner viniculturalist Seowoon-myon, Kyungki-do, Republic of Korea, 1985—88. Author: Historic Factors Influencing Korean Higher Education, 2000, Korean Higher Education: A Confucian Perspective, 2002, Educational Credentialism in Korean Society: Origin and Development, 2003, The Encyclopedia of New Religion: Guide to New Religions and Alternative Spiritualities, 2004; contbr. articles to publs. Pastor Seventh Day Adventist Ch., Deoksong-ri, Kyungki-do, Republic of Korea, 1978—79; expert adviser Future Unification Instn., Seoul, 1999—; columnist, expert adviser Korean U. Newspaper, Seoul, 2003—. Henderson scholar, U. Tex., Austin, 1996, Academic Competitive scholar, 1996—97. Mem.: Assn. Asian Studies, Korean Soc. Study of Ednl. Adminstrn. (assoc.), Phi Kappa Phi. Avocations: reading, writing, travel, meditation. Home: 16621-19 Ave Surrey BC Canada V3S 9R4 Office Phone: 604-323-6980. Personal E-mail: jeongkyuk@hotmail.com.

LEE, JEROME G., lawyer; b. Chgo., Feb. 23, 1924; m. Margo B. Lee, Dec. 23, 1947; children: James A., Kenneth M. BSChemE, U. Wis., 1947; JD, NYU, 1950. Bar: N.Y. 1950, U.S. Supreme Ct. 1964. Assoc. Jeffery, Kimball, Eggleston, NYC, 1950-52, Morgan, Finnegan, Durham & Pine, NYC, 1952-59; ptnr. Morgan, Finnegan, Pine, Foley & Lee, NYC, 1959-86; sr. ptnr. Morgan & Finnegan, NYC, 1986-95, of counsel, 1995—. Lectr. in field. Author (with J. Gould): Intellectual Property Counseling and Litigation, 1988; author: USPTO Proposals to Change Rule 56 and the Related Rules Regarding a Patent Applicant's Duty of Candour, Patent World, 1992; contbr. articles to legal jours. Mem. Planning and Zoning Bd., Longboat Key, Fla., 1994—2005, chmn., 1999—2003. Fellow: Am. Bar Found.; mem.: ABA (mem. coun. intellectual property law sect., chmn. com. fed. practice and procedure, chmn. com. Ct. Appeals Fed. Cir., chmn. com. ethics and profl. responsibility, mem. stds. com., mem. fed. cir. adv. com. 1992—97), ATLA, others, N.Y. Patent, Trademark and Copyright Law Assn. (bd. dirs. 1975—80, pres. 1981), N.Y. County Bar Assn., Assn. Bar City of N.Y., N.Y. Bar Assn., Found. Creative Am. (bd. dirs.), Internat. Fedn. Indsl. Property Attys., Am. Judicature Soc., Am. Intellectual Property Law Assn. (bd. dirs. 1984—90, pres. 1991). Office: Morgan and Finnegan 3 World Financial Ctr New York NY 10281-2101 Home: 1299 N Tamiami Trail #628 Sarasota FL 34236 Office Phone: 212-415-8700.

LEE, JHEMON HOM, physician; b. Redwood City, Calif., July 1, 1970; s. Billy Tom and Yuen Han Lee. BA in Engring. summa cum laude, Harvard U., 1990; MD cum laude, U. Md., 1994. Diplomate Nat. Bd. Med. Examiners. Resident in diagnostic radiology U. Chgo., 1994—98, chief resident, 1997—98; fellow in abdominal imaging Brigham and Women's Hosp./Harvard Med. Sch., Boston, 1998—99; vice chair, radiology dept. Los Alamitos Med. Ctr., Los Alamitos, Calif.; radiologist, ptnr. MemRAD Med. Group, Long Beach, Calif., 1999—2006; ptnr. Los Alamitos Radiology Group, 2006—. Bd. dir. Radiologic Practice Mgmt., Inc., 2004—05. Editor-in-chief UMAB news, 1993; news editor East Wind, 1987-90; contbr. articles to profl. jours. Mem. steering com. United Asian Am. Orgns., Chgo., 1996-98; mem. Leadership Ctr. for Asian Ams., Chgo., 1997-98. Named one of Am. Top Radiologists, Consumers' Rsch. Coun. of Am., 2002—03, Am. Top Physicians, 2004—05; recipient Chgo. Chpt. Recognition award, Nat. Assn. of Asian Am. Profl., 1998, Lifetime Achievement award, 2002. Mem. Radiol. Soc. N.Am., Nat. Assn. Asian Am. Profls. (nat. pres., 1998-2000, exec. v.p. 2002-04), Chgo. Radiol. Soc., Asian Pacific Am. Med. Students Assn. (pres. adv. bd.), Asian Profl. Exch. (chair Healthcare Spl. Interest Group, dir. profl. devel. 2000-01), Orgn. Chinese Ams. (pres. Orange County chpt. 2003-06), Cold Tofu Improv, East West Players Actors Conservatory, Phi Beta Kappa, Alpha Omega Alpha. Avocations: computers, Asian American culture, writing, films. Home: 13710 Alderton Ln Cerritos CA 90703 Office Phone: 562-799-3294. Business E-Mail: jhemon@post.harvard.edu.

LEE, JIMMY CHE-YUNG, urban planner; b. Canton, China, May 29, 1946; came to U.S., 1969. s. Che Dui and Fong-Yee (Leung) Lee; m. Annie On-Lin Chan, Nov. 29, 1970 (div. 1987); m. Eileen Oi Ping Cheung, Dec. 16, 1987 (div. 1990); m. Sara Yeuk Siu, June 21, 1994; children: Grace Yeuk Won, Michelle Yeuk Shun. Grad., Sir. Robert Black Coll. Edn., Hong Kong; BA, U. Tex., 1973, MA, 1975. Tchr. English and Chinese Asbury Meth. Primary Sch., Hong Kong, 1966-69; asst. mgr. Trader Vic's Restaurant Dallas Hilton Inn, 1971-75; planner Dallas County Community Action Agy., 1975, dir. projects and resource devel. div., 1975—77; pres. U-Asia Corp., Hong Kong, 1975; owner Dragon Inn Restaurant, 1975; contr. food and beverage div. Plaza of Am. Hotel, 1979-82; comptr. Carlyle Hotels & Restaurants Inc., Harold Farb Co., 1982; founder, chief exec. officer Lee & Lee Fine Linens, Inc., 1982—; v.p. Asiatex Inc., 1987—, Titan Real Estate Devel. & Investment Group, Inc., 1993—. Bd. dirs. Crown Chpt. Nat. Bank Dallas. Pres. North Tex. Cantonese Assn., 1986-88, hon. pres., 1989—; dir. Dallas chpt. Friends of Hong Kong and Macau; v.p., dir. North Tex. Chinese Culture Divination Soc. Mem. Am. Inst. Planners (assoc.), Tex. Assn. Community Action Agys., Hong Kong Registered Tchrs. Assn. Baptist. Home: 629 Killarney Richardson TX 75081-5157 E-mail: jimcylee@aol.com.

LEE, JOHN CHAESEUNG, nuclear engineering educator; b. Seoul, July 29, 1941; came to U.S., 1965; s. Kwanhee and Chinbae (Kim) L.; m. Theresa Sungock Lee, June 26, 1971; 1 child, Nina. BS, Seoul Nat. U., 1963; PhD, U. Calif., Berkeley, 1969. Sr. engr. Westinghouse Nuclear Energy Systems, Pitts., 1969-73, GE, San Jose, Calif., 1973-74; asst. prof. nuc. engring. U. Mich., Ann Arbor, 1974-78, assoc. prof., 1978-81, prof., 1981—, chmn. dept., 1994—2004. Cons. U.S. Nuc. Regulatory Commn., Washington, 1975-94; mem. NAS separations tech. and transmutations systems transmutation subpanel, 1991-95—; vis. scientist Julich (Fed. Republic Germany) Nuc. Rsch. Ctr., 1981-82; generation IV roadmap working group US Dept. Energy, 2000-02. Contbr. numerous articles on nuc. sci. and engring. to profl. jours. Recipient Disting. Svc. award U. Mich. Class of 1938E, 1979. Fellow Am. Nuc. Soc.; mem. AAAS. Roman Catholic. Home: 3850 Wynnstone Dr Ann Arbor MI 48105-2879 Office: U Mich Dept Nuc Engring Ann Arbor MI 48109 Office Phone: 313-764-9379. Business E-Mail: jcl@umich.edu.

LEE, JOHN JIN, lawyer; b. Chgo., Oct. 20, 1948; s. Jim Soon and Fay Yown (Young) L.; m. Jamie Pearl Eng, Apr. 30, 1983. BA magna cum laude, Rice U., 1971; JD, MBA, Stanford U., 1975. Bar: Calif. 1976. Assoc. atty. Manatt Phelps & Rothenberg, LA, 1976-77; asst. counsel Wells Fargo Bank N.A., San Francisco, 1977-79, counsel, 1979-80, v.p., sr. counsel, 1980, v.p., mng. sr. counsel, 1981-98, v.p., asst. gen. counsel, 1998—2001; gen. counsel, sec. Westlake Realty Group, San Mateo, Calif., 2002—. Mem. governing com. Conf. on Consumer Fin. Law, 1989-93. Bd. dirs. Asian Bus. League San Francisco, 1980—, gen. counsel, 1980—81, chmn., 2004—. Fellow Am. Coll. Consumer Fin. Svcs. Lawyers, Inc. (bd. regents 1995-96); mem. ABA (chmn. subcom. housing fin., com. consumer fin. svcs., bus. law sect. 1983-90, vice chmn. securities products, consumer fin. svcs., bus. law sect. 1995-96, chmn. subcom. elec. banking, com. consumer fin. svcs., bus. law sect. 1996-2000, co-chmn. joint subcom. elec. fin. svcs., bus. law sect. 1997-2000, co-chmn. directory com. minority in-house counsel group 1995-98), Consumer Bankers Assn. (lawyers com.), Soc. Physics Students, Stanford Asian-Pacific Am. Alumni/ae Club (bd. dirs. 1989-93, v.p. 1989-91). Democrat. Baptist. Office: PO Box 1304 San Carlos CA 94070-7304 Home Phone: 650-368-1106; Office Phone: 650-579-1010 157. Business E-Mail: johnjinlee@stanfordalumni.org.

LEE, JOHN JOON, research scientist, minister; s. Young Mo and Sang Yeon Lee; m. Amy Hye-Sook Kim, Aug. 10, 1991. BS in Biology, U. Mich., 1986; MDiv, Princeton Theol. Sem., 1993; PhD in Ednl. Psychology, UCLA, 1999. Sr. rschr. Ctr. for Rsch. on Evaluation, Standards, and Student Testing, UCLA, 1994—; tentmaking pastor Cmty. Presbyn. Ch. Bellflower, Calif., 2001—. Developer (software) Quality School Portfolio. Mem.: Am. Ednl. Rsch. Assn. Office: Ctr Rsch Evaluation Stds Student Tchg UCLA Ste 1400 10945 Le Conte Blvd Los Angeles CA 90095 Office Phone: 310-794-9155. Business E-Mail: johnjn@ucla.edu.

LEE, JOHN LAWRENCE, JR., educational administrator; b. Pitts., Oct. 4, 1956; s. John Lawrence Sr. and Helen Marie (Kenny) L. BS in Edn., Duquesne U., 1978, MS in Edn., 1982; prin. cert., Indiana U. of Pa., 1989. Cert. reading specialist, elem. prin. Tchr. Assumption Sch., Pitts., Avonworth Sch. Dist., Pitts.; tchr. grade 5 Seneca Valley Sch. Dist., Mars, Pa.; prin. Southmoreland Sch. Dist., Alverton, Pa. Mem. ASCD, NAESP, Pa. ASCD, Pa. Assn. Elem. Sch. Prins. Office: Scottdale Elem Sch 421 N Chestnut St Scottdale PA 15683-1058 Home: 121 N Mulberry Dr Mount Pleasant PA 15666-3401 Office Phone: 724-887-2020.

LEE, JOHN MARSHALL, mathematics professor; b. Phila., Sept. 2, 1950; s. Warren W. and Virginia (Hull) L.; m. Pm Weizenbaum, May 26, 1984; children: Nathan Lee Weizenbaum, Jeremy Lee Weizenbaum. AB, Princeton U., 1972; student, Tufts U., 1977-78; PhD, MIT, 1982. Systems programmer Tex. Instruments, Princeton, NJ, 1972-74; Geophys. Fluid Dynamics Lab., GFDL/NOAA, Princeton, 1974-75; tchr. math. and physics Wooster Sch., Danbury, Conn., 1975-77; programmer and cons. info. processing svcs. MIT, Cambridge, Mass., 1978-82; asst. prof. math. Harvard U., Cambridge, 1982-87, U. Wash., Seattle, 1987-89, assoc. prof. math., 1989-96, prof. math., 1996—. Sr. tutor Harvard U., Cambridge, 1984-87. Author: Riemannian Manifolds: An Introduction to Curvature, 1997, Introduction to Topological Manifolds, 2000, Introduction to Smooth Manifolds, 2002; contbr. articles to profl. jours. Rsch. fellow NSF, 1982. Mem. Am. Math. Soc. (Centennial fellow 1989). Avocations: hiking, wine tasting, music. Office: Univ Wash Math Dept PO Box 354350 Seattle WA 98195-4350 Home Phone: 206-524-6346; Office Phone: 206-543-1735. E-mail: lee@math.washington.edu.

LEE, JONATHAN OWEN, financial services company executive, lawyer; b. Boston, Mar. 12, 1951; s. Herbert C. and Mildred (Schiff) L.; m. Barbara Ruth Cole, Mar. 24, 1984; children: Suzanna Cole, Alexander Philip. AB in Architecture, U. Calif., Berkeley, 1973; JD, Boston Coll., 1976. Bar: Mass. 1976. Staff atty. SEC, NYC, 1976-79; pres. Lee Capital Holdings, LLC, Boston, 1979—. Chmn. bd. dirs. Globe Metall., Inc., Cleve., 1986—, HSC Hospitality, Inc., Dallas, 1995—, Heritage Brands, LLC, Wilton, Conn., 1997, Hafslund Metall.As, Sarpsborg, Norway, 1998, Fesil Asa, Oslo, Norway, 1998; bd. dirs. So. Energy Homes, Inc., Adison, Ala., 1st Security Svcs., Inc., Boston, Mass., P.A.R. Assocs., Inc., Boston, Citizens Capital, Inc., Boston. Bd. dirs. Combined Jewish Philanthropies, Boston, 1987—, The Park Sch., Brookline, Mass, 1998—, Wang Ctr. Performing Arts, Boston, 1998—, Project Hope, Dorchester, Mass., 1999; mem. bd. overseers Mus. Fine Arts, Boston. Mem. Young Presidents Orgn., Explorers Club.

LEE, JONG HYUK, accountant; b. Hamheung, Korea, May 6, 1941; s. Jung Bo and Wol Sun Lee; m. Esther Kim, Jan. 24, 1970. BA, Sonoma State U., Rohnert Park, Calif., 1971; MBA in Taxation, Golden Gate U., 1976; DBA, Argosy U., 2007. CPA, Calif. Cost acct., internal auditor Foremost-McKesson Co., San Francisco, 1971-74; sr. acct. Clark, Wong, Foulkes & Barbieri, CPAs, Oakland, Calif., 1974-77; pres. J.H. Lee Accts. Corp., Oakland, 1977-97, J. Lee Assocs., Oakland, 1997—. Instr. Armstrong Coll., Berkeley, Calif., 1977-78; lectr. acctg., dir. Sch. Bus., U.S. Korea Bus. Inst., San Francisco State U., cross cultural seminars info. tech. industry major U.S. cities, France, Mex.; mem. adv. bd. Ctr. Korean Studies, Insts. East Asian Studies, U. Calif., Berkeley; adj. faculty Argosy U., 2007; bd. dirs. United Labor Bank, Oakland, Internat. Found. Ewha Women's U. Columnist tax and bus. column Korea Times, 1980. Commr. Calif. OEO, 1982—86; regional chmn. Adv. Coun. on Peaceful Unification Policy, Republic of Korea; commr. Asian Art Mus., San Francisco, 1988—91, Oakland Cmty. and Econ. Devel., 1997; bd. dirs., dir. East Bay Asian Local Devel. Corp.; pres. Oakland Masonic Ctr., Communities United Com., Korean Am. Dem. Network, Dem. Nat. Fin. Coun.; chmn. caucus Calif.-Nev. Ann. Conf. United Meth. Ch., 1977; bd. dirs. Korean Residents Assn., 1974, Multi-Svc. Ctr. for Koreans, 1979, BBB, 1984—87. Cpl. Korean Marine Corp, 1961—64, 1st lt. Calif. Mil. Res. Named March 5, 2004 Jong H. Lee Day, Mayor of Oakland. Mem. AICPA, Nat. Assn. Asian Am. CPAs (bd. dirs.), Am. Acctg. Assn., Nat. Assn. Accts., Internat. Found. Employee Benefit Plans, Calif. Soc. CPAs, Oakland C of C., Korean Am. C. of C. (pres. Pacific North Coast), Rotary. Home: 180 Firestone Dr Walnut Creek CA 94598-3645 Office: 369 13th St Oakland CA 94612-2636 Office Phone: 510-836-7400. Business E-Mail: jlee@jhleecpa.com.

LEE, JONG Y., medical scientist, educator; b. Seoul, Korea; MD, PhD in Pathology, U. Minn., 1987. Postdoctoral fellowship U. Minn., Mpls., 1987—92, educator, 1992—; pres. LGen Medtech, Ltd., Mpls., 1996—. Pres. Korean Scientists and Engrs. Assoc., Mpls., 1993—94; com. Bus. Cooperation, Dept. of Commerce, U.S. Govt., Washington, 1996—99. Author: (pioneering achievements/researcher) Brain microsurgery methodology: the central nervous system and hypertension (Am. Heart Association's Internat. Fellowship Award, 1990); contbr. articles to profl. jours. Recipient Scholastic achievement, Phi Kappa Phi, 1986, Outstanding Leadership Achievement Nat. award, Korean Scientist and Engrs. Assoc., 1994, Outstanding Leadership Achievement award, Govt. of State of Minn., 1994, Coun. of Asian Pacific Minnesotans, 1994, Most Outstanding Manuscript Award of Yr., Assn. for Advancement of Med. Instrumentation, 1998, Young Investigator's award mentorship honor, 1998. Mem.: Am. Heart Assn., Amerian Soc. of Hypertension, Twin Cities Catholoc Chorale, U. of Minn. Pres. Club (life), Phi Kappa Phi (life Academic excellence GPA 4.0/4.0 1986). Roman Catholic. Achievements include patents for expression vector using human gene to purify pure protein and its antobody; R&D and trials on invention of products; patents pending for differential diagnostic test kits for clinical use; invention product for hypertension; research in brain microsurgery, methodology, hypertension, the central nervous system, salt generic hypertension and chronobiological hypertension. Avocations: music, gardening, reading, travel, camping. Home: 828 Spring St NE Apt 2001 Minneapolis MN 55413-2673 Home Phone: 612-379-2467.

LEE, JOOHAN, materials scientist; BS, Yonsei U., Seoul, Republic of Korea, 1996; MS, U. Md., Coll. Pk., 1999, PhD, 2001. Prin. applications engr. GSI Group, Wilmington, Mass., 2001—. Contbr. over 20 articles to profl. jours. Recipient Excellent Performance award, GSI Group, 2003. Mem.: IEEE. Achievements include over 10 patents including pending patents in laser-material interaction and laser processing. Office: GSI Group 60 Fordham Rd Wilmington MA 01887 Home Phone: 857-222-1103; Office Phone: 978-661-4567. Office Fax: 978-988-9353. Personal E-mail: lee_joohan@yahoo.com.

LEE, JOSEPH WILLIAM, sales executive; b. Florence, SC, Sept. 19, 1943; s. Warner Lou and Rosalee (Hyman) L.; m. Rita Martin, Sept. 8, 1962; children: Mark Stephen, Allison Lynette. Grad. high sch., Florence. Clk. Atlantic Coast Line R.R., Florence, 1962-69; sales rep. Durham (N.C.) & So. Rwy., 1969-74; dist. sales mgr. Westmoreland Coal Sales Co., Charlotte, NC, 1974-82, v.p. purchasing Phila., 1982-85, v.p. purchasing distbn., 1985-88, v.p. purchasing and northern sales, 1988-91, sr. v.p., 1991, pres., 1991-95; v.p. sales TECO Coal Corp., 1995. Mem., trustee So. Coals Conf., Inc., 1989—92. Mem. N.C. Coal Inst., Charlotte C. of C. Republican. Personal E-mail: jlee17@carolina.rr.com.

LEE, KATHERINE See JOEL, KATIE

LEE, KATHLEEN MARY, health facility administrator, nursing executive; b. Phila., Apr. 12, 1948; d. Daniel Joseph and Mary Ann (Daly) Glackin; m. Gary Douglas MacClay, May 2, 1970 (div. 1980); 1 child, Jeffrey Daniel; m. Glenn Patrick Lee, Feb. 14, 1981. RN diploma, Phila. Gen. Hosp., 1969; BS, St. Joseph Coll., 1985; M Health Svcs. Adminstrn., St. Josephs Coll., 1990; PhD in Health Svcs., Walden U., 1992. RN, Ga., R.I., Pa., Miss.; cert. nursing adminstr. Head nurse, nursery Jeanes Hosp., Phila., 1969-78; administrv. supr. Roger Williams Hosp., Providence, 1981-83; head nurse, nursery svcs. King Fahad Hosp., Rivadh, Saudi Arabia, 1983-85; charge nurse psychiatric N.E. Ga. Med. Ctr., Gainesville, 1986-87; v.p. patient svcs. St. Joseph's Hosp., Dahlonega, Ga., 1987-95, Coffee Regional Med. Ctr., Douglas, Ga., 1996-98; assoc. adminstr. Nursing and Profl. Svcs., Ocean Springs, Miss., 1998—. Founder, UNITE, Parent Support Group, Phila., 1976; co-founder, Neonatal Soc. San Antonio, 1979. Capt. USAF, 1978-81. Fellow: Am. Coll. Healthcare Execs.; mem.: ANA, Ga. Nurses Assn. (Ga. Nurses Make a Difference award 1991, dist. honoree 1992), Am. Orgn. Nurse Execs., Miss. Nurses Assn. (Dist. Specialty Nurse of Year award 2000), Sigma Theta Tau (Excellence in Nursing Adminstrn. award Zeta Gamma chpt. 2005). Democrat. Roman Catholic. Home: 1509 Amberjack Dr Gautier MS 39553-7133 Office: Nursing and Profl Svcs 3109 Bienville Blvd Ocean Springs MS 39564-4361 Home Phone: 228-497-5772; Office Phone: 228-818-1193. Business E-Mail: k_lee@srhsealth.com.

LEE, KATIE N., biochemistry and chemistry scholar; d. Joe and Patricia L. BS in Biochemistry, Chemistry, Univ. Minn., 2007; DPhil student in Biochemistry, Oxford Univ., 2007—. Rhodes Scholar. Achievements include entering univ. at age 15; conducting rsch. on human papilloma virus at Harvard Med. Sch. Avocation: violin.*

LEE, KATRINA LASHAWN, health insurance business consultant; b. Jacksonville, Fla., June 20, 1966; d. Kelly Lucas and Hattie Lee. AA, Fla. C.C., 1987; AS in Med. Lab. Tech., Fla. Jr. Coll., 1986; BS in Health Sci., U. North Fla., 1992, M in Health Adminstrn., 1997. Cert. Clin. Lab. Scientist Nat. Cert. Agy. Med. Lab. Personnel, Med. Lab. Tech. Am. Soc. Clin. Pathologists Bd. Registry. Sr. med. tech. U. Med. Ctr., Jacksonville, Fla., 1987—97; project cons. Blue Cross, Blue Shield Fla., Jacksonville, 1997—; adj. prof. Fla. Met. U., Orange Park, 2004—. Sec. U. North Fla. Coll. Health Alumni Assn., Jacksonville, 2005—. Mem.: Am. Alliance Health, Phys. Edn., Recreation, Dance (assoc.). Home Phone: 904-771-9806.

LEE, KENNETH STUART, neurosurgeon, educator; b. Raleigh, NC, July 23, 1955; s. Kenneth Lloyd and Myrtie Lee (Turner) L.; m. Cynthia Jane Anderson, May 23, 1981; children: Robert Alexander, Evan Anderson. BA, Wake Forest U., 1977; MD, East Carolina U., 1981. Diplomate Nat. Bd. Med. Examiners, Am. Bd. Neurol. Surgeons; med. lic. N.C., Ariz. Intern, then resident in neurosurgery Wake Forest U. Med. Ctr., Winston-Salem, N.C., 1981-88; fellow Barrow Neurol. Inst., Phoenix, 1988-89; clin. asst. prof. neurosurgery East Carolina U., Greenville, NC, 1989-93, clin. assoc. prof. neurosurgery, 1994—2001, clin. prof. neurosurgery, 2001—, adj. assoc. prof. health edn., 1997—. Assoc. editor Current Surgery, 1990—; contbr. 30 articles to profl. jours. and 6 chpts. to books. Mem. Ethicon Neurosurgical Adv. Panel, 1989-95. Bucy fellow, 1988. Fellow ACS, Am. Heart Assn. (stroke coun.); mem. AMA, N.C. Med. Soc., Am. Assn. Neurol. Surgeons, Am. Soc. Stereotactic and Functional Neurosurgery, So. Med. Assn., Congress Neurol Surgeons, N.C. Neurosurg. Soc. (sec.-treas. 1991-93, pres. 1994-95), So. Neurosurg. Soc., Leksell Gamma Knife Soc., Alpha Omega Alpha. Republican. Baptist. Achievements include research on the efficacy of certain surgical procedures, particularly carotid endarterectomy, in the prevention of strokes. Home: 792 Lexington Dr Greenville NC 27834 Office: Ea Carolina Neurosurg 2325 Stantonsburg Rd Greenville NC 27834-7534 Home Phone: 252-355-4860; Office Phone: 252-752-5156.

LEE, KICHOON, animal scientist, educator; s. Sang-Oh Lee and Moon-Ja Choi; m. Yeunsu Suh; 1 child, Eugene. PhD, U. Ga., Athens, 1997. Rsch. asst. U. Ga., Athens, 1991—99; rschr. U. Calif., Berkeley, 1999—2002; rsch. instr. Pennington Biomed. Rsch. Ctr., Baton Rouge, 2002—04; asst. prof. Ohio State U., Columbus, 2004—. Contbr. articles to profl. jours. Home: 7388 Tullymore Dr Dublin OH 43016 Office: Ohio State Univ 2029 Fyffe Rd Columbus OH 43210 Home Phone: 614-733-0526; Office Phone: 614-688-7963.

LEE, KUO-HSIUNG, medicinal chemistry professor; b. Kaohsiung, Taiwan, Jan. 4, 1940; came to U.S., 1965; s. Ching-Tsung Lee and Chin-Yeh Yang; m. Lan-Huei Chen; children: Thomas Tung-Ying, Catherine Tung-Ling. BS, Kaohsiung Med. Coll., Taiwan, 1961; MS, Kyoto U., Japan, 1965; PhD, U. Minn., 1968. Postdoctoral scholar dept. chemistry UCLA, 1968-70; asst. prof. Sch. Pharmacy, U. N.C., Chapel Hill, 1970-74, assoc. prof., 1974-77, prof. medicinal chemistry, 1977-91, dir. natural products rsch. labs., 1983—, Kenan prof. medicinal chemistry, 1992—, chair divsn. med. chem. and natural products, 1998-99. Adj. prof. Kaohsiung Med. Coll., 1977—; mem. devel. therapeutics contract rev. com. Nat. Cancer Inst., NIH, 1984-88, Bio-organic and natural products chemistry study sect., 1990-94, mem. reviewers res., 1994-98; external assessor, res grants coun., Hong Kong, 1994—; cons. natural products program divsn. life scis. NSC, Taiwan, 1986-87, Food and Drug Bur., Dept. Health, Exec. Yuan of Republic of China, Taiwan, 1986-92, Genelabs, Inc., Redwood City, Calif., 1988-00, Nat. Rsch. Inst., Chinese Medicine, Taiwan, 1989—, Sphinx Pharms. Corp., Durham, N.C., 1990-94; sci. advisor Nat. Lab. Foods and Drugs, Dept. Health, Exec. Yuan of Republic of China, Taiwan, 1990—; mem. sci. adv. bd. Pharmagenesis, 1992-03; mem. acad. adv. com. planning sect. Nat. Health Rsch. Inst., Dept. Health, 1992-95, mem. recruitment and adv. com., 1996-00, mem. sci. rev. and sci. coun. com. pharm. and biotech. sect., 1996—; mem. internat. adv. com. Biotech. Rsch. Inst., Hong Kong U. Sci. and Tech., 1997—; mem. strategic adv. panel Hong Kong Jockey Club Inst. Chinese Medicine, 2002-; mem. adv. com. Inst. Plant and Microbial Biology Academia Sinica, Taiwan, 2001-, Genomic Rsch. Ctr., Academia Sinica, 2004-, Inst. Cellular and Organismic Biology Academia Sinica, 2004-, Nat. Health Rsch. Insts., 2007—, Nat. Sci. Coun.'s Nat. Sci. and Tech. Program in Pharmacy and Tech., Taiwan, 2002-; chair sci. adv. bd. Plantaceutica, Inc., Research Triangle Park, N.C., 2001-04; chair com. for promotion of Chinese herbal medicine industry and tech. Ministry of Econ. Affairs, Taiwan, 2000-05; hon. advisor Chinese Medicinal Material Rsch. Ctr., Chinese U. of Hong Kong, 1999—, hon. prof. Inst. Med. Plant Devel., Chinese Acad. Med. Scis., 1999. Mem. editl. adv. bd. Abstracts of Chinese Medicines, 1986-, Oriental Healing Arts Internat. Bull., 1987-, Bot. Bull. Academia Sinica, 1988-, The Chinese Pharm. Jour., 1988-, Jour. Pharm. Sci., 1990-92, Jour. Chinese Medicine, 1990-, Internat. Jour. Oriental Medicine, 1989-, Kaohsiung Jour. Med. Sci., 1992-, Internat. Jour. Pharmacognosy, 1991-, Jour. Nat. Prod., 1994-, Jour. Asian Nat. Prod. Rsch., 1998-, Jour. Med. Chem., 1999-2003, Jour. Biomed. Sci., Current Med. Chemistry - Anticancer Agents, 2005-, Current Bioactive Compounds, 2005-; contbr. more than 600 articles to profl. jours. Grantee NIH, Am. Cancer Soc., U.S. Army, 1971—; recipient Soine Meml. award U. Minn., 1990, Achievement award Genelabs, 1993, Lifu Acad. award Chinese Medicine, 1994, T.M. Tu Sci. award, 1995, Merit award Nat. Health Rsch. Insts., 1996, Editor's award Japan Oil Chem. Soc., 1997; named Hon. Prof., Shanghai Inst. Materia Medica, 1996-; recipient Outstanding Achievement award U. Minn., 1999, Achievement award Taiwanese-Am. Found. Sci. and Engring., 2003, Kitasato Microbial Chemistry medal, Japan, 2005. Fellow AAAS, Am. Assn. Pharm. Scientists, Acad. Pharm. Sci.; mem. Am. Chem. Soc., Chem. Soc., Am. Soc. Pharmacognosy, Am. Assn. Pharm. Sci., Am. Assn. Coll. Pharm., Phytochemistry Soc. N.Am., Soc. Syn. Organic Chemistry, Am. Assn. Cancer Rsch., Academia Sinica (academician). Achievements include more than 50 patents on synthesis of anti-cancer drugs, anti-fungal agts., anti-AIDS compounds, discovery of more than 2,000 novel plant anti-tumor agts. and synthetic analogs; elucidation of structure-activity relationships, mechanisms of action of bioactive products, herbal medicine including Chinese herbal medicine. Office: U NC Sch Pharmacy Chapel Hill NC 27599-7360 Office Phone: 919-962-0066. Business E-Mail: khlee@unc.edu.

LEE, KWAN MIN, communications educator, consultant; s. Youngduck and Sohyun Lee; m. Jihye Mo, Dec. 25, 1998. BA, Sogang U., Republic of Korea, 1994; MA, Mich. State U., East Lansing, 1998; PhD, Stanford U., Calif., 2002. Rschr. IBM T. J. Watson Rsch. Ctr., Hawthorn, NY, 2000—00; rsch. behavior analyst Quack.com (now merged to AOL), San Jose, Calif., 2001—01; cons. Samsung, Seoul, 2002—04; prof. U. So. Calif., LA, 2002—. Mem. adv. bd. World Cyber Edugames, Seoul, 2005, Beijing, 05. Mem. editl. bd.: Jour. Comm., Human Comm. Rsch., Comm. Theory, Korean Prospect, 2005. Fellow, Stanford U., 1999; grantee, Annenberg Found., 2003, Ministry Edn., 2004; Lily M. and Henry J. Budde fellow, Stanford U., 2001. Mem.: ACM (assoc.), Korean Am. Comm. Assn. (v.p. 2005—), Nat. Comm. Assn. (assoc.), Internat. Comm. Assn. (assoc.). Achievements include research in human-computer interaction; media psychology. Office: U So Calif Annenberg Sch Comm Los Angeles CA 90089 Home Phone: 310-205-8927; Office Phone: 213-740-3935. Business E-Mail: kwanmin.lee@usc.edu.

LEE, KWANGIL, electrical engineer, researcher; b. Susan, Chungchung South, Korea (South), June 3, 1970; s. YiSun Lee and Sunbun Kim; m. Hyejin Kim, May 12, 2001; 1 child, Isaac Sungjun. BS, Chungnam Nat. U., Daejeon, Korea, 1993, MS, 1996, PhD, 2001. Guest rschr. NIST, Gaithersburg, Md., 2000—02; rsch. assoc. U. Md., College Park, Md., 2002—04; vis. prof. U. of Tex., El Paso, 2005, rsch. assoc. Dallas, 2005—06; sr. rschr. Elec. and Telecomm. Rsch. Inst., Yuseung, Daejeon, Republic of Korea, 2006—. Contbr. articles to profl. jours. Grantee Student Travel grantee, IEEE Globecom, 1997; scholar Best Student scholar, Chungnam Nat. U., 1988—92. Mem.: IEEE (assoc.). Christian. Achievements include patents pending for connection management scheme with VLAN for UPnP; QoS switching between heterogeneous QoS Networks in home environments; QoS switching between non-QoS and QoS Networks in home environments; QoS extensions for home network middleware. Avocations: travel, bowling, soccer, ping pong/table tennis. Home: Guamdong Chorong APT 3-705 Daejeon Yuseung 305-801 Republic of Korea Office: Elec and Telecomm Rsch Inst 161 Gajeong-dong Daejeon Yuseung 305-700 Republic of Korea Office Phone: 82-42-860-5025. Office Fax: 82-42-860-5218; Home Fax: 82-42-860-5218. Business E-Mail: leeki@etri.re.kr.

LEE, KYO RAK, radiology educator; b. Seoul, Korea, Aug. 3, 1933; s. Ke Chong and Ok Hi (Um) L.; came to U.S., 1964, naturalized, 1976; MD, Seoul Nat. U., 1959; m. Ke Sook Oh, July 22, 1964; children: Andrew, John. Intern, Franklin Sq. Hosp., Balt., 1964-65; resident U. Mo. Med. Center, Columbia, Mo., 1965-68; instr. dept. radiology U. Mo., Columbia, 1968-69, asst. prof., 1969-71; asst. prof. dept. radiology U. Kans., Kansas City, 1971-76, assoc. prof., 1976-81, prof., 1981—. Served with Republic of Korea Army, 1950-52. Diplomate Am. Bd. Radiology (cert. added qualification in pediat. radiology). Recipient Richard H. Marshak award Am. Coll. Gastroenterology, 1975. Fellow Am. Coll. Radiology; mem. Radiol. Soc. N.Am., Am. Roentgen Ray Soc., Assn. Univ. Radiologists, Kans. Radiol. Soc., Greater Kansas City Radiol. Soc., Wyandotte County Med. Soc., Korean Radiol. Soc. N.Am., Soc., Soc. Pediat. Radiology. Contbr. articles to med. jours. E-mail: klee@kumc.edu. Home: 9800 Glenwood St Shawnee Mission KS 66212-1536 Office: U Kans 39th St and Rainbow Blvd Kansas City KS 66103 Office Phone: 913-588-6832. Business E-Mail: klee@kumc.edu.

LEE, LELA A., dermatology educator, researcher; b. Gorman, Tex., Sept. 7, 1950; d. J.H. and Pauline (Lemaster) L.; m. Norman Erling Wikner, June 24, 1984. BA, Rice U., 1972; MD, Southwestern Med. Sch., Dallas, 1976. Diplomate Am. Bd. Internal Medicine, Am. Bd. Dermatology. Resident in medicine Temple U. Hosp., Phila., 1976-79; resident in dermatology U. Colo., Denver, 1980-83, immunodermatology fellow, 1983-85, asst. prof. dermatology and medicine, 1985-91; staff physician V.A. Hosp., Denver, 1985-91; prof. dermatology U. Okla. Sch. of Medicine, 1991-97; chief dermatology Denver Health Med. Ctr., 1997—. Mem. test com. Am. Bd. Dermatology, 1993-97, dir., 2001—; prof. dermatology and medicine U. Colo. Sch. Medicine, 1997—; vis. lectr. Kyoto U., 1991, Keio U. Sch. Medicine, Tokyo, 1991, Tyndale lectr. U. Utah, 1994; mem. adv. bd. Neonatal Lupus Nat. Registry, N.Y.C., 1995—; dir. Am. Bd. Dermatology, Neonatal Lupus Internat. Symposium, Aspen, Colo., 1996. Contbr. articles to med. jours.; chief assoc. editor: Jour. Investigative Dermatology, 1990-92. Mem. adv. com. Lupus Found. Colo., Denver, 1999—. Recipient Stelwagon award Coll. Physicians of Phila., 1983, Clin. Investigator award NIH, 1985-90; VA merit rev. grantee, 1991-97; fellow Exec. Leadership in Acad. Medicine, Phila., 2000-01; Bill Reed Traveling fellow Friends of Bill Reed Com., 1984; named Carl Herzog Prof. of Dermatology, 1991. Fellow: Am. Acad. Dermatology; mem.: Am. Bd. Dermatology (bd. dirs. 2001—), Colo. Dermatol. Soc., Am. Dermatol. Assn., Soc. Investigative Dermatology (bd. dirs. 1985—87), Med. Dermatology Soc. (pres. 1998—99), Southwestern Med. Sch. Alumni Assn., Assn. Rice Alumni. Avocations: puzzles, music, hiking. Office: Denver Health Med Ctr 660 Bannock St M/C 4000 Denver CO 80204

LEE, LEONARD S., health facility administrator; b. Canton, China, Oct. 10, 1939; US, 1957; s. Man-Kei and Wen-Yee Fung Lee; m. Diana C. Lee, Aug. 23, 1963; children: Laurence L., Janice D. BS in Biology, East Tex. Bapt. U., 1961; MS in Biochemistry, N. Mex. Highlands U., 1964. Registered Environmental Specialist. Quality control specialist Merck and Co. Inc., South San Francisco, 1962—63, sr. rsch. scientist, 1964—83; tchr. San Francisco Unified Sch. Dist., 1984—86; health inspector Contra Costa Dept. of Health, Richmond, Calif., 1986—90; environ. specialist Santa Clara County, San Jose, Calif., 1990—2004; pres., founder San Bruno Chinese Sr. Ctr., Calif., 2004—. Food safety trainer Stanford U. Food Svc., Calif., 1990—2004; food trainer for state cert. Pacific Rim Environ. Health, San Francisco, 1993—; conf. spkr. World Congress in Environ. Health, Kaula Lumpur, Malaysia, 1994. Elder San Bruno Chinese Ch., 1993—98; deacon San Bruno Chinese Bapt. Ch. Inc., 1999—; cert. trainer AARP Sr. Driver Safety Program, Millbrae, Calif., 2000—; pres., founder San Bruno Chinese Sr. Ctr., 2004—; dir. Pacific Rim Environ. Health Assn., 1995—. Recipient Disting. award, Calgon Corp., 1983, Award of Excellence, Stanford U. Food Svc., 1999—2004, City Proclamation: Leonard Lee Day, South San Francisco, 2004. Mem.: Calif. Assn. of Environ. Health, Nat. Assn. Environ. Health, Am. Chem. Soc. Achievements include patents in field. Avocations: reading, writing, music, sports. Home: 476 Alta Vista Dr South San Francisco CA 94080

LEE, LESLIE WARREN, marketing executive, educator; b. Mpls., Nov. 21, 1949; s. Adolph Orlando and Eunice Celia (Akerson) L.; m. Kathleen Karen Frie, June 2, 1973; children: Megan Christine, Maren Elisabeth, Matthew Warren. BA in History magna cum laude, Augsburg Coll., Mpls., 1971. CLU, ChFC. Dir. YMCA, Mpls., 1971-73; dist. sales mgr. Chrysler Mtr. Corp., Marshfield, Wis., 1973-75; agt. Northwestern Mut. Life, Marshfield, 1975-81; mgr. advanced underwriting The Rural Co., Madison, Wis., 1981-83; advanced life mktg. specialist Am. Family Ins., Madison, 1983-95; nat. sales dir., v.p. mktg. Flexsystem, Madison, 1995-98; specialist Farmers Ins. Group Life, 1999—; trainer Farmers Fin. Svc., 1999—. Instr. dept. bus. U. Wis., Madison, 1981-82, instr. dept. econs., Stevens Point, 1978-81; lectr., cons. in field. Mem. Nat. Assn. Ins. & Fin. Advisors, Madison Assn. Ins. and Fin. Adv., Nat. Spkrs. Assn., Wis. Profl. Spkrs. Assn., Soc. Fin. Svc. Profls. Republican. Lutheran. Avocation: stamp collecting/philately. Office: Motivation and Tng for Arena Life PO Box 620305 7522 E Hampstead Ct Middleton WI 53562-3609 Office Phone: 608-831-4857. E-mail: leslee@itis.com.

LEE, LESTER P., JR., historian; b. Boston, Aug. 30, 1949; s. Rose Frances and Lester Preston Lee. BA in History, Antioch Coll., Yellow Springs, Ohio, 1972; MA in Internat. Rels., Johns Hopkins U., Washington, DC, 1975; MA in History, Harvard U., Cambridge, Mass., 1976. Asst. coop. edn. faculty coord. Northeastern U., Boston, 1998—2005; vis. asst. prof. history Salem State Coll., Mass., 2005—. Mem. Dem. City Com., Cambridge, Mass., 2000—. Recipient Peace and Justice award, Cambridge Peace Commn., 1996, Arthur Morgan Disting. Alumni award, Antioch Coll., 1998; W.E.B. DuBois fellowship, Harvard U., 1977 - 78. Fellow: Mass. Hist. Soc. Democrat-Npl. Home: 6 Agassiz St Cambridge MA 02140 Home Phone: 617-492-1894. Personal E-mail: lesterpleejr@verizon.net.

LEE, LEWIS SWIFT, retired lawyer; b. Dallas, Nov. 19, 1933; s. Lenoir Valentine and Margaret Louise (Clendon) L.; m. Frances Ann Childress, Mar. 16, 1956; children; Frances Ann Lee Webb, Lewis S. Jr., George Childress, Lenoir Valentine Lee II. AB, U. South, 1955; postgrad., Washington & Lee U., 1954-55; MA, Emory U., 1956, LLB (replaced by JD), 1960. Bar: Fla. 1960. Trainee Citizens & So. Nat. Bank, Atlanta, 1956, 58-59; assoc. Adair, Ulmer, Murchison, Kent & Ashby, Jacksonville, Fla., 1960-63; shareholder Ulmer, Murchison, Ashby & Ball, Jacksonville, 1963-95; of counsel LeBoeuf, Lamb, Greene & MacRae, LLP, Jacksonville, 1996-99, Martin, Ade, Birchfield & Mickler, PA, Jacksonville, 2000, McGuire Woods LLP, Jacksonville, 2001—05; pres. Longleaf, Inc., 2005—; gen. ptnr. Longleaf LLLP, 2005—. Gen. counsel Fla. Rock Industries, Inc., Jacksonville, Fla., 1972—2004, Patriot Transp. Holdings, Inc., 1989—2004; mgr. Kanapaha Ranch, 1974—. Dir. Fla. Sch. Book Depository, Jacksonville, 1990—2005. 1st lt. US Army, 1956—58. Mem. ABA, Jacksonville Bar Assn., Ponte Vedra Inn & Club, Timuquana Country Club, Fla. Yacht Club, The River Club, Haile Plantation Golf & Country Club (Gainesville). Republican. Episcopalian. Avocations: hiking, skiing, swimming, hunting, travel. Home: 3733 Ortega Blvd Jacksonville FL 32210-4347 Office: McGuire Woods LLP 50 N Laura St Ste 3300 Jacksonville FL 32202

LEE, LORRIN L., internet marketing entrepreneur, architect, writer; b. Honolulu, July 22, 1941; s. Bernard Chong and Betty (Lum) L.; m. Nina Fedoroscko, June 10, 1981. BArch, U. Mich., 1970; MBA, Columbia Pacific U., 1981, PhD in Psychology, 1981. Registered Hawaii. Arch. Skidmore, Owings & Merrill Archs., Hawaii, 1967, Clifford Young AIA, Honolulu, 1971-72, Aotani & Oka AIA, Honolulu, 1972—73, Naramore, Bain, Brady & Johansen, Hawaii, 1974, Geoffrey Fairfax FAIA, Honolulu, 1974-76; seminar leader Lorrin Lee Program, Honolulu, 1976-81; star grand master coord. Enhance Corp., 1981-83; 5-diamond supr. Herbalife Internat., LA, 1983—, mem. Global Expansion Team, 1993—; presdl. dir. Uni-Vite Internat., San Diego, 1989-92; agt. Internat. Pen Friends, 1995—; mgr. Cyber Media Sales, 1996-2000; dealer Cajun Country Candies, 2000—05; pearl distributor Tahitian Noni Internat., 2002—; agt. Friend-Finder, 2001—; assoc. My World Plus, 2007—. Author: Here is Genius, 1980, How to be Rich and Happy, How to Have an Ideal Relationship, Live a Memorable Life. Editor Honolulu Chinese Jaycees, Honolulu, 1972, v.p., 1983; active Makiki Cmty. Ctr., Honolulu, 1974. 1st lt. U.S. Army, 1967-70, Okinawa, 2nd Logistical Command. Recipient Braun-Knect-Heimann award, 1959, 1st Prize in Design Kidjel Cali-Pro Internat., 1975, Kitchen Design award Sub-Zero Contest, 1994; named Honolulu Chinese Jaycee of Yr., Honolulu Chinese Jaycees, 1973. Mem. Nature Conservancy, Sierra Club. Avocations: international travel, hiking, desktop publishing, photography, reading. Office: 500 University Ave #2415 Honolulu HI 96826 Office Phone: 808-949-5000. Personal E-mail: lorrin@lorrinlee.com.

LEE, LOW KEE, electronics engineer, consultant; b. Feb. 12, 1916; s. Hing Wing and Yan Hai (Louie) L.; m. Alice Jing, Nov. 29, 1953; children: Elliott James, Elizabeth Joanne. BS, U. Calif., Berkeley, 1937, MS, 1939; PhD, Calif. Western U., 1977. Group leader Aerophysics Lab., LA, 1946—50; lab. mgr. Stanford Rsch. Inst., Menlo Park, Calif., 1950—55; asst. to dir. Gen. Mills, Mpls., 1955—57; dept. mgr. product engring. TRW, Redondo Beach, Calif., 1957—62, asst. dir. product assurance, 1962—78; ret., 1978. Cons. Omni Corp., Rancho Santa Fe, 1983—, Control Data Inc., City of Industry, Calif. Co-author: Design and Construction of Electronic Equipment, 1961; contbr. to books, encys. Fellow: IEEE; mem.: Chinese Am. Inst. Engrs. and Scientists (pres. San Francisco 1945—46, trustee 1979—81, 1989—91, Meritorious award 1985), Masons. Home: 33 Linda Ave 1301 Oakland CA 94611 Home Phone: 510-985-0452. Personal E-mail: lowlee@comcast.net.

LEE, MARGARET BURKE, college president, language educator; b. San Diego, Dec. 28, 1943; d. Peter John and Margaret Mary (Brown) Burke; m. Donald Harry Lee, June 30, 1973 (dec. June 2002); children: Katherine Louise, Kristopher Donald. BA summa cum laude, Regis Coll., 1966; MA with honors, U. Chgo., 1970, PhD, 1978; IEM Cert., Harvard U., 1992, Seminar for New Pres., 1996. Asst. to humanities MIT, Cambridge, 1969; instr. Dover-Sherborn H.S., Dover, 1973-75, Alpena (Mich.) C.C., 1975-80, dean liberal arts, 1980-82; dean instrn. Kalamazoo Valley C.C., 1982-85; v.p. Oakton C.C., Des Plaines, Ill., 1985-95, pres., 1995—. Vice chair Am. Coun. on Internat. Intercultural Edn., 2000—, chair, 2002-05; cons., field faculty Vt. Coll., Montpelier, 1982-85; admissions com. Ill. Math and Sci. Acad., 1988—; bd. govs. North Cook Ednl. Svc. Ctr., 1988-2004, vice chair, 1990-91, chair, 1992-94, bd. dirs.; bd. dirs. Academic Search Cons. Svcs., Internat. Chair Acad. Bd. edn. Dist. 39, Wilmette, Ill., 1990-92, Des Plaines Sister Cities, 1995—; mem. 50th ann. leadership cir. Sister Cities Internat.; bd. dirs. Ill. C.C. Atty.'s Assn., 1994—; mem. Career Edn. Planning Dist., Kalamazoo, 1982, Kalamazoo Forum/Kalamazoo Network, 1982, Needs Assessment Task Force, 1984. Ford Found. fellow, 1969—73, Woodrow Wilson Found. fellow, 1975, fed. grantee, 1978—84. Mem. Am. Assn. CC (bd. dirs. 2000-04, exec. com. 2002-04), Am. Assn. Cmty. and Jr. Colls., Mich. Assn. C.C. Instrnl. Adminstrs. (pres. 1983-85), Mich. Occupl. Deans Adminstrs. Coun. (exec. bd. 1983-85), Mich. Women's Studies Assn. (hons. selection com. 1984), North Ctrl. Assn. Acad. Deans (pres. 1988-90, cons. evaluator Chgo., 1982—, commr.-at-large, 1988-92, commn. on inst. of higher edn. bd. dirs. 1992—, vice chair, 1996-98, chair 1998-2001, v.p.), Kalamazoo Consortium Higher Edn. (pres.'s coun. coord. com. 1982-85), Kalamazoo C. of C. (vocat. edn. subcom. indsl. coun. 1982), North Ctrl. Assn. Acad. Deans (v.p., pres. 1985-87), Des Plaines C. of C. (bd. dirs. 1995—). Democrat. Lutheran. Avocations: quilt collecting, reading, listening to classical music, sports spectating, theatre-going. Home: 2247 Lake Ave Wilmette IL 60091-1410 Office: Oakton CC 1600 E Golf Rd Des Plaines IL 60016-1234 Business E-Mail: plee@oakton.edu.

LEE, MARGARET NORMA, artist; b. Kansas City, Mo., July 7, 1928; d. James W. and Margaret W. (Farin) Lee; PhB, U. Chgo., 1948; MA, Art Inst. Chgo., 1952. Lectr., U. Kansas City, 1957-61; cons. Kansas City Bd. Edn., Kansas City, Mo., 1968-86; guest lectr. U.Mo.-Columbia, 1983, 85, 87, 89, 91, 93-95, 97; one-woman shows Univ. Women's Club, Kansas City, 1966, Friends of Art, Kansas City, 1969, Fine Arts Gallery U. Mo. at Columbia, 1972, All Souls Unitarian Ch. Kansas City, Mo., 1978; two-Woman show Rockhurst Coll., Kansas City, Mo., 1981 exhibited in group shows U. Kans., Lawrence, 1958, Chgo. Art Inst., 1963, Nelson Art Gallery, Kansas City, Mo., 1968, 74, Mo. Art Show, 1976, Fine Arts Gallery, Davenport, Iowa, 1977; represented in permanent collections Amarillo (Tex.) Art Center, Kansas City (Mo.) Pub. Library, Park Coll., Parkville, Mo. Mem. Coll. Art Assn. Roman Catholic. Contbr. art to profl. jours.; author booklet. Home: 4109 Holmes St Kansas City MO 64110-1127

LEE, MARILYN MODARELLI, lawyer, retired law library director; b. Jersey City, Dec. 8, 1934; d. Alfred E. and Florence O. Modarelli; m. Alfred McClung Lee III, June 8, 1957 (div. July 1985); children: Leslie Lee Ekstrand, Alfred McClung IV, Andrew Modarelli. BA, Swathmore Coll., Pa., 1956; JD, Western New Eng. Sch. of Law, 1985. Bar: Mass. 1986. Claims rep., supr. region II Social Security Adminstrn., Jersey City, 1956—59; law libr. County of Franklin, Greenfield, Mass., 1972—78; head law libr. Mass. Trial Ct., Greenfield, 1978—2001. Mem. Franklin County Futures Lab Project (Mass. Cts.), 1994—. Vice chmn. Greenfield Planning Bd., 1987—95; mem. bldg. com. Greenfield Sch., 1995—2003, clerk, 2002—03; mem. Greenfield Bd. Registrar of Voters, 2003—, Jennie L. Bascom Fund, 2004—05, Franklin Regional Planning Bd., 1988—98; moderator All Souls Unitarian Ch., 1996—2000, asst. treas., 1997—98, 2006—, treas., 1998—2001; chmn. Franklin County Tech., Turners Falls, Mass., 1974—76, bldg. com. chair, 1974—76, clk., 1976—81; exec. bd. Franklin Regional Planning Bd., 1992—95; mem. Greenfield C.C. Found., 1990—, Franklin Regional Transp. Com., 1992—; mem. alumni coun. Swarthmore Coll., 1994—97. Mem. Franklin County Bar Assn. (chmn. lawyer referral com. 1992-94, 97-99, vice-chmn. 1994-97, chmn. libr. com. 1992—), Law Librs. of New Eng. (treas. 1993-97), Am. Assn. Law Librs. (mem. state ct. and county law librs. sect. 1972—, bylaws com. 1996-99, chair bylaws com. 1997-98), Greenfield Charter (commn. clk. 1979-83), Mass. Soc. Prevention of Cruelty to Children (mem. we. regional bd. 2002-06), We. Mass. Libr. Club (bd. clk. 2003—). Avocations: swimming, gardening, travel.

LEE, MARTHA, artist, writer; b. Chehalis, Wash., Aug. 23, 1946; d. William Robert and Phyllis Ann (Herzog) L.; m. Peter Reynolds Lockwood, Jan. 25, 1974 (div. 1982). BA in English Lit., U. Wash., 1968; student, Factory of Visual Art, 1980-82. Reporter Seattle Post-Intelligencer, 1970; personnel counselor Theresa Snow Employment, 1971-72; receptionist Northwest Kidney Ctr., 1972-73; proprietress The Reliquary, 1974-77; travel agt. Cathay Express, 1977-79; artist, 1980—. Painter various oil paintings; exhibited in numerous one-woman shows; numerous group shows including most recently: Baker Bay Gallery, Ilwaco, Wash.; author: To The Beach and Other Poems, 1998. Avocations: horseback riding, reading, music. Home: PO Box 1157 Ocean Park WA 98640-1157 Office Phone: 360-665-4579.

LEE, MINNIE JOYCELYN See ELDERS, JOYCELYN

LEE, MORDECAI, political scientist, educator; b. Milw., Aug. 27, 1948; s. Jack Harold and Bernice (Kamesar) L.; 1 child, Ethan. BA, U. Wis., Madison, 1970; MPA, Syracuse U., NYC, 1972, PhD, 1975. Guest scholar Brookings Instn., Washington, 1972-74; legis. asst. to Congressman Henry Reuss Washington, 1975; asst. prof. polit. sci. U. Wis.-Whitewater and Parkside, 1976; mem. Wis. Ho. Reps., 1977-82, Wis. Senate, 1982-89; exec. dir. Milw. Jewish Coun. Cmty. Rels., 1990-97; asst. prof. govt. U. Wis.-Milw., 1997—2002, assoc. prof., 2002—06, prof., 2006—. Author: The First Presidential Communications Agency: FDR's Office of Government Reports, 2005, Institutionalizing Congress and the Presidency: The U.S. Bureau of Efficency, 1916-1933, 2006. Grantee, Franklin and Eleanor Roosevelt Inst., 2002, Hoover Presdl. Libr. Assn., 2003, IBM Ctr. for Bus. of Govt., 2003. Mem.: ASPA (co-chair program com. 64th conf. 2003, exec. com. sect. pub. adminstrn. edn. 1998—2003), Assn. for Rsch. on Nonprofit Orgns. and Voluntary Action (vice-chair sect. tchg. 2001—03). Business E-Mail: mordecai@uwm.edu.

LEE, MYUNG WOO, accountant, financial secretary; b. Republic of Korea; arrived in U.S., 1972, naturalized; s. Sung S. and Sea (Oh) L.; m. Chan Soo Kim, Nov. 15, 1960; children: Francis S., Sang-Gil P., Monica E. BSBA, Chung-Ang U., Seoul, Republic of Korea, 1960; MBA in Fin., Oklahoma City U., 1994. CPA, Series 6 stock broker. Chief acct., bd. mem. Hwa Sung Ind. Co. Ltd., Seoul, 1965-72; assembler, support person, internal auditor ISO 9002, logistics coord., tng. GM Plant, Oklahoma City, 1979—2006; fin. sec. UAW Local 1999, Oklahoma City, 1995-98; owner Lee's CPA, Moore, Okla., 1999—. Chmn. bd. Armstrong Lee Scholarship Fund, Inc. V.p. Chung Ang Econ. Rsch. Club, Seoul, 1958-60; bd. mem. Korean Soc. Oklahoma City, 1996; treas. North Cleveland County Dem. Club, Moore, Okla., 1997; chmn. election com., Korean Soc. of Oklahoma City, 1998; parish coun. chair Korean Martyrs Cath. Ch., Oklahoma City, 1998—. Mem.: AICPA, Okla. Soc. CPAs. Avocations: swimming, ping pong/table tennis, golf. Home and Office: 801 S Bouziden Dr Moore OK 73160-7324 Office Phone: 405-204-3566. Personal E-mail: moneywiselee@sbcglobal.net.

LEE, NANCY RANCK, management consultant; b. Yonkers, NY, Oct. 31, 1932; d. William Edward and Marion Edna Ranck; children: John Gregory, Paul Edward. BS, Cornell U., 1953; postgrad., Boston U., 1974-75. Social worker Tompkins County, Ithaca, N.Y., 1953-54; pers. adminstr. GE Advanced Electronics Ctr., Ithaca, 1954-55; fashion publicist Macy's, NYC, 1956-59; mgr. advt. and pub. rels. Josiah Wedgwood & Co., NYC, 1959-65; dir. comms. Gregory Fosella Assocs., Boston, 1969-71; dir. mktg. Kuras & Co., Boston, 1971-73; internat. sales mgr. Laser Focus Mag., Boston, 1973-75; pres. Lee Assocs., Boston, 1975-82; exec. v.p. Infotech, Boston, 1982-92; pres. Requisite Orgn. Assoc., Sarasota, Fla., 1992—. Lectr. Simmons Coll. Author: Targeting the Top: Everything a Woman Needs to Know to Succeed in Business, 1980, The Practice of Managerial Leadership, 2007. Mem. Cornell Cb, Ivy League Club, Phi Kappa Phi. Avocation: skiing. Home: 1590 1st St Sarasota FL 34236

LEE, NELDA S., art appraiser, art dealer, film producer; b. Gorman, Tex., July 3, 1941; d. Olan C. and Onis L.; 1 dau., Jeanna Lea Pool. AS (Franklin Lindsay Found. grantee), Tarleton State U., Tex., 1961; BA in Fine Arts, N. Tex. State U., 1963; postgrad., Tex. Tech. U., 1964, San Miguel de Allende Art Inst., Mexico, 1965. Head dept. art Ector H.S., Odessa, Tex., 1963-68. Group exhbns. include El Paso, Tex., New Orleans; contbr. articles to profl. jours. Bd. dir. Odessa YMCA, 1970, bd. dirs. Am. Heart Assn., Odessa, 1975; fund raiser Easter Seal Telethon, Odessa, 1978-79; bd. dir. Ector County (Tex.) Cultural Ctr., Tex. Bus. Hall of Fame, 1980-85; bd. dir., mem. acquisition com. Permian Basin Presdl. Mus., Odessa, 1978; bd. dir., chairperson acquisition com. Odessa Art Mus., 1979—; pres. Mega-Tex. Prodns., TV and movie prodrs.; pres. Ector County Dem. Women's Club, 1975, Nelda Lee, Inc., Odessa; appointee Tex. Commn. Arts, 1993—. Recipient Designer-Craftsman award El Paso Mus. Fine Arts, 1964. Mem. Am. Soc. Appraisers (sr.), Nat. Tex. Assn. Art Dealers (pres. 1978—), Odessa C. of C. Office Phone: 432-366-8426. Personal E-mail: neldasl@cableone.net.

LEE, PALI JAE (POLLY JAE STEAD LEE), retired librarian, writer; b. Nov. 26, 1925; d. Jonathan Everett Wheeler and Ona Katherine (Grunder) Stead; m. Richard H.W. Lee, Apr. 7, 1945 (div. 1978); children: Catherine Lani Honcoop, Karin Elizabeth Robinson, Ona G., Laurie Brett, Robin Louise Halbert; m. John K. Willis, 1979 (dec. 1994). Student, U. Hawaii, 1944-46, Mich. State U., East Lansing, 1961-64. Cataloguer and processor US Army Air Force, 1945-46; with US Weather Bur. Film Library, New Orleans, 1948-50, FBI, Wright-Patterson AFB, Dayton, Ohio, 1952, Ohio Wholesale Winedealers, Columbus, Ohio, 1956-58, Coll. Engring., Ohio State U., Columbus, 1959; writer tech. manual Annie Whittenmeyer Home, Davenport, Iowa, 1960; with Grand Rapids Pub. Libr., Mich., 1961-62; dir.

Waterford Twp. Librs., Mich., 1962-64; acquisition librarian Pontiac Pub. Librs., Mich., 1965-71, dir. East Side br. Mich., 1971-73; rsch. asst. dept. anthropology Bishop Mus., Honolulu, 1975-83; pub. Night Rainbow Pub., Honolulu, 1984—. Author: HIstory of Wine Growing in America, 1952, House Parenting at its Best, 1960, Mary Dyer, Child of Light, 1973, Giant: Pictorial History of the Human Colossus, 1973, History of Change: Kaneohe Bay Area, 1976, English edit., 1983, Tales of the Night Rainbow, 1981, rev. edit., 1988, Mo'olelo O Na Pohukaina, 1983, Ka Ipu Kukui, 1994, Ho'opono, 1999, rev. edit., 2007, Remembrance: The History of a Family, 2003; contbr. articles to profl. jours. Chmn. Oakland County br. Multiple Sclerosis Soc., 1972-73, co-chmn. Pontiac com. of Mich. area bd., 1972-73; sec. Ohana o Kokua, 1979-83, Paia-Willis Ohana, 1982-91, Ohana Kame'ekua, 1988-91; bd. dirs. Detroit Multiple Sclerosis Soc., 1971; mem. Mich. area bd. Am. Friends Svc. com., 1961-69; mem. consumer adv. bd. Libr. for Blind and Physically Handicapped, Honolulu, 1997—, bd. dirs. 1999—; pres. consumer 55 plus Hawaii Ctr. for Ind. Living, 1990-94, pres., 1995-96; pres. Honolulu chpt. Nat. Fedn. of Blind, 1991-93, 1st v.p. #93 state affiliate, 1991-93, editor Na Na Maka Aloha newsletter, 1990-94 Recipient Mother of the Yr. award Quad City Bus. Men, 1960, Bowl of Light award Cmty. Hawaii, 1989. Mem. Soc. Friends, Talking Book Readers Club (1st v.p. Hawaii chpt. 1994-95, pres., 1996, corr. sec. 2000-05), Hahamenalima Club (chmn. youth outreach com.), Peace and Social Concerns Soc. Friends (corr. dinajor, peace sub com.). Personal E-mail: palijae@juno.com, palijae@hawaii.rr.com.

LEE, PAMELA ANNE, bank executive, accountant, financial analyst; b. San Francisco, May 30, 1960; d. Larry D. and Alice Mary (Reece) L. BBA, San Francisco State U., 1981. CPA Calif. Typist, bookkeeper, tax acct. James G. Woo, CPA, San Francisco, 1979-85; tutor bus. math. and stats. San Francisco State U., 1979-80; from teller to ops. officer Gibraltar Savs. and Loan, San Francisco, 1978-81; sr. acct. Price Waterhouse, San Francisco, 1981-86; corp. acctg. mgr. First Nationwide Bank, Daly City, Calif., 1986-89, v.p., 1989-91, v.p., project mgr., 1991-92; sr. conversion and bus. analyst, 1992-93; sr. bus. analyst, asst. v.p. Bank of Am., 1993—98, mktg. cons., v.p. San Francisco, 1998-99, sr. cons. bus. automation, v.p., 1999-2001, sr. v.p., 2001—. Acctg. cons. New Performance Gallery, San Francisco, 1985, San Francisco Chamber Orch., 1986; treas. Golden Gate chpt. Team Bank of Am., 2000-02, co-chmn., 2003-04, treas, 2005—. Founding mem., chair bd. trustees Asian Acctg. Students Career Day, 1988-89; vol. Mickaboo Cockatiel Rescue, 1998—, CFO, 2002-. Mem.: AICPA, Calif. Soc. CPAs, Toastmasters Internat. (co-v.p. membership Tower of Talk chpt. 2000—01, co-v.p. edn. 2001, competent toastmaster status 2001, v.p. membership 2002, competent leader status 2002, advanced toastmaster silver status 2004, pres. Everybody Speaks chpt. 2004—, v.p. edn. United We Speak chpt. 2005—06). Republican. Avocations: reading, music, personal computing, crafting. Office: 1455 Market St 13th Fl San Francisco CA 94103

LEE, PATRICK A., physics educator; b. Hong Kong, Sept. 8, 1946; m. Jeanne M. Tran, June 7, 1969; children: Eric, Brian. BS, MIT, 1966, PhD, 1970. Gibbs instr. Yale U., New Haven, 1970-72; asst. prof. U. Wash., Seattle, 1973-74; mem. tech. staff Bell Labs., Murray Hill, N.J., 1974-82; prof. physics MIT, Cambridge, 1982—. Fellow Am. Phys. Soc. (Oliver Buckley prize 1991); mem. NAS, Am. Acad. Arts and Scis. Office: MIT 77 Massachusetts Ave Cambridge MA 02139-4307

LEE, PAUL LAWRENCE, lawyer; b. NYC, Mar. 7, 1946; AB, Georgetown U., 1969; JD, U. Mich., 1972. Bar: N.Y. 1974. Editor-in-chief Mich. Law Rev., 1971-72; law clk. to Hon. Walter R. Mansfield US Ct. Appeals (2d cir.), 1973-74; spl. asst. to gen. counsel US Treasury Dept., 1977-78, exec. asst. to dep. sec., 1978-79; dep. supt. and counsel NY State Banking Dept., 1980-81; ptnr. Shearman & Sterling, NYC, 1982-94; exec. v.p., gen. counsel Republic N.Y. Corp., NYC, 1994-2000; sr. exec. v.p., gen. counsel HSBC USA Inc., NYC, 2000—04; ptnr., head Banking Practice, mem. Fin. Insts. Group Debevoise & Plimpton LLP, NYC, 2004—. Office: Debevoise & Plimpton LLP 919 Third Ave New York NY 10022 Office Phone: 212-909-6955. Office Fax: 212-521-7955. Business E-Mail: pllee@debevoise.com.

LEE, PAUL P., ophthalmologist, educator, lawyer; b. Taipei, Taiwan, Sept. 1960; s. Pei-Fei and Julia Lee. BA, U. Mich., 1981, MD, 1986; JD, Columbia U., 1986. Bar: Md. 1987, D.C. 1988. Congl. intern U.S. House Select Commn. on Aging, Washington, 1980; biologist NASA, Cape Canaveral, Fla., 1981; med. intern Beth Israel Hosp., Boston, 1986—87; resident ophthalmology Johns Hopkins Hosp., Balt., 1987—90; fellow glaucoma Mass. Eye & Ear Infirmary, Boston, 1990—91; asst. prof. U. So. Calif., LA, 1991—95, assoc. prof., 1995—97; prof. Duke U., Durham, NC, 1997—, James Pitzer Gills III, MD and Joy Gills prof. ophthalmology, 2003—. Health scis. program Rand Corp., Santa Monica; bd. dirs. Blind Children's Ctr.; chair Duke Eye Care, LLC; cons. WHO. Mem. editl. bd. Archives Ophthalmology, Evidence-Based Ophthalmology, Chinese Jour. Ophthalmology; contbr. articles to profl. jours. Rsch. fellowship Brookdale Inst. on Aging, 1985; sr. fellow Ctr. Aging Duke U., Ctr. for Clin. Health Policy Rsch. Duke U.; Stone scholar Columbia U. Law Sch., 1985 Mem. AMA, ABA, Am. Acad. Ophthalmology (bd. trustees 2000-04), Assn. Health Svcs. Rsch., Chinese-Am. Ophthalmology Soc., Assn. for Rsch. in Vision and Ophthalmology Office Phone: 919-681-2793. Business E-Mail: lee00106@mc.duke.edu.

LEE, PETER JAMES, bishop; b. Greenville, Miss., May 11, 1938; s. Erling Norman and Marion (O'Brien) L.; m. Kristina Knapp, Aug. 28, 1965; children: Stewart, Peter James Jr. AB, Washington and Lee U., 1960; LittD, U. of the South, 1999; MDiv, Va. Theol. Sem., 1967; postgrad, Duke U. Law Sch., 1963-64; DD (hon.), Va. Theol. Sem., 1984, St. Paul's Coll., Lawrenceville, Va., 1985, U. of the South, 1993; LittD, Washington and Lee U., 1997. Ordained priest Episc. Ch., 1968, bishop, 1984. Newspaper reporter, editor, Pensacola, Fla., Richmond, Memphis, 1960-63; deacon St. John's Cathedral, Jacksonville, Fla., 1967-68; asst. min. St. John's Ch. LaFayette Sq., Washington, 1968-71; rector Chapel of the Cross, Chapel Hill, NC, 1971-84; bishop coadjutor Episcopal Diocese of Va., Richmond, 1984-85, bishop, 1985—. Pres. trustees of the funds Diocese of Va., 1985—; dir. Presiding Bishop's Fund for World Relief, 1986-93. Rector bd. trustees Episcopal H.S., Alexandria, Va., 1985—; chmn. Meml. Trustees, Richmond; trustee Wash. Nat. Cathedral, Ch. Pension Fund, 1999—, Berkeley Div. Sch. at Yale, 1999-2002. Recipient duPont Fund Lifetime Achievement award, 1997. Mem. Phi Beta Kappa, Omicron Delta Kappa. Episcopalian. Office: Diocese Va 110 W Franklin St Richmond VA 23220-5010 Home Phone: 804-288-9009. Business E-Mail: pjlee@thediocese.net.

LEE, PETER JOHN, research engineer; BSc in Metallurgy & Materials Sci., U. Birmingham, UK, 1977—80, PhD in Metallurgy & Materials, 1980—83. Sr. scientist Applied Superconductivity Ctr., U. Wis., Madison, 1994—2006, Applied Superconductivity Ctr., Nat. High Magnetic Field Lab., Fla. State U., Tallahassee, 2006—. Mem. Condr. Adv. Com. for Superconducting Super Collider, 1990—92, Condr. Adv. Com. for High Energy Physics High Field Magnets, 1999—; bd. mem. Applied Superconductivity Conf., 2002—, Internat. Cryogenic Materials Commn., 2004—, vice-chair, 2005—. Editor: (technical book) Engineering Superconductivity, Composite Superconductors. Mem.: Microscopy Soc. Am. Achievements include patents for artificial and multiple phase microelectropolishing. Office: Nat High Magnetic Field Lab Applied Superconductivity Ctr 2031 E Paul Dirac Dr Tallahassee FL 32310

LEE, RAEJIN, music educator, soprano; b. Seoul, Korea, Nov. 18, 1976; arrived in US, 1995; d. Duk Ku Lee and Ja Kyung Suh; m. Justin Lee, May 28, 2005; 1 child, Ashley. MusB, Ind. U., Bloomington, 1999, MusM, 2001; postgrad., Rutgers U., New Brunswick, NJ, 2002—; artist diploma, Cleve. Inst. Music, 2003. Tchg. asst. Rutgers U., New Brunswick, 2002—05; asst. prof., dir. vocal studies La Sierra U., Riverside, Calif., 2005—. Soloist Euclid Meth. Ch., Cleve., 2001—02, Calvary Meth. Ch., East Brunswick, NJ, 2002—05; music dir. Union Evang. Ch., West Covina, Calif., 2005—. Recipient Italian Art Song prize, Italian Am. Cultural Found., Cleve., 2002. Mem.: Coll. Music Soc., Nat. Assn. Tchrs. of Singing. Home: 22887 Canyon View Rd Diamond Bar CA 91765 Office: La Sierra U 4500 Riverwalk Pky Riverside CA 92515

LEE, RAPHAEL CARL, plastic surgeon, biomedical engineer; b. Sumter, SC, Oct. 29, 1949; s. Leonard Powell and Jean Maurice (Langston) L.; m. Kathleen Kelley, Feb. 11, 1983; children: Rachel, Catherine. BS, U. SC, 1971, DSc (hon.), 2000; MS, Drexel U., 1975; MD, Temple U., 1975; ScD, MIT, 1979. Diplomate Am. Bd. Plastic Surgeons, Am. Bd. Surgery. Chief resident gen. surgery U. Chgo. Hosps., 1980-81; chief resident plastic surgery Mass. Gen. Hosp., 1982-83; dir. Elec. Trauma Rsch. Program, 1991—; med. dir. U. Chgo. Burn Unit, 1991-97. Asst. prof. surgery Harvard Med. Sch., 1984—89; VanTassel asst. prof. elec. and bioengring. MIT, 1983—89; asst. prof. bioengring. and surgery Harvard MIT, Divsn. Health Scis. and Tech., 1983—89; prof. surgery, medicine, molecular medicine, anatomy and bioengring. U. Chgo., 1992—; chmn. bd. dirs. Avocet Polymers Techs., Inc., 1996—; exec. com. Biomed. Engring. Inst., Ill. Inst. Tech.; founder, dir. Maroon Biotech., Inc.; founder, chmn. bd. dirs. Electrokinetics Signal Rsch., Inc.; founder, dir. Renacyte BioMolecular Tech., Inc. Author: Electrical Injury, Multidisciplinary Approach, 1994, Occupational Electrical Injury, 1999; editor: Electrical Trauma, Pathophysiology, 1992; assoc. editor Bioelectromagnetics, 1993—; contbr. more than 200 articles to profl. jours. Recipient Alumni Achievement award Class of 1975 Temple Med. Sch., 1995, Searle Scholar award The Searle Found., 1985-88, Disting. Engring. Sch. Alumnus award U. SC, 1998, award for advancing safety and health Am. Electric Power Assn.; named Ams. 100 Brightest Young Scientists Sci. Digest, 1984; MacArthur Prize fellow John D. and Catherine T. MacArthur Found., 1981-86. Fellow ACS (Schering scholar in Surgery 1978), Am. Inst. Med. and Biol. Engring.; mem. IEEE, AAAS, Am. Burn Assn. (Lindberg award), Am. Phys. Soc., Am. Soc. for Cell Biology, Am. Assn. Plastic Surgeons (James Barrett Brown award 1988), Biophys. Soc., Nat. Med. Assn. (plastic surgery sect. chmn. 1989-91), Soc. for Phys. Regulation in Biology and Medicine (pres. 1995), Soc. Univ. Surgeons, Surg. Biology Club III, Tau Beta Pi, Alpha Omega Alpha, Sigma Xi. Achievements include 12 patents. Office: U Chgo Hosps Pritzker Sch Medicine-Surgery MC6035 5841 S Maryland Ave Chicago IL 60637-1463 Office Phone: 773-702-6302, 815-609-2170. Business E-Mail: r-lee@uchicago.edu, rlee@avocetcorp.com.

LEE, RICHARD DIEBOLD, lawyer, educator; b. Fargo, ND, July 31, 1935; s. Sidney Jay and Charlotte Hannah (Thompson) L.; m. Patricia Ann Taylor, June 17, 1957; children: Elizabeth Carol, Deborah Susan, David Stuart. BA with distinction, Stanford U., 1957; JD, Yale U., 1960. Bar: Calif. 1961, U.S. Dist. Ct. (no. dist.) Calif. 1961, U.S. Ct. Appeals (9th cir.) 1961. Dep. atty. gen. Office of Atty. Gen., Sacramento, 1960-62; assoc. McDonough, Holland, Schwartz, Allen & Wahrhaftig, Sacramento, 1962-66, ptnr., 1966-69; asst. dean U. Calif. Sch. Law, Davis, 1969-73, assoc. dean, 1973-76; assoc. prof. law Temple U. Sch. Law, Phila., 1976-77, vis. prof., 1975-76, prof., 1977-89; dir. profl. devel. Baker & McKenzie, Chgo., NYC, 1981-83; dir. Am. Law Inst.-ABA In-House, Phila., 1985—89, mem. adv. bd., 1989—; dir. profl. devel. Morrison & Foerster, San Francisco, 1989—93; dir. Continuing Edn. of the Bar, Berkeley, Calif., 1993—97; v.p. JusLaw.com, 2000—01, LawyersTV Continue Learning Networks L.L.C., 2002. Mem. Grad. and Profl. Fin. Aid Coun., Princeton, NJ, 1974-80; trustee Law Sch. Admissions Coun., Washington, 1976-78; mem. internat. adv. com. Internat. Juridical Orgn., Rome, 1977-88; mem. bd. advisors Lawyer Hiring and Tng. Report, Chgo., 1983-95. Author: (coursebook) Materials on International Efforts to Control the Environment, 1977, 78, 79, 80, 84, 85, 87; co-editor: Orientation in the U.S. Legal System annual coursebook, 1982-92; contbr. articles to profl. jours. Trustee Grad. Theol. Union, Berkeley, 1991—2000, vice chair, 1994—99; mem. bd. of coun. Episc. Cmty. Svcs., Phila., 1984—88; trustee Grace Cathedral, San Francisco, 1989—2004, chair bd. trustees, 1992—95; trustee Coll. of Preachers, Washington Nat. Cathedral, 1999—2004, mem. cathedral coll. bd., 2004—06; adv. bd. Ch. Div. Sch. of the Pacific, 2000—; bd. dirs. Lung Assn. of Sacramento-Emigrant Trails, 1962—69, pres., 1966—68; bd. dirs. Sacramento County Legal Aid Soc., 1968—74, pres., 1971—72; chmn. bd. overseers Phila. Theol. Inst., 1984—88, bd. overseers, 1979—80, 1984—88; mem. bd. visitors John Marshall Law Sch., Chgo., 1989—93; bd. dirs. Earplay, 2004—06; chair, bd. dirs. The Ghiberti Found., 2002—04, bd. dirs., 2004—, San Francisco Contemporary Music Players, 2007—. Mem. ABA (chmn. various coms., spl. cons. on continuing legal edn. MacCrate Task Force on Law Schs. and the Profession: Narrowing the Gap, 1991-93, standing com. on specialization 1998-2001, standing com. paralegals 2003-06), State Bar Calif. (chair standing com. on minimum continuing legal edn. 1990-92, com. mem. 1990-93), Bar Assn. San Francisco (legal ethics com., conf. of delegates 1987—), Profl. Devel. Consortium (co-founder, chair 1990-93), Am. Law Inst., Yale Club (N.Y.C., San Francisco). Democrat. Episcopalian. Home and Office: 2001 Sacramento St Ste 4 San Francisco CA 94109-3342 Home Phone: 415-673-9929. Personal E-mail: RichardDLee@earthlink.net.

LEE, RICHARD FRANCIS JAMES, evangelical clergyman, media consultant, lawyer; b. Yakima, Wash., Sept. 13, 1967; s. Richard Francis and Dorothy Aldean (Blackwell). Diploma, Berean Coll., Springfield, Mo., 1989; BA, U. Wash., Seattle, 1990; JD, Gonzaga Sch. Law, 1997; MDiv, Fuller Theol. Seminary, 2001. Bar: Wash. 2002; ordained Assemblies of God, So. Calif. dist., 1999. Lic. clergyman N.W. dist. Assemblies of God, Seattle, 1989. Author: Tell Me the Story 1982, The Crimson Detective Motion Picture 1996. Named Most Likely to be Pres. Franklin High Sch. Seattle 1986. Mem.: Soc. Pentecostal Studies. Pentecostal. Avocations: collector, writing, filmmaking. Home: 2604 E Boone Ave Spokane WA 99202-3718 Office Phone: 509-536-0986. Business E-Mail: info@richardleeministries.org. E-mail: L5RC@comcast.net.

LEE, RICHARD H(ARLO), lawyer; b. Glen Falls, NY, June 5, 1947; s. Donald D. and Jeanne M. (Uthus) L.; m. Mary Ahearn, June 10, 1972; children: Christine Marie Ahearn Lee, Andrea Elizabeth Ahearn Lee. BS with honors, Mich. State U., 1972; JD magna cum laude, Ariz. State U., 1976. Bar: Ariz. 1977, U.S. Ct. Appeals (6th cir.) 1977, U.S. Dist. Ct. Ariz. 1978, U.S. Ct. Appeals (9th cir.) 1981. Law clk. to Judge George Edwards U.S. Ct. Appeals (6th cir.) Ohio, Cin., 1976-77; assoc. Sparks & Siler, Scottsdale, Ariz., 1977-78, Murphy & Posner, Phoenix, 1979-82, ptnr., 1983-86; assoc. Storey & Ross, Phoenix, 1986-88; prin. McDaniel & Lee, Phoenix, 1989-91, Law Office of Richard H. Lee, Phoenix, 1982—; of counsel Martin & Patterson, Ltd., 1992-98, Martin & Assocs., 1998-99. Comment and notes editor Ariz. State U. Law Jour., 1975-76; bd. editors Maricopa County Lawyer, 1990-91. Chmn. Ariz. Canal Divershion Channel task force City of Phoenix, 1985—86, mem. exec. com., mem. citizens bond com., 1975, chmn. solid waste bond com., 1987—88, mem. bond adv. com., 1988—2000; mem. adv. com. City of Phoenix Neighborhood Orgn. Divsn., Ariz., 1974—75; vo. VISTA Crow Indian Tribe, Crow Agy., Mont., 1969—71; state committeeman Ariz. Dem.s, Phoenix; bd. dirs. Valley of the Sun Sch. and Habilitation Ctr., 1991—95, treas., 1992—93, chair fin. com., 1993—94. Mem. Ariz. Bar Assn. (chmn. com. on CLE bankruptcy sect. 1985-87, chmn. bankruptcy sect. 1987-88), Ariz. State U. Coll. Law Alumni Assn. (pres. 1981), Ariz. State U. Alumni Assn. (bd. dirs. 1981-82), Kappa Sigma. Home: 331 W Orangewood Ave Phoenix AZ 85021-7249 Office: PO Box 7749 Phoenix AZ 85011-7749 Home Phone: 602-395-0405; Office Phone: 602-231-0595. Business E-Mail: lee@azbar.org.

LEE, RICHARD KENNETH, software company executive; b. Birmingham, Eng., Dec. 10, 1942; came to U.S., 1964; s. Kenneth Jesse Lee and Eleanor Margaret (Bellsham) Dean; m. Melinda Elena Noback, Aug. 20, 1966; children: Sonja Eleanor, Alyssa Claire. BSc with upper 2d class honours, No. Poly. U. London, 1964; MS in Inorganic Chemistry, Northwestern U., 1965; PhD in Inorganic Chemistry, U. London, 1968. Various corp. rsch. positions UOP Inc., Des Plaines, Ill., 1965-74, mgr. catalyst R & D automotive products divsn., 1974-77; v.p., gen. mgr. portable battery div. Gould Inc., St. Paul, 1977-82; v.p., gen. mgr. Elgar Corp., an Onan/McGraw Edison Co., San Diego, 1982-85; v.p. R & D, Pharmaseal div. Baxter Healthcare Corp., Valencia, Calif., 1985-88; v.p. strategic bus. ops. Manville Sales Corp., Denver, 1988-92; pres., chief exec. officer Rocklite Inc., Denver, 1992-99; prin. LeeVarage Internat., Castle Rock, 1993-00; chmn., pres., CEO Value Innovations, Inc., Denver, 1999—; mng. dir. Edgeguard Internat. Ltd., Castle Rock, 2002—03. Adj. prof. masters tech. program U. Coll., U. Denver, 1993-95; bd. dirs. Q.E.D., Denver; mem. adv. bd. Kodiak, Denver, 1998-99. Author: (videotape) U.S. Competitiveness—A Crisis?, 1992; patentee for vehicle emission control system. Chmn. Summit 91, Denver, 1991, mem. organizing com. Summit 92, Pacoima, Calif., 1992; bd. dirs. Indsl. Rsch. Inst., Inc., Washington, 1991-92, chmn. emeritus, 2003-04. Recipient IR-100 award, Indsl. R & D, 1978; Fulbright travel scholar, 1964—65. Mem. Rocky Mountain World Trade Ctr. (vice chmn. 1992-94, exec. com. 1992-94, bd. dirs. 1990-95). Office Phone: 303-688-4143. Business E-Mail: dick_lee@valueinnovations.net. *The quality of life for U.S. citizens in the early 21st Century will be primarily determined by the results of U.S. industry and government efforts to improve our ability to commercialize technology successfully.*

LEE, RICHARD VAILLE, internist, educator; b. Islip, NY, May 26, 1937; s. Louis Emerson and Erma Natalie (Little) L.; m. Susan Bradley, June 25, 1961; children: Matthew, Benjamin. BS, Yale U., 1960, MD cum laude, 1964. Diplomate Am. Bd. Internal Medicine, Am. Bd. Family Practice. Intern Grace-New Haven Hosp., 1964-65, asst. resident in internal medicine, 1965-66, 69-70; fellow in inflammatory disease Yale U., New Haven, 1970-71, asst. prof. medicine, 1971-74, assoc. prof. clin. medicine, 1974-76; practice medicine specializing in internal medicine New Haven, 1969-76, Buffalo, 1976—; family practice Poplar, Mont., 1966-68, Chester, Mont., 1968-69; prof. medicine SUNY, Buffalo, 1976—, prof. pediat., 1985—, adj. prof. anthropology, 1989—, prof. obstetrics, 1992—, chief divsn. gen. internal medicine, 1979-82, chief divsn. maternal and adolescent medicine, 1982—, chief divsn. geog. medicine, 1991—; dir. primary care ctr. Yale-New Haven Hosp., 1975-76, dir. med. clinics, 1971-75; chief med. svc. Buffalo VA Hosp., 1976-79; head dept. medicine Children's Hosp. Buffalo, 1979-96; fellow WHO Collaborating Ctr. for Health in Housing, 1985—, chief med. officer, 1995—. Cons. internal medicine N.Y. Zool. Soc., 1973—; cons. physician Buffalo Zool. Soc., 1980—2001; aviation med. examiner, 1980—2001; med. dir. Ecology and Environment, Inc., Lancaster, NY; mem. N.Y. State Bd. for Medicine, 1995—2002; mem. com. Nat. Bd. Med. Examiners, 1999—; mem. N.Y. State Office for Profl. Med. Conduct, 2001—. Author: Outside Rounds, 2005; editor: When I Was a Boy in China, 2003; sr. editor: Current Obstetric Medicine, 1989—95; corr. editor Jour. Obstetrics and Gynecology, London, 1989—; mem. editl. bd.: Internat. Jour. Environ. Health, 1994—; cons. editor Am. Jour. Medicine, 1976—86, chair editl. bd. Obstetric Medicine; contbr. chapters to books on obstetrics and toxicology, articles to profl. jours. Served with USPHS, 1966-68. Recipient C.G. Barnes award, Internat. Soc. Obs. Medicine, 2006—. Fellow: ACP (sr. editor Med. Care of the Pregnant Patient 2000, Laureate award 2002), Royal Soc. Asian Affairs, Royal Geog. Soc., Explorers Club N.Y.C.; mem.: AMA, Am. Coll. Occupl. and Environ. Medicine, Internat. Soc. of Travel Medicine, Soc. Obstetric Medicine (pres. 1991—93, C. G. Barnes award for disting. svc. to obstetric medicine 2006), Infectious Disease Soc. Am., Am. Soc. Tropical Medicine and Hygiene, Gen. Internal Medicine, Am. Fedn. Clin. Rsch. Soc., N.Y. Acad. Sci., Yale China Assn. (trustee 1992—2001, sec. 1995—2001), Nat. Bd. Med. Examiners, Am. Soc. History of Medicine, Royal Soc. Medicine, Great Lakes Interurban Clin. Club, Alpha Omega Alpha. Achievements include editing and reprinting, with introduction and photographs, his grandfather's book When I Was a Boy In China, 2003. Home: 7664 East Quaker Rd Orchard Park NY 14127-2015 Office Phone: 716-684-8060.

LEE, ROBERT ANTHONY, church musician, accompanist; b. Washington, Dec. 21, 1936; s. Charles Foster and Cornelia McAllister Lee. Organist St. Michael and All Angels Episcopal Ch., Adelphi, Md., 1961—67; organist, choir master St. John's Episcopal Ch., Boulder, Colo., 1968—70, assoc. organist, 2005—; organist St. Aidan's Episcopal Ch., Boulder, 1971—2004. Rehearsal accompanist Ars Nova Singers, Boulder, 1986—, Boulder Chorale, 2005—. Composer: (choral work) Jesu dulcis memoria, 1996. Fellow, Coll. Ch. Musicians, 1964—67. Mem.: Am. Guild Organists (assoc.). Home: PO Box 419 Lafayette CO 80026 Personal E-mail: ranthlee@hotmail.com.

LEE, ROBERT ERICH, Internet company executive, information technology consultant, biomedical imaging researcher; b. Spokane, Wash., Dec. 26, 1955; s. Robert Edward Lee and Edith Freida (Klasen) Moore; m. Vicky Ann Rowland, Jan. 31, 1981 (div. June 1998); children: Erich Rowland, Christopher Michael; m. Heidi LaVerne Christensen, Sept. 13, 1998. Student in Biomed. Engring., Vanderbilt U., Nashville, 1973—77, B in Biomed. Engring., 2005; ME in Biomed. Engring., Vanderbuilt U., Nashville, 2007. Mgr., instr. Neptune Equipment Co., Nashville, 1976—77; customer engr. Hewlett-Packard Co., LA, 1977—82, dist. svc. mgr., 1982—85, region svc. adminstrn. mgr. North Hollywood, 1985—86; dir. mgmt. info. Tova Corp., Beverly Hills, 1986—87; dir. info. tech. PrimeSource/Sequoia Supply, Inc., Irvine, 1987—92; pres. Results From Tech.!, 1992—; v.p. info. tech. Triton Soc., 1998—; founder OurSeas.org, 2003—; co-founder Lee-Cobb, 2007—. Spkr. in field. Author: The ISDN Consultant, 1996; author: (columnist) Interex Press, 1995—97; author: (writer) Interact, 1995—97, Sun World Online, 1996—99. Active Irvine Children's Fund; honors Eagle Scout, Cub Scout Woodbadge. Mem.: Am. Acad. Underwater Sci., Internat. Soc. for Magnetic Resonance in Medicine, Soc. for Imaging Informatics in Medicine. Republican. Avocations: skiing, scuba diving, travel, hiking, bicycling. Home and Office: 1046 Walnut Bend Ln Brentwood TN 37027 Business E-Mail: rlee@roblee.com.

LEE, ROBERT HUGH, management executive; b. Honolulu, Jan. 3, 1950; s. Hugh Sebastian and Margaret Carol (Bennett) L.; m. Lois Ann Brown, Jan. 31, 1981. BA in Communications, Coll. St. Francis, 1972; MBA, No. Ill. U., 1977. Pres., owner Robert Hugh Lee Pub., Lockport, Ill., 1973-76; pres. Robert Hugh Lee, MBA and Assocs., DeKalb, Ill., 1978—; pres., chmn. bd. dirs., treas. Lee, Williams, Rogers & Assocs., Inc., Freeport, Ill., 1988—. Lectr., tchr. bus. strategy, mktg. and fin. at several univs. in Midwest. Author: King of Laoise's Crusade, A Board Game of War and Strategy, 2002; creator: board game King of Laoise's Crusade, 2002. Dem. candidate Clk. of Cir. Ct., McLean County, Ill., 1980, Treas. DeKalb County, Ill., 1986, DeKalb County bd., 1988, Ill. Gen. Assembly, 1988; Dem. ward capt. cen. com., Blackhawk County, Iowa, 1982-85; trustee DeKalb County Regional Sch. Bd., 1987-95. Mem.: NRA (life). Avocations: carpentry, touch football, golf. Home and Office: 530 Woodlyn Dr Aurora IL 60505-9759 Home Phone: 630-264-2477; Office Phone: 630-264-2477.

LEE, RONALD DEMOS, demographer, economist, educator; b. Sept. 5, 1941; s. Otis Hamilton and Dorothy (Demetracopoulou) Lee; m. Melissa Lee Nelken, July 6, 1968; children: Sophia, Isabel, Rebecca. BA, Reed Coll., 1963; MA, U. Calif., Berkeley, 1967; PhD, Harvard U., 1971; D (hon.), Lund U., Sweden, 2004. Postdoctoral fellow Nat. Demographic Inst., Paris, 1970-71; asst. prof. to prof. U. Mich., Ann Arbor, 1971-79; prof. demography and econs. U. Calif., Berkeley, 1979—. Dir. Berkeley Ctr. Econs. and Demography Aging; chair com. population NAS, 1993—97; cons. in field. Author, editor: Population Patterns in the Past, 1977, Econometric Studies of Topics in Demographic History, 1978, Population, Food, and Rural Development, 1988, Economics of Changing Age Distributions in Developed Countries, 1988, Population Change in Asia: Transition, Development and Aging, 2000, Demographic Change and Fiscal Policy, 2000, United States Fertility: New Patterns, New Theories, 1996; contbr. articles to profl. jours. Vol. Peace Corps, Ethiopia, 1963—65. Recipient Mindel C. Sheps award, Population Assn. Am. and U. N.C. Sch. Pub. Health, 1984, MERIT award, Nat. Inst. Aging, 1994—2003, 2005—, Taeuber award, Population Assn. Am. and Princeton U., 1999; fellow, Social Sci. Rsch. Coun., 1970—71; NIH fellow, 1965—67, NSF fellow, 1968—69, NIH grantee, 1973—, Guggenheim fellow, 1984—85. Mem.: AAAS, NAS, Am. Philos. Soc., Internat. Union Sci. Study Population, Am. Acad. Arts and Scis., Am. Econ. Assn., Population Assn. Am. (pres. 1987), Brit. Acad. (corr.). Democrat. Home: 2933 Russell St Berkeley CA 94705-2333 Office: U Calif Dept Demography 2232 Piedmont Ave Berkeley CA 94720-2120 E-mail: rlee@demog.berkeley.edu.

LEE, RONALD DEREK, lawyer; s. Frank B. and Mary Lee. AB, Princeton U., NJ, 1980; M of Philosophy, Oxford U., 1982; JD, Yale U., 1985. Bar: N.Y. 1986, D.C. 1987, Calif. 1991. Law clk. to Judge Abner J. Mikva U.S. Ct. Appeals (D.C. cir.), Washington, 1985-86; law clk. to Justice John Paul Stevens U.S. Supreme Ct., Washington, 1986-87; assoc. Arnold & Porter, Washington, 1987-91, LA, 1991-92, ptnr., 1993-94; gen. counsel Nat. Security Agy., 1994—98; chief of staff CIA, 1996; assoc. dep. atty. gen. U.S. Dept. Justice, Washington, 1998—2000; ptnr., Nat. Security Law & Policy Practice group Arnold & Porter LLP, Washington, 2001—. Rhodes scholarship Rhodes Trust, 1980. Mem. Phi Beta Kappa. Avocations: tennis, table tennis. Office: Arnold & Porter LLP 555 Twelfth St NW Washington DC 20004-1206 Office Phone: 202-942-5380. Office Fax: 202-942-5999. Business E-Mail: ronald.lee@aporter.com.

LEE, RUBY BEI-LOH, multimedia and computer systems architect; b. Singapore; came to the U.S., 1970, naturalized, 1996; m. Howard F. Lee, July 27, 1974; children: Patrick, Josephine. AB in Computer Sci. and Comparative Lit. with distinction, Cornell U., 1973; MS in Computer Sci., Stanford U., 1975, PhDEE, 1980. Asst. prof. elec. engring. Stanford (Calif.) U., 1980-81; lead architect Hewlett Packard Co., Palo Alto, Calif., 1982-84, lead designer microprocessors, 1984-86, project mgr. Cupertino, Calif., 1987-90, chief arch. computer sys. architecture, multimedia, security, 1991-97; chief arch. Security Architecture, Cupertino, Calif., 1997-98; Forrest G. Hamrick prof. elec. engring. Princeton (N.J.) U., 1998—. Cons. assoc. prof. elec. engring. Stanford U., 1990-95, cons. prof., 1995-98. Designer PA-RISC (Precision Architecture Reduced Instrn. Set Computer) architecture, Multimedia Acceleration EXtensions (MAX) architecture; contbr. articles to profl. jours.; inventor, patentee in field, including 22 U.S. patents and more than 93 foreign ones. Fellow IEEE (mem. exec. com., mem. tech. com. on microprocessors, mem. program com. Compcon conf. San Francisco 1991-97, program chairperson Hot-Chips Symposium, Stanford 1992-93, assoc. editor-in-chief IEEE Micro Spectrum, mem. editl. bd. IEEE Spectrum, guest editor spl. issues IEEE MICRO 1994, 96), Assn. for Computing Machinery; mem. Phi Beta Kappa, Alpha Lambda Delta. Methodist. Office: Princeton U Dept Elec Engring Princeton NJ 08544-0001 E-mail: rblee@princeton.edu.

LEE, SALLY A., editor-in-chief; m. Rob Niosi. Grad., Durham U., Eng.; MA, Clark U., Mass. Tchr. writing and lit. Clark U.; reporter Worcester (Mass.) Telegram; mng. editor Worcester (Mass.) Monthly; spl. features editor Woman's World mag., NYC; articles editor Woman's Day mag., NYC; sr. editor Redbook mag., NYC; editor-in-chief YM, NYC, 1994—96, Fitness Mag., NYC, 1996—98, Parents Mag., NYC, 1998—; editl. dir. YM mag., NYC, 2004. Corr. E! Entertainment Network. Author: The Best Advice I Ever Got, 2001. Bd. dirs. Room to Grow, Women for Women Internat. Mem.: Parenting Network. Office: Parents Mag 375 Lexington Ave Fl 10 New York NY 10017-5514 Office Phone: 212-499-2050, 212-449-2083.

LEE, SAMUEL SANGWON, civil engineer, environmental engineer, agricultural engineer; b. Seoul, Republic of Korea, June 11, 1961; naturalized; s. Sungchan and Chunyun Lee; m. Youngsin Kim, July 16, 1988; 1 child, Michael Gyunghwan. BA, Chunbuk Nat. U., Chunju, South Korea, 1984; MS, Northeastern U., Boston, 1996; PhD, U. RI, Kingston, 1999. Rschr. Korea Mag. Rsch. Inst., Seoul, 1987—88; rsch. asst. Va. Tech, Blacksburg, 1988—90, Northeastern U., Boston, 1990—96, U. RI, 1996—2000; sr. hydrogeologist Lee County Regional Water Supply Auth., Fort Myers, Fla., 2000; hydraulic engr. US Army Corps Engrs., Jacksonville, Fla., 2000—03; civil engr. Fed. Energy Regulatory Commn., San Francisco, 2003—. Cons. Vadose Dot Net, Palo Alto, Calif., 1992—2000. Actor: Chonju, R.O. Korea, 1981; author: (book) Korean Essay Book, 2005; contbr. articles to profl. jours. Recipient Patriot Merit for contbg. human rights, South Korean Pres. Dae-Jung Kim, 2003. Mem.: ASCE (assoc.), Nat. Ground Water Assn. (assoc.). Democrat. Achievements include development of vadose zone leaching and saturated zone mixing model 2.0 developed for USEPA; 2, 3-D FDM seepage models devloped for USDOD and USDOE; a vadose and groundwater model; research in improved free space optics and laser marking. Avocations: gardening, music, sports card collecting, golf, reading. Home: 855 Bruce Dr Palo Alto CA 94303 Office: US Dept Energy Fed Energy Regulatory Cmmn D2SI San Francisco Regional Office 901 Market St Ste 350 San Francisco CA 94103 Office Phone: 415-369-3393. Personal E-mail: sam@vadose.net.

LEE, SANDRA, food service executive, product designer, chef; Grad., U. Wis., 1992. CEO Sandra Lee Semi-Homemade Corp. Product designer Target, Wal-Mart, QVC Shopping Network-USA, QVC-U.K., QVC-Germany; guest lectr. Dynamic Women in Bus. Conf., Harvard Bus. School. Host (TV series) Semi-Homemade Cooking with Sandra Lee, Food Network; author: Sandra Lee Semi-Homemade Cooking, 2002 (NY Times Best-Seller), Sandra Lee Semi-Homemade Desserts, 2003, Sandra Lee Semi-Homemade Cooking II, 2005, Sandra Lee Semi-Homemade Grilling, 2006, Sandra Lee Semi-Homemade Cooking Made Light, 2006, Sandra Lee Semi-Homemade Cool Kids Cooking, 2006; guest appearances Today, Entertainment Tonight, Extra, CNN, The View, Fox News Live, Good Day Live, featured in TV Guide, Brandweek, Women's World, Time mag., Newsweek, Gourmet mag., Better Homes and Gardens, Family Circle, Ladies Home Journal. Bd. trustee Project Angel Food, Children's Hospital; bd. dir. Southern Calif. Chpt. US Fund for UNICEF. Named Achiever of Yr., Wallcoverings, Windows & Interior Fashion award; recipient Home Decorating Product of Yr. award, Profitable Craft Merchandising. Office: TV Food Network GP 1180 Ave of Americas 11th Fl New York NY 10036*

LEE, SANG M., management educator; b. Seoul, Republic of Korea, Apr. 1, 1939; arrived in U.S., 1961; s. Chang Woo Lee and Duck Soon Bahng; m. Joyce A. Sturm, Mar. 16, 1991; children: Tosca Lee, Amy L. BA in Econs., Seoul Nat. U., 1961; MBA, Miami U., Oxford, Ohio, 1963; PhD, U. Ga., 1969; degree (hon.), U. Tirana, 1998; PhD (hon.), Cheongju U., 2001, Bangkok U., 2002, Chungbuk U., 2004. Prof. bus. Va. Poly. Inst., Blacksburg, 1968—76; disting. prof., chair U. Nebr., Lincoln, 1976—. Cons. Omaha Pub. Power, 1983—86, Ssang Yong Corp., Seoul, 1984—97; project dir. U.S. Agy. Internat. Devel., 1991—2003; sr. scientist Gallup, 2001—. Author: Operations Management, 1995, Management Science, 4th edit., 1995, World Class Organization, 1996, others. Recipient Valley Forge Leavy award, Freedoms Found., 1995. Fellow: Decision Scis. Inst. (pres. 1984—85), Pan Pacific Bus. Assn. (pres. 1985—), Acad. Mgmt. Republican. Office: Univ Nebr 209 CBA Lincoln NE 68588 Office Phone: 402-472-3915. Business E-Mail: slee1@unl.edu.

LEE, SEAN S., dentist, researcher; m. Iris S. Kang; children: Christopher, Stephen. DDS, UCLA, 1988. Lic. dentist Calif., 1988. Dir. Ctr. Dental Rsch., Loma Linda, Calif., 2003—. Recipient Pres. Bush award, Phys. Award Com., 2005. Mem.: ADA, Iadr. Office: Ctr Dental Rsch 24876 Taylor St Loma Linda Univ Loma Linda CA 92407 Home Phone: 909-938-7770; Office Phone: 909-558-8178.

LEE, SE-HEE, electrical engineer, researcher; b. Yechon, Kyungbuk, Korea, Aug. 3, 1971; s. Sang-Seop Lee and Sun-Deok Kim; m. In-Sook Heo, June 19, 1975; 1 child, Eun-Jae. PhD, Sungkyunkwan U., 2002. Part-time lectr. Daelim Coll., Anyang, Kyunggi-Do, Republic of Korea, 1998—99; vis. lectr. ANSOFT Korea Corp., Seoul, 1999—2000; sr. rschr. Sungkyunkwan U., Suwon, Kyunggi-Do, Republic of Korea, 2002—, part-time lectr., 2003; post-doctoral fellow MIT, Cambridge, 2003—04, post-doctoral assoc., 2004—. Contbr. articles to profl. jours. Post-doctoral Fellowship, Korea Sci. and Engring. Found., 2003—04. Mem.: Korea Inst. Elec. Engrs. Office: Massachusetts Institute of Technology 155 Massachusetts Ave BldgN10 Cambridge MA 02139 Home Phone: 617-661-4940; Office Phone: 617-253-5019. Personal E-mail: shlees@mit.edu.

LEE, SEOKWOO S., periodontist, educator; b. Seoul, Republic of Korea, Feb. 25, 1959; s. Jong-Bae Lee and Bong-Sun Han; m. Eunkyung E. Kim, Jan. 13, 1962; children: Paul S., Stephanie S. DDS, Seoul Nat. U., 1983; MS, U. Mich., Ann Arbor, 1988; PhD, U. Fla., Gainesville, 1995. Asst. prof. U. Md., Balt., 1998—2004; assoc. prof. Columbia U., NYC, 2004—07. Lt. Korean Air Force, 1983—86. Grantee, NIH, 1998, 2004. Mem.: Am. Soc. Microbiology (assoc.). Conservative. Office Phone: 212-342-5244. Office Fax: 212-305-9313.

LEE, SEONG-JAE, research scientist; b. Kwangyang, Chunnam, South Korea, Apr. 30, 1963; s. Yong-Dae Lee and Il-Lim Suh; m. Sung-Hye Yoon; children: Sharon, Amy. BS, Yonsei U., Seoul, 1986, MS, 1988; PhD, Iowa State U., 1998. Rsch. asst. Iowa State U., Ames, 1993—98, rsch. assoc., 1998—2003, rsch. scientist Ctr. for Nondestructive Evaluation, 2004—. Contbr. articles to profl. jours. Mem.: Sigma Xi. Home: 240 Raphael Apt 21 Ames IA 50014 Office: Iowa State U Ames Lab 258H Metals Devel Bldg Ames IA 50011 Office Phone: 515-294-9066. Business E-Mail: sjlee@ameslab.gov.

LEE, SEON-HWA, professional golfer; b. Chonnan, South Korea, Feb. 10, 1986; Profl. golfer, 2000—; mem. LPGA, 2006—. Mem. Korean Team Pinx Cup, 2003. Achievements include finishing first on Futures Tour money list, 2005; winner, Albany FUTURES Pro Golf Classic on the Futures Tour, 2005; winner, ShopRite LPGA Classic, 2006, HSBC Women's World Match Play Championship, 2007; winner, Korean LPGA tour events including McSquare Championship, 2001, HiMart Championship, 2003, Hite Championship, 2005; youngest player to win on Korean LPGA tour. Office: c/o Ladies Profl Golf Assn 100 Internat Golf Dr Daytona Beach FL 32124-1092

LEE, SHAU KEE, real estate developer; b. Shunde, Guangdong, China, Jan. 29, 1928; 5 children. DBA, DSSc, LLD. With Henderson Land Devel., Hong Kong; chmn. Hong Kong & China Gas; chmn., mng. dir. Henderson Land Group, 1976—, Henderson Investment Ltd.; chmn. Henderson Cyber Ltd., Miramar Hotel and Investment Co. Ltd.; vice chmn. Sun Hung Kai Properties; dir. Hong Kong Ferry (Holdings) Co. Ltd., Bank of East Asia Ltd., Henderson Devel. Ltd., Believegood Ltd, Cameron Enterprise Inc. Named one of World's Richest People, Forbes mag., 2005—. Avocation: golf. Office: 23d Fl 363 Java Rd Northpoint Hong Kong Hong Kong*

LEE, SHUISHIH SAGE, pathologist; b. Soo-chow, Kiang su, China, Jan. 5, 1948; came to U.S., 1972, naturalized, 1979; m. Chung Seng Lee; children: Yvonne Claire, Michael Chung. MD, Nat. Taiwan U., 1972; PhD, U. Rochester, 1976. Resident in pathology Strong Meml. Hosp., Rochester, NY, 1976-78, Northwestern Meml. Hosp., Chgo., 1978-79; dir. cytology and electron microscopy Parkview Meml. Hosp., Ft. Wayne, Ind., 1979—. Clin. prof. Ind. U. Med. Sch. Contbr. articles to profl. jours. Fellow: Am. Soc. Clin. Pathologists, Coll. Am. Pathologists; mem.: AMA, Internat. Assn. Chinese Pathologists (pres. 1999—2001), Ft. Wayne Acad. Physicians and Surgeons (pres. 1990), Ft. Wayne Med. Soc. (pres. 2001—02, chair bd. 2002—), Electron Microscopy Soc. Am., Internat. Acad. Cytology, Internat. Acad. Pathology, Am. Soc. Cytology, Am. Assn. Pathologists, N.Y. Acad. Scis., Ind. Assn. Pathologists, N.E. Ind. Pathologists Assn. (sec. 1984), Ind. Med. Assn. Home: 5728 The Prophets Pass Fort Wayne IN 46845-9659 Office: Parkview Meml Hosp 2200 Randallia Dr Fort Wayne IN 46805-4699

LEE, SIDNEY PHILLIP, chemical engineer, state senator; b. Pa., Apr. 20, 1926; s. Samuel L. and Mollie (Heller) L. B.Sc., U. Pa., 1939; McMullin fellow, Cornell U., 1939-40, then M.Ch.E. Chem. engr. Atlantic Richfield Co., 1938-42; sr. chem. engr., 1942-45; pres. Dallas Labs., 1945—, Asso. Labs., Dallas, 1945—, West Indies Investment Co., 1957—; chmn. exec. com. West Indies Bank & Trust Co. Dir., mem. exec. com. Am. Ship Bldg. Co.; prin. West Indies Investment Co., St. Croix, 1956— Writer of Lee Lets Loose column for local Carribean newspapers. Mem. V.I. Senate, 1976—, now v.p.; chmn. com. govt., chmn. com. on fin. ops. V.I. Govt. Dem. nat. committeeman for V.I., 1969—; mem. V.I. Bd. Edn., 1969-76; mem. Gov.'s Blue Ribbon Commn. for Econ. Devel., 1995—; commr. V.I. Port Authority, 1997—. Fellow Am. Inst. Chemists; mem. AIChE (sr.), AIME (sr.), AARP (chmn. legis. com. 1984—), St. Croix C. of C. (v.p. 1995), Rotary (pres. 1971-73), Lions (pres. 1960), Tau Beta Pi, Sigma Tau, Beta Sigma Rho. Home and Office: 135 E 54th St Apt 11C New York NY 10022-4511 Office: PO Box 130 St Croix VI 00821-0130 *In retrospect, elation from supposed triumphs or defeats is blurred in memory; and of greater importance is the quality of one's life or how one played the game.*

LEE, SOO-HOON, human resources specialist; d. Chin-Quan Lee and Choon-Kiew Tan; m. Phillip H. Phan, Feb. 13, 1988. BBA with honors, Nat. Singapore U., 1986; PhD, U. Wash., Seattle, 1993. Pres. Core Competence Cons. Inc., Toronto, 1993—97; asst. prof. Nat. U., Singapore, 1997—2000; vis. asst. prof. Rensselaer Poly. Inst., Troy, NY, 2000—02; asst. prof. Morgan State U., Balt., 2002—04, Old Dominion U., Norfolk, Va., 2004—. Fellow, U. Wash., 1988—93; grantee, Nat. U., Singapore, 1997—2000, Rensselaer Poly. Inst., 2000—02, Morgan State U., 2002—04, Rsch., Old Dominion U., 2004—06. Home Phone: 410-637-3428.

LEE, SOOJEONG, music educator, soprano; b. Seoul, Republic of Korea, Apr. 23, 1970; arrived in US, 1992; d. Eun-Kil Lee and Keum-Sun Ji; m. Jung-Woo Kim; 1 child, Erin Kim. MusB in Voice Performance, Seoul Nat. U., 1992; MusM in Voice Performance, Manhattan Sch. Music, NYC, 1995, profl. study diploma, 1996; D in Musical Arts in Vocal Performance, U. Ill., 2003. Cert. tchr. Republic of Korea. Asst. prof., head voice and opera U. North Ala., Florence, 2001—. Asst. stage dir. Seoul Nat. U. Alumni Opera, NYC, 1995; founder Manhattan Singers, NYC, 1995—96; opera, musical theatre dir. U. North Ala., Florence, 2001—. Soloist: numerous prodns., concerts and numerous performances including at Carnegie Hall and Lincoln Center. Adjudicator scholarship competition Florence Music Club, 2002, 2004; adjudicator Solo and Ensemble Festival Vocal Assn., 2002; adjudicator auditions Ala. Music Tchrs. Assn., 2004; soloist So-Myung Ch. Choir, LI, 1992—95; mem. Milal Missionary Choir, NYC, 1992—96; soloist New Life Ch., Urbana, Ill., 1996—2001, tchr. Bible study, 2000—01. Recipient Outstanding Performance Excellence award, L. Douglas Wilder Arts Ctr., Norfolk, Va., 2002; grantee, U. North Ala., Coll. Arts and Scis., 2002, 2005, 2006, Ala. Coun. Arts, Kennedy Douglass Arts Ctr., 2004; scholar, Seoul Nat. U., 1988—92. Mem.: Ala. Fedn. Music Clubs, Nat. Assn. Tchrs. Singing, Coll. Music Soc., Phi Kappa Lambda, Phi Kappa Phi. Achievements include research in Korean folk songs and modern art songs; Jane Bathori and the early twentieth century French mélodie. Avocations: travel, cooking, yoga. Home: 215 Crownridge Dr Madison AL 35756 Office: Univ N Ala Dept Music 5040 Florence AL 35632

LEE, SOO-KYUNG, molecular biologist, educator; BS, Chonnam Nat. U., South Korea, 1997, MS, 1999, PhD, 2001. Postdoctoral rschr. Salk Inst. Biol. Studies, Calif., 2001—04; asst. prof. depts. molecular and cellular biology and molecular and human genetics Baylor Coll. Medicine Huffington Ctr. Aging, Houston, 2004—. Contbr. articles to profl. jours. Pew Scholar, 2005. Office: Dept Molecular & Cellular Biology Baylor Coll Medicine One Baylor Plz 132 C Houston TX 77030 Office Phone: 713-798-8524. Office Fax: 713-798-0545. E-mail: sklee@bcm.edu.*

LEE, SPIKE (SHELTON JACKSON LEE), film director and producer; b. Atlanta, Mar. 20, 1957; s. William James Edwards and Jacqueline (Shelton) L.; m. Tonya Lewis, Oct. 2, 1993; children: Satchel, Jackson BA, Morehouse Coll., 1979; MFA, NYU, 1982. Owner, 40 Acres & a Mule Filmworks, 1986-, 40 Acres & a Mule Musicworks, 1987-94, Spike's Joint, 1994-, chmn., Spike/DDB, 1996-; moderator, Moorehouse Coll. Black Athletes Forum, 2007. Actor, dir., prodr., writer (films) She's Gotta Have It, 1986 (New Generation award L.A. Film Critics, Prix de Jeunesse, Cannes Film Festival 1986), School Daze, 1988, Do the Right Thing, 1989, Mo' Better Blues, 1990, Jungle Fever, 1991, Malcolm X, 1992, Crooklyn, 1994, Clockers, 1995, Summer of Sam, 1999; actor, dir., prodr. Girl 6, 1996, The Original Kings of Comedy, 2000; dir., prodr., writer (films) Joe's Bed-Stuy Barbershop: We Cut Heads, 1983 (student dir. award Acad. Motion Pictures Arts and Scis.), He Got Game, 1998, Bamboozled, 2000, She Hate Me, 2004; dir., prodr. (films) Original Kings of Comedy, 2001, 25th Hour, 2002,; actor, prodr. (films) 3 A.M., 2001; dir. only (films) Last Hustle in Brooklyn, 1977, The Answer, 1980, Sarah, 1981, Inside Man, 2006(Dir. of Motion Picture, TV Movie, NAACP Image Awards, 2007); prodr. only (films) The Best Man, 1999, Love and Basketball, 2000; exec. prodr. only (films) Drop Squad, 1994, New Jersey Drive, 1995, Tales from the Hood, 1995, Home Invaders, 2001; dir., prodr. (documentaries) Get on the Bus, 1996, 4 Little Girls, 1997, A Huey P. Newton Story, 2001, Jim Brown: All American, 2002, When the Levees Broke: A Requiem in Four Acts, 2006 (2006 George Polk award for Documentary TV); (short films) Jesus Children of America, 2005, All the Invisible Children, 2005; (TV films) Sucker Free City, 2004; dir. (TV movies) Freak, 1998; actor (TV appearances) Into the Comics: Part 1, 1992; dir. (TV series) Shark (pilot), 2006; author: Spike Lee's Gotta Have It: Inside Guerilla Filmmaking, 1987, Uplift the Race: The Construction of School Daze, 1988, Do the Right Thing: A Spike Lee Joint, 1989, Mo' Better Blues, 1990, By Any Means Necessary: The Trials and Tribulations of the Making of "Malcolm X", 1992; co-author: (with Ralph Wiley) Best Seat in the House, 1997, (with Tonya Lewis Lee) Please, Baby Please, 2002, (with Kaleem Aftab) Thats My Story and I'm Sticking to It, 2005. Trustee Morehouse Coll., 1992- Recipient French Acad. Cinema award, 2002, Filmmaker Trumpet award, 2003, Ossie Davis Humanitarian award, Black Movie awards, 2006, Spl. Achievement award, African-American Film Critics Assn., 2006. Fellow Am. Acad. Arts & Scis. Office: 40 Acres & a Mule 124 Dekalb Ave Ste 2 Brooklyn NY 11217-1200*

LEE, STAN (STANLEY MARTIN LIEBER), cartoon publisher, writer; b. NYC, Dec. 28, 1922; s. Jack and Celia (Solomon) Lieber; m. Joan Clayton Boocock, Dec. 5, 1947; 2 children, Joan C., Jan (dec.). Degree (hon.), Bowling Green State U. Copy writer, then asst. editor, editor Timely Comics, NYC, 1939—42; editor, creative dir. Atlas Comics (formerly Timely Comics), 1945—61; with Marvel Comics, 1961—72, pub., editl. dir., 1972—78; creative dir. Marvel Prodns., 1978—89, chmn. Marvel comics; partnered with DC Comics, 2000—. Founder, Stan Lee Media. Creator, former writer and editor Fantastic Four, Incredible Hulk, Amazing Spiderman, numerous others; author: Origins of Marvel Comics, 1974, Son of Origins, 1975, Bring On The Bad Guys, 1976, Mighty Marvel Strength & Fitness Book, 1976, Mighty Marvel Superheroes Fun Book, 1976, The Marvel Comics Illustrated Version of Star Wars, 1977, The Amazing Spiderman Vol. No. 3, 1977, The Superhero Women, 1977, The Mighty World of Marvel Pin-up Book, 1978, The Mighty Marvel Superhero Fun Book Vol. No. 3, 1978, The Silver Surfer, How to Draw Comics the Marvel Way, 1978, Marvel's Greatest Superhero Battles, 1978, Incredible Hulk, 1978, Marvelous Mazes to Drive You Mad, 1978, Fantastic Four, 1979, Doctor Strange, 1979, Complete Adventures of Spider-Man, 1979, Captain America, 1979, The Best of the Worst, 1979, Marvel Word Games, 1979, Omnibus Fun Book, 1979, Dunn's Conundrum, 1985, The Best of Spider-Man, 1986, Marvel Team-Up Thrillers, 1987, The Amazing Spider-man, No. 2, 1980, Hulk Cartoons, 1980, Marvel Masterworks Vol. 2: Fantastics Four, 1987, X-Men, 1987, Marvel Masterworks, Vol. 1: Amazing Spider-Man, 1987, Masterworks, Vol. 6: Fantastic Four, 1988, Silver Surfer: Judgement Day, 1988, Silver Surfer: Parable, 1988, Spider-Man, 1988, Avengers, 1988, The God Project, 1990, Silver Surfer: The Enslavers, 1990, Marvel Masterworks, Vol. 13: Fantastic Four, 1990, Best of Marvel Comics, 1991, Night Cat, 1991, Marvel Masterworks, Vol. 17: Daredevil, 1991, Marvel Masterworks, Vol. 18: Thor, 1991, Spider-Man Wedding, 1991, Spider-Man Masterworks, 1992, Uncanny X-Men Masterworks, 1993, Marvels Greatest Super Battles, 1994, The Ultimate Spider-man, 1994, The Very Best of Spiderman, 1994, The Incredible Hulk: A Man-Brute Berserk, 1995, others; creator (TV series), Iron Man, 1966, Hulk, 1966, Spider-Man, 1994-98, The Fantastic Four, 1994, The Incredible Hulk, 1996-97, Avengers, 1999-2000, Spider-Man: The New Animated Series, 2003, Striperella, 2003; cameos in several movie adaptations of comic book characters including X-Men, 2000, Spider-Man, 2002, Daredevil, 2003, Hulk, 2003, Spider-Man 2, 2004, Fantastic Four, 2005; guest appearences include (voice) The Incredible Hulk, 1997, (voice) Spider-Man, 1998, 2003, Turn Ben Stein On, 2001, To Tell the Truth, 2001, (voice) The Simpsons, 2002, Mad TV, 2003, 2004, and several talk shows. With Signal Corps US Army, 1942—45. Recipient Alley Award, 1963-68; Comic Art Award, Soc. for Comic Art Rsch. & Preservation, 1968; Eureka Award, Il Targa 1970; Publisher of the Year, Periodical & Book Assn. of America, 1978; ann. award Popular Culture Assn., 1974 Mem. (founder), Acad. Comic Book Arts (award 1973), Nat. Acad. TV Arts and Scis., Nat. Cartoonists Soc., AFTRA. Clubs: Friars (N.Y.C.). Office: Marvel Comics Group Wilshire Blvd Ste 1400 Los Angeles CA 90024 Mailing: Attn: Ross Fineman William Morris Agency 151 ElCamino Dr Beverly Hills CA 90212 Address: Attn: Gill Champion POW! Entertainment 9440 Santa Monica Blvd Ste 620 Beverly Hills CA 90210 Office: Marvel Enterprises Inc 417 5th Ave Fl 2 New York NY 10016-2204

LEE, STEPHEN W., lawyer; b. New Castle, Ind., Oct. 25, 1949; s. Delmer W. Lee and Loma F. (Thurston) McCall; m. Pamela A. Summers, Aug. 2, 1969; children: Erin E., Stephanie M. BS, Ball State U., 1971; JD summa cum laude, Ind. U., 1977. Bar: Ind. 1977, U.S. Dist. Ct. (so. dist.) Ind. 1977, U.S. Ct. Appeals (7th cir.) 1977, U.S. Supreme Ct. 1982. Officer, lt.(j.g.) USNR, Phila., 1971-74; law clk. U.S. Dist. Ct. (no. dist.) Ind., Ft. Wayne, 1977-78; assoc. Barnes, Hickam, Pantzer & Boyd, Indpls., 1978-

82, Barnes & Thornburg, Indpls., 1982-83, ptnr., 1984—. Dir. The Julian Ctr., Indpls., 1999-2005; mem. Ind. U. Sch. of Law Bd. of Visitors, 1999—. Editor-in-chief: Indiana Law Jour., 1976-77. Dir. Ind. Repertory Theatre, Indpls., 1986-91; exec. coun. Ind. U. Alumni Assn., Bloomington, 1989; dir. Ind. U. Sch. of Law Alumni Assn., Bloomington, 1984-90, pres., 1991-92; mem. Ball State U. Coll. Bus. Alumni Bd., 1991-2000, Ball State U. Entrepreneurship Adv. Bd., 1994-2002; mem. United Way Ctrl. Ind. Projects Commn., 1996—. Mem. Ind. State Bar Assn., Indpls. Bar Assn. (chmn. bus. sect. 1985), Highland Golf & Country Club. Republican. Avocation: golf. Office: Barnes & Thornburg 11 S Meridian St Indianapolis IN 46204-3535 Office Phone: 317-231-7200. Business E-Mail: slee@btlaw.com.

LEE, STEVE CHI KONG, bank executive; b. Taipei, Taiwan, Sept. 11, 1951; s. Shih Hwa and Ming Ling Lee; m. Judy Chow, July 3, 1982; children: Andrew Chow Lee, Mike Chow Lee. BA, Soo Chow U., Taipei, 1979; MBA, Woodbury U., LA, 1983. Cert. stock exch. broker United World Chinese Comml. Bank, Taipei, 1979—80; officer Am. Asian Bank, Beverly Hills, Calif., 1981—84; asst. v.p. Sumitomo Bank, LA, 1984—89; v.p. Mitsubishi Bank, LA, 1989—93; sr. v.p. Tokai Bank, LA, 1993—2001; exec. v.p. Far East Nat. Bank, LA, 2001—. Recipient Achievement proclamation, Mayor and Councelmen of City of Cerritos, Calif., 2000. Mem.: City Club. Buddhist. Avocations: photography, fishing, golf, ping pong/table tennis, basketball.

LEE, STEVEN C., lawyer; CPA; bar: Ohio 1989. Atty. Calfee, Halter & Griswold, Cleve., 1989—95; asst. v.p., corp. counsel Premier Farnell Corp., Independence, Ohio, 1995—97; v.p., gen. counsel TravelCenters Am., Westlake, Ohio, 1997—2005, sr. v.p., gen. counsel, asst. sec., 2005—. Office: TravelCenters of America Ste 200 24601 Center Ridge Rd Westlake OH 44145 E-mail: lee.steven@tatravelcenters.com.*

LEE, STEVEN XAVIER, museum director, artist and environmentalist; b. Balt., Dec. 25; s. Francis Xavier Lee and Dolores Carroll Lee Lucas. BFA, Howard U., 1974; MS, Pratt Inst., 1977. News reporter WHUR Radio, Washington, 1972—74; exhbn. designer Manasse Assocs., NYC, 1975—77, Warren Displays, NYC, 1976—77; art dir. The Continental Group, NYC, 1978—80; art and animation dir. Le Centre Bossuet, Paris, 1980—81; lectr./assoc. prof. U. Md., Baltimore County/College Park, 1982—87; asst. curator Office of the Mayor, Balt., 1988—91; dir. The Heritage Mus., Balt., 1991—, Benjamin Banneker Hist. Pk. and Mus., Oella, Md., 1997—. Dir. The Found. for Minority Film, Balt., 1984—90; art and culture com. chmn. Balt. Cable Access Corp., 1984—94; instr. Md. Inst. Coll. Art, Balt., 1985—86; adj. assoc. prof. U. Balt., 1988—90; bd. dirs. Friends of the Gwynns Falls/Leakin Pk., Balt., 1989—, Consortium African and Am. Museums Md., Annaplolis, 2002—. Co-author: Understanding & Exploring Community-Based Approaches to Ecosystem Management in the U.S.; prodr., author: exhibition Remember Maryland - A History of Free African American and Native Americans in the Making of Early Maryland (Md. Humanities Coun. award, 1995), hist. exhbn. Smithsonbian Mus. for the Native Am., prodr., interviewer: public radio program Living Voices/Voces Vivas; commentator, historian (pub. TV prodn.) American Almanacs - A Living History; book (non-fiction), Windsor Hills - A Century of History 1895 to 1995, digital painting, Embers - Tribute to Haile Gerima (Sigraph Art Show award, 1986), exhbn., Design (Design Excellence award, 1979), History of Trade Shows (First Pl. in Hist. Exhbn., 1977). Task force appointee Mayor's Task Force for the Gwynns Falls Greenway, Balt., 1993—96; com. mem. Md. Stream ReLeaf Coordinating Com., Annapolis, 1998—2002; steering com. mem. Revitalizing Balt., 1995—2000; monument com. chmn. Balt. Cultural Alliance, 1999—2005; dir. Gwynns Falls Conservancy, Balt., 1993—2005. Named Living Maker of History, Gov. Paris Glendening & Iota Phi Lambda, Baltimore County Trailblazer, The Links, Inc., 2006; recipient Stream Action award, Md. Save Our Streams, 1995, Hose Resolution - In Recognition of Exceptional Achievement in the Devel. Diverse Cultural Arts, Md. Ho. Dels., 1997, CityArts award, Mayor's Adv. Com. on Art and Culture, 1998, Tralblazer award, Links, Inc., 2006. Mem.: Internat. Coun. Museums, Am. Assn. Museums. Achievements include design of modular pneumatic exhibition structures; development of The Heritage Museum - first organization for the combined development of African, African American, Carribean, Latin American and Native American cultures; The Gwynns Falls Conservancy - minority organization for environmental education and conservation. Office: Benjamin Banneker Hist Park and Mus 300 Oella Ave Baltimore MD 21228 Office Phone: 410-887-1081. Office Fax: 410-203-2747. Business E-Mail: sxlee@baltimorecountymd.gov.

LEE, SUL HI, library administrator, dean; b. Taegu, Korea, July 13, 1936; s. Sang Moo and Won Nim L.; m. Seol Bong Ryu, Sept. 6, 1962; 1 child, Melissa Jemee. BA, Bowling Green State U., 1961; MA, U. Toledo, 1964, U. Mich., 1966. Reference libr. Toledo Pub. Libr., 1961-67; supr. info. analysts Owens-Ill., Inc., 1967-68; dir. U. Toledo Ctr. Libr. and Info. Systems, 1968-70; assoc. dir. librs. Ea. Mich. U., Ypsilanti, 1970-73, U. Rochester, NY, 1973-75; dean libr. svcs. Ind. State U., Terre Haute, 1975-78; dean univ. librs. U. Okla., Norman, 1978—, adj. prof. Sch. Libr. and Info. Studies, 1988—. Author: Library Orientation, 1972, A Challenge for Academic Libraries, 1973, Planning-Programing-Budgeting System, 1973, Library Budgeting, 1977, Emerging Trends in Library Organization, 1978, Serials Collection Development: Choices and Strategies, 1981, Reference Service: a Perspective, 1983, Library Fundraising, 1984, Issues in Acquisitions, 1984, Access to Scholarly Information, 1985, Pricing and Cost of Monographs and Serials, 1987, Acquisitions, Budgets and Materials Costs, 1988, The Impact of Rising Costs of Serials and Monographs on Library Services and Programs, 1989, Library Material Costs and Access to Information, 1990, Budgets for Acquisitions, 1991, Vendor Evaluation and Acquisitions Budgets, 1992, Collection Assessment and Acquisitions Budgets, 1993, The Role and Future of Special Collections in Research Libraries, 1993, Declining Acquisitions Budgets, 1994, Access, Ownership and Resource Sharing, 1995, Emerging Pattern of Collection Development in Expanding Resource Charing, Electronic Information and Network Environment, 1996, Economics of Digital Information: Collection, Storage and Delivery, 1997, Challenges of Collection Development: Digital Information, Internet and Print Materials, 1998, Collection Development in the Electronic Environment: Shifting Priorities, 1999; editor: Collection Management, 1996-98, Jour. Libr. Adminstrn., 1987—. Mem. ALA (com. on accreditation 1981-83, mem. coun. 1986-90, coun. com. on coms. 1988-89), Assn. Rsch. Librs. (chair com. mgmt. rsch. librs. 1987-89, bd. dirs. 1991-94), Greater Midwestern Rsch. Librs. Consortium (chair 1994-95), U. Mich. Sch. Libr. Sci. Alumni Soc. (pres. 1983-84, mem. edtl. com. CAUSE 1995-98). Office: U Okla Univ Librs 401 W Brooks St Norman OK 73019 Office Phone: 405-325-2611. Office Fax: 405-325-7550. E-mail: shlee@ou.edu.*

LEE, SUNG HO, psychiatrist; b. Seoul, June 28, 1934; s. Suk K. Lee and Chung Won Kim; m. Myung H. Lee, Nov. 17, 1959; children: Benjamin, May. Student, Yonsei U., 1953-55, MD, 1959; MSc, Ohio State U., 1967; postgrad. med. cert., UCLA, 1968. Diplomate Am. Bd. Psychiatry and Neurology, Korean Bd. of Psychiatry and Neurology. Psychiat. resident Brentwood Psychiat. Hosp., VAMC, LA, 1967-68, Ohio State U. Hosp., Columbus, 1965-67; neurology resident Cin. Gen. Hosp., 1964-65; psychiat. resident Yonsei U. Hosp., Seoul, 1960-62, staff psychiatrist, 1968-69; chief psychiatrist Ewha U. Hosp., Seoul, 1969-70; clin. dir. unit B Broughton State Hosp., Morganton, NC, 1970-71; chief psychiatrist VA Med. Ctr., Dayton, Ohio, 1971-79; staff psychiatrist Eastway Cmty. Mental Health Ctr., Dayton, 1975-95; med. dir. South Cmty. Inc., Centerville, Ohio, 1990-95; pvt. practice Dayton, 1975-95; chief psychiatrist Kyung Hee Pundang CHA Gen. Hosp., Seoul, 1995-96; staff psychiatrist Accord Behavioral Healthcare, Dayton, 1996—2004; staff psychiatrist, dep. med. dir. Eastway Corp., Dayton, 1996—2004. Cons. psychiatrist South Cmty Inc., Centerville, 1980-90, Dayton Mental Health Ctr., 1975-95, Eastway Cmty. Mental Health Ctr., 1975-79; assoc. clin. prof. Wright State U., Dayton, 1979—, asst. clin. prof., 1975-79; prof. Kyung Hee U., 1975-76; asst. clin. prof. Ohio State U., Columbus, 1971-75; asst. prof. Ewha U. Coll. of Medicine, 1969-70; instr. Yonsei U. Coll. of Medicine, 1968-69, 1961-64. Home: 13230 Palm Pl Cerritos CA 90703-1345 Office: 1490 Central Ave Chino CA 91710 E-mail: sungl_1@msn.com.

LEE, SUNGHO H., education educator, consultant, academic administrator; b. Kyonggi-do, Republic of Korea, Nov. 3, 1946; s. Kiwon and Imae (Song) L.; m. Hwadong Kim, Feb. 17, 1973; children: Haichung, Haiseok. BA, Yonsei U., Seoul, Rep. of Korea, 1970, MA, 1975; student, Ruhr U., Bochum, Germany, 1976-77; EdD, George Washington U., 1980. Instr. Yonsei U., 1975-76, asst. prof., 1981-85, assoc. prof., 1986-90, prof., 1991—, dean Coll. Edn., 1998-2000, dean Grad. Sch., 2000—02, v.p., 2002—04. Asst. min. Ministry of Edn., Rep. of Korea, 1993; dir. univ. evaluation Korean Coun. for Univ. Edn., Korea, 1983-90; mem. Presdl. Commn. 21st Century, 1989-93. Author: Shaking Parents and Straying Children, 1997 (award Chosun Daily Newspaper Co. 1997); co-author: Scientific Development and Higher Education, 1989 (award NSF 1986), Academic Profession in the World, 1995, Teaching Methods in Schools, 1999; contbr. chpts. to books. Cons. New Cmty. Devel. Movement Assn., Korea, 1996-99; mem. Nat. Commn. UNESCO, Korea, 1993-95; bd. trustees Nat. Inst. Curriculum Devel., 1998-99; mem. nat. adv. com. for edn. policy, Korea, 1996-99; mem. standing com. Presdl. Com. for Rebuilding Korea, 1998-2000; mem. adv. com. Korean Air Force, 2001—; chmn. Nat. Edn. Policy Adv. Com., 2001-2003. Sgt. US I Corps., 1970-73. Decorated U.S. Army Commendation medal, Order of Svc. Merit Pres. of Korea; recipient award, Nat. Carnegie Found., 1992; grantee, Nat. Assn. Trade and Tech. Schs., 1980, Ford Found., 2001. Mem. Korean Soc. for Study Edn. (bd. trustees 1981-83, 86-90, 98-2000), Korean Higher Edn. Assn. (bd. trustees 1994—). Evangelical. Avocation: golf. Office: Yonsei U Dept Edn Shinchon-dong 134 Sodaemoon-ku Seoul 120-749 Republic of Korea Office Phone: 2-2123-3176. Business E-Mail: leesh@yonsei.ac.kr.

LEE, TABIA (T. LEE), social studies educator; b. Lodi, Calif. d. Lloyd Laughlin and Ann Melton. BA in Sociology, U. Calif., Davis, 1999; MA in Edn., U. Phoenix, 2004; EdD, U. Calif., Irvine, 2006—, Calif. State U., LA, 2006—. Cert. Social Studies Tchr. Nat. Bd. Profl. Tchg. Stds., 2004. Tchr. LA Unified Sch. Dist., 1999—. Profl. reviewer Corwin Press, Thousand Oaks, 2004—. Mem.: ACLU, United Tchrs. LA, Internat. Reading Assn., Nat. Coun. Social Studies, Assn. Supervision and Curriculum Devel., Pi Lambda Theta. Avocations: reading, writing, music, dance, cooking. Home Phone: 323-467-7784. Personal E-mail: nbctresearch@aol.com.

LEE, THEODORE BO, real estate developer; b. Stockton, Calif., Dec. 28, 1932; s. Wong Bo and Daisy (Lum) L.; m. Doris Shoong, June 14, 1969; children: Gregory T.H., Ernest T.H. BA, Harvard Coll., 1954; JD, U. Calif., Berkeley, 1959, MBA, 1966. Bar: Hawaii 1962, Calif. 1960. Jr. lectr. U. Singapore, 1960—61; legal assoc. Fong, Miho, etal, Honolulu, 1961—62; assoc. dir. East West Ctr., Honolulu, 1962—64; real estate atty. Urban Cons., San Francisco, 1964—82; chmn. Urban Group, San Francisco, 1971—. Dir. Ind. Nev. Casino Operators, Las Vegas, Nihonmachi Cmty. Devel. Corp., San Francisco. Author: Laws of the Commonwealth (Singapore), 1961. Pres. St. Pauls Parents Assn., Concord, N.H., 1980-88; trustee, vice chair Berkeley Found., 1984-97. Recipient internat. legal fellowship U. Calif., Berkeley, 1959, Wheeler Oak award Berkeley Found., 1985. Mem. Harvard Alumni Assn. (trustee, dir. 1982-85, overseer 1994-2000, alumni award), Boalt Hall Alumni Assn. (pres.). Avocation: foreign travel. Office: Urban Land Nev 3271 S Highland Dr Ste 704 Las Vegas NV 89109-1051 Home Phone: 702-735-4567; Office Phone: 702-369-9595.

LEE, THERESA K., lawyer, chemicals executive; b. Gary, W.Va., Nov. 21, 1952; BS in Polit. Sci. and Hist., East Tenn. State U., 1974; JD, U. Tenn., 1977; postgraduate student, Harvard U., 1999. Staff atty. Legal Svcs. Upper East Tenn., 1977—79; sr. law clk. to Judge H. Emory Widener, Jr. US Ct. Appeals (4th cir.), 1979—87; atty. Eastman Chem., 1987—91, asst. to pres., 1991—92, asst. sec., sr. counsel Tex. Eastman divsn., 1992—93, asst. sec., asst. gen. counsel legal dept. health safety and environ. grp., 1993—95, asst. sec., asst. gen. counsel legal dept., corp. grp., 1995—97, v.p., sec., asst. gen. counsel, 1997—2000, chief legal officer, 2000—; sr. v.p. Eastman Chem. Co., 2002—. Recipient Outstanding Alumna award, East Tenn. State U. Nat. Alumni Assn., 2002. Mem.: ABA (gen. counsel com.), Soc. Corp. Secs. & Governance Profls., Kingsport Bar Assn., Tenn. Bar Assn. (ho. of dels.), Am. Corp. Counsel Assn. (bd. dirs.). Office: Eastman Chem Co PO Box 431 Kingsport TN 37662-5280

LEE, THOMAS ALEXANDER, accountant, educator; b. Edinburgh, May 18, 1941; s. Thomas Henderson and Dorothy Jane (Norman) L.; m. Ann Margaret Brown, Sept. 14, 1963; children: Sarah Ann, Richard Thomas. Chartered acct., Inst. Chartered Accts.Scotland, Edinburgh, 1964; tax acct., Inst. Tax, Glasgow, Scotland, 1965; MS, U. Strathclyde, Glasgow, Scotland, 1969, DLitt, 1984. Audit asst., Edinburgh, 1959-64, Glasgow, 1964-66; lectr. U. Strathclyde, 1966-69, U. Edinburgh, 1969-73, prof. Eng., 1976-90, U. Liverpool, Eng., 1973-76; dir. rsch. Inst. Chartered Accts. Scotland, 1983-84; prof. U. Ala., 1990—2001, dir. PhD program, 1991—2001, emeritus prof., 2001—; hon. prof. U. Newcastle, 2003—. Vis. prof. U. Md., 1986, U. Utah, 1987-88, U. Edinburgh, 1991-94, Deakin U., 1994—, U. Newcastle; hon. prof. U. Dundee, Scotland, 1995—, U. St. Andrews, Scotland, 2006-. Editor: Internat. Jour. Auditing; mem. editl. bd. various jours., 1971—. Acad. Acctg. Historians, pres., 1999, past pres., 2000. Recipient Burnum award U. Ala., 1997. Mem. Inst. Chartered Accts. Scotland (coun. 1989-90), Inst. Taxation, Brit. Acctg. Assn. (Lifetime Achievement award 2004, Hall of Fame 2005). Presbyterian. Avocations: church, road running, cricket history. Home: 5 Alderston Gardens Haddington EH41 3RY England Office: Sch Mgmt Univ St Andrews St Andrews Scotland KY16 9SS Office Phone: 011441334461969. Personal E-mail: leeatom@aol.com.

LEE, THOMAS E., emergency physician; BA, Stanford U., Palo Alto, Calif., 1988; MD, U. Calif., Irvine, 1993; MPH, U. Ill., Chgo., 1999. Attending physician Mercy Hosp., Chgo., 1997—2000, Calif. Emergency Physicians, Visalie, 2000—06, Northwest Permanente Hosp., Portland, 2006—. Editor: Iraqi Jour. Medicine, 2004. Fellow: Am. Coll. Emergency Physicians; mem.: Spl. Operation Med. Assn.

LEE, THOMAS F., art association administrator; Exec. com. Fedn. of Musicians, Local 161-710, Washington, 1980, sec.-treas., 1990; mem. internat. exec. bd. Am. Fedn. Musicians, 1991, v.p., 1995—99, sec., treas., 1999—2001, pres., 2001—. Mem. exec. com. Am. Fedn. Musicians; pianist US Marine Band. Office: Am Fedn Musicians 1501 Broadway Ste 600 New York NY 10036 Office Phone: 212-869-1330. Office Fax: 212-764-6134. E-mail: presoffice@afm.org.*

LEE, THOMAS H., investment company executive; b. 1944; m. Ann Tenenbaum; children: Stephen Zachary, Robert Schiff. B, Harvard U., 1965. With First Nat. Bank Boston, 1966—74, mgr. high tech. leading grp., 1968—74, v.p., 1973—74; chmn. T.H. Lee Mezzanine; chmn., CEO THLee Putnam Ventures; founder, chmn., CEO Thomas H. Lee Ptnrs., Boston, 1974—2005, Lee Equity Ptnrs. LLC, NYC, 2006—. Nat. adv. bd. JP Morgan; dir. Metris Cos. Inc., Miller Import Corpn., Wyndham Internat. Inc., Snapple Beverage Corpn., Gen. Nutrition Cos., Playtex Products Inc., Vail Resorts Inc., 1993—, Safelite Glass Corpn., Vertis Holdings Inc., First Security Svcs. Corpn. Established Henry Rosovsky Fund, Faculty of Arts and Scis., Harvard U., 1984; trustee Intrepid Mus., Lincoln Ctr. for Rockefeller U., NYU Med. Ctr., Mus. Modern Art, NYC; v.p. bd. Whitney Mus. Am. Art. Named one of Top 200 Collectors, ARTnews mag., 2003—06. Avocation: Collector of Modern and contemporary art; Egyptian art.*

LEE, THOMAS HENRY, internist, cardiologist, healthcare executive; b. Schenectady, NY, Dec. 2, 1953; Grad., Harvard Coll., 1975; MD, Cornell U., 1979; MSc, Harvard U., 1987. Bd. cert. internal medicine 1982, bd. cert. cardiovasc. disease. Intern Harvard Med. Sch., Boston, 1980—82; resident Brigham and Women's Hosp., Boston, 1982—84, cardiology fellow, 1984—85, internist, cardiologist; assoc. prof. dept. health policy and mgmt. Harvard Med. Sch., Boston; chief med. officer Partners Cmty. Healthcare, Inc., network pres., 2004—, CEO, 2004—. Bd. dirs. Mass. Quality Partnership, Bridges to Excellence; dir. Partners Signature Initiatives. Assoc. editor: The New England Journal of Medicine, editor-in-chief: The Harvard Heart Letter, author numerous scholarly articles. Office: Partners Cmty Health Care Inc Prudential Twr Ste 1150 800 Boylston St Boston MA 02199 also: Brigham Internal Medicine Assoc 75 Francis St Boston MA 02115

LEE, THOMAS TEHWEN, neurosurgeon; b. Tainan, Taiwan, Dec. 27, 1967; s. Chang Kuei and Shiu-Hoa Shu L.; m. Margaret Yu, Aug. 31, 1993. BA magna cum laude, U. Calif., Berkeley, 1989; MD, UCLA, 1993; MBA, George Washington U., DC, 2007. Diplomate Am. Bd. Neurol. Surgery, Nat. Bd. Med. Examiners. Resident in neurosurgery U. Miami - Jackson Meml. Med. Ctr., 1993-99; attending neurosurgeon Westchester Med. Ctr., NY, 1999—; chief sect. neurosurgery St. John's Riverside Hosp., 2001—; clin. asst. prof. Mt. Sinai Sch. Medicine, NYC, 2005—. Credentials com. Phelps Meml. Hosp., Sleepy Hollow, NY, 2001—; med. bd. St. John's Riverside Hosp., Yonkers, NY, 2003—05, bd. dirs., chmn. auditing com., mem. fin. com., 2007; co-chair legis. com., bd. dirs. Westchester County Med. Soc., 2007—. Mem. editl. rev. bd. The Spine, 1999—; contbr. articles to profl. jours., chpt. to books in field. Mem. med. response team Championship Auto Racing Team, 1995-99. Dean's scholar, UCLA, 1993. Fellow: ACS; mem.: AMA, Congress Neurol. Surgeons (med. edn. liaison, mem. com. on edn., mem. sci. program com.), Am. Assn. Neurol. Surgeons, N.Am. Spine Soc., Phi Beta Kappa, Golden Key. Avocations: movie poster collection, swimming, tennis, target shooting. Office Phone: 914-631-9207. Personal E-mail: thomastleemd@aol.com.

LEE, TIMOTHY EARL, international agency executive, paralegal; b. Seattle, May 23, 1947; s. Charles Augusta and Esther Letty (Young) L.; m. Marcia Lea Wulff, July 6, 1968 (div. May 1976); children: Vincent Dean, Dante' Claude; 1 stepson, Kevin Paul McCorkle; m. Jayne Elizabeth Ashley, Apr. 28, 1984 (div. Apr. 1995). Cert., Ivy Tech., 1981, Am. Inst. Paralegal Studies, 1988. Mgr. Gen. Fin. Corp., Evanston, Ill., 1970-74, FBT Capital Corp., South Bend, Ind., 1974-76; owner Lee's Internat. Investigative Rsch. Agy., Ft. Wayne, Ind., 1978—. Mem. Heritage Foun., Citizens Against Govt. Waste; spl. adv. Allen Superior Ct. With U.S. Army, 1966-68, Vietnam. Recipient Cert. of Appreciation, DAV, 1968. Mem. VFW, Ind. Assn. Pvt. Detectives (v.p. N.E. region Ind. 1984—), Ind. Sheriff's Assn., Ft. Wayne Allen County Security Assn., Coun. for Inter-Am. Security, Nat. Security Ctr., Nat. Def. Inst., 27th Field Artillery Assn. (v.p., founding father), Am. Legion, Vietnam Vets, Internat. Platform Assn., Concord Coalition. Address: PO Box 15028 Fort Wayne IN 46885-5028 Office Phone: 260-437-7167. E-mail: Liira@gte.net.

LEE, TOM STEWART, judge; b. 1941; m. Norma Ruth Robbins; children: Elizabeth Robbins Maron, Tom Stewart Jr. BA summa cum laude, Miss. Coll., 1963; JD cum laude, U. Miss., 1965. Ptnr. Lee & Lee, Forest, Miss., 1965—84; pros. atty. Scott County, Miss., 1968—71; judge Scott County Youth Ct., Forest, 1979—82, US Dist. Ct. (so. dist.) Miss., Jackson, 1984—96, chief judge, 1996—2003, sr. judge, 2006—. Asst. editor: Miss. Law Jour. Pres. Forest Pub. Sch. Bd., Scott County Heart Assn.; bd. trustees Miss. Coll. Named one of Outstanding Young Men Am. Fellow: Found. of Fed. Bar Assn. (life); mem.: 5th Cir. Jud. Coun. (CACM com. Jud. Conf., Disting. Svc. award), Fed. Judges Assn., Fed. Bar Assn., Hinds County Bar Assn., Scott County Bar Assn., Miss. Bar Assn., Ole Miss. Alumni Assn. (pres.), Am. Legion. Office: US Dist Ct 245 E Capitol St Ste 110 Jackson MS 39201-2414 Office Phone: 601-965-4963. Business E-Mail: tom_lee@mssd.uscourts.gov.

LEE, TONG HUN, economics professor; b. Seoul, Republic of Korea, Nov. 20, 1931; arrived in U.S., 1955, naturalized, 1968; s. Chong Su and Yun L.; m. Yul Jah Ahn, June 11, 1960; children: Bruce Keebeck, James Keewon. BS, Yonsei U., 1955; PhD, U. Wis., 1961. Asst. prof. econs. U. Tenn., Knoxville, 1962-64, assoc. prof., 1964-67; prof. econs. U. Wis., Milw., 1967-96, chmn. dept. econs., 1978-82; disting. prof. econs. Ajou U., Suwon, Republic of Korea, 1997—. Author: Interregional Intersectoral Flow Analysis, 1973; contbr. articles to profl. jours. NSF grantee, 1965-67, 73-75. Mem. Am. Econ. Assn., Am. Fin. Assn., Am. Statis. Assn., Econometric Soc. Home: 55 W Delaware Pl Apt 1021 Chicago IL 60610-6073 Office: Ajou U Sch Bus Adminstrn 5 Wonchon-Dong Paldal-Gu Suwon 442-749 Republic of Korea Personal E-mail: tonghunlee2000@yahoo.co.kr. *Success comes from determination, persistence and hard work, but the ultimate measure of success is derived from the inner life of a person.*

LEE, TONÍA RENEÉ, entertainer, former government agent, educator; b. Colorado Springs, Mar. 27, 1963; d. Ernest and Claudine (Brunt) L. BA in Oral Communication, U. Central Okla., 1983; postgrad., Tex. So. U., 1983, Oral Roberts U., 1984-85; MPA, U. So. Calif., 1987, cert. in jud. adminstrn., 1987; postgrad., Saybrook Inst., 1988-89, U. West Los Angeles, 1986-87, U. La Verne, 1990-92. Cert., registered hypnotherapist. Spl. agt. US Dept. Def., Gardena, Calif., 1986-93. Vol. cons. Tulsa County Juvenile Bur., 1985; adj. prof. Union Inst. and U., 1999-2002; talent agent Dale Garrick Internat. Talent Agency, Hollywood, Calif.; literary agent, talent mgr., music promoter Big Dogg Plus Sports & Entertainment LLC, Oklahoma City. Author: Slavery Without Chains and Other Selected Poems, Big Mom's and Little Mom's Cook Book. Vol. ARC, 1980; mem. Young Democrats, 1981-83, NAACP (LA chpt. 1990-92). Recipient Editor's Choice award Nat. Libr. of Poetry, 1994; named to Outstanding Young Women of Am., 1985. Mem. AAUW, NAFE, SAG, Pre-Law Club (sec.-treas. 1982-83), Am. Bus. Women's Assn., Creating Mobility and Independence for People With Disabilities, NCO Wives Club (ednl. scholarship 1980), Ctrl. State U. Alumni Assn., U. So. Calif. Alumni Assn., Internat. Fedn. U. Women, Nat. Assn. U. Women, Kappa Delta Pi, Delta Sigma Theta (golden life mem., ednl. scholarship 1980). Democrat. Baptist. Avocations: acting, travel, writing, poetry. Office Phone: 405-942-7844. E-mail: toniatinseltown@aol.com.

LEE, TSUNG-DAO, physicist, researcher; b. Shanghai, Nov. 24, 1926; arrived in U.S., 1946; s. Tsing-Kong L. and Ming-Chang (Chang); m. Jeannette Chin, June 3, 1950; children: James, Stephen. Student, Nat. Chekiang U., Kweichow, China, 1943-44, Nat. S.W. Assoc. U., Kunming, China, 1945-46; PhD, U. Chgo., 1950; DSc (hon.), Princeton U., 1958; LLD (hon.), Chinese U., Hong Kong, 1969; DSc (hon.), CCNY, 1978. Rsch. assoc. in astronomy U. Chgo., 1950; rsch. assoc. Yerkes Astron. Obs., Lake Geneva, Wis., 1950; rsch. assoc., lectr. physics U. Calif., Berkeley, 1950—51; mem. Inst. Advanced Study, Princeton U., NJ, 1951—53, prof. physics, 1960—63; asst. prof. Columbia U., NYC, 1953—55, assoc. prof., 1955—56, prof., 1956—60, adj. prof., 1960—62, Enrico Fermi prof. physics, 1963—, univ. prof., 1984—. Loeb lectr.

Harvard U., Cambridge, Mass., 1957, Cambridge, 64. Editor: Weak Interactions and High Energy Nutrino Physics, 1966, Particle Physics and Introduction to Field Theory, 1981; contbr. articles to profl. jours. Decorated grande ufficiale Order of Merit (Italy); recipient Albert Einstein Sci. award Yeshiva U., 1957, (with Chen Ning Yang) Nobel prize in physics, 1957, Ettore Majorana-Erice-Sci. for Peace prize, 1990. Mem. NAS, Acad. Sinica, Am. Acad. Arts and Scis., Am. Philos. Soc., Acad. Nazionale dei Lincei, Acad. Sci. China. Achievements include investigation of the so-called parity laws that have led to important discoveries regarding the elementary particles. Office: Columbia U Dept Physics 829 Pupin Hall 120th St New York NY 10027

LEE, V. PAUL, entertainment software company executive; B in Commerce, U. BC. Prin. Distinctive Software, Inc.; with Elec. Arts, Redwood City, Calif., 1991—, gen. mgr. Canada, COO, CFO sports, v.p. fin. and adminstrn., sr. v.p., COO Redwood City, Calif., 1998—2002, exec. v.p., COO, 2002—05, pres. worldwide studios, 2005—. Office: Elec Arts 209 Redwood Shores Pky Redwood City CA 94065 Office Phone: 650-628-1500.

LEE, VANILLA R., school system administrator, educational consultant; d. Garland Lee and Vivian Lenore Brown. BS, Kans. State U., Manhattan, 1971, MS, 1977; Ednl. Specialist, U. Mo., Kansas City, 1995; EdD, George Washington U., Washington, 2002. Curriculum coord., sch. liaison Kansas City Sch. Dist., Mo., 1990—96, program adminstr., 1996—97, dir. higher edn. partnerships, 2004—06; grad. asst., rsch. asst. Grad. Sch. Edn., George Washington U., 1997—2000; vice prin. Grandview Sch. Dist., Mo., 2000—03; assoc. project dir. Nat. Coun. Accreditation Tchr. Edn., Washington, 2003—04. Mem. adv. bd. Avila U., Kansas City, 2005—06, William Jewell Coll. Sch. Edn., Liberty, Mo., 2006; mem. profl. devel. consortium Pk. U., Parkville, Mo., 2005—06; presenter in field. Asst. supt. Sunday sch. 2d Bapt. Ch., Kansas City, 1977—79; editor newsletter Grace Bapt. Ch., Kansas City, 1993—99, 2000—, personnel com., 2006—. Recipient Excellence in Edn. award, Westport-Hyde Pk. Optimist Club, Kansas City, 1992, Time Well Spent award, United Minority Media Assn., 2006. Mem.: AAUW, ASCD, Phi Delta Kappa. Baptist. Avocations: reading, writing, walking, sewing.

LEE, VERNON ROY, minister; b. Jackson, Miss., Feb. 1, 1952; s. Samuel Rayford and Evie Mae (Abel) L.; m. Rhonda Sue Parker, Nov. 6, 1970; 1 child, Shannon Grant. Pastor Mt. Moriah Bapt. Ch., Junction City, Ark., 1971-72, Pleasant Grove Bapt. Ch., El Dorado, Ark., 1972-74, Pilgrims Rest Bapt. Ch., Spearsville, La., 1974-76, Bethany Bapt. Ch., Bastrop, La., 1976-78, 1st Bapt. Ch., Taylor, Ark., 1978-83, Farmington Bapt. Ch., Corinth, Miss., 1983-86, Wyatt Bapt. Ch., El Dorado, 1986—. Trustee Southeastern Bapt. Coll., Laurel, Miss., 1983-86, Ctrl. Bapt. Coll., Conway, Ark., 1992-96, 99—, asst. chmn. bd. trustees, 1993-95, 2001—03, chmn., 1995-96, 2004-; vol. Boy's Clubs, El Dorado, 1986-91, YMCA, Corinth, 1983-86. Mem. Bapt. Missionary Assn. Am. (v.p. 1986-88, 2000-02, pres. 1990-92, clk. missionary com. 1989-91, asst. ch. adv. com. 1992-95, v.p. pastors and laymen's conf. 1996-98, pres. pastors and laymen's conf. 1998-2000, chmn. adv. com. 2000—, asst. chmn. missionary com. 2002—), Miss. Bapt. Assn. (pres. 1984-86), Bapt. Missionary Assn. Ark. (v.p. 2000-02, pres. 2002—, asst. chmn. missionary com. 2002—). Avocations: golf, fishing, basketball, softball. Home: 625 Royal Oak El Dorado AR 71730 Office: Wyatt Bapt Ch 4621 W Hillsboro El Dorado AR 71730-6768

LEE, VIRGINIA M. -Y., medical educator, health science association administrator; PhD, U. Calif., San Francisco, 1973; MBA, U. Pa., 1984. Prof. dept. pathology and lab. medicine U. Pa. Sch. Medicine, co-dir. neurodegenerative disease rsch., 1992—2002, dir. neurodegenerative disease rsch., 2002—. Mem. grant rev. com. NIH Study Sect., others; mem. med./sci. adv. com. Alzheimer's Assn., S.E. Pa.; mem. coun. Nat. Inst. on Aging. Contbr. papers to profl. jours. Recipient John H. Ware 3d Chair for Alzheimer's Disease Rsch., Stanley N. Cohen Biomed. Rsch. award, 2000. Mem.: Inst. Medicine, Soc. for Neurosci. (elected councilor). Achievements include research in Alzheimer's disease; neuronal cytoskeleton. Office: Ctr for Neurodegenerative Disease Rsch 3d Fl Maloney Bldg 4283 3600 Spruce St Philadelphia PA 19104-4283

LEE, VIVIAN S., radiologist; MD with hon., Harvard Med. Sch.; PhD, Oxford Univ. Gen. surgery resident Duke Univ., Chapel Hill, NC, 1992—93, chief resident diagnostic radiology, 1993—97; fell. in Body and Cardiovascular Magnetic Resonance Imaging NYU, 1997, mem. med. faculty, 1998—, named vice chmn. research, dept. Radiology, 2002, prof., depts. Radiology, Physiology, Neuro Science. Vis. prof., lectr. several nat. univ. Contbr. articles to numerous profl. med. jours.; mem. edl. bd.: Jour. Computer Assisted Tomography. Named one of 40 Under 40, Crain's NY Bus. Jour., 2006; recipient Orloff award, NYU, 2001. Mem.: Internat. Soc. Magnetic Resonance in Medicine (elected to bd. 2002, v.p. 2005, chmn. 2005). Office: Tisch Hospital Rusk 225 530 First Ave New York NY 10016

LEE, WENDY WAN-KI, music educator; arrived in US, 1999; d. Vincent Hon-Sang Lee and Beatrice Shuk-Yee Foo. Assoc. Royal Conservatory Music in Piano, Royal Conservatory Music, Toronto, 1994; licentiate in Piano, Trinity Coll. Music, London, 1998, licentiate in Piano, 1999; MusB in Composition with honors, U. Toronto, Ont., Can., 1999; MusM in Composition, U. Mich., Ann Arbor, 2001, PhD in Music Composition and Theory, 2006. Instr. Mobile Music, Inc., Toronto, 1996—99, Merriam Sch. Music, Toronto, 1996—97, Classical Music Conservatory, Toronto, 1997—98; grad. student instru., theory tutor U. Mich., Ann Arbor, 2000—04; vis. instr. Oberlin Coll. Conservatory Music, 2004—05; asst. prof. SUNY, Binghamton, 2006—. Mem. adminstrv. com. Oberlin Coll. Conservatory Music, 2005; lectr. in field. Composer: A Stormy Night, 1998, Sonic Chains, 2003, 'Tis a Little Journey, 2003, (albums) Wheels of Life: In Reminiscence, 2006; guest composer: U. Ark., 2007, arranger: to Benjamin Pierce, to Yi-Pei Lee, to Yee-Hong Chow, to Paula Seo. Pianist DareArts Found., 1996; piano accompanist Dexter Mid. and HS, Mich., Ann Arbor Sch. Performing Arts; piano accompanist sems. and opera rehearsals U. Mich., 2001—04; guest organist St. James United Ch., St. Luke's Episcopal Ch., Federated Ch. Grass Lake, Mich. Recipient Glenn Gould Composition award, 1997; scholar Ont. Grad. scholar, 1999; Music Alumni scholar, U. Toronto, 1996, Robert and Jean McBroom scholar, 1998, Donald Matheson Springer fellow, 2000—02, Alumnae Coun. Women scholar, U. Mich., 2000—04, Grad. fellow, 2000—03, Rackham Travel grantee, 2003—05, Rackham Discretionary grantee, 2005, Rackham Predoctoral fellow, 2005—06, Travel grantee, 2006, Michael Iovenko Meml. scholar, Florence Gould Found., 2003, others. Mem.: ASCAP, Soc. Music Theory, Soc. Composers, Royal Conservatory Music Affiliate Tchrs. Orgn., Music Theory Midwest, Mich. Tchrs. Nat. Assn., Internat. Alliance Women in Music, Coll. Music Soc., Am. Music Ctr., Pi Kappa Lambda, Golden Key. Office: SUNY Binghamton Music Dept Vestal Pky E Binghamton NY 13902-6000

LEE, WILLIAM CHARLES, judge; b. Ft. Wayne, Ind., Feb. 2, 1938; s. Russell and Catherine (Zwick) L.; m. Judith Anne Bash, Sept. 19, 1959; children: Catherine L., Mark R., Richard R. AB, Yale U., 1959; JD, U. Chgo., 1962; LLD (hon.), Huntington Coll., 1999. Bar: Ind. 1962. Ptnr. Parry, Krueckeberg & Lee, Ft. Wayne, Ind., 1964—70, chief dep., 1966-69; U.S. atty. No. Dist. Ind., Ft. Wayne, 1970-73; ptnr. Hunt, Suedhoff, Borror, Eilbacher & Lee, Ft. Wayne, 1973-81; U.S. dist. judge U.S. Dist. Ct. (no. dist.) Ind., Ft. Wayne, 1981—; dep. pros. atty. Allen County Ind., 2006. Instr. Nat. Inst. Trial Advocacy; lectr. in field. Co-author: Business and Commercial Litigation in Federal Courts, 1998; author: Volume I Federal Jury Practice and Instructions, 1999; contbr. to numerous publs. in field. Co-chmn. Fort Wayne Fine Arts Operating Fund Drive, 1978; past bd. dirs., v.p., pres. Fort Wayne Philharm. Orch.; past bd. dirs., v.p. Hospice of Fort Wayne, inc.; past bd. dirs. Fort Wayne Fine Arts Found., Fort Wayne Civic Theatre, Neighbors, Inc., Embassy Theatre Found.; past bd. dirs., pres. Legal Aid of Fort Wayne, Inc.; past mem. chm. coun., v.p. Trinity English Lutheran Ch. Coun.; past trustee, pres. Fort Wayne Cmty. Schs., 1978-81, pres., 1980-81; trustee Fort Wayne Mus. Art, 1984-90; past bd. dirs., pres. Fort Wayne-Allen County Hist. Soc. Griffin Scholar, 1955-59; chmn. Fort Wayne Cmty. Schs. Scholarship Com.; bd. dirs. Arts United of Greater Fort Wayne, Fort Wayne Ballet. Weymouth Kirkland scholar, 1959-62; named Ind. Trial Judge of Yr., 1988; recipient Nat. Conservative award Izack Walter League of Am., Jorgenson Leadership award Sagamore of the Wabash, Nieman citation excellence and professionalism. Fellow Am. Coll. Trial Lawyers, Ind. Bar Found.; mem. ABA, Allen County Bar Assn., Ind. State Bar Assn., Fed. Bar Assn., Seventh Cir. Bar Assn., Benjamin Harrison Am. Inn of Ct., North Side High Alumni Assn. (bd. dris., pres.), Fort Wayne Rotary Club (bd. dirs.), Phi Delta Phi (chmn. Indian Pro Bono Commn.). Republican. Lutheran. Office: US Dist Ct 2145 Fed Bldg 1300 S Harrison St Fort Wayne IN 46802-3495

LEE, WILLIAM F., lawyer; b. 1950; BA magna cum laude, Harvard U., 1972; MBA with distinction, Cornell U., 1976, JD magna cum laude, 1976. Bar: Mass. 1977, US Supreme Ct. Assoc. counsel to Lawrence E. Walsh Ind. Counsel in Iran-Contra Investigation, 1987—89; joined Hale & Dorr, LLP, Boston, 1976, mng. ptnr., 2000—04; co-mng. ptnr. Wilmer, Cutler, Pickering, Hale & Dorr, LLP, Boston, 2004—. Vis. prof. Harvard U. Law Sch.; appointed by chief judge Ct. Appeals Fed. Cir. to Ct. Adv. Com., 2000; Ct. Adv. Com. US Dist. Ct. Mass., Com. to Evaluate Adminstrn. Criminal Justice Act, Merit Selection Panel Magistrate Judges; Intellectual Property Adv. Com. US Dist. Ct. Del.; spl. Jud. Nominating Com. Mass. Supreme Jud. Ct. Named one of Top 10 Trial Lawyers in Am., Nat. Law Jour., 1996, 2005, 100 Most Influential Lawyers in Am., 2000, 2006, Top Boston lawyers, Boston Mag., 2002, Top 10 Super Lawyers in Mass., 2004. Fellow: Am. Coll. Trial Lawyers; mem.: Cornell Law Sch. (vis. com.), Harvard U. (bd. overseers 2002), Tenacre Country Day Sch. (chmn. bd. trustees). Order Coif. Office: Wilmer Cutler Pickering Hale & Dorr LLP 60 State St Boston MA 02109 Office Phone: 617-526-6556. Office Fax: 617-526-5000. Business E-Mail: william.lee@wilmerhale.com.*

LEE, WILLIAM FRANKLIN, III, composer, musician; b. Galveston, Tex., Feb. 20, 1929; s. William Franklin Jr. and Anna Lena (Keis) Lee; children: William Franklin IV, Robert Terry, Patricia Lynn, Peggy Ann. MusB, N. Tex. State U., 1949, MS, 1950; MusM, PhD, U. Tex., 1956. Prof. music St. Mary's U., San Antonio, 1952-55; asst. to dean fine arts U. Tex., 1955-56; chmn. dept. music Sam Houston State Coll., 1956-64; dean Sch. Music U. Miami (Fla.), 1964-82, provost, exec. v.p., 1982-86, disting. prof., composer in residence, 1986-88; dir. arts Fla. Internat. U., Miami, 1988-90; dean coll. fine arts and humanities U. Tex., San Antonio, 1990-94; exec. dir. Internat. Assn. Jazz Educators, 1994-98, ret., 1998. Performances with Houston, Dallas symphony orchs., performances with Gene Krupa and Artie Shaw, guest clinician, condr., composer, 1952—; composer, author, arranger more than 100 published works.; author: Music Theory Dictionary, 1962, American Big Bands, 2006, The Melody is Highly Overrated, 2006; also articles, music publs.; biographer, discographer of Stan Kenton, 1981, Maynard Ferguson, 1997, Bill Evans, 2000, America's Big Bands, 2002, Taylor Made (biography., discograpy of Billy Taylor), 2003; editor, co-founder: Southwestern Brass Jour., 1958, Belwin New Dictionary of Music and Musicians, 1988. Mem. AAUP, ASCAP (recipient ann. awards 1968— including Deems Taylor awards 1981, 85), Nat. Assn. Am. Composers and Condrs., Music Educators Nat. Conf., Am. Fedn. Musicians, Music Tchrs. Nat. Assn., Pi Kappa Lambda, Kappa Kappa Psi, Phi Mu Alpha.

LEE, WILLIAM JOHN, petroleum engineering educator, consultant; b. Lubbock, Tex., Jan. 16, 1936; s. William Preston and Bonnie Lee (Cook) L.; m. Phyllis Ann Bass, June 10, 1961; children: Anne Preston, Mary Denise. B in Chem. Engring., Ga. Inst. Tech., 1959, MSChemE, 1961, PhD in Chem. Engring., 1963. Registered profl. engr., Tex. Sr. rsch. specialist Exxon Prodn. Rsch. Co., Houston, 1962-68; assoc. prof. petroleum engring. Miss. State U., Starkville, 1968-71; tech. advisor Exxon Co., Houston, 1971-77; prof. petroleum engring. Tex. A&M U., College Station, 1977—, holder Noble chair in petroleum engring., 1985-93, Peterson chair in petroleum engring., 1993—. Dir. Crisman Inst. for Petroleum Reservoir Mgmt. at Tex. A&M U., 1987-93; exec. v.p. S.A. Holditch & Assocs., Inc., College Station, 1979-99. Author: Well Testing, 1982, Gas Reservoir Engineering, 1996, Pressure Transient Testing, 2003. Recipient award of excellence Halliburton Edn. Found., 1982, Meritorious Engring. Tchg. award Tenneco, Inc., 1982, 2000, Disting. Tchg. award Assn. Former Students Tex. A&M U., 1983, Continuing Edn. award, 2001; Tex. Engring. Experiment Sta. fellow, 1987-88, sr. fellow, 1990, Crawford Svc. award, 2005; named to Dream Team, Tex. Soc. Profl. Engrs., 2001. Mem. Soc. Petroleum Engrs. (hon., disting., chmn. edn. and accreditation com. 1985-86, disting. lectr. 1980, Disting. Faculty Achievement award 1982, Reservoir Engring. award 1986, Regional Svc. award 1987, Disting. Svc. award, 1992, Carll award 1995, dir. 1996-99, disting. lectr. 2005-06, Lucas medal 2003, DeGolyer Disting. Svc. medal 2004), Am. Inst. Mining Metal. and Petroleum Engrs. (hon.), Nat. Acad. Engring., Russian Acad. Natural Scis. Presbyterian. Avocation: travel. Home: 9310 Lake Forest Ct S College Station TX 77845-8758 Office: Tex A&M U Dept Petroleum Engring 3116 TAMU College Station TX 77843-3116 Office Phone: 979-845-2208. Business E-Mail: john.lee@pe.tamu.edu.

LEE, WILLIAM JOHNSON, lawyer; b. Jan. 13, 1924; s. William J. and Ara (Anderson) L. Student, Akron U., 1941—43, Denison U., 1943—44, Harvard U., 1944—45; JD, Ohio State U., 1948. Bar: Ohio 1948, Fla. 1962, US Dist. Ct. (no. dist.) Ohio 1960, US Dist. Ct. (so. dist.) Fla. 1965, US Dist. Ct. (so. dist.) Ohio 1970. Rsch. asst. Ohio State U. Law Sch., Columbus, 1948—49; asst. dir. Ohio Dept. Liquor Control, chief purchases, 1956—57, atty. examiner, 1951—53, asst. state permit chief, 1953—55, state permit chief, 1955—56; asst. counsel, staff Hupp Corp., 1957—58; spl. counsel City Attys. Office, Ft. Lauderdale, Fla., 1963—65; pvt. practice Ft. Lauderdale, 1965—66; asst. atty. gen. Office Atty. Gen. State of Ohio, 1966—70; administr. State Med. Bd. Ohio, Columbus, 1970—85. Mem. Federated State Bd.'s Nat. Commn. for Evaluation of Fgn. Med. Schs., 1981-83; mem. Flex 1/Flex 2 Transitional Task Force, 1983-84; acting mcpl. judge, Ravenna, Ohio, 1960; instr. Coll. Bus. Adminstrn., Kent State U., 1961-62. chmn. legal aid com. Portage County, Ohio, 1960. Mem. editl. bd. Ohio State Law Jour., 1947—48; contbr. articles to profl. jours. Mem. pastoral rels. com. Epworth United Meth. Ch., 1976; chmn. troop awards Boy Scouts Am., 1965; mem. ch. bd. Melrose Park Meth. Ch., Fla., 1966. Served with USAAF, 1943-46. Mem. ATLA, Fla. Bar Assn., Ohio State Bar Assn., Broward County Bar Assn., Franklin County Trial Lawyers Assn., Columbus Bar Assn., Akron Bar Assn., Exptl. Aviation Assn. S.W. Fla., Am. Legion, Delta Theta Phi, Phi Kappa Tau, Pi Kappa Delta. Home: Apple Valley 704 Country Club Dr Howard OH 43028-9530

LEE, WILLIAM MARSHALL, lawyer; b. NYC, Feb. 23, 1922; s. Marshall McLean and Hazel (Letts) L.; m. Lois Kathryn Plain, Oct. 10, 1942; children: Marsha Derynck, William Marshall Jr., Victoria C. Nelson. Student, U. Wis., 1939-40; BS, Aero. U., Chgo., 1942; postgrad., UCLA, 1946-48, Loyola U. Law Sch., LA, 1948-49; JD, Loyola U., Chgo., 1952. Bar: Ill. 1952, U.S. Supreme Ct., 1972. Thermodynamicist Northrop Aircraft Co., Hawthorne, Calif., 1947-49; patent agt. Hill, Sherman, Meroni, Gross & Simpson, Chgo., 1949-51, Borg-Warner Corp., Chgo., 1951-53; ptnr. Hume, Clement, Hume & Lee, Chgo., 1953-72; pvt. practice Chgo., 1973-74; ptnr. Lee and Smith (and predecessors), Chgo., 1974-89, Lee, Mann, Smith, McWilliams, Sweeney & Ohlson, Chgo., 1989—2002; ind. expert intellectual property Barrington, Ill., 1999—. Cons. Power Packaging, Inc., 1982-2002, spkr. in field. Contbr. articles to profl. jours. Pres. Glenview (Ill.) Citizens Sch. Com., 1953-57; v.p. Glenbrook High Sch. Bd., 1957-63. Lt. USNR, 1942-46, CBI. Recipient Pub. Svc. award Glenbrook High Sch. Bd., 1963 Mem. ABA (chmn. sect. intellectual property law 1986-87, sect. fin. officer 1976-77, sect. sec. 1977-80, sect. governing coun. 1980-84, 87-88), Ill. Bar Assn., Chgo. Bar Assn., 7th Fed. Cir. Bar Assn., Am. Intellectual Property Law Assn., Intellectual Property Law Assn. Chgo., Licensing Execs. Soc. (pres. 1981-82, treas. 1977-80, trustee 1974-77, 80-81, 82-83, internat. del. 1980—), VFW, Phi Delta Theta, Phi Alpha Delta. Republican. Office: 84 Otis Rd Barrington IL 60010-5128

LEE, WINNIE SITA, dentist; b. Loma Linda, Calif., Mar. 20, 1978; d. Stanley Tak and Rita Sook Lee. BA in Applied Scis., U. of Pacific, Calif., 2003; DDS, U. Pacific Sch. Dentistry, Calif., 2001. Dental Lic. Calif., 2001. Pre-clin. instr. U. Pacific Sch. Dentistry, San Francisco, 2002—04; dentist pvt. practice, Sunnyvale, 2003—. Presenter in field. Recipient Athena award, San Jose Alumni Panhellenic, Calif., 1996. Fellow: Internat. Congress Oral Implantologists, Am. Acad. Implant Dentistry (assoc.); mem.: Acad. Gen. Dentistry, Santa Clara Dental Soc., Alpha Lambda Delta. Avocations: running, exercise. Office Phone: 408-830-0888.

LEE, WON GYU, chemical engineer, educator; b. Samchuck, Kangwon, Republic of Korea, Aug. 20, 1962; s. Hee Kyung Lee and Soon Oak Jin; m. Young Rhan Yeom; children: Sun Chul, Doo Hyun. PhD, Korea Advanced Inst. Sci. and Tech., Daejeon, Korea, 1995. Prin. engr. Hynix Semiconductor Inc., Icheon, KyungKi, Republic of Korea, 1985—2002; assoc. prof. dept. chem. engring. Kangwon Nat. U., Chunchon, Republic of Korea, 2002—. Dir. Rsch. Ctr. Surface Cleaning Tech., Chunchon, Kangwon, Republic of Korea, 2004—; vis. prof. dept. chem. engring. U. Fla., 2006—07. Mem.: Korean Inst. Chem. Engrs. (assoc.). Avocations: skiing, running, golf. Office: Kangwon Nat U 192-1 Hyoja2-Dong Kangwon Chuncheon 200-701 Republic of Korea Office Phone: 82-33-250-6337. Office Fax: 82-33-251-3658. Business E-Mail: wglee@kangwon.ac.kr.

LEE, WON JAY, radiologist; b. Seoul, Korea, Feb. 2, 1938; arrived in U.S., 1965; s. Kang Sei and Choon Ja (Park) L.; m. Moon Jung, Feb. 24, 1968; children: Julie, Lisa, Jennifer. MD, Yonsei U., Seoul, 1962. Diplomate Am. Bd. Radiology, Am. Bd. Nuclear Medicine. Intern Wyckoff Heights Hosp., Bklyn., 1965-66; resident in radiology N.Y. U. Med. Ctr., NYC, 1966-69; fellow, asst. radiologist L.I. Jewish Med. Ctr., New Hyde Park, 1969-71, staff radiologist, 1975-82, chief uroradiology, 1983—2001, hon. staff, 2001—; assoc. radiologist Binghamton Gen. Hosp., 1971-75. Asst. prof. SUNY, Stony Brook, 1975-86, assoc. prof. radiology, 1987-89; prof. radiology Albert Einstein Coll. Medicine, 1989-2002, prof. emeritus radiology, 2002-; clin. prof. diagnostic radiology Yonsei U. Coll. Medicine, Seoul, 1996—; cons. in field. Asst. editor: Jour. Endourology, 1987-96; assoc. editor: Jour. Korean-Am. Med. Assn., 1995-98, editor-in-chief, 1999-2000; contbr. chpts. to books and articles to profl. jours. First lt. Republic of Korea Army M.C., 1962-65. Recipient Sci. Paper award Soc. Uroradiology, 1994, Clin. award Can. Assoc. Radiologists, 1979, Disting. Svc. award Yonsei U. Col. Med. Alumni Assn., 1998. Fellow Am. Coll. Radiology, Soc. Interventional Radiology (emeritus), Soc. Uroradiology (emeritus); mem. AMA, Am. Roentgen Ray Soc. (Merit award 1983), Radiol. Soc. N.Am., Korean-Am. Med. Assn. (chmn. sci. and edn. divsn. 1996), Korean Radiol. Soc. N.Am., Severance Alumni Assn. Am. (pres. 1997). Democrat. Presbyn. Avocations: gardening, travel. Office: Lee Radiol Cons 6306 Adirondack Ct Gainesville VA 20155 Office Phone: 703-743-1382. Personal E-mail: wjaylee@yahoo.com.

LEE, WON SUK, engineering educator; b. Seoul, Korea; m. In Ok Kim; children: Jae Young, Katie J. BS, Seoul Nat. U., Suwon, Korea, 1986, MS, 1988; PhD, U. Calif., Davis, 1998. Grad. rsch. asst. Seoul Nat. U., Suwon, Republic of Korea, 1986—88, U. Calif., Davis, 1993—98; postdoctoral rsch. assoc. Tex. A&M U., College Station, 1998—2000; asst. prof. U. Fla., Gainesville, 2000—06, assoc. prof., 2006—. Contbr. articles to profl. jours. Deacon Korean Bapt. Ch. of Gainesville, Gainesville, Fla., 2000—06. Mem.: Fla. State Hort. Soc., Soc. Photo-Optical Instrumentation Engrs., Am. Soc. Agrl. and Biol. Engrs. (vice chair, chair 2004—06). Achievements include patents pending for Soil phosphorus sensing system. Office: University of Florida Rogers Hall Museum Rd Gainesville FL 32611-0570 Office Phone: 352-392-1864. E-mail: wslee@ufl.edu.

LEE, XIAOYANG, scientist; b. Beijing, July 23, 1956; came to the U.S., 1985; s. Yi-Minn and Shu-Zhi (Zhang) L.; m. Amy Lee; children: James, Joan. BSEE, Beijing U. Post and Telecom., 1982; MSEE, Columbia U., 1987. Design engr. Berkeley Varitronics Sys., Metuchen, NJ, 1987-91; engr. Rsch. Inst. Telecom. Transmission, MPT, Beijing, 1982-85; sr. scientist Panasonic Techs., Inc., Princeton, NJ, 1991-2000; prin. sys. engr. Nokia-Siemens Networks, Boca Raton, Fla., 2000—. Mem.: IEEE (sr.). Achievements include patents for frequency measuring system, asynchronous data transmitting and receiving systems, combination brouter and cluster controller, audio/video distribution systems, asynchronous data transmitting and receiving systems, method and apparatus for increasing system efficiency of TDMA system by reducing time slos guard time. Home: 12 Essex Dr Monmouth Junction NJ 08852-2502 Office: Siemens 5000 T-Rex Ave Ste 300 Boca Raton FL 33431 Home Phone: 732-438-9476; Office Phone: 561-322-7007. E-mail: xiaoyang_lee@yahoo.com.

LEE, YEU-TSU MARGARET, surgeon, educator; b. Xian, Shensi, China, Mar. 18, 1936; m. Thomas V. Lee, Dec. 29, 1962 (div. 1987); 1 child, Maxwell M. AB in Microbiology, U. S.D., 1957; MD, Harvard U., 1961. Diplomate Am. Bd. Surgery. Assoc. prof. surgery Med. Sch., U. So. Calif., LA, 1973-83; commd. lt. col. U.S. Army Med. Corps, 1983, advanced through grades to col., 1989; chief surg. oncology Tripler Army Med. Ctr., Honolulu, 1983-98; ret. U.S. Army, 1999; assoc. clin. prof. surgery Med. Sch., U. Hawaii, Honolulu, 1984-92, clin. prof. surgery, 1992—. Author: Malignant Lymphoma, 1974; author chpts to books; contbr. articles to profl. jours. Pres. Orgn. Chinese-Am. Women, L.A., 1981, Hawaii chpt., 1988; active U.S.-China Friendship Assn., 1991—. Decorated Nat. Def. Svc. medal, Army Commendation medal, Army Meritorious Svc. medal, Army Humanitarian Svc. medal; recipient Chinese-Am. Engrs. and Scis. Assn., 1987; named Sci. Woman Warrior, Asian-Pacific Womens Network, 1983. Mem. ACS, Soc. Surg. Oncology, Assn. Women Surgeons. Avocations: classical music, movies, hiking, ballroom dancing. Address: PO Box 29726 Honolulu HI 96820 E-mail: ytm_lee@hotmail.com.

LEE, YOON MO, state official; arrived in US, 1970; m. Hwa Kim; 2 children. BS in Agricultural Sci., Seoul Nat. U.; MDiv in Christian Social Ethics, Seoul Methodist Theological Seminary; DPh, Asbury Theological Seminary; MA in Sociology, PhD in Sociology, Loyola U. Former reporter, mng. editor & chief editor Korea Times, Chicago; former CEO Korean Am. TV of Chicago; chief rsch., planning and develop., fed. grant project dir. & webmaster Ill. Dept. of Human Rights, 2000—. Lead rsch. adv. Asian Am. Inst. of Chicago. Author: Seventy Years' History of the First Korean United Methodist Church of Chicago, 1995. Office: Ill Dept of Human Rights James R Thompson Ctr 100 W Randolph St Ste 10-100 Chicago IL 60601

LEE, YOUNG WOO, neurosurgery educator; b. Ulsan City, Republic of Korea, Mar. 9, 1937; s. Jong Kap and Myung Ran (Choi) L.; m. Kyung Ja Kim, Nov. 3, 1969; children: Sang Min, Soon Jeong. MD, Pusan Nat. U.,

1962, MSc, 1965, PhD, 1973. Lic. med. practice Ministry Social Welfare, Republic of Korea, 1962, cert. diplomate Korean Bd. Neurosurgery, 1967; lic. radioactive isotope use Korean Atomic Ministry, 1964, marriage counsellor 2004, drug preventive consulting dir. 2004. Intern Pusan Nat. U. Hosp., 1962-63, resident in surgery and neurosurgery, 1963—65, resident in neurosurgery, 1965—67; prof. neurosurgery Pusan Nat. U. Sch. Medicine, Pusan Nat. U. Hosp., 1971—2002, chmn. dept neurosurgery, 1975—2002; rsch. fellow dept. neurology U. Ala., Birmingham Sch. Medicine and Med. Ctr., 1974—75; fellow Dept. Neurosci. LI Coll. Hosp., Bklyn., 1980—81; fellow dept. neurosurgy McGill U., Montreal Neurol. Inst., Canada, 1998—99; prof. emeritus Pusan Nat. U. Hosp., 2002—; hon. supt. Dong-Rae Bong Seng Hosp., 2002—, chmn., 2002—. Co-author: The Great Medical Encyclopedia, 1991; contbr. chapters to books. Maj. Korean Army, 1967—70. Decorated Viet-Nam War medal Pres. Republic of Korea, Merit Viet-Nam Korean Comdr. Viet-Nam War, First Technique Decoration medal Viet-Nam Gov., Civil Decoration medal; recipient award, Pfizer's Med. Co., 1977, Ednl. award, Korean Tchr. Assn., 2001, Pusan Tchr. Assn., 2001, Acad. award, Pusan Med. Assn., 2002, Ockjo award, Korean Gov., 2002. Mem.: AAAS, Korean Vet. Soc., Mil. Medalist Assn., World Fedn. Neurosurgeons, Korean Soc. Med. and Biol. Engring., Korean Radioisotope Soc., Korean Soc. Neurobiology and Neurosci., NY Acad. Sci., Am. Assn. Electrodiagnositc Medicine, Korean Med. Assn., Korean Neurosurg. Soc. (v.p. 1988—89, pres. 1987—88). Home: Lucky Apt 19-1205 707 Oncheon 2-dong Tong-rae ku Busan 607-753 Republic of Korea Office: Busan Nat U Sch Medicine and Pusan Nat U Hosp Dept Neurosurgery 1-10 Ami-dong Busan 602-739 Republic of Korea Office Phone: 82-51-247-0244.

LEE, YUAN TSEH, chemistry professor; b. Hsinchu, Taiwan, China, Nov. 19, 1936; arrived in U.S., 1962, naturalized, 1974; s. Tsefan and Pei (Tasi) Lee; m. Bernice Wu, June 28, 1963; children: Ted, Sidney, Charlotte. BS, Nat. Taiwan U., 1959; MS, Nat. Tsinghua U., Taiwan, 1961; PhD, U. Calif., Berkeley, 1965; PhD (hon.), U. of Waterloo, 1986. From asst. prof. to prof. chemistry U. Chgo., 1968—74; prof. emeritus U. Calif., Berkeley, 1974—, former prin. investigator Lawrence Berkeley Lab., 1974—97, Miller Professorship, 1981—82; pres. Academia Sinica, Taiwan, 1994—. Hon. prof. Chinese Acad. Sci., 1980, Fudan U., Shanghai, 1980; Sherman Fairchild Disting. Scholar Calif. Inst. Tech., 1983; hon. prof. Chinese U. Sci. & Tech., Hofei, Anhuei, 1986. Contbr. articles to profl. jours. on chem. physics. Recipient Nobel Prize in chemistry, 1986, Ernest O. Lawrence award, Dept. Energy, 1981, Nat. Medal of Sci., 1986, 1990, Peter Debye award for phys. chemistry, 1986, Harrison Howe award, 1983, Sherman Fairchild Disting. Scholar, Calif. Inst. Tech., 1983; fellow, Alfred P. Sloan, 1969—71, John Simon Guggenheim Found., 1976—77, Amer. Acad. of Arts and Sciences, 1975; scholar Tchr. scholar, Camille and Henry Dreyfus Found., 1971—74. Fellow: Am. Phys. Soc.; mem.: Academia Sinica, 1980, Am. Chem. Soc., Am. Acad. Arts and Scis., AAAS, NAS. Office: Acad Sinica Pres Office 128 Academia Rd Sec 2 Nankang Taipei 11529 Taiwan

LEE, YU-JIN, retired military physician; b. Taipei, Taiwan, Feb. 13, 1934; arrived in US, 1966; s. Siong Ai and Sun Lu Chow Lee; m. Marie Louise Willing, Aug. 23, 1969; children: Heather N., Math-Yu E., Jin-Nefer M. MD, Nat. Taiwan U., Taipei, 1961. Lic. physician Del., 1974, Md., 1999. WHO fellow States Serum Inst., Copenhagen, 1961—62; asst. prof. dept. microbiology Nat. Taiwan U., Taipei, 1962—66; rotating intern Toledo Hosp., 1966—67; resident Maryview Hosp., Portsmouth, Va., 1967—68, Wilmington Med. Ctr., Del., 1968—70; pub. health physician II Del. State Bd. Health, Newark, 1970—74; dir. med. svcs. US Naval Hosp., Japan, 1980—82, 1985—89, USN Med. Clinic, Quantico, Va., 1983—85, Naval Hosp., Great Lakes, Ill., 1985—86. Capt. USN, 1974—98. Mem.: AMA. Avocations: swimming, gardening. Home: 902 Song Sparrow Ct Arnold MD 21012

LEE, YUNG-KEUN, physicist, researcher; b. Seoul, Sept. 26, 1929; came to U.S., 1953, naturalized, 1968; s. Kwang-Soo and Young-Sook (Hur) L.; m. Ock-Kyung Pai, Oct. 25, 1958; children: Ann, Arnold, Sara, Sylvia, Clara. BA, Johns Hopkins, 1956; MS, U. Chgo., 1957; PhD, Columbia, 1961. Research scientist Columbia U., NYC, 1961-64; prof. physics Johns Hopkins U., Balt., 1964—2004, prof. emeritus physics, 2004—. Vis. mem. staff Los Alamos Sci. Lab., 1971; vis. rschr. Inst. Nuc. Scis., Grenoble, France, 1975; cons. Idaho Nat. Engring. Lab., 1988-91; mem. Brahms collaboration Brookhaven Nat. Lab., 1996-2005. Contbr. articles to profl. jours. Mem.: Johns Hopkins Club. Democrat. Methodist. Home: 1318 Denby Rd Baltimore MD 21286-1627 Office: Johns Hopkins U 34th and Charles Sts Baltimore MD 21218 Office Phone: 410-516-7355. Business E-Mail: yklee@jhu.edu.

LEE, YUN-SHIK, physics professor; PhD, U. Tex., Austin, 1992—97. Rsch. fellow U. Mich., Ann Arbor, 1998—2001; asst. prof. Oreg. State U., Corvallis, 2001—06, assoc. prof., 2006—. Contbr. articles to profl. jours. Recipient CAREER award, NSF, 2005. Mem.: Optical Soc. Am. Achievements include research in terahertz pulse shaping. Office: Oregon State Univ Physics Dept 301 Weniger Hall Corvallis OR 97331 Office Phone: 541-737-5057. Office Fax: 541-737-1683. Business E-Mail: leeys@physics.oregonstate.edu.

LEEBENS, PATRICIA KAY, psychiatrist; b. Austin, Minn., Aug. 21, 1951; d. William Moore and Jean Elizabeth (Stubbee) Leebens. BA in English and Psychology, Grinnell Coll., 1973; MAT in English Edn., Brown U., 1974; MA in Psychology, U. No. Colo., 1978; MD, U. Colo., 1986; postgrad., Yale U., 1986—94. Diplomate Am. Bd. Psychiatry and Neurology. English tchr., guidance counselor Charles M. Russell Jr. HS, Colorado Springs, 1974—77, 1978—79, 1981—82; resident psychiatry Yale U. Sch. Medicine, New Haven, 1986—90, fellow child psychiatry, 1990—94; unit chief dept. children and families Riverview Hosp., Middletown, Conn., 1994—2000; dir. psychiatry Dept. Children and Families, State Conn., Hartford, 2001—05; cons. child and adolescent psychiatrist Family and Children's Aid, Danbury, Conn., 2005—. Warden Trinity Episcopal Ch. on the Green, New Haven, 1997—2001; bd. dirs. Elm City Girls Choir, New Haven, 1995—99. Democrat. Avocations: reading, gardening, travel, movies. Office: Family and Children's Aid 75 West St Danbury CT 06108 Office Phone: 203-748-5689. Personal E-mail: patricia.leebens@verizon.net.

LEEBENS-MACK, JAMES H., biologist; b. Milw., Wis., Jan. 15, 1963; s. James H. and Mary C. Mack; m. Michelle A. Leebens; children: Heather M., Ian J. PhD, U. Tex., Austin, 1995. Rsch. asst. prof. Pa. State U., University Park, 2002—06; asst. prof. U. Ga., Athens, 2006—. Office: Univ Ga Dept Plant Biology Athens GA 30602 Office Phone: 706-583-5573.

LEEBRON, DAVID WAYNE, academic administrator, law educator; b. Phila., Feb. 12, 1955; m. Y. Ping Sun; children: Daniel, Merissa. BA, Harvard U., 1976, JD, 1979. Bar: Hawaii 1980, Pa. 1981, NY 1982. Law clk. to Judge Shirley Hufstedler US Ct. Appeals Ninth Cir., LA, 1979—80; adj. prof. UCLA Sch. Law, Los Angeles, Calif., 1980; assoc. Cleary, Gottlieb, Steen & Hamilton, NYC, 1981—83; prof., dir. Internat. Legal Studies Program NYU Sch. Law, NYC, 1983—89; prof. Columbia U. Sch. Law, NYC, 1989—2004, dean, Lucy G Moses Prof. of Law, 1996—2004; pres. Rice U., Houston, 2004—, prof. polit. sci., 2004—. Vis. fellow Max Planck Inst. Fgn. and Internat. Pvt. Law, Hamburg, Germany, 1988; Jean Monnet vis. prof. law, Bielefeld, Germany, 1992—93; mem. editl. bd. Found. Press; bd. dirs. IMAX Corp. Co-editor: Human Rights, 1999. Pres. Columbia Cmty. Services. Mem.: Coun. Fgn. Rels., Assn. of the Bar of the City of NY, Am. Soc. of Internat. Law, Am. Law Inst., Am. Law Deans Assn., ABA, Am. Assn. of Law Schools. Office: Rice U Office of Pres 6100 Main St Houston TX 77005 E-mail: president@rice.edu.*

LEECH, CHARLES RUSSELL, JR., lawyer; b. Coshocton, Ohio, July 29, 1930; s. Charles Russell and Edna (Henry) L.; m. Patricia Ann Tubaugh, June 20, 1953; children— Charles Russell III, Timothy David (dec.), Beverly Ann. AB cum laude, Kenyon Coll., 1952; JD, Ohio State U., 1955; MA, U. Toledo, 1969. Bar: Ohio 1955. Assoc. Fuller & Henry Ltd. and predecessors, Toledo, 1957-64, ptnr., 1964-97, counsel, 1997-99. Mng. editor: Ohio State Law Jour, 1955. Mem. exec. com. alumni council Kenyon Coll., 1967-72, trustee coll., 1974-80. Served with USNR, 1955-57. Fellow Ohio State Bar Found.; mem. ABA, Ohio Bar Assn., Kenyon Coll. Alumni Assn. Maumee Valley (past pres.), Beta Theta Pi, Phi Delta Phi. Republican. Home: 20285 Zion Rd Gambier OH 43022-9643

LEECH, FREDERICK C., lawyer; b. Pitts., Aug. 21, 1954; BA with high honors, U. Mich., 1976; JD, Northeastern U., Boston, 1980. Bar: Pa. 1980. Joined Reed Smith LLP, Pitts., 1980, now ptnr., practice group leader investment mgmt. group, 2002—. Hearing officer Pa. Disciplinary Bd. Mem.: Allegheny County Bar Assn., Pa. Bar Assn. Office: Reed Smith LLP 435 Sixth Ave Pittsburgh PA 15219 Office Phone: 412-288-4178. Office Fax: 412-288-3063. Business E-Mail: fleech@reedsmith.com.

LEECH, JAMES WILLIAM, investment company executive; b. St. Boniface, Man., Can., June 12, 1947; s. George Clarence and Mary Elizabeth (Gibson) L.; m. Deborah Barrett; children: Jennifer Hilton Cumming, Joanna Marjorie Thiessen, James Andrew Douglas. BS in Math. and Physics with hons., Royal Mil. Coll. Can., 1968; MBA, Queen's U., Can., 1973; grad., Inst. Corp. Dirs., 2004. Exec. asst. to pres. Commerce Capital Corp., Ltd., Montreal, Que., Canada, 1973-74, v.p., 1974-75; exec. v.p. Commerce Capital Trust Co., Calgary, Alta., Canada, 1976-78; sr. v.p. Eaton/Bay Fin. Services Ltd., Toronto, Ont., Canada, 1979; pres., bd. dirs. Unicorp Canada Corp., Toronto, 1979-88; pres., CEO, bd. dirs. Union Energy, Inc., Toronto, 1985-93, Disys Corp., Toronto, 1993-96; vice-chmn., bd. dirs. Kasten Chase Applied Rsch. Ltd., Mississauga, Ont., Canada, 1996-99; pres., CEO, bd. dirs. InfoCast Corp., Toronto, 1999-2001; sr. v.p. Tchrs. Pvt. Capital, Ont. Tchrs. Pension Plan, Toronto, 2001—. Bd. dirs. CTV Globe Media, Maple Leaf Sports & Entertainment, WorldSpan Techs., Cadillac Fairview Corp. Vice-chmn. adv. coun. sch. bus. Queens U., 1979-83, chmn. 1998-2001, mem. gen. coun., 1978-97, mem. investment com. bd. trustees, 1980-97, trustee, 1984-96, mem. fund coun., 1988-97; bd. dirs., chmn., pres., mem. exec. com. Can. Stage Co., 1989-94; v.p., bd. dirs. Toronto Arts Coun., 1994-2000; trustee Toronto Gen. and Western Hosp. Found., 1996—; bd. govs. Stratford Festival of Can., 2002—; bd. dirs. Right to Play, 2002—. Capt. Can. Armed Forces, 1968—71. D.I. McLeod scholar, 1971-73; Seagram rsch. fellow, 1983, Samuel Bronfman Found. fellow, 1973, Transp. Devel. Agy. fellow, 1972, Gold Medalist, Canadian Securities Course, 1974. Mem. World Pres. Orgn., The Nat. Club, Muskoka Lakes Golf and Country Club, Canadian Club Toronto (bd. dirs. 2004—06). United Ch. Can. Home: 51 Mathersfield Dr Toronto ON Canada M4W 3W4 E-mail: jim_leech@otpp.com.

LEECH, KATHARINE (KITTY LEECH), costume designer, educator; b. Phila., Jan. 10, 1957; d. Noyes and Louise Leech; m. Scot Campbell Galliher, Sept. 20, 1986. BA, U. Pa., Phila., 1979; MFA, NYU, NYC, 1983. Resident costume designer, costume coord. NYU Tisch Sch. Arts, NYC, 1984—2002; resident costume designer Opera Festival NJ, Princeton, 1985—88, Emelin Libr. Theatre, Mamaroneck, NY; tchr. Parson's Sch. Design, NYC, 1995—98, Playwright's Horizon's Theatre sch., 1999—2004; assoc. tchr. NYU Tisch Sch. Arts, 2002—. Chair costume design exam com. IATSE United Scenic Artists Local 829, NYC, 1988—; mem. Theatre Devel. Fund Costume Collection Adv. Com., 1995—; guest artist Am. Internat. Sch., Salzburg, Austria, 2002; guest lectr. Pratt Inst. Design, NYC, 2003—04. Costume designer (plays) Gross Indecency, The Three Trials Of Oscar Wilde, Waitng for My Man, The Novelist, A Romantic Portrait Of Jane Austen, The Gas Heart, (musical) Goblin Market, The Beautiful Lady written and directed by Elizabeth Swados, exhibitor (exhibition) The Leech- Gallagher Family Three Generations/ Five Artists, The Family Bus. Susan Teller Gallery, 2005, San Francisco Print Fair (Achenbach Found. Curator's Choice, 2002), World Stage Design; contbr. on line exhibition; costume designer (concert series) Lyrics and Lyricists, designer (window display) Greenberg and Hammer. Recipient award, U. Pa. Alumnae Club, 1979. Mem.: Soc. Children's Books Writers and Illustrators, NY Women Film and TV, Children's Book Illustrating Group. Avocations: children's book writing and illustration, photography. Office: New York University 721 Broadway New York NY 10003

LEECH, NOYES ELWOOD, lawyer, educator; b. Ambler, Pa., Aug. 1, 1921; m. Louise Ann Gallagher, Apr. 19, 1954; children: Katharine, Gwyneth. AB, U. Pa., 1943, JD, 1948. Bar: Pa. 1949. Assoc. Dechert, Price & Rhoads (and predecessors), Phila., 1948-49, 51-53; mem. faculty law sch. U. Pa., Phila., 1949-57, prof., 1957-78, Ferdinand Wakeman Hubbell prof. law, 1978-85, William A. Schnader prof. law, 1985-86, prof. emeritus, 1986—. Co-author: The International Legal System, 3d edit., 1988; gen. editor: Jour. Comparative Bus. and Capital Market Law, 1978-86. Mem. Order of Coif, Phi Beta Kappa. Home: 6300 Greene St 505 Philadelphia PA 19144-2510

LEEDER, ELLEN LISMORE, literature and language professor, literary critic; b. Vedado, Havana, Cuba, July 8, 1931; came to U.S., 1959; d. Thomas and Josefina (Jorge) Lismore; m. Robert Henry Leeder, Dec. 20, 1957 (dec. 1994); 1 child, Thomas Henry. D of Pedagogy, U. Havana, Cuba, 1955; MA, U. Miami, 1966, PhD, 1973. Lang. tchr. St. George's Sch., Havana, 1952—59; from part-time instr. to full prof. Spanish Barry U., Miami Shores, Fla., 1960—75, prof. Spanish, 1975—2006, chmn. dept. fgn. lang., 1975—76, coord. fgn. lang., 1976—89, dir. Spanish immersion program, 1986—88, prof. emerita, 2006—. Part-time prof. Miami-Dade C.C., 1974-75; vis. prof. U. Madrid, 1982; prof. Forspro Program Studies Abroad, 1989, 90; cons. HEH, 1981-83; judge Asociación Críticos y Comentaristas del Arte, Miami, 1985—; judge Silver Knight Awards, 1979-83; oral examiner juror Dade County Pub. Schs., Miami, 1986-87. Author: El Desarraigo en Las Novelas de Angel María de Lera, 1978, Justo Sierra y el Mar, 1979, Dimensión Existencial en la Narrativa de Lera, 1992; co-editor: El arte narrativo de Hilda Perera, 1996. Bd. dirs. Vis. Nurse Assn., 1978-80. Mem. MLA, South Atlantic MLA, Am. Coun. Tchg. Fgn. Langs., Am. Assn. Tchrs. Spanish and Portuguese (pres. 1978-84, v.p. 1984-87, pres. Southeastern Fla. chpt.), Fla. Fgn. Assn., Círculo de Cultura Panamericano, Assn. Internat. Hispanistas, Assn. Cubana de Mujeres Universitarias (pres.), Cuban Women Club, Phi Alpha Theta, Kappa Delta Pi, Sigma Delta Xi, Alpha Mu Gamma, Coral Gables Country Club. Avocations: tennis, piano, singing, coin collecting/numismatics. Home: 830 SW 101st Ave Miami FL 33174-2836 Personal E-mail: eleeder@mail.barry.edu.

LEEDOM, JOHN NESBETT, manufacturing executive, state legislator; b. Dallas, July 27, 1921; BSEE, Rice U., Houston, 1943. Engr. Naval Rsch. Lab., Washington, 1943-45; asst. sales mgr. Sprague Products Co., North Adams, Mass., 1945-50; founder, CEO Wholesales Electronic Supply Inc., Dallas, 1950—. Pres. Levco, Inc., 1973—; mem. Tex. Senate, 1980-96. Author: The Group and You, 1994, Whose Water, 2002, Words of God, 2004, What's What, 2005. Chmn. Dallas County Rep. Com., 1962-66, mem. state exec. com., 1966-68; mem. Dallas City Coun., 1975-80. Served to lt. (j.g.) USNR, 1943-45. Mem.: Nat. Assn. Wholesale Distbrs. (pres. 1972—73), Nat. Electronic Distbrs. Assn. (pres. 1971—72), Weather Modification Assn. (chmn. legis. com. 2001—), Mil. Order World Wars, Navy League, Tau Beta Pi. Office: Wholesales Electronic Supply Inc 1225 Roundtable Rd Dallas TX 75277 Office Phone: 214-969-9400 ext. 200.

LEEDS, BARRY HOWARD, literature and language professor; b. NYC, Dec. 6, 1940; s. Andrew Samuel and Paula (Stark) Leeds; m. Robin Leigh Flowers, Apr. 20, 1968 (div. Dec. 2000); children: Brett Ashley, Leslie Lion(dec.). BA, Columbia U., 1962, MA, 1963; PhD, Ohio U., 1967. Lectr. CUNY, 1963-64; instr. U. Tex., El Paso, 1964-65; asst. prof. Cen. Conn. State U., New Britain, 1968-71, assoc. prof., 1971-76, prof., 1976-91; disting. prof., 1991—. Cons. Am. lit. Choice mag., Middletown, Conn., 1968—; vis. faculty Yale U., 1984-85. Author: The Structured Vision of Norman Mailer, 1969, Ken Kesey, 1981, The Enduring Vision of Norman Mailer, 2002; editor: Conn. Rev., 1989-92, mem. editl. bd., 1986-95; contbg. editor D.C. Heath Anthology Am. Lit., 1986—; contbr. articles to profl. jours. incl. Saturday Rev., Modern Fiction Studies, Jour. Modern Lit. Alumni interviewer Columbia Coll., N.Y.C., 1982-95. Conn. State U. grantee, 1986-2003; recipient Disting. Svc. award Cen. Conn. State U., 1982. Mem.: Norman Mailer Soc. (v.p. 2002—), Conn. Acad. Arts and Scis. Avocations: scuba diving, weightlifting, ballroom dancing, competition target shooting. Home: 200 Blakeslee St Apt 121 Bristol CT 06010-8800 Office: Cen Conn State U Dept English 1615 Stanley St New Britain CT 06053-2439 Office Phone: 860-832-3208. Personal E-mail: bhleeds01@snet.net.

LEEDS, CHARLES ALAN, publishing executive; b. Mpls., Aug. 20, 1951; s. Charles Phillips and Irene (Pollard) L.; m. Karen Sue Biggs, Aug. 2, 1986; children: Charles Austin, Tyler Dixon. BA, Drake U., 1973, MPA, 1978. Mktg. coord. Register and Tribune Syndicate Inc., Des Moines, Iowa, 1973-79; sales mgr. Washington Post Writers Group, Washington, 1979-89; pres. and editorial dir. L.A. Times Washington Post News Svc., Washington, 1989—. Asst. professorial lectr. George Washington U., Washington, 1986, 88. Mem. nat. adv. bd. Sch. Journalism and Mass Comm. Drake U., 1996—2001, chmn. Bus. Basics, 1999—2003. Recipient Best in Bus. award Am. Journalism Rev., 1995. Mem. Internat. Press Inst. (assoc.), Soc. Profl. Journalists, Sigma Delta Chi (dir. 2007-), Kappa Tau Alpha. Presbyterian. Avocations: jogging, tennis, golf. Home: 4714 17th St N Arlington VA 22207-2031 Office: LA Times-Washington Post News Svc 1150 15th St NW Washington DC 20071-0001

LEEDS, DOUGLAS BRECKER, advertising executive, theater producer; b. NYC, Mar. 15, 1947; s. Richard Henry and Nancy Ann (Brecker) L.; m. Christine (Anki) Castler, Jan. 14, 1980; 1 child, Victoria Brecker. BS, Babson Coll., 1970. V.p., dir. Auto Data Systems, Inc., Natick, Mass., 1970-72; dir. leasing Beacon Cos., Inc., Boston, 1972-77; account exec. Thomson-Leeds Co., Inc. divsn. The WPP Group, NYC, 1977-84, exec. v.p., 1985-88, pres., 1988-97, chmn., CEO, 1989—2002; CEO StoreBoard Media LLC, 2006—, 2005—. Chmn. ednl. rels. com. Point of Purchase Advt. Inst., 1986—, bd. dirs., vice chmn., 1994—; pres. Tori Group, Inc., 2002—. Co-prodr.: (Broadway musical) Streetheat, 1985; assoc. prodr.: (Broadway play) Sleight of Hand, 1986; patentee in field. Chmn., founder Lobby Gallery Assocs. Whitney Mus. Am. Art, NYC, 1983-90; trustee Guild Hall of East Hampton (Mus. and Theatre), 1990-92, John Drew Theatre; chmn. men's com. Boys Club NY, 1989; bd. dirs. chmn. Friends Henry Street Settlement House, NYC, 1977-80; trustee Whitney Mus. Am. Art, 1992-99, co-chmn. membership com., 1993—, Worcester Acad., 1982-85, trustee emeritus; trustee Babson Coll., 1979-86, co-chmn. devel. and pub. affairs com.; dream team Meml. Sloan-Kettering Cancer Ctr.; bd. dirs. Checker Board Found., Am. Theatre Wing, 1991—, vice chmn., treas., sec. bd. dirs., pres., 2004—, adminstrn. com. Tony Awards; mem. coun. Frick Collection, 2000—. Mem. Union Club, Doubles Club, Royal Tennis Court Club (Middlesex, Eng.). Office Phone: 212-682-3300. Business E-Mail: doug@storeboards.net.

LEEDS, JENNIFER ALYSON, bacteriologist, researcher; d. Michael Alan Leeds and Dorian Kay Fine; m. Robert Alan Hess, Sept. 7, 1996; children: Tjaden Adam Hess, Maximilian Joseph Hess. BS, Cornell U., Ithaca, NY, 1991; PhD, U. Wis., Madison, 1996. Postdoctoral fellow Harvard Med. Sch., Boston, 1996—2001; sr. scientist Dyax Corp., Cambridge, Mass., 2001—03; rsch. investigator Novartis Inst. Biomed. Rsch., Cambridge, 2003—. Achievements include invention of novel antibacterial compounds.

LEEDS, NANCY BRECKER, sculptor, lyricist; b. NYC, Dec. 22, 1924; d. Louis Julius and Dorothy (Faggen) Brecker; m. Richard Henry Leeds, May 9, 1945; children: Douglas Brecker, Constance Leeds Bennett. BA, Pine Manor Coll., 1944. Pres. Roseland Ballroom, NYC, 1977-81. One-woman shows include Andrew Crispo Gallery, N.Y.C., 1979, Jeannette McIntyre Gallery Fine Arts, Palm Springs, Calif., 1987-88; exhibited in group shows at Bond St. Gallery, Great Neck, N.Y., Gallery Ranieri, N.Y.C., 1978, Country Art Gallery, 1984, Nature Conservatory Show, Country Art Gallery, 1985, Bonwit Teller, Manhasset, N.Y., 1985, Jeanette C. McIntyre Gallery, Palm Springs, Calif., 1987, The Empire Collection, N.Y.C., 1988, 89, Nassau County Mus. of Art, 1992, Chrysalis, East Hampton, 1998, Christmas Miniature Art Show at Chelsea, Nassau County Mus. of Art "Dance Dance", 2000; represented in permanent collections at New Orleans Mus. Art; writer lyrics for musical Great Scot, 1965, score for Scrooge Musical Theatre of Ariz., 1989; lyricist for popular music; lyricist for off-Broadway children's show, 2004. Trustee Floating Hosp., N.Y.C., 1975—, v.p.; mem. Upper Brookville (L.I., N.Y.) Planning Bd., 2000-01. Mem. ASCAP, Dramatist Guild, Songwriters Guild.

LEEDS, NORMAN E., medical educator, radiologist; b. Jersey City, June 9, 1928; m. Bette G. Leeds, June 12, 1953; children: Frederick G., Patrice G. BA, Yale Coll., 1948; MD, NY Med. Coll., 1953. Diplomate in radiology and in neuroradiology Am. Bd. Radiology. Asst. prof. radiology U So. Calif. Sch. Medicine, LA, 1961—63; asst. prof. U. Pa. Grad. Sch. and Grad. Hosp., Phila., 1962—64, U. Pa. Children's Hosp., 1964—69, Albert Einstein Hosp. Temple U., 1964—69; assoc. prof. Albert Einstein Coll. Medicine, Montefiore Hosp., Bronx, 1969—74, prof., 1974—85, Mt. Sinai Sch. of Medicine, NYC, 1985—90; chair dept. radiology Beth Israel Hosp., NYC; prof., Kennedy chair U. Tex. M.D. Anderson Cancer Ctr., Houston, 1991—2003; clin. prof. Mt. Sinai Sch. Medicine, Mt. Sinai Hosp., 2003—. With USPHS, 1955—57. Fellow: Am. Heart Assn., Am. Coll. Radiology; mem.: Am. Soc. Neuroradiology (pres. 1973, Gold medal 2003). Home: 50 Sutton Pl S Apt 5E New York NY 10022 E-mail: norman.leeds@msnyuhealth.org.

LEEDS, RICHARD, computer marketing executive; BS, NYU, 1982. Chmn., CEO Systemax Inc. (formerly Global DirectMail), Port Washington, NY, 1995—. Bd. mem. North Shore LIJ Hosp. Office: Systemax 11 Harbor Park Dr Port Washington NY 11050-4656*

LEEDS, ROBIN LEIGH, transportation executive; b. Athens, Ohio, Jan. 4, 1942; d. Clarence Thomas and Jean B. (Foster) Flowers; m. John A Cornwell, Oct. 28, 1957 (div. Jan. 1968); children: Michael John, Brian Arthur; m. Barry H. Leeds, Apr. 20, 1968 (div. Dec. 2000); children: Brett Ashley, Leslie Robin; m. Arthur A. Tanner, Apr. 29, 2006. BS in Edn., Ohio U., 1967. Cultural arts dir. Regional Sch. Dist. # 10, Burlington, Conn., 1978-81; exec. dir. Conn. Sch. Transp. Assn., Newington, Conn., 1982, ret. Exec. sec. N.E. Sch. Transp. Safety Inst., West Hartford, 1987-04; regulatory liaison Nat. Sch. Transp. Assn., Alexandria, Va., 2000-; columnist Sch. Transp. News, Redondo Beach, Calif., 2002—; bd. dir., Pupil Transportation Safety Inst., Syracuse, NY, 2003-, chmn. Conn. Sch. Transp. Safety Commn., 1990-94; state del. Nat. Standards Congress, Warrensburg,

1990, 95, 00, 05; mem. Gov.'s Motor Carrier Adv. Com., Conn., 1989-04, Dept. Motor Vehicles Safety Task Force, Conn., 1991-96; prin. Leeds Consulting, 2004-. Contbr. articles to profl. jours.; mem. adv. bd. Sch. Transp. News, 1994—. Chmn. gifted edn. task force, Regional Sch. Dist., 1976-78; arbitrator Dept. Consumer Protection, Conn., 2002—. Named Contractor of Yr., Sch. Bus Fleet Mag., 1990, Exec. of Yr., Conn. Soc. Assn. Execs., 1993. Mem. Nat. Sch. Transp. Assn., Nat. Assn. Pupil Transp., Nat. Safety Coun., Transp. Rsch. Bd. (Assn. Exec. of Yr. award). Avocation: ballroom dancing. Home: 36 Church St Groton CT 06340 Personal E-mail: robinleeds@comcast.net.

LEEDY, WALLACE CURTIS, former educator; b. Dinuba, Calif., Nov. 15, 1924; s. Walter Boston Leedy and Stella Eunace Fields; m. Barbara Mace, July 1, 1945 (dec. June 1999); 1 child, Dawn Caroline Leedy Guest. BA, Fresno State Coll., 1951; Tchr. Cert., 1952. Cert. tchr. secondary sch. Tchr. L.A. City Schs., 1952-56, N.Am. Aviation, 1956-85; ind. rschr., writer social behavioral sci. and biology. Mem. Social Sci. Honor Soc., Edn. Honor Soc., Arabian Horse Assn. of San Fernando Valley (past pres.). Avocation: Arabian horses. Home: 1400 Victoria Ave Apt 120 Oxnard CA 93035-2113

LEE JOEL, KATIE See JOEL, KATIE

LEEK, ANNE CARLIN, music educator; b. Augusta, Ga., June 13, 1954; d. Joseph Hugh and Frances Carlin Leek; 1 child, Miriam Elisabeth. MusB, Julliard, N.Y.C., 1975, MusM, 1977; MusD, Julliard, N.Y.C., 1989. Prin. oboist Orch. Rheinland-Pfalz, Germany, 1979—89; acting prin. oboist Pitts. Symphony, 1989—91; assoc. prof. oboe Ariz. State U., Phoenix, 1991—92; acting prin. oboist San Diego Symphony, 1992; assoc. prin. oboist Houston Symphony, 1992; assoc. prof. oboe Ind. U., Blommington, 1999—2001; prof. oboe U. Houston, 1998—. Artistic dir. Greenbriar Consortium, Houston, 1994—. Musician: (recording) Mozart Oboe Concerto, 1989, Baird Oboe Concerto, 1988. Recipient Top prize, Geneva Internat. Music Competition, 1984, Special Mozart award, 1984. Unitarian. Avocation: needlecrafts. Personal E-mail: draleek@hotmail.com.

LEEK, JAY WILBUR, management consultant; b. Albany, Ind., Apr. 24, 1928; s. Cecil and Hazel (Lindley) Leek; m. Laurayne M. DelaHunt, Sept. 22, 2001; children from previous marriage: Roderick Jay, Stacy LeAnn, Scott Lee, Timothy Lane, Debra Jan, Marilynn Sue, James Jay. BS Indsl. Engring., Pacific We. U., 1969, MS Indsl. Engring., 1976, D Bus. Adminstrn., 1980. Registered profl. engr., Calif. Mgr. Nutone, Inc., Cin., 1951—53, Bulova Watch Co., NYC, 1953—59, Martin Marietta Corp., Orlando, Fla., 1959—75; v.p. Northrop Corp., LA, 1975—80; pres., COO Philip Crosby Assocs., Winter Park, Fla., 1980—87, also bd. dirs.; mgmt. cons. Ft. Myers, 1987—91; pres., CEO Carchi-Resources, Inc., Ocala, Fla., 1991—. Bd. dirs. So. Bank, Longwood, Fla., Electro-World, Orlando Author: Workmanship Standards, 1974; co-author: (with others) AMA Management Handbook, 1986, Quality Management Handbook, 1986 Trustee Orlando Sports Inc., 1985-87, Fla. State U. Found., Tallahassee, 1986-96; bd. dirs. Fla. Citrus Sports Assn., Orlando, 1984-90. With USN, 1944-46 Recipient Academician award Internat. Acad. for Quality, Grobenzell, Germany, 1985; named to Wall of Fame, Am. Mgmt. Assn., 1979 Fellow: Am. Soc. Quality Control (pres. 1980—81); mem.: Sawgrass Country Club, Ponte Vedra Golf Country Club, Shriners, Masons. Republican. Avocations: golf, travel. Home: 951 Spinnakers Reach Dr Ponte Vedra Beach FL 32082 E-mail: bearj824@aol.com.

LEEKLEY, JOHN ROBERT, lawyer, consumer products company executive; b. Phila., Aug. 27, 1943; s. Thomas Briggs and Dorothy (O'Hora) L.; m. Karen Kristin Myers, Aug. 28, 1965 (dec. Mar. 1997); children: John Thomas, Michael Dennis; m. Gerry Lee Gildner, June 5, 1999. BA, Boston Coll., 1965; LLB, Columbia U., 1968. Bar: NY 1968, Mich. 1976. Assoc. Curtis, Mallet-Prevost, Colt & Mosle, NYC, 1968-69, Davis, Polk & Wardwell, NYC, 1969-76; asst. corp. counsel Masco Corp., Taylor, Mich., 1976-77, corp. counsel, 1977-79, v.p., corp. counsel, 1979-88, v.p., gen. counsel, 1988-96, sr. v.p., gen. counsel, 1996—. Bd. visitors Columbia U. Law Sch., NYC, 1994-96; mem. Freedom Twp. Bd. Tax Appeals, 1984-85. Mem. ABA (com. long range issues affecting bus. practice 1976-96), Mich. State Bar Assn. Democrat. Roman Catholic. Avocations: percheron horse breeding, hunting, fishing, outdoor activities. Office: Masco Corp 21001 Van Born Rd Taylor MI 48180-1300

LEEMAN, DANIEL J., otolaryngologist; MD. Cert. Am. Bd. Otolaryngology, Am. Acad. Facial Plastic & Reconstructive Surgery. Pvt. practice Comprehensive ENT Ctr. Tex., Austin, Tex., 2000—. Recipient Austin Under 40 award for Health Care, 2006. Office: Comprehensive ENT Ctr Tex Ste 205 1015 E 32nd St Austin TX 78705 Office Phone: 512-478-2273.

LEEMAN, EVE, psychiatrist; b. Boston, May 29, 1960; d. Cavin Philip and Susan (Epstein) Leeman; m. Alberto Jose Villar, June 23, 1990; children: Elena, Claudia, Alejandro. BA magna cum laude, Harvard U., 1982, MD, 1987. Diplomate Am. Bd. Psychiatry and Neurology. Intern Overlook Hosp., Summit, NJ, 1987—88; psychiat. chief resident Columbia U., NYC, 1991; pvt. practice psychiatry NYC, 1991—; instr. clin. psychiatry Columbia U., NYC, 1991—94, asst. clin. prof. psychiatry, 1994—; psychiatrist Washington Heights Cmty. Svc., NYC, 1991—2000. Rschr. NY State Psychiat. Inst. Rsch. Found., NYC, 2000—; psychotherapy supr. residency program NY State Psychiat. Inst., NYC, 1991—; presenter in field. Contbr. revs., articles to profl. publs. Recipient Horowitz award for clin. excellence, NY State Psychiat. Inst., 1991; Laughlin fellow, Am. Coll. Psychiatrists, 1990. Mem.: Am. Acad. Psychoanalysis and Psychodynamic Psychiatry, Am. Psychiat. Assn. Avocations: tennis, jogging, reading. Office: 161 Fort Washington Ave New York NY 10032 Office Phone: 212-781-2237. Business E-Mail: el7@columbia.edu.

LEEMAN, STACY N., artist, education educator; b. Columbus, Ohio, Mar. 27, 1972; d. Bary Alan and Roni Jean Leeman; m. Gary Mark Liebesman, July 1, 2001; 1 child, Yaakov. BA, Oberlin Coll., 1994; MFA, Rutgers U., 2001. Adj. faculty Columbus State Cmty. Coll., Ohio, 2001—, Ohio U., 2002—. Artist Sharon Weiss Gallery, Columbus, Ohio, 2002—. Bd. mem. Am. Friends of Nishmat, NYC, 2001—05. Recipient Merit award, Rosewood Gallery, 2003; grant, Vt. Studio Ctr., 2002. Mem.: Phila. Watercolor Soc., Coll. Art Assn. Democrat. Jewish. Avocations: swimming, gardening, walking, reading. Home: 215 S Roosevelt Ave Columbus OH 43209

LEEMANS, WIM PIETER, physicist; b. Gent, Belgium, June 7, 1963; BS in Elec. Engring., Free U. Brussels, 1985; MS in Elec. Engring., UCLA, 1987, PhD in Elec. Engring., 1991. Teaching asst. UCLA, 1986-87, rsch. asst., 1987-91; staff scientist Lawrence Berkeley Lab., Berkeley, Calif., 1991—. Group leader exptl. beam physics group, 1994—; chair ICFA panel on advanced and novel accelerators; presenter numerous seminars. Contbr. articles to profl. jours. Recipient Simon Ramo awd., Am. Physical Soc., 1992; grad. scholar IEEE Nuclear and Plasma Soc., 1987. Fellow Belgian Am. Ednl. Found., Francqui Found.; mem. IEEE (Nuclear and Plasma scis. soc. grad. scholar 1987), Soc. Photo-Optical Instrument Engrs., Am. Phys. Soc., Royal Flemish Engrs. Soc. Achievements include research in high intensity laser-plasma interaction, interaction of relativistic electrons with lasers and plasmas, novel radiation sources, advanced accelerator concepts, non-linear dynamics of free electron lasers. Office: Lawrence Berkeley Lab Divsn Accelerator Fusion Rsch 1 Cyclotron Rd Ms 71 259 Berkeley CA 94720-0001

LEEMPUTTE, PETER G., manufacturing executive; BS in chem. engring., Wash. U.; MBA, U. Chgo. Grad. Sch. of Bus. Product devel. engr. Proctor & Gamble Co.; fin. Armco Inc., FMC Corp., BP Amoco; v.p., ptnr. Mercer Mgmt. Cons., 0196—1998; Exec. v.p., CFO, admin. officer Chgo. Title Corp., 1998—2000; v.p., contr. Brunswick Corp., Lake Forest, Ill., 2000—03, sr. v.p., CFO, 2003—. Office: Brunswick 1 N Field Ct Lake Forest IL 60045-4811*

LEENEY, ROBERT JOSEPH, newspaper editor; b. New Haven, May 10, 1916; s. Patrick Joseph and Mary Alice (Ross) L.; m. Anne King Coyne, June 28, 1941; children: Robert Joseph, David Coyne, Anne Patricia. Student pub. and pvt. schs.; L.H.D. (hon.), U. New Haven, 1983, Albertus Magnus Coll., 1985. Reporter, book page editor, drama critic New Haven Register, 1940-47, editorial writer, 1947-55; editor editorial page New Haven Jour.-Courier, New Haven Register, 1956-61, exec. editor, 1961-72, editor, 1972-81, editor emeritus, 1981, v.p., dir., 1970—. V.p., sec. Register Pub. Co.; dir. Conn. Savs. Bank.; examiner adminstrv. reports, editor Ofcl. Digest State Reports, Conn., 1951-52 Author: New Haven in the 20th Century, 2000; columnist. Conn. pub. info. chmn. Am. Cancer Soc.; v.p. Arts Council Greater New Haven; mem. Conn. Edn. Council, Edn. Commn. of States, Conn. Commn. on Freedom of Info., 1981-86; bd. dirs. St. Raphael's Hosp. Found., Long Wharf Theatre, New Haven, 1990; trustee Albertus Magnus Coll., 1984, Conn. Found. Open Govt. Served with USAAF, World War II. Named to New Eng. Journalism Hall of Fame, 1977; recipient Seal of the City award for disting. cmty. svc., 1994; named Hon. Capt. 2d Co. Gov.'s Footguard 1775. Mem. SAR (hon. mem., Humphreys br. 2005), Nat. Conf. Editl. Writers, Am. Soc. Newspaper Editors, New Eng. Soc. Newspaper Editors (pres. 1961), New Eng. AP News Execs. Assn. (pres. 1977), Conn. Editl. Assn., Conn. Cir. AP (pres.), New Haven C. of C. (v.p., dir., Disting. Svc. award), Outer Circle, NH Colony Hist. Soc., Kiwanis, Woodbridge Club, Mory's Club, Quinnipiak Club, Sigma Delta Chi (pres. Conn. chpt. 1963-69). Home: R 69 424 Carrington Rd Bethany CT 06524-3160 Office: New Haven Register 40 Sargent Dr New Haven CT 06511-5939 E-mail: rjleeney@snet.net.

LEENMAN, WILLEM P., mental health services professional, director; b. Rheden, Netherlands, Jan. 9, 1950; arrived in US, 1967; s. Bas Leenman and Teuntje Remmers; children: Eva, Gabriel, Eleanor, Theo. M in Human Svcs. Adminstrn., Antioch New Eng. Grad. Sch., Keene, NH. Dir. Forty Seven Main St., Inc., Castleton, Vt., 1985—. Supr. Rutland County Solid Waste Dist., Vt., 1988—96; chair sch. bd. West Haven Elem. Sch., Vt., 1990—99; vice-chair, sec., mem. Eugen Rosenstock-Hvessy Fund, Norwich, Vt., 1994—; mem., vice chair, chair Town Dem. Party, West Haven, 1988—; chair bd. dirs. Therapeutic Cmty. Ctr., Inc., West Haven, Vt., 1980—; chair exec. bd. Am. Residential Treatment Orgn., Stockbridge, Mass., 2000—03; bd. dirs. Fair Haven Rescue Squad, Vt., 2004—; chair bd. dirs. FSM Supportive Living, Inc., Castleton. Mem.: Am. Residential Treatment Assn. (chair 2000—03). Home: 523 Main Rd West Haven VT 05743 Office: Forty Seven Main St Inc 706 Main St Castleton VT 05735-0038

LEEPER, KATHLEEN MARIE, elementary school educator; b. LA, Dec. 5, 1962; d. Carl L. and Mary E. (Parker)_L. BA, Calif. Poly. Inst., 1985, MEd, 1988. Cert. adminstrn. 2001. Tchr. New Lexington Sch., El Monte, Calif., 1985—2001; asst. prin. Frank M. Wright Elem. Sch., El Monte, Calif., 2001—06; co-prin. Columbia Sch., El Monte, 2006—. Mem. leadership team New Lexington Sch.; tchr. transition English, 1990-2001; grant writer El Monte City Sch. Dist., 1990-2001. Sunday sch. tchr. El Monte 1st Presbyn. Ch., 1980-2001, elder; mem. Village Presbyn. Ch., 2005-. Mem. Delta Kappa Gamma. Presbyterian. Avocations: travel, reading, swimming, walking, spanish.

LEEPER, RAMON JOE, physicist; b. Princeton, Mo., Apr. 1, 1948; s. Joe Edd and Jeanne (Gaul) Leeper; m. Sumiko Yasuda, Dec. 21, 1976; 1 child, Joe Eric. BS, MIT, 1970; PhD, Iowa State U., 1975. Rsch. assoc. Ames (Iowa) Lab. U.S. Dept. Energy, 1975-76; mem. tech. staff Sandia Nat. Labs., Albuquerque, 1976-86, dept. mgr. diagnostics and target physics dept., 1986—. Guest scientist Argonne Nat. Lab., Ill., 1971—76; invited lectr. NATO Advanced Study Inst., Italy, 1983, Internat. Sch. Plasma Physics, Italy, 2001. Contbr. articles to profl. jours. Recipient Outstanding Tchg. award, Iowa State U., 1973; fellow NDEA, 1971—73. Mem.: IEEE (session chmn. 1984), Am. Phys. Soc. (chmn. high temperature plasma diagnostics conf. 1992), Sigma Xi. Republican. Achievements include patents in field. Home: 6905 Rosewood Rd NE Albuquerque NM 87111-1021 Office: Diagnostics & Target Physics Dept 1677 Sandia Nat Labs Albuquerque NM 87185 E-mail: rjleepe@sandia.gov.

LEER, STEVEN F., mining executive; b. Vermillion, SD; m. Beverly Uhl; 1 child. BSEE, Univ. Pacific, 1975; MBA, Washington Univ., 1977; D (hon.), Univ. Pacific, 1993. Exec. mgmt. positions Ashland Inc., Ashland Coal, Valvoline Co.; pres., CEO Arch Mineral Corp., Arch Coal Inc., St. Louis, 1997—2006, chmn., CEO, 2006—. Bd. dir. Norfolk Southern Corp., USG Inc., Mineral Info. Inst., We. Bus. Roundtable; bd. dir., past chmn. Nat. Coal Council, Ctr. for Energy & Econ. Develop., Nat. Mining Assn.; delegate Coal Ind. Adv. Bd. Internat. Energy Agency, Paris. Mem.: Bus. Roundtable, NAM. Office: Arch Coal 1 City Pl Saint Louis MO 63141*

LEES, ALFRED WILLIAM, former magazine editor, writer; b. Kansas City, Kans., June 12, 1926; s. Alfred Whitaker and Blanche (Pontius) L. BA, Stanford U., 1950. Editor and writer Home Craftsman, NYC, 1953—59, Family Handyman, 1960, Popular Sci., NYC, 1960—62, sr. editor and writer, 1967—71; editor and writer Popular Mechanics, 1962—66; home care columnist Cosmopolitan, 1965—67; group editor reader activities Popular Sci., 1972—88; dir. and judge nat. ann. design competition Am. Plywood Assn., Tacoma, 1976—86. Pres. Nat. Assn. Home and Workshop Writers, 1990—92. *Upon retiring from his 35-year career as a how-to writer-editor, Lees tackled a book unlike the six he'd already published: an anthology of autobiographies by committed male couples across America. It took four years to find a publisher — not because the accounts were sensational, but because they were not. Even publishers with "gay lists" had scant interest in solid-citizen couples, preferring to present from-another-planet stereotypes. When Haworth Press bought the manuscript, the 28 authors — including Lees himself and his partner Ronald Nelson — persisted in telling their tales without compromise, resulting in a book that pioneered the marriage equality movement.* Author: Leisure Homes, 1980, 67 Prizewinning Plywood Projects, 1984; co-author: Wood Finishing and Painting, 1955, DIY Projects for Your Own Backyard, 1978, 2d edit., 1984, What's Wrong with My Car?, 1990, Decks and Sunspaces, 1991, Longtime Companions, 1999, Year of the B's: An Illustrated Chronicle of '04, 2005. With USAAF, 1944—45. Mem. Delaware Valley Arts Alliance, Dutch Treat Club, Traveler's Century Club (130 countries visited). Avocations: world travel, photography. Home: 140 Nassau St Apt 9B New York NY 10038-1548

LEES, FRANCIS, economics professor; b. Bklyn., Jan. 19, 1931; s. Roy A. and Mary (Ozustowicz) L.; m. Kathryn V. Murphy, June 6, 1959; children: Veronica Ann, Francis, Daniel, Jeannette Marie. BA, Bklyn. Coll., 1952; MA, St. Louis U., 1953; PhD, NYU, 1961. Instr. Fordham U., NYC, 1956-60; asst. prof. St. Johns U., Jamaica, NY, 1960-61; fin. analyst Dominick & Dominick, NYC, 1961-62; assoc. prof. St. John's U., 1962-68, prof., 1968—. Cons. Conf. Bd., 1979-86, U.S. Govt., 1985 fin. analyst, Internat. Report, 1982-84, CIA, 1985-86; prof. global fin. St. John's U., 1999—. Author: Capital Controls and the US Balance of Payments, 1968, International Banking and Finance, 1974, International Financial Markets, 1975, Foreign Banking and Investment in the United States, 1976, Economic and Political Development of the Sudan, 1977, International Lending, Risk, and the Euromarkets, 1979, Foreign Multinational Investment in the U.S., 1986, Banking and Financial Deepening in Brazil, 1990, Global Finance, 1995, 98, Foreign Participation in China's Banking and Securities Markets, 1996, China Superpower, 1997, The Euro, Capital Markets and Dollarization, 2002, Russia Inc., 2005; founder, co-editor Jour. Emerging Markets, 1996—; contbr. articles to profl. jours. Served with AUS, 1953-56. Am. Bankers Assn. Summer Rsch. fellow, 1969; Fulbright rsch. scholar, 1987-88. Office: St Johns U Grand Central And Utopia Pkwy Jamaica NY 11439-0001 Home: 12 Leland St East Northport NY 11731 Office Phone: 718-990-7305.

LEES, WILLIAM GLENWOOD, retired finance and retail executive; b. Flat River, Mo., Nov. 18, 1916; m. Mary Louise Meier, Aug. 22, 1937; children: Graham (dec.), Van P.G. Grad. high sch., Flat River, 1934. Office clk. Schramm Grocery Co., Flat River, 1934—36; asst. mgr. Wetterau Grocery Co., Desloge, Mo., 1936—39; owner Lees Food Market, Flat River, 1939—48, Lees Tom Boy Store, Farmington, Mo., 1948—55; pres. Lees Shopping Ctr. Inc., Farmington, 1955—80, So. Acceptance Corp., Inc., Farmington, 1961—98; ret., 1998; pres. Lees Home Furnishings Inc., Farmington, 1990—2007; ret., 2007. Pres. Presbyn. Home for Children, Farmington, 1958-70; v.p. Camp Penuel, Inc., Ironton, Mo., 1977—; elder Presbyn. Ch., Farmington, 1958-70, Penuel Fellowship,Ironton, 1977—. With U.S. Army, 1943-46. Mem. C. of C. (bd. dirs. 1956-58), Masons, Shriners (pres. 1963). Republican. Avocations: golf, travel. Home: 18 Airline Dr Farmington MO 63640-1106

LEESON, PETER J., IV, lawyer; b. Honolulu; s. Peter J. and Grace C. Leeson; m. Nichole Snook; children: Ella Cuvee, Mia Nichole. BS in Agrl. Bus., Calif. State U., San Luis Obispo; JD cum laude, U. San Diego. Law clk. Hon. Alan M. Ahart, US Bankruptcy Ct., Ctrl. Dist. Calif.; atty. Kirkland and Ellis LLP; dep. city atty. Hermosa Beach, Calif.; atty. Luce, Forward, Hamilton & Scripps LLP; atty., mng. shareholder Leeson Law Group, P.C., Pasadena. Editor: Norton Bankruptcy Law and Practice: Retiree Benefits Under 1114 and 1129(a)(13), 2003, 2004; pro bono exec. bd., editor-in-chief San Diego Internat. Law Jour. Mem.: ABA, LA County Bar Assn., Pasadena Bar Assn., Internat. Assn. Restructuring, Insolvency and Bankruptcy Profls., Am. Bankruptcy Inst. (bankruptcy litigation, distressed M&A sects.), U. San Diego Sch. Law Alumni Assn. (founding mem. LA chpt.), Order of the Coif. Office: Leeson Law Group PC 600 S Lake Ave Ste 401 Pasadena CA 91106

LEESTMA, ROBERT, retired federal agency administrator, educational association administrator; b. Detroit, Oct. 15, 1927; s. Richard and Jeanne (Nivarre) L.; m. Margaret Elizabeth Bell, Aug. 13, 1955 (dec. 1982). AB, U. Mich., 1949, AM, 1951, PhD, 1956. Rsch. teaching asst., cmty. adult edn. program U. Mich., Ann Arbor, 1949-50; tchr. English and social studies Ann Arbor pub. schs., 1950-51; asst. dir. Audio-Visual Edn. Ctr., lectr. sch. edn. U. Mich., 1951-55, assoc. prof., dir. Peace Corps tng. program, 1961-64; ICA edn. and mass. comm. advisor Govt. of Vietnam, 1955-58; edn. adviser Govt. of Thailand, 1958-61; dep. chief edn. div. Bur. Africa, AID, 1964-65; dir. Office Multilateral Policy and Programs, Multilateral Policy Planning Staff, Bur. Ednl. and Cultural Affairs, Dept. State, 1965-67; asst. to asst. sec. edn. for internat. edn. HEW, 1967-68; dir. Inst. Internat. Studies, assoc. commr. internat. edn. U.S. Office Edn., 1968-74, assoc. commr. instl. devel. and internat. edn., 1974-79; dep. dir. planning and implementation Office Edn. for Overseas Dependents, U.S. Dept. Edn., 1980-82; assoc. dir. dissemination and improvement of practice Nat. Inst. Edn., 1982-83, assoc. dir. field initiated and internal studies, 1984—85; dir. U.S. study edn. in Japan, Office Ednl. Rsch. and Improvement Dept. Edn., 1986—89; v.p. internat. programs Am. Assn. State Colls. and Univs., Washington, 1989-91; dir. spl. studies staff U.S. Dept. Edn. Office Ednl. Rsch. and Improvement, 1991-94; also sr. policy advisor Edn. Rsch. and Devel. Bur. AID, 1992-94; interim dir. Nat. Libr. Edn., 1994; edn. cons., 1995—. Mem., chmn. and/or adviser U.S. dels. internat. confs.; U.S. rep., chmn. edn. com. OECD; U.S. rep. governing coun. Internat. Bur. Edn., UNESCO; mem. Indo-U.S. Subcommn. on Edn. and Culture, U.S.-Egyptian Joint Working Group on Edn. and Culture, U.S.-Japan Culcon Edn. Com., U.S. Nat. Commn. for UNESCO; alt. mem. U.S.-Japan Friendship Commn., also Am. panel Joint Culcon Com.; mem. adv. com. Hanna Collection, Hoover Instn., Com. on Edn. and Successor Generation of Atlantic Coun. U.S.; bd. dirs. Pericles Inst., Abraham A. Low Inst. Author, co-author and/or editor books, chpts. and articles in profl. jours., including Japanese Education Today, 1987, Japanese Educational Productivity, 1992. With AUS, 1946-47. Payne scholar U. Mich., 1951-52, Hinsdale scholar, 1953-54. Mem. Comparative and Internat. Edn. Soc., Assn. Asian Studies, Phi Delta Kappa. Home: 2712 George Mason Pl Alexandria VA 22305-1620 Office Phone: 703-549-0509.

LEET, KENNETH H.M., automotive executive; married; 4 children. Grad., Brown U.; MBA, Harvard U. Lending officer Manufacturers Hanover Trust; principal Odyssey Partners; assoc. mergers & acquisitions dept. Goldman Sachs, v.p. leverage fin. / principal investing, mng. dir. mergers & acquisitions dept., mng. dir. investment banking divsn.; head corp. and investment banking corporate for Europe, the Middle East and Africa Bank of America, London, 2005—06; strategic advisor to Bill Ford Ford Motor Co., 2006—. Bd. dirs. Dana-Farber Cancer Inst.; founder Immunotherapy Rsch. Fund; trustee Rudolph Rupert Found.; bd. dirs., trustee The Old Vic, London. Avocation: piano. Office: Ford Motor Co 1 American Rd Dearborn MI 48126-2798

LEET, MILDRED ROBBINS, social welfare administrator, consultant; b. NYC, Aug. 9, 1922; d. Samuel Milton and Isabella (Zeitz) Elowsky; m. Louis J. Robbins, Feb. 23, 1941 (dec. 1970); children: Jane, Aileen; m. Glen Leet, Aug. 9, 1974 (dec. 1998). BA, NYU, 1942; LHD (hon.), Coll. Human Svcs., 1988; LLD honoris causa, Marymount Coll., Tarrytown, NY, 1991; HHD, Lynn U., 1993; D Humanitarian Svc. (hon.), Norwich U., 1994; DHL, Conn. Coll., 1996; DHL (hon.), Wilson Coll., 2003. Pres. women's div. United Cerebral Palsy, NYC, 1951-52, bd. dirs., 1953-55; rep. Nat. Coun. Women U.S. at UN, 1957-64, 1st v.p., 1959-64, pres., 1964-68, hon. pres., 1968-70; sec., v.p. conf. group U.S. Nat. Orgns. at UN, 1961-64, 76-78, vice chmn., sec., 1962-64, mem. exec. com., 1961-65, chmn. hospitality info. svc., 1960-66; vice chmn. exec. com. NGO's UN Office Public Info., 1976-78, chmn. ann. conf., 1977; chmn. com. on water, desertification, habitat and environment Conf. NGO's with consultative status with UN/ECOSOC, 1976-77; mem. exec. com. Internat. Coun. Women, 1960-73, v.p., 1970-73; chmn. program planning com., women's com. OEO, 1967-72; chmn. com. on natural disasters N.Am. Com. on Environment, 1973-77; N.Y. State chmn. UN Day, 1975; ptnr. Leet & Leet (cons. women in devel.), 1979—98. Co-founder Trickle Up Program, 1979—, pres., 1991—2000, chair, 2001—; mem. task force on Africa UN, 1995—. Contbr. articles to profl. jours.; editor UN Calendar & Digest, 1959-64, Measure of Mankind, 1963; editorial bd.: Peace & Change. Co-chmn. Vols. for Stevenson, N.Y.C., 1956; vice chmn. task force Nat. Dem. Com., 1969-72; commr. N.Y. State Commn. on Powers Local Govt., 1970-73; chmn. Coll. for Human Svcs. Audrey Cohen Coll., 1985-2000; former mem. bd. dirs. Am. Arbitration Assn., New Directions, Inst. for Mediation and Conflict Resolution, Spirit of Stockholm; bd. dirs. Hotline Internat.; v.p. Save the Children Fedn., 1986-93 rep. Internat. Peace Acad. at UN, 1974-77, Internat. Soc. Cmty. Devel., 1977-98, del. at large 1st Nat. Women's Conf., Houston, 1977; chmn. task force on internat. interdependence N.Y. State Women's Meeting, 1977; mem. Task Force on Poverty, 1977; chmn. Task Force on Women, Sci. and Tech. for Devel., 1978; U.S. del. UN Status of Women Commn., 1978, UN Conf. Sci. and Tech. for Devel., 1979, Brazzaville Centennial Celebration, 1980; mem. global adv. bd. Internat. Expn. Rural Devel., 1981—; mem. Coun. Internat. Fellows U. Bridgeport, 1982-88; trustee overseas edn. fund LWV, 1983-91; v.p. U.S.

Com. UN Devel. Fund for Women, 1983-94, trustee, 1998-2000; mem. Nat. Consultative Com. Planning for Nairobi, 1984-85; co-chmn. women in devel. com. Interaction, 1985-91; mem. com. of cooperation Interam. Commn. of Women, 1986; bd. dirs. Internat. Devel. Conf., 1991-2001; mem. UN task force informal sector devel. Africa, 1995—. Recipient Crystal award Coll. Human Svcs., 1983, Ann. award Inst. Mediation and Conflict Resloution, 1985, Woman of Conscience award Nat. Coun. Women, 1996, Temple award Inst. Noetic Scis., 1987, Presdl. End Hunger award, 1987, Giraffe award Giraffe Project, 1987, Woman of the World award Eng.'s Women Aid, 1989, Mildred Robbins Leet award Interaction, 1995; co-recipient Rose award World Media Inst., 1987, Human Rights award UN Devel. Fund for Women, 1987, Leadership award U.S. Peace Corps, Woman of Vision award N.Y.C. NOW, 1990, Matrix award Women in Comm., Inc., Spirit of Enterprise award Rolex Industries, 1990, Ann. Bush's Ann. Points of Light award, 1992, Internat. Humanity award ARC Overseas Assn., 1992, Excellence award U.S. Com. for UNIFEM, 1992, Champion of Enterprise award Avon, 1994, Achievement award NYU-Washington Sq. Coll. Alumni. Assn., 1995, Lizette H. Sarnoff Vol. Svc. award Yeshiva U., 1996, Disting. Svc. award N.Y. African Studies Assn., 1996, Disting. Svc. award 50th Anniversary United Cerebral Palsy, 1997, Eleanor Schnurr award UN Assn./USA, Women of Distinction honoree Birmingham So. Coll., Spirit award Nat. Assn. Women Bus. Owners, 1998, Nat. Caring Inst. award, 2001, Nat. Women's Hall of Fame, 2003, Met. Coll. NY Leadership award, 2004, Philippine Kalayan award, 2004, Global Summit of Women Internat. Hall of Fame award, 2005. Mem. AAAS, Women's Forum, Coun. on Fgn. Rels., Cosmopolitan Club, Princeton Club. Home and Office: 54 Riverside Dr New York NY 10024-6509 E-mail: millieleet@aol.com.

LEET, RICHARD EUGENE, artist, museum director; b. Waterloo, Iowa, Sept. 11, 1936; s. Arthur John and Gladys Fern Leet; m. Kay Annette Whitney, June 26, 1960; children: Kimberly Renee, Todd Whitney. BA, U. Northern Iowa, Cedar Falls, 1958, MA, 1965. Art instr. Oelwein Cmty. Sch. Sys., Iowa, 1958—65; artist Oelwein, 1958—; founding dir. Charles H. MacWidner Mus., Mason City, Iowa, 1965—2001. Mem. Iowa Arts Coun., Des Moines, 1970—76. Author (editor): (book) Bilbaird...He Pulled Lots of Strings, 1988, 25 Selections American Art: Charles H. MacNider Museum, 1991; exhibitions include Charles H. MacNider Mus., Mason City, Brunnier Gallery, Iowa, 1994—96, Arts Coun. and LA Divsn. Tourism, 1997—98, many other group and invitational exhbns., one-man shows include MacNider Mus., 1995—97, Cornell Coll., Mt. Vernon, Iowa, Tweed Mus. Art, U. Minn., Duluth, Sioux City Art Ctr., Iowa, Represented in permanent collections Iowa State Meml. Union, Iowa State U., Coll. Southern Idaho, Twin Falls, The Pillsbury Corp. Coll., Mpls., The Dubuque Art Assn. Mem. First United Meth. Ch., Mason City, 1965—, pastor/parish com. chair; pres. United Meth. Men, 1991—92; trustee, bd. chair North Ctrl. Regional Libr., Mason City, Iowa, 1976—82; bd. mem. Mason City Sesquicentennial Bd., 1999—2003. Recipient Lifetime Distinguished Svc. award, Assn. Midwest Mus., 1995. Mem.: Mason City Sister City Orgn., Iowa Watercolor Soc. (touring exch. chair 1989—91), Iowa Mus. Assn. (life pres. 1978—2001, Hall Fame 2001), Mason City Rotary (program chair 1970—71, bd. dirs. 1971—73, program chair 1979—80, v.p. 1981—82, pres. 1982—83, bd. mem., Paul Harris Fellow 1999). Methodist. Avocations: fishing, music, golf. Home: 1149 Manor Dr Mason City IA 50401 Office: Studio Richard Leet Artist 103 E State St Ste 425 Mason City IA 50401

LEET, RICHARD HALE, oil industry executive; b. Maryville, Mo., Oct. 11, 1926; s. Theron Hale and Helen Eloise (Rutledge) L.; m. Phyllis Jean Combs, June 14, 1949; children: Richard Hale II, Alan Combs, Dana Ellen. BS in Chemistry, N.W. Mo. State Coll., 1948; PhD in Phys. Chemistry, Ohio State U., 1952. Rsch. chemist Standard Oil Co., Whiting, Ind., 1953-64; dir. long-range and capital planning, mktg. dept. Am. Oil Co., Chgo., 1964-68, mgr. ops. planning, mfg. dept., 1968-70, regional v.p. Atlanta, 1970-71, v.p. supply Chgo., 1971-74; v.p. planning and adminstrn. Amoco Chems. Corp., Chgo., 1974-75, v.p. mktg., 1975-77, exec. v.p., 1977-78, pres., 1978-83; dir. Amoco Corp., Chgo., 1983-91, vice chmn., 1991-92. Bd. dirs. emeritus Gt. Lakes Chem., Vulcan Materials Corp., ITW, Landauer, Inc. Former chmn. bd. mgrs. Met. YMCA, Chgo.; former pres. Boy Scouts Am.; former chmn. bd. Am. Indsl. Health Coun.; former bd. visitors Emory U., 1970-71; hon. v.p. found. bd. Ohio State U; trustee Brenau U. With USNR, 1944-46. Mem. Chem. Mfrs. Assn. (dir.), Phi Sigma Epsilon, Gamma Alpha. Office: Lighthouse Acres 3631 Lantern Dr Gainesville GA 30504-5420

LEETCH, BRIAN JOSEPH, retired professional hockey player; b. Corpus Christi, Tex., Mar. 3, 1968; m. Mary Beth Leetch; 3 children. Attended, Boston Coll., 1986—87. Defenseman NY Rangers, 1988—2004, Toronto Maple Leafs, 2004—05, Boston Bruins, 2005—06. Mem. USA Olympic Hockey Team, Calgary, Alta., Canada, 1988, Nagano, Japan, 98, Salt Lake City, 2002, Team USA, Canada Cup, 1991, Team USA, World Cup of Hockey, 1996, 2004; player NHL All-Star game, 1990—92, 1994, 1996—98, 2001—02. Named to NHL All-Rookie team, 1989, First All-Star team, NHL, 1992, 1997; recipient Calder Meml. Trophy, 1989, James Norris Meml. Trophy, 1992, 1997, Conn Smythe Trophy, 1994. Achievements include being a member of Stanley Cup Champion New York Rangers, 1994; being a member of World Cup Champion Team USA, 1996; being a member of silver medal winning USA Hockey Team, Salt Lake City Olympics, 2002.*

LEETE, WILLIAM WHITE, retired artist; b. Portsmouth, Ohio, June 12, 1929; s. Bernard Emerson and Lois Trowbridge (Denison) L.; m. Doris Louise Knight, Sept. 19, 1952; children: Amy MacDonald, Robin Schodt. BA, Yale U., 1951, BFA, 1955, MFA, 1957. Mem. faculty dept. art U. R.I., Kingston, 1957-95, prof. emeritus, 1995, acting dept. chmn., 1968, 69-70, 76. Represented in permanent collections, De Cordova Mus., Lincoln, Mass., Cleve. Mus., Worcester Mus., Bank Am., also various pvt. collections. With USMC, 1951—53. Mem.: Coll. Art Assn. Home: 202 Silver Lake Ave Wakefield RI 02879-4231 Personal E-mail: wleete@aol.com.

LEETMAA, ANTS, environmental services administrator, educator; m. Anu Leetmaa. BS in Physics, U. Chgo., 1965; PhD in Oceanography, MIT, 1969. Rsch. assoc., postdoctoral studies MIT, Cambridge, Mass., 1969—72; researcher NOAA, Atlantic Oceanographic Meteorological Lab., Miami, Fla., 1972—86; oceanographer to Chief, Coupled Model Project, to sr. scientist Nat. Ctr. for Environ. Prediction, 1986—97; dir. NOAA Climate Prediction Ctr., Camp Springs, Md., 1997—2001; lead climate forecaster in the US, 1997—2000; lectr. with rank of prof., geosciences & atmospheric and oceanic sciences Princeton Univ. Forrestal Campus, Princeton, NJ, 2001—, dir., NOAA Geophysical Fluid Dynamics Lab., 2001—. Mem. steering com. Climate Variability and Predictability, chmn. upper ocean panel. Contbr. articles to profl. jours. Mem.: Am. Geophysical Union. Office: NOAA /220 GFDL Princeton U Forrestal Campus 201 Forrestal Rd Princeton NJ 08540 Office Phone: 609-452-6502. Business E-Mail: aleetmaa@NOSPAMprinceton.edu.*

LEETS, PETER J., consulting firm executive; b. London, Mar. 12, 1946; came to U.S., 1948; s. Earl Edward and Doris Eileen L.; m. Anne E. Shahinian, May 15, 1982. BS in Mktg., Ind. U., 1969. Salesman Ortho Pharm. Corp., Raritan, NJ, 1969-74; account mgr. Revlon Inc., Indpls., 1974-76, regional dir. Cleve., 1976-79, field sales mgr. Bay Village, Ohio, 1979-83; N.Am. field sales mgr. Binney & Smith, Bethlehem, Pa., 1983-85; v.p., dir. sales Dell Pub. Co., Inc., NYC, 1985-87; exec. v.p. Geneva Corp., Irvine, Calif., 1987-88; pres. Geneva Cos., Costa Mesa, Calif., 1988-90; exec. v.p. Exec. Assets Corp., Irvine, Calif., 1990-91, pres., 1992-94; reg. mng. prin. Right Mgmt. Cons., Irvine, Calif., 1994—2003; mng. ptnr. The Leets Consortium, 2003—. Bd. dirs. Career Beginnings, Career Transition Ptnrs., Constl. Rights Found., Prof. Coaches Mentors Assn., Juvenile Diabetes Rsch. Found. Orange County. Chairperson Orange County Econ. Outlook Conf.; bd. dirs. Forum for Corp. Dirs., PIHRA Found., Chapman U. Named Susan G. Komen Pink Tie Guy, 2007. Fellow Mgr. Inst. of Career Devel.; mem. Internat. Assn. Career Mgmt. Profls. (bd. dirs.), Ind. U. Alumni (life), Delta Chi. Office: 4695 MacArthur Ct Ste 930 Newport Beach CA 92660 Home: 30441 Via Ventana San Juan Capistrano CA 92675-1731 Office Phone: 949-260-0300. Business E-Mail: peter@leelsconsortium.com.

LEEVES, JANE, actress; b. Ilford Essex, England, Apr. 18, 1961; m. Marshall Coben, Dec. 21, 1996; 2 children. Actress (TV series) The Benny Hill Show, 1983-84, Double Trouble, 1984, Throb, 1986-88, Murphy Brown, 1989-1993, Just Deserts, 1992, Frasier 1993-2004 (Emmy award nom. sup. actress, 1998, SAG award outstanding performance ensemble, 2000); (TV movies) Red Dwarf, 1992, Pandora's Clock, 1996, Just Deserts, 1999; (films) The Hunger, 1983, To Live and Die in L.A., 1985, Miracle on 34th Street, 1994, The Meaning of Life, 1983, Mr. Write, 1994, James and the Giant Peach (voice), 1996, Don't Go Breaking My Heart, 1999, Music of the Heart, 1999, Adventures of Tom Thumb and Thumbelina (voice), 2002, The Event, 2003, Garfield: A Tail of Two Kitties (voice), 2006; (TV guest appearances) Murder, She Wrote, 1987, It's a Living, 1989, Hooperman, 1989, Mr. Belvedere, 1989, My Two Dads, 1990, Who's the Boss?, 1990, Blossom, 1991, Seinfeld, 1992-93, 98, Caroline in the City, 1995, Hercules (voice), 1998, The Simpsons, 2003; (Broadway show) Cabaret, 2002. Avocations: reading, cooking, sports, dance. Office: Talent Group Inc 5670 Wilshire Blvd #820 Los Angeles CA 90036-5602

LEEWER, WILLIAM GEORGE, JR., education educator; b. Camden, NJ, Nov. 17, 1950; s. William George Leewer, Sr. BA in Lit., R. Stockton State Coll. NJ, Pomona, 1975; MEd in Curriculum and Instrn., U. So. Miss., Hattiesburg, 1987, PhD in Edn., 2000. Cert. English tchr. grades K-12 NJ, secondary lang. arts Colo., AAAA edn. lic. secondary edn. Miss., advanced ops. aerial NJ State Fire Coll. Sr. grad. rsch. asst. So. Edn. Consortium and State Sch. Ctr., Hattiesburg, 1997—99; faculty chair, head trainer Koch Crime Inst., St. Mary's, Kans., 1999—2001; lang. arts tchr. Adams City H.S., Denver, 2001—02; asst. vis. prof. edn. U. So. Miss., Hattiesburg, 2002—03, trainer,. F. Karnes Ctr. Gifted and Talented Edn., 2002—; asst. prof. edn. Miss. State U., Meridian, 2003—, grad. coord., 2004—. Participant NJ State- China Tchr. Exch. Program, 1988; cons., trainer, editor So. Edn. Consortium, Meridian, 1997—, U. Ctrl. Ark. Grad. Sch., Conway, 2003—; cons., trainer East Miss. Ctr. Edn. Devel., Meridian, 2003—; invitee Oxford Round Table on Poverty and Depravation, England, 2007, Oxford Round Table on Ch. and State, 2007. Editor: School Safety and Security Legal News, 1999—, Legal Update: Southern Education Consortium, 2002—, Legal Update for C.C., 2003—. Founding mem., mem. leadership coun. Wall of Tolerance, So. Poverty Law Ctr., 2002; mem. Commanders Club DAV, 2003; founding mem. Nat. WWII Meml., Washington, 2004; charter mem. Nat. WWII Mus., New Orleans, 2005; ptnr. Spl. Olympics, 2004—06. Named Bronze Leader, DAV, 2003, Good Samaritan of Yr., 2005, Silver Leader Comdr.'s Club, 2007, Miss. Donor of Yr., WWII Veterans Com., 2004, Disting. Donor, VFW, 2005, Miss. Donor of Yr., Help Hospitalized Veterans, 2005, Donor of Yr., 2007, Patriot of Yr., 2007; named one of Outstanding Young Men Am., 1975—76; named to The Wall Soc., Vietnam Veterans Meml., 2007—; recipient cert. appreciation, Easter Seals, 2005, 2006. Mem.: ACLU, So. Poverty Law Ctr., The Wall Soc. (disting. donor 2004), Kappa Delta Pi, Pi Delta Kappa (hon.). Avocations: fishing, stamp collecting/philately, etymology. Office: Miss State Univ 1000 Hwy 19 N Meridian MS 39307 Office Phone: 601-484-0496.

LEFAR, MARC P., former telecommunications industry executive; b. Dec. 28, 1963; BS in Commerce, U. Va. Positions in fin., brand mgmt. Procter & Gamble; sr. advisor WWC Capital, Washington; chief mktg. officer Cable & Wireless Global; v.p., wireless internet, data svcs., and e-enablement GTE Wireless, v.p., mktg.; chief mktg. officer AT&T Wireless (formerly Cingular Wireless), Atlanta, 2003—07. Recipient Marketing 50 award.*

LEFAVE, RICHARD T.C., telecommunications industry executive; BS, Boston Univ.; MBA, Univ. Puget Sound; MS, Univ. So. Calif. CIO Boston Co., Thomas Cook Travel, So. New Eng. Telephone, Nextel Communications, 1999—2005, Sprint Nextel, Reston, Va., 2005—. Served US Army. Office: Sprint Nextel 2001 Edmund Halley Dr Reston VA 20191*

LEFCO, KATHY NAN, law librarian; b. Bethesda, Md., Feb. 24, 1949; d. Ted Lefco and Dorothy Rose (Fox) Harris; m. Stephen Gary Katz, Sept. 2, 1973 (div. May 1984); m. John Alfred Price, Nov. 24, 1984 (dec. Jan. 1989); m. Richard Louis Edmonds, Apr. 12, 2002. BA, U. Wis., 1971; MLS, U. Wis., Milw., 1975. Rsch. asst. Ctr. Auto Safety, Washington, 1971-73; asst. to dir. Ctr. Consumer Affairs, Milw., 1973-74; legis. libr. Morgan, Lewis & Bockius, Washington, 1976-78; dir. library Mulcahy & Wherry, Milw., 1978; paralegal Land of Lincoln Legal Assistance, Springfield, Ill., 1979-80; reference and interlibrary loan libr. So. Ill. U. Sch. Medicine, Springfield, 1980; reader svcs. libr. Wis. State Law Library, Madison, 1981-83; ref. libr. Mudge Rose Guthrie Alexander & Ferdon, NYC, 1983-85; sr. legal info. specialist Cravath, Swaine & Moore, NYC, 1985-86; asst. libr. Kaye, Scholer, Fierman, Hays & Handler, NYC, 1986-89; head libr. Parker Chapin Flattau & Klimpl, NYC, 1989-94; dir. libr. svcs. Winston & Strawn LLP, Chgo., 1994—. Author: (with others) Mobile Homes: The Low-Cost Housing Hoax, 1973. Mem. bd. visitors LaFollette Sch. Pub. Affairs, U. Wis., Madison, 2007—. Mem. Chgo. Assn. Law Librs., Am. Assn. Law Librs. Democrat. Jewish. Avocations: biking, backgammon, politics. Home: 543 Oakdale Ave Glencoe IL 60022 Office: Winston & Strawn LLP 35 W Wacker Dr Ste 4200 Chicago IL 60601-1695 Home Phone: 847-242-0309; Office Phone: 312-558-5813. E-mail: klefco@winston.com.

LEFCOURT, GERALD B., lawyer; b. NYC, June 1, 1942; s. Albert Lefcourt and Ethel (Saltzman) L.; children: Jeffrey Michael, Karen Elizabeth. BS, NYU, 1964; JD, Bklyn. Law Sch., 1967. Bar: N.Y. 1967, U.S. Dist. Ct. (ea. and so. dists.) N.Y., U.S. Ct. Appeals (2nd and D.C. cirs.), U.S. Supreme Ct. Staff atty. Legal Aid Soc., NYC, 1967-68; legislative dir. Nat. Emergency Civil Liberties Com., NYC, 1968-69; sole practice NYC, 1971—. Adj. prof. law Hofstra U., 1978; adv. bd. dirs. Law Sch. NYU, 1985—. Author various legal publs. Mem. ABA (ho. of dels., lawyers coalition for criminal justice), ACLU, NACDL (past pres., Robert C. Heeney Meml. award 1993), Nat. Coll. Criminal Def. Attys., N.Y. State Bar Assn. (Outstanding Practitioner award 1985, 93), N.Y. Criminal Bar Assn. (past pres.), founder, mem. N.Y. State Assn. Criminal Defense Lawyers (Thurgood Marshall Lifetime Achievement award 1997). Office: 148 E 78th St New York NY 10021-0406 Office Phone: 212-737-0400. E-mail: lefcourt@aol.com.*

LEFEBER, EDWARD JAMES, JR., internist, educator; b. Galveston, Tex., Jan. 12, 1941; s. Edward James Lefeber and Ellie Hancock Weisiger; m. Faith Linn Gabrielsen, Oct. 18, 1967; 1 child, Karin. BA cum laude, U. South, Sewanee, Tenn., 1962; MD with honors, U. Tex., Galveston, 1966. Cert. internal medicine 1976, 1997, geriatric medicine 1988, 1997. Staff dept. internal medicine William Beaumont Army Hosp., 1971—72; pvt. practice Casa Blanca Med. Grp., Mesa, Ariz., 1972—73; staff physician VAMC, Phoenix, 1973—82, chief gen. internal medicine, dept. medicine, 1982—95; staff physician Temple VAMC, 1995—96, tchg. svc., 1996—98; attending physician Good Samaritan Phoenix VAMC Internal Medicine, 1974—95; acting chief tchg. svc., 1998—99; mem. clin. staff UTHSCSA, 1999—. Asst. prof. internal medicine Texas A&M Med. Sch., Tex., 1996—99; credentials com. mem. U. Physicians Grp., 1999—. Col. USAR, 1966—2001, gen. med. officer US Army, 1967—69, Vietnam, hosp. cmdr. US Army, 403 Combat Support Hosp., active duty US Army, 1970—72, active duty US Army, 1990—91, commdg. officer, major assignment, 1988—92, Phoenix, Saudi Arabia. Decorated Bronze Star Medal US Army, Meritorious Svc. medal. Fellow: Am. Coll. Physicians; mem.: ACLS, Alpha Omega Alpha. Avocations: hiking, history. Office: UT Medicine Diagnostic Pavilion 4647 Medical Dr San Antonio TX 78229 Business E-Mail: leferber@uthscsa.edu.

LEFEBVRE, EUGENE ALLEN, zoology educator, ecologist; b. St. Paul, Oct. 18, 1929; s. Clarence J. and Lucille (Willy) LeF.; m. Mary Ellen Schultz, Aug. 26, 1966; children: Ann Marie, Charles Allen. MS, U. Minn., 1956, PhD, 1964. Rsch. fellow U. Minn., Mpls., 1960—61, rsch. assoc., 1961—66; asst. prof. So. Ill. U., Carbondale, 1966—72, assoc. prof., 1972—91, emeritus prof., 1991—. Chair nominating com. Nature Conservancy, Mpls., 1962-66; cons. in field. Author: (chpt.) Energy Cost of Free Flight in Columbia, 1976; contbr. articles to profl. jours. Mem. com. planning ten yr. program IBHE, Cardondale, 1970; mem. com. Nat. Environ. Leadership Coun., 1990; bd. dirs. Nature Conservancy, Mpls., 1964-66, So. Ill. Bird Obs., Carbondale, 1976-82, chair bd. dirs., 1978-82. With U.S. Army, 1954-56, ETO. Grantee Ill. Dept. of Conservation, NSF, NRA, So. Ill. U. Mem. Ecol. Soc. Am., Cooper Wilson Ornithology Soc., Soc. Conservation Biologists, Sigma Xi. Achievements include research in perceptions of HEP, laysan albatross breeding, energy expenditure of flight, thermal modeling of Canada geese; design of flight time integrator, micro-syringe technique. Office: So Ill U Dept Of Zoology Carbondale IL 62901 Personal E-mail: the-pack@woofhaven.name.

LEFEBVRE, JULIE AGUILAR, not-for-profit fundraiser; b. Baton Rouge, Aug. 28, 1976; d. Stephen M. Wilson and Marilyn Gay Aguilar, Rodolfo Jesus Aguilar (Stepfather); m. Joshua James LeFebvre, Mar. 20, 2004. BA in Mass Comm., La. State U., Baton Rouge, 1998. Spl. events mgr., devel. officer, A.B. Freeman Sch. Bus. Tulane U., New Orleans, 2001—03; account exec. Hayes & Assocs., McLean, Va., 2003—04; account mgr. GES Expn. Svcs., Landover, Md., 2004—05; devel. dir. Ballet Austin, Tex., 2006—. Vol. mem. advance team White Ho., DC, 2004—06. Mem.: Assn. Fundraising Profls. (assoc.; philanthropy day com. mem. 2006—07). Office: Ballet Austin 501 W 3rd St Austin TX 78701 Office Fax: 512-476-3973. Business E-Mail: julie.lefebvre@balletaustin.org.

LEFEBVRE, LUDOVIC, chef; b. France, 1972; Trained at L'Esperance, France, Pierre Gagnaire, France, L'Arpege, Paris; chef Le Grand Vefour; personal chef for Def. Min. of France; exec. chef L'Orangerie; head chef Bastide, LA. Named one of LA's Rising Stars, StarChefs.com, 2006. Office: Bastide Restaurant 8475 Melrose Pl West Hollywood CA 90069 Office Phone: 323-651-5950.*

LEFEMINE, ARMAND ANGELO, thoracic surgeon, educator; b. Windsor Licks, Conn., Sept. 14, 1926; s. Vito and Mary (Casarola) L.; m. Natalie Jenckes, June 10, 1952; children— Stephen, Linda, David, Carolyn. B.S., Holy Cross Coll., 1948; M.D., Harvard U., 1952. Diplomate Am. Bd. Surgery, Am. Bd. Thoracic Surgery. Intern USPHS Hosp., Brighton, Mass., 1952-53; resident Boston VA Hosp., 1953-57, Rutland Heights VA Hosp., 1957-58, Peter Bent Brigham Hosp.-Mt. Auburn Hosp., 1958-60; assoc. in surgery Peter Bent Brigham Hosp., Boston, 1960-66; staff surgeon Hartford Hosp., Conn., 1966-69; chief cardiothoracic surgery St. Elizabeth Hosp., Boston, 1969-78; chief surgery VA Med. Ctr., Johnson City, Tenn., 1978, prof. surgery, 1978—; assoc. chmn. dept. surgery East Tenn. State U., Johnson City, 1983—. Author: Surgery and Acquired Lesions of the Heart and Pericardum, 1978. Contbr. articles to profl. jours. Served with USN, 1944-45. Grantee Conn. Heart Assn. 1966-67, Tenn. affiliate Am. Heart Assn. 1979-80, Mass. Heart Assn. 1971-72, VA merit rev., 1984—. Fellow ACS; mem. Am. Assn. Thoracic Surgery, Soc. Thoracic Surgeons, Internat. Coll. Vascular Surgeons. Roman Catholic. Avocation: painting. Office: Ctrl Office Dir Surg 111 810 Vermont Ave NW Washington DC 20420-0001

LEFER, ALLAN MARK, physiologist; b. NYC, Feb. 1, 1936; s. I. Judah and Lillian G. Lefer; m. Mary E. Indoe, Aug. 23, 1959; children: Debra Lynn, David Joseph, Barry Lee and Leslie Ann (twins). BA, Adelphi Coll., 1957, Western Res. U., 1959; PhD, U. Ill., 1962. Instr. physiology, USPHS-NIH fellow Western Res. U., 1962-64; asst. prof. physiology U. Va., 1964-69, assoc. prof., 1969-71, prof., 1972-74; vis. prof. Hadassah Med. Sch., Jerusalem, 1971-72; prof., chmn. dept. physiology Jefferson Med. Coll., Thomas Jefferson U., Phila., 1974—2001, prof. emeritus, 2001—; dir. Ischemia-Shock Rsch. Inst., 1980-95. Cons. Merck & Co., Upjohn Co., Genentech Inc., Syntex, Inc., Ciba-Geigy, NIH, Nitromed, IBEX Technologies, Bristol-Myers Squibb, Cytel Corp., Wellcome Found.; vis. prof. 1985-86, Pfizer vis. prof. cardiovasc. medicine, 1995; Nat. Bd. of Med. Examiners, Step 1, 1993-95; vis. prof. U. Calif., San Diego, 1995-96. Author: Pathophysiology and Therapeutics of Myocardial Ischemia, 1977, Prostaglandins in Cardiovascular and Renal Function, 1979, Cellular and Molecular Aspects of Shock and Trauma, 1983; Leukotrienes in Cardiovascular and Pulmonary Function, 1985; mng. editor: Eicosanoids, 1988-93; cons. editor Circulatory Shock, 1973-80; field editor Jour. of Pharmacology and Exptl. Therapeutics Cardiovasc., 1994-2000; mem. editl. bd. Critical Care Medicine, Shock Am. Jour. Physiology, Endothelium, Cardiovasc. Pathology, Drug News and Perspectives; contbr. to World Book Ency. Sci. Yearbook, 1979, Cardiovasc. Drug Reviews, Circulation Rsch. Drugs Today; contbr. over 600 articles to profl. jours. Chmn. United Jewish Appeal of Charlottesville, Va., 1973-74; coach basketball and baseball Huntingdon Valley Athletic Assn., 1975-78. Recipient Pres. and Visitor's prize in rsch. U. Va., 1970, Disting. Alumnus award U. Ill., 1996, Disting. Svc. award Coll. Grad. Studies, Thomas Jefferson U., 1999; NSF fellow U. Ill., 1960-62. Fellow Am. Coll. Cardiology; mem. AAAS, Am. Physiol. Soc. (Carl J. Wiggers award 2003), Am. Soc. Pharmacology and Exptl. Therapeutics, Internat. Heart Rsch. Soc., Am. Heart Assn. (established investigator 1968-73, fellow circulation coun., nat. grant rev. com. 1993-95), Pa. Heart Assn. (rsch. com.), Shock Soc. (hon. life, chmn. membership com., pres. 1983-84, chmn. devel. com. 1985-89, chmn. internat. rels. com. 1993), Internat. Fed. Shock Socs. (coun. 1994-2002, pres. 4th internat. shock congress 1996-99), Soc. Exptl. Biology and Medicine, Soc. Leukocyte Biology, Israel Soc. Physiology and Pharmacology, Phila. Physiol. Soc. (pres. 1978-79), Sierra Club, B'nai B'rith (Charlottesville chpt., v.p. 1967-68, chmn. Va. Hillel 1970-71), Sigma Xi. Democrat. Home: 57 Oyster Reef Dr Hilton Head Island SC 29926 E-mail: allefer@aol.com.

LEFEVRE, DAVID, chef; b. Wis., 1974; Attended, U. Wis.; grad., Culinary Inst. Am., 1995. Tournant Charlie Trotter's, Las Vegas, 1995; apprentice La Côte d'Or, France, Restaurant Jean Bardet, France, le Moulin de Mougins, France; line cook Charlie Trotter's, Chgo., 1996, sous chef, exec. sous chef; exec. chef Water Grill, LA, 2004—. Co-prodr.: (TV series) Kitchen Sessions with Charlie Trotter. Office: Water Grill 544 S Grand Ave Los Angeles CA 90071 Office Phone: 213-891-0900.*

LEFEVRE, DAVID E., lawyer, business executive; b. Cleve., Oct. 25, 1944; s. Fay A. and Mary (Eaton) LeF. BA, Yale U., 1966; JD, U. Mich., 1971. Bar: N.Y., U.S. Dist. Ct. (so. and ea. dists.) N.Y. Assoc. Reid & Priest, NYC, 1971-78, ptnr., 1979-92; owner Houston Astros Baseball Club, 1979-84, Cleve. Indians Baseball Club, 1984-86. Bd. govs. NHL and NHL Pension Soc., 1992—97; bd. dirs. Fla. Sports Found., 1996—99. Vol. Peace Corps, Uruguay, 1966—68. Recipient Tenth Ann. award Mayor's Beautification Program, Tampa, 1999, Spl. award Tampa Sports Club;

named Hon. Alumnus, Cleve. State U., 1985. Mem. ABA, Sports Lawyers Assn., Canyon Club (past pres. Armonk, N.Y. 1986—), Palma Ceia Golf and Country Club. Address: 303 E 57th St New York NY 10022-2947

LEFEVRE, THOMAS VERNON, retired utilities executive; b. Dallas, Dec. 5, 1918; s. Eugene H. and Callie E. (Powell) L.; m. Lillian Herndon Bourne, Oct. 12, 1946; children: Eugene B., Nicholas R., Sharon A., Margot P. BA, U. Fla., 1939, LLB, 1942; LLM, Harvard U., 1946. Bar: Fla. 1945, N.Y. 1947, D.C. 1951, Pa. 1955, U.S. Supreme Ct. 1953. Atty. IRS and various firms, NYC, Washington, and Phila., 1946-55; ptnr. Morgan, Lewis & Bockius, Phila., 1956-79; pres., chief exec. officer UGI Corp., Valley Forge, Pa., 1979-85, chmn., 1983-89. Chmn. G.P. Hospitality, Inc., 1981—; mem. Commr.'s Adv. Group IRS, 1976-77. Bd. dirs. Zool. Soc. Phila., 1982-91, WHYY Inc., 1982-96; chmn. U. Arts, 1986-89; trustee Franklin Inst., 1980-89, Fox Chase Cancer Ctr., 1979-88. With USMC, 1942-46. Fellow ABA (vice chmn. govt. rels. sect. of taxation 1976-79), Am. Bar Found.; mem. Pa. Bar Assn., Merion Cricket Club, Merion Golf Club, Sankaty Head Golf Club, Nantucket Yacht Club. Episcopalian. Office: 5 Radnor Corp Ctr Wayne PA 19087-4526 Office Phone: 610-964-8131.

LEFF, ALAN RICHARD, medical educator, researcher; b. May 23, 1945; s. Maurice D. and Grace Ruth (Schwartz) Leff; m. Donna Rae Rosene, Feb. 14, 1975; children: Marni, Karen, Alison. AB cum laude, Oberlin Coll., 1967; MD, U. Rochester, 1971. Diplomate Am. Bd. Internal Medicine, Am. Bd. Pulmonary Disease. Intern U. Mich. Hosp., Ann Arbor, 1971—72, resident, 1974—76; fellow U. Calif., San Francisco, 1976—77, postdoctoral fellow, 1977—79; asst. prof. medicine U. Chgo., 1979—85, assoc. prof. medicine and clin. pharm., 1985—89, prof. medicine, anesthesia, critical care and clin. pharm., 1989—, prof. cell physiology, 1992—, prof. pediats., neurobiology, physiology, 1999—, dir. pulmonary medicine svc., 1984—87, dir. Pulmonary Function Lab., 1979—87, chief sect. pulmonary and critical care medicine, 1987—2000, sr. dir. R&D biol. scis., 2000—02. Dir. NIAID Asthma and Allergic Disease Coop. Rsch. Ctr., Chgo., 1993—97; co-chair asthma sect. NIAID Task Force on Immunology, 1996—98; advisor San Francisco Dept. Pub. Health, 1977—79, Chgo Dept. Health, 1979—89; dir. Ctr. of Excellence in Asthma Glaxo Smith Kline, 2000—. Cons. editor, mem. editl. bd. Jour. Clin. Investigation, mem. editl. bd. Am. Jour. Physiology, Jour. Applied Physiology; editor: Am. Jour. Respiratory Critical Care Medicine, 1994—99, Procs. Am. Thoracic Soc., 2004—; editor, assoc. editor: Am. Rev. Respiratory Diseases, 1989—94, Pulmonary Pharmacology, 1987—92, assoc. editor: European Respiratory Jour., 2006—; contbr. articles to profl. jours. Bd. dirs. Chgo. Lung Assn., 1984—93. With USPHS, 1972—74. Recipient Citation of Merit, Chgo. Lung Assn., 1974, Am. Lung Assn., 1998; fellow, Leopold Schepp Found., 1967—69. Fellow: Am. Coll. Chest Physicians; mem.: Am. Assn. Immunologists, Ctrl. Soc. for Clin. Investigation, Am. Thoracic Soc. (Spl. Citation 1999), Assn. Am. Physicians, Am. Physiol. Soc., Am. Soc. Clin. Investigation, Am. Fedn. Clin. Rsch. (councilor 1983—86), Sigma Xi. Avocation: music. Home: 5730 S Kimbark Ave Chicago IL 60637-1615 Office: U Chgo Pritzker Sch Medicine Div Biological Scis MC 6076 5841 S Maryland Ave Chicago IL 60637-1463 Home Phone: 773-955-9555. Business E-Mail: aleff@medicine.bsd.uchicago.edu.

LEFF, DEBORAH, foundation administrator; b. Washington, Oct. 25, 1951; d. Sam and Melitta Leff. AB, Princeton U., NJ, 1973; JD, U. Chgo., 1977. Trial atty. Civil Rights divsn. U.S. Dept. Justice, Washington, 1977-79; dir. office of pub. affairs Fed. Trade Commn., Washington, 1980-81; sr. producer Nightline-ABC News, Washington and London, 1983-89, World News Tonight-ABC News, NYC, 1990-91; pres. The Joyce Found., Chgo., 1992-99; pres., CEO Am.'s Second Harvest, Chgo., 1999-2001; dir. John F. Kennedy Presdl. Libr., Boston, 2001—06; pres. Pub. Welfare Found., Washington, 2006—. Bd. dirs. Sound Portraits; chmn. Midwest Rhodes Scholars Selection Com., Chgo., 1992. Bd. dirs. Am. Bd. Internal Medicine Found. Office: Pub Welfare Found 1200 U St NW Washington DC 20009-4943

LEFF, ILENE J(AFNEL), corporate executive, federal official; b. NYC, Mar. 29; d. Abraham and Rose (Levy) L. BA cum laude, U. Pa., 1964; MA with honors, Columbia U., 1969. Statis. and computer analyst McKinsey & Co., NYC, 1969—70, rsch. cons., 1971—74; mgmt. cons. NYC and Europe, 1974—78; dir. exec. resources Revlon, Inc., NYC, 1978—81, dir. human resources, 1981—83, dir. pers., 1983—86; cons. APM Inc., 1986—88; mgmt. cons. The Estee Lauder Cos., 1988—92; dep. asst. sec. for mgmt. HUD, Washington, 1993—94; pres. Leff Mgmt., NYC, 1995—97, 2000—03; mng. dir. Eisner LLP, NYC, 1997—2000; pres. Jafnel Advisors, 2004—. Rsch. asst. U. Pa., Phila., 1964-65; employment counselor State of N.J., Newark, 1965-66; tchr., Newark, 1966-69; lectr. Grad. Program in Pub. Policy, New Sch. for Social Rsch., Wharton Sch., Duke U.; chmn. com. on employment and unemployment, mem. exec. com. Bus. Rsch. Adv. Coun., U.S. Bur. Labor Stats., 1980; sr. del. econ. rels. and trade Sino-U.S. Conf., 1986; mem. nat. adv. bd. First Book. Contbr. issues papers and program recommendations to candidates for U.S. Pres., U.S. Senate and Congress, N.Y. State gov., mayor N.Y.C. Mem. ops. coun. Jr. Achievement Greater N.Y., 1975-78; cons. Com. for Econ. Devel., N.Y. Hosp., Regional Plan Assn., Am. Cancer Soc.; vol. for dep. mayor for ops. N.Y.C., 1977-78 Mem. N.Y. Human Resource Planners (treas. 1984), Fin. Women's Assn. N.Y. (exec. bd. 1977-78, 83-84), Fashion Group (treas. 1989). Office Phone: 212-674-1140. Personal E-mail: ileneleff@aol.com.

LEFF, JOSEPH NORMAN, yarn manufacturing company executive; b. NYC, Dec. 17, 1923; s. Phillip and Lillian (Wiesen) L.; m. Joyce Hochberg, June 12, 1954 (div. 1958); 1 child, Julie; m. Juanita Hughey, Dec. 17, 1967; 1 child, Valerie. BS, Columbia U., 1944, AB, 1946. Treas. Nat. Spinning Co. Inc., NYC, 1949-63, pres., CEO, 1963-83, chmn., CEO, 1983-97, chmn. bd. dirs. Mem. bd. visitors Columbia Coll., N.Y.C., 1987-92; trustee Park Ave. Synagogue, N.Y.C., 1987-95; bd. dirs., pres. 92d St. YM/YWHA, N.Y.C., 1994-97, chmn., 1997—; bd. dirs. Inst. Textile Tech., Va., 1982-97; mem. Purchase Coll. Found., 1999—. With U.S. Army, 1944-45. Mem. Harmonie Club (pres. 1974-75) (N.Y.C.), Quaker Ridge Golf Club (Scarsdale, N.Y.), Boca Rio Country Club (Boca Raton, Fla.), Regency Whist Club. Jewish. Home Phone: 914-285-9182; Office Phone: 212-382-6411.

LEFFEK, KENNETH THOMAS, retired chemist, educator; b. Nottingham, Eng., Oct. 15, 1934; emigrated to Can., 1959, naturalized, 1966; s. Thomas and Ivy Louise (Pye) L.; m. Janet Marilyn Wallace, Sept. 26, 1958; children: Katharine, Geoffrey. BS, Univ. Coll., London, 1956, PhD, 1959. Asst. prof. chemistry Dalhousie U., Halifax, N.S., 1961-67, assoc. prof., 1967-72, prof., 1972-94, dean grad. studies, 1972-90, prof. chemistry, 1990-94, ret., 1994. Chmn. Atlantic Provinces Interuniv. Com. on Scis., 1975-77. Author: Sir Christopher Ingold, a Biography; contbr. articles on phys.-organic chemistry to profl. jours. Leverhulme fellow U. Kent (Eng.), 1967-68 Fellow Chem. Inst. Can., Royal Soc. Arts (London; chmn. Atlantic Can. chpt. 1987-91); mem. Chem. Soc. London, Chem. Inst. Can. (nat. dir. tech. and sci. affairs 1980-83, nat. v.p. 1985-86, pres. 1986-87) Home: 980 Kentwood Ter Victoria BC Canada V8Y 1A6 Home Phone: 250-658-1329. E-mail: kleffek@vanisle.net.

LEFFELL, DAVID JOEL, dermatologist, surgeon, writer, photographer, medical school administrator, educator; b. Montreal, Feb. 28, 1956; came to U.S., 1973; s. Allen Bernard and Freda (Deckelbaum) L. BS, Yale U., 1977; MD, McGill U., Montreal, 1981. Diplomate Am. Bd. Dermatology, Am. Bd. Internal Medicine. Resident in internal medicine Meml. Sloan-Kettering Cancer Ctr., NYC, 1981-84; instr. medicine Cornell U. Sch. Medicine, NYC, 1983-84; resident in dermatology Yale U. Sch. Medicine, New Haven, 1984-86; lectr., fellow dermatologic surgery U. Mich., Ann Arbor, 1987-88; chief Mohs micrographic surgery and laser surgery Yale U. Sch. Medicine, New Haven, 1988—, dir. Yale skin cancer detection program, 1988—, med. dir. faculty practice plan, 1996-98, prof. dermatology, plastic surgery and otolaryngology, 1998—, assoc. dean clin. affairs, 1999-2000; dir. Yale Med. Group, New Haven, 1999—; sr. assoc. dean clin. affairs Yale U. Sch. Medicine, New Haven, 2001—05, dep. dean clin. affairs, 2005—. Sci. advisor Nat. Hereditary Hemorrhagic Telangiectasia Found., New Haven, 1991—99; bd. dirs. Am. Coll. Mohs Micrographic Surgery and Cutaneous Oncology, Artspace. Author: Manual of Skin Surgery, 1996, Total Skin: The Definitive Guide to Whole Skin Care for Life, 2000; contbg. editor Jour. Dermatologic Surgery and Oncology, 1992-97; assoc. editor Med. and Surg. Dermatology; mem. editl. bd. Archives of Dermatology, Jour. Aesthetic Dermatology and Cosmetic Surgery, 1999—; assoc. editor Skin and Aging, 1996-98; editor: Faculty of 1000; inventor laser fluorescence device to measure photoaging; patent: PTC skin cancer gene, 2003. Bd. dirs. Conn. Pub. TV, 2001-04, Artspace, NH, 2007-. Recipient Frederic Mohs award Skin Cancer Found., 1988, 91. Mem. Conn. Dermatology Soc. (pres.). Home: 460 St Ronan St New Haven CT 06511-2251 Office: Yale Sch Medicine PO Box 208059 New Haven CT 06520-8059 Office Phone: 203-785-7999. Business E-Mail: david.leffell@yale.edu.

LEFFERTS, GEORGE, television producer; b. Paterson, NJ; BA in English, U. Mich., 1942. Exec. prodr., writer, dir. NBC, 1947-57; pres. George Lefferts Assocs., 1968—; exec. prodr. ABC, 1966-67, Time-Life Films, 1980-81; tchr. John Hopkins U., Balt., 1989-90, Rutgers U., 1992—; prodr., writer, dir. Network for Continuing Med. Edn., 1990—95. Program cons. ABC, 1981. Exhibited sculpture, Sculpture Gallery, N.Y.C., 1960; producer: series Report from America, U.S. Dept. State, Tactic, Am. Cancer Soc., others; (Recipient Nat. Media award 1961, Fame award 1962, Fgn. Press award 1963, Golden Globe award 1967, Plaudit award Producers Guild 1968, 69, Cine Golden Eagle award 1974, Peabody award 1970, 75, 1st prize San Francisco Film Festival 1970; nominee Humanitas Prize 1988); author: plays Nantucket Legend, 1960, The Boat, 1968, Hey Everybody, 1969; columnist N.Y. Observer, Litchfield County Times, 1984-87 (1st place New England Journalism award, 1984, 85); also author mag. articles, works on piano method, syndicated columns, others; prodns. include Biographies in Sound (Peabody award 1956), NBC Theatre, (Ohio State award 1955), Kraft Theatre, Armstrong Circle Theatre, Studio One, Lights Out, Frank Sinatra Show; spl. program Pain, 1971, Bravo Picasso!, 1972, What Price Health; program NBC Investigative Reports, 1972 (Albert Lasker award), CBS, Ben Franklin Series (Peabody award 1975, Emmy award 1975), Ryan's Hope, 1977 (Emmy award 1977), Purex Specials, 1966 (Emmy award 1966), The People vs. Jean Harris, 1981; exec. prodr., writer, dir., NBC, Spls. for Women (2 Emmy awards 1965); series (Emmy award 1962), 1961 (Golden Globe award 1961); exec. prodr.: series Breaking Point, 1962-64 (Prodrs. Guild Plaudit award 1963), CBS, Smithsonian Spls., 1974-75, ABC, Wide World of Entertainment, 1973-74, Bing Crosby Prodns., 1962-64; exec. prodr.: Wolper Prodns., 1974-75, Time/Life Films, 1978-79; original films produced include: The Living End, 1959, The Stake, 1960, The Teenager, 1965, The Harness, 1972, The Night They Took Miss Beautiful, 1977, Bud & Lou, 1978, Mean Dog Blues, 1979, The Search for Alexander the Great, 1981, Dressed to Kill, 1980; prodr.: series Hallmark Hall of Fame, 1969-70, Never Say Goodbye, 1987 (Emmy award 1988, Humanitas award nomination 1988), TV play Teacher, Teacher, 1974 (Emmy award 1974). With AUS, 1942-45. William Rose scholar Drew U., 1940. Mem. NATAS, Am. Acad. Motion Picture Arts and Scis., Christopher Morley Knothole Assn. Clubs: South Bay Cruising (Babylon, (N.Y.).

LEFFERTS, GILLET, JR., architect; b. NYC, May 6, 1923; s. Gillet and Helen Willets (Lambert) L.; m. Lucia Beverly Hollerith, Apr. 21, 1951; children: Helena Gillet (dec.), Robert Beverly, John Willets, Sarah Fox, David Hollerith. AB, Williams Coll., 1947; MFA, Princeton, 1950. Apprentice Moore & Hutchins, NYC, 1947-48, 50-55, assoc., 1955-66, ptnr., 1967-72, Hutchins, Evans & Lefferts, NYC, 1972-89; mem. The Hall Partnership, Archs., LLP, NYC, 1990—. Instr. Mechanics Inst., N.Y.C., 1955-58. Prin. works include SUNY-Binghamton, Buffalo, master plan Coll. Agr., Malaya, St. Johnland Nursing Home, L.I., N.Y., Clark Gymnasium, Cooperstown, N.Y., Nat. Baseball Hall of Fame and Mus. Expansion, Cooperstown, Scholes Libr. Coll. Ceramics, Alfred U., Ice Arena, Broome CC, Binghamton. Mem. zoning bd. appeals Town of Darien, Conn., 1961-69, mem. planning and zoning commn., 1969-77, chmn., 1973-77, mem. bd. selectmen, 1983-89; bd. dirs. Darien Hist. Soc., 1978-83, pres., 1982-83; trustee Darien Pub. Libr., 1991-97; bd. dirs. Darien Nature Ctr., 1997-2004, pres., chmn. 1999-2001. With USAAF, 1943-46. Decorated Air medal with oak leaf cluster. Fellow AIA; mem. Fairfield County Alumni Assn. Williams Coll. (v.p. 1965-67), Nat. Inst. Archtl. Edn. (chmn. bd. trustees 1963-65, treas. 1970-73), Soc. Alumni Williams Coll. (exec. com. 2004-07), Williams Club N.Y.C., Delta Psi. Episcopalian. Office: 42 E 21st St New York NY 10010-7216 Home Phone: 203-655-2327; Office Phone: 212-777-2090. Business E-Mail: glefferts@hallarchitect.com.

LEFFERTS, WILLIAM GEOFFREY, internist, educator; b. Towanda, Pa., Mar. 24, 1943; s. William LeRoy and Beatrice (Smith) L.; m. Susan Lynn Hiles, Oct. 31, 1970. BA, Hamilton Coll., 1965; MD, Hahnemann Med. Coll., 1969. Intern Hahnemann Hosp., 1969-70; resident in internal medicine Cleve. Clinic Hosp., 1970-73, chief med. resident, 1972-73; asst. prof. internal medicine Hahnemann Med. Coll., 1973-77; assoc. prof. Med. Coll. Pa., 1978-82, dir. primary care unit, 1978-82, dir. div. gen. internal medicine, 1979-82; staff physician Cleve. Clinic Found., 1982—. Fellow ACP. Office: 9500 Euclid Ave Cleveland OH 44195-0001

LEFFLER, CAROLE ELIZABETH, retired women's and mental health nurse; b. Sidney, Ohio, Feb. 18, 1942; d. August B. and Delores K. Aselage; children: Veronica, Christopher. ADN, Sinclair C.C., Dayton, Ohio, 1975. Cert. psychiat. nurse supr. Nurse Grandview Hosp, Dayton, 1961—76; substitute sch. nurse Fairborn City Schs., Ohio, 1981—82; dir. nursing Fairborn Nursing Home, 1983; supr. psychiat. nurse Twin Valley Behavioral Health Ctr., 1984—; ret., 2006. Mem. exec. bd. 1199; chmn. disaster mental health com. ARC Ohio. Vol., instr., disaster health nurse ARC, chmn. State of Ohio disaster mental health com.; officer, leader, camp nurse for Girl Scouts, Boy Scouts; Ch. Parish Coun. Recipient Fleur de Lis award Girl and Boy Scouts, Svc. award ARC, Fairborn Mayor's Cert. of Merit for Civic Pride, State of Ohio Govs. award Innovation Ohio, Ohio State Gov.'s award for assistance in N.Y.C. disaster, 2001. Mem. ANA, Ohio Nurses Assn., BPOE and Women of the Moose. Home: 1711 Port Jefferson Rd Sidney OH 45365-1939

LEFFLER, JEAN RIISE, religious organization administrator; b. NYC, Mar. 5, 1949; d. Morris Mike and Muriel Rita Riise; m. David Lawrence Leffler, Oct. 17, 1946; children: Catherine, Virginia. AA in Comml. Art, Palm Beach C.C., 1968; BS in Bus. magna cum laude, Ctrl. Baptist Coll., 2002; BA in Theology, St. Gregory's U., 2003. Sr. citizen meal site supr. West Ctrl Ind. Econ. Devel. Dist., Terre Haute, Ind., 1983—86; sr. citizen ctr. dir. Shelby Sr. Svcs., Shelbyville, 1986—93; tech. writer Leisure Arts, Little Rock, 1993—95; activity dir. St. Andrews Pl., Conway, Ark., 1995—97; asst. cmty. dir. Outlook Pointe Assisted Living, Maumelle, Ark., 1997—98; social svc., mktg. dir. Faulkner Nursing & Rehab. Ctr., Conway, Ark., 1998—2000; dir. religious edn. St. Joseph Cath. Ch., Conway, Ark., 2000—. Profl. workshop leader, facilitator, Ark., 1998—2004. Author (designer): (nat. publs.) Crafts, Crafting Traditions, Etc., 1978—99, (booklet) Leisure Arts Publications, 1995, newspaper articles. Leadership at county and state level 4-H, Ind., 1988—93; com. chair Ptnrs. for Pinnacle, Little Rock, 1993—99; sec. Union Pacific Employees Club #54, Little Rock, 1998—2000; adv. coun. Hospice Home Care, Conway, Ark., 2002—; profl. workshop leader Diocese of Little Rock, 2002—. Republican. Roman Catholic. Avocations: historical reenactment 1840s, gardening, writing. Home: 33 Bernard Dr Conway AR 72032 Office: St Joseph Cath Ch 1115 College Ave Conway AR 72032 Office Phone: 501-513-6812.

LEFFLER, MARVIN, foundation administrator, writer; s. Saul Leffler and Bertha Cohen; m. Charlotte K. Frank, Dec. 23, 1989; m. Shirley Schleicher, Sept. 3, 1944 (dec. Sept. 15, 1988); children: Bruce, Nancy. BS, NYU, 1942, MBA, 1951. Pres. Continous Sales Corp., LI, NY, 1945—92, Flexible Fabricators, Inc., Port Jervis, NY, 1954—90, Town Hall Found., NYC, 1978—. Pres. Nat. Coun. Sales Orgn., NYC, 1960—85. Author: How To Become A Successful Sales Rep, 1951, How To Increase Your Sales Volume, 1954. Mem. policy com. for disciplinary com. first appellate divsn. Ct. of Appeals, 2004—; mem. midtown com. Mayor, NYC, 1980—. Sgt. US Army, 1942—46. Named Disting. Alumnus award, NYU, 2005; recipient Presdl. citation, 1990. Mem.: NYU Alumni Assn. (pres. 1984, exec. com., pres. 2000), Am. Arbitration Assn. (panelist 1970—), Fenway Golf Club (dir. 2004—). Avocations: golf, travel, writing. Office: Town Hall 123 West 43rd St New York NY 10036 Business E-Mail: MLeffler@the-townhall-nyc.org.

LEFFLER, MELVYN P., history professor; b. NYC, May 31, 1945; s. Louis and Mollie (Fuchs) L.; m. Phyllis Koran, Sept. 1, 1968; children: Sarah Ann, Elliot. BS, Cornell U., 1966; PhD, Ohio State U., 1972. Asst. prof. Vanderbilt U., Nashville, 1972-77, assoc. prof., 1977-86; Coun. Fgn. Rels. internat. affairs fellow Dept. Def., Washington, 1979-80; prof. U. Va., Charlottesville, 1986-94, Edward R. Stettinius prof. history, 1994—, chmn. hist. dept., 1990-95, Edward R. Stettinius prof. history dept., 1995-97, dean Coll. and Grad. Sch. Arts and Scis., 1997-2001. Harmsworth prof. Am. history Oxford (Eng.) U., 2002-03; Henry Kissinger chair Libr. Congress, 2005. Author: The Elusive Quest, 1979, A Preponderance of Power, 1992 (Bancroft, Ferrell & Hoover prizes 1993), The Specter of Communism, 1994; contbr. articles to profl. jours. Fellow Woodrow Wilson Internat. Ctr., 1979, 2001-02, Am. Coun. Learned Socs., 1984, Nobel Peace Inst., 1994, 98, U.S. Inst. Peace, 2004-2005. Mem. Am. Hist. Assn., Orgn. Am. Hists., Soc. Hists. Am. Fgn. Rels. (v.p. 1993, pres. 1994, Bernath Article prize 1984). Jewish. Home: 1612 Concord Dr Charlottesville VA 22901-3135 Office: U Va Dept History PO Box 400180 Charlottesville VA 22904-0180

LEFKOW, JOAN HUMPHREY, federal judge; b. Kans., Jan. 9, 1944; d. Otis L. and Donna Grace (Glenn) Humphrey; m. Michael F. Lefkow (dec. 2005), June 21, 1975 AB, Wheaton Coll., 1965; JD, Northwestern U., 1971. Bar: Ill. 1971, U.S. Dist. Ct. (no. dist.) Ill. 1972, U.S. Ct. Appeals (7th cir.) 1972, U.S. Ct. Appeals (5th cir.) 1980. Law clerk to Hon. Thomas E. Fairchild U.S. Ct. Appeals (7th cir.), 1974—75; atty. Legal Assistance Found. Chgo., 1975—79; adminstrv. law judge Ill. Fair Employment Practices Commn., 1975—77; instr. sch. law U. Miami, Fla., 1980—81; exec. dir. Cook County Legal Assistance Found., 1981—82; magistrate judge U.S. Dist. Ct. (no. dist.) Ill., 1982—96; judge U.S. Bankruptcy Ct. (no. dist.) Ill., 1997—2000. Mem. editl. bd. Northwestern U. Law Rev. Mem. Chgo. Bar Assn. (Alliance for Women 1992—), Chgo. Coun. Lawyers (gov. bd. 1975-77), 7th Cir. Bar Assn. Episcopalian. Office: Everett McKinley Dirksen Bldg Ste 1956 219 S Dearborn St Chicago IL 60604

LEFKOWITZ, ALAN ZOEL, retired lawyer; b. Pitts., Dec. 1, 1932; s. Curtis and Lily Rose Lefkowitz; m. Francine Marcia Kaplan, Feb. 5, 1956; children: Curtis Robert, Gail Ann, David Edward. AB, U. Pitts., 1953; JD, U. Mich., 1955. Bar: Pa. 1956, U.S. Supreme Ct. 1959, U.S. Ct. Appeals (3d cir.), U.S. Dist. Ct. (we. dist.) Pa., U.S. Tax Ct. Assoc. Kaplan, Finkel & Roth, Pitts., 1955-72; mng. ptnr. Kaplan, Finkel, Lefkowitz, Roth & Ostrow, Pitts., 1972-82, Finkel Lefkowitz Ostrow & Woolridge, Pitts., 1982-88; ptnr., head corp. sect. Tucker Arenberg, P.C., Pitts., 1988-93; dir. Kabala & Geeseman, Pitts., 1993-99. Adj. prof. arts and law Heinz Sch. Pub. Policy and Adminstrn./Carnegie Mellon U., instr. Shakespeare and digital photography 2001—,Acad. Lifelong Learning, bd. dirs., 2003—, treas., 2007—,; sec. TPC Comm., Inc., Pitts., 1970-91, Computer Rsch., Inc., Pitts., 1969-92, Star-Tron Tech., Inc., Pitts., 1986-92. Active Pitts. Coun. Internat. Visitors; trustee United Jewish Fedn. Pitts., 1964-68, Rodef Shalom Congregation, Pitts., 1962-64, 90-98; bd. dirs., treas., v.p. Jewish Family and Childrens Svcs., Pitts., 1967-68; chair adv. com. Rauh Jewish Archives, 2004-07; bd. dirs. Family Resources, 1986, U.S. Counter-Intelligence Corp. With U.S. Army, 1956-59. Mem. AAAS (trustee 2005—, pres. 2007—), ABA, Internat. Assn. Fin. Planners (Pitts. chpt. v.p. ethics regulation), Internat. Assn. Jewish Lawyers, Pa. Bar Assn., Allegheny County Bar Assn. (former chair arts law sect., former chair, coun. corp. sec., chair securities regulation com., former chair internat. com.), Photo-imagers Guild, Acad. Arts and Scis. (pres. photography sect. 2007—, bd. dirs. 1994), Silver Eye Ctr. for Photography (trustee, sec.). Avocations: photography, theater. Personal E-mail: alllaw@hotmail.com.

LEFKOWITZ, DAVID S., lawyer; b. NYC, Nov. 3, 1960; BS, Northwestern U., 1982; JD cum laude, Georgetown U., 1986. Bar: NY 1987. Ptnr. Weil, Gotshal & Manges, NYC, co-head capital markets group. Named a Leading Capital Markets Lawyer, Chambers USA, 2005; named an Am. Lawyer Dealmaker of Yr., 2004; named one of 40 Under 40 for Rising Stars in Law, Nat. Law Jour., 1995. Office: Weil Gotshal & Manges 767 Fifth Ave New York NY 10153 Office Phone: 212-310-8000. Office Fax: 212-310-8007. Business E-Mail: david.lefkowitz@weil.com.

LEFKOWITZ, HOWARD N., lawyer; b. Utica, NY, Oct. 28, 1936; s. Samuel I. and Sarah Lefkowitz; m. Martha Yelon, June 16, 1958; children: Sarah, David. BA, Cornell U., 1958; LLB, Columbia U., 1963. Bar: N.Y. 1963. Ptnr. Proskauer Rose LLP, NYC, 1963—. Cons. in field. Co-author: New York LLC and LLP Forms and Practice Manual, Data Trace, rev. edit. 2003; co-author: Transactional Lawyers Deskbook: Advising Business Entities West, 2001; editor Columbia Law Rev., 1963; contbg. editor Encyclopedia of Private and Venture Capital. Lt. (j.g.) USN, 1958-61. Kent scholar, Columbia U. Law Sch. Mem.: Tri Bar Opinion Com., N.Y. Pvt. Investment Funds Forum (chmn. 2004), N.Y. County Lawyers Assn. (chmn. com. on comm. entertainment and arts-related law 1983—86), Assn. Bar City of N.Y. (chmn. com. on corp. law 1990—93, com. on corp. law 1997—2000), ABA (mem. partnership and uninc. bus. orgns. 1993—, legal opionions 1995—). Office: Proskauer Rose LLP 1585 Broadway Fl 23 New York NY 10036-8299

LEFKOWITZ, IVAN MARTIN, lawyer; b. Winston-Salem, NC, Jan. 4, 1952; s. Ernest W. and Matilda C. (Center) L.; m. Fern Deutsch, Apr. 14, 1972; children: Aaron M., Shira B. BBA, U. Ctrl. Fla., Orlando, 1973; JD, U. Miami, Coral Gables, 1976; LLM Estate Planning, 1980. Bar: Fla. 1979, US Dist. Ct. (mid. dist.) 1980, US Tax. Ct. 1980; CPA, Fla. Sr. acct. Alexander Grant & Co. CPA, Orlando, Fla., 1974-76; assoc. Gray, Harris & Robinson P.A., Orlando, 1980-82; pvt. practice, Orlando, 1982-88; ptnr. Lefkowitz & Miner, P.A., Orlando, 1988-93; sr. ptnr. Lefkowitz & Bloom, P.A., Orlando, 1993—2005, Lefkowitz & Shaw, P.A., 2005—. Adj. prof. Am. Coll., Denver, 1984-90, Mgmt. Inst., U. Ctrl. Fla., Orlando, 1988—; sec., dir. Employee Benefits Coun. Fla., 1987-89, pres., 1990. Mem. dean's exec. coun. U. Ctrl. Fla. Coll. of Bus., 2000—; mem. governing bd. Princeton Hosp., Orlando, 1997—98; mem. Ctrl. Fla. Estate Planning Coun.; treas. Holocaust Meml. Resource and Edn. Ctr. Ctrl. Fla., 2000—01; mem. U. Ctrl. Fla. Found. Orlando, 1981—96, 2001—; U. Ctrl. Fla. Found. Orlando, 1981—96; bd. dirs., pres. Nat. Kidney Found. Ctrl. Fla., Orlando and Tampa, 1984—91. Recipient Induction to Coll. of Bus.

Adminstrn. Hall of Fame, U. Ctrl. Fla., 2001. Democrat. Office: 430 N Mills Ave Orlando FL 32803-5746 Home Phone: 407-647-6573; Office Phone: 407-425-1974. Business E-Mail: firm@orlandolaw.org, lefkowitz@orlandolaw.org.

LEFKOWITZ, JEROME, lawyer; b. NYC, Mar. 24, 1931; s. Jack and Sue (Horowitz) L.; m. Myrna Judith Weishaut, Aug. 12, 1956; children: Jay, Mark, Miriam, Alan. Student, Jewish Theol. Sem., NYC, 1948-51; BA, NYU, 1952; JD, Columbia U., 1955. Bar: NY 1955, US Dist. Ct. (so. and ea. dists.) NY 1990. Asst. atty. gen. NY State Dept. Law, Albany, 1958-60; counsel, dep. commissioner NY State Dept. Labor, NYC, 1960—67, Albany, 1960—67; dep. chmn., mem. NY Pub. Rels. Bd., Albany, 1967—87; dep. counsel Civil Svc. Employment Assn., Albany, 1987—2007; chmn. Pub. Employment Relations Bd., Albany, 2007—. Adj. faculty Albany Law Sch., Columbia U., NYC, 1968-89; cons. in field. Author: Public Employee Unionism In Israel, 1971; editor: Public Sector Labor & Employment Law, 1988, 2d edit., 1998, The Evolving Process--Collective Negotiations In Public Employment, 1985. Chmn. cmty. rels. com. Albany Jewish Fedn., 1980-84, 86-87; pres. Massad Hebrew Speaking Camps. Mem. NY State Bar Assn. (chmn. com. on pub. sector labor rels. 1975-79, chmn. com. on legis. 1980-83, chmn. labor law sect. 1991-92). Republican. Avocations: tennis, skiing, reading, history. Home: 54 Maxwell St Albany NY 12208-1639 Office: Pub Employment Relations Bd 80 Wolf Rd 5th Fl Albany NY 12205 Home Phone: 518-482-7169; Office Phone: 518-457-2578. Business E-Mail: jlefkowitz@perb.state.ny.us.

LEFKOWITZ, ROBERT JOSEPH, biomedical researcher, educator; b. NYC, Apr. 15, 1943; s. Max and Rose (Levine) Lefkowitz; m. Lynn Tilley, May 26, 1991. BA, Columbia Coll., NYC, 1962; MD, Columbia U. Coll. Physicians and Surgeons, NYC, 1966. Diplomate Am. Bd. Internal Medicine. Assoc. prof. medicine Duke U. Med. Ctr., Durham, NC, 1973—77, prof. medicine, 1977—, James B. Duke prof. medicine, 1982—, prof. biochemistry, 1985—. Investigator Howard Hughes Med. Inst., Durham, 1976—; vis. prof. NYU, 1996. Author: Receptor Binding Studies in Adrenergic Pharmacology, 1978, Receptor Regulation, 1981, Principles of Biochemistry, 1983. Named Am. Heart Assn. established investigator, 1973—76; recipient Basic Rsch. prize, 1990, Young Scientist award, Passano Found., 1978, George Thorn award, Howard Hughes Med. Inst., 1979, Oppenheimer award, 1982, Gordon Wilson medal, Am. Clin. and Climatol. Assn., 1982, Lita Annenberg Hazen award, 1983, Outstanding Rsch. award, Internat. Soc. Health Rsch., 1985, H.B. van Dyke award, Coll. Physicians and Surgeons Columbia U., 1986, Steven C. Beering award, Ind. U. Sch. Medicine, 1986, NC award in sci., 1987, Internat. award, Gairdner Found., 1988, Novo Nordsk Biotechnology award, 1990, Biomedical Rsch. award, Assn. Am. Med. Colls., 1990, City of Medecin award, NC, 1991, Alumnus award for disting. achievement in cardiovasc. rsch., Columbia U. Coll. of Physicians and Surgeons, 1992, The Giovani Lorenzini prize for basic biomedical rsch., 1992, Joseph Mather Smith prize, Columbia U. Coll. Physicians and Surgeons, 1993, The Endocrine Soc. Gerald D. Aurbach Lectr. award, Inst. of Medicine NAS, 1995, J. David Gladstone Insts. Disting. Lecture award, 1996, Ciba award, Hypertension Rsch. award, 1996, Glorney-Raisbeck award in cardiology, N.Y. Acad. Medicine, 1997, Novartis/Drew award in biomed. rsch., 2000, F.E. Shideman-Sterling award, U. Minn., 2001, Louis and Artur Lucian award for rsch. in circulatory disease, 2001, Peter Harris Disting. Scientist award, Internat. Soc. for Heart Rsch., 2001, 15th Ann. Pasarow Cardiovasc. Rsch. award, The Robert J. and Claire Pasarow Found., 2002, Bio/Tech. Winter Symposia Feodor Lynen award, Medal of Merit, Internat. Acad. Cardiovasc. Scis., 2003, IPSEN Endocrinology prize, Found. IPSEN, Paris, 2003, Found. Lefoulon-Delalande Grand Prize for Sci. award, Inst. France, 2003, Founding Disting. Scientist award, Am. Heart Assn., 2003, Herbert Tabor Lecture award, Am. Soc. Biol. Chemistry and Molecular Biology, 2004, Shaw prize, Life Sci. and Medicine, Shaw Prize Found., 2007;, Internat. Acad. Cardiovasc. Scis., 2002. Mem.: NAS (coun. mem., Jessie Stevenson Kovalenko medal 2001), Am. Heart Assn. Basic Rsch. Soc., Am. Acad. Arts and Scis., Am. Fedn. Clin. Rsch. (mem. nat. coun. 1978—83, sec.-treas. 1980—83), Endocrine Soc. (Fred Conrad Koch award 2001), Am. Soc. Pharmacology and Exptl. Therapeutics (John J. Abel award 1978, Goodman and Gilman award 1986), Assn. Am. Physicians (treas. 1989—94, Francis Gilman Blake award 2001), Am. Soc. Clin. Investigation (counselor 1982—85, pres.-elect 1986—87, pres. 1987—88), Am. Soc. Biol. Chemists, Japanese Biochemical Soc. (hon.). Office: Duke U Med Ctr 467 Carl Bldg PO Box 3821 Durham NC 27710 Office Phone: 919-684-2974. Office Fax: 919-684-8875. E-mail: lefko001@receptor-biol.duke.edu.*

LEFLER, SHERRY LYNETTE, elementary school educator; d. Charles William and Mary Jones Ridge; m. David Donald Lefler, July 28, 1973; children: Jamie Lynn Irvin, Jacob Alan. BS in Edn., SW Tex. State U., 1972; M in Elem. Edn., Prairie View A&M U., Tex., 1977. Kindergarten endorsement SW Tex. State U. Educator Needville (Tex.) Consol. Ind. Sch. Dist., 1973—82, Lamar Consol. Ind. Sch. Dist., Rosenberg, Tex., 1982—. Trainer NJ. Writing Project in Tex., Rosenberg, 1999—; mem. Districtwide Student Improvement Coun. Lamar Consol. Ind. Sch. Dist., Rosenberg, 2002—. Named Tchr. of Yr., Travis Elem. Sch., 1992. Mem.: West Houston Area Coun. Tchrs. English (pres. 2004—), Tex. State Tchrs. Assn. (rec. sec. 1973—74), Tex. Classroom Tchrs. Assn. (assoc.), Delta Kappa Gamma (rec. sec. 1993—95). Home: 1500 Band Rd Rosenberg TX 77471 Office: Lamar Consolidated Independent School Di 3911 Avenue I Rosenberg TX 77471 Home Phone: 281-232-2324.

LEFLER, WADE HAMPTON, JR., ophthalmologist; b. Statesville, NC, Feb. 27, 1937; s. Wade Hampton and Eunice Trudye (Chilcoat) L.; m. Katherine Webb Davis, Apr. 1, 1961; children: Elizabeth Ashley Wilson, Rosemary Kirsten, Ririe. AB, U. NC, 1959; MD, Bowman Gray Sch. Medicine, 1963. Diplomate Am. Bd. Ophthalmology. Intern N.Y. Hosp./Cornell Med. Ctr., 1963-64; resident in ophthalmology Duke U. Med. Ctr., Durham, N.C., 1966-69; practice medicine specializing in ophthalmology, Hickory, N.C., 1969—; ptnr. Graystone Eye, Ear, Nose and Throat Ctr., Hickory, 1974—; clin. assoc. prof. ophthalmology Duke Med. Ctr., 1969—. Mem. staff Catawba Meml. Hosp., Hickory, Frye Regional Med. Ctr., Hickory, Western Carolina Center, Morganton, N.C., Duke Eye Center, Durham, N.C., Oteen VA Hosp., Asheville, N.C. Trustee Catawba Meml. Hosp., 1990-94. Served to capt. M.C., U.S. Army, 1964-66. Duke U. Med. Ctr. grantee, 1968-70. Mem. AMA, N.C. Med. Soc., Catawba County Med. Soc., Med. Alumni Assn. Bowman Gray Sch. Medicine (pres. 1993, Disting. Svc. award 1995), Lake Hickory Country Club, Phi Beta Kappa, Alpha Omega Alpha. Presbyterian. Home: 1260 6th St NW Hickory NC 28601-2408 Office: PO Box 2588 Hickory NC 28603-2588 E-mail: khlefler@charter.net.

LEFRAK, EDWARD ARTHUR, cardiovascular and thoracic surgeon; b. Newark, Apr. 21, 1943; s. Bernard David and Lillian (Hollander) L.; m. Trudy Glaser, Aug. 8, 1973; children: Lisa, Allison, Shayna, Ashley, Mikaela. BA cum laude, SUNY, Buffalo, 1965; MD, Ind. U., 1969. Diplomate Am. Bd. Surgery, Am. Bd. Thoracic Surgery. Intern in gen. surgery Baylor Coll. Medicine Affiliated Hosps., Houston, 1969-70, resident in gen. surgery, 1970-75; resident cardiopulmonary surgery U. Oreg. Med. Sch., 1975-77; med. dir. cardiac surgery Inova Heart and Vascular Inst., Falls Church, Va., 1977—; assoc. dir. cardiac surgery rsch. Inova Heart Ctr. at Fairfax Hosp., Falls Church, Va.; pres. Cardiovascular and Thoracic Surgery Assocs., P.C., Annandale, Va.; med. dir. cardiac surgery Inova Heart and Vascular Inst., Falls Church, Va.; clin. assoc. profl. surgery Uniformed Svcs. U. Health Scis., Bethesda, Md.; asst. clin. prof. surgery Georgetown U. Sch. Medicine, Washington; active staff Cardio-Thoracic Surgery Svc. Nat. Naval Med. Ctr., Bethesda; prof. surgery Inova campus Va. Commonwealth U. Sch. Medicine, Falls Church. Asst. prof. surgery U. Oreg. Med. Sch., 1977; mem. courtesy staff Alexandria (Va.) Hosp.; active staff Arlington (Va.) Hosp., Alexandria (Va.) Hosp.; cons. Clin. Ctr. NIH, Bethesda; mem. med. adv. com. Washington Regional Transplant Consortium; dir. heart and lung transplantation Va. Heart Ctr. Fairfax, 1986-96; mem. critical care com. Fairfax Hosp., 1978-93; jour. cons. Chest, Cancer Chemotherapy Reports, Ann. Thor. Surg. Author: Cardiac Valve Prostheses, 1979; prodr. films in field; contbr. articles to profl. publs. Fellow ACS, Am. Coll. Cardiology, Am. Coll. Chest Physicians, Internat. Coll. Surgeons; mem. AMA, Am. Heart Assn. (bd. dirs. No. Va. chpt. 1978), Albert Starr Surg. Soc., Fairfax County Med. Soc., Med. Soc. Va., Met. Washington Soc. Thoracic and Cardiovascular Surgeons, Michael E. DeBakey Internat. Cardiovascular Soc., Soc. Thoracic Surgeons, Internat. Soc. for Heart and Lung Transplantation, So. thoracic Surg. Assn., Washington Area Transplant Soc., Am. Assn. Thoracic Surgery, Colegio Interamericano de Médicos y Cirujanos. Address: 2921 Telestar Ct Falls Church VA 22042 Office Phone: 703-280-5858. Business E-Mail: edward.lefrak@inova.com.

LEFTON, IRA S., lawyer; b. Pitts., June 23, 1952; BA in English cum laude, Yale U., 1974; JD with honors, U. NC, 1978. Bar: Pa. 1978. Joined Reed Smith LLP, 1978, now ptnr., chair firmwide pro bono com. Phila. Sec. bd. dirs. Citizens for the Arts in PA. Rotary Internat. Found. Grad. Fellow, 1974—75. Mem.: Allegheny County Bar Assn. (co-founder & past pres. arts and law com.), Pa. Bar Assn. Office: Reed Smith LLP 2500 One Liberty Pl 1650 Market St Philadelphia PA 19103 Office Phone: 215-851-8236. Office Fax: 215-851-1420. Business E-Mail: ilefton@reedsmith.com.

LEFTON, LESTER ALAN, academic administrator, psychology professor; b. Brookline, Mass., July 27, 1946; s. Bernard and Sylvia (Bernstein) L.; m. Linda J. Levine, June 7, 1969; children: Sarah, Jesse. BA in Psychology, Northeastern U., 1969; PhD in Psychology, U. Rochester, NYC, 1974. Asst. prof. psychology U. SC, Columbia, 1972—75, assoc. prof., 1975—80, prof., 1980—82, dir. grad. studies, 1982-84, dir. undergraduate edn., 1985-87, chmn. Psychology Dept., 1986-94, dean Coll. Liberal Arts, 1994—97; prof., dean Columbian Sch. Arts and Scis. George Washington U., Washington, 1997—2001; provost, sr. v.p. academic affairs Tulane U., New Orleans, 2001—06; pres. Kent State U., Ohio, 2006—. Mem. Harvard Univ.'s Mgmt. Devel. program; mem. Coun. Acad. Deans; mem. Coun. Colls. Arts and Scis. Author: Introductory Psychology, 6th edit., 1996; co-author: Mastering Psychology, 4th edit., 1992. Pres. Tree of Life Congregation, Columbia, 1983-84. Fellow: APA; mem. Optical Soc. Am., Psychonomic Soc., Southeastern Psychol. Assn. Jewish. Avocations: bicycling, photography. Office: Kent State U Office of Pres Kent OH 44242 Office Phone: 330-672-2210. E-mail: lefton@kent.edu.

LEFTWICH, BYRON ANTRON, professional football player; b. Jan. 14, 1980; Quarterback Jacksonville Jaguars, Fla., 2003—. Finalist Offensive Player of Yr award, Walter Camp Nat.; recipient Vern Smith Leadership award, Mid-Am. Conf., Offensive Player of Yr. award. Office: Jacksonville Jaguars 1 Alltel Stadium Pl Jacksonville FL 32202

LEFURGY, RICH, advertising executive; BS, Syracuse U. With Starwave Corp., 1995; co-founder Interactive Advt. Bur., 1996, chmn., 1996—2001, mem. exec. com., chmn. emeritus; ptnr. WaldenVC, San Francisco, 1999—2005; prin. Archer Advisors; chmn. bd. X+1, NYC, 2005—. Founding chmn. Bay Area Interactive Group; dir. Web Clients; bd. mem. Adtech Adv. Bd. Named to Interactive Hall of Fame, Advertising Age, 2000. Office: Archer Advisors One Bush St 12th Fl San Francisco CA 94104 also: X+1 470 Park Ave S Ste 7N New York NY 10016 E-mail: rich@archeradvisors.com.

LEGATES, JOHN CREWS BOULTON, information scientist; b. Boston, Nov. 19, 1940; s. Eber Thomson and Sybil Rowe (Crews) LeGates; m. Nancy Elizabeth Boulton, Apr. 28, 1993. BA in Math., Harvard U., 1962. Edn. svcs. mgr. Bolt Beranek & Newman, Cambridge, Mass., 1966-67; v.p. Washington Engring. Svcs., Cambridge, 1967-69; v.p., co-founder Cambridge Info. Systems, 1968-69; v.p., founder Computer Adv. Svc. to Edn., Wayland, Mass., 1966-72; exec. dir. Educom Interuniversity Communications Coun., Boston, 1969-72; founder, mng. dir. Program on Info. Resources Policy Harvard U., 1973—, founder, pres. Ctr. Info. Policy Rsch., 1978—. Mem. Arpanet NWG, core Arpanet/Internet design team, 1970-72; U.S. del. First World Conf. on Computer Comms., Amsterdam, 1970; cons. in field; pioneer ednl. computing. Photo exhbn., Boston Mus. Fine Arts; contbr. articles to profl. jours. Bd. dirs. Nat. Telecommunications Conf., Washington, 1979. Kent fellow, 1964. Mem. NAS/NRC (panelist), IEEE, NSF, Soc. for Values in Higher Edn., Nashoba Valley Hunt Club (pres. 1974-80). Unitarian Universalist. Achievements include pioneering educational computers, building world's first hospital integrated information system at Mass. Gen. Hosp. Corp. Bds. Avocations: sailing, foxhunting, mountain climbing, classical music. Home: PO Box 6331 Lincoln MA 01773-6331 Office Phone: 617-495-4114.

LEGENDRE, LOUIS, oceanographer, educator, research scientist; b. Montreal, Que., Can., 1945; s. Vianney and Marguerite Legendre. BA, U. Montreal, 1964, BSc, 1967; PhD, Dalhousie U., Halifax, 1971; Doctorat honoris causa, U. Liege, 1997. Postdoctoral fellow U. Paris VI, Villefranche-sur-Mer, France, 1971-73; rsch. assoc. U. Laval, Quebec City, Que., Canada, 1973, asst. prof., 1974-77, assoc. prof., 1977-81, prof., 1981-2000, emeritus prof., 2001—; rsch. prof. CNRS, France, 2000—; dir. Villefranche-sur-Mer Oceanography Lab., 2001—; dep. sci. dir. European Network Excellence EUR-OCEANS, 2004—. V.p. Groupe Interuniversitaire de Recherches Océanographiques du Que., 1989—2000; group chmn. Natural Scis. and Engring. Rsch. Coun. Can., Ottawa, 1989—92; mem. sci. adv. group Intergovernmental Oceanographic Commn., 2005—. Author (with P. Legendre): (book) Numerical Ecology, 1983, 1998; author: Scientific Research and Discovery: Process, Consequences and Practice, 2004; contbr. articles to profl. jours. V.p. Model Environ., Liege, Belgium, 1993—; mem. standing adv. group Nuclear Applications Internat. Atomic Energy Agy., 2005—. Decorated Knight of Malta; recipient Léo-Pariseau award, Assn. Canadienne-Française pour l'Avancement des Scis., 1985, Michel-Jurdant award, 1986, Que. Sci. prize, Pure and Applied Scis., 1997, Excellence in Ecology prize, Internat. Ecology Inst., 2001; fellow Killam Rsch., Can. Coun., 1996—98. Fellow: Internat. Ecology Inst., Royal Soc. Can.; mem.: European Geosci. Union, Am. Geophys. Union, Am. Soc. Limnology and Oceanography (G. Evelyn Hutchinson award 2002). Office: LOV BP 28 06234 Villefranche-sur-Mer Cedex France Office Phone: 33 4 9376 3836. Business E-Mail: legendre@obs.vlfr.fr.

LEGG, BENSON EVERETT, federal judge; b. Balt., June 8, 1947; s. William Mercer Legg and Beverly Mason; m. Kyle Prechtl Legg; children: Jennifer, Charles, Matthew. BA in English Lit. magna cum laude, Princeton U., 1970; JD, U. Va., 1973. Bar: Md. 1973. Summer assoc. Venable, Baetjer & Howard, 1971, Goodwin, Procter & Hoar, Boston, 1972; law clk. to Hon. Frank A. Kaufman, Balt., 1973-74; assoc. Venable, Baetjer & Howard, Balt., 1975-81, ptnr., 1982-91; judge U.S. Dist. Ct., Dist. Md., Balt., 1991—2003, chief judge, 2003—. Faculty mem. Md. Inst. for Continuing Profl. Edn. of Lawyers; instr., Trial Advocacy Inst. U. Va. Editl. bd. Va. Law Review, 1971—73. Adv. bd. Nat. Aquarium, Balt., 1987—2003; trustee, mem. exec. com. and fin. com. Md. Zool. Soc., 1990—2004. Mem.: Order of Coif. Office: US Dist Ct 101 W Lombard St Ste 7A Baltimore MD 21201-2605 Office Phone: 410-962-0723.

LEGG, J. IVAN, academic administrator; BA in Chemistry, Oberlin Coll., 1960; PhD in Chemistry, U. Mich., 1965. Faculty Wash. State U., 1966—87, chair chemistry, 1978—86; dean sci. and math. Auburn U., 1987—92; provost U. Memphis, 1992—2001; exec. v.p., provost No. Ill. U., DeKalb, 2001—. NIH fellow, Harvard Med. Sch., 1972, 1973. Office: No Ill U Office Of Provost Dekalb IL 60115-2886 Office Phone: 815-753-0493. Business E-Mail: ilegg@ntu.edu.

LEGG, WILLIAM JEFFERSON, lawyer; b. Enid, Okla., Aug. 20, 1925; s. Garl Paul and Mabel (Gensman) L.; m. Eva Imogene Hill, Dec. 16, 1950; children: Melissa Lou, Eva Diane, Janet Sue. Grad., Enid Bus. Coll., 1943; student, Pittsburg State U., 1944; BBA, U. Tex., Austin, 1946; JD, U. Tulsa, 1954. Bar: Okla. 1954, US Dist. Ct. (we. dist.) Okla., US Ct. Appeals (10th cir.), US Supreme Ct. With aviation sales Phillips Petroleum Co., 1946-48; atty. Marathon Oil Co., 1954-61; pvt. practice Oklahoma City, 1962—; with Andrews Davis Legg Bixler Milsten & Price, Inc. and predecessor firms, Oklahoma City, 1962—2002, pres., 1983—86, also dir., 1973-77, 80-81, 83-86, 90, sec., 1975-80, 82-83, 90; sr. counsel, 1991—2002. Adj. prof. law Oklahoma City U., 1975-80; lectr. Okla. U. Law Sch., 1986; dir., v.p. Woods Petroleum Corp. subs., Turkey, Australia, Brunei, 1965-82; client rep. Can., Singapore, Hong Kong, Japan, China, Switzerland, Italy, England, 1968-81; USA nat. agent of Kamera Tourism, Istanbul travel agy., 1970-; dir., gen. counsel NJR Energy Corp., Wall, NJ, 1986-91; rsch. fellow The Ctr. for Am. and Internat. Law (formerly Southwestern Legal Found.), Dallas, 1989—, CLE adv. bd., 1998—; lectr. in field. Contbr. articles to profl. jours. Legal com. Okla. Gov.'s Energy Adv. Coun., 1973, Okla. Blue Ribbon Com. on Natural Gas Well Allowables, 1983; dir. Skillpath, Inc., Kansas City, Mo., 1994—98; ordained Cmty. of Christ (formerly Reorganized Ch. of Jesus Christ of Latter Day Saints), 1964, dist. pres., 1975—80, br. pres., 1986—91, evangelist, 1993—; missionary rep. in Germany, The Netherlands, England, Can. Australia, New Zealand, Tahiti, 1971—75; trustee Am. Inst. Discussion, 1962—88, chmn., 1969—72; trustee Restoration Trails Found., 1975, Jenkins Found. Rsch.; sec. Graceland U., Lamoni, Iowa, 1975—81, trustee, 1986—2000, exec. com., chmn. bus. affairs com., 1988—98, investment com., 1998—2000, trustee emeritus, 2007—; trustee Met. Lib. Endowment Trust, 1986—99, treas., 1988—99, chmn. investment com. With USN, 1943—46, lt. (j.g.) USNR, 1946—66. Mem. ABA, English Speaking Union US, Okla. Bar Assn. (past com. chmn.), Oklahoma County Bar Assn. (past com. chmn.), Internat. Bar Assn., Internat. Assn. Energy Econs., Econ. Club Okla., Men's Dinner Club, Petroleum Club. Home: 3017 Brush Creek Rd Oklahoma City OK 73120-1855

LEGGE, CHARLES ALEXANDER, federal judge; b. San Francisco, Aug. 24, 1930; s. Roy Alexander and Wilda (Rampton) L.; m. Janice Meredith Sleeper, June 27, 1952; children: Jeffrey, Nancy, Laura. AB with distinction, Stanford U., 1952, JD, 1954. Bar: Calif. 1955. Assoc. Bronson, Bronson & McKinnin, San Francisco, 1956-64, ptnr., 1964-84, chmn., 1978-84; U.S. Dist. Ct. judge U.S. Dist. Ct. (no. dist.) Calif., San Francisco, 1984—. Served with U.S. Army, 1954-56. Fellow Am. Coll. Trial Lawyers; mem. Calif. Bar Assn. (past chmn. adminstrn. justice com.). Clubs: Bohemian, World Trade (San Francisco); Orinda (Calif.) Country. Republican.

LEGGE KEMP, DIANE, architect, landscape consultant; b. Englewood, NJ, Dec. 4, 1949; d. Richard Claude and Patricia (Roney) L.; m. Kevin A. Kemp; children: Alloy Hudson, McClelland Beebe, Logan Roney. BArch, Stanford U., 1972; MArch, Princeton U., 1975. Registered arch., Ill., landscape arch., Ill. Arch. Northrop, Kaelber & Kopf, Rochester, NY, 1971—73, Michael Graves, Architect, Princeton, NJ, 1973—75, The Ehrenkrantz Group, NYC, 1975-77; ptnr. Skidmore Owings & Merrill, Chgo., 1977-89; pres. Diane Legge Kemp Architecture and Landscape Consulting, Riverside, Ill., 1993—, DLK Architecture, 1993—, DLK Civic Design. Mem. bd. govs. Sch. of Art Inst., Chgo., 1991—; dir., past pres. Soc. for Contemporary Art, Chgo., 1991—. Office: DLK Civic Design 410 S Michigan Ave Chicago IL 60605-1308 Office Phone: 312-322-2550. Business E-Mail: dleggekemp@dlkinc.com.

LEGGETT, ANN VAUGHAN, artist; b. NYC, Oct. 6, 1941; d. Stanton and Barbara Vaughan Leggett. Student, Sarah Lawrence Coll., Bronxville, NY, 1958—60, Art Student's League, 1960—63, Japan Soc. Toyota Lang. Sch., 1999—. One-woman shows include Nat. Arts Club, NY, Avery Hall, Columbia U., Edward Merrin Gallery, NY, Princeton U., C.G. Rein Gallery, Scottsdale, Ariz., Alan-Mayhew Gallery, Martha's Vineyard, Stuart Brent, Chgo., Wabash Coll., Norfolk Acad., Onslow county Arts Coun., NC, Block Island Hist. Soc., RI, Union League Club, NYC, others. Recipient Montague award, Pastel Soc. Am., NYC, 1975, Bruce Stevenson award, Nat. Arts Club, NYC, 1976. Mem.: Japanese Artists Assn. NY, Asia Soc., Japan Soc. Avocations: gardening, Japanese language and culture. Home and Office: 13-22 Jackson Ave Long Island City NY 11101 Office Phone: 718-786-9261.

LEGGETT, ANTHONY JAMES, physics professor, researcher; b. London, 1938; Student, Balliol Coll., Oxford, Eng.; degree in physics, Merton Coll., Oxford, PhD in Theoretical Physics. Mem. faculty U. Sussex (UK), 1967-71, reader, 1971-78, prof., 1978-83; John D. and Catherine T. Macarthur prof. U. Ill., Urbana-Champaign, 1983—. Rschr. Urbana, Ill., Kyoto, Japan; lectr. in field. Author: The Problems of Physics, 1987, Quantum Tunnelling in Condensed Media, 1992; contbr. articles to profl. jours. Recipient Maxwell Medal and Prize, Inst. Physics, UK, 1975, Simon Meml. prize, 1981, Fritz London Meml. award, 1981, Paul Dirac Medal and prize, Inst. Physics, UK, 1992, John Bardeen prize, 1994, Wolf prize in physics, Wolf Found., Israel, 2003, Nobel prize in physics, 2003. Fellow: American Physical Soc., Inst. Physics, UK (hon.), Royal Soc., UK; mem.: Russian Acad. of Sciences, Nat. Acad. of Sciences (assoc.), Am. Acad. Arts & Sciences, Am. Philol. Soc. Achievements include research in condensed matter physics, high-temperature superconductivity, foundations of quantum mechanics. Office: U Ill 1110 W Green St Urbana IL 61801-9013 E-mail: aleggett@uiuc.edu.

LEGGETT, GLORIA JEAN, minister; b. Buffalo, June 6, 1941; d. Richard Howard and Mary Alice (Jumper) Pope; m. Arthur William Leggett, June 17, 1961; children: Wendy Irene, Pamela Jean. MusB, Va. Commonwealth U., 1986; MDiv, Wesley Theol. Sem., 1991. Ordained to ministry Christian Ch., 1991. Choir dir. St. Mark's United Meth. Ch., Richmond, Va., 1974-80; vol. hosp. chaplain Johnston-Willis Hosp., Richmond, Va., 1991—; interim minister Westville Christian Ch., Mathews, Va., 1992-93, Crewe (Va.) Christian Ch.; vol. police chaplain Chesterfield County (Va.) Police Dept., 1995—; pastor Westside Christian Ch., Richmond, Va., 1997—, Ind. Christian Ch., Ashland, Va., 1998—; interim Unity Christ Ch. of Bon Air, 1999; min. Colonial Christian Ch., Colonial Heights, Va., 1991—2005. Tchr. music, Richmond, 1972—; supply preacher, keynote spkr. Main Line Denomination Chs., Va., 1990—. Counselor rape crisis YWCA, Richmond, 1992; bd. dirs. Va. Wildlife Fedn., 1986—92. Recipient Achievement award, Dale Carnegie Course, 1979. Mem.: NOW, AAUW, Phi Kappa Phi. Avocations: travel, crossword puzzles, music, camping, pets. Home and Office: 9216 Groomfield Rd Richmond VA 23236-3402 E-mail: revgjleggett@aol.com.

LEGGETT, JAMES DANIEL, bishop; b. Williamston, NC, Oct. 21, 1939; s. James S. and Hazel Louise (Wynn) Leggett; m. Clara Faye Watts, June 25, 1961; children: James Jr., Joseph Talmadge, Cynthia Faye, John David. BA, Pembroke State U.; ThB, Holmes Coll. of the Bible; doctorate (hon.), Holmes Coll. Bible, 1988. Ordained to minstry Pentecostal Holiness Ch., 1960. Pastor Swan Quarter Pentecostal Holiness Ch., 1962-64, Pinetown Pentecostal Holiness Ch., 1962-64, Mt. Olive Pentecostal Holiness Ch., Pembroke, 1964-70, Culbreth Meml. Pentecostal Holiness Ch., Falcon, 1970-86; supr. N.C. Conf. Pentecostal Holiness Ch., 1986-89; asst. gen. supt. Internat. Pentecostal Holiness Ch., Bethany, Okla., 1989-93, gen. supt., bishop, 1989—97, vice chmn., 1993—. Exec. dir. Evangelism USA, 1989—97; pres. Extension Loan Fund, 1989—97; mem. exec. com. Pentecostal/Charismatic Chs. N.A.; bd. dirs. Nat. Assn. Evangs.; chmn. Pentecostal World Fellowship; mem. exec. coun. Internat. Charismatic Consultation; mem. Mission Am.; former mem. Evang. Curriculum Commn.; writer Sunday Sch. lit., instr. extension classes Holmes Coll. of the Bible, Emmanuel Coll. Sec. bd. trustees Holmes Coll. of the Bible, past bd. dirs. Office: Pentecostal Holiness Ch 7300 NW 39th Expy Bethany OK 73008-2340 Office Phone: 405-787-7110 x 3302. Business E-Mail: jleggett@iphc.org.

LEGGETT, ROBERTA JEAN (BOBBI LEGGETT), retired social services administrator; b. Kankakee, Ill., Nov. 30, 1926; d. Clyde H. and Sybil D. (Billings) Karns; m. George T. Leggett, Aug. 25, 1956. Sec. Cardov div. Chemetron Corp., Chgo., 1951-60; sec., asst. mgr. Ravisloe Country Club, Homewood, Ill., 1961-65; sec. Nationwide Paper Co., Chgo., 1966-68; exec. dir. Am. Bd. Oral and Maxillofacial Surgery, Chgo., 1969-87. Mem. Chgo. Soc. Assn. Execs., Conf. Med. Soc. Execs. of Greater Chgo., Profl. Secs. Internat. Methodist.

LEGGETT, SCOTT, chef, consultant; s. Joseph and Mary Leggett. B, Johnson & Wales, Providence, 1982; A, U. Colo., Boulder, 1984. Cert. exec. chef Am. Culinary Fedn., 1986. Exec. chef, design cons. Gallery 101 Bistro, Buffalo, 1998—99; corp. chef US Foodsvc., Rosemont, Ill., 2000—. Contbr. (food show) Profl. Chef's Assn. Niagara Culinary Salon, (ice sculpture) Nat. Ice Carving Assn.Winter Nats., (culinary demonstration) Rocky Mountain Food and Wine Festival, (culinary salon) Indpls. Chef's De Cuisine (3 Gold medals, 1983). Mem.: Rsch. Chefs Am. (assoc.), Am. Culinary Fedn. (assoc.). Avocations: kite flying, travel. Office: Monarch Foods US Foodsvc 6133 N River Rd Rosemont IL 60018 Home Phone: 716-649-2749.

LEGGETT, WILLIAM C., biology professor, academic administrator; b. Orangeville, Ont., Can., June 25, 1939; s. Frank William and Edna Irene (Wheeler) L.; m. Claire Holman, May 9, 1964; children: David, John. BA, Waterloo U. Coll., 1962; MSc, U. Waterloo, 1965, DSc, 1992; PhD, McGill U., 1969, DSc, 2001; LLD, Wilfred Laurier U., 1994, Queen's U., 2005; DSc, Laval U., 1996. From rsch. sci. to rsch. assoc. Essex (Conn.) Marine Lab., 1965-73; asst. prof. McGill U., Montreal, Que., Canada, 1970-72, assoc. prof., 1972-79, prof., 1979—2004, chmn. dept. biology, 1981-85, dean of sci., 1986-91, acad. v.p., 1991-94; prin., vice chancellor Queen's U., Kingston, Ont., Canada, 1994—2004, prin. emeritus, prof. emeritus, 2004—; chmn. bd. Huntsman Marine Lab., 1980-89; pres. Quebec Inter univ. Oceanographic Rsch. Group, 1986-91; fellow Sch. Policy Studies Queens U., 2004—; prin. ptnr. Tancho Innovation Capital, 2005—; gen. ptnr. Tancho Investment Capital, 2006—; chmn. bd. Can. Found. Innovation, 2007—. Chmn. grant selection com. for population biology Natural Scis. and Engring. Rsch. Coun. Can., 1980-81, chmn. grant selection com. for oceans, 1986-87; exec. com. Coun. Ontario Univs., 1996-2004, vice-chair, 2002-04; mem. com. internationalization Assn. Univ. Colls. Can., 2001-04; bd. dirs. Office for Partnerships for Advanced Skills, 2000-04; chair Ont. Commn. on Interuniv. Athletes, 2002-04; bd. dirs., sec. Conn. River Ecol. Study Found., 2004-. Mem. editl. bd.: Can. Jour. Fisheries and Aquatic Sciences, 1980-85, Le Naturaliste Canadien, 1980-91, Can. Jour. Zoology, 1982-86; contbr. articles in field. Chair svc. learning adv. com. McConnell Found., 2004—. Recipient Fry medal Can. Soc. Zoologists, 1990, Outstanding Biologist award Can. Coun. Biol. Chmn., 1993, John Orr award, 2003, Queen's U., Disting. Svc. award, 2004, Stirling medal, 2004, Isi Highly Cited Rschr. award, 2004—; Paul Harris fellow Rotary Internat., 2004; grantee in field. Fellow Rawson Acad., Royal Soc. Can., Order of Can.; mem. Am. Fisheries Soc. (pres. North-East divsn. 1977-78, Dwight D. Webster award 1989, EO Sette award 1996, Excellence award 1997, Award for Excellence for Fisheries Edn. 1990), Can. Com. for Fishery Rsch., Can. Soc. Zoologists, Am. Soc. Limnology and Oceanography, Am. Soc. Naturalists. Office: Queen's U Dept Biology Kingston ON Canada K7L 3N6 Office Phone: 613-533-6534. Business E-Mail: wleggett@post.queensu.ca.

LEGLER, KRISTIN M., music educator; b. West Plains, Mo., Jan. 10, 1981; d. Robert E. and Rebecca L. Legler. BS in Edn. - Music, Mo. State U., 2003; postgrad., U. Ark., 2005—. Tchr. music Green Forest Pub. Schs., 2003—04; piano tchr. United Meth. Ch., Harrison, Ark., 2004—05; tchr. music Gravette Pub. Schs., 2005—; band dir. Decatur Pub. Schs., 2005—. Presenter in field. Mem. Ark. Winds Cmty. Band, Ozark Bronze Handbell Choir. Recipient Lowell K. Fleenor scholarship, Mo. State U., 2002, 2003, Soloist Showcase award, 2002. Mem.: Ark. Sch. Band & Orch. Assn., Ark. Bandmasters Assn., Music Educators Nat. Conf., Mo. Music Educators Assn., Ark. Music Educators Assn., Pi Kappa Lambda, Mu Phi Epsilon, Kappa Kappa Psi. Independent. Avocations: travel, music, handbells. Office: 500 8th St SW Gravette AR 72736 Home Phone: 479-200-8841; Office Phone: 479-787-4140. Personal E-mail: klegler@gmail.com. Business E-Mail: klegler@lions.k12.ar.us.

LEGO, PAUL EDWARD, retired manufacturing executive; b. Centre County, Pa., May 16, 1930; s. Paul Irvin and Sarah Elizabeth (Montgomery) L.; m. Ann Sepety, July 7, 1956; children: Paul Gregory, Debra Ann, Douglas Edward, Michael John. BS in Elec. Engring, U. Pitts., 1956, MS, 1958. With Westinghouse Electric Corp., 1956-93, gen. mgr. Westinghouse semiconductor div. Pitts., 1970-74, gen. mgr. electronic tube div. Elmira, NY, 1974-75, bus. unit gen. mgr. electronic components divs. Pitts., 1975-77, v.p., gen. mgr. lamp divs. Bloomfield, NJ, 1977-80, exec. v.p. electronics and control group Pitts., 1980-83, exec. v.p. control equipment, 1983-85, sr. exec. v.p. corp. resources, 1985-87, pres., COO, 1988-90, chmn., CEO, 1990-93, also bd. dirs.; ret., 1993; pres. Intelligent Enterprises, Pitts., 1993—; chmn. bd. Commonwealth Industries, Inc., Louisville, 1995—2004. Bd. dirs. Aleris, Internat. Trustee U. Pitts.; mem. bd. visitors U. Pitts. Sch. Engring. With U.S. Army, 1948-52. Recipient Westinghouse Order of Merit 1975, Disting. Alumni award U. Pitts. Sch. Engring., 1986, Bicentennial Medallion of Distinction award U. Pitts., 1987, Legacy Laureate award U. Pitts., 2000. Mem. Am. Soc. Corp. Execs., Valley Brook Country Club, Duquesne Club, The Club Pelican Bay (Naples, Fla.), Laurel Valley Golf Club, Rolling Rock Club (Ligonier, Pa.), Golf Club of Everglades (Naples). Republican. Roman Catholic. Office: Exec Assocs One PPG Pl Ste 2970 Pittsburgh PA 15222 Office Phone: 412-263-3344. E-mail: plego10@aol.com. *I believe that every individual should take ownership of his or her job and have the authority and responsibility to make continuous improvements in the processes by which the objectives of that job are accomplished.*

LEGOHN, LISA MARIE, vocational school educator; d. Lawrence John and Lucille Gladys Legohn; m. Keith Lamont Stephens (div. Oct. 8, 2001); 1 child, Lisa Marie Hamilton. Completion cert., L.A. Trade Tech. Coll., 1981; Vocat. edn. instr. credential, Calif State U., Long Beach, 1987; Calif C.C. instr. credential, UCLA Ext., LA, 1984, UCLA, 1984. Welder Komax Systems, Inc, Long Beach, 1981—87; welding instr. Compton (Calif.) C.C., 1983—2003; welder fabricator Unique Ennocations, Inglewood, Calif., 1987—89; assoc. prof. L.A. C.C. Dist., 1990—. Welding dept. adv. bd. Compton C.C., 1983—2003; constrn. tech. adv. bd. L.A. Trade Tech. Coll., 1994—; risk mgmt. cons. J. Paul Getty Mus., LA, 2005. Welder, fabricator and builder (documentaries) BIG, welder, fabricator & builder Monster Garage. Active Jerusalem Missionary Bapt. Ch., LA, 1999—2006. Named Welder of the Yr., L.A. Trade Tech. Coll. Catercraft Award, 1981, Tchr. of Yr., L.A. Trade Tech. Coll. Tools for Success, 1998. Mem.: Am. Welding Soc. (assoc.). Achievements include nine Guiness World Records. Avocations: cooking, swimming, investments. Office: L A Community College District LATTC 400 West Washington Blvd Los Angeles CA 90012 Home Phone: 323-644-8179; Office Phone: 213-763-3942. Business E-Mail: legohnlm@lattc.edu.

LEGRAND, MICHEL JEAN, composer; b. Paris, Feb. 24, 1932; came to U.S., 1955; s. Raymond and Marcelle Legrand; children: Hervé, Benjamin, Eugénie, Dominique. Diploma, Conservatoire Nationale Superieur de Musique, Paris, 1951. Composer, condr., pianist, 1965—. Composer: (score, song, adaptation) I Will Wait for You, 1965 (3 Acad. award nominations), Windmills of Your Mind, 1968 (Acad. award 1968), film scores include Summer of 42, 1970 (Acad. award 1970), Brian's Song, 1971, Lady Sings the Blues, 1972, The Three Muscateers, 1973, Ode to Billy Joe, 1975, The Other Side of Midnight, 1977, Atlantic City, 1980, The Mountain Men, 1980, Never Say Never Again, 1983, Yentl, 1984 (Acad. award 1984), The Pickle, 1993, Ready to Wear, 1994, Madeline, 1998, also over 100 albums; arranger (album) I Love Paris, 1954; contbr. jazz pianist with numerous orchs. including Pitts. Symphony, Minn. Orch., Buffalo Philharm.; collaborated with various artists including Barbra Streisand, Sarah Vaughan, Jack Jones, Lena Horne, Dame Kiri Te Kanawa, Ray Charles, Miles Davis, Neil Diamond, Johnny Mathis, Jessye Norman; dir. (film) 5 Days in June, 1989. Mem. Dramatists Guild, Songwriters Guild of Am., Am. Fedn. Musicians, AFTRA, ASCAP, Acad. Motion Picture Arts and Scis. (Oscar award 1967, 70, 83). Avocations: boating, airplane pilot, tennis, horseback riding. Office: care Jim DiGiovanni PO Box 2040 New York NY 10101-2040 E-mail: jjosie157@aol.com.

LEGRAND, SUSAN BUCHANAN, palliative medicine physician, educator; b. Columbia, SC, Oct. 11, 1952; d. Talmadge Moore and Charlotte Buchanan LeGrand. MD, U. SC, Columbia, 1983. Diplomate Am. Bd. Internal Medicine, 1986, Am. Bd. Med. Oncology, 1989, Am. Bd. Hospice and Palliative Medicine, 2003. Staff physician Cleve. Clinic Taussig Cancer Ctr., 1998—; dir. edn. Harry R. Horvitz Ctr. Palliative Medicine, Cleve., 1998—. Fellow: Am. Acad. Physicians; mem.: Am. Acad. Hospice and Palliative Medicine (nominating com. 2007—, alt. del. to AMA 2002—06), Am. Soc. Clin. Oncology, Phi Beta Kappa. Democrat. Episcopalian. Avocations: reading, travel. Office: Cleve Clinic 9500 Euclid Ave R35 Cleveland OH 44195 Office Phone: 216-444-4523.

LEGRO, PATRICE, museum director; b. Dec. 1953; m. Alan Legro. BA in Art History, Old Dominion U., 1977; MA in internat. transaction, George Mason U., 1996. Program officer Office Internat. Affairs Nat. Acad., Wash., DC, 1987—93, mgr. Nat. Sci. Edn. Standards Project, co-study dir. Tchg. About Evolution and Nature of Sci., 1998, dir. Divsn. Comm. and Special Projects Ctr. Sci., Math., and Engring. Edn., 1998, dir. Philanthropy Svcs., 1998—2002; dir. Marian Koshland Sci. Mus. Nat. Acad. Scis., Wash., DC, 2002—. Office: Marian Koshland Sci Mus Nat Acad 500 Fifth St NW Washington DC 20001 Office Phone: 202-334-2728.

LEGROS, JAMES, actor; b. Mpls., Apr. 27, 1962; m. Kristina Loggia, 1992; 2 children. Movies include Solarbabies, 1986, Fatal Beauty, 1987, Phantasm II, 1988, Drugstore Cowboy, 1989, Blood and Concrete, 1991, Leather Jackets, 1991, Point Break, 1991, Guncrazy, 1992, Where the Day Takes You, 1992, Mrs. Parker and the Vicious Circle, 1994, Destiny Turns on the Radio, 1995, Boys, 1996, Infinity, 1996, Countdown, 1996, Wishful Thinking, 1997, The Myth of Fingerprints, 1997, The Pass, 1998, LA Without a Map, 1998, Thursday, 1998, There's No Fish Food in Heaven, 1998, Enemy of the State, 1998, Psycho, 1998, Jump, 1999, Drop Back Ten, 2000, If You Only Knew, 2000, Scotland, Pa., 2001, Lovely & Amazing, 2001, World Traveler, 2001, November, 2004, Catch That Kid, 2004, Straight Into Darkeness, 2005, Trust the Man, 2005, The Last Winder, 2006, Zodiac, 2007, (TV films) The Ratings Game, 1984, Ace Hits the Big Time, 1985, Marshal Law, 1996, Pronto, 1997, Border Line, 1999, Common Ground, 2000, Big Shot: Confessions of a Campus Bookie, 2002, Damaged Care, 2002, The Street Lawyer, 2003, Paradise, 2004, (TV series) Ally McBeal, 2000-01. Office: IFA Talent Agy 8730 W Sunset Blvd Ste 490 Los Angeles CA 90069-2248*

LEGUEY-FEILLEUX, JEAN-ROBERT, political scientist, educator; b. Marseilles, France, Mar. 28, 1928; came to U.S., Aug. 1949; s. E. Feilleux and Jeanne (Leguey)Levassort; m. Virginia Louise Hartwell, Sept. 19, 1953; children— Michele, Monique, Suzanne, Christiane. MA, Ecole Superieure de Commerce, France, 1949; Diplome Superieur d'Etudes Coloniales, U. d'Aix-Marseille, France, 1949; MA, U. Fla., 1951; PhD, Georgetown U., 1965. Lectr. Sch. Foreign Service Georgetown U., Washington, 1957-66; dir. research Inst. World Polit. Georgetown U., 1960-66; asst. prof. St. Louis U., 1966-70, assoc. prof., 1970—2000, chmn. polit. sci. dept., 1983-96, prof., 2000-, dir. foreign svcs. program, 2006-; vis. scholar Harvard Law Sch., Cambridge, Mass., 1974-75; chmn. Fulbright Commn. for France Inst. Internat. Edn., NYC, 1974-76; vis. researcher UN, NYC, 1981; mem. academic delegation, Jordan, 1988, Israel, 1990, Syria, Bahrain, Kuwait, 1991, Kuwait, Syria, 1992, Syria, 1993—. Yemen, 1995, Morocco, Tunisia, Spain, 1996, Tunisia, 1997, Yemen, 1998, Saudia Arabia, 1999, United Arab Emirates and Oman, 2005. Author (with others): Law of Limited International Conflict, 1965. Contbr. chpt. to books Implications of Disarmament, 1977, Democracy in a High-technology Society, 1988, The External Environment, 1991, Proceedings of First Gobal Village Conference, 1992, Great Events from History II: Human Rights, 1992, Science and Politics of Food: World Food Diplomacy, 1995, Morocco's Development Experience, 1999, Leadership and Development, 2002, Lessons of Moroccan Foreign Policy, 2002, Political Implications of Globalization, 2004. Contbr. articles to profl. jours. Author testimony Pres.'s Commn. on 25th Anniversary of UN, 1970. Recipient Medaille d'Or Institut Comml., France, 1949, Fulbright award U.S. State Dept., 1950, Cert. Disting. Service Inst. Internat. Edn., 1976; named Outstanding Educator Nutshell Mag., 1982; Malone fellow in Jordan, 1988. Mem. UN Assn. (mem. nat. coun. chpt. and div. pres. 1972-73, steering com. 1973-75), Am. Biog. Inst. (named to Hall of Fame, 1986), Internat. Human Rights Task Force (chmn. 1975-81), Character Research Assn. (pres. 1980-83, 89-90), Acad. Coun. on UN System, Am. Coun. for UN Univ., Georgetown U. Gold Key Soc., Alpha Sigma Nu, Phi Alpha Theta, Pi Sigma Alpha, Delta Phi Epsilon, Pi Delta Phi. Roman Catholic. Home: 6139 Kingsbury Ave Saint Louis MO 63112-1101 Office: St Louis U Dept Polit Sci 3500 Lindell Blvd Saint Louis MO 63103-1024 Office Phone: 314-977-3033. Business E-Mail: legueyf@slu.edu.

LEGUILLON, ROLANDE LUCIENNE, French educator; b. Etréchy, Essonne, France, Mar. 4, 1924; came to U.S., 1946; d. Marcel Charles and Fernande Léone (Mansion) Pipereau; m. Harry Sylvain Leguillon, Aug. 24, 1946; children: Philippe, Catherine Leguillon Conrad, Michael. BA, U. St. Thomas, Houston, 1962; MA, U. Houston, 1966; PhD, Rice U., 1970. Tchr. Lamar High Sch., Houston Ind. Sch. Dist., 1962-66; instr. Tex. So. U., Houston, 1966-68; prof. French U. St. Thomas, 1968—, chmn. dept., 1970—, dir. French Program, 1980—, chmn. modern lang. dept., 1981-90. Lectr. various univs. in SW U.S., 1974—. Contbr. articles to profl. jours. Spkr. various Alliances Françaises, S.W. U.S., 1970—, pres., Houston, 1981-82, 96—, bd. dirs., 1988—. Decorated chevalier Palmes Acadèmiques (France), decorated officier Palmes Acadèmiques, 1995; recipient Coll. Tchr. of Yr. award Tex. Fgn. Lang. Assn., 1993-94. Mem. Am. Assn. Tchrs. French (regional rep. 1974-80), Fedn. French Alliance in U.S. (bd. dirs. 1987-2002, dir. scholarships Houston chpt. 1987—, oral examiner baccalaureate 1982-93), Houston Assn. Tchrs. French Lang. (pres. 1975-76), Houston French Alliance (bd. dirs. 1970—, pres. 1982-83, 1994—), Pi Delta Phi (nat. v.p. 1981-91, pres.-elect 1991, nat. pres. 1992-1998, reader advanced program in French 1987-94, spkr. at meetings 1981—). Avocations: movies, theater, travel. Office: U St Thomas 3800 Montrose Blvd Houston TX 77006-4626 Office Phone: 713-525-3216. Business E-Mail: rolandel@stthom.edu.

LE GUIN, URSULA KROEBER, writer; b. Berkeley, Calif., Oct. 21, 1929; d. Alfred Louis and Theodora (Kracaw) Kroeber; m. Charles A. Le Guin, Dec. 22, 1953; children: Elisabeth, Caroline, Theodore. BA, Radcliffe Coll., 1951; MA, Columbia, 1952; 9 hon. degrees. Vis. lectr. or writer in residence numerous workshops and univs., U.S. and abroad. Author: Planet of Exile, 1966, Rocannon's World, 1966, City of Illusion, 1967, A Wizard of Earthsea, 1968, The Left Hand of Darkness, 1969, The Tombs of Atuan, 1970, The Lathe of Heaven, 1971, The Farthest Shore, 1972, The Dispossessed, 1974, The Wind's Twelve Quarters, 1975, A Very Long Way from Anywhere Else, 1976, Orsinian Tales, 1976, The Word for World is Forest, 1976, The Language of the Night, 1979, rev. edit., 1992, Leese Webster, 1979, Malafrena, 1979, The Beginning Place, 1980, Hard Words, 1981, The Compass Rose, 1982, The Eye of the Heron, 1983, Cobbler's Rune, 1983, King Dog, 1985, Always Coming Home, 1985, Buffalo Gals, 1987, Wild Oats and Fireweed, 1988, A Visit from Dr. Katz, 1988, Catwings, 1988, Solomon Leviathan, 1988, Fire and Stone, 1989, Catwings Return, 1989, Dancing at the Edge of the World, 1989, Tehanu, 1990, Searoad, 1991, Fish Soup, 1992, A Ride on the Red Mare's Back, 1992, Blue Moon Over Thurman Street, 1993, Wonderful Alexander and the Catwings, 1994, Going Out With Peacocks, 1994, A Fisherman of the Inland Sea, 1994, Four Ways to Forgiveness, 1995, Unlocking the Air, 1996; author: (with Diana Bellessi) The Twins, The Dream, 1997; author: Lao Tzu: Tao Te Ching: A Book About the Way and the Power of the Way, 1997, Steering the Craft, 1998, Jane on Her Own, 1999, Sixty Odd, 1999, The Telling, 2000, The Other Wind, 2001, Tales From Earthsea, 2001, The Birthday of the World, 2002, Tom Mouse, 2002, Kalpa Imperial, 2003; translator: Selected Poems of Gabriela Mistral, 2003;; author: Changing Planes, 2003, The Wave in the Mind, 2004, Gifts, 2004, Incredible Good Fortune, 2006, Voices, 2006, Powers, 2007, short stories, numerous poems, screenplays; contbr. articles to profl. jours. Recipient Locus Readers award novel, 1973, collection, 1984, 96, story, 1995, 2003, story and novel, 2001, 02, Jupiter award 1975-76, Lewis Caroll Shelf award 1979, Internat. Fantasy award 1988, Howard D. Vursell award Am. Acad. Arts and Letters, 1991, Pushcart prize, 1991, Boston Globe-Hornbook award for excellence in juvenile fiction, 1968, Newbery Honor medal, 1972, Nebula award (novel) 1969, 75, 90, (story) 1975, Hugo award (novel) 1969, 75, (story) 1974, 88, Gandalf award, 1979, Kafka award, 1986, Nat. Book award, 1972, H.L. Davis award Oreg. Inst. Literary Arts, 1992, Hubbub annual poetry award, 1995, Asimov's Reader's award, 1995, 03, James Tiptree Jr. award, 1995, 97, Retrospective award, 1996, Theodore Sturgeon award (story), 1995, Prix Lectures-Jeunesse award, 1987, Bumbershoot Arts award, Seattle, 1998, Lifetime Achievement award Robert Kirsch/L.A. Times, 2000, Lifetime Achievement award Pacific NW Booksellers Assn., 2001, Endeavor award, 2001, 03, Willamette Writers Lifetime Achievement award, 2002, PEN/Malamud award for short fiction, 2002, World Fantasy award, 2002, Grand Master award SFW, 2003, Margaret A. Edwards award, 2004, Literary award PEN Ctr. USA, 2005, Maxine Cushing Gray award for literary achievement, 2006, CES Wood Disting. Writers award, 2006, Gallun award for outstanding contbn. to the genre of sci. fiction, 2007; Arbuthnot lectr. ALA, 2004. Mem. NARAL, Amnesty Internet. USA, Environ. Def. Fund, Nat. Resources Def. CTEE, Planned Parenthood Fedn. Am., Oreg. Nature Conservancy, Sci. Fiction Rsch. Assn., Sci. Fiction Writers Assn. (Grand Master 2003), Authors League, PEN (PEN/USA award 2005), Writers Guild West, Phi Beta Kappa. Office: care Virginia Kidd Lit Agy PO Box 278 Milford PA 18337-0278 also: c/o William Contandi 244 Madison Ave #E1 New York NY 10016-4702

LEGUIZAMÖ, JOHN, actor, comedian; b. Bogota, Columbia, July 22, 1964; s. Alberto and Luz Leguizamo; m. Yelba Osorio, Sept. 1994 (div. Nov. 1996); m. Justine Mauer, July 5, 2003; children: Allegra Sky, Ryder Lee. Studied, Sylvia Leigh's Showcase Theater, NY, Lee Strasberg Inst., HB Studio; studied Theater, NYU. Actor (films) Mixed Blood, 1985, The Burning Question, 1988, Casualties of War, 1989, Street Hunter, 1990, Gentille alouette, 1990, Revenge, 1990, Die Hard 2, 1990, Poison, 1991, Hangin' with the Homeboys, 1991, Out for Justice, 1991, Regarding Henry, 1991, Time Expired, 1992, Whispers in the Dark, 1992, Night Owl, 1993, Super Mario Bros., 1993, Carlito's Way, 1993, A Pyromaniac's Love Story, 1995, To Wong Foo, Thanks for Everything, Julie Newmar, 1995, Executive Decision, 1996, The Fan, 1996, Romeo & Juliet, 1996, The Pest, 1996, A Brother's Kiss, 1997, Spawn, 1997, Frogs for Snakes, 1998, Body Count, 1998, (voice only) Doctor Doolittle, 1998, Joe the King, 1999, Summer of Sam, 1999, (voice only) Titan A.E., 2000, Moulin Rouge!, 2001, What's the Worst That Could Happen?, 2001, King of the Jungle, 2001, Empire, 2002, Zigzag, 2002, (voice only) Ice Age, 2002, Spun, 2002, Crónicas, 2004, Sueño, 2005, Assault on Precinct 13, 2005, The Honeymooners, 2005, Land of the Dead, 2005, The Alibi, 2006, (voice only) Ice Age: The Meltdown, 2006; actor (TV films) Words in Your Face, 1991, N.Y.P.D. Mounted, 1991, Arabian Nights, 2000, Point of Origin, 2002, Undefeated, 2003, (also exec. prodr., dir., writer); (TV series) House of Buggin, 1995 (also writer, prodr.), The Brothers Garcia (voice), 2000, ER, 2005-06; (TV appearances) Miami Vice, 1986, 1987, 1989; actor (music video for Madonna) Borderline, 1984, Madonna: The Immaculate Collection, 1990; co-exec. prodr. Piñero, 2001; exec. prodr. Nuyorican Dream, 1999; writer (one person show) Freak: A Semi-Demi-Quasi-Autobiographical Comedy, 1997 (Tony award nomination), John Leguizamo LIVE, Sexaholix...A Love Story, 2001 (also prodr.); writer (TV film) Mambo Mouth, 1991, Spic-O-Rama, 1993; author: Pimps, Hos Playa Hatas and All the Rest of My Hollywood Friends, 2006 Recipient OBIE award for Mambo Mouth, 1991, Tony award for play Freak, 1998, Entertainer of Yr. ALMA, 2002 Office: William Morris Agy 151 S El Camino Dr Beverly Hills CA 90212-2775

LEGUM, JEFFREY ALFRED, holding company executive; b. Balt., Dec. 16, 1941; s. Leslie and Naomi (Hendler) L.; m. Harriet Cohn, Nov. 10, 1968; children: Laurie Hope, Michael Neil. BS in Econs., Wharton Sch. U. Pa., 1963; grad., Chevrolet Sch. Merchandising and Mgmt., 1966. With Park Circle Motor Co. DBA Pk. Cir. Investments, Balt., 1963—, exec. v.p., 1966—77, pres., 1977—, CEO, 1982—; pres. and dir. Legum Chevrolet-Nissan, 1977—89; ltd. ptnr. Pkwy. Indsl. Ctr., Dorsey, Md., 1965-91, Circle Ltd. Partnership, Glen Burnie, Md., 1991—99; v.p., dir. P.C. Parts Co., 1967—, pres., 1995—, One Forty Corp., Westminster, Md., 1972—97; pres. and CEO Westminster Motor Co., 1973—. Dir., exec. com. United Consol. Industries, 1970-73; dist. chmn. Chevrolet Dealers Coun., 1975-77; chmn. Washington zone, 1982-83. Exec. com. Balt. Mus. Art, 2006—; chmn. transp. divsn. Assoc. Jewish Charities, Balt., 1966—69; investment com. Balt. Hebrew Congregation, 1980—99, 2002—, bd. electors, 1990—93; bd. dirs. Assoc. Placement Bur. (Jewish Vocat. Svc.), Balt., 1964—76, v.p., 1972—76; adv. bd. Competitive Edge, Albuquerque, 1977—81; mem. Md. Svc. Acad. Rev. Bd., 1975—77, Bus. Adv. Bd. to Atty. Gen., 1985—87; trustee Balt. Mus. Art, 1992—, fine arts accessions com., 1992—, chair legal panel, 1996—99, investment com., 1992—, chair, 1996—98, chair fine arts accessions com., 2001—04, mem. exec. com., 1993—, mem. fin. com., 1996—, sec.-treas., 1996—2001, sec., 2001—04; pres.'s com. U. Toronto, 1983—99, The Park Sch., Balt., 1979—94, chmn. investment com., 1980—96, mem. exec. com., chmn. fin. com. and treas., 1981—91; trustee The Legum Found., 1967—; trustee, mem. fin. com. Johns Hopkins Med. Insts., 1997—; mem. inst. rev. bd. for human subjects rsch. Johns Hopkins Bayview Med. Ctr., 1992—98; steering com. Govt. House Trust, 1996—2002; v.p. Preakness Celebration, Inc., 1988—89; sponsor endowment for Jeffrey and Harriet Legum professorship in acute neurol. medicine Johns Hopkins U.; adv. coun. Wilmer Eye Inst., The Johns Hopkins Hosp., 1991—. Recipient award of honor, Assn. Jewish Charities of Balt., 1967, 1968, Cadillac Master Dealer award, 1980—88, 1991, Cadillac Pinnacle of Excellence award, 1986, Young Pres.'s Orgn. Cert. Appreciation, 1984, Nissan Nat. Merit Master award, annually, 1979—89, Sales Giant award, Automotive News, 1987, Minute of Gratitude, The Park Sch. Bd. Trustees, 1994. Mem. Young Pres. Orgn. (pres.'s forum 1977-92), World Pres.' Orgn., Benjamin Franklin Assocs., Johns Hopkins Assocs., Md. Hist. Soc. (exec. com. Library of Md. History 1981-90), Suburban Club (Balt. County), U. Pa., Center Club. Home: 10 Stone Hollow Ct Baltimore MD 21208-1860 Office: 1829 Reisterstown Rd Baltimore MD 21208-6320

LEGUM, JUDD, think-tank executive, editor; B in Pub. Policy Analysis, Pomona Coll., So. Calif., 2000; JD, Georgetown U. Law Ctr. Rsch. asst. for former chief of staff John Podesta; dep. rsch. dir. Ctr. for American Progress, Washington, rsch. dir.; editor ThinkProgress.org; co-editor The Progress Report newsletter, editor; rsch. dir. Hillary Clinton presdl. campaign, 2007—. Published writings in numerous publications including The Nation, The San Diego Union-Tribune, DC Examiner, Salon and American Prospect Online, guest appearances Al Franken Show, Bill Press Show. Mem.: Md. Bar. Office: Hillary Clinton for President 4420 N Fairfax D Arlington VA 22203 Office Phone: 202-682-1611.*

LEGVOLD, ROBERT, political science professor; b. Mpls., Feb. 26, 1940; s. Oscar and Hazel Legvold; m. Gloria Dee Welch, Mar. 17, 1940; children: Nancy Diane Rubbico, Nathan Cameron. BA, U. SD, 1962; MA, Tufts U., 1962—67, MA in Law and Diplomacy, 1964, PhD, 1967; LLD (hon.), U. SD, 1989. From asst. to assoc. prof. Tufts U., Medford, Mass., 1967—77; sr. fellow Coun. on Fgn. Rels., NYC, 1979—84; from assoc. prof. to prof. Columbia U., NYC, 1984—2006, Marshall D. Shulman profl. polit. sci., 2006—. Author: Soviet Policy in West Africa, 1971; editor: Belarus at the Crossroads, 1999, Thinking Strategically: The Major Powers, Kazakhstan, and the Central Asian Nexus, 2002, Swords and Sustenance: The Economics of National Security in Belarus and Ukraine, 2004, Statehood and Security: Georgia After the Rose Revolution, 2005, Russian Foreign Policy in the 21st Century and the Shadow of the Past, 2007. Active Carnegie Endowment for Internat. Peace, Washington, 1993—2005; mem. and com. chair Watson Inst., Brown U., Providence, 1998—2005. Named one of 500 Most Influential People in U.S. in Field of Fgn. Policy, World Affairs Couns. of Am., 2004; recipient Disting. Svc. to Profession award, Tufts U., 1991. Fellow: AAAS, Am. Acad. Arts and Scis.; mem.: Coun. on Fgn. Rels. Avocations: tennis, gardening, carpentry. Home: 11 Fenwick Rd Winchester MA 01890 Office: Columbia Univ New York NY 10027 Home Phone: 781-729-8247; Office Phone: 212-854-5426. Office Fax: 212-666-3481. Business E-Mail: rhl1@columbia.edu.

LEHAN, JONATHAN MICHAEL, judge; b. LA, Apr. 25, 1947; s. Bert Leon and Frances (Shapiro) L.; m. Annett Jean Garrett, Aug. 1, 1970; children: Joshua Michael, Melanie Janine. BA, Calif. State U., Fullerton, 1968; JD, Calif. Western Sch. Law, 1971; grad., Nat. Drug Ct. Inst., 2000, Nat. Ctr. for State Cts., Williamsburg, Va. Bar: Calif. 1972, U.S. Dist. Ct. (no. dist.) Calif. 1973, U.S. Supreme Ct. 1975. Law clk. to presiding and assoc. justice Calif. Dist. Ct. Appeals, San Bernardino, 1971-73; dep. dist. atty. Mendocino County, Ukiah, Calif., 1973-76, coast asst. dist. atty. Fort Bragg, Calif., 1976-83; pvt. practice Fort Bragg, 1983-84; ptnr. Lehan & Kronfeld, Fort Bragg, 1984-90; judge Mendocino County Superior Ct., Ft. Bragg, 1990—. Instr. Barstow C.C., Calif., 1972, Mendocino C.C., Ukiah, 1974-75, Coll. Redwoods, Ft. Bragg, 1981-82; seminar faculty Calif. Jud. Coll., U. Calif., Berkeley, 1993; faculty Calif. Judges Assn. Mid-Year Conf., 1998, ann. conf., 1999; contbr. Calif. Drunk Driving Law, Kuwatch, 1995; mem. juvenile dependency atty. working group Jud. Coun. Calif., 2004. Bd. dir. Salmon Restoration Assn., Fort Bragg, Gloriana Opera Co., Mendocino, Mendocino Art Ctr. Editor Calif. Western Sch. Law Law Rev., 1971. Mem. ABA, Mendocino County Bar Assn. (pres. 1989), Phi Delta Phi, Mendocino C. of C. (bd. dir.). Democrat. Avocations: violist Mendocino string quartet, violist Osprey string quartet. Office: Mendocino Superior Ct 700 S Franklin St Fort Bragg CA 95437-5464 Home Phone: 707-964-9343; Office Phone: 707-964-3192. E-mail: judgejon@judgejon.com.

LEHANE, DENNIS, writer; b. Dorchester, Mass., Aug. 4, 1965; Author: A Drink Before the War, 1994, Darkness Take My Hand, 1996, Sacred, 1997, Gone, Baby, Gone, 1998, Prayers for Rain, 1999, Mystic River, 2001 (Anthony award, Barry award, Mass. Book award), Shutter Island, 2003.

LEHMAN, ARNOLD LESTER, museum official, art historian; b. NYC, July 18, 1944; s. Sidney and Henrietta F. L.; m. Pamela Gimbel, June 21, 1969; children— Nicholas Richard, Zachary Gimbel. BA, Johns Hopkins, 1965, MA, 1966, Yale U., 1968, PhD, 1973. Chester Dale fellow Met. Mus. Art, NYC, 1969-70; lectr. art history Cooper Union and Hunter Coll., 1969-72; dir. Urban Improvements Program, NYC, 1970-72, Parks Council of N.Y.C., 1972-74, Met. Mus. and Art Centers, Miami, Fla., 1974-79, Balt. Mus. Art, 1979-97, Bklyn. Mus. Art, 1997—. Adj. prof. dept. art history Johns Hopkins U., 1986-97; dir. or trustee several corps. and non-profit orgns. Author: The Architecture of Worlds Fairs 1900-1939, 1972, The New York Skyscraper: A History of its Development 1870-1939, 1974, various mus. catalogues; editor: Oskar Schlemmer, 1986; exhibitions include. Mem. Bklyn. Arts Coun.; trustee Am. Fedn. Arts, NY, several non-profit orgns.; mem. exec. planning com. The Bard Grad Ctr. for Studies in the Decorative Arts. Mem.: Assn. Art Mus. Dirs. (trustee 1987—93, pres. 1990—91). Office: Bklyn Mus Art 200 Eastern Pkwy Brooklyn NY 11238-6052

LEHMAN, DENNIS DALE, chemistry professor, department chairman; b. Youngstown, Ohio, July 15, 1945; s. Dale Vern and Coryn Eleanor (Neff) L.; m. Maureen Victoria Tierney, July 19, 1959 (div. Mar. 1981); children: Chris, Hillary; m. Kathleen Kim Kuchta, May 15, 1983. BS, Ohio State U., 1967; MS, Northwestern U., 1968, PhD, 1972. Prof. chemistry, chmn. dept. Chgo. City Colls., 1968—, chmn. dept. phys. sci., 2000—, chmn. combined biology and phys. scis. dept., 2003—. Prof. chemistry Northwestern U., Evanston, Ill., 1974-98, dir. Rsch. Experience for Tchrs., 2002—, lectr. biochemistry Med. Sch., Chgo., 1979-90, lectr. chemistry, 1998; cons. Chgo. Bd. Edn.; disting. prof. Harold Washington Coll, 2004-2005; cmty. coll. coord Caspie Project; dir. speech project Washington Coll., 2005—. Author: Chemistry for the Health Sciences, 1981, 8th edit., 1998, Laboratory Chemistry for the Health Sciences, 1981, 8th edit., 1998 Named Disting. Prof., Harold Washington Coll., 2004—05; Sr. fellow, Sencer Project. Mem. AAAS, Am. Chem. Soc., Sigma Xi. Home: 5918 Tomlinson Dr Mchenry IL 60050-1715 Office: Chgo City Colls 30 E Lake St Chicago IL 60601-2403 Home Phone: 815-759-1724; Office Phone: 312-553-5787. Business E-Mail: dlehman@ccc.edu.

LEHMAN, DONALD RICHARD, physicist, educator, academic administrator; b. York, Pa., Dec. 13, 1940; s. Frederick Hinkle and Wilhelmina Emma (Ruesskamp) Lehman; m. Elyse Joan Brauch, Aug. 24, 1962. BA in Physics, Rutgers U., 1962; PhD in Theoretical Physics, George Washington U., 1970. NAS NRC postdoctoral rsch. assoc. Nat. Bur. Stds., Gaithersburg, Md., 1970-72; from asst. to assoc. prof. physics George Washington U., Washington, 1972-82, prof., 1982—2002, George Gamow prof. theoretical physics, 2003—, dep. chair physics, 1986-87, chair physics, 1987-93, dir. ctr. nuclear studies, 1990-93, assoc. v.p. rsch. and grad. studies, 1993-96, v.p. acad. affairs, 1996—2002, exec. v.p. acad. affairs, 2003—. Guest worker Nat. Bur. Stds., Gaithersburg, 1972—89, program analyst, 1974; vis. staff mem., collaborator Los Alamos (N.Mex.) Nat. Lab., 1973—2001; spkr. internat. confs. Contbr. articles to profl. jours. Grantee, Rsch. Corp., N.Y., 1974—76, Dept. Energy, Germantown, Md., 1979—98, NATO, Belgium, 1987—91. Fellow: Am. Phys. Soc.; mem.: Southeastern Univs. Rsch. Assn. (trustee 1993—, chair bd. trustees 2002—03, mem. exec. com. 1996—). Achievements include elucidation of the physics of the 3 body structure of 6Li; unraveling of the physics underlying the role of exact three body continuum states in the photodisintegration of 3He. Office: George Washington U Academic Affairs 2121 I St NW Washington DC 20037-2353 Home Phone: 703-281-7558; Office Phone: 202-994-6510.

LEHMAN, EDWARD WILLIAM, social studies educator, researcher; b. Regensburg, Germany, Feb. 7, 1936; arrived in US, 1939; s. William and Kate (Hoffman) Lehman; m. Ethna V O'Flannery, May 26, 1962; 1 child, Robert (dec.). BS, Fordham U., 1956, MA, 1959; PhD, Columbia U., 1966. Lectr. Fordham U., 1958-59; vis. research sociologist dept. psychiatry Montefiore Hosp., Bronx, NY, 1959-61; lectr. Sch. Nursing, Columbia U., NYC, 1964-67; research sociologist Cornell U. Med. Coll., NYC, 1961-67; asst. prof., then assoc. prof. sociology NYU, 1967-78; prof., 1978—; chmn. dept., 1978-84, 93-96. Assoc dir Ctr Policy Research, New York, NY, 1976—85, sr research assoc, 1969—89; mem minority adv comt NY State Dept Mental Hygiene, 1981—90. Author: (book) Coordinating Health Care: Explorations in Interorganizational Relations, 1975, Political Society: A Macrosociology of Politics, 1977, The Viable Polity, 1992; editor (with others): A Sociological Reader in Complex Organizations, 1980, Autonomy and Order: A Communitarian Anthology, 2000. Served to capt US Army, 1957. Mem.: Soc. for Advancement of SocioEcons., Am. Polit. Sci. Assn., Am. Sociol. Assn. Democrat. Roman Catholic. Home: Apt 8B 1 Washington Square Village New York NY 10012-1632 Home Phone: 212-475-4390; Office Phone: 212-998-8379. Business E-Mail: ewl1@nyu.edu.

LEHMAN, I(SRAEL) ROBERT, biochemist, educator; b. Tauroggen, Lithuania, Oct. 5, 1924; arrived in U.S., 1927; s. Herman Bernard Lehman and Anne Kahn; m. Sandra Lee, July 5, 1959; children: Ellen, Deborah, Samuel. BA, Johns Hopkins U., 1950, PhD, 1954; MD (hon.), U. Gothenberg, Sweden, 1987; DSc, U. Paris, 1992. Asst. prof. Stanford (Calif.) U., 1959-62, assoc. prof., 1962-67, prof. biochemistry, 1967—, chmn. dept. biochemistry, 1974—79. Mem. sci. adv. bd. U.S. Biochem., Cleve., 1984-98, RPI Pharms., Boulder, Colo., 1991-96, Genetrol, Oakland, Calif., 1998-2003; cons. Abbott Labs, Chgo., 1990-94. Author: Principles of Biochemistry, 7th edit., 1984. Sgt. U.S. Army, 1943-46, ETO. Recipient Merck award Am. Soc. Biochemistry and Molecular Biology, 1994. Fellow: Am. Acad. Arts and Scis.; mem.: Am. Soc. Biochemistry and Molecular Biology (pres. 1995), Nat. Acad. Scis. Democrat. Jewish. Office: Sch of Medicine Stanford U Stanford CA 94305

LEHMAN, JEFFREY SEAN, academic administrator; b. Bronxville, NY, Aug. 1, 1956; s. Leonard and Imogene (McAuliffe) L.; m. Kathy Okun; children: Rebecca Colleen, Jacob Keegan, Benjamin Emil. AB, Cornell U., 1977; M of Pub. Policy, U. Mich., 1981, JD, 1981. Bar: DC 1983, US Ct. Appeals (fed. cir.) 1984, US Ct. Appeals (D.C. cir.) 1987, US Supreme Ct. 1987. Law clk. to chief judge US Ct. Appeals (1st cir.), Portland, Maine, 1981-82; law clk. to assoc. justice US Supreme Ct., Washington, 1982-83; assoc. Caplin & Drysdale, Chartered, Washington, 1983-87; asst. prof. U. Mich. Law Sch., Ann Arbor, 1987-92, prof., 1992-93, prof. law and pub. policy, 1993—2003, dean, 1994—2003; pres. Cornell U., Ithaca, NY, 2003—05; sr. scholar Woodrow Wilson Internat. Ctr. for Scholars, Washington, 2005—. Vis. prof. Yale U., 1993, U. Paris II, 1994. Co-author: Corporate Income Taxation, 1994; editor-in-chief: Mich. Law Rev., 1979-80. Office Phone: 313-483-3080. Business E-Mail: jlehman@china.us.law.org.

LEHMAN, JOAN ALICE, real estate company executive; b. Jamaica Queens, NY, May 8, 1938; d. Hans Newman and Margot (Deutsch) Senen; m. Eugene Lehman, June 17, 1956 (div. Mar. 1990); children: Joel, Peter, Alan, Ira, Helen Ann, Helen Beth, Robert, Jacqueline, John, Steven, Robin, Elizabeth, Jody, Lisa, David, Andy, Jeremy, Jay. AA, Nassau C.C., East Meadow, NY, 1971; BS, Nova U., 1982. Lic. real estate broker, Fla. Owner Joan Lehman Real Estate Mgmt. Co., Old Bethpage, NY, 1961-82; tchr. Broward County Schs., Ft. Lauderdale, Fla., 1982-86; owner Joan Lehman Real Estate, Pompano Beach, Fla., 1986—; pres. Jo Al 1 Inc., Pompano Beach. Mem. Sunset Sch. Adv. Bd., Ft. Lauderdale, 1994-96; pres. The Pointe Condo Assn., 2001—; bd. dirs. Property Owners Ctrl. Lauderhill, Fla., 1996; den mother Boy Scouts Am., Old Bethpage, N.Y.; leader Girl Scouts U.S., Old Bethpage. Avocations: bowling, travel, theater.

LEHMAN, JOHN F., JR., private equity executive; b. Phila., Sept. 14, 1942; s. John F. and Constance (Cruice) L.; m. Barbara Wieland, 1975; children: John F., Alexandra, Grace. BS in Internat. Rels., St. Joseph's Coll., 1964; BA in Law with honors, MA in Internat. Law and Diplomacy, Cambridge U., 1967; PhD in Internat. Rels., U. Pa., 1974. Sr. staff mem. NSC, 1969-74; dep. dir. US Arms Control & Disarmament Agy., 1975-77; pres. Abingdon Corp., 1977-81; sec. Dept. Navy US Dept. Def., Washington, 1981-87; mng. dir. Paine Webber, 1988-91; chmn. J.F. Lehman & Co., NYC, 1991—, OAOT Corp., 2001—. Bd. dirs. Ball Corp., ISO, Inc.; commr. The Nat. Commn. on Terrorist Attacks Upon the U.S. (The 9-11 Commn.), 2002—04. Author: Command of the Seas, 1989, Making War, 1992, On Seas of Glory, 2001. Capt. USNR, 1968—93.

LEHMAN, LAWRENCE HERBERT, consulting engineering executive; b. NYC, Apr. 30, 1929; s. Samuel and Shirley (Freiberg) L.; m. Susan E. Green, June 29, 1957; children: Scott Jeffrey, Christopher Adam. BCE, NYU, 1949; MBA, Iona Coll., 1978. Registered profl. engr., N.Y., N.J., Ky., Ill., Mass., Conn., Ind., Pa., Md., Fla. Project engr. Andrews & Clark (Cons. Engrs.), NYC, 1951-57; project mgr. Barstow, Mulligan & Vollmer (Cons. Engrs.), NYC, 1957-59; chief engr., ptnr. Vollmer Assos. (Cons. Engrs.), NYC, 1959-67; CEO, dir. Berger, Lehman Assos. (P.C.), Rye, NY, 1967—. Trustee Rye Libr. Recipient Third award U.S. Steel Corp., 1966, Bridge award Pre-stressed Concrete Inst., 1975, Honor award Nat. ACEC, 1995, nat. awards USDOT, 2000, Am. Cons. Engrs. Coun., 2000, others. Fellow ASCE (life); mem. NSPE, Am. Cons. Engrs. Coun., Soc. Am. Mil. Engrs., Transp. Rsch. Bd., Am. Ry. Engring. Assn., Internat. Assn. Bridge and Structural Engrs., Inst. Transp. Engrs., Am. Arbitration Assn. (nat. panel arbitrators), N.Y. Assn. Cons. Engrs. (Engring. Excellence awards 1975, 79, 90, 95), Conn. Engrs. in Pvt. Practice, West County Profl. Engrs. Soc. (Engr. of Yr. award 1991), The Moles. Home: 10 Chester Dr Rye NY 10580-2204 Office: 411 Theodore Fremd Ave Rye NY 10580-1410 Office Phone: 914-967-5800. E-mail: blalehman@aol.com.

LEHMAN, LEONARD, retired lawyer, consultant; b. Bklyn., July 5, 1927; s. Samuel and Marcy (Dolgenas) Lehman; m. Imogene McAuliffe, June 11, 1954; children: Jeffrey, Toby, Amy, Zachary. BA, Cornell U., 1949; JD, Yale U., 1952. Bar: N.Y. 1953, U.S. Supreme Ct. 1969, D.C. 1979, U.S. Ct. Internat. Trade 1981, U.S. Ct. Appeals (fed. cir.) 1982. Atty.-advisor U.S. Tax Ct., Washington, 1952—55; practice NYC, 1955—63; sr. counsel Office Tax Legis. Counsel, U.S. Dept. Treasury, Washington, 1963—65; asst. to chief counsel U.S. Customs Svc., 1965—67, dep. chief counsel, 1968—71, asst. commr., 1971—79; ptnr. Barnes, Richardson and Colburn, NYC, Washington and Chgo., 1979—89, counsel, 1989—95; mem. industry functional adv. com. on customs/trade policy U.S. Dept. Commerce, 1989—95. Contbr. articles to profl. jours. Recipient Meritorious Svc. award, U.S. Dept. Treasury, 1971, Exceptional Svc. award, 1979, U.S. Customs Honor award, 1977. Mem.: ABA (standing com. on customs law 1974—80, chmn. 1980, customs and tariff com., adminstrv. law sect. 1971—88, vice chmn. 1981—83, chmn. 1984—88), Phi Kappa Phi, Phi Beta Kappa. Home and Office: 18 Rich Branch Ct North Potomac MD 20878-2461

LEHMAN, MARK E., lawyer; b. Bklyn., Mar. 14, 1951; s. Edward Berton and Aileen Sally (Tarrow) L.; m. Diane Carol Goller, Aug. 15, 1976; children: David, Abigail. BA, Columbia Coll., 1973; JD, NYU, 1976. Bar: N.Y. 1977, U.S. Dist. Ct. (so. dist.) N.Y. 1977. Litigation atty. Merrill Lynch, Pierce, Fenner & Smith, Inc., NYC, 1976-79; gen. coun. Bear Stearns & Co. Inc., NYC, 1986—2004, spl. advisor to c.e.o., 2004—. Arbitrator Am. Stock Exchange, Nat. Assn. Securities Dealers. Mem. Securities Industry Assn., Future Industry Assn. Office: 245 Park Ave New York NY 10167-0002

LEHMAN, MICHAEL EVANS, information technology executive; BBA in Acctg., U. Wis., Madison, 1974. Sr. mgr. Price Waterhouse, San Francisco; asst. corp. contr., external reporting mgr. Asian subs. Sun Microsystems, Inc., Hong Kong, dir. fin. and adminstrn. Asian subs., v.p., corp. contr., v.p., CFO, 1994—98, v.p. corp. resources, CFO, corp. exec. officer, 1998-2000, exec. v.p. corp. resources, CFO, 2000—02, 2006—. Bd. dirs. Sun Microsystems, Inc., 2002—06. Mem. deans adv. bd. Grad. Sch. Bus., U. Wis., Madison. Mem. Am. Electronics Assn. (exec. com.). Office: Sun Microsystems Inc 4150 Network Cir Santa Clara CA 95054 Office Phone: 650-960-1300.*

LEHMAN, RICHARD WILLIAM, electrical engineer; s. Delos Richard and Vernet LaRue Lehman; m. Patricia Bradley Lehman, Apr. 30, 1988. Design engr. Clair Bros. Audio, Inc., Lititz, Pa., 1985—. Cons. in field. Mem.: Audio Engring. Soc. Achievements include patents in field. Home: 120 Hoffer Way Manheim PA 17545 Office: Clair Brothers Audio Enterprises Inc 1 Ellen Ave Lititz PA 17543 Home Phone: 717-358-0119; Office Phone: 717-626-4000.

LEHMAN, ROBERT WYLIE, music educator; b. Pitts., July 23, 1960; s. Raymond Walter and Elizabeth Wylie Lehman; m. Allison Hunt, Oct. 10, 1987; children: Meredith Delaney, Elizabeth Farrington. BFA, Carnegie Mellon U., Pitts., Pa., 1982; MusM, Westminster Choir Coll., Princeton, N.J., 1985. Ordained FCM Protestant Episcopal Cathedral Found., 1986; cert. AAGO SUNY, 1982, ChM SUNY, 1982. Asst. organist, choirmaster Wash. Nat. Cathedral, Washington, 1985—91; music dir., condr. The Woodley Ensemble, Washington, 1990—97; organist, choirmaster Christ Ch. Episcopal, New Haven, 1994—; music dir., condr. Phoenix Vocal Ensemble, N.Y.C., 1997—. Fellow: Davenport Coll.-Yale U. Office: Christ Ch Episcopal 84 Broadway New Haven CT 06511-3412 Office Phone: 203-865-6354. Home Fax: 203-865-6354. Personal E-mail: rwlehman@mac.com.

LEHMAN, TOM (THOMAS EDWARD LEHMAN), professional golfer; b. Austin, Minn., Mar. 7, 1959; m. Melissa; children: Rachael, Holly, Thomas. Student, U. Minn. Profl. golfer PGA, 1982—. Named Ben Hogan Tour Player of Yr., 1991; named to Pres. Cup team, 1994;; won Reflection Ridge, Gulf Coast Classic, S.C. Classic, Santa Rosa Open, The Meml. Tournament, 1994, Colonial Invitational, 1995, Brit. Open, 1996, The Tour Championships, 1999, Phoenix Open, 2000, 12 straight seasons in top 100 on money list, 1992-2003. Office: Signature Sports Group Ste 110 4150 Olson Memorial Hwy Minneapolis MN 55422-4804

LEHMANN, CORINNE E., medical educator; d. Terry W. and Hannah Lehmann; 1 child, Miro Calderas. BS in Chemistry, Ohio State U., 1988; MS in Chemistry, Yale U., New Haven, Conn., 1989; MD, U. Cin., 1993, MEd, 2005. Intern, resident internal medicine, pediat. U. Cin., 1993—97; physician West Suburban Hosp., Oak Park, Ill., 1998—2000; assoc. prof. dept. internal medicine, pediat. U. Cin., 2000—04, assoc. prof., 2006—; dir. resident edn. divsn. adolescent medicine Cin. Children's Hosp., 2002—. Mem. admissions com. U. Cin., Coll. Medicine, 2003—04; fellow adolescent medicine Cin. Children's Hosp. Med. Ctr., 2000—02. Grantee, U. Cin., 2003, 2004. Fellow: Am. Acad. Pediat.; mem.: ACP, Ohio Med. Pediat. Assn., Soc. Adolescent Medicine (sec., treas. 2004). Avocations: tennis, music, art. Office: Cin Childrens Hosp Med Ctr Divsn Adolescent Medicine 3333 Burnet Ave ML 40000 Cincinnati OH 45229 also: U Pediat Internal Medicine Assoc 234 Goodman Ave ML 665X Cincinnati OH 45219 Office Phone: 513-636-4681. E-mail: corinne.lehmann@uc.edu.

LEHMANN, DORIS ELIZABETH, retired elementary school educator; b. Ramsey, NJ, Aug. 17, 1933; d. Alfred Harrison and Anna Elizabeth (Gerhold) Rockefeller; m. Victor S. Lehmann, June 25, 1955; children: Joanne E. Cathy Lynn, Victor A., Kristie Sue. BS in Edn. magna cum laude, Wagner Coll., 1955; student in edn., Columbia U., summers 1988-91, Jersey City State, 1990—, William Paterson, 1971. Elem. tchr. Sch. St. Sch., Ramsey, 1955-56; bedside instr. N. Bergen County schs., NJ, 1966-71; elem. tchr. Edith A. Bogert Sch., Upper Saddle River, NJ, 1971-2000; ret., 2000. Author numerous poems; author: (with others) Curriculum for Values Education in New Jersey, 1991. Indian cons. Bergen County Mus. Art Sci., Paramus, NJ, 1983—. Recipient Fellowship Life award Luth. Layman's Movement, 1955. Fellow Upper Saddle River Edn. Assn. (social sec. 1972-73, v.p. 1974-75, 84-85, liaison to USR hist. soc. 1986—) NJ Edn. Assn., NJ North Edn. Assn., VFW Aux. (historian, 1st v.p. 2000—), Alpha Omicron Pi (life, treas. 1954, v.p. 1955). Republican. Lutheran. Personal E-mail: vlcco@aol.com.

LEHMANN, MICHAEL STEPHEN, film director; b. San Francisco, Mar. 30, 1957; s. Herbert and Minette L.; m. Holland Sutton; children: Alexander, Natalie. BA, Columbia U., 1978; MFA, U. So. Calif., 1985. Mgr. electronic cinema div. Zoetrope, Hollywood, Calif., 1981-83. Dir. (films) Heathers, 1989 (Best First Feature award Ind. Feature Project 1990), Meet the Applegates, 1991, Hudson Hawk, 1991, Airheads, 1994, The Truth About Cats and Dogs, 1996, My Giant, 1998, 40 Days and 40 Nights, 2002, Because I Said So, 2007, (TV series), Pasadena, 2001, Watching Ellie, 2002, Wonderfalls, 2004; exec. prodr. (films) Ed Wood, 1994, (TV series) Century City, 2004. Office: Creative Artists Agy 9830 Wilshire Blvd Beverly Hills CA 90212-1825*

LEHMANN, RUTH, geneticist, educator; PhD, U. Tubingen, Germany. Assoc. prof. Dept. Biology MIT; assoc. investigator Howard Hughes Med. Inst.; dir. devel. genetics group Skirball Inst. NYU Med. Ctr. Sr. mem. Whitehead Inst. Biomedical Rsch. Mem.: NAS (fgn. assoc.). Office: The Lehmann Lab Devel Genetics Program 540 First Ave 4th Floor New York NY 10016 Office Phone: 212-263-7595. E-mail: lehmann@saturn.med.nyu.edu.

LEHMANN, WILLIAM LEONARDO, electrical engineer, educator; b. Milw., Dec. 17, 1924; s. William Christian and Johanna Alma (Schrumpf) L.; m. Barbara Taylor, June 29, 1948; children: Johanna, William, Katherine, Wendy, Christianne. AB, Haverford Coll., Pa., 1944; MS, Syracuse U., NY, 1948, PhD, 1953. Registered profl. engr., Ohio. Prof. physics acting dean Air Force Inst. Tech., 1951-66; lectr. Ohio State U., 1957-60; dir. for labs. Office Asst. Sec. Air Force Research and Devel., 1966-74; dir. Air Force Office Sci. Research, 1974-78, Air Force Weapons Lab., Kirtland AFB, N.Mex., 1978-81; chief scientist Combat Devel. Experimentation Ctr. U.S. Army Sci. Support Lab, Ft. Ord, Calif., 1982-85; sr. sci. analyst N.Mex. Engring. Research Inst., 1985-93; prof. elec. engring. U. N.Mex., Albuquerque, 1988-93; sr. assoc. Ctr. for Occupational R & D, 1993—. Vis. prof. U. N.Mex., 1981-82, also adv. bd. Coll. Engring.; Past mem. Gov. N.Mex. Tech. Excellence Com.; mem. USAF Scientific Adv. Bd., 1985-92. Patentee solar orientation device. Mem. Beaver Creek (Ohio) Sch. Dist. Bd., 1965-66; trustee Lovelace Med. Found. Served with AUS, 1944-45. Recipient Air Force Exceptional Civilian Service medal with three oak leaf cluster, 1981, Ohio Engr.'s award, 1966, award Ohio Soc. Profl. Engrs., 1965 Fellow AAAS; mem. Air

Force Assn. (citation honor 1978), Am. Soc. Engring. Edn., AIAA, Am. Def. Preparedness Assn., Sigma Xi, Sigma Pi Sigma, Tau Beta Pi. Lodges: Rotary. Republican. Episcopalian. Home: 700 Island Retreat Rd Port Aransas TX 78373-6012 Office: Port Aransas High Sch PO Box 1297 Port Aransas TX 78373-1297 Office Phone: 361-749-7136. E-mail: bblehmann@aol.com.

LEHMANN-HAUPT, CHRISTOPHER CHARLES HERBERT, book reviewer; b. Edinburgh, June 14, 1934; arrived in US, 1934; s. Hellmut Otto Emil and Letitia Jane H. (Grierson) Lehmann-H.; m. Natalie Robins, Oct. 3, 1965; children: Rachel Louise, Noah Christopher. BA, Swarthmore Coll., 1956; MFA in Theatre History and Dramatic Criticism, Yale U., 1959. Editor A.S. Barnes & Co., Inc., NYC, 1961-62, Holt, Rinehart & Winston, NYC, 1962-63; sr. editor Dial Press, 1963-65; mem. staff NY Times Book Review, 1965-69; sr. daily book reviewer NY Times, 1969-95, daily book reviewer, 1995-2000, chief obituary writer, 2000—. Asst. prof. lit. CUNY, 1973—75. Author: Me and Di Maggio, 1986, A Crooked Man, 1995, The Mad Cook of Pymatuning, 2005. Bd. trustees Putney Sch. Mem.: Century. Office: New York Times 229 W 43rd St New York NY 10036-3959 Office Phone: 212-556-1706. Business E-Mail: clhaupt@nytimes.com.

LEHMBECK, JOHN PIERCE, journalist, writer; b. Pinehurst, Ga., Nov. 26, 1936; s. John Wesley Sullivan and Jewell Ellen Powell, Norman Gene Lehmbeck (Stepfather); m. Karen Barbara Armel, June 18, 1998; m. Nancy Jane Voss, June 12, 1959 (div. Nov. 26, 1980); children: Cynthia Lynne, John Pierce Jr., Michael Sean. BS in Journalism, Fla. State U., 1958. Newsman The AP, 1955—76, chief bur. Albany, NY, 1968—72, NYC, 1972—76; account exec. Hill & Knowlton Inc., NYC, 1976—77; bus. svcs. ombudsman N.Y. State Dept. Commerce, Albany, 1977—79, dir. state info., 1980; editor Fin. News & Daily Record, Jacksonville, Fla., 1980—84; mng. editor Clay TODAY, Orange Park, 1986—88; reporter, columnist St. Augustine Record, 1994—98; pres. Media Lehmbeck, Jacksonville, 1998—2002, O'Sullivan Gold, 2002—. Bd. mem. Journalism Adv. Bd., St. Bonaventure U., Olean, NY, 1968—72; supervising dir. NYC Election Svc., 1972—76. Author: (novels) Sullivan Road, 2004. With US Army N.G., 1959—76. Recipient Gold Key Scholastic and Leadership Soc., Fla. State U., 1958, Outstanding Contbn. Journalism, for creation of Empire Audio, NY State Broadcasters Assn., 1971—72, Outstanding Contributions Journalism, Morrisville State U., 1972, Outstanding Contributions Broadcast Journalism, NY State AP Broadcasters Assn., 1972; Grantland Rice Meml. scholar, Fla. State U., 1958. Independent. Avocations: post-graduate study, special education, reading, writing, sports. Home: 8767 Como Lake Dr Jacksonville FL 32256 Home Phone: 904-620-8643. Personal E-mail: plehmbeck@hotmail.com.

LEHMBERG, ROBERT HENRY, retired research physicist; b. Phila., Dec. 4, 1937; s. Henry and Marguerite Elenore (Schock) L.; m. Norma Geder, Dec. 29, 1966; 1 child, Karl Robert. BSc, Pa. State U., State College, 1959; MSc, U. Ariz., Tucson, 1961; PhD, Brandeis U., Waltham, Mass., 1968. Rsch. physicist Naval Air Devel. Ctr., Warminster, Pa., 1966-72, Naval Rsch. Lab., Washington, 1972—2006, ret., 2006, part-time contractor, 2006—07. Chmn. program com. Conf. on Lasers and Electro-Optics, Washington, 1991. Contbr. articles to profl. jours.; patentee in field. Recipient E.O. Hulbert Ann. Sci. award Naval Rsch. Lab., 1997. Fellow Am. Phys. Soc. (Excellence in Plasma Physics Rsch. award 1993); mem. IEEE, Sigma Xi. Achievements include development of optical beam smoothing techniques for laser fusion, optical design of the Naval Research Laboratory's Nike laser facility, and research in nonlinear optics, excimer laser physics and laser-plasma interaction physics. Office: Naval Rsch Lab Plasma Divsn 4555 Overlook Ave SW Washington DC 20375-0001 Business E-Mail: lehmberg@this.nrl.navy.mil.

LEHMBERG, STANFORD EUGENE, historian, educator; b. McPherson, Kans., Sept. 23, 1931; s. Willard Eugene and Helen (Stanford) L.; m. Phyllis Barton, July 23, 1962; 1 son, Derek Grantham. BA, U. Kans., 1953, MA, 1954; PhD, Cambridge U., Eng., 1956, DLitt, 1990. Mem. faculty U. Tex., Austin, 1956-69; mem. faculty U. Minn., 1969-98, prof. history, 1967-98, chmn. dept., 1979-85. Author: Sir Thomas Elyot, Tudor Humanist, 1960, Sir Walter Mildmay and Tudor Government, 1966, The Reformation Parliament, 1970, The Later Parliaments of Henry VIII, 1977, The Reformation of Cathedrals, 1988, The People of the British Isles to 1688, 1991, 2d edit., 2001, Cathedrals Under Siege, 1996, (with Ann M. Pflaum) The University of Minnesota, 1945-2000, 2001, Holy Faith of Santa Fe, 2004, English Cathedrals: A History, 2005, Churches for the Southwest: The Ecclesiastical Architecture of John Gaw Meem, 2005; contbr. articles, revs. to profl. jours. Fulbright scholar, 1954—56, Guggenheim fellow, 1965—66, 1985—86. Fellow Royal Hist. Soc., Soc. of Antiquaries; mem. Am. Hist. Assn., Midwest Conf. Brit. Studies (pres. 1982-84), Renaissance Soc. Am., Am. Soc. Reformation Research. Episcopalian. Home: 1005 Calle Largo Santa Fe NM 87501-1068 Personal E-mail: lehmberg@earthlink.net.

LEHN, JEAN-MARIE PIERRE, chemistry professor; b. Rosheim, Bas-Rhin, France, Sept. 30, 1939; s. Pierre and Marie (Salomon) Lehn; m. Sylvie Lederer, 1965; 2 children. Grad., U. Strasbourg, France, 1960, PhD, 1963; PhD (hon.), U. Jerusalem, 1984, U. Autonoma, Madrid, 1985, U. Göttingen, 1987, U. Brussels, 1987, U. Herakliou, Greece, 1989, U. Bologna, 1989, Charles U., Prague, 1990, U. Twente, 1991, U. Sheffield, 1991, U. Athens, 1992, U. Polytech. Athens, 1992, Poly. U. Bucharest, 1994, Ill. Wesleyan U., 1995, U. Montreal, 1995, Bielefeld U., 1998, USTC, Hefei, 1998, Southeast U., Nanjing, 1998, Weizmann Inst., Rehovoth, 1998; DSc (hon.), U. Brussels, 1999, U. Nagoya, 2000, U. Sherbrooke, 2000, U. Trieste, 2001, Jiao Tong U., Shanghai, 2003, Nanjing U., 2003, KTH, 2003, U. St. Andrews, 2004, St. Petersburg U., 2005, Mazaryk U., 2005, Heriot Watt U., 2005. Various positions Nat. Ctr. Sci. Rsch., France, 1960—66; postdoctoral rsch. assoc. Harvard U., Cambridge, Mass., 1963—64; asst. prof. U. Strasbourg, France, 1966—69; assoc. prof. U. Louis Pasteur of Strasbourg, 1970, prof. of chemistry, 1970—79; prof. Coll. France, Paris, 1979—. Vis. prof. chemistry Harvard U., 1972—74, E.T.H., Zurich, Switzerland, Cambridge (Eng.) U., 1984, Barcelona (Spain) U., 1985, Fankfurt (Germany) U., 1985—86; Heinrich-Hertz Gast prof. Karlsruhe U., 1989; Woodward vis. prof. Harvard U., Cambridge, Mass., 1997; Newton-Abraham vis. prof. Oxford U., 1999—2000. Contbr. articles to sci. publs. Decorated commandeur Légion d'Honneur, officer Order Nat. du Mérite, Ordre pour le Mérite for Scis. and Arts, Austrian Cross of Honor for Sci. and Art, First Class; recipient Bronze, Silver and Gold medals, Ctr. Nat. Sci. Rsch. (CNRS), Pontifical Acad. Sci., 1981, Swiss Chem. Soc., 1982, von Humboldt prize, 1983, Nobel prize for chemistry, 1987, Karl-Ziegler prize, 1989, Bonner Chemiepreis, 1993, Ettore Majorana-Erice-Sci. for Peace prize, 1994, Gold medal, Soc. Acad. Arts, Scis., Lettres, 1995, Davy medal, Royal Soc., 1997, Lavoisier medal, SFC, 1997, A.R. Day award, 1998, others. Mem.: Chinese Acad. Scis., Acad. Bibliotheca Alexandrinae (pres.), Slovenian Acad. Arts and Scis., Hungarian Acad. Scis., Russian Acad. Scis., Royal Irish Acad., Acad. Scis. Torino, Pontifical Acad. Scis., Third World Acad. Scis., The Czech Learned Soc., Korean Acad. Sci. and Tech., Royal Soc., Acad. Roumaine, Inst. Grand Ducal (Luxembourg), Acad. Scis. Ukraine, Acad. Arts and Scis. P.R., Royal Acad. Scis., Letters and Fine Arts (Belgium), Polish Acad. Scis., Indian Acad. Scis., Yugoslav Acad. Arts and Scis. Zagreb, Acad. Wissenschaften, Acad. Wissenschaften Literalur-Mainz, Acad. Europaea, Am. Philos. Soc. (Phila., fgn. mem.), Royal Netherlands Acad., Acad. Nazionale dei Lincei, Deutsche Acad. der Naturforscher Leopoldina, Inst. de France, AAAS (fgn.) (hon.), NAS (fgn.) (assoc.). Home: 6 rue des Pontonniers 67000 Strasbourg France Office: Coll France 11 pl Marcelin Berthelot 75005 Paris France also: ISIS U Louis Pasteur 8 allee Gaspard Monge 67000 Strasbourg France

LEHNER-QUAM, ALISON LYNN, library administrator; b. Oak Harbor, Wash., Apr. 25, 1960; d. Paul Elias and Johanna Marie (Vinson) Q.; m. Matthias Karl-Eugen Lehner, Oct. 3, 1997; 1 child, Peter Elias Bernhard Lehner. BA, U. Wash., 1983; cert. tech. theater, Yale U., 1985; MS in Libr. Sci., Columbia U., 1991. Freelance costumer various prodns., NYC, 1984-90; cataloging asst. Fashion Inst. of Tech., NYC, 1986-91; intern Bank St. Sch., NYC, 1991; asst. dir. Columbia Children's Lit. Inst., NYC, 1990; libr. dir. Lincoln Ctr. Inst., NYC, 1991—. Project dir. Arts Edn. Reference Window on the Work, 1992—. Pub. mgr.: (periodical) The Institute View, 1996—, website mgr. www.lcinstitute.org, 2000—; resource round-up editor Teaching Artist Jour., 2002-2003. Vol. mgr. Lincoln Ctr. Inst., N.Y.C., 1995-2001. Recipient Dirs.' Emeriti award Lincoln Ctr. for Performing Arts, 1997; scholar Sch. Libr. Svcs., Columbia U., 1989, 90. Mem. ALA, N.Y. Arts in Edn. Roundtable (steering com. 1995-98), Theater Libr. Assn., Beta Phi Mu (bd. dirs. Theta chpt. 1997-2004, v.p. 1994-96). Avocations: reading, the arts. E-mail: alquam@lincolncenter.org.

LEHOCZKY, JOHN PAUL, statistics educator; b. Columbus, Ohio, June 29, 1943; s. Paul Nicholas and Thelma Marie (Heisterkamp) L.; m. Mary Louise Zimmerman, Sept. 10, 1966; children: Jennifer Lynne, Jessica Augusta. BA, Oberlin Coll., 1965; MS, Stanford U., 1967, PhD, 1969. Asst. prof. stats. Carnegie Mellon U., Pitts., 1969-73, assoc. prof., 1973-81, prof., 1981-96, head dept., 1984-95, Thomas Lord prof. stats., 1997—, dean humanities & social scis., 2000—; assoc. editor IEEE Transactions on Computers, 1995-98. Cons. in field. Dept. editor Mgmt. Sci., 1981-86; assoc. editor Jour. Real-Time Systems, 1989—; contbr. articles to profl. jours. Fellow INFORMS, Am. Statis. Assn. (statistician of yr. Pitts. chpt. 1987), Inst. Math. Stats.; mem. IEEE (Tech. Leadership award, Tech. Com. on Real-Time Sys., 2004), AAAS, Assn. for Computing Machinery, Internat. Statis. Inst. (elected), Sigma Xi, Phi Beta Kappa. Office: Carnegie Mellon Univ Dept Stats Pittsburgh PA 15213 Business E-Mail: jpl@stat.cmu.edu.

LEHR, JEFFREY MARVIN, immunologist, allergist; b. NYC, Apr. 29, 1942; s. Arthur and Stella (Smellow) L.; m. Suzanne Kozak, June 10, 1946; children: Elisa, Alexandra, Vanessa, Ryan. BS, City Coll., Bklyn., 1963; MD, NYU, 1967. Intern, resident Beth Israel Hosp., NYC, 1967-69; resident in allergy/immunology, internal medicine Roosevelt Hosp., NYC, 1969-72; chief of allergy/immunology USAF, Wright Patterson AFB, Ohio, 1972-74; allergist, immunologist Monterey, Calif., 1974—. Chmn. Monterey Bay Ari Pollution Hearing Bd., 1982-95; v.p. Lyceum of Monterey, 1977-83. Fellow Am. Acad. Allergy/Immunology, Am. Coll. Allergy/Immunology, Am. Assn. Cert. Allergists; mem. Am. Lung Assn. (v.p. 1989-91), Monterey County Med. Soc. (pres. 1988-89). Avocations: tennis, jogging, golf, hiking, backpacking. Office: 798 Cass St Monterey CA 93940-2918 Office Phone: 831-649-6340. Personal E-mail: lehrallergy@sbcglobal.net.

LEHR, MICHAEL L., lawyer; b. NYC, Mar. 8, 1948; s. Hanns and Friederike (Gross) L.; children: Jackson M., Samuel G., Genevieve E. BA, U. Pa., 1969; JD, Harvard U., 1973. Bar: Pa. 1973, U.S. Dist. Ct. (ea. dist.) Pa. 1973, U.S. Ct. Appeals (3d cir.) 1975, D.C. 1976, U.S. Ct. Appeals (D.C. cir.) 1977, U.S. Tax Ct. 1984. Assoc. Ballard Spahr Andrews & Ingersoll, Phila., 1973-74, 79-82; asst. spl. prosecutor Watergate Spl. Prosecution Office, Washington, 1974-76; asst. U.S. atty. U.S. Atty.'s Office, Washington, 1976-79; ptnr. Ballard Spahr Andrews & Ingersoll, 1982—; now mng. shareholder, co-chair nat. public fin. practice Greenberg Traurig, LLP, Phila. Dir. Pub. Interest Law Ctr. of Phila., 1992—. Office: Greenberg Traurig LLP Two Commerce Sq Ste 2700 2001 Market St Philadelphia PA 19103 Office Phone: 215-988-7800. Office Fax: 215-988-7801. Business E-Mail: lehrm@gtlaw.com.

LEHRER, JAMES CHARLES, reporter, journalist; b. Wichita, Kans., May 19, 1934; s. Harry Frederick and Lois Catherine (Chapman) Lehrer; m. Kate Staples, June 4, 1960; children: Jamie, Lucy, Amanda. AA, Victoria Coll., 1954; BJ, U. Mo., 1956. Reporter Dallas Morning News, 1959—61; reporter, columnist, city editor Dallas Times Herald, 1961—70; exec. prodr., corr. Sta. KERA-TV, Dallas, 1970—72; pub. affairs coord. PBS, Washington, 1972—73; corr. NPACT-WETA-TV, Washington, 1973—; exec. editor, anchor The NewsHour with Jim Lehrer, 1995—; instr. creative writing Dallas Coll., So. Meth. U., 1967—68. Author: (novels) Viva Max, 1966, Kick the Can, 1988, Crown Oklahoma, 1980, The Sooner Spy, 1990, Lost and Found, 1991, Short List, 1992, Blue Hearts, 1993, Fine Lines, 1994, The Last Debate, 1995, White Widow, 1997, Purple Dots, 1998, The Special Prisoner, 2000, No Certain Rest, 2002, Flying Crows, 2004, The Franklin Affair, 2005, The Phony Marine, 2006, (memoirs) We Were Dreamers, 1975, A Bus of My Own, 1992, (plays) Chili Queen, 1986, Church Key Charlie Blue, 1987, The Will and Bart Show, 1992. With USMC, 1956—59. Named to Acad. TV Arts and Scis. Hall of Fame, 1999; recipient Columbia-Dupont award, George Polk award, Peabody award, Emmy award, Nat. Humanities medal, 1999. Fellow: Soc. Am. Historians; mem.: Coun. on Fgn. Rels., Tex. Inst. Letters, Dramatists Guild, Authors Guild, Am. Acad. Arts and Scis. Office: Sta WETA-TV 3620 27th St S Arlington VA 22206-2302

LEHRER, KENNETH EUGENE, economic consulting company executive; b. NYC, Apr. 17, 1946; s. Charles Carlton and Evelyn Estelle (Rosenfeld) L.; m. M. Newman, 1981 (div. 1988); m. Geraldine Trudy Fishman, Mar. 18, 1994. BS, NYU, 1967, MBA, 1969, MA, 1972, D in Pub. Adminstrn., 1980. Registered investment advisor; lic. real estate appraiser, real estate broker. Asst. treas. Banker's Trust Co., NYC, 1970-73; dir. devel. Coventry Devel. Corp., NYC, 1974-77; asst. v.p. Affiliated Capital Corp., Houston, 1977-80; dir. fin. Allison/Walker Interests, Houston, 1980-82; mng. dir. Lehrer Fin. and Econ. Adv. Svcs., Houston, 1982—; sr. economist Aztec Oil & Gas, Houston, 2005—, dir., 2005—. Prof. real estate fin. U. Houston Grad. Sch. Bus. Adminstrn., 1984-2002; adj. prof. econ. and fin. U. Phoenix (Houston div.) 2003—; chmn., bd. dirs. Acadia Savings and Loan Assn., Crowley, La., French Market Homestead Savs. Assn., Metairie, La., Twin City Savs. Bank, West Monroe, La., 1st Savs. La., LaPlace, 1988-89, Integrated Resource Techs., Inc., 1992-95. Pres. Cornerstone Mcpl. Utilities Dist. 1978-85; bd. dirs. Ft. Bend County Mcpl. Utility Dist #106, 1987-98, Houston Caliber Fin. Group chmn. 1994-96; Tex. Rep. Assn., Rep. Senatorial Inner Cir. (life, Medal of Freedom 1994). Mem. Am. Horse Show Assn. (life), Nat. Steeplechase and Hunt Assn. (life), U.S. Tennis Assn. (life), Am. Real Estate and Urban Econs. Assn., Am. Real Estate Soc., Nat. Assn. Bus. Economists, NYU Money Marketeers, Nat. Forensic Ctr., Nat. Assn. Corp. Dirs., Am. Acad. Econ. and Fin. Experts, Internat. Coll. Real Estate Cons. Profls., Internat. Assn. Corp. Real Estate Execs., Nat. Assn. Forensic Economists, Am. Arbitration Assn., Houston Bus. Economists, Western Econ. Assn., Fin. Club N.Y.C., Real Estate Educators Assn., Am. Econ. Assn., N. Am. Econs. and Fin. Assn., So. Econ. Assn., NYU Alumni Fedn. (bd. dirs. 1974-77), Houston C. of C. (mem. govtl. rels. com.), Princeton Club (N.Y.), St. James's Club (London), Capitol Hill Club (Washington), Royal Oaks Country Club (Houston). Episcopalian. Home: 5555 Del Monte Dr Unit 802 Houston TX 77056-4117 Office: Lehrer Fin & Econ Adv Svcs 1775 Saint James Pl Ste 110 Houston TX 77056-3403 Office Phone: 713-972-7912. Business E-Mail: drken@lehecoserv.com.

LEHRER, STANLEY, magazine publisher, editorial director, museum exhibitor; b. Bklyn., Mar. 18, 1929; s. Martin and Rose L.; m. Laurel Francine Zang, June 8, 1952; children: Merrill Clark, Randee Hope. BS in Journalism, NYU, 1950; postgrad. in Edn., San Antonio Coll., 1952. Editor and pub. Crossroads mag., Valley Stream, NY, 1949-50; youth svc. editor Open Road mag., NYC, 1950—51; mng. editor School & Society, NYC, 1953-68, v.p., 1956-68; pub. School & Society Books, NYC, 1963-86; pres., pub. School & Society mag., NYC, 1968-72; founder, pres., pub. Intellect mag., NYC, 1972-78, editl. dir., 1974-78; founder, pres., pub., editl. dir. USA Today, Valley Stream, 1978—99, Newsview newsletter, 1979—99, Your Health newsletter, 1980-99; pres., pub., editl. dir. The World of Sci. newsletter, 1980-99. Cons. Child Care Publs., NYC, 1955; guest spkr. Midwestern Writers' Conf., Chgo., 1950, Writers and Artists Group Nat. Music Camp, Interlochen, Mich., 1950, World of the Little Mag., Sta. WNYC-AM, NYC, 1977, Titanic Symposium Mariners' Mus., Newport News, Va., 1998, Titanic Revealed, Nat. Geog. Ch., 2004, Auction Adventure, Fine Living Network, Time-Warner Ch., 2005; prodr., commentator Report on Edn. radio program Sta. WBAI-FM, NYC, 1960—61; internat./nat. mus. exhibitor. Author: John Dewey: Master Educator, 1959, Countdown on Segregated Education, 1960, Religion, Government, and Education, 1961, A Century of Higher Education: Classical Citadel to Collegiate Colossus, 1962, Automation, Education, and Human Values, 1966, Conflict and Change on the Campus: The Response to Student Hyperactivism, 1970, Leaders, Teachers, and Learners in Academe: Partners in the Educational Process, 1970, Education and the Many Faces of the Disadvantaged: Cultural and Historical Perspectives, 1972, Titanic: Fortune & Fate, 1998; contbr. articles to nat. mags., newspapers, and profl. jours.; collector (exhibitions) NY Yacht Club, 1983, Forbes Mag. Galleries, NYC, 1989—90, French Embassy, NYC, 1992, On Normandie, Bass Mus. Art, Miami, 1993, PaineWebber Art Gallery, NYC, 1994—95, Nat. Maritime Mus., London, 1994—95, Water St. Gallery Seamen's Ch. Inst., NYC, 1996, 2001—02, Mariners' Mus., Newport News, Va., 1998, World Trade Ctr., Boston, 1998, Union Depot, St. Paul, 1998—99, US Courthouse, NYC, 1999, Tropicana, Atlantic City, NJ, 1999, 2000, Better Living Ctr., Toronto, Ont., Can., 1999—2000, Fair Park, Dallas, 2000, Mus. Sci. and Industry, Chgo., 2000, Mus. Ctr., Cin., 2000, Opryland Hotel, Nashville, 2001, Kansas City Mus., Union Station, 2001, (exhibits) Hoboken Hist. Mus., NJ, 2002, (exhibitions), Orlando, Fla., 2002—04, Belfast City Hall, No. Ireland, 2004, World's Largest Mus. Attraction, Branson, Mo., 2005—, Lunt-Fontanne Theatre, NYC, 1997; performer: An Evening with "Mr. Titanic," Stanley Lehrer, 2004; official transfer of Stanley Lehrer Ocean Liner Collection to South St. Seaport Mus., NYC, 2006, as ref. resource to the pub., collector (photographs and artifacts featured in books including) On Board The Titanic, 1996, Lost Liners, 1997, Titanic: Legacy of the World's Greatest Ocean Liner, 1997, Titanic: Fortune & Fate, 1998, Titanic, Nat. Geog. Soc., 1998, Eyewitness: Titanic, 1999, Molly Brown: Unraveling the Myth, 1999, The Lost Ships of Robert Ballard, 2005, (photographs and artifacts featured in videos including) Titanica, 1998, Steamboats: On the Hudson, 2004. Donor Stanley Lehrer Ocean Liner Collection South St. Seaport Mus., NYC, 2006; v.p. Garden City Park Civic Assn., NY, 1961-63; treas. Citizens' Com. Edn., Garden City Park, 1962; mem. nat. jr. book awards com. Boys' Clubs Am., 1954; mem. nat. hon. com. for Richard H. Heindel Meml. Fund, Pa. State U., 1979-80. With Signal Corps, U.S. Army, 1951-53. Recipient non-fiction awards Midwestern Writers Conf., Chgo., 1948, 1950; honoree South Street Seaport Mus., Explorers Club, NYC, 2006. Mem. New Hyde Park C. of C., NY, (dir. 1961-62), Titanic Hist. Soc., S.S. Hist. Soc. Am., Titanic Internat., Soc. Advancement of Edn. (treas. 1953-99, trustee 1963-99, pres. 1968-99), Ocean Liner Mus. (1983-2002), NYC, Psi Chi Omega. Home: 82 Shelbourne Ln New Hyde Park NY 11040-1044

LEHRMAN, MARGARET MCBRIDE, broadcast executive, television producer; d. John P. and Ruth A. McBride; m. Michael L. Lehrman, June 27, 1970. BA, U. Oreg., 1966; MS, Columbia U., 1970. Staff Peace Corps, Washington, 1966-69; with The Morning News Co., Washington, 1970-72; radio and newspaper reporter Albright Comms., Washington, 1973-74; tv assignment editor ABC News, Washington, 1974; press asst. Senator Robert P. Griffin, Washington, 1975-79; rschr. Today Show, NBC News, Washington, 1979, assoc. prodr., 1979—83, Washington prodr., 1983-89, dep. bur. chief, 1989-95, sr. Washington prodr. spl. coverage and events, 1995—. Trustee U. Oreg. Found., 1990-2000; Internat. Women's Media Found., Women's Fgn. Policy Group, World Affairs Coun. Recipient Edwin M. Hood award for diplomatic reporting (China), Nat. TV News Emmy award. Office: NBC News 4001 Nebraska Ave NW Washington DC 20016-2733 Home Phone: 202-483-1369. Business E-Mail: margaret.lehrman@nbc.com.

LEHTIHALME, LARRY K. (LAURI LEHTIHALME), financial planner; b. Montreal, Que., Can., Feb. 26, 1937; came to U.S., 1964; s. Lauri Johann and Selma Maire (Piispanen) L.; m. Elizabeth Speed Smith, Sept. 9, 1961; children: Tina Beth, Shauna Lyn. Student, Sir George Williams U., Montreal, 1960-64, Mission Coll., San Fernando, Calif., 1978-80, Pierce Coll., Woodland Hills, Calif., 1990-92. Lic. in variable annuity, life and disability ins., Calif.; lic. securities series 7 SEC, series 63. Acct., customer svc. cons. No. Electric, Montreal, 1957—64; salesman Remington Rand Systems, Wilmington, Del., 1964—67; account exec., comm. cons. Pacific Tel. & Telegraph Co., LA, 1968—84; tech. customer support specialist AT&T, LA, 1984—85; fin. advisor Ameriprise Fin. Svcs., Inc., LA, 1987—. Mem. L.A. World Affairs Coun., 1998—. Mem. ctrl. com. Calif. 39th Assembly Dist. Rep. Com., 1976-81, 12th dist. adv. com. City of LA, 1976-02, chmn. recreation and pks. 12th dist. subcom. City of LA, 1976-83; pres. North Hills Jaycees, 1969-70; sec.-treas. Com. Ind. Valley City and County Govt., 1978-82; subchmn. allocations United Way, Van Nuys, Calif., 1990; fundraiser North Valley YMCA, 1986-98; formerly active numerous comty. and polit. orgns. in San Fernando Valley. Named Jaycee of Yr., Newark (Del.) Jaycees, 1966, Granada Hills Jaycees, 1971; recipient cert. of merit U.S. Ho. of Reps., 1973, award of merit, City of L.A., 1970, cert. appreciation, 1980, 84, tribute, 2003, State of Calif., 20th senate dist., 1983, Comty. Spirit award, 1990. Mem. L.A. Olympic Organizing Com. Alumni Assn., Jr. Chamber Internat. (life, senator 1973), U.S. Jaycees (life, Jaycee of Yr. 1965, Outstanding Local Jaycee 1965-66, Presdl. award Honor 1967, Jaycee of Month 1966-67, state dir. North Hollywood chpt. 1970-71, Cert. Merit 1971, Outstanding State Chmn. Calif. dist. 22 1973-74), State of Calif. Jaycees (asst. gen. chmn. 1970-71, state gen. chmn. 1971-72, 72-73, Granada Hills C. of C. (bd. dirs. 1976-83, Man of Yr. award 1973), Granada Hills Jr. C. of C. Episcopalian. Avocation: community service. Home: 11408 Haskell Ave Granada Hills CA 91344-3959 Office: Ameriprise Fin Svcs Inc 17050 Chatsworth St Ste 235 Granada Hills CA 91344-5898 Office Phone: 818-360-0390. Personal E-mail: llehti@aol.com. Business E-Mail: lauri.k.lehtihalme@ampf.com.

LEI, HUI, computer scientist; b. Wuhan, Hubei, China, Oct. 14, 1966; s. Zichao Lei and Shuzheng Yao; m. Huiwei Wu, July 6, 1995; children: Ethan children: Jason Hui. BS, Zhongshan U., Guangzhou, China, 1987; MS, NYU, 1989; MPhil, Columbia U., 1995, PhD, 1997. Sr. software engr. Syncsort Inc., Woodcliff Lake, NJ, 1990—93; rsch. staff mem. IBM T. J. Watson Rsch. Ctr., Yorktown Heights, NY, 1998—. Chair Mobile Computing Profl. Interests Cmty., IBM Rsch., 2002—; program co-chair Second ACM Internat. Workshop on Mobile Commerce, 2002; conf. chmn. internat. conf. on mobile data mgmt. IEEE, 2004, program co-chair, internat. conf. on e-bus. engring., 05. Guest editor: jour. spl. issue IEEE Pervasive Computing, IEEE Wireless Comm., ACM/Baltzer Mobile Networks and Applications; arch. comml. software; contbr. articles to profl. jours. Achievements include patents for the system and method for performing joins and self-joins in a database system; the system and method for disconnected database access by heterogeneous clients; patents pending for the method and apparatus for content prefetching and preparation; the method and apparatus for providing a flexible and scalable context service; the method and apparatus for providing extensible scalable transcoding of multimedia content; the system and method for sorting embedded content in Web pages; system and method for enabling disconnected Web access; the method and apparatus for fusing context data; the system and method for web services QoS observation and dynamic selection; the method and system for context-aware unified communication; the system and method for pervasive enablement of buisness processes; the apparatus and method of semantic-based publish-subscribe systems. Avocations: music, travel, volleyball. Home: 15 Clarendon Pl Scarsdale NY 10583 Office: IBM T J Watson Rsch Ctr Route 134 Yorktown Heights NY 10598 Office Phone: 914-945-3624. E-mail: hlei@us.ibm.com.

LEIBEL, STEVEN ARNOLD, radiologist; MD, U. Calif., San Francisco, 1972. Bd. cert. radiation oncology, bd. cert. therapeutic radiology. Intern U. Calif., San Francisco, 1972—73, resident radiation oncology, 1973—76, assoc. prof. radiation oncology, 1982—88; vice chmn., clin. dir. dept. radiation oncology Meml. Sloan-Kettering Cancer Ctr., NYC, 1988—98; chmn. radiation oncology Meml. Sloan Kettering Cancer Ctr., NYC, 1998—. Mem.: Am. Bd. Radiology (pres.). Office: Stanford Cancer Ctr 875 Blake Wilbur Dr Mc 5827 Stanford CA 94305-5827

LEIBER, GERSON AUGUST, artist; b. Bklyn., Nov. 12, 1921; s. William and Rebecca (Margulis) L.; m. Judith Maria Peto, Feb. 5, 1946. Student art, Art Students League, NYC, 1947-52, Bklyn. Mus. Art Sch., 1952-53; DFA (hon.), Bar Ilan U., Israel, 1993. Instr. Newark Sch. Fine and Indsl. Arts; v.p. Judith Leiber, Inc., NYC, 1963—. One-man shows Oakland (Calif.) Mus., 1960, N.Y.C., 1961, 62, 63, 64, 68, 69, 72, 76, 85, 95, 96, 98, 99, Fine Arts Mus. L.I. (N.Y.), 1991, Steinbaum-Kraus Gallery, 1998, Denise Bibro Gallery, East Hampton, 2001, 2003, Guild Hall Mus., 2003, Leiber Gallery, East Hampton, N.Y.; exhibited in numerous nat. and internat. group shows, prints and paintings represented in pvt. and permanent collections With US Army, 1942-47. Recipient numerous prizes including Bklyn. Mus. Purchase awards, 1953-66, 2d prize of $1,000, Assoc. Am. Artists Nat. Print Exhbn., 1959, Soc. Washington Printmakers prize, 1962, purchase award Hunterdon County Art Center 6th nat. print exhbn., 1962, Audubon medals of Honor for Graphics, 1963, 65, Sonia Watter award Am. Color Print Soc., 1968, 1000 Purchase award Assn. Am. Artists, 1968, John Taylor Arms Meml. prize NAD, 1971, Lifetime Achievement award Soc. Am. Graphic Artists, 2006; Tiffany fellow, 1957, 60 Mem. NAD (assoc. 1978-91, academician 1991-, Soc. Am. Graphic Artists (past pres., Lifetime Achievement award 2006), Art Students League N.Y. Studio: 36 E 31st St New York NY 10016 Home Phone: 212-679-5870; Office Phone: 212-481-3436.

LEIBER, JUDITH MARIA, designer, manufacturer; b. Budapest, Hungary, Jan. 11, 1921; came to U.S., 1947, naturalized, 1949; d. Emil and Helen (Spitzer) Peto; m. Gerson Leiber, Feb. 6, 1946. Student pvt. schs., Hungary and Eng.; DFA (hon.), Internat. Fine Arts Coll., 1993; PhD (hon.), Bar Ilan U., Israel, 1993, Internat. Fine Arts Coll., Miami, Fla., 1993. Master handbag maker, Hungary, 1942; pattern maker, designer Nettie Rosenstein, NYC, 1947-60, Koret, NYC, 1960-61; owner, mgr. Judith Leiber, Inc., NYC, 1963—. Author: (Book) Judith Leiber, The Artful Handbag; (Designer) Retrospective exhbn. 30 yrs. F.I.T. Mus., N.Y.C., 1993—94, Retrospective exhbn. Corcoran Mus., Washington, 2002, designer Bush Libr., College Station, 2004, Walton Art Ctr., Fayetteville, Ark., 2004, Newark Mus., 2004. Recipient Swarovski award and Am. Handbag Designer award, Leather Industries Am., 1970, Hall of Fame award, Accessory Coun., 2001, George Washington award, Am. Hungarian Found., 2001, Coty award, Am. Fashion Critics, 1973, Neiman-Marcus award, 1980, Women Who Made a Difference award Fashion Group, 1986, Lifetime Achievement award, Dallas Mart, 1991, Am. Acad. Achievement award, 1992, FAAB Lifetime Achievement award, 1992, Ellis Island Medal Honor, 1993, Lifetime Achievement award, Coun. Fashion Designers Am., 1993, Fashion Hall of Fame award, Shannon Rodgers & Jerry Silverman Sch. Fashion Design and Merchandising, Kent State U., 1995, featured Retrospective of Work New Orleans Mus. Mem. Nat. Handbag Authority (dir. 1972—) Achievements include pioneering woman master handbag maker, Hungary; first woman patternmaker Am. handbag industry.

LEIBERT, BURTON M., lawyer; b. Bklyn., Sept. 6, 1945; AB, Franklin & Marshall Coll., 1966; JD, Georgetown U., 1969, LLM, 1973. Bar: Va. 1969, DC 1970, NY 1981. Asst. dir. Div. Investment Mgmt. SEC; counsel ERISA Regulation and Fiduciary Responsibility US Dept. Labor; ptnr. Corp. and Fin. Svcs. Dept. Willkie Farr & Gallagher LLP, NYC. Mem.: ABA, Assn. Bar of City NY. Office: Willkie Farr & Gallagher LLP 787 Seventh Ave New York NY 10019 Office Phone: 212-728-8238. Office Fax: 212-728-9238. E-mail: bleibert@willkie.com.

LEIBHOLZ, STEPHEN WOLFGANG, physicist, information technology executive, entrepreneur; b. Jan. 28, 1932; s. Ernest S. and Louise (Stern) L.; m. Ann Esther Greenberg, May 29, 1958; children: Judith, Robert, Daniel. BA in Physics, NYU, 1952. Prin. engr. Repub. Fairchild Co., Farmingdale, NY, 1957-60; mgr. sys. design and analysis Auerbach Corp., Phila., 1960-67; founder, CEO Analytics Inc., 1967—90, ACS, Inc., 1987—90, Chesapeake TechLabs Inc., 1986—, Gensor Inc., 1996—; co-founder, vice chmn., chief scientific officer VizorNet, Inc., 2002—. Spl. employee, US Govt.; former bd. mem., Military Ops. Rsch. Soc.; former bd. visitors Marine Biological Lab.; sr. fellow Fgn. Policy Rsch. Inst. Author and editor 7 books; contbr. papers, articles to profl. publs. Bd. dirs. Jenkintown Music Sch., 1970-74; advisor Kansas City Camerata Chamber Orch. Cons. U. Arts, Pa. Conv. Ctr.; mem. adv. bd. Inst. for Adv. Psychology; former trustee Cheltenham Ctr. for Arts. Fellow Fgn. Policy Rsch. Inst. (sr.); mem. AAAS, IEEE (life), SPIE, Mil. Ops. Rsch. Soc. (past bd. dirs.), Marine Biol. Soc. (past mem sci. bd.), Inst. for Advanced Psychology (mem. sci. bd.), NY Composers Cir. (chmn.), Assn. Old Crows, Cosmos Club Washington. Avocations: composing music, photography. Office: 2333 Huntingdon Pike Huntingdon Valley PA 19006-6109 Office Phone: 215-938-7800. Business E-Mail: swl@techlabs.com.

LEIBLER, KENNETH ROBERT, finance company executive; b. NYC, Feb. 21, 1949; s. Max and Martha (Dales) L.; m. Marcia Kate Reiss, July 15, 1973; children: Jessica Hope, Andrew Ethan. BA magna cum laude, Syracuse U., 1971; postgrad., U. Pa., 1972. Mgr. options Lehman Bros., 1972-75; v.p. options Am. Stock Exchange, NYC, 1975-79, sr. v.p. adminstrn. and fin., 1979-81, exec. v.p. adminstrn. and fin., 1981-85, sr. exec. v.p., 1985-86, pres., 1986-90, Liberty Fin. Cos., Boston, 1990—2001; chmn. Boston Stock Exchange, 2001—03, Boston Options Exchange, 2004—. Instr. N.Y. Inst. Fin.; bd. dirs. Ruder Finn Group, Optimun Funds, Northwest Utilities; trustee Putman Funds. Contbg. author: Handbook of Financial Markets: Securities, Options Futures, 1981. Trustee Beth Israel Deaconess Med. Ctr. Mem. Securities Industry Assn., Phi Beta Kappa, Phi Kappa Phi.

LEIBOLD, ARTHUR WILLIAM, JR., lawyer; b. Ottawa, Ill., June 13, 1931; s. Arthur William and Helen (Cull) L.; m. Nora Collins, Nov. 30, 1957; children: Arthur William III, Alison Aubry, Peter Collins. AB, Haverford Coll., 1953; JD, U. Pa., 1956. Bar: Pa. 1957. With Dechert, Price & Rhoads, Phila., 1956—69, ptnr., 1965—69, Washington, 1972—97. Gen. counsel Fed. Home Loan Bank Bd. and Fed. Savs. & Loan Ins. Corp., Washington, 1969-72, Fed. Home Loan Mortgage Corp., 1970-72; lectr. English St. Joseph's Coll., Phila., 1957-59 Contbr. articles to profl. publs. Mem. Pres. Kennedy's Lawyers Com. Civil Rights, 1963, Adminstrv. Conf. U.S., 1969-72; bd. dirs. Marymount Coll. Va., 1974-75; Mem. Phila. Com. 70, 1965-74, Fellowship Commn. Mem. ABA (mem. ho. dels. 1967-69, 79-88, treas. 1979-83, mem. fin. com., mem. bd. govs. 1977-83), Fed. Bar Assn. (mem. nat. coun. 1971-80), D.C. Bar Assn., Phila. Bar Assn., Am. Bar Found. (treas. 1979-83), Am. Bar Ret. Assn. (dir. 1978-83), Am. Bar Endowment (bd. dirs. 1984-97, pres. 1995-97), Am. Bar Ins. (bd. dirs. 1999—, treas.), Chester River Yacht and Country Club (Chestertown, Md.), Tequesta CC, Fla., Skating Club Phila., Order of Coif, Phi Beta Kappa. Republican. Roman Catholic. Office: Dechert 1775 Eye St NW Ste 1100 Washington DC 20006-2424 Office Phone: 202-261-3301. Personal E-mail: leibold1@aol.com. Business E-Mail: aleibold@dechert.com.

LEIBOVICH, SIDNEY, engineering educator; b. Memphis, Apr. 2, 1939; s. Harry and Rebecca (Palant) L.; m. Gail Barbara Colin, Nov. 24, 1962; children: Bradley Colin, Adam Keith. BS, Calif. Inst. Tech., Pasadena, 1961; PhD in Theoretical and Applied Mechanics, Cornell U., 1965. NATO postdoctoral fellow U. Coll., London, 1965-66; asst. prof. thermal engrng. Cornell U., Ithaca, NY, 1966-70, assoc. prof. thermal engring., 1970-78, prof. mech. and aerospace engring., 1978-89, Samuel B. Eckert prof. mech. and aerospace engring., 1989—, S.C. Thomas Sze dir. Sibley Sch. Mech. and Aerospace Engring, 1998—2005. Chmn. U.S. Nat. Com. for Theoretical and Applied Mechanics, 1990—92. Editor: Nonlinear Waves, 1974; assoc. editor: Jour. Fluid Mechanics, 1982-93; co-editor: Acta Mechanica, 1986-92; mem. editl. bd. Ann. Revs. of Fluid Mechanics, 1989-93; gen. editor Cambridge U. Press Monographs on Mechanics, 1994-04. Disting. lectr. Naval Ocean Rsch. Devel. Activity, 1983. Recipient MacPherson prize Calif. Inst. Tech., 1961. Fellow ASME (chmn. applied mechanics div. 1987-88), Am. Phys. Soc. (chmn. div. fluid dynamics 1987-88), Am. Acad. Arts and Scis.; mem. Nat. Acad. Engring. Office: Cornell U 246 Upson Hall Ithaca NY 14853 Office Phone: 607-255-3477. E-mail: SL23@cornell.edu.

LEIBOVITZ, ANNIE, photographer; b. Waterbury, Conn., Oct. 2, 1949; children: Sarah, Susan Anna, Samuelle Edith. BFA, San Francisco Art Inst., 1971. Photographer Rolling Stone, 1970-83, chief photographer, 1973-83; photographer Conde Nast Vanity Fair, Vogue, 1980—; proprietor Annie Leibovitz Studio, NYC. Works exhibited in various galleries and mus. including the National Portrait Gallery, Washington DC, 1991, The Corcoran Gallery, 1999; author: Photographs: Annie Leibovitz 1970-1990, 1992, Olympic Portraits: Annie Leibovitz, 1996, Annie Leibovitz: Women,(with essay by Susan Sontag) 1999, American Music, 2003, A Photographer's Life: 1990-2005, 2006; creator offcl. portfolio for 26th Olympic Games, Atlanta, 1995. Recipient Photographer of Yr. award Am. Soc. Mag. Photographers, 1984, Innovation in Photography award Am. Soc. Mag. Photographers, 1987, Clio award, 1987, Campaign of Decade award Advt. Age mag., 1987, Infinity award for applied photography Internat. Ctr. for Photography, 1990; named one of Top 10 Living Artists, ARTnews mag., 1999. Achievements include first woman and second photographer to have a solo exhibit at The National Portrait Gallery. also: Art & Commerce Care Jim Moffat 755 Washington St New York NY 10014-1746 Office: Annie Leibovitz Studio 311 W 11th St New York NY 10014-2368 E-mail: als@leibovitzstudio.com.

LEIBOW, RONALD LOUIS, lawyer; b. Santa Monica, Calif., Oct. 4, 1939; s. Norman and Jessica (Kellner) L.; m. Linda Bengelsdorf, June 11, 1961 (div. Dec. 1974); children: Jocelyn Elise, Jeffrey David, Joshua Aaron; m. Jacqueline Blatt, Apr. 6, 1986. AB, Calif. State U., Northridge, 1962; JD, UCLA, 1965. Bar: Calif. 1966, U.S. Dist. Ct. (cen. dist.) Calif. 1966, U.S. Dist. Ct. (no., so. and ea. dists.) Calif. 1971. Spl. asst. city atty. City of Burbank, Calif., 1966-67; from assoc. to ptnr. Meyers, Stevens & Walters, LA, 1967-71; ptnr. Karpf, Leibow & Warner, Beverly Hills, Calif., 1971-74, Volk, Newman Gralla & Karp, L.A., LA, 1979-81, Spector & Leibow, LA, 1982-84, Stroock & Stroock & Lavan, LA, 1984-94, Kaye Scholer LLP, LA, 1994—, mng. ptnr., 1996-97. Lectr. law UCLA, 1968-69, Practicing Law Inst., 2001-; asst. prof. Calif. State U., Northridge, 1969-71, faculty, Practising Law Inst., 2001-. Contbr. articles to profl. jours. Pres. Jewish Cmty. Ctr., Greater LA, 1983-86; vice chair Jewish Cmty. Ctr. Assn. N.Am., NYC, 1988—; vice chair Jewish Fedn. Greater LA, 1988—, chair planning and allocations com., 1998-01, chair Jewish Cmty. Rels. Com., 2006-; chair internat. bd., exec. com. Starlight Children's Found., co-chair exec. com., 2005-06; vice chair Modern and Contemporary Arts Coun., LA County Mus. Art, 2003-. Mem. ABA (bus. bankruptcy com.), Phi Alpha Delta. Avocations: writing, tennis, skiing, travel. Office: Kaye Scholer LLP 1999 Avenue Of The Stars Fl 17 Los Angeles CA 90067-6022 Office Phone: 310-788-1220. Business E-Mail: rleibow@kayescholer.com.

LEIBOWITZ, HERBERT AKIBA, literature and language professor, writer; b. SI, NY, Apr. 26, 1935; s. Morris and Rose (Rabinowitz) L.; m. Susan Yankowitz, May 3, 1978; 1 son, Gabriel. BA, Bklyn. Coll., 1956; MA, Brown U., Providence, 1958; PhD, Columbia U., NYC, 1966. Asst. prof. English Columbia U., 1967-70; asst. prof. humanities Richmond Coll., SI, NY, 1971-73, assoc. prof., 1973-76; assoc. prof. English Coll. SI, 1976-81; prof. English Coll. SI, CUNY and Grad. Ctr., CUNY, 1981—; prof. English emeritus, 1991—. Fannie Hurst vis. prof. Washington U., St. Louis, 1995; Fulbright prof. U. Barcelona, 1999, U. Autonoma, 1999. Author: Hart Crane: An Introduction to the Poetry, 1968, Fabricating Lives, 1989; editor: Selected Music Criticism of Paul Rosenfeld, 1970, Parnassus: Poetry in Review, 1972, Parnassus: Twenty Years of Poetry in Review, 1994, Asphodel, That Greeny Flower and Other William Carlos Williams Love Poems, 1994. Recipient Fels award for edil. distinction Coordinating Coun. Lit. Mags., 1975, Elizabeth Kray award Poets House, 2002; postdoctoral fellow U. Ill. Ctr. Advanced Study, 1968-69, Chamberlain fellow Columbia U., 1970, fellow NY Inst. Humanities, 1987—, Mellon Seminar fellow NYU, 1988, Guggenheim fellow, 1991-92. Mem. PEN (Nora Magid award for disting. editing of lit. mag. 1995), Nat. Book Critics Circle (bd. dirs. 1988-94, pres. 1992-94). Jewish. Home: 205 W 89th St New York NY 10024-1828 Office: Poetry Rev Found 205 W 89th St Apt 8F New York NY 10024-1835 Personal E-mail: parnew@aol.com.

LEIBOWITZ, JACK RICHARD, physicist, educator; b. Bridgeport, Conn., July 21, 1929; BA, MS, NYU; PhD in Physics, Brown U., Providence, RI, 1962. Rsch. physicist MIT Lincoln Lab., 1956—61, Westinghouse Rsch. Labs., Pitts., 1961—64; asst. prof. U. Md., College Park, 1964—69; assoc. prof. physics Cath. U. Am., Washington, 1969—73, prof. physics, 1974—95, prof. physics emeritus, 1995—, assoc. dean for grad. studies, 1988—93, chmn. art dept., 1982—86, acad. senate. Contbr. articles to profl. jours., chapters to books. Fellow: Washington Acad. Scis., Am. Phys. Soc.; mem.: Sigma Xi. Achievements include research in condensed matter physics; superconductivity, electron-phonon interaction, band structure. Address: PO Box 31761 Santa Fe NM 87594-1761 Personal E-mail: jrleib@earthlink.net.

LEIBOWITZ, JON, commissioner; m. Ruth Marcus; children: Emma, Julia. BA, U. Wis., 1980; JD, NYU, 1984. Atty. pvt. practice, Washington, 1984—86; counsel to Senator Paul Simon, 1986—87; chief counsel to Senator Herb Kohl, 1989—2000; chief counsel, staff dir. Senate Subcommittee on Juvenile Justice, 1991—94, Senate Subcommittee on Terrorism and Tech., Washington, 1995—96; Dem. chief counsel, staff dir. Senate Antitrust Subcommittee, Washington, 1997—2000; v.p. Congl. affairs Motion Picture Assn. of Am., 2000—04; commr. FTC, 2004—. Mem.: Phi Beta Kappa. Democrat. Office: FTC 600 Pennsylvania Ave, NW Washington DC 20580 Office Phone: 202-326-3400. Business E-Mail: jleibowitz@ftc.gov.

LEIBOWITZ, JONATHAN STEWART See STEWART, JON

LEIBOWITZ, MARK ALAN, lawyer; b. NYC, Jan. 22, 1950; s. Philip and Muriel Shirley Leibowitz; m. Ann, Nov. 30, 2002; children: Joan, Jonathan. BA, Syracuse U., 1972; JD, U. Miami, 1975. Bar: Fla. 1975, U.S. Dist. Ct. (so. dist.) Fla. 1976, Colo. 1994. Lawyer Wolfson & Diamond, Miami Beach, Fla., 1976-82, Wolpe & Leibowitz, Miami, Fla., 1982—2002, Wolpe, Leibowitz, Alvarez & Fernandez LLP, 2002—. Named one of Best Lawyers in South Fla., South Fla. Legal Guide, 2005, 2006, 2007. Mem.: Dade County Trial Lawyers Am. Bar Assn., Dade County Bar Assn., Fla. Bar Assn. (bd. cert. civil trial lawyer). Avocations: skiing, hiking, golf. Office: Wolpe Leibowitz Alvarez & Fernandez LLP 44 W Flagler Penthouse Miami FL 33130-4400 Office Phone: 305-372-0060. Business E-Mail: mleibowitz@wlaf-law.com.

LEIBOWITZ, MARTIN L., financial services company executive; m. Sarah Leibowitz. BA, U. Chgo., 1955, MS in Physics, 1956; PhD in Math, NYU. Mng. dir., dir. rsch. fixed income and equities, mem. exec. com. Salomon Bros., Inc.; vice-chmn., chief investment officer TIAA-CREF, NYC, 1995—2004; mng. dir. US equity strategy team Morgan Stanley, NYC, 2004—. Author: Franchise Value: A Modern Approach to Security Analysis, 2004; co-author: Inside the Yield Book, 1972. Bd. trustees Carnegie Corp. of NY, 1998—, vice chair, 2002—; trustee Inst. Advanced Studies, Princeton, NJ, 1995—, vice-chmn. bd. trustee, serves on fin. and nominating com. of the bd. and endowment campaign task force. Recipient Nicholas Molodovsky Award, CFA Inst., 1995, James R. Vertin Award, 1998, Award for Profl. Excellence, 2005. Fellow: Am. Acad. Arts and Sciences. Office: Morgan Stanley 1585 Broadway New York NY 10036

LEIBOWITZ, MARVIN, lawyer; b. Phila., Jan. 24, 1950; s. Aaron and Ethel (Kashoff) L.; m. Faye Rebecca Liepack, Nov. 12, 1983; children: Cheryl Renée, Ellen Paulette. BA, Temple U., 1971, postgrad., 1971-72; JD, Widener U., 1976. Bar: Pa. 1977, N.J. 1977, U.S. Dist. Ct. N.J. 1977, U.S. Dist. Ct. (we. dist.) Pa. 1980. Atty.-advisor SSA, Pitts., 1977-95, sr. atty., 1995—2001; quality assurance reviewer Office of Program and Integrity Revs., 1997; pvt. practice Pitts., 1979—. Apptd. quality assurance rev. and arbitrator US Dist. Ct. for We. Dist. Pa.; mem. equal opportunity rev. commn. City of Pitts. Active Phila. Dem. Com., 1973—77. Pa. State Scholar Pa. Higher Edn. Assistance Agy., Harrisburg, 1967-71; recipient U.S. Dept. Health and Human Svcs. Assoc. Commr.'s citation, 1994. Mem. ABA, Nat. Treasury Employees Union (regional steward 1982-99, regional v.p. 1999-2001), Pa. Bar Assn., Allegheny County Bar Assn. Democrat. Jewish. Home: 6501 Landview Rd Pittsburgh PA 15217-3000 Office Phone: 412-391-1191. Personal E-mail: marvleibo@yahoo.com.

LEIBRECHT, MURL EDWIN, preventive medicine physician, consultant, retired military officer; b. Spokane, Wash., June 21, 1945; s. Frank John and Minnie Louise Leibrecht; m. Karen Rae Kappel, Aug. 12, 1967. BA, Whitman Coll., Walla Walla, Wash., 1967; MD, U. Utah Coll. Medicine, Salt Lake City, 1971; MPH, Harvard U., Boston, 1986. Diplomate Nat. Bd. Med. Examiners, 1972, preventive/aerospace medicine Am. Bd. Preventive Medicine, 1988. Chief physician aeromedical svcs. McChord AFB Clinic, Tacoma, 1977—80; clinic dir. and embassy med. advisor USAF Clinic, Oslo, 1980—85; command chief physician aerospace medicine SAC, Omaha, 1987—90; program dir. residency in aerospace medicine USAF Sch. Aerospace Medicine, San Antonio, 1990—93; chief physician/command surgeon USAF Space Command, Colorado Springs, 1993—96; clinic dir. Bad Aibling Sta. Clinic, Germany, 1996—2004; cons. physician Landstuhl Regional Med. Ctr., 2004—. Med. advisor US Embassy, Oslo, 1980—85; asst. prof. Uniformed Svcs. U. Health Sciences, Bethesda, Md., 1990—96; chmn. dept. aerospace medicine USAF Sch. of Aerospace Medicine, San Antonio, 1992; med. mem.astronaut selection bd. USAF Astronaut Selection Bd., Washington, 1993—96; mem. and med. advisor USAF Space Shuttle Support Team, Patrick Air Force Base, Fla. Editor: (report) Integrating Women into High Altitude Reconaissance Aircraft Flight Operations; contbr. scientific papers. Working mem. Habitat for Humanity, San Antonio, 1990—. Col. USAF, 1972—96. Decorated Legion of Merit USAF; recipient First prize, Student AMA Sci. Rsch. Competition, 1971. Fellow: Am. Coll. of Preventive Medicine (life), Aerospace Med. Assn. (life); mem.: Soc. of Air Force Flight Surgeons (pres. 1995—96), Nat. Wildlife Fedn. (life), Nat. Audubon Soc. (life), Order of Waiilatpu (life), Tau Kappa Epsilon (life). Independent. Avocations: travel, photography, skiing, creative writing, gardening. Home: En Bout Tournus 71700 France Office: Landstuhl Regional Medical Ctr CMR 402 Box 1147 APO AE 09180 Home Phone: 01133 38532 1265; Office Phone: 01149 637186 8048. Business E-Mail: murl.leibrecht@lnd.amedd.army.mil.

LEIBY, ARTHUR DANIEL, accountant; b. Easton, Md., Apr. 6, 1951; s. Marion George Leiby and Marian Belle Kendall. BA, Morningside Coll., Sioux City, Iowa, 1973; MA, West Chester U., Pa., 1975, Wash. Coll., Chestertown, Md., 1983. Revenue specialist Comptr. of the Treasury, Motor Vehicle Fuel Tax Divsn., Annapolis, Md., 1978—88; intermittent specialist, unemployment ins. and job svc. Md. Dept. Labor, Licensing and Regulation, Chestertown, 1991—97; fiscal accounts clk. II Kent County Office of Child Support, Kent County Dept. of Social Svcs., Chestertown, 1997—. Mem. Nat. Eagle Scouts Assn., Boy Scouts of Am., 1980—2006, Hist. Soc. Kent County, Inc, Chestertown, 1985—2006; life mem. Confraternity of the Blessed Sacrament (Anglican devotional soc.), 1986—2006; mem. Nat. Episcopal Historians and Archvists, Swarthmore, Pa., 1986—2006, Episcopal Women's History Project, 1986—2006, Hist. Soc. of the Episcopal Ch., 1986—2006; founding mem. Gen. Conf. Hist. Soc. of the United Meth. Ch., 1988—2006; mem. Order of St. Vincent, 1985—2006; diocesan archivist Episcopal Diocese Easton, 1986—2006, diocesan coun. mem., 1987—90, lic. lay reader, 1973—2006, chalicist, 1973—2006, lay eucharistic min., 1973—2006; founding mem. Peninsula-Del. Conf. Hist. Soc., United Meth. Ch., Dover, 1986—2006, former rec. sec., former mem. exec. com.; mem. Upper Shore Geneal. Soc. Md., Inc., Easton, 1983—2004, former bd. dirs.; sec., trustee Salem M.E.Ch., Centreville, Md., 1974—2006; trustee Queen Anne's County Hist. Soc., Inc., Centreville, Md., 1980—2006, sec., 1980—2006, life mem., 1980—2006, newsletter editor, 1985—89. Mem.: Am. Guild of Organists. Democrat. Episcopalian. Avocations: genealogy, historic preservation. Home Phone: 410-648-5586; Office Phone: 410-810-7773. Office Fax: 410-810-8931. Business E-Mail: aleiby@dhr.state.md.us.

LEIBY, BRUCE RICHARD, retired secondary school educator, writer; b. Media, Pa., Aug. 30, 1947; s. Edward Charles and Margaret Ellen (Strawbridge) L.; m. Linda Pauline Flounders, June 26, 1971. BSBA, Tusculum Coll., Greeneville, 1969; postgrad., West Chester U., Pa., 1970-72. Tchr. Interboro Sch. Dist., Prospect Park, Pa., 1969-70, Delaware County C.C., Media, 1974; acct., tchr. info. processing Upper Darby Adult Sch., Pa., 1970-88, Upper Darby Sch. Dist., Pa., 1970—2006; ret., 2006. Staff asst. Upper Darby H.S., 1987-2006, mem. bus. edn. adv. bd., co-sponsor Bus. Club, 1987-2006; mem. bus. edn. curriculum com., 1992-2006. Author for Greenwood Press, Westport, Conn., 1988—; author: Gordon Macrae--A Bio-Bibliography, 1991, Howard Keel--A Bio-Bibliography, 1995; co-author: A Reference Guide to Television's Bonanza, 2001, The Scribner Encyclopedia of American Lives, 2007. Co-lay leader Meth. ch.; mem. Praise Team. Named to Contemporary Authors, 2007. Mem. NEA, Pa. Edn. Assn., Upper Darby Edn. Assn. (past membership chmn.), Internat. Friends of Gordon Macrae, Internat. Doris Day Soc., Michael Crawford Fan Club, Michael Ball Fan Club. Republican. Avocations: music, reading, collecting performing arts memorabilia, acting. Home: 13 E 6th St Media PA 19063-2501

LEICH, JEFFREY R., museum director; b. Wash., DC, May 13, 1949; s. Harold Herbert and Cora McIver Leich; m. Martha H. Leich, Sept. 16, 1990; children: Alexander H., Emily A. BA, Dartmouth Coll., Hanover, NH, 1971. Asst. mgr. Ea. Mountain Sports, N.Conway, NH, 1972—74; area shop mgr. Jack Frost Shop, NH, 1977—82; golf course supt. Eagle

Mountain Ho., Jackson, 1978—86; ski shop mgr. Ski Rack, Alta, Utah, 1983—86; park ranger Mt. Wash. State Pk., Gorham, NH, 1986—96; ski patrol dir. Wildcat Mountain, Jackson, 1994—97; exec. dir. New Eng. Ski Mus., Franconia, 1997—. Mem. editl. bd. Skiing Heritage, 2001—. Editor: Jour. New Eng. Ski Mus., 1997—; author: (books) Over the Headwall, 1999, Tales of the 10th, 2003. Sec. Friends of Tuckerman, N.Conway, 1999—; v.p. NH Outdoor Council, 2001—. Recipient Good Buddy award, 10th Mountain Divsn, 2003, Bill Whitney award, Ski NH, 2006, Curatorial award, Internat. Skiing History Assn., 2007. Mem.: Ea. Ski Writers Assn. Home: 3480 W Side Rd North Conway NH 03860 Office: New Eng Ski Mus PO Box 267 Franconia NH 03580 Office Phone: 603-823-7177. Business E-Mail: jeff@skimuseum.org.

LEICHTLING, MICHAEL ALFRED, lawyer; b. NYC, Mar. 30, 1943; s. Stanley Arthur and Roslyn Priscilla (Fuhr) L.; m. Arlene Dorf, July 30, 1966; children: Julie Karen Nacos, Nina Anastasia, Noah James. BA, SUNY, Binghamton, 1963; JD, Northwestern U., 1966; postgrad., Columbia U., 1968. Bar: N.Y. 1969, U.S. Ct. Appeals (2d cir.) 1969. Assoc. Aranow Brodsky Bohlinger Einhorn & Dann, NYC, 1966, Parker Chapin & Flattau, NYC, 1969-77; ptnr. Parker Chapin Flattau & Klimpl, LLP, NYC, 1977-2001, Jenkens & Gilchrist Parker Chapin LLP, NYC, 2001—05, Troutman Sanders LLP, NYC, 2005—, mem. exec. com. Bd. dir. H. Warshow & Sons Inc., N.Y.C. Editor Northwestern U. Law Rev., 1965-66, Equipment Leasing Jour., 1986—; co-editor Commercial Finance Guide, 1997—, Commercial Loan Documentation Guide, 1997—. Bd. dir., exec. com. Friends of Israel Disabled Vets., N.Y.C., 1986—; bd. trustees, chmn., exec. com. Equipment Leasing and Fin. Found., Arlington, Va., 1998—. With U.S. Army, 1966-68; Vietnam. Decorated Bronze Star; Regents scholar, 1963, Newman scholar, 1963-66. Mem. N.Y. State Bar Assn. (corp. law sect.), N.Y. County Lawyers Assn. (banking law com., secured lending com.), Equipment Leasing and Fin. Assn. (bd. dir. 2001-2004, exec. com. 2007, industry future coun.), Ea. Assn. Equipment Lessors (gen. counsel 1986—) Avocations: reading, painting, swimming, golf. Home: 148 Quinn Rd Briarcliff Manor NY 10510-2133 Office: 405 Lexington Ave New York NY 10174-0002 Office Phone: 212-704-6257. Business E-Mail: michael.leichtling@troutmansanders.com.

LEIDEL, KATHERINE, journalist, newscaster; b. Vienna, June 28, 1954; arrived in U.S., 1956; d. Donald Charles and Beverly (Broy) Leidel; 1 child, David Michael Harris. Student, Santa Clara U., Calif., 1972-73, Inst. European Studies, Madrid, 1973, George Washington U., 1974; BS in Orgnl. Mgmt., Palm Beach Atlantic Coll., 1998. Mgr./developer The Country Store, Knoxville, 1976-77; cons. Southeastern Sight & Sound, Raleigh, 1977-79; producer Capitol Broadcasting Co., Raleigh, 1979-80; newsanchor Mann Media Broadcasting, Raleigh, 1980-81, Fairbanks Broadcasting, West Palm Beach, Fla., 1981-83; writer West Communications, Orlando, Fla., 1987-88; artist-in-residence Sch. Arts Palm Beach County, Fla., 1991-94; writer WeekDay Newspaper, Palm Beach Gardens, Fla., 1996-97. Mgr. Nutrition World, 1996—98; writer WeekDay Newspaper, Palm Beach Gardens, Fla., 1996—97; pub. rels. dir. Am. Lung Assn. S.E. Fla., 1998—2004; dir. comm. Am. Lung Assn. Fla., 2003—04; instr. N.Am. Riding for Handicapped Assn. Contbr. articles to profl. jours. Vol. Nassau County Humane Soc. Recipient Working Women's award, The White House, 1980. Mem.: Fla. Motion Picture and TV Assn. (v.p. 1987—88, bd. dirs. 1988—91, pres. Palm Beach area chpt. 1990, state v.p. 1991, pres.), Palm Beach County Film Adv. Coun. (hon.; chmn. 1991—93), Fla. Congress Lung Assn. Staff. Avocations: horseback riding, skiing, travel.

LEIDEN, JEFFREY MARC, venture capitalist, molecular biologist, cardiologist; b. Chgo., Oct. 12, 1955; s. Irving and Rosemary (Rebelsky) Leiden; m. Lisa Leyland, June 23, 1982; children: Benjamin Bradford, Alexander Dow. BA in Biol. Sci. with honors, U. Chgo., 1975, MD with honors, 1979, PhD, 1981. Diplomate Am. Bd. Internal Medicine, Am. Bd. Cardiovascular Diseases, lic. cardiologist Mass., Ill. Chief cardiology, Frederick H. Rawson prof. medicine and pathology U. Chgo.; Elkan R. Blout prof. biological sciences Harvard Sch. Public Health; prof. medicine Harvard Medical Sch.; founder Cardiogene, Inc.; bd. dirs. Abbott, 1999, sr. v.p., chief scientific officer, 2000, exec. v.p. pharmaceuticals, 2000, pres., COO pharmaceutical products group, 2001—06; ptnr. Clarus Ventures, 2006—. Cons. Pfizer, Bristol Meyers-Squibb, Boston Scientific Inc. Bd. dirs. Chgo.'s Mus. Sci. and Industry, Ravinia Festival, Keystone Symposia. Fellow: Am. Acad. Arts and Sciences; mem.: Am. Assn. Physicians, Am. Soc. Clinical Investigation, IOM. Office: Clarus Ventures One Memorial Drive Ste 1230 Cambridge MA 02142*

LEIDENIX, MONTE JOHN, ophthalmologist, researcher; b. Bismark, ND, Nov. 7, 1963; s. John and Gladys Leidenix. BS in Microbiology, chemistry, SD State U., Brookings, 1986; MS in Microbiology, Molecular Genetics, U. ND, Grand Forks, 1988, MD, 1992. Cert. Am. Bd. Ophthalmology, 2000, lic. ND, 1997, SD, 1997, Mont., 1997. Fellow ophthalmic pathology rsch. U. Utah, Salt Lake City, 1992—93, intern, 1993—94; resident ophthalmology U. N. Tex. Med. Br., Galveston, Tex., 1994—96, chief resident ophthalmology, 1996—97; ophthalmologist Eye Clinic ND, Bismark, 1997—. Contbr. articles to profl. jours. Grantee, Alcon Labs., Inc., 1992—; Amdahl Med. scholar, U. ND, 1989, Duggin Med. scholar, 1991. Mem.: AMA, Am. Acad. Ophthalmology. Achievements include patents in field; research in intra-ocular lenses. Avocations: basketball, football, softball, water sports, volleyball. Office: Eye Clinic ND 620 N 9th St Bismarck ND 58501-4112

LEIDY, CHARLOTTE, military officer; d. Edward and Mary Ellen Bartholomew. BA, Susquehanna U., Selinsgrove, PA, 1977—81; MS, Naval Postgraduate Sch., Monterey, Calif., 1989. Commd. ensign USN, 1982, advanced through grades to Capt.; plans and exercise officer US Naval Sta., Keflavik, Iceland, 1982—84; chief computer ops. divsn. Navy Regional Data Automation Ctr., Washington, 1985—87; head pers-4 computer sys. and networks Bur. of Naval Pers., Arlington, Va., 1989—93; officer in charge Pers. Support Detachment Crystal City, Arlington, 1994—96; comm. officer and dep. J6 Iceland Def. Force, Keflavik, 1996—97; exec. officer Dept. of Navy Info. Network Program Office, Washington, 1997—98; commdg. officer Naval Computer and Telecom. Sta., Diego Garcia, 1998—99; dep. dir., command control comm., and computer sys. Mil. Sealift Command, Washington, 2000—03; divsn. chief, net-centric capabilities divsn. Joint Chiefs of Staff, Washington, 2003—07. Stephen ministry vol. Faith Luth. Ch., Arlington, 2003—06. Decorated Navy Achievement medal Sec. of Navy, Navy Meritorious Svc. medal, Navy Commendation medal Chief of Naval Ops., Def. Meritorious Svc. medal Comdr., Iceland Def. Force, Def. Superior Svc. medal Sec. of Def. Avocations: golf, travel, bicycling.

LEIER, CARL VICTOR, internist, cardiologist; b. Bismarck, ND, Oct. 20, 1944; married; 3 children. Grad., Creighton U., MD cum laude, 1969. Diplomate Am. Bd. Internal Medicine, Cardiovascular Medicine, Critical Care Medicine, Geriatric Medicine, Electrocardiography, Nat. Bd. Med. Examiners; lic. med., surgical Nebr., med. Ohio. Intern Ohio State U. Coll. Medicine, Columbus, 1969-70, med. resident (instr.) dept. medicine, 1971-73, chief resident (instr.), 1973-74, fellowship divsn. cardiology, 1974-76; pathology resident dept. pathology St. Vincent Hosp., Worcester, Mass., 1970-71; trainee NIH Tng. Grant, 1974-75; asst. prof. medicine cardiology dept., Ohio State U. Coll. Medicine, Columbus, 1976-80, asst. prof. pharmacology, 1976-80, assoc. prof., 1980-84, faculty mem. grad. sch., 1980—, dir. rsch. divsn. cardiology, 1980-83, James W. Overstreet prof. of medicine, 1983—, prof. of medicine divsn. cardiology, 1984—, prof. pharmacology, dept. pharmacology, 1984—, dir. divsn. cardiology, 1986-98. Mem. rsch. com. ctrl. Ohio chpt. Am. Heart Assn., 1977-84, bd. trustees, 1979-88, exec. rsch. com., 1979-84, vice chmn. rsch. com., 1980-82, chmn. rsch. peer rev. com., 1982-84, v.p., 1984-86, pres. elect, 1986-88; numerous other coms.; cons. AMA on Drugs and Tech., 1985—, FDA Cardiorenal adv. com. 1986-92; mem. chmn. Annual Sci. Sessions of the Am. Coll. of Cardiolog, 1996-97; vis. prof., lectr. and presenter at numerous sci. confs., insts. in U.S. and internationally. Editor: (book) Cardiotonic Drugs, 1986, 2d rev. edit., 1991; co-author: (with H. Boudoulas) CardioRenal Disorders and Diseases, 1986, 2d edit., 1992 (with J. Vincent) Critical Care Medicine: Recent Advances in Cardiovascular Medicine, 1990; contbr. more than 40 chpts. to other medical books and almost 200 articles to peer reviewed jours. including: Circulation, Brit. Heart Jour., Jour. Clin. Investigation, Jour. Am. Coll. Cardiology, Am. Jour. Cardiology, Chest, Am. Jour. Medicine, Am. Heart Jour., Annals of Internal Medicine and others; editor in chief Congestive Heart Failure: Index and Revs., 1988-94; mem. editorial bds. of ten medical jours. concerned with heart diseases, the review bds. of others including New Eng. Jour. Medicine, Internat. Jour. Cardiology, Jour. of Lab. and Clin. Medicine. Recipient Upjohn award, 1969, Lange Scholar award, 1969, Golden Apple Student Tchg. award, 1973, 75, Young Investigator award Ctrl. Ohio Heart Chpt., Am. Heart Assn., 1976-78, Rsch. Recognition award, 1978. Fellow Am. Heart Assn., Am. Coll. Cardiology, Am. Coll. Physicians, Coun. on Geriatric Cardiology; mem. AAAS, Am. Fedn. for Clin. Rsch., Ctrl. Soc. for Clin. Rsch., Am. Soc. Clin. Investigation, Assn. Univ. Cardiologists. Office: Ohio State U Med Ctr Divsn Cardiology 473 W 12th Ave Columbus OH 43210-1250 Office Phone: 614-293-8963.

LEIFER, EDGAR, physician, retired medical educator; b. NYC, Aug. 20, 1918; s. Moses and Rose (Greenfield) Leifer; m. Violet S. Beerman, June 17, 1945; 1 child, Dana. BS, CCNY, 1937; PhD, Columbia U., 1941, MD, 1946. Diplomate Am. Bd. Internal Medicine. Rsch. chemist Corning (N.Y.) Glass Works, 1941—43; radiobiologist Los Alamos (N.Mex.) Sci. Lab., 1947—48; chief Isotope Lab. Walter Reed Med. Ctr., Washington, 1948—49; resident physician Presbyn. Hosp., NYC, 1949—51, attending physician, 1951—, dir. med. affairs, 1977—83. Prof. clin. medicine Columbia Presbyn. Med. Ctr., NYC, 1951—2000, prof. emeritus, 2000—03. Contbr. articles to profl. jours. Capt. US Army, 1947—49. Office: Presbyn Hosp 161 Ft Washington Ave New York NY 10032

LEIFERT, TERENCE, engineer; b. Torrington, Conn., May 31, 1967; s. John and Marva Leifert; m. Melanie Bruorton, Aug. 20, 1995; 1 adopted child, Conner 1 child, Brady. Assoc. in Engring., Palm Beach CC, Palm Beach Gardens, Fla., 1998; degree in Bus. Mgmt., U. Phoenix, 2001. Project engr. UTC Pratt and Whitney, East Hartford, Conn., 1995—2002; project mgr. Siemens, Cromwell, Conn., 2002—. Mem.: Mensa. Home Phone: 407-382-2531. Personal E-mail: tleifert@cfl.rr.com.

LEIGH, ANDREW KEITH, economist, researcher; b. Sydney, Aug. 3, 1972; s. Michael and Barbara Leigh; m. Gweneth Newman Leigh, Jan. 18, 2004. BA with hons., U. Sydney, Sydney, Australia, 1994, LLB with hons., 1996; PhD, Harvard U., Cambridge, Mass., 2004. Bar: NSW, Australia 1998. Law clk. Justice Michael Kirby, High Ct. Australia, Canberra, Australia, 1997—98; sr. trade adviser Australian Senate, Canberra, 1998—2000; rsch. fellow Australian Nat. U., Canberra, 2004—. Author: Imagining Australia: Ideas for Our Future, 2004; editor: The Prince's New Clothes: Why do Australians Dislike Their Politicians?, 2002, Kennedy School Rev., 2001. Frank Knox fellowship, Harvard U., 2000—04. Mem.: Am. Econ. Assn. Office: Australian Nat U Spear Rsss Hackett ACT 0200 Australia Office Phone: 011 612 6125 1374. Office Fax: 011 612 6125 0182. Business E-Mail: andrew_leigh@ksg02.harvard.edu.

LEIGH, HOYLE, psychiatrist, educator, writer; b. Seoul, Korea, Mar. 25, 1942; came to U.S., 1965; m. Vincenta Masciandaro, Sept. 16, 1967; 1 child, Alexander Hoyle. MA, Yale U., 1982; MD, Yonsei U., Seoul, 1965. Diplomate Am. Bd. Psychiatry and Neurology. Asst. prof. Yale U., New Haven, 1971-75, assoc. prof., 1975-80, prof., 1980-89, lectr. in psychiatry, 1989—. Dir. Behavioral Medicine Clinic, Yale U., 1980-89; dir. psychiat. cons. svc. Yale-New Haven Hosp., 1971-89; chief psychiatry VA Med Ctr., Fresno, Calif., 1989—; prof., vice chmn. dept. psychiatry U. Calif., San Francisco, 1989—, head dept. psychiatry, 1989—; cons. Am. Jour. Psychiatry, Archives Internal Medicine, Psychosomatic Medicine. Author: The Patient, 1980, 2d edit., 1985, 3d edit., 1992; editor: Psychiatry in the Practice of Medicine, 1983, Consultation-Liaison Psychiatry: 1990's & Beyond, 1994, Biopsychosocial Approaches in Primary Care: State of the Art and Challenges for the 21st Century, 1997. Fellow ACP, Internat. Coll. Psychosomatic Medicine (v.p.), Am. Acad. Psychosomatic Medicine; mem. AMA, AAUP, World Psychiat. Assn. Avocations: reading, music, skiing. Office: U Calif Dept Psychiat 2615 E Clinton Ave Fresno CA 93703-2223

LEIGH, JANIS, clinician; d. Andrew Gordon Williamson and Delores Marie Hilliard; m. Michael Brian Lee, Aug. 3, 2005; 1 child, Charles Kristofer Petersen. BA in Psychology magna cum laude, U. Wash., Seattle, 2004; postgrad., Ind. State U., 2005—. V.p. sales Bell-Anderson Agy. Inc., Kent, Wash., 1981—2001; rsch. coord. U. Wash. Med. Ctr., Seattle, 2004—05; rsch. asst. Ind. State U., Terre Haute, 2005—. Contbr. articles to profl. jours. Youth shelter vol. Auburn Youth Resources, Wash., 1993—94; motivational spkr. Wash. Women's Employment and Edn., Kent, 1993—96; emotional clarity facilitator Internat. Clarity Inst., Fresno, Calif., 2001—03; group therapist Meditation-Based Eating Awareness Therapy, 2006—; pres., CEO 2bme, Inc., Seattle, 2001—06. Mem.: Assn. Behavioral and Cognitive Therapies (assoc.), Golden Key, Phi Beta Kappa. Conservative. Buddhist. Avocations: reading, meditation, yoga, gardening, travel. Home: 4802 E Brentview Ave Terre Haute IN 47805 Office: Ind State U Root Hall 555 S 7th St Terre Haute IN 47809 Home Phone: 812-466-7767; Office Phone: 812-237-3488. Personal E-mail: janisleigh@comcast.net. E-mail: jleigh1@indstate.edu.

LEIGH, JENNIFER JASON (JENNIFER LEIGH MORROW), actress; b. LA, Feb. 5, 1962; d. Barbara Turner and Vic Morrow; m. Noah Baumbach, Sept. 3, 2005. Student, Lee Strasberg Inst. Appearances include (films) Eyes of a Stranger, 1980, Fast Times at Ridgemont High, 1982, Wrong is Right, 1982, Easy Money, 1983, Grandview U.S.A., 1984, Flesh & Blood, 1985, The Hitcher, 1986, The Men's Club, 1986, Sister, Sister, 1987, Under Cover, 1987, Heart of Midnight, 1988, The Big Picture, 1989, Last Exit to Brooklyn, 1989 (Critic Soc. award 1990), Miami Blues, 1990 (Critic Soc. award 1990), Fire Princess, 1990, Crooked Hearts, 1991, Backdraft, 1991, Rush, 1992, Single White Female, 1992, The Prom, 1992, Short Cuts, 1993, The Hudsucker Proxy, 1994, Mrs. Parker and the Vicious Circle, 1994, Dolores Claiborne, 1994, Georgia, 1995, Kansas City, 1996, Bastard Out of Carolina, 1996, A Thousand Acres, 1997, Washington Square, 1997, eXistenZ, 1998, The King is Alive, 2000, Skipped Parts, 2000, Beautiful View, 2000, The Quickie, 2001, The Anniversary Party, 2001, Hey Arnold! The Movie, (voice) 2002, Road to Perdition, 2002, In the Cut, 2003, The Machinist, 2004, Palindromes, 2004, Childstar, 2004 (Genie award 2005), The Jacket, 2005, Easter Sunday, 2005, Rag Tale, 2005; (TV movies) Angel City, 1980, I Think I'm Having a Baby, 1981, The Killing of Randy Webster, 1981, The Best Little Girl in the World, 1981, The First Time, 1982, Have You Ever Been Ashamed of Your Parents?, 1983, Girls of the White Orchid, 1983, Picnic, 1986, Buried Alive, 1990, The Love Letter, 1998, Crossed Over, 2002 (mini series) Thanks of a Grateful Nation, 1998; prodr., actress Georgia, 1995; writer, dir., prodr., actor The Anniversary Party, 2001; TV guest appearances include The Waltons, 1972, Tracey Takes On..., 1996, King of the Hill, 1997; (TV series) Hercules (voice), 1998; appeared in music video Last Cup of Sorrow by Faith No More; (theatre) Cabaret, Proof, Abigail's Party, 2005. Named one of America's 10 Most Beautiful Women, Harper's Bazaar mag., 1989. Office: ICM c/o Tracey Jacobs 8942 Wilshire Blvd Beverly Hills CA 90211-1934 also: care Elaine Rich 2400 Whitman Pl Los Angeles CA 90068-2464

LEIGH, MIKE, film director; b. Salford, England, Feb. 20, 1943; s. A.A. and P.P. (Cousin) Leigh; m. Alison Steadman, 1973 (div. 2001); 2 children. Student, Royal Acad. Dramatic Art, London, Camberwell Sch. Arts and Crafts, Cen. Sch. Art and Design, London Film Sch. Writer, dir.: (plays) The Box Play, 1965, My Parents Have Gone to Carlisle, The Last Crusade of the Five Little Nuns, 1966, Nenaa, 1967, Individual Fruit Pies, Down Here and Up There, Big Basil, 1968, Epilogue, Glum Victoria and the Lad with Specs, 1969, Bleak Moments, 1970, A Rancid Pong, 1971, Wholesome Glory, The Jaws of Death, Dick Whittington and His Cat, 1973, Babies Grow Old, The Silent Majority, 1974, Abigail's Party, 1977, Ecstasy, 1979, Goose-Pimples, 1981 (Critics' Choice Best Comedy award London Evening Std. 1981, Critics' Choice Best Comedy award Drama London 1981), Smelling A Rat, 1988, Greek Tragedy, 1989, It's a Great Big Shame!, 1993, (feature films) Bleak Moments, 1971 (Golden Leopard award Locarno Film Festival 1972, Golden Hugo award Chgo. Film Festival 1972), High Hopes, 1988 (Internat. Critic's prize Venice Film Festival 1988, Best Film Coup de Coeur Geneva 1989, Peter Sellers Best Comedy Film award London Evening Std. 1990), Life is Sweet, 1990, Naked, 1993 (Best Dir. award Cannes Internat. Film Festival 1993), Secrets and Lies, 1996 (Palme d'Or Cannes 1996), Career Girls, 1997, Topsy-Turvy, 1999, All or Nothing, 2002, Vera Drake, 2004; (TV films) A Mug's Game, Hard Labour, 1972, The Permissive Society, The Birth of the 2001 F.A. Cup Final Goalie, Old Chums, Probation, A Light Snack, Afternoon, 1975, Nuts in May, 1976, Knock for Knock, 1976, The Kiss of Death, 1977, Abigail's Party, 1977, Who's Who, 1978, Grown Ups, 1980, Home Sweet Home, 1981, Meantime, 1983, Four Days in July, 1984, The Short and Curlies, 1987, A Sense of History, 1992, (radio play) Too Much of a Good Thing, 1979. Address: Peters Fraser & Dunlop Drury House 34-43 Russell London WC2B 3HA England

LEIGH, VINCENTA M., health administrator; b. NYC, June 27, 1947; d. Emanuel and Ines Masciandara; m. Hoyle Leigh, Sept. 16, 1967; 1 child, Alexander. BA, Lehman Coll., 1968; MSN, Yale U., 1973. Psychiat. clinician Jacobi Hosp., Bronx, NY, 1971; pediatric nurse Conn. Mental Health Ctr., New Haven, 1971-73; instr. in psychiat. nursing Yale U., New Haven, 1973-77; asst. dir. mental health nursing edn. Conn. Valley Hosp., Middletown, 1980-81; nurse coord. Inst. of Living, Hartford, Conn., 1981-85, asst. dir. nursing, 1985-89; asst. clin. profl. psychiatry U. Calif., San Francisco, 1989—; coord. Intensive outpatient program Kaiser Permanent, Fresno, Calif., 1996—. Contbr. articles to profl. jours. Mem. ANA, Am. Psychosomatic Soc., Internat. Coll. Psychosomatic Medicine, Am. Orthopedic Assn., Jr. League. Avocations: piano, reading, trombone, skiing.

LEIGHTON, ALBERT CHESTER, history educator; b. Chester, N.H., Sept. 6, 1919; s. Arthur Edmund and Sarah Elizabeth (Edwards) L.; m. Estella Ruth Dietel, Jan. 17, 1958; children: Cedric Edmund George. AB, U. Calif., Berkeley, 1960, MA, 1961, PhD, 1964. Enlisted U.S. Army, 1937, commd. 2d lt., 1946, advanced through grades to capt., 1953, ret., 1957; ops. officer, Germany, 1947-50, staff officer Hdqrs., Washington, 1950-53, 55-57, ops. officer, Korea, Japan, Taiwan, 1954-55; assoc. prof. history SUNY-Oswego, 1964-69, prof., 1969-85, prof. emeritus, 1985—; adj. prof., lectr. U. Tex. at San Antonio, 1987—; Fulbright Rsch. prof. U. Munich, 1978-79; faculty exchange scholar SUNY, 1981-85; coord. internat. rsch. in hist. cryptanalysis, 1969—; speaker Internat. Congress, St. Petersburg formerly Leningrad, 1970, Moscow, 1971, Tokyo, 1974, Edinburgh, 1977. Author: Transport and Communication in Early Medieval Europe, 1972; contbr. Ency. Americana; contbr. articles to profl. jours. Rsch. fellow Ctr. Medieval and Renaissance Studies UCLA, 1984, Medieval Insts. fellow Duke U., 1976, SUNY Binghamton fellow, 1985. Mem. Am. Hist. Assn., Medieval Acad. Am., Am. Cryptogram Assn., Beale Cypher Soc., Ancient and Honorable Arty. Co. Mass., New Eng. Hist. and Genealogical Soc., Ret. Officers Assn. Home: 8406 Burwell San Antonio TX 78254-2538

LEIGHTON, CHARLES MILTON, retired specialty consumer products executive; b. Portland, Maine, June 4, 1935; s. Wilbur F. and Elizabeth (Loveland) L.; children: Julia Loveland, Anne Throop; m. Roxanne Brooks McCormick, May 23, 1992. AB, Bowdoin Coll., 1957, LLD (hon.), 1989; MBA, Harvard U., 1960. Product lines mgr. Mine Safety Appliances Co., Pitts., 1960-64; instr. Harvard Bus. Sch., 1964-65; group v.p. Bangor Punta Corp., Boston, 1965-69; chmn., CEO CML Group, Inc., Acton, Mass., 1969-97; pvt. investor, cons. mergers and acquisitions Bolton, Mass., 1997—. Exec. dir. U.S. Sailing, 2005—; bd. dirs. Met. Life Ins. Co., N.Y.; trustee Lahey Clinic; chmn. Lahey Clinic Pension Fund. Past pres. Alumni Coun. Harvard Bus. Sch., Cambridge, Mass.; past pres. trustees Concord Acad., Mass. Mem. N.Y. Yacht Club (commodore 1993-94, chmn. trustees Am.'s Cup 2000 Challenge), Chatham (Mass.) Yacht Club (vice commodore 1957), Harvard of N.Y.C., Harvard Faculty Club, Tarratine Club, Carnegie Abby Golf Club. Republican. Episcopalian. Home: 330 Gray Craig Rd Middletown RI 02842 Office Phone: 401-683-0800. E-mail: cleighton@ussailing.org.

LEIGHTON, FRANK T., mathematics professor; BS summa cum laude, Princeton U.; PhD in Math., MIT. Prof. applied math. MIT, head Algorithms Group, Artificial Intelligence Lab., 1996—; co-founder Akamai Technologies, 1998. Chmn. Pres. Info. Tech. Adv. Com. (PITAC), 2003—. Contbr. articles to profl. jours. Fellow: AAAS; mem.: NAE, Assn. Computing Machinery (former chair). Office: MIT Rm 2-377 77 Massachusetts Ave Cambridge MA 02139-4307 Office Phone: 617-253-3662. E-mail: ftl@math.mit.edu.

LEIGHTON, GEORGE NEVES, retired judge; b. New Bedford, Mass., Oct. 22, 1912; s. Antonio N. and Anna Sylvia (Garcia) Leitao; m. Virginia Berry Quivers, June 21, 1942; children: Virginia Anne, Barbara Elaine. AB, Howard U., 1940; LLB, Harvard U., 1946; LLD, Elmhurst Coll., 1964; LLD., John Marshall Law Sch., 1973; LLD, U. Mass., 1975, New Eng. U. Sch. Law, 1978, R.I. Coll., 1992, So. New Eng. Sch. Law, 2000; LLD (hon.), Loyola U., Chgo., 1989. Bar: Mass. 1946, Ill. 1947, U.S. Supreme Ct. 1958. Ptnr. Moore, Ming & Leighton, Chgo., 1951-59, McCoy, Ming & Leighton, Chgo., 1959-64; judge Cook County Circuit Ct., Chgo., 1964-69, Ill. Appellate Ct. (1st dist.), 1969-76; U.S. dist. judge U.S. Dist. Ct. (no. dist.) Ill., 1976-86, sr. dist. judge, 1986-87; ret.; of counsel Earl L. Neal & Assocs., 1987—. Adj. prof. John Marshall Law Sch., Chgo., 1965—; commr., mem. character and fitness com. for 1st Appellate Dist., Supreme Ct. Ill., 1955-63, chmn. character and fitness com., 1961-62; joint com. for revision Ill. Criminal Code, 1959-63; chmn. Ill. adv. com. U.S. Commn. on Civil Rights, 1964; mem. pub. rev. bd. UAW, AFL-CIO, 1961-70; Asst. atty. gen. State of Ill., 1950-51; pres. 3d Ward Regular Democratic Orgn., Cook County, Ill., 1951-53; v.p. 21st Ward, 1964; spl. counsel to chmn. bd. Chgo. Transit Authority, 1988. Contbr. articles to legal jours. Bd. dirs. United Ch. Bd. for Homeland Ministries, United Ch. of Christ, Grant Hosp., Chgo.; trustee U. Notre Dame, 1979-83, trustee emeritus, 1983—; bd. overseers Harvard Coll., 1983-89. Capt., inf. AUS, 1942-45. Decorated Bronze Star; recipient Civil Liberties award Ill. div. ACLU, 1961, U.S. Supreme Ct. Justice John Paul Stevens award, 2000, Father Agustus Tolton award Cath. Archdioceses Chgo., 2000; named Chicagoan of Year in Law and Judiciary Jr. Assn. Commerce and Industry, 1964, Laureate, Acad. Ill. Lawyers, 2000; named Main US Post Office Bldg. in his honor, New Bedford, Mass., 2005 Fellow ABA (chmn. coun. 1976, mem. coun. sect. legal edn. and admissions to bar, medal 2005), Am. Coll. Trial Lawyers;

mem. NAACP (chmn. legal redress com. Chgo. br.), John Howard Assn. (bd. dirs.), Chgo. Bar Assn., Ill. Bar Assn. (joint com. for revision jud. article 1959-62, sr. counselor 1996), Nat. Harvard Law Sch. Assn. (mem. coun.), Howard U. Chgo. Alumni Club (chmn. bd. dirs.), Phi Beta Kappa. Office: Neal & LeRoy LLC 203 N LaSalle Ste 2300 Chicago IL 60601-1213 Home Phone: 312-580-0286; Office Phone: 312-641-7144. Business E-Mail: gleighton@nealandleroy.com.

LEIGHTON, JACK RICHARD, retired small business owner, education educator; b. Boise, Idaho, May 10, 1918; s. Ralph Waldo and Lucia Marie (Strub) L.; m. Helen Louise Wirtenberger, July 24, 1942; 1 child, James Carl. Student, U. Wash., 1938—39; BS, U. Oreg., 1941, MS, 1942, PhD, 1954; postgrad., U. Iowa, 1950. Dir. phys. edn. and athletics Montpelier HS, Idaho, 1941-42; exec. asst. phys. medicine rehab. svc. Vancouver VA Hosp., Wash., 1946-50; assoc. prof. phys. edn. Pa. State U., State College, 1952-53; assoc. prof. Ea. Wash. U., Cheney, 1953-56, prof., 1956-81, dir. divsn. health, phys. edn., recreation and athletics, 1953-81; pres. Leighton Flexometer Co. Inc., Spokane, Wash., 1985—2007; ret., 2007. Mem. com. on secondary sch. health and phys. edn. Idaho Dept. Edn., Boise, 1942; cons. state adv. com. on sch. activity and phys. edn. Wash. Dept. Pub. Instrn., Olympia, 1954-55, mem. com. on phys. edn. curriculum guide, 1957-58. Author: Physical Education for Boys, 1942, Objective Physical Education, 1946, Progressive Weight Training, 1961, Fitness, Body Development & Sports Conditioning Through Weight Training, 1983; assoc. editor Rsch. Quar. AAHPERD, 1960-63, Jour. Health, Phys. Edn. and Recreation, 1967-68; editor Jour. Assn. for Phys. and Mental Rehab., 1963-67; mem. editl. bd. Am. Corrective Therapy Jour., 1972-79; contbr. articles to profl. jours., chpts. to books; patentee instrument to measure range of joint motion. Mem. Ea. Wash. U. Retirees Bd., 1996-99; mem. Spokane County Cmty. Svcs. Devel. Disabilities Adv. Bd., 2000-2005. With AUS, 1942-46. Fellow Am. Coll. Sports Medicine; mem. AAHPERD (necrology com. 1955-58, chmn. fitness sect. 1960-61, mem. rsch. coun., com. to study purpose and propose revisions of structure and procedures gen. divsn. 1960-61; mem. N.W. dist. honor awards com. 1955-57, 76-79, chmn. 1976-77, mem. constn. com. 1957-60, chmn. rsch. sect. 1957-58, v.p. phys. edn. 1957-58, chmn. fitness sect. 1963-64, pres. 1971-72), Wash. Assn. Health, Phys. Edn. and Recreation (phys. fitness steering com. 1955-57, constn. com. 1957-58, chmn. tchr. tng. sect. 1956-57, phys. fitness steering com. 1957-59, v.p. ea. dist. 1957-58, pres. 1959-60), Spokane United Sch. Groups (Ea. Wash. U. rep. 1957-60), Spokane Area C. of C. (small bus. coun. 1993—2003), Phi Delta Kappa, Phi Epsilon Kappa. Home: 3118 E Chaser Ln Spokane WA 99223-7267

LEIGHTON, LAWRENCE WARD, investment banker; b. NYC, July 1, 1934; s. Sidney and Florence (Ward) Leighton; m. Mariana Stroock, June 21, 1959; children: Sandra L. Galvin, Michelle S. BSE, Princeton U., 1956; MBA, Harvard U., 1962. V.p. Kuhn Loeb & Co., NYC, 1962-69, Clark, Dodge & Co., Inc., 1970-74; dir. Norton-Simon, Inc., 1974-78; ltd. ptnr. Bear, Stearns & Co., 1978-82; mng. dir. Chase Investment Bank, 1983-88; pres., CEO Union d'Etudes et d'Investissements Mcht. Bank of Credit Agricole, 1989-93; vice-chmn. 2I, Inc., 1993-94; mng. dir. LM Capital Corp., 1994-96, Bentley Assocs., LP, NYC, 1997—. Chmn. Princeton Schs. Com. NY, 1965—85. Mem. exec. com. alumni coun. Lawrenceville Sch., 1999—2002; mem. nat. fin. com. Pete DuPont for Pres., 1986—88; mem. exec. com. alumni coun. Princeton U., NJ, 1975—80, vice-chmn. nat. schs. com., 1980—; chmn. Harvard Bus. Sch. Fund. NY, 1964—65; trustee Waterford Inst., 1985—; dir. Delve Group, 2004—. Lt. (j.g.) USN, 1957—60. Mem.: Mid Ocean Club (Bermuda), Coral Beach and Tennis Club (Bermuda), Princeton Club NY (mem. scholarship com. 1970—, bd. govs. 1989—96), Stanwich Club (Greenwich, Conn.). Avocations: flying, golf, photography. Home and Office: Bentley Assocs 360 Lexington Ave 3rd Fl New York NY 10014 Office Phone: 212-763-0374. Business E-Mail: lwleighton@bentleylp.com.

LEIGHTON, RICHARD FREDERICK, retired dean; BA, Western Md. Coll., 1951; MD, U. Md., 1955; ScD (hon.), Med. Coll. Ohio, Toledo, 2000. Diplomate Am. Bd. Internal Medicine (Specialty Cardiovascular Disease). Intern U. Hosp., Balt., 1955—56; flight surgeon USN, 1956—58; resident Ohio State U. Hosp., 1959—61, resident, cardiology fellow, 1961—64; from asst. prof. to assoc. prof. medicine Coll. Medicine Ohio State U., 1965—74, dir. coronary care unit, 1968—69, dir. cardiac catheterization labs., 1970—74; prof. medicine, chief cardiology Med. Coll. Ohio, 1974—90, acting chmn. dept. medicine, 1988, vice chmn., 1988—90, v.p. acad. affairs, dean Sch. Medicine, 1990—95, sr. v.p. acad. affairs, dean Sch. Medicine, 1995—96, emeritus, ret., 1997; prof. medicine Mercer U. Med. Sch., 1998—; chmn. instnl. rev. bd. Meml. Health U. Med. Ctr., 1998—. Editl. bd. La Lettre du Cardiologue, 1985—; contbr. numerous articles to profl. jours. Fellow ACP, Am. Coll. Cardiology (gov. Ohio chpt. 1985-88), Am. Heart Assn (coun. circulation, epidemiology, clinical cardiology, coun. rep. Ohio 1977-80), Royal Soc. Medicine; mem. Ctrl. Soc. Clin. Rsch., U. Md. Med. Alumni Assn. (Honor award, Gold Key 2005), Societe Francaise Cardiologie (corr.), Alpha Omega Alpha. Office: Meml Health U Med Ctr Dept Internal Med Edn PO Box 23089 Savannah GA 31403-3089 Business E-Mail: leighril@memorialhealth.com. E-mail: rflfsl@bellsouth.net.

LEIGHTON, ROBERT JOSEPH, lawyer; b. Austin, Minn., July 7, 1965; s. Robert Joseph Sr. and JoAnn (Mulvihill) L. BA, U. Minn., 1988; JD, U. Calif., Berkeley, 1991. Minn. state rep. Dist. 27B, 1995—2002; atty. Nolan, MacGregor, Thompson & Leighton, St. Paul, 2002—. Presdl. and Waller scholar U. Minn., 1988. Mem. Minn. Bar Assn., Minn. Trial Lawyers Assn., Phi Beta Kappa. Home: 4243 Wexford Way Eagan MN 55122 Office: Nolan MacGregor Thompson & Leighton Lawson Commons Ste 710 380 St Peter St Saint Paul MN 55102 Home Phone: 651-686-4467; Office Phone: 651-227-6661. Business E-Mail: rleighton@nmtlaw.com.

LEIJONHUFVUD, AXEL STIG BENGT, economics professor; b. Stockholm, Sept. 6, 1933; came to U.S., 1960; s. Erik Gabriel and Helene Adelheid (Neovius) L.; m. Marta Elisabeth Ising, June 10, 1955 (div. 1977); m. Earlene Joyce Craver, June 18, 1977; children— Carl Axel, Gabriella Helene, Christina Elisabeth Fil. kand., U. Lund, Sweden, 1960; MA, U. Pitts., Pa., 1961; PhD, Northwestern U., 1967; Fil. Dr. (hon.), U. Lund, Sweden, 1983; Dr. (hon.), U. Nice, Sophia-Antipolis, France, 1995. Acting asst. prof. econs. UCLA, 1964-67, assoc. prof. econs., 1967-71, prof. econs., 1971—, chair dept. econs., 1980-83, 90-92; dir. Ctr. for Computable Econs., 1992-97; prof. monetary theory and policy U. Trento, Italy, 1995—. Co-dir. summer workshops Siena Internat. Sch. Econ. Rsch., 1987-91; dir. program in econ. dynamics U. Trento, 2000—; participant profl. confs.; cons., lectr., vis. prof. econs. various colls. and univs.; cons. Republic of Tatarstan, 1994. Author: On Keynesian Economics and the Economics of Keynes: A Study in Monetary Theory, 1968, Keynes and the Classics: Two Lectures, 1969, Information and Coordination: Essays in Macroeconomic Theory, 1981; co-author (with D. Heymann): High Inflation, 1995, Macroeconomic Instability and Coordination, Selected Essays, 2000; editor: Monetary Theory as a Basis for Monetary Policy, 2001, Monetary Theory and Policy Experience, 2001, Informazione, coordinamento e instabilità macroeconomica: a cura di Elisabella de Antoni, 2004, Organizacion e instabilidad economica: ensayos elgidos, 2006. Econ. expert com. of pres. Kazakhstan, 1991-92. Brookings Instn. fellow, 1963-64; Marshall lectr. Cambridge U., Eng., 1974; Overseas fellow Churchill Coll., Cambridge, 1974; Inst. Advanced Study fellow, 1983-84 Mem. Am. Econ. Assn., Western Econ. Assn., History of Econs. Soc. Business E-Mail: axel@ucla.edu.

LEIKEN, EARL MURRAY, lawyer; b. Cleve., Jan. 19, 1942; s. Manny and Betty G. L.; m. Ellen Kay Miner, Mar. 26, 1970; children: Jonathan, Brian. BA magna cum laude, Harvard U., 1964, JD cum laude, 1967. Asst. dean, assoc. prof. law Case Western Res. U., Cleve., 1967-71; ptnr. Hahn, Loeser, Freedheim, Dean & Wellman, Cleve., 1971-86, Baker & Hostetler, Cleve., 1986—. Adj. faculty, lectr. law Case Western Res. U., 1971-86. Pres. Shaker Heights (Ohio) Bd. Edn., 1986-88, Jewish Community Ctr., Cleve., 1988-91, Shaker Heights Family Ctr., 1994-97; mem. Shaker Heights City Coun., 2000—. Named one of Greater Cleve.'s 10 Outstanding Young Leaders, Cleve. Jaycees, 1972; recipient Kane award Cleve. Jewish Community Fedn., 1982. Mem. ABA, Greater Cleve. Bar Assn. (chmn. labor law sect. 1978). Home: 20815 Colby Rd Cleveland OH 44122-1903 Office: Baker & Hostetler 3200 Nat City Ctr 1900 E 9th St Ste 3200 Cleveland OH 44114-3475

LEIN, ED, research scientist; BS in Biochemistry, Purdue U., 1993; PhD in Neurobiology, U. Calif., Berkeley, 1999. Postdoctoral work Salk Inst. for Biol. Studies; dir., neuroscience Allen Inst. for Brain Sci., Seattle, contbr., Allen Brain Atlas project. Co-recipient Rave award-Science, WIRED Mag., 2007. Office: Allen Inst for Brain Sci 551 N 34th St Seattle WA 98103

LEINART, MATT, professional football player; b. Santa Ana, Calif., May 11, 1983; s. Bob and Linda Leinart; 1 child, Cole. BA in Sociology, U. So. Calif., 2006. Quarterback Ariz. Cardinals, Phoenix, 2006—. Named Pac-10 Offensive Player of the Yr., 2003, Rose Bowl MVP, 2003; named to All-American first team, 2003, 2004, 2005, All-Pac-10 first team; recipient Manning award, 2004, Heisman Meml. Trophy, Heisman Trophy Trust, 2004, Johnny Unitas Golden Arm award, 2005. Achievements include quarterback, co-Nat. Champions U. So. Calif. Trojan's, 2004, Nat. Champions, 2005; set Orange Bowl record with 5 touchdown passes, 2005. Office: Ariz Cardinals PO Box 888 Phoenix AZ 85001*

LEINENWEBER, HARRY D., federal judge; b. Joliet, Ill., June 3, 1937; s. Harry Dean and Emily (Lennon) L.; m. Lynn Morley Martin, Jan. 7, 1987; 5 children; 2 stepchildren. AB cum laude, U. Notre Dame, 1959; JD, U. Chgo., 1962. Bar: Ill. 1962, U.S. Dist. Ct. (no. dist.) Ill. 1967. Assoc. Dunn, Stefanich, McGarry & Kennedy, Joliet, Ill., 1962-65, ptnr., 1965-79; city atty. City of Joliet, 1963-67; spl. counsel Village of Park Forest, Ill., 1967-74; spl. prosecutor County of Will, Ill., 1968-70; spl. counsel Village of Bolingbrook, Ill., 1975-77, Will County Forest Preserve, 1977; mem. Ill. Ho. of Reps., Springfield, 1973-83, chmn. judiciary I com., 1981-83; ptnr. Dunn, Leinenweber & Dunn, Joliet, 1979-86; fed. judge U.S. Dist. Ct. (no. dist.) Ill., Chgo., 1986—. Bd. dirs. Will County Bar Assn., 1984-86, State Jud. Adv. Coun., 1973-85, sec. 1975-76; tchr. legis. process seminar U. Ill., Chgo., 1988-2001; coord. U. Ill. Disting. Lecture Series, 2002--; mem. U. Ill. Inst. Govt. and Pub. Affairs Nat. Adv. Com., 1998-2001. Bd. dirs. Will County Legal Assistance Found., 1982-86, Good Shepard Manor, 1981—, Am. Cancer Soc., 1981-85, Joliet (Ill.) Montessori Sch., 1966-74; del. Rep. Nat. Conv., 1980; precinct committeeman, 1966-86; mem. nat. adv. com. U. Ill. Inst. Govt. and Pub. Affairs, 1998-2001. Recipient Environ. Legislator Golden award. Mem. Will County Bar Assn. (mem. jud. adv. coun., 1973-85, sec. 1975-76, bd. dirs. 1984-86), Nat. Conf. Commrs. on Uniform State Laws (exec. com. 1991-93, elected life mem. 1996), The Law Club of Chgo. (bd. dirs. 1996-98). Roman Catholic. Office: US Dist Ct 219 S Dearborn St Ste 1946 Chicago IL 60604-1801 Home Phone: 773-935-4205; Office Phone: 312-435-7612. E-mail: harry_leinenweber@ilnd.uscourts.gov.

LEINICKE, KRIS GAYMAN, museum director, educator; d. Robert Francis and Emma Elizabeth Gayman; m. William H. Leinicke (dec.); 1 child, Samuel D. BA in History with highest honors, U. Del., 1977; MA in History Mus. Studies, SUNY, Oneonta, 1986. Vis. instr. Augustana Coll., Rock Island, Ill., 1982—; exhibits specialist John M. Browning Meml. Mus., Rock Island Arsenal, 1983—85; curator of collections Rock Island Arsenal Mus., 1985—99, mus. dir., 1999—. US Army mus. cert. inspector US Army Ctr. Mil. History, Ft. McNair, DC, 1997—, mus. planning com. Nat. Mus. US Army, 2001—03. Troop com. Boy Scouts Am., Rock Island, 2005—; event com. Alternatives for the Older Adult, Moline, Ill., 2005—. Recipient Achievement medal for civilian svc., Dept. of the Army, 2000, Comdr.'s award for civilian svc., 2002, 2004, Cmty. Svc. Award, 2007. Mem.: Phi Beta Kappa. Office: Rock Island Arsenal Mus 1 Rock Island Arsenal Rock Island IL 61299-5000 Office Phone: 309-782-3518. Office Fax: 309-782-3598. E-mail: muse1905@mchsi.com.

LEINIEKS, VALDIS, classicist, educator; b. Liepaja, Latvia, Apr. 15, 1932; came to U.S., 1949, naturalized, 1954; s. Arvid Ansis and Valia Leontine (Brunaus) L. BA, Cornell U., 1955, MA, 1956; PhD, Princeton U., 1962. Instr. classics Cornell Coll., Mount Vernon, Iowa, 1959-62, asst. prof. classics, 1962-64; assoc. prof. classics Ohio State U., 1964-66, U. Nebr., Lincoln, 1966-71, prof. classics, 1971—2005, chmn. dept. classics, 1967-95, chmn. program comparative lit., 1970-86, interim chmn. dept. modern langs., 1982-83, prof. emeritus, 2005—. Author: Morphosyntax of the Homeric Greek Verb, 1964, The Structure of Latin, 1975, Index Nepotianus, 1976, The Plays of Sophokles, 1982, The City of Dionysos, 1996; contbr. articles to profl. jours. Mem. AAUP, Am. Philol. Assn Home: 2505 A St Lincoln NE 68502-1841 Office: U Nebr Dept Classics Lincoln NE 68588-0337

LEINOFF, ANDREW MORRIS, lawyer; b. Paterson, NJ, Mar. 28, 1950; s. Benjamin B. and Rhoda Leinoff; m. Ellen Judith Cohen, Aug. 19, 1973; children: Paul, Alexis, Max. BA, Ohio State U., 1971; JD, U. Miami, 1974. Bar: Fla. 1974, US Dist. Ct. (so. dist. Fla.) 1975, US Ct. Appeals (5th cir.) 1975; cert. Fla. Bar Bd. Legal Specialization and Edn. (matrimonial and family law). Assoc. Adams, Beeabe, Wood, Shuir & Mampson, P.A., Miami, Fla., 1974-75, Storace, Idri & Hauser, Miami, 1975-77; ptnr. Marks, Aronovitz & Leinoff, Miami, 1978-88; pvt. practice atty. Coral Gables, Fla., 1988; ptnr. Leinoff & Lemos, P.A., South Miami, Fla. Contbr. articles to profl. publs. Named one of Top 100 Attys., Worth mag., 2005—06. Fellow Am. Acad. Matrimonial Lawyers (frequent lectr., pres. Fla. chpt. 1989-99); mem. ABA (family law sect.), Fla. Bar (family law sect.), Dade County Bar Assn., Internat. Acad. Matrimonial Lawyers, Am. Inns Ct. (master chpt. 181), Phi Delta Phi. Office: Leinoff & Lemos PA 7301 SW 57th Ct Ste 545 South Miami FL 33143-5317 Home Phone: 305-667-3942; Office Phone: 305-661-1556. Office Fax: 305-665-2555.*

LEIPER, ROBERT DUNCAN, local government official; b. Houston, July 22, 1953; s. William Harper Leiper and Frances Ann (Wright) Freeman; m. Glynna Dell Wilson, May 18, 1985; children: Kelsey Allison, Chad Wilson. AAS in Fire Protection, San Jacinto Coll., 1983; BA in Pub. Mgmt., U. Houston, 1988; MS in Pub. Adminstrn., Grand Canyon U., Phoenix, 2003. Master fire fighter, Tex.; cert. fire protection specialist. Lt. Spring Br. Fire Dept., Houston, 1973-75; asst. svc. mgr. Archer Motor Sales, Houston, 1975-77; fire fighter Baytown (Tex.) Fire & Rescue, 1977-80, driver, 1980-83, lt., 1983-88, capt., 1988-92, fire chief, 1992—2002; asst. city mgr. City of Baytown, 2002—04, deputy city mgr., 2004—. Instr. Tex. A & M U., College Station, 1988-92, Lamar U., Beaumont, Tex., 1990-92. Chmn. bd. Baycoast Med. Ctr., Baytown, Tex., 1994-95. Named Exec. Fire Officer, Nat. Fire Acad.; recipient Fire Fighter of Yr. award VFW, 1987, 90. Mem. Nat. Fire Protection Assn., Tex. Fire Chief's Assn. (dir.), Hispanic C. of C., Baytown C. of C., Kiwanis Club (pres. 1994, Rookie of Yr. award 1989). Avocations: wood working, camping, photography. Office: City of Baytown PO Box 424 Baytown TX 77522-0424 Home Phone: 281-428-2697. E-mail: bfrs@earthlink.net.

LEIPOLD, CRAIG L., professional sports team executive; m. Helen; children: Chris, Kyle, Conner, Curtis, Bradford. Grad., Hendrix Coll. With Kimberly-Clark Corp., Neenah, Wis.; founder Ameritel Corp.; owner Rainfair Corp., 1987; owner, gov. Nashville Predators Hockey Team, 1998—; chmn. Gaylord Entertainment, Nashville. Bd. dirs. Rainfair Corp. Named Sports Person of the Year, 1999, Father of the Year, Nashville Father's Day Coun., 1999, Nashvillian of the Year, Easter Seals, 1999; named to Seton Society, St. Thomas Health Services, 2004. Office: c/o Nashville Predators 501 Broadway Nashville TN 37203-3932

LEIPOLD, JAMES G., lawyer; BA magna cum laude, Brown U.; JD magna cum laude, Temple U. Law Sch. Dir. admissions Temple U. Law Sch.; sr. mgmt. team Law Sch. Admissions Council, asst. dir. Admissions, Edn. and Pre-law Programs, dir. Electronic Services Support and asst. dir. Edn. and Pre-law; exec. dir. Nat. Assn. for Law Placement, 2004—. Office: Nat Assn for Law Placement 1025 Connecticut Ave Ste 1110 Washington DC 20003-5413 Office Phone: 202-835-5413. Office Fax: 202-835-1112. Business E-Mail: jleipold@nalp.org.

LEIPZIG, ARTHUR, photographer, retired educator; b. Bklyn., Oct. 25, 1918; s. Julius M. and Esther Pearl (Rubin) L.; m. Mildred Levin, Mar. 21, 1942; children: Joel Myron, Judith Anne. Student, Photo League, 1942-43, Paul Strand Photo Workshop, 1946. Staff photographer PM newspaper, NYC, 1942-46, Internat. News Photos, NYC, 1946; freelance photographer, Sea Cliff, N.Y., 1946-68; prof. art, dir. photography C.W. Post Sch. of Arts, L.I. U., Greenvale, N.Y., 1968-90, prof. emeritus, 1990—. Contbr. photographs to Fortune, Look, Parade, Life, Natural History, Sunday Times, also indsl. mags.; guest editor Infinity Mag., N.Y.C., 1970, mem. editorial bd., 1973-75; interview and photographs included Life Documentary Photo Book, N.Y.C., 1972, 83; exhibited works Mus. Modern Art, 1946-51, 55-58, Met. Mus. Art, 1961, 62, Nassau Mus. Art, 1975, Queens Mus. Art, 1982, Transco Gallery, Houston, 1985, Daniel Wolf Gallery, N.Y.C., Houston Foto Fest, 1986, Photo Find Gallery, Woodstock, Coll. Art Gallery, New Paltz, N.Y., Smithsonian Mus., Washington, 1987, Mus. of the City of N.Y., Children's Games, 1988, Photofind Gallery, N.Y.C., 1990, ICP, Bklyn., 1992; one-man shows include Midtown Y Gallery, 1978, Henry St. Settlement, Arts for Living Ctr., 1986, Frumkin Adams Gallery, N.Y.C., 1990, 92, Photofind Gallery, 1990, Howard Greenberg Gallery, 1991, 98, Salena Gallery, Bklyn., 1992, Port Washington Libr., 1994, Mus. of the City of N.Y., 1995, 96, Albin O. Kuhn Gallery, Balt., Md., Milw. Inst. Art & Design, 1998, Firehouse Gallery, Nassau C.C., 2001, Columbus Mus. Art, 2005-06, Hillwood Mus., 2006, Nat. Portrait Gallery, 2007; Arthur Leipzig: A Tribute to Influence; group shows include Balt. Mus. Art, 1998, Whitney Mus. Am. Art, 1999, Am. Embassy, Copenhagen Art in Embassies, 1999, The Jewish Mus., The Changing Face of Family, 1999, N.Y.: Capital of Photography, The Jewish Mus., 2002; represented in permanent collections Mus. Modern Art, Bklyn. Mus., Eastman House, Nat. Gallery Art, Nassau Mus. Art, Houston Mus. Fine Arts, Midtown Y Gallery, Visual Studies Workshop, Pablo Casals Mus., Internat. Ctr. Photography, Nat. Mus. Am. Art, Washington, Consol. Freightways, San Francisco, Bank of Am. Art Program, San Francisco, Bibliotheque Nationale, Paris, The Jewish Mus., N.Y.C., Mus. Folkwang, Essen, Germany, Nat. Portrait Gallery, Washington, The Gilman Paper Co., Queens Coll., N.Y., Madison Art Ctr., Wis., U. Tex., Dallas, Dreyfus, N.Y.C., Soho Grand Hotel, Columbus Mus. Art, Nassau C.C., Kresge Mus. Art, East Lansing, Mich., Milbank Meml. Fund, Santa Barbara Mus. Art, BAlt. Mus. Art; retrospective exhbn. Hillwood Gallery, Brookville, N.Y., 1989, Musée De La Civilisation, Quebec City, 1990, Balt. Mus. Art, Reader's Digest Corporate Art Gallery; featured on World of Photography, Sta. WABC-TV; pub. Classic Photographs from the Brooklyn Museum Collection, 1987, Sarah's Daughters, 1988, Master Photographs Photography in Fine Arts Exhbt. Internat. Ctr. Photography, 1988, 92, The Nat. Portrait Gallery, 1992, High Mus., Altlanta, 1992, Mus. of the City of N.Y., 1995; photographer: (books) Shari Lewis Puppet Book, Sarah's Daughter, 1987, Growing Up in N.Y., 1995, On Assignment with Arthur Leipzig, 2005; photos included in 2007 Women of Our Time. Adv. bd. Midtown Y Gallery, 1983; bd. dirs. Nassau Mus. Fine Art, 1973-75. Recipient Nat. Urban League award, 1962, ORT award, 1976, Nassau County Office Cultural Devel. award, 1982, Award for Scholarly Achievement, L.I. U. Trustees, 1983, 89, David Newton Excellence in Tchg. award, 1989, Lucie award for fine art Photography Awards, 2004. Mem. Am. Soc. Mag. Photographers (bd. govs., trustee 1960-65, treas. 1965). E-mail: aleipzig@optonline.net. *My photography is very personal, my focus the human condition, exploring people, their humanity and inhumanity. I am not a cerebral photographer. My Images come as intuitive responses and they deal with my feelings about life. Through my work I have learned about myself and the world.*

LEIPZIG, MELVIN, art educator; b. Bklyn., May 23, 1935; s. Irving and Anne Leipzig; m. Mary Jo Michelessi, Sept. 14, 1968; children: Francesca Leipzig Picone, Joshua Michael. 3-yr. cert., The Cooper Union, 1956; BFA, Yale U., 1958; MFA, Pratt Inst., 1972. Instr. Columbia U., NYC, 1968—70, Queens (N.Y.) Coll., 1968—73; prof. Mercer County C.C., Trenton, NJ, 1968—. Bd. dirs. Trenton Artists Workshop Assn., 1979—, Assn. Art Edn. N.J., 1986—, N.J. Sch. for Arts, 2001—. Recipient grant for painting, NEA, 1995, award, Louis Comfort Tiffany, 1959, grant to Paris, Fulbright Found., 1958; grantee, N.J. State Coun. on Arts, 1982, 1986, 1992, 2002. Office: Mercer County C C 1200 Old Trenton Rd Trenton NJ 08690 Office Phone: 609-586-4800 3353.

LEISEY, DONALD EUGENE, learning materials executive; b. Pa., Sept. 23, 1937; s. Alvin L. and E. Marie Leisey; m. Patricia M. Leisey; children: Kristen, Kendra. BS in Edn., West Chester U., Pa., 1959; MA in Adminstrn., Villanova U., Pa., 1962; cert. in bus. adminstrn., U. So. Calif., 1972, EdD in Adminstrn., 1973. Cert. gen. adminstrv., gen. secondary, gen. elem. Calif. Tchr., Coatesville, Pa., 1959—62; prin. Downingtown, Pa., 1962—64, Dept. Def. Dependent Schs., Japan, 1964—67; asst. supt. Lennox Schs., Inglewood, Calif., 1967—71; dir. adminstrv. svcs. San Rafael City Sch. Dist., Calif., 1971—73, supt. schs., 1973—79; instr. Dominican Coll., 1973—79; v.p., regional mgr. Am. Learning Corp., Huntington Beach, Calif., 1979—80; v.p., treas. Kittredge Sch. Corp., San Francisco, 1980—83; instr. Calif. State U., Hayward, 1981; chmn., CEO, Merryhill Schs., Inc., Sacramento, 1981—89; pres., chmn. bd., CEO, The Report Card, Citrus Heights, Calif., 1990—; co-dir. Internat. Acad. Ednl. Entrepreneurship, 2000—. Apptd. bd. councilors U. So. Calif., Rossier Sch. Edn., 1999; trustee Found. Bd. West Chester U., 2000. Co-author: The Educational Entrepreneur: Making a Difference, 2000. Apptd. to Gov.'s Child Care Task Force, Calif., 1984, Gov.'s Child Devel. Program Adv. Com., Calif., 1985—. Recipient Disting. Svc. award, LA County Sheriff, 1969, Hon. Svc. award, PTA, 1970, Disting. Alumnus award, West Chester U., 1983. Home and Office: 23 Peacock Dr San Rafael CA 94901-8301 Office: 6366 Tupelo Dr Citrus Heights CA 95621-1700 Personal E-mail: delaplus@aol.com.

LEISH, KENNETH WILLIAM, retired publishing company executive; b. Cambridge, Mass., Dec. 31, 1936; s. Frank and Lillian (Kargir) L.; m. Barbara Lynn Ackerman, Nov. 27, 1966; children: Matthew, Emily, Adam. AB magna cum laude, Harvard U., 1958; MS in Journalism, Columbia U., 1959. Interviewer Oral History Office, Columbia, 1960; free lance drama reviewer Variety, 1961-66; editor Am. Heritage Pub. Co., Inc., NYC, 1961-69, v.p., gen. mgr. book div., 1971-77; editor-in-chief Am. Heritage Press, 1970-71; mgr. large-format paperbacks Bantam Books Inc., NYC, 1977-81; editor-in-chief Grolier Inc. Project Editorial Group, 1981-87; v.p., dir. product devel. Grolier Internat., Inc., Danbury, Conn., 1988-91; v.p. new product devel. Grolier Inc., Danbury, Conn., 1992-95; v.p., mng. editor

Grolier Ednl., Danbury, Conn., 1996—2003. Author: The White House, 1972, A History of the Cinema, 1974. Served with U.S Army, 1959-60. Home: PO Box 1681 White Plains NY 10602-1681 E-mail: leishbk@msn.com.

LEISING, DAVID MICHAEL, industrial engineer; b. Buffalo, Jan. 18, 1950; s. Lawrence Valentine and Patricia (Masterson) L.; m. Mary Kathleen Coyle, July 19, 1969; 1 child, Michelle. AAS, Jamestown CC, NY, 1977; BS, Rochester Inst. Tech., 1992. Indsl. engr. Weber Knapp Co., Jamestown, NY, 1977-99; steam engr. Chautauqua Belle, Mayville, NY, 1999—; mfg. engr. Blackstone Bus. Enterprises, Jamestown, 2000—. Capt. summer wind tour boat, 2003—. Capt. Chautauqua Belle Steambot and Summer Wind Tour Boat. With USN, 1969—73. Mem.: ASME, Am. Assn. Indsl. Engrs., Waltonians (bd. dirs. 1993—94). Roman Catholic. Avocations: hunting, fishing, carpentry, camping, sailing. Home: 2756 Tompkins Rd Jamestown NY 14701

LEISNER, ANTHONY BAKER, publishing company executive; b. Evanston, Ill., Sept. 13, 1941; s. A. Paul and Ruth (Solms) L.; children: Justina, William, Sarah; m. Patricia Anne Leisner, 1996. MBA, Northwestern U., 1983; PhD, Walden U., 2005. Salesman Pitney Bowes Co., 1976-77; with Quality Books Inc., Lake Bluff, Ill., 1968—, v.p., 1972—, gen. mgr., 1979—91. Adj. faculty Lake Forest Sch. Mgmt., Ill., 1983-92, Kellogg Grad. Sch. Mgmt. Northwestern U., Evanston, Ill.; assoc. prof. internat. mktg. Schiller Internat. U., Dunedin, Fla., 1995—,faculty, Walden U. 2005-; head global strategic planning, spl. asst., CEO Dawson Group, Folkestone, Eng. pres. Watersedge Properties Inc., Tarpon Springs, Fla.; ptnr. Wikle Properties Mgmt., Palm Harbor, Fla.; bd. dirs. Highland Properties, Inc., Palm Harbor; mem. Pinellas Workforce Bd., Pinellas County, Fla. Author: Official Guide to Country Dance Steps, 1980; contbr. articles to jours. Pres. bd. dirs. Lake Villa Pub. Libr., 1972-78; bd. dirs. No. Ill. Libr. Sys., 1973-78, St. Petersburg Coll. Found., Fla., PACE Ctr. Pinellas County, Fla.; chmn. Leepa-Rattner Mus., Libertarian Party Lake County, Ill., 1980-81, 02, Econ. Devel. Tarpon Springs, Fla.; probation officer Lake County CAP, 1981. Mem.: ALA (councilor, del. pub. com. White House conf. on librs. and info. svcs.), World Future Soc., Am. Mktg. Assn., Acad. Mgmt., Ill. Libr. Assn. (Gerald L. Campbell award 1980), Tarpon Springs C. of C. (chmn. econ. devel.), World Isshin Ryu Karate Assn., Tarpon Springs Yacht Club. Home and Office: 1350 Riverside Ave Tarpon Springs FL 34689-6614 Business E-Mail: aleisner@waldenu.edu.

LEISTNER, MARY EDNA, retired secondary school educator; b. Evanston, Ill., Apr. 13, 1929; d. Joseph W. and Edna C. (Moe) Cox; m. Delbert L. Leistner, Sept. 30, 1950; children: David, Martha, Joseph. BS Chemistry, Purdue U., 1950; MEd, Miami U., Oxford, Ohio, 1964. Tchr. sci. and math. Ctrl. Jr. H.S., Sidney, Ohio, 1962—66; tchr. chemistry, biology, advanced chemistry Sidney H.S., 1966—93; ret., 1993. Mem. high sch. chemistry test com. Am. Chem. Soc., 1983-85 Exec. com. Ohio Dist. Luth. Women's Missionary League, Columbus, 1978-82, conv. chmn., 1988; pres. Miami Valley zone, 1985-87; pres. Redeemer Ladies Soc., Sidney, 1980-91, 94-98, treas., 1998-2003, St. John's Luth. Joy Circle 2003—, Thrift & Shop Leader 2005—; mem. gift shop com. Wilsom Meml. Hosp., Sidney, 1994-96, aux. sec., 1997-98, membership chair, aux. v.p., 1999, aux. pres., 2000 Mem. NSTA (Cadre 100 award, H.S. chemistry test com.), We. Ohio Sci. Tchrs. Assn. (pres. 1972-73), Sci. Edn. Coun. Ohio (dist. rep. exec. bd. 1984-86, treas. 1986-90, pres. elect 1991-92, pres. 1992-93, immediate past pres. 1993-94, chair retirees/hist. com. 1995-2000), Sidney Edn. Assn. (treas. 1980-82, 85-86, Tchr. of Yr. 1988), Ohio Acad. Scis. (Jerry Acker Outstanding Tchr. of Yr. award 1988-89, Exemplar 1993), Shelby Co. Ret. Tchrs. Assn. (v.p. 2003-2004, pres. 2005-2006), Delta Kappa Gamma (2d v.p. 1992-94, 1st v.p. 1994-96, pres. 1996-98, past pres. 1998—) Republican. Lutheran.

LEISURE, PETER KEETON, federal judge; b. NYC, Mar. 21, 1929; s. George S. and Lucille E. (Pelouze) L.; m. Kathleen Blair; Feb. 27, 1960; children: Lucille K. (dec.), Mary Blair, Kathleen K. BA, Yale U., 1952; LL.B., U. Va., 1958. Bar: N.Y. 1959, U.S. Supreme Ct. 1966, D.C. 1979, U.S. Dist. Ct. Conn. 1981. Assoc. Breed, Abbott & Morgan, 1958-61; asst. U.S. atty. So. Dist. N.Y., 1962-66; partner firm Curtis, Mallet-Prevost, Colt & Mosle, 1967-78; ptnr. Whitman & Ransom, NYC, 1978-84; judge U.S. Dist. Ct. (So. Dist.), NYC, 1984—, sr. judge, 1997—. Bd. dirs. Retarded Infants Svcs., 1968-78, pres., 1971-75; bd. dirs. Community Coun. of Greater N.Y., 1972-79, Youth Consultation Svcs., 1971-78; trustee Ch. Club of N.Y., 1973-81, 87-90; mem. jud. ethics com. Jud. Conf., 1990-93, fin disclosure com. 1st lt. USAR, 1953-55. Recipient Ellis Island medal of honor, 2000. Fellow: Am. Coll. Trial Lawyers, Am. Bar Found.; mem.: ABA, Fed. Bar Coun. (trustee, v.p. 1973—78), D.C. Bar Assn., Am. Judges Assn., Fed. Judges Assn., Am. Law Inst., Nat. Lawyers Club (hon.). Office: US Dist Ct 1910 US Courthouse 500 Pearl St New York NY 10007-1316 Office Phone: 212-805-0226.

LEIT, DAVID EDWARD, lawyer; b. Edison, NJ, Sept. 1, 1969; s. Norman and Carol Fonorow Leit; m. Karyn Boosin, Jan. 8, 1969; children: Benjamin Michael, Margery Emma. AB, Stanford U., Calif., 1991; JD, Coumbia U., NYC, 1995. Bar: N.J. 1995, N.Y. 1996. Assoc. Sattelee Stephens Burke & Burke LLP, NYC, 1995—2000, Brobeck Phleger & Harrison LLP, NYC, 2000—02; mem. of firm Lowenstein Sandler PC, Roseland, NJ, 2000—. Office: Lowenstein Sandler PC 65 Livingston Ave Roseland NJ 07068 Office Phone: 973-597-2500. Business E-Mail: dleit@lowenstein.com.

LEITCH, DAVID G., automotive executive, lawyer; b. 1960; m. Ellen Leitch; 3 children. Grad., Duke U., 1982; JD, U. Va. Sch. Law, 1985. Law clk. to Hon. J. Harvie Wilkinson III US Ct. Appeals (4th Cir.); law clk. to Chief Justice William H. Rehnquist US Supreme Ct.; dep. asst. atty. gen., sr. counsel, Office Legal Counsel US Dept. Justice, Washington; assoc. Hogan and Hartson, LLP, Washington, 1987—94, ptnr., 1994—2001; chief counsel FAA, Washington, 2001—02; counsel, Transition Planning Office US Dept. Homeland Security, Washington; dep. asst. to the Pres, dep. counsel The White House, Washington, 2002—05; gen. counsel, sr. v.p. Ford Motor Co., Dearborn, Mich., 2005—. Office: Ford Motor Co 1 Am Rd Dearborn MI 48126

LEITER, EDWARD HENRY, cell biologist, researcher; b. Columbus, Ga., Apr. 17, 1942; m. Susan Shaw, Sept. 5, 1964. BS, Princeton U., 1964; MS, PhD in Cell Biology, Emory U., 1968. Fellow U. Tex., Austin, 1968-71; asst. prof. in Genetics of Diabetes and Inflammatory Bowel Disease CUNY, Bkyn., 1971-74; assoc. staff scientist Jackson Lab., Bar Harbor, Maine, 1974-75, staff scientist, 1975-90, sr. staff scientist, 1990—. Recipient rsch. award, Juvenile Diabetes Found., 1994. Achievements include research in include research in genetics and immunology of diabetes. Office: Jackson Lab 600 Main St Bar Harbor ME 04609-1500 Office Phone: 207-288-6370.

LEITER, MICHAEL E., government agency administrator; BA, Columbia U.; JD, Harvard Law Sch. Law clerk Chief Judge Michael Boudin, US Ct. of Appeals, First Cir., Assoc. Justice Stephen G. Breyer, US Supreme Ct.; asst. US atty. Dept. of Justice, Ea. Dist. of Va., 2002—05; dep. gen. coun., asst. dir. President's Commn. on the Intelligence Capabilities of the US Regarding Weapons of Mass Destruction; dep. chief of staff Office of the Dir. of Nat. Intelligence (ODNI); prin. dep. dir. Nat. Counterterrorism Ctr. Naval Flight Officer USN, 1991—97, former Yugoslavia, Iraq. Office: Nat Counterterrorism Ctr Mc Lean VA 22101*

LEITER, RICHARD ALLEN, law librarian, educator; b. Sacramento, Mar. 21, 1952; s. Lionel and Lois Rose Leiter; m. Wendy Ellin Werges, Dec. 30, 1978; children: Emily Grace, Madeline Rose, Anna Joy, Rebecca Hope. BA in Anthropology and Religious Studies with honors, U. Calif., Santa Cruz, 1976; JD, Southwestern U., Georgetown, Tex., 1981; M of Libr. and Info. Sci., U. Tex., 1986. Libr. asst. Irell & Manella, LA, 1977-78; libr. Hopkins, Mitchell & Carley, San Jose, Calif., 1982-84; head of reference Law Sch., U. Tex., Austin, 1984-86; pub. svcs. libr. Law Sch., U. Nebr., Lincoln, 1986-88; head libr. Littler, Mendelson, Fastiff & Tichy, San Francisco, 1988-91; dir. law libr., assoc. prof. law Regent U. Sch. Law, Virginia Beach, Va., 1991-94; assoc. prof. law Howard U. Sch. Law, A.M. Daniels Law Libr., Washington, 1994-98, dir. law libr., 1994—2000; assoc. dean, prof. Howard U., Washington, 1998-2000; dir. Schmid Law Libr., prof. law U. Nebr., Lincoln, 2000—. Mem. Westlaw Acad. Adv. Bd., 1990-93; sec. bd. dirs. StoneBridge Sch., 1993-94; mem. adv. bd. Oceana Publs., Inc., 1994-98. Editor: (book sect.) Yellow Pads to Computers, 1986, 91; author: (bibliography) New Frontiers of Forensic & Demonstrative Evidence, 1985; editor: Automatome, 1987-89, The Spirit of Law Librarianship, 1991, 2d edit., 2005, National Survey of State Laws, 5th edit., 2005; (with A. White) Concordance of Federal Legislation, 1999; editor Southwestern U. Law Review; contbr. articles to profl. jours. Mem. adv. com. StoneBridge Ednl. Found. Mem. ABA, Am. Assn. Law Librs. (so. chpt., automation and sci. devel. spl. interest sect. 1986—, chair 1989-90, indexing of periodical lit. adv. com. 1990-91, 2001-04, chair 1990-91, mem. spl. com. to promote development of resources for legal info. cmty. 1994-96, recruitment com. 1995-97, chair rsch. com. 1998-99, mem. adv. com. Law Libr. Jour./Spectrum 2005-07, chair 2005-06), San Francisco Pvt. Law Librs. (steering com. 1989), Mid Am. Law Sch. Libr. Consortium, Scribes. Avocations: bicycling, reading, running. Home: 1301 N 37th St Lincoln NE 68503-2015 Office: U Nebr Schmid Law Libr Coll Law Lincoln NE 68583-0902 Business E-Mail: rleiter@unl.edu.

LEITER, ROBERT ALLEN, journalist, editor, writer; b. Phila., Apr. 21, 1949; s. Samuel Simon and Beverly (Agins) L.; m. Barbara Ann Field, May 6, 1973; children: Lauren, James, Rebecca. BA in English and Creative Writing with honors, U. Iowa, 1970. Freelance writer short stories, book revs., feature articles The Nation, The New Republic, Redbook, Am. Scholar, N.Y. Times, Partisan Rev., The Forward, others, 1973—; mng. editor, book columnist Inside mag., Phila., 1983-87; gen. reporter, book editor Jewish Exponent, Phila., 1987-98. Co-editor Friday, lit. supplement newspaper Jewish Exponent, Phila., 1983-87, mgn. editor Jewish Exponent 100th Anniversary edit., 1987, editor Extra Extra, weekly mag. sect., 1987-94; news editor Jewish Exponent, 1994-95, lit. supplement editor, 1995-98, interim editor-in-chief, 1998-99, lit. editor, 1999—; editor-in-chief, Inside Mag., 2000—; contbr. editor Am. Poetry Rev., Phila., 1987—; instr. writing, Am. lit., theater Cheltenham (Pa.) Adult Sch., 1983-87; instr. Jewish Am. lit., Jews in politics Daroff Campus Adult Studies, Pa., 1984, 99-2001; mem. selection com. Ann. Chaim Potok Lit. Award. Author: (with others) Jewish Profiles, 1992. Asst. to vice chmn. U.S. Commn. on Civil Rights, Washington, 1987-88. Recipient Smolar award for excellence in N.Am. Jewish journalism for article series, 1989, Simon Rockower award, 1990, (2), 1993, 1996, 1998, 2000, Keystone Press award, 1994, 2003, Soc. Profl. Journalists award, 1996, 2001. Mem. Phi Beta Kappa. Jewish. Avocations: collecting books, antique furniture and paintings. Home: 1002 Prospect Ave Elkins Park PA 19027-3058 Office: Phila Jewish Exponent 2100 Arch St Philadelphia PA 19103-1300 Home Phone: 215-635-6893; Office Phone: 215-832-0726. E-mail: bleiter@jewishexponent.com.

LEITER, SAMUEL L., theater educator; b. Bkyn., July 20, 1940; s. Joseph and Frieda Leiter; m. Marcia Frieda Lerner, Dec. 26, 1942; children: Bambi Lani Falvo, Justin Leigh. BA, Bklyn Coll., 1962; MFA, U. Hawaii, Honolulu, 1964; PhD, NYU, NYC, 1968. Disting. prof. theatre Bklyn Coll., CUNY, 1965—2006. Chair Theatre Dept., Bklyn Coll., 2002—06. Author: (book) The Art of Kabuki: Famous Plays in Performance, From Belasco to Brook: Representative Directors of the English-Speaking Stage (Choice Outstanding Academic Book, 1991), New Kabuki Encyclopedia: A Revised Adaptation of Kabuki Jiten; editor: Japanese Theatre in the World, Zeami and the No Theatre in the World, Japanese Theatre and the International Stage; translator: The Man Who Saved Kabuki: Faubion Bowers and Theatre Censorship in Occupied Japan; editor: A Kabuki Reader: History and Performance, Kabuki Plays On Stage: Brilliance and Bravado, Kabuki Plays on Stage: Villainy and Vengeance, Kabuki Plays On Stage: Darkness and Desire; author: Kabuki Encyclopedia: An English-Language Adaptation of Kabuki Jiten, Frozen Moments: Writings on Kabuki, 1966-2001; editor: Kabuki Plays On Stage: Restoration and Reform, Masterpieces of Kabuki: Eighteen Plays On Stage; author: Historical Dictionary of Japanese Traditional Theatre, The Encyclopedia of the New York Stage, 1920-1930; editor: Shakespeare around the Globe; author: Ten Seasons: New York Theatre in the Seventies, The Encyclopedia of the New York Stage, 1930-1940, From Stanislavsky to Barrault: Representative Directors of the European Stage, The Encyclopedia of the New York Stage, 1940-1950, The Great Stage Directors: 100 Distinguished Careers of the Theatre; editor: (newsletter) Asian Theatre Bulletin, Encyclopedia of Asian Theatre; contbr. articles to profl. jours., chapters to books. Recipient Outstanding Academic Book, Choice Mag., 1991, Tow award, Claire and Leonard Tow Found., 1995—96, Excellence Creative Achievement award, Bklyn Coll., 2001, Excellence Editing award, Assn. Theatre Higher Edn., 2005; fellow, East-West Ctr., 1962—64, Fulbright Found., 1974—75, Wolfe Inst., 1999—2000; grantee Profl. Staff Congress Rsch. Grant, Profl. Staff Congress, 1986—88, Profl. Staff Congress Award, 1991—93. Fellow: Coll. Fellows Am. Theatre; mem.: Am. Soc. Theatre Rsch. (exec. com. 1999—2002), Assn. Theatre Higher Edn., Assn. Asian Performance, Phi Beta Kappa (hon.). Jewish. Avocations: travel, reading, walking, Japanese language study, baseball. Home: 137-29 79 St Howard Beach NY 11414 Home Phone: 718-843-2799. Personal E-mail: sleiter@nyc.rr.com.

LEITH, CECIL ELDON, JR., retired physicist; b. Boston, Jan. 31, 1923; s. Cecil Eldon and Elizabeth (Benedict) L.; m. Mary Louise Henry, July 18, 1942; children: Ann, John, Paul. AB, U. Calif. at, Berkeley, 1943, PhD, 1957. Exptl. physicist Lawrence Radiation Lab., Berkeley, 1946-52, theoretical physicist Livermore, Calif., 1952-68; sr. scientist Nat. Center for Atmospheric Research, Boulder, Colo., 1968-83, div. dir., 1977-81; physicist Lawrence Livermore Nat. Lab. (Calif.), 1983-90. Symons Meml. lectr. Royal Meteorol. Soc., London, 1978; chmn. com. on atmospheric scis. NRC, 1978-80, sci. program evaluation com. Univ. Corp. for Atmospheric Rsch., 1991-96; mem. joint sci. com. world climate research program World Meteorol. Organ. and Internat. Council Sci. Unions, 1976-83; mem. program adv. com. Office Advanced Sci. Computing, NSF, 1984-85. Served with AUS, 1944-46. Fellow Am. Phys. Soc., Am. Meteorol. Soc. (Meisinger award 1967, Rossby research medal 1982) Home: 627 Carla St Livermore CA 94550-2316 Office: Lawrence Livermore Nat Lab PO Box 808 Livermore CA 94551-0808 Office Phone: 925-423-1612.

LEITHMANN, DAVID EDWARD, music educator; b. Phila., Oct. 27, 1943; s. Joseph Parker and Eleanor Philapena Leithmann; m. Laraine Beam Leithmann, Aug. 28, 1965; children: Dana M. Cottle, Darci L. Giovan. BS, West Chester U., Pa., 1965, MEd, 1969; student, Temple U., 1971—73, Peabody Inst., 1980—84, Millersville U., Pa., 1991. Tchr. music Ephrata (Pa.) Sch. Dist., 1965—67; dir. orchestra Hempfield Sch. Dist., Landisville, Pa., 1967—96; tchr. music Lancaster (Pa.) Conservatory Music, 1999—. Prof. music Elizabethtown (Pa.) Coll., 1974—2004; condr. Lancaster County Youth Symphony, 1985—; dir. Music in the Sch. Lancaster/Lebanon Counties, 1998—. Home: 111 Broad St Akron PA 17501-1105 E-mail: leithmannmusic@aol.com.

LEITMANN, GEORGE, mechanical engineer, educator; b. Vienna, May 24, 1925; arrived in U.S., 1940, naturalized, 1944; s. Josef and Stella (Fischer) Leitmann; m. Nancy Lloyd, Jan. 28, 1955; children: Josef Lloyd, Elaine Michèle. BS, Columbia U., 1949, MA, 1950; PhD, U. Calif., Berkeley, 1956; D Engring. honoris causa, Tech. U. Vienna, 1988; D honoris causa, U. Paris, 1989, Tech. U. Darmstadt, 1990. Physicist, head aeroballistics sect. U.S. Naval Ordnance Sta., China Lake, 1950-57; mem. faculty U. Calif., Berkeley, 1957—, prof. engring. sci., 1963—, first acad. ombudsman, 1968—70, prof. grad. sch., 1995—, assoc. dean acad. affairs, 1981-90, assoc. dean rsch., 1990-94, acting dean, 1988, chair faculty, 1994-98, assoc. dean internat. rels., 2003—. Cons. to aerospace industry and govt.; lectr. in field. Author: (book) An Introduction to Optimal Control, 1966, Quantitative and Qualitative Games, 1969, The Calculus of Variations and Optimal Control, 1981; editor: (jour.) Math Analysis Applications, 1985—2002; assoc. editor Optimization Theory Applications; contbr. 300 articles to profl. jours.; assoc. editor, mem. editl. bd. (to 11 jour.); translator: The Mantle of Dreams. Chmn. bd. dirs. ARTSHIP Found.; master knight Order of Knights of Vine; mem. Acad. Italiana della Cucina. With AUS, 1944—46, ETO, combat engrs., special agent CIC. Decorated Croix de Guerre France, Fourragere Belgium, Comdr.'s Cross, Order of Merit Germany, commendatore Order of Merit Italy; named Miller Rsch. prof., 1966; recipient Pendray Aerospace Lit. award, AIAA, 1979, Mechanics and Control of Flight award, 1984, Von Humboldt U.S. Sr. Scientist award, Von Humboldt Found., 1980, Levy medal, Franklin Inst., 1981, Berkeley citation, U. Calif.-Berkeley, 1991, von Humboldt medal, von Humboldt Found., 1991, Rufus Oldenburger medal, ASME, 1995, Distng. Engring. Alumni award, 2002, Disting. Emeritus of Yr., 2004, 1st recipient Isaacs award, Internat. Soc. Dynamic Games, 2004, Werner Heisenberg medal, von Humboldt Found., 2005; Berkeley fellow, 2002. Mem.: NAE, World Innovation Found., Georgian Acad. Sci., A. V. Humboldt Assn. Am. (pres. 1994—97), Bavarian Acad. Sci., Georgian Acad. Engring., Russian Acad. Natural Sci., Argentine Nat. Acad. Engring., Internat. Acad. Astronautics, Acad. Sci. Bologna. Avocations: art, swimming, oenology, international relations. Office: U Calif Coll Engring Berkeley CA 94720-0001 Business E-Mail: gleit@berkeley.edu.

LEITNER, ALFRED, retired mathematical physicist, educator, educational film producer; b. Vienna, Nov. 3, 1921; came to U.S., 1938, naturalized, 1944; s. Philipp and Lona (Machlup) L.; m. Marzia O'Neil, Nov. 24, 1948 (dec. 2005); children: Kathleen, Deborah Jones, David. BA, U. Buffalo, 1944; MS, Yale U., 1945, PhD, 1948. Research assoc. Courant Inst. Math. Scis., N.Y. U., 1947-51; from asst. prof. to prof. physics Mich. State U., 1951-67; prof. physics Rensselaer Poly. Inst., 1967-88, prof. emeritus, 1988—; research assoc. Harvard U., 1965-66. Cons. Harvard project physics, 1966-68; vis. prof. U.S. Mil. Acad., West Point, 1983-85. Author papers on theory spl. functions, boundary value problems, antennas, history of sci., teaching.; Films Liquid Helium, 1963, Superconductivity, 1966, Project Physics, 1965-68; Dispersion, 1973, Fraunhofer (2 films), 1974, A Story of Research, 1981; (videotapes) Our Favorite Physics Demonstrations, 1987. Guggenheim fellow, 1958-59; Deutscher Akademischer Austauschdienst fellow, 1977 Fellow Am. Phys. Soc.; mem. Phi Beta Kappa, Sigma Xi. Home: 1201 8th Ter N Naples FL 34102-5411

LEITNER, JAMES, finance company executive; m. Sandra Leitner. BS Econ., Yale U.; MS Internat. Fin., Columbia U.; JD, Fordham U. Law Sch., 1982. Mng. dir. Bankers Trust, Global Trading Dept.; v.p. of propriety trading Shearson Lehman; chief dealer Bank of Am. Internat.; FX trader Morgan Guaranty; pres. Falcon Mgmt. Corp. Mem.: Dean's Planning Coun. and the Crowley Adv. Com. at Fordham U. Law Sch., Dean's Coun. of the Sch. of Internat. and Pub. Affairs at Columbia U., Yale Investment Com. Office: Straumur Investment Bank Borgartun 25 IS — 105 Reykjavik Iceland Office Phone: 354 580 91 00. Office Fax: 354 580 91 01. E-mail: straumur@straumur.net.*

LEITNER, PAUL REVERE, lawyer; b. Winnsboro, SC, Nov. 11, 1928; s. W. Walker and Irene (Lewis) L.; m. Jeannette C. Card, Mar. 16, 1985; children by previous marriage: David, Douglas, Gregory, Reid, Cheryl. AB, Duke U., Durham, NC, 1950; LLB, McKenzie Coll., 1954. Bar: Tenn. 1954; cert. civil trial specialist Nat. Bd. Trial Advocacy and Tenn. Commn. on CLE and Specialization. Pvt. practice law, Chattanooga, 1954; assoc. Leitner, Williams, Dooley & Napolitan and predecessor firms, 1952-57; ptnr. Leitner, Williams, Dooley & Napolitan and predecessor firms, 1957—. Tenn. chmn. Def. Rsch. Inst., 1978-89. Bd. dirs. Family Service Agy., 1957-63, Chattanooga Symphony and Opera Assn., 1986-89, sec., 1987-89, Prison and Prevention Ministries, 1992—, chmn. 1996-99; mem. Chattanooga-Hamilton County Community Action Bd.; mem. Juvenile Ct. Commn., Hamilton County, 1955-61, chmn., 1958-59; chmn. Citizens Com. for Better Schs.; mem. Met. Govt. Charter Commn. Served with U.S. Army, 1946-47. Named Young Man of Yr. Chattanooga Area, 1957. Fellow Am. Coll. Trial Lawyers, Tenn. Bar. Found, Chattanooga Bar Found. (founding), Am. Bar Found.; mem. ABA, Tenn. Bar Assn., Jaycees (Chattanooga, pres. 1956-57), Chatanooga Bar Assn., Fed. Bar Assn., Fed. Def. Corp. Counsel, Internat. Assn. Def. Coun., Trial Attys. Am., Tenn. Def. Lawyers Assn. (pres. 1975-76), Am. Bd. Trial Advs. (advocate), U.S. Sixth Cir. Jud. Conf. (life), Am. Inns of Ct. Methodist. Home: 3926 Windward Ln Soddy Daisy TN 37379 Business E-Mail: paul.leitner@leitnerfirm.com.

LEITZ, PAULA HELEN, education educator; d. Wayne and Hazel Greer; m. Steven James Leitz, May 8, 1993; children: Aaron Morgan, Christopher Lee Rallo, Ty Joseph Rallo. BS in Child Devel., U. Calif., Davis, 1971; MA in Spl. Edn., Calif. State U., Sacramento, 1976; PhD in Spl. Edn., U. Wash., Seattle, 1988. Cert. tchr. OSPI/Wash., 1980. Tchr. spl. edn. San Juan Unified Sch. Dist., Sacramento, 1972—78, 1978—82; rsch. asst., 1982—86; asst. prof. St. Martin's U., Lacey, Wash., 1986—89; tchr. spl. edn. U. Wash., 1989—94; assoc. prof. Sch. Edn., Pacific Luth. U., Tacoma, 1994—, assoc. dean, 2001—06. Spl. edn. coord. Peninsula Sch. Dist., Gig Harbor, Wash., 1991—94. Bd. mem. Namibian Ednl. Found., Gig Harbor, Wash., 2002. Mem.: Internat. Assn. Spl. Edn. (treas.), Coun. for Exceptional Children (assoc.; mem.-at-large 1996—98, tchr. edn. divsn. 1994—). Lutheran. Avocations: travel, hiking, reading, wine making. Office: Pacific Luth Univ Sch Edn 121 Hauge Adminstrn Tacoma WA 98447 Office Phone: 253-535-7112. Office Fax: 253-535-7184. Business E-Mail: leitzph@plu.edu.

LEITZEL, JEFFREY DALE, psychology professor; s. James Dale and Judith Dressler Leitzel; m. Jacklyn ann Robinson, June 14, 1998; children: Tara, Meredith Hudak, Jonathan Hudak. BS in Psychology, Pa. State U., 1987; MA in Psychology, Marywood Coll., 1993; PhD in Human Devel., Marywood U., 2000. Lic. psychologist Pa. Rsch. assoc. Mil. Family Inst., Scranton, Pa., 1993—99; asst. prof. Bloomsburg U., Pa., 1999—. Staff psychologist Scranton Counseling Ctr., 1990—; dir. rsch. Behavioral Health Rsch. Inst., Scranton, 1998—2000, exec. dir., 2000—; steering com. Inst. Rsch., Edn. and Tng. in Addictions, Pitts., 2002—; rsch. cons. child abuse tng. program U. Pitts., Mechanicsburg, Pa., 2005—. Proposal reviewer NE Behavioral Healthcare Consortium, Wilkes-Barre, Pa., 2005. Recipient McGowan medal, Marywood U., 2000. Fellow: Pa. Psychol. Assn.; mem.: APA, Assn. for Psychol. Sci. Avocations: cycling, weightlifting, music. Office: Bloomsburg Univ Dept Psychology 400 E Second St Bloomsburg PA 17815

LEITZEL, JOAN RUTH, retired academic administrator; BA in Math., Hanover Coll., 1958; MA in Math., Brown U., 1961; PhD in Math., Ind. U., 1965. Instr. math. Oberlin (Ohio) Coll., 1961-62; asst. prof. math. Ohio State U., Columbus, 1965-70, assoc. prof., 1970-84, prof., 1984-92, vice-chmn. dept., 1973-79, acting chmn., 1978, assoc. provost, 1985-90;

prof. dept. math. and stats. U. Nebr., Lincoln, 1992-96, sr. vice chancellor for acad. affairs, 1992-96, interim chancellor, 1995-96; pres. U. N.H., Durham, 1996—2002, pres. emerita, 2002—. Adv. com. Griffith Ins. Found., 1979-82; cons. Ohio Dept. Edn., 1980-83; participant Am. Coun. on Edn., 1980, 82; cons. Nat. Commn. on Excellence in Edn., U.S. Dept. Edn., 1982; univ. math. edn. del. to China, 1983; dir. divsn. materials devel., rsch. and info. sci. edn. NSF, 1990-92; presenter in field, 1980—; bd. dirs. Am. Assn. Higher Edn., chmn.-elect, 1996-97, chmn., 1997-98; mem. interpretive reports adv. bd. Nat. ssessment Ednl. Progress, 1995-98; trustee Consortium on Math. and Its Applications, 1994-95; mem. exec. coun. com. on acad. affairs Nat. Assn. State Univs. and Land-Grant Colls., 1994-96, bd. dirs., 1997-99, chmn. com. on faculty, 1994-96; coord. coun. for edn. NRC, 1993-95, mem. bd. on math. scis. edn., 1985-87, math. scis. edn. bd., chmn. 2000-05. Bd. dirs. United Way Lincoln, 1995-96, 1st Plymouth Ch., 1996, Lincoln Partnership for Econ. Devel., 1996, N.H. Charitable Found., 1998-02, Durham Cmty. Ch., 1996-02. Recipient Disting. Alumni award Hanover Coll., 1986, dir.'s award for mgmt. excellence NSF, 1991; Disting. Tchg. award Ohio State U., 1982, Disting. Svc. award Ohio State U., 2002, Pettee medal U. N.H., 2002; grantee NSF, 1976-798, 84-88, Battelle Found., 1981-83, SOHIO, 1983-85. Mem. AAAS (edn. com. 1981-84), Am. Math. Soc. (com. on excellence in scholarship 1993-95), Assn. for Women in Math., Math. Assn. Am. (nominatinig com. 1978-79, com. on tchr. tng. and accreditation Ohio sect. 1976-79, nat. com. on undergrad programs 1982-85, chmn. joint task force on curriculum for grades 11-13 with Nat. Coun. Tchrs. Math. 1986-88), Nat. Coun. Tchrs. Math., Mortar Bd., Sigma Xi, Phi Kappa Phi. Business E-Mail: joan.leitzel@unh.edu.

LEITZELL, TERRY LEE, lawyer; b. Williamsport, Pa., Apr. 15, 1942; s. Ernest Richard and Inez Mae (Taylor) L.; m. Lucy Acker Emmerich, June 18, 1966; children: Thomas Addison, Charles Taylor, Robert Davies. AB, Cornell U., 1964; JD, U. Pa., 1967. Bar: DC 1967. Consular officer Dept. State, Bombay, India, 1968-70, atty.-adv. for oceans affairs Washington, 1970-77, chief U.S. negotiator UN law of sea negotiations Geneva, also NYC, 1974-77; asst. adminstr. for fisheries and dir. Nat. Marine Fisheries Service, NOAA, Dept. Commerce, Washington, 1978-81; practice law Washington, 1981-92, Seattle, 1992—; gen. counsel Icicle Seafoods, Seattle. Mem.: Wash. Bar Assn. Democrat. Home: 3150 W Laurelhurst Dr NE Seattle WA 98105-5346 Office: Icicle Seafoods 4019 21st Ave W Ste 300 Seattle WA 98199-1299 Office Phone: 206-281-5372. Business E-Mail: terryl@icicleseafoods.com.

LEIVE, CYNTHIA, editor-in-chief; m. Howard Bernstein; 1 child, Lucy. BA in English Literature, Swarthmore Coll., 1988. With The Paris Rev, The Saturday Rev.; editl. asst., then dep. editor Glamour Mag., 1988—99; editor-in-chief Self Mag., 1999—2001, Glamour Mag., 2001—. Named one of Top 40 Under 40 Executives in NY, Crain's NY Bus., 2002; recipient Matrix award for magazine work, NY Women in Comm. Inc., 2006, Nat. Mag. award for Personal Svc. journalism, Am. Soc. Mag. Editors, 2007. Mem.: Am. Soc. Mag. Editors (bd. dirs. 2001—, pres. 2006—). Mailing: Glamour Mag 4 Times Square 17th Floor New York NY 10036*

LEKAS, MARY DESPINA, retired otolaryngologist; b. Worcester, Mass., May 13, 1928; d. Spyridon Peter and Merciny S. (Manoliou) Lekas; m. Harold William Picozzi (dec.). Student, Boston U.; BA, Clark U., 1949, DSc, ScD, Clark U., 1997; MD, Athens U., Greece, 1957; MA, Brown U., 1986. Diplomate Am. Bd. Otolaryngology. Sci. instr. Hahnemann Hosp. Sch. Nursing; rotating intern Meml. Hosp., Worcester, 1957-58; resident in otolaryngology R.I. Hosp., Providence, 1958-62; resident in otolaryngology and otorhinolaryngology U. Pa. Grad. Sch. Medicine, 1960; surgeon in chief, dept. otolaryngology R.I. Hosp., 1984-96, surgeon-in-chief emerita; pvt. practice Providence, 1962—. Chmn. dept. otolaryngology Brown U., Providnce, 1984, clin. prof. emerita surgery divsn. otolaryngology, head and neck; cons. Cleft Palate Clin. and Craniofacial of R.I. Hosp., 1964—, VA Hosp., Providence, 1967—, St. Joseph Hosp., Providence, 1983—, Miriam Hosp., Providence, 1984—; lectr. profl. orgns.; mem. Project Hope in Columbia, Ceylon/Sri Lanka, SS Hope Hosp. Ship, People-to-People, Inc., Washington, 1968-69. Mem. editl. bd. Am. Jour. Rhinology, 1987—; contbr. articles to profl. jours. Mem. alumni coun. Clark U.; pres. Providence Med. Assn., 1987-88. Named R.I. Woman Physician of Yr., 1992, Endowed Chair in her name, Clark U., 1997; recipient Disting. Svc. award, Providence Med. Assn., 1996, Emeriti award, Brown U., 1999, Outstanding Svc. award, Brown Med. Alumni Assn., 1999, Cert. of Recognition, People-to-People, Inc.; Jonas Clark fellow. Fellow ACS, Soc. Univ. Otolaryngologists-Head and Neck Surgeons, Triological Soc. (ea. sect. sec., Presdl. Citation 1993), Am. Acad. Otolaryngology-Head and Neck Surgeons (gov. R.I. chpt. bd. of govs. 1985-), Am. Acad. Facial Plastic and Reconstructive Surgeons, Am. Acad. Broncho-Escophalogy (treas., v.p. 1990); mem. AMA, Assn. Acad. Dept. Otolaryngology-Head and Neck Surgery, Deafness Rsch. Found., Am. Cleft Palate Assn., Am. Med. Women's Assn. (R.I. Woman Physician of Yr. 1992), Am. Broncho-Esophagological Assn. (hon.), New Eng. Otolaryng. Soc. (pres. 1987-88, Cert. of Recognition 1980-81), Centurion Club. Greek Orthodox. Avocations: bicycling, swimming, church choir. Home: 129 Terrace Ave Riverside RI 02915-4726 Home Fax: 401-433-0941.

LEKBERG, BARBARA, sculptor; BFA, MA, Univ. Iowa; DFA (hon.), Simpson Coll. Instr. Univ. of the Arts, Phila., Nat. Acad. Sch. of Fine Arts, NYC. Exhibitions include Sculpture Ctr., NYC, Marmara Manhattan, NYC, Mt. Holyoke Coll, Glass Art Gallery, Toronto, Pa. Acad. Fine Arts, Whitney Mus. Am. Art, Mus. Modern Art; represented in collections of NAD, Whitney Mus. Am. Art, George Washington Univ., Des Moines Art Ctr., General Electric Corp., Birmingham Mus. Art, New Sch. Univ., NY, Bayfield Clark Collection, Bermuda, Michener Mus., Pa., Brookgreen Gardens, SC. Grantee 2 Guggenheim Fellowships, Inst. Arts & Letters, Richard Florsheim Art Fund. Mem.: Century Assn., NAD (academician, Saltus Gold medal 1990), Nat. Sculpture Soc. (sec., Gold medal 1991, Fellow). Studio: Apt 2A 195 Stanton St New York NY 10002 Office Phone: 212-529-8370. E-mail: blekberg@yahoo.com.

LELAND, JOY HANSON, retired anthropologist, researcher; b. Glendale, Calif., July 29, 1927; d. David Emmett and Florence (Sockerson) Hanson; m. David A. Riegert, Nov. 14, 1993. BA in English Lit., Pomona Coll., Claremont, Calif., 1949; MBA, Stanford U., 1960; MA in Anthropology, U. Nev., 1972; PhD in Anthropology, U. Calif., Irvine, 1975. Sec. Office Spl. Rep., Paris, 1951—53; dir. pers. Libyan Am. Tech. Assistance Svc., Tripoli, Libya, 1953—56; with Desert Research Inst. U. Nev., 1961—; asst. research prof. Desert Research Inst., U. Nev., 1975-77, assoc. research prof., 1977-79, rsch. prof., 1979-89, rsch. prof. emerita, 1990—. Author: Smithsonian Handbook of North American Indians; contbr. articles to profl. jours., chpts. to books. Founding trustee Robert and Joy Leland Charitable Trust (now Robert and Joy Leland Endowment Native Am. Rights Fund), 1992—2005. NIMH grantee, 1972-73; Nat. Inst. Alcohol Abuse and Alcoholism grantee, 1974-75, 79-81 Mem. Am. Anthrop. Assn., Southwestern Anthrop. Assn., Soc. Applied Anthropology, Soc. Med. Anthropology, Gt. Basin Anthrop. Conf., Phi Kappa Phi. Address: 6126 Carriage House Way Reno NV 89519

LELAND, MARC ERNEST, trust company executive, consultant, lawyer; b. San Francisco, Apr. 20, 1938; s. Herbert and Sarah Betty (Robinson) L.; m. Elisabeth Gustava De Rothschild, July 7, 1970 (div. Sept. 1980); children: Natasha Hanna, Olivia Mitzi; m. Jacqueline de Botton, 1989. AB in Govt., Harvard U., Cambridge, Mass., 1959; MA in Law, St. John's Coll.-Oxford U., Eng., 1961; JD, U. Calif.-Berkeley, 1963. Ford Found. fellow Inst. Comparative Law-U., Paris, 1963-64; assoc. Cerf Robinson & Leland, San Francisco, 1964-68, ptnr., 1972-76; faculty fellow Harvard U. Law Sch., Boston, 1968-70; gen. counsel Peace Corps, Washington, 1970-71, ACTION, Washington, 1971-72; ACDA rep. Force Reduction Talks, Vienna, Austria, 1976-78; resident ptnr. Proskauer Rose Goetz & Mendelsohn, London, 1978-81; asst. sec. internat. affairs Dept. Treasury, Washington, 1981-84; pres. Marc E. Leland & Assocs., Washington, 1984—. Republican. Jewish. Office: 1001 19th St N Ste 1700 Arlington VA 22209-1725

LELAND, RICHARD G(UY), lawyer; b. Oceanside, NY, Jan. 25, 1949; s. Arnold Joseph and Eunice (Himlyn) L.; m. Jane E. Schwartz; children: Jennifer Schultz, David Jarett. BS, Cornell U., Ithaca, NY, 1971; JD with distinction, Hofstra U., Hempstead, NY, 1974. Bar: NY 1975, US Ct. Appeals (2nd cir.) 1975, US Dist. Ct. (so., ea., no. and we. dists.) NY 1976, US Supreme Ct. 1979. Assoc. Winer, Neuburger & Sive, NYC, 1974-76; law sec. to Justice Douglas F. Young Supreme Ct. NY Nassau County, Mineola, 1976-79; assoc. Ruskin, Schlissel, Moscou & Evans, P.C., Mineola, 1979-82, ptnr., 1982-89, Rosenman & Colin LLP, NYC, 1989—2002, Kramer Levin Naftalis & Frankel LLP, NYC, 2002—07, Fried, Frank, Harris, Shriver & Jacobson LLP, NYC, 2007—. Spl. prof. Hofstra U., Hempstead, 1991—; mem. Real Estate Bd. of NY, Inc.; chair Commn. on Environ. Law. Contbr. articles to profl. jours. Mem.: Assn. Bar City NY, NY State Bar Assn. (task force downtown redevelopment, land use and energy com. 2002), Hofstra Law Sch. Alumni Assn. (pres. 1995—99). Office: Fried Frank Harris Shriver & Jacobson LLP One NY Plaza New York NY 10004 Home Phone: 201-964-1403; Office Phone: 212-859-8978. Business E-Mail: richard.leland@friedfrank.com.

LELAND, TIMOTHY, retired newspaper executive; b. Boston, Sept. 24, 1937; s. Oliver Stevens and Frances Chamberlain (Ayres) L.; m. Natasha Bourso, Sept. 26, 1964 (div. 1981); children: Christian Bourso, London Chamberlain; m. Julie S. Hatfield, Nov. 23, 1984. AB cum laude, Harvard U., 1960; MS with honors, Columbia Sch. Journalism, 1961. Med. editor Boston Herald, 1963-64; sci. editor Boston Globe, 1965-66, State House bur. chief, 1966-67, asst. city editor, 1968-69, investigative reporter, 1970-71, asst. mng. editor, 1972, mng. editor (Sunday), 1976-81, mng. editor (daily), 1981-82, asst. to pub., 1984-97, asst. to chmn., 1997-98, v.p., 1990—. Bd. dirs. Boys and Girls Clubs of Boston. Recipient Am. Polit. Sci. award, 1968; Pulitzer Prize for investigative reporting, 1972; Sigma Delta Chi award for civic service (reporting), 1972; award for pub. service A.P. Mng. Editors, 1974; Sevellon Brown award, 1974; U.S.-South African Leader Exchange Program traveling grantee, 1969; Internat. fellow Columbia, 1961. Mem. Harvard Club. Office: 617 Tremont St Boston MA 02118

LELAS, SNJEZANA, pharmacologist, researcher; b. Zagreb, Croatia, Apr. 29, 1971; d. Srdan and Jasmina Lelas. BA, U. Oxford, 1989—92, DPhil, 1993—96. Postdoctoral fellow La. State U. Med. Ctr., New Orleans, 1996—98, Harvard Med. Sch., Southborough, Mass., 1999—2001; sr. rsch. investigator Bristol-Myers Squibb, Wallingford, Conn., 2001—. Contbr. articles to profl. jours. Scholar, U. Oxford, 1991. Mem.: Am. Soc. for Pharmacology and Exptl. Therapeutics, Behavioral Pharmacology Soc., Soc. for Neuroscience. Avocations: travel, writing, sports, theater. Home: 3B Oak Hill Dr Clinton CT 06413 Office: Bristol-Myers Squibb 5 Research Pkwy Wallingford CT 06492 Home Phone: 860-669-7752; Office Phone: 203-677-7441. Office Fax: 203-677-7569. Business E-Mail: snjezana.lelas@bms.com.

LELE, AMOL SHASHIKANT, obstetrician, gynecologist; b. Chhindnara, India, May 23, 1944; came to US, 1970; d. Gajanan S. and Sarala S. (Manjrekar) Karande; m. Shashikant Lele, Feb. 28, 1970; children: Kedar, Rajal. MBBS, Bombay U., 1967, MD, 1970; D Ob-Gyn., Coll. Physicians, Bombay, 1969. Diplomate Am. Bd. Ob-Gyn. Clinician ob-gyn. clinic St. Luke's Hosp., Cleve., 1974; instr. SUNY, Buffalo, 1974-76, asst. prof., 1976-84, clin. assoc. prof., 1984—; fellow Children's Hosp., Buffalo, 1976-78, dir. women's svcs., 1976—, dir. outreach program, 1991—; dir. prenatal care Erie County Med. Ctr., Buffalo, 1979-97; clin. chief ob-gyn. CHOB Kaleida Health Sys., 1999—. Mem. health com. Planned Parenthood, Buffalo, 1992-97; mem. infant mortality task force Health Systems Agy., Buffalo, 1994-97. Avocations: reading, theater, music. Home: 75 Nottingham Ter Buffalo NY 14216-3620 Office: 11 Summer St Buffalo NY 14209-2256 Home Phone: 716-873-1513; Office Phone: 716-881-0400.

LELEU, JONATHAN PAUL, lawyer; b. Chgo., Feb. 10, 1974; s. Henri Ignatious and Inalynn Marie Leleu; m. Jacquelyn Sue Dietz, Nov. 3, 2001. BA, Loyola U., Chicago, 1996; JD, Coll. of Law DePaul U., Chgo., 1999. Bar: Nev. 2000, Ill. 2000. Atty. Zenoff & Zenoff, Chartered, Chgo., 1999—2001, Rawlings Olson Cannon Gormley & Desruisseaux, Las Vegas, Nev., 2001—03, Kummer Kaempfer Bonner & Renshaw, Las Vegas, 2003—. Legis. intern U.S. Senator Carol Moseley Braun, Chgo., 1995—96. Mem.: ABA (assoc.), Clark County Bar Assn. (assoc.), Nev. Am. Inn of Ct. (assoc.), Pi Alpha Delta (life). Roman Catholic. Avocations: baseball, hockey, culinary arts, travel. Office: Kummer Kaempfer Bonner & Renshaw 7th Fl 3800 Howard Hughes Pkwy Las Vegas NV 89109 Home Phone: 702-240-0620; Office Phone: 702-792-7000. Office Fax: 702-796-7181. E-mail: jleleu@kkbr.com.

LELYVELD, GAIL ANNICK, actress; b. Boston, May 22, 1948; d. Edward I. and Beatrice Elizabeth (Hewitt) L. BA in Polit. Sci., Boston U., 1970; MA in Polit. Sci., Goddard Coll., 1974; studied with Paul Barry, Peter Donat, Ray Reinhardt, Darrell Lauer, others. Actress, 1970—; tech. staff USA Prodns. and Midseason, Hempstead, NY, 1986-87, prodn. stage mgr., 1987—. Tech. staff Gray Wig, Hempstead, 1986, 87; cons. Talking With prodn. M.A., C.W. Post. Appeared in numerous films including Frances, Halloween III, Children On Their Birthdays, Project 1917, Rocky II, Happy Endings, Seeds of Innocence, Bonfire of the Vanities, The Music of the Heart, The Bird's Eye View, Insomnia, Monster Math, The Lesson, I'm Not Rappaport, City Hall, The House of the Venus Flytrap (ind. film), Believe for Hofstra University (film), Baby Buyer (NYU short film); (TV): Archie Bunker's Place, Mister Clown Says, White Noise, The Gentle Creature, (ABC Afterschool Spl.) Summer Stories: The Mall, Mathnet, Bill Cosby Murder Mystery, Cosby: You're OK, I'm Hilton, Upright Citizen Brigade; actor: Alice in Wonderland, Not So Grimm Fairytale Players; actress (Littletop Theater Co.) Toby Tyler, Marmalade Gumdrops, Bohemian Lights, King Lear - Tenant, Doctor & Knight Plainedge Playhouse, The Hostage, USA Prodns., The Cherry Orchard, Broadhollow Theater Bay Way Art Ctr., The House of Blue Leaves, The Lady of Larkspur Lotion, Broadhollow Theatre Bay Way Arts Ctr., Sarah Good and the Voice of Martha Corey, BDR Repertory Co., The Worst Play in the World, Women's Theatrical Collective, The Man Who Came to Dinner, U.S.A. Prodns., Holocaust Survivor-Columbia U.; Singer: Gospel Oedipus at Colonus evangelist, townsperson, choir, Musicum Collegium Hofstra U., Pala Opera Assn., St. Patrick's Cathedral Choir, Temple Emanuel New Hyde Park Choir; singer and leader Christmas Carols Garden City Group Christmas Party, Garden City Group Chorus Holiday Songs and Soloist; soloist piano recital, solo singer Ecumenical Thanksgiving Svc.; one-person performance, Dona Gracia Nasi, Memoirs of Glüchel of Hameln, Temple Emanuel of New Hyde Park, Karen Finley Workshop Performance Arts, Actors Bootcamp, Purple Rose Theatre Co.; theater tech. involvement includes stage mgr., sound asst. Wings; sound asst. Danton's Death; asst. stage mgr. props, fx, dresser Accomplice; cons. on reading The Sisters Rosenweig; writer Tom Berenger Online Newsletter. Reader Ynm Kippur svcs. Temple Emanuel, San Francisco. Mem. AFTRA Jewish. Avocations: reading, knitting, walking. Home: 205 C St NE Washington DC 20002 Personal E-mail: berrydoor863@yahoo.com.

LELYVELD, JOSEPH SALEM, former newspaper editor, news correspondent, writer; b. Cin., Apr. 5, 1937; s. Arthur Joseph and Toby (Bookholtz) L.; m. Carolyn Fox, June 14, 1959 (dec. May, 2004); children: Amy, Nita. BA summa cum laude, Harvard Coll., 1958, MA, 1959; MS in Journalism, Columbia U., 1960. Reporter, editor N.Y. Times, 1963—2001, fgn. corr., Johannesburg, New Delhi, Hong Kong, London, 1965-86, columnist mag., staff writer, 1977, 84-85, fgn. editor, 1987-89, mng. editor, 1990-94, exec. editor, 1994—2001, interim exec. editor, 2003. Author: Move Your Shadow, 1985 (Pulitzer prize, L.A. Times Book prize, Sidney Hillman award, all 1986), Omaha Blues: A Memory Loop, 2005. Recipient George Polk Meml. award, 1972, 84; Guggenheim fellow, 1984. Mem. Coun. Fgn. Rels., The Century Assn. E-mail: lelyveld@nytimes.com.

LEMAIRE, ELIZABETH GRIFFIN, parochial school educator; b. Bklyn., May 27, 1948; d. Gerald Aloysius Griffin and Mary Elizabeth Broekman; m. Asa Conrad LeMaire, Apr. 24, 1971; children: Brian Joseph, Lisa Marie. BA in Secondary Edn., Polit. Sci. and History, Our Lady the Lake U., San Antonio, 1970. Tchr. St. Thomas More Sch., Houston, 1979—. Social studies dept. chair St. Thomas More Sch., 1989—, student coun. adv., 1990—. Mem.: Nat. Cath. Edn. Assn.

LEMAIRE, JACQUES, professional hockey coach; b. Lasalle, Que., Can., Sept. 7, 1945; Player Montreal Canadiens, 1967-79, head coach, 1983-85; head coach, player Sierre Hockey Club, Switzerland, 1979-81; asst. coach SUNY Coll., Plattsburgh, 1981-82; coach Longueuil Chevaliers, maj. jr. league, Que., 1982-83; dir. of hockey pers. Montreal Canadiens, 1985-87, asst. to mng. dir., 1987-93, cons. to gen. mgr., 1998-00; head coach NJ Devils, 1993-98, Minnesota Wild, Saint Paul, 2000—. Mem. Stanley Cup Championship teams, 1968, 69, 71, 73, 76-79; coach 1995. Named NHL Coach of Yr., Sporting News, 1993, 94; inducted into Hockey Hall of Fame, 1984; recipient Jack Adams Award, NHL, 2003. Home: Minn Wild 317 Washington St Saint Paul MN 55102

LEMAISTRE, CHARLES AUBREY, retired internist, epidemiologist, educator; b. Lockhart, Ala., Feb. 10, 1924; s. John Wesley and Edith (McLeod) LeM.; m. Joyce Trapp, June 3, 1952 (dec. Dec. 2003), Andreae Preyer Behlen, Jan. 29, 2005; children: Charles Frederick, William Sidney, Joyce Anne, Helen Jean; m. Andreae Preyer Behlen, Jan. 29, 2005. BA, U. Ala., 1943, LLD (hon.), 1971; MD, Cornell U., 1947; LLD (hon.), Austin Coll., 1970; DSc (hon.), U. Dallas, 1978, Southwestern U., 1981; D honoris causa, U. Guadalajara, Mex., 1989. Intern, then resident in medicine N.Y. Hosp., 1947-49; rsch. fellow infectious diseases Cornell U. Med. Coll., 1949-51, mem. faculty, 1951-54, asst. prof. medicine, 1953-54; mem. faculty Emory U. Sch. Medicine, 1954-59, prof. preventive medicine, chmn. dept., 1957-59; prof. medicine U. Tex. Southwestern Med. Sch., 1959-78, assoc. dean, 1965-66; vice chancellor health affairs U. Tex. Sys., Austin, 1966-68, exec. vice chancellor, 1968-69, dep. chancellor, 1969-70, chancellor, 1971-78, prof. medicine, 1978-96; pres. M.D. Anderson Cancer Ctr. U. Tex., 1978—96, internist M.D. Anderson Cancer Ctr., 1978—96, prof. M.D. Anderson Cancer Ctr., 2006—. Cons. epidemiology Communicable Disease Ctr., USPHS, 1953-69; cons. medicine VA, 1954-59; area med. cons. VA (Atlanta area), 1958-59; vis. staff physician Grady Meml. Hosp., Atlanta, 1954-59, Emory U. Hosp., 1954-59; sr. attending staff mem. Parkland Meml. Hosp., Dallas, 1959-66; med. dir. chest divsn. Woodlawn Hosp., Dallas, 1959-65; mem. Surgeon Gen.'s Adv. Com. Smoking and Health, 1963-64, AMA-Edn. Rsch. Found. com. rsch. tobacco and health, 1964-66; chmn. Gov. Tex. Com. Tb Eradication, 1963-64; cons. internal medicine Baylor U. Med. Ctr., Dallas, 1962-66, St. Paul Hosp., Dallas, 1966; cons. divsn. hosp. and med. facilities USPHS, 1966; mem. N.Y.C. Task Force on Tb, 1967; cons. Bur. Physician, HEW, 1967-70; mem. grad. med. edn. nat. adv. com. Health Resources Adminstrn., 1977-80; mem. Tex. Legislature Dept. Health, Edn. and Welfare, 1967, Tex. Legislature Com. on Organ Transplantation, 1968, Carnegie Commn. on Non-Traditional Study, 1971-73; mem. bd. commrs. Nat. Commn. on Accrediting, 1973-76; mem. joint task force on continuing competence in pharmacy Am. Pharm. Assn.-Am. Assn. Coll. in Pharmacy, 1973-74; mem. exec. com. Legis. Task Force on Cancer in Tex., 1984-86; adv. bd. 6th World Conf. on Smoking and Health. Contbr. articles to med. jours.; contbg. author: A Textbook of Medicine, 10 and 11th edits, 1963, Pharmacology in Medicine, 1958; translating author: The Tubercle Bacillus, 1955; mem. editl. bd. Am. Rev. Respiratory Diseases, 1955-58. Mem. President's Commn. White House Fellows, 1971; chmn. subcom. on diversity and pluralism Nat. Coun. on Ednl. Rsch., 1973-75; bd. dirs. Assn. Tex. Colls. and Univs., 1974-75; mem. devel. coun. United Negro Coll. Fund, 1974-78; mem. nat. adv. coun. Inst. for Svcs. to Edn., 1974-78; mem. exec. com. Assn. Am. Univs., 1975-77; mem. Project HOPE com. on Health Policy, 1977; chmn. steering com. Presbyn. Physicians for Fgn. Missions, 1960-62; mem. Ministers Cons. Clinic, Dallas, 1960-62; trustee Austin Coll., 1979-83, Stillman Coll., 1978-84; bd. dirs. Ga. Tb Assn., 1955-59; bd. dirs. Damon Runyon-Walter Winchell Cancer Fund, 1976-85, chmn. exec. com., v.p., 1978, pres., 1979-83; trustee Biol. Humanics Found., Dallas, 1973-82; chmn. health manpower com. Assn. Am. Univs., 1975-78; sec. Coun. So. Univs., Inc., 1976-78, pres., 1977-78; hon. life trustee Menninger Found.; host com. Houston Econ. Summit, 1990. Recipient Cornell Univ. Alumni of Distinction award, 1978, Disting. Alumnus award U. Alabama Sch. Medicine, 1982, Pres.' award Am. Lung Assn., 1987, Gibson D. Lewis award for Excellence in Cancer Control Tex. Cancer Coun., 1988, award of Honor Am. Soc. Hosp. Pharmacists, 1988, Svc. to Mankind award Leukemia Soc. Am. Tex. Gulf Coast chpt., 1991, People of Vision award Tex. Soc. to Prevent Blindness, 1991, Outstanding Tex. Leader award 7th Ann. John Ben Sheppard Pub. Leadership Forum, 1991; Inst. Religion's Caring Spirit Tribute, 1993, AMA Disting. Svc. award, 1995, Ala. Acad. of Honor, 1998, Disting. Svc. award NASA, 1998, Charles A. LeMaiste Clinic Bldg. U. Tex. M.D. Anderson Cancer Ctr., Houston, 1997; named Houstonian of Yr., Houston Sch. for Deaf Children, 1987, Lamar award Assn. Tex. Colls. and Univs., 2000; named to Ala. Healthcare Hall of Fame, 1999. Mem. AMA, (Disting. Svc. award 1995), NASA, NIH (chair joint adv. com. behavioral rsch. 1992), Am. Thoracic Soc. (past v.p.), So. Thoracic Soc. (past pres.), Nat. TB Assn., Tex. Med. Assn., Ga. Med. Assn., Soc. Assn. Oncology (bd. dirs.), Am. Cancer Soc. (Tex. bd. dirs. 1977-89, med. and sci. com. 1974, chmn. study com. on tobacco and cancer 1976, pub. edn. com. 1976-87, chmn., mem. various nat. coms., v.p., pres. 1986, med. dir.-at-large 1977-89, Ted C. Mars award 1998, medal of Honor 1998, Biennial Symposium Founders award 2006), Houston C. of C. (dir. 1979-89), Philos. Soc. Tex. (pres. 1980-81), Greater Houston Partnership (bd. dirs. 1989-96), Alpha Omega Alpha. Presbyterian. Mailing: Box 90449 San Antonio TX 78209 Personal E-mail: cajtlem@satx.rr.com. E-mail: clemaistre@gmail.com.

LEMAN, EUGENE D., meat industry executive; b. Peoria, Ill., Dec. 1, 1942; s. Vernon L. and Viola L. (Beer) L.; m. Carolyn Leman, June 14, 1964; children— Jill C., Jennifer A. BS, U. Ill., 1964. Dir. various depts. Wilson Foods, Oklahoma City, 1964-78, v.p. fresh and processed pork, 1978-80, v.p. fresh meat group, 1980-81; group v.p. IBP, Inc., Dakota City, Nebr., 1981-86, exec. v.p., 1986—95, CEO, exec. v.p., 1986—95, pres. Allied Group, 1996—98; pres. IBP Fresh Meats, Dakota City, Nebr., 1998, CEO, 2000, sr. group v.p., 2001, Tyson Fresh Meats, Dakota City, Nebr., 2003. Bd. dirs. Wells Fargo Bank, Dakota Valley Bus. Coun.; bd. trustees BSA Mid-Am. Coun. Bd. mem. United Way of Siouxland, 2003—05, campaign chmn., 2004—05; bd. trustees Siouxland Cmty. Found. Mem. Am. Meat Inst. (chmn. pork com. 1980-81), Nat. Pork Producers Council (packer rep. Pork Value Task Force 1981-82, 88, pork export com. 1985) Clubs: Sioux City Country (Iowa), Dakota Dunes Country Club. Republican. Office: Tyson Fresh Meats Ste 820 800 Stevens Port Dr Dakota Dunes SD 57049-5005 E-mail: gene.leman@tyson.com.

LEMAN, LOREN DWIGHT, former lieutenant governor, civil engineer; b. Pomona, Calif., Dec. 2, 1950; s. Nick and Marian (Broady) L.; m. Carolyn Rae Bratvold, June 17, 1978; children: Joseph, Rachel, Nicole. BSCE, Oreg. State U., 1972; MS in Civil, Environ. Engring., Stanford U., 1973; studied Arctic engring., U. Alaska, Anchorage. Registered profl. engr., Alaska. Project mgr. CH2M Hill, San Francisco, 1973, Reston, Va., 1973-74, Ketchikan, Alaska, 1974-75, Anchorage, 1975-87; owner Loren Leman, P.E., Anchorage, 1987—; mem. Alaska Ho. of Reps., 1989-93, Alaska State Senate, Dist. G, Juneau, 1993—2003; lt. gov State of Alaska, Juneau, 2003—07. Mem. Anchorage Hazardous Materials Commn., Local Emergency Planning Com., 1989-93. Contbr. articles to profl. jours. Mem. Breakthrough Com., Anchorage, 1978; del. to conv. Rep. Party of Alaska, 1976-90; basketball coach Grace Christian Sch., Anchorage, 1985-88; commr. Pacific States Marine Fisheries Commn.; past chmn. Pacific Fisheries Legis. Task Force. Mem. ASCE, Alaska Water Mgmt. Assn., Am. Legis. Exch. Coun., Water Environment Fedn., Toastmasters (pres.). Republican. Avocations: reading, fishing, bicycling, music, basketball. Office Phone: 907-465-3520.*

LEMANN, THOMAS BERTHELOT, lawyer; b. New Orleans, Jan. 3, 1926; s. Monte M. and Nettie E. (Hyman) L.; m. Barbara M. London, Apr. 14, 1951 (dec. 1999); children: Nicholas B., Nancy E.; m. Sheila Bosworth Bell, June 1, 2000. AB summa cum laude, Harvard U., 1949, LLB, 1952; MCL, Tulane U., 1953. Bar: La. 1953. Assoc. Monroe & Lemann, New Orleans, 1953-58, ptnr., 1958-98; of counsel Liskow & Lewis, New Orleans, 1998—. Bd. dirs. B. Lemann & Bro., Mermentau Mineral and Land Co., Avrico Inc. Contbr. articles to profl. publs. Mem. coun. La. State Law Inst., sec. trust adv. com.; chmn. Mayor's Cultural Resources Com., 1970-75; pres. Arts Coun. Greater New Orleans, 1975-80, bd. dirs.; mem. vis. com. art museums Harvard U., 1974-80; trustee Metairie Park Country Day Sch., 1956-71, pres., 1967-70, New Orleans Philharm. Symphony Soc., 1956-78, Flint-Goodridge Hosp., 1960-70, La. Civil Svc. League, pres., 1974-76, New Orleans Mus. Art, 1986-92; bd. dirs. Zemurray Found., Hever Found., Hawkins Found., Parkside Found., Azby Fund, Azby Art Fund, Greater New Orleans Found., 1996-05, Arts Coun. New Orleans, Musica da Camera. Served with AUS, 1944-46, PTO. Mem. ABA, La. Bar Assn. (bd. govs. 1977-78), New Orleans Bar Assn., Assn. Bar City N.Y., Am. Law Inst., Soc. Bartolus, New Orleans Country Club, Wyvern Club (New Orleans), Phi Beta Kappa. Jewish. Home: 6020 Garfield St New Orleans LA 70118 Office: Liskow Lewis APLC 701 Poydras St Ste 5000 New Orleans LA 70139-5099 Office Phone: 504-581-7979. Business E-Mail: tblemann@liskow.com.

LEMANSKE, ROBERT F., JR., allergist, immunologist; b. Milw., 1948; MD, U. Wis., 1975. Diplomate Am. Bd. Pediats., Am. Bd. Allergy and Immunology. Intern U. Wis. Hosp., Madison, 1975-76, resident in pediats., 1976-78, prof. pediats. medicine, divsn. head pediat. allergy, immunology & rheumatology. Fellow: Am. Acad. Allergy and Immunology, Am. Acad. Pediat. Office: Clin Sci Ctr Rm K4/916 600 Highland Ave Madison WI 53792-0001 Office Phone: 608-265-2206.

LEMANSKI, LARRY FREDRICK, medical educator, academic administrator; b. Madison, Wis., June 5, 1943; s. Fredrick Everett and Marjery Ulila (Hill) L.; m. Sharon Lee Wulf, Aug. 6, 1966; children: Scott Fredrick, Jennifer Lee. BS, U. Wis., Platteville, 1966; MS, Ariz. State U., 1968, PhD, 1971. Asst. prof. U. Calif., San Francisco, 1975-77; assoc. prof. U. Wis., Madison, 1977—79, prof., 1979—83; prof. and chmn. dept. anatomy and cell biology SUNY, Syracuse, 1983—97, cell and molecular biology doctoral tng. program and consortium, 1987—97; rsch. prof. biology Syracuse U., 1988-97; assoc. v.p. for rsch., acting v.p. Tex. A&M. U., College Station, 1997—2001; prof. biomed. sci., biology and chemistry Fla. Atlantic U., 2001—, v.p. rsch. and grad. studies, pres., CEO of FAU Rsch. Corp. Chmn. spl. study sect. NIH; v.p., dean grad. programs Fla. Atlantic U., 2001—05; mem. bd. dirs. NIH rev. panel Roadmap Rsch. Programs, 2004—05; bd. dirs. Ctr. Human and Machine Cognition, 2004—; founder divsn. rsch. Fla. Atlantic U.; bd. dirs. Fla. Rsch. Consortium, Fla. Space Rsch. Inst.; mem. Gov.'s Team Fla. in Germany and Switzerland, 2005—; mem. govs. Enterprise Fla. Trade Mission to UK and other ednl. visits for rsch. collaborations, 2006—. Adult leader Boy Scouts Am., mem. nat. staff Boy Scout Jamboree, 1989, coun. tng. chmn., 1992—94; bd. dirs. Oak Ridge Assn. Univs., 1999—2002, 2004—07, Inst. Human and Machine Cognition, gov.'s appointee, 2004—; bd. dirs. I.B.M Latin Am. Grid, 2005—, bd. govs., 2006—; Fla. del. Enterprise Fla. Team Trade Missions to U.K., Germany, Switzerland, and Israel, 2005—07; rsch. acad. Trade Missions to China and Japan, 2007; bd. dirs. Fla.-Israeli Inst., 2006—. Officer USAR, 1965—69. Recipient Pres'. award Rsch. SUNY HSC, 1987, Disting. Alumnus award U. Wis., Platteville, 1990, Profl. Excellence award N.Y. State/United Univ. Professions, 1990, 95, SUNY Pres.'s award for affirmative action, 1995, Outstanding Rschr. award SUNY Coll. of Medicine, 1997; NIH fellow, 1968-71, 71-73, Muscular Dystrophy fellow, 1973-75; grantee NIH, 1975—. Mem. AAAS, Am. Heart Assn. (Wis. affiliate rsch. com. 1982-83, peer review panel, Louis N. Katz Rsch. prize 1978, Outstanding Rsch. award 1982, Established Investigator award 1976-81, symposium chair Internat. Soc. Heart Rsch. Conf., Brisbane, Australia, 2004, Fla.-Puerto Rican rsch. com. 2004-), Electron Microscopy Soc. Am., Tex. Soc. for Biomed. Rsch. (bd. dirs. 1999-2001), Am. Assn. Anatomy, Cell Biology, and Neurobiology (chair nat. coun. 1997—), Am. Assn. Anatomists, Am. Soc. Cell Biology (congrl. liaison com.), Soc. Devel. Biology, Am. Assn. Anatomy Chmn., NY Acad. Scis., Masons (3d degree master), Sigma Xi, Beta Beta Beta, Phi Beta Delta. Christian. Avocations: gardening, fishing, boating, camping, music. Home: 6762 Camille St Boynton Beach FL 33437 Office: Fla Atlantic U 777 Glades Rd PO Box 3091 Boca Raton FL 33431-0991 Office Phone: 561-752-0698. Business E-Mail: lemanski@fau.edu.

LEMARBE, EDWARD S., marketing and engineering executive; b. Chicago Heights, Ill., June 30, 1952; s. Gerald Joseph and Irene Helen (Jelen) LeM.; m. Patricia Ann Czyz, May 28, 1977; children: Kyle Bradford, Randall Jered. BS in Mech. Tech., Purdue U., 1976; MBA, Lewis U., 1984. Field engr. Morrison Constrn. & Engring., Hammond, Ind., 1976-78; sr. engr. Miner Enterprises, Inc., Geneva, Ill., 1978-85; mgr. product devel. Alco Dispensing Systems div. Alco Standard, Torrington, Conn., 1985-88; v.p. engring. Jet Spray Corp., Norwood, Mass., 1988-92; sr. dir. Engring. Multiplex Co., Ballwin, Mo., 1992-95; sr. dir. key accounts mktg., R&D Multiplex Co., Ballwin, 1995-97, v.p. nat. accounts, 1997—2000, dir. bus. devel., 2000—03; dir. sales engring. Duke Mfg. Co., St. Louis, 2003—. Mem. pres.' staff Alco Dispensing/Selmix-Alco, Torrington, 1986-88; mem. exec. com. Jet Spray Corp., Norwood, 1988-92; mem. resource allocation com. Multiplex Co. Inc., 1992-96, mem. strategic planning, 1996—. Mem. ASTM (subcom. 1988—), Am. Mgmt. Assn. (assoc.), Internat. Food Svc. Mfrs. Assn. (corp. mem.), Hickory Bend Condo Assn. (bd. dirs. 1984-85). Republican. Roman Catholic. Avocations: golf, tennis, scuba diving. Office Phone: 314-231-1130 322. E-mail: elemarbe@charter.net, elemarbe@dukemfg.com.

LE MASTER, DENNIS CLYDE, retired forester, economist, educator; b. Startup, Wash., Apr. 22, 1939; s. Franklin Clyde and Delores Ilene (Schwartz) Le M.; m. Kathleen Ruth Dennis, Apr. 4, 1961; children: Paul, Matthew. BA, Wash. State U., Pullman, 1961; MA, Wash. State U., 1970, PhD, 1974. Asst. prof. dept. forestry and range mgmt. Wash. State U., Pullman, 1972-74, assoc. prof., 1978-80, prof., chair dept., 1980-88; prof., head dept. forestry and natural resources Purdue U., West Lafayette, Ind., 1998—2004; dir. resource policy Soc. Am. Foresters, Bethesda, Md., 1974-76; staff counsel subcom. on forests Ho. of Reps., Washington, 1977-78, ret., 2005. Cons. USDA Forest Svc., Washington, 1978—, Com. on Ag., Ho. of Reps., 1979-80, Forest History Soc., Durham, N.C., 1979-83, The Conservation Found., 1989-90, Office Tech. Assessment, Washington, 1989-91, Consultative Group on Biol. Diversity, 1991, Colo. State Forest Svc., 2006-07. Author: Decade of Change, 1984; co-editor 8 books; contbr. articles to profl. jours. Bd. dirs. Pinchot Inst. for Conservation, treas., 1996-97, vice-chair, 1998-99, chair, 2000-01. Sr. fellow, Pinchot Inst. for Conservation. Mem. AAAS, Soc. Am. Foresters (chair ho. of dels. 1982, coun. 1999), Inst. Forest Biotech., Internat. Union Forest Rsch. Orgns., Beta Gamma Sigma, Epsilon Sigma Phi, Omicron Delta Epsilon, Xi Sigma Pi. Democrat. Episcopalian. Avocation: fishing. Home: 626 40th Pl Everett WA 98201 Office: Purdue U Dept Forestry and Natural Resources West Lafayette IN 47907 Home Phone: 425-252-1391; Office Phone: 425-252-1391. Personal E-mail: dclmstr@comcast.net.

LEMASTER, JOSEPH WILLIAM, physician, epidemiologist; s. Luella Mattox and Joseph Woodford LeMaster; m. Judith Anne Nichols; children: Luke Pemba, Claire Elizabeth. MD, U. Kans., Kansas City, 1985; MS in Pub. Health in Developing Countries, London Sch. Hygiene and Tropical Medicine, 1994; MPH in Epidemiology, U. Wash., Seattle, 2002. Family medicine resident John Peter Smith Hosp., Ft. Worth, 1985—88; staff emergency rm. physician St. Francis Hosp. and Med. Ctr., Topeka, 1988—90; sr. med. pub. health officer Okhaldhunga Hosp. and Primary Health Care Program, Nepal, 1990—96; dep. health svcs. dir. United Mission to Nepal, Kathmandu, 1996—99; sr. rsch. scientist, epidemiologist Anandaban Leprosy Hosp., Kathmandu, Nepal, 1999—2000; asst. prof. dept. family and cmty. medicine Sch. Medicine, U. Mo., Columbia, 2002—. Contbr. articles to med. jours. Missionary physician Interserve USA, Okhaldhunga and Kathmandu, Nepal, 1990—2000. Recipient Alumni Academic award, Boise State U., 1981, Howard Matzke Anatomy award, U. Kans., 1985, Berket Sandoz Family Practice award, 1985;, State of Idaho scholar, 1975, Academic scholar, NW Nazarene Coll., 1977—79, Merck Academic scholar, U. Kans., 1985. Mem.: Am. Acad. Family Physicians, Am. Diabetes Assn., Alpha Delta Sigma. Achievements include research in current randomized controlled trial (Feet First study) investigates the role of weight-bearing exercise regarding the risk of foot ulcers for people with diabetes mellitus and insensitive feet; participating in community-based project for better self-management of diabetes. Office: Dept Family and Cmty Medicine DC03200 Sch Medicine U Mo Columbia MO 65212 Home Phone: 573-875-1423; Office Phone: 573-884-4534. Office Fax: 573-882-9096. Business E-Mail: lemasterj@health.missouri.edu.

LEMAY, HARRY ADRIAN, artist, educator; b. Lewiston, Pa., Dec. 19, 1929; s. Joseph Adrian LeMay and Edna May Price; m. Yves Lindsay, July 24, 1954 (dec. Dec. 28, 1974); children: Nina(dec.), Peter(dec.); m. Nancy Potenzano, Jan. 24, 1986. BS with honors, U.S. Mcht. Marine Acad., 1952; diploma, Cooper Union, NYC, 1958; diploma in vocat. edn., CUNY, 1976. Cert. tchr. N.Y.C., LA. Art dir. Mann Assoc., NYC, 1960—63; designer, art dir. Rapid Art, NYC, 1963—65; mgr. art & prodn. RCA Victor Record Club, 1965—67; v.p. creative Capitol Record Club, 1967—69; tchr. HS Art & Design, NYC, 1972—91; pres. LeMay Co., NY, Calif., 1975—. Judge Suburban Art League, JP Morgan Estate, NY, 1965. Exhibited in group shows, NYC, LA, 1955—2005, one-man shows include, Saratoga Springs, 1970, LA, 1970—2004, NYC, 1980—91; pub.: Keynotes Mag., 1967—69, Calif. Quarterly, UC Davis, 1981, Kiplinger's Personal Fin. Mag., 1998; guest (TV series) You're Part of Art, 1971—72; lighting design, tech. dir.: Folklorico Philipino Dance Performances, 1973, 1974; designer, pub.: Day of the Wounded Eagle (Daisy Alden), 1990. U.S. rep. Donatello Awards, Italy, 1962—63. Lt. (j.g.) USN, 1953—55. Mem.: Art Students League (life), Acad. Magical Arts, Inc., Am. Philatelic Soc. Avocations: stamp collecting/philately, collecting movie posters, collecting books. Home: 357 S Curson Ave #6B Los Angeles CA 90036 Personal E-mail: halemay@ca.rr.com.

LEMAY, JACQUES, lawyer; b. Quebec City, Can., July 10, 1940; s. Gerard and Jacqueline (LaChance) LeMay. BA, Que. Sem., 1959; LL.L., Laval U., 1962; postgrad., U. Toronto, 1964; D.E.S., 1965. Bar: Que. 1963. Practice in, Quebec City, 1964—; mem. firm Prevost, Gagne, Flynn, Chouinard & Jacques, 1964-67; ptnr. Flynn, Rivard, Jacques, Cimon, Lessard & LeMay, 1968-86, Flynn, Rivard, 1986—2003, Desjardins, Ducharme, Quebec, 2003—. Legal adv. Soc. des Ajusteurs d'Assurance, 1969. Named one of Best Lawyers, 2006; recipient, 2007. Mem.: Soc. des Etudes Juridiques (pres. 1969), Cercle de la Garnison (Que.). Home: 265 ch duBout de l'Ile Sainte-Petronille PQ Canada G0A 4C0 Office: 70 Dalhousie Ste 300 Quebec City PQ Canada G1K 4B2 Office Phone: 418-640-4450. Business E-Mail: jacques.lemay@ddsm.ca.

LE MAY, MOIRA KATHLEEN, retired psychology educator; b. NYC, Apr. 12, 1934; d. Bernard Howard and Kathleen (Sullivan) Fitzpatrick; m. Joseph Albert Le May, June 14, 1958; children: Valerie H. (Le May) Teal, Joseph B. BS, Queens Coll., 1956; MS, Pa. State U., 1960, PhD, 1970. Engring. psychologist USN Rsch. Lab., Washington, 1960-62, ITT Fed Labs., Nutley, N.J., 1962-64; instr. psychology Manhattanville Coll., Purchase, N.Y., 1964-68; asst. prof. Skidmore Coll., Saratoga Springs, N.Y., 1968-70; prof. Psychology Montclair State Coll., Upper Montclair, NJ, 1970—98; ret. Cons. in engring. psychol. USAF-WPAFB, Human Resources Lab., Dayton, Ohio, 1978-79, NASA Calif. Tech. Jet Propulsion Lab., Pasadena, 1982-83, USN Air Devel. Ctr. Warminster, Pa., 1986-87, NASA Langley Rsch. Ctr., Hampton, Va., 1989-90, NASA-Ames Rsch. Ctr., Moffett Field, Calif., 1994 Contbr. numerous artticles to profl. jours and papers to sci. meetings. Campaign worker, Ridgewood (N.J.) Dem. Orgn., 1974-89, com. rep. corresponding sec. 1978-86. Fellow Am. Psychol. Soc.; mem. IEEE, AAAS, APA, Human Factors Soc. (liaison to AAAS 1984-91). Roman Catholic. Avocations: historical preservation, antiques, architecture. Home: 1023 Hillcrest Rd Ridgewood NJ 07450-1030

LEMAY, NICHOLAS K., broadcast executive; b. Mount Vernon, Ill., June 14, 1983; s. Kent A. LeMay and Sharon L. Richardson. AA, Rend Lake Coll., Ina, Ill., 2003; BS cum laude, So. Ill. U., Carbondale, 2005. Stringer reporter CBS Radio; asst. news dir. WMIX AM/FM, Mount Vernon, 1999—2002; weekend news dir. WDML-FM, Mount Vernon, 1999—2002, news dir., 2002—; regional news dir. Mount Vernon, 2002—. Dir. publicity and media rels. Jefferson County Toys for Kids, Mount Vernon, 2001—06; bd. dirs. Am. Cancer Soc., Marion, Ill., 2004—. Recipient Ill. Silver Dome award for Excellence in Broadcasting, Ill. Broadcasting Assn., 2007, US Presdl. Vol. Svc. award, USA Freedom Corps, 2007. Mem.: Nat. Broadcasting Soc. (life; proffesional mem., Life induction 2005), Gamma Beta Phi, Golden Key, Alpha Epsilon Rho, Phi Theta Kappa. Office: Withers Broadcasting Companies 3501 Broadway St Mount Vernon IL 62864 Home Phone: 618-266-7205; Office Phone: 618-242-3500. Personal E-mail: nicklemay@yahoo.com.

LEMBARK, CONNIE WERTHEIMER, art consultant; b. Omaha, Mar. 8, 1934; d. Sam Wertheimer and Elinor (Livingston) Wertheimer-Dombrowsky; m. Daniel Lembark, July 10, 1955; 1 child, Steven. Student, U. Ariz. Docent UCLA, 1964-71; owner, art cons. Connie W. Lembark, Nashville, 1992—2000, LA; owner, founding ptnr. Art Posters Ltd., LA, 1971-82; art cons., 1983—. Founder Mus. Contemporary Art LA; spkr., lectr. in field. Author: The Prints of Sam Francis, 1992; organizer (one-man shows) Tenn. State Mus., presenter The Life of Frank Stella, San Francisco Mus. Art, 2005, Walker Art Mus., 2006, Albright Knox Mus., 2007. Recipient Herb Alpert honors, Lincoln Ctr., NYC, 2001, honors, Vanderbilt Med. Ctr., 2006. Personal E-mail: clembark@earthlink.net.

LEMBERG, LOUIS, cardiologist, educator; b. Chgo., Dec. 27, 1916; s. Morris and Frances Lemberg; m. Dorothy Feinstein, 1940 (dec. 1969); children: Gerald, Laura Bott, Paula Saltzman; m. Miriam Mayer, Jan. 29, 1971. BS, U. Ill., Chgo., 1938; MD, U. Ill., 1940. Intern Mt. Sinai Hosp., Chgo., 1940-41, resident, 1945-48, asst. prof. med., 1955-58, assoc. prof. med., 1958-70; prof. clin. cardiology U. Miami (Fla.) Sch. Medicine, 1970—, dir. coronary care unit, 1965-75. Chief cardiology Mercy Hosp., 1974-79; chief staff Nat. Children's Cardiac Hosp., 1959-66; cons. cardiology VA Hosp., Miami, 1953-64; dir. cardiology Dade County Hosp., 1953-64, dir. Heart Sta. and Electrocardiography, U. Miami Jackson Meml. Med. Ctr., 1952-75, program dir. Courses in Coronary Care for Practicing Physician, 1970-2003, Courses in Coronary Care for Nurses, 1970-90; Master Approach to Cardiovascular Problems, 1972-82, Cardiology Update for Intensive Care Nurses, Am. Coll. Cardiology, 1978-92, Cardiology Update, 1987-2002. Author: Vectorcardiography, 1969, 2d edit., 1975, Electrophysiology of Pacing and Cardioversion, 1969; editor-in-chief Current Concepts in Cardiovascular Disorders, 1984-86; contbr. to med. publs. Served to maj. AUS, 1941-55, ETO. Recipient U. St. Torres (Phillippines) Luis Guerrero hon. lectr. award, 1977, Recognition award U. Miami Sch. Medicine, Lifetime Achievement award Jackson Meml. Med. Ctr. U. Miami, 1997, Key to City of Miami Beach, Fla., Nurses Pioneering Spirit award Am. Assn. Critical Care, 2000, Physicians Recognition awards AMA. Fellow ACP, Am. Coll. Cardiology (editl. bd. jour.); mem. Heart Assn. Greater Miami (pres.), Fla. Heart Assn. (pres.), Am. Heart Assn. (fellow coun. clin. cardiology). Democrat. Jewish. Achievements include pioneer in development Demand Pacemaker, 1964, a chair in cardiology established at the U. Miami Sch. of Medicine entitled The Louis Lemberg Professor of Cardiology, 1990. Home: 720 NE 69th St Apt 18 South Miami FL 33138-5738 Office: U Miami Sch Medicine Divsn Cardiology PO Box 016960 Miami FL 33101 Office Phone: 305-243-3515.

LEMBERGER, LOUIS, pharmacologist; b. Monticello, NY, May 8, 1937; s. Max and Ida Lemberger; m. Myrna Sue Diamond, 1959; children: Harriet Felice Schor, Margo Beth. BS magna cum laude, Bklyn. Coll. Pharmacy, LI U., 1960; PhD in Pharmacology, Albert Einstein Coll. Medicine, 1964, MD, 1968; Doctorate (hon.), LI U., 1994. Pharmacy intern VA Regional Office, Newark, summer 1960; postdoctoral fellow Albert Einstein Coll. Medicine, 1964-68; intern in medicine Met. Hosp. Ctr., NY Med. Coll., NYC, 1968-69; rsch. assoc. NIH, Bethesda, Md., 1969-71; clin. pharmacologist Lilly Lab. for Clin. Rsch., Eli Lilly & Co., Indpls., 1971-75, chief clin. pharmacology, 1975-78, dir. clin. pharmacology, 1978-89, clin. rsch. fellow, 1982-93; asst. prof. pharmacology Ind. U., 1972-73, asst. prof. medicine, 1972-73, assoc. prof. pharmacology, 1973-77, assoc. prof. medicine, 1973-77, prof. pharmacology, 1977—, prof. medicine, prof. psychiatry, 1977—, mem. grad. faculty, 1975—; adj. prof. clin. pharmacology Ohio State U., 1975-86; physician Wishard Meml. Hosp., 1976-98. Cons. US Nat. Commn. on Marijuana and Drug Abuse, 1971-73, Can. Commn. Inquiry into Non-Med. Use of Drugs, 1971-73; mem. Pharm. Mfrs. Assn. Commn. on Medicines for Drug Dependence and Abuse, 1990-93, Ind. Optometric Legend Drug Adv. Com., 1991-96; guest lectr. various univs., 1968—; lectr. U. Minn., 1993—; mem. adv. com. Faseb Life Scis. Rsch. Office, 1993-96. Author: (with A. Rubin) Physiologic Disposition of Drugs of Abuse, 1976; contbr. numerous articles on biochemistry and pharmacology to sci. jours.; editorial bd.; Excerpta Medica, 1972-96, Clin. Pharmacology and Therapeutics, 1976-96, Communications in Psychopharmacology, 1975-91, Pharmacology, Internat. Jour. Exptl. and Clin. Pharmacology, 1978-94, Drug and Alcohol Abuse Rsch., 1979-86, Drug Devel. Rsch., 1980-87, Trends in Pharmcol. Scis., 1980-85. Post adviser Crossroads of Am. coun. Boy Scouts Am., 1972-77; comdr. Jewish War Vet. Post 114, 2005—06. Lt. comdr. USPHS, 1969-71. Recipient Disting. Alumnus award, Albert Einstein Coll. Medicine, 1989, LI U., 1990, Pres. award, 1998, Cornerstone award for Outstanding Lifetime Achievement in Health Scis., Am. Drugstore Mus., 2000. Fellow ACP, AAAS, Am. Coll. Neuropsychopharmacology (chmn. credentials com. 1993), Am. Coll. Clin. Pharmacology; mem. Am. Soc. Pharmacology and Exptl. Therapeutics (com. div. clin. pharmacology 1972-78, chmn. com. 1978-83, coun. 1980-83, chmn. long-range planning com. 1984-86, pres. 1987-88, ASPET award in Therapeutics, 1985, Harry Gold award for rsch. and teaching excellence in clin. pharmacology 1993), Am. Soc. Clin. Pharmacology and Therapeutics (chmn. sect. neuropsychopharmacology 1973-80, chmn. fin. com. 1976-83, 89-92, v.p. 1981-82, pres. 1983-84, dir. 1975-81, 84-87, Rawls-Palmer award 1986, Henry Elliot Disting. Svc. award 1992, Oscar B. Hunter award for outstanding achievement in exptl. therapeutics 2003), Am. Soc. Clin. Investigation, Collegium Internat. Neuro-Psychopharmacologicum, Am. Fedn. Clin. Rsch. Ctrl. Soc. Clin. Rsch., Soc. Neuroscis., Jewish War Vets (comdr. Post 114 2005-06), Sigma Xi, Alpha Omega Alpha, Rho Chi. Jewish. Achievements include being first person to administer and study the actions in humans of the antidepressant drug Prozac (fluoxetine), Permax (pergolide) the drug used to treat Parkinson's disease, and the cannabinoid drug Cesamet (nabilone) utilized for the treatment of nausea and vomiting secondary to cancer chemotherapy and Zyprexa (Olanzepine) the drug utilized in schizophrenia and Strattera (atomoxetine) the drug utilized in attention deficit hyperactivity disorder; responsible for directing and spearheading the clinical development of Prozac, Permax and Cesamet through clinical trials, regulatory approval and eventually into the marketplace. Home: 3315 Walnut Creek Dr N Carmel IN 46032-9038 Office: Ind Univ Sch Medicine Dept Pharmacology and Medicine Indianapolis IN 46202

LE MENAGER, LOIS M., incentive merchandise and travel company executive; b. Cleve., Apr. 25, 1934; d. Lawrence M. and Lillian C. (Simicek) Stanek; m. Charles J. Blabolil (dec. 1982); children: Sherry L., Richard A.; m. Spencer H. Le Menager, Mar. 23, 1984. Grad. high sch. Travel counselor Mktg. Innovators Internat. Inc., Rosemont, Ill., 1978-80, mktg. dir., 1980-82, chmn., CEO, owner, 1982—. Dir. Northwest Commerce Bank, Rosemont. Featured in (articles) Crain's Chgo. Bus. Recipient Entrepreneurial Success award U.S. Small Bus. Adminstrn., 1999; named Supplier of Yr., J.C. Penney Co., Inc. Mem. NAFE, Am. Inst. Entrepreneurs (Entrepreneur of Yr. 1988), Am. Mktg. Assn., Internat. Soc. Mktg. Planners, Soc. Incentive Travel Execs., Am. Soc. Travel Agts., Nat. Fedn. Ind. Bus., Nat. Assn. Women Bus. Owners, Des Plaines C. of C., Rosemont C. of C., Chicagoland C. of C. (dir.), The Chgo. Network, Exec. Club (Chgo.). Congregationalist. Office: Mktg Innovators Internat Inc 9701 W Higgins Rd Rosemont IL 60018-4717 Office Phone: 847-696-1111.

LEMENS, WILLIAM VERNON, JR., banker, finance company executive, lawyer; b. Austin, Tex., Oct. 26, 1935; s. William Vernon and Lylia (Engberg) L.; m. Jean Lemens, May 31, 1959; children: William Vernon III, Shandra Christine. BA, U. Tex., 1958, LLB, JD, U. Tex., 1962. Bar: Tex. 1962; lic. real estate broker, Tex. Pvt. practice, Austin, 1962—; pres. Standard Fin. Co., Austin, 1963-67, First State Loan, Austin, 1967—; chief exec. officer Southwest Computer Svcs., Inc., Austin, 1965—. Pres., chief instr., mgmt. cons. Decision Dynamics, Inc., Austin, 1965-75; exec. v.p., atty. Northwest Savs. Assn., Austin, 1975-78; chmn. bd. First State Bank, Jarrell, Tex., 1975-87; pres., chief exec. officer First Am. Fin. Co., Ft. Worth, 1982—, Eagle Bank, Jarrell, 1987—. Author: Elements of Objective Orientation, 1971, SSAM-The Power of Perfect Decisions, 1972, Successful Financial Institution Operation, 1978, National Standard Financial Company Operations, 1981. Pres. Ballet Austin, 1967, Southwest Regional Ballet Assn., 1968; deacon Univ. Bapt. Ch., Austin, 1979—. Mem. State Bar Tex., Austin Bd. Realtors, Tex. Fin. Inst. (bd. dirs. 1975—), Tex. Consumer Fin. Assn. (bd. dirs. 1995—). Office: 1509 Guadalupe St Ste 200 Austin TX 78701-1608 Office Phone: 512-476-2608. E-mail: vlemens@aol.com.

LEMER, ANDREW CHARLES, engineer, economist; b. Maxwell Field, Ala., Dec. 25, 1944; s. Samuel Theodore and Carol (Oppenheimer) L.; m. Patricia Spear, Aug. 1967 (div. Dec. 1981); m. Janet Felsten, Aug. 1992;

children: Elizabeth Catherine, Daniel Evan, Rebekah Simone. SB, MIT, 1967, SM, 1968, PhD, 1971. Assoc. Alan M. Voorhees & Assoc., Inc., McLean, Va., 1971-76; sr. assoc. PRC Planning & Econs., Inc., McLean, 1976-80; chief planner PRC (Nigeria) Ltd., Lagos, 1980-82; divsn. v.p. PRC Engring., Inc., McLean, 1982-85; pres. Matrix Group, LLC, Balt., 1985—; dir. bldg. rsch. bd. Nat. Acad. Scis., Washington, 1988—93. Cons. Fed. Rail Adminstrn., Washington, 1975, FAA, Washington, 1986-90, World Bank, Washington, 1980—, Abell Found., Balt., 1993-94, Transp. Rsch. Bd., Washington, 1993—; vis. prof. civil engring. Purdue U., West Lafayette, Ind., 1995-96; adj. faculty Johns Hopkins U., Balt., 1994—, Am. Planning Assn., 2005—. Prin. author: In Our Own Back Yard: Principles for Improving the Nation's Infrastructure, 1993, Toward Infrastructure Improvement: A Research Agenda, 1994, Solving the Innovation Puzzle: Challenges Facing the U.S. Design and Construction Industry, 1996, Getting the Most Out of Your Infrastructure Assets, 2002; editl. adv. bd. Jour. Infrastructure Sys., Constrn. Bus. Rev., Constrn. Mgmt. and Econs., Pub. Works Mgmt. and Policy. Loeb fellow Harvard U., 1992-93. Mem. ASCE, The Am. Soc. Macroengring. (bd. dirs. 1997—, pres. 2000—), Cosmos Club (Washington), 14 W. Hamilton St. Club (Balt.), Lambda Alpha Internat (pres. Balt. chpt. 2002—06). Office: 4701 Keswick Rd Baltimore MD 21210-2322

LEMIEUX, JACOB E., biochemist; b. NYC, 1985; BS in Biochemistry, Stanford Univ., Palo Alto, 2007; PhD student in Biochemistry, Oxford Univ., 2007—. Recipient award for saving a jogger's life, Palo Alto Fire Dept., 2005; Rhodes Scholar. Achievements include organizing a program to provide smokeless stoves to villages in India to limit smoke-induced respiratory illness; leading an effort to est. and support a girls' sch. in a Tanzanian village.*

LEMIEUX, LINDA DAILEY, museum director; b. Cleve., Sept. 6, 1953; d. Leslie Leo LeMieux Jr. and Mildred Edna (Dailey) Tutt. BA, Beloit Coll., 1975; MA, U. Mich., 1979; A cert., Mus. Mgmt. Program, Boulder, Colo., 1987. Asst. curator Old Salem, Inc., Winston-Salem, NC, 1979-82; curator Clarke House, Chgo., 1982-84, Western Mus. Mining and Industry, Colorado Springs, Colo., 1985-86, dir., 1987—. Author: Prairie Avenue Guidebook, 1985; editor: The Golden Years--Mines in the Cripple Creek District, 1987; contbr. articles to mags. and newspapers. Fellow Hist. Deerfield, Mass., 1974—. Rsch. grantee Early Am. Industries Assn., 1978. Mem. Am. Assn. Mus., Am. Assn. State and Local History, Colo.-Wyo. Mus. Assn., Colo. Mining Assn., Mountain Plains Assn. Mus., Women in Mining, Colo. Mont. Wyo. State Conf. Edn. Com. NAACP. Mem. First Congl. Ch. Home: 1337 Hermosa Way Colorado Springs CO 80906-3050 Office: Western Mus Mining & Industry 1025 N Gate Rd Colorado Springs CO 80921-3018 E-mail: director@wmmi.org, lindalemieux1@aol.com.

LEMIEUX, MARIO, professional sports team executive and retired hockey player; b. Montreal, PQ, Can., Oct. 5, 1965; m. Natalie Asselin, June 26, 1993; children: Lauren, Stephanie, Austin, Alexa. Player Pitts. Penguins, 1984—97, 2000—06, CEO, 1998—2006, owner, chmn., 1998—. Mem. Team Can., Olympic Games, Salt Lake City, 2002, Team Can., World Cup of Hockey, 2004. Named Player of the Yr., Can. Hockey League, 1983—84, MVP, NHL All-Star game, 1985, 1988, 1990; named to NHL All-Star game, 1986—89, 1990, 1992—93, 1996—97, 2001; recipient Calder Memorial Trophy, 1985, Hart Meml. trophy for most valuable player, 1988, 1993, 1996, Conn Smythe Trophy, 1991—92, Art Ross Meml. trophy, 1988—89, 1992—93, 1996—97, Michel Briere trophy, 1983—84, Jean Beliveau trophy, 1983—84, Michael Bossy trophy, 1983—84, Guy LaFleur trophy, 1983—84, Bill Masterson Meml. trophy, 1993. Achievements include being only player in NHL history to score a goal 5 different ways in a single game, 1988; being a member of Stanley Cup Champion Pittsburgh Penguins, 1991-92; being inducted to Hockey Hall of Fame without mandatory 3 year waiting period, 1997; being a member of gold medal Canadian Hockey Team, Salt Lake City Olympic games, 2002; being a member of World Cup Champion Team Canada, 2004. Office: Pitts Penguins Mellon Arena 66 Mario Lemieux Dr Pittsburgh PA 15219

LE MIN, THOMAS FRANCIS, law enforcement official, educator; s. Joseph D. and Rita R. Le Min; m. Charupin Charoenthep. BA in Polit. sci., Widener U., Chester, Pa., 1983—87; MS in Criminal Justice, U. Ala., Tuscaloosa, 1996—98. Cert. Assessor Commn. on Accreditation for Law Enforcement Agencies, 1995, Master Police Instructor Del. Coun. on Police Tng., 1995, Nationally Credentialed Law Enforcement Officer Nat. Law Enforcement Credentialing Bd., 1997. Asst. prof., mil. sci. U. Del., Newark, 1994—2003; adminstrv. divsn. comdr. Newark Police Dept., Del., 1990—; adj. prof., criminal justice Wilmington Coll., New Castle, Del., 2000—. Contbr. articles to profl. jours. Decorated Parachutist Badge U.S. Army Inf. Ctr. and Sch., Army Achievement Medal U.S. Army; recipient Police Officer of Yr., Newark Lion's Club, 1993, Police Officer of Yr. Award, VFW, Post 475, 1994. Mem.: FBI Law Enforcement Exec. Devel. Assn., European Assn. for Forensic Entomology. Office: Newark Police Dept 220 Elkton Rd Newark DE 19711 Office Phone: 302-366-7111. E-mail: tlemin@comcast.net, tlemin@newarkpd.state.de.us.

LEMIRE, RONALD JOHN, pediatrician, educator; b. Portland, Apr. 20, 1933; s. Lucile Frances Morelock; m. Kathy H. Brazeau, Aug. 1, 1993; children: Gregory, Suzy McNabb, Jennifer, Anne Kondra, Alisa Brooks, Brian Brazeau, Leisa Houlahan. Undergrad., U. Wash., 1958, MD, 1962. Internship King County Hosp., 1962—63; resident pediatrics U. Wash., 1965—67; chief resident pediatrics Children's Orthopedic Hosp., 1967—68; prof. pediatrics U. Wash. Sch. Medicine, Seattle, 1977—; dir. impatient svcs. Children's Hosp. & Regional MEd. Ctr., 1978—. Author: Normal and Abnormal Development of the Human Nervous System, 1975, Anencephaly, 1978, Mental Retardation and Congenital Malformations of the Central Nervous System, 1981, Holoprosencephaly: An Overview and Atlas of Cases, 1990, Catalog of Teratogenic Agents, 12th edit., 2007; mem. editl. bd.: Jour. Child Neurology, 1985—91, Pediatric Neurosci., 1985—91, Pediatric Neurosurgery, 1992—2002. With USN, 1951—55. Mem.: AAUP, Soc. Pediatric Rsch., Teratology Soc. Avocations: flying, fishing. Home: 10037 NE 127th Pl Kirkland WA 98034 Office: Childrens Hosp and Regional Med Ctr 4800 Sand Point Way NE Seattle WA 98105 Office Phone: 206-987-2025. Business E-Mail: ron.lemire@seattlechildrens.org.

LEMKE, CAROL ANN, music educator, pianist, accountant; b. Crivitz, Wis. d. Martin G. and Una B. (Dupey) Larson; m. Allan J. Lemke, 1968; children: Blake Betsy, Allan J. II. BMus, Wis. Conservatory of Music, 1965; degree in liberal arts, Marquette U., 1966, postgrad., U. Wis. Cert. piano tchr. Am. Coll. Musicians. Instr. Wis. Conservatory of Music, Milw., 1965—71; comptroller IGIC, Milw., 1969—71; pvt. piano and voice tchr., 1963—2006. Music judge. Performer of piano & voice. Founder North Shore Music Festival. Named to, ACM Hall of Fame, 1989. Mem.: Wis. Sch. Music Assn., Nat. Music Tchrs. Assn., Nat. Guild Piano Tchrs., Wis. Fedn. Music (bd. dirs.), Wis. Music Tchrs. Assn., Milw. Music Tchrs. Assn. (bd. dirs. 1978—2006, pres. 1986—92).

LEMKE, HERMAN ERNEST FREDERICK, JR., retired elementary school educator, consultant; b. Argo, Ill., July 13, 1919; s. Herman and Augusta Victoria (Statt) L.; m. Geneva Octavene Davidson, Sept. 5, 1942 (dec.); children: Patricia, Herman E.F. III, Gloria, John, Elizabeth. BA, George Peabody Coll., 1949, MA, 1952. Cert. social sci. tchr., Tenn., elem. tchr., Calif. Tchr. Cadd Parish Sch., Shreveport, La., 1950-55, Pacific Sch. Dist., Sacramento, 1956-58, Sacramento (Calif.) Sch. Dist., 1958-89; part-time tchr. Sacramento (Calif.) County Sch., 1974-84, ret., 2002. Substitute tchr., 1989—. Co-author: Natural History Guide, 1963, (field guide) Outdoor World of Sacramento Region, 1975; contbr. articles to profl. jours. Asst. dist. Commn. Boys Scouts Am., Shreveport, 1954, cubmaster, 1954; leader 4-H Club, Shreveport, 1950-54; elder Faith Luth. Ch., Fair Oaks, Calif., 1981-88. Recipient Scouter award, Boy Scouts Am., Shreveport, 1954, Honorary Svc. award Am. Winn Sch. PTA, 1982, Calif. Life Diploma Elem. Schs., 1961. Mem. Calif. Congress Parents Tchrs. Inc. (life). Democrat. Avocations: backpacking, coin collecting/numismatics, stamp collecting/philately, antiques, fishing. Home: 5901 Belmont Park Fair Oaks CA 95628 Personal E-mail: hermanlemke@worldnet.att.net.

LEMKE, JAMES UNDERWOOD, physicist; b. Grand Rapids, Mich., Dec. 26, 1929; s. Andrew Bertram and Frances (Underwood) L.; m. Ann Stickley, Aug. 1, 1953; children: Catherine, Susan, Michael. BS in Physics, Ill. Inst. Tech., 1959; MS in Physics, Northwestern U., 1960; PhD in Physics, U. Calif., Santa Barbara, 1966. From assoc. to tech. v.p. Armour Rsch. Found., Chgo., 1957-60; dir. Bell & Howell Rsch. Labs., Pasadena, Calif., 1960-68; pres. Spin Physics, Inc. subs. Eastman Kodak, San Diego, 1968-82; fellow rsch. labs. Eastman Kodak, Rochester, NY, 1982-86; pres. Rec. Physics, Inc., San Diego, 1986—; founder, dir. Visqus Corp., 1989. Adj. prof. U. Calif. at San Diego, LaJolla, 1982—. Contbr. numerous sci. and tech. articles to phys. jours.; patentee in field. Bd. dirs. San Diego Aero-Space Mus., 1982—. Recipient Revelle medal U. Calif. San Diego. Fellow IEEE (Reynold Johnson medal, 1995), AAAS; mem. NAE, AAAS, Am. Phys. Soc., Magnetic Soc. Democrat. Avocation: airplane pilot. Office Phone: 858-535-9920 222. E-mail: james@lemke.com.

LEMKE, JUDITH A., lawyer; b. New Rochelle, NY, Sept. 28, 1952; d. Thomas Francis and Sara Jane (Blish) Fanelli; m. W. Frederick Lemke, Apr. 1, 1980; 1 child, Morgan Frederick. Student, Manhattanville Coll., Purchase, NY, 1970-72; BA, Case Western Res. U., Cleve., 1974, MA, 1975, JD, 1978. Sr. cert. pub. acct. Price Waterhouse, Cleve., 1978-81; assoc. Benesch Friedlander Coplan & Aronoff, Cleve., 1981-85; adj. faculty Cleve. Marshall Coll. Law, 1982-86; ptnr. Benesch Friedlander Coplan & Aronoff, Cleve., 1986-94; prin. Kahn Kleinman Yanowitz & Arnson Co., Cleve., 1994-95; tax mgr. N.Am./L.Am. tax planning and compliance Chiquita Brands Internat., Cin., 1995-97, tax mgr. Europe, Colombia, Panama, 1998—, asst. v.p. taxation, 1998-99; v.p. tax Pepsi Bottling Group, Somers, NY, 1999—2005, Alltel Corp., Little Rock, 2005—06, sr. v.p. tax, 2007—. Adj. faculty Case Western Res. U. Sch. of Law, 1993-95. Recipient Elijah Watt Sells award for highest distinction AICPA, N.Y.C. 1979. Mem. ABA, Ohio State Bar Assn., Internat. Fiscal Assn., Case Western Res. U. Undergrad. Alumni Assn. (exec. com. 1987-95, trustee 1987-95, chmn. spl. events com. 1989-90, pres. 1990-92, v.p. 1993-94). Avocations: wilderness canoe camping, guitar. Office: Alltel Corp One Allied Dr MS B4F06-SA Little Rock AR 72202 Home: 18 Chenal Cir Little Rock AR 72223 Office Phone: 501-905-5094. Office Fax: 501-905-5096. Personal E-mail: jude.lemke@alltel.com.

LEMKE, SHERRY ELLEN, therapist; b. Mpls., Sept. 8, 1946; d. Henry Lloyd Oscar Dietz and Virginia Jean (Aument) Hennis; m. Ronald Herbert Erwin, July 31, 1965; children: Lorra Jeanne Prabhakar, Peter Christian, Kirra Lynne Denten. BM, DePaul U., 1980; MA, Roosevelt U., 1987. Lic. clin. profl. counselor Ill., cert. addictions specialist; profl. compulsive gambling therapist Ill., nat. cert./registered music therapist, Carl Orff cert. for music profls. in edn. Music therapist, instr., Arlington Heights, Ill., 1980—; family therapist Luth. Child and Family Svcs., Arlington Heights, 1987-94; family therapist, dir. Crossroads Cmty. Counseling, Arlington Heights, 1994—2006, Lake Geneva, Wis., 2006—. Mem. adv. bd. for pers. No. Ill. Dist. of Mo. Synod Luth. Ch., Hillside, Ill., 1994-2003. Recipient Monetary award Webb Found., 1994-99, monetary grantee, 1995. Mem. ACA, Am. Assn. Christian Counselors, Ill. Mem. Counseling Assn., Christian Profl. Women's Group at Crossroads Cmty. Counseling (founder), 116/120 Eastman Women's Group (co-founder), Cen. Bus. Dist. Lutheran. Achievements include cofounding new theory model Therapy within the Christian Context. Home: 786 Timber Ridge Rd Fontana WI 53125-1601 Office: Crossroads Cmty Counseling W3743 Orlando Dr Lake Geneva WI 53147 Office Phone: 262-348-9081.

LEMKE, STACY J., secondary school educator; d. Richard W. and Barbara J. Lemke; m. James W. Krehbiel, July 8, 1989. MusB in Edn. summa cum laude, U. Cin., 1983; MEd, Ashland U., Columbus, Ohio, 1999. Orch. dir., music dept. chair, suzuki violin tchr. Del. City Schs., Ohio, 1984—. Violin instr. Suzuki, 1984—; adjudicator Ohio Music Edn. Assn., 2005—. Mem.: Ohio Music Educators Assn., Ohio Edn. Assn., Ohio String Tchr. Assn., NEA, Am. String Tchrs. Assn., Suzuki Assn. of the Ams., Music Educators Nat. Conf. Avocations: mountain climbing, travel. Office: Rutherford B Hayes HS 289 Euclid Ave Delaware OH 43015 Home Phone: 740-369-0408; Office Phone: 740-833-1000 ext. 2863. Office Fax: 740-833-1899. Business E-Mail: lemkest@dcs.k12.oh.us.

LEMKE, THOMAS P., lawyer, brokerage house executive; s. Richard Lemke; m. Sarah Elizabeth O'Neil, Jan. 18, 1986. JD, Am. U., 1979; BA magna cum laude, SUNY, Albany. Chief counsel SEC Div. Investment Mgmt., Washington; gen. counsel & COO Strong Capital Mgmt.; ptnr. Morgan Lewis Bockius LLP, Washington, 2000—05; sr. v.p. & gen. counsel Legg Mason, Balt., 2005—. Mem. bd. gov. Investment Co. Inst.; mem. NASD Mutual Fund Task Force, NASDR Investment Cos. com. Co-author: Regulation of Investment Companies, Regulation of Investment Advisers, Soft Dollars and Other Brokerage Arrangements, How To Read a Mutual Fund Prospectus. Office: Legg Mason 100 Light St PO Box 1476 Baltimore MD 21202-1476

LEMLE, ROBERT SPENCER, lawyer; b. NYC, Mar. 6, 1953; s. Leo Karl and Gertrude (Bander) L.; m. Roni Sue Kohen, Sept. 5, 1976; children: Zachary, Joanna. AB, Oberlin Coll., 1975; JD, NYU, 1978. Bar: N.Y. 1979. Assoc. Cravath, Swaine & Moore, NYC, 1978—82; assoc. gen. counsel Cablevision Sys. Corp., Bethpage, NY, 1982—84, v.p., gen. counsel, 1984—86, sr. v.p., gen. counsel, sec., 1986—94, bd. dirs., 1988—2003, exec. v.p., gen. counsel, sec., 1994—2001, vice chmn., gen. counsel, sec., 2001—02, vice chmn., sec., 2002—03; vice chmn. Madison Sq. Garden, NYC, 1999—2002. Bd. editors Cable TV and New Media Law and Fin., N.Y.C., 1983-99. Trustee L.I. Children's Mus., 1990—, pres., 1996-2006, co-chair, 2006—; trustee Oberlin Coll., 1996-2006, vice-chair, 2001-05, chair, 2005—. Mem. ABA, N.Y. State Bar Assn. Avocation: real estate. Office: Ste 400 50 Charles Lindbergh Blvd Uniondale NY 11553 Office Phone: 516-390-4775. E-mail: rlemle@optonline.net.

LEMLEY, MARK ALAN, law educator; b. St. Louis, Nov. 20, 1966; s. Alan Norman Lemley and Linda Leigh (Allen) Huheey; m. Rose Anne Hagan, Mar. 11, 1995. AB in Econs. and Polit. Sci., Stanford U., 1988; JD, U. Calif., Berkeley, 1991. Bar: Calif. 1991, US Ct. Appeals 9th Cir. 1991, US Ct. Appeals 7th Cir. 1996, US Ct. Appeals Fed. Cir. 1997, U.S. Ct. Appeals 2nd Cir., U.S. Supreme Ct. 2002. Law clk. to Judge Dorothy W. Nelson US Ct. of Appeals 9th Cir., Pasadena, Calif., 1991-92; atty. Brown & Bain, Palo Alto, Calif., 1992-93, Fish & Richardson P.C., Menlo Park, Calif., 1993—94, of counsel Austin, Tex., 1995—2001, Keker & Van Nest, San Francisco, 2001—; asst. prof. U. Tex. Sch. Law, Austin, 1994-98, prof., 1998—99, Marrs McLean prof. law, 1999—2000; prof. law Boalt Hall Sch. Law, U. Calif., Berkeley, 2000—04, co-dir. Berkeley Ctr. for Law & Tech., 2000—04, Elizabeth Josslyn Boalt Chair in Law, 2003—04; William H. Neukom prof. law Stanford Law Sch., 2004—, dir. Program in Law, Sci. & Tech., 2004—. Vis. prof. Boalt Hall Sch. Law, U. Calif., Berkeley, 1998, Stanford Law Sch., 2003; bd. editors Am. Intellectual Property Law Assn. Quarterly Jour., 1994-2000; mem. No. Dist. Calif. Working Com. on Model Patent Jury Instruction, 2000-, Calif. Blue Ribbon Task Force on Nanotechnology, 2004-05. Co-author: Antitrust, 1996, 2004, Intellectual Property in the New Technological Age, 1997, 4th edit., 2006, Software and Internet Law, 2000, 3d edit., 2006, IP and Antitrust, 2001. Adv. bd. Electronic Frontier Found., 2004-. Named Young Alumnus of Yr., Boalt Hall Sch. Law, 2002, World Econ. Forum Young Global Leader, 2007; named one of 100 Most Influential Lawyers, Nat. Law Jour., 2006, Litigation's Rising Stars, The Am. Lawyer, 2007; recipient Thelen Marrin Prize, Boalt Hall Sch. Law, Order of the Coif. Mem. Am. Intellectual Property Law Assn., Am. Law and Economics Assn., U. Coop. Soc. (bd. dirs. 1995-99), Assn. of Am. Law Schools (chair law and computers sect. 1997, chair antitrust sect. 2006). Avocations: cooking, hiking. Office: Stanford Law Sch Crown Quadrangle 559 Nathan Abbott Way Stanford CA 94305 Office Phone: 650-723-4605. Office Fax: 650-725-0253. Business E-Mail: mlemley@law.stanford.edu.

LEMLICH, ROBERT, chemical engineer, educator; b. Bklyn., Aug. 22, 1926; s. Marcus S. and Mary L.; m. Elizabeth Ann Murphy, Jan. 31, 1976. B Chem. Engring. summa cum laude, NYU, 1948; M Chem. Engring., Poly. Inst. Bklyn., 1951; PhD, U. Cin., 1954. Registered profl. engr., N.Y., Ohio. Rsch. chem. engr. Allied Chem. & Dye Corp., 1948-49; mem. faculty U. Cin., 1952—, prof. chem. engring., 1962-85, prof. emeritus, 1985—; fellow U. Cin. Grad. Sch., 1971—, chmn. fellows, 1976-78. Fulbright lectr., Israel, 1958-59, Argentina, 1966, USSR, 1991, rschr., cons. in field. Rsch. Corp. grantee, 1954-55, NSF grantee, 1956-59, 73, 77-81, 85-88, NIH grantee, 1959-69, P & G grantee, 1976-77. Editor: Adsorptive Bubble Separation Techniques, 1972; editor, originator: Jour. Chem. Engring. Edn, 1962-65. Served in USN, 1944-46. Recipient Sigma Xi award disting. rsch. U. Cin., 1969. Fellow AAAS, AIChE (named Chem. Engr. of Yr. Ohio Valley sect. 1979); mem. Am. Chem. Soc., Am. Soc. Engring. Edn., Mensa, Ky. Cols., Sigma Xi, Tau Beta Pi, Phi Lambda Upsilon.

LEMLY, THOMAS ADGER, lawyer; b. Dayton, Ohio, Jan. 31, 1943; s. Thomas Moore and Elizabeth (Adger) L.; m. Kathleen Brame, Nov. 24, 1984; children: Elizabeth Hayden, Joanna Marsden, Isabelle Stafford, Kate Brame. BA, Duke U., 1970; JD with honors, U. N.C., 1973. Bar: Wash. 1973, U.S. Dist. Ct. (we. dist.) Wash. 1973, U.S. Ct. Appeals (9th cir.) 1975, U.S. Supreme Ct. 1980. Assoc. Davis Wright Tremaine, Seattle, 1973-79, ptnr., 1979—. Contbg. editor Employment Discrimination Law, 1984-87, 94—; editor Wash., Oreg., Alaska and Calif. Employment Law Deskbooks, 1987—. Chmn. Pacific Coast Labor Conf., Seattle, 1983; trustee Plymouth Congregational Ch., 1980-84, Seattle Opera Assn., 1991—. Fellow Am. Coll. Trial Lawyers; mem. ABA (labor employment law sect. 1975—, subcom. chmn. 1984-90, govt. liaison com. 1982-94), Seattle-King County Bar Assn. (chmn. labor sect.), Assn. Wash. Bus. (sec.-treas. 2002-03, trustee 1992—, vice chair 2003-2004, bd. chair 2004-2005, chmn. human resources coun. 1993-2002, chmn. employment law task force 1987-93), U. N.C. Bar Found. (bd. dirs. 1973-76), Seattle Duke Alumni Assn. (pres. 1979-84), Order of Coif, Wash. Athletic Club (Seattle), Rotary. Republican. Presbyterian. Home: 1614 7th Ave W Seattle WA 98119-2919 Office: Davis Wright Tremaine 2600 Century Sq 1501 4th Ave Seattle WA 98101-1688 Office Phone: 206-628-7716. E-mail: tomlemly@dwt.com.

LEMMER, WILLIAM C., lawyer; BA, Mich. State U., 1966; JD, U. Va., 1971. Assoc. Bigham, Englar, Jones & Houston, NY, 1971—76; staff atty. Overseas Pvt. Investment Co., 1976—79; various sr. mgmt. positions Sunoco, Inc., 1979—88; chief counsel Oryx Energy Co., 1988—94, v.p., gen. counsel, corp. sec., 1994—99; v.p., gen. counsel, sec. Cameron Internat. Corp., Houston, 1999—. Office: Cameron Internat Corp 1333 W Loop South Ste 1700 Houston TX 77027-9109 Office Phone: 713-513-3300. Office Fax: 713-513-3421.

LEMNIOS, ANDREW ZACHERY, aerospace engineer, educator, researcher; b. Newburyport, Mass., Nov. 23, 1931; s. Zaharias Vasilios and Evangelia (Malamoglou) L.; m. Aspasia Soula Hanos, Sept. 26, 1954; children: Karen Eve, Keith Harold. SB, MIT, 1953, SM, 1954; PhD, U. Conn., 1967; grad. advanced mgmt. program, Harvard U., 1983; grad. mgmt. program, Rensselaer Poly. Inst., 1970. Rsch. engr. United Techs. Rsch., East Hartford, Conn., 1954—60; sr. analytical engr. Kaman Aerospace Corp., Bloomfield, Conn., 1961—63, chief fluid mechanics, 1963—68, chief rsch. engr., 1969—76, dir. rsch. and tech., 1976—89, asst. v.p. rsch. and tech. programs, 1989—93; mem. rotorcraft adv. com. Rensselaer Poly. Inst., Troy, NY, 1985—92, clin. prof., dir. Rotorcraft Tech. Ctr., 1993—99; v.p., dean Rensselaer at Hartford, 1999—2002, adj. prof., 2002—03. Adj. prof. Western New Eng. Coll., Springfield, Mass., 1956-76, U. Mass., Amherst, 1976-78, U. Hartford, Conn., 1997-99; mem. aeronautics adv. com. NASA, Washington, 1979-84; mem. rotorcraft adv. com. U. Md., College Park, 1985-92, Ga. Inst. Tech., Atlanta, 1985-92. Patentee controllable twist rotor, rotor trim tab. Fellow AIAA (assoc.), Am. Helicopter Soc. (hon.). Republican. Greek Orthodox. Avocations: carpentry, gardening, music, reading. Home: 144 Primrose Dr Longmeadow MA 01106-2534 E-mail: andrewlemnios@comcast.net.

LEMOI, BRIAN ANDRÉ, religious organization administrator, religious studies educator, writer; b. Warwick, RI, July 7, 1959; s. Leo Joseph and Oglor Doris (Dionne) Lemoi. BA magna cum laude, Iona Coll., New Rochelle, NY, 1981; MA, U. St. Thomas, St. Paul, Minn., 1995. Cert. Profl. Tchng. Fla., Social Scis. and Bible Fla. 6th grade tchr. St. Cecelia Sch., NYC, 1981—84; 5th grade tchr. Iona Grammer Sch., New Rochelle, NY, 1984—85; 5th and 6th grade tchr. St. Peter Claver Sch., Tampa, Fla., 1985—86; 9-12 grade tchr. Tampa Cath. HS, 1986—90; prin. St. Anthony Sch., San Antonio, 1990—93, Sacred Heart Sch. Elem., Pinellas Pk., 1993—96; diocesan dir. Evangelization & Lifelong Faith Formation Cath. Diocese St. Petersburg, 1996—. Chair Fla. Conf. Diocesan Dirs. of Religious Edn., 2003—05; mem. U.S. Cath. Conf. Bishops; nat. adv. com. Adult Religion Edn.; lectr. in field. Contbr. column mag. Treas. South Seminole Heights Neighborhood Assn., 1999—2003; sec. Lake forest Homeowners Assn., 1990—92. Nat. Catechetical Scholar, Nat. Cath. Edn. Assn., 1999—2000. Mem.: Cath. Edn. Assn., Chief Adminstrs. Cath. Edn., Nat. Conf. Catechetical Leadership. Office: Cath Diocese St Petersburg PO Box 40200 Saint Petersburg FL 33743 Office Phone: 727-341-6849.

LEMOINE, DAVID G., state official; b. Waterville, Maine, May 25, 1957; m. Karen Lemoine; 2 children. BA, Colby Coll., 1979; JD, Maine Law Sch., 1988. Staff US Senator Edmund Muskie, 1979—82, US Senator George J. Mitchell, 1982—85; rep. Maine Ho. Rep., 1998—2004; state treas. State of Maine, 2004—. Chmn. Old Orchard Beach Dem. Com., 1996—98; vice chmn. York County Dem. Com., 1997—98. Adv. bd. Salvation Army. Mem.: ABA, Maine Bar Assn., Saco Bay Rotary Club. Democrat. Office: State Treas 39 State House Sta Augusta ME 04333-7630 Office Phone: 207-624-7477. Office Fax: 207-287-2367. Business E-Mail: state.treasurer@Maine.gov.*

LEMOLE, GERALD MICHAEL, surgeon; b. SI, NY, Dec. 17, 1936; s. Joseph Michael and Mary (Boylan) L.; m. Emily Jane Asplundh, Dec. 8, 1962; children: Lisa Jane, Laura Leigh, Emily Anne, Gerald Michael Samantha Mary, Christopher Robin. BS in Biology, Villanova U., 1958; MD, Temple U., 1962. Diplomate Am. Bd. Surgery, Am. Bd. Thoracic Surgery. Intern S.I. Hosp., 1962-63; resident Temple U., Phila., 1963-67, Baylor Affiliated Hosps., Houston, 1967-69; practice medicine specializing in throacic surgery Phila., 1969—, Browns Mills, NJ, 1972-84; W.L. Samuel CArpenter III disting. chmn. cardiovascular surgery Christiana Care Health Sys., 2006—; assoc. med. dir. Christiana Care Ctr. for Heart and Vascular Health, 2006—. Chief sect. cardiac and thoracic surgery Temple U. Hosp., Phila., 1970-77; prof. surgery Temple U. Health Scis. Ctr., 1975-77; chmn. dept. surgery Deborah Heart and Lung Ctr., Phila., 1972-84; chief sect. cardiovascular surgery Med. Ctr. Del.; vis. prof.

cardiac surgery U. Dublin, Ireland, 1974, u. Istanbul, Turkey, 1982, Mil. Med. Coll., Ankara, Turkey, 1985, Beijing Heart Inst., 1991; clin. prof. surgery U. Pa., 1979, Rutgers Med. Sch., Thomas Jefferson U., 1999—; rschr. in field. Contbr. numerous articles on cradiovascular surgery and disease to med. jours. Recipient Disting Alumnus award Villanova U., 1987. Fellow ACS, Coll. Cardiology, Am. Coll. Chest Physicians (cardiovascular com. 1974—); mem. AMA, Am. Assn. Thoracic Surgery, Am. Fedn. Clin. Rsch., Pan Am. Thoracic Soc., Am. Heart Assn. (cardiovascular coun. 1973—, pres. Del. chpt. 1991, chmn. bd. dirs. 1992), Pa. Med. Soc., Pa. Assn. Thoracic Surgery (program chaor 1975—),, Pa. Assn. Thoracic Surgeons, Phila. County Med. Soc., Phila. Acad. Surgery, Phila. Acad. Cardioloby (pres. 1976-79, chmn. exec. com. 1976—), Phila. Coll. Physicians, Internat. Cardiovascular Soc., Assn. Acad. Surgeons, Soc. Casvular Surgery, Denton A. Cooley Cardiovascular Surg. Soc. Home: 404 Tomlinson Rd Huntingdon Valley PA 19006-4818 Office: Med Ctr Del 4745 Ogletown Stanton Rd # 20 Newark DE 19713-2067 Personal E-mail: gmlmd17@aol.com.

LEMON, LESLIE GENE, retired diversified financial services company executive, lawyer; b. Davenport, Iowa, June 14, 1940; BS, U. Ill., 1962, LLB, 1964. Bar: Ill. 1964, Ariz. 1972. Asst. gen. counsel Am. Farm Bur. Fedn., Chgo., 1964-69; sr. atty. Armour and Co., Chgo., 1969-71; with Viad Corp (formerly The Dial Corp and Greyhound Corp.), Phoenix, 1971-99; gen. counsel The Dial Corp (formerly Greyhound Corp.), Phoenix, 1977-96, v.p., 1979-99; ret., 1999; chmn. State of Ariz. Citizens Clean Elections Commn., 1999—2003. Vestryman All Saints Episcopal Ch., Phoenix, 1975-81; trustee Phoenix Art Mus., 1985-98; bd. dirs. Phoenix Children's Hosp., 1985-98; bd. visitors U. Calif. Med. Sch., Davis, 1983—. Mem. ABA, Nat. Conf. Uniform Law Commrs., Assn. Gen. Counsel, Maricopa County Bar Assn., State Bar Ariz., Phoenix C. of C. (bd. dirs. 1989-95), Am. Arbitration Assn. (bd. dirs. 1996-2004). Home: 1136 W Butler Dr Phoenix AZ 85021-4428 E-mail: l.lemon@azbar.org.

LEMON, LESLIE ROY, radar meteorologist; b. Greenville, SC, Jan. 19, 1947; s. Carlson Howard and Diora Elizabeth (Hyre) L.; m Betty Louise Vest, June 15, 1968; children: Kirsten M., Allison M., Jonathan M. BS, postgrad., Okla. U., 1970. Phys. sci. aide Nat. Severe Storms Lab., Norman, Okla., 1968-70, rsch. meteorologist, 1975-76; mem. NOAA Commn. Corps, 1970—75; meteorologist, forecaster Nat. Severe Storms Forecast Ctr., Kansas City, Mo., 1976, rsch. meteorologist techniques devel. unit, 1976-81; mgr. Nexrad ops. compatibility assurance Sperry Corp., Great Neck, NY, 1981-89; NEXRAD rsch. meteorologist, program control mgr. Unisys Corp., Great Neck, NY, 1989-95; chief meteorologist, mgr. advanced weather sys., rsch. ops. Loral Def. Sys. East, 1995-96; chief meteorologist, mgr. advaned weather sys. Lockheed Martin Tactical Def. Sys., 1996-97; chief meteorologist, weather and ATC programs Lockheed Martin Ocean, Radar & Sensor Sys., Syracuse, NY, 1997-99; radar and severe storms meteorologist, cons., 1999—2001, 2005—06; rsch. meteorologist Basic Commerce and Industry, Inc., Moorestown, NJ, 2001—05; rsch. assoc. Coop. Inst. Mesoscale Meteorol. Studies U. Okla., 2006—. Cons. USAF, Scott AFB, Ill., Tech. Svc. Corp., Corp., Silver Spring, Md., 1984, 91, TV Sta. tng. weather radar use and interpretation, 1990—, domestic and internat. weather radar interpretation, 1996—; vis. prof. China Meteorol. Adminstrn., 2000-. Designer/creator nat. severe thunderstorm radar warning technique The Lemon Technique; co-discoverer Doppler Weather Radar Tornadic Vortex Signature; contbr. chpt. to textbook, articles to profl. jours. Mem. sch. bd. Blue Ridge Christian Sch., Kansas City, 1984; mem. ch. bd. Blue Ridge Bible Ch., Kansas City, 1977-81. Lt. (s.g.) NOAA, 1970-75; bd. trustees Calvary Bible Coll., 2004—. Fellow U. Okla., 1997—, Am. Meteorol. Soc. Fellow Am. Meteorol. Soc. (Outstanding Contbn. to the Advance of Applied Meteorology award 1997), Nat. Weather Assn. (pres. local chpt. 1989, councillor 1998, v.p. 1999, pres. 2001), Sigma Tau. Republican. Achievements include conducting the first storm damage survey in Romanian history; discovering and documenting the first recorded tornado in Romanian history in 2003. Avocations: cosmology, walking, public speaking, reading. Home: 16416 S Cogan Dr Independence MO 64055-2257 Personal E-mail: lrlemon@comcast.net.

LEMON, WILLIAM JACOB, lawyer; b. Covington, Va., Oct. 25, 1932; s. James Gordon and Elizabeth (Wilson) L.; m. Barbara Inez Boyle, Aug. 17, 1957; children: Sarah E. Lemon Ludwig, William Tucker, Stephen Weldon. BA, Washington & Lee U., 1957, JD, 1959. Bar: Va. 1959. Assoc. Martin, Martin & Hopkins, Roanoke, Va., 1959-61; ptnr. Martin, Hopkins & Lemon, Roanoke, 1962—. Trustee Washington and Lee U., Lexington, Va., 1988-97, North Cross Sch., Roanoke, 1995-2006; pres. Specific Reading and Learning Difficulties Assn. Shedd Early Learning Ctr., 1985-86, George C. Marshall Found., Lexington, Va., 1997-2004. With U.S. Army, 1952-54. Mem. Va. Bar Assn., Roanoke Bar Assn. (pres. 1982-83), Va. State Bar, Shenandoah Club. Presbyterian. Avocations: farming, hunting, travel. Office: Martin Hopkins Lemon Wachovia Tower 10 S Jefferson St Ste 1000 Roanoke VA 24011-1314 also: PO Box 13366 Roanoke VA 24033-3366

LEMONE, MARGARET ANNE, atmospheric scientist; b. Columbia, Mo., Feb. 21, 1946; d. David Vandenberg and Margaret Ann (Meyer) LeMone; m. Peter Augustus Gilman; children: Patrick Cyrus, Sarah Margaret. BA in Math., U. Mo., 1967; PhD in Atmospheric Scis., U. Wash., 1972. Postdoctoral fellow Nat. Ctr. for Atmospheric Rsch., Boulder, Colo., 1972-73, scientist, 1973-92, sr. scientist, 1992—; chief scientist Globe, 2003—. Mem. bd. on atmospheric sci. and climate NRC, 1993-97, 2001-04; mem. sci. adv. com. U.S. Weather Rsch. Program, 1997-99. Contbr. articles to profl. jours.; contbg. author: D.C. Heath Earth Science, 1983-93; editor Jour. Atmospheric Scis., 1991-95. Woodrow Wilson fellow, NSF fellow, NDEA fellow, 1967. Fellow AAAS, Am. Meteorol. Soc. (councillor, mem. exec. com. 1992-96, Editor's award, Charles Anderson award); mem. Am. Geophys. Union, Nat. Acad. Engring. Achievements include research in dynamics of linear convection (roll vortices) in daytime atmospheric boundary layer and its relationship to clouds; demonstrating that bands of deep convection (like squall lines) can increase the vertical shear of horizontal wind (contrary to conventional wisdom at that time); developing technique to estimate small fluctuations in air pressure from aircraft flying over land, used to estimate pressure field around clouds and storms. Home: 2048 Balsam Dr Boulder CO 80304-3618 Office: Nat Ctr Atmospheric Rsch PO Box 3000 Boulder CO 80307-3000 Business E-Mail: lemone@ucar.edu.

LEMONS, DONALD W., state supreme court justice; b. Feb. 22, 1949; BA, U. Va., JD, 1976. Bar: Va. 1976. Former asst. dean U. Va. Law Sch.; judge Richmond Circuit Ct., 1995—2000; justice va. Supreme Ct., 2000—. Mem. Commn. on Family Violence Prevention. Mem.: ABA, Va. Bar Assn., Am. Inns of Ct. (trustee). Office: Supreme Ct Bldg 100 N Ninth St, 5th Floor Richmond VA 23219 also: PO Box 1315 Richmond VA 23218-1315*

LE MONS, KATHLEEN ANN, securities company executive, portfolio manager, investment officer; b. Trenton, NJ, Apr. 6, 1952; d. Albert Martin and Veronica Grace (Kern) LeM.; m. Walter Everett Faircloth, Apr. 15, 1978 (div. Dec. 1988); m. Jeffery West Benedict, June 29, 1991. Student, Rollins Coll., 1970-71, Fla. State U., 1971-76; BSBA magna cum laude, Christopher Newport U., 1995; MBA in Fin., Coll. William and Mary, 1998; postgrad., U. Pa., 2005—, Wharton Sch. Bus., 2005—. Registered rep. NASD/NYSE; registered investment advisor; cert. portfolio mgr.; accredited asset mgmt. specialist. Sci. rsch. assoc. NASA, Hampton, Va., 1973-76; fin. cons. Merrill Lynch Pierce Fenner Smith, Hampton, 1985-88; investment officer, portfolio mgr. Wheat First Butcher Singer (now Wachovia Securities), Newport News, Va., 1988—; sr. v.p. Wachovia Securities (formerly First Union Securities), investment officer, br. mgr. Life mem. Capital Dist. Found., 1992; mem. exec. panel fund distbn. Va. Peninsula United Way, 1996-97; Hampton Rds. chair March of Dimes Walk Am., 1996-98; bd. dirs. Greater Hampton Rds. March of Dimes Found., 1997—. George F. Hixson fellow Kiwanis Internat., 1996. Mem. Am. Mktg. Assn., Va. Peninsula C. of C. (transp. task force 1993-97, govtl. affairs task force 1993-99), Rotary, Oyster Point Kiwanis (charter, pres. 1991-92, 98-99), Coll. of William and Mary Part-Time MBA Assn. (charter, curriculum com. chair 1995-97, v.p. 1996-97, bd. dir.), Christopher Newport U. Pres.' Coun., Christopher Newport Univ. Alumni Soc. (bd. dirs., v.p. bd. dirs. 1998—), Mensa, James River Country Club (9-hole golf group), Smithfield Women's Club, Smithfield Rotary Club, Kiwanis Internat. (life), Alpha Chi. Republican. Avocations: golf, snowskiing. Home: 20454 Gatling Pointe Pkwy S Smithfield VA 23430-5756 Office: Wheat First Butcher Singer 11817 Canon Blvd Newport News VA 23606-2569

LEMONS, L. JAY, academic administrator; b. Chadron, Nebr., Aug. 30, 1959; s. Larry Dean and LaVana Lee (Smith) L.; m. Marsha Louise Schone Lemons, May 27, 1984; children: Olivia Jaye, Magdalene Marie, Thomas Potter, Meredith. BS in phys. edn. and health edn., Nebr. Wesleyan U., 1983, BA in philosophy, 1983; MEd in ednl. psychology and coll. student devel., U. Nebr., 1985; PhD in higher edn. adminstrn., U. Va., 1991. Cert. phys. edn. tchr., health edn. tchr. Hall dir. office residence life Nebr. Wesleyan U., Lincoln, 1982-84; grad. asst. to dir. admissions office admissions and advising U. Nebr., Lincoln, 1984-85; asst. area coord. dept. student affairs Tex. A&M U., College Station, 1985-86, area coord. dept. student affairs, 1986-88; grad. asst. to dean Curry Sch. Edn. U. Va., Charlottesville, 1988-89, intern Curry Sch. Edn. Found., 1989, intern office of pres., 1989-90, asst. to pres., 1990—92; chancellor U. Va. Coll. at Wise, 1992—2001; pres. Susquehanna U., 2001—. Contbr. articles to profl. jours. Recipient Outstanding Young Men of Am. award, 1986, Gov.'s fellowship, 1988-90, Annette Gibbs Rsch. and Publ. award, 1990. Mem. Am. Assn. Counseling and Devel., Am. Coll. Personnel Assn. (presenter nat. conf. 1986), Nat. Assn. Student Personnel Adminstrs. (participant new profl.'s inst. region III 1987, local arrangements com. mem. fall conf. 1988, registration chair Tex. state conf. 1988, program coord. state conf. 1989, 90, presenter region IV west conf. 1986, nat. conf. 1988, region III chief student affairs officers workshop 1988, ann. conf. 1991, Outstanding New Profl. award region III 1987), Assn. Study Higher Edn., So. Assn. Coll. Student Affairs (registration chair devel. theories workshop 1988, presenter ann. conf. 1987), Blue Key Nat. Honor Soc., Kappa Delta Pi (Outstanding Edn. Student award 1983). Office: Susquehanna U 514 Univ Ave Selinsgrove PA 17870-1025*

LEMOS, ARTHUR, retired music educator; b. Mt. Vernon, NY, Feb. 1, 1932; s. Antonio Tavares de Lemos and Silvina de Almeida Santos. BS, NYU, 1953; MA, Montclair State U., NJ, 1956. Cert. Music Tchr. N.J. Edn. Dept., 1953, N.Y. State Edn. Dept., 1956, Elem. Sch. Prin. N.Y. State Edn. Dept., 1956. Music tchr. Paterson Pub. Schs., NJ, 1953—56, New Hyde Pk. Pub. Schs., NY, 1956—67, Brentwood Pub. Schs., NY, 1967—68, Scarsdale Pub. Schs., NY, 1968—69, Lakeland Pub. Schs., Shrub Oak, NY, 1969—92; ret., 1992. Tuba player Mt. Vernon Symphony, NY, 1949—50, Mt. Vernon Mcpl. Band, Mt. Vernon, NY, 1950—65, Herricks Cmty. Band, NY, 1956—67, Lynbrook Symphony, NY, 1957—58; conductor New Hyde Park Adult Edn. Band, 1965—66; tuba player Mamaroneck Cmty. Band, NY, 2001—06, Westchester Seasonal Pops Band, Larchmont, NY, 2001—02, Pleasantville Fire Dept. Band, 2001, Merry Tuba Christmas Band, Rockefeller Ctr., NYC, 2001, Bronxville Pops Concert Band, NY, 2002—06; pres. New Hyde Pk. Rd. Sch. Tchrs. Assn., NY, 1960—63; nominating com. mem. Sole Supervisory Dist. Tchrs. Assn., Floral Park, NY, 1961—66; del. NY State Tchrs. Assn., Albany, NY, 1961—66, resolutions com. mem., NY, 1962—65, activities com. mem., Albany, NY, 1966—66, activities com. chmn., NY, 1966—66; del. NY State Tchrs. Retirement Sys., Albany, NY, 1962—66; salary com. mem. New Hyde Pk. Tchrs. Assn., New Hyde Park, NY, 1964—66, treas., 1964—67, Sole Supervisory Dist. Tchrs. Assn., Floral Park, NY, 1965—66, v.p., 1966—67; substitute pianist and organist 1st Presbyn. Ch., 1983—. Author: A Speck of Dust, 2001; musician (musical composition): (paso doble for concert band) El Hillside, 1960, El Pancho, 1961, El Torero, 2003, El Vencedor, 2004, El Vigo, 2007, (march for concert band) The Mount Vernon Band March, 1960, (composition) The Hartley Park March, 1960, Mercer Community Band Fanfare, 2007, Fanfare for Band, 2007, (vocal or piano solo) O Destino, 1974, A Tristeza, 2003, Solitude, 2003, Saudades de Portugal, 2004, (vocal solo) A Bright White Star, 1960, The United States of America, 2001; corr. Portuguese Heritage Jour., 1991—93, Mundo Portugues, 1994—95. Mem. citizens adv. com. City of Mt. Vernon, NY, 1985—88, mem. city centennial com., 1992; deacon First Presbyn. Ch., Mt. Vernon, NY, 1975—77, Mount Vernon, NY, 1980—82, 1988—89, elder Mt. Vernon, NY, 1983—85, 1990—92, 1997—2001, worship and music com. chmn., 1984—85, mem. centennial com., 1987—87, mem. centennial plus ten, com., 1997—97, missions com. mem., 1993—94, nominating com. mem., 1997—98. Decorated Medal of the Order of Merit Govt. of Portugal; recipient Honored vol. svc., 1994. Mem.: Berkeley Coll. (Arthur Lemos Scholarship award 1994), NEA (life; del. 1965—66, 1967), Am. Found. for Charities of Portugal (assoc.; mem. bd. dirs. 1984—88), Westchester County Stamp Club (assoc.; sec. 1984—85), Portuguese Civic Assn. of NY (life; sec. 1978—95, Elected Man of Yr. 1986, Elected Hon. mem. 1984), Portuguese Am. Club (life; sec. 1976—94, hon. 1983, Elected Meritorious mem. 1992). Conservative. Presbyterian. Avocations: travel, photography, computer, movies, current events. Personal E-mail: arthur13@netzero.net.

LEMOV, MICHAEL R., lawyer; b. NYC, Jan. 21, 1935; BA in Polit. Sci. magna cum laude, Colgate U., 1956; LLB, Harvard U., 1959. Bar: NY 1960, DC 1971, Md. 1995. Gen. counsel Nat. Commn. on Product Safety; spl. counsel consumer protection subcom. US Ho. of Reps., 1972—75, chief counsel interstate and fgn. commerce subcom. on oversight and investigation, 1975—77; ptnr. Leighton Lemov Jacobs & Buckley, Washington; named exec. dir. Food Rsch. and Action Ctr., Washington, 1984; ptnr. Winston & Strawn, Washington; dep. gen. counsel Office Compliance US Congress; of counsel Jackson Kelly PLLC, Washington, 2004—. Author: Consumer Product Safety Commn. Regulatory Manual, 1981. Bd. dirs. John E. Moss Found. Office: Jackson Kelly PLLC 2401 Pennsylvania Ave NW Washington DC 20037 Office Phone: 202-973-0200. Business E-Mail: mlemov@jacksonkelly.com.

LEMPERT, DENNIS ALAN, lawyer; b. NYC, Mar. 18, 1943; s. Hyman and Bertha Lempert; m. Joy Ellen Lempert, June 6, 1964; children: Hamilton H., Scott S., Macey M. BS, NY U., NYC, 1963; LLB, Bklyn. Law Sch., 1966, JD, 1967. Bar: NY 1966, Calif. 1967. Estate tax atty. IRS, San Francisco, 1966—67; sr. dep. dist. atty. Santa Clara County, San Jose, 1967—77; pvt. practice Santa Clara, Calif., 1978—. Mem.: Santa Clara County Bar Assn. (Salsman award 1975), Calif. Bar Assn. Office: 100 Saratoga Ave Santa Clara CA 95051 Office Phone: 408-249-5152. Office Fax: 408-248-5972. Business E-Mail: dennis@crimelaw.com.

LEMPERT, PHILIP, advertising executive, writer, news correspondent; b. East Orange, NJ, Apr. 17, 1953; s. Sol and Lillian E. L.; m. Laura Gray; 1 son BS in Mktg., Drexel U., 1974; degree in Package Design, Pratt Inst., 1978. With Lempert Co., Belleville, NJ, 1974—89; pres. Consumer Insight, Inc., 1990—; sr. v.p., sr. ptnr. AGE Wave Inc., 1991—93; pres., CEO Supermarketguru.com, 1993—. Founder, CEO Supermarket Alliance, 1993—; adj. prof. Fairleigh Dickinson U., Seton Hall U. Pub., editor newsletter The Lempert Report; editor Factus, Figures and the Future e-Newsletter; lectr. in field Author: Phil Lempert's Supermarket Shopping and Value Guide, 1996, Top Ten Trends for Baby Boomers for Business, 1997, Being the Shopper: Understanding Consumer Choices for the Second Millenium, 2002; columnist Chgo. Tribune, 1993-98, Knight-Ridder/Tribune Syndicate, L.A. Times, 2000-02, Progressive Grocer mag., 2003—; editor (newsletter) Facts, Figures and the Future, Xtreme Retail 23; food editor, corr. Today Show, KNBC-TV, BBC Radio 5; talk show host WOR Radio Network; news corr. Discovery Health Network Chmn. Tribune Food Task Force, 1996-98; bd. dirs. Powerhouse Theatre, Partnership for Food Safety; adv. bd. Partnership for Food Safety Mem. Am. Assn. Advt. Agys. (bd. govs. 1986-88, legis. liason 1988-90, legis. coord. 1987-90), Nat. Food Brokers Assn. (chmn. food svcs. com.) Office: Consumer Insight Inc 3015 Main St Ste 320 Santa Monica CA 90405-6401 Office Phone: 323-860-3070.

LEMPERT, RICHARD OWEN, lawyer, educator; s. Philip Leonard and Mary (Steinberg) L.; m. Cynthia Ruth Willey, Sept. 10, 1967 (div.); 1 child, Leah Rose; m. Lisa Ann Kahn, May 26, 2002. AB, Oberlin Coll., 1964; JD, U. Mich., 1968, PhD in Sociology, 1971. Bar: Mich. 1978. Asst. prof. law U. Mich., Ann Arbor, 1968-72, assoc. prof., 1972-74, prof. law, 1974—, prof. sociology, 1985—, Francis A. Allen collegiate prof. law, 1990—2001, acting chair dept. sociology, 1993-94, chair dept. sociology, 1995-98, dir. life scis., values and society program, 2000—04, Eric Stein Disting. Univ. prof. law and sociology, 2001—; dir. divsn. social and econ. scis. NSF, 2002—06. Mason Ladd disting. vis. prof. U. Iowa Law Sch., 1981; vis. fellow Centre for Socio-Legal Rsch., Wolfson Coll., Oxford (Eng.) U., 1982; mem. adv. panel for law and social sci. div. NSF, 1976-79, mem. exec. com. adv. com. for social sci., 1979; mem. com. law enforcement and adminstrn. of justice NRC, vice chmn., 1984-87, chmn., 1987-89; mem. adv. panel NSF program on Human Dimensions of Global Change, 1989, 92-94; mem. com. on DNA technology in forensic sci. NRC, 1989-92, com. on drug testing in workplace, 1991-93; vis. scholar Russell Sage Found., 1998-99; vis. scholar Russell Sage Found., 1998-99. Author: (with Stepehn Saltzburg) A Modern Approach to Evidence, 1977, 2d edit., 1983, 3d edit. (with Sam Gross and James Liebman), 2000; (with Joseph Sanders) An Invitation to Law and Social Science, 1986, Under the Influence, 1993; editor: (with Jacques Normand and Charles O'Brien) Under the Influence? Drugs and the American Work Force, 1994, Evidence Stories, 2006; editorial bd. Law and Soc. Rev., 1972-77, 89-92, 98—, editor, 1982-85; mem. editl. bd. Evaluation Rev., 1979-82, Violence and Victims, 1985—, Jour. Law and Human Behavior, 1980-82; contbr. articles to profl. jours. Fellow Ctr. for Advanced Study in Behavioral Scis., 1994-95; vis. scholar Russell Sage Found., 1998-99. Fellow Am. Acad. Arts and Scis.; mem. Am. Sociol. Assn. (chair sect. sociology of law 1995-96, mem. coun. 2005-), Am. Assn. Advancement Sci. (sec. sect. K 2006-) Law and Society Assn. (trustee 1977-80, 90-93, 06-, exec. com. 1979-80, 82-87, pres. elect, 2006-07; Harry Kalven Jr. Prize), Order of Coif, Phi Beta Kappa, Phi Kappa Phi. Jewish. Personal E-mail: rol25@hotmail.com.

LENAGH, THOMAS HUGH, lawyer, financial advisor; b. Lawrence, Mass., Nov. 1, 1920; s. Frank Albert and Bethia (Coultar) L.; m. Leila Semple Fellner; children: Katherine, Thomas C., Jessie W. BA, Williams Coll., 1941; LLB, Columbia U., 1948. Analyst Cyrus J. Lawrence, NYC, 1953-59; mgr. research service Goodbody & Co., NYC, 1959-61; asst. treas. Ford Found., NYC, 1961-64, treas., 1964-78; fin. v.p. Aspen Inst., NYC, 1978-80; chmn., chief exec. officer Greiner Engring., Los Angeles, 1982-85; chmn. bd. Photonics Products Group. Bd. dirs. Adams Express, Petroleum & Resources Fund, Photonics Products Group, Cornerstone Strategic Fund, Cornerstone Total Rerun Fund. Chmn. N.Y. YWCA, N.Y.C., 1975-92. Served with USN, 1941-46, capt. USNR, 1950-53. Mem. Chartered Fin. Analysts, N.Y. Soc. Security Analyst, Conn. Bar Assn., Williams Club. Republican. Home: 13 Allens Corner Rd Flemington NJ 08822-5620

LENARD, GEORGE DEAN, lawyer; b. Joliet, Ill., Aug. 26, 1957; s. Louis George and Jennie (Helopoulos) L. BS, Ill. State U., 1979; JD, Thomas Cooley Law Sch., 1984. Bar: Ill. 1984, U.S. Dist. Ct. (no. dist.) Ill. 1984, U.S. Ct. Appeals (6th cir.) 1998, U.S. Supreme Ct. 1990, Mich. 1998, Ariz. 1999, Calif. 2001, Fla. 2003. Asst. states atty. Will County States Attys. Office, Joliet, 1984-88; pvt. practice law Joliet, 1988—. Mem. ABA (mem. Ill. capital litigation trial bar, lead counsel), ATLA, Nat. Assn. Criminal Def. Lawyers, State Bar Ariz., State Bar Mich., State Bar Calif., State Bar Fla., Phi Alpha Delta (Isaac P. Christiancy chpt.). Avocation: golf. Office: 81 N Chicago St Ste 206 Joliet IL 60432-4383 Office Phone: 815-723-9016. Business E-Mail: lenardlaw@aol.com.

LENARD, MARY JANE, finance educator; b. York, Pa., July 8, 1955; d. Martin and Anne Ruth (Zimmerman) Kondor; m. Robert Louis Lenard, July 9, 1977 (div. 2004); children: Kevin, Kelsey. BS in Econ. and Adminstrv. Sci., Carnegie Mellon U., 1977; MBA in Fin., U. Akron, 1982; PhD in Bus. Adminstrn., Kent State U., 1995. Cert. mgmt. acct. Mgmt. trainee Equibank, NA, Pitts., 1977-78; acct., auditor Goodyear Tire and Rubber Co., Akron, Ohio, 1978-86; instr. U. Akron, 1986-93; mem. adj. faculty Cleve. State U., 1994-97; assoc. prof. Barton Coll., Wilson, NC, 1997—2001; asst. prof. U. N.C., Greensboro, 2001—05; assoc. prof. Meredith Coll., Raleigh, NC, 2005—. Author procs.; contbr. articles to profl. jours. Pres. Hillcrest Elem. PTA, Richfield, Ohio, 1992—93; v.p. Summit County PTA, Akron, 1994—96; mem., newsletter dir. Wakefield Mid. Sch. PTSA, 2000—02; coord. Vol. Income Tax Assistance, Barton Coll., Wilson, 1998—2001; active Revere Schs. Computer Curriculum Com., 1994—95; mem. Wakefield HS PTSA, 2002—; mem. and chair IT Com. for Acctg. Dept. at UNC, 2001—05; mem. Bryan Sch., UNC Greensboro Planning Com., 2002—05, Bryan Sch., UNC Greensboro Faculty Develop. Com., 2002—05, Bryan Sch., UNC Greensboro Undergraduate Programs Com., 2004—05. Grantee Faculty Devel. grant, Barton Coll., 1997, 1999. Mem.: Assn. Cert. Fraud Examiners, Decision Scis. Inst., Akron Women's Network, Assn. for Info. Systems, Inst. Mgmt. Accts. (dir. mem. retention 1994—96), Am. Acctg. Assn. (Best Paper award 1998), Beta Gamma Sigma. Home: 3049 Imperial Oaks Dr Raleigh NC 27614-7001 Office: Meredith Coll Sch Business Raleigh NC 27607 E-mail: lenardmj@meredith.edu.

LENDSEY, JACQUELYN L., foundation administrator; BS in Edn., Adelphi U.; MEd, Howard U. With pub. sch. sys., Prince George County, Md.; v.p. corp. and cmty. devel. Greater S.E. Healthcare; v.p. pub. policy Planned Parenthood Fedn. Am., NYC, 1998—2001; pres., CEO Women in Cmty. Svc., Alexandria, Va., 2001—07; CEO EdBuild, Washington, 2007—. Bd. dirs. Nat. Assembly Health and Human Svcs. Orgns., Reproductive Health Tech. Project. Mem.: Leadership Washington. Office: EdBuild 1411 K St NW Ste 503 Washington DC 20005 Office Phone: 202-589-1150. Office Fax: 202-589-1140.*

LENDVAY, THOMAS SEAN, pediatric urologist, medical educator; b. Phila., July 25, 1973; s. Joseph Alan and Jutta Lendvay; m. Kathleen Clare Gilpin, May 29, 1999. BA, Rice U., Houston, 1995; MD, Temple U., Phila., 1999. Lic. Medicine and Surgery Ga. and Wash. Med. Bds., 2000, Gen. Surgery Internship Emory U., Urology Emory U., 2004, Pediatric Urology U. Wash., 2006. Pediatric urology fellowship U. Wash., Seattle, 2004—06, asst. prof. pediatric urology, 2006—. Contbr. chapters to books, articles profl. jours. Scholar Pfizer Scholars in Urology, Pfizer Parmaceutical Co., 2003. Mem.: Inst. Surg. and Interventional Simulation (expert mem. 2005—), Am. Assn. Pediatric Urologists, Internat. Pediatric Endosurgical Group, Endourological Soc., Soc. Fetal Urology, Soc. Pediatric Urology, Am. Urol. Assn. Liberal. Achievements include discovery of Fibroblast Growth Factor-10 is a compensatory mechanism of the urinary bladder to healing in response to urinary tract injury. Avocations: travel, golf, skiing, piano, racquetball. Home: 2826 11th Ave E Seattle WA 98102 Office: Childrens Hosp 4800 Sand Point Way NE Seattle WA 98105 Home Phone: 206-329-5656; Office Phone: 206-987-1270.

LENEHAN, JAMES T., former pharmaceutical executive; married; 3 children. BA in econs., U. Akron, 1971; MBA in mktg., Northwestern U. With golf divsn. Wilson Sporting Goods; mktg. positions, McNeil Consumer Products Co. Johnson & Johnson, 1976—90; pres., 1990—94; group chmn. Johnson & Johnson, 1993—94, worldwide chmn. consumer pharms. and professional group, 1994—99, mem. exec. com., 1994—2004, worldwide chmn. med. devices and diagnostic group, 1999—2004, vice chmn., 2001—04, pres., 2002—04. Bd. dir. Medtronic, Inc, 2007—. Office: MedTronic Inc 710 Medtronic Pkwy Minneapolis MN 55432-5604*

LENEY, GEORGE WILLARD, retired consulting engineer; b. Nov. 13, 1927; s. Bert and Iva Irene (Skoog) L.; m. Arax G. Tefankjian, June 25, 1955 (dec. Aug. 1983); children: Sara Ann, Janet Ellen, John Alan, Ruth Alison. BS, U. Mich., 1950, MS, 1952, MA, 1955. Tchg. fellow U. Mich., 1951—53, 1953—55; geophysicist Gulf Oil Co., Harmarville, Pa., 1955—56; chief geophysicist Hanna Mining Co., Cleve., 1956—64; staff geophysicist Shell Oil Co., Houston, 1964—66; chief geologist H.K. Porter Co., Inc., Pitts., 1966—76; cons., 1976—77, 1981—86; regional geologist U.S. Dept. Energy, 1977—81; adminstr. air pollution Allegheny County Health Dept., Pa., 1986—97; ret., 1997. Organizer minerals exploration programs for asbestos, iron ore, base metals, gold, oil and gas, and uranium in the US, Can., Brazil and Cameroon; v.p. Pacific Asbestos Corp., 1970—75. With USN, 1946—48. Recipient Robert Peele Meml. award AIME, 1965 for pioneering work in geophysical exploration of iron ore. Mem. Soc. Econ. Geologists, Am. Inst. Mining Engrs., Soc. Exploration Geophysicists, Geologic Soc. Am., Pa. Acad. Sci., Air and Waste Mgmt. Assn. Achievements include rsch. in mineral exploration and mining geophysics, emissions inventory and ozone planning; discovery of Pilot Knob iron ore body in Missouri; on canoe reconnaissance in Labrador and the Northwest Territories in Can. Home: 5335 Tomfran Dr Pittsburgh PA 15236-2477

LENFANT, CLAUDE JEAN-MARIE, physician, director; b. Paris, Oct. 12, 1928; arrived in U.S., 1960, naturalized, 1965; s. Robert and Jeanine (Leclerc) Lenfant; children: Philipe, Bernard, Martine Lenfant Wayman, Brigitte Lenfant Martin, Christine. BS, U. Rennes, France, 1948; MD, U. Paris, 1956; DSc (hon.), SUNY, 1988. Asst. prof. physiology U. Lille, France, 1959—60; from clin. instr. to prof. medicine physiology and biophysics U. Wash. Med. Sch., 1961—72; assoc. dir. lung programs Nat. Heart, Lung and Blood Inst. NIH, Bethesda, Md., 1970—72, dir. divsn. lung diseases, 1972—80; dir. Fogarty Internat. Ctr. NIH, 1980—82, assoc. dir. internat. rsch., 1980—82; dir. Nat. Heart, Lung and Blood Inst., 1982—2003, disting. scientist emeritus, 2003—; pres. World Hypertension League, 2000—06; exec. dir. Global Initiative Asthma, and Global Initiative Chronic Obstructive Lung Disease, 2005—. Mem. editl. bd.: Undersea Biomed. Rsch., 1973—75, Respiration Physiology, 1971—78, Am. Jour. Physiology and Jour. Applied Physiology, 1970—76, Am. Rev. Respiratory Disease, 1973—79, Jour. Applied Physiology, 1976—82, Am. Jour. Medicine, 1979—82; editor: Lung Biology in Health and Disease. Elected mem., planning group Alliance Against Chronic Respiratory Disease/WHO, 2007—; apptd. mem., advisory panel WHO Etpest, 2007—. Recipient Nathan Davis award, AMA, 1998, Gold Heart award, Am. Heart Assn., 2002, European Lung Found. award, 2002. Fellow: Royal Soc. Medicine, Royal Coll. Physicians; mem.: French Nat. Acad. Medicine, USSR Acad. Med. Scis., Inst. Medicine of NAS, Undersea Med. Soc., NY Acad. Scis., Am. Physiol. Soc., French Physiol. Soc., Am. Soc. Clin. Investigation, Assn. Am. Physicians, Alpha Omega Alpha. Home: PO Box 83027 Gaithersburg MD 20883-3027 Personal E-mail: lenfantc@prodigy.net.

LENFEST, HAROLD FITZGERALD, former cable television executive, lawyer; b. Jacksonville, Fla., May 29, 1930; s. Harold Churchill and Herrena (FitzGerald) L.; m. Marguerite Brooks, July 9, 1955; children: Diane, H. Chase, Brook. AB, Washington and Lee U., 1953, DHL (hon.), 2004; LLB, Columbia U., 1958; DHL (hon.), Ursinus Coll., 2000, Temple U., 2002, Widener U., 2006. Bar: N.Y. 1959. Assoc. Davis Polk & Wardwell, NYC, 1958-65; assoc. counsel Triangle Publs., Phila., 1965-70, mng. dir. comm. divsn. NYC, 1970-74; editorial dir., pub. Seventeen mag., NYC, 1970-74; pres. Suburban Cable TV Co.; pres., CEO Lenfest Comm., Inc., 1974-2000. Bd. dirs. TCI West, Inc., Seattle, Liberty Media Corp., Cable Advt. Bur., Vidéopole, France, Australis Media Ltd., Australia, Voice FX, Inc.; chmn. Video JukeBox, Inc.; CEO Cable AdNet, Inc., 1981—92, StarNet, Inc., 1989—2001, TelVue, Inc., 1990—, CAM Sys., 1995—2001. Trustee Walter Kaitz Found., Oakland, Calif., 1986-1988, Columbia U., 2000-; nat. campaign chmn., trustee Washington and Lee U., 1990—1998, hon. chair campaign, 2000-2004; mem. bd. regents Mercersburg Acad., 1989-1997, pres., 1994—1997; bd. dirs., v.p. Columbia U. Sch. Law, NYC, 1960—1965, 1974—1978, mem. bd. visitors, 1992—; mem. James Madison Coun. Libr. of Congress, 1989—2007, chair, 2007—, bd. trustees, 2007—; mem. Phila. Children's Commission 2004-; bd. trustees Phila. Mus. Art, 1993—; trustee, exec. com. Chesapeake Bay Found., 1995—; bd. dirs. C-SPAN, 1995—2000, Smithsonian, 2003—2004; chair bd. trustees Phila. Mus. Art, 2001—, Curtis Inst. Music, 2006—; chmn. bd. Bus. Leaders for Cath. Schs., 2005—2007; chair bd. dir. Am. Revolution Ctr., 2006—; mem. bd. dir. Nat. Park Found., 2007-. Capt. USNR, 1953—76, active duty USNR, 1953—56, active duty USNR, 1962. Named Man of Yr., Phila. Area Easter Seal Soc., 1992, Citizen of Yr., PenJerDel Coun., 2004, Individual Philanthropist of Yr., Assn. Fundraising Profls., Phila. Chpt., 2004; named one of 50 Most Generous Philanthropists, BusinessWeek, 2005; recipient Disting. Achievement award, Columbia U. Sch. Law, 1997, Individual Leadership award, Phila. Arts and Bus. Coun., 2002, Patron of Yr. award, Gov. of Pa., 2002, Russell H. Conwell award, Temple U., 2003, Vision for Phila. award, Phila. Hospitality, Inc., 2003, Americanism award, Anti-defamation League, 2004, Woodrow Wilson award for pub. svc., Internat. Ctr. Scholars of Smithsonian Instn., 2005, Internat. Outstanding Philanthrophist award, Assn. Fundraising Profls., 2005, Robert P. Casey medal for commitment to ind. higher edn., Assn. Ind. Colls. and Univs. Pa., 2005, Horatio Alger award, 2006, Joseph C. Donchess Disting. Svc. award, Wyo. Sem., 2006; fellow, Phila. Coll. Physicans, 2005. Mem. Pa. Cable TV Assn. (bd. dirs., officer 1976-79), Mayflower Soc., Athenaeum of Phila., Coun. on Fgn. Relations, Am. Philos. Soc., Soc. Colonial Wars, Order of the Coif. Office: The Lenfest Group 300 Barr Harbor Dr Ste 460 West Conshohocken PA 19428 Business E-Mail: gerry@lenfestgroup.com.

LENGEMANN, FREDERICK WILLIAM, retired physiology educator; b. NYC, Apr. 8, 1925; s. Peter and Dorathea Johanna (Wolter) L.; m. J. Joan Doremus, Dec. 23, 1950; children: Frederick William Jr., David Munson. Student, N.Y. State Sch. Agr., Farmingdale, 1942—43; BS with distinction, Cornell U., 1950, M in Nutrition Sci., 1951; PhD, U. Wis., 1954. Rsch. assoc. U. Tenn.-AEC Agrl. Rsch. Program, Oak Ridge, 1954-55; asst. prof. dept. chemistry U. Tenn. Med. Sch., Memphis, 1955-59; prof. dept. physiology N.Y. State Coll. Vet. Medicine, Cornell U., 1959-88, prof. physiology emeritus, 1988—; biochemist divsn. biology and medicine AEC, 1962-63. Cons. FAO-IAEA, Vienna, Austria, 1966-67, 76-77, Fed. Radiation Coun., 1964-65, NRC, 1970-73, Nat. Com. on Radiation Protection, 1970-73, 79, 82; IAEA expert U. Nacional Agraria, Peru, 1978; lectr., dir. tng. courses. Contbr. articles to profl. jours. Mem. planning bd. Town of Dryden, NY, 1963-68; treas. Rome (Pa.) Presbyn. Ch. Active duty USN, 1943—46, with USNR, 1946—50. Decorated Air medal with 2 stars. Fellow AAAS; mem. Coun. Agrl. Sci. and Tech., Am. Dairy Sci. Assn., Am. Nutrition Soc., Fed. Am. Socs. for Exptl. Biology, Nat., N.Y. State Christmas Tree Growers Assns., Sigma Xi, Phi Kappa Phi. Home: RR3 Box 3000J Rome PA 18837 Office: Cornell U NY State Coll Vet Medicine Dept Physiology Ithaca NY 14853

LENGER, JOHN RICHARD, journalism educator; b. Washington, Mo., Jan. 26, 1964; s. Richard and Bev (stepmother) Lenger and Joan and Craig (stepfather) Hart; m. Maria Cristina Caballero, Aug. 5, 2000; 1 child, Juan Rafael Lenger BJ, U. Mo., 1986, BA in Polit. Sci., 1986; MEd, Harvard U., 2002. Editor The LaBelle (Mo.) Star, 1986, Suburban Newspapers Greater St. Louis, 1986-90; Sunday editor The Post-Star, Glens Falls, NY, 1990-92; copy editor Gazette Newspapers, Schenectady, NY, 1992-93; freelance editor, writer Foxboro, Mass., 1993-94; asst. editor Harvard U. Gazette, Cambridge, Mass., 1994-95, editor-in-chief, 1995-98; publs. dir. Harvard U. Office News & Pub. Affairs, Cambridge, 1998—; instr. journalism Harvard U., Cambridge, 1997—. Bd. dirs. New England Press Assn. Co-author: (chpt.) The Writer's Handbook, 2001, Living Ethics: Developing Values in Mass Communication, 1996; editor: The Harvard Guide, 2000, 2002; contbr. articles to profl. jours. Mentor Graham & Parks Alternative Pub. Sch., Cambridge, 1995—2002; bd. dirs. New England Press Assn., 2005—. Recipient James E. Conway Excellence in Tchg. Writing award, Harvard U., 2005. Mem. Soc. Profl. Journalists, New Eng. Press Assn. (vol. coord. 1999—, bd. dirs. 2005). Office: Harvard U News & Pub Affairs 1060 Holyoke Ctr Cambridge MA 02138 E-mail: john_lenger@harvard.edu.

L'ENGLE, MADELEINE (MRS. HUGH FRANKLIN), writer; b. NYC, Nov. 29, 1918; d. Charles Wadsworth and Madeleine (Barnett) Camp; m. Hugh Franklin, Jan. 26, 1946 (dec., 1986); children: Josephine Franklin Jones, Maria Franklin Rooney, Bion. AB, Smith Coll., 1941; postgrad., New Sch., 1941-42, Columbia U., 1960-61; holder 19 hon. degrees. Tchr. St. Hilda's and St. Hugh's Sch., 1960—; mem. faculty U. Ind., 1965-66, 71; writer-in-residence Ohio State U., 1970, U. Rochester, 1972, Wheaton Coll., 1976—, Cathedral St. John the Divine, NYC, 1965—. Author: The Small Rain, 1945, Ilsa, 1946, Camilla Dickinson, 1951, A Winter's Love, 1957, And Both Were Young, 1949, Meet the Austins, 1960, A Wrinkle in Time, 1962, The Moon by Night, 1963, The 24 Days Before Christmas, 1964, The Arm of the Starfish, 1965, The Love Letters, 1966, The Journey with Jonah, 1968, The Young Unicorns, 1968, Dance in the Desert, 1969, Lines Scribbled on an Envelope, 1969, The Other Side of the Sun, 1971, A Circle of Quiet, 1972, A Wind in the Door, 1973, The Summer of the Great-Grandmother, 1974, Dragons in the Waters, 1976, The Irrational Season, 1977, A Swiftly Tilting Planet, 1978, The Weather of the Heart, 1978, Ladder of Angels, 1980, A Ring of Endless Light, 1980, Walking on Water, 1980, A Severed Wasp, 1982, And It Was Good, 1983, A House Like a Lotus, 1984, Trailing Clouds of Glory, 1985, A Stone for a Pillow, 1986, Many Waters, 1986, Two-Part Invention, 1988, A Cry Like a Bell, 1987, Sole Into Egypt, 1989, From This Day Forward, 1988, An Acceptable Time, 1989, The Glorious Impossible, 1990, Certain Women, 1992, The Rock That Is Higher: Story As Truth, 1993, Anytime Prayers, 1994, Troubling a Star, 1994, Penguins and Golden Calves, 1996, A Live Coal in the Sea, 1996, Glimpses of Grace, 1996, Wintersong, 1996, Mothers and Daughters, 1997, Friends for the Journey, 1997, Bright Evening Star: Mystery of the Incarnation, 1997, The Other Dog, 2001, Madeleine L'Engle Herself: Reflections on a Writing Life (with Carole Chase), 2001 Pres. Crosswicks Found. Recipient Newbery medal, 1963, Sequoyah award, 1965, runner-up Hans Christian Andersen Internat. award, 1964, Lewis Carroll Shelf award, 1965, Austrian State Lit. award, 1969, Bishop's Cross, 1970, U. South Miss. medal, 1978, Regina medal, 1985, Alan award Nat. Coun. Tchrs. English, 1986, Kerlan award, 1990, Margaret Edwards award, 1998; collection of papers at Wheaton Coll. Mem. Authors Guild (mem. council), Authors League (mem. council), Writers Guild Am. Episcopalian. Office: Cathedral Libr St John the Divine 1047 Amsterdam Ave New York NY 10025-1747 also: care Random House Children's Media 1540 Broadway New York NY 10036-4039 *Over the years I've worked out a philosophy of failure which I find extraordinarily liberating. If I'm not free to fail, I'm not free to take risks, and everything in life that's worth doing involves a willingness to take a risk and involves the risk of failure. Each time I start a new book I am risking failure. Although I have had over 60 books published, there are at least 6 full unpublished books which have failed, but which have been necessary for the book which then gets published. The same thing is true in all human relationships. Unless I'm willing to open myself up to risk and to being hurt, then I'm closing myself off to love and friendship.*

LENGYEL, ALFONZ, art history, archeology and museology educator; b. Godollo, Hungary, Oct. 21, 1921; arrived in US, 1957; s. Aurel and Margit (Furedy) Lengyel; m. Hongying Liu. Degree in mil. sci., Miskolc Law Acad., Budapest, 1944, degree in law and polit. sci., 1948; MA, San Jose State Coll., 1959; PhD, U. Paris, 1964; LLD (hon.), London Inst. Applied Rsch., 1973. Asst. prof. San Jose State Coll., Calif., 1961-63; faculty U. Md. European Div., Paris and Heidelberg, Germany, 1963-68; intern museology Ecole du Louvre, Paris, 1965-66; prof. Wayne State U., Detroit, 1968-72, No. Ky. U., Highland Heights, 1972-77; dean, prof. Inst. Mediterranean Art and Archaeology, Cin., 1977-82; coord. art history Rosemont Coll., Pa., 1982-86; rsch. prof. art history, dir. Goebel's Print Collection, Ea. Coll., St. Davids, Pa., 1986—88; pres. Fudan Mus. Found., China, 1988—. Adj. curator Detroit Inst. Arts, 1968-72; cons. Paris Am. Acad., 1963—; dir. UPAO, Washington, 1983-87; adv. prof. Fudan U., Shanghai, People's Republic of China; cons. prof. Xian Jiaotong U., Xian, People's Republic of China, founder Sino-Am. Field Sch. Archaeology; mem. Sarasota County Arts Coun., Fla., 1995—. Author: Pub. Rels. for Mus., 1992, Archaeology for Museologists, 1993, Chinese Chronological History, 1993, Field Work in Archaeology, 2001, Chinese Chronological History, 2001; co-author: The Archaeology of Roman Pannonia, 1983; contbr. numerous articles to profl. jours. Bd. dirs. Hungarian-Am. Fedn., Cleve., 1983-91, exec. v.p., Ft. Lauderdale, Fla., 1991-2005; mem. Rep. Presdl. Task Force, Washington, 1982-86; mem. adv. bd. U.S. Dept. Interior Nat. Pk. Svc., 1987-91; bd. dirs. Mus. Asian Art, Sarasota, Fla., 2001-05; officer Cross of Honor, Hungarian Republic, 1992. Grantee Rockefeller Found., 1957, Govt. France, 1962-63, Smithsonian Instn., 1968, HEW, 1971.; S.H. Kress Found. lectureship Denison U., Ohio, 1967-68; Named Man of Yr., Am. Biog. Inst., 2006 Fellow Internat. Acad. Sci. and Letters, Arpad Acad. (pres. 1982—), Szechenyi Acad., Am. Assn. Swiss, German, Austrian Profs.; mem. Internat. Coun. Mus., Renaissance Soc. Am., Coll. Art Assn. Am., Archaeol. Inst. Am., Nat. Fedn. Hungarian-Ams., Soc. Architectural Historians, NY Acad. Scis., Hungarian Acad. Scis., Mich. Acad. Scis. and Letters, Register of Profl. Archaeologists, Christopher Giest Hist. Soc., Detroit Classical Assn., Mich. Acad. Arts and Scis., Am. Assn. Mus. Republican. Roman Catholic. Home: 4206 73d Terrace E Sarasota FL 34243 Office: Sino-Am Field Sch Archaeology Fudan Mus Found Sarasota FL 34243 Personal E-mail: fmfsafsa@juno.com.

LENHART, CHERYL HAYES, nursing administrator, consultant; b. Pitts., Apr. 18, 1952; d. William Pearse and Virginia Englert Hayes; m. William Terry Lenhart, June 12, 1976; children: Matthew Pearse, Erin Elizabeth. Nursing Diploma, Pitts. Hosp. Sch. Nursing, 1973; BSN, Pa. State U., State College, 1981; M in Human Resource Mgmt., LaRoche Coll., 1998. Staff nurse Allegheny Gen. Hosp., Pitts., 1973—75, nurse mgr., 1975—78, asst. DON, 1978—81, Montefiore Hosp., Pitts., 1981—88, nurse mgr. emergency dept., 1988—91, The Western Pa. Hosp., Pitts., 1991—93, nurse mgr. outpatient ctr. and intravenous therapy, 1991—, nurse mgr. oncology unit, 2000—. Nurse spkr./cons. in field, 2000—. Associate editor: nursing publ. Profl. Paradigms (Merit Award for In Ho. Publications for Hospitals of 500+ Beds, 2005); contbr. articles to profl. jours. Pres. Women's Guild, Pitts., 2002—05. Mem.: Intravenous Nursing Soc., Nat. Oncology Nursing Soc., Oncology Nursing Soc. (pres. 2005—, Greater Pitts. chpt. 2004—05). Achievements include research in relative dose intensity of chemotherapy administration; preventing complications of central venous access devices; use of saline flush only (vs. Heparin) in preventing central line clotting. Office: The Western Pennsylvania Hosp 4800 Friendship Ave Pittsburgh PA 15224 Home Phone: 412-922-1862; Office Phone: 412-578-7113. Business E-Mail: clenhart@wpahs.org.

LENHART, CYNTHIA RAE, conservation organization executive; b. Cheverly, Md., Nov. 3, 1957; d. Donald Edward and Vesta Jean Lenhart. BS in Environ. Studies, Coll. William & Mary, 1979; MS in Environ. Sci., SUNY, Syracuse, 1983. Asst. to pres. Environ. Policy Inst., Washington, 1979-81; wildlife policy analyst Nat. Audubon Soc., Washington, 1984-90; exec. dir. Hawk Mountain Sanctuary, Kempton, Pa., 1990—2004; prin., owner Salamander, Saluda, NC, 2004—. Bd. dirs. Am. Bird Conservancy, Washington, Pa. Environ. Coun., Phila. Contbr. chpts. to Audubon Wildlife Report, 1985, 87, 88, 89. Chair Everglades Coalition, Washington, 1986-88. Home Phone: 828-749-3466.

LENHOFF, HOWARD MAER, biological sciences educator, academic administrator; b. North Adams, Mass., Jan. 27, 1929; s. Charles and G. Sarah Lenhoff; m. Sylvia Grossman, June 20, 1954; children: Gloria, Bernard. BA, Coe Coll., 1950, D.Sc. (hon.), 1976; PhD, Johns Hopkins U., 1955. USPHS fellow Loomis Lab., Greenwich, Conn., 1954-56; vis. lectr. Howard U., Washington, 1957-58; rsch. assoc. George Washington U., Washington, 1957-58; postdoctoral fellow Carnegie Instn., Washington, 1958; investigator Howard Hughes Med. Inst., Miami, 1958-63; prof. biology, dir. Lab. for Quantitative Biology U. Miami, Coral Gables, 1963-69; prof. biol. scis. U. Calif., Irvine, 1969—96, prof. polit. sci., 1986, assoc. dean biol. scis., 1969-71, dean grad. div., 1971-73, faculty asst. to vice chancellor of student affairs, 1986-88, 90-96, chair faculty senate, 1988-90, prof. emeritus, rsch. prof., 1993—; adj. prof. psychology U. Mass., Amherst, 2001—03. Adj. prof. biology U. Miss., Oxford, 2001—; vis. scientist, Louis Lipsky fellow Weizmann Inst. Sci., Rehovot, Israel, 1968-69; vis. prof. chem. engring., Rothschild fellow Israel Inst. Tech., 1973-74; vis. prof. Hebrew U., Jerusalem, spring 1970, fall 1971, 77-78; Hubert Humphrey Inst. fellow Ben Gurion U., Beersheva, Israel, 1981; sr. rsch. fellow Jesus Coll., U. Oxford, 1988; dir. Nelson Rsch. & Devel. Co., Irvine, 1971-73; bd. dirs. BioProbe Internat., Inc., Tustin, Calif., 1983-89, chmn. bd., 1983-86. Editor/author: Biology of Hydra, 1961, Hydra, 1969, Experimental Coelenterate Biology, 1972, Coelenterate Biology— Review and Perspectives, 1974, Hydra: Research Methods, 1983, Enzyme Immunoassay, 1985, From Trembley's Polyps to New Directions in Research on Hydra, 1985, Hydra and the Birth of Experimental Biology, 1986, Biology of Nematocysts, Conception to Birth, 1988, Williams-Beuren Syndrome, 2006, The Strangest Song, 2006, Black Jews, Jews and Other Heroes, 2007; mem. editl. bd. Jour. Solid Phase Biochemistry, 1976-80. Vice chmn. So. Calif. div. Am. Assn. Profs. for Peace in Middle East, 1972-80; bd. dirs. Am. Assn. for Ethiopian Jews, 1974-93, pres., 1978-82; bd. govs. Israel Bonds Orange County, Calif., 1974-80, Dade County Heart Assn., Miami, 1958-61, So. Calif. Technion Soc., 1976; pres. Hillel Coun. of Orange County, 1976-78; nat. chmn. faculty div. State of Israel Bonds, 1976; mem. sci. adv. bd. Am. Friends of Weizman Inst. Sci., 1980-84; bd. dirs. Hi Hopes Identity Discovery Found., Anaheim, Calif., 1982-87, pres. bd. govs., 1983-85, William Syndrome Found., trustee, 1992, 99—, pres., bd. dirs., 1993-95, exec. v.p., 1995-99; v.p. edn. Williams Syndrome Assn., 1994, bd. dirs., 1993-94, mem. adv. bd., 2001—; founder, mem. adv. bd., founder Berkshire Hills Music Acad., 2000—; founder, mem. adv. bd. Guardian Angel Initiative, 2004—. 1st lt. USAF, 1956-58. Recipient Career Development award USPHS, 1965-69; Disting. fellow Iowa Acad. Sci., 1986. Fellow AAAS; mem. Soc. Physics and Natural History of Swiss Acad. Scis. Geneva (hon.), Am. Chem. Soc., Am. Biophys. Soc., Am. Soc. Zoologists, History of Sci. Soc., Am. Soc. Cell Biologists, Am. Soc. Biol. Chemists, Biophysics Soc., Soc. Gen. Physiologists, Soc. Growth and Devel. Home: 304 Dogwood Dr Oxford MS 38655-9670 Office: U Calif Sch Biol Scis Irvine CA 92697-2300 Office Phone: 949-824-7259. Business E-Mail: hlenhoff@uci.edu.

LENK, EDWARD C. (TOBY), retail executive; BA in Econs. and Govt. summa cum laude, Bowdoin Coll., Brunswick, Maine; MBA, Harvard U. Stragegy cons. LäEäK Partnership; v.p. corp. strategic planning Walt Disney Co.; founder eToys, Inc., Santa Monica, Calif., 1997, pres., CEO, uncle of the bd., 1997—2001; co-founder, CEO GameFly, 2002—03; pres. Gap Inc. Direct Gap, Inc., San Francisco, 2003—. Office: Gap Inc 2 Folsom St San Francisco CA 94105 Office Phone: 650-952-4400.*

LENKE, JOANNE MARIE, publishing executive; b. Chgo., Aug. 27, 1938; d. August Julian and Dorothy Anna (Gold) L. BS, Purdue U., 1960; MS, Syracuse U., 1964, PhD, 1968. Tchr. pub. schs., Evanston, Ill., 1960-63; editor Test Dept. Harcourt, Brace & World, Inc., NYC, 1967-70; rsch. psychologist Harcourt Brace Jovanovich, Inc., NYC, 1970-73, exec. editor, 1973-75; asst. dir. ednl. measurment divsn. The Psychol. Corp., NYC, 1975-83, dir. ednl. measurement and psychometrics Cleve., 1983-85, San Antonio, 1986, v.p. dir. measurement divsn., 1986-88, sr. v.p., 1988-91, exec. v.p., 1991-97, pres., 1997-99; cons., 1999—2002; assoc. v.p. Ednl. Testing Svc., 2002—06, v.p., 2006—. Field reader U.S. Office Edn., 1972. Adv. editor Jour. Ednl. Measurement, 1974-78. NSF grantee, 1963-64. Mem. APA, Nat. Coun. Measurement in Edn., Am. Ednl. Rsch. Assn. Home: 2534 Winding VW San Antonio TX 78258-7257 Personal E-mail: jlenke@usa.net.

LENKE, LAWRENCE GERALD, orthopedic surgeon, educator; b. Harvey, Ill., June 28, 1960; m. Beth Lenke; children: Lauren, Bradley, Erin. BS summa cum laude in Pre-Profl. studies, U. Notre Dame, Ind., 1982; MD, Northwestern U., Chgo., 1986. Cert. Am. Bd. Orthop. Surgery, 2005. Intern Washington U. Sch. Medicine/Barnes Hosp./Children's Hosp., St. Louis, 1986—87; resident orthop. surgery Washington U. Sch. Medicine Affiliated Hosps., 1987—91, fellow pediatric and adult spinal surgery, 1991—92; instr. orthop. surgery Washington U. Med. Ctr., 1991—92, asst. prof., 1992—97, assoc. prof., 1997—2001, co-dir. orthop. residency program, 1999—2006, prof. orthop. surgery, 2001, Jerome J. Gilden prof. orthop. surgery, 2001—, co-chief pediatric and adult spinal, scoliosis and reconstructive surgery, 2004—, prof. neurosurgery, 2006—; dir. spinal surgery Shriners Hosp. Children, St. Louis, 1993—. Spine cons. US Olympic Festival, St. Louis, 1994, NFL St. Louis Rams, 1995—, NHL St. Louis Blues, 1997—, Maj. League Baseball St. Louis Cardinals, 1998—2006. Contbr. articles to med. jours., chapters to books; editor: Spinal Deformity: Guide to Surgical Planning and Management, and the Radiographic Measurement Manual. Named one of Best Drs., St. Louis Mag., 2000—06; recipient Spinal Cord Rsch. award, Group Internat. Cotrel-Dubousset, France, 1994. Fellow: Scoliosis Rsch. Soc. (Russell L. Hibbs award 1991, John H. Moe award 1995, Louis A. Goldstein award 2005), Am. Acad. Orthop. Surgeons; mem.: AMA, St. Louis Orthop. Soc., St. Louis Guild of Cath. Med. Assn., Russell Hibbs Soc., Pediatric Orthop. Soc. N.Am., Mo. State Orthop. Assn., Am. Spinal Injury Assn., Am. Orthop. Assn. (Best Clin. Rsch. Paper 2000, Regional Zimmer Travel award 2000), North Am. Spine Soc. (Outstanding Paper award 1999), Phi Beta Kappa. Achievements include being one of the world's foremost leaders in spinal deformity surgery. Office: Dept Orthop Surgery Washington U Campus Box 8233 660 S Euclid Ave Saint Louis MO 63110 Office Phone: 314-747-2535. Office Fax: 314-747-2599.

LENKOSKI, LEO DOUGLAS, retired psychiatrist, educator; b. Northampton, Mass., May 13, 1925; s. Leo L. and Mary Agnes (Lee) L.; m. Jeannette Teare, July 12, 1952; children— Jan Ellen, Mark Teare, Lisa Marie, Joanne Lee. AB, Harvard, 1948, spl. student, 1948-49; MD, Western Res. U., 1953; grad., Cleve. Psychoanalytic Inst., 1964. Intern Univ. Hosps., Cleve., 1953-54, resident in psychiatry, 1956-57, dir. psychiatry, 1970-86, chief of staff, 1982-90; dir. profl. services Horizon Ctr. Hosp., 1980; asst. resident in psychiatry Yale U., New Haven, 1954-56; teaching fellow Case Western Res. U., Cleve., 1957-60, from instr. to prof. psychiatry, 1960-93; prof. emeritus, 1993—; assoc. dean Sch. Medicine Case Western Res. U., Cleve., 1982-93, dir. Substance Abuse Ctr., 1990-93. Cons. Cleve. Ctr. on Alcoholism, DePaul Maternity and Infant Home, St. Ann's Hosp., Def. Dept., Cleve. VA Hosp., Psychiat. Edn. br. NIMH; mem. Cuyahoga County Mental Health and Retardation Bd., 1967-73, 94-2002, 2004—, Health Planning and Devel. Commn., 1967-73, Ohio Mental Health and Retardation Commn., 1976-78; mental health advisor Jewish Family Svcs. Assocs., 2003—. Contbr. articles to profl. jours. Bd. dirs. Hough-Norwood Health Ctr., Hitchcock Ctr., Hopewell Inn, Woodruff Found, 2001—. 1st lt. USAAF, 1943-46. Decorated D.F.C., Air medal with oak leaf cluster.; Career Tchr. grantee NIMH, 1958-60 Fellow Am. Psychiat. Assn. (life), Am. Coll. Psychiatrists, Am. Coll. Psychoanalysts (pres. 1988-89); mem. AMA, AAAS, Ohio Psychiat. Assn. (pres. 1974—), Am. Psychoanalytic Assn., Assn. Am. Med. Colls., Cleve. Acad. Medicine (bd. dirs. 1987-90), Ohio Med. Assn., Pasteur Club, Am. Assn. Chairmen Depts. Psychiatry (pres. 1978-79), Alpha Omega Alpha. Home: 1 Bratenahl Pl Apt 1010 Cleveland OH 44108-1155 Office: 11000 Euclid Ave Cleveland OH 44106-1714

LENMAN, BRUCE PHILIP, historian, educator; b. Aberdeen, Scotland, Apr. 9, 1938; s. Jacob Philip and May (Wishart) L. MA in History with 1st class honors, Aberdeen U., 1960; MLitt, U. Cambridge, 1965, LittD, 1986. Asst. prof. U. Victoria, B.C., Canada, 1963; lectr. Queen's Coll., Dundee, Scotland, 1963—67, U. Dundee, 1967—72, U. St. Andrews, Scotland, 1972—78, sr. lectr., 1978—83, reader, 1983—92, prof. modern history, 1992—2003, emeritus, 2003—. James Pinckney Harrison prof. history Coll. William and Mary, Williamsburg, Va., 1988-89; Bird prof. history Emory U., Atlanta, 1998; mem. humanities com. Coun. for Nat. Acad. Awards, London, 1985-87. Author: From Esk to Tweed, 1975, Economic History of Modern Scotland, 1977 (Scottish Arts Coun. award 1977), The Jacobite Risings 1689-1746, 1980 (Scottish Arts Coun. award 1980), Scotland 1746-1832, 1981, 2d edit., 2007, The Jacobite Clans of the Great Glen, 1984, The Jacobite Cause, 1986, The Eclipse of Parliament, 1992, England's Colonial Wars, 2000, Britain's Colonial Wars, 2001; co-author: (with John S. Gibson) The Jacobite Threat, 1990; editor: Chambers Dictionary of World History, 1993, 3d edit., 2005. Brit. Acad.-Newberry Library fellow, 1982, John Carter Brown Library fellow, 1984, Mellon fellow Va. Hist. Soc., 1990, Mayers fellow Huntington Libr., 1996, Hill fellow, 2004, Folger Libr. fellow, 1997. Fellow Royal Hist. Soc., Royal Soc. Edinburgh; mem. 18th Century Scottish StudiesSoc., Soc. for History of Discoveries, Hakluyt Soc., Royal Commonwealth Club (London). Avocations: golf, hill walking, swimming, scottish country dancing, curling. Home and Office: Apt 4 55 Victoria Pl Stirling FK8 2QT Scotland E-mail: bl@st-andrews.ac.uk.

LENNAN, ANNE CELESTE, trade association and educational software company executive; b. Englewood, NJ, June 14, 1963; d. John Ross and Blanche Coffey Lennan; m. Greg Glynn Bardwell, May 23, 1993. BA, Vanderbilt U., Nashville, 1986. Cert. employee benefit specialist. Dir. fed. affairs Soc. Profl. Benefit Adminstrs., Chevy Chase, Md., 1986—90; v.p., mem. bd. Cognitive Techs. Corp., IBA Math Realm, Rockville, Md., 1996—2005; v.p. Soc. Profl. Benefit Adminstrs., 1990—. Editor, pub. (software) The Trig Explorer, 1977, Alegebra World, 1998, Pre-Algebra World, 1998, Algebra Explores, 2003. Contbr. Jr. League Washington DC, 1992—2000. Recipient Tech. and Leasing Excellence award, Media and Methods Mag., 2001, Portfolio award, 2001, 2003, 2004. Mem.: Internat. Soc. Cert. Employee Benefit Specialists. Avocations: hiking, bicycling, sailing. Office: Soc Profl Benefit Administrs Two Wiscosin Cir Ste 670 Chevy Chase MD 20815

LENNARZ, WILLIAM JOSEPH, research biologist, educator; b. NYC, Sept. 28, 1934; s. William and Louise (Richter) L.; m. Roberta S. Lozensky, June 16, 1956 (div. June 1973); children: William, Matthew, David; m. Sheila Jackson, July 13, 1973. BS, Pa. State U., 1956; PhD, U. Ill., 1959; research fellow, Harvard, 1959-62. Mem. faculty Johns Hopkins Sch. Medicine, 1962-83, assoc. prof. biochemistry, 1966-70, prof., 1971-83; R.A. Welch prof. and chmn. dept. biochemistry and molecular biology U. Tex. Cancer Ctr., M.D. Anderson Hosp., Houston, 1983-89; disting. prof., chmn. dept. biochemistry and cell biology SUNY, Stony Brook, 1989—; dir. Inst. for Cell and Devel. Biology, Stony Brook, 1990—. Cons. NIH, Seminars in Cell and Developmental Biology; sec. adv. bd. Ceptor Corp.; sci. adv. bd. Whitney Lab., 2005—. Co-editor in chief: Encyclopedia of Biological Chemistry, 2005, mem. editl. bd.: Biochem. Biophys. Rsch. Commn. Clayton Found. scholar, 1962-64; grantee NIH, 1963-2005, Lederle, 1965-67; recipient Disting. Young Scientist award Md., 1967. Mem. NAS, Am. Chem. Soc., Am. Soc. Biol. Chemistry and Molecular Biology (pres. 1989-90, coun. 2002—), Am. Soc. Cell Biology (pub. affairs com.), Am. Med. Grad. Sch. Dept. Biochemistry (pres. 1993), Internat. Union Biochemistry and Molecular Biology (exec. com.), Worcester Found. (sci. adv. bd.), Soc. Glycobiology (pres. 1993, Karl Meyer award 2004), Sigma Xi, Phi Kappa Phi, Alpha Chi Sigma. achievements include rsch. in biosynthesis and degradation of glycoproteins and of fertilization. Home: 43 Erland Rd Stony Brook NY 11790-1124 Office: SUNY at Stony Brook 450 Life Sci Stony Brook NY 11790 Office Phone: 631-632-8560. Business E-Mail: wlennarz@notes.cc.sunysb.edu.

LENNIX, HARRY JOSEPH, III, actor; b. Chgo., Nov. 16, 1964; s. Harry Joseph Jr. and Lillian Cleo (Vines) L. BS, Northwestern U., 1986. Former tchr. Chgo. Pub. Schools. Dir. Pegasus Players Theater, Chgo., 1987-88; artistic dir. Legacy Prodns., Chgo.; artistic cons. David C. Waite Mgmt., Chgo. Actor: (films) The Package, 1989, The Five Heartbeats, 1991, Mo' Money, 1992, Bob Roberts, 1992, Guarding Tess, 1994, Notes in a Minor Key, 1994, Comfortably Numb, 1995, Clokers, 1995, Get on the Bus, 1996, Chicago Cab, 1998, The Unspoken, 1999, Titus, 1999, Love & Basketball, 2000, All or Nothing, 2001, Home Invaders, 2001, Pumpkin, 2002, Collateral Damage, 2002, Don't Explain, 2002, Never Get Outta the Boat, 2002, Black Listed, 2003, The Matrix Reloaded, 2003, The Human Stain, 2003, The Matrix Revolutions, 2003, Chrystal, 2004, Barbershop 2: Back in Business, 2004, Suspect Zero, 2004, Ray, 2004, Trespass, 2005, Sharif Don't Like It, 2006, Stomp the Yard, 2007, (TV series) Commander in Chief, 2005-06, (TV films) A Mother's Courage: The Mary Thomas Story, 1989, Perry Mason: The Case of the Defiant Daughter, 1990, In The Best Interest of the Children, 1992, Vanishing Son II, 1994, Vanishing Son IV, 1994, Nothing But the Truth, 1995, Friends 'Til the End, 1997, Too Close to Home, 1997, Since You've Been Gone, 1998, Keep the Faith, Baby, 2002; appeared on stage Ma Rainey's Black Bottom, 1988, Statements, 1989, The Meeting, 1990, A Midsummer Night's Dream, The Great Gatsby, MacBeth; Broadway productions include Radio Golf, 2007. Vol. Chgo. Urban League, 1987. Mem. SAG, Actor's Equity Assn. Avocations: jazz piano, saxophone, pool.*

LENNON, JOSEPH LUKE, retired academic administrator, priest; b. Providence, Sept. 21, 1919; s. John Joseph and Marjorie (McCabe) L. AB, Providence Coll., 1940; STB, Immaculate Conception Coll., 1946; MA, U. Notre Dame, 1950, PhD, 1953; LLD, Bradford Durfee Coll. Tech., 1963; LittD (hon.), U. Southeastern Mass., 1975; DHL (hon.), Roger Williams Coll., 1980. Ordained priest Roman Cath. Ch., 1947; instr. U. Notre Dame, 1948-50; mem. edn. dept. Providence Coll., 1950-51, 53-56, asst. dean men, 1953, dean of men, 1954-56, dean of coll., 1956-68, v.p. community affairs, 1968-88, ret., 1988. Dir. Tchrs. Guild of Thomistic Inst., 1953—56, Pennywise Shop; bd. trustees So. New Eng. Sch. of Law, 1994—. Author: The Role of Experience in the Acquisition of Scientific Knowledge, 1952, The Dean Speaks, 1958, College is for Knowledge, 1959; rev. as 30 Ways to Get Ahead at College, 1964. Mem. adv. council Citizens Ednl. Freedom; adv. bd. Perceptional Edn. and Research Center; co-chmn. Easter Seals, 1968; arbitrator R.I. Bd. Labor; adv. com. Mental Retardation, R.I.; chmn. Nat. Library Week, 1962; mem. R.I. Adv. Com. Vocational Edn.; ann. lectr. Psychology and Everyday Life, WJAR-TV, 1960-75; mem. Gov. R.I. Com. to Study R.I. State Inst. at, Howard; chmn. speaker's bur. United Fund Campaign, 1971; coordinator Civil Rights Affirmative Action Program, 1970-78; mem. Com. Future Jurisprudence in, R.I; com. clergy renewal Diocese Providence; mem. Com. for CROP-Community Hunger Appeal of Ch. World Service, 1974-75; mem. subcom. on family law Gov.'s Commn. on Jurisprudence of Future; mem. membership com. Cancer Control Bd., R.I., 1977; mem. Gov.'s Commn. on Consumer's Council, 1977, Gov.'s Leadership Conf. on Citizen Participation.; bd. dirs. Blue Cross and Blue Shield, Progress for Providence, R.I. Legal Services, Fed. Hill House, Pawtucket YMCA, The Samaritans, Handgun Alert, Vols. in R.I. Schs., Meeting St. Sch., Big Sisters, Big Bros. Assn. R.I., R.I. Easter Seal, Blackstone Valley Surgicare, R.I. Heart Assn.; chmn. 1975 Heart Fund campaign; trustee R.I. chpt. Leukemia Soc. Am.; adv. bd. Parents Without Partners; bd. govs. John E. Fogarty Found., Irish Scholarship Found.; bd. dirs., trustee Big Sisters Assn., R.I.; bd. dirs. Diabetes Assn.; adv. bd. St. Joseph's Merged Hosps.; mem. corp. R.I. Hosp.; trustee Emma Pendleton Bradley Hosp., 1984—, Southern New Eng. Sch. Law, 1994—; chmn. Laborer's Internat. Union North Am. Scholarship Program, 1995—; mem. adv. council Quirk Inst.; mem. Spl. Legis. Commn. Created on Catastrophic Health Ins., 1979-82, Gov.'s Screening Com. for the Judiciary, 1980-89; mem. Save the Bay, 1986-88; bd. dirs. John Burke Scholarship Found., 1973— Scholarship Funds of the Laborers' International Union of North America. Recipient Seal of Approval, RI Automobile Dealers Assn., 1978, Father Lennon O.P. Park established in his honor, City of Providence, 1998, inducted into RI Heritage Hall of Fame, 1999. Mem. Nat. Cath. Edn. Assn., Am. Cath. Sociol. Soc., Nat. Soc. Study Edn., Am. Philosophers Edn. Assn., New Eng. Ednl. Assn., New Eng. Guidance and Personnel Assn., Greater Providence Epilepsy Assn., Nat. Soc. Study Edn., Am. Arbitration Assn., Alpha Epsilon Delta, Delta Epsilon Sigma (pres. 1966-69) Home Phone: 401-865-2221.

LENNON, SEAN TARO ONO, musician; b. NYC, Oct. 9, 1975; s. John Lennon and Yoko Ono. Touring bassist with Cibo Matto; signed to Capitol Records, 2001—. Musician: (albums) Into the Sun, 1998, Half Horse, Half Musician, 1999, Friendly Fire, 2006, collaborator on albums by Yoko Ono, Lenny Kravitz, Cibo Matto, Soulfly, and others. Office: c/o Capitol Records Inc 1750 Vine St Los Angeles CA 90028

LENNON, THOMAS FURNEAUX, television producer, writer; b. Washington, Nov. 3, 1951; BA magna cum laude, Yale U., 1973. Adminstrv. dir. Assn. Ind. Video and Filmmakers, NYC, 1975-78; assoc. prodr./writer ABC News, NYC, 1979-83, prodr.-dir., writer, 1983-87, Thomas Lennon Prodns., NYC, 1987; prodr. China AIDS Media Project, NYC. Guest lectr. Columbia Sch. Journalism, NYC, 1990. Prodr., dir., writer: (TV Documentaries) ABC News: To Save Our Schools, 1984 (Emmy award); ABC News: Growing Old in America, 1985; ABC News: At a Loss for Words, 1986 (Christopher award); Frontline: Seven Days in Bensonhurst, 1990 (Outstanding Documentary Script of 1990, Writers Guild, Best Current Events Documentary, San Francisco Film Festival, Writers Guild Am. award, Documentary-Current Events, 1991); Frontline: The Choice, 1992 (Writers Guild Am. award, Documentary-Current Events, 1994); Frontline: Tabloid Truth, 1994; The American Experience: The Battle of the Bulge: World War II's Deadliest Battle, 1994 (George Foster Peabody award, 1994, Dupont-Columbia award, 1996); The American Experience: The Battle Over Citizen Kane, 1996 (George Foster Peabody award, 1996); Frontline: Jefferson's Blood, 2000; Becoming American: The Chinese Experience: Between Two Worlds, 2003; prodr.: Frontline: Racism 101, 1988 (Nat. Black Prodrs. award), Julia's Story, 2005; prodr., dir.: The American Experience: Demon Rum, 1989 (Blue ribbon, Am. Film and Video Festival, CINE Golden Eagle, History, 1990); sr. prodr. Frontline: The Pilgrimage of Jesse Jackson, 1996; prodr., writer The American Experience: The Hurricane of '38, 2001; prodr., series prodr., writer, dir. Becoming American: The Chinese Experience: No Turning Back, 2003; series prodr., writer, dir. Becoming American: The Chinese Experience: Gold Mountain Dreams, 2003; series prodr. Becoming American: The Chinese Experience: Becoming American: Personal Journeys, 2003; prodr.: (TV Segments) 20/20: The Favored Few, 1986, 20/20: Shoplifters, 1988; prodr., writer, dir.: (TV miniseries) The Irish in America: Long Journey Home, 1998; prodr., dir.: (documentaries) Unchained Memories: Readings from the Slave Narratives, 2003; prodr.: The Blood of Yingzhou District, 2006 (Acad. award, Best Documentary, Short Subjects, 2007). Vol. The Fourth World Movement, NYC, 1990. Recipient Humanitas award, 1985. Mem. Writers Guild Am., Dirs. Guild Am. Office: c/o China AIDS Media Project Sesame Workshop 1 Lincoln Plz 2nd Fl New York NY 10022 Office Phone: 212-875-6181. E-mail: tl@thomaslennonfilms.com.*

LENNOX, DONALD D(UANE), retired automotive and housing components company executive; b. Pitts., Dec. 3, 1918; s. Edward George and Sarah B. (Knight) L.; m. Jane Armstrong, June 11, 1949; children: Donald D., J. Gordon. BS with honors, U. Pitts., 1947. CPA, Pa. With Ford Motor Co., 1950-69, Xerox Corp., 1969-80, corp. v.p. and sr. v.p. info. tech. group Rochester, N.Y., 1969-73, group v.p. and pres. info. tech. group, 1973-75, group v.p., pres. info. systems group, 1975-80, sr. v.p., sr. staff officer Stamford, Conn., 1973-74; sr. v.p. ops. staff Navistar Internat. Corp., Chgo., 1980-81, exec. v.p., 1981-82, pres., chief operating officer, 1982, chmn., chief exec. officer, 1983-87, also bd. dirs.; chmn., chief exec. officer Schlegel Corp., Rochester, N.Y., 1987-89; chmn. Internat. Imaging Materials, Inc., Amherst, N.Y., 1990-97; ret., 1997. Bd. dirs. Prudential-Securities Mut. Funds, Gleason Corp. Served with AC USN, 1942-45. Decorated D.F.C. with 2 gold stars, Air medal with 4 gold stars. Mem. Rochester Area C. of C. (pres. 1979), Country Club of Rochester, Genesee Valley Econ. Club, Chgo. Club, Order of Artus, Beta Gamma Sigma. Republican. *What modest success I have enjoyed is the result of hard work and dedication to the success of the organization public or private. Rarely is one's contribution to the success of the organization not recognized or rewarded.*

LENNOX, HEATHER, lawyer; b. Cleve., Sept. 22, 1967; d. Rand Tru and Leilani Marie L.; m. Douglas Robert Krause, Sept. 17, 1994. BA summa cum laude, John Carroll U., 1989; JD cum laude, Georgetown U., 1992. Bar: Ohio 1992, US Dist. Ct. (no. dist.) Ohio 1993, US Ct. Appeals (6th cir.) 2006. Ptnr. Jones Day, Cleve., 1992—. Contbr. articles to profl. jours. Named an Outstanding Young Prof., Turnarounds & Workouts, 2006, Ohio Super Lawyer, Law Politics & Pubs. of Cin. mag., 2005, 2006, Law Politics & Pubs. of Cin. Mag., 2007; named one of The Best Lawyers in Am., 2006, 2007. Mem.: Am. Bankruptcy Inst., Cleve. Bar Assn. Office: Jones Day N Point 901 Lakeside Ave E Cleveland OH 44114-1190 Office Phone: 216-586-7111. Office Fax: 216-579-0212. Business E-Mail: hlennox@jonesday.com.

LENNOX, PAMELA CHATTERTON, academic administrator; b. LA; BA, MA, Calif. State U., Long Beach; EdD, UCLA. Adj. prof., coll. profl. studies U. San Francisco, 1986—91; dir. coop. edn. Calif. State U., Stanislaus, 1987—91; exec. dir. Higher Edn. Consortium of Ctrl. Calif., 1991; dir., profl. experience and career planning Long Island U., 1992—95, assoc. provost, 1995—. Mem., bd. dirs. Girl Scouts of Nassau County, 1999—2004; membership com. chair Coop. Edn. Assn., 1989—90; mem., conf. planner Stanislaus County Literacy Network, 1989—91; bd. mem., vol Brookville Park Found., 1999—2002, bd. v.p., vol., 2002—; higher edn. grants field reader U.S. Dept. Edn., 1991—. Recipient Vol. Merit Award, Jr. League of Long Island, 1999, 90 Women for 90 Years Award, Girl Scouts of Nassau County, 2002, "Thanks" Badge, 2004, Mentor Award, Nassau County Edn. Leadership Ctr., 2003. Office: CW Post Campus Long Island Univ 720 Northern Blvd Greenvale NY 11548 Office Phone: 516-299-2824.

LENNOX, WILLIAM JAMES, JR., retired military officer; BS, U.S. Mil. Acad., 1971; MLitt, Princeton U., DLitt, 1982; student, Command & Gen. Staff Coll., Ft. Leavenworth, Kans., 1985—86. Commd. 2d lt. US Army, 1971, advanced through grades to lt. gen., 2001, forward observer later exec. officer, C battery, later Fire Support Officer, 1st bn., 29th field arty., 4th infantry (mechanized) Ft. Carson, Colo., 1972—74, aide de camp to the asst. divsn. comdr. for support, 4th infantry divsn. (mechanized), 1974—75; instr., later asst. prof. english US Mil. Acad., West Point, NY, 1979—82; S-3 (ops.) later exec. officer, 2nd bn., 41st field arty., 3rd infantry divsn. (mechanized) US Army, Germany, 1982—85, comdr. B battery, 2nd bn., 20th field arty., 4th infantry divsn. (mechanized) Ft. Carson, Colo., 1975—76, comdr. 5th bn. 29th field arty., 4th infantry divsn. (mechanized), 1988—90, spl. asst. to sec. Washington, 1991—92, comdr., divsn. arty. 24th Infantry divsn. Ft. Stewart, Ga., 1992—94, exec. officer for dep. chief of staff ops. and plans Washington, 1994—95; dep. commdg. gen. US Army Field Arty. Ctr., Ft. Sill, Okla., 1995—97, asst. comdt., 1995—97; chief of staff III Corps, Ft. Hood, Tex., 1997—98; asst. chief of staff, C-3/J-3, UN Command/ Combined Forces Command US Forces Korea, commdg. gen., 8th Army US Army, Republic of Korea, 1998—99; chief legis. liaison, Office Sec. Army The Pentagon, Washington, 1999—2001; supt. US Mil. Acad., West Point, NY, 2001—06. Decorated Legion of Merit with 4 oak leaf clusters, Def. Disting. Svc. medal, D.S.M. with oak leaf cluster, Meritorious Svc. medal with oak leaf cluster, Army Commendation medal with two oak leaf clusters, Army Achievement medal, Korean Order of Mil. Merit, Inheon medal, French Legion of Honor.

LENNY, RICHARD HERBERT, food products executive, marketing professional; b. Atlanta, Jan. 5, 1952; s. Julian I. and Helen (Prozan) L.; m. Roxanne Hager, Jan. 1985. BBA in Mktg. magna cum laude, Ga. State U., 1974; MBA in Mktg. with distinction, Northwestern U., 1977. Research assoc. Atlanta Newspapers, Inc., 1974-76; market analyst Kraft, Inc., Chgo., 1977-78, asst. mktg. mgr., 1978-80, brand mgr. Glenview, Ill., 1980-82, group brand mgr., 1982-84, v.p. mktg. Celestial Seasonings Boulder, Colo., 1985-87, corp. v.p. sales and mktg. promotion Glenview, 1987—97; pres., CEO Hershey Foods Corp., 2001—, chmn., 2002—. Bd. dirs. Sunoco Inc., McDonald's Corp., 2005-. Recipient Disting. Scholar award Northwestern U., 1977, Advt. Age Mag. award 1986, Rising Young Advt. Clients award, 1986. Mem. Northwestern Alumni Assn. (fund raising chmn. 1984, adminstrv. bd. mgmt. alumni 1985—), Am. Mktg. Assn, Grocery Mfrs. Am. (chmn.). Office: Hershey Foods Corp 100 Crystal A Dr Hershey PA 17033*

LENO, JAY (JAMES DOUGLAS MUIR LENO), talk show host, comedian, writer; b. New Rochelle, NY, Apr. 28, 1950; s. Angelo and Cathryn Leno; m. Mavis Nicholson Nov. 30, 1980. Grad., Emerson Coll., 1972. Worked as Rolls-Royce auto mechanic and deliveryman. Stand-up comedian playing Carneigie Hall, Caesar's Palace, others; numerous appearances on Late Night with David Letterman; exclusive guest host The Tonight Show, NBC-TV, 1987-92, host, prodr., writer, 1992— (Emmy award, 1995, People's Choice award, favorite late night talk show host, 2006); host, prodr. Showtime Spl. Jay Leno and the American Dream, 1986, Saturday Night Live, 1986, Jay Leno's Family Comedy Hour (Writers Guild Am. nomination), 1987, Our Planet Tonight; film appearances include: The Silver Bears, Fun with Dick and Jane, 1977, American Hot Wax, 1978, Americathon, 1979, Collision Course, 1989, Dave, 1993, Wayne's World 2, Major League 2, The Flintstones, 1994, The Birdcage, 1996, (voice) What's up Hideous Sun Demon?, We're Back! A Dinosaur's Story, 1993, The Flinstones, 1994, (voice) Robots, 2005, Ice Age: The Meltdown, 2006, Cars, 2006, The Astronaut Farmer, 2007; (TV series) The Fairly Odd Parents (voice only), 2001; prodr. (TV films) Roadside Attractions, 2002; writer: (TV series) Good Times, 1974-79; author: Leading with my Chin, 1996, If Roast Beef Could Fly, 2004, How to be the Funniest Kid in the Whole Wide World (or Just in your Class), 2005 Named one of 100 Most Powerful Celebrities, Forbes.com, 2007. Avocation: antique motorcycles and automobiles.*

LENO, SAM R., corporate financial executive; BS in Acctg., North Ill. U.; MBA, Roosevelt U. Various financial mgmt. roles Baxter Internat. (and its predecessor, Am. Hosp. Supply), 1971—94; CFO, exec. v.p. Corp. Express Inc., Broomfield, Colo., 1995-1999; CFO, sr. v.p. Arrow Electronics, Inc., Melville, NY, 1999—2001; sr. v.p. Zimmer Holdings, Inc., 2001—03, exec. v.p. corp. fin. operations, 2003—07, CFO, 2003—07; exec. v.p. fin. & info. systems, CFO Boston Scientific Corp., Natick, Mass., 2007—. Bd. dirs. TomoTherapy Inc., 2006—. Office: Boston Scientific Corp One Boston Scientific Pl Natick MA 01760*

LENOBEL, JEFFREY A., lawyer; b. Bklyn., 1951; BA, Gettysburg Coll., 1973; JD cum laude, Cumberland Sch. Law, 1978. Bar: NY 1979. Assoc. Demov & Morris, 1978—84, ptnr., 1985—87, Mudge Rose Guthri Alexander & Ferdon, 1987—90, Baker & McKenzie, 1990—94, Orrick Herrington & Sutcliffe LLP, 1994—97; chmn., real estate dept. Schulte Roth & Zabel LLP, 1997—, ptnr. Adv. bd. Chgo. Title Ins. Co., 1994—, Stewart Title Ins. Co., 2001—, First Am. Title Ins. Co., 2002—04. Assoc. editor Cumberland Law Rev., 1976—77, exec. editor, 1977—78; contbr. articles to profl. jour.; spkr. in field. Exec. com. UJA-Fedn. Real Estate Lawyers Div., Fund to Cure Asthma, Nat. Jewish Med. Rsch. Ctr.; commr. Village of Scarsdale Cable TV Commn., 1994—2001, chmn., 1998—2000; mem. Internat. Coun. Shopping Ctrs. Named to Best Lawyers, Super Lawyers; recipient Burton Award legal achievement, 2003. Mem.: Am. Coll. Real Estate Lawyers, Comml. Mortgage Securities Assn., Mortgage Bankers Assn., ABA (securitized mortgage lending 1998—2002, chmn., pension fund investments com. 2002—), NY State Bar Assn. (cooperatives & condominiums com. 1986—), Assn. Bar City NY (housing & urban devol. com. 1986—89, 1991—94), Phi Alpha Delta. Office: Schulte Roth & Zabel LLP 919 Third Ave New York NY 10022 Office Phone: 212-756-2444. Office Fax: 212-593-5955. Business E-Mail: jeffrey.lenobel@srz.com.

LENOIR, GLORIA CISNEROS, secondary school educator, consultant; b. Monterrey, Nuevo Leon, Mex., Aug. 18, 1951; arrived in US, 1956, naturalized; d. Juan Antonio and Maria Gloria (Flores) Cisneros; m. Walter Frank Lenoir, June 6, 1975; children: Lucy Gloria, Katherine Judith, Walter Frank IV. Student, Inst. Am. Univs., 1971-72; BA in French Art, Austin Coll., 1973, MA in French Art, 1974; MBA in Fin., U. Tex., 1979, postgrad., 2001—. Cert. region XIII behavior mgmt. coach Tex., 2006, mediator Tex., 2006. French tchr. Sherman HS, Tex., 1973-74; French/Spanish tchr, dept. chmn. Lyndon Baines Johnson HS, Austin, Tex., 1974-77; legis. aide Tex. State Capitol, Austin, 1977-81; stock broker Merrill Lynch, Austin, 1981-83, Schneider, Bernet and Hickman, Austin, 1983-84; bus. mgr. Holleman Photographic Labs., Inc., Austin, 1984-87, 88-90; account exec., stock broker Eppler, Guerin & Turner, 1987-88; ind. distbr. Austin, 1990-93; owner, cons. Profl. Cons. Svcs., Austin, 1991—2001; adj. faculty Spanish for internat. trade St. Edwards U., 1991-99; bilingual interviewer Gallup Orgn., 1997-98; Spanish tchr., club sponsor Hyde Park Bapt. Schs., 1997-99; tchr. computer applications Travis HS Comm. Acad., 1999-2000, 9th grade coord., 2000—01; tchr. langs. Travis HS, 2001—, chmn. dept. langs. other than English, 2005—, cons. region XIII, 2006—. Group counselor, organizer Inst. Fgn. Studies U. Strasbourg, France, 1976; mktg. intern IBM, Austin, 1978; mktg. cons. Creative Ednl. Enterprises, Austin, 1980—81; hon. spkr. Mex.-Am. U. Tex., Austin, 1984; coord. small bus. workshops, 85; group sponsor, advisor Travel Selections, 1997—2003, Explorica, Inc., 2003—06; mem. campus adv. coun. Travis HS, 1999—2002; S.W. area rep. Travel Selections, Campbell, Calif., 2000—03; presenter Space Econs. NASA Educator's Conf. Space Exploration, 2006—; spkr. in field. Photograhs pub. in Review, 1968, Women in Space, 1979; Exhibited in group shows, Tex. and US, 1979, 1988—89, 1999, 2005. Neighborhood capt. Am. Cancer Soc., Austin, 1982—86, 1990, Am. Heart Assn., 1989; active Advantage Austin, 1988; dep. registrar Travis County, 2004—; peer panelist Maj. Art Insts., Austin; megaskills leader Austin Ind. Sch. Dist., 1991—96; bd. dirs. Magnet Parents Coalition, 1995—98; participant NASA Urban and Rural Cmty. Enrichment Program, 2002; mem. smaller learning cmtys. com. Travis HS, Austin, 2002—04, mem. partnership behavior success com., 2003—, mem. com. HS redesign, 2005—06; active Inst. Civility Govt., 2005—; elder Ctrl. Presbyn. Ch., 1988—90, 2000—02, 2006—, tchr. HS Sunday sch., 2002—03; mem. PTA; liaison leads program Austin Coll., 1983—2000. Recipient Night on the Town award, IBM, 1978. Mem.: NEA, Am. Edn. Rsch. Assn., Tex. Fgn. Lang. Assn., Edn. Austin, Kappa Delta Pi, Pi Lambda Theta. Democrat. Home and Office: 1801 Lavaca St Apt 11E Austin TX 78701-1331 Personal E-mail: glenoir@mail.utexas.edu.

LENÔTRE, MARIE, dean; B in Psych., U. Houston; B in Drama, U. Athens; M in Pub. Health Edn., U. Tex.; M in English and Creative Writing, U. Houston. Dir. Culinary Inst. Alain & Marie LeNôtre, Houston, 1998—. Founder Culinary Endowment & Scholarship. Mem.: Les Dames d' Escoffier, Houston Chpt. (pres. 2005—06). Office: Culinary Inst Alain & Marie LeNotre 7070 Allensby Houston TX 77022*

LENOX, ADRIANE, actress; b. Memphis, Sept. 11, 1956; m. Zane Mark; 1 child, Crystal Joy. Grad., Lambuth U. Performer: (Broadway plays) Ain't Misbehavin', 1978—82, Dreamgirls, 1981—85, How To Succeed in Business Without Really Trying, 1995—96, The Gershwins' Fascinating Rhythm, 1999, Kiss Me, Kate, 1999—2001, Caroline, or Change, 2004, Doubt, 2005— (Outer Critics Circle award nomination for Outstanding Featured Actress in a Play, 2005, Drama Desk award for Outstanding Featured Actress in a Play, 2005, Tony award for Best Performance by a Featured Actress in a Play, 2005), Buddy Holly Story, Chicago, 2007, (off-broadway plays) Spunk, 1981, The American Play, 1994, Merrily We Roll Along, 1994, Identical Twins from Baltimore, 1995, The Venus, 1995, Broken Sleep: Three Plays, 1997, Dinah Was, 1998 (Obie award for Performance, 1998, Audelco award), The Broadway Musicals of 1943, 2001, Miss Evers Boys, 2002, Crowns, 2002, Our Town, 2002, Cavedweller, 2003, Caroline, or Change, 2004, Beehive, 1986, On the Town, 1989 (Helen Hayes award for Outstanding Lead Actress in a Musical), The Color Purple, 2004, Doubt, 2004 (Lucille Lortel award for Outstanding Featured Actress, 2005); actress (TV series) Third Watch, 2000, 2004, Law and Order, 1999, Law and Order: Special Victims Unit, 2001, 2003, (films) Forever, Lulu, 1987, On the One, 2005, Griffin & Phoenix, 2006, Black Snake Moan, 2006, (TV films) Double Platinum, 1999. Mem.: Actors Equity Assn. Office: Walter Kerr Theatre PO Box 944 New York NY 10108-0944*

LENOX, GINA MARIE, music educator; b. Meadowbrook, Pa., July 12, 1979; d. David Richard and Eileen Marie Lenox. BS cum laude in Music Edn., Ind. U. of Pa., 2001. Cert. tchr. Pa., 2002. Tchr. gen. music Coun. Rock Sch. Dist., Holland, Pa., 2002; tchr. instrumental music Centennial Sch. Dist., Warminster, Pa., 2002—. Musician: Warminster (Pa.) Symphony Orch., 2001—, Ea. Wind Symphony, 2001—, Landis Mills Quintet, 2003—05, Anemos Winds, 2004—. Fellow, U. North Tex., 2006—, U. Minn., 2001. Mem.: Nat. Band Assn. (fellow 2005), Bucks County Music Educators Assn., Pa. Music Educators Assn., Music Educators Nat. Conf., Sons of Italy, Sigma Alpha Iota (life; pres. 1999—2001, corr. sec. 1999—2001, Sword Honor award 2001, Sword of Honor 2001). Home: 662 Paddock Drive Southampton PA 18966 Home Phone: 215-962-3000.

LENOX, WILLIAM F., literature and language professor; m. Sharom McKenna; children: William Jr., Lauren McKenna. BA, Providence Coll. Prof. english Johnson & Wales Univ., Providence, 2000—07. Pres. Scituate Scholarship Found., 1998. Office: Johnson & Wales Univ 8 Abbott Park Pl Providence RI 02903 Home Phone: 401-598-1879; Office Phone: 401-598-1879. Business E-Mail: wlenox@jwu.edu.

LENSKI, RICHARD EIMER, evolutionary biologist, educator; b. Ann Arbor, Mich., Aug. 13, 1956; BA in Biology, Oberlin Coll., 1976; PhD in Zoology, U. NC, 1982. Postdoctoral rsch. assoc. dept. zoology U. Mass., Amherst, 1982-85; vis. asst. prof. Dartmouth Coll., Hanover, NH, 1984; asst. prof. dept. ecology and evolutionary biology U. Calif., Irvine, 1985—88, assoc. prof., 1988-91; Hannah prof. of Microbial Ecology Mich. State U., East Lansing, 1991—. Vis. asst. prof. dept. biol. scis. Dartmouth Coll., Hanover, N.H., 1984; mem. NRC Commn. on Life Scis., 1990-96, NRC Bd. Biology, 1990-96. Assoc. editor Evolution, 1990-93; editorial bd. Microbial Ecology, 1991-93; contbg. author: Coevolution, 1983; contbr. articles to Sci., Nature, Ecology, Am. Naturalist. NSF fellow, 1977-81; Presdl. Young Investigator NSF, 1988-93; rsch. fellow Guggenheim Found., 1992-93; vis. fellow All Souls Coll., Oxford U., 1992-93; McArthur fellow, 1996. Fellow Am. Acad. Arts Sci.; mem. Am. Soc. Microbiology, Am. Soc. Naturalists, Ecol. Soc. Am.(com. on environ. applications genetically engineered organisms 1988), Genetics Soc. Am., Soc. Study Evolution, Sigma Xi, NAS. Achievements include research on ecology, genetics and evolution of microbial populations including studies on coevolution of bacteria, viruses and plasmids, causes of mutation. Office: Ctr Microbial Ecology Mich State U 288 Plant And Soil Science East Lansing MI 48824-1325 Office Phone: 517-355-3278. E-mail: lenski@msu.edu.

LENT, JOHN ANTHONY, journalist, educator; b. East Millsboro, Pa., Sept. 8, 1936; s. John and Rose (Marano) L.; children: Laura, Andrea, John, Lisa, Shahnon. BS, Ohio U., 1958, MS, 1960; PhD, U. Iowa, 1972; cert., Press Inst. of India, Sophia U., Tokyo, U. Oslo, Guadalajara, Mex., Summer Sch. Dir. pub. rels., instr. English W.Va. Tech., Montgomery, 1960-62, asst. prof., 1965-66; Newhouse rsch. asst. and asst. to dir. comm. rsch. Syracuse (NY) U., 1962-64; lectr. De La Salle Coll., Manila, 1964-65; asst. prof. journalism U. Wis., Eau Claire, 1966-67; asst. prof. journalism, head tchrs.' journalism sequence Marshall U., Huntington, W.Va., 1967-69. Vis. assoc. prof. U. Wyo., Laramie, 1969—70; asst. editor Internat. Comm. Bull., Iowa City, 1970—72; coord. mass comm. U. Sains Malaysia, Penang, 1972—74; assoc. prof. comm. Temple U., Phila., 1974—76, prof. comm. journalism, 1976—95, prof. comm. broadcasting, telecom. and mass media, 1995—, Benedum vis. disting. prof., 1987; Rogers disting. prof. U. Western Ont., Canada, 2000; guest prof. Shanghai U., 2002—, China Comm. U., 2004—, hon. chair Asian Rsch. Ctr. Animation and Comic Art, 2005—; guest prof. Animation Sch., Jilin Coll. Arts, China, 2006—; mem. Pulitzer Prize Nominating Jury, 2007. Author: Asian Newspapers Reluctant Revolution, 1971, Asian Mass Communications: A Comprehensive Bibliography, 1975, 2d edit., 1978, Third World Mass Media and Their Search for Modernity, 1977, Broadcasting in Asia and Pacific, 1978, Topics in Third World Mass Media, 1979, Caribbean Mass Communications: A Comprehensive Bibliography, 1981, Asian Newspapers: Contemporary Trends and Problems, 1982, Videocassettes in the Third World, 1989, Asian Film Industry, 1990, Caribbean Popular Culture, 1990, Caribbean Mass Communications, 1990, Transnational Communications, 1991, Women and Mass Communications: An International Annotated Bibliography, 1991, Bibliographic Guide to Caribbean Mass Communications, 1992, Bibliography of Cuban Mass Communications, 1992, Cartoonometer, 1994, Animation, Caricature, and Gag and Political Cartoons in the U.S. and Canada: An International Bibliography, 1994, Comic Art of Europe: An International, Comprehensive Bibliography, 1994, Comic Books and Comic Strips in the United States: An International Bibliography, 1994, Asian Popular Culture, 1995, A Different Road Taken, 1995, Comic Art in Africa, Asia, Australia and Latin America: A Comprehensive, International Bibliography, 1996, Global Productions, 1998, Themes and Issues in Asian Cartooning, 1999, Pulp Demons, 1999, Women and Mass Communications in the 1990's, 1999, Illustrating Asia, 2001, Animation in Asia and the Pacific, 2001, Cartooning in Africa, 2006, Comic Art in Africa, Asia, and Latin America Through 2000: An Internat. Bibliography, 2004, Comic Art of Europe Through 2000: An Internat. Bibliography, 2 vols., 2003, Cartooning in Latin America, 2005, Centennial Reflections on Cinematic China, 2005, Comic Art of the United States Through 2000: Animation and Cartoons, 2005, Cartooning in Africa, 2007, others; founding editor: Berita, 1975—2002, Internat. Jour. Comic Art, 1998—, founding mng. editor: WittyWorld, 1987—; editor: Westview Press Internat. Comm. series, 1992—95, Asian Cinema, 1994—, Hampton Books Popular Culture series, Hampton Books Comic Art series. Recipient Benedum award, 1968, 2 Broadcast Preceptor awards, 1979, Paul Eberman Outstanding Rsch. award, 1988, Ray and Pat Browne Nat. Book award, 1995, Temple U. Exceptional award, 1995, John Buscena Lifetime Achievement in Comics award, 2006; Anchor Hocking scholar, 1954-58, U. Oslo scholar, 1962, Fulbright scholar, Philippines, 1964-65; established John A. Lent Scholarship ICAF, 2003, John A. Lent award Malaysia/Singapore/Brunei Studies Group, 2007—. Mem. Malaysia/Singapore/Brunei Studies Group (founding chmn. 1975-82), Caribbean Studies Assn., Assn. Asian Studies, Internat. Assn. Mass Comm. Rsch. (visual and comic art organizer, chair 1984—), Asian Cinema Studies Soc. (chmn. 1994—), Popular Culture Assn. (founding chmn. Asian popular culture group 1996—), Asian Media and Info. Commm. Ctr. (Lifetime Achievement award 2006), Sigma Delta Chi, Sigma Tau Delta, Kappa Tau Alpha, Phi Alpha Theta. Home: 669 Ferne Blvd Drexel Hill PA 19026-3110 Office: Temple Univ Broadcasting/Telecom Dept Philadelphia PA 19122 Business E-Mail: jlent@temple.edu. *I have cherished the principles of hard work over long hours, accuracy, comprehensiveness, and honesty in my intellectual and scholarly endeavors. I have considered it important to set and meet goals, to share my work with others, to remain untainted by organizations or individuals who, I feel, are not working for the good of humankind. I also cherish, and protect and use, my right to speak out on those issues which I feel are offensive to the public; the result has been that my writings have incurred the wrath of government ministers in at least two countries.*

LENT, MICHAEL STEPHEN, artist, curator; b. Jackson, Miss., June 22, 1976; s. Stephen Douglas Lent and Patricia Pendleton; life ptnr. Jared William Vassillius Pappas-Kelley. BFA, Temple U., Elkins Park, Pa., 2000. Pub. Toby Rm., Tacoma, 2001—; curator, v.p. ArtRod, Tacoma, 2003—; curator Tollbooth Gallery, Tacoma, 2003—, Critical Line, Tacoma, 2006—. Devel. staff Tacoma Art Mus., 2004—. Numerous exhibitions including most recently, exhibitions include Sota Gallery, Tacoma, Wash., 2002, Tollbooth Gallery, 2004, 2005, Basil-Hallward Gallery, Portland, Oreg., 2006. Recipient Amocat Arts Genius aard - Individual Innovators, Mayor, City Coun., Arts Commn. of Tacoma, 2005; grantee Arts Project grantee, Tacoma Arts Commn., 2004—06, Project Support grantee, Wash. State Arts Commn., 2005, Cmty. grantee, Greater Tacoma Cmty. Found., 2004—06, Google grantee, Google.com, 2005. Mem.: Ams. for the Arts, Coll. Art Assn., Am. Assn. of Mus. Independent. Jewish. Avocations: travel, reading, vegan cooking, music. Home: 820 South Ainsworth Ave Tacoma WA 98405 Home Phone: 253-222-3942; Office Phone: 253-444-2741. Business E-Mail: michael@artrod.org.

LENT, NORMAN FREDERICK, JR., former congressman; b. Oceanside, NY, Mar. 23, 1931; s. Norman Frederick and Ellen (Bain) L.; m. Barbara Ann Morris, Aug. 4, 1979; children from previous marriage: Norman Frederick III, Barbara Anne, Thomas Benjamin (dec.). BA, Hofstra U., 1952; JD, Cornell U., 1957; LLD (hon.), Kyung Hee U., Seoul, Republic of Korea, 1975, Molloy Coll., 1985, Hofstra Coll., 1988. Bar: N.Y. 1957, Fla. 1976. Assoc. police judge, East Rockaway, NY, 1958-60; confidential law sec. to N.Y. State Supreme Ct., 1960-62; mem. N.Y. State Senate, 1963-70, chmn. joint legislative com. public health, 1966-70; mem. 92nd Congress 5th Dist. N.Y., 1971-73; mem. 93rd-102d Congresses 4th Dist. N.Y., 1973-93; vice chmn. Energy and Commerce com. 100th-102nd Congresses U.S. Ho. Reps., 1986-93, vice chmn. Mcht. Marine subcom., 1987-93; cons. Lent Scrivner & Roth, Washington, 1993—. Lt. (j.g.) USNR, 1952—54. Recipient George Estabrook Disting. Service award Hofstra U., 1967, Israeli Prime Minister's medal, 1977, Disting. Achievement medal N.Y.C. Holland Soc., 1987, Tree of Life award Jewish Nat. Fund, 1987, Anatoly Sharansky Freedom award L.I. Com. for Soviet Jewry, 1983. Republican. Office: Lent Scrivner & Roth 1420 New York Ave NW Washington DC 20005-2302 Personal E-mail: nlent@lentdc.com.

LENT, ROBERT WILLIAM, counseling psychologist; b. Bklyn. Apr. 1, 1953; s. Jack Harvey and Gladys (Unger) L. BA, SUNY-Albany, 1975; MA, Ohio State U., 1977, PhD, 1979. Lic. psychologist. Teaching assoc. Ohio State U., Columbus, 1976-77; psychology intern Mpls. VA Hosp., 1977-78; psychology intern Ohio State U., 1978-79; asst. prof. student counseling bur., U. Minn., 1979-84, assoc. prof., 1984-85; asst. prof. counseling psychology Mich. State U., East Lansing, 1985-86, assoc. prof., 1986-93, prof., 1993-95; prof. counseling psychology U. Md, College Park, 1995-. Mem. Am. Psychol. Assn., Am. Psychol. Soc., Phi Beta Kappa. Co-author profl. publs., tng. films; co-editor Handbook of Counseling Psychology, Convergence in Career Development Theories: Implications for Science and Practice, Career Development and Counseling: Putting Theory and Research to Work. Office: U Md Dept Counseling and Pers Svcs 3214 Benjamin Bldg College Park MD 20742

LENTINI, FRANCINE, retired physical education educator; b. Bklyn., Dec. 6, 1950; d. Jack and Ida Cutinella Morales; m. Joseph Lentini (div. 1983); 1 child, Christopher; m. John Andreacchio (dec. Sept. 11, 2001). BA, Hunter Coll., 1972; MS in Phys. Edn., Bklyn. Coll. Cert. in adminstrn. and supervision in edn. Tchr. sci., health, phys. edn. St. Mary Elem. Sch., Brooklyn, 1972—73; tchr. health, phys. edn. and gymnastics coach Bishop Kearney HS, 1973—74; tchr. health, phys. edn. Wingate HS, 1974—76, Erasmus Hall HS, 1983—96; A.P. coord. health, phys. edn. EHC: HS for Humanities, 1996—2006. Author: (book) Heart and Soul - A Poetic Journey Since 9/11, 2003. Recipient N.Y.C. Recognition Award, 1989, N.Y.C. Zone Excellence in PE Award, 1989. Mem.: The Acad. Am. Poets. Democrat. Roman Catholic. Avocations: writing, poetry, reading, exercise. Personal E-mail: Francilen4@aol.com.

LENTINI, JOSEPH CHARLES, retired webmaster, systems analyst; b. Washington, Oct. 2, 1943; s. Joseph and Pearl (Crosman) L.; m. Colleen Gail Sargent, Dec. 5, 1983; children: Randolph, Lois, Stephen, Suzanne, Richard. AA cum laude, Prince Georges C.C., Largo, Md., 1977; BS cum laude, U. Md., 1982; MS Pub. Adminstrn., Am. U., 1991; CIO cert., Info. Resources Mgmt. Coll., 1997. Owner, operator N.Am. Van Lines, Ft. Wayne, Ind., 1974—79; materiel bus. adminstr. E-Sys. Inc., Falls Church, Va., 1979—81; adminstrv. mgr. MA/COM, Inc., Rockville, Md., 1981—83; computer specialist VA, Washington, 1983—89; webmaster, mgmt. analyst, IRM expert EPA, Washington, 1989—2005. Mem. adv. com. Nat. Multiple Sclerosis Soc., Washington, 1993-95. Served with USN, 1961-69. Decorated Purple Heart, Presdl. Unit citation, Combat Action ribbon. Mem. DAV, VFW, Am. Legion, Fleet Res., Vets. Honor Guard Tenn., Mil. Order of the Purple Heart, Rotary. Democrat. Avocations: biking, reading, US travel, music, photography. Home: 6502 Pleasant Ridge Rd Sparta TN 38583 E-mail: lentini.joseph@gmail.com.

LENTON, ROBERTO LEONARDO, environmental services administrator; b. Buenos Aires, Feb. 28, 1947; s. Leonard Gersham and Katie (McCulloch) L.; m. Julia Anne Frend, June 11, 1971; children: Alexandra, James, Christopher, Jessica. Civil Engr., U. Buenos Aires, 1971; SM in Civil Engring., MIT, 1973, PhD in Water Resources Systems, 1974. Planning asst. Ministry Pub. Works, Buenos Aires, 1970-71; vis. rsch. engr. MIT, Cambridge, 1971-72, rsch. asst., 1972-74, asst. prof., 1974-77; project specialist Ford Found., New Delhi, 1977-80, program officer, 1980-83, NYC, 1983-86; dep. dir. gen. Internat. Irrigation Mgmt. Inst., Kandy, Sri Lanka, 1986-87, dir. gen. Colombo, Sri Lanka, 1987-94; dir. sustainable energy and environ. divsn. UN Devel. Programme, NYC, 1995-2000; sr. advisor for internat. affairs Internat. Rsch. Inst. for Climate and Soc., Columbia U., NYC, 2001—. Co-author: Applied Water Resources Systems Planning, 1979, Health, Dignity and Development: What Will it Take?, 2005. Bd. dirs., treas. Am. Embassy Sch., New Delhi, 1981-83; bd. dirs. Overseas Children's Sch., Colombo, 1989-93; trustee Iwokrama Internat. Ctr. for Rain Forest Conservation and Devel., Georgetown, Guyana, 1998-2001; chair Water Supply and Sanitation Collaborative Coun., Geneva, 2005—. Mem. ASCE, Am. Geophys. Union, Centro Argentino Ingenieros. Avocations: windsurfing, tennis, running. Home: 48 Rye Rd Rye NY 10580-2231 Office: IRI Lamont-Doherty Earth Observatory Columbia U Lamont Hall Palisades NY 10964-8000 Office Phone: 845-680-4414. Business E-Mail: rlenton@iri.columbia.edu.

LENTS, DON GLAUDE, lawyer; b. Kansas City, Mo., Nov. 4, 1949; s. Donald Victor and Helen Maxine (Draper) L.; m. Peggy Lynn Iglauer, Aug. 27, 1972; children: Stacie Lee, Kelsey Lynn. BA magna cum laude, Harvard Coll., 1971; JD magna cum laude, Harvard Law Sch., 1974. Bar: Mo. 1974, U.S. Dist. Ct. (ea. dist.) Mo. 1975, U.S. Ct. Appeals (8th cir.) 1975. Jr. ptnr. Bryan Cave LLP, St. Louis, 1974-81, ptnr., 1982, 84—, London, 1982-84, mem. exec. com., 1988—, mgr. internat. dept., 1984-88, mgr. corp. and bus. dept., 1988-95, chair corp. and bus. dept., 1995-96, head transactions group, 1996—2002, vice chmn., 2003—04, chmn., 2004—. Instr. law Washington U., 1979-80, adj. prof., 2002-03. Co-author: Missouri Corporate Law and Practice, 1989, 5th edit., 2007, and ann. supplements. Bd. dirs. Leadership St. Louis, Inc., 1978-81, 86-91, pres., 1989-91; bd. dirs. Coro Found., St. Louis, Inc., 1986-91, gen. counsel, sec., 1988-90; vol. St. Louis Lawyers and Accts. for Arts, 1988-93, v.p., 1990-92, pres., 1992-93; bd. dirs. Brit. Am. Project, 1989-94, pres., 1993-94; bd. dirs., exec. com. Confluence St. Louis, 1995-96; bd. dirs., exec. com. Focus St. Louis, 1996-2000; bd. dirs. Grand Ctr., Inc., 2002—, chmn. bd., 2004—; bd. dirs. St. Louis Regional Chamber and Growth Assn., 2005-; exec. bd. dirs. St. Louis coun., Boy Scouts Am., 2004—; bd. dirs. United Way Greater St. Louis, 2007—. Sheldon fellow Harvard U., 1974-75. Mem. ABA, Mo. Bar Assn. (coun. corp. and bus. law sect. 1987-93, vice chmn. 1988-92), Met. St. Louis Bar Assn. (sec. bus. law sect. 1980-81), Harvard Alumni Assn. (regional dir. 1993-96), Hasty Pudding Club, Harvard Club (exec. com. St. Louis Club 1978-82, v.p. 1987-92, pres. 1992-93). Office: Bryan Cave One Metropolitan Sq 211 N Broadway Saint Louis MO 63102-1705 Office Phone: 314-259-2119. Office Fax: 314-259-2020. Business E-Mail: dglents@bryancave.com.

LENTS, PEGGY IGLAUER, marketing professional; b. St. Louis, Apr. 14, 1950; d. Hank S. and Elizabeth Ruth (Metzger) Iglauer; m. Don G. Lents, Aug. 27, 1972; children: Stacie Lee, Kelsey Lynn. BA magna cum laude, Tufts U., 1971; MPA, Harvard U., 1974. Legis. aide Congressman Symington, Washington, 1971; adminstrv. mgr. May Co., London, 1974; buyer Famous Barr subs. May Co., St. Louis, 1976-78; gen. mdse. mgr. Roman Co., St. Louis, 1978-80, mktg. dir., 1981-82, v.p., 1982; mktg. cons., 1983-86; ptnr. Andrew & Lents, St. Louis, 1987-89; pres. Lents & Assocs., St. Louis, 1990—. Cons. Human Resources Adminstrn., NYC; cons. in field. Chmn. nat. leadership program Nat. Coun. Disability, 1974; v.p. planning and devel. Nat. Coun. Jewish Women, 1986—90, adv. bd., 2000—; chmn. adv. bd. Alzheimer's Assn., 1993—; adv. bd. Metro Link Arts Transit; counsel Direct Mktg. Assn., 2001—; v.p. St. Louis Forum, 2005—, 2005—; adv. bd. Ctr. Contemporary Arts, 1989—; bd. dir. Springboard to Learning, 1987—2006, Mo. Bot. Garden, 1988—92; sr. v.p. comm. Mo. Botanical Garden, 2002—, dir. comm., 2004—; bd. dir. Jewish Family and Children's Svcs., 1998—2005, v.p., 2004—05; devel. bd. univ. fellow Tufts U., 1971; chancellor's com. arts U. Mo., St. Louis, 1999—2004. Named one of Top 25 Most Influential Women, St. Louis Bus. Jour., 2003; grantee, Harvard U., 1974; Tchg. fellow, Tufts U., 1971—72. Mem.: Directory Group (U.K.), Women in Bus., Direct Mktg. Assn. (sr. cons. 2000—), Am. Mgmt. Assn., Jewish Hosp. Sch. Nursing Alumni Assn. (life), Westwood Country Club, Pioneers. Address: 1750 S Brentwood Blvd Ste 552 Saint Louis MO 63144-1302 Office Phone: 314-968-3060. Business E-Mail: plents@lentsandassoc.com.

LENTZ, DAVID, chef; m. Suzanne Goin. Intern Clivedon, Taplow, England; saucier The Heights, San Francisco; chef China Grill, Miami, Blue Door restaurant, Delano Hotel; exec. chef China Grill, Las Vegas, Campanile, LA, Opaline, LA; co-owner, exec. chef Hungry Cat, LA. Named one of LA's Rising Stars, StarChefs.com, 2006. Office: Hungry Cat 1555 N Vine St Los Angeles CA 90082*

LENTZ, EDWARD ALLEN, consultant, retired health administrator; b. Superior, Wis., May 30, 1926; s. Otto Albert and Martha Mary Ann (Gruhel) L.; m. Margaret Ann Denier, May 30, 1952; 1 child, Elizabeth Ann Clark. BS, U. Cin., 1951; MHA, Wayne State U., Detroit, 1957. Asst. dir. Pub. Health Fedn., Cin., 1954-57; dir. health planning United Cmty. Coun., Columbus, Ohio, 1957-62; asst. dir. Columbus Hosp. Fedn., 1962-65; assoc. exec. dir. Ohio Hosp. Assn., Columbus, 1965-69; exec. dir. Health Planning Assn. of Ohio River Valley, Cin., 1969-70; asst. prof. grad. program in health svcs. adminstrn. Coll. of Medicine, Ohio State U., Columbus, 1970-72, adj. assoc. prof. preventive medicine, 1957—; dep. dir. med. care adminstrn. Ohio Dept. Health, Columbus, 1972-75; pres., CEO Med. Advances Inst., Columbus, 1975-79; v.p. corp. devel. Mt. Carmel Health System, Columbus, 1979-95, cons., 1995-97. Cons. cmty. health planning USPHS; bd. dirs. Scioto Valley Health Sys. Agy. Contbr. articles to profl. jours. Mem., chair Ohio Dept. Jobs and Family Svcs./Ohio Med. Care Adv. Com., Columbus, 1975—; bd. dirs., vice chair Netcare Corp., Columbus, 1989-2006. Served with USN, 1944-46; 1st lt. U.S. Army, 1951-53, Korea. Recipient Spl. Citation for hosp. planning and mktg. in Ohio and Delbert L. Pugh Conf., Ohio State U. Coll. Medicine and Ohio Hosp. Assn., 1991. Fellow Am. Pub. Health Assn. (bd. dirs., vice chmn. bd. trustees 1979-83); mem. Ohio Pub. Health Assn. (pres. 1969-70), Am. Assn. Areawide Planning Agencies (pres. 1969-70), Ohio Hosp. Assn. Soc. for Hosp. Planning and Mktg. (pres. 1987-88), Columbus Rotary (com. chair). Presbyterian. Avocations: fishing, photography, tennis. Home: 585 Keyes Ln Worthington OH 43085-3503 Personal E-mail: lentz43085@gmail.com.

LENTZ, MARY A., lawyer, educator; b. Cleve., May 17, 1942; BA, Ursuline Coll., Cleve., 1964; MA, Georgetown U., 1968; JD, Cleve. State U., 1973. Bar: Ohio 1973, Pa. 1984, U.S. Dist. Ct. (no. and ea. divsns.) Ohio 1974, U.S. Ct. Appeals (6th dist.) 1975, U.S. Ct. Appeals (D.C. cir.) 1986, U.S. Supreme Ct. 1977; cert. secondary tchr., Ohio. Tchr. Cleve. Pub. Schs., 1965-74; legal counsel Ohio State Dept. Edn., Columbus, 1974-76; asst. pros. atty. criminal divsn. Cuyahoga County, Cleve., 1976-78; atty., ptnr. Weston, Hurd, Fallon, Paisley & Howley, Cleve., 1978-92; police prosecutor City of Westlake (Ohio), Ohio, 1994—96; ptnr. Walter & Haverfield, Cleve.; pvt. practice Chagrin Falls, Ohio, 1999—. Lectr. and presenter in field. Editor Ohio Sch. Jour., 1977—; author: Lentz School Security, 2004, 07. Recipient FBI Dir.'s Cmty. Leadership award, 1999. Mem. ABA, Ohio State Bar Assn., D.C. Bar Assn.

LENTZ, THOMAS LAWRENCE, biomedical educator, dean, researcher; b. Toledo, Mar. 25, 1939; s. Lawrence Raymond and Kathryn (Heath) L.; m. Judith Ellen Pernaa, June 17, 1961; children: Stephen, Christopher, Sarah. Student, Cornell U., 1957-60; MD, Yale U., 1964. Instr. in anatomy Yale U. Sch. Medicine, New Haven, 1964-66, asst. prof. anatomy, 1966-69, assoc. prof. cytology, 1969-74, assoc. prof. cell biology, 1974-85, prof. cell biology, 1985—, asst. dean for admissions, 1976-2000, assoc. dean for admissions, 2000—03, assoc. dean admissions and fin. aid, 2003—, vice chmn. cell biology, 1992—. Mem. cellular and molecular neurobiology panel NSF, 1987-88, mem. cellular neurosci. panel, 1988-90; mem. neurology B-1 study sect. Nat. Inst. Neurol. Disorders and Stroke, NIH, 1996, 98; mem. exptl. virology study sect. Nat. Inst. Allergy and Infectious Disease, NIH, 1997, 98. Author: The Cell Biology of Hydra, 1966, Primitive Nervous Systems, 1968, Cell Fine Structure, 1971; contbr. over 100 articles to sci. publs. Vice chmn., chmn. Planning and Zoning Commn., Killingworth, Conn., 1979—; active Killingworth Hist. Soc. Recipient Conn. Fedn. Planning and Zoning Agys. award, 1995, Citizen of Yr. award Killingworth Lions Club, 1993, Pub. Svc. award Sec. of State, 2002; fellow Trumbull Coll., Yale U.; grantee NSF, 1968-92, Dept. Army, 1986, NIH, 1987-2000. Mem. AAAS, Am. Soc. Cell Biology, Soc. for Neurosci., Appalachian Mountain Club (trails com., Warren Hart award, Pychowska award, White Mountain Four Thousand Footer Club), Fla. Trail Assn., Appalachian Trail Conf., Mt. Washington Obs., Alpha Omega Alpha. Republican. Mem. United Ch. of Christ. Achievements include study of primitive nervous systems, identification of neurotoxin binding site on the acetylcholine receptor, identification of cellular receptor for rabies virus. Office: Yale U Sch Medicine Dept Cell Biol 333 Cedar St PO Box 208002 New Haven CT 06520-8002

LENTZ, THOMAS W., museum director, curator; m. Mary Pfeifer Lentz. BA, Claremont Men's Coll.; MA in Near Eastern studies, U. Calif., Berkeley; MA in Islamic art, Harvard U., PhD in fine arts, 1985. Curator Asian art RISD; from asst. curator to curator and head Dept. Ancient and Islamic Art LA County Mus. Art; asst. dir. rsch. and collections Freer and Sackler Galleries Smithsonian Inst., Washington, DC, 1992, dep. dir. to dir. internat. art mus. div.; Elizabeth and John Moors Cabot Dir. Harvard U. Art Mus., Cambridge, Mass., 2003—. Curator Timur and the Princely Vision: Persian Art and Culture in the 15th Century, LA Co. Mus. Art. Fellow: Am. Acad. Arts & Scis. Office: Harvard U Art Mus 32 Quincy St Cambridge MA 02138 Office Phone: 617-459-9400.*

LENZ, DOLLY (IDALIZ DOLLY LENZ), real estate broker; b. Bronx, NY, Feb. 1957; d. Manuel and Lucy Camino; m. Aaron D. Lenz, 1980; children: Joseph, Jenny. Student in Acctg., Baruch Coll.; M in Acctg & Mgmt. Auditing, The New Sch. Auditor United Artists; with Sotheby's Internat. Realty; mng. dir. Prudential Douglas Elliman Real Estate, NYC, 2000—. Achievements include fluency in English, French, Italian, Portuguese, and Spanish; number one real estate broker in the U.S. from 2004-07. Avocation: running. Office: Prudential Douglas Elliman Real Estate 575 Madison Ave New York NY 10022 Office Phone: 212-891-7113. E-mail: DLenz@elliman.com.*

LENZ, EDWARD ARNOLD, trade association administrator, lawyer; b. White Plains, NY, Sept. 28, 1942; s. Fritz and Hildegard (Bunzel) L.; m. Anna Maria Bartusiak, Mar. 21, 1987; children: Scott, Eric. BA, Bucknell U., 1964; JD, Boston Coll., 1967; LLM, NYU, 1968. Bar: N.Y. 1968, D.C. 1973, Mich. 1982. Trial atty. U.S. Dept. Justice, Washington, 1970-72; assoc. gen. counsel litigation U.S. Cost of Living Coun., Exec. Office of the Pres., Washington, 1973; assoc. Miller & Chevalier, Washington, 1973-80; counsel Health Ins. Assn. Am., Washington, 1980-82; v.p., asst. gen. counsel Kelly Svcs. Inc., Troy, Mich., 1982-89; chmn. legis. com. Am. Staffing Assn., Alexandria, Va., 1985-89, sr. v.p., gen. counsel, 1989-93, sr. v.p. legal and govt. affairs, 1993-99, sr. v.p. pub. affairs, gen. counsel, 1999—. Author: Co-employment--Employer Liability Issues in Third-Party Staffing Arrangements, 1994, 6th edit., 2007. Capt. U.S. Army, 1968-70, Vietnam. Decorated Bronze Star. Fellow Coll. Labor and Employment Lawyers; mem. ABA, N.Y. Bar Assn., D.C. Bar Assn., Pi Sigma Alpha, Sigma Alpha Epsilon. Home: 818 S Lee St Alexandria VA 22314-4334 Office: Am Staffing Assn 277 S Washington St Ste 200 Alexandria VA 22314-3675 Office Phone: 703-253-2020.

LENZ, HENRY PAUL, management consultant; b. NYC, Nov. 24, 1925; s. Ernest and Margaret (Schick) L.; m. Norma M. Kull, Jan. 25, 1958; children: Susan, Scott, Theresa. AB, U. N.C., 1946; MBA, Coll. Ins., 1974. Underwriter U.S. Casualty Co., NYC, 1948-55; underwriting mgr. Mass. Bonding & Ins. Co., NYC, 1955-60; with Home Ins. Co., NYC, 1960-85, sr. v.p., 1972-75, exec. v.p., dir., 1975-85; chmn. bd. Lenz Enterprises Ltd., Chatham, NJ, 1985—. Former pres., dir. Home Indemnity Co.; pres., dir. Home Ins. Co. Ind., Home Ins. Co. Ill., City Ins. Co., Home Group Risk Mgmt.; chmn. bd. Home Reins. Co., Scott Wetzel Services Inc.; chmn., pres. Cityvest Reins. Ltd., City Ins. Co. (U.K.) Ltd.; trustee Am. Inst. Property and Liability Underwriters, Ins. Inst. Am. Served with USNR, 1944-47, 52-53. Decorated Army Commendation medal. Mem. Soc. CPCU's, Phi Beta Kappa, Sigma Nu. Office Phone: 973-377-2949.

LENZEN, DANA DIANE, social studies educator; b. St. Louis, June 4, 1959; d. William and Barbara Ann (O'Connor) Gerdemann; m. Jeff G. Lenzen, July 11, 1986; children: Bonnie, Alexandra, Claire. BS Elem. Edn., SE Mo. State U., Cape Girardeau, 1981; MA Tchg. Social Studies, Webster U., Webster Groves, Mo., 1989; MEd Elem. Counseling, U. Mo. St. Louis, 1997. Tchr. 2d grade Little Flower of St. Theresa, Richmond Heights, Mo., 1981—85; tchr. 1st grade Lindbergh Sch. Dist., St. Louis, 1985—89, tchr. 4th & 5th grade Social Studies, 1989—. Mem.: NEA, Nat. Conf. Social Studies Tchrs. Roman Catholic. Home: 4879 Gatesbury Dr Saint Louis MO 63128 Office: Kennerly Elem Sch 10025 Kennerly Rd Saint Louis MO 63128 Office Phone: 314-729-2440 x 4020. Business E-Mail: dlenzen@lindberghschools.edu.

LEO, JACQUELINE M., editor-in-chief; Feature writer AP; sr. editor Modern Bride; co-founder Child, NYC, 1986, editor-in-chief, 1987-88, Family Circle, NYC, 1988-94; editl. dir. women's mags. group N.Y. Times Co., NYC, 1994, dir. mag. and media devel., 1994-95; editl. dir. Good Morning America ABC-TV News, NYC, 1995—97; editl. dir. Consumer Reports, 1997-99; v.p., editl. dir. Interactive Media/Meredith Corp., 1999—2001; v.p., US editor-in-chief Reader's Digest, Pleasantville, NY, 2000—. Author: New Woman's Guide To Getting Married. Recipient Matrix award Women in Comm., 1993. Mem. Am. Soc. Mag. Editors (bd. dirs., pres.), N.Y. Acad. Scis. (bd. govs.). Office: Office of Editor-in-Chief Reader's Digest Reader's Digest Rd Pleasantville NY 10570 Office Phone: 914-238-1000, 914-244-5567. Fax: 914-244-5900; Office Fax: 914-238-4559. E-mail: jacqueline_leo@rd.com.*

LEO, LEONARD A., legal association administrator, lawyer; b. 1965; m. Sally Leo; children: Margaret, Anthony, Elizabeth, Thaddeus. AB, Cornell U., 1987, JD, 1989. Cons. various legis. and litigation projects; exec. v.p. Federalist Soc. Law and Pub. Policy Studies, Washington; mem. U.S. govt. delegation to UN Commn. on Human Rights. Co-chmn. Rep. Nat. Com. Cath. Outreach; Cath. strategist Bush-Cheney campaign, 2004. Contbr. articles to profl. jours.; co-editor: Presidential Leadership: Rating the Best and Worst in the White House, 2004. Bd. dirs. Nat. Cath. Prayer Breakfast, Youth Leadership Found., Men's Leadership Found., Cath. Action Network. Office: The Federalist Soc 1015 18th St NW Ste 425 Washington DC 20036 Office Phone: 202-822-8138.

LEO, MARTHA E., advocate, counselor; b. Bronxville, NY, May 26, 1955; d. Joseph S. Leo, Robert (Stepfather) and Nancy (Lombard) Hudock. B in Social Work, R.I. Coll., Providence, 1983; MS in Counseling, So. Conn. State U., New Haven, 1989. Lic. profl. counselor Conn., cert. substance abuse counselor, rehab. counselor Nat. Rehab. Counseling Assn. Statisician Dept. Transp., Wethersfield, Conn., 1983—84; counselor Ctr. Ind. Living, Bridgeport, Conn., 1984—86; trainer mentally retarded Easter Seals, New Haven, 1986; vocat. rehab. counselor State. of Conn. Dept. Social Svcs., New Haven, 1987—2001; advocate and investigator Children in Placement, New Haven, 2006—. Guardian ad litem, 2006—. Commr. Office Handicap Svcs. and Advocacy City of New Haven, 1995—97; vol. raising svc. animals. Recipient Dedicated Svcs. to Individuals with Disabilities award, State of Conn. Dept. Social Svcs., 2001. Mem.: Am. Counseling Assn. Avocations: literature, writing, dance, travel, baking. Home: 361 Lenox St New Haven CT 06513

LEO, PETER ANDREW, columnist, educator; b. Aug. 3, 1943; s. Maurice Matthew and Mary (Trincellita) L.; m. Sylvia Weed, July 26, 1970; children: Steven, Jane. AB, U. Toronto, 1966; MA, NYU, 1967. Tchr. H.S. Peace Corps, Nairobi, Kenya, 1968-69; reporter AP, NYC, 1970, Greenboro (N.C.) Record, 1971-72, Wilmington (Del.) News Jour., 1973-78; reporter, asst. city editor, columnist, assoc. editor Pitts. Post-Gazette, 1978—. Instr. U. Pitts., 1999—. Recipient Headliners award Atlantic City Press Club, 1972, Golden Quill award Pitts. Press Club, 1980, 95, Keystone award Pa. Newspaper Pubs. and Editors Assn., 1984. Home: 5266 Beelermont Pl Pittsburgh PA 15217-1010 Office: PG Pub Co 34 Blvd Of The Allies Pittsburgh PA 15222-1200

LEOGRANDE, WILLIAM MARK, political science professor, writer; b. Utica, NY, July 1, 1949; s. John James and Patricia Ann (Ryan) LeoG; m. Martha J. Langelan AB, Syracuse U., 1971, MA, 1973, PhD, 1976. Asst. prof. Hamilton Coll., Clinton, NY, 1976-78; dir. polit. sci. Am. U., Washington, 1980-82, asst. prof. polit. sci., 1978-83, assoc. prof., 1984-89, prof., 1989—, chair dept. govt., 1992-96, dean Sch. Pub. Affairs, 1997-99, 2002—. Mem. profl. staff U.S. Senate, 1982-83, cons., 1984-85 Author: Cuba's Policy in Africa, 1980; editor: (with Morris Blachman) Confronting Revolution; Security Through Diplomacy in Central America, 1986, (with Louis Goodman) Political Parties and Democracy in Central America, Our Own Backyard: The United States in Central America, 1998; dir. Latin Am. Rsch. Rev., 1982-86, World Policy Jour., 1983-93. Dir. svc. com. Unitarian-Universalist Ch., Boston, 1983-86; mem. staff Michael Dukakis Presdl. Campaign, 1988. Council Fgn. Relation Internat. Affairs fellow, 1982-83, Pew Faculty fellow, 1994-95. Mem. Coun. Fgn. Rels., Am. Polit. Sci. Assn., Latin Am. Studies Assn. (exec. council 1984-87) Democrat. Home: 7215 Chestnut St Bethesda MD 20815-4051 Office: Am U Sch Pub Affairs Ward Cir Washington DC 20016 Business E-Mail: wleogra@american.edu.

LEON, ARTHUR SOL, research cardiologist, exercise physiologist; b. Bklyn., Apr. 26, 1931; s. Alex and Anne (Schrek) L.; m. Gloria Rakita, Dec. 23, 1956; children: Denise, Harmon, Michelle. BS in Chemistry with high honors, U. Fla., 1952; MS in Biochemistry, U. Wis., 1954, MD, 1957. Intern Henry Ford Hosp., Detroit, 1957-58; fellow in internal medicine Lahey Clinic, Boston, 1958-60; fellow in cardiology Jackson Meml. Hosp.-U. Miami (Fla.) Med. Sch., 1960-61; dir. clin. pharmacology research unit Hoffmann-La Roche Inc.-Newark Beth Israel Med. Ctr., 1969-73; from instr. to assoc. prof. medicine Coll. Medicine and Dentistry N.J., Newark, 1967-73; from assoc. prof. to prof. div. epidemiology U. Minn., Mpls., 1973—, H.L. Taylor prof. exercise sci. and health enhancement, dir. lab. physiol. hygiene and exercise sci., div. kinesiology, Coll. Edn., 1991—, dir. applied physiology and nutrition, 1973-91. Mem. med. eval. team Gemini projects NASA, 1964-67. Editor Procs. of the NIH Consensus Conf. on Phys. Activity and Cardiovasc. Health, 1997; assoc. editor Surgeon Gen.'s Report on Health Benefits of Exercise, 1996; contbr. numerous articles to profl. publs. Trustee Vinland Nat. Sports Health Ctr. for Disabled, 1978—; mem. gov.'s coun. physical fitness sports, 1979-90. Served as officer M.C. U.S. Army, 1961-67, 90-91, col. Res. 1978-92, ret. Recipient Meritorious Svc. medal U.S. Army, 1993, Anderson award AAHPER, 1981, Presdl. award for exercise sci. rsch. Internat. Olympic Com., 1999; Am. Heart Assn. fellow, 1960-61 Fellow Am. Coll. Cardiology, Am. Coll. Chest Physicians, Am. Coll. Clin. Pharmacology, N.Y. Acad. Scis., Am. Coll. Sports Medicine (trustee 1976-78, 82-83, v.p. 1977-79, pres. Northland chpt. 1975-76, Citation award 1995), Am. Assn. Cardiovasc. and Pulmonary Rehab. (trustee 1989-90), Am. Acad. Kinesiology and Phys. Edn.; mem. Am. Physiol. Soc., Am. Soc. Pharmacology and Exptl. Therapeutics, Am. Inst. Nutrition, Am. Heart Assn. (v.p. Hennepin County divsn. 1980-81, pres. 1982-83), Am. Coll. Nutrition, Am. Fedn. Clin. Rsch., Minn. Lung Assn. (trustee 1978-81), Phi Beta Kappa, Phi Kappa Phi. Jewish. Home: 5628 Glen Ave Minnetonka MN 55345-6610 Office: U Minn Sch Kinesiology 202 Cooke Hall Minneapolis MN 55455-0136 Home Phone: 952-937-5271; Office Phone: 612-624-8271. Business E-Mail: leonx002@umn.edu.

LEON, ARTURO SEGUNDO, civil engineer, researcher; b. Ayacucho, Ayacucho, Peru, Jan. 26, 1976; s. Cirilo Leon and Victoria Cuba. BS in Civil Engring., Nat. U. San Cristobal de Huamanga, Ayacucho, 1996; MS in Hydraulic Engring., Nat. U. Engring., Lima, Peru, 1998; PhD in Civil and Environ. Engring., U. Ill., Urbana, 2006. Cert. Profl. Engr., Colegio de Ingenieros del Peru, Lima, 2000. Tchg. asst. Nat. U. Engring., Lima, 1997—98, course instr., 1999—2002; hydraulic engr. Cosapi S.A., Juliaca, Peru, 1999—2000, Knight Piesold Consuting S.A., Lima, 2001—02; rsch. asst. U. Ill., 2002—06, tchg. asst., 2004—05; project engr. Engrs. Without Borders (USA), Enugu, Nigeria, 2006—. Author: (book) Local scour around cylindrical piers in non-cohesive beds, Spanish translation, 1998, (book (in Spanish) The hydraulic design of a bottom rack-type intake in supercritical regime, 2000. Grantee Travel Grant, U. Ill., 2004, 2006. Mem.: Internat. Assn. for Hydraulic Rsch., Internat. Water Resources Assn., Colegio de Ingenieros del Peru (assoc.), Engrs. Without Borders. Achievements include development of computationally efficient model for the transient analysis of free surface, pressurized and simultaneous occurrence of free surface and pressurized flows in closed conduit systems; numerical model to determine the hydraulic capacity in tunnels; research in formulation of Godunov-type schemes for modeling one and two-phase waterhammer flows. Office: U Ill 2519 Hydrosystems 205 N Mathews Ave Urbana IL 61801 Home Phone: 217-979-2706; Office Phone: 217-333-6178. Office Fax: 217-333-0687. Personal E-mail: artuleon@gmail.com. Business E-Mail: asleon@uiuc.edu.

LEON, BRUNO, architect, educator; b. Van Houten, N.Mex., Feb. 18, 1924; s. Giovanni and Rosina (Cunico) L.; m. Louise Dal-Bo, Sept. 4, 1948 (dec. 1974); m. Bonnie Bertram, Sept. 12, 1976; children: Mark Jon, John Anthony, Lisa Rose. Student, Wayne State U., 1942, U. Detroit, 1945-48, LHD (hon.), 1984; BArch, N.C. State U., 1953. Registered architect, Mich., N.C., Mass., N.Y., N.Mex., Fla. Head design staff Fuller Research Found., Raleigh, NC, 1954-55; archtl. designer I.M. Pei & Assos., NYC, 1955-56; instr. Mass. Inst. Tech., 1956-59; designer Catalano & Belluschi (architects), Cambridge, Mass., 1958-59; asst. prof. U. Ill., Urbana, 1959-61; dean Sch. Architecture, U. Detroit, 1961-93, dean emeritus, 1993; pvt. practice architecture, 1956—. With USAAF, 1942-45. Fellow AIA (dir. Detroit 1963-64); mem. Alpha Sigma Nu (hon.), Phi Kappa Phi. Home: 9 Redondo Ct Santa Fe NM 87508-8308 Office Phone: 505-466-1961. Personal E-mail: volterra@newmexico.com. *I believe the integral quality of the human spirit to be the ability to dream rather than to rationalize.*

LEON, MARTIN BERT, cardiologist, educator; b. Bklyn., Sept. 5, 1950; MD, Yale Univ., 1975. Cert. Internal Medicine, Cardiovascular Disease. Intern Yale-New Haven Hosp., 1975—76, resident, 1976—78, clin. fellow, cardiology, 1980—82; dir. clin. rsch. Washington Cardiology Ctr., Washington Hosp. Ctr.; clin. prof. medicine Georgetown Univ. Med. Ctr., Washington; founding physician Cardiovascular Rsch. Found., NYC, chmn. emeritus; assoc. dir. Ctr. for Interventional Vascular Therapy; practicing interventional cardiologist NY-Presbyterian Hosp./Columbia Univ. Med. Ctr. Prin. investigator for numerous clin. trials in the field of interventional vascular medicine (STARS, Gamma-1 and SIRIUS trial); dir., founder Transcatheter Cardiovascular; clin. assoc., sr. investigator, dir., catheterization lab., cardiology branch Nat. Heart, Lung, & Blood Inst., NIH, Bethesda, Md.; founder Washington Cardiology Ctr., Cardiology Rsch. Found., Washington. Contbr. articles to profl. jours. Office: Cardiovascular Rsch Found 55 E 59th St and 111 E 59th St New York NY 10022-1122 also: 161 Fort Washington Ave New York NY 10032 Address: 177 Fort Washington Ave New York NY 10032 Office Phone: 212-851-9300, 212-305-7060, 212-305-3640. Office Fax: 212-305-4285, 212-305-7060.*

LEON, NELLIE, health educator; d. Jesus Leon and Celia Rivas; m. Joachim M. Brown, Oct. 9, 2004. BS in Kinesiology and Health Promotion, Calif. State Poly. U., Pomona, 2003; M in Health Scis., Western U. Health Scis., Pomona, 2005; postgrad., Loma Linda U., Calif., 2005—. Grad. rsch. asst. Loma Linda U., Calif., 2005—; svc. learning instr. Western U. Health Scis., Pomona, 2005—. Health edn. cons. Calif. State Poly. U. Pomona, 2006—. Recipient Outstanding Health Promotion Grad. award, Calif. State Poly. Pomona U., 2003, Judy Ann Oliver Meml. award, Western U. Health Scis., 2005, Outstanding Thesis/Spl. Project award, 2005; Hilda Solis scholar, Calif. State Poly. Pomona U., 2005. Mem.: APHA, Am. Coll. Health Assn., Soc. Pub. Health Edn. Home Phone: 951-235-3364.

LEON, RICHARD J., federal judge; b. South Natick, Mass., Dec. 3, 1949; s. Silvano B. and Rita (O'Rorke) L.; m. M-Christine Costa; Nicholas Cavanagh. AB, Holy Cross Coll., 1971; JD cum laude, Suffolk Law Sch., 1974; LLM, Harvard U., 1981. Bar: R.I. 1975, U.S. Ct. Appeals (2d cir.) 1977, U.S. Dist. Ct. R.I. 1976, U.S. Supreme Ct. 1984, D.C. 1991, U.S. Dist. Ct. D.C. 1991, U.S. Ct. Appeals (D.C. cir.) 1991. Law clk. to justices Superior Ct. Mass., 1974-75, to justice R.I. Supreme Ct., 1975-76; spl. asst. U.S. atty. U.S. Attys. Office (so. dist.) N.Y., 1977-78; asst. prof. law St. John's U. Law Sch., 1979-83; adj. prof. law Georgetown U. Law Ctr., 1997—; sr. trial atty., criminal sect., tax div. U.S. Dept. Justice, Washington, 1983-87, dep. asst. U.S. atty. gen. environment and natural resources divsn., 1988-89; ptnr. Baker & Hostetler, Washington, 1989-99,Vorys, Sater, Seymour and Pease, Washington, 1999-2002; judge U.S. Dist. Ct., 2002—; dep. chief minority counsel House Select "Iran-Contra" Com., 1987; active Jud. Conf. D.C. cir., 1991—, mem. Pres.'s Commn. on White House Fellowships, 1990-93; chief minority counsel House Fgn. Affairs Com. 'October Surprise' Task Force, 1992; spl. counsel House banking com. "Whitewater investigation", 1994; spl. counsel House ethics reform task force, 1997; mem. Jud. Rev. Commn. on Fgn. Asset Control, 2000-01. Author: (chpt.) Environmental Crime, Lawyers' Desk Book on White Collar Crime, 1991; contbr. articles to legal jours. Trustee Suffolk U., 1990-98. Mem. ABA, Order of Barristers, R.I. Bar Assn., Fed. Bar Coun., Suffolk Law Sch. Assn. Met. N.Y. (past pres.), Suffolk Law Sch. Assn. Met. Washington (past pres.), Chevy Chase Club. Republican. Roman Catholic. Office: US Courthouse 333 Constitution Ave NW Washington DC 20001

LEON, ROBERT LEONARD, psychiatrist, educator; b. Denver, Jan. 18, 1925; s. Louis and Rae (Brown) L.; m. Willena Lee, Sept. 14, 1947; children: Alexis Kay, Mark Robert, Jeffrey Clayton, Stacy Lee. MD, U. Colo., 1948. Diplomate Am. Bd. Psychiatry and Neurology. Intern U. Mich. Hosp., Ann Arbor, 1948-49; resident in psychiatry U. Colo. Med. Ctr., Denver, 1949-52, child psychiatry fellow, 1951-52, Bur. Mental Hygiene, New Haven, Conn. Dept. Health/Student Health Svc., Yale U., 1952-53; asst. dir., acting dir. child psychiatry Greater Kansas City Mental Health Found., 1953-54; instr. psychiatry U. Kans. Sch. Medicine, Kansas City, 1956-57; asst. prof. psychiatry U. Tex. Health Sci. Ctr. at Dallas, Southwestern Med. Sch., 1957-61, assoc. prof., 1961-65, prof., 1965-67; prof., chmn. dept. psychiatry Sch. Medicine U. Tex. Health Sci. Ctr., San Antonio, 1967-95, interim chmn., 1995-96; Ashbel Smith prof. U. Tex. Health Sci. Ctr., San Antonio, 1990—2003, prof. emeritus, 2003—. Chief psychiatry U. Health Sys., Bexar County, San Antonio, 1967-96; mem. Am. Assn. Chmn. Depts. Psychiatry, 1967-96, pres., 1982-83; cons. psychiatry Audie Murphy Vet.'s Hosp., 1973—; cons. Mental Health Orgn., region IV, HEW, 1957-73; mem. Psychiat. Tng. Rev. NIMH, Rockville, Md., 1970-74; hon. cons. World Health Orgn., Geneva, 1996. Author: Psychiatric Interviewing: A Primer, 1982, 2d edit., 1989; contbr. articles to profl. jours. Sr. surgeon USPHS, 1954-57. Fellow ACP (pres. 1987-88), Am. Psychiat. Assn. (life), Am. Orthopsychiat. Assn. (life), Am. Acad. Child and Adolescent Psychiatry (life), Am. Assn. Social Psychiatry (pres. 1990-92); mem. Benjamin Rush Soc., World Assn. for Social Psychiatry. Avocation: photography. Home: 6866 Stonykirk St San Antonio TX 78240-2743 Office: U Tex Health Sci Ctr 7703 Floyd Curl Dr MS 7792 San Antonio TX 78229-3900 Home Phone: 210-696-3962; Office Phone: 210-567-5408. Business E-Mail: leon@uthscsa.edu.

LEONA, ESAKI See ESAKI, LEO

LEONARD, ANGELA MICHELE, librarian, educator; b. Washington, June 26, 1954; d. Walter Jewell and Betty (Singleton) L. AB, Harvard U., 1976; MLS, Vanderbilt U., 1982; MPhil, George Washington U., 1987, PhD, 1994; postgrad., Dartmouth Sch. Criticism and Theory, 1996, NEH Inst., 1998, Chesapeake Regional Scholars Inst., 1999, Gilder Lehman Inst. Am. History, 2003. Cons. Seigenthaler Assocs., Nashville, 1979-81; instr. Trevecca Nazarene Coll., 1979, Nashville State Tech. Inst., 1980-81; rschr., learning libr. program Fisk U. Libr., 1981-82; cataloguer Howard U. Librs., 1983; reference libr. Founders Grad. Libr., 1983-89; tchg. asst. George Washington U., 1986-90; lectr. Bowdoin Coll., 1990-91; instr. St. Cloud State U., 1991; asst. prof. Dickinson Coll., 1992-94, Bucknell U., 1994-95; lectr. UMCP, 1995; asst. prof. Loyola Coll., Md., 1996—. Vis. prof. Johns Hopkins U., 1998; corp. and spl. ref. libr., 1988-90, 95-97; vis. scholar Wolfson Coll., Oxford U., 2005. Copy editor Am. Quarterly, 1988-90; editor: Boorstin Bibliography, Antislavery Materials; contbr. articles to books, profl. jours. Coolidge scholar, 2003, Hedgebrook fellow, 2006. Fellow Oxford Round Table; mem. ALA, NAACP, AAUW, Am. Hist. Assn., Orgn. Am. History, Semiotics Soc. Am., Nat. Soc. Exptl. Edn., Nat. Urban League, Assn. Black Women Historians (eastern regional dir.), Assn. Study African Am. Life and History, Links, Inc., Nat. Assn. Women Cath. Higher Edn., Translantic Studies Assn., Am. Soc. Environ. Historians, Black and Asian Studies Assn., Alpha Kappa Alpha, Beta Phi Mu. Roman Catholic. Office: Loyola Coll Dept Hist 4501 N Charles St Baltimore MD 21210-2601 E-mail: aleonard@loyola.edu.

LEONARD, SISTER ANNE C., school system administrator; b. NYC, Dec. 22, 1936; d. Patrick A. and Mary T. (McAlpin) L. BS in Edn. and Social Sci., Fordham U., 1962, MA, 1965; CAGS, Boston U., 1972; postgrad., Hunter Coll., U. San Francisco, U. Northern Ill., Notre Dame U. Cert. tchr. K-12, adminstr. N.Y. Tchr., asst. prin., prin. Notre Dame Acad., Staten Island, NY, 1957-68; prin. Maternity B.V.M. Sch., Bourbonnais, Ill., 1968-69, St. Jude the Apostle Sch., South Holland, Ill., 1969-78; dir. Cath.

Elem. Schs. Archdiocese of Chgo., 1978-83, dir. ednl. svcs., mem. Cardinal Bernadin's cabinet, 1983-90, exec. officer commn. ednl. svcs., 1983-90; supt. schs., dir. edn. Archdiocese of Okla. City, 1990-96; U.S. province leader Congregation of Notre Dame, Ridgefield, Conn., 1996—2005, leadership team Montreal, Canada, 2006—. Chair edn. divisn. Cath. Conf. Ill., 1988-90; del. gen. chpt. Congregation Notre Dame, mem. provincial coun., mem. leadership team, 2006—; mem. edn. com. U.S. Cath. Conf. Bishops, Washington, 1985-88; mem. Nat. Cath. Bishops' Millennium Com.; spkr. in field; lectr., presenter workshops; mem. Fortune 500 panel edn. and bus.; devel. mission statement, just principles compensation, new models compensation for prins., 1987-91; initiated, organized Dirs. Edn. Wis., Ill., Ind., Ohio, Mich.; attended symposia in field; mem. com. prep. Office of Cath. Edn. Conciliation Process; exec. officer local sch. bds.; initiated individually guided edn. program St. Jude Sch. Cons. textbooks William H. Sadlier, Inc.; contbr. articles to profl. jours. Trustee DePaul U., 1986—; trustee Midwestern U., 1999—, bd. dirs., vice chair acad. affairs com.; bd. dirs. Jr. Achievement, Chgo., 1984-90, Oklahoma City, 1991-96; mem. NCCJ, 1992-96, Gov. Ill. adv. com. on non-pub. schs., Springfield, 1978-82, planning com. Big Shoulders Project, officer Leadership Conf. of Women Religious (Region I), 1997-2005; mem. Congregation of Notre Dame, 2006. Mem. ASCD, Nat. Cath. Ednl. Assn. (pres. chief adminstrs. Cath. edn. 1991-94, v.p. 1989-91, vice chair bd. 1991-94, task force 1990-91, centennial com. 1997—2002, supervision, pers., curriculum, Educator of Yr. award 1990), Archdiocesan Prins. Assn. (pres. 1973-78), Nat. Religious Retirement Bd. (grant com.), Chgo. Coun. Fgn. Rels., Phi Delta Kappa (Educator of Yr. 1984). Avocations: reading, swimming, travel. Home Phone: 514-933-0142; Office Phone: 514-931-5891. Business E-Mail: aleonard@cnd-m.com.

LEONARD, BETSY ANN, director, writer; d. Herbert Douglas Baker, Jessie Lee and Beverly W. Koeppel (Stepfather); m. Dale Forrest Leonard, Nov. 7, 1981. BS, Fla. State U., Tallahassee, 1975; M in Curriculum and Instrn., San Diego State U., 1992. Cert. tchr. Calif. Calif. coord. Golden State Environ. Edn. Consortium, Sacramento, 1997—98; environ. edn. coord. San Diego Nat. History Mus., 1997—2001; project leader Calif. Inst. for Biodiversity, Oakland, 2002; project coord. hs curriculum project Tijuana River Nat. Estuarine Rsch. Res., Imperial Beach, Calif., 2003—05. Cons. in field. Coord. US Info. Agy., San Diego, 1997; EE grant evaluator Calif. State Dept. Edn., Sacramento, 1993—97; chair edn. com. Project Wildlife, 1986—90; del. U.S./Spain Joint Conf. Edn., Barcelona, 1995; scorer Ednl. Testing Svc., 2003; coord. North Am. Assn. Environ. Edn., 2000. Recipient 1st Pl. Nat. award, YMCA Armed Svcs., 1981, Outstanding Leadership award, Calif. Alliance Enviorn. Edn., 1997. Mem.: Nat. Assn. for Interpretation (bd. dirs. 1997—98, cert., chair environ. edn. sect. 1992—99, Environ. Edn. Svc. award 2002). Democrat. Episcopalian. Avocations: skiing, reading, writing, bicycling. Home: 71 River View Pl Parachute CO 81635 Personal E-mail: betsleon@msn.com.

LEONARD, BILL (J. WILLIAM LEONARD), federal agency administrator; BA History, St. John's U., NYC; MA Internat. Rels., Boston U. Indsl. security rep., NYC; command security officer US Dept. Def.; instr. Def. Indsl. Security Inst., Richmond; dir. Office of Indsl. Security Internat., Brussels, 1989—92; asst. dep. dir. Def. Investigative Service (DIS) US Dept. Def., 1992—96, dir. security programs, 1996—98, dep. asst. sec. (security & info. ops.), 1998—2000, prin. dir. Office Asst. Sec. for Security & Info. Ops., 2000—02; dir. Info. Security Oversight Office (ISOO) The US Nat Archives & Records Adminstrn, Washington, 2002—. Dep. of def. mem. Interagency Security Classification Appeals Panel, 1998—2002. Recipient DIS Exceptional Svc. award, 1987, 1996, DIS Meritorious Svc. award, 1989, 1993, Office Sec. Def. Medal for Meritorious Civilian Svc., US Dept. Def., 2000, Medal for Disting. Civilian Svc., 2001, US Dept. Def, 2002, Presdl. Rank of Meritorious Exec., The White House, 2002. Office: Info Security Oversight Office he US Nat Archives & Records Adminstrn 700 Pennsylvania Ave NW Rm 500 Washington DC 20408-6001 Office Phone: 202-357-5250. E-mail: bill.leonard@nara.gov.*

LEONARD, CHARLES H. (CHUCK LEONARD), air transportation executive; b. 1949; Controller Tex. Ea. Products Pipeline Co., LLC, 1988—89, v.p., 1988—90, CFO, 1989—90, sr. v.p., CFO, 1990—2005, treas., 1996—2002; CFO Eagle Global Logistics (EGL), Inc., Houston, 2006—. Office: EGL Inc Intercontinental Airport 15350 Vickery Dr Houston TX 77032 Office Phone: 281-618-3100, 800-888-4949.

LEONARD, DAVID MORSE, lawyer; b. Akron, Ohio, Dec. 4, 1949; s. Frank O. and Barbara J. Leonard. BS in Chem. Engring., Purdue U., 1972; JD, Emory U., 1975. Bar: Ga. 1975, N.Y. 2005, U.S. Ct. Appeals (4th, 5th and 11th cirs.), U.S. Dist. Ct. (no., mid. and so. dists.) Ga., U.S. Dist. Ct. (so. dist.) Ala., U.S. Dist. Ct. (we. dist.) La.; registered atty. U.S. Patent and Trademark Office. Assoc. Montet & Smith, Atlanta, 1975-79, Hurt, Richardson, Garner, Todd & Cadenhead, Atlanta, 1979-83, ptnr., 1983-85; of counsel Lord, Bissell & Brook LLP, Atlanta, 1985—87, ptnr., 1987—. Mem. panel of arbitrators Am. Arbitration Assn., 1995—, arbitrator, mediator. Mem. ABA (litigation sect., intellectual property sect., tort and ins. practice sect.), Profl. Liability Underwriting Soc., Atlanta Lawyers Club, Atlanta C. of C., Am. Arbitration Assn. (panel of arbitrators). Office: Lord Bissell & Brook LLP Ste 1900 1170 Peachtree St NE Atlanta GA 30309-7675 Office Phone: 404-870-4676.

LEONARD, EDWIN DEANE, lawyer; b. Oakland, Calif., Apr. 22, 1929; s. Edwin Stanley and Gladys Eugenia (Lee) L.; m. Judith Swatland, July 10, 1954; children: Garrick Hillman, Susanna Leonard Hill, Rebecca Leonard McCauley, Ethan York. BA, The Principia, 1950; LLB, Harvard U., 1953; LLM, George Washington U., 1956. Bar: D.C. 1953, Ill. 1953, N.Y. 1957. Assoc. Davis Polk Wardwell Sunderland & Kiendl, NYC, 1956-61; ptnr. Davis Polk & Wardwell, NYC, 1961-97, sr. counsel, 1998—. Trustee the Brearley Sch., N.Y.C., 1980-90; pres. Millbrook Equestrian Ctr., 1983-98. Served to 1st lt. JAGC, 1953-56. Mem. ABA, N.Y. Bar Assn., N.Y. County Bar Assn., Assn. of Bar of City of N.Y. (chmn. various coms.). Home: 157 Conklin Hill Rd Stanfordville NY 12581-5639 Office: Davis Polk & Wardwell 450 Lexington Ave New York NY 10017-3982 Personal E-mail: deaneleonard@worldnet.att.net.

LEONARD, ELMORE JOHN, writer, scriptwriter; b. New Orleans, Oct. 11, 1925; s. Elmore John and Flora Amelia (Rivé) L.; m. Beverly Claire Cline, Aug. 30, 1949 (div. 1977); children: Jane, Peter, Christopher, William, Katherine; m. Joan Leanne Lancaster, Sept. 15, 1979 (dec. 1993); m. Christine Kent, Aug. 19, 1993. PhB, U. Detroit, 1950. Author over 30 novels including Hombre, 1961, Swag, 1976, Unknown Man No. 89, 1977, City Primeval, 1980, Split Images, 1982, Cat Chaser, 1982, La Brava, 1983, Stick, 1983, Glitz, 1985, Bandits, 1987, Touch, 1987, Freaky Deaky, 1988, Killshot, 1989, Get Shorty, 1990, Maximum Bob, 1991, Rum Punch, 1992, Pronto, 1993, Riding the Rap, 1995, Out of Sight, 1996 (Edgar Allan Poe award 1999), Tishomingo Blues, 2002, Mr. Paradise, 2004, The Hot Kid, 2005 (Publishers Weekly Hardcover Bestseller list, 2005); author of screenplays including The Moonshine War, 1970, Joe Kidd, 1972, Mr. Majestyk, 1974, (with Joseph Stinson) Stick, 1985, (with John Steppling) 52 Pick-Up, 1986, (with Fred Walton) The Rosary Murders, 1987, (with Jim Borrelli and Alan Sharp) Cat Chaser, 1990, Jackie Brown, 1997, Cuba Libre, 1998, Be Cool, 1999; cons. (ABC TV) Karen Sisco, 2003—. With USN, 1943-46. Recipient Mystery Writers of Am. Grand Master award, 1992. Mem. Writers Guild of Am., Authors Guild, Mystery Writers of Am., Western Writers of Am. Roman Catholic.

LEONARD, GEOFFREY PORTER, lawyer; m. Sandy Sevier Simmons, July 9, 1988. BA, Trinity Coll., 1978; JD, Georgetown U., 1981. Bar: NY 1982, Calif. 1992. Corp. assoc. Cravath, Swaine & Moore, NYC, 1986—92; ptnr. Orrick, Herrington & Sutcliffe LLP, Menlo Park, Ropes & Gray LLP, San Francisco, 2006. Mem.: NY Bar. Assn., State Bar of Calif. Office: Ropes & Gray LLP One Embarcadero Ctr Ste 2200 San Francisco CA 94111 Office Phone: 415-315-6364. Office Fax: 415-315-4833.*

LEONARD, GEORGE EDMUND, bank executive, credit manager, marketing professional; b. Phoenix, Nov. 20, 1940; s. George Edmund and Marion Elizabeth (Fink) L.; m. Gloria Jean Henry, Mar. 26, 1965 (div. Feb. 1981); children: Tracy Lynn McKinney, Amy Theresa Blanchard, Kristin Jean Steel; m. Mary C. Short, Sept. 22, 1990. Student, Ariz. State U., 1958—60; BS, U.S. Naval Acad., 1964; postgrad., Pa. State U., 1969—70; MBA, U. Chgo., 1073. Commd. ensign USN, 1964, advanced through grades to lt. comdr., 1975; v.p. 1st Nat. Bank Chgo., 1970-75; exec. v.p., chief banking, CFO, chief lending officer Mera Bank, Phoenix, 1975-90, also bd. dirs., 1982-90; pres., CEO Ctrl. Savs., San Diego, 1985-87; chmn., CEO AmBank Holding Co. of Colo., Scottsdale, Ariz., 1990-91, Consumer Guarantee Corp., Phoenix, 1996; pres., CEO Diversified Mgmt. Svcs., Inc., Phoenix, 1991-96, GEL Mgmt. Inc., Phoenix, 1991—; v.p. CFO Western Pacific Airlines, Colorado Springs, 1996-98, bd. dirs., 1996-98; exec. v.p., CFO, treas., sec., dir. fin. Radi Sys. Microware Sys. Corp., Des Moines, 1998—2002, COO, bd. dirs., 2000—01; sr. v.p., chief credit officer Harris Bank N.A., Scottsdale, Ariz., 2002—. Active Phoenix Thunderbirds, 1979—; bd. dirs. Maricopa C.C.s Found., treas., 2nd v.p., 1991-93, 1st v.p., 1993-94, pres., 1994-95, past pres., 1995-96, Camelback Charitable Trust, 1991-92, The Samaritan Found., 1993-96, chmn. fin. com., 1994-96, vice chmn., 1996; bd. dirs. Westminster Village, Inc., 2003—, sec., 2004—; bd. trustees Desert Bot. Gardens, 2004—; mem. City Scottsdale Housing Bd., 2005-. Mem. Phoenix Met. C. of C. (bd. dirs. 1975-82), Inst. Fin. Edn. (bd. dirs. 1980-87, nat. chmn. 1985-86), Ariz. State U. Coll. of Bus. Deans Coun. of 100, Paradise Valley Country Club (bd. dirs. 1991-98, treas. 1992-95, pres. 1995-97), White Mountain Country Club (bd. dirs. 2005—), Kiwanis. Republican. Roman Catholic. Office: Harris Bank NA 6720 N Scottsdale Rd Ste 111 Scottsdale AZ 85253 Home: 11113 E North Ln Scottsdale AZ 85259-4853 Office Phone: 480-951-4616. Personal E-mail: geljr@aol.com.

LEONARD, GUY MEYERS, JR., international holding company executive; b. Bluefield, W.Va., Sept. 22, 1926; s. Guy Meyers and Mabel (Bonham) L.; m. Pat Kirby, June 28, 1949; children: Calvin David, Dinah Lynn. AB, BS, Morris Harvey Coll., 1949; BDiv, Southwestern Bapt. Sem., 1952; STM, Harvard U., 1957. Commd. ensign USN, 1952, advanced through grades to capt., 1968, ret., 1972; dir. R&D Ency. Britannica Ednl. Corp., Chgo., 1972-76; pres. Communication Programming Svcs., inc., Charleston, SC, 1976—; pres. and CEO First Don Trading Co., 1982—. Chmn. and CEO Transocean Ltd., Internat. Holding Co., 1982—86, Marti Div. Co., 2004—; pres. GHL, Inc., Pacific Rim, South Africa, 1991—2004; chmn. Point of Pines Real Estate Devel. Co., 2004—. Cons. drug control programs for schs., cons. Ency. Britannica, Home Mission Bd. and Brotherhood Commn. So. Bapt. Conv. Sec., U.S. Power Squadron, Charleston, 1969; chmn. Spl. Commn. on Drug Abuse for Armed Forces, 1970-72; active Conn. coun. Boy Scouts Am., 1959-62; chmn. stewardship com. Episc. Diocese of S.C., 1994-95; bd. dir. CWA Found. Ch. Adv. Bd. CWA. Decorated Legion of Merit, Meritorious Svc. medal, Navy Commendation medal, Disting. Svc. medal; recipient Disting. Svc. award City of Louisville, 1963. Mem. Harvard Club S.C., C. of C., Trident Chamber (Charleston), Navy League U.S., Ret. Officers Assn., Kiwanis (spl. projects chmn. 1964-65). Achievements include the design and prodn. with Harvard U. and sta. WGBH, Boston, mediated coll. curriculum leading to BS degree for use by naval personnel. Home: 2331 Vanderbilt Dr Charleston SC 29414

LEONARD, HASSE A., psychologist, educator; 1 child, Bianca. BA with honors, U. Hawaii, Manoa, Oahu, 1996; PhD, Calif. Sch. Profl. Psychology, 2001. Adj. prof. Calif. Sch. Profl. Psychology, San Francisco, 2003—; tng. dir. A Better Way, Inc., Berkeley, Calif., 2005—. Cons. Bd. Psychology, Sacramento, 2004—05. Multicultural Ednl. Rsch. Intervention and Treatment grantee, Calif. Sch. Profl. Psychology, 2000. Mem.: APA. Home Phone: 510-932-6460; Office Phone: 510-932-6460. Personal E-mail: hpagel@sbcglobal.net.

LEONARD, HERMAN BEUKEMA (DUTCH), public finance, management, and leadership educator; b. Carlisle Barracks, Pa., Dec. 26, 1952; s. Charles Frederick and Margery Alden (Beukema) L.; m. Kathryn Anne Angell, Oct. 9, 1983; children: Whitney Angell, Dana Angell. AB summa cum laude, Harvard U., 1974, AM, 1976, PhD, 1979. Asst. prof. pub. policy John F. Kennedy Sch. Govt., Harvard U., Cambridge, Mass., 1979-83, assoc. prof., 1983-86, George F. Baker, Jr. prof. pub. mgmt., 1986—, acad. dean for curriculum and instrn., 1992—96, acad. dean for teaching programs, 1996—2000; Eliot I. Snider and Family prof. bus. adminstrn. Harvard Bus. Sch., Harvard U., Cambridge, Mass., 2004—. Co-author: Discrimination in Rural Housing, 1976, The Federal Budget and the States, 1993-99; author: Checks Unbalanced: The Quiet Side of Public Spending, 1986, By Choice or By Chance? Tracking the Values in Massachusetts Public Spending, 1992; contbr. numerous articles on pub. fin. and mgmt. to jours. in field. Mem. Gov.'s Coun. Econ. Policy, Alaska, 1980—82; chmn. Gov.'s Task Force on Coll. Opportunity, Mass., 1987—88; mem. adv. bd. NYC Debt Mgmt., 1990—94; mem. Mass. Performance Enhancement Commn., 1997—98; bd. dirs. Hitachi Found., 2004—, Mass. Health and Ednl. Facilities Authority, 1988—99, Civic Investments, 1992—2005, Harvard Pilgrim Health Care, 2000—, ACLU-Mass., 2005—. Recipient grad. fellowship NSF, 1974; jr. fellow Soc. Fellows, Harvard U., 1976-79; Presdl. scholar, 1970. Mem. Phi Beta Kappa. Office: Harvard U John F Kennedy Sch Govt 79 JFK St Cambridge MA 02138-5801 also: Harvard U Harvard Bus Sch Soldier's Field Rd Boston MA 02163 Business E-Mail: dutch_leonard@harvard.edu.

LEONARD, J. RICH, federal judge, educator; b. 1949; AB, U. N.C., 1971, MEd, 1973; JD, Yale U., 1976. Bar: N.C. 1976. Law clk. to Hon. Franklin T. Dupree, Jr., U.S. Dist. Ct., 1976-78; assoc. Sanford, Adams, McCullough & Beard, 1978-79; magistrate judge for ea. dist. N.C., U.S. Magistrate Ct., 1981-92; bankruptcy judge for ea. dist. N.C., U.S. Bankruptcy Ct., Wilson, 1992-99; chief US bankruptcy judge US Bankruptcy Ct. (ea. dist.) N.C., NC, 1999—. Adj. prof. civil procedure N.C. Ctrl. U. Sch. Law, 1985-86, adj. prof. bankruptcy law, 1995-97; adj. profl. U. N.C., Law Sch., Chapel Hill, 1995; dir., sec.-treas. Nat. Inst. for Dispute Resolution. Mem. ABA, FBA (N.C. adv. coun.), N.C. Bar Assn. (v.p. 1995), Wake County Bar Assn., 4th Circuit Jud. Conf. (com. on case mgmt. and ct. adminstrn.), N.C.-Fed. Jud. Coun. Office: US Bankruptcy Ct E Dist NC 1760 A Parkwood Blvd W Wilson NC 27893-3564 Office Phone: 919-856-4033, 252-237-0248.

LEONARD, J. WAYNE, energy executive; BA in Acctg., Ball State U., 1973; MBA, Ind. U., 1987. CPA, Ind. Various positions PSI Energy, sr. v.p., CFO, 1989-94; group v.p., CFO, Cinergy, 1994-96, pres. energy commodities strategic bus. unit, 1996-98; pres. Cinergy Capital and Trading, 1996-98; pres., COO domestic bus. units, in-charge for internat. ops. Entergy Corp., New Orleans, 1998, CEO, 1999—2006, chmn., CEO, 2006—. Leader BusinessLINC, Mississippi River Delta bus.-to-bus. mentoring. Mem. AICPA. Office: Entergy Corp 639 Loyola Ave New Orleans LA 70113*

LEONARD, JACQUELYN ANN, retired elementary school educator; b. Hollister, Okla., Apr. 2, 1931; d. Alex and Dolly M. (McCurty) McKinney; m. Malvin Paul Leonard, Feb. 6, 1952 (div. Apr. 1993); children: Diana, Andrea. BA in Art Edn. and Pub. Sch. Music, Ctrl. State U., 1955; postgrad., U. Mich., 1955—62, Mich. State U., 1955—62. Pres. Jacquelyn-Jackie Leonard Corp., Lake Orion, Mich., 1994—. Contbr. articles to profl. jours. Contbr. Am. Cares, The Law Enforcement Officers Meml. Fund, Washington. Mem.: Mich. Assn. Ret. Personnel, Nat. Trust. Avocations: reading, singing, piano, swimming. Home: 3091 Oakridge Ct Lake Orion MI 48360

LEONARD, JAMES, law librarian, educator; b. High Point, NC, June 27, 1954; s. Burgess Guy Jr. and Irene (Meekins) L.; m. Judy Ryan, Aug. 17, 1974; children: Jamie Ryan, Burgess Guy III, Sarah Ann Leonard. BA, U. NC, 1975, MSLS, 1980, JD, 1986. Bar: Ohio 1987, D.C. 1988, U.S. Ct. Appeals (6th cir.) 1989, U.S. Supreme Ct. 1990. Tech. svcs. libr. Wake Forest U. Law Libr., Winston-Salem, NC, 1981—83, acting library dir., 1984; dir. Law Libr. Ohio No. U. Pettit Coll. Law, Ada, 1986—97, dir. Legal Writing and Rsch. Program, 1986—92; prof. law, dir. Bounds Law Libr. U. Ala. Sch. Law, Tuscaloosa, 1998—. Mem. ABA, Am. Assn. Law Libraries, Ohio Region Assn. Law Libraries, Ohio State Bar Assn. Democrat. Office: Bounds Law Libr U Ala Sch Law Box 870383 Tuscaloosa AL 35487-0383 Office Phone: 205-348-5927. E-mail: jleonard@law.ua.edu.*

LEONARD, JEFFREY S., lawyer; b. Bklyn., Sept. 14, 1945; m. Maxine L. Bortnick, Dec. 28, 1967; children: Deborah, Jennifer. AB in History, U. Rochester, 1967; JD, U. Ariz., 1974. Bar: Ariz. 1974; U.S. Dist. Ct. Ariz. 1974, U.S. Ct. Appeals (9th cir.) 1974, U.S. Supreme Ct. 1985. Law clk. to judge US Dist. Ct. Ariz., 1974—75; atty. Sacks Tierney P.A., Scottsdale, Ariz., 1975—. Mem. editl. bd. Ariz. Law Rev., 1973-74. Mem. Order of Coif. Office: Sacks Tierney PA 4th Fl 4250 N Drinkwater Blvd Scottsdale AZ 85251-3693 Office Phone: 480-425-2652. Business E-Mail: leonard@sackstierney.com.

LEONARD, JOHN, film and literature critic; b. Wash., DC, Feb. 25, 1939; divorced; children: Andrew, Amy; m. Sue Leonard; 1 stepchild, Jen Nessel. Attended, Harvard U.; BA, U. Calif. Berkeley. Former writer Nat. Review Mag.; former dir. drama and lit. KPFA Radio; lit. critic New York Times Book Review, 1967—71, 1975—, exec. editor, 1971—75; co-editor, books section The Nation Mag., 1995—98. Contbr. articles to newspapers and mags. incl. The Nation, The New Republic, NY Times Review Books, Harper's, Atlantic Monthly, Playboy, Esquire, Harper's Bazaar, Vogue, Newsweek, The Village Voice, and Washington Post; author: (books) The Naked Martini, 1964, Wyke Regis, 1966, Crybaby of the Wetern World, 1969, Black Conceit, 1972, This Pen for Hire, 1973, Private Lives in the Imperial City, 1979, The Last Innocent White Man in America, 1994, Smoke and Mirrors: Violence, Television, and Other American Cultures, 1997, When the Kissing Had to Stop: Cult Studs, Khmer Newts, Langley Spooks, Techno-Geeks, Video Drones, Author Gods, Serial Killers, Vampire Media, Alien Sperm Suckers, Satanic Therapists and Those of Us Who Hold a Left-Wing Grudge in, 1999, Lonesome Rangers: Homeless Minds, Promised Lands, Fugitive Cultures, 2002. Recipient Ivan Sandrof Lifetime Achievement award, Nat. Book Critics Circle, 2007. Office: NY Mag 14th Fl 444 Madison Ave New York NY 10022*

LEONARD, JOSEPH B., airline company executive; b. 1943; BS, Auburn U., 1967. V.p. ops. svcs. Eastern Air Lines, Inc., Miami, Fla., 1984-85, sr. v.p. ops. svcs., 1985, exec. v.p., gen. mgr. airline ops., 1985-86, pres., COO, 1986—91; mgmt. positions through sr. v.p., pres. & CEO aerospace mktg. sales & svc. Allied Signal, 1993—99; chmn., CEO Airtran Holdings, Inc., Orlando, Fla., 1999—. Bd. dir. Walter Industries Inc. Bd. dir. Metro Atlanta C. of C. Mem.: Commerce Club (bd. dir.), The Wings Club (pres.). Office: 9955 AirTran Blvd Orlando FL 32827*

LEONARD, JOSEPH HOWARD, staff specialist; b. Cambridge, Md., Oct. 20, 1952; s. Joseph Francis and Catherine (Hill) L.; m. Jacquelyn Lee McCall, June 7, 1975 (div. Dec. 1981); m. Margaret Ann Shenton, June 26, 1982 (div. Dec. 2004); children: Stephanie Kristina, Jacquelyn Margaret. BA in Psychology, Salisbury State U., 1976; MA in Rehab. Counseling, Gallaudet U., 1979; postgrad., Washington Coll., 1984, Wasington Coll., 1988, U. Md., 1986—87, San Diego State U., 1996, Johns Hopkins U., 1998. Cert. profl. counselor, Md. Instr., program coord. Dorchester Devel. Unit, Inc., Cambridge, 1976—77; rehab. counselor Tex. Rehab. Commn., Austin, 1979; instr. Am. Sign Lang., develop. disabilities Chesapeake Coll., Wye Mills, Md., 1979—90; case mgr., coord. spl. programs Dorchester County Health Dept., Cambridge, 1979—90; ind. interpreter Am. Sign Lang. Md., 1979—; exec. dir. Deaf Ind. Living Assn., Inc., Salisbury, Md., 1990—2005; adj.faculty, interpreter tng. program Catonsville C.C., Md., 1995—2000; state coord. deaf svcs. divsn. Rehab. Svcs., Balt., 2005—. V.p., bd. dirs. Deaf Ind. Living Assn., Inc., Md., 1984-90; trustee Md. Sch. for the Deaf, 1985-02, pres., 1996-97; adv. bd. Devel. Disabilities program Chesapeake Coll., 1986-90; mem. Gov.'s Commn. on the Hearing Impaired, Md., 1984-90; surveyor Applied Rsch. and Evaluation U., U. Md., 1988-89; mental health adv. com. for deaf and hearing impaired, Md., 1986—; adv. coun. Office for the Deaf and Hard of Hearing, Md., 2001—, chair 2003—. Contbr. articles to profl. jours. Asst. scoutmaster Boy Scouts Am., Cambridge, 1973-78; v.p. bd. dirs. Dorchester County Family YWCA, 1985; pres. bd. dirs. Dorchester Assn. for Devel. Disabled, 1979-88; bd. dirs. Ea. Shore Ctr. Ind. Living, 1998-2005, v.p., 2003-04, Md. Assn. of Deaf, 1982-86; bd. dirs. Md. Assn. of Cmty. Svcs., 1992-02; pres. Trappe Little League Baseball and Softball Assn., 2000-02. With USN, 1970-73, with USCGR, 1975-86. Recipient Founder's award Gallaudet U., 1993, Disting. Svc. award Md. Assn. of the Deaf, 1995, Agy. Innovation award Md. Assn. Cmty. Svcs., 1996. Mem. Am. Deafness and Rehab. Assn., Md. Rehab. Assn., Nat. Assn. Deaf, Registry of Interpreters for the Deaf (bd. dirs. Potomac chpt. 1996-2000), Chi Sigma Iota, Psi Chi, Rho Sigma Chi. Roman Catholic. Avocations: photography, boating, canoeing, sailing, woodcarving. Home: 32655 Meadowlark Ln Easton MD 21601 Office: Divsn Rehab Svcs Workforce and Tech Ctr 2301 Argonne Dr Baltimore MD 21218 Home Phone: 410-822-8071. Business E-Mail: jhleonard@dors.state.md.us.

LEONARD, JUDITH PRICE, educational advisor; b. Milw., July 10, 1941; d. Ralph H. and Sylvia (Shames) Price; m. Richard Black Leonard Jr., Dec. 15, 1962 (dec. Dec. 1978); m. Norman Crasilneck, Aug. 31, 1991. BS in Math., Antioch U., Yellow Springs, Ohio, 1963; MS in Math., St. Louis U., 1970. Tchr. math. Ferguson Florissant Schs., Mo., 1963—94, coord., 1971—73; mentor, co-dir., faculty advisor Engelmann Math. & Sci. Inst., U. Mo., St. Louis, 1988—96; supr. student tchrs. U. Mo., St. Louis, 1995—96; coord. Regional Inst. Sci. Edn., St. Louis, 1996—2000; evaluator and cons. math. programs St. Louis Pub. Schs., 1994—2005, 2007; cons. math. programs Riverview Gardens Schs., 2006—07; faculty advisor NSF Young Scholars, U. Mo, St. Louis, 1997, NSF Students & Tchrs. as Rsch. Scientists, U. Mo., St. Louis, 1998—99. Co-dir. Post Dispatch and Monsanto Greater St. Louis Sci. Fair, 1998—99; adv. bd. Greater St. Louis Sci. Fair, 1997—2007, Intel Internat. Sci. and Edn. Fair, 1996—99, adults in charge, 1997—99, fair dir., 1999, mem. leadership coun., 2005—07; chair Discovery Young Scientist Challenge, St. Louis, 1999—2007; sec. exec. bd. Math. Educators Greater St. Louis, 2001—07; mem. Math. Sci. Network of Greater St. Louis, 1995—2007; math. cons. U. Mo., St. Louis, 2002—03; presenter, judge, chmn. judges for math. computer sci., physics and engring. Jr. Sci., Engring. and Humanities Symposium, 1995—2001, 2003—06. Author: Word Problems, Basic Skills Instructional Fair, 1996; author, editor: (brochure) Teacher Linking Collaborative, 1997, 2002; editor 3 Math. Books, 2002, 5th and 6th Pre Algebra, 2002. Hon. Engelmann scholar Engelmann Math. and Sci. Inst., St. Louis, 1993, NSF Young scholar U. Mo., St. Louis, 1997; recipient Math. Edn. award Math. Educators Greater St. Louis, 1994, NSF STARS award U. Mo., St. Louis, 2000, Recognition award Acad. Sci. St. Louis, 2006. Mem. NEA, Nat. Coun. Tchrs. Math., Nat. Coun. Suprs. Math., Mo.

Coun. Tchrs. Math. (life), Ferguson Florissant NEA (life). Avocations: tennis, biking, walking. Home: 22 Bellerive Acres Saint Louis MO 63121-4321 Personal E-mail: judy@judyleonard.net.

LEONARD, KURT JOHN, retired plant pathologist, director; b. Holstein, Iowa, Dec. 6, 1939; s. Elvin Elsworth and Irene Marie (Helkenn) L.; m. Maren Jane Simonsen, May 28, 1961; children: Maria Catherine, Mary Alice, Benjamin Andrew. BS, Iowa State U., 1962; PhD, Cornell U., 1968. Plant pathologist Agrl. Rsch. Svc. USDA, Raleigh, NC, 1968-88, dir. Cereal Disease Lab. U. Minn. St. Paul, 1988—2001. Author: (with others) Annual Review of Phytopathology, 1980; co-editor: Plant Disease Epidemiology, vol. 1, 1986, vol. 2, 1989, Fusarium Head Blight of Wheat and Barley, 2003; editor-in-chief: Phytopathology, 1981-84, Am. Phytopathol. Soc. Press, 1994-97; contbr. over 130 articles to profl. jours., chpts. to books. Fellow Am. Phytopathol. Soc. (coun. 1981-84, 94-97); mem. Am. Mycol. Soc., Internat. Soc. Plant Pathology (councilor 1982-93), Brit. Soc. Plant Pathology, Phi Kappa Phi, Sigma Xi, Gamma Sigma Delta. Achievements include description of new species and genera of plant pathogenic fungi; research on spread of disease through crop mixtures, on relationships between virulence and fitness in plant pathogenic fungi. Office: U Minn Dept Plant Pathology Saint Paul MN 55108

LEONARD, LAURA L., lawyer; b. 1956; AB, U. Calif., Davis, 1978; JD, Loyola U., Chgo., 1983. Bar: Ill. 1983. With Sidley & Austin, Chgo., 1983—, ptnr., 1991—. Lectr. on environ. aspects of bus. trans., including Northwestern U. Kellogg Grad. Sch. Mgmt.; mem. adv. bd. BNA's Environ. Due Digigence Guide. Office: Sidley & Austin Bank One Plz 10 S Dearborn St Chicago IL 60603 Fax: 323-853-7620. E-mail: lleonard@sidley.com.

LEONARD, MICHAEL A., retired automotive executive; b. Cadillac, Mich., Aug. 3, 1937; s. Hugel A. and Mildred (Johnson) L.; m. Frances Erickson, June 18, 1960; children: Kristin, Anne. MA, Alma Coll., 1959; MBA, Wayne State U., 1964; MS, MIT, 1971. Exec. Chrysler Corp., Highland Park, Mich., 1959—75; group v.p. Bendix Corp., Southfield, Mich., 1975—83; v.p., group exec. Allied Signal Automotive, Bloomfield Hills, Mich., 1983—91; pres. Harman, Inc., Southfield, 1991—94; mng. ptnr. Exec. Resources Inc., Bloomfield Hills, 1994—2002. Bd. dirs. Kalyani Brake Co., Pune, India, Bendix France, Paris, Bendix Italy, and fgn. subs. Trustee Alma (Mich.) Coll.; chmn. Presbyn. Villages of Mich. Sloan fellow, MIT. Mem. Soc. Automotive Engrs., Delta Sigma Phi (pres. 1958-59). Presbyterian. Avocations: swimming, golf, boating. Home: 37215 S Summit Crest Ct Tucson AZ 85739-1438 Personal E-mail: bordertwo@aol.com.

LEONARD, MICHAEL STEVEN, industrial engineering educator; b. Salisbury, NC, Feb. 2, 1947; s. Charles Thomas and Dorothy Francis (Loflin) L.; m. Mary Elizabeth Stewart, June 21, 1969; children: Dorothy Elizabeth, Amanda Brooke, Gabrielle Francis. B in Engring., U. Fla., 1970, M in Engring., 1972, PhD, 1973. Registered profl. engr., Mo., S.C. Asst. prof. health systems rsch. ctr. Georgia Tech, Atlanta, 1973-75; asst. prof. indsl. engring. U. Mo., Columbia, 1975-79, assoc. prof. indsl. engring., 1979-82, prof. indsl. engring., 1982-90, dept. chmn. indsl. engring., 1985-90; chmn. dept. indsl. engring. Clemson (S.C.) U., 1990—95, 2001—03; sr. assoc. dean Mercer U., Sch. Engring., Ga., 2004—. Bd. dirs. Accreditation Bd. Engring. and Tech., Balt., 1999-2005. Editor Jour. Soc. for Health Systems, 1989-91; contbr. articles to profl. jours. Evaluation adv. com. Am. Blood Commn., Washington, 1977-80; bd. dirs. Am. Cancer Soc. Boone County Mo. unit, Columbia, 1978-90. Mem. Soc. Health Systems (bd. dirs. 1989-94, pres. elect 1991-92, pres. 1992-93), Inst. Indsl. Engrs. (nat. dir. career guidance 1987-95, v.p. acad. affairs 1995-97, bd. trustees 2006—), Mo. Soc. Profl. Engrs (cen. chpt. treas. 1988-89, v.p. 1989-90). Office: Mercer Univ Sch Engring Macon GA 31207-0001 Office Phone: 478-301-2520. Business E-Mail: leonard_ms@mercer.edu.

LEONARD, NAOMI EHRICH, aerospace engineer, educator; BSE, Princeton U., NJ, 1985; MS, U. Md., College Park, 1991, PhD, 1994. Engr. elec. power ind.; asst. prof., mech. and aerospace engring. Princeton U., 1994—99, assoc. prof., 1999—2003, prof., 2003—. Author: of numerous sci. jour. articles, including Journal of Dynamical Control Systems, Physica D, and Automatica. Named a MacArthur Fellow, 2004. Office: Dept Mech and Aerospace Engring D 234 Engring Quadrangle Princeton Univ Princeton NJ 08544 Office Phone: 609-258-5129. Office Fax: 609-258-6109. Business E-Mail: naomi@princeton.edu.

LEONARD, R. MICHAEL, lawyer; b. Atlanta, Feb. 27, 1953; s. Charles C. and Catherine (Martin) L.; m. Margaret Ellen Mead, June 29, 1985 (div. 1993); 1 child, Sarah Marie; m. Michelle Merritt, May 27, 2001, 1 child, Eleanor Iris. AB, U. N.C., 1975, JD with honors, 1978. Bar: Ala. 1978, N.C. 1987. Assoc. Cabaniss, Johnston, Gardner, Dumas & O'Neal, Birmingham, Ala., 1978-85, ptnr., 1985-86; assoc. Womble Carlyle Sandridge & Rice, Winston-Salem, N.C., 1986-88, ptnr., 1988—. Author: Trail and Naturalist's Guide to Oak Mountain State Park, Alabama, 1982. Bd. dirs. Ala. Conservancy, Birmingham, 1981-85, Ruffner Mountain Nature Ctr., Birmingham, 1982-86, pres. 1985-86, Nature Sci. Ctr., Winston-Salem, N.C., 1987-91, Piedmont Land Conservancy, Greensboro, N.C., 1989-91; bd. dirs. Ala. Trails Assn., Birmingham, 1985—, founder, pres., 1985-87; trustee N.C. Nat. Heritage Found., Raleigh, 1989-92; gov.'s appointee bd. trustees N.C. Natural Heritage Trust Fund, 1994—, Ala. scenic Byways Program Adv. Coun., 2000-02; nat. adv. coun. Trust for Pub. Land, San Francisco, 1991—; mem. adv. coun. N.C. Yr. of the Mtns., 1995-96; mem. Nat. Coun. Conservation Fund, Arlington, Va., 1997—; pres. Bethania (N.C.) Hist. Property Owners Assn., Inc., 1996—; founding chmn. Ga. Pinhoti Trail Assn., Rome, 1996—; bd. dirs. Bethania Historical Assn., 1996—, Coalition for the Blue Ridge Pkwy, Asheville, N.C., 1997-2000, Bethabara Hist. Park, Winston-Salem, 2001—, Conservation Fund, 2004—; adv. coun. Blue Ridge Pkwy. Found., Winston-Salem, 1998—, High Country Conservancy, Boone, N.C., 1999-2003; bd. visitors Warren Wilson Coll., Black Mtn., N.C., 1999—, U. N.C., Chapel Hill, 1999—. Recipient Chevron Conservation award, San Francisco, 1998, Leon E. Rice Cmty. Svc. award, Winston-Salem, 1998, E-Town E-chievement award, Boulder, Colo., 1997, Pres.'s Conservationist of Yr. award Conservation Fund, Arlington, 1996, Oak Leaf award Nature Conservancy, Washington, 1991, Sol Feinstone Environ. award Coll. Environ. Sci. & Forestry, SUNY, Rochester, 1991, Chpt. Svc. award N.C. Chpt. Sierra Club, 1990, Malcolm Stewart Conservationist of Yr. award Ala. Conservancy, Birmingham, 1983, N.C. Wildlife Fedn. Environ. Essay award, 1970. Mem. Ala. Bar Assn., N.C. Bar Assn., Forsyth County Bar Assn., Winston-Salem Rotary Club, Carolina Club, Order of Coif, Phi Beta Kappa, Phi Eta Sigma. Democrat. Avocations: writing, hiking, mountain climbing, camping, turkey hunting. Office: Womble Carlyle Sandridge & Rice One West Fourth St Winston Salem NC 27101-4019

LEONARD, RAYMOND W., historian, educator; b. Wichita, Kans., May 19, 1959; BA in History, Wichita State U., Kans., 1981, MA in History, 1985; MA in Soviet and East European Studies, U. Kans., Lawrence, 1987, PhD in History, 1997. Instr. dept. history and anthropology U. Ctrl. Mo., Warrensburg, Mo., 1998—2003, asst. prof. history dept. history and anthropology, 2003—. Actor: (game) Purged in Blood; contbr. numerous book reviews, articles to encyclopedias. Recipient Oswald P. Backus II Meml. award, U. Kans., 1998; fellow, Ky. U. Ctr. Russian and East European Studies, 1998, Nat. Holocaust Edn. Found., 2000. Office: Univ Ctrl Mo 136 Wood Warrensburg Mo 64093 Home Phone: 660-422-6980; Office Phone: 660-543-4595. Business E-Mail: leonard@cmsu1.cmsu.edu.

LEONARD, RICHARD HART, journalist, educator; b. NYC, May 23, 1921; s. Richard Barstow and Stella Burnham (Hart) L.; m. Barbara Klausner, July 11, 1948; children: Laurie, Lisa. BA, U. Wis., 1947. Reporter Milw. Jour., 1947, picture editor, 1948, with Madison (Wis.) bur., 1949-50, state desk, 1951-52, state editor, 1953-62, mng. editor, 1962-66; editor, v.p. Milw. Jour. Co., 1967-85; ret., 1986; editor-in-residence East-West Ctr., Honolulu, 1987. Sr. fellow East-West Ctr., 1988-89; mem. Pulitzer Prize Bd., 1976-86; Nieman prof. journalism Marquette U., 1989-99, emeritus, 1999—. With AUS, 1942-46. Recipient Carr Van Anda award, Ohio U., 1972, Disting. Svc. award, U. Wis., 1973, East-West Ctr., 1989. Mem. Am. Soc. Newspaper Editors, Internat. Press Inst. (chmn. 1984-86), Milw. Press Club (pres. 1965, elected Hall of Fame), Sigma Delta Chi (nat. pres. 1976), Phi Kappa Phi. Presbyterian. Personal E-mail: dickleonard@wi.rr.com.

LEONARD, THOMAS, lawyer; b. Phila., Sept. 5, 1946; s. Thomas Aloysius and Mary Teresa (Kelly) Leonard; m. Kathleen Mary Duffy; children: Sarah, Mary Kate, Tom. BS, Drexel U., 1968; JD, Temple U., 1971. Bar: Pa., U.S. Supreme Ct., U.S. Ct. Appeals (3d cir.), U.S. Dist. Ct. (ea., mid., we. dists.) Pa., U.S. Dist. Ct. (so. dist.) N.J., U.S. Dist. Ct. Utah, U.S. Dist. Ct. (so. dist.) N.Y. Assoc. Dilworth, Paxson, Kalish & Kauffman, Phila., 1972-76, ptnr., 1976—79, 1983—91, sr. ptnr., mem. exec. com., 1979—83; controller City of Phila., 1991—; chmn. litigation dept., sr. ptnr., permanent mem. mgmt. com. Obermayer, Rebmann, Maxwell and Hippel, Phila., 1991—. Bd. dirs. Fed. Nat. Mortgage Assn., Independence Blue Cross, World Affair Coun. Phila., Cora Social Svcs., Pa. Bus. Bank, U.S. Facilities, Hahnemann Hosp.; chmn. Permalith Plastics. Mem. editl. bd. Amran's Pa. Practice, 1972; contbr. articles to profl. jours. Vice chmn. Phila. Gas Commn., 1979—83; register wills City of Phila., 1976—79; mem. disciplinary bd. Supreme Ct., Pa., 1991—95, vice chmn., 1995—96, chmn., 1996—, Delaware Valley Real Estate Investment Fund, 1999—, Crowley Chemical, 2007; mem. coun. Phila. Orch., 1981—86; mem. Dem. Nat. Com., Washington, 1976—83, mem. fin. com., 1988, vice chair fin., 1993—, Pa. fin. chair, 1993—, bd. dirs.; del. Dem. Nat. Conv., 1976, 1980, 1992, 1996; chmn. Pa. fin. com. Clinton for Pres., 1992, 1996; co-chair Rendell for Mayor, 1991, 1995; bd. dirs. Acad. Scis., Phila., 1981—85; pres. Pa. chpt. Irish Am. Partnership. Capt. US Army, 1971—77. Recipient Man of the Yr. award, Emerald Soc., 1979, Korean-Am. Friendship Soc., 1982, Carmel Humanitarian award, Haifa U., 1981, Merit award, Chapel of Four Chaplains, 1983. Mem.: ABA, Phila. Bar Assn. (bd. govs. 1979—82), Pa. Bar Assn., Sierra Club (past pres.), Racquet Club, Union League. Roman Catholic. Office: Obermayer Rebmann Maxwell and Hippel 1617 John F Kennedy Blvd Fl 19 Philadelphia PA 19103-1821 Office Phone: 215-665-3220. Business E-Mail: thomas.leonard@obermayer.com.

LEONARD, THOMAS C., librarian, dean; BA (hon.), Univ. Mich., 1966; PhD in History, Univ. Calif., 1973. Prof., former assoc. dean, grad. sch. journalism U. Calif., Berkeley, Calif., interim univ. libr., 2000—01, libr. dir., 2001—. Spkr., cons. in field. Author: Above the Battle: War-Making in America from Appomattox to Versailles, 1978, The Power of the Press: The Birth of American Political Reporting, 1986, News for All: America's Coming of Age with the Press, 1995; contbr. numerous articles to profl. jours. Office: U Calif Berkeley Libr 245 Doe Libr MC 6000 Berkeley CA 94720-6000 Office Phone: 510-642-3773. Business E-Mail: tleonard@library.berkeley.edu.*

LEONARD, TIMOTHY DWIGHT, judge; b. Beaver, Okla., Jan. 22, 1940; s. Dwight and Mary Evelyn Leonard; m. Nancy Louise Laughlin, July 15, 1967; children: Kirstin Dione, Ryan Timothy, Tyler Dwight. BA, U. Okla., 1962, JD, 1965; student, Mil. Naval Justice Sch., 1966. Bar: Okla. 1965, U.S. Dist. Ct. (no. and we. dists.) Okla. 1969, U.S. Ct. Appeals (10th cir.) 1969, U.S. Supreme Ct. 1970. Asst. atty. gen. State of Okla., 1968-70; mem. Okla. Senate, 1979-88; ptnr. Blankenship, Herrold, Russell et al, Oklahoma City, 1970-71, Trippet, Leonard & Kee, Beaver, 1971-88; of counsel Huckaby, Fleming et al, Oklahoma City, 1988-89; U.S. atty. Western Dist. Okla., 1988-92; judge U.S. Dist. Ct. (we. dist.) Okla., 1992—. Guest lectr. Oklahoma City U., 1988—89; mem. U.S. Atty. Gen.'s Adv. Com., 1990—92, chmn. office mgmt. and budget subcom., 1990—92, jud. conf. com. on fin. disclosure, 1998—2006, jud. coun. of 10th cir., 1999—2001, 10th cir. adv. coun., 2002—05; adj. prof. Okla. U. Sch. Law, 2000—05. Co-author: 4 Days, 40 Hours, 1970. Rep. Party candidate for lt. gov. of Okla., 1986; minority leader Okla. State Senate, 1985-86; White House mil. aide, Washington, 1966-67; ex officio mem. Okla. State Fair Bd., Oklahoma City, 1987-90; mem. Gov.'s Coun. on Sports and Phys. Edn., Oklahoma City, 1987-89; mem. Donna Nigh Found., Edmond, Okla., 1987-89. Lt. USN, 1965-68. Named Outstanding Legislator, Okla. Sch. Bd. Assn., 1988. Fellow ABA; mem. Okla. Bar Assn., Okla. County Bar, Phi Alpha Delta, Beta Theta Pi. Republican. Presbyterian. Avocations: golf, basketball, running, reading. Office: US Courthouse 200 NW 4th St Ste 5012 Oklahoma City OK 73102-3031 Office Phone: 405-609-5300.

LEONARD, WALTER RAYMOND, retired biology professor; b. Scott County, Va., July 5, 1923; s. Homer Stanley and Minnie Eunice (Neal) L.; m. Alice Ann McCaskill, Sept. 1, 1951; children— Leslie Ann, Walter Raymond. BA, Tusculum Coll., Greeneville, Tenn., 1946; MA, Vanderbilt U., 1947, PhD, 1949. Mem. faculty Wofford Coll., Spartanburg, S.C., 1949-93, John M. Reeves prof. biology, 1954-87, William R. Kenan Jr. prof. biology, 1987-93, William R. Kenan Jr. prof. emeritus, 1993—. Instl. rev. bd. mem. Spartanburg Regional Med. Ctr., 1994-98; faculty athletic rep. NCAA. With USAAF, 1942—43. Named to Sports Hall of Fame, Tusculum Coll., 1983; Walter Raymond Leonard scholarship created Wofford Coll., 1973; W. Ray Leonard award established Beta Beta Beta, 1993; W. Ray Leonard Retirement Fund established Former Students Wofford Coll., 1993, disting. citizen award Wofford Coll. Nat. Alumni Assn., 1999. Mem. AAAS, S.C. Acad. Sci., Scabbard and Blade (hon.), Lamda Chi Alpha (named to Hall of Fame 1996), Letterman's Club (hon.). Methodist. Achievements include rsch. on cell metabolism. Home: 228 Arbours Coommons Ct Spartanburg SC 29307-2938 Office: Wofford Coll N Church St Spartanburg SC 29301 Personal E-mail: wrleonard2006@yahoo.com.

LEONARD, WILLIAM, automotive supplies and retired food services company executive; BA, NYU; MBA, U. Chgo., 1965. Pres. ARATEX services Aramark Corp., Phila., 1984—92, pres. uniform services, 1992—93, exec. v.p., pres. global food & support services, 1993—96, pres., COO, 1997—2003, pres., CEO, 2004—05; non-exec. chmn. The Pep Boys-Manny, Moe & Jack, Phila., 2006—, interim CEO, 2006—07. Bd. dirs. The Pep Boys-Manny, Moe & Jack, 2002—. Office: The Pep Boys-Manny Moe & Jack 3111 W Allegheny Ave Philadelphia PA 19132*

LEONARDO, ANN ADAMSON, marketing and sales consultant; b. Hamilton, Lanark, Scotland, Jan. 4, 1944; d. James Walker and Margaret Patterson (Burnside) Adamson; m. John Constantine Leonardo, Jr., Mar. 29, 1975; 1 child, Elizabeth Margaret. BA in Bus., McGill U., Montreal, Que., Can., 1970. Market rsch. mgr. MacLaren Advt., Toronto, Ont., Can., 1965-70; group product mgr. Menley & James, Montreal, 1970-74; mktg. mgr. Maybelline divsn. Plough, Toronto, 1074-75; v.p. mktg. Van De Kamp's Bakery, Glendale, Calif., 1976-80; v.p. mktg. and sales Cal West Periodicals, Oakland, 1980-84; mktg. cons., San Francisco, 1984-87; pes., owner MicroCosmic Rsch., Ketchum, Idaho, 1988—. Founding dir., bd. dirs. Family House Inc., San Francisco, 1981—90. Bd. dirs. Sagebrush Equestrian Training Ctr. Handicapped, Hailey, Idaho, 2004—, Sun Valley Summer Symphony, Idaho, 2005—. Home: 77 6516 Alii Drive Kailua Kona HI 96740 Personal E-mail: AAL5711@aol.com.

LEONARDO, JAMES M., hematologist, educator, oncologist, director; b. Staten Island, Ny, Oct. 22, 1954; m. Kathleen Dorrian Leonardo, Sept. 26, 1981; children: Michael, Anne. PhD in Biology, Temple U., Phila., 1980; MD, U. Miami, Fla., 1990. Diplomate Am. Bd. Internal Medicine, 1993, in hematology Am. Bd. Internal Medicine, 1996, in oncology Am. Bd. Internal Medicine, 1997. Assoc. prof. medicine Brody Sch. Medicine, Greenville, NC, 1996—2004; assoc. dir. Bassett Regional Cancer Program, Bassett Healthcare, Cooperstown, NY, 2005—; clin. assoc. prof. medicine Columbia U. Coll. Physicians and Surgeons, NYCV, NY, 2005—. Fellow: ACP; mem.: Am. Soc. Law, Medicine and Ethics, European Soc. Med. Oncology, Am. Soc. Clin. Oncology. Home: 83 Chestnut St Cooperstown NY 13326 Office: Bassett Healthcare 1 Atwell Rd Cooperstown NY 13326 Home Phone: 607-547-6076; Office Phone: 607-547-7887. Business E-Mail: james.leonardo@bassett.org.

LEON AZOFEIFA, PEDRO, molecular biologist; b. Costa Rica; Grad., Baylor U., U. Oreg. Tchr. to prof. dept. physiology U. Costa Rica Cell and Molecular Biology Rsch. Ctr., San Jose, 1975—, dir.; dir. Ctr. Advanced Technologies Univ. Couns. Pub. Univs., Costa Rica. Contbr. articles to sci. jours. Founding mem., pres. Nat. Parks Found. Recipient George Burch award, Smithsonian Instn., Biology prize, Third World Acad. Scis., 2006; grantee Guggenheim Found. fellowship. Mem.: NAS (fgn. assoc.), Costa Rica Acad. Scis., Orgn. Tropical Studies (pres. exec. com.). Office: U Costa Rica Ciudad Univ Rodrigo Facio Brenes San Pedro de Montes de Oca San José Costa Rica E-mail: pleon@conare.ac.cr.

LEONE, JOSEPH M., finance company executive; BBA, CUNY; student in Mgmt., Harvard U. From mem. staff to sr. v.p., controller Mfrs. Hanover Corp., 1982—87, sr. v.p., controller, 1987—91; exec. v.p. Sales and Fin. Unit CIT Group, Livingston, NJ, 1991—95, exec. v.p., CFO, 1995—2003, vice-chmn., CFO, 2003—. Vice chmn. Children's Specialized Hosp. Found., Mountainside, NJ; bd. trustees Ramapo Coll. Found. Mem.: AICPA, Fin. Execs. Inst., N.Y. Soc. CPAs. Office: CIT Group 1 CIT Drive Livingston NJ 07039*

LEONE, LAWRENCE JOSEPH, real estate broker; b. Kansas City, Nov. 18, 1945; s. Joseph Lawrence Leone and Vera Thellis McCann; m. Janine Marie Wagner; children: Theresa Marie, Anita Jo, Lawrence Joseph, Joseph Vincent. Grad. high sch., Kansas City. Mechanic, tech. Trans World Airlines, Kansas City, 1968—97; sales Victor-Ross Realtoes, Kansas City, 1972—76, Century 21, Kansas City, 1976—82; broker Era Martin Ho. Realty, Platte City, 1982—94, Realty Execs., Kansas City, 1997—. Mem., pres. CLS Multiple Listing Svc., Kansas City, 1985—90. Vol. Habitat for Humanity, Kansas City, 1998—; bd. dirs. Platte County Hwy. G.P., Platte County Regional Sewer, 1994—96. Sgt. USAF, 1964—68. Mem.: Mensa. Republican. Mem. Assembly God Ch. Avocations: golf, scuba diving, travel, tennis. Office: Realty Execs Area Realtors 100 NW Englewood Rd Kansas City MO 64118

LEONE, STEPHEN JOSEPH, language educator, computer technician, consultant; b. Nyack, NY, Sept. 24, 1953; s. Anthony John and Anne Helen (Renella) L.; m. Dee Ann Hammond, July 15, 1989; children: Stephanie Kara, Rebecca Dawn. BA in English and Edn., LaSalle U., Phila., 1975; MA in English, Villanova U., 1982; DArts in English, St. John's U., Queens, NY, 2006. Cert. educator NY, Pa. Tchr. Bishop Egan HS, Cath. Schs. of Phila., Fairless Hills, Pa., 1975-82, Sewanhaka HS, Ctrl. HS Dist., Elmont, NY, 1982-85, Farmingdale HS, Farmingdale, NY, 1985-88, Manhattanville Coll., Purchase, NY, 1990-94, Westchester CC, Valhalla, NY, 1989—, program adminstr., 2001—; tchr. Rockland CC, Suffern, NY, 1993—. Computer cons. Nyack Fire Dept., 1993—; adv. lit. mag. Bishop Egan H.S., 1978-80; adv. drama club Sewanhaka H.S. Ctrl. H.S. Dist., Elmont, N.Y., 1982-85; English curriculum coord. Verizon Next Step Program, 2001—. Editor D.A. Report, 1996-98. Founding mem. Rockland County YMCA Youth Svcs., Nyack, 1985-88; chmn. Nyack YMCA Bd. Mgrs., 1986-88; chair Mazeppa Planning Com., Nyack, 1985-95; sec. Mazeppa Engine Co. #2, Nyack, 1982-91, pres., 1991-97. Named Am. Legion Good Citizen, Nyack; Recipient Outstanding Programs in English award, Two Year College Assn.-Natl. Coun. Tchrs. of English, 2002. Mem. MLA, Nat. Coun. Tchrs. of English, Conf. on Coll. Composition, Alliance Computers and Writing, LaSalle Edn. Alumni Assn. Home: 118 Helene Rd Valley Cottage NY 10989-2623 Office: Westchester CC 75 Grasslands Rd Valhalla NY 10595 Office Phone: 914-606-6658. Personal E-mail: sjleone@juno.com. Business E-Mail: steve.leone@sunywcc.edu.

LEONE, WILLIAM CHARLES, retired manufacturing executive; b. Pitts., May 3, 1924; s. Joseph and Fortuna (Sammarco) L.; m. Sara Jane Hollenback, Aug. 26, 1950; children: William Charles, David M., Patricia Ann, Mary Jane. BS, Carnegie Inst. Tech., 1944, MS, 1948, DSc, 1952. Asst. prof. engring. Carnegie Inst. Tech., Pitts., 1946-53; mgr. Indsl. Sys. divsn. Hughes Aircraft, LA, 1953-59; v.p., gen. mgr., dir. Rheem Califone, LA, 1960, Rheem Electronics, LA, 1960-68; group v.p. Rheem Mfg. Co., 1968-71, exec. v.p. NYC, 1971-72, pres., 1972-76, also dir.; pres. City Investing Co. Internat., Inc., 1972-76; pres., dir. Farah Mfg. Co., El Paso, Tex., 1976-77; bus. cons., 1977-79; acting vice chmn. McCulloch Oil Corp. (MCO), LA, 1979-80, also bd. dirs.; pres., dir. MAXXAM Inc. (formerly MCO Holdings, Inc.), 1980-90; vice chmn. MAXXAM Inc., 1990-92. Chmn., CEO, dir. Pacific Lumber Co., 1986-90, Horizon Corp., 1984-89. Author: Production Automation and Numerical Control; contbr. articles to tech. jours.; patentee in field. Trustee Carnegie Mellon U., 1986-92. Lt. (j.g.) USN, 1944—46. Mem. ASME, IEEE, Am. Inst. Aerospace and Aeronautics, Sigma Xi, Tau Beta Pi, Pi Tau Sigma, Theta Tau, Pi Mu Epsilon. Home: 2209 Chelsea Rd Palos Verdes Peninsula CA 90274-2603 Personal E-mail: wcle@aol.com.

LEONE, WILLIAM J., lawyer, former prosecutor; b. Trinidad, Colo., Oct. 16, 1956; BA in Polit. Sci., Colo. State U., Ft. Collins, 1978; JD, U. Colo., 1981. Bar: Colo. Assoc. Sparks Dix Enoch Suthers, Colorado Springs, Colo., 1985-86; assoc., officer, dir. Ireland, Stapleton, Pryor, Denver, 1982—94; ptnr. Cooley Godward Castro, Denver, 1994—2001; first asst. US atty. dist. Colo. US Dept. Justice, Denver, 2001—04, US atty., 2005—06; ptnr. Faegre & Benson LLP, Denver, 2006—. Author: Immunity to a Direct Action: Is It a Defense, 1978. Active Colo. and Adams County Rep. Orgn., 1978—; bd. dirs. Cath. Cmty. Svcs., Colorado Springs, 1985; pres. Brandy Chase East Homeowner's Assn., Aurora, Colo., 1981-84. Mem. ABA, Colo. Bar Assn., Denver Bar Assn., Order of Coif, Denver Athletic Club, Phi Beta Kappa. Avocations: basketball, golf. Office: Faegre & Benson LLP 3200 Wells Fargo Ctr 1700 Lincoln St Denver CO 80203 Home Phone: 303-726-6606; Office Phone: 303-607-3595. Business E-Mail: wleone@faegre.com.

LEONETT, ANTHONY ARTHUR, banker; b. Summit, NJ, Jan. 4, 1929; s. Joseph J. and Margaret (DiGuglielmo) L.; m. Ann Marino, Oct. 6, 1974; 1 son by previous marriage, Anthony Arthur. BS, Seton Hall U., 1950; cert., Am. Inst. Banking, 1956; postgrad., U. Wis., 1962. Mgr. First Nat. Bank & Trust Co., Summit, 1950-56; sr. v.p., auditor Nat. State Bank, Elizabeth, NJ, 1956-91; ret., 1991. Instr. principles of auditing and bank ops. Am. Inst. Banking; mem. faculty N.J. Data Processing Sch., Princeton, Bank Adminstrn. Sch. of U. Wis. Bd. dirs. N.J. affiliate Am. Heart Assn. With U.S. Army, 1951-53. Recipient Irving Grabiel award for outstanding leadership in banking, 1979 Mem. Am. Inst. Banking (dir. chpt.), Bank Adminstrn. Inst. (N.J. state dir. 1977-79, pres. N.J. chpt., dist. dir. 1979-81) Clubs: K.C., Minisink (Chatham). Republican. Roman Catholic. Home: 102 N Hillside Ave Chatham NJ 07928-2825

LEONG, ALBIN B., pediatric pulmonologist, allergist, educator; b. Astoria, Oreg., Nov. 8, 1950; BS in Biology, Trinity Coll., Hartford, Conn., 1973; MD, U. Calif., La Jolla, Calif., 1977. Diplomate Nat. Bd. Medical Examiners, 1979, Am. Bd. Pediatrics, 1982, Am. Bd. Allergy & Immunology, 1983. Resident Children's Hosp. of L.A., 1977-79; resident in pediat. U. Calif., San Diego, 1979-80, fellow in pediat. pulmonology, immunology and allergy, 1980-82; pediat. pulmonologist and allergist Sacramento Kaiser Found. Hosp., 1993—. Contbr. articles to profl. jours. Grantee Travel grant, Am. Acad. Alelrgy, 1981, 2004—05, 2006—. Mem.: Calif. Thoracic Soc., Am. Thoracic Soc., Am. Acad. Pediatrics. Office: Sacramento Kaiser Found Hosp Pediatric Pulmonology & Allergy 2025 Morse Ave Sacramento CA 95825 Office Phone: 916-973-7324. Office Fax: 916-973-7338. Business E-Mail: albin.leong@kp.org.

LEONG, BELINDA, chef; Grad., San Francisco City Coll. Internship Aqua, 1998, Gary Danko, San Francisco, 1999, exec. pastry chef, 2001—; stage Restaurant Daniel, NYC, Aureole, Citrella, NYC, Fauchon, NYC; chef Thomas Haas Chocolates, Vancouver. Named one of San Francisco's Rising Stars, StarChefs.com, 2007. Office: Gary Danko 800 N Point St San Francisco CA 94103 Office Phone: 415-749-2060.*

LEONG, CHIA KEN, mechanical engineer; b. Georgetown, Penang, Malaysia, June 9, 1979; arrived in U.S., 1999; s. Foot Sung Leong and Poh Hong Teoh; m. Chia Sia Teh. BSME, SUNY, Buffalo, 2001, MSME, 2003, PhD, 2005. Grad. rsch. asst., grad. tchg. asst. SUNY, Buffalo, 2001—05; sr. flip chip packaging engr. Advanced Micro Devices, Sunnyvale, Calif., 2005—. Grad. rsch. asst. Composite Materials Rsch. Lab., Buffalo, 2001—05. Recipient Alana Acad. Achievement award, SUNY-Buffalo, 2003, Circle of Excellence Scholarship award, 1999. Mem.: Internat. Microelectronics and Packaging Soc. Achievements include invention of low cost carbon black invention for use as thermal interface materials for electronic packaging industry; patents pending for. Avocations: reading, tennis, basketball. Home: 3612 Flora Vista Ave Apt 257 Santa Clara CA 95051 Office: Advanced Micro Devices One AMD Pl PO Box 3453 MS103 Sunnyvale CA 94088-3453 Office Phone: 408-749-2122. Business E-Mail: chiaken.leong@amd.com.

LEONG, STEPHANIE MEI, financial planner; b. Stockton, Calif., July 21, 1947; d. Edward G. and Ly H. (Ng) L.; m. Truman D. Wong, Aug. 24, 1969 (div. Mar. 1995); 1 child, Alexandra G.; m. Raymond Tom, June 17, 1995. BA, Mills Coll., 1970. Software cons. ComputerLand, San Francisco, 1983-86; trainer acctg. software Data Integrity, San Francisco, 1986-88; fin. cons. Shearson Lehman Bros., San Francisco, Larkspur, Calif., 1988-92, FN Investment Ctr., San Francisco, 1992-95; wealth mgr. Assoc. Securities Corp., Santa Rosa, Calif., 1995-99, Investment Architects, Inc., 1999—. Vol. Donaldina Cameron House, San Francisco, 1962-83; mem. fin. com. Santa Rosa Symphony Assn., 1996-2003, bd. dirs., 1998-2004; bd. dirs. Jr. League Napa-Sonoma, 1996-1997, San Francisco Opera Guild, 1998—; docent coun. Asian Art Mus., San Francisco, 2000—, bd. dirs., 2003-2007 alumnae admissions rep. Mills Coll., 2000-2003. Named to Golden Scale Coun., Putnam Investments, Boston, 1993. Mem. Internat. Assn. Fin. Planning, Kiwanis (bd. dirs. Santa Rosa, suburban chmn. interclub 1996-98, Outstanding Achievement award 1998). Presbyterian. Avocations: sailing, art, classical music, dance, travel. Office Phone: 415-479-8997. Personal E-mail: stephanieleong@yahoo.com.

LEON-GUERRERO, JILLETTE TORRE, nonprofit organization executive, consultant, writer; d. Justo Torre and Sally Jean (Wessel) Leon-Guerrero; m. Jean Paul Lescure, Mar. 17, 1989; children: Christopher Shawn, Island Bernard Lescure. BA in Anthropology, U. Guam, 1981; MA in Human Rels., U. Okla., 1991. Cert. in advanced news editing U. So. Calif., 1985. Comm. officer South Pacific Commn., Noumea, New Caledonia, 1987—89; exec. dir. Guam Humanities Coun., Tamuning, 1991—95, Hagatna, 1999—2005, dir. mktg. and devel., 2005—; exec. dir. Consortium for Pacific Arts and Cultures, Honolulu, 1996—97; COO ARC Guam Chpt., Hagatna, 1997—98. Writer Pacific Daily News, Hagatna, 1985—91; comm. cons. UN Devel. Programme, Suva, Fiji, 1989—91; nonprofit cons., Hagatna, 1990—. Author, co-producer (video production) Guam Paradise Island (First Guam Produced Video Prodn. Feature, Guam Visitor's Bur., 1985), prodr., writer Challenge to Change: A Documentary of the Fourth Regional Women's Conference in Suva, Fiji, 1987; prodr.: (exhibit, video presentation) Families Under Siege: Stories of Family Life in Japanese-occupied Guam, 2005 (Humanities Project of Yr., Guam Humanities Coun., 2005). Founding bd. mem. Guam Humanities Coun., Hagatna, 1990—91. Recipient Governor's Guahan award for improving and making a positive impact on the island of Guam, Gov. of Guam, 2005, Legislative Resolution Commending for Lifetime of Contbn. to Cmty., 28th Guam Legislature, 2005. Mem.: Am. Assn. State and Local History, Guam Women's Club (v.p. 2005—06, pres. 2006—07). Home: PO Box 5763 Hagatna GU 96932 Office: Guam Humanities Coun 111 Chalan Santo Papa Ste 711 Hagatna GU 96910 Home Phone: 671-477-1265. Office Fax: 671-472-4465; Home Fax: 671-472-4460. Personal E-mail: jillette@guam.net. Business E-Mail: jillette@guampedia.com.

LEONHARDT, CLIFTON ANDREW, lawyer, public information officer; b. New Orleans, Dec. 27, 1947; s. Robert Crawford and Mary Gay (Labrot) L.; m. Mary Alice Leonhardt, Dec. 18, 1988 (div. Jan. 2004); children: Theodore Lawrence, Christine Alexandra AB cum laude, Cornell U., 1969; JD, Harvard U., 1972; postgrad., Balliol Coll., Oxford U., Eng., 1972—73. Assoc. Robinson & Cole, Hartford, Conn., 1973—74; legis. counsel Com. on Govt. Ops., U.S. Senate, Washington, 1974—75; dep. sec. State of Conn., Hartford, 1975—79, state senator, 1979—83; assoc. Wiggin & Dana, New Haven, 1984—89; chairperson Dept. Pub. Utility Control State of Conn., 1991—93; prin. de Fontenay, Savin & Kiss, Greenwich, Conn., 1994—95; chief counsel Freedom of Info. Commn., State of Conn., 1996—. Law lectr. U. Conn., Hartford, 1983—85; dir. Atlantic Wood Industries, Savannah, Ga., 1978—85, La. Fruit Co., Belle Chasse, 2006—. Contbr. articles to profl. jours. Del. Dem. Nat. Conv., San Francisco, 1984; bd. dirs. Conn.Correctional Ombudsman, Hartford, 1994—; corporator Renbrook Sch., West Hartford, 2000—05. Mem. N.Y. Yacht Club, Hartford Tennis Club, Phi Beta Kappa Democrat. Episcopalian. Avocations: tennis, reading. Home: 46 Mountain Spring Rd Farmington CT 06032 Office: Freedom of Info Commn 18-20 Trinity St Hartford CT 06106 Home Phone: 860-676-1113; Office Phone: 860-566-3234 ext. 311. Business E-Mail: clifton.leonhardt@ct.gov.

LEONHARDT, FREDERICK WAYNE, lawyer; b. Daytona Beach, Fla., Oct. 26, 1949; s. Frederick Walter and Gaetane Laura Leonhardt; m. Victoria Ann Cook, Dec. 27, 1975; children: Ashley Victoria, Frederick Whitaker. BA, U. Fla., 1971, JD, 1974. Bar: Fla. 1974, N.C. 1984, D.C. 1985; cert. real estate lawyer, Fla. Gen. counsel Fla. Ho. of Reps., 1974—75; ptnr. Cobb, Cole and Bell, Daytona Beach, 1975-79; pres. Leonhardt & Upchurch, 1979-87; ptnr. Holland & Knight, Orlando, Fla., 1987-93, Gray Robinson, Orlando, Fla., 1993—. Chmn. bd. dirs. Orlando/Orange County Compact, 1989-90, Orlando/Orange County Civic Facilities Authority, 1998-2000; founder Leadership Daytona Beach; grad. Leadership Fla., mem. bd. regents, 1995—, chmn. state program, 1997-98, chair-elect, 1999, chair, 2000-2001; active Leadership Ctrl. Fla., Leadership Orlando; past chmn. Ctrl. Fla. Sports Commn., bd. dirs., 1992-98; bd. dirs. Enterprise Fla., Orlando/Orange County Conv. and Visitors Bur., Celebration Health Found., Ctr. for Drug Free Living, Prevent Blindness Fla., Fla. Bank Commerce; mem. Orange County Civic Facilities Authority, 1998-2001; founder VCARD; past gen. campaign mgr. Volusia County United Way; mem. Gov.'s Growth Mgmt. Study Commn.; exec. com. Floridians for Better Transp., 2000—, chair, 2002, 03; treas. U. Ctrl. Fla. Found., 2000—; bd. dirs. Econ. Devel. Commn. Mid-Fla., 2001—, vice chmn., 2006; bd. dirs. Ctrl. Fla. Boy Scouts Am., 2000—, chair, 2005; bd. dirs. Ctrl. Fla. Tiger Bay Club, chair, 2006; mem. adv. bd. Ronald McDonald House; trustee U. Fla. Law Sch. Mem.: ABA (chmn. state and local govt. law sect. 1997—98, editor sect. newsletter 1991—94), Fla. Coun. of 100, Fla. C. of C. (bd. dirs. 1984—90, 1993—, chair 2004), Daytona Beach Area C. of C. (pres. 1985), Greater Orlando C. of C. (chmn. 1991—92), Orange and Volusia Counties Bar Assn., Delta Chi, Phi Alpha Delta. Office: Gray Robinson PA PO Box 3068 301 E Pine St Ste 1400 Orlando FL 32801-2731 Office Phone: 407-244-5655. Business E-Mail: fleonhardt@gray-robinson.com.

LEONHARDT, THOMAS WILBURN, librarian, library director; b. Wilmington, NC, Feb. 7, 1943; s. Thomas Beauregard and Rachel Virginia (Callicutt) L.; m. Margaret Ann Pullen, Sept. 19, 1966; children: Hilary, Thomas, Rebecca, Benjamin. AA, Pasadena City Coll., Calif., 1968; AB, U. Calif., Berkeley, 1970, MLS, 1973. Head gift and exch. div. Stanford U. Librs., Calif., 1973-76; head acquisition dept. Boise State U. Libr., Idaho, 1976-79, Duke U. Librs., Durham, NC, 1980-82; asst. univ. libr. U. Oreg., Eugene, 1982-87; dean librs. U. of the Pacific, Stockton, Calif., 1987-92; dir. tech. svcs. U. Okla. Librs., Norman, 1992-97; libr. dir. Oreg. Inst. Tech., Klamath Falls, 1997—2001; founding libr. Internat. U., Bremen, Germany, 2001; cons., 2002—; dir. Scarborough-Phillips Libr./St. Edward's Univ., Austin, Tex., 2002—. Editor RTSD Newsletter, Chgo., 1986-89, Info. Tech. & Librs., Chgo., 1990-95. Editor Advances in Collection Development and Resource Management, JAI Press, 1994-97, Internat. Leads, 2004-05; publisher, editor Callicutt Family Chronicle; contbr. articles to profl. jours. Bd. dirs. No. Regional Libr. Facility, Richmond, Calif., 1988-92, Feather River Inst. for Libr. Acquisitions, Blairsden, Calif.; del. Online Computer Libr. Ctr. AMIGOS Bibliog. Coun., Inc., 1996-97; chair Orbis Coun., 1999-2001; mem. Klamath Symphony, 1997-2001; chair Am. Libr. Assn. Com. on Accreditation, 2005—. Mem. ALA (chair com. on accreditation 2005—), Assn. Coll. Rsch. Librs., Libr. and Info. Tech. Assn. (pres. 1997-98), Assn. for Libr. Collections and Tech. Svcs., Ctrl. Assn. Librs. (bd. dirs. Stockton chpt. 1987-92). Democrat. Avocations: trumpet, guitar. Office Phone: 512-448-8470. Personal E-mail: twleonhardt@earthlink.net. Business E-Mail: thomasl@admin.stedwards.edu.

LEONHART, MICHELE MARIE, federal agency administrator; BS in Criminal Justice, Lakewood CC, Minn., 1978. Police officer Balt. Police Dept., Md.; spl. agt. Drug Enforcement Adminstrn., Mpls., 1980—85, spl. agt. recruiter St. Louis, 1986—88, group supr., intelligence supr. San Diego, 1988—93, OPR (internal affairs) inspector Arlington, Va., 1993—94, bd., 1994—95, asst. spl. agt. in charge of field divsn. LA, 1995—96, sr. exec. svc. mem. spl. agt. recruitment program, 1996—97, spl. agt. in charge field divsn. San Francisco, 1997—98, LA, 1998—2003, acting dep. adminstr. Alexandria, 2003—04, dep. adminstr., 2004—. Office: Drug Enforcement Adminstrn Mailstop AXS 2401 Jefferson Davis Hwy Alexandria VA 22301

LEONI, TEA (ELIZABETH TEA PANTALEONI), actress; b. NYC, Feb. 25, 1966; m. Neil Tardio, Feb. 1992 (div. Oct. 1995); m. David Duchovny, May 6, 1997; children: Madeline West, Kyd Miller. Attended, Sarah Lawrence Coll. Actor (TV series): Santa Barbara, 1989, Flying Blind, 1992-93, The Naked Truth, 1995-98; (TV movies) The Counterfeit Contessa, 1994; (films) Switch, 1991, A League of Their Own, 1992, Wyatt Earp, 1994, Bad Boys, 1995, Flirting with Disaster, 1996, Deep Impact, 1998, There's No Fish Food in Heaven, 1998, The Family Man, 2000, Jurassic Park 3, 2001, Hollywood Ending, 2002, People I Know, 2002, House of D, 2004, Spanglish, 2004, Fun with Dick and Jane, 2005, You Kill Me, 2007. Recipient Saturn award best actress for "The Family Man", 2001.*

LEON-PORTILLA, MIGUEL, historian, educator; b. Mexico City, Mex., Feb. 22, 1926; s. Miguel and Luisa (Portilla) L.; m. Ascension Hernandez Treviño, May 2, 1965; 1 child, Marisa. BA, Loyola U., LA, 1948, MA, 1951; PhD, Nat. U. Mex., 1956; PhD (hon.), So. Meth. U., 1980; DHL (hon.), U. Tel Aviv, 1987, So. Calif. U., 1989, Toulouse U., France, 1990, Colima U., San Andres, 1994, U. La Paz, Bolivia, 1994, Brown U., 1996; PhD (hon.), U. Carolina, Prague, 2000, Calif. State U., San Diego, 2002, U. Iberoamericana, Mexico City, 2002, Cath. U., Peru, 2003, La Habama, 2006. Sec. Interam. Indian Inst., Mexico City, 1955-58, asst. dir., 1958-60, dir., 1960-66; prof. faculty philosophy Nat. U. Mex., 1957—, dir. Inst. Hist. Rsch., 1966-76; researcher emeritus Inst. Hist. Rsch. Nat. Univ. Mexico, Mexico City. Sec.-gen. Internat. Congress Americanists, Mexico City, 1962; disting. lectr. Am. Anthrop. Assn., 1974. Author: La Filosofia Nahuatl estudiada en sus fuentes, 10th edit., 2001, Vision de las Vencidos, 18th edit., 2001, Broken Spears-Aztec Account of Conquest of Mexico, 10th edit., 1994, Aztec Thought and Culture, 1964, 20th edit., 2003, Le Crepuscule des Azteques, 1965, Trece Poetas del Mundo Azteca, 1967, Pre-Columbian Literatures of Mexico, 1969, Testimonios Sudcaliforníanos, 1970, Religion de los Nicaraos, 1972, Time and Reality in the Thought of the Maya, 1972, The Voyages of Francisco de Ortega to California, 1932-36, 1972, Historia Natural y Cronica de la Antiqua California, 1973, Il Rovescio della Conquista, Testimoniaze Asteche Maya e Inca, 1974, Anthropology and the Endangered Cultures, 1976, New Light on the Sources of Torquemada's Monarchia Indiana, 1979, Native Mesoamerican Spirituality, 1980, Toltecayotl, Aspectos de la Cultura Nahuatl, 1980, The Natural History of Baja California, 1980, The Testaments of Culhuacan, 1984, La Pensèe Azteque, 1985, Time and Reality in the Thought of the Maya, 1988; editor: Monarquia Indiana (Father Juan de Torquenada), 1975, Hamnotzejim Jazon, 1976, Culturas en peligro, 1976, Indian Place Names in Baja California, 1977, Los manifiestos en nahuatl de Emilian Zapata, 1978, Native Mesoamerican Spirituality, Ancient Myths, Discourses, Stories, Doctrines, Hymns, Poems from the Aztec, Yucatec, Quichè-Maya, and Other Sacred Traditions, 1980, The Natural History of Baja California, 1980, Place Names in Nahuatl: Their Morphology, 1981, Fifteen Poets of the Aztec World, 1992, Aztec Image of Self and the Others, 1994, Tonantzin Guadalupe, 2000, El Retorno de Quetzalcoatl, 2002; (with Earl Shorris) In the Language of Kings, 2002, The Ancient Books of the New World, 2003, Antigua y Nueva Palara, 2004. Bd. regents Nat. U. Mex., 1976-86; amb. of Mex. to UNESCO, 1987-92, permanent del., Paris, 1987-92. Decorated Order of Great Cross, Alfonso X the Wise (Spain), Palmes Academiques (France), Great Cross Civil Merit, Spain, 2003; recipient Elias Sourasky prize in Humanistic Rsch. Mex. Sec. Edn., 1966; recipient Serra award of the Ams., 1978, Nat. prize in Social Scis. Govt. of Mex., 1981, Gamio award, 1983, Raphael Heliodoro Valle prize in History, 1984, Nat. U. Mex. prize, 1994, Alfonso Reyes Internat. prize, Mex., 2000, Menédez Pelayo Internat. prize, Santander, 2001, B. de las Casas prize, 2001, Tlamatine prize, 2005, Chiapas prize, 2005; Guggenheim fellow, 1969; Fulbright fellow, 1975. Mem. NAS (fgn.), Mex. Acad. History (pres. 1996), Royal Spanish Acad. Lang., Smithsonian Coun., Am. Hist. Assn. (hon.), Sociètè des Americanistes de PAris, Inst. Different Civilizations, Sociedad Mexicana de Antropologia, Am. Anthrop. Assn., El Colegio Nacional Mex., Royal Acad. Letters of Extremadura, Nat. Acad. of Sci., Wash., DC. Home: Coyoacán 103 Alberto Zamora 04000 Mexico City Mexico Office: Ciudad U Inst de Investig Históricas 04510 Mexico City Mexico Home Phone: 52-55-5554-0802; Office Phone: 52-55-5665-4417, 55-56-650-070. Fax: 52-56-650-070. Business E-Mail: portilla@servidor.unam.mx.

LEONSIS, TED, media and professional sports team executive; b. Bklyn., Jan. 8, 1956; BA magna cum laude, Georgetown U., 1976; postgrad., Suffolk U. Law Sch., 1980. Copywriter, advt. mgr. Wang Labs., Inc., 1976-78, corp. publicity/pub. rels. dir., 1978-81; dir. mktg. comm. Harris Corp., Melbourne, Fla., 1981-83; founder, CEO Redgate Pub. Co., Vero Beach, Fla., 1983—, also dir.; founder, CEO Redgate Comm. Corp., 1986-94; pres. Am. Online Svcs. Co., 1994-96, vice chmn., 2002—, pres. AOL audience bus., 2002—06; pres., CEO AOL Studios, Vienna, 1996—; majority owner Washington Capitals; founder Lincoln Holdings; minority shareholder Washington Wizards. Founder Collegiate Entrepreneurs Fund; dir. Preview Travel Inc., Thrive, Interzine, The Hub, Digital City, Planet Out, Tribune Interactive, Best Buddies, Georgetown U. Internat. TV & Radio Soc., Brevard Venture Fund. Chmn. Author: Software Master for the IBM Pc, Mastering the IBM Assistant Series, Software Master for PFS, Blue Magic; pub. The Macintosh Buyer's Guide, Apple II Rev., The Apple IIGS Buyer's Guide, COMPAQ, FYI, The Harris Mag. ofr INfo. Mgmt.; contbr. articles to profl. jours. Chmn. United Fund campaign, Wang Labs. Inc., 1980; bd. dirs. Big Bros. Brevard County, 1981, Brevard Art Ctr. and Mus., Brevard Coun. of Arts, 1981, Juvenile Employment Project, Lowell, Mass., Merrimack Regional Theatre. Named one of entrepreneurs of yr. Chivas Regal, 1989, one of 200 global leaders of tomorrow World Econ. Forum, 1993; recipient Andrew Heiskell Community Service Award. Mem. Pub. Rels. Soc. Am. (cert.), Publicity Club Boston, Bus. Profl. Advt. Adminstrs., Am. Mktg. Assn. Office: AOL Studios 490 Sea Oak Dr Vero Beach FL 32963-3245 also: c/o Washington Capitals 401 9th St NW Ste 750 Washington DC 20004-2132

LEOPOLD, BLAKE, music educator; b. Spring Valley, Ill., Oct. 1, 1955; s. William Leopold; m. Esther Mae Brautigam, Aug. 28, 1976; children: Amanda Jo Cabannas, Rachael Anne Garnett, Travis Andrew. Voice tchr., owner The Leopold Sch. Voice, Tampa, Fla., 2000—. Dir. Opera Breve. Mem.: Nat. Assn. Tchrs. Singing. Home: 10848 May Apple Ct Land O Lakes FL 34638 Office: The Leopold School of Voice 108 S Armenia Ave Tampa FL 33609 Home Phone: 813-253-3339; Office Phone: 813-253-3339.

LEOPOLD, MARK F., lawyer; b. 1950; s. Paul F. and Corinne (S.) L.; m. Jacqueline, June 9, 1974; children: Jonathan, David. BA, Am. U., Washington, 1972; JD, Loyola U., 1975. Bar: Ill. 1975, U.S. Dist. Ct. (no. dist.) Ill. 1975, Fla. 1976, U.S. Ct. Appeals (7th cir.) 1976, U.S. Ct. Appeals (8th cir.) 1979, U.S. Supreme Ct., 2003. Assoc. McConnell & Campbell, Chgo., 1975-79; atty. U.S. Gypsum Co., Chgo., 1979-82, sr. litigation atty., 1982-84, USG Corp., Chgo., 1985-87, corp. counsel, 1987, sr. corp. counsel, 1987-89; asst. gen. counsel G.D. Searle & Co., 1989-93, Household Internat., Inc., Prospect Heights, Ill., 1993—2004; dep. gen. coun. HSBC Fin. Corp., Prospect Heights, Ill., 2004—; asst. gen. counsel HSBC N.Am. Holdings Inc., 2004—. Mem. adv. bd. Roosevelt U. Legal Asst. Program, 1994-2000; legal writing instr. Loyola U. Sch. Law, Chgo., 1978-79. Pres., bd. dirs. Internat. Policyholders Assn., 1992-93; del. candidate Rep. Nat. Conv., 1996; mem. Lake County Study Commn. II, Waukegan, Ill., 1989-90; commr. Lake County, Waukegan, 1982-84, Forest Preserve, Libertyville, Ill., 1982-84, Pub. Bldg. Commn., Waukegan, 1980-82; chmn. Deerfield Twp. Rep. Cen. Com., Highland Park, Ill., 1984-86, officer, 1981-89; vice chmn. Lake County Rep. Cen. Com., Waukegan, 1982-84; bd. dirs. Am. Jewish Com., Chgo., 1988-91; bd. dirs. A Safe Place, Lake County, Ill., 2001—, treas., 2004-06, chmn. fin. com., 2004-06, v.p. 2006-; chmn. amicus sub-com. Civil Justice Reform, bus. roundtable, 2002-05; bd. dirs. Civil Justice Assn. Calif., 2005-. Recipient Disting. Svc. award Jaycees, Highland Park, 1983. Mem. ABA (antitrust com. 1976—, litigation com. 1980—, torts and ins. practice com. 1989-2005), Pi Sigma Alpha, Omicron Delta Kappa. Republican. Office: HSBC-NAm 2700 Sanders Rd Prospect Heights IL 60070-2701

LEOS, KATHLEEN, federal agency administrator; 5 children. BA with high honors, George Washington U. Dir. Dallas Svcs. for Visually Impaired Children, 1988—89; trustee, pres., v.p., chair Bus., Personnel, and Edn. Coms. Dallas Sch. Bd., Tex., 1995—2002; assoc. dep. sec., sr. policy advisor Office of English Language Acquisition, US Dept. Edn., Washington, 2002—05, asst. dep. sec., dir., 2005—. Founder Basic English Inc. Recipient Internat. Altrusa Cmty. Svc. Award, 1995, Tex. Women of Spirit Award, 1995, Velma Schmidt Early Childhood Award, 1996, Advocate of Yr. Award, 1996, Hispanic Salute Award, Ford Motor Co., 1999, President's Award for Excellence in Edn. for Hispanic Students, League of United Latin Am. Citizens, 2003. Office: US Dept Edn 400 Maryland Ave SW Washington DC 20202*

LEPAGE, EILEEN MCCULLOUGH See MCCULLOUGH, EILEEN

LEPAGE, ROBERT, actor, playwright; b. Quebec City, Can., 1957; Cert. in acting, Conservatoire d'Art Dramatique, Quebec, 1978; studied with Alain Knapp, Paris, 1978; PhD in Arts (hon.), Univ. Laval, Que., 1994; PhD in Lit. (hon.), McGill U., Montreal, 1997, U. Toronto, 1997; PhD in Law (hon.), Concordia U., Monteal, 1999. Actor Ligue Nationale d'Improvisation, 1984—88; artistic co-dir., actor Théâtre Repère, Que, 1986—89; founder, pres. Robert Lepage Inc., Que., 1988; artistic dir. French theatre Nat. Arts Ctr., Ottawa, 1989—93; founder, pres., artistic dir. Ex Machina, Que., 1994—. In Extremis Images, Inc., Montreal, 1995; founder La Caserne Dalhousie, Que, 1997; v.p. Ex Aqueo Films Inc., Que., 2004. Dir. Nat. Theatre Sch. Can., Montreal, 1990—91; gen. commr. Le Printemps du Québec en France, 1999; cons. New Millennium Dome Experience, 1999. Dir., set designer Et Drömspel, 1994, dir., actor (adapted French version) Elseneur, 1995, writer, dir., actor (one-man shows) Needles and Opium, 1991, La face cachée de la Lune, 2000, (films) Far Side of the Moon, 2003, (plays) Le projet Andersen, 2005; dir.: Los Cincos soles, 1991, Macbeth, 1992, (French version) La Tempêtê, 1992, A Midsummer Night's Dream, 1992, Alanienouidet, 1992, Le cycle de Shakespeare: Macbeth, Coriolan et La tempêtê, 1992, National Capitale Nationale, 1993, (Japanese version) Macbeth and La Tempêtê, 1993, Shakespeare's Rapid Eye Movement, 1993, Noises, Sounds and Sweet Airs, 1994, Le songe d'une nuit d'été, 1995, (Japanese version) The Polygraph, 1996, (adapted English version) Elsinore, 1997, (Swedish version) La Celestina, 1998, (Spanish version), 2004, Kindertotenlieder, 1998, La tempête, 1998, Jean-sans-nom, 1999, Zulu Time, 1999, (original French version) La Casa Azul, 2001; co-writer, dir. La géométrie des miracles, 1998, The Seven Streams of the River Ôta, 1994, (Spanish and Italian versions) The Polygraph, 2000, La trilogie des dragons, 2003, co-writer, dir., actor Les plaques tectoniques, 1991, numerous other plays; actor: (TV series) Court-circuit, 1984, Les grands Esprits, 1987; (films) Jesus de Montreal, 1988, Montreal vu par..., 1991, Ding et Dong, le film, 1992, Stardom, 2000; player Ligue Nationale d'Improvisation, 1984; dir.: Le groupe Sanguin, prise I, 1986, Le groupe Sanguin, prise II, 1987, (ads) Loto-Quebec, 1988, Syndicat de la Fonction Publique du Quebec, 1988, (video) Diane Dufrene's L'Enfant lumière, 1999; (films) Possible Worlds, 2000; (Operas) Bluebeards Castle, 1992, Erwartung, 1992, Die Dreigroschenoper, 2002, The Busker's Opera, 2004, 1984, 2005, Peter Gabriel's Secret World Tour, 1993, Peter Gabriel's Growing Up Tour, 2002; stage dir. La damnation de Faust, 1999, creator, dir. KÀ, 2004, co-writer, actor (films) Suspect No. 1, 1989, scriptwriter, dir. (screenplays) The Confessional, 1995, The Polygraph, 1996, Nô, 1997. Nominee Oscar for Best Fgn. Lang. Feature Film, 2004; recipient Pierre Curzi trophy, Ligue Nationale d'Improvisation, 1985, Profil du Public award, 1986, O'Keefe trophy, 1987, People's Choice award, La Presse Newspaper, Montreal, 1985, Best Directing award, Fondation de Théâtre du Trident, 1986, Conseil de la culture de Quebec award, Vinci, 1986, Best dir., best prodn., best sound realization awards, Que. Theatre Critics Assn., 1986, Best Show of Yr. award, 1987, Nat. Bank award, 1992, Best Show of Yr. award, Le Cercle des critiques de la Capitale, 1987, Grand prize, Festival de Théâtre des Amériques, 1987, Coup de Pouce award, 1987, Dora Mavor Moore award, Toronto Theatre Alliance, 1988, Dora Maver Moore award, 1990, Gascon-Roux award, 1988, 1989, 2003, 2006, Knight of the Order of Arts and Lit., Le Ministère de la Culture, 1990, Floyd S. Chalmers award, 1991, 1995, award, Nat. Arts Ctr., 1994, Genie award for best motion picture, 1995, Officer of Order of Can., Gov. Gen. Can., 1995, Best Screenplay award, SARDEC, 1996, Internat. Critics award, Istanbul Internat. Film Festival, 1997, City TV award, Toronto Internat. Film Festival, 1998, Best Can. Film award, Sudbury's Internat. Film Festival, 1999, Spl. Jury award, La Semana de Cine exptl. de Madrid, 2001, Chevalier of Legion of Hon., French Embassy, 2002, Queen's Golden Jubilee medal, Dept. Can. Heritage, 2002, Prix Denise-Pelletier, 2003, Hans Christian Andersen prize, 2004, Bayard d'Or, 19th Namur Internat. French-Speaking Film Festival, 2004, Audience prize, Festival of Theatre Spotkania, 2004, Cooper Wing award, Phoenix Film Festival, 2005, 2007, numerous others. Fax: 418-692-5400. Business E-Mail: rli@exmachina.qc.ca.

LEPELSTAT, MARTIN L., lawyer; b. Bklyn., Apr. 10, 1947; s. Larry and Nana L.; m. Audrey A. Fireman, Jan. 18, 1975; children: Rachel M., Michael H. BBA, CCNY, 1968; JD, Cornell U., 1971; MBA, U. Mich., 1970; LLM, NYU, 1976. Bar: NJ 1978, NY 1972, Fla. 1972. Tax cons. Touche Ross, NYC, 1971-73; assoc. Weil, Gotshal & Manges, NYC, 1973-78, Greenbaum, Rowe, Smith, Woodbridge, NJ, 1978—. Bd. dirs. Winston Towers 300 Assn., Inc., Cliffside Park, NJ, 1978-86. Fellow Am. Coll. of Trust and Estate Counsel, 1991—; mem. ABA (tax and real estate probate com.), NJ State Bar Assn., Middlesex County Bar Assn. (pres. tax com. 1987-88, pres. probate com. 1986-87, trustee 1988-92), Fla. Bar Assn. Home: 20 Snoden Ln Watchung NJ 07069-6253 Office: Greenbaum Rowe Smith PO Box 5600 Woodbridge NJ 07095-0988 Office Phone: 732-549-5600. Business E-Mail: mlepelstat@greenbaumlaw.com.

LEPKOWSKI, SUZANNE JOY, language educator; b. Newfane, NY, Dec. 27, 1971; d. Rockwood K. and Rose M. Chambers; m. David C. Lepkowski, 1997. BS in English, SUNY Brockport, 1997, MS in English Edn., 2003. Cert. tchr. English NY. Reading tchr. Charlotte Mid. Sch., Rochester, NY, 1997—98; tchr. English Gates-Chili Sr. HS, Rochester, 1998—99, Holley Jr. HS, NY, 1999—. Student tchr./mentor SUNY Brockport, 2002; sr. class advisor Holley Jr. HS, 2001—, tchr. SAT prep course, 2005. Recipient Florence Brasser scholarship, United Meth. Ch. North Chili, NY, 1992. Mem.: United Meth. Women (pres., sec. 2002). Republican. United Methodist. Avocations: gardening, reading. Home: 667 Whittier Rd Spencerport NY 14559 Office: Holley Jr HS 3800 N Main St Holley NY 14470

L'EPLATTENIER, NORA SWEENY HICKEY, nursing educator; b. NYC, Mar. 16, 1945; 1 child, Brendan Sweeny Hickey. Diploma, Bellevue Mills Sch. Nursing, 1965; BS Health Sci. summa cum laude, Bklyn. Coll., 1978; MS Psychiat.-Mental Health Nursing, Adelphi U., 1982, PhD, 1988. RN NY, bd. cert. clin. specialist adult psychiat. mental health, Am. Nurses Credentialing Ctr., bd. cert. advanced practice holistic nursing, Am. Holistic Nurses Assn., lic. nurse practitioner in psychiatry, NY, Reiki therapist, cert. in group psychotherapy. Dir. psychiat. staff devel. Bellevue Hosp. Ctr., NYC, 1980—82; group psychotherapist Jewish Inst. Geriatric Care, New Hyde Park, NY, 1983; staff psychotherapist New Hope Guild, NYC, 1984; prof. LI U. Bklyn., 1986—. Pvt. practice, NYC, 1982—2000; nurse rschr. Maimonides Med. Ctr., Bklyn., 1992—94, Englewood Hosp. and Med. Ctr., NJ, 1994—97; psychiat. nurse practitioner Alternatives Counseling Project, Riverhead, NY, 2000—04. Maj. USAR, 1977—2003. Am. Legion scholar, 1962, Isabel McIsaac scholar, 1983. Mem.: NY State Homeopathy Assn., Soc. Rogerian Scholars, Sigma Theta Tau. Business E-Mail: nhickey@liu.edu.

LEPLEY, RICK ALLEN, consumer products company executive; b. Lewistown, Pa., Apr. 16, 1950; s. Robert Kenneth and Eva Louise L.; m. Deborah Gail Ohmer, Sept. 8, 1982; children: Robert O., Lauren A. BA in Polit. Sci., Lycoming Coll., 1972. Field sales mgr. Chrysler Corp., Detroit, 1977-78, asst. zone mgr., 1978-79, regional sales mgr. Los Angeles, 1979-80; gen. sales mgr. Mid-Atlantic Toyota, Glen Burnie, Md., 1980-81, corp. mktg. mgr., 1981-82; dir. eastern ops. Mitsubishi Motor Sales Am., Inc., Bridgeport, N.J., 1982-87, gen. sales mgr. Fountain Valley, Calif., 1987-88, v.p. to sr. v.p., sales and marketing Cypress, Calif.; former pres. Retail Investment Concepts, Inc., Fla.; pres. Office Depot- Japan, 2001—. Mem. Am. Internat. Automotive Dealers Assn., S. Jersey C. of C. Republican. Avocations: golf, history, baseball.

LEPORE, FREDERICK EVERETT, neurologist, educator; b. NYC, Nov. 23, 1949; s. Michael Joseph and Ardean Clough (Everett) L.; m. Adlynn McKeel Gordon, Sept. 9, 1978; children: Adlynn Everett, Meredith Ardean. AB, Princeton U., 1971; MD, U. Rochester, 1975. Diplomate Am. Bd. Psychiatry and Neurology. Intern in internal medicine U. Mich., Ann Arbor, 1975-76; resident in neurology U. Va., Charlottesville, 1976-79; fellow in neuro-ophthalmology Bascom Palmer Eye Inst.-U. Miami, Fla., 1979-80; asst. prof. neurology U. Med. & Dentistry N.J./Rutgers Med. Sch., Piscataway, 1980-86; assoc. prof. neurology U. Med. and Dentistry/Robert Wood Johnson Med. Sch., Piscataway, 1986-94, prof. neurology, 1994—, prof. ophthalmology, 1998—; acting chmn. dept. neurology U. Med. and Dentistry Robert Wood Johnson Med. Sch., Piscataway, 1995—97. Attending physician Robert Wood Johnson Univ. Hosp., New Brunswick, N.J., 1980—; chief neurology svcs., 1994-98; cons. VA Hosp., East Orange, N.J., 1982—. Guest editor (jour.) Seminars in Neurology, 1986; designer Optic Nerve Test Card, 1985. Fellow Am. Acad. Neurology; mem. AAUP (pres. coun. chpts. 2004-06), Am. Neurol. Assn., Assn. for Rsch. in Nervous and Mental Disease, Queen Square Alumnus Assn. Presbyterian. Avocations: photography, running. Office: Robert Wood Johnson Med Sch Dept Neurology 97 Paterson St New Brunswick NJ 08901-1928 Home Phone: 609-865-7579; Office Phone: 732-235-7731. Business E-Mail: leporefe@umdnj.edu.

LEPORE, LISA, principal; d. Ann Nancy and Anthony Nicholas Lepore. BA, R.I. U., Providence, 1981, MA, 1987. Cert. tchr. R.I., 2000. Tchr. St. Leo the Gt. Sch., Pawtucket, RI, 1985—2001, prin., 2001—. Substance abuse coord. St. Leo the Gt. Sch., Pawtucket, RI, 1987—. Pres. Girls Softball League; appeals com. chairperson Cath. Athletic League, Providence, 2003. Named Coach of Yr., Cath. Youth Orgn. League, 1995. Mem.: Nat. Cath. Edn. Assn. Home: 32 Cambridge Cir Smithfield RI 02917 Office: St Leo the Great Sch 723 Central Ave Pawtucket RI 02861 E-mail: llepore@cox.net.

LEPORE, RALPH THOMAS, III, lawyer; b. Framingham, Mass., Oct. 11, 1954; s. Ralph Thomas Jr. and Barbara (Ablondi) L.; m. Marianne Moruzzi, June 20, 1986; children: Cristina Marie, Timothy James. BA in Polit. Sci., U. Mass., 1976; JD, Boston Coll., 1979; LLD (hon.), Framingham State Coll., 2002. Bar: Mass. 1979, U.S. Dist. Ct. Mass. 1980, U.S. Ct. Appeals (1st, 5th and fed. cirs.), U.S. Supreme Ct. 2006, pro hac vice admissions RI, NJ, Md., Maine, Pa., Ala., Conn., Vt. Fla., Tex., Calif., N.Y. Assoc. Sheridan, Garrahan & Lander, Framingham, 1978—81, Warner & Stackpole, Boston, 1981—88, ptnr., 1987—98, Holland & Knight LLP, Boston, 1998—, mem. dir. com. Mem. Mass. Jud. Nominating Coun., 1991-97, vice chmn., 1994-. Co-editor: Massachusetts Liability Insurance Manual, 2000, 2004. Trustee Framingham State Coll., 1991-2001, chmn., 1995-1997, 1999-2001, bd. advisors found. bd. 1992-; bd. advisors Christa McAuliffe Ctr. 1998-; served fundraising activities Jimmy Fund 1988-, S. Middlesex Legal Svcs.1999-; mem. Framingham Town Mtg. 1986-91. Mem. ABA, Mass. Bar Assn., Boston Bar Assn., Justinian Law Soc., Def. Rsch. Inst., Framingham Country Club (mem. bd. dirs. 1995-97, v.p. 1998-99, pres. 2000-2001. Democrat. Roman Catholic. Avocation: golf. Home: 7 Gaslight Ln Framingham MA 01702-5539 Office: Holland & Knight LLP 10 St James Ave 11th Fl Boston MA 02116 Office Phone: 617-523-2700. Business E-Mail: ralph.lepore@hklaw.com.

LEPOW, MARTHA LIPSON, pediatric educator, consultant; b. Mar. 28, 1927; d. Harry A. and Anna (Miller) Lipson; m. Irwin H. Lepow, Feb. 7, 1958 (dec. 1984); children: Lauren, David, Daniel. BA, Oberlin Coll., 1948; MD, Case Western Res. U., 1952. Intern, resident in pediats. Case Western Res. U., Cleve., 1952—56, fellow, asst. prof. pedit., 1958—67; from assoc. prof. to prof. pediats U. Conn., Farmington, 1967—78; prof. pediats. Albany (NY) Med. Coll., 1978—, dir. Clin. Studies Ctr., 1979—87, vice chmn. pediats, 1981—94, chmn. pediats., 1994—97; attending physician Albany Med. Ctr. Hosp., NY, 1979—. Cons. pediat. infectious disease St. Peter's Hosp., 1978—82; spl. fellow USPHS, Oxford, England, 1961—62; bd. dirs. Albany Coll. Pharmacy, 1987—89; mem. study sect. NIH Epidemiology & Disease Control, 1972—76. Contbr. more than 95 articles to profl. jours.; mem. editl. bd.: Pediats., 1976—81. Sec. HEW Task Force on Immunization Practices, 1977—78; mem. Conn. Acad. Sci. and Engring., 1977; mem. adv. com. Inst. Allergy and Infectious Disease, NIH, 1978—82; bd. dirs. Whitney Youhg Health Ctr., Albany, 1985—2004; mem. profl. adv. com. Ctr. for Disabled, Albany; bd. dirs. WYHCR Found., 2005—06. Mem.: Infectious Diseases Soc., Am. Soc. for Microbiology, Am. Pediat. Soc., Am. Soc. Pediat. Rsch., Am. Soc. Immunology (com. on status of women 1982—85), Com. on Vaccines, Inst. Medicine, Capital Dist. Pediat. Soc., Am. Acad. Pediats. (com. infectious diseases 1985—91, assoc. editor report), Alpha Omega Alpha, Sigma Xi. Home: 217 Milner Ave Albany NY 12208 Office: Albany Med Coll MC 88 47 New Scotland Ave Albany NY 12208 Office Phone: 518-262-5332.

LEPPARD, RAYMOND JOHN, conductor, musician; b. London, Aug. 11, 1927; arrived in U.S., 1976; s. Albert Victor and Bertha May (Beck) Leppard. MA, U. Cambridge, Eng., 1955; DLitt (hon.), U. Bath, Eng., 1973; PhD (hon.), U. Indpls., 1991, Purdue U., 1992, Butler U., 1994, Wabash Coll., 1995; MusD (hon.), Ind. U., 2001. Fellow Trinity Coll., Cambridge; lectr. music U. Cambridge, 1958—68; music dir. English Chamber Orch., London, 1959—77; prin. condr. BBC Philharm., Manchester, England, 1972—80; condr. symphony orchs. in Am. and Europe, Met. Opera, NYC, Santa Fe Opera, N.Mex., San Francisco Opera, Calif., Covent Garden, Glyndebourne, Paris Opera, Paris; prin. guest condr. St. Louis Symphony Orch., St. Louis, 1984—90; music dir. Indpls. Symphony Orch., 1987—2001, condr. laureate, 2001—. Music dir. European tours, 1993, 97. Rec. artist, composer numerous film scores; author: Authenticity in Music, 1989, Raymond Leppard on Music/An Anthology of Critical and Personal Writings, 1993; composer: (film scores) Lord of the Flies, Laughter in the Dark, Hotel New Hampshire. Decorated Commendatore Della Republica Italiana, comdr. Order Brit. Empire; recipient Gov.'s Arts Award, 1997, Deutsche Schallplattenpreis, Grammy award, Grand Pro/Am Music Prix du Disque, Edison prize. Office: care Michal Schmidt 59 E 54th St Ste 83 New York NY 10022 also: Indianapolis Symphony Orchestra 32 E Washington St Ste 600 Indianapolis IN 46204-3585

LEPPARD, STEPHANIE JEAN, systems analyst, artist; b. Fairbury, Nebr., Nov. 18, 1943; d. Robert Lee (Stepfather) and Marjorie Bloyd Martin, William Flavel Peters; m. Ronald Francis Aaron, Oct. 15, 1963 (div. May 12, 1965); m. Larry Dee Leppard, Feb. 21, 1967 (div. May 25, 1975); children: Adrian Allen Aaron, Michael Jay, Danielle Lynn Leppard-Gullo. Student, Riverside City Coll., 1961—64. Pub. Svc. Supr. San Bernardino Valley Coll., 1980. Eligibility worker San Bernardino Dept. of Pub. Social Svcs., Calif., 1969—71; automated sys. analyst ISAWS - Calif. State Wide Automated Sys., Sacramento; eligibility worker supr. San Bernardino Dept. Pub. Social Svcs., 1972—75; quality control supr. San Bernardino Count Dept. of Pub. Social Svcs., San Bernardino, Calif., 1975—76; staff devel. - trainer San Bernardino County Dept. of Pub. Social Svcs., 1976—79, program mgr., 1979—93; sys. analyst State of Calif. NAPAS Automated Welfare Sys., Napa, Calif., 1993—96, San Bernardino County Dept. of Pub. Social Svcs., San Bernardino, 1996—2000, LA County LEADER Automated Sys., LA, 2000—01, CalWIN Automated Sys., Sacramento, 2001—. Tng. cons. Imperial County, Calif., 1997. Colored pencil, paintings, Haley's Bath, pencil, The Egg and the Sea Horse, colored pencil, Man In Boat, The Christmas Tree, Decorated Joshua Tree, Pippen in Trouble, Self Portrait - My grandmother, Myself, The Vacationer, water color, Sea Turtle for Noelle. Dir. Beginning Experience, San Bernardino, Calif., 1980—90; bishop's coun. mem. San Bernardino Diocese, 1990—91; peer councilor Beginning Experience, 1980—90, coord., 1980—90. Mem.: Daughter's of Am. Revolution. Avocations: needlework, colored pencil artist, consultant. Home Phone: 916-990-9162.

LEPPER, MARK ROGER, psychologist, educator; b. Washington, Dec. 5, 1944; s. Mark H. and Joyce M. (Sullivan) L.; m. Jeanne E. Wallace, Dec. 22, 1966; 1 child, Geoffrey William. BA, Stanford U., Calif., 1966; PhD, Yale U., 1970. Asst. prof. psychology Stanford U., 1971-76, assoc. prof., 1976—82, prof., 1982—, chmn., 1990—94, 2000—04, Albert Ray Lang prof. psychology, 2004—. Fellow Ctr. Advanced Study in Behavioral Scis., 1979-80; chmn. mental health behavioral scis. rsch. rev. com. NIMH, 1982-84, mem. basic sociocultural rsch. rev. com., 1980-82. Co-editor: The Hidden Costs of Reward, 1978; cons. editor Jour. Personality and Social Psychology, 1977-85, Child Devel., 1977-86, Social Cognition, 1981-84, Jour. Ednl. Computing Rsch., 1983—, Media Psychology, 1999—; contbr. articles to profl. jours. Recipient Cattell Found. award, 1999; Woodrow Wilson fellow, 1966-67, NSF fellow, 1966-69, Sterling fellow, 1969-70, Mellon fellow, 1975; grantee NSF, 1978-82, 86-88, 2004, NIMH, 1978-86, 88, 2005—, Nat. Inst. Child Health and Human Devel., 1975-88, 90-98, U.S. Office Edn., 1972-73. Fellow APA, AAAS, Am. Psychol. Soc., Soc. Personality and Social Psychology, Soc. Psychol. Study Social Issues, Am. Acad. Arts and Scis.; mem. Am. Ednl. Rsch. Assn., Soc. Exptl. Social Psychology, Soc. Rsch. in Child Devel. Home: 1544 Dana Ave Palo Alto CA 94303-2813 Office: Stanford U Dept Psychology Jordan Hall Bldg 420 Stanford CA 94305-2130

LEPPERT, CYNTHIA L., lawyer; b. Balt., Nov. 26, 1956; d. Peter and Mary R. Leppert; m. Douglas J. Stanley, Sept. 30, 2001. BA with honors, Johns Hopkins U., 1978; JD, UCLA, 1982. Bar: Md. 1982. Assoc. Semmes, Bowen & Semmes, Balt., 1982—83; staff atty. FTC, Washington, 1983—86; from assoc. to ptnr. Frank, Bernstein, Conaway & Goldman, Balt., 1986—92; prin. Neuberger, Quinn, Gielen, Rubin & Gibber, P.A., Balt., 1992—. Mem., peer rev. panel Atty. Grievance Com., Md., 1998—; mem. faculty professionalism course Md. State Bar Assn., 2002—. Comments editor UCLA Law Rev., 1981—82. Mktg. and comm. com. Jr. Achievement Ctrl. Md., Inc., Balt., 2005—; mem. policy com. Alzheimer's Assn. Ctrl. Md., 2000—01; commr. Md. Commn. for Women, Annapolis, 2002—; bd. dirs. Wakefield Improvement Assn., Timonium, Md., 2003—06, v.p., 2005—06. Named one of Md.'s Top 100 Women, Daily Record, 2006; recipient Leadership in Law award, Daily Record, Md., 2005; Regents' fellow in econs., UCLA, 1978—79. Fellow: Litig. Counsel Am., Balt. City Bar Found., Md. Bar Found.; mem.: ABA, Nat. Assn. Women Bus. Owners (sec. Balt. chpt. 2005—07, edn. chair Balt. chpt. 2007—), Bar Assn. Balt. City (exec. coun. 2005, chair continuing legal edn. com. 2005—06, chair mem. com. 2006—), Balt. Women's Bar (exec. com. 1996—2001, sec. 1998—99, pres. 1999—2000), Bankruptcy Bar Assn. Md., Md. State Bar Assn., Women's Bar Assn. Md. (chair jud. selections com. 2000—04, bd. dirs. 2000—05, treas. 2004—05, v.p. 2005—06, pres.-elect 2006—07, pres. 2007—, Pres.'s award 2004, 2006, 2007). Office: Neuberger Quinn Gielen Rubin & Gibber One South St 27th Fl Baltimore MD 21202

LEPPERT, PHYLLIS CAROLYN, obstetrician, gynecologist; b. Phila., July 7, 1938; d. Walter Jennings and Alice (Brubach) Leppert. BS, Columbia U., 1961, MS, 1964, PhD, 1986; MD, Duke U., 1973; DSc (hon.), DePauw U., 2000. Diplomate Nat. Bd. Med. Examiners, Am. Bd. Ob-Gyn. Clin. scholar Duke U., Durham, NC, 1973-74, resident in pediatrics Med. Ctr., 1974-76; resident in ob-gyn. Med. Sch. Yale U., New Haven, 1976-79; assoc. in ob-gyn. Columbia U., NYC, 1979-81, asst. prof. ob-gyn., 1981-88; chmn. dept. ob-gyn. Rochester (N.Y.) Gen. Hosp., 1989-95; from assoc. prof. to prof. Sch. Medicine and Dentistry U. Rochester, 1989-95; prof. SUNY, Buffalo, 1996-98, chmn. ob-gyn., 1996-98; chief reproductive scis. br. Nat. Inst. Child Health and Devel./NIH, Bethesda, Md., 1999—2006, sr. staff scientist reproductive endocrinology unit reproductive biology and medicine br., 1999—2006; prof. ob-gyn., vice chmn. rsch. in ob-gyn. Duke U., Durham, NC, 2006—. Vis. prof. Tokyo Coll. Pharmacy, 1989, St. Louis U., 1999—; mem. adv. com. women's health initiative program NIH, 1993—97, mem. ad hoc study sect., mem. Buffalo Vanguard Ctr. Women's Initiative, 1996—98; mem. N.Y. State Coun. Grad. Med. Edn., 1994—99, Bd. Profl. Med. Conduct, NY, 1990—99; founder Internat. Confs. Extra Cellular Matrix Reproductive Tract; program dir. We. N.Y. Perinatal Database, 1997—98; adj. prof. Uniform Svcs. U., Bethesda, 2000—06. Co-editor: (book) The Extracellular Matrix of the Reproductive Tract, 1992; sr. editor: book Primary Care for Women, 1996, 2d edit., 2004; contbr. articles to profl. jours. Mem. adv. com. Office Tech., U.S. Congress, 1984; mem. Monroe County Bd. Health, 1992—96, St. Albans Ch., Washington; mem. vestry Christ Ch. Riverdale, Bronx, NY, 1984—86; mem. St. Stephen Ch., Durham, NC, 2006—; bd. dirs. Riverdale Mental Health Assn., 1986—89, St. Luke/Roosevelt Hosp., NYC, 1986—88, Maternity Ctr. Assn., NYC, 1988—96, Preferred Care, Rochester, 1990—94. Fellow: ACOG (past mem. com. underserved, mem. com. acad. rsch. fellowship, past mem. gynecol. practice com., mem. obstetrics practice com., mem. genetics com.), Am. Coll. Nurse Midwives; mem.: AAAS, Am. Soc. Matrix Biology, Am. Soc. Reproductive Medicine, Soc. Study Reproduction, Am. Soc. Profs. Ob-gyn. (region I rep. to coun. grad. med. edn. ob-gyn. 1999), Soc. Gynecol. Investigation (mem. coun. 2003—, chmn. publs. com. 2006—), N.Y. Obstet. Soc., Soc. Exptl. Biology and Medicine, Coun. Resident Edn. Ob-gyn. (rep. region I 1999—, mem. residency rev. com. ob-gyn.), Am. Gynecol. Obstet. Soc., Alpha Omega Alpha. Avocations: gardening, reading, singing, music, Scottish Country Dancing. Mailing: DUMC Dept Ob-gyn Baker House 212 Box 3279 Durham NC 27710

LEPPERT, THOMAS C., mayor, former construction executive; b. 1954; m. Laura Leppert; 3 children. BA in Econ. and Acctg., Claremont McKenna Coll., 1977; MBA, Harvard Bus. Sch., 1979. Prin. McKinsey & Co.; nat. ptnr. Trammell Crow Co.; dir. Castle & Cooke, Inc.; pres., CEO Castle & Cooke Hawaii, 1989—96, Castle & Cooke Properties, Inc., 1989—96; vice-chmn. Bank of Hawaii and Pacific Century Fin. Corp., 1996—97; trustee Estate of James Campbell, 1998—99; chmn., CEO The Turner Corp., 1999—2006; mayor City of Dallas, 2007—. Bd. mem. West Dallas Initiative, Dallas Zoological Soc., The Dallas Citizens Coun., Episc. Sch. of Dallas, Trinity Trust, Willis M. Tate disting. Lecture Series at So. Meth. U., TX Environ. Rsch. Consortium, Circle Ten Coun. of the Boy Scouts of Am., U.S. Chamber of Commerce; CEO adv. coun. U.S. Green Bldg. Coun. (USGBC); bd. mem. Washington Mutual, Inc., Leighton Holdings Ltd., Outrigger Hotel & Resorts, Baylor U. Healthcare System; vice-chmn. bd. of trustees, exec. com. Claremont McKenna Coll. Mem. exec. com. Greater Dallas Chamber; chmn. Dallas Com. on Fgn. Rels.; mem. TX Gov. Bus. Coun. Recipient Global Cross Millennium Award for Corp. Environ. Leadership, Global Green USA, 2006, Torch of Conscience Award, Am. Jewish Congress, 2006. Mem.: Alumni Bd. of Dirs., Harvard Bus. Sch., Chief Executives Orgn., World Presidents Orgn., Young Presidents Orgn. Republican. Office: Dallas City Hall 1500 Marilla St Rm 5EN Dallas TX 75201-6390 Office Phone: 214-670-4054. Office Fax: 214-670-3409.*

LEPPIK, ILO E., neurologist, educator; b. Tartu, Estonia, Aug. 18, 1942; arrived in U.S., 1950; s. Elmar Emil and Lilly (Hanson) L.; m. Margaret Ann White, June 18, 1967; children: Peter, David, Karina. BS, Haverford Coll., Pa., 1964; MD, U. Pa., 1968. Diplomate Am. Bd. Neurology and Psychiatry, Am. Bd. Clin. Neurophysiology. Rsch. fellow Montreal Neurol. Inst., McGill U., Que., Canada, 1974-76; asst. prof. neurology U. Minn., Mpls., 1976-80, assoc. prof. neurology, 1980-87, prof. neurology, 1987-89, clin. assoc. prof. pharmacy, 1986-89, clin. prof. pharmacy, 1987—2004, prof. pharmacy, 2004—; dir. rsch. MINCEP Epilepsy Care, Mpls., 1990—. Adj. prof. neurology U. Minn., 1989—. Author: Contemporary Diagnosis and Management of the Patient with Epilepsy, 1993, 6th edit., 2006, Epilepsy: A Guide to Balancing Your Life, 2006; founding editor Jour. Epilepsy Rsch., 1986—2006; contbr. articles to profl. jours. Bd. dirs. Am. Bd. Clin. Neurophysiology, 1992-94; prin. investigator NIH program epilepsy in elderly, 1997-; mem. ctrl. com. Rep. Party Minn. Maj. USAF, 1969-71. Fellow Am. Acad. Neurology; mem. Am. Epilepsy Soc. (pres. 1992-94, treas. 1983-86), Ctrl. Soc. Neurol. Rsch. (pres. 1991-92), Assn. Neurologists of Minn. (pres. 1983-89), Epilepsy Found. Am. (chmn., profl. adv. bd. 1989-91, bd. dirs. 1982-92). Unitarian Universalist. Achievements include development of new drugs for treatment of epilepsy. Avocation: cross country skiing. Office: 7-115 Weaver Densford Hall Univ Mn Coll Pharmacy 308 Harvard St SE Minneapolis MN 55455 Home Phone: 763-546-3328; Office Phone: 612-625-7139. Business E-Mail: leppi001@umn.edu.

LEPPIK, MARGARET WHITE, municipal official; b. Newark, June 5, 1943; d. John Underhill and Laura (Schaefer) White; m. Ilo Elmar Leppik, June 18, 1967; children: Peter, David, Karina. BA, Smith Coll., 1965. Rsch. asst. Wistar Inst., U. Pa., Phila., 1967-68, U. Wis., Madison, 1968-69; mem. Minn. Ho. Reps., St. Paul, 1991—2003, chair higher edn. fin. com.; mem. Met. Coun., 2003—. Active Golden Valley (Minn.) Planning Commn., 1982—90, Golden Valley Bd. Zoning Appeals, 1985—87; commr. Midwest Higher Edn. Commn., 1999—2003; bd. dirs. Minn. Partnership Action Against Tobacco, 1998—2003. Named Citizen of Distinction, Hennepin County Human Svcs. Planning Bd., 1992, Legislator of Yr., U. Minn. Alumni Assn., 1995, 1998—2001, Minn. State U. Student Assn., 1999; recipient Presdl. medallion, North Hennepin CC, 2003. Mem.: LWV (v.p., dir. 1984—90), Hubert H. Humphrey Inst. (adv. coun. 2003—), Nature Conservancy (bd. trustees 2003—), Minn. Opera Assn. (pres. 1986—88), Optimists, Rotary. Republican. Avocations: gardening, bicycling, canoeing. Home: 7500 Western Ave Golden Valley MN 55427-4849 Personal E-mail: peggy@leppik.net.

LEPPO, LISA MARIE, forensic anthropologist; b. Lebanon, Pa., Oct. 12, 1956; d. George W. and Mildred S. Hoshower; m. Jeffrey Francis Leppo, Dec. 18, 1999; 1 child, Cassandra Estella. BS, Pa. State U., 1978; MS, U. Ill., 1989; PhD, U. Fla., Gainesville, 1992. Diplomate Am. Bd. Forensic Anthropology, 1997. Police officer Pa. State Capitol Police, Harrisburg, Pa., 1978—84; forensic anthropologist U.S. Army Ctrl. Identification Lab., Hickam Air Force Base, Hawaii, 1994—2000, UN Internat. Criminal Tribunal for the Former Yugoslavia, Sarajevo, Bosnia-Herzegovina, 2000—01; sr. forensic anthropologist Internat. Commn. on Missing Persons, Sarajevo, 2002; mortuary affairs specialist US Army, Ft. Lee, Va., 2002—. Faculty mem. Va. Inst. Forensic Sci. and Medicine, Richmond; anthrop. cons. Office of the Chief Med. Examiner, Richmond, Charlottesville Police Dept., Va. Contbr. chapters to books, articles to profl. jours. Fellow: Am. Acad. Forensic Scis. Office: US Army Mortuary Affairs Center 1201 22nd St Fort Lee VA 23801-1601 Office Phone: 804-734-3748. Office Fax: 804-734-4758. Business E-Mail: lisa.leppo@lee.army.mil.

LEPRINO, JAMES G., food products executive; b. 1937; married; 2 children. With Leprino Foods Co., Denver, 1955—, chmn. bd., CEO. Named one of 400 Richest Americans, Forbes, 2005—. Office: Leprino Foods Co 1830 W 38th Ave Denver CO 80211-2200

LE QUÉRÉ, JEAN FRANÇOIS MARIE, scientific instrumentation researcher; b. Pabu, France, Apr. 7, 1933; s. Yves Marie and Yvonne Marie Rose (Olivier) Le Quéré; m. Jacqueline Marie Le Colas, Mar. 26, 1964; children: Anne Marie, Isabelle Marie, Jean-Yves Marie, Blandine Marie. Upper tech. diploma, Nat. Conservatory Arts-Trade, Paris, 1965, engr. physicist grad., 1968; DEng, U. Pierre and Marie Curie, Paris, 1983. Electrician Regie Renault, Paris, 1950-61; lab. technician, Paris, 1961-65; lab. upper rsch. technician, 1965-68; engr. physicist U. Paris 6, 1968-72, engr. rschr., 1972-96; mem. faculty U. Paris 7, 1972-94, engr. rschr., 1972—. Contbr. articles to profl. jours. With French Army, 1953. Mem. Assn. Tchg. (pres. 1996). Home: 22 rue Pierre Brossolette 93160 Noisy-le-Grand France

LE QUESNE, PHILIP WILLIAM, chemistry educator, researcher; b. Auckland, New Zealand, Jan. 6, 1939; came to U.S., 1967; s. Ernest W. B. and Bettie A. (Colwill) Le Q.; m. Mary E. Kinloch, 1965 (dec. 1988); children: Elizabeth Ruth, Martin James. BS, U. Auckland, 1960, MS, 1961, PhD, 1964, D.Sc. (hon.), 1979. Asst. prof. U. Mich., Ann Arbor, 1967-72; assoc. prof. Northeastern U., Boston, 1973-78, prof., 1978—, chmn. dept. chemistry, 1979-87, vice provost for rsch. and grad. edn., 1991-93. Assoc. dir. Barnett Inst. for Chem. analysis and Materials Sci., 1993-97. Mem. editl. bd. Bioactive Natural Products, 2004—, Novel Bioactive Compounds, 2005—, Current Bioactive Compounds, 2005—; contbr. articles on chemistry to profl. jours. Sr. warden Ch. of the Advent, Boston, 1990-96; mem. bd. The Living Ch. Found., 2005— Home: 17 Stafford Rd Newton Center MA 02459-1818 Office: Northeastern U Chemistry Dept 360 Huntington Ave Boston MA 02115-5000 Office Phone: 617-373-2858. E-mail: p.lequesne@neu.edu.

LERACH, WILLIAM S., lawyer; b. Pitts., Mar. 14, 1946; m. Star Soltan. BA, U. Pitts., 1967, JD magna cum laude, 1970. Bar: Pa. 1970, Calif. 1976. Ptnr. Reed Smith Shaw & McClay, Pitts., Milberg, Weiss, Bershad, Hynes & Lerach LLP, San Diego, Lerach Coughlin Stoia Geller Rudman & Robbins LLP, San Diego. Mem. US Holocaust Meml. Coun.; presenter numerous seminars, confs. Contbr. articles to profl. jours. Named Legacy Laureate, U. Pitts.; named one of 100 Most Influential Lawyers, Nat. Law Jour., 2006; recipient Lifetime Achievement award, ACLU So. Calif., 2003. Mem. ABA, Assn. Trial Lawyers Am., Pa. Bar Assn., State Bar Calif., Calif. Trial Lawyers Assn., San Diego Bar Assn., San Diego County Trial Lawyers Assn., Order of Coif. Office: Lerach Coughlin Stoia Geller Rudman & Robbins LLP 655 W Broadway Ste 1900 San Diego CA 92101 E-mail: wsl@lerachlaw.com.*

LEREAH, DAVID ALAN, economist; b. NYC, June 3, 1953; s. Jack and Lee (Arditti) L.; m. Wendy Joy Knepper; children: Abbey, Jeffrey, Jenna. BA in Econs. & Mktg., Am. U., Washington, 1976; PhD in Econs., U. Va., Charlottsville, 1983. Asst. prof. U. Va., Charlottsville, 1979, Grad. Sch. Mgmt., Rutgers U., Newark, N.J., 1980-82; fin. economist FDIC, Washington, 1983-85; chief economist, 1st v.p. Sovran Bank (Nation's Bank), Richmond, Va., 1986-89; mng. prin., CEO Vantage Fin. Group, Inc., Fredericksburg, Va., 1990-91; chief economist, sr. v.p. Mortgage Banker's Assn., Washington, 1992—2000; pres., CEO Lender Technologies Corp. (subsidiary of Mortgage Banker's Assn.); chief economist, sr. v.p. Nat. Assn. Realtors, Washington, 2000—07; exec. v.p. Move, Inc., Westlake Village, Calif., 2007—. Mem. econ. adv. coun. Am. Banker's Assn., Washington, 1987-89; mem. investment com. Sovran Bank, Richmond, 1986-89. Contbr. numerous articles to profl. jours. Recipient Ednl. scholarship U. Va., 1978. Office: Move Inc 30700 Russell Ranch Rd Westlake Village CA 91362

LERER, NEAL M., lawyer; b. Chelmsford, Mass., June 20, 1954; m. Rose P. Meegan, July 28, 1991; children: Scott Harold, Benjamin Joseph. BA, Brown U., 1976; JD, Duke Law Sch., 1979. Bar: Mass. 1979, U.S. Dist. Ct. Mass. 1980, U.S. Ct. Appeals (1st cir.) 1991. Atty. Martin, Magnuson, McCarthy & Kenney, Boston, 1980-96; mng. atty., pvt. practice Chelmsford, Mass., 1996—. Corporator Lowell (Mass.) 5 Cents Savings Bank, 1985—. Co-author: Personal Injury and Death, 1980, Damages in Massachusetts, 1990, Personal Injury Litigation in Massachusetts, 1991, Premises Liability, 1994. Reader Recording for the Blind, Cambridge, Mass., 1987-94; bd. dirs. Goodwin Fund; dir. Town of Chelmsford Scholarship Com., pres., 2003-06; cubmaster Pack 45, Chelmsford, Mass., 2004-06. Mem. Mass. Bar Assn., Mass. Bar Found., Greater Lowell Bar Assn., Brown Club of Boston (bd. dirs., co-pres. 1998-2000). Home: 4 Manahan St Chelmsford MA 01824-2844 Office Phone: 978-244-1114. Personal E-mail: neallerer@aol.com.

LERITZ, LAWRENCE R., choreographer, singer, dancer; b. Alton, Ill., Sept. 26, 1952; s. Leonard Henry and Marcella Rose (Fravle) L. Student, Harkness Ballet Sch., 1973-74, Sch. Am. Ballet, 1975-76. Debut: State Fair, St. Louis Muny Opera, 1969, appeared in Can Can, 1983; TV appearances include Capitol, 1982, All My Children, 1981-85, Home Sweet, Homeless; Rodney Dangerfield: It's Lonely at the Top, HBO, 1992, various commls.; guest expert on various talk shows including Rolonda, Charles Perez, Maury Povich, Show Biz Today, Am. Muscle Mag., Rosie O'Donnell Show; film debut: Stardust Memories, 1979; appeared in Easy Money, 1982, Stag, 1997; star Leritz and His Girls, 1983-85; headliner Las Vegas Stardust Hotel, 2006; Broadway appearances include: Fiddler on the Roof, 1981, Fonteyn and Nureyev on Broadway, 1975; prodr., choreographer Boobs!, N.Y.C., N.Y., 2000, Boobs! The Musical, off Broadway, 2003-04; appeared Met. Opera telecast of Manon Lescaut, 1980; choreographer feature film musical The Last Dragon, 1984; choreographer, co-star home video Treehouse Trolls Birthday Day, 1993; dancer with Harkness Ballet, Paris Opera, Hamburg Ballet, Chgo. Ballet, world wide guest star; dir., choreographer own co. Dance Celebration which represented U.S. at Internat. Choreographic Competitions, Paris, 1979; dir. mus. numbers for Shields and Yarnell; creator mus. indsls. for Lily of France, Bausch & Lomb, Christian Dior; pres. Leritz Prodns., Ltd., N.Y.C. and L.A., 1983—; star exercise cruise on Queen Elizabeth II, 1995; rec. artist: It Takes Two to Tango, 1984, Crank It Up, 1989, Bright Light, 1992; song lyricist, composer; East coast prodr. Day of Compassion, 1995-97; choreographer, guest dancer Placido Domingo's L.A. Music Ctr. Opera, 1987. Writer Muscular Devel. mag., Ironman mag., Men's Fitness mag., Muscle & Fitness mag.; creator, star of video Total Stretch! with Lawrence Leritz, 1992. Full scholar Sch. Am. Ballet, Harkness Ballet Sch.; Lawrence R. Leritz Day declared; recipient Key to City, Wood River, Ill., 1983, Alton, Ill., 1987; appeared on cover Dance Pages mag., fall 1987, spring 1989 Time Mag.'s Local Hero, 1996. Mem. AFTRA, ASCAP (Pop Music awards for songwriting 1985—), SAG (film nominating com. 1996), Actors Equity Assn., Am. Guild Musical Artists (bd. govs. 1979-92, 94—, prodn. supr./choreographer 50th Ann. Gala 1986, Life Membership award for disting. svc. 1991). Office: 318 W 45th St # 3 New York NY 10036 Home Phone: 212-765-4523. E-mail: lleritz@aol.com.

LERMAN, KENNETH BARRY, marketing professional, consultant; b. Bklyn., Apr. 15, 1947; s. Albert J. and Dorithee (Goldman) Lerman; m. Geri Anne Appel, Apr. 24, 1976. BA, Coll. of Emporia, 1972; MBA, Emporia State U., 1976. Product mgr. H. J. Heinz, Pitts., 1976-77; sr. product dir. Johnson & Johnson, New Brunswick, N.J., 1977-81; mktg. dir. Pizza Hut/Pepsico, Inc., Wichita, Kans., 1981-83, Taco Tico, Inc., Wichita, 1983-85; owner Kenneth B. Lerman, Cons., Wichita, 1985—; pres., owner North Am. Mktg., Wichita, 1989—. Presenter in field. Contbr. articles to publs. Elected del. pres. White House Conf. Small Bus., 1995; bd. dirs. Botanica, Wichita Gardens, 1994—96, Nat. Found. Tchg. Entrepreneurship, 1994—95, Crime Stoppers, Wichita, 1987—88, Wichita River Festival, 1985—88, Huntingdon's Disease Found., Wichita, 1987—88; bd. dirs., founder Music Theatre Young People, Wichita, 1985—88; founder, pres. Wichita chpt. Planning Forum, Inc., 1985—88; bd. dirs. Wichita Conv. and Visitors Bur., 2003—, chair, 2005. Decorated Navy Combat Action medal, Navy Unit Commendation medal. Mem.: Downtown Rotary Club Wichita. Christian Scientist. Avocations: cooking, travel. Address: North American Marketing 1668 N Sagebrush St Wichita KS 67230-7010 Office Phone: 316-733-5800.

LERMAN, MARK JEFFREY, nephrologist, medical administrator; b. Wharton, Tex., Jan. 6, 1947; s. Sol and Lillian Lerman; m. Ray Ann Lerman, June 28, 1970; children: Marci, Marshall. BA, U. Tex., 1969; MD, U. Tex., Galveston, 1973. Diplomate Am. Bd. Internal Medicine. Nephrologist Dallas Nephrology, 1978—; med. dir. Med. City Hosp., Dallas, 1998—. Chmn. com. med. stds. Drs. Hosp., Dallas, 1982. Author: (book chpt.) Pancreas Transplantation, 1999; contbr. articles to med. jours. Fellow ACP; mem. Internat. Soc. Nephrology, Internat. Soc. Heart and Lung Transplantation, Am. Soc. Nephrology, Am. Soc. Transplantation, Tex. Transplant Soc., Phi Beta Kappa, Alpha Omega Alpha. Avocations: computers, golf, travel. Home: 6928 Sparky Branch Ct Dallas TX 75248 Office: Dallas Nephrology Assocs 13154 Coit Rd Dallas TX 75240-5773 E-mail: mjl972@aol.com.

LERMAN, ZAFRA MARGOLIN, science educator, public policy professor; b. Haifa, Israel, Jan. 27, 1937; came to U.S., 1969; d. Lipa and Sara (Chervinsky) Jacobi; 1 child, Yoav Margolin. BSc in Chemistry, Technion-Israel Inst. Tech., Haifa, 1960, MSc in Chemistry, 1964; PhD in Chemistry, Weizmann Inst. Sci., Rehovot, Israel, 1969. Rsch. assoc. Cornell U., Ithaca, NY, 1969-72, Northwestern U., Evanston, Ill., 1972-76; vis. scholar Swiss Fed. Inst. Tech., Zurich, Switzerland, 1976-77; mem. faculty sci. and math. dept., chmn. dept. Columbia Coll., Chgo., 1977-91, disting. prof. sci. & pub. policy, head Inst. Sci. Edn. & Sci. Communication, 1991—. Mem. organizing com. Albert Einstein Peace Prize Found., participant Internat. Conf. on Arid Lands, Corsica, France, 1981-82, mem. exec. com., 1981—; mem. Pyramid Conf. on Sci. Edn., 1984, Triangle Coalition on Sci. Edn., 1984-85; symposia and seminar lectr. Contbr. articles to profl. jours. Bd. dirs. Com. Concerned Scientists, 1989—. Recipient gold medal Coun. for Advancement and Support Edn., 1989, Nat. Catalyst award Chem. Mfrs. Assn., 1990, Jose Vasconcelos World Award in Edn., World Cultural Coun., 2000; grantee NSF, 1990. Mem. AAAS, Am. Chem. Soc. (bd. dirs. Chgo. sect. 1983-84, 87—, com. on internat. activities div. chem. edn. 1990—), Internat. Union Pure and Applied Chemistry, Am. Inst. Chemists, Nat. Sci. Tchrs. Assn., Am. Soc. for Technion (bd. dirs. 1986—), Chgo. Coun. on Fgn. Rels., Execs. Club Chgo., Sigma Xi. Office: Columbia Coll 600 S Michigan Ave Chicago IL 60605-1900 Office Phone: 312-344-7180. Office Fax: 312-344-8051.

LERNER, ABRAM, museum director, artist; b. NYC, Apr. 11, 1913; s. Hyman and Sarah (Becker) L.; m. Pauline Hanenberg, Oct. 7, 1940; 1 child, Aline. BA, NYU, 1935; student, Ednl. Alliance, Art Students League, Bklyn. Mus.; pvt. studies, Florence, Italy. Asso. dir. A.C.A. Gallery and Artist's Gallery, NYC, 1945-57; curator Joseph H. Hirshhorn Collection, NYC, 1957-66; dir. Hirshhorn Mus. and Sculpture Garden, Washington, 1967-85; founding dir. emeritus, ret. Hirshhorn Mus. and Sculpture Garden, Smithsonian Instn., Washington, 1985. Adv. bd. Archives Am. Art, 1970— Author: Hirshhorn Museum and Sculpture Garden - Inaugural Book, 1974, Gregory Gillespie, 1977; contbr. to mags., mus. catalogues.; one man show, Davis Gallery, N.Y.C., 1958, Corcoran Gallery, Washington, 2007; group shows include, A.C.A. Gallery, Peridot Gallery, Bklyn.-Mus., Pa. Acad., Davis Gallery; represented in pvt. collections. Decorated comdr. Order Oranje-Nassau (Netherlands); chevalier Order Arts and Letters (France). Home: 77 S Canaan Rd Apt 239 Canaan CT 06018-2521

LERNER, ALEXANDER ROBERT, insurance company executive; b. Chgo., June 26, 1946; s. Peter Lerner and Lillian Orlinsky Joseph; m. Marianne Ryan, Apr. 21, 1979; 1 child, Lindsey Anne. BS, No. Ill. U., 1970. Adminstrv. asst. Gov. of Ill., 1970-72; adminstrv. asst. spkr. Ill. Ho. of Reps., Springfield, 1973-74; asst. dir. pub. affairs divsn. AMA, Chgo., 1974-75; dir. Ill. State Med. Soc., Chgo., 1975-78; pres. Govtl. Affairs, Inc., Chgo., 1978—81; CEO ISMIE Mut. Ins. Co., Chgo., 1981—. Mem. adv. com. to dir. Ctrs. Disease Control and Prevention, 2001—04, NIH. Bd. dirs. Lincoln Park Zoo; chmn. Ill. Sports Facilities Authority, 1992—2004; mem. 2016 olympics com. Chgo. Fellow: Inst. Medicine Chgo.; mem.: Assn. Forum Chgo., Chgo. Soc. Assn. Execs., Am. Soc. Assn. Execs., Am. Assn. Med. Soc. Execs., Conway Farms Golf Club, Execs. Club of Chgo., Michigan Shores Club, Chgo. Yacht Club, Union League Club. Avocations: nautical antiques, presidential history, travel, golf. Office: Ill State Med Soc 20 N Michigan Ave Ste 700 Chicago IL 60602-4811 Home Phone: 842-835-0604; Office Phone: 312-580-2412.

LERNER, BARBARA, writer, researcher; b. Chgo., Mar. 31, 1935; d. Jacob Israel and Mary (Turen) Lerner. BA with honors, U. Ill., 1956; MA, U. Chgo., 1961, PhD, 1965, JD, 1977. Bar: Ill. 1977. Intern U. Chgo. Hosp. and Clinic, 1962-63; instr. Coll. Medicine U. Ill., 1963-64; clin. psychologist Ill. Mental Health Ctr., Chgo., 1965-68; assoc. prof. Ohio U., Athens, 1968-70; pvt. practice clin. psychologist Chgo., 1970-78; assoc. prof. Roosevelt U., Chgo., 1972-74; study dir. Nat. Acad. Scis., Washington, 1977-78; pres. Lerner Assocs., Princeton, NJ, 1981-96. Vis. scholar Ednl. Testing Svc., Princeton, 1978—79, sr. rsch. scientist, 1980—81; expert witness fed. cts. Debra P. vs. Turlington, Tampa, Fla., Marshall vs. Ga., 1983; vis. prof. U. Tex., Austin, 1989. Author: Therapy in the Ghetto, 1972, Minimum Competence, Maximum Choice, 1980; assoc. editor: U. Chgo. Law Rev., 1975—77, columnist: Phila. Inquirer, 1992—93; contbr. articles to profl. jours., newspapers and mags. Mem. U.S. Commn. Civil Rights, NJ, 1985—87; Pres. nominee U.S. Dept. of Edn., Washington, 1986. Recipient Cert. of Appreciation award for outstanding svc., U.S. Dept. of Edn., 1985. Mem.: Sigma Xi, Phi Beta Kappa. Avocation: gardening. Office: 5050 S East End Ave Chicago IL 60615-5901 E-mail: xlerner@ameritech.net.

LERNER, BETH M., non-profit consultant; b. Phila., Dec. 9, 1972; d. Craig and Zena Lerner; m. Kartik Krishnaiyer. BA, Temple U., 1995. Cmty. svc. coord. SE Fla. chpt. Alzheimer's Assn., Palm Beach, 2001—02; resource devel. dir. United Way of Palm Beach County, Boynton Beach, Fla., 2002—04; polit. cons. JKRB Inc., Coral Springs, Fla., 2003—04; legis. asst. State Rep. Mary Brandenburg, Palm Beach, Fla., 2004—05; non-profit cons. Am. Cancer Soc., 2005—; v.p. Palm Cons. Group, 2004—. Exec. com., Jewish cmty. rels. coun. Jewish Fedn. South Palm Beach County, Boca Raton, 2004; pub. affairs com. Planned Parenthood of Palm Beaches and Treasure Coast, West Palm Beach, 2004; team devel. chair Am. Cancer Soc., West Palm Beach, 2004; pres. Palm Beach County Young Democrats, Boynton Beach, Fla., 2003—05, Lake Worth (Fla.) Dem. Club, 2005; precinct capt. Palm Beach County Dem. Party, Lantana, Fla., 2002—; bd. dirs. Children's Case Mgmt. Orgn., Inc., West Palm Beach, 2005—. Recipient Svc. Award, Fla. Young Democrats, 2003. Mem.: NOW, AAUW, Nat. Assn. Notaries, LWV. Democrat. Jewish. Avocations: travel, politics, history. Home Phone: 561-706-3701. Personal E-mail: bethrenrel@aol.com.

LERNER, DAVID EVAN, mathematician; b. Kansas City, Mo., Mar. 21, 1944; s. George and Florence Rosen Lerner; m. Esther Priscilla Hahn, Oct. 11, 1969; 1 child, Michael George. BA, Haverford Coll., Pa., 1964; PhD, U. of Pitts., 1972. Vol. U.S. Peace Corps, Mlanje, Malawi, 1964—66; post-doctoral assoc. physics dept. Syracuse (N.Y.) U., 1973—75; post-doctoral assoc. Math. Inst., U. of Oxford, 1976—77; prof. of math. U. of Kans., Lawrence, 2000—. Contbr. scientific papers to profl. jours. Dir. Lawrence (Kans.) Amateur Golf Assn., 2001—06. Recipient support for sci. rsch. grant, NSF, NIH/NINDS, NIH/NIDCD, Dept. of Def., 1975—. Achievements include patents for Detecting Changes Of State In The Brain. Office: U Kans Dept Math Lawrence KS 66045 Office Phone: 785-864-5181. Office Fax: 785-864-5255. E-mail: lerner@ku.edu.

LERNER, ERIC M., lawyer; b. Bklyn., July 18, 1957; BA cum laude, SUNY, Binghamton, 1979; JD, U. Chgo., 1982. Bar: NY 1983. Ptnr. Katten Muchin Zavis Rosenman, NYC. Mem.: ABA (mem. Bus. Law Sect.), Pi Sigma Alpha, Phi Beta Kappa. Office: Katten Muchin Zavis Rosenman 575 Madison Ave New York NY 10022 Office Phone: 212-840-7157. Office Fax: 212-940-8776. E-mail: eric.lerner@kmzr.com.

LERNER, FREDERIC HOWARD, finance executive, educator; b. Bklyn., Feb. 10, 1957; s. Irving and Judith (Zarchin) L.; m. Sheryl Ann Gorman, June 5, 1983 (div. Jan. 2003); children: Jacklyn Michele, Allison Genna. BS in Acct., SUNY, Albany, 1979. Staff acct. Kipnis & Karchmer, NYC, 1979-81; fin. analyst Bank Leumi Trust Co., NYC, 1981-84; asst. sec. N.J. Trust Co., Jersey City, 1984-91; asst. v.p. The CIT Group/Bus. Credit Inc., NYC, 1991-94, v.p., 1994-96, Congress Fin. Corp., NYC, 1996-97; sr. mgr. Deloitte and Touche LLP, NYC, 1997-98; audit mgr. Transam. Bus. Credit Corp., Rye, N.Y., 1998-99; CPAs sr. mgr. Marden, Harrison & Kreuter, CPAs, White Plains, N.Y., 1999-2001; v.p. Wells Fargo Bus. Credit, NYC, 2001—. Prof. NYU, 1983—; pvt. practice, NYC, 1984—; cons. in field. Contbr. articles to profl. jours. Recipient Teaching award for excellence, 1987, Svc. to Univ. award NYU, 1987. Mem. Nat. Comml. Fin. Assn., Cert. Fraud Examiners. Office: Wells Fargo Business Credit Fl 16 119 W 40th Street New York NY 10018 Business E-Mail: frederic.h.lerner@wellsfargo.com.

LERNER, HARRY JONAS, publishing executive; b. Mpls., Mar. 5, 1932; s. Morris and Lena (Liederschneider) Lerner; m. Sharon Ruth Goldman, June 25, 1961 (dec. 1982); m. Sandra Karon Davis, Aug. 24, 1996. Student, U. Mich., 1952, Hebrew U., Jerusalem, 1953-54; BA, U. Minn., 1957. Founder Lerner Publs. Co., Mpls., 1959, chief exec. officer, 1959—; founder Muscle Bound Bindery, Inc., 1967, chief exec. officer, 1967—; founder Carolrhoda Books, Inc., 1969; gen. mgr. Interface Graphics Inc., 1969—, CEO, 1993—. Bd. visitors U. Minn. Press; chmn. N. Loop Bus. Assn., Mpls., 1972—79, Minn. Books Pubs. Roundtable, 1974; del. White House Conf. Libr. and Info. Svcs., 1979; bd. overseers Hill Monastic Manuscript Libr. St. John's U., Collegeville, Minn., 1986—89; bd. dirs., libr. dir. Jewish Cmty. Ctr.; mem. adv. coun. small bus. and labor Fed. Res. Bank, Mpls., 2006—. Pres. Twin City chpt. Am. Jewish Com., 1980—85; bd. dirs. Fgn. Policy Assn. Minn., 1970—71, Children's Book Coun., NYC, 1991—94, Minn. Libr. Assn. Found., 1997; bd. advisors Books for Africa, 1996. Recipient Brotherhood award, NCCJ, 1961, Kay Sexton award, 2002, numerous graphic arts awards, Minn. Innovative Communicator award, Minn. State U., 2004. Mem.: Jewish Hist. Soc., St. Paul-Mpls. Com. Fgn. Affairs, Walker Art Ctr., Mpls. Inst. Art, Daybreakers Breakfast Club (Mpls.), Upper Midwest Ampersand Club. Home: 2215 Willow Ln N Minneapolis MN 55416-3862 Office: Lerner Pub Group 241 1st Ave N Minneapolis MN 55401-1676 Business E-Mail: hjl@lernerbooks.com.

LERNER, HERBERT J., tax consultant; b. Newark, Aug. 19, 1938; s. Morris David Lerner and Evelyn L. (Shapiro) Kaplan; m. Dianne Joan Prag, Aug. 23, 1959; children— Joy Ellen, Mark Allen. BS, Rutgers U., 1959; LL.B., Georgetown U., 1963. Bar: D.C. 1964; C.P.A., D.C. With Ernst & Young, Washington, 1963-96, ptnr., 1970-83, 83-89, vice chmn. tax Washington, 1990—96, nat. dir. tax policy and standards; ret. Mem. IRS Commrs. Adv. Group, 1982-83, 96-98; treas., trustee Am. Tax Policy Inst., 1990-97 Author: (with others) Federal Income Taxation of Corporations Filing Consolidated Returns, 4 vols., 1975, with ann. supplement thru 1997; contbr., editor pvt. letter rulings column Jour. Taxation Mem. AICPA (exec. com. tax divsn. 1979-82, 85-89, past chmn., bd. dirs. 1990-94, co-chmn. nat. conf. lawyers and CPAs 1992-95), ABA, George Town Club. Office Phone: 202-333-8632. E-mail: Herblerner@aol.com.

LERNER, JONATHAN J., lawyer; b. Bklyn., 1948; BA, SUNY, Binghamton, 1970; JD magna cum laude, St. John's U., Jamaica, NY, 1973. Bar: NY 1974. Ptnr., corp., securities and commercial litigation Skadden, Arps, Slate, Meagher & Flom, LLP, NYC. Lectr. bus. judgement rule and fed. practice and procedure Practising Law Inst. and bar associations confs.; lectr. at law Columbia U. Sch. of Law, 1989—92; mem. Dept. Disciplinary Com., Appellate Divsn., First Jud. Dept., 1983—90, 1993, hearing panel chmn., 1984—90, 1992—; adj. prof. Bklyn. Law Sch., 2000—. Published numerous articles on the liability of corp. dirs., corp. takeovers, litigation strategy and legal ethics. Mem.: Assn. of the Bar City NY (mem. com. on profl. and jud. ethics 1981—84, mem. com. on the fed. courts 1989—92, chmn. 1999—2002). Office: Skadden Arps Slate Meagher & Flom LLP 4 Times Sq New York NY 10036 Office Phone: 212-735-2550. Office Fax: 917-777-2550. Business E-Mail: jlerner@skadden.com.

LERNER, LAURENCE M., college administrator; b. NYC, Aug. 21, 1939; s. Meyer Philip and Rose (Goss) L.; m. Susan Goodstein, sept. 8, 1963; children: Elisabeth, Marc. BA, NYU, 1961; MA, U. Wis., 1963, PhD, 1970. Asst. adminstr. history U. Wis., Madison, 1964-66; instr. Hofstra U., Hempstead, N.Y., 1967-68; sr. assoc. Drummond Assocs., Inc., NYC, 1968-71; lectr. Am. history Barnard Coll., NYC, 1971; asst. editor Bus. Internat., Inc., NYC, 1972-73, asst. editor mgmt. practices, 1972-73; dir. rsch. United Jewish Appeal, NYC, 1973-79; dir. devel. Am. Jewish Congress, NYC, 1979-80; exec. v.p. Alumni Fedn. of NYU, Inc., NYC, 1980-89; sr. v.p., spl. asst. to the pres. Manhattan Coll., Riverdale, 2000—02, v.p. coll. advancement, 1989-95, sr. v.p. capital campaign, 1996—2000. Bd. dirs. Hamilton-Madison House, N.Y.C., 1985-91, U.S. Com./Sports for Israel, N.Y.C., 1979-81; mem. historian's com. Am. Mus. Immigration, N.Y.C., 1982—; bd. advisors Coun. of Mcpl. Performance, N.Y.C., 1977-84; bd. trustees Horace Mann-Barnard Sch., Riverdale, 1979-82. Mem. NYU Alumni Assn. (bd. dirs. 1996—), Alumni Fedn. NYU (bd. dirs. 1982-96), NYU Club (ex-officio bd. govs. 1983-89), Univ. Glee Club of N.Y.C. Democrat. Jewish. Avocation: singing.

LERNER, MARTIN, museum curator; b. NYC, Nov. 14, 1936; s. Joseph and Rose (Kolberg) L.; m. Roberta M. Rubenstein, Feb. 26, 1968; children: Benjamin Louis, Seth Laurence, Jocelyn Ann. BA, Bklyn. Coll., 1959; postgrad., Inst. Fine Arts, NYU, 1961-65. Asst. prof. U. Calif., Santa Barbara, 1965-66; asst. curator Oriental art Cleve. Mus. Art, 1966-72; asst. prof. Case Western Res. U., 1968-72; vice chmn. charge Far Eastern art Met. Mus. Art, NYC, 1972-75, curator Indian and S.E. Asian art, 1978—2004, curatorial advisor for South and S.E. Asian art, 2004—. Adj. prof. Columbia U., 2004, art adv. assoc., 2005;cons. Christie's, 2003-, others in field; internat. lectr. Author: Bronze Sculptures from Asia, 1975, Blue and White: Early Japanese Export Ware, 1978, The Flame and the Lotus, 1984, (with W. Felten) Cambodian and Thai Sculpture: From the 6th to the 14th Century, 1989, Entdeckungen: Skulpturen der Khmer und Thai, 1989, (with S. Kossak), The Lotus Transcendent, 1991, Ancient Khmer Sculpture, 1994; contbr. articles to profl. jours. Served with U.S. Army, 1959-61. Mem.: East India; Devonshire (London). Home: Giglio Ct Croton On Hudson NY 10520 Office: Met Mus Art 82nd & Fifth Ave New York NY 10028 Personal E-mail: mlerneraaa@aol.com.

LERNER, MAX KASNER, lawyer; b. NYC, Dec. 27, 1916; s. Louis Lerner and Beckie Kasner; m. Lila Schachner, Oct. 5, 1943 (dec.); children: Helene, Beth. LLB, Bklyn. Law Sch., 1939. Bar: N.Y. 1940, U.S. Supreme Ct. 1952. Author: ABA Journal of Limitations Imposed on Radio and TV, 1949. Home: 350 1st Ave New York NY 10010-4902 Office Phone: 212-732-9000.

LERNER, MICHAEL, rabbi; BA, Columbia U.; studied, Jewish Theological Seminary. Ordained Rabbi 1995. Chmn. Free Students Union, 1966—68; chmn., Berkeley Chapter Students for a Democratic Soc.; lectr., Philosophy of Law San Francisco State U.; founder Seattle Liberation Front; prof., Dept. Philosophy Trinity Coll., 1972; prof., Field Study U. Calif., Berkeley, 1975—77; found. Inst. Labor and Mental Health, 1977; rabbi ALEPH: Alliance For Jewish Renewal, 1995—. Founder, current editor Tikkun Mag. Named one of The Top 50 Rabbis in America, Newsweek Mag., 2007; recipient Gandhi, King, Ikeda Community Builders Prize, Moorehouse Coll., 2005. Mem.: Atid (past pres.). Office: Tikkun Mag Ste 1200 2342 Shattuck Avenue Berkeley CA 94704 Fax: 510-644-1255.*

LERNER, RANDOLPH D., finance company executive; s. Alfred and Norma Lerner. BA, Columbia U., 1984, JD, 1987. Bar: N.Y., D.C. With Bear Stearns; ptnr. Securities Advisors, L.P., 1991—2001; dir. MBNA Corp., 1993—2006, vice chmn., 2002, chmn., 2002—06; owner, chmn. Cleve. Browns, 2002—. Chmn. bd. trustees NY Acad. Art, 1998—2003; trustee Hosp. for Spl. Surgery, NYC. Named one of 400 Richest Americans, Forbes, 2006. Mem.: D.C. Bar Assn., N.Y. State Bar Assn. Office: Cleveland Browns Stadium 100 Alfred Lerner Way Cleveland OH 44114

LERNER, RICHARD E., lawyer; b. Queens, NY, May 19, 1961; BA, SUNY, Albany, 1985; JD, St. John's U., 1989. Bar: Conn. 1989, NY 1989, US Dist. Ct. Ea. Dist. NY, US Dist. Ct. So. Dist. NY, US Ct. Appeals 2nd Cir., US Ct. Appeals DC Cir. Ptnr. Wilson, Elser, Moskowitz, Edelman & Dicker LLP, NYC. Mem.: Queens County Bar Assn., Assn. of the Bar of the City of NY, NY State Bar Assn. Office: Wilson Elser Moskowitz Edelman & Dicker LLP 23rd Fl 150 E 42nd St New York NY 10017-5639 Office Phone: 212-490-3000 ext. 2414. Office Fax: 212-490-3038. Business E-Mail: lernerr@wemed.com.

LERNER, SANDRA, artist; one-woman shows: Mercer Gallery, N.Y.C., 1969, Nassau County Mus. Fine Arts, Roslyn, N.Y., 1976, Soho Ctr. Visual Artists, N.Y.C., 1977, Betty Parsons Gallery, N.Y.C., 1982, Kampo Mus., Kyoto, Japan, 1983, 84, Gallery Don, Fukuoka, Japan, 1984, Tokyo Mus. Art, 1984, 86, 87, 89, Kampo Mus., Kyoto, 1984, 93, June Kelly Gallery, N.Y.C., 1992, 92, 96, 99-2000, June Kelly Gallery, NYC, 2004, Washington Assn. Gallery, Conn., 2005; group shows include: NAD, 1966, 72, 73, Heckscher Mus., Huntington, N.Y., 1963, 68, 69, 74, Guild Hall Mus., Easthampton, N.Y., 1974, N.Y. Carlsberg Blyptotek Mus., Copenhagen, 1980, N.Y.C. Cultural Ctr., 1983, Mus. Stoney Brook, NY, 1996, Zimmerli Mus., NEw Brunswick, N.J., 1999, Jeollabuk-do, Republic Korea, 2003, Art in Embassies Program, Bangladesh, Washington, 2004; represented in permanent collections: Aldrich Mus. Contemporary Art, Kampo Mus., Fukuoka, Japan, Zimmerli Mus., Rutgers U., Heckscher Mus., Huntington. ICA lectr., Japan, 1981; stage designer LAND Dance Performance, 1991, slide image for ECHO Japan Soc., 1995. Recipient Purchase award Nassau Community Coll., 1970, 74, Anne Eisner Putnam prize Nat. Assn. Women Artists, 1973, Benjamin Altman prize NAD, 1972; grantee ICA, 1981. Mailing: 10 E 18th St 6th Fl New York NY 10003 Home Phone: 212-929-2721; Office Phone: 212-929-2721. E-mail: sandralerner@aol.com, sandra@sandralearner.com.

LERNER, STEPHEN ALEXANDER, microbiologist, physician, educator; b. Chgo., Oct. 4, 1938; s. David G. and Florence (Trace) L.; m. June 6, 1963 (div. 1990); children: Deborah, Daniel, Susan; m. Aug. 18, 1991; children: Helena, Thomas. AB magna cum laude, Harvard U., 1959, MD magna cum laude, 1963. Intern, then resident Peter Bent Brigham Hosp., 1963-65; rsch. assoc. NIH, 1965-68; postdoctoral fellow Stanford (Calif.) U., 1968-71; asst. prof. then assoc. prof. U. Chgo., 1971-86; prof. medicine and infectious diseases Wayne State U., Detroit, 1986—, assoc. dean faculty affairs, 2002—. Convenor Soviet-Am. Symposium Antibiotics and Chemotherapy, Moscow, 1988; mem. merit rev. subcom. on infectious disease VA, 1998-2001; co-chair exec. coun. Mich. Antibiotic Resistance Reduction Coalition, 1999—. Editor: Aminoglycoside Ototoxicity, 1981; mem. editl. bd. Antimicrobial Agts. and Chemotherapy, 1981—, European Jour. Clin. Microbiology and Infectious Diseases, 1992-2005, Antibiotic Resistance Updates, 1997—; contbr. articles to profl. jours. With USPHS, 1965-67. Recipient Borden Rsch. award, 1963. Fellow Infectious Disease Soc. Am., Am. Acad. Microbiology (com. on awards 1993-96); mem. Am. Soc. Microbiology (chmn. antimicrobial chemotherapy 1987-88, divsn. group rep. 1990-92, councillor 1990-92, chmn. confs. com. 1993-96, internat. com. 1993-2005, chmn. 1996-2003, prof. devel. com. 2005-07), Inter-Am. Soc. for Chemotherapy (pres. 1986-88, bd. dirs., chmn. 1988-93), Internat. Union Microbiol. Socs. (U.S. nat. com. 2001-06, chmn. 2005-06), Internat. Soc. Chemotherapy (exec. com. 1987-93), Phi Beta Kappa, Sigma Xi, Alpha Omega Alpha. Democrat. Jewish. Avocations: travel photography, russian language, collecting antique maps. Office: Harper Hosp Div Infectious Diseases 3990 John R St Detroit MI 48201-2097 Office Phone: 313-577-9877. Business E-Mail: slerner@med.wayne.edu.

LERNER, THEODORE, real estate company executive; b. 1925; m. Annette Lerner; 3 children. BA, George Washington Univ., 1947. Real estate developer, 1950—; owner, prin., pres. Lerner Enterprises, Wash., DC; owner Washington Nationals (MLB), 2006—. Developer Wheaton Plaza Shopping Mall, 1960, Tysons Corner Shopping Ctr., 1968. Founder Annette M. and Theodore N. Lerner Found. Named one of 400 Richest Americans, Forbes, 2006; named to DC Bus. Hall of Fame, 2004. Office: Lerner Enterprises 11501 Huff Ct North Bethesda MD 20895-1094

LERNER, VLADIMIR SEMION, computer scientist, educator; b. Odessa, Ukraine, Sept. 12, 1931; arrived in U.S., 1990; s. Semion N. and Manya G. (Grosman) L.; m. Sanna K. Gleyzer, Sept. 28, 1954; children: Alex, Tatyana, Olga. BSEE, Odessa Poly. Inst., 1954; MEE, Inst. Problem's Controls, Moscow, 1959; PhD in Elec. Engring., Moscow Power Inst., 1961; D Sci. in Systems Analysis, Leningrad State U., 1974. Prof. elec. engring. Kishinev (Moldova) State U., 1962-64; prof. elec. engring. and control systems Kishinev Poly. Inst., 1964-79; sr. scientist in applied math. Acad. Sci., Kishinev, 1964-79; dir. math. modeling and computer sci. lab. Rsch. Inst., Odessa, 1979-89; sr. lectr. UCLA, 1991-93, rschr., 1993—; chmn. computer sci. dept. West Coast U., LA, 1993-97, Nat. U., LA, 1997-99. Mem. adv. bds. Acad. Sci., Kishinev, 1964—79, Poly. Inst. Kishinev, 1964—79; vis. prof. Leningrad State U., 1971—73; cons., mem. adv. bd. Poly. Inst. Odessa, 1979—89. Author: Physical Approach to Control Systems, 1969, Superimposing Processes in Control Problems, 1973, Dynamic Models in Decision Making, 1974, Special Course in Optimal and Self Control Systems, 1977, Lectures in Mathematical Modelling and Optimization, 1995, Mathematical Foundations of Informational Macrodynamics, 1996, Lectures in Informational Macrodynamics, 1996, Information Systems Analysis and Modelling: An Informational Microdynamics Approach, 1999, Variation Principle in Informational Macrodynamics, 2003, Introduction to Information Systems Theory, 2004. Recipient Silver medal for rsch. achievements, Moscow, 1961, outstanding achievements in edn., Kishinev, 1975. Achievements include development of new scientific discipline Informational Macrodynamics. Avocations: bicycling, travel. E-mail: vslerner@yahoo.com.

LERNER, WARREN, historian, educator; b. Boston, July 16, 1929; s. Max and Rebecca (Rudnick) L.; m. Francine Sandra Pickow, Aug. 16, 1959; children: Suzanne Rachel Knuiman, Amy Florence Coyle, Daniel Joseph. BS, Boston U., 1952; MA and cert. of Russian, Inst. Columbia U., 1954, PhD, 1961. Asst. prof. history Roosevelt U., 1959-61; asst. prof. Duke U., 1961-65, assoc. prof., 1965-72, prof., 1972—2002, chmn. dept., 1985-90, prof. emeritus, 2002—. Cons. NEH, 1974—80. Author: Karl Radek: The Last Internationalist, 1970, A History of Socialism and Communism in Modern Times, 1982, rev. edit., 1993; editor: The Development of Soviet Foreign Policy, 1973, (with Clifford M. Foust) The Soviet World in Flux, 1967; contbr. articles to profl. jours.; mem. editl. bd. Studies in Comparative Communism, 1973-91. Served with U.S. Army, 1954-56. Am. Philos. Soc. fellow, 1972, 82; NEH, 1974-75; Am. Council Learned Socs.-Social Svc. Rsch. Coun. fgn. area fellow. Mem. Conf. Slavic and East European History (exec. council 1978-80, pres. 1986-87), So. Conf. Slavic Studies (Outstanding Svc. award, 2003) Jewish. Office: Duke U Dept History PO Box 90719 Durham NC 27708-0719 Home Phone: 919-489-4362. Business E-Mail: wlerner@duke.edu.

LERNER, WAYNE M., healthcare executive; b. Chicago, Ill. BS, U. Ill.; MHA, U. Mich., DPH, 1988. Adminstrv. positions Rush Presbyterian St. Luke's Med. Ctr., Chicago; pres. Jewish Hosp., St. Louis, 1991—96; developer. exec. v.p. BLC Health System, 1993—96; v.p. Lash Group, Bannockburn, Ill., 1996; pres., CEO Rehab. Inst. Chgo., 1997—. Chmn. Am. Hosp. Assn. Com. of Commissioners; mem. exec. com., bd. of commissioners Joint Commn. on Accreditation of Healthcare Orgn. Fellow Am. Coll. of Healthcare Executives. Office: Rehab Inst Chgo 345 E Superior St Chicago IL 60611-2654 Office Phone: 312-908-2720.

LERNER, WILLIAM C., lawyer; b. Phila., July 17, 1933; m. G. Billie Campbell, Aug. 15, 1957; children: Bonnie, Edwina. BA, Cornell U., 1955; LLB, NYU, 1960. Bar: NY 1961, Pa. 1992. Counsel SEC, 1960—65; asst. v.p., compliance officer Am. Stock Exch., 1965—68; sr. v.p., sec., compliance officer Carter, Berlind & Weill, Inc., NYC, 1968—71; pvt. practice Buffalo, 1971—85; counsel Snow, Becker & Krauss, PC, NYC, 1990—95; pvt. practice Pitts., 1991—. V.p., gen. counsel The Geneva Cos., Irvine, Calif., 1986—89, Hon. Devel. Co., Laguna Hills, Calif., 1990—91; pub. arbitrator Nat. Assn. Securities Dealers, 1995—2006; bd. dirs. Reich and Tang Complex Money Market Funds including Daily Income Fund, Calif. Daily Tax Free Income Fund, Conn. Daily Tax Free Income Fund and NJ Daily Mcpl. Income Fund, Coach Industries Group, Inc., MTM Techs., Inc. Chmn. Erie County Pub. Utilities Task Force, 1974—75; mem. Art Coll. Coun. Cornell U., 1977—85; mem. NY Gov.'s Hazardous Waste Facilities Task Force, 1983—85. 1st. lt. Q.M.C. US Army, 1955—57. Mem.: Assn. SEC Alumni, Am. Soc. Corp. Secs. and Governance Profls. Office: 423 E Beau St Washington PA 15301-3605 Office Phone: 724-225-7177.

LERNER-LAM, EVA I-HWA, transportation executive; b. NYC, Dec. 27, 1954; d. Sau-Wing and Jean (Lu) Lam; m. Arthur Lawrence Lerner-Lam, Sept. 4, 1977; children: Timothy Chi-Wen, Matthew Ta-Wen, Katherine I-Wen. AB, Princeton U., 1976; MS, MIT, 1978. Asst. planner County of San Diego, San Diego, 1977-78; dir. transp. planning group PRC Toups/Voorhies, La Jolla, Calif., 1978-79; assoc. planner Orange County Transit Dist., Garden Grove, Calif., 1979-80, San Diego Met. Transit Devel. Bd., 1980, sr. planner, 1981, dir. planning and ops., 1982-84; gen. mgr. Regency Motors, Montclair, NJ, 1984-85; asst. v.p., dir. planning and adminstrn. The Dah Chong Hong Trading Corp., NYC, 1985-88; prin., cons. The Palisades Cons. Group Inc., Tenafly, NJ, 1988—; transport sys. advisor Economist Confs. Group, 1994—; co-founder ChinaTransport.net, 2000—. Mem. coun. on Fgn. Rels., 1996—, bd. adv. ENO Transp. Found., 1997—; chair Transit Cooperative Rsch. Program Transit-IDEA, Transp. Rsch. Bd., 1998—; bd. dirs. Transit Stds. Consortium, Inc. Founder, coord. Asian-Am. Admissions Vols. Group, Princeton, N.J., 1985—; chmn. bd. dirs. Si-Yo Music Soc. Found., N.Y.C., 1988—; bd. dirs. Princeton U., 1984-88, founder, bus. mgr. and condr. Princeton U. Jazz Ensemble, 1973-76; mem. Coun. on Fgn. REls., 1996—; bd. advisors Eno Transp. Found., 1997—. Outstanding student fellow State Farm Cos., Princeton, 1974; recipient Outstanding Achievement award Tribute to Women in Industry, San Diego, 1983; named Auto Dealer of Yr., N.J. Living Mag., 1985. Mem. NSF (transp. rsch. bd.), ASCE (vice chmn. planning com. urban transp. divsn. 1987-91, vice chairperson exec. com. 1991-92, chmn. exec. com. 1992-93, Frank M. Masters Transp. Engring. award 1998), Am. Planning Assn., Inst. Transp. Engrs. (best paper award 61st ann. meeting 1991, Innovative Intermodal Solutions for Urban Transp. award 1993, Ivor S. Wisepart Engr. award 1995), IVHS Am. (founding mem.), Asian Alumni of Princeton (mem. exec. com. Beijing 2000—, Outstanding Achievement award 1988), Campus Club (bd. dirs. 1984-94), San Diego Princeton Club (pres. 1983-84). Avocations: piano, swimming, running, bicycling, hiking. E-mail: elernerlam@palisadesgroup.com.

LEROY, CLAUDE, physics professor, researcher; b. Charleroi, Hainaut, Belgium, Sept. 30, 1947; s. Bernard and Renée (Jacobeus) L. Mathématique Spéciale, Faculté St. Louis, Brussels, 1967; Lic. en Sci., U. Louvain, Belgium, 1971, D in Scis., 1976. Rsch. assoc. McGill U., Montréal, 1977-80; attaché de rsch U. Montréal, 1978-80; rsch. assoc. Northwestern U., Evanston, Ill., 1980-81; chercheur du fonds du devel. scis. U. Louvain, 1981-83; rsch. scientist Inst. Particle Physics, Montréal, 1983-90; assoc. prof. physics McGill U., 1983-90; titular prof. physics U. Montréal, 1990—, dir. nuc. physics lab., 1991—94, 2000—; assoc. dir. Lab. Advanced Detector Devel. Can. Found. for Innovation, 2002—. Vis. rsch. fellow U. Southampton, Eng., 1976-77; sci. assoc. Ctr. European Rsch. Nuc. physics, Geneva, Switzerland, 1980—, dept. energy U. Florence, 1995-97; hon. prof. Nat. U. Peru, 1994—; mem. bd. mgmt. Inst. for Exptl. and Applied Physics, Prague, TRIUMF Can.'s Nat. Lab. for Particle and Nuc. Physics, Ctr. Exptl. Nuc. Physics and Astrophysics, Prague. Contbr. over 400 articles to profl. jours. Recipient prize for Achievements in Physics, Sci. Coun. Joint Inst. Nuclear Rsch., Moscow, 2000; Killam Rsch. fellow, The Can. Coun., 1993—95. Fellow Royal Soc. Can. (Rutherford prize for physics, 1988, mem. Acad. Scis.); mem. Inst. Particle Physics Can., Can. Assn. Physicists. Roman Catholic. Avocations: Chinese language, hieroglyphics, history, fishing. Home: 335 Hauterive Laval PQ Canada H7G 4L5 Office: U Montréal Nuclear Physics Lab CP 6128 succursale Centre-ville Montreal PQ Canada H3C 3J7 Office Phone: 514-343-6722. Personal E-mail: claude.leroy@cern.ch. Business E-Mail: leroy@lps.umontreal.ca.

LEROY, DAVID HENRY, lawyer; b. Seattle, Aug. 16, 1947; s. Harold David and Lela Fay (Palmer) L.; 2 children. BS, U. Idaho, 1969, JD, 1971; LLM, NYU, 1972; JD (hon.), Lincoln Coll., 1993. Bar: Idaho 1971, NY 1973, US Supreme Ct. 1976. Law clk. Idaho 4th Dist. Ct., Boise, 1969; legal asst. Boise Cascade Corp., 1970; assoc. firm Rothblatt, Rothblatt, Seijas & Peskin, NYC, 1971-73; dep. prosecutor Ada County Prosecutor's Office, Boise, 1973-74, pros. atty., 1974-78; atty. gen. State of Idaho, Boise, 1978-82, lt. gov., 1983-87; ptnr. Runft, Leroy Coffin & Matthews, 1983-88, Leroy Law Offices, 1988—. Candidate for Gov. of Idaho, 1986, US Congress, 1994; US nuc. waste negotiator, 1990-93; US Presdl. elector, 1992; chmn. com. on improving practices for regulatory and mng. low-activity radioactive waste NAS, 2002--; lectr., cons. in field. Mem. State Task Force on Child Abuse, 1975; mem. Ada County Coun. on Alcoholism, 1976; del. Rep. Nat. Conv., 1976, 80, 84, 2004; chmn. Nat. Rep. Lt. Gov.'s Caucus, 1983-86; bd. dirs. United Fund, 1975-81; del. Am. Coun. Young Polit. Leaders, USSR, 1979, Am. Coun. for Free Asia, Taiwan, 1980, U.S./Taiwan Investment Forum, 1983; del. leader Friendship Force Tour USSR, 1984; legal counsel Young Reps., 1974-81; candidate for Gov. Idaho, 1986; presdl. elector, 1992; candidate U.S. Ho. Reps. 1st Dist., Idaho, 1994; Idaho Abraham Lincoln Bicentennial Commn. Com. 2006—. Mem. Nat. Dist. Attys. Assn., Idaho Prosecutors Assn., Am. Trial Lawyers Assn., Idaho Criminal Defense Lawyers Assn., Nat. Assn. Attys. Gen. (chmn. energy subcom., exec. com., del to China 1981), Western Attys. Gen. Assn. (vice chmn. 1980-83, chmn. 1981), Nat. Lt. Govs. Assn. (exec. bd. 1983), Idaho Bar Assn., Ada County Lincoln Day Assn. (pres. 2000), Am. Lung Assn. Idaho, Found. for Idaho History (pres. 2001-05), NAS (chmn. com. on improving practices for regulating and mng. low activity radioactive waste 2002-06), Idaho State Repub. Conv. (vice chmn. 2004, chmn. Idaho Abraham Lincoln bicentenniel com. 2006—, governor's coun. US Abraham Lincoln bicentenniel commn., 2007-), Sigma Alpha Epsilon. Presbyterian. Office: The Leroy Offices PO Box 193 Boise ID 83701-0193 Office Phone: 208-342-0000.

LEROY, G. PALMER, art dealer; b. NYC, July 15, 1929; s. John Minturn and Georgiana Kip (Palmer) LeR.; m. Kyra Hawkins, June 18, 1955; children: Kyra, Nina, Pamela. BA, Harvard U., 1951. With N.Y. Times, 1951-52, Frank Best & Co., NYC, 1952-53, Kenyon & Eckhardt, Inc., NYC, 1953-55, Inmont Corp., U.S. and Europe, 1955-83; v.p. sales Inmont Internat., Inc., NYC, 1974-83; ptnr. Clinton R. Howell, Inc. Antiques, Pound Ridge, N.Y., 1984-85; mng. dir. Met. Opera Guild, Inc., NYC, 1985-94; pub. Opera News, NYC, 1985-94; dealer 19th and 20th Century Am. Art Palmer LeRoy Fine Art, Nantucket, Mass., 1994—. Mem. industry sector adv. com. chem. industry U.S. Commerce Dept., 1976-83. Pres. Friends of John Jay Homestead, Inc., Katonah, N.Y., 1977-95, chmn., 1995-98, chmn. emeritus, 1998—; bd. dirs. The Bedford Assn., 1972-85, pres., 1975-80, bd. dirs. emeritus, 1986-97; bd. dirs. Wildlife Preservation Trust Internat., Inc., Phila., 1983-94, pres., 1990-93, emeritus coun., 1994—; bd. dirs. N.Y. br. English Speaking Union, 1993-98, chmn., 1994-97; sr. warden St. Matthew's Ch., Bedford, 1985-89.

LEROY, MISS JOY, model, apparel designer; b. Riverdale, Ill., Sept. 8, 1927; d. Gerald and Dorothea (Wingebach) Reasor. BS, Purdue U., 1949. Model, sales rep. Jacques, Lafayette, Ind., 1950; book dept. sales rep. Loebs, 1951-52; window trimmer Marshall Fields and Co., Evanston, Ill., 1952-53; sales and display rep. Emerald House, 1954-55. Model, narrator, designer J. L. Hudson Co., GM Corp., Coca Cola Co., Hoover Vacuum Co., Jam Handy Orgn., Rambler and Kelvinator divsn. Am. Motors Corp., Speedway Petroleum Corp., Ford Motor Co., auto, tractor & implement divsn., Sykes Co., Detroit, 1956—61; tour guide, model, freelance writer Christian Sci. Publ. Soc. and Monitor; spl. events coord. Prudential Ins. Co.; model Copley 7, Boston, 1962—70. Author: Puzz-its, 1986—2006. Founding angel Asolo Theatre, Sarasota, 1960; mem. Ft. Lauderdale Internat. Film Festival, 1990, Mus. of Art, 1978, Fla. Conservation Assn., Rep. Senatorial Com. Inner Cir., 1990, Rep. Nat. Hall of Honor, 1992, Congl. Com., 1990, Nat. Trust for Hist. Preservation, 1986, Fla. Trust for Hist. Preservation, 1987; one of founding friends 1000 Friends of Fla., 1991; life mem. Rep. Presdl. Task Force, 1993; mem. Grand Club Rep. Party Fla., 1996; v.p. of recognition bd. World Congress of Arts, Sci., and Comms., Washington, 2007. Named Internat. Visual Artist of Yr., Woman of Yr., Ambassador Gen., ABI, Hon. Dir., Gen., Life Patron, Global Yr. of Excellence Gold Medal, IBA, Noble and Genius Laureate, 2005, Amb., Internat. Order Merit, 2007; named one of Top 100 Artist; named to Order of Am. Ambassadors; recipient Rep. Presdl. Legion Honor medal, 1993, Rep. medal of Freedom and Wall of Honor, 1994, Disting. 20th Century Rep. Leader, 1994, 1998, Founder's Wall award, 1995, World Laureate of Eng., 1999, Rep. Presdl. Roundtable, 2000—07, Internat. Order of Merit, Am. Order of Excellence, 2000, Order of Internat. Ambs., 2000, Congl. medal of excellence, 2002, Hallmark medal of honor, 2002, Rep. Senatorial Millennium Medal of Freedom and Star, Lifetime Achievement award, World Congress of Arts, Sci. and Comm., Medal of Honor, Internat. Hall of Fame, Masters, World Acad. of Letters, Statesman award, DaVinci Diamond, 50th Crystal Platinum, 2004, Sci. and Comm. 100 Life Achievement award, World Congress of Arts, Salute to Greatness Gold Medal, Gold Medal of Freedom, Gold Medal for USA, Republican Senatorial Am. Spirit award, 2006, World Record Holder, ABI, Achievement and Excellence in Art decree, Internat. Biog. Assn., 2007, Pres. Cup award, World Forum, Oxford, England, 2007. Mem.: Friends of Fla. 1000, Am. Rivers, Am. Queen Inaugural Soc., Stratford Shakespearean Festival of Can., Libr. of Congress (nat. mem.), Wilderness Soc., Heritage Found., The Crystal Soc., Ellis Island Found. (charter), Cousteau Soc., Heralds of Nature Soc., Purdue U. Alumni Assn. (pres.'s coun.), USS Constn. Mus., Paddlewheel Steamboatin' Soc. Am., Nat. Corvette Owners Assn., Soc. Honorary Mariners, INTRAV-Pinnacle-Elite Explorer Club, Internat. Gov.'s Club (continental gov.), Maupin Travelers Club, Platinum Captain's Cir., Ducks Unltd., Skald Club, Seabourn Club, Cunard World Club, Magic Kingdom Entertainment Club, Zeta Tau Alpha. Avocations: travel, art, education, design, photography. Home: 2100 S Ocean Ln Apt 2104 Fort Lauderdale FL 33316-3827

LEROY, SPENCER, III, lawyer; b. Oak Park, Ill., Apr. 13, 1946; s. Spencer and Priscilla LeRoy; m. Barbara LeRoy. AB with high honors, U. Mich., 1968, JD, 1974. Bar: Ill. 1974, US Dist. Ct. No. Dist. Ill. 1974. Assoc. Lord, Bissell & Brook, 1974—82, ptnr., 1982—92; sr. v.p., sec., gen. counsel Old Republic Internat. Corp., Chgo., 1992—. Sgt. US Army, 1970—73. Mem.: Ill. State Bar Assn., ABA, Phi Beta Kappa. Office: Old Republic International Corp 19th Fl 307 N Michigan Ave Chicago IL 60601

LESAR, DAVID J., oil industry executive; b. 1954; BS, U. Wis., 1975, MBA, 1978. Ptnr. in charge of energy mfg. and retail practices Arthur Andersen & Co., Dallas, 1978—93; exec. v.p. fin. & adminstrn. Halliburton Energy Services, 1993—95; pres., CEO Brown and Root, Inc., 1996—97; exec. v.p., CFO Halliburton Co., 1995—96, pres., COO, 1997—2000, chmn., pres., CEO, 2000—. Bd. dirs. Lyondell Chemical Co., Mirant Co., 2000—. Mem.: Am. Petroleum Inst., Upstream Com. Office: Halliburton Co 5 Houston Ctr 1401 McKinney Ste 2400 Houston TX 77020*

LESAVOY, MALCOLM ALAN, plastic surgeon; b. Allentown, Pa., June 27, 1942; BA, U. NC, 1964; MD, Chgo. Med. Sch., 1969. Diplomate Am. Bd. Plastic Surgery 1977. Resident gen. surgery U. Chgo., 1969—74; resident plastic and reconstructive surgery U. Miami, 1974—76; chief plastic surgery Harbor-UCLA Med. Ctr., Torrance, 1976—99; plastic surgeon Encino Outpatient Surgery Ctr., Calif., 1999—. Prof. plastic and reconstructive surgery UCLA Sch. Medicine, LA, 1976—99, clin. prof. plastic and reconstructive surgery, 1999—; nat. pres. Millard Plastic Surgery Soc., 1987—89; Frank Hawkins Kenan vis. prof. dept. surgery Duke U., Durham, NC, 2003; Kazanjian vis. prof. divsn. plastic and reconstructive surgery Harvard U., Boston, 2003; Courtemanche vis. prof. U. BC, Vancouver, 2004; vis. prof. Baylor Coll. Med., Houston, 2005. Author: Reconstruction of the Head and Neck, 1981, Hand Surgery Review, 1981, 2d edit., 1985, over 25 book chpts., over 70 articles to profl. jours. in field. Nat. pres. Reconstructive Surgeons Vol. Program, 1990—92. With USAR, 1969—76. Named a Disting. Alumnus, Chgo. Med. Sch., 1983; recipient Excellence in Clin. Tchg. award, UCLA Sch. Medicine, 1978, 1992, 1993, 2004. Mem.: ACS, World Soc. Reconstructive Microsurgery, Plastic Surgery Rsch. Coun., Plastic Surgery Ednl. Found. (bd. dirs. 1984—93, pres. 1991—92), Internat. Coll. Surgeons, Am. Soc. Plastic Surgeons (bd. dirs. 1990—94, chmn. bd. trustees 1995—96), Am. Soc. Maxillofacial Surgeons, Am. Assn. Plastic Surgery (named Clinician of Yr. 2002). Office: 16311 Ventura Blvd Ste 555 Encino CA 91436 Office Phone: 818-986-8270. Business E-Mail: mlesavoy@surgicalrenaissance.com.

LESBO, PAULA MAE, elementary and secondary education educator; b. Ft. Collins, Colo. d. Vernon E. and Mae Pauline (Topolka) Johnson; m. Barnard J. Lesbo, Jan. 3, 1969; children: Crystal, Michael. Degree in edn., Loretto Heights Coll., Denver; BA, U. Nev., Reno, 1970. Lic. tchr., Nev., Ariz. Tchr. Nev. Youth Tng. Ctr., Elko, Nev. Office: Nev Youth Tng Ctr 100 youth Ctr Rd Elko NV 89803-0469

LESCH, ANN MOSELY, political scientist, educator; b. Washington, Feb. 1, 1944; d. Philip Edward and Ruth (Bissell) Mosely. BA, Swarthmore Coll., 1966; PhD, Columbia U., 1973. Rsch. assoc. Fgn. Policy Rsch. Inst., Phila., 1972-74; assoc. Middle East rep. Am. Friends Svc. Com., Jerusalem, 1974-77; Middle East program officer Ford Found., NYC, 1977-80, program officer Cairo, 1980-84; assoc. Univs. Field Staff Internat., 1984-87; prof. Villanova U., 1987—2004, assoc. dir. ctr. Arab and Islamic studies, 1992-95; dean humanities & social scis. Am. U. Cairo, 2004—. Author: The Politics of Palestinian Nationalism, 1973, Arab Politics in Palestine, 1979, Political perceptions of the Palestinians on the West Bank and Gaza, 1980, (with Mark Tessler) Israel, Egypt and the Palestinians, 1989, Transition to Palestinian Self-Government, 1992, (with D. Tschirgi) Origins and Development of the Arab-Israeli Conflict, 1998, 2d edit., 2006, The Sudan: Contested National Identities, 1998, (with Steven Wondu) Battle for Peace in Sudan, 2000, (with Osman Fadl) Coping with Torture: Images from Sudan, 2004, (with Ian Lustick) Exile & Return, 2005; contbr. articles to profl. jours. Co-chair Middle East Program Com., Am. Friends Svc. Com., 1989—94; mem. Quaker UN Com., 1979—80; U.S. adv. com. Interns for Peace, 1978—82; bd. dirs. Am. Near East Refugee Aid, 1980—86, Middle East Report, 1989—93, Human Rights Watch/Middle East, 1989—. Fellow Catherwood Found., 1965; NDFL, 1967-71; Am. Rsch. Ctr. grant Egypt, 1988, U.S. Inst. of Peace Rsch. grants, 1990-91, 97, 2002-03, Wilson Ctr. Guest scholar Smithsonian, 1990, Rockefeller Fdn. Bellagio Ctr., 1996, Fulbright scholar, Cairo, 1999-2000, Beirut, 2003. Mem.: Palestinian Am. Rsch. Ctr. (co-chair 1998—2001, U.S. dir. 2001—04), Coun. on Fgn. Rels., Sudan Studies Assn. (sec. 1993—96, pres. 1998—2000), Am. Polit. Sci. Assn., Mid. East Inst., Mid. East Studies Assn. (bd. dirs. 1988—91, pres. 1993—96, bull. editor 1997—99). Unitarian Universalist. Office: American Univ HUSS Dean 113 Qasr al-Aini Cairo Egypt

LESCH, MICHAEL, cardiologist; b. NYC, June 30, 1939; s. Maurice and Rose (Linn) L.; m. H. Bella Samuels, June 25, 1961; children— Leah Deura, Ian Samuel. AB, Columbia U., 1960; MD, Johns Hopkins U., 1964. Diplomate: Am. Bd. Internal Medicine, Am. Bd. Cardiology. Intern, then resident in medicine Johns Hopkins Hosp., 1964-66; physician USPHS, 1966-68; chief resident physician, fellow cardiology, asst. prof., then asso. prof. medicine Harvard U. Med. Sch.-Peter Bent Brigham Hosp., 1968-76; Magerstadt prof. medicine Northwestern U. Med. Sch., 1976-89; clin. prof. medicine, chmn. dept. medicine, Henry Ford Hosp. U. Mich., Detroit, 1989—; prof. Medicine Case Western U., Cleve., 1994—. Mem. life scis. adv. com. NASA, 1980 Editor: Progress in Cardiovascular Diseases, 1971—; editorial bd. profl. jours. Fellow A.C.P., Am. Coll. Cardiology; mem. Am. Soc. Clin. Investigation, Am. Heart Assn. (gov. 1978-81), Chgo. Heart Assn. (pres. 1982-83)

LESCH, MICHAEL OSCAR, lawyer; b. Berlin, May 28, 1938; came to U.S., 1940, naturalized, 1946; s. Adolf F. and Maria E. Leschnitzer; m. Judith Willis, Aug. 31, 1965; children: Sara, Benjamin. AB, Columbia U., 1958; LLB, Harvard U., 1961. Bar: N.Y. 1961, U.S. Dist. Ct (so. dist.) N.Y. 1963, U.S. Dist. Ct (ea. dist.) N.Y. 1965, U.S. Ct. Appeals (2d cir.) 1968, U.S. Supreme Ct. 1975, U.S. Ct. Appeals (3d cir.) 1979, U.S. Ct. Appeals (7th cir.) 1979, U.S. Ct. Appeals (9th cir.) 2001. Assoc. Shea & Gould and predecessors, NYC, 1961-69, ptnr., 1970-94, LeBoeuf, Lamb, Greene & MacRae, NYC, 1994—. Dir. Apple Bank for Savs., NYC, 2001—. Contbr. articles to profl. jours. Mem. ABA, N.Y. State Bar Assn., Assn. Bar City N.Y., Fed. Bar Coun., Am. Arbitration Assn. (panel of arbitrators). Office: LeBoeuf Lamb Greene & MacRae 125 W 55th St New York NY 10019-5369 Home Phone: 914-834-9370. Business E-Mail: michael.lesch@llgm.com.

LESCROART, JOHN THOMAS, writer, composer, singer; b. Houston, Jan. 14, 1948; s. Maurice Eugene and Loretta Therese (Gregory) L.; m. Leslee Ann Miller, 1976 (div. 1978); m. Lisa Sawyer, Sept. 2, 1984; children: Justine Rose Lescroart, John Jack Sawyer Lescroart. BA in English Lit. with honors, U. Calif., Berkeley, 1970. Author: Sunburn, 1981 (Joseph Henry Jackson award, 1978), Son of Holmes, 1986, Rasputin's Revenge, 1987, Dead Irish, 1989, The Vig, 1990, Hard Evidence, 1993, The 13th Juror (NY Times Best Seller 1995), A Certain Justice, 1995, Guilt (NY Times Best Seller 1998), The Mercy Rule (NY Times Best Seller 1999), Nothing But The Truth (NY Times Best Seller 2001), The Hearing (NY Times Best Seller 2002), The Oath (NY Times Best Seller 2002), The First Law (NY Times Best Seller 2003), The Second Chair (NY Times Best Seller 2004), The Motive (NY Times Best Seller 2006), The Hunt Club (NY Times Best Seller 2006) The Suspect (NY Times Best Seller 2006), Whiskey and Roses, 2007; composer (album) Date Night, 2003; composer and singer As The Crow Flies, 2003, Whiskey and Roses, 2007. Bd. trustees U. Calif., Davis. Mem. El Macero Country Club, Wine & Food Soc. Sacramento/San Joaquin. Avocations: fishing, baseball, food and wine. Personal E-mail: jles@calweb.com.

LESEBERG, DIETER WOLFGANG MICHAEL, mathematician; b. Berlin, Mar. 26, 1947; s. Wilhelm and Kathie Leseberg; m. Sirpa Maritta Laitinen, Nov. 21, 1975; children: Nora, Anna. Diploma, Free U., Berlin, 1974, Doctorate, 1980, habilitation, 1995. EDP organizer Siemens AG, Berlin, 1974; lectr. high sch., Berlin, 1974—76; reference libr. GHB, Kassel, 1979—80, L-Sch., Frankfurt, 1980—81; with Inst. Care Monuments, Hannover, 1983—85; lectr. U. Hannover, 1984; sci. libr. Tech. U., Braunschweig, 1985—; lectr. Free U. Berlin, 1990—95, asst. prof., 1995—. Contbr. articles to profl. jours. Mem. Vol. Fire Brigade, 1995. Mem.: Berlin Math. Soc. Office: U B Braunschweig Pockelsstrasse 13 38106 Braunschweig Germany Office Phone: 49 (531) 391-5006. Business E-Mail: d.leseberg@tu-bs.de.

LESER, ANNE ELIZABETH, education educator; d. Stark William and Ann Moloney Leser. BA, Ohio No. U., 1972; MA, Ohio State U., 1984, PhD, 1989. Cert. elem. and secondary tchr. Tchr. Gallipolis (Ohio) City Schs., 1973—74, Hancock Hardin Wyandot Putman Head Start, Findlay, Ohio, 1974—76, edn. dir., 1976—81; cons. Upper Sandusky, Ohio, 1981—83; grad. asst. Ohio State U., Columbus, 1984—88; asst. prof. U. Fla., Gainesville, 1988—89; faculty devel. Ohio State U., Columbus, Ohio, 1989—90, U. Ill., Champaign, 1990—92; from asst. to assoc. prof. Maryville U., St. Louis, 1992—2003; assoc. prof., dir. Early Childhood Studies Bowling Green State U.-Firelands, Huron, Ohio, 2003—. Condr. workshop for tchrs. Amy Biehl Found., Cape Town, South Africa, 1999, 2005; cons. pub. schs., Cape Town, South Africa, 00; presenter nat. confs., 1994—. Co-author: (handbook) Handbook for Clinical Instructors, 1990. Mem. ACLU, So. Poverty Law Ctr., Birmingham, Ala.; vol. Rape Crisis Ctr., St. Louis, 1995—98, CASA, Ohio, 2005—, ct. apptd. spl. adv.; leader student group Cape Town, South Africa, 2005. Mem.: Nat. Assn. Multicultural Edn., Ohio Assn. Early Childhood Tchr. Edn. (pres.), Nat. Assn. Early Childhood Tchr. Edn., Nat. Assn. Edn. Young Children, Ohio State Alumni Club (pres. 2001, sec. 2002), Phi Delta Kappa. Avocations: travel, social justice activities, reading. Office: Bowling Green State U-Firelands 1 University Dr Huron OH 44839 Office Phone: 419-372-0928. Business E-Mail: aleser@bgnet.bgsu.edu.

LE SHANA, DAVID CHARLES, retired academic administrator; b. Lucknow, India, Nov. 15, 1932; came to U.S., 1949; naturalized, 1958; s. Newman John and Gwendolyn Beatrice (White) Le S.; m. Rebecca Ann Swander, June 8, 1951; children: Deborah Lynn, James David, Catherine Ann, Christine Joy. AB, Taylor U., Upland, Ind., 1953; AM in Edn, Ball State U., 1959; PhD, U. So. Calif., 1967; LHD (hon.), George Fox Coll., 1982; EdD (hon.), Taylor U., 1996; DD (hon.), Western Evang. Sem., 1996. Ordained to ministry Friends Ch., 1953; pastor Ypsilanti (Mich.) Friends Ch., 1953-54; dir. pub. relations, chaplain Taylor U., 1954-61; pastor 1st Friends Ch., Long Beach, Calif., 1961-67; mem. staff George Fox Coll., Newberg, Oreg., from 1967, acting pres., 1967—68, exec. v.p., 1968—69, pres., 1969-82, pres. emeritus, 1996—; pres. Seattle Pacific U., 1982-91, pres. emeritus, 1991—; pres. Western Evang. Sem., Portland, Oreg., 1992-96, pres. emeritus, 1996—. Min. Pacific N.W. Conf. of Free Meth. Ch.; bd. dirs. Coun. Ind. Colls., 1971-80, chmn., 1976-78; chmn. commn. higher edn. Nat. Assn. Evangelicals, 1973-75; chmn. Oreg. Ind. Colls. Assn., 1971-72, 81-82; mem. So. Calif. Radio and TV Commn., 1963-67; bd. dirs. Christian Coll. Consortium, chmn., 1984-86; mem. fact-finding group to Bangladesh, 1972; mem. adv. bd. Oriental Missionary Soc.Internat.; bd. advs. Latin Am. Mission, 1984-2002, Friends Ctr., Azusa Pacific U., 1986—; mem. capital campaign com. Taylor U., 1995-2000; bd. dirs. N.W. Christian Cmty. Found., 1999—, Westlake Home Owners Assn., KWI Found., 1984-2000. Author: Quakers in California, 1969; Rec.: album Songs of Discipleship, 1965. Bd. dirs. Oreg. Ind. Coll. Found., 1969-82, 92-96, George Fox Coll. Found., 1971-82, Herbert Hoover Found., Oreg., 1975-82, Ind. Colls. of Wash., 1982-91, Wash. Friends of Higher Edn., 1982-91, Latin Am. Mission, 2002-06, Significant Living, 2002-06; bd. assocs. Pacific Sci. Ctr., 1989-92; mem. Wash. Gives Leadership Coun., 1989-92, mem. edn. commn. States Task Force on State Policy and Ind. Higher Edn., 1986-89; trustee CRISTA Ministries, 1982-88, 90-96, bd. dirs., 1982—; chmn. bd. Christian Coll. Coalition, 1991; trustee Azusa Pacific U., 2003—. Recipient Alumni Service award Taylor U., 1961, Chamber of Achievement award, 1978; Tchr. of Yr. award Ball State U., 1978 Mem. Nat. Assn. Evangs. (bd. dirs. 1980-99, chmn. theology com. 1992-94).

LESHER, JOHN LEE, JR., consulting services company executive; b. Harrisburg, Pa., Feb. 7, 1934; s. John Lee and Mary Alice (Watkeys) L.; m. Nancy Smith, July 11, 1970; children by previous marriage: John David, James Elam, Andrew Gwynne. BA cum laude, Williams Coll., 1956; MBA, Harvard U., 1958. Budget dir., asst. sec. The Barden Corp., Danbury, Conn., 1958-61; cons. Booz, Allen & Hamilton Inc., NYC, 1961-64, assoc., 1964-66, v.p., 1966-76, pres., 1976-85, Mars & Co. Cons. Inc., Greenwich, Conn., 1985-87, Home Group Fin. Services, NYC, 1987-88; v.p. Cresap, McCormick & Paget, NYC, 1988-89; mng. dir. Korn/Ferry Internat., NYC, 1989-93; pres. Jack Lesher & Assocs., Greenwich, Conn., 1993—. Mem.: Harvard Bus. Sch., Watch Hill Yacht, Misquamicut (Watch Hill, R.I.), Round Hill (Greenwich, Conn.), River (N.Y.C.), Coral Beach (Bermuda). Home Phone: 203-531-2879; Office Phone: 203-531-2803.

LESHER, WILLIAM RICHARD, retired academic administrator; b. Carlisle, Pa., Nov. 14, 1924; s. David Luther and Carrie LaVerne (Adams) L.; m. Veda E. Van Etten, June 16, 1946; children— Eileen Fern, Martha Zoe Lesher Keough Th.B., Atlantic Union Coll., South Lancaster, Mass., 1946; MA, Andrews U., 1964; PhD, NYU, 1970. Ordained to ministry Seventh-day Adventist Ch., 1951. Pastor No. New Eng. Conf. Seventh-day Adventists, 1946-56; pastor, mission dir. Delta sect. Nile Union Seventh-day Adventists, Alexandria, Egypt, 1957-58; prin. Nile Union Acad., Cairo, Egypt, 1959-61; sec. Middle East Div. Seventh-day Adventists Beirut, Lebanon, 1962-64; assoc. prof. religion, dir. summer sch., asst. to pres. Atlantic Union Coll., 1964-71; assoc. dir. Sabbath sch. dept. Gen. Conf. Seventh-day Adventists, Washington, 1971-79; dir. Bibl. Research Inst., Gen. Conf. Seventh-day Adventists, Washington, 1979-84; gen. v.p. Gen. Conf. Seventh-day Adventists, Washington, 1981-84; pres. Andrews U., Berrien Springs, Mich., 1984-94; ret., 1994. Author: Tips for Teachers, 1979; editor adult Sabbath Sch. lessons, 1971-79, studies in sanctuary and atonement, 1980-81; contbr. articles to religious jours. Recipient Founders Day award NYU, 1970 Home: 4703 Greenfield Dr Berrien Springs MI 49103-9566 Business E-Mail: lesher@andrews.edu.

LESHNER, ALAN IRVIN, science administrator; b. Lewisburg, Pa., Feb. 11, 1944; s. Saul S. and Martha (Schmidt) L.; m. Agnes Farkas, May 18, 1969; children: Sarah, Michael. AB, Franklin and Marshall Coll., 1965; MS, Rutgers U., 1967, PhD, 1969. Asst. prof. psychology Bucknell U., 1969-73, assoc. prof., 1973-78, prof., 1978-82; program assoc. divsn. behavioral and neural scis. NSF, Washington, 1979-80, dep. dir. divsn. behavioral and neural scis., 1983-85, dir. divsn. precoll. materials devel. and rsch., 1984-85, exec. officer biol., behavioral and social scis., 1985-87; project mgr. Office Dir., 1980-82; dep. exec. dir. Commn. on Precoll. Edn., Nat. Sci. Bd., 1982-83; dep. dir. NIMH, 1988-90, acting dir., 1990-92; dir. Nat. Inst. Drug Abuse NIH, Wash., DC, 1994—2001; CEO AAAS, Wash., DC, 2001—. Vis. scientist U. Wis., 1976-77, lectr. Weizmann Inst. Sci., Rehovoth, Israel, 1977-78; Am.-Hungarian Acads. Sci. exchange scientist Postgrad Med. Sch., Budapest, 1974; mem. bd. dirs. NSF Nat. Sci. Bd., 2004-. Author: An Introduction to Behavioral Endocrinology, 1978; exec. publisher Jour. Sci., 2001-; contbr. chpts. to books, numerous articles on roles of hormones in behavior, sci. and tech. policy, higher edn. to profl. publs. Fulbright scholar Weizman Inst. Sci.; recipient Nat. Rsch. Svc. award, 1976, Pres. Merit Exec. Rank award, 1990, Pres. Dist. Exec. Rank award, 1996. Fellow AAAS, APA, Am. Psychological Soc., N.Y. Acad. Scis., Internat. Soc. Rsch. on Aggression; mem. I.O.M., Phi Beta Kappa. Democrat. Jewish. Office: AAAS 1200 New York Ave NW Washington DC 20005 Office Fax: 202-371-9526.

LESHNER, ROBERT THEODORE, neurologist; b. Bklyn., Oct. 19, 1944; s. Theodore and Genevieve (Thomas) L.; m. Elizabeth Ann Weckesser, Dec. 28, 1968 (div. July 1991); m. Deborah C. Goodman, May 30, 1992; children: David Daniel, Elizabeth Tuttle, Thomas Weckesser. BA, Cornell U., 1965, MD, 1969. Intern Med. Ctr. Hosp. of Vt., 1969-70; resident in neurology U. Colo., 1970-74; Asst. prof. neurology Med. Coll. Ga., Augusta, 1978-80; assoc. prof. Med. Coll. Va., Richmond, 1980-88, prof. neurology & pediatrics, 1988—. Dir. neuromuscular sect. Med. Coll. Va., 1993—, dir. muscular dystrophy clinic, 1980—. Lt. comdr. USNR, 1974-78. Mem. Am. Assn. Electrodiagnostic Medicine (com. chari 1993), Am. Acad. Neurology, Deep Run Hunt Club. Avocations: skiing, equestrian events, scuba diving. Office: Med Coll Va PO Box 980599 Richmond VA 23298-0599

LESHNER, STEPHEN I., lawyer; b. NYC, Sept. 26, 1951; s. Leo and Gloria (Perlman) L.; m. Mary Ann Relles, Oct. 28, 1978; children: Samuel Joseph, Harry Jacob. BA, SUNY, Stony Brook, 1973; JD, Northeastern U., 1976. Bar: Ariz. 1976, U.S. Dist. Ct. Ariz. 1977, U.S. Ct. Appeals (9th cir.) 1981, U.S. Supreme Ct. 1980, U.S. Ct. Fed. Claims, 2006. Assoc. Legal Clinic Bates & O'Steen, Phoenix, 1977; ptnr. O'Steen Legal Clinic, Phoenix, 1977-80, Van, O'Steen and Ptnrs., Phoenix, 1980—2004; of counsel Plattner Verderame, PC, Phoenix, 2004—05, Stephen I. Leshner, P.C., Phoenix, 2005—. Criminal law specialist, Ariz. Bd. Legal Specialization, 1982-95, injury and wrongful death litigation specialist, 1991—; judge pro tem Maricopa County Superior Ct., 1993—. Mem. Assn. Trial Lawyers Am., Ariz. Trial Lawyers Assn. (bd. dirs., pres. 1999), Am. Bd. Trial Advocates, Million Dollar Advocates Forum, State Bar Ariz. Assn., Nucleus Club (chmn. 1995-96). Office: Stephen I Leshner PC 1440 E Missouri Ave Ste 265 Phoenix AZ 85014 Office Phone: 602-266-9000. Business E-Mail: steve@steveleshner.com.

LESHY, JOHN DAVID, lawyer, solicitor, educator; b. Winchester, Ohio, Oct. 7, 1944; s. John and Dolores (King) L.; m. Helen M. Sandalls, Dec. 15, 1973 (div. 2005); 1 child, David Alexander. AB cum laude, Harvard U., 1966, JD magna cum laude, 1969. Trial atty. civil rights divsn. Dept. Justice, Washington, 1969-72; atty. Natural Resources Def. Coun., Palo Alto, Calif., 1972-77; assoc. solicitor energy and resources Dept. Interior, Washington, 1977-80, solicitor (gen. counsel), 1993-2001; prof. law Ariz. State U., Tempe, 1980—2002; spl. counsel to chair Natural Resources Com. US Ho. Reps., Washington, 1992-93. Cons. Calif. State Land Commn., N.Mex. Atty. Gen., Western Govs. Assn., Congl. Rsch. Svc., Ford Found., Hewlett Found., Pew Charitable Trusts, Wyss Found.; mem. com. Onshore Oil & Gas Leasing, NAS Nat. Rsch. Coun., 1989-90; vis. prof. Sch. Law U. San Diego, 1990; disting. vis. prof. law U. Calif. Hastings Coll. Law, 2001-02, Harry D. Sunderland disting. prof. real property, 2002-; vis. prof. Harvard Law Sch., 2004, 06, 07. Author: The Mining Law: A Study in Perpetual Motion, 1987, The Arizona State Constitution, 1993; co-author Federal Public Land and Resources Law, 6th edit., 2007, Legal Control of Water Resources, 4th edit., 2006; contbr. articles, book chpts. to profl. jours., environ. jours. Bd. dirs. Ariz. Ctr. Law in Pub. Interest, 1981—86, Grand Canyon Trust, 1987—92, 2002—, Natural Heritage Inst., 2002—, Ariz. Raft Adventures, 1982—92, 2002—; mem. Gov.'s Task Force Recreation on Fed. Lands, 1985—86, Gov.'s Task Force Environ. Impact Assessment, 1990, City of Phoenix Environ. Quality Commn., 1987—90; pres. Wyss Found., 2002—07, vice-chair bd., 2007—. Robinson Cox vis. fellow U. Western Australia Law Sch., Perth, 1985, rsch. fellow U. Southampton, Eng., 1986; Ford Found. grantee, Resources for the Future grantee. Democrat. Avocations: piano, hiking, whitewater rafting, photography. Office: Calif Hastings Coll Law 200 McAllister St San Francisco CA 94102-4978 Business E-Mail: leshyj@uchastings.edu.

LESIKAR, JAMES DANIEL, II, physicist, engineer; b. Houston, Texas, Feb. 24, 1954; s. James Daniel and Ludine Luella (Kosel) L.; m. Sara Goeller, Dec. 9, 1995. BSME cum laude, Rice U., 1976, MME, 1978, MA, 1981, PhD in Physics, 1982. Registered profl. engr., Va., Md., Tex. Rsch. asst. T.W. Bonner Nuc. Labs. Rice U., Houston, 1976-81; asst. prof. physics US Naval Acad., Annapolis, Md., 1984-85; sr. analyst fed. sector civil group Computer Sci. Corp., Lanham, Md., 1986—2003; prin. engr. Sparta Inc., Columbia, Md., 2003—06; sr. prin. ops. rsch. analyst L-3 Commn. Titan Group, Reston, Va., 2006—. Mem. Md. State Bd. for Profl. Engr., 1996-2001, vice-chmn., 1998-2001; chair Md. Profl. Engr. Complaints Com., 1996-2001; spkr. in field; adj. faculty Anne Arundel CC, Arnold, Md., 2001-2002; evaluator Aerospace Programs (Engring. Accrediation Commn./ABET), 2003-; with Practicing Inst. Engring., Troy, NY, 2004-. Author (with others) NASA reports, 1987—; author of scope of practice for the design professions bill which was signed into law in Md., 2001; contbr. articles to Physics Letters, Phys. Rev., Phys. Rev. Letters. Co-moderator Math Counts Program, Annapolis, Md., 1991, 95, 96, 98, 99, 2000, 01, 02, 03, 06, 07; judge Hubble Space Telescope Engring. Competition, 1998, Solar and Heliospheric Observatory Engring. Competition, 1999; spkr. Nat. Engr. Week, Duval HS, Lanham, Md., 1999-; proctor Md. Mathcounts, 1996, 99, 2002, 03, 04, 06; sci. fair judge St. John the Evangelist Sch., Severna Park, Md., 2000-02; Internat. Sci. and Tech. Fair, U. Ctrl. Fla., 2004. Capt. US Army, 1981—85, lt. col. USAR, 1988—2006. Decorated Bronze Cross for Achievement Legion of Valor, Nat. Def. Svc. medal, Army Parachutist Badge; recipient Outstanding Teamwork award Goddard Space Flight Ctr., 2000; grad. fellow Rice U., Houston, 1976-77, Nettie S. Autrey Meml. fellow in sci., 1978-79; Order of the Engr., 1998; NCEES, NE Zone Distinguished Svc. Cert., 2003. Fellow AIAA (life assoc., guidance navigation and control tech. com. 2001—, mem. ethical conduct panel 2004-07, chair 2006-07, tech. area chair GNC Confs. 2003-07, tech. program chair GNC Conf. 2008); mem. ASME (life; chair profl. practice and ethics com. Balt. sect. 1998-2001, mem. bd. profl. practice and ethics 2003-05, mem. ethics and tech. program com. 2005-06, com. ethical stds. and review 2005—, nat. nom. com., 2006-), AAAS, fellow, NSPE (sec.-treas. Annapolis chpt. 1994-97, v.p. Md. 2001-02, pres.-elect Md. 2002-03, pres. Md. 2003-04, mem. bd. ethical rev. 2003—, N.E. regional v.p. 2005-06), Nat. Coun. Examiners for Engring. and Surveying (mem. com. on examination audit 1998-99, com. on uniform procedures and legis. guidelines 2000-04, mech. exam group 2000-02), coun. engring. and sci. specialty bds., bd. dir. 2004-), Am. Phys. Soc. (life), Soc. of Am. Mil. Engr. (sec. Houston chpt. 1978), Nat. Def. Indsl. Assn. (life), Optimists (bd. dir. East Lawton Okla. chpt. 1983-84), Sigma Xi (life), Sigma Pi Sigma (pres. Rice U. chpt. 1976-77). Achievements include supervision and participation with flight dynamics support team for the Cosmic Background Explorer, POLAR and Fast Auroral Snapshot Telescope Sci. Satellites, GOES-10, Goes 11 and GOES-12 Weather Satellites, Earth Observing System AM-1/Terra and PM-1/Aqua Environmental Monitoring Satellites; research in high energy spin-dependence of hadron interactions. Home: 463 Yorkshire Dr Severna Park MD 21146-1650 Office Phone: 703-571-0005. Personal E-mail: lesikarj@asme.org. Business E-Mail: james.lesikarii@js.pentagon.mil.

LESJAK, CATHERINE A., computer company executive; b. 1959; B in Biology, Stanford U., Calif.; MBA, U. Calif., Berkeley. With Hewlett Packard Co., Palo Alto, Calif., 1986—, various fin. and risk mgmt. positions, 1986—2000, contr. HP software solutions, 2000—02, v.p. fin. HP enterprise mktg. & HP software, 2002—03, sr. v.p., treas., 2003—06, exec. v.p., CFO, 2006—. Office: Hewlett Packard Co 3000 Hanover St Palo Alto CA 94304*

LESK, ANN BERGER, lawyer; b. NYC, Feb. 7, 1947; d. Alexander and Eleanor A. (Dickinson) Berger; m. Michael E. Lesk, June 30, 1968. AB cum laude, Radcliffe Coll., 1968; JD with high honors, Rutgers U., 1977. Bar: NY 1979. Law clk. to justice NJ Supreme Ct., Mountain, 1977-78; assoc. Fried, Frank, Harris, Shriver & Jacobson LLP, NYC, 1978—84, ptnr., 1984—. Editor-in-chief Rutgers Law Rev., 1976—77. Dir. Appalachian Mountain Club, 2004—; mem. profl. adv. coun. Met. Mus. Art; mem. profl. advisors com. Mus. Art and Design. Fellow: Am. Coll. Trusts and Estates Counsel; mem.: ABA, Am. Coll. Trusts and Estates Counsel, Assn. of the Bar of City of NY (com. trusts, estates and surrogates cts. 1992—95, com. estate and gift taxation 1997—2000, com. trusts, estates and surrogates cts. 2000—03, com. estate and gift taxation 2004—06, com. trusts, estates and surrogates' cts. 2006—), NY State Bar Assn. (mem. house of dels. 2003—07), New York County Lawyers Assn. (co-chair com. trusts and estates legislation and govtl. affairs 1995—98, co-chair com. trusts and estates sect. 1998—2001, bd. dirs. 2001—04, sec. 2004—06, v.p. 2006—07, pres.-elect 2007—). Office: Fried Frank Harris Shriver & Jacobson LLP 1 New York Plz Fl 22 New York NY 10004-1980 Office Phone: 212-859-8113. Business E-Mail: ann.lesk@friedfrank.com.

LESK, MICHAEL E., library and information science educator; b. May 21, 1945; BA in Physics and Chemistry, Harvard Coll., 1964; PhD in Chem. Physics, Harvard U., 1969. Mem. staff Computing Sci. Rsch. Ctr. Bell Labs., 1969-83, exec. dir. computer sci. rsch. dept., 1983-95; chief rsch. scientist Info. Scis. Rsch. Lab. Bellcore; head Div. Info. and Intelligent Sys. NSF, 1998—2002; prof. libr. and info. studies, chair Dept. Libr. and Info. Sci. Sch. Comm., Info. and Libr. Sci., Rutgers U., New Brunswick, NJ, 2002—. Vis. prof. computer sci. U. Coll. London, vis. fellow librarianship and archive studies; mem. vis. com. Harvard U. Libr.; mem. tech. assessment adv. com. Commn. Preservation and Access; adj. lectr. computer sci. Columbia U., 1983-85. Author: Practical Digital Libraries: Books, Bytes and Bucks, 1997; editor Information Systems book series, 1983-90; contbr. articles to profl. jours. Sr. Rsch. fellow Brit. Libr., 1987. Fellow: Assoc. Computing Machinery; mem.: NAE. Home: 424 Summit Rd Mountainside NJ 07092-1516 Office: Rutgers U Rm 306, SCILS 4 Huntington St New Brunswick NJ 08901 Office Phone: 732-932-7500 8230. Office Fax: 732-932-6916. Personal E-mail: lesk@acm.org. Business E-Mail: lesk@scils.rutgers.edu.*

LESKE, M. CRISTINA, medical researcher, educator; MD with highest honors, U. Chile, 1964; MPH, Harvard U., 1966; DSc (hon.), U. West Indies, 2004. Resident preventive medicine Harvard Sch. Pub. Health, Boston, 1966; resident pub. health Mass. Dept. Pub. Health, Boston, 1966—67, asst. dir. divsn. local health svcs., 1967—68; resident preventive medicine U. Rochester, NY, 1974, asst. prof. preventive medicine, 1975; asst. clin. prof. epidemiology and biostats. SUNY Coll. Optometry, NYC, 1976—77, assoc. clin. prof., 1977—79; asst. prof. preventive medicine SUNY Sch. Medicine, Stony Brook, 1979—82, assoc. prof., 1982—89, prof. preventive medicine and ophthalmology, 1989—97, disting. svc. prof., 1997—, disting. prof., 2001—, head divsn. epidemiology, 1986—2002, chair dept. preventive medicine, 1991—2002; med. staff Univ. Hosp., Stony Brook, 1981—. Nat. adv. eye coun. NIH, 1987—91. Contbr. over 300 articles to profl. jours. Named Woman of the Yr. in Health, Three Village Times, N.Y., 1996, Outstanding Woman of Yr. in Sci., Town of Brookhaven, N.Y., 1998, Local Legend, Am. Med. Women Assn.; recipient Bicentennial medal, U. Cath. Chile, 1988, Disting. Achievement award in rsch., N.Y. Optometric Assn., 2000, Alumni Merit award, Harvard Sch. Pub. Health, 2004; Pub. Health fellow, Orgn. Am. States, 1965—67. Fellow: Am. Coll. Epidemiology, Am. Coll. Preventive Medicine; mem.: Inst. of Medicine of NAS. Achievements include research in in breast cancer; epidemiology of eye diseases, especially open-angle glaucoma and cataract. Office: 086L3 Health Sciences Ctr Stony Brook NY 11794-8036

LESKO, JOHN J., retail executive; Sr. v.p. info. sys. Jack Eckerd Corp., 1997; various mgmt. positions Kohl's Corp., Menomonee Falls, Wis., 1997—2000, exec. v.p. adminstrn., 2000—. Office: Kohls Corp N56 W17000 Ridgewood Dr Menomonee Falls WI 53051-5660 Office Phone: 262-703-7000.*

LESKO, LEONARD HENRY, historian, educator, writer; b. Chgo., Aug. 14, 1938; s. Matthew Edward and Josephine Bernice (Jaszczak) L.; m. Barbara Jadwiga Switalski, Dec. 29, 1966. BA, Loyola U., Chgo., 1961, MA, 1964; PhD, U. Chgo., 1969; MA ad eundem, Brown U., 1983. Tchr. Quigley Prep. Sem. South, Chgo., 1961—64; Egyptologist, epigrapher, epigraphic survey Oriental Inst., U. Chgo., Luxor, Egypt, 1964—65; acting instr. U. Calif. Berkeley, 1966—67, acting asst. prof., 1967—68, asst. prof., 1968—72, assoc. prof., 1972—77, prof. Egyptology, 1977—82, dir. Ctr. Near Ea. Studies, 1973—75, chmn. dept., 1975—77, 1979—81, chmn. grad. program in ancient history and Mediterranean archaeology, 1978—79, chmn. humanities coun., 1980—81, dir. Seila project, 1981; C.E. Wilbour prof. Egyptology, chmn. dept. Brown U., 1982—2005, prof. emeritus, 2005—. Author: The Ancient Egyptian Book of Two Ways, 1972, Glossary of the Late Ramesside Letters, 1975, King Tut's Wine Cellar, 1977, Index of the Spells on Egyptian Middle Kingdom Coffins and Related Documents, 1979; co-author: Religion in Ancient Egypt, 1991, Pharoah's Workers: The Villagers of Deir el-Medina, 1994; editor: A Dictionary of Late Egyptian, vol. I, 1982, vol. II, 1984, vol. III, 1987, vol. IV, 1989, vol. V, 1990, 2d edit., Vol. I, 2002, Vol. II, 2004, Egyptological Studies in Honor of Richard A. Parker, 1986, Exodus: The Egyptian Evidence, 1997, Ancient Egyptian and Mediterranean Studies in Memory of William A Ward, 1998; co-editor: Joseph Lindon Smith: Paintings from Egypt, 1998; contbr. articles to profl. publs. and encys. Active Friends of Libr., Brown U.; assoc. John Carter Brown Libr. Recipient award computer oriented rsch. in humanities Am. Coun. Learned Socs., 1973; NEH fellow, 1970-71, grantee, 1975-79, co-dir. Summer Inst., 1995; FIAT faculty fellow U. Torino, 1990; grantee RI Com. for the Humanities, 1998. Mem.: Soc. Francaise d' Egyptologie, Found. Egyptologique Reine Elizabeth, Egypt Exploration Soc., Archaeol. Inst. Am. (pres. San Francisco chpt. 1976—78, pres. Narragansett chpt. 1994—95), Am. Oriental Soc., Am. Rsch. Ctr. in Egypt (gov. 1973—75), Maserati Club Internat., US Lighthouse Soc., Chevalier de Confrèrie de la Chaine des Rotisseurs (vice chargè de presse 1999), RI Acad. of Wine, John Russell Bartlett Soc. (pres. 1997—98), Chevalier de Ordre Mondial des Gourmets Dègustateurs, Lighthouse Preservation Soc., Ferrari Club Am., Rolls Royce Owners Club, The Club of Odd Vols. (Boston), Univ. Club (Providence), Explorers' Club (N.Y.). Office: Brown U Dept Egyptology PO Box 1899 Providence RI 02912-1899 Business E-Mail: Leonard_Lesko@Brown.edu.

LESKO, NEWLAND A., paper company executive; b. 1945; BA, Colby Coll., 1965. Staff Internat. Paper Co., Stamford, 1967, staff v.p., dir. quality mgmt., 1990, v.p., coated papers, 1990—92, v.p., gen. mgr., specialty indsl. papers, 1992, sr. v.p., indsl. packaging, chmn., leadership coun., exec. v.p., 2003—. Office: Internat Paper Co 400 Atlantic St Stamford CT 06921*

LESLIE, ALFRED, painter, filmmaker; b. Bronx, NY, Oct. 29, 1927; Attended, N.Y.U., 1947—49. Vis. artist Amherst Coll., Youngstown State Univ.; vis. prof. painting Boston Univ. Exhibitions include Mus. Fine Arts, Boston, Hirshhorn Mus., Washington, Mus. Contemporary Art, Chgo., Butler Inst. Am. Art, 1984, Newport Harbor Art Mus., 1985, Boca Raton Mus. Art, 1989, St. Louis Art Mus., 1991, Joseloff Gallery, Univ. Hartford, 1991, Oil & Steel Gallery, N.Y., 1992, Manny Silverman Gallery, L.A., 1995; represented in collections of Met. Mus. Art, NYC, Stedelijk Mus., Amsterdam, Kunstmuseum, Basel, Moderna Museet, Stockholm; films include Pull My Daisy, 1959, The Last Clean Shirt, 1963, The Cedar Bar, 2002; author of 100 Views Along the Road, 1988; founding editor, The Hasty Papers, 1959. Recipient lifetime achievement award, Chgo. Underground Film Festival; grantee Guttman Found. for Avant-Garde Film, 1962. Mem.: Am. Acad. Arts and Letters, NAD (academician 1994—). Business E-Mail: aleslie@nyc.rr.com.

LESLIE, GREGG P., lawyer; b. 1963; BA, JD, Georgetown U. Bar: DC 1990. Writer, rsch. dir Wash. mag.; staff atty. Reporter Com. for Freedom of the Press, 1994—, legal defense dir. Office: Reporters Com for Freedom of Press 1101 Wilson Blvd Ste 1100 Arlington VA 22209*

LESLIE, HENRY ARTHUR, lawyer, retired bank executive; b. Troy, Ala., Oct. 15, 1921; s. James B. and Alice (Minchener) L.; m. Anita Doyle, Apr. 5, 1943; children: Anita Lucinda Leslie Bagby, Henry Arthur Jr. BS, U. Ala., 1942, JD, 1948; JSD, Yale U., 1959; grad., Rutgers U., 1964. Bar: Ala. 1948. Asst. prof. bus. law U. Ala., 1948-50, 52-54; prof., asst. dean U. Ala. Sch. Law, 1954-59; v.p. trust officer Birmingham Trust Nat. Bank, 1959-64; sr. v.p., trust officer Union Bank & Trust Co., Montgomery, Ala., 1964-73, sr. v.p., sr. loan officer, 1973-76, exec. v.p., 1976-78, pres. CEO, 1978-91, bd. dirs.; ret., 1991; pvt. practice Montgomery, 1991—. Mem. Ala. Oil and Gas Bd., 1984-85. Pres. Downtown Unltd., 1983-84; mem. Ala. Bd. Bar Examiners, 1973-78, bd. dirs. YMCA, 1992—; mem., vice-chmn. Ala. Jud. Campaign Oversight Com., 1999-2001; mem. Bus. Com. Arts, 2003—. With US Army, WWII, with USAR, retired as ltd. col. JAGC Res., 1970. Decorated Bronze Star for heroic svc. in France. Mem. ABA, Ala. Bar Assn., Montgomery Bar Assn. (Liberty Bell award 1989), Ala. Ind. Bankers (chmn. 1983-84), Ala. Bankers Assn. (trust div. pres. 1963-65), Ind. Bankers Assn. Am. (dir. 1983-90), Ala. World Affairs Coun. (past pres.), Farrah Order Jurisprudence (pres. 1973), Order of Coif Alumni, Montgomery C. of C. (dir. 1983-84, pres. 1987-88), Maxwell Officers Club, Montgomery Country Club, Kiwanis, Delta Sigma Pi, Phi Delta Phi, Omicron Delta Kappa, Pi Kappa Phi. Episcopalian (past sr. warden). Home: 3332 Boxwood Dr Montgomery AL 36111-1702 Office Phone: 334-269-2740.

LESLIE, JACQUES ROBERT, JR., journalist; b. LA, Mar. 12, 1947; s. Jacques Robert and Aleen (Wetstein) L.; m. Leslie Wernick, June 21, 1980; 1 child, Sarah Alexandra. BA, Yale U., 1968. Tchr. New Asia Coll., Chinese U., Hong Kong, 1968-70; free-lance journalist Washington, 1970-71; fgn. corr. L.A. Times, Saigon, 1972-73, Phnom Penh, 1973, Washington, 1974, chief New Delhi (India) bur., 1974-75, Madrid, 1975-76, chief Hong Kong bur., 1976-77; freelance journalist, 1977—; contbg. writer Wired Mag., 1993—2002. Author: The Mark: A War Correspondent's Memoir of Vietnam and Cambodia, Deep Water: The Struggle Over Dams, Displaced People and the Environment, 2005 (named one of Top Sci. Books, Discover mag., 2005). Recipient Best Fgn. Corr. award Sigma Delta Chi, 1973, citation for reporting Overseas Press Club, 1973, J. Anthony Lukas Book-in-Progress award 2002, Drunken Boat Panliterary Nonfiction award 2005; Individual Artist grantee Marin Arts Coun., 1999, 2003; grantee, William and Flora Hewlett Found., 2001, Fred Gellert Family Found., 2001; finalist Nonfiction Book award No. Calif., 2006. Home: 124 Reed St Mill Valley CA 94941-3448 Office Phone: 415-380-1875. Personal E-mail: jacques@well.com.

LESLIE, JOHN FRANKLIN, pathologist, educator; s. Frank Reid and Peggy Shelton Leslie; m. Ingelin Lono, Jan. 10, 1976; children: Timothy Franklin, Inger Leslie Talbot. BA, U. Dallas, Irving, 1971—75; MS, U. Wis., Madison, 1975—77, PhD, 1977—79. Postdoctoral rschr. genetics Stanford U., Palo Alto, Calif., 1979—81; microbiologist Internat. Minerals & Chemicals Corp., Manhattan, Kans., 1981—84; asst. prof. plant pathology Kans. State U., Manhattan, 1984—90, assoc. prof. plant pathology, 1990—96, prof. plant pathology, 1996—2006, prof., head plant pathology, 2006—. Vis. sr. rsch. assoc. Stanford U., Palo Alto, Calif., 1992—93; vis. prof. Universidad Nacional de Rio Cuarto, Argentina, 1996; fungal genetics stock ctr. adv. bd. Fungal Genetics Stock Ctr., Kans. City, 1999—; sr. fulbright scholar U. Sydney & Royal Botanic Gardens, Sydney, 2001—02; hon. rsch. assoc. Royal Botanic Gardens, Sydney, 2002—; visitng prof. genetics Coll. U. Tech. & Mgmt. Malaysia, Kuala Lumpur, Selangor, 2003—; hon. academic fellow St. Paul's Coll., U. Sydney, 2004—. Author: (book) The Fusarium Laboratory Manual; editor: (books) Sorghum and Millets Diseases, Fusarium: Paul E. Nelson Memorial Symposium, Disease Analysis through Genetics and Biotechnology: Interdisciplinary Bridges to Improved Sorghum and Millet Crops; assoc. editor Phytopathology, 1988—90, Mycologia, 1994—97; editor: Applied and Environ. Microbiology, 1997—2006, Food Additives and Contaminants, 2006—; contbr. articles to profl. jours. Achievements include patents for flocculation of phosphate slimes. Office: Kans State Univ 4024A Throckmorton Plant Scis Ctr Manhattan KS 66506-5502 Home Phone: 785-537-8708.

LESLIE, JOHN WILLIAM, public relations and advertising executive; b. Indpls., Nov. 22, 1923; s. John Edward and Catherine (Harris) L.; m. Joan Williams, Dec. 26, 1970; 1 dau. by previous marriage, Catherine Alexandra. Student, U.S. Naval Acad., 1943-44, George Washington U., 1949, Indsl. Coll. Armed Forces, 1956. Dep. excise adminstr., Ind., 1946-47; pvt. pub. relations bus., 1947-49; dir. pub. relations Ind. Democratic State Central Com., 1948-49, Ind. Dept. Vets. Affairs, 1949; press officer Dept. Labor, 1949-51, acting asst. dir. info., 1951-52, asst. dir., 1952-56, dep. dir., 1956-59, dir., 1959-81; sr. assoc. Kamber Group, Washington, 1981-84, counselor, 1984-88, exec. v.p., COO, 1988-96, vice chmn., sec., 1997-98, pub. rels. cons., 1998—, also bd. dirs. Mem., dir. pub. D.C. Com. Employment Physically Handicapped, 1952-53; charter mem. U.S. Sr. Exec. Svc., 1979—. Author numerous articles in field. Advt. cons. Pres.'s Com. on Youth Employment, 1964-80; U.S. del Internat. Graphic Design Coun., Japan, 1973; trustee Washington chpt. Leukemia Soc. Am., 1976-82; chmn. Pub. Printers Adv. Com. on Printing and Publs, 1977-79. Served with USN and USNR, 1941-46. Recipient commendation President's Com. Employment Physically Handicapped, 1954; Disting. Service award Dept. Labor, 1962; citation outstanding service Navy Dept., 1964; Presdl. citation, 1966; Merit award Internat. Labor Press Assn., 1969; Disting. Career Service award Dept. Labor, 1973; Communications award Ga. chpt. Pub. Relations Soc. Am., 1972; Sec. Labor's Recognition award, 1974; Communicator of Yr. award Nat. Assn. Govt. Communicators, 1981 Mem. Am. Assn. Polit. Cons., Am. League Lobbyists, Nat. Press Club, English Speaking Union, Univ. Club (Winter Park, Fla.), Stag Club of Winter Park. Episcopalian. Home and Office: Sweetwater Country Club 2433 Orchard Dr Apopka FL 32712-2562 E-mail: TwoLeslies@aol.com.

LESLIE, LISA DESHAUN, professional basketball player; b. Gardena, Calif., July 7, 1972; d. Christine Leslie-Espinoza; m. Michael Lockwood; 1 child, Lauren Jolie Lockwood. Student, U. So. Calif., 1990—94, grad. in Comm., 1997. Player Sicilgesso, Italy, 1994—95, USA Women's Nat. Team, 1996, LA Sparks, 1997—. Mem. gold medal winning 1994 Goodwill Games Team, US Women's Basketball Team, Athens Olympics, 2004; color commentator U. So. Calif. Basketball Games; guest corr. NBA Inside Stuff. Named USA Basketball Female Athlete of Yr., 1993, WNBA All-Star Game MVP, 1999, 2001, 02, WNBA MVP, 2001, 04, 06, WNBA Finals MVP, 2001, 02, Sportswoman of Yr. for a team sport, Women's Sports Found., 2003, WNBA Defensive Player of Yr., 2004; named to All-WNBA First Team, 1997, 2000, 01, 02, 03, 04, 06, WNBA All-Defensive Team, 2006, WNBA All-Decade Team, 2006; recipient Gold medal Atlanta Olympics, 1996, Sydney Olympics 2000, Athens Olympics, 2004. Achievements include winning WNBA Championships as a member of the Sparks, 2001, 02. Mailing: LA Sparks 888 S Figueroa St Ste 2010 Los Angeles CA 90017*

LESLIE, MAE SUE, writer; b. Forrester, Ark., Dec. 22, 1940; d. Doyle Joseph and Ruby Estelle (Stewart) Davis; m. Gerald Robert Leslie, Sept. 2, 1967; children: Neal R., Denise. Student, Instituto Allende, San Miguel Allende, Mex., 1960-61; BA in Journalism, Sam Houston State U., 1966. Cert. nursing home social worker, Tex. Sec. Am. Gen. Ins. Co., Houston, 1966-67; social worker Harris County, Houston, 1968; sec. temp. agys. Houston, 1977-81; freelance writer, 1981—. Author: (novel) Canadian Capers, 1998; author of three childrens books and screenplay; freelance cartoonist. Pianist, Sunday sch. tchr. Riverside (Tex.) Bapt. Ch., 1963-65. Recipient 3d pl. for article Fla. State Writing Competition, 1994, 2d pl. for short story Manuscripts Guild, 1994, 3d pl. for nonfiction, 1994. Mem. Nat. Writer's Union, Houston Screenwriters, Nat. Honor Soc. for Journalism Students. Democrat. Baptist. Home: 5326 De Lange Ln Houston TX 77092-4208

LESLIE, MAUREEN HEELAN, university director; b. Bronx, NY; d. James Joseph, Sr. and Evelyn (McDonald) H.; m. Bruce Allan Leslie; children: James Christopher, Michael Patrick. BA in Bus. Mgmt. cum laude, Molloy Coll., 1997. Adminstrv. asst., A placement dir., counselor Berkeley Coll., NYC, 1965—71; entrepreneur The Silk Floral Gallery, Huntington, 1984-86; gen. orgn. treas. South Huntington Sch. Dist., 1984-98; devel. assoc. Molloy Coll., Rockville Ctr., 1998-99, dir. alumni rels., 1999—2002; exec. dir. L.I. (N.Y.) Ctr. Bus. and Profl. Woemn, 2003—04; asst. dir. off-campus programs Adelphi U., Garden City, NY, 2004—. Mem. industry adv. bd. South Huntington Sch. Dist., 1998—, Mt. Sinai (N.Y.) Sch. Dist., 1999—; bd. dirs. L.I. (N.Y.) Ctr. Bus. and Profl. Women V.p. St. Hugh of Lincoln Sch. Bd., Huntington Sta., N.Y., 1983; mem. LIA/Long Isalnd Works Coalition, Melville, N.Y., 1998—. Mem. AAUW (mem. com. industries initiatives 2005—), Exec. Women's Golf Assn., Long Island Women's Agenda, Long Island Ctr. Bus. and Profl. Women, L.I. Regional C. of C. to Bus. Partnership (mem. industry adv. bd. 2001—), Young Profls. C. of C. (mem. industry adv. bd. 1998—, edn. and tng. com. 2005—), Soc. Human Resource Profls., Delta Epsilon Sigma, Delta Epsilon Pi, Lambda Pi Eta, Phi Delta Kappa Roman Catholic. Avocations: tennis, golf, swimming, dance, reading.

LESLIE, ROBERT LORNE, lawyer; b. Adak, Ala., Feb. 24, 1947; s. J. Lornie and L. Jean (Conelly) L.; children: Lorna Jean, Elizabeth Allen. BS, U.S. Mil. Acad., 1969; JD, U. Calif., San Francisco, 1974. Bar: Calif. 1974, D.C. 1979, U.S. Dist. Ct. (no. dist.) Calif. 1974, U.S. Ct. Claims 1975, U.S. Tax Ct. 1975, U.S. Ct. Appeals (9th and D.C. cirs.) 1974, U.S. Ct. Mil. Appeals 1980, U.S. Supreme Ct. 1980. Commd. 2d lt. U.S. Army, 1969, advanced through grades to maj., 1980; govt. trial atty. West Coast Field Office, Contract Appeals, Litigation and Regulatory Law divsns., Office JAG, Dept. Army, San Francisco, 1974-77; sr. trial atty., team chief Office of Chief Trial Atty., Dept. of Amry, Washington, 1977-80; ptnr. McInerney & Dillon, Oakland, Calif., 1980—, 1980—. Lectr. on govt. contracts CSC, Continuing Legal Edn. Program; lectr. in govt. procurement U.S. Army Material Command. Served to col. USAR, ret. Decorated Purple Heart, Silver Star. Mem. ABA, Fed. Bar Assn., Associated Gen. Contractors, The Beavers. Office: McInerney & Dillon 1999 Harrison St Ste 1700 Oakland CA 94612

LESLIE, SEAVER, artist; b. Boston, Aug. 22, 1946; s. John Frederick and Joan (Warland) L.; m. Anne Cleland Rogers; children: Genevieve, Marion, Frances. BFA, RISD, 1969, MEd, 1970. Instr. painting RISD, Providence, 1971-81, 97-2000, Parsons sch. Design, NYC, 1980-82, Wellesley (Mass.) Coll., 1983-84; artist-in-residence U Calif., San Diego, 1984-85,1987-88. Exhibited in shows at Hirschl & Adler Gallery, N.Y.C., 1981, Tatistcheff Gallery, N.Y.C., 1982, DeCordova Mus., Lincoln, Mass., 1989, Maine Coast Artists, Rockport, 1993, 2000, Portland (Maine) Mus. Art, 1993, 2000; author: 12 Points: Putting the Case for Customary Measure, 1979, Why America Should Not Go Metric, 1993. Founder Ams. for Customary Weight and Measure, N.Y.C., The Morris Farm Trust; co-founder Maine Trans. Coalition, Wicasset. Studio: PO Box 248 Old Stone Farm Wiscasset ME 04578

LESLIE, SEYMOUR MARVIN, communications executive, director; b. NYC, Dec. 16, 1922; s. Harry and Fay (Goldstein) L.; m. Barbara Miller, Mar. 30, 1947; children: Ellen, Jane, Carol. EE, Syracuse U., 1945; grad., Advanced Mgmt. Program, Harvard U., 1971; DHL, Hofstra U., 1974; Mus D, 5 Towns Coll. Music and Pa., 2005. Sales mgr. Voco, Inc., NYC, 1946-52; founder, chmn. Pickwick Internat., Inc., Woodbury, NY, 1953, chmn. bd., pres., 1953-77; chmn. Leslie Group, Inc., 1977—; pres. CBS Video Enterprises div. CBS, Inc., NYC, 1980-82; chmn., CEO MGM/UA Home Entertainment Group, Inc., 1982-87; co-chmn. Leslie/Linton Entertainment Corp., 1993—. Vice chair Songwriters Hall of Fame; vis. disting. prof. Syracuse U. Sch. Music, 1984. Active Boy Scouts Am., 1947-50; mem. corp. adv. coun. Syracuse U.; mem. coun. Hofstra U.; bd. govs. Anti Defamation League, 1960—; v.p., dir. T.J. Martell Found.; pres. Friars Found.; vice chmn., bd. dirs. Songwriter's Hall of Fame. Sgt. U.S. Army, 1942-46, PTO. Recipient Presdl. award Nat. Assn. Record Merchandisers, 1976, Disting. Svc. award, 1977, Outstanding Arendts Alumnus award Syracuse U., 1978; named Man of Yr. Time Mag., 1987; named to Video Hall of Fame, 1987. Mem. ASCAP, N.Y. Coun. for Humanities (dir.), Record Industry Assn. Am. (profl. group), B'nai B'rith, Friars Club, Harvard Club, Harvard Bus. Club. Office: Leslie Group Inc Ste 1103 50 W 57th St New York NY 10019-4651 E-mail: Cyleslie01@aol.com.

LESLIE, WILLIAM BRUCE, history professor; b. Orange, NJ, July 21, 1944; s. William and Annette (Riedell) L.; stepmother, Dorothy Kaul; children: William Andrew, Sarah Acton. BA, Princeton U., 1966; PhD, Johns Hopkins U., 1971. Asst. prof. history SUNY, Brockport, 1970—79, assoc. prof., 1979—96, prof., 1996—; vis. prof. Jordanhill Coll., Scotland, 1972, dir. grad. studies in history, 1984—90, 1997—99. Vis. scholar U. Cambridge, 2003, 05; co-dir. SUNY Social Sci. Program, London, 1978-79, 82-83, 89; cons. in field. Author: Gentlemen and Scholars, 1993, 2d edit., 2005; mem. editl. bd. History of Higher Edn. Ann., 1991—, History Edn. Quar., 2006—; contbr. articles and revs. to profl jours. Fulbright scholar, Denmark, 1996-97. Mem.: Hist. of Edn. Soc., Am. Hist. Assn., Orgn. Am. Historians, U. Cambridge, Wolfson Coll., Princeton Club NY. Democrat. Avocations: camping, travel, gardening. Office: SUNY History Dept Brockport NY 14420-2956 Home: 2 Doctors Lodge Metfield Suffolk IP20 0LH England Office Phone: 585-395-5691. E-mail: bleslie@alumni.princeton.edu.

LESMAN, MICHAEL STEVEN, lawyer; b. NYC, May 26, 1953; s. Herman and Estelle (Levy) L.; m. Gail R. Grossman, May 26, 1980; children: Adam, Laura. BA magna cum laude, CUNY, 1975; JD, Bklyn. Law Sch., 1982. Bar: NY 1983. Assoc., supervising atty. Jacobowitz & Lysaght, NYC, 1983-88; atty. record, mng. atty. Jacobowitz, Garfinkel & Lesman, NYC, 1989—. Staff counsel Am. Internat. Cos., NYC, 1989—. Mem. ABA, NY State Bar Assn., NY County Lawyers Assn., Def. Rsch. Inst., NY State Trial Lawyers Assn. Office: Fiedelman, Garfinkel & Lesman 110 William St Fl 17 New York NY 10038-3914 Home Phone: 516-242-1812; Office Phone: 212-891-0888. Personal E-mail: lesmanlaw@gmail.com. Business E-Mail: mlesman@fojp.com.

LESMES, STEPHANIE BROOKS, lawyer; b. Stuttgart, Germany, Sept. 16, 1971; BS summa cum laude, Tex. Christian U., 1994; JD, Tex. Tech U. Sch. Law, 1998. Bar: Tex. 1998, US Dist. Ct. (no., we. and so. dists. Tex.). Atty. Baron & Budd, P.C., Dallas, 2001—. Named a Rising Star, Tex. Super Lawyers mag., 2006. Mem.: ABA, Am. Trial Lawyers Assn., Dallas Assn. Young Lawyers, Trial Lawyers for Pub. Justice, Dallas Trial Lawyers Assn., Tex. Trial Lawyers Assn., Assn. Trial Lawyers of Am., Dallas Bar Assn. (mem. judiciary com.), Phi Beta Kappa. Avocations: art, travel, horseback riding. Office: Baron & Budd PC 3102 Oak Lawn Ave Ste 1100 Dallas TX 75219 Office Phone: 214-521-3605. E-mail: slesmes@baronbudd.com.*

LESONSKY, RIEVA, editor-in-chief; b. NYC, June 20, 1952; d. Gerald and Muriel (Cash) L. BJ, U. Mo., 1974. Rschr. Doubleday & Co., NYC, 1975-78, Entrepreneur Mag., LA, 1978-80, rsch. dir., 1983-84, mng. editor, 1985-86, exec. editor, 1986-87, editor Irvine, Calif., 1987-90; sr. v.p., editor dir. Entrepreneur Media, Inc., Irvine, 1990—; rsch. dir. LFP Inc., LA, 1980-82; editor-in-chief Entrepreneur Mag., Irvine. Spkr., lectr. in field. Author: Start Your Own Business, 1998, 4th edit., 2007, Young Millionaires, 1998, Get Smart!, 1999, 303 Marketing Tips, 1999, Ultimate Guide to Franchises, 2004; editor: Complete Guide to Owning a Home-based Business, 1990, 168 More Businesses Anyone Can Start, 1991, 111 Businesses You Can Start for Under $10,000, 1991; contbr. articles to mags. Mem. adv. bd. disting. counselors Women's Leadership Exch.; nat. adv. coun. SBA, 1994—2000; bd. dirs. Students in Free Enterprise, Jr. Achievement, Orange County. Named Dist. Media Adv. of Yr., SBA, 1993, Dist. Women in Bus. Adv., SBA, 1995; Bus. Luminaries award. Mem. Women's Network for Entrepreneurial Tng. (bd. dirs., advisor, nat. steering com.). Avocations: books, magazines, baseball. Office: Entrepreneur Media Inc 2445 Mccabe Way Irvine CA 92614-6244 Office Phone: 949-261-2325. Business E-Mail: rieva@entrepreneur.com.

LESOURD, NANCY SUSAN OLIVER, lawyer, writer; b. Atlanta, Aug. 22, 1953; d. Carl Samuel and Jane (Meadows) Oliver; m. Jeffrey Alan LeSourd, Oct. 18, 1986; children: Jeffrey Luke, Catherine Victoria. BA in Polit. Sci., Agnes Scott Coll., 1975; MA in History, Edn., Tufts U., 1977; JD, Georgetown U., 1984. Bar: Pa. 1985, D.C. 1986, Va. 1992, Fed. Cir. Ct. Appeals., 1988, U.S. Claims Ct., 1988, U.S. Supreme Ct. Instr. Newton H.S., Mass., 1976—78, Stony Brook Sch., NY, 1978—81; assoc. Gammon and Grange, Washington, 1984—88; shareholder Gammon and Grange, P.C., 1988—; mgr. Marshall-LeSourd L.L.C., 1996—. Legal commentator (radio shows) UPI News, Washington, 1985-91, Focus on the Family (Washington corr.), Colorado Springs, Colo., 1987-94; legal columnist Christian Mgmt. Rev., Downers Grove, Ill., 1987-90; spkr. in field. Author: No Longer The Hero, 1992, Liberty Letters: Underground Railroad, 2003, Liberty Letters: The Story of Pocahontas, 2003, Liberty Letters: Civil War Spies, 2004, Liberty Letters: Pearl Harbor, 2004, Christy: Christmastime in Cutter Gap, 2003; editor: Georgetown Law Jour., 1982-84; contbr. articles to profl. jours.; cons., prodr. three TV movies based on Christy, 2000—. Founder, vice-chmn. bd. trustees Ambleside Sch., 1998—2001; Bd. dirs. Arlington County Equal Employment Opportunity Commn., 1985. William Robertson Coe fellow SUNY, Stony Brook, 1978. Mem. D.C. Bar Assn., Va. Bar Assn., Christian Legal Society (bd. dirs. 1990-93). Republican. Office: Gammon and Grange PC 8280 Greensboro Dr Fl 7 Mc Lean VA 22102-3807 Home: 18456 Lincoln Rd Purcellville VA 20132 Office Phone: 703-761-5000. Business E-Mail: nol@gg-law.com.

LESOWITZ, JESSICA R., lawyer; b. LA, Calif., Sept. 4, 1976; BA, Univ. Calif., Berkeley, 1998; JD, Pepperdine Univ., 2001. Bar: Calif. 2001, US Dist. Ct. No., Ea., Ctrl., So. Calif. Atty., family law practice, Beverly Hills. Named a Rising Star, So. Calif. Super Lawyers, 2006. Mem.: State Bar Calif., Beverly Hills Bar Assn., LA County Bar Assn., Santa Monica Bar Assn. Office: Jessica R Lesowitz 9663 Santa Monica Blvd Beverly Hills CA 90210 Office Phone: 310-288-1601. Office Fax: 310-858-8504. Business E-Mail: jrl@jrlesowitzlaw.com.

LESS, ANTHONY ALBERT, retired naval officer; b. Salem, Ohio, Aug. 31, 1937; s. Joseph Anthony and Mildred Gertrude (Bair) L.; m. Leanne Carol Kuhl, Mar. 3, 1962; children: Robyn, Pamela, Theresa, Christina. BS in Chemistry, Heidelberg Coll., 1959. Designated naval aviator. Commd. ensign USN, 1960, advanced through grades to vice adm., 1991, ret., 1994; comdg. officer USS Wichita (AOR-1), 1979-81, USS Ranger (CV-61), 1982-83; chief of staff Comdr. 7th Fleet, Yokosuka, Japan, 1983-84; dir. Polit. Mil Br. JCS, Washington, 1985-87; comdr. Carrier Group One, Pacific, 1987-88, Mid. East Force, Manama, Bahrain, 1988-89; dir. Plans and Policy Navy Staff, Washington, 1989-91; comdr. Naval Air Force Atlantic Fleet, Norfolk, Va., 1991-94; pres. Assn. Naval Aviation, Washington, 1995. Cons. Kaman Aerospace, Bloomfield, Conn., 1994-2003; v.p. govt. programs Kaman Aerospace, Arlington, Va.; sr. v.p. navy programs Burdeshaw Assocs., Ltd., Bethesda, Md., 2003—. Mem. Assn. Naval Aviation (pres. 1994), Soc. Naval Engrs. Roman Catholic. Avocations: racquetball, farming, reading. Office: Burdeshaw Assocs Ltd 4701 Sangamore Rd Bethesda MD 20816-2500 Home Phone: 703-998-9358; Office Phone: 301-229-5800. Business E-Mail: tonyless@burdeshaw.com.

LESSARD, MICHEL M., finance company executive; b. Quebec City, Can., Aug. 31, 1939; s. Maurice and Jacqueline (Lacasse) Lessard; children: Eric, Christine. BA, Laval U., Que., Can., 1958, B in Commerce, 1961, M in Commerce, 1962; MBA, Harvard U., 1967. With Can. Ingersoll Rand, Allied Chem. Can., DomGlass Ltd., Montreal, Que., Canada; with Credit Foncier, Montreal, 1970-86, asst. gen. mgr., treas., 1978-79, sr. asst. gen. mgr., 1979-80, exec. v.p., 1980-81, pres., dir., mem. exec. com., 1981-86, pres., CEO, 1984-86; pres. Sogexfi Inc., 1986—; pres., CEO Immobiliere Natgen Inc., 1993-95; gen. mgr. Hippodrome De Montreal Inc., 1997-99; pres. Domaine de L'isle au oyes Inc., 2000—. Bd. dirs. Azura Furniture, Hydro-Mobile Inc., Fonds de Solidarite FTQ, Montreal Port Authority. Fellow: Trust Cos. Inst.; mem.: Club de Golf de la Vallee du Richelieu, Winchester Club. Home: 11 O'Reilly Apt 1503 Verdun PQ Canada H3E 1T6 E-mail: mlessard@sogexfi.ca.

LESSENCO, GILBERT BARRY, retired lawyer; b. Balt., June 19, 1929; s. Jacob David and Sarah (Bank) L.; m. Elaine Beitler, Sept. 3, 1952; children: Susan Donna, Amy Gail, Robert Howard. BS, Johns Hopkins U.; JD, Harvard U. Bar: D.C. 1953, Md. 1955. Atty. Wilner and Bergson, Washington, 1955; ptnr. Wilner & Scheiner, Washington, 1960—90, Semmes, Bowen & Semmes, Washington, 1990—95, mng. ptnr., 1992—95; of counsel Thompson & Hine, Washington, 1995—2006; ret., 2006. Prof. bus. law and mktg. law Johns Hopkins U. Carey Sch. Bus., 1997—; prof. law course Eotvos Lorand, Budapest, Hungary, 2007. Chmn. Internat. Visitors Svc. Coun., 1965; bd. dirs. Mental Health Assn. Montgomery County, 1996, pres., 1981—82; mem. Johns Hopkins U. Com. for Washington, 1996; trustee Meridian Internat. Ctr., 1965—75; commr. Washington Suburban San. Commn., 1987—93, chmn., 1989—90; co-chmn., fundraiser St. Luke's Ho., 1989; mem., treas. Dem. Ctrl. Com., Montgomery County, Md., 1970—74; bd. dirs. Jewish Social Svc. Agy. Greater Washington, 1978—, pres., 1984—86. Lt. USAF, 1953—55. Named Outstanding Young Lawyer of Yr., D.C. Jr. Bar, 1965, St. Luke's Ho. Cmty. Leadership award, 2002. Mem.: Phi Sigma Delta (v.p.). Home: 10731 Gloxinia Dr Rockville MD 20852-3442 E-mail: gilandelaine@comcast.net.

LESSER, HENRY, lawyer; b. London, Feb. 28, 1947; came to US, 1976; s. Bernard Martin and Valerie Joan (Leslie) L.; m. Jane Michaels, June 29, 1969. BA with honors, Cambridge U., Eng., 1968, MA with honors, 1972; LLM, Harvard U., 1973. Bar: Eng. 1969, N.Y. 1977, U.S. Dist. Ct. (so. and ea. dists.) N.Y. 1977, Calif. 1984, U.S. Dist. Ct. (cen. dist.) Calif. 1984. Pvt. practice, London, 1969-71; assoc. Spear & Hill, NYC and London, 1974-75, Webster & Sheffield, NYC and London, 1976-77, Wachtell, Lipton, Rosen & Katz, NYC, 1977-80, ptnr., 1980-83, Gibson, Dunn & Cutcher, LA, 1983-87, Fried, Frank, Harris, Shriver & Jacobson, LA, 1987-91, Irell & Manella, LLC, LA, 1991-97, Heller, Ehrman, White & McAuliffe, Palo Alto, Calif., 1997-2000, Gray, Cary, Ware & Friedenrich, Ea. Palo Alto, 2000—04; ptnr., co-chmn. Private Equity practice group DLA Piper Rudnick Gray Cary, Ea. Palo Alto, Calif., 2005—. Lectr. law Oxford (Eng.) U., 1968-69, Cambridge U., 1970-71, UCLA, 1989. Editor-in-chief emeritus (bi-monthly) Corporate Governance Adviser; contbr. articles to profl. publs. Chmn. bd. Schola Cantorum, Mountain View, Calif.; bd. mem. Redwood Symphony Orch. Harkness fellow Commonwealth Fund, N.Y., 1971; named one of No. Calif. Top 100 Super Lawyers, San Francisco mag., 2004. Mem. ABA, Internat. Bar Assn., Calif. Bar Assn. (chmn. corps. com. 1990-91, vice chmn. bus. law sect. exec. com. 1993-94), Am. Law Inst., Assn. Bar City N.Y. Avocations: running, golf. Office: DLA Piper Rudnick Gray Cary 2000 University Ave East Palo Alto CA 94303 Home Phone: 650-036-0539; Office Phone: 650-833-2425. Office Fax: 650-833-2001. Business E-Mail: henry.lesser@dlapiper.com.

LESSER, JOAN L., lawyer; b. LA; BA, Brandeis U., 1969; JD, U. So. Calif., 1973. Bar: Calif. 1973, U.S. Dist. Ct. (cen. dist.) Calif. 1974. Assoc. Irell and Manella LLP, LA, 1973-80, ptnr., 1980—. Bd. dirs. In2Books.org; spkr. profl. confs. Trustee Windward Sch., 1994-00, bd. dirs. UCLA Design for Sharing, 2005—, v.p. fin. Mem. Orgn. Women Execs. (past pres., bd. dirs.), Order of Coif. Office: Irell & Manella LLP 1800 Avenue Of The Stars Los Angeles CA 90067-4276 Office Phone: 310-203-7577. Business E-Mail: jlesser@irell.com.

LESSER, LAURENCE, musician, educator; b. LA, Oct. 28, 1938; s. Moses Aaron and Rosalyne Anne (Asner) L.; m. Masuko Ushioda, Dec. 23, 1971; children— Erika, Adam AB, Harvard U., 1961; student of Gaspar Cassadó, Germany, 1961-62; student of Gregor Piatigorsky, 1963-66. Mem. faculty U. So. Calif., Los Angeles, 1963-70, Peabody Inst., Balt., 1970-74, New Eng. Conservatory Music, Boston, 1974—, pres., 1983-96, pres. emeritus, 1997—, interim CEO, 2006—07. Former vis. prof. Eastman Sch. Music, Rochester, NY; vis. prof. Toho Gakuen Sch. Music, Tokyo, 1973—95; performed with New Japan Philharm., Boston Symphony, London Philharm., L.A. Philharm. and Marlboro, Spoleto, Casals, Santa Fe, Banff and Orford festivals; rec. artist. Trustee emeritus WGBH Ednl. Found. Recipient prize Tchaikovsky Competition, Moscow, 1966; Fulbright scholar, 1961-62; Ford Found. grantee, 1972. Mem. Am. Acad. Arts and Scis., Harvard Mus. Assn., Phi Beta Kappa, Pi Kappa Lambda, Sigma Alpha Iota. Jewish. Home: 26 Walker St Cambridge MA 02138-2404 Office: New Eng Conservatory Music 290 Huntington Ave Boston MA 02115-5018 Personal E-mail: ldlesser@comcast.net.

LESSER, RICHARD G., retired apparel executive; Pres. The Marmaxx Group, 1995—2001, chmn., 2001; other executive and merchandising positions The TJX Cos. Inc., Framingham, Mass., 1981—93, COO, 1994—99, exec. v.p., 1999—2001, sr. corp. advisor, 2001—05, also bd. dirs., ret. Bd. dir. A.C. Moore Arts & Crafts, Inc., Dollar Tree Stores, Inc. Office: The TJX Cos Inc 770 Cochituate Rd Framingham MA 01701-4672*

LESSER, ROBERT LEWIS, ophthalmologist; m. Ruth E. Lesser. MD, Cornell U., NY, 1967. Clin. prof. dept. ophthalmology, visual sci. and neurology sch. medicine Yale U., New Haven, 1970—. Staff assoc. USPHS, 1968—70. Recipient Honor cert., Am. Acad. Ophthalmology, 1996. Avocations: opera, tennis, travel. Office: The Eye Care Group 40 Temple St New Haven CT 06510 Office Phone: 203-597-9100.

LESSER, WENDY, editor, writer, consultant; b. Santa Monica, Calif., Mar. 20, 1952; d. Murray Leon Lesser and Millicent Dillon; m. Richard Rizzo, Jan. 18, 1985; 1 child, Nicholas 1 stepchild, Dov Antonio. BA, Harvard U., 1973; MA, Cambridge U., Eng., 1975; PhD, U. Calif., Berkeley, 1982. Founding ptnr. Lesser & Ogden Assocs., Berkeley, 1977-81; founding editor Threepenny Rev., Berkeley, 1980—. Bellagio resident Rockefeller Found., Italy, 1984. Author: The Life Below the Ground, 1987, His Other Half, 1991, Pictures at an Execution, 1994, A Director Calls, 1997, The Amateur, 1999, Nothing Remains the Same, 2002, The Pagoda in the Garden, 2005; editor: Hiding in Plain Sight, 1993, The Genius of Language, 2004. Fellow, NEH, 1983, Guggenheim Found., 1988, NEH, 1992, ACLS, 1996, Open Soc. Inst., 1998, Columbia U., 2000—01, Am. Acad. Berlin, 2003, Remarque Inst., 2004, Cullman Ctr. for Scholars and Writers, 2005—06. Democrat. Office: The Threepenny Rev PO Box 9131 Berkeley CA 94709-0131

LESSER, WILLIAM HENRI, marketing educator; b. NYC, Dec. 19, 1946; s. Arthur and Ethel (Boissevain) L.; m. Susan Elizabeth Bailey, Dec. 27, 1975; children: Andrew, Jordan. BA in Geography, U. Wash., 1968; MS in Resource Econs., U. R.I., 1974; PhD in Agrl. Econ., U. Wis., 1978. From asst. to assoc. prof. mktg. Cornell U., Ithaca, NY, 1978—91, prof., 1991—, dir. undergrad. program, 1998—99, dept. chmn., 2003—, Susan E. Lynch prof. in sci. and bus., 2006—. With Internat. Acad. Environ., Geneva, 1993-94, FAO vis. scientist, 2002; grad. field rep. Dept. Agrl. Econs., Ithaca, 1985-88; dir. Cornell Western Socs. Program, 1991-93; cons. World Bank, Washington, US/AID, Winrock Internat., Morrilton, Ark. Editor: Animal Patents: The Legal Economic and Social Issues, 1990; author: Equitable Patent Protection in the Developing World, 1991, Marketing Livestock and Meat, 1993, Sustainable Use of Genetic Resources under the Convention on Biological Diversity, 1998. Zone capt. Dem. com. Town of Ithaca, 1985-90, mem. planning bd., 1987-93, councilman, 1999-2005. Nat. fellow, Kellogg Found., 1988—91. Mem. Am. Agrl. Econ. Assn., Patent and Trademark Office Soc. Avocations: gardening, painting, antique cars. Home: 406 Coddington Rd Ithaca NY 14850-6012 Office: Cornell U Dept Applied Econs & Mgmt 154 Warren Hall Ithaca NY 14853-7801 Office Phone: 607-255-4576. Business E-Mail: whl1@cornell.edu.

LESSEY, SAMUEL KENRIC, JR., foundation administrator; b. Newark, Oct. 9, 1923; s. Samuel Kenric and Ruth (Turner) Lessey. BS, US Mil. Acad., 1945; student, Vanderbilt U., 1945; LLB, Harvard U., 1951; postgrad., George Washington U., 1951—52, U. Md., 1951—53; MBA, Harvard U., 1956; postgrad., Air War Coll., 1974—75. Bar: NY, US Dist. Ct. DC, S. Ct. Claims, US Tax Ct., US Ct. Mil. Appeals, US Ct. Appeals (DC cir.), US Supreme Ct. Commd. USAF, 1945, advanced through grades to brig. gen., active duty, 1942-54, 76-78; with USAFR, 1954-83; v.p., bd. dirs. Nat. Aviation Corp. Investment Trust, 1957-68; v.p. Shearson Hammill and Co., Inc., 1968-74; moblzn. asst. to dir. Fed. Emergency Mgmt. Agy., 1979-82; insp. gen. US Synthetic Fuels Corp., 1982—86; dir. Selective Svc. System, 1987-91. Civilian aide to Sec. of Army, 1992; bd. visitors US Mil. Acad., West Point, NY, 2003—, vice chmn., 2007. Bd. dirs. Nat. Stroke Assn., 1991—, chmn. bd., 1994—2000, chmn. emeritus, 2001—; bd. dirs. Dwight D. Eisenhower Soc., 2004—, vice chmn., 2006—. Decorated Legion of Merit with Oak Leaf Cluster, Army Outstanding Civil Svc. award, Selective Svc. Disting. Svc. medal, WWII Victory medal, Occupation medal, Nat. Def. Svc. medal, Am. Campaign medal, UN Svc. medal, Air Force Outstanding Unit award; Korean Svc. medal. Mem. AIAA, IEEE, Aerospace Analysts Soc. (past pres.), Am. Fighter Pilots Assn., Air Force Assn. (past v.p. Iron Gate chpt.), Am. Astronautical Soc., Am. Def. Preparedness Assn., Am. Helicopter Soc., Assn. US Army (NH pres.), Aviation Space Writers Assn., Elec. and Electronic Analysts Group, Chartered Fin. Analysts Inst., NY Soc. Security Analysts, Mil. Order of World Wars, Res. Officers Assn., Air Force Pub. Affairs Alumni Assn., Am. Assoc. Royal Acad. Arts, Def. Orientation Conf. Assn. (dir.), Wings Club (past bd. dirs.), Ctr. for Mil. Readiness (adv. bd.), Nat. Aviation Club, NY Athletic Club, Lincoln's Inn Soc., Capitol Hill Club, Army & Navy Club. Avocations: skiing, tennis, swimming, traditional jazz, antiques. Home: Brimstone Corner PO Box 57 Hancock NH 03449-0057 Office: Nat Stroke Assn 9707 E Easter Ln Centennial CO 80112-3754

LESSICK, MIRA LEE, nursing educator; d. Jack H. and Shirley E. (Frumkin) Lessick. Diploma in Nursing, Albany Med. Coll., NY, 1969; BSN, Boston U., 1972; MS, U. Colo., 1973; PhD, U. Tex., 1986. Staff nurse Boston City Hosp. and Mass. Gen. Hosp., 1969-72; instr. to asst. prof. nursing, genetics clinician U. Rochester, NY, 1973-79; asst. prof. nursing, practitioner Rush U. Coll. Nursing, Chgo., 1986-91, assoc. prof. nursing, 1992—2001, project dir. genetic health nursing program, 1993—2001; assoc. prof. U. Toledo, 2001—. Human genome rsch. initial rev. group, ethical, legal, and social implications subcom. Nat. Human Genome Rsch. Inst., NIH, 1996-99; peer reviewer Bur. Health Professions, HHS, 2001-02, Nat. Inst. Nursing Rsch., NIH, 2004—. Mem. editl. bd. Nursing for Women's Health (formerly AWHONN Lifelines), 1999-2007; manuscript rev. panel, Rsch. in Nursing and Health Jour., MEDSURG Nursing, 2005—, Advanced Critical Care Jour., 2002—; genetics column editor Medsurg Nursing: Jour. Adult Health, 2001-05; contbr. articles to profl. jours.; chpts. to books. Recipient Bd. of Govs. award, Excellence in Pediatric Nursing award Albany Med. Ctr., 1969, Outstanding Nurse Recognition award March of Dimes Birth Defects Found., 1991, Recognition award for Individual Contbn. to Maternal-Child Health Nat. Perinatal Assn., 1993, Founders Award in Edn., Internat. Soc. Nurses in Genetics, 1997, Urologic Nursing Jour. Literary Writers award, 2004. Mem. Internat. Soc. Nurses in Genetics (chair rsch. com. 1993-2002, co-chair rsch. com. 2003—05, mem. Genetic Nursing Credentialing Commn., 2001-2004, mem. web site editl. bd. 2001-05, mem. rsch. com. 2005—, hon. mention Genetic Nursing Writer's award 2002), Assn. Women's Health, Obstetric, and Neonatal Nurses, Am. Soc. Human Genetics, Chgo. Nurses Assn. (legis. com. 1990-91), Midwest Nursing Rsch. Soc., Sigma Theta Tau (Luther Christman award for excellence in published writing 1993, Luther Christmas award Excellence Pub. Writing 1998), Phi Kappa Phi. Achievements include development of a genetic health area of concentration within a graduate level nursing program. Office: Univ Toledo Coll Nursing Bancroft Campus Toledo OH 43606-3390 Home Phone: 419-534-5403.

LESSIG, L. LAWRENCE, III, lawyer, educator, writer; b. Rapid City, SD, June 3, 1961; m. Bettina Neuefeind, 1999; 1 child, Willem Dakota Neuefeind. BA in Econs., U. Pa., 1983, BS in Mgmt., 1983; MA in Philosophy with honors, Trinity Coll., 1986; JD, Yale U., 1989. Law clk. to Hon. Richard Posner US Ct. Appeals 7th cir., 1989—90; law clk. to Hon. Antonin Scalia US Supreme Ct., 1990—91; asst. prof. law U. Chgo., 1991—95, prof. law, 1995—97, co-dir. Ctr. for the Study of Constitutionalism in Ea. Europe; prof. law Harvard U., Cambridge, 1997—2000, Jack N. and Lillian R. Berkman Prof. Entrepreneurial Legal Studies, 1998; prof. law Stanford U., 2000—, founder, exec. dir. Ctr. for Internet and Soc., 2000—, Wilson Faculty Scholar Calif., 2002, John A. Wilson Disting. Faculty Scholar Calif., 2003—. Vis. prof. law Yale U., 1995, Harvard U., 1997; bd. mem. RedHat Ctr. for Pub. Domain, 2000—01; bd. dirs. Electronic Frontier Found., San Francisco, Pub. Knowledge, Washington, Free Software Found.; mem. Penn Nat. Commn. Soc., Culture and Cmty. U. Pa., Phila.; moderator Constl. Law Discussion Group Lexis Counsel Connect, 1994—95; editl. adv. bd. Lexis-Nexis Electronic Authors Press, 1995—97; monthly columnist The Industry Standard, 1998—2001, Wired Mag., 2003—; bi-monthly columnist Red Herring, 2002—03; columnist CIO Insight, 2002—03; lectr. in field. Author: Code, and Other Laws of Cyberspace, 1999, The Future of Ideas: The Fate of the Commons in a Connected World, 2001 (Editor's Choice Award for Best Non-Tech. Book, Linux Jour., 2002), Free Culture: How Big Media Uses Technology and the Law to Lock Down Creativity, 2004. Chmn. bd. dirs. Creative Commons, Stanford, 2001—; bd. dirs. Pub. Libr. Sci., San Francisco, 2003—. Named one of Top 25 eBiz Leaders, BusinessWeek, 2000, 2001, 100 Most Influential Lawyers, Nat. Law Jour., 2000, 2006, Top 50 Innovators, Sci. Am., 2002; recipient Annual Award, Internat. Tech. Network, 2001, World Tech. Award for Law, 2001, Free Software award, Free Software Found., 2002; fellow Program on Ethics and the Professions, Harvard U., 1996—97, Wissenschaftskolleg zu Berlin, Germany, 1999—2000. Fellow: Am. Acad. Arts & Sciences, World. Acad. Art and Sci. Office: Stanford Law Sch Crown Quadrangle 559 Nathan Abbott Way Stanford CA 94305-8610*

LESSIN, LAWRENCE STEPHEN, hematologist, oncologist, educator; b. Washington, Oct. 14, 1937; s. Maurice and Anna (Brodsky) L.; m. Judith Ann Lustok, Dec. 23, 1961; children: Jennifer Lynn, Jonathan Lustok, Martine Rose. Student, U. Mich., 1955-58; MD, U. Chgo., 1962. Diplomate Am. Bd. Internal Medicine (assoc. mem. 1976-82). Intern, resident in internal medicine, chief resident, fellow in hematology Hosp. U. Pa., 1962-67; spl. fellow Nat. Heart Inst., Inst. for Cell Pathology, Paris, 1967-68; asst. prof. medicine Duke U., 1968-70; assoc. prof. medicine and pathology George Washington U., 1970-74, prof. medicine and pathology, dir. div. hematology and oncology, 1974—; dir. George Washington U. Cancer Ctr., Washington, 1991-93; med. dir. Washington Cancer Inst. Washington Hosp. Ctr., 1993—2007. Vis. physician medicine br. Nat. Cancer Inst., 1971-74; cons. hematology Washington VA Hosp., 1971—; cons. ARC Blood Bank, 1972—, Nat. Naval Med. Ctr., Bethesda, Md., 1974—, NHLBI, 1974, Walter Reed Army Med. Ctr., 1978—; mem. NASA Biomed. Rev. Panel, 1981-88; chmn. div. blood diseases and resources adv. com. Nat. Heart, Blood and Lung Inst., NIH, 1985-86, mem. inst. sci. rev. com., 1997-99; mem. data safety monotoring bd. NHLBI, NIH, 2000—; chmn., program dir. Assn. Hematology-Oncology, 1983-87; vol. spl. emphasis panel Comprehensive Sickle Cell SCOR Applications, 1997-99; mem. FDA panel on spongiform encephalopaties, cons. panel on oncology drugs, ODAC; mem. internat. adv. bd. King Hussein Cancer Ctr., Amman, Jordan, 2003—; mem. sci. adv. bd. Capital Tech. Info. Svcs., 2004—; bd. dirs. Internat. Spirit of Life Found., Rockville, Md., 2002—, Ceylinco Health, Colombo, Sri Lanka, 1999—. Editorial reviewer: Annals of Internal Medicine, 1969—, Nouvelle Revue de Hematologie, 1970—, Blood, Jour. Hematology, 1971—, Archives of Internal Medicine, 1972—, Nature, 1973, Jour. Clin. Investigation, 1973—, New Eng. Jour. Medicine; mem. editorial Blood Cells, 1979—, Hematologic Pathology, 1985—; contbr. articles to profl. jours., chpts. to books. Served to capt. M.C. USAR, 1963-69. Named Intern of Year U. Pa. Hosp., 1963; nominee for Golden Apple award, 1975; Nat. Heart Inst. spl. fellow Paris, 1967-68 Master ACP (chair Hematology Med. Knowledge Self-Assessment program 1992-); fellow Internat. Soc. Hematology; mem. Am. Soc. Hematology, Am. Fedn. Clin. Rsch., Am. Soc. Clin. Oncology (pub. info. com. 1999-2003, oncology manpower task force 2003-), Am. Blood Commn., Am. Soc. Internal Medicine, D.C. Med. Soc., Internat. Blood Cells Club, Am. Soc. Clin. Oncology (mem. oncology manpower coms., 2004-), Cosmos Club (Washington), Annapolis Yacht Club, Sigma Xi, Alpha Omega Alpha. Office: Washington Cancer Inst 110 Irving St NW Washington DC 20010-2976 Office Phone: 202-877-8111. Business E-Mail: lawrence.lessin@medstar.net.

LESSING, BRIAN REID, actuary; b. Miami, Fla., Feb. 2, 1954; s. Kenneth Oliver Ralph and Margaret (Takash) L. AB magna cum laude, Princeton U., NJ, 1976; MS, NYU, 1979. Cert. FSA, Soc. Actuaries, 1989, CLU, Am. Coll., 1992. Tech. asst. Mut. of NY, 1980-84; from actuarial asst. to v.p. AXA Equitable Life Ins. Co., NYC, 1984—98, v.p., 1998—. Adj. instr. NY Inst. Tech., 1979, Pace U., NYC, 1979, 80; adj. asst. prof. The Coll. of Ins., NYC, 1989-91; rsch. asst. NYU, 1976-80. Mem. ch. coun. exec. com. Cmty. Ch. of NY, 1984-87, fin. com., 1989-99. Fellow Soc. of Actuaries; mem. Soc. Fin. Svc. Profls., Am. Acad. Actuaries, Phi Beta Kappa. Unitarian Universalist. Office: AXA Equitable Life Ins Co 14th Fl Location 14 093 1290 Avenue Of The Americas New York NY 10104-0101

LESSING, DORIS (DORIS MAY), writer; b. Kermanshah, Persia, Oct. 22, 1919; d. Alfred Cook Tayler and Emily Maude McVeagh; m. Frank Charles Wisdom, 1939 (div. 1943); m. Gottfried Anton Nicholas Lessing, 1945 (div. 1949); children: John W. (dec.), Jean W., Peter L. Educated in, So. Rhodesia; DLitt (hon.), Princeton U., 1989, Durham U., 1990; D Fellow in Lit., Sch., Eng. Am. Studies, U. East Anglia, 1991; DLitt (hon.), Warwick U., 1994; LittD (hon.), Bard Coll., 1994, Harvard U., 1995, Open Univ., 1999, Univ. London, 1999. Author: (nonfiction) In Pursuit of the English, 1961, Particularly Cats, 1967, Going Home, 1968, Prisons We Choose to Live Inside, 1987, The Wind Blows Away Our Words...and Other Documents Relating to the Afghan Resistance, 1987, Particularly Cat and More Cats, 1989, Particularly Cats and More Cats...And Rufus, 1991, African Laughter: Four Visits to Zimbabwe, 1992, Under My Skin: Volume One of My Autobiography, to 1949, 1994, Walking in the Shade: Volume Two of My Autobiography, 1949-62, 1994, On Cats, 2002, (novels) The Grass is Singing, 1950, Five Short Novels, 1953, Retreat to Innocence, 1959, The Golden Notebook, 1962 (Prix Medicis award, 1976), Children of Violence, 5 vols., 1964—69, Briefing For a Descent Into Hell, 1971, The Summer Before the Dark, 1973, The Memoirs of a Survivor, 1975, Shikasta, 1979, Marriages Between Zones Three, Four and Five, 1980, The Sirian Experiments, 1981, The Making of the Representative for Planet 8, 1982, Documents Relating to the Sentimental Agents in the Volyen Empire, 1983, The Good Terrorist, 1985 (W.H. Smith Lit. award, 1986, Palermo prize, 1987, Premio Internazionale Monello, 1987), The Libretto of the Making of the Representative for Planet 8, 1988, The Fifth Child, 1988, Playing the Game, 1995, Love, Again, 1996, Mara and Dann, 1999, Ben, In The World, 2000, The Old Age of El Magnifico, 2001, The Sweetest Dream, 2001, Love Child, 2003, The Grandmothers, 2003, Mara and Dann, 2005, The Story of General Dann and Mara's Daughter Griot and the Snow Day, 2006, The Cleft, 2007, (essays) Time Bites, 2004; author: (under pseudonym Jane Somers) Diary of a Good Neighbour, 1983, and If the Old Could..., 1984; author: (short stories) This Was the Old Chief's Country, 1952, The Habit of Loving, 1957, A Man and Two Women, 1963, African Stories, 1965, The Temptation of Jack Orkney and Other Stories, 1978, The Story of a Non-Marrying Man, 1972, Collected African Stories, 1978, The Sun Between Their Feet, 1981, London Observed: Stories and Sketches (U.K.)/The Real Thing (U.S.), 1992, (collections) To Room 19, vols. 1 and 2, 1978, The Doris Lessing Reader, 1990, (plays) Each in His Own Wilderness, 1958, Play with a Tiger, 1973, The Singing Door, 1973, (essays) A Small Personal Voice, 1974, (poetry) Fourteen Poems, 1959, (Operas) (music by Philip Glass) The Making of the Representative for Planet 8, 1988; contbr. columns in newspapers. Recipient Somerset Maugham award Soc. of Authors, 1954, Austrian State prize for European Lit., 1981, Shakespeare prize, Hamburg, 1982, Grinzane Cavour award,

Italy, 1989, David Cohen prize, 2001, Golden PEN award for Lifetime Distingushed Services, 2002; named Woman of Yr. Norway, 1995, awarded Premi Internatl. Catalunya, 1999, Principe de Asturias, Spain, 2001. Fellow MLA (hon.); mem. Nat. Inst. Arts and Letters., Am. Acad. Arts & Letters (assoc. mem. 1974), Inst. Cultural Rsch. (Companion of Honor 2000). Office: care Jonathan Clowes Ltd 10 Iron Bridge House London NW1 8BD England

LESSING, STEPHEN M., finance company executive; m. Sandra Lessing; children: Steve, Caroline, Lawrence, Jack. BA, Fairfield U., 1975; MBA, Fordham U., 1979. With Chem. Bank, NYC, 1975—80; assoc., fixed income divsn. Lehman Brothers Holdings Inc., 1980—82, N.Y. sales mgr. for money markets, 1982—83, nat. sales mgr., 1983—86, head, global sales for mortgages, 1986—89, head, mortgage bus., 1989—92, head, global fixed income sales, 1992—96, head, global capital markets' sales and rsch., 1996—2000, sr. global client relationship mgr. and head, pvt. client group, 2000—02, mng. dir., mem. exec. com., head client relationship mgmt., 2002—. Mem. exec. com., bd. dirs. Internat. Tennis Hall of Fame; mem. investment com. Archdiocese of N.Y.; mem. bd. dirs. Lessing's Inc. Bd. trustees Fairfield U., 2000—; mem. pres. adv. council Dartmouth Coll.; pres. bd. gov. Bond Club of N.Y.; bd. dir. Dorothy Rodbell Cohen Found.; mem. nat. adv. bd. Youth Inc.; trustee Univ. Richmond, 2002—, Cold Spring Harbor Lab., Alfred E. Smith Found. Mem.: Securities Industry Assn. (v. chmn., bd. dirs.). Office: Lehman Brothers Holdings Inc 745 Seventh Ave New York NY 10019*

LESSLY, CHRIS ANN, music educator, director, conductor; d. Claude William and Jessie Geraldine Lessly. MusB in Edn., U. Ctrl. Mo., Warrensburg, 1980; MusM in Edn., U. Kans., Lawrence, 1987, PhD, 1996. Orff-Schulwerk Level I Iowa, 1993, World Music Drumming Curriculum Levels 1, 2, 3 Wis., 2004. Music educator Mo. Pub. Schs., Rolla, 1981—85; grad. tchg. asst. U. Kans., Lawrence, 1986—89; asst. prof. music U. Montevallo, Ala., 1989—91; asst. prof music Luther Coll., Decorah, Iowa, 1992—93; prof. music edn. Ind. Wesleyan U., Marion, 1993—. Musical dir. The Heart Ind. Children's Choir, Marion, 1997—; dir. contemporary svc. First Christian Ch., Marion, 1998—2002. Musician: (solo recitals) Clarinet Standard Classical Repertoire, (clarinetist) Civic Theatre Productions. Chair, bd. elders First Christian Ch., Marion, 2004—06; north ctrl. MENC rep. Soc. Gen. Music, Reston, Va.; bd. mem. Marion Philharm. Orch., Ind., 2000—01. Mem.: Nat. Assn. Coll. Wind and Percussion Instructors, Ind. Music Educators Assn. (licentiate), Orff-Schulwerk Assn. (licentiate), Nat. Assn. For Music Edn. (life). Home: 1709 N Denver Dr Marion IN 46952 Office: Ind Wesleyan U 4201 S Washington St Marion IN 46953 Personal E-mail: chris.lessly@indwes.edu.

LESSNAU, KLAUS-DIETER KARL, pulmonologist, director, medical educator; b. Nuremberg, Bavaria, Germany, Jan. 22, 1955; s. Lothar and Magda Lessnau; m. Cynthia DeLuise, July 26, 1995; 1 child, Mikaela Zoe. MD, Friedrich Alexander U., Erlangen, West Germany, 1985; grad., Friedrich-Alexander U. Diplomate Germany, 1985. Resident Cabrini Med. Ctr., 1988—91; mem. staff Lenox Hill Hosp. NYU Med. Ctr., NYC, 2001—, med. dir. Pulmonary Physiology Lab., 2001—; asst. clin. prof. medicine NYU Sch. Medicine, 2002—. Contbr. articles to profl. jours. Named Best Tchg. Physician, Med. Residents Bklyn Hosp. Ctr., 2001; fellow, Cabrini Med. Ctr., 1991—93, Mt. Sinai Med. Ctr., 1993—94, SUNY, Bklyn., 1994—95. Mem.: AMA, Soc. Critical Care Medicine, Am. Thoracic Soc., Am. Coll. Chest Physicians. Achievements include patents for pulmonary artery catheter. Home: 300 East 93rd 18B New York NY 10128 Office: Lenox Hill Hospital 100 East 77th Street New York NY 10021 Home Phone: 212-996-3357; Office Phone: 212-434-3490. Personal E-mail: klessnau@pol.net.

LESTENKOF, AQUILINA DEBBIE, environmental advocate; Co-dir. Ecosystem Conservation Office Tribal Govt. of St. Paul Island, Alaska. Dir. Pribilof Islands Stewardship Prog., 1994; mem. steering com. Pacific Northwest Crab Industry Adv. Com. Recipient Conservation Merit award, WWF, 2001, Eva Haller award for humanity, Wings WorldQuest Women of Discovery Awards, 2006. Mem.: Aleut Internat. Assn. Office: Ecosystem Conservation Office Tribal Govt St Paul PO Box 107 Saint Paul Island AK 99660 E-mail: aquilina@tdxak.com.

LESTER, ALICIA LOUISE, financial analyst; b. Niagara Falls, NY, Aug. 28, 1955; d. Belmira Hinto Harris and James Lester; children: Deláno Thompson, Michael, Jr. Thompson. BS in Commerce, Niagara U., 1977. Underwriting cert. Robert Morris Assn., 1997. Mktg., acctg. analyst Carborundum Abrasives Co., Niagara Falls, NY, 1978—87; pvt. practice contractor Buffalo, 1990—96; comml. fin. analyst Fleet Boston Financial - Corp. Banking, Buffalo, 1996—2000; fin. analyst Motorola Inc., Elma, NY, 2000—02; fin. analyst II, banking officer M & T Bank, Buffalo, 2002—05; sr. fin. analyst, asst. v.p. fin. ops. Hong Kong and Shanghai Banking Corp. Ltd., Bank NA, Buffalo, 2005—. Owner Thunder Solutions Programming and Mktg., Buffalo, 1997—. Bd. dirs. Buffalo Prenatal-Perinatal Network, 2005—; chair Clark Acad. Performing Arts, 1990—. Mem.: Inst. Mgmt. Accts., Harriet Tubman 300, Inc., Fin. Women Internat. (comm. chair 1997—99), The Links, Inc. (Niagara Falls chp., co-chair tech. 1997—2002, chair arts facet 1997—2002, fin. sec. 2003—). Office Phone: 716-447-9400. Personal E-mail: A.Lester@verizon.net.

LESTER, ANDREW WILLIAM, lawyer; b. Mpls., Feb. 17, 1956; s. Richard G. and Marion Louise (Kurtz) L.; m. Barbara Regina Schmitt, Nov. 22, 1978; 1 child, Susan Erika. Student, Ludwig-Maximilians U., Munich, 1975-76; BA, Duke U., Durham, NC, 1977; MS in Fgn. Svc., Georgetown U., Washington, 1981, JD, 1981. Bar: Okla. 1981, DC 1985, Tex. 1990, US Supreme Ct. 1992, Colo. 1995. Cons. Dresser Industries, Inc., Washington, 1979-81; assoc. Conner & Winters, Tulsa, 1981-82; asst. atty. City of Enid, Okla., 1982-84; ptnr. various law firms Enid, Oklahoma City, 1984-96; ptnr. Lester, Loving & Davies PC, Edmond, 1996—. Adj. prof. Okla. City Univ. Sch. of Law; lectr. in field; US magistrate judge Western Dist. Okla., 1988-96; constl. law specialist Ctrl. and East European Law Initiative, ABA, Ukraine, Belarus and Moldova, 1993; adj. scholar Okla. Coun. Pub. Affairs. Author: Constitutional Law and Democracy, 1994; contbr. book revs. and articles to profl. jours. Intern Office of Senator Bob Dole, Washington, 1977-78; mem. transition team EEOC Office Pres.-Elect Reagan, Washington, 1980-81; chmn. law enforcement and corrections transition team, mem. budget and fin. transition team Office of Gov.-Elect Brad Henry, 2002-03; chmn. Enid Police Civil Service Commn., 1985-87; bd. dirs. Enid Habitat for Humanity, 1986-88, Booker T. Washington Cmty. Ctr., Enid, 1987-90, St. Mary's Episcopal Sch. of Edmond, 1999-2001; bd. dirs. U. Ctrl. Okla. Found., 2005—; mem. bd. advisors Oklahoma City Command Salvation Army, 2002—; mem. Martin Luther King, Jr. Holiday Commn. of Enid, 1988-91; deacon First Bapt. Ch. of Oklahoma City. Fellow Okla. Bar Found.; mem. Okla. Bar Assn., Colo. Bar Assn., Okla. Assn. Mcpl. Attys. (bd. dirs. 1987-91, 94-98, 00-, gen. counsel 1987-88, pres. 1988-90), Okla. County Bar Assn., Def. Rsch. Inst. (govt. liability com.), Federalist Soc. (vice chmn. civil rights practice group 1996—, pres. Ctrl. Okla. chpt. 1996-99), Hist. Soc. of Tenth Jud. Cir. (bd. dirs. 2005—, pres. 2006—). Republican. Avocations: german language, cartography. Office: Lester Loving & Davis PC 1701 S Kelly Ave Edmond OK 73013-3623 Office Phone: 405-844-9900. Office Fax: 405-844-9958. Business E-Mail: alester@lldlaw.com.

LESTER, BILL (WILLIAM ALEXANDER LESTER), race car driver; b. Wash., DC, Feb. 6, 1961; m. Cheryl Lester; 1 child, William Alexander IV. BS in Elec. Enging., Computer Sci., Univ. Calif., Berkeley. Software engr., project mgr. Hewlett-Packard, 1982—98; profl. race car driver, 1998—. Mem. NACAR Diversity Coun., 1998—. Finalist Regional Road Racing Championship, SCCA GT-3, 1986, Four Hour Endurance Championship, RDC, 1989; recipient Rookie Yr., SCCA No. Calif. Region, 1985. Achievements include being first black driver to qualify for race in NASCAR's top series in 20 yrs., 2006.

LESTER, CHARLES TURNER, JR., lawyer; b. Plainfield, NJ, Jan. 31, 1942; s. Charles Turner and Marlyn Elizabeth (Tate) L.; m. Nancy Hudmon Simmons, Aug. 19, 1967; children: Susan Hopson, Mary Elizabeth. BA, Emory U., 1964, JD, 1967. Bar: Ga. 1966, U.S. Dist. Ct. (no. dist.) Ga. 1967, D.C. 1970, U.S. Ct. Appeals (5th cir.) 1967, U.S. Ct. Appeals (11th cir.) 1982, U.S. Ct. Appeals (10th cir.) 1984, U.S. Supreme Ct. 2001. Assoc. Sutherland, Asbill & Brennan, Atlanta, 1970-77, ptnr., 1977—. Mem. Leadership Atlanta, 1980-81; pres. Atlanta Legal Aid Soc., 1979-80. Lt. JAGC, USNR, 1967-70. Fellow Am. Bar Found; mem. ABA, State Bar of Ga. (pres. young lawyers sect. 1977-78, bd. govs. 1977-78, 80-93, chmn. formal adv. opinion bd. 1987-90, exec. com. 1977-78, 1987-93, pres. 1991-92), Atlanta Bar Assn., Am. Judicature Soc., Lawyers Club Atlanta (treas. 1982-83, exec. com. 1982-90, 2d v.p. 1986-87, 1st v.p. 1987-88, pres. 1988-89), D.C. Bar Assn., Ga. C. of C. (bd. dirs. 1994-2000), Lawyers Com. for Civil Rights Law (bd. dirs., vice-chmn. S.E. region, co-chair 1999-2001). Democrat. Methodist. Home: 1955 Musket Ct Stone Mountain GA 30087-1703 Office: Sutherland Asbill & Brennan LLP 999 Peachtree St NE Ste 2300 Atlanta GA 30309-3996 Home Phone: 770-938-2533; Office Phone: 404-853-8116. Business E-Mail: charles.lester@sablaw.com.

LESTER, HELEN DOUGHTY, writer; b. Evanston, Ill., June 12, 1936; d. William Howard and Elizabeth Sargent Doughty; m. Robin Lester, Aug. 26, 1967; children: Robin Debevoise, James Robinson. BA, Wheelock Coll., Boston, 1959. Cert. elem. tchr. State of Mass. Elem. tchr. Lexington (Mass.) Pub. Schs., 1959—62; children's book author Houghton, Mifflin Co., Boston, 1981—; elem. tchr. San Francisco, 1987—89, Francis W. Parker Sch., Chgo., 1962—69, 1991—95. Author: (children's books) Tacky the Penguin, 1988, Fluffy the Porcupine, 1986, Princess Penelope's Parrot, 1996, Three Cheers for Tacky, 1994, The Wizard, the Fairy and the Magic Children, 1983, It Wasn't My Fault, 1984, Hooray for Wodney Wat (Winner of state Children's Choice awards in Calif., Colo., Del., Ga., Ind., Ky., Md., Mo., Nebr., Nev., N.C., N.D., S.C., Tenn. Utah, Va., Wash., Wyo., 1990), Me First, 1992, Listen Buddy, 1995, A True Story, 1997, Tacky in Trouble, Score One for the Sloths, 2004, Tacky and the Emperor, 2001, Tacklocks and the Three Bears, 2002, Something Might Happen, 2003, Hurty Feelings, 2004, Tacky and the Winter Games, 2005 (Smithsonian Notable Book, 1997, Parenting Mag. Reading Magic award, 1997, 1999, Sch. Libr. Jour. Best Books of 1997, Sch. Libr. Jour. Best Books of 1999, others), Batter Up, Wombat, 2006, The Sheep in Wolf's Clothing, 2007. Vol. dir., arts and crafts Bedford (N.Y.) Correctional Instn. for Women, 1998—2005. Named Adm. in the Nebr. Navy, Gov. of the State of Nebr., 1994. Mem.: Soc. of Children's Book Authors and Illustrators. Avocations: travel, hiking, cooking, reading. Home: PO Box 63 Pawling NY 12564 Home Phone: 845-855-9762.

LESTER, HENRY ALLEN, biology professor; AB, Harvard Coll., 1966; PhD, Rockefeller U., 1971. Asst. prof. Calif. Inst. Tech., Pasadena, 1973—76, assoc. prof., 1976—83, prof., 1983—2000, Bren prof. biology, 2000—. Contbr. articles to sci. jours. Fellow: Am. Acad. Arts & Scis. Office: Calif Inst Tech Divsn Biology Mail Code 156-29 1200 E Calif Blvd Pasadena CA 91125 E-mail: lester@caltech.edu.

LESTER, JAMES D., III, insurance company executive; m. Faye Lester. B in math., Emory U.; MS in computer sci., Ga. Inst. Tech. Joined Aflac Inc., 1999, sr. v.p. info. tech. rsch. and devel., 1999, chief tech. officer, 2000—, chief info. officer, 2002, now sr. v.p. global tech. strategy. Mem. bd. Ga. Tech. Authority, 2000—, chmn., 2002—. Served USN. Named one of Premier 100 IT Leaders, Computerworld, 2005, top 25 CTOs, InforWorld Media Group, 2005. Office: Aflac Inc 1932 Wynnton Rd Columbus GA 31999 Office Phone: 706-323-3431. Office Fax: 706-324-6330.

LESTER, JULIUS B., author; b. St. Louis, Jan. 27, 1939; s. W.D. and Julia (Smith) L.; m. Milan Sabatini; children: Jody Simone, Malcolm Coltrane, Elena Milad, David Julius, Lian Sifuentes. BA, Fisk U., Nashville, 1960. Prof. Judaic studies U. Mass., Amherst, 1971—2003, prof. emeritus, 2004—. Profl. musician and singer, recording for Vanguard Records, folklorist and writer, dir., Newport Folk Festival, 1966-68; author: (with Pete Seeger) The 12-String Guitar as Played by Leadbelly, 1965, Look Out, Whitey, Black Power's Gon' Get Your Mama, 1968, To Be a Slave, 1968 (Newberry Honor book 1968), Black Folktales, 1969, Revolutionary Notes, 1969, Search for the New Land, 1970, The Knee-High Man and Other Tales, 1972, Long Journey Home: Stories from Black History, 1972, Two Love Stories, 1972, Who I Am, 1974, All Is Well, 1976, This Strange New Feeling, 1982, Do Lord Remember Me, 1985, The Tales of Uncle Remus: The Adventures of Brer Rabbit, 1987, The Tales of Uncle Remus, The Further Adventures of Brer Rabbit, 1988, Lovesong: Becoming a Jew, 1988, How Many Spots Does A Leopard Have?, 1989, Further Tales of Uncle Remus, 1990, Falling Pieces of the Broken Sky, 1990, Last Tales of Uncle Remus, 1994, And All Our Wounds Forgiven, 1994, The Man Who Knew Too Much, 1994, John Henry, 1994 (Boston Globe-Horn Book award 1995), Othello: A Novel, 1995, Sam and the Tigers, 1996, From Slave Ship to Freedom Road, 1998, Black Cowboy, Wild Horses, 1998, What A Truly Cool World, 1999, When the Beginning Began, 1999, Pharaoh's Daughter, 2000, Albidaro and the Mischievous Dream, 2000, The Blues Singers: Ten Who Shook the World, 2001, Ackamarackus: Julius Lester's Sumptuosly Silly Fantastically Funny Fables, 2001, When Dad Killed Mom, 2001, Why Heaven is Far Away, 2002, Shining, 2003, Let's Talk About Race, 2004, On Writing for Children and Other People, 2004, The Autobiography of God, 2004, Day of Tears, 2005 (Coretta Scott King award), The Old African, 2005, Cupid: A Novel, 2007; editor: Seventh Son: The Thoughts and Writings of W.E.B. DuBois, vol. 1 and 2, 1971; assoc. editor: Sing Out, 1964-69; contbg. editor: Broadside of New York, 1964-70. Personal E-mail: jbles@charter.net. *The older I become, the greater the mystery of my life. I think I see my life as journey into mystery, in awe and fear, with joy and apprehension. Whatever my accomplishments, my life is more than and other than, and finally, best expressed by the silence of winter snow, prairie skies, or a feathered serpent. To be as true and eloquent as a drop of water hanging from a twig— that is my ideal.*

LESTER, JUNE, library and information scientist, educator; b. Sandersville, Ga., Aug. 25, 1942; d. Charles DuBose and Frances Irene (Cheney) L.; 1 child, Anna Elisabeth Engle. BA, Emory U., 1963, M in Librarianship, 1971; D in Libr. Sci., Columbia U., 1987, cert. in advanced librarianship, 1982. Asst. prof., cataloger U. Tenn. Libr., Knoxville, 1971-73; libr. divsn. libr. and info. mgmt. Emory U., Atlanta, 1973-81, asst. prof. div. libr. and info. mgmt., 1976-80, assoc. prof., 1980-87; accreditation officer Am. Libr. Assn., 1987-91; assoc. dean, assoc. prof. Sch. Libr. and Info. Scis. U. North Tex., Denton, 1991—93; prof. U. Okla., Norman, 1993—, dir. Sch. Libr and Info. Studies, 1993—2000. UCLA sr. fellow, 1987. Mem. ALA (coun. mem. 1987), Assn. for Libr. and Info. Sci. Edn. (bd. dirs. 1985-87, 94-97, pres. 1995-96), Am. Soc. Info. Sci. and Tech. (treas., 2004-2007, bd. mem., 2004-2007), Okla. Libr. Assn., Phi Beta Kappa, Beta Phi Mu. Unitarian Universalist. Home: 2006 Trailview Ct Norman OK 73072-6654 Office: U Okla Sch Libr and Info Studies 401 W Brooks St Norman OK 73019-6030 Office Phone: 405-325-3921. E-mail: jlester@ou.edu.

LESTER, MARK CHARLES, neurosurgeon; b. Pitts., Sept. 23, 1952; AB, Cornell U., 1973; MD, U. Pitts., 1977; MBA, U. Pa., 2002. Diplomate Am. Bd. Neurol. Surgery, cert. physician exec. Intern gen. surgery U. Health Ctr. Hosps., Pitts., 1977—78, resident in neurological surgery, 1978—83; neurosurgeon Allentown, Pa., 1983—2004; chief divsn. neurol. surgery Lehigh Valley Hosp., Allentown, 1992—2001, vice-chmn. opers. dept. surgery, 1999—2004, med. dir. oper. rm., 1999—2004; clin. assoc. prof. Pa. State Coll. Medicine, Hershey, 1995—2004, Mich. State Coll. Human Medicine, Lansing, 2004—; chief med. officer St. Mary's Mich. Med. Ctr., Saginaw, 2004—. Adj. clin. asst. prof. Hahnemann U., Phila., 1988—2004. Fellow: ACS; mem.: Am. Coll. Physician Execs., Am. Assn. Neurol. Surgeons.

LESTER, PAMELA ROBIN, lawyer, consultant; b. NYC, Aug. 5, 1958; d. Howard M. and Patricia B. Lester; married; 1 child. Student in Russian language program, Princeton U., 1978—79; BA in Comparative Lit., cum laude, Amherst Coll., Mass., 1980; JD, Fordham U., 1983. Bar: NY 1984, DC 1985, NJ 2007. With Advantage Internat., Inc., Washington, 1984—89, gen. counsel, 1987—89; assoc. Akin, Gump, Strauss, Hauer & Feld, Washington, 1989—90; sr. v.p. bus. affairs and gen. counsel Time Warner Sports, NYC, 1991—99; COO HBO Properties, 1998—2000; pres. Lester Sports and Entertainment, Inc., 2001—; pvt. practice, 2007—. Adj. lectr. sports law Am. U. Law Sch., Washington, 1989—91; adj. faculty sports law 1992-96 Fordham U. Law Sch., Bronx, NY, 1992—96; bd. advisors Ctr. Protection of Athletes Rights, 1994—97; co-chair Am. Law Inst.-ABA Entertainment, Arts and Sports Law Program, LA, 2006—. Contbr. chpts. on athletic mktg. and endorsement contracts to books. Head girls varsity lacrosse coach and vol. asst. field hockey coach Montgomery H.S., NJ, 2001—04; mid. sch. lacrosse coach Princeton Day Sch., Princeton, NJ, 2005—06. Recipient Profl. Sports Lawyer of Yr., Fordham Law Sch., 2004. Mem. ABA (program and sports divsn. chair forum entertainment and sports industries' governing com. 1992-96, chair elect 1996, chair 1997-99, immediate past chair 1999-01, governing com. standing com. on forum-coms. 1994; Ed Rubin award, Forum on Entertainment and Sports Industries 2007), Assn. Bar City NY (sports law com. 1991-94, 04—), NJ State Bar Assn., Sports Lawyers Assn. (bd. dir., pres.-elect 2000-01, pres. 2001-03), NY State Bar Assn., Women's Sports Found. (bd. adv. 1991-99), Va. Commonwealth U. Sportscenter (adv. bd. 1999-00), US Field Hockey (mktg. com. mem.), Acad. TV Arts and Sci. Achievements include being the first woman to serve as president of Sports Lawyers Association; first woman to chair ABA forum on Entertainment and Sports Industries. Office: Lester Sports and Entertainment, Inc PO Box 481 Hopewell NJ 08525 Business E-Mail: pam.lester@lestersports.com.

LESTER, RICHARD GARRISON, radiologist, educator; b. NYC, Oct. 24, 1925; s. L. I. and Pauline (Smolan) L.; m. Marion Louise Kurtz, Jan. 17, 1949; children: Elizabeth P., Andrew W. AB, Princeton U., 1946; MD, Columbia U., 1948. Intern N.Y.C. Hosp., 1948-49; asst. resident radiology Stanford Hosp., 1950-51, 53-54; from instr. to asso. prof. radiology U. Minn., 1954-61; prof. radiology, chmn. dept. Med. Coll. Va., 1961-65, Duke Sch. Medicine, 1965-76; prof. radiology U. Tex. Med. Sch., Houston, 1976-84, chmn. dept., 1977-81; interim pres. Meharry Med. Coll., Nashville, 1981-82; dean Eastern Va. Med. Sch., Norfolk, 1984-89, prof. radiology, 1984-93, chmn. dept., 1989-91, prof. emeritus, 1993—; v.p. acad. affairs Med. Coll. of Hampton Roads (formerly Eastern Va. Med. Authority), Norfolk, 1984—89. Trustee Meharry Med. Coll., 1975—. Author: (with others) Congenital Heart Disease, 1965, Exposure of the Pregnant Patient to Diagnostic Radiations, 1985, 2d edit., 1997; also numerous articles. Deacon Freemason St. Bapt. Ch. Capt. USAF, 1951-53. Fellow Am. Coll. Radiology, Am. Coll. Chest Physicians; mem. Assn. Univ. Radiologists, Am. Roentgen Ray Soc., Soc. Pediatric Radiology, Radiol. Soc. N.Am. (dir. 1976—, chmn. bd. 1981, pres. 1983). Home: 1362 De Bree Ave Norfolk VA 23517-2131 Office: Ea Va Med Sch PO Box 1980 Norfolk VA 23501-1980 Office Phone: 757-446-6037. Personal E-mail: rglester@aol.com.

LESTER, ROBIN DALE, historian, educator, writer, former headmaster; b. Holdrege, Nebr., Mar. 1, 1939; s. Earl L. and Evelyn Grace (Robinson) L.; m. Helen Sargent Doughty, Aug. 26, 1967; children: Robin Debevoise, James Robinson. Student, St. Andrews U., Scotland, 1960—61; BA, Pepperdine U., 1962, MA, 1963; MAT, U. Chgo., 1966, PhD, 1971. Resident head, dean of students U. Chgo., 1964-72, Ferdinand Schevill fellow dept. history, 1966-68; asst. prof. history Columbia Coll., Chgo., 1966-70, chmn. social scis. dept., 1970-72; chmn. history dept. Collegiate Sch., NYC, 1972-75; headmaster Trinity Sch., NYC, 1975-86, San Francisco U. Sch., 1986-88, Latin Sch. of Chgo., 1989-92; tchr. Francis W. Parker Sch., Chgo., 1994-97; interim head Blake Sch., Mpls., 1997—98. Adj. prof. Columbia Coll., Chgo., 1992-95; interim head Blake Sch., Mpls., 1997-98. Author: Dictionary of American Biography, 1978, Stagg's University, 1995, Wuzzy Takes Off, 1995, Roy Foy, 1996, Going to School and Awww!, 1997; contbg. author: Problems in American Sports History, 1997; contbr. to NY Times, Chgo. Sun Times, Jour. Am. History, Chgo. Tribune, Jour. Sports History, History Edn. Quar., U. Chgo. mag. Mem. Manhattan Borough Dem. Com., NYC, 1977-86; commr. Commn. on Ednl. Issues, 1980-84; trustee, treas. St. Andrews U. Am. Found., 1985-2004, emeritus, 2004-; mem. edn. com. Chgo. Hist. Soc., 1991-95; mem. Chgo.-Prague Sister Cities Com., 1991-97; mem. NYC Prep for Prep Adv. Bd., 1998-2005; sect. Pauling Cmty. Found., 2004-05; precinct capt. Dem. Party, Chgo., 1964. Lauder fellow Aspen Inst., 1985. Mem. Am. Hist. Assn., Am. Studies Assn., N. Am. Soc. Sport Historians (Book of the Yr. award 1995), Orgn. Am. Historians, Headmaster's Assn., Univ. Club NYC, Quadrangle Club Chgo., Pawling Garden Club (mem. exec. com.). Episcopalian. Business E-Mail: rl1709@hotmail.com.

LESTER, ROY DAVID, lawyer; b. Middletown, Ohio, Jan. 16, 1949; s. Edgel Celsus and Norma Marie (Elam) L.; children: Justin David, Benjamin, Jackson, Caroline. BS, We. Ky. U., 1970; JD, U. Ky., 1975. Bar: Ky. 1975, U.S. Tax Ct. 1979, U.S. Dist. Ct. (ea. dist.) Ky. 1976, U.S. Supreme Ct. 1979. With Stoll, Keenon, Ogden PLLC, Lexington, Ky., 1975—. Mem. YMCA (Lexington), Fayette County Bar Assn., Order of Coif, Lexington Country Club. Republican. Office: Stoll Keenon Ogden PLLC 300 West Vine St Ste 2100 Lexington KY 40507-1380 Home Phone: 859-299-3494; Office Phone: 859-231-3082. Business E-Mail: david.lester@skofirm.com.

LESTER, VIRGINIA LAUDANO, academic administrator; b. Phila., Jan. 5, 1931; d. Edmund Francis and Emily Beatrice (Downes) Laudano; children: Pamela Lester Golde, Valerie Lester Greer. BA, Pa. State U., 1952; MEd, Temple U., 1955; PhD, Union Grad. Sch., 1972; JD, Stanford U. Law Sch., 1988. Tchr. pub. schs., Abington, Pa., 1952-55, Greenfield Center, NY, 1956; instr. edn. dept. Skidmore Coll., Saratoga Springs, NY, 1962-64, dir. ednl. research, 1967-72, asst. to the pres., 1968-72; asst. dir. Capitol Dist. Regional Supplementary Edn. Ctr., Albany, NY, 1966-67; assoc. dean, asst. prof. state-wide programs Empire State Coll., State U. NY, Saratoga Springs, 1973-75, sr. assoc. dean, assoc. prof., 1975-76, acting dean state-wide programs, 1976; pres., prof. interdisciplinary studies Mary Baldwin Coll., Staunton, Va., 1976-85, cons. to bd. trustees, 1985-88; assoc. Hunton & Williams, Richmond, Va., 1988-90; interim pres. Friends World Coll., Huntington, NY, 1990-91; dir. presdl. search consultation svc. Assn. of Governing Bds. of Univs. and Colls., 1991-94; of counsel spl. projects office of exec. dir. Am. Assn. Retired Persons, 1994—2001. Mem. cons. core faculty Union Grad. Sch., Union for Experimenting Colls. and Univs., Cin., 1975—82; vis. faculty fellow Harvard U. Grad. Sch. Edn., 1976; bd. dirs. So. Bankshares, So. Bank, Coun. Advancement of Small Colls., 1977—81, Am. Council Edn., 1983-85; adj. faculty mem. Grad. Sch. George Washington U., 1996, 2002—; cons. Nat. Exec. Svc. Corp., 1991—; state legis. lobbyist AARP, 2004—05. Mem. com. on criminal sexual assault Va. State Crime Commn., 1976; v.p. Costume Collection,

Inc., 1971-73; v.p. Warren, Washington, Saratoga Counties Planned Parenthood, 1972-74, bd. dirs., 1970-74; mem. Saratoga Springs Housing Bd. Appeals, 1966-76, Commn. on Future of Va., 1982-84; bd. dirs. Nat. Urban League, 1979-86; pres. commn. NCAA, 1984-85. Mem. Am. Acad. Polit. and Social Scis., Va. Found. Ind. Colls. (trustee, exec. com.), Va. Council Ind. Colls., Am. Council on Edn. (commn. on women in higher edn. 1977-80, bd. dirs. 1981-85), Nat. Assn. Ind. Colls. and Univs. (dir.), Assn. Va. Colls. (sec.-treas. 1978-79, pres. 1980-81, dir.), Assn. Ch. Related Colls. and Univs. of South (pres. 1983), Pi Lambda Theta, Pi Gamma Mu, Chimes. Mem. Soc. Of Friends. E-mail: vlester55@msn.com.

LESTER, W. HOWARD, retail executive; Attended, Univ. Okla. V.p. Computer Sciences Corp.; founder Centurex Corp.; CEO Williams-Sonoma Inc., San Francisco, 1978—2001, 2006—, chmn., 1986—. Bd. dir. Harold's Stores, Inc. Mem. adv. bd. Haas Sch. Bus., Univ. Calif., Berkeley, Retail Mgmt. Inst., Santa Clara Univ.; mem. exec. council Univ. Calif., San Francisco; bd. mem. Mus. Modern Art, San Francisco. Named Bus. Leader of the Yr., Haas Sch. Bus. Univ. Calif. Berkeley, 2003; named to Okla. Hall of Fame, 2001. Mem.: Internat. Assoc. Shopping Centers (assoc.). Office: Williams-Sonoma Inc 3250 Van Ness Ave San Francisco CA 94109*

LESTER, WILLIAM ALEXANDER, JR., chemist, educator; b. Chgo., Apr. 24, 1937; s. William Alexander and Elizabeth Frances (Clark) L.; m. Rochelle Diane Reed, Dec. 27, 1959; children: William Alexander III, Allison Kimberleigh. BS, U. Chgo., 1958, MS, 1959; postgrad., Washington U., St. Louis, 1959-60; PhD, Cath. U. Am., 1964. Phys. chemist Nat. Bur. Stds., Washington, 1961-64; asst. dir. Theoretical Chemistry Inst./U. Wis., Madison, 1965-68; rsch. staff IBM Rsch. Lab., San Jose, Calif., 1968-75, mgr., 1976-78; tech. planning staff IBM T.J. Watson Rsch. Ctr., Yorktown Heights, NY, 1975-76; dir. Nat. Resource for Computation in Chemistry, Lawrence Berkeley (Calif.) Lab., 1978-81, also assoc. dir., staff sr. scientist, 1978-81, faculty sr. scientist, 1981—; prof. chemistry U. Calif., Berkeley, 1981—, assoc. dean Coll. Chemistry, 1991-95. Lectr. chemistry U. Wis., 1966-68; cons. NSF, 1976-77, chem. divsn. adv. panel, 1981-83, adv. com. Office Advanced Sci. Computing program, 1985-87, chmn., 1987, sr. fellow for sci. and engring., asst. to dir. for human resource devel., 1995-96; US nat. com. Internat. Union Pure and Applied Chemistry, 1976-79; com. on recommendations for U.S. Army Basic Sci. Rsch. NRC, 1984-87, steering com., 1987-88; chemistry rsch. evaluation panel AF Office Sci. Rsch., 1974-78; chmn. Gordon Conf. Atomic and Molecular Interactions, 1978; mem. NRC panel on chem. physics Nat. Bur. Stds., 1980-83; com. to survey chem. scis. NRC, 1982-84, Fed. Networking Coun. Adv. Com., 1991-95; blue ribbon panel on high performance computing NSF, 1993; com. on high performance computing and comm.: status of a major initiative NRC, 1994-95, com. on math. challenges from theoretical computational chemistry, NRC, 1994-95; tech. assessment bd. Army Rsch. Lab., NRC, 1996-99; coun. mem. Gordon Rsch. Conf., 1997-2000, selection and scheduling com., 2000-06, bd. trustees, 2006—; adv. bd. Model Instns. Excellence Spelman Coll., 1997-2004; external vis. com. Nat. Partnership Advanced Computational Infrastructure, 1999-2002; pres. com. Nat. Medal Sci., 2000-02; dept. energy adv. com. on advanced sci. computing, 2000-04; bd. on chem. scis. and tech. NRC, 2004-06. Editor: Procs. of Conf. on Potential Energy Surfaces in Chemistry, 1971, Recent Advances in Quantum Monte Carlo Methods, 1997; co-editor (with J. Govaerts and M.N. Houkonnou): Contemporary Problems in Mathematical Physics, 2000; co-editor: (with S.M. Rothstein and S. Tanaka) Recent Advances in Quantum Monte Carlo Methods, Part II, 2002; co-author (with Brian L. Hammond and Peter J. Reynolds): Monte Carlo Methods in Ab Initio Quantum Chemistry, 1994; mem. editl. bd. Jour. Phys. Chemistry, 1979—81, Jour. Computational Chemistry, 1980—87, Computer Physics Comm., 1981—86, mem. adv. bd. Sci. Yr., 1989—93, Comms. on Analysis, Geometry and Physics, 1997—, Jour. Chem. Physics, 2006—. Recipient Alumni award in sci. Cath. U. Am., 1983; named to U. Chgo. Athletics Hall of Fame, 2004. Fellow AAAS (com. on nominations 1988-91, nat. bd. dirs. 1993-97, coun. del. chemistry sect.), Calif. Acad. Scis., Am. Phys. Soc. (chmn. divsn. chem. physics 1986); mem. Am. Chem. Soc. (sec.-treas. Wis. sect. 1967-68, chmn. divsn. phys. chemistry 1979, treas. divsn. computers in chemistry 1974-77), Nat. Orgn. Black Chemists and Chem. Engrs. (Percy L. Julian award 1979, Outstanding Tchr. award 1986, exec. bd. 1984-87), Sigma Xi (lectureships com. 1993-2002, chair 1998-2000, bd. dirs. 1998-99, com. on devel. 1999-2006, U. Calif. Berkeley chpt. v.p. 1998-2000, pres. 2000-01), Internat. Acad. Quantum Molecular Sci. Home: 4433 Briar Cliff Rd Oakland CA 94605-4624 Office: U Calif Dept Chemistry Berkeley CA 94720-1460 Home Phone: 510-635-9782; Office Phone: 510-643-9590. Business E-Mail: walester@lbl.gov. *Perseverance is the watchword-the will to hold on.*

LESTER, WILSON A., JR., retail executive; BS in Indsl. Engring., Hampton U., Va. Sr. v.p. logistics Office Max, Cleve., Sports Authority, Ft. Lauderdale, Ga., JoAnn Stores, Hudson, Ohio; gen. mgr. Tamco Distbrs.; various positions including regional distbn. mgr. Abbott Labs., Chgo.; v.p. distbn. Gray Drug Fair, Cleve.; with Peoples Drug Stores, Inc., Revco Drug Stores; sr. v.p. ops Petstore.com; sr. v.p. supply chain Rite Aid Corp., Camp Hill, Pa., 2001—. Chmn. logistics com. Nat. Assn. Chain Drug Stores. Office: Rite Aid Corp 30 Hunter Lane Camp Hill PA 17011 Office Phone: 717-761-2633.*

LESTON, PATRICK JOHN, judge; b. Maywood, Ill., May 2, 1948; s. John R. and Lorraine (McQueen) L.; m. Kristine Brzezinski; children: Alison, Adam. BS in Comm., U. Ill., 1970; JD cum laude, Northwestern U., Chgo., 1973. Bar: Ill. 1973, U.S. Dist. Ct. (no. dist.) Ill. 1973, U.S. Ct. Appeals (7th cir.) 1973. Ptnr. Jacobs & Leston, Villa Park, Ill., 1973-79; atty. Patrick J. Leston Ltd., Glen Ellyn, Ill., 1979-89; ptnr. Keck, Mahin & Cate, Oakbrook Terrace, Ill., 1989-95; judge 18th Cir. Ct., DuPage County, Ill., 1995—. Presiding judge juvenile divsn. DuPage County, 2006-, supervising judge juvenile ct.; presenter at profl. confs. Editor Ill. State Bar Assn./Young Lawyers Divsn. Jour., 1983-85. Class rep. Northwestern U. Law Sch. Fund, 1982-88; organizer DuPage County (Ill.) Law Explorers. Fellow ABA (Ill. del. to ABA/Young Lawyers divsn. assembly 1982-85), Ill. Bar Assn. (chmn. fellows 1991-92, bd. govs. 1990-97, chmn. young lawyers divsn. 1985, chmn. agenda com. 1986, del. to 18th jud. cir. assembly 1982-88), Ill. Judges Assn. (bd. dirs. 1997-2004, chmn. benefits and pension com. 1999—, chmn. govt. affairs 2004—), Ill. Bar Found. (charter), Am. Bar Found.; mem. DuPage County Bar Assn. (bd. dirs. 1979-84, pres. 1987, chmn. judiciary com. 1988, gen. counsel 1989), Lions, Chi Psi. Avocations: volleyball, skiing, scuba diving, travel, golf. Office: 18th Jud Cir Ct 505 N County Farm Rd Wheaton IL 60187-3907 Home Phone: 630-469-0977; Office Phone: 630-407-8860. Business E-Mail: patrick.leston@dupageco.org.

LESZINSKE, WILLIAM O., investment company executive; Chief investment officer Texas Commerce Investment Mgmt. Co.; sr. ptnr. and and equity portfolio mgr. Harris Investment Mgmt. Inc., Harris Bankcorp., Inc., Chgo., 1995, pres., chief investment officer, 1966—. Office: Harris Bankcorp Inc 190 S Lasalle St Chicago IL 60603-3410

LETHEM, JONATHAN ALLEN, writer; b. NYC, Feb. 19, 1964; Attended, Bennington Coll., 1982—84. Author: (novels) Gun, with Occasional Music, 1994, Amnesia Moon, 1995, As She Climbed Across the Table, 1997, Girl in Landscape, 1998, Motherless Brooklyn, 1999, The Fortress of Solitude, 2003, Thirsty People, 2005, You Don't Love Me Yet, 2006, (short stories) The Wall of the Sky, the Wall of the Eye, 1996, Men and Cartoons, 2005, Disappointment Artist: Essays, 2005; editor: The Vintage Book of Amensia, 2000. Named a MacArthur fellow, John D. and Catherine T. MacArthur Found., 2005; recipient CWA Silver Dagger award, The Salon Book award, Nat. Book Critics Circle award.

LETICHE, JOHN MARION, economist, educator; b. Uman, Kiev, Russia, Nov. 11, 1918; came to U.S., 1941, naturalized, 1949; s. Leon and Mary (Grossman) L.; m. Emily Kuyper, Nov. 17, 1945; 1 son, Hugo K. BA, McGill U., 1940, MA, 1941; PhD in Econs, U. Chgo., 1951. Rockefeller fellow Council Fgn. Relations, NYC, 1945-46; Smith-Mundt vis. prof. U. Aarhus and U. Copenhagen, Denmark, 1951-52; spl. tech. econ. adv. UN ECA, Africa, 1961-62; prof. U. Calif. at Berkeley, 1960—. Cons. AID, U.S. Depts. State, Labor, HUD and Treasury, 1962—; emissary to Japan and Korea, Dept. State, 1971; cons. Econ. Coun. Can., 1972—, World Bank, 1981—, Bank of Eng., London, Bundesbank, Frankfurt, Germany; lectr. Stockholm, Paris, Uppsala, Hamburg, Kiel, Oxford (Eng.), 1973—, joint session Calif. legis., 1975, Vancouver, Toronto, Montreal, Zagreb, 1983, Frankfurt, Bonn, Moscow and Nakhodka Acad. Scis. USSR, 1986, Hong Kong, Shanghai, Wuhan, Beijing, London, Bonn, Frankfurt, De Hague, 1987, Bundesbank, 1992-93, 99, China, Beijing, Shanghai, 1988, 90, 94, New Delhi, Addis Ababa, Kuala Lumpur and Seoul, 1996, 99, U.S. War Coll., Quintico, Va., 1997, Acad. Scis., Taipei, 1989, Moscow, 2001, Buenos Aires, 2005; ext. examiner adv. degrees U. Hong Kong, U. Calcutta, India. Author: Reciprocal Trade Agreements in the World Economy, 1948, in Japanese, 1951, System or Theory of the Trade of the World, 2d edit., 1957, Balance of Payments and Economic Growth, 2d edit., 1976, A History of Russian Economic Thought, 2d edit., 1977, The Key Problems of Economic Reconstruction and Development in Nigeria, 1970, Dependent Monetary Systems and Economic Development, 1974, Lessons of the Oil Crisis, 1977, Gains from Trade, 1979, Controlling Inflation, Recession, Federal Deficits and the Balance of Payments, 1980, The New Inflation and Its Urban Impact, 1980, Monetary Systems of Africa in the 1980s, 1981, International Economic Policies and Their Theoretical Foundations, 1982, 2d edit., 1992; Russian Statecraft: An Analysis and Translation of Iuril Krizhanich's Politika, 1985, Economics of the Pacific Rim, 1989; editor Royer Lectures, 1980-90, Toward a Market Economy in China, 1992, China's Emerging Monetary and Financial Markets, 1995, India's Economic Reforms, 1996, Causes of the Financial and Economic Crisis in Southeast Asia, 1998, Lessons from the Euro Zone for the East Asian Economies, 2000, Writ of Certiorara, Supreme Court of the U.S., 2004, Economic Incentives New Behavioral Economics and Successful Economic Transitions, 2006, Russia Moves into the Global Economy, 2007; contbr. articles to profl. jours. Supervisory bd. Sch. Econs., St. Petersburg, Russia, 1994—. Recipient certificate merit Ency. Brit., certificate merit Inst. World Affairs, certificate merit Internat. Legal Center, U. Mich., U.S. Office Personnel Mgmt. Sr. Fed. Govt. Execs. and Mgrs., U. Calif.-Berkeley, Adam Smith medal U. Verona, 1977, Medal, Ioffe Inst. Physics and Tech., 1998, Laureate Living Sci. award NBC Cambridge, Eng., 2004; Guggenheim fellow, 1956-57. Mem. Am. Econ. Assn. (nominating com. 1968-69), Econometric Soc., Royal Econ. Soc., U.S.-Asian Econ. Com. (bd. dirs. 1983—), African Studies Assn., Am. Soc. Internat. Law (bd. 1969-72). Home: 968 Grizzly Peak Blvd Berkeley CA 94708-1549 Business E-Mail: letiche@econ.berkeley.edu.

LETO, JARED JOSEPH, actor, singer; b. Bossier City, La., Dec. 26, 1971; Co-founder, vocalist & guitarist 30 Seconds to Mars, 1998—. Actor: (TV series) Camp Wilder, 1992, My So-Called Life, 1994—95; (TV films) Cool & the Crazy, 1994; (films) How to Make an American Quilt, 1995, The Last of the High Kings, 1996, Prefontaine, 1997, Switchback, 1997, Basil, 1998, Urban Legend, 1998, The Thin Red Line, 1998, Black & White, 1999, Fight Club, 1999, Girl, Interrupted, 1999, American Psycho, 2000, Requiem for a Dream, 2000, Sunset Strip, 2000, Highway, 2002, Panic Room, 2002, Alexander, 2004, Lord of War, 2005, Lonely Hearts, 2006, Chapter 27, 2007; co-prodr.: Sol Goode, 2001; musician: (albums) 30 Seconds to Mars, 2002, A Beautiful Lie, 2005, (songs) The Kill, 2005 (MTV2 award, MTV Video Music awards, 2006, mtvU Woodie award for Best Live-Action Video, 2006). Named one of 50 Most Beautiful People, People mag., 1996, 1997. Office: Immortal Records Ste 120 10585 Santa Monica Blvd Los Angeles CA 90025*

LETO, SHARON ANN, secondary school educator, consultant; d. Martin and Sheradene (Collins) Ralph; m. Nicholas Charles Leto, Mar. 18, 1978; children: Carla Michelle, Gina Marie. BA in Natural Sci., U. South Fla., Tampa, 1979, BA in Secondary Edn., 1979; MS in Edn., Walden U., Mpls., 2006. Cert. tchr. Fla. Sci. educator Brandon (Fla.) HS, 1979—80, biology educator, 1995—2002; sci. educator Turkey Creek Jr. HS, Plant City, Fla., 1980—83, Christ the King Cath. Sch., Tampa, 1988—89, McLane Jr. HS, Brandon, 1989—95; biology educator George S. Middleton Magnet HS, Tampa, 2002—. Cons. Hillsborough County Pub. Schs., Tampa, 1996—; textbook reviewer Pearson Edn./Benjamin Cummings Pub., San Francisco, 2004. Recipient Shining Star award, Hillsborough County Pub. Schs., 2005. Mem.: NEA, NSTA, Hillsborough Classroom Tchrs. Assn., Nat. Assn. Biology Tchrs., Nat. Wildlife Fedn. Republican. Roman Catholic. Avocations: photography, nature, reading, swimming, travel. Office: Hillsborough County Pub Schs 4801 N 22nd St Tampa FL 33610 Home Phone: 813-689-8882; Office Phone: 813-233-3360. Personal E-mail: nleto@tampabay.rr. com. Business E-Mail: sharon.leto@sdhc.k12.fl.us.

LETOURNEAU, JEAN-PAUL, professional society administrator; b. St.-Hyacinthe, Que., Can., May 4, 1930; s. Eugene and Annette (Deslandes) L.; m. Claire Paquin, Sept. 26, 1956. Counsellor in Indsl. Relations, U. Montreal, Que., 1953; cert. c. of c. adminstrn., U. Syracuse, 1962; cert. advanced mgmt. U.S. C. of C, 1965. Mcpl. sec. Mont St.-Hilaire, Que., 1950-53; personnel mgr. Dupuis Freres (mail order house), 1953; editor Jeune Commerce, weekly tabloid Fedn. Que. Jr. C's. of C., 1953. Sec. gen. Montreal Jr. C. of C., 1953-56; asst. gen. mgr. Province Que. C. of C., Montreal, 1956-59, gen. mgr., 1959-71, exec. v.p., 1971-90. Author: Quebec, The Price of Independence, 1969, Report on Corporate Social Responsibilities, 1982. Mem. C. of C. Execs. Can. (pres. 1982-83, mem. coun. excellence 1986), Corp. Consellors in Indsl Rels. of Que., Am. C. of C. Execs. (bd. dirs. 1982-83), Can. Exec. Svc. Orgns. (bd. dirs. 1991-95, vice chair 1993-95), Office Persons Handicapped of Que. (bd. dirs. 1992-98, exec. com. 1994-98). Roman Catholic. Office: 165 Cote Ste-Catherine #202 Outremont PQ Canada H2V 2A7 *Liberty is priceless; but liberty imposes responsibility, and if one is not responsible he will lose his liberty.*

LETSINGER, ROBERT LEWIS, chemistry professor; Student, Ind. U., 1939-41; BS in Chemistry, MIT, 1943, PhD in Organic Chemistry, 1945; DSc (hon.), Acadia U., Can., 1993. Research assoc. MIT, 1945-46; research chemist Tenn. Eastman Corp., 1946; faculty Northwestern U., 1946—, prof. chemistry, 1959—, chmn. dept., 1972-75, joint prof. biochemistry and molecular biology, 1974—92, Clare Hamilton Hall prof. chemistry, 1986—91, Clare Hamilton Hall prof. emeritus chemistry, 1991—; co-founder Nanosphere Inc., 2000—; adj. prof. Ind. U., 2002—. Med. and organic chemistry fellowship panel NIH, 1966-69, mem. physiol. chemistry review group, 1984, bio-organic and natural products chemistry study sect., 1985, chmn. spl. proposal rev. com., 1992; medicinal chem. A study sect., 1971-75; bd. on chem. scis. and tech. NRC, 1987-90, chmn. site visit NRC rsch. assocs., Frank J. Seiler rsch. lab, 1990; mem. steering com. Inst. Medicine Workshop; mem. AIDS project concept rev. panel, 1987; mem. program rev. divsn. biochem. and biophysics, FDA; mem. spl. rev. com. human genome program, 1992; mem. spl. emphasis panel for nat. coop. drug discovery groups for treatment of HIV infection. Bd. editors: Nucleic Acids Rsch., 1990—2002, Oligonucleotides, 2002—. Recipient Rosenstiel medallion, 1985, MIH merit award, 1988, Arthur C. Cope scholar award, 1993, B.F. Goodrich Collegiate Inventors award, 1997, Humboldt prize, Germany, 1989; Guggenheim Fellow, 1956, JSPS fellow, Japan, 1978. Fellow AAAS, Am. Acad. Arts and Scis., Nat. Acad. Scis., Am. Assn. Arts and Scis.; mem. Am. Chem. Soc. (bd. editors 1969-72, adv. bd. for bioconjugate chemistry 1992—, editl. bd. oligonucleotides, 2004—), Sigma Xi, Phi Lambda Upsilon (hon. mem.). Achievements include development of base for efficient automated synthesis of gene fragments that has facilitated rapid development of molecular biology; introduction of rapid chemical methods for synthesis of DNA segments, including solid phase synthesis and application of phosphite intermediates. Avocations: golf, hiking. Home: 1034 Sassafras Cir Bloomington IN 47408

LETTEN, JAMES B., prosecutor; b. New Orleans; married; 2 children. Degree, U. New Orleans, 1976; JD, Tulane Law Sch., 1979. With New Orleans Dist. Attys. Office, 1979—82; with Organized Crime and Racketeering Strike Force US Dept. Justice, La., 1982—94, 1st asst. US atty. New Orleans, 1994—2005, interim US atty. (ea. dist.) La., 2000—05, US atty. (ea. dist.) La., 2005—. Advanced through ranks to comdr. USNR, 1986—. Office: US Attys Office 500 Poydras St Rm B210 New Orleans LA 70130*

LETTERIE, KATHLEEN, broadcast executive; Head, talent WB Network, 1994—97, sr. v.p. talent and casting Burbank, Calif., 1997—2001, exec. v.p. talent and casting, 2001—.

LETTERMAN, DAVID, talk show host, producer, comedian, writer; b. Indpls., Apr. 12, 1947; s. Joseph and Dorothy L.; m. Michelle Cook, 1969 (div. 1977); 1 child. Grad., Ball State U., 1969. Weatherman and TV announcer, 1970—74; radio talk show host, 1974—75. Co-owner Rahal Letterman Racing. Performer The Comedy Store, Los Angeles, 1975; appearances on TV include (variety series) Mary, 1978, frequent guest host The Tonight Show; host (morning comedy/variety program) David Letterman Show, NBC, 1980 (2 Daytime Emmy awards), Late Night with David Letterman, NBC, 1982-1993, (5 Emmy awards) The Late Show with David Letterman, CBS, 1993— (also writer, exec. prodr.) (Emmy award for Outstanding Variety, Music or Comedy Program, 1994, 1998, 1999, 2000, 2001 and 2002); host, Emmy Awards, 1991, Academy Awards, 1995; writer for TV including Bob Hope Special, Good Times, Paul Lynde Comedy Hour, John Denver Special; author: (with others) The Late Night with David Letterman Book of Top Ten Lists, 1990, An Altogether New Book of Top Ten Lists, 1991; film appearances include: Cabin Boy, 1994; prodr. Worldwide Pants Inc.(TV series) The Bonnie Hunt Show, 1995-96, The Late Late Show With Tom Synder, 1995-99, The High Life, 1996, Everybody Loves Raymond, 1996-2005, Late Late Show with Craig Kilburn, 1999-2005, Welcome to New York, 2000-01, Ed, 2000-04, Late Late Show with Craig Ferguson, 2005-. Named one of 100 Most Powerful Celebrities, Forbes.com, 2007. Avocations: baseball, basketball, auto racing, running.*

LETTIERI, RICHARD J. (RICHARD JOSEPH LETTIERI), lawyer; b. Chelsea, Mass., May 29, 1947; s. Rosario and Genevieve Helen (Sokoloski) L. AB in History, Villanova U., 1969; JD, Boston Coll., 1974. Bar: Mass. 1975, U.S. Dist. Ct. Mass. 1975, U.S. Ct. Appeals (1st cir.) 1979, U.S. Ct. Appeals (D.C. cir.) 1985. Pvt. practice, Boston, 1975-77; staff atty. Mass. Port Authority, Boston, 1977-81, chief legal counsel, 1981-86; assoc. Ropes & Gray, Boston, 1987-90, ptnr., 1990—. Mem. Boston Bar Assn., Justinian Law Soc. Office: Ropes & Gray 1 International Pl Fl 4 Boston MA 02110-2624 Office Phone: 617-951-7000. E-mail: rlettieri@ropesgray.com.

LETTOW, CHARLES FREDERICK, federal judge; b. Iowa Falls, Iowa, 1941; s. Carl Frederick and Catherine L.; m. Sue Lettow, 1963; children: Renee, Carl II, John, Paul. BSChemE, Iowa State U., 1962; LLB, Stanford U., 1968; MA, Brown U., 2001. Bar: Calif. 1969, Iowa 1969, DC 1972, Md. 1991. Law clk. to Hon. Ben C. Duniway US Ct. Appeals (9th cir.), San Francisco, 1968-69; law clk. to Hon. Warren E. Burger US Supreme Ct., Washington, 1969-70; counsel Coun. Environ. Quality, Washington, 1970-73; assoc. Cleary, Gottlieb, Steen & Hamilton, Washington, 1973-76, ptnr., 1976—2003; judge US Ct. Fed. Claims, Washington, 2003—. Contbr. articles to profl. jours. Trustee Potomac Sch., McLean, Va., 1983-90, chmn. bd. trustees, 1985-88. 1st lt. US Army, 1963-65. Mem. ABA, Am. Law Inst., DC Bar, Iowa Bar Assn., Order of Coif, Univ. Club. Office: US Ct Fed Claims 717 Madison Pl NW Washington DC 20005 Office Phone: 202-357-6588.

LETTOW, LUCILLE JANE, school librarian, education educator; b. Eldora, Iowa, Mar. 8, 1942; d. Emily Barnhart and Harold W. C. Ziesman; m. Gary J. Lettow, July 25, 1964; 1 child, Karl Josef. BA, U. No. Iowa, 1964; MLS, U. Mo., 1969; M in English, U. No. Iowa, 1984. Iowa Permanent Profl.Tchg. Cert. 1973, Mo. Permanent Profl. Tchg. Cert. 1970. Jr. high tchr. Yale-Jamaica-Bagley Cmty. Schs., Iowa, 1964—66; sch. libr. media specialist Cedar Falls Cmty. Schools, Iowa, 1969—79; youth collection libr. and prof. U. No. Iowa, Cedar Falls, 1980—. Co-director, uni children's lit. workshops U. of No. Iowa, 1986—. Co-author: (profl. book) Picture Books to Enhance the Curriculum; contbr. articles to profl. jours. Recipient IEMA/SIRS Intellectual Freedom award, Iowa Ednl. Media Assn., 1990, Lamplighter award, 2000. Mem.: Assn. for Childhood Ednl. Internat., Internat. Reading Assn., ALA, Iowa Ednl. Media Assn. (pres. 1994—95, Presdl. Citation 1995). Office: Rod Library University of Northern Iowa 1227 West 27th St Cedar Falls IA 50613 Business E-Mail: lucille.lettow@uni.edu.

LETTS, LINDSAY GORDON, pharmacologist, educator; b. Warragul, Victoria, Australia, Jan. 9, 1948; came to US, 1987; m. Barbara Dawn Hawkey, Sept. 13, 1969; children: Michelle Maree, Kathryn Jane, David Gordon. BS, Monash U., Australia, 1971; PhD, Sydney U., 1980. Tutor Sydney U., 1976-80; rsch. scientist Royal Coll. Surgeons Eng., London, 1980-82; sr. rsch. fellow Merck Frosst Can. Inc., 1982-87; dir. pharmacology Boehringer Ingelheim Pharms., Inc., Ridgefield, Conn., 1987-93; v.p. rsch. NitroMed Inc., Cambridge, Mass., 1993-96, chief sci. officer, sr. v.p. R&D, 1997—2007. Adj. assoc. prof. Yale U. Sch. Medicine, New Haven, 1991-94; bd. dirs. IPS Pharma. Editor Mediators of Inflammation, 1992-98, Pulmonary Pharmacology and Therapeutics, 1992-2004; sect. editor Prostaglandins, 1986-2003; editor Inflammation Rsch., 1994-2002. Bd. dirs. Nat. Inst. for Community Health Edn., Quinnipiac Coll., Hamden, Conn., 1990-94, Conn. United Rsch. Excellence, Wallingford, 1991-94. Mem.: Internat. Assn. Inflammation Socs. (v.p. 2001—04, pres. 2004—07), Inflammation Rsch. Assn. (bd. dirs. 1992—2000, pres. 1996—98). Office: NitroMed Inc 45 Hayden Ave Ste 3000 Lexington MA 02421

LETWIN, JEFFREY WILLIAM, lawyer; b. Pitts., Nov. 26, 1953; s. Myron Harvey and Phyllis Harriet (Unatin) L.; m. Roberta Lee Rosenbloom, July 24, 1983; children: Ari, Andrew, Amanda. BA in History and Lit., U. Pitts., 1975; JD, Am. U., 1979. Bar: Pa. 1980, D.C. 1980. Staff atty. Dept. Justice, Washington, 1979-80; assoc. Gilloti, Goldberg & Capristi, Pitts., 1980-83, Finkel, Lefkowitz & Ostrow, Pitts., 1983-85, Rosenberg & Kirshner, Pitts., 1986-94; assoc. v.p. Doepken Keevican & Weiss, Pitts., 1994—2001, bd. dirs.; mng. ptnr. Pitts. office Schnader Harrison Segal & Lewis, 2002—. Lectr. Pa. Bar Inst., 1983, 87, 88; mem. Pitts. High Tech. Council, 19855, Enterprise Group, Pitts., 19855; arbitrator N.Y. Stock Exch; solicitor Allegheny County Airport Authority, 19995. Commr. City of Pitts. Planning Commn., 1965; vice chair C.C. of Allegheny County Edn. Found., 1965; mem. Young Leadership Cabinet USA, 1984-87; chmn. young bus. and profl. divsn., 1985-87, chmn. exec. and profl. divsn., 1987-88; participant Leadership Pitts., 1995; bd. dirs., vice chmn. Pitts. Film Office, 1995-2003; solicitor Allegheny County Airport Authority, 1999-; bd. dirs. Leadership Pitts., Allegheny County Sanitary Authority, 2000-04; chmn. Greater Pitts. Conv. and Visitors Bur., 2004—, Port Authority of Allegheny County, 2005—; mem. steering com., PGN Commn., mem. legal com. steering group, Airports Coun. Internat.; bd.

dirs. Jewish Assn. on Aging, 1975, Holocaust Commn., Pitts., 1983, Jewish Family and Children's Svc., Pitts., 1983-86, United Jewish Fed., Pitts., 1984-86, mem. exec. com. United Jewish Fedn., 1975; chmn. Holocaust Commn. of Greater Pitts., 1991-94, Pitts. Israel C. of C. 1991-97. Named one of Outstanding Young Men in Am., 1985, One of Pa.'s Super Lawyers, Laqw & Politics Pub., 2004; recipient Stark Young Leadership award, 1989. Mem. ABA, Pa. Bar Assn., D.C. Bar Assn., Alleghany County Bar Assn. (bus., banking, and comml. sect., continuing legal edn. com.), Nat. Assn. Securities Dealers (arbitrator, mem. steering com. legal com. duprols coun. internat. 2002—). Democrat. Jewish. Avocations: golf, running, films. Office: Schnader Harrison Segal Lewis LLP 270 5th Ave Pittsburgh PA 15222-3010

LETWIN, LEON, law educator; b. Milw., Dec. 29, 1929; s. Lazar and Bessie (Rosenthal) L.; m. Alita Zurav, July 11, 1952; children— Michael, Daniel, David PhB, U. Chgo., 1950; LLB, U. Wis., 1952; LLM, Harvard U., 1964. Bar: Wis. 1952, Calif. 1969. Teaching fellow Harvard Law Sch., Boston, 1963-64; faculty Law Sch. UCLA, 1964—, prof., 1968-92, prof. emeritus, 1993—. Coord. Native-Am. Grave Protection and Repatriation Act, UCLA, 1998—2002. Contbr. articles to profl. jours. Active ACLU. Mem. Lawyers Guild, State Bar Calif. Home: 2226 Manning Ave Los Angeles CA 90064-2002 Office: UCLA Law Sch 405 Hilgard Ave Los Angeles CA 90095-9000 Business E-Mail: letwin@ucla.edu.

LETZIG, BETTY JEAN, financial consultant; b. Feb. 18, 1926; d. Robert H. and Alina Violet (Mayes) L. BA, Scarritt Coll., 1950, MA, 1968. Ednl. staff The Meth. Ch. Ark., Okla., Tex., 1953-60; with Internat. Deaconess Exch. Program, London, 1961-62; staff exec. nat. divsn. United Meth. Ch., NYC, 1962-95, cons. current and deferred giving, 1995—. Coord. Mission Pers. Support Svcs., 1984-88; exec. sec. Deaconess Program Office, 1989-95. Contbr. articles to profl. jours. Bd. dirs. Global Health Action, Atlanta, 1974-88, Vellore Christian Med. Coll., N.Y.C., 1984-94; mem. U.S. com. Internat. Coun. Social Welfare, Washington, 1983-89; active Nat. Interfaith Coalition on Aging, Athens, Ga. and Washington, 1972—, pres., 1981-85. Mem.: LWV, AAUW, Older Women's League, Nat. Coun. Social Welfare, Nat. Voluntary Orgns. Ind. Living for Aging, Nat. Coun. Aging. Avocations: travel, photography, needlecrafts. Home: 266 Merrimon Ave Asheville NC 28801

LEUBERT, ALFRED OTTO PAUL, management consultant; b. NYC, Dec. 7, 1922; s. Paul T. and Josephine (Haaga) L.; m. Celestine Capka, July 22, 1944 (div. 1977); children: Eloise Ann Cronin, Susan Beth; m. Hope Sherman Drapkin, June 4, 1978 (div. 1982). Student, Dartmouth Coll., Hanover, NH, 1943; BS, Fordham U., Bronx, NY, 1946; MBA, NYU, 1950. Account mgr. J.K. Lasser & Co., NYC, 1948-52; controller Vision, Inc., NYC, 1952-53, Old Town Corp., 1953-54, sec., controller, 1954-56, sec.-treas., 1956-57, v.p., treas., 1957-58; dir. subsidiaries Old Town Corp. (Old Town Internat. Corp., Old Town Ribbon & Carbon Co., Inc.), Mass. and Calif., 1955-58; v.p., controller Willcox & Gibbs, Inc., NYC, 1958-59, v.p., treas., 1959-65, pres., dir., CEO, 1966-76; founder, pub., pres. Leubert's Compendium of Bus. (Fin. and Econ. Barometers), 1978-82; pres. Alfred O.P. Leubert Ltd., 1981-82, chmn. CEO, 1993—; chmn., CEO Solidyne, Inc., 1982; chmn. bd., pres., CEO, dir. Chyron Corp., 1983-91; dir. K & R Real Estate Ltd., China, 1994-96; chmn. bd. CEO Leubert & Co. (H.K.) Ltd., 1994-98; dir. Laser-Pacific Media Corp., 1995-96; chmn. bd., CEO, bd. dirs. Chyron Group (U.K.) Ltd., 1985-89; dir., vice chrmn. Advanced Definition Systems, Inc., 1996-97; chmn. bd., CEO, bd. dirs. CMX Corp., 1983-91; strategic advisor PlasmaNet, Inc., 1999—, Tru-You.Com, Inc., 2000—01, Dir. Media, Inc., 2000—01, Planet Playier, Inc., 2001—. CEO, dir. CGS Units, Inc., 1988-90, chmn. bd., 1989-90; bd. dirs. Digital Svcs. Corp.; vice chmn. bd. dirs. CMX Laser Sys., Inc., 1988-93; instr. accountancy Pace Coll., 1955-57. Bd. dirs. United Fund of Manhasset, 1963-69, pres., 1964-65; bd. dirs. Actor's Studio, 1972-76; adv. bd. St. Anthony's Guidance Clinic, 1967-69. Served to capt. USMCR, 1943-46. Decorated Bronze Star; recipient Humanitarian award Hebrew Acad., NYC, 1971 Mem. AICPA, NY State Soc. CPAs, Fordham U. Alumni Assn., NY Athletic Club. Roman Catholic. Home and Office: 1 Lincoln Plz New York NY 10023-7129 Office Phone: 212-595-4900.

LEUBSDORF, CARL PHILIPP, publishing executive; b. NYC, Mar. 17, 1938; s. Karl and Bertha (Boschwitz) Leubsdorf; m. Carolyn Cleveland Stockmeyer, Mar. 26, 1963 (div. 1978); children: Carl Philipp Jr., Loma Stockmeyer, E. William Stockmeyer Jr., C. Cleveland Stockmeyer, Claire C. Goodwin; m. Susan Page, May 23, 1982; children: Benjamin Page, William Page. BA in Govt., Cornell U., 1959; MS in Journalism, Columbia U., 1960. Staff writer AP, New Orleans, 1960—63, Washington, 1963—75; corr. Balt. Sun, Washington, 1976—81; Washington bur. chief Dallas Morning News, Washington, 1981—. Recipient Columbia Journalism Sch. Alumni award, 1999. Mem.: Nat. Press Club (Washington), White Ho. Corrs. Assn. (pres. 1995—96), Gridiron Club (sec. 2004—06, v.p. 2007—), Phi Beta Kappa. Office: Dallas Morning News 1325 G St NW Ste 250 Washington DC 20005-3115 Business E-Mail: cleubsdorf@dallasnews.com.

LEUCHOVIUS, DEBORAH, advocate, special education services professional, consultant; b. Litchfield, Minn., Dec. 22, 1954; d. David Robert Leslie and Corinne Ardell Shiell; m. James Raphael Poole, Aug. 18, 1979; 1 child, Frederick Winston Leuchovius Poole. BA, Hamline U., 1978; MA, Rutgers U., 1981. Americans with Disabilities Act specialist PACER Ctr., Inc., Mpls, tech. assistance specialist Mpls., 1994—96, project dir. TATRA project, 1996—, nat. coord., transition tech. assistance programs, 2001—. Cons. Change Agy., St. Paul, 1990—. Editor: (newsletter) Point of Departure, (book) The Americans with Disabilities Act: A Guide for People with Disabilities, Their Families and Advocates. Advisor to nat. leadership team Assn. Sci. and Tech. Ctrs., Mus. and Access; mem. Spina Bifida Assn. Minn., 1994—, sec., 2000; advisor VSA Arts Minn., Mpls., 1995—99; advisor to access com. Walker Art Ctr.; bd. dirs. ADA Minn., St. Paul, 1992—95; founding mem. Minn. Ind. Scholars Forum, 1981—89. Mem.: Nat. Rehab. Assn., Coun. Exceptional Children (parent rep. divsn. career devel. 1997—99). Office: PACER Ctr 8161 Normandale Blvd Minneapolis MN 55437 Office Phone: 952-838-9000. Business E-Mail: pacer@pacer.org.

LEUCHTMAN, STEPHEN NATHAN, lawyer; b. Detroit, Oct. 14, 1945; s. Alexis C. and Frances J. (Boucher) L.; m. Jacque Ward, Nov. 29, 1991; children: Stephen, John II, Lucinda. BA, U. Mich., 1967, JD, 1970. Bar: Mich. 1970, Calif. 1993, U.S. Dist. Ct. (ea. and so. dists.) Mich. 1970, U.S. Ct. Appeals (6th cir.) 1982. Assoc. Eggenberger, Eggenberger, McKinney & Weber, Detroit, 1970-75, Tyler & Canham, Detroit, 1975-80; ptnr. Sommers, Schwartz, Silver & Schwartz, Southfield, 1980-97; founding ptnr. Trowbridge Law Firm, P.C., Detroit, 1997-2001; atty. Stephen N. Leuchtman, P.C., Detroit, 2001—; of counsel Ravid & Assocs., 2005—. Contbr. articles to profl. jours. Mem. ABA, ATLA, Am. Bd. Trial Advocates, Million Dollar Advocates Forum, Consumer Attys. of Calif., Mich. Bar Assn., Calif. Bar Assn. Democrat. Avocations: writing, golf, travel. Office: 23855 Northwestern Hwy Southfield MI 48075 Office Phone: 248-948-9696 ext. 143. Personal E-mail: joiedDieu@wowway.com.

LEUENBERGER, BETTY LOU, psychologist, educator; b. Detroit, Sept. 21, 1947; d. Stanley Ray and Lillian Elizabeth Nichols; m. Jerry Lee Leuenberger, Aug. 10, 1968; children: Cameron Lee, Justin L. BS in Edn., Ctrl. Mich. U., Mt. Pleasant, 1969, MA in Health Edn./Adminstrv. Curriculum Design, 1987. Tchr. Hemlock Pub. Schs., Mich., 1969—71, Meridian Pub. Schs., Sanford, Mich., 1971—77; tchr. adult edn. Kingsley Pub. Schs., Mich., 1978—93; tchr. jr. and sr. HS Traverse City Area Pub. Schs., Mich., 1978—. Mem. dist. adv. bd. Traverse City Area Pub. Schs., 1985—95, site leader, chair dept. social studies, 1985—2005. Named Tchr. of Yr., Traverse City Area Pub. Schs., 1989; named to, Nat. Honor Roll Am. Tchrs. Mem.: NCSS, ASCAID. Democrat. Avocations: motorcycling, gardening, gourmet cooking, travel. Office: Traverse City Ctrl HS PO Box 32 Traverse City MI 49685 Office Phone: 231-933-3500. Business E-Mail: leuenberbe@csh.tcaps.net.

LEULIETTE, CONNIE JANE, secondary school educator; d. Audie Nelson and Sadie Laura (Gregory) Ware; m. Charles Benjamin Leuliette, Jr., Sept. 5, 1964; 1 child, Eric Wesley. BS, W.Va. U., 1963, MA, 1965. Tchr. grades 1-4 Point Mountain Elem. Sch., Webster Springs, W.Va., 1959-60; tchr. gen. sci. Webster Springs (W.Va.) High Sch., 1963-64; tchr. 2d grade Norwood Elem. Sch., Clarksburg, W.Va., 1965-66, tchr. 6th grade, 1966-67; circulation clk., librarian Clarksburg-Harrison Pub. Library, 1981-83, reference librarian, 1983-89; tchr. sci. South Harrison High Sch., Lost Creek, W.Va., 1989-90, Roosevelt-Wilson Middle Sch., Nutter Fort, W.Va., 1990-96, Washington Irving Mid. Sch., Clarksburg, W.Va., 1996—2003. Pres. Nutter Fort PTA, 1978-79; elder Presbyn. Ch. NSF grantee, 1964-65. Mem. NEA, AAUW (sec. W.Va. divsn. 1981-83, conv. chmn. 1978-80, treas. 1992-96, br. pres. 1983-85, chair W.Va. Ednl. Found. 2000-02, chair W.Va. internat. rel. 2006—), W.Va. Sci. Tchrs. Assn., W.Va. Assn. Parliamentarians (unit sec. 1986-90, treas. 1991-94, 99-01, 1st v.p. 2005-), W.Va. Fedn. Woman's Club (chmn. edn. dept. 1982-86, continuing edn. divsn. 1990-92, cmty. improvement program 1992-94, dist. edn. dept. 1990-92, dist. treas. 1994-98, dist. 2d v.p. 1998-2000, dist. 1st v.p. 2000-02, dist. pres. elect 2002-04, North Ctrl. dist. pres. 2004-2006, chmn. conservation dept. 2006—), Woman's Club Nutter Fort (pres. 1990-92), Alpha Delta Kappa (W.Va. chpt. v.p. 1992-94, chpt. pres. 1994-96, state historian 2000-02, state treas. 2002-2006, state chaplain 2006—). Democrat. Presbyterian. Avocations: reading, crosswords, walking, photography, stamp collecting/philately. Home: 107 Arbutus Dr Clarksburg WV 26301-4301

LEULIETTE, TIMOTHY D., automotive executive; m. Cindy Leuliette; 4 children. BSME, MBA, U. Mich. Engring. & planning positions Ford Motor Co.; exec. dir. prod. planning Am. Motors; group v.p. Bendix Electronics group Allied Signal Automotive; pres., CEO Siemens Automotive L.P.; corp. v.p. Siemens AG; pres., CEO ITT Automotive Inc., 1991—96; pres., COO Penske Corp., 1996—2001; founding ptnr., sr. mng. dir. Heartland Indsl. Ptnrs.; pres., CEO Metaldyne, 2001—, chmn., 2002—. Past chmn. bd. Detroit (Mich.) Br. The Fed. Res. Bank Chgo.; bd. dir. Collins & Aikman, TriMas Corp. Mem. Citizen's Rsch. Coun. Mich.; mem. citizens adv. com. U. Mich., Dearborn, Mich.; bd. mem. Karmanos Cancer Inst., Vattikuti Urology Inst., Henry Ford Health Systems. Named World Trader of Yr., Detroit (Mich.) Regional C. of C. Mem.: Engring. Soc. Detroit, Soc. Automotive Engrs., Detroit (Mich.) Econ. Club (bd. dir.). Office: Metaldyne Corp 47659 Halyard Dr Plymouth MI 48170

LEUNG, FIRMAN, investment bank executive; b. NYC, Nov. 15, 1957; s. Kwok Choy and Moo-Kit (Tsui) L.; m. Mary Elizabeth Gose, July 23, 1988; children: Anthony, Philip. BS, The Wharton Sch., 1979; MBA, Amos Tuck Sch., 1985. Product mgr. Citibank, N.A., NYC, 1979-80; assoc. Morgan Stanley & Co. Inc., NYC, 1980-83; v.p. Merrill Lynch & Co., NYC, 1985-91; mng. dir. Serfin Securities, NYC, 1991-94; dir. Salomon Bros. Inc., NYC, 1994—2001; mng. dir. Sandler O'Neill & Partners, NYC, 2001—. Mem. N.Y. Athletic Club, Leewood Country Club. Republican. Home: 28 Meadow Rd Scarsdale NY 10583-7640 Office: Sandler O'Neill & Partners 919 Third Ave New York NY 10022

LEUNG, FRANKIE FOOK-LUN, lawyer; b. Guangzhou, China, 1949; (div.); 1 child. BA in Psychology with honors, Hong Kong U., 1972; MS in Psychology, Birmingham U., Eng., 1974; BA, MA in Jurisprudence, Oxford U., Eng., 1976; JD, Coll. of Law, London, 1977. Bar: Calif. 1987. Barrister Eng. and Hong Kong, 1977—. Lectr. Chinese law for businessmen Hong Kong U., 1984-85, 85-86; vis. scholar Harvard U. Law Sch., 1983; barrister, solicitor Supreme Ct. of Victoria, Australia, 1983—, Calif. Bar, 1987—; cons. prof. Chinese Law Diploma Program, U. East Asia, 1986-87; adj. prof. Loyola Law Sch., L.A., 1988-2000, Pepperdine U. Law Sch., 1989-90; lectr. Stanford U. Law Sch., 1995-96, U. So. Calif. Law Sch., 1998-2003. Author books on Chinese and Hong Kong law, Asian politics, Asian trade and bus. mgmt.; contbr. numerous articles to profl. jours., and 6 books. Bd. advisors Hong Kong Archives Hoover Instn.-Stanford U., 1988—; adv., Ctrl. Policy Unit, Hong Kong govt., 1997-99, dir. YMCA, Pasadena, Calif., 1997-99. Mem. Am. Arbitration Assn. (bd. dirs.), Calif. State Bar (mem. exec. coun. internat. sect. 1989-92, Wiley W. Manuel award 1993), Hong Kong Bar Assn., European Assn. for Chinese Law (mem. exec. coun. 1986—, country corr. 1985—), Am. C. of C. (chmn. subcom. on Chinese intellectual property law 1985-86), Am. Soc. Internat. Law (judge moot ct. 1984-2005). Office: 444 S Flower St Ste 3010 Los Angeles CA 90071-2901 Home Phone: 213-952-8511; Office Phone: 213-228-8922. Personal E-mail: frankieleunglaw@aol.com.

LEUNG, KA-CHEONG, engineering educator; B in Engring. in Computer Sci., Hong Kong U. Sci. and Tech., 1994; MSEE in Computer Networks, U. So. Calif., 1997, PhD, 2000. Rsch. asst. U. Hong Kong, 1998—2000, vis. asst. prof. dept. elec. engring., 2005—; sr. rsch. engr. Nokia Rsch. Ctr., Irving, Tex., 2001—02; asst. prof. Tex. Tech U., 2002—05. Ind. cons. Tex. Internat. Edn. Consortium, 2004. Contbr. articles to profl. jours. Mem.: IEEE. Office: U Hong Kong Dept EEE Pokfulam Rd Hong Kong Hong Kong Personal E-mail: kcleung@eee.hku.hk. Business E-Mail: kcleung@ieee.org.

LEUNG, PRUDENCE MARGUERITE, pharmacist; b. Sacramento, Calif., Feb. 24, 1957; d. Chung S. and Katherine Chin; m. Henry K. Leung, Nov. 25, 1989; children: Jamie Nicole, David Hoang Cheung. BA, U. Calif., Santa Barbara, 1982; PharmD, U. Calif., San Francisco, 1986. Registered pharmacist Calif. Bd. Pharmacy, 1986. Clin. pharmacist Dept. Veterans Affairs, San Francisco, 1987—90; pharmacist Payless Drug Stores, Pittsburg, 1990—96, Kaiser Permanente, Mountain View, 1997—98, South San Francisco, 1998—2005; clin. pharmacist First DataBank, San Bruno, 2005—. Mem.: Am. Coll. Clin. Pharmacy. Office: First DataBank Ste 350 1111 Bayhill Dr San Bruno CA 94066 Office Phone: 800-633-3453.

LEUNG, SANDRA, pharmaceutical executive, lawyer; b. 1960; married; 2 children. Grad., Tufts U., 1981; JD, Boston Coll. Law Sch., 1984. Asst. dist. atty. NYC; with Bristol-Myers Squibb, 1992—, corp. sec., 1999—2002, v.p., corp. sec., 2002—07, interim gen. counsel, 2006—07, sr. v.p., gen. counsel, 2007—. Office: Bristol-Myers Squibb 345 Park Ave New York NY 10154

LEUNG, SIMON, lawyer, electronics executive; BA, U. Calif., Davis; JD, U. Minn. Atty. Fotenos & Suttle, PC, 1995—99, Paul, Hastings, Janofsky & Walker LLP, 1999—2000; corp. counsel SYNNEX Corp., Fremont, Calif., 2000—01, gen. counsel, corp. sec., 2001—. Office: SYNNEX Corp 44201 Nobel Dr Fremont CA 94538 Office Phone: 510-656-3333.*

LEUPOLD, HERBERT AUGUST, physicist; b. Bklyn., Jan. 6, 1931; s. August John and Josefa (Thalmayr) L. BS in Physics, CUNY-Queens Coll., 1953; AM in Physics, Columbia U., 1958, PhD in Physics, 1964. Instr. physics CUNY-Queens Coll., Flushing, 1957; fellow Lawrence Livermore Lab., Livermore, Calif., 1964-67; instr. physics Monmouth Coll., West Long Branch, NJ, 1967-70, 84-85; instr. chemistry Trenton (N.J.) State Coll., 1984-85; rsch. physicist U.S. Army Rsch. Lab., Ft. Monmouth, NJ, 1967-97, U.S. Army Rsch. Lab. at U.S. Mil. Acad., West Point, NY, 1997—2000; ret., 2000; cons. Gen. Tech. Svcs., Wall Township, NJ, 2001—. Sr. technologist U.S. Army, 1995. Co-author: Rare Earth-Iron Permanent Magnetics, 1996; contbr. over 100 articles to profl. jours.; over 120 patents in fields of magnetics and electronics. With U.S. Army, 1953-55. Fellow IEEE (mem. assoc. editors of IEEE transactions), Army Rsch. Lab.; mem. Magnetics Soc. of IEEE (mem. adminstrv. com. 1991-93, mem. various conf. organizing coms.), Am. Phys. Soc., Sigma Xi. Roman Catholic.

LEUPP, EDYTHE PETERSON, retired education educator; b. Mpls., Nov. 27, 1921; d. Reynold H. and Lillian (Aldridge) Peterson; m. Thomas A. Leupp, Jan. 29, 1944 (dec.); children: DeEtte(dec.), Patrice, Stacia-(dec.), Roderick, Braden. BS, U. Oreg., Eugene, 1947, MS, 1951, EdD, 1972. Tchr. various pub. schs., Idaho, 1941-45, Portland, Oreg., 1945-55; dir. tchr. edn. N.W. Nazarene Coll., Nampa, Idaho, 1955-61; sch. adminstr. Portland Pub. Schs., 1963-84; dir. tchr. edn. George Fox Coll., Newberg, Oreg., 1984-87; ret., 1987. Vis. prof. So. Nazarene U., Bethany, Okla., 1988—95, Asia Pacific Nazarene Theol. Sem., 1996, prof., 2000; adj. prof. Warner Pacific Coll., Portland, 1996—97; pres. Portland Assn. Pub. Sch. Adminstrs., 1973—75; dir.-at-large Nat. Coun. Adminstrv. Women Edn., Washington, 1973—76; state chmn. Oreg. Sch. Prins. Spl. Project, 1978—79; chair Confdn. Oreg. Sch. Adminstrs. Ann. Conf.; rschr. 40 tchr. edn. programs in colls. and univs.; designer tchr. edn. program George Fox Coll. Author: tchr. edn. materials. Pres. Nampa PTA, 1958, Idaho State Aux. Mcpl. League, 1957. Named Honored Tchr. of Okla., 1993; recipient Golden Gift award, 1982; fellow, Charles Kettering Found., 1978, 1980, 1987, 1991, 1992, 1993, 1994; scholar Hazel Fishwood, 1970. Mem.: Am. Assn. Colls. Tchr. Edn., Pi Lambda Theta, Phi Delta Kappa, Delta Kappa Gamma (pres. Alpha Rho State 1986—88). Republican. Nazarene. Avocations: travel, crafts, photography. Home: 8100 SW 2nd Ave Portland OR 97219-4602

LEUTHOLD, RAYMOND MARTIN, agricultural economics professor; b. Billings, Mont., Oct. 13, 1940; s. John Henry and Grace Irene L.; m. Jane Hornaday, Aug. 20, 1966; children— Kevin, Gregory. Student, Colo. U., 1958-59; BS, Mont. State U., 1962; MS, U. Wis., 1966, PhD, 1968. Faculty U. Ill., Urbana-Champaign, 1967—, now prof. emeritus dept. agrl. econs., T.A. Hieronymus disting. prof. Vis. scholar Stanford U., 1974, Chgo. Mercantile Exch., 1990, 91. Co-author: The Theory and Practice of Futures Markets, 1989; editor: Commodity Markets and Futures Prices, 1979; co-editor: Livestock Futures Research Symposium, 1980. With US Army, 1962—64. Fulbright research scholar Institute de Gestion Internationale Agro-Alimentaire, Cergy, France, 1981 Mem. Am. Econ. Assn., Am. Agrl. Econs. Assn. (Disting. Policy award 1980, Outstanding Instr. award 1986, 88, 90, 92, College Funk award 1993). Office: 305 Mumford Hall 1301 W Gregory Dr Urbana IL 61801-9015

LEVADA, WILLIAM JOSEPH CARDINAL, archbishop emeritus, cardinal; b. Long Beach, Calif., June 15, 1936; s. Joseph and Lorraine (Nunez) Levada. BA, St. John's Coll., Camarillo, Calif., 1958; STL, Gregorian U., Rome, 1962, STD, 1971. Ordained priest in St. Peter's Basilica, Rome, 1961; assoc. pastor Archdiocese of LA, 1962—67; prof. theology St. John's Sem., Camarillo, Calif., 1970—76; exec. dir. Calif. Cath. Conf. of Bishops, Sacramento, 1982—84; ordained bishop, 1983; Titular Bishop of Capri & Aux. Bishop of LA, 1983—86; episcopal vicar Santa Barbara County, 1984—86; chancellor & moderator of the curia Archdiocese of LA, 1986; archbishop of Portland, Oreg., 1986—95; coadjutor to archbishop of San Francisco, 1995, archbishop, 1995—2005, archbishop emeritus Calif., 2005—; apostolic adminstr. Diocese of Santa Rosa, Calif., 1999—2000; elevated to Cardinal by Pope Benedict XVI, 2006—; prefect Congregation for the Doctrine of the Faith, 2005—. Mem. editl. com. Commn. for the Catechism of the Cath. Ch., 1986—93; ofcl. Congregation for the Doctrine of the Faith, 1976—82, mem., 2000—, prefect, 2005—; co-chair Anglican-Roman Cath. dialogue in the US, 2000; pres. Internat. Theological Comm., 2005—, Pontifical Biblical Comm., 2005—. Mem.: US Cath. Conf. Bishops (chmn. com. on doctrine 2003—05). Office: Congregation for Doctrine of Faith Piazza del Sant'Uffizio 11 00193 Rome Italy

LEVAI, PIERRE ALEXANDRE, art gallery executive; b. Paris, Mar. 6, 1937; came to U.S., 1967; s. Paul Victor and Jeanne (Illa) L.; m. Rosemary Hare, Aug. 22, 1969; children: Paula, Max. Degree in bus. and polit. sci., Inst. d'Etudes Politiques, 1959. With Marlborough Gallery, London, 1964-67, pres., dir. NYC, 1967—. Decorated chevalier dans l'ordre des Arts et des Lettres. Mem. Chelsea Arts Club (London). Roman Catholic. Office: Marlborough Gallery 40 W 57th St Fl 2 New York NY 10019-4069

LEVAL, PIERRE NELSON, federal judge; b. NYC, Sept. 4, 1936; s. Fernand and Beatrice (Reiter) L. BA cum laude, Harvard U., 1959, JD magna cum laude, 1963. Bar: NY 1964, US Ct. Appeals (2nd cir.) 1964, US Dist. Ct. So. Dist. NY 1966. Law clk. to Hon. Henry J. Friendly, US Ct. Appeals, 1963—64; asst. U.S. atty. So. Dist. NY, 1964—68, chief appellate atty., 1967—68; assoc. firm Cleary, Gottlieb, Steen & Hamilton, NYC, 1969—74; ptnr. firm, 1973—75; 1st asst. dist. atty. Office of Dist. Atty., NY County, 1975—76, chief asst. dist. atty., 1976—77; U.S. dist. judge So. Dist. NY, NYC, 1977—93; judge US Ct. of Appeals (2nd cir.), NYC, 1993—2002, sr judge, 2002—. Adj. faculty NYU Sch. of Law. Contbr. articles to profl. jours. With US Army, 1959. Recipient Learned Hand Medal, Fed. Bar Council, 1997; grantee Fowler Harper Mem. Fellowship, Yale Law Sch., 1992; Melville Nimmer Lectureship, UCLA Law Sch., 1997, Intellectual Property Keynote Lecturship, U. Conn Sch. of Law, 2001. Mem.: NY County Lawyers Assn., Assn. Bar City NY, Am. Law Inst. (coun.). Office: US Courthouse 40 Foley Sq New York NY 10007-1502*

LEVALLEY, AMBER NOEL, school psychologist; b. Missoula, Mont., Jan. 13, 1978; d. Brent and Shirley Hinther; m. Thomas LeValley, Oct. 7, 2006. BA, U. Mont., Missoula, 2001, MA, 2002, Edn. Specialist, 2004. Cert. sch. psychologist Oreg. Sch. psychologist Somerton Sch. Dist., Ariz., 2003—. Mem.: Ariz. Assn. Sch. Psychologists, NASP (cert.), Psi Chi. Office Phone: 541-440-4038.

LEVAN, MARTIN DOUGLAS, chemical engineering professor; b. Chattanooga, Aug. 30, 1949; s. Martin Douglas and Charlotte Irene (McAmis) LeV.; m. Barbara Lynn Verkins, Sept. 24, 1977; children: Theodore Douglas, Gregory William. BSChemE, U. Va., 1971; PhD in Chem. Engring., U. Calif., Berkeley, 1976. Sr. research engr. Amoco Prodn. Co., Tulsa, 1976-78; asst. prof. chem. engring. U. Va., Charlottesville, 1978-83, assoc. prof., 1983—89, prof., 1989—96; Centennial prof. and chair chem. engring. Vanderbilt U., Nashville, 1997—2003, J. Lawrence Wilson prof. engring., 2004—. Cons. Amoco Prodn. Co., Tulsa, 1984—, Amoco Chems. Co., Chgo., 1986—; vis. prof. Perpignan U., France, 1994. Contbg. author: Perry's Chemical Engineer's Handbook, 1984; contbr. more than 140 articles to profl. jours. and procs. Cub scout officer Boy Scouts Am., Charlottesville, 1986—; coach boys and girls soccer, Charlottesville, 1987—. Fulbright sr. scholar Coun. for Internat. Exchange of Scholars, U. Porto, Portugal, 1985-86, CNRS-LIMSI, Orsay, France, 1993-94; grantee NSF, Petroleum Research Fund of Am. Chem. Soc., others. Mem. Am. Inst Chem. Engrs. (chmn. com. on absorption and ion exchange 1985-87, chmn. symposia 1981—), Am. Chem. Soc., Alpha Chi Sigma, Phi Eta Sigma, Tau Beta Pi, Sigma Xi. Avocations: golf, art. Office: Vanderbilt U Dept Chem Enging Va Station B 351604 Nashville TN 37235 Business E-Mail: m.douglas.levan@vanderbilt.edu.

LEVANDER, ANDREW JOSHUA, lawyer; b. NYC, Aug. 15, 1953; s. Seymour S. and Ellenore B. L.; m. Carol A. Loewenson, Sept. 18, 1983; children: Samuel, Benjamin. BA summa cum laude, Tufts U., 1973; JD, Columbia U., 1977. Bar: NY 1978, DC 1978, US Supreme Ct., US Ct. Appeals (2nd, 3rd, 4th, 5th, 7th and 10th DC cirs.), US Dist. Ct. (so. and ea. dists. NY). Law clk. to Judge Wilfred Feinberg US Ct. Appeals, NYC, 1977-78; asst. Solicitor Gen.'s Office US Dept. Justice, Washington, 1978-81; asst. US atty. securities and commodities fraud unit So. Dist. NY, NYC, 1981-85; ptnr. Shereff, Friedman, Hoffman & Goodman, NYC, 1985-98; assoc. ind. counsel Washington, 1987; ptnr. Swidler, Berlin, Shereff & Friedman, LLP, Washington, 1998—2004, Dechert, LLP, NYC, 2005—, mem. policy com. Bd. dirs. Swidler, Berlin, Shereff & Friedman, exec. com., 1998-2004. Co-author: The Prosecution and Prevention of Computer and High Technology Crime, 1986, Settling Commercial Litigation, 1999; contbr. articles to profl. jours. Chmn. scholar com. Westside Youth Soccer League, NYC, 1996-2003. Named one of Top 10 Trial Lawyers in Am., Nat. Law Jour., 2005. Mem. ABA (White Collar Com. 1997-99, lectr. white collar convention 2002), Bar Assn. City of NY (securities regulation com. 1997-99). Avocations: tennis, travel, coaching. Office: Dechert LLP 30 Rockefeller Plz New York NY 10112-2200 Office Phone: 212-698-3683. Office Fax: 212-698-3599. E-mail: andrew.levander@dechert.com.*

LEVANDOWSKI, BARBARA SUE, education educator; b. Mar. 16, 1948; d. Earl F. and Ann (Klee) L. BA in Edn. and Spanish, North Park Coll., 1970; MS in Elem. Edn., No. Ill. U., 1975, degree in curriculum and supervision/, 1977, EdD, 1979. cert. elem. tchr.; cert. secondary tchr.; cert. in administrv. with supt. endorsement; cert. sr. reviewer, Ill. Tchr. Round Lake (Ill.) Sch. Dist., 1970-75, Schaumburg (Ill.) Sch. Dist., 1975-87, asst. prin., 1977-87; prin., staff devel. dir. Dist. 200 Northwood Elem. Sch., Woodstock, Ill., 1987-94, dir. curriculum and instrn., 1994—2002; developer, dir. Woodstock Mentor-Instrn. for Tchrs., 1998—2002; prof. Sch. Edn., North Park U., Chgo., 2003—. Curriculum cons. Spring Grove Sch. Dist., Ill., 1980-81; instr. various courses, Schaumburg, 1984-86; dir. Einstein Sch. Writing Project, 1986-87; dir. Dist. 200 Thinking Thinking Skills, 1988—; co-instr. Dist. 200 Tchg. Thinking Skills Across the Curriculum, 1992—, dir. curriculum and instrn.; chair north ctrl. assn. visitation team Huntley Sch. Dist, 1989; co-developer 4 yr. tchr. mentor program, 1994—. Mem. editorial bd. Ill. Sch. R & D Jour., 1981—; contbr. articles to profl. jours. Chair Computer/Tech. Strategic Action Team, Woodstock, 1988-89. Recipient numerous awards for excellence in teaching, Those Who Excel award State of Ill., 1979, Plato award, 2006; fed. grantee. Mem. NAESP, NAFE, ASCD (insvc. presenter 1984—, presenter state and nat. conv. 1989—), Am. Biog. Rsch. Assn. (bd. dirs. 1985—, publs. com. 1983), Nat. Staff Devel. Coun., Nat. Coun. of States for Insvc., Ill. Staff Devel. Coun., Ill. Assn. for Supervision and Curriculum Devel. (chair rsch. com. 1982), Ill. Computer Educators, Inst. Ednl. Rsch. (editorial bd. advisors, co-chair effective teaching characteristics observation 1990—, Omega award), Ill. Prin. Assn. Phi Delta Kappa, Delta Kappa Gamma. Home: 426 Normandie Ln Round Lake IL 60073-3711 Office: North Park Univ 3225 W Foster Ave Chicago IL 60625 Office Phone: 773-244-5789. E-mail: blevandowski@northpark.edu.

LEVANT, BRIAN, film director; b. Highland Park, Ill., Aug. 6, 1952; m. Alison Logan. Grad., U. N.Mex. Dir. (TV series) Married...With Children, 1987-97; dir. (films) Problem Child 2, 1991, Beethoven, 1992, The Flintstones, 1994, Jingle All the Way, 1996, Flintstones in Viva Rock Vegas, 2000, It's a Dog's Life, 2001, Snow Dogs, 2002, Are We There Yet?, 2005; writer (TV series) Happy Days, 1974-84, Mork & Mindy, 1978-82; prodr. (TV series) The Bad News Bears, 1979-80, Still The Beaver, 1985-89; writer, exec. prodr. (TV films) Poonchinski, 1990, The Adventures of Captain Zoom in Outer Space, 1995. also: United Talent Agy 9560 Wilshire Blvd Fl 5 Beverly Hills CA 90212-2401

LEVASSEUR, GUY J., lawyer; b. Amityville, NY, Sept. 3, 1965; BA, Dowling Coll., 1987; JD, Thomas E. Cooley Law Sch., 1991. Bar: Mich. 1992, NY 1993, Conn. 1993, US Dist. Ct. Ea. Dist. NY, US Dist. Ct. So. Dist. NY, US Ct. Appeals 2nd Cir., US Supreme Ct. Legal clk. Legal Aid of Ctrl. Mich., 1990—91; ptnr. Wilson, Elser, Moskowitz, Edelman & Dicker LLP, White Plains, NYC. Mem.: ABA (torts, ins. & compensation sect., litig. sect.), Ins. Brokers Assn. NY, NY Self Insurers Assn., Transp. Lawyers Assn., NY State Bar Assn. (torts, ins. & compensation sect.), Delta Theta Phi. Office: Wilson Elser Moskowitz Edelman & Dicker LLP 3 Gannett Dr White Plains NY 10604 Office Phone: 914-323-7000. Office Fax: 914-323-7001. Business E-Mail: levasseurg@wemed.com.

LEVASSEUR, LEE ALLAN, artist; b. Hartford, Conn., Apr. 8, 1950; s. Euclid Roland and Beatrice Marie (Daigle) LeVasseur; m. Evelyn M. Tucker, June 30, 1973 (div. Mar. 1986); 1 child, Robert Aaron. BS in Art Edn., So. Conn. State U., 1973. Cert. art tchr. K-12. Artist Organic Surrealism, Branford, Conn., 1989—, prodr., dir., 1991; custom picture framer APN Gallery, Branford, Conn., 1990-92, Off the Wall Gallery, Madison, Conn., 1992-93; archival picture framer Northlight Gallery, Branford, 1995—; fine arts restoration Brandon Gallery, Madison, Conn., 1995—2004. Lectr. Rotary, Guilford, Conn., 1990; co-prodr., dir. Am. 500 Quintcentennial, Buenos Aires, New Haven, Boston, NYC, 1992. Exhibitions include Festival of Arts and Ideas, New Haven, 1999, Brandon Gallery, Madison, Conn., 2001—04. Recipient cert. Excellence Artitudes, Internat. Art Competition, NYC, 1989, Blue ribbon, Branford Festival, 1991, prize E, SoHo Internat. Art Competition, 1992, 1st pl. mixed media, Cheshire Art League, 2000. Mem.: Art Coun. New Haven, Shoreline Alliance Artists, Branford C. of C. Democrat. Roman Catholic. Avocations: hiking, herbalism, camping, gardening, environmental conservator. Personal E-mail: leelevasseur@aol.com.

LEVASSEUR, MARK, dean; BA, Coll. of Atlantic; A of Occupl. Sci. in Culinary Arts, Culinary Inst. Am. With The Mayflower Inn, Balsams Grand Resort Hotel, Le Cirque; dean culinary arts Le Cordon Bleu Coll. Culinary Arts, Las Vegas. Office: Le Cordon Bleu Coll of Culinary Arts 1451 Center Crossing Rrd Las Vegas NV 89144*

LEVCHIN, MAX, Internet company executive; b. Kiev, Ukraine, 1975; BS in Computer Sci., Univ. Ill. at Urbana-Champaign, 1997. Founder PayPal, Slide personal media-sharing service, 2004—. Creator Gausebeck-Levchin test; prin. investor Yelp; co-founder Net Meridian Software, SponsorNet New Media. Achievements include designing innovative anti-fraud methods for PayPal in early stages.*

LEVE, ALAN DONALD, electronics executive; b. LA, Dec. 15, 1927; s. Milton Lewis and Etta L.; m. Annette Einhorn, Sept. 3, 1962; children—Laura Michelle, Elise Deanne. BS, UCLA, 1951. CPA, Calif. Staff acct., mgr. Joseph S. Herbert & Co. (C.P.A.s), Los Angeles, 1951-57, ptnr., 1957-63; CFO, sec., treas. Mica Corp., Culver City, Calif., 1963-82, also bd. dirs., 1963-82, chmn. bd., chief exec. officer, 1982-83; v.p., bd. dirs. Micaply Internat. Inc., 1968-1982; v.p. Micaply AG, Switzerland, 1972-83, also bd. dirs., chief exec. officer, also bd. dirs., 1982-83; v.p., bd. dirs. Micaply Internat., Ltd., U.K., 1971-82; chmn. bd., mng. dir., chief exec. officer Micaply Internat. Ltd., U.K., 1982-83; v.p., bd. dirs. Titan Chem. Corp., Edgecraft Corp., Culver Hydro-Press, Inc., LA, 1963-75; chmn. bd., pres., chief exec. officer Ohmega Techs., Inc., Culver City, Calif., 1983—, Ohmega Electronics, Inc., Culver City, 1986—. Served with USAAF, 1946-47. Home: 16430 Dorado Dr Encino CA 91436-4118 Office: 4031 Elenda St Culver City CA 90232-3723

LEVEEN, PAULINE, retired history professor, government professor; b. NYC, Mar. 5, 1925; d. Aaron and Sophie (Karp) Ugelow; m. Seymour Leveen, Nov. 5, 1944; children: David Ian, Amy Frances, Adriane Beth. Student, Coll. City N.Y., 1941-44; BA, Elmira Coll., 1963, MS, 1965; postgrad., Cornell U., 1967, 71-72, Syracuse U., 1981-82. Cert. tchr. permanent secondary social studies. Substitute tchr. Elmira (N.Y.) Sch. Dist., 1960-65; prof. history and govt. Corning (N.Y.) C.C., 1965-92, prof. emeritus, 1992—, dir. paralegal program, 1975-93, chmn. div. social scis., 1984-91, liaison Accelerated Coll. Edn. Lectr. Elderhostel, Painted Post, N.Y., 1982—. Mem. AAUW (chair Elmira-Corning br., 1989-1996, pres., 2003-06, chair edn. & econ. equity 2004—), Phi Alpha Theta, Beta Chi/Delta Kappa Gamma Corning (profl. affairs 1968, 75, legis. 1989—). Avocation: reading. Home: 60 Ohio Ave Elmira NY 14905-1822

LEVEEN, ROBERT FREDERICK, radiologist; b. Jersey City, July 24, 1946; s. Harry Henry and Jeanette Lois (Rubricius) LeV.; m. Sandra Sue Hickstein, May 28, 1974; children: Emily, Rob. BA, Grinnell Coll., Iowa, 1968; MD, U. Nebr., Omaha, 1974. Diplomate Am. Bd. Radiology. Intern dept. surgery U. Wash., 1974-75; resident in radiology Coll. Medicine U. Nebr., 1975-78; asst. prof. radiology U. Nebr. Med. Ctr., Omaha, 1978-80; from asst. prof. radiology to assoc. prof. U. Pa., Phila., 1980-90; rsch. assoc. VA Med. Ctr., Phila., 1980-83, clin. investigator, 1985-90; coord. angiography rsch. Dept. Radiology U. Pa., 1985-90; assoc. prof. radiology U. Nebr. Med. Ctr., 1991-99; chief radiology svc. VA Med. Ctr., Omaha, 1991-99; assoc. prof. U. Fla., Gainesville, 1999—. Recipient Career Devel. award, VA, 1985; Stauffer award, Assn. U. Radiologists, 1986. Fellow Am. Coll. Radiology; mem. Soc. Cardiovasc. and Interventional Radiology, Radiologic Soc. N.Am., Assn. U. Radiologists, Nebr. Radiol. Soc. (pres. 1998-99), Fla. Radiol. Soc. Presbyterian. Office: U Fla Coll Medicine Dept Radiology PO Box 100374 Gainesville FL 32610-0374 Office Phone: 352-376-1611 x 6396. E-mail: leveer@radiology.ufl.edu.

LEVEILLE, GILBERT ANTONIO, food products executive; b. Fall River, Mass., June 3, 1934; s. Isidore and Rose (Caron) L.; divorced; children: Michael, Kathleen, Edward; m. Carol A. Phillips, Aug. 7, 1981. B in Vocat. Agr., U. Mass, 1956; MS, Rutgers U., 1958, PhD in Nutrition and Biochemistry, 1960; DSc (hon.), Purdue U., West Lafayette, Ind., 2007. Prof. nutritional biochemistry U. Ill., Urbana, 1965-71; chmn. dept. food sci. and human nutrition Mich. State U., East Lansing, 1971-80; dir. nutrition and health sci. Gen. Foods Corp., Tarrytown, NY, 1980-86; v.p. for rsch. and tech. svcs. Nabisco Inc., East Hanover, NJ, 1986-96; pres. Leveille Assocs., Denville, NJ, 1996-99, 2004—; v.p. worldwide, sci. and regulatory affairs McNeil Consumer Healthcare, Fort Washington, Pa., 1999—2001; v.p. tech. food sys. design, dir. food tech. devel. ctr. Cargill, Inc., 2002—04; exec. dir. Wrigley Sci. Inst. William Wrigley Jr. Co., Chgo., 2005—. Author: The Set Point Diet, 1985 (Nonfiction Bestseller, NY Times); contbr. articles to profl. jours. Served to 1st lt. U.S. Army, 1960-62. Recipient rsch. award Poultry Sci. Assn., 1965, Disting. Faculty award Mich. State U., 1980, Chancellor's Medal, U. Mass., 2000. Mem. AAAS, Am. Chem. Soc., Am. Soc. for Nutrition (pres. 1988-89, Mead Johnson rsch. award 1971, Elvehjem award 2002), Inst. Food Technologists (pres. 1983-84, fellow 1983, Carl Fellers award 1992, Indsl. Scientist award 2004). Personal E-mail: leveilleg@optonline.net.

LEVEL, LEON JULES, investor, director; b. Detroit, Dec. 30, 1940; s. Leon and Madeline G. (Mayea) L.; m. Constance Kramer, June 25, 1966; children— Andrea, Aileen BBA, U. Mich., 1962, MBA, 1963. CPA, Mich. Asst. accountant Deloitte Haskins & Sells, Detroit, 1963-66, sr. accountant, 1966-69, prin., 1969-71; asst. corp. controller Bendix Corp., Southfield, Mich., 1971-81; v.p. fin. planning Burroughs Corp., Detroit, 1981-82, v.p., treas., 1982-86, Unisys Corp., Blue Bell, Pa., 1986-89; CFO, v.p. Computer Scis. Corp., 1989—2006. Mem. adv. bd. U. Mich., Ann Arbor, 1984-90, Providence Hosp., Southfield, Mich., 1984-86, Western FM Global Ins., 1995-06; bd. dirs. Allied Waste Industries, Inc., UTi Worldwide, Inc., Levi Strauss & Co. Trustee Walnut St. Theatre, Phila., 1988-89, Autry Nat. Ctr., 2000. Mem. Fin. Execs. Inst. (sec. Detroit chpt. 1983-85, v.p. 1985-86, pres. 1986-87, bd. dirs. 2001), Am. Inst. C.P.A.s, Mich. Assn. C.P.A.s, Inst. Mgmt. Accts.

LEVELL, EDWARD, JR., retired airport director, aviation consultant; b. Jacksonville, Ala., Apr. 2, 1931; m. Rosa M. (Casellas) L, Aug. 3, 1951 (dec.); children: Edward III (dec.), Ruben C., Kenneth W. (dec.), Randy C., Raymond C. (dec.), Cheryl D. Levell Rivera, Michael K. BS, Tuskegee Inst., 1953; MA in Urban Sociology, U. Northern Colo., 1972; M in Mgmt., Indsl. Coll./Air War Coll., 1974. Commd. 2d lt. USAF, 1953, advanced through grades to col., 1978, various flight tng., air ops. and command positions, 1953-69; comdr. cadet group, then dep. commandant cadet wing USAF Acad., 1969-73; dep. comdr., vice comdr., wing comdr. 1st spl. ops. wing USAF, 1973-77, wing comdr. 58th tactical air command tng. wing, 1977-78, col., vice comdr., comdr. 20th air divsn., 1978-83, ret., 1983; dep. commr. aviation City of Chgo. Dept. Aviation, 1983-89; dep. dir. aviation, fin. and adminstrn. City of New Orleans Dept. Aviation, 1989-90, dep. dir. aviation, ops. and maintenance, 1990-92, dir. aviation, 1992—99; ret., 2000. Bd. dirs. Tourist & Conv. Commn., New Orleans; trustee Dryades YMCA, New Orleans; mem. transp. com. World Trade Ctr. Decorated Legion of Merit, D.F.C. (2), Meritorious Svc. Medal (2), Air Medal (8), Air Force Commendation Medal; recipient Disting. Svc. award Jacksonville, Ala., 1974, State of Fla. Commn. Human Rels. award for spl. recognition, 1977, Air Force Assn. Spl. Citation of Merit, 1977, Disting. Svc. award City of Chgo. Dept. Aviation, 1986, 87, 88; inducted in Tuskegee Univ. Hall of Fame, 1991. Mem. Airport Ops. Coun. Internat. (task force chmn. ann. conf. New Orleans 1991), Am. Assn. Airport Execs., Gulf Coast Internat. Hispanic C. of C. Home: 13881 Cinch Ln Gainesville VA 20155 Personal E-mail: eddielevell@aol.com, eddielevell@comcast.net.

LEVEN, ANN RUTH, financial consultant; b. Canton, Ohio, Nov. 1, 1940; d. Joseph J. and Bessie (Scharff) L. AB, Brown U., 1962; cert. with distinction in Bus. Adminstrn., Harvard-Radcliffe U.s, 1963; MBA, Harvard U., 1964. Product mgr. household products div. Colgate-Palmolive, NYC, 1964-66; account exec. Grey Advt., 1966-67; fin. asst. Met. Mus. Art, 1967-69, asst. treas., 1970-72, treas., 1972-79; v.p., sr. corp. planning officer Chase Manhattan Bank, 1979-83; pres. ARL Assoc., 1983—; treas. Smithsonian Instn., Washington, 1984-90; dep. treas. Nat. Gallery Art, 1990-94, treas. and CFO, 1994-99. Adj. asst. prof. Grad. Sch. Bus. Columbia U., NYC, 1975—77, adj. assoc. prof., 1977—79, adj. prof., 1980—93; exec.-in-residence Amos Tuck Sch. Dartmouth Coll., Hanover, NH, 1976, 84; bd. dir. Del. Group Family of Funds, Systemax; bd. gov. Investment Co. Inst., 1997—2004. Artist (awarded prizes for painting and graphic arts); contbr. articles to profl. jours. Exec. bd. new leadership divsn. Fedn. Jewish Philanthropies, 1968-70; coun. mem. N.Y. Pub. Libr., exec. com., 1976-79; mus. adv. panel N.Y. State Coun. Arts, 1977-79; bd. dirs. Camp Rainbow, 1970-84, v.p., 1976-78, treas., 1982-84; bd. overseers Amos Tuck Sch., 1978-84, chmn. ednl. affairs com., 1979-84; trustee Brown U., 1976—, fin. and budget com., student life com., devel. com., adv. and exec. coms., bd. dirs. Ctr. Fgn. Policy Devel.; bd. dirs. Am. Arts Alliance, 1990-92, Twyla Tharp Dance Found., 1982-87, Reading Is Fundamental, 1987-91, adv. coun., 1991-94; trustee Carnegie Corp. N.Y., 1981-1987, Artists' Choice Mus., 1979-87; vis. com. Harvard U. Bus. Sch., 1979-84; bd. overseers Hood Mus.-Hopkins Ctr. Dartmouth Coll., 1984-91, chmn., 1988-91; trustee ARC Endowment Fund, 1985-90, N.Y. Sch. Interior Design, 1996—, Andy Warhol Found., 1999—; staff Presdl. Task Force on Arts and Humanities, 1981. Recipient Young Leadership award Council Jewish Fedns. and Welfare Funds, 1968; named N.Y. State's Outstanding Young Woman, 1976. Mem. Harvard Bus. Sch. Alumni Assn. (exec. coun. 1976-79, v.p. 1978-79), Women's Fin. Assn., Women's Forum, Econ. Club of N.Y., Cosmopolitan Club, Harvard Bus. Sch. Club, Radcliffe Club, Brown Club, Art Table, Century Assn. Home: 785 Park Ave New York NY 10021-3552

LEVEN, CHARLES LOUIS, economics professor; b. Chgo., May 2, 1928; s. Elie H. and Ruth (Reinach) R.; m. Judith Danoff, 1950 (div. 1970); m. Dorothy Wish, 1970 (div. 1999); children: Ronald L., Robert M., Carol E., Philip W., Alice S. Student, Ill. Inst. Tech., 1945-46, U. Ill., 1947; BS, Northwestern U., 1950, MA, 1957, PhD, 1958. Economist Fed. Res. Bank of Chgo., 1950-56; asst. prof. Iowa State U., 1957-59, U. Pa., 1960—62; assoc. prof. U. Pitts., 1962-65; chmn. dept. econs. Washington U., St. Louis, 1975-80, prof. econs., 1965-91, 2005—, prof. emeritus, 1991—; dir. Inst. Urban and Regional Studies, 1965-85. Disting. prof. U. Mo., St. Louis, 1991—2001; disting. vis. prof. George Mason U., 2007; cons. EEC, Ill. Auditor Gen., Polish Ministry of Planning and Constrn., St. Louis Sch. Bd., Ukrainian Ctr. for Markets and Entrepreneurship, City of Chgo.; mem. internat. adv. bd., com. spatial econ. and regional planning Polish Acad. Sci. Author: Theory and Method of Income and Product Accounts for Metropolitan Areas, 1963, Development Benefits of Water Resource Investment, 1969, An Analytical Framework for Regional Development Policy, 1970, Neighborhood Change, 1976, The Mature Metropolis, 1978. Served with USNR, 1945-46. Ford Found. fellow, 1956, Weiner Sch. Real Estate Fin. and Urban Econ. hon. fellow, 2005; recipient Disting. Alumni award Sullivan HS, Chgo., 2002; grantee Social Sci. Rsch. Coun., 1960, Com. Urban Econ., 1965, NSF, 1968, 73, Merc. Bancorp., 1976, HUD, 1978, NIH, 1985, 2001 Mem.: Am. Econ. Assn., Regional Sci. Assn. (pres. 1964—65, Walter Isard award for disting. scholarship 1995), Western Regional Sci. Assn. (pres. 1974—75, Disting. Fellow 1999), So. Regional Sci. Assn. (Disting. Fellow 1991). Office: Washington U Box 1208 1 Brookings Dr Saint Louis MO 63130-4899 Home: 1111Ontario Apt 1007 Oak Park IL 60302 Personal E-mail: charlessleven@yahoo.com. *Achievement is satisfying, but especially so when one can win without others losing. At the same time, it appears unnecessary to be a failure to prove one's sincerity.*

LEVEN, STEPHEN H., retired human resources specialist; BS, Cornell U.; MBA, So. Meth. U. Adminstr. Tex. Instruments, Dallas, 1973-80, employee rels. profl., 1980-82, mgr. human resources, 1982-92, sr. v.p. human resources semiconductor group, 1992-98, sr. v.p. and mgr. worldwide human resources, 1998; ret., 1998.

LEVENBACK, KAREN L., librarian, archivist, educator, writer, editor; b. NYC, Nov. 11, 1951; d. Gerald and Gloria Adele Levenback; m. Michael John Neufeld, June 14, 1994. BA, SUNY, Stony Brook, 1972; MA, Georgetown U., 1974; postgrad., Cornell U., 1974-75; PhD, U. Md., 1981; MLIS, Cath. U., 2004. Instr. Anatolia Coll., Thessaloniki, Greece, 1981-83; prof. Sch. Bus. Adminstrn. and Liberal Arts, Thessaloniki, 1981-83; lectr. George Washington U., Washington, 1984-2000. Author: Annual Bibliography of Woolf Scholarship, 1987-90, Virginia Woolf and the Great War, 1999; mem. editl. bd. GW Forum, 1998-99; book rev. editor Virginia Woolf Miscellany, 1999—; assoc. editor Woolf Studies Ann., 1994-99; contbr. essays to Anne Tyler as Novelist, 1994, Virginia Woolf and War, 1991; contbr. articles and revs. to profl. jours. Ombudsman, bd. dirs. Thessaloniki Players, 1981-83; sec. Takoma Pk. Arts and Humanities Commn., 2005—. Mem. MLA, ALA, Soc. Am. Archivists, Mid-Atlantic Regional Archives Conf., Internat. Virginia Woolf Soc. (sec.-treas. 1988-90, pres. 1991-93)

LEVENDUSKY, PHILIP GEORGE, psychologist, academic administrator, educator; b. Lowell, Mass., Oct. 21, 1946; s. Harry George and Phyllis Mary (Cowgill) Levendusky; m. Cynthia Ann Becton; children: Jason Philip, Anya Prentiss, Katya Sprague. BA magna cum laude, U. Mass, 1968; MS, Wash. State U., 1971, PhD, 1973. Diplomate Am. Bd. Profl. Psychology. Asst. to dir. Human Rels. Ctr., Wash. State U., Pullman, 1971-73; asst. psychologist McLean Hosp., Belmont, Mass., 1974-82, assoc. psychologist, 1982-92, psychologist, 1992—, dir. cognitive behavior therapy unit, 1974-94, dir. ambulatory care, 1991-95, asst. gen. dir., 1993-95, v.p. network devel., 1995—, dir. dept. psychology, dir. clin. tng., 1996—; instr. psychiatry Harvard Med. Sch., Boston, 1974-88, asst. prof., 1988-97, assoc. prof., 1997—; dir. Levendusky and Assocs., Arlington, Mass., 1980—. Cons. VA Hosp., Boston, 1977—85, Boston Cardiovasc. Health, 1983—85, Mass. Dept. Mental Health, 1987—90, Mass. Dept. Mental Retardation, 1997—2004; bd. dirs. Bain & Co., Employee Consultation, Boston, 1987—, Parthenon Group Mem. Assistance Program; mem. Mass. Bd. Psychology, 1988—93. Contbr. articles to profl. jours., mags., newspapers, chapters to books; guest numerous TV and Radio programs, Boston. Mem. Sch. Bd., Manchester, Mass., 1999—2002; bd. dirs. Feeding Ourselves, 1980, Anorexia Bulimia Care, 1991—93. Mem.: APA, New Eng. Soc. Behavior Analysis and Therapy (bd. dirs. 1991), Assn. Advancement Behaviour Therapy, Blue Hill Country Club, Phi Beta Kappa. Republican. Roman Catholic. Avocations: skiing, jogging. Office: McLean Hosp 115 Mill St Belmont MA 02478-1048 E-mail: levendp@mclean.harvard.edu.

LEVENFELD, MILTON ARTHUR, lawyer; b. Chgo., Mar. 18, 1927; s. Mitchell A. and Florence B. (Berman) Levenfeld; m. Iona R. Wishner, Dec. 18, 1949; children: Barry, David, Judith. Ph.B., U. Chgo., 1947, JD, 1950. Bar: Ill. 1950. Ptnr. Altman, Levenfeld & Kanter, Chgo., 1961-64, Levenfeld and Kanter, Chgo., 1964-80, Levenfeld, Eisenberg, Janger & Glassberg, Chgo., 1980-99; of counsel Levenfeld Pearlstein, Chgo., 1999—. Lectr. in fed. taxation. Contbr. articles to profl. jours. Co-gen. chmn. Chgo. Jewish United Fund, 1977, vice chmn. campaign, 1979; gov. mem. Orchestral Assn. Chgo. Symphony Orch.; bd. dirs. Jewish Fedn. Chgo., 1975—84, Spertus Coll. Judaica; mem. vis. com. U. Chgo. Law Sch., 1989—91. With USNR, 1944—45. Recipient Keter Shem Tov award, Jewish Nat. Fund, 1978. Mem.: ABA, Chgo. Bar Assn., Ill. Bar Assn., Am.-Israel C. of C. (pres. Met. Chgo. 1993—95, 1996—98, bd. dirs., 1st nat. v.p., chmn. legacies and endowments com. 1982—84). Home: 866 Stonegate Dr Highland Park IL 60035-5145 Office: 400 Skokie Blvd Ste 400 Northbrook IL 60062 Office Phone: 312-476-7531. Business E-Mail: mlevenfeld@lplegal.com.

LEVENICK, STUART L., manufacturing executive; BS, Univ. Ill.; MS, MIT. Mgmt. positions Caterpillar Inc., Peoria, Ill., 1977—89, div. mgr., 1989—95, regional mgr. Asia, 1995—98, gen. mgr. ops. CIS, 1998—2000, v.p. Asia Pacific & chmn. Shin Caterpillar Mitsubishi Ltd. Tokyo, 2000—04, group pres. Peoria, Ill., 2004—. Bd. dir. Entergy Corp., W.W. Grainger Inc., Heartland Partnership. Sloan Fellow. Mem.: U.S. Japan Bus. Council, U.S. China Bus. Council (dir.). Office: Caterpillar Inc 100 NE Adams St Peoria IL 61629*

LEVENS, DORSEY (HERBERT LEVENS), professional football player; b. Syracuse, NY, May 21, 1970; Student, U. Notre Dame, Ga. Poly. U. Running back Green Bay (Wis.) Packers, 1994—2001, Phila. Eagles, 2002—, New York Giants, 2003—04; co-owner Premier K-9 Inc.; owner World Gym, Atlanta. Named to Pro-Bowl, 1997. Achievements include being a member of Super Bowl XXXI Championship Team, 1996.

LEVENSON, ALAN IRA, psychiatrist, physician, educator; b. Boston, July 25, 1935; s. Jacob Maurice and Frances Ethel (Biller) Levenson; m. Myra Beatrice Katzen, June 12, 1960 (div. 1993); children: Jonathan, Nancy; m. Linda Ann Nadell, Jan. 30, 1994. AB, Harvard U., 1957, MD, 1961, MPH, 1965. Diplomate Am. Bd. Psychiatry and Neurology. Intern U. Hosp., Ann Arbor, Mich., 1961-62; resident in psychiatry Mass. Mental Health Ctr., Boston, 1962-65; staff psychiatrist NIMH, Chevy Chase, Md.,

1965-66, dir. divsn. mental health svc. programs, 1967-69; prof. psychiatry U. Ariz. Coll. Medicine, Tucson, 1969-2000, prof. emeritus, 2000—, head dept. psychiatry, 1969-89; CEO Palo Verde Mental Health Svcs., Tucson, 1971-91, chief med. officer, med. dir., 1991-93; chmn. bd. dirs., CEO Psychiatrists' Purchasing Group, 1991—; chmn. bd. dirs. Psychiatrists' Risk Retention Group, 1991-2000. Author: (book) The Community Mental Health Center: Strategies and Programs, 1972; contbr. papers and articles to profl. jours. Bd. dirs. Tucson Urban League, 1971—78, Pima Coun. Aging, 1976—83, 2006—. With USPHS, 1965—69. Fellow: Am. Coll. Mental Health Adminstrn. (v.p. 1980—82, pres. 1982—83), Am. Coll. Psychiatrists (regent 1980—83, v.p. 1983—85, pres.-elect 1985—86, pres. 1986—87), Am. Psychiat. Assn. (treas. 1986—90); mem.: Group Advancement Psychiatry, Harvard Alumni Assn. (bd. dirs. 1988—91). Office: 75 E Calle Resplendor Tucson AZ 85716-4937

LEVENSON, BRUCE, professional sports team owner, communications executive; m. Karen Levenson; 3 children. BA in Polit. Sci., Washington U., St. Louis; law degree, Am. U., Washington. Writer Washington Star and Observer Pub.; co-founder, ptnr. United Comm. Grp., Rockville, Md., 1977—; owner minority interest Washington Capitals, Washington Wizards, Capital Ctr. and MCI Ctr., 1994—99; prin. Atlanta Spirit, LLC (parent co. of NBA Atlanta Hawks and NHL Atlanta Thrashers). Bd. dirs. Newsletter and Electronic Pubs. Assn., TechTarget.com. Past. pres. I Have a Dream Found.; bd. dirs. Hoop Dreams Found. Office: United Comm Grp Ste 1100 11300 Rockville Pike Rockville MD 20852-3030*

LEVENSON, JACOB CLAVNER, language educator; b. Boston, Oct. 1, 1922; s. Joseph Mayer and Frances (Hahn) L.; m. Charlotte Elizabeth Getz, June 6, 1946; children: Anne L. Brown, Jill L. Eisenberg, Paul G. AB, Harvard U., 1943, PhD, 1951. Tutor in history and lit. Harvard, 1946-50, vis. lectr. English and gen. edn., 1951-52; instr. English U. Conn., 1950-54; asst. prof. to prof. English U. Minn., 1954-67; Edgar Allan Poe prof. English U. Va., Charlottesville, 1967-99, chmn. dept., 1971-74, prof. emeritus Charlottesville, 1999—; faculty Salzburg (Austria) Seminar in Am. Studies, 1947, 49. Mem. Com. of Cons., Notable Am. Women, 1607-1950, 63-72. Author: The Mind and Art of Henry Adams, 1957, Hist. and Critical Introductions The Works of Stephen Crane, II-V, VII, 1969-76; editor: Stephen Crane: Prose and Poetry, 1984, Mark Twain Life on the Mississippi, 1967, Discussions of Hamlet, 1960, The Letters of Henry Adams I-III, 1982, IV-VI, 1988; mem. editorial bd.; Am. Quar., 1964-70, Va. Quar. Rev., 1968-99, New Literary History, 1969-2000, Am. Lit., 1988-91; contbr. articles to profl. jours. Served with AUS, 1943-45. Decorated Bronze Star; Guggenheim fellow, 1958-59; Am. Council Learned Socs. fellow, 1961-62; Am. Philos. Soc. Penrose grantee, 1956; recipient E. Harris Harbison award for disting. teaching Danforth Found., 1966 Mem.: MLA, Am. Studies Assn., U. Va. Soc. Fellows (hon.), Signet Soc., Phi Beta Kappa. Home: 1581 Belvedere Dr Charlottesville VA 22901-1862

LEVENSON, MARC DAVID, optics and lasers specialist, editor; b. Phila., May 28, 1945; s. Donald William and Ethyl Jean Levenson; m. Naomi Francis Matsuda, Oct. 24, 1971. SB, MIT, 1967; MS, Stanford U., 1968, PhD, 1971. Rsch. fellow Harvard U., Cambridge, Mass., 1971-74; asst. prof. physics U. So. Calif., LA, 1974-77, assoc. prof., 1977-79; mem. rsch. staff IBM Rsch. div., San Jose, Calif., 1979-93, head mgr. OSC, 1987, mgr. quantum metrology, 1990; v.p. Focused Rsch., Inc., Sunnyvale, Calif., 1993-95; propr., cons. Marc D. Levenson Optics, Saratoga, 1993—. Vis. fellow Joint Inst. for Lab. Astrophysics, U. Colo., Boulder, 1995-96; vis. prof. Rice U., Houston, 1996. Author: Introduction to Nonlinear Laser Spectroscopy, 1988; editor: Lasers, Spectroscopy, New Ideas, 1987, Resonances, 1991; contbg. editor Solid State Tech. mag., 1993—; editor-in-chief Microlithography World Mag., 1995—; contbr. articles to profl. jours. Alfred Sloan rsch. fellow, 1975. Fellow IEEE, Optical Soc. Am. (Adolph Lomb medal 1976), Am. Phys. Soc., Bay Area Chrome Users Soc./Soc. Photog. and Instrumentation Engrs. (award 1991); mem. NAE. Avocations: gardening, reading. Home Phone: 408-867-1746; Office Phone: 650-941-3438 x26. Business E-Mail: marcl@pennwell.com.

LEVENSON, MILTON, chemical engineer, consultant; b. St. Paul, Jan. 4, 1923; s. Harry and Fanny M. Levenson; m. Mary Beth Novick, Aug. 27, 1950 (dec.); children: James L., Barbara G., Richard A., Scott D., Janet L. BChemE, U. Minn., 1943. Jr. engr. Houdaille-Hershey Corp., Decatur, Ill., 1944; research engr. Oak Ridge Nat. Lab., 1944-48; with Argonne (Ill.) Nat. Lab., 1948-73, assoc. lab. dir., 1973; dir. nuclear power div. Electric Power Research Inst., Palo Alto, Calif., 1973-80; exec. cons. Bechtel Power Corp., San Francisco, 1981-88; v.p. Bechtel Internat., 1984-89; pvt. exec. cons., 1990—. Lectr. in field. Contbr. over 150 articles to profl. jours., chpts. to 8 books; patentee in field. Served with C.E. U.S. Army, 1944-46. Bechtel fellow, 1981-89. Fellow AIChE (Robert E. Wilson award 1975), NAE, Am. Nuclear Soc. (pres. 1983-84). Office: 2319 Sharon Rd Menlo Park CA 94025-6807 E-mail: mlevenso@nas.edu.

LEVENSON, ROBERT MONTIE, retired physician; b. Yakima, Wash., Jan. 10, 1921; s. Montie T. and Ellen (Sharkey) L.; m. Marie E. Hofmeister, Sept. 21, 1947; children: Robert Jr., Albert D., David A., Nancy, Linda, Mary. MD, U. Louisville, 1946. Diplomate Am. Bd. Internal Medicine, 1955. Intern King County Hosp., Seattle, 1946-47; pvt. practice in internal medicine Seattle, 1954-88; resident Providence Hosp., Seattle, 1949-51, U. Calif. Hosp., San Francisco, 1951-52. Clin. prof. U. Wash. Med. Sch., Seattle, 1974—. Trustee Swedish Hosp. Med. Ctr., Seattle, 1985-88, King County Med. Blue Shield, Seattle, 1985—, J.L. Locke Trust, Seattle, 1974—. Fellow Am. Coll. Cardiology, Am. Coll. Physicians, Council Clin. Cardiology; mem. Am. Heart Assn. (award of merit 1982). Home: 3406 72nd Pl SE Mercer Island WA 98040-3342

LEVENSON, STANLEY RICHARD, public relations and advertising executive; b. Cin., Dec. 28, 1933; s. Irven Philip and Dorothy (Aftel) L.; m. Barbara Lind, July 23, 1962; children: Laura, Amy. BA, U. Mich., 1956; postgrad., Am. U. S.W. sales and promotion mgr. DOT Records, Hollywood, Calif., 1959-62; S.W. sales and mktg. rep. Pickwick Internat. Co., 1963-65; pres., chmn. bd. Stan Levenson Assos., Dallas, 1966-76; exec. v.p., gen. mgr. public relations div. S.W., Bozell & Jacobs, Dallas, 1976-81; pres., CEO Levenson & Levenson, Dallas, 1981-83; CEO Levenson Pub. Rels., 1984—; dir. Fidelity Nat. Bank, Dallas. Adj. prof. in pub. relations mgmt. So. Meth. U., 1987-88, mem. adv. bd. Pub. Rels. sequence studies. Group leader comm. task force Dallas Police Dept.; assoc. mem. Dallas Assembly; bd. dirs. Dallas Arboretum, Vis. Nurses Assn., Family Place, Dallas Coun. World Affairs, Dallas Urban League, 2001, Dallas Trees and Parks Found., Thanksgiving Found.; mem. adv. bd. Crystal Charity Ball; co-chmn. Dallas Mayor's Task Force on Mktg.; mem. exec. com., bd. dirs. Ctrl. Downtown Assn., Dallas, 1993-94; mem. Dallas Citizens Coun., 1997—; arts adminstrn. and corp. comm. adv. bd. So. Meth. U., 2000—; trustee TACA, 1980, bd. dirs., 2000; trustee Dallas Alliance, 1988; mem. exec. com. Ctrl. Dallas Assn.; state com. chmn. March of Dimes, 2002, bd. dirs. North Tex. Commn. With U.S. Army, 1956-58. Recipient A. Maceo Smith Cmty. Aware award for support and leadership in the African Am. Cmty., Dallas, 2005. Mem. Pub. Rels. Soc. Am. (accredited, North Tex. Teich award), Soc. Profl. Journalists, Am. Heart Assn. (bd. dir., com. chmn. 2002—), Greater Dallas Chamber (mktg. and comm. adv. coun. 2000—). Home: 4545 Mill Run Rd Dallas TX 75244-6432 Office: 717 N Harwood 20th Fl Dallas TX 75201-7484 Office Phone: 214-932-6076. Business E-Mail: s.levenson@levensonbrinkerpr.com.

LEVENTHAL, BENNETT LEE, psychiatry and pediatrics educator, academic administrator; b. Chgo., July 6, 1949; s. Howard Leonard and Florence Ruth (Albert) L.; children: Matthew G., Andrew G., Julia G. Student, Emory U., Atlanta, 1967—68; BS, La. State U., New Orleans, 1972, MD, 1974. Diplomate Am. Bd. Psychiatry and Neurology in Psychiatry, Am. Bd. Psychiatry and Neurology, Child Psychiatry; lic. physician NC, La., Ill., Va. Undergrad. rsch. assoc. Lab. Prof. William A. Pryor dept. chemistry La. State U., 1968-70; house officer I Charity Hosp. at New Orleans, 1974; resident in psychiatry Duke U. Med. Ctr., Durham, NC, 1974-78, chief fellow divsn. dept. psychiatry, 1976-77, chief resident dept. psychiatry, 1977-78, clin. assoc. dept. psychiatry, 1978-80; staff psychiatrist, head psychiatry dept. Joel T. Boone Clinic, Virginia Beach, Va., 1978-80; staff psychiatrist, faculty mem. dept. psychiatry Naval Regional Med. Ctr., Portsmouth, Va., 1978-80; asst. prof. psychiatry and pediats. U. Chgo., 1978-85, dir. Child Psychiatry Clinic, 1978—2005, dir. Child and Adolescent Psychiatry Fellowship tng. program, 1979-88, Irving B. Harris prof. child and adolescent psychiatry, 1998—, emeritus, 2005—, dir. Sonia Shankman Orthogenic Sch., 2002—05; prof. psychiatry, dir. Ctr. Child Mental Health U. Ill., Chgo., 2005—. Psychiat. cons. Caledonia State Prision/Halifax Mental Health Ctr., Tillery, NC, 1976-77, Fed. Correctional Inst., Butner, NC, 1977-78; cons. Norfolk Cmty. Mental health Ctr., 1978-80; adj. prof. psychology, biopsychology, and devel. psychology U. Chgo., 1990, adj. assoc. prof. dept. psychology and com. on biopsychology, 1987-90; meed. dir. Child Life and Family Edn. program Wyler Children's Hosp. of U. Chgo., 1983-95; dir. child and adolescent programs Chgo. Lakeshore Hosp., 1986-2000; Pfizer vis. prof. dept. psychiatry U. PR, 1992; examiner Am. Bd. Psychiatry and Neurology in Gen. Psychiatry and Child Psychiatry, 1982—; mem. steering com. Harris Ctr. for Devel. Studies, U. Chgo., 1983—; mem. com. on evaluation of GAPS project AMA, 1993-97; treas. Chgo. Consortium for Psychiat. Rsch., 1994; pres. Ill. Coun. Child and Adolescent Psychiatry, 1992-94; vis. scholar Hunter Inst. Mental Health and U. New Castle, NSW, Australia, 1995; mem. Gov.'s Panel on Health Svcs., 1993-94; prof. psychiatry & pediats. U. Chgo., 1990-2005, chmn. dept. psychiatry, 1991-98, Irving B. Harris prof. child & adolescent psychiatry, 1998-2004; presenter in field. Mem. editl. bd. Univ. Chgo. Better Health Letter, 1994-96; cons. editor: Jour. Emo tional and Behavioral Disorders, 1992-96; reviewer: Archives of Gen. Psychiatry, 1983—, Biol. Psychiatry, 1983—, Am. Jour. Psychiatry, 1983—, Jour. AMA, 1983—, Jour. Am. Acad. Child and Adolescent Psychiatry, 1983—, Sci., 1983—; book rev. editor Jour. Neuropsychiatry and Clin. Neuroscis., 1989-92, mem. editl. bd., 1989-92; contbr. articles to profl. jours. Lt. comdr. MC USNR, 1978—80. Recipient Crystal Plate award Little Friends, 1994, Individual Achievement award Autism Soc. Am., 1991, Merit award Duke U. Psychiat. Resident's Assn., 1976, Bick award La. Psychiat. Assn., 1974; Andrew W. Mellon Found. faculty fellow U. Chgo., 1983-84; John Dewey lectr. U. Chgo., 1982. Fellow Am. Acad. Child and Adolescent Psychiatry (Outstanding Mentor 1988, dep. chmn. program com. 1979—, chmn. arrangements com. 1979—, new rsch. subcom. for ann. meeting 1986—, mem. work group on rsch. 1989—), Am. Psychiat. Assn. (Falk fellow, mem. Ittleson Award Bd. 1994-97, mem. Am. Psychiat. Assn./Wisniewski Young Psychiatrists Rsch. Award Panel 1994—), Am. Acad. Pediats., Am. Orthopsychiat. Assn.; mem. AAAS, Am. Coll. Psychiatrists, Brain Rsch. Inst., Ill. Coun. Child and Adolescent Psychiatry, Ill. Psychiat. Soc., Soc. for Rsch. in Child Devel., Soc. of Profs. of Child and Adolescent Psychiatry, Soc. Biol. Psychiatry, Nat. Bd. Med. Examiners, Mental Health Assn. Ill. (profl. adv. bd. 1991—), Sigma Xi. Office: Inst for Juvenile Rsch Dept Psychiatry (M/C 747) U Ill at Chgo 1747 W Roosevelt Rd Rm 155 Chicago IL 60608 Office Phone: 312-355-3026. Business E-Mail: bll@uic.edu.

LEVENTHAL, CARL M., neurologist, consultant, retired government agency administrator; b. NYC, July 28, 1933; s. Isidor and Anna (Semmel) L.; m. Brigid Penelope Gray, 1962 (dec. 1994); children: George Leon, Sarah Elizabeth Roark, Dinah Susan, James Gray. AB cum laude, Harvard Coll., 1954; MD, U. Rochester, NY, 1959. Diplomate: Am. Bd. Psychiatry and Neurology. Fellow in anatomy U. Rochester, 1956—57; intern, then asst. resident in medicine Johns Hopkins Hosp., 1959-61; asst. resident, then resident in neurology Mass. Gen. Hosp., Boston, 1961-64; commd. officer USPHS, 1963-96, asst. surgeon gen., 1979-83; asso. neuropathologist Nat. Inst. Neurol. Diseases and Blindness, 1964-66; neurologist Nat. Cancer Inst., 1966-68; asst. to dep. dir. sci., 1968-73; acting dep. dir. sci. NIH, 1973-74; dep. dir. bur. drugs FDA, Rockville, Md., 1974-77; dep. dir. Nat. Inst. Arthritis, Diabetes and Digestive and Kidney Diseases, 1977-81; div. dir. Nat. Inst. Neurol. Disorders and Stroke, 1981-96; sr. policy analyst for life scis. Office of Sci. and Tech. Policy, Exec. Office of Pres., 1983; sr. dir. med. affairs INC Rsch., Inc., 2005—. Asst. clin. prof. neurology Georgetown U. Med. Sch., 1966-76 Recipient Commendation medal USPHS, 1970, Meritorious Svc. medal, 1974, 77, 91, Outstanding Svc. medal, 1988, dir's. award NIH, 1992, Disting. Svc. medal, 1997. Fellow Am. Acad. Neurology; mem. Am. Assn. Neuropathologists, Am. Neurol. Assn., Am. Soc. for Exptl. Neurotherapeutics, Alpha Omega Alpha. Home: 10924 Brewer House Rd Rockville MD 20852-3422

LEVENTHAL, ELAINE A., internist; MD, U. Wis., 1974; PhD, Yale U., 1966. Diplomate Am. Bd. Internal Medicine. Resident in gynecology U. Hosps., Madison, Wis., 1974—77; resident in internal medicine Mt. Sinai Med. Ctr., Milw., 1977—79; fellow in geriat. Williams S. Middleton Vets. Meml., Madison, 1979—81; prof. divsn. gen. internal medicine Robert Wood Johnson U. Med. Group, New Brunswick, NJ, 1988—. Office: Robert Wood Johnson U Med Group Clinical Acad Bldg 125 Paterson St Ste 5100A New Brunswick NJ 08901-1977 Home Phone: 732-247-7944; Office Phone: 732-235-6577. Business E-Mail: eleventh@umdnj.edu.

LEVENTHAL, ELLEN IRIS, portfolio manager; b. NYC; d. Harry and Laura (Schapira) L. BA, Barnard Coll., NYC, 1971; MA, Columbia U., 1973; MBA, NYU, 1978; student, Harvard U., 1968. Registered rep. NASD. Sr. investment analyst Comptrollers Office, City of N.Y., 1978-79; asst. investment officer Chem. Bank, NYC, 1980-81; v.p., portfolio mgr. E.F. Hutton, NYC, 1981-87, Shearson Lehman Bros., NYC, 1987-89, Ellaure Corp., NYC, 1989—. Portfolio mgr. Delta Capital Mgmt., 1993—. Mem. Investment Tech. Assn., N.Y. Soc. Security Analysts, NYU Bus. Forum, NYU Fin. Club, Money Marketeers of NYU, Princeton Club of N.Y., Barnard Coll. Club of N.Y., City Club of N.Y., Women's City Club of N.Y., Kappa Delta Pi. Avocations: golf, piano, ballet, tennis.

LEVENTHAL, HOWARD, health psychology educator, researcher; b. Bklyn., Dec. 7, 1931; s. Elias and Mildred (Turetsky) L.; m. Elaine A. Silverman, June 6, 1954; children: Edith A. Leventhal Burns, Sharon G. Student, CCNY, 1948-50; BS, CUNY, 1952; MA, U. N.C., 1954, PhD, 1956. Asst. prof. psychology Yale U., New Haven, 1958-64, assoc. prof., 1964-67; prof. depts. psychology and sociology U. Wis., Madison, 1967-88, dir. social and personality grad. program, 1967-77, acting dir. Inst. on Aging, 1986-87, chmn. dept. psychology, 1987-88; bd. govs., prof. dept. psychology Rutgers U., New Brunswick, NJ, 1988—, chmn. div. on health, assoc. dir. for program devel. Inst., 1988—97. Vis. lectr. Justus Liebig U., Giessen, Germany, summer 1981, U. Tilberg, The Netherlands, summers 1989-90, Rijks U., Leiden, The Netherlands, summer 1992; mem. adv. com. on cancer control Fox Chase Cancer Ctr., Phila., 1980—, mem. sci. adv. com., Phila., 1987—, mem. behavioral medicine study sect. NIH, 1986-90, chmn. 1990-91, mem. nat. reviewer res., 1991—, mem. sci. adv. bd. USAF Project Heart; reviewer Behavioral Medicine, Health Psychology, Psychol. Bull., Psychol. Rev., numerous others. Assoc. editor Health Psychology, 1982-87, mem. editl. bd., 1992; adv. editor Contemporary Psychology, 1987-91; mem. editl. bd. jour. Personality and Social Psychology, 1969-70, cons. editor, 1989; mem. editl. bd. Jour. Applied Social Psychology, 1981—, Motivation and Emotion, Psychosomatic Medicine, 1991—; former mem. editl. bd. Jour. Personality, Jour. Exptl. Social Psychology, Social Psychology; mem. editl. adv. bd. Cognition and Emotion; others; contbr. over 250 articles to psychol. and med. jours. Lt. USPHS, 1956-58. Recipient Disting. Alumnus award U. N.C. at Chapel Hill Carolina Psychology Alumni Assn., 1984, merit award Nat. Inst. on Aging, 1990, Bd. Trustees award for excellence in rsch. Rutgers U., 1992; grantee nat. Heart, Lung and Blood Inst. 1979-83, Nat. Inst. Aging, 1982-90, 93—, Nat. Cancer Inst., 1983-86, Nat. Inst. on Drug Abuse, 1984-87. Fellow AAAS, APA (fellow divsns. 1, 8, 38, pres.-elect divsn. 38 1995, pres. 1995—, Sr. Investigator award 1987), Am. Psychol. Soc., Acad. Behavioral Medicine Rsch. (adv. bd. 1988-91); mem. Inst. Medicine NAS, Am. Psychosomatic Soc., Soc. Exptl. Social Psychologists, Internat. Soc. Rsch. in Emotion, Sigma Xi. Office: Rutgers U Inst for Health 30 College Ave New Brunswick NJ 08901-1283

LEVENTHAL, LAWRENCE JAY, rheumatologist, educator; b. NYC, June 5, 1958; s. Samuel and Anne Leventhal; m. Linda Currao, May 15, 1988; 2 children. BA in Biology magna cum laude, Brandeis U., 1980; MD, Hahnemann U., 1984. Resident in internal medicine Albert Einstein Med. Ctr., Phila., 1984-87; fellow in rheumatology U. Pa., Phila., 1987—90, clin. assoc. in medicine, 1989—91, clin. asst. prof. medicine, 1989—97; clin. asst. prof. Med. Coll. Pa., Phila., 1990—; assoc. prof. medicine Hahnemann U., 1997. Dir. arthritis rsch. edn. Presbyn. Hosp., Phila., 1990—93; assoc. chief rheumatology Grad. Hosp., Phila., 1993—98, chief rheumatology, 1998—, vice chair dept. medicine, 2001—03, chair of medicine, 2003—. Author: Primer of Rheumatic Disease, 1994; editor: Jour. Clin. Rheumatology; contbr. articles to profl. jours. Named one of Best Drs. in Am., Ctr. for the Study Svcs., 1996—2006. Fellow ACP, Am. Coll. Rheumatology, Phila. Coll. Physicians; mem. AMA (physicians recognition award 1987—), Am. Soc. Internal Medicine, Phila. Rheumatism Soc. (pres. 1996), Arthritis Found. (exec. bd.). Office: Grad Hosp 1800 Lombard St Philadelphia PA 19146-1497 Personal E-mail: ljlmd@yahoo.com.

LEVENTHAL, NORMAN B., entrepreneur; b. Boston; BS, MIT, 1938; PhD (hon.), Hebrew Coll., Brandeis Univ. Co-founder, chmn. Beacon Cos., 1946—. Bd. dir. Doubletree Corp., 1993—97, GQHP, 1992—93, Picower Inst. Med. Rsch. Author: Mapping Boston, 1999. Fellow: Am. Acad. Arts & Scis.; mem.: Corp. of MIT (life). Office: Beacon Cos 490 Portion Rd Ronkonkoma NY 11779 Office Phone: 800-472-9201.*

LEVENTHAL, WILLIAM E. (WILLY) SIEGEL, writer; b. Staten Island, NY, Oct. 15, 1946; s. Bernard Leventhal and Eugenia Grace Siegel, Enid Firebaugh Leventhal (Stepmother). BA, UCLA, 1970, MA, 1972. Polit. staff, presdl. campaigns Senator George McGovern, Senator Henry M. Jackson and Pres. Jimmy Carter Presdl. Campaigns, 1972—80; pub. sch. tchr. LA Unified Sch. Dist. & Oxnard Unified Sch. Dist., 1991—2001; sociology prof. Troy U., Ala., 2002—04; pub., writer, editor Challenge Pub., Montgomery, Ala., 2005—; polit. and adminstrv. aide. Cons., ofcl. commn. reporter Martin Luther King, Jr. Fed. Holiday Commn., Washington and Atlanta, 1986—93. Author: (book) The SCOPE of Freedom: The Leadership of Hosea Williams with Dr. King's Summer '65 Student Volunteers, 2005, Brothers, Bats, and Balls...and Other Life Lessons in Sports, 2007; author: (and editor) (book) The Children Coming On: A Retrospective of the Montgomery Bus Boycott, 1998. Mem., writer for mag. So. Christian Leadership Conf., Atlanta, 1995—2003. Recipient Legacy award, E.D. Nixon Found., 2005. Mem.: Atlanta Internat. City Peace (assoc.; founding bd. mem. 2006). Conservative. Jewish. Avocations: softball, bicycling, surfing, baseball. Office: Challenge Publishing PO Box 1342 Montgomery AL 36102 Office Phone: 805-403-3638.

LEVER, JACK Q., JR., lawyer; b. Washington, July 8, 1948; BSME emphasis electrical engring., Clemson U., 1970; JD, Catholic U., 1974. Bar: Md. 1974, U.S. Ct. Customs and Patent Appeals 1975-82, D.C. 1978, U.S. Ct. Appeals (fed. and D.C. cirs.) 1982, U.S. Dist. Ct. D.C. 1990, U.S. Dist. Ct. Md. 1990, U.S. Ct. Appeals (8th cir.) 1990; registered to practice U.S. Patent and Trademark Office. Patent examiner U.S. Patent and Trademark Office, 1970-76; patent atty. Dept. Energy, 1976-81, dep. gen. counsel patents, 1980-82; atty. Willian, Brinks, Olds, Gilson & Lione PC, Washington, 1982; ptnr., chmn. firm intellectual property dept. McDermott Will & Emery LLP, Washington. Spl. counsel and rep. office tech. assessment, U.S. Congress, 1981. Editor: U.S. Intellectual Property Legislative Review: An Annual Review (Clark Boardman); contbr. articles to profl. jours. Mem. ABA (mem. sect. patent trademark and copyright law, litigation, corp banking and bus. law, antitrust), Am. Intellectual Property Law Assn., Inter-Am. Bar Assn., D.C. Bar, Bar Assn. D.C., Md. State Bar Assn., Internat. Trade Commn. Trial Lawyers Assn. Office: McDermott Will & Emery LLP 600 13th St NW 12th Fl Washington DC 20005-3096 Office Phone: 202-756-8365. Office Fax: 202-756-8087. Business E-Mail: jlever@mwe.com.

LEVERETT, DAWN R., disability education consultant; d. George R. and Wilma J. Leverett; life ptnr. Der Hsien Chang, May 10, 1997. AA, Yuba CC, Marysville, Calif., 1993; BA in Social Work, Calif. State U., Sacramento, 1996; MS in Edn., Nat. U., Sacramento, 2000; MS in Counseling, Calif. State U., Sacramento, 2007—. Disability counselor New Directions Edn. Ctr., Sacramento, 1998—99; disability edn. cons. Yuba County Office Edn., Marysville, 2000; tech. support agt. Earthlink, Inc., Sacramento, 2000—01; resource specialist tchr. (long -term substitute) Marysville H.S., 2001—02; after hours help desk agt. Volt Info. Sciences-Hewlett Packard, Roseville, Calif., 2003—04; disability edn. cons. A.C.E. Consulting, Yuba City, 2004—; vocat. rehab. rsch. asst. Calif. Dept. Rehab., Sacramento, 2005. Associated Students Inc. rep. U. Com. for Disabled Persons, Calif. State U., Sacramento, 2005—; vocat. rehab. counselor intern Calif. State U. Ctr., Sacramento, 2006; career counselor intern Yuba CC, 2006—07. Author: (manual) The Diabetes Survival Guide for K-12 Teachers, The Guide to Pre-Diabetes, Type 1 Diabetes, and Type 2 Diabetes for Vocational Rehabilitation Counselors. CPR and first aid instr. ARC, Yuba City, 1991—93; leader Girl Scouts USA, Tierra Del Oro Girl Scout Coun., Olliyuma Svc. Unit, Yuba City, 1992—93; mem. Sutter County Hist. Soc., Yuba City, Calif., 2004—06. Recipient Appreciation award, Girl Scouts USA, Olliyuma Svc. Unit, Troop 1187, 1991—92, Support and Dedication award, Girl Scouts USA, Olliyuma Svc. Unit, Troop 1239, 1992—93, Adult Leadership Devel. Pin, Girl Scouts USA, 1993, Adult Leadership Devel. Leaf, 1993. Mem.: ACA, Nat. Rehab. Assn., Nat. Rehab. Counseling Assn. (pres. 2004—06), Am. Rehab. Counseling Assn., Nat. Career Devel. Assn., Chi Sigma Iota. Office: ACE Consulting Ste 630 #315 1282 Stabler Ln Yuba City CA 95993 Home Phone: 530-790-7096; Office Phone: 530-701-7335. Personal E-mail: blu_mu@yahoo.com. Business E-Mail: leverett.aceconsulting@gmail.com.

LEVERICH, DENIS, protective services official, educator; b. Twin Falls, Idaho, Apr. 11, 1955; s. Thomas Lewis and Viola May Leverich; children: Brenda King, Joseph, Greggory, Christopher, Jeremie, Rachel. Certificate, Crowder Coll., Neosho, Mo., 1974; AGS, Ctrl. Tex. Coll., Kaleen, 1981; student, Kaplan U., Davenport, Ohio, 2004. Enlisted U.S. Army, Boise, Idaho, 1976; rose through ranks to Master Sgt. 101st Airborne; retired, 2002; correctional officer Clallam Bay Correctional Ctr., Wash., 1993—96, Cedar Creek Correctional Ctr., 1996—2000; list sgt. Stafford Creek Correctional Ctr., Aberdeen, Wash., 2000—, list lt. (acting), 2004, Washington Corrections Ctr., 2005—. Field tng. officer Dept. Corrections, Aberdeen, Wash., 2000; fire arms instructor Section Law Enforcement, 1995. Master sgt. Washington State Nat. Guard 2nd Bn. 146th FA, 1993—2002. Mem.: VFW, Correctional Peace Officers Foundation, Western Correctional Assn., Am. Legion, Skookun Rotary Club. Home: 607 Grandview Shelton WA 98584 Office: Dept Corrections W 2321 Dayton Airport Rd Shelton WA 98584 Office Phone: 360-426-4433. Personal E-mail: ariesdenis@yahoo.com.

LEVERIDGE, RICHARD J., lawyer; b. Jamestown, NY, June 14, 1956; BA magna cum laude, Providence Coll., 1978; JD cum laude, Georgetown U., 1981. Bar: DC 1981, US Dist. Ct. DC 1982, US Supreme Ct. 1986, US Ct. Appeals (4th cir.) 1988, US Ct. Appeals DC 1988, NY 1997, US Dist. Ct. (ea. dist.) NY 1998, US Dist. Ct. (so. dist.) NY 1998. Assoc. Dickstein Shapiro Morin & Oshinsky LLP, Washington, ptnr., group leader, Litig. & Dispute Resolution Group; mng. ptnr. Dickstein Shapiro LLP, Washington, 2006—. Mem.: ABA (litig. sect.), DC Bar (litig. sect.). Office: Dickstein Shapiro LLP 1825 Eye St NW Washington DC 20006 E-mail: leveridger@dicksteinshapiro.com.*

LEVERING, KATHRYN H., lawyer; b. Providence, Apr. 6, 1950; BA, Wheaton Coll., 1972; MA, Byrn Mawr Coll., 1973; JD, U. Pa., 1976. Bar: Pa. 1976. Joined Drinker, Biddle & Reath, Phila., 1976, sr. ptnr., labor, employment practice group, mng. ptnr., mem. mgmt. com., and chair, litig. dept., 2002—. Mem.: ABA (mem., labor, employment sect.), Phi Beta Kappa. Office: Drinker Biddle & Reath One Logan Sq 18th & Cherry Sts Philadelphia PA 19103-6996 Office Phone: 215-988-2919. Office Fax: 215-988-2757. Business E-Mail: kate.levering@dbr.com.

LEVERMORE, MONIQUE A., psychologist, educator; b. Montreal, Quebec, Can., Oct. 29, 1966; d. Oswald and Claudette Levermore; m. Mark Bartolone, Oct. 17, 1998; children: Nino, Kai. BA, U. Miami, Fla., 1988, MS in Edn., 1990; MS, Howard U., Washington, 1993, PhD, 1995. Cert. Fellow Am. Bd. Psychol. Specialties. Clin. fellow Harvard U., Cambridge, Mass., 1994—95; resident Psy-Eckerd Youth Devel. Ctr., Okeechobee, Fla., 1995—96; asst. prof. Palm Beach Atlantic U., West Palm Beach, Fla., 1996—97; pvt. practice Melbourne, Fla., 1997; asst. prof. Fla. Inst. Psychology, Melbourne, 1998—2004; pres. Adolescent Behavioral Inst., Melbourne, 2004—. Pres. Martique Corp. Chmn. adv. bd. With a Brush of Love, Md., 2002—; active Together in Partnership, Broward County, Fla., 2001—, Links, Inc., Brevard County, Fla., 2003; founder Growing Into Young Ladies Successfully; bd. dirs. Salvation Army, Melbourne, Fla., 2002—. Miami Tchg. fellow, 2006. Mem.: APA, ACFEI (jour. editor). Democrat. Episcopalian. Avocations: singing, flute. Office Phone: 321-724-2161. Personal E-mail: drl@levermore.com.

LEVESON, IRVING FREDERICK, economist; b. NYC, June 28, 1939; s. Hyman Wolf and Minnie L.; m. Barbara Diane Wurtzelman, Jan. 28, 1961; children: Stephen Martin, Scott Owen. BA (NY State Regents scholar), CCNY, 1960, MBA, 1963; PhD, Columbia U., 1968. Rsch. analyst, rsch. asst. Nat. Bur. Econ. Rsch., 1963-67; rsch. economist NYC Health Svcs. Adminstrn., 1967-68; economist RAND Corp., 1968-69; dir. rsch. Office Comprehensive Planning, NYC, Planning Commn., 1969-71; asst. adminstr. health systems planning NYC Health Services Adminstrn., 1971-74; sr. profl. staff, dir. econ. studies Hudson Inst., NY, 1974-84; sr. v.p., dir. rsch. Hudson Strategy Group, NYC, 1984-90; pres. Leveson Cons., Jackson, NJ, 1990—, ForecastCenter.com, LLC, Jackson, NJ, 1999—. Cons. Aerospace Corp.; adj. fellow Hudson Inst.; lectr. in field. Author: The Future of the Financial Services Industry, 1982, American Challenges, 1991; editor: Quantitative Explorations in Drug Abuse Policy, 1980; co-editor: Western Economies in Transition, 1980, Analysis of Urban Health Problems, 1976. Mem. Am. Meteorol. Soc., Am. Econ. Assn., Nat. Assn. Bus. Econs., Inst. Navigation. Jewish. Home and Office: 10 Inverness Ln Jackson NJ 08527-4047

LEVESON, NANCY G., aeronautical engineer; PhD, UCLA, 1980. Prof. computer sci. U. Calif., Irvine; Boeing prof. computer sci. and engring. U. Wash., 1993; prof. aeronautics and astronautics MIT, Cambridge. Author: Safeware: System Safety and Computers, 1995; contbr. articles to profl. jours.; past editor-in-chief IEEE Transactions on Software Engring. Recipient Info. Sys. award AIAA, 1995. Fellow ACM (mem. com. on computers and pub. policy, Allen Newell award 1999); mem. IEEE, NAE, Internat. Coun. on Sys. Engring. (past bd. dirs.), Computing Rsch. Assn., NRC (commn. on engring. and tech. sys., liaison to aeronautics and space engring. bd.), NASA Langley Adv. Subcom. on Air Frame Sys. Rsch. Achievements include research in software safety, which is concerned with the problems of building software for real-time systems where failures can result in loss of life or property. Office: Dept Aeronautics and Astronautics Rm 33-406 MIT 77 Mass Ave Cambridge MA 02139 E-mail: leveson@mit.edu.

LEVESQUE, PAUL JOSEPH, religious studies educator; b. Santa Monica, Calif., June 17, 1962; s. Ray Levesque and Marianna L. BA in Philosophy, Cath. U. of Am., DC, 1984, MA in Philosophy, 1985; BA in Religious Studies, Katholieke Universiteit Leuven, Belgium, 1987, MA in Religious Studies, Sacrae Theologiae Baccalaureatus, Katholieke Universiteit Leuven, Belgium, 1988, M in Morals and Religious Scis., 1989, PhD in Religious Studies, 1995. Lectr. Calif. State U., Fullerton, 1997—2001, asst. prof., 2001—07, assoc. prof., 2007—. Author: (book) Symbols of Transcendence: Religious Expression in the Thought of Louis Dupré, 1997, (essay in book) The Presence of Transcendence, 2001; contbr. articles to profl. jours. Theodore T. Basselin scholar, Sch. of Philosophy Honors Program, The Cath. U. of Am., 1982-1985. Mem.: Assn. for Sociology of Religion (assoc.), N.Am. Assn. for the Study of Religion (assoc.), Soc. for Sci. Study of Religion (assoc.), Am. Acad. of Religion (assoc.). Office: Calf State Univ Comparative Religion PO Box 6868 Fullerton CA 92834-6868 Office Phone: 714-278-5902. Personal E-mail: plevesque@fullerton.edu.

LEVETON, IAN SINCLAIR, civil engineer; b. Birmingham, Eng., Nov. 27, 1942; came to U.S., 1953; s. Eric Karl and Zena (Altman) L. BA in Physics and Econs., NYU, 1965; cert. of achievement, Orange Coast Coll., Costa Mesa, Calif., 1990. Computer programmer trainee Bklyn. Union Gas Co., 1969; computer programmer Elizabeth Arden Sales Corp., NYC, 1970; electronics expeditor Bendix Navigation & Controls, Teterboro, NJ, 1971; inventory control supr. Roman Products Inc., South Hackensack, NJ, 1972; nuclear mech. engr. Pub. Svc. N.J., Newark, 1973; mech. engr. Chemplant Designs divsn. DuPont, NYC, 1974-78, Holmes and Narver, Inc., Orange, Calif., 1978-82; tech. writer nuclear safety So. Calif. Edison, Rosemead, Calif., 1983-85; civil engr. tech. City of Santa Ana, Calif., 1985—. Cons. Islian Assocs., Teaneck, N.J., 1970-71. Mem. Teaneck Bicentennial Com., 1976; coord. United Way, City Pub. Works Agy., Santa Ana, 1992. Mem. KP (sec. 1974-76). Avocations: tennis, boating, reading, music, travel. Home: 19302 Steven Ln Huntington Beach CA 92646-2711

LEVETOWN, ROBERT ALEXANDER, lawyer; b. Bklyn., July 20, 1935; s. Alfred A. and Corinne L. (Cohen) L.; m. Roberta S. Slobodkin, Oct. 18, 1959. Student, U. Munich, Fed. Republic Germany, 1954-55; AB, Princeton U., 1956; LLB, Harvard U., 1959. Bar: D.C. 1960, N.Y. 1982, Va. 1984, Pa. 1985. Assoc. Pierson, Ball & Dowd, Washington, 1960-62; asst. U.S. atty. Washington, 1962-63; atty. Chesapeake & Potomac Telephone Cos., Washington, 1963-66, gen. atty., 1966-68, gen. solicitor, 1968-73, v.p., gen. counsel, 1975-83; exec. v.p., gen. counsel Bell Atlantic, 1983-91, vice chmn., 1991-92, also bd. dirs., 1989-92. Chmn. H.R. com., 1995-99; bd. dirs. Telecom NZ. Mem. ABA (vice chmn. comm. com., pub. utility law sect. 1986-93), Washington Met. Corp. Counsels' Assn. (bd. dirs. 1981-83), Nat. Legal Ctr. (legal adv. coun. 1986-92). Republican. Jewish. Address: PMB 606 10645 N Tatum Blvd #200 Phoenix AZ 85028-3053

LEVETT, TODD A., government agency administrator; s. Barry and Susie Levett. BA, Am. U., Washington. Feature editor The Plain Dealer, NEXT Sect., Cleveland, Ohio, 1998—2000; spl. asst. Office of the U.S. Ho. Dem. Leader/Office of Congressman Richard A. Gephardt, Washington, 2002—04; policy & comm. fellow U.S. Ho. Com. on Homeland Security, Washington, 2005—06; pres. & chief talent officer TAL Entertainment Group, Cleveland, Ohio, 1999—2002; profl. staff mem. U.S. Ho. Com. on Homeland Security, Minority Staff, Washington, 2006—06; advisor for policy & outreach, prin. advisor for homeland def. U.S. Ho. Com. on Homeland Security, Majority Staff, Washington, 2006—; projects asst. to the leader Office of the U.S. Ho. Dem. Leader, Washington, 2001—02. Truman assoc. Truman Nat. Security Project, Washington, 2005—. Spokesman Juvenile Diabetes Rsch. Found., Cleve., 1997—2001; bd. mem. Saltzman Philanthropy Bd. of Jewish Fedn., Cleve., 2000—00; surrogate scheduling coord. Gephardt for Pres., Washington, 2003—04. Recipient Performance award, Enterprise Rent-A-Car Northeastern Ohio, 2000, Michael Dively Govt. award, U. Sch., 2001, Appreciation cert., US Dept. State, 2004. Liberal. Avocations: tennis, bicycling. Office: US House Com on Homeland Security 176 Ford House Office Bldg Washington DC 20515 Business E-Mail: todd.levett@mail.house.gov.

LEVEY, GERALD SAUL, dean, internist, educator; b. Jersey City, Jan. 9, 1937; s. Jacob and Gertrude (Kantoff) Levey; m. Barbara Ann Cohen, June 4, 1961; children: John, Robin. AB, Cornell U., 1957; MD, N.J. Coll. Medicine, 1961. Diplomate Am. Bd. Internal Medicine. Med. intern Jersey City Med. Ctr., 1961—62, asst. med. resident, 1962—63; postdoctoral fellow dept. biol. chemistry Harvard U. Med. Sch., 1963—65; med. resident Mass. Gen. Hosp., Boston, 1965—66; clin. assoc. clin. endocrinology br. Nat. Inst. Arthritis and Metabolic Diseases NIH, Bethesda, Md., 1966—68, clin. assoc. Nat. Heart and Lung Inst., 1968—69, sr. investigator Nat. heart and Lung Inst., 1969—70; assoc. prof. medicine U. Miami Sch. Medicine, Fla., 1970—73, prof. medicine Fla., 1973—79; prof., chmn. dept. medicine U. Pitts. Sch. Medicine, 1979—91; physician-in-chief Presbyn.-Univ. Hosp., Pitts., 1979—91; sr. v.p. for med. and sci. affairs Merck and Co., Inc., Whitehouse Sta., NJ, 1991—94; prof., dept. medicine UCLA, dean, David Geffen Sch. of Medicine, 1994—, vice chancellor med. scis., 1994—. Harold Jeghers lectr. N.J. Coll. Medicine, 1977; Marian Blankenhorn lectr. Cin. Soc. Internal Medicine, 1982—; co-prin. investigator Nat. Study of Internal Medicine Manpower, 1984—. Mem. editl. bd.: Endocrinology, 1972—76, Am. Jour. Physiology, 1972—76, Jour. Applied Physiology, 1972—76, Annals of Internal Medicine, 1981—84, cons. editor: Hosp. Medicine, 1981—91; contbr. articles to profl. jours. Mem. United Jewish Fedn. Pitts. Leadership Devel., 1981—82; bd. dirs. Jewish Family and Children's Svcs., 1982—83, Am. Jewish Com., Miami, 1975—79. Grantee, NIH, 1971—91, Fla. Heart Assn., 1971—74. Fellow: ACP; mem.: AMA, Assn. Am. Physicians, Soc. Gen. Internal Medicine, So. Soc. Clin. Investigation, Assn. Profs. Medicine (chmn. ad hoc com. for use of animals in rsch. 1982—85, chmn. task force on internal medicine manpower 1983—90, nat. pres. 1990—91), Endocrine Soc., Am. Soc. Clin. Investigation, Am. Fedn. Clin. Rsch. (councillor so. sect. 1973—76, pres. so. sect. 1977—78), Am. Thyroid Assn. (mem. membership com. 1977—80), Alpha Omega Alpha. Office: UCLA Deans Office Sch Medicine 10833 Le Conte Ave Los Angeles CA 90095-3075

LEVEY, ROBERT FRANK, columnist, not-for-profit fundraiser; b. NYC, June 2, 1945; s. Stanley Victor and Sylvia Rose (Frank) L.; m. Jane Ellen Freundel, May 17, 1980; children: Emily Susanna, Alexander Freundel. BA, U. Chgo., 1966. Reporter Albuquerque Tribune, 1966-67; reporter, editor Washington Post, 1967-81, columnist, 1981—2004; sr. v.p. for devel. Washington Hosp. Ctr. Found., 2004—. Vis lectr. Duke U., Durham, N.C., 1979—; adviser journalism Cath. U. Am., Washington, 1979-81. Co-author: Washington Album, 2000; talk show host Sta. WRC, 1981—83, Sta. WBAL, 1988—92, Sta. WJLA-TV, 1984—86, Sta. WETA-FM, 1985—90, Sta. WTOP, 1997—2001, Newschannel 8, 2000—02. Woodrow Wilson fellow. Mem. Reporters Com. for Freedom of the Press, Newspaper Guild (chmn. Washington Post unit 1972-75), AFTRA, U. Chgo. Alumni Assn. (bd. govs. 1992-2000, pres. 1998-2000), Sigma Delta Chi. Jewish. Office Phone: 202-877-7983. Personal E-mail: bob.levey@comcast.net. Business E-Mail: bob.levey@medstar.net.

LEVEY, STUART A., federal agency administrator; b. 1963; Grad. summa cum laude, Harvard Coll., 1986; grad. magna cum laude, Harvard U., 1989. Bar: 1990. Law clerk U.S. Ct. Appeals (DC cir.), 1989—90; pvt. practice Miller, Cassidy, Larroca & Lewin LLP (now Baker Botts LLP), 1990—2001; with US Dept. Justice, Washington, 2001—04, assoc. dep. atty. gen., chief of staff to dep. atty. gen., prin. assoc. dep. atty. gen.; under sec. terrorism & fin. intelligence US Dept. Treasury, Washington, 2004—, head Office Terrorism and Fin. Intelligence, 2004—, head Office Intelligence & Analysis. Office: US Dept Treasury 1500 Pennsylvania Ave Washington DC 20220

LEVI, DANILO, sociologist, educator, director; m. Margaret Gaffney; children: Christian A., Gianni G. BA in Sociology, U. New Orleans, 1978, MA in Sociology, 1981; PhD, Tulane U., New Orleans, 1997. Asst. prof. sociology Southeastern La. U., Hammond, 1997—, interim dir. Internat. Initiatives Office.

LEVI, DAVID F., federal judge; b. 1951; BA, Harvard U., MA, 1973; JD, Stanford U. Bar: Calif. 1983. US atty. ea. dist. State of Calif., Sacramento, 1986-90; judge US Dist. Ct. (ea. dist.) Calif., Sacramento, 1990—, chief judge, 2003—. Chmn. task force on race, religious and ethnic fairness U.S. Ct. Appeals (9th cir.), 1994-97, mem. jury com., 1993-95. Adv. com. on Civil Rules, 1994—2003, chair, 2000—2003; chair Standing com.on Rules Practice and Procedure, 2003-; vis. com. U. Chgo. Law Sch., 1995-98. Fellow Am. Acad. Arts & Scis.; mem. Am. Law Inst. (mem. coun. 2004—), Milton L. Schwartz Inn of Ct. (pres. 1992-95). Office: US Dist Ct Rom 14-230 501 I St Sacramento CA 95814-7300*

LEVI, HERBERT WALTER, biologist, educator; b. Frankfurt, Germany, Jan. 3, 1921; came to U.S., 1938, naturalized, 1945; s. Ludwig and Irma (Hochschild) L.; m. Lorna Rose, June 13, 1949; 1 child, Frances. Student, Art Students League, NYC, 1938-39; BS, U. Conn., Storrs, 1946; MS, U. Wis., 1947, PhD, 1949; MA (hon.), Harvard U., Cambridge, Mass., 1970. Instr., then asst. prof. to assoc. prof. zoology, extension div. U. Wis., 1949-56; asst. curator arachnology Mus. Comparative Zoology Harvard U., 1956-57, assoc. curator, 1957-66, curator, 1966-91, prof. biology, 1970-91, Agassiz prof. zoology, 1972-91, prof. emeritus, 1991—. Sec. Rocky Mountain Biol. Lab., 1959—65; vis. prof. Hebrew U., Jerusalem, 1975; bd. govs. Nature Conservancy, 1959—62; taxonomic cons. Smithsonian project, 1979. Author (with L.R. Levi): Spiders and Their Kin, 1968, 2002; author: Aranas y especies afines, 1971; contbr. articles to profl. jours.; translator, editor: Invertebrate Zoology (Kaestner), bd. reviewers: Pacific Insects, 1980—85, bd. editors: Psyche, 1957—92, Zoomorphology, 1980—85, Sci. Bull. de Mus., 1980, Annales Zoologici Warszawa Poland, 1993, Memorias do Instituto Butantan, 1994. Fellow AAAS; mem. Am. Soc. Zoologists, Soc. Study Evolution, Soc. Systematic Zoology (councillor 1967-69), Am. Micros. Soc. (bd. reviewers 1973-94), Am. Arachnol. Soc. (hon. mem., bd. editors 1974—, dir. 1975-83, pres. 1979-81), Am. Ecol. Soc., Am. Inst. Biological Scis., Wildlife Soc., Am. Ornithol. Union, Assn. Systematics Collections (council nat. systematic collections and resources 1975), British Arachnological Soc., Cambridge Entomology Club, Internat. Soc. Arachnology (v.p. 1965-68, pres. 1980-83, hon. mem. 1995—), Japanese Arachnological Soc. (hon.), Soc. Systematic Biologists, Spider Club So. Africa (hon.), Wilson Ornithological Soc., Wilderness Soc. Home: 45 Wheeler St Pepperell MA 01463-1025 Office: Harvard U Mus Comparative Zoology Cambridge MA 02138-2902 Office Phone: 617-495-2447. Business E-Mail: levi@fas.harvard.edu.

LEVI, JAMES HARRY, real estate executive, investment banker; b. Boston, Oct. 28, 1939; s. Robert Emmett and Doris (Cohen) L.; m. Constance Jo Adler, Dec. 30, 1967; children: James H. II, Andrew R., Deanne D., Constance Jo. AB, Harvard U., 1961, MBA, 1964. Past pres. Value Properties Inc., NYC; now pres. Levi Co., Larchmont, NY. Chmn. bd. dirs. New Millenium Energies, Inc., St. Louis; pres. Gt. Train Store co., Dallas, others; prof. Bus. Sch. Columbia U., N.Y.C.; past pres. Oppenheimer Properties, Inc., N.Y.C.; exec. v.p., mem. exec. com. Oppenheimer & Co., Inc.; pres., chmn. bd. dirs. numerous affiliated cos. Mem. Bus. Sch. coun. Tulane U., N.Y.; mem. bd. govs. Hebrew Union Coll./Jewish Inst. Religion; mem. bd. overseers Sch. Architecture, Ill. Inst. Tech.; mem. exec. bd. Westchester Putnam coun. Boy Scouts Am.; mem. traffic commn. Village of Larchmont, N.Y.; mem. joint planning commn. Villages of Larchmont and Mamaroneck; trustee Larchmont Hist. Soc. Ensign USN, 1961-62. Named Man of Yr., St. Louis Rabbinical Coll., 1986. Mem. Real Estate Securities and Syndication Inst. (former gov.), Nat. Assn. Realtors, Nat. Assn. Rev. Appraisers (cert.), Soc. for Indsl. Archeology, Soc. Archtl. Historians, Nat. Assn. Security Dealers (registered prin.), Sheldrake Yacht Club (past treas.). Avocations: boating and sailing, collecting antiques, travel, opera, kinetic sculpture. Home: 85 Larchmont Ave Larchmont NY 10538-3748 Office: Levi Co 85 Larchmont Ave Larchmont NY 10538-3748 Office Phone: 917-834-5500. Business E-Mail: jameshlevi@cs.com.

LEVI, JOHN G., lawyer; b. Chgo., Oct. 9, 1948; s. Edward H. and Kate (Sulzberger) L.; m. Jill Felsenthal, Oct. 7, 1979; children: Benjamin E., Daniel F., Sarah K.H BA honors, U. Rochester, 1969; JD, Harvard U., 1972, LLM, 1973. Bar: Ill. 1973, U.S. Dist. Ct. (no. dist.) Ill. 1973, U.S. Ct. Appeals (7th cir.) 1973, U.S. Supreme Ct. 1977. Ptnr. Sidley Austin LLP, Chgo., 1973—. Chmn. bd. Francis W. Parker Sch., Chgo.; bd. dirs. Chgo. Child Care Soc., U. Chgo. Brain Rsch. Found., Jane Addams Juvenile Ct. Found., Ctr. for Wrongful Convictions, Chgo. Inst. for Psychoanalysis, High Jump Mem. ABA, Ill. Bar Assn., Chgo. Bar Assn., Lawyers Club Chgo Office: Sidley Austin LLP One S Dearborn St Chicago IL 60603

LEVI, JOSEF ALAN, artist; b. New York, Feb. 17, 1938; s. Jacob and Evelyn D. (Speizer) L. BA, U. Conn., 1959; postgrad., Columbia U., 1960. Artist in residence Appalachian State U., N.C., 1969, vis. prof. art, Pa. State U., 1976 One-man shows of paintings include Stable include N.Y.C., 1966, 67, 68, 69, 70, Arts Club of Chgo., 1967, J.B. Speed Art Mus., Louisville, Ky., 1968, Appalachian State U., Boone, N.C., 1969, Lambert Gallery, Los Angeles, 1971, Gertrude Kasle Gallery, Detroit, 1971, Jacobs Ladder Gallery, Washington, 1972, Images Gallery, Toledo, Ohio, 1972, A.M. Sachs Gallery, N.Y.C., 1975, 76, 78, O.K. Harris Gallery, N.Y.C., 1983, 85, 87, 90, 92, 94, 96, 99, Adams-Middleton Gallery, Dallas, 1986, Harmon Meek Gallery, Naples, Fla., 1996, 2001; numerous group shows, 1965—, latest being, Balt. Mus. Art, 1975, Mus. Art, R.I. Sch. Design, 1976, Art Mus., U. N.C., Greensboro, 1977, Russell Sage Coll., Troy, N.Y., 1977, Washington U., St. Louis, 1977, Whitney Mus., N.Y.C., 1978-79, Meml. Art Gallery, U. Rochester, N.Y., 1979, Aldrich Mus. Contemporary Art, Ridgefield, Conn., 1980, Western Assn. Art Museums, 1981, Worcester (Mass.) Art Mus., 1981, Palace Theatre of Arts Gallery, Stamford, Conn., 1984, Randolph Macon Coll., Ashland, Va., 1985, Robert I. Kidd Galleries, Birmingham, Mich., 1985, Elaine Benson Gallery, Bridgehampton, N.Y., 1985; others; represented in numerous permanent collections including, Aldrich Mus. Contemporary Art, Albright-Knox Gallery, Buffalo, N.Y., Mus. Modern Art, N.Y.C., Krannert Art Mus., U. Ill., Urbana, Va. Mus. Fine Arts, Richmond, AT&T, N.Y.C., Corcoran Gallery, Washington, U. Md., College City, Chrysler Corp., Detroit., Spellman Coll., Atlanta, Exxon Corp., N.Y.C., Minolta Corp., N.Y.C., Des Moines Art Ctr., Newark Mus., Dartmouth Coll., Hanover, N.H., Storm King Art Ctr., Mountainville, N.Y., U. Notre Dame Art Gallery, South Bend, Ind., J. B. Speed Art Mus., Louisville, Bank of N.Y., N.Y.C., Lewis and Clark Coll., Portland, Oreg., Technimetrics Inc., N.Y.C., Best Products Corp., Ashland, Va., Southland Corp., Dallas, TRW Corp., Cleve., Bklyn. Mus. Art, Worcester (Mass.) Art. Mus., Nat. Gallery of Art, Washington, Albion (Mich.) Coll., Prudential Ins. Co. Am., Newark. Served to 1st. lt. Adj. Gen. Corps U.S. Army, 1959-60. Mem. N.Y. Artist Equity Assn.

LEVICK, RICHARD SCOTT, communications executive, lawyer, consultant, educator; b. NYC, Dec. 10, 1957; s. Robert Richard and Marlene (Rosenblatt) L. BA, U. Md., 1979; JD, Am. U., 1987; MS, U. Mich., 1988. Exec. dir., chief lobbyist Pub. Interest Rsch. Group in Mich., Detroit and Lansing, 1979-84; pub. affairs cons. AFSCME, Washington, 1985; law clk. Fed. Bur. of Prisions U.S. Dept. of Justice, Washington, 1986; law clk. Fed. Bur. of Prisons Marian Baurely, P.C., Washington, 1987; chief exec. officer Nat. Cons. Strategies, Silver Spring, Md., 1987-90; ptnr. Jaffe Assocs., Washington, 1991; pvt. practice, 2006—. Spl. counsel Foley and Co., Washington, 1989—; cons. Potter for County Exec., Montgomery County, Md., 1990; prof. lectr. Am. U., Washington, 1990—. Co-author: Stop the Presses: The Litigation PR Desk Reference and 365 Marketing Meditations: Daily Lessons for Marketing & Communications Professionals; prodr. (TV comml.): Woodstock Commercial, 1989; contbr. articles to profl. jours. Mem. Ballot Question Com., Montgomery County, 1990; co-chair Dem. Task Force, Montgomery County, 1991—, Dist. 15 Caucus Issues Com., Montgomery County, 1991—. Named Pub. Rels. Profl. of Yr. US Agys. pub. rels. week, 2002, Crisis Agy. of Yr. The Holmes Report, 2005-; finalist Ernst & Young Entrepreneur of Yr., 2005. Mem. ABA, Nat. Assn. Law Firm Assn., Md. Bar Assn., Montgomery County Bar Assn., Montgomery County C. of C. (vice chair 1990—). Jewish. Avocations: running, swimming, biking, hiking. Business E-Mail: rlevick@levick.com.

LEVICOFF, VALERIE ANN, music educator; b. Phila., Feb. 13, 1961; d. Edward Joseph and Maryann (nee Adams) Lynch; m. Jerold Stephen Levicoff, Aug. 11, 1990; children: Alexander William, Edward Justin. BA in violin performance, Phila. Coll. of Perfoming Arts, 1983; MA in edn., La Salle U., Phila., 1990. Cert. music edn. K-12 Pa. Dept. Edn. Section violinist N.Y. Harlem Opera Co., 1985—86; social rehab. counselor Charles Drew Mental Health, Phila., 1986—87; asst. prin., 2d violinist Reading Symphony Orch., Pa., 1986—; music educator Sch. Dist. of Pa., Phila., 1987—; concert mistress Warminster Symphony, Pa., 1996—; adj. prof. music Arcadia U., Glenside, Pa., 2003—. Judge, adjudicator Warminster Symphony, Pa., 1997—, Reading Youth Symphony, Pa., 2001—; validator, benchmark Nat. Bd. Profl. Tchg. Stds., Phila. and San Antonio, 2003. Contbg. author (curriculum material) Sounds of Learning, Phila. Opera Co., 2005, 2006; editor: String Quartet Arranging, 2001—; facilitator Reading Symphony Orch., 2001—; musician (violinist): (TV commercial) Reading Symphony, 1999—; musician: (first violinist) Strings Fantastique, 1990. Nominee Tchr. of Yr., Phila. Sch. Dist., 2004; recipient Am. Legion award, 1975, Outstanding Educator Rose Lindenbaum award, 2005. Mem.: MENC, Pa. Music Educators Assn., ASTA, Reading Musician's Union, Phila. Fedn. Musicians. Avocations: travel, knitting, reading, music, art. Home: 1979 Audubon Dr Dresher PA 19025 Personal E-mail: violinval@comcast.net.

LEVIE, HOWARD S(IDNEY), lawyer, educator; b. Wolverine, Mich., Dec. 19, 1907; s. J. Walter and Mina (Goldfarb) L.; m. S. Blanche Krim, July 24, 1934 AB, Cornell U., 1928, JD, 1930; LL.M., George Washington U., 1957. Bar: N.Y. 1931, Mo. 1965, U.S. Dist. Ct. (ea. dist.) N.Y. 1934, U.S. Dist. Ct. (so. dist.) N.Y. 1935, U.S. Supreme Ct. 1947, U.S. Ct. Appeals (D.C. cir.) 1949, U.S. Ct. Mil. Appeals 1953. Assoc. Weit & Goldman, NYC, 1931-42; with JAGC, U.S. Army, 1942, advanced through grades to col., 1954; staff officer UN Command Armistice Del., Korea, 1951-52; chief internat. affairs div. Office of JAG, 1954-58; legal adviser U.S. European Command, Paris, 1959-61; ret., 1963; prof. law St. Louis U., 1962—72, prof. emeritus, 1972—; prof. U.S. Naval War Coll., Newport, RI, 1972—73, Charles H. Stockton prof. internat. law, 1972—73; instr. internat. law Salve Regina Coll., Newport, RI, 1984-88. Adj. prof. Naval War Coll., 1991—. Author: Prisoners of War in International Armed Conflict (Internat. Soc. for Mil. Law and the Law of War Ciardi prize

1982), 1979, Documents on Prisoners of War, 1980, Protection of War Victims, 4 vols., 1979-81, The Status of Gibraltar, 1983, The Code of International Armed Conflict, 1986, The Law of Non-International Armed Conflict, 1987, The Law of War and Neutrality: A Selected English-Language Bibliography, 1988, Mine Warfare at Sea, 1992, Terrorism in War: The Law of War Crimes, 1993; editor vols. 7-12: Terrorism: Documents of International and Local Control, 1997, Levie on the Law of War, 1998. Decorated Legion of Merit, Bronze Star; grantee Ctr. for Advanced Rsch., Naval War Coll., 1980-82, U.S. Inst. Peace, 1991; Howard S. Levie Mil. Chair of Operational Law established by U.S. Naval War Coll., 1994; recipient Outstanding Civilian Svc. medal Dept. of the Army, 1995; named Disting. Mem. of Judge Advocate Gen.'s Corps Regiment, 1995, The Col. Howard S. Levie Libr., established at the Army Judge Advocate's School is named in his honor. Mem. ABA, Am. Soc. Internat. Law (exec. coun. 1969-70), Internat. Law Assn., Ret. Army Judge Advs. Assn., Internat. Soc. for Mil. Law and Law of War, Phi Beta Kappa. Home and Office: 125 Quaker Hill Ln Apt 316 Portsmouth RI 02871-4075 Personal E-mail: hlevie41@aol.com.

LEVIE, JOSEPH HENRY, lawyer, banker; b. NYC; s. Mortimer Joseph and Pearl (Seelig) L.; m. Hallie Ratzkin, Jan. 26, 1963; children: Matthew Benjamin, Jessica Ruth. AB, Columbia U., 1949, LLB, 1951. Bar: N.Y. 1952, U.S. Supreme Ct. 1954. Assoc. Laporte & Meyers, NYC, 1955-59; asst. gen. counsel Loew Theatres Inc., NYC, 1959-63; from assoc. to ptnr. Rathheim, Hoffman, Kassel & Levie, NYC, 1964-81; ptnr. Rogers & Wells, NYC, 1982-94, ret., 1994, sr. counsel, 1995—. Arbitrator N.Y. Stock Exch., NASD; former dir. Chinese Am. Bank N.Y. Contbr. articles to profl. jours. With JAGC, U.S. Army, 1952-55. Fellow: Am. Coll. Comml. Fin. Attys. Home: 131 Riverside Dr New York NY 10024-3713 Personal E-mail: leviej@verizon.net.

LEVIE, MARK ROBERT, lawyer; b. Chgo., Sept. 2, 1951; s. Harold M. and Muriel L.; m. Gail M., Aug. 19, 1973; children: Melissa, Allison, David. BA in Rhetoric and Composition, U. Ill., 1973; JD magna cum laude, Harvard U., 1976. Bar: Calif. 1978, U.S. Dist. Ct. (no. dist.) Calif. 1978. Clk. to Hon. James R. Browning, chief judge U.S. Ct. Appeals (9th cir.), San Francisco, 1976-77; assoc. Orrick, Herrington & Sutcliffe, San Francisco, 1977-82, ptnr., 1983—, mem. exec. com., mng. dir. transactional practices. Bd. dirs., mem. audit com. Legal Aid Soc.-Employment Law Ctr., 2006—. Mem. ABA (corp. banking and bus. law sect., com. devel. bus. fin., sub-com. on securitization of assets, fin. task force), State Bar of Calif., San Francisco Bar Assn., San Francisco Lawyers Com. for Civil Rights (treas. 1995-1998). Avocations: golf, reading. Office: Orrick Herrington & Sutcliffe LLP 405 Howard St San Francisco CA 94105 Office Phone: 415-773-5955. Office Fax: 415-773-5759. Business E-Mail: mlevie@orrick.com.

LEVIEN, DAVID HAROLD, surgeon; b. N.Y.C., Aug. 4, 1948; s. Maurice Berryl and Gloria Anita (Siff) L.; m. Merril Ann Lirette, Aug. 6, 1977; children— Michael, William, Rachel. BA, Johns Hopkins U., 1970; MD, Georgetown U., 1974. Diplomate Am. Bd. Surgery, Am. Bd. Med. Examiners. Resident Mt. Sinai Hosp., N.Y.C., 1974-76; coordinated surg. resident U. Mass., 1976-79; surg. edn. coordinator New Rochelle Hosp., N.Y., 1980-90; instr. surgery N.Y. Med. Coll., Valhalla, 1980-83, asst. prof. surgery, 1983-90, clin. assoc. prof., 1990-91; cons. in surgery Castle Point VA Hosp., 1980-90; clin. assoc. prof. surgery Med. Coll. Pa./Hahnemann U., 1991—, clin. prof. surgery Jefferson Med. Coll., 1996—; dir. surgery Episcopal Hosp.; chmn. surgery St. Vincent's Med. Ctr., Bridgeport, Conn., 2000-03; prof. clin. surgery NY Med. Coll., 2001-03; surgeon Houlton (Maine) Regional Hosp., 2003-06; chmn. surgery St. Agnes Hosp., Balt., 2006—. Author textbook on surgery; contbr. articles to profl. jours. Mem. alumni admissions com. Johns Hopkins U., Balt., 1984-90. Fellow ACS, Am. Soc. Colon and Rectal Surgeons; mem. AMA, Soc. Critical Care Medicine, Assn. Acad. Surgery, Pa. Soc. Colon and Rectal Surgery (pres. 1997-98), Acad. Surgery Phila. (sec. 1998-99), Phila. Acad. Surgery (v.p. 2000), Balt. Acad. Surgery. Office: St Agnes Hosp 900 Caton Ave Box 207 Baltimore MD 21229 Home: 4404 Bedford Pl Baltimore MD 21208 Home Phone: 443-388-9681; Office Phone: 410-368-2745. Personal E-mail: dlevien@stagnes.org.

LEVIEN, ROGER ELI, strategy and innovation consultant; b. Bklyn., Apr. 16, 1935; s. Abraham Mark and Rosalind (Horowitz) L.; m. Carla Johanna Sherow, Oct. 9, 1960; children: Royce Adam, Alisa Tova. BS, Swarthmore Coll., Pa., 1956, MS, 1958; PhD, Harvard U., Cambridge, Mass., 1962. Mem. rsch. staff RAND Corp., Santa Monica, Calif., 1960-67, head sys. scis. dept., 1968-71, dir. Washington domestic program Washington, 1971-74; program leader Internat. Inst. Applied Sys. Analysis, Laxenburg, Austria, 1974-75, gen. dir., 1975-81; dir. strategic sys. analysis Xerox Corp., Stamford, Conn., 1981-85, corp. v.p. strategy office, 1985-92, corp. v.p. strategy and innovation, 1992-97. Adj. prof. UCLA, 1970-81; mem. adv. bd. Carnegie-Bosch Inst., Pitts., 1995-2002, Poly. U., Bklyn., 1995-97; chmn. com. on internet addressing and the domain name sys. NRC, 2000-05. Author: The Emerging Technology, 1972, Research and Development Management, 1975, Taking Technology to Market, 1997, NRC Report Signposts in Cyberspace, 2005; contbr. chpts. to books. Bd. dirs. Nat. Corp. Theatre Fund, N.Y.C., 1985-2003, Conn. Grand Opera and Orch., Stamford, 1994—2005. Recipient Ehrenkreuz First Class in Arts and Sci. award Austrian Govt., 1982. Mem. Mfrs. Alliance Coun. on Strategy (chmn. 1990-91), Coun. Planning Execs. (conf. bd.), Coun. on Mgmt. of Innovation and Tech. (chmn. conf. bd. 1996-97), Phi Beta Kappa, Sigma Xi, Tau Beta Pi. Avocations: skiing, photography, collecting north american indian art, musical theater. E-mail: rlevien@aol.com.

LEVI-MONTALCINI, RITA, neurobiologist, researcher; b. Turin, Italy, Apr. 22, 1909; came to U.S., 1947; naturalized, 1956; d. Adamo Levi and Adele Montalcini. MD, U. Turin, 1936. Asst. in neurology Inst. Anatomy, Neurology Clinic, Turin Sch. Medicine, 1936—37; researcher Neurol. Inst. Brussels, 1939; with Allied Health Svc., Italy, 1944—45; resident, assoc. zoologist Washington U., 1947—51, assoc. prof., 1951—58, prof., 1958—81, prof. emeritus St. Louis, 1977; dir. neurobiology rsch. program CNR (Nat. Rsch. Coun.), Rome, 1961—69, dir. cellular biology lab., 1969—79, guest prof. cellular biology lab., 1979—89; pres. Inst. della Enciclopedia Italiana Treccani, 1993—98. Pres. Ency. Italiana, 1993, Italian Nat. Commn. of United World Colls., 1993. Author: In Praise of Imperfection: My Life and Work, 1988. Named Sen. for Life, Italian Parliament, 2001; recipient Albert Lasker Med. Rsch. award, 1986, Nobel prize in physiology or medicine for work on chemical growth factors which control growth and development in humans and animals, 1986, Lewis S. Rosenstiel award, U.S. Nat. Medal of Sci. Mem. AAAS, Soc. Devel. Biology, Am. Assn. Anatomists, Tissue Culture Assn., NAS, Pontifical Acad., Nat. Acad. dei Lincei, Harvey Soc., Am. NAS, Belgian Royal Acad. Medicine, NAS of Italy, European Acad. Scis., Arts and Letters, Acad. Arts and Scis. of Florence. Office: European Brain Rsch Inst EBRI Via del Fosso di Fiorano 64 65 00143 Rome Italy

LEVIN, A. LEO, law educator, retired government official; b. NYC, Jan. 9, 1919; s. Issaachar and Minerva Hilda (Shapiro) L.; m. Doris Feder, Dec. 28, 1947; children— Allan, Jay Michael BA, Yeshiva Coll., 1939; JD, U. Pa., 1942; LLD (hon.), Yeshiva U., 1960, NY Law Sch., 1980, Quinnipiac Coll., 1995; PhD (hon.), Bar-Ilan U., Israel, 1990. Bar: N.Y. 1947, U.S. Supreme Ct. 1982. Instr., then asst. prof. law U. Iowa, 1947-49; law faculty U. Pa., Phila., 1949-69, 70-89, Meltzer prof. law, 1987-89, Meltzer prof. emeritus, 1989—, vice provost, 1965-68; v.p. for acad. affairs Yeshiva U., NYC, 1969-70; dir. Fed. Jud. Ctr., Washington, 1977-87. Chmn. Pa. State Legis. Reapportionment Commn., 1971-73; founding dir. Nat. Inst. Trial Advocacy, 1971-73; conf. coord. Nat. Conf. on Causes of Popular Dissatisfaction with Adminstrn. of Justice (Pound Conf.); chmn. bd. cert. Circuit Execs., 1977-87; mem. adv. bd. Nat. Inst. Corrections, 1977-87. Author: (with Woolley) Dispatch and Delay: A Field Study of Judicial Administration in Pennsylvania, 1961; (with Cramer) Problems on Trial Advocacy, 1968; editor: (with Schuchman and Yablon) Cases on Civil Procedure, 1992, Supplement, 1997. Hon. trustee Bar Ilan U., Ramat Gan, Israel, 1967—; hon. pres. (former pres.) Jewish Publ. Soc. Am. Served to 1st lt. USAF, 1942-46, ETO Recipient Mordecai Ben David award Yeshiva U., 1967, Disting. Svc. award U. Pa. Law Sch. Alumni, 1974, Bernard Revel award Yeshiva Coll., 1963, Justice award Am. Judicature Soc., 1995; White lectr. La. U., 1970, Jeffords lectr., N.Y. Law Sch., 1980, Murrah Lectr. U. Pa. Law Sch., 1989. Fellow Am. Acad. Arts and Scis.; mem. Am. Law Inst., Am. Judicature Soc. (pres. 1987-89), Order of Coif (nat. pres. 1967-70) Jewish.

LEVIN, ALAN M., television journalist; b. Bklyn., Feb. 28, 1926; s. Herman and Shirley (Levinstein) L.; m. Hannah Alexander, Oct. 30, 1948; children: Marc, Nicole, Danielle, Juliet. BA, Wesleyan U., Middletown, Conn., 1946. Reporter, columnist Plainfield (N.J.) Courier News, 1957-60; statehouse corr. AP, Trenton, N.J., 1960-61; writer N.Y. Post, 1961-63; press sec. Sen. Harrison Williams, Washington, 1963-64; news producer, writer WABC-TV, NYC, 1965-67; owner Levin Mediaworks Inc., producers documentaries for comml. and pub. TV, NYC; sr. prodr. Blowback Prodns. Documentary film maker, NET, N.Y.C., 1968-69, documentary film maker, pub. affairs, news writer, dir., producer, WNET-TV, N.Y.C., 1969-82 Served with AUS, 1944-46. Recipient numerous awards including George Polk Meml. award, Dupont Columbia award, Emmy awards. Home: 88 Claremont Ave Maplewood NJ 07040-2024 Office: Levin Prodns 601 W 26th St Fl 17 New York NY 10001-1101 E-mail: avanti11@comcast.net.

LEVIN, ALAN SCOTT, pathologist, allergist, immunologist, lawyer; b. Chgo., Jan. 12, 1938; s. John Bernhard and Betty Ruth (Margulis) L.; m. Vera S. Byers, June 15, 1971. BS in Chemistry, U. Ill., Champaign-Urbana, 1960; MS in Biochemistry, U. Ill., Chgo., 1963, MD, 1964; JD, Golden Gate U., 1995. Diplomate Am. Bd. Allergy and Immunology, Am. Bd. Pathology; bar: Calif. 1995, Tex. 1996, Nev. 1999, U.S. Patent Office 2002. Intern Children's Hosp. Med. Ctr., Boston, 1964-65; postdoctoral fellow Harvard U., Boston, 1965-66; adj. instr. pediatrics U. Calif., San Francisco, 1971-72, asst. prof. immunology dept. dermatology, 1972-78, adj. assoc. prof., 1978-88; dir. lab. immunology U. Calif. & Kaiser Found. Rsch. Inst. Joint Program Project, San Francisco, 1971-74; attending physician dept. medicine Mt. Zion/U. Calif. San Francisco Hosps., 1971—; dir. div. immunology Western Labs., Oakland, Calif., 1974-77; med. dir. MML/Solano Labs. Div. Chemed-W.R. Grace, Inc., Berkeley, Calif., 1977-79; med. dir. Levin Clin. Labs., Inc., San Francisco, 1979-81; pvt. practice San Francisco, 1981—. Contbr. articles to profl. jours., chpts. to books. Lt. USN, 1966-69, Vietnam. Decorated Silver Star medal, Bronze Star medal with Combat V, 4 Air medals; Harvard Med. Sch. traineeship grantee, 1964, USPHS hematology tng. grantee U. Calif., San Francisco Med. Ctr., 1969-71; recipient Faculty Rsch. award Am. Cancer Soc., 1970-74. Fellow Coll. Am. Pathologists, Am. Coll. Emergency Physicians, Am. Soc. Clin. Pathologists; mem. AMA, Am. Acad. Allergy and Immunology, Am. Coll. Allergy and Immunology, Am. Assn. Clin. Chemists, Am. Acad. Environ. Medicine, Calif. Med. Assn., San Francisco Med. Soc. Jewish. Home Phone: 775-771-9076; Office Phone: 775-831-5603. E-mail: flitequack@aol.com.

LEVIN, ALEXANDER B., mathematics professor; b. Moscow, Sept. 25, 1952; came to U.S., 1993; s. Boris I. Levin and Mariam S. Yanskaya; m. Tatyana I. Fedorova, Aug. 8, 1986. MS in Math., Moscow State U., 1974, PhD in Math., 1984. Cert. acad. status of assoc. prof. higher math., Ministry Higher Edn., USSR, 1987; cert. good work in field of math edn., Russia, 1989. Assoc. prof. math. Moscow Metall. Inst., 1986-92; math. instr. Montgomery Coll., Rockville, Md., 1993-95; from asst. prof. math. to assoc. prof. Cath. U. Am., Washington, 1995—2003, prof. math., 2003—. Author: 15 textbooks in fourier series, math. programming, difference and differential algebra, other topics; contbr. articles. Mem.: Am. Math. Soc. Avocation: chess. Home: 10619 Pine Haven Ter Rockville MD 20852-3434 Office Phone: 202-319-5221. Business E-Mail: levin@cua.edu.

LEVIN, ALLEN JAY, lawyer; b. Bridgeport, Conn., May 27, 1932; s. Simon H. and Adele Miriam (Rossinoff) L.; m. Judith Ann Rubinstein, Aug. 18, 1957 (div. 1987); children: Jennifer Suzanne, Miriam Adele, David Newmark, Michael Aaron; m. Gabrielle Hasson-Azar, Feb. 24, 1995. BA, NYU, 1954; postgrad., Boston U., 1954-55; JD, U. Miami, 1957. Bar: Fla. 1957, Conn. 1958, U.S. Dist. Ct. Conn. 1960, U.S. Dist. Ct. (so. dist.) Fla. 1962, U.S. Dist. Ct. (mid. dist.) Fla. 1969, U.S. Ct. Appeals (11th cir.) 1981, U.S. Supreme Ct. 1972. Small claims ct. judge County of Charlotte, Punta Gorda, Fla., 1962-72; legal counsel Port Charlotte-Charlotte Harbor (Fla.) Fire Control Dist., 1965-86; mcpl. judge City of North Port, Fla., 1973-76, city atty., 1977-87; pvt. practice Charlotte, Fla. Legal counsel Charlotte County Habitat for Humanity, Inc. Mem.: ABA, Port Charlotte-Charlotte County C. of C., Charlotte County Bar Assn., Fla. Bar Assn. (probate law com., real property probate and trust laws sect.), Port Charlotte-Charlotte County Bd. of Realtors (assoc.), Kiwanis (pres. 1984—85, youth svcs. chmn. Port Charlotte Club 1986—, pres. 1998—99, lt. gov.- elect divsn.18 so. Fla. dist. 1999—2000, lt. gov. 2000—01, dist. chair com. on bylaws, practice & procedure, protocol Fla. Dist. 2002—03, trustee Fla. dist. found. 2002—, dist. chmn. laws and regulations Fla. Dist. 2006—), Elks. Avocation: stamp collecting/philately. Office: 3440 Conway Blvd Ste 1A Port Charlotte FL 33952 Home: 1238 Vermeer Dr Nokomis FL 34275 Office Phone: 941-625-4189.

LEVIN, ALLEN JOSEPH, lawyer; b. Lewistown, Pa, Jan. 17, 1948; s. Norman Lewis and Dorothy Sanford (Herbster) L.; m. Mary Gwendolyn McAdoo, Aug. 14, 1974. Cert., Ecole d'art Americaines, Fontainebleau, France, 1968; BA, Dickinson Coll., 1969; JD, Dickinson Sch. Law, 1974. Bar: Pa. 1974, US Supreme Ct., US Ct. Appeals (3d cir.), US Dist. Ct. (Mid. Dist. Pa.). Assoc. Brugler & Levin Law Offices, Lewistown, 1974-80, ptnr., 1980-2000, Levin Law Offices, Lewistown, 2000—. Counsel Mifflin County Ind. Devel. Corp., Lewistown, 1978—, Mifflin County Ind. Devel. Authority, Lewistown, 1980—; pres. Pa. Sch. Bd. Solicitors Assn., 1989; v.p., assoc. gen. counsel Pocono Mountain R.R., Scranton, Pa., 1994-96; pres. Lewistown Ctrl. R.R. Co., Mt Union Connecting R.R. Co. Pres. Greater Lewistown Corp., 1983-95, v.p., 1995-99. Recipient Outstanding Svc. to Edn. award Pa. Sch. Bd. Assn., 1989. Mem. Pa. Bar Assn., Mifflin County Bar Assn. (pres. 1992-93), Juniata Valley C. of C. (pres. 1983-85), Rotary Club Lewistown, Elks (# 663). Jewish. Avocations: fishing, reading. Home: 9 N Grand St Lewistown PA 17044-2040 Office: Levin Law Offices 27 West 3d St Lewistown PA 17044-0231 Office Phone: 717-247-3577.

LEVIN, ANDREW W., lawyer, communications executive; CPA. Fin. mgr. Bell Atlantic Corp.; Dem. counsel US House Energy and Commerce Com., Washington, DC; sr. v.p. govt. affairs Clear Channel Comm. Inc., Washington, DC, 2002—04, exec. v.p. law and govt., chief legal officer San Antonio, 2002—. Office: Clear Channel Comm Inc 200 E Basse Rd San Antonio TX 78209 E-mail: AndyLevin@clearchannel.com.*

LEVIN, BARRY STEVEN, lawyer; b. St. Louis, Dec. 16, 1954; AB, Washington U., St. Louis, 1976; JD, Northwestern U., 1979. Bar: Calif. 1979. Atty. Heller Ehrman White & McAuliffe, LLP, San Francisco, 1979—, chmn. ins. coverage practice group, 1995—97, chmn. litigation dept., 1997—99, shareholder, chmn., 1999—2005. Lectr. in ins. coverage and law firm mgmt. Named one of Leading Ins. Coverage Attorneys in Calif., Chambers & Partners America's Leading Bus. Lawyers, 2003, 2004; recipient Atty. of Yr. award, Calif., 2003. Mem. ABA, Order of Coif, Bar Assn. San Francisco, Phi Beta Kappa. Office: Heller Ehrman White & McAuliffe 333 Bush St San Francisco CA 94104-2806 Office Phone: 415-772-6646. Fax: 415-772-6268. E-mail: blevin@hewm.com.

LEVIN, BERNARD, physician; b. Johannesburg, Apr. 1, 1942; came to U.S., 1966, naturalized, 1972; m. Ronelle DuBrow; children: Adam, Katherine. MB, BCh, U. Witwatersrand, 1964. Resident Presbyn. St. Lukes Hosp. Chgo., 1966-68; rsch. fellow U. Chgo., 1968-71, NIH fellow, 1971-72, instr. medicine, 1971-73, asst. prof. medicine, 1973-78, assoc. prof., 1979-84; prof. medicine, chmn. dept. gastro. oncology and digestive U. Tex. Med. Ctr./M.D. Anderson Hosp., Houston, 1984-94, Robert R. Herring prof., 1986-91, Ellen F. Knisely chair, 1991-94, v.p. for cancer prevention, 1994—, Betty Marcus chair, 1994—. Mem. large bowel cancer working group Nat. Cancer Inst., 1984-85; cons. spl. study sect. Nat. Cancer Inst., 1976-84, chair nat. adv. com. on colorectal cancer, 1990—; chair Nat. Colorectal Cancer Roundtable, 1998—. Mem. editl. bd. Jour. Nat. Cancer Inst., Cancer Epidemiology, Biomarkers, Prevention; contbr. articles to profl. jours. Grantee USPHS, 1976-80, Melamid Found. grantee U. Chgo., 1978-83, NCI grantee, 1980-84, 1994; recipient award for sci. excellence in medicine Am. Italian Cancer Found., 2001, Janssen-Cilag Masters in Gastroenterology award Am. Gastroenterological Assn., 2005, Charles A. LeMaistre MD Outstanding Achievement award in cancer M.D. Anderson Cancer Ctr., 2007. Fellow ACP, Am. Coll. Nutrition; mem. AAAS, Am. Assn. Cancer Rsch., Am. Gastroenterol. Assn., Am. Soc. Gastrointestinal Endoscopy, Am. Pancreatic Assn., Am. Soc. Preventive Oncology, Am. Soc. Clin. Oncology (chmn. cancer prevention com. 2002-04, award 2004), Am. Cancer Soc. (chair nat. adv. com. on colorectal cancer, award 2004), Sigma Xi. Jewish. Office: UT M D Anderson Cancer Ctr 1155 Pressler St Unit 1370 Houston TX 77030-4009

LEVIN, BURTON, diplomat; b. NYC, Sept. 28, 1930; s. Benjamin and Ida (Geller) L.; m. Lily Lee, Jan. 4, 1960; children: Clifton, Alicia. BA, CUNY, 1952; M Internat. Affairs, Columbia U., 1954; postgrad., Harvard U., 1964; LLD (hon.), Carleton Coll., 1993. Commd. fgn. service officer Dept. State, 1954; counselor/econ. officer Am. Embassy, Taipei, Taiwan, 1954-56, polit. officer, 1969-74; intelligence research specialist Dept. State, Washington, 1956-58, dir. Republic China affairs, 1974-77; polit. officer Am. Embassy, Jakarta, Indonesia, 1959-63, Am. Consulate Gen. Hong Kong, 1965-69, dep. chief mission, 1977-78, consul gen., 1981-86; dep. chief mission Am. Embassy, Bangkok, Thailand, 1978-81; amb. to Burma, 1987-90; dir. Asia Soc. Hong Kong Ctr., 1990-95. Vis. prof. Carleton Coll., 1995; vis. fellow Stanford U., 1974; vis. lectr. Harvard U., 1986, Carleton Coll., 1994; bd. dirs. Mansfield Found., Noble Resources Ltd.; mem. coun., chmn. emeritus Hopkins-Nanjing U. Ctr. for Chinese and Am. Studies Johns Hopkins U. Mem. Am. Fgn. Service Assn. Clubs: Am., Hong Kong Country. Home: 314 2nd St E Northfield MN 55057-2204 Office Phone: 507-645-0086. Personal E-mail: burtlevin@comcast.net.

LEVIN, CARL MILTON, senator; b. Detroit, June 28, 1934; m. Barbara Halpern, 1961; children: Kate, Laura, Erica. BA in Polit. Sci., Swarthmore Coll., 1956; LLB, Harvard U., 1959. Bar: Mich. 1959. Ptnr. Grossman, Hyman & Grossman, Detroit, 1959-64; asst. atty. gen., gen. counsel Mich. Civil Rights Commn., 1964-67; chief appellate defender City of Detroit, 1968-69, mem. coun., 1970-73, pres. coun., 1974-77; ptnr. Schlussel, Lifton, Simon, Rands & Kaufman, 1971—73, Jaffe, Snider, Raitt, Garratt & Hever, 1978—79; US Senator from Mich., 1979—. Past instr. Wayne State U., U. Detroit; chmn. Armed Svcs. Com., Homeland Security and Govtl. Affairs Com., Com. on Small Bus., Senate Dem. Steering & Coordination Com., Senate Select Com. on Intelligence, Congressional-Executive Commn. on China. Mem. ABA, Mich. Bar Assn., Detroit Bar Assn., Democrat. Jewish. Office: US Senate 269 Russell Senate Ofc Bldg Washington DC 20510-2202 also: Patrick V McNamara Fed Bldg Rm 1860 477 Michigan Ave Detroit MI 48226-2576 Office Phone: 202-224-6221, 313-226-6020. Office Fax: 202-224-1388, 313-226-6948. E-mail: senator@levin.senate.gov.*

LEVIN, CHARLES EDWARD, lawyer; b. Chgo., Oct. 6, 1946; m. Barbara Serwer, Dec. 28, 1975. BA with high honor, DePaul U., 1968; JD cum laude, Northwestern U., Chgo., 1971. Bar: Ill. 1971. Asst. instr. legal writing and rsch. Northwestern U. Law Sch., 1970-71; assoc. D'Ancona & Pflaum, Chgo., 1971-76, ptnr., 1977-90, Jenner & Block, Chgo., 1990-2000, McDermott, Will & Emery, Chgo., 2000—. Governing bd. Comml. Fin. Assn. Edn. Found., 1990-2000; asst. instr. legal writing, rsch. Northwestern U., 1970-71. Mem. bd. editors Northwestern U. Law Rev., 1970-71. Aux. bd. Chgo. Architecture Found., 1989-99; founders leadership coun. C omml. Fin. Assn. Edn. Found., NY. Mem. ABA (bus. sect. 1992—), Chgo. Bar Assn. (vice chmn. architecture and law com. 1974-75, vice chmn. divsn. D, mem. exec. com. fed. tax com. 1983-84, comml. fin. and trans. com. 1990—, Article 9 drafting subcom.), East Bank Club Chgo. Avocations: acquisition fine arts, support arts organizations, jogging. Office: McDermott Will & Emery LLP 227 W Monroe St Ste 4400 Chicago IL 60606-5016

LEVIN, CHARLES LEONARD, state supreme court justice; b. Detroit, Apr. 28, 1926; s. Theodore and Rhoda (Katzin) L.; children: Arthur, Amy, Fredrick. BA, U. Mich., 1946, LLB, 1947; LLD (hon.), Detroit Coll. Law, 1980. Bar: Mich. 1947, N.Y. 1949, U.S. Supreme Ct. 1953, D.C. 1954. Pvt. practice law, NYC, 1948-50, Detroit, 1950-66; ptnr. Levin, Levin, Garvett & Dill, Detroit, 1951-66; judge Mich. Ct. Appeals, Detroit, 1966-73; assoc. justice Mich. Supreme Ct., 1973-96. Mem. Mich. Law Revision Commn., 1966 Trustee Marygrove Coll., 1971-77, chmn., 1971-74; mem. vis. coms. to Law Schs., U. Mich., U. Chgo., 1977-80, Wayne State U. Mem. Am. Law Inst. Office: Mich Supreme Ct 500 Woodward Ave Fl 20 Detroit MI 48226-5498

LEVIN, DONALD ROBERT, business and finance executive, motion picture producer, professional sports team owner; b. Chgo., Oct. 17, 1947; s. Jack Levin and Henrietta (Wolf) Berman; m. Kathleen Ann Fitzsimmons; 1 child, Robert James. Student pub. schs., Chgo. Pres. Adams Apple Distbg. Co., Chgo., 1969-82, Republic Tobacco, Inc., Chgo., 1982—, D.R.L. Mgmt. Svcs., Chgo., 1982—; CEO Adams Apple Film Co., Chgo., 1982—, Republic Techs., Perpignan, France. Chmn. Top Tobacco Co.; chmn., CEO Chgo. Wolves hockey team; bd. dirs. Republic Entertainment Internat., Chgo., Dr. Levin Family Found.; chmn. D.D.M. Film Co., Altesse Firstenfeld Austere, Republic Group, Glenview, Ill. With USMCR, 1965-71. Jewish. Office: DRL Mgmt Svcs Inc 2301 Ravine Way Glenview IL 60025-7627

LEVIN, EDWARD JESSE, lawyer; b. Balt., Oct. 31, 1951; s. Cyril and Virginia Lee (Kremer) Levin; m. Cheri Wyron, Feb. 18, 1973; children: Paul Clifford, Benjamin Lawrence. BA, Johns Hopkins U., 1973; JD, U. Va., 1976. Bar: Md. 1976, U.S. Supreme Ct. 1980. Assoc. Piper & Marbury, Balt., 1976-84; ptnr. DLA Piper US LLP (formerly DLA Piper Rudnick Gray Cary US LLP), Balt., 1984—. Co-author: Maryland Real Estate Leasing Forms and Practice, 1988. 1st v.p. Balt. Bd. Jewish Edn., 1987—89, pres., 1989—91; trustee Hebrew U., Balt., 1999—2000. Fellow: Am. Bar Found., Am. Coll. Real Estate Lawyers (chmn. atty.'s opinions com. 1992—99); mem.: Md. Mortgage Bankers Assn. (Mortgage Assoc. of Yr. 2004), Balt. City Bar Assn. (co-chmn. spl. joint com. lawyers' opinions comml. transactions 1989—90), Md. State Bar Assn. (chmn. sect. real property, planning and zoning 1988—90, co-chmn. spl. joint com. lawyers' opinions comml. transactions 1989—90, Disting. Md. Real Property Practitioner of Yr. 2006—07). Democrat. Jewish. Office: DLA Piper US LLP 6225 Smith Ave Baltimore MD 21209 Office Phone: 410-580-4700. E-mail: edward.levin@dlapiper.com.

LEVIN, EDWARD M., lawyer; b. Chgo., Oct. 16, 1934; s. Edward M. and Anne Meriam (Fantl) L.; children from previous marriage: Daniel Andrew, John Davis; m. Margot Aronson, Apr. 4, 1993. BS, U. Ill., 1955; LLB, Harvard U., 1958. Bar: Ill. 1958, U.S. Supreme Ct. 1968. Mem. firm Ancel, Stonesifer, Glink & Levin and predecessors, Chgo., 1958, 61-68; draftsman Ill. Legis. Reference Bur., Springfield, 1961; spl. asst. to regional adminstr. HUD, Chgo., 1968-71, asst. regional adminstr. community planning and mgmt., 1971-72; asst. dir. Ill. Dept. Local Govt. Affairs, Chgo., 1973-77; of counsel Holleb, Gerstein & Glass, Ltd., Chgo., 1977-79; chief counsel Econ. Devel. Adminstrn., U.S. Dept. Commerce, Washington, 1979—85, 1997—2001; sr. fellow Nat. Gov's. Assn., 1985-86; sr. counsel U.S. Dept. Commerce, Washington, 1987-96. Lectr. U. Ill., 1972—73, adj. assoc. prof. urban scis., 1973—79; lectr. Loyola U., 1976—79, No. Va. Law Sch., 1988; instr. Mgmt. Concepts, Inc., Vienna, 2001—. Assoc. editor Assistance Mgmt. Jour., 1990-95; mem. editl. adv. bd. Fed Grants Mgmt. Handbook, 2005—; contbr. articles to profl. jours. Mem. Ill. Nature Preserves Com., 1963-68, Northea. Ill. Planning Commn., 1974-77, Ill.-Ind. Bi-State Commn., 1974-77; bd. dirs. Cook County Legal Assistance Found., 1978-79, D.C. Appleseed Ctr., 1994—; bd. dirs. Ill. divsn. ACLU, 1965-68, 77-79, v.p., 1977-78; chmn. ABA fed. assistance com., 1995-96. With AUS, 1958-60. Recipient Lincoln award Ill. Bar Assn., 1977, Gold medal U.S. Dept. Commerce, 2000, Corrigan award Econ. Devel. Adminstrn., 2000. Mem. FBA (chmn. fed. grants com. 1991-95), Nat. Grants Mgmt. Assn. (bd. dirs. 1988-92, Pres.'s award 1994), Appleseed Found. (bd. dirs. 1994—, mem. exec. com. 1994-2002). Home and Office: 3201 Porter St NW Washington DC 20008-3212 Office Phone: 202-363-0558. Personal E-mail: elevin111@erols.com.

LEVIN, EVANNE LYNN, lawyer, educator; b. LA, Nov. 6, 1949; d. Marshall Levin and Rose (Tolchin) Levin Albert; m. Jeffrey Neal Oliver, 1992 (div. 1996); m. Al Gerisch Jr., Sept. 2005. BA in Polit. Sci. cum laude, UCLA, 1971; JD, Loyola Law Sch., LA, 1974. Bar: Calif. 1995; lic. real estate broker Calif. Assoc. Ervin, Cohen & Jessup, Beverly Hills, Calif., 1977-78, Mason & Sloane, LA, 1978-82; atty. Orion Picturs Corp., LA, 1982-84; v.p. TV prodn. legal affairs Twentieth Century Fox Film Corp., Beverly Hills, 1986-89; of counsel Weinberg, Zipser, Arbiter & Heller, LA, 1990; v.p., gen. counsel Zodiac Entertainment, Studio City, Calif., 1991-95; prin., owner Law Offices Evanne L. Levin, LA, 1995—; instr. entertainment law UCLA, 1999—; prin. Levin Realty, 2004—. Instr. personal mgmt. pub. and music career courses Learning Network, 1985—86; instr., asst. atty. UCLA, Learning Network, Entertainment Law Tng. Program, 1999—; devel. and fundraising cons. Acad. for Jewish Religion, Calif., 2004—05; prin. ELG Design, 2006—. Contbr. articles to profl. jours.; columnist: LA Women in Music Newsletter, 1986—88. Mem. Planned Giving Round Table So. Calif., Sherman Oaks Neighborhood Coun., 2006, River Oaks Chorus; maj. gifts officer Woodbury U., 2002—04; v.p. event chair City Live!, 2003; bd. dir. arts festival Hollywood Women's Coalition, 1985, bd. dir., 1985—86; bd. mem. and officer Woodman Manor Homeowners Assn., 1988—2005; mem. exec. bd. Wellness Guild; mem. exec. com. bd. dir. Weingart Ctr. Assn. Ptnrs., 2001—04. Mem.: Interior Deisgn Soc., Calif. Copyright Conf., LA Women Music (bd. dirs. 1986—88, mem. adv. com.), Women Entertainment Law, Beverly Hills Bar Assn. (former bd. govs., barristers bd. govs., founding mem./co-chair com. arts, mem. entertainment law com., del. to state bar and ABA convs.), LA County Bar Assn. (vols. in parole, exec. bd. intellectual property sect.), Assn. Profl. Fundraisers, Coun. Advancement Support Edn., Sherman Oaks Homeowners Assn. Avocations: scuba diving, collecting kaleidoscipes, travel. Office: 14937 Rhinestone Dr 1st Fl Sherman Oaks CA 91403 Personal E-mail: ellesq@adelphia.net. E-mail: ellesq@yahoo.com.

LEVIN, EZRA GURION, lawyer; b. Bklyn., Feb. 10, 1934; s. Harry and Bertha Levin; m. Batya Ann Schaefer, June 19, 1960; children: Zachary Abraham, Ayala Deborah Levin-Kruss. AB, Columbia U., 1955; postgrad., U. Chgo., 1955-56; LLB, Columbia U., 1959. Bar: NY 1961. Assoc., then ptnr. Marshall, Bratter, Greene, Allison & Tucker, NYC, 1961-79; ptnr., co-chair Kramer Levin Naftalis & Frankel LLP, NYC, 1979—. Bd. dirs. MAXXAM, Inc., Houston, 1988-2006; adj. prof. sociology Columbia U., 1973-77, 87, 93; adj. faculty U. Conn. Law Sch., 1970-73; vis. prof. U. Wis. Law Sch., 1967, 98. Contbr. articles to profl. jours. Mem.-at-large Jewish Cmty. Rels. Coun., NYC, 1983—, pres., 2001—04; vice chmn. Coalition for Soviet Jewry, NYC, 1984—93, co-chair, 1994—2001; counsel Am. Friends Sarah Herzog Meml. Hosp.-Jerusalem, Inc., NYC, 1975—; sec., bd. dirs. Scholarship, Edn. and Def. Fund for Racial Equality, NYC, 1961—70; founding chair Solomon Schechter High Sch. N.Y., 1992—96. Mem.: Hebrew Free Loan Soc. (pres. 2004—06, bd. dirs.), Law and Soc. Assn., ABA. Avocation: tennis. Office: Kramer Levin Naftalis & Frankel LLP 1177 Ave of the Americas New York NY 10036 Office Phone: 212-715-9227. Business E-Mail: elevin@kramerlevin.com.

LEVIN, FRANCES R., psychiatrist, educator; b. Newton, Mass., Nov. 29, 1959; m. Howard Robert Levin; children: Allison Paula, Tamara Stephanie, Charles Jacob. BS magna cum laude, Brown U., 1981; MD, Cornell U., 1985. Diplomate Am. Bd. Psychiatry and Neurology. Q.J. Kennedy assoc. prof. clin. psychiatry Columbia U.; assoc. attending psychiatry N.Y. Presbyn. Hosp.; resident in psychiatry N.Y. Hosp., Payne Whitney Clinic, NYC, 1985—89, asst. unit chief, 1988—89; rsch. and addiction psychiatry fellow Nat. Inst. on Drug Abuse, U. Md., Balt., 1989—90; asst prof. dept. psychiatry U. Md. Med. Ctr., 1990—92; asst. prof. clin. psychiatry dept. psychiatry Columbia U. Coll. Physicians and Surgeons, 1992—99, assoc. pro. clin. psychiatry dept. psychiatry, 1999—; assoc. attending psychiatrist N.Y. Presbyn. Hosp., 1992—99, assoc. attending psychiatrist, 1999—. Mem. numerous panels and coms.; presenter in field. Reviewer: numerous profl. jours., mem. editl. bd.: Am. Jour. on Addictions, 2000; contbr. over 70 articles to profl. jours. Recipient Connie Guion scholarship, 1983, AMA-ERF Rock Sleyster Meml. scholarship, 1985; numerous rsch. grants. Fellow: N.Y. Acad. Medicine, Am. Psychiat. Assn.; mem.: AMA, Group for Advancement of Psychiatry, Coll. on Problems of Drug Dependence, Am. Soc. Addiction Medicine (N.E. region subcom. 1991), Assn. for Med. Edn. and Rsch. in Substance Abuse, Md. Psychiat. Soc. (com. on addiction 1989), Am. Acad. Addiction Psychiatrists (chair area dirs. 2001, bd. dirs. 2001), Sigma Xi, Phi Beta Kappa. Office: NYSPI Columbia Univ 1051 Riverside Unit 66 New York NY 10032 Office Phone: 212-543-5896. Business E-Mail: frl2@columbia.edu.

LEVIN, FRANK S., physicist, educator; b. NYC, Apr. 14, 1933; s. James J. and Celia (Aronovitch) L.; m. Madeline Carol McMurrough, Apr. 1973; 4 children. BA, Johns Hopkins U., 1955; PhD, U. Md., 1961. Rsch. assoc. Rice U., Houston, 1961-63, Brookhaven Nat. Lab., Upton, NY, 1963-66, U.K. Atomic Energy Authority, Harwell, England, 1965-67; mem. faculty Brown U., Providence, 1967—, prof. physics, 1977-98, emeritus prof., 1998—. Co-organizer 9th Internat. Conf. on Few-Body Problems, 1980. Author: An Introduction to Quantum Theory, 2002, Calibrating the Cosmos: How Cosmology Explains Our Big Bang Universe, 2006; co-editor (series): Finite Systems and Multiparticle Dynamics. Recipent Sr. U.S. Scientist award Alexander von Humboldt Stiftung, 1979. Fellow Am. Phys. Soc. (founder, 1st chmn. topical group on few body systems and multiparticle dynamics) Office: Brown U Physics Dept PO Box 1843 Providence RI 02912-1843

LEVIN, FREDRIC GERSON, lawyer; b. Pensacola, Fla., Mar. 29, 1937; s. Abraham I. and Rose (Lefkowitz) L.; m. Marilyn Kapner, June 14, 1959; children: Marci Levin Goodman, Debra Levin Dreyer, Martin, Kimberly Levin Brielmayer. BSBA, U. Fla., Gainesville, 1958, JD, 1961. Bar: Fla. 1961, US Dist. Ct. (no. dist.) Fla., US Ct. Appeals (5th cir.). Assoc. Levin, Papantonio, Thomas, Mitchell, Echsner & Proctor, PA, Pensacola, 1961—. Counsel Fla. Senate, 1981-82. Author: Effective Opening Statements, 1983; contbr. articles to profl. jours. Fellow Acad. Fla. Trial Lawyers (dir. 1977-84), mem. Inner Circle of Advocates. Democrat. Jewish. Office: Levin Papantonio Thomas Mitchell Echsner & Proctor PA 316 S Baylen St Pensacola FL 32501-5900 Home: 3400 N 18th Ave Pensacola FL 32503-4137 Office Phone: 850-435-7123. Business E-Mail: flevin@levinlaw.com.

LEVIN, GAIL, writer, educator, photographer; d. Barron and Shirley Levin. BA, Simmons Coll., 1969, D (hon.), 1996; MA, Tufts U., 1970; PhD, Rutgers U., 1976. Instr. New Sch. for Social Rsch., NYC, 1973—75, Baruch Coll., CUNY, 1974; asst. prof. art history Conn. Coll., New London, 1975—76; vis. prof. art history Grad. Ctr. CUNY, 1979—80; curator Whitney Mus. Am. Art, NYC, 1976—84; vis. prof. Nesbit Coll. Design, Drexel U., 1985—86; asst. prof. art Baruch Coll. CUNY, 1986—87, assoc. prof. art, 1988—89, prof., 1990—. Will and Ariel Durant prof. humanities St. Peter's Coll., Jersey City, 1987—88; chair excellence U. Tenn., Chattanooga, 1995—96. Prodr., host Art at Issue, Manhattan Cable TV, 1985—86; author: Synchromism and American Color Abstraction, 1910-25, 1978, Edward Hopper: The Complete Prints, 1979, Edward Hopper as Illustrator, 1979, Edward Hopper: The Art and the Artist, 1980, Edward Hopper, 1984, Twentieth Century American Painting The Thyssen-Bornemisza Collection, 1987, Edward Hopper: An Intimate Biography, 1995, 2007, Edward Hopper: A Catalogue Raisonné, 1995, Becoming Judy Chicago: A Biography of the Artist, 2007; co-author: Abstract Expressionism: The Formative Years, 1978, Aaron Copland's America: A Cultural Perspective, 2000, Theme and Improvisation: Kandinsky and The American Avant-garde 1912-1950; co-editor, contbr.: Ethics and the Visual Arts, 2006; editor: The Poetry of Solitude: A Tribute to Edward Hopper, 1995, Silent Places: A Tribute to Edward Hopper, 2000; author, photographer Hoppers Places, 1985, Marsden Hartley in Bavaria, 1989, film Edward Hopper, 1981; contbr. articles to profl. jours. and exhibition catalogues; one-woman shows include Kingston Artists Group, Gallery Rondout, 1984, Kennedy Galleries, Inc., N.Y.C., 1985, Jane Voorhees Zimmerli Art Mus., 1985, Meml. Art Gallery, U. Rochester, 1985, Fay Gold Gallery, Atlanta, Barridoff Gallery, Portland, 1986, Cedar Rapids Art Mus., 1986, Hopper House Art Ctr., Nyack, NY, 1986, Hilton Head Art League, SC, 1986, U. Iowa Art Mus., 1987, St. Peter's Coll. Art Gallery, Jersey City, 1987, Pa. Acad. of Fine Arts, 1987, Ariz. State U., Tempe, 1988, Emerson Gallery, Hamilton Coll., Clinton, NY, 1989, Milw. Art Mus., 1990, Bowdain Coll. Art Mus., 1990, Cress Gallery U. Tenn., Chattanooga, 1995, Trustman Art Gallery Simmons Coll., Boston, 1995, Provincetown (Mass.) Monument Mus., 1996, Cape Cod Mus. Art, 2007, exhibited in group shows at Catskill Ctr. for Photography in Woodstock, N.Y., 1985, A.I.R. Gallery, N.Y.C., 1985, 1986, 1987, 2002, The 9th Precinct Gallery, 1986, Baruch Coll. Art Gallery, 1987. Named Disting. Fulbright chmn., Roosevelt Ctr., 2007; recipient Alumnae Achievement award, Simmons Coll., 1986, The Hadassah Internat. Rsch. Inst. on Jewish Women at Brandeis U. Rsch. award, 2001—02, Rsch. award, Schlesinger Libr. Harvard U., 2005—, award for biography and art history, Nat. Assn. Women Artists, 2007; fellow, Pollock-Krasner/Stonybrook Found., 2006—07; grantee, Rockefeller Found., 1993, Smithsonian Inst., 1993; Rsch. grantee, NEH, 1984, 1989, 1992, 1993—95, Am. Coun. Learned Socs., 1988, U. Prof. fellow, NEH, 1998—99, 2006—, Fulbright Sr. scholar, 2006. Mem.: Catalogue Raisonné Scholars Assn. (pres. 1991—97), Coll. Art Assn., Pen Freedom to Write, Internat. Assn. Art Critics. Address: CUNY Baruch Coll B7-235 1 Bernard Baruch Way New York NY 10010-5518 Home Phone: 212-689-5260; Office Phone: 646-312-4062. Business E-Mail: gail_levin@baruch.cuny.edu.

LEVIN, GEOFFREY ARTHUR, botanist; b. Los Alamos, N.Mex., Dec. 7, 1955; s. Jules Samuel and Jane Walden (Settle) L.; children: Tobias, Madeline; m. Lori E. Davis, 2001. BA, Pomona Coll., 1977; MS, U. Calif., Davis, 1980, PhD, 1984. Asst. prof. Ripon (Wis.) Coll., 1982-84; curator, chmn. botany dept. San Diego Natural History Mus., 1984-93; lectr. U. San Diego, 1984-90; asst. profl. scientist Ill. Natural History Survey, Champaign, 1994-96, assoc. profl. scientist to profl. scientist, dir. Ctr. for Biodiversity, 1996—. Adj. asst. prof. dept. plant biology U. Ill., 1995—; rsch. assoc. Mo. Bot. Garden, 1994—. Contbr. articles to jours. in field. Bd. dirs. Fond du Lac Audubon Soc., 1983-84, San Diego Audubon Soc., 1986-87; pres. Summit Unitarian Universalist Fellowship, El Cajon, Calif., 1989-91; treas. Unitarian Universalist Ch., Urbana, Ill., 1996-98, moderator, 1998-2000. Recipient Jesse M. Greenman award. Mo. Bot. Garden, 1987; NSF grad. fellow, 1977-81. Mem. Am. Inst. Biol. Scis., Am. Soc. Plant Taxonomists, Bot. Soc. Am., Soc. Systematic Biologists, Calif. Bot. Soc. (bd. editors 1992-95), Phi Beta Kappa, Sigma Xi. Democrat. Office: Illinois Natl History Survey Ctr Biodiversity 1816 S Oak St Ste A Champaign IL 61820-6954 Business E-Mail: glevin@inhs.uiuc.edu.

LEVIN, GEORGE MARTIN, association and organization administrator, aeronautical engineer; b. Atlantic City, Oct. 21, 1940; m. Patricia Anne Sever; children: Courtney Anne Avnaim, Suzanne Michelle Griffin. BS, U. of MD, 1962, MS, 1967; diploma, Inst. Von Karman de Dynamique Des Fluides. Dir. Aero. and Space Engring. Bd. Nat. Acad. Scis., Washington, 1997—; engr. Goddard Space Flight Ctr. NASA, 1962—71, mgr. devel. Hubble Space Telescope, 1972—81, mgr. devel.secondary payloads Space Shuttle and Delta II, 1981—97, program mgr. orbital debris, 1990—97. Mem.: Internat. Acad. of Astronautics. Office: Nat Academies 500 5th St NW Washington DC 20001 Home Phone: 703-273-1205; Office Phone: 202-334-2858. Business E-Mail: glevin@nas.edu.

LEVIN, GERALD M. (JERRY LEVIN), former media and entertainment company executive; b. Phila., May 6, 1939; m. Carol Levin (div.); children: Jonathan(dec.), Leon, Michael, Laura, Anna; m. Barbara J. Riley (div.); m. Laurie Perlman. BA, Haverford Coll., 1960; LLB, U. Pa., 1963; LLD (hon.), Tex. Coll., 1985; LLD (hon.), Middlebury Coll., 1994; LHD (hon.), U. Denver, 1995. Assoc. Simpson, Thacher & Bartlett, NYC, 1963-67; gen. mgr., COO Devel. and Resources Corp., NYC, 1967-71; rep. Internat. Basic Economy Corp., Tehran, Iran, 1971-72; v.p. programming Home Box Office, NYC, 1972-73, pres., CEO, 1973-76, chmn., CEO, 1976-79; group v.p. video Time Inc., NYC, 1979-84, exec. v.p., 1984-88, vice chmn., dir., 1988-90; vice chmn. Time Warner Inc., NYC, 1990—93, COO, 1991-92, chmn., CEO, 1992—2000, AOL Time Warner, Inc., NYC, 2000—02. Trustee emeritus Hampshire Coll.; bd. dirs. Moonview Sanctuary, Santa Monica. Bd. dirs., treas. N.Y. Philharm., Ctr. for Comm., A Living Meml. to the Holocaust—Mus. of Jewish Heritage. Mem.: The Trilateral Commn., Coun. on Fgn. Rels., Nat. Cable TV Ctr. and Mus., The Aspen Inst., N.Y. City Partnership, Phi Beta Kappa. Office: Moonview Sanctuary PO Box 1518 Santa Monica CA 90406*

LEVIN, GILBERT VICTOR, biotechnology company executive; b. Balt., Apr. 23, 1924; s. Henry I. and Lillian R. (Richman) L.; m. Karen Bloomquist, Oct. 25, 1953; children: Ron L., Henry L., Carol Y. BE, Johns Hopkins U., 1947, MS, 1948, PhD, 1963. Registered profl. engr., D.C., Md. With Md. State Dept. Health, 1948-50, Calif. Dept. Health, 1950-51, D.C. Dept. Pub. Health, 1951-55; v.p. Resources Research, Inc., Washington, 1955-63; dir. life systems div. Hazleton Labs., Inc., Reston, Va., 1963-67; CEO, chmn. bd. Spherix Inc. (formerly Biospherics, Inc.), Beltsville, Md., 1967—2003, exec. officer for sci., chmn. bd., 2003—. Contbr. 120 articles to profl. jours.; mem. editorial bd. BioScience, 1960-63; over 100 patents in field. Trustee John Hopkins U., 1982-85. Merchant Marine USCG, 1944-46. Recipient Pub. Svc. medal NASA, 1977; Whiting medal Johns Hopkins U., 1987, Disting. Alumnus award, 1995. Fellow Am. Pub. Health Assn.; mem. ASCE, AAAS (Newcomb Cleveland prize 1977), Am. Water Works Assn., Water Pollution Control Fedn., Am. Soc. Microbiology, N.Y. Acad. Scis. Clubs: Cosmos. Achievements include being NASA experimenter Mariner 9 mission, 1971; Viking Mission Labeled Release Life Detection experiment producing evidence of extant microbial life in Martian soil, 1976; mem. team Mars oxidant expt. for Russian Mars lander, 1996; inventor PhoStrip process for wastewater nutrient removal, microbial radiorespirometry, nonfattening sweeteners, use of D-tagatose as antihyperglycemic agent and in diabetes treatment; applications of chiral chemistry to foods and environmental products; application of firefly bioluminescent assay for adenosine triphosphate to biomass determination and to microbial enumeration. Office Phone: 410-224-3319. Business E-Mail: glevin@spherix.com. *Man's ability to accumulate information through learning and to pass it on to his descendents frees his generations from endless repetition. He may hope to understand the universe and his place in it.*

LEVIN, GOLAN, artist, composer, engineer; BS in Art and Design, MIT, 1994, MS in Media Arts and Scis., 2000. Mem. rsch. staff Interval Rsch. Corp., 1994—98; undergraduate rsch. asst. MIT Media Lab., 1990—94, rsch. asst., 1998—2000; cons. Design Machine, NY, 2000—02; adj. prof. Columbia U., 2000; vis. artist and lectr. Cooper Union Sch. Art, 2001—02; adj. faculty Parsons Sch. Design, 2001—03; asst. prof., electronic time-based media, dept. art, sch. art Carnegie Mellon U., 2004—. Invited lectr. in field; interface design cons. Boston Digital Corp., Woburn, Mass., 1993—94; cons. Design Machine, NYC, 2000—02. Composer numerous interactive and multimedia compositions, performances, recordings and other works.; artist with Paul Debevec Rouen Revisited, 1996, artist with Gregory Shakar and Scott Gibbons Scribble, 2000, artist with Gregory Shakar, Scott Gibbons, Yasmin Sohrawardy Dialtones: A Telesymphony, 2001—02, artist with Jonathan Feinberg and Cassidy Curtis Alphabet Synthesis Machine, 2001, artist with Jonathan Feinberg, S. Wynecoop, M. Wattenberg The Secret Lives of Numbers, 2002, artist with Zachary Lieberman RE:MARK, 2002, The Hidden Worlds of Noise and Voice, 2002, The Manual Input Sessions, 2004, artist with Zachary Lieberman, Jooap Blonk, Joan La Barbara Messa di Voce, 2003; exhibitions include Mus. of Innovation, San Jose, Calif., 1999, NY Digital Salon Exhbn., NYC, 2000, MoMA Contemporary Art Ctr., 2001, Am. Mus. of the Moving Image, 2002, Microwave Internat. Media Art Festival, Hong Kong, 2003, Whitney Biennial, Whitney Mus. Am. Art, 2004, Neuberger Mus. of Art at SUNY, Purchase, NY, 2005, and several others, Represented in permanent collections Am. Mus. of the Moving Image, Rouen Revisited, NYC, Ars Electronica Mus. of the Future, Linz: AVES, Australian Ctr. for the Moving Image, Sydney:AVES, Computer Fine Arts Collections: Blobby (Tiles), Zeum.org, San Francisco: Meshy, Whitney Mus. of Am. Arts:Axis, Ars Electronica Mus. of the Future, Linz: Hidden Worlds, Am. Mus. of the Moving Images, Floccus, NYC. Named New Artist Under 30, Print Mag., 2002; named one of Top 100 Young Innovators Under 35, MIT Tech. Review, 2004; recipient Bronze Medal, ID Mag. Interaction Design Award, 2002, Award Distinction, Net Art, Prix Ars Electronica, 2004; grantee Artist's grant emerging fields category, Creative Capital Found., 2006. Fellow: World Tech. Network. Achievements include co-holder three US patents; winner ASCI Digital2000 Competition, 2000; winner Comm. Arts Interactive Design Annual 6, 2000; finalist, Adobe Pub. Art Commn. Competition, 2003. Office: Carnegie Mellon U Sch Art CFA 300 5000 Forbes Ave Pittsburgh PA 15213-3890 Office Phone: 917-520-7456. Office Fax: 412-268-7817. Business E-Mail: golan@flong.com.

LEVIN, HARVEY JAY, financial institution design and construction specialist, developer, auctioneer; b. Fitchburg, Mass., Apr. 27, 1936; Student, Brandeis U., Boston U., U. Md., Harvard U.; BBA in Fin., U. Mass., 1960; MA in Econs., U. N.H., 1970; PhD in Philosophy Bus. Mgmt., LaSalle U., 1996. Lic. real estate broker Mass., NH, RI, comml. pilot FAA, auctioneer Maine, Mass., Fla., NH, RI, Vt., accredited auctioneer real estate Ind. U., cert. auctioneer Cert. Auction Inst., 1993. Pres. Ctrl. Tool Warehouse, Leominster, Mass., 1959—66; dir. mktg. and sales Spacemakers, Canton, Mass., 1970—72, New Eng. Homes, Biddeford, Mass., 1973—74; gen. mgr. Great No. Homes, Boston, 1966—70; cons. svc. mgr. Bank Bldg. Corp., St. Louis, 1974—80; v.p. Shelter Resources, Birmingham, Ala., 1972—73, Fin. Concepts, Natick, Mass., 1980—85; pres. Am. Bank Design, Inc., and Credit Union Bldg. Corp., New Castle, NH, Harv Levin, Inc., Auctioneers, 1986—. Gen. ptnr. Hazel Dell LLC; cons. Republic Homes, Truro, Canada, 1974. Author, lectr. personal and profl. seminars. Chmn. Sch. Bldg. Com., Kensington, NH, 1985; pres. Pheasant Run Condominium Assn., 1993—95; chairperson Parents Fund U. N.H., 1993—95, pres.-elect Parents Coun., 1995. With US Army, 1955—57. Named Hon. Lt. Col. Aide-de-Camp, Gov. Ala., 1978; recipient Honor award, Bank Bldg. Corp. Am., 1976, 1st Pl. Design award, 1977, Best Mktg. and Sales Plan award, Automation in Housing Assn., 1972, FMHA award for Best Elderly Housing Project. Mem.: Aircraft Owners and Pilots Assn., Nat. Auctioneers Assn. (life), Wentworth By the Sea Country Club, Hampton River Boat Club, The River Club Kennebunkport, Maine, Portsmouth Power Squadron Club, Masons, Phi Sigma Kappa. Office: Am Bank Design Inc PO Box 2114 New Castle NH 03854-2114 Office Phone: 603-436-8488. Business E-Mail: info@auctionsnewengland.com.

LEVIN, HENRY MORDECHAI, economist, educator; b. NYC, Dec. 7, 1938. BS cum laude, NYU, 1960; MA, Rutgers U., 1962, Ph.D., 1966. assoc. research scientist, Grad. Sch. Pub. Adminstrn., NYU, 1965-66; research assoc. social econs. Econ. Studies div. Brookings Inst., Washington, 1966-68; asst. prof. edn. and econs. Stanford U., Calif., 1968-69, assoc. prof. econs., 1969-75, prof. econs. and edn., 1975—, David Jacks Prof. of Higher Edn. and Econs., 1992—. William Heard Kilpatrick prof. econ. and edn., Tchrs. Coll., Columbia U.; fellow Ctr. for Advanced Studies in Behavioral Scis., 1976-77, dir. Inst. Research on Ednl. Fin. and Governance, 1978-84; Fulbright prof. U. Barcelona, 1989; vis. scholar Russell Sage Found., 1996-97. Office: Tchrs Coll Columbia U Box 181 525 W 120th St New York NY 10022 E-mail: hl361@columbia.edu.

LEVIN, HERBERT, retired diplomat, foundation administrator; b. NYC, Jan. 14, 1931; s. Sol and Kate (Gottlieb) Levin; m. Cornelia Rose, Feb. 21, 1954; children: Martha, Jonathan C. BA, Harvard U., Cambridge, Mass., 1952; MA, Fletcher Sch. Law Diplomacy, Medford, Mass., 1956. With U.S. Fgn. Svc., 1956—91; internat. economist U.S. Dept. State, Washington, 1956—58, Chinese lang. and area tng. Taichung, Taiwan, 1959—61, econ. officer Am. Consulate Gen. Hong Kong, 1961—64, polit. officer Am. Embassy Taipei, Taiwan, 1964—67, Tokyo, 1967—70; staff mem. for East Asia, NSC, 1970—71; dep. dir. Japanese affairs U.S. Dept. State, Washington, 1971—74, dep. chief mission Am. Embassy Dar-es-Salaam, Tanzania, 1975—78, Colombo, Sri Lanka, 1977—79, New Delhi, 1979—81; asst. nat. intelligence officer East Asia East and South Asia Nat. Intelligence Coun., Washington, 1981—83; staff mem. policy planning coun. U.S. Dept. State, 1983—85; diplomat-in-residence and dir. studies Asia Found., San Francisco, 1986—88; spl. asst. office of sr. rep. strategic tech. policy U.S. Dept. State, Washington, 1988—90, exec. asst. amb.-at-large and spl. asst. sec. of state non-proliferation and nuc. energy affairs, 1990—91; spl. advisor to under-sec. gen. Ji Chaozhu U.N., NYC, 1991—94; exec. dir. Am.-China Soc., 1994—99. Adviser U.S. del. 14th Gen. Assembly UN, NYC, 1985; staff dir. subcom. Asian and Pacific Affairs U.S. Ho. Reps., Washington, 1985; assoc. in rsch. Fairbank Ctr. East Asian Rsch. Harvard U., Cambridge, Mass.; mem. Nat. Com. U.S.-China Rels., Nat. Com. on Am. Fgn. Policy. With Far East Command US Army, 1953—55. Fellow, Ctr. Internat. Affairs, Harvard U., 1974—75.

Fellow: Atlantic Coun. (assoc. sr. mem.), Am.-China Forum; mem.: UN Assn. N.Y., Diplomatic and Consular Officers Ret. (life), Am. Fgn. Svc. Assn. (life), Assn. Asian Studies (life), Coun. Fgn. Rels., Asia Soc., Cosmos Club, Harvard Club N.Y., Lake Mansfield Trout Club (life), Hong Kong Cricket Club (life), Sri Lanka Hill Club (life), Dar-es-Salaam Yacht Club (life). Home: 650 Park Ave Apt 4A New York NY 10065-6115 Office Phone: 212-861-8758. Personal E-mail: herbertlevin@cs.com.

LEVIN, HERVEY PHILLIP, lawyer; b. Oct. 22, 1942; s. Julius L. and Gertrude (Cohen) L.; m. Madeleine J. Raskin, Sept. 22, 1970; children: Arianne, Nicole, David. BBA, U. Mich., 1964, MBA, 1968; JD, DePaul U., 1969. Bar: Ill. 1969, Tex. 1979, US Dist. Ct. (no. dist.) Ill. 1970, US Ct. Appeals (5th cir.) 1981, US Ct. Appeals (7th cir.) 1971, US Supreme Ct. 1972. Assoc. Potts Randall & Horn, Chgo., 1970—71; assoc., jr. ptnr. Mehlman, Ticho, Addis, Susman, Spitzer, Randall, Horn & Pyes, Chgo., 1971—75; pvt. practice Chgo., 1975—78, Dallas, 1979—. Dir. Leedal Inc., Chgo.; cons. labor stds. subcom., house edn. and labor com. US Congress; cons. in workers' compensation, occupl. disease and gen. practice. Bd. dirs. Solomon Schecter Acad. Dallas, Cong. Shearith Israel, Dallas, 1981-88, Am. Jewish Congress, Dallas, 1980-85, Nat. Assn. Mortgage Planners, 1995-00. Named Ky. Col. Fellow Coll. Worker's Compensation Lawyers (pres.); mem. ABA (workers compensation com. torts and ins. practices sect., chmn. 1989-90, coun. mem. tort trial and ins. practices sect. 1995-98, 1999-05, ho. of dels. 1999-05, various adminstrv. coms., tort trial and ins. practices sect. 1990—, liaison to Internat. Assn. Indsl. Accident Bds. and Comms. 1989-1995), Ill. Bar Assn., Tex. Bar Assn., Dallas Bar Assn., Chgo. Bar Assn. Office: 6918 Blue Mesa Dr Ste 115 Dallas TX 75252-6140 Home Phone: 972-733-0663; Office Phone: 972-733-3242. Office Fax: 972-733-3269. Personal E-mail: hervey@airmail.net.

LEVIN, IAN, radiologist; arrived in US, 1996; s. Joseph and Rochelle Levin; m. Paula Levin, Nov. 15, 1992; 1 child, Michael. MB, BChir, U. Witwatersrand, Johannesburg, 1987; MBA, U. BC, Vancouver, Can., 1994. Cert. Am. Bd. Radiology, 2000, Can. Bd. Radiology, 2000, with added qualification in vascular and interventional radiology. Gen. and family practice, Canada, 1989—91; resident internal medicine Toronto Gen. Hosp., Canada, 1991—92; mgmt. cons. Deloitte & Touche, Vancouver, 1994—95; dir., bus. devel. officer VSM Medtech, Vancouver, 1995—96; diagnostic radiology resident U. So. Calif., LA, 1996—2000, fellow vascular and interventional radiology, 2000—01; pvt. practice radiology Citrus Med. Imaging, West Covina, Calif., 2002—06, Image Guided Therapeutics, San Francisco, 2006—. Chair elect dept. radiology Queen of Valley Hosp., West Covina, 2004, chair dept. radiology, 05. Fellow: Royal Coll. Physicians Can.; mem.: Radiol. Soc. N.Am., Am. Coll. Radiology, Royal Coll. Physicians and Surgeons Can. (licenciate).

LEVIN, IRA, writer, playwright; b. NYC, Aug. 27, 1929; s. Charles and Beatrice (Schlansky) L.; m. Gabrielle Aronsohn, Aug. 20, 1960 (div. 1968); children: Adam, Jared, Nicholas; m. Phyllis Finkel, Aug. 26, 1979 (div. 1982). Student, Drake U., Des Moines, 1946-48; AB, N.Y. U., 1950. Freelance writer, 1950—; author: A Kiss Before Dying, 1953, Rosemary's Baby, 1967, This Perfect Day, 1970, The Stepford Wives, 1972, The Boys from Brazil, 1976, Sliver, 1991, Son of Rosemary, 1997; playwright: No Time for Sergeants, 1955, Interlock, 1958, Critic's Choice, 1962, General Seeger, 1962, Drat! the Cat, 1965, Dr. Cook's Garden, 1967, Veronica's Room, 1973, Deathtrap, 1978, Break a Leg, 1979, Cantorial, 1989, Sliver, 1991, Son of Rosemary: The Sequel to Rosemary's Baby, 1997. Served with U.S. Army, 1953-55. Recipient Edgar Allan Poe award, 1953, 80, Bram Stoker award, 1997, Grand Master award, Mystery Writers of Am., 2003. Mem. Dramatists Guild (council mem. 1980—). Office: c/o Harold Ober Assocs 425 Madison Ave New York NY 10017-1110

LEVIN, JACK, physician, biomedical investigator, educator; b. Newark, Oct. 11, 1932; s. Joseph and Anna (Greengold) L.; m. Francine Corthesy, Apr. 13, 1975. BA magna cum laude, Yale U., 1953, MD cum laude, 1957. Diplomate: Am. Bd. Internal Medicine. Intern in medicine Grace-New Haven Hosp., 1957-58, asst. resident in medicine, 1960-62; chief resident in medicine Yale-New Haven Med. Ctr., 1964-65; clin. assoc. Nat. Cancer Inst., Bethesda, Md., 1958-60; fellow in hematology Johns Hopkins U. Sch. Medicine and Hosp., Balt., 1962-64, mem. faculty, 1965-82, prof. medicine, 1978-82; prof. lab. medicine, prof. medicine U. Calif. Sch. Medicine, San Francisco, 1982—; dir. hematology lab. and blood bank San Francisco VA Med. Ctr., Calif., 1982-93, dir. flow cytometry facility Calif., 1987-90; dir. Anticoagulation Clinic, San Francisco VA Med. Ctr., San Francisco, 1996—. Cons. in field. Author: (with P.D. Zieve) Disorders of Hemostasis, 1976; editor: (with E. Cohen and F.B. Bang) Biomedical Applications of the Horseshoe Crab (Limulidae), 1979, (with S.W. Watson and T.J. Novitsky) Endotoxins and Their Detection with the Limulus Amebocyte Lysate Test, 1982, Detection of Bacterial Endotoxins with The Limulus Amebocyte Lysate Test, 1987, (with others) Bacterial Endotoxins. Structure, Biomedical Significance, and Detection with the Limulus Amebocyte Lysate Test, 1985, Megakaryocyte Develop. and Function, 1986, Bacterial Endotoxins. Pathophysiological Effects, Clinical Significance, and Pharmacological Control, 1988, Molecular Biology and Differentiation of Megakaryocytes, 1990, Bacterial Endotoxins: Cytokine Mediators and New Therapies for Sepsis, 1991, Bacterial Endotoxin: Recognition and Effector Mechanisms, 1993, Bacterial Endotoxins: Basic Sci. to Anti-Sepsis Strategies, 1994, Bacterial Endotoxins: Lipopolysaccharides from Genes to Therapy, 1995; mem. editorial bd. Blood, Jour. Endotoxin Rsch.; contbr. numerous articles to profl. jour; editor-in-chief, Jour. Endotoxin Rsch., 1998-2004; developer (with F.B. Bang) Limulus test for bacterial endotoxins. Mem. Yale Alumni Sch. Com. for Md., 1967-82, for San Francisco, 1986-1997; mem. sci. adv. bd. Nat. Aquarium, Balt., 1978-82; mem. corp. Marine Biol. Lab., 1965—; trustee Marine Biol. Lab., 1988-93; mem. panel ind. assessors for rsch. project grants awards Nat. Health and Med. Rsch. Coun. Australia, 1982—. Served with USPHS, 1958-60. Markle scholar, 1968-73; recipient USPHS Rsch. Career Devel. award, 1970-75; Royal Soc. Medicine fellow Oxford (Eng.) U., 1972; Josiah Macy Jr. Found. faculty scholar, 1978-79; fellow, Found. for Med. Rsch., Paris, France, 1998; Fonds Nat. de la Rechorche Scientifique (FNRS) fellowship, Liege (Belg.), 2003; Frederik B. Bang award for rsch. in bacterial endotoxins, 1986. Fellow ACP; mem. Am. Soc. Hematology, Am. Soc. Clin. Investigation, Internat. Soc. Hematology, Internat. Soc. Explt. Hematology, Am. Soc. Investigative Pathology, Am. Fedn. Clin. Rsch., Soc. Exptl. Biology and Medicine, Internat. Endotoxin Soc., So. Soc. Clin. Investigation, Western Assn. Physicians, Soc. Invertebrate Pathology, Soc. Analytical Cytology, Cell Kinetics Soc., Internat. Soc. Artificial Cells, Blood Substitutes and Immobilization Biotech., Calif. Acad. Medicine, Phi Beta Kappa, Sigma Xi. Clubs: 14 W Hamilton St, Tudor and Stuart; Yale (San Francisco). Office Phone: 415-750-6913. Business E-Mail: levinj@medicine.ucsf.edu.

LEVIN, JACK S., lawyer; b. Chgo., May 1, 1936; s. Frank J. and Judy G. (Skerball) L.; m. Sandra Sternberg, Aug. 24, 1958; children: Lisa, Laura, Leslie, Linda. BS summa cum laude, Northwestern U., 1958; LL.B. summa cum laude, Harvard U., 1961. Bar: Ill. 1961; C.P.A. (gold medalist), Ill., 1958. Law clk. to chief judge U.S. Ct. of Appeals 2d Circuit, NYC, 1961-62; asst. for tax matters to Solicitor Gen. of U.S., Washington, 1965-67; assoc. law firm Kirkland & Ellis, Chgo., 1962-65, ptnr., 1967—. Frequent lectr. legal aspects of pvt. equity and venture capital transactions, mergers, acquistions, buyouts, workouts, fed. income tax matters; vis. com. Harvard Law Sch., 1987-93, lectr., 1997—; lectr. Law Sch. U. Chgo., 1988—. Author book on structuring venture capital, pvt. equity and entrepreneurial transactions; co-author 4-volume treatise on mergers, acquisitions and buyouts; case editor Harvard Law Rev., 1959-61; contbr. numerous articles to legal jours. and chpts. to law books. Parliamentarian Winnetka (Ill.) Town Meetings, 1974-83, 89, 93-96; chmn. nat. fundraising drives Harvard Law Sch., 1985-86, 90-91, 95-96, 2001, 03-06, chmn. lawyer's divsn. Jewish United Fund Chgo., 1993-95. Recipient Learned Hand award, Am. Jewish Com., 2000, Fellows award, Ill. Venture Capital Assn., 2002, Chambers Internat. Lifetime Achievement award, 2005, Humanitarian award, Ill. Holocaust Mus., 2005. Mem. ABA (chmn. subcom. 1968-79), Fed. Bar Assn., Chgo. Bar Assn. (tax sect. exec. com. 1985-00), Am. Jewish Com. (nat. bd. govs. 2005—, Midwest bd. dirs., exec. com. 2003-), Am. Coll. Tax Counsel, Mid-Am. Club (bd. dirs. 1985-88), Birchwood Club (pres. 1980-82). Home: 985 Sheridan Rd Winnetka IL 60093-1558 Office: Kirkland & Ellis 200 E Randolph St 57th Fl Chicago IL 60601-6608 Office Phone: 312-861-2004. Business E-Mail: jlevin@kirkland.com.

LEVIN, JANNA J., physicist, educator; b. 1968; BS in Astronomy and Physics, Barnard Coll., 1988; PhD in Theoretical Physics, MIT, 1993. Postdoctoral fellow Canadian Inst. for Theoretical Astrophysics, 1993—95; postdoctoral fellow, Ctr. for Particle-Astrophysics U. Calif. Berkeley, 1995—98; advanced fellow, Dept. of Applied Mathematics and Theoretical Physics (DAMTP) Cambridge U., 1999—2003; Nat. Endowment for Sci. Technol. and Arts (NESTA) fellow, Astophysics Dept. Oxford U., 2003; asst. prof. astronomy & physics Barnard Coll., NYC, 2004—. NESTA Dream Time Fellow, Scientist-in-Residence Ruskin School of Drawing and Fine Art, Oxford, 2003. Author: How the Universe Got Its Spots: Diary of a Finite Time in a Finite Space, 2002, (novels) A Madman Dreams of Turing Machines: A Story of Coded Secrets and Psychotic Delusions, of Mathematics and War Told by a Physicist Obsessed by the Lives of Turing & Gödel, 2006. Recipient Kilby award, 2003. Achievements include first official scientist in residence at the Ruskin School of Drawing and Fine Art at Oxford U. Office: Barnard Altschul 505 Dept Physics & Astronomy 3009 Broadway New York NY 10027 Business E-Mail: jlevin@barnard.edu.

LEVIN, JOSHUA ZEV, computer scientist, consultant, transportation engineer; b. Cambridge, Mass., Feb. 5, 1949; s. Betty Louise Zimmermann and Herschel Levin; m. Susan Evelyn Goldsmith, 1982 (div. 2003); children: Barry Naphtali, David Reuven. PhD, Rensselaer Poly. Inst., 1980; MSEE, NYU, 1974; BA, CUNY, Flushing, 1971. Chief computer scientist Epoch Engring., Lower Gwynedd, Pa., 1988—94; cons. in field. Mem. MetaNexus Inst., Phila., 2002—03, Beth Sholom Congregation, Elkins Park, Pa., 2000—03. Mem.: IEEE, Soc. for Automotive Engring., Soc. Indsl. Applied Math., Assn. Computing Machinery, Phi Beta Kappa. Democrat. Jewish. Achievements include development of software pricing engine; theatre anti-submarine warfare war gaming program; algorithm for tracing intersection curves of quadric surfaces; design of the Levi Car maglev vehicle; high speed personal transportation systemusing modular cars. Mailing: 106 Mansfield Blvd S Cherry Hill NJ 08034-3613 Office Phone: 866-538-4227. Personal E-mail: josh-levin@ieee.org.

LEVIN, LAWRENCE DANIEL, lawyer; b. Chgo., May 10, 1959; s. Sandra Morrison, June 22, 1986; children: Phillip David, Laura Michelle. BS in Accountancy, U. Ill., 1981, JD, 1985. Bar: Ill. 1985, U.S. Dist. Ct. (no. dist.) Ill. 1985. Ptnr. Katten Muchin Rosenman LLP, Chgo., 1985—. Mem. ABA, Chgo. Bar Assn. (chmn. securities law com. 1996-97). Office: Katten Muchin Rosenman LLP 525 W Monroe St Ste 1900 Chicago IL 60661-3693

LEVIN, LAWRENCE SCOTT, plastic surgeon; b. Phila., Apr. 1, 1955; MD, Temple U., Phila., 1982. Cert. Nat. Bd. Med. Examiners, 1983, Am. Bd. Orthop. Surgery, 1993, Am. Bd. Plastic and Reconstructive Surgery, 1993. Hand and microsurgery fellow Christine Kleinert Inst., Louisville, 1988; resident, gen. surgery Duke U. Med. Ctr., 1982—84, resident, orthopedic surgery, 1984—88, resident, plastic and reconstructive surgery, 1984—91, hand surgery fellow, 1989, chief, divsn. of plastic and reconstructive surgery, 1996—, assoc. prof., orthopedics and plastic surgery, 1997—2001, assoc. prof., plastic, reconstructive, maxillofacial and oral surgery, 1997—2001, prof. surgery, 2001—. Capt. 3274th Med. Corps Res. US Army, 1989—98. Mem.: Am. Soc. Plastic and Reconstructive Surgeons, Am. Soc. Surgery of the Hand, Am. Soc. Reconstructive Microsurgery, Am. Orthop. Foot & Ankle Soc., Am. Orthop. Assn., Am. Israeli Orthop. Soc., Am. Assn. Plastic Surgeons, Am. Acad. Orthop. Surgeons. Office: 3945 Duke Univ Med Ctr Durham NC 27710-0001*

LEVIN, MARK REED, radio personality, legal foundation administrator; b. Phila., Sept. 21, 1957; s. Jack Eugene and Norma (Rubin) Levin; m. Kendall Edwards, Aug. 24, 1985. BA magna cum laude, Temple U., 1977, JD, 1980. Asst. counsel Tex. Instruments, Inc., Dallas, 1980-81; adminstrv. asst. Action Agy., Washington, 1981-82; dep. asst. sec. for elementary & secondary edn. US Dept. Edn., Washington, 1982-84; assoc. dir. for Presdl. personnel The White House, Washington, 1984-85; dep. solicitor US Dept. Interior, Washington; chief of staff to atty. gen. US Dept. Justice, Washington; dir. legal policy Landmark Legal Found., Leesburg, Va., pres.; radio talk show host The Mark Levin Show, WABC-NY, 2003—. Legal analyst MSNBC. Author: Men in Black: How the Supreme Court is Destroying America, 2005. Mem. Cheltenham Twp. Sch. Bd., Pa., 1977-80 Recipient Ronald Reagan award, Am. Conservative Union, 2001. Mem.: Pa. Bar Assn., Phi Beta Kappa. Republican. Jewish. Office: Landmark Legal Found 19415 Deerfield Ave Ste 312 Leesburg VA 20176 Office Phone: 703-554-6100. Office Fax: 703-554-6119. E-mail: marklevinshow@abc.com.*

LEVIN, MARVIN EDGAR, physician; b. Terre Haute, Ind., Aug. 11, 1924; s. Benjamin A. and Bertha Levin; m. Barbara Yvonne Symes; 3 children. BA, Washington U., St. Louis, 1947; MD, Washington U., 1951. Diplomate Am. Bd. Internal Medicine. Intern Barnes Hosp., St. Louis, 1951-52, asst. resident in internal medicine, 1952-53; Nat. Polio Found. fellow in metabolism and endocrinology Sch. Medicine, Washington U., St. Louis, 1953-55; adj. prof. medicine Washington U. Sch. Medicine, St. Louis, 1980—98. Vis. prof. endocrinology and diabetes People's Republic of China, 1982, Jakarta, Indonesia, Cairo, 92, Taipei, 94, Malvern, England, 96; med. dir. Harry and Flora D. Freund Meml. Found., adj. prof. medicine endocrine, diabetes and metabolism, 2000—. Co-author: Levin and O'Neal's The Diabetic Foot, 7th edit., 2007; co-editor: The Uncomplicated Guide to Diabetes Complication, 3d edit.; contbr. articles to profl. jours., book chpts. Recipient Disting. Alumni award, Washington U., 1989, Arts and Scis. Disting. award, 1998. Fellow ACP, Soc. Vascular Medicine and Biology, Am. Coll. Endocrinology; mem. AMA, Am. Diabetes Assn. (nat. bd. dirs. 1984-86, chmn. publ. com. 1986-87, bd. dirs. Mo. chpt. 1987-93, editor in chief Clin. Diabetes 1988-93, co-editor Diabetes Spectrum 1988-93, Outstanding Clinician award 1979, Outstanding Physician Educator award 1991), Am. Dietetic Assn. (hon., Marvin E. Levin, MD Scholarship Program for rsch. in diabetic lower extremity disease named for him), St. Louis Clin. Diabetes Assn. (pres. 1965-66), Am. Thyroid Assn., Endocrine Soc., St. Louis Soc. Internal Medicine, St. Louis Internist Club (pres. 1972), Sigma Xi, Alpha Omega Alpha. Avocations: golf, art. Office: 732 Fairfield Lake Dr Town And Country MO 63017-5928 Office Phone: 314-469-6918. Personal E-mail: blevin0001@aol.com.

LEVIN, MARVIN EUGENE, lawyer; b. Antigo, Wis., June 20, 1924; s. Jacob and Lillian (Goldberg) L.; m. Ruth Ganzfried, June 10, 1948; children: Randal Mark, Gregary. BS, U. So. Calif., 1948, JD, 1951. Bar: Calif. 1952. Pvt. practice, LA, Santa Monica, Calif., 1952-68; sr. ptnr. Levin & Freedman, Santa Monica, 1968-97, of counsel, 1997—2003; arbitrator and mediator Santa Monica, Calif., 2004—. Lectr. in field. Bd. dirs., founding mem. NCCJ, Santa Monica, 1959-2003, chmn., 1965, So. Calif. regional bd., 1984-92; regional bd. Anti-Defamation League, 1958—, exec. com., 1960-81, 87-2003; pres. Santa Monica Family YMCA, 1985-86, trustee endowment trust, 1985—, bd. dirs., 1987—, chmn. endowment com., 1990-2004; bd. dirs. U. Synagogue, West LA, Calif., 1970-74. Capt. USAAF, 1943-46. Decorated Air medal with oak leaf cluster; recipient Brotherhood award Santa Monica Bay Area chpt. NCCJ, 1968. Fellow Am. Coll. Trust and Estate Counsel; mem. ABA (sect. dispute resolution, real property, probate and trust law, sr. lawyers divsn.), State Bar Calif. Assn. (sect. real property, probate, trust law), LA County Bar Assn., Santa Monica Bay Dist. Bar Assn. (trustee 1971-74, pres. 1973-74, chmn. sect. real property law 1982-84), Am. Arbitration Assn. (panel of arbitrators 1968-90), Rotary Internat. Found. (chmn. world cmty. svc. Santa Monica chpt. 1985-98, chmn, 2001—, dir. internat. svc. 2005-06, bd. dirs. 2005-06) Office: 2530 Wilshire Blvd Ste 200 Santa Monica CA 90403 Home Phone: 310-454-3032. Business E-Mail: mandrlevin@verizon.net.

LEVIN, MICHAEL JOSEPH, lawyer; b. Detroit, Feb. 1, 1943; s. Bayre and Lydia Ruth (Kahn) L.; m. Adah Hanson, Aug. 3, 1974; children: Andrew, Stephen. BA, Johns Hopkins U., 1964; JD, U. Mich., 1967. Bar: Mich. 1968, N.Y. 1973. Assoc. Milbank, Tweed, Hadley & McCloy, NYC, 1971-86; ptnr. Boyle, Vogeler & Haimes, NYC, 1986-93, Sutherland, Asbill & Brennan, NYC and Washington D.C., 1993-97; of counsel Menaker & Herrmann LLP, NYC, 1997-2000, Barger & Wolen LLP, NYC, 2000—. Served to lt. col. USMCR, 1963-90. Mem. Mich. Bar Assn., N.Y. State Bar Assn., Assn. of Bar of City of N.Y. Office: Barger & Wolen LLP 10 East 40th St New York NY 10016 Home Phone: 908-561-5889; Office Phone: 212-557-2800.

LEVIN, MICHAEL STUART, steel company executive; b. NYC, Aug. 2, 1950; s. Morton Sheldon and Ruth Jean (Leff) Levin; m. Laurence Diane Daisy deBardon deSegonzac, Dec. 13, 1984; children: Alex-Rene-Phillippe, Max-André Simon, Sebastien Pierre. BA (hon.), U. Wis., 1972; MBA, Harvard U., 1974. Asst. trader Titan Indsl. Corp., NYC, 1974—75, trader, 1975—76, export mgr., 1976—78, v.p., 1978—80, sr. v.p., 1980—82, pres., 1982—98, chmn., 1988—; CEO, chmn., founder e-STEEL, NYC, 1999—. Bd. dirs. Mus. Modern Art, NYC. Mem.: Coun. of Fgn. Rels., Explorers Club, Mashomack Fish and Game Preserve, River Club, Millbrook Golf and Tennis Club, N.Y. Yacht Club. Avocations: polo, sailing, skiing, shooting. E-mail: mlevin@titansteel.com.

LEVIN, MORTON D(AVID), artist, printmaker, educator; b. NYC, Oct. 7, 1923; s. Louis and Martha (Berusch) L. BS in Art Edn, CCNY, 1948; student in painting, Andre LHote, Paris, 1950; in sculpture, Ossip Zadkine, 1950; etching and engraving, Federico Castellon, NYC, 1948, Stanley W. Hayter, Paris, 1951; student in lithography, Pratt Graphic Art Center, NYC, 1966. Founder, dir., instr. printmaking, painting Morton Levin Graphics Workshop, San Francisco, 1972-91. One-man shows include Galerie Breteau, Paris, 1952, Winston Gallery, San Francisco, 1972, 80, 83, 85-97, 98-2003, 2005-06; exhibited in group shows at Seattle Art Mus., 1946-49, Libr. of Congress, Washington, 1946, 49, Pa. Acad. Fine Arts, 1948, Mus. Modern Art, Paris, 1951, Pallazzo del Academia, Genoa, Italy, 1951; represented in permanent collections at N.Y. Pub. Libr., Libr. of Congress, History of Medicine Divsn. Nat. Libr. Medicine; work featured in Jour. Erotic Arts, Yellow Silk #34, 1990. Served with inf. U.S. Army, 1943-45. Recipient Bryan Meml. prize Villager Travel Exhbn., N.Y.C., 1964, prize Washington Sq. Art Exhbn., 1964 Office Phone: 415-392-8824. Personal E-mail: mlevin@mortonlevin.com. *My goal has been to define our world and the primal forces of desire, love, procreation, death, and rebirth. To this end, I have created a universe in my art inhabited by the natural and fantastic. Humans, birds, and beasts, male and female, interact and strive on an elemental level. In a romantic expressionistic style, I have attempted to illuminate the human condition.*

LEVIN, MURRAY SIMON, lawyer; b. Phila., Feb. 8, 1943; s. Sidney Michael and Eva (Goldstein) L.; m. Jalond Marie Robinson, June 9, 1968; children: Adrianne Lesley, Alexandra Amber-Rose. BA, Haverford Coll., 1964; MA, LLB, Harvard U., 1968; cert., Hague Internat. Acad. Law, 1967. Bar: Pa. 1968, U.S. Dist. Ct. (ea. dist.) Pa. 1970, U.S. Ct. Appeals (3d cir.) 1970, U.S. Supreme Ct. 1979. Instr. English Harvard U., 1965-68; law clk. to U.S. Dist. Ct. Judge, 1968-70; instr. govt. Haverford Coll., 1970-71; litigation ptnr. Pepper, Hamilton LLP, Phila., 1970—, mem. firm exec. com., 1993-95. Mem. mng. bd. dirs. Atlas Pipeline Ptnrs., 2003-2005; overseas lectr., U.K., Sweden, Germany, Senegal, Kenya, Cameroon, Morocco, Israel, Vietnam, Italy, Portugal, Spain, Brazil1988—; law seminar spkr. Weekly commentator radio Sta. WCAU Dick Clayton Show, TV program Morningside, 1973-76; weekly host, interviewer Sta. WHYY, 1974-79; TV commentator O.J. Simpson trial, 1995; contbr. articles to profl. jours. Chmn. Phila. Coun. Experiment in Internat. Living, 1968—70; mem. Phila. Urban Coalition Housing Task Force, 1968—80; chmn. coll. divsn. Allied Jewish Appeal, 1968—70; pres. Ctrl. Phila. Reform Dems., 1973—74; candidate for Dem. Party nomination for U.S. Senate from Pa., 2000; chair Dem. Party Lower Merion/Narberth, 2003—06; del. Dem. Nat. Conv., 2004; mem. Pa. Dem. Party State Com., 2002—; bd. dirs. Grad. Hosp. Phila., 1976—96, mem. patient safety com., 2002—07; bd. dirs. Friends Ctrl. Sch., 1988—96, divsn. Fgn. Policy Rsch. Com. Mid. East Coun., 1992—94; mem. mng. bd. dirs. Mid. East Forum, 1994—; bd. dirs. French Internat. Sch. Phila., 2002—, Jewish Family and Children's Svc. Greater Phila., 2003—, Resource Capital Corp., 2005—, Atlar Pipeline Ptnrs., 2001—05. Root-Tilden fellow, 1964. Mem. ABA, Pa. Bar Assn. (ho. of dels.), Phila. Bar Assn. (young lawyers exec. bd. 1973, bd. govs. 1985-88, zone del. 1988—, chmn. profl. guidance com. 1989-92, co-chmn. internat. human rights com. 1990-91), Phila. Trial Lawyers Assn., Assn. Internat. des Jeunes Avocats Brussels (bd. dirs. 1981-85, 1st Am. pres. 1985-88), Union Internationale des Avocats Paris (advisor to pres., mem. exec. com. 1993—, pres. Am. chpt. 1995-97, congress pres. 1997, pres. tort law commn. 2003—), Am. Law Inst., Am. Judicature Soc., Phi Beta Kappa. Office: Pepper Hamilton LLP 3000 2 Logan Sq 18th & Arch Sts Philadelphia PA 19103-2799 Office Phone: 215-981-4335. Business E-Mail: levinm@pepperlaw.com.

LEVIN, PETER S.W., lawyer; b. 1952; BA, Yale U., 1974; JD, NYU, 1981. Bar: N.Y. 1982. Assoc. Davis, Polk & Wardwell, NYC, 1981—83, 1986—88, ptnr., 1989—, coord. credit practice group, assoc. Paris, 1984—86. Office: Davis Polk & Wardwell 450 Lexington Ave New York NY 10017 Office Phone: 212-450-4630. Office Fax: 212-450-3630. Business E-Mail: peter.levin@dpw.com.

LEVIN, RICHARD I., dean, cardiologist, researcher; b. Long Branch, NJ, July 28, 1948; s. Jack and Sally (Stark) L.; m. Jane Ellen Bressman, June 21, 1970; children: Emily, Jordan, Jennifer Kate. BS in Biology, Yale U., 1970; MD, NYU, 1974. Diplomate Am. Bd. Internal Medicine, Am. Bd. Internal Medicine/Cardiovascular Diseases. Instr. NYU Sch. of Med., NYC, 1978-83, asst. prof., 1983—2006, prof. medicine, vice dean edn.; vis. instr. Cornell U. Med. Coll., NYC, 1979-81, vis. asst. prof., 1981-83; founder, v.p., med. dir. Q-Med, Inc., Clark, NJ, 1983—; vice prin. health affairs, dean medicine, prof. McGill U., Montreal, 2006—. Bd. dirs., Q-Med, Inc.; lectr. Ciba-Geigy, Inc., Summit, N.J., 1985—; cons. Lipsome Co., Princeton, 1988—. Contbr. articles to profl. jours.; patentee in field. Bd. dirs. Am. Heart Assn., NYC Affiliate, 1988—. Recipient clinical investigator award, Nat. Inst. of Health, Bethesda, Md., 1980, Valentine Matt medal, NYU, Sch. of Med., NYC, 1974, Grant-in-Aid, Am. Heart Assn., 1988. Fellow Am. Coll. Physicians, Am. Coll. Cardiology; mem. Am. Fedn. for Clinical Research (councilor 1986-88), The Harvey Soc., N.Y. Heart Assn. (peer rev. council, 1986-89). Jewish. Avocations: tennis, skiing, theater. Office Phone: 212-263-8300, 212-263-6554. Office Fax: 212-263-3297. E-mail: richard.levin@med.nyu.edu.

LEVIN, RICHARD LOUIS, retired language educator; b. Buffalo, Aug. 31, 1922; s. Bernard and Meta (Block) Levin; m. Muriel Abrams, June 22, 1952; children: David, Daniel. BA, U. Chgo., 1943, MA, 1947, PhD, 1957. Mem. faculty U. Chgo., 1949-57, asst. prof. English, 1953-57; prof. English, SUNY, Stony Brook, 1957—, acting chmn. English dept., 1960-63, 65-66, ret., 1994. Mem. adv. bd. World Ctr. Shakespeare Studies; mem. acad. adv. coun. Shakespeare Globe Ctr.; Fulbright lectr., 1984—85. Editor: Tragedy: Plays, Theory and Criticism, 1960, The Question of Socrates, 1961, Tragedy Alternate, 1965, Michaelmas Term (Thomas Middleton), 1966, The Multiple Plot in English Renaissance Drama, 1971, New Readings vs. Old Plays: Recent Trends in the Reinterpretation of English Renaissance Drama, 1979, Looking for an Argument: Critical Encounters with the New Approaches to the Criticism of Shakespeare and His Contemporaries, 2003. Served to lt. (j.g.) USNR, 1943—46, ETO. Recipient Explicator award, 1971; fellow, Am. Coun. Learned Socs., 1963—64; Rsch. fellow, SUNY, 1961, 1965—68, 1971, 1973, Faculty Exch. scholar, NEH Sr. fellow, 1974, Guggenheim fellow, 1978—79, Nat. Humanities Ctr. fellow, 1987—88. Mem.: MLA (mem. adv. com. publs., mem. del. assembly), Medieval and Renaissance Drama Soc. (mem. coun.), Shakespeare Assn. Am. (trustee), Internat. Shakespeare Assn., Columbia U. Shakespeare Seminar, Joseph Crabtree Found. Democrat. Jewish. Home: 26 Sparks St Melville NY 11747-1727 Office: SUNY English Dept Stony Brook NY 11794-5350 Personal E-mail: rlevin@ms.cc.sunysb.edu.

LEVIN, RICK (RICHARD CHARLES LEVIN), academic administrator, economist; b. San Francisco, Apr. 7, 1947; s. D. Derek and Phylys M. (Goldstein) Levin; m. Jane Ellen Aries, June 24, 1968; children: Jon, Daniel, Sarah, Rebecca. BA, Stanford U., 1968; LittB, Oxford U., Eng., 1971; PhD, Yale U., 1974; LLD (hon.), Princeton U., 1993, Harvard U., 1994; D in Civil Law (hon.), Oxford U., 1998; Doctorate (hon.), Peking U., 2003. With Yale U., New Haven, 1974—, chmn. econs. dept., 1987—92, Frederick William Beinecke prof. econs., 1992—, dean Grad. Sch., 1992—93, pres., 1993—. Rsch. assoc. Nat. Bur. Econ. Rsch., Cambridge, Mass., 1985—90; program dir. Internat. Inst. Applied Sys. Analysis, Vienna, 1990—92; trustee Tanner Lectures on Human Values; bd. dir. Am. Express, 2007—; cons. numerous law and bus. firms. Trustee Hopkins Sch., New Haven, 1988—95, Yale-New Haven Hosp., 1993—, Univs. Rsch. Assn., 1994—99; bd. dirs. Yale-New Haven Health Svcs. Corp., Inc., 1993—; mem. bd. sci., tech. and econ. policy Nat. Rsch. Coun.; bd. mem. The William and Flora Hewlett Found.; mem. presdl. commn. U.S. Postal Svc., 2003; mem. Commn. on the Intelligence Capabilities of the U.S. Regarding Weapons of Mass Destruction, 2004. Fellow, Merton Coll. Oxford U., 1996. Fellow: Am. Acad. Arts and Scis.; mem.: Satmetrix, Econometric Soc., Am. Econ. Assn. Democrat. Jewish. Office: Yale U Office of Pres 105 Wall St New Haven CT 06511-6608 also: Yale University Office of Public Affairs 265 Church Street, Suite 901 New Haven CT 06511 Office Phone: 203-432-2550. Business E-Mail: richard.levin@yale.edu.

LEVIN, ROBERT EUGENE, food scientist, educator; b. Boston, Dec. 1, 1930; s. Jacob Levin and Etta Lillian Levine; m. Lenora L. Schiff, Dec. 13, 1952; children: David Eugene, Steven Phillip. BS, Calif. State Coll., LA, 1952; MS, U. So. Calif., LA, 1954; PhD, U. Calif., Davis, 1963. Asst. prof. Oreg. State U., Corvallis, 1963—64; from asst. to prof. environ. toxicology, food microbiology U. Mass., Amherst, 1964—2006. Contbr. articles to profl. jours. With US Army, 1954—56. Grantee, NIH, 1966—2006, USDA, 1966—2006, NOOA, 1966—2006. Achievements include development of methodology for molecular detection and enumeration of low numbers of infectious bacteria in foods. Home: 10 Wildflower Dr Amherst MA 01002 Office: U Mass 100 Holdsworth Way Amherst MA 01003 Home Phone: 413-256-0976; Office Phone: 413-545-0187. Office Fax: 413-545-1262. Business E-Mail: relevin@foodsci.umass.edu.

LEVIN, ROBERT J., finance company executive; BA in Econs. with high honors, U. N.C.; MBA, U. Chgo. With Fannie Mae, Washington, 1981—, various positions including sr. v.p. mktg. and mortgage-backed securities and sr. v.p. corp. fin., exec. v.p. mktg., 1990—98, exec. v.p. housing and cmty. devel., 1998—2005, interim CFO, 2004—06, exec. v.p., chief bus. officer, 2005—. Trustee Morehouse Coll. Exec. Program Club fellow, U. Chgo. Mem.: Phi Beta Kappa. Office: Fannie Mae 3900 Wisconsin Ave NW Washington DC 20016-2892

LEVIN, ROBERT JOSEPH, food products executive; b. Everett, Mass., Mar. 19, 1928; s. Edward A. and Rose E. L.; m. Carrol Silverman, June 21, 1948; children: Richard J., Cathy Levin Shuman. BA cum laude, U. Wis., 1948. From dir. store ops. and purchasing to pres., treas. C.B. Perkins Tobacco Co., Boston, 1948-73; from dir. store ops. and purchasing to pres., treas. C.B. Perkins Tobacco Co. (co. merged with Stop & Shop), Boston, 1970; v.p., then pres. Medi Mart div. Stop & Shop, 1971-75; group v.p. Stop & Shop Cos., Inc., Boston, 1975-79, sr. v.p., 1979-82, vice. chmn., 1982—, also dir. Bd. dirs. S.A.Y. Industries, Sterling Inc.; chmn. bd. S.A.Y. Packaging, 1988—. Bd. dirs. U. Wis. Found. Mem. Nat. Mass Retailing Inst. (dir.) Jewish. Home: 4762 Exeter Estate Ln Lake Worth FL 33467-8105 Office: 1776 Heritage Dr Quincy MA 02171-2119 also: PO Box 369 Boston MA 02101-0369

LEVIN, RONALD MITCHELL, geriatrician; b. Phila., July 29, 1958; s. Herbert A. and Marlene (Axelrod) L.; m. Carol Lynn Most, June 17, 1979; children: Jay Samuel, Marc Andrew, Eric Brian. BA cum laude, LaSalle U., 1980; MD with hons. in Pediats., distinction in medicine, Hahnemann U., 1984. Diplomate Am. Bd. Internal Medicine, Nat. Bd. Med. Examiners; cert. of advanced qualifications in geriatric medicine, Am. Bd. Internal Medicine, 1994, 2004. Intern, resident internal medicine Bryn Mawr Hosp., Phila., 1984-87; physician Lawndale Family Practice, Phila., 1987-88; pvt. practice Phila., 1988—95, 2001—03; clin. instr. medicine Hahnemann MCP Sch. Medicine, 1993—2003, Allegheny U. Health Scis., 1993—2003; internist Abington Meml. Hosp., 1995-2001; med. dir. U.S. Homecare, Phila., 1991-94; staff physician Salisbury Va. Med. Ctr., 2003—06, West Palm Beach VA Med. Ctr., Fla., 2006—. Interviewer med. sch. admissions com. Hahnemann Med. Coll. Pa. Sch. Medicine, 1995-97. Fellow ACP; mem. AMA (Physician's Recognition award 1991, 94, 97, 2000, 03, 06), Am. Geriatric Soc. Home: 7912 Sonoma Springs Cir Apt 101 Lake Worth FL 33463 Office: West Palm Beach VA Medical Ctr 7305 N Military Trail West Palm Beach FL 33410 Home Phone: 561-966-1595; Office Phone: 561-422-8262. Personal E-mail: rmlmdfacp@aol.com.

LEVIN, SANDER MARTIN, congressman, lawyer; b. Detroit, Sept. 6, 1931; s. Saul R. and Bess (Levinson) L.; m. Victoria Schlafer, 1957; four children. BA, U. Chgo., 1952; MA in Internat. Relations, Columbia U., 1954; LLB, Harvard U., 1957. Atty. priv. practice, 1957—64; supr. Oakland County Bd. Suprs., Mich., 1961-64; mem. Mich. Senate, 1965-70; atty. priv. practice, 1971—77; fellow Kennedy Sch. Govt., Inst. Politics, Harvard U., Cambridge, Mass., 1975; asst. adminstr. Agency for Internat. Develop., Washington, 1977-81; mem. U.S. Congresses from 12th (formerly 17th) Mich dist., 1983—; mem. ways and means com. Adj. prof. law Wayne State U., Detroit, 1971—74. Chmn. Mich. Dem. Com., 1968-69; Dem. Candidate for Gov., 1970, 74. Recipient Public Policy award, Am. Soc. Tng. and Devel. award, 1997. Democrat. Jewish. Office: US House Reps 2300 Rayburn House Office Bldg Washington DC 20515-0001 also: District Office 27085 Gratiot Ave Roseville MI 48066-2947 Office Phone: 202-225-4961, 586-498-7122. Office Fax: 202-226-1033, 586-498-7123.*

LEVIN, SIMON, lawyer; b. Newark, Aug. 4, 1942; m. Barbara Leslie Lasky; children: David, Jennifer Menken, Yale, Michael, Jacob. BS cum laude, Lehigh U., 1964; JD, NYU, 1967, LLM in Taxation, 1974. Bar: N.J. 1967, U.S. Tax Ct. 1971, U.S. Ct. Claims 1972, N.Y. 1980. Assoc. Shanley & Fisher, Newark, 1970, Hannoch Weisman, Newark, 1970-73; ptnr. Robinson, Wayne, Levin, Riccio & La Sala, Newark, 1973-88; mem., chmn. tax dept. Sills Cummis Radin Tischman Epstein & Gross, Newark, 1988—. Civillian aide to Sec. Army for N.J., 1992-95; mem. N.J. Dept. Treasury Transition Team for Gov. Christine Todd Whitman, 1993-94; mem. Treas. Adv. Group N.J. Dept. of Treasury, 1995—; lectr., panelist numerous orgns. Co-author: Taxation Investors in Securities and Commodities, 1983, 2d edit., 1984, supplement, 1986, Estate Planning and Administration in New Jersey, 1987; contbr. articles to profl. jours. Trustee, mem. exec. com. Jewish Comty. Found., MetroWest, Whippany, N.J., pres., 1979-83; trustee, mem. exec. com. Israel Bond Campaign MetroWest, Livingston, N.J., chmn., 1988-89; trustee Monmouth Healthcare Ctr. Found., 1997—, N.J. Vietnam Vets. Meml. and Edn. Ctr. Found., Holmdel, 1994—. Capt. U.S. Army, 1968-69, Vietnam. Recipient Cohn Leadership award Jewish Fedn. MetroWest, 1982, Endowment Achievement award Coun. Jewish Fedns., 1986, N.J. Meritorious Svc. medal, 1995. Fellow Am. Coll. Tax Counsel; mem. ABA, N.J. Bar Assn. (chmn. commodities sect. 1982-86), Essex County Bar Assn. (chmn. sect. taxation 1974-76), Monmouth County Bar Assn., Phi Delta Phi. Avocations: tennis, skiing, politics, opera, community service. Office: Sills Cummis Radin Tischman Epstein & Gross 1 Riverfront Plz Fl 10 Newark NJ 07102-5401

LEVIN, SIMON ASHER, mathematician, ecologist, educator; b. Balt., Apr. 22, 1941; s. Theodore S. and Clara G. L.; m. Carole Lotte Leiffer, Aug. 4, 1964; children: Jacob, Rachel. BA in Math., Johns Hopkins U., Balt., 1961; PhD in Math. (NSF fellow), U. Md., College Park, 1964; DSc (hon.), Ea. Mich. U., Ypsilanti, 1990. Teaching asst. U. Md., 1961-62, research assoc., 1964, visitor, 1968; NSF fellow U. Calif., Berkeley, 1964-65; asst. prof. math. Cornell U., 1965-70, assoc. prof. applied math., ecology, theoretical and applied math., 1971-77, Charles A. Alexander prof. biol. scis., 1977—92, adj. prof., 1992—, chmn. sect. ecology and systematics div. biol. scis., 1974-79, dir. Ecosystems Rsch. Ctr., 1980-87, dir. Ctr. for Environ. Rsch., 1987-90; George Moffett prof. biology Princeton U., 1992—, associated faculty applied math., 1992—, dir., Princeton Environ. Inst., 1993-98, dir., Del. Ctr. for Biocomplexity, 2001—. Vis. scholar U. Wash., 1973-74, Inst. for Advanced Study, 1999; vis. scientist Weizmann Inst., Rehovot, Israel, 1977, 80; hon. prof. U. B.C., 1979-80; Lansdowne lectr. U. Victoria, 1981; disting. vis. scientist SUNY, Stony Brook, 1984; vis. fellow All Souls Coll., U. Oxford, 1988; vis. scientist, Woods Hole Oceanographic Instn., Geophysical Fluid Dynamics Summer Prog., 1994; Ostrom lectr. Wash. State U., Pullman, 1994; lectr. Third Annual Stanislaw Ulam Meml., Santa Fe Inst., 1996; The Per Brinck Lecture, U. Lund, Sweden, 1999, Chesley Lecture, Carleton Coll., 2002; co-chmn. Gordon Conf. on Theoretical Biology, 1970, chmn. Gordon Conf. on Theoretical Biology and Biomath., 1971; chmn. Am. Math. Soc./ Soc. Indsl. and Applied Maths. Com. on Maths. in Life Scis., 1973-79; mem. core panel on math. in biol. scis., program com. Internat. Congress Mathematicians, 1977-78; co-convenor Biomath. Conf., Oberwolfach, West Germany, 1978; co-dir. Internat. Ctr. for Theoretical Physics Autumn Course on Math. Ecology, Trieste, Italy, 1988, 92, 96, 2000; mem. adv. com. divsn. environ. scis. Oak Ridge Nat. Lab., 1978-81; vice chmn. math. Com. Concerned Scientists, N.Y.C., 1979—; mem. sci. panel Hudson River Found., 1982-86, chmn., 1985-86, bd. dirs., 1986-96; mem. Commn. on Life Scis., NRC, 1983-89, mem. com. ecosys. mgmt. of sustainable marine fisheries ocean studies bd., 1995-98; mem. Health and Environ. Rsch. Adv. Com. Dept. of Energy, 1986-90; prin. lectr. Conf. Bd. on Math. Scis. course on math. ecology, 1985; mem. oversight rev. bd. U.S. Nat. Acid Precipitation Assessment Program; spkr. commencement address Ea. Mich. U., 1990; sci. bd. Santa Fe Inst., 1991—, chair, 2006-, Inst. Med. Bio Math., Bene Ataroth, Israel, 1999—; bd. dirs. Beijer Inst., 1994-99, chmn. 1997-99; The H. John Heinz III Ctr. for Sci., Econs. and the Environment, 1994-99; tech, adv. bd. Brit. Petroleum, 2001—; mem. sci. adv. bd. Gordon and Betty Moore Found., 2006-. Author: Fragile Dominion: Complexity and the Commons, 1999; editor: Lectures on Mathematics in Life Sciences, vols. 7-12, 1974-79, Ecosystem Analysis and Prediction, 1974, (with R.H. Whittaker) Niche: Theory and Application, 1975, Studies in Mathematical Biology, 2, vols., 1978, New Perspectives in Ecotoxicology, 1983, Mathematical Population Biology, 1984, Mathematical Ecology, 1984, Math Ecology: An Introduction, 1986, (with others) Mathematical Ecology, 1988, Ecotoxicology: Problems and Approaches, 1989, Perspectives in Theoretical Ecology, 1989, (with T. Hallam and L. Gross) Applied Mathematical Ecology, 1989, (with T. Powell and J.H. Steele) Patch Dynamics, 1993, Frontiers in Mathematical Biology, 1994, (with Abe and Higashi) Biodiversity: An Ecological Perspective, 1997 (with A. Okubo) Diffusion and Ecological Problems,2d edit.2001, (with P. Kareiva) The Importance of Species, 2003; editor-in-chief Ecological Applications, 1988-95, Ency. of Biodiversity, 1997-2000; Mathematical and Computational Biology Book Series, 1997-2000; editor: Ecology and Ecol. Monographs, 1975-77, Princeton Series in Theoretical and Computational Biology, 2000; editor Jour. Math. Biology, 1976-79, mng. editor, 1979-95; mng. editor Biomath., 1976-95, Lecture Notes in Biomath., 1973-95; mng. editor Princeton U. Press, Monographs in Population Biology, 1992—; assoc. editor Theoretical Population Biology, 1976-84; mem. editl. bd. Evolution Theory, 1976—, Ecol. Issues, 1995—, Conservation Ecology, 1995—, Discrete Applied Math., 1978-87, Internat. Jour. Math. and computer Modelling, 1979—, SIAM Rev., 1997—, Santa Fe Inst., 1998—, Philosophical Transactions of the Royal Soc., Series B, 1998—, Jour. Biomath., 1999, Procs. Nat. Acad. of Scis., 2000—; mem. editl. bd. Princeton U. Press, Complexity series, 1992—; mem. adv. bd. Jour. Theoretical Biology, 1977—, Ecological Rsch., 1996—, Ecosystems, 1996—; also various other editl. positions; contbr. articles to profl. jours. Bd. dirs. N.J. chpt. Nature Conservancy, 1995-97. Recipient Robert MacArthur award, Ecol. Soc. Am., 1988, Disting. Statis. Ecologist award, Internat. Assn. Ecology, 1994, Okubo award, Japanese Assn. for Math. Biology/Soc. for Math. Biology, 2001, A.H. Heineken prize for Environ. Scis., Royal Netherlands Acad. Arts and Scis., 2004, Kyoto prize (Basic Scis.), Inamori Found., 2005, Cmty. Lectr. award, Soc. Indsl. and Applied Math. I.E. Block, 2006, Disting. Scientist award, Am. Inst. Biol. Scis., 2007; fellow, Guggenheim, 1979—80, Japanese Soc. Promotion of Sci., 1983—84. Fellow AAAS (bd. dirs. 1994-98), Am. Acad. Arts and Scis.; mem. Ecol. Soc. Am. (chmn. Mercer awards subcom. 1976, mem. coun. 1977-77, ad hoc com. to evaluate ecol. consequences of nuclear war 1982-83, pres. 1990-91, MacArthur award 1988, Disting. Svc. citation 1998, chmn. MacArthur award com. 1999-2000), Soc. and Indsl. and Applied Math. (mem. coun. 1977-79, coun. exec. com. 1978-79, coun. rep. to bd. trustees 1978-79, chmn. human rights com. 1980-83, mng. editor Jour. Applied Math. 1975-79), Am. Inst. Biol. Scis., Am. Soc. Naturalists, Soc. Math. Biology (pres. 1987-89), Soc. for Conservation Biology, Brit. Ecol. Soc., Soc. Study Evolution, Japaneses Soc. Theoretical Biology (Okuba Lifetime Achievement award), U.S. Com. for Israel Environ., Sigma Xi. Jewish. Home: 11 Beechtree Ln Princeton NJ 08540-7428 Office: Princeton U Dept Ecology & Evolutionary Biology Eno Hall Princeton NJ 08544-1003

LEVIN, STEVEN JONATHAN, physician; b. Providence, Dec. 21, 1959; Grad., Brown U.; MD, Emory U. Sch. Medicine, 1985. Resident, family medicine Med. U. SC, Charleston, SC, 1985—88, fellow, family medicine, 1988—89; faculty develop. fellow U. NC; clin. asst. prof. U. Medicine and Dentistry NJ (UMDNJ)-Robert Wood Johnson Med. Sch., New Brunswick, NJ, now assoc. prof.; med. dir., sole physician St. John's Health Ctr., New Brunswick, NJ, 1989—. Mentors and educates family medicine residents and med. students U. Medicine and Dentistry NJ-Robert Wood Johnson Med. Sch.; chief faculty adv. Homeless and Indigent Population Health Outreach Project. Named Family Physician of Yr., NJ Acad. Family Physicians, 2005, 2007 Physician of Yr., Am. Acad. Family Physicians. Achievements include committing life to providing medical care to underserved populations; as a result of dedication to community service a group of his students formed the nationally recognized Homeless and Indigent Population Health Outreach Project in 1992; helping another group of medical students from UMDNJ-Robert Wood Johnson Medical School establish the Promise Clinic. Business E-Mail: slevin@umdnj.edu.*

LEVIN, SUSAN BASS, state agency administrator, lawyer; b. Wilmington, Del., July 18, 1952; d. Max S. and Harriet C. (Rubin) Bass; children: Lisa, Amy. BA, U. Rochester, 1972; JD, George Washington U., 1975. Bar: DC 1975, U.S. Ct. Claims 1975, N.J. 1976, Pa. 1981, U.S. Ct. Appeals (3d cir.) 1983, U.S. Supreme Ct. 1984. Law clk. to assoc. justice US Ct. Claims, Washington, 1975—76; assoc. Covington & Burling LLP, Washington, 1976—79; pvt. practice Cherry Hill, NJ, 1979—87; counsel Ballard, Spahr, Andrews & Ingersoll, Phila., Camden, 1993—96, Pepper Hamilton LLP, Phila. and Cherry Hill, 1996—2000; spl. counsel Fox Rothschild OBrien Frankel, 2001—02; commr. NJ Dept. Cmty. Affairs, 2002—07; dep. dir. The Port Authority of NY & NJ, 2007—. Chair N.J. Redevel. Authority, 2002—; COO Corzine for Gov., 2005; mem. Corzine Transition Team, 2005. Trustee N.J. Coalition Small Bus. Orgns., 1985—87; del. to Pres.'s Summit Am.'s Future, chair Pam's List; chair N.J. Coun. Affordable Housing; del. Dem. Presdl. Conv., 1992, 1996, 2000, 2004; pres. Cherry Hill Twp. Coun., 1986—88; mayor City of Cherry Hill, 1988—2002; bd. dirs. N.J. Alliance Action, S. Jersey Devel. Coun., U.S. Holocaust Coun., Big Bros./Big Sisters, Boys and Girls Club, trustee; bd. dirs. N.J. League Municipalities. Recipient Woman of Achievement award, Camden County Girl Scouts, 1986, Barbara Boggs Sigmuno award, N.J. Women Polit. Caucus, 1996, Gov.'s award on volunteerism, 1998. Mem.: N.J. Assn. Women Bus. Owners (state pres. 1984—85, named Woman of the Yr. 1985), Tri County Women Lawyers (pres. 1984—85), Order of Coif, Phi Beta Kappa. Office: The Port Authority of NY & NJ 225 Park Ave S New York NY 10003 Personal E-mail: brook@voicenet.com, brook168@comcast.net.

LEVIN, WARREN MAYER, family practice physician; b. Phila., Aug. 20, 1932; s. Israel and Clara Deborah (Cherim) L.; m. Marsha Ann Beinstein, Dec. 24, 1955 (div. 1975); children: Beth Ann, Julie Ruth; m. Frances Susan Teitler, Mar. 20, 1982; 1 child, Erika Alexandra. BS, Ursinus Coll., 1952; MD, Jefferson Med. Coll., 1956. Diplomate Am. Bd. Family Practice, Am. Bd. Bariatric Medicine, Am. Bd. Environ. Medicine, Am. Bd. Chelation Therapy, Internat. Bd. Advanced Longevity Medicine; cert. homeopath. Intern U.S. Naval Hosp., Newport, RI, 1956-57; pvt. practice SI, NY, 1959-74; founder, med. dir. Heights Holistic Health Ctr., Bklyn., 1974-79, World Health Med. Group, NYC, 1979-94; physician Physicians for Complementary Medicine, NYC, 1994-97, Comprehensive Med. Svcs., NYC, 1998—2000, Americas Med. Ctr., Ridgefield, Conn., 1998—2000; founder, med. dir. Interactive Medicine Conn., Wilton, 2001—03, with NYC office, 2001—04; physician Issels Med. Ctr., Phoenix, 2004—05, pvt. practice, Scottsdale, Ariz., 2005—06, Fairfax, Va., 2006—. Mem. bd. examiners Internat. Bd. Advanced Longevity Medicine, 1998—2000; founder & med. dir. Integrative Medicine of Conn., 1998—2004, Longevity Med. Ctr., Phoenix, 2004—05; pvt. practice, Scottsdale, Ariz., 2005—06. Contbr. to books Nutrition in Pregnancy, 1981, to books Challenging Orthodoxy, 1991, to books Alternative Medicine, 1994, to books The Cholesterol Hoax, 1998, to books Whole Body Dentistry, 1999. Bd. govs. Internat. Coll. Applied Nutrition, 1974-76; chmn. med. adv. bd. Survive Until a Cure, advisory coun.-Chemical Awareness Rsch. Educ. & Solutions; prin. investigator-A Study on Use of Human Growth Hormone. Lt. M.C., USNR ret. Recipient Disting. Pioneer in Alternative Medicine award Found. for Advancement of Innovative Medicine Fund, 1995, Presdl. Commendation, Am. Coll. for Advancement in Medicine, 1995. Fellow: Am. Acad. Family Pactice, Am. Coll Nutrition, Am. Acad. Environ. Medicine (bd. dirs. 2003); mem.: Am. Soc. Bariatric Medicine (v.p. 1980—82), Am. Coll. Advancement Medicine (treas.). Avocations: ice skating, sailing, swimming. Home: 11743 English Mill Ct Oakton VA 22124 Office Phone: 703-255-0313. Personal E-mail: drwmlevin@aol.com.

LEVIN, WILLIAM EDWARD, lawyer; b. Miami, Fla., June 13, 1954; s. Harold A. and Phyllis (Wolfson) L.; m. Mary Catherine Egan, June 25, 1994; children: Sean Alexander, Troy Andrew. Student, Conn. Coll., 1972-74; BA, Emory U., Atlanta, 1976; JD, U. Miami, 1979. Bar: Fla. 1979, Calif. 1982; lic. real estate broker, Calif. Distbr. N.Y. Times, Atlanta, 1975-76; legis. intern Congressman William Lehman, Washington, 1974; law clk. Superior Ct. Hillsborough County, Tampa, Fla., 1974; legal asst./law clk. U. Miami Sch. Law, 1977-78; law clk. Shevin, Shapo & Shevin, Miami, 1977-79; assoc. Law Offices of John Cyril Malloy, Miami, 1979-82; assoc./ptnr. Flehr, Hohbach, Test, Albritton & Herbert, San Francisco, 1982-87; ptnr. Cooper, White & Cooper, San Francisco, 1987-88; pvt. practice trademark and copyright law San Francisco, 1988-92, Irvine, Calif., 1993-96; broker/sole proprietor Levin Realty, San Francisco, 1987-92; of counsel Goldstein & Phillips, San Francisco, 1988-91, Hawes & Fischer, Newport Beach, Calif., 1992-93, Gauntlett & Assocs., Irvine, Calif., 1995-96; mng. partner Levin & Gluck, Laguna Beach, Calif., 1996-97; founding ptnr. Levin & Hawes, Laguna Beach, Calif., 1997—2003; founder Levin Intellectual Property Group, 2003—. Co-chmn. trademark com. San Francisco Patent & Trademark Assn., 1985-86; moot ct. judge Giles Rich Moot Ct. Competition, San Francisco, 1986; ofcl. arbitrator Am. Arbitration Assn., 1987-96; mem. exec. com. L.A. Complex Inns of Ct., 1994-96; lectr. in field. Author: Trade Press Protection, 1996; mem. editorial bd. Trademark World, London, 1987-90, Trademark Reporter, 1987-89, 93-2000, Trademark Reporter Task Force, 1994-97, San Francisco Atty., 1986-89; mem. adv. bd. United States Patents Quarterly, 2000—; contbr. articles to profl. jours. Mem. adminstrv. bd. Californians for Missing Children, San Francisco, 1989-92, Hebrew Inst. Law, San Francisco, 1986-88; atty's. steering com. Jewish Cmty. Fedn., San Francisco, 1987-88; fin. com. Temple Emanu-el, San Francisco, 1985-86; bd. dirs. Ctr. 500, Orange County Performing Arts Ctr. Support Group, 1996, Anti-Defamation League Orange County and Long Beach Region, 1998—; trustee Shir Ha Ma'lot Temple, 1997-2002; mem. intellectual property adv. bd. Whittier Law Sch., 2002—; bd. dirs. Laguna Outreach Cmty. Arts, 2003-04. Named Rep. of Yr., Nat. Rep. Congl. Com., 2001. Mem. ABA, Internat. Trademark Assn., Orange County Bar Assn., Orange County Patent Law Assn. Jewish. Lead trial counsel in case resulting in $143 million trademark infringement jury verdict, largest award of this type in the world, Oct. 1999. Office Phone: 949-497-7676. Personal E-mail: williamlevin@cox.net.

LEVIN, WILLIAM ROBERT, art historian; b. Newton, Mass., Oct. 22, 1948; s. Robert Fink and Louise (Oppenheimer) Levin; m. Maria Grazia Nardelli, July 18, 1981; children: Chiara Maria, Elena Stella. BA, Northwestern U., Evanston, Ill., 1970; MA, U. Mich., Ann Arbor, 1973, PhD, 1983. Instr. Assoc. Colls. Midwest, Florance, Italy, 1977—81; asst. prof. Mankato State U., Minn., 1983—86, Centre Coll., Danville, Ky., 1986—92, assoc. prof., 1992—2001, prof., 2001—, H.W. and Adele Stodghill rsch. prof., 2006. Author: Images of Love and Death in Late Medieval and Renaissance Art, 1976, The Allegory of Mercy at the Misericordia in Florence: Historigraphy, Context, Iconography, and the Documentation of Confraternal Charity in the Trecento, 2004; contbr. articles to profl. publs. Mem. governing bd. Mankato Area Arts Coun., 1984—86; sec. Danville Archtl. Rev. Bd., 2000—05; mem. facilities and exhibits com. Cmty. Arts Ctr., Danville, 2003—. Study fellow, Internat. Telephone and Telegraphi Corp., Florence, 1976—77, Centre scholar, Centre Coll., 2001—03. Mem.: Coll. Art Assn., Italian Art Soc. (mem. program com. 2004—07), SE Coll. Art Conf. (bd. dirs. 1997—2003), Phi Beta Kappa. Office: Centre Coll 600 W Walnut St Danville KY 40422

LEVINE, A. KENNETH, lawyer; b. Charleston, W. Va., June 21, 1965; BS in Mgmt., Tulane U., New Orleans, 1987, JD, 1990. Bar: Fla. 1990, DC 1991, US Dist. Ct. (no., mid. and so. dists.) Fla., US Ct. Appeals (2nd, 4th, 5th, 6th, 7th, 9th, 11th cirs.), US Ct. Appeals (DC cir.), US Ct. Appeals (fed. cir.), US Claims Ct., US Supreme Ct., cert.: ins. mediator. Extern for Judge Robert F. Collins U.S. Dist. Ct. (ea. dist.) La., New Orleans, 1989—90; atty. Fla. Dept. Ins. and Treas., Tallahassee, 1990—92, sr. atty., 1992—95; gen. counsel ACSI, Inc., Clearwater, Fla., 1995; assoc. Blank, Rigsby & Meenan, P.A., Tallahassee, 1996—98; ptnr. Pennington, Moore, Wilkinson, Bell & Dunbar, P.A., Tallahassee, 1998—2001, Tew Cardenas LLP, Tallahassee, 2001—05, Broad and Cassel, Tallahassee, 2006—. Gen. counsel Am. Mfrs. Warranty Assn., Inc.; mem. adv. coun. Calif. Bur. Electronic and Appliance Repair, mem. svc. contract task force. Editor: Tulane Environ. Law Jour.; contbr. articles to profl. jours. Named to, Nat. Order of the Barristers. Mem.: ABA, Assn. Insurance Compliance Profls., Internat. Assn. Insurance Receivers, Tulane Bus. Assn., Govs. Club. Office: The Levine Law Group 1615 Village Sq Blvd Ste 7 Tallahassee FL 32309-2769 Office Phone: 850-841-7770. Business E-Mail: klevine@levinelawgroup.net.

LEVINE, ADAM NOAH, singer; b. LA, Mar. 18, 1979; Band mem. Kara's Flowers (name changed to Maroon 5 in 2001), 1995—; signed to Reprise Records, 1997—99, Octone Records, 2001—. Performer (as Kara's Flowers): (albums) Fourth World, 1997; performer: (as Maroon 5) Songs About Jane, 2002, 1.22.03.Acoustic, 2004, Live Friday the 13th, 2005, It Won't Be Soon Before Long, 2007, (songs) Harder to Breathe, 2003, This Love, 2004 (MTV Video Music award for Best New Artist, 2004, Grammy award for Best Group Pop Performance, 2006), She Will Be Loved, 2004, Sunday Morning, 2004, Shiver, 2005, contbr. Spider-Man 2 soundtrack, 2004; performer: (duets) Wild Horses with Alicia Keys, 2005. Recipient World Music award for Best New Group, 2004, MTV Europe award for Best New Act, 2004, Grammy award for Best New Artist (with Maroon 5), 2005. Address: Maroon 5 PO Box 884564 San Francisco CA 94188 Office: Octone Records Rm 500 560 Broadway New York NY 10012 Office Phone: 646-613-0200. E-mail: maroon5@maroon5.com.

LEVINE, ALAN, lawyer; b. Middletown, NY, Jan. 17, 1948; s. Jacques and Florence (Tananbaum) L.; m. ALison Newman; children: Emily Jane, Malcolm Andrew. BS in Econs., U. Pa., 1970; JD, NYU, 1973. Bar: N.Y. 1974, U.S. Dist. Ct. (so. dist.) N.Y. 1974, U.S. Dist. Ct. (ea. dist.) N.Y. 1980, U.S. Tax Ct. 1980, U.S. Ct. Appeals (2d cir.) 1975, U.S. Supreme Ct. 2000. Law clk. to Hon. Lee P. Gagliardi US Dist. Ct. (so. dist.) N.Y., NYC, 1973-75; asst. U.S. atty. (so. dist.) NY US Dept. Justice, NYC, 1975-80; assoc. Kronish, Lieb, Weiner & Hellman LLP, NYC, 1980-82, ptnr., 1982—98, mng. ptnr., 1998—2006; ptnr., mem. exec. com. Cooley Godward Kronish LLP, NYC, 2006—. Bd. dirs. Legal Aid Soc., NYC, mem. exec. com., 2003—, chair bd. dirs., 2006—; chmn. lawyers divsn. United Jewish Appeal Fedn. NY, 2004—; mem. NY Commn. Pub. Authority Reform, NY, 2005—. Chmn. bd. dirs. Park Ave. Synagogue, N.Y.C., 1993-98; bd. dirs. Jewish Theol. Sem., 1998-, mem. exec. com.; law chmn. N.Y. County Rep. Com., 1991-93. Recipient Atty. Gen. Dirs. award U.S. Dept. Justice, 1980, Torch of Learning award Am. Friends Hebrew U., 1995, Human Rels. award Anit-Defamation League, 2001, Robert Morgenthau award Police Athletic League, 2006. Fellow Am. Bar Found., Am. Coll. Trial Lawyers; mem. ABA (ho. of dels. 1983-84, chmn. spl. com. for youth edn. for citizenship, 1988-91, vice chmn. white collar crime com. 1996—), N.Y. State Bar Assn. (chmn. com. on citizenship edn. 1979-84, ho. of dels. 1982-84, award of achievement 1984), Sunningdale Country Club (bd. trustees 1988-90 Scarsdale, N.Y.), Mask and Wig Club (Phila.). Republican. Jewish.

LEVINE, ALISON, entrepreneur, leadership development consultant, adventurer; b. Apr. 5, 1966; Undergraduate degree, U. Ariz.; MBA, Duke U., 2000. Positions in sales and mktg. in the healthcare industry in US and Asia, 1989—2000; with Goldman Sachs, 2000—03; founder, pres. Daredevil Strategies, San Francisco, 2003—. Dep. fin. dir. for Arnold Schwarzenegger, 2003; invited spkr. Guest appearences on Today Show, CNN, CNBC, Fox ABC News, CBS Evening News and other nat. programs, subject of articles in Oprah Mag., National Geographic, Lifetime Mag., Sports Illustrated Women, Outside and other publications, host of blog womenclimbhigh.spaces.inc.com, featured in More Than 85 Broads, Smart Moves; performer: The Vagina Monologues, Calif. Theater, 2005. Participant North Pole Leadership Challenge, 2004; founder The Climb High Found., 2005—; founding mem. World Wildlife Fund's Young Partners in Conservation. Named one of San Francisco's Top Bus. Leaders Under 40, Arizona's Most Interesting People; recipient Courage in Sports award, Anaheim Angels, 2003. Mem.: Assn. of Women MBAS, 85 Broads (co-chair). Achievements include climbing mountains in 1998 after a second heart surgery to repair a life threatening condition called Wolff Parkinson White Syndrome; serving as team captain of the first American Women's Everest Expedition in 2002; climbed highest peaks on six continents-Kilimanjaro, Aconcagua, Elbrus, Carstensz Pyramid, McKinley and Vinson, also Rainier, Muir, Whitney and Shasta, Cotopaxi (Ecuador), Ixta and Orizaba (Mexico); skied more than 100 miles to reach the top of the world-the North Pole; created Climb High Foundation for improving the lives of jobless women in third-world countries by training them to be trekking guides or porters for the local mountains; involvment in Western Uganda was groundbreaking because it was the first time the local women had climbed mountains because it was forbidden due to cultural beliefs (subordinate status of women); raised funds to build two schools in Nepal; helped to fund the construction of a school for AIDS orphans in Uganda. Avocations: mountaineering, adventure travel, philanthropy, women's initiatives, theater, reading. Office: Daredevil Strategies 1538 Filbert St #4 San Francisco CA 94123 Office Phone: 415-595-3966. Business E-Mail: alison@daredevilstrategies.com.

LEVINE, ARTHUR ELLIOTT, former academic administrator, educator; b. NYC, June 16, 1948; s. Meyer and Katherine (Kalman) L.; m. Linda Christine Fentiman, Aug. 18, 1974; children: Jamie Sloan Fentiman, Rachel Elizabeth Fentiman. BA in Biology, Brandeis U., 1970; PhD, SUNY-Buffalo, 1976; PhD (hon.), St. Thomas Aquinas Coll., 2001; LHD (hon.), U. Puget Sound, 1981, William Jewell Coll., 1995, U. NH, 1995; DHL (hon.), U. New Eng, Biddeford, Maine, 1983, Unity Coll., Maine, 1984, Bradford Coll., 1989, Capitol U., 1991, Taitung Nat. Tchrs. Coll., Taiwan, 1991, Albright Coll., 1993, U. NH, 1995, William Jewell Coll., 1995, Mt. Union Coll., 1995, Niagara U., 1996, LaGuardia CC, 1998, Wilmington Coll., 1998, Elmhurst Coll., 2006; LittD (hon.), Greensboro Coll., 1988, Jewish Theol. Seminary, 1996, others. Sr. fellow Carnegie Council on Policy Studies in Higher Edn., Berkeley, Calif., 1975-80, Carnegie Found., Washington, 1980-82; pres. Bradford Coll., Mass., 1982-89; chmn. Inst. for Edn. Mgmt. Harvard U., Cambridge, Mass., 1989-94; pres., prof. edn. Tchrs. Coll., Columbia U., NYC, 1994—2006. Cons. to numerous colls., univs., U.S. Co-author: Reform of Undergraduate Education, 1973 (Am. Coun. on Edn. Book of Yr. award 1974), Quest for Common Learning, 1982, Opportunity in Adversity, 1985, Shaping Higher Education's Future, 1989, Higher Learning in America, 1993, Beating the Odds, 1996, When Hope and Fear Collide, 1998; author: Handbook on Undergraduate Curriculum, 1978, Why Innovation Fails, 1980, When Dreams and Heroes Died, 1980. Pres. Woodrow Wilson Nat. Fellowship Found. Recipient Edn. Press Assn. Am. award, 1981, 89, 90, 94; book named Book of Yr., Am. Coun. on Edn., 1974; Spencer fellow, 1979. Fellow: Am. Acad. Arts & Sciences.

LEVINE, ARTHUR M., law educator; b. NYC, Apr. 14, 1939; s. Mervin Levine and Elsie Klein. BA, Princeton U., NJ, 1960; JD, Yale U., New Haven, Conn., 1963. Assoc. atty. McGlaughlin & Stern, NYC, 1965—66; civil rights atty. Dept. of Justice, Washington, 1966—67; underwriter Ladenburg Thalmann, NYC, 1968—70; investment analyst Lehman Bros., NYC, 1971—73; prof. ethics and legal studies Calif. State U., Coll. Bus. Adminstrn., Long Beach, Calif., 1974—. Host, exec. prodr. (TV series) Straight Talk, 1992—. Bd. dirs. Long Beach Transit, 1988—96, Ctr. for Water Edn., Hemet, Calif., 2004—. Lt. USN, 1964—70. Recipient Dist. Faculty Tchg. award, Calif. State U., Long Beach, 2003. Mem.: State Bar NY, State Bar Calif. Office: Calif State Univ Coll Bus Adminstrn 1250 Bellflower Blvd Long Beach CA 90840

LEVINE, ARTHUR SAMUEL, pediatric hematologist, dean, educator, oncologist, researcher; b. Cleve., Nov. 1, 1936; s. David Alvin and Sarah Ethel (Rubinstein) L.; m. Ruth Eleanor Rubin, Oct. 14, 1959; children: Amy Elizabeth, Raleigh Hannah, Jennifer Leah. AB, Columbia U., 1958; MD, Chgo. Med. Sch., 1964. Diplomate Am. Bd. Pediatrics, Am. Bd. Pediatric Hematology-Oncology. Intern in pediatrics U. Minn., Mpls., 1964-65, resident in pediatrics, 1965-66, USPHS fellow in hematology and genetics, 1966-67; capt. USPHS, 1967-92, rear adm., asst. surgeon gen., 1992-98; clin. assoc. div. cancer treatment Nat. Cancer Inst., Bethesda, Md., 1967-69, sr. staff fellow, 1969-70, sr. investigator, 1970-73, head sect. infectious disease, pediatric oncology br., 1973-75, chief pediatric oncology br., 1975-82; sci. dir. Nat. Inst. Child Health and Human Devel., Bethesda, 1982-98; sr. vice chancellor for health scis., dean Sch. Medicine, U. Pitts., 1998—, prof. medicine and molecular genetics and biochemistry, 1998—. Clin. prof. medicine and pediatrics Georgetown U., Washington, 1975-98; clin. prof. pediatrics Uniformed Svcs. U. Health Scis., Bethesda, 1983-98; vis. prof. Cold Harbor Spring Lab., N.Y., 1973, Benares Hindu U., India, 1975, U. Minn., 1974, Hebrew U., Israel, 1981, U. Bologna, 1989, Northwestern U., 1992, Moscow State U., 1996; Karon meml. lectr. U. So. Calif., 1983; Seham lectr. U. Minn., 1983; Harris lectr. Va. Commonwealth U., 1995; Markey lectr. Wash. U., 1996; Green lectr. European Molecular Biology Lab. Heidelberg, 1997; Walter Rubin meml. lectr. Drexel U., 2003; John Conley lectr. in med. ethics Am. Acad. Otolaryngology, 2003; vis. dean U. Mich., 2003. Author: Cancer in the Young, 1982; editor-in-chief The New Biologist, 1989-92; contbr. articles to profl. jours. Recipient Disting. Alumnus award Chgo. Med. Sch., 1972, NIH Dir.'s award, 1984, Meritorious Svc. award USPHS, 1987, Disting. Svc. award, 1991, Surgeon Gen.'s Exemplary Svc. award, 1993. Mem. AAAS, Am. Soc. Clin. Investigation, Soc. Pediatric Research, Am. Assn. Cancer Research, Am. Soc. Hematology, Am. Soc. Clin. Oncology, Am. Fedn. Clin. Research, Am. Soc. Microbiology, Am. Soc. Pediatric Hematology/Oncology, Alpha Omega Alpha. Office: U Pittsburgh 3550 Terrace St Pittsburgh PA 15261-0001 Home Phone: 412-687-4007; Office Phone: 412-648-8975. Business E-Mail: alevine@hs.pitt.edu.

LEVINE, AUDREY PEARLSTEIN, foundation administrator; b. NYC, July 6, 1934; d. Irving and Flora Malkin Pearlstein; m. Arthur Levine, Mar. 15, 1958; children: Michael S., Charles T., Andrew S. Student, Hofstra U., 1952, student, 1957. Sec., treas. Pearlstein Found., 1976—2006, pres., 2007—; gen. ptnr. Adams County Realty LLP, McSherrystown, Pa., 2003—. Specialist trade shows Stone Care Internat. Inc., Owings Mills, Md., 1991—; adminstr., gen. ptnr. Pearlstein Partnership, Palm Beach, Fla., 1998—; gen. ptnr. Audrey Realty, Pikesville, Md., 2003—07. V.p. PTA Ft. Garrison Sch., Pikesville, Md., 1968—69; chmn. Hadassah Ho. & Garden Tour, Balt., Palm Beach, 1969, 1970, 1999, Booster Club Pikesville H.S., Pikesville, 1970, 1971, 1975—76, 1980—82; v.p. PTA Pikesville Sr. HS, Pikesville, 1970, 1976, 1980—82; v.p. parents-student bd. Am. U., Washington, 1978—79, 1984—86; chmn. Save Ft. Garrison, Pikesville, 1965—66, 2001; mem. com. Senator Henry Jackson Save Soviet Jews, Washington, 1972—73; v.p. Jewish Nat. Fund Women, Balt., 1973—75; pres. Balt. Suburban Hadassah, 1963—64; dedication chmn. Jerusalem stone wall for peace and freedom and for victims of 9-11 Har Sinai Congregation, Owings Mills, 2005; bd. dirs. Women's Aux. Sinai Hosp., Balt., 1985—88, Nat. Coun. Johns Hopkins, Balt., 1990—92, Pikesville Recreation Coun., Pikesville, 1968—71; chmn. Rededication of Fort Garrison, Pikesville, Md. Mem.: Nat. Mus. Women in the Arts (charter). Republican. Jewish. Avocations: sculpting, painting, flower arranging, boating, tennis. Home (Winter): Bldg 1 Apt 2A 2500 S Ocean Blvd Palm Beach FL 33480 Home (Summer): 3421 Garrison Farms Rd Pikesville MD 21208 Office: Audrey Levine Trust 2500 S Ocean Blvd Apt 2A Palm Beach FL 33480-5401 Personal E-mail: levineaa@verizon.net.

LEVINE, BENJAMIN, lawyer; b. May 22, 1931; s. George and Frances (Levovsky) L.; m. Arleen Ella Rosenblatt, Jan. 14, 1962; children: Joshua, Sarah. BA, U. Conn., 1953; JD, Rutgers U., 1963. Bar: N.Mex. 1964, N.Y. 1965, N.J. 1967, U.S. Supreme Ct. 1980; cert. trial atty., 1986; diplomate Nat. Bd. Trial Advocacy, 1989. Law clk. N.Mex. Sup. Ct., 1963-64; spl. asst. N.J. Commr. Conservation and Econ. Devel., 1965-67; dep. atty. gen. State of N.J., 1967-70; pvt. practice Newark and NYC, 1970—. Adj. prof. law Ramapo Coll., Mahwah, N.J., 1978-80; arbitrator U.S. Dist. Ct. N.J., 1989. Author: Medical Malpractice; Zoning Guide for Local Officals; contbr. articles to profl. jours. Pres. Environ. Action Inst. N.J., 1977-80; chmn. North Plainfield (N.J.) Environ. Commn., 1974-76; trustee South Branch Watershed Assn., 1976-80, Rabbinical Coll. Am., 1994—. Lt. (j.g.) USN, 1956-60. Mem.: ATLA, Million Dollar Advocates Forum, NY County Lawyers Assn. (chmn. state legis. com. 1976—80, mem. com. on constn., com. on civil cts. 1980—82), Am. Arbitration Assn. (nat. panel arbitrators 1973—), NJ Bar Assn. (bd. dirs. med.mal.com, cert. trial lawyers sect.). Office: 111 Dunnell Rd Maplewood NJ 07040 Office Phone: 973-378-8850. Office Fax: 973-378-8852. Personal E-mail: levine@ix.netcom.com.

LEVINE, C. BRUCE, lawyer; b. Liberty, NY, Aug. 20, 1945; Student, Stanford U.; AB magna cum laude, UCLA, 1967; JD cum laude, Harvard U., 1971. Bar: Calif. 1971, US Tax Ct. Mem. Greenberg, Glusker, Fields, Claman & Machtinger, LA, 1971—; ptnr. Greenberg Glusker, LA. Spkr. in various fields. Mem. State Bar Calif., LA County Bar Assn. (chmn. income tax com. tax sect. 1979-80), Beverly Hills Bar Assn. (chmn. taxation com. 1977-78), Phi Beta Kappa, Pi Gamma Mu. Office: Greenberg Glusker 1900 Ave of Stars 21st Fl Los Angeles CA 90067 Office Phone: 310-201-7440. Business E-Mail: blevine@ggfirm.com.

LEVINE, DANIEL, historian, educator; b. NYC, Dec. 31, 1934; s. Morris Simeon and Margaret (Hirsch) L.; m. Susan Rose, July 29, 1954; children— Timothy, Karen. BA in History, Antioch Coll., 1956; PhD in History (Woodrow Wilson fellow, Social Sci Research Council fellow), Northwestern U., 1961. Asst. prof. history Earlham Coll., 1960-63; asst. prof. Bowdoin Coll., Brunswick, Maine, 1963-66, assoc. prof., 1966-72, prof., 1972—, Thomas Bracket Reed prof. history and polit. sci., 1974—. Fulbright sr. lectr., Munich, 1979-80; vis. prof. U. Copenhagen, 1991. Author: Varieties of Reform Thought, 1964, Jane Addams and the Liberal Tradition, 1971, Poverty and Society, 1988, Bayard Rustin and the Civil Rights Movement, 2000; contbr. articles to profl. jours; editl. bd.: Explorations in Entrepreneurial History, 1962-70. Bd. dirs. Maine Civil Liberties Union, 1988-94. Fulbright lectr. Denmark, 1969-70; mem. jury Ralph Waldo Emerson prize Phi Beta Kappa, 1973-74; Guggenheim fellow, 1972-73. Mem. Am. Hist. Assn., Orgn. Am. Historians, AAUP, Social Welfare History Group (v.p. 1975-76), Arbeitskreis: Geschichte Sozialer Sicherung un Sozialer Disziplinierung. Democrat. Home: 785 Mere Point Rd Brunswick ME 04011 Office: Bowdoin Coll History Dept Brunswick ME 04011 Office Phone: 207-725-3293. Business E-Mail: dlevine@bowdoin.edu.

LEVINE, DANIEL BLANK, classical studies educator; b. Cin., July 22, 1953; s. Joseph and Elizabeth (Blank) L.; m. Judith Robinson, Aug. 14, 1984; children: Sarah Ruth, Amy Elizabeth. Student, Am. Sch. Classical Studies, Athens, 1974, student, 1978—79; BA in Greek and Latin magna cum laude, U. Minn., 1975; PhD in Classics, U. Cin., 1980. Seymour fellow Am. Sch. Classical Studies, 1978-79; asst. prof. U. Ark., 1980-84, assoc. prof., 1984-98, prof., 1998—. Dir. Summer Session Am. Sch. Classical Studies, Athens, 1987, 95, 2006; dir. study tour in Greece Vergilian Soc., 1990, Greece Univ. Ark., 2000-01, 03, 05, 07; referee Classical Jour., 1984-88, Helios, 1984-88, Cornell U. Press, 1988-89, 91—, Classical Outlook, 1988-89; panelist NEH, Washington, 1986; co-dir., instr. gifted and talented HS students summer program State of Ark. Dept. Edn. Grant, 1988; mng. com. Am. Sch. Classical Studies Athens, 1991—. Contbr. articles to profl. jours. Grantee NEH 1981-84, 92; recipient Outstanding Tchr. award Mortar Bd. Sr. Honor Soc., U. Ark., 1991, Master Tchr. award Fulbright Coll., 1995. Mem. Am. Philological Assn. (Excellence in Teaching Classics award 1992), Am. Classical League, Classical Assn. Mid. West and South (Ovatio 1996, v.p. com. promotion Latin in Ark. 1980-86, 91-95, chmn. regional rep. com. for promotion Latin, Outstanding State V.P. for 1982-83), U. Ark. Teaching Acad., Golden Key, Phi Beta Kappa. Home: 904 Park Ave Fayetteville AR 72701-2027 Office: U Ark Dept Fgn Langs 425 Kimpel Hall Fayetteville AR 72701 Business E-Mail: dlevine@uark.edu.

LEVINE, DAVID, artist; b. Bklyn., Dec. 20, 1926; s. Harry L.; children: Matthew, Eve. B.F.A., Temple U., 1949, BS in Edn, 1949; postgrad., Hans Hoffman Sch. Paintings, 1950. One-man shows Forum Gallery, N.Y.C., 1966—, Ga. Mus. Art, 1968, Calif. Palace Legion of Honor, 1968-69, 71-72, 83, Wesleyan U., 1970, Bklyn. Mus., 1971, Princeton U., 1972, Galerie Yves Lambert, Paris, 1972, Yale U., 1973, Hirshhorn Mus. and Sculpture Garden, Washington, 1976, Galerie Claude Bernard, 1979, Phillips Gallery, 1980, Pierpont Morgan Library, 1981, Santa Fe East Gallery, 1983, Ash Molean Mus., Meredith Long, Houston, 1984; represented by Forum Gallery; author: The Man From M.A.L.I.C.E., 1966, Pens and Needles, 1969, No Known Survivors, 1970, The Arts of David Levine, 1978, Aesop's Fables. Served with U.S. Army, 1945-46. Recipient Tiffany award, 1955, Isaac N. Maynard prize, 1958, Julius Halligarten prize, 1960, Thomas B. Clark prize, 1962, George Polk award, 1965, Childe Hassam Purchase prize 1972, Benjamin Altman prize, 1973, Gold medal for Graphic Work, Am. Acad. Inst. Arts and Letters, 1992, Thomas Nast award, 1995; Guggenheim fellow, 1967. Mem. AAAL, Century Assn. Address: care Forum Gallery 745 5th Ave New York NY 10151-0099 Office Phone: 718-522-1808.

LEVINE, DAVID ETHAN, lawyer; b. Niagara Falls, NY, Feb. 28, 1955; s. Morree Morell Levine and Marbud Juel (Gagen) Prozeller; m. Ann Lee Ruhlin, May 23, 1981. BS in Bus., Miami U., 1977; JD, Capital U., 1981. Bar: N.Y. 1982, U.S. Dist. Ct. (we. dist.) N.Y. 1982. Assoc. Grossman, Levine and Civiletto, Niagara Falls, 1981-89, Cummings and Levine, Niagara Falls, 1989-92; pvt. practice Niagara Falls, 1992—. Mem. N.Y. State Bar Assn., Pitt. Ski Club., Recumbenteers Bicycle Club, Adirondack Mountain Club. Unitarian Universalist. Avocations: skiing, photography, bicycling, hiking. Home: 22 Hemlock Dr Grand Island NY 14072-3315 Office: PO Box 456 669 Main St Niagara Falls NY 14302 Home Phone: 716-775-3325; Office Phone: 716-284-2306. E-mail: del14072@aol.com.

LEVINE, ELLEN R., editor-in-chief; b. NYC, Feb. 19, 1943; d. Eugene Jack and Jean (Zuckman) Jacobson; m. Richard U. Levine, Dec. 21, 1964; children: Daniel, Peter. Student, Wellesley Coll. Reporter The Record, Hackensack, NJ, 1964—70; editor Cosmopolitan mag., NYC, 1976—82; editor-in-chief Cosmopolitan Living mag., NYC, 1980—81, Woman's Day mag., NYC, 1982—91, Redbook mag., NYC, 1991—94, Good Housekeeping, NYC, 1994—2006; editorial cons. O, The Oprah Mag., 2000—; editl. dir. Hearst Magazines, NYC, 2006—. Commr. U.S. Atty. Gen.'s Commn. on Pornography, 1985—86; bd. dirs. Finlay Enterprises, Inc., Lifetime TV; bd. adv. NY Women in Comm.; bd. dir. Gaylord Entertainment, 2004—. Author: Planning Your Wedding, Waiting for Baby, Rooms That Grow With Your Child; mem. editl. bd. O mag.; contbr. articles to profl. jours. Bd. dirs. Lifetime TV, Christopher Reeve Paralysis Found., NY Restoration Project. Named to Writers Hall of Fame, 1981, Acad. Women Achievers, YWCA, 1982; recipient Outstanding Profl. Achievement award, N.J. Fedn. Women's Clubs, 1984, Matrix award, N.Y. Women in Comm., Inc., 1989, Am. Health Found., 1996, 2d Century award, Columbia U. Sch. Nursing, 1997, Nat. Mag. award for personal svc., 1999. Mem.: Am. Soc. Mag. Editors (named to Hall of Fame). Achievements include being first woman named editor-in-chief of Good Housekeeping. Office: Hearst Magazines 959 8th Ave New York NY 10019 E-mail: elevine@hearst.com.

LEVINE, FELICE J., educational association administrator; AB in Psychology, U. Chgo., AM in Sociology and Psych., PhD in Psychology. Sr. rsch. social scientist Am. Bar Found., 1974—79; prog. dir. law and social sci. NSF, 1979—91; exec. officer Am. Sociol. Assn., Washington, 1991—2002; exec. dir. Am. Ednl. Rsch. Assn., Washington, 2002—. Mem. nat. human rsch. protections adv. com. HHS, co-chair social and behavioral sci. working group; exec. com. Consortium Social Sci. Assns., chair, 1997—2000; mem. adv. com. Decennial Census; bd. mem. Nat. Humanities Alliance; mem. adv. com. Nat. Consortium Violence Rsch. Fellow: AAAS, Am. Psychol. Soc. Office: Am Ednl Rsch Assn 1230 Seventeenth St NW Washington DC 20036 Office Phone: 202-223-9485. Office Fax: 202-775-1824.*

LEVINE, GAIL CARSON, writer; b. NYC, Sept. 17, 1947; d. David and Sylvia Carson; m. David Matthew Levine, Sept. 2, 1967. BA, CCNY, 1969. Employment interviewer NY State Dept. of Labor, NYC, 1970—82; adminstrv. asst. NY State Dept. of Commerce, NYC, 1982—86; welfare adminstr. NY State Dept. of Social Services, NYC, 1986—96. Author: (children's books) Ella Enchanted, 1997 (Newbery Honor Book, 1998), Dave at Night, 1999, The Fairy's Mistake, 1999, The Princess Test, 1999, Princess Sonora and the Long Sleep, 1999, The Wish, 2000, Cinderellis and the Glass Hill, 2000, The Two Princesses of Bamarre, 2001, For Biddle's Sake, 2002, The Fairy's Return, 2002, (children's picture book) Betsy Who Cried Wolf, 2002, Fairy Dust and the Quest for the Egg, 2005. Mem.: Soc. Children's Book Writers and Illustrators, PEN, Author's Guild. Office: HarperCollins Children's Books 1350 Ave of Americas New York NY 10019

LEVINE, GEORGE LEWIS, literature and language professor, critic; b. NYC, Aug. 27, 1931; s. Harris Julius and Dorothy Sara (Podolsky) L.; m. Margaret Bloom, Aug. 19, 1956; children: David Michael, Rachel Susan. BA, NYU, 1952; MA, U. Minn., 1953, PhD, 1959. Instr. Ind. U., Bloomington, 1959-62, asst. prof., 1962-65, assoc. prof., 1965-68; prof. English Rutgers U., New Brunswick, NJ, 1968—2006, chmn. dept., 1979-83, Kenneth Burke prof., 1985—2006, prof. emeritus, 2006—. Vis. prof. U. Calif.-Berkeley, 1968, Stanford U., Calif., 1974-75; vis. rsch. fellow Girton Coll., Cambridge U., Eng., 1983; Avalon prof. lit. Northwestern U., 1998; dir. Ctr. Critical Analysis of Contemp. Culture, 1998-2006; disting. vis. scholar, NYU, 2007-. Author: Boundaries of Fiction, 1968, The Endurance of Frankenstein, 1975, The Realistic Imagination, 1981, One Culture, 1987, Darwin and the Novelists, 1988, Lifebirds, 1995, Dying to Know, 2002, Darwin Loves You, 2006; author, editor: The Art of Victorian Prose, 1968, Mindful Pleasures, 1975, Constructions of the Self, 1992, Realism and Representation, 1993, Aesthetics and Ideology, The Politics of Research, 1994, Cambridge Companion to George Eliot; editor Victorian Studies, 1959-68. With US Army, 1953—55. Guggenheim Found. fellow, 1971-72; NEH fellow, 1978-79; Rockefeller Found. fellow, 1983; Rockefeller Found. Bellagio fellow, 1996, Bogliasco Found. fellow, 1999, 2004. Mem. MLA, AAUP Democrat. Jewish. Home: 108 Wesley Ave Atlantic Highlands NJ 07716 E-mail: georlevine@gmail.com.

LEVINE, GEORGE RICHARD, language educator; b. Boston, Aug. 5, 1929; s. Jacob U. and Rose Lillian (Margolis) L.; m. Joan Adler, June 8, 1958 (div. 1977); children— David, Michael; m. Linda Rashman, Apr. 17, 1977. BA, Tufts Coll., Medford, Mass., 1951; MA, Columbia, 1952, PhD, 1961. Lectr. English Columbia, 1956-58; instr. Northwestern U., 1959-63; mem. faculty SUNY, Buffalo, 1963—2001, prof. emeritus, 2001—; prof. English State U. N.Y., 1970—, dean faculty arts and letters, 1975-81. Author: Henry Fielding and The Dry Mock, 1967; editor: Harp on the Shore: Thoreau and the Sea, 1985, Jonathan Swift: A Modest Proposal and Other Satires, 1995; contbr. articles to profl. jours. Chmn. bd. dirs. Youth Orch. Found., Buffalo, 1974-75; trustee Buffalo Chamber Music Soc., Arts Devel. Svcs.; bd. dirs. Buffalo Philharm. Orch., 1992-97; pres. Arts in Edn. Inst. Western N.Y. With AUS, 1952-54. Univ. fellow Columbia U., 1958-59, Faculty Research fellow SUNY, 1966-67; Fulbright lectr. W. Ger., 1969-70; recipient Chancellor's award excellence in teaching SUNY, Buffalo, 1973-74. Mem. MLA, Am. Soc. 18th Century Studies, Internat. Assn. Univ. Profs. English, Adirondack Mountain Club. Jewish. Home: 66 Woodbury Dr Snyder NY 14226 Business E-Mail: grlevine@buffalo.edu.

LEVINE, HARVEY DAVIS, retired dentist; b. Bklyn., Dec. 22, 1920; s. William and Minnie Levine; m. Sylvia Shulman, Aug. 17, 1945; children: James Daniel, Matthew Paul. BA, Bklyn Coll., 1944; DDS, NYU, NYC, 1945. Pvt. practice, NYC, 1946—87. Sr. clin. asst. dept. dentistry Poly. Hosp., NYC, 1946—52; instr. crown and bridge dept. NYU Coll. Dentistry, NYC, 1946—52. Photographer (exhibitions) NY Scenes, Fla. Maritime Mus. Lt. USNR, 1945—46, lt. USNR, 1952—54. Mem.: ADA, First Dist. Dental Soc., Omicron Kappa Upsilon. Avocations: kayaking, sailing, canoeing, boat building. Home: 3410 Winding Oaks Dr Longboat Key FL 34228-4125 Office: Florida Maratime Museum at Cortez 4415 119th St West Cortez FL 34215

LEVINE, HARVEY ROBERT, lawyer; b. NYC, Aug. 17, 1944; married; 2 children. BS, LI U., 1966; JD, St. Mary's U., 1970, NYU, 1972, JSD, 1974. Bar: Calif, (NY), (Tex.). Ptnr. Levine Steinberg Miller & Huver LLP. Prof. law U. San Diego, 1972—92; bd. dirs. Children's Advocacy Inst., San Diego County Bar Found., YMCA Youth & Family Services. Author: (Law Guide) Ins. Bad Faith Litigation, 1984, Calif. Practice Guide: Bad Faith, 1986, Levine on Trial Advocacy: Jury Selection, 2004, Levine on Trial Advocacy: Opening Statement, 2005; editor: Bad Faith Law Update, 1986; contbr. articles to profl. jours. Named a Trial Lawyer of the Year, San Diego Trial Lawyers Assn., 1981, 1986, Consumer Atty. of San Diego, 2002; named an Outstanding Trial Lawyer, San Diego Trial Lawyers Assn., 1981, 1987, 1990; recipient Bernard E. Witkin Award, San Diego, 2000, Robert E. Cartwright, Sr. Award, 1999, Spl. Recognition for Consumer Advocacy, Consumer Attorneys of San Diego, 1998, 2000. Office: Levine Steinberg Miller & Huver LLP 550 W C St Ste 1810 San Diego CA 92101-8596 Office Phone: 619-231-9449. Office Fax: 619-231-8638. E-mail: hlevine@levinelaw.com.*

LEVINE, HENRY DAVID, lawyer; b. NYC, June 7, 1951; s. Harold Abraham and Joan Sarah (Price) L.; m. Barbara Wolgel, Aug. 28, 1976; children: David, Rachel, Daniel. AB, Yale U., 1972; JD, Harvard U., 1976, M in Pub. Policy, 1976. Bar: N.Y. 1977, D.C. 1978, U.S. Supreme Ct. 1980. Assoc. Wilmer, Cutler & Pickering, Washington, 1976-80, Morrison & Foerster, Washington, 1981-83, ptnr., 1983-92, Levine, Blaszak, Block & Boothby LLP, Washington, 1993—. Cons. to GSA on FTS2001 and successor programs, 1994-; chmn. bd. TechCaliber, LLC, 1999-; mem. exec. bd. NY Telecon Reliability Adv. Coun., 2005-. Bd. dirs. Washington Hebrew Congregation, 1996—, pres., 2006—; bd. dirs. Appleseed Found., 2001—. Named one of the twenty-five most powerful people in networking Network World, 1996. Mem. ABA, Fed. Communication Bar Assn., Forum Com. on Comm. Law. Home: 5208 Edgemoor Ln Bethesda MD 20814-2342 Office: Levine Blaszak Block & Boothby 2001 L St NW Ste 900 Washington DC 20036-4940 Office Phone: 202-857-2550. Business E-Mail: hlevine@lb3law.com.

LEVINE, HERBERT, lawyer; b. June 5, 1924; s. Barnet and Mollie (Morris) L.; m. Pearl H. Kahn, Mar. 30, 1946; children: Barbara, Susan, Deborah, Steven. BBA, JD, U. Wis., 1950. Bar: Wis. 1950, U.S. Dist. Ct. (ea. dist.) Wis. 1950. Pvt. practice, Milw., 1950-66; assoc. Bernstein, Wessel & Lewis, Milw., 1967-75; shareholder Stupar, Schuster & Cooper S.C., Milw., 1976-2000; sole practitioner Milw., 2000—. Instr. Am. Inst. Banking, Milw., 1964-88; lectr. Marquette U., 1968-79, Milw. Bd. Realtors, 1961. Pres. Bayside PTA, Wis., 1965-66; active Indian Guides, Bayside, Wis., 1972-73. Sgt. USAAF, 1943-46. Mem. Wis. Bar Assn., Milw. Bar Assn. Home: 9055 N King Rd Milwaukee WI 53217-1848 Office: 633 W Wisconsin Ave Milwaukee WI 53203-1918 Office Phone: 414-271-8833. E-mail: ssc@ssclaw.com.

LEVINE, HOWARD ARNOLD, judge; b. Mar. 4, 1932; m. Barbara Joan Segall, July 25, 1954; children: Neil Louis, Ruth Ellen, James Robert. BA, Yale U., 1953, LLB, 1956; LLD (hon.), Union U., 1994. Bar: N.Y. 1956. Asst. in instrn., research assoc. in criminal law Yale Law Sch., 1956-57; assoc. firm Hughes, Hubbard, Blair, Reed, NYC, 1957-59; practiced in Schenectady, 1959-70; asst. dist. atty. Schenectady County, NY, 1961-66, dist. atty., 1967-70; judge Schenectady County Family Ct., 1971-80; acting judge Schenectady County Ct., 1971-80; adminstrv. judge family cts. N.Y. State 4th Jud. Dist., 1974-80; assoc. justice appellate div. 3d dept. N.Y. State Supreme Ct., 1982-93; assoc. judge N.Y. Ct. of Appeals, 1993—2003; sr. counsel Whiteman, Osterman & Hanna, Albany, NY, 2003—. Vis. lectr. Albany Law Sch., 1972-81; mem. N.Y. Gov.'s Panel on Juvenile Violence, N.Y. State Temp. Commn. on Child Welfare, N.Y. State Temp. Commn. on Recodification of Family Ct. Act, N.Y. State Juvenile Justice Adv. Bd., 1974-80; mem. ind. rev. bd. N.Y. State Div. for Youth, 1974-80; mem. rules and adv. com. on family ct. N.Y. State Jud. Conf., 1974-80 Contbr. articles to law revs. Bd. dirs. Schnecatady County Child Guildance Ctr., Carver Community Ctr., Freedom Forum of Schnectady. Mem. ABA, Am. Law Inst., N.Y. State Bar Assn. (chmn. spl. com. juvenile justice), Assn. Family Ct. Judges State N.Y. (pres. 1979-80) Home: 2701 Rosendale Rd Niskayuna NY 12309-1300 Office: Whiteman Osterman & Hanna One Commerce Plz Albany NY 12210 Office Phone: 518-487-7684.

LEVINE, HOWARD R., retail executive; b. 1959; With merchandising dept. Family Dollar Stores, Matthews, NC, 1981-87, v.p., gen. merchandise mgr. softlines, 1996, sr. v.p. merchandising and advt., 1996-97, pres., COO, 1997-98, CEO, 1998—2003, chmn., CEO, 2003—. Office: Family Dollar Stores PO Box 1017 Charlotte NC 28201-1017*

LEVINE, IRVING R., commentator, dean, writer, educator; b. Pawtucket, RI; s. Joseph and Emma (Raskin) L.; m. Nancy Cartmell Jones, July 12, 1957; children— Jeffrey Claybourne Bond, Daniel Rome, Jennifer Jones. BS, Brown U., Providence, RI, 1944, LHD (hon.), 1969; MS, Columbia U., NYC, 1947; LHD (hon.), Bryant Coll., Smithfield, RI, 1974; D.Journalism (hon.), Roger Williams Coll., 1985; LLD (hon.), U. RI, Kingston, 1988; LHD (hon.), Lynn U., Boca Raton, Fla., 1992; LLD (hon.), Northeastern U., Boston, 1993; D.Journalism (hon.), RI Coll., Providence, 1996. Writer obits. Providence Jour., 1940-43; fgn. news editor Internat. News Service, 1947-48; chief Vienna (Austria) bur., 1948-50; with NBC, 1950-95, war corr. in Korea, 1950-52; radio anchor World News Roundup, NYC, 1953-54; chief corr. NBC, Moscow, 1955-59, Rome, 1959-71, London, 1967-68, chief econs. corr. Washington, 1971-95; dean emeritus Coll. Internat. Comms., Lynn U., Boca Raton, Fla., 1995—. Commentator Consumer News and Bus. Channel Cable TV affiliate svc. NBC TV News, 1990-96; commentator Pub. Broadcasting Sys. TV, Nightly Bus. Report, 1997—; spl. writer London Times, 1955-59; covered assignments in Can., China, Czechoslovakia, Bulgaria, Poland, Japan, Vietnam, Formosa, Thailand, Eng., France, Germany, Switzerland, Algeria, Congo, Israel, Turkey, Tunisia, Greece, Yugoslavia, Union of South Africa, Denmark, Sweden, Ireland; press group with pres. Ford, Carter, Reagan, Bush, Clinton; attended G-7 Econ. Summits, 1975-95; world affairs lectr. Holland Am. Cruise Line. 1995-97, Cunard Cruise Line, 1998-2001, Radisson Seven Seas Cruise Line, 2000-04, Celebrity Cruise Lines, 2004—; lectr. univs., bus. groups, cruise ships; writer Internet World Traveler Column, 1997-99; moderator Bus. Update TV Program, Fla. TV programs, 1998-99; nat. spokesperson First Penn-Pacific Life Ins. Co., 1997-99; anchor Bus. Trends TV program, 2000. Author: Main Street, USSR, 1959, Travel Guide to Russia, 1960, Main Street, Italy, 1963, The New Worker in Soviet Russia, 1973; contbr. articles to nat. mags.; guest on numerous TV shows including Johnny Carson, 1960, Murphy Brown, 1989, David Letterman Show, 1990, Jay Leno Show, 1990. 2d lt. Signal Corps, U.S. Army, 1943-46, Philippines, Japan. Recipient award for best radio-TV reporting from abroad Overseas Press Club, 1956, award for outstanding radio network broadcasting Nat. Headliners Club, 1957, 50th Anniversary award Columbia Sch. Journalism, 1963, Emmy citation 1966, Martin R. Gainsbrugh award for best econ. reporting, 1978, William Rogers award Brown U., 1988, Silver Circle award Nat. Acad. TV Arts and Scis., 1990; named one of 10 Outstanding Young Men, U.S. Jaycees, 1956; named to R.I. Hall of Fame, 1972, Pawtucket Hall of Fame, 1986, Nat. Broadcasters Hall of Fame Lifetime Achievement award, 1995, TJFR and Master Card award as one of 100 top bus. news luminaries, 2000; named Among 100 Most accomplished Grads. 20th Century Brown Alumni mag., 2000; honoree Loyola Coll.'s Beta Gamma Sigma, 1994, Mem. Coun. on Fgn. Rels. (fellowship 1952-53), Cosmos, Phi Beta Kappa, Beta Gamma Sigma. Office: Lynn U 3601 N Military Trail Boca Raton FL 33431-5598

LEVINE, JACK, artist; b. Boston, Jan. 3, 1915; s. Samuel Mayer and Mary (Grinker) L.; widowed; 1 child, Susanna Levine Fisher. AFD, Colby Coll., Waterville, Maine, 1956. One-man shows include Downtown Gallery, N.Y.C., 1938, Artists, 1942, Mus. Modern Art, N.Y.C., 1943; exhibited in group shows at Jeu de Paume, Paris, 1938, Carnegie Internat. exhbns., 1938-40, Artists for Victory, Met. Mus., N.Y.C., 1942, retrospective at Jewish Mus., N.Y.C., 1978-79, Bklyn. Mus., 1999; represented in permanent collections Mus. Modern Art, Met. Mus. Art, N.Y.C., William Hayes Foggs Mus., Harvard U., Addison Gallery, Andover, Mass., Mus. Vatican, D.C. Moore Gallery, N.Y., DeYoung Mus., San Francisco. With AUS, 1942-45. Mem. Am. Acad. Arts and Letters (pres., chancellor), Inst. Arts and Letters (pres. 1993), Nat. Acad. Design, Century Club.

LEVINE, JACK ANTON, lawyer; b. Monticello, NY, Dec. 23, 1946; s. Milton and Sara (Sacks) L.; m. Eileen A. Garsh, Sept. 7, 1974; children: Matthew Aaron, Dara Esther. BS with honors, SUNY, Binghamton, 1968; JD with honors, U. Fla., 1975, LLM in Taxation, 1976. Bar: Fla. 1975, U.S. Ct. Appeals (11th cir.) 1981, U.S. Tax Ct., 1982. Tax atty. legis. and regulations divsn. Office chief counsel IRS, Washington, 1977-81; assoc. Holland & Knight, Tampa, Fla., 1981-83, ptnr., 1984—. Lectr. in field. Contbr. articles to profl. jours. Mem. ABA, Fla. Bar Assn. (sect. taxation exec. coun. 1984-2003, chmn. partnership com. 1985-88, chmn. taxation regulated pub. utilities com. 1988-92, co-chmn. corps. and tax-exempt orgns. com. 1992-2001, bd. cert. in tax law 1984—). Democrat. Jewish. Avocations: golf, reading, travel. Home: 10905 Carrollwood Dr Tampa FL 33618-3903 Office: Holland & Knight Ste 4100 100 N Tampa St Tampa FL 33602-3644 Home Phone: 813-933-9877; Office Phone: 813-227-6531. E-mail: jack.levine@hklaw.com.

LEVINE, JAMES, conductor, music director, pianist; b. Cin., June 23, 1943; s. Lawrence M. and Helen (Goldstein) Levine. Studied theory and interpretation with Walter Levin, studied piano with Rosina Lhevinne and Rudolf Serkin, studied conducting with Jean Morel, Fausto Cleva and Max Rudolf; student, Juilliard Sch. Music, 1961—64; degree (hon.), U. Cin., New Eng. Conservatory, Northwestern U., SUNY, Potsdam, The Juilliard Sch. Debut as pianist Cin. Symphony Orch., 1953; debut as condr. Aspen (Colo.) Music Festival, 1961; asst. condr. Cleve. Orch., 1964—70; condr. The Met. Opera, NYC, 1971—73, prin. condr., 1973—75, music dir., 1976—85, 2004—, artistic dir., 1986—2004; chief condr. Munich Philharm., 1999—2004; music dir. UBS Verbier Festival Orch., 2000—04, Boston Symphony Orch., Boston, 2004—, Ravinia Festival, Highland Park, Ill., 1973—93, Cin. May Festival, 1974—78; guest condr. Vienna Philharm. Orch., Berlin Philharm. Orch., Chgo. Symphony Orch., Phila. Orch., Boston Symphony Orch., NY Philharm. Orch., Dresden Staatskapelle, Philharmonia Orch., Israel Philharm. Orch., Bayreuth Festival, Salzburg Festival. Recipient Nat. Medal of Arts, 1997, Kennedy Ctr. Honors, 2002, 8 Grammy awards. Office: The Met Opera Lincoln Ctr New York NY 10023

LEVINE, JANICE R., clinical psychologist; b. Cleve., Mar. 4, 1954; d. Bennett and Lenore (Tracht) L.; m. Brian Richard Igoe, Aug. 31, 1980; children: Brennan Joseph, Sarah Ann. BA cum laude, Yale U., 1976; MA, Harvard U., 1979, PhD, 1983. Lic. psychologist, Mass. Sr. ptnr., cons. Cambridge Consortium, Mass.; staff psychologist Ayer Clinic, Mass.; lectr. psychology Harvard U., Cambridge, Mass. Sch. Profl. Psychology, Boston; pvt. practice clin. psychologist Lexington, Mass. Lectr., pub. speaker, workshop leader, cons. in field. Author: (book) The Couples' Health Program; co-author: (books) Beyond the Chuppah, 2000, (with Howard Markman) Why Do Fools Fall in Love, 2001. Founder Third Thursday Parent Edn. Series, Lexington, dir.; bd. dirs. Terezin Chamber Music Found. Margaret Yardley fellow, 1980, Devel. Trainee fellow NIH, 1978-79. Mem. APA, MPA. Office: 76 Bedford St Ste 19 Lexington MA 02420-4640

LEVINE, JEFFREY E., real estate developer; BS in Architecture, CUNY City Coll. Sch. Arch. Pres. Levine Builders, 1979—; prin. Douglaston Develop. Mem. bd. gov. Real Estate Bd. N.Y.; bd. mem. Citizens Housing and Planning Coun., NY Housing Conf. Named Assoc. Builders and Owners Greater NY Develop. Yr., 1997; recipient Nat. Assn. Homebuilders Pillars of Industry, 1997, Entrepreneur Yr., Ernst & Young, 1997, Develop. Yr., NY Housing Conf., 2000, Cmty. Builder award, Phipps Houses, 2003. Mem.: Nat. Assn. Homebuilders (BUILD-PAC trustee). Office: Levine Builders 42-09 235th St Douglaston NY 11363 Office Phone: 718-224-7147. Office Fax: 718-224-1397.

LEVINE, JENNY, library and information scientist, writer; MLS, U. Ill., Urbana-Champaign, 1992. Tech. coord. Grande Prairie Pub. Libr. Dist., Hazel Crest, Ill., 1996; internet devel. specialist Met. Libr. Sys. (formerly Suburban Libr. Sys.), Burr Ridge, Ill.; internet devel. specialist, strategy guide info. tech. and telecommunication svcs. and pub. ALA, 2006—. Creator (websites) Librarians' Site du Jour, 1995; blogger: ALA TechSource, 2005— (named one of 10 Blogs to Read in 2006, Libr. and Info. Sci. News), The Shifted Librarian. Office: ALA 50 E Huron St Chicago IL 60611 Office Phone: 312-280-2461. Business E-Mail: jenny@theshiftedlibrarian.com, jlevine@ala.org.

LEVINE, JEROME, psychiatrist, educator; b. NYC, July 10, 1934; s. Abraham and Sadie (Glowatz) L.; children: Ross W., Lynn R., Andrew R. BA, U. Buffalo, 1954, MD, 1958. Intern, then psychiat. resident E.J. Meyer Meml. Hosp., Buffalo, 1958-61; sr. psychiat. resident St. Elizabeth's Hosp., Washington, 1961-62; staff psychiatrist USPHS Hosp., Lexington, Ky., 1962-64; research psychiatrist, asst. chief psychopharmacology research br. NIMH, 1964-67, chief of br., 1967-81, chief pharmacologic and somatic treatments research br., 1981-84; research prof. psychiatry U. Md. Sch. Medicine, Balt., 1985-94; dep. dir. Nathan Kline Inst. for Psychiat. Rsch., Orangeburg, NY, 1994—; rsch. prof. psychiatry NYU, 1994—. Instr. psychiatry Johns Hopkins Med. Sch., 1964-72; vis. prof. U. Pisa, Italy, 1977 Author books and papers on psychopharmacology, clin. trial methodology, somatic treatment assessment for psychiat. disorders. Mem. Soc. Clin. Trials, Am. Psychiat. Assn. (Hofheimer Research prize 1970), Am. Coll. Neuropsychopharmacology, Collegium Internationale Neuropsychopharmacologicum, Am. Soc. Clin. Pharmacology and Therapeutics. Home: 15 Stony Hollow Chappaqua NY 10514-2014 Office: Nathan Kline Inst Bldg 35 140 Old Orangeburg Rd Ste 35 Orangeburg NY 10962-1159 Office Phone: 845-398-5503. E-mail: levine@nki.rfmh.org.

LEVINE, JEROME L., lawyer; b. LA, July 20, 1940; m. Maryanne Shields, Sept. 13, 1966; children: Aron Michael, Sara Michelle. BA, U. So. Calif. San Francisco State U., 1962; JD, U. Calif. Hastings Law Coll., 1965. Bar: Calif. 1966, U.S. Dist. Ct. (Ctrl. Dist. Calif.) 1966, U.S. Ct. Appeals (9th Cir.) 1985, U.S. Supreme Ct. 1986, U.S. Dist. Ct. (Ea. Dist. Calif.) 1988, U.S. Ct. Appeals (Fed. Cir.) 1989. Dir. operational svcs., assoc. dir. Western Ctr. on Law and Poverty, LA, 1968-72; assoc. Swerdlow, Glikbarg & Shimer, Beverly Hills, Calif., 1972-77; ptnr. Lans Feinberg & Cohen, LA, 1977-79, Albala & Levine, LA, 1980-83, Neiman, Billet, Albala & Levine, LA, 1983-90, Levine & Assocs., LA, 1991-2000, Holland & Knight LLP, LA, 2000—, exec. ptnr. L.A. office, 2006—. Lectr. U. So. Calif. Law Ctr. 1970, Loyola U. Sch. Law 1971; corp. counsel Nat. Indian Gaming Assn.(NIGA)(chmn. task force on IGRA regulations, mem. NIGA-Nat. Congress American Indians Tribal-State negotiating team (NCAI)), Calif. Nations Indian Gaming Assn. (CNIGA), Wash. Indian Gaming Assn.(WIGA); mem. bd. dir. Law and Legis. Com. 1988-92, co-chmn. 1992-95; mem. dir. com. Holland & Knight LLP, L.A., 2004—; spkr. in field. Contbr. articles to profl. jours.; regular contbr. Indian Gaming Mag., 1990—97, Internat. Gaming and Wagering Mag., oversees editing and publication Indian Gaming Handbook. Mem. ABA (sects. on corp., banking and bus. law, litig., patent, trademark and copyright law, mem. forum com. on the entertainment and sports industries 1979), Beverly Hill Bar Assn. (mem. corp. and commerical law com. 1977-, entertainment law com. 1977-), LA County Bar Assn. (mem. antitrust sect.), Fed. Bar Assn. (indian law sect.), State Bar Calif., Internat. Assn. Gaming Lawyers, Internat. Masters Gaming Law Assn. Office: Holland & Knight LLP 633 W 5th St 21st Fl Los Angeles CA 90071 Office Phone: 213-896-2565. Business E-Mail: jerry.levine@hklaw.com.

LEVINE, JOSHUA H., medical products executive; BA in Comm., U. Ariz. Various exec. level sales and mktg. positions to v.p., gen. mgr., Home Health Care Divsn. Kinetic Concepts, Inc., San Antonio, 1989—96; v.p., sales and aesthetic products Mentor Corp., Santa Barbara, Calif., 1996—98, v.p., sales and mktg., aesthetic products, 1998—2000, v.p., domestic sales and mktg., aesthetic products, 2000—01, head of global aesthetic sales and mktg., 2001—02, sr. v.p., global sales and mktg., 2002—03, pres., COO, 2003—04, pres., CEO, 2004—, also bd. dir.; chief develop. officer The Plastic Surgery Co., 2000. Office: Mentor Corp 201 Mentor Dr Santa Barbara CA 93111

LEVINE, JUDY KENDALL, real estate broker, interior designer, writer; d. Allen Harvern Emerman and Serena Roth; m. Ira Bradley Levine, Jan. 10, 1975; children: Jonathan Alexander, Ross Stewart. BA, Finch Coll., 1972. Sales broker Gumley Haft Kleier, NYC, 1997—; interior designer Kendall Assocs., Inc, NYC, 1980—; v.p. Douglas Elliman, NYC, 2003—. Poetry studies N.Y. Pub. Libr., NYC, 2000—02; advisor emergency housing for victims of Sept.11th, NYC, 2001. Author; (poetry) A Childs' Prayer, 2001. Pediatric dir. donor affairs N.Y. Presbyn. Hosp., N.Y. Weil Cornell Med. Ctr., NYC, 1989—93. Mem.: Soc. Libr., Real Estate Bd. of N.Y., Soc. of Journalists & Authors. Avocations: cultural activities, charitable affilations, crafts, golf. Office: Douglas Elliman 575 Madison Ave New York NY 10022

LEVINE, LAURENCE HARVEY, lawyer; b. Cleve., Aug. 23, 1946; s. Theodore and Celia (Chaikin) Levine; m. Mary M. Conway, May 13, 1978; children: Abigail, Adam, Sarah. BA cum laude, Case Western Res. U., 1968; JD, Northwestern U., 1971. Bar: Ill. 1971, U.S. Dist. Ct. (no. dist.) Ill. 1972, U.S. Ct. Appeals (6th, 7th, 10th, 11th and D.C. cirs.), U.S. Ct. Claims 1997, U.S. Ct. Appeals (fed. cir.) 2000. Law clk. to presiding judge U.S. Ct. Appeals (6th cir.), Detroit, 1971-72; assoc. Kirkland & Ellis, Chgo., 1972-76; ptnr. Latham & Watkins, Chgo., 1976—. Bd. editors Northwestern Law Rev., 1968-71. Mem. ABA, Chgo. Bar Assn., Mid-Am. Club. Office: Latham & Watkins Sears Tower Ste 5800 Chicago IL 60606-6306 E-mail: laurence.levine@lw.com.

LEVINE, LOUIS D., museum administrator, archaeologist; b. NYC, June 4, 1940; s. Moe Wolf and Jeanne Levine; m. Dorothy Abrams, Dec. 30, 1962 (div. 1991); children: Sarra L., Samuel E.; m. Pat Molholt, May 25, 1997. Student, Brandeis U., 1960; BA with honors, U. Pa., 1962, PhD with distinction, 1969. Instr. of Hebrew U. Pa., Phila., 1966-69; asst. curator Royal Ont. Mus., Toronto, Can., 1969-75, assoc. curator, 1975-80, curator, 1981, assoc. dir., 1987-90; asst. commr., dir. N.Y. State Mus., Albany, 1990-98; dir. collections & exhbns. Mus. Jewish Heritage, NYC, 1998—. Vis. sr. lectr. Hebrew U., Jerusalem, 1975-76; vis. prof. U. Copenhagen, 1985; asst. prof. U. Toronto, 1969-74, assoc. prof. U. Toronto, 1974-81, prof., 1981-90; dir. Seh Gabi Expdn., western Iran, 1971-73, dir. Mahidasht Project, western Iran, 1975-79. Author: The Neo-Assyrian Zagros, 1974; editor: Scream the Truth at the World, 2001, Lives Remembered, 2002; exhbn. prodr.: Our Fight for American Jews in the Second World War, 2003; contbr. articles to profl. jours. NDEA fellow U. Pa., 1962-65, Fulbright fellow, 1965, W.F. Albright fellow, Am. Schs. of Oriental Rsch., 1966, fellow Inst. for Advanced Studies, Hebrew U. Mem. Brit. Inst. of Persian Studies, Brit. Sch. of Archaeology in Iraq, Am. Assn. Mus., Am. Oriental Soc. Jewish. Office: Mus Jewish Heritage 36 Battery Pl New York NY 10280 Home Phone: 914-725-2011; Office Phone: 646-437-4249. E-mail: llevine@mjhnyc.org.

LEVINE, MACY IRVING, physician; b. Johnstown, Pa., May 19, 1920; s. Elliott B. and Ida (Leuin) L.; m. Evelyn B. Levine, June 28, 1948 (dec. July 1996); children: Alan, Amy, Paul, Robert. BS, U. Pitts., 1940, MD, 1943. Diplomate Am. Bd. Internal Medicine, Am. Bd. Internal Medicine and Allergy. Intern U. Pitts. Med. Ctr., 1944; resident in allergy VA Hosp., Aspinwall, Pa., 1947-48, resident in medicine, 1948-49; fellow in medicine Lahey Clinic, Boston, 1950-51; USPHS postdoctoral fellow in medicine Peter Bent Brigham Hosp.-Harvard Med. Sch., Boston, 1951-52; pvt. practice Pitts., 1952—. Clin. prof. medicine U. Pitts. Sch. Medicine. Editor: Monograph on Insect Allergy, 4th edit., 2003; editor Bull. of the Allegheny County Med. Soc., 1975-86, Pitt Medicine Med. Alumni Assn., U. Pitts., 1987-99; contbr. more than 70 articles to profl. jours. Bd. dirs. Self Help Group Network, 1989-95, B'nai Israel Congregation, Pitts., 1965-71, Hebrew Free Loan Assn. Pitts., 1980—. Capt. U.S. Army, 1944-46, PTO. Recipient Disting. Svc. award Am. Acad. Allergy and Immunology, 1987, Frederick M. Jacob, M.D. Physician Merit award for Outstanding Svc. Allegheny County Med. Soc., 1988. Fellow Am. Acad. Allergy, Asthma and Immunology (v.p. 1982-83, Outstanding Vol. Clin. Faculty award 1996), Pa. Allergy Assn. (pres. 1970-71, Spl. Recognition award 1989), fellow, ACP; mem. Pitts. Allergy Soc. (pres. 1959-61), U. Pitts. Med. Alumni Assn. (pres. 1976-77), U. Pitts. Alumni Assn. (pres. 1984-85). Avocations: tennis, bridge. Home: 220 N Dithridge St Apt 400 Pittsburgh PA 15213-1421 Office Phone: 412-621-2393.

LEVINE, MADELINE GELTMAN, literature and language educator, translator; b. NYC, Feb. 23, 1942; d. Herman and Nettie (Kritman) Geltman; m. Steven I. Levine; children: Elaine, Daniel. BA, Brandeis U., 1962; MA, Harvard U., 1964, PhD, 1971. Asst. prof. Eng. Sch. CUNY, NYC, 1971-74; assoc. prof. U. NC, Chapel Hill, 1974-80, prof., 1980-94, Kenan prof. Slavic lits., 1994—, chmn. dept. Slavic langs., 1979-87, 94-99, interim dean, 2006—. Chmn. joint com. on Ea. Europe, Am. Coun. Learned Socs.-Social Sci. Rsch. Coun., 1989-92; chmn. bd. govs. U. N.C. Press, 1999-2005. Translator: A Memoir of the Warsaw Uprising (Miron Bialoszewski), 1977, 2d edit. 1991, The Poetry of Osip Mandelstam: God's Grateful Guest (Ryszard Przybylski), 1987, Beginning With My Streets: Essays and Recollections (Czeslaw Milosz), 1992, A Year of the Hunter (Czeslaw Milosz), 1994, Bread for the Departed (Bogdan Wojdowski), 1997, Lost Landscapes: In Search of Isaac Bashevis Singer and the Jews of Poland (Agata Tuszynska), 1998, Milosz's ABCs (Czeslaw Milosz), 2001, The Woman from Hamburg and Other True Stories, (Hanna Krall), 2005, Legends of Modernity: Essays and Letters From Occupied Poland, 1942-1943, 2005; translator with Francine Prose: A Scrap of Time and Other Stories (Ida Fink), 1986, 2d edit., 1995; author: Contemporary Polish Poetry, 1925-75, 1981; co-editor (with Bogdana Carpenter): To Begin Where I Am: Selected Essays (Czeslaw Milosz), 2001. NEH fellow, 1984, 2000; recipient (with Francine Prose) award for lit. translation PEN-America, 1988. Mem. Am. Assn. for Advancement of Slavic Studies, Polish Inst. of Arts and Scis. Am., Am. Assn. Tchrs. of Slavic and East European Langs., Am. Literary Translators Assn., Pen-Am. Home: 5001 Whitehorse Rd Hillsborough NC 27278-9399 Office: U NC CB # 3165 425 Dey Hall Chapel Hill NC 27599-3165 Office Phone: 919-962-7553. Business E-Mail: mgl@unc.edu.

LEVINE, MARCI ROBYN, lawyer; b. LA, Dec. 7, 1962; BA, UCLA, 1986; JD, Southwestern U., 1990. Bar: Calif. 1990, US Dist. Ct. 1990. Ptnr. Freid & Goldsman, L.A. Asst. acct. (films) White Fang, 1991, first asst. acct. What About Bob, 1991, prodn. acct. Capt. Ron, 1992, prodn. auditor (films) Life with Mikey, 1993, prodn. acct. The Hunchback of Notre Dame, 1996, prodn. rep. for Disney A Bug's Life, 1998, Toy Story 2, 1999, assoc. prodr. Valiant, 2005; co-prodr.: (films) 9, 2007—. Recipient Super Lawyer in Family Law, So. Calif., 2005, 2006, Achievement Award in Writing, Southwestern U. Mem.: Beverly Hills and LA Bar Assn. Office: Freid & Goldsman 2029 Century Pk E Ste 860 Los Angeles CA 90067 Office Phone: 310-552-2700. Office Fax: 310-552-2770.*

LEVINE, MARK DAVID, science administrator, director; b. Cleve., May 26, 1944; s. Hyman and Rebecca (Spector) Levine; m. Irma Herrera, June 1990. AB summa cum laude, Princeton U., 1966; PhD, U. Calif., Berkeley, 1975. Staff scientist Ford Found. Energy Policy Project, Washington, 1972-73; sr. energy policy analyst SRI Internat., Menlo Park, Calif., 1974-78; staff scientist Lawrence Berkeley Lab., Berkeley, 1978-84, dept. program leader, 1984-86, leader energy analysis program, 1986-96, dir. environ. energy techs. divsn., 1996—2006, leader China energy group, 2006—. Cons. Ford Found., TEM, Inc., Pacific Gas & Electric Co., QED Rsch., Inc., Energy Found., Peabody Energy; adv. bd. China Energy Conservation Investment Corp., 1994—98, Dow Chem. Co.; adv. bd. energy efficiency ctr. U. Calif., Davis, 2007—. Contbr. articles to profl. jours.; mem. editl. bd.: Energy Policy, Building Research and Information. Bd. dirs. Am. Coun. Energy Efficient Econ., Ctr. Clean Air Policy, Ctr. Resource Solutions, chair; bd. dirs. Calif. Clean Energy Fund, Shanghai Pacific Energy Ctr. Fulbright scholar, 1966. Fellow: Calif. Coun. Sci. and Tech.; mem.: Consortium Electricity Reliability (vice-chair). Jewish. Home: 5701 Barrett Ave El Cerrito CA 94530-1408 Office: Lawrence Berkeley Lab Bldg 90 Room 3125 Berkeley CA 94720 Business E-Mail: mdlevine@lbl.gov.

LEVINE, MELDON EDISES, lawyer, retired congressman; b. LA, June 7, 1943; s. Sid B. and Shirley B. (Blum) L.; children: Adam Paul, Jacob Caplan, Cara Emily. AB, U. Calif., Berkeley, 1964; MPA, Princeton U., 1966; JD, Harvard U., 1969. Bar: Calif. 1970, D.C. 1972. Assoc. Wyman, Bautzer, Rothman & Kuchel, 1969-71; legis. asst. U.S. Senate, Washington, 1971-73; ptnr. Levine Krom & Unger, Beverly Hills, Calif., 1973-77; mem. Calif. Assembly, Sacramento, 1977-82, 98th-102d Congresses from 27th Calif. dist., Washington, 1983-93; ptnr. Gibson, Dunn & Crutcher, LA, 1993—. Author: The Private Sector and the Common Market, 1968; contbr. articles to various publs. Mem. governing bd. U.S.-Israel Sci. and Tech. Commn., U.S. Holocaust Meml. Mus.; mem. amateur baseball team Hollywood Stars, 1971—. Mem.: LA Bar Assn., Calif. Bar Assn. Office: Gibson Dunn & Crutcher 2029 Century Park E Ste 4000 Los Angeles CA 90067-3032 Office Phone: 310-557-8098. Business E-Mail: mlevine@gibsondunn.com.

LEVINE, MICHAEL, public relations executive, author, television and radio personality; b. NYC, Apr. 17, 1954; s. Arthur and Virginia (Gaylor) L. Student, Rutgers U., 1978. Owner, operator TV News Mag., Los Angeles, 1977-83; owner Levine/Schnieder Pub. Rels., now Levine Comms. Office, Los Angeles, 1982—. Gov.'s adv. bd. State Calif., Sacramento, 1980-82; pres., owner Aurora Pub., LA, 1986—; moderator Thought Forum; lectr. in field; founder, moderator LA Media Roundtable; founder LBN ELERT Breaking News Newsletter; media expert KFWB Radio; radio host Access LA, Spiritual Seeker, Inside/Out Author: The Address Book: How to Reach Anyone Who's Anyone, 1984, The New Address Book, 1986, The Corporate Address Book, 1987, The Music Address Book, 1989, Environmental Address Book, 1991, Kid's Address Book, 1991, Guerrilla P.R., Lessons at Halfway Point, 1995, Take It From Me, Selling Goodness, 1998, The Princess & The Package, 1998, Guerrilla PR Wired, A Branded World, 2003, The 7 Life Lessons of Noah's Ark, 2004, Charming Your Way to the Top, 2004, Broken Windows, Broken Business, 2005; composer: Never, 2007; editor (newsletter): For Consideration. Mem. Ronald Reagan Pres.'s Libr.; founder The Actor's Conf., Aurora Charity, 1987; bd. dir. Felice Found., Micah Ctr.; adv. bd. Dare America; moderator U. Judaism Thought Forum. Mem. TV Acad. Arts and Scis., Entertainment Industries Coun., Musician's Assistance Program, West Hollywood C. of C. (bd. dirs. 1980-82). Jewish. Office: 1180 S Beverly Dr 301 Los Angeles CA 90035 Office Phone: 310-300-0950 ext 230. Office Fax: 310-300-0951. Business E-Mail: mlevine@lcoonline.com.

LEVINE, MICHAEL J., sports products company executive; BA in History, Cornell Univ. Jr. publicist, media rels. dept. CBS Sports; mgr., talent mktg. divsn. The Marquee Group; sr. dir., mktg. sponsorship SFX Sports Group; v.p., bus. devel. SportsCapsule, Inc.; now pres. Van Wagner Sports Group, LLC. Guest lectr. NYU's Sch. Continuing Edn. Named one of 40 Under 40, Sports Bus. Jour., 2006. Home: Van Wagner Sports Group 28th Fl 800 Third Ave New York NY 10022*

LEVINE, NAOMI BRONHEIM, academic administrator; b. NYC, Apr. 15, 1923; d. Nathan and Malvina (Mermelstein) Bronheim; m. Leonard Levine, Apr. 11, 1948; 1 child, Joan. BA, Hunter Coll., 1944; LLB, Columbia, 1946, JD, 1970. Bar: N.Y. 1946. With Scaadrett, Tuttle & Chalaire, NYC, 1946-48, Charles Gottleib, NYC, 1948-50, Am. Jewish Congress, 1950-78, exec. dir., 1972-78; v.p. to sr. v.p. external affairs NYU, NYC, 1978—2002, spl. advisor to pres., 2002—; chmn., dir. Heyman Ctr. for Philanthropy and Fund Raising, 2002—. Asst. prof. law and police sci. John Jay Coll., NYC, 1969—73, L.I. U., 1965—69. Author: (book) Schools in Crisis, 1969, The Jewish Poor-an American Awakening, 1974, Politics, Religion and Love, 1990; mem. editl. bd. Columbia Law Rev., 1945—46; author: For Her Days Not Her Nights. Chmn. N.Y.U. Bronfman Ctr., N.Y.U. Ctr. for Israeli Studies; com. on character and fitness N.Y. Supreme Ct.; co-chair Taub Ctr. for Israel Studies, NYU; bd. dirs. N.Y. Ctr. Philanthropy and Fund Raising. Named to Hunter Coll. Hall of Fame, 1972; recipient NY U. Presdl. medal, 2005. Office: NYU 29 Washington Square West New York NY 10011 Home Phone: 212-260-5674; Office Phone: 212-998-2380, 212-998-2384.

LEVINE, NORMAN, physician; b. Detroit, May 18, 1945; BA, U. Mich., 1966, MD, 1970. Cert. Dermatologist. Intern internal medicine Montefiore Hosp., Bronx, 1970-71; gen. med. officer U.S.A.F., Wright-Patterson AFB, OH, 1971-73; rsch. fellow Einstein Coll. Medicine, Bronx, 1973-75, resident dermatology, 1975-77, asst. prof. medicine, 1977-78; asst. prof. dermatology U. Ariz., 1978-83, assoc. prof. dermatology, 1983-86, prof./chief dermatology, 1986—2003, prof. dermatology, 2003—06. Editorial advisory bd. Dermatology Times, Cleve., 1988—, exam writing com. Am. Bd. Dermatology, Detroit, 1992-96. Editor: Pigmentation and Pigmentary Disorders, 1993; author: Skin Healthy, 1995. Capt. USAF, 1971-73. Fellow Am. Acad. Dermatology. Avocations: sports, computers, reading. Office: 5639 E Grant Rd Tucson AZ 85712 Office Phone: 520-615-3444. Business E-Mail: derm318@gmail.com.

LEVINE, PAMELA, film company executive; Pres. Marketcast, 1985—95; sr. v.p. mkting., planning and rsch. Twentieth Century Fox Film Corp., 1995—2002, co-pres. domestic theatrical mktg. LA, 2002—. Named one of 100 Most Powerful Women in Entertainment, Hollywood Reporter, 2006. Office: Twentieth Century Fox Film Corp 10201 W Pico Blvd Los Angeles CA 90035 Office Phone: 310-277-2211. Office Fax: 310-203-1558.*

LEVINE, PAUL MICHAEL, paper company executive, consultant; b. Bklyn., Apr. 15, 1934; s. Isaac Bert and Jessie Sue (Palevsky) L.; m. Lois Jaffin, June 11, 1954 (div.); children: Daniella Sarah, Julie Ann, Carl Joseph; m. 2d Noelle Tenedou, July 14, 1974; children: Simone Allana, Alexander Owen. AB in Econs., Harvard Coll., 1954; A.M. in Internat. Econs., Fletcher Sch. Internat. Law and Diplomacy, 1955. Sales mgr. U.S. Industries, Stamford, Conn., 1956-61; chief exec. officer subs. cos. Parsons and Whittemore-Black Clawson, NYC, 1962-69; dep. adminstr. City of N.Y., 1970-72; v.p. S&S Corrugated Paper Machinery Co., Bklyn., 1973-76, Continental Group, Stamford, Conn., 1977-83; chmn. New Lehigh Corrugated Products, Farmingdale, NY, United Container Corp., Phila. Lectr., fellow Yale U., U. Conn., Fordham U., 1979-90; Neeltran Inc., New Milford, Conn., Shulz Electric Corp., New Haven, Conn., Gulf Copper Mfg. Co., Port Arthur, Tex., Gas Tech Engring., Tulsa, Okla. Author: Proceedings 6th World Forestry Congress, 1966; editor: Study of Peoria County Model Program, 1970, Practical Exporting, 1962, The Role of Venture Capital in Europe and the World Trustee Hartman Regional Theatre, Stamford, 1981-82; bd. dirs. Ridgefield Orch., 1978-83, Bklyn. Arts and Culture Assn., 1973-92. Mem. Turnaround Mgmt. Assn., Explorers Club. Democrat. Jewish. Office: Paul M Levine & Assocs 466 Ridgebury Rd Ridgefield CT 06877-1228 E-mail: levassoc@aol.com. *Creativity, innovation and laughter are the glories of the world.*

LEVINE, PHILIP, classics educator; b. Lawrence, Mass., Sept. 8, 1922; s. Samuel and Jennie (Derdak) L.; m. Dinnie Moseson, June 19, 1955; children— Jared Elliott, Harlan Alcon. AB, Harvard, 1946, A.M., 1948, PhD, 1952; DHL (hon.), U. Judaism, 1986. Instr., asst. prof. classics Harvard, 1952-59; assoc. prof. classical langs. U. Tex. at Austin, 1959-61; assoc prof., prof. classics UCLA, 1961-91, prof. emeritus, 1991—, dean div. humanities, 1965-83; Biggs resident lectr. Washington U., 1993. Info. officer Coun. U. Calif. Emeriti Assn. Author: Lo Scriptorium Vercellese da S. Eusebio ad Attone, 1958, St. Augustine, City of God, Books 12-15, 1966; editor: Latin lt. sect. Twayne World Author Series, 1964—; adv. editor, U. Calif. Publs. in Classical Studies, 1963-72; assoc. editor, contbr. to U. Calif. Studies in Classical Antiquity, 1967-75, sr. co-editor, 1975-78; mem. editorial bd. Classical Antiquity, 1986-93. Mem. rev. com., sr. fellowship program Nat. Endowment for Humanities, 1966-70; bd. govs. U. Judaism, 1968-90, coun. visitors, 1990-94, acad. adv. coun., 1994—. With AUS, 1943-46. Sheldon fellow Italy; Guggenheim fellow; Fulbright Research grantee; recipient Bromberg Humanities award; decorated Cavaliere dell' Ordine al Merito della Repubblica Italiana. Mem. Am. Philol. Assn. (dir. 1968-70), Mediaeval Acad. Am. (exec. council 1969-72), Renaissance Soc., Am. Philol. Assn., Pacific Coast (chmn. gen. lit. 1964-65), Phi Beta Kappa. Home: 224 S Almont Dr Beverly Hills CA 90211-2507 Office: U Calif Dept Classics Los Angeles CA 90095-0001 Office Phone: 310-825-4171. Business E-Mail: levine@humnet.ucla.edu.

LEVINE, RAPHAEL DAVID, chemistry professor; b. Alexandria, Egypt, Mar. 29, 1938; brought to U.S., 1939; s. Chaim S. and Sofia (Greenberg) L.; m. Gillah T. Ephraty, June 13, 1962; 1 child, Ornah T. MSc, Hebrew U., Jerusalem, 1959; PhD, Nottingham U., Eng., 1964; DPhil, Oxford U., Eng., 1966; PhD honoris causa, U. Liege, Belgium, 1991, Tech. U., Munich, Germany, 1996. Vis. asst. prof. U. Wis., 1966-68; prof. theoretical chemistry Hebrew U., Jerusalem, 1969—, chmn. research ctr. molecular dynamics, 1981—, Max Born prof. natural philosophy, 1985—; disting. prof. dept. chemistry and biochemistry UCLA, 1990—, prof. molecular and med. pharmacology, 2007—. Battelle prof. chemistry and math. Ohio State U., Columbus, 1970-74; Brittingham vis. prof. U. Wis., 1973; adj. prof. U. Tex., Austin, 1974-80, MIT, 1980-88, UCLA, 1989—; Arthur D. Little lectr. MIT, 1978; Miller rsch. prof. U. Calif., Berkeley, 1989, A.D. White prof. at large Cornell U., 1989-95. Author: Quantum Mechanics of Molecular Rate Processes, 1969, Molecular Reaction Dynamics, 1974, Lasers and Chemical Change, 1981, Molecular Reaction Dynamics and Chemical Reactivity, 1986, Algebraic Theory of Molecules, 1995, Molecular Reaction Dynamics, 2005; mem. editorial bds. several well known scientific jours.; contbr. articles to profl. jours. With US Army, 1960—62. Co-recipient Wolf prize in chemistry, Wolf Found., 1988; named Ramsay Meml. fellow, 1964—66, Alfred P. Sloan fellow, 1970—72; recipient Ann. award, Internat. Acad. Quantum Molecular Sci., 1968, Landau prize, 1972, Israel prize in exact scis., 1974, Weizman prize, 1979, Rothschild prize, 1992, Max Planck prize for internat. cooperation, 1996, EMET prize, 2002, MOLEC award, 2004. Fellow Am. Phys. Soc.; mem. Israel Chem. Soc., Israel Acad. Scis., Max Planck Soc. (fgn. mem.), Academia Europaea (fgn.), Am. Acad. Arts and Scis. (fgn. hon. mem.), Am. Philos. Soc. (fgn.), Royal Danish Acad. Scis. and Letters (fgn.), Natl. Acad. of Sci., US, (fgn.). Office: UCLA Dept Chemistry & Biochemistry 607 Charles E Young E Dr Los Angeles CA 90095-1569 also: Hebrew U Jerusalem Fritz Haber Rsch Ctr Molecular Dynamics Jerusalem 91904 Israel Office Phone: 310-206-0476.

LEVINE, RICHARD E., lawyer; b. Flushing, NY, Aug. 6, 1950; s. Sol and Betty Levine; m. Lori A. Balter, Oct. 28, 1979; 1 child, Jamie Balter. BS in Mech. Engring., Bucknell U., 1972; JD, U. Md., 1975; LL.M. in Taxation, Georgetown U., 1978. Bar: Md. 1975, U.S. Tax Ct. 1979, D.C. 1980, U.S. Supreme Ct. 1983, U.S. Ct. Appeals (4th cir.) 1984. Assoc. Miles & Stockbridge, Balt., 1978-83, prin., 1983—2001; ptnr. DLA Piper LLP, Balt., 2002—. Adj. prof. U. Md. Law Sch., Balt., 1988. Contbr. articles to profl. jours. Bd. dirs. Har Sinai West Sr. Citizens Housing, Balt., 1983—92; trustee McDonogh Sch., 2002—. Fellow Am. Coll. Tax Counsel; mem. ABA (tax sect., chair partnerships 1990-92), Md. State Bar Assn. (tax sect. coun. 1983-86), The Center Club (house com. 1990—, bd. govs. 1996—). Avocations: golf, music. Office: DLA Piper US LLP 6225 Smith Ave Baltimore MD 21209-3600

LEVINE, RICHARD JAMES, publishing executive; b. NYC, Jan. 24, 1942; s. Irving Joseph and Dorothy Joyce (Thome) L.; m. Neil Ann Stuckey, June 1, 1963; children: Jonathan Donald, Russell Neilan. BS, Cornell U., 1962; MS in Journalism with high honors, Columbia U., 1963. Gen. assignment reporter Wall St. Jour., Washington, 1966—67, labor corr., 1967—70, mil. writer, 1970—75, chief econ. writer, outlook columnist, 1976—80; editl. dir., data base pub. Dow Jones & Co., Princeton, NJ, 1980—87, v.p. info. svcs. group, 1987—89, v.p. and editl. dir. info. svcs. group, mem. mgmt. com., 1989—92, v.p., mng. editor info svcs. segment, mem. mgmt. com. NYC, 1992—95; v.p. fin. info. svcs. group, mng. editor Dow Jones News Svcs., NYC, 1995—97; v.p., mng. editor Dow Jones Newswires, Jersey City, 1997—2001, v.p., exec. editor Jersey City and Princeton, NJ, 2001—05, v.p., news and staff devel. Princeton, NJ, 2005—06; pres. Dow Jones Newspaper Fund, Inc., 2005—. Dep. chmn. VWD GmbH, 1996—2004. Author: (with others) The Wall Street Journal Views America Tomorrow, 1977. Trustee Opera Festival NJ, 1998-2003, McCarter Theatre Ctr., Princeton, NJ, Princeton Symphony Orch.; dir. Nat. Jr. Tennis League Trenton; 1st lt. US Army, 1964-66. Pulitzer fellow, 1963—64. Mem. Cornell U. Coun., Cornell U. Tower Club, Soc. Profl. Journalists, Cornell Club (NYC), Princeton Indoor Tennis Ctr. Home: 108 Parkside Dr Princeton NJ 08540-4815 Office: Dow Jones and Co PO Box 300 Princeton NJ 08543-0300

LEVINE, ROBERT A., cardiologist; b. NYC, Jan. 29, 1953; s. Jules and Shirley (Krupnick) L. AB summa cum laude, Harvard Coll., 1974; MD, Harvard Med. Sch., 1978. Diplomate Am. Bd. Internal Medicine. Intern, resident in medicine Beth Israel Hosp., Boston, 1978-81; fellow in cardiology Mt. Sinai Hosp., NYC, 1981-83; clinical & rsch. fellow Mass. Gen. Hosp., Boston, 1983-85; instr. in medicine Harvard Med. Sch., Boston, 1985-87, from asst. prof. to assoc. prof. medicine, 1987-2000, prof., 2000—. Staff physician cardiac unit Mass. Gen. Hosp., Boston, 1985—, dir. cardiac ultrasound labs., 1995—; sci. session abstract chmn. Am. Soc. Echocardiography, 1993-95, program chmn., 1996-98, bd. dirs.; adj. prof. bioengring. Ga. Inst. Tech., Atlanta, 1995—; program leader mitral valve disease Leducq Found. Transatlantic Network of Excellence, 2007-. Editl. bd. Jour. Am. Coll. Cardiology, 1991-95, 99-2001, Circulation, 1996—2002, Jour. Amer. Soc. Ech., 1998-2002. Recipient awards NIH, 1985, 87, 95, 98, 2001, 02, 03, 04, 07, Israel Heart Soc., 1999, Doris Duke Charitable Found. Innovations Med. Rsch. award, 2000, Richard Popp award for mentoring Am. Soc. Echocardiography, 2002, Henry N. Neufeld award US-Israel Binational Sci. Found., 2002; named clinician-scientist, established investigator Am. Heart Assn., 1986, 91; Atna Found. Quality Care Rsch. Fund, 2001. Office: Mass Gen Hosp Cardiac Ultrasound YOCC5068 Boston MA 02114 E-mail: rlevine@partners.org.

LEVINE, ROBERT ARTHUR, economist, educator, policy writer; b. Bklyn., July 7, 1930; s. Isaac Bert and Jessie Sue (Palevsky) L.; m. Esther Carol Knudsen, Mar. 2, 1953; children: David Knudsen, Peter Kemmerer, Joseph Karl. BA, Harvard U., Cambridge, Mass., 1950, MA, 1951; PhD, Yale U., New Haven, Conn., 1957. Economist Rand Corp., 1957-61, sr. economist, 1962-65, 69-73, 87—, sr. economist emeritus, cons., 1994-98, 98—; research assoc. Harvard U. Center Internat. Affairs, 1961-62; asst. dir. for research, plans, programs and evaluation OEO, Washington, 1966-69; pres. N.Y.C.-Rand Inst., 1973-75; dep. dir. Congl. Budget Office, Washington, 1975-79; v.p. System Devel. Corp., Santa Monica, Calif., 1979-85; pres. Canyon Analysts, 1985—. Sr. fellow Nat. Security Studies Program, UCLA, 1964-65; vis. prof. public policy Stanford U. Grad. Sch. Bus., 1972; adj. prof. econs. Pepperdine U. Sch. Bus. and Mgmt., 1984 Author: The Arms Debate, 1963, The Poor Ye Need Not Have With You, 1971, Public Planning: Failure and Redirection, 1972, Evaluation Research and Practice, 1981, Still the Arms Debate, 1990, Turmoil and Transition in the Atlantic Alliance, 1991. With USN, 1951—54. Ford Found. grantee, 1969, 1985, German Marshall Fund grantee, 1979, Carnegie Corp. grantee, 1986. Clubs: Beverly Glen Democratic. Home and Office: 10321 Chrysanthemum Ln Los Angeles CA 90077-2812 Personal E-mail: ralev@adelphia.net. Business E-Mail: ral@rand.org.

LEVINE, ROBERT H., medical educator, psychiatrist; b. NYC, Apr. 27, 1939; s. Max Levine and Edythe Eisenstein-Levine; children: Joshua Matthew, Zori Levine-Goldstein, Max Paul. BA, U. Pa., Phila., 1961; MD, NYU, 1965. Diplomate Am. Bd. Psychiatry and Neurology, 1972. Asst. prof. NYU Coll. Medicine, NYC, 1971—75, assoc. prof. clin. psychiatry, 1990—; clin. asst. prof. Cornell Sch. Medicine, 1978—80. Prin. investigator Neuropsych Rsch. Assocs., NYC, 1990—. Contbr. articles scientific publs.; editor: (magazine) New Beginnings, 1993—94. Capt. USAF, 1969—71. Named one of Best Drs. in Am., 2005—06; recipient A.E. Bennett award, Soc. Biol. Psychiatry, 1969, Charles C. Colt award, Nat. Alliance for Mental Ill, 1992, Disting. Psychiatrist, 1993. Fellow: Marcan Psychiat. Assn. (life). Office: Robert Levine MD PC 1236 Park Ave New York NY 10128 Office Phone: 212-722-6604.

LEVINE, ROBERT JAY, lawyer; b. Hackensack, NJ, Aug. 7, 1950; s. Nathan R. and Naomi (Bendel) Levine; m. Joan Beth Mirviss, Aug. 10, 1975. AB, Brown U., 1972; JD, U. Pa., 1975. Bar: N.Y. 1976, U.S. Dist. Ct. (so. and ea. dists.) N.Y. 1976. Assoc. Davis Polk & Wardwell, NYC, 1975-82, ptnr., 1983—2002, sr. counsel, 2003—. Pres., bd. dirs. Sylvan Winds, Inc. Trustee NY Youth Symphony, Inc. Mem.: ABA, Internat. Bar Assn., Assn. Bar City of N.Y., N.Y. State Bar Assn., Brown Club N.Y.C., Phi Beta Kappa. Democrat. Jewish. Avocations: golf, travel, cooking, films. Home: 115 Central Park W New York NY 10023-4153 Office: Davis Polk and Wardwell 450 Lexington Ave New York NY 10017-3982 Home Phone: 212-799-4025; Office Phone: 212-450-4000.

LEVINE, ROBERT JEFFREY, lawyer; b. Miami Beach, Fla., Nov. 27, 1956; s. I. Stanely and Elaine (Martz) L. BSBA magna cum laude, U. Fla., 1978; JD, George Washington U., 1981. Bar: Fla. 1981, U.S. Dist. Ct. (so. dist.) Fla. 1981, U.S. Ct. Appeals (5th and 11th cirs.) 1981, U.S. Supreme Ct. 1986; cert. civil mediator, Fla. Supreme Ct.; lic. sea capt. USCG. Assoc. Barron, Lehman & Cardenas, Miami, 1981-82; ptnr. Haves & Levine, Miami, 1982-83; pvt. practice law Miami, 1983-85; ptnr. Toland & Levine, Miami, 1985-90, Levine & Geiger, P.A., Miami, 1990-94, Levine & Ptnrs., P.A., Miami, 1994—. Mem.: ATLA, Acad. Fla. Trial Lawyers, Fla. Bar Assn. Avocations: diving, fishing, skiing, golf, tennis. Office: Levine & Ptnrs PA 1110 Brickell Ave 7th Fl Miami FL 33131-3132 E-mail: RJL@levinelawfirm.com.

LEVINE, ROBERT JOHN, internist, medical educator, ethicist; b. NYC, Dec. 29, 1934; s. Benjamin Bernard and Ruth Florence (Schwartz) L.; m. Jeralea Fooshee Hesse, Nov. 28, 1987; children from previous marriage: John Graham, Elizabeth Hurt Braun; stepchildren: Stephen B. Hesse, Katherine F. Hesse. Student, Duke U., 1951—54; MD with distinction, George Washington U., 1958. Diplomate Am. Bd. Internal Medicine. Med. house officer Peter Bent Brigham Hosp., Boston, 1958-59, asst. resident in medicine, 1959-60; clin. assoc. Nat. Heart Inst., Bethesda, Md., 1960-62, investigator, 1963-64; chief med. resident VA Hosp., West Haven, Conn., 1962-63; mem. faculty depts. medicine and pharmacology Yale U., New Haven, 1964-73, chief sect. clin. pharmacology, 1966-74, prof. medicine, lectr. pharmacology, 1973—, co-chair exec. com. interdisciplinary program bioethics, 1999—2005; mem. med. staff Yale-New Haven Med. Ctr., 1964-68, attending physician, 1968—, co-dir. Ctr. Interdisciplinary Rsch. on AIDS, Law, Policy and Ethics Core, 1997—2000, dir., 2000—; co-dir. Yale U. Interdisciplinary Ctr. Bioethics, 2005—. Mem. Conn. Adv. Com. on Foods and Drugs, 1967-82, sec. 1969-71, chmn., 1971-73; mem. adv. com. AIDS program U.S. HHS, 1989-95; cons. Nat. Commn. Protection of Human Subjects of Biomed. and Behavioral Rsch., 1974-78; bd. dirs. Medicine in the Pub. Interest, Inc., 1976-2002, sec., 1983-2002; mem. ethics subcom. of dir.'s adv. com. Ctrs. for Disease Control and Prevention, 1997-2001, 05—; HIV prevention scis. working group NIH: Office of AIDS Rsch., 1998-2002; mem. adv. com. Nat. Human Rsch. Protections, 2000-02. Author: Ethics and Regulation of Clinical Research, 1981, 2d edit., 1986; editor Clin. Rsch., 1971-76, IRB: Rev. Human Subjects Rsch., 1978-2000, chairperson editl. bd., 2000—; contbr. numerous articles to profl. jours. Mem. Conn. Humanities Coun., 1983-89, chmn. 1988-89, Coun. Internat. Orgn. Med. Scis., co-chmn. steering com. revision internat. ethical guidelines for biomed. rsch. involving human subjects, 1991-93, chmn., 1998-02; chair working group for revision of Declaration of Helsinki, World Med. Assn., 1998-99. Recipient Outstanding Achievement medal, Office Human Rsch. Protection US Dept. Health and Human Svcs.,

2004, Lifetime award Excellence in Human Rsch. Protection, Health Improvement Inst., 2004, Lifetime Achievement award Excellence in Rsch. Ethics, Pub. Responsibility in Medicine and Rsch., 2005; grantee Multiple rsch. grants. Fellow ACP, The Hastings Ctr., AAAS (coun. del. 1987-91); mem. Am. Soc. Clin. Investigation, Am. Soc. Clin. Pharmacology and Therapeutics (bd. dirs. 1981-85), Am. Fedn. Clin. Rsch. (nat. coun. 1967-76, exec. com. 1971-76), Am. Soc. Pharmacology and Exptl. Therapeutics (exec. com. 1974-77), Am. Soc. Law, Medicine and Ethics (bd. dirs. 1986-96, pres. 1989-90, 94-95), Pan Am. Health Orgn. (internat. bioethics adv. bd. 2000-03), Pub. Responsibility in Medicine and Rsch. (bd. dirs. 1984—), Soc. for Bioethics Consultation (bd. dirs. 1988-94), Nat. Inst. Mental Health (human subjects rsch. coun. working group 1999—), Sigma Xi, Alpha Omega Alpha. Office: Yale Univ Interdisciplinary Ctr Bioethics PO Box 208209 New Haven CT 06520-8209 Office Phone: 203-432-8807. Personal E-mail: levinerj@sbcglobal.net.

LEVINE, ROBERT SIDNEY, chemical engineer, consultant; b. Des Moines, June 4, 1921; s. George Julius and Betty (Dennen) L.; m. Sharon Lorraine White; children: George, Gail, Tamara, Michelle, James. BS in Chem. Engring, Iowa State U., 1943; S.M. (Std. Oil Co. Ohio fellow 1947-48), M.I.T., 1946, Sc.D., 1949. With Rocketdyne div. Rockwell Internat. Co., 1948-66; assoc. research dir. NASA, 1966-74; chief liquid rocket tech. Nat. Bur. Stds., Washington, 1974-97; chief fire dynamics Nat. Bur. Stds. (now Nat. Inst. Stds. and Tech.), Washington, 1975-97. Mem. faculty UCLA, 1962-64, George Washington U., 1977; pres. Combustion Inst., 1974-78; chmn. Am. and Soviet Com. on Fire Rsch. in Housing, 1977-82. Author papers in field; mem. Washington editl. rev. bd. NIST, 1976-97. Named Engr. of Year Los Angeles sect. Am. Inst. Chem. Engrs., 1961 Mem. Am. Chem. Soc., AIAA, Nat. Fire Prevention Assn. Home: 19017 Threshing Pl Gaithersburg MD 20886-3143 Home Phone: 301-926-8868; Office Phone: 301-926-8868. Personal E-mail: rslevine@erols.com.

LEVINE, RONALD JAY, lawyer; b. Bklyn., June 23, 1953; s. Louis Leon and Marilyn Priscilla (Markovich) L.; m. Cindy Beth Israel, Nov. 18, 1979; children: Merisa, Alisha. BA summa cum laude, Princeton U., 1974; JD cum laude, Harvard U., 1977. Bar: NY 1978, US Dist. Ct. (so. and ea. dists.) NY 1978, DC 1980, NJ 1987, US Supreme Ct. 1982, US Ct. Apeals (2d cir.) 1983, NJ 1987, US Dist. Ct. NJ 1987, US Dist. Ct. (we. dist.) NY 1991, US Ct. Appeals (3d cir.) 1991, Pa. 1995. Assoc. Phillips, Nizer, Benjamin, Krim & Ballon, NYC, 1977-80, Debevoise & Plimpton, NYC, 1980-84, Herrick, Feinstein, NYC, 1984-85, ptnr., 1985—. Arbitrator Small Claims Ct. of Civil Ct. of City of NY, 1983-85; chmn. fee arbitration com. Mercer County, NJ; mem. NJ-Israel Commn., 2003-; sustaining mem. Product Liability Adv. Coun. Editor: Product Liability: Law and Strategy. Mem. Site Plan Rev. Adv. Bd., West Windsor, NJ, 1986, planning bd., 1987. Mem. ABA (litigation sect.), NY State Bar Assn. (chmn. com. on legal edn. and bar admission 1982-92, com. on profl. discipline 1989-90), NJ State Bar Assn. (product liability com. 1991—, profl. responsibility com. 1992-96, 2007—), Assn. of Bar of City of NY (coun. jud. adminstrn. 1994-95, com. on profl. responsibility 1980-83, 2006—, com. on legal assistance 1983-86, product liability com. 1987-91, trustee career devel. awards 1989-90), Phi Beta Kappa. Home: 6 Arnold Dr Princeton Junction NJ 08550-1521 Office: Herrick Feinstein 2 Park Ave Fl 20 New York NY 10016-9302 Business E-Mail: rlevine@herrick.com.

LEVINE, SAMUEL MILTON, lawyer, retired judge, arbitrator, mediator; b. Syracuse, NY, Feb. 24, 1929; s. Joseph and Sophie Levine; m. Leona Miller, Sept. 9, 1950; children: Judith, Donald, Gary. BBA, Syracuse U., 1950; JD, Bklyn. Law Sch., 1953. Bar: N.Y. 1953, U.S. Supreme Ct. 1960, U.S. Dist. Ct. (ea. and so. dists.) N.Y. 1962; cert. mediator, arbitrator. Assoc. Law Office of William S. Miller, Esq., NYC, 1954-62, Law Office of Ferdinand I. Haber, Esq., Mineola, N.Y., 1958-62; pvt. practice Nassau County, N.Y., 1962-65; counsel English, Cianciulli, Reisman & Peirez, 1962-65; supt. of real estate Nassau County, 1965-84; pvt. practice Garden City, N.Y., 1984—. Pres., past pres. bd. of judges Dist. Ct. Nassau County; N.Y. state hearing officer; lectr. in field. Contbr. articles to profl. jours. Past chmn. Sch. Aid Coun. L.I., Citizens Com. for Elmont Schs., N.Y.; former counsel, trustee Temple Bnai Israel, Elmont; former bd. visitors Pilgrim State Hosp.; treas., counsel N.Y. State Coun. Orgns. for Handicapped; past pres. Nassau County Epilepscy Found.; former chmn. Health and Welfare Coun. Nassau County; former mem. Nassau-Suffolk Health Sys. Agy.; del. White House Conf. on Children and Youth, 1960; candidate N.Y. State Senate, 1964; Dem. candidate Dist. Ct. Judge, 1985; candidate N.Y. State Supreme Ct., 1990; counsel Health Advs., Voice for Handicapped, Fedn. Parent Orgns., League of Voters for Handicapped; del. White House Conf. on Disabilities, 1970, White House Conf. on Sr. Citizens, 1980, White House Conf. on Mental Health, 1999. With U.S. Army, 1948. Recipient Adv. of Yr. award L.I. Coun. Fedn. Parents Orgns., 1978. Mem. Nat. Acad. Elder Law Attys., N.Y. State Bar Assn., Nassau County Bar Assn. (former chmn. social svc. and health law com., legis. com.), Syracuse U. Alumni Club, Kiwanis, Knights of Pythias, B'nai B'rith. Home: 711 Shore Rd Apt 2E Long Beach NY 11561-4707 Office Phone: 516-889-0496. E-mail: askjdgsamny@aol.com.

LEVINE, SANFORD HAROLD, lawyer; b. Troy, NY, Mar. 13, 1938; s. Louis and Reba (Semegren) L.; m. Margaret R. Appelbaum, Oct. 29, 1967; children: Jessica Sara, Abby Miriam. AB, Syracuse U., 1959, JD, 1961. Bar: NY 1961, US Dist. Ct. (no. dist.) NY 1961, US Dist. Ct. (we. dist.) NY 1979, US Dist. Ct. (ea. and so. dists.) NY 1980, US Ct. Appeals (2d cir.) 1962, US Supreme Ct. 1967. Law asst. to assoc. judge NY Ct. Appeals, Albany and to justice NY Supreme Ct., 1962-66, NY Ct. Appeals, Albany, 1964; asst. counsel NY State Temporary commn. on Constl. Conv., NYC, 1966-67; assoc. counsel SUNY System, Albany, 1967-70, dep. univ. counsel, 1970-78, acting counsel, 1970-71, acting univ. counsel, 1978-79, univ. counsel, vice chancellor legal affairs, 1979-97, prof. Sch. of Edn., dir. program in edn. and law, 1997—. Adj. prof. Sch. of Edn. SUNY, Albany, 1992—97; mem. paralegal curriculum adv. com. Schenectady County Community Coll., 1975—. Editl. bd. Syracuse U. Law Rev., 1960-61; editl. adv. bd. Jour. Coll. and Univ. Law, 1977-81. Fellow Am. Bar Found., NY Bar Found., State Acad. for Pub. Adminstrn.; mem. ABA (ho. dels. 1987-89), NY State Bar Assn., Albany County Bar Assn., Nat. Assn. Coll. and Univ. Attys. (exec. bd. 1979-82, bd. dirs. 1982-89, pres. 1986-87), Am. Soc. Pub. Adminstrn. Home: 1106 Godfrey Ln Schenectady NY 12309-2712

LEVINE, SHEPARD, painter, educator; s. Jacob and Betty Levine; m. Gloria Lucienne Eisen, Aug. 25, 1951 (dec.); children: Josh, Kate. BA with honors, U. N.Mex., Albuquerque, 1950; MA, U. N. Mex., Albuquerque, 1951; postgrad., U. Toulouse, France, 1951—52. Prof. art Oreg. State U., Corvallis, 1953—91. Exhibited in numerous national, publ. and pvts. collections. With USCG, 1943—45. Home: 3750 NW Hayes Ave Corvallis OR 97330

LEVINE, SHERRIE, conceptual artist; b. Hazelton, Pa. BFA, U. Wis., 1969, MFA, 1973. Exhibitions include Newborn galerie deux Co., Ltd., Tokyo, 1995, Hiram Butler Gallery, Houston, 1995, 2003, Mus. Contemporary Art, LA, 1995, Galerie Jablonka, Cologne, Germany, 1996, Frac des Pays de la Loire, Nantes, France, 1996, Mus. Modern Art, NYC, 1996, 1999, 2000, 2001, Whitney Mus., 1996, Phila. Mus. Art, 1996, Mus. Fine Arts, Boston, 1996, Campbell-Thiebaud Gallery, San Francisco, 1997, Margo Leavin Gallery, LA, 1997, 1999, 2000, 2001, XXIV Bienal de Sao Paulo, 1998, Hamburger Kunstverein, Hamburg, 1998, Pitts. Ctr. for the Arts, Pitts., 1998, Mus. Ludwig, Cologne, 1998, Walker Art Ctr., Mpls., 1998, 2002, 2005, Whitechapel Art Gallery, London, 1999, Rena Bransten Gallery, NYC, 1999, Paula Cooper Gallery, 1999, 2000, 2002, Coll. New Rochelle, NJ, 2001, Getty Rsch. Inst., LA, 2001, Centre des Arts Saidye Bronfman, Montreal, 2002, MIT List Visual Arts Ctr., Cambridge, Mass., 2003, Faggionato Fine Arts, London, 2004, Bard Coll., Annandale-on-Houston, NY, 2005, numerous others. Office: c/o Paula Cooper Gallery 534 & 521 W 21st St 2d Floor New York NY 10011

LEVINE, STANLEY WALTER, chemical company executive; b. Boston, Dec. 13, 1929; s. Bernard T. and Sonia (Spector) L.; m. Tochia Levine; children: Robert, Douglas, Elizabeth. BS in Journalism, Butler U., 1952; postgrad., Boston Coll., 1967; grad., FBI Citizens Acad. Nat. mktg. dir. Bates Mfg. Co., NYC, 1965-68; mgmt. cons. Frederick Chusid Co., NYC, 1971-76, Fashioncade, NYC, 1968-71; pres., CEO Internat. Coating & Chem. Co. Inc., Fairfield, Conn., 1976—. Contbr. articles to Nat. Chem. Weekly, Harpers. Mem. Nat. Republican Congl. Com., Rep. Com. Fairfield County (Conn.); bd. dirs. Butler U., So. Poverty Law Ctr., Ariz. and Nat. regional rep., Ariz. Humane Soc., Phoenix Meml. Hosp.; trustee Butler Univ.; bd. mem. Audubon Soc., Arthritis Found., Home Base for Homeless Kids, Anti-Defamation League, St. Joseph Hosp.-Barrow Neurological, Boys Scouts of Am., Ariz. Animal Welfare League; capt. posse edivsn., spl. dep. Sheriff's Dept. Maricopa County; pres. Am. Jewish Com.; mem. Phoenix Environ. Quality Commn.; apptd. mem. Phoenix Arts and Culture Commn., Appellate Ct. Appointments Commn. Served to capt. USAF, 1952-55. Decorated Korean Honor medal, Disting. Svc. to Cmty. award Salvation Army. Mem. Am. Mgmt. Assn., Chem. Week Contbrs., Pres.'s Club N.Y., Nat. Chem. Club, N.Y. Acad. Scis., Internat. Platform Assn., Harmonie Club, Paradise Valley Country Club, Plaza Club (bd. dirs.), Rolls Royce Club (chmn. pres. S.W. region), Coddington Landing Assn. (bd. dirs.), Camelback Estates I (bd. dirs.), Gainey Ranch Country Club (bd. dirs.), Alexis de Tocqueville Soc., Sigma Delta Chi, Sigma Alpha Mu, Alpha Phi Omega. also: PO Box 6345 Scottsdale AZ 85261-6345 Office Phone: 480-948-8089. E-mail: stantoch@aol.com.

LEVINE, STEVEN ALAN, lawyer; Counsel Pub. Svc. Commn. Wis. Mem.: Wis. Bar Assn. (pres. 2006—07). Office: Office of General Counsel Public service Commn PO Box 7854 Madison WI 53707-7854 Office Phone: 608-267-2890. E-mail: steven.levine@psc.state.wi.us, steven.levine@charter.net.

LEVINE, SUZIN NANCY LEAH, religious organization administrator; b. LA, Mar. 5, 1952; d. Ciprano C. Ortega and Wanda Laurie Murphy; m. Ronald Stuart Levine, Oct. 23, 1972; children: Jason, Elizabeth, Justin, Joshua. Grad., Willow Glen H.S., San Jose, Calif., 1969. Dir. I Care Ministry, Visalia, Calif., 1995—; tchr. Cath. Apostles of Christ, Visalia, 1999—. Author: Don't Cry Anymore, 1995, This is How I Pray, 2000, God Awaits Us, 2003; pub. Chaplet of Reconciliation, Cath. Apostle of Christ Handbook, originator Spiritual Care Packets. Home and Office: I Care Ministry PO Box 7164 Visalia CA 93290 E-mail: jle1172801@hotmail.com.

LEVINE, T. BARRY, cardiologist, educator; s. Jacob Levine. BS in Med. Scis., Free U. Brussels, 1969, MD, 1973. Diplomate Am. Bd. Cardiology. Prof. medicine Drexel U. Sch. Medicine, Pitts., 2003—. Avocation: philosophy. Office: ABLE Med Cons 5624 Bartlett St Pittsburgh PA 15217

LE VINE, VICTOR THEODORE, retired political science professor; b. Berlin, Dec. 6, 1928; came to U.S., 1938; s. Maurice and Hildegard (Hirschberg) LeV.; m. Nathalie Jeanne Christian, July 19, 1958; children: Theodore, Nicole. BA, UCLA, 1950, MA, 1958, PhD, 1961. Research assoc. UCLA, 1958-60; prof., head dept. polit. sci. U. Ghana, Legon, 1969-71; Fulbright prof. U. Yaounde, Cameroon, 1981-82; prof. polit. sci. Washington U., St. Louis, 1961—2003, prof. emeritus, 2003—. Cons. U.S. Dept. State, Dept. Def., 1971—; lectr. USIA, 1981—; mem. U.S. Nat. Commn. UNESCO, 1964; dir. Office Internat. Studies, Washington U., 1975-76; vis. lectr. Fudan U., U. Nanjing (China), 1987, Ibn Saud and King Abdulazziz Univs., Saudi Arabia, 1990; mem. Carter Ctr. Internat. monitoring team to Ghana nat. elections, 1992; vis. prof. Hebrew U., Jerusalem, 1978, U. Tex., Austin, 1980, Sabanci U., Turkey, 2003, Athens U., Greece, 2003. Author: Cameroons: Mandate to Independence, 1964, 70, Cameroon Federal Republic, 1971, Political Corruption: Ghana, 1975, (with Timothy Luke) Arab-African Connection, 1979; (with Heidenheimer and Johnston) Political Corruption: A Handbook, 1990; Conceptualizing Ethnicity and Ethnic Conflict: A Controversy Revisited, 1997 Parapolitics: Mapping The Terrain of Informal Politics, 2002, Politics in Francophone Africa, 2004. Mem., dir. UN Assn., St. Louis, 1964-74; mem. Coun. on World Affairs, 1969-2000; pres. Ctr. for Internat. Understanding, 1988-2000. With U.S. Army, 1951-54. Ford. Found. fellow Cameroon, 1960-61; Hoover Instn. fellow, 1974; Lester Martin fellow Truman Instn., Jerusalem, 1978; Fulbright lectr. U.S. Fulbright Commn., Yaounde, Cameroon, 1981-82, Greece and Turkey, 2003. Mem. Am. Polit. Sci. Assn., African Studies Assn., Mideast Studies Assn., Midwest Polit. Sci. Assn., Mo. Polit. Sci. Assn. Office: Washington U Dept Polit Sci Saint Louis MO 63130 Office Phone: 314-935-5867. Business E-Mail: vlevine@wustl.edu.

LEVINE, WILLIAM MICHAEL, lawyer; b. Rockville Ctr., NY, May 21, 1952; s. Leonard and Regina (Bloom) L.; m. E. Chouteau Levine, Feb. 29, 2004; children: Katie M., Diana R. BA, Northwestern U., Evanston, Ill., 1974; JD, Suffolk U., 1978. Bar: Mass. 1978, U.S. Dist. Ct. Mass. 1978, U.S. Ct. Appeals (1st cir.) 1981; U.S. Tax Ct. 1982. Asst. regional counsel Dept. Pub. Welfare, Boston, 1978-80; dep. regional counsel Dept. Social Svcs., Boston, 1980-81; assoc. Atwood & Wright, Boston, 1981-83, Peabody & Arnold, Boston, 1983-85, Bowser & Lee (now Lee & Levine LLP), Boston, 1985-87, ptnr., 1987-88, Lee & Levine (formerly Lee, Levine & Bowser), Boston, 1988—. Contbg. author: Massachusettes Family Law Manual, 1986-88; contbr. articles to profl. jours. Named one of Boston's top lawyers, Boston Mag., 2002, 2004, 2005, 2006, Top 100 Lawyers, Worth mag., 2005. Fellow Internat. Acad. Matrimonial Lawyers, Am. Acad. Matrimonial Lawyers (bd. mgrs. 1988-91, chpt. pres., pres.-elect, v.p., treas. 1997-2005, arbitration com. chair 2005-06); mem. Mass. Bar Assn. (family law sect. coun. 1987-88), Boston Bar Assn. (chmn. family law sect. 1988-91). Office: Lee & Levine LLP 222 Berkeley St Ste 1400 Boston MA 02116-3750 Office Phone: 617-266-6262. Office Fax: 617-266-8250.*

LEVINE, WILLIAM SILVER, electrical engineer, educator; b. Bklyn., Nov. 19, 1941; s. Louis Nathan and Gertrude (Silver) Levine; m. Shirley Johannesen, Feb. 14, 1963; children: Bruce Jonathan, Eleanor Joan. BEE, MIT, 1962, MEE, 1965, PhD in Elec. Engring., 1969. Project engr. Data Tech. Inc., Cambridge, Mass., 1962—64; grad. asst. MIT, Cambridge, 1964—69; asst. prof. U. Md., College Park, 1969—73, assoc. prof., 1973—81, prof., 1981—. Cons. IBM Fed. Sys. divsn., Gaithersburg, Md., 1972—75, Computational Engring. Inc., Laurel, Md., 1980—90. Co-author: Using MATLAB to Analyze and Design Control Systems, 1992, 2d edit., 1995; editor: The Control Handbook, 1996, Control Engineering Series, 1996—; co-editor: Handbook of Networked and Embedded Control Systems, 2005; contbr. articles to profl. jours. Rsch. grantee, 1969—. Fellow: IEEE, IEEE Control Sys. Soc. (pres. 1990, disting. mem. 1990); mem.: Soc. Indsl. and Applied Math., Am. Automatic Control Coun. (v.p. 2002—03, pres. 2004—05). Office: U Md Dept Elect & Computer Engring College Park MD 20742-0001 Business E-Mail: wsl@eng.umd.edu.

LEVINE, ZACHARY THOMAS, neurosurgeon; b. New Haven, Conn., July 30, 1967; s. Stephen Maxwell Levine, Rhea JC Levine; m. Jennifer Avellino, Aug. 18, 1991; children: Julia, Leah. AB Biology, Dartmouth Coll., 1993. Diplomate Board Medical Examiners 1996, cert. neurological surgery 2004. Resident George Washington U. Med. Ctr., Washington, 1994—99, chief resident, 1999—2000; dir. functional neurosurgery Washington Hosp. Ctr., DC, 2004. Rsch. com. Parkinson's Found., Nat. Capital Area, Fairfax, 2001—. Mem.: Am. Assn. Neurol. Surgeons (assoc.). Achievements include invention of method of cellular transplantation into the brain, 1992. Avocations: sailing, fly fishing, skiing, reading, cooking. Office: Washington Brain & Spine Inst 4927 Auburn Ave Bethesda MD 20814 Home Phone: 301-263-1003; Office Phone: 301-718-9611. Personal E-mail: zlevine@brainsurgery.com. Business E-Mail: info@brainsurgery.com.

LEVINE SIMON, SARAH ANN, music educator; b. Pitts., Dec. 18, 1945; d. Jules D. and Maita Sivitz Levine; m. Roger Hendricks Simon, Oct. 8, 1972; children: Noah Simon, Daniel Hendricks Simon, Abigail Simon. Student, Oberlin Coll., Ohio, 1963—66, Juilliard Sch., NYC, 1968—72; BA, Columbia U., NYC, 1994, postgrad., 1995. Voice tchr., 1968—; comm. tchr. Dutchess CC, Poughkeepsie, NY, 2004. Adj. instr. NY Inst. Tech., NYC, 1999—2000; writing tchr. Bklyn. Coll., 1997—99; playwright Plays for Living, NYC, 1995. Author: (plays) Bernardo's Farewell, 1994, Rule of Thumb, 1995, Mouse Music, 1996, singer numerous solo recitals, operas; dir.: Jewish Heritage Ensemble. Chmn. Hudson Valley Philharm. String Camp, Poughkeepsie, 2006—07; advisor on arts Office of Mayor, Poughkeepsie, 2004—05; condr. choir 1st Presbyn. Ch., Poughkeepsie; bd. dirs. Cappella Festival, Poughkeepsie, 2006. Recipient Hon. Mention, Montage, NY, 1999; Kathryn Long grantee, Met. Opera, NY, 1972—74. Mem.: Nat. Assn. Tchrs. Singing, NY Singing Tchrs. Assn. Democrat. Jewish. Avocations: cooking, pilates, yoga, reading, gardening. Home: 109 Hooker Ave Poughkeepsie NY 12601

LEVINGER, JOSEPH SOLOMON, physicist, researcher; b. NYC, Nov. 14, 1921; s. Lee J. and Elma (Ehrlich) Levinger; m. Gloria Edwards, Aug. 14, 1943 (dec. Jan. 20, 1987); children: Sam, Laurie, Louis, Joe; m. Hedi McKinley, Sept. 4, 1998. BS, U. Chgo., 1941, MS, 1944; PhD, Cornell U., 1948. Physicist Metall. Lab., U. Chgo., 1942-44, Franklin Inst., Phila., 1945; instr. Cornell U., 1948-51, vis. prof., 1961-64; from asst. prof. to prof. La. State U., 1951-61; prof. physics Rensselaer Poly. Inst., 1964-92, prof. emeritus, 1992—; Fulbright fellow, asso. prof. U. Paris— Sud, 1972-73. Author: Nuclear Photo-Disintegration, 1961, Secrets of the Nucleus, 1967, The Two and Three Body Problem, 1974. Guggenheim fellow, 1957—58. Fellow: Am. Phys. Soc. Home: PO Box 411 Altamont NY 12009-0411 Office: Rensselaer Poly Inst Dept Physics Troy NY 12180 Personal E-mail: levinj@rpi.edu.

LEVINGER, MATTHEW B., historian; s. George and Ann Levinger; m. Livia Nicolescu; children: Alexandra, Isaac. BA, Haverford Coll., 1983; MA, U. Chgo., 1986, PhD, 1992. History tchr. Hackley Sch., Tarrytown, 1983—85; lectr. in history Stanford U., Stanford, Calif., 1991—94; asst. prof. history Lewis & Clark Coll., Portland, 1994—2000, assoc. prof. history, 2000—05; dir., acad. for genocide prevention US Holocaust Meml. Mus., Washington, 2005—. Author: Enlightened Nationalism: The Transformation of Prussian Political Culture, 1806-1848, 2000; author: (with Charles Breunig) (textbook) The Revolutionary Era, 1789-1850, 3d edit., 2002. William C. Foster fellowship, U.S. Dept. of State, 2003—04, Berlin Program doctoral fellowship, Social Sci. Rsch. Coun., 1988—90. Mem.: Am. Hist. Assn. Office: United States Holocaust Meml Mus 100 Raoul Wallenberg Pl SW Washington DC 20024 Home Phone: 301-656-6999; Office Phone: 202-488-6191. E-mail: mlevinger@ushmm.org.

LEVINGS, THERESA LAWRENCE, lawyer; b. Kansas City, Mo., Oct. 24, 1952; d. William Youngs and Dorothy (Neer) Frick; m. Darryl Wayne Levings, May 25, 1974; children: Leslie Page, Kerry Dillon. BJ, U. Mo., 1973; JD, U. Mo., Kansas City, 1979. Bar: Mo. 1979, U.S. Dist. Ct. (we. dist.) Mo. 1979, U.S. Ct. Appeals (8th cir.) 1982, U.S. Ct. Appeals (10th cir.) 1986, U.S. Dist. Ct. (ea. dist.) Mo. 1989, U.S. Dist. Ct. Kans. 1995. Copy editor Kansas City Star, 1975-78; law clk. to judge Mo. Supreme Ct., Jefferson City, 1979-80; from assoc. to ptnr. Morrison & Hecker, Kansas City, 1980-94; founding ptnr. Badger & Levings, L.C., Kansas City, 1994—. Mem. fed. practice com. U.S. Dist. Ct. (we. dist.), 1990-95; mem. fed. adv. com. U.S. Ct. Appeals (8th cir.), 1994-97, Kans. 2005, U.S. Supreme Ct. 2006. Mem. ABA (house dels., 2006—), Mo. Bar (bd. govs. 1990—03, pres. 2001-02), Assn. Women Lawyers Greater Kansas City (pres. 1986-87, Woman of Yr. 1993), Kansas City Met. Bar Assn. (chair civil practice and procedure com. 1988-89, chair fed. practice com. 1990-91, Inns of Court (master 1996-2000, 2002-06). Office: Badger & Levings LC Ste 1920 920 Main St Kansas City MO 64105 Office Phone: 816-421-2828. Business E-Mail: tlevings@badgerlevings.com.

LEVINGSTON, ERNEST LEE, engineering company executive; b. Pineville, La., Nov. 7, 1921; s. Vernon Lee and Adele (Miller) L.; m. Kathleen Bernice Bordelon, June 23, 1944; children: David Lewis, Jeanne Evelyn, James Lee. BME, La. State U., 1960. Registered profl. engr., La., Tex., Miss., Ark., Tenn., Pa., Md., Del., N.J., D.C., Okla., Colo. Gen. forman T. Miller & Sons, Lake Charles, La., 1939-42; sr. engr., sect. head Cities Svc. Refining Corp., Lake Charles, 1946-57; group leader Bovay Engrs., Baton Rouge, 1957-59; chief engr. Augenstein Constrn. Co., Lake Charles, 1959-60; pres. Levingston Engrs., Inc., Lake Charles, 1961-85; gen. mgr. SW La. Austin Indsl., 1985-88; pres. Levingston Engrs., Lake Charles, 1989-96, chmn. bd., 1996-2000, pres., chmn. bd., 2000—. Mem. Lake Charles Planning and Zoning Commn., 1965-70; adv. bd. Sowela Tech. Inst., 1969—; mem. Regional Export Expansion Coun., 1969-70, chmn. code com., 1966—; mem. La. Bd. Commerce and Industry, 1978—; bd. dirs. Lake Charles Meml. Hosp.; bd. dirs., regional chmn. La. Chem. Industry Alliance, 1990—. With USNR, 1942-46. Named Jaycee Boss of Yr., 1972. Mem. La. Engring. Soc. (pres. 1967-68, state bd. dirs. 1967-68, 90-91), Nat. Inst. Cert. Engring. Technologists (past trustee, mem. exam. com.), La. Assn. Bus. and Industry, Lake Area Industries/McNeese Engring., Lake Charles C. of C. (dir. 1969-73). Baptist (deacon 1955—). Office: PO Box 1865 Lake Charles LA 70602-1865 Office Fax: 337-474-3789.

LEVINS, JOHN RAYMOND, investment advisor, educator, management consultant; b. Jersey City, Aug. 4, 1944; s. Raymond Thomas and Catherine (Kelly) L. BS in Acctg., U. NH, 1973; MBA, U. NH, Plymouth, 1976. Registered investment advisor; cert. mgmt. cons., enrolled to practice IRS; cert. licensing instr., real estate and multiple lines ins. broker, comml. arbitration panelist; accredited tax advisor; cert. mediator; registered securities prin. Office Supervisory Jurisdiction, Nat. Securities Bur. Mgmt. risk analyst Express Treaty Mgmt. Corp., NYC, 1962-67; asst. risk mgr. Bigelow-Sanford, Inc., NYC, 1967-71; cons., broker BYSE, Inc., Laconia, NY, 1971-74; asst. prof. Nathaniel Hawthorne Coll., Antrim, NH, 1975-82, Keene State Coll., NH, 1982—; prin. Levins & Assocs., Concord, NH, 1986—; investment advisor Reality Techs., Internat. Fin., Concord, 1991—; prin. Levins & Assocs. Dir. Small Bus. Inst. Keene State Coll., 1982-86; exec. seminar leader Strategic Mgmt. Group, Inc., 1986—, Boston U., 1976-99; mem. bd. advisors Am. Biog. Inst.; pvt. practice real estate, ins. cons., Concord, 1981; panelist securities arbitration Nat. Assn. Security Dealers, Am. Stock Exch., NY Stock Exch., Gen. Securities Prin.; consumer affair mediator Dept. Justice, Office of Atty. Gen., NH, NASA Svc. Bureau-Compliance; mortgage banker; comml. financing broker; mem. SEC, spkr., seminar leader in field; fin. faculty grad. programs Boston U., 1996 fin. and investment provider Dun & Bradstreet, 1997; expert witness investments and securities WestLaw.com, FindLaw.com, Martindale and Hubbelle; compliance NASD Svc. Bureau; sr. v.p. Investment Source Captial Group, Inc.; sr. v.p. gen. securities Prin. Source Capital Group. Author: Finance and Accounting, 1979 (Excellence award 1980), Financial Analysis, 1981 (Excellence award 1980), Managing Cash Flow, 1988 (Excellence award 1988), Finance and Management, 1989. Incorporator Spaulding Youth Ctr., Tilton, NH, 1990; colleague Found. for

Acctg. Edn., assoc., profl. standing, 1988; mem. Nat. Consortium Edn. and Tng., Madison, Wis., 1989. With USN, 1969-71, SE Asia. Named Outstanding Support Leader US Small Bus. Adminstrn., Concord, 1985, Outstanding Svc. Leader Community Leaders Am., NH, 1990, One of Outstanding Young Men Am. US Jaycees Bd. Adv.'s, 1983. Mem. AICPA (mem. Profl. Devel. Inst., sponsor trainer 1988-89), Found. Acctg. Acctg., Investment Co. Inst. (assoc., nat. standing 1987), Inst. Mgmt. Cons. (assoc., nat. standing 1985, cert. profl. cons. to mgmt.), Nat. Soc. Pub. Accts. (del., profl. standing 1985), Nat. Soc. Non-Profit Orgns. (svc. provider 1989, colleague), Accreditation Coun. for Accountancy (fed. taxation accreditation 1987, colleague), NASD Svc. Bur. Compliance. Avocations: boating, teaching, community service, athletics. Office Phone: 603-629-0056. Personal E-mail: levinsjohnr@comcast.net.

LEVINSKY, FRIEDA LIBBY, language educator; b. Belz, Poland, Jan. 25, 1932; came to U.S., 1949; d. Moses and Esther Bodenstein; m. Ely S. Levinsky, May 24, 1953 (div. Oct. 1980); children: Steven A., Jeff L. BA in History and Spanish, San Diego State U., 1969, postgrad., 1972. Tchr. Clairemont Adult Sch., San Diego, 1960-61, 64-65; tchr. Spanish and English adult edn. program San Diego C.C. Dist., 1971-91; tutor Kate Sessions Elem. Sch., San Diego, 1991; tutor ESL La Jolla (Calif.) Elem. Sch., 1992. Owner rental units, San Diego, 1980-2006; appeared on KPBS radio, and TV Channel 8; tutor English U. Calif., San Diego, 1994; asst. judge poetry contest Women in Lit., 1999. Editor: Women, Gifted Gazette, Gifted Gazette, 1972-74; poem housed at Nat. Mus. Woman in Arts, Brandeis U., Stanford U., San Diego (Calif.) Pub. Libr.; publ. judge (poetry manuscript by Pat Clark) North of Wandering; author Enlightened Ambiance, 2006; exhibitions include Down Town San Diego Pub. Libr., 2007. Publicity chmn. North Shores chpt. B'nai B'rith Women, San Diego, 1974-78, chmn. adult edn. com., 1972-74; publicity chmn. Coun. Jewish Women, 1980-84; mem. Sisterhood Congregation Beth El, Congregation Adut Yeshurun; chmn. reporting com. San Diego Assn. Gifted Students, 1971-72; nat. women's com. Braindeis U., 1999; mem. Pacific Beach Town Coun. Recipient Golden Poet award World of Poetry, 1986, 87, 88, 90, 91, Mentor Poetry award N.Am. Mentor, Friendly Exch. cert. Farmers Ins. Mag., Prose award Dana Lit. Soc., award San Diego County Apt. Assn. Mem. Acad. Am. Poets, Nat. Collegiate Fgn. Lang. Soc., Poets and Writers, Pacific Beach Town Coun., Adams Avenue Bus. Assn., Friends La Jolla Libr., Atheaneum Libr., La Jolla Hist. Soc., Nat. Collegiate Fgn. Lang. Soc., Bar-Illan U. Calif. Sheriff's Assn., Hadassah Brandeis U. (life), Mingee INternat. Mus., Weitzman Inst. Sci., Alpha Mu Gamma. Independent. Jewish. Achievements include invention of crime deterrent sign.

LEVINSOHN, GARY, producer; b. 1959; Prodr., prin. Mutual Film Co. (with Mark Gordon), LA, 1996—. Exec. prodr. films including: Blue Ice, 1992, The Real McCoy, 1993, Twelve Monkeys, 1995, Angus, 1995, The Relic, 1997, The Jackal, 1997, (TV) The Ripper, 1997, Black Dog, 1998, A Simple Plan, 1998, Virus, 1999, All the Rage, 1999, Isn't She Great? 2000, Timeline, 2003; prodr. Hard Rain, 1998, Paulie, 1998, Saving Private Ryan, 1998, Primary Colors, 1998, Man on the Moon, 1999, The Patriot, 2000, Timeline, 2003, Life of the Party, 2005, Casanova, 2005, Snakes on a Plane, 2006, The Hoax, 2006.*

LEVINSON, ARNOLD IRVING, allergist, immunologist; b. Balt., 1944; MD, U. Md. Sch. Medicine, 1969. Diplomate Am. Bd. Internal Medicine, Am. Bd. Allergy and Immunology. Intern Balt. City Hosps., 1969-70, resident internal medicine, 1970-71; prof. medicine and neurology U. Pa., Phila., 1987—. Fellow, U. Pa., Phila., 1971—72, U. Calif., San Francisco, 1972—73. Fellow Am. Acad. Allergy, Asthma and Immunology, Am. Assn. Immunologists, Am. Fedn. for Clin. Rsch., Am. Soc. for Clin. Investigation; mem. Clin. Immunology Soc. Office: U Pa Hospital 3400 Spruce St Philadelphia PA 19104-4206

LEVINSON, BARRY L., film director; b. Balt., Apr. 6, 1942; Student, Am. U., Washington; D of fine arts (hon.), Am. U., 1999. Film writer, actor: Silent Movie, 1976, High Anxiety, 1978; writer: ...And Justice for All, 1979, Inside Moves, 1980, Best Friends, 1982, Unfaithfully Yours, 1984; dir.: The Natural, 1984, Young Sherlock Holmes, 1985, Good Morning Vietnam, 1987, Rain Man, 1988 (Academy award 1989, Dirs. Guild Am. award 1989); screenwriter, dir.: Diner, 1982, Tin Men, 1987, Avalon, 1990 (Writers Guild Am. award 1990); co-prodr., dir. Bugsy, 1991, Disclosure, 1994, Wag the Dog, 1997, Sphere, 1998, An Everlasting Piece, 2000, Bandits, 2001, Envy, 2004; co-writer, dir., prodr. Toys, 1992; prodr. Donnie Brasco, 1997, An Everlasting Piece, 2000, Bandits, 2001, Possession, 2002; exec. prodr. Analyze That, 2002, Deliver Us from Eva, 2002; writer, dir., prodr. Jimmy Hollywood, 1994 (also actor), Sleepers, 1996, Liberty Heights, 1999; actor: Quiz Show, 1994; dir., exec. prodr. (TV) Homicide: Life on the Street, 1993 (Emmy award, Outstanding Individual Achievement in Directing in a Drama Series, 1993, Peabody award 1993, Humanitas award, 1999); exec. prodr. (TV) Oz, 1997, American Tragedy, 2000, Shot in the Heart, 2001, Baseball Wives, 2002, Strip Search, 2004; dir, and prodr. (TV), The Beat, 2000, The Jury, 2004. Recipient ACE Golden Eddie Filmmaker of Yr. award, 2002. Mem. Dirs. Guild Am., Writers Guild Am. Address: c/o Baltimore Pictures 8306 Wilshire Blvd PMB 1012 Beverly Hills CA 90211

LEVINSON, DANIEL RONALD, federal agency administrator, lawyer; b. Bklyn., Mar. 24, 1949; s. Gerald Sam and Risha Rose (Waxer) L.; m. Luna Frances Lambert, Sept. 13, 1980; children: Luna Claire, Hannah Louise. AB, U. So. Calif., 1971; JD, Georgetown U., 1974; LLM, George Washington U., 1977. Bar: N.Y. 1975, Calif. 1976, D.C. 1976, U.S. Supreme Ct. 1978; cert. fraud examiner. Law clk. appellate divsn. N.Y. Supreme Ct., Bklyn., 1974-76; assoc. McGuiness & Williams, Washington, 1977-81, ptnr., 1982-83; dep. gen. counsel U.S. Office Personnel Mgmt., Washington, 1983-85; gen. counsel U.S. Consumer Product Safety Commn., Washington, 1985-86; chmn. U.S. Merit Sys. Protection Bd., Washington, 1986-93; of counsel Shaw Bransford & O'Rourke, Washington, 1993-94; chief of staff U.S. Rep. from Ga. Bob Barr, Washington, 1995-98; prin. Law Offices of Daniel R. Levinson, Washington, 1998—2000; insp. gen. General Svc. Admin., Washington, 2001—05; acting insp. gen. U.S. Dept. Health & Human Services, Washington, 2004—05, insp. gen., 2005—. Adj. lectr. Am. U., Washington, 1981-82, Cath. U. Am., Washington, 1982. Editor-in-chief Jour. Pub. Inquiry, 2002-05; notes and comments editor Am. Criminal Law Rev., 1973-74; contbr. articles to profl. jours. Bd. dirs. Washington Hebrew Congregation, 1993-96; prin. Coun. for Excellence in Govt., 1993-94. Mem. Adminstrv. Conf. U.S. (govt. mem. 1984-93), Phi Beta Kappa Office: US Dept Health and Human Services 330 Independence Ave SW Rm 5250 Washington DC 20201 Office Phone: 202-619-3148. Business E-Mail: daniel.levinson@oig.hhs.gov.

LEVINSON, DAVID MATTHEW, engineering educator, civil engineer; s. Lawrence Jacob and Roslyn Levinson; m. Trinh Ann Levinson, June 3, 2002; children: Benjamin Levinson Carpenter, David. B in Civil Engring., Ga. Inst. Tech., 1988; MSc, U. Md., 1992; PhD, U. Calif., Berkeley, 1998. Cert. Am. Inst. Cert. Planners, 1993. Asst. prof. U. Minn., Mpls., 1999—2004, assoc. prof., 2005—. Chair transportation engring. Braun, 2006—. Author: (book) Financing Transportation Networks, 2002, The Transportation Experience, 2005; editor: Assessing the Benefits and Costs of Intelligent Transportation Systems, 2004, Access to Destinations, 2005. Recipient Tiebout prize, Western Regional Sci. Assn., 1995, Career award, NSF, 2003—, New Faculty Mem. award, Coun. U. Transp. Ctrs. Am. Rd. and Transp. Bldrs. Assn., 2005. Mem.: Inst. Transp. Engrs. Office: Univ Minn 500 Pillsbury Dr SE Minneapolis MN 55455 Home Phone: 612-625-6354; Office Phone: 612-625-6354. Office Fax: 612-626-7750. Business E-Mail: levin031@umn.edu.

LEVINSON, HARRY, psychologist, educator; b. Port Jervis, NY, Jan. 16, 1922; s. David and Gussie (Nudell) L.; m. Roberta Freiman, Jan. 11, 1946 (div. June 1972); children— Marc Richard, Kathy, Anne, Brian Thomas; m. Miriam Lewis, Nov. 23, 1990. BS, Emporia State U., Kans., 1943, MS, 1946; PhD, U. Kans., 1952; DHL (hon.), Mass. Sch. Profl. Psychology, 2004. Coordinator profl. edn. Topeka State Hosp., 1950-53, psychologist, 1954-55; dir. div. indsl. mental health Menninger Found., Topeka, 1955-68; vis. prof. MIT, 1961-62, U. Kans. Bus. Sch., 1967, Texas A&M U., 1976; Thomas Henry Carroll-Ford Found. distinguished vis. prof. Harvard Grad. Sch. Bus., Boston, 1968-72; adj. prof. Coll. Bus. Adminstrn., Boston U., 1972-74; lectr. Harvard Med. Sch., 1972-85; adj. prof. Pace U., 1972-83; clin. prof. psychology Harvard Med. Sch., 1985-92, emeritus prof., 1992—; head sect. orgnl. mental health Mass. Mental Health Ctr., 1983-92; pres. The Levinson Inst., 1968-91, chmn. bd., 1991—97. Mem. Am. Bd. Profl. Psychology, 1972-80, chmn., 1978-80; Ford Found. prof. Mathur Inst., Jaipur India, 1974; conducted internat. course on social psychiatry Finnish Govt. Inst., 1979. Author: Emotional Health In the World of Work, 1964, Executive Stress, 1970, The Exceptional Executive (McKinsey Found. and Acad. Mgmt. awards), 1968 (James A. Hamilton Hosp. Adminstrs. Book award), Organizational Diagnosis, 1971, The Great Jackass Fallacy, 1973, Psychological Man, 1976, Casebook for Psychological Man; (with S. Rosenthal) CEO: Corporate Leadership in Action (Am. Coll. Health Care Adminstrs. Book award 1986), 1984, Ready, Fire, Aim, 1986, Designing and Managing Your Career, 1989, Career Mastery, 1992, Organizational Assessment, 2002. Chmn. Kans. adv. com. U.S. Civil Rights Commn., 1962-68; chmn. Topeka Human Relations Commn., 1967-68. Served with F.A. AUS, 1944-46. Recipient Perry Rohrer Cons. Psychology Practice award, 1984, Career award Mass. Psychol. Assn., 1985, Disting. Svc. award Soc. Consulting Psychology, 2004, First award Soc. Psychologists in Mgmt.; Eminent scholar in bus. Fla. Atlantic U., 1995. Fellow APA (award for disting. profl. contbn. to knowledge 1992, Gold medal for life achievement in the application of psychology 2000), Am. Psychol. Found. Address: 4889 Pineview Cir Delray Beach FL 33445-4318 Personal E-mail: hlevinson@bellsouth.net.

LEVINSON, HERBERT SHERMAN, civil and transportation engineer; b. Chgo., Sept. 25, 1924; s. Israel and Tillie (Gash) Levinson; m. Sally Farver, July 3, 1977. BSCE, Ill. Inst. Tech., 1949; cert. in hwy. traffic, Yale U., 1952. Jr. traffic engr. Chgo. Park Dist., 1949-51; from assoc. to sr. v.p. Wilbur Smith & Assocs., New Haven, 1952-80; prin. Herbert S. Levinson Transp. Cons., New Haven, 1980—; prof. civil engring. U. Conn., Storrs, 1980-86; prof. transp. Poly. Inst. of N.Y., NYC, 1986-88. UTRC mentor CCNY, 1999—; vis. lectr. Yale U., New Haven, 1961—80. Author: Future Highways and Urban Growth, 1961, Parking in the City Center, 1965, Transportation and Parking for Tomorrow's Cities, 1966; author: (with D. Votaw) Elementary Sampling for Traffic Engineers, 1961; author: (with R. Weant) Urban Transportation Perspectives and Prospects, 1983, Parking, 1990; contbr. numerous articles to profl. jours. Cpl. USAF, 1943—46. Recipient Presdl. Design award, Nat. Endowment for Arts, 1988, Leadership award, XIII Pan-Am. Conf. Traffic and Transp. Engring., 2004. Fellow: ASCE (Benjamin Wright award 1993, Wilbur S. Smith award 1997, Frank Turner lectr. 2003), Inst. Transp. Engrs. (hon., Transp. Engr. of Yr. 1976, Tech. Coun. award 1982, Theodore M. Matson award 1997); mem.: NAE (nat. assoc.), Conn. Acad. Sci. and Engring. (Disting. Svc. award 2003), Am. Planning Assn., Transp. Rsch. Bd. (Roy W. Crum award 1997). Home Phone: 203-389-0041; Office Phone: 203-389-2092. Personal E-mail: hslevinson@aol.com.

LEVINSON, JOHN MILTON, obstetrician, gynecologist; b. Atlantic City, Aug. 17, 1927; m. Elizabeth Carl Bell; children: Patricia Anne, John Carl, Mark Jay. BA, Lafayette Coll., Easton, Pa., 1949; MD, Thomas Jefferson U., 1953. Diplomate Am. Bd. Ob-Gyn. Intern Atlantic City Hosp., 1953-54; Am. Cancer Soc. clin. fellow Jefferson Med. Coll. Hosp., Phila., 1954-55; resident in ob-gyn. Del. Hosp., Wilmington, 1955-57; pvt. practice ob-gyn. Wilmington, 1957-85; prof. dept. ob-gyn. Jefferson Med. Coll., Thomas Jefferson U., Phila., hon. clin. prof., 1990—; sr. attending physician emeritus Med. Ctr. Del., Wilmington, 1986—; attending chief dept. ob-gyn. St. Francis Hosp., Wilmington, chief emeritus, 1986-92. Founder, pres. Aid for Internat. Medicine, Inc., 1966—; med. dir., chief surgeon Quark Expeditions, 1991-95; cons. Riverside Hosp., 1972-86, Wilmington Pa. Blue Shield, 1982—: cons. gynecology U.S. VA, 1974-85; founding mem., treas., bd. dirs. Physicians Health Svcs., Del., Ltd., 1985-87; vis. prof., cons., ship's surgeons, practicing physician various orgns. in Africa, Antarctica, Arctic regions, Ctrl. Am., Europe, S.E. Asia, S.W. Asia, 1963—; lectr. in field; internat. med. cons. to Sen. Edward M. Kennedy, 1967—; chmn. Antarctic expdns. study group to advise NSF, 1992-93; co-chmn. Com. for Safety in Arctic and Antarctic Frontier Expeditions, 1992-93. Author: Shorebirds: The Birds, the Hunters, the Decoys, 1991, Safe Passage Questioned: Medical Care and Safety for the Polar Tourist, 1998, Advanced First Aid Afloat, 2000; assoc. prodr. 3 films on explorer Ernest Shackleton; contbr. articles to profl. jours., chpts. to books. Bd. dirs. Del. com. Project H.O.P.E., 1965-75, ARC, 1968-70, Charles A. Lindbergh Fund, Inc., 1985-90; trustee Blue Cross/ Blue Shield Del., Inc., 1968-86, Brandywine Coll., 1972-77; bd. dirs. Nat. Assn. Blue Shield Plans, 1971-77; mem adv. com. Trinity Alcohol and Drug Program, 1978-85; mem. Del. Gov.'s Commn. on Health Care Cost Mgmt., 1985-87; bd. dirs. founding mem. World Affairs Coun. Wilmington Inc, v.p., 1981-86; pres. Rockland Mills Cmty. Assn., 1992-94; mem. bd. advisors World Sportsmen Ctr., Orlando, 1997—, With USN, 1945-47; col. M.C., USAFR, 1984-87. Recipient Brandywine award Brandywine Coll., 1968, cert. of appreciation for med. svcs. Ministry of Health, Republic of Vietnam, 1963-66, commendation Pres. of U.S., 1971, The Eisenhower award People to People Internat., 1986, Commemorative medal Charles A. Lindbergh Fund, 1987, Phila. Explorers award 1987, Citation for Outstanding Contbn. to People of Del., Med. Soc. Del., 1992. Fellow Am. Coll. Ob.-Gyn., Royal Geog. Soc. London; mem. AMA, Am. Assn. Gyn. Laporoscopists (founding, bd. dirs.), Del. Obstetric Soc. (pres. 1980-82), Phila. Obstetric Soc., Med. Soc. Del. (Citation of Merit award 1992), New Castle County Med. Soc., Soc. Ob-Gyn. Vietnam (hon.), Ducks Unltd. (sponsor, mem. Del. com. 1980-92), Explorers Club (fellow 1966—, chmn. Phila. chpt. 1983-85, bd. dirs. 1981-88, pres. N.Y.C. 1985-87), Univ. and Whist Club Wilmington (life, bd. govs. 1961-64), Rotary (bd. dirs. local club 1991-93), Theta Chi (pres. 1945) Phi Beta Pi (pres. 1952), Kappa Beta Phi (pres. 1952). Avocations: hunting, polar history, sailing, carving bird decoys. Home: 55 Millstone Ln Rockland DE 19732

LEVINSON, JOSEPH E., retired internist, rheumatologist, educator; b. Cin., Apr. 7, 1920; s. Samuel W. and Rebecca (Lewin) L.; m. Mimi Freiberg, Mar. 21, 1945 (dec. Apr. 1992); children: Steven Henry, Henry Samuel, Richard Peter (dec.); m. Carol Weihl, Oct. 10, 1993 (dec. Mar. 1999); m. Sophia Ralson, Nov. 10, 2001. Student, Columbia U., NYC, 1937-40; BA, Stanford U., Calif., 1941; MD, U. Cin., 1944. Clin. and rsch. fellow in medicine Harvard U./Mass. Gen. Hosp., Boston, 1950-52; instr. medicine U. Cin., 1953-61, assoc. prof. medicine, 1961-73, prof. medicine and pediatrics, 1973-85, dir. divsn. pediatric rheumatology, 1975-86, assoc. dir. Multipurpose Arthritis Ctr., 1978-82, prof. emeritus medicine and pediatrics, 1985—. Dir. arthritis tchg. svc. Cin. Gen. Hosp., 1960-64. Contbr. chapters to books, articles to profl. jours. Bd. dirs. Seven Hills Sch., Cin., 1993-2001, Cancer Family Care, Cin., Anthem Found. of Ohio, 1999-2004, Friends of the Spl. Treatment Ctr.; bd. dirs. Planned Parenthood S.W. Ohio Region, 2000— Master Am. Coll. Rheumatology Avocations: tennis, horse and mule wilderness pack trips, travel. Office: Children's Hosp Med Ctr 3333 Burnet Ave Cincinnati OH 45229-3026 Home: Apt 802 2121 Alpine Pl Cincinnati OH 45206-3697 Office Fax: 513-636-5568. Personal E-mail: jelevinson@fuse.net.

LEVINSON, LAWRENCE EDWARD, lawyer; b. NYC, Aug. 25, 1930; s. Samuel Keever and Sara Lee (Tarvin) L.; m. Margaret Anne Bishop, Aug. 20, 1989; children: Elizabeth, Suzanne, Lucia. BA magna cum laude, Syracuse U., 1952; LLB, Harvard U., 1955. Bar: N.Y. 1957, D.C. 2002; U.S. Supreme Ct. 1958. Atty. Office Sec. Air Force, Washington, 1957-63; spl. assignments Office Sec. Def., Washington, 1963-65; dep. counsel to Pres. US, Washington, 1965-69; sr. v.p. Paramount Communications, Inc., NYC, 1969-94; sr. Washington counsel VIACOM Internat., 1994-95; ptnr. Verner, Liipfert, Bernhard, McPherson and Hand, Washington, 1995—2002, DLA Piper Rudnick, Washington, 2002—04, DLA Piper Rudnick Gray Cary, Washington, 2005—. Mem. Nat. Council on Health Planning and Devel., Washington, 1978-84; host pub. affairs TV program Capital Notebook, 1991-95. Mem. bd. visitors Syracuse U. Coll. Arts and Scis., 1981—; mem. bd. dir. Assn. Am. Publishers. Served with Judge Adv. div. U.S. Army, 1955-57. Mem. N.Y. State Bar Assn., Assn. Am. Pubs. (bd. dirs. 1989-95), Army-Navy Country Club (Washington), Phi Beta Kappa. Home: 5715 Little Falls Rd Arlington VA 22207-1554 Office: 1200 Nineteenth St NW Washington DC 20036-2412 Office Phone: 202-861-6463. Office Fax: 202-689-8568. Business E-Mail: lawrencelevinson@dlapiper.com.

LEVINSON, MICHAEL R., lawyer; b. Chgo., May 25, 1954; BS summa cum laude, Claremont Men's Coll., 1976; JD, Harvard U., 1979; MBA, U. Chgo., 1997. Bar: Ill. 1979, U.S. Dist. Ct. (no., ctrl. dists.) Ill. 1979, US Supreme Ct., Ill. Supreme Ct., US Ct. of Appeals (fed., 6th & 7th cirs.), US Dist. Ct. (so. dist.) Indiana, US Dist. Ct.(ea. dist.) Wisconsin. Mem. Seyfarth, Shaw, Fairweather & Geraldson, Chgo.; ptnr. Seyfarth Shaw LLP. Adj. prof. coll. law DePaul U., 1982-85; arbitrator Nat. Assn. Securities Dealers, chmn. Seyfarth, mem. CPR Dispute Resolution Disting. Panels Neutrals, adj. prof. Chgo. Kent Coll. Law, spkr. in feilds. Contbr. Mem. (bd. trustees) Roycemore Sch., Evanston, Ill. Recipient Ill. Super Lawyer, Ill. Leading Lawyer. Mem. ABA, Nat. Inst. Trial Advocacy, Chgo. Bar Assn., Nat. Assn. Securities Dealers (arbitrator). Office: Seyfarth Shaw LLP 131 S Dearborn St Ste 2400 Chicago IL 60603-5577 Office Phone: 312-460-5868. Office Fax: 312-460-7868. Business E-Mail: mlevinson@seyfarth.com.

LEVINSON, PAUL HOWARD, lawyer; b. NYC, Nov. 9, 1952; s. Saul and Gloria (Samson) L.; m. Susan Norine Morley, May 29, 1983; children: Lauren Hope, David Ross. BA in Sociology, Northwestern U., 1973; JD, Columbia U., 1977. Bar: NY 1978; US Dist. Ct. (so. dist.) NY 1983, US Dist. Ct. (no. dist.) NY 1992, US Dist. Ct. (ea. dist.) Pa. 2007, US Ct. Appeals (2d cir.) 1986, US Ct. Appeals (3rd cir. 1987), US Supreme Ct. 1986, US Dist. Ct. (ea. dist.) NY 2007. Asst. dist. atty., supervising sr. trial atty. Kings County, Bklyn., 1977-84; assoc. Blodnick, Schultz & Abramowitz, P.C., Lake Success, N.Y., 1984-85; ptnr. Leavy, Rosensweig & Hyman and predecessor firms, NYC, 1985-99, McLaughlin & Stern, LLP, NYC, 2000—. Trustee Cmty. Synagogue, Rye, N.Y., 1996-2002, mem. exec. com., corr. sec., 2000-04; mem. adv. coun. parks and recreation Village of Rye Brook, N.Y., 1994-97. Harlan Fiske Stone scholar. Mem. ABA, NY State Bar Assn., Assn. of Bar of City of NY (com. on criminal justice ops. and budget 1992-94, com. on criminal cts. 1995-97, chmn. sub-com. on the NYC civilian complaint rev. bd., moderator, com. on state cts. of superior jurisdiction 2002—), Bklyn. Bar Assn. (CLE seminars in criminal trial advocacy and matrimonial practice), Columbia Law Sch. Alumni Assn., Northwestern U. Entertainment Alliance East (treas. 1998—, pres. 2000-2002), Northwestern U. Alumni Assn., Northwestern U. Alumni Club NYC. Democrat. Jewish. Avocations: tennis, skiing, swimming. Home: 312 Betsy Brown Rd Rye Brook NY 10573-1901 Office: McLaughlin & Stern LLP 260 Madison Ave 18th Fl New York NY 10016 Office Phone: 212-448-6279. Business E-Mail: plevinson@mclaughlinstern.com.

LEVINSON, PETER JOSEPH, retired lawyer; b. Washington, June 11, 1943; AB in History cum laude, Brandeis U., Waltham, Mass., 1965; JD, Harvard U., Cambridge, Mass., 1968. Summer supr. Harvard Legal Aid Bur., Cambridge, Mass., 1968; rsch. asst. Harvard Law Sch., 1968-69; tchg. fellow Osgoode Hall Law Sch. York U., Canada, 1969-70, rsch. assoc., 1969-70, asst. prof., 1970-71; dep. atty. gen. State of Hawaii, 1971-75; vis. fellow Harvard U., 1976-77; ptnr. Levinson and Levinson, Honolulu, 1977-79; spl. asst. to dir. office program support Legal Svcs. Corp., Washington, 1979; cons. Select Commn. on Immigration and Refugee Policy, Washington, 1980-81; minority counsel subcom. on immigration, refugees and internat. law com. on judiciary US Ho. of Reps., Washington, 1981-85, minority counsel subcom. monopolies and comml. law, 1985-89, minority counsel subcom. econ. and comml. law, 1989-95, counsel com. on judiciary, 1995-2001, ret., 2001. Mem.: ABA.

LEVINSON, ROBERT ALAN, textiles executive; b. Balt., July 26, 1925; s. Louis and Frieda Levinson; m. Patricia S. Schulte, Apr. 23, 1954; children: Margot, Andrew, John. AB, MBA, Dartmouth Coll., 1946; postgrad., London Sch. Econs., 1946-47. With Burlington Industries, NYC, 1949-51; v.p., dir. Bangor Punta, Inc., NYC, 1964-68; chmn. bd. Duplan Corp., NYC, 1968-79. Trustee Bklyn. Mus., chmn., 1972—84; trustee governing com. New Sch. U. Gen. Studies, Bklyn., 2006; bd. dirs. World Policy Inst., Nat. Dance Inst., Nat. Commn. US-China Rels., mem. exec. com.; trustee Inst. Current World Affairs, 2007; bd. mem. Arrow Rsch. Develop. Corp., 2007; vice-chmn. Nat. Acad. Mus. With USNR, 1943—45, with USNR, 1952—54. Home: 1035 5th Ave New York NY 10028-0135 Office: 1065 Avenue of the Americas Fl 28 New York NY 10018

LEVINSON, SHAUNA T., financial services executive; b. Denver, Aug. 1, 1954; d. Charles E. and Geraldine D. Titus; m. Kenneth L. Levinson, Dec. 21, 1986. BA cum laude, U. Puget Sound, 1976; M in Bank Mktg. with honors, U. Colo., 1986; M in Nonprofit Mgmt. with distinction, Regis U., Denver, 2002. Cert. fin. planner. Fin. planning analyst Swift and Co., Chgo., 1977-79; from credit analyst to asst. v.p. Ctrl. Bank of Denver, 1979-84; v.p. fin. svcs. First Nat. Bank S.E. Denver, 1984-94; dir. mktg. First Nat. Banks, 1991-94; pres., CEO Fin. Directions, Inc., Denver, 1994—, Levinson Resources, Inc., Denver, 1994—, Ranchos Los Prados, 2005—. Dir. Colo. Planned Giving Roundtable. Contbr. articles to profl. jours. Chmn. human resources com., mem. adminstrv. coun. Jr. League Denver, 1983—; cmty. assistance fund, placement adv. com. Jr. League, Denver; fundraiser Women's Libr. Assn., U. Denver, 1990—94, 1996—98, Good Shepherd Cath. Sch., 1986—95, Jewish Cmty. Ctr., Denver, 1990—95, St. Mary's Academy, 1995—99; active Allied Jewish Fedn. Colo., 2000—02; bd. dirs. Colo. Planned Giving Roundtable, 2004—. Recipient Gold Peak award Am. Bankers Assn.-Bank Mktg. Assn., 1987; named Businessperson of Week Denver Bus. Jour., 1995. Mem.: Jr. League Denver (sustaining), Bonfils Blood Ctr. Legacy Soc., Betty Baur Lambert Soc. (life), St. Andrews Soc. (life), U. Denver Pioneer Hockey, Crestmoor Gardeners (treas. 1994—2000), Phi Chi Theta, Phi Kappa Phi, Kappa Alpha Theta (Chgo. NW alumnae 1977—79, Denver alumnae 1980—, rush adv. com. 2000—, program com. 2004—). Address: 1745 Lafayette St Denver CO 80218

LEVINSON, STEPHEN, television producer; Talent agent InterTalent, 1991, UTA, Dolores Robinson Entertainment; founder Leverage Mgmt. (agent for Mark Wahlberg, Doug Ellin, Julian Farino, Adrian Grenier, Jerry Ferrara, Samaire Armstrong), 1996. Exec. prodr.: (films) Kissing A Fool, 1998; (TV series) Entourage, 2004— (Producers Guild award, 2006). Mailing: Home Box Office Entourage 1100 Ave of the Americas New York NY 10036

LEVINSON, STEPHEN ELIOT, electrical engineer, educator; b. NYC, Sept. 27, 1944; s. Benjamin Adler and Doris Ruth (Goldstein) L.; m. Diana

Elaine Sheets, June 6, 1976. AB, Harvard U., 1966; MS, U. R.I., 1972, PhD, 1974. J.W. Gibbs instr. Yale U., New Haven, 1974-76; Disting. mem. tech. staff Bell Labs., Murray Hill, N.J., 1976—, head linguistics rsch. dept., 1990-97; prof. elec. computer engring. Beckman Inst. U. Ill., Urbana, 1997—. Vis. researcher NTT Labs., Tokyo, 1979; vis. fellow Cambridge U., U.K., 1984. Editor Computer Speech and Language jour., 1986—; patentee in speech recognition field. Fellow IEEE, Acoustical Soc. Am.; mem. AAAS, Assn. for Computing Machinery, N.Y. Acad. Sci., Sigma Xi (rsch. award U. R.I. chpt. 1973). Avocations: violin, sailing, skiing.

LEVINSON, STEVEN HENRY, state supreme court justice; b. Cin., June 8, 1946; BA with distinction, Stanford U., 1968; JD, U. Mich., 1971. Bar: Hawaii 1972, U.S. Dist. Ct. Hawaii 1972, U.S. Ct. Appeals (9th cir.) 1972. Law clk. to Hon. Bernard H. Levinson Hawaii Supreme Ct., 1971-72; pvt. practice Honolulu, 1972-89; judge Hawaii Cir. Ct. (1st cir.), 1989-92; assoc. justice Hawaii Supreme Ct., Honolulu, 1992—. Staff mem. U. Mich. Jour. Law Reform, 1970-71. Active Temple Emanu-El. Recipient Allies for Justice award, Nat. Lesbian and Gay Law Assn., 2006. Mem. ABA (jud. divsn. 1989—), Hawaii State Bar Assn. (dir. young lawyers divsn. 1975-76, dir. 1982-84), Am. Judges Assn., Am. Judicature Soc. Jewish. Office: Supreme Ct Hawaii Aliiolani Hale 417 S King St Honolulu HI 96813-2912 Home Phone: 808-988-7868; Office Phone: 808-539-4735. Business E-Mail: steven.h.levinson@courts.state.hi.us.

LEVINSON, WARREN MITCHELL, broadcast journalist; b. Bklyn., Feb. 23, 1953; s. Abraham and Roslyn Anne (Bell) L.; m. Debra Lynn Galant, Sept. 1, 1985; children: Margot, Noah. BA, Duke U., 1975. Reporter Sta. WCHL Radio, Chapel Hill, NC, 1974-77; news dir. Sta. WBLG/WKQQ Radio, Lexington, Ky., 1977-78; newswriter AP, NYC, 1979-82; corr. AP Radio and Video, NYC, 1982—. Co-host (radio talk program) Newsweek on Air, 1985-2005. Recipient Silver medal for News Mag. Internat. Radio T.V. Soc., 1989, Crystal award of Excellence, Nat. Communicator Awards, 2000, Edward R. Murrow award Radio TV News Dirs. Assn., 2007. Avocations: bicycling, poetry. Office: Associated Press 450 W 33rd St New York NY 10001 Home Phone: 973-680-4435. Business E-Mail: wlevinson@ap.org.

LEVINSTEIN, MARK STEVEN, lawyer, educator; b. Pitts., June 17, 1958; s. Hyman Joseph and Myrna Carol (Cohen) L.; m. Teresa K. Wellman, Aug. 31, 1991; children: Brian Philip, Kimberly Jael, Carly Ann. BA with honors, U. Va., 1979; JD, Harvard U., 1982. Bar: D.C. 1983, N.J. 1983, Md. 1983, U.S. Dist. Ct. N.J. 1983, Va. 1985, U.S. Dist. Ct. (ea. dist.) Va. 1985, U.S. Dist. Ct. D.C. 1985, U.S. Dist. Ct. Md. 1986, U.S. Ct. Appeals (4th cir., D.C. cir.) 1986, U.S. Ct. Appeals (9th cir.) 1989, U.S. Supreme Ct. 1990. Law clk. to presiding justice U.S. Dist. Ct. Mass., Boston, 1982-83; assoc. Williams & Connolly, Washington, 1983-90, ptnr., 1991—. Adj. prof. law Cath. U., Washington, 1985-92, George Washington U., Washington, 1991-94, Georgetown U., Washington, 1992-1999; chmn. Laws Jour.-Seminars Press Sports Law Program, 1996-2000. Co-author: Sports and the Law: Cases and Materials, 1997, 2d edit., 2007; contbr. articles to profl. jours. Founder Athletes for Hope, chair, 2006—. Named one of Best Lawyers in Am., 2007; Echols scholar. Mem. ABA, Md. Bar Assn., Va. Bar Assn., D.C. Bar Assn., Assn. Trial Lawyers Am., Sports Lawyer Assn., Raven Soc., Phi Beta Kappa, Omicron Delta Kappa. Home: 8609 Meadow Edge Ter Fairfax Station VA 22039-3349 Office: Williams & Connolly LLP 725 12th St NW Washington DC 20005-5901 Home Phone: 703-690-2339; Office Phone: 202-434-5012. E-mail: mlevinstein@wc.com.

LEVIS, DONALD JAMES, psychologist, educator; b. Cleve., Sept. 19, 1936; s. William and Antoinette (Stejskal) L.; children: Brian, Katie. PhD, Emory U., 1964. Postdoctoral fellow clin. psychology Lafayette Clinic, Detroit, 1964-65; asst. prof. psychology U. Iowa, Iowa City, 1966-70, assoc. prof., dir. research and tng. clinic, 1970-72; prof. SUNY-Binghamton, 1972—. Author: Learning Approaches to Therapeutic Behavior Modification, 1970, Implosive Therapy, 1973; cons. editor: Jour. Abnormal Psychology, 1974-80, Jour. Exptl. Psychology, 1976-77, Behavior Moedifications, 1977-81, Behavior Therapy, 1974-76, Clin. Behavior Therapy Rev., 1978—; contbr. articles to profl. jours. Served to capt. AUSR, 1958-66. Fellow Behavior and Therapy Research Soc. (charter, clin.), Am. Psychol. Assn.; mem. Assn. Advancement Behavior Therapy (publ. bd. 1979-82), AAAS, Psychonomic Soc., N.Y. State Psychol. Assn., Sigma Xi Home: 48 Riverside Dr Binghamton NY 13905-4402 Office: SUNY at Binghamton Dept Psychology Binghamton NY 13901 Office Phone: 607-772-9710.

LEVIS, WILLIAM, utilities executive; BS in Marine Engring., US Naval Acad., Annapolis, Md. Lic. profl. engr., 1985; cert. sr. reactor operator. With GE Nuc. Svcs., Westec Svcs., NRC; with Brunswick facility Carolina Power & Light; with Pickering Plant Ont. Hydro; Byron Sta. mgr. Exelon, 1998—99, v.p. Byron Sta., 1999—2001, v.p. Limerick Generating Sta., 2001; v.p. Mid-Atlantic ops. Exelon Nuc.; sr. v.p., chief nuc. officer Nuc. Oper. Svcs. Agreement between PSEG and Exelon Nuc.; pres., chief nuc. officer PSEG Nuc., 2007—; pres., COO PSEG Power, 2007—. Served in USN, ret. comdr. USNR. Office: PSEG PO Box 570 Newark NJ 07101 Office Phone: 973-430-7000.*

LEVIT, HÉLOÏSE B. (GINGER LEVIT), art historian, journalist, art dealer, consultant; b. Phila., Apr. 2, 1937; d. Elmer and Claire Frances (Schwartz) Bertman; m. Jay Joseph Levit, July 14, 1962; children: Richard Bertman, Robert Edward, Darcy Francine Honker. BA in French Literature, U. Pa., 1959; MA in French Literature, U. Richmond, 1975; MA Art History, Va. Commonwealth U., Richmond, 1998; Cert., Alliance Française, Paris, 1991, Chambre de Commerce et d'Industrie de Paris, 1991, La Sorbonne, Paris, 1994, Istituto Lorenzo di Medici Firenze, Italy, 1996, Ecole du Louvre, 1998, Cert., 2005. Arts broadcaster, Richmond, Va., 1976-82; dir. Fine Arts Am., Inc., Richmond, 1982-84; tchr. Henrico County Pub. Schs., Richmond, 1984-88; dir. devel. Sta. WVST-FM Va. State U., Petersburg, 1987-88; mgr., dir. devel. Richmond Philharm. Orch., 1988-99; fine arts and media cons. Art-I-Facts, Richmond, 1988—; cons., 1997-98. Author: Moments, Monuments & Monarchs, 1986 (Star award, 1986); arts writer: Richmond Rev., 1989—90, Mid Atlantic Antiques mag., Mid-Atlantic Antiques News, Washington Jewish Week, Tidewater Women, Va. Jewish News; anchor, prodr. (syndicated radio series) Va. Arts Report, 1978—83, Va. Women, 1984. V.p. Va. Mus. Collectors Cir., Richmond, 1986-91, mem. steering com.; pres. Richmond Area Dem. Women's Club, 1992-93; mem. Va. Mus. Coun., Richmond; rec. sec. Richmond Symphony Orch. League, 1998-2000, dir. pub. rels., 2000—, guest condr., 2000. Mem. Va. Press Women (2d pl. award 2001, 02, 03), U. Pa. Alumni Club (v.p. 1980-90, Ben Franklin award 1990), Am. Symphony Orch. League, L'Accueil Francais, Alliance Francaise, La Table Francaise (chmn. 1996—), World Affairs Coun. Avocations: antiques, art collecting, classical music, travel. Home and Office: Art-I-Facts 419 Dellbrooks Pl Richmond VA 23238-5559 Home Phone: 804-740-1471; Office Phone: 804-740-1471. Business E-Mail: ginger@vcu.org.

LEVIT, JAY J(OSEPH), lawyer; b. Phila., Feb. 20, 1934; s. Albert and Mary Levit; m. Heloise Bertman, July 14, 1962; children: Richard Bertman, Robert Edward, Darcy Francine. AB, Case Western Res. U., Cleve., 1955; JD, U. Richmond, Va., 1958; LLM, Harvard Law Sch., Cambridge, Mass., 1959. Bar: Va. 1958, US Ct. Appeals (DC cir.) 1962, US Ct. Appeals (4th cir.) 1967, US Ct. Appeals (11th cir.) 1989, US Supreme Ct. 1961. Trial atty. US Dept. Justice, Washington, 1960-64; sr. atty. Gen. Dynamics Corp., Rochester, NY, 1965-67; ptnr. Stallard & Levit, Richmond, Va., 1968-77, Levit & Mann, 1978—2006, Jay J. Levit Law Office, 2006—. Instr. U. Mich. Law Sch., Ann Arbor, 1964—65; adj. assoc. prof. U. Richmond Law Sch., 1974—77; adj. lectr. Va. Commonwealth U., Richmond, 1970—85; lectr. in field. Contbg. editor The Developing Labor Law, 4th edit., Bur. Nat. Affairs, 1974—, guest columnist on labor and employment Va. Lawyers Weekly. Recipient ABA and Bur. Nat. Affairs Books cert. of appreciation for significant contbns. to advancement of the law, 1999—2006. Mem.: ABA (labor com.), Fed. Bar Assn. (labor and employment com.), Va. Bar Assn. (labor and employment com., Chair's award for extraordinary contbns. to labor and employment law sect. 1999). Avocations: art collecting, jogging, swimming, travel. Home: 419 Dellbrooks Pl Richmond VA 23238-5559 Office: 10132 West Broad St Glen Allen VA 23060-3303 Office Phone: 804-270-4600. Business E-Mail: jaylevit@msn.com.

LEVIT, LAWRENCE A., lawyer; b. Columbus, Ohio, Aug. 18, 1945; BA with honors, U. Chgo., 1966; JD cum laude, Harvard U., 1969. Bar: DC 1972. Ptnr. Arent Fox Kintner Plotkin & Kahn, Washington, Arent Fox LLP, Wash., DC. Mem. D.C. Bar (mem. steering com. real estate, housing and land use divsn. 1974-75, vice-chmn. real estate com. 1975-76), Phi Beta Kappa. Office: Arent Fox LLP 1050 Connecticut Ave NW Washington DC 20036 Office Phone: 202-857-6215. Office Fax: 202-857-6395. Business E-Mail: levit.lawrence@arentfox.com.

LEVIT, MAX, wholesale distribution and food service executive; s. Joe and Dora Levit. V.p., 1958-1993; pres. Grocers Supply Co., Houston, 1993—. Recipient Torch of Liberty award, Anti-Defamation League, 2001. Office: Grocers Supply Co 3131 E Holcombe Blvd Houston TX 77021

LEVIT, WILLIAM HAROLD, JR., lawyer; b. San Francisco, Feb. 8, 1938; s. William Harold and Barbara Janis Kaiser L.; m. Mary Elizabeth Webster, Feb. 13, 1971; children: Alison Jones Baumler, Alexandra Bradley Kovacevich, Laura Elizabeth Fletcher, Amalia Elizabeth Webster Todryk, William Harold, III. BA magna cum laude, Yale U., 1960; MA Internat. Rels., U. Calif., Berkeley, 1962; LLB, Harvard U., 1967. Bar: N.Y. 1968, Calif. 1974, Wis. 1979. Fgn. service officer Dept. State, 1962-64; assoc. Davis Polk & Wardwell, NYC, 1967—73; assoc. ptnr. Hughes Hubbard & Reed, NYC., L.A., 1973-79; sec. and gen. counsel Rexnord Inc., Milw., 1979-83; ptnr., chair internat. practice group, loss prevention ptnr., former dir and chair litigation practice group Godfrey & Kahn, Milw., 1983—. Substitute arbitrator Iran-U.S. Claims Tribunal, The Hague, 1984-88; lectr. Practicing Law Inst., ABA, 7th Cir. Bar Assn., Nat. Assn. Corp. Dirs., Calif. Continuing Edn. of Bar, State Bar of Wis.; trustee State of Wis. Investment Bd., 2003—. Chmn. Bd. Ad Oversight Supreme Ct. Wis. Office Lawyer Regulation, 2000—06; bd. dirs. Wis. Humane Soc., 1980—90, pres., 1986—88; bd. dirs. Vis. Nurse Corp., Milw., 1980—90, chmn., 1985—87; bd. dirs. Vis. Nurse Found., 1986—95, chmn., 1986—91; bd. dirs. Aurora Health Care Inc., 1988—93, Aurora Health Care Ventures, 1993—2004, chair, 1998—2000, 2002—03; trustee Columbia Coll. Nursing, 1992—, chair, 2002—04; trustee Mt. Mary Coll., 2002—04; dir. adv. bd. Med. Coll. Wis. Cardiovasc. Ctr., 1994—, chmn., 1999—2002; rep. Assn. Yale Alumni, 1976—79, 1981—84, 1990—93; pres. Yale Club So. Calif., 1977—79; neutral advisor panel, gen. counsel, franchise and ins. panels Internat. Inst. for Conflict Prevention and Resolution. Ford Found. fellow, U. Pa., 1960—61, NDEA fellow, U. Calif., Berkeley, 1961—62. Fellow: Wis. Law Found., Am. Bar Found., Chartered Inst. Arbitrators (London) (chartered arbitrator); mem.: ABA, Internat. C. of C. (arbitration panel), Am. Arbitration Assn. (comml., internat., large complex case, and mediation panels), Inst. Jud. Adminstrn., Am. Soc. Internat. Law, N.Am. Coun. London Ct. of Internat. Arbitration, N.Y. Stock Exch. (panel arbitrators 1988—), Nat. Assn. Security Dealers (panel arbitrators 1988—), Am. Br. Internat. Law Assn., Bar Assn. 7th Cir. (pres. 2002—03), State Bar Wis. (dir. internat. bus. transactions sect. 1985—92, dist. 2 Wis. Supreme Ct. bd. attys. profl. responsbility com. 1985—94, chmn. 1993—94), L.A. County Bar Assn. (ethics com. 1976—79), State Bar Calif. (com. on continuing edn. of bar 1977—79), Assn. Bar City N.Y., Am. Soc. Corp. Secs. (dir. 1981—92, pres. Wis. chpt. 1982—83), Am. Law Inst., Mountain Lake Club, Milw. Athletic Club, Town Club, Phi Beta Kappa. Office: 780 N Water St Ste 1200 Milwaukee WI 53202-3512 Office Phone: 414-273-3500. Business E-Mail: wlevit@gklaw.com.

LEVITAN, DAVID M(AURICE), lawyer, educator; b. Tver, Lithuania, Dec. 25, 1915; (parents Am. citizens); m. Judith Morley; children: Barbara Lane Levitan, Stuart Dean Levitan. BS, Northwestern U., 1936, MA, 1937; PhD, U. Chgo., 1940; JD, Columbia U., 1948. Bar: N.Y. 1948, U.S. Dist. Ct. (so. dist.) N.Y. 1948, U.S. Supreme Ct. 1953. Various U.S. Govt. adminstrv. and advisory positions with Nat. Youth Adminstrn., Office Price Adminstrn., War Prodn. Bd., Fgn. Econ. Adminstrn. Supreme Hdqrs. Allied Expeditionary Force, and Cen. European div. Dept. State, 1945—46; cons., sec. joint-com. of 5th and 6th coms., 2d Gen. Assembly, dir. com. of experts for establishing adminstrv. tribunal UN, 1946-47; cons. pub. affairs dept., producer series of pub. affairs programs on TV and radio ABC, 1946-53; pvt. practice NYC, 1948-66; counsel Hahn & Hessen, NYC, 1966-68, ptnr., 1968-86, counsel, 1986-96; instr. U. Chgo., 1938-41; adj. prof. public law Columbia U., 1946-65; adj. prof. John Jay Coll. Criminal Justice, CUNY, 1966-75; adj. prof. polit. sci. Post Coll., 1964-66; adj. prof. law Cardozo Sch. Law, 1978-82; pvt. practice, NYC, 1996—. Asst. to Ill. state adminstr. Nat. Youth Adminstrn., chief budget sect., Washington, 1940-41; mgmt. analyst Office of Price Adminstrn., 1941; spl. asst. to chmn. War Prodn. Bd., 1942-43; chief property control divsn. Fgn. Econ. Adminstrn., Washington, 1944-45; with U.S. Group of Control Coun. for Germany at SHAEF, London, 1944; advisor Ctrl. European divsn. U.S. Dept. State, 1945; cons. UN, 1946-47, Sect. Joint Com. 5th and 6th Coms., 1946-47, 2d session of 1st Gen. Assembly, 1946-47; dir. Com. of Experts on Establishment of Adminstrn. Tribunal, 1946-47; cons. pub. affairs dept. ABC, 1946-53. Contbr. articles to legal jours. Mem. Nassau County (N.Y.) Welfare Bd., 1965-69; chmn. Planning Bd., Village of Roslyn Harbor, N.Y., 1965-66; chmn. Bd. of Zoning Appeals, Village Roslyn Harbor, 1967-86. Recipient Demobilization award Social Sci. Rsch. Coun., 1946-48. Fellow Am. Coll. Trust and Estate Counsel; mem. ABA, Am. Polit. Sci. Assn., Am. Soc. Internat. Law, Am. Law Inst., Assn. Bar City N.Y. Office: Ste 704 455 North End Ave New York NY 10282 Office Phone: 917-522-1301.

LEVITAN, GUTMAN, research and development company executive, communications engineer; b. Kramatorsk, Ukraine, July 31, 1937; arrived in US, 1987, naturalized, 1992; s. Israel Levitan and Kelia Konovalova; m. Olga Wexler Levitan, Jan. 4, 1964; 1 child, Gary. Diploma in Elec. Engring., Poly. Inst., Kharkov, Ukraine, 1959; PhD in Computer Sci., Inst. of Comms., Moscow. Russia, 1972. Sr. rsch. fellow Ctrl. Inst. Automation, Moscow, 1964—86; sr. software engr. Syllogy Corp., Hackensack, NJ, 1987—92; sr. analyst Trecom Bus. Sys., NYC, 1992—97; pres. Virtel Corp., Stamford, Conn., 1997—. Leader Trust Group, Moscow, 1985—86. Mem.: IEEE. Jewish. Achievements include patents on inventions that facilitate convergence of television and the Internet. Avocations: philosophy, religion. Home: Apt 11 101 Grove St Stamford CT 06901 Office Phone: 203-359-6970. Office Fax: 203-359-0198. Business E-Mail: gl@virtelnet.com.

LEVITAN, LAURENCE, lawyer, retired state senator; b. Oct. 22, 1933; s. Maurice and Nathlie (Rosenthal) L.; m. Barbara E. Levin, 1957; children: Jennifer, Michelle, Lisa. BS, Washington and Lee U., 1955; JD, George Washington U., 1958. Bar: Md. 1964. With Levitan, Cramer & Weinstein, 1959-72, Levitan Ezrin, West & Kenxton, 1973-85, Beckett Cromwell & Goldman, 1990-92; of counsel Baker & Hostetler, 1992-95; ptnr. Rifkin, Livingston, Levitan and Silver, LLC, Annapolis, Md., 1995—. Mem. Md. Ho. of Dels., 1971-74; mem. Md. Senate, 1975-94, chmn. budget and taxation com., policy com., spending affordability com, mem. joint com. on mgmt. pub. funds, legis. com. on budget and audit, gov.'s commn. to rev. state taxes and taxes structure, joint legis. com. on tax refrm, govtl. commn. to revise annotated code of Md., joint subcom. on program open space, chmn. drunk and drugged driving task force, chmn. joint com. on ins. tax reform; mem. Montgomery County Exec.'s Commn. for Higher Edn. in High Tech.; past mem. Gov.'s Commn. to Study Unification of Cir. Ct., Gov.'s Commn. to Study Condominium Laws, Gov.'s Commn. Law Enforcement and Adminstrn. Justice, Gov.'s Subcom. on Revenue Structure of Task Force to Study State-Local Rels.; mem. Gov.'s Commn. to Study Feasability of Biennial Budget, Gov.'s Task Force on Real Property Closing Costs, Task Force to Study Md. Tax Ct., Gov.'s Commn. Sch. Funding, Joint Task Force on Md.'s Procurement Law; apptd. co-chmn. transition team on budget rev. Gov. Glendening; chmn. Gov.'s Jud. Compensation Commn., 1998—; mem. Commn. on Md.'s Fiscal Structure, 2002-03. Bd. regents Morgan State U., 2006—. Mem. ABA, D.C. Bar Assn., Md. Bar Assn., Nat. Conf. State Legislatures (mem. subcom. on fed. budget and taxation com., fiscal affairs govt. oversight com.), So. Legis. Conf. (chmn. fiscal affairs and govt. ops. steering com. 1992-93), Am. Legis. Exch. Coun. (tax task force, chmn. jud. compensation commn. 2003-2009). Democrat. Jewish. Office: 225 Duke Of Gloucester St Annapolis MD 21401-2506 also: 11426 Georgetowne Dr Potomac MD 20854-3722 Home Phone: 301-299-1356; Office Phone: 410-269-5066. E-mail: checkoffLL@aol.com, llevitan@rlls.com.

LEVITAN, MAX FISHEL, anatomist, geneticist, educator; b. Tverai, Telsiu Aps, Lithuania, Mar. 1, 1921; came to U.S., 1928; s. Solomon Leib and Hannah (Siev) Levitan; m. Beth Sheva German, Oct. 25, 1947; children: Eve Leah Gerber, Sara Anne, Marjorie Ruth Gross. AB, U. Chgo., 1944; MA, U. Mich., 1946; PhD, Columbia U., 1951. Asst. in zoology Columbia U., NYC, 1946—49; assoc. prof. biology Va. Poly. Inst., Blacksburg, 1949—55; asst. prof. anatomy Woman's Med. Coll. Pa., Phila., 1955—58, assoc. prof., 1958—60, prof. anatomy and med. genetics, 1960—66, acting chmn. anatomy dept., 1964—66; prof. biology, chmn. dept. George Mason U., Fairfax, Va., 1966—68; assoc. prof. anatomy Mt. Sinai Sch. Medicine, NYC, 1968—70, prof. anatomy, 1970—, prof. human genetics, 1995—. Author: Textbook of Human Genetics, 1971, 3rd edit. 1988; contbng. author: Clinical Genetics, 1973, Genetics and Biology of Drosophila, 1982, Drosophila Inversion Polymorphism, 1992, Encyclopedia of Human Biology, 1992, 1997, Encyclopedia of Science and Technology, 1992, 1997, Genetics of Natural Populations, 1995; assoc. editor Evolution, 1977-79; contbr. articles to profl. jours. Named Edward Everett Just Meml. lectr. Howard U., Washington, 1968; recipient Rsch. Career Devel. award NIH, 1963. Fellow AAAS; mem. Genetics Soc. Am., Soc. for Study of Evolution, Am. Soc. Naturalists, Sigma Xi (sec. VPI chpt. 1954-55, sec.-treas. Mt. Sinai chpt. 1975—). Jewish. Achievements include research in linkage disquilibria in inversion systems, unique chromosomal breakage factor, suppressor systems in evolution, climatic changes and inversion systems, frequency changes under global warming. Home: 1212 5th Ave New York NY 10029-5210 Office: Mt Sinai Sch Medicine 1 Gustave L Levy Pl New York NY 10029-5216 Home Phone: 212-722-1732; Office Phone: 212-241-4576. Fax: 212-824-9485. Business E-Mail: max.levitan@mssm.edu.

LEVITAN, NATHAN, internist, hematologist, medical oncologist; b. Beverly, Mass., June 21, 1954; BA, Brandeis Univ., Waltham, Mass., 1976; MBA, Weatherhead Sch. Mgmt., Case Western Reserve Univ., 1996; MD, Tufts Univ. Sch. Medicine, Boston, Mass., 1980. Intern, resident internal medicine Boston VA Med. Ctr., 1980—83, clin. fellowship, hematology/oncology, 1983—84; clin. & rsch. fellow, blood banking and immunohematology Univ. Mass. Med. Ctr., 1984—85, clin. fellow, hematology/oncology, 1985—86; prof. medicine Case Western Reseve U.; chief med. officer Univ. Hosps. Case Med. Ctr.; med. dir., clin. cancer prog. Ireland Cancer Ctr. & Univ. Hosps. Health Sys. Contbr. articles to profl. jours. Achievements include being the lead surgeon in conjoined twins' surgery in Ohio, 2007. Office: Case Western Reserve Univ Dept Medicine 11100 Euclid Ave Cleveland OH 44106*

LEVITAN, STEVE, lawyer; b. Bklyn., June 14, 1960; s. Irving and Blanche (Karp) L. AB, Dartmouth Coll., 1982; JD, MBA, U. Chgo., 1986. Bar: N.Y. 1987, D.C. 2004, U.S. Dist. Ct. (ea. and so. dists.) N.Y. 1987, U.S. Ct. Appeals (D.C. cir.) 1990, U.S. Supreme Ct. 1990; CPA, Ill. Intern Internat. Peace Acad. UN, NYC, 1982; chmn. Univ. Student Fed. Credit Union, Chgo., 1983-86; intern Ernst & Whinney, Chgo., 1984; assoc. Simpson Thacher & Bartlett, NYC, 1986-90, Weil Gotshal & Manges, NYC, 1990-92; counsel Stroock & Stroock & Lavan LLP, NYC, 1996—2002; ptnr. McKee Nelson, LLP, NYC, 2002—. Cons. Bus. Adv. Group, Washington, 1993-95. Mng. editor U. Chgo. Legal Forum, 1984-86. Mem. Kingsway Jewish Ctr., Bklyn., 1987—; Dem. candidates campaign mgr., 1992-95. Mem. ABA, AICPA, Ill. Soc. CPA's, Assn. Bar City N.Y., MENSA, Kappa Kappa Kappa. Avocations: scuba diving (master), skiing, travel. Home: 1524 E 35th St Brooklyn NY 11234-3439 Office: McKee Nelson LLP One Battery Pk Plz 35th Fl New York NY 10004 Office Phone: 917-777-4200.

LEVITAS, ANDREW STEPHEN, child psychiatrist, educator; b. Bklyn., Feb. 17, 1948; s. Louis and Laura (Perlman) L.; m. Phyllis Malin, Apr. 19, 1970; children: Joshua, Matthew. BS, Union Coll., 1968; MD, Albert Einstein Coll. Medicine, 1972. Diplomate Am. Bd. Psychiatry and Neurology. Intern Montefiore Hosp. and Med. Ctr., Bronx, 0972—1973; resident in psychiatry Downstate-Kings County Hosp. Ctr., Bklyn., 1973—75; fellow in child psychiatry U. Colo. Health Scis. Ctr., Denver, 1975—77, asst. clin. prof., 1982—86; staff psychiatrist Denver Children's Hosp., 1977—79; pvt. practice Denver, 1979—86; asst. prof. U. Nebr. Med. Ctr., Omaha, 1986—88, U. Medicine and Dentistry N.J. Sch. Osteo. Medicine, Cherry Hill, 1988—96, assoc. prof. psychiatry, 1996—; med. dir. divsn. prevention and treatment of devel. disorders Sch. Osteo. Medicine, Cherry Hill, 1992—. Cons. psychiatrist T.I.M. House, Devel. Pathways, Aurora, Colo., 1982-86; mem. sci. adv. bd. Fragile-X Soc. Assoc. editor: Mental Health Aspects of Developmental Disabilities, 1997—; contbr. numerous articles to profl. jours. Mem. MLA, Am. Psychiat. Assn., Am. Acad. Child and Adolescent Psychiatry. Office: U Medicine and Dentistry NJ Sch Oste Medicine Dept Psy 101 Laurel Rd Stratford NJ 08084-1352

LEVITCH, JOSEPH See LEWIS, JERRY

LEVITE, LAURENCE A., publishing executive; b. Buffalo, Apr. 26, 1940; s. Samuel and Estelle (Tishman) L.; m. Sharon Cohen, Aug. 15, 1965; children: Adam, Joshua. Student, U. Pa., 1958-60; grad., Am. Acad. Dramatic Arts, 1962; student, U. Buffalo Law Sch., 1965. Gen. mgr. McLendon Broadcasting, WYSL and WPHD Radio, Buffalo, 1970-74; exec. v.p., gen. mgr. Queen City Radio Corp., WEBR Radio, Buffalo, 1974-77; founder, pres., CEO Algonquin Broadcasting Corp., Buffalo, 1977-94; chmn. bd. dirs., pres. Algonquin Comm., Inc., Buffalo, 1995—; chmn., pub. Buffalo Spree Publishing, Inc., Williamsville, NY, 1998—. Bd. govs. Jewish Fedn. Buffalo, 1982—; chmn. media divsn. United Way campaign, 1985; mem. adv. bd. Jr. League, 1981, Medaille Coll., 1980, Jewish Ctr. of Buffalo, 1979-82, Episcopal Charities, 1981-83; bd. dirs. Bryant and Stratton Coll., 1998—, Shea's Buffalo Theatre, 1998—. Mem. Profl. Communicators of Western N.Y. (pres.), Buffalo Radio Assocs. Group (pres. 1972), N.Y. Broadcasters, N.Y. State Broadcasters Assn. (bd. dirs. 1983—, chmn. 1987), Nat. Assn. Broadcasters, Radio Advt. Bur., Buffalo Exec. Assn., Buffalo Club. Jewish. also: Buffalo Spree Publishing Inc 6215 Sheridan Dr Williamsville NY 14221 Office Phone: 716-634-0820 x 2220.

LEVITIN, YELENA, surgeon; b. Kharkov, Ukraine, Jan. 20, 1969; arrived in U.S., 1987; 2 children. BA, Northwestern U., Evanston, Ill., 1991; MD, Northwestern Med. Sch., Chgo., 1996. Cert. FACS. Surg. resident St. Luke's, Chgo., 1995—2000; gen. surgeon Chgo. Surg. Clinic, Wheeling, Ill., 2000—. Fellow: ACS, Soc. Am. Gastrointestinal and Endoscopic Surgeons. Office: Chgo Surgical Clinic 201 E Strong St Ste 7 Wheeling IL 60090 Office Phone: 847-215-0530.

LEVITON, ALAN EDWARD, curator; b. NYC, Jan. 11, 1930; s. David and Charlotte (Weber) L.; m. Gladys Ann Robertson, June 30, 1952; children: David A., Charlotte A. Student, NYU, 1948; postgrad., Columbia U., 1948; AB, Stanford U., 1949, MA, 1953; student, U. Nebr., 1954; PhD, Stanford U., 1960. Asst. curator herpetology Calif. Acad. Scis., San Francisco, 1957—60, assoc. curator, 1960—61, chmn., curator, 1962—82, 1989—92, 2001—, curator, 1983—88, 1993—2000, chmn. computer svcs., 1983—92, editor sci. publs., 1994—; assoc. curator zool. collections Stanford U., 1962—63, lectr. biol. sci., 1963—70; professorial lectr. Golden Gate U., 1953—63; adj. prof. biol. sci. San Francisco State U., 1967—2000, rsch. prof., 2000—. Rsch. assoc. nat. mus. natural history Smithsonian Instn., Washington, 2005—. Author: North American Amphibians, 1970, Reptiles of the Middle East, 1992, T.H. Hittel's California Academy of Sciences, 1997; contbr. articles to profl. jours. Grantee Am. Philos. Soc., 1960, NSF, 1960-61, 77-79, 80, 83-89, 91-93, 2002—, Belvedere Sci. Fund, 1958-59, 62; recipient Fellows' medal Calif. Acad. Scis., 1999. Fellow AAAS (coun. 1976-97, com. coun. affairs 1983-85, sec.-treas. Pacific divsn. 1975-79, exec. dir. 1980-98, 2000-2001, pres.-elect 1998, pres. 1999-2000, counselor 2001—), Calif. Acad. Scis., Geol. Soc. Am. (vice-chmn. history geology divsn. 1989-90, chmn. 1990-91); mem. Am. Soc. Ichthyologists and Herpetologists (mem. bd. govs. 1960-84), Soc. Systematic Zoology (sec.-treas. Pacific sect. 1970-72), Forum Historians of Sci. Am. (coord. com. 1986-88, sec.-treas. 1988-90), Herpetologists League (pres. 1961-62), History of Sci. Soc. Home: 571 Kingsley Ave Palo Alto CA 94301-3225 Office: Calif Acad Scis 875 Howard St San Francisco CA 94103

LEVITSKY, MELVYN, former ambassador; b. Sioux City, Iowa, Mar. 19, 1938; s. David and Mollie (Schwartz) L.; m. Joan Daskovsky, Aug. 12, 1962; children: Adam, Ross Josh. BA, U. Mich., 1960; MA, U. Iowa, 1963. Polit. officer U.S. Embassy, Moscow, 1972-75; officer-in-charge Soviet-U.S. bilateral relations Dept. State, Washington, 1975-78, dep. dir. UN polit. affairs, 1978-80, dir. UN polit. affairs, 1980-82, dep. asst. sec. for human rights and humanitarian affairs, 1982-83; dep. dir. Voice of Am., Washington, 1983-84; U.S. amb. to Bulgaria, 1984-87; exec. sec., spl. asst. to sec. Dept. State, Washington, 1987-89, asst. sec. state internat. narcotics matters, 1989-94, U.S. amb. to Brazil Brasilia, 1994—; prof. Internat. Relations & Pub. Adminstrn. Maxwell School of Citizenship & Pub. Affairs, Syracuse U., Syracuse, NY; Disting. Fellow of Moynihan Inst. of Global Affairs Syracuse U., Syracuse, NY, 1998—2006; professorial lectr. Johns Hopkins U. Sch. Advanced Internat. Studies, Washington, 2001—05. UN Econ. and Social Coun. elected mem. Internat. Narcotics Control Bd., 2002—; lectr., sr. fellow Internat. Policy Ctr., Gerald R. Ford Sch. Pub. Policy U. Mich., 2006—. Bd. dirs. Drug Free Am. Found. Recipient Meritorious Honor award Dept. State, 1968, Superior Honor award Dept. State, 1975, 82, Presdl. Meritorious Svc. awards, 1986-91. Mem. Am. Fgn. Svc. Assn., Am. Acad. Diplomacy, Washington Inst. Fgn. Affairs. Office: Joan and Sanford Weill Hall Ste 3310 735 S State St Ann Arbor MI 48109 Address: 2427 Moors Ct Ann Arbor MI 48108 Office Phone: 734-615-4262. Business E-Mail: levitsky@umich.edu.

LEVITT, ARTHUR, JR., investment company executive, former federal agency administrator; b. Bklyn., Feb. 3, 1931; s. Arthur and Dorothy (Wolff) L.; m. Marylin Blauner, June 12, 1955; children: Arthur III, Lauri. BA, Williams Coll., 1952, LLD (hon.), 1980, Pace U., 1980, Hamilton Coll., 1981, L.I. U., 1984, Hofstra U., 1985; LLD (hon.), Columbia U., 1999. Asst. promotion dir. Time, Inc., NYC, 1954-59; exec. v.p., dir. Oppenheimer Industries, Inc., Kansas City, Mo., 1959-62; with Shearson Hayden Stone Inc. (now Citigroup), NYC, 1962-78, pres., 1969-78; chmn., CEO, Am. Stock Exch., NYC, 1978-89; chmn. Levitt Media Co., NYC, 1989-93, NYC Econ. Devel. Corp., NYC, 1989—93, SEC, Washington, 1993—2001; sr. adv. The Carlyle Group, NYC, 2001—, WisdomTree Investments, NY, 2006—; spl. advisor Am. Internat. Group Inc., NYC, 2005—. Co-chair Promontory Fin. Group, 2006—. Co-author (with Paula Dwyer): Take on the Street: What Wall Street and Corporate America Don't Want You To Know, 2003. Chmn. President's Pvt. Sector Survey on Cost Control, 1982-84, President's Task Force on Pvt. Sector Initiatives, 1981-82, White House Small Bus. Conf. Commn., 1978-80; mem. N.Y. State Coun. on Arts, 1969—; chmn. bd. dirs. Spl. Adv. Task Force on Future Devel. West Side Manhattan, President's Base Closure and Realignment Commn.; former trustee Williams Coll.; bd. dirs. Bloomberg LLP, Rand Corp. With USAF, 1952—54, maj. res. Recipient Medal of Excellence Bd. Regents State of NY. Mem. Am. Bus. Conf. (chmn. 1980-89), Phi Beta Kappa. Office: The Carlyle Group 520 Madison Ave New York NY 10022 Business E-Mail: arthur.levitt@carlyle.com.*

LEVITT, BRIAN MICHAEL, consumer products company executive, lawyer; b. Montreal, Que., Can., July 26, 1947; s. Eric and Rya Levitt; m. Claire Gohier, Jan. 25, 1992; children: Marie-Anne, Katherine. BASc, U. Toronto, Ont., Can., 1969, LLB, 1973. Spl. asst. to provost U. Toronto, 1969-73; dir. interpretation Anti-Inflation Bd. Govt. Can., Ottawa, 1975-76; assoc. Osler, Hoskin & Harcourt, Toronto, 1976-79, ptnr., 1979-91; pres. Imasco Ltd., Montreal, 1991—, COO, 1993—, CEO, 1995—, also bd. dirs. Bd. dirs. First Fed. Savs. & Loan Assn., Rochester, N.Y., CT Fin. Svcs., Inc., Westbury Can. Life Ins. Co., BCE, Inc., Montreal, Bell Can.; mem. adv. bd. faculty mgmt. McGill U., Montreal. Contbr. articles to profl. jours. Bd. dirs. Montcrest Schs.; mem. adv. coun. Soc. Ednl. Visits and Exchanges in Can. Mem. ABA (bus. law subsect.), Can. Bar Assn., Law Soc. Upper Can., Caledon Ski, Toronto Club, Mt. Royal Club, Donalda Club, Mt. Bruno Country Club. Avocations: skiing, riding, sailing.

LEVITT, GEORGE, retired chemist; b. Newburg, NY, Feb. 19, 1925; m. Julie Zeto; children: Barbara Klein, Jeffrey, David, Gregory. BS, Duquesne U., 1950, MS, 1952; PhD, Mich. State U., 1957. Rsch. chemist Exptl. Sta. E.I. du Pont de Nemours & Co., Inc., 1956—63, rsch. chemist Stine Lab., 1963—66, rsch. chemist Exptl. Sta., 1966—68, sr. rsch. chemist, 1968—80, rsch. assoc., 1981—86. Instr. Del. Tech. and C.C., 1975—80. Pres. Ronald McDonald House of Del, 1986—87, bd. dirs., 1986—94. Recipient Internat. pesticide rsch. award, Swiss Soc. Chem. Industries, 1982, award, Chesapeake chpt. Nat. Agrl. Mktg. Assn., 1987, disting. alumni award, Duquesne U. Coll. Arts and Sci., 1988, Nat. Medal of Tech., 1993, Disting. Inventor award, Intellectual Property Owners Am., 1983. Mem.: AAAS, Internat. Union Pure & Applied Chemistry, Am. Chem. Soc. (Creative Invention award 1989, Kenneth Spencer award 1991, internat. award for rsch. in agrochems. 1998, Hero of Chem. award 1999), Sigma Xi. Achievements include research in organic syntheses, herbicides, fungicides, medicinals, pesticides; synthesis of heterocyclic compounds; characterization and identification of novel organic compounds for biological evaluation; defined and optimized chemical structure-biological activity relationships and sulfonylurea herbicides. Home: 82 Via del Corso Palm Beach Gardens FL 33418-3773 Personal E-mail: gleanr@msn.com.

LEVITT, GERALD STEVEN, engineering executive; b. Bronx, Mar. 21, 1944; s. Charles and Beatrice (Janet) L.; m. Natalie Lillian Hoppen; children: Mark, Roy. B in Mgmt. Engring., Rensselaer Poly. Inst., 1965; MBA, DePaul U., 1972. Registered profl. engr., Ill. Tech. rep. Worthington Air Conditioning Co., Ampere, NJ, 1965-67; indsl. sales engr. Peoples Gas Light & Coke Co., Chgo., 1967-71; planning specialist Peoples Gas Co., Chgo., 1971-72; v.p. Stone & Webster Mgmt. Cons., Inc., NYC, 1972-82; exec. v.p., chief staff officer South Jersey Gas Co., Folsom, NJ, 1982-98; v.p., CFO South Jersey Industries, Inc., Folsom, NJ, 1987-98; sr. v.p., treas., CFO, bd. dirs. Greenhorne & O'Mara, Inc., Laurel, Md., 1998—. Past bd. dirs. Camden County coun. Boy Scouts Am., West Collingswood, N.J., Rowan Coll. Found. Mem. Greater Atlantic City C. of C. (past bd. dirs.), N.J. State C. of C. (past bd. dirs.), Greenhorne O'Mara, Inc. (bd. dirs.). Office: Greenhorne & O'Mara Inc 6110 Frost Pl Laurel MD 20707 Home Phone: 410-379-6254; Office Phone: 301-982-2800. Business E-Mail: glevitt@g-and-o.com.

LEVITT, HARRY, speech and hearing scientist; b. Johannesburg, May 19, 1937; came to U.S., 1964; s. Boris and Thelma (Kagan) L.; m. Eleanor Claire Sosnow, June 15, 1969 (dec. Sept. 2000); 1 child, David Avrum. BSc, U. Witwatersrand, Johannesburg, 1958; PhD, Imperial Coll. Sci. and Tech., London, 1964. Tech. staff mem. AT&T Bell Labs., Murray Hill, NJ, 1964-69; assoc. prof., prof., disting. prof. CUNY, 1969-2000. Cons. AT&T Bell Labs., 1980-99, BBN, 1970—85, Audimax, 1970—, various univs.; reviewer NIH, NSF, Office Edn., VA, 1970—. Beit fellow, 1960-63; fellow Acoustical Soc. Am., 1970, Am. Speech and Hearing Assn., 1980; recipient Nat. Winner for Computing to Aid the Handicapped Johns Hopkins, 1981, N.Y.C. Mayor's award for contbns. to sci. and tech., 1999, Lifetime Achievement award Am. Auditory Soc., 2001, James Jerger Career award in audiology, 2006. Achievements include introducing computer assisted adaptive testing to the field of audiology; helped develop first digital hearing aid. Office: CUNY Grad Sch 365 5th Ave New York NY 10016-4334 Home: PO Box 610 Bodega Bay CA 94923-0610 E-mail: harrylevitt@earthlink.net.

LEVITT, JERRY DAVID, medical educator; b. Phila., 1941; s. Abraham and Nettie L.; m. Julie Meranze, 1967; children: Rachel, Daniel, Gabriel. BA, U. Pa., 1962, MD, 1966. Diplomate Am. Bd. Anesthesiology, Pain Mgmt.; lic. physician, Pa., Maine. Intern Mt. Sinai Hosp., NYC, 1966—67; resident in anesthesia U. Pa. Hosp., Phila., 1967—69, rsch. fellow, 1971—72; instr. anesthesia U. Pa., Phila., 1972—73, asst. prof. anesthesia, 1973—82; assoc. prof. anesthesiology Med. Coll. Pa. Hahnemann Sch. Medicine, Phila., 1982—2002, Drexel U. Coll. of Medicine, Phila., 2002—. Author: (with others) Basic Pharmacology in Medicine, 1990; contbr. articles to profl. jours. With USPHS, 1969-71. Avocations: photography, sailing, music, motorcycles. Office: Hahnemann Univ Hosp Broad & Vine Sts Philadelphia PA 19102 Office Phone: 215-762-3544.

LEVITT, ROBERT E., gastroenterologist; b. Phila., Oct. 22, 1948; s. Martin E. and Miriam G. (Elson) L.; m. Linda Levitt, Mar. 13, 1976; children: Adam, Ashley. BA summa cum laude, Temple U., 1970, MD, 1974. Diplomate Am. Bd. Internal Medicine, Am. Bd. Gastroenterology. Chief hepatology and gastrointestinal rsch. Presbyn. U. of Pa. Med. Ctr., Phila., 1979-88, staff gastroenterologist, 1979—, assoc. dir. Inst. Gastroenterology, 1981-89; chief svc. gastroenterology Bryn Mawr (Pa.) Hosp., 1985—, chief gastrointestinal sect. dept. medicine, 1988—, dir. endoscopy ste., 1988—; asst. prof. medicine U. Pa. Sch. Medicine, 1979—; dir. endoscopy suite Bryn Mawr Hosp., 1988—. Clin. assoc. prof. medicine, Jefferson Med. Coll., Thomas Jefferson U., Phila. Contbr. articles to med. jours., chpts. to med. books; mem. editorial adv. bd. Post-Grad. Medicine. Fellow ACP, Am. Gastroenterol. Assn.; mem. AMA (Physicians Recognition award 1978, others), Am. Coll. Gastroenterology, Am. Soc. for Gastrointestinal Endoscopy, Pa. Soc. Gastroenterology, Med. Club Phila., Phi Eta Sigma, Alpha Omega Alpha. Office: 933 E Haverford Rd Bryn Mawr PA 19010-3819

LEVITT, SEYMOUR HERBERT, radiologist, educator; b. Chgo., July 18, 1928; s. Nathan E. Levitt and Margaret (Chizever) D.; m. Phillis Jeanne Martin, Oct. 31, 1952 (div. Oct. 1981); children: Mary Jeanne, Jennifer Gaye, Scott Hayden; m. Solveig I. Ostberg, Feb. 6, 1983. BA, U. Colo., 1950, MD, 1954, DSc (hon.), 1997. Diplomate Am. Bd. Radiology. Intern Phila. Gen. Hosp., 1954-55; resident in radiology U. Calif. at San Francisco Med. Center, 1957-61; instr. radiation therapy U. Mich., Ann Arbor, 1961-62, U. Rochester, NY, 1962-63; asso. prof. radiology U. Okla., Oklahoma City, 1963-66; prof. radiology, chmn. div. radiotherapy Med. Coll. Va., Richmond, 1966-70; prof., head dept. therapeutic radiology U. Minn., Mpls., 1970—99. Cons. in field. Exec. bd. Am. Joint Com. for End Result Reporting and Cancer Staging; com. radiation oncology studies Nat. Cancer Inst.; trustee Am. Bd. Radiology, 1977-89; chmn. bd. dirs. Found. for Rsch. and Edn.; fgn. adj. prof. Karolinska Inst., Stockholm, 2002. Bd. dirs., mem. exec. com. Am. Cancer Soc., 1990-95. With M.C., AUS, 1955-57. Recipient Disting. Svc. award U. Colo., 1988, Gold Medal award Gilbert Fletcher Soc., 1987, Silver and Gold award Med. Sch., U. Colo., 1992. Fellow: Am. Soc. Therapeutic Radiologists (exec. bd. 1974—78, pres. 1978—79, chmn. bd. 1979—80, Gold medal 1991), Am. Coll. Radiology (bd. chancellors, Gold medal 1995), Royal Coll Radiology (hon.); mem.: Am. Soc. Clin. Oncology, Soc. Nuclear Medicine, Internat. Soc. Radiation Oncology (pres. 1981—85), Soc. Chmn. Acad. Radiation Oncology Programs (pres. 1974—76), German Soc. Radiation Oncology (hon.), European Cong. Radiology (hon.), German Soc. Radiology (hon.), Am. Roentgen Ray Soc., Am. Cancer Soc. (pres. Minn. divsn. 1979—80, nat. bd., exec. com.), Am. Assn. Cancer Rsch., Radiol. Soc. N.Am. (bd. dirs. 1991—2000, chmn. bd. dirs. 1997—98, pres.-elect 1998, pres. 1999—, Gold medal 2004), Am. Radium Soc. (sec. 1981—83, pres. 1983—84, Janeway medal 1989), Alpha Omega Alpha, Sigma Xi, Phi Beta Kappa.

LEVITT, STEVEN D., economics professor; BA in Econ. summa cum laude, Harvard Univ., 1989; PhD in Econ., MIT, 1994. Mgmt. cons. Corporate Decisions, Inc., 1989—91; Jr. Fellow Harvard Soc. of Fellows, 1994—97; Rsch. Fellow Am. Bar Found., 1997—; asst. prof., econ. Univ. Chgo., 1997—98, assoc. prof., 1998—99, prof., 1999—2002, Alvin H. Baum prof., 2002—. Assoc. editor Quarterly Jour. Econ., 1998—99; editor: Jour. Polit. Economy, 1999—; co-author (with Stephen J. Dubner): Freakonomics: A Rogue Economist Explores the Hidden Side of Everything, 2005 (NY Times Bestseller list, Publishers Weekly Bestseller list, Quills award-business book, 2005). Co-recipient Duncan Black Prize, Public Choice, 2000; named one of 100 Most Influential People, Time mag., 2006; recipient Nat. Sci. Found. CAREER award, 1999, Nat. Sci. Found. Presdl. Early Career award for scientists and engrs., 2000, John Bates Clark Medal for best Am. economist under 40; grantee Faculty Rsch. Fellow, Nat. Bur. Econ. Rsch., 1994—, John M. Olin Rsch. Fellow in law and econ., Harvard Law Sch., 1995—97, Nat. Fellow, Harvard Univ. Program in Inequality and Social Policy, 1998—, Alfred P. Sloan Rsch. Fellowship, 1999. Fellow: Ctr. for Adv. Study Behavioral Sci., Stanford, Calif., Am. Acad. Arts and Sci.; mem.: Phi Beta Kappa. Office: Dept Econ Univ Chgo 1126 E 59th St Chicago IL 60637 Business E-Mail: slevitt@midway.uchicago.edu.

LEVITTE, JEAN-DAVID, ambassador; b. Moissac, France, June 14, 1946; married; 2 children. Grad., Inst. Polit. Scis. With Secs. Fgn. Affairs (the East), 1970—71; vice consul Hong Kong, 1971; 3rd sec. Peking, 1972—74; dir. econ. affairs Min. Fgn. Affairs, 1974—75; sec. gen., 1975—81; permanent mission France UN, 1981—84; sub-mgr. West Africa Min. Fgn. Affairs, 1984—86; dir. asst. Cabinet Fgn. Min., 1986—88; amb. France UN, Geneva, 1988—90; dir. Asia and Oceania Min. Fgn. Affairs, 1990—93, gen. mgr. cultural rels., sci. and tech., 1993—95; diplomatic adv. Pres. Sherpa, 1995—2000; amb. France UN, NYC, 2000—; amb. to the U.S. France, 2003—. Office: French Embassy 4101 Reservoir Rd NW Washington DC 20007

LEVITZ, PAUL ELLIOT, publishing executive; b. Bklyn., Oct. 21, 1956; s. Alfred Lazarus and Hannah (Brenner) L.; m. Jeanette Francine Cusimano, Nov. 2, 1980; children: Nicole, Philip, Garret. Student, N.Y. U., 1973-76. Editor, pub. The Comic Reader, Bklyn., 1971-73; writer, asst. editor Nat. Periodical Publs., Inc., NYC, 1973-76; editor, editorial coordinator, writer DC Comics, NYC, 1976-80, mgr. bus. affairs, 1980-82, v.p. ops., 1982-84, exec. v.p., 1984-89, exec. v.p., pub., 1989—2002, MAD mag., 1993—2002; pres. & publ. DC Comics & MAD mag., 2002—. Jewish. Home: 23 Stony Hollow Rd Chappaqua NY 10514-2014 Office: DC Comics 1700 Broadway New York NY 10019-5905 Office Phone: 212-636-5555. E-mail: paul.levitz@dccomics.com.

LEVKOVICH, TOBIAS M., financial analyst, investment advisor; BA, Concordia Univ., Montreal; attended, Grad. Sch. Bus. Boston Univ. Asst. v.p. rsch. dept. L.F. Rothschild; securities analyst engring. construction & machinery Salomon Smith Barney, NYC, 1988—2001; mng. dir., chief U.S. equity strategist Citi Smith Barney, NYC, 2001—. Named one of Power 30, SmartMoney Mag.; named to All-Am. Rsch. Team, Institutional Investor mag. Office: Citi Smith Barney 388 Greenwich St New York NY 10013*

LEVMORE, SAUL, dean, law educator; b. 1953; BA, Columbia Coll., 1973, PhD, 1978; JD, Yale U., 1980; LLD (hon.), Ill. Inst. Tech. Chgo.-Kent Law Sch., 1995. Bar: Va. 1983. Dean Jonathan Edwards Coll. Yale U., 1979-80; asst. prof. U. Va., Charlottesville, 1980-84; prof. U. Va., Charlottesville, 1984—98, Brokaw prof. of law; William B. Graham prof. law U. Chgo. Law Sch., 1998—, dean, 2001—. Lectr. econs. Yale U., 1976-80, vis. prof., 1986-87; vis. prof. Harvard U., 1990-91, U. Chgo., 1993. Author: (book) Superstrategies for Puzzles and Games, 1981. Recipient Alumni Assn. Teaching Award, U. Va., 1984, Traynor Award, 1997. Mem.: Am. Law Deans Assn. (pres.), Am. Acad. of Arts and Sciences. Office: U Chgo Law Sch 1111E 60th St Chicago IL 60637 Office Phone: 773-702-9590. Office Fax: 773-702-0730. Business E-Mail: s-levmore@uchicago.edu.*

LEVOIR, LURESE CHERENE, dietetic technician; b. Garden Grove, Calif., June 10, 1960; d. Clive Ellsworth and Grace Marie LeVoir. BS in Nutritional Sci., San Jose State U., Calif., 2003. Registered dietetic tech. Dietetic technician Regional Med. Ctr. San Jose, 1989—. Chair of delegates for calif. Am. and Calif. Dietetic Assn., Calif., 2003—05. Mem.: Calif. Dietetic Assn. (assoc.; pres. San Jose chpt. 1998—99, Dietetic Technician of Yr. 1996, Excellence in Tech. Practice award 1995), Ameican Dietetic Assn. (assoc.; registered dietetic technician, chmn. dels. Calif. 2003—05). Avocation: travel. Home: 39 Finger Ave Redwood City CA 94062 Home Phone: 650-704-6658; Office Phone: 650-704-6658. Personal E-mail: levoir_l@yahoo.com.

LEVOVITZ, PESACH ZECHARIAH, rabbi; b. Poland, Sept. 15, 1922; came to U.S., 1923; s. Reuben and Leah Zlate (Kustanowitz) L.; m. Bluma D. Feder, Feb. 5, 1945 (dec. 1970); children: Sivya, Yaakov; m. Eleanore Herman Klugmann, 1972 (dec. Nov. 1980); children: Maurice, Danny, Renee, Jackie; m. Frayde Twersky Perlow, Dec. 18, 1989; stepchildren: Yitzchok, Faige, Joseph. BA, Yeshivah U., 1942. Rabbi Mesivtha Tifereth Jerusalem Rabbinical Sem., 1943, Congregation Sons of Israel, Lakewood, N.J., 1944—; founder, 1945; since dean Bezalel Day Sch.; Pres. Rabbinical Council Am., 1966-68, chmn. commn. on internat. affairs, 1972; asso. chmn. Soviet Jewry commn., 1980. Mem. exec. com. Synagogue Coun. Am., 1953—; standing com. Conf. European Rabbis and Asso. Rabbis, 1964—; steering com. World Conf. Ashkenazi and Sephardi Synagogues; Co chmn. rabbinic cabinet Bonds for Israel, 1972; chaplain Lakewood Police Dept., 1950—; vis. chaplain Naval Air Sta., Lakehurst, N.J., 1945—; nat. chmn. ann. conv. Rabbinical Coun. Am., 1971, chmn. internat. conf., 1966; v.p. Religious Zionists Am., 1974; nat. chmn. Vaad Haroshi Religious Zionists Am., 1975; pres. Beth Din of Am., 1986; rsch. prof. U. Tenn. Mem. adv. bd. Lakewood Housing Council, Nat. Cmty. Rels. Adv. Coun., United Jewish Appeal; chmn. bd. Sons of Israel Sr. Citizens Housing Inc., 1980; mem. N.J. Drug Utilization Coun.; chmn. adv. coun. on protection kosher legislation to Atty. Gen., State of N.J.; mem. exec. Ocean County Jewish Fedn., 1988, chmn. Jewish Family and Children Svc., 1997; co-chmn. Blue Ribbon Panel Lakewood Twp., 1992—; apptd. Jewish chaplain Vis. Nurses Assn. Ctrl. N.J. Hospice Program, 2000. Recipient Revel Meml. award in religion and religious edn. Yeshivah Coll. Alumni Assn., 1967; award for outstanding rabbinic leadership Union of Orthodox Jewish Congregations Am., 1969; Nat. Assn. Hebrew Day Schs., 1980; chief Rabbi Issas Halevi Herzog Torah Fellowship award Religious Zionists Am., 1972; chmn. nat. conv., 1974; named Rabbi of Yr., Israel Bond Orgn., 1991. Mem. Conf. Presidents Nat. Jewish Orgns., Am. Conf. Soviet Jewry, Vis. Nurses Assn. (spiritual counselor 2000). Home: 403 6th St Lakewood NJ 08701-2705 Office: Congregation Sons of Israel Madison Ave Lakewood NJ 08701

LEVOX, GARY (GARY WAYNE VERNON JR.), country/rock singer; b. July 10, 1970; m. Tara Levox; children: Brittany Kay, Brooklyn Leigh. Performer Printers Alley, Nashville; founder, singer Rascal Flatts, 2000—. engr.: (albums) Gospel, 1998; singer Rascal Flatts, 2000, Melt, 2002, Feels Like Today, 2004 (Group/Duo Video of Yr., Country Music Television Music awards, 2005), Me and My Gang, 2006; performer: (songs) "Walk the Llama Llama", Emperor's Last Groove (Original Soundtrack), 2000. Recipient Vocal Group Yr., Country Music Assn., 2002, 2004—06, Song Yr. for I'm Movin On, Acad. Country Music Awards, 2002, Top Vocal Group, 2003, 2005—07, Country Song Yr. for Bless the Broken Road, Radio Music Awards, 2005, Best Country Song, Grammy Awards, 2006, Group/Duo Video of Yr. for Skin (Sarabeth), Country Music TV Awards, 2006, Group Video of Yr. for What Hurts the Most, 2007, Favorite Country Band, Am. Music Awards, 2006, Favorite Song from a movie & Favorite Remake-Life is a Highway, People's Choice Awards, 2007. Avocations: hunting, fishing. Office: Lyric Street Records 1100 Demonbreun St Nashville TN 37203-3108 Office Phone: 615-963-4848.

LEVOY, MYRON, author; b. NYC, Jan. 30, 1930; s. Bernard and Elsie Levoy; m. Beatrice Fleischer, Jan. 27, 1952; children: David, Deborah. BS in Chem. Engring., CCNY, 1952; MS in Chem. Engring., Purdue U., 1953. Engr. Pratt & Whitney Aircraft Co., East Hartford, Conn., 1953-56; project engr. Reaction Motors Inc., Rockaway, NJ, 1956-67; engr. specialist Polytech. Design, Livingston, NJ, 1973-81; writer, 1955—. Author: A Necktie in Greenwich Village, 1968, Penny Tunes and Princesses, 1972, The Witch of Fourth Street and Other Stories, 1972 (Book World Honor Book, 1972, Children's Book Showcase award, 1973), Alan and Naomi, 1977 (Boston Globe-Horn Book award, Honor Book, 1978, Jane Addams Honor Book award, 1978, Nat. Book award finalist, 1980, Silver Pencil award The Netherlands, 1981, Austrian State prize for children's lit, 1981, German State prize for young adult lit., 1982, Buxtenhuder Bulle award Fed. Republic Germany, 1982), A Shadow Like a Leopard, 1981 (ALA Best Book for Young Adults, 1981), Three Friends, 1984, The Hanukkah of Great-Uncle Otto, 1984, Pictures of Adam, 1986 (ALA Best Book for young adults, 1986, Internat. Reading Assn. young adult choice, 1986), The Magic Hat of Mortimer Wintergreen, 1988 (Jr. Lit. Guild selection, 1988), Kelly 'N' Me, 1992, Eine Liebe in Schwarz-weiss, 1999, poetry and plays. Mem. PEN, The Authors Guild, The Dramatists Guild. Jewish. Avocations: tennis, cross country skiing, swimming, museums, films. Office: Writers House Inc 21 W 26th St New York NY 10010 Office Phone: 212-685-2400.

LEVY, ALAN M., lawyer; b. Milw., Nov. 10, 1940; s. Sam and Emma (Gold) L.; m. Tee Gee Azine, Mar. 3, 1964; children: Shawn, Joshua, Pamela, Jonathan. AB, U. Chgo., 1963, JD, 1965. Bar: Wis. 1965, U.S. Dist. Ct. (ea. dist.) Wis. 1965, U.S. Ct. Appeals (2d, 5th, 6th, 7th, 8th, 9th and 10th cirs.) 1968, U.S. Dist. Ct. (ctrl. dist.) Ill. 1969, U.S. Supreme Ct. 1980, Ill. 1982, U.S. Dist. Ct. (no. dist.) Ill. 1982, U.S. Dist. Ct. (we. dist.) Mich. 2001, U.S. Dist. Ct. (we. dist.) Wis., 2004. Ptnr. Goldberg, Previant, Uelman, Gratz, Miller et al, Milw., 1965-82; sr. legal counsel, dir. plan devel./compliance Ctrl. States, S.E. and S.W. Areas Pension Fund, Chgo., 1982-85; assoc. O'Neil, Cannon & Hollman, S.C., Milw., 1985-91, Lindner & Marsack, S.C., Milw., 1991—. Bd. incorporators Commonwealth Mut. Savs. Bank, Milw., 1977-82; adj. prof. labor law U. Wis., Milw., 1974—, Marquette U., 2007-. Contbr. articles to profl. jours. Chmn. Iron Mask, 1963-64, U. Chgo. Alumni Schs. Com., Milw., 1987-2003, U. Chgo. Alumni Assn. Milw., 1996-98; trustee Congregation Emanu-El B'Ne Jeshurun, Milw., 1978-82, 86-92; campaign co-chmn. Urban Day Sch., Milw., 1988; active ACLU, Milw., 1966-82. Named Page scholar, U. Chgo., 1961. Mem. ABA (labor law sec. 1967—), Wis. Bar Assn. (labor law sect. chmn. 1979-80), Ill. Bar Assn., U. Chgo. Alumni Assn. (bd. govs. 1998-2004, v.p. 2002-04). Office: Lindner & Marsack SC 411 E Wisconsin Ave Ste 1800 Milwaukee WI 53202-4416 Office Phone: 414-273-3910. Business E-Mail: alevy@lindner-marsack.com. *Notable cases include: Phillips vs. Alaska HERE Pension Fund, 11 EBC 1929 W.D. Wash., 1989, which involved class action regarding eligibility criteria as structural defect in a multiemployer pension fund; I-Mark Industries, Inc., et al vs. Arthur Young & Co., et al, 148 Wis. 2d 605, 436 N.W. 2d 311, 1989, which involved third party borrower's liability to plaintiff lender for malpractice by defendant acct.; Teamster's Local 348 Health and Welfare Fund, et al vs. Kohn Beverage Co., 749 F. 2d 315 6th Cir., 1984, which involved the enforcement of benefit fund contribution obligations regardless of union activity; Loran W. Robbins, et al vs. The Pepsi-Cola Met. Bottling Co., et al, 7 EBC 2033 N.D. Ill, 1986, which involved the withdrawal liability obligations to multiemployer pension fund; Wardle vs. Cen. States, S.E. and S.W. Areas Pension Fund, 627 F. 2d 820 7th Cir., 1980, which involved the right to jury trial and standard of rev. in pension benefit claim; Inland Trucking Co. vs. NLRB, 440 F. 2d 562 7th Cir., 1971, which involved the use of replacement employees during a single employer lock-out.*

LEVY, ALBERT, physician; b. Stanleyville, Congo, Nov. 8, 1948; arrived in US, 1977; s. Moise and Eugenie J. (Menache) Levy; m. Linda Vertannes; children: Antonia G., Eric M. MD, Fed. U. Brazil, Rio de Janeiro, 1973, MS in Field Medicine, 1976. Diplomate Am. Bd. Family Physicians, Am. Bd. Family Practice, Am. Bd. Geriatric Medicine. Chief family medicine sect. Our Lady of Mercy Hosp., Bronx, NY, 1989-96; pvt. practice family medicine Manhattan Family Practice, NYC, 1990—; physician Montefiore Med. Ctr., Bronx, 1994—; asst. clin. prof. dept. family medicine Albert Einstein Coll. Medicine, Bronx, 1994—; asst. prof. NY Med. Coll., Valhalla, 1994—; asst. prof. medicine Mt. Sinai Sch. Medicine, 1999—. With Beth Israel Med. Ctr., 1986, St. Luke's/Roosevelt Med. Ctr., 1986, Lenox Hill Hosp., 1995, Mt. Sinai Med. Ctr., 1999. Fellow: NY Acad. Medicine, Royal Soc. Medicine (Eng.), Am. Acad. Family Physicians; mem.: AMA, Soc. Tchrs. Family Medicine, NY County Acad. Family Physicians (v.p. 1992), Med. Soc. State of NY, NY Acad. Scis., Acads. Family Physicians, World Orgn. Nat. Colls., Am. Geriatric Soc. Jewish. Avocations: tennis, opera, travel, windsurfing. Home: 25 Sutton Pl S Apt 7N New York NY 10022-2441 Office: Manhattan Family Practice 911 Park Ave New York NY 10021-0337 Office Phone: 212-288-7193. Home Fax: 212-832-6774. Personal E-mail: alevymd@earthlink.net.

LEVY, ARNOLD S(TUART), real estate company executive; b. Chgo., Mar. 15, 1941; s. Roy and Esther (Scheff) L.; m. Eva Cichosz, Aug. 8, 1976; children: Adam, Rachel, Deborah. BS, U. Wis., 1963; MPA, Roosevelt U., 1970. Dir. Neighborhood Youth Corps, Chgo., 1966-68; v.p. Social Planning Assn., Chgo., 1968-70; planning dir. Office of Mayor, Chgo., 1970-74; dep. dir. Mayor's Office Manpower, Chgo., 1974-75; sr. v.p. Urban Investment & Devel. Co., Chgo., 1975-93; pres., CEO Stone-Levy, LLC, Chgo., 1994—. Mem. S-L Hospitality Group, LLC, 1995—; pres. JMB/Urban Hotels, Hotel and Resort Devel. Group, JMB/Urban Devel. Co., 1985-93; mem. Urban Land Inst. Pres. Ark, Chgo., 1970-72, Parental Stress Svcs., Chgo., 1978-79; past lectr. DePaul U., Roosevelt U., Loyola U.; v.p. Inst. Urban Life, 1983-2005, Urban Land Inst., Chgo. Co-editor: The Professionals' Guide to Commercial Property Development, 1988. Bd. dirs. Mus. Broadcast Comms., Am. Shalom; pres. Ill. Humane Soc.; steering com. Radio Hall of Fame; chmn. Spertus Inst. Jewish Studies, Glencoe Plan Commn.; bd. dirs. Inst. for Computers in Jewish Life, mem. United Way of Glencoe. Mem.: Hospitality Asset Mgrs. Assn., Glencoe Golf Club (chmn. adv. com. 2005—), Twin Orchard Club, Glen Club. Home: 535 Park Ave Glencoe IL 60022-1501 Office: Stone-Levy LLC 630 Dundee Rd Ste 220 Northbrook IL 60062-2750

LEVY, ARTHUR JAMES, public relations executive, writer; b. Bklyn., Dec. 23, 1947; s. Bernard and Bernice (Lipner) L.; m. Andrea Susan Hall, May 11, 1980; children: Zoe Jess, Jake Benjamin. BA, Brandeis U., 1969. Account exec., disc jockey Sta. WBUS-FM, Miami Beach, Fla., 1971; pop music critic Magic Bus Newspaper, Miami Beach, 1971; sr. editor, writer Zoo World mag., Ft. Lauderdale, Fla., 1971-74; chief writer Atlantic Records, NYC, 1975-78; assoc. dir. Press and Pub. Info. dept. Columbia Records, NYC, 1978-88, nat. dir. media services, publicity dept., 1988-93; v.p. Sony Music Entertainment Comms. Dept., NYC, 1993-95. So. regional v.p. Rock Writers of the World, 1973-74; seminar panelist United Jazz Coalition, N.Y.C., 1983—, CMJ Folk, 1987—, New Music Seminar Folk, 1989—; ind. music publicity cons., writer, 1995—; prodr. (ann. concert series) A Klezmer Rave, 1997-98. Writer, rschr. album and video liner notes for Sammy Davis, Jr., Rolling Stones, Eric Andersen, Johnny Cash, Herbie Mann, Taj Mahal, Al Kooper, Robert Johnson, Jan Hammer, Julio Iglesias, Joan Baez, Manfred Mann, Jimmy Webb, Pete Seeger, Burl Ives, Montreux Festival '77, Elvis Presley: Golden Celebration, 1985 (Grammy nomination), Songs of the Civil War, Iggy Pop; appeared on album session (Finnadar Records) Idil Biret's New Line Piano, 1978, (Columbia) Jaroslav Jakubovic's Checkin' In, 1978, Sony Music 100 Years: Soundtrack For A Century (Folk, Gospel and Blues) (Grammy nomination), 1999; exec. prodr.: Abe Schwartz--The Klezmer King, 2002, Tanz! With Dave Taras and the Musiker Bros., 2002, From Avenue A to the Great White Way (various artists), 2002. Named Publicist of Yr. Columbia Records, 1982, 87, Media Man of Yr. Record World mag., N.Y.C., 1981. Mem. NARAS (gov. N.Y. chpt., Grammy voting com., Liner Notes com., Hist. Album Com.), Rock and Roll Hall of Fame (nominating com., mus. experts com.), Nat. Acad. Popular Music. Avocation: record collecting. Office Phone: 718-601-4239. Office Fax: 718-601-1399. Personal E-mail: mortedart@aol.com.

LEVY, BERN, communications executive, optical applications consultant; b. Oct. 28, 1929; m. Anne Marilyn King, June 22, 1958; children: Leah, Janna, Matthew. AA, Fairleigh Dickinson U., 1950. Cinematographer Sta. WKNY-TV, Kingston, NY, 1953-56, Sta. WNBC-TV, West Hartford, Conn., 1956-59, United Aircraft Rsch. Lab., East Hartford, Conn., 1959-65; mktg. mgr. Radiant-Pathé, Morton Grove, Ill., 1965-68, Angenieux Corp. Am., Bohemia, NY, 1968-84; cons. Bern Levy Assocs., Northport, NY, 1984—. Cons. Insight Vision Systems, Gt. Britain, 1985-86, Tamron Optics, Port Washington, N.Y., 1985-86, Cinema Products Corp., L.A., 1984—, Century Precision Optics, L.A., 1984—. Author: (indsl. photography) Cine Lens Glossary, 1973, A Guide to Depth-of-Field/Field-of-View for 16mm Cine Lenses, 1974, Getting Closer with Diopter Lens Attachments, 1987, (video systems) Lens Reality, 1987, (broadcast mgmt., engring.) Lenses: Maintaining Your Image, 1987; co-author: American Cine Manual. Home and Office: 21 Whippoorwill Ln Palmyra VA 22963-2252

LEVY, CESAR, mechanical engineer, educator; s. Albert and Ida Levy; m. Lois Zalkind, June 7, 1954; children: Menachem, Yehuda. BS in Aerospace Engring., Poly. Inst. Bklyn, 1972; MA in Applied Math., NYU, NYC, 1974; PhD, Stanford, Palo Alto, Calif., 1983. Lt. col. US Army, 1974—78, US Army Res., 1978—99; prof. Fla. Internat. U., Miami, 1985—; prof. (sabbatical) Coll. Judea and Samaria, Ariel, Israel, 1999—2001. Dir. ALLSTAR Network, Miami, Fla. Assoc. editor: Internat. Jour. Modeling and Simulation, 1995—99, mem. editl. bd.: Nat. Acad. Advising Jour., 1990—93. Mem. governing bd. Cong. Shaaray Tefila, N. Miami Beach, Fla., 2004—06. Capt. US Army, 1974—78. Recipient Tchg. award, Fla. Internat. U., 1989, Advising award, 1990, Svc. award, 1992, Rsch. award, 1994; fellowship, Technion Israel Inst. Tech., Haifa, 1983—85. Mem.: ASME, Tau Beta Pi, Sigma Xi (assoc.). Achievements include development of aeronautics/aviation website with materials in history, science principles and career information related to those fields; research in the effects of erosion and cracks in thickwalled, partially and fully autofrettaged, pressurized tubes; the effects of viscoelastic materials, shape memory alloys, and carbon nanotubes on vibration attenuation of structures. Office: Florida International University Department of Mech and Matl's Eng Miami FL 33199 Office Phone: 305-348-3643. Business E-Mail: levyez@fiu.edu.

LEVY, CLIFFORD J., reporter; b. New Rochelle, NY, June 15, 1967; married; 3 children. Degree in pub. policy and internat. affairs, Princeton U., 1989. Reporter N.Y. bur. UP Internat.; news asst. N.Y. Times, 1990—92, reporter, 1992—2000, chief Albany bur., polit. reporter, City Hall corr., Newark corr., spl. projects reporter met. desk, 2000—. Recipient George Polk award for local reporting, 1998, Pulitzer prize for investigative reporting, 2003. Office: 229 W 43d St New York NY 10036-3959*

LEVY, DANY, publishing executive; b. 1973; BA, Brown U., 1994. Intern, columnist, Gotham Style page editor NY mag., 1994—98; editor Self, Lucky; founder, chmn. & editor-in-chief DailyCandy, 2000—. Named one of 40 Under 40, Crain's NY Bus., 2007. Office: Daily Candy Inc c/o Brown Raysman et al LLP 900 3rd Ave New York NY 10022*

LEVY, DAVID, retired lawyer, insurance company executive, consultant; b. Bridgeport, Conn., Aug. 3, 1932; s. Aaron and Rachel (Goldman) L. BS in Econs., U. Pa., Phila., 1954; JD, Yale U., New Haven, 1957. CPA Conn.; bar: Conn. 1958, US Supreme Ct. 1963, DC 1964, Mass. 1965, NY 1971, Pa. 1972. Acct. Arthur Andersen & Co., NYC, 1957-59; sole practice Bridgeport, 1959-60; specialist tax law IRS, Washington, 1960-64; counsel State Mut. Life Ins. Co., Worcester, Mass., 1964-70; assoc. gen. counsel taxation Penn Mut. Life Ins. Co., Phila., 1971-81; sole practice Washington, 1982-87; v.p., tax counsel Pacific Life Ins. Co., Newport Beach, Calif., 1987-2001; ret., 2001. Author: (with others) Life Insurance Company Tax Series, Bureau National Affairs Tax Management Income Tax, 1970-71. Mem. adv. bd. Tax Mgmt., Washington, 1975-90, Hartford Inst. on Ins. Taxation, 1990-97; bd. dirs. Citizens Plan E Orgn., Worcester, 1966-70. With AUS, 1957. Mem. ABA (vice-chmn. employee benefits com. 1980-86, ins. cos. com. 1984-86, torts and ins. practice sect., subcom. chair ins. cos. com. tax sect. 1994—), Assn. Life Ins. Counsel, AICPA, Beta Alpha Psi. Jewish.

LEVY, DAVID LAWRENCE, retired lawyer, legal association administrator; b. NYC, Nov. 7, 1936; s. Arthur Morgan and Shirley (Lanz) L.; 1 child from previous marriage, Justin; m. Virginia Carey, May, 1974 (div. 1980); m. Ellen Dublin, Dec., 1984; 1 child, Diana. BA, U. Fla., 1958, JD, 1961. Bar: D.C. 1968, U.S. Supreme Ct. 1983. Lawyer U.S. Copyright Office, Libr. Congress, Washington, 1962-69, 77-97, ret., 1997; co-founder, CEO Children's Rights Coun., Washington, 1985—. Author: Potomac Conspiracy, 1976; editor: The Best Parent Is Both Parents, 1993; editor-in-chief student newspaper, U. Fla., 1957-58 (recipient awards). Chmn. Students for Kennedy for Pres., 1959, 60. Recipient Civic award Prince George's County (Md.) Civic Fedn., 1989, Disting. Svc. to Children award Parents Without Ptnrs. Internat., 1996, Lifelong Achievement award for untiring efforts on behalf of children U.S. Fed. Child Support Office, 2000, Svc. to Children award N.J. Coun. for Children's Rights, 2000. Mem.: U.S. Supreme Ct. Bar, D.C. Bar Assn., Supervised Visitation Network (bd. dirs.), Stepfamily Assn. Am. (bd. dirs.), Masons, Elks. Jewish. Office: Childrens Rights Coun 8181 Professional Pl Ste 240 Friendship MD 20758 Home Phone: 301-927-1897; Office Phone: 301-559-3120. Personal E-mail: davidlevy1@juno.com.

LEVY, DAVID WILLIAM, history educator; b. Chgo., May 6, 1937; s. Roy A. and Helen (Loeffler) L.; m. Lynne Ellen Hunt, Sept. 7, 1969; children: Beth Ellen, Benjamin Robert. BA, U. Ill., 1959; MA, U. Chgo., 1961; PhD, U. Wis., 1967. Instr. Ohio State U., Columbus, 1964-67; asst. prof. history U. Okla., Norman, 1967—71, assoc. prof., 1971-84, prof., 1984—, David Ross Boyd prof. Am. history, 1987—, chmn. faculty senate, 1985-86. Author: Herbert Croly of the New Republic, 1985; co-editor: Letters of Louis D. Brandeis, 5 vols., 1971-78, Debate over Vietnam, 1991, 2d edit., 1995, University of Oklahoma: A History, 3 vols., 2004—; contbr. numerous articles to scholarly, popular and legal jours. Chmn. Norman Planning Commn. Recipient Regents award for disting. teaching U. Okla., 1973, Students Assn. award for outstanding teaching, 1985; grantee NEH, 1967, 68, 69, 72-74, 84-87; fellow Rockefeller Found., 1980-81, Southwestern Bell, 1988; Danforth teaching assoc. Mem. AAUP (pres. Okla. conf. 1975-76), Orgn. Am. Historians. Home: 914 Hoover St Norman OK 73072-6153 Office: U Okla History Dept 455 W Lindsey St Norman OK 73019-2000 Business E-Mail: dwlevy@ou.edu.

LEVY, DEBORAH, security company executive; b. Chgo. d. Sam and Ruth Gadlin; m. Barry W. Levy (dec.); children: Scott B., Todd B. Student, So. Ill. U. Exec. v.p., sec., officer, dir. Levy Security Corp., Chgo., until 1994, chair, CEO, 1994—. Mem. Women Bus. Enterprise Initiative (Mem. of Yr. award 1997), Nat. Assn. Women Bus. Owners, Am. Soc. Indsl. Security. Achievements include being listed in Working Woman 500 Magazine. Office: Levy Security Corp Ste 1200 8750 W Bryn Mawr Ave Chicago IL 60631-3560 Home Phone: 847-392-0343; Office Phone: 773-867-9204. Business E-Mail: dlevy@levysecurity.com.

LEVY, DONALD HARRIS, chemistry professor; b. Youngstown, Ohio, June 30, 1939; s. Gabriel and Minnie (Lerner) L.; m. Susan Louise Miller, June 14, 1964; children— Jonathan G., Michael A., Alexander B. BA, Harvard U., 1961; PhD, U. Calif.-Berkeley, 1965. Asst. prof. chemistry U. Chgo., 1967-74, assoc. prof., 1974-78, prof., 1978—, chmn. dept. chemistry, 1983-85, Ralph and Mary Otis Isham prof., 1994-97, Albert A. Michelson Dist. Svc. prof., 1997—, v.p. rsch. and nat. labs. Mem. chemistry adv. com. NSF; Lady Davis vis. prof. The Technion, Haifa, Israel, 1998; Jeremy Musher Meml. lect. Hebrew U., Jerusuem, Israel, 2002; Powell lectr. U. Richmond, 2006. Assoc. editor Jour. Chem. Physics, 1983-98; editor Jour. Chem. Physics, 1998—. Fellow AAAS, Am. Phys. Soc. (Plyler prize 1987, Bright Wilson award 2006), Optical Soc. Am. (Ellis A. Lippencott award 2000—); mem. Am. Chem. Soc.(E. Bright Wilson award in Spectroscopy, 2006), Am. Acad. Arts and Scis., Nat. Acad. Scis. Office: U Chgo Dept Chemistry 5640 S Ellis Ave Chicago IL 60637-1433 Business E-Mail: levy@silly.uchicago.edu.

LEVY, ELAINE ANN, music educator; b. Fall River, Mass., Mar. 20, 1927; d. Max and Sarah Brodsky Ritter; m. Jack Kirstein Levy, Aug. 18, 1951 (dec. Nov. 1981); children: Steven Mark, Richard Allan. Diploma in Theory & Music, N.Eng. Conservatory Music, 1942; student, Boston U., 1945; AA, Cin. Coll. Music, 1948; MusB, Calif. State U., Fullerton, 1972. Cert. music tchr. Calif., 1990, Music Tchrs. Nat. Assn., 1990. Music tchr. Indep. Music Tchrs. Assn., La Palma, Calif., 1940—. Music aide Thomas M. Erwin Sch., La Puente, Calif., 1958—65; pres. Musical Arts Orange County, La Palma, 1978—80; adv. bd. Music Tchrs. Assn. Calif., Long Beach, Calif., 1988—97. Composer music for Music Tchrs. Assn. Calif. Regional chairperson So. Calif. Jr. Bach Festival, LA and Orange County, 1963—2004, regional advisor, 2004—; active Dem. Party, La Puente, 1964. Mem.: AAUW, Mu Phi Epsilon. Avocations: dance, bowling, swimming, walking, reading. Home: 7811 Norann Circle La Palma CA 90623-1648

LEVY, EUGENE, actor, film director, screenwriter; b. Hamilton, Ont., Can., Dec. 17, 1946; m. Deborah Divine, 1977; 2 children. Appearences include (films) Cannibal Girls, 1972, Running, 1979, Nothing Personal, 1980, Heavy Metal, 1981, Strange Brew, 1983, Going Berserk, 1983, National Lampoon's Vacation, 1983, Splash, 1984, Armed and Dangerous, 1986, The Canadian Conspiracy, 1986, Club Paradise, 1986, Speed Zone, 1989, Father of the Bride, 1991, Once Upon A Crime, 1992, Stay Tuned, 1992, I Love Trouble, 1994, Father of the Bride, Part II, 1995, Waiting for Guffman, 1996, Multiplicity, 1996, Waiting for Guffman (also wrote), 1996, Dogmatic, 1996, Creature Crunch (voice only), 1996, Almost Heroes, 1998, Richie Rich's Christmas Wish, 1998, Akbar's Adventure Tours, 1998, The Secret Life of Girls, 1999, American Pie, 1999, Best in Shown (also wrote), 2000, The Ladies Man, 2000, Silver Man, 2000, Down to Earth, 2001, American Pie 2, 2001, Serendipity, 2001, Repli-Kate, 2002, Like Mike, 2002, Bringing Down the House, 2003, A Mighty Wind (also wrote), 2003, Dumb and Dumberer: When Harry Met Lloyd, 2003, American Wedding, 2003, New York Minute, 2004, The Man, 2005, Cheaper by the Dozen 2, 2005, Curious George, 2006, Over the Hedge (voice), 2006, For Your Consideration, 2006; actor: (TV) Second City TV, 1977-81, Lovebirds, 1979, From Cleveland, 1980, George Burn's Comedy Week, 1985, SCTV Network, 1981-83, The Last Polka, 1985, Dave Thomas: The Incredible Time Travels of Henry Osgood, 1986, Billy Crystal-Don't Get Me Started, 1986, Bride of Boogedy, 1987, Ray Bradbury Theatre, 1988, Autobiographies: The Enigma of Bobby Bittman, 1988, Hiller and Diller, 1997, Hercules (voice only), 1998, D.O.A., 1999, The Sports Pages, 2001, Club Land, 2001, Committed (TV series), 2001, The Kid, 2001, Greg the Bunny (TV series), 2002; dir.: (TV) Second City's 50th Anniversary Special, 1988, Once Upon a Crime..., 1992, Partners in Love, 1992, Sodbusters, 1994. Office: United Talent Agy 9560 Wilshire Blvd Ste #500 Beverly Hills CA 90212*

LEVY, EUGENE HOWARD, planetary sciences and astrophysics educator, researcher; b. NYC, May 6, 1944; s. Isaac Philip and Anita Harriet (Guttman) L.; children: Roger P., Jonathan S., Benjamin H. AB in Physics with high honors, Rutgers U., 1966; PhD in Physics, U. Chgo., 1971. Teaching asst. dept. physics U. Chgo., 1966-69, rsch. asst. Enrico Fermi Inst., 1969-71; postdoctoral fellow dept. physics and astronomy U. Md., 1971-73; asst. prof. physics and astrophysics Bartol Rsch. Found., Franklin Inst., Swarthmore, Pa., 1973-75; asst., then assoc. prof. U. Ariz., Tucson, 1975-83, prof. planetary scis., 1983—2000, mem. faculty applied math. program, 1981—2000, head dept. planetary scis., dir. lunar and planetary lab., 1983-94, mem. theoretical astrophysics program, 1985—2000, dean coll. of sci., 1993—2000, dir. NASA-Ariz. Spacegrant Coll. Consortium Tucson, 1989—2000, prof. physics, 1996—2000; prof. physics and astronomy Rice U., Houston, 2000—, Howard R. Hughes Provost, 2000—. Mem. com. on planetary and lunar exploration of space sci. bd., Nat. Acad. Scis., 1976-79, chmn., 1979-82, co-chair Space Sci. Bd. Study on Exploration Primitive Solar-System Bodies, 1978, mem. Space Sci. Bd., 1979-82, head U.S. del., co-chair Nat. Acad. Scis.-European Sci. Found. Joint Working Group on Cooperation in Planetary Exploration, 1982-84, mem. steering group com. on major directions for space sci. 1995-2015, 1984-86, chair adv. com. on internat. cooperation for Mars sample return, 1986-88; mem. Comet Halley Sci. Working Group, NASA, 1977, mem. spacelab phys. sci. rev. panel space sci. steering com., 1979, mem. rev. panel on origin plasmas in Earth's neighborhood, 1980, mem. solar system exploration com. of Adv. Coun., 1980-83, mem. Ames Rsch. Ctr. Planetary Detection Study, 1983, Solar System Exploration Mgmt. Coun., 1983-87, mem. com. on future space-sta. sci. projects, 1985, mem. Space Sta. Sci. Users' Working Group, 1985-86, Space and Earth Sci. Adv. Com., 1985-88, chair Comet Rendevous and Asteroid Flyby Rev. Panel, 1986, mem. Mars Exploration Strategy Adv. Group, 1986, Mars Rover Sample Return Sci. Working Group, 1987—; sci. cons. Rockwell Internat. Corp., 1980; mem. COSPAR Internat. Tech. Panel on Comets, 1980-82; U.S.-NASA del. to discussions on internat. cooperation investigations of Comet Halley, Padua, Italy, 1981, to U.S.-USSR Joint Working Group on Near-Earth Space, the Moon and Planets, 1981; mem. program adv. bd. Internat. Conf. on Cometary Exploration, Budapest, Hungary, 1982; mem. exec. com. univs.' space sci. working group Assn. Am. Univs., 1982-86; study panel U.S.-Soviet cooperation in space sci. U.S. Cong. Office of Tech. Assessment, 1984; chair planetary exploration panel Pacific Rim Nations Internat. Space Yr. Conf., Kona, Hawaii, 1987; mem. working group planetary systems sci. NASA, 1988—, rev. panel lunar and planetary, 1988-90, rev. panel origins solar systems programs, 1990-91; chair formation/detection group, 1993-95; mem. astronomy and astrophysics survey com., sci. opportunities panel NAS, 1989-90; mem. study panel on robotic exploration of Moon and Mars, U.S. Cong. Office Tech. Assessment, 1991; chmn. coun. of instns., bd. dirs. U.S. Space Rsch. Assn., 1991-98, vice-chmn. bd. dirs. 1993-98; NASA Origins of Solar Syss. Mgmt. Working Group (chair 1994-96), chmn. NASA Origins of Solar Syss. Planet Formation and Detection Rev. Panel, 1993-95, Am. Astron. Soc. (com. on pub. edn., 1994-95), Internat. Sci Found. Astronomy Rev. Panel, 1993-94, NASA Origins of Solar Syss. Mgmt. Ops. Working Group, 1994—, Am. Astron. Soc. Com. on Pub. Edn., 1994; chair Discovery-4 Space Flight Mission Selection Bd., NASA, 1995, mem. Keck Observatory Telescope Allocation Com., 1998-2000, mem. astronomy and astrophysics survey com. NRC/NAS Found., 1999, chair external review com. dept. of space physics and astronomy, Rice U., 1999, bd. dirs. Nat. Space Grant Alliance, 1999-2000, bd. trustees Associated Univs., Inc., 2001-; mem. planetary protection adv. com. NASA, 2002-06, chmn. 2005-06, chair nuc. sys. initiative sci. definition team NASA, 2002, mem. jovian icy mmons tour review bd. NASA, 2002; former mem. adv. coun. sci. com., NASA, 2005-06; cons. and lectr. in field. Am. Geophys. Union (frmr), Am. Phys. Soc. (frmr), Internat. Astron. Union. Editor: Protostars and Planets III, 1993; contbr., author articles for gen. pub., adv. reports for Congl. Record, abstracts, book revs., others. Bd. dir. Nat. Space Biomed. Rsch. Inst., 2004—; bd. trustees Associated Univs., 2001, exec. com., 2001—; mem. Space Telescope Inst. Coun., 2003—. Recipient Disting. Pub. Svc. medal NASA, 1983, Alexander von Humboldt-Stiftung Sr. Scientist award Fed. Republic Germany, 1989; Disting. vis. scientist Jet Propulsion Lab., Calif. Inst. Tech., 1985-91; NASA predoctoral fellow U. Chgo., 1966-69, fellow Ctr. for Theoretical Physics, U. Md., 1971-73; rsch. grantee NASA, NSF. Mem.: AAAS, Phi Beta Kappa, Sigma Xi. Achievements include research in theoretical cosmical physics, planetary geophysics, magnetohydrodynamics, space and solar physics, magnetic field generation, physical processes associated with the formation of stars and planetary systems. Office: Provost Office MS2 430 Allen Ctr Rice Univ 6100 Main St Houston TX 77005 Office Phone: 713-348-4026. Business E-Mail: ehl@rice.edu.

LEVY, EUGENE PFEIFER, architectural firm executive, architect; b. Little Rock, Dec. 14, 1936; s. Emmanuel Gabe and Elizabeth (Pfeifer) L.; m. Candy Sue Hood, Sept. 21, 2004; children: Edwin Cromwell, Andrew Stewart, Charles Pfeifer. B.Arch., U. Va., 1959. Registered architect, Ark., Calif., Ga., Tex. Apprentice Erhart, Eichenbaum, Rauch & Blass, Little Rock, 1959-60; arch., pres. Cromwell, Truemper, Levy, Thompson & Woodsmall, Inc., Little Rock, 1962-85, chmn., CEO, 1985—2002; v.p. State Bd. Archs., 1998—; chmn. emeritus Cromwell Archs. Engrs.,

2002—. Bd. dirs. Little Rock Boys' Club, 1973—, Temple B'nai Israel, Little Rock, 1975-78; chmn. Ctrl. Ark. chpt. ARC, 1989; mem. Fifty for Future. Capt. U.S. Army, 1960-62. Recipient numerous awards including: U.S. Corps. of Engrs. 1985 Design award for Resident Office and Visitors Ctr., Greers Ferry Lake, Ark., USAG 1985 First Honor award for commissary, Camp Foster, Okinawa, Japan, AIA 1980 Design award for Master Plan and First Phase Design for Multi Agy. Office Bldg., State of Ark. Capitol Ground, Little Rock, AIA Honorable Mention award for Systematics, Inc., Corp. Hdqrs., 1982, AIA Design award for Winthrop Rockefeller Meml. Gallery Ark. Arts Ctr., Little Rock, 1982, Little Rock Riverfront Belvedere, AIA Design award, 1987, AIA Design award for Itzkowitz residence, Little Rock, 1991. Fellow AIA (Design award Commissary USAF, UAMS Stephens Spine and Neurosci. Inst. 2004); mem. Greater Little Rock C. of C. (com. 1983-84). Office: Cromwell Archs Engrs Cromwell Bldg 101 S Spring St Little Rock AR 72201-2413 Home: 1911a W 2d Little Rock AR 72205

LEVY, EZRA CESAR, aerospace scientist, real estate agent; b. Habana, Cuba, Sept. 22, 1924; s. Mayer D and Rachel Levy; m. Margot Webb, 2000; children from previous marriage: Daniel M, Diana M Levy Friedman, Linda R Levy Brenden. MS, UCLA, 1951. Sect. head Douglas Aircraft Co., Santa Monica, Calif., 1951—54; dept. head Lockheed Aircraft Co., Van Nuys, Calif., 1954—56, Librascope, Glendale, Calif., 1956—57, Radioplane, Van Nuys, 1957—58; asst. dept. mgr. Space Tech. Labs., Redondo Beach, Calif., 1958—60; asst. divsn. dir. TRW, Redondo Beach, Calif., 1960—74; now real estate broker, owner Jaunty Real Estate, Valencia, Calif., 1984—. Rschr. ECG analysis Heart Rsch. Found, 1953—68; spec traffic consult South Bay Cities, 1960—65; tchr. Real Estate. Author: (book) Laplace Transform Tables, 1958, Selling Your Property?, 1995, Sample Contractual (Real Estate) Terms, 1996, A Glossary of Real Estate Terms, 1998, A Glossary of Real Estate Terms, 2d ed, 2000, Masonry in Los Angeles Silver Trowel Lodge, 2001; contbr. articles to profl jours. With US Army, 1944—46. Mem.: Temple City C. of C. (bd. dirs. 1992—97, pres. 2000—01), Eastern Star (past patron), Masons (past master and sec.). Democrat. Jewish. Avocations: art, music, philately. Home and Office: 24688-A Brighton Dr Valencia CA 91355 Office Phone: 818-259-3549. E-mail: levymasonman@aol.com.

LEVY, GERHARD, pharmacologist; b. Wollin, Germany, Feb. 12, 1928; came to U.S., 1948, naturalized, 1953. s. Gotthold and Eliesabeth (Luebeck) L.; m. Rosalyn Mincer, June 8, 1958; children: David, Marc, Sharon. BS, U. Calif., San Francisco, 1955, Pharm.D., 1958; Dr. honoris causa, Uppsala U., Sweden, 1975, Phila. Coll. Pharmacy and Sci., 1979, L.I. U., 1981, U. Ill., 1986, Hoshi U., Japan, 1996, Ohio State U., 1998, U. Minn., 2001. Asst. prof. pharmacy U. Buffalo, 1958-60; assoc. prof. pharmacy State U. N.Y. at Buffalo, 1960-64, prof. biopharmaceutics, 1964-72, distinguished prof. pharmaceutics, 1972-75, chmn. dept. pharmaceutics, 1966-70, univ. disting. prof. emeritus, 1995. Vis. prof. Hebrew U., Jerusalem; cons. WHO, 1966, Bur. Drugs Adv. Panel System, FDA, 1971-74; mem. com. on problems of drug safety NRC, 1971-75; mem. pharmacol.-toxicol. com. NIH, 1971-75 Mem. editorial bd. Jour. Pharm. Sci, 1970-75, Clin. Pharmacology and Therapeutics, 1969-2002, Internat. Jour. Clin. Pharmacology, 1968-78, Drug Metabolism and Disposition, 1973-78, Jour. Pharmacokin Biopharm, 1972-97, Internat. Jour. Pharm., 1977-95, Jour. Pharmacobi-Dynamics, 1979-93, Pharm. Res., 1983-95; contbr. articles to profl. jours. Served with AUS, 1950-51. Recipient Ebert prize, 1969, Am. Pharm. Assn. Research Achievement award, 1969, McKeen Cattell award Am. Coll. Clin. Pharmacology, 1978, Host-Madsen medal Internat. Pharm. Fedn., 1978, Oscar B. Hunter award in exptl. therapeutics Am. Soc. Clin. Pharmacology and Therapeutics, 1982, Volwiler Research Achievement award Am. Assn. Colls. Pharmacy, 1982, Scheele award Swedish Acad. Pharmaceutical Scis., 1992, 1st Lifetime Achievement in the Pharm. Scis. award Internat. Pharm. Assn., 1994; named Alumnus of Year U. Calif. Sch. Pharmacy Alumni Assn., 1970 Fellow Am. Pharm. Assn., Acad. Pharm. Scis. (Takeru Higuchi Research prize 1983), AAAS; mem. Inst. Medicine of Nat. Acad. Scis., Am. Assn. Pharm. Scientists (Dale E. Wurster Rsch. award 1992), Am. Soc. Exptl. Pharmacology and Therapeutics. Home: 4832 Peregrine Point Cir W Sarasota FL 34231-2335 Office Phone: 941-925-3655. Personal E-mail: glevypkpd@aol.com.

LEVY, GREGG H., lawyer; b. Jan. 18, 1953; AB, Harvard U., 1974, JD cum laude, 1977. Bar: DC 1977. Ptnr. Covington & Burling LLP, Washington, 1977—, co-chmn., Litig. Practice Group, chmn. Sports Practice Group; outside counsel NFL. Outside counsel Nat. Football League (NFL). Mem.: Conflict Prevention & Resolution Inst. (Panel of Distinguished Neutrals). Office: Covington & Burling LLP 1201 Pennsylvania Ave NW Washington DC 20004-2401 Office Phone: 202-662-5292. Office Fax: 202-662-6291. Business E-Mail: glevy@cov.com.*

LEVY, HAROLD DAVID, psycholinguist; b. Rochester, NY, Aug. 25, 1938; s. Barnet Lewis and Ada Sylvia (Zimmerman) L.; m. Jan Patricia Schwartz, Mar. 3, 1959 (div. 1961); 1 child; m. Natalie Miller, Nov. 27, 1969 (div. 1982); 1 child; m. Judy Weiner, Sept. 9, 1987. BS in Gen. Studies, U. Rochester, 1969, MA in Edn., 1971. Permanent cert. to teach French, grades 7-12. Sociotherapist Convalescent Hosp. for Children, Rochester, 1971-72; tutor spl. edn. City Sch. Dist., Rochester, 1973-83; editor, ednl. dir. Operaton Friendship, Rochester, 1983-88; pvt. tutor home and social agencies Rochester, 1982-91; vol. and activities asst. therapist Genesee Hosp., Rochester, 1983-93. Dramatics instr. Hochstein Music Sch., Rochester, 1972; lang. tchr. Harley Sch. and Talmudical Inst. Upstate N.Y., 1974-75. Author: Forced Categories: A Taxonomy for Languages, 1971, Languages: Their Common Elements, 1990, Language Learning by Slices, 1990, Linguistics: The Binary System, 1990, Psycholinguistic Interpretation of Names as Language Field Universals, 1995, Lexical Transformations: The Brain's Code, 1996, The Psycholinguistic Development of Terminal Information Systems, 1997; contbr. articles to sci. jours. Avocations: jazz piano, mental health education, nutrition. Home: 111 East Ave Apt 719 Rochester NY 14604-2542 Personal E-mail: hlevy@rochester.rr.com.

LEVY, HERBERT MONTE, lawyer; b. NYC, Jan. 14, 1923; s. Samuel M. and Hetty D. L.; m. Marilyn Wohl, Aug. 30, 1953; children: Harlan A., Matthew D., Alison Jill. BA, Columbia U., 1943, LLB, 1946. Bar: N.Y. 1946, U.S. Dist. Ct. (so. dist.) N.Y. 1946, U.S. Ct. Appeals (2d cir.) 1949, U.S. Dist. Ct. (ea. dist.) N.Y. 1949, U.S. Supreme Ct. 1951, U.S. Ct. Appeals (10th cir.) 1956, U.S. Tax Ct. 1973, U.S. Ct. Appeals (4th cir.) 1988. Assoc. Rosenman, Goldmark, Colin & Kaye, 1946-47, Javits & Javits, 1947-48; staff counsel ACLU, 1949-56; pvt. practice, 1956-64; ptnr. Hofheimer, Gartlir, Hofheimer, Gottlieb & Gross, 1965-69; pvt. practice NYC, 1969—. Bd. dirs. Music Outreach; faculty N.Y. County Lawyers Assn.; past lectr. Practising Law Inst. Author: How to Handle an Appeal (Practicing Law Inst.), 1968, 4th edit., 1999, now pub. annually; contbr. articles to profl. jours. Exec. com. on law and social action Am. Jewish Congress, 1961-66; trustee Congregation B'nai Jeshurun, 1987-98, chmn. bd. trustees, 1988-91, gen. counsel bd. trustees, 1991-92. Mem. Fed. Bar Coun. (past trustee), Bar Assn. City N.Y., N.Y. County Lawyers Assn., 1st Amendment Lawyers Assn. Democrat. Home: 285 Central Park W Apt 12W New York NY 10024-3006 Office: 230 Park Ave Ste 1000 New York NY 10169 Office Phone: 212-370-4950. Personal E-mail: hmlnyc@aol.com.

LEVY, I. RICHARD, lawyer; b. Albuquerque, Apr. 19, 1959; s. Joseph Leon and Paula Maxine (Block) L.; m. Kathyrn Hasson, 1997; children: Steven Randall, Daniel Lawrence, Simon Michelle, Dena Raquel. BA cum laude, Yale U., 1981; JD with honors, U. Tex., 1986. Bar: Tex. 1986, US Dist. Ct. (no., so. and ea. dists.) Tex. 1986, US Ct. Appeals (5th cir.) 1992; bd. cert. in bankruptcy law, Tex. Bd. Legal Specialization, 2005, Am. Bd. Certification, 2005; Bar Register Preeminent Lawyers, 2004-. Assoc. Akin, Gump, Strauss, Hauer & Feld, Dallas, 1986-92; spl. counsel Gibson, Dunn & Crutcher, 1992—99; shareholder Gerard, Singer & Levick, P.C., 1999—2003; pvt. practice I. Richard Levy PC, 2003—. Pres. mem. com. Yale U. Alumni Schs., Dallas, 1982; cubmaster Boy Scouts Am.; active Am. Jewish Congress, Dallas, 1988. Henry N. Mallon scholar Yale U., 1977-81. Mem. ABA, Am. Bankruptcy Inst., Assn. Yale Alumni, Dallas Yale Club (v.p. & chmn.). Avocations: golf, travel, gardening. Office: 5050 Quorum Dr Ste 700 Dallas TX 75254 Business E-Mail: levy@irlevylaw.com.

LEVY, JACK, investment banker; b. 1955; MBA, Stanford U., 1978. With Merrill Lynch, 1978—91, global head merger bus. NYC, 1991—2000; co-chmn., global mergers & acquisitions Goldman Sachs Group, Inc., NYC, 2000—. Named a Top Dealmaker, Dealmaker mag., 2006; named to New Stars of Fin. list, Bus. Week mag., 1997. Office: Goldman Sachs Group Inc 85 Broad St SC Level New York NY 10004 Office Phone: 971-343-8000.*

LEVY, JEROME, dermatologist, retired military officer; b. Bklyn., Aug. 17, 1926; s. Alexander and Pauline (Wollkof) L.; m. Leona Elsie Eligator, June 6, 1948; children: Andrew B., Eric J., Peter C., David J. Student, Wesleyan U., 1944—45, postgrad., 1952—54; BA, Yale U., 1947; MD, Albany Med. Coll., 1958. Diplomate Am. Bd. Dermatology. Commd. ensign USN, M.C., 1957, advanced through grades to capt., 1972; intern U.S. Naval Hosp., Newport, RI, 1958—59; resident Phila. (Pa.) Naval Hosp., 1960—62, U. Pa. Grad. Sch. Medicine, Phila., 1962—63, chief dept. dermatology Memphis, 1963—67, Yokosuka, Japan, 1967—70, Long Beach, Calif., 1974—75; head outpatient dermatology clinic San Diego Naval Hosp., 1970—72; sr. med. officer Keflavik, Iceland, 1972—74; ret., 1975; med. dir. dermatology Westwood Pharm. Co., Buffalo, 1975—82; acting chief dermatology dept. Buffalo Gen. Hosp., 1981—82; practice medicine specializing in dermatology Coronado, Calif., 1982—90. Cons. Erie County Health Dept., 1979-82; clin. assoc. prof. SUNY, Buffalo Med. Sch., 1980-82. Contbr. articles to med. jours. and popular mags. Decorated Navy Commendation medal, Joint Svc. Commendation medal; Knight's Cross of the Order of Falcon (Iceland). Fellow ACP, Am. Acad. Dermatology; mem. AMA, So. Med. Assn., Assn. Mil. Surgeons, U.S. Navy League, City Club San Diego, Univ. Club San Diego, Yale Club N.Y.C., Alpha Omega Alpha. Democrat. Jewish. Home: 3352 Lucinda St San Diego CA 92106-2932 Personal E-mail: zitzapper@aya.yale.edu.

LEVY, JILL SONDRA, educational association administrator; b. Bronx, NY, July 13, 1938; d. Abe and Ruth (Fischer) Waltzer; m. Joseph Wilbur Levy, June 14, 1957; children: Allan Mark, Bruce Michael. BA, Queens Coll., 1959; MS, Hunter Coll., 1973; postgrad., Columbia U., 1991. Cert. sch. adminstr. and supr., NY. Tchr., dir. early childhood Hilltop Village, Queens, N.Y., 1962-65; tchr. NYC Bd. Edn., 1959-62, tchr., coord. spl. edn., 1975-81, supr. spl. edn., 1981-89; coord. Supervisory Support Program, NYC, 1989-94; treas. Am. Fedn. Sch. Adminstrs., Washington, 2000—03, exec. v.p., 2003—06, nat. pres., 2006—; v.p. Coun. of Suprs. and Adminstrs., NYC, 1989—92, exec. v.p., 1992—2000, pres., 2000—06. Mem. exec. bd. NY State Fedn. Sch. Adminstrs., NYC, 1994—; dir. Leadership Inst. for Educators, NYC, 1991—; mem. adv. bd. Annenberg Found., NYC, 1996—; cons. Life Skills Coop., Great Barrington, Mass., 1990—. Editor newsletter ANIBIE; creator/author audio tape; author articles. Trustee Page and Otto Marx Jr. Found., NYC, 1996—; mem. labor subcom. Pres.'s Com. on Employment of Poeple with Disabilities, Washington, 1996—; mem. NY State Regents Select Com. on Disabilities, 1989-96. Recipient Outstanding Ednl. Leadership award Adminstrv. Women in Edn., 1993, Edn. Leadership award Jewish Tchrs. Cmty. Chest, 1990, 94, Outstanding Leadership award Joint Assn. Suprs., 1992, 93, Disting. Svcs. award Assn. Jewish Profls., 1997. Mem. ASCD, Coun. for Exceptional Children, Assn. for Neurologically Impaired/Brain Injured Children (pres., dir. 1975-92). Office: Am Fedn Sch Adminstrs 1101 17th St NW Ste 408 Washington DC 20036

LEVY, JON D., state supreme court justice; Grad., Syracuse U., West Va. U. Coll. of Law. Law clerk U.S. Dist. Ct., Charleston, W.Va., court monitor; chief judge Dist. Ct., deputy chief judge; judge Dist. Ten; assoc. justice Maine Supreme Ct., 2002—. Chmn. Maine Family Law Adv. Commn., 1996—2000; ct. liaison Adv. Com. on Professional Responsibility, CASA Adv. Bd., Com. on Jud. Responsibility & Disability; chair Jud. Resource Team. Author: (book) Maine Family Law, 1988. Office: Maine Supreme Ct 142 Federal St PO Box 368 Portland ME 04112-0368*

LEVY, JOSEPH, lawyer; b. NYC, June 9, 1928; s. Morris Joseph and Dora (Cohen) L.; m. Gertrud C. Roeder, Jan. 20, 1967; children— Diana N., Susan R. BBA cum laude, CCNY, 1950; JD cum laude, NYU, 1954. Bar: N.Y. 1955, D.C. 1968. Asso. Parker, Chapin and Flattau, NYC, 1954-62; ptnr. firm Rivkin, Sherman & Levy (and predecessors), NYC, 1962-84, Schnader, Harrison, Segal & Lewis, 1984-93; v.p., sec., dir. Trecom Bus. Sys., Inc., Edison, NJ, 1993-97. Sec., dir. Horizons Comms. Corp., 1970-78, Quad Typographers, Inc., 1965-79; sec. Savin Bus. Machines Corp., 1959-84, On-Line Systems, Inc., 1968-78, Lambda Tech., Inc., 1970-78, Programming Methods, Inc., 1969-72, Kreisler Mfg. Cor., 1969-72, Peck & Peck, 1970-73, v.p., sec., dir. Trecom Bus. Systems, Inc., 1985-97, Business Edge Solutions, Inc., Edison, N.J., 1999—. Served to capt. AUS, 1951—53. Home: 254 University Way Paramus NJ 07652-5516

LEVY, KENNETH, music educator; b. NYC, Feb. 26, 1927; s. Meyer and Sylvia Levy; m. Clara Brooks Emmons, Jan. 25, 1956; children: Robert Brooks, Helen Gardner. AB, Queens Coll., 1947; MFA, Princeton U., 1949, PhD, 1956; Doctorate (hon.), U. Athens, 2004. Instr. music Princeton (N.J.) U., 1952-54; from asst. prof. to Fredrick R. Mann. prof. Brandeis U., Waltham, Mass., 1954-66; prof. music Princeton U., 1966—, chmn. dept. music., 1967-70, 88, Scheide prof. music history, 1988-95. Author: Music: A Listener's Introduction, 1983, Gregorian Chant and the Carolingians, 1998; assoc. editor: Anthologie de la Chanson Parisienne au Seizieme Siecle, 1953; Festschrift: The Study of Medieval Chant: In Honor of Kenneth Levy (edited by P. Jeffery), 2001; mem. editl. bd. Monumenta Musicae Byzantinae, 1968—, Grove's Dictionary, 6th edit, Early Music History, 1980—; contbr. articles to profl. jours. With USNR, 1945-46. Recipient Fulbright award Italy, 1962-63, Howard T. Behrman award for disting. achievements in humanities, 1983, Deems Taylor award ASCAP, 1989, Pres.'s Disting. Teaching award Princeton U., 1995; Guggenheim fellow, 1955-56, Am. Coun. Learned Socs. fellow, 1970-71, sr. fellow Dumbarton Oaks, Harvard U., 1992-96; vis. fellow Cambridge U., 1995. Fellow Medieval Acad. Am.; mem. Am. Philos. Soc., Am. Musicological Soc. (hon.). Office: Princeton U Dept Music Woolworth Ctr Mus Studies Princeton NJ 08544-0001

LEVY, KENNETH, computer company executive; BS in Engring., MS in Engring. Founder KLA Instruments Corp., 1976; former CEO KLA-Tencor, San Jose, Calif., chmn., 1999—2006, chmn. emeritus, 2006—. Dir. emeritus Semiconductor Equipment Materials Inst. Recipient numerous awards. Mem.: NAE. Office: KLA-Tencor Corp One Technology Dr Milpitas CA 95035

LEVY, KENNETH JAY, psychology professor, academic administrator; b. Dallas, Sept. 18, 1946; s. Reuben and Ruth (Okon) L.; children: Ryan S., Scott D. BA, U. Tex., 1968, MA, 1969; PhD, Purdue, 1972. Asst. prof. psychology SUNY, Buffalo, 1972-75, assoc. prof., 1976-78, prof., 1979—, chmn. dept. psychology, 1976-78, dean social scis., 1978-82, various adminstrv. positions, 1985—, assoc. provost, 1987—92, sr. vice provost, 1992—. Contbr. numerous articles to profl. jours.; editorial cons. Psychometrika. Home: 39 Shire Dr S East Amherst NY 14051-1816 Office: SUNY at Buffalo 353 Park Hall Buffalo NY 14260 Office Phone: 716-645-3650 ext. 353.

LEVY, LEAH GARRIGAN, federal official; b. Miami, Fla., Apr. 29, 1947; d. Thomas Leo and Mary (Flaherty) Garrigan; m. Roger N. Levy, May 2, 1977; children: Philip, Aaron. BA in Polit. Sci., George Mason U., 1998, MA, 2007. Mem. legis. staff U.S. Ho. Reps., 1973-75; mem. scheduling staff U.S. Senate, 1975-77, mem. administrv. scheduling staff, 1977-81; staff asst. pub. liaison The White House, 1982-84; spl. asst. U.S Dept. Transport, Washington, 1984-89, U.S. Dept. Housing, Washington, 1989—; scheduling asst. Empower Am., Washington, 1993-94; scheduler majority leader Dick Armey U.S. Ho. of Reps., Washington, 1995-2001; dir. scheduling and advance Sec. of Labor, Washington, 2001—03, spl. asst. Office of the Sec., 2002—03; dir. scheduling U.S. Senator Elizabeth Dole, Washington, 2003—; v.p. devel. Empower Am., Washington, 2003—05; dir. scheduling and advance US Dept. Labor, Washington, 2005—, dir. operations, 2007—. Contbr. to Rep. Nat. Com., Washington. Contbr. Rep. Nat. Conv. Va. Rep. Party, Washington; del. Va. State GOP Conv., Richmond, 1994. Mem. Alpha Chi. Roman Catholic. Avocations: tennis, golf, reading. Personal E-mail: thelevys@aol.com.

LEVY, LESLIE ANN, application developer; b. NYC, Dec. 25, 1941; d. Paul and Ruth Candace (Tachna) Bauman; m. Marc Gersan Gerard Levy, Oct. 1962 (div.); children: Benjamin Gerard, Remy Marcel Gerard. BA summa cum laude in philosophy and history, Smith Coll., 1962; MBA, Harvard U., Boston, 1976, DBA, 1980. Cert. French Fashion Acad., 1964. Tchg. asst. in philosophy UCLA, 1962-63; pres. Commonwealth Collaborative, Inc., Cambridge and Sarasota, Fla., 1976—99; sr. rsch. assoc. Harvard Sch. Bus. Adminstrn., Boston, 1979-81; asst. prof. mgmt. policy, industry analysis Case Western Res. U., Cleve., 1981-84; pres., CEO Acad. for Corp. Governance, Fordham U. Grad. Sch. Bus., 1990-91; pres., dir., treas., sec. Directors, Data, Inc., 1999—; pres., sec. Life Choices and Death Wishes, 2000—. Sr. advisor, pres., dir. Inst. Rsch. on Bd. Dirs., 1998-; with Honeywell Info. Sys., Boston, 1971-75; former cons. and lectr. in field. Author: Director Motivation: Incentives and Disincentives to Board Service, 1996, Separate Chairmen of the Board: Their Roles, Legal Liabilities, and Compensation; editor, co-author: Boards of Directors Part II; columnist: Directors and Boards, 1996-97; contbr. aricles to profl. jours. Mem. Boston and Tampa Bay Com. on Fgn. Rels. Acad. Corp. Governance rsch. fellow; Fulbright scholar. Mem. Am. Soc. Corp. Secs., Nat. Assn. Corp. Dirs., Acad. Mgmt. (article reviewer), Nat. Investor Rels. Inst., Inst. of Dirs., Federalist Soc., Women in Pensions, So. Fin. Assn., Harvard Club of Sarasota, Am. Jewish Com., Am. Jewish Congress, Nat. Coun. Jewish Women. Avocations: hiking, art history, construction, whitewater canoeing. E-mail: dirsdata@drleslielevy.com, irbd@drleslielevy.com.

LEVY, LOUIS EDWARD, retired accounting firm executive; b. Cleve., Nov. 16, 1932; s. Jerome and Bessie (Goldberg) L.; m. Sandra Harris, Mar. 4, 1956; children: Jerold, Richard, Lawrence. BBA, Case Western Res. U., 1956. CPA, N.Y. Agt. IRS, Cleve., 1956; ptnr., vice chmn. KPMG Peat Marwick, NYC, 1958-90. Chmn. bd. dirs. ISI Mut. Funds; former mem. emerging issues task force Fin. Acctg. Standards Bd.; former adj. prof. Columbia U. Grad. Sch. Bus.; former dir. Kimberly-Clark, Household Internat., Scudder Mutual Funds. Trustee, chmn. Nat. Multiple Sclerosis Soc., NYC, 1978-2000; trustee New Coll. Fla. Found., Sarasota, 2003—, Sarasota Meml. Healthcare Found., 2005—. With US Army, 1956—58. Recipient Braden award Weatherhead Sch. Mgmt. Case Western Res. U., 1984, Community Svc. award Brandeis U., 1980; fellow Brandeis U., Boston, 1981—. Mem. AICPA (former chmn. quality control inquiry com.), Maplewood Country Club (N.J.), Longboat Key Country Club. Republican. Jewish. Avocations: tennis, boating, golf. E-mail: loulevy@msn.com.

LEVY, MARK IRVING, lawyer; b. Chgo., June 28, 1949; s. Kenneth Warren and Arleen (Langhaus) L.; m. Judith Jarrell Levy, Sept. 8, 1979; children: Elizabeth Sara, Mitchell Bennett. BA summa cum laude with distinction, Yale U., New Haven, 1971; JD, Yale U., New Haven, Conn., 1975. Bar: DC 1976, US Dist. Ct. D.C. 1977, US Supreme Ct. 1980, Ill. 1986, US Ct. Appeals (DC cir.) 1990, US Ct. Appeals (6th, 7th and 8th cirs.) 1990, US Tax Ct. 1990, US Ct. Appeals (9th cir.) 1993, US Ct. Appeals (2d, 4th and 10th cirs.) 1994, US Ct. Appeals (3d, 5th, 11th and Fed. cirs.) 1996, US Ct. Appeals (1st cir.) 2000. Law clk. Judge Gerhard A. Gesell, Washington, 1975-76; assoc. Covington & Burling, Washington, 1976-79, 81-83; asst. to solicitor gen. US Dept. Justice, Washington, 1979-81, 83-86; ptnr. Mayer, Brown & Platt, Chgo., 1987-93; dep. asst. atty. gen. (Appellate) Civil Divsn. US Dept. Justice, Washington, 1993-95; ptnr. Howrey & Simon, Washington, 1995—2003; of counsel Kilpatrick Stockton LLP, 2004—. Adj. faculty, appellate sem. U. Va. Sch. Law, 1999-2002, 2004-; mem. adv. com. fed. rules of appellate procedure, former mem. adv comm. on procedures DC Cir. Exec. editor Yale Law Jour., 1974-75; columnist Nat. Law Jour. Recipient Israel H. Peres prize Yale Law Sch., 1975; named one of the Best Lawyers in Am. Fellow Am. Acad. Appellate Lawyers; mem. Lawyers Club of Chgo., Yale Law Sch. Alumni Assn. (former treas., exec. com. mem. 1987-90), Edward Coke Appellate Am. Inn of Ct. (master), Phi Beta Kappa (fellow). Home: 7609 Winterberry Pl Bethesda MD 20817-4847 Office: Kilpatrick Stockton LLP 607 14th St NW Ste 900 Washington DC 20005-2018 Office Phone: 202-824-1437. Business E-Mail: mlevy@kilpatrickstockton.com.

LEVY, MARK RAY, lawyer; b. Denver, Mar. 2, 1946; s. Richard C. and Hilde (Lindauer) L.; m. Patricia Loeb, June 13, 1971; children: Betsy, Robert. BA, U. Colo., 1968, JD, 1972. Bar: Colo. 1972, U.S. Dist. Ct. Colo, 1972. Assoc. Holland & Hart LLP, Denver, 1972-78, ptnr., 1978—. Adj. prof. the lawyering process U. Denver Law Sch., 1990-93; mem. spl. adv. com. Colo. Securities Bd., 1996-97. Author: (with others) Colorado Corporations Manual, 1987, Colorado Corporation Law and Practice, 1990. Trustee Congregation Emanuel, Denver, 1984-90, mem. legal com., 2005-06; chmn. Denver Alumni Phonathon U. Colo. Law Sch., 1989-90, mem. alumni bd., 1992-96, chmn. alumni bd., 1994-95; trustee Nat. Repertory Orch., 1995-96. Mem. ABA, Colo. Bar Assn. (Blue Sky Law task force 1980-81, co-chmn. Colo. securities law rev. com. 1988-91, Article 8 of UCC com. 1995-96, chmn. ann. conv. com. 1999-00, mem. annual conv. com. 1998-02, mem. planning com. annual bus. law inst. 2000, mem. bd. dirs. Am. Jewish com. 2005-, v.p. Colo. chpt. 2005-), Denver Bar Assn. Office: Holland & Hart LLP 555 17th St Ste 3200 Denver CO 80202-3950 E-mail: mlevy@hollandhart.com.

LEVY, MARV (MARVIN DANIEL), professional football team executive and retired coach; b. Chgo., Aug. 3, 1925; m. Mary Frances Levy; 1 child, Kimberly. BA, Coe Coll., Cedar Rapids, Iowa, 1950; MA, Harvard U., 1951. High sch. coach, St. Louis, 1951-52; asst. coach Coe Coll., Cedar Rapids, Iowa, 1953-55, U. N.Mex., 1956—58, head coach, 1958—59, U. Calif. Golden Bears, Berkeley, 1960-63, Coll. William & Mary, Williamsburg, Va., 1964-68; kicking teams coach Phila. Eagles, 1969; spl. teams coach LA Rams, 1970, Wash. Redskins, 1971-72; head coach Montreal Alouetts, Can. Football League, 1973-77, Kans. City Chiefs, 1978-82, Chgo. Blitz, US Football League, 1984, Buffalo Bills, 1986—97, v.p., 1995—97, gen. mgr., v.p. football ops., 2006—. Author: Marv Levy: Where Else Would You Rather Be?, 2004. Served Army Air Corps., 1943—46. Named AFC Coach of the Yr., 1988, 1993, 1995, NFL Coach of the Yr., UPI, 1988, 1995; named to The Pro Football Hall of Fame, 2001; recipient Annis Stukus trophy (Coach of the Yr.), Can. Football League,

1974. Achievements include leading the Buffalo Bills to four consecutive Super Bowl appearances, 1990-94. Office: Buffalo Bills Rich Stadium 1 Bills Dr Orchard Park NY 14127-2296

LEVY, MAURICE, retired education educator, researcher; b. Chgo., Aug. 15, 1933; s. Eugene and Jean Belle (Anshel) L.; m. Loris Belle Rissman, Sept. 11, 1955, (dec. Nov. 25, 2005); children: Arden Lynn, Andrea Hilary, James Michael. BS, U. Ill., 1956, EdM, 1959; EdD, U. Ga., 1968. Asst. prof. Ga. State U.-Atlanta, 1968-69; postdoctoral fellow U. So. Calif., LA, 1969-70; assoc. prof. Med. Coll. Ga., Augusta, 1970-73, prof. ednl. rsch., dir., 1976-86, prof. pediatrics, 1986-97, assoc. dean faculty devel., 1990, prof. emeritus, 1997—; prof., dir. So. Ill. U. Sch. Medicine, Springfield, 1973-76. Author: Introduction to Pediatric Cardiology, 1975, Physicians Assistants Exam Review, 1980; contbr. articles to profl. jours. Bd. dirs. Am. Cancer Soc., Springfield, Ill., 1974, Health Info. Services, Virginia Beach, Va., 1982—; trustee Augusta County Day Sch., 1972-80; chmn. Med. Coll. Ga. United Fund, Augusta, 1980. Recipient Outstanding Sci. Exec. award Am. Acad. Family Practice, 1974; Gold Cert. award Am. Acad. Pediatrics, 1973; Boss of Yr. award Am. Bus. Women's Assn., 1978. Mem. Am. Acad. Phys. Assts. (bd. advisors 1975-85, Significant Contbns. award 1980-83), Health Scis. Commn. Assn. Jewish. Clubs: Augusta Track, Torch (vice chmn. 1972-73). Home: 1 Lookout Hilton Head Island SC 29928-5265 Personal E-mail: mlevyedd@mindspring.com.

LEVY, MICHAEL, electronic manufacturing company executive; b. Gainesville, Fla., Dec. 19, 1946; s. Leon and Geneva (Shore) Levy; m. Jo-Lynn Nelson, July 3, 1986; children: Susan Elizabeth, Amanda Christine. BSEE, Ga. Inst. Tech., 1969. Design engr. Harris Corp., Melbourne, Fla., 1969—73; mgr. engrng. Racal-Milgo, Inc., Miami, Fla., 1973—78; chmn., CEO Lexicon Corp., Ft. Lauderdale, Fla., 1978—93, Scope Inc. subs. Lexicon, Reston, Va., 1985—93; pres., CEO SportsLine USA (now CBS.SportsLine.com Inc.), Ft. Lauderdale, 1994—. Bd. dirs. Sports-Tech Internat. Inc. subs. Lexicon, Ft. Lauderdale, Cosmo Comm. Corp., Miami. Named Named hon. Ky. Col.; named one of 100 Most Powerful People in Sports (3 times), Sporting News. Mem.: Mem. Am. Electronics Assn. Republican. Achievements include patents for electronic dictionary, five others. Office: SportsLine 2200 W Cypress Creek Rd Fort Lauderdale FL 33309-1825

LEVY, MICHAEL B., business educator; b. Balt., July 12, 1947; m. Bonny B. Wolf; 1 child. BA, Brown U., 1969; PhD, Rutgers U., 1979. Tchr. social studies, coach Loyola High Sch., Balt., 1969—72; teaching asst. Rutgers U., New Brunswick, NJ, 1973—76, instr., 1978; asst. prof. Tex. A&M Univ., College Sta., 1978-84, assoc. prof. polit. sci., 1984-85; economist joint econ. com. U.S. Congress, Washington, 1985-87; adminstrv. asst. to Sen. Lloyd Bentsen U.S. Senate, Washington, 1987-93; asst. sec. legis. affairs U.S. Dept. Treasury, Washington, 1993-95; adj. instr. Georgetown U., Washington, 1986-93, disting. prof., 1995—; sr. advisor to U.S. Treas. Sec. Robert Rubin U.S. Dept Treas., Washington, 1995. Policy dir. Brownstein, Hyatt, Farber & Schreck, Denver and Washington, 1995—. Editor: Political Thought in America, 1981, 87, (with Philip Abbott) The Liberal Future in America: Essays in Renewal, 1985, (with Edward Portis) Handbook of Political Theory and Policy Sciences, 1989; contbr. articles to profl. jours. Bevier fellow Rutgers U., 1979; R.J. Reynolds fellow for So. High Sch. Tchrs. Office: Georgetown U Sch Bus 411 Ol North Washington DC 20057-0001 Business E-Mail: levymb@msb.edu, mlevy@bhfs-law.com.

LEVY, MURRAY, business educator; b. NYC, May 8, 1944; d. Leon and Mollie Levy; m. Sally Kilby, May 15, 1979 (div. Dec. 20, 1999); children: Justin, Megan. BBA, CUNY, NYC, 1971; MBA, Fordham U., NYC, 1979; EdD, U. So. Calif., LA, 1993. Communication cons. Western Union Internat., NYC, 1969—72; mgr. Hersey Co., NYC, 1973—75; mktg. mgr. Nestle Co., NYC, 1976—80; traffic cons. Sys. 99, Pico Rivera, Calif., 1981—84; prof. Glendale Coll., Calif., 1984—. Bd. dirs. Chancellor's Statewide Occupl. Com., Sacramento, 1997—2001. Author: (films) Bloody Movie, 1987. Vice chair Natural Resource Commn., South Pasadena, Calif., 2001—04; docent LA Zoo, 2001—; outing leader Sierra Club, 2001—; chair Libertarians, Pasadena, 2006; Libertarian candidate Dist. 22 Calif. State Senate, 2006. With US Army, 1965—71. Mem.: Mktg. Educators Assn. (bd. dirs. 1997—2000), Calif. Assn. Internships (pres., bd. dirs. 1998—2002), Am. Legion. Jewish. Avocations: opera, history, travel, racquetball. Home: 1141 Pine St #10 South Pasadena CA 91030 Office: Glendale Coll 1500 N Verdugo Rd Glendale CA 91208

LEVY, NAOMI, rabbi; m. Robert Eshman; children: Adin, Noa. BA summa cum laude, Cornell U. Cert. ordained Rabbi Jewish Theological Seminary. Founder, spiritual leader Nashuva. Spkr. in field of Judaism and Spirituality. Author: (Religious Books) To Begin Again, Talking to God; TV appearances: Oprah Winfrey Show; NBC's Today Show; featured Red Book, Self Mag., LA Times, The Boston Globe. Named one of The Top 50 Rabbis in America, Newsweek Mag., 2007. Office: Nashuva PO Box 64196 Los Angeles CA 90064*

LEVY, NELSON LOUIS, immunologist, educator, surgeon; b. Somerville, NJ, June 19, 1941; s. Myron L. and Sylvia (Cohen) L.; m. Joanne Barnett, Dec. 21, 1963 (div. 1972); children: Scott, Erik, Jonathan; m. Louisa Douglas Stiles, Dec. 21, 1974; children: Michael, Andrew, David. BA/BS summa cum laude, Yale U., 1963; MD, Columbia U., 1967; PhD, Duke U., 1972. Diplomate Am. Bd. Allergy and Immunology. Intern U. Colo. Med. Ctr., Denver, 1967-68; resident Duke U. Med. Ctr., Durham, NC, 1970-73; rsch. assoc. NIH, Bethesda, Md., 1968-70; asst. prof. immunology Duke U. Med. Ctr., Durham, 1972-75, assoc. prof. immunology and neurology, 1975-80, prof., 1980-81; dir. biol. rsch. Abbott Labs., Abbott Park, Ill., 1981, v.p. rsch., 1981-84; pres. Fujisawa Pharm., Deerfield, Ill., 1992-93; CEO Ill. Tech. Devel. Corp., 1993-95, The Core Techs Corp., Lake Forest, Ill., 1984—92, chmn. bd. dirs., CEO, 1995—. Chmn. bd. dirs. Horizon Quest Inc., Laguna Hills, Calif., 1996—97, ColesCraft Corp., 1997—, IMM UVA Corp., New Orleans, 1997—, ChemBridge Pharms., Inc., 2006—; bd. dirs. ChemBridge Corp., San Diego, Targeted Genetics Corp., Seattle, Biona PTY Ltd., Laguna Beach, Cary Pharm. Co., Bethesda, Md., ChemBridge Rsch. Labs., LLC, San Diego, zuChem, Inc., Chgo.; chmn. sci. adv. bd. Neoprobe Corp., First Horizon Pharms., Inc.; mem. sci. adv. bd. Ligand Pharms. Inc.; cons. Alcide Corp., 1991—, Ameritech, 1993—, U.S. Dept. Treasury, FTC, 1999—; others. Contbr. chapters to books, articles to profl. jours. Mem. Gov.'s Task Force on Econ. Devel., 1993-98; mem. corp. adv. bd. Family Svc. of South Lake County, 1991—; commr. Lake County, Ill., 1998—. Surgeon USPHS, 1968-70. Grantee Am. Cancer Soc., 1970-75, NIH, 1971-81, Nat. Multiple Sclerosis Soc., 1974-81, Ill. Dept. Commerce and Cmty. Affairs, 1993—. Mem. Am. Assn. Immunologists, Am. Assn. Cancer Rsch., Licensing Execs. Soc., Rotary, Phi Beta Kappa, Sigma Xi, Alpha Omega Alpha, Phi Gamma Delta. Avocations: triathlons, biking, rhythm 'n blues. Office: 1391 Concord Rd Lake Forest IL 60045-1506

LEVY, NORMAN B., psychiatrist, educator; b. NYC, 1931; s. Barnett Theodore and Lena (Gulnick) L.; m. Lya Weiss (dec.); children: Karen, Susan, Joanne; m. Carol Lois Spiegel, 1 son, Robert Barnett. BA cum laude, NYU, 1952; MD, SUNY. Diplomate Am. Bd. Psychiatry and Neurology (examiner). Intern Maimonides Med. Center, Bklyn.; resident physician in medicine U. Pitts.-Presbyn. Hosp.; resident in psychiatry Kings County Hosp. Center, Bklyn.; instr. psychiatry SUNY Downstate Med. Ctr. Coll. Medicine, Bklyn., asst. prof., assoc. prof.; prof. State U. N.Y. Downstate Med. Center Coll. Medicine, 1980-95; presiding officer faculty SUNY Downstate Med. Ctr. Coll. Medicine, assoc. dir. med-psychiat. liaison service, 1965-80; prof. psychiatry, medicine, surgery and coordinator psychiat. liaison services NY Med. Coll., 1980-95; clin. prof. psychiatry, adj. prof. of medicine Health Science Ctr. SUNY, Bklyn., 1996—2007; dir. psychiatry Kingsboro Psychiat. Ctr., Bklyn., 2000—06; prof. psychiatry U. So. Calif., 2007—. Dir. liaison svcs. psychiatry divsn. Westchester County Med. Ctr., 1980-95, mem. exec. com. med. staff, 1981-85, 89-92, NY Med. Coll., 1980-95; clin. prof. psychiatry, adj. prof. medicine health sci. ctr. SUNY, Bklyn., 1996—; dir., consultation-liaison and emergency psychiatry Coney Island Hosp., Bklyn., 1996-2000; vis. prof. psychiatry and medicine So. Ill. U. Sch. Medicine; vis. prof. psychiatry John A. Burns Sch. Medicine, U. Hawaii, 1981; coord. 1st Internat. Conf. Psychol. Factors in Hemodialysis and Transplantation, 1978, 2d-9th Internat. Confs. on Psychonephrology; cons. NIMH; chief med. svcs. USAF Hosp., Ashiya, Japan; clin. prof. psychiatry, adj. prof. medicine SUNY Health Sci. Ctr., Bklyn., 1996. Author: (with others), editor: Living or Dying: Adaptation to Hemodialysis, 1974, Psychonephrology I: Psychological Factors in Hemodialysis and Transplantation, 1981, Men in Transition: Theory and Therapy, 1982, Psychonephrology II: Psychological Problems in Kidney Failure and their Treatment, 1983; contbr. articles to jours., chpts. to textbooks in field.; assoc. editor: Gen. Hosp. Psychiatry, 1978-82, sect. editor, 1982-2005; sect. editor: Internat. Jour. Psychiatry in Medicine, 1977-78; mem. editl. bd., book rev. editor Jour. Dialysis and Transplantation, 1979-97, Facta Universitatis, 1997—; mem. editl. bd. Resident and Staff Physician, 1981-91, Internat. Jour. Artificial Internat. Organs, 1983-93, Geriatric Nephrology and Urology, 1990—, Kidney: A Current Survey of World Literature, 1990—, Dialysis and Transplantation, 1979—. Served to capt. M.C. USAF. Recipient William A. Console Master Tchr. award, SUNY, Bklyn., 1991. Fellow ACP, Am. Coll. Psychiatrists, Am. Psychiat. Assn. (pres. Kings County dist. br. 1981-82), Acad. Psychosomatic Medicine (Thomas P. Hackett award 1993); mem. AAAS, Am. Psychosomatic Soc. (coun. 1994-97), NY Acad. Scis., Psychonephrology Found. (pres. 1978—), Internat. Soc. Nephrology, Am. Soc. Nephrology, Soc. Liaison Psychiatry (bd. dirs. 1979-80, sec. 1980-81, pres.-elect 1991-92, pres. 1992-94, bd. dirs. 1995-98, award 1998), Serbian Acad. Medicine, Phi Beta Kappa, Sigma Xi. Office Phone: 646-331-6280. Personal E-mail: nephropsyc@aol.com.

LEVY, PETER A., lawyer; b. Apr. 17, 1949; BA, U. Ill., Urbana-Champaign, 1971; JD, U. Chgo., 1974. Bar: Ill. 1974. Ptnr., co-chmn. Lodging & Timeshare practice group DLA Piper Rudnick Gray Cary, Chgo. Lectr. Practicing Law Inst., Georgetown Univ. Law Ctr. Co-author: Ill. Real Estate Forms. Mem.: ABA, Ill. State Bar Assn., Chgo. Bar Assn., Phi Beta Kappa. Office: DLA Piper Rudnick Gray Cary 203 N LaSalle St Chicago IL 60601-1293 Office Phone: 312-368-4068. Office Fax: 312-630-5342. Business E-Mail: peter.levy@dlapiper.com.

LEVY, RALPH, engineering executive, consultant; b. London, Apr. 12, 1932; came to U.S., 1967, naturalized, 1978; s. Alfred and Esther L.; m. Barbara Dent, Dec. 12, 1959; children: Sharon E., Mark S. BA, Cambridge U., 1953, MA, 1957; PhD, Queen Mary Coll. U. London, 1966. Mem. sci. staff GEC, Stanmore, Middlesex, Eng., 1953-59; mem. sci. staff Mullard Research Labs., Redhill, Eng., 1959-64; lectr. dept. elec. and electronic engrng. U. Leeds, 1964-67; v.p. research Microwave Devel. Labs., Inc., Natick, Mass., 1967-84; v.p. engrng. KW Engrng., San Diego, 1984-88; v.p. research Remec Inc., San Diego, 1988-89; R. Levy Assocs., 1989—. Author: (with J.O. Scanlan) Circuit Theory, 1970, 2d vol., 1973; contbr. articles in field; patentee in field. Fellow IEEE (editor Transactions on Microwave Theory and Techniques 1986-88, Career award IEEE Microwave Theory and Techniques Soc. 1997); mem. Instn. Elec. Tech. (London). Office: 1897 Caminito Velasco La Jolla CA 92037-5725 Office Phone: 858-459-2286. E-mail: r.levy@ieee.org.

LEVY, ROBERT A., academic administrator; BA, Ohio Wesleyan U.; MA in English, Temple U. Asst. to v.p. acad. affairs U. Tenn., Knoxville, 1973—85, assoc. v.p., 1985—2004, v.p. acad. affairs, 2004—. Office: Univ Tenn 810 Andy Holt Tower 1331 Circle Pk Knoxville TN 37996*

LEVY, ROBERT EDWARD, retired management consultant; b. Cin., May 23, 1939; s. Aaron F. and Elizabeth W. (Hirsch) L.; m. Candace Ann Wolfe, June 20, 1970; children: Brian D., Jessica A. BChemE, Cornell U., 1962; PhDChemE, U. Calif., Berkeley, 1967. Various positions, including mgr. synthetic fuels devel., rsch. and engring. Exxon Co., Florham Park, NJ, 1967-80, 84-86; mgr. tech. dept. Lago Oil & Transport Co., Esso Interam. divsn. Exxon Co., Aruba, Netherlands Antilles, 1980-84; v.p., dir. tech. devel. M.W. Kellogg Co., Houston, 1987-93; v.p. govt. and regulatory affairs Energy Biosystems Corp., The Woodlands, Tex., 1993-97; mgmt. cons. Houston, 1997-99; sr. v.p. Allan F. Dow & Assocs., Houston, 1998-99, UniPure Corp., Houston, 2000—04, dir., 2001—04; pres., CEO AstroVelos, LLC, Houston, 2005—07. Cons. in field. Patentee in field. Indsl. mem. Com. for Prevention of Shoreline Pollution by Oil, Aruba, 1982—84; founder Industry Profls. for Clean Air, Houston, 2004. Mem. AIChE, Indsl. Rsch. Inst. (bd. editors 1992-95, pre-coll. edn. com. 1995-2000, chmn., 1996-97), Galveston Houston (Tex.) Assn. Smog Prevention (bd. dirs. 2005—), Sigma Xi (pres. Kellogg chpt. 1991-92). Avocations: tennis, jogging, sailing. Personal E-mail: boblevy@houston.rr.com.

LEVY, ROBERT S., lawyer; b. NYC, May 27, 1932; s. Harry Victor and Betty Ruth L.; m. Lorna Iris Klein, June 30, 1957; children— Jill Arden, Kenneth Arlan. BS cum laude, NYU, 1954, LLB cum laude, 1955. Bar: NY 1956, NJ US Dist. Ct. (so. and ea. dists.) NY 1962, US Supreme Ct. 1967, US Ct. Appeals (2d cir.) 1973. Assoc., Nordlinger, Reigelman, Benetar & Charney, NYC, 1955-59; sr. assoc. Reich, Spitzer & Feldman, NYC, 1959-64; pvt. practice, NYC, 1964-78; gen. counsel Audiovox Corp., Hauppauge, NY; mem. nat. panel arbitrators Am. Arbitration Assn., NYC, 1961—. Author: Guide to Franchise Investigation and Contract Negotiation, 1967; Woman's Guide to Franchises, 1967; Directory of State and Federal Funds for Business, 1968. Mem. NY State Bar Assn., Phi Beta Kappa.Tam O'Shanter (Brookville, NY). Office: Levy Stopol & Camelo LLP 1425 Reckson Plaza Uniondale NY 11556-1425 Office Phone: 516-802-7008.

LEVY, ROCHELLE FELDMAN, artist; b. NYC, Aug. 4, 1937; d. Harry and Eva (Krause) Feldman. m. Robert Paley Levy, June 4, 1955; children: Kathryn Tracey, Wendy Paige, Robert Paley, Angela Brooke, Michael Tyler. Student, Barnard Coll., 1954—55, U. Pa., 1955—56; BFA, Moore Coll. Art, 1979, HHD (hon.), 1998. Mgmt. cons. Woodlyn Sch., Rosemont, Pa., 1983—2003; ptnr. Phila. Phillies, 1981—94; sr. ptnr. DRT Interiors, Phila., 2006—. One-woman shows include Watson Gallery Wheaton Coll. Norton, Mass., 1977, U. Pa., 1977, Med. Coll. Pa. Phila., 1982, Aquaduct Race Track, 1982, Phila. Art Alliance, 1983, Paley Gallery, Moore Coll. Art and Design, 1984, 2003, Art Alliance, 1994, Frost & Reed Gallery, Saratoga, NY, 2000-05, Frost & Reed Ltd, NYC, 2004, Cross Gate Gallery, Saratoga, 2005, 06, 07, Reef Gallery, Ocean Reef, Fla., 2006. Pres. League of Children's Hosp. Phila., 1969-70; bd. overseers Ctr. for Judaic Studies U. Pa., 1993-96; bd. mgrs. Moore Coll. Art and Design, 1970—, chmn. exec. com., 1982-99, trustees 1979-99, chmn. emerita bd. trustees, 1999-2004. Recipient G. Allen Smith Prize Woodmere Art Gallery, Chestnut Hill, Pa., 1979, Disting. Alumni award Moore Coll. Art, 2005, Woman honoree Samuel Paley Day Care Ctr., Phila., 1990, Jefferson Bank Declaration award, 1991, Nat. Philanthropy honoree Nat. Soc. Fund Raising Execs. Greater Phila. chpt., 1994, Hon. Alumni award Moore Coll. Art, 2005. Mem. Pa. Acad. Fine Arts (selections and acquisitions com. 1970—, bd. mgrs. 1975—, chmn. exec. com. 1982—, trustee 1990—), Artist's Equity, Phila. Art Alliance, Phila. Mus. Art (assoc.), Phila. Print Club. Office: 200 W Montgomery Ave Ardmore PA 19003

LEVY, RONALD, medical educator, researcher; b. Carmel, Calif. BS, Harvard U., 1963; MD, Stanford U., 1968. Cert. Internal Medicine, 1973, Med. Oncology, 1979, lic. Commonwealth Mass., 1970, State Calif. Med. License, 1975. Intern, internal medicine Mass. Gen. Hosp., Boston, 1968-69, residency, internal medicine, 1969-70; clin. assoc., immunology branch Nat. Cancer Inst., 1970—72; Helen Hay Whitney Found. fellow in dept. chem. immunology Weizmann Inst. Sci., Rehovot, Israel, 1973-75; fellow, dept. medicine, divsn. oncology Stanford U. Sch. Medicine, 1972—73, mem. faculty Calif., 1975—, asst. prof. medicine, divsn. oncology Calif., 1975—81, assoc. prof. dept. medicine-oncology Calif., 1981—87, prof. medicine, divsn. oncology Calif., 1987—, Robert K. Summy and Helen K. Summy prof. Calif., 1987—; Frank and Else Schilling Am. Cancer Soc. Clin. Rsch. prof., 1987—; chief divsn. oncology Stanford U. Sch. Medicine, Calif., 1993—. Investigator Howard Hughes Med. Inst., 1977—82; chmn., bd. scientific counselors, divsn. cancer treatment NIH, 1989—93; mem. scientific advisory bd. Fred Hutchinson Cancer Rsch. Ctr., 1994—, Coley Pharm. Group, 2001, XTL Therapeutics, Rehovoth, Israel, Therion Inc., Cambridge, Mass., Xeyte Therapeutics, Seattle, Agensys, Santa Monica, Calif., Pointilliste, Mountain View, Calif., Cell Genesis, Foster City, Calif., Five Prime, South San Francisco, Calif.; Woodward vis. prof. Meml. Sloan Kettering Cancer Ctr., NY, 1994; Morton Mason lecture U. Tex. Southwestern, 1995; vis. prof. U. Minn. Cancer Ctr., 1996, U. Nebr. Cancer Ctr., 1999; lectr. in field. Contbr. articles to profl. jours.; Author, co-author of several books and publs. Mem. Dorothy P. Landon Am. Assn. for Cancer Rsch. Translational Cancer Rsch. com., 2001; bd. dir. Damon Runyon Cancer Rsch. Fund, 2002—; mem., Conflict of Interest Com. Stanford U. Sch. Medicine, 2001—; mem. Am. Assn. Med. Sch. Task Force on Fin. Conflicts of Interest in Clin. Rsch., 2001, GM Cancer Rsch. Found. Awards Assembly, 1992—96, 2001—. Recipient Armand Hammer award for Cancer Rsch., 1982, Ciba-Geigy/Drew award in Biomedical Rsch., 1983, Dr. Josef Steiner prize for Cancer Rsch., 1989, Karnofsky award, Am. Soc. Clin. Oncology, 1999, Charles F. Kettering award, GM Cancer Rsch. Found., 1999, Centeon award, 6th Internat. Conf. on Bispecific Antibodies, 1999, C. Chester Stock award, Meml. Sloan-Kettering Cancer Ctr., 2000, Medal of Honor, Am. Cancer Soc., 2000, Key to the Cure award, Cure for Lymphoma Found., 2000, Evelyn Hoffman Meml. award, Lymphoma Rsch. Found. Am., 2001, Jeffrey A. Gottlieb Meml. award, M.D. Anderson Cancer Ctr, 2003, Discovery Health Channel Med. Honors, 2004. Mem. ACP, Am. Soc. Clin. Oncology, Am. Cancer Soc. (chmn. immunology study sect., 1988-92, mem., rsch. coun., 2003-), Am. Soc. Clin. Investigation, Assn. Am. Physicians, Am. Assn. for Cancer Rsch. (chmn., Joseph H. Burchinal award com., 2002, Joseph H. Burchenal Clin. Cancer Rsch. award, 1997), Am. Assn. Immunology (program com. and block chmn. for tumor immunology, 1992-96), Am. Fed. for Clin. Rsch., Am. Soc. Hematology, Western Soc. Medicine, Acad. of Cancer Immunology. Achievements include first to the development of idiotype-based therapeutic vaccines for the treatment of non-Hodgkin's B-cell lymphoma. Office: Levy Lab Divsn Oncology 269 Campus Dr CCSR 1126 Stanford CA 94305-5151 Address: Stanford Sch Medicine 300 Pasteur Dr M207 Stanford CA 94305 Office Phone: 650-725-6452. Office Fax: 650-725-1420. E-mail: levy@stanford.edu.

LEVY, SALOMON, mechanical engineer; b. Jerusalem, Apr. 4, 1926; arrived in U.S., 1945; s. Abraham Isaac and Sultana Claire (Elyachar) Levy; m. Eileen Dolores Jaques, Oct. 14, 1951; children: Marshall Douglas, Linda C. BSME, U. Calif., Berkeley, 1949, MME, 1951, PhD in Mech. Engring., 1953. Engr. GE, Schenectady, NY, San Jose, Calif., 1953—59, mgr. heat transfer, 1959-66, mgr. sys. engring., 1966-68, mgr. design engring., 1968-71, gen. mgr. fuel, 1971-75, gen. mgr. boiling water reactor ops., 1975-77; chmn. S. Levy Inc., Campbell, Calif., 1977-98; owner Levy & Assocs., 1998—. Adj. prof. UCLA, 1986—87; Springer prof. U. Calif., Berkeley, 1979—80; bd. dirs. IES Industries, Inc. Author: Two-Phase Flow in Complex Systems, 1999. Fellow: ASME (hon.; chmn. heat transfer divsn. 1964—65, Heat Transfer Conf. award 1963, Heat Transfer Meml. award 1966, 50th Ann. Heat Transfer Divsn. award 1988), Am. Nuc. Soc. (chmn. thermal hydraulics divsn. 1985—86, Thermal Hydraulics Divsn. Achievement award 1987, Power Divsn. Walter H. Zinn award 1989); mem.: AIChE (Donald Kern award 1993), NAE, Inst. Nuc. Power Ops. (mem. adv. coun.). Democrat. Unitarian Ch. Achievements include patents in field. Avocations: racquetball, golf. Home: 1829 Dry Creek Rd San Jose CA 95124-1002 Office: Levy and Assocs Ste 225 3425 S Bascom Ave Campbell CA 95008 Office Phone: 408-369-6500. Personal E-mail: slevy112@aol.com.

LEVY, SHAWN ANTHONY, writer; b. NYC, Oct. 22, 1961; s. Jerome Sanford and Agnes Madeline (Shand) L.; m. Mary Elizabeth Bartholemy, Dec. 30, 1985; children: Vincent Bartholemy Levy, Anthony Augustine Levy. BA, U. Pa., 1982; MFA, U. Calif., Irvine, 1985, MA, 1989. Assoc. editor Box Office Mag., LA, 1989-90; sr. editor Am. Film Mag., LA, 1990; film critic Portland Oregonian. Author: (books) King of Comedy: The Life and Art of Jerry Lewis, 1997, Rat Pack Confidential: Frank, Dean, Sammy, Peter, Joey and the Last Great Show Biz Party, 1998, Ready, Steady, Go! The Smashing Rise and Giddy Fall of Swinging London, 2003, The Last Playboy: The High Life of Porfirio Rubirosa, 2005. Office: Author Mail InkWell Mgmt 26th fl 521 Fifth Ave New York NY 10175

LEVY, STANLEY HERBERT, lawyer; b. Phila., Apr. 11, 1922; s. Max and Rose (Cohen) L.; m. Gloria Kamber, Dec. 20, 1953; children: Steven M., Peter B. BA, Cornell U., 1943; LL.B., Harvard U., 1968, JD, 1968. Bar: N.Y. 1949, U.S. Dist. Ct. (ea. and so. dists.) N.Y., U.S. Treasury 1949, U.S. Supreme Ct. 1961. Practiced in N.Y.C., 1949—. Mem. Republican Town Com., Scarsdale, 1963-65, Temple Emanu-el, Westchester, N.Y. Served to 1st lt. F.A., AUS, 1943-47. Mem. Assn. Bar City N.Y., Confrérie des Chevaliers du Tastevin (officier commandeur), Commanderie de Bordeaux (comdr.), Harvard Club, Yale Club, Century Country Club (Purchase, N.Y.). Home: 3 Richbell Rd Scarsdale NY 10583-4421 Office: 551 Fifth Ave New York NY 10176-0003 Home Phone: 914-723-5306; Office Phone: 212-672-1500 ext. 206. Business E-Mail: stanley@kamberllc.com.

LEVY, STEPHEN H., computer scientist, educator; b. Phila., Oct. 24, 1945; s. Emanuel and Mae Levy; m. Beryl W. Levy, 1977; 1 child, Darren. BA in English lit., cum laude, Temple U., Phila., 1966; MA in philosophy, Duke U., Durham, NC, 1968; PhD in logic and philosophy of math., Fordham U., NYC, 1981. Tchg. fellow philosophy Johns Hopkins U., Balt., 1968—71; prof. philosophy SW Mo. State U., Springfield, 1971—73; prof. math. Spring Garden Coll., Phila., 1975; computer scientist US Naval Command, Washington, 1975—76; prof. math. Pa. State U., Media, 1977—78; prof. computer sci. Pace U., Pleasantville, NY, 1979—81; mgmt. scientist Irving Trust Co., NYC, 1982—83; sr. computer cons. AT&T Bell Labs., Summit, Holmdel, NJ, 1985—91; prof. philosophy, religion Coll. Morris, Randolph, NJ, 1994—; prof. philosophy St. Peter's Coll., Jersey City, 2001—. Judge essay contests US Inst. Peace, Washington, 1998—; book reviewer Prentice Hall Pubs., Englewood Cliffs, NJ, 2002—, McGraw-Hill Pubs., NYC, 2006—. Screenwriter, prodr. (screenplay) The Field of Honor: The Hamilton/Burr Duel, 1974; editor: (computer newsletter US Naval Command) WOW - Words of Wisdom, 1976; author: (computer sci. book) The Unix Ada Programmer's Manual, 1987 (AT&T Ada Tech. award, 1987); contbr. articles to profl. jours. Co-founder McGovern for Pres., Springfield, Mo., 1971—72, Student Lecture Series, Temple U., Phila., 1965—66; spkr. on lit., philosophic, religious topics, 1993—2007. Recipient Acad. Excellence award, Coll. Morris, 1997; fellow, NSF, 1966-1968, Linguistic Soc. Am., 1971; grantee, NEH, 1995, US Inst. Peace, 1997, NJ Coun. Humanities, 1998, 1999. Mem.: ACLU, So. Poverty Law Ctr., Nat. Resources Def. Coun., Assn. Computing Machinery, Charles S. Peirce Soc., Am. Philos. Assn., Am. Assn. Philosophy Tchrs., Amnesty Internat. Jewish. Achievements include discovery of new methods for solving two and three valued logic problems. Avocations: singing, playing saxophone, tennis, coaching Little League, acting. Home Phone: 908-317-6837; Office Phone: 973-328-5468. Personal E-mail: stephlevy@netzero.com.

LEVY, STEPHEN RAYMOND, retired data processing executive; b. Everett, Mass., May 4, 1940; m. Sandra Helen Rosen, Aug. 26, 1961; children: Phillip, Susan. BBA, U. Mass., 1961, LLD (hon.), 2001. Chmn., CEO Bolt Beranek and Newman Inc., Cambridge, Mass., CEO, 1976—94; gen. ptnr. Levy Venture Ptnrs. LP. Chmn. bd. dirs. Kaon Interactive Corp. Bd. dirs. Pharos LLC. Decorated Army Commendation medal. Mem. Am. Electronics Assn. (chmn. 1986), Mass. High Tech. Coun. (chmn. 1987-89), Mass. Network Comms. Coun. (chmn. 1996), Common Angels (chmn. 2004). Home: 300 Boylston St Apt 1204 Boston MA 02116-3940 Office: Levy Venture Ptnrs LP 20 Pk Plz Ste 436 Boston MA 02116-2322

LEVY, STEVE, sports anchor, studio host; b. Mar. 12, 1965; BS in Comms., SUNY, Oswego, 1987. Reporter Sta. WTOP-TV, Oswego, NY, 1983-87, sports dir., 1986-87; play-by-play commentator Oswego State's hockey team Sta. WOCR-Radio, Oswego, NY; part-time reporter various sports events Sta. WABC-Radio, 1987; prodr., host pre-game show NHL Radio Network, 1988-89; host intermission updates for N.Y. Rangers and Knicks' games Sta. WNBC-Radio, NYC, 1987-88; weekend sports reporter, host The NFL in Action Sta. WFAN-Radio, NYC, 1986-93; sports anchor/reporter Sta. WCBS-TV, NYC, 1992-93; host Sports Desk Madison Sq. Garden Network, NYC, 1989; SportsCenter anchor ESPN, 1993—, NHL studio host, 1993—2004, Sports Radio GameDay anchor, 1993—, host Nat. Hockey Night, 1993—2004, NFL co-host Sports Radio's Game Day, 1993—. Guest appearance Fever Pitch, 2005. Office: c/o ESPN ESPN Pla Bristol CT 06010

LEVY, STEVE A., county official, former state legislator; b. Glendale, NY, Aug. 25, 1959; m. Colleen West Levy; stepchildren: Shannon, Erin. BA in Polit. Sci. and History, SUNY, Stony Brook, 1981; JD, St. John's U. Sch. Law, 1984. Legis. Suffolk County, NY, 1985—2000; mem. NY State Assembly from Dist. 5, 2001—03; county exec. Suffolk County, NY, 2004—. Standing com. Aging, Consumer Affairs and Protection, Election Law and Real Property Taxation. Recipient Excellence in Govt. award, Suffolk County Independance Party, Innovation in Govt. award, Nat. Assn. of Counties. Office: Office County Exec H Lee Dennison Bldg 100 Veterabs Meml Hgwy PO Box 6100 Hauppauge NY 11788*

LEVY, STUART ARTHUR, pulmonologist, consultant; b. NYC, June 4, 1937; s. Philip and Adeline Levy; m. Nancy J. Kaufmann, June 19, 1965; children: Lenore Aileen Day, Kenneth Michael. B of Chem. Engring., Cooper Union Sch. Engring., 1959. Lic. physician Wis. Intern N.C. Meml. Hosp., Chapel Hill, 1965—66, jr. med. resident, 1966—67; sr. med. resident, pulmonary fellow Hosp. of U. of Pa., Phila., 1967—69; med. dir., pres. med. staff Transitional Hosp. of Milw. and Kindred Hosp. of Milw., 1994—2001. Clin. prof. medicine Med. Coll. Wis., 1982—; clin. asst. prof. medicine U. Wis. Med. Sch., 1984—2006. Contbr. chapters to books. Capt. USAF, 1969—71. Fellow: ACP (life), Am. Coll. of Chest Physicans (life). Home: 9509 N Wakefield Ct Milwaukee WI 53217 Home Phone: 414-351-1530.

LEVY, STUART B., molecular biologist, educator, science administrator, researcher; b. Wilmington, Del., Nov. 21, 1938; m. Cecile Pastel, 1983; 3 children. AB, Williams Coll., 1960; MD, U. Pa., 1965; Degree in Biology (hon.), Wesleyan U., 1998; Degree in Sci. (hon.), Des Moines U., 2001. Intern, med. resident Mt. Sinai Hosp., NYC, 1965-67, rsch. fellow dept. cellular biology, 1966-67; from asst. prof. to assoc. prof. Tufts U., Boston, 1971-80, prof. medicine molecular biology & microbiology Med. Sch., 1980—; dir. Ctr. Adaptation Genetics & Drug Resistance, 1992—. Rsch. fellow dept. microbiology U. Milan, Italy, 1962, Keio U., Tokyo, 1964; publiker nutrition fellow Kenyatta Nat. Hosp., Nairobi, 1964; staff assoc. NIH, Italy, 1967-70, Pasteur Inst., Paris, 1976; fellow hematology New Eng. Med. Ctr., Boston, 1970-71; collaborator East African Viral Inst., Entebbe, Uganda, 1971; staff physician NE Med. Ctr. Hosp., Boston, 1976—; staff scientist Cancer Rsch. Ctr. Med. Sch. Tufts U., 1976—; sci. adv. Biomed. Rsch. Ctr. U. Nat. Pedro Henriquez Urena, Santa Domingo, Dominican Republic, 1977-83; cons. FDA, Washington, 1978-80, 85-87; adv. Fate of the Earth, Inc., 1981—; pres. Alliance for the Prudent Use of Antibiotics, 1981—, Boston Blood Club, 1984; overseas vis. Bd. Postgrad. Med. Edn. Royal Melbourne Hosp., Australia, 1983-84; gen. chmn. Int. Task Forces on Use of Antibiotics Worldwide Fogarty Int. Ctr. NIH, 1983-86; mem. subcom. Gram-Negative Facultatively Anaerobic Rods Am. Soc. Metals, 1985-88; subcom. health & antibiotic resistance EPA, 1988—; lectr. Am. Soc. Microbiology Found., 1989-90, Australian Soc. Microbiology, 1990—; mem. sci. evaluation com. Pasteur Inst., Paris, 1990; dir. Ctr. for adaptation genetics and Drug Resistance, Tufts U. Sch. Medicine. Mem. Am. Assn. Cancer Rsch., Am. Soc. Biochem. & Molecular Biology, Am. Soc. Clin. Investigation, Am. Soc. Hematology, Infectious Disease Soc. of Am., Am. Soc. Microbiology (collection com. on genetic & molecular microbiology 1986, mem. com. environ. microbiology 1989—, pres. 1998—, Hoechst-Roussel award 1995), Am Soc. Microbiology. Achievements include research in resistance to antibiotics and anticancer drugs. Office: Tufts U Sch Medicine Molecular Biology & Microbiology Dept 136 Harrison Ave Boston MA 02111-1817

LEVY, TODD ROBERT, musician, educator; b. Somerville, NJ, Jan. 7, 1962; s. Douglas Marshall and Berna Ann Levy; m. Patricia Ann Niemi. MusB, The Juilliard Sch. Music, 1984, MusM, 1985. Prin. clarinet The Stamford Symphony, Conn., 1980—2000, The NEw World Symphony, Miami, Fla., 1988—93, Solisti N.Y. Chamger Orch., NYC, 1989—2000, The Eos Orch., 1994—2000, Northeastern Pa. Phil., Wilkes Barre, Pa., 1995—2000, The Santa Fe Opera, 1999—, The Milw. Symphony Orch., 2000—. Asst. prof. clarinet U. Milw., 2000—. Named Grammy award, Nat. Acad. Rec. Arts and Scis., 2001; recipient, 2000, 2002. Avocations: photography, skiing, basketball.

LEW, GINGER EHN, investment company executive, lawyer; b. San Mateo, Calif., Nov. 3, 1948; d. Bing and Suey Bow (Ng) Lew; m. Carl Lennart Ehn Lew, Feb. 2, 1984; children: Melissa, Jeremy. BS, UCLA, 1970; JD, U. Calif., Berkeley, 1974. Bar: Calif. 1974, DC 1980. Dep. city atty. City of Los Angeles, 1974—75; asst. regional counsel US Dept. Energy, San Francisco, 1975—77, chief counsel, 1978—80; dep. asst. sec. for East Asia & Pacific Islands US Dept. State, Washington, 1980—81, spl. adv., 1981—82; ptnr. Stovall, Spradlin, Armstrong & Isreal, Washington, 1983—86, Arthur Young Co., Washington, 1986—93; gen. counsel US Dept. Commerce, Washington, 1993—96; dep. adminstr., COO Small Bus. Adminstrn., 1996—98; mng. dir. Telecommunications Investment Fund, 1998—2005; CEO Three Oaks, LLC, 2005—. Bd. dirs. ATS Corp., 2007—. Recipient Outstanding Achievement award, Dept. State, 1980, Meritorious Svc. award, 1981. Mem.: Nat. Lawyers, Orgn. of Chinese-Am., Women's Bar Assn., Asian Pacific Am. Bar Assn., ABA, Commonwealth, Pi Sigma Alpha.*

LEW, JACOB, public administration educator; b. NYC, Aug. 29, 1955; married; 2 children. AB, Harvard U., 1978; JD, Georgetown U., 1983. Bar: D.C., Mass. Legis. aide, Washington, 1973—75; prin. domestic policy advisor Spkr. Thomas P. O'Neill Jr. Ho. of Reps., 1979—87, asst. dir., then exec. dir. Dem. steering and policy com.; pvt. practice law, 1987—91; spl. asst. to pres. Office Mgmt. & Budget Exec. Office of the Pres., Washington, 1993—94, exec. assoc. dir., assoc. dir. legis. affairs, 1995, dep. dir., 1995—98, dir., 1998—2001; vis. prof. Georgetown U. Pub. Policy Inst., 2001; exec. v.p. and prof. pub. admin. NYU, 2001—. Exec. dir. Ctr. Mid. East Rsch. Dep. dir. office program analysis City of Boston Office Mgmt. and Budget, 1978; issues dir. Dem. Nat. Com. Campaign '88. Office: NYU Office of Exec VP 70 Washington Sq S Rm 1219 New York NY 10012

LEW, JOYCELYNE MAE, actress; b. Santa Monica, Calif., Feb. 25, 1962; d. George and Mabel Florence (Lum) L. BA in Theatre Arts, UCLA, 1981, teaching credential, 1982; MA in Urban Edn., Pepperdine U., 1984; bilingual cert., U. So. Calif., 1983; postgrad., Stella Adler Acad., 1988; studied with, The Groundlings Improv Group, 1987. Exec. com. Acad. T.V. Arts & Scis., 2000-01. Appeared in films Tai-Pan, 1987, Fatal Beauty, 1989, The Royal Affair, 1993, Shattered Image, 1993, Dr. Boris and Mrs. Duluth, 1994, Hindsight, 1996, Fire in My Heart, 1996, Ginseng Power, 1998; TV programs The Young and the Restless, 1990, Phil Donahue Show, 1993, Hard Copy, 1994, Current Affair, 1995, Gordon Elliott, 1995, Married With Children, 1997, True Hollywood Stories, 1997, Nat. Enquirer TV, 2000, Arrest & Trial, 2000, Extra, 2001, Men are from Mars, Women are from Venus, 2001, Sins of Hollywood, 2002; (theater) Mary Tape, 2000; voice over artist, mag. model, body double, dancer; appeared in comml. Good Seasons, 1996, Pillsbury Doughboy, 1996, Pacific Bell, 1996, Beefsteak Rye Bread, 1998, Miller Beer, 1998; co-writer film script They Still Call Me Bruce, 1986 (award); song lyricist Nighttime Blues (award Allure Mag., 2002). Mem. judging com. for film grants Nat. Endowment for Arts, 1986; mem. L.A. Beautiful, 1993. Mem. AFTRA, SAG, AEA, ATAS (exec. com. performer's branch, 2000, blue ribbon com. for Emmy awards 1986-96), Assn. Asian Pacific Am. Artists (treas. 1983-89), Nat. Asian Am. Telecomms. Assn., Am. Film Inst. Conservatory Workshop, Calif. PTA (life). Avocations: calligraphy, makeup art and hair, charcoals, fashion and interior design. Home and Office: 1952 N Van Ness Ave Los Angeles CA 90068-3625 E-mail: Joycelyne@finalprint.com.

LEW, ROGER ALAN, manufacturing executive; b. NYC, Mar. 16, 1941; s. Louis Arthur and Estelle Bebe (Marcus) L.; m. Marilyn Drourr, May 29, 1962; children— William, Jeffrey, Richard. BS in Fin, NYU, 1963. With Franklin Nat. Bank, NYC, 1963-66; sr. v.p. Security Nat. Bank, NYC, 1966-75; v.p. NVF Co., NYC, 1975-78, sr. v.p., 1978-81, treas., 1979-81; pres., dir. Wormuth Bros. Foundry, Inc., Athens, NY, 1981—2003, Richmond Builders LLC, Sag Harbor, NY, 2004—. Pres., bd. dirs. Mirage Fin., Inc., 1985-2003, transmission Gear Sales, Inc., 1985-2003; former sr. v.p., treas. Sharon Steel Corp., Pa. Engring. Corp., DWG Co., Southeastern Pub. Svc. Co.; former sr. v.p., treas., Wilson Bros.; former mem. small bus. and agr. adv. coun. to NY Fed. Res. Bank; former v.p. Security Mgmt. Corp. Trustee Universal Housing & Devel. Co., former exec. v.p. With USAR, 1958—66. Mem. Am. Iron and Steel Inst. Clubs: Sag Harbor (NY) Yacht. E-mail: mirage700@aol.com.

LEW, SALVADOR, radio station executive; b. Camajuani, Las Villas, Cuba, Mar. 6, 1929; s. Berko and Clara (Lewinowicz) Lew; 1 child, Esther Maria. JD magna cum laude, U. Havana, 1952. Editor Sch. Mural Newspaper, Camajuani, Cuba, 1941-43; pres. youth sect., nat. sect. Cuban People's Party, 1948-53; Lat. Am. cons. Waltes, Moore & Costanzo, Miami, 1961-72; news dir. Sta. WMIE and Sta. WQBA, Miami, 1961-70; gen. mgr., news dir. Sta. WRHC, Miami, 1973-89; host talk show, 1989—2001, 2005—. Pres. adv. bd. Cuba Broadcasting, 1992—2001; dir. Office of Cuba Broadcasting, Radio & TV Marti, appointed by President Geroge W. Bush; sr. cons. Everet Clay Assocs., 1989—2001. Trustee, dir. United Way, 1985—. Recipient Lincoln Marti award, Sec. HEW, 1964, FBI award for cmty. svcs., 1983, cmty. svc. awards, various orgns. Mem.: Cuban Lawyers Assn., Exile. Jewish. Home: 2863 SW 23rd St Miami FL 33145-3309

LEWANDOSKI, ROBERT HENRY, editor, publisher; b. NYC, Jan. 21, 1951; BA, Pace U., NYC, 1972. Editor, pub. The Former Presidents Quar., RHL Enterprises, Fullerton, Calif., 1993—; freelance author Model Ship Builder, Cedarburg, Wis., 1981-92. Avocations: model ship building, autograph collecting. Office: RHL Enterprises PO Box 6443 Fullerton CA 92834-6443

LEWANDOWSKI, ANDREW ANTHONY, utilities executive, consultant; b. Kiel, Germany, Nov. 29, 1946; arrived in US, 1949; s. Kazlmierz and Emily Lewandowski; m. Mary Ann Zuza; 1 child, Adam Christopher. Student, Rutgers U., 1964-66; BSME, N.J. Inst. Tech., 1969; postgrad., Pa. State U., 1969-70; MSME, N.J. Inst. Tech., 1973. Registered profl. engr., N.J.; cert. profl. planner N.J. NSF trainee NJ Inst. Tech., 1970—72; Engr. I DeLeuw, Cather & Co., Newark, 1970; from gas utilities engr. to chief specifications DeLeuw, Cather & Co. of NY, Inc., NYC, 1972—75; from supv. engr. to mgr. planning, budgets Elizabethtown Gas Co., Iselin, NJ, 1976—86, internal cons., computer mgmt. Elizabeth, NJ, 1986-87, internal cons. ops., engring. Iselin, NJ, 1987-89, from internal cons. engring., budgets to sr. planning engr. Union, NJ, 1989—98, sr. planning engr. Stewartsville, 2004—05; sys. adminstr. NUI/Utility Bus. Svcs., Union, NJ, 1998-99, mgr. applications, 2000—04; sr. engr. AGLR/Elizabethtown Gas Co., Union, 2005; cons. GIS expert, 2005—06; sr. corrosions apps. engr. Pub. Svc. Electric and Gas, Newark, 2007—. Editor: Jaycee newsletter, 1979—80, Rep. newsletter, 1986; contbr. articles to publs. Den leader, asst. cubmaster Boy Scouts Am., sec. troop com., merit badge counselor. Named to South Plainfield HS Hall of Fame, 1997; recipient Dir. of Yr. award, South Plainfield Jaycees, 1972, Disting. Svc. award, 1975, Outstanding Young Man of the Yr. award, 1976, N.J. Jaycees, 1975, Den Leader award, Boy Scouts Am., 1994. Mem.: KC, ASME, NSPE, Film Music Soc., South Plainfield Polish Nat. Home. Republican. Roman Catholic. Home: 1910 Murray Ave South Plainfield NJ 07080-4713 Office Phone: 973-430-6620. Personal E-mail: el_cid@att.net.

LEWANDOWSKI, JEROME L., physicist; b. Rennes, France, Sept. 22, 1968; arrived in US, 1999; s. Raymond Lewandowski and Laurent Sylvette; m. Kanugo Hemamalini. BS, Sherbrooke U, Sherbrooke, 1990; MS, U Montreal, Montreal,Can., 1993; PhD, Australian Nat. U, Canberra, 1998. Rsch. physicist Princeton U, NJ, 2000—06. Mem.: Math. Assn. Am., Am. Physicist Soc., Soc. for Indsl. and Applied Math. Office: ExxonMobil Upstream Rsch Corp Houston TX 77098 Home: 3000 Bissonnet St Apt 4203 Houston TX 77005 Personal E-mail: jlvlewandowski@yahoo.com. Business E-Mail: jlewando@pppl.gov.

LEWCOCK, RONALD BENTLEY, architect, educator; b. Brisbane, Australia, Sept. 27, 1929; s. Harry Kingsley and Ena (Orrock) L.; m. Barbara Sansoni, Aug. 8, 1981. Student, U. Queensland, 1947-49; BArch, Cape Town U., South Africa, 1951; PhD, U. Cape Town, South Africa, 1961; MA, Cambridge U., Eng., 1970; DArch (hon.), Natal U., South Africa, 1999. Pvt. practice architecture, 1951—; Whitehead research fellow Clare Hall, Cambridge U., Eng., 1970-72, ofcl. fellow, 1976-84; research officer Middle East Centre, Cambridge U., Cambridge, 1973-80; Aga Khan prof. architecture for Islamic culture, dir. program in architecture for Islamic socs. MIT, Cambridge, 1984-91; chmn. Aga Khan program for Islamic architecture MIT and Harvard U., 1985-87; prof. architecture Ga. Inst. Tech., Atlanta, 1991—. Cons. UNESCO, 1978-98, Habitat, World Bank, British Coun., Am. Rsch. Ctrl., Egypt, 1978-83; lectr. U. Natal, 1952-57, sr. lectr., 1958-69; lectr., examiner Cambridge U., 1973-85; unit leader design in developing world Archtl. Assn., London, 1977-81; lectr. Archtl. Assocs. Sch., London, 1971-82; vis. prof. grad. sch. architecture Ga. Inst. Tech., 1979-84, Harvard, 1984, Louvain U., 1984; vis. Aga Khan prof., MIT, 1991-93, UQT, Australia, 1996. Author: Early 19th Century Architecture in South Africa, 1963, Traditional Architecture in Kuwait and the Northern Gulf, 1978, 2d edit. 81, Wadi Hadramawt and the Walled City of Shibam, 1986, web edit., 2003, The Old City of San'a', 1986, web edit., 2000, The Architecture of an Island-Sri Lanka, 1998; editor: (with R.B. Serjeant) San'a' an Arabian Islamic City, 1983; contbr. articles to profl. jours., Architecture in the Islamic World, 1976, New Grove Dictionary of Music and Musicians, 1980, 97. Mem. coun. Inst. History and Archaeology East Africa, London, 1976-86, Middle East Centre, Cambridge, Eng., 1981-88, British Sch. Archaeology in Jerusalem, London, 1981-98; tech. coord. Internat. Campaign for the Conservation of Sana'a in Yemen Arab Rep. and Shibam and Wadi Hadramaut in Peoples Dem. Rep. of Yemen, 1978-93, UNESCO/UNDP Campaign for Conservation of Monuments and Cities in Uzbekistan, 1994-97; steering com. mem. Aga Khan award, 1990-93, Aga Khan Trust for Culture, Geneva, 1993—. Eliza Howard vis. fellowship Columbia U., 1963. Mem. Royal Inst. Brit. Archs. (assoc.). Office: Georgia Inst of Technology 225 North Ave NW Atlanta GA 30332-0002 also: 13 Norwich St Cambridge CB2 1ND England

LEWCZYK, DAVID C., military officer; b. South Charleston, W.Va., Nov. 15, 1976; s. Lawrence M. Lewczyk and Laura L. Stocks, Elizabeth A. Lewczyk (Stepmother); m. Kimberly J. Lewczyk, Oct. 14, 2000; children: Samuel R., Isaiah L. AAS in Criminal Justice, Wilkes CC, Wilkesboro, NC, 2005. Cert. intermediate law enforcement NC Criminal Justice Tng. and Stds., 2005. Airborne inf. squad leader B Co 1/325 AIR, Ft Bragg, NC, 1995—99; asst. scout squad leader Va. Army N.G., Pulaski, 1999—2000; criminal investigator Wilkesboro Police Dept., NC, 2000—06; constrn. engr. supr. NC Army N.G., Taylorsville, NC, 2000—. Decorated NCO Profl. Devel. ribbons US Army, Parachutist badge, Humanitarian Svc. medal, Expert Infantryman badge, Army Achievement medals, Nat. Def. Svc. medals, NCNG Meritorious Svc. medal NC N.G., Army Commendation medal US Army, Armed Forces Res. medal, Combat Action badge. Office: Detachment 1 882nd Engring Co 40 National Guard Armory Rd Taylorsville NC 28681 Home Phone: 336-667-3969; Office Phone: 828-632-6237.

LEWELLEN, WILBUR GARRETT, management educator, consultant; b. Charleroi, Pa., Jan. 21, 1938; s. Anthony Garrett and Cozie Harriett (Watson) L.; m. Jean Carolyn Vanderlip, Dec. 8, 1962 (div. 1982); children— Stephen G., Jocelyn A., Jonathan W., Robyn E.; m. Eloise Evelyn Vincent, Mar. 5, 1983 BS, Pa. State U., University Park, 1959; MS, MIT, Cambridge, 1961, PhD, 1967; LhD (hon.), Budapest U. of Econ. Scis., 1996. Asst. prof. mgmt. Purdue U., West Lafayette, Ind., 1964-68, assoc. prof. mgmt., 1968-72, prof., 1972-83, Loeb prof. mgmt., 1983-88, Krannert disting. prof. mgmt., 1988—, dir. exec. edn. programs, 1985—2006. Cons. Bank Am., San Francisco, 1975—90, Ind. Bell Tel. Co., Indpls., 1976—90, Am. Water Works Co., Wilmington, Del., 1978—94, Indpls. Power and Light Co., 1993—99, NiSource, Inc., 2000—; bd. dirs. Indsl. Dielectrics, Inc. Author: Executive Compensation in Large Industrial Corporations, 1968, Ownership Income of Management, 1971, The Cost of Capital, 1981, Financial Management: An Introduction to Principles and Practice, 2000. Recipient Salgo-Noren award as Outstanding Tchr. in Grad. Profl. Programs, Salgo-Noren Found., 1973, 77, 79, 84. Mem. AAUP, Fin. Mgmt. Assn. (v.p. 1973-74), Am. Fin. Assn., Western Fin. Assn. Methodist. Office: Purdue Univ Grad Sch Mgmt West Lafayette IN 47907 Office Phone: 765-494-4493.

LEWENSTEIN, BRUCE VOSS, science historian; b. Palo Alto, Calif., Sept. 18, 1957; s. Harry and Marion (Marcus) L.; m. Claudia Voss, May 29, 1983; children: Joel, Gabriel, Ari. AB, U. Chgo., 1980; MA, U. Pa., 1985, PhD, 1987. Chief researcher U.S. News Books, Washington, 1980-82; advt. copywriter SS&W, McLean, Va., 1982-83; editorial coord. History Sci. Soc., Phila., 1983-85; pub. edn. officer Ctr. for History Chemistry, 1985-87; asst. prof. depts. communication, sci. & tech. studies Cornell U., Ithaca, NY, 1987-93, assoc. prof., 1993—2007, prof., 2007—. Cons. in field. Editor: Public Understanding of Sci., 1998-2003, When Science Meets the Public, 1992; contbr. numerous articles to profl. jours. Recipient Disting. Tech. Communication award Soc. for Tech. Communication, 1986. Fellow AAAS; mem. Assn. for Edn. in Journalism and Mass Communication, Forum for History of Sci. in Am., History of Sci. Soc., Nat. Assn. Sci. Writers, Soc. for Social Studies of Sci. Office: Cornell Univ 321 Kennedy Hall Ithaca NY 14853-4203

LEWIE, REVA GOODWIN, artist, educator; b. Balt., Feb. 14, 1930; d. William Milton Goodwin Sr. and Edith Elizabeth (Koon) Goodwin; m. Lemuel Arthur Lewie Jr., Aug. 28, 1948; 1 child, Reva Marcia Lewie-Thompson, MD. BS, Morgan State U., 1956; MA, NYU, 1961; postgrad., U. Md., Towson State U. Tchr. art and geography Balt. City Pub. Schs., 1956, coord. art, 1966; instr. art Morgan State U., 1968; tchr. art resource Balt. City Pub. Schs., 1959—67, chair art dept., 1967—71, head art dept., 1971—87; v.p. Lewie Consol. Enterprises, 1990—. Docent Walters Art Mus., Balt., 1993—2004, mem. adv. bd. African Am. steering com., 1990—98, docent emeritus, 2004—; mem. Baltimore County Commn. Arts and Scis., 1990—2004. Represented in permanent collections James E. Lewis Collection, Morgan State Univ., Balt., Md., exhibitions include Loeb Ctr., NYC, Washington County Mus., Hagerstown (Artists Equity Shows), Md., State Capital, Annapolis, Md., James E. Lewis Mus. Morgan State Univ., Balt., Md., Walters Art Mus., commn., Madison Med. Ctr., Balt., Md, DHIS Inst., Lanham, Md., Garwyn Med. Ctr., Balt., Md., Mercy Med. Ctr. Mem. WAM Womens Com., 1993—. Named Woman of Yr. Cmty. Svc. award, U.S. Senator Barbara Mikulski, 2003; recipient Tchr. of the Yr. award, Nat. Art Edn. Assn., 1985, Md. Art Edn. Assn. award, 1986, Walters Art Gallery award, 1996, NAACP ACTSO award, 1992, Mary Fritzpatrick award, Federated Garden Clubs of Md. Inc., 1998, 2001, 2004, Patapsco River Links Art award, 1999, Woman of the Yr. in Cultural Arts, Balt. City's Mayoral award, City Coun. awards, Md. State awards, 1998—2003. Mem.: Md. Ret. Tchrs. Assn., Nat. Educators Assn., Les Grandes Dames (pres. 1999—2004), The Pierians, Inc. of Baltimore County, Nat. Coalition of 100 Black Women, Inc., Beautiful Balt. (bd. dirs.), Federated Garden Clubs Md. (sec. 2000), The Links (charter), For-Win-Ash Garden Club (pres. 2000—04), Zeta Phi Beta Sorority, Inc. Avocations: travel, flower arranging, art. Personal E-mail: rglewie@verizon.net.

LEWIN, JOHN CALVERT, medical association administrator; b. Camden, NJ, Jan. 8, 1946; s. John Edward and Ruth Beatrice (Calvert) L; m. Sandra Patricia Smith, June 17, 1972; children: Jennifer, John, Josanna. BA, U. Calif., Irvine, 1967; MD, U. So. Calif., 1971. Physician, svc. unit dir. US Pub. Health Svc. (USPHS), Kayenta, Ariz., 1972-75; exec. dir., founder the Navaho div. Health Improvement Svcs., Window Rock, Ariz., 1976-79; physician, med. dir. Kula Hosp., Hawaii, 1979-86; dir. health State of Hawaii, 1987—94; exec. v.p., CEO Calif. Med. Assn., 1995—2006; CEO Am. Coll. Cardiology, Washington, 2006—. Office: Am Coll Cardiology Heart House 2400 N St NW Washington DC 20037 also: 9111 Old Gerogetown Rd Bethesda MD 20814-1699 Office Phone: 916-444-5532.

LEWIN, PETER ANDREW, electrical engineer, educator; b. Oct. 27, 1945; BSc and MSc, U. Denmark, 1969, PhD, 1979. Project leader Bruel & Kjaer Naerum, Copenhagen, Denmark, 1969-78; project mgr. Danish Inst. Biomed. Engring., Copenhagen, 1978-80; rsch. fellow U. Denmark, 1980-83; prof. dept. elec. and computer engr. Drexel U., 1983—, Richard B. Beard disting. prof. Fellow IEEE (mem. tech. com. IEEE Ultrasonics Symposium 1985, mem. stds. subcom. on ultrasonics, sensors, session chmn. IEEE Ultrasonics Symposia, session chmn./organizer, Lithotripsy, Engring. in Medicine and Biology conf. 1990, co-chmn. med. ultrasound track EMBS conf. 1990, co-chmn. indsl. exhibits com. EMBS conf. 1990, co-editor IEEE Med. Ultrasound Parameter Measurement Guide 1984-88, reviewer IEEE Transactions, co-editor spl. issue IEEE Transactions on

Ultrasonics, Frequency and Frequency Control 1988), Acoustical Soc. Am., Am. Inst. Ultrasound in Medicine, Am. Inst. for Med. Biol. Engring. Office: Drexel U Dept Electrical & Computer Eng Philadelphia PA 19104

LEWIN, RALPH ARNOLD, biologist; b. London, Apr. 30, 1921; arrived in US, 1947; s. Maurice and Ethel Lewin; m. Joyce Mary Chismore, June, 1950 (div. 1965); m. Cheng Lanna, June 3, 1969. BA, Cambridge U., Eng., 1942, MA, 1946; PhD, Yale U., 1950; ScD, Cambridge U., Eng., 1973. Instr. Yale U., New Haven, Conn., 1951-52; sci. officer Nat. Rsch. Coun., Halifax, N.S., Can., 1952-55; ind. investigator NIH, Woods Hole, Mass., 1956-59; from assoc. prof. to prof. U. Calif., La Jolla, 1960—. Editor: Physiology and Biochemistry of Algae, 1962, Genetics of Algae, 1976, Biology of Algae, 1979, Biology of Women, 1981, (poems) Origins of Plastids and Other Animals, 1993, Internacia Vortaro de Mikroba Genetiko, 1994; co-editor: Prochloron, a microbial enigma, 1989; transl. Winnie-La-Pu (Esperanto), 1972, La Dektri Horlogoj, 1993, Merde, 1999, (poems) Abacus & Swallows, 2000, Poems on Politics, Pollution and Religion, 2003, (poems) Blue Green, 2003. Served with British Army, 1943-46. Mem. Phycological Soc. Am. (pres. 1970-71, Darbaker prize 1963). Avocations: languages, recorder, badminton. Home: 8481 Paseo Del Ocaso La Jolla CA 92037-3024 Business E-Mail: rlewin@ucsd.edu.

LEWIN, ROBERT, lawyer; b. NYC, July 11, 1952; BA with honors, Johns Hopkins U., 1974; JD, NYU, 1977. Bar: NY 1978. Ptnr., insurance/reinsurance litig. Stroock & Stroock & Lavan LLP, NYC, chmn., pro bono com. Arbitrator Reinsurance Assn. Am. Mem.: ABA, Assn. Internationale de Droit des Assurances, Assn. Bar City NY, NY Lawyers for Pub. Interest (bd. dir.). Office: Stroock & Stroock & Lavan LLP 180 Maiden Ln New York NY 10038-4982 Office Phone: 212-806-5643. Office Fax: 212-806-6006. Business E-Mail: rlewin@stroock.com.

LEWIN, TAMAR (KATHERINE LEWIN), reporter; b. Cleve., Dec. 6, 1949; d. David Victor and Doris Lewin; m. Robert L. Krulwich, June 29, 1980; children: Nora, Jesse. BA, Barnard Coll., NYC, 1971; JD, Columbia U., NYC, 1974. Bar: NY 1975, DC 1978. Reporter Bergen Record, Hackensack, NJ, 1975-77; investigative rschr. Common Cause, Washington, 1977-78; Washington Bur. chief Nat. Law Jour., 1978-80, mng. editor NYC, 1980-82; legal affairs reporter, nat. corr. NY Times, NYC, 1982-86, nat. corr., 1989—, nat. edn. reporter. Office Phone: 212-556-1015. Office Fax: 212-556-3758. Business E-Mail: lewin@nytimes.com.

LEWINE, MARK SAUL, anthropology professor; b. Jan. 29, 1946; Prof. anthropology, sociology and urban studies, dir. Ctr. for Community Rsch. Cuyahoga CC, Cleve. Recipient President's Award, Soc. for Anthropology in CC, US Professors of Yr. Award for Outstanding CC Prof., Carnegie Found. for Advancement of Tchg. and Coun. for Advancement and Support of Edn., 2006. Office: Cuyahoga CC Metro Campus 2900 Community College Ave Cleveland OH 44115 E-mail: Mark.Lewine@tri-c.edu.*

LEWINS, STEVEN, financial analyst, investment company executive, legislative staff member, retired military officer; b. NYC, Jan. 22, 1943; s. Bruno and Kaethe (Czhoeck) L.; m. Rayna Lee Kornreich, July 4, 1968 (div. 1991); children: Shani Nicole, Scott Asher. BA, Queens Coll., CUNY, 1964, MA in Diplomatic-Econ. History, 1966; postgrad. in pub. adminstrn., NYSCSC, SUNY, 1967; MBA, CUNY, 1972; postgrad. in info. tech., U. Va., 1979. Park ranger, historian Nat. Park Svc., Statue of Liberty, NYC, 1964-66; traffic asst. AT&T, White Plains, NY, 1966; adminstrv. intern NY State, Albany, 1966-67; asst. to commr. NY State Narcotics Addiction Control Commn., NYC, 1967—69; security analyst Value Line Investment Survey, NYC, 1969-71, assoc. rsch. dir., 1971-74, rsch. dir., directing editor, 1975-80; creator Value Line Fin. Database, NYC, 1974; v.p. Arnold Bernhard & Co., NYC, 1975-80, dir., 1976-80, mem. exec. com., 1977-80; ptnr. Ray-Lux Products, NYC, 1978-80; pres. RayLux Assocs., NYC, 1980-81, dir., 1980-86; with Gruntal & Co., LLC, NYC, 1986—. Founder RayLux Fin. Svc., 1980; v.p. unit head investment divsn. Citibank N.A., 1981-86, v.p. Citicorp Investment Mgmt., Inc., 1986-88; v.p. transp. and aerospace investment mgmt; chancellor Capital Mgmt., 1988-92; mng. dir., rsch. dir., head of equity First Capital Advisers/F.C. Fin. Svcs., N.Y.C., 1992-93; v.p. Investment Rsch. Gruntal & Co., Inc., 1994-00; adv. corp. disclosure com. SEC, 1977-78, ICC, 1982-92, Dept. Transp., 1982-00, interval funds investment cons., 1997-00, Dept. Justice, 1982-92, 95-96, 03, Dept. State, 1986-92, Surface Transp. Bd. Legal Panel, 1996-97; advisor surface transport. bd., 1965-2000, Fed. Res. Bd., 1996-00, 2003, dept. treasury, 2003, infrastructure com. U.S. Ho. of Reps., 1997-00, Summit Bank, 1998-00; spkr. in field. Author: Fashoda Crisis of 1898, 1966, Knowing Your Common Stocks, 1979, The Social Overhaul of the USSR, 1986, Economic Reform in the U.S.S.R., 1990, USA: 21st Century World Transportation Crossroads, 1994, U.S. Needs World-Class Transportation System, 1994, Transports as Economic Indicators, 1995, The New Union Pacific, 1996, Transportation Trends into the 21st Century, 1996, The Global Terrorist Threat, 1996, The Boeing Company: Firing on All Cylinders, 1997, U.S. Transportation "Consolidations" and "Surprise," 1997, Secular Trends in Global Transportation, 1997; co-author: (with Parkanskii) US-USSR Summit Agenda, 1995, (with Bogdanov and Bobrakov) US-USSR Anti-International Terrorist Protocol, 1989, Rights of Terrorists, 1990, (with Semenov) US-USSR Sub-Orbital Space Cooperation, 1990; editor: Megatrends, 1980, Witch Doctor of Wall Street, 1990; creator Global Transportation and Orbital Space Transport Investment Trust, Gruntal & Co., L.L.C., 1998-2000. Participant U.S.-USSR Emigration/Jackson Vanek, 1984-91, U.S.-USSR Pan Am.-Aeroflot Aviation Agreement, 1985, USSR Student Exch., 1985-86, U.S.-USSR Anti-Internat. Terrorism, 1985-91, U.S.-USSR Rights of Terrorists, 1985, U.S.-USSR Trans-Siberian-CSX Corp. Initiative, 1989, TRW, Inc-Energia N.P.O. Look Down Satellite Agreement, 1989-90, U.S.-USSR Sub-Orbital Space Coop. Agreement, 1989-90, U.S.-USSR Def. Conv. Projects, 1990-93, Reagan-Gorbachev Summit Preparations, 1986-88, Bush-Gorbachev Summit Preparations, 1990, U.S.-USSR AMR Corp.-Aeroflot Bilateral Discussion, 1989, U.S.-USSR Spl. Mission/Secure Info. Negotiation, 1983-92, U.S.-Japan airline bilateral negotiation, 1996, CSX Corp./CIS indsl. negotiation, 1996-97; sponsor U.S.-USSR Pace U., rsch. exch., 1990; Citicorp liaison USSR mission to UN, 1982-88, Inst. U.S. and Can., Acad. Scis. USSR, 1985-88, econs. dept. Acad. Scis. USSR, 1988; liaison Chancellor Capital Mgmt., USSR, 1988-92; overseas fact-finding visits include Saudi Arabia, Egypt, Jordan, Israel, 1979, Peoples Republic of China, Japan, Hong Kong, 1981, USSR, 1985-86, 89-90, Georgia SSR, 1985, 90, Uzbekistan SSR, 1986, Baykhal, Irkutsk, Olha, Siberia, 1989, Kazakhstan SSR, Republic of Georgia, Baykonour-Soyuz Launch Ctr., 1990, Bangkok, Thailand, 1988, Rio de Janeiro, Brazil, 1990, Athens, Greece, 1998, Constantinople, Turkey, 1998; mem. Croton-on-Hudson Narcotics Guidance Coun., 1972-75, Cortland Indsl. Com., 1975-77; dist. leader Dem. Party, 1979-83; founding mem. Challenger Found., 1987, Nat. Space Mus., Dallss, Tex. 1998. Recipient Commendation citations for Gulf War, 1992, Reagan-Gorbachev Summit preparartions and diplomatic achivements, 1990, USSR Supreme Soviet Red Bannerr election for 50th birthday anniversary award in svc. to USSR for peace, 1990. Fellow Fin. Analyst Fedn.; mem. N.Y. Soc. Security Analysts (sr. security analyst, membership com., computer applications symposium, airline splinter group, motor carrier splinter group, aerospace splinter group), Bus. Economists Coun., Washington Transp. Roundtable, Assn. Computer Users, Internat. Platform Assn., N.Y. Assn. Bus. Economists, Nat. Assn. Bus. Economists, Nat. Planetary Soc., Nat. Space Soc., Nat. Air and Space Mus., Nat. Air and Space Soc. (founding mem. 1998), Tau Delta Phi (pres. 1963, 64, Undergrad. of Yr. 1963, Spl. Student Senate Recognition 1964, Coll. Distinction medal French 1964). Democrat.

LEWIS, ALAN JAMES, pharmaceutical executive, pharmacologist; b. Newport Gwent, UK; BSc, Southampton U., Hampshire, 1967; PhD in Pharmacology, U. Wales, Cardiff, 1970. Postdoctoral fellow biomedical sci. U. Guelph, Ont., Can., 1970-72; rsch. assoc. lung rsch. ctr. Yale U., 1972-73; sr. pharmacologist Organon Labs., Ltd., Lanarkshire, Scotland, 1973-79; rsch. mgr. immunoinflammation Am. home products Wyeth-Ayerst Rsch., Princeton, N.J., 1979-82, assoc. dir. exptl. therapeutics, 1982-85, dir., 1985-87, asst. v.p., 1987-89, v.p. rsch., 1989-93; pres. Signal Pharms. Inc., San Diego, 1994-96, pres., CEO, 1996-2000; pres. signal rsch. divsn. Celgene Corp., 2000—. Editor allergy sect. Agents & Actions & Internat. Archives Pharmacodynamics Therapy; reviewer Jour. Pharmacology Exptl. Therapy, Biochemical Pharmacology, Can. Jour. Physiol. Pharmacology, European Jour. Pharmacology, Jour. Pharm. Sci. Mem. Am. Soc. Pharmacological and Exptl. Therapeutics, Am. Rheumatism Assn., Mid-Atlantic Pharmacology Soc. (v.p. 1991-93, pres. 1993-94), Pulmonary Rsch. Assn., Inflammation Rsch. Assn. (pres. 1986-88), Pharm. Mfrs. Assn., Internat. Assn. Inflammation Socs. (pres. 1990-95), Bio Bd. Achievements include research in mechanisms and treatment of inflammatory diseases including arthritis and asthma cardiovascular diseases, metabolic disorders, central nervous system diseases, osteoporosis and viral diseases. Office: Celgene Signal Research 4550 Towne Centre Ct San Diego CA 92121-1900 E-mail: alewis@signalpharm.com.

LEWIS, ALVIN BOWER, JR., lawyer; b. Pitts., Apr. 24, 1932; s. Alvin Bower Sr. and Ethel Weidman (Light) L.; m. Elizabeth Therese O'Shea; children: Alvin B. III, Judith W., Robert B. II. BA, Lehigh U., 1954; LLB, Dickinson Sch. Law, 1957. Bar: Pa. 1957, U.S. Dist. Ct. (mid. and ea. dists.) Pa. 1958, U.S. Ct. Appeals (3d cir.) 1958, D.C. 1979. Ptnr. Lewis & Lewis, Lebanon, Pa., 1957-66, Lewis, Brubaker, Whitman & Christianson, Lebanon, 1967-76; spl. counsel, acting chief counsel, dir. select com. on assassinations of M.L. King, and J.F. Kennedy U.S. Ho. of Reps., Washington, 1976-77; ptnr. Lewis & Kramer, Phila., 1977-78, Hartman, Underhill & Brubaker, Lancaster, Pa., 1979-95, Sprague & Lewis, Ltd., Lancaster, 1995-99, Stevens & Lee, Lancaster, 1999—. Dist. atty. County of Lebanon, Pa., 1962-70; chmn. Gov.'s Justice Commn., Pa., 1969-74; mem., chmn. Pa. Crime Commn., Pa., 1979-85. Fin. chmn., mem. exec. com. Rep. County Com., Lebanon, 1959-76; chmn. Lancaster City Rep. Com., 1994-98; co-chmn. Lancaster Crime Commn., 2000-03; mem. Rep. State Com., 1998-2000; bd. dirs., chmn. adv. com., mem. nominating com. Urban League Lancaster County, 1986-91; elected Rep. State Com., 1998—; co-chmn. Lancaster Crime Commn., 2000; chmn. Lehigh U. Scholar-Athletes Fund Drive, 1990-94; bd. govs. Lancaster County Found. Recipient Furtherance of Justice award Mercyhurst Coll., 1979, Dist. Service award Ho. of Reps. Pa., 1982, Award of Distinction Pa. Senate, 1982, Outstanding Service award Gov. and Atty. Gen. Pa., 1974, Alumni of the Yr. award Lehigh U., 1999. Fellow Fgn. Policy Assn.; mem. ABA, Pa. Bar Assn. Lancaster County Bar Assn. (chmn. trial law sect. 1995—), Preservation Pa. (bd. dirs. 1982-92, bd. advisors 1992-2003), Lebanon County Bar Assn. (pres. 1974-76, bd. dirs. 1982-90), Nat. Dist. Attys. Assn. (bd. dirs. 1966-68), Pa. Dist. Attys. Assn. (officer, pres., bd. dirs. 1964-68), Lancaster County Found. (bd. govs.), Masons. Lutheran. Avocations: pilot, small airplanes. Office: Stevens & Lee One Penn Sq Lancaster PA 17602-1594 Home Phone: 717-393-3826; Office Phone: 717-393-3826. Personal E-mail: aande136@comcast.net. Business E-Mail: abl@stevenslee.com.

LEWIS, ANDRÉ LEON, performing company executive; b. Hull, Que., Can., Jan. 16, 1955; s. Raymond Lincoln and Theresa Lewis. Student, Classical Ballet Studio, Ottawa, Royal Winnipeg (Man.) Ballet Sch., 1975; studies with David Moroni, Arnold Spohr, Rudi van Dantzig, Jiri Kylian, Peter Wright, Hans van Manen, and Alicia Markova, among others. Mem. corps de ballet Royal Winnipeg (Man.) Ballet, 1979-82, soloist, artistic coord., 1984-89, interim artistic dir., 1989-90, assoc. artistic dir., 1990-96, artistic dir., 1996—. Staged Danzig's Romeo and Juliet, Teatro Comunale, Florence, Italy, Greek Nat. Opera, Athens. Dancer soloist (ballets) Song of a Wayfarer, Fall River Legend, Nuages, Lento A Tempo E Appassionatto, Nutcracker, Four Last Songs, Romeo and Juliet, The Ecstasy of Rita Joe, (TV films) Belong, Romeo and Juliet, The Big Top, Firebird, (ballets) performed at many events including the opening Gala in Jackson Miss., Le Don Des Etoiles, Montreal, spl. gala honoring Queen Beatrix of Holland and at a Gala performance in Tchaikovsky Hall, Moscow, appeared as a guest artist throughout, N.Am., the Orient and USSR. Avocation: listening to opera. Office: Can Royal Winnipeg Ballet 380 Graham Ave Winnipeg MB Canada R3C 4K2 Office Phone: 204-956-0183. E-mail: ballet@rwb.org.*

LEWIS, ANDREW LINDSAY, JR., (DREW LEWIS), former transportation and natural resources executive; b. Phila., Nov. 3, 1931; s. Andrew Lindsay and Lucille L. (Bricker); m. Marilyn S. Stoughton, June 1, 1950; children: Karen Lewis Sacks, Russell Shepherd, Andrew Lindsay IV. BS, Haverford Coll., Pa., 1953; MBA, Harvard U., 1955; postgrad., MIT, 1968. With Henkels & McCoy, Inc., Blue Bell, Pa., 1955-60, Am. Olean Tile Co., Inc., Lansdale, Pa., 1960-68, Nat. Gypsum Co., Buffalo, 1960-70; chmn. Simplex Wire & Cable Co., Boston, 1970-74, chief exec. officer, 1972-74; pres., chief exec. officer Snelling & Snelling, Inc., Boston, 1972-74; fin. and mgmt. cons. Lewis & Assocs., Plymouth Meeting, Pa., 1974-81; sec. US Dept. Transp., Washington, 1981-83; chmn. Warner Amex Cable Communications Inc., NYC, 1983-86; chmn., chief exec. officer Union Pacific R.R., Omaha, 1986; pres. Union Pacific Corp., NYC, 1986-87, chmn., CEO Bethlehem, Pa., 1987-97. Bd. dirs. Am. Express, Millenium Bank, FPL Group Inc., Gannett Co., Inc., Union Pacific Resources, Inc., Ford Motor Co., SmithKlein Beckman Corp.; trustee Com. for Econ. Devel. Mem. Rep. Nat. Com., 1976—90; dep. chmn. Rep. Nat. Com., 1980; Rep. candidate for gov., Pa., 1974; dep. polit. dir. Reagan-Bush Campaign Com., 1980; co-chmn. Nat. Econ. Commn., 1988—89; mem. nat. exec. bd. Boy Scouts of Am.; chmn. The Bus. Roundtable, 1990—99. Mem.: Loblolly Pines Golf Club (HobeSound, Fla.), Bohemian Club (San Francisco), Saucon Valley Country club (Bethlehem, Pa.), Sunnybrook Golf Club (Plymouth Meeting, Pa.), Phila. Club.

LEWIS, ANN FRANK, former government official; b. Jersey City, Dec. 19, 1937; d. Samuel and Elsie (Golush) Frank; m. Myron Sponder, 1989; children from previous marriage: Patricia Fay, Beth Ellen Susan Jane. Student, Radclffe Coll., 1954-55. Asst. to mayor City of Boston, 1968-75; dep. campaign mgr. Bayh for Pres., 1975-76; adminstrv. asst. to Congressman Stan Lundine, U.S. Ho. of Reps., Washington, 1976-81, adminstrv. asst. to Congresswoman Barbara Mikulski, 1978-81; polit. dir. Dem. Nat. Com., Washington, 1981-85; nat. dir. Ams. for Dem. Action, Washington, 1985-87; nat. affairs columnist MS mag., 1988-92; analyst Monitor Radio and Sta. WHDH-TV, 1992; v.p. for pub. policy Planned Parenthood Fedn. Am.; pres. Politics, Inc.; co-chmn. Back to Bus. Com., 1994; dep. campaign mgr. Clinton-Gore, 1996; dep. dir. comm. and strategic planning The White House, Washington, 1997, counselor to Pres., dir. comm. and strategic planning, 1997-2000. Inst. Politics of Kennedy Sch. Govt. fellow Harvard U., 1989. Office: Office of the President Rm GLF, West Wing White House Washington DC 20500

LEWIS, ANNE MCCUTCHEON, architect; b. New Orleans, Oct. 15, 1943; d. John Tinney and Susan (Dart) McCutcheon; m. Ronald Burton Lewis, Oct. 2, 1971; children: Matthew, Oliver. BA magna cum laude, Radcliffe Coll., 1965; MArch, Harvard U., 1970. Registered architect, D.C., Md., Va., Pa. Architect Skidmore, Owings & Merrill, Washington, 1969—72, Keyes, Lethbridge & Condon, Washington, 1972—75; ptnr. McCartney Lewis Architects, Washington, 1981—98; prin. Anne McCutcheon Lewis AIA, Washington, 1976—81, 1999—. Mem. Harvard U. Grad. Sch. Design Alumni Coun., Cambridge, Mass., 1979-82; bd. dirs. Friends Non-Profit Housing, Washington, 1981-98, Washington Humane Soc., 1990—2006, D.C. Hist. Preservation Rev. Bd., 2003—. Fellow: AIA (dir.-at-large Washington chpt. 1982—84, Design awards 1979, 1983, 1989, 1990, 1991, 1992, 1993, 1996, 1998, 2000, 2001). Office: Anne McCutcheon Lewis FAIA 3400 Reservoir Rd NW Washington DC 20007-2328

LEWIS, ANTHONY, columnist, educator; b. NYC, Mar. 27, 1927; s. Kassel and Sylvia (Surut) L.; m. Linda Rannells, July 8, 1951 (div.); children: Eliza, David, Mia; m. Margaret H. Marshall, Sept. 23, 1984 AB, Harvard U., 1948. Deskman Sunday dept. NY Times, 1948-52, reporter Washington bur., 1955-64, chief London bur., 1965-72, editl. columnist (column Abroad at Home), 1969—2001; staff Dem. Nat. Com., 1952; reporter Washington Daily News, 1952-55. Lectr. on law Harvard U., 1974-89; James Madison vis. prof. Columbia U., 1983—. Author: Gideon's Trumpet, 1964 (Mystery Writers Am. Award for best factual crime book of yr.), Portrait of a Decade: The Second American Revolution, 1964, Make No Law: The Sullivan Case and the First Amendment, 1991; contbr. articles to profl. jours. Recipient Heywood Broun Award, 1955, Pulitzer Prize for Nat. Reporting, 1955, 63, Presdl. Citizens' Medal, 2001; Nieman Fellow, Harvard U., 1956-57. Mem.: Am. Acad. Arts and Scis., Am. Philos. Soc., Tavern Club. Home Phone: 617-661-0860; Office Phone: 617-354-2229. Personal E-mail: tlewis@galaxy.net.

LEWIS, AYLWIN B., retail executive, former food service company executive; m. Noveline Lewis. BS in Bus. Mgmt. & English Lit, Houston U., MBA. Sr. v.p. mktg. & ops. devel. KFC, PepsiCo, Inc., 1995—96; sr. v.p. ops. Pizza Hut, Inc., 1996—97, COO, 1997—99; exec. v.p. ops. & new bus. devel. YUM! Brands, Inc., 2000, COO, 2000—03, pres., chief multi-branding & oper. officer, 2003—04; pres., CEO, bd. dirs. Kmart Holding Corp., Troy, Mich., 2004—05; pres., CEO Sears Holdings Corp., Hoffman Estates, Ill., 2005—. Bd. dirs. Halliburton Co., 2001—05, The Walt Disney Co., 2004—. Office: Sears Holding Corp 3333 Beverly Rd Hoffman Estates IL 60179*

LEWIS, BARBARA SUE, chemist; b. Washington, Mar. 6, 1951; d. William Wesley and Hazel Lewis Smith; m. John Gregory Lewis, Mar. 20, 1976; children: Jessica, J G, Wesley. BS, Radford U., Va., 1973. Lab. technician Litton Bonetics, Frederick, Md., 1973—74; chemist AH Robins Pharms., Richmond, Va., 1974—76, Bell Pharmacal, Greenville, SC, 1976—79; lab. instr. Greenville Tech., Greenville, 1980—95, Clemson (S.C.) U., 1995—2003, lab. coord., 2003—. Priest Comty. of Christ Ch., 1992—. Avocations: reading, gardening, cooking, health and nutrition. Home: 450 Newton Rd Pickens SC 29671 Office: Clemson U 269 Hunter Labs Clemson SC 29634

LEWIS, BENJAMIN PERSHING, JR., pharmacist, retired public health service officer; b. Danville, Ky., June 2, 1942; s. Benjamin Pershing Lewis and Juanita Elizabeth Applewhite; m. Patricia Glover, 1968; children: Laura, Jason. BS in Pharmacy, Auburn U., 1966, MS in Pharmacy, 1972; PhD of Health Svcs. Mgmt., Century U., 1989; postgrad., Johns Hopkins U., 1993. Registered pharmacist Ky., Ala. Instr. Auburn U. Sch. Pharmacy, Ala., 1972—73, now affiliate asst. prof.; commd. lt. comdr. USPHS, 1976, advanced through grades to capt., 1985; pharmacy officer Bur. Drugs FDA, Rockville, Md., 1976—82, health scientist adminstr. orphan products devel., 1982—87, AIDS coord., 1987—89, spl. asst. to assoc. dir. Ctr. Biologics Evaluation-Rsch. Bethesda, Md., 1989—92, dir. regulatory ops. divsn. of transfusion and emerging transmitted diseases Ctr. Biologics Evaluation and Rsch. Rockville, 1993—2002; mng. dir. Brand Inst., Inc., Rockville, 2002—03; v.p. regulatory affairs Prestwick Pharm., Inc., Washington, 2003—. Adj. prof. San Diego State U., 1998. Co-author: Veterinary Drug Index, 1982; editor: FDA Role in AIDS, 1988, The International Ramifications of Drug Development, 1988, Report of the Criticism Task Force on Career Development, 1989; co-editor: Poliovirus Attenuation: Molecular Mechanisms and Practical Aspects, 1993, Combined Vaccines and Simultaneous Administration, 1995; contbr. articles to profl. jours. Officer U.S. Army, 1972-76. Recipient letter of appreciation Sec. Md. Dept. Econ. and Employment Devel., 1991, Secs. award for disting. svc. Dept. HHS, 2001, PHS Meritorious Svc. medal FDA, 2002. Mem. COA of USPHS, Regulatory Affairs Profl. Soc. (Cert. Appreciation 1993), Drug Info. Assn., Am. Pharm. Assn., Am. Acad. Pharm. Rsch. and Sci., Drug Info. Assn., FDA Alumni Assn., Sigma Xi. Methodist. Achievements include assignment by FDA to San Diego State U. to create one of the first Master of Science degrees in Regulatory Affairs in the U.S., 1998. Office: 1825 K St NW Ste 1475 Washington DC 20006 Office Phone: 202-296-1400. Business E-Mail: benl@prestwickpharma.com.

LEWIS, BERNARD, retired social studies educator; b. London, May 31, 1916; s. H. Lewis; m. Ruth Helene Oppenhejm, 1947 (div. 1974); 2 children. BA, PhD, U. London; postgrad., Univs. of London and Paris; doctorate (hon.), Hebrew U., Jerusalem, 1974, Tel Aviv U., 1979, SUNY, Binghamton, 1987, U. Pa., 1987, Hebrew Union Coll., 1987, Yeshiva U., 1991, Haifa U., 1991, Bar-Ilan U., 1992, Brandeis U., 1993, Ben-Gurion U., 1996, Ankara U., 1996, New Sch. U., NY, 2002, Princeton U., 2002, Northwestern U., Evanston, Ill., 2003, U. Judaism, LA, 2004. Asst. lectr. in Islamic history Sch. Oriental Studies U. London, 1938, prof. history Near and Mid. East, Sch. Oriental and African Studies (formerly named Sch. Oriental Studies), 1949-74; Cleveland E. Dodge prof. near ea. studies Princeton (NJ) U., 1974-86, prof. emeritus, 1986—, hon. Ataturk prof., 1992-93; A.D. White prof. at large Cornell U., 1984-90; dir. Annenberg Rsch. Inst., Phila., 1986-90. Vis. prof. history UCLA, 1955-56, Columbia U., 1960, Ind. U., 1963; vis. prof. College de France, 1980, Ecole des Hautes Etudes, Paris, 1983-86; Class of 1932 lectr. Princeton U., 1964; vis. mem. Inst. for Advanced Study, Princeton, NJ, 1969, long-term mem., 1974-86, U. Chgo., 1985; Gottesman lectr. Yeshiva U., 1974; Jefferson lectr. NEH, 1990; Tanner lectr. Oxford U., 1990; Weizmann lectr. in humanities, 1991; Henry M. Jackson meml. lectr., 1992; Siemens Stiftung lectr., Munich, 1993; Merle-Curti lectr., Madison, Wis., 1993; lectr. NY Pub. Libr., 1993. Author: The Origins of Ismailism, 1940, Turkey Today, 1940, British Contributions to Arabic Studies, 1941, Handbook of Diplomatic and Political Arabic, 1947, The Arabs in History, 1950, new edit., 1993, Notes and Documents from the Turkish Archives, 1952, The Emergence of Modern Turkey, 1961, 3rd edit. 2002, (transl. from Ibn Gabirol) The Kingly Crown, 1961, rev. edit. 2003, Istanbul and the Civilization of the Ottoman Empire, 1963, The Middle East and the West, 1964, The Assassins, 1967, Race and Color in Islam, 1971, Islam in History, 1973, new edit., 1993, Islam from the Prophet Muhammad to the Capture of Constantinople, 2 vols., 1974, History Remembered, Recovered, Invented, 1975, Studies in Classical and Ottoman Islam, 7th-16th centuries, 1976, The Muslim Discovery of Europe, 1982, The Jews of Islam, 1984, Semites and Anti-Semites, 1986, rev. edit., 1997, The Political Language of Islam, 1988, Race and Slavery in Islam, 1990, Islam and the West, 1993, The Shaping of the Modern Middle East, 1994, Cultures in Conflict: Christians, Muslims and Jews in the Age of Discovery, 1995, The Middle East: A Brief History of the Last 2000 Years, 1996, The Future of the Middle East, 1997, The Multiple Identities of the Middle East, 1999, A Middle East Mosaic: Fragments of life, letters and history, 2000, Music of a Distant Drum, 2001, What Went Wrong? Western Impact and Middle Eastern Response, 2002, The Crisis of Islam: Holy War and Unholy Terror, 2003, From Babel to Dragomans: Interpreting the Middle East, 2004; (with Amnon Cohen) Population and Revenue in the Towns of Palestine in the Sixteenth Century, 1978; author, editor: Land of Enchanters, 1948, 3d edit. (with Stanley Burstein) 2001, The World of Islam: Faith, People, Culture, 1976; author, co-editor: Historians of the Middle East, 1962, Ency. of Islam, 1956-87; editor: (with others) The Cambridge History of Islam, vols. 1-11, 1971; co-editor: Muslims in Europe, 1992, Religionsgespräche im

Mittelalter, 1992; also articles. Served with Royal Armoured Corps and Intelligence Corps, Brit. Army, 1940-41; with dept. Fgn. Office, 1941-45. Recipient Cert. of Merit for svcs. to Turkish culture, Turkish Govt., 1973, Harvey prize, 1978, Ataturk Peace prize, 1998, Golden Plate award, Acad. Achievement, 2004, Nat. Humanities Medal, NEH, 2006, Irving Kristol award, 2007; Univ. Coll. of London fellow, 1976, hon. fellow U. London. 1986. Fellow Brit. Acad., Royal Hist. Soc., Turkish Hist. Soc. (hon.), Sch. of Oriental and African Studies (hon.); mem. Am. Acad. Arts and Scis., Am. Philos. Soc., Am. Hist. Assn., Soc. Asiatique (hon.), Inst. d'Egypte (Cairo, assoc.), Inst. de France (corr.), Turkish Acad. Scis. (hon.). Office: Near East Studies Dept Princeton U Princeton NJ 08544-1008

LEWIS, BRIAN KREGLOW, retired physiologist, computer scientist; b. Durban, Rep. South Africa, Sept. 2, 1932; s. Arthur Armington and Isabel (Kreglow) L.; m. Mary Helen Kidwell, July 14, 1953; children: Brian E., James A., Charles A., Carol J., Robert E., Sharon H. BS secondary sci. edn., Ohio State U., 1950—54; PhD med. physiology, Tufts U., 1966—71. Biology tchr. Lincoln-Sudbury (Mass.) Regional High Sch., 1965-66; rsch. assoc. May Inst. for Med. Rsch., Cin., 1971-75; from asst. to assoc. prof. health sci. Grand Valley State U., Allendale, Mich., 1975-81; assoc. prof. Ponce Sch. Medicine, PR, 1981—84, prof. chmn. physiology, 1987—91; prin. Lewis Assocs., Sarasota, Fla., 1984—2003, ret., 2004. Adj. asst. prof. physiology Cin. Coll. Medicine, 1972-75; assoc.; instr. Macintosh computer for beginners Sarasota County Tech. Inst., 1995-97. Editor: Search of Far Horizons; developer business and edn. software, 2004; contbr. articles to profl. jours Cubmaster, scoutmaster Boy Scouts Am., 1963-78; mem. Choral Polifonica, Ponce, PR, 1982-84, ch. choir, St. Andrew Ch., Sarasota, 1984—, mem. fin. com., 1991-98, treas., 1999-2001, chmn. fin. com. 2005—; bd. dirs. Sarasota chpt. Soc. Preservation and Encouragement Barbershop Quartet Singing in Am., 1994, sec., 1995-99; active Village Voices, Greenhills, Ohio, 1972-75; active Meadows Chorus, 1996—; mem. Manatee chpt. SPEBSQSA, 2002—, treas., 2005— Lt. supply corps USN, 1954—62. NIH fellow, 1965-71. Mem. Endocrine Soc., Soc. for Study Reproduction, Soc. for Study Fertility, Sarasota PC Users Group (spreadsheet SIG leader 1993-94, software reviewer 1992—, moderator TechForum 1996-2003, author monthly TechTalk, 1995—), Sigma Xi. Personal E-mail: bwsail@yahoo.com.

LEWIS, BROCK, investment company executive; b. New Bedford, Mass., July 16, 1930; s. Frank Edward and Mary (Brock) L.; m. Susan Wahl, Sept. 4, 1954 (div.); children: Juliana D., Christopher B., Josiah E., Victoria D. BA, Dartmouth Coll., 1952; LLB, Boston U., 1955; postgrad., NYU, 1959-61. Asst. v.p. Fidelity Union Trust Co., Newark, 1955-64; v.p., trust officer County Nat. Bank, Poughkeepsie, NY, 1964-67, Capital Nat. Bank, Houston, 1967-69; v.p. Lionel D. Edie & Co., Houston, 1969-72, Dominick Mgmt. Co., NYC, 1972-75, Marine Midland Bank, NYC, 1975-80; 1st v.p. Lehman Mgmt. Co., NYC, 1980-82; owner, pres. Brock Lewis Assocs. Ltd., Nantucket, Mass., 1982—; pres. Living Daylight, Inc., Nantucket, Mass., 2004—. Cons. State of N.J. Adminstrn. Office of Cts., Trenton, 1993—; dir. Inst. Social and Econ. Policy Middle East, Cambridge, Mass., 1993-99. Pres. Greater Trenton Symphony, 1993-2001, pres. emeritus, 2001—; dir. Steinway Soc., Princeton, 1990-2000; trustee emeritus Tabor Acad., Marion, Mass.; mem. Republican Presdl. Roundtable, 2000—. Mem. Nat. Assn. Bus. Economists, Tabor Acad. Alumni Assn. (chmn. 1995-98, trustee 1995-98), Dartmouth Rowing Club, Nantucket Hist. Assn

LEWIS, CALVIN FRED, architect, educator; b. Chgo., Mar. 27, 1946; s. Howard George and Fern Teresa (Voelsch) L.; m. L. Diane Johnson, Aug. 24, 1968; children: Nathan, Miller, Cooper, Wilson. BArch, Iowa State U., 1969. Architect Charles Herbert and Assocs., Des Moines, 1970-86; prin. Herbert Lewis Kruse Blunck Architecture, Des Moines, 1987—2004; prin., owner Lewis Studio, Des Moines, 2005—; prof. Iowa State U., 2000—, chmn. Dept. Arch., 2000—. Peer reviewer Design Excellence Program GSA, 2003—; lectr., awards juror. More tha 50 projects published in profl. jours. Recipient Best in Design award Time mag.; named one of Top Young Architects in Country, Met. Home mag.; firm named Nat. AIA Firm of Yr., 2001. Fellow AIA (over 70 Design awards 1972—, 3 Nat. Honor awards 1997, 2002), Internat Design award Bus. Week/Archtl. Record 1998, Internat. Design mag. awards 1998-99, Nat. Design award AIA-AISC 1999). Avocations: sports, photography. Office: Dept Arch Iowa State U 156A Coll of Design Ames IA 50011 Office Phone: 515-294-2665. E-mail: calewis@iastate.edu.

LEWIS, CARL (FREDERICK CARLTON LEWIS), Olympic track and field athlete; b. Birmingham, Ala., May 1, 1961; s. William McKinley Lewis, Jr. and Evelyn (Lawler) Lewis. Student, U. Houston. Mem. U.S. Olympic Team, 1980, 1984, 1988, 1992, 1996. Musician: (albums) Break it Up, 1986. Founder Carl Lewis Found. Recipient James E. Sullivan award best amateur athlete, 1981, Jesse Owens award, 1982, Athlete of Yr. award Assoc. Press Sports, 1983; named World Athlete of the Decade Track & Field News, 1980-89, Olympic Athlete of the Century, 2000, U.S. Athlete of the Yr., 1981, 82, 83, 84, 87, 88, 91, World Athlete of the Yr., 1982, 83, 84, named to U.S. Olympic Hall of Fame, 1985. winner 1 Bronze medal Pan Am. Games, 1979, 2 Gold medals, 1981, 1 Gold medal World Cup, 1981, 3 Gold medals, 100m, long jump, 400m relay, World Championships, 1983, 1987, 9 Olympic Gold medals, Long Jump 1984, 1988, 1992, 1996, 100m, 1984, 1988, 200m, 1980, 4x100m relay, 1984, 1992, Silver medal, 200m, 1988; world record holder in 4x100m relay, 1981, 83, 84, 91, 92, in 4x200m relay, 1989, 100 meter dash, 1991; Am. record holder in 4x100 relay, 1981, 83, 84, 90, 91, in 200 meter dash, 1983, 100 meter dash, 1987, 88, 91, 4x200m relay, 1989; world and Am. indoor record holder in long jump, 1981, 82, 84, in 60 yd. dash, 1983, holds current world record of 37.40 seconds in the 4x100m relay, 1992-. Office: 528 Palisades Dr Ste 525 Pacific Palisades CA 90272

LEWIS, CARLA SUSAN, psychology educator; b. Bklyn. d. Harry Aaron and Mildred Lewis. BA summa cum laude, Fordham U., 1979; MA in Psychology, CUNY, 1984, MPhil, 1986, PhD in Psychology, 1988. Asst. rsch. scientist N.Y. State Psychiat. Inst., NYC, 1987-88; rsch. scientist Columbia Sch. Pub. Health, NYC, 1988-90; adj. asst. prof. MA in program in forensic psychology John Jay Coll. Criminal Justice, NYC, 1990; mem. faculty psychology rsch. lab. Princeton U., NJ, 1992-93; adj. asst. prof. psychology Fordham U., NYC, 1993-95, dep. exec. dir. planning, evaluation and QI, 1995—2004; dir. planning Project Hospitality, SI, NY, 2004—. Rsch. scientist, cons. Columbia Sch. Pub. Health, N.Y.C., 1993-94; rsch. cons. dept. environ. medicine NYU Med. Ctr., 1994, Nat. Devel. and Rsch. Inst., Insts. for Therapeutic Cmty. Rsch., N.Y.C., 1995; sr. rsch. analyst Beth Israel Medical Ctr., 2000-02; presenter in field; chief evaluator Urban Resource Inst., 2002-06, Domestic Violence Shelters U. R.I.; Mt. Sinai Pub. Advocate, 2002; presenter in field. Contbr. articles to profl. jours. Mem. task force against domestic violence City NY; mem. HIV prevention planning group NYC Dept. Health, chairperson intervention behavioral sci. com.; mem. quality care steering com. NY AIDS Inst. Recipient Disting. Rsch. award Psi Chi Nat. Honor Soc., 1991. Mem.: APA. Office: Porject Hospitality 100 Park Ave Staten Island NY 10302 Office Phone: 718-448-1544 x 158. Business E-Mail: carla_lewis@projecthospitality.org.

LEWIS, CHARLES A., foundation administrator; b. Orange, NJ, Oct. 23, 1942; s. F. Donald and Edna H. L.; m. Gretchen Smith, July 1967 (div.); m. Penny Bender Sebring, June 9, 1984. BA, Amherst Coll., 1964; MBA, U. Pa., 1966; LHD (hon.), Amherst Coll., 2003. Asst. to pres. Computer Tech., Inc., Skokie, Ill., 1969-70; 1st v.p. White, Weld, & Co., 1970-78; vice chmn. investment banking Merrill Lynch & Co., Chgo., 1978—2004. Mem. adv. com. Database of Black Performers of Instrumental Concert Music, 1999—. Life trustee Amherst Coll., Folger Shakespear Libr., 1989—; life trustee, vice chair Chgo. Symphony Orch., 1989—; life dir. Juvenile Diabetes Rsch. Found. Ill.; vis. com. divsn. social scis. U. Chgo.; trustee Ravinia Festival, 1995—98; leadership coun. Chgo. Pub. Edn. Fund, 2000—; governing bd. North Kenwood/Oakland Charter Sch., 2000—03; co-chair The Amherst Coll. Campaign, 1993—2001; mem. policy bd. Ctr. Urban Sch. Improvement U. Chgo., 2003—; bd. dirs. Juvenile Diabetes Rsch. Found. Internat., 1994—95. Named to, Shaker H.S. Sports Hall of Fame, 2003; recipient Cmty. Ptnr. award, People's Music Sch., 2002. Mem. Chgo. Club, Glen View Club. Office: Coach House Capital and Lewis-Sebring Family Found 2735 Sheridan Rd Evanston IL 60201 Home Phone: 847-328-4310; Office Phone: 847-864-9615. E-mail: calewis@lewissebringff.org.

LEWIS, CHARLES JEREMY (JERRY LEWIS), congressman; b. Spokane, Wash., Oct. 21, 1934; BA, UCLA, 1956. Former life ins. underwriter; field rep. for former U.S. Rep. Jerry Pettis; mem. Calif. State Assembly, 1968-78; vice chmn. rules com., chmn. subcom. on air quality; mem. U.S. Congress from 41st (formerly 35th) Calif. dist., 1979—; mem. appropriations com.; chmn., 2005—. Former chmn. VA-HUD subcom., mem. defense subcom., select com. on intelligence, chmn. subcom. on human intelligence; co-chair Calif. Congl. Delegation, 1996-2001. Republican. Presbyterian. Office: US Ho Reps 2112 Rayburn Ho Office Bldg Washington DC 20515

LEWIS, CHARLES JOSEPH, journalist; b. Bozeman, Mont., July 10, 1940; s. Vern Edward James and Mary (Brooke) L.; m. Sarah Withers (div. 2002); children: Peter, Patrick, Barbara; m. Vivian Chen, July 14, 2007. BS in Humanities with Honors, Loyola U., Chgo., 1962; JD, Columbia U., 1965. Bar: Ill. 1965. Atty. McDermott, Will & Emery, Chgo., 1965-67; reporter City News Bur., Chgo., 1967-68; reporter, editor Chgo. Sun-Times, 1968-73; with AP, 1974-89, reporter, editor, Washington, 1974-78, reporter, editor, L.A., 1978-80, personnel mgr., N.Y.C., 1981-83, bur. chief, Hartford, Conn., 1980-81, bur. chief, Washington, 1984-89; bur. chief Hearst Newspapers, Washington, 1989—. Bd. dirs. Nat. Press Found., Washington, 1985-2003, treas., 1987-88, vice chmn., 1988-90, chmn., 1990-92; dir. Reporters Com. for Freedom of the Press, 1993-98, SDX Found. Washington, 1996—; mem. adv. bd. Paul Miller Washington Reporting Fellowships, 1999—. Lance cpl. USMCR, 1963-67. Named to Hall of Fame, SPJ, 2006. Mem. Am. Soc. Newspaper Editors, Gridiron Club, Sigma Delta Chi (v.p. Washington chpt. 1988-89). Office: Hearst Newspapers 1850 K St NW Ste 1000 Washington DC 20006 Office Phone: 202-263-6400, 202-263-6411.

LEWIS, CHARLES LEONARD, psychologist; b. Wellsville, Ohio, Jan. 6, 1926; s. Cleo L. and Charlotte (Hahn) L.; m. Charlotte J. Wynn, Sept. 8, 1948 (dec. Mar. 1987); children: Stephen C., Janet J., Judith A.; m. Jane E. McCormick, Oct. 1, 1988. BS in Edn. with honors, Ohio U., 1949; MA, U. Minn., 1953, PhD, 1955. Asst. dean of men Ohio U., 1948-50; assoc. dir. activities U. Minn., 1950-55; dean student affairs, assoc. prof. psychology U. N.D., 1955-62; exec. dean, assoc. prof. ednl. psychology U. Tenn., 1962-67; v.p. student affairs Pa. State U., 1967-72; exec. dir. Am. Personnel and Guidance Assn., Washington, 1972-74, exec. v.p., 1974-83, exec. v.p. emeritus, 1984—; pres. Charles L. Lewis & Assocs., Annandale, Va., 1983-85, Chuck Lewis et al, Lancaster, Pa., 1985—. Guest prof. U. Md., 1973; mem. Nat. Adv. Com. for Devel. Guidance Components-Career Edn., 1972-76. Founding editor Jour. Coll. Students Pers., 1958-64; mem. editl. bd. Pers. and Guidance Jour., 1954-57. Mem. Pres.'s Com. for Handicapped, 1972-80; bd. dirs. Ctr. Cmty. Hosps., Bellefonte, Pa. With U.S. Army, 1944-47. Named Outstanding Alumnus, Coll. Edn. Ohio U., 1988; recipient George Hill Disting. Alumni award, Ohio U., 1981. Mem.: AAUP, APA, Willow Valley Computer Sig. (pres. 1999—2001), Ohio U. Alumni Soc. and Friends Coll. Edn. (coun. 1985—92, bd. dirs. 1986—92), Coun. Advancement of Stds. (bd. dirs.), Am. Assn. Univ. Adminstrs. (dir. 1973), Am. Pers. and Guidance Assn. (dir. 1967—70), Nat. Assn. Woman Deans and Counselors, Nat. Assn. Student Pers. Adminstrs., Am. Coll. Pers. Assn. (pres. 1968—69, honoree Diamond Anniversary 1999, Lifetime Achievement award 2001), Am. Assn. Higher Edn., Psi Chi, Chi Sigma Iota (founding dir. 1984—90), Beta Theta Pi, Kappa Delta Pi. Episcopalian. Home Phone: 717-464-6225. E-mail: clewis26@dejazzd.com.

LEWIS, CHARLES RAYMOND, II, traffic engineer, consultant; b. Charleston, W.Va., May 29, 1947; s. Charles Raymond and Jane Ann (Veazey) L.; m. Constance Maria Gratop, Aug. 29, 1970; 1 child, Brian Anthony. BSCE, Ohio U., Athens, 1970; MEng in Civil Engring., Pa. State U., University Park, 1971. Registered profl. engr., W.Va., profl. surveyor, W.Va.; lic. master electrician, W.Va. Asst. planning and rsch. engr. W.Va. Dept. Hwys., Charleston, 1970-73; planning and rsch. engr. Dept. Transp. Traffic Engr. Divsn. W.Va. Divsn. Hwys., Charleston, 1973—2004; ADA compliance officer Dept. of Transp., W.Va., 2002—, staff engr. traffic rsch. and spl. projects traffic engring. divsn. W.Va. divsn. hwys., 2004—; value engring coord. Dept. of Transp., 1994—. Com. mem. Transp. Rsch. Bd., Washington, 1983—, com. chmn., 1984-90; project and synthesis panel mem. Nat. Coop. Hwy. Rsch. Program, Washington, 1991—; adj. instr. Marshall U., 2003—. Asst. scoutmaster Boy Scouts Am., Charleston, 1991—; co-clerk Charleston Friends Meeting, 2001—. Fellow Automotive Safety Found.; recipient Silver Beaver award Boy Scouts Am., 1998, Lifetime Achievement award W.Va. Operation Lifesaver, 2001. Fellow Inst. Transp. Engrs. (joint com. on hwy.-rail grade crossings 2003—); mem. Am. Ry. Engring. and Maintenance of Way Assn. (mem. coms.). Avocations: photography, geology, amateur astronomy. Office: Traffic Engring Divsn WVa Dept Transp 1900 Kanawha Blvd E Charleston WV 25305-0009 Business E-Mail: rlewis@dot.state.wv.us.

LEWIS, CHIP, lawyer; b. 1969; BA, U. Tex., Austin; JD, U. Houston; grad., Nat. Coll. of Dist. Attys. Career Procecutor Course. Bar: Tex. 1994, Fed. Dist Ct. Tex., US Supreme Ct. Asst. dist. atty. Harris County Dist. Atty.'s Office, 1994—2000; pvt. practice Houston, 2000—. Recipient Karen Kaough Award. Mem.: Harris County Criminal Lawyers Assn., Tex. Criminal Defense Lawyers Assn. (featured speaker), Nat. Assn. Criminal Defense Lawyers, Order of Barristers. Office: 2120 Welch St Houston TX 77019

LEWIS, CHRIS A., manufacturing executive; b. Apr. 22, 1931; BA, Wittenberg U. CPA. With KPMG Peat Warwick; US contr. Peek PLC, 1989—95; treas. Jabil Circuits, 1995—96, CFO, 1996—2004, v.p. global bus. units, 2004—. Recipient CFO Excellence award for planning and performance mgmt., CFO Mag., 2001. Office: Jabil Cir 10560 9th St N Saint Petersburg FL 33716

LEWIS, CHRISTA MARIE, music educator; b. Fond du Lac, Wis., Apr. 17, 1977; d. Duane Carl and Elaine Mary Rebek; m. Christopher Lee Lewis, Aug. 5, 2006. BS in Music and Theatre, Ripan Coll., Wis., 1999. Gen. music tchr. FACES, Fond du Lac, Wis., 2001—; drama dir. St. Mary's Springs HS, Fond du Lac, 2002—, band dir., 2003—, acting tchr., 2004—. Condr. music liturgy St. Mary's Springs HS, 2003—06; asst. dir., music dir. BRAVO, Fond du Lac, 2003—05. Mem.: MENC. Roman Catholic. Avocations: singing, trumpet, scrapbooks.

LEWIS, CLAUDIA, film company executive; BA in Film, UC Berkeley; MFA, UCLA. V.p. prodn. Avenue Pictures; prodr. Addis Wechsler; with Fox Searchlight Pictures, 1995—, exec. v.p. prodn., pres. prodn., 2006—. Named one of 100 Most Powerful Women in Entertainment, Hollywood Reporter, 2006. Office: Fox Searchlight Pictures 10201 W Pico Blvd Bldg 38 Los Angeles CA 90035 Office Phone: 310-369-4402. Office Fax: 310-369-2359.*

LEWIS, CYNTHIA, law librarian; b. Athens, Greece; m. Jason Lewis; 2 children. BA, Wellesley Coll., 1985; MSLIS, Simmons Coll., 1991; JD, Franklin Pierce Law Ctr., 2001. Law libr., Boston; reference/computer rsch. libr. Franklin Pierce Law Ctr., Concord, NH; electronic resources libr. Hugh and Hazel Darling Law Libr., UCLA Sch. Law, 2001, assoc. law libr., acting dir., 2006—, tchr. advanced legal rsch. Contbr. articles to law jours. Office: UCLA Box 951476 Los Angeles CA 90095-1476 Office Phone: 310-267-4468. E-mail: lewis@law.ucla.edu.*

LEWIS, DAN ALBERT, education educator; b. Chgo., Feb. 14, 1946; s. Milton and Diane (Sabath) L.; m. Stephanie Riger, Jan. 3, 1982; children: Matthew, Jake. BA cum laude, Stanford U., 1968; PhD, U. Calif., Santa Cruz, 1980. Rsch. assoc. Arthur Bolton Assocs., Sacramento, 1969-70; survey contr. Sci. Analysis Corp., San Francisco, 1971; dir. Stanford Workshops on Polit. and Social Issues Stanford (Calif.) U., 1971-74; projects adminstr. Ctr. Urban Affairs and Policy Rsch., Northwestern U., Evanston, Ill., 1975-80, asst. prof. edn., 1980-86, assoc. prof. edn., 1986-90, assoc. dir., chair grad. program human devel./social policy, 1987-90, prof. edn., 1990—. Vis. scholar Sch. Edn., Stanford U., 1990-91; mem. task force on restructuring mental health svcs. Chgo. Dept. Health, 1982; mem. human rights authority Ill. Guardianship and Advocacy Commn., 1980-82; adv. mem. com. on planning and inter-agy. coordination Commn. Mental Health and Devel. Disabilities, 1979; interim adv. com. on mental health City of Chgo., 1978; adv. mem. Gov.'s Commn. to Revise Mental Health Code Ill., 1975-77;dir. Univ. Consortium on Welfare Reform, 1999-2003; presenter at profl. confs.; presenter workshops. Editor: Reactions to Crime, 1981; co-author: Fear of Crime: Incivility and the Production of a Social Problem, 1986, The Social Construction of Reform: Crime Prevention and Community Organizations, 1988, The Worlds of the Mentally Ill, 1991, The State Mental Patient in Urban Life, 1994, Race and Educational Reform, 1995; contbr. articles, book revs. to profl. publs. Bd. dirs. Designs for Change, Ill. Mental Health Assn.; rsch. adv. com. Chgo. Urban League, Chgo. Panel Pub. Sch. Finances, 1989-91; needs assessment tech. com. United Way Chgo., 1989-90; ednl. coun. Francis W. Parker Sch., Chgo., 1988-90; task force on restructuring mental health svcs. Chgo. Dept. Health, 1982; com. on mentally disabled Ill. State Bar Assn., 1983-89; dir. U. Consortium on Welfare Reform, 1999-2002; rsch. policy com. Ill. Dept. Mental Health, 1978; bd. dirs. Mental Health Assn. Greater Chgo., 1977-84, v.p. pub. policy, 1979-83 Recipient Excellence in Tchg. award Northwestern U. Alumni Assn., 1998; named to Faculty Honor Roll Associated Student Govt., 2001-04. Office: Northwestern Univ 2040 Sheridan Rd Evanston IL 60208-0855 Business E-Mail: dlewis@northwestern.edu.

LEWIS, DANIEL MARTIN, lawyer; b. NYC, Feb. 3, 1944; s. David W. and Muriel (Osafs) L.; m. Claudia Vera Dean, Oct. 2, 1971; children: Matthew, Ethan, Jennifer. BA, Yale U., 1966, LLB, 1969. Bar: D.C., U.S. Ct. Appeals (9th, 5th and 4th cirs.). Legis. asst. U.S. senator Joseph D. Tydings, Md., 1969-70; chief legis. asst. U.S. senator Edmund S. Muskee, Maine, 1971-72; assoc. Arnold & Porter, Washington, 1973-79, ptnr., Antitrust and Trade Regulation Practice Group, 1979—. Office: Arnold & Porter 555 12th St NW Washington DC 20004-1206 Office Phone: 202-942-5661. Office Fax: 202-942-5999. Business E-Mail: daniel.lewis@aporter.com.

LEWIS, DAVE, professional hockey coach, retired professional hockey player; b. Kindersley, Sask., Can., July 3, 1953; m. Brenda Lewis; children: Ryan, Meagan. Defenseman NY Islanders, 1973—80, LA Kings, 1980—83, NJ Devils, 1983—86, Detroit Red Wings, 1986—88, asst. coach, 1988—97, assoc. coach, 1997—2002, head coach, 2002—05, scout, 2005—06; head coach Boston Bruins, 2006—07; asst. coach LA Kings, 2007—. Achievements include being associate coach of Stanley Cup Champion Detroit Red Wings, 1997, 1998, 2002. Office: LA Kings Hockey Club 1111 S Figueroa St, Ste 3100 Los Angeles CA 90015*

LEWIS, DAVID BAKER, lawyer; b. Detroit, June 9, 1944; BA, Oakland U., 1965; MBA, U. Chgo., 1967; JD, U. Mich. Law Sch., 1970. Bar: Mich. 1970. Law clk. to Honorable Theodore Levin, US Dist. Ct., Ea. Dist. Mich., 1970—71; pres. Lewis, Clay & Munday, Detroit, 1972—82, chmn. corp. svcs. practice group, 1982—, founder, shareholder; assoc. prof. law, law and social change Detroit Coll. Law, 1973—78. Mem., sec. State of Mich. Atty. Discipline Bd., 1978—83; mem. steering com. Bond Attys. Workshop, 1979, 89; mem. exec. com. Met. Ctr. High Tech., 1983—90, bd. dirs., 1983—90; mem. exec. com. HGH Health Sys., 1984—88, bd. trustees, 1984—88, Inst. Am. Bus., 1985—, mem. exec. com., 1985—; mem. Met. Affairs Corp., 1985—91, vice-chmn., 1989—91, bd. dirs., 1989—91, Booker T. Washington Bus. Assn., 1989—91, Consolidated Rail Corp. (Conrail), 1989—, mem. audit com., 1989—, mem. fin. com., 1989—; mem. audit com. LG&E Energy Corp., 1992—, mem. devel. com., 1992—, bd. dirs., 1992—, TRW, Inc., 1995—, mem. compensation com., 1995—, mem. retirement funding com., 1995—; mem. audit and legal com. Comerica Bank, Mich., 1995—, mem. trust and investment com., 1995—, bd. dirs., 1995—; life mem. Sixth Circuit Judicial Conf. Mem. Greater Detroit Area Hosp. Coun., Inc., 1977—79, 1983—87, Detroit Inst. Arts Dir. Search Com., 1983—85, Greater Detroit and Windsor Japan-Am. Soc., 1989; bd. trustees Harper-Grace Hosp., 1979—88, mem. exec. com., 1979—88; bd. trustees Oakland U., 1970—81, vice chmn. bd. trustees, 1976—78, chmn. bd. trustees, 1978—80, trustee emeritus bd. trustees; pres. Franklin-Wright Settlement, Inc., 1975—76; v.p. Mich. Assn. Governing Bds. Colls. and Univs., 1977—79; chmn. com. vis. U. Mich. Law Sch.; bd. trustees Ctr. Creative Studies, 1983—95, Grosse Pointe Acad., 1984—87, 1993—94; bd. dirs. Detroit Symphony, 1983—, Detroit. Zoological Soc., 1983—89, Musical Hall Ctr. Performing Arts, 1983—94, Founders Soc., Detroit Inst. Arts, 1984—89, Greater Detroit Interfaith Round Table, Nat. Conf. Christian and Jews, Inc., 1990—, Detroit Club, 1989—95, sec., 1989—95. Named one of Am. Top Black Lawyers, Black Enterprise Mag., 2003. Mem.: Nat. Assn. Securities Profl., Inc. (sec. 1985—87, chair-elect 1987, chair 1988, exec. com.), Nat. Assn. Bond Lawyers (bd. dirs. 1993—95). Office: Lewis & Munday 2490 First Nat Bldg 660 Woodward Ave Detroit MI 48226-3531 Home Phone: 313-823-0471; Office Phone: 313-961-2550 4110. Business E-Mail: dlewis@lewismunday.com.

LEWIS, DAVID CARLETON, medical educator, academic administrator; b. Hartford, Conn., May 19, 1935; s. Theodore and Lillian (Levin) L.; m. Eleanor Grace Levinson, Aug. 23, 1959; children: Deborah, Steven. AB magna cum laude, Brown U., 1957; MD, Harvard U., 1961. Intern Beth Israel Hosp., Boston, 1961-62, jr. resident, 1962-63, chief med. resident, 1966-67, dir. emergency unit and med. outpatient dept., 1969-71; sr. resident U. Hosps. Cleve., 1963-64, Parkland Meml. Hosp., Dallas, 1964-66; fellow U. Tex. Southwestern Med. Hosp., Dallas, 1964-66; Sloan Found. fellow Harvard Med. Sch., Boston, 1971-72; med. dir. Washingtonian Ctr. for Addictions, Boston, 1972-77; dir. div. alcohol and substance abuse Roger Williams Gen. Hosp., Providence, 1976-82; dir. program in alcoholism and drug abuse Brown U., Providence, 1976-82, prof. medicine and community health, 1982—, Donald G. Millar prof. alcohol and addiction studies, 1987—, chmn. dept. community health, 1981-86, dir. Ctr. Alcohol and Addiction Studies, 1982-2000. Nat. adv. coun. Nat. Alcohol Inst., Rockville, Md., 1981-85, cons. to dir., 1985-93; sci. adv. bd. Children of Alcoholics Found., 1985-95; cons. WHO, 1986-2000, cocaine global adv. com., 1992-95; chair Physician Consortium on Substance Abuse Edn., 1989—99; mem. Carnegie Substance Abuse Adv. com., 1989-92; scholar-in-residence Nat. Inst. Med., 1991-92; adv. panel to U.S. Pharmacopoeia, 1995—99; mem. Drug Strategies Nat. Adv. Panel, 1994—2000, dir. WHO Collaborating Ctr. at Brown U., 1995-2000; nat. adv. com. Robert Wood Johnson Found. Fighting Back program,

1996—2002; bd. dirs. Nat. Coun. Alchoholism and Drug Dependence, 1995-, dep. chair 2002-04, chair, 2004—; bd. dirs. Drug Policy Alliance. Author: The Drug Experience: Data for Decision Making, 1970; editor: Providing Care for Children of Alcoholics, 1986; editor Brown U. Digest of Addiction Theory and Application, 1986—2001; exec. editor Substance Abuse jour., 1984—; contbr. numerous articles to profl. jours. Med. dir. Beacon Hill Free Clinic, Boston, 1968—71; chmn. Mayor's Coun. on Drug Abuse, Boston, 1972—80; project dir. Physician Leadership on Nat. Drug Policy, 1997—2004; bd. dirs. Physicians and Lawyers for Nat. Drug Policy, 2004—. Grantee Nat. Alcohol and Drug Insts., 1986—, Robert Wood Johnson Found., 1996—, John D. and Catherine T. MacArthur Found., 1997—99, Open Study Inst., 1997—99; Edward John Noble fellow Harvard U. Med. Sch., 1957-91; receipient Assn. Med. Edn. and Rsch. in Substance Abuse award for Excellence in Medical Edn., 1986, Norman E Zinberg Meml. Lectr. award Harvard Med. Sch., 1996, AMA award, 1997, Excellence in Med. Edn. AMA-ERF, 1997. Fellow: ACP; mem.: NAS, Assn. for Edn. and Rsch. in Substance Abuse (bd. dirs. 1985—), Brown Med. Alumni Assn. (pres. 1974—76), Assn. Med. Edn. and Rsch. in Substance Abuse (pres. 1983—88, Excellence in Medicine award 1986), Inst. Medicine Study on Treatment Alcohol Problems, Am. Acad. on Physician and Patient (bd. dirs. 1998—2001), Am. Soc. Addiction Medicine (bd. dirs. 1995—2005, sec. 2003—05, John P. McGovern award 2004), Sigma Xi, Phi Beta Kappa. Avocations: choral singing, sailing, photography. Office: Brown Univ Ctr Alcohol & Addiction Studies Box G Providence RI 02912 Office Phone: 401-863-6639. E-mail: David_Lewis@brown.edu.

LEWIS, DAVID JOHN, lawyer; b. Zanesville, Ohio, Feb. 4, 1948; s. David Griff and Barbara Ann (Hoy) L.; m. Susan G. Smith; 1 child, Ann Elizabeth. BS in Fin., U. Ill., 1970, JD, 1973. Bar: Ill. 1973, D.C. 1974. Law clk. to Judge Philip W. Tone U.S. Dist. Ct. For North Dist. Ill., Chgo., 1973-74; assoc. Sidley Austin LLP, Washington, 1974-80, ptnr., 1980—. Comml. arbitrator Am. Arbitration Assn.; mem. Washington panel CPR Inst. Dispute Resolution. Mem. ABA. Office: Sidley Austin LLP 1501 K St NW Washington DC 20005 Office Phone: 202-736-8183. E-mail: dlewis@sidley.com.

LEWIS, DAVID L., lawyer; b. NYC, Aug. 11, 1954; s. Albert B. and Sara Anne (Beresniakoff) L.; m. Carol Hayward, Dec. 21, 1983; children: Alexandra Hayward, Andrew Chase. BA, NYU, 1976; JD, Fordham U., 1979. Bar: NY 1980, US Dist. Ct. (ea. and so. dists. NY) 1980, US Ct. Appeals (2nd cir.) 1981, US Supreme Ct. 1983. Counsel to spk. pro tem NY State Assembly, Albany, 1980-83; ptnr. Lewis & Fiore, NYC, 1980; pvt. practice atty. Assoc. counsel to Senator Ray M. Goodman NY State Senate, 2000, chief counsel, 2001. Columnist Decor mag., 1980-88. Mem. law com. Kings County Dem. Com., Bklyn., 1980; pres. Bensonhurst Redevelopment Corp., Bkyn., 1981-82. Mem. ATLA (author text on plea bargaining and settlement), NADCL (past bd. dirs.), NY State Bar Assn., Assn. Bar City NY, NY County Lawyers Assn., NY State Assn. Criminal Def. Lawyers (bd. dirs., past pres.). Jewish.*

LEWIS, DAWNN, actress; b. Bklyn., Aug. 13, 1961; m. Johnny Newman, Dec. 2004 (separated). Grad. in voice and mus. theater magna cum laude, U. Miami, 1982; grad., N.Y. High Sch. Music and Art. Actress (films) I'm Gonna Git You Sucka, 1988, SPider-Man: Sins of the Fathers, 1996, Bruno the Kid: The Animated Movie, 1996, Bad Day on the Block, 1997, The Wood, 1999, Nicolas, 2001, Before Now, 2002, Charlotte's Web 2: Wilbur's Great Adventure, 2003, Gladius, 2003, X-Men Legends II: Rise of Apocalypse, 2005, True Crime: NYC, 2005, The Adventures of Brer Rabbit, 2006, I Was a Network Star, 2006, Holly Hobbie and Friends: Christmas Wishes, 2006, Marvel: Ultimate Alliance, 2006, Dreamgirls, 2006, The Last Sentinel, 2006, (TV films) Stompin' at the Savoy, 1992, Yuletide in the 'hood, 1993, A Cool Like That Christmas, 1994, Race to Freedom: The Underground Railroad, 1994, The Cherokee Kid, 1996, The Poof Point, 2001, (TV series) A Different World, 1987—92, Hangin' With Mr. Cooper, 1992—93, C-Bear and Jamal, 1996, Bruno the Kid, 1996, Spider-Man, 1995—97, The 10th Kingdom, 2000, Any Day Now, 2000—02, appeared on The Steve Harvey Show, 1997, Sliders, 1997, The Parent 'Hood, 1997, Nash Bridges, 1999, King of the Hill, 1997, Buzz Lightyear of Star Command, 2000, Andy Richter Controls the Universe, 2002, Strong Medicine, 2003, Futurama, 1999—2003, Girlfriends, 2003, NYPD Blue, 2004, actress (plays) Money Notes, Shades of Harlem, (nat. tour plays) Tap Dance Kid, (plays) Sister Act, 2006; singer: (albums) Worth Waiting For, 2006; composer (lyrics): A Different World theme song, 1987. Spokesperson United Negro Coll. Fund, Office of Substance Abuse, Nat. Assn. Social Workers. Avocation: horseback riding. Office: Carsey-Werner Co 4024 Radford Ave Studio City CA 91604-2101 E-mail: talk2me@dawnnlewis.com.*

LEWIS, DENNIS CARROLL, writer, publishing executive; b. Milw., Jan. 7, 1940; s. Carroll and Alyce Lewis Paxton; m. Marie Benedicte Denizet, Nov. 1, 1973 (div. Dec. 1982); m. Dasha Trebichavska, Mar. 5, 2007; 1 child, Benoit. Student, U. Wis., 1957-61; BS, San Francisco State U., 1967. Computer programmer, analyst Levi Struass, San Francisco, 1969-72; freelance book editor San Francisco, 1972-73; book editor Miller Freeman Pub. Co., San Francisco, 1973-76; pub. rels. account exec. Paul Purdom & Co., San Francisco, 1977-81; ptnr. Hi-Tech. Publicity, San Francisco, 1981-84; pres. Hi-Tech. Pub. Rels., Inc. (acquired by Shandwick Plc, 1988), San Francisco, 1984-90. Owner Mountain Wind Pub., San Francisco, 1996—; Healing Tao instr. and Chi Nei Tsang practitioner, 1993—; instr. B.K. Frantzis Energy Arts, 1997—. Author: The Tao of Natural Breathing, 1997, 2005, Breathing as a Metaphor for Living, 1998, Free Your Breath, Free Your Life, 2004; co-editor: Sacred Tradition and Present Need, 1975, On the Way to Self Knowledge, 1976; co-pub., editor Computer Publicity News, 1981-90; pub., editor Inner Alchemy jour., 1997-99; contbr. articles to newspapers and profl. jours. Mem. San Francisco Tennis Club. E-mail: info@authentic-breathing.com.

LEWIS, DENNIS M., federal agency administrator, former hospital administrator; Payroll clk. Ctrl. Office Veterans Heath Adminstrn., US Dept. Veterans. Affairs, Washington, asst. dep. under sec. for health & ops., acting dep. under sec. for health & ops., 2005—. Dir. VA Hosp., Hines, Ill. Contbr. articles to profl. jours. Recipient Meritorious Presdl. Rank Award. Fellow: Am. Coll. Healthcare Execs.; mem.: Fed. Healthcare Execs. Inst. (life), Leadership VA Alumni Assn. (life; past pres.). Office: US Dept Veterans Affairs Vets Health Adminstrn 810 Vermont Ave NW Washington DC 20420 Office Phone: 202-273-5400.

LEWIS, DONALD EMERSON, banker; b. Orange, NJ, Apr. 3, 1950; s. Donald Emerson Lewis and Marie (Gannon) Slaght; m. Suzanne Kimm, Oct. 12, 1974; children: Andrew Gannon, Meredith Marie, Carolyn Ann. AB, Villanova U., 1972; MBA, Boston Coll., 1974. V.p. Citibank N.A., NYC, 1974-85, Boston Safe Deposit & Trust Co., NYC, 1985-87; sr. v.p. United Jersey Banks, Princeton, NJ, 1987-91; v.p. Fleet Bank, N.A., Bridgewater, NJ, 1991-2000; ptnr. Wachovia Wealth Mgmt. Group, Summit, NJ, 2000—. Mem.: Canoe Brook Country. Republican. Roman Catholic. Avocations: golf, platform tennis. Office: Wachovia Bank NA 190 River Rd Summit NJ 07901-1412 Home Phone: 973-635-9226; Office Phone: 908-598-3705. E-mail: donald.lewis@wachovia.com.

LEWIS, DONALD SYKES, JR., artist; b. Norfolk, Va., Dec. 13, 1947; s. Donald Sykes and Beverly Porter Lewis; m. Elizabeth Caldwell McCauley, Jan. 15, 1993; children: Davidson, Byron, Peyton. BA in Fine Arts, Randolph-Macon Coll., 1970; MA in History of Art, U. Va., 1973. V.p. Auslew Gallery Inc., Norfolk, Va., 1974—86; instr. Old Dominion U., Norfolk, Va., 1975—76, Hermitage Mus., Norfolk, Va., 1978—79; pres. Auslew Gallery Inc., Norfolk, Va., 1987—93; dir., sec., treas. Granby & Main Corp., Norfolk, Va., 2004—05, pres., 2006—. One-man shows include Auslew Gallery, Norfolk, Va., 1982, Art Works, 1994, Hermitage Found. Mus., 1996, Warm Springs (Va.) Gallery, 2000, 2006, exhibited in group shows at Randolph-Macon Coll., Ashland, Va., 1985, exhibitions include Springville (Utah) Mus. Art, 1981, Gallery Mayo, Richmond, Va., 1983—95, 20th Century Gallery, Williamsburg, Va., 1985, Peninsula Fine Arts Ctr., Newport News, Va., 1997, Salmagundi Club, N.Y.C., 2002, Pleiades Gallery, 2002, Am. Artist and Profl. League, 2003, Salmagundi Club, 2003; author: (exhbn. catalog) Brandywind Mus., 1992; contbr. articles to profl. jours. Chmn. fundraising com. Chrysler Mus., Norfolk, Va., 1982—84; v.p. alumni bd. Randolph-Macon Acad., Front Royal, Va., 1983—87; advisor Va. Opera Assn., Norfolk, 1988. Home: 708 Cavalier Dr Virginia Beach VA 23451

LEWIS, DOUGLAS, retired art historian; b. Centreville, Miss., Apr. 30, 1938; s. Charles Douglas and Beatrice Fenwick (Stewart) L. BA in History; BA in History of Art, Yale U., 1960, MA, 1963, PhD, 1967; BA in Fine Arts, Clare Coll., Cambridge U., Eng., 1962; MA, Clare Coll., Cambridge (Eng.) U., 1966. Asst. in instrn. Yale U., 1962-64; asst. prof. art Bryn Mawr Coll., 1967-68; vis. lectr. U. Calif., Berkeley, spring 1970, fall 1979; adj. prof. Johns Hopkins U., 1973-77; curator sculpture and decorative arts Nat. Gallery Art, Washington, 1968—2004; dir. rsch. mus svcs. Neal Auction Co., New Orleans, 2005—. Professorial lectr. Georgetown U., 1980-93; adj. prof. U. Md., 1988-91, 93-2003; mem. art adv. coms. Mt. Holyoke Coll. Art Mus., 1978-2003, U. Va. Art Mus., 1995-2005, Lawrenceville Sch.; adv. coun. Humanities West, San Francisco, 1991-98; adv. bd. Centro Palladiano, Vicenza, Italy, Audubon and Rosedown (La.) State Hist. Sites, Natchez Lit. and Cinema Celebration; mem. nat. citizens stamp adv. com. U.S. Postal Svc., 1979-2005, chmn., 2004-05. Author: The Late Baroque Churches of Venice, 1979, The Drawings of Andrea Palladio, 1981, rev. and enlarged edit., 2000, intro. to Renaissance Master Bronzes, 1986. Mem. Am. fellowship com. Belgian-Am. Ednl. Found., 1971—. Recipient Copley medal Nat. Portrait Gallery, 1981; Chester Dale fellow; David E. Finley fellow Nat. Gallery Art, 1964-67; Rome Prize fellow Am. Acad. Rome, 1964-66, Bruce Curatorial fellow Nat. Gallery Art, 1997-98. Mem. Coll. Art Assn. Am., Soc. Archtl. Historians, Nat. Trust Historic Preservation, Manuscript Soc. Clubs: Yale (N.Y.C.); Falcons (Cambridge U.). Episcopalian.

LEWIS, EARL, academic administrator; b. Va. m. Susan Whitlock. BA in History and Psychology magna cum laude, Concordia Coll., Moorhead, Minn., 1978; MA in Am. History, U. Minn., 1981, PhD in History, 1984. Various positions U. Calif., Berkeley, 1984—89; mem. faculty U. Mich., 1989—2004, dir. Ctr. for Afroamerican and African Studies, 1990—93, interim dean Rackham Grad. Sch., 1997—98, dean, vice provost Rackham Grad. Sch., 1998—2004; provost Emory U., Atlanta, 2004—. Chair bd. dirs. Coun. Grad. Schs., 2002. Author: In Their Own Interests: Race, Class and Power in Twentieth-Century Norfolk, 1993; co-author: Love on Trial: An American Scandal in Black and White, 2001, Defending Diversity, 2004; contbr. articles to publs.; co-author: The African American Urban Experience, 2004. Recipient Disting. Achievement award, U. Minn., 2001. Office: Office of Provost Emory Univ Atlanta GA 30322

LEWIS, E(ARL) B(RADLEY), artist, illustrator; b. Phila., Dec. 16, 1956; Student, Temple Univ. Sch. Art League; BFA in Graphic Design & Illustration and Art Edn., Temple Univ., 1979, MFA. Art tchr., freelance artist; now adj.assoc. prof. Univ. of the Arts, Phila. Illustrator: (children's books) Fire on the Mountain, 1994, Down the Road, 1995, Magid Fasts for Ramadan, 1996, Creativity, 1997, The Bat Boy and His Violin, 1998, I Love My Hair!, 1998, The Jazz of Our Street, 1998, Dirt on Their Skirts, 2000, Bippity Bop Barbershop, 2002, Talkin' About Bessie, 2002 (Coretta Scott King award, 2003), Coming On Home Soon, 2004, others. Mem.: Soc. Illustrators, NYC. Office: Illustration Univ of the Arts 320 S Broad St Philadelphia PA 19102 E-mail: eblewis@eticomm.net.

LEWIS, EDDIE, professional soccer player; b. Cerritos, Calif., May 17, 1974; m. Marisol Lewis; 2 children. Attended, UCLA. Defender San Jose Earthquakes, 1996—2000, Fulham FC, England, 2000—02, Preston North End, England, 2002—05, Leeds United, England, 2005—. 69 caps, 8 goals U.S. Nat. Soccer team, 1996—; mem. U.S. World Cup team, 2002, 06. Named to All-Star team, Major League Soccer, 1999. Mailing: US Soccer Fedn 1801 S Prairie Ave Chicago IL 60616

LEWIS, EDWIN REYNOLDS, biomedical engineering educator, academic administrator; b. LA, July 14, 1934; s. Edwin McMurtry and Sally Newman (Reynolds) L.; m. Elizabeth Louise McLean, June 11, 1960; children: Edwin McLean, Sarah Elizabeth. AB in Biol. Sci., Stanford U., 1956, MSEE, 1957, Engr., 1959, PhD in Elec. Engring., 1962. With research staff Librascope div. Gen. Precision Inc., Glendale, Calif., 1961-67; mem. faculty dept. elec. engring. and computer sci. U. Calif., Berkeley, 1967—, dir. bioengring. tng. program, 1969-77, prof. elec. engring. and computer sci., 1971-94, prof. grad. sch., 1994-99, prof. emeritus, 1999—, assoc. dean grad. div., 1977-82, assoc. dean interdisciplinary studies coll. engring., 1988-96. Chair joint program bioengring. U. Calif., Berkeley and San Francisco, 1988-91. Author: Network Models in Population Biology, 1977, (with others) Neural Modeling, 1977, The Vertebrate Inner Ear, 1985, Introduction to Bioengineering, 1996; contbr. articles to profl. jours. Grantee NSF, NASA, 1984, 87, Office Naval Rsch., 1990-93, NIH, 1975-2001; Neurosci. Rsch. Program fellow, 1966, 69; recipient Disting. Tchg. citation U. Calif., 1972, Berkeley citation, 1997; Jacob Javits Neurosci. investigator NIH, 1984-91. Fellow IEEE, Acoustical Soc. Am.; mem. AAAS, Assn. Rsch. in Otolaryngology, Soc. Neurosci., Toastmasters (area lt. gov. 1966-67), Sigma Xi. Office: U Calif Dept Elec Engring & Computer Scis Berkeley CA 94720-1770 Business E-Mail: lewis@eecs.berkeley.edu.

LEWIS, ELEANOR ROBERTS, lawyer; b. Detroit, Jan. 5, 1944; m. Roger Kutnow Lewis, June 24, 1967; 1 child, Kevin Michael. BA, Wellesley Coll., 1965; MA, Harvard U., 1966; JD, Georgetown U., 1974. Bar: DC 1975. Atty. HUD, Washington, 1974-76, asst. gen. counsel, 1979-82; atty. Brownstein Zeidman & Schomer, Washington, 1976-79; chief counsel internat. commerce US Dept. Commerce, Washington, 1982—2006. Author, editor (with others): book Street Law, 1975; contbr. chapters to books, articles to legal and fin. jours. Bd. dirs. Dana Pl. Condominium, Washington. Mem.: ABA, Sr. Execs. Assn., DC Bar Assn. Home: 5034 1/2 Dana Pl NW Washington DC 20016-3441

LEWIS, EMANUEL RAYMOND, historian, psychologist, retired librarian; b. Oakland, Calif., Nov. 30, 1928; s. Jacob A. and Rose Lewis; m. Joan R. Wilson, Feb. 7, 1954; 1 son, Joseph J.; m. Eleanor M. Gamarsh, Aug. 24, 1967. BA, U. Calif., Berkeley, 1951, MA, 1953; PhD, U. Oreg., 1962. Asst. prof. psychology We. Oreg. U., 1961-62, Oreg. State U., 1962-67; project mgr. System Devel. Corp., Falls Church, Va., 1968-69; vis. postdoctoral research asso. in Am. history Smithsonian Instn., Washington, 1969-70; chief historian, dir. rsch. Contract Archeology, Alexandria, Va., 1971-73; libr. US Ho. of Reps., Washington, 1973-95, libr. emeritus, 1995. Author: Seacoast Fortifications of the United States, 1970, 2d edit. 1979, 3d edit. 1993; editor: The Educational Information Center, 1969. Served with M.I. U.S. Army, 1954-56. NIMH research fellow, 1960

LEWIS, EVAN LARSON, urologist; b. Birmingham, Ala., Nov. 28, 1920; s. Robert Ash Lewis and Freeda Larson; m. Bernardine Buck Lewis, Feb. 26, 1994; children: Sharon, Griffith. BA, Howard Coll., Birmingham, Ala., 1942; MD, Johns Hopkins, Balt., 1945. Intern Johns Hopkins Hosp., Balt., 1946; resident urology Walter Reed Med. Ctr., Washington, 1948—52; chief of surgery 21st EVAC Hosp., Pusan, Republic of Korea, 1953; chief of urology Tokyo Gen. Hosp., 1953—60, Letterman Gen. Hosp., San Francisco, 1956—60, Madigan Gen. Hosp., Tacoma; dep. surgeon 8th Army, Seoul; chief of urology Fitsimmons Gen. Hosp., Denver, 1964—69, Walter Reed Gen. Hosp, Washington, 1969—70; occpl. health Rocky Mountain Arsenal, Denver, 1980—85. Contbr. articles to profl. jours. Col. US Army, 1943—73. Fellow: ACS; mem.: AMA, Am. Urological Assn. Achievements include invention of Lewis Stowe forcep. Home: 4043 S Newport Denver CO 80237

LEWIS, EVERETT D., oil industry executive; B in Chem. Engring., Iowa State U.; MBA, U. Hawaii. Sr. v.p. strategic projects Tesoro Corp., San Antonio, 1999—2001, sr. v.p. planning and risk mgmt., 2001—03, sr. v.p. planning and optimization, 2003—04, sr. v.p. corp. strategic planning, 2004, exec. v.p. strategy and asset mgmt. Office: Tesoro Corp 300 Concord Plz San Antonio TX 78216-6999 Office Phone: 210-283-2000.

LEWIS, FELICE FLANERY, retired lawyer, educator; b. Plaquemine, La., Oct. 5, 1920; d. Lowell Baird and E. Elizabeth (Lee) Flanery; m. Francis Russell Lewis, Dec. 22, 1944. BA, U. Wash., 1947; PhD, NYU, 1974; JD, Georgetown U., 1981. Bar: N.Y. 1982. Dean Liberal Arts and Scis. L.I. Univ., Bklyn., 1974-78; assoc. Harry G. English, Bklyn., 1983-85, 91-01; adj. prof. polit. sci. L.I. Univ., Bklyn., 1983—2001; ret., 2001. Author: Literature, Obscenity and Law, 1976; co-editor: Henry Miller, Years of Trial & Triumph, 1962-64, 1978. Home: 28 Whitney Cir Glen Cove NY 11542-1316

LEWIS, FLOYD WALLACE, former electric utility executive; b. Lincoln County, Miss., Sept. 23, 1925; s. Thomas Cassidy and Lizzie (Lofton) L.; m. Jimmie Etoile Slawson, Dec. 27, 1949; children: Floyd Wallace, Gail, Julie, Ann, Carol, Michael Paul. BBA, Tulane U., 1945, LL.B., 1949. Bar: La. 1949. With New Orleans Pub. Service Inc., 1949-62, v.p., chief fin. officer, 1960-62; v.p. Ark. Power & Light Co., Little Rock, 1962-63, sr. v.p., 1963-67; exec. v.p., dir. La. Power & Light Co., New Orleans, 1967-68, pres., 1968-70, chief exec. officer, 1968-71, chmn. bd., 1970-72; pres. Middle South Utilities, Inc., 1970-79, 80-85, chmn. bd., 1979-85, also dir., chief exec. officer, 1972-85. Pres., dir. Middle South Services, Inc., New Orleans, 1970-75, chmn., 1975-85, chief exec. officer, 1972-79; pres., dir. Middle South Energy, Inc., 1974-85; chmn. bd. System Fuels, Inc., 1972-85; dir. New Orleans br. Fed. Res. Bank, 1974-75, chmn., 1975; past dir. Fed. Res. Bank of Atlanta, Breeder Reactor Corp., New Orleans Pub. Service Inc., Ark. Power and Light Co., La. Power & Light Co., Miss. Power and Light Co., U.S. Chamber Commerce; mem. adv. com. Elec. Cos. Advt. Program, 1969-72, chmn., 1970-71; mem. electric utility adv. com. to Fed. Energy Adminstrn., 1975-76; chmn. Edison Electric Inst., 1976-77, mem. exec. com., 1974-78; mem. exec. com. Assn. Edison Illuminating Cos., 1973-80; dir. Electric Power Research Inst., 1977-82, chmn., 1979-81; dir. Am. Nuclear Energy Council, 1982-86; pres. Provident Housing Corp., 1999-2001. Mem. exec. bd. New Orleans area coun. Boy Scouts Am., 1967-80, v.p., 1970-74, pres., 1975-76, mem. regional exec. com., 1968-80; v.p. Com. for a Better La., 1975-76, sr. v.p., 1976-77, pres., 1977-78; bd. dirs. La. World Expn. Inc., 1976-89, chmn., 1980-81, 83-89, pres., 1981-83; chmn. Utility Nuc. Power Oversight Com., 1979-81; vice chmn. campaign United Fund, New Orleans, 1970, chmn., 1971; bd. dirs. New Orleans Symphony Soc., 1974-75, Atomic Indsl. Forum, 1982-86, vice chmn., 1985-86; bd. dirs. Pub. Affairs Rsch. Coun. La.; pres. New Orleans Bapt. Sem. Found., 1973-76, 91-92; trustee La. Coll., 1984-90; New Orleans Baptist Theol. Sem., 1954-62, 1968-78, v.p., 1970-78; bd. adminstrs. Tulane U., 1973-88, bd. visitors, 1968-71; bd. govs. Med. Ctrs., 1969-73, vice chmn., 1969-71; chmn. alumni adv. council Grad. Sch. Bus., 1970-73; bd. dirs. U.S. Com. Energy Awareness, 1982-85, vice-chmn., 1983-84, chmn., 1985; v.p. Internat. House, 1970; trustee Com. Econ. Devel., 1972-87; mem. bd. Ochsner Med. Found., 1976-96, mem. exec. com., 1977-96; 1st chmn. Parents Coun., Furman U.; mem. Parents Coun., Wake Forest U., 1980-81; trustee La. Bapt. Found., 1995-2000, chmn. 1996; chmn. Kaken-Am. Found., 1999-2007. Served to ensign USNR, 1945-46. Recipient Oliver Townsend medal Atomic Indsl. Forum, Outstanding Alumni award Grad. Sch. Bus., 1970, Disting. Alumnus award Tulane U., 1983. Mem. Order of Coif, Beta Gamma Sigma, Omicron Delta Kappa, Beta Theta Pi, Phi Delta Phi. Baptist (deacon).

LEWIS, FRANK LEROY, electrical engineering educator, researcher; b. Wurzburg, Germany, May 11, 1949; s. Frank Leroy and Ruth Evangeline (Shirley) L.; MBA in Elec. Engring. and Physics, Rice U., 1971, MEE, 1971; MS in Aero. Systems, U. West Fla., 1977; PhD in Elec. Engring., Ga. Tech., 1981. asst. prof. elec. engring. Ga. Inst. Tech., Atlanta, 1981-86, assoc. prof. 1986-90, prof., 1990; Moncrief-O'Donnell prof. electrical engring. U. Tex., Arlington, 1990—; cons. Lockheed-Ga., Marietta, 1983-87; cons./lectr. UN Umbrella Project, Warsaw, Poland, 1991. Author: Optimal Control, 1986, 2d edit. 1995; Optimal Estimation, 1986, Aircraft Simulation and Control, 1992, Applied Optimal Control and Estimation, 1992, Robot Control, 1992, Control of Robot Manipulators, 1993, Neural Network Control, 1999, High-Level Feedback Control Using Neurol Nets, 1999; editor Automatica, 1999; mem. editl. bd. Internat. Jour. Intelligent Control and Systems, 1995—, others; contbr. over 120 articles to profl. jours. Lt. USN, 1971-77. NSF grantee, 1982, 86, 88, 90, 92, 94-95, 98; Fulbright scholar, 1988; recipient Terman award Am. Soc. Engring. Edn., 1989, best faper award ARRI, 1992, 93, Excellence in Tchg. award Eta Kappa Nu, 1981. Fellow IEEE (Engr. of Yr. award Ft. Worth sect. 1995, other awards); mem. AAAS, NAE (com. on space sta. 1995—), Control Systems Soc. of IEEE (bd. govs. 1995, Best Paper award Dallas-Ft. Worth chpt. 1994), Sigma Xi (M. Ferst awards 1981, 84, Monie A. Ferst Best Paper award 1990). Achievements include rsch. in intelligent control, robotics, manufacturing, systems engineering, automation. Home: 2015 Hill Country Ct Arlington TX 76012 Home Phone: 817-277-6360.

LEWIS, FRANK RUSSELL, JR., surgeon; b. Willards, Md., Feb. 23, 1941; m. Janet Christensen, 1996. AB in Physics, Princeton U., 1961; MD, U. Md., 1965; postgrad. in med. physics, U. Calif., Berkeley, 1970. Surg. dir. M/SICU San Francisco Gen. Hosp., 1973-80, dir. emergency dept., 1980-83, chief of staff, 1983-85, asst. chief of surgery, 1981-86, chief of surgery, 1986-92; prof. surgery Case We. Res. U., Cleve., 1994—2002; chmn. dept. surgery Henry Ford Hosp., Detroit, 1992—2002; former exec. dir. Am. Bd. Surgery. Fellow: ACS (gov. 1988—93, 1st v.p. 1995—96); mem.: So. Surg. Assn., Shock Soc. (coun. 1978—, pres.), We. Surg. Soc., Ctrl. Surg. Soc., Am. Assn. for Surgery of Trauma (pres. 1999—2002), Am. Surg. Assn. Office: Am Bd Surgery 1617 JFK Blvd Ste 860 Philadelphia PA 19130 Home Phone: 267-514-1125; Office Phone: 215-568-4000. Business E-Mail: flewis@absurgery.org.

LEWIS, GENE EVANS, retired medical equipment company executive; b. Terrell, Tex., May 17, 1928; s. John Evans and Helen Elizabeth (Patterson) L.; m. Sonya Dolishny, Jan. 21, 1950; children: Robert, Melissa. BSEE, Tex. A&M U., 1949. Sales, mktg. and engring. mgr. GE, Schenectady, Dallas, Pittsfield, Holyoke, Lynn, 1950-68, gen. mgr. various bus. Milw., 1970-77; group product mgr. Picker X-Ray, Cleve., 1968-70; pres. sci. instruments div. Am. Optical Corp., Southbridge, Mass., 1977-78, pres. internat. div., 1978-79, pres., 1979—84, Baker Instruments Corp., Allentown, Pa., 1985—88; bd. mem. Novecon Technologies, 1994—99. CEO Sterling Semicondr., Inc., 1996-2001. With Signal Corps U.S. Army, 1949. Mem.: Sea Pines Country Clubc, Calibogue Club. Home: 25 Spartina Cres Hilton Head Island SC 29928-2925 Personal E-mail: gelsl@aol.com.

LEWIS, GEORGE RALPH, consumer goods company executive; b. Burgess, Va., Mar. 7, 1941; s. Spencer Harcum and Edith Pauline (Toulson) L.; m. Lillian Charlotte Glenn, Oct. 11, 1963; children: Tonya, Tracey. BS, Hampton U., 1963; MBA, Iona Coll., 1968. Product analyst Gen. Foods Corp., White Plains, N.Y., 1963-66; fin. analyst W.R. Grace, NYC, 1966-67; corp. analyst Philip Morris Inc., NYC, 1967-69, sr. planning analyst, 1969-70, mgr. fin. rels., 1970-72, mgr. fin. svcs., 1972-73, asst. treas., 1973-75; v.p. fin. and planning, treas. Philip Morris Indsl., Milw., 1975-82; v.p., treas. Philip Morris Cos., Inc., NYC, 1984—; v.p. fin. The Seven Up Co., St. Louis, 1982-84. Bd. dirs. Ctrl. Fidelity Bank, Richmond, Va., Kemper Nat. Ins. Cos., Ceridian Corp.; nat. adv. com. Profl. Golfers' Assn. Am. Trustee Hampton (Va.) U.; bd. dirs. Nat. Urban League, N.Y.C. Recipient Arthur A. Loftus Achievement award in Fin., Iona Coll., 1981, Outstanding Twenty Yr. Alumnus award Hampton U., 1983. Mem. Nat. Corp. Treas. Assn., Nat. Bankers Assn. (corp. adv. bd.), Omega Psi Phi, Sigma Pi Phi.

LEWIS, GERALD JORGENSEN, judge; b. Perth Amboy, NJ, Sept. 9, 1933; s. Norman Francis and Blanche M. (Jorgensen) L.; m. Laura Susan McDonald, Dec. 15, 1973; children by previous marriage: Michael, Marc. AB magna cum laude, Tufts Coll., 1954; JD, Harvard U., 1957. Bar: D.C. 1957, N.J. 1961, Calif. 1962, U.S. Supreme Ct. 1968. Atty. Gen. Atomic, La Jolla, Calif., 1961-63; ptnr. Haskins, Lewis, Nugent & Newnham, San Diego, 1963-77; judge Mcpl. Ct., El Cajon, Calif., 1977-79, Superior Ct., San Diego, 1979-84; assoc. justice Calif. Ct. of Appeal, San Diego, 1984-87; of counsel Lathan & Watkins, 1987-97. Adj. prof. evidence Western State U. Sch. Law, San Diego, 1977-85, exec. bd., 1977-89; faculty San Diego Inn of Ct., 1979—, Am. Inn of Ct., 1984—; bd. dirs. Cardium Therapeutics Inc., Tennenbaum Opportunities Fund V. Cons. editor: California Civil Jury Instructions, 1984. City atty. Del Mar, Calif., 1963-74, Coronado, Calif., 1972-77; counsel Comprehensive Planning Orgn., San Diego, 1972-73; trustee San Diego Mus. Art, 1986-89; bd. dirs. Air Pollution Control Dist., San Diego County, 1972-76. Served to lt. comdr. USNR, 1957-61. Named Trial Judge of Yr., San Diego Trial Lawyers Assn., 1984; recipient Heritage award, Am. Ireland Fund, 2004. Mem. Am. Judicature Soc., Soc. Inns of Ct. in Calif., Confrerie des Chevaliers du Tastevin, Order of St. Hubert (knight comdr.), Friendly Sons of St. Patrick (Irishman of Yr. 2000), The Irisn 50 Aztec Big 50, Bohemian Club, La Jolla Country Club (dir. 1980-83), Prophets, The K Club (County Kildare), Pauma Valley Country Club. Republican. Episcopalian. Home: PO Box 325 Pauma Valley CA 92061 also: 600 W Broadway Ste 1800 San Diego CA 92101-8197 Home Phone: 858-539-2283; Office Phone: 619-238-2843.

LEWIS, GLENN C., lawyer; b. NYC, Oct. 20, 1952; BA in Politics and Pub. Affairs, U. Miami, 1973; JD, George Mason U., 1977. Bar: Va. 1977, U.S. Dist. Ct. (ea. dist.) Va. 1977, U.S. Ct. Appeals (4th cir.) 1977, DC 1978, U.S. Dist. Ct. DC 1978, U.S. Ct. Appeals (DC cir.) 1978, Md. 1999. Prin. The Lewis Law Firm PC, Washington. Moderator Va. Bar Leader's Inst., Richmond, 1997; neutral case evaluator Fairfax Cir. Ct.; spkr. in field. Exec. prodr., host (TV series) Law Weekly, Washington. Mem. task force domestic rels. delay reduction Fairfax Cir. Ct., 1988—90; mem. Adv. Work Group Legis. Implementation Family Ct., Va., 1992; trustee William B. Fitzgeralad Scholarship Fund. Recipient Telly award for Outstanding Ednl. Series, Local Cable TV Industry, 1990, Outstanding Live Cable Talk Show, Nat. Fedn. Local Cable Programmers, 1991. Mem.: Fairfax County Bar Assn. (mem. family law sect. 1988—, bd. dirs. 1991—, mem. budget com. 1994—, mem. child advocacy task force, mem. legis. com. 1994—, pres. 1995—96, others, Pres.'s award for outstanding svc., Exceptional Svc. award 1990), DC Bar (mem. chief judge's task force maintaining ofcl. ct. record 1994—, mem. domestic rels. counsel, mem. family law com., mem. civil litig. com.), Va. Bar Assn. (bd. govs. family law sect. 1989—93, chair family law sect. 1992—93, mem. coun., mem. domestic rels. counsel, pres. 2006—07, Oustanding Achievement award 1990, award of merti 1996, Local Bar Leader of the Yr. award 1997). Office: The Lewis Law Firm PC 805 15th St NW Ste 200 Washington DC 20005 Office Phone: 202-408-0655. Office Fax: 202-408-9826. E-mail: glewis@lewislawfirm.com.*

LEWIS, GORDON GILMER, golf course architect; b. Shawnee, Okla., Sept. 7, 1950; s. Ted Eugene and Janet Garvin (Panner) Lewis; m. Karen Louise McKenzie, June 2, 1973 (div. Dec. 1981); children: Melanie Marie Lewis-Lehr, Katie McKenzie Lewis-Lehr; m. Susette Mamie London, June 11, 1988; children: London Marshall, Sarah June Victoria. B in Landscape Architecture, Kans. State U., 1974. Registered landscape arch., Ala., Kans., Fla. Golf course architect David Gill, St. Charles, Ill., 1974-75; golf course arch. Charles M. Graves Orgn., Atlanta, 1975-78, Gordon G. Lewis, Naples, Fla., 1978—. Prin. works include Meadowbrook Links, Rapid City, S.D. (Top 50 Pub. Courses in U.S.), Hulman Links at Los Creek, Terre Haute, Ind. (Top 50 Pub. Courses in U.S.), Lagoon Pk., Montgomery, Ala. (Top 75 Pub. Courses in U.S.), The Forest, Ft. Myers, Fla., The Vines, Estero, Fla. (One of Top New Courses Golf Digest, 1986), Worthington, Bonita Springs, Fla., Tsai-Hsing, Taipei, Taiwan, others. Republican. Presbyterian. Avocation: golf. Home: 5980 Golden Oaks Ln Naples FL 34119

LEWIS, GUY A., prosecutor; b. Chattanooga, Tennessee; m. Loyda Lewis; 1 child, Rose Marie. BS, U. Tennessee, 1983; Juris Doctor, U. Memphis Sch. of Law, 1986. Law clerk Hon. Thomas E. Scott, U.S. Dist. Ct., Fla., Hon. William Cowen. U.S. Ct. Appeals, Federal Circuit, Washington; prosecutor State's Atty.'s Office, 1988—, first asst.; U.S. atty. so. dist. U.S. Dept. Justice, 2000—02; dir. Exec. Off. for U.S. Atty., 2002—. Co-counsel trial U.S. vs. Gen. Manuel Noreiga, Matthew Block Prosecution; deputy chief Narcotics Section. Office: EOUSA 950 Pennsylvania Ave NW Rm 2616 Washington DC 20530

LEWIS, HENRY RAFALSKY, manufacturing executive; b. Yonkers, NY, Nov. 19, 1925; s. Jasper R. and Freda (Rafalsky) L.; m. Barbara Connolly, June 15, 1957; children: Peter, Susan, Abigail. AB, Harvard U., 1949, MA, 1951, PhD, 1957. Group head Ops. Evaluation Group, Washington, 1955-57; staff electronic rsch. lab. RCA, Princeton, NJ, 1957-66, dir., 1966-70; v.p. R & D Itek Corp., Lexington, Mass., 1970-74; pres. Optel Corp., Princeton, NJ, 1974; sr. v.p. Dennison Mfg. Co., Waltham, Mass., 1974-85, vice-chmn., 1986-91, also bd. dirs.; CEO Celadon Scis. Inc., Boston, 1996-98. Bd. dirs. Dyax Corp., Cambridge, Pericor, Waltham. Contbr. articles to profl. jours. Chmn. investment com. Powers (Mass.) Music Sch., 1978-90; mem. Harvard Grad. Sc. Coun., 1992-95. With U.S. Army, 1944-46. Mem. IEEE, Am. Phys. Soc., Harvard Club, Phi Beta Kappa, Sigma Xi. Home: 975 Memorial Dr # 805 Cambridge MA 02138 Office Phone: 617-576-1498. Personal E-mail: hhrrlewis@aol.com.

LEWIS, HOMER DICK, retired nuclear engineer; b. Covington, Ky., Oct. 4, 1926; s. Homer Dewey and Viola Mabel Lewis; m. Marjorie Louise Hacker; children: Homer Daniel, Holly J., Laurel Marion Williams, Heather Eileen Wheat. BS Metallurgical Engring., U. Cin., 1952; MS Nuclear Engring., U. N.Mex., 1964, MSc Materials Sci., 1971. Lic. profl. engr., N.Mex., 1957. Staff mem. Los Alamos Sci. Lab., N.Mex., 1952—57; lead engr. Boeing Airplane Co., Seattle, 1957—58; staff mem. Los Alamos Sci. Lab./Los Alamos Nat. Lab., 1958—86; lab. assoc./staff mem. Los Alamos Nat. Lab., 1986—94. Sect. leader - enriched uranium casting sect. Los Alamos Sci. Lab., 1953—57, prin. investigator/experimenter measurement of high temperature phys., chem., properties of lmfbr fuels and fuel/clad interactions, 1975—79; lead engr. - manufacturing/welding rsch. Boeing Airplane Co., Seattle, 1957—58; rep. Nat. Task Group for Fast Breeder Reactor Fuels Properties US Dept. of Energy, Los Alamos Nat. Lab., 1977—80; sect. leader nonferrous and enriched uranium melting casting tech. sect. Los Alamos Nat. Lab., 1981—86. Contbr. articles to profl. jours. Instr./ assoc. dir. Los Alamos Ski Sch. at Pajarito Mtn., 1967—71. With USNR, 1944—49, capt. USAF Res., 1952—68. Named to Covington Ky. Ind. Schs. Hall Disting. Alumni, Holmes HS, 2002. Mem.: NRA (life), San Juan Wildlife Fed. (life), Am. Soc. Metals (life), Rocky Mtn. Ski Instrs. Assn., Profl. Ski Instrs. Am. (life), Single Action Shooting Soc. (life), Los Alamos Ski Club (pres. 1962—63), Knights Templar (comdr. 1970—71), Masons (life), Phi Kappa Phi (life). Achievements include patents for powder metallurgy. Personal E-mail: marjlulew@obii.net.

LEWIS, HUEY (HUGH ANTHONY CREGG III), singer, composer, bandleader; b. NYC, July 5, 1951; s. Hugh Anthony II and Magda Cregg; m. Sidney Conroy, 1983; children: Kelly, Austin. Student, Cornell U. Mem. Clover, 1972-77; singer, composer leader Huey Lewis and the News, 1978—. Rec. artist: (with Clover) Clover, 1977, Unavailable, 1977, Love on the Wire, 1977, (with Huey Lewis and the News) Huey Lewis and the News, 1980, Picture This, 1982, Sports, 1983, Fore, 1986, Small World, 1988, Hard at Play, 1991, Best of Huey Lewis and the News, 1992, Four Chords and Several Years Ago, 1994, Time Flies...The Best of Huey Lewis, 1996, Original Gold, 2000; hit singles include Do You Believe in Love?, Workin' for a Living, I Want a New Drug, The Heart of Rock 'n' Roll (Grammy award for Best Music Video 1985), Heart and Soul, Walking on a Thin Line, Hip To Be Square, I Know What I Like, (single from Back to the Future soundtrack) The Power of Love; contbr. (single and video) We Are the World, 1984; (films) Back to the Future, 1985, Short Cuts, 1993, Sphere, 1998, Shadow of Doubt, 1998, Duets, 2000; (TV films) Dead Husbands, 1998, video: Twister: A Ritual Reality, 1994; (Broadway actor) Chicago, 2006. Office: c/o Capitol EMI Records 1750 Vine St Hollywood CA 90028-5209*

LEWIS, HUNTER, investment advisor, writer; b. Dayton, Ohio, Oct. 13, 1947; s. Welbourne Walker and Emily (Spivey) L.; m. Elizabeth Sidamon-Eristoff, July 3, 1993. AB magna cum laude, Harvard U., 1969. Asst. to office of pres. Boston Co., 1970, v.p., 1972-73; prs. Boston Co. Fin. Strategies, Inc., 1971-72; co-founder Cambridge Assocs., Inc., Boston, 1973—. Author: A Question of Values, 1990, many other books; contbr. articles to N.Y. Times, Atlantic Monthly, Washington Post, others mags. and newspapers; author monographs on specialized fin. subjects. Dir. Peabody Sch.; former dir. Worldwide Fund Nature; former mem. pension fin. com. World Bank; former chmn., bd. dirs. Nat. Environ. Trust; former dir., chmn. fin. com. Groton Sch.; former chmn. adv. bd. Dumbarton Oakes affil. of Harvard U.; former chmn. Worldwatch Inst.; former treas., dir. emeritus World Wildlife Fund; former dir. Thomas Jefferson Found., Monticello, Va., Pierpont Morgan Libr., NYC, Rockefeller Bros. Fund; pres. emeritus, dir. Am. Sch. Classical Studies at Athens; chmn. bd. Inst. Edn. Foster Children. With USMC, 1969—70. Mem. Univ. Club (N.Y.C.), Knickerbocker Club (N.Y.C.), Met. Club (Washington).

LEWIS, JACK (CECIL PAUL LEWIS), publishing executive, editor; b. North English, Iowa, Nov. 13, 1924; s. Cecil Howell and Winifred (Warner) L.; children: Dana Claudia, Brandon Paul, Scott Jay, Suzanne Marie. BA, State U. Iowa, 1949. Publicist savs. bonds U.S. Treasury Dept., Des Moines, 1948-49; reporter Santa Ana (Calif.) Register, 1949-50; motion picture writer Monogram Pictures, 1950; reporter Daily Pilot, Costa Mesa, Calif., 1956-57; editor Challenge Pub., North Hollywood, Calif., 1957-60; pres. Gallant/Charger Publs. Inc, Capistrano Beach, Calif., 1960-98; editor, pub. Gun World, 1960-97. Author: (autobiography) White Horse, Black Hat, 2002, 14 novels, 31 other books, 11 TV shows, 8 motion pictures; editor 27 books; contbr. articles to mags. Served to lt. col. USMCR, 1942-46, 50-56, 58, 70. Decorated Bronze Star, Air medal (4), Meritorious Service medal, Navy Commendation medal. Mem. Writers Guild Am., U.S. Marine Corps Combat Corrs. Assn. (pres. 1970-71, 73-74, 80-81, chmn. bd. 1972-78), Sigma Nu, Sigma Delta Chi. Republican. Home: RR 2 Box 4784 Pahoa HI 96778-9779 Personal E-mail: wanderer@hilo.net.

LEWIS, JAMAL, professional football player; b. Atlanta, Aug. 29, 1979; Degree, U. Tenn. Running back Balt. Ravens, 2000—07, Cleve. Browns, 2007—. Named NFL Offensive Player of Yr., 2003; named to Am. Football Conf. Pro-Bowl Team, 2003. Achievements include being a member of Super Bowl XXXV Champion Baltimore Ravens, 2001; setting an NFL record for single game rushing (295 yards), 2003; led NFL in rushing yards (2,066), 2003. Mailing: Cleve Browns 76 Lou Groza Blvd Berea OH 44017*

LEWIS, JAMES BELIVEN, state official; b. Roswell, N.Mex., Nov. 30, 1947; m. Armandie Johnson; children: Terri, James Jr., Shedra, LaRon. BS in Edn., Bishop Coll., 1970; MA in Pub. Adminstrn., U. N.Mex., 1977, BS in Bus. Adminstrn., 1981; chief staff cert., Duke U.; student minority leaders program, U. Va. Chief adminstrn. officer City of Albuquerque; dir., asst. sec. US Dept. Energy; coord., counselor pub. svcs. careers program N.Mex. State Personnel Office, Albuquerque; adminstr. consumer affairs div., investigator white collar crime sect., then dir. purchasing div. Bernalillo County Dist. Atty.'s Office, 1977—83; adminstr., educator U. Albuquerque; county treas. Bernalillo County, 1982-85; state treas. State of N.Mex., 1985-90, 2007—; chief of staff Gov. Bruce King, 1991—94; chief clerk N.Mex. State Corp. Commn., 1995—96; city adminstr. Rio Rancho, 1996; dir. oil, gas, and mineral divsn. N.Mex. Commn. Pub. Lands, 1995. Mem. State Investment Coun., Coun. Govs. (policy advisor); apptd. to U.S. Magistrate Merit Selection Panel, 1994; spkr Washington Area State Rels. Group; invitee Governance Mag. Reinventing Govt. (Va./Calif.). Mem. adv. bd. Victims of Domestic Violence; past chmn. Dem. precincts and ward, Albuquerque; mem. N.Mex. State Bd. of Fin., Edn. Found. Bd., State Investment Coun., Oil and Gas Ad-Hoc Com., NAACP. With U.S. Army, 1970-72. Recipient Toll Fellowship Coun. State Govt., Lexington, Ky. Mem. Nat. State Treas.'s Assn. (v.p.), Western State Treas.'s Assn. (pres.), Western Gov.'s Assn. Staff Coun., Pub. Employees Retirement Assn., Edn. Retirement Assn., Mortgage Fin. Authority, N.Mex. Assn. of Counties (past pres. treas.'s affiliate), Nat. Assn. County Treas. and Fin. Officers (chmn. membership com., bd. dirs.), Am. Soc. for Pub. Adminstrn. (past treas. N.Mex. chpt., pres. 1989), mem. Coun. State Govts. Internat. Com., Coun. Gov. Policy Advisors (Disting. Pub. Svc. award, pres. coun. govt. policy advs. 1994-95, apptd. U.S. magistrate merit selection panel 1994, spkr. Wash. area state rels. group), 1994, Am. GI Forum, Am. Legion, Internat. Alumni Assn. Bishop Coll., Taylor Ranch Neighborhood Assn., Western State Treas.'s Assn. (pres.), Kiwanis, Masons, Omega Psi Phi (life), Alpha Beta Psi. Office: Office of State Treas 2019 Galisteo St Bldg K PO Box 608 Santa Fe NM 87504-0608 Office Phone: 505-955-1120. Office Fax: 505-955-1195.*

LEWIS, JAMES EARL, investor; b. Chgo., Aug. 1, 1939; s. J. Earl and Elsie L. (Danneberg) Lewis; m. Patricia Ann Martin, Jan. 19, 1980. BA, DePauw U., 1961; MBA, U. Chgo., 1966. Analyst Harris Trust & Savs. Bank, Chgo., 1966-68; v.p. Paine, Webber, Jackson & Curtis, Boston, 1968-70; mgr. corp. loan component Gen. Electric Credit Corp., Stamford, Conn., 1971-77; v.p. Rauscher Pierce Refsnes Inc., Dallas, 1978-82; sr. v.p., mgr. corp. fin. dept. First Okla. Bancorp. Inc., Dallas and Oklahoma City, 1982-84; v.p., mgr. corp. fin. group PNC Mcht. Banking Co., Phila., 1984-87; v.p., dir. corp. fin. Ferris & Co., Inc., Washington, 1987-88; v.p. Washington Sq. Capital Markets Inc., Bala Cynwyd, Pa., 1988-90; pres., founder Mid. Atlantic Capital, Wayne, Pa., 1990-94; founder, pres. PFI Fin. LLC, 1993—. Bd. dirs. PFI Fin. LLC, chmn. bd. dirs., 2002—04. With US Army, 1962—64. Mem.: Internat. Factoring Assn. Office: 3650 Winding Way Newtown Square PA 19073 Home: 200 Garden Pl Radnor PA 19087 Office Phone: 610-355-1770. Business E-Mail: jim@pfifinancial.com.

LEWIS, JAMES KEVIN, music educator; s. James and Minnie J. Lewis; m. Margaret Dorothy Heater, July 17, 2004. BA in History, Va. Poly. Inst. and State U., Blacksburg, Va., 1995, BA in Music, 1999. Cert. tchr. Md. Bd. Edn., 2004, Va. Bd. Edn., 2004. Dir. band Orange (Va.) County H.S., 2000—04; dir. band and choral Frederick (Md.) H.S., 2004—. Adj. prof., dir. jazz ensemble Hood Coll., Frederick, 2005—. Mem.: NEA, Md. State Tchrs. Assn., Internat. Assn. Jazz Educators, Md. Choral Dirs. Assn., Md. Band Dirs. Assn., Md. Music Educators Assn., Frederick County Tchrs. ASsn., Music Educators Nat. Conf. Home Phone: 301-668-3059; Office Phone: 240-236-7020.

LEWIS, JAMES LEE, JR., actuary; b. Toungoo, Burma, June 11, 1930; s. James Lee and Lilly (Ryden) L.; m. Tamra Dell Johns, June 30, 1954; children: James Lee III, David Alexander, Stephen John, Susan Kim, Michael Ryden. BA, U. Mich., 1952, MA, 1956. Actuary Lincoln Nat. Life Ins. Co., Ft. Wayne, Ind., 1956-74; sr. v.p. Mutual Security Life Ins. Co., Ft. Wayne, 1974-83; v.p., actuary Montlife Corp., Itaska, Ill., 1983-84; v.p., sr. actuary Covenant Life Ins. Co., Phila., 1984-94; actuary provident Mut. Life Ins. Co., Phila., 1994-96; ret., 1996. Pres. Associated Chs., Ft. Wayne., 1982; chmn. Project Commitment, Ft. Wayne, 1969. With U.S. Army, 1952-54. Fellow: Soc. of Actuaries (com. chmn. 1988—91); mem.: Am. Acad. Actuaries (charter). Baptist. Avocations: racquetball, barbershop singing.

LEWIS, JAMES (JIM) M., lawyer; b. Richmond, Va., Feb. 21, 1946; BA, U. Va., 1968, JD, 1974. Bar: Va. 1974, U.S. Ct. Appeals (4th Cir.), 1975, U.S. Supreme Ct., 1983; cert. specialist, bus. bankruptcy law, Am. Bankruptcy Bd. of Certification. Joined Boothe, Prichard and Dudley (merged with McGuire, Woods, LLP), Va.; ptnr. McGuire, Woods, LLP, Va.; exec. ptnr. Holland & Knight LLP, McLean, Va., 2000—. Gen. counsel 1998 World Congress on Info. Tech., 1996—99, Va. Chamber Orchestra; mem., gen. counsel World Info. Tech. and Svcs. Alliance, 1998—, Internat. Trade Assn. No. Va., 1995—; former mem., panel of bankruptcy trustees U.S. Bankruptcy Ct. (Ea. Dist. Va.), 1983—90; served Internat. Adv. Com., 2000 World Congress on Info. Tech., Taiwan, 2000; mem. steering com. Global Internet Summit, George Mason U., 2000. Exec. bd. advisors to the Nat. Ctr. for Tech. George Mason U. Sch. Law. Lt. USNR, 1968—71. Mem.: Info. Tech. Assn. Am. (mem. legal roundtable, "Yr. 2000 Challenge"), Omicron Delta Kappa. Office: Holland & Knight LLP 1600 Tysons Blvd Ste 700 Mc Lean VA 22102 Office Phone: 703-720-8638. Business E-Mail: james.lewis@hklaw.com.

LEWIS, JASON ALVERT, JR., communications executive; b. Clarksville, Tex., Aug. 17, 1941; s. Jason Allen and Mary (Dinwiddie) L. Student, Stockton Coll., 1959-60, San Jose Jr. Coll., 1962-63. Field engr. telephone tech. Pacific Bell, San Francisco, 1983-84; systems technician AT&T, San Francisco, 1984—. Patentee in field. With U.S. Army, 1964-66. Mem. Internat. Platform Assn., Cousteau Soc., Astron. Soc. Pacific, San Francisco Zool. Soc., Planetary Soc., U.S. Naval Inst. Democrat. Avocations: photography, astronomy. Home: 139 Pecks Ln South San Francisco CA 94080-1744

LEWIS, JEFFREY E., dean, law educator; BA, Duke U., 1966, JD, 1969. Asst. prof. law U. Akron Sch. Law, 1970—72, U. Fla. Coll. Law, 1972—75, assoc. prof., 1975—77, prof., 1977—99, prof. emeritus, 1999—, assoc. dean, 1982—88, dean, 1988—96, dean emeritus, 1996—; dean. prof. law Saint Louis U. Sch. Law, 1999—. Vis. prof. law Escuela Libre de Derecho, 1996, Johann Wolfgang Goethe U., 1997, U. Ala., 1999. Contbr. articles to law jours. Fellow: ABA; mem.: Omicron Delta Kappa, Phi Kappa Phi. Office: St Louis U Sch Law 3700 Linden Blvd Saint Louis MO 63108 E-mail: lewisje@slu.edu.

LEWIS, JERRY (JOSEPH LEVITCH), comedian; b. Newark, Mar. 16, 1926; s. Danny and Rae Levitch; m. Patti Palmer, 1944 (div., 1982); children: Gary, Ron, Scott, Chris, Anthony, Joseph; m. Sandra Pitnick, 1983; 1 child, Danielle Sara. DHL (hon.), Mercy Coll., 1987. Prof. cinema U. So. Calif.; pres. JAS Prodns., Inc., P.J. Prodns., Inc. Began as entertainer with record routine at Catskill (NY) hotel; formed comedy team with Dean Martin, 1946-56, The Martin and Lewis Show, 1949-53, performed at Copa, 1948, 1950, Las Vegas Performances, 1952; performer with Sammy Davis Jr., Playboy Afterdark, 1969; performed as a single, 1956—, The Diamond Jubilee of the Royal Variety Performance, The Palladium, London, 1966 (for Her Majesty Queen Elizabeth The Queen Mother), 1966, (Her Majesty The Queen Elizabeth II), 1969, Olympia, 1976; formed Jerry Lewis Prodns. Inc., prod., dir., writer, star, 1956; films include: How to Smuggle a Hernia Across the Border, 1949 (also dir., writer), My Friend Irma, 1949, My Friend Irma Goes West, 1950, At War with the Army, 1950, That's My Boy, 1950, Sailor Beware, 1951, The Stooge, 1952, Jumping Jacks, 1952, Road to Bali, 1952, The Stooge, 1953, Scared Stiff, 1953, The Caddy, 1953, Money From Home, 1954, Three Ring Circus, 1954, Living it Up, 1954, You're Never Too Young, 1955, Artists and Models, 1955, Pardners, 1956, Hollywood or Bust, 1956, The Delicate Delinquent, 1957(also prodr.), The Sad Sack, 1957, The Geisha Boy, 1958 (also prodr.), Rock-a-bye Baby, 1958 (also prodr.), The Jazz Singer, 1959, Don't Give Up the Ship, 1959, Li'l Abner, 1959, It's a Mad, Mad, Mad, Mad World, 1959, Visit to a Small Planet, 1960, The Bellboy, 1960 (also writer, dir., prodr., co-author), Cinderfella, 1960 (also prodr.), The Ladies Man, 1961(also dir., prodr., co-author), It's Only Money, 1962, The Errand Boy, 1962 (also dir., composer, co-author), The Nutty Professor, 1963(also dir., co-author), Who's Minding The Store, 1963, The Patsy, 1964 (also dir., co-author), The Disorderly Orderly, 1964, Ben Casey, 1964 (also dir., one episode), The Family Jewels, 1965 (also dir., prodr., co-author), Boeing-Boeing, 1965, Three On A Couch (also dir., prodr.), 1966, Way...Way...Out, 1966, The Big Mouth, 1967 (also dir., prodr., co-author), Don't Raise the Bridge, Lower the River, 1968, Hook, Line and Sinker, 1969 (also prodr.), One More Time, 1969 (also dir.), Which Way To the Front?, 1970 (also dir., prodr.), The Day the Clown Cried, 1972 (also dir., co-author), Hardly Working, 1981 (also dir., co-author), King of Comedy, 1983, Smorgasbord, 1983 (also dir., co-author), Cracking Up, 1983 (also dir., writer), Slapstick of Another Kind, 1984, To Catch A Cop, 1984, How Did You Get In?, 1985, Fight for Life, 1987, Cookie, 1989, Boy, 1990 (also writer, dir.), Arrowtooth Waltz, 1991, Arizona Dream, 1991, Mr. Saturday Night, 1992, Funny Bones, 1994, Miss Cast Away, 2004; appeared on Broadway in Damn Yankees, 1995, on nat. tour, 1995-1997, internat. tour., 1997; (TV series) Wiseguy, 1988-89; dir. (TV Series) The Bold Ones: The New Doctors, 1969, Good Grief, 1991, Super Force, 1993; writer, exec. prodr. (films) Nutty Professor, 1996, Nutty Professor II: The Klumps, 2000; writer (TV Series) The Jerry Lewis Show, 1963; author: The Total Film-Maker, 1971, Jerry Lewis in Person, 1982, (with James Kaplan) Dean & Me, 2005; guest appearances include: Toast of the Town, 1948, 1960-62, 1961, What's My Line?, 1954, 1956, 1960-62, 1966, This is Your Life, 1956, Rowan & Martin's Laugh-In, 1968, Saturday Night Live, 1983, Mad About You, 1993, (voice) The Simpsons, 2003, and several famous talk shows 1970-; principal TV appearances include master of ceremonies ann. Labor Day Muscular Dystrophy Telethon, 1966-. Comdr. Order of Arts & Letters, France, 1984; nat. chmn. Muscular Dystrophy Assn. Recipient most promising male star in TV award Motion Picture Daily's 2nd Ann. TV poll, 1950, (as team with Dean Martin), one of TV's top 10 money making stars award Motion Picture Herald - Fame poll, 1951, 53-54, 57, The Number One Top Money Actors, Independent Film Jour., 1953, best comedy team award Motion Picture Daily's 16th annual radio poll, 1951-53, Top Men in the Movies, Look Mag., 1953, Nobel Peace Prize nomination, 1978, French Legion of Honor, 1984, Lifetime Achievement award, Am. Comedy Awards, 1998, Governors award, Creative Arts Primetime Emmy Awards, 2005; Honored by the Eleanor Roosevelt Inst. for Cancer Rsch. Mem.

Screen Producers Guild, Screen Dirs. Guild, Screen Writers Guild. also: William Morris Agy Inc 151 S El Camino Dr Beverly Hills CA 90212-2704 Office: Jerry Lewis Films Inc 2820 W Charleston Blvd Ste D33 Las Vegas NV 89102

LEWIS, JERRY LEE, country-rock singer, musician; b. Ferriday, La., Sept. 29, 1935; s. Elmo and Mary Ethel L.; m. Kerrie Lee; children: Phoebe, Jerry Lee Jr. Student, Waxahachie Bible Inst., Tex. Rock and roll performer, recs. on Sun Records label, Whole Lotta Shakin' Goin' On, 1957, Great Balls of Fire, Mercury/Phonogram, 1963-78, Elektra Records, 1978-81; shifted to country and rock repertoire: recs. include Golden Hits, Odd Man In, Country Class, Roll Over Beethoven, High Heel Sneakers, Jerry Lee Lewis, Southern Roots, Good Rockin' Tonight, Taste of Country, Sunday After Church, Rural Route #1, Drinkin Wine Spo Dee O Dee, Golden Cream of Country, Monsters, Old Tyme Country Music, Rockin with From the Vaults of Sun; appeared in films American Hot Wax, Disc Jockey Jamboree, High School Confidential; albums include Sold Gold, 1986, The Killer Rocks On, 1987, Rocket, 1988, 1992, Killer: The Mercury Years Vol. One, Vol. Two, Vol. Three, 1989, Great Balls of Fire, 1989, Whole Lotta Shakin' Goin' On, 1992, Rockin' My Life Away, 1992, Heartbreak, 1992, All Killer, No Filler: The Anthology, 1993, Young Blood, 1995, Back to Back, 1996, By Invitation Only, 2000. Named to Rock and Roll Hall of Fame, 1986; recipient Lifetime Achievement Grammy Award, 2005. Office: Warner Bros Records 75 Rockefeller Plz New York NY 10019-6908

LEWIS, JERRY M., psychiatrist, educator; b. Utica, NY, Aug. 18, 1924; s. Jerry M. and Margaret (Miller) L.; m. Patsy Ruth Price, Sept. 24, 1949; children: Jerry M., Cynthia Lewis-Reynolds, Nancy Minns, Tom. MD, Southwestern Med. Sch., Dallas, 1951. Diplomate Am. Bd. Psychiatry and Neurology. Staff psychiatrist Timberlawn Psychiat. Hosp., Dallas, 1957-63, chief women's svc., 1963-66, chief adolescent svcs., 1966-70, dir. profl. edn., 1970-79, psychiatrist-in-chief, 1979-88, dir. rsch., 1988-93. Dir. rsch. and tng. Timberlawn Psychiat. Rsch. Found., Dallas, 1967-88, sr. rsch. psychiatrist, 1988—; clin. prof. psychiatry, family practice and cmty. medicine Southwestern Med. Sch.; cons. in psychiatry Baylor U. Med. Ctr., Dallas. Author: No Single Thread, 1976, How's Your Family, 1978, To Be a Therapist, 1979, The Long Struggle, 1983, Swimming Upstream: Teaching Psychotherapy in a Biological Era, 1991, The Monkey-Rope, 1995, Marriage as a Search for Healing: Theory, Assessment & Therapy, 1997, (with John Gossett, Ph.D.) Disarming the Past: How an Intimate Relationship Can Heal Old Wounds, 1999, Reflections on the Good Life: A Psychotherapist Writes to His Grandchildren, 2005, Famous Marriages: What They Can Teach Us, 2006. Served with USN, 1943-45. Fellow Am. Coll. Psychiatrists (pres. 1985), Am. Psychiat. Assn., So. Psychiat. Assn. (pres. 1979); mem. Group for Advancement of Psychiatry (pres. 1987), Benjamin Rush Soc. (pres. 1994-95), AMA, Tex. Med. Assn. Office: PO Box 270789 Dallas TX 75227-0789 Office Phone: 214-275-4001.

LEWIS, JESSE, editor; b. 1955; Joined Wall St. Jour., 1987, nat. copy chief, 1997—2002, global copy chief, 2002—03; dep. mng. dir. Wall St. Jour. Europe, Brussels, 2003—06, mng. dir., 2006—. Office: Wall St Journal Europe Boulevard Brand Whitlock 87 1200 Brussels Belgium Office Phone: 02-741-12-11. Office Fax: 02-732-11-02.

LEWIS, JODI A., secondary school educator, theater educator; b. Mount Vernon, Ill., Aug. 29, 1981; d. Brian L. and Kim Renee (Ashland) Lewis. BA in Theatre, Lindenwood U., St. Charles, Mo., 2004, BA in Performing Arts, 2004, secondary tchg. cert., 2004, M in Theatre, 2006. Cert. secondary tchr. in theatre and speech Mo. Theatre tchr. Parkway North H.S., St. Louis, 2004—. Dir. prodns. Parkway North Repertory, St. Louis, 2004—. Avocations: crafts, films, photography, musical theatre. Office: Parkway North High School 12860 FeeFee Rd Saint Louis MO 63146

LEWIS, JOHANNA MILLER, historian, educator; b. Balt., Jan. 18, 1961; d. Norvell Elliott and Josephine Carlson Miller; m. Michael Harold Lewis, May 19, 1984. AB, Salem Coll., 1983; MA, Wake Forest U., 1985; PhD, Coll. William and Mary, 1991. Asst. prof. history U. Ark., Little Rock, 1991—95, assoc. prof., 1995—2000, prof. history, 2000—, chair history, 2001—05. Dir., chair hist. Ark. Women's History Inst., Little Rock, 2000—05; grad. coord. Ark. Women's History Instr., Little Rock, 2005—; pres. Ctrl. High Mus., Inc., Little Rock, 2002—05. Author: Artisans in the North Carolina Backcountry; co-author: Women of the American South: A Multicultural Reader, Essays on Women and Freedom in Early America; curator (exhibitions) Against Their Will; Japanese Americans in World War II, Arkansas, Undaunted Courage, Proven Loyalty: Japanese American Soldiers in World War II, Women of the Central High Crisis: The Politics of Gender and Desegregation, 'The Finest High School for Negro Boys and Girls': Dunbar High School in Little Rock, 1929-1955 (Cert. Commendation. Am. Assn. State and Local History, 1999), 'All the World is Watching Us': Little Rock and the '57 Crisis (Cert. Commendation. Am. Assn. State and Local History, 2000, Instl. Progress award Ark. Mus. Assn., 2000), Arkansas Fights World War I, 'The Sun Never Sets on the Mighty Jeep': The Jeep During World War II; contbr. articles to profl. jours. Recipient America's Best Tchrs. award, 1996, 1998, 2004, Outstanding Ark. Working Woman for the Achievement of Excellence in Edn., Ark. Bus. & Profl. Women, 2001, Faculty Excellence award in Pub. Svc., U. Ark. at Little Rock, 2004; grantee, Ark. Humanities Coun., 1995, 1996, Little Rock Edn. Commn., 1996, Ark. Natural and Cultural Resources Coun., 2000, 2003, Winthrop Rockefeller Found., 2002—04, 2002; scholar, Coll. of William and Mary, 1985—89; Rsch. fellow, 1990, Archie K. Davis fellow, North Caroliniana Soc., 1991, Rsch. grantee, Ark. Humanities Coun., 2000, 2001, Edn. grantee, Little Rock Edn. Commn., 1996. Mem.: Am. Assn. of State and Local Hist. (Cert. of Merit 2005), Nat. Trust Hist. Preservation, Orgn. Am. Historians, So. Hist. Assn., Phi Alpha Theta. Office: U Ark 2801 S University Little Rock AR 72204-1099 Office Phone: 501-569-3216. Office Fax: 501-569-3059. Business E-Mail: jmlewis@ualr.edu.

LEWIS, JOHN BRUCE, lawyer; b. Poplar Bluff, Mo., Aug. 12, 1947; s. Evan Bruce and Hilda Kathryn (Kassebaum) L.; m. Diane F. Grossman, July 23, 1977; children: Samantha Brooking, Ashley Denning. BA, U. Mo., 1969, JD, 1972; LLM in Labor and Employment Law, Columbia U., 1978; diploma, Nat. Inst. Trial Advocacy, 1982. Bar: Mo. 1972, U.S. Ct. Appeals (8th cir.) 1973, U.S. Dist. Ct. (ea. dist.) Mo. 1974, U.S. Dist. Ct. (no. dist.) Ohio 1979, Ohio 1980, U.S. Ct. Appeals (6th cir.) 1982, U.S. Dist. Ct. (ea. dist.) Mich. 1983, U.S. Ct. Appeals (3d cir.) 1987, U.S. Supreme Ct. 1987, U.S. Dist. Ct. (no. dist.) Calif. 1987, U.S. Ct. Appeals (7th cir.) 1990, U.S. Dist. Ct. (so. dist.) Ohio 2003. Assoc. Millar, Schaefer & Ebling, St. Louis, 1972-77, Squire, Sanders & Dempsey, Cleve., 1979-85; ptnr. Arter & Hadden, Cleve., 1985-2001, Baker & Hostetler, Cleve., 2001—, chair nat. employment and civil rights class action team, 2005—. Lectr. in field. Author: Employment Practices Self-Assessment Guide, 3d edit., 2006; contbr. articles to legal jours. Mem. Cleve. Council on World Affairs. Fellow: Coll. Labor and Employment Lawyers; mem. ABA (sec. labor and employment law, com. EEO law, comm. law forum), Ohio State Bar Assn. (sec. labor and employment law), Cleve. Bar Assn. (sec. labor law), St. Louis Met. Bar Assn., Am. Law Inst., Selden Soc., Ohio C. of C. (employment law com.), William K. Thomas Inn of Ct. (master bencher). Office: Baker & Hostetler LLP 3200 Nat City Ctr 1900 E 9th St Cleveland OH 44114-3485 Office Phone: 216-861-7496. Business E-Mail: jlewis@bakerlaw.com.

LEWIS, JOHN CHRISTOPHER, allergist; b. Boston, Oct. 15, 1950; MD, Loyola U., Maywood, 1982. Asst. prof. medicine Mayo Clinic Coll. Medicine (formerly Mayo Med. Sch.), Scottsdale, Ariz. Office: Mayo Clinic Scottsdale 13400 E Shea Blvd Scottsdale AZ 85259-5499 Home Phone: 480-451-8753; Office Phone: 480-301-8227.

LEWIS, JOHN FRANCIS, lawyer; b. Oberlin, Ohio, Oct. 25, 1932; s. Ben W. and Gertrude D. Lewis; m. Catharine Monroe, June 15, 1957; children: Ben M., Ian A., Catharine G., William H. BA, Amherst Coll., 1955; JD, U. Mich., 1958. Bar: Ohio 1958, U.S. Dist. Ct. (no dist.) Ohio 1959, U.S. Supreme Ct. 1972. Assoc. firm Squire, Sanders & Dempsey, Cleve., 1959—67; ptnr. Squire, Sanders & Dempsey LLP, 1967—2002, mng. ptnr. Cleve. office to sr. coun., 1985—2002, sr. coun., 2002—. Co-author: Baldwin's Ohio School Law, 1980-91, Ohio Collective Bargaining Law, 1983. Hon. life trustee Found. for Sch. Bus. Mgmt., Leadership Cleve., 1977—78; trustee Playhouse Sq. Found., chmn., 1980—85; chair Cleve. Initiative for Edn., 1988—95; chmn. Cleanland Cleve., 1992—95; trustee Ohio Found. Ind. Colls. Case Western Res. U., chmn., 1995—2006; trustee, chmn. Ohio Aerospace Coun., 2001—03; trustee Ohio Aerospace Inst., Inst. for Rsch. on Unlimited Love. Recipient Malcolm Daisley Labor-Mgmt. Rels. award, 1991, Tree of Life award Jewish Nat. Fund, 1993, NCCJ award, 1995, Franklin D. Roosevelt March of Dimes award, 1999, Case Western Reserve U. Presdl. medal, 2001, Goff award The Cleveland Found., 2005. Mem.: ABA, Ohio Coun. Sch. Bd. Attys. (founding chair), Ohio Assn. Sch. Bus. Ofcls. (Marion McGehey Edn. Law award 1996), Edn. Law Assn. (past pres.), Nat. Sch. Bd. Assn., Ohio Bar Assn., Cleve. Bar Assn., Edn. Law Inst., Fifty Club of Cleve. Episcopalian. Home: 2 Bratenahl Pl Ste 7ef Bratenahl OH 44108-1183 Office: Squire Sanders & Dempsey 4900 Key Tower 127 Public Sq Ste 4900 Cleveland OH 44114-1304 Office Phone: 216-479-8553. Personal E-mail: capeoceans@aol.com. Business E-Mail: Jlewis@ssd.com.

LEWIS, JOHN HARDY, JR., lawyer; b. East Orange, NJ, Oct. 31, 1936; s. John Hardy and Sarah (Ripley) L.; m. Mary Ann Spurgeon, June 25, 1960; children: Peter, David, Mark. AB magna cum laude, Princeton U., 1958; JD cum laude, Harvard U., 1961. Bar: Pa. 1962. Assoc. Morgan, Lewis & Bockius, Phila., 1965-69, ptnr., 1969-99, Montgomery McCracken Walker & Rhoads, LLP, Phila., 1999—. Trustee Blair Acad., Blairstown, N.J. Served to maj. USAF, 1962-65. Fellow Am. Coll. Trial Lawyers. Office: Montgomery McCracken Et Al 123 S Broad St Philadelphia PA 19109-1029 Home: 1112 Robin Rd Gladwyne PA 19035 Home Phone: 610-527-4384; Office Phone: 215-772-7596.

LEWIS, JOHN MILTON, cable television company executive; b. Slocomb, Ala., Mar. 29, 1931; s. Phil Truman and Vermell Beatrice (Avery) L.; m. Mary Lee Robledo, June 9, 1951; children: Janet Lee, Lee Michael. Grad. high sch., Panama City, Fla. With Gulf Power Co., Panama City, Fla., 1949-56; self-employed Vehicle Svc. Co., Panama City, 1956-58; dir. Burnup & Sims of Fla., Inc., W. Palm Beach, 1958-70; pres., bd. dirs. Wometco Cable Corp., Miami, Fla., 1970-94; pres., CEO SP1 Holding, Inc., Richardson, Tex., 1988-89; bd. dirs., CEO Spectradyne, Inc., Richardson, 1988-89; pres. Key Capital Group, Inc., Miami, 1995—, St. Joe Comms., Inc., Port St. Joe, Fla., 1996—2000. Bd. dirs. Allied Waste Mgmt., Phoenix; pres. St. Joe Telephone Co., Inc., Port St. Joe, Fla.; cons. in field. Recipient Tower Club award So. TV Assn. Mem. Cable TV Pioneers, Masons. Office: Key Capital Group Inc PO Box 561009 9500 S Dadeland Blvd Ste 603 Miami FL 33156-2848

LEWIS, JOHN PRIOR, economist, educator; b. Albany, NY, Mar. 18, 1921; s. Leon Ray and Grace (Prior) L.; m. June Estelle Ryan, July 12, 1946; children— Betsy Prior, Sally Eastman, Amanda Barnum. Student, St. Andrews U., Scotland, 1939-40; AB, Union Coll., Schenectady, 1941; M.Pub. Adminstrn., Harvard, 1943, PhD in Polit. Economy and Govt, 1950; D.C.L., Union Coll., 1970. Instr., asst. prof. econs. and govt. Union Coll., Schenectady, 1946-50; mem. staff, asst. to chmn. Council Econ. Advisers, Exec. Office of Pres., Washington, 1950-53; cons. UN Korean Reconstrn. Agy., Pusan, Korea, 1953; assoc. prof. Ind. U., 1953-56, prof. bus. econs. and pub. policy, 1956-64, disting. service prof. bus. econs. and pub. policy, 1964, chmn. dept., 1961-63; mem. Council Econ. Advisers, Exec. Office of Pres., Washington, 1963-64; minister-dir. USAID mission to India, 1964-69; dean Woodrow Wilson Sch. Pub. Affairs, 1969-74; prof. econs. and internat. affairs Princeton (N.J.) U., 1969-91, prof. emeritus, 1991—; on leave as chmn. devel. assistance com. OECD, Paris, 1979-81, as DAC chmn. ann. OECD vols. on devel. cooperation, 1979-81; sr. advisor Overseas Devel. Coun., 1981—99. Sr. staff mem. in India Brookings Instn., Washington, 1959-60; mem. UN Com. on Devel. Planning, 1970-83, rapporteur, 1972-78 Author: Business Conditions Analysis, 1959, 2d edit., (with R.C. Turner), 1967, Quiet Crisis in India: Economic Development and American Policy, 1962, (with Ishan Kapur) The World Bank, Multilateral Aid, and the 1970's, 1973, (with V. Kallab) U.S. Foreign Policy and the Third World, 1983, Development Strategies Reconsidered, 1986, Strengthening the Poor, 1988, India's Political Economy, 1995, (with Devesh Kapur and Richard Webb) The World Bank: Its First Half Century, 1997, The Goliath Problem: The Wages of Hegemony, 2004, Development Corporation, 2006. Served to lt. USNR, 1943-46, PTO. Home: 12 Valencia Ct Skillman NJ 08558-2354 Office: Princeton U Woodrow Wilson Sch Princeton NJ 08544-0001

LEWIS, JOHN ROBERT, congressman; b. Troy, Ala., Feb. 21, 1940; m. Lillian Miles, 1968; 1 child, John-Miles. BA in Theology, Am. Bapt. Theol. Sem., Nashville, 1961; BA in Religion & Philosophy, Fisk U., 1963. Mem. City Coun., Atlanta, 1983—86, U.S. Congress from 5th Ga. dist., Washington, 1987—, former chief dep. majority whip; community affairs dir. Nat. Consumer Coop. Bank, 1980—82. Founder, chair Student Non-Violent Coordination Com., 1963—66; assoc. dir. Field Found., 1966—67; dir. Voter Edn. Project, 1970—77; assoc. dir. ACTION, 1977—80; bd. dirs. African Am. Inst., Friends of VISTA, Martin Luther King Jr. Ctr. for Social Change; bd. dirs Nat. Democratic Inst. for Internat. Affairs; bd. dirs. Robert F. Kennedy Meml. Author: Walking With the Wind: A Memoir of the Movement, 1998 (Robert F. Kennedy Book award, 1999). Mem. Martin Luther King Ctr. for Social Change, African Am. Inst., Robert F. Kennedy Meml. Recipient Eleanor Roosevelt award for Human Rights, 1998, Pinnacle award for Lifetime Achievement, ACDelco, 1999, Martin Luther King Jr. Non-Violent Peace Prize, 1999, Raoul Wallenberg medal, U. Mich., 2000, Helen Keller Achievement award for Advocacy, Am. Found. for the Blind, 2001, We the People award, Nat. Constitution Ctr, 2001, John F. Kennedy Profile in Courage Award, 2001, Springarn award, NAACP, 2002, William Mott Jr. Parks Leadership award, Nat. Parks Conservation Assn., 2002, Edwin T. Dahlberg award, Am. Baptist Churches USA, 2003, Allies for Justice award, Nat. Lesbian and Gay Law Assn., 2004, Golden Plate award, Acad. Achievement, 2004, Most Influential Black Americans, Ebony mag., 2006. Mem.: Faith & Politics Inst., Americans for Democratic Action (pres. 1993—95). Democrat. Baptist. Office: US House Reps 343 Cannon 40 B Washington DC 20515-1005 Office Fax: 202-225-0351.*

LEWIS, JOHN WILSON, political science professor; b. King County, Wash., Nov. 16, 1930; s. Albert Lloyd and Clara (Lewis) Seeman; m. Jacquelyn Clark, June 19, 1954; children: Cynthia, Stephen, Amy. Student, Deep Springs Coll., 1947-49; AB with honors, UCLA, 1953, MA, 1958, PhD, 1962; degree (hon.), Morningside Coll., 1969, Lawrence U., 1986, Russian Acad. Sci., 1996. Asst. prof. govt. Cornell U., 1961-64, assoc. prof., 1964-68, asst. prof. govt., 1961-64; prof. polit. sci. Stanford U., 1968-97, William Haas prof. Chinese politics, 1972-97, William Haas prof. emeritus, 1997—, co-dir. arms control and disarmament program, 1971-83, co-dir. NE Asia U.S. Forum on Internat. Policy, 1980-90, co-dir. Ctr. for Internat. Security and Arms Control, 1983-91, sr. fellow, 1991—; dir. Project on Peace and Cooperation in the Asian-Pacific Region, 1990—; coord. Five-Nation Project on Asian Regional Security and Econ. Cooperation, 2001—; chmn. Internat. Strategic Inst., 1983-89; chmn. joint com. on contemporary China Social Sci. Rsch. Coun.-Am. Coun. Learned Socs., 1976-79; mng. dir. Generation Ventures, 1994-99. Former vice chmn. Nat. Com. on U.S.-China Rels.; cons. Senate Select Com. on Intelligence, 1977-81, Los Alamos Nat. Lab., 1987-92, Lawrence Livermore Nat. Lab., 1982-2002, Dept. of Def., 1994-96; mem. Def. Policy Bd., 1994-96; chmn. com. advanced study in China Com. Scholarly Comm. with People's Republic of China, 1979-82; com. on internat. security and arms control Nat. Acad. Scis., 1980-83; organizer first univ. discussion arms control and internat. security matters Chinese People's Inst. Fgn. Affairs, 1978, first academic exch. agreement Dem. People's Repb. of Korea, 1988; negotiator first univ. tng. and exch. agreement People's Rep. of China, 1978; coord. Five-Nation Project on Asian Regional Security and Econ. Devel., 2002-05; co-chmn. Nat. Com. North Korea, 2004. Author: Leadership in Communist China, 1963, Major Doctrines of Communist China, 1964, Policy Networks and the Chinese Policy Process, 1986; co-author: The United States in Vietnam, 1967, Modernization by Design, 1969, China Builds the Bomb, 1988, Uncertain Partners: Stalin, Mao, and the Korean War, 1993, China's Strategic Seapower: The Politics of Force Modernization in the Nuclear Era, 1994, Imagined Enemies: China Prepares for Uncertain War, 2006; editor: The City in Communist China, 1971, Party Leadership and Revolutionary Power in China, 1970, Peasant Rebellion and Communist Revolution in Asia, 1974; contbr.: Congress and Arms Control, 1978, China's Quest for Independence, 1979, others; mem. editl. bd. Chinese Law and Govt., China Quarterly. Served with USN, 1954-57. Recipient Helios award, 2001. Home: 541 San Juan St Stanford CA 94305-8432 Office: Stanford U Encina Hall Stanford CA 94305-6105 Office Phone: 650-723-9627. Business E-Mail: jwlewis@stanford.edu.

LEWIS, JONATHAN JOSEPH, surgical oncologist, molecular biologist, educator, entrepreneur; b. Johannesburg, May 23, 1958; s. Myer Philip and Maisie (Bagg) Lewis; m. Nanci Lynn Vicedomini, May 20, 1990. MB BCH, Witwatersrand U., Johannesburg, 1982; PhD, Yale U., 1990. Registrar in surgery Witwatersrand U. Sch. Medicine, Johannesburg, 1982-87; postdoctoral assoc. Yale U. Sch. Medicine, New Haven, 1987-90, chief resident, surgery, 1990-92; fellow dept. surgery Meml. Sloan-Kettering Cancer Ctr., NYC, 1992-94, attending surgeon, 1994—, asst. mem., 1994-99, assoc. mem., 1999—; chmn., CEO, pres. Ziopharm, NYC, 2004—. Asst. prof. surgery Cornell U. Med. Coll., 1994—99, assoc. prof., 1999—; chief med. officer Antigenics Inc., NYC, 2000—03. Contbr. articles to profl. jours. Recipient Abelheim medal, Med. Coun., 1982, Trubshaw medal, Coll. Surgeons, Johannesburg, 1984, OHSE award, Yale U., 1989, Outstanding Tchr. award, Meml. Sloan-Kettering Cancer Ctr., 1997; Winston fellow, Sloan-Kettering Inst., 1994—95. Fellow: ACS, Royal Coll. Surgeons; mem.: N.Y. Acad. Scis., Soc. Surg. Oncology, Assn. Acad. Surgeons, Am. Soc. Clin. Oncology (Young Investigator award 1994), Am. Assn. Cancer Rsch., Am. Soc. Cell Biology. Jewish. Achievements include research in oncogenes; growth factors; signal transduction; immunotherapy; gene therapy. Office: ZIOPHARM Oncology Inc 1180 Avenue of the Americas 19th Flr New York NY 10036 Home Phone: 203-256-0422.

LEWIS, JUDITH SUSANNA, artist; b. Ithaca, Ohio, Apr. 16, 1940; d. Kenneth William and Mildred Pauline Coates; m. Harry Robert Lewis, Aug. 18, 1967; children: Lucianna Doré, Brishen Marie. BS, Miss. State Coll. for Women, 1962; MS, Ind. U., 1966. Cert. tchr., Miss., Ind. Elem. tchr. Seymour (Ind.) Cmty. Schs., 1963-74. Muralist pub. schs. and bldgs. One-woman shows include Shaker Seed Box Co. Gallery, Mariemont, Ohio, 1991, Bloomington, Ind., 2005, exhibited in group shows at Madison (Ind.) Fine Arts Gallery, 1997, exhibitions include So. Ind. Ctr. Arts, Seymour, 1997, 2002 (Best of Show, 1st place), 2005 (Best of Show, Merit award), Columbia Club, Indpls., 1999, Hilbert Cir. Theatre, 2000, Hoosier Salon, New Harmony, Ind., 2003, 2005 (Merit award, Purchase award), Hoosier Salon-Broad Ripple, Indpls., 2003, Ind. Heritage Arts, 2004 (Merit award), 2005 (Merit award, 2007, Purchase award, 2007), Represented in permanent collections The Honeywell Found., Inc., Wabash, Ind., Lilly Found., Indpls., Ind. U. Found., Evansville Art Mus. Recipient 1st pl. award, Madison Art Club Exhibit, Ind., 1999, 2005, 2006, Best of Show and 1st pl. award, 2002, 1st pl. and Best of Show awards, Brown County Art Gallery Patrons Show, Nashville, Ind., 1998, 1999, Merit award, Hoosier Salon, 2004, Hoosier Soc., 2005. Mem.: Small Painting Soc. of Brown County, Oil Painters of Am., Brown County Art Assn., Southside Art League (Merit award 2000), Ind. Heritage of the Arts (Merit award and Purchase award 2007, Merit award 1999), Plein Air Painters, Hoosier Salon (Merit award and Purchase award 2000, Best Traditional Oil Painting award 2001, Best Oil Painting award, Purchase award 2002), So. Ind. Ctr. for the Arts. Avocations: travel, writing, photography, plays and musicals. Home: 602 N Walnut St Seymour IN 47274-1539

LEWIS, JULIETTE, actress; b. San Fernando Valley, Calif., June 21, 1973; d. Geoffrey L. and Glenis Batley; m. Stephen Berra, Sept. 9, 1999. TV appearances include The Wonder Years, 1987, The Facts of Life, 1988, Dharma & Greg, 2001; TV films include Homefires, 1987, I Married Dora, 1988, Too Young To Die, 1989, A Family For Joe, 1990, My Louisiana Sky (Emmy nominee), Hysterical Blindness, 2002, Chasing Freedom, 2004; films include My Stepmother is an Alien, 1988, Runnin' Kind, 1989, Meet the Hollowheads, 1989, National Lampoons Christmas Vacation, 1989, Cape Fear, 1991 (Academy Award and Golden Globe nomination best supporting actress 1991), Crooked Hearts, 1991, Husbands and Wives, 1992, Kalifornia, 1993, That Night, 1993, What's Eating Gilbert Grape, 1993, Romeo is Bleeding, 1994, Natural Born Killers, 1994, Mixed Nuts, 1994, Strange Days, 1995, The Basketball Diaries, 1995, Audition, 1996, From Dusk Till Dawn, 1996, The Evening Star, 1996, Full Tilt Boogie, 1997, Somegirl, 1998, The 4th Floor, 1999, The Other Sister, 1999, Way of the Gun, 2000, Room to Rent, 2000, Picture Claire, 2001, Gaudi Afternoon, 2001, Armitage: Dual Matrix, 2001, Enough, 2002, Old School, 2003, Cold Creek Manor, 2003, Blueberry, 2004, Starsky & Hutch, 2004, Grilled, 2005, Aurora Borealis, 2005, Daltry Calhoun, 2005, Lightfield's Home Videos, 2006, The Darwin Awards, 2006, Catch and Release, 2006; singer, Juliette Lewis and the Licks, albums include Like a Bolt of Lightning, 2005, You're Speaking My Language, 2005, Four on the Floor, 2006. Involved with Fight for Kids. Office: William Morris Agy care Norman Brokaw 151 S El Camino Dr Beverly Hills CA 90212-2775 Home: 8687 Melrose Ave West Hollywood CA 90069-5701*

LEWIS, KAY, interior designer, consultant; b. Greenbackville, Va., July 11, 1921; d. Charles E. Lewis and Catharine E.B. Sharpley; m. Mano G.G. Eftimiadi, Dec. 20, 1967; 1 child, Peter Gibb Cropper Nemiroff. Diploma, Lycoming Coll., Williamsport, Pa., 1940; BA, Pa. State U., University Park, 1942. Jr. exec. squad Macy, NYC, 1942—44; designer Scott Wilson Indsl. Design Studio, NYC, 1944—47; assoc. stylist Seneca Textile Co., NYC, 1947—48; stylist Elmer P. Scott Co., NYC, 1948—49, Mead and Montague, Linen Guild, Inc., NYC, 1949—53; head textile design dept. Moore Inst. Art., Phila., 1954—60; pres. Kay Lewis Inc., NYC, 1959—79; textile design instr. Arts Students League NY, NYC, 1959—79; dir. design Dalbolt, Inc., NYC, 1962—65; v.p., dir. product and design United Merchants, NYC, 1978—81. Art show judge Art Inst. and Gallery, Salisbury, Md., 1987—, Ea. Shore Art League, Onancock, Va., 1999—; Tiffany, Ford and Fulbright Founds., NYC; spkr. in field. One-woman shows include Ea. Shore Art League, Onancock, Va., 1998, watercolors and oil paintings, Textile Designs and Fabrics, 1944—2003. Recipient Disting. Alumna award, Pa. State U., 1978, Alumna of Yr., Lycoming Coll., 1979. Mem.: Nat. Soc. Daus. of Am. Revolution (2d vice regent 1998—2003, regent ea. shore Va. chpt. 2007—), Colonial Dames 17th Century, Pa. State U. Alumni Assn. Democrat. Home: PO Box 185 Greenbackville VA 23356-0185 Personal E-mail: kaylewis23356@peoplepc.com.

LEWIS, KENNETH D., bank executive; b. Meridian, Miss., Apr. 9, 1947; BS, Ga. State U., 1969. Pres. NCNB Nat. Bank Fla., 1986-88, NCNB Tex., Dallas, NC, 1988-90, Gen. Bank NationsBank, Atlanta, 1991-93, NationsBank Corp., Charlotte, NC, 1993-99; pres., COO Bank Am. Corp. (formerly NationsBank Corp.), Charlotte, NC, 1999—2001; chmn., pres., CEO Bank Am. Corp. (merged with FleetBoston), Charlotte, NC, 2001—04; pres., CEO, chmn. Bank Am. Corp., Charlotte, NC, 2004—. Bd. dir. Health Mgmt. Assocs., Inc. Naples, Fla., 1991-2004, Lowe's Companies, Inc., 2000-2004, Fin. Svcs. Roundtable. Past chmn. bd. United Way Cen. Carolinas Inc., Charlotte; dir. Homeownership Edn. and Counseling Inst.; chmn. bd. trustees Nat. Urban League; chmn. Arts and Sci. Coun., campaign dr., Charlotte, 1998; bd. dirs. Presbyn. Hosp. Found., Charlotte. Named Banker of the Year, Am. Banker, 2002, Top CEO, US Banker, 2002; named one of The World's Most Influential People, TIME mag., 2007. Office: Bank Am Corp Ctr 100 N Tryon St Fl 58 Charlotte NC 28255-0001 Office Phone: 704-386-5666. Office Fax: 704-386-4578.*

LEWIS, KEVIN PAUL, lawyer; BA, Yale U., 1983; JD, Harvard Law Sch., 1986. Bar: Tex. 1986, NY 1988. Ptnr. Vinson & Elkins, Singapore, 1995—98, Houston, 1998—. Chmn. Interfaith Care Ptnrs., Houston, 2001—03; exec. com. mem. Asia Soc. Tex., 2004—; trustee Congregation Beth Israel, 2004—; chmn. Career & Recovery Resources, 1993—94. Named one of Best Lawyers in Am., Woodward, White, Inc., 2005, 2006; recipient Best Energy Lawyers award, Euromoney, 1999, Best Project Fin. Lawyers award, 2000, 2002, 2004, 2006, Best Structured Fin. Lawyers award, 2005, Super Lawyer award, Tex. Lawyer, 2005, 2006. Office: Vinson & Elkins 1001 Fannin St Ste 2300 Houston TX 77002 Office Phone: 713-758-3884.

LEWIS, LAWRENCE M., emergency physician, researcher; s. Alfred David and Pauline Lewis; m. Marlene Tendrich, June 25, 1972; 1 child, Marissa Anne. AA, U. Miami, 1972, MD, 1976. Cert. Am. Bd. Internal Medicine, 1979, Am. Bd. Emergency Medicine, 1985. Internal medicine resident Jewish Hosp. of St. Louis, Wash. U. Med. Ctr., 1976—79; instr. depts. surgery and medicine St. Louis U., Health Scis. Ctr., 1979—81, asst. prof. surgery and medicine, 1981—89, assoc. chief emergency medicine divsn., 1983—85, chief emergency medicine, 1985—94; assoc. prof. emergency medicine Barnes-Jewish Hosp., Wash. U., St. Louis, 1994—. Oral examiner Am. Bd. Emergency Medicine, 1996—; chair rsch. com. Soc. Academic Emergency Medicine, Lansing, Mich., 1998—2000; dir. rsch. emergency medicine divsn. Wash. U., 2002—07; step III item writer US Med. Licensing Exam., 2005—07. Contbr. chapters to books. Editl. bd. Academic Emergency Medicine, Lansing, Mich., Geriatric Emergency Medicine Reports, 1999—; bd. mem. Mo. Coll. of Emergency Physicians, Jefferson City, Mo., 1985—2003; chair continuing edn. com. Mo. Coll. Emergency Physicians, Jefferson City, Mo., 1993—95, chair govt. affairs com., 1994—96, pres., 1997—99. Grantee, Alzheimer's Disease Rsch. Ctr., 2003—04, Found. Edn. and Rsch. in Neurologic Emergencies/Emergency Medicine Found., 2004—05; Biomarkers in Traumatic Brain Injury Rsch. grant, Mo. Coll. Emergency Physicians, 2006. Fellow: Am. Coll. Emergency Physicians (mo. counselor 1992—98); mem.: St. Louis Emergency Physicians Assn. (founder, pres. 1989—95). Achievements include research in traumatic brain injury; abdominal pain in seniors; disparities in healthcare and access to healthcare. Office: Wash Univ 660 S Euclid Ave Saint Louis MO 63110 Home Phone: 341-961-0590. Office Fax: 314-362-0478; Home Fax: 314-362-0478. Business E-Mail: lewisl@msnotes.wustl.edu.

LEWIS, LESLIE JOY, music company executive, consultant; b. Glendale, Calif., May 28, 1968; d. Thomas Reynolds and Linda Lewis. Dir. arts & repertoire RCA Records/BMG, LA, 1991—94; co-founder Grammy Recordings Record Label Nat. Acad. Recording Arts & Scis., 1994—95; dir. and product mgr. artists & repertoire PolyGram Soundtracks, 1995—98; v.p. artists and repertoire A&M Records (now Interscope/Geffen/A&M), 1998—99; v.p. motion picture music Miramax Film Corp., 1999—2000; dir. prodrs. and engrs. wing Nat. Acad. Recording Arts & Scis., 2000—05; owner and pres. Leslie Lewis Consulting, 2006—. Cons. Musicians Inst., 1997, Grammy Concert Series, 1998, Interscope Records, 1998; prodr. albums and cds. Prodr.: (albums) James Bond 18: Tomorrow Never Dies, 1999 (Golden Globe nomination, 1999), Sheryl Crow: The Globe Sessions, 1999 (2 Grammy awards, 1999); assoc. prodr. and coord.: albums The Songs of West Side Story, 1994—95, contbr.: films Scream III, Scary Movie, Boys & Girls, The Titanic, Truth About Cats & Dogs, Tomorrow Never Dies, Mr. Holland's Opus, Romeo & Juliet, Slingblade, Grosse Pointe Blank, Life Soundtrack, City High, Sheryl Crow. Nominee Grammy, Nat. Acad. Recording Arts & Scis., 1995—2006, Latin Grammy, 2001—04. Office Phone: 310-271-1003. E-mail: info@leslielewisconsulting.com.

LEWIS, LINDA KATHRYN, librarian; BA, U. Okla., 1968, MLS, 1969. Reference libr. U. N.Mex., Albuquerque, 1969-88, dir. collection devel., 1988—. Co-author: The Complete Guide to Acquisitions Management, 2003; contbr. chpts. to books, articles to profl. jours. Mem. ALA, N.M. Libr. Assn., N.Am. Serials Interest Group, Assn. Coll. and Rsch. Librs Office: U N Mex MSC 05 3020 Univ Libr Albuquerque NM 87131-0001 Business E-Mail: llewis@unm.edu.

LEWIS, LORRAINE, former federal agency administrator; b. Springfield, Mass., Feb. 25, 1956; d. Richard N. and Janet Claire (Howard) Pratte; m. Jacob M. Lewis, Sept. 28, 1985; 2 children. BA in History magna cum laude, Yale Coll., 1978; JD, Harvard Law Sch., 1981. Bar: D.C., Ill., 1982. Field atty. NLRB, Chgo., 1982-84; assoc. Feder & Edes, Washington, 1984-85; vol. atty. Washington Lawyer's Com. for Civil Rights, 1986; staff asst. Sen. John Glenn, 1986; asst. counsel then counsel and gen. counsel sen. com. on govtl. affairs, 1987-93; gen. counsel Office of Personnel Mgmt., 1993—; with United Mineworkers Funds, Wash., DC. Office: United Mineworkers Funds 2121 K St NW Washington DC 20037 Office Phone: 301-320-9384. Business E-Mail: llewis20817@aol.com.

LEWIS, MARGARET MARY, marketing professional; b. Bridgeport, Conn., Sept. 27, 1959; d. Raymond Phillip and Catherine Helen (Gayda) Palovchak; m. William A. Lewis Jr., Oct. 4, 1980. BS summa cum laude, Sacred Heart U., 1986; postgrad., U. Bridgeport; AS, Katherine Gibbs Sch., 1980. Program mgr. sales svc. group Newspaper Coop. Couponing, Inc., Westport, Conn., 1985-87; sales adminstr. Supermarket Communication Sys., Inc., Norwalk, 1987—88, mgr. mktg. support, 1988—89; asst. project mgr. sales promotion Mktg. Corp. Am., Westport, 1989—91, account exec., 1991—92; mgr. program svcs. Ryan Partnership, 1992—93, sr. program mgr., 1993—95, mng. dir., 1995—96; account dir. Creative Alliance, 1996—97; promotion mktg. cons. CSC Weston Group, Wilton, 1997—98; account dir. TLP Inc., 1998—2000, group account dir., 2000—01; sr. dir. Source Mktg., Westport, 2001—02; mng. dir. Ryan Partnership, Wilton, 2002—04, v.p., 2004—05; exec. v.p., ptnr. Catapult Mktg. subs. D.L. Ryan Cos., Wilton, 2005—. Democrat. Roman Catholic. Home: 16 Nickel Pl Monroe CT 06468-3010 Office: Catapult Mktg 55 Post Rd W Westport CT 06880 E-mail: mlewis@catapultmarketing.com.

LEWIS, MARJORIE, librarian; b. NYC, May 3, 1929; d. Leon Schwartz and Julie Rudomin; m. Philip Lewis; children: Victoria, Laura, David, James. BA, Russell Sage Coll., Troy, NY, 1949; MLS, Rutgers U., New Brunswick, NJ, 1970. Advt. and editl. asst. Fred Kogos Publ., NYC, 1949—51; asst. Nate Fine Advt., NYC, 1949—51; film prodr. CBS-TV, NYC, 1951—55, ARC, NYC, 1956, Compton Advt., NYC, 1956—58; libr. Brookside Sch., Montclair, NJ, 1963—71, Scarsdale Pub. Libr., NY, 1974—76, Scarsdale Jr. High, 1976—94. Co-editor: Waltzing on Water; author: children's books, numerous profl. books, articles, revs. Mem.: ALA, Am. Assn. Mus., Beta Phi Mu. Democrat. Jewish. Avocations: politics, cooking. Home: PO Box 186 Canaan NY 12029 Personal E-mail: marglew68@aol.com.

LEWIS, MARJORIE EHRICH, lawyer; b. Nov. 21, 1954; BA magna cum laude, Tufts U., Mass., 1976; JD, NYU, 1979. Bar: Calif. 1979. Law clk. to Hon. Warren J. Ferguson U.S. Ct. Appeals (9th cir.), 1979-80; joined Gibson, Dunn & Crutcher, 1981—, ptnr. bus. litig. LA, 1988—, now ptnr.-in-charge, LA and Century City offices. Mem. exec. com. Gibson Dunn & Crutcher, 1996—2000, mem. mgmt. com., 1999—2000. Mem. NYU Law Rev., 1977—78. Office: Gibson Dunn & Crutcher 333 S Grand Ave Ste 4400 Los Angeles CA 90071-3197 Office Phone: 213-229-7462. Office Fax: 213-229-6462. Business E-Mail: mlewis@gibsondunn.com.

LEWIS, MARK K., lawyer; b. Bellmore, NY, Aug. 8, 1965; BS magna cum laude, U. Md., 1987; JD magna cum laude, Georgetown U., 1990. Bar: Md. 1990, D.C. 1991. Ptnr., mem. exec. com. & dep. chmn. global projects dept. Baker Botts LLP, Washington. Mem.: Assn. Internat. Petroleum Negotiators, Energy Bar Assn. Office: Baker Botts LLP The Warner 1299 Pennsylvania St NW Washington DC 20004-2400 Office Phone: 202-639-7732. Office Fax: 202-639-7890. Business E-Mail: mark.lewis@bakerbotts.com.

LEWIS, MARK KEVIN, history professor, minister; b. Kountze, Tex., Sept. 29, 1954; s. Mason Audrey and Doris Francis Lewis; m. Debbie Lynn Hohmann, May 29, 1986. BA in History, Angelo State U., San Angelo, Tex., 1976; BA in Bible, Freed-Hardeman U., Henderson, Tenn., 1977; MEd in History, SW Tex. State U., San Marcos, 1990; postgrad., Tex. Tech U., Lubbock, 1994—95. Cert. profl. Microsoft, Calif., 2000, profl., plus Internet Microsoft, Calif., 2000, Microsoft Certified Systems Engineer Microsoft, Calif., 2000, cert. A+ computer Comp TIA, 2000; lic. 3rd Class Radio Operator Tex., 1975. Instr. ESL Shanghai Tchrs. Tech. Coll., 1990—91; instr. history Asian divsn. U. Md., Seoul, Republic of Korea, 1991—93; computer instr. New Horizons Computer Learning Ctr., Bakersfield, Calif., 2000; assoc. faculty history Allan Hancock Coll., Santa Maria, Calif., 2001—; instr. history Bakersfield Coll., Calif., 2004—. Guest lectr. ch. history Four Seas Coll., Singapore, 1998. Staff writer (religious jour.) Contending for the Faith; contbr. chapters to books, articles to profl. jours. Min. Ch. of Christ, Cache, Okla., 1978—79, Visalia, Calif., 1979—83, San Marcos, Tex., 1983—84, Peterborough, England, 1985—86, Banbury, England, 1988—90, Bakersfield, Calif., 1997—2000, Lamont, Calif., 2000—. Named one of Outstanding Young Men Am., US Jaycees, 1982. Mem.: Phi Alpha Theta (life). Office: Allan Hancock College 800 S College Dr Santa Maria CA 93454 Office Phone: 805-922-6966. Personal E-mail: mklewis929@msn.com.

LEWIS, MARTIN EDWARD, transportation executive, oil trader, foreign government concessionary; b. Chgo., Dec. 27, 1958; s. Martin Luther and Anna Adlene (Gaines) L. BA, Johns Hopkins U., 1981; postgrad., Rush Med. Coll., 1983-85. Chmn. bd., chief exec. officer Internat. Financier Inc., Chgo., 1987—; co. rep. Assn. S.E. Asia Nations Secretariat Gen., Jakarta, Indonesia, 1995—. Co. rep. OPEC, Vienna, 1988—, Supreme Coun. States of Cooperation Coun., Summit Confs. Countries of Cooperation Coun. for Arab States of Gulf, Secretariat Gen., Riyadh, Saudi Arabia, 1989—; corp. amb. plenipotentiary GM Overseas Ops., NYC, 1977, Adam Opel, Russelsheim, Fed. Republic Germany, 1977. Mem. Asia Soc., Japan Soc. Republican. Avocations: golf, tennis, yachting, scuba diving. Home Phone: 773-783-0071. Business E-Mail: info@ifiworld.com, ifiworld1@yahoo.com, ifiworldbiz@yahoo.com.

LEWIS, MARTIN R., paper company executive, consultant; b. Feb. 14, 1929; s. William and Ida (Goldman) L.; m. Renee Raines, Aug. 13, 1950 (div.); children: Jeffrey, Wendy, Lisa; m. Diane Carol Brandt, July 4, 1975. BA, NYU, 1949, LLB, 1951; LLM, U. Mich., 1952. CEO Williamhouse-Regency, Inc., NYC, 1955-95; vice-chmn. DIMAC Corp., NYC, 1998-99; owner Martin Lewis Assocs., NYC, 1999—. Cons. in field. Mem. Envelope Mfg. Assn., Paper Club N.Y., N.Y. Jewish. Office Phone: 212-253-6474. Business E-Mail: marty@mlewis.cc.

LEWIS, MARVIN, professional football coach; b. Pittsburgh, Pa, Sept. 23, 1958; m. Peggy Lewis; 2 children. BS physical ed., Idaho State U., 1981, MA athletic admin., 1982. Linebackers coach Idaho State U., 1981—84, Long Beach State U., 1985—86, NM State U., 1987—89, U. of Pittsburgh, 1990—91, Pittsburgh Steelers, 1992—96; defensive coordinator Balt. Ravens, 1996—2002, Wash. Redskins, 2002; head coach Cin. Bengals, 2003—. Achievements include coaching 2000 Super Bowl Champion team, Baltimore Ravens. Office: c/o Cincinnati Bengals 1 Paul Brown Stadium Dr Cincinnati OH 45202

LEWIS, MARY JANE, retired elementary school educator; b. Hot Springs, SD, Dec. 11, 1939; d. LeRoy Allen and Mary Jane (Casey) Y.; m. Robert Melroy Lewis; children: Patrick, Christopher, Timothy, Eric. BS, U. Wyo., 1962, MA in Curriculum and Instrn., 1979. Cert. elem. tchr., reading specialist (kindergarten through twelfth grades). Elem. tchr. 2nd and 3rd grade, Medicine Bow, Wyo., 1962-63; elem. tchr. 3rd and 4th grade Shirley Basin, Wyo., 1964—66; jr. high reading, study skills tchr. Laramie, Wyo., 1967—98; reading dept. head, 1967—98; ret., 2003. Adj. prof. undergrad. studies U. Wyo. Coll. Edn., 1998—2003, student tchr. cons.; presenter, spkr. in field. Sect. vice-chair Albany County Reps., Laramie, 1990-92, sect., 1986-90; mem. Albany County United Way; v.p. Little League Baseball; cub scout leader; chpt. vol. Red Cross Mothers, March of Dimes. State Innovative grant State Dept. Wyo., 1989. Mem. IRA Snowy Range Internat. Reading Assn. (pres.), NRA Nat. Reading Assn., U. Wyo. Alumni Assn. (life), Phi Delta Kappa, Alpha Delta Kappa (chaplain, v.p., co-pres.), Delta Kappa Gamma (sect. v.p.), Alpha Kappa PEO(guard). Episcopalian. Avocations: reading, golf, bridge. Home: 203 Arrowhead Rd Torrington WY 82240

LEWIS, MARY JANE, film producer, film director, scriptwriter; b. Kansas City, Mo., July 22, 1950; d. J.W. Jr. and Hilda (Miller) L. BA, Stephens Coll., Columbia, Mo., 1971; MA, NYU, 1984, PhD, 1996. Office mgr. Crazy Shirts, Inc., Honolulu, 1974-79; creator Exotic Exports, Honolulu, 1979-80; asst. buyer Bloomingdale's, NYC, 1980-82; office mgr., media dir. Andiamo, Inc., NYC, 1982-85; freelance stylist Condé Nast, Inc., NYC, 1985-86; tchg. fellow NYU, 1988-90, adj. prof., 1990-92. Adj. faculty Fashion Inst. Tech., NYC, 1983; lectr. U. Hawaii, creator adult edn. programs and credit classes, 1986—97; lectr. NYU Sch. Cont. Edn., 1991—94; freelance video stylist, asst. prodr. State of Hawaii, Honolulu, 1994—2003; TV prodr. Office of the Mayor, City and County of Honolulu, 1998; video prodr. Olelo Cmty. TV, Honolulu. Author: Careers in Fashion Manual, 1992, (screenplays) The Last Rose of Summer, 1992, (TV movie scripts) The Mustard Seed, 1992 (Maui Writers Conf. Screenwriting Competition award, 1998); prodr., dir., writer, narrator (video) Learning Through Community Service, 1998 (Communicator award, 1998, Videographer award, 1999); prodr.: (live TV show) City Lights, Honolulu City Lights, 1998; prodr., dir., writer (documentary) Sarah Josepha Hale and The Godey Girls, 2000—. Mem. Friends of the Richards Free Libr., Newport, NH; sponsor Women Make Movies. Mem. AAUW, The Fashion Group Internat., Inc., NYU Alumni Assn., Nat. Trust for Historic Preservation, Nat. Women's History Project, Kappa Alpha Theta Alumni (pres. pledge class 1968), Elks Club. Avocations: psychic tarot readings, harpsicord, sailing, gardening, cats. Home: 91-513 B Hapalua St Ewa Beach HI 96706 Home Phone: 808-689-4225; Office Phone: 808-689-4225.

LEWIS, MICHAEL, writer, journalist; b. New Orleans, 1960; m. Tabitha Soren, Oct. 4, 1997; children: Quinn Tallulah, Dixie. BA in Art History, Princeton U.; M in Econ., London Sch. Economics. Former bond salesman Salomon Brothers, London; writer. Contbr. articles The New Republic, NY Times Mag., Bloomberg; author: (non-fiction) Liar's Poker: Rising Through the Wreckage of Wall Street, 1989, The Money Culture, 1992, Trail Fever, 1997, The New New Thing, 1999, Next: The Future Just Happened, 2001, Moneyball: The Art of Winning an Unfair Game, 2003, Coach: Lessons on the Game of Life, 2005, The Blind Side: Evolution of a Game, 2006. Office: Bloomberg 731 Lexington Ave New York NY 10022*

LEWIS, MICHAEL ROBERT, medical researcher, educator; b. Madison, Wis., Sept. 29, 1962; s. Robert Glenn and Sue Ann Lewis; m. Varyanna Chryzhtjanok Ruthengael, Sept. 28, 1991. PhD, City of Hope Grad. Sch. of Biol. Scis., Duarte, Calif., 1994—97. NIH post doc. fellow Wash. U., St. Louis, 1997—2000; asst. prof. U. of Mo. Columbia, 2000—. Study sect. reviewer NIH, Bethesda, Md., 2002—; ad hoc reviewer Bioconjugate Chemistry Internat. Jour. Pharmaceutics, Jour. Nuclear Medicine; mem. bd. dirs. Radiopharmaceutical Scis. Coun. Grantee, Dept. Health and Human Svcs. Nat. Cancer Inst., 2003—, Dept. of Def., 2001—, 2002—, Dept. of Vet. Affairs, 2005—. Mem.: AAAS, Soc. of Radiopharmaceutical Chemistry and Biology, Soc. of Nuc. Medicine (bd. dirs.), Am. Chem. Soc., Alpha Chi Sigma. Office: U MO Columbia 379 E Campus Dr Columbia MO 65211 Business E-Mail: lewismic@missouri.edu.

LEWIS, NED LEHMON, secondary school educator; b. Shreveport, La., June 1, 1953; s. John Whorley and Juanita Choyce Lewis. BS, Fisk U., 1974; MusM, U. Mich., 1976. Instr. Tuskegee (Ala.) U., 1976—79; min. music Mount Gilead Bapt. Ch., Washington, 1979—82; educator Capitol Hill Cluster Schs., Washington, 1982—92, Dunbar H.S., Washington, 1992—96, High Point H.S., Beltsville, Md., 1996—. Nat. choral adjudicator Heritage Music Festival, Va., 2002—, Md., 2002—; cons. Md. State Arts Coun., Balt., 2003—05. Named Outstanding Educator, Prince George's Sch. Sys., Beltsville, 2000, Disting. Faculty Member, High Point H.S., 2005, 2006. Mem.: Am. Choral Dirs. Assn. Avocations: weightlifting, reading, concerts.

LEWIS, NORMAN G., academic administrator, researcher, consultant; b. Irvine, Ayrshire, Scotland, Sept. 16, 1949; came to U.S., 1985; s. William F. and Agnes H. O. L.; m. Christine I. (div. Oct. 1994); children: Fiona, Kathryn; m. Laurence Beatrice Davin, July 1997; 1 child, Sebastien. BSc in Chemistry with honors, U. Strathclyde, Scotland, 1973; PhD in Chemistry 1st class, U. B.C., 1977. NRC postdoctoral fellow U. Cambridge, Eng., 1978-80; rsch. assoc. chemistry dept. Nat. Rsch. Coun., Can., 1980; asst. scientist fundamental rsch. divsn. Pulp and Paper Rsch. Inst. Can., Montreal, 1980-82, group leader chemistry and biochemistry of woody plants, grad. rsch. chemistry divsn., 1982-85; assoc. prof. wood sci. and biochemistry Va. Poly. Inst. and State U., Blacksburg, 1985-90; dir. Inst. Biol. Chemistry, Wash. State U., Pullman, 1990—; Eisig-Tode disting. prof. Wash. State U., Pullman. Cons. NASA, DOE, USDA, NIH, NSF, Am. Inst. Biol. Sci., other industries, 1985—; mem. sci. adv. bd. Ctr. for Marine Sci., U. NC, 2004—, Thad Cochran Nat. Ctr. for Natural Products Rsch., U. Miss., Oxford, 2003—, Donald Danforth Plant Sci. Ctr., St. Louis, 2002—. Mem. editl. bd. Holzforschung, 1986, TAPPI, 1986, 89, Jour. Wood Chemistry and Tech., 1987, Polyphenols Actualities, 1992—; mem. editl. bd. Wood Sci. and Tech., 2001-, The Ams., Asia regional editor Phytochemistry, 1992—; exec. editor Advances in Plant Biochemistry and Molecular Biology, 2007-; monitoring editor Plant Physiology, 2005-; author or co-author more than 200 publs., books, articles to profl. jours. Hon. mem. Russian Assn. Space and Mankind. Recipient ICI Merit awards Imperial Chem. Industries, 1968-69, 69-70, 70-71, 71-72, ICI scholar, 1971-73, Chemistry awards Kilmarnock Coll., 1969-70, 70-71; NATO/SRC scholar U. B.C., 1974-77; named Local Hero, Prestwick Acad., Ayrshire, Scotland. Mem. TAPPI, Am. Chem. Soc. (at-large cellulose divsn., organizer symposia, programme subcom. cellulose, paper and textile divsn. 1987-90, editl. bd.), Am. Soc. Plant Biologists, Am. Soc. Gravitational and Space Biology (pres. 1998-99), Phytochem. Soc. N.A. (phytochem. bank com. 1989—, pres. 2006—), Chem. Inst. Can. (treas. Montreal divsn. 1982-84, Am. Inst. Chemists and Chem. Inst. Can. Montreal conf. 1982-84), Can. Pulp and Paper Assn., Societe de Groupe Polyphenole, Gordon Rsch. Conf. (vice-chmn. renewable resources com. 1993). Presbyterian. Achievements include numerous patents in field; consultant on a project on bioprospecting in Brazil (funded by FAPESP), which has goals of bioassay-guided fractionation, as well as studying biosynthetic pathways and ecological interactions. Home: 1710 NE Upper Dr Pullman WA 99163-4624 Office: Washington State U Inst Biol Chemistry Clark Hall Pullman WA 99164-6340 Office Phone: 509-335-8382. Office Fax: 509-335-8206. Business E-Mail: lewisn@wsu.edu.

LEWIS, ORME, JR., real estate company executive, land use adviser; b. Phoenix, Apr. 26, 1935; s. Orme and Barbara (Smith) L.; m. Elizabeth Bruening, Oct. 17, 1964; children: Joseph Orme, Elizabeth Blaise Hazelblood. BS, U. Ariz., Tucson, 1958. Assoc. Coldwell Banker, Phoenix, 1959-64; v.p. Braggiotti Constrn., Phoenix, 1964-65; pvt. practice investment brokerage Phoenix, 1966-69; dep. asst. sec. Dept. Interior, Washington, 1969-73; dir. devel. Ariz. Biltmore Estates, 1973—76; exec. World Resources Co., Phoenix and McLean, Va., 1978-91; mng. mem. Applewhite Laflin & Lewis, Phoenix, 1979-96; gen. ptnr. Equity Interests, Phoenix, 1982—; mng. dir. Select Investments, Phoenix, 1996—. Co-chmn. U.S. Adv. Com. on Mining and Mineral Rsch., Washington, 1982-94; mem. U.S. Emergency Minerals Adminstrn., 1987-01, Gov.'s Regulatory Rev. Coun., 1992-95, State Plant Site Transmission Line Com., Phoenix, 1974-85; co-chmn. Biomed. Rsch. Commn., 1995-2002; adv. bd. U.S. Minerals Mgmt. Svcs., 2002—. Mem. Ariz. Senate, 1966-70 (chmn. Phoenix Children's Hosp., 1981—; mem. bds. Boyce Thompson Arboretum, 1999—); mem. governing bd. Polycystic Kidney Disease Found., Kansas City, Mo., 1983-2002, Ariz. Cmty. Found., 1986-91, Ariz. Parks and Conservation Coun., 1985-96, Ariz. State U. Found., Tempe, 1981-2006, Ariz. Hist. Found., 1984—, Desert Bot. Garden, 1987-89, Men's Art Coun., 1962-. Recipient Dept. Interior Conservation Svc. award, 1996; inductee Wisdom Hall of Fame, 1997. Mem. Ariz. C. of C. (dir. 1990-96), Met. Club (Washington), Ariz. Valley Field Riding and Polo Club, Paradise Valley Country Club (Scottsdale), Rotary. Republican. Home: 4325 E Palo Verde Dr Phoenix AZ 85018-1127 Office: Select Investments LLC 5070 N 40th St Ste 140 Phoenix AZ 85018-2193 Office Phone: 602-952-8800. Personal E-mail: adviser_az@msn.com.

LEWIS, PATRICIA MOHATT (PATTY), special education educator; children: Christopher Brian, Ginger Louise, Katie Elizabeth Smolen, David Patrick. BS, U. Okla., Norman, 1965. Prin., tchr. Holy Family Cathedral Sch. Diocese Okla., Tulsa, 1995—99; coord. student svcs. Oral Roberts U., Tulsa, 1999—2001; tchr. spl. edn. inclusion Tulsa Pub. Schs., 2001—. Named Tchr. of Yr., Chester W. Nimitz Mid. Sch., 2002—03; recipient Customer Svc. award, Oral Roberts U., 2000, Diligent Svc. Faculty award, 2001. Mem. Rhema Bible Ch. Office: Tulsa Public Schools 3331 E 56th Street Tulsa OK 74105 Home Phone: 918-951-3209.

LEWIS, PERRY JOSHUA, investment banker; b. San Antonio, Feb. 11, 1938; s. Perry Joshua and Zelime L. L.; m. Memrie Taylor Mosier, May 12, 1962 (div. 1994); children— Perry Joshua, IV, Memrie Fraser; m. Basha Szymanska, May 15, 1997. BA, Princeton U., NJ, 1959. Registered rep.

Lee Higginson Corp., NYC, 1960-63; comml. project mgr. Parsons & Whittemore, Inc., NYC, 1964-67; sr. v.p., mgr. corp. fin. div. Smith Barney, Harris Upham & Co. Inc., NYC, 1967-79; pres. MacKay-Lewis Inc., NYC, 1980-81; ptnr. Morgan Lewis Githens & Ahn, Conn., 1982—2004; sr. mng. dir. Heartland Indsl. Ptnrs., Greenwich, Conn., 2000—01, 2006—; adv. dir. CRT Capital Group LLC, Stamford, Conn., 2002—06. Bd. dirs. Clear Channel Comm., Inc., San Antonio, Superior Essex Inc., Atlanta, Springs Global Participacoes, S.A., Sao Paulo, Brazil, Springs Industries, Inc., Middleton, Wis., Gangagen Inc., Ottawa, Can. With U.S. Army, 1959-60, 61-62. Mem.: Knickerbocker of NY. Business E-Mail: perryjlewis@yahoo.com.

LEWIS, PETER BENJAMIN, insurance company executive; b. Cleve., Nov. 11, 1933; s. Joseph M. and Helen (Rosenfeld) Lewis; children: Ivy, Jonathan, Adam. AB, Princeton U., NJ, 1955. Underwriting trainee Progressive Ins. Cos., 1955; exec. trainee Progressive Casualty Ins. Co., pres., CEO, 1965-94, The Progressive Corp., Ohio, 1965-2000, chmn. bd., 2000—. Served on bd. trustees Solomon R. Guggenheim Mus. Named one of Top 200 Collectors, ARTnews Mag., 2004, Forbes' Richest Ams., 2006. Achievements include a contribution to Princeton University, which allowed the university to establish a science library and the Lewis-Sigler Institute for Integrative Genomics; one of the most significant benefactors in all of Princeton University's history in 2006, recent contribution will allow for the expansion of the creative & performing arts program. Avocation: Collector of Contemporary art including Am. conceptualism. Office: Progressive Corp 6300 Wilson Mills Rd Cleveland OH 44143-2109 Office Phone: 440-461-5000. E-mail: peter_lewis@progressive.com.*

LEWIS, PETER CUSHMAN, electric company executive; b. Cleve., June 9, 1934; s. Dudley C. and Elizabeth (Seymour) L.; m. Mary Louise Earthrowl, Dec. 22, 1956; children: Peter Cushman, Kimberly, Geoffrey Seymour. Student, Deerfield Acad., 1950-52; BA, Williams Coll., 1956; LL.B., U. Va., 1962. Bar: Hawaii 1962. Practice in, Honolulu, 1962-68; dep. atty. gen. State of Hawaii, 1962-68; asst. sec. Hawaiian Electric Co., Honolulu, 1968, sec., 1968-86, asst. treas., 1971-74, treas., 1974-75, asst. v.p., 1975-77, v.p., adminstrn. sec., 1977-86, v.p. adminstrn., 1986—99, v.p. adminstrn., corp. sec., 1999—. Per diem dist. judge, Honolulu, 1970-94; dir. Honolulu Fed. Savs. & Loan Assn., Constl. Conv. Hawaii, 1968, del., 1978. Served to 1st lt. USAF, 1956-59. Mem. ABA (past mem. exec. council young lawyers sect.), Hawaii Bar Assn. (sec. young lawyers sect., past pres., v.p. adminstrn. 1986—), Am., Hawaii Econ. Assn., Hawaiian Employment Council, Delta Kappa Epsilon, Phi Alpha Delta. Clubs: Hawaii Big Game Fishing (past pres.), Pacific. Democrat. Home: 3929 Old Pali Rd Honolulu HI 96817-1001 Office: Hawaiian Electric Industries Inc PO Box 730 Honolulu HI 96808-0730

LEWIS, PRUDENCE FOX, Christian science practitioner; b. Wilkensburg, Pa., Apr. 9, 1943; d. Clarence Cole and Mildred Charlotte Ives. BA, Principia Coll., Elsah, Ill., 1965. Internat. negotiator NOAA, Washington, 1967—99; Christian Sci. practitioner Alexandria, Va., 2004—. Sunday sch. tchr. Christian Sci. Ch., Fairfax, Va., 1978—2007. Recipient Bronze medal, U.S. Dept. of Commerce, 1999. Mem.: Principia Club (sec. 1995—2007, chair jointly maintained Christian sci. reading rm. 2007). Christian Science. Achievements include aided in concluding agreements on international trade in endangered species, whale conservation through the Internationl Whaling Commission; elimination of foreign fishing in the U.S. 200 mile zone; conservation of fish and marine species and trade measures for conservation objectives. Home: 203 Yoakum Pky #1125 Alexandria VA 22304 Office: Christian Sci Practitioner 1050 17th St NW Washington DC 20036 Office Phone: 703-370-0029. Personal E-mail: pruelewis@aol.com.

LEWIS, R. FRED, state supreme court justice; b. Beckley, W.Va., Dec. 14, 1947; m. Judith Lewis, 1969; children: Elle, Lindsay. Grad. cum laude, Fla. So. Coll., 1969; JD cum laude, U. Miami, 1972; grad., U.S. Army A.G. Sch.; PhD in Public Service (hon.), Fla. So. Coll., 2000; LLD (hon.), St. Thomas U., 2002. Pvt. practice, Miami; justice Fla. Supreme Ct., 1998—, chief justice, 2006—. Mem. Fla. Commn. on Legal Needs of Children; active in Justice Teaching Inst.; liaison Fla. Bd. of Bar Examiners, Judicial Management Council; mem. Fla. Supreme Ct. Com. on Rules of Civil Procedure, Fla. Supreme Ct. Com. on Standard Civil Jury Instructions, Fla. Supreme Ct. Code & Rules of Evidence Com. Contbr. pubs. Continuing Edn. Legal Program. Bd. dirs. Miami Children's Hosp.; inventory atty. The Fla. Bar. Recipient Friends of Justice award ABOTA, 1999, Jud. Pub. Trust and Confidence award FLREA, 2001, Citizen Yr. award, Fla., 2001, Everyday Hero award for outstanding contbn. to cmty. svc. in Fla., Justice R. Fred Lewis award U. Ctrl. Fla., 2002, Great Am. Law in Edn. award, 2005, Guardian of the Constitution award, 2006, Ed. for Democracy award, 2006, Judge Wilke Ferguson award for protector of disabled Easter Seals, 2005-06, Guardian of the Constitution Citizenship award for Law-Related Edn., Equal Opportunities in Jud. award 2007, Edn. for Justice award, 2007, Justice Thurgood Marshall award, 2007, others; named Fla. Jurist of Yr., Fla. ABOTA, 2007; grantee NCAA, 1969. Mem. Omicron Delta Kappa, Psi Chi, Sigma Alpha Epsilon. Address: Fla Supreme Ct 500 S Duval St Tallahassee FL 32399-6556 Office Phone: 850-488-0007. E-mail: supremecourt@mail.flcourts.org.

LEWIS, RANDALL J., healthcare insurance company executive; BS in Acctg., Purdue U., MBA; grad., GE fin. mgmt. prog., Northwestern U. Kellogg Sch. Mgmt. exec. devel. prog., Inst. Mgmt. Devel. bus. mgmt. course. Various fin. and ops. roles GE; mng. dir. corp. devel. Wells Fargo and Co., exec. v.p., chief auditor; sr. v.p. internal audit, process improvement, chief compliance officer Anthem, Inc., 2003—04; sr. v.p. internal audit and chief compliance officer WellPoint, Inc. Bd. dirs. Purdue Alumni Assn., Ind. Repertory Theatre, Legacy Fund. Mem.: Blue Cross Blue Shield Assn. (audit com. mem.), Indpls. C. of C. (bd. dirs.). Office: WellPoint Inc 120 Monument Cir Indianapolis IN 46204

LEWIS, RANDOLPH VANCE, molecular biologist, researcher; b. Powell, Wyo., Apr. 8, 1950; s. William (Jack) Fredrick and Evelyn Jean (Vonburg) L.; m. Lorrie Dale Emery, May 27, 1972; children: Brian, Daryl (dec.), Karren. BS in Chemistry, Calif. Inst. Tech., 1972; MS in Chemistry, U. Calif., San Diego, 1974; PhD in Chemistry, U. Calif., 1978. Postdoctoral fellow Roche Inst. Molecular Biology, Nutley, N.J., 1978-80; asst. prof. molecular biology U. Wyo., Laramie, 1980-84, assoc. prof., 1984-89, head dept., 1986-91, prof., 1989—; dir. NSF EPSCOR Program, 1990—. Cons. NIH, Bethesda, Md., 1985—91, Hoffman-LaRoche, Nutley, NJ, 1990—93, DuPont, Wilmington, Del., 1990—94, Protein Polymer Techs., San Diego, 1988—94, Nexia, 1999—; pres. Wyobigen, Laramie, Wyo., 1994—; bd. dirs. Wyo. Bus. Devel. Ctr. Author chpts. to books; contbr. articles to profl. jours. Mem. Jr. Livestock Sale Com., Laramie, 1991-98; pres. Albany County 4-H Coun., Laramie, 1994-98. Sloan Found. fellow, 1985; recipient Research Career Devel. award NIH, 1985, Jr. Faculty award Am. Cancer Soc., 1985, Burlington-North Faculty award U. Wyo., 1986. Mem. Am. Chem. Soc., Am. Soc. Biochemists and Molecular Biologists, N.Y. Acad. Scis., Protein Soc. Republican. Baptist. Achievements include discovery of opioid peptide precursor; sequencing of first spider silk protein genes; five product licenses; 4 patents. Home: 1948 Howe Rd Laramie WY 82070-6889 Office: U Wyo 1000 E University Dept 3944 Laramie WY 82071-3944 Office Phone: 307-766-2147. Business E-Mail: silk@uwyo.edu.

LEWIS, RASHARD QUOVON, professional basketball player; b. Pineville, La., Aug. 8, 1979; Forward Seattle SuperSonics, 1998—2007, Orlando Magic, Fla., 2007—. Named Player of Yr., Parade mag., 1998; named to All-USA First Team, USA Today, 1998, Western Conf. All-Star Team, NBA, 2005. Mailing: Orlando Magic 8701 Maitland Summit Blvd Orlando FL 32810*

LEWIS, RAY, professional football player; b. May 15, 1975; children: Ray Anthony Lewis, Jr., Rayshad, Dymond Deseree. Degree in arts and scis. Profl. football player Balt. Ravens, 1996—. Vol. charitable orgns. Named NFL Defensive Player of the Yr., 2000, 2003, Super Bowl XXV MVP, 2000; named to NFL Pro-Bowl, 1998—2000, 2003—04. Achievements include being the second player in NFL history to win both NFL Defensive MVP and Super Bowl MVP; being a member of Super Bowl XXXV Champion Balt. Ravens, 2000; leading NFL in defensive tackles (210), 1997. Avocations: fishing, camping, swimming, basketball. Office: Balt Ravens Ravens Stadium 1101 Russell St Baltimore MD 21230 E-mail: inquiries@baltimoreravens.com.*

LEWIS, RICHARD B., manufacturing and logistics executive; b. London, Nov. 18, 1957; m. Mary Echizenya Mitchell; children: Sabrina Nichol Mitchell, Edward Alger Mitchell, Jason Richard, Jarod Simon. BA in Econs., U. Mass., 1979. Material planning supr. Sunstrand Inc., Phoenix, 1984—93; prodn. control mgr. Celwave Inc., Phoenix, 1993—95; mfg. and ops. mgr. Acme Inc., Tempe, Ariz., 1995—96; v.p. mfg. and logistics AeroVironment, Inc., Simi Valley, Calif., 1996—. Mem.: Am. Production and Inventory Control Soc., Assn. Mfg. Excellence (assoc.). Avocations: soccer, travel. Home: 4808 Beaumont St Simi Valley CA 93063 Office: AeroVironment Inc 900 Enchanted Way Simi Valley CA 93063 Home Phone: 805-584-3442; Office Phone: 805-581-2187. Personal E-mail: skystone@earthlink.net. E-mail: lewis@aerovironment.com.

LEWIS, RICHARD M., lawyer; b. Gallipolis, Ohio, Dec. 11, 1957; s. Denver E. and Mary Esther (Mobley) L. BA in Polit. Sci., Ohio State U., 1979; JD, Capital U., 1982. Bar: Ohio 1982, U.S. Dist. Ct. (so. dist.) Ohio 1984, U.S. Supreme Ct. 1986, U.S. Ct. Appeals (6th cir.) 1999; cert. civil trial advocacy Nat. Bd. Trial Advocacy. Pvt. practice law, 1982-83; assoc. Mary Bone Kunze, Jackson, Ohio, 1983-85; pvt. practice Jackson, 1985-86, 2000—; ptnr. Ochsenbein, Cole & Lewis, Jackson, 1986-96, Cole & Lewis, Jackson, 1996-2000. Lectr. in field; expert witness; appt. to Ohio Sup. Ct. Commn. Cert. of Attys. as Specialists, 2002-06. Named one of Ohio's Super Lawyers, Law and Politics, 2006, 2007. Mem. ABA, ATLA, Ohio State Bar Assn. (com. Ind. Judicracy and Unjust Criticism of Judges, 2001—), Jackson County Bar Assn. (past pres.), Ohio Acad. Trial Lawyers (trustee 1993—, budget com. 1993-94, Supreme Ct. screening com. 1994, 2004, vice-chair family law com. 1994-95, chair family law com. 1995-96, exec. com., chair mem. com. 1996-97, co-chair regional CLE seminars 1997, chair ADOPT task force 1998, co-editor Book of Complaints 2002, co-editor Book of Motions 2004, co-chair consumer law sect. 2006-07). Home: 603 Reservoir Rd Jackson OH 45640-8714 Office: The Law Firm of Richard M Lewis 295 Pearl St Jackson OH 45640-1748 Office Phone: 740-286-0071.

LEWIS, RICHARD PHELPS, cardiologist, educator; b. Portland, Oreg., Oct. 26, 1936; s. Howard Phelps and Wava Irene (Brown) L.; m. Penny A. Brown, Oct. 12, 1982; children: Richard Phelps, Heather Brown. BA, Yale U., 1957; MD, U. Oreg., 1961. Intern Peter Bent Brigham Hosp., Boston, 1961-62, resident, 1962-63; Howard Irwin fellow in cardiology U. Oreg., Portland, 1963-65; sr. resident Stanford U., 1965-66, instr. dept. medicine, 1968-69; asst. chief cardiology Madigan Gen. Hosp., Tacoma, 1966-68; asst. prof. medicine div. cardiology Ohio State U., 1969-71, assoc. prof., 1971-75, prof., 1975-2000, dir. Divsn. Cardiology, 1972-86, dir., 1972-86, assoc. chmn. for hosp. and clin. affairs, 1980-86, prof. emeritus, 2000—. Mem. cardiovascular sect. Am. Bd. Internal Medicine, 1981-87, critical care medicine, 1988-92. Contbr. articles to profl. jours. Served with M.C. U.S. Army, 1966-68, col. res. Decorated Army Commendation medal Master Am. Coll. Cardiology (Ohio gov. 1988-91, chmn. bd. govs. 1990-91, trustee 1991-2000, editor self assessment program ACCSAP, 1991-96, 2000—, v.p. 1994-95, pres.-elect 1995-96, pres. 1996-97); fellow ACP (gov. Ohio chpt. 1976-80, chmn. MKSAP cardiovascular sect. 1989-82, master tchr. 1998), Am. Heart Assn. (coun. on clin. cardiology), Am. Clin. and Climatological Assn.; mem. Am. Fedn. Clin. Rsch., Ctrl. Soc. Clin. Rsch., Laennec Soc., Am. Heart Assn., Assn. U. Cardiologists, Alpha Omega Alpha. Republican. Episcopalian. Home: 5088 Stratford Ave Powell OH 43065-8771 Office: 473 W 12th Ave Columbus OH 43210-1240 E-mail: richard.lewis@osumc.edu.

LEWIS, RITA HOFFMAN, plastic products manufacturing company executive; b. Phila., Aug. 6, 1947; d. Robert John and Helen Anna (Dugan) Hoffman; 1 child, Stephanie Blake. Student, Jefferson Med. Coll. Sch. Nursing, 1965—67, Gloucester County Coll., 1993—. Gen. mgr. Sheets & Co., Inc. (now Flower World, Inc.), Woodbury, NJ, 1968—72; dir., exec. v.p., treas. Hoffman Precision Plastics, Inc., Blackwood, 1973—. Ptnr. Timber Assocs. Author: The Part of Me I Never Really Meant to Share, 1979, In Retrospect: Caught Between Running and Loving; editor: SPOTLIGHTER; columnist: Innovative Singles Mag., 1989—. Commr. N.J. Expressway Authority, 1990—, sec., 1990—91, treas., 1991—, chmn. pers., 1991—; apptd. mem. N.J. Senate Forum on Budget and Revenue Alternatives, 1991; guest spkr. various civic groups, 1974; active Coun. for Citizens of Glen Oaks, NJ, 1979—, Cloucester Twp. Econ. Devel. Com., 1981—, Cloucester Twp. Day Scholar Com., 1984—; adv. coun. Gloucester Twp. Econ. Adv. Coun., 1985—; chair Gloucester Twp. Day Scholar Found., 1985—96; bd. dirs. Diane Hull Dance Co. Recipient Winning Eagle award, 1982, Mayor's award for Womens' Achievement, 1987, Outstanding Cmty. Svc. award Mayor, Coun. and Com., 1987, Don L. Stackhouse Achievement award, 1996. Mem.: NAFE, Soc. Plastic Engrs., Blackwood Businessmen's Assn., Sales Assn. Chem. Industry, White Horse Rotary Club (sargent-at-arms 2003, sec. 2004, dist. RYLA com. 2004, 2005, pres. 2005—06, dist. family of rotary chair 2006—, membership chair, sgt.-at-arms 2007—, dist. grants com. 2007, Presdl. citation dist 7640 2006, Paul Harris fellow 2007). Roman Catholic.

LEWIS, ROBERT DAVID, ophthalmologist, educator; b. Thomasville, Ga., Aug. 27, 1948; s. Ralph N. and E. Margaret (Klaus) L.; m. Cathleen Ann Polster, May 26, 1996. BS, St. Louis Coll. Pharmacy, 1971; MD, St. Louis U., 1975. Diplomate Am. Bd. Ophthalmology; registered pharmacist. Intern, Cardinal Glennon Hosp. Children, St. Louis, 1975-76; resident St. Louis U., 1976-79; dir. pediatric ophthalmology St. Louis U., 1980-82, 85, asst. prof., 1980-88, assoc. prof., 1988-97, clin. prof. ophthalmology, 1998; pres. St. Louis Ophthalmological Soc., 1991-92; dir. pediatric ophthalmology Cardinal Glennon Hosp. for Children, St. Louis, 1980-82, 85; adv. bd. Delta Gamma Found. for Visually Handicapped Children. Recipient St. Louis U. Award for Teaching, 1982. Fellow ACS; mem. AMA, Mo. Med. Assn., St. Louis Med. Soc., Am. Acad. Ophthalmology, Contact Lens Assn. Ophthalmology, Internat. Assn. Ocular Surgeons, Am. Intraocular Implant Soc., St. Louis Ophthalmol. Soc. (pres. 1991-92), Am. Bd. Club. (pres. 1991-92). Office: 12700 Southfork Rd Ste 205 Saint Louis MO 63128-3201 Office Phone: 314-842-0582.

LEWIS, ROBERT DAVID GILMORE, retired editor; b. Chgo., Jan. 16, 1932; s. James Lee and Betty (Ryden) Lewis; m. Georgia Demopoulos, Aug. 4, 1956 (div. July 1988); children: Peter, Sarah, Mary, John, Elizabeth, Daniel, Susan; m. Jacqueline McGregor, July 15, 1988; children: Jill, Katy, Sara. BA, Mich. State U., 1955. Reporter, city editor Galesburg (Ill.) Register-Mail, 1955-59; reporter, bus. editor Kalamazoo Gazette, 1960-64; state capitol corr. Booth Newspapers, Lansing, Mich., 1964-66, Washington corr., 1966-87, Newhouse Newspapers, 1987-91; sr. editor Am. Assn. Ret. Persons Bull., Washington, 1991-99; ret., 1999; mng. dir. Lewis Properties, 2000—. Bd. visitors Les Aspin Ctr. Govt. Marquette U., 1996—. Mem.: Nat. Press Club (chmn. bd. govs. 1975—77), White Ho. Corr. Assn., Soc. Profl. Journalists (chmn. freedom info. com. 1978—83, sec.-treas., pres.-elect to pres. 1983—86, Key award 1980), U.S. Capital Hist. Soc., Supreme Ct. Hist. Soc., Cosmos Club. Avocations: antique furniture collecting, fishing. Home: 301 Constitution Ave NE Washington DC 20002-5921

LEWIS, ROBERT EDWIN, JR., pathology and immunology educator, researcher; b. Meridian, Miss., Mar. 11, 1947; s. Robert Edwin and Cecille (Ryan) Lewis. BA in Biology and Chemistry, U. Miss., 1969, MS in Microbiology, 1973, PhD in Pathology, 1976; specialty tng., Barnes Hosp., U. Miami Med. Ctr., U. Tenn. Ctr. for Health Scis., City of Memphis Hosps., St. Jude Children's Research Hosp. Instr. pathology, anesthesiology U. Miss. Med. Ctr., Jackson, 1976-77, asst. prof. pathology, 1977-84, asst. prof. anesthesiology, 1977-85, asst. dir. clin. immnuopathology lab., 1978-81, assoc. dir. tissue typing lab., 1980-84, dir. paternity testing lab., 1981—, assoc. dir. clin. immunopathology lab., 1981-84, asst. prof. nurse anesthesiology, 1981-85, assoc. prof. pathology, 1984-91, prof., 1991—, dir. clin. immunology, tissue typing lab., 1984—, mem. grad. council, 1981—, prof., 1991—. Co-author: Illus. Dictionary of Immunology, 1995, 2003, Atlas of Immunology, 1999, 2d edit., 2004; co-author: (with J.M. Cruse) Immunology Guidebook, 2004, Historical Atlas of Immunology, 2005; editor (with J.M. Cruse): Concepts in Immunopathology, Vols. 1-8, 1985—91; editor: The Yr. in Immunology-1984-85, 1985, The Yr. in Immunology-1986-8, 1987, The Yr. in Immunology-1988, 1989, The Yr. in Immunology-1989-90, 1990, Progress in Exptl. Tumor Rsch. Vol. 32, 1987, Contributions to Microbiology and Immunology, Vol. 8, 1986, Vol. 9, 1987, Vol. 10, 1989, Vol. 11, 1989, The Yr. in Immunopathology, 1987, Complement Profiles, Vol. 1, 1992, Historical Atlas of Immunology, 2004; sr. editor Immunologic Research, 1981, Pathology and Immunopathology Rsch., 1982—90, Pathobiology, 1990—98, Pathology, 1990—98, Transgenics, 1993, Exptl. and Molecular Pathology, 1999, series editor Concepts in Immunopathology, The Yr. in Immunology, Contributions to Microbiology and Immunology, vol. editor Progress in Exptl. Tumor Rsch, immunology editor Dorland's Illus. Med. Dictionary, 26th and 27th edits., dep. editor-in-chief Pathobiology, 1990—98; contbr. chpts. to books. Am. Cancer Soc. grantee, NIH grantee, Wilson Found. grantee, 1990-2002. Fellow Royal Soc. Health, Royal Soc. Medicine; mem. AAAS, Am. Assn. Pathologists, Am. Assn. Immunologists, Clin. Immunology Soc., Can. Soc. Immunology, Reticuloendothelial Soc., Am. Soc. Microbiology, Am. Soc. Histocompatibility and Immunogenetics (chmn. publs. com. 2000-03, bd. dirs. 2004—), Exptl. Biology and Medicine, N.Y. Acad. Scis., Miss. Acad. Scis., Sigma Xi. Office: U Miss Med Ctr Pathology Dept Dept Pathology 2500 N State St Jackson MS 39216-4500 Home Phone: 601-856-5045; Office Phone: 601-984-1562. Business E-Mail: rlewis@pathology.umsmed.edu.

LEWIS, ROBERT ENZER, editor, educator; b. Windber, Pa., Aug. 12, 1934; s. Robert Enzer and Katharine Torrence (Blair) L.; m. Julie Fatt Cureton, May 14, 1977; children: Perrin Lewis Rubin, Torrence Evans Lewis; stepchildren: Sarah Cureton Kaufman, James S. Cureton. BA, Princeton U., 1959; MA, U. Pa., 1962, PhD, 1964. Tchr. English Mercersburg (Pa.) Acad., 1959-60; teaching fellow U. Pa., Phila., 1961-63; lectr. Ind. U., Bloomington, 1963-64, asst. prof., 1964-68, assoc. prof., 1968-75, prof. English, 1975-82, U. Mich., Ann Arbor, 1982—2003, prof. emeritus, 2004—. Author: (with A. McIntosh) Descriptive Guide to the Manuscripts of the Prick of Conscience, 1982, (with others) Index of Printed Middle English Prose, 1985; editor: De Miseria Condicionis Humane (Lotario dei Segni), 1978; co-editor: Middle English Dictionary, 1982-83, editor-in-chief: vols. 8, 9, 10, 11, 12, 13, 1984-2001; gen. editor: Chaucer Libr., 1970—, chmn. editl. com., 1978-89, 97—. Bd. regents Mercersburg Acad., 1975-87. U.S. Army, 1954-56. Recipient Sir Israel Gollancz Meml. prize for English studies Brit. Acad., 2003; vis. rsch. fellow Inst. Advanced Studies in the Humanities, U. Edinburgh, 1973-74; Am. Coun. Learned Socs. fellow, 1979-80. Fellow: Dictionary Soc. N.Am. (mem. nominating com. 2005—); mem.: Medieval Acad. Am. (mem. publs. com. 1987—92). Episcopalian. Office: U Mich Dept English 3187 Angell Hall Ann Arbor MI 48109-1003 Business E-Mail: relewis@umich.edu.

LEWIS, ROBERT JOHN CORNELIUS KOONS, retired library director; b. Feb. 15, 1938; s. Frank Ashby and Dorothy Elaine (Koons) L.; m. Martha Marie Popejoy, Dec. 22, 1957 (div. 1964); 1 child, Stephen Ashley; m. Helena Barbara Vaughn Schumacker, Sept. 11, 1968 (div. 1976); children: Matthew, Randolph; m. Marguerita S. Kris, July 28, 1985 (dec. Feb. 2001). BA in History of Religion, George Washington U., 1961, MA in Secondary Edn., 1966; MSLS, Cath. U. Am., 1974. Intelligence analyst CIA, Washington, 1958-62; tech. libr. supr. Bell Aerospace, Tucson, 1968-70; info. officer Ambionics Inc., Washington, 1970-73; law libr. Patton, Boggs & Blow, Washington, 1973-75; rschr. George Washington U., Washington, 1976-78; libr. dir. Benjamin Franklin U., Washington, 1979—2003; ret. Oriental art cons. Silverman Galleries, Alexandria, Va., 1978—; libr. dir. Cushman, Darby & Cushman, 1988-90, Nat. Geneal. Soc., 1990-93; libr. Met. Club, 1994—. Author, compiler: Brief History of the Rose Mount Branch of the Surles (Searles) Lewis Family of Virginia, 1976, collected poems: Quatrains based on the Love Poems of the 6th Dalai Lama and other poems, 1979, Lewis Patriarchs of Early Va. and Md., 1989, rev. edit., 1991, rev. 3d. edit., 1998, Welsh Family Coats of Arms, 1995. With U.S. Army, 1963-65. Awarded title of Gyalwa Karma Lozang Dondrup, by Kalu Rinpoche of Darjeeling, 1977; hon. grantee of arms Coll. of Arms, London, 1998. Mem. ALA (pres. com. 1982), Assn. Former Intelligence Officers, Spl. Librs. Assn., Nat. Geneal. Soc. (councilor 1990-93), Soc. Geneal. of London, Jamestowne Soc., The Augustan Soc., Mahikari of Am. Club, Subud Club, Theosophical Soc. Club, Sigma Phi Epsilon. Episcopalian. Home: 18612 Sage Way Germantown MD 20874-2041 Office Phone: 301-972-9211. E-mail: robertjcklewis@aol.com.

LEWIS, ROBERT KAY, JR., fundraising executive; b. Danville, Ky., Aug. 10, 1935; s. Robert K. and Mona (Hyden) L.; m. Wendy Gardiner, June 18, 1960; children: Mary Elizabeth, Mona Hyden, Robert K. III. BA, Ctr. Coll., Danville, 1957; MS, George Washington U., 1972. Advanced through ranks to lt. U.S. Navy, 1958—63; dir. alumni/annual giving Ctr. Coll., Danville, 1963—67; served to capt. U.S. Navy, 1967—81; dir. alumni/pub. affairs Ctr. Coll., 1981—83; dir. pub. affairs Va. Tech., Blacksburg, 1983—87; sr. v.p. Host Comm., Lexington, 1987—89; pres. Ky. C. of C., Frankfort, 1990; chmn., CEO Global Advancement, Lexington, 1991—. Trustee Severn Sch., Severna Park, Md., 1979-83; bd. visitors McCallie Sch., Chattanooga, 1983-86; bd. dirs. Ky. Adv. for Higher Edn., Lexington. Mem. Assn. Fund Raising Profls. (bd. dirs. Bluegrass chpt. 1991-2003), Henry Clay Found. (bd. dirs. Lexington, 1994-2005, chmn. emeritus), Nat. Press Club, Coun. Advancement and Support of Edn. (bd. dirs. Ky. chpt. 1991-98), Assn. Philanthropic Counsel (nat. bd. dirs., exec. com. 2000-05), Lexington Rotary Endowment (bd. dirs. 1995-2001), Giving Inst. (nat. bd. dirs. 2006—). Presbyterian. Home: Forest Hill Farm 2667 Lexington Rd Danville KY 40422 Office: Global Advancement 333 W Vine St Ste 300 Lexington KY 40507-1626 Office Phone: 859-231-8575. Business E-Mail: Bob@global-advt.com.

LEWIS, ROBERT LEE, lawyer; b. Oxford, Miss., Feb. 26, 1944; s. Ernest Elmo and Johnice Georgia (Thirkield) L.; children: Yolanda Sherice, Robert Lee Jr., Dion Terrell, Viron Lamar, William Lovell, Tremaine Donnell Lewis. BA, Ind. U., 1970, JD, 1973; M in Pub. Service, West Ky. U., 1980. Bar: Ind. 1973, Ky. 1979, U.S. Ct. Claims, U.S. Ct. Internat. Trade, U.S. Tax. Ct., U.S. Ct. Mil. Appeals, U.S. Ct. Appeals (fed. cir.),

U.S. Supreme Ct. Sole practice, Evansville, Ind., 1973-75, Gary, Ind., 1980—; atty., army officer U.S. Army, Ft. Knox, Ky., 1975-78; appellate referee Ind. Employment Security Div., Indpls., 1978-80. Mem. adv. com. Vincennes (Ind.) U., 1983—; bd. dirs. Opportunities Industrialization Ctr., Evansville, 1973-75. Served to sgt. JAGC, USMC, 1962-66, Vietnam, sgt. U.S. Army, 1975-78, lt. col. USAR. Named Ky. Col. Mem. ABA, Ind. Bar Assn., Ky. Bar Assn., Nat. Bar Assn., Ind. Bd. Realtors, Ind. U. Alumni Assn., Phi Alpha Delta. Methodist. Home and Office: 2148 W 11th Ave Gary IN 46404-2306

LEWIS, ROBERT V., JR., computer programmer; b. Amarillo, Tex., Feb. 14, 1966; s. Robert Vernon and Jackie Lynn Lewis; m. Ronda Lynn Craig, Sept. 26, 1992; children: Amanda Marie, BriAna Nicole, Kyle Robert. B in Applied Sci., ITT Tech. Inst., Aurora, Colo., 1995. Computer technician IBM/Eduquest, Denver, 1992—93; sr. computer technician Ultimate Electronics, Wheatridge, Colo., 1993—96; field svc. engr. Digital Equipment Corp., Englewood, Colo., 1996—97; tech. trainer III TEK Systems, Balt., 1997—2002; programmer/SQL DBA CPI Qualified Plan Consultants, Great Bend, Kans., 2002—. Microsoft small bus. specialist Plato Consulting LLC, Claflin, Kans., 2000—. Served with USN, 1984—89. Mem.: IEEE. Office: Plato Consulting LLC PO Box 317 Claflin KS 67525 Home Phone: 620-786-4369; Office Phone: 620-786-4369. Personal E-mail: roblewis963@hotmail.com.

LEWIS, RODERIC W., electronics executive, lawyer; b. Nyssa, Oreg., May 17, 1955; BA in Econs. and Asian studies, Brigham Young U., 1980; JD, Columbia U., 1983. Bar: Utah 1983. Assoc. LeBoeuf, Lamb, Leiby & MacRae, NYC, 1983-89, Rogers, MacKay, Price & Anderson, 1989-91; asst. gen. counsel Micron Tech., Inc., Boise, 1991-95, v.p. legal affairs, gen. counsel, corp. sec., 1996—; v.p., gen. counsel, corp. sec. Micron Electronics, Inc., 1995—96. Vice-chmn. Utah Bus. Corp. Act Revision Com. Mem. ABA, Idaho State Bar, Utah State Bar (chmn. bus. law sect. 1988-89). Office: Micron Technology Inc PO Box 6 8000 S Federal Way Boise ID 83716-9632 Office Phone: 208-368-4500. E-mail: rodlewis@micron.com.*

LEWIS, ROGER KUTNOW, architect, educator, author; b. Houston, Jan. 9, 1941; s. Nathan D. and Betty K. Lewis; m. Eleanor Draper Roberts, June 24, 1967; 1 child, Kevin Michael. BArch, MIT, 1964, MArch, 1967. Registered architect, D.C., Va., Md. Vol. architect Peace Corps, Nabeul, Tunisia, 1964-66; designer Wilkes & Faulkner, Washington, 1967-68; ptnr. Chavarria/Lewis Assocs., Washington, 1968-71; prin. Roger K. Lewis AIA & Assocs., Washington, 1971-80; pres. Pecla Corp., Washington, 1971-81; ptnr. Chesapeake Design Group, Balt., 1980-81; prin. Roger K. Lewis FAIA, Architect & Planner, Washington, 1981—; prof. U. Md. Sch. Arch., 1968—2006, prof. emeritus, 2006—. Mem. D.C. Com. on Design Arts, Washington, 1988-92; design advisor City of Alexandria, Va.; nat. peer profl. Gen. Svcs. Adminstrn. Pub. Bldg. Svc. Design Excellence Program. Author: Architect? A Candid Guide to the Profession, 1985, revised edit., 1998, Shaping the City, 1987; co-author Growth Management Handbook, 1989; author articles in jours.and periodicals, chpts. in books, encys.; columnist The Washington Post, 1984—. Trustee Nat. Children's Mus. Recipient Fed. Design Achievement award Nat. Endowment for the Arts, Washington, 1988, numerous awards Am. Planning Assn., AAUW, 1985—. Fellow AIA (numerous design awards 1973—, Presdl. citation 2003); mem. Faberge Arts Found. (bd. advs.), Cosmos Club. Home: 5034 1/2 Dana Pl NW Washington DC 20016-3441 Personal E-mail: rogershome@aol.com.

LEWIS, RON, congressman; b. Greenup County, Ky., Sept. 14, 1946; m. Kayi Gambill, 1966; children: Ronald Brent, Allison Faye. Student, Morehead State U.; BA in History and Polit. Sci., U. Ky., 1969; MA in Higher Edn., Morehead State U., 1981; student, USN Officer Candidate Sch. Ordained to ministry Bapt. Ch. With Ky. Hwy. Dept., Ea. State Hosp.; with sales various cos.; tchr. Watterson Coll., 1980-85; pastor White Mills Bapt. Ch.; owner small bus. Elizabethtown, Ky.; mem. US Congress from 2d Ky. Dist., 1994—, mem. ways & means com., subcoms., mem. govt. reform com. Past pres. Hardin and Larue County Jail Ministry. Named Guardian of Srs.' Rights, Tax Fairness Srs.; League Pvt. Property Rights, Coun. Citizens Against Govt. Waste, Nat. Fed. Ind. Bus. Mem. Severns Valley Ministerial Assn., Elizabethtown C. of C. Republican. Office: US Ho Reps 2418 Rayburn Ho Office Bldg Washington DC 20515-1702 Office Phone: 202-225-3501.*

LEWIS, SAMUEL WINFIELD, retired federal agency administrator, diplomat; b. Houston, Oct. 1, 1930; s. Samuel Winfield and Sue Roselle (Hurley) L.; m. Sallie Kate Smoot, June 20, 1953; children: Pamela Gracelle, Richard Winfield. BA magna cum laude, Yale U., 1952; MA, Johns Hopkins U., 1954; PhD (hon.), Tel Aviv U., 1985, Hebrew U. Jerusalem, 1985, Weizman Inst. Sci., 1985; DHL (hon.), Hebrew Union Coll., 1986, Balt. Hebrew U., 1988; LLD (hon.), Salem-Teikyo U., 1991. Exec. asst. Am. Trucking Assn., Washington., 1953-54; fgn. svc. officer Dept. State, Washington, 1954-85; consular officer Naples, Italy, 1954-55; consul Florence, Italy, 1955-59; officer-in-charge Italian affairs Washington, 1959-61; spl. asst. to undersec. state, 1961; spl. asst. to spl. rep. of pres., 1961-63; dep. asst. dir. US AID Mission to Brazil, Rio de Janeiro, 1964-65; exec. officer embassy, Rio de Janeiro, 1965-67; dep. dir. Office Brazil Affairs, Washington, 1967-68; sr. staff mem. for Latin Am. Affairs Nat. Security Council, White House, Washington, 1968-69; spl. asst. for policy planning Bur. Inter-Am. Affairs, Washington, 1969; spl. asst. to dir. gen. Fgn. Svc., 1970-71; dep. chief mission and counselor embassy Kabul, Afghanistan, 1971-74; dep. dir. policy planning staff Dept. State, 1974-75, asst. sec. state for internat. orgn., 1975-77; U.S. ambassador to Israel, 1977-85; lectr., diplomat-in-residence Johns Hopkins Fgn. Policy Inst., Washington, 1985-86; pres. U.S. Inst. of Peace, Washington, 1987-93; dir. policy planning staff U.S. Dept. State, Washington, 1993-94, cons., 1994-95. Sr. internat. fellow The Dayan Ctr., Tel Aviv U., 1986-87; chmn. bd. overseers Harry S. Truman Rsch. Inst. for Advancement of Peace, Hebrew U., 1986-91; guest scholar The Brookings Inst., Washington, 1987; mem. bd. advisors Washington Inst. Near East Policy, 1986-93, 98—, counselor, 1995-98; adv. com. Search for Common Ground in the Mid. East, Washington, 1994—, chmn., 2005—; vis. prof. Hamilton Coll., spring 1995, fall 1997, adj. prof. Sch. Fgn. Svc., Georgetown U., 1996; sr. advisor Israel Policy Forum, 1998—; profl. lectr. Nitze Sch. Advanced Internat. Studies, Johns Hopkins U., 2006; lectr. in field. Author: Making Peace Among Arabs and Israelis, 1991; contbg. author: The Middle East: Ten Years After Camp David, 1988, Soviet-American Competition in the Middle East, 1988, Israel: The Peres Era, 1987, The United States and Israel: Evolution of an Unwritten Alliance, 1999; contbr. articles to profl. jours., also NY Times, Washington Post. Bd. dirs. Inst. for Study Diplomacy, Georgetown U., 1994—; vice chmn. Ctr. Preventive Action, Coun. Fgn. Rels., 1994-97. Recipient William A. Jump award for outstanding service in pub. adminstrn., 1967, Meritorious Honor award Dept. State, 1967, Meritorious Honor award AID, 1967, Pres.' Mgmt. Improvement cert., 1971, Distinguished Honor award Dept. State, 1977, 85, Disting. Alumnus award Johns Hopkins U., 1980, Wilbur J. Carr award Dept. State, 1985; vis. fellow Princeton U., 1963-64. Mem. Am. Acad. Diplomacy (bd. dirs. 1995-, vice chmn. bd. dirs. 1995-99), Am. Fgn. Svc. Assn., US Interreligious Com. for Peace in the Middle East, UN Assn., Middle East Inst., Assn. Diplomatic Studies and Tng. (bd. dirs. 1995-2005, 2006—), Inst. World Affairs (bd. dirs. 1996-2005), Ptnrs. for Dem. Change (bd. dirs. 2004-), Cousteau Soc., Sierra Club, Phi Beta Kappa. Episcopalian. Office Phone: 703-448-1997. Personal E-mail: sixtymeter@aol.com.

LEWIS, SANDRA COMBS, research psychologist, writer; b. Troup County, Ga., Oct. 8, 1939; d. Robert Milton and Imogene (Richardson) Combs; children: Virginia Susan Lewis, Charles James III. AB, Wesleyan Coll., 1961; MEd, Mercer U., 1972, Ga. State U., 1976; PhD, U. Ga., 1980. Personnel asst. Sears Roebuck & Co., Atlanta, 1961—62; rsch. asst. bd. regents U. Sys. Ga., 1962—63; asst. psychol. svcs. Bibb County Bd. Edn., Macon, 1972—73; instr. Macon Jr. Coll., 1973, 1982, Wesleyan Coll., 1973—75, 1981; psychometrist Middle Ga. Psychoednl. Ctr., 1975—76; instr. Mercer U., 1980—82. Presenter at profl. confs. Co-author: Christian Love and Problems of Living, 1992, God and Positive Christianity, 1998, Psychology for Life, 2000, A Revolutionary View of Education and Teaching for the Third Millennium, 2002; assoc. editor Truth Seekers Newsletter, 1998-2006, editor, 2007—. Pres. Macon Wesleyan Alumnae Club, 1973-74; bd. dirs. Family Counseling Ctr., Macon, 1975-76; ruling elder, clk. of session Northminster Presbyn. Ch., Macon, 1988-90, 94-96, vice moderator Presbyn. Women, 1989-90, 2002, moderator Presbyn. Women, 1990-91, 2003; v.p. Fore(In)Sight Found., 1991-2006; pres. Fore(In)Sight Found., 2006—. Mem.: APA (life), Mid. Ga. Psychol. Assn., Ga. Psychol. Assn. (life). Avocations: gardening, photography. Home and Office: 4976 Oxford Rd Macon GA 31210-3059 Office Phone: 478-474-3869. Business E-Mail: foreignsight@excite.com.

LEWIS, SCOTT P., lawyer; b. Chgo., 1950; BA in Econs. magna cum laude, Yale U., 1971; JD cum laude, Harvard U., 1974. Bar: Mass. 1974. Mem. Palmer & Dodge LLP, Boston, 1974—2006; ptnr. Anderson & Kreiger LLP, Cambridge, Mass., 2006—. Chair Lawyers Com. (civil Rights under law), Boston. Named Super Lawyer; recipient Beale Prize. Office: Anderson & Kreiger LLP 1 Canal Pk Ste 200 Cambridge MA 02141 Office Phone: 617-621-6560. Office Fax: 617-621-6660. Business E-Mail: slewis@andersonkreiger.com.

LEWIS, SHARYN LEE, sculptor; b. Carmel, Calif., July 31, 1946; d. William Albert and Hazel Elisabeth Lewis; m. Robert John Western, Mar. 22, 1986. Asst. art tchr. Benin (Nigeria) Coll., 1974-76; comml. artist KTT Art Svc., Campbell, Calif., 1976-77; graphic artist, illustrator Intersil Corp., Santa Clara, Calif., 1977-80; sr. artist, graphic designer Pro-Log Corp., Monterey, Calif., 1980-83; freelance graphic designer Monterey, 1983-92; sculptor, 1992—. Exhibitions include Mystic Maritime Gallery, Mystic Seaport, Conn., 1995-2006, Big Horn Galleries, Carmel, 1995-96, Fifth Ann. Loveland (Colo.) Sculpture Invitational, 1996, Monterey Peninsula Art Found., 1997, Monterey Mus. Art, 1998-2003, Maritime Gallery, Mystic, Conn., 2004, Pk. Ave. Atrium Gallery, NYC, 2003-04, Brookgreen Gardens, SC, 2003, Monterey Gallery, Calif., 1994-2006, Chirstopher Bell Gallery, 1994-2006; pvt. collections. Mem. Internat. Sculpture Ctr., Washington, Nat. Sculpture Soc. (NYC), Nat. Mus. Women in Art (Washington), Met. Mus. Art (NYC), Monterey Mus. Art. Personal E-mail: sharynlewis@comcast.net.

LEWIS, SHELDON NOAH, technology consultant; b. Chgo., July 1, 1934; s. Jacob Joseph and Evelyn (Mendelsohn) Iglowitz; m. Suzanne Joyce Goldberg, June 17, 1957; children: Sara Lynn, Matthew David, Rachel Ann. BA with honors, Northwestern U., 1956, MS (Univ. fellow), 1956; PhD (Eastman Kodak fellow), UCLA, 1959; postgrad. (NSF fellow), U. Basel, Switzerland, 1959-60; postgrad. cert. in research mgmt, Indsl. Research Inst., Harvard U., 1973. With Rohm & Haas Co., 1960-78, head lab., 1963-68, research supr., 1968-73, dir. splty. chem. research, 1973-74; gen. mgr. DCL Lab. AG subs., Zurich, Switzerland, 1974-75; dir. European Labs. Valbonne, France, 1975-76; corp. dir. research and devel. worldwide for polymers, resins and monomers Spring House, Pa., 1976-78; with The Clorox Co., Oakland, Calif., 1978-91, v.p. R&D, 1978, group v.p., 1978-84, exec. v.p., 1984-91, also bd. dirs.; pres. SNL Inc., Lafayette, Calif., 1991—. Mem. indsl. panel on sci. and tech. NSF. Referee: Jour. Organic Chemistry; patentee in field; contbr. articles to profl. publs. Mem. Calif. Inst. Adv. Bd., World Affairs Council, UCLA Chemistry Adv. Council, Bay Area Sci. Fair Adv. Bd., Mills Coll. Adv. Council for Sci. and Math. Recipient cert. in patent law Phila. Patent Law Assn., 1962, Roon award for coatings research Fedn. Socs. Coatings Tech., 1966, cert. of service Wayne State U. Polymer Conf. Series, 1967, cert. in mgmt. by objectives Am. Mgmt. Research, Inc., 1972 Mem. Soap and Detergent Assn. (bd. dirs.), Chem. Ind. Inst. of Toxicology (bd. dirs.), Indsl. Rsch. Inst., Am. Chem. Soc. (chmn. Phila. polymer sect. 1970-71), Soc. Chem. Industry London, Sigma Xi. Jewish. Office: SNL Inc 3711 Rose Ct Lafayette CA 94549-3030

LEWIS, SHIRLEY JEANE, retired psychologist; b. Phoenix, Aug. 23; d. Herman and Leavy (Hutchinson) Smith; m. Edgar Anthony Lewis (div.); children: Edgar Anthony (dec.), Roshaun, Lucy Ann Jonathan. AA, Phoenix C.C., 1957; BA, Ariz. State U., 1960; MS, San Diego State U., 1975, MA, 1985, Azusa Pacific U., 1982; PhD, U. So. Calif., 1983. Cert. tchr. Calif. Recreation leader Phoenix Parks and Recreation Dept., 1957-62; columnist Ariz. Tribune, Phoenix, 1958-59; tchr. phys. edn. San Diego Unified Schs., 1962—; adult educator San Diego C.C., 1973—94; counselor San Diego County Schs., 1979—97; assoc. prin. Oceanside (Calif.) Unified Sch. Dist., 1997—98; head counselor Gomper Secondary Sch. San Diego (Calif.) Unified Schs., 1998—2003, ret. Gomper Secondary Sch., 2003. Instr. psychology, health, Black studies, 1977—, counselor, 1981—; cmty. counselor S.E. Counseling and Cons. Svcs. and Narcotics Prevention and Edn. Sys., Inc., San Diego, 1973-77; counselor educator, counselor edn. dept. San Diego State U., 1974-77; marriage, family, child counselor Counseling and Cons. Ctr., San Diego, 1977—; inservice educator San Diego Unified and San Diego County Sch. Dists., 1973-77; Fulbright Exch. counselor, London, 1994-96; instr. San Diego (Calif.) C.C., 1977-94, counselor, 1981-94; lectr. in field. Contbr. articles to profl. jours. Girl Scout phys. fitness cons., Phoenix, 1960-62; vol. cmty. tutor for high sch. students, San Diego, 1963; sponsor Tennis Club for Youth, San Diego, 1964-65; troop leader Girl Scouts U.S., Lemon Grove, Calif., 1972-74; vol. counselor USN Alcohol Rehab. Ctr., San Diego, 1978; mem. sch. coun.'s adv. bd. San Diego State U. Named Woman of Yr., Phoenix, 1957, One of Outstanding Women of San Diego, 1980; recipient Phys. Fitness Sch. award and Demonstration Sch. award Pres.'s Coun. on Phys. Fitness, Taft Jr. H.S., 1975, Excel award Corp. Excellence Edn., 1989; Delta Sigma Theta scholar, 1957-60; Alan Korrick scholar, 1956. Mem. NEA, Calif. Tchrs. Assn., San Diego Tchrs. Assn., Assn. Marriage and Family Counselors, Am. Personnel and Guidance Assn., Calif. Assn. Health, Phys. Edn. and Recreation (v.p. health), Am. Alliance of Health, Phys. Edn. and Recreation, Assn. Black Psychologists (corr. sec. 1993), Assn. African-Am. Educators, Delta Sigma Theta (Delta of Yr. 1987). Democrat. Baptist. Home: 1226 Armacost Rd San Diego CA 92114-3307 *Personal philosophy: High self-esteem, responsibility, self-discipline and striving to achieve personal goals are necessary for a healthful lifestyle regardless of one's personal, historical circumstances. The initial access to such characteristics, in reality, may only be in one's invention of fantasy.*

LEWIS, STEPHEN E., lawyer; b. Rock Hill, SC, 1966; BS with honors, U. NC, 1988, JD with high honors, 1991. CPA NC, 1988; bar: Ga. 1991. Assoc. Troutman Sanders LLP, Atlanta, 1991—98, ptnr., corp. and securities group leader, 1999—, hiring ptnr., 2002. Mem. NC Law Rev., 1989—90. Named a Super Lawyer, Atlanta Mag., 2004, Legal Elite in corp. law, Ga. Trend Mag., 2004. Mem.: Beta Alpha Psi, Phi Beta Kappa, Order of Coif. Office: Troutman Sanders LLP One Union Sq Ste 5200 600 Peachtree St Atlanta GA 30308-2216 Office Phone: 404-885-3448. Office Fax: 404-962-6616. Business E-Mail: stephen.lewis@troutmansanders.com.

LEWIS, STEPHEN RICHMOND, JR., economist, educator; b. Englewood, NJ, Feb. 11, 1939; s. Stephen Richmond and Esther (Magan) Lewis; m. Judith Frost, 1996; children from previous marriage: Virginia, Deborah, Mark. BA, Williams Coll., 1960, LLD, 1987; MA, Stanford U., 1962, PhD, 1963; LHD, Doshisha U., 1993, Macalester Coll., 2002; LLD, Carleton Coll., 2002. Instr. Stanford U., 1962—63; research advisor Pakistan Inst. Devel. Econs., Karachi, 1963—65; asst. prof. econs. Harvard U., 1965—66, Williams Coll., 1966—68, assoc. prof., 1968—73, prof., 1973—76, Herbert H. Lehman prof., 1976—87, provost of coll., 1968—71, 1973—77, spl. asst. to pres., 1979—80, dir. Williams-Botswana Project, 1982—88, chmn. dept. econs., 1984—86; vis. sr. research fellow Inst. Devel. Studies, Nairobi, Kenya, 1971—73; econ. cons. to Ministry of Finance and Devel. Planning, Govt. of Botswana, 1975—; vis. fellow Inst. Devel. Studies, Sussex, England, 1986—87; pres., prof. econs. Carleton Coll., Northfield, Minn., 1987—2002, pres. emeritus, 2002—; chmn. RiverSource Funds, 2007—, also bd. dirs. Trustee Carnegie Endowment for Internat. Peace, 1988—, Minn. Humanities Commn., 2004—; bd. dirs. William Mitchell Coll. Law, XDX Innovative Refrigeration, Inc., Xenomosis, LLC, Valmont Industries, Inc.; cons. in field. Author (with others): Relative Price Changes and Industrialization in Pakistan, 1969; author: Economic Policy and Industrial Growth in Pakistan, 1969, Pakistan: Industrialization and Trade Policy, 1970, Williams in the Eighties, 1980, Taxation for Development, 1983, South Africa: Has Time Run Out?, 1986, Policy Choice and Development Performance in Botswana, 1989, The Economics of Apartheid, 1989; editor: Very Brave or Very Foolish? Memoirs of an African Democrat, 2006; mem. editl. bd.: Jour. Econ. Lit., 1985—87; contbr. chapters to books, articles to profl. jours. Mem. chmn.'s coun. No. Star coun. Boy Scouts Am., 1989—. Decorated Presdl. Order of Meritorious Svc. Botswana; recipient Disting. Eagle Scout award, 1993; fellow, Danforth Found., 1960—63, Ford Found., 1962—63. Mem.: Am. Econ. Assn., Nat. Tax Assn., Coun. on Fgn. Rels., Phi Beta Kappa. Office: 901 Marquette Ave S Ste 2810 Minneapolis MN 55402

LEWIS, SUFORD, computer scientist, consultant; b. Washington, Feb. 20, 1943; d. Robert Ogden and Thelma Jensen Hereford; m. Anthony Richard Lewis, Apr. 7, 1968; 1 child, Alice Naomi Sophronia. BA in English, cum laude, Harvard Coll., 1965; MS in Math., Northeastern U., Boston, 1972. Cert. data processor Inst. for the Certification of Computer Profls., 1972. Programmer Wolf R&D, Inc., West Concord, Mass., 1965—66; mem. tech. staff Arthur D. Little, Inc., Cambridge, Mass., 1966—74; sr. systems programmer Signal Processing Systems, Waltham, Mass., 1974—77; sr. software engr. Softech, Waltham, Mass., 1977—80; prin. software engr. Digital Equip. Corp., Maynard, Mass., 1980—85; sect. mgr. AlphaTech, Burlington, Mass., 1985—88; project leader Computer Link, Wilmington, Mass., 1988—89; ind. cons. Mass., 1988—94; project leader AEG Schneider Automation, North Andover, Mass., 1994—96, Atex Media Solutions, Bedford, Mass., 1997, Applied Lang. Techs. (now Speechworks), Boston, 1997—98; project mgr. P I A Investment Trading Co., Newton, Mass., 1998—99, Availant, Inc, Cambridge, Mass., 1999—2001; cons. Suford's Solutions, Natick, Mass., 2001—. Editor: (video) Noreascon 3 Masquerade, (photo souvenir book) The Noreascon Two Memory Book, (tarot deck, each by a different artist) The Fantasy Tarot; editor: (also interviewer, author of 3 articles) (collection of short stories and essays) Dreamweaver's Dilemma; prodn. editor seven other books. Marcher NOW, NARAL, Washington, 1989, 2004. Fellow: New Eng. Sci. Fiction Assn. (founding mem.); mem.: AAUW, Soc. Women Engrs., Software Process Improvement Network, Women Entrepreneurs in Sci. and Tech., IEEE Computer Soc., Assn. Computing Machinery, Assn. Women in Computing (pres. 2003—05, sec. 2005—06, del. leader trip to China with People to People 2006), Arthur D. Little Alumni Assn. Jewish. Avocations: science fiction, singing, acting. Home Phone: 508-314-3802. Personal E-mail: consultant@sufordssolutions.com.

LEWIS, SUZANNE, parks director; b. 1956; BA magna cum laude, U. W. Fla., 1978. Various positions including seasonal park supt., park tech. park historian, supervisory park ranger, mgmt. asst. to supt. Glacier Nat. Park Gulf Islands Nat. Seashore, 1978—89; acting supt. Christiansted Nat. Historic Site, Buck Island Reef Nat. Monument U.S. Virgin Islands; supt. Timucuan Ecological and Historic Preserve, 1990—97, Chattahoochee River Nat. Recreation Area, Atlanta, 1997—2000, Yellowstone Nat. Park, 2002—. Named Mgr. of Year for Partnerships, Nat. Parks and Conservation Assn., 1994; recipient Woman of Distinction award, Girl Scout Councils of Am., 1997, Sec. of Interior Bronze Exec. Leadership award, 2004, others. Office: Yellowstone Nat Park PO Box 168 Yellowstone National Park WY 82190-0168*

LEWIS, SYLVIA DAVIDSON, foundation executive; b. Akron, Ohio, Apr. 28, 1927; d. Harry I. and Helen E. (Stein) Davidson; m. Allen D. Lewis, Oct. 12, 1947; children: Pamela Lewis Kanfer, Randy, Daniel, Cynthia Lewis Lagdameo. Student, U. Mich., 1945—47, U. Akron, 1961—62. Editor Akron Jewish News, 1948-50; tchr. Revere Rd. Congregation, Akron, 1964-70; office mgr. Acme Lumber & Fence Co., Akron, 1970-85; nat. pres. NA'AMAT USA (Movement of Working Women & Vols.), NYC, 1993-97. Pres. Planned Parenthood Summit Portage and Medina Counties, 1999-2001; founding mem. Govt. Affairs Com., Columbus, Ohio, 1981—, exec. com., 1988-89; v.p. Akron Jewish Cmty. Fedn., 1988-94, pres. women's divsn., 1987-90; elect mem. Akron Jewish Cmty. Bd., 1999-2006; nat. v.p. Na'amat USA, 2004—. Named Woman of Distinction, YWCA Summit County, 2001; named one of No. Ohio's Top Women Profls., No. Ohio Live mag., 1997; named to Ohio Women's Hall of Fame, 1995; recipient Golden Rule award, J.C. Penney, 1994, Vol. of Yr. award, Lippman Cmty. Day Sch., 1992, Commendation of Honor award, Ohio Gen. Assembly, 1993, Women of Achievement award, YWCA of Summit County, 1999. Democrat. Jewish. Avocations: reading, writing, travel. Home: 4389 Everett Rd Richfield OH 44286 Personal E-mail: syllewis1@aol.com.

LEWIS, TOM E., JR., architect; m. Cynthia Lewis; 2 children. BS and BArch, MArch, Ga. Inst. Tech.; law student, Fla. State U. Pvt. practice arch.; spl. asst. Adminstrn. of Fla. Gov. Bob Graham; asst. sec. Fla. Dept. Transp.; sec. Fla. Dept. Cmty. Affairs; dir. residential devel., v.p. cmty. devel. Disney Devel. Co. (later Walt Disney Imagineering), chmn. celebration cmty. devel. dist.; v.p. devel. Walt Disney World Co.; sec. Fla. Dept. Mgmt. Svcs.; spl. cons. Pennington, Moore, Wilkinson, Bell & Dunbar, P.A., Tallahassee, 2007—. Arch., mgr., mem. Air Force Design Adv. Coun. USAF. Fellow: AIA. Office: Pennington Moore Wilkinson Bell & Dunbar 215 S Monroe St 2nd Fl Tallahassee FL 32301 Office Phone: 850-222-3533. Office Fax: 850-222-2126. E-mail: tom@penningtonlaw.com.

LEWIS, W. WALKER, strategic and financial advisory company executive; b. Middletown, Ohio, Sept. 15, 1944; s. W. Walker Jr. and Emily S. (Spivy) L.; m. Ellen Anschuetz, Mar. 30, 1970; children: Walker, Alexandra (Sasha), Morgan. AB, Harvard U., 1967. Mgr. Boston Cons. Group, 1970-72; chmn. Strategic Planning Assocs., Washington, 1972-92; pres. Avon Products, NYC, 1992-94; mng. dir. Kidder Peabody, NYC, 1994-96; sr. advisor Dillon Read & Co., NYC, 1997—; chmn. Devon Value Advisers, NYC, 1997—. Mem. Coun. on Fgn. Rels., Washington Inst. Fgn. Affairs. Office: Devon Value Advisers 399 Park Ave Fl 38 New York NY 10022-4616 Business E-Mail: wlewis@devonvalue.com.

LEWIS, WALTER DAVID, historian, educator; b. Towanda, Pa., June 24, 1931; s. Gordon Cleon and Eleanor Esther (Tobias) L.; m. Carolyn Wyatt Brown, June 12, 1954 (div. 1980); children: Daniel Kent, Virginia Lorraine, Nancy Ellyn; m. Patricia L. Freeman, Apr. 26, 1986. BA cum laude, Pa. State U., 1952, MA, 1954; PhD, Cornell U., 1961. Instr. pub. speaking Hamilton Coll., Clinton, NY, 1954-57; fellowship coordinator Eleutherian Mills-Hagley Found., Wilmington, Del.; also lectr. history U. Del., 1959-65; assoc. prof. history SUNY, Buffalo, 1965-71, prof., 1971; Hudson prof. history and engrng. Auburn (Ala.) U., 1971-95, disting. Univ. prof., 1994—. Dir. univ. project tech., human values and so. future, 1974-79; doctoral fellow in Am. civilization Cornell U., 1958-59; vis. prof. history U. Tex.-Dallas, summer 1982, 83, 84; pres., dir. conf. on history of civil and comml. aviation (ICCA 92), Swiss Transport Mus., Lucerne, Switzerland, 1992; Charles A. Lindbergh prof. of aerospace history Nat. Air and Space Mus., 1993-94. Exec. co-prodr. (documentary film): About Us: A Deep South Portrait, 1977; author: From Newgate to Dannemora: The Rise of the Penitentiary in New York, 1965, Iron and Steel in America, 1976, Sloss Furnaces and The Rise of the Birmingham District: An Industrial Epic, 1994, Eddie Rickenbacker: An American Hero in the Twentieth Century, 2005; co-author: Delta: The History of an Airline, 1979, Hopewell Furnace, 1983, The Airway to Everywhere: A History of All American Aviation, 1937-53, 1988; contbg. author: The Professions in America, 1965, Technology in Western Civilization, 1967, The Development of an American Culture, 1969, Notable American Women, 1971, Great Engineers and Pioneers in Technology, 1981, Technology in America, 2d edit., 1990, Science-Technology Relationships, 1993, Eli Whitney's Cotton Gin, 1793-1993, 1994, Bring History Alive, 1996, Reconsidering A Century of Flight, 2003, Realizing the Dream of Flight, 2005; editor: Fighting the Flying Circus, 1997, Airline Executives and Federal Regulation: Case Studies in American Enterprise from the Airmail Era to the Dawn of the Jet Age, 2000, The Americanization of Edward Bok, 2000; co-editor: Economic Change in the Civil War Era, 1965, The Southern Mystique: Technology and Human Values in Changing Region, 1977; gen. editor Procs. of the Internat. Conf. on the History of Civil and Commercial Aviation, 1995; contbr. articles to profl. jours. Grantee NEH, 1973-79, 80-82, Delta Airlines Found. 1973-79, Eleutherian Mills Hist. Libr., 1970-73, 80; postdoctoral fellow Nat. Humanities Inst., U. Chgo., 1978-79, Mellon fellow Va. Hist. Soc., 1988, 89, 92; recipient Leonardo da Vinci medal, Soc. Hist. Tech., 1993. Mem. Soc. History Tech., Hist. Soc., Internat. Congress for History of Tech., Phi Beta Kappa. Episcopalian. Home: 210 Lee Dr Auburn AL 36832-6722 Office Phone: 334-844-4360. Personal E-mail: lewiswd@mindspring.com. Business E-Mail: lewiswd@auburn.edu.

LEWIS, WAYNE H., investment company executive; b. NYC, July 8, 1931; s. Harry Wayne and Eleanor (Diegoli) L.; m. Mary Jane Durnford, June 18, 1956; 1 child, Laura Alane. AB, Harvard U., 1953. Sales, instr. Exxon Corp., Boston, 1956-59; sales Conn. Gen. Life Ins. Co., Hartford, Conn., 1959-62; mgr. Mass. Gen. Life Ins. Co., Boston, 1962-67; v.p. sales Integon Corp., Winston-Salem, NC, 1967-69; v.p. Lionel D. Edie & Co., NYC, 1969-72; v.p. fin. planning 1st Pa. Bank, Phila., 1970-72; pres., owner Investor Svcs. Ltd., Villanova, Pa., 1972—. Chmn., bd. trustees Anthony Wayne Found., Paoli, 1991—; pres. Wayne Family Orgn., Paoli, 1988—; mem., oper. com. Wayne Mus., Paoli, 1984—. Mem. Union League Pa. (life), Merion Cricket Club, Desert Mountain Club, The Estancia Club, Chaine des Rotisseurs (officer exec. com. 1982—). Avocations: aerobics, hiking, sightseeing. Office: Investor Svcs Ltd PO Box 310 Villanova PA 19085-0310 Home: 1404 Mount Pleasant Rd Villanova PA 19085-2111

LEWIS, WILBUR H., educational management consultant; b. Belmont, Ohio, Sept. 16, 1930; s. Charles W. and Lily B. (Dunfee) L.; m. Jean E. Lewis, Aug. 23, 1958; children— David, Deretta, Denise, Dawn, Darrin-(dec.). Student, Miami U., Oxford, Ohio, 1948-51; BSBA, Ohio State U., 1953; M.Ed., Ohio U., 1961, PhD, 1964. Tchr. pub. schs., Scioto County, Ohio, 1957; tchr., adminstr. public schs. Belmont County, Ohio, 1958-60; grad. asst. Ohio U., 1960-61; prin. high sch., adminstrv. asst. to supt. public schs. Athens, Ohio, 1961-64; asst. prof., adviser to Govt. of Nigeria, 1964-66; asst. supt. pub. schs. Athens, Ohio, 1966-67; prin. high sch. public schs. Wilmington, Ohio, 1967-68; with Parma (Ohio) City Schs., 1968-77, asst. to supt., 1968-70, asst. supt., 1970-72, assoc. supt., 1972-75, supt., 1975-77, Tucson Unified Sch. Dist., 1977-79; cons. ednl. mgmt. Tucson, 1979—. Vice chmn. nat. adv. coun. Edn. Disadvantaged Children, 1972-80; supt. Ariz. State Schs. for Deaf and Blind, 1994-98; semi-ret. edn. cons., 2002. Planning divsn. United Way, Tucson, 1978-80; bd. dirs. Jr. Achievement, 1978-80. 1st lt. QMC, U.S. Army, 1954-56. Recipient numerous civic awards for community service; Kettering Found. fellow, 1970 Mem. Am. Assn. Sch. Adminstrs., Buckeye Assn. Sch. Adminstrs., Masons, Shriners, Rotary Internat. (v.p. Tucson 1987—, past pres., dist. gov.'s rep. group study exch. dist. 9120 Nigeria, dist. 5500, chmn. group study exch. dist. 5490 1991-93), Phi Delta Kappa, Lambda Chi Alpha, Sigma Phi Epsilon. Achievements include rsch. in orgnl. devel., adminstrv. behavior patterns, tchr. job satisfaction, student achievement. Home: 10481 E Barbara Pl Tucson AZ 85748 *To achieve one must aspire. To aspire one must dream. But if dreams and aspirations are to become achievements one must persevere. The perseverance necessary to turn dreams and aspirations into achievements has always been made easier for me knowing that children and youth were the benefactors of my efforts.*

LEWIS, WILLIAM ARTHUR, artist, educator; b. Detroit, Mar. 20, 1918; s. Arthur Ernest and Anna Bertha Lewis; m. Ethel Kudrna (div.); children: Susan Amy, Clayton Arthur; m. Garland Anne Sorenson, Dec. 22, 1984. B of Design, U. Mich., Ann Arbor, 1948. Tech. illustrator U. Mich. Engring. Ctr., Willowrun, 1951—57; instr. art U. Mich., Coll. Arch. and Design, Ann Arbor, 1949—50, 1952—53, asst. prof. art, assoc. prof., 1957, 1964, prof. art, 1967, assoc. dean, 1967—74, U. Mich. Sch. Art, Ann Arbor, 1974—76, 1984—85, prof. art emeritus, 1985—. Exhibitions include U. Mich, 1995, USN Gallery, 1997. With USN, 1938—45. Fellow: Nat. Assn. Sch. Art & Design (life; v.p. 1971—75, dir. accreditations com. 1971—75); mem.: William Clements Libr. Am. History, Mich. Watercolor Soc. Avocations: photo history, naval history and ship design. Home: 2550 Traver Blvd Ann Arbor MI 48105 Office Phone: 734-662-7443. Personal E-mail: william.a.lewis@worldnet.att.net.

LEWIS, WILLIAM HEADLEY, JR., manufacturing executive; b. Washington, Sept. 29, 1934; s. William Headley and Lois Maude (Bradshaw) L.; m. Susan M. Simpson, Apr. 25, 2006; children: Teresa Lynne, Bret Cameron, Charles William, Kevin Marcus. BS in Metall. Engring., Va. Poly. Inst., 1956; postgrad. Grad. Sch. Bus. Adminstrn., Emory U., 1978. Registered profl. engr., Calif. Various positions Lockheed Corp., Marietta, Ga., 1956-87, mgr. engring. tech. services, 1979-83, dir. engring. Getex divsn., 1983-86; mgr. Inspection Systems divsn. Lockheed Air Terminal, Inc., 1986-87; CEO Measurement Sys. Inc., Atlanta, 1987—. Chmn. Lockheed Corp. Task Force on NDE, 1980-86; mem. Com. to Study Role of Advanced Tech. in Improving Reliability and Maintainability of Future Weapon Systems, Office of Sec. of Def., 1984-85; co-founder Applied Tech. Svcs., Inc., 1967—; pres., CEO Applied Tech. Fin. Corp., Atlanta, 1983-86; mng. ptnr. Tech. Fin. Co., LLC; lectr. grad. studies and continuing edn. Union Coll., Schenectady, N.Y., 1977-82. Editor: Prevention of Structural Failures: The Role of Fracture Mechanics, Failure Analysis, and NDT, 1978; patentee detection apparatus for structural failure in aircraft. Served to 1st lt. USAF, 1957-60. Fellow: Am. Soc. for Nondestructive Testing (nat. dir. 1976—78, chmn. nat. tech. coun. 1977—78, chmn. aerospace com. 1972—74, nat. nominating com. 1982—85); mem.: NAS (mem. com. on compressive fracture 1981—83), AIAA, Am. Soc. for Metals, Brotherhood of the Knights of the Vine, Grand Haven Golf Club, Country Club Sapphire Valley, St. Ives Country Club. Home: 4 Jasmine Dr Palm Coast FL 32137 Personal E-mail: bill@whlewis.com.

LEWIS, WILLIAM HENRY, JR., lawyer; b. Durham, NC, Nov. 12, 1942; s. William Henry Sr. and Phyllis Lucille (Phillips) L.; m. Jo Ann Whitsett, Apr. 17, 1965 (div. Sept. 1982); 1 child, Kimberly N.; m. Peyton Cockrill Davis, Nov. 28, 1987. Student, N.C. State U., 1960-63; AB in Polit. Sci., U. N.C., 1965, JD with honors, 1969. Bar: Calif., D.C., U.S. Dist. Ct. (cen. dist.) Calif., U.S. Ct. Appeals (D.C. cir., 2nd and 5th cirs.), U.S. Supreme Ct. Assoc. Latham & Watkins, Los Angeles, 1969-74; exec. officer Calif. Air Resources Bd., Los Angeles and Sacramento, Calif., 1975-78; dir. Nat. Com. on Air Quality, Washington, 1978-81; counsel Wilmer, Cutler & Pickering, Washington, 1981-84; ptnr. Morgan, Lewis & Bockius LLP, Washington, 1984—2004, mgr. nat. environ. practice, 1999—2000, sr. counsel, 2004—. Spl. advisor on environ. policy State of Calif., L.A. and Sacramento, 1975; lectr. Law Sch. U. Va., 1993-97. Bd. dirs. For Love of Children, Inc., Washington, 1985-95, pres., 1987-91; bd. dirs. Advs. for Families, Washington, 1985-87, Hillandale Homeowners Assn., Washington, 1986-87, Thurgood Marshall Ctr. Trust, Washington, 1989-95; mem. EPA Clean Air Act Adv. Com., 1994-2005; chmn. bd. dirs., co-founder The Montpelier Found., 1998-2006, chmn. emeritus, 2006—. Mem. ABA. Home: 3900 Georgetown Ct NW Washington DC 20007-2127 also: 18454 Monteith Farm Rd Gordonsville VA 22942-7560 Office: Morgan Lewis and Bockius LLP 1111 Pennsylvania Ave NW Washington DC 20004 Office Phone: 202-739-5145. Business E-Mail: wlewis@morganlewis.com.

LEWIS, WILLIAM JOHN, aerospace engineer; b. Moncton, NB, Can., Sept. 3, 1959; s. Ronald Lloyd and Marion Elizabeth (Dodge) L.; m. Shane Andrea Martin, July 16, 1983; children: Theodore William Dodge, Benjamin Peter Dodge. B in Engring., Royal Mil. Coll., Kingston, Ont., Can., 1981, M in Nuc. Engring., 1988; MBA, U. Man., Winnipeg, Can., 1985; B in Edn., Queen's U., Kingston, 1990, MEd, 1991; PhD in Nuc. Engring., Pacific Western U., 1992. Registered profl. engr., Ont. and Man. Commd. 2d lt. Can. Air Force, 1981, advance through grades to lt. col., 1994; aerospace engring. officer Dept. Nat. Def., Winnipeg, 1982-85, Ottawa, 1985-86, maintenance analysis officer Trenton, Ont., 1991-94, aerospace engring. officer, 1994-97, Ottawa, 1997—2001, Trenton, 2001—; lectr. engring. Royal Mil. Coll., 1985-88, asst. prof., then assoc. prof., 1988-91, adj. prof., 1991—. Cons., pres. Software Aide, Kingston and Trenton, 1985—; mem. postgrad. adv. bd. Royal Mil. Coll., 1988-91. Contbg. author: Neutron Radiography, 3rd edit., 1990, 5th edit., 1997, Radiation Measurements and Applications, 1991. Scout leader Boy Scouts Am., 1994—. Grantee, Chief of Rsch. and Design, Ottawa, 1986—; recipient Can. 125 medal Govt. of Can., 1993, Can. Order of Mil. Merit, Govt. Can., 1999. Mem. AIChE, Am. Soc. for Engring. Edn., Can. Soc. Chem. Engring., Can. Soc. for Non-destructive Testing, Can. Neutron-Radiography Assn. (mem. conf. organizing com. 1990), Can. Nuc. Soc. (conf. organizing com. 1991), Masons, Shriners. Mem. United Ch. of Can. Achievements include design, installation and commission of world's first neutron radiography facility using small research reactor as neutron source; pioneer in investigation of advanced metal ceramics and composite aircraft flight controls using neutron radiography. Home: 49 Oak Ridge Dr RR #4 Brighton ON Canada K0K 1H0 Office: Royal Mil Coll Can Chem Eng PO Box 17000 Stn Forces Kingston ON Canada K7K 5L0 E-mail: bstblewis@sympatico.ca, lewis-w@rmc.ca.

LEWIS, WILLIAM M., diversified financial services company executive; b. Richmond, Va., Apr. 30, 1956; s. William M. and Essie Lewis; m. Carol Sutton. BA in Economics, Harvard U., 1978, MBA, 1982. Fin. analyst Morgan Stanley, NYC, 1978—80, with, 1982—99, co-head global banking dept., 1999—2004; mng. dir., co-chmn. investment banking Lazard Freres & Co. LLC, NYC, 2004—. Bd. dirs. Cancer Rsch. Inst., 2003—, Freddie Mac, 2004—, Darden Restaurants, Inc., 2005—. Chmn. NAACP Legal Def. & Ednl. Fund; bd. mem. Carnegie Endowment for Internat. Peace. Named one of The Top 50 African-Americans on Wall St., Black Enterprise, 2002. Office: Lazard Freres & Co LLC 30 Rockefeller Plz Fl 59 New York NY 10112*

LEWIS, WILLIAM RAYMOND, art educator, artist; b. Osceola, Iowa, Sept. 23, 1920; s. Frank Raymond and Pearle Darlene Lewis; m. Marian Joan Lewis; children: Steven, Robert, Donald, Douglas. BFA, Drake U., DesMoines, 1949; postgrad., U. Wash., Seattle, 1949—50; MA in Art Edn., Ariz. State U., Tempe, 1951. Art tchr. Madison Dist., Phoenix, 1951—52, Whittier-Phoenix, 1952—54; art dept. chair South Mountain H.S., Phoenix, 1954—78. Art instr. Phoenix Coll., 1956—78; charter mem. Ariz. Watercolor Assn., Phoenix, 1960. Cpl. US Army, 1942—45. Decorated Bronze Star US Army. Avocations: collecting juice boxes, collecting Golden Age radios. Home: 313 E 15th St Tempe AZ 85281

LEWIS-WHITE, LINDA BETH, elementary school educator; b. Fresno, Calif., June 30, 1950; d. Lloyd Ernest and Anne Grace (Barkman) Lewis; m. Francis Everett White, Feb. 15, 1975; children: Anna Justine, Christopher Andrew Arthur. BA in Home Econs., Calif. State U., Sacramento, 1972, MA in Social Scis., 1973; postgrad., Tex. Women's U., 1976-79; PhD in Reading, East Tex. State U., 1994. Cert. bilingual and elem. edn. tchr., Tex. Tchr. bilingual Arlington Sch. Dist., 1977-96; prof. reading Eastern Mich. U., 1996—. Adj. prof. reading Tex. Women's U., Denton, 1989, adj. prof. ESL East Tex. State U., 1993; mem. tchr. trainer cadre, Dallas Ind. Sch. Dist., 1985-92; freelance cons., 1987—; presenter TESOL Internat. Conf., San Antonio, 1989. Cons., writer (book) Ciencias-Silver Burdett, 1988. Troop leader Girl Scouts U.S., Dallas, 1980-82. Recipient Ronald W. Collins Disting. Faculty award, Eastern Mich. U., 2007. Mem. Nat. Reading Conf., Nat. Writing Project, Internat. Reading Assn., Tchrs. of English to Spkrs. of Other Langs. (nominating com. 1990-91), TEXTESOL V (chair elem. edn. com. 1989-91), Tex. Assn. Bilingual Edn., Phi Delta Kappa, Phi Mu. Mem. Christian Ch. Avocations: sewing, knitting, quilting, reading, gourmet cooking. Office: Eastern Mich U 313A Porter Bldg Ypsilanti MI 48197-2210 Business E-Mail: llewiswh@emich.edu.

LEWITT, MILES MARTIN, computer engineering company executive; b. NYC, July 14, 1952; s. George Herman and Barbara (Lin) L.; m. Susan Beth Orenstein, June 24, 1973; children: Melissa, Hannah. BS summa cum laude, CCNY Engring., 1973; MS, Ariz. State U., 1976. Software engr. Honeywell, Phoenix, 1973-78; architect iRMX line ops. systems, x86 line microprocessors Intel Corp., Santa Clara, Calif., 1978; engring. mgr. Intel, Hillsboro, Oreg., 1978-80, 1981-89, corp. strategic staff, 1981-82, engring. mgr. Israel, 1980-81; v.p. engring. Cadre Techs., Inc., Beaverton, Oreg., 1989-91; v.p. rsch. and devel. ADP, Portland, Oreg., 1991—2001; v.p. tech. group Intuit, San Diego, 2001—. Instr. Maricopa Tech. Coll., Phoenix, 1974-75; spkr., keynote spkr. at confs. Contbr. articles to profl. jours. Bd. dirs. Portland Computer Tng. Inst., 1995—98; mem. adv. bd. Data Intensive Sys. Ctr., Portland State U., Oreg. Grad. Inst. Recipient Engring. Alumni award CCNY, 1973, Eliza Ford Prize CCNY, 1973, Advanced Engring. Program award, Honeywell, 1976, Product of Yr. award Electronic Products Mag., 1980. Mem. IEEE (sr.), IEEE Computer Soc. (voting mem.), Assn. Computing Machinery (voting mem.), Am. Electronics Assn. (exec. com. Oreg. Coun.), Am. Soc. for Quality (sr.). Democrat. Avocations: photography, travel, walking.

LEWITTES, DON JORDAN, psychologist; b. Bklyn., Jan. 21, 1950; s. Morton H. and Laura C. L.; 1 child, Jason D.; m. Deborah Steiner, Oct. 30, 2005. BA, NYU, 1971; PhD, SUNY, Albany, 1976. Diplomate Am. Bd. Med. Psychotherapists, Am. Bd. Forensic Examiners, Am. Bd. Forensic Medicine, Am. Bd. Psychol. Specialities. Instr. dept. psychiatry Albany Med. Coll., 1976-78; clin. affiliate, prof. of psychology St. John's U., 1983-85; sr. psychologist Schenectady Shared Svcs., Ellis Hosp., 1976-77; dir. adminstrv. and clin. inpatient svcs. South Richmond-South Beach Psychiat. Ctr., SI, NY, 1977-81; chief psychologist South Nassau Cmty. Hosp., Oceanside, NY, 1982-87; cons. Nassau Coalition on Child Abuse and Neglect, Hempstead, NY, 1989-98. Psychol. cons. Gracie Sq. Hosp., N.Y.C., 1989-91; expert cons. N.Y.C. Office Legal Affairs/ACS, 1991—, Kings County and Bronx County Dist. Atty's. Office, 1994—; adjunct faculty Grad. Sch. Social Svc. Fordham U., 1995-96; intern dept. psychiatry Rutgers Med. Sch., Piscataway, N.J., 1974-75. Contbr. articles to profl. jours. Mem. Am. Psychol. Soc., Am. Profl. Soc. on the Abuse of Children. Office: Ste 150 30 Hempstead Ave Rockville Centre NY 11570-4033 Office Phone: 516-763-1631.

LEWRIS, BASIL J., lawyer; b. Manhattan, NY, Feb. 26, 1949; BChE cum laude, CUNY, 1972; JD with high honors, George Washington U., 1977, LLM in Patent and Trade Regulation Law, 1980. Bar: Va. 1977, US Ct. Fed. Claims 1978, DC 1979, US Supreme Ct. 1981, US Ct. Appeals (Fed. Cir.) 1982, registered: US Patent & Trademark Office. Law clerk to assoc. judge Donald E. Lane US Ct. Customs and Patent Appeals, 1977-79; lectr. Patent Resources Group, Inc., 1982-91; ptnr. Finnegan, Henderson, Farabow, Garrett & Dunner LLP, Washington, mem. exec. com. Co-author (with Matthew Bender): Patent Law Perspectives, 1984—88. Named one of best lawyers in intellectual property law, Best Lawyers in Am., 2005—06. Mem.: Order of Coif, Va. State Bar Assn., Fed. Cir. Bar Assn., DC Bar, Assn. Trial Lawyers Am., ABA, Am. Intellectual Property Law Assn., Omega Chi Epsilon, Tau Beta Pi, Delta Theta Phi. Office: Finnegan Henderson Farabow Garrett & Dunner LLP 901 New York Ave NW Washington DC 20001-3315 Office Phone: 202-408-4000. Office Fax: 202-408-4400. Business E-Mail: bill.lewris@finnegan.com.

LEWY, ROBERT MAX, physician; b. NYC, Oct. 18, 1945; s. Martin and Ellen (Newmark) L.; m. Barbara, Oct. 4, 1987; children: Jennifer, Sarah. AB, U. Rochester, 1967; MD, U. Medicine and Dentistry N.J., Newark, 1971; MPH, Columbia U., 1977. Diplomate Nat. Bd. Med. Examiners, Am. Bd. Family Practice. Intern Dartmouth Affiliated Hosps., Hanover, NH, 1971-72; resident Maine-Dartmouth Family Practice Program, Augusta, 1974-75; clin. scholar Columbia U., NYC, 1975-77; dir. employee health svcs. Presbyn. Hosp., Columbia-Presbyn. Med. Ctr., NYC, 1977-88, dir. office physician affairs, 1988-91, sr. v.p. med. affairs, 1991-98; assoc. prof. medicine Columbia U., NYC, 1991—, sr. assoc. dean health affairs, 1998—. Author: Preventive Primary Medicine, 1981, Employees at Risk, 1991; contbr. articles to profl. jours. With USPHS, 1972-74. Fellow Am. Occupational Med. Assn. (sec. chmn. 1984-88), Am. Coll. Preventive Medicine; mem. Am. Pub. Health Assn., N.Y. Occupational Med. Assn. (bd. dirs. 1985—). Home: 864 Bradley Pky Blauvelt NY 10913-1127 Office: Columbia U Box 100 630 W 168th St New York NY 10032-3795 E-mail: rl10@columbia.edu.

LEWYN, ANN SALFELD, retired English as a second language educator; b. NYC, Dec. 1, 1935; d. Henry and Betty (Ahrens) Salfeld; m. Thomas Mark Lewyn, July 15, 1955; children: Alfred Thomas, Mark Henry. BA, Hunter Coll., 1967, MA, 1982. Mem. faculty UN Hospitality Extension Lang. Program, NYC, 1974-86; adj. instr. ESL NYU, 1986-90, adj. asst. prof., 1990-95, adj. assoc. prof., 1995-2000, adj. prof., 2001—02; ret., 2003—. Editor-in-chief (Newsletter) UN Hospitality Com., 1967-86. Mem. exec. bd. Small Press Ctr., N.Y.C., 1990-98; mem. adv. coun. Hospitality Com. for UN Dels. Inc., 1991-98; bd. dirs. Hunter Coll. Scholarship and Welfare Fund, N.Y.C., 1992—, sec., 1998-2000, 3d v.p., 2000-2001, 2d v.p., 2001-06, 1st v.p., 2006—. Mem. Teachers of English as Second Lang. (author in Aug. 1990 newsletter), N.Y. State Tchrs. of English as Second Lang., Pi Sigma Alpha, Kappa Delta Pi. Avocations: travel, tennis, needlepoint, photography, golf. Home: 911 Park Ave New York NY 10075

LEWYN, THOMAS MARK, lawyer; b. NYC, July 2, 1930; s. Oswald and Agnes (Maas) L.; m. Ann Salfeld, July 15, 1955; children— Alfred Thomas, Mark Henry. BA, Stanford, 1952, postgrad., 1952-54; LL.B., Columbia, 1955. Bar: N.Y. 1957. Assoc. Simpson, Thacher & Bartlett, NYC, 1957-64, ptnr., 1965-75, sr. ptnr., 1976-90, of counsel, 1991—95. Bd. dirs. Metro-Goldwyn-Mayer, Inc. Contbr. articles to profl. jours. Served to 1st lt., F.A. AUS, 1955-57. Mem. ABA, Assn. of Bar of City of N.Y., N.Y. State Bar Assn. Home: 911 Park Ave New York NY 10021-0337 Office: Simpson Thacher & Bartlett 425 Lexington Ave Fl 15 New York NY 10017-3954 Office Phone: 212-455-2820. Personal E-mail: tomlewyn@aol.com.

LEY, RONALD, psychologist, educator; b. Buffalo, Oct. 19, 1929; s. August Andreas and Marie (Jerge) L.; m. Carmen De Brito, Jan. 16, 1965; 1 child, Jessica Elizabeth. BA, U. Buffalo, 1951; PhD, Syracuse U., 1963. Rsch. dir. Madison Area Project, Syracuse, 1962—63; asst. prof. psychology No. Ill. U., DeKalb, 1963—64; asst. prof. grad. faculty New Sch. U., NYC, 1964—66; prof. psychology and stats. SUNY Albany, 1966—99, rsch. prof., 1999—. Cons. Nat. Inst. for Occupational Safety and Health; vis. prof. psychology U. P.R., 1969, cardiac dept., Charing Cross Hosp., London, 1988. Author: A Whisper of Espionage, 1990, Rumores de Espionaje: Wolfgang Köhler y los Monos en Tenerife, 1995; co-editor: Behavioral and Psychological Approaches to Breathing Disorders, 1994; mem. editl. bd. Jour. Behavior Therapy and Exptl. Psychiatry, 1983—, Applied Psychophysiology and Biofeedback, 1997—, Behavior Modification, Jour. Anxiety Disorders, guest editor Biofeedback and Self-Regulation, 1994; guest editor: Behavior Modification, 2001; guest editor Behavior Modification, 2003; contbr. articles to profl. jours. and encys. Bd. dirs. Father's Assn. of the Albany Acad. for Girls, 1981-84. Rsch. fellow SUNY, 1967-68, 70, 74, 76, 78, 91, Rsch. grantee, 1967-72, 74-76, 78, 87-88, 91-92, 96-97, Nat. Inst. Occupl. Safety and Health grantee, 1982-83, 87-88, others. Fellow Am. Psychol. Soc., Behavior Therapy and Rsch. Soc.; mem. APA, Anxiety Disorders Assn. Am., Am. Statis. Assn., Assn. for Psychol. Sci., Assn. Advancement Behavior Therapy, Assn. Applied Psychophysiology and Biofeedback (chmn. sect. applied respiratory psychophysiology 1998-99), Authors Guild, Authors League Am., Ea. Psychol. Assn., Internat. Soc. Advancement Respiratory Psychophysiology (co-founder, pres. 1994-96), Psychol. Assn. Northeastern N.Y. (sec. 1967-68, pres. 1983-84, Disting. Psychologist award 1996), Soc. Psychophysiol. Rsch., Psychonomic Soc., Sigma Xi. Home: 22 Marion Ave Albany NY 12203-1823 Office: Univ at Albany SUNY 233 ED Bldg 1400 Washington Ave Albany NY 12222-1000 Office Phone: 518-442-5055.

LEY, TIMOTHY JAMES, hematologist, molecular biologist; b. Buffalo Ctr., Iowa, June 17, 1953; s. William Dean and Clara Ruth (Odland) L.; m. Patricia Ann Hohn, Aug. 21, 1986; children: Amelia, James, Anna. BA, Drake U., 1974; MD, Washington U., St. Louis, 1978. Diplomate Am. Bd. Internal Medicine and Hematology. Resident in medicine Mass. Gen. Hosp., Boston, 1978-80; fellow in hematology NIH, Bethesda, Md., 1980-83, sr. investigator, 1984-86; fellow in hematology and oncology Washington U. Med. Sch., St. Louis, 1983-84, asst. prof. medicine and genetics, 1986-90, assoc. prof. medicine, 1990-93, prof. medicine and genetics, 1993—. Assoc. dir. Basic Rsch. Siteman Cancer Ctr., 1999—. Mem. Gasconade County R2 Sch. Bd., Mo., 2000—. With USPHS, 1980—86. Fellow AAAS; mem. Inst. of Medicine, NAS, Am. Soc. Hematology, Am. Soc. Biochemistry and Molecular Biology, Am. Soc. for Clin. Investigation (pres. 1997-98), Am. Assn. Physicians (coun. 2007—), Phi Beta Kappa, Alpha Omega Alpha. Democrat. Mem. United Ch. Christ. Achievements include rsch. in practical feasibility of manipulating fetal hemoglobin production in patients with hemoglobinopathies; development of mouse models of human leukemias, and determination of roles of proteases in immune effector cell functions. Office: Washington U Med Sch Box 8007 660 S Euclid Ave Saint Louis MO 63110-1010 Home Phone: 573-437-5497; Office Phone: 314-362-8831. Business E-Mail: tley@im.wustl.edu.

LEYDEN, MICHAEL JOSEPH, II, (LEI JIE MING), finance educator, entrepreneur, writer; b. Wash., Feb. 26, 1950; s. Lawrence Ignatius and Wilma LaVerne Gugliemette Eriksen; m. Michele Theresa Vespier, 1972 (div. 1987); children: Sophia Dion, Søren Nicholas; m. Zhong Yu (Ivy) Xu, Nov. 1991; 1 child, Sophia Qian Yu. AA in Econs., Wenatchee Valley Coll., 1970; student, Charlotte Amailie, St. Thomas U. V.I., 1970—71; BA in Philosophy and Psychology, Ctrl. Wash. U., 1972; MA in Philosophy, Wash. State U., 1974; various mktg. diplomas, U. Hawaii, 1975-89; DBA, Newport U., Utah and Beijing, 1997; postgrad., U. N.B., Fredericton, Can. Corp. mgr., tng. dir. Colwell Bankers-Davenport Inc., Wenatchee, Wash.,

1977—81; v.p. sales and mktg. John's Real Estate and Securities Corp., Bellevue, Wash., 1981—82; pres., founder Aero-Brokers Inc., Aero-Brokers Trading Co., Inc., Aero-Brokers Internat. Securities Co., ABI Comm. Group Svcs. Co., Aero-Brokers Internat. Real Estate Corp., Honolulu, Hawaii, Long Beach, Calif., Wenatchee, Wash., 1983—86; gen. mgr. Tadashi & Sons Ltd., (Truk) Chuuk Islands, Micronesia, 1987; CEO, adminstrv. and fin. mgr. Zorro's Pizza and Italian Restaurants (4 branches), Honolulu, 1988; gen mgr., tile and marble import wholesaler Coast Enterprises Hawaii Inc., Honolulu, 1990; exec. v.p., gen. mgr. Eternity (Tianjin) Internat. Trade Devel. Co., Ltd., Honolulu, 1992—93; prof. Sch. Internat. Bus. Nankai U., Tianjin, China, 1994; prof. dept. internat. politics Sch. Internat. Rels. Beijing U., China, 1995; prof. dept. econ. and mgmt. Qinghua (Tsinghua) U., Beijing, 1996; internat. bus. affairs dir. Michael Trading and Cons. Co. Ltd., Beijing City, 1997; prof. dept. econ. and mgmt. Shanghai U., China, 1998; dean, adminstrn. and devel. and CFO Coll. Marshall Islands, Majuro, Micronesia; project dir. employment, tng. coord. not for profit orgn. Honolulu Cmty. Action Program, Inc., Honolulu, 1999—2000; prof. grad. sch. mgmt. Tianjin Polytechnic U., 2002; acting dean Coll. Bus. Adminstrn. Kazakhstan Inst. Mgmt. Econs. Strategic Policy, Almaty, Kazakhstan, 2004; dean Coll. Continuing Edn. Kazakhstan Inst. Mgmt., Econs. Strategic Policy, Almaty, 2004—05; prof. fin., econs. and banking Internat. Edn. Ctr. Shandong U. Scis. and Tech., Tai'an, China, 2006. Spl. asst. to commr. edn. and rsch., statistician No. Marianas Islands Pub. Sch. Sys., 1991; program mgr. edn. and tng. Workforce Investment Act, Samoan Svc. Providers Assn., Honolulu, 2001—; dep. vice gen. mgr. Beijing (Peking) and Prosperity Advt. Co., Ltd., Tianjin, 2003; prof., provost, v.p. acad. affairs Tianjin Pacific Profl. Coll., 2004-05, corp. sec. Santee H.H.H. (U.S.A.) Corp., Honolulu, prof. Beijing Wuzu U., China, 2006; invited prof. Shanjiang Normal U., 2006, St. John's Tech. U., 2007, Emirates Aviation Coll., Dubai, United Arab Emirates, 2007-; advisor GLC Cons. Contbr. articles and revs. in field, poems to pubs. Recipient Pres.'s medal for leadership, 1970, Sophia Newspaper Editors award, 1973, Honolulu Mayor's award bus. honour, 1975, INDEPEX, 1997, Internat. Philatelic Exbn., New Dehli, 1997, Bronze medal in Philatelic Lit., CCNY Jour., Large Silver medal Bangkok Internat. Philatelic Exhibit philatelic lit., 2003, Tianjin Mcpl. Archive Hon. Achievement award to First Foreigner, Dir. Sun, Silver medal, Chgo. PEX, 2003, Silver medal, Postal History Lit. Book APS Stamp Show, Columbus, OH, 2003, Large Silver medal, No. 1 of 56 Philatelic entries, ACPF Nat. Expn. Chong Qing City, Tianjin-Beijin Phil. Soc. Gold, 2007. Mem. Am. Mgmt. Assn. (mem. pres. club 1980, 87, 92), N.Ctrl. Wash. Oriental Rug Soc. (editor Oriental Textile newsletter 1977-80), Shanghai Am. C. of C. Edn.-Pub. Com. (chmn. 1997-99), All China Philatelic Fed. Beijing Assn., Tianjin Philatelic Assn., Royal Philatelic Soc. London, Am. Philatelic Soc., China Stamp Soc., NC Wash. Writers Guild, BCC Hawaii, Collectors Club (NY), Lions, Rotary, Inernat. Honolulu Downtown Club, SESCAL, So. Calif. Philatelic Soc., COLOPEX, Cath. Charismatic Conf., GLC Ecex. Coun. Avocations: writing, sports, history. Home: Ouya Hua Yuan European Asian Gardens Tower Dr 4 Ste 1205 Penthouse Binshui Rd Tianjin 300060 China Home (Winter): PO Box 22124 Honolulu HI 96823-2124 Home Phone: 862288353948; Office Phone: 8613902129012. Office Fax: 862288354496. Personal E-mail: michaelleyden@yahoo.com.

LEYDORF, FREDERICK LEROY, lawyer; b. Toledo, Ohio, June 13, 1930; s. Loftin Herman and Dorothy DeRoyal (Cramer) L.; m. Mary MacKenzie Malcolm, Mar. 28, 1953; children: Robert Malcolm, William Frederick, Katherine Ann, Thomas Richard, Deborah Mary. Student, U. Toledo, 1948-49; BBA, U. Mich., 1953; JD, UCLA, 1958. Bar: Calif. 1959, U.S. Supreme Ct. 1970. Assoc. Hammack & Pugh, LA, 1959-61; ptnr. Willis, Butler, Scheifly, Leydorf & Grant, LA, 1961-81, Pepper, Hamilton & Scheetz, LA, 1981-83, Hufstedler & Kaus, LA, 1983-95. Lectr., cons. Calif. Continuing Edn. of Bar, 1965-92; mem. planning com. Probate and Trust Conf., U. So. Calif., 1984-92. Contbg. author: California Non-Profit Corporations, 1969; contbr. articles to profl. jours. Chmn. pub. adminstr.-pub. guardian adv. commn. Los Angeles County Bd. Suprs., 1972-73; v.p. J.W. and Ida M. Jameson Found., 1995—, bd. dirs., 1967—; bd. dirs. Western Ctr. on Law and Poverty, Inc., 1980-82, L.A. Heart Inst., 1988-90; mem. legal com. Music Ctr. Found., 1980-95; mem. lawyers adv. coun. Constl. Rights Found., 1982-85; mem. devel. adv. bd. U. Mich. Sch. Bus. Adminstrn., 1984-90; mem. adv. bd. UCLA-CEB Estate Planning Inst., 1979-92; Lt. USNR, 1953-55. Mem. Libbey H.S. Hall of Fame (Toledo), 1999. Mem. L.A. County Bar Assn. (bd. trustees 1973-75), State Bar Calif. (chmn. conf. dels. 1977, Alumnus of Yr. award, conf. of dels. 1983, mem. exec. com. estate planning, trust and probate law sect. 1979-80), L.A. County Bar Found. (pres. 1977-79, bd. dirs. 1975-87), Internat. Acad. Estate and Trust Law (v.p. N.Am. 1978-82), Life Ins. and Trust Coun. L.A. (pres. 1983-84), UCLA Law Alumni Assn. (pres. 1982), L.A. World Affairs Coun. (mem. internat. cir.), Chancery Club (pres. 1991-92), Jonathan Club, Laguna Woods Golf Club, Sunrise Country Club (Rancho Mirage, Calif.), Phi Delta Phi, Phi Delta Theta. Republican. Lutheran. Home: 75 Majorca Dr Rancho Mirage CA 92270-3826

LEYDORF, MARY MALCOLM, physician, writer; b. Manila, Philippines; d. Justice George Arthur and Lucille Margaret Malcolm; m. Frederick Leroy Leydorf, 1953; children: Robert, William, Katherine, Thomas, Deborah. MD, UCLA, 1957. Cert. pediatrics, exec. mgmt. Claremont Grad. Sch. Intern Harbor Gen. Hosp., Torrance, Calif., 1957—58, resident pediatrics, 1958—61; fellow devel. medicine Brain Rsch. Inst., UCLA, 1967—68; asst. clin. prof. pediatrics UCI, Irvine, Calif., 1971—73; physician-in-charge L.A. Med. Treatment Unit Calif. Children's Svc., physician-in-charge Glendale Med. Treatment Unit; commr. lic. divsn. Med. Bd. Calif.; physician L.A. County Pub. Health, Calif. State U., LA; attending physician child devel. clinic UCI Med. Ctr., Orange, Calif., White Meml. Hosp., LA; sch. physician El Monte, San Gabriel, Temple City Sch. Dists. Founder, dir. Leydorf Med. Clinics, Inc., 1969—89. Editor: (quarterly newsletter) Dev. Disability Rsch. Rev., 1987—89; co-author: (articles) Jour. Spl. Edn., Jour. Western Medicine, Pediatrics. Mem. Rotary Internat., 2000, Zonta Internat.; vol. physician YMCA, So. Pasadena, San Marino, Calif., Spastic League, Pasadena. Mem.: Am. Acad. Pediatrics, AMA, Calif. Scholarship Fedn., Palm Springs Writers Guild, Kappa Alpha Theta. Avocations: horseback riding, breeding thoroughbred horses. Home: 75 Majorca Dr Rancho Mirage CA 92270 Personal E-mail: malcolmpub@aol.com.

LEYHANE, FRANCIS JOHN, III, lawyer; b. Chgo., Mar. 29, 1957; s. Francis J. and Mary Elizabeth (Crowley) L.; m. Diana M. Urizarri, May 8, 1982; children: Katherine, Francis J. IV, Joseph, Brigid Rose, James Matthew. BA, Loyola U., Chgo., 1977, JD, 1980. Bar: Ill. 1980, U.S. Dist. Ct. (no. dist.) Ill. 1980, U.S. Ct. Appeals (7th cir.) 1986. Assoc. Condon, Cook & Roche, Chgo., 1980-87; ptnr. Condon & Cook, Chgo., 1988-98, Boyle & Leyhane, Ltd., Chgo., 1998—2003, Leyhane & Assocs. Ltd., 2003—. Contbr. articles to profl. jours. Mem. Sch. bd. Immaculate Conception Parish, Chgo., 1993-96. Fellow Ill. Bar Found.; mem. Appellate Lawyers Assn. Ill., Ill. State Bar Assn. (mem. assembly 1987-90), Chgo. Bar Assn., Blue Key. Office: Leyhane and Assocs Ltd 205 West Randolph St Ste 1320 Chicago IL 60606 Home Phone: 773-763-9027. Business E-Mail: leyhane329@aol.com.

LEYLAND, JIM (JAMES RICHARD LEYLAND), professional baseball manager; b. Toledo, Dec. 15, 1944; m. Katie Leyland. Player various minor league teams Detroit Tigers, 1964-69, coach minor league system, 1970-71, mgr. minor league system, 1971-81; coach Chgo. White Sox, 1981-85; mgr. Pitts. Pirates, 1985-96, Fla. Marlins, Miami, 1997-98, Colo. Rockies, Denver, 1998—99, Detroit Tigers, 2005—. Christmas chmn. Salvation Army, 1990-91. Named Nat. League Mgr. Yr. Baseball Writers' Assn., 1988, 1990, 2006; Sporting News, 1990, Man of Yr. Arthritis Found., 1989, Epilepsy Found., 1991; lead Detroit to playoffs two years after having worst record in Major League Baseball, 2006 Office: Detroit Tigers Comerica Pk 2100 Woodward Ave Detroit MI 48201

LEZAK, CAROL SPIELMAN, communications executive, editor, writer, design consultant, medical librarian; b. NYC, Oct. 24, 1949; d. Murray and Sylvia Zeena (Ruderman) Spielman; m. Jeffrey Mayer Lezak, Mar. 2, 1975; 1 child, Jessica Lilli. BA in Fine Arts and Art History, Boston U., 1971; MA in Libr. Sci., U. Mich., 1972. Cataloguer of books Ryerson and Burnham Librs., Art Inst. Chgo., 1972-76, acting head tech. svcs., 1976-77; head tech. svcs. Gilpin Libr., Chgo. Hist. Soc., 1977-79; asst. editor Gen. Learning Comm., Highland Park, Ill., 1982-83, assoc. editor, 1983-84, mng. editor, 1984-92, sr. editor Northbrook, Ill., 1992-99, editor Eleven mag. for WTTW Chgo., 1995-99; editl. dir. Bounty SCA Worldwide, Chgo., 1999—2001; mgr. corp. comm. Walgreen Co./Walgreens Health Initiatives, Deerfield, Ill., 2001—04; sr. med. writer Walgreens Health Svcs., Deerfield, Ill., 2004—05; health content mgr. Walgreens.com Health Libr., Deerfield, 2005—. Book reviewer Libr. Jour., 1977-00, Elle mag., 2005, Obituary, 2007; freelance bookbinder, Highland Park, 1980—; owner North Woods Writing, Highland Park, 1994-06. Author: Medication Matters Series, 2002—05; author, editor: Clara's Bakery Cookbook, 1995, Chicago Historical Society 5 Year Cumulative Index to Chicago History mag., The Better Health Booklets, 1995—99, Mrs. Applegate's Boarding House Cookbook, 1995; editor: Maturity Matters/Your Healthy Best, 1992—99 (award Soc. Nat. Assn. Publs., 1995), Your Health Report, 1992—99, The Good Health Sourcebook, 1996, Good Health Sourcebook Annual Calendar, Tobacco Free Clinical Care Management Program, 2005, Walgreens Health Initiatives Outlook Trend Report, 2005, Walgreens Ask a Pharmacist Series, 2005—; editor design cons.: mag. Your Health and Fitness, 1984—99; editl. cons. (video) Breast Self-Exam Guide, 1993;, author poetry. Vol., writing lab. tutor Highland Park Pub. Schs., 1994-96. Recipient Ednl. Press Assn. awards, 1988-1995, 1st pl. award logo design Sister Cities Found., 1990, hon. mention awards Gardeners of the North Shore, 1995, Internat. Corp. SMART award for adminstrv. excellence, 6 Mercury 2000 awards of excellence. Avocations: writing, reading, gardening. Office: Walgreen Co Dept 1458 104 Wilmot Rd Deerfield IL 60015 Home Phone: 847-433-6202. Business E-Mail: carol.lezak@walgreens.com.

L'HEUREUX, RICHARD ALLEN, academic administrator, consultant; b. International Falls, Minn., Mar. 6, 1953; s. John Joseph and Agnes Frances L'heureux; m. Meeta Goel; children: Autumn Paige, Brea Elizabeth, Samuel Hsing, Kyle Praveen Singhal, Maia Natalya Goel-L'heureux. BS in Polit. Sci., U. Minn., 1975; MS in Acquisition Mgmt., Air Force Inst. Tech., 1988; PhD in Bus. Adminstrn., Fla. State U., 1994. Commd. 2d lt. USAF, 1980, advanced through grades to lt. col., with San Antonio, 1978—99; exec. v.p. New West Strategies, Helena, Mont., 1999—; provost Mountain State U., Beckley, Minn., 2000—. Contbr. articles to profl. jours. Vol. Spl. Olympics, 1980—99, Habitat for Humanity, Beckley, W.Va., 2000—04; com. mem. Beckley (W.Va.) C. of C., 2003—04; tchr. St. Francis de Sales, Beckley. Recipient Ezra Kotcher award for Curriculum Devel., Air U., 1998. Mem.: Nat. Contract Mgmt. Assn. (cert. profl. contract mgr. 1990). Roman Catholic. Avocations: skiing, golf, canoeing, camping, Native American art. Office: New West Strategies Inc Butte MT 59701 Home: 55 Mily Way Butte MT 59701

LHUILLIER, (DIANE) MONIQUE, apparel designer; b. Philippines; m. Tom Bugbee. Grad., Fashion Inst. of Design and Merchandising, Los Angeles. Founder, designer Monique Lhuillier & Co., Los Angeles, 1996—; opened Monique Lhuillier Boutique, Beverly Hills, 2001—. Designs featured in numerous magazines including W, In Style, Modern Bride, Elle. Recipient Glamorous Bridal Designer award, 2001, Avant Garde Bridal Designer award, Wedding Dresses Mag., 2002. Mem.: Council of Fashion Designers of Am. Office: Monique Lhuillier & Co 1201 S Grand Ave 3rd Fl Los Angeles CA 90015

LI, CHENGLONG, biophysicist, educator; b. Susong, Anhui, China, Apr. 24, 1965; s. Youde Li and Zhonghua Wu; m. Dahao Ling, Dec. 7, 1967; children: Glenna Gelan, Patricia Yumei. BS, Beijing U., 1985, MS, 1988; PhD, Cornell U., Ithaca, NYC, 2000. Rsch. assoc. Inst. Biophysics, Beijing, 1988—90, Burnham Inst., La Jolla, Calif., 2000—02, Scripps Rsch. Inst., La Jolla, 2002—05; asst. prof. Ohio State U., Columbus, 2005—. Cons. Glycopep, Chgo., 2006—. Fellow, US Dept. Def., 2002—04. Mem.: Am. Assn. Cancer Rsch., Am. Crystallographic Assn., Am. Chem. Soc. Achievements include development of suicide gene therapy prodrugs; first to determin the largest crystal substructure of anomalous scatterers; design of a novel hierarchical computational drug design method; discovery of a novel protein structure fold and a novel ATP binding motif; invention of a novel anti-cancer drug disabling oncogene STAT3. Home: 6068 Round Tower Ln Dublin OH 43017 Home Phone: 614-761-3729; Office Phone: 614-247-8786. Office Fax: 614-292-2435. Business E-Mail: li.728@osu.edu.

LI, CHIANG J., pharmaceutical executive, physician scientist; s. Tian-En Li and Ailian Liu; m. Liz; children: Linda, William, Charles. Diploma in health sci. and tech., MIT, Cambridge, 1996; MD magna cum laude, Harvard U., Boston, 1998. Diplomate Am. Bd. of Internal Medicine, 2001. Head ArQule Biomed. Inst., Woburn and Norwood, Mass., 2003—07; chief sci. officer, exec. v.p. ArQule Inc., Woburn, Mass., 2003—; chmn., CEO Boston Biomedical, Inc., 2007—. Adj. prof. SE U., Nanjing, China, 1999—; adj. faculty Med. Sch. Harvard U., Boston, 2000—; prin. investigator, gi cancer lab. Harvard-Beth Israel Deaconess Med. Ctr., Boston, 2000—; chmn., joint r&d com. ArQule-Roche Oncology Partnership, 2004—. Singer (songwriter): Searching for You (Best Score, NY Film and Video Festival, 2005). Recipient Richard A. Smith award, Harvard-Dana-Farber Cancer Inst., 1993; grantee, Nat. Rsch. Svc., 1993—94; scholar, Merck, 1996; Internat. Monbushu scholar, Japanese Ministry of Sci. and Edn., 1989, Lyman and Grew scholar, Harvard U., 1996—97. Mem.: Am. Soc. Clin. Oncology, Am. Gastroenterology Assn., Am. Assn. Cancer Rsch. Achievements include first to propose and pursue activated checkpoint pathway therapy for cancers and other diseases; discovery of how HIV kills T cells and Tat as AIDS Vaccine Target; invention of use of beta-lapachone to treat cancers; transkingdom RNA interference; the world's first selective C-met oncogen inhibitor drugs. Office: Boston Biomedical Inc 333 Providence Hwy Norwood MA 02062 Office Phone: 781-278-0900. Business E-Mail: cli@bostonbiomedical.com.

LI, CHING-CHUNG, electrical engineering educator; b. Changshu, Kiangsu, China, Mar. 30, 1932; arrived in U.S., 1954, naturalized, 1972; s. Lung-Han and Lien-Tseng (Hwa) L.; m. Hanna Wu, June 10, 1961; children: William Wei-Lin, Vincent Wei-Tsin. BSEE, Nat. Taiwan U., 1954; MSEE, Northwestern U., 1956, PhD, 1961. Jr. engr. analytical dept. Westinghouse Electric Corp., East Pittsburgh, Pa., 1957; inst. fellow Northwestern U., Evanston, Ill., 1957-59; asst. prof. elec. engring. U. Pitts., 1959-62, assoc. prof., 1962-67; vis. assoc. prof. elec. engring. U. Calif.-Berkeley, 1964; vis. prin. scientist Alza Corp., Palo Alto, Calif., 1970; faculty rsch. participant Pitts. Energy Tech. Ctr., Dept. Energy, 1982, 83, 85, 88, 89; mem. Ctr. Multivariate Analysis, 1982-87, Ctr. for Parallel and Distributed Intelligent Systems, 1986—96; sabbatical leave Lab. for Info. and Decision Systems, MIT, 1988, Robotics Inst., Carnegie Mellon U., 1999, Advanced Multimedia Processing Lab., Carnegie Mellon U., 2006; prof. computer sci. U. Pitts., 1977—, prof. elec. engring., 1967—. Mem. sci. adv. com. Horus Therapeutics, Inc., 1995-97. Guest editor: Jour. Cybernetics and Info. Sci., 1979, Computerized Med. Imaging and Graphics, 1991, assoc. editor: Pattern Recognition, 1985—2001, mem. editl. bd.: Internat. Jour. Image and Graphics, 2000—, Jour. Wavelet Theory and Applications, 2007—; contbr. articles to profl. jours. Co-recipient cert. of merit Radiol. Soc. N.Am., 1979; rsch. grantee NSF, 1975-81, 85-87, Pa. Dept. Health, 1977-79, We. Pa. Advanced Tech. Ctr., 1983-84, 86-88, Health Rsch. and Svc. Found., 1985-86, Air Force Office Sci. Rsch., 1990-93, Pitts. Digital Greenhouse, Inc., 2000-02. Fellow IEEE (tech. com., com. chmn. 1967—), Internat. Assn. for Pattern Recognition; mem. AAAS, Biomed. Engring. Soc., Pattern Recognition Soc., Sigma Xi, Eta Kappa Nu. Home: 2130 Garrick Dr Pittsburgh PA 15235-5033 Office: U Pitts Dept Elec and Computer Engring Pittsburgh PA 15261 Office Phone: 412-624-9679. Business E-Mail: ccl@engr.pitt.edu.

LI, CHU-TSING, art historian, educator; b. Canton, China, 1920; came to U.S., 1947; m. Yao-wen; children: Ulysses, Amy. BA, U. Nanking, 1943; MA in English Lit., U. Iowa, 1949, PhD in Art History, 1955. Instr. U. Iowa, 1954-55, 56-58, asst. prof., 1958-62, assoc. prof., 1962-65, rsch. prof., 1963—64, prof., 1965-66; prof. art history U. Kans., Lawrence, 1966-78, dept. chmn., 1972-78, Judith Harris Murphy Disting. prof., 1978-90, prof. emeritus, 1990—, dir. NEH summer seminar on Chinese art history, 1975, 78, coord. Mellon faculty seminar, 1979; acting asst. prof. Oberlin Coll., 1955-56; asst. prof. Ind. U., summer 1956; coord. N.Y. state faculty seminar on Chinese Art History, SUNY, 1965; rsch. curator Nelson Gallery of Art, Kansas City, 1966—. Vis. prof. fine arts Chinese U., Hong Kong, 1972-73, summer 1971, leader China visit group, 1973; vis. prof. Grad. Inst. Art History, Nat Taiwan U., 1990; vis. Andrew W. Mellon prof. U. Pitts., 1995; dir. NEH Summer Inst. Modern Chinese Art and Culture, 1991; participant Internat. Symposiums on Chinese Painting, Nat. Palace Mus., Taipei, 1970, Cleve. Mus. Art, 1981, Huangshan Sch. Painters, Hefei, Ahnui, Rep. China, 1984, on Words and Images in Chinese Painting, Met. Mus. Art, N.Y.C., 1985, on the Elegant Brush: Chinese Painting under the Qianlong Emperor, Phoenix Art Mus., 1985, to celebrate 60th anniversary Nat. Palace Mus., Taipei, Taiwan, 1985, on History of Yuan Dynasty, Nanjing U., China, 1986, on art of Badashanren (Chu Ta), Nanchang, China, 1986; on Dunhuang Grottoes, China, 1987; on the Four Monk Painters, Shanghai Mus., 1987; on art of Chang Dai-chien, Nat. Mus. History, Taipei, 1988; Symposium on Contemporary Artistic Development, Nanjing, 1988; Symposium on Chinese Painting of Ming Dynasty Chinese U. Hong Kong, 1988; Symposium on Chinese Painting of the Ming and Qing Dynasties from the Forbidden City, Cleve. Mus. Art, 1989, Symposium on Hist. Studies, since 1911, Nat. Taiwan U., 1989, Symposium on 40th Anniversary of Founding of Liaoning Provincial Mus., Shenyang, China, 1989, Symposium on Painting of Wu Sch., Palace Mus., Beijing, 1990; Internat. Colloquium on Chinese Art History, Nat. Palace Mus. Taipei, 1991, Internat. Symposium on Art of Four Wangs, Shanghai, 1992, VIIeme Colloque Internat. de Sinologie, Chantilly, France, 1992, Symposium Painting at Close Qing Empire, Phoenix, 1992, Symposium on Ming & Qing Painting, Beijing, 1994, Symposium on Art of Zhao Meng-fu, Shanghai, 1995, Symposium on 20th Century Chinese Painting, Hong Kong Mus. Art, 1995, Symposium on Contemporary Chinese Painting, Biennale of Shanghai Art Mus., 1998; spl. cons. Chinese U., Hong Kong, 1971, Symposium on Painting and Calligraphy by Ming Loyalists, Early Ch'ing Period, 1975, Symposium on the Art of Liu Kuo-sung, Mus. of History, Beijing, 2002, Palace Mus., Beijing, 2007, Symposium on Chinese Painting of 1850-1950, Kaohshing Mus. of Art, Taiwan, 2007. Author (books and exhbn. catalogues): The Autumn Colors on the Ch'iao and Hua Mountains, A Painting by Chao Meng-fu, 1254-1322, 1965; author: Liu Kuo-sung: The Development of a Modern Chinese Artist, 1970, A Thousand Peaks and Myriad Ravines: Chinese Paintings in the Charles A Drenowatz Collection, 2 vols., 1974, Trends in Modern Chinese Painting, 1979; co-author: History of Modern Chinese Painting, Part 1: Late Qing, 1998, Part 2: Republican China, 2001, Part 3: Contemporary, 2003, Tradition and Transformation: Studies in Chinese Art in Honor of Chu-Tsing Li, 2005; editor: Artists and Patrons: Some Social and Economic Aspects of Chinese Painting, 1990; co-editor: Chinese Scholar's Studio: Artistic Life in Late Ming, Asia Soc., 1987; contbr. articles to profl. jours. Ford Found. Fgn. Area Tng. fellow, 1959-60; grantee Am. Coun. Learned Socs. and Social Sci. Rsch. Coun., 1963-64, NEH, 1975, 78, 91, Com. for Scholarly Communication with People's Republic of China NAS, 1979, Am. Coun. Learned Socs., 1980, Asian Cultural Coun., N.Y., 1981, Kans. U., summers 1966-80; Fulbright-Hayes faculty fellow, 1968-69 Mem. Coll. Art Assn. Am., Assn. for Asian Studies, Midwest Art History Soc., Min-chiu Soc. Hong Kong, Phi Tau Phi, Phi Beta Kappa (hon.), Phi Beta Delta. Home: 1108 Avalon Rd Lawrence KS 66044-2506 Office: Univ Kans Kress Found Dept Art History Lawrence KS 66045-0001 Personal E-mail: ctsli@earthlink.net. Business E-Mail: ctsli@ku.edu.

LI, DONG, economics professor; b. Wuhan, Hubei, China, 1969; BS in Quantitative Econs., Huazhong U. Sci. & Tech., Wuhan, China, 1991, MS in Quantitative Econs., 1994; PhD, Tex. A&M U., College Station, 2000. Asst. prof. East Carolina U., Greenville, NC, 2000—01, Kans. State U., Manhattan, 2001—06, assoc. prof., 2006—. Office: Kan State Univ 327 Waters Hall Manhattan KS 66506-4001 Office Phone: 785-532-4572.

LI, GONG, actress; b. Shenyang, Liaoning, China, Dec. 31, 1965; m. Ooi Wei Ming, Feb. 15, 1996. Grad., Ctrl. Drama Acad., Beijing, 1989. Mem. tchg. staff Ctrl. Drama Acad., Beijing; spokesperson Shanghai Tang Clothing line; actress advt. L'Oreal. Appearances include (films) Red Sorghum, 1987, Operation Cougar, 1989, The Empress Dowager, 1989, Mr. Sunsshine, 1989, The Terracotta Warrior, 1989, The Puma Action, 1989, Ju Dou, 1990, Raise The Red Lantern, 1991, The Banquet, 1991, Back To Shanghai, 1991, Mary From Beijing, 1992, The Story of Qiu Ju, 1992, Flirting Scholar, 1993, Farewell, My Concubine, 1993 (New York Film Critics award, Golden Globe award), 8 Guardians of Buddhism, 1994, The Great Conqueror's Concubine, 1994, To Live, 1994, The Godfather's Mistress, Shanghai Triad, 1995, Soul of a Painter, 1995, Temptress Moon, 1996, Chinese Box, 1997, Breaking the Silence, 1999, The Emperor and the Assassin, 1999, Zhou Yu's Train, 2002, "2046", 2004, Eros, 2004, Memoirs of a Geisha, 2005 (Best Supporting Actress, Nat. Bd. Review, 2005), Miami Vice, 2006, Curse of the Golden Flower, 2006, Hannibal Rising, 2007. Recipient Volpi Cup Venice Internat. Film Festival, 1992, Best Actress award The Story of Qui Ju, 1992, N.Y. Film Critics award Farewell My Concubine, 1993, Best Supporting Actress award Nat. Bd. Rev., 2005.*

LI, JAMES CHEN MIN, materials science educator; b. Nanking, China, Apr. 12, 1925; came to U.S., 1949; s. Vei Shao and In Shey (Mai) L.; m. Lily Y.C. Wang, Aug. 5, 1950; children: Conan, May, Edward. BS, Nat. Ctrl. U., China, 1947; MS, U. Wash., 1951, PhD, 1953. Rsch. assoc. U. Calif., Berkeley, 1953-55; supr. Mfg. Chemists Assn. project Carnegie Inst. Tech., Pitts., 1955-56; phys. chemist Westinghouse Elec. Co., Pitts., 1956-57; sr. scientist U.S. Steel Corp., Monroeville, Pa., 1957-69; mgr. strength physics Allied Chem. Co., Morristown, NJ, 1969-71; A.A. Hopeman prof. engring. U. Rochester (N.Y.), 1971—. Vis. prof. Columbia U., N.Y.C., 1964-65, adj. prof., 1965-71; adj. prof. Stevens Inst. Tech., Newark, 1971-72; vis. prof. Ruhr U., Bochum, Fed. Republic Germany, 1978-79. Author 1 book; editor 3 books; contbr. 350 articles to profl. jours.; holder 5 patents in 6 countries. Recipient Alexander Von Humboldt award, 1978, Acta Metallurgica Gold medal, 1990, Grad. Teaching award U. Rochester, 1993. Fellow TMS/AIME (Robert F. Mehl medal and lectr. 1978, Champion H. Mathewson Gold medal 1972, Structural Materials Divsn. luncheon spkr. 1993, chmn. phys. mutall. com. 1992-95), ASM Internat. (chmn. materials sci. divsn. 1982-84), Am. Phys. Soc.; mem. ASME, NAE, Materials Rsch. Soc., Chinese Soc. Materials Sci. (Lu Tse-Hon medal 1988). Office: U Rochester Dept Mech Engring PO Box 270132 Rochester NY 14627-0133 Office Phone: 585-275-4038. E-mail: li@me.rochester.edu.

LI, JET (LI LIAN JIE, LEI LIN-GIT), actor; b. Beijing, Apr. 26, 1963; m. Qiuyan Huang, 1987 (div. 1990); 2 children; m. Nina Li Chi, Sept. 19, 1999; 2 children. Former mem. Beijing Wu Shu team. Actor: (films) Shao Lin tzu, 1979, Shao Lin xiao zi, 1983, Nan bei Shao Lin, 1986, Shao Lin Hai Deng da shi, 1988, Long zai tian ya, 1988, Long xing tian xia, 1989, Wong Fei-hung, 1991, Yi tian tu long ji zhi mo jiao jiao zhu, 1993, Shu dan long wei, 1995, Gei ba ba de xin (The Enforcer), 1995, Mo him wong, 1996, Hak hap (Black Mask), 1996, Sat sau ji wong, 1998, Lethal Weapon 4, 1998, Romeo Must Die, 2000, The One, 2000, Ying xiong (Hero), 2002, Cradle 2 the Grave, 2003, Fearless, 2006, War, 2007; actor & prodr. (films) Wong Fei-hung tsi sam: Siwong tsangba, 1993, Wong Fei-hung chi tit gai dau neung gung, 1993, Fong Sai-Yuk, 1993, Tai ji zhang san feng, 1993, Zhong Nan Hai bao biao, 1994, Jing wu ying xiong, 1994, Hong Xiguan zhi Shaolin wu zu, 1994, Danny the Dog (Unleashed), 2005, actor, writer, assoc. prodr. Kiss of the Dragon, 2001, actor, dir. Zhong hua ying xiong, 1986. Recipient 15 gold medals, 1 silver medal, Chinese Wu Shu championships.*

LI, JIANLIANG, engineer; m. Yanrong Kang. PhD, U. Rochester, NY, 1998—2004. Rsch. assoc. U. Rochester, 2004—06; sr. r&d engr. Synopsys Inc., Hillsboro, Oreg., 2006—. Mem.: IEEE (assoc.). Achievements include patents for an innovative way of calculating the effect of assist feature on a device layout; correlating physical model representation to pattern; a detector of 2-dimensional features; transferring optical proximity correction (OPC) effect into optical mode. Office Phone: 503-547-6224. Business E-Mail: lijianliang05@gmail.com.

LI, JOHN K.H., pathologist, department chairman; b. Nanking, China, Nov. 19, 1932; arrived in U.S., 1949; s. Ti-Tsun and Nora Tsuei (Ju) Li; m. Lorraine L. Yuan, June 29, 1959; children: Dina Wan, Roger M.K. AB, Harvard U., 1954, MD, 1958. Diplomate in anat. pathology and clin. pathology Am. Bd. Pathology. Dir. pathology and labs. Morrisania City Hosp., NYC, 1966—76, North Ctrl. Bronx Hosp., NYC, 1976—92; chmn. dept. pathology L.I. Coll. Hosp., Bklyn., 1992—; assoc. clin. prof. pathology SUNY, Bklyn., 1993—. Pres. Pathologists' Club of N.Y., NYC, 1989, NYC, 90; co-founding physician Chinatown Health Clinic, NYC, 1971—. Contbr. articles to profl. jours. Pres. Chinese Am. Med. Soc., NYC, 1992, 1993. Recipient Cmty. Svc. award, Chinese Am. Med. Soc., 1998, Ann. Recognition award, Othmer Cancer Ctr., 2001. Fellow: Am. Soc. Clin. Pathology, N.Y. Acad. Medicine, Coll. Am. Pathologists. Democrat. Avocations: reading, writing, sailing. Office: LI Coll Hosp 339 Hicks St Brooklyn NY 11201 Home Phone: 212-737-0018; Office Phone: 718-780-1005. E-mail: johnli@chpnet.org.

LI, KAI, chemist, research scientist; b. Jiangyin, Jiangsu, China, Aug. 16, 1962; arrived in U.S., 1997, permanent resident; s. Fuxin Li and Xiubao Zhou; m. Linda Yanping Qin, Mar. 21, 1986; children: Tony Zhen, Daniel Lin, Vincent. MSc, Soochow U., Suzhou, China, 1985, U. BC, Vancouver, Can., 1992, PhD, 1996. Post-doctoral fellow U. Hawaii at Manoa, Honolulu, 1997—99, U. Wis., Milw., 1999—2000. Sr. rsch. scientist Pharm. Products Devel., Inc, Middleton, Wis., 2000—. Mem.: Am. Chem. Soc. Home: 7625 Sawmill Road Madison WI 53717 Home Phone: 608-827-2982; Office Phone: 608-827-9400. Office Fax: 608-827-8807; Home Fax: 608-827-2982. Personal E-mail: likai97@gmail.com.

LI, KA-SHING, international entrepreneur; b. Chaozhou, Guangdong, China, 1928; m. Yuet-ming Chong (dec.); children: Victor, Richard. LLD (hon.), U. Hong Kong, 1986, U. Calgary, Can., 1989, Chinese U. Hong Kong, 1997, Cambridge U., 1999; doctorate (hon.), Peking U., 1992; doctorate in Social Scis. (hon.), Hong Kong U. Sci. and Tech., 1995, City U. Hong Kong, 1998, Open U. Hong Kong, 1999. Advanced from wholesale salesman to gen. mgr., 1945—47; founder Cheung Kong Plastics Factory, 1950, Li Ka Shing Found. Ltd., 1980, Shantou Univ., 1981; chmn. Cheung Kong (Holdings) Ltd., Hong Kong, 1972—; acquired Hutchison Whampoa Ltd., Hong Kong, 1979, Hong Kong Elec. Holdings, Ltd., 1985, Cheung Kong Infrastructure Holdings, Ltd. (listed), 1996; owner, shareholder numerous cos. Mem. drafting com. basic law Hong Kong Spl. Adminstrv. Region, 1985—90, mem. prep. com., 1995—97; advisor Hong Kong Affairs, 1992—97; mem. Internat. Bus. Adv. Coun. of U.K., 2006. Named a Justice of the Peace, 1981, Grand Officer, Order of Vasco Nuñez de Balboa, Panama, 1982, Comdr., Order of Brit. Empire, 1989, Knight Bachelor, 2000, Comdr., Leopold Order, Belgium, 2000, Legion of Honor, France, 2005, Order of the Crown Belgium, 1986; named an Hon. Citizen, Cities of Shantou, Guangzhou, Shenzhen, Nanhai, Foshan, Zhuhai, Chaozhou, Beijing, Winnipeg (Can.); named one of World's Richest People, Forbes Mag., 2007; recipient Entrepreneur of Millennium award, The Times, Ernst & Young, UK, 1999, Internat. Disting. Entrepreneur award, U. Man., Can, 2000, Grand Bauhinia medal, Hong Kong SAR, 2001, Malcolm S. Forbes Lifetime Achievement award 2006, Spl. Hon. award for econ. contbn., CCTV, 2007, Lifetime Achievement award for philanthropy, PRC Ministry Civil Affairs, 2007, Presdl. award, TESOL, Inc., 2007. Office: Cheung Kong (Holdings) Ltd 70/F 2 Queen's Rd Ctrl Hong Kong China

LI, LI, research scientist; s. Benmao Li and Yichun Huang; m. Shaoqin Liang; children: Kathleen B., Abby J. BS, Wuhan U., China, 1984; MS, Beijing U. of Posts and Telecom., Beijing, China, 1984—87; PhD, U. Wash., Seattle, 1995. Scientist Caelum Rsch. Corp., Rockville, Md., 1995—97; sr. scientist Jet Propulsion Lab., Pasadena, Calif., 1997—2004; rsch. scientist Naval Rsch. Lab., Washington, 2004—. Recipient Tech. Excellence award, Jet Propulsion Lab., 2002, Group Achievement award, NASA, 2002, Outstanding Contbn. award, Naval Rsch. Lab., 2005; scholar RAP grad. fellow, Nat. Ctr. for Atmospheric Rsch., Boulder, Colo., 1993—95. Mem.: IEEE, Am. Geophys. Union, Eta Kappa Nu. Presbyterian. Achievements include research in developing various satellite remote sensing techniques for land, ocean and atmospheric applications. Office: Naval Research Laboratory 4555 Overlook Ave SW Washington DC 20375 Home Phone: 703-425-2502; Office Phone: 202-767-0849. Office Fax: 202-767-9194. Business E-Mail: li.li@nrl.navy.mil.

LI, LIDE, mathematician, econometrician, consultant; arrived in US, 1982, naturalized, 1993; s. Yuchen Li and Aichun Luo; m. Quanyi Zhang, Sept. 10, 1996; children: Sherrie, Janice. PhD in Math., U. Ark., Fayetteville, 1985; MSc, U. Chgo., 1990, PhD in Computer Sci., 1993. Rschr. Lehman Bros., Chgo., 1994—97; sr. cons. Exelon Corp., Kennett Square, Pa., 1997—. Reviewer math. reviews Am. Math. Soc., Providence, 1985—93; tchr. risk mgmt. courses Incisive Media Risk Jour., Houston, 1996; author Ctr. Rsch. Regulated Industries, Newark, 2002—06; referee Energy Jour., Toronto, Ontario, Canada, 2005—06; presenter in field. Contbr. articles to profl. jours. Rsch. grant for rsch. in theoretical computer sci., NSF, 1992—93. Achievements include design of numerous algorithms simulating electric power and load for risk management and portfolio analyses; effective calculation tools for financial instruments; apply ring/group theory to the complexity structure; effectively characterized inverse semigroup using algebraic equations; applied econometrics theory to the energy world, including electric load instruments and power price simulation model. Avocations: music, gardening. Business E-Mail: Lide.Li@exeloncorp.com.

LI, LINDA (LINDA JIAN-YUH LI), plastic surgeon; b. Morgantown, WV, Sept. 26, 1969; m. Bill Fulcher; 1 child. BA/MD (six yr. program) cum laude, Boston U., 1993. Cert. Am. Bd. Plastic Surgery, 2002. Intern, plastic surgery U. So. Calif., LA, 1993—94, resident, surgery, 1994—98; fellow Cornell Med. Ctr., NYC, 1998—2000; attending physician Hosp. Good Samaritan, LA, 2000; private practice Beverly Hills, Calif., 2000—. Featured on Dr. 90210, 2005—. Fellow: Am. Coll. Surgeons; mem.: Calif. Soc. Plastic Surgeons, Am. Soc. Plastic Surgery, Soc. Grad. Surgeons of LA County/U. So. Calif. Med. Ctr. Avocations: exercise, yoga. Office: 433 N Camden Dr Ste 1190 Beverly Hills CA 90210 Office Phone: 310-273-6252. Office Fax: 310-273-6050.

LI, MARIA, neurosurgeon; d. Pierre and Sharon Li. MD, CM, McGill U., Montreal, Quebec, Can., 1990. Diplomate Am. Bd. Neurol. Surgery, 2003. Postdoctoral fellow U. Calif., San Francisco, 1997—99; neurosurgeon City of Hope, Duarte, Calif., 1999—2000, Meritcare Health Sys., Fargo, ND, 2000—02, GroupHealth Coop., Seattle, 2003—04; cerebrovascular fellow Swedish, Seattle, 2005; neurosurgeon Presbyn. Health Sys., Albuquerque, 2005—. Named one of Am. Top Physicians, Surgeons, Consumer's Rsch. Coun. Am., 2004—05, 2007, Albuquerque's Top Drs., Albuquerque The Mag., 2007. Mem.: Congress Neurol. Surgery, Am. Assn. Neurol. Surgeons. Home Phone: 505-897-3221; Office Phone: 505-563-6682.

LI, MING, oceanographer; s. Zongyao Li and Guifang Wu; m. Xiaohong Sophie Wang, July 18, 1992; children: Michael, Marvin. BEng, Hohai U., Nanjing, China, 1983; PhD in Applied Math., U. Oxford, Eng., 1991. Rsch. scientist Inst. of Ocean Sciences, Sidney, BC, Canada, 1996—2001; rsch. assoc. U. Victoria, BC, 1991—96; assoc. prof. U. Md., Cambridge, Md., 2001—. Mem.: Oceanography Soc., Am. Meteorol. Soc., Am. Geophys. Union. Achievements include research in several areas of oceanography such as air-sea interaction, estuarine/coastal circulations, biological-physical interactions, ocean mixing processes and marine pollution. Home Phone: 410-749-5934; Office Phone: 410 221 8420. Business E-Mail: mingli@hpl.umces.edu.

LI, MIN-TANG, systems engineer; s. Ing-Chou and Chun-Hsia Wang Li; m. Lee-Fang Chow, Dec. 29, 1993; 1 child, Andrew. BA in Transp. Engring. & Mgmt., Nat. Chiao-Tung U., Hsinchu, Taiwan, 1985—89; MS in Civil Engring., U. Fla., Gainesville, 1992—95, PhD in Civil Engring., 1996—99. Cert. engr.-in-tng., Fla. Bd. Profl. Engrs., 2005, profl. engr., Fla. Bd. Profl. Engrs., 2006. Asst. transp. planner Asian Tech. Cons., Inc., Taipei, Taiwan, 1991—92; grad. rsch. asst. Transp. Rsch. Ctr., dept. civil & coastal engring., U. Fla., 1993—99, rsch. engr., 1999; sr. rsch. assoc. Lehman Ctr. Transp. Rsch., dept. civil & environ. engring. Fla. Internat. U., Miami, 2000—05; sr. transp. analyst Fla. Dept. Transp., Dist. 4, Ft. Lauderdale, 2005—06, sr. systems engr., 2006—. Contbr. articles to profl. jours. Recipient Value Engring. Recognition award, Fla. Dept. Transp., 2005—06, Dist. Team of Yr. award, 2005—06, Monthly Employee award, 2006. Master: SE Fla. FSUTMS Users Grp. (corr.). Avocations: travel, golf. Office: Fla Dept Trans-D4 3400 W Commercial Blvd Fort Lauderdale FL 33309 Office Fax: 954-777-4671. Business E-Mail: min-tang.li@dot.state.fl.us.

LI, NORMAN N., chemicals executive; b. Shanghai, Jan. 14, 1933; naturalized, US, 1969; s. Lieh-wen and Amy H. Li; m. Jane C. Li, Aug. 17, 1963; children: Rebecca H., David H. BSChemE, Nat. Taiwan U., Taipei, 1955; MS, Wayne State U., 1957; PhD, Stevens Inst. Tech., 1963. Sr. scientist Exxon Rsch. and Engring. Co., Linden, NJ, 1963-81; dir. separation sci. and tech. UOP, Des Plaines, Ill., 1981-88; dir. engineered products and process tech. Allied-Signal Inc., Des Plaines, Ill., 1988-92, dir. rsch. and tech., 1993-95; pres., CEO NL Chem. Technology, Inc., 1995—. Mem. NRC, 1985-89; lectr. AIChE, 1975-86. Editor 20 books on separation sci. and tech.; contbr. articles to profl. jours.; patentee in field. Fellow: AIChE (dir. divsn. food, pharms. and bioengring. 1988—91, bd. dirs. 1992—94, founder award for Outstanding Contributions to Chem. Engring. field 2006, Alpha Chi Sigma rsch. award 1988, Ernest Thiele award 1995, Chem. Engring. Practice award 2000, Lifetime Achievement award 2001, Gerhold award in separation tech. 2002); mem.: Acad. Sinica, Chinese Acad. Scis., N.Am. Membrane Soc. (pres. 1991—93, Perkin medalist 2000), Am. Chem. Soc. (Separation Sci. and Tech. award 1988), NAE. Home: 620 N Rolling Ln Arlington Heights IL 60004-5820 Office Phone: 847-824-2888. Personal E-mail: NLChem@aol.com.

LI, PETER WAI-KWONG, mathematics professor; b. Hong Kong, Apr. 18, 1952; came to U.S., 1971; s. Chun Tat and Lai Mui (Sum) L.; m. Glenna Marie Seaver, Oct. 30, 1982; children: Tiana, Natasha, Talia. BA, Calif. State U., 1974; MA, U. Calif., Berkeley, 1977, PhD, 1979. Rsch. mem. Inst. for Advanced Study, Princeton, N.J., 1979-80; asst. prof. Stanford (Calif.) U., 1980-83; assoc. prof. Purdue U., West Lafayette, Ind., 1983-85; prof. U. Utah, Salt Lake City, 1985-89, U. Ariz., Tucson, 1989-91, U. Calif., Irvine, 1991—, chmn. math. dept., 1993—96, 1999—2001, Chancellor's prof. math, 2003—. Editor Rocky Mountain Jour. Math., 1989-91, Procs. of Am. Math. Soc., 1991—; editor-in-chief Comm. in Analysis and Geometry, 1992-2002, editor, 2002—. Named Highly Cited Rschr., ISI, 2003—; NSF grantee, 1980—; Sloan fellow, 1982-83, Guggenheim fellow, 1989-90. Fellow Am. Acad. Arts & Scis.; mem. Am. Math. Soc., Phi Beta Kappa. Avocations: swimming, skiing, cooking, wine-tasting. Office: Dept Math U Calif Irvine Irvine CA 92697-3875 Office Phone: 949-824-7049. Business E-Mail: pli@math.uci.edu.

LI, QIN, news anchor, reporter, television director and producer; came to U.S., 1999:; d. Jinkui and Hong Li. BA in Law, Chinese Youth Coll. Polit. Sc., Beijing, 1992; MS in Econs., Chinese Acad. Social Sci., Beijing, 1998; MS in Journalism, Columbia U., 2000. Cert. in pub. affairs. Reporter People's Daily, Beijing, 1992-94, editor, reporter Shanghai, 1994-99; TV anchor, prodr., news reporter Sino TV, Inc., NYC, 2001—. Dep. editor-in-chief New Asia Culture Found. and Pub. House, Hong Kong, 1999—. Prodr.: (TV news documentary) Blue Sky Station: 8th Avenue-New York's 3d Chinatown, 2000 (Emmy award NATAS, 2000); dir., prodr. (TV documentary) A Hole in Chinatown's Heart-Rebuild Chinatown after 9/11, 2003; contbg. author: First-Hand Experience with China's Hope Project in One Hundred Counties, 1991; co-author: Japan: Another Miracle in the 21st Century?, 1993; contbr. feature stories to internat. publs. Mem. selection com. Internat. Fanzhian Scholarship, Hong Kong, 1998-2001 Recipient Best News award Chinese Nat. Journalists Assn. and Chinese Disability Assn., 1994, Best News award Chinese People's Polit. Consultative Conf., 1993; featured in Selected Works of Outstanding Chinese Editors and Reporters, 1996. Mem. Soc. Profl. Journalists, Nat. Acad. TV Arts and Scis. Home Phone: 917-291-4800; Office Phone: 212-625-2877. Office Fax: 212-965-8917. Personal E-mail: qlinyc@gmail.com. Business E-Mail: ql20@columbia.edu.

LI, QINGDI QUENTIN, physician, research scientist, medical educator; b. Guilin, Guangxi, China, Apr. 18, 1956; m. Li Ding; 1 child, Jueli Maggie. MA, MD, Guangxi Med. U., 1987; MS, PhD, U. Md., 2000. Microbiologist, immunologist Guangxi Med. U., Nanning, China, 1983—87; dermatologist Sun Yat-sen Univ. Sch. Medicine, Guangzhou, Guangdong, China, 1987—91; postdoctoral fellow Nat. Cancer Inst., Bethesda, Md., 1996—98; rsch. scientist Balt. VA Med. Ctr., 1998—2000; asst. prof. Sch. Medicine and Health Sci. Ctr. W.Va. U., Morgantown, 2000—06, rsch. coord. MBR Cancer Ctr., 2000—06; rsch. scientist Nat. Cancer Inst., NIH, Bethesda, Md., 2006—. Vis. prof. Wuhan U., China, 2002—, Guangxi Med. U., Nanning, China, 2002—, SE U., Nanjing, China, 2003—, Tongji Med. Coll., Ctrl. China Univ. Sci. and Tech., Wuhan, 2004—, Nanjing Med. U., China, 2006—. Recipient Intramural Rsch. Award, Nat. Cancer Inst., 1996-1998, Nat. Svc. Award, NIH, 1998-2000. Mem.: AAAS, Chinese Soc. Microbiology, Am. Soc. Microbiology, NY Acad. Sci., Am. Assn. Cancer Rsch., Chinese Med. Assn. Home: 216 Watkins Pond Blvd Rockville MD 20850-5622 Office: Nat Cancer Inst NIH Bethesda MD 20892-5065 Home Phone: 301-208-1945; Office Phone: 301-435-7869. Business E-Mail: liquenti@mail.nih.gov, quentinli2004@yahoo.com.

LI, RAO, mathematician, computer scientist; b. Fushun, Liaoning, China, May 3, 1965; arrived in U.S., 1993; s. Jingyuan Li and Liangzhi Zhu; m. Yan Wu, Apr. 27, 1966; 1 child, Dorothy. BS, Huaibei Tchr. Coll., 1985; MS, Harbin Inst. Tech., 1988; MA, U. Pitts., 1994; MS in Computer Sci., U. Memphis, 1999, PhD in Math., 1999. Asst. prof. Fushun Petroleum Inst., Liaoning, China, 1988—91, lectr., 1991—92; asst. prof. Ga. Southwestern State U., Americus, 1999—2001, U. SC, Aiken, 2001—06, assoc. prof., 2006—. Contbr. articles to profl. jours. Mem.: Assn. for Computing Machinery, Am. Math. Soc. Home: 775 Locks Way Martinez GA 30907 Office: University of South Carolina at Aiken 471 University Parkway Aiken SC 29801 Office Phone: 803-641-3264. Business E-Mail: raol@usca.edu.

LI, RICHARD T., retired library director, secondary school educator; b. Quidong, Hunan Province, China, Aug. 19, 1929; naturalized, U.S., 1977; s. Town and Pan-Chin Li; m. Felisa T. Tan, Oct. 25, 1964; children: Ray, Joy. BA in English, Tamkang Coll. Arts and Sci., Taipei, Taiwan, 1965; MA in English, S.E. Mo. Coll., 1970; MLS, Kans. State Tchrs. Coll. Emporia, 1971; EdD, U. Kans., 1978. Tchg. cert. Kans. Engring. officer, army capt. Chinese Army, Taiwan, 1954—59; tchr. KW Tech Sch., Taichung, Taiwan, 1959—61, Keelung 5th Mid. Sch., Keelung, Taiwan, 1965—67; tchr., libr. Eastern Heights H.S., Agra, Kans., 1973—74; head libr. media specialist Atchison (Kans.) H.S., 1974—78; asst. prof. Southwestern Okla. State U., Weatherford, 1978—80; Title III project officer Cameron U., Lawton, Okla., 1980—81; asst. dir. learning resources ctr. Tarrant County Jr. Coll., Fort Worth, 1982—97; ret., 1997. Author: Education and Career: An Immigrant's Journey in the Promised Land with Survival Tips, 1999, Where Can I Find It? A Sources Handbook for New Immigrants, 2000, My God, It Missed Me! A Young Soldier's Accounts in the War Torn China 1940-50s, 2002, The Golden Lotus, 2004, Haipin, the student's wife, a common immigrant, a hardworking citizen, 2005, The Rough Journey, A War-Time Romance, 2006. Home: 4554 Rose Tree Ct Fort Worth TX 76137 Personal E-mail: w007745@airmail.net.

LI, ROWENA LIU-PING, media specialist; d. XingYun and YanQiu Li; m. Bohong Li, Apr. 15, 1987; children: Rusi Woody, Oliver. BA, Nankai U., Tianjin, China, 1985; MLS, CUNY, 1997; postgrad., U. N.Tex., 2004. Cert. sch. media specialist N.Y. State Edn. Dept., 2002. Lectr. Nankai U., Tianjin, China, 1985—90; journalist Chinese Cmty. Weekly, Flushing, NY, 1991; sec. Queens Coll., CUNY, Flushing, 1993—99, rschr., 1999—2000; sr. reference libr. Queens Borough Pub. Libr., Jamaica, NY, 2001; sch. media specialist Bayside HS Libr., 2001—. Reviewer Improving Literacy through Sch. Librs. US Dept. Edn., 2007—; presenter in field. Contbr. articles and posters. Recipient Conf. Sponsorship award, EBSCO, 2005; fellow, Inst. Mus. and Libr. Svcs., 2004—06; scholar, U. N.Tex., 2004—06. Mem.: ALA, Assn. Libr. and Info. Sci. Edn., Am. Soc. Info. Sci. and Tech., Phi Kappa Phi. Office: Bayside High Sch Libr 32-24 Corporal Kenedy St Bayside NY 11361 Home Phone: 718-428-1590; Office Phone: 718-229-7600 3014.

LI, SHUYU, research scientist; PhD, U. Tex. Southwestern Med. Ctr., Dallas, 1999. Sr. rsch. scientist Eli Lilly & Co., Indpls., 2002—. Office: Eli Lilly & Co Lilly Corporate Ctr Indianapolis IN 46285 Business E-Mail: li_shuyu_dan@lilly.com.

LI, TIEN-SHUN, obstetrician, gynecologist, educator; b. Kaohsiung, Taiwan, Nov. 13, 1932; arrived in U.S., 1968; MD, Nat. Taiwan U., 1960. Diplomate Am. Bd. Ob-Gyn. From intern to resident ob-gyn. Nat. Taiwan U. Hosp., Taipei, 1961—64; resident ob-gyn. St. Barnabas Med. Ctr., Livingston, NJ, 1971—73; clin. asst. prof. U. Medicine and Dentistry N.J., 1978—; pvt. practice Ft. Lee, NJ, 1978—. Attending staff Meadowlands Hosp. Med. Ctr., Secaucus, NJ, 1985—. Fellow: ACOG. Office: 2231 Lemoine Ave Fort Lee NJ 07024-6115 Office Phone: 201-944-1008.

LI, TINGYE, electrical engineer; b. Nanjing, China, July 7, 1931; arrived in U.S., 1953, naturalized, 1963; s. Chao and Lily Wei-peng (Sie) L.; m. Edith Hsiu-hwei Wu, June 9, 1956; children: Deborah Chunroh, Kathryn Dairoh. BSEE, U. Witwatersrand, South Africa, 1953; MS, Northwestern U., Evanston, Ill., 1955, PhD, 1958; DEng (hon.), Nat. Chiao Tung U., Hsinchu, Taiwan, 1991. Mem. tech. staff AT&T Bell Labs., Holmdel, NJ, 1957-67; dept. head repeater techniques research dept. Bell Labs., 1967-76, lightwave media research dept., 1976-84, lightwave systems research dept., 1984-96; dept. head lightwave networks rsch. dept. AT&T Labs.-Rsch., Holmdel, NJ, 1996, divsn. mgr. Middletown, NJ, 1997-98, ret., 1998; ind. cons. Boulder, Colo., 1999—. Hon. prof. Tsinghua U., Shanghai Jiao Tong U., Beijing U. Posts and Telecomms., U. Electronic Sci. and Tech. of China, Qufu Normal U., Beijing Jiao Tong U., Tianjin U., Nankai U., Fudan U., S.E. U., Nat. Chiao Tung U., Nat. Taiwan U. Assoc. editor Optics Letters, 1977-78, topical editor, 1989-91; assoc. editor Jour. of Lightwave Tech., 1983-86; editor book series: Optical Fiber Telecommunications IV, Optical Fiber Communications, OSA Trends in Optics and Photonics Series; mem. editl. bd. Procs. IEEE, 1974-83, Microwave and Optical Tech. Letters, 1987-90, Internat. Jour. High Speed Electronics, 1990-95; contbr. articles on microwave antennas and propagation, lasers, coherent optics, optical comms., optical-fiber transmission, systems and networks to sci. jours., chpts. in books; patentee in field. Recipient Alumni Merit award Northwestern U., 1981, Sci. and Tech. medal AT&T, 1997. Fellow IEEE (W.R.G. Baker prize 1975, David Sarnoff award 1979, Photonics award 2004), AAAS, Internat. Engring. Consortium, Photonics Soc. Chinese-Ams. (Achievement award 1998), Optical Soc. Am. (chmn. optical comms. tech. group 1979-80, bd. dirs. 1985-87, chmn. internat. activities com. 1988-90, chmn. photonics divsn. 1991-92, v.p. 1993, pres.-elect 1994, pres. 1995, John Tyndall award 1995, Frederic Ives medal/Quinn Endowment 1997); mem. NAE, Chinese Inst. Engrs. U.S.A. (bd. dirs. 1974-78, Achievement award 1978), Academia Sinica (Taiwan), Chinese Acad. Engring., Chinese Am. Acad. and Profl. Assn. (bd. dirs. 1985-89, Achievement award 1983), Electromagnetics Acad., Sigma Xi, Eta Kappa Nu, Phi Tau Phi (pres. chpt. 1991-93).

LI, TZE-CHUNG, lawyer, educator; b. Shanghai, China, Feb. 17, 1927; came to U.S., 1956; s. Ken-hsiang Li and Yun-hsien (Chang) Li; m. Dorothy In-lan Wang, Oct. 21, 1961; children— Lily, Rose LL.B., Soochow U., Shanghai, 1948; Diploma, Nat. Chengchi U., Nanking, 1949, China Research Inst. of Land Econs., Taipei, 1952; M.C.L., So. Meth. U., Dallas, 1956; LL.M., Harvard U., Cambridge, 1958; MS, Columbia U., NYC, 1965; PhD, New Sch. for Social Research, NYC, 1963. Judge Hwa-lien Dist. Ct., Hwa-lien, Taiwan, Republic of China, 1949-51; dist. atty. Ministry of Justice, Tapei, 1951-52; chief law sect. Ministry of Nat. Def., Tapei, 1952-56; asst. prof. library sci. Ill. State U., Normal, 1965-66; asst. prof. polit. sci., library sci. Rosary Coll., River Forest, Ill., 1966-69, assoc. prof. library sci., 1969-70, 72-74, prof. library sci., 1974-82, dean, prof. Grad. Sch. Library and Info. Sci., 1982-88; prof. Dominican U., River Forest, Ill., 1988-99, dean, prof. emeritus, 2000—; vis. assoc. prof. law Nat. Taiwan U., 1969; vis. assoc. prof. polit. sci. Soochow U., Taipei, 1969; dir. Nat. Central Library, Taipei, 1970-72. Chmn. Grad. Inst. Library Sci., Nat. Central Library, Taipei, 1970-72; commr. Ministry of Examination, Examination Yuan, Taipei, 1971; chmn. com. on library standards, Ministry of Edn., Taipei, 1972; library cons. Soochow U., Nat. Chengchi U., Dr. Sun Yat-sen Meml. Library; mem. library adv. com. Ency. Britannica, 1982-95; hon. prof. library and info. sci. Jiangxi U., People's Republic of China, 1985—; vis. prof. law Suzhou U., Peking U., 1991, Nat. Taiwan U., 1991; hon. cons. univ. library, 1985—; hon. cons. Jiangxi Med. Coll., 1985—; adv. prof. East China Normal U., 1987—; cons. Nova U., 1987-88; mem. ad hoc adv. com. Chgo. Pub. Library Bldg. Planning, 1987-88; CEO LLD Group, 1972—; bd. chmn. Li Ednl. Found., 1977—; legacy leader Nat. Conf. Asian Pacific Am. Librarians, 2001. Author books including: Social

Science Reference Sources, 1980, 3d edit., 2000, Mah Jong, 1982, 2d edit., 1991, An Introduction to Online Searching, 1985; also numerous articles in profl., scholarly jours.; founding editor Jour. Library and Info. Sci., 1975-80, mem. editl. bd. 1986-90; founding chmn., mem. editl. bd. Internat. Jour. of Revs., 1984-89; editor: World Libraries, 1996-99. Pres. Chinese Am. Ednl. Found., Chgo., 1968—70. Recipient Govt. Citation Republic of China, 1956, 1972, Philip D. Sang Excellence in Teaching award Rosary Coll., 1971, Disting. Service award Phi Tau Phi, Chgo., 1982, Service award HUD, Chgo. region, 1985, Disting. Service award Chinese Am. Librarians Assn., 1988. Mem. Chinese Am. Librarians Assn. (founding pres. 1976-80), China Assn. Libr. and Info. Sci. Edn. (hon.), Library Assn. China (Taipei), Phi Tau Phi (pres. 1985-87) Roman Catholic. Home: 135 E 54th St 11H New York NY 10022 Business E-Mail: richard@chamonline.org.

LI, WEIYE, ophthalmologist, educator, biochemist; b. Zhejiang, China, Oct. 10, 1946; arrived in U.S., 1990; s. Zhao-ji and Qin (Yue) Li; m. Xinru Liu, Apr. 12, 1986; 1 child, Yafeng. MD, Peking Second Med. Coll., China, 1970; postgrad., Acad. Med. Scis., China, 1978—80; PhD, U. Pa., 1984. Intern Chao Young Hosp., Peking, 1970—71, resident ophthalmology, 1971—78; rsch. fellow dept. ophthalmology and biochem. grad. sch. Sch. Medicine U. Pa., Phila., 1981—84, postdoctor, asst. prof. dept. ophthalmology Scheie Eye Inst. Sch. Medicine, 1984—85; asst. prof., attending physician ophthalmology Peking Union Med. Coll. Hosp., 1985—86, assoc. prof. ophthalmology, 1986—88, prof. ophthalmology, 1988—, chmn. dept. ophthalmology, 1989—99; prof. ophthalmology, dir. rsch. dept. ophthalmology Hahnemann U., Phila., 1990—; attending physician, retinal specialist Riddle Memory Hosp., Pa., 2003—. Recipient Rsch. award, Internat. Juvenile Diabetes Found., 1984—86, 1st Class Sci. and Tech. Advances prize, Chinese Ministry Pub. Health, 1988; fellow, Internat. Juvenile Diabetes Found., 1982—84; grantee, NIH, 1981—82, 1986—2000, Fight for Sight Inc., 1982—83, Am. Diabetes Assn., 1990—2001. Mem.: Assn. Chinese Ophthalmology Soc., Assn. Rsch. in Vision and Ophthalmology. Avocations: ping pong/table tennis, bicycling, classical music. Office: Sinclair Retina Assocs 311 E Baltimore Pike Media PA 19063 Office Phone: 610-892-1708. Business E-Mail: weiye.li@drexelmed.edu.

LI, XIANG-YANG, science educator; b. TaiXin, China, Oct. 28, 1971; s. KaiWen Li and LanHua Wu; m. Min Chen, May 31, 1996; children: Sophia, Kevin. PhD, U. Ill., Urbana, 2000. Asst. prof. Ill. Inst. Tech., Chgo., 2000—06, assoc. prof., 2006—. Chgo. chpt. pres. Soc. Chinese Am. Profs. and Scientists, 2006. Recipient Young Rschr. Golden award, Jiang Su Province, YangZhou City, China, 1990. Mem.: IEEE (assoc.), Assn. Computing Machinery (assoc.). Achievements include design of the firsts theoretical method for producing well-shaped 3D mesh that is crucial for some numerical simulation. Office Phone: 312-567-5207.

LI, Y. CHARLES, mathematician, educator; m. Sherry Yeh, Sept. 4, 1966; 1 child, Brandon Ziqi. BSc, Peking U., China, 1986; PhD, Princeton U., NJ, 1993. Hedrick asst. prof. UCLA, 1993—96; instr. MIT, Cambridge, 1996—98; prof. U. Mo., Columbia, 1999—. Chief editor: Journal: Dynamics of Partial Differential Equations (Guggenheim Fellowship, 1999). Named Centennial fellow, Am. Math. Soc., 1998; fellow, Am. Math. Soc. Centennial, Inst. For Advanced Study, Princeton, NJ, 1998—99, Am. Math. Soc. Centennial, Harvard U., Cambridge, 1998—99, Am. Math. Soc. Centennial, Math. Inst., Berkeley, Calif., 1998—99, Guggenheim Found., 1999; grantee, DOE, 2006. Mem.: Am. Math. Soc. Office: U Mo Dept Math Columbia MO 65211 Office Phone: 573-884-0622. Office Fax: 573-882-1869. E-mail: cli@math.missouri.edu.

LI, YANYAN, mathematician, educator; arrived in U.S., 1984; s. Xiongfei Li and Yunming Ye; m. Marjorie Lee, May 2, 1992; children: Rachel Ruiqi Lee, Alvin Ruiwen Lee. BS, U. Sci. and Tech. of China, 1982; MS, Academia Sinica, China, 1984; PhD, NYU, 1988. Instr. Princeton U., NJ, 1988—90; asst. prof. Rutgers U., New Brunswick, NJ, 1990—93, assoc. prof., 1993—97, prof. math., 1997—. Mem. overseas adv. com. Morningside Inst. Math., 1996—; mem. sci. com. Inst. Math. Jejiang U., China, 1995—98; mem. sci. com. Internat. Math. Ctr., Beijing, 2006—; mem. sci. com. Ctr. Partial Differential Equations Academia Sinica, Beijing, 2006—; prof. Beijing Normal U., 2005—. Mem. editl. bd.: Acta Mathematica Scientia, 1996—, Differential and Differential and Integral Equations, 2001—, J. Partial Differential Equations, 2001—, Nonlinear Differential Equations and Applications, 2001—, Comm. on Pure and Applied Analysis, 2001—04, Advanced Nonlinear Studies, 2003—, Discrete and Continuous Dynamical Systems - Series A, 2004—. Recipient K. O. Friedrichs prize, Courant Inst. Math., NYU, 1989; fellow, The Alfred P. Sloan Found., 1987—88, 1993—95, Rutgers U., 1990—92, 1993. Mem.: Am. Math. Soc. (mem. com. on coms. 1999—2000, chmn. mem. fan fund com. 2003—04, mem. fan fund com. 2000—04). Office: Rutgers U Dept Math 110 Frelinghuysen Rd Piscataway NJ 08854 Office Phone: 732-445-3483. Office Fax: 732-445-5530. Business E-Mail: yyli@math.rutgers.edu.

LI, YONG-GANG FRANK, research scientist, educator; b. Shanghai, China, Jan. 23, 1945; s. Zhiping Li and Yueying Wang; m. Yungyung Nancy Wang, Oct. 6, 1973; 1 child, Thomas. BS, Fudan U., 1967, MS, 1968; PhD, U. So. Calif., LA, 1988. Rschr. Inst. Marine Geology & Geophysics, Shanghai, 1968—81; rsch. assoc. U. So. Calif., LA, 1982—88, rsch. prof., 1989—. Contbr. scientific papers to profl. jours. Grantee, NSF, 1990—2005. Fellow: Am. Chinese Scholar Assn. So. Calif. (corr.), Fudan U. Alumni Assn. So. Calif. (corr.); mem.: Am. Geophys. Union, Soc. of Exploration Geophysicists, Seismol. Soc. of Am. Achievements include discovery of Fault-Zone Seismic Trapped Waves And Post-Earthquake Fault Healing. Home: 290 Bloom Dr Monterey Park CA 91755 Office: Univ So Calif Dept Earth Scis University Park Los Angeles CA 90089 Home Phone: 323-722-6999; Office Phone: 213-740-3556. Office Fax: 213-740-8801. Business E-Mail: ygli@usc.edu.

LIACOURAS, PETER JAMES, academic administrator, lawyer, arbitrator, educator; b. Phila., Apr. 9, 1931; s. James Peter and Stella (Lagakos) L.; m. Ann Locke Myers, Sept. 5, 1959; children: Lisa Ann, James Peter, Stephen Myers, Gregory Locke. Student, Coll. William and Mary, 1950-51; BS, Drexel U., 1953; JD, U. Pa., 1956; MA, Fletcher Sch. Law and Diplomacy, 1958; LLM, Harvard U., 1959; postgrad. (Sterling fellow), Yale U. Law Sch., 1964-65; LLD (hon.), Dropsie U., 1982; LHD (hon.), Drexel U., 1984. Bar: Pa. 1957. Atty. Defender Assn. Phila., 1956-57, 59; research assoc. Duke U. Law Sch. Rule of Law Research Center, 1959-63; asst. prof. law Temple U., 1963-65, asso. prof., 1965-67, prof., 1967—, dean Sch. Law, 1972-82, univ. pres., 1982—2000, chancellor, 2000—, prof., 2000—. Spl. dist. atty., Phila., 1969, 70; chmn. Select Commn. on Pa. Bar Exam. Procedures, 1970; co-chmn. sect. legal edn. World Peace Through Law Center, 1973-74; chmn. confidentiality com. Pa. Gov.'s Justice Commn., 1974-78; lectr. law schs., India, 1967, Rome, 1974, 75, Ghana, 1975; lectr. law schs. Hebrew U., Jerusalem, 1975, 76, 77, 78, 79, Tel Aviv, 1981, Greece, 1977, 78, 79, 81, internat. law. Author: The International Court of Justice, 2 vols, 1962; contbr. numerous articles to law jours., 1957—. Abroad residing mem. Acad. Athens, 2003—. Recipient Human Rights award Nat. Conv. Women in Law, 1976, Ann. Human Relations award Am. Jewish Com., Phila., 1978, Disting. Am. award Am. Found. for Negro Affairs, 1987, Great Am. Traditions award, B'nai B'rith, 1999. Mem. ABA (Post-Bakke Task Force 1978-80), Phila. Bar Assn., Acad. Athens. Democrat. Greek Orthodox. Office: Temple University Barrack Hall Suite 300 1819 N Broad St Philadelphia PA 19122*

LIAN, BONG H., mathematics professor, department chairman; BA, U. Toronto, Can., 1985; PhD in Physics, Yale U., 1991. Math. and sci. tutor Yale Coll. Yale U., 1988—90, postdoctoral fellow dept. math. and physics, 1993; postdoctoral instr. dept. math. U. Toronto, 1991—93; postdoctoral fellow dept. math. Harvard U., 1994—95; asst. prof. dept. math. Brandeis U., Waltham, Mass., 1995—97, assoc. prof., 1997—2001, full prof., 2001—, undergrad. advisor, 1997—99, grad. advisor, 2001—02, chmn. dept. math., 2002—. Vis. assoc. prof. Nat. U. Singapore, 2001. Contbr. articles to profl. jours. Fellow, John Simon Guggenheim Meml. Found., 2003; A.P. Sloan Grad. Dissertation fellow in math., 1990—91. Mem.: Internat. Congress Chinese Mathematicians (sci. com. mem. 1999—), Internat. Sci. Found. Cambridge (sec. 1998—). Achievements include research in representation theory and semi-infinite cohomology; mirror symmetry and Calabi-Yau geometry; string theory. Office: Brandeis Univ Dept Math Goldsmith Bldg Rm 314 MS 050 415 South St Waltham MA 02454-9110 Office Phone: 781-736-3069. Office Fax: 781-736-3085. E-mail: lian@brandeis.edu.*

LIANG, BAILIN, immunologist; s. Furen Liang and Xiulin Wu; m. Suk Liang; children: Kaley, Landon. Degree in Food Engring., S. China Agrl. U., Guangzhou, 1990; PhD, U. Ariz., Tucson, 1996. Clin. document quality specialist Wyeth, Collegeville, Pa., 2002; sr. rsch. scientist Johnson & Johnson, Radnor, Pa., 2002—. Investigator Glaxosmithkline, Collegeville, 2001—02. Fellow, Arthritis Found. Am., 1998—2000; grantee, Ethel F. Donaghue Found., 2000—01. Mem.: Am. Assn. Immunologists (assoc.). Independent. Home: 2868 Marietta Way Gilbertsville PA 19525 Office: Johnson & Johnson 145 King of Prussia Rd Radnor PA 19087 Office Phone: 610-240-8597. Business E-Mail: bliang1@cntus.jnj.com.

LIANG, CHENJU, engineering educator; s. Y. T. Liang and Y. H. Tseng; m. C. H. Wang, Jan. 12, 2000; children: T. G., S. G. B in Engring., Tam-Kang U., Taipei, 1994; MS in Environ. Engring., U. Mass., Lowell, 1998, D in Engring., 2002. Instr. Merrimack Coll., North Andover, Mass., 2003—03; rsch. assoc. U. Mass., Lowell, 2003—04; asst. prof. dept. environ. engring. Nat. Chung Hsing U., Taichung City, Taiwan, 2004—. Cons. Xpert Design and Diagnostics, Stratham, NH, 2003—03, TETRA TECH, Inc., Oak Ridge, Miss., 2003—04. Grantee, Grad. Student Assn., U. of Mass., Lowell, 2000. Achievements include patents for Chemical Oxidation of Organic and Inorganic Contaminants by Chelated Transition Metals Catalyzed Persulfate. Office: Nat Chung Hsing U Dept Environ Engring 250 Kuo-Kuang Rd Taichung 402 Taiwan Office Phone: 886-4-22856610. Office Fax: 886-4-22856610. E-mail: cliang@dragon.nchu.edu.tw.

LIANG, EDISON PARKTAK, astrophysicist, plasma physicist, educator, researcher; b. Canton, Republic of China, July 22, 1947; came to U.S., 1964; s. Chi-Sen and Siu-Fong (Law) L.; m. Lily K. Yuen, Aug. 7, 1971; children: Olivia, James, Justin. BA, U. Calif., Berkeley, 1967, PhD, 1971. Rsch. scientist U. Tex., Austin, 1971-73; assoc. instr. U. Utah, Salt Lake City, 1973-75; asst. prof. Mich. State U., East Lansing, Mich., 1975-76, Stanford U., Calif., 1976-79; physicist, group leader Lawrence Livermore Nat. Lab., Livermore, Calif., 1980-88, assoc. div. leader, 1988-91; prof. space physics and astronomy Rice U., Houston, 1991-2001, Andrew Hays Buchanan prof. astrophysics, 2001—, assoc. chmn., dept. physics and astronomy, 2001—; assoc. dir. Rice Space Inst., Houston, 2001—. Mem. NASA and NSF Rev. Panels, Washington, 1988—. Editor: (book) Gamma Ray Bursts, 1986. Named Sci. fellow and Anthony scholar U. Calif., Berkeley, 1967-69. Fellow Am. Phys. Soc. (chair topical group in plasma astrophysics 2003, Lawrence Livermore Sabbatical award 2004); mem. Am. Astron. Soc., Internat. Astron. Union, Phi Beta Kappa, Sigma Xi. Office: Rice U Herman Brown Hall 6100 Main St MS108 Houston TX 77005-1892 Business E-Mail: liang@spacibm.rice.edu.

LIANG, JEROME ZHENGRONG, radiology educator; b. Chongging, China, June 23, 1958; arrived in U.S., 1981; BS, Lanzhou U., China, 1982; PhD, CUNY, 1987. Rsch. instr. Albert Einstein Coll. Medicine, Bronx, NY, 1986—87; rsch. assoc. Duke U. Med. Ctr., Durham, NC, 1987—89, asst. med. rsch. prof., 1990—92; asst. prof. SUNY, Stony Brook, 1992—97, assoc. prof., 1997—2000, prof., 2000—, co-dir. biomed. engring., 1996—. Mem. adv. bd. MDOL, Inc., 1999—; bd. dirs., v.p. R&D, founder Viatronix, Inc., 2000—. Contbr. articles to profl. jours.; mem. editl. bd.: IEEE Transactions on Med. Imaging, 1999—. Recipient NIH awards, 1990—, AHA award, 1996—2001, N.Y. State Biotech. award, 1996—98, E-Z-EM award, 1997—98; grantee, Soc. Thoracic Radiology, 1994—95, ADAC Rsch. Lab., 1994—95. Achievements include development of Bayesian image processing, quantitative emission computed tomography, tissue segmentation from magnetic resonance images, virtual endoscopy, virtual realities in radiology. Avocations: swimming, exercise, tennis. Office: SUNY Stony Brook Dept Radiology 4th Fl Rm 120 Stony Brook NY 11794-8460 Office Phone: 631-444-7837. Business E-Mail: jerome.liang@sunysb.gov.

LIANG, JIANMING, computer scientist, researcher; B in Engring., U. Sci. and Tech., Beijing, 1987; M in Engring., N.China Inst. Computing Tech., Beijing, 1990; PhD, U. Turku, Finland, 2000. Natural Sci. and Engring. Rsch. Coun. indsl. rsch. fellow Analogy Design Automation, Inc (aquired by Synopsys), Ottawa, Ont., Canada, 2001—02; rsch. scientist Siemens Med. Solutions USA, Inc., Malvern, Pa., 2002—. Contbr. articles to profl. jours. Recipient Faculty Rsch. award, Faculty Math. and Natural Sci., U. Turku, 2000; grantee, Chinese 8-5 Program, 1991. Mem.: IEEE (sr.), IEEE Computer Soc. (sr.), Assn. Computing Machinery (sr.). Achievements include patents pending for system and method for the detection of shapes in images; a system and method for toboggan based object segmentation using divergent gradient field response in images; dynamic fast tobogganing; toboggan-based object segmentation using distance transform; object characterization of toboggan-based clusters; medical diagnostic ultrasound characterization of cardiac motion. Office: Siemens Med Solutions USA Inc 51 Valley Stream Pkwy Malvern PA 19355 Office Phone: 610-448-1460.

LIANG, JUNXIANG, retired aeronautics and astronautics engineer, educator; b. Hangzhou, Zhejiang, China, Aug. 17, 1932; s. Yigao and Yunruo (Yu) L.; m. Junxian Sun, Jan. 27, 1960; 1 child, Song Liang. Grad., Harbin Inst. Tech., 1960. Head control dept. Shenyang Jet Engine R & D Inst., 1960—70, China Gas Turbine Establishment, Jiangyou, Sichuan, China, 1970—78, assoc. chief engr., 1979—83; vis. scientist MIT, Cambridge, 1984—86; prof. China Aerospace Inst. Sys. Engring., Beijing, 1986—2003; grads. supr. Beijing U. Aero-Astronautics, 1986—2003; chief engr. Full Authority Digital Elec. Engine Control China Aerospace Industry Ministry, Beijing, 1986—93; ret., 2003. Mem. China Aerospace Sci. and Tech. Com., Beijing, 1983-94, Aero-engine R & D Adv. Bd., Beijing, 1991-95; bd. dirs. China Aviation Ency. Editl. Bd., Beijing, 1991-95; tech. support supr., mgmt. info. svc. dir. Am. PC, Inc., Union City, Calif., 1993—. Author: Nonlinear Control System Oscillation, 1964; contbr. articles to Jour. Aeronautics and Astronautics, Jour. Propulsion Tech., Internat. Aviation, Acta Aeronautica et Astronautica Sinica. Recipient Nat. Sci. and Tech. 2d award, China Nat. Sci. and Tech. Com., Beijing, 1965, Sci. and Tech. Progress award, China Aerospace Industry Ministry, 1991, Nat. Outstanding Sci. and Tech. Contbn. award, 1992. Mem. AIAA (sr.), Chinese Soc. Aero. and Astronautical Engine Control (commn. com. 1987—). Achievements include solution of oscillation problem on nonlinear control system; formulation of aircraft overall strategy, study and control of High Thrust/Weight Engine Research Program.

LIANG, LEE Z., biology professor; s. Jin Liang and Mei Zhu; m. Amy Xiao, June 29, 1985; children: Jiang H., Kevin. BS in Plant Pathology, China; MS in Botany and Plant Pathology, Mich. State U., E. Lansing, 1991. Cert. seed pathology Danish Govt. Inst. Seed Pathology, 1986. Seed pathologist Beijing Vegetable Rsch. Ctr., 1982—89; rsch. asst. Mich. State U., 1989—95; biol. scientist U. Of Fla., Belle Glade, Fla., 1995—2006; assoc. prof. Palm Beach Cmty. Coll., W. Palm Beach, Fla., 2006—. Vis. scientist Seed Path. Inst., Copenhagen, 1985—87; com. mem. Campus Sustainability, Palm Beach Cmty. Coll., Belle Glade, Fla., 2007—. Contbr. scientific papers to profl. jours. Grantee Profl. Tchg. & Learning Rsch. grant, Palm Beach Cmty. Coll., 2006—07. Mem.: Fla. Assn. Cmty. Colls. (assoc.). Achievements include discovery of a new fungal subspecies. Office: Palm Beach Cmty Coll 1977 College Dr Belle Glade FL 33430

LIANG, QINGQING, electronics engineer; b. Changsha, Hunan, China, Sept. 20, 1977; s. Xuegong Liang and Fan Huang; m. Jinghong Ma, Aug. 14, 2002; 1 child, Michelle. BS hons., Fudan U., Shanghai, China, 1997, MS, 2000; PhD, Ga. Inst. Tech., Atlanta, 2005. Grad. rsch. asst. Ga. Inst. Tech., Gatech Elec. Design Ctr., Atlanta, 2002—05; semiconductor device engr. IBM Semiconductor & Rsch. Ctr., Hopewell Junction, NY, 2005—. Grad. rsch. asst. Fudan U., Integrated Circuit Tech. Computer-Aided-Design Lab., Shanghai, 1997—2000, Auburn U., Ala. Microelectronic Sci. & Tech. Ctr., Ala., 2000—02. Fellow, Auburn U., 2001—02. Mem.: Silicon Radio Frequency Symposium Com., Semiconductor Rsch. Corp., IEEE. Achievements include patents pending for new semiconductor device structure; first to radio-frequency circuit design methodology; microwave devices or circuits characterization methodology; device nonlinear modeling methodology; development of next generation high performance logic device. Home Phone: 347-325-0804; Office Phone: 845-892-8058.

LIANG, TYNG-YEU, engineering educator; BEE, Nat. Cheng-Kung U., Taiwan, 1992, MEE, 1994, PhD in Elec. Engring., 2000. Lectr. math. Nat. Tainan Tchrs. Coll., 1997—2000; asst. prof. computer sci. and info. engring. Leader U., Taiwan, 2002—03; asst prof. elec. engring. Nat. Kaohsiung U. Applied Sci., 2003—. Contbr. scientific papers, articles to profl. jours. Mem.: IEEE (mem. task force cluster computing 2003—). Office: Kaohsiung Univ Applied Sci 415 Chien-Kung Rd Kaohsiung 807 Taiwan Office Phone: 886-7-3814526 ext. 5508. Business E-Mail: lty@mail.ee.kuas.edu.tw.

LIANGOS, ORFEAS, nephrologist, researcher; m. Agnieszka Liangos. MD, Free U. Berlin, 1995. Cert. internist Am. Bd. Internal Medicine, 2001, nephrologist Am. Bd. Internal Medicine, 2003. Resident internal medicine Benjamin Franklin U. Clinic, Berlin, 1996—97, Cleve. Clinic Found., 1998—2001; clin. fellow nephrology Tufts-New Eng. Med. Ctr., Boston, 2001—03, clin. rsch. fellow nephrology, 2003—05; staff physician, divsn. nephrology Caritas St. Elizabeth's Med. Ctr., Boston, 2005—. Dir., acute renal failure rsch., kidney & dialysis rsch. lab. Caritas St. Elizabeth's Med. Ctr., Boston, 2005—. Nat. Scientist Devel. grant, Am. Heart Assn., 2005, Charlton Rsch. grant, Tufts U. Sch. Medicine, 2005. Fellow: Am. Soc. Nephrology; mem.: Am. Soc. Internal Medicine, Am. Coll. Physicians. Office: Caritas St Elizabeths Med Ctr 736 Cambridge St Boston MA 02135 Office Phone: 617-562-7654.

LIAO, MARTHA, geneticist; b. Leeds, Eng., Feb. 9, 1948; came to U.S., 1967; d. Chung-Chou and Shirley Liao; m. Haojiang Tian, Mar. 18, 1991. BA, Bryn Mawr Coll., 1970; PhD, U. Pa., 1974. Inst. fellow Eleanor Roosevelt Inst., Denver, 1979-86; asst. prof. U. Colo. Health Scis. Ctr., Denver, 1982-88; sr. fellow Eleanor Roosevelt Inst., Denver, 1986-94; assoc. prof. dept. pediat. U. Colo. Med. Sch., Denver, 1988-95. Chmn. sci. adv. bd. Cancer League of Colo., Denver, 1989-91; reviewer VA Merit Rev. Bd., Washington, 1988-92; vis. assoc. prof. Albert Einstein Coll. Medicine, Bronx, N.Y., 1992-96; presenter in field. Contbr. articles to Porceedings NAS. Pres. Asian Performing Arts Colo., Denver, 1986—; chmn. rev. com. Denver Cultural Dist., 1989-91; bd. dirs. Asian Arts Assn., Denver Art Mus., 1989-91. Rsch. scholar to China NAS, 1981-82; Rsch. grantee NSF, 1984-86, Am. Cancer Soc., 1981-82, NIH, 1980-94. Mem. Am. Soc. Human Genetics, Am. Soc. for Cell Biology, AAAS, Soc. Chinese Bioscientist in Am. (rep. Denver 1988—), Assn. Chinese Geneticists in Am. (sec. 1989-91). Achievements include research in human chromosome 12 by molecular and cell genetics, human protein and its gene that helps AIDS virus multiply in humans. Home: 451 W Jamison Pl Littleton CO 80120-4264 Office: 150 Columbus Ave Apt 18D New York NY 10023-5969

LIAO, PAUL FOO-HUNG, electronics executive; b. Phila., Nov. 10, 1944; s. Tseng Wu and Tung Mei (Lin) L.; m. Karen Ann Pravetz, Aug. 31, 1968; children: Teresa S., Joanna S. BS, MIT, 1966; PhD, Columbia U., 1973. Rsch. assoc. Columbia U., NYC, 1972-73; mem. tech. staff Bell Labs., Holmdel, N.J., 1973-80, dept. head., 1980-83; div. mgr. Bell Communications Rsch., Red Bank, N.J., 1984-89, asst. v.p., 1989-93, gen. mgr., 1993-95, v.p., 1995-96; v.p., chief tech. officer Panasonic Corp. N.Am., 1996—. Co-editor: Academic Press Quantum Electronics Book Series, 1980-96; contbr. over 75 articles to profl. jours.; holder over 12 patents in field. Bd. trustees Brookdale C.C. Fellow IEEE (Millennium medal 2000), Optical Soc. Am. (editor jour.), Am. Phys. Soc.; mem. Lasers and Electro Optic Soc. of IEEE (pres. 1987). Office: Panasonic Corp N Am One Panasonic Way Secaucus NJ 07094

LIAO, SHUTSUNG, biochemist, molecular oncologist; b. Tainan, Taiwan, Jan. 1, 1931; s. Chi-Chun Liao and Chin-Shen Lin; m. Shuching Liao, Mar. 19, 1960; children: Jane, Tzufen, Tzuming, May. BS in Agrl. Chemistry, Nat. Taiwan U., 1953, MS in Biochemistry, 1956; PhD in Biochemistry, U. Chgo., 1961. Rsch. assoc., 1960-63; asst. prof. U. Chgo., 1964-69; assoc. prof. dept. biochemistry and molecular biology Ben May Lab. Cancer Rsch., U. Chgo., 1969-71; prof. depts. biochemistry, molecular and cancer biology Ben May Inst. for Cancer Rsch., 1972—; dir. Tang Ctr. Herbal Medicine Rsch., 2000—02. CEO, chmn. bd., Anagen Therapeutic Co., 2000—; cons. in field. Mem. editl. bd. Jour. Steroid Biochemistry and Molecular Biology, The Prostate, Receptors, Signal Transduction, J. Formosan Med. Assoc., Biomedical Sci.; assoc. editor Cancer Rsch., 1982-89; contbr. over 250 articles to profl jours. V.p. Chgo. Formosan Fed. Credit Union, 1977-79; trustee Taiwanese United Fund in U.S., 1981-85; mem. adv. com. Taiwan-U.S. Cultural Exch. Ctr., 1984-87. Recipient Sci-Tech. Achievement prize Taiwanese-Am. Found., 1983, Pfizer Lecture fellow award Clin. Rsch. Inst. Montreal, 1972, Gregory Pincus medal and award Worcester Found. for Exptl. Biology, 1992, Tzongming Tu award Formosan Med. Assn., 1993, C.H. Li Meml. Lecture award, 1994; NIH grantee, 1962—; Am. Cancer Soc. grantee, 1971-81. Fellow Am. Acad. Art and Scis.; mem. Am. Soc. Biochemistry and Molecular Biology, Am. Assn. Cancer Rsch., Endocrine Soc., N.Am.-Taiwanese Profs. Assn. (pres. 1980-81, exec. dir. 1981—), Nat. Acad. Taiwan. Achievements include discovery of androgen activation mechanism and androgen receptors; cloning and structural determination of androgen receptors and other novel nuclear receptors, and their genes, and receptor gene mutation in hereditary abnormalities and cancers; rsch. on regulation of hormone-dependent gene expression and cell growth, molecular bases of cancer cell growth and progression, chemoprevention, and therapeutic treatment of hormone-sensitive and insensitive cancers and diseases, molecular bases of cholesterol modulation and control in cardiovascular and neurodegenerative diseases and cancer progression. Home: 5632 S Woodlawn Ave Chicago IL 60637-1623 Office: U Chgo Ben May Inst Cancer Rsch 929 E 57th St Chicago IL 60637

LIASHKOV, PETER, artist, educator; b. Rouen, France, Oct. 7, 1939; came to U.S., 1955; s. Maxim and Olga (Veger) L.; m. Ann Harvey; 1 child, Alexina. MFA, Otis Art Inst., LA, 1968. Sr. instr. Art Ctr. Coll. of Design, Pasadena, Calif., 1975—. One-man shows include Spruce Street Forum, San Diego, 1996, Oculorum Gallery, L.A., Julie Rico Gallery, Santa Monica, Calif., 1999; exhibited in group shows at Kuhn Galerie, Aachen,

West Germany, 1971, San Francisco Art Inst., 1977, 86, Baum-Silverman Gallery, L.A., 1980, 81, Koplin Gallery, L.A., 1984, Mcpl. Art Gallery, L.A., 1979, 86, 87, Bliss Gallery, Pasadena, 1989, Marble Palace, St. Petersburg, Russia, 1992, F. Riestra Gallery, Mexico City, 1993, Riverside (Calif.) Mus. of Art, 1996, San Diego Mus. Contemporary Art, 1997, others; represented in permanent collections Bklyn. Mus., Ill. Inst. Tech., Chgo., Pa. Acad. Fine Arts, Phila., AT&T, Chgo., N.Y. Pub. Libr., others. Office: Art Ctr Coll Design 1700 Lida St Pasadena CA 91103-1924

LIASSON, MARA, news correspondent; BA in Am. History, Brown Univ. Mng. editor, anchor Calif. Edition; journalist The Vineyard Gazette; gen. assignment reporter, newscaster Nat. Public Radio (NPR), 1985, nat. polit. corr., 1985—, White House corr., 1992—2000, congl. corr., 1989—92; political correspondent FOX News Channel, 1997—. Regular contbr., Special Report with Brit Hume FOX News Channel, panelist, FOX News Sunday. Contbr. reports to All Things Considered and Morning Edition. Recipient Merriman Smith award, White House Correspondents' Assn., 1994, 1995, 1997; fellow Bagehot Fellowship in Economics and Business Journalism. Office: FOX News Channel 400 N Capitol St NW Ste 550 Washington DC 20001

LIAU, GENE, medical educator; b. Hsing-Chu, Taiwan, Nov. 28, 1954; came to U.S., 1965; BS in Biology, U. NC, 1977; DPhil, Vanderbilt U., 1982. Postdoctoral fellow Lab. Molecular Biology, Nat. Cancer Inst. NIH, Bethesda, Md., 1982-85; assoc. mem. dept. cell biology Revlon Biotech. Rsch. Ctr., Rockville, Md., 1985-87; scientist I dept. molecular biology Am. Red Cross Jerome H. Holland Lab., Rockville, 1987-90, scientist II, 1990-96, sr. scientist, 1996-98; assoc. prof. dept. anatomy George Washington U. Med. Ctr., Washington, 1995—; unit head metabolic and vascular disease group Genetic Therapy Inc., Gaitersburg, Md., 1998—; adj. prof. molecular biology Holland Lab., 1998—, sr. scientist, 1998—. Mem. AHA Vascular Wall Biology Rsch. Study Com., 1992-96, Pathology A Study Sect. NIH, 1994-98; invited spkr. in field. Contbr. articles to profl. jours. Arthritis Found. fellow, 1982-85; pub. health svc. grantee, 1988—; recipient Nat. Rsch. Svc. award NIH, 1977-81, Rsch. Career Devel. award, 1990-95. Mem. AAAS, Am. Soc. Cell Biology, Am. Heart Assn. Coun. Basic Sci. (Established Investigator 1990, Grant-in-Aid 1992-95, 95-98), Soc. Chinese Bioscientists, Sigma Xi. Office: Genetic Therapy Inc 100 Technology Sq Cambridge MA 02139-3585

LIBASSI, FRANK PETER, lawyer; b. NYC, Apr. 20, 1930; s. Frank G. and Mary (Marino) Libassi; m. Mary Frances Steen, July 10, 1954; children: Thomas, Timothy, Jennifer. BA in Polit. Sci. cum laude, Colgate U., Hamilton, NY, 1951; LLB, Yale U., New Haven, 1954. Bar: N.Y. 1955, Conn. 1980. Enforcement atty. NY State Housing and Rent Commn., 1954-56; regional dir. NY State Commn. Human Rights, Albany, 1956-62; dep. staff dir. US Commn. Civil Rights, 1962-66, spl. asst. to sec., dir. office for civil rights, 1966-68; gen. counsel US Dept. Health Edn. & Welfare, Washington, 1977-79; exec. v.p. Urban Coalition, Washington, 1968—71; v.p. Am. City Corp., Columbia, Md., 1971-72; pres., CEO Greater Hartford (Conn.) Process Inc. (Greater Hartford Cmty. Devel. Corp.), 1971-77; ptnr. Verner, Liipfert, Bernhard and McPherson, Washington, 1979-82; sr. v.p. Travelers Corp., Hartford, 1982-93; of counsel Verner, Liipfert, Bernhard & McPherson, Washington, 1993-95; dean Barney Sch. of Bus. and Pub. Adminstrn., U. Hartford, West Hartford, Conn., 1993-96; pres. Children's Fund Conn., Hartford, 1996—2001, Child Health and Devel. Inst. Conn., Hartford, 1997—2001. Mem. Urban Land Inst., 1971—77; v.p. Ctr. Global Bus. Studies, Paris, 1996—97; adv. bd. Bur. Nat. Affairs Housing and Cmty. Devel. Reporter, 1972—77; vis. lectr. Anderson Coll., Chatham Coll., Goddard Coll., Ohio Wesleyan U., 1974—76; adj. faculty Grad. Sch. Bus. and Pub. Adminstrn. U. Hartford, Hartford, 1976—77. Author: The Negro in the Armed Forces, 1963, Family Housing and the Negro Serviceman, 1963, Equal Opportunity in Farm Programs, 1965, Revitalizing Central City Investment, 1977. Mem. nat. consumer adv. com. Am. Health Care Assn., 1985—86; mem. Nat. Retirees Vol. Ctr., 1988—90; chmn. Ct. Cmty. Care, Inc., 1980—86; mem. com. aging soc. NAS, 1982—86; mem. exec. com. Downtown Coun. Hartford, 1983—86, Greater Hartford Arts Coun., 1983—86; chmn. Gov.'s Commn. Financing Long Term Care, 1986—87; mem. com. elderly people living alone Commonwealth Fund, 1985—91; mem. Sec. Bowen's Task Force Long-Term Health Care Policies Health Care Financin Adminstrn., 1986—87; bd. dirs. Alliance Aging Rsch., 1986—91; mem. Pew Commn. Future Health Profls., 1990—93, Pub. Affairs Rsch. Coun. Conf. Bd., 1990—93, United Srs. Health Coop., 1990—91; mem. com. predicting future diseases Inst. Medicine, 1991—93; trustee Conn. Pub. Expenditure Coun., 1991—96; mem. adv. com. health care reform Commonwealth Fund, 1993—98; bd. dirs. Duncaster Cmty., 1993—97, Conn. Health Found., 1999—2004, Conn. Appleseeds, 2004—, Hartford Symphony Orch., 2005—; bus. adv. bd. Conn. Commn. Children, 1998—2004; mem. adv. com. Dem. Nat. Com., 1974—77; bd. dirs. Hartford Sem., 2002—06; bd. dirs. legis. com. Am. Coun. Life Ins., 1987—90; bd. dirs., mem. exec. com. Ins. Inst. Hwy. Safety, 1984—88; adv. bd. Nat. Acad. Aging, 1992—96, U. Conn. Sch. Nursing, 1996—2002; bd. dirs. The Bushnel, 1998—2006; incorporator Inst. Living, 1973—2004, Hartford Hosp., 1973—2004, St. Francis Hosp., 1990—2004, Wheeler Clinic, 1996—. Recipient Superior Performance award, U.S. Commn. Civil Rights, 1963, Meritorious Svc. award, 1965, Sec.'s Spl. citation, 1967, Disting. Svc. award, HEW, 1968, award, Friend La Casa de P.R., Hartford, 1992, Exec. Dirs. award, Conn. Assn. Human Svcs., 1996, John Filer award for Philanthropy, 2004; Woodrow Wilson Sr. fellow, 1973—77. Mem.: Greater Hartford C. of C. (bd. dirs. 1985—93, mem. exec. com.), Am. Assn. Ret. Persons (mem. nat. steering com. new roles in soc. 1987—90), Hartford Club. Office Phone: 860-726-2227. Personal E-mail: libassi@comcast.net. Business E-Mail: peter@libassi.org.

LIBBY, DANIEL M., pulmonologist; b. NYC, Sept. 9, 1949; s. Nathan and Shirley Rebecca (Stats) Libby; m. Nancy Ellen Kemeny, May 22, 1977; children: Jacqueline, Laura, Victoria. AB, Columbia U., NYC, 1971; MD, Baylor U., Waco, Tex., 1974. Diplomate Am. Bd. Internal Medicine, Am. Bd. Pulmonary Medicine, Am. Bd. Critical Care Medicine. Intern N.Y. Hosp.-Cornell Med. Ctr., 1974—75, resident, 1975—77; fellowship pulmonary disease Cornell U. Med. Coll., 1977—79; attending physician NY Presbyn. Hosp., NYC, 1979—; clin. prof. medicine Weill Med. Coll., Cornell U., NYC, 1979—, bd. dirs. Mem.: AOA, N.Y.C. Physician Golfing Assn. (pres. 2002—03), River Club NY. Avocations: tennis, golf, travel. Home: 333 E 68th St New York NY 10021 Office: 407 E 70th St New York NY 10021 Office Phone: 212-628-6611. Personal E-mail: dmlibbyoo@aol.com.

LIBBY, GARY RUSSELL, museum director emeritus, writer; b. Boston, June 7, 1944; s. Charles W. and Sylvia P. Libby. BA, U. Fla., 1967, MA (NDEA fellow), 1968; MA, Tulane U., 1972. Instr. English Tulane U., 1968-71; asst. prof. Stetson U., Deland, Fla., 1972-77, vis. prof., 1977-86; dir. Mus. Arts and Scis., Daytona Beach, Fla., 1977—2001, 2004—05, dir. emeritus, 2002—. Reviewer Inst. Mus. Svcs.; panelist Mus. Assessment Program; reviewer Accreditation Commn. of Am. Assn. Mus.; cons. in field. Author: Two Centuries of Cuban Art, 1985, Cuba: A History in Art, 1997, Coast to Coast: The Contemporary Landscape in Florida, 1998, A Treasury of American Art, 2002; editor: Archipenko: Themes and Variations, 1989, Chihuly: Form From Fire, 1994 (Southeastern Mus. Conf. award, 1994), A Century of Jewelry and Gems, 1995, Celebrating Florida, 1995, Illustrated Dictionary of Florida Art, 2007—. Trustee Cuban Found.; mem. artists in edn. panel, visual arts panel, youth and children's mus. panel, sci. mus. panel Fla. Arts. Coun., 2006—07; panelist Challenge Grant Program, Cultural Instns. Program; mem. hist. mus. grants panel Fla. Divsn. History; mem. Halifax Area Advt. Authority, 1999—; mem. adv. bd. Daytona Beach Econ. Devel., 1999—2004; vice chmn. Mainstreet Redevel. Bd., 2004—06; mem., chmn. adv. bd. Environ., Cultural, Hist., and Outdoors, 2001—05, chmn., 2007—; mem. Cultural Coun. Volusia County, 2002—03, Daytona Beach Charter Rev.; mem. mayor's cabinet City of Daytona Beach, 2007; v.p. Hist. Pinewood, 2005—07; chmn. arts and entertainment Halifax Area Advt. Authority, 2003—; bd. dirs. Mus. Arts and Scis. Mem.: Cuban Found. (v.p. 2006—07), Fla. Cultural and Ednl. Alliance (bd. dirs. 1995), Fla. Assn. Mus. (bd. dirs. 1992—98, sec. 1995—98), Fla. Art Mus. Dirs. Assn. (govt. liaison 1990—95, pres. 1995—97). Home and Office: 723 N Oleander Ave Daytona Beach FL 32118-3826 Business E-Mail: grlibby@moas.org.

LIBBY, WENDY B., academic administrator; m. Richard Libby; children: Glenn, Gregg. BS in Biology, Cornell U., 1972; MBA, Johnson Grad. Sch. of Mgmt. at Cornell U., 1977; PhD in Ednl. Adminstrn., U. Conn., 1994. Dir. adminstrn. pub. mgmt. program Johnson Grad. Sch. of Mgmt. at Cornell U., Ithaca, NY, 1979—80; dir. adminstrv. ops. Coll. of Architecture, Art and Planning, Ithaca, NY, 1980—84; adminstrv. mgr. Coll. Edn. Ohio State U., Columbus, 1984—85, adminstrv. assoc. Office of Fin., 1984—85; asst. dir. U. Conn. Med. Ctr. John Dempsey Hosp., Farmington, Conn., 1985—87, asst. to assoc. exec. dir., 1985—87; spl. asst. to pres. and sr. human resources officer U. Hartford, Conn., 1987—89; chief fin. and bus. officer Westbrook Coll., Portland, Maine, 1989—95; v.p. bus. affairs and CFO Furman U., Greenville, SC, 1995—2003; pres. Stephens Coll., Columbia, Mo., 2003—. Founding bd. dirs. Tuition Plan Consortium, Caribbean Inst. Tech.; bd. dirs. Greenville Literacy Assn., Women's Coll. Coalition. Mem.: Soc. Coll. and U. Planning, So. Assn. of Coll. and U. Bus. Officers, Ea. Assn. of Coll. and U. Bus. Officers (bd. dirs.), Nat. Assn. of Coll. and U. Bus. Officers. Office: Stephens Coll 1200 E Broadway Columbia MO 65215

LIBBY-BARTH, JENNIFER, social studies educator; b. Bennington, Vt., Jan. 7, 1975; d. Sandra Gonyeau; m. Michael Barth, Oct. 12, 2002; children: Trevor Barth, Owen Barth. BA, Syracuse U., Utica, NY, 1997. Social studies tchr. Craftsbury Acad., Craftsbury Commons, Vt., 1998—99, St. Francis H.S., Atlanta, 1999—2001, Timberlane Regional H.S., Plaistow, NH, 2001—. Student coun. advisor Timberlane Regional H.S., Plaistow, NH, 2003—. Mem.: Nat. Coun. Social Studies (assoc.). Home: 18 Dolliver Ln Kingston NH 03848 Office: Timberlane Regional HS 36 Greenough Rd Plaistow NH 03865 Home Phone: 603-475-8862; Office Phone: 603-382-6541. Office Fax: 603-382-8086. Business E-Mail: jlibby@timberlanehs.com.

LIBCHABER, ALBERT JOSEPH, physics professor; b. Paris, Oct. 23, 1934; came to US, 1983; s. Charles and Cyrla (Markowska) L.; m. Irene Gelman, Sept. 11, 1955; children: Jacques, Remy, David BS, U. Paris, 1956; MS, U. Ill., 1959; PhD, Ecole Normale Superieure, Paris, 1965. Matre de Recherche Nat. Ctr. Sci. Rsch. (CNRS), Ecole Normale, Paris, 1967-74, dir. rsch., 1974-83; prof. physics U. Chgo., 1983-91, Paul Snowden Disting. Svc. prof., 1987; prof. dept. physics Princeton U., NJ, 1991-94; prof. Rockefeller U., NYC, 1994—, Detlev W. Bronk prof., 1995—. Officer French Army, 1959—61. Recipient Wolf prize in physics, Wolf Found., Israel, 1986, MacArthur Found. Fellow, 1986-91. Fellow NEC Rsch. Inst. Princeton; mem. Am. Phys. Soc., French Phys. Soc. (Silver medal 1971, prix Ricard 1979), Am. Acad. Arts & Scis., NAS. Jewish. Office: Lab Exptl Condensed Matter Physics Rockefeller U 1230 York Ave New York NY 10021 Office Phone: 212-327-8000. E-mail: libchbr@rockefeller.edu.*

LIBERATI, MARIA THERESA, lifestyle company executive, cooking expert, writer; b. Phila., July 16, 1965; Student, Laval U., Que., Can., 1984; BS in Fgn. Lang. Edn., Temple U., 1986. Pres., bd. dirs. Sierra Ctr., Feasterville, Pa., 1988—; pres. M.T.L. Prodns., Phila., 1989—; exec. pres. Art of Living, Prima Media, 2004—. Spokesperson for Sparkling Cards, 2005—. Author: Fashion, Fun and Fitness, 1989, The Model's Guide, 1998, The Basic Art of Italian Cooking, 2006; editor mag. Better Nutrition for Today's Living, 1990—. Named Miss Pa., 1985, Miss World, 1986; recipient Merit award Actors and Artists Assn., Rome. Mem. AFTRA, NAFE (adv. bd. 1988—). Avocations: reading, cooking. E-mail: marialib@hotmail.com, marialiberati@liberaticorporation.com, lacucinadimaria@yahoo.com.

LIBERATO, LYNNE, lawyer; b. Pensacola, Fla., Dec. 22, 1953; BS in Journalism, Sam Houston State U.; MS in Journalism, Tex. A&M Commerce; JD, South Tex. Coll. Law. Bar: Tex. 1981, admitted to practice: US Ct. Appeals (5th Cir.) 1982, US Dist. Ct. (So. Dist.) Tex. Reporter/photographer Huntsville (Tex.) Item, 1974-75, Commerce Jour., 1975-76, Sta. KHOU-TV, Houston, 1976; with pub. affairs dept. Shell Oil Co., Houston, 1976-81; ptnr., Civil Appeals Haynes and Boone LLP, Houston. Chief staff atty. First Ct. Appeals, Houston, 1981-90; mem. adminstrv. oversign com. State Bar of Tex., 1995-96, gen. counsel oversight com., 1995-96, adv. com. legal svcs. corp., 1995-96, others; examiner Tex. Bd. Legal Specialization, 1989, appellate adv. bd. 1990-92; sec. Com. for Harris County Benchbook, 1993-97; speaker in field. Contbr. articles to numerous profl. jour.; author: Reason for Reversal in Texas Courts of Appeals (Outstanding Law Rev. Article Award, Tex. Bar Found., 2004). Chmn. Bd. United Way of Tex. Gulf Coast, 1996—, chmn. allocations rev. team, fund distbrn. subcom. 1997, chmn. implementation redesign com. 1996-97, steering com. for fund distbrn. redesign adv.com. 1994-95; mem. torch relay judging com. U.S. Olympics, 1996; v.p. Neighborhood Justice Ctr., 1981-85; mem. adv. bd. U. Houston Inst. for Urban Edn., 1997. Named Comml. Prosecutor of yr. Internat. Comml. Litigation mag., 1997, One of Ten Women on the Move, Houston Post, 1992, Woman of Year in Law, YWCA, 1993, Top Notch Appellate Lawyer, Tex. Lawyer, 2002, True Texan Award, Muscular Dystrophy Assn., 2002, Woman of Yr., United Way of Tex. Gulf Coast, 2004, one of top 100 Tex. Super Lawyers, Top 50 Female Lawyers, Top 100 Houston Lawyers, Tex. Montly Mag., 2003, 2004. Fellow Tex. Bar Found., Houston Bar Found.; mem. Am. Law Inst., Fedn. of Houston Profl. Women (Woman of Excellence 1994), Houston Bar Assn. (pres. 1993-94, editor jour. 1990-91, chmn. campaign for homeless 1991-92, legal edn. com. 1989-90, others), State Bar Tex. (chmn. client security fund com. 1995-96, exec. com. 1994-97, chmn. nominations and elections com. 1997-98, chmn. bd. dirs. 1996-97, pres. 2000-2001), Supreme Ct. Hist. Soc., Tex. Assn. Civil Trial and Appellate Specialists (bd. dirs. 1992-93). Office: Haynes and Boone LLP 1 Houston Ctr 1221 McKinney Ste 2100 Houston TX 77010 Office Phone: 713-547-2017. Office Fax: 713-236-5538. Business E-Mail: lynne.liberato@haynesboone.com.

LIBERMAN, GAIL JEANNE, editor; b. Neptune, NJ, Feb. 26, 1951; d. Si and Dorothy (Gold) L.; m. Alan Lavine, Dec. 20, 1991. BA, Rutgers U., 1972. Youth editor AP, NYC, 1972-73; writer United Feature Syndicate, NYC, 1973; reporter, broadcast editor UPI, Phila. and Hartford, Conn., 1973-75; reporter Courier-Post, Camden, NJ, 1976-80, Bank Advt. News, North Palm Beach, Fla., 1981-82; editor Bank Rate Monitor, North Palm Beach, 1982-97. Author: Improving Your Credit and Reducing Your Debt, 1994 (endorsed Inst. CFPs), The Complete Idiot's Guide to Making Money With Mutual Funds, 1996, Love, Marriage and Money, 1998, Rags to Riches: Motivating Stories of How Ordinary People Achieved Extraordinary Wealth, 2000, Short and Simple Guide to Life Insurance, 2000, More Rags to Riches: All New Stories of How Ordinary People Achieved Extraordinary Wealth, 2002, Rags to Retirement, 2003, Quick Steps to Financial Stability, 2006; columnist: Boston Herald, 1994—, America Online, 1996—, Investor Square, 1996—, Mutual Funds Interactive, 1996—, Quicken, 1998—, Palm Beach Daily News, 1998—, CNBC.com, 2000, Fasttrack mag., 2001, Pitts. Post-Gazette, 2001—, Dow Jones Market Watch, 2006—; contbr. articles to profl. jours. Mem. Soc. Am. Bus. Editors and Writers. Personal E-mail: mwliblav@aol.com.

LIBERMAN, MEGAN ROSE, editor; b. 1968; d. Micheline Blum and Donald Liberman, Dr. Michael Jaker (Stepfather) and Anya Luchow-Liberman (Stepmother); m. Edward Lewine, Sept. 19, 1998. BA cum laude, Barnard Coll.; M in journalism cum laude, Columbia U. Exec. dir. Swing mag., 1996—99; exec. editor Us Weekly, 1999—2000; arts editor NY Times, 2000—02; editor NY Times mag., 2002—. Office: NY Times 229 W 43rd St New York NY 10036 Office Phone: 212-556-8330. Office Fax: 212-556-3830.

LIBERMAN, ROBERT PAUL, psychiatry educator, researcher, writer; b. Newark, Aug. 16, 1937; s. Harry and Gertrude (Galowitz) L.; m. Janet Marilyn Brown, Feb. 16, 1973; children: Peter, Sarah, Danica, Nathaniel, Annalisa. AB summa cum laude, Dartmouth Coll., 1959, diploma in medicine with honors, 1960; MS in Pharmacology, U. Calif., San Francisco, 1961; MD, Johns Hopkins U., 1963. Diplomate Nat. Bd. Med. Examiners, Am. Bd. Psychiatry and Neurology. Intern Bronx (N.Y.) Mcpl. Hosp.-Einstein Coll. Medicine, 1963-64; resident psychiatry Mass. Mental Health Ctr., Boston, 1964-68; postdoctoral fellow in social psychiatry Harvard U., 1966-68, tchg. fellow in psychiatry, 1964-68; mem. faculty group psychotherapy tng. program Washington Sch. Psychiatry, 1968-70; asst. clin. prof. psychiatry UCLA, 1970-72, assoc. clin. prof., 1972-73, assoc. rsch. psychiatrist, 1973-76, rsch. prof. psychiatry, 1976-77, prof. psychiatry, 1977—. With nat. Ctr. Mental Health Svc., Tng. and Rsch., St. Elizabeths Hosp., also mem. NIMH Clin. and Rsch. Assocs. Tng. Program, Washington, 1968-70; dir. Camarillo-UCLA Clin. Rsch. Unit, 1970-97, dir. Clin. Rsch. Ctr. Schizophrenia and Psychiat. Rehab., 1977-2001; chief Rehab. Medicine Svc., West L.A. VA Med. Ctr., Brentwood divsn., 1980-92; cons. divsn. mental health and behavioral scis. edn. Sepulveda (Calif.) VA Hosp., 1975-80; practice medicine specializing in psychiatry, Reston, Va., 1968-70, Thousand Oaks, Calif., 1977—; staff psychiatrist Ventura County Mental Health Dept., 1970-75, Ventura County Gen. Hosp.; mem. med. staff UCLA Neuropsychiat. Inst. and Hosp., 1971—, Ventura Gen. Hosp., Camarillo State Hosp., 1970-97, West L.A. VA Med. Ctr.; dir. Rehab. Rsch. and Tng. Ctr. Mental Illness, 1980-85; prof. psychiatry, dir. psych. rehab. program UCLA Sch. Medicine. Author: (with King, DeRisi and McCann) Personal Effectiveness: Guiding People to Assert Their Feelings and Improve Their Social Skills, 1975, A Guide to Behavioral Analysis and Therapy, 1972, (with Wheeler, DeVisser, Kuehnel and Kuehnel) Handbook of Marital Therapy: An Educational Approach to Treating Troubled Relationships, 1980, Psychiatric Rehabilitation of Chronic Mental Patients, 1987, (with DeRisi and Mueser) Social Skills Training for Psychiatric Patients, 1989, (with Kuehnel, Rose and Storzbach) Resource Book for Psychiatric Rehabilitation, 1990, Handbook of Psychiatric Rehabilitation, 1992, (with Yager) Stress in Psychiatric Disorders, 1993, (with Corrigan) Behavior Therapy in Psychiatric Hospitals, 1994, International Perspectives on Skills Training with the Mentally Disabled, 1998; mem. editl. bd. Jour. Applied Behavior Analysis, 1972-78, Jour. Marriage and Family Counseling, 1974-78, Jour. Behavior Therapy and Exptl. Psychiatry, 1975-2000, Behavior Therapy, 1979-84, Assessment and Intervention in Devel. Disabilities, 1980-85; assoc. editor Jour. Applied Behavior Analysis, 1976-78, Schizophrenia Bull., 1981-87, Internat. Rev. Psychiatry, 1988—, Psychiatry, 1993—; contbr. over 300 articles to profl. jours. and chpts. to books. Bd. dirs. Lake Sherwood Cmty. Assn., 1978—, pres., 1979-81, 90-92, v.p., 1992-95, sec., 1995-97; mem. Conejo Valley Citizens Adv. Bd., 1979-81. Served as surgeon USPHS, 1964-68. Recipient Noyes award for Rsch. in Schizophrenia, 1992, Kolb award in Schizophrenia, 1994, Human Rights award Psychosocial Rehab., Lilly Reintegration prize, Human Rights award WHO, 2000, Reintegration award Eli Lilly, 2000, Disting. Investigator award Nat. Alliance for Rsch. in Schizophrenia and Depression, 2000-01; rsch. grantee NIMH, SSA, NIDA, VA, 1972—. Mem. Assn. Advancement Behavior Therapy (exec. com. 1970-72, dir. 1972-79), Am. Psychiat. Assn. (Hibbs and Van Ameringen awards, Inst. Psychiat. Svcs. Significant Achievement award), Assn. Clin. Psychosocial Rsch. (mem. coun. 1985-98, pres. 1995-97), Phi Beta Kappa. Home: 528 Lake Sherwood Dr Thousand Oaks CA 91361-5120 Office: UCLA Neuropsychiatric Inst 760 Westwood Plz Los Angeles CA 90095

LIBERT, DONALD JOSEPH, lawyer; b. Sioux Falls, SD, Mar. 23, 1928; s. Bernard Joseph and Eleanor Monica (Sutton) L.; m. Jo Anne Murray, May 16, 1953; children: Cathleen, Thomas, Kevin, Richard, Stephanie. BS magna cum laude in Social Scis., Georgetown U., 1950, LLB, 1956. Bar: Ohio. From assoc. to ptnr. Manchester, Bennett, Powers & Ullman, Youngstown, Ohio, 1956-65; various positions to v.p., gen. counsel and sec. Youngstown Sheet & Tube Co., 1965-78; assoc. group counsel LTV Corp., Youngstown and Pitts., 1979; v.p. and gen. counsel Anchor Hocking Corp., Lancaster, Ohio, 1979-87; pvt. practice Lancaster, 1987—. Served to lt. (j.g.) USN, 1951-54. Mem. Ohio Bar Assn., Fairfield County Bar Assn., Lancaster Country Club, Rotary. Republican. Roman Catholic. Home: 2198 William T Cir Lancaster OH 43130-1087

LIBERT, NANCY PORTA, retired elementary school educator; b. Bay Shore, NY, Nov. 6, 1936; d. Frank and Anna Klenner Porta; m. Calvin Clifford Libert, Sept. 19, 1959; children: Darien Libert Logan, Leslie Libert Cain. Student, Hofstra U., 1954—59; BA Elem. Edn., Stony Brook U., 1973; MA Elem. Edn., Adelphi U., 1977; MA Linguistics, SUNY, Stony Brook, 1985. Cert. TESOL. Tchr. 1st grade Cordello Ave. Sch., Central Islip, NY, 1973—74, tchr. 3d grade, 1974—78, tchr. 5th grade, 1978—79; tchr. ESL Mulligan Sch., Central Islip, 1980—81; tchr. 6th grade Mulligan and O'Neill Schs., Central Islip, 1980—99; ret., 1999. Tchr. English phonology SUNY, Stony Brook, 1984—85; presenter in field. Author: The Western Civ Rap, 1994; editor, writer: bi-monthly newsletter Neighborhood News, 1988—2000, monthly newsletter Lamplighter, 1979—. Co-founder Old South Islip Civic Assn., 1980—, past-pres., 1980—, editor, 1980—2002, com. chmn., 1980—; tutor, mentor L.I. Youth Mentoring, Deer Park, NY, 2001—; co-founder Islip Sch.-Age Child Care, 1985—93, bd. dirs., 1985—93, publicity chair, 1985—93; co-chmn. annual auction benefit Presbyn. Ch. Islip, 2002—05. Mem.: Hist. Soc. Islip Hamlet (co-founder 1993, site designation com., edn. liaison, corr. sec. 2004), Central Islip Ret. Tchrs. Assn. (exec. bd. del. 2001—). Democrat. Presbyterian. Avocations: collecting adolescent literature series, local historical research, running. Home: 88 Monell Ave Islip NY 11751

LIBERTH, RICHARD FRANCIS, lawyer; b. Bklyn., Mar. 1, 1950; s. S. Richard and Frances J. (Falconer) L.; m. Lisa M. Feenick, June 8, 1974; children: Andrew R., Erica M. BS in Bus. Adminstrn., U. Denver, 1972; JD, Bklyn. Law Sch., 1976. Bar: NY 1977, US Dist. Ct. (so. and ea. dists.) NY 1981, US Dist. Ct. (no. dist.) NY 1991. Staff atty. Mental Health Legal Svcs., Poughkeepsie, NY, 1976-78; sr. asst. dist. atty. Rockland County Dist. Attys. Office, NYC, 1978-81; prin. Tarshis Catania Liberth Mahon & Milligram PLLC, Newburgh, NY, 1981—. Atty. Fraternal Order of Police Lodge #957. Dir. Legal Aid Soc. Orange County, Goshen, NY, 1982-84, Orange County Cerebral Palsy Assn., Goshen, 1986-89; mem. Rep. Nat. Com., Washington, 1990—; Rep. chmn. Town of Woodbury, 1997-99; trustee Orange Regional Med. Ctr. Found., 2005—. Mem. NY Bar Assn., Newburgh Bar Assn. (pres. 1991), Orange County Bar Assn. (v.p. 1995, pres. 1997), Woodbury Lions Club (Central Valley, NY) (past pres.). Avocations: golf, tennis, reading, collecting. Home: 134 Hasbrouck Rd Goshen NY 10924 Office: Tarshis Catania Liberth Mahon & Milligram PLLC One Corwin Ct Newburgh NY 12550 Business E-Mail: rliberth@tclmm.com.

LIBERTO, JOSEPH SALVATORE, retired bank executive; b. Balt., Apr. 26, 1929; s. Cosimo and Anna (Serio) L.; m. Mary Jane Colandro, May 20, 1962; children— Joseph C., Grace Ann. Student, Balt. City Coll., 1945-47; certificate accounting, Balt. Coll. Commerce, 1949; grad., Nat. Assn. Bank Auditors, and Comptrollers Sch. Banking, U. Wis., 1968. With Signet Bank, Md., Balt., from 1954; auditor Union Trust Co. Md., 1963-98, asst. v.p., security officer, 1979-98; ret. Served with AUS, 1951-53, Japan. Mem. Bank Adminstrn. Inst. (pres. Balt. 1968—), Inst. Internal Auditors. Home: 3219 Hiss Ave Parkville MD 21234-4724 Office: Wachovia Bank Baltimore St Baltimore MD 21202-1603

LIBERTY, ARTHUR ANDREW, judge; b. Oak Park, Ill., Nov. 7, 1954; s. Arthur and Patricia (Horton) L.; m. Jean Liberty, Nov. 22, 1980; children: Rebecca, Rachael. BS, Excelsior Coll., Albany, 1983; JD with honors, Ill. Inst. Tech., Chgo., 1987. Bar: Ill. 1987, U.S. Dist. Ct. (no. dist.) Calif. 1988, U.S. Dist. Ct. (no. dist.) Ill., 1992, U.S. Dist. Ct. (cen. dist.) Ill., 1995, U.S. Ct. Appeals (7th cir.) 1992, U.S. Ct. Appeals (9th cir.) 1989. Asst. dist. counsel U.S. Immigration and Naturalization Service, San Francisco, Chgo., 1987-88, 91-92; sector counsel U.S. Border Patrol, Livermore, Calif., 1988-91; ptnr. Azulay & Azulay, Chgo., 1992-95; pvt. practice Chgo. and Joliet, Ill., 1995-97; U.S. adminstrv. law judge Office of Hearings and Appeals, Detroit, 1997-98, chief U.S. adminstrv. law judge Evansville, Ind., 1998—2002, Dept. of Housing and Urban Devel., Washington, 2002—. Spl. asst. U.S. atty. ea dist. Calif., Fresno, 1988—91; instr. law and legal proc. Fed. Law Enforcement Tng. Ctr., Artesia, N.Mex., 1989—91; Assn. Pres. Hearing Office Chief Judges, 2001—02; law and jud. proc. Office Hearings and Appeals Nat. Tng. Cadre, Falls Church, Va., 2001—02; instr. fair housing litig. skills tng. program John Marshall Law Sch., Chgo., 2002—; instr. law and legal procedure Dept. Housing Urban Devel., 2002—. Contbr. articles to profl. books. Lt. col., pilot, comdr. Evansville sr. squadron Civil Air Patrol, 1999—2002, dep. comdr. Group I Md. Wing, 2002—06. Mem. Fed. Bar Assn. (jud. divsn. chair-elect 2005-06, chair 2006-07). Avocations: flying, music, cooking. Office: HUD OALJ 1707 H St NW 11th Fl Washington DC 20006 Office Phone: 202-254-0000. Business E-Mail: arthur.a.liberty@hud.gov.

LIBESKIND, DANIEL, architect; b. Poland, 1946; naturalized, U.S., 1965; married; 3 children. Student of music, Israel; degree in architecture, Cooper Union, 1970; postgrad., Sch. of Comparative Studies, Essex, Eng., 1972; doctorate (hon.), Humboldt U., Berlin, 1997, Essex U., England, 1999, U. Edinburgh, 2002, DePaul U., 2002, U. Toronto, 2004. Cert. arch., Germany. Head dept. architecture Cranbrook Acad., 1978—85; head Inst. Architecture and Planning, Milan, 1986—89; architect Berlin, 1990—2003, New York, 2003—. Sr. scholar John Paul Getty Ctr.; scholar Royal Danish Acad.; Louis Sullivan prof., Chgo.; Bannister Fletcher prof. U. London; Louis Kahn prof. Yale U., New Haven; Frank O'Gehry Chair U. Toronto; Cret chair U. Pa.; prof. Hochschule fur Gestaltung, Karlsruhe, Germany; guest prof. Harvard U., Cambridge, Mass., UCLA, Hochschule Weisensee, Germany; writer in field; first cultural amb. for architecture CultureConnect program U.S. Dept. State. Prin. works include Jewish Mus. Berlin, 1989—99 (German Architecture prize, 1999), Felix Nussbaum Mus., Osnabrueck, 1995—99, Danish Jewish Mus., 1996—2004, Victoria and Albert Mus. Ext., London, 1996—, Imperial War Mus. North, Manchester, Eng., 1997—2002 (award Royal Inst. Brit. Architects, 2004), Jewish Mus. San Francisco, 1998—, Denver Art Mus. Ext., 2000—06, Westside Shopping and Leisure Centre, Brunnen, Switzerland, 2001—, Bar-Ilan U. Wohl Conv. Centre, Tel Aviv, 2000—05, German Mil. Mus., Dresden, 2002—, Dali Mus., Prague, 2004, London Met. U. Grad. Student Centre, 2002—04 (award Royal Inst. Brit. Architects, 2004), World Trade Ctr. site, 2003—, responsible for sets, costumes lights, also dir., St. Francis of Assisi Opera, Berlin Opera, 2003, sets and costumes, Tristan, Opera Saarbrueken, 2001; author: Daniel Libeskind: The Space of Encounter, 2001, Breaking Ground: Adventures in Life and Architecture, 2004. Recipient Golden Lion, Venice Biennale, 1985, award for architecture, Am. Acad. Arts and Letters, 1996, Citizen of Berlin Culture prize, 1996, Goethe Medallion for Cultural Contbn., 2000, Hiroshima Art prize, 2001; scholar, Am. Israel Cultural Found. Mem.: European Acad. Arts and Letters, Acad. of the Arts, Fedn. German Architects. Office: Studio Daniel Libeskind 2 Rector St 19th Fl New York NY 10006

LIBIN, LAURENCE ELLIOT, retired curator; b. Chgo., Sept. 19, 1944; s. Aaron L. and Vera Maye (Sugerman) Zimmerman; m. Genevieve Vaughn, July 26, 1970 (div. 1983); m. Kathryn Shanks, Dec. 31, 1988. Mus. B., Northwestern U., 1966; Mus.M., Kings Coll., U. London, 1968; postgrad., U. Chgo., 1966-67, 68-71. Asst. prof. Ramapo Coll., Mahwah, NJ, 1972-73; curator dept. mus. instruments Met. Mus. Art, NYC, 1973—2006, endowed chair, 1989—, rsch. curator, 1999—2006; emeritus hon. curator Steinway & Sons, 2006—. Freelance profl. harpsichordist, 1964-. Author: American Musical Instruments, 1985; contbr. articles to profl. lit. Travel and rsch. grantee Nat. Mus. Act, 1979-80, Catherine Lorillard Wolfe Fund, Theodore Rousseau Meml. Fund, 1981; rsch. grantee Nat. Endowment for Arts and NEH, 1976-80, 89. Fellow Royal Soc. Arts; mem. Am. Recorder Soc. (editl. bd. 1979-89), Am. Mus. Instrument Soc. (bd. dirs. 1977-87, v.p. 1987-91), Am. Musicological Soc., Am. Organ Archives (gov. 1993—), Internat. Com. Mus. and Collections of Musical Instruments, Organ Hist. Soc. (v.p.), Galpin Soc. (Anthony Baines Meml. prize 2006). Home: 126 Darlington Ave Ramsey NJ 07446-1443 Home Phone: 201-327-8426.

LIBIN, PAUL, theater producer and director; b. Chgo., Dec. 12, 1930; m. Florence Rowe, Sept. 25, 1956; children: Charles, Claire, Andrea. Student, U. Ill.; B.F.A., Columbia U., 1956. Producing dir., v.p. Jujamcyn Theaters, NYC, 1990—. Producer (plays) including The Crucible, 1958, Six Characters in Search of an Author, 1963, Royal Hunt of the Sun, 1965, Circle in the Sq. Theatre, N.Y.C., 1965-90; co-producer (plays) Uncle Vanya, 1973, The Iceman Cometh, 1973, Death of a Salesman, 1975, The Lady from the Sea, 1976, The Night of the Iguana, 1976, The Club, 1976, Tartuffe, 1977, The Inspector General, Man and Superman, Spokesong, Loose Ends, 1978, Major Barbara, Past Tense, The Man Who Came to Dinner, 1979, The Bacchae, John Gabriel Borkman, The Father, Scenes and Revelations, 1980, Candida, MacBeth, Eminent Domain, 1981, Present Laughter, The Queen and the Rebels, The Misanthrope, 1982, The Caine Mutiny Court-Martial, Heartbreak House, Awake and Sing, 1983, Design for Living, 1984, Arms and the Man, Marriage of Figaro, 1985, You Never Can Tell, 1986, Coastal Disturbances, 1987, A Streetcar Named Desire, Juno and the Paycock, 1988, The Night of the Iguana, 1988, The Devil's Disciple, 1988, Ghetto, 1989, Sweeney Todd, 1989, Zoya's Apartment, 1990, The Miser, 1990; producing dir. plays I Hate Hamlet, 1991, Secret Garden, 1991, La Bete, 1991, Two Trains Running, 1992, Jelly's Last Jam, 1992, Tommy, 1993, Angels in America, 1993, My Fair Lady, 1993, Grease, 1994, Love! Valour! Compassion!, 1995, Smokey Joe's Cafe, 1995, My Thing of Love, 1995, Moon Over Buffalo, 1995, Patti LuPone on Broadway, 1995, Seven Guitars, 1996, A Funny Thing Happened on the Way to the Forum, 1996, Present Laughter, 1996, David Copperfield, Dreams and Nightmares, 1996, Annie, 1997, Young Man from Atlanta, 1997, The Sound of Music, 1998, Forever Tango, 1998, The Beauty Queen of Leenane, 1998, Death of a Salesman, 1999, The Civil War, 1999, The Weir, 1999, Swing, 1999, A Moon for The Misbegotten, 2000, Proof, 2000, King Hedley II, 2001, The Crucible, 2002, Sixteen Wounded, 2004, Caroline, or Change, 2004, Gem of the Ocean, 2004. With US Army, 1953—55. Recipient Obie award The Club, Village Voice, 1977, Tony award, 1976, 92, 93, 94, 95, medal Eugene O'Neill Soc., 2003, TAO House award Eugene O'Neill Found., 2004. Mem. 2d League Off Broadway Theatres and Producers (pres. emeritus), 1st League Am. Theatres and Producers (officer, exec. com., bd. govs.), Circle in the Square Theatre (owner, operator), Broadway Cares Equity Fights AIDS (pres.). Office: Jujamcyn Theaters St James Theatre 246 W 44th St New York NY 10036-3971

LIBOFF, RICHARD LAWRENCE, physicist, researcher; b. NYC, Dec. 30, 1931; s. William and Sarah (Mell) L.; m. Myra Blatt, July 4, 1954; children: David, Lisa. AB, Bklyn. Coll., 1953; PhD, NYU, 1961. Asst. prof. physics NYU, 1961-63; prof. applied physics, applied math. and elec. engring. Cornell U., 1964—2005; prin. investigator Air Force Office Sci. Research, 1978-83, Army Research Office, 1984—; disting. prof. physics U. Ctrl. Fla., Orlando, 2005—. Cons. Batelle Columbus Lab. Author: Introduction to the Theory of Kinetic Equations, 1969, 1979, Russian edit., 1974, Introductory Quantum Mechanics, 1980, Korean edit., 1992, 4th edit., 2003, Waveguides, Transmission Lines and Smith Charts, 1984, Kinetic Theory: Classical, Quantum and Relativistic Descriptions, 1990, 3d edit., 2003, Primer for Point and Space Groups, 2003. Served with Chem. Corps U.S. Army, 1953-55. Recipient Founders Day cert. N.Y. U., 1961; Solvay fellow, 1972; Fulbright scholar, 1984 Fellow Am. Phys. Soc.; mem. Sigma Xi. Office: U Ctrl Fla Physics-Math Bldg Orlando FL 32816-2385 Home Phone: 407-695-4172. Business E-Mail: rll@physics.ucf.edu.

LIBONATI, MICHAEL ERNEST, law educator, writer; b. Chgo., May 25, 1944; s. Roland V. and Jeannette K. Libonati; m. Yvonne M. Barber, Sept. 30, 1967; children: Michael, Emma. LLB, Yale U., 1967, LLM, 1969. Bar: D.C. 1968, Ill. 1975, Pa. 1976. Prof. law Temple U., Phila., 1972-90, Carnell prof., 1990—; cons. U.S. Adv. Commn. Intergovernmental Rels. Vis. prof. law U. Ala., Tuscaloosa, 1976, Cornell U., Ithaca, NY, 1977, Coll. William and Mary, Williamsburg, Va., 1987. Author (with Sands and Martinez): Local Government Law, 4 vols., 1981—82; author: (with Hetzel and Williams) Legis. Law and Statutory Interpretation, 3d edit., 2001; author: Local Govt. Autonomy, 1993, Local Govt. Autonomy, Japanese edit., 1997, Local Govt. Autonomy, Spanish edit., 2000; author: (with Martinez) State and Local Govt. Law, 2000; asst. editor articles: Am. Jour. Legal History, 1971—82. Named Hon. Editor, Temple U. Law Quar., vol. 59, 1986; recipient Williams prize for Excellence in Tchg., 1985, 1990. Mem.: NAS (nat. rsch. bd., hwy. law project adv. commn.), Am. Law Inst. Office: Temple U Sch Law 1719 N Broad St Philadelphia PA 19122-6002 Home Phone: 215-247-5069; Office Phone: 215-204-7872. Business E-Mail: michael.libonati@temple.edu.

LIBONATI-RITZ, GENENE MARIE, lawyer; b. Hazleton, Pa., May 1, 1969; d. Francis Paul and Jacquelyn Ann Libonati; m. Robert Joseph Ritz Jr., June 22, 1996; children: Isabelle Rose Ritz, Franklin Joseph Ritz. BA in English with honors, King's Coll., Wilkes-Barre, Pa., 1991; MA in English with honors, U. Scranton, Pa., 1995; JD with honors, Dickinson Sch. Law, Carlisle, Pa., 1997. Bar: Pa. 1997; cert. secondary edn. tchr. Pa., 1991. Assoc. Law Office of Michael Beltram, Hazleton, 1997—99; law clk. Schuylkill County Common Pleas, Pottsville, Pa., 1998—2000, Superior Ct. Pa., Hazleton, 2005—; prof. Wilkes U., Hazleton and Wilkes-Barre, 1999—2003; English tchr. Hazleton Area HS, 2000—06; prof. English Pa. State U., Hazleton, 2001—02. Mem.: Dickinson Sch. Law Wolsack Soc. (Outstanding Achievement award), Delta Epsilon Sigma. Democrat. Roman Catholic. Avocations: running, knitting, reading, writing. Home: 5 Captain Cir Conyngham PA 18219 Office: Office of Correale F Stevens Superior Ct Pa 300 Laurel Professional Ctr Hazleton PA 18202

LIBOWSKY, STEPHEN DAVID, lawyer; b. Atlanta, Dec. 3, 1957; m. Sue Ellen Berman, Nov. 5, 1983; children: Samuel Louis, Sarah Ellerie, Ruth Lily. BA, Vanderbilt U., 1979; JD, U. Ga., 1982. Bar: Ga. 1982, Ill. 1984. Law clk. to Hon. G. Ernest Tidwell, Atlanta, 1982—84; assoc. Reuben & Proctor, Chgo., 1984—86, Katten Muchin Rosenman, Chgo., 1986—89, ptnr., 1989—2002, Howrey LLP, Chgo., 2002—. V.p., bd. dirs. Pub. Interest Law Initiative, Chgo., 1995; active Am. Youth Soccer Orgn., Highland Park, Ill., 2002. Home: 3023 Greenwood Ave Highland Park IL 60035-1429 Office: Howrey LLP 321 N Clark St Ste 3400 Chicago IL 60610 Home Phone: 847-432-3481; Office Phone: 312-595-2252. Office Fax: 312-264-0372; Home Fax: 847-432-3981. Personal E-mail: libers4@aol.com. Business E-Mail: libowskys@howrey.com.

LIBRETTO, JOHN CHARLES, television director; b. NYC, Oct. 16, 1947; s. Charles and Esther (Boccuzzi) LiB.; m. Kristin Stromquist, Sept. 1, 1983; children: Katharine, Charles. BA in History, C. W. Post Coll., 1968. Mgr. NBC TV Network, NYC, 1968-75, assoc. dir., 1975-85; dir. NBC Sports, NYC, 1985-87, NBC News, NYC, 1987-98, 2000—, ABC-TV, NYC, 1998-2000; sr. dir. NBC News, 2000—. Lectr. NATAS, N.Y.C., 1989. Dir.; (TV shows) World Championship Track and Field, 1983 (Monitor award 1984), Wimbledon Preview, 1983-86, Baseball Pre-Game, 1983-86, NFL Football, 1983-88, Donahue, 1985, Internat. Amateur Athletics Fedn. Track and Field, 1986, NBC Nightly News, 1987-88, XXIV Olympics, 1988, Decisions '88, '92, '96, '00 and '04, Today Show and Weekend Today, 1989-98, Rights and Lives, 1989, A Closer Look, 1991, Presidential Debates, 1992,2004, Pope John Paul II in Central Park, 1995, The Faith Daniels Show, Ricki Lake Show, Tempestt, In Person With Maureen O'Boyle, Good Morning America, 1998-99, Dateline NBC, 2000—, Presdl. Innauguration, 2005, convs. and elections, 2000, 2004, Upfront Presentations, 2001— Sgt. USAF, 1969-71, Vietnam. Recipient Emmy award, 1984, 88, Emmy award nomination, 1979-80, 88, 96. Mem. NATAS, Dirs. Guild Am. Episcopalian. Avocations: music, travel, sports. Office: NBC 30 Rockefeller Plz New York NY 10112-0036 Office Phone: 212-664-7897. Business E-Mail: john.libretto@nbcuni.com.

LIBUTTI, PATRICIA O'BRIEN, university librarian; BA, Seton Hill Coll., Pa., 1966; MEd, Temple U. Tyler Art Sch., 1980; PhD, Temple U., 1978; MLS, Rutgers U., 1988. Edn. subject specialist Fordham U. Librs., NY; social studies/edn. libr. emerita Rutgers U. Librs., NJ. Editor: Librarians as Learners, Librarians as Teachers: The Diffusion of Internet Expertise in Academic Libraries, 1999, Digital Resources & Librarians: Case Studies in Innovation, Invention & Implementation, 2004; co-editor: Teaching Information Retrieval & Evaluation Skills to Education Students & Practitioners: A Casebook of Applications, 1995. Mem.: ALA (Edn. & Behavioral Sciences sect. 1991—), Assn. Coll. & Rsch. Librs. (pub. bd., Disting. Edn. & Behavioral Sciences Libr. award 2007), Spl. Librs. Assn. (Edn. Divsn. 1999—, webmaster 2002, guest editor Edn. Librs. 2003, divsn. chair 2004—05, Anne Galler award for Profl. Excellence 2007). Office: Archibald S Alexander Libr Rutgers The State U of NJ 169 College Ave CAC New Brunswick NJ 08901-1163

LICATA, ARTHUR FRANK, lawyer; b. NYC, June 16, 1947; BA in English, Le Moyne Coll., 1969; postgrad., SUNY, Binghamton, 1969—71; JD cum laude, Suffolk U., 1976. Bar: Mass. 1977, NY 1985, U.S. Ct. Appeals (1st cir.) 1977, U.S. Dist. Ct. Mass. 1977, admitted Frank B. Murray, Jr. Inns of Ct. 1990-92. Assoc. Parker, Coulter, Daley & White, Boston, 1977-82; prin. Arthur F. Licata P.C., Boston, 1982—. Prin. Ardlee Internat. Trading Co., Ea. and Ctrl. Europe and Russia, 1989-99; del. White House Conf. on Trade and Investment in Ctrl. Europe, Cleve., 1995; lectr. Mass. Continuing Legal Edn., Boston, 1982-2001, mem. trial adv. com., 1984-88; mem. working group on drinking and drunk driving Harvard Sch. Pub. Health Ctr. for Health Comms., 1986; spkr. Conv. Nat. Fedn. Paralegal Assns., Boston, 1987; del. U.S.-China Joint Session on Trade, Investment and Econ. Law, Beijing, 1987; co-sponsor Estonian legal del. visit to Mass. and NH correctional instns., 1990; Boston host former Soviet legal del. visit, 1989; legal advisor Czech Anglo-Am. Bus. Inst., Prague, Czech Republic, 1989—, Russian Children's Fund, 1992-94, Estonia Acad. for Pub. Safety, 1992-94; adv. bd. Ford Found.'s Legal Resource Ctr., Czech Republic, 1994-96; participant U.S.-Russian Investment Symposium, Harvard U.; spkr. Conf. on Proposed Tobacco Settlement and Tort Law, Harvard Law Sch., 1997; guest WGBH-Ch 2, TV, Greater Boston With Emily Rooney, 1999, 2001; chair seminar Mass. CLE, Boston, 2000. Panel mem. sta. WBZ TV, Boston; contbr. articles to profl. jours. U.S. Del. 6th People to People Juvenile Justice Program to USSR, Moscow, 1989; legal advisor Mass. chpt. MADD, Plymouth County, 1984-87; mem. State Adv. Com. Med. Malpractice, Boston, 1985; bd. dirs. Boston Ctr. for the Arts, 1990-94; mem. profl. adv. bd. Mass. Epilepsy Assn., 1986-93; counsel state coord. commn. MADD, Mass., 1984-86; participant Harvard Law Sch. Seminar Program on Negotiation and Mediation, 2000-01; mem. Congress Fellow, Ctr. Internat. Legal Studies, Salzburg, 2004. Recipient Outstanding Citizen award MADD, 1986, Sacred Angelic Imperial Constanian Order of Saint George awarded by the Duke of Parma, Italy, 2000; named Super Lawyer, Boston Mag., 2006, Super Lawyer Mass., Super Lawyer website, 2006. Fellow Mass. Bar Found. (life); mem. ATLA, Mass. Acad. Trial Attys. (bd. dirs. 1991-99, exec. com. 1997-99), Nat. Bd. Trial Advocacy (bd. cert. civil trial adv. 1992-). Avocation: travel. Office: Fed Res Plz 600 Atlantic Ave 25th Fl Boston MA 02210-2211 Office Phone: 617-523-9977. Fax: 617-523-7743. Personal E-mail: arthur@alicata.com, licata@att.net.

LICHLITER, WARREN EUGENE, surgeon, educator; b. Murphysboro, Ill., Jan. 24, 1952; s. Gene Estel and Dorothy Colleen (Williams) L.; m. Carol Jane Loftin, Nov. 3, 1979; children: Gary Edward, Christopher Warren, Adrienne Leigh, Abigail Meredith. BA, U. Tenn., 1974; MD, U. Tex., Galveston, 1978. Intern and resident in gen. surgery Baylor U. Med. Ctr., Dallas, 1979-83, resident in colon rectal surgery, 1983-84, mem. attending staff dept. colon rectal surgery, 1984—, assoc. dir. surg. edn., 1984—, program dir. dept. colon rectal residency, 2000—, chief dept. colon rectal surgery, 2000—; clin. asst. prof. surgery health sci. ctr. U. Tex., Dallas, 1990—. Fellow: ACS (pres. North Tex. chpt. 2007), Am. Soc. Colon Rectal Surgeons; mem.: Dallas County Med. Soc. (sec.-treas. 2001—02, pres. 2004), Dallas Soc. Surgeons, Tex. Surg. Soc., Alpha Omega Alpha. Avocations: running, bicycling, sailing, kayaking, swimming. Office: 3409 Worth St Ste 500 Dallas TX 75246-2057

LICHSTEIN, EDGAR, cardiologist; b. NYC, Nov. 27, 1936; s. Joseph and Ruth (Weisner) L.; m. Marilyn Dorf, June 19, 1966; children: Adam Robert, Amy Ruth. AB, Columbia Coll., 1957; MD, SUNY, Bklyn., 1961. Diplomate Am. Bd. Internal Medicine, Am. Bd. Cardiovascular Disease. Intern Lenox Hill Hosp., NYC, 1961-62, resident in medicine, 1962-63, NYU, NYC, 1963-64; fellow in cardiology NYU-Nat. Heart Inst., 1964-66; chief cardiology Mt. Sinai Med. Services Elmhurst, NYC, 1971-77; dir. cardiology Maimonides Med. Ctr., Bklyn., 1977-89, chmn. dept. medicine, 1989—; prof. medicine SUNY Downstate, 1980—2004, Mt. Sinai Sch. Medicine, 2004—. Bd. dirs. Maimonides Rsch. and Devel. Found., Bklyn., N.Y. Heart Assn. Author: Hemodynamict's Reference File, 1971; contbr. articles to profl. jours. Mem. New Rochelle (N.Y.) Sch. Bd., 1977-81; bd. dirs. New Rochelle Youth Soccer League, 1976. Served to capt. USAF, 1966-68. Fellow ACP, Am. Coll. Cardiology, Am. Coll. Chest Physicians, Coun. Clin. Cardiology; mem. N.Y. Heart Assn. (chmn. coun. cmty. programs, bd. dirs. 1983—). Jewish. Avocation: swimming. Office: Maimonides Med Ctr 4802 10th Ave Brooklyn NY 11219-2844 Office Phone: 718-283-7074.

LICHT, RICHARD A., lawyer; b. Providence, Mar. 25, 1948; s. Julius M. Licht and Irene (Lash) Olson; m. Roanne Sragow; children: Jordan David, Jeremy Michael, Jaclyn Rose, Jacob Adam. AB cum laude, Harvard U., 1968, JD cum laude, 1972; LLM in Taxation, Boston U., 1975. Law clk. to chief justice R.I. Supreme Ct., Providence, 1973-74; ptnr. Letts, Quinn & Licht, Providence, 1974-84; mem. R.I. Senate, Providence, 1975-84, chmn. judiciary com. and rules com., 1984; lt. gov. State of R.I., Providence, 1985-89; mng. ptnr. Tillinghast, Licht, Perkins, Smith & Cohen LLP, Providence, 1989—. Former chmn. R.I. Commn. on Racial, Religious and Ethnic Harrassment, Dr. Martin Luther King Jr. Holiday Commn., State Energy and Tech. Study Commn. rules com.; chmn. Coun. of State Govt., Intergovtl. Affairs Com., Nat. Focus Team, Bd. Gov. Higher Edn.; bd. regents Elem. and Secondary Edn.; mem. Pub. Telecom. Authority R.I., Univ. R.I. Found., Community Coll. R.I. Found. Bd. dirs., mem. corp. Roger Williams Hosp.; advisor Community Prep. Sch.; corporator Roger Williams Hosp.; trustee Save the Bay, Inc., Emma Pendleton Bradley Hosp.; bd. dirs. Temple Emanuel, Providence, Jewish Fedn. R.I., Samaritans; chmn. Small Bus. Adv. Council, Task Force on Teenage Suicide Prevention, CD Civil Preparedness Adv. Council, Urban League R.I., 1980-82, John Hope Settlement House, 1976-81; chair Am. Cancer Soc. Ball, 1989, Jewish Fedn. R.I. Passage to Freedom, 1989; chair R.I. chpt. Anti-Defamation League; mem. Women and Infants Corp., Dorcas Place, PARI, UNITAM, NCLG task force of Youth Suicide Prevention, Jewish Home for the Aged of R.I., bd. govs. for the handicapped; active YWCA of Greater R.I., Vols. in Action, Inc., Big Sister Assn. of R.I., Big Bros. R.I.; coordinator vols. gubernatorial campaigns Frank Licht, 1968, 70; active Jewish Community Ctr., Providence, 1975-83, East Side Sr. Citizens Ctr., 1975-76, R.I. Youth Guidance Ctr., Inc., 1987, Block Island Conservancy, Inc., Notre Dame Health Care Corp., 1987; Dem. candidate for U.S. Senate, 1988; chmn. ann. campaign Meeting Street Sch., 1990-91, mem. steering com. for capital fund drive, 1989-92; mem. corp. Womens and Infants Hosp.; Dem. candidate U.S. Senate, 2000. Named an Outstanding Young Man of R.I., R.I. Jaycees, 1979; recipient David Ben Gurion award State of Israel Bonds, 1977, Outstanding Pub. Service award Temple Torat Yisrael, 1985, Disting. Services to the Hispanic Community award Casa Puerto Rico, 1985, Hon. Pub. Service award Meeting St. Sch., 1986, Recognition award R.I. Day Care Dirs. Assn., 1986, award of Appreciation Child Care/Human Services, 1986, Govtl. Services award Ocean State Residences for the Retarded, 1987. Mem. R.I. Bar Assn., Hosp. Assn. R.I. (bd. dirs. 1997). Democrat. Office: Tillinghast Licht LLP 10 Weybosset St Providence RI 02903-2818 Fax: 401-456-1210. E-mail: rlicht@tllaw.com.

LICHTBLAU, ERIC, journalist; b. Syracuse, NY; BA in english & polit. sci., Cornell U., 1987. With LA Times, 1987—99, Justice Dept. staff writer Washington, 1999—2002; Justice Dept. corr. NY Times, Washington, 2002—. Recipient Pulitzer Prize for nat. reporting, 2006. Office: NY Times Washington Bur 7th Fl 1627 I St Washington DC 20006 Office Phone: 202-862-0396. Office Fax: 202-862-0340. E-mail: ericl@nytimes.com.

LICHTBLAU, JOHN H., retired economist; b. Vienna, June 26, 1921; came to U.S., 1939; s. Ernst and Alice (Fischer) Lichtblau-Lind; m. Charlotte M. Adelberg, Apr. 12, 1944; 1 child, Claudia L. Payne. B in Social Sci., CCNY, 1949; postgrad., NYU, 1950-53. Economist US Dept. Labor, Washington, 1951-53, Conf. Bd., NYC, 1953-54, Walter J. Levy Assocs., NYC, 1955-56; research dir. Petroleum Ind. Research Found. Inc., NYC, 1956-61, exec. dir., 1961-72, chmn., 1972—2006, PIRA Energy Group, NYC, 1977—2006; ret., 2006. Bd. mem. The Energy Forum NYU. Contbr. articles to profl. jours., book chpts. Served with U.S. Army, 1944-47, ETO. Mem. Am. Petroleum Inst., Nat. Petroleum Coun., 1968-2002, Am. Econ. Assn., Internat. Assn. for Energy Economics (5th Ann. award for outstanding contbns. 1986), Coun. on Fgn. Rels.

LICHTE, ARTHUR J., career military officer; b. Bronx, NY, Apr. 20, 1949; BS in Bus. Adminstrn., Manhattan Coll., 1971; M in Systems Mgmt., U. Southern Calif., 1978; student, Nat. War Coll., 1989, JFK Sch. Govt., 1994, Naval Postgraduate Sch., 2002. Commd. 2d lt. USAF, 1971, advanced through grades to lt. gen., 2003; pilot, EC-121 552nd Airborne Early Warning and Control Wing, McClellan AFB, Calif., 1972-75; co-pilot, aircraft comdr., flight comdr. 380th Air Refueling Squadron, Plattsburgh AFB, NY, 1975-81; various positions Hdqrs. Strategic Air Command, Offutt AFB, Nebr., 1981-85; KC-10A flight comdr., ops. officer to comdr. 9th Air Refueling Squadron, March AFB, Calif., 1985-88; dep. chief Office of Strategic Forces divsn. Hdqrs. USAF, The Pentagon, Washington, 1989-90, exec. officer, dep. chief of staff for programs/resources, 1990-91; asst. dep. comdr. for ops. 2nd Bombardment Wing, Barksdale AFB, La., 1991-92; comdr. 458th ops. group 22nd Air Refueling Wing, Barksdale AFB, La., 1992-93; exec. officer to comdr. chief U.S. Transp. Command, comdr. Air Mobility Command, Scott AFB, Ill., 1993-95; comdr. 92nd Air Refueling Wing, Fairchild AFB, Wash., 1995-96, 89th Airlift Wing, Andrews AFB, Md., 1996-99; dir. global rsch. Office Asst. Sec. Air Force for Acquisition USAF, Arlington, Va., 1999—2000; dir. plans & programs Hdqs. Air Mobility Command Air Mobility Command, Scott AFB, Ill., 2000—02; vice comdr. USAF Europe USAF Europe, Ramstein AFB, Germany, 2002—05; asst. vice chief of staff USAF, Washington, 2005—. Decorated Legion of Merit with oak leaf cluster, Disting. Svc. medal, Def. Superior Svc. medal, Meritorious Svc. medal with three oak leaf clusters, Nat.Order of Merit Office: 1670 Air Force Pentagon Washington DC 20330

LICHTENBAUM, PETER, lawyer, former federal agency administrator; b. 1965; BA, Princeton U., 1986; MPP, JD, Harvard U., 1990. Ptnr. Steptoe & Johnson LLP, Washington, 1999—2003, 2006—; asst. sec. for export adminstrn. US Dept. Commerce, Washington, 2003—06, acting under sec. for industry & security, 2005, acting dep. under sec. for internat. trade adminstrn., 2005—06. Mem. Def. Trade Adv. Group US Dept. State, 2006—.

LICHTENBERG, MAGGIE KLEE, publishing executive; b. NYC, Nov. 19, 1941; d. Lawrence and Shirley Jane (Wickman) Klee; m. James Lester Lichtenberg, Mar. 31, 1963 (div. 1982); m. William Shaw Jones, July 2, 2000; children: Gregory Lawrence, Amanda Zoe. BA, U. Mich., 1963; postgrad., Harvard U., 1963. Cert. profl. coach Internat. Coach Fed. Book rev. editor New Woman mag., 1972-73; assoc. editor children's books Parents Mag. Press, 1974; editor, rights dir. Books for Young People, Frederick Warne & Co., NYC, 1975-78; sr. editor Simon & Schuster, NYC, 1979-80; dir. sales promotion Grosset & Dunlap, NYC, 1980-81; ednl. sales mgr. Bantam Books, NYC, 1982-84; dir. mktg. and sales Grove Press, NYC, 1984-86, dir. of sales, 1986-87; dir. sales Weidenfeld & Nicolson, NYC, 1986-87; mktg. dir. Beacon Press, Boston, 1988-95; bus. and pub. coach, 1995—. Freelance critic, 1961—. Author: The Open Heart Companion: Preparation and Guidance for Open-Heart Surgery Recovery, 2006 (finalist, Book of Yr. awards, ForeWord Mag., 2006); contbr. articles, essays, stories, poetry, revs. to mags. newspapers and anthologies. Bd. dirs. Children's Book Council, 1978. Recipient 2 Avery Hopwood awards in drama and fiction, 1962, 2 in drama and poetry, 1963; coll. fiction contest award Mademoiselle mag., 1963; Woodrow Wilson fellow, 1963. Mem. Women's Nat. Book Assn. (past pres. N.Y. chpt.), Internat. Coach Fedn. (cert.), The Coaching Collective, PMA Independent Book Pubs. Assn. (bd. dirs.), N.Mex. Book Assn., PEN N.Mex., Adult Congenital Heart Assn. Home and Office: 4 Cosmos Ct Santa Fe NM 87508-2285 Office Phone: 505-986-8807. Business E-Mail: maggie@openheartcoach.com, maggie@maggielichtenberg.com.

LICHTENSTEIN, ELISSA CHARLENE, legal association executive; b. Oct. 23, 1954; d. Mark and Rita (Field) L. AB cum laude, Smith Coll., Northampton, Mass., 1976; JD, George Washington U., 1979. Bar: D.C. 1980, U.S. Dist. Ct. (D.C. dist.) 1980, U.S. Ct. Appeals (D.C. cir.) 1980. Law clk. U.S. EPA, Washington, 1978-79; staff dir. ABA, Washington, 1979—, assoc. dir. pub. svcs. divsn., 1981-85, dir., 1985—. Editor, contbr.: Common Boundary/Common Problems: The Environmental Consequences of Energy Production, 1982, Exit Polls and Early Election Projections, 1984, The Global Environment: Challenges, Choices and Will, 1986, (newsletter) Environ. Law; co-editor, contbr. The Environ. Network; co-editor: Determining Competency in Guardianship Proceedings, 1990, Due Process Protections for Juveniles in Civil Commitment Proceedings, 1991, Environmental Regulation in Pacific Rim Nations, 1993, The Role of Law in the 1992 UN Conference on Environment and Development, 1992, Trade and the Environment in Pacific Rim Nations, 1994, Public Participation in Environmental Decisionmaking, 1995, Endangered Species Act Reauthorization: A Biocentric Approach, 1996, Sustainable Development in the Americas: The Emerging Role of the Private Sector, 1996, Environmental Priorities in Southeast Asian Nations, 1997, Law School Public Interest Law Programs, 1995, 99; prodn. contbg. editor American Justice Through Immigrants' Eyes, 2004, A Judge's Guide to Immigration Law in Criminal Proceedings, 2004. Named Outstanding Young Woman of Am., 1982. Mem.: NAFE, ABA, Greater Washington Soc. Assn. Execs., D.C. Bar Assn., Met. Washington Environ. Profls. (pres. 1986—96), Assn. Women in Comms., Am. Soc. Assn. Execs., Environ. Law Inst. (assoc.). Democrat. Jewish. Office: ABA Div Pub Svcs 740 15th St NW 9th Fl Washington DC 20005-1019

LICHTENSTEIN, HARVEY, performing arts association administrator; b. Bklyn., Apr. 9, 1929; s. Samuel and Jennie (Meiner) Lichtenstein; m. Phyllis Holbrook, Nov. 14, 1971; children: Saul, John. BA, Bklyn. Coll., 1951, LHD (hon.), 1986; postgrad., Bennington Coll., Vt., 1953; ArtsD (hon.), L.I. U., 1989; MusD (hon.), Mannes Coll. Music, 1989; LHD (hon.), Pratt Inst., 1993, Juilliard Sch., 1999, Bard Coll., 1999; DFA (hon.), Princeton U., 1999. Subscription and group sales mgr. N.Y.C. Ballet, also N.Y.C. Opera, 1965-67; pres., exec. producer Bklyn. Acad. Music, 1967-99, chmn. local devel. corp. NYC, 1999—2007; Am. dir. Spoleto Festival, Italy, 1971—73; chmn. cultural dist. planning downtown Bklyn. Partnership, 2007—. Decorated officer Legion of Honor France; recipient Disting. Svc. to Arts award, Am. Acad. Arts and Letters, 1999, Nat. Medal of Arts, 1999. Mem.: Century Assn. (N.Y.C.). Office Phone: 718-403-1609.

LICHTENSTEIN, NATALIE G., lawyer; b. NYC, Sept. 17, 1953; d. Abba G. and Cecile (Geffen) L.; m. Willard Ken Tom, June 10, 1979. AB summa cum laude, Radcliffe Coll., 1975; JD, Harvard U., 1978. Bar: DC 1978. Atty., advisor US Dept. Treasury, Washington, 1978-80; prin. counsel World Bank, Washington, 1980-94, chief counsel East Asia and Pacific divsn. Legal Dept., 1994-99, adviser to v.p. legal, 1999-2001, chief counsel instnl. affairs, 2001—04, asst. gen. counsel, 2004—. Adj. prof. Chinese law Georgetown U., Washington, 1982-86. Contbr. articles on Chinese and Vietnamese law to profl. jours.

LICHTENSTEIN, ROBERT, Education executive; Bar: NY, NJ, US Supreme Ct. Assoc. adj. prof. NYU Real Estate Inst.; dir. real estate NYU, U. Nev.; v.p., gen. counsel Kumon North Am., 2007—. Office: Kumon Norht America Inc Glenpointe Ctr E 5th Fl 300 Frank W Burr Blvd Teaneck NJ 07666 Office Phone: 201-928-0444. Office Fax: 201-928-0044.*

LICHTENSTEIN, ROBERT JAY, lawyer; b. Phila., Jan. 23, 1948; s. Irving M. and Marjorie J. (Weiss) L.; m. Sandra Paley, Aug. 14, 1971; children: David P., Kate. BS in Econs., U. Pa., 1969; JD, U. Pitts., 1973; LLM in Taxation, NYU, 1974. Bar: Pa. 1974, U.S. Tax Ct. 1978, U.S. Dist. Ct. (ea. dist.) Pa. 1979, U.S. Ct. Appeals (3rd cir.) 1982, U.S. Ct. Appeals (4th cir.) 1987. Assoc. Morgan, Lewis & Bockius, Phila., 1974-78; ptnr., leader employee benefits & exec. compensation practice group Morgan, Lewis & Bockius LLP, Phila., 1988—; ptnr. Saul, Ewing, Remick & Saul, 1978-88; dir. Maritrans Inc., 1995—2006. Instr. Main Line Paralegal Inst., Wayne, Pa., 1984-87, Paralegal Inst., Phila., 1987-90; adj. prof. law Villanova U. Sch. Law, 1991—, U. Pa. Sch. of Law, 1999—. Trustee Temple Brith Achim, King of Prussia, Pa., 1986-91. Mem.: ABA, Phila. Bar Assn. Democrat. Avocations: skiing, tennis, reading. Office: Morgan Lewis Bockius LLP 1701 Market St Philadelphia PA 19103-2903 Office Phone: 215-963-5726. Office Fax: 215-963-5001.

LICHTENSTEIN, SALLY (ALI) TUCKER, small business owner, writer, English and women's studies educator; d. A. Richard Tucker and Orenadel Pitney; m. John E. Lichtenstein, May 1982; children: Evan, Jesse, Samar, Eli. BA Cultural Studies and Philosophy, Vt. Coll., 1999, MA Rhetoric and Women's Studies, 2001; PhD Interdisciplinary Arts and Sci., Union Inst. and U., 2006. Founder, dir. Empty Bowl Writers, Marlborough, NH, 1998—. Instr. Keene State Coll., NH, 1999—; chmn. Monadnock Arts in Edn., Keene, 2000—03. Contbg. author: Writing Alone and With Others, 2003. Mem.: AAUW, Nat. Coun. Tchrs. English, Nat. Women's Studies Assn. Avocations: hiking, travel, writing, photography. Office: Keene State College 202 Parker Hall 229 Main St MS 1402 Keene NH 03435-1402 Office Phone: 603-358-8888 4176. Business E-Mail: alichten@keene.edu.

LICHTENSTEIN, STEVEN JAY, ophthalmologist; b. Phila., July 29, 1952; s. Albert and Mildred Lichtenstein; m. Pamela Ann Davenport, Aug. 31, 1997; children: Adam Kenton Elder, Ariana Ronit, Andrew (Drew) Gregory. BA, La Salle Coll., Phila., 1976; MS in Anatomy, U. Louisville, 1979, MD, 1983. Bd. cert. Am. Bd. Ophthalmology, 1990. Intern U. Louisville, Sch. Medicine, Dept. Internal Medicine, 1983—83; resident Yale U. Sch. Medicine, Dept. Ophthalmology and Visual Sciences, New Haven, 1984—87; pediatric ophthalmologist pvt. practice, Louisville, 1988—89; chief of pediatric ophthalmology Louisville Children's Eye Specialists, P.S.C., Louisville, 1990—2005; pediatric ophthalmologist Ill. Eye Ctr., Peoria, 2005—; clin. assoc. prof. U. Ill. Coll. Medicine, Depts. Surgery and Pediat., 2005—. Mem., pediatric adv. com. Prevent Blindness Am., Chicago, Ill., 2002—. Contbr. articles to profl. jours. and monographs. Bd. mem. Joint Commn. Allied Health Pers. Ophthalmology Found., 2005—; mem. Louisville Zoo Found., 1988—90; lead ophthalmologist, med. mission Romania NW Med. Teams, Portland, 1994—94; vol. ophthalmologist Louisville Zoo, 1988—2005. Recipient Physician's Recognition award, AMA, 1989, 1992, 1998, 2001, 2004, Physician's Recognition award with commendation, 2007, Golden Apple award, Jefferson County Pub. Schs., 1993, Lifelong Edn. Ophthalmologist award, Am. Acad. Ophthalmology, 1997, 2000, 2004, Honor award, Am. Assn. Pediatric Ophthalmology and Strabismus, 2004; fellow, Harvard Med. Sch., Boston Children's Hosp., 1987—88. Fellow: ACS, Am. Acad. Pediat. (mem. exec. com. sect. ophthalmology 1996—2002, chair sect. ophthalmology 2002—04, mem. surg. adv. panel 2002—06), Am. Acad. Ophthalmology (mem. leadership devel. program 2002—03, mem. councilor coun. 2002—04, mem. ophthalmic tech. assessment com. 2006—); mem.: Peoria Med. Soc. (chair program com. 2005—, program chair, bd. dirs. 2005—, bd. dirs. 2006—), Ill. State Med. Soc. (mem. coun. membership & advocacy 2005—07), Am. Assn. Pediatric Ophthalmology and Strabismus (chair bylaws com. 2004—06). Achievements include research in pediatric population of Levofloxacin ophthalmic antibiotic; pediatric population of Moxifloxacin ophthalmic antibiotic. Office: Illinois Eye Center 8921 North Wood Sage Rd Peoria IL 61615 Office Phone: 309-243-2400. Office Fax: 309-243-5376. Personal E-mail: eyedoc44@aol.com.

LICHTENSTEIN, SUSAN R., lawyer, medical products executive; BA, Univ. Minn.; JD, Northwestern Univ. Ptnr. Schiff Hardin & Waite; dep. corp. counsel City of Chgo.; mgmt. positions through sr. v.p., sec., gen. counsel Ameritech, 1994—2000; sr. v.p., sec., gen. counsel Tellabs Inc., 2000—02; gen. counsel to Ill. Gov. Rod Blagojevich, 2003—04; ptnr. McDermott Will & Emery, 2004—05; corp. v.p., gen. counsel Baxter Internat. Inc., Deerfield, Ill., 2005—. Bd. mem. StarFarm Productions Inc. Bd. mem. Temple Sholom, Chgo., Lyric Opera, Chgo., Olin-Sang-Ruby Union Inst., Facing History & Ourselves; co-founder, past co-chair Women in Bus., Politics & Powers symposium series. Mem.: Sr. Businesswomen's Forum (mem. steering com.), Chgo. Network. Office: Baxter Internat 1 Baxter Pkwy Deerfield IL 60015-4625*

LICHTENSTEIN, WARREN G., investment company executive; BA in Economics, U. Pa. Analyst Para Partners LP; acquisition/arbitrage analyst Ballantrae Partners LP; co-founder Steel Partners I LLC, 1990, chmn., sec., and mng. mem., 1996—; co-founder Steel Partners II Ltd, 1993, CEO, pres., 1999—; CEO SL Industries Inc., 2002—05. Dir. United Indsl. Corp., 2001—, chmn.; dir. Layne Christensen Co., 2004—, BKF Capital Group Inc., 2005—; chmn. bd. WHX Corp., 2005—; dir. WebFinancial Corp., SL Industries Inc., 1993—97, chmn., 2002—. Office: Steel Partners LP 590 Madison Ave New York NY 10022

LICHTER, ALLEN S., oncologist, educator, dean; BS, U. Mich., 1968, MD, 1972. Intern St. Joseph Hosp., Denver; resident U. Calif., San Francisco, 1976; former dir. radiation therapy sect. radiation oncology br. Nat. Cancer Inst.; dir. breast oncology program Comprehensive Cancer Ctr., U. Mich., Ann Arbor, 1984-91, chmn. dept. radiation oncology, 1984-97, interim dean Med. Sch., 1998-99, prof. radiation oncology, 1999—, dean Med. sch., 1999—. Bd. dirs. Accreditation Coun. for Grad. Med. Edn. Assoc. editor Jour. Clin. Oncology; editl. bd. Jour. Nat. Cancer Inst., Internat. Jour. Radiation Oncology; co-editor Clinical Oncology, 1995, 2d edit., 1999. Mem.: Am. Soc. Therapeutic Radiology and Oncology (bd. dirs.), Am. Soc. Clin. Oncology (past pres.). Achievements include research in effective breast cancer treatment. Office: U Mich M4101 Med Science Bldg I-C Wing MSI 0624, 1301 Catherine St Ann Arbor MI 48109

LICHTER, PAUL RICHARD, ophthalmology educator; b. Detroit, Mar. 7, 1939; BA, U. Mich., 1960, MD, 1964, MS, 1968. Diplomate Am. Bd. Ophthalmology. Asst. to assoc. prof. ophthalmology U. Mich., Ann Arbor, 1971-78, prof., chmn. dept. ophthalmology and visual scis., 1978—. Chmn. Am. Bd. Ophthalmology, 1987. Editor-in-chief Ophthalmology jour., 1986-94; assoc. editor Am. Jour. Ophthalmology, 2004—. Served to lt. comdr. USN, 1969-71. Fellow: Am. Acad. Ophthalmology (bd. dirs. 1981—97, pres. 1996, sr. hon. award 1986, Lifetime Achievement award 2001); mem.: Acad. Ophthalmologica Internat. (sec.-gen. 2002—), Assn. Univ. Profs. Ophthalmology (trustee 1986—93, pres. 1991—92), Mich. Ophthalmol. Soc. (pres. 1993—95), Washtenaw County Med. Soc., Mich. State Med. Soc., Pan Am. Assn.Ophthalmology (bd. dirs. 1988—, sec.-treas. English-speaking countries 1991—95, pres. 1999—2001), Am. Ophthalmol. Soc. (pres. 2000—01), AMA, Alpha Omega Alpha. Office: U Mich Med Sch Kellogg Eye Ctr 1000 Wall St Ann Arbor MI 48105-1912 Business E-Mail: Plichter@umich.edu.

LICHTER, STEPHEN MARC, oncologist; b. NYC, Feb. 13, 1949; MD, Univ. Health Scis./Chgo. Med. Sch., 1975. Diplomate Am. Bd. Internal Medicine, Am. Bd. Med. Oncology. Intern Brookdale Hosp. Med. Ctr., NY, 1975—76, resident NY, 1976—78, fellow NY, 1978—80; assoc. chief hematology/oncology Beth Israel Med. Ctr., Bklyn.; asst. clin. prof. mediicine SUNY Health Sci. Ctr., Bklyn. Fellow: ACP; mem.: NY State Soc. Med. Oncologists, Kings County Med. Assn., NY State Med. Assn., Am. Soc. Hematology, Am. Coll. Clin. Oncology. Office: 2558 E 18th St Brooklyn NY 11235 Home Phone: 516-678-2584; Office Phone: 718-616-0801. Business E-Mail: lichter@hemoncare.com.

LICHTERMAN, MARTIN, history professor; b. NYC, July 18, 1918; s. Joseph Aaron and Esther S. (Schacknowitz) L.; m. Charlotte Rottenberg, Oct. 7, 1945; children: Joshua David, Andrew Marc. BS, Harvard U., 1939, A.M., 1947; PhD, Columbia U., 1952. Instr. Rutgers U., Newark, 1948-51; instr., lectr. Princeton U., 1953-55; mem. research staff Princeton U. (Center for Research on World Polit. Instns.), 1951-53; asst. prof. M.I.T., 1955-60; dir. research to gov. Mass., 1959-60; exec. sec., dir. New Eng. Bd. Higher Edn., Winchester, Mass., 1961-66; dean Center Humanities and Social Scis. Union Coll., Schenectady, 1966-71; acting dean faculty Union Coll., 1971-72, dean faculty, 1972-76; prof. history Center Humanities and Social Scis. Union Coll., 1966-76, distinguished prof. history and higher edn., 1976-78; dean Empire State Coll., 1978-82, prof. history, 1982-83, prof. emeritus, 1983—; pres. Alternative Lifelong Learning, Berkeley, Calif., 1989-91. Cons. 20th Century Fund, N.Y.C., 1955-57, Friends World Coll., 1984-86; mem. Mass. Bd. Collegiate Authority, 1961-66; history docent Oakland Mus. of Calif., 1999-2006. Author: To the Yalu and Back, 1963; co-author: Political Community in the North Atlantic Area, 1957; contbr. articles to profl. jours. Vice chmn. bd. Mass. Com. Children and Youth, 1963-66, mem. exec. bd., 1961-66; adv. bd. Civil Liberties Mass., 1963-66; chmn. bd. New Eng. Council Advancement Sch. Adminstrn., 1961-63; vice chmn. Capital Dist. Civil Liberties Union, 1966-67; chmn. Freedom Forum, Inc., 1970-71, Schnectady Renewals, Inc., 1972-76; bd. dirs. Suffolk County chpt. N.Y. Civil Liberties Union, 1981-87; bd. dirs. Della Corte Internat., Inc., 1983-88; history docent Oakland Mus. of Calif., 1999—; co-founder Alternative Lifelong Learning Berkeley. Home: The Stratford at Countrywood 1545 Pleasant Hill Rd Lafayette CA 94549 E-mail: mlichty1@comcast.net.

LICHTIG, LEO KENNETH, health economist; b. Bklyn., Oct. 20, 1953; s. Samuel and Alyne Norma (Strauss) L.; m. Susan Mary Walsh, May 15, 1977; children: Brielle Joy, Danica Jill. BS, MS, Rensselaer Poly. Inst., 1974, PhD, 1976. Asst. prof. SUNY, Albany, 1976—77; project specialist, econometrician N.J. State Dept. Health, Trenton, 1977—82; dir. utilization econs. and rsch. Empire Blue Cross/Blue Shield, Albany, 1982—90; v.p. rsch. and demonstration Health Care Rsch. Found., Albany, 1982—90; v.p. Network, Inc., Randolph, NJ, 1990—94, sr. v.p., chief info. officer Somerset, NJ, Latham, NY, 1994—2002; v.p. life sci. group Aon Consulting, Inc., Somerset, 2002—. Nat. diagnosis related group steering com. health care fin. adminstrn. Yale U., Washington, 1979-81; adj. faculty Russell Sage Grad. Sch. Health Adminstrn., Albany, 1986-94, Union Coll. Grad. Mgmt. Inst., Schenectady, NY, 1991-92; expert reviewer Health Care Financing Adminstrn., Washington, 1987, 89; panelist Rand Corp., 2006-07; mem. tech. expert panel Medicare Org. refinement Rand Corp., 2006-07; cons. in field. Author: Hospital Information Systems for Case Mix Management, 1986; contbg. editor (newsletter) Nat. Report on Computers & Health, 1982-85; contbr. articles to profl. jours. Mem. tech. adv. com. Statewide Planning and Rsch. Coop. Sys., N.Y. State Dept. Health; mem. N.Y. State Universal Data Set Specifications Task Force, 1998-2002, N.Y., State Uniform Billing Com., 2002—, N.Y. State Data Protection Rev. Bd., 2003-. Mem. Assn. for Health Svcs. Rsch., Am. Statis. Assn. (com. on privacy and confidentiality 1981-84, subcom. on quality and productivity measures 1988-90), Acad. for Health Svcs. Rsch. and Health Policy, Healthcare Fin. Mgmt. Assn., Internat. Arthurian Soc. (N.Am. br.). Avocation: arthurian legends. Office: Aon Consulting Inc 270 Davidson Ave Somerset NJ 08873-4140 Office Phone: 732-537-4057. Business E-Mail: lichtl@rpi.edu.

LICHTIN, LEON (JUDAH LEON LICHTIN), retired pharmaceutical educator; b. Phila., Mar. 5, 1924; s. Aaron and Rosa (Rosenberg) L.; m. Beverly I. Cohen, Aug. 6, 1950; children— Benjamin Lloyd, Alan Eli. BS in Pharmacy, Phila. Coll. Pharmacy and Sci., 1944, MS in Pharmacy, 1947; PhD in Pharm. Chemistry, Ohio State U., 1950. Asst. prof. pharmacy U. Cin., 1950-51, assoc. prof., 1951-64, prof., 1964-71, Andrew Jergens prof. pharmacy, 1971-91, Andrew Jergens prof. pharmacy emeritus, 1991—. Cons. in cosmetic sci. Composer string music, vocal music, prodr. (CDs) JuChriLam in Celebration of Jerusalem 3000, Ezekiel, Chapter 37, Verses 1-14 "The Valley of Dry Bones; contbr. articles to pharm. jours. Past pres. No. Hills Synagogue, Cin. Fellow AAAS, Soc. Cosmetic Chemists; mem. Rho Chi. Achievements include patents in field. Home: 801 Cloverview Ave Cincinnati OH 45231-6017 Personal E-mail: leon.lichtin@uc.edu.

LICHTIN, NORMAN NAHUM, chemistry professor; b. Newark, Aug. 10, 1922; s. James Jechiel and Clara (Greenspan) L.; m. Phyllis Selma Wasserman, May 30, 1947; children— Harold Hirsh, Sara Marjorie Boyd, Daniel Albert. BS, Antioch Coll., 1944; MS, Purdue U., 1945; PhD, Harvard U., 1948. Faculty Boston U., 1947-93, prof. chemistry, 1961-93, prof. emeritus, 1993—, univ. prof., 1973-93, chmn. dept. chemistry, 1973-84, dir. divsn. engrng. and applied sci., 1983-87; chief scientist Synlize, Inc., 1987-90, Project Sunrise Inc., 1990-92, Photox Corp., Boston, 1993-97; chief sci. adviser, bd. dirs. NanoTek, Inc., Tucson, 1998—2004. Vis. chemist Brookhaven Nat. Lab., Upton, N.Y., 1957-58, research collaborator, 1958-70; guest scientist Weizmann Inst. Sci., Rehovoth, Israel, 1962-63; vis. prof. Inst. Phys. and Chem. Research, Wako, Japan, 1980, Hebrew U., Jerusalem, 1962-63, 70-71, 75-76, 80; Coochbehar lectr. Indian Assn. Cultivation of Sci., Calcutta, 1980 Assoc. editor Solar Energy, 1976-93; rsch. and publs. on mechanisms of chem. reactions including reaction of atomic nitrogen with organic compounds, influence of high energy radiation on organic compounds and photoredox reactions of dyes; photochem. conversion solar energy, ionization processes and ionic reactions in solutions in liquid sulfur dioxide, photo assisted solid-catalysis; catalytic and photocatalytic decomposition of organic and inorganic pollutants of air and water. Mem. alumni bd. Antioch Coll., 1996—2002. NSF sr. fellow, 1962-63. Fellow AAAS; mem. Am. Chem. Soc., Sigma Xi, Phi Beta Kappa (hon.) Home: 195 Morton St Newton MA 02459-1522 E-mail: norlichtin@aol.com.

LICHTINGER, MOISES, obstetrician, gynecologist; arrived in U.S., 1976; s. Kuba Lichtinger and Teresa Waisman-Lichtinger; m. Rina B. Lichtinger, Nov. 26, 1978; children: Liza, Alexis. BS, Escuela de la Ciudad de Mexico, Mexico City, 1969; MD, Nat. U. Mexico, Mexico City, 1975. Ho. officer ob-gyn. Gynccobstretras S.Q., Mexico City, 1976; intern Jackson Meml. Hosp., Miami, Fla., 1976, resident dept. ob-gyn., 1976—80, fellow dept. ob-gyn. divsn. oncology, 1980—82; instr. dept. ob-gyn. U. Miami, 1980—81, jr. attending in gynecology and gynecologic oncology, 1981—82, asst. prof. dept. ob-gyn., 1982—86, 1982—87, asst. prof. dept. oncology, 1984—87; asst. prof. dept. med. oncology U. Miami Sch. Medicine, 1982—87, clin. asst. prof. dept. med. oncology, 1986—87, clin. asst. prof. dept. ob-gyn., 1986—90, vol. faculty, 1990—93; physician in charge gyn-oncology Mt. Sinai Med. Ctr., Miami Beach, 1986—87, assoc. attending dept. ob-gyn., 1986—88; chmn. peer rev. ob-gyn. Holy Cross Hosp., Ft. Lauderdale, Fla., 1998—2001, chmn. dept. ob-gyn., 2002—. Chmn. ob-gyn. dept. Holy Cross Hosp., Ft. Lauderdale; rschr. in field; presenter in field. Contbr. articles to profl. jours. Named Best Med. Student of Mexico, Pres. Luis Ecteravia, 1976, Best Chief Resident Tchr., U. Miami Sch. Medicine, 1980. Mem.: BCMA, ACOG (2nd best video on gynecol. surgery award 2002), ACS, Philharmonic Soc., Opera Soc. (Father of Yr. award). Avocation: yoga instructor. Office: Holy Cross Med Group 4701 N Federal Hwy Fort Lauderdale FL 33308

LICHTMAN, ADAM DAVID, anesthesiologist, educator; b. NYC, July 16, 1968; s. Arthur and Celia Lichtman; m. Jaquelline Perlman-Lichtman, May 30, 1993. BA, Tulane U., New Orleans, 1990; MD, Med. Coll. Pa., Phila., 1994. Diplomate Am. Bd. Anesthesiology, 2000, cert. perioperative transehopegeal echocardiography Nat. Bd. of Echocardiographers, 2000, ATLS ACS, 2002, ACLS Am. Heart Assn., 1997. Chief resident dept. anesthesiology Columbia Presbyn. Med. Ctr., NYC, 1997; instr. anesthesiology Mt. Sinai Sch. Medicine, NYC, 1998—99, asst. prof. anesthesiology, 1999—2003, Weill Cornell Med. Ctr., NYC, 2003—. Contbr. articles to med. jours. Comdr. USN, 2003. Decorated Navy and Marine Corps Achievement medal. Mem.: Mil. Anesthesia Soc., Naval Res. Assn., Wilderness Med. Soc., Spl. Opperations Med. Soc., NY Soc. Anesthesiologists, Am. Soc. Anesthesiologists, NY State Fraternal Order Police. Office: Weill-Cornell Med Ctr 525 E 68th St New York NY 10021-4870

LICHTMAN, ALLAN JAY, historian, educator, consultant; b. Bklyn., Apr. 4, 1947; s. Emanuel and Gertrude Louise (Cohen) L.; m. Katherine Martin Crane, June 6, 1970 (div.); 1 child, Kara Martin; m. Shelia

Bradford, 1980 (div.); m. Karyn Lynn Strickler, June 8, 1991; 1 child, Samuel Allan. BA magna cum laude, Brandeis U., 1967; PhD, Harvard U., 1973. Dir. forensics Brandeis U., Waltham, Mass., 1968-71, Harvard U., Cambridge, Mass., 1971-72; asst. prof. history The Am. U., Washington, 1973—77, assoc. prof. history, 1977-78, prof. of history, 1978—, assoc. dean faculty and curricular devel. coll. arts & scis., 1985-87, chair dept. history, 1997—. Instr. Brandeis U., 1970; cons. Smithsonian Instn., 1974-79, John Anderson campaign for Pres., 1980, George Washington U., 1983, U.S. Dept. Justice, Washington, 1983—, V.P. Albert Gore, Jr., Washington, 1994-95; advisor Ted Kennedy for Pres. campaign, 1980; cons., commentator NBC spl. project on the history of the Am. Presidency; news cons. CBS; polit. commentator NBC News Nightside, Voice of Am., USIA, Am.'s Talking Cable Network; expert witness Com. for Civil Rights Under Law, 1983—, U.S. Dept. Justice, 1983—, pvt. attys., 1986—, various state, mcpl. and county jurisdictions, 1986—, ACLU, 1987—, So. Poverty Law Ctr., 1990, Legal Def. Fund, 1991, Puerto Rican Legal Def. and Edn. Fund, 1991—, NAACP, 1993-94, Reform Party, 1996, 2000, Reuters News Svc., 1996, 2000; columnist Montgomery Jour., Rockville, Md., 1990-98; columnist Montgomery Gazette, Gaithersburg, Md., 1998—; appeared on various radio and TV programs; spkr. at more than 50 confs. Author: Your Family History: How to Use Oral History, Personal Family Archives, and Public Documents to Discover Your Heritage, 1978, Prejudice and the Old Politics: The Presidential Election of 1928, 1979, The Keys to the White House, 1996; co-author (with Valerie French) Historians and the Living Past: The Theory and Practice of Historical Study, 1978, (with Laura Irwin Langbein) Ecological Inference, 1978; co-editor (with Joan Challinor) Kin and Communities: Families in America, 1979, (with Ken DeCell) The 13 Keys to the Presidency, 1990; series editor: Studies in Modern American History, 2000—; contbr. articles to profl. jours. and popular mags. Tchg. fellow Harvard U., 1969-73; rsch. grantee Am. U., 1978, 82; recipient Outstanding Young Men of Am. award U.S. C. of C. 1979-80, Top Spkr. award Nat. Conv. Internat. Platform Assn., 1983, 84, 87; Sherman Fairchild Distinguished Visiting scholar Calif. Inst. Tech., 1980-81; defeated twenty opponents on TIC TAC DOUGH, 1981. Mem. Am. Historian Assn., Orgn. Am. Historians, Social Sci. History Assn., Fed. City Club, Phi Alpha Phi, Phi Beta Kappa. Democrat. Jewish. Home: 9219 Villa Dr Bethesda MD 20817-3365 Office: The Am Univ Washington DC 20016

LICHTMAN, DAVID MICHAEL, orthopedist, health facility administrator, educator, retired military officer; b. Bklyn., Jan. 14, 1942; s. Harry S. and Frances (Rubin) L.; m. Frances Lubin; children: James Matthew, Elisabeth Jill. Student, Tufts Coll., 1962; MD, SUNY, Bklyn., 1966. Diplomate Am. Bd. Orthop. Surgery. Intern U. Minn. Hosp., 1966-67, Naval Aerospace Med. Inst., Pensacola, Fla., 1967; commd. lt. USN, 1967, advanced through grades to rear adm., 1988, flight surgeon Air Wing 3, 1968-69; mem. staff orthop. svc. Nat. Naval Med. Ctr., Bethesda, Md., 1974-77, chmn. dept. orthop. surgery, head, hand surgery svc., 1984-87, dir. orthop. residency program, 1984-87, asst. chmn. dept. orthop. surgery, 1975-77, chmn. dept. orthop. surgery, head hand surgery svc., dir. orthop. residency program, 1984-87; chmn. dept. orthop. surgery and rehab. Naval Hosp., Oakland, Calif., 1977-83, dir. orthop. residency program/dir. navy hand fellowship, 1977-83, head hand and microsurgery svc., 1977-83, mem. staff orthop. surgery, sr. hand/microsurgery cons., 1988-91, commdg. officer, 1989-91; comdr. San Francisco Med. Command, Oakland, 1988-91; promoted to Rear Adm. (lower half), 1989; Rear Adm. (upper half), 1991; ret. USN, 1994; John Dunn prof. orthop. hand surgery Baylor Coll. Medicine, Houston, 1994-98; chmn. dir. orthop. residency tng. John Peter Smith Hosp., Ft. Worth, 1998—; clin. prof. orthop. Southwestern Coll. Medicine, Dallas, 1998—2005; chmn. Dept. Orthop. Surgery Health Scis. Ctr. U. North Tex., Ft. Worth, 2005—. Cons. orthop. surgery asst. sec. def. for health affairs Dept. Def., Washington, 1988-94; specialty advisor naval surgeon gen. for orthop. surgery and hand surgery Bur. Medicine and Surgery Dept. Navy, Washington, 1983-86; prof. surgery and head divsn. orthop. surgery Uniformed Svcs. U. of Health Scis., Bethesda, 1984-94, ex-officio mem. bd. regents, 1991-94' examiner Am. Bd. Orthopaedic Surgery. Editor: The Wrist and Its Disorders, 1988, 2d edit., 1997, Hand and Wrist Sect. Current Opinion in Orthopaedics; contbr. articles to profl. jours. Mem. ACS (bd. govs. 1987-96), Am. Acad. Orthop. Surgeons, Am. Soc. Surgery of Hand (coun. 1999-2002, pres. 2005—, AMA del. 2001-06), Am. Orthop. Assn. (hon.), Mil. Surgeons U.S. (Philip Hench award 1982), Tex. Med. Assn. (del. Tarrant County 2003), Soc. Naval Flight Surgeons, Soc. Med. Consultants to the Armed Forces (coun. 1994—, pres. 2002-03), Soc. Mil. Orthop. Surgeons (bd. dirs. 1987-90), Orthopaedic RRC of the ACGME, Fedn. Ctrl. and N.Am. Hand Surgery and Therapy Soc. (pres.-elect 2007). Home: 4958 Overton Woods Ct Fort Worth TX 76109-2433 Office: John Peter Smith Hosp Dept Orthopedic Surgery 1500 S Main St Fort Worth TX 76104-4917 Home Phone: 817-763-5089; Office Phone: 817-920-6903.

LICHTMAN, EMILY ANN, radiologist; BA, NYU, NYC, 1965; MD, SUNY Downstate Med. Ctr., Bklyn., 1970. Diplomate Am. Bd. Radiology. Intern Maimonides Med. Ctr., Bklyn., 1970—71; resident SUNY Downstate Med. Ctr., Bklyn., 1971—74; fellow Hosp. Joint Diseases, NYC, 1974—75; radiologist Dept. Vets Affairs Med. Ctr., NYC, 1975—2006. Clin. asst. prof. radiology NYU Sch. Medicine, 1981—. Mem.: Radiol. Soc. N.Am., Am. Coll. Radiology.

LICHTMAN, MARSHALL ALBERT, hematologist, educator, researcher; b. NYC, June 23, 1934; s. Samuel and Vera Lichtman; m. Alice Jo Maisel, June 23, 1957; children: Susan, Joanne, Pamela. AB, Cornell U., 1955; MD, U. Buffalo, 1960. Diplomate Am. Bd. Internal Medicine. Resident in medicine Strong Meml. Hosp., 1960-63; surgeon USPHS, 1963-65; postdoctoral rsch. assoc. Sch. Pub. Health, U. N.C., 1963-65; chief resident, instr. medicine Strong Meml. Hosp., 1965-66; sr. instr. medicine, rsch. trainee in hematology U. Rochester (NY) Sch. Medicine, 1966-67, asst. prof. medicine, 1968-70, spl. postdoctoral rsch. fellow hematology, 1968-70, assoc. prof. medicine and biophysics, 1971-74, prof. medicine and biophysics, 1974—95, prof. medicine, biochemistry and biophysics, 1996—, chief hematology unit dept. medicine, 1975-77, co-chief, 1977-89, sr. assoc. dean for acad. affairs and rsch., 1979-89, dean Sch. Medicine and Dentistry, 1990-95; exec. v.p. rsch. and med. affairs Leukemia & Lymphoma Soc., 1996—2007. Mem. sci. coun. Am. Nat. Red Cross, 1987-95; vis. prof. univs.; lectr. in field. Editor: Abnormalities of Granulocytes and Monocytes, 1975, Hematology for Practitioners, 1978, Hematology and Oncology, 1980; (with W.J. William, E. Beutler, A.J. Erslev) Hematology, 3d edit., 1983; (with E. Beutler, B. Coller, T.J. Kipps, U. Seligsohn), 7th edit., 2006; (with H.J. Meiselman and P.L. LaCelle) White Cell Mechanics: Basic Science and Clinical Aspects, 1984, Hematology: Landmark Papers of the Twentieth Century, 2000; (with E. Beutler, T.J. Kipps, W.J. Williams) Williams Manual of Hematology, 2003; (with J. Shafer, R. Felgar, N. Wang) Atlas of Hematology, 2007; mem. editl. bd. Blood Cells, 1978-84, Stem Cells, 1981-83, 93—, Blood, 1983-87, Internat. Jour. Cell Cloning, 1983-92, Exptl. Hematology, 1990-93, Blood Cells, Molecules and Diseases, 1995—, editor-in-chief, 2000—, Am. Jour. Hematology, 2000-07; contbr. articles to profl. jours. Bd. govs. ARC, 1990-96, chair sci. coun., 1987-95. Recipient contracts U.S. Army Rsch., 1972-78, U.S. Dept. Energy, 1972-80; USPHS grantee, 1971-95. Master ACP; mem. NIH (hematology study sect. 1982-86), AAAS, Am. Fedn. Med. Rsch., Am. Soc. Hematology (pres. 1989), Internat. Soc. Hematology, N.Y. Acad. Scis., Am. Soc. Clin. Investigation, Assn. Am. Physicians, Am. Assn. for Cancer Rsch., Am. Physiol. Soc., Soc. Leuk Biology, Am. Soc. Cell Biology. Home: 64 Woodbury Pl Rochester NY 14618-3445 Office: U Rochester Sch Medicine & Dentistry Box 610 601 Elmwood Ave Rochester NY 14642-0001 Office Phone: 585-275-2205. E-mail: mal@urmc.rochester.edu.

LICHTWARDT, ROBERT WILLIAM, mycologist; b. Rio de Janeiro, Nov. 27, 1924; s. Henry Herman and Ruth Moyer Lichtwardt; m. Elizabeth Thomas, Jan. 27, 1951; children: Ruth Elizabeth, Robert Thomas. AB, Oberlin Coll., 1949; MS, U. Ill., 1951, PhD, 1954. Postdoctoral fellow NSF, Panama, Brazil, 1954-55; postdoctoral rsch. assoc. Iowa State U., Ames, 1955-57; asst. prof. U. Kans., Lawrence, 1957-60, assoc. prof., 1960-65; sr. postdoctoral fellow NSF, Hawaii, Japan, 1963-64; prof. U. Kans., Lawrence, 1965-94, prof. emeritus, 1994—. Author: The Trichomycetes, Fungal Associates of Arthropods, 1986; contbr. 130 articles to profl. jours. Mem. Mycological Soc. Am. (life, pres. 1971-72, editor-in-chief 1965-70, William H. Weston award for tchg. excellence in mycology 1982, Disting. Mycologist award 1991), Brit. Mycological Soc. (hon.), Japan Mycological Soc. (hon.). Office: U Kans Dept Ecology Evol Biology Lawrence KS 66045-7534 Business E-Mail: licht@ku.edu.

LICHTY, WARREN DEWEY, JR., lawyer; b. Colorado Springs, Dec. 17, 1930; s. Warren D. and Margaret (White) L.; m. Margaret Louise Grupy, Dec. 8, 1962. Student, Chadron State Coll., Nebr., 1948—50; BS in Law, U. Nebr., Lincoln, 1952, JD, 1954. Bar: Nebr. 1954, US Dist. Ct. Nebr. 1954, US Ct. Appeals (8th cir.) 1973, US Supreme Ct. 1979. Spl. agt. CIC, 1955—58; county judge Dawes County, Nebr., 1958—61; spl. asst. atty. gen. Nebr. Dept. Justice, Lincoln, 1961—69; mng. asst. atty. gen., chief counsel Nebr. Dept. Roads, Lincoln, 1969—97. Lectr. law Chadron State Coll., 1959-60; mem. com. on eminent domain and land use, transp. rsch. bd. NAS–NRC, 1973-90. With US Army, 1954—58. Decorated United Grand Imperial Coun., Red Cross Constantine, Grand Sovereign, 2001-02. Mem. Nebr. Bar Assn., Lincoln Bar Assn., Am. Assn. State Hwy. and Transp. Ofcls. (subcom. on legal affairs 1969-97), Scottish Rite Rsch. Soc. (pres. 1990-95, bd. dirs.), Am. Legion, Internat. Supreme Coun. (hon., Order DeMolay), Hiram Club (past pres.), Masons (33d degree, grand master Nebr. 1979, vice chmn. conf. Grand Masters N.Am. 1980, bd. dirs. Home Corp. Nebr. 1979-90, pres. George Washington Nat. Meml. Assn. 2002-05), Shriners, Royal Order Scotland, Scottish Rite (Grand Chancellor, supreme coun. so. jurisdiction, U.S. and sovereign grand insp. gen. in Nebr. 1991—, bd. dirs. Found. Nebr. 1981-90, pres. bd. dirs. Found. Nebr. 1990—) Republican. Episcopalian. Home and Office: PO Box 22559 Lincoln NE 68542-2559

LICK, DALE WESLEY, educational leadership educator, mathematician; b. Marlette, Mich., Jan. 7, 1938; s. John R. and Florence M. (Baxter) L.; m. Marilyn Kay Foster, Sept. 15, 1956; children: Lynette (dec.), Kitty (dec.), Diana, Ronald. BS with honors, Mich. State U., East Lansing, 1958, MS in Math, 1959; PhD in Math, U. Calif., Riverside, 1965. Research asst. physics Mich. State U., East Lansing, 1958, teaching asst. math., 1959; instr., chmn. dept. math. Port Huron (Mich.) Jr. Coll., 1959-60; asst. to comptroller Mich. Bell Telephone Co., Detroit, 1961; instr. U. Redlands, 1961-63; teaching asst. math. U. Calif., Riverside, 1964-65; asst. prof. math. U. Tenn., Knoxville, 1965-67; postdoctoral fellow Brookhaven Nat. Lab., Upton, NY, 1967-68; assoc. prof. U. Tenn., 1968-69; assoc. prof., head dept. math. Drexel U., Phila., 1969-72; adj. assoc. prof. dept. pharmacology Med. Sch., Temple U., Phila., 1969-72; v.p. acad. affairs Russell Sage Coll., Troy, NY, 1972-74; prof. math. and computing scis. Old Dominion U., Norfolk, Va., 1974-78; also dean Old Dominion U. (Sch. Scis. and Health Professions); pres., prof. math. and computer sci. Ga. So. Coll., Statesboro, 1978-86; pres., prof. math. U. Maine, Orono, 1986-91, Fla. State U., Tallahassee, 1991-93, Univ. prof. Learning Sys. Inst. and Dept. Edn. Leadership, 1993—. Certs. in tng. and cons., mng. orgnl. change. Author: Fundamentals of Algebra, 1970, (with C. Murphy) Whole-Faculty Study Groups: A Powerful Way to Change Schools and Enhance Learning, 1998, (with C. Mullen) New Directions in Mentoring: Creating a Culture of Synergy, 1999, (with C. Murphy) Whole-Faculty Study Groups: Creating Student-Based Professional Development, 2001, Whole-Faculty Study Groups: Creating Professional Learning Communities That Target Student Learning, 2005, (with C. Murphy) The Whole-Faculty Study Groups Fieldbook: Improving Schools and Enhancing Student Learning, 2006; contbr. articles to profl. jours. Bd. dirs. Statesboro/Coll. Symphony, 1978-86, Statewide Health Coordinating Coun. Va., 1976-78, United Way of the Big Bend, 1992-98; chmn. higher edn. adv. bd. Cmty. of Christ, 1986-2004; mem. planning com. Bulloch Meml. Hosp., 1979-86; v.p., mem. Coastal Empire coun. Boy Scouts Am., 1982-86, Katalidin coun., 1986-91; bd. dirs. Health Care Ctrs. Am., Virginia Beach, Va., 1978, Ea. Va. Health Systems Agy., 1976-78; chmn., bd. dirs. Assembly Against Hunger and Malnutrition, 1977-78, pres., 1977-78; mem., high priest Cmty. of Christ. Named one of 40 Alumni Who Make a Difference, U. Calif. Riverside, 1954—94; recipient Disting. Alumni award, Mich. State U., 2006. Mem. AAUP, AAAS, Am. Math. Soc., Math. Assn. Am., Am. Assn. Univ. Adminstrs., Am. Soc. Allied Health Professions, Am. Assn. State Colls. and Univs. (chmn. com. agr. resources and rural devel. 1981-86), Am. Assn. Higher Edn., Nat. Staff Devel. Coun., Sigma Xi, Phi Kappa Phi, Pi Mu Epsilon (governing coun. 1972-77), Beta Gamma Sigma, Pi Sigma Epsilon. Office: Fla State U Learning Systems Inst C-4600 University Ctr Tallahassee FL 32306-2540 Home Phone: 850-553-4080; Office Phone: 850-553-4080. Business E-Mail: dlick@lsi.fsu.edu.

LICK, WILBERT JAMES, mechanical engineering educator; b. Cleve., June 12, 1933; s. Fred and Hulda (Sunntag) L.; children— James, Sarah. BAE., Rensselaer Poly. Inst., 1955, MAE., 1957, PhD, 1958. Asst. prof. Harvard, 1959-66; sr. research fellow Calif. Inst. Tech., 1966-67; mem. faculty Case Western Res. U., 1967-79, prof. earth scis., 1970-79, chmn. dept., 1973-76; prof. mech. engring. U. Calif.-Santa Barbara, 1979—, chmn. dept., 1982-84. Home: 1236 Camino Meleno Santa Barbara CA 93111-1007 Office: U Calif Dept Mech & Environ Engring Santa Barbara CA 93106 Office Phone: 805-893-4295. Business E-Mail: willy@engineering.ucsb.edu.

LICKE, WALLACE JOHN, lawyer; b. Bemidji, Minn., Jan. 23, 1945; s. George John and Lois (Sanford) L.; m. Martha Miriam Eddy, Dec. 19, 1969; children: Loriann, Paul. BA, U. Minn., 1967, MA, 1970, JD cum laude, 1973. Bar: Minn. 1973, U.S. Dist. Ct. Minn. 1973, U.S. Ct. Appeals (8th cir.) 1981, U.S. Supreme Ct. 1981. Instr. Itasca C.C., Grand Rapids, Minn., 1968—; assoc. Helgesen, Peterson, Engberg & Spector Attys. at Law (now Peterson, Engberg & Peterson), Mpls., 1972-75; sec., gen. counsel Blandin Paper Co. and UPM-Kymmene Inc., subs. UPM-Kymmene Corp., a Finnish Co., Helsinki, 1975—2002; pvt. practice, 2002—. Bd. dirs. Vol. Atty. Program Super Bd., Judy Garland Mus. and Children's Discovery Mus.; chmn. bus. retention and expansion strategies program U. Minn.; mem. panel of arbitrators Am. Arbitration Assn. Mem. bd. editors Minn. Law Rev. Area rep. Minn. awareness project Minn. Internat. Ctr./World Affairs Ctr.; Bd. dirs., pres. hon. bd. dirs. Itasca County Family YMCA, Itasca County Family YMCA, Grand Grand Rapids; bd. dirs., v.p., pres. Itasca County unit Am. Cancer Soc.; bd. dirs., pres. Myles Reif Performing Arts Ctr.; chmn., sec. post com. computer-small bus. explorer post Boy Scouts Am.; adult leader 4-H program Agrl. Extension Svc. U. Minn., St. Paul; mem. Bass Brook Twp. (Minn.) Econ. Devel. Com.; mem. promotion and prospecting com. Itasca Devel. Corp.; trustee Grand Rapids area community found; chmn. coop. solutions adv. bd. Grand Rapids, Minn.; trustee Libr. Found., Grand Rapids, Minn., bd. dirs.; trustee Cmty. Libr. Found.; class rep. U. Minn. Law Sch.; bd. dirs. Judy Garland Mus. and Children's Discovery Mus., Grand Rapids, Minn. Recipient William Spurgeon III award Boy Scouts Am., 1988; NDEA Title IV fellow, 1967, Paul Harris fellow. Mem. ABA (com. mem.), Fed. Bar Assn., Minn. Bar Assn. (del., planning com.), Itasca County Bar Assn. (past sec., pres.), Minn. 15th Dist. Bar Assn. (com. mem.), Am. Corp. Counsel Assn. (charter), Am. Soc. Corp. Secs., Grand Rapids C. of C. (chmn. com., bd. dirs.), Rotary (bd. dirs., pres., sec. Grand Rapids, dist. rep.), Order of Ski U Mah, Phi Beta Kappa. Office Phone: 218-743-6564. Personal E-mail: john_licke@yahoo.com.

LICKHALTER, MERLIN, architect; b. St. Louis, May 4, 1934; s. Frank E. and Sophia (Geller) L.; m. Harriet Braen, June 9, 1957; children: Debra, Barbara. BArch, MIT, 1957. Registered arch., Mo., Calif., Fla., Man. Ptnr. Drake Partnership, Architects, St. Louis, 1961-77; pres. JRB Architects, Inc., St. Louis, 1977-81; sr. v.p., mng. dir. Stone, Marraccini & Patterson, St. Louis, 1981-93; sr. v.p., dir. Cannon, 1993—2002; pres. Lickhalter & Assocs. LLC, 2003—. Owner, pres. mgmt. program Harvard U. Bus. Sch., 1992; cons. Dept. Def., Washington, 1977-78; lectr. Washington U. Sch. Medicine, 1989—. Prin. projects include The Mayo Clinic, Jacksonville, Fla., Washington U. Med. Ctr., St. Louis, U.S. Army Hosp., Frankfurt, Germany, Nat. AIDS Rsch. Ctr., NIH, Washington, Evanston (Ill.) Hosp., Loma Linda (Calif.) U. Med. Ctr., U. Mo. Health Scis. Ctr., Columbia, St. Louis U. Health Scis. Ctr., Children's Hosp. Rsch. Inst., New Orleans, U. Ala. Birmingham Sch. Medicine, U. Ala. Sch. Optometry. Trustee United Hebrew Congregation, St. Louis, 1980-88, 93-98, 2000—; exec. com. bd. dir. Arts & Edn. Coun. St. Louis, 1991-2002; pres. Acad. Architecture for Health Found., 2002-06; exec. com., bd. dir. United Arts Coun. Collier County, 2003—, pres. elect, 2007. Capt. U.S. Army, 1957-59. Recipient Renovation Design award St. Louis Producers Coun., 1976, USAF Europe Design Award, 1990. Fellow: AIA (pres. nat. acad. arch. for health 1993, bd. dir. 2003—, exec. com.), Am. Coll. Healthcare Architects; mem.: Acad. Arch. Health Found. (pres. and trustee 2000—), United Arts Coun. (dir. (Naples, Fla.)), MIT Club Southwest Fla. (dir. 2005—), Club Pelican Bay. Jewish. Home and Office: 6825 Grenadier Blvd Naples FL 34108 Personal E-mail: mlickhalter.hsfa@comcast.net.

LICKLITER, TODD, men's college basketball coach; b. Apr. 17, 1955; s. Arlan Lickliter; m. Joez Lickliter; children: Ry, Garrett, John. A, Ctrl. Fla. CC, 1977; BS in Secondary Edn., Butler U., 1979. Head coach Pk. Tudor HS, Indpls., 1979—87, Danville HS, Ind., 1987—88, 1989—92, Ah Ahli Sports Club, Jeddah, Saudi Arabia; asst. coach Butler U., 1988—89, 1999—2001, adminstrv. asst., 1996—97, head coach, 2001—07, U. Iowa, 2007—; asst. coach Ea. Mich. U., Ypsilanti, 1997—99. Named Horizon League Coach of Yr., 2006, 2007, Divsn. I Coach of Yr., Nat. Assn. Basketball Coaches, 2007. Office: Iowa Basketball 240 Carver Hawkeye Arena Iowa City IA 52242-1020 Office Phone: 319-335-9444.*

LICKTEIG, MARY JOAN, elementary school educator; b. Algona, Iowa, Jan. 2, 1929; d. Ambrose John Lickteig and Rose Annette McMahon. BA, Clarke Coll., Dubuque, Iowa, 1963; MA, Clarke Coll., 1967; PhD, U. Iowa, 1980. Cert. tchr. Iowa. Tchr. St. Columbkille Sch., Dubuque, 1952—61; prin. Resurrection Sch., Dubuque, 1961—68, literacy coord., 1998—; ednl. cons. Archdiocesan Edn. Office, Dubuque, 1968—77; prof. Clarke Coll., Dubuque, 1977—98. Home: 2360 Carter Rd Dubuque IA 52001-2933 Office Phone: 563-583-9488. Personal E-mail: joanlickteig@hotmail.com. Business E-Mail: jlickteig@hf.dbg.pvt.k12.ia.us.

LID, GLENN DAVID, chemistry educator; b. Chgo., Oct. 25, 1957; s. Robert Charles and Joan Edith Lid; m. Carol Gail Lid. BS, Elmhurst Coll., Ill., 1979; MA, Concordia Coll., River Forest, Ill., 1985. Tchr. chemistry Proviso E. H.S., Maywood, Ill., 1979—. Coach asst. varsity wrestling Proviso E. HS, Maywood, 1979—, coach varsity baseball. Named H.S. Tchr. of Yr., Disney Corp., 2004, Ill. Golden Apple Tchr. of Distinction, 2007; recipient Presdl. award, Ill. Sci. Tchrs. Assn., 1993, Alumni Merit award, Elmhurst Coll., 2005, Chem. Industry Coun. Ill. Davidson award, 2007. Mem.: NSTA, Chem W. Office: Proviso E HS 807 S First St Maywood IL 60153 Office Phone: 708-449-9539.

LIDDELL, CHRISTOPHER P., computer software company executive; married; 2 children. BS in Engring. with honors, Auckland U., New Zealand; MA in Philosophy, Oxford U., Eng. CFO to CEO Carter Holt Harvey, 1995—2002; v.p., fin. Internat. Paper Co., Stamford, Conn., 2002—03, sr. v.p., CFO, 2003—05; CFO Microsoft Corp., 2005—. Office: Microsoft Corp 1 Microsoft Way Redmond WA 98052*

LIDDELL, W. KIRK, specialty contracting company executive; b. Lancaster, Pa., July 24, 1949; m. Pamela E. Trow; four children. AB in Econs. magna cum laude, Princeton U., 1971; MBA, JD, U. Chgo., 1976. Assoc. Covington & Burling, Washington, 1976-80; gen. counsel, v.p. AC and S Inc/Irex Corp., Lancaster, 1980-83; pres., CEO Irex Corp., 1984—. Bd. dirs. High Industries Inc., Splty. Products & Insulation Co., PCI Ins., Inc.; chmn. Lancaster City Partnership, 1986, Lancaster C. of C. and Industry, 1991; pres. Econ. Devel. Co. Lancaster County, 1997—98; chmn. Lancaster Alliance, 2002—04. Campaign chmn. United Way of Lancaster County, 1995. Lt. USAR, 1971—73. Leon Carol Marshall scholar U. Chgo. Grad. Sch. Bus., 1974-76; named Scholar-Athlete Nat. Football Found. Mem.: NAM (bd. dirs., asbestos steering com., exec. com., chmn. legal issues policy group), Nat. Insulation Assn. (chmn. long range planning 1998—2004), Pa. C. of C. & Industry (chmn.). Office: Irex Corp 120 N Lime St Lancaster PA 17602-2923

LIDDLE, ALAN CURTIS, retired architect; b. Tacoma, Mar. 10, 1922; s. Abram Dix and Myrtle (Maytum) L. B.Arch., U. Wash., 1948; postgrad., Eidgenoissche Technische Hochschule, Zurich, Switzerland, 1950-51. Asst. prof. architecture U. Wash., 1954-55; prin. Liddle & Jones, Tacoma, 1957-67, Alan Liddle (architects), Tacoma, 1967-90, Liddle & Jacklin, Tacoma, 1990-98; ret., 1999. Architect oceanography bldgs, U. Wash., 1967, Tacoma Art Mus., 1971, Charles Wright Acad., Tacoma, 1962, Pacific Nat. Bank Wash., Auburn, 1965. Pres. bd. Allied Arts Tacoma, 1963-64, Civic Arts Commn. Tacoma-Pierce County, 1969; commr. Wash. Arts Commn., 1971; Bd. dirs. Tacoma Art Mus., Tacoma Zool. Soc., Tacoma Philharmonic, Inc. Served with AUS, 1943-46. Fellow A.I.A. (pres. S.W. Wash. chpt. 1967-68); mem. Wash. Hist. Soc., U. Wash. Alumni Assn. (all life) Home: 12735 Gravelly Lake Dr SW Lakewood WA 98499-1459 Office: 703 Pacific Ave Tacoma WA 98402-5207 Home Phone: 353-588-4525; Office Phone: 253-272-3155.

LIDDLE, JEFFREY L., lawyer; b. Aurora, Ill., Apr. 21, 1949; s. Harry Edward and Vera E. (Trippon) L.; m. Tara Liddle; children: Alexa, Harry. BS, Cornell U., 1971; JD, NYU, 1976. Bar: NY 1977, U.S. Dist. Ct. NY (so. and ea. dist.) 1977, U.S. Ct. Appeals (2d cir.) 1979, U.S. Supreme Ct. 1980, DC 1980, U.S. Tax Ct. 1984, U.S. Dist. Ct. NY (no. dist.) 1993, U.S. Ct. Appeals (sixth cir.) 1995, U.S. Ct. Appeals (first cir.) 1999. Assoc. Baer Marks & Upham, NYC, 1976—79; founding ptnr. Liddle & Robinson LLP (formerly Liddle, McMillin & Henze), NYC, 1979—. Co-author: Labor and Employment in NY: A Guide to New York Laws, Regulations, and Practices; contbr. articles to profl. jours.; lectr. in field. Mem. ABA, Fed. Bar Council, Assn. of Bar of City of NY (mem. arbitration com. 2002-). Office: Liddle Robinson Llp 800 3rd Ave New York NY 10022-7601

LIDDLE, SIDNEY GEORGE, retired mechanical engineer, researcher; b. Salt Lake City, Feb. 27, 1933; s. Clare Maynard and Rozella (Gater) L.; m. Johanna Funkhouser, May 8, 1987 (dec. Aug. 1988). BSME, U. Utah, 1956; PhD in Mech. Engring., U. N.S.W., Sydney, Australia, 1970. Design engr. Rocketdyne divsn. N.Am Aviation, Canoga Park, Calif., 1956-64; tchg. fellow U. N.S.W., Sydney, 1965-69; sr. engr. Rsch. Lab. GM, Warren, Mich., 1969-77, CalTech, Pasadena, Calif., 1977-85; project engr. Rand Co., Santa Monica, Calif., 1985-89; dir. Calif. Engring. Rsch. Inst., Pasadena, 1989-90; propulsion engr. GE Astro-Space, Princeton, NJ,

1990-92; ret., 1992. Contbr. numerous papers to profl. publs. Mem. ASME, AIAA, Soc. Automotive Engrs., Sigma Xi, Tau Beta Pi, Pi Tau Sigma. Achievements include 5 patents. Home: PO Box 2928 Running Springs CA 92382 Personal E-mail: sidliddle@earthlink.net.

LIDDY, EDWARD M., insurance company executive; b. New Brunswick, NJ, Jan. 28, 1946; m. Marcia Liddy; 3 children. BA, Cath. U. Am., 1968; MBA, George Washington U., 1972. With Internat. Harvester Co., Ford Motor Co., Ryder Systems Inc., 1968-79; sr. v.p. G.D. Searle & Co., Skokie, Ill., 1979-85; exec. v.p., CFO ADT Inc., NYC, 1986-88; CFO Sears, Roebuck and Co., 1988-94; pres., COO The Allstate Corp. and Allstate Ins. Co., Northbrook, Ill., 1994-98, chmn., pres., CEO, 1999—2005, chmn., CEO, 2005—06, chmn., 2007—. Bd. dirs. The Kroger Co., 3M, Ins. Information Inst., Goldman Sachs Group, Inc. Chmn. elect, nat. gov. Boys & Girls Clubs Am.; bd. dirs. Northwestern Meml. Hosp., Jr. Achievement of Chgo. Mem.: Catalyst, Bus. Roundtable, Fin. Svcs. Forum. Office: The Allstate Corp 2775 Sanders Rd Northbrook IL 60062-6127

LIDE, DAVID REYNOLDS, editor-in-chief; b. Gainesville, Ga., May 25, 1928; s. David Reynolds and Laura Kate (Simmons) L.; m. Mary Ruth Lomer, Nov. 5, 1955 (div. Dec. 1988); children: David Alston, Vanessa Grace, James Hugh, Quentin Robert; m. Bettijoyce Breen, 1988. BS, Carnegie Inst. Tech., 1949; AM, Harvard U., 1951, PhD, 1952. Physicist Nat. Bur. Stds., Washington, 1954-63, chief molecular spectroscopy sect., 1963-69, dir. std. reference data Gaithersburg, Md., 1969-88; editor-in-chief Handbook of Chemistry and Physics, CRC Press, 1988—. Pres. Com. on Data for Sci. and Tech., Paris, 1986-90. Author: Basic Laboratory and Industrial Chemicals, 1993, Handbook of Organic Solvents, 1995; (with G.W.A. Milne) Handbook of Data on Organic Compounds, 3rd edit., 1993, Names, Synonyms, and Structures of Organic Compounds, 1995; (with H.V. Kehiaian) Handbook of Thermophysical and Thermochemical Data, 1994; (with Milne) Handbook of Data on Common Organic Compounds, 1995, Properties of Organic Compounds and Properties of Organic Solvents Databases, 1996; (with G. L. Trigg and E. R. Cohen) AIP Physics Desk Reference, 2002, A Century of Excellence in Measurements, Standards and Technology, 2001, Handbook of Chemistry and Physics on CD-ROM, 2007; founding editor Jour. Phys. and Chem. Reference Data, 1972-92. Recipient Skolnik award for Chem. Info., Am. Chem. Soc., 1988, Patterson-Crane award, 1991, Presdl. Rank award in sr. exec. svc., 1986. Mem. NAS (nat. assoc.), Internat. Union Pure and Applied Chemistry (pres. phys. chemistry divsn. 1983-87). Achievements include research in microwave spectroscopy for studying molecular structure and hindered internal rotation, explanation of HCN laser, development of electronic databases of physical and chemical properties. Home and Office: 13901 Riding Loop Dr North Potomac MD 20878-3879

LIDE, VINTON DEVANE, lawyer; b. Greenville, SC, May 4, 1937; s. Theodore Ellis and Mary Elizabeth (DeVane) L.; m. Carol Jean Keisler, July 8, 1979; children: Wade Patrick, Emily Elizabeth. AB, Davidson Coll., 1959; LLB (now JD), U. Va., 1962. Bar: Va. 1962, S.C. 1962, U.S. Ct. Appeals (4th cir.) 1974, U.S. Ct. Appeals (9th cir.) 2001, U.S. Supreme Ct. 1980. Assoc. Shand & Wilmeth, Hartsville, SC, 1962-64; ptnr. Shand & Lide, Hartsville, SC, 1964-78; pub. defender Darlington County, SC, 1969-76; exec. asst./legal advisor to gov. S.C., 1978-79; asst. atty. gen. State of S.C., 1978-79; gen. counsel S.C. Dept. Social Svcs., 1979-81; chief counsel, staff dir. Com. on the Judiciary, U.S. Senate, Washington, 1981-85; adminstrv. asst. to U.S. Senator Strom Thurmond Washington, 1985—. Mcpl. ct. judge, Hartsville, 1963—69; U.S. atty. Dist. of S.C., 1985—89. Recipient cert. of Appreciation, Drug Enforcement Adminstrn., U.S. Dept. Justice, 1980. Mem. ABA (ho. dels. 1978-82), S.C. Bar Assn., Va. Bar Assn. Republican. Lutheran. Office: Vinton D Lide & Assocs LLC 5179 Sunset Blvd Lexington SC 29072 Office Phone: 803-808-1799. E-mail: dee@lidelaw.com.

LIDEN, HANNA, photographer; b. Stockholm, 1976; BFA in Photog., Parsons Sch. Design, NYC, 2002. Exhibited in group shows at You're Just a Summer Love but I'll Remember You When Winter Comes, 2005, one-man shows include and her shadow Death, Rivington Arms Gallery, NYC, exhibited in group shows at Be In, The Volta Show, 2006, Noctambule, NYC, The Whitney Biennial, Whitney Mus. Art, NYC, 2006.

LIDGE, BRAD, professional baseball player; b. Sacramento, Calif., Dec. 23, 1976; Attended, Notre Dame Univ., So. Bend, Ind. Relief pitcher Houston Astros, 2002—. Mem. Team USA, World Baseball Classic, 2006. Named to NL All-Star Team, 2005; recipient Nat. Good Guy award, Colo. Chapter National Baseball Writers Assn. Office: Minute Maid Park PO Box 288 Houston TX 77001-0288

LIDICKER, WILLIAM ZANDER, JR., zoologist, educator; b. Evanston, Ill., Aug. 19, 1932; s. William Zander and Frida (Schroeter) L.; m. Naomi Ishino, Aug. 18, 1956 (div. Oct., 1982); children: Jeffrey Roger, Kenneth Paul; m. Louise N. DeLonzor, June 5, 1989. BS, Cornell U., 1953; MS, U. Ill., 1954, PhD, 1957. Instr. zoology, asst. curator mammals U. Calif., Berkeley, 1957-59, asst. prof., asst. curator, 1959-65, assoc. prof., assoc. curator, 1965-69; assoc. dir. Mus. Vertebrate Zoology, 1968-81, acting dir., 1974-75, prof. zoology, curator mammals, 1969-89, prof. integrative biology, curator of mammals, 1989-94, prof., curator emeritus, 1994—. Adj. rsch. scientist Inst. Ecology U. Ga., 1989-. Dancer Westwind Internat. Folk Ensemble, 1994-2000, Jubilee Am. Dance Theater, 1999—; contbr. articles to profl. jours. Bd. dir. No. Calif. Com. for Environ. Info., 1971-77; bd. trustees BIOSIS, 1987-92, chmn., 1992; N.Am. rep. steering com., sect. Mammalogy IUBS, UNESCO, 1978-89; chmn. rodent specialist group Species Survival Comm., IUCN, 1980-89; mem. sci. adv. bd. Marine World Found. at Marine World Africa USA, 1987-98; pres. Dehnel-Petrusewicz Meml. Fund, 1985-97, sec.-treas., 1999. Fellow AAAS (life, 50 Yr.), Calif. Acad. Scis., Polish Acad. Scis. (fgn. mem., 50 Yr. Anniversary medal and diploma 2004), Explorers Club; mem. Internat. Fedn. Mammalogists (bd. dir. 2006—, pres. 2007—), Am. Soc. Mammalogists (dir. 1969—, 2d v.p. 1974-76, pres. 1976-78, C.H. Merriam award 1986, hon. mem. 1995), Am. Soc. Naturalists, Berkeley Folk Dancers Club (pres. 1969, tchr. 1984—, hon. mem. 2000), Nat. Folk Orgn. (bd. trustees 2005—), Folk Dance Fedn. Calif. (pres. 2007—). Office: U Calif Mus Vertebrate Zoology Berkeley CA 94720-0001 Business E-Mail: wlidicker@berkeley.edu.

LIDMAN, TOMAS ERIK, national archivist; b. Stockholm, June 30, 1948; s. Ivar and Gunhild (Andersson) L.; m. Kerstin Gårdbro, Aug. 19, 1972; children: Erica, Carl-Fredrik, Charlotte. PhD, U. Stockholm, 1979. Asst. libr. Royal Libr., Stockholm, 1971-79; sr. libr. Stockholm U. Libr., 1979-80; head dept. Delegation for Sci. Info., Stockholm, 1980-84; libr. Nordic Mus., Stockholm, 1984-85; dir. Nat. Libr. Psychology and Edn., Stockholm, 1985-92; libr. Stockholm U. Libr.; 1992-95; nat. libr. Royal Libr., Stockholm, 1995—2003, nat. archivist, 2003—. Chmn. U. Borås, 1998—2003, Royal U. Coll. Fine Arts, 2004-; bd. dirs. Nordic Coun. Sci. Info., chmn., 2003; v.p. Internat. Coun. on Archives, 2006. Author: Party Politics in the House of Nobility in the 19th Century, 1979, Libraries in Sweden, 1990, Essays on Books and Libraries, 2003; co-author: Litteratursociologi, 1995; editor: Svenska Antikvariat, 1986. Mem. Swedish Assn. Bibliophiles (pres. 1992-97), Swedish Assn. Rsch. Librs. (pres. 1989-94), Scandinavian Fedn. Rsch. Librs. (pres. 1992-94). Avocations: art, music, sports, travel. Office: Nat Archives PO Box 12541 S-10229 Stockholm Sweden Business E-Mail: tomas.lidman@riksarkivet.ra.se.

LIDSKY, ELLA, retired law librarian; b. Wilno, Poland; arrived in US, 1962; d. Leib and Sheina (Izygzon) Cwik; m. Alexander Lidsky, Feb. 20, 1963 (dec. Mar., 1996); 1 son, David Abraham. BA, Pedagogical Inst. Odessa, USSR; MS, Columbia U., NYC, 1966, MA, 1973. Cert. Russian and Hebrew lang. tchr. Tchr. high sch., Poland, 1948-51; elem. sch. Israel, 1961-62; asst. cataloger Tchrs. Coll. Columbia U., NYC, 1966-68; cataloger Fairleigh Dickinson U., Teaneck, NJ, 1968-69, asst. dir. tech. services Madison, NJ, 1973-84; head cataloger Ramapo Coll., Mahwah, NJ, 1971-73; asst. libr. U.S. Ct. Internat. Trade Law Libr., NYC, 1985-2000. Mem. Am. Assn. Law Libraries, Law Librarians of Greater N.Y., N.Y. Tech. Services Librarians, N.J. Law Librarians Assn. Democrat. Jewish. Avocations: music, travel. Personal E-mail: ella64@rcn.com.

LIDSTONE, HERRICK KENLEY, JR., lawyer; b. New Rochelle, NY, Sept. 10, 1949; s. Herrick Kenley and Marcia Edith (Drake) L.; m. Mary Lynne O'Toole, Aug. 5, 1978; children: Herrick Kevin, James Patrick, John Francis. AB, Cornell U., 1971; JD, U. Colo., 1978. Bar: Colo. 1978, U.S. Dist. Ct. Colo. 1978. Assoc. Roath & Brega, P.C., Denver, 1978—85, Brenman, Epstein, Raskin & Friedlob, P.C., Denver, 1985—86; shareholder Brenman, Raskin & Friedlob, P.C., Denver, 1986—94; mem. Friedlob Sanderson Raskin Paulson & Tourtillott, LLC, Denver, 1995—98, Norton Lidstone, P.C., Greenwood Village, Colo., 1998—2002, Burns, Figa & Will, P.C., Englewood, Colo., 2002—. Adj. prof. U. Denver Coll. Law, 1985-2000; mem. state securities bd. Colo. Dept. Regulatory Agys., 1999—, vice chmn., 2000-01, 04-05, chmn., 2001-02, 05-06; spkr. in field. Author: Federal and State Securities Regulation for the General Practitioner in Colorado, 2000, Securities Law Deskbook, 2006, supplement, 2007; editor U. Colo. Law Rev., 1977-78; co-author: Federal Income Taxation of Corporations, 6th edit.; contbg. author: Legal Opinion Letters Formbook, 1996, supplement, 2006, The Practioner's Guide to Colorado Business Organizations, 2006; contbr. articles to profl. jours. Served with USN, 1971-75, with USNR, 1975-81. Mem. ABA (Am. Law Inst.), Colo. Bar Assn., Arapahoe County Bar Assn., Denver Assn. Oil and Gas Title Lawyers. Avocation: languages. Office: Burns Figa & Will PC Ste 1000 6400 S Fiddlers Green Cir Greenwood Village CO 80111 Office Phone: 303-796-2626. Business E-Mail: hklidstone@bfw-law.com.

LIDSTROM, MARY E., chemical engineering and microbiology professor; BS in Microbiology, Ore. State Univ., 1973; MS in Bacteriology, Univ. Wis., Madison, 1975; PhD in Bacteriology, Univ. Wis., 1977. Prof., environ. engrng. sci. Calif. Tech. Inst.; Frank Jungers Chair, Engrng. Univ. Wash., and prof. chem. engrng, prof. microbiology, assoc. dean for new initiatives in engrng. Rsch. prof. Howard Hughes Med. Inst., 2002—. Editl. bd. Jour. Bacteriology; contbr. articles to profl. journals. Recipient Prather award for Young Women in Sci., CalTech award for Excellence, NSF Faculty award for Women, Howard Hughes Med. Inst. grant, 2002. Fellow: Am. Acad. Microbiology. Office: 263 Benson Univ Wash Box 351750 Seattle WA 98195-1750 Office Phone: 206-616-5282. Office Fax: 206-616-5721. Business E-Mail: lidstrom@u.washington.edu.

LIDSTROM, NICKLAS, professional hockey player; b. Vasteras, Sweden, Apr. 28, 1970; Defenceman Detroit Red Wings, 1991—, capt., 2006—; player NHL All-Rookie Team, 1992, NHL All-Star Game, 1996, 1998—2004. Named to All-Rookie Team, NHL, 1992, First All-Star Team, 1998—2003, 2006, 2007; recipient James Norris Meml. Trophy, 2001, 2002, 2003, 2006, 2007, Conn Smythe Trophy, 2002. Achievements include being a member of Stanley Cup Champion Detroit Red Wings, 1997, 1998, 2002; being a member of gold medal winning Swedish Hockey Team, Torino Olympics, Italy, 2006; over 600 assists, 2006. Office: Detroit Red Wings Joe Louis Arena 600 Civic Ctr Detroit MI 48226*

LIDTKE, DORIS KEEFE, retired computer science educator; b. Bottineau County, ND, Dec. 6, 1929; d. Michael J and Josephine (McDaniels) Keefe; m. Vernon L Lidtke, Apr. 21, 1951. BS, U. Oreg., 1952, PhD, 1979; MEd cum laude, Johns Hopkins U., 1974. Programmer analyst Shell Devel. Co., Emeryville, Calif., 1955—59, U. Calif., Berkeley, 1960—62; asst. prof. Lansing (Mich.) C.C., 1963—68; ednl. specialist Johns Hopkins U., Balt., 1968; assoc. program mgr. NSF, Washington, 1984—85, program dir., 1992—93; sr. mem. tech. staff Software Productivity Consortium, Reston, Va., 1987—88; asst. prof. computer sci. Towson U., Balt., 1968—80, assoc. prof., 1980—90, prof., 1990—2002, prof. emerita, 2002—; adj. accreditation dir. computing ABET Inc., 1999—. V.p. Computing Scis. Accreditation Bd., 1993—95, pres., 1995—97. Fellow: CSAB, ABET (formerly Accreditation Bd. Engrng. and Tech.), Assn. Computing Machinery (edn. bd. 1980—98, coun. 1984—86, spl. interest group bd. 1985—99, chmn. 1994—98, coun. 1994—98, Recognition Svc. award 1978, 1983, 1985, 1986, 1990, 1991, Outstanding Contbn. award 1995, Outstanding Svc. award 2004); mem.: Assn. Edn. Data Sys. (named Outstanding Educator 1986), Nat. Edn. Computer Conf. (steering com., vice-chmn. 1983—85, chmn. 1985—89, Outstanding Svc. award 1999, Outstanding Leadership award 1999), Computer Soc. of IEEE (Outstanding Contbn. award 1986, 1992, Golden Core). Home: 4806 Wilmslow Rd Baltimore MD 21210-2328 Office: Towson U Computer and Info Scis Baltimore MD 21252-0001 also: ABET Inc 111 Market Pl Baltimore MD 21202 Office Phone: 410-347-7700. Business E-Mail: dlidtke@abet.org, lidtke@towson.edu.

LIDTKE, VERNON LEROY, history professor; b. Avon, SD, May 4, 1930; s. Albert William and Aganeta (Boese) Lidtke; m. Doris Eileen Keefe, Apr. 21, 1951. BA, U. Oreg., 1952, MA, 1955; PhD, U. Calif., Berkeley, 1962. Tchr. high sch., Riddle, Oreg., 1953-55; instr. social sci. U. Calif., Berkeley, 1960-62; asst. prof. history Mich. State U., 1962-66, asso. prof., 1966-68; vis. asst. prof. U. Calif., Berkeley, 1963; asso. prof. Johns Hopkins U., 1968-73, prof., 1973—2001, chmn. dept. history, 1975-79, prof. emeritus, 2001—; pres. Friends of the German Historical Inst., Washington, 1991-94. Author: (book) The Outlawed Party: Social Democracy in Germany, 1878-1890, 1966, The Alternative Culture: Socialist Labor in Imperial Germany, 1985; mem ed bd: Jour Modern Hist, 1973—76, Cent European Hist, 1982—89, Int Labor and Working Class Hist, 1984—89; contbr. articles to profl jours. Fellow Fulbright Research, 1959—60, 1966—67, Nat Endowment Humanities, 1969—70, Davis Ctr Hist Studies, Princeton Univ, 1974—75, Wissenschaftskolleg zu Berlin, 1987—88, Max-Planck-Institut für Geschichte, Göttingen, 1996. Mem.: AAUP, Conf Group German Polit (officer 1975—83), Conf Group Cen European Hist (vpres 1985, pres 1986), Col Art Asn, Am Hist Asn (chair modern European sect 1992, Eugene Asher Distinguished Teaching Award 1999), Johns Hopkins Club. Home: 4806 Wilmslow Rd Baltimore MD 21210-2328 Office: Johns Hopkins U Dept History Baltimore MD 21218

LIE, ERIK, finance educator; b. 1968; s. Rolf Lie. BS summa cum laude, U. Ore., 1990, MBA, 1991; PhD, Purdue U., 1996. Asst. prof. bus. Coll. William & Mary, Williamsburg, Va., 1996—2002, Wilson P. and Martha Claiborne Stephens assoc. prof., 2002—04; assoc. prof., Henry B. Tippie rsch. fellow U. Iowa, Iowa City, 2004—. Contbr. articles to profl. jours. Served with Norwegian Navy, Norwegian Coast Guard, 1991—92. Named one of The World's Most Influential People, TIME mag., 2007; recipient Alumni Fellowship award for Excellence in Teaching, Coll. William & Mary, 2002. Office: Henry B Tippie Coll Bus U Iowa Iowa City IA 52242-1000 Office Phone: 319-335-0846. Office Fax: 319-335-3690. E-mail: erik-lie@uiowa.edu.*

LIEB, ELLIOTT HERSHEL, physicist, mathematician, educator; b. Boston, July 31, 1932; s. Sinclair M. and Clara (Rosenstein) L.; m. Christiane Fellbaum; children: Alexander, Gregory. BSc, MIT, 1953; PhD, U. Birmingham, Eng., 1956; DSc (hon.), U. Copenhagen, 1979; D (hon.), Ecole Poly. Fed. Lausanne, Switzerland, 1995, U. Munich, 2004; DSc (hon.), U. Birmingham, Eng. With IBM Corp., 1960-63; sr. lectr. Fourah Bay Coll., Sierra Leone, 1961; mem. faculty Yeshiva U., 1963-66, Northeastern U., 1966-68, MIT, Cambridge, 1968-75, prof. physics, 1963-68, prof. math., 1968-73, prof. math. and physics, 1973—, Princeton (N.J.) U., 1975—. Author: (with D.C. Mattis) Mathematical Physics in One Dimension, 1966, (with B. Simon and A. Wightman) Studies in Mathematical Physics, (with M. Loss) Analysis; also articles. Recipient Boris Pregel award chem. physics N.Y. Acad. Scis., 1970, Dannie Heineman prize for mathematical physics Am. Inst. Physics and Am. Phys. Soc., 1978, Prix Scientifique, Union des Assurances de Paris, 1985, Birkhoff prize Am. Math. Soc. and Soc. Indsl. Applied Math., 1988, Max-Planck medal German Phys. Soc., 1992, Boltzmann medal Internat. Union of Pure and Applied Physics, 1998, Onsager medal Norwegian U. Sci. and Tech., 1998, Rolf Schock prize in math. Swedish Acad. Scis., 2001, Levi L. Conant prize of Am. Math. Soc., 2002, Austrian medal Sci. Art, 2002, Poincare prize Internat. Assn. Math. Physics, 2003; Guggenheim Found. fellow, 1972, 78. Fellow AAAS, Am. Phys. Soc.; mem. NAS, Austrian Acad. Scis., Danish Royal Acad., Am. Acad. Arts and Scis., Internat. Assn. Math. Physics (pres. 1982-84, 97-99). Office: Princeton U Jadwin Hall-Physics Dept PO Box 708 Princeton NJ 08544-0708

LIEB, L. ROBERT, lawyer; b. Jersey City, July 15, 1941; s. Nathan Philip and Elizabeth (Blum) Lieb; m. Sherry Young, Sept. 11, 1971; children: Elizabeth Ann, Nathan Young. BA, U. Buffalo, 1962; LLB, NYU, 1965. Bar: N.J. 1967, N.Y. 1970, U.S. Dist. Ct. (so. and ea. dists.) N.Y. 1970. Law clk., appellate divsn. Superior Ct. N.J., 1965—66; sr. ptnr. Kimmelman, Lieb, Wolf & Samson, West Orange, NJ, 1972—77; chmn. Mountain Devel. Corp., West Paterson, NJ, 1978—, Bretton Woods Corp., NH, 1980—84. Chmn., bd. dirs. NorCrown Bank of Roseland, 1987; bd. chmn. Pub. Health Rsch. Inst., 2004. Pres. The Children's Inst., Livingston, NJ, 1995; trustee Passaic County 200 Club, YMCA of the Oranges, Livingston Edn. Found.; co-chmn. Bryant Park Mgmt. Corp. Served 1st lt. JAGC USAF, 1966—72. Harry Rudin scholar, NYU, 1963—65. Mem.: Essex County Bar Assn., Green Brook Country Club (North Caldwell, N.J.). Office: Mountain Devel Corp PO Box 1069 100 Delawanna Ave Ste 100 Clifton NJ 07014-1069 Office Phone: 973-279-9000. Business E-Mail: blieb@mountaindevelopment.com.

LIEB, PETER, lawyer; BA, Yale U.; JD, U. Mich. Law clk. to Chief Justice Warren Burger US Supreme Ct.; asst. atty. US Dist. Ct. (so. dist. NY); ptnr. Jones, Day, Reavis & Pogue; asst. gen. counsel GTE Svc. Corp.; v.p., dep. gen. counsel Internat. Paper Co., 1998—2003; sr. v.p., gen. counsel, sec. Symbol Technologies, Inc., Holtsville, NY, 2003—06; sr. v.p., gen. counsel NCR Corp., 2006—. Adj. prof. Fordham U. Office: NCR Corp 1700 S Patterson Blvd Dayton OH 45479 Office Phone: 631-738-4765. Office Fax: 631-738-5980.*

LIEB, RICHARD JAY, investment banker; b. 1959; m. Ellen Susan Munt, Oct. 18, 1986. Grad., Wesleyan U.; MBA, Harvard U. Various positions Goldman Sachs, NYC, 1984—2000, head, real estate investment banking group, 2000—05; mng. dir. real estate industry group Greenhill & Co., NYC, 2005—. Named a Top Dealmaker, Dealmaker mag., 2006. Office: Greenhill & Co 300 Park Ave Fl 23 New York NY 10022-7405 Office Phone: 212-389-1597. Office Fax: 212-389-1797.*

LIEBELER, SUSAN WITTENBERG, lawyer; b. July 3, 1942; d. Sherman K. and Eleanor (Klivans) Levine; m. Wesley J. Liebeler, Oct. 21, 1971 (dec.); 1 child, Jennifer. BA, U. Mich., 1963, postgrad., 1963-64; LLB, UCLA, 1966. Bar: Calif. 1967, Vt. 1973, DC 1988. Law clk. Calif. Ct. of Appeals, 1966-67; assoc. Gang, Tyre & Brown, 1967-68, Greenberg, Bernhard, Weiss & Karma, L.A., 1968-70; assoc. gen. counsel Rep. Corp., 1970-72; gen. counsel Verit Industries, 1972-73; prof. Loyola Law Sch., LA, 1973—85; spl. counsel, chmn. John S. R. Shad, SEC, Washington, 1981-82; commr. U.S. Internat. Trade Commn., Washington, 1984-88, vice-chmn., 1984-86, chmn., 1986-88; ptnr. Irell & Manella, LA, 1988-94; pres. Lexpert Rsch. Svcs., LA, 1995—. Vis. prof. U. Tex., summer 1982; cons. Office of Policy Coordination, Office of Pres.-elect, 1981-82; cons. U.S. Ry. Assn., 1975, U.S. EPA, 1974, U.S. Price Commn., 1972; mem. Adminstrv. Conf. U.S., 1986-88. Mem. editl. adv. bd. Regulation mag. CATO Inst.; sr. editor UCLA Law Rev., 1965-66; contbr. articles to profl. jours. Mem. adv. bd. U. Calif. Orientation in USA Law; bd. govs. Century City Hosp., 1992—2002, vice chair, 1997—99, chair, 1999—2001. Stein scholar UCLA, 1966. Mem. State Bar Calif. (treas., vice chair, chair exec. com. internat. law sect.), Practicing Law Inst. (Calif. adv. com.), Washington Legal Found. (acad. adv. bd.), Order of Coif. Jewish. Office Phone: 310-589-5546. Business E-Mail: lexpert@lexpertresearch.com.

LIEBEN, THOMAS GEOFFREY, lawyer; b. Omaha; s. Theodore Jack and Eileen (Brooks) L.; m. Anne C., June 26, 1971; children: Elizabeth, Caroline, Andrew. BA, Creighton U., 1968; JD, NYU, 1971. Bar: Nebr. 1971, U.S. Dist. Ct. Nebr. 1971, U.S. Ct. Appeals (8th cir.) 1972, U.S. Tax Ct. 1972. Ptnr. Fitzgerald & Brown, Omaha, 1971-88; prin. Lieben, Whitted, Houghton, Slowiaczek & Cavanagh, P.C., Omaha, 1988—. Dir. Financial Dynamics Inc., Omaha, 1988-99. Contbr. articles to profl. jours. Recipient Order of the Coif award NYU, 1971; fellow Nebr. Bar Found., Lincoln, 1994; named in Best Lawyers in Am., 1983—. Fellow Am. Bar Found.; mem. Omaha Bar Assn., Nebr. Bar Assn., ABA, Omaha Estate Planning Coun., Omaha Pension Coun., Employee Benefits Roundtable. Democrat. Avocation: tennis. Office: Lieben Whitted Houghton Slowiaczek & Cavanagh PC 2027 Dodge St Ste 100 Omaha NE 68102-1238 Business E-Mail: jlieben@liebenlaw.com.

LIEBENBERG, ROBERTA D., lawyer; b. Washington, 1949; BA, Univ. Mich., 1970; JD, Cath. Univ., 1975. Bar: Pa. 1980, Va. 1975, DC 1976, U.S. Supreme Ct. 1980. Law clerk U.S Ct. Appeals, Pa., 1975—77; atty. Fine, Kaplan & Black, Phila., 2000—. Bd. dir. Anti-Defamation League, Phila. chpt., Women's Way, Pa. Named one of Top 50 Female Super Lawyers, Philadelphia Magazine, 2004, Top 100 Lawyers in Pa., 2004, The 50 Most Influential Women Lawyers in Am., Nat. Law Jour., 2007; recipient Woman of Distinction, Philadelphia Business Journal, 2003. Fellow: Am. Bar Found., Pa. Bar Assn. (bd. govs. 2000—03, Lynette Norton award 2003); mem.: Am. Law Inst., ABA (bd. govs. 2003—05, mem. standing com. fed. judiciary). Office: Fine Kaplan & Black 28th Fl 1835 Market St Philadelphia PA 19103 Home Phone: 215-947-2773; Office Phone: 215-567-6565. Business E-Mail: rliebenberg@finekaplan.com.*

LIEBENSON, GLORIA KRASNOW, interior design executive, freelance writer; b. Chgo., Apr. 6, 1922; d. Henry Randolph and Margaret (Rivkin) Krasnow; m. Herbert Liebenson, Mar. 11, 1944 (dec.); children: Lauren Ward, Lynn Liebenson Green. Student, Internat. Inst. Interior Design, Washington, 1961; B Am. Studies, Dunbarton Coll., Washington, 1974. Numerous positions Journalism, Advt., editing, 1942-62; interior design exec. Creative Interiors, 1962—. Tchr. interior design YMCA, Washington, 1980-82. Mem. editorial staff Champlin Encyclopedia, 1945-47; journalist Shreveport Jour., 1944; author: Corned Beef on Lies: the Laugh Track From My 83-Year Life Trek, 2005 Bd. dirs. Jewish Social Svc. Agy., Washington, 1983-85, Nat. Coun. Jewish Women, 1982-84; pres. Friends Nat. Museum African Art, 1983-85, D.C. Mental Health Assn., 1986-88. Democrat. Jewish. Avocations: theater, concerts, Scrabble, reading, travel. Home: Ste 615 4200 Massachusetts Ave NW Washington DC 20016-4734 Personal E-mail: glor15@verizon.net.

LIEBENSON, JEFFREY M., lawyer; b. NYC, Mar. 14, 1953; AB, U. Calif., Berkeley, 1975; JD, NYU, 1978, LLM, 1982. Bar: NY 1979. Ptnr. Katten Muchin Rosenman, NYC. Mem.: Copyright Soc. of USA. Office: Katten Muchin Rosenman 575 Madison Ave New York NY 10022 Office Phone: 212-940-8597. Office Fax: 212-894-5597. E-mail: jeff.liebenson@kattenlaw.com.

LIEBER, CHARLES, chemistry professor, researcher, materials scientist; b. Phila., Apr. 9, 1959; BS in Chemistry, Franklin & Marshall Coll., 1981; PhD in Chemistry, Stanford U., 1985; postdoctoral study, Calif. Inst. Tech., 1985—87. Postdoctoral rsch. California Inst. of Tech., 1986; assist. prof. chemistry Columbia U., 1987—91; prof. chemistry, chemical biology & Mark Hyman prof. chemistry div. of engring. & applied sci. Harvard U., 1991—. Scientific founder and mem. scientific adv. bd. Nanosys, Inc. Author numerous scientific articles in professional journals & mags. including: Jour. of Am. Chemistry Soc., Applied Physics Letters, Scientific American, Jour. of Physical Chemistry, Nature, Science. Named one of Brilliant 10, Popular Sci. mag., 2002; recipient Pure Chemistry award, Am. Chemical Soc., 1992, Creativity award, Nat. Sci. Found., 1996, Feynman award in nanotechnology, 2001, MRS medal, 2002, Harrison-Howe award, 2002, APS McGroddy prize for new materials, 2003, Inventor of the Yr., NY Intellectual Property Law Assn., 2003, World Tech. award in materials, 2003, Scientific American award in nanotechnology & molecular electronics, 2003, Chemistry of Materials award, Am. Chemical Soc., 2004. Fellow: Am. Physical Soc.; mem.: Optical Soc. Am., Materials Rsch. Soc., Internat. Soc. Optical Engring., Am. Chem. Soc., AAAS, NAS. Developed and applied a new chemically sensitive microscopy for probing organic and biological materials at nanometer to molecular scales. Office: Harvard U Dept Chemistry & Chemical Biology 12 Oxford St Cambridge MA 02138 Business E-Mail: cml@cmlliris.harvard.edu.

LIEBER, CHARLES SAUL, internist, educator; b. Antwerp, Belgium, Feb. 13, 1931; came to U.S., 1958, naturalized, 1966; s. Isaac and Lea (Maj) L.; m. M. A. Leo; children: Colette, Daniel, Leah, Samuel, Sarah. Candidate in natural and med. sci., U. Brussels, 1951; MD, 1955. Cert. Am. Bd. Clin. Nutrition, 1967. Intern, resident U. Hosp., Brugmann, Belgium, 1954—56; research fellow med. found. Queen Elizabeth, 1956-58; research fellow Thorndike Meml. Lab. Harvard Med. Sch., Boston, 1958—60, instr., 1961; assoc. Harvard U., 1962; assoc. prof. medicine Cornell U., 1963-68; dir. liver disease and nutrition unit Bellevue Hosp., NYC, 1963-68; chief sect. liver disease, nutrition and alcohol Tng. Program VA Hosp., Bronx, NY, 1968—97; prof. medicine Mt. Sinai Sch. Medicine, NYC, 1969—, prof. pathology, 1976—, dir. Alcohol Rsch. and Treatment Ctr., 1977—. Assoc. vis. physician Cornell Med. div. Bellevue, Meml., James Ewing hosps., 1964-69; Am. Coll. Gastroenterology disting. lectr., 1978, Henry Baker lectr., 1979. Recipient award of Belgian Govt. for rsch. on gastric secretion, 1956, Rsch. Career Devel. award NIH, USPHS, 1964-68, E.M. Jellinek Meml. award, 1976, A. Boudreau award Laval U., 1977, W.S. Middleton award highest honor for med. rsch. Dept. Vets. Affairs, 1977, Leahy Rsch. award highest honor for outstanding investigator, 1994, first Mark Keller award NIAAA-NIH, 1996, AMA Sci. Achievement award The Christopher D. Smithers Found., 1998, R. Brinkley Smithers award in rsch. and edn. in alcohol 2003. Master ACP; fellow AAAS, Am. Soc. Nutritional Sci., Am. Gastroent. Assn. (Disting. Achievement award 1973, Hugh R. Butt award for liver/nutrition 1992); mem. Assn. Am. Physicians, N.Y. Gastroent. Assn. (pres. 1974-75), Am. Soc. Biochemistry and Molecular Biology, Am. Soc. Addictive Medicine (pres. 1974-77, Sci. Achievement award 1989, Disting. Scientist award 1996), Assn. Clin. Biochemists (Kone award 1994), Am. Soc. Clin. Nutrition (McCollum award 1973, pres. 1975-76, Robert H. Herman Meml. award 1993), Am. Soc. Clin. Investigation, Am. Soc. Pharmacol. Exptl. Therapy, Rsch. Soc. on Alcoholism (pres. 1977-79, Sci. Excellence award 1980, Disting. Svc. award 1992), Am. Coll. Nutrition (Outstanding Achievement award 1990). Home: 6 Johnson Ave Englewood Cliffs NJ 07632-2107 Office: James J Peters VA Med Ctr 130 W Kingsbridge Rd Bronx NY 10468-3904 Office Phone: 718-741-4244. Personal E-mail: liebercs@aol.com.

LIEBER, DAVID LEE, university president; b. Stryj, Poland, Feb. 20, 1925; came to U.S., 1927, naturalized, 1936; s. Max and Gussie L.; m. Esther, June 10, 1945; children: Michael, Daniel, Deborah, Susan. BA, CCNY, 1944; B of Hebrew Lit., Jewish Theol. Sem. Am., 1944, M of Hebrew Lit., 1948, D of Hebrew Lit., 1951; MA, Columbia U., 1947; postgrad., U. Wash., 1954—55, UCLA, 1961—63; LDH (hon.), Hebrew Union Coll., 1982. Ordained rabbi, 1948. Rabbi Sinai Temple, LA, 1950-54; dir. B'nai B'rith Hillel, Seattle, Cambridge, 1954-56; dean students U. Judaism (now The Am. Jewish U.), LA, 1956—63, Samuel A. Fryer prof. Bible, pres., 1963—92, Skovron Disting. Svc. prof. Bibl. lit., 1990—, pres. emeritus, 1992—; lectr. Hebrew UCLA, 1957-90; vice chancellor Jewish Theol. Sem., 1972-92. Mem. exec. coun. Rabbinical Assembly, 1966-69, v.p., 1994-96, pres., 1996-98; vice chmn. Am. Jewish Com., L.A., 1972-75; bd. dirs. Jewish Fedn. Coun., L.A., 1980-86. Mem. editl. bd. Conservative Judaism, 1968-70; sr. editor (bibl. commentary) ETZ Hayim. Served as chaplain USAF, 1951-53. Recipient Torch of Learning award Hebrew U., 1984, Simon Greenberg award U. Judaism, 2002, Book of Yr. award Nat. Jewish Book Coun., 2002, Tomech Torah award Nat. Jewish Edn. Assn., 2004. Mem. Assn. Profs. Jewish Studies (dir. 1970-71), Phi Beta Kappa. Office: The Am Jewish U 15600 Mulholland Dr Los Angeles CA 90077-1519 Office Phone: 310-440-1288. Personal E-mail: dllieber@aol.com.

LIEBER, LOLA, artist; b. Mukaoevo, Czechslovakia, Mar. 15, 1923; arrived in US, 1947; d. Lazar and Shari Leser; children: Hershel, Joseph, Madeline. Art tchr. Lola's Art Studio Gallery, Bklyn., 1951—. Represented in permanent collections Art Mus. San Francisco, Yad Vashem in Jerusalem, Vets. Mus. Las Vegas, exhibitions include Lutka Pink Gallery, Paris, Gordon Gallery, Tel Aviv. Jewish. Home: 1530 54th St Brooklyn NY 11219 Office: Lolas Art Studio Gallery 4813 16th Ave Brooklyn NY 11204

LIEBER, MICHAEL RANDALL, biochemist, educator; b. St. Louis, June 21, 1955; s. John Warren Sr. and Matilda V. Lieber; m. Chih-Lin Hsieh, Jan. 1, 1990. BA, BS, U. Mo., 1977; PhD, U. Chgo., 1981, MD, 1983. Diplomate Am. Bd. Pathology. Resident in pathology NIH, Bethesda, Md., 1983-86, postdoctoral fellow, 1986-89; asst. prof., then assoc. prof. Stanford (Calif.) U., 1989-94; assoc. prof. pathology Washington U., St. Louis, 1994-97; prof. U. So. Calif., 1997—. Editl. bd. Molecular and Cellular Biology, JBC, DNA Repair; contbr. over 130 articles to profl. publs., including Nature, Cell, Sci., EMBO Jour., Genes & Devel. Recipient Faculty Scholar award Leukemia Soc. Am., 1994-99, Ed Heitz Meml. Rsch. Fund award Leukemia Soc. Am., 1998, award Warner-Lambert/Parke-Davis, 1998; Stohlman scholar Leukemia Soc. Am., 1999. Mem. AAAS, Am. Soc. Investigative Pathology. Achievements include patents in field. Home: 245 W Palm Dr Arcadia CA 91007 Office: USC Sch Medicine ME 9176 1441 Eastlake Ave Los Angeles CA 90089-9176

LIEBER, RICHARD LOUIS, biomedical engineering scientist, educator; b. Walnut Creek, Calif., Dec. 14, 1956; s. Richard and Janet Elizabeth (Stone) L.; children: Katelyn Suzanne, Kristin Michelle; m. Dina Lieber, Oct. 2004. BS with honors, U. Calif., Davis, 1978, PhD, 1982. Sr.rsch. career scientist VA Med. Ctr., San Diego, 1983—; prof. orthopaerics & bioengring. U. Calif., 1985—. Cons. Pref Med. Products Inc., 1987—. Contbr. sci. papers to profl. publs.; inventor surgical myometer, 1985, adaptive muscle stimulator, 1987. Faculty advisor Inter-Varsity Christian Fellowship, San Diego, 1984—. Recipient Presdl. award Am. Acad. Cerebral Palsy, 1984, Nicolas Andry award Am. Bone & Joint Inst., 1998; State of Calif. Gov.'s scholar, 1974. Mem. IEEE, Orthopaedic Rsch. Soc., Biophys. Soc. (Talbot award 1981), Rehab. Engring. Soc. N.Am., Soc. Neursci., Am. Soc. Biomechanics, Am. Physiol. Soc. Republican. Achievements include patent for surgical myometer; development of techniques used involving computer controlled muscle contraction and optical sensors for structure monitoring; research on skeletal muscle properties in normal and diseased muscles. Home: 10471 Mira Montana Dr Del Mar CA 92014 Office: U Calif Dept Orthopaedics V 151 San Diego CA 92161-0001 Office Phone: 858-552-8585 x 7016. Business E-Mail: rlieber@ucsd.edu.

LIEBER, ROBERT C., investment company executive; b. Aug. 4, 1954; BA, U. Colo., 1977; MBA, The Wharton Sch., 1984. Joined Lehman Brothers, NYC, 1984, mem., Real Estate Investment Banking Grp., mng. dir., 2006—07, prin., Equity Funds, 2006—07; pres. NYC Econ. Devel. Corp., 2007—. Affiliated with Fisher Ctr. for Real Estate and Urban Economics, U. Berkeley Haas Sch. Bus., Zell/Lurie Real Estate Ctr., U. Pa. Trustee Urban Land Inst. Office: NYC Economic Development Corp 110 William St New York NY 10038*

LIEBER, ROBERT JAMES, political science professor; b. Chgo. m. Nancy Lieber; 2 children. BA in Polit. Sci. with high honors, U. Wis., 1963; postgrad. in Polit. Sci., U. Chgo., 1963-64; PhD in Govt., Harvard U., 1968. Asst. prof. Polit. Sci. U. Calif., Davis, 1968-72, assoc. prof., 1972-77, chmn. dept. Polit. Sci., 1975-76, 77-80, prof., 1977-81; postdoctoral rschr. St. Antony's Coll. Oxford (Eng.) U., 1969-70; prof. Georgetown U., Washington, 1982—, chmn. dept. govt., 1990-96, acting chmn. dept. psychology, 1997-99. Vis. prof. Oxford U., 1969, Fudan U, Shanghai, 1988; rsch. assoc. Ctr. Internat. Affairs, Harvard U., 1974—75; cons. U.S. Dept. State and Dept. Def., 1975—. Author: British Politics and European Unity, 1970, Theory and World Politics, 1972, Oil and the Middle East War: Europe in the Energy Crisis, 1976, The Oil Decade: Conflict and Cooperation in the West, 1983, No Common Power: Understanding International Relations, 1988, 4th edit., 2001, The American Era: Power & Strategy for the 21st Century, 2005 rev. expanded edit., 2007; co-author: Contemporary Politics: Europe, 1976; editor, contbg. author: Eagle Adrift: American Foreign Policy at the End of the Century, 1997, Eagle Rules? Foreign Policy and American Primacy in the 21st Century, 2002; co-editor, contbg. author: Eagle Entangled: U.S. Foreign Policy in a Complex World, 1979, Eagle Defiant: U.S. Foreign Policy in the 1980s, 1983, Eagle Resurgent? The Reagan Era in American Foreign Policy, 1987, Eagle in a New World: American Grand Strategy in the Post-Cold War Era, 1992; editor: Will Europe Fight for Oil?, 1983; contbr. articles to Harper's, Commentary, Politique étrangère, N.Y. Times, Washington Post, Christian Sci. Monitor, L.A. Times, others, and profl. jours. Advanceman nat. campaign staff McCarthy for Pres., 1968; fgn. policy advisor various Presdl. campaigns, 1980—2000. Woodrow Wilson fellow, 1963, fellow NDEA, 1963-64, grad. prize fellow Harvard U., 1964-68, Social Sci. Rsch. Coun., 1969-70, Coun. Fgn. Rels., 1972-73, Guggenheim fellow, 1973-74, Rockefeller Found., 1978-79, Wilson Ctr. Smithsonian Inst., 1980-81, 99-00, Ford Found., 1981; vis. fellow Atlantic Inst. Internat. Affairs, Paris, 1978-79; guest scholar Brookings Inst., 1981. Mem.: Coun. on Fgn. Rels., Phi Beta Kappa. Office: Georgetown U Dept Of Government Washington DC 20057-1034 Office Phone: 202-687-5920. Business E-Mail: lieberr@georgetown.edu.

LIEBER, STANLEY MARTIN See LEE, STAN

LIEBERFARB, WARREN N., digital media pioneer; b. Mar. 1943; BS, U. Penn; MBA, U. Mich. Financial analyst Ford Motor Co.; exec. asst. to pres. Paramount Pictures; v.p., telecommunications 20th Century Fox Film, 1973—75; sr. v.p., sales & mktg. Warner Bros., 1982—84; pres. Warner Home Video, Burbank, Calif., 1984—2002; chmn. Lieberfarb & Assoc.

LIEBERG, OLAF U., orthopaedic surgeon; arrived in U.S., 1951; s. Ulrich J. and Lisa Lieberg; m. Elaine Ann Willower, Sept. 9, 1994; children: Tanya, Kirk, Melanie, Summer, Michelle, Daniel, Angelena. AA, Lake Mich. Coll., 1962; BA, Western Mich. U., 1964; MS in Zoology, U. Mich., 1965, MD, 1969. Bd. cert. orthopaedic surgery Am. Acad. Orthopaedic Surgery. Resident in orthopaedic surgery U. Mich., Ann Arbor, 1974; orthopaedic surgeon Geneva Orthopaedics PC, 1974—82, in solo practice, 1982—2004, Interlakes Orthopaedic Surgery, Geneva, 2004—06; orthopaedic surgeon, ptnr. Finger Lakes Bone and Joint Ctr., Geneva, 2006—. Ptnr. Microtel of Seneca Falls, 2002—; owner Blue Stone Properties, Geneva Mini-Storage; owner, pres. Liberty Laserwash, Geneva Laserwash, E-Z Car Wash of Geneva, Liberty Commons Plz., Kentucky Fried Chicken of Canandaigua. Capt. USAR, 1970—76. Recipient Clarence Beckwith Disting. Alumni award, Lake Mich. Coll., 1999. Fellow: Am. Acad. Orthopaedic Surgeons (diplomate). Avocations: sailing, fishing. Home: 4437 Clarks Point Geneva NY 14456 Office: Finger Lakes Bone and Joint Ctr 875 Pre Emption Rd Geneva NY 14456 Office Phone: 315-789-5061.

LIEBERMAN, ANNE MARIE, retired financial executive; b. Jersey City, Aug. 28, 1946; d. Ralph Norman and Kathleen Celestine (Dooris) L.; m. Stephen Bruce Oshry, Sept. 21, 1986. BA, Sonoma State U., 1968; MLS, U. Calif., 1970, MBA, 1977. Cert. fin. planner; cert. fund specialist. V.p. Bank of Am., San Francisco, 1977-81, Lawrence A. Krause & Assocs., San Francisco, 1982-86; pres. Lieberman Assocs., San Rafael, Calif., 1986-98, ret., 1998; facilitator Lefkoe Belief Process, 2007—. Bd. dirs. Sonoma (Calif.) State U. Found. Author: Marketing Your Financial Planning Practice, 1986, Mastering Money, 1987; contbg. author: Financial Planning Can Make You Rich, 1987, The Expert's Guide to Managing a Successful Financial Planning Practice, 1988, About Your Future, 1988; columnist North Bay Bus. Jour., 2005. Bd. dirs. Marin Gen. Found. Hosp., 1995; mem. pres.'s adv. bd. Sonoma State U., 2000; active Sonoma State U. Found. Bd., 2005. Selected by Worth mag. as one of 250 best fin. advisors in U.S., 1997, 98. Mem. Inst. Cert. Fin. Planners (Fin. Writer's award 1986), Nat. Endowment for Fin. Edn. (bd. dirs. 1996-2002). Avocations: singing, ballroom dancing. E-mail: annelieberman@comcast.net.

LIEBERMAN, CAROL, healthcare marketing communications consultant; b. St. Louis, June 14, 1938; d. Norman Leonard and Ethel (Silver) Mistachkin; m. Malcolm P. Cooper, Aug. 25, 1962 (div. June 1977); children: Lawrence, Edward, Marcus; m. Edward Lieberman, Apr. 1992. BS, U. Wis., 1959; MA, N.Y. Inst. Tech., 1992; CTEFL, CTBE, Worldwide Tchr.'s Inst., 2000; postgrad. in Health Care Sci., Nova Southeastern U., 2007—. Cert. tchr. english as foreign lang., tchr. of bus. english. Media buyer Lennen and Newell, LA, 1959-61; advt. mgr. Hartfield-Zodys, LA, 1961-62, Haggarty's, LA, 1962-63; sales rep. Abbott Labs., Bklyn., 1974-75; edn. dir. N.Y. and NJ Regional Transp. Program, NYC, 1975-78; account exec. Med. Edn. Dynamics, Woodbridge, NJ, 1978-79; dir. program devel. Kallir, Phillips & Ross Info. Media, NYC, 1979-81; exec. v.p. sales and mktg. Audio Visual Med. Mktg., NYC, 1981-85; exec. v.p. Park Row Pubs./John Wiley & Sons Med. Div., NYC, 1985-88; pres., prin. Pk. Row Pub., NYC, 1988-91; pvt. practice healthcare mktg. comms. cons. Dix Hills, NY, 1991—. Prof. N.Y. Inst. Tech., 1991—95; exec. sec. cardiopulmonary bypass consensus panel Bayer Corp., 1993—2002; asst. prof. Southampton Coll. L.I. (N.Y.) U., 2000—03; facilitator U. Phoenix, 2001—; instructional specialist U. Phoenix Online, 2003—05; internet pub. Am. Assn. Thoracic Surgery, 1999—2003. Pub. CME Press. Mem. TESOL, IATEFL, Am. Women in Radio and TV, Soc. Tchr. Family Medicine (cons.), Pharm. Advt. Council, Nat. Council Jewish Women, Hadassah. Avocations: tennis, writing, piano. Home and Office: 7101 Grassland Ct Sarasota FL 34241 Personal E-mail: carolli@optonline.net.

LIEBERMAN, CHARLES, economist; b. Landsburg, Bavaria, Germany, July 25, 1948; s. Leo and Tola (Melcer) L.; m. Anne Rosenberg, Aug. 26, 1972; children: David, Michael, Jeremy. BS, MIT, 1970; AM in Econs., U. Pa., 1972, PhD in Econs., 1974. Asst. prof. U. Md., College Park, 1974-79; vis. assoc. prof. Northwestern U., Evanston, Ill., 1978-79; economist Fed. Res. Bank N.Y., NYC, 1979-81; sr. economist Morgan Stanley, NYC, 1981-83; v.p., sr. economist Shearson Lehman Bros., NYC, 1983-86; mng. dir., dir. fin. market rsch. Chem. Securities Inc./Mfrs. Hanover Securities Corp., NYC, 1986-96; chief economist The Global Bank, Chase Manhattan Bank, 1996-97; mng. ptnr. Strategic Investors, NYC, 1997—99; mng. mem. Lieberman Asset Mgmt. LLC, 1999—; chief investment officer Advisors Capital Mgmt., 2001—. Econs. commentator CNBC; bd. dirs. Bookrags, Inc., C3i, Inc. Author: (newsletter) Market Commentary; contbr. articles to profl. jours. Sgt. U.S. Army Res., 1970-76. Stonier fellow, 1973, NSF fellow, 1971. Mem. Forecasters Club N.Y. (treas. 1987-89, v.p. 1990-91, pres. 1991-92), Money Marketeers NYU (bd. govs., v.p., pres. 1992-93). Jewish. Avocations: tennis, skiing, classical music. Office: Advisors Capital Mgmt 115 W Century Rd Paramus NJ 07652 Office Phone: 201-986-1900. *Work hard, play hard, and enjoy life.*

LIEBERMAN, DAVE, chef; b. Pa. Grad., Yale U., 2003. Chef (cooking shows) Campus Cuisine, Good Deal, Food Network, Eat This; author: Young and Hungry: Making the Most of Fresh and Affordable Food. Office: The Home of Food Network 75 9th Ave New York NY 10011

LIEBERMAN, DOUGLAS MARK, lawyer; b. Flushing, NY, Aug. 17, 1960; s. Harvey Jack and Sandra Ann (Silver) Lieberman; m. Lori Ilene Nadel, Oct. 18, 1987. BA, SUNY, Plattsburgh, 1981; MA, U. Md., 1983; JD, Hofstra U., 1986. Bar: N.J. 1986, U.S. Dist. Ct. N.J. 1986, N.Y. 1987, U.S. Dist. Ct. (so. and ea. dists.) N.Y. 1987. Assoc. Zane & Rudofsky, NYC, 1986-90; ptnr. Markotsis & Lieberman, Hicksville, NY, 1990—. Editor-in-chief: newspaper Conscience, 1985—86, articles editor: Hofstra Labor Law Jour., 1985—86, assoc. editor: Nassau Lawyer, 2000—02, co-editor-in-chief:, 2002—04, chpt. editor: book Mechanics of Beginning, 1994; contbr. articles to profl. jours.; assoc. editor: Nassau Lawyer, 2004—. Scholar Alumni, Plattsburgh Coll. Found. SUNY, Rotary Club. Mem.: ABA, Nassau County Bar Assn., N.Y. State Bar Assn., Alpha Epsilon Rho, Phi Kappa Phi, Phi Alpha Delta. Democrat. Jewish. Avocations: ice hockey, golf, road racing, stamp collecting/philately. Office: 183 Broadway Ste 210 Hicksville NY 11801-4240

LIEBERMAN, EDWARD JAY, lawyer; b. Evansville, Ind., Apr. 8, 1946; s. Heiman George and Anna Sharp (Blacker) L.; m. Ellen Ackerman Wegusen, June 1, 1969; 1 child: Laura Amy. BSBA, Washington U., St. Louis, 1968, JD, 1971. Bar: Mo. 1971. Jr. ptnr. Bryan Cave, St. Louis, 1972-76; assoc. counsel 1st Nat. Bank in St. Louis, 1976-80; ptnr. Lowenhaupt, Chasnoff, Armstrong & Mellitz, St. Louis, 1980-84, Husch & Eppenberger, LLC, St. Louis, 1984—. Mem. ABA, Mo. Bar, Bar Assn. Met. St. Louis, Am. Coll. Mortgage Attys., Nat. Health Care Lawyers Assn. Office: Husch & Eppenberger LLC 190 Carondelet Plz Ste 600 Saint Louis MO 63105 E-mail: ed.lieberman@husch.com.

LIEBERMAN, GAIL FORMAN, financial consultant; b. Phila., May 26, 1943; d. Joseph and Rita Forman. BA in Physics and Math., Temple U., 1964, MBA in Fin., 1977. Dir. internat. fin. Std. Brands Inc., NYC, 1977-79; staff v.p. fin. and capital planning RCA Corp., 1979-82; CFO, exec. v.p. Scali McCabe Sloves, Inc., 1982-93; v.p. fin., CFO, mng. dir. Moody's Investors Svc., NYC, 1994-96; CFO TFPPG Thomson Corp., Boston, 1996-99; CEO Liquid Alternatives Inc., 2000; mng. ptnr. Rudder Capital LLC, 2001—. Bd. dirs. I-TRAX Corp., TriPath Imaging Ic., Breeze Eastern Corp. Mem. Fin. Execs. Inst. Office Phone: 917-207-4969. Personal E-mail: liebermang@earthlink.net.

LIEBERMAN, JAMES SANFORD, physiatrist, neurologist; b. Mpls., Apr. 24, 1938; BS, U. Calif., 1960, MD, 1963. Diplomate in neurology Am. Bd. Psychiatry and Neurology, in phys. medicine and reahb. Am. Bd. Phys. Medicine and Rehab. Instr., asst. prof. neurology SUNY, Downstate, 1967—71; asst. prof. neurology Columbia U., 1971—72; from asst. prof. to prof. phys. medicine and rehab. and neurology U. Calif., Davis, 1972-91, chmn. phys. medicine and rehab., 1982—91; prof., chmn. rehab. medicine Columbia U., NYC, 1991—, sr. assoc. dean, 1996—, asst. v.p. health sci., 1996—; prof. divsn. head rehab. medicine Cornell U., NYC, 2000—; physiatrist-in-chief NY Presbyn. Hosp., 2000—. Mem. NAS Inst. Medicine, Am. Acad. Clin. Neurophysiology, Am. Acad. Neurology, Am. Acad. Phys. Medicine and Rehab. Office: Columbia U 630 W 168th St Unit 38 New York NY 10032-3795 Home Phone: 914-725-5740; Office Phone: 212-305-4818. Office Fax: 212-305-3916. Business E-Mail: jsl12@columbia.edu.

LIEBERMAN, JANET ELAINE, academic administrator; b. NYC, Oct. 21, 1921; d. Samuel and Ida (Schubert) Rubensohn; m. Allen L. Chase, July 9, 1940 (div. 1954); children: Gary Andrew, Randolph H.; m. Jerrold S. Lieberman, June 30, 1957. Student, Vassar Coll., 1939-40; BA, Barnard Coll., NYC, 1943; MA, City Coll., NYC, 1946; PhD, NYU, NYC, 1965. Asst. prof. Hunter Coll., NYC, 1965-70; prof. LaGuardia C.C., Long Island City, NY, 1970-72, asst. dean faculty, 1972-74, prof. psychology, 1974-86, asst. to pres., 1986—, prof. emeritus, 2005. Cons. Ford Found., 2004, Woodrow Wilson Found., 2005. Recipient Innovation in Higher Edn. award Charles A. Dana Found., N.Y.C., 1989, Break the Mold award U.S. Dept. Edn., Washington, 1992, LaGuardia medal of honor, 2002, Disting. Alumni award NYU, 2003, McGraw Hill Ednl. Achievement award, 2004. Office: LaGuardia CC 31-10 Thomson Ave Long Island City NY 11101-3071 Office Phone: 718-482-5049.

LIEBERMAN, JOE (JOSEPH ISADORE LIEBERMAN), senator; b. Stamford, Conn., Feb. 24, 1942; s. Henry and Marcia (Manger) L.; m. Betty Haas, 1965 (div. 1981) children: Matthew, Rebecca; m. Hadassah Freilich, Mar. 20, 1983; 1 child Hana, 1 stepson Ethan BA in Politics & Economics, Yale U., 1964, JD, 1967; LLD (hon.), Trinity Coll., 2001. Bar: Conn. 1967. Atty. Wiggin & Dana, New Haven, 1967—69; co-chmn. Senator Robert F. Kennedy presdl. campaign, 1968; mem. Conn. State Senate, Hartford, Conn., 1971-81, majority leader, 1975-81; ptnr. Lieberman, Segaloff & Wolfson, New Haven, 1972-83; atty. gen. State of Conn., Hartford, Conn., 1983-89; US Senator from Conn., 1989—. Mem. armed svcs. com., environment & pub. works com., homeland security & govtl. affairs com., small bus.& entrepreneurship com.; chmn. Dem. Leadership Coun., 1995-2001; Dem. nominee for v.p. US, 2000; bd. dirs. Nixon Ctr. Peace & Freedom. Author: The Power Broker: A Biography of John M. Bailey, Modern Political Boss, 1966, The Scorpion and the Tarantula: The Struggle to Control Atomic Weapons, 1970, The Legacy, 1981, Child Support in America: Practical Advice for Negotiating-and Collecting-A Fair Settlement, 1986; co-author (with Michael D'Orso) In Praise of Public Life, 2000, (with Haddash Lieberman and Sarah Crichton) An Amazing Adventure: Joe and Hadassah's Personal Notes on the 2000 Campaign, 2003. Recipient Henry M. Jackson Disting. Svc. award, Jewish Inst. for Nat. Security Affairs, 1997, Disting. Am. award, John F. Kennedy Library, 2001, Human Rels. award, Nat. Conf. for Community & Justice, 2001, Congl. Leadership award, Am. Jewish Com., 2001, Founders Circle award, TechNet, 2002. Independent. Jewish. Office: 706 Hart Senate Office Bldg Washington DC 20510-0001*

LIEBERMAN, JOSEFA NINA, retired psychologist, writer; b. Jaroslaw, Poland, May 16, 1921; came to U.S., 1946; d. David Samuel and Rosa Zerline (Leinwand) Margules; m. Meyer Frank Lieberman, Feb. 12, 1956. BS, Columbia U., 1957, MA, 1959, PhD in Ednl. Psychology, 1964. Lic.

psychologist, N.Y. Lectr. Bklyn. Coll., 1964-65, asst. prof., 1965-71, assoc. prof., 1972-79, prof., 1979-83, prof. emerita, 1983—. Spkr. in field. Author: Playfulness: Its Relationship to Imagination and Creativity, 1977, Japanese translation, 1981, He Came to Cambridge, 1982, (chpt.) I Came Alone, 1990, The Salzburg Connection: An Adolescence Remembered, 2004; contbr. articles to profl. jours. and newspapers. Mem., chair Hillel Found., Bklyn., 1964—83; founding mem. Solomon Schechter H.S.l, Bklyn., 1971; mem. Sr. Recreation, Woodstock, NY, 1984—; vol. Jewish Family Svc.; pen pal RSV. Recipient fellowships and rsch. grants NIMH, 1958-78. Mem. APA, Phi Beta Kappa, Sigma Xi. Democrat. Avocations: languages, music, chess. Home: 648 Zena Rd Woodstock NY 12498 Personal E-mail: jnina@aol.com.

LIEBERMAN, JUDITH L., retired special education educator; b. Waukegan, Ill., Mar. 31, 1945; d. Norton E. and Esther Landfield; children: Jonathan, Natalie. BS in Speech Correction, U. Ill., 1967; MA in Speech Pathology, 1968. Spl. edn. tchr. Los Angeles Unified Sch. Dist., Sylmar, Calif.; speech pathologist Camarillo State Hosp., Calif., Fullerton Sch. Dist., Calif.; hearing clinician Spl. Sch. Dist., St. Louis. Mem. clinician Calif. Readers, Granada Hills. Mem. Holocaust ednl. bd. mem. Anti Defamation League, Los Angeles; v.p. legal adv. fund Am. Assn. U. Women. Home: 247 Odebolt Dr Thousand Oaks CA 91360

LIEBERMAN, LAURA CROWELL, arts administrator, artist, critic; b. Oak Ridge, Tenn., Apr. 7, 1952; d. Bernard and Lisbeth (Crowell) L.; m. William R. Gignilliat, III, Mar. 20, 1984; children: William R. Gignilliat, IV, Elizabeth Ann Gignilliat. BA in English Lit., Swarthmore Coll., 1974. Tchr. remedial reading Paulding County Schs., Dallas, Ga., 1974-75; critic, writer Atlanta, 1976-77, 89-92; artist-in-residence Atlanta Women's Art Collective, 1977-78; editor-in-chief Art Papers, Atlanta, 1979-84; arts editor So. Accents Mag., Atlanta, 1985-88; dir. Arts Clearinghouse Bur. Cultural Affairs, Atlanta, 1992—. Publicist Gt. Am. Gallery, Atlanta, 1988-92; lectr. Ala. Attists Gallery, Montgomery, 1991; cons., juror, panelist and lectr. in field. Contbr. articles to Afterimage, Atlanta Mag., Am. Ceramics, Atlanta Jour.-Constn., Fulton County Daily Report, So. Homes, So. Accents, Southpoint, others. Founding bd. dirs. Whittier Mills Village Neighborhood, 1990—, S.E. Arts Exch., 1984-85; bd. dirs. Atlanta Art Workers Coalition, others. Home: 3 Spring Cir NW Atlanta GA 30318-1024

LIEBERMAN, LAURENCE, poet, educator; b. Detroit, Feb. 16, 1935; s. Nathan and Anita (Cohen) L.; m. Bernice Clair Braun, June 17, 1956; children— Carla, Deborah, Isaac. BA, U. Mich., 1956, MA in English, 1958; postgrad., U. Calif.-Berkeley. Prof. English Coll. V.I., 1964-68; prof. English and creative writing U. Ill., Urbana, 1968—. U. Ill. Ctr. for Advanced Study Creative Writing fellow, Japan, 1971-72 Author: The Unblinding, 1968, The Achievement of James Dickey, 1969, The Osprey Suicides, 1973, Unassigned Frequencies: American Poetry in Review (1964-77), 1977, God's Measurements, 1980, Eros At the World Kite Pageant, 1983, The Mural of Wakeful Sleep, 1985, (poems) The Creole Mephistopheles, 1989, The Best American Poetry, 1991 (award), New and Selected Poems (1962-92), 1993, The St. Kitts. Monkey Feuds, 1995, Beyond the Muse of Memory: Essays on Contemporary Poets, 1995, Dark Songs: Slave House and Synagogue, 1996, Compass of the Dying, 1998, The Regatta in the Skies: Selected Long Poems, 1999, Flight From the Mother Stone, 2000, Hour of The Mango Black Moon, 2004, Carib's Leap: Selected and New Poems, 2005, numerous poems; poetry editor U. Ill. Press, 1970—. Recipient award for Best Poems of 1968, Nat. Endowment for Arts, 1969, Jerome P. Shestack award Am. Poetry Rev., 1986; creative writing fellow U. Ill. Ctr. for Advanced Study, 2000—, Nat. Endowment Arts, 1986-87. Office: U Ill English Dept 608 S Wright St Urbana IL 61801-3630

LIEBERMAN, LESTER ZANE, engineering company executive; b. Newark, July 4, 1930; s. Herman P. and Cecile A. (Ashenfeld) Lieberman; m. Judith Mazor, Aug. 11, 1957; children: Susan, Jane. BSME, Newark Coll. Engring., 1951, postgrad., 1953—58; DHL (hon.), Clarkson U., 1991, U. Medicine and Dentistry NJ, 2005. Registered profl. engr., N.J., Pa. Pres. Crest Engring. Inc., Newark, 1955—60; chmn., pres. Atmos Engring. Co. Inc., Kenilworth, NJ, 1960—78; pres., CEO, Clarkson Industries, Inc., NYC, 1978—90; real estate investment and development Dowel Assoc., 1990—; partner, cons. Construction HVAC, 1990—. Bd. dirs. Lazard Fund, Cives Steel Corp. Chmn. Beth Israel Med. Ctr., Newark, 1970—96, N.J. Healthcare Found., 1996—, Irvington Gen. Hosp., 1992—96; mem. coun. N.J. Performing Arts Ctr., Pub. Health Rsch. Inst., N.J. Med. Sch.; trustee Clarkson U., Potsdam, NY. Named Alumnus of the Yr., Newark Coll. Engring., 1980; recipient Friendship award, Best Friends Newark, 1999, Humanitarian award, St. Barnabas' Burn Found., 1999, Citizens award, N.J. Acad. Medicine, 2000, Cmty. award, Y Camps N.J., 2000, Humanitarian award, United Jewish Cmtys., 2004. Mem.: NSPE, ASHRAE, Am. Acad. Environ. Engrs. (diplomate), N.J. Soc. Profl. Engrs., Cornell Club (N.Y.), Mountain Ridge Country Club (N.J.), Stockbridge Country Club (Mass.), Masons, Tau Beta Pi (Key award 1982). Jewish. Avocations: skiing, sailing, tennis, golf. Home: 685 Spring Valley Rd Morristown NJ 07960-7011 Office: 25 Lindsley Dr Morristown NJ 07960-4455 Office Phone: 973-401-0070. Personal E-mail: leszl@aol.com.

LIEBERMAN, LOUIS (KARL LIEBERMAN), artist; b. Bklyn., May 7, 1944; s. Abraham and Jeannette (Feinberg) L. BFA, R.I. Sch. Design, 1969; cert., Bklyn. Mus. Art Sch., 1964; BA, Bklyn. Coll., 1966. Adj. lectr. Bklyn. Coll., 1971-78, Lehman Coll., Bronx, NY, 1972-75; vis. artist Ill. State U., Normal, 1978, Hamilton Coll., Clinton, NY, 1982. One-man shows include Vancouver Art Gallery, B.C., Can., 1969, James Yu Gallery, N.Y.C., 1973, 74, Nina Freudenheim Gallery, Buffalo, 1976, Root Art Ctr., Hamilton Coll., Clinton, N.Y., 1980, Harm Bouckaert Gallery, N.Y.C., 1981, John Davis Gallery, Akron, Ohio, 1983, 85, Columbus Mus. Art, Ohio, 1983, John Davis Gallery, N.Y.C., 1986; group shows include Aldrich Mus. Contemporary Art, Ridgefield, Conn., 1973, 74, Johnson Mus. Art, Ithaca, N.Y., 1981, Fine Arts Mus. L.I., Hempstead, N.Y., 1982, Cleve. Inst. Art, 1982, Met. Mus. Art, N.Y.C., 1983, Byer Mus. Art, Evanston, Ill., 1982, Visual Arts Ctr., Beer-Sheva, Israel, 1985, Kunsthauses, Zurich, Switzerland, McNay Art Mus., San Antonio, Phila. Mus. of Art, 1988, Erie (Pa.) Art Mus., 1988, Art Mus. of Santa Cruz, Calif., 1988, Hunter Mus., Chattanooga, 1989, others; represented in permanent collections including Kenan Ctr., Lockport, N.Y., Aldridge Mus. Contemporary Art, Ridgefield, Conn., Met. Mus. Art, N.Y.C., Phila. Mus. Art, Stamford (Conn.) Mus., Bklyn. Mus., Mus. Fine Arts, Budapest, Hungary, Istvan Kiraly Mus., Budapest, Ackland Art Mus., Chapel Hill, N.C.; art critic N.Y. Arts Jour., 1978-79. Recipient Sculpture award Creative Artist Pub. Service Found., 1971-72, Graphics award Creative Artist Pub. Svc. Found., 1980-81, Graphics award N.Y. Found. Arts, 1984-85; visual arts fellow Nat. Endowment for Arts, 1979-80; Pollack-Krasner Found. fellow, 1987; Adolf and Esther Gottlieb Found. grantee, 1989. Achievements include development of Aqua-Resin polymer product.

LIEBERMAN, MARVIN SAMUEL, lawyer; b. NYC, Apr. 26, 1935; s. Abe and Gertrude (Connelly) L.; m. Kathryn Fuhrer, Aug. 10, 1963; children: Kathryn, Willis. BA, Lafayette Coll., 1955; JD, Rutgers U., 1962. Bar: NJ 1962, US Ct. Appeals (3d cir.) 1965; cert. civil trial atty., NJ. Assoc. Jacob, Alfred & Richardson Levinson, Perth Amboy, NJ, 1962-69; ptnr. Levinson, Conover, Lieberman & Fink, Perth Amboy, NJ, 1969-71, Lieberman & Ryan, Somerville, NJ, 1971-83, 88-95, Lieberman, Ryan, Richardson, Welaj & Miller, Somerville, NJ, 1983-87, Lieberman, Ryan & Forrest, Somerville, NJ, 1995—2006, Lieberman, Ryan, Forrest & Voorhees, 2007—. With USAF, 1955-58. Mem. ATLA, NJ Bar Assn., NJ Trial Lawyers Assn., Middlesex County Trial Lawyers Assn., NJ Lawyers Assn., Am. Bd. Trial Advs. Home: 14 Riverview Terr Hillsborough NJ 08844 Office: Lieberman Ryan Forrest & Voorhees 141 W End Ave Somerville NJ 08876-1809 also: 84 Park Ave Flemington NJ 08822 Office Phone: 908-231-8844. Business E-Mail: liryfo@aol.com. E-mail: mlieberman@liryfo.com.

LIEBERMAN, MICHAEL J., lawyer; b. 1951; BA summa cum laude, SUNY Albany, 1972; JD, Harvard U., 1976; LLM, NYU, 1984. Bar: NY 1976, Mass. 1995. Atty., leader Tax Practice Group Fine & Ambrogne; ptnr., chmn. & mgr., Tax Sect. Mintz Levin Cohn Ferris Glovsky & Popeo PC, Boston. Office: Mintz Levin Cohn Ferris Glovsky & Popeo PC One Financial Ctr Boston MA 02111 Office Phone: 617-348-1682. Office Fax: 617-542-2241. Business E-Mail: mlieberman@mintz.com.

LIEBERMAN, NANCY ANN, lawyer; b. NYC, Dec. 30, 1956; d. Elias and Elayne Hildegarde (Fox) L.; m. Mark Ellman, Sept. 6, 1997. BA summa cum laude, U. Rochester, 1977; JD, U. Chgo., 1979; LLM in Taxation, NYU, 1981. Bar: N.Y. 1980. Intern White House, Washington, 1975; law clk. Hon. Henry A. Politz U.S. Ct. Appeals (5th cir.), Shreveport, La., 1979-80; assoc. Skadden Arps Slate Meagher & Flom LLP, NYC, 1981-87, ptnr., 1987—. Trustee U. Rochester, 1994-2004, 2007-, Citizens Budget Commn., 2007-; bd. dirs. Pacific Coun. Internat. Policy, 2003-. Mem. ABA, Assn. Bar City N.Y., Coun. Fgn. Rels., Phi Beta Kappa. Republican. Jewish. Office: Skadden Arps Slate Meagher & Flom LLP 4 Times Sq New York NY 10036-6595 Home: 435 E 52d St New York NY 10022 Office Phone: 212-735-2050. Business E-Mail: nlieberman@skadden.com.

LIEBERMAN, ROCHELLE PHYLLIS, small business owner; b. Bklyn., June 27, 1940; d. Solomon and Freda (Shapiro) Beller; m. Melvyn Lieberman, June 10, 1961; children: Eric Neil, Marc Evan. BA, Bklyn. Coll., 1961; MEd, Duke U., 1977. Tchr. Bklyn. pub. schs., 1961-64; instr. Carolina Friends, Durham, NC, 1967-70; grad. intern Duke U., Durham, 1974-75, faculty adviser, 1975-76; sales assoc. Kelly Matherly, Durham, 1978-81; pres. Shelli, Inc., Durham, 1981—. Treas. Duke Forest Assn., Durham, 1980—85; pres. Bus. Commn., 2004; mem. Predl. Bus. Commn., 2005, Nat. Rep. Congl. Com., Congl. Bus. Adv. Coun. Named NRCC Businesswoman of Yr., Duke-Durham Campaign, 2006. Mem. LWV, Durham and Chapel Hill Bd. Realtors, Women's Council of Realtors (sec. 1980-81), Duke U. Eye Ctr. (adv. bd.), Kappa Delta Pi. Clubs: Duke Faculty, Duke Campus (Durham). Jewish. Avocations: piano, walking, knitting, writing, reading. Office: Shelli Inc 1110 Woodburn Rd Durham NC 27705-5738 Home Phone: 919-493-3640; Office Phone: 919-489-8829. Personal E-mail: shelliinc@aol.com.

LIEBERMAN-CLINE, NANCY, sports commentator, former professional basketball coach and player; b. July 1, 1958; m. Tim Cline, 1988; 1 child, Timothy Joseph. Grad., Old Dominion U., 1981. Guard WBL's Dallas Diamonds, 1980-86, USBL's L.I. Knights, 1986-87, Washington Generals, 1987-88, Athletes in Action, 1996-97, WNBA - Phoenix Mercury, 1997; head coach, gen. mgr. WNBA - Detroit Shock, 1998—2000; now sports commentator. Women's basketball analyst NBA Broadcasting, ESPN, ABC, ESPN 2, Fox Sports Network, NBC. Recipient Broderick Cup, 1979, 80, Wade Trophy (2), U.S. Olympic Silver medal, 1976; named All- Am., 1978-80, ODU Outstanding Female Athlete of Yr., 1977-80; mem. Women's Am. Basketball Championship team, 1985; Named to Basketball Hall of Fame, 1996. Home: 2636 Creekway Dr Carrollton TX 75010-4227

LIEBERMANN, LOWELL, composer, conductor, pianist; b. NYC, Feb. 22, 1961; D in Musical Arts, Juilliard Sch.; studied with David Diamond, Vincent Persichetti, Jacob Lateiner, Laszlo Halasz. Composer-in-residence Dallas Symphony, 1999-2002. Composer (orchestra) War Songs for Bass Voice and Orch. Op. 7, 1981, Concertino for Cello and Chamber Orch. Op. 8, 1982, Symphony No. 1 Op. 9 (BMI award, 1st prize Juilliard Orch. Competition 1987), 1982, Three Poems of Stephen Crane Op. 11 for baritone, string orch., two horns, harp (Devora Nadworney award Nat. Fed. Music Clubs 1986) 1983, Concerto No. 1 for Piano and Orch. Op. 12, 1983, Sechs Gesaenge Nach Gedichten Von Nelly Sachs Op. 18 for soprano and orch., 1986, The Domain of Arnheim Op. 33, 1990, Concerto No. 2 for Piano and Orch. Op. 36, 1992, Flute Concerto Op. 39, 1992, Revelry for Orch. Op. 47, 1995, Concerto for Flute, Harp, and Orch. Op. 48, 1995; (opera) The Picture of Dorian Gray Op. 45, 1995, (chorus) Two Choral Elegies Op. 2 for SATB a capella (Fred Waring Choral award Nat. Fed. Music 1978), 1977, Missa Brevis Op. 15 for SATB chorus, tenor and baritone solos, organ (3d prize Ch. and Artist Composers Competition 1987), 1985; (piano solo) Piano Sonata Op. 1 (Outstanding Composition award Yamaha Music Found. 1982, 1st prize Nat. Composition Contest Music Tchrs. Nat. Assn. 1978), 1977, Piano Sonata No. 2 Sonata Notturna Op. 10, 1983, Variations on a Theme by Anton Bruckner Op. 19, 1987, Nocturne No. 1 Op. 20, 1987, Four Apparitions Op. 17, 1987, others; (chamber music) Sonata for Violoncello and Piano Op. 3, 1978, Two Pieces for Violin and Viola Op. 4, 1978, Sonata for Viola and Piano Op. 13 (1st Place Victor Herbert/ASCAP awards Nat. Fed. Music Clubs 1986, Brian Israel prize Soc. for New Music 1986), 1984, Sonata for Contrabass and Piano Op. 24, 1987, Fantasy on a Fugue by J.S. Bach Op. 27 for flute, oboe, clarinet, horn, bassoon, piano, 1989, Quintet for Piano and Strings Op. 34 for piano and string quartet, 1989, Concert for Trumpet and Orchestra Op. 64, 1999, Symphony No. 2 Op. 67, 1999, Three Impromptus Op. 68)Grand prize Van Cliburn Internat. Piano Competition 2001, First Am. Composers Invitational prize); others; recordings: Piano Concerto on Hyperion with pianist Stephen Hough, James Galway plays Lowell Liebermann on BMG Classics; also organ music, voice and piano. Nominee Grammy award for best classical contemporary composition for Piano Concerto No. 2, 1997. Mem. ASCAP, NARAS. Office: c/o Theodore Presser Co 588 North Gulph Rd King Of Prussia PA 19406 Business E-Mail: lowelll@lowellliebermann.com.

LIEBERSON, PETER, composer; b. NYC, Oct. 25, 1946; s. Goddard Lieberson and Vera Zorina; m. Lorraine Hunt Lieberson. BA in English, NYU; degree, Columbia U.; PhD, Brandeis U. Prodn. engr. WNCN-FM radio, NY; dir. Shambhala Training Internat., Halifax, exec. dir., 1989; tchr. Harvard U., 1984—88. Composer: Piano Concerto, 1983 (Contemporary Music award Opus mag., 1985), Drala, 1986, Fire, 1996, Variations for Violin and Piano, 1996, Horn Concerto, 1999, Free and Easy Wanderer, Piano Quintet, Piano Concert No. 3, Red Garuda, 1999, Ah, Six Realms, 2000, Piano Fantasy, 2000, The Ocean that has no West and no East, 2000, (Operas) King Gesar, Ashoka's Dream, 1997. Recipient Brandeis Creative Arts award. Mem.: AAAL.

LIEBERSON, STANLEY, sociologist, educator; b. Montreal, Que., Can., Apr. 20, 1933; s. Jack and Ida (Cohen) L.; m. Patricia Ellen Beard, 1960; children— Rebecca, David, Miriam, Rachel (dec.). Student, Bklyn. Coll., 1950-52; MA, U. Chgo., 1958, PhD, 1960; MA (hon.), Harvard U., 1988; LHD (hon.), U. Ariz., 1993. Assoc. dir. Iowa Urban Cmty. Rsch. Ctr., U. Iowa, 1959-61, instr., asst. prof. sociology, 1959-61; asst. prof. sociology U. Wis., 1961-63, assoc. prof., 1963-66, prof., 1966-67; prof. sociology U. Wash., 1967-71, dir. Ctr. Studies Demography and Ecology, 1968-71; prof. sociology U. Chgo., 1971-74, assoc. dir. Population Rsch. Ctr., 1971-74; prof. sociology U. Ariz., Tucson, 1974-83, head dept., 1976-79; prof. sociology U. Calif., Berkeley, 1983-88, Harvard U., Cambridge, Mass., 1988—91, Abbott Lawrence Lowell prof. sociology, 1991—2007, Abbott Lawrence Lowell rsch. prof. sociology, 2007—. Vis. prof. Stanford U., summer 1970; Claude Bissell disting. vis. prof. U. Toronto, 1979-80; Christensen fellow Oxford U., St. Catherine's Coll., 2001; mem. com. on sociolinguistics Social Sci. Rsch. Coun., 1964-70; mem. sociology panel NSF, 1978-81 Author: (with others) Metropolis and Region, 1960, Ethnic Patterns in American Cities, 1963; editor: Explorations in Sociolinguistics, 1967, (with Beverly Duncan) Metropolis and Region in Transition, 1970, Language and Ethnic Relations in Canada, 1970, A Piece of the Pie, 1980, Language Diversity and Language Contact, 1981, Making It Count, 1985, (with Mary C. Waters) From Many Strands, 1988, A Matter of Taste, 2000 (co-winner book award culture sect. Am. Sociol. Assn. 2001, Mirra Komarovsky book award Ea. Sociol. Soc. 2002); assoc. editor: Social Problems, 1965-67, Sociol. Methods and Research, 1971-96; editorial cons. Sociol. Inquiry, 1965-67; adv. editor: Am. Jour. Sociology, 1969-74; editorial bd. Lang. in Society, 1972-74, Internat. Jour. Sociology of Lang, 1974-2000, Canadian Jour. Sociology, 1975-2000, Social Forces, 1980-83; adv. council Sociol. Abstracts, 1972-73, Language Problems and Language Planning, 1984-87; mem. editorial com. Ann. Rev. Sociology, 1992-96. Recipient Colver Rosenberger Ednl. prize, 1960, Paul F. Lazarsfeld award, 2007; Guggenheim fellow, 1972-73, fellow Ctr. for Advanced Study in Behavioral Scis., 1995-96, Sackler Inst. for Advanced Study, Tel Aviv U., 1999, Stanfor U. Ctr. Study Poverty and Inequality. Fellow: NAS, Am. Acad. Arts and Scis.; mem.: Am. Philos. Soc., Am. Sociol. Assn., Ea. Sociol. Soc. (Mirra Komarovsky Book award 2002), Am. Name Soc., Sociol. Rsch. Assn. (exec. com. 1976—81, pres. 1981), Phi Beta Kappa (hon.), Pacific Sociol. Assn. (v.p. 1984—85, pres. 1986—87), Internat. Population Union, Population Assn. Am. (dir. 1969—72), Am. Sociol. Found. (trustee 1992—96), Am. Sociol. Assn. (coun. mem. 1985—87, pres. 1990—91, Disting. Contbn. to Scholarship award 1982, co-winner culture sect. award 2001). Office: Harvard U Dept Sociology William James Hall Cambridge MA 02138 Office Phone: 617-495-3818. E-mail: SL@WJH.harvard.edu.

LIEBERT, LYNN LANGENBACH, psychologist, educator; b. Bayshore, NY, June 1, 1962; d. Herbert John and Joan Charlotte Langenbach; m. Robert Mandel Liebert (dec.); children: Rachel Lynn, Richard Karl. BA in Psychology, State U. NY-Stony Brook, 1987, MA in Psychology, 1990, PhD in Clin. Psychology, 1995. Consulting psychologist neurology SUNY at Stony Brook, 1995—99; psychologist Sagamore Children's Psychiat. Ctr., Dix Hills, 2001—03; psychology instr. Suffolk County C.C., Brentwood, 2003—, asst. acad. chair social scis. dept. Co-author: (book) Personality: Strategies and Issues, 8th ed., 1998, Science and Behavior: An Introduction, 1995; contbr. articles to profl. jours. Elder First Presbyterian Ch. Port Jefferson, 2005—. Mem.: APA, Nat. Parent Tchr. Assn. Avocations: drawing, painting, poetry. Office: Suffolk County CC Social Sci Dept Crooked Hill Rd Brentwood NY 11717

LIEBESKIND, RICHARD, lawyer; b. New Haven, June 11, 1958; AB magna cum laude, Duke U., 1980; JD, Columbia U., 1984. Bar: NY 1985, DC 2002, US Dist. Ct. (DC, so. & ea. dist. NY), US Ct. Appeals (DC cir.). Assoc. Cravath Swaine & Moore, NYC; trial atty. and asst. chief, antitrust div. U.S. Dept. Justice, Washington; dep. asst. dir. Mergers III div. FTC, Washington, asst. dir. Bureau of Competition; ptnr. antitrust and competition practice Pillsbury Winthrop Shaw Pittman, Washington, 2002—. Contbr. articles to profl. jours. Recipient Rand Dixon award, FTC, 1998; Harlan Fiske Stone scholar. Mem.: ABA. Office: Pillsbury Winthrop Shaw Pittman 2300 N St NW NW Washington DC 20037 Office Phone: 202-663-9238. Office Fax: 202-513-8264. Business E-Mail: richard.liebeskind@pillsburylaw.com.

LIEBHABER, MYRON I., allergist; b. Dec. 28, 1943; MD, U. Ariz., 1972. Allergist Coll. Hosp., Santa Barbara, Calif. Assoc. vis. clin. prof. UCLA. Office: Sansum Med Found Clinic 215 Pesetas Ln Santa Barbara CA 93110-1416 Home Phone: 805-963-8033; Office Phone: 805-681-7635. Business E-Mail: mliebhab@sansumclinic.org. E-mail: mil1258@pol.net.

LIEBLING, DEBBIE (DEBORAH LIEBLING), film company executive; Grad., Boston U., 1981. Exec. FX, MTV; west coast exec. prodn. Nickelodeon; sr. v.p. original programming and develop. Comedy Central, 1996—2002; exec. v.p. prodn. 20th Century Fox, 2002—07; pres. prodn. Fox Atomic, 2007—. Co-prodr.: (films) South Park: Bigger, Longer and Uncut. Named one of 100 Most Powerful Women in Entertainment, Hollywood Reporter, 2006; recipient Two CableAce awards. Office: Fox Atomic 20th Century Fox Film Corp 10201 W Pico Blvd Los Angeles CA 90064*

LIEBLING, JEROME, photographer, educator; b. NYC, Apr. 16, 1924; s. Maurice and Sarah (Goodman) L.; married, Nov. 11, 1949 (div. 1969); children: Madeline, Tina, Adam, Daniella, Rachel Jane. Student, Bklyn. Coll., 1942, 46, 48, New Sch. for Social Research, NYC, 1948-49; LLD (hon.), Portland Sch. Art, Maine, 1989. Prof. photography U. Minn., Mpls., 1949-69; prof. SUNY-New Paltz, 1957-58, Yale U., New Haven, 1976-77, Hampshire Coll., Amherst, Mass., 1970—. Author, photographer: Jerome Liebling Photographs (Best of Yr. 1982), Aperture, N.Y.C., 1988, The People Yes, The Photographs of Jerome Liebling, Aperture, 1995; editor: Photography-Current Perspective, 1977, Jerome Liebling: The Minnesota Photographs, 1997, The Dickinsons of Amherst, 2001. Served with U.S. Army, 1942-45, ETO, Africa. Fellow Mass. Arts Found., 1975, Nat. Endowman Arts, 1979, Guggenheim, 1977, 81; recipient Umhoefer prize Arts and Humanities Found., 2002; named The Jerome Liebling Ctr. for Film, Photography andVideo, Hampshire Coll., Amherst, Mass., 2004. Mem.: Soc. Photog. Edn. (named Educator of Yr. 2004). Home: 39 Dana St Amherst MA 01002-2208 Office: Hampshire Coll West St Amherst MA 01002-2954 Office Phone: 413-549-5507. Personal E-mail: jliebling@verizon.net. Business E-Mail: rnordstrom@hampshire.edu.

LIEBMAN, GREGG, communications executive; b. 1970; BS in Mgmt., State U. of NY, Binghamton. Sr. rsch. analyst Foote, Cone & Belding; mgr., Ad Sales Rsch. MTV, 1995—98; media rsch. dir., ptnr. J. Walter Thompson, NY; mgr., rsch. dept. DoubleClick; rsch. dir. Team One, Hal Riney & Partners, Saatchi & Saatchi, ZGPE; sr. v.p. rsch. dir. Zenith Media Optomedia; v.p., Ad Sales Rsch. CNN. Named one of 40 Executives Under 40, Multichannel News, 2006. Office: Cable News Network Lp LLLP 1 CNN Ctr Atlanta GA 30303

LIEBMAN, JUDITH RAE STENZEL, retired operations research specialist; b. Denver, July 2, 1936; d. Raymond Oscar and Mary Madelyn (Gallop) Stenzel; m. Jon Charles Liebman, Dec. 27, 1958; children: Christopher Brian, Rebecca Anne, Michael Jon. BA in Physics, U. Colo., Boulder, 1958; PhD in Ops. Rsch., Johns Hopkins U., 1971. Successively asst. prof., head indsl. systems, assoc. prof. U. Ill., Urbana, 1972-84, prof., 1984-96, prof. emerita, 1996—, acting vice chancellor for rsch., 1986-87, vice chancellor for rsch., 1987-92, acting dean Grad. Coll., 1987-92, dean, 1987-92. Vis. prof. Tianjin (China) U., 1983; charter mem. Ill. Gov.'s Sci. Adv. Com., Ill. Exec. Com., 1989-92; mem. adv. com. for engring. NSF, 1988-92, chmn., 1991-92; mem. NRC Bd. Engring. Edn., 1997-2001, Army Sci. Bd., 1997-99. Author: Modeling and Optimization with GINO, 1986; author numerous articles in field. Bd. dirs. United Way, Champaign, Ill., 1986-91, U. Colo. Found., 1999-2003; bd. dirs. East Cen. Ill. Health Systems Agy., Champaign, 1977-82, pres., 1980-82; trustee U. Colo. Found., 2003—. Mem. Ops. Rsch. Soc. Am. (pres. 1987-88), INFORMS, Nat. Assn. State Univs. and Land Grant Colls. (exec. bd. 1990-92), Rotary, Sigma Xi, Sigma Pi Sigma, Alpha Pi Mu, Phi Kappa Phi. Home: 110 W Whitehall Ct Urbana IL 61801-6664

LIEBMAN, LANCE MALCOLM, law educator; b. Newark, Sept. 11, 1941; s. Roy and Barbara (Trilinsky) L.; m. Carol Bensinger, June 28, 1964; children: Jeffrey, Benjamin. BA, Yale U., 1962; MA, Cambridge U., 1964; LLB, Harvard U., 1967. Bar: DC 1968, Mass. 1976, NY, 1995. Asst.

to Mayor Lindsay, NYC, 1968-70; asst. prof. law Harvard U., 1970-76, prof., 1976-91, assoc. dean, 1981-84; dean, Lucy G. Moses prof. law Columbia U. Sch. Law, NYC, 1991-96, prof., dir. Parker Sch. Fgn. Law, 1996—, Williams S. Beinecke prof. law, 1998—; dir. Am. Law Inst., 1998—. Successor trustee Yale Corp., 1971-83 Office: Columbia U Sch Law 435 W 116th St New York NY 10027-7297 Office Phone: 212-854-5699. E-mail: lliebman@law.columbia.edu.

LIEBMAN, PAMELA, real estate company executive; b. NYC; Grad., U. Mass., Amherst; attended, European Bus. Sch., London. Broker The Corcoran Group, 1985—90, dir., downtown office, 1989—90, ptnr., founder mktg. div., 1990—2000, pres., CEO, 2000—. Lecturer NYU, 92nd St. Y, NY Real Estate Bd. Mem. Young President's Org.; founding bd. mem. Wipe Out Leukemia Forever Found.; bd. mem. Leukemia and Lymphoma Soc. Named one of 50 Most Powerful Women in NY, NY Post, 2003. Office: Corcoran Group 36 E 12th St New York NY 10003*

LIEBMAN, RONALD STANLEY, lawyer; b. Balt., Oct. 11, 1943; s. Harry Martin and Martha (Altgenug) L.; m. Simma Liebman, Jan. 8, 1972; children: Shana, Margot. BA, McDaniel Coll., Westminster, 1966; JD, U. Md., 1969. Bar: Md. 1969, U.S. Dist. Ct. Md. 1970, U.S. Ct. Appeals (4th cir.) 1972, D.C. 1977, U.S. Dist. Ct. D.C. 1982, U.S. Ct. Appeals (D.C. cir.) 1982, U.S. Ct. Appeals (5th cir.) 1985, U.S. Ct. Appeals (2nd cir.) 1988, U.S. Ct. Appeals (11th cir.) 1991, U.S. Ct. Appeals (9th cir.) 1992, U.S. Dist. Ct. (no. dist.) Calif. 1994, U.S. Supreme Ct. 1995, U.S. Ct. Appeals (7th cir.) 1996, U.S. Dist. Ct. (ea. dist.) Tex. 1999, U.S. Ct. Appeals (10th cir.) 2003. Law clk. to chief judge U.S. Dist. Ct. Md., 1969-70; assoc. Melnicove, Kaufman & Weiner, Balt., 1970-72; asst. U.S. atty. Office of U.S. Atty., Dept. Justice, Balt., 1972-78; ptnr. Sachs, Greenebaum & Tayler, Washington, 1978-82; ptnr., Litigation & Dispute Resolution, White Collar Criminal Def. practices Patton Boggs LLP, Washington, 1982—, mem. exec. com. Author: Grand Jury, 1983, Shark Tales, 2000; co-editor: Testimonial Privileges, 1st edit., 1983. Recipient spl. commendation award U.S. Dept. Justice, 1978. Mem. ABA, DC Bar Assn., Md. Bar Assn. Office: Patton Boggs LLP 2550 M St NW Washington DC 20037-1350 Office Phone: 202-457-6310. Office Fax: 202-457-6315. Business E-Mail: rliebman@pattonboggs.com.

LIEBMAN, SARAH, artist, educator; b. Bklyn. Student, Bklyn. Mus. Art Sch., 1963—69; BA cum laude, CUNY, Bklyn., 1976; MEd, Pratt Inst., Bklyn., 1977; MFA, CUNY, Bklyn., 1978; EdD, Columbia U., NYC, 1990. Illustrator Dorcelle Creations, Inc., NYC, 1967—70; recreational dir. Bayview Manor, Bklyn., 1970—71; artist-in-residence Bklyn. Coll. Early Childhood Ctr., 1977; instr. art Bklyn. Coll. Inst. Ret. Profls., 1979—80; tchr. art Ssephardic Cmty. Ctr., Bklyn., 1981—83; lectr., tchr. art Bronx Emanuel Camps, Copake, NY, 1984; instr. art Bklyn. Coll., 1983—87; lectr., tchr. art U. Conn., Stamford, 1991—92. One-woman shows include Bklyn. Mus., 1967—69, 1979, Darcia Gallery, NYC, 1978, 1979, Audubon Artiss, Inc., 1979, Salmagundi Art Club, 1980, Nat. Assn. Woman Artists, 1981, 1982, 1983, 1984, Catherine Loriland Wolf Art Club, 1982, Nat. Coun. Art Jewish Life, 1983. Fellow, Pratt Inst. Mem.: Kappa Delta Pi.

LIEBMAN, THEODORE, architect; b. Newark, May 7, 1939; s. Edward and Miriam (Applebaum) Liebman; m. Nina Roskin, Oct. 27, 1968; children: Sophie, Hanna, Tessa. B.Arch., Pratt Inst., 1962; M.Arch., Harvard U., 1963. Registered architect, Mass, NY, Colo, Ind, Fla, NJ, Pa. Project design officer Boston Redevel. Authority, Mass., 1963-64; project dir. David A. Crane, Architect, Phila., 1966-69; chief architect N.Y. State Urban Devel. Corp., NYC, 1969-75; prin. urban design and archtl. adviser Harvard Inst. Internat. Devel., Tehran, Iran, 1975-77; pres. HAUS Internat., Inc., NYC, 1977-79, The Liebman Melting Partnership, Architects and Planners, NYC, 1979—. Bd advisers Inst Urban Design, New York, NY, 1980—84; assoc prof urban design Pratt Inst, Brooklyn, NY, 1983—88; land develop mgr Russian Fed Housing Project-World Bank, 1995—96. Mem ed bd: Metropolis, 1981—88; contbr. articles to mags. Fellow, Am Acad, Rome, 1966, Wheelwright Travelling, Harvard Univ, 1971. Fellow: AIA (pres NY chpt 1983—84); mem.: Urban Land Inst (mem int coun). Office: The Liebman Melting Partnership 330 W 42nd St New York NY 10036-6902 Office Phone: 212-239-8080. Business E-Mail: liebman@liebmanmelting.com.

LIEBMAN, WILMA B., federal agency administrator; b. Phila., 1950; BA, Barnard Coll., NYC; JD, George Washington U., Washington. Staff atty. NLRB, 1974—80; legal counsel Internat. Brotherhood of Teamsters, 1980—89; labor counsel Bricklayers and Allied Craftsmen, 1990—93; asst. to dir. Fed. Mediation and Conciliation Svc., 1994—96, dep. dir.; mem. NLRB, Washington, 1997—. Mem.: Coll. of Labor and Employment Lawyers, Inc. (exec. bd.), Indsl. Rels. Rsch. Assn. (exec. bd.). Office: NLRB 1099 14th St NW Washington DC 20570-0001*

LIEBMANN, GEORGE W., lawyer; b. NYC, June 20, 1939; s. William Liebmann and Margaret (Hirschman) Cook; m. Anne-Lise Grimstad, Apr. 29, 1967; children: Pamela, George, Franklin. AB, Dartmouth Coll., 1960; JD, U. Chgo., 1963. Bar: Md. 1964, Ill. 1964. With Chaucer Head Book Shop, Inc., NYC, 1958-59; law clk. to chief judge Ct. Appeals Md., 1963-64; with Frank, Bernstein, Conaway and Goldman, Balt., 1964-79; asst. atty. gen. State of Md., Balt., 1967-69; exec. asst. to Gov. Md., Annapolis, 1979-80; prin. Liebmann and Shively, P.A., Balt., 1980—. Lectr. U. Md. Law Sch., 1977—78, Johns Hopkins U., 1991—92; mem. Gov.'s Commn. to Revise Annotated Code Md., 1974—83; alt. mem. State Planning Coun. on Radioactive Waste Mgmt., 1980—82; chmn. Gov.'s Task Force on Local Govt. Antitrust Liability, 1982—83, Gov.'s Commn. Health Care Providers' Profl. Liability Ins., 1983—84; gen. counsel Md. Econ. Devel. Corp., 1985—; vis. fellow U. Salford, England, 1996, Wolfson Coll., Cambridge, 1996, 1998—99, 2002—03, 2005—06; panelist U.S. Bankruptcy Trustee, 1980—. Author: Maryland District Court Law and Practice, 2 vols., 1976, Maryland Civil Practice Forms, 2 vols., 1984, The Little Platoons: Sub-Local Governments in Modern History, 1995, The Gallows in the Grove: Civil Society in American Law, 1997, Solving Problems Without Large Government, 1999, reprint Neighborhood Futures, 2004, Six Lost Leaders: Prophets of Civil Society, 2001, The Common Law Tradition: A Collective Portrait of Five Legal Scholars, 2005; editor: The Trimmer's Almanac: Ten Years of the Calvert Institute 1996-2006, 2007; mng. editor U. Chgo. Law Rev., 1962-63. Trustee Hist. Annapolis Found., 1991—99; exec. dir. Calvert Inst. Policy Rsch., 2001—; sec. Coalition Against the SST, Washington, 1969; Rep. primary candidate U.S. Senate, 1998. Simon indsl. and profl. fellow U. Manchester, Eng., 1993-94. Mem. Am. Law Inst., Fed. Jud. Conf. 4th Cir., Libr. Co. Balt. Bar (bd. dirs. 1967—, pres. 1975-77, 2006—), Engring. Soc. Md. (assoc.) Office: 8 W Hamilton St Baltimore MD 21201-5020 Office Phone: 410-752-5887. Personal E-mail: george.liebmann2@verizon.net.

LIEBMANN, JEFF S., lawyer; AB cum laude, Princeton U., 1971; JD cum laude, Harvard U., 1978. Bar: NY 1979. Ptnr. & co-chmn. insurance group Dewey Ballantine LLP, NYC. Mem.: ABA, N.Y. State Bar Assn., Soc. of Actuaries (assoc.). Office: Dewey Ballantine LLP 1301 Ave of the Americas New York NY 10019-6092 Office Phone: 212-259-6230. Office Fax: 212-259-6333. Business E-Mail: jliebmann@dbllp.com.

LIEBMANN, SEYMOUR W., construction executive, consultant; b. NYC, Nov. 1, 1928; s. Isidor W. and Etta (Waltzer) L.; m. Hinda Adam, Sept. 20, 1959; children: Peter Adam, David W. BSME, Clarkson U., 1948; grad., Indsl. Coll. Armed Forces, 1963, U.S. Army Command and Gen. Staff Coll., 1966, U.S. Army War Coll., 1971. Registered profl. engr., N.Y., Mass., Ga. Area engr. constrn. divsn. E.I. DuPont de Nemours & Co., Inc., 1952-54; constrn. planner Lummus Co., Inc., 1954-56; prin. mech. engr. Perini Corp., 1956-62; v.p. Boston Based Contractors, 1962-66, A.R. Abrams, Inc., Atlanta, 1967-74, pres., 1974-78, also bd. dirs. Founder Liebmann Assocs., Inc., Atlanta, 1979—; nat. adv. bd. Am. Security Coun.; steering com. Atlanta Engring. Acad. Author: Military Engineer Field Notes, 1953, Prestressing Miter Gate Diagonals, 1960; contbr. articles to publs. Active USO Coun., Atlanta, 1968—, v.p., 1978, exec. com., 1975-79; active Nat. UN Day Com., 1975; sr. army coord., judge Sci. Fair, Atlanta Pub. Schs., 1979-88, 92-2004, 06; asst. scoutmaster Atlanta area coun. Boy Scouts Am., 1980-87, Explorer advisor, 1982-86, unit commr., 1985, commr. North Atlanta dist., 1988-90, asst. coun. commr., 1990-95, North Atlanta dist. com., 1996-1998; faculty Commrs. Coll., 1985-88, 92; alumni adv. com. Clarkson Coll. Tech., 1981—, alumni bd. govs., 1983-94, Disting. Alumni Golden Knight award, 1983; exec. com., zoning chmn. neighbor planning unit "A" City of Atlanta, 1982-2006, chmn., 1988, 95-2006, vice-chmn., 1989; pres. West Paces/Northside Neighborhood Assn., 1991-2007; apptd. civil engr. mem. to City of Atlanta Water and Sewer Appeals Bd., 1992—; apptd. mem. to Mayor's Bond Oversight Com. City of Atlanta, 1995-96; mem. Atlanta, Cobb County regional mil. affairs com., 2001—; chair City of Atlanta Nancy Creek Tech. Tunnel Adv. Com., 2002-06; mem. blue ribbon panel Fulton County Juvenile Ct., 2001-04; mem. Philmont Fall Adventure Trek, 2002; apptd. mem. Mayor's Svc. Commn., 2002—. Col. AUS Ret. Corps Engrs., 1948-52, Korea, Germany. Decorated Legion of Merit, Meritorious Svc. medal, USAR Achievement medal with oak leaf cluster; named to Old Guard of Gate City Guard, 1979; recipient cert. achievement, Dept. Army, 1978, Bronze DeFleury medal, U.S. Army Engr. Regiment, 1997, USO Recognition award, 1979, Order of Arrow award, Boy Scouts Am., 1983, 1987, Scouters Key, 1988, North Atlanta Dist. Merit award, 1989, Silver Beaver award, 1991, Disting. Commr. award, 1991, Engring. Profl. award, Am. Inst. Plant Engrs., 1987, Hands Across Atlanta award, 1997, Medal of Honor award, Ga. Engring. Found., 2004, Proclamation of Honor, Atlanta City Coun., 2006. Fellow: Soc. Am. Mil. Engrs. (life; program chmn. Atlanta post 1980—81, v.p. 1982, pres. 1983, chmn. readiness com. 1986—2000, bd. dirs. 1986—, program chmn. 1988, nat. meeting, asst. regional v.p. for readiness So. region 1991—, life dir. Atlanta Post 1994, James Lucas Chair Atlanta Post 1994, elected nat. dir. 1994—97, program chmn. S.Ea. regional site tng. conf. 1999, Nat. award of Merit 1982—83, Atlanta Post Leadership award 1988); mem.: NRA, NSPE, ASTM, Internat. Concrete Repair Inst. (awards com. 2000), Internat. Concrete Restoration Inst. (judge awards com. 2002), Am. Arbitration Assn. (panel arbitrators 1979—, constrn. adv. com. 1984—), Engrs. Club Boston, Met. Atlanta Engrs. (chmn. Engrs. Week 2000 and 2001 awards com.), Jt. Ga. Soc. Profl. Engrs. and Am. Counsel of Engring. Cos. (chmn. state licensing com. 2002—03, bd. dirs. Buckhead chpt., state ethics com., Engr. of Yr. in Pvt. Practice 1990, Ga. Engr. Yr. 1991, Lifetime Achievement award for engring. excellence 2001), Am. Concrete Inst., Army Engr. Assn. (life), U.S. Army Hist. Found., Atlanta Area Mil. Affairs Com., Vets. of the 1st U.S.Army Engr. Combat Bn., Atlanta Hist. Soc., Ga. Conservancy, Benyton Mackaye Trail Assn., Appalachian Trail Conf., Order of Engr., Mil. Order World Wars, Atlanta C. of C. (mil. affairs com. 1999), Downtown Atlanta Kiwanis, Cobb C. of C., Assn. U.S. Army (v.p. exec. com. local chpt. 1998—2000), Nat. Def. U. Found., U.S. Army War Coll. Alumni Assn. (life), Def. Preparedness Assn. (life), U.S. Army War Coll. Found. (life; Alumni Assn. Disting. Alumni Selection Com. 1997—), Res. Officers Assn. (life), Soc. 1st U.S. Inf. (life), Heros of 76, Civitan, Elks, Nat. Sojourners, Shriners, Masons (32d degree). Republican. Jewish. Office: Liebmann Assocs Inc 1266 W Paces Ferry Rd NW Box 518 Atlanta GA 30327

LIEBOWITZ, DANIEL S.F., retired medical educator; b. NYC, Nov. 26, 1921; s. David and Emily Liebowitz; m. Florence Evans Liebowitz, 1978 (dec. Feb. 2006); children: Peter, Sylvie, Danny P. BA, Columbia U., 1943; MD, NYU, 1946. Diplomate internal medicine. Postgrad. tng. Goldwater Meml. Hosp., NY, Crile VA Hosp., Case We. Res. U., Cleve., 1950—52; clin. prof. medicine emeritus Stanford U. Sch. Medicine, 1963—96; dir. med. edn. emeritus Sequoia Hosp., Redwood City, Calif., 1963—99. Lectr. in field. Author: (novels) The Lion and The Flame, 1992, (biography) The Physician and the Slave Trade, The Livingstone Expeditions and the Crusade Against Slavery in East Africa, 1999; co-author: Cook to Your Heart's Content on a Low Fat Low Salt Diet, 1970; co-author: (with Charles Pearson) The Last Expedition - Stanley's Mad journey Through the Congo, 2005; contbr. articles to profl. jours. Capt. US Army, 1949—50. Fellow: ACP, Royal Geog. Soc.; mem.: AMA, Am. Soc. Gastrointestinal Endoscopy, Am. Gastroenterology Assn., Explorers Club. Avocations: hiking, camping, photography, exploration. Personal E-mail: eminpasha@aol.com, eminpasha@yahoo.com.

LIEBOWITZ, LARRY ARNOLD, electroceramics materials engineer; b. Brooklyn, June 19, 1943; s. Max and Estelle L. BSChemE, City Coll. of N.Y., 1965; MSChemE, N.Y. Univ., 1968. Engring. group leader MEPCO divsn. NA Philips, Morristown, NJ, 1965—68; product mgr. Nytronics, Inc., Berkeley Heights, NJ, 1968—71; engring. mgr. KDI Pyrofilm Corp., Whippany, NJ, 1971—75; pres. LAL Technol. Corp., East Brunswick, NJ, 1975—. Founder, CEO Advanced Materials Tech. Corp., NJ. Mem. Soc. Plastic Engr. (chmn. elec. and electronic divsn. 1970-71), Am. Chem. Soc., Am. Ceramics Soc. Achievements include devel. of monolithic multilayer ceramic capacitors, superior ceramic materials and chip structures and mfg. techniques for electronic components and microcircuits which allow their use at microwave frequencies and in broad band wireless comm. applications, log slope method of predicting high frequency performance of electronic devices, water based binders for electronic ceramics, replacing ones based on environment unfriendly volatile organic solvents; inventor split plate constrn. to promote flux cancellation for reduced inductance in multilayer capacitor chips; patent buried layer chip architecture for chips in microwave applicatons, patent in manufacturing process of single layer ceramic capacitors with dielectric thickness less then .001 inch; development of SAFETURF (artificial turf engineered to reduce leg injuries). Mailing: PO Box 412 East Brunswick NJ 08816-0412 Office Phone: 732-251-5446. Personal E-mail: laltec@optonline.net.

LIEBOWITZ, NEIL ROBERT, psychiatrist; b. Bklyn., Feb. 5, 1956; s. Harold and Gertrude Liebowitz; m. Judith Linda, Oct. 21, 1952; children: Sarah Michelle, Daniel Geoffery BA, U. Va., 1978; MD, SUNY, Stony Brook, 1982. Cert. Am. Bd. Psychiatry and Neurology; cert. in clin. psychopharmacology Am. Soc. Clin. Psychopharmacology. Intern Greenwich Hosp. Assn., Greenwich, Conn., 1982-83; psychiatry fellow Yale Dept. Psychiatry, New Haven, 1982-86; chief resident psychiatry Yale New Haven Hosp., 1985-86; dir. consultation liaison psychiatry Newington VA Med. Ctr., Newington, Conn., 1986-87, chief mental hygiene clinic, 1986-88; asst. prof. psychiatry U. Conn., Farmington, 1986-92, asst. clin. prof. psychiatry, 1993—; dir. inpatient psychiatry Newington VA Med. Ctr., 1988-89; dir. ambulatory psychiatry John Dempsey Hosp., Farmington, 1989-91. Cons. psychiatrist Rocky Hill (Conn.) Vets. Home and Hosp., 1987-88; attending New Britain Gen. Hosp., 1992—; dir. Conn. Anxiety & Depression Treatment Ctr., Farmington, 1994—; founding mem., bd. dirs. PsychCare, Inc., 1996-98; bd. dirs. Psych Mgmt Contbr. articles to profl. jours.; co-investigator clin. research Clin. Psychopharmacology, 1988—; mem. Integrated Neuroscis., Inc., 1999-2002 Mem. Am. Psychiat. Assn., Conn. Psychiat. Soc., Hartford Psychiat. Soc. (pres. 1997), Phi Beta Kappa Office: Conn Anxiety & Depression Treatment Ctr Farmington CT 06032

LIEBOWITZ, RONALD D., academic administrator; m. Jessica Liebowitz; children: David Heschel, Shoshana, Ezra. AB, Bucknell U.; PhD in Geography, Columbia U., 1985. Instr. geography Middlebury Coll., 1984—88, assoc. prof. geography Vt., 1988—93, prof. geography Vt., 1993—, dean of faculty Vt., 1993—95, v.p. Vt., 1995—97, provost, exec. v.p., 1997—2004, acting pres. Vt., 2002, pres. Vt., 2004—. Editor: Gorbachev's New Thinking: Prospects for Joint Ventures, 1988; co-editor: Perestroika and East-West Economic Relations: Prospects for the 1990s, 1989, Russia and Eastern Europe after Communism: The Search for New Political, Economic and Security Systems, 1996. Fellowship, Nat. Coun. on Soviet and East European Rsch., Internat. Rsch. and Exchange Bd., Social Sci. Rsch. Coun., George F. Kennan Inst., Woodrow Wilson Ctr. for Internat. Scholars. Avocations: world metro/subway riding, reading, squash. Office: Office of Pres Middlebury Coll Middlebury VT 05753 E-mail: liebowit@middlebury.edu.

LIEBRANDT, PAUL, chef; Commis chef L'Escargot, London, 1992—94, Marco Pierre White, London, 1994—96; chef de partie Le Manoir aux Quat' Saisons, Oxford, England, 1996—97, Pierre Gagnaire, Paris, 1998—99; sous chef Bouley Bakery, NYC, 1999—2000; exec. chef Atlas, NYC, 2000—01; dir. Papillon Restaurant, NYC, 2001—02; personal chef for Lord Rothschild, 2002, Prince Andrew; founder, cons. Veda Grp., NYC, 2003—; chef dir. Gilt, NYC, 2005—06. Named one of NYC's Rising Stars, StarChefs.com, 2006; recipient Three Stars, NY Times.*

LIEBSCHER, GREGORY J., plastic surgeon; Grad., U. Notre Dame, 1983; MD, Bowman Gray Sch. Medicine, Wake Forest U., Winston-Salem, NC, 1987. Cert. Gen. Surgery Am. Bd. Surgery, 1993, Am. Bd. Plastic Surgery, 1996. Gen. surgery resident St. Louis U. Med. Ctr., 1987—92; plastic & reconstructive surgery fellow Mayo Clinic, Rochester, Minn., 1992—94; pvt. practice Colorado Springs, Colo. Named El Paso County's "Top Doc, Plastic Surgery", Colo. Springs Bus. Jour., 2004. Fellow: Am. Coll. Surgery. Office: Audubon Med Campus 3030 N Circle Dr Ste 214 Colorado Springs CO 80909 Office Phone: 719-634-2503. Office Fax: 719-634-2686.*

LIEFF, ROBERT LAWRENCE, lawyer; b. Bridgeport, Conn., Sept. 29, 1936; BA, U. Bridgeport, 1958; JD, MBA, Columbia U., 1962. Bar: Calif. 1966, U.S. Dist. Ct., No. Dist. Calif. 1969, U.S. Ct. Appeals, Ninth Cir. 1969, U.S. Supreme Ct. 1969, U.S. Ct. Appeals, Seventh Cir. 1972, U.S. Tax Ct. 1974, U.S. Dist. Ct., Dist. of Hawaii 1986. Founding ptnr. Lieff, Cabraser, Heimann & Bernstein, LLP, 1972—2006, of counsel, 2007—; founding ptnr. Lieff Global, 2007—. Bd. visitors Columbia Law Sch., 1992—2004. Mem.: ABA (mem. Section on Corp., Banking and Bus. Law), Assn. Trial Lawyers of Am., Consumer Attys. Calif., Calif. Trial Lawyers Assn., San Francisco Trial Lawyers Assn., Lawyers Club of San Francisco, State Bar of Calif., Bar Assn. of San Francisco. Office: Lieff Cabrasser Heimann & Bernstein Embarcadero Ctr W 275 Battery St Ste 3000 San Francisco CA 94111 Office Phone: 415-965-1000. E-mail: rlieff@lchb.com, relieff@lieffglobal.com.*

LIEGL, DOROTHY M., library director; Libr. SD State Libr., Pierre, 1972—82, dep. state libr., 1982—2004, state libr., 2004—. Mem.: ALA, SD Libr. Assn. (Disting. Svc. award 1999), Chief Officers of State Libr. Agencies, Western Coun. State Librs., Mountain Plains Libr. Assn., SD Libr. Network. Office: SD State Libr Mercedes MacKay Bldg 800 Governors Dr Pierre SD 57501-2294 Office Phone: 605-773-3131. Office Fax: 605-773-6962. Business E-Mail: dorothy.liegl@state.sd.us.*

LIEGLER, ROSEMARY MENKE, dean; b. Fairfield, Iowa, Aug. 21, 1939; d. Vincent Thomas and Catherine Lucille Menke; m. Donald G. Liegler, June 8, 1963; children: Katherine, Jerry. BSN, St. Ambrose Coll., 1961; MS in Nursing, Marquette U., 1962; PhD, Claremont Grad. Sch., 1994. Asst. prof. Miami (Fla.)-Dade Jr. Coll., Georgetown U., Washington, U. Miami; prof., dean Sch. Nursing Azusa (Calif.) Pacific U. Bd. dirs. Huntington East Valley Hosp. Mem. ANA, Calif. Assn. Colls. Nursing, East San Gabriel Valley Vis. Nurses' Assn. (cmty. bd. 1995), Sigma Theta Tau. Home: 3226 E Whitebirch Dr West Covina CA 91791-3037 Office: Azusa Pacific U Sch Nursing 901 E Alosta Ave Azusa CA 91702-2769

LIEM, TIMOTHY K., surgeon; BA in Bioengring., U. Calif., LaJolla, 1986; MD, U. So. Calif., LA, 1990. Asst. prof. surgery U. Mo., Columbia, 1997—2001; clin. assoc. prof. surgery Oreg. Health & Sci. U., Portland, 2001—05, assoc. prof. surgery, 2005—. Adj. asst. prof. radiology U. Mo.; adj. assoc. prof. radiology Oreg. Health & Sci. U. Mem.: Alpha Omega Alpha. Office: Oreg Health & Sci I Divsn Vascular Surgery 3181 SW Sam Jackson Pk Rd Portland OR 97239

LIEN, JOHN DONOVAN, lawyer; b. LaCrosse, Wis., Dec. 30, 1943; s. Arthur Marvin and Alverda (Larson) L.; m. Kathleen MeHenry, June 17, 1967 (div. Mar. 1983); m. Molly Warner, Apr. 2, 1983. BA, U. Wis., 1965; JD, Harvard U., 1968. Bar: Wis. 1968, Ill. 1972, U.S. Dist. Ct. (no. dist.) Ill. 1972, U.S. Ct. Appeals (7th cir.) 1977. Assoc. Wilson & McIlvaine, Chgo., 1972-77, ptnr., 1978-86, Antonow & Fink, Chgo., 1986-88, Foley & Lardner LLP, Chgo., 1988—, chmn. construction practice group. Trustee Village of Winnetka, Ill., 1997-2001, Winnetka Libr. Dist., 1985-93. Capt. USAF, 1968-72. Republican. Episcopalian. Office: Foley & Lardner LLP One IBM Plz Chicago IL 60611 Office Phone: 312-832-4370. Business E-Mail: jlien@foley.com.

LIEN, TING-TING, music educator; b. Kaohsiung, Taiwan, July 3, 1965; arrived in U.S., 1983; d. Johnny Y.D. and Lily Lien; m. Jun Peng, June 27, 1995; children: Jacquelyn Ting, Charlene Ting. MusB, New Eng. Conservatory of Music, 1989; MusM, Rider U., 1996. Instr. music Westminster Conservatory Music, Princeton, 1992—98; adj. prof. Westminster Choir Coll. Rider U., Princeton, 2001—. Choir dir. Princeton Christian Ch., 1994—98; adjudicator Shore Music Educators Assn., NJ, 2002—, NJ Music Tchrs. Assn., 1998—. Mem.: Nat. Cert. Tchrs. Music, Kindermusick Nat., N.J. Music Tchrs. Assn., Piano Tchrs. Forum. Home: 6 Walden Pond Way Monmouth Junction NJ 08852-2900 Office Phone: 732-274-2082. Personal E-mail: tinglien@comcast.net.

LIENEMANN, DELMAR ARTHUR, SR., accountant, real estate developer; b. Papillion, Nebr., May 17, 1920; s. Arthur Herman and Dorothea M. (Marth) L.; m. Charlotte Peck, Jun 17, 1944 (dec. Mar. 1995); children: Delmar Arthur Jr., David (dec.), Diane, Douglas, Dorothy, Daniel, Denise. BS, U. Nebr., 1941. CPA, Nebr. Acct. Wickstrom Supply, Lincoln, Nebr., 1941, L.L. Coryell & Sons, Lincoln, 1942, Lester Buckley, CPA, Lincoln, 1943-45; pvt. practice Lincoln, 1945—. Pres., v.p., sec., treas., bldg. chmn., charter mem. Christ Luth. Ch., Lincoln, 1949-70; co-commr. Lancaster County, Lincoln, 1954-58; pres. Lincoln Symphony Orch. Found., 1984—, Ethel S. Abbott Charitable Found. Mem. AICPA, N.E. Soc. CPA, Colo. Soc. CPA, Tex. Soc. CPA, Sertoma (sec.-treas. Lincoln chpt. 1952-68, Internat. Sertoman of Yr. 1962), Nebr. Soc. CPA (Pub. Svc. award, 2003), Hillcrest Country Club, Nebr. Club, Nebr. Chancelors Club, Nebr. Touchdown Club, Nebr. Power Club, Nebr. Rebounders Club. Republican. Avocation: travel. Office: PO Box 81407 Lincoln NE 68501-1407

LIENERT, CHRISTOPH, physical education educator; b. Berlin, Jan. 12, 1963; s. Wolfgang and Marlies L. BA, MA, Free U. Berlin, Germany, 1993, We. Mich. U., Kalamazoo, 1990; PhD, Tex. Woman's U., Denton, Tex., 1998. Cert. tchr. Tex. Asst. prof. U. Maine, Presque Isle, Maine, 1998—2001; assoc. prof. Manhattan Coll., Bronx, NY, 2001—. Pres. Maine Task Force on Adapted Phys. Edn., Maine, 2000—01; German lang. editor Internat. Coun. for Health, Phys. Edn., Recreation, Sport and Dance, 1994—2007, mem. adapted phys. edn. commn., 2004—05, jour. reviewer, 2005—07. Mem. editl. bd.: Adapted Phys. Activity Quarterly, 2006—. Recipient Biennial Award for Disting. Contbn., Internat. Coun. for Health, Phys. Edn., Recreation, Sport, and Dance, 1997, Kitty Winter Magee Most

Promising Profl. award, Tex. Woman's U., 2001. Mem.: AAHPERD, Internat. Fedn. Adapted Phys. Activity (rep. N.Am. Fedn. on Adapted Phys. Activity 2000—04, Elly D. Friedmann Outstanding Young Profl. award 2001), Coun. Exceptional Children, Internat. Soc. Comparative Phys. Edn. and Sport, Phi Kappa Phi (life). Office: Manhattan Coll 4513 Manhattan College Pkwy Bronx NY 10471 Office Phone: 718-862-7518. Business E-Mail: christoph.lienert@manhattan.edu.

LIENERT, JAMES M., oil industry executive; BS in Acctg., SUNY, Buffalo; MBA, SUNY Buffalo. CPA Tex. With Occidental Chem. Corp., Niagara Falls, NY, 1974, v.p. fin., 1998, sr. v.p. chlor-alkali bus., 2000, sr. v.p. vinyls bus., 2002, pres., 2004—06; v.p. Occidental Petroleum Corp., 2004—06, exec. v.p. fin. and planning, 2006—. Office: Occidental Petroleum 10889 Wilshire Blvd Los Angeles CA 90024-4201 Office Phone: 310-208-8800.*

LIENHARD, JOHN HENRY, IV, mechanical engineer, educator; b. St. Paul, Aug. 17, 1930; s. John Henry and Catherine Edith Lienhard; m. Carol Ann Bratton, June 20, 1959; children: John Henry V, Andrew Joseph. AS, Multnomah Jr. Coll., 1949; BS, Oreg. State Coll., 1951; MSME, U. Wash., 1953; PhD in Mech. Engring., U. Calif., Berkeley, 1961; DHL (hon.), U. Houston, 2002, Sacred Heart U., 2002. Assoc. prof. mech. engring. Wash. State U., Pullman, 1961-67; prof. mech. engring. dept. U. Ky., Lexington, 1967-80; prof. mech. engring. U. Houston, 1980-89, M.D. Anderson prof. mech. engring. and history, 1989—2000, prof. emeritus, 2000—. Clyde chair prof. U. Utah, Salt Lake City, 1981. Author (with C. L. Tien): Statistical Thermodynamics, 1971, 1979; author: (with J. H. Lienhard V) A Heat Transfer Textbook, 1981, 1987; author: (with E. T. Layton) History of Heat Transfer, 1988; author: The Engines of Our Ingenuity, 2000, Inventing Modern, 2003, How Invention Begins, 2006; author, host (radio) The Engines of Our Ingenuity; contbr. articles to profl. jours. Mem.: ASME (hon. Heat Transfer Meml. award, Charles Russ Richards award, Engr. Historian award 1998), Nat. Acad. Engring., Am. Soc. Engring. Edn. (Ralph Coates Roe Tchg. medal). Episcopalian. Home: 3719 Durhill St Houston TX 77025-4006 Office: U Houston Dept Mech Engring Houston TX 77204-4006 Home Phone: 713-663-7705; Office Phone: 713-743-4518. Business E-Mail: jhl@uh.edu.

LIEPMANN, DORIAN, engineering educator; b. LA, Nov. 21, 1957; s. Hans Wolfgang and Dietland (Goldschmidt) L.; m. Kathleen Mary Toups, July 10, 1992; 1 child, Colin Wolfgang. BA, Occidental Coll., 1981; BS, Calif. Inst. Tech., 1981, MS, 1983; PhD, U. Calif., San Diego, 1990. Engr. Jet Propulsion Laboratory, Pasadena, Calif., 1983—84; rsch. scientist Technol. Rsch. Group Sci. Applications Internat. Corp., San Diego, 1984—92; rsch. engineer, Inst. for Non-Linear Sci. U. of Calif. San Diego, 1986—92; asst. prof. mechanical engring. U. of Calif. Berkeley, 1992—98, assoc. prof. departments of bioengineering and mechanical engring., 1998—2003; mem. faculty joint grad. group U. of Calif. Berkeley and U. of Calif. San Francisco, 1993—; Lester John and Lynne Dewar Lloyd Disting. Prof. Bioengineering U. of Calif. Berkeley, 2001—, prof. bioengineering and mechanical engring., 2003—, vice chair undergraduate affairs, dept. bioengineering, 2003—, chair dept. bioengineering, 2004—. Dir. Berkeley Sensor and Actuator Ctr. U. of Calif. Berkeley, 1998—. Mem. ASME, Am. Phys. Soc. Office: U Calif 483 Evans Hall 1762 Berkeley CA 94720-1741 Business E-Mail: liepmann@me.berkeley.edu.

LIEPMANN, HOLGER A., pharmaceutical executive; B in Psychology, Dartmouth Coll., Hanover, NH; MBA, Stanford U., Calif. Mktg. mgr. Europe Cutter Labs. (subs. of Bayer AG); bus. devel. mgr. Abbott Internat. Abbott Labs., 1986, various mgmt. positions including divisional v.p. and regional dir., Europe, gen. mgr. Spain Internat. divsn. and v.p. Japan Ops., sr. v.p. Abbott Internat., exec. v.p. Pharm. Products Group, exec. v.p. global nutrition, 2006—. Office: Abbott Labs 100 Abbott Park Rd Abbott Park IL 60064-6400 Office Phone: 847-937-6100.*

LIES, VALERIE SHARP, foundation administrator; b. Buffalo, Sept. 18, 1948; d. Osborne Kenneth and Norma (Taylor) Sharp; m. Brian P. Lies, July 25, 1970; 1 child, Taylor. BA, Vassar Coll., 1970; MSW, U. Minn., 1974. Human resources planner Minn. State Planning Agy., St. Paul, 1973-74; exec. dir. Otto Bremer Found., St. Paul, 1974-82; v.p. Pub. Edn. Fund, Pitts., 1983-87; pres. Donors Forum Chgo., 1987—. Chmn. bd. Women and Founds., N.Y.C., 1988—, bd. dirs. philanthropy sect., 1985—, 1st Non Profit Risk Pooling Trust, Chgo., 1988—. Chair Nat. Ctr. for Family Philanthropy. Office: Donors Forum Chgo 208 S LaSalle St, Ste 740 Chicago IL 60604 E-mail: vlies@donorsforum.org.

LIESS, BENJAMIN D., otolaryngologist; b. St. Louis, Dec. 10, 1977; s. Gary and Shari Liess; m. Angela Liess; children: Hannah, Jacob. MD, U. Mo., Columbia, 2004. Lic. otolaryngologist head and neck surgeon Mo. Physician U. Mo. Hosp. & Clinic, 2004—. Contbr. chapter to book, articles to profl. jours. Mem.: Am. Laryngol., Rhinol. and Otol. Soc., Am. Acad. Otolaryngology Head and Neck Surgery, Mortar Bd. Achievements include research in airway difficulty.

LIETO, TIM, information technology executive; BSBA in Fin. magna cum laude, Boston U., 1980. With Data Gen., Chipcom, Prominet, Lucent; sr. v.p. worldwide sales Pirus Networks; pres., CEO, sr. v.p. worldwide sales and svc. Sandial Systems; sr. v.p. Ams. sales Sun Microsystems, Inc., Santa Clara, Calif., 2005—. Office: Sun Microsystems Inc 4150 Network Cir Santa Clara CA 95054 Office Phone: 650-960-1300.*

LIETZ, JEREMY JON, educational administrator, writer; b. Milw., Oct. 4, 1933; s. John Norman and Dorothy B. (Drew) L.; m. Cora Fernandez, Feb. 24, 1983; children: Cheryl, Brian, Angela, Andrew, Christopher, Jennifer. BS, U. Wis., Milw., 1961; MS, U. Wis., Madison, 1971; EdD, Marquette U., 1980. Tchr. Milw. Pub. Schs., 1961-63, diagnostic counselor, 1968-71, sch. adminstr., 1971-95, hearing panel ombudsman, 1999—, acting student svcs. coord., 1999—2003; tchr. Madison Pub. Sch., Wis., 1964-65; rsch. assoc. U. Wis., Madison, 1965-67; instr. Marquette U., Milw., 1980-82, Milw. U. Sch., 2000—02. Lectr. HEW Conf. on Reading, Greeley, Colo., 1973, NASP Conf. on Reading, St. Louis, 1974, various state and nat. orgns.; co-founder, bd. dirs., cons. Ednl. Leadership Inst., Shorewood, Wis., 1980—; dir. Religious Edn. Program, Cath. Elem. East, Milw., 1985-86. Author: The Elementary School Principal's Role in Special Education, 1982; contbr. numerous articles, chpts., tests, revs. to profl. jours. V.p. PTA, 1961-62. With U.S. Army, 1954-56, ETO. Recipient Cert. of Achievement award NAESP, 1974. Mem. AAAS, Assn. Wis. Sch. Adminstrs. (mem. state planning com. 1977-79, lectr. 1982), Adminstrs. and Suprs. Coun. (mem. exec. bd. dist. 1977-79, mem. contract negotiations com. 1991-95), Filipino Am. Assn. Wis., U. Wis. Alumni Assn. (Madison), Milw. Mcpl. Chess Assn., U.S. Chess Fedn., Phi Delta Kappa. Home: 424 Susan Ln Thiensville WI 53092-1451 Office: Ednl Leadership Inst PO Box 11411 Shorewood WI 53211-0411 Personal E-mail: lietz1012@yahoo.com.

LIETZAU, WILLIAM KENDALL, career officer, lawyer; b. Annapolis, Md., Nov. 9, 1960; s. Karl Ernest and Janice Mae L.; m. Diane Michelle, May 19, 1984; children: Rachel Anne, Zachary Thomas. BS, US Naval Acad., 1983; JD, Yale U., 1989; LLM, US Army JAG Sch., 1995; MS, Nat. War Coll., 2004. Bar: Conn. 1989, Ct. Mil. Appeals 1990, U.S. Supreme Ct. 1995. Rifle co. comdr. USMC, Kaneohe Bay, Hawaii, 1984-87, spl asst. U.S. atty. Jacksonville, N.C., 1989-91, lt. col., 1995; chief prosecutor Camp Lejeune, N.C., 1991-92; chief def. counsel Iwakuni, Japan, 1992-93; dep. sta. judge adv., 1993-95; head law armed conflict br. Navy JAG, Washington, 1996-97; dep. legal counsel to chmn. Joint Chiefs Staff Washington, 1997-99; chief mil. judge Atlantic cir., 1999-2000; cmdg. officer 1st RTBn., San Diego, 2000—02; spl. asst. to Dept. Def. gen. counsel, 2002; staff judge advocate US European Command, 2005—. Adj. prof. Georgetown U., Washington, 1998-2000; spkr. in field. Contbr. articles to profl. jours. U.S. del. Ottawa Conv. Banning Landmines, Terrorist Bombing Conv., Nuc. Terrorism Conv., Rome Treaty Internat. Criminal Ct., Hague Cultural Property Protocol. Recipient Major Gen. Pugh award, 1995; named Career Mil. Lawyer of the Yr. Judge Adv. Assn., 1998. Avocations: running, biking, lifting. Office: HQ USEUCOM/ECJA Unit 30400 APO AE 09131 Office Phone: (49) 711 680 8001. Personal E-mail: wklietzau@hotmail.com. Business E-Mail: lietzauw@eucom.mil.

LIEWENDAHL, BO KRISTIAN, retired pathologist, nuclear medicine physician; b. Helsinki, Aug. 21, 1941; s. Ernst August and Irina (Semenov) Liewendahl; 1 child, Kari Peter Nikolai. MD, U. Helsinki, 1966, PhD, 1968. Diplomate. Resident in clin. chemistry Helsinki U. Hosp., 1966-69, resident in medicine, 1969-72, cons. lab. dept., 1974-82; asst. prof., lectr. U. Helsinki, 1977-96, prof., 1996—; chief physician divsn. nuclear medicine Helsinki U. Hosp., 1983-99; NIH fellow U. Calif., San Francisco, 1972-73. Vis. scientist U. Wis., Madison, U. Va., Charlottesville, 1982; dir. nuc. medicine rsch. group Minerva Inst. Found., Helsinki, Finland, 1977—2002; sec. gen. Minerva Found., 1997—2002, bd. dirs., 2002—04; pres. European Nuc. Medicine Congress, Helsinki, 1984, Scandinavian Congress Nuc. Medicine, Helsinki, 1998; chmn. European Congress Clin. Chemistry, Tampere, Finland, 1995; del. nuc. medicine sect. European Union Med. Spltys., 1994—2002; del. European Bd. Nuc. Medicine, 1995—2002. Author, editor: Scandinavian Jour. Clin. Lab. Investigation, 1986—96; mem. editl. bd. European Jour. Nuclear Medicine, 1991—2002; contbr. articles to profl. jours. Recipient J. W. Runeberg prize, Finnish Med. Soc., 1969, Ann. Lecture prize, 1973, T. Heiskanen Meml. prize, Finnish Radiol. Soc. and Finnish Nuc. Medicine Soc., 1985, Gold medal, Minerva Found., 1989. Mem.: NY Acad. Scis., Soc. Nuc. Medicine NY, World Fedn. Nuc. Medicine and Biology (del. 1988—2003, organizing com. 8th World Congress, Santiago, Chile 2002), Finnish Soc. Nuc. Medicine (pres. 1996—98), European Thyroid Assn. (sec. Helsinki congress 1976), European Assn. Nuc. Medicine (del. 1988—95, mem. organizing com. Copenhagen congress 1996, v.p. organizing com. Helsinki congress 2004, Congress prize 1991). Lutheran. Achievements include research in thyroid function tests, particularly accurate assays for free thyroid hormone concentrations in blood, nuclear medicine procedures for diagnosis of oncological, hematological and neurological diseases. Avocation: history. Office: Minerva Found Inst Biomedicum Helsinki Haartmansgatan 8 00290 Helsinki Finland

LIFF, ZANVEL A., psychologist; b. NYC, Oct. 31, 1927; s. Samuel and Lena Liff; m. Sylvia Barchenko, June 30, 1957; children: Sharon, Janet. BS in Social Sci., City Coll. N.Y., NYC, 1948, MA, 1949; PhD, NYU, NYC, 1955. Diplomate clin. psychologist Am. Bd. Profl. Psychology, 1977, psychoanalysis Am. Bd. Profl. Psychology, 1996; lic. psychologist N.Y., 1958. Pvt. practice, NYC, 1958—; dir. psychology Postgraduate Ctr. Mental Health, NYC, 1970—90. Vis. prof. New Sch. U., NYC, 1973—79. Editor: The Leader in the Group, 1975, Internat. Jour. Group Psychotherapy, 1979—84. Named Disting. Practioner, Nat. Acad. Practice Psychology, 1988. Fellow: Am. Group Psychotherapy Assn., Am. Acad. Psychoanalysis; mem.: APA (pres. psychoanalysis divsn. 1988—89). Home and Office: 55 E 86th St New York NY 10028 Personal E-mail: zansyliff@aol.com.

LIFSCHITZ, JUDAH, lawyer; b. NYC, Nov. 28, 1952; s. Morris and Edna (Love) L.; m. Marilyn Feder, Dec. 8, 1974; children: Lisa, Ira, Tamar. BA magna cum laude, Yeshiva U., 1974; JD, George Washington U., 1977. Bar: Md. 1977, D.C. 1978, U.S. Dist. Ct. D.C. 1980, U.S. Claims Ct. 1980, U.S. Ct. Appeals (D.C. cir.) 1980, U.S. Ct. Appeals (4th cir.) 1982, U.S. Ct. Appeals (fed. cir.) 1985, U.S. Supreme Ct. 1985. Assoc. Hudson, Creyke, Koehler & Tacke, Washington, 1980, Epstein, Becker, Borsody & Green, Washington, 1980-83; ptnr., chmn. govt. contracts dept. Washington Perito & Dubuc, Washington, 1983-91; ptnr. Shapiro, Lifschitz and Schram, P.C., Washington, 1991—. Author: Heaven Sent Stories of Faith and Effort, 1997, Stories for Sahuli, 1999, The Klausenberger Rebbe, The War Years, 2003. Washington counsel Nat. Coun. Young Israel, N.Y.C., 1980—95; pres. Yeshiva of Greater Washington, 1985-89; bd. dirs. Jewish Community Coun., Washington, 1980—90, United Jewish Appeal Fedn., Washington, 1985. Recipient Shofar award Nat. Coun. Young Israel, 1980, Kesser Torah award Yeshiva of Greater Washington, 2000. Mem. ABA, Md. State Bar Assn. Office: Shapiro Lifschitz and Schram PC 1742 N Street NW Washington DC 20036

LIFSON, KALMAN ALAN, retired retail and bank executive, portfolio manager; b. Mpls., Oct. 15, 1926; s. Maurice Kalman and Gertrude (Shulkin) L.; m. Irene Londer, June 17, 1950 (dec. July 1968); m. Judith Abrams, Sept. 3, 1969; children: Valerie Leftwich; Kipp, Ione Spear, Stacey Kivowitz, Grant Dorfman. BS in Naval Tech., U. Minn., 1946, MBA, 1949; PhD in Psychology, Purdue U., 1951. Commd. ensign USN, 1945, lt. (j.g), 1952; engring. officer Panama Canal Zone, 1945-46; supr. indsl. engring. Temco Aircraft, Dallas, 1951-52; mgmt. engring. officer USN, Washington, 1953-54, resigned; prin. Lifson, Wilson, Ferguson & Winick, Dallas, 1954-94, Pers. Decisions, Inc., Dallas, 1995-99; chmn. Harris'Dept. Stores, San Bernadino, Calif., 1980-94, Tex. Rsch. and Electronic Corp. and successors, Dallas, 1962-94, Electronic Mgmt. Info. Sys., 1970-94; chmn. emeritus B.R. Blackmarr & Assocs., Dallas, 1986-99; ret., 1999; portfolio mgr. Delphi/EMSS Bank Fund, Dallas, 2005—. Chmn. Fed. Home Loan Bank of 9th Dist., Little Rock, 1979-80; portfolio mgr. Delphi Emis Bank Fund, 2005-; spkr. fields of psychology, retailing, banking, ops. rsch. Contbr. articles to profl. jours. Chmn. Congl. Commn. on Guaranteed Student Loans, Washington, 1975, Commn. on Orgn. of U.S. Dept. Labor, Washington, 1976; mem. Tex. Commn. on State Employee Productivity, Austin, Tex., 1985. Mem. APA, World Pres. Orgn., Columbian Club (treas. 1950-54), Crescent Club, Sigma Xi. Jewish. E-mail: klifson906@aol.com. *"Winners" are those who can make the big play, who can turn the game around, who can conceive and institute dramatic changes. Those few of us who have been so endowed and developed must use our winnership to effect significant improvements to the well-being of those within our spheres of influence.*

LIFTIN, JOHN MATTHEW, lawyer; b. Washington, June 25, 1943; children: Eric, Hilary, Sam. AB, U. Pa., 1964; LLB, Columbia U., 1967. Bar: N.Y. 1967, D.C. 1974, U.S. Dist. Ct. D.C. 1975, U.S. Ct. Appeals (D.C. cir.) 1975, U.S. Supreme Ct. 1980. Assoc. Sullivan & Cromwell, NYC, 1967-71; spl. counsel to chmn. SEC, Washington, 1971-72, assoc. dir. market reg. div., 1972-74; ptnr. Rogers & Wells, Washington, 1974-85; pres. Quadrex Securities Corp., NYC, 1985-87; sr. v.p., gen. counsel Kidder, Peabody Group Inc., NYC, 1987-96; independent cons. Prudential Fin., Newark, 1997—98; sr. v.p., gen. counsel Prudential Insurance, 1998—2000, Prudential Fin., 2000—05; vice-chmn., gen counsel Bank of NY, NYC, 2005—07; mng. dir., gen counsel D.E.Shaw Group, NYC, 2007—. Mem. adv. bd. securities regulation and law reports Bur. Nat. Affairs, Inc., Washington, 1979—; mem. N.Y. Stock Exch. Legal Adv. Com., 2000—. Mem. ABA, Univ. Club. Office: DE Shaw Group 39th Fl Tower 45 120 W 45th St New York NY 10036

LIFTON, PAUL SAMUEL, theater educator; s. David and Bernice Lorber Lifton. BA in English, Pomona Coll., Claremont, Calif., 1971; PhD, U. Calif., Berkeley, 1985. Asst. prof. theatre Agnes Scott Coll., Decatur, Ga., 1985—88; assoc. prof. theatre arts N.D. State U., Fargo, ND, 1988—. Author: Vast Encyclopedia: The Theatre of Thornton Wilder, 1995. Fellow, Asian Cultural Coun., 2005. Mem.: Assn. Asian Performance, Phi Beta Kappa. Home Phone: 701 293-9516; Office Phone: 701 231-7785.

LIFTON, RICHARD P., medical educator, researcher; b. 1953; BA summa cum laude in Biology, Dartmouth Coll., Hanover, NH, 1975; MD, Stanford U., Palo Alto, Calif., 1982, PhD in Biochemistry, 1986. Diplomate Am. Bd. Internal Medicine. Resident internal medicine Brigham and Women's Hosp., Boston, 1983—86, chief med. resident, 1986—87; instr. medicine Brigham and Women's Hosp. and Harvard Med. Sch., 1987—91, asst. prof., 1991—93; asst. prof. medicine and genetics Yale U., New Haven, 1993—94, assoc. prof., 1994—97, prof. medicine, genetics and molecular biophysics & biochemistry, 1997—, chmn. dept. genetics, 1998—; asst. investigator Howard Hughes Med. Inst., 1994—96, assoc. investigator, 1997—; dir. cardiovasc. genetics prog. Boyer Ctr. Molecular Medicine, 1996—; dir. NIH Specialized Ctr. Rsch. in Hypertension, 1996—. Contbr. articles to profl. jours. Recipient SmithKline-Beecham Young Investigator award, Internat. Soc. Hypertension, 1994, Homer Smith award, Am. Soc. Nephrology, 1998, Novartis award, Am. Heart Assn., Med. Rsch. award, Pasarow Found., Earnest H. Starling Disting. lectureship, Am. Physiol. Soc., 2002, Alfred Newton Richards award, Internat. Soc. Nephrology, 2007. Mem.: NAS. Office: Lifton Lab Yale U Sch Medicine BCMM 147 295 Congress Ave New Haven CT 06510 Office Phone: 203-737-4420. E-mail: richard.lifton@yale.edu.*

LIFTON, ROBERT KENNETH, manufacturing executive; b. NYC, Jan. 9, 1928; s. Benjamin and Anna (Pike) L.; m. Loretta J. Silver, Sept. 5, 1954; children: Elizabeth Gail Lifton Hooper, Karen Grace Lifton Healy. BBA magna cum laude, CCNY, 1948; LLB, Yale U., New Haven, Conn., 1951; doctorate (hon.), Bar Ilan U., 1993. Bar: NY 1952. Assoc. Kaye, Scholer, Fierman, Hays & Handler, NYC, 1955—56; asst. to pres. Glickman Corp., NYC, 1956—57; pres. Robert K. Lifton, Inc., NYC, 1957—61; chmn. bd. Terminal Tower Co., Inc., Cleve., 1959—63; pres. Transcontinental Investing Corp., NYC, 1961—72, chmn. bd., 1969—72; ptnr. Venture Assocs., 1972—89; pres. Preferred Health Care Ltd., 1983—88; chmn. bd. dirs. Marcade Group, Inc., 1986—91, Medis El, 1993—, Cell Diagnostics, Inc., 1992—99, Cell Kinetics Ltd., 2006—; chmn. bd. dirs., CEO Medis Techs., Ltd., NYC, 1999—. CEO, chmn. bd. dirs. Team Am., Inc., 1983-85; treas. Consol. Accessories Corp., 1980-88, Caron's Connection, Inc., 1985-89; bd. dirs. exec. investment com. Bank Leumi USA, NYC, 2005; bd. dirs. Leumi Investment Svcs., Inc., 2005-06; mem. faculty Columbia U. Law Sch., 1973-78, Yale U. Law Sch., 1972-75; guest lectr. Practicing Law Inst., Yale Law Sch., Pace Inst., NYU; founder Nat. Exec. Conf., Washington, Inc.; chmn. oversight com. for Masters Degree, NYU Real Estate Inst., 1987-88. Author: Practical Real Estate: Legal Tax and Business Strategies, 1978; contbr. articles to profl. jours. and handbooks (Graham and Dodd award for best article Fin. Analyst Jour. 1967). Mem. McGovern econ. adv. com., 1972-73; chmn. parents com. Barnard Coll., 1976-78; mem. com. of the collection Whitney Mus., 1976-79; trustee Yale U. Sch. Fund, 1974-77, NYU Real Estate Inst., 1983-89; chmn., bd. dirs. Fund for Religious Liberty, 1987-88; pres. Am. Jewish Congress, 1988-94; chmn. Internat. Bd. U.S. Mid. East Project coun. fgn. rels., 1994—; pres. Israel Policy Forum, 1994—96, chmn. bd., 1996-97, chmn. emeritus, 1997—; bd. dirs. HIAS, 1990-96, Builders for Peace, 1993—, Abraham Fund, 1993—2006, Besa Inst., 1994—, Tel Aviv Mus., 1996-00, Georgia O'Keeffe Mus., 1999-02; mem. exec. com. AIPAC, 1990—93; vice-chmn. NJCRAC, 1994—96; exec. com. AIPAC, 1993-96; co-chmn. U.S. Middle East Project, Coun. on Foreign Relations, 1994—, Internat. Ctr. Pub. Health, 1999-05; trustee Am. Friends of Bar Ilan U., 1996-02, mem. global bd. trustees, 1997—05; bd. dirs. Pub. Health Rsch. Inst., 1996-05, vice chmn., 1997-98, chmn., 1998-04, chmn. emeritus, 2004—. Served to lt. (j.g.) USN, 1952-55. Recipient Achievement award Sch. Bus. Alumni Soc. CCNY, 1984, James Madison award Fund for Religious Liberty, 1987, Stephen S. Wise award Am. Jewish Congress, 1993; named Tech. Pioneer World Econ. Forum, 2003, 2004 Mem. Order of Coif, Beta Gamma Sigma. Home: 983 Park Ave New York NY 10028-0808 Office: 805 3rd Ave New York NY 10022-7513 Business E-Mail: rlifton@medistechnologies.com, robertl@medistechnologies.com.

LIGAN, WARREN J., corporate financial executive; BBA, Walsh Coll.; JD, Detroit Coll. Law; LLM in taxation, DePaul Univ. Sr. v.p., CFO Chiquita Brands Internat.; v.p. global taxation, then sr. v.p., corp. controller Solectron Corp., Milpitas, Calif., 2000—, interim CFO, 2005. Office: Solectron Corp 847 Gibraltar Dr Milpitas CA 95035

LIGETT, WALDO BUFORD, chemist; b. Middletown, Ohio, Nov. 2, 1916; s. Waldo Buford and Mabel Louise (Berkley) L.; m. Ann Elizabeth Hartwell, Aug. 29, 1940; children: Robert A., John D., Michael T., Steven D., Daniel L. BS, Antioch Coll., Yellow Springs, Ohio, 1939; MS, Purdue U., West Lafayette, Ind., 1941, PhD, 1944, DSc (hon.), 1965; grad. in Advanced Mgmt., Harvard U., Cambridge, Mass., 1967. Chemist Eastman Kodak Co., Rochester, N.Y., 1935-38; research supr. Ethyl Corp., Detroit, 1944-51, asst. dir. chem., 1951-52, asso. dir. chem., 1952-62, dir. research and devel., 1962-63; v.p. Celanese Chem. Co., Corpus Christi, Tex., 1963-64, v.p. tech. and mfg., 1964-66; tech. dir. Celanese Corp., NYC, 1966-67, v.p., 1967-72, Franklin Inst., Phila., 1973-81; pres. Franklin Inst. Research Labs., 1975-81. Dir. Franklin-Hahnemann Inst., 1974-81 Contbr. articles to profl. jours. Mem.: Am. Chem. Soc. Achievements include patents in field. Home: 700 Carolina Meadows Apt 232 Chapel Hill NC 27517

LIGETY, TED, Olympic athlete; b. Salt Lake City, Aug. 31, 1984; Mem. US Ski Team, 2003—; skier US Men's Olympic Team, Torino, Italy, 2006. Achievements include winner, Gold Medal, Men's Combined, Torino Olympic Games, 2006.

LIGGETT, HIRAM SHAW, JR., retired diversified financial services company executive; b. St. Louis, Jan. 12, 1932; s. Hiram Shaw and Lucille (Gardner) L.; m. Margaret McGinness, Jan. 21, 1961; children: Lucille Gardner, Frances Shelby. BA, Colo. Coll., 1953; LLD (hon.), Maryville U., 1991. Cashier Brown Group, Inc., St. Louis, 1957-64, asst. treas., 1964-68, treas., 1968—, v.p., 1983-86 (ret.). Bd. dirs. Roosevelt Fed. Savs. and Loan, St. Louis Past trustee, vice chmn. bd. dirs. McKendree Coll., Lebanon, Ill., 1980-88; trustee, past chmn. bd. trustees Maryville U., St. Louis, 1982-91; past chmn. Provident Counseling, 1983; past v.p., bd. dirs. Jr. Achievement Miss. Valley, 1983; past dir. bi-state chpt. ARC, 1983; bd. dirs., pres. Cardinal Ritter Inst.; bd. dirs., chmn. devel. bd. Paraquad. Capt. USNR, 1953-79. Mem. Fin. Execs. Inst. (pres., dir. 1983—), St. Louis Coun. Navy League (bd. councilors 1982), Univ. Club (St. Louis, chmn. house com. 1975-78), Strathalbyn Farms Club (chmn. house com., pres. bd. dirs.), Alpha Kappa Psi, Tau Kappa Alpha. Republican. Presbyterian. Office: Liggett-Black & Co 8000 Bonhomme Ave #320 Saint Louis MO 63105 Home: 14304 Quiet Meadow Ct E Chesterfield MO 63017 Personal E-mail: hligg498@aol.com.

LIGGETT, LAWRENCE MELVIN, vacuum equipment manufacturing company executive; b. Denver, June 22, 1917; s. Thomas Harrison and Mary Deacon (Taylor) L.; m. Edith Irene Harris, June 20, 1943; children: Pamela Jane Liggett Schwartz, Betty Sue Liggett Brooks El Gammal. AB, Ctrl. Coll., Pella, Iowa, 1938; PhD in Chemistry, Iowa State Coll., 1943. Rsch. chemist NDRC, Iowa State Coll., 1941-43; plant mgr. Cardox Corp., Claremore, Okla., 1943-48; dir. inorganic rsch. Wyandotte Chems. Corp., 1948-55; dir. rsch., v.p. tech. dir. Airco Speer divsn. Airco, Inc., 1955-70, pres. Airco Electronics divsn., 1970-75; pres. Airco Temescal divsn. BOC

Group, Berkeley, Calif., 1975-82; cons. bus. and tech., 1982—. Author; patentee in field. Mem. Am. Chem. Soc., Electronic Industries Assn. Republican. Home: 1856 Piedras Cir Alamo CA 94507-2820

LIGGETT, THOMAS JACKSON, retired seminary president; b. Nashville, May 27, 1919; s. Thomas Jackson and Lola Cleveland (Ballentine) L.; m. Virginia Corrine Moore, Aug. 12, 1941; children: Thomas Milton, Margaret Moore Liggett. AB, Transylvania U., 1940; MDiv, Lexington Theol. Sem., 1944, postgrad., 1950-52; LLD, Interam. U., 1965, Culver-Stockton Coll., 1959, Butler U., 1975; DHL, Transylvania U., 1969; DD, Eureka Coll., 1971, Phillips U., 1989, Christian Theol. Sem., 2002. Ordained to ministry Christian Ch., 1940; pastor in Danville, Ky., 1943-45; missionary Argentina, 1946-57; prof. Union Theol. Sem., Buenos Aires, 1948-57; pres. Evang. Sem. of P.R., 1957-65; exec. sec. for Latin Am. Christian Ch., 1965-67, chmn. div. world mission, 1967-68; pres. United Christian Missionary Soc., 1968-74, Christian Theol. Sem., Indpls., 1974-86, ret., 1986. Del. World Coun. Chs. assembly in Uppsala, 1968, adviser assembly, Nairobi, Kenya, 1975; mem. governing bd. Nat. Council Chs., 1969-75; moderator Disciples of Christ, 1985-87. Author: Where Tomorrow Struggles to be Born, 1970; Editor: Cuadernos Teologicos, 1954-55. Co-chmn. McGovern Task Force on Fgn. Policy in Latin Am., 1972, Democratic precinct committeeman, 1970-72. Mem. Disciples of Christ Hist. Soc. (life), Theta Phi. Home: 522 Bradford Ct Claremont CA 91711 E-mail: tjl222@peoplepc.com.

LIGGETT, TWILA C., broadcast executive, educator; b. Pipestone, Minn., Mar. 25, 1944; d. Donald L. Christensen and Irene E. (Zweigle) Christensen Flesher. BS, Union Coll., Lincoln, Nebr., 1966; MA, U. Nebr., Lincoln, 1971, PhD, 1977; DHL (hon.), Marymount Manhattan Coll., 2000. Dir. vocal and instrumental music Sprague (Nebr.)-Martell Pub. Sch., 1966-67; tchr. vocal music pub. schs., Syracuse, Nebr., 1967-69; tchr. Norris Pub. Sch., Firth, Nebr., 1969-71; cons. fed. reading project pub. schs., Lincoln, Nebr., 1971-72; curriculum coord. Westside Cmty. Schs., Omaha, 1972-74; dir. state program Right-to-Read Nebr. Dept. Edn., 1974-76; asst. dir. Nebr. Commn. on Status of Women, 1976-80; asst. dir. project adminstrn./devel. Great Plains Nat. Instructional TV Libr. U. Nebr., Lincoln, 1980-97, 2002—05; sr. v.p. for edn. Lancit Media Ent., Ltd. a Junior Net Co., NY, 1998—2001; exec. prodr. Reading Rainbow/Nebr. Ednl. TV Network/GPN, 1980—2005, Nebr. Ednl. TV Network/GPN, 2001—05; pres. Twila Liggett Media, Inc., 2005—07; asst. prof. literacy Marymount Manhattan Coll., 2006—. Cons. U.S. Dept. Edn., 1981; cons. Far West Regional Lab. Nebr. Edn. TV Network, San Francisco, 1978—79; panelist, presenter in field; Blue Ribbon panelist NATAS, 1991—2006; final judge Nat. Cable Ace Awards, 1991—92, 1997. Author: Reading Rainbow's Guide to Children's Books: The 101 Best Titles, 1994, rev. edit., 1996. Bd. dirs. Planned Parenthood, Lincoln, 1979-81. Recipient Grand award, N.Y., 1993, Gold medal, Internat. Film and TV Festival, 1996, 1999, World Gold medal, N.Y. Internat. Film and TV, 1995, Golden Eagle award, Coun. on Non-theatrical Events, 1995, Image award, NAACP, 1994, 1996, 1999, 2002, 26 Nat. Emmy awards, 10 for Outstanding Children's Series, 1985—2006. Mem. NATAS, Internat. Reading Assn. (panelist, presenter, Spl. award Contbns. Worldwide Literacy 1992), Am. Women in Film and TV, Phi Delta Kappa. Presbyterian. Home: 37 Crescent Pl Matawan NJ 07747 Office Phone: 212-774-4852. Business E-Mail: rrainbow1@aol.com.

LIGGINS, ALFRED C., III, broadcasting company executive; b. Omaha, 1965; MBA, Wharton Sch. Bus. U. Penn, 1995. Pres., treas., CEO Radio One Inc., Lanham, Md., 1996—; chmn. TV One LLC, 2003—. Bd. dirs. iBiquity; mem., adv. com. on diversity for comm. in the digital age FCC. Office: Radio One Inc 8th Floor 5900 Princess Garden Pkwy Fl 8 Lanham Seabrook MD 20706-2925

LIGGIO, CARL DONALD, lawyer; b. NYC, Sept. 5, 1943; AB, Georgetown U., 1963; JD, NYU, 1967. Bar: N.Y. 1967, D.C. 1967, Wis. 1983, Ill. 1998. Cons. Arent, Fox, Kintner, Plotkin & Kahn, Washington, 1968-69; assoc. White & Case, NYC, 1969-72; gen. counsel Arthur Young & Co., NYC, 1972-89, Ernst & Young, NYC, 1989-94; ptnr. Dickinson, Wright, Moon, Van Dusen & Freeman, Chgo., 1995-97, of counsel, 1998-99, McCullough, Campbell & Lane, 1999—; CFO, gen. counsel, dir. Tempico, Inc., 1998—, Ethics Point, Inc., 2002—. Bd. dirs. Fios, Inc.; mem. Brookings Civil Justice Reform Task Force, 1988. Trustee Fordham Prep. Sch., 1988-96. Mem. ABA, Am. Corp. Counsel Assn. (chmn. bd. dirs. 1984, mem. exec. com. 1982-95), Am. Judicature Soc. (bd. dirs. 1988-92), Coll. Law Mgmt., N.Y. State Bar Assn., Wis. Bar Assn., Ill. Bar Assn., D.C. Bar Assn. Home: 233 E Walton St Chicago IL 60611-1510 Office: 205 N Michigan Ave Ste 4100 Chicago IL 60601 Office Phone: 312-923-4103. Business E-Mail: cliggio@mcandl.com.

LIGGIO, JEAN VINCENZA, adult education educator, artist; b. NYC, Nov. 5, 1927; d. Vincenzo and Bernada (Terrusa) Verro; m. John Liggio, June 6, 1948; children: Jean Constance, Joan Bernadette. Student, N.Y. Inst. Photography, 1965, Elizabeth Seton Coll., 1984, Parsons Sch. of Design, 1985. Hairdresser Beauty Shoppe, NYC, 1947-65; instr. watercolor N.Y. Dept. Pks., Recreation and Conservation, Yonkers, 1985-89, Bronxville (N.Y.) Adult Sch., 1989—. Substitute tchr. cosmetology Yonkers Bd. Edn., 1988-89; tchr. watercolor painting J.V.L. Watercolor Workshop of Fine Arts, Jakes Art Ctr., Mt. Vernon, N.Y. Paintings pub. by Donald Art Co., C.R. Gibson Greeting Card Co., Enesco Corp., 1996; paintings for Avon Calendar, Avon Cosmetics Co., 1994, 96, Avon-Can. Publ., 1996-97; greeting cards published by C.R. Gibson Co. Publ., 1996-1997, boxed notecards by C.R. Gibson; painting on cover of C.R. Gibson Jour., 2000, C.R. Gibson Inspirational Jour.; pub. Friends Jour. Mag., Phila.; exhibitor numerous shows, 1981— (more than 267 awards). Mem.: Art Soc. Old Greenwich, Hudson Valley Art Assn., New Rochelle Art Assn., Scarsdale Art Assn. (publicity chmn. 1984—89), Mt. Vernon Art Assn. (pres. membership com. 1983—). Avocation: antiques. Home and Office: 166 Helena Ave Yonkers NY 10710-2524 Office Phone: 914-779-3882. Business E-Mail: jean@jvlwatercolor.com.

LIGH, JONATHAN KENNARD, ophthalmologist; m. Melanie Pamela Wilson. MD, NYU, 1978. Sr. attending surgeon NY Eye and Ear Infirmary, NYC, 1984—; sr. clin. instr. ophthalmology Mount Sinai Sch. Medicine, NYC, 1984—; asst. clin. prof. ophthalmology NYU Sch. Medicine, NYC, 1987—; dir. ophthalmology NY Downtown Hosp., NYC, 2001—, attending, 2001—. Bd. dirs. Kress Vision, NYC. Chmn. bd. dirs. Mus. of the Chinese in Am., NYC, 2004—. Fellow: ACS, Am. Acad. Ophthalmology. Avocation: travel. Office: 345 E 37th St Ste 315 New York NY 10016 Office Phone: 212-983-4510.

LIGHT, ALFRED ROBERT, law educator; b. Dec. 14, 1949; s. Alfred M. Jr. and Margaret Francis (Asbury) L; m. Mollie Sue Hall, May 28, 1977; children: Joseph Robert, Gregory Andrew. Student, Ga. Inst. Tech., 1967-69; BA with highest honors, Johns Hopkins U., 1971; PhD, U. N.C., 1976; JD cum laude, Harvard U., 1981. Bar: D.C. 1981, Va. 1982. Tax clk. IRS, 1967; lab technician Custom Farm Svcs. Soils Testing Lab, 1968; warehouse asst. State of Ga. Mines, Mining and Geology, 1970; clk.-typist systems mgmt. divsn., def. contract adminstrv. Def. Supply Agy., Atlanta, 1971; rsch. and teaching asst. dept. polit. sci. U. N.C., Chapel Hill, 1971-74; rsch. asst. Inst. Rsch. in Social Sci., 1975-77; program analyst Office of Sec. Def., 1974; asst. prf. polit. sci., rsch. scientist Ctr. Energy Rsch. Tex. Tech. U., Lubbock, 1977-78; rsch. asst. grad. sch. edn. Harvard U., 1978-79; assoc. Butler, Binion, Rice, Cook & Knapp, Houston, 1980, Bracewell & Patterson, Washington, 1980; Hunton & Williams, Richmond, Va., 1981-89; of counsel, 1989-93, 95-96; assoc. prof. St. Thomas U. Sch. Law, Miami, Fla., 1989-93, prof., 1993—. Interim dean, 1993-94; bd. advisors Toxics Law reporter, Bur. Nat. Affairs, Washington, 1987—. Contbr. articles to profl. jours. Charter mem. West Broward Cmty. Ch. Capt. USAR, 1971-85. Grantee NSF, Inst. Evaluation Rsch., U. Mass., Ctr. Energy Rsch., Tex. Tech. U., 1977-78, U.S. EPA, 2003-06; recipient William Anderson award Am. Polit. Sci. Assn., 1977. Mem. ABA (vice-chmn.) tort and ins. practice sect. 1988-97, nat. res. and environ. sect. 1993-95, chmn. 1995-2000), Fed. Bar. Assn., Va. Bar Assn., Richmond Bar Assn., Phi Beta Kappa, Phi Eta Sigma. Democrat. Home: 1042 Woodfall Ct Weston FL 33326-2832 Office: St Thomas U Sch Law 16401 NW 37th Ave Miami Gardens FL 33054-6313 E-mail: alight@stu.edu.

LIGHT, ARTHUR HEATH, bishop; s. Alexander Heath and Mary Watkins (Nelson) L.; m. Sarah Ann Jones, June 12, 1953; children: William Alexander, Philip Nelson, John Page, Sarah Heath. BA, Hampden-Sydney Coll., 1951, DD, 1987; MDiv, Va. Theol. Sem., 1954, DD, 1979, St. Paul's Coll., 1979. Ordained priest Episcopal Ch., 1955. Rector West Mecklenburg Cure, Boydton, Va., 1954-58, Christ Ch., Elizabeth City, NC, 1958-63, St. Marys Ch., Kinston, NC, 1963-67, Christ and St. Luke's Ch., Norfolk, Va., 1967-79; bishop Diocese of Southwestern Va., Roanoke, 1979-96; pres. Province III Episcopal Ch., 1984-93. Mem. adv. coun. to presiding bishop, 1985-93; nominating com. 25th presiding bishop of the Episcopal Ch., 1994-97. Author: God, The Gift, The Giver, 1984. Bd. dirs. United Cmty. Fund, 1969-79, Norfolk Seamen's Friends Soc., 1969-79, Tidewater Assembly on Family Life, 1970-79, Friends of Juvenile Ct., 1975-79, Va. Inst. Pastoral Care, 1971-72; bd. dirs., exec. com. Va. Coun. Chs., 1979-97; bd. dirs. Roanoke Valley Coun. Cmty. Svcs., 1980-83, Virginians Organized for Informed Cmty. Effort, 1981-86; bd. dirs. Appalachian People's Svc. Orgn., 1981-91, pres., 1981-85, v.p., 1989-91; bio-med. ethics com. Ea. Va. Med. Sch., 1973-79, Lewis Gale Hosp., Salem, 1988-2003, Cmty. Hosp. Roanoke Valley, 1990-94; trustee Va. Episc. Sch., Lynchburg, 1979-96, Episc. H.S., Alexandria, 1979-96, Boys' Home, Covington, 1979-96, Stuart Hall Sch., Staunton, 1979-96, St. Paul's Coll., Lawrenceville, 1979-88; chmn. com. on continuing edn. Va. Theol. Sem., Alexandria, 1985-96, v.p. bd. trustees, 1987-96; bd. dirs., co-chmn. rural residency program Appalachian Ministries Ednl. Resource Ctr., Berea, Ky., 1985-87; mem. coord. cabinet Va. Coun. Churches, 1988-96, chmn. com. on church and soc., 1989-92; mem. Am. com. Kyosato Ednl. Experiment Project, 1990—2004, v.p., 1991-2004; mem. Gen. Conv. Standing Com. on World Mission, 1988-94, chmn., 1991-94; trustee Kanuga Conf. Ctr., 1991-95; bd. dirs. Conflict Resolution Ctr., 1996-98; cmty. rels. task force City of Roanoke, 1995—; bd. dirs. Habitat for Humanity, 1997-2000, Roanoke Valley Pastoral Counseling Ctr., 1998-2003, pres., 1999-2001; bd. dirs. Nat. Conf. for Cmty. and Justice, 2001-03, Regional End of Life Partnership Care Com.; asst. bishop Diocese So. Va., 2006-07. Named One of Outstanding Men of Yr., Jaycees, 1961, 63; fellow St. George's Coll., Jerusalem, 1978, 89, fellow in biomed. ethics U. Va., 1989; recipient humanitarian award Nat. Conf. Cmty. and Justice, 2002; Va. State Srs. Tennis Doubles champion, 2001, 04. Democrat. Episcopalian.

LIGHT, BETTY JENSEN PRITCHETT, retired dean; b. Omaha, Sept. 14, 1924; d. Lars Peter and Ruth (Norby) Jensen; m. Morgan S. Pritchett, June 27, 1944 (dec. 1982); children: Randall Wayne, Robin Kay Pritchett Church, Royce Marie Pritchett Bishop; m. Kenneth F. Light, Nov. 23, 1985 (dec. 2003). BS, Portland State U., 1965; MBA, U. Oreg., 1966; Ed.D., Oreg. State U., 1973. Buyer Rodgers Stores, Inc., Portland, Oreg., 1947-62; chmn. bus. div. Mt. Hood Community Coll., Gresham, Oreg., 1966-70, dir. evening coll., 1970-71, assoc. dean instn., 1972-77, dean humanities and behavioral scis., 1977-79, dean devel. and spl. programs, 1979-83, dean communication arts, humanities and social scis., 1983-86. State com. for articulation between cmty. colls. and higher edn., 1976-78; mem. Gov.'s Coun. on Career and Vocat. Edn., 1977-86; owner Effective Real Estate Mgmt., 1982-2002. Author: Values and Perceptions of Community College Professional Staff in Oregon, 1973; contbg. author: The Pritchett Study in Retailing, An Economic View, 1969. Mem. Gresham City Council, 1983-86. Mem.: Am. Vocat. Assn., Danish Brotherhood, N.W. Danish Found., Danish Heritage Soc. Home: 1635 NE Country Club Ave Gresham OR 97030-4432

LIGHT, CHRISTOPHER UPJOHN, freelance/self-employed writer, photographer; b. Kalamazoo, Jan. 4, 1937; s. Richard and Rachel Mary (Upjohn) L.; m. Lilykate Victoria Wenner, June 22, 1963 (div. 1986); children: Victoria Mary, Christopher Upjohn Jr.; m. Margo Ruth Bosker, Jan. 2, 1994. AB, Carleton Coll., 1958; MS, Columbia U., 1962; MBA, We. Mich. U., 1967; PhD, Washington U., St. Louis, 1971. Editor, pub. Kalamazoo Mag., 1963-66; pres. Mich. Outdoor Pub. Co., Kalamazoo, 1965-68; product planner Upjohn Co., Kalamazoo, 1967-68; asst. prof. U. Utah, Salt Lake City, 1971-72; assoc. prof., chmn. fin. dept. Roosevelt U., Chgo., 1975-78; vis. prof. fin. No. Ill. U., 1978-79; freelance writer, computer musician, 1979—. Editor: Charles Dickens' Village Coquettes, 1992; mgr. spl. projects Sarasota Music Archive, 1992-96. Contbr. articles to profl. and microcomputer jours.; composer: Ten Polyrhytmic Etudes, 1991, Piano Sonata #1, 1992, (albums) Apple Compote, One-Man Band, 1985, Ultimate Music Box, Vol. I, 1988, Ultimate Music Box, Vol. II, 1993; Aspects of Flowers, Ann Arbor, Mich., 1996, East Lansing, Mich., 1997, Kalamazoo, 1997, Aspects of Flowers II, Ann Arbor, 1997, Aspects of Flowers III, Fontana Festival, 1998, Portraits of Engines, Kalamazoo, 1998, Aspects of Flowers: Selections, Ann Arbor, 1999, Pathways, Kalamazoo, 1999, Aspects of Flowers IV, 2001, Landscapes, 2001, Aspects of Flowers, Sarasota, Fla., 2005, Portraits of Engines, Kalamazoo, 2006. Trustee Harold and Grace Upjohn Found., 1965-85, 94-2002, pres., 1997-2002; trustee, bd. dirs. Kalamazoo Symphony Orch. Assn., 1990-99; trustee Sarasota Music Archive, 1990-95, Kalamazoo Coll., 1991-93; bd. dirs. Am. Symphony Orch. League, 1992-2000, sec., 1996-99; bd. dirs. Fontana Chamber Arts, 2002—. Recipient ann. press award Mich. Welfare League, 1967. Mem. ASCAP, NARAS (voting com.), Fin. Mgmt. Assn., Soc. Profl. Journalists, Univ. Club Chgo., Sarasota Concert Assn. (bd. dirs. 1998—, v.p., 2003—), Gull Lake Country Club, Columbia U. Club. N.Y. Home: 1808 Greenlawn Ave Kalamazoo MI 49006-4325

LIGHT, JANE ELLEN, library director; b. Crosby, ND, May 4, 1948; d. Ralph W. and Ethel S. (Cady) Johnson; children: Jessica, David. BA, Calif. State U., Sacramento, 1973; MLS, U. Calif., Berkeley, 1974. Project mgr. Peninsula Libr. Sys., San Mateo, Calif., 1974-78, sys. dir., 1979-83; prog. mgr. Coop. Libr. Authority, San Jose, Calif., 1978-79; asst. libr. dir. Redwood City Pub. Libr., Calif., 1983-84, libr. dir., 1984-97; city libr. San Jose Pub. Libr., Calif., 1997—. Del. On-line Computer Libr. Ctr. User's Coun., 1993—2000; chair exec. bd. Urban Librs. Coun., 2005—06. Bd. dirs. Child Care Coordinating Coun., San Mateo, 1988-97, pres. 1992-93; bd. dirs. YMCA of Santa Clara Valley, 2001—. Mem. ALA, Calif. Libr. Assn., Pub. Libr. Assn. (Charlie Robinson award 2004), Rotary Club San Jose. Office: San Jose Pub Libr Sys 150 E San Fernando St San Jose CA 95112 Office Phone: 408-808-2150. E-mail: jane.light@sjlibrary.org.

LIGHT, JO KNIGHT, stockbroker; b. DeQueen, Ark., Mar. 15, 1936; d. Donald R. and Auda (Waltrip) Knight; m. Jerry T. Light, June 21, 1958 (dec. 1979); m. Victor E. Menefee Jr., Nov. 18, 1981; 1 child, Jerry T. Jr. BA cum laude, U. Ark., 1958. CFP. Travel cons. Comml. Nat. Bank, Little Rock, 1971-76; dist. mgr. Am. Express Co., NYC, 1976-82; fin. advisor and retirement planning specialist Morgan Stanley, NYC, 1982—, registered investment advisor, 1996—, sr. v.p. investments, 1999—. Mem. Jr. League of Little Rock Sustainers; vol. Happiness Singers. Mem. Fin. Planning Assn., Internat. Assn. Fin. Planners (bd. dirs. 1992-98, pres. bd. 1995-96), U. Ark. Alumni Assn. (bd. dirs. 1974-77), Morgan Stanley Pres.'s Club, Morgan Stanley Dir.'s Club, Phi Beta Kappa, Kappa Kappa Gamma. Avocations: music, tennis, sailing, skiing. Office: Morgan Stanley 425 W Capitol Ave Ste 200 Little Rock AR 72201-3440 E-mail: jo.light@morganstanley.com.

LIGHT, JOHN RICHARD, sculptor; b. Kalamazoo, Oct. 11, 1940; s. Richard Light and Rachel Mary (Upjohn) L.; m. Frances Mary Hesser, June 21, 1969; 1 child, Aimee Upjohn. BA, Yale U., 1962. Asst. advt. mgr. Verson Allsteel Press Co., Chgo., 1967-68; pub. relations copywriter Barton Brands, Chgo., 1970; investment cons. Chgo., 1972-86; sculptor, 1986—. Editor: Impact Machining, 1968; exhbns. include Skokie (Ill.) Fine Arts Commn., 1991, Iron Feather Gallery, Sedona, Ariz., 1993, Auburn (Calif.) Art Ctr., 1994, Art Guild, Farmington, Conn., 1995, Art at Parkview Hills, Kalamazoo, 2000; represented in permanent collections Goulandris Mus. Cycladic Art, Athens, Greece, Harvard Med. Sch., Cambridge, Mass., Nat. Gallery Art, Washington, Nat. Mus. Ireland, Dublin, Pushkin Mus. Art, Moscow, U. Chgo., Yale U., New Haven. Bd. dirs. Juvenile Protective Assn., Chgo., 1975—, Kalamazoo Child Guidance Clinic, 1969—, Lakeside Boys and Girls Home, 1979—. Recipient Distinguished Service award Publicity Club Chgo., 1972. Mem. Internat. Sculpture Ctr., Nat. Sculpture Soc., Publicity Club (Chgo.) (dir. 1975-77, mgr. club publs. 1972-73, chmn. seminar com. 1976-77), Kiwanis (Kalamazoo and Chgo.). Roman Catholic. Home: 4020 Old Field Trl Kalamazoo MI 49008-3339

LIGHT, RICHARD JAY, statistician, educator; b. NYC, Sept. 10, 1942; s. Solomon Julius and Muriel (Szwarcman) L.; m. Patricia Kahn, June 27, 1965; children: Jennifer Susan, Sarah Elizabeth. BS, U. Pa., 1962, AM, 1964; PhD, Harvard U., 1969; LLD (hon.), U. Winnipeg, Can., 1991. Mem. faculty Harvard U., Cambridge, Mass., 1969—, prof. stats., 1975—. Dir. faculty studies John F. Kennedy Inst. Politics, 1971-76; mem. Bd. on Testing and Assessment, 2000—; mem. panel children's and family policy Nat. Acad. Scis., 1977—, chmn. panel on evaluation, 1982; panel program evaluation Social Sci. Research Council, 1977—; bd. dirs Huron Inst., Cambridge, Mass., 1971—; cons. World Bank, 1975—; dir. Harvard Assessment Seminar, Cambridge, 1986—; bd. testing and assessment Nat. Rsch. Coun. Co-author: Data for Decisions, 1982, Summing Up, 1984, By Design, 1990, Meta-analysis for Explanation, 1992; editor: Learning from Experience, 1982, Evaluation Studies Rev., 1983; author: Making the Most of College, 2001. Trustee Buckingham, Browne and Nichols Sch., Cambridge, 1977—, Wellesley Coll., 1998—; mem. policy adv. group Mass. Office of Children, 1977—; bd. dirs. Fund for Improvement Post-Secondary Edn., 1992-95. N.Y. State Advanced Coll. Teaching fellow, 1965; vis. fellow Ctr. Analysis Health Practices, Harvard U. Sch. Pub. Health, 1977-78; Sr. Research award Spencer Found., Chgo., 1978-84; research fellow Ford Found., N.Y.C., 1981; recipient Paul Lazarsfeld award for contbns. to sci., 1992. Fellow Am. Acad. Arts and Scis.; mem. Am. Assn. Higher Edn. Assn., Am. Ednl. Rsch. Assn., Am. Sociol. Assn., Am. Evaluation Assn. (pres. 1986), Coun. Applied Social Rsch., Evaluation Rsch. Soc. (Paul Lazarsfeld award 1991), Am. Assn. for Higher Edn. (nat. bd.), Fund for Improvement Postsecondary Edn. (nat. bd.). Home: 31 Dunbarton Rd Belmont MA 02478-2458 Office: John F Kennedy Sch Govt Harvard U Cambridge MA 02138 Office Phone: 617-495-1183. Business E-Mail: richard_light@harvard.edu.

LIGHT, TERRY RICHARD, orthopedic hand surgeon; b. Chgo., June 22, 1947; BA, Yale U., 1969; MD, Chgo. Med. Sch., 1973. Diplomate in orthopedic surgery and in hand surgery Am. Bd. Orthopaedic Surgery. Asst. prof. Yale U., New Haven, 1977-80, Loyola U., Maywood, Ill., 1980-82, assoc. prof., 1982-88, prof., 1988-90, Dr. William M. Scholl prof., chmn. orthop. surgery and rehab, 1991—. Attending surgeon Hines (Ill.) VA Hosp., 1980—, Shriner's Hosp., Chgo., 1981—, Foster McGaw Hosp., Maywood, 1980—; hand cons. Chgo. White Sox, 1986-2003; bus. mgr. Jour. Hand Surgery, 1995-99. Editor Am. Acad. Orthop. Surgeons Hand Surgery Update, 1999, 2d edit. V.p. Frank Lloyd Wright Home and Studio Found., Oak Park, Ill., 1985-88, pres., 1988-90; chmn. bd. Fairfield Pub. Gallery, Sturgeon Bay, Wis., 1998-99; bd. dirs. Loyola U. Health Sys., 1999—. Fellow: ACS, Am. Acad. Orthop. Surgeons (editor Instrnl. Cruise Lects. vol. 55 2006); mem.: Am. Orthop. Assn. (2d v.p. 2004—05, 1st v.p. 2005—06, pres. 2006—), Ill. Orthop. Soc. (v.p. 1995, pres.-elect 1996, pres. 1997), Twenty-First Century Orthop. Assn. (pres. 1979—), Acad. Orthopaedic Soc. (pres. 2001—02), Chgo. Soc. for Surgery of Hand (sec. 1985—87, pres.-elect 1987—88, pres. 1988—89), Am. Assn. Hand Surgery (bd. dirs. 1989—91), Am. Soc. for Surgery of Hand (chair Jour. Hand Surgery com. 1995—99, treas. 1999—2002, v.p. 2002—03, pres. 2004—05), Alpha Omega Alpha. Avocation: collecting American arts and crafts and pottery. Office: Loyola U Med Ctr 2160 S 1st Ave Maywood IL 60153-3304 Office Phone: 708-216-4570. Personal E-mail: tlight1320@aol.com. Business E-Mail: tlight@lumc.edu.

LIGHTBURN, ANITA LOUISE, dean, social work educator; b. San Diego, Jan. 2, 1946; d. Kenneth E. and Ann Lorraine (Rosepiler) Schimp; m. Kenneth Dale Lightburn, Aug. 25, 1973; children: Tiffany, Kara. BA, Wheaton Coll., 1968; MS, Columbia U., 1972, MEd, 1988, EdD, 1989. Social worker Mass. Divsn. Child Guardianship, Boston, 1968-70; supr. psychiat. social work McMahon Meml. Shelter, NYC, 1972-73; lectr. Flinders U., Adelaide, Australia, 1973-85; asst., then assoc. prof. Columbia U., NYC, 1989-94; dean, prof. Sch. Social Work Smith Coll., Northampton, Mass., 1994—. Vis. prof. U. Conn., West Hartford, 1985, Columbia U., N.Y.C., 1986-88; cons., clinician, therapist in field. Author chpts. to books; contbr. articles to profl. jours. Mem. NASW. Office: 17 Hillcrest View Hartsdale NY 10530 Home: 17 Hillcrest Vw Hartsdale NY 10530-3106

LIGHTFOOT, ALBERT J., clergyman; b. Birmingham, Ala., July 2, 1926; s. Albert and Odessa Lightfoot; m. Catherine Kidd; children: Calvin, Cornelius, Reggie, Ronald, Phillip, Nedra, Phyllis. Student, U. Mich., 1960-62, Liberty Bible Coll., 1965-68, Union Bapt. Sem., 1975. Ordained to ministry Bapt. Ch., 1965. Organizer, pastor New Hope Bapt. Ch., Ann Arbor, Mich., 1965—, also gen. supt. Sunday sch., trustee clk., deacon, organizer Kangaroo Day Care Program. Moderator Huron Valley Dist. Assn., 1996; mem. Wolverine State Conv., Nat. Bapt. Conv. USA Inc. Mem. Ypsilanti-Ann Arbor Vicinity Ministerial Alliance (pres.). Home: 700 Braeside Pl Ann Arbor MI 48103-6149 Office: New Hope Bapt Ch 218 Chapin St Ann Arbor MI 48103-3390

LIGHTFOOT, ALFRED J., retired education educator; b. Shawano, Wis., July 23, 1936; BS, U. Wis., Milw., 1958; MA, Marquette U., 1966, EdD, 1968; ScD (hon.), London Insti. Applied Rsch., 1972. Cert. tchr. Calif., Wis. Prof. edn. Loyola Marymount U., LA, 1968—94; asst. prof. edn. Calif. State U., LA, 1969—71; ret., 1994. Dir. urban edn. Loyola Marymount U., LA, 1972—94; sr. lectr. edn. and psychology U. Wis., Waukesha, 2001—02; cons. in field. Author: The Culturally Disadvantaged, 1970, Inquiries into the Social Foundations of Education, 1972, American Urban Education: Inquiries into Changing Patterns, 1973, Socio-Psychological Dimensions of Learning, 1973, Robert Owen: Schools and Society for a New Age, 1976, Urban Education in Social Perspective, 1976 (Alumnus of Yr., Sch. Edn., Marquette U., 1995), Schools, Cities, and Teaching, 1980, Schools in Crisis: A Socio-Psychological View, 1983, Sociology of Education: Issues, Problems, Perspectives, 1986, Sociology of Education: The Culturally Different, 1990, Socio-Cultural Foundations of Education, 1993; editor: Schools and Society, 1969; contbr. articles to profl. jours. Home: PO Box 2266 Waukesha WI 53187-2266 Personal E-mail: al72336@aol.com. E-mail: light5859@sbcglobal.net.

LIGHTFOOT, EDWIN NIBLOCK, JR., retired chemical engineering educator; b. Milw., Sept. 25, 1925; married 1949, 5 children. BS, Cornell U., 1947, PhD in Chem. Engring., 1951; D in Tech. (hon.), Tech. U. Norway, 1985, Tech. U. Denmark, 2000. Asst prof., prof. biochem engr. U. Wis., Madison, 1953-80, prof. chem. engr., 1980-95, prof. emeritus, 1995—. Vis. prof. Tech. U. Norway, 1962, Stanford U., 1971, U. Canterbury, New Zealand, 1972. Author 14 books; contbr. articles to profl. jours. Recipient William H. Walker award Am. Inst. Chem. Engrs., 1975, Food, Pharm. and Bioengring. award, 1979, Warren K. Lewis award, 1991, Nat. medal sci. in engring., 2004, James E. Bailey award Soc. Biol. Engring., 2006. Mem. NAS, AAAS, Nat. Acad. Engr., Royal Norwegian Soc. Sci. and Letter, Am. Inst. Chem. Engr., Am. Chem. Soc. (E.V. Murphree award, 1994). Achievements include research on physical separation technology mass transfer and biomedical engineering. Office: U Wis 3639 Engineering Bldg 1415 Engineering Dr Madison WI 53706-1691 Business E-Mail: lightfoot@engr.wisc.edu.

LIGHTFOOT, JAMES ELLISON, researcher, director; b. Syracuse, NY, May 23, 1944; s. Robert and Evelyn Lightfoot; m. Pamela Joyce Endicott, Aug. 14, 1976; children: Stephen, Philip. BS in Geography & History, Bradley U., Peoria, Ill., 1962—65; MS in Geography, U. Calif., Riverside, 1976—78; PhD in Geography, U. Calif., LA, 1978—85. Cert. project mgmt. profl. Project Mgmt. Inst., 2000. Asst. prof. geography U. Ctrl. Ark., Conway, 1985—90; nat. security fellow, Nat. Security Program, Kennedy Sch. Govt. Harvard U., Cambridge, Mass., 1990—91; spl. projects officer N.G. Bur., 1993—95; sr. gen. mgr. Northrop Grumman Info. Tech.-Logicon, DC, 1995—2002; sr. geospatial analyst Northrop Grumman Info. Tech., DC, 2002—04; assoc. dir. Ctr. Strategic Intelligence Rsch. Nat. Def. Intelligence Coll., DC, 2004—; command sponsored rschr. Airpower Rsch. Inst. Air U., Maxwell Air Force Base, Ala. Dep. comdr. resources 164th Airlift Grp., Tenn. Air N.G., Memphis Internat. Airport, 1987—89. Editor: (books) Shooting the Front: Allied Aerial Reconnaissance and Photographic Interpretation on the Western Front - World War I, Learning With Professionals: Selected Works from the Joint Military Intelligence College; author: (govt. publ.) Electronic Imaging Standards for Archiving Records, (book) Mobilizing the Air National Guard for the Persian Gulf War: Lessons and New Directions; prodr.: (video) National Guard Aviation. Decorated Meritorious Svc. medal USAF. Mem.: Wash. Map Soc. (bd. dirs. 2006—), Rotary (pres. 2006—, Paul Harris Fellow 2006). Home: 2305 Knotweed Ct Waldorf MD 20603-4946 Office: National Defense Intelligence College Bldg 6000 Bolling AFB Washington DC 20340-5100 Home Phone: 301-932-9004. Personal E-mail: jelightfoot@comcast.net.

LIGHTFOOT, WILLIAM P., JR., lawyer; b. Jan. 3, 1950; m. Cynthiana Lightfoot; children: Ariana, B.J. BA, Howard U., 1972; JD, Wash. U., 1977. Bar: Pa. 1977, DC 1980, US Dist. Ct. Dist. Md., cert.: Nat. Bd. Trial Advocacy. Mng. ptnr. Koonz, McKenney, Johnson, DePaolis & Lightfoot, Washington. Lectr. in field; chairperson DC Cable TV Design Commn., 1983—84; mem.-at-large DC Coun., 1988—96; mem. ABA-ALI Restatement of Law, 1994—; diplomat Nat. Coll. Advocacy. Bd. dirs. Children's Advocacy Ctr.; mem. DC Jury Project, 1998—2000, DC Judicial Tenure and Disabilities Commn. Named Trial Lawyer Yr., Trial Lawyers Assn. Met. Wash. DC, 2003; named one of Am. Top Black Lawyers, Black Enterprise Mag., 2003; recipient Cmty. Svc. award, Leadership Wash., 2002. Mem.: Charlotte Rae Am. Inn Ct., Am. Law Inst., Trial Lawyers Assn. Met. Wash., Assn. Trial Lawyers Am., ABA, Bar Assn. DC, DC Bar. Office: Koonz Mckenney Johnson 2001 Pennsylvania Ave NW Ste 450 Washington DC 20006-1824 Office Phone: 202-659-5500. Business E-Mail: wlightfoot@koonz.com.

LIGHTFORD, KIMBERLY A., state legislator; BA in Pub. Comm., Western Ill. U.; MPA, U. Ill., Springfield. Mem. Ill. Senate, Springfield, 1998—, chair edn. com., vice chair higher edn. com., mem. fin. instns. com., mem. pub. health com., mem. revenue com. Former trustee Village of Maywood. Democrat. Address: 10001 W Roosevelt Rd Ste 202 Westchester IL 60154 Office Phone: 217-782-8505, 708-343-7444. Business E-Mail: klightford@senatedem.ilga.gov.

LIGHTHIZER, ROBERT E., lawyer; b. Ashtabula, Ohio, 1947; BA, Georgetown U., 1969, JD, 1973. Bar: DC 1973. Ptnr., practice leader internat. trade and transactions Skadden, Arps, Slate, Meagher & Flom, Washington, practice leader, legislative/lobbying. Chief of staff US Senate Com. Fin., 1981-83; dep. US Trade Rep. rank of amb.; treas. Republican Presdl. Campaign, 1996; spkr. on trade and tax issues, politics and other developments in Washington, DC; bd. dir. for several charitable and polit. groups. Contbr. articles to profl. publs. and jours. Mem. Internat. Bar Assn. Office: Skadden Arps Slate Meagher & Flom 1440 New York Ave NW Ste 600 Washington DC 20005 Office Fax: 202-661-8225. Business E-Mail: rlighthi@skadden.com.

LIGHTMAN, ALAN PAIGE, writer, physicist, educator; b. Memphis, Nov. 28, 1948; s. Richard Louis and Jeanne (Garretson) L.; m. Jean Greenblatt, Nov. 28, 1976; children: Elyse, Kara. AB, Princeton U., 1970; PhD in Physics, Calif. Inst. Tech., 1974; LittD (hon.), Bowdoin Coll., 2005; DFA (hon.), Memphis Coll. Arts, 2006; DHum (hon.), U. Md. Baltimore County, 2006. Postdoctoral fellow Cornell U., Ithaca, NY, 1974-76; asst. prof. Harvard U., Cambridge, Mass., 1976-79; staff scientist Smithsonian Astrophys. Obs., Cambridge, 1979-88; prof. sci. and writing MIT, Cambridge, 1988-95, John E. Burchard prof. humanities, 1995—2001, adj. prof. humanities, 2001—. Chair sci. panel NRC Astron. and Astrophys. Survey for 1990s. Author: Problem Book in Relativity and Gravitation, 1974, Radiative Processes in Astrophysics, 1976, Time Travel and Papa Joe's Pipe, 1984, A Modern Day Yankee in Connecticut Court, 1986, Origins: The Lives and Worlds of Modern Cosmologists, 1990, Ancient Light, 1991, Great Ideas in Physics, 1992, Time for the Stars, 1992, Einstein's Dreams, 1993, Good Benito, 1995, Dance for Two, 1996, The Diagnosis, 2000, Reunion, 2003, A Sense of the Mysterious: Science and the Human Spirit, 2005, The Discoveries, 2006. Recipient Most Outstanding Book in Phys. Sci., Assn. Am. Pubs., 1990 (Origins); Runner up PEN New England/Boston Globe Book Award, 1993 (Einstein's Dreams); Lit. Light of Boston Pub. Libr., 1995; Gemant award Am. Inst. of Physics, 1996, Gyorgy Kepes prize in the arts, MIT, 1998; Finalist Nat. Book Award in Fiction, 2000 (The Diagnosis); Disting. Alumnus Award Calif. Inst. Tech., 2003, McGovern Sci. and Soc. award Sigma Xi, 2006. Fellow AAAS, Am. Acad. Arts and Scis., Am. Phys. Soc.; mem. Am. Astron. Soc. (chmn. high energy astrophysics divsn. 1991).

LIGHTMAN, HAROLD ALLEN, marketing executive; b. Gloucester, Mass., Oct. 23, 1925; s. Abraham and Gertrude (Chait) L.; m. Irma Shorell, Feb. 19, 1954; children: Timothy, Chip, Stacey. Student, Norwich U., 1943; student, Cambridge U., Eng., 1946; BBA, U. Miami, 1949; postgrad., Oxford U., Eng., 1996. Acct. exec. Grant Advt., Miami, Fla., 1948-50; advt. dir. Sears Roebuck & Co., Tampa, Fla., 1950-51; acct. exec. Robert Otto Internat., NYC, 1952-53; acct. exec., field supr. Amos Parish & Co., NYC, 1954-56; acct. exec. Dowd, Redfield & Johnstone, NYC, 1957-59; chmn. bd. dirs. H. Allen Lightman Inc., NYC, 1959—. Bd. dirs. Irma Shorell Inc., N.Y.C.; pres., bd. dirs. Ind. Cosmetic Mfg. and Distbrs. U.S.A., v.p. nat. legis. affairs, 1974—; exec. v.p. Alfin Fragrances, Inc., 1985-87; pres. I.S. Labs. Inc., 1987-2000. Columnist: Seen & Heard, 1965-83; producer: Cable TV program Seen & Heard, 1978-87. Sgt. U.S. Army, 1943-46, ETO. Decorated Purple Heart, Bronze Star, European-African-Mid. Ea. Campaign medal with 3 battle stars, Combat Inf. Badge; recipient Pub. Rels. Gold Key award, 1987, Wisdom award Wisdom Soc. for Advancement of Knowledge, Learning and Rsch. in Edn., 2001; eminent Wisdom fellow of Wisdom Hall of Fame, 2001. Fellow Winston Churchill Meml. Libr., Harry S. Truman Meml. Libr.; mem. Nat. Fedn. Ind. Bus. (del. 1979), Internat. Platform Assn., Alpha Delta Sigma (founder, 1st pres. 1947-48), Miami Jr. C. of C. (publicity, pub. rels. dir. 1948-50), DAV, Am. Legion (vice comdr. 1948-49), Vets. of the Battle of the Bulge, The Jockey Club, Nat. Assn. Cosmetic Entrepreneurs (pres. 1997-98), lifetime character mem. Nat. WWII Meml., Wash. D.C., Tribute to a Generation, 2004. Office Phone: 212-535-9471.

LIGHTSTONE, JOHN B., finance company executive; b. England; s. Hyman and Golda Lightstone; m. Linda E. Lightstone; children: Leah Elbaum, Emily. BA, Cambridge U., England, 1962; PhD, Harvard U., Cambridge, Mass., 1968, NYU, NY, 1979. Pres. Lightstone Capital Mgmt. LLC, White Plains, NY, 1998—. Adj. prof. Lubin sch. bus. Pace U., White Plains, NY, 1991—. Vol. Meals on Wheels, White Plains, NY. Achievements include patents in field. Office: Lightstone Capital Mgmt LLC 16 Midchester Ave Ste 301 White Plains NY 10606-3605 Home Phone: 914-4761-5131; Office Phone: 914-761-9091. Personal E-mail: jbl@post.harvard.edu.

LIGHTSTONE, RONALD, lawyer; b. NYC, Oct. 4, 1938; s. Charles and Pearl (Weisberg) L.; m. Nancy Lehrer, May 17, 1973; 1 child, Dana. AB, Columbia U., 1959; JD, NYU, 1962. Atty. CBS, NYC, 1967-69; assoc. dir. bus. affairs CBS News, NYC, 1969-70; atty. NBC, NYC, 1970; assoc. gen. counsel Viacom Internat. Inc., NYC, 1970-75, v.p., gen. counsel, sec., 1976-80; v.p. bus. affairs Viacom Entertainment Group, Viacom Internat., Inc., 1980-82, v.p. corp. affairs, 1982-84, sr. v.p., 1984-87; exec. v.p. Spelling Entertainment Inc., LA, 1988-91, CEO, 1991-93; chmn. Multimedia Labs. Inc., 1994-97; CEO, pres. New Star Media Inc., 1997-99, vice chmn., 1999-2000. Lt. USN, 1962—66. Mem. ABA (chmn. TV, cable and radio com.), Assn. of Bar of City of N.Y., Fed. Comm. Bar Assn. Home Phone: 310-474-9120. Business E-Mail: ron@sagpond.com.

LIGLER, FRANCES SMITH, biochemist; b. Louisville, June 11, 1951; d. George Frederick and Mary Frances (Hagan) Smith; m. George Todd Ligler, Aug. 19, 1972; children: Amy Elizabeth, Adam George. BS, Furman U., Greenville, SC, 1972; DPhil, Oxford U., Eng., 1977. Postdoctoral fellow U. Tex. Health Sci. Ctr., San Antonio, 1975-76; instr., asst. instr. Southwestern Med. Sch., Dallas, 1976-80; group leader cellular immunology DuPont, Glenolden, Pa., 1980-85; head biosensors and biomaterials Naval Rsch. Lab., Washington, 1985—. Cons. Potomac (Md.) Biotech, 1985—. Contbr. articles to profl. jours. Recipient Alan Berman Rsch. Publ. award, 1988, manuscript award 3M/Am. Assn. Med. Instrumentation ann. mtg. 1988, chemistry div. award Superior Tech. Publ., 1989, NLR tech. transfer award, 1991, 93, tech. transfer award Office of Drug Control Policy, 1992, ACS Hillebrand award, 1993, Edison patent award, 1992, 94. Mem. NAE, Am. Assn. Immunologists, Am. Assn. Pathologists, Am. Chem. Soc., Chem. Soc. Washington (bd. dirs. 1988—), Dept. of Def. Tech. Working Group, Dept. of State Tech. Task Group L. Avocations: horseback riding, soccer. Office: US Navel Rsch Lab 4555 Overlook Ave, SW Washington DC 20375

LIGOCKI, GORDON MICHAEL, artist, educator; b. Hammond, Ind., Sept. 7, 1943; s. Michael and Regina (Hlodnicki) L.; m. Rita K. Herdaliska, Jan. 25, 1968 (div. June 1980); 1 child, Ian Gabriel; m. Linda Lee Heinsen, Oct. 30, 1994. BFA, Ohio Wesleyan U., 1965; MA in Drawing, U. Iowa, 1967; MFA in Sculpture, U. Ill., 1968; postgrad., Gov.'s State U., 1987-92. Writer Arts Ind., Indpls., 1987-91; writer, art critic Hammond (Ind.) Times, 1985-93; instr. life drawing Art Barn, Valparaiso, Ind., 1989—; assoc. prof. Purdue U., Hammond, 1992-97; gallery dir., adj. prof. Ind. U. N.W., Gary, 1992—2001; assoc. prof. Valparaiso U., 1990—2001; asst. prof. Ancilla Coll., 2003—. Panelist Ind. Arts Commn., Indpls., 1989; cons. on drawing Collegiate Press, Alta Loma, Calif., 1995; curator individual shows Midwest Mus. of Am. Art, Elkhart, Ind., 1991, No. Ind. Art Assn., Munster, Ind., Gary Comty. Mental Health, Hammond Pub. Libr. One-person shows include R.H. Love Gallery, Chgo., 1992, Herr Chambliss Gallery, Hot Springs, Ark., 1992, Uncle Freddies Gallery, Highland, Ind., 2003-06; contbr. articles to newspapers and profl. pubs. Named Friend of the Arts in Edn., Ind. Art Edn. Assn., 1991. Mem.: Internat. Soc. of Visual Sociology. Avocation: gardening. Home: 2142 N 125 E Winamac IN 46996-8520 Office: Tortuga Inn Bed & Breakfast 2142 N 125 E Winamac IN 46996-8520 Office Phone: 574-936-8898 256. Business E-Mail: gligocki@ancilla.edu.

LIGON, DEMOND L., SR., sales executive; b. Gary, Ind., Feb. 25, 1972; s. Terry Tyrone Ligon and Corleatha Marie Moore; m. Marion A. Gant, Aug. 16, 1996; 1 child, Demond L. Ligon, Jr. BS in Bus., Tri-State U., Angola, Ind., 2006. Cert. info. tech. Ind., 2002. Package handler FedEx Ground, Hammond, Ind., 1995—97, territory mgr., 1997—2001; svc. mgr. FedEx Home Delivery, Griffith, Ind., 2002—04; gen. mgr. Exel Direct Logistics, Thornton, Ill., 2004—06; ops. mgr. Am. Port Svcs., Inc., Elwood, Ill., 2007—; sales account exec. Insignia Stone, Inc., New Lenox, Ill., 2007—. Mem.: Leadership NW Ind., Alpha Beta Gamma, Omega Psi Phi Frat. Inc. Achievements include development of operations management; tact & finesse communication; interaction management. Office: 26453 Center Point Dr Elwood IL 60421 Personal E-mail: demondligon@aol.com.

LIGON, DUKE R., lawyer; b. May 16, 1941; BS, Westminister Coll., 1963; JD, U. Tex., 1969. Bar: Okla. 1969, D.C. 1973, U.S. Supreme Ct. 1974, N.Y. 2004. Ptnr. Bracewell & Patterson, Corcoran, Hardesty, Whyte, Hemphill & Ligon, Washington, DC; various positions US Dept of Interior, Dept. of Treas., Dept. of Energy; sr. v.p., mng. dir. for investment banking Bankers Trust Co., NYC, 1985—95; ptnr. Mayer, Brown & Platt, NYC, 1995—97; v.p., gen. counsel Devon Energy Corp., 1997—99, sr. v.p., gen. counsel, 1999—2006. Mem.: ABA, Okla. State Bar Assn., N.Y. Bar Assn., N.Y. State Bar Assn., Phi Alpha Delta.

LIGORANO, MICHAEL KENNETH, lawyer; b. Morristown, NJ, July 24, 1954; s. Michael Thomas and Virginia J. Ligorano; m. Debra Ann Baumann, Aug. 12, 1978. BA cum laude, Rutgers U., Newark, 1975; JD, Western New Eng. Law Sch., Springfield, Mass., 1978. Bar: N.J. 1978, U.S. Dist. Ct. N.J. 1978, Fla. 1980, U.S. Ct. Appeals (3d cir.) 1980, U.S. Tax Ct. 1980, U.S. Supreme Ct. 1985, N.Y. 1990; lic. real estate sales N.J. Assoc. Charles M. Lee, Washington, N.J., 1978-79, Hogan Folk Mahon & Simms, Flemington, Somerville, N.J., 1979-82, ptnr., 1982-83, Mahon Moeller & Ligorano, Flemington, 1983-84, Schaff Motiuk et al, Flemington, Trenton, 1984-87, Ligorano & Sozansky P.C., Flemington, 1987-98, Archer & Greiner, P.C., Flemington, Princeton, 1998—2001, Norms, McLaughlin & Marcus, Somerville, 2001—. Atty. Mine Hill Twp. Bd. Adjustment, 1978-88; asst. Hunterdon County counsel, 1979-82; legal counsel Hunterdon County Bd. Recreation Commrs., 1980-2000; atty. Alexandria Twp. Bd. Adjustment, 1983-84; spl. counsel Solid Waste, Hunterdon County, 1984; atty. Readington Twp. Planning Bd., 1985-91, Readington Twp., 1991-96, Clinton Twp., 1996, Clinton Twp. Planning Bd., 1997-99, Glen Gardner Bd. Edn., 1996-98; spl. title counsel High Bridge Bd. Edn., 1996; mem. Dist. XIII Ethics Com., 1987-91, chair, 1990-91; mem. Dist. XIII Fee Arbitration Com., 1991-2000; mem. N.J. Supreme Ct. Complementary Disput Resolution Project, 1995-98; instr. N.J. Inst. Continuing Legal Edn., 1995-97; adv. bd. Summit Bank, 1990-92, First Cmty. Bank, 1992-94; gen. counsel The Blue Army, U.S.A., World Apostolate of Fatima, 1999—. Environ. commr. Denville Twp., 1973-75; legis. aide N.J. Assembly, 1974-75; mem. N.J. Natural Areas Coun., 1983-84; mem. Glen Gardner Bd. Health, 1993-95; bd. dirs. Hunterdon chpt. ARC, 1982-84, Glen Gardner Youth Ctr., 1988-90; mem. Hunterdon County Rep. Com., 1983-97; mem. Leukemia Soc. of Am. Team in Tng. Alaska Marathon, 1997, San Diego Marathon, 1999; adv. bd. ARC, 1994—. Recipient Vol. of Yr. award, ARC of NJ, 2004. Mem. N.J. State Bar Assn. (gen. coun. 1993-94, sects. on land use, real property, probate and trust, dispute resolution), N.Y. State Bar Assn. (sect. on real property, probate and trust), The Fla. Bar (sect. on land use, real property, probate and trust), Am. Immigration Lawyers Assn., Hunterdon County Bar Assn. (sec. 1991-92, v.p. 1992-93, pres. 1993-94, trustee 1994-97, equity settlement panel 1994—, chair com. on professionalism 1996—), Hunterdon C. of C. (bd. dirs. 1981-86), Hunterdon/Somerset Realtors Assn., Nat. Geneology Soc., Knights of Columbus. Avocations: genealogy, long distance running. Office: PO Box 1018 Somerville NJ 08876-1018 E-mail: mkligorano@nmmlaw.com.

LIGUORI, PETER, broadcast executive; b. Bronx, NY, 1960; m. Hannah Cox, Jan. 16, 1988; 2 children. BA in History, Yale U., 1982. Advt. exec. Ogilvy & Mather, Saatchi & Saatchi; v.p. consumer mktg. HBO, v.p. to sr. v.p. mktg. home video divsn.; sr. v.p. mktg. Fox/Liberty Networks News Corps., 1996—98, pres., CEO FX Networks, 1998—2005; pres. entertainment Fox Broadcasting Co., LA, 2005—07, chmn. entertainment, 2007—. Assoc. prodr. (films) Big Night, 1996. Bd. trustees Entertainment Industries Coun. Office: Fox Broadcasting Co 10201 W Pico Blvd Los Angeles CA 90035 Office Phone: 310-369-1000. Office Fax: 310-369-1049.*

LIGUORI, ROBERT, lawyer, insurance company executive; b. Bklyn, Jan. 7, 1954; AA, Nassau Cmty. Coll., 1973; BA, SUNY, Binghamton, 1975; JD, Potomac Sch. Law, Washington, 1980. Bar: Ga. 1981, Md. 1982, Mass. 2001, US Dist. Ct. (no. dist. Ga. 1981), US Ct. Appeals (5th cir. 1982), US Tax Ct. 1982. Former sr. v.p., co-gen. counsel Mass. Mutual Fin. Group, Springfield, Mass. Bd. trustees We. New Eng. Coll. Mem.: ABA, Md. State Bar Assn., DC Bar, State Bar Ga.

LIJOI, PETER BRUNO, lawyer; b. Suffern, NY, Sept. 2, 1953; s. Salvatore and Josephine (Gentile) L.; m. Christine Louise Confroy, Aug. 19, 1978; children: Jonathan Peter, Christopher Andrew. BA in History and Econs., Montclair State U., 1975; postgrad. in urban planning, Rutgers U., 1975-76; JD, Pace U., 1979; postgrad., Harvard U., 1992. Bar: NJ 1981, NY 1988; cert. tax assessor NJ. Rsch. intern N.J. Dept. Edn., Trenton, 1976; intern Office US Atty., NYC, 1977-78; energy coord. Rockland County, 1979-80; dep. dir., of counsel Pvt. Industry Coun., Pearl River, NY, 1980-91; pvt. practice law Summit, NJ, 1981—; dir., counsel County of Rockland Indsl. Devel. Agy., 1981-95; v.p., gen. counsel Rockland Econ. Devel. Corp., Pearl River, 1990-91. Cons. US Dept. Energy, Washington, 1980; mem. program of instrn. lawyers Law Sch., Harvard U., 1992; legal counsel and land acquisition mgr. K. Hovnanian Cos. North Jersey, Inc., 1993—95, K. Hovnanian Cos. Northeast, Inc., 1995—2001; sr. v.p. land acquisition and legal counsel D.R. Horton Inc., NJ, 2001—06; legis. counsel to Assemblyman Eric Munoz, NJ State Legis.; sr. area devel. ptnr., legal counsel Fairfield Residential LLC, Summit, 2006—. Guest writer The Bond Buyer. Pres. Washington Elem. Sch. PTA, Summit, 1986—88; mem. Summit Planning bd.; desegregation grant adv. and facilities coms. Summit Bd. Edn., 1992—; commr. tax bd. Union County, NJ, 1999—; pres. Summit Soccer Club, 2002—04; bd. dirs. Rockland County coun. Girl Scouts US, 1982—92. Mem. ABA, N.J. Bar Assn., N.Y. Bar Assn., Union County Bar Assn., Assn. Trial Lawyers Am., Nat. Assn. Bond Lawyers, Summit Soccer Club (pres. 2002—). Roman Catholic. Avocations: running, coaching youth soccer. Home and Office: Fairfield Residential LLC 124 Canoe Brook Pkwy Summit NJ 07901-1436 Office: 28 Beechwood Rd Summit NJ 07901 Office Phone: 732-682-1403. Business E-Mail: plijoi@ffres.com.

LIKENS, GENE ELDEN, biology and ecology educator; b. Pierceton, Ind., Jan. 6, 1935; s. Colonel Benjamin and Josephine (Garner) L.; m. Phyllis Craig; children: Kathy, Gregory, Leslie. BS, Manchester Coll., Ind., 1957, DSc (hon.), 1979; MS, U. Wis., 1959, PhD, 1962; DSc (hon.), Rutgers U., 1985, Plymouth State Coll., U. N.H., 1989, Miami U., 1990; LHD (hon.), Union Coll., 1991; DSc (hon.), U. Bodenkultur, Vienna, Austria, 1993, Marist Coll., 1993, Wageningen Agrl. U., Netherlands, 1998, U. Conn., 2004. Asst. zoology Manchester Coll., 1955-57; grad. tchg. asst. U. Wis., 1957-59, vis. lectr., 1963; instr. zoology Dartmouth Coll., 1961, instr. biol. scis., 1963, asst. prof., then assoc. prof., 1963-69; mem. faculty Cornell U., 1969-83, prof. ecology, 1972-83, Charles A. Alexander prof. biol. scis., 1983, adj. prof., 1983—; v.p. N.Y. Bot. Garden, 1983-93; dir. Inst. Ecosystem Studies, Millbrook, NY, 1983—2007, pres., 1993—2007; G. Evelyn Hutchinson chair in ecology Inst. Ecosys. Studies, Millbrook, NY, 2000—05; dir. Mary Flagler Cary Arboretum, 1983—93; prof. biology Yale U., 1984—; prof. grad. field of ecology Rutgers U., 1985—. Vis. prof. Ctr. Advanced Rsch., dept. environ scis. U. Va., Charlottesville, 1978-79, SUNY, Albany, 2004-; vis. disting. rsch. prof. U. Conn., Storrs, 2005—; chmn. New Eng. divsn. task force conservation aquatic ecosystems U.S. Internat. Biol. Program, 1966-67; vis. assoc. ecologist Brookhaven Nat. Lab., 1968; C.P. Snow lectr. Ithaca Coll., 1979, 89; Rilett vis. scholar Ill. State U., 1985; vis. scholar James Madison U., 1988; Class of 1960 vis. scholar, Williams Coll., Williamstown, Mass., 1988; William V. Kaesar Meml. scholar U. Wis., Madison, 1991; vis. disting. ecologist, Colo. State U., 1994; Walker Ames prof., U. Wash., Seattle, 2001; Miegunyah fellow U. Melbourne, Australia; cons., panelist, lectr. in field Contbr. articles to profl. jours. Recipient Conservation award Am. Motors Corp., 1969, 75th Anniversary award U.S. Forest Svc., 1980, Disting. Achievement award Lab. Biomed. and Environ. Studies, UCLA, 1982, Regents medal SUNY, 1984, NY Acad. Scis. award, 1986, Internat. ECI prize for Limnetic Ecology, 1989, Disting. Svc. award N.Y. Bot. Garden, 1989, Am. Inst. Biol. Scis., 1990, Lifetime Accomplishment award, 2000, Disting. Svc. award Hudson River Environ. Soc., 1997, The Garden Club Am. Spl. Citation, 1992, Tyler World Environment prize U. So. Calif., 1993, Australia prize, 1994; Sr. fellow NATO, 1969, Guggenheim fellow, 1972-73; grantee NSF, EPA, Dept. Energy, USDA Forest Svc., NOAA, Disting. Svc. award Hudson River Environ. Soc., Inc., 1997, Vollenweider award and lectureship, Canada Ctr. for Inland Waters, Nat. Water Rsch. Inst., 1998, Storm King award Scenic Hudson Inc., 1998, Excellence award Nat. Coun. State Garden Clubs Inc., 1999, Nat. Medal Sci., 2001, Blue Planet prize, 2003; Miequnyah Disting. fellow U. Melbourne, Australia, 2004. Fellow: AAAS, Am. Philos. Soc.; mem.: NAS (chmn. sect. 27 1986—89), Inst. Biology (London), Royal Danish Acad. Sci., Am. Inst. Biol. Scis. (pres. 2002—03, Lifetime Accomplishment award 2000, Huxley medal, Inst. Biology (UK) 2001), Austrian Acad. Scis., Australian Soc. Limnology, Internat. Water Resources Assn. (charter), Internat. Assn. Gt. Lakes Rsch., Freshwater Biol. Assn., Internat. Water Acad. (life), Am. Water Resources Assn. (hon.), Brit. Ecol. Soc. (hon.), Explorers Club, Am. Polar Soc., Royal Swedish Acad. Scis., Internat. Assn. Theoretical and Applied Limnology (v.p. 1998, pres. 2001—04, 2004—07, Naumann-Thienemann medal 1995), Am. Soc. Limnology and Oceanography (v.p. 1975—76, pres. 1976—77, 1st G.E. Hutchinson award for excellence in rsch. 1982), Ecol. Soc. Am. (chmn. study com. 1971—74, v.p. 1978—79, pres. 1981—82, Eminent Ecologist award 1995), Am. Acad. Arts and Scis., Sigma Xi, Phi Sigma, Gamma Alpha. Methodist. Office: Inst Ecosys Studies Box AB Millbrook NY 12545 Business E-Mail: likensg@ecostudies.org.

LIKENS, JAMES DEAN, economics professor; b. Bakersfield, Calif., Sept. 12, 1937; s. Ernest LeRoy and Monnie Jewel (Thomas) L.; m. Janet Sue Pelton, Dec. 18, 1965 (div.); children: John David, Janet Elizabeth; m. Karel Carnohan, June 4, 1988 (div.); m. Christine Irons, Feb. 8, 2003. BA in Econs., U. Calif., Berkeley, 1960, MBA, 1961; PhD in Econs., U. Minn., 1970. Analyst Del Monte Corp., San Francisco, 1963; economist 3M Co., Mpls., 1968-71; asst. prof. econs. Pomona Coll., 1969-75, assoc. prof. econs., 1975-83, prof. econs., 1983-85, Morris B. and Gladys S. Pendleton prof. econs., 1989—, dept. chair, 1998-2001. Vis. asst. prof. econs. U. Minn., 1970, 71, vis. assoc. prof., 1976-77; pres., dean Western CUNA

Mgmt. Sch., Pomona Coll., 1975—; chmn. bd. First City Credit Union, 1978—; coord. So. Calif. Rsch. Coun., LA, 1980-81, 84-85; adv. coun. Western Corp. Fed. Credit Union, 1993—; cons. in field. Author: (with Joseph LaDou) Medicine and Money, 1976, Mexico and Southern California: Toward A New Partnership, 1981, Financing Quality Education in Southern California, 1985; contbr. articles to profl. jours. Served with USCG, 1961-67; dir. Centennial, Pomona Coll., 1987-88. Named Dir. of Yr., Calif. Credit Union League, 1997, Credit Union Exec. Soc., 2001; recipient Leo H. Shapiro Lifetime Achievement award, Calif. Credit Union League, 2001, Herb Wegner Lifetime Achievement award, Nat. Credit Union Found., 2005; grantee rsch. grantee HUD-DOT, Haynes Found. Mem.: ABA, Western Econ. Assn., Am. Econ. Assn. Avocations: painting, clarinet, golf. Home: 725 W 10th St Claremont CA 91711-3719 Office: Pomona Coll Dept Econs Claremont CA 91711 Office Phone: 909-821-8998. Business E-Mail: jlikens@pomona.edu.

LIKINS, PETER WILLIAM, retired academic administrator; b. Tracy, Calif, July 4, 1936; s. Ennis Blaine and Dorothy Louise (Medlin) L.; m. Patricia Ruth Kitsmiller, Dec. 18, 1955; children: Teresa, Lora, Paul, Linda, Krista. BCE, Stanford U., 1957, PhD in Engring. Mechanics, 1965; MCE, MIT, 1958; PhD (hon.), Lafayette Coll., 1983, Moravian Coll., 1984, Med. Coll. Pa., 1990, Lehigh U., 1991, Allentown St. Francis de Sales, 1993, Czech Tech U., 1993. Devel. engr. Jet Propulsion Lab., Pasadena, Calif., 1958-60; asst. prof. engring. UCLA, 1964-69, assoc. prof., 1969-72, prof., 1972-76, asst. dean, 1974-75, asso. dean, 1975-76; dean engring. and applied sci. Columbia U., NYC, 1976-80, provost, 1980-82; pres. Lehigh U., Bethlehem, Pa., 1982-97, U. Ariz., Tucson, 1997—2006. Cons. in field. Author: Elements of Engineering Mechanics, 1973, Spacecraft Dynamics, 1982; Contbr. articles to profl. jours. Mem. US Pres.'s Coun. Advisors Sci. and Tech., 1990-93. Ford Found. fellow, 1970-72; named to Nat. Wrestling Hall of Fame. Fellow AIAA; mem. Nat. Acad. Engring., Phi Beta Kappa, Sigma Xi, Tau Beta Pi. Office Phone: 520-298-0820. E-mail: plikins@arizona.edu.

LIKINS, ROSE MARIE, former federal agency administrator, ambassador; b. Andrews AFB, Md., Jan. 22, 1959; d. Eugene Aloysius and Merlyn (Houghland) McCartney; m. John Foster Likins, MAy 30, 1981; children: James, Kevin. BA in Internat. Affairs, Mary Washington Coll., Fredericksburg, Va., 1981, BA in Spanish, 1981. Joined Fgn. Svc., U.S. Dept. State, Washington, 1981—, previous fgn. svc. assignments Honduras, Paraguay, Bulgaria, U.S. amb. to El Salvador El Salvador, 2000—03, acting asst. sec. Bur. of Polit.-Military Affairs, 2005. Rm. mother Tuckahoe Elem. Sch., Arlington, Va., 1993-94. Mem. Am. Fgn. Svc. Assn., Mortar Board (pres. chpt. 1980-81), Phi Beta Kappa. Roman Catholic. Achievements include fluent in Spanish and Bulgarian.

LIKOVA MINEVA, LORA T., research scientist; d. Tzvetko T. Likov and Angelina B. Tzvetkova; m. Kristyo N. Mineff; 1 child, Zlatko K. Minev. MSc in Computer Sci., Tech. U., Sofia; PhD in Cognitive Neuroscience, Ctrl. and East-European Ctr. Cognitive Scis., New Bulgarian U., Sofia; postgrad., U. Nat. and World Econs., Sofia; fMRI (functional MRI) tng., MIT/HMS/MGH Ctr. for Biomedical Imaging, Boston. Asst. prof. Ctrl. Inst. of Computer Technique, Sofia, Bulgarian Acad. Scis., Sofia, Inst. for Microprocessing Technique, Sofia; rsch. scientist Smith-Kettlewell Eye Rsch. Inst., San Francisco, postdoctoral fellow; vis. scientist U. Warwick, Coventry, England. Hon. prof. Tech. U., Sofia; head Non-Standard Think Group/Computer Inst. Contbr. articles to profl. jours. Recipient award, Nat. Patent Inst.; fellow fellow for European Conf. on Visual Perception, Oxford, Eng., Brit. Coun.; Rachel C. Atkinson fellow, Smith-Kettlewell Eye Rsch. Inst., San Francisco, fellow European Conf. on Visual Perception, Helsinki, Finland, Soros Open Soc. Found. Mem.: Cognitive Neuroscience Soc., Vision Sci. Soc., Orgn. for Human Brain Mapping, Soc. for Neuroscience. Achievements include patents for magnetic head; discovery of new brain areas: first brain imaging studies (fMRI) on dynamic stereovision; discovering a new brain areas for 3D-motion processing; eye disease diagnosis: discovering a fundamental blind-spot related mechanism and inventing a clinical method (Blue Light Papillometry) for early diagnosis of blinding diseases; depth-motion phenomenon: discovering of a new category of perceived 3D-motion in 3D displays (Monopolar Depth Motion); the transient asynchrony/synchrony is a critical organizational factor in visual perception of dynamic world; for the first time in the human brain a figure/ground mechanism based on top-down suppression of the background representation in retinotopic visual areas. Avocations: philosophy, yoga, hiking, drawing, poetry. Office: Smith-Kettlewell Eye Rsch Inst 2318 Fillmore St San Francisco CA 94115 Office Phone: 415-345-2066. Business E-Mail: lora@ski.org.

LI-LAN, artist; b. NYC, Jan. 28, 1943; d. Yun Wing and Helen Charlotte (Zimmer) Gee.; m. Masuo Ikeda, 1969 (div. 1980). One-man shows include Nantenshi Gallery, Tokyo, 1971, 1974, 1977, 1980, 1985, OK Harris Gallery, NYC, 1983, 1985, 1987, Franz Bader Gallery, Washington, 1989, Asher/Faure Gallery, LA, 1980, 1982, Robert Miller Gallery, NYC, 1978, James Yu Gallery, 1974, William Benton Mus. Art, Storrs, Conn., 1990, New Arts Program, Kutztown, Pa., 1991, Amelie A. Wallace Gallery SUNY-Old Westbury, 1992, Benton Gallery, Southampton, N.Y., 1992, 1993, Art Projects Internat., NYC, 1994, 1996, Lin & Keng Gallery, Taipei, Taiwan, 1995, 1997, 2001, 2006, Rutgers U., New Brunswick, N.J., 2002, DoubleVision Gallery, LA, 2003, Nabi Gallery, NY, 2004, Jason McCoy Inc., 2006, exhibited in group shows, East Hampton, 1973, Guild Hall Mus., 1975, 1976, 1978, 1979, 1997, Randolph Macon Women's Coll., Lynchburg, Va., 1974, Philbrook Art Ctr., Tulsa, 1975, Phoenix Art Mus., 1979, Am. Acad. and Inst. Arts and Letters, NYC, 1983, 1987, Sydney and Frances Lewis Found. Collection travelling exhbn., 1978—, Norton Ctr. for Arts, Danville, Ky., 1987, Southampton Campus Fine Arts Gallery, L.I. U., 1988, Parrish Art Mus., Southampton, 1988, 1992, 1993, 2000, Internat. Travelling Exhbn., Mex., S.Am., Spain, Portugal, 1989—90, Travelling Exhbn. including Blum Helman Gallery, NY, 1989—90, U. Okla. Mus. Art, Norman, 1989—90, Grand Rapids Art Mus., 1989—90, Mich. U. Art Gallery, 1989—90, U. North Tex., Denton, 1989—90, Hillwood Art Gallery, Brookville, N.Y., 1989—90, Heckscher Mus., Huntington, N.Y., 1992, Huntington, 1995, 1996, PS 1 Mus., Long Island City, N.Y., 1984, Long Island City, 1992, New Mus. Contemporary Art, NYC, 1994, Eretz Israel Mus., Tel Aviv, 1996, Weatherspoon Art Gallery, Greensboro, NC, 1977, 2001, 2007, Smithsonian Instn., Washington, 2001, Pace Wildenstein Gallery, NYC, 2003, Lin-Keng Gallery, Beijing, China, 2007, Represented in permanent collections Sezon Mus. Modern Art, Karuizawa, Japan, Modern Art Mus., Toyama, Sydney and Frances Lewis Found. Collection, Richmond, Vassar Coll. Art Gallery, Poughkeepsie, N.Y., Estee Lauder, Inc., NYC, Security Pacific Nat. Bank, L.A., Atlantic Richfield Co., Dallas, Ohara Mus. Art, Kurashiki, Japan, Guild Hall Mus., East Hampton, Mobil Oil Corp., NYC, Virlane Found., New Orleans, Va. Mus. Fine Arts, Richmond, Visconsi & Jacobs, Cleve., Seattle 1st Nat. Bank, Chermayeff and Geismar Assocs., NY, Parrish Art Mus., Southampton, William Benton Mus. Art, Storrs, Westfield State Coll., Mass., Lifetime TV, NYC, Ark. Arts Ctr., Little Rock, Fisher Pharm. Ltd., Tel Aviv, San Diego Mus. Art, Balt. Mus. of Art; author: Canvas with An Unpainted Part: An Autobiography, 1976. Avocations: photography, writing.

LIL' BOW WOW, See MOSS, SHAD

LILENFELD, LISA RACHELLE, psychology professor, psychologist; b. NYC, Nov. 1, 1968; d. Donald Lilenfeld and Bette Jo Paluzzi; m. Lawrence Philip Riso, June 27, 1999; children: Alana Lilenfeld Riso, Hannah Lilenfeld Riso, Alec Lilenfeld Riso. BS, Cornell U., Ithaca, NY, 1990; PhD, U. Minn., Mpls., 1995. Assoc. prof. psychology Ga. State U., Atlanta, 1998—2006, Argosy U., Washington, 2007—. Assoc. dir. clin. tng. Ga. State U., Atlanta, 2004—06. Contbr. articles to profl. jours. Fellow, Western Psychiat. Inst. & Clinic, Pitts., 1995—98. Fellow: Acad. Eating Disorders. Jewish. Avocations: running, piano. Office: Argosy Univ Clinical Psychology Program 1550 Wilson Blvd Ste 600 Arlington VA 22209 Office Phone: 703-526-5878. Business E-Mail: llilenfeld@argosy.edu.

LILES, CLIFTON ROY, retired application developer; b. San Antonio, Jan. 28, 1944; s. Roy Clifton and Lucy Mae Liles. BS in Physics, U. Houston, 1978. Software engr. Tex. Instruments, Richardson, Tex., 1978-90, Unisys, Houston, 1990-96; mem. computer sci. staff, software designer United Space Alliance, Houston, 1996—2006; ret., 2006. With US Army, 1967—71. Mem.: IEEE, Assn. Computing Machinery, Am. Geophys. Union. Home: 2310 Longwood Dr Pearland TX 77581 Personal E-mail: lilescr@acm.org, c.liles@sbcglobal.net.

LILES, KEVIN, music company executive; b. Balt., Feb. 27, 1968; 3 children. Student, Morgan St. U. Mem. group Numarx, 1989—91; co-founder, co-pres. Marx Bros. Records, 1991—92; intern Def Jam Records, 1992, gen. mgr. promotions, 1994—96, gen. mgr., v.p. promotions, 1996—98, pres., 1998—2004; exec. v.p. Island Def Jam Music Group, 2002—04, Warner Music Group, 2004—. Writer: songs Girl You Know It's True (performed by Milli Vanilli); author (with Sammantha Marshall): Make It Happen: The Hip Hop Generation Guide to Success, 2005. Recipient Vibe award, Power Broker of the yrear, 2005. Office: Warner Music Group 75 Rockefeller Plz New York NY 10019

LILEY, PETER EDWARD, retired engineering educator; b. Barnstaple, North Devon, Eng., Apr. 22, 1927; came to U.S., 1957; s. Stanley E. and Rosa (Ellery) L.; m. Elaine Elizabeth Kull, Aug. 16, 1963; children: Elizabeth Ellen, Rebecca Ann. BSc, U. London, 1951, PhD in Physics, 1957, DIC, 1957. With Brit. Oxygen Engring., London, 1955-57; asst. prof. mech. engring. Purdue U., West Lafayette, Ind., 1957-61, assoc. prof., 1961-72; assoc. sr. researcher Thermophys. Properties Research Ctr., Purdue U., West Lafayette, Ind., 1961-72, prof. mech. engring., 1972-98; sr. rschr. Ctr. for Info. and Numerical Data Analysis and Synthesis, Purdue U., West Lafayette, Ind., 1972-92; ret., 1997. Cons. in field. Author: Sect. 2 Perry's Chemical Engineers Handbook, 7th edit., 1997; author: (with Hartnett et al.) Handbook of Heat Transfer Fundamentals, 2d edit., 1985; author: (with others) Marks Mechanical Engineers Handbook, 11 edit., 2006, Schaums 2000 Solved Problems in Mechanical Engineering Thermodynamics, 1995, Kutz Mechanical Engineers Handbook, 3d edit., 2006; co-author: Steam and Gas Tables with Computer Equations, 1985, Thermal Conductivity of Nonmetallic Liquids and Gases, 1970;: Properties of Nonmetallic Fluid Elements, 1981, Properties of Inorganic and Organic Fluids, 1988; editor, mem. editl. bd. Internat. Jour. Thermophysics, 1980—86; contbr. chpts. to handbooks in field, articles to profl. jours.; reviewer profl. jours. Served with Royal Corps Signals, Brit. Army, 1945-48. Lutheran. Home: 3608 Mulberry Dr Lafayette IN 47905-3937 E-mail: peterelliley@insightbb.com.

LILIENSTERN, O. CLAYTON, lawyer, educator; b. Houston, Nov. 13, 1943; s. Oscar C. and Suzanne (Haughton) L.; m. Rebecca D. L.; children: Robert, Susan, Kelli, Melanie. AB, U. Ala., 1965; JD, U. Houston, 1968, MBA, 1992; LLM, George Washington U., 1972; MTS, So. Meth. U., 2002. Bar: Tex. 1968, U.S. Dist. Ct. (so. dist.) Tex. 1973, U.S. Tax Ct. 1975, U.S. Supreme Ct. 1976, U.S. Dist. Ct. (we. dist.) Tex. 1978, U.S. Dist. Ct. (ea. dist.) Tex. 1987, U.S. Dist. Ct. (no. dist.) Tex. 1988, U.S. Ct. Appeals (5th, 9th, 11th and fed. cirs.); cert. civil trial law Tex. Bd. Legal Specialization. Assoc. Andrews & Kurth, Houston, 1972-79, ptnr., 1979-97, Hicks, Thomas & Lilienstern LLP, Houston, 1997—2001, of counsel, 2001—; asst. head sch. Episcopal HS, Bellaire, Tex., 2004—07; head of sch. U. Sch. Jackson, Tenn., 2007—. Mem. Leadership Houston, 1989—. Capt. JAGC, U.S. Army, 1968-72. Decorated Joint Svc. Commendation medal; NAIS/E.E. Ford fellow, 2005-06. Fellow Tex. Bar Found., Houston Bar Found.; mem. ABA, State Bar Tex., Houston Bar Assn., A.A. White Soc., U. Houston Law Ctr., U. Houston Law Alumni Assn. (pres. 1982-83, life), Houston Law Rev. Alumni Assn. (pres. 1991-92), Jasons Soc., Briar Club (bd. dirs., pres. 2004) Delta Tau Delta, Omicron Delta Kappa, Phi Alpha Delta.

LILJEBERG, GENEVIEVE BROCATO, artist; b. Shreveport, La., Dec. 12, 1939; d. Samuel Charles and Rosalie Pittari Brocato; m. Robert Louis Liljeberg, June 4, 1960; children: Roxanne, Robert, Sam, Hans, Heidi Student, Loyola U., 1957—60. One-woman shows include St. Jude Hosp., Kenner, La., 1989, On Four Gallery, New Orleans, 1991, Sylvia Schmidt Gallery, 1994, 1995, 1998, 1999, Entergy Ctr., New Orleans, 1997, Zeigler Mus., Jennings, La., 1993, Beresford Sporting Gallery, Saratoga, N.Y., Collector's Gallery, Lexington, Ky., Linda Howell & Assocs., Oklahoma City, 1996, Sportsman Gallery, Vail, Colo., 1998, Ctr. for Arts Invitational, Mt. Kisco, N.Y., 1998, exhibitions include New Orleans Acad. Art, 2003, Sportsmans Gallery, Marietta, Ga., Union Art Gallery, Baton Rouge, 2006, La. Invitational; featured artist Cadwell Arts Coun., 2000; New Orleans Opera Ball poster, 2003, poster and cover 2003 opera program; contbr. articles to profl. jours. Recipient Best in Show award Mus. of Horse, 1997 Mem. Am. Acad. Equine Art (assoc.) Republican. Roman Catholic. Avocations: jogging, swimming, volleyball, horse racing, opera. Home: 1506 Milan St New Orleans LA 70115-3825 Studio: 832 Baronne St New Orleans LA 70113-1103

LILJEGREN, FRANK SIGFRID, art association administrator, artist, educator; b. NYC, Feb. 23, 1930; s. Josef Sigfrid and Ester (Davidsson) L.; m. Donna Kathryn Hallam, Oct. 12, 1957. Student, Art Students League, NYC, 1950—55. Instr. painting, drawing, composition Westchester County Ctr., White Plains, NY, 1967-77, Art Students League, 1974-75, Wassenberg Art Ctr., Van Wert, Ohio, 1978-80, Wright State U. Br. Western Ohio Campus, Celina, 1981—. Corr. sec. Allied Artists Am., N.Y.C., 1967, exhbn. chmn., 1968-, pres., 1970-72, also bd. dirs. Exhibited at Suffolk Mus., Stonybrook, NY, Springfield (Mass.) Mus., Marion Kugler McNay Art Inst., San Antonio, Philbrook Mus., Tulsa, NAD, NYC, New Britain (Conn.) Mus. Art, Ft. Wayne (Ind.) Mus. Art; represented in permanent collections Art Students League, Univ. Mus., S.E. Mo. State U., Cape Girardeau, Manhattan Savs. Bank, NYC, Am. Ednl. Pubs. Inst., NYC, New Britain Mus. Am. Art, Conn., U. St. Francis, Ft. Wayne, Ft. Wayne Mus. Art. With AUS, 1951. Recipient numerous awards for still life oil paintings. Mem. Fine Arts fedn. N.Y, Art Students League (life), Acad. Artists Assn., Allied Artists Am. (life), Coun. Am. Artists Socs., Artists Fellowship, Salmagundi. Home Phone: 419-238-1159. *The best advice I could give young artists is to first learn their craft to the fullest so that they can then be free to express themselves in what ever style and medium they then choose to work. Last but not least, they should have self-respect and great love for what they are doing.*

LILLARD, JOHN FRANKLIN, III, lawyer; b. Bladensburg, Md., Aug. 2, 1947; s. John Franklin Lillard Jr. and Madeline Virginia (Berg) Lillard; m. Kim Leslie Oliver, June 1, 1991 (div.); 1 child, John Franklin Lillard IV. BA, Washington and Lee U., 1969, JD, 1971. Bar: NY 1972, DC 1974, Md. 1975. Assoc. Donovan, Leisure, Newton & Irvine, NYC, 1971-74, Pierson, Ball & Dowd (merged into Reed, Smith,. McClay & Lynch), 1974—76; ptnr. Lillard & Lillard, Washington, 1977—; trial atty. civil divsn. Dept. Justice, Washington, 1976-77. Instr. Dale Carnegie Course, 1988—97. Notes and comments editor: Washington and Lee Law Rev., 1970. Vice chair Village Coun. Friendship Heights, Chevy Chase, Md., 1975—77; chair Am. Solar Energy Assn.; founding mem. Nat. Adv. Coun. Ctr. for Study of the Presidency, 1970—99, Md. State Adv. Bd. on Spl. Tax Dists., 1976—77; alcoholic beverage adv. bd. Montgomery County, 1977—79; chair Eisenhower Centennial Meml. Com., 1990—97; candidate US Congress 5th dist., Md., 1981. Recipient Eastman award, Am. Arbitration Assn., 1971. Mem.: Anne Arundel County Bar Assn., Prince George's County Bar Assn., Md. Bar Assn., Tred Avon Yacht Club (Oxford, Md.), Met. Club. Republican. Episcopalian. Office: 8 Loudon Ln Annapolis MD 21401-1219 Home Phone: 410-268-8456; Office Phone: 410-268-1900. Personal E-mail: johnlillard@toad.net.

LILLARD, MARK HILL, III, engineering consultant, retired military officer; b. Jacksonville, Fla., Sept. 1, 1943; s. Mark Hill Jr. and Cornelia Kingman (Callaway) L.; m. Marie-Jacques Le Guyader, June 3, 1972; children: Mark Hill IV, Michael Robert. BA, Bowling Green U., 1965; MS, St. Mary's U., San Antonio, 1976; MBA, Auburn U., 1977. Commd. 2d lt. USAF, 1965, advanced through grades to brig. gen., 1991; ret., 1991; exec. v.p. Pilot Rsch. Assocs., Inc., Vienna, Va., 1991—2001, also bd. dirs.; regional v.p. RCM Technologies, Inc., Bethesda, Md., 2001—04; sr. assoc. Booz Allen Hamilton, McLean, Va., 2004; v.p. Seta Corp., McLean, 2005—06; sr. v.p. Dewberry & Davis LLC, 2006—. Author: Simulation, 1976. Decorated Legion of Merit, Def. Superior Svc. medal, Def. Meritorious Svc. medal; Samil medal (Republic of Korea). Mem. Air Force Assn., Lions, Kiwanis, Phi Delta Theta. Republican. Avocations: tennis, golf. Home: 9516 Locust Hill Dr Great Falls VA 22066-2021 Office: 8401 ARlington Blvd Fairfax VA 22031 Personal E-mail: mlillard@dewberry.com.

LILLEHAUG, DAVID LEE, lawyer; b. Waverly, Iowa, May 22, 1954; s. Leland Arthur and Ardis Elsie (Scheel) L.; m. Winifred Sarah (Smith), May 29, 1982; one child, Kara Marie. BA, Augustana Coll., Sioux Falls, SD, 1976; JD, Harvard U., 1979. Bar: Minn., 1979, US Dist. Ct. Minn., 1979, DC, 1981, US Ct. Appeals (8th cir.), 1981, US Dist. Ct. DC, 1982. Law clk. to presiding judge US Dist. Ct., Mpls., 1979-81; assoc. Hogan and Hartson, Washington, 1981-83, 84-85; issues aide, exec. asst. to Walter Mondale, Washington, 1983-84; assoc. Leonard, Street, and Deinard, Mpls., 1985-87, ptnr., 1988—93, 1998—99; US atty. Dist. of Minn., 1994-98; atty. Fredrikson & Byron, P.A., Mpls., 2002—. Candidate, US Senate, 1999-2000. Recipient Outstanding Alumnus award, Augustana Coll., 2006; Mondale Policy Forum fellow, U. Minn., 1990—91. Mem. Minn. Bar Assn. (past chair constrn. law sect., Author's Award 1990). Lutheran. Avocations: fishing, golf. Office: Fredrikson & Byron PA 200 S Sixth St Minneapolis MN 55402 Home: 6701 Parkwood Ln Edina MN 55436 Office Phone: 612-492-7000. Business E-Mail: dlillehaug@fredlaw.com.

LILLEHOFF, PIPER, psychiatrist; d. Harvest and adopted d. Foster Eubank. BA in Psychology, U. Calif., Irvine, 1989; MD, Drexel U., Phila., 1996. Resident adult psychiatry Oreg. Health Scis. U., Portland, 1996—99; fellow child psychiatry U. Calif., Irvine, 1999—2001; child and adolescent psychiatrist County of Orange, Health Care Agy., Costa Mesa, Calif., 2002—. Mem. physician content rev. bd. Healthcasts/Profl. TV Network, NYC, 2005—. Author poetry. Mem. Universalist-Unitarian Ch., Laguna Beach, Calif., 2006. Finalist Flute Competition, Calif. Music Tchrs. Assn.; recipient Youth Leadership award, Hugh O'Brien Found.; scholar, Mills Coll., U. Calif., Irvine; Rock Sleyster scholar for Outstanding Med. Student Performance in Psychiatry, AMA. Mem.: Physician's Com. For Responsible Medicine, Am. Psychiat. Assn., Am. Acad. Child and Adolescent Psychiatry, Internat. Libr. Poetry (hon.; Am. amb. poetry), Phi Beta Kappa, Psi Chi. Universalist-Unitarian. Avocations: music/art therapy (flute/poetry), movement therapy (dance/yoga), animal-assisted therapy (canine). Home Phone: 949-679-4920. Personal E-mail: pprlhf@yahoo.com.

LILLESAND, THOMAS MARTIN, engineer, educator; b. Laurium, Mich., Oct. 1, 1946; m. Theresa Hofmeister, 1968; children: Mark, Kari, Michael. BS, U. Wis., 1969, MS, 1970, PhD in Civil Engring., 1973. Prof. remote sensing SUNY, Syracuse, 1973-78, U. Minn., 1978-82, U. Wis., Madison, 1982—. Cons., 1973—. Recipient SAIC/Estes Meml. Tchg. award, 2005. Mem. Am. Soc. Photogrametry and Remote Sensing (pres. 1998-99, Alan Gordon award 1979, 93, Talbert Abrams award 1984, Fennell award 1988, SAIC/Estes Meml. Tchg. award 2005). Office: U Wis Environ Remote Sensing Ctr 1225 W Dayton St Rm 1239B Madison WI 53706-1612

LILLESTOL, JANE BRUSH, educational consultant; b. Jamestown, ND, July 20, 1936; d. Harper J. and Doris (Mikkelson) Brush; m. Harvey Lillestol, Sept. 29, 1956; children: Kim, Kevin, Erik. BS, U. Minn., 1969, MS, 1973, PhD, 1977; grad. Inst. Ednl. Mgmt., Harvard U., 1984. Dir. placement, asst. to dean U. Minn., St. Paul, 1975-77; assoc. dean, dir. student acad. affairs ND State U., Fargo, 1977-80; dean Coll. Human Devel. Syracuse U., NY, 1980-89, v.p. for alumni rels., 1989-95, project dir. IBM Computer Aided Design Lab., 1989—92; prin. Lillestol Assocs.; emeritus faculty Syracuse U., 1995—; faculty U. Phoenix, 2002—, curriculum devel. specialist, 2003. Charter mem. Mayor's Commn. on Women, 1986-90; NAFTA White House Conf. for Women Leaders, 1993. Bd. dirs. Univ. Hill Corp. Syracuse, 1983-93; mem. steering com. Consortium for Cultural Founds. of Medicine, 1980-89; trustee Manlius Pebble Hill Sch., 1990-94, Archbold Theatre, 1990-95, ND State U., 1992—. Recipient award US Consumer Product Safety Commn., 1983, Woman of Yr. award AAUW, 1984, svc. award Syracuse U., 1992; named among 100 Outstanding Alumni Over Past 100 Yrs., U. Minn. Coll. Human Ecology, 2001. Home: 3207 Casa Marina Rd NW Alexandria MN 56308-4613

LILLEY, ALBERT FREDERICK, retired lawyer; b. Harrisburg, Pa., Dec. 21, 1932; s. Frederick Anthony and Jane Sander (Ingham) L.; m. Judith Carter Pennock, Sept. 1, 1956; children: Kirk Anthony, Kristin Sander, James Alexander. AB, Bowdoin Coll., 1954; LLB, U. Va., 1959. Assoc. Milbank, Tweed, Hadley & McCloy, NYC, 1959-67, ptnr., 1967-96; ret., 1997. Trustee No. Highlands Regional H.S., Allendale, N.J., 1964-65; mem. Allendale Bd. Zoning Adjustment, 1965-66; bd. overseers Bowdoin Coll., 1976-88, overseer emeritus, 1988—; trustee Valley Hosp., Ridgewood, N.J., 1978-92, vice chmn. bd., 1985-89, chmn. bd., 1989-92; bd. dirs. Valley Care Corp., 1992-97, Valley Home and Cmty. Health Care, Inc., 1992-97, Chapel Hill-Carrboro Arts Ctr., 2001—, vice chmn. bd. 2005-06, chmn. bd. 2006-07; mem. alumni coun. U. Va. Law Sch., 1991-94, U.S. Can. Law Project Adv. Bd., 1990-95. 1st lt. U.S. Army, 1954-56. Recipient Alumni Svc. award, Bowdoin Coll., 2004. Mem. ABA, Am. Law Inst., U. Va. Law Sch. Alumni Assn. (class mgr. annual giving campaign), Chapel Hill Rotary Club (vocat. svc. dir. 1998-99, treas. 1999-2000, sec. 2000-01, v.p. 2001-02, pres. 2002-03),. Home: 204 Laurel Hill Rd Chapel Hill NC 27514-4325 E-mail: afl@nc.rr.com.

LILLEY, DAVID, chemicals executive; MA in Chem. Engring., Cambridge U. Former v.p., mem. exec. com. Am. Cyanamid Co.; v.p. Am. Home Products Corp., 1994-97; pres., COO, bd. dirs. Cytec Industries, Inc., West Paterson, NJ, 1997-98, pres., CEO, 1998—99, chmn., pres., CEO, 1999—. Office: Cytec Industries 5 Garret Mountain Plz West Paterson NJ 07424*

LILLEY, JOHN MARK, academic administrator; b. Converse, La., Mar. 24, 1939; s. Ernest Franklin and Sibyl Arrena (Geoghagan) L.; children: Sibyl Elizabeth, Myles Durham; m. Geraldine Mills; stepchildren: Benjamin Murphy, Jason Murphy. B in Music Edn., Baylor U., 1961, MusB, 1962, MusM, 1964; D of Musical Arts, U. So. Calif., 1971. Mem. faculty Claremont McKenna, Harvey Mudd, Pitzer and Scripps Colls., Claremont, Calif., 1966-76; asst. dean faculty Scripps Coll., 1973-76; asst. dean arts and scis. Kans. State U., Manhattan, 1976-80; provost, dean Pa. State U., Erie, 1980—2001; pres. U. Nev., Reno, 2001—05, Baylor U., Waco, Tex.,

2006—. Bd. dirs. Erie Conf., 1997-01; mem. N.W. Pa. Indsl. Resource Ctr., 1987-01, Forum for a Common Agenda, 2001-03, Econ. Devel. Authority of West Nev., 2001-05. Condr. 1st performances Kubik, 1972, 76, Ives, 1974, (recording) Kubik, 1974. Bd. dirs., v.p. So. Calif. Choral Music Assn., L.A., 1971-76, Reno Philharm., 2004-05; mem. Archtl. Commn., Claremont, 1974-76; bd. dirs. Erie Philharm., 1980-86, Reno Philharm., 2004-, Sta. WQLN Pub. Broadcasting of N.W. Pa., 1992-01; bd. dirs. United Way of Erie County, 1981-01, chair, 1998-99; mem. Regents Commn. on Nursing Edn., Kansas City, Kans., 1978-79; pres. Pacific S.W. Intercollegiate Choral Assn., L.A., 1969-70; mem. Pa. Gov.'s Tuition Account Program Adv. Bd., 1996-2001. NEH grantee, 1978. Mem. Am. Assn. Higher Edn., Coll. Music Soc., Am. Choral Dirs. Assn., Am. Assn. State Colls. and Univs. (vice chair confs. and profl. devel. com. 1989, 97, chair 1990, bd. dirs. 1995-97), Las Vegas C. of C. (bd. advisors 2004—), Rotary (pres. and bd. dirs. Manhattan club 1979-80, Erie club 1981-20018), Ridgewood Club, Phi Mu Alpha Sinfonia, Omicron Delta Kappa. Republican. Baptist. Avocation: golf. Office: Baylor U Office of Pres Waco TX 76798 Office Phone: 254-710-3555.

LILLEY, MILI DELLA, insurance company executive, entertainment management consultant; b. Valley Forge, Pa., Aug. 29; d. Leon Hanover and Della Beaver (Jones) L. MBA, Tenn. Christian U., 1957, PhD, 1959. Various positions G & G Cons. Inc., Ft. Lauderdale, Fla., 1971-75; v.p. AMEX, Inc., Beverly Hills, Calif. and Acapulco, Mex., 1976-80; pres. The Hanover Group, Ft. Lauderdale, 1981—; personal and bus. mgr. entertainers including Ink Spots, Ft. Lauderdale, 1984—, Lanny Poffo, Ft. Lauderdale, 1990—. Dist. agt. ITT Life Ins. Corp., also other leading cos. Named to All Stars Honor Roll Nat. Ins. Sales Mag., 1989. Mem. Fla. Assn. Theatrical Agts., Fla. Guild of Talent Agts., Mgrs., Prodrs. and Orchs. Office: The Hanover Group PO Box 70218 Fort Lauderdale FL 33307-0218 Home Phone: 954-772-2074; Office Phone: 954-491-1101.

LILLEY, WILLIAM, III, business executive, consultant; b. Phila., Jan. 14, 1938; s. William, Jr. and Ida Weaver (Macklin) L.; m. Eve Auchincloss, Mar. 12, 1977; children: Buchanan Morgan, Brooke Carole, Whitman Elisa, Justin Weaver BA magna cum laude, U. Pa., 1959; MA, Yale U., 1961, PhD, 1965. Asst. prof. history Yale U., New Haven, 1962-69; prof. govt. U. Va., Charlottesville, 1977; co-founder, editor Nat. Jour., Washington, 1969-73; dep. asst. sec. HUD, Washington, 1973-75; dep., then dir. Council Wage and Price Stability, Washington, 1975-77; staff dir. Com. on Budget, Ho. of Reps., Washington, 1977-78; v.p. CBS, Inc., Washington, 1980-81, v.p. corporate affairs NYC, 1981-84, sr. v.p. corporate affairs, 1985-86; pres. Am. Bus. Conf., 1986-88, Policy Communications Inc., Washington, 1988-2000; chmn., CEO InContext, Inc., 1992-2000, iMap Data Inc., 2000—04; exec. dir. govt. mkts. ChoicePoint Inc., 2005—. Co-author: New Technologies Affecting Broadcasting, 1981, Economic and Social Impacts of Media Advertising, 1989, Impact of Advertising on the Competetive Structure of the Media, 1990, Impact of Media Advertising on International Competetiveness, 1991, Geographic Distribution of U.S. Businesses Which Advertise Heavily, 1991, Almanac of State Legislatures, 1994, State Atlas of Political and Cultural Diversity, 1996, State Legislative Elections: Voting Patterns and Demographics, 1997, The Sports That Make Communities Rich: An Inquiry into the Economics of Professional Sports, 1997, Almanac of State Legislatures: Changing Patterns, 1990-97, 1998, The Economic Impact of the European Grands Prix, 1999; contbr. articles to profl. jours. Bd. dirs. Stanford U. Social Sci. History Inst., 2000—, Woodrow Wilson Nat. Fellowship Found., 2002—, Yale U. Alumni Assn., 2006—. Recipient U.S. Govt. Disting. Svc. award 1975, 76; Samuel F.B. Morse Rsch. fellowship, 1967-68; George Washington Eggleston prize; Woodrow Wilson Fellowship, 1959-61. Mem.: River Club, Yale Club. Office Phone: 732-659-1073. Business E-Mail: wlilley@imapdata.com.

LILLIE, JOHN CANFIELD, III, lawyer; b. Rochester, Minn., May 7, 1970; m. Shelley Lillie; 1 child. BA, Hope Coll., 1992; JD, Hamline U. Sch. Law, 1998. Bar: Minn. 1998. Atty. Dudley and Smith, P.A., St. Paul. Named a Rising Star, Minn. Super Lawyers mag., 2006. Mem.: Nat. Assn. Criminal Def. Lawyers, Minn. Assn. Criminal Def. Lawyers, Washington County Bar Assn., ABA, Minn. State Bar Assn., Ramsey County Bar Assn. Office: Dudley & Smith PA 2602 US Bank Ctr 101 E 5th St Saint Paul MN 55101 Office Phone: 651-291-1717. E-mail: jcl@dudleyandsmith.com.*

LILLISTON, ANDREW WILSON, JR., lawyer; b. Washington, Nov. 18, 1946; s. Andrew Wilson and Mary (D.) Lilliston; m. Elaine Alling Lilliston, Aug. 9, 1969; children: Jennifer Lilliston Hindman, Andrew W. III, Cortlin Alling, Kimberly Lilliston Roberts. BS in Bus., Ind. U., 1968; JD, U. Va., 1975. Bar: Ind. 1975, US Dist. Ct. (so. dist.) Ind. 1975, US Ct. Appeals (7th cir.) 1976, US Supreme Ct. 1992. Assoc. Ice Miller, Donadio & Ryan, Indpls., 1975—78; staff atty. Burger Chef Sys. Inc., Indpls., 1978—81, sr. atty., 1981—83; sr. corp. atty. Hardee's Food Sys., Inc., Rocky Mount, NC, 1983—87, asst. gen. counsel, 1987—90; spl. counsel Golden Corral Corp., Raleigh, NC, 1991—94, dep. gen. counsel, asst. sec., 1994—. Capt. US Army, 1968—72, Vietnam. Decorated Bronze Star. Mem.: Lions (pres. Fuquay-Varina Lions club 2001—02, dist. zone chmn. 2002—03, region chmn. 2003—04, humanities/white cane chmn. 2004—05, Progressive Melvin Jones fellow 2005, Jack Stickley fellow 2003), "I" Men's Assn., Raven Soc., Beta Gamma Sigma, Kappa Delta Rho, Phi Delta Phi. Methodist. Avocations: kayaking, hiking, softball. Office: Golden Corral Corp 5151 Glenwood Ave Raleigh NC 27612 Business E-Mail: alilliston@goldencorral.net.

LILLY, EDWARD GUERRANT, JR., retired utilities executive; b. Lexington, Ky., Oct. 29, 1925; s. Edward Guerrant and Elisabeth Read (Frazer) L.; m. Nancy Estes Cobb, Nov. 25, 1961; children: Penelope Read, Edward Guerrant III, Collier Cobb (dec.), Steven Clay. BS, Davidson Coll., 1948; MBA, U. Pa., 1949. Credit analyst Citizens and So. Nat. Bank, Charleston, SC, 1949-50; asst. v.p. Wachovia Bank and Trust Co., Charlotte, 1952-55, v.p., loan adminstrv. officer Wilmington, NC, 1956-60, sr. v.p., area exec. Kinston, NC, 1961-62, Durham, NC, 1963-70, sr. v.p., mgr. trust investment svcs. dept. Winston-Salem, NC, 1970-71, also bd. dirs., 1971-88; sr. v.p., group exec. Carolina Power and Light Co., Raleigh, NC, 1971-76, sr. v.p., chief fin. officer, 1976-81, exec. v.p., chief fin. officer, 1981-90, also bd. dirs. Bd. dirs. N.C. Enterprise Corp. Mem. U. N.C. bd. visitors, 1974-87; bd. dirs. Gen. Telephone Co. S.E., 1965-1972, Rsch. Triangle Found., Research Triangle Park, CSC Industries, 1990-95; trustee Davidson Coll., 1976-88, Union Theol. Seminary. Lt. USNR, 1950—52. Mem. Edison Electric Inst. (chmn. fin. group 1979) Lodges: Rotary (Raleigh). Presbyterian.

LILLY, EVANGELINE, actress; b. Fort Saskatchewan, Alberta, Can., Aug. 3, 1979; Attended, U. Brit. Columbia. Actor: (TV series) Judgment Day, 2002, Lost, 2004— (Outstanding Performance by an Ensemble in a Drama Series, Screen Actors Guild award, 2006); (TV miniseries) Kindgom Hospital, 2004; (films) The Long Weekend, 2005; (TV series, guest appearance) Smallville, 2002, Tru Calling, 2003. Address: ABC TV c/o Lost 77 W 66th St New York NY 10023-629

LILLY, JAMES EDWARD, lawyer; b. Birmingham, Ala., Aug. 5, 1960; s. Joseph Lanahan and Mildred Irene (Gorman) L.; m. Dawn Patrice Lee, June 6, 1981; children: Justin Patrick, Mary Jessica, Kaitlin Elizabeth. BA summa cum laude in Bus. Adminstrn. and Polit. Sci., Birmingham-Southern Coll., 1982; JD with high honors, Duke U., 1985. Bar: NC 1985, Ga. 1991. Joined Womble Carlyle Sandridge & Rice PLLC, Winston-Salem, NC, 1985, mem. Atlanta, Charlotte, NC, leader capital markets practice group, 2001—. Mem.: ABA (sect. bus. law). Republican. Roman Catholic. Avocations: golf, basketball, reading. Office: Winston Carlyle Sandridge & Rice PLLC One Wachovia Ctr Ste 3500 301 S College St Charlotte NC 28202-6037 Office Phone: 704-331-4969. Office Fax: 704-338-7854. Business E-Mail: jlilly@wcsr.com.

LILLY, JOHN RICHARD, II, lawyer; b. Phila., July 20, 1962; s. John Richard Sr. and Elizabeth Anne (Brown) Lilly; m. Amy Katherine Scribner; children: John Richard III, Cameron Lewis, Jason Benjamin, Robyn Deborah. BA, Geoge Washington U., 1987; JD, U. Balt., 1991. Bar: Md. 1992, US Dist. Ct. Md. 1995. Law clk. 7th Jud. Cir. Md., Upper Marlboro, 1991-92; asst. state's atty. State's Atty.'s Office Prince George's County Md., Upper Marlboro, 1992-98; asst. atty. gen. Md. Atty. Gen.'s Office, Balt., 1998-2001; pvt. practice Ellicott City, Md., 2001—; of counsel Baker and Gaffigan, Lanham, Md., 2005—; intelligence specialist Naval Criminal Investigative Svc., Washington, 2003—05. Adj. prof. U. Balt. Sch. Law, 1999-00. Comments editor U. Balt. Jour. Environ. Law. Chmn. Oakland Mills Village Bd., Columbia, Md., 1990-92; pres. St. Stephen's Area Civic Assn., Crownsville, Md., 1994-95; soccer coach Severna Park Ath. Assn., 2000-03. Lt. comdr. USNR, 1988—. Avocations: tennis, sailing, reading, photography. Office: 3545 Ellicott Mills Dr Ellicott City MD 21043 Home: 4413 Cross Country Dr Ellicott City MD 21042 Personal E-mail: jrlillyesq@aol.com.

LILLY, KEVIN L., lawyer, manufacturing executive; BA, JD, U. Notre Dame. Staff atty. US Ct. Appeals (7th cir.), Chgo.; ptnr. Jamieson, Moore, Peskin & Spicer, Archer & Greiner; gen. counsel Inrange Technologies Corp. SPX Corp., Charlotte, NC, 2003, group gen. counsel tech. and industrial sys. bus., assoc. gen. counsel bus. ops., v.p., gen. counsel, sec., 2006—, sr. v.p., 2007—. Office: SPX Corp 13515 Ballantyne Corporate Pl Charlotte NC 28277 Office Fax: 704-752-4400.*

LILLY, LUELLA JEAN, retired academic administrator; b. Newberg, Oreg., Aug. 23, 1937; d. David Hardy and Edith (Coleman) Lilly. BS, Lewis and Clark Coll., 1959; postgrad., Portland State U., 1959—61; MS, U. Oreg., 1961; PhD, Tex. Woman's U., 1971; postgrad., various univs., 1959—72. Tchr. phys. edn. and health, dean girls Ctrl. Linn Jr.-Sr. H.S., Halsey, Oreg., 1959—60; tchr. phys. edn. and health, coach swimming, tennis, golf Lake Oswego H.S., Oreg., 1960—63; instr., intramural dir., coach Oreg. State U., Corvallis, 1963—64; instr., intercollegiate coach Am. River Coll., Sacramento, 1964—69; dir. women's phys. edn., athletics U. Nev., Reno, 1969—73, assoc. prof. phys. edn., 1971—76, dir. women's athletics, 1973-75, assoc. dir. athletics, 1975—76; dir. women's intercollegiate athletics U. Calif., Berkeley, 1976—97; ret., 1997. Organizer, coach Lue's Aquatic Club, 1962—64; v.p. PAC-10 Conf., 1990—91. Author: An Overview of Body Mechanics, 1966, 3d rev. edit., 1969. Vol. instr. ARC, 1951; vol. Heart Fund and Easter Seal, 1974—76, Am. Heart Assn., 1991—95, Multiple Sclerosis Soc., 1999—2004; vol. ofcl. Spl. Olympics, 1975; mem. LA Citizens Olympic Com., 1984; bd. dirs. Las Trampas, 1993—98, sec., 1996—98. Named to Athletic Hall of Fame, Lewis and Clark Coll., 1988, First 125 Yrs. Women of Honor, U. Calif., Berkeley, 1995, Athletic Hall of Fame, 2005; recipient Mayor Anne Rudin award, Nat. Girls' and Women's Sports, 1993, Lifetime Sports award, Bay Area Women's Sports Found., 1994, Golden Bear award Vol. of Yr., 1995, Su Stauffer Firend of Edn. award, 2002, Pride of Nev. award, 2006, Lifetime Sport and Leadership award, 2006. Mem.: AAUW, AAHPERD (life), No. Calif. Athletic Conf. (pres. 1979—82, sec. 1984—85), Nev. Assn. Health Phys. Edn. and Recreation (state chmn. 1974), No. Calif. Intercollegiate Athletic Conf. (volleyball coord. 1971—72), No. Calif. Women's Intercollegiate Conf. (sec., basketball coord. 1970—71), Nev. Bd. Women Ofcls. (chmn. basketball sect. 1969, chmn. bd. dirs., chmn. volleyball sect.), Calif. Assn. Health, Phys. Edn. and Recreation (chmn.-elect jr. coll. sect. 1970), Ctrl. Calif. Bd. Women Ofcls. (basketball chmn. 1968—69), Oreg. Girls' Swimming Coaches Assn. (pres. 1960, 1963), We. Assn. Intercollegiate Athletics Women (exec. bd. dirs. 1973—75, 1979—82), We. Soc. Phys. Edn. Coll. Women (membership com. 1971—74, program adv. com. 1972, exec. bd. 1972—75), Coun. Collegiate Women Athetics Adminstrs. (membership com. 1989—92), Women's Athletic Caucus, Nat. Assn. Coll. Women Athletic Adminstrs. (divsn. 1-A women's steering com. 1991—92, Lifetime Achievement award 1999), Women's Sports Found. (awards com. 1994—2007), Nat. Soc. Profs., Soroptomists (v.p. 1989, 1992—93, sec. 1993—95, 1st v.p. 1996—97, corr. sec. 1997—98, pres. 1998—2000, sec. 2001—02, pres. 2006—07, bd. dirs., Women Helping Women award 1991, Women of Distinction award 2002), Theta Kappa, Phi Kappa Phi. Avocation: swimming. Home and Office: 60 Margrave Ct Walnut Creek CA 94597-2511 Home Phone: 925-934-3868; Office Phone: 925-934-3868.

LILLY, MARTIN STEPHEN, retired university dean; b. New Albany, Ind., Aug. 31, 1944; s. Raymond John and Amy Elizabeth (Peake) L.; m. Marilyn Ann MacDougall, Jan. 8, 1966; children— Matthew William, Mark Christopher, Rachel Marie, Martin Stephen, Jason Wood BA, Bellarmine Coll., Louisville, 1966; MA, Peabody Coll., Nashville, 1967, Ed.D., 1969. Instr. dept. spl. edn. Peabody Coll., 1967-69; asst. prof. edn. U. Oreg., 1969-71; research coordinator N.W. Regional Spl. Edn. Instructional Materials Center, 1969-71; research coordinator div. research Bur. Edn. for Handicapped U.S. Office Edn., 1971-72; assoc. prof. dept. spl. edn. U. Minn., Duluth, 1972-75; assoc. prof., chmn. dept. spl. edn. U. Ill., Urbana-Champaign, 1975-79, prof., chmn., 1979-81, assoc. dean grad. studies Coll. Edn., 1981-84; dean Coll. Edn. Wash. State U., Pullman, 1984-90, Calif. State U., San Marcos, 1990—2004; ret. Cons. in field; U.S. Office Edn. fellow, 1966-69; pres. Tchr. Edn. Coun. State Colls. and Univs.; commr. Calif. Commn. on Tchr. Credentialing, 2002-05. Author: Children with Exceptional Needs: A Survey of Special Education, 1979, (with C.S. Blankenship) Mainstreaming Students With Learning and Behavior Problems, 1981; assoc. editor: Exceptional Children, 1969-79; cons. editor: Edn. Unltd, 1979-81; reviewer: Jour. Tchr. Edn, 1980—; mem. editorial bd. Tchr. Edn. and Spl. Edn, 1980-83, co-editor, 1983-84; contbr. chpts. to books, articles to profl. jours. Trustee Vista (Calif.) Unified Sch. Dist., 2004—. Democrat. Roman Catholic. Office: Calif State U San Marcos CA 92096-0001 Home Phone: 760-598-3304; Office Phone: 760-750-4310. Business E-Mail: slilly@csusm.edu.

LILLY, MICHAEL ALEXANDER, lawyer, writer; b. Honolulu, May 21, 1946; s. Percy Anthony Jr. and Virginia (Craig) L.; m. Cindy Lilly; children: Michael Jr., Cary J., Laura B., Claire F., Winston W. AA, Menlo Coll., Menlo Park, Calif., 1966; BA, U. Calif., Santa Cruz, 1968; JD with honors, U. of Pacific, 1974. Bar: Calif. 1974, U.S. Dist. Ct. (no., so., ctrl. and ea. dists.) Calif. 1974, U.S. Ct. Appeals (9th cir.) 1974, Hawaii 1975, U.S. Dist. Ct. Hawaii 1975, U.S. Ct. Appeals (D.C. cir.) 1975, U.S. Supreme Ct. 1978, U.S. Ct. Appeals (7th cir.) 1979. Atty. Pacific Legal Found., Sacramento, 1974-75; dep. atty. gen. State of Hawaii, Honolulu, 1975-79, 1st dep. atty. gen., 1981-84, atty. gen., 1984-85; ptnr. Feeley & Lilly, San Jose, Calif., 1979-81, Ning, Lilly & Jones, Honolulu, 1985—. Author: If You Die Tomorrow-A Layman's Guide to Estate Planning. Dir. Diamond Head Theatre, U.S.S. Mo. Meml. Assn.; Lt. USN, 1968-71, Vietnam; capt. USN, ret. Named hon. Ky. col.; decorated Legion of Merit medal, 1997. Mem. Nat. Assn. Attys. Gen., Navy Res. Assn. (pres. 14th dist. 1986-89), Navy League (dept. judge adv. to bd. Honolulu coun.), Outrigger Canoe Club. Office: Ning Lilly & Jones 707 Richards St Ste 700 Honolulu HI 96813-4623 Office Phone: 808-528-1100. Business E-Mail: michael@nljlaw.com. *Personal philosophy: Always do what you are afraid to do. Never give up. Forgive your enemies.*

LILLY, THOMAS GERALD, retired lawyer; b. Belzoni, Miss., Sept. 17, 1933; s. Sale Trice and Margaret Evelyn (Butt) Lilly; m. Constance Ray Holland, Dec. 29, 1962; children: Thomas Gerald Jr., William Holland, Carolyn Ray. BBA, Tulane U., New Orleans, 1955; LLB, U. Miss., 1960, JD, 1968. Bar: Miss. 1960. Assoc. firm Stovall & Price, Corinth, Miss., 1960—62; asst. U.S. atty. No. Dist. Miss., Oxford, 1962—66; assoc. Wise Carter Child & Caraway (and predecessor), Jackson, Miss., 1966—67, ptnr., 1967—94, Lilly & Wise, Jackson, 1994—2000, of counsel, 2001—03; ret., 2003. Del. 19th World Methodist Conf., Seoul, Republic of Korea, 2006. With USNR, 1955—88, rear adm. USNR. Decorated Legion of Merit, Navy Commendation medal. Fellow: Found. Fed. Bar Assn. (life); mem.: FBA (nat. coun. 1972—, rec. sec. 1975—76, gen. sec. 1976—77, 2d v.p. 1977—78, pres.-elect 1978—79, pres. 1979—80), Ulster Geneal. and Hist. Guild, Family Rsch. Assn. Miss. (1st v.p. 2004, pres. 2005), Miss. Geneal. Soc., Democracy Devel. Inst. (bd. dirs. 1995—2003), Miss. Bar Found., Miss. State Bar, Hinds County Bar Assn., Salt & Light Ministry Found. (gen. sec. 2005—06, bd. dirs. 2005—), Miss. Com. Employer Support Guard and Res. (coord. navy svc.), Jackson Civil War Roundtable, Navy Supply Corps Assn., Mil. Officers Assn. Am., Res. Officers Assn. (pres. Miss. dept. 1982—83), Naval Res. Assn., Naval Order US, Navy League (pres. Ctrl. Miss. coun. 1993), Naval Hist. Soc., Chester Dist. Geneal. Soc., Internat. Trade Club Miss. (bd. dirs. 1995—96), Nat. Lawyers Club (bd. govs. 1976—81), Scabbard and Blade, Mil. Order World Wars, Lamar Order, Delta Sigma Pi, Sigma Nu, Phi Delta Phi (pres. Mayes Inn 1959—60), Omicron Delta Kappa. United Methodist. Personal E-mail: tglilly@vista-express.com.

LILLY, THOMAS JOSEPH, lawyer; b. Bklyn., Feb. 17, 1931; s. Frank A. and Mary Ellen (Kelly) L.; m. Margaret Mary Doherty, June 28, 1959; children: Thomas J., Mary Jo, Joseph, Sean. BA, St. John's Coll., 1953; JD, Fordham U., 1961; LLM, NYU, 1967. Bar: N.Y. 1962, U.S. Dist. Ct. (ea. and so. dists.) N.Y. 1963, U.S. Ct. Appeals (2d cir.) 1965. Dir. rsch. Office and Profl. Employees Internat. Union AFL-CIO, NYC, 1960-62; asst. U.S. atty. U.S. Dist. Ct. (ea. dist.) N.Y., Bklyn., 1962-66; ptnr. Doran, Colleran, O'Hara, Pollio & Dunne, NYC, 1966-79, Quinn & Lilly, P.C., NYC and Garden City, N.Y., 1979-89; pvt. practice O'Donnell, Schwartz, Glanstein, & Lilly, Garden City, 1989—. Adj. prof. N.Y. State Indsl. and Labor Rels. Sch., Cornell U., 1980-81; arbitrator U.S. Dist. Ct. (ea. dist.) N.Y.; mem. Nassau County Pub. Employment Rels. Bd., 1994-2002. With USN, 1953-57. Mem. ABA, N.Y. Bar Assn., Nassau County Bar Assn., Sea Cliff Yacht Club, Prestwick Golf Club. Home: 136 8th Ave Sea Cliff NY 11579-1308 Office: 245 Hillside Ave Williston Park NY 11596 Office Phone: 516-794-9460. Business E-Mail: ThomasJLillySr@LillyandAssociates.net.

LILLY, WESLEY COOPER, marine engineer; b. Phila., May 23, 1933; s. Richard Gladstone and Margaret Jane Lilly; m. Barbara Joan Newton (div. Nov. 24, 1978); children: Pamela Lynn, Barbara Joan. BS in Engring., Temple U., Phila., 1956; student, Pa. Mil. Coll. (now Widener U.), Chester, 1956—61, Georgetown U., Washington. Apprentice machinist Phila. Naval Shipyard, 1951-53, prodn. shipbuilding, 1955-66, planning, design divsn., 1966-68; shipbuilding specifications and testing staff Naval Weapons Svc. Office, 1968—70; procurement prodn. Navy Dept. Navsea, Washington, 1970-86; pres., founder Saturn Marine Engring., St. Augustine, Fla., 1986—. Programmer Basic, Fortran, and Cobol rev. bus. computech programs. With US Army, 1953—55. Mem.: Soc. Naval Archs. and Marine Engrs. (chmn. com. for small and medium shipyards/shipbldg.), Christian Motorcycle Assn., Island Motorcycle Assn. Achievements include design of Fast Tanker 04 double hull tanker; copyrights for marine engineering; co-design of today's modern accounting system. Avocations: computers, boating, motorcycling. Home: 2757 1st Ave Fernandina Beach FL 32034-2345 Office: Saturn Marine Engineering Amelia Island FL 32034 Personal E-mail: abcmarine2@hotmail.com.

LILLY-HERSLEY, JANE ANNE FEELEY, nursing researcher; b. Palo Alto, Calif., May 31, 1947; d. Daniel Morris Sr. and Suzanne (Agnew) Feeley; children: Cary Jane, Laura Blachree, Claire Foale; m. Dennis C. Hersley, Jan. 16, 1993. BS, U. Oreg., 1968; student, U. Hawaii, 1970; BSN, RN, Sacramento City Coll., 1975. Cert. ACLS, BCLS. Staff and charge nurse, acute rehab. Santa Clara Valley Med. Ctr., San Jose, Calif., staff nurse, surg. ICU and trauma unit; clin. project leader mycophenolate mofetil program team Syntex Rsch., Palo Alto. Pres. Rsch. Consultation Inc., Santa Cruz, Calif, cons. med. rsch. pharmaceutical rsch. Featured in: BBC documentary; appearances: nat. TV and radio broadcasts, pub. presentations. Co-founder, CFO, dir. scientific rsch. Citizens United Responsible Environmentalism, Inc., (CURE). Mem. AACN, Nature Conservancy, Nat. Wildlife Fedn., Monterey Bay Aquarium, World Wildlife Fund., Smithsonian Assn., Nature Plant Soc., Nat. Sludge Alliance. Achievements include research and education in mold exposure and human mycotoxicoses. Personal E-mail: jhersley@comcast.net.

LILLYMAN, WILLIAM JOHN, language educator, academic administrator; b. Sydney, Apr. 17, 1937; came to US, 1963, naturalized, 1974; s. John and Christina Mary (Munro) L.; m. Ingeborg Wolz, Sept. 14, 1962; children: Gregory, Christina. AB, U. Sydney, 1959; PhD, Stanford U., Calif., 1964. Asst. prof. Stanford U., 1964-67; assoc. prof. U. Calif., Santa Cruz, 1967-72, prof. German Irvine, 1972—, dean humanities, 1973-81, vice chancellor acad. affairs, 1981-82, exec. vice chancellor, 1982-88, 98-00. Author: Otto Ludwig's Zwischen Himmel und Erde, 1967, Otto Ludwig: Romane und Romanstudien, 1977, Reality's Dark Dream The Narrative Fiction of Ludwig Tieck, 1979, Goethe's Narrative Fiction, 1983; co-editor; Probleme der Moderne, 1983, Horizonte Festschrift für H. Lehnert, 1990, Critical Architecture and Contemporary Culture, 1994. Recipient Extraordinarius award, U. Calif.-Irvine, 1988, UCI medal, 2000. Mem. MLA, Am. Assn. Tchrs. German. Office: U Calif Exec Vice Chancellors Office 509 Administrn Bldg Irvine CA 92697-1000 Business E-Mail: wjlillym@uci.edu.

LILYHORN, GREGORY DEAN, security firm executive; s. Jack L. and Betty J. Lilyhorn; m. Polly H. Hammond, June 25, 1999; m. Ranita Jean Lindstorm, Nov. 24, 1979 (div. May 16, 1995); 1 child, Patricia K. Lilyhorn - Martin. BS, U. Nebr., 1982. Cert. Homeland Security Profl. Am. Coll. Forensic Examiners Inst., 2003, Profl. Instr. Nat. Acad. Higher Edn., 2003, Fed. Security Risk-Mgr. Applied Rsch. Assocs. Inc, 1989, Instr. Crisis Prevention Inst., 2006, Protection Profl. ASIS, 2006, Health & Pub. Safety Internat. Healthcare & Security Assn., 2006, Law Enforcement Officer Tex., Kans., & Nebr., Fed. Law Enforcement Officer Fed. Law Enforcement Tc, 1983. Sr. fed. law enforcement & security specialist U.S. Dept. Homeland Security, Bur. Immigration and Customs Enforcement Fed. Protective Svc., Washington, 1983—2003; corp. security specialist Tenet Healthcare Corp., Dallas, 2005—. Security cons., Dallas, 2003—; instr. police acad. Dallas County C.C., Dallas, 2003—; instr. Police Acad., Dallas, 2003—. Co-author: Downtown Dallas Emergency Mgmt. Manual. Adv. bd. Security Intelligence for Total Corp. Alignment Inc, Dallas, 2003; mem. adv. bd. Tex. Homeland Security Alliance, Dallas, 2003; program devel. adv. bd. Eastfield Coll. Police Acad., Dallas, 2003. Enlisted Mil. Police USAF, 1973—75. Recipient Nat. Law Enforcement Accreditation, Commn. on Profl. Law Enforcement Stds., 1979, J. Edgar Hoover Meml. Award for Disting. Pub. Svc., Am. Police Hall of Fame, 2002, Honor award for Disting. Achievement in Pub. Svc., 2002, Nat. Police Patriotism award. Mem.: Am. Soc. Indsl. Security (assoc.), Assn. Healthcare Security & Safety (assoc.), Assn. Cert. Fraud Examiners (assoc.), Am. Coll. Forensic Examiners Inst. (assoc.). Conservative-R. Achievements include Federal Security Building & Facilities Assessments; Protection of Federal Building DayCare Centers; Emergency Operations Planning Federal Facilities; Development of Hospital Emergency Security Operations Plans. Avocations: travel, research, education, history. Office: Tenet Healthcare Corporation 13737 Noel Rd Ste 100 Dallas TX 75240 Office Phone: 469-893-6271. Business E-Mail: greg.lilyhorn@tenethealth.com.

LIM, ALAN YOUNG, plastic surgeon; b. St. Louis, Apr. 11, 1953; MD, U. Calif., San Diego, 1979. Plastic surgeon Kaiser-Permanente, Sacramento, Calif. Assoc. clin. prof. U. Calif. Davis Office: Plastic Surg 1020 29th St Sacramento CA 95816 Office Phone: 916-733-9588.

LIM, ALEXANDER RUFASTA, neurologist, clinical investigator, clinical neurophysiologist, educator, writer; b. Manila, Philippines, Feb. 20, 1942; s. Benito Pilar and Maria Lourdes (Cuyegkeng) Lim; m. Norma Sue Hanks, June 1, 1968; children: Jeffrey Allen, Gregory Brian, Kevin Alexander, Melissa Gail. Student, U. Santo Tomas, Manila, 1959, MD, 1964. Intern Bon Secours Hosp., Balt., 1964-65; resident in internal medicine Scott and White Clinic Tex A&M U., Health Sci. Ctr. Coll. Medicine, Temple, Tex., 1965-67; resident in neurology Cleve. Clinic, 1967-69, chief resident in neurology, 1969-70, fellow clin. neurophysiology, 1970-71; clin. assoc. neurologist Cleve. Clinic Hosp., 1971-72; neurologist-in-chief, co-founder, co-mng. ptnr. Neurol. Clinic, Corpus Christi, Tex., 1972—; pres., CEO Neurology, P.A., Corpus Christi, 1972-92. Chief neurology dept. Meml. Med. Ctr., Corpus Christi, Tex., 1975—90, Spohn Hosp., Corpus Christi, 1974—90, Reynolds Army Hosp., Ft. Sill, Okla., 1990—91; clin. assoc. prof. Sch. Medicine U. Tex. Health Sci. Ctr., San Antonio; cons., reviewer Tex. Medicine, 1995—. Reviewer: Am. Acad. Neurology; mem. editl. bd. Coastal Bend Medicine, 1988—95, NEURO Ctrl., 1999—. Active mentorship program for gifted and talented srs. South Tex. Area H.S. Lt. col. med. corps US Army, 1990—91, Desert Shield/Desert Storm. Decorated Army Commendation medal, Nat. Def. medal U.S. Army; recipient Best doctors in Am., 1988, 1989, 1990, Am. Top Physicians, 2005. Mem.: KC, AMA, Tex. Neurol. Soc. (sec. 1986—88, pres. 1989—90), Tex. Med. Assn. (chmn. neurology 1985—86), So. Electroencephalographic Soc., Soc. Behavioral and Cognitive Neurology, Am. Acad. Immunotherapy, Am. Clin. Neurophysiology Soc., Am. Epilepsy Soc. (editl. bd. mem. Neurocentral), Am. Acad. Neurology (spkrs. bur., mem. physicians com. for responsible medicine), Internat. Soc. Poets, Acad. Am. Poets, Internat. Platform Assn. Republican. Roman Catholic. Avocations: tennis, stamp collecting/philately, essay and poetry writing, skiing, bonsai. Home: 4821 Augusta Cir Corpus Christi TX 78413-2711 Office: Neurol Clinic Corpus Christi Med Towers 1521 South Staples St Ste 402 Corpus Christi TX 78404 Home Phone: 361-992-2261; Office Phone: 361-883-1731. Office Fax: 361-883-1440. Personal E-mail: anlim8@hotmail.com. Business E-Mail: lima@neurologypa.com.

LIM, BYUNG-JOON LUCAS, language educator, department chairman; s. Gil Sang Lim and Man Ja Park; m. Jung Sook Lee; children: Minju, John. MA in Econs., U. Mich., Ann Arbor, 1990—91; MA in Linguistics, U. Ga., Athens, 1993—95, PhD in Linguistics, 1995—2001. Instr. U. Ga., 1995—2001; prof. Korean lang. Def. Lang. Inst., Monterey, Calif., 2002—, dept. chairperson, 2004—, assoc. prof., 2007—. CEO Lucas Ministry, Pacific Grove, Calif., 2002—; paper reviewer Am. Coun. Tchg. Fgn. Langs., Alexandria, Va., 2005—. Author: (language book) Common Korean Phrases into English, Colloquial English Expressions, 2007. Decorated Army Achievement medal Sec. Army, Army Commendation medal. Mem.: Am. Assn. Tchrs. Korean (exec. sec. 2004—06, bd. mem. 2006—). Home: 702 Grove St Pacific Grove CA 93950 Home Phone: 831-373-7159. Personal E-mail: open24hours@hotmail.com.

LIM, EDWARD CHOL, chemistry professor, researcher; b. Gaesong, Korea, 1932; came to U.S., 1952; s. Kwang Un and Chang Soon L. m. Bee Tuan Uy, June 23, 1958; children: Diane Marie, Janice Catherine. BS in Chemistry, St. Procopium College, 1954; MS in Phys. Chemistry, Oklahoma State U., 1957, PhD in Phys. Chemistry, 1959. Instr. chemistry Loyola U., Chgo., 1959-61, asst. prof. chemistry, 1961-63, assoc. prof. chemistry, 1963-66, prof. chemistry, 1966-68; prof. phys. chemistry Wayne State U., Detroit, 1968-89; Goodyear prof. chemistry U. Akron, Ohio, 1989—. Editor: Excited States, 1974—, Lasers in Chemistry, 1992—. Recipient Ho-Am Found. prize in Sci., 2001. Fellow Am. Phys. Soc.; mem. Am. Chem. Soc. Office: U Akron Dept Chemistry 319 Knight Chemical Lab Akron OH 44325-0001 Office Phone: 330-972-5297. Business E-Mail: elim@uakron.edu.

LIM, HENRY WAN-PENG, dermatologist; b. Bandung, Indonesia, July 19, 1949; s. Budiman Ruslim and Nietje Tedjasuryani; m. Mamie Wong, July 20, 1975; children: Christopher T., Kevin T. BS in Biochemistry with honors, McGill U., 1971; MD cum laude, SUNY, Bklyn., 1975. Diplomate Am. Bd. Dermatology, Nat. Bd. Med. Examiners. Intern Albert Einstein Coll. Medicine, Bronx, NY, 1975-76; resident dept. dermatology NYU Sch. Medicine, NYC, 1976-79, NIH fellow in dermatology, 1979, Dermatology Found. fellow, 1979-80, from instr. to assoc. prof. dermatology, 1979-93, prof. dermatology, 1993-97, asst. dean vet. affairs, 1993-97; chmn., Clarence S. Livingood chair dermatology Henry Ford Hosp., Detroit, 1997—, dir. acad. programs, 2002—03, v.p. for acad. affairs, 2003—; assoc. dean Wayne State U./Henry Ford Health Sys., Wayne State U. Sch Medicine, Detroit, 2004—. Chief dermatology svc. N.Y. VA Med. Ctr., NYC, 1985—94, chief staff, 1993—97, staff physician dermatology svc., 1994—97; prof. pathology Sch. Medicine Wayne State U., Detroit, 2003—. Editor: Photodermatology, Photoimmunology & Photomedicine, 2000—03; assoc. editor: Jour. Investigative Dermatology, 2003—; mem. editl. bd. Jour. Am. Acad. Dermatology, 1993—. Recipient numerous awards; scholar, McGill U., 1968—70. Mem.: AMA, AAAS, Internat. Union Photobiology (v.p. 2004—), Photomedicine Soc. (pres. 1992—99), Am. Assn. Immunologists, Am. Soc. Photobiology (councilor 1998—2001, pres. 2002—03, chair sci. program com. 2003—04), Am. Fedn. for Clin. Rsch., Assn. Profs. Dermatology (bd. dirs. 2000—03), Am. Dermatology Assn. (chair membership com. 2002—03, program com. 2005—, bd. dirs. 2006—), Dermatology Found. (trustee 2003—), Soc. Investigative Dermatology, Am. Acad. Dermatology (bd. dirs. 2002—06, exec. com. 2004—, v.p. 2007—), Alpha Omega Alpha. Avocation: travel. Office: Henry Ford Med Ctr New Ctr One Dept Dermatology 3031 W Grand Blvd Dept Ste 800 Detroit MI 48202-2689 Home Phone: 313-886-5002; Office Phone: 313-916-4060. Business E-Mail: hlim1@hfhs.org.

LIM, JUNG YUL, biomedical engineer; b. Seoul, Republic of Korea, Feb. 14, 1970; BS, Seoul Nat. U., 1992, MS, 1994, PhD, 1999. Postdoc. fellow, biomaterials rsch. ctr. Korea Inst. Sci. and Tech., Seoul, 1999—2002; postdoctoral fellow dept. orthopaedics and rehab. Pa. State Coll. Medicine, Hershey, 2002—06, instr., 2006—. Contbr. articles and papers to profl. jours. and pubs. Mem.: Orthopaedic Rsch. Soc. (assoc.). Achievements include patents for development of high strength bioabsorbable implants. Office: Penn State Coll Medicine Ortho 500 University Dr Hershey PA 17033 Office Phone: 717-531-6696. Business E-Mail: jlim@psu.edu.

LIM, PHILLIP, apparel designer; b. 1974; Designer Katayone Adeli; head designer Development; founder, head designer 3.1 clothing line, NYC, 2005—. Finalist Fashion Fund award, Coun. Fashion Designers Am./Vogue, 2006; recipient First place in Women's Designer Rising Star, Fashion Grp. Internat., Swarovski award for Emerging Talent in Womenswear, Coun. Fashion Designers Am., 2007. Office: 260 W 39th St 9th Fl New York NY 10018*

LIM, RALPH WEI HSIONG, finance educator; b. NYC, Oct. 3, 1953; s. Yuen and Huan Lim. BSE, Princeton U., NJ, 1975; MBA, U. Pa., Wharton, 1977. CFA. Fin exec. Internat. Paper Co., NYC, 1977-82; cons. Synergy Assocs. LLC, Darien, Conn., 1982—; prof. Sacred Heart U., Fairfield, Conn., 1984—, v.p. academic assembly, 2005—06, pres. academic assembly, 2006—; faculty cons. Charter Oak State Coll., New Britain, Conn., 2000—, mem. acad. coun., 2004—, chmn. bus. com., 2005—. Vis. fellow Yale U., New Haven, 1988—89. Contbr. articles to profl. jours. Mem. CAP, Ark., 1978-80, Conn., 1980—; rep. Darien Town Legis., Darien, 1988-89; commr. Darien Housing Authority, 1991-96. Mem. CFA Inst., Stamford CFA Soc. (bd. dirs. 1995-2001, pres. 1998-99), Fin. Execs. Internat. Republican. Avocations: aircraft pilot, acting. Home: PO Box 938 Darien CT 06820-0938

LIM, RAMON (KHE-SIONG LIM), neuroscience educator, researcher; b. Cebu City, Philippines, Feb. 5, 1933; came to U.S., 1959, naturalized, 1973; s. Eng-Lian and Su (Yu) L.; m. Victoria K. Sy, June 21, 1961; children: Jennifer, Wendell, Caroline. AB, U. Santo Tomas, Manila, 1953; MD cum laude, U. Santo Tomas, 1958; PhD in Biochemistry, U. Pa., 1966. Diplomate Am. Bd. Psychiatry and Neurology. Rsch. neurochemist U. Mich., Ann Arbor, 1966-69; asst. prof. biochemistry U. Chgo., 1969-76, assoc. prof. Brain Rsch. Inst., 1976-81; prof. dept. neurology U. Iowa, Iowa City, 1981—2005, dir. divsn. neurochemistry and neurobiology, 1981—2005, prof. emeritus, 2005—. Career investigator VA, 1983; adv. internat. writing program U. Iowa, 2002—05. Mem. editl. bd. Internat. Jour. Devel. Neurosci., 1984-91, Neurochem. Rsch., 1997—2006, Handbook of Neurochemistry and Molecular Neurobiology, 2005-; contbr. numerous articles to sci. jours. Grantee NIH, 1971—, NSF, 1979—, VA, 1981—; recipient 3d prize Art Assn. Philippines, 1957, 3d prize 8th Internat. Calligraphy Competition, Shanghai, China, 2005; named Outstanding Overseas Young Chinese, Fedn. Overseas Chinese Orgns., 1961. Mem. Am. Soc. Biochem. Molecular Biology, Internat. Soc. Neurochemistry (vis. lectureship 1986), Am. Soc. Neurochemistry, Soc. Neurosci., Am. Soc. Cell Biology. Achievements include research in isolation and characterization of regulatory brain proteins; growth and differentiation of brain cells; brain chemistry and molecular biology. Avocations: calligraphy, painting, writing, music. Home: 118 Richards St Iowa City IA 52246-3516 Office: U Iowa Iowa City IA 52242 Office Phone: 319-335-8527. E-mail: ramon-lim@uiowa.edu.

LIM, SALLYJANE, financial planner, diversified insurance and financial advisor, realtor; b. Manila; arrived in U.S., 1990; d. Teddy and Sonia (Yii); children: Robin Michael, Rodney Jovin, Romelle Gavin Lim Velasco. AB-BSC magna cum laude, Coll. of the Holy Spirit, Manila. CPA Philippines; CLU; CFP, chartered sr. fin. planner. Ins. rep. Insular Life Assurance Co., Makati, 1972-82; project analyst Pvt. Devel. Corp. of The Philippines, Makati, 1972—78; account exec. Genbancor Devel. Corp., Makati, 1978-80; risk mgr. Filcapital Devel. Corp., Makati, 1978-82; pres. and gen. mgr., ins. broker Sally-Jane Multiline Insce. Consulting, Inc., Manila, 1978-90; real estate broker Sally-Jane Realty, Inc., Manila, 1980-90; ins. rep. and v.p. Macaulay Club Sun Life of Can., 1982-91; ind. ins. broker John Hancock Life Ins. Co., Blue Cross/Blue Shield Calif., 1998—; ind. broker Allianz Life, Lincoln Nat. Life, 2001—; rep. Prudential Ins. Co. of Am., NYLIFE Securities, Inc., Pasadena, Calif., 2000—01; registered rep. Pruco Securities Corp., L.A. Dist., South Pasadena, Calif., 1990-91, Asian Pacific Dist., Calif., 1991-98, John Hancock Variable Life Ins. Co., 1998-2000, Signator Investors, Inc., 2001—04, AIG Am. Gen. Life, 2004—, Sunlife Fin., 2005—. Flagbearer The Philippines Opening Ceremonies, Million Dollar Round Table 58th Ann. Meeting, San Francisco, 1985; guest fashion model A Company of Women Carnegie's Highlands Golf & Country Club, Idaho, 1999. Recipient Ann. Nat. Consumers' award Golden Trophy Most Outstanding Ins. Sales Exec. of the Philippines, Consumers' Union of the Philippines, 1983, 1988, Plasma 1 Million trophies, Dept. Ins. the Philippines, 1988, 1989, Young Achiever award, Young Achiever Found., Quezon City, Philippines, 1988, Golden Scroll award, Philippine Ednl. Youth Devel., Inc., Quezon City, 1988, Twelve Outstanding Profl. Svc. (T.O.P.S.) awards, Nat. Achievement Rsch. Soc., Manila, 1988, Internat. Quality award (IQA) (Five Yrs. Qualification), Life Ins. Mktg. and Rsch. Assn., Hartford, 1989, Lahing Kayumanggi award Outstanding Lady Bus. Exec., Sons and Daughters Charity, Inc., the Philppines, 1988, Young Famous Celebrity Mother's trophy, Golden Mother/Father Found., Quezon City, Philippines, 1990, 8th Ann. Women of Achievement award, San Gabriel Valley YWCA, 1992, Grand Achievement award for Profl. Sector, People's Choice awards, Ateneo U., the Philippines, 1998, Parangal ng Bayan awardee, Nat. Consumers Coun. the Philippines, 1998, numerous others. Fellow: Life Underwriter Tng. Coun.; mem.: Assn. Chartered Sr. Fin. Planners, Calif. Assn. Ins. and Fin. Advisors (qualifying), Million Dollar Round Table (life; 20 yrs.), Nat. Assn. Ins. and Fin. Advisors (Pasadena). Avocations: broadway musicals, ballet, fashion shows, concerts, ballroom dancing. Home and Office: 1006 Royal Oaks Dr Ste A Monrovia CA 91016-3737 Office Phone: 626-358-2809. E-mail: starSJLim@aol.com, starSJLim@yahoo.com.

LIM, SEONG BAE, business educator; b. Yongin, Kyonggido, Republic of Korea, Sept. 23, 1969; arrived in U.S., 1994; s. Young Sam Lim and Young Soon Lee; m. Yoo Rim Choi, Mar. 16, 2002. BA, Kyonggi U., 1997; MA, Sogang U., Seoul, 1999; PhD, U. Nebr., 2003. Instr. U. Nebr., Lincoln, 2002—03; asst. prof. SUNY, Geneseo, 2003—. Mem. editl. bd.: Internat. Jour. Info. Tech. and Mgmt., 2005—06; contbr. articles and papers to profl. jours.; reviewer: Jour. Electronic Commerce Rsch., 2005—. Recipient Outstanding Grad. Rsch. award, U. Nebr., 2003, Asst. award, 2002, 2001. Mem.: Decision Sci. Inst., Assn. for Info. Sys., Pan-Pacific Bus. Assn. Home: 120 Caversham Woods Pittsford NY 14534 Office: SUNY S 103 1 College Cir Geneseo NY 14454

LIM, SUNG KYU, computer scientist, educator; s. Sook Hee Lim; m. Jee Eun Byon, May 4, 2002; children: Yuna children: Mina. BS in Computer Sci., UCLA, 1994, MS in Computer Sci., 1997, PhD, 2000. Asst. prof. Ga. Inst. Tech., Atlanta, 2001—. Office: Ga Inst Tech 777 Atlantic Dr NW Atlanta GA 30332 Office Phone: 404-894-0373. E-mail: limsk@ece.gatech.edu.

LIM, YOON-MI, muisc director, organist; b. Busan, Republic of Korea, Aug. 10, 1974; d. Dong-Kyu Lim and Kyung-Hae Baik. D in Musical Arts in Organ Performance and Lit., Ind. U., Bloomington, 2000—. Organist, bell choir dir. Fairview United Meth. Ch., Bloomington, 2000—03; music dir., organist Fairlawn Presbyn. Ch., Columbus, Ind., 2003—. Artist Concert Artist Coop., Sebastopol, Calif., 2006—, Karen McFarlane Artists, Inc., Cleve., 2004—06. Musician: (organ performance competition) National Young Artists Competition in Organ Performance, 2004 (winner), (organ scholarship competition) John Rodland Scholarship Competition, Arthur Poister Scholarship Competition, (CD rec.) Gifts from Above, Gifts from Above, Pro Organo #7205. Mem.: Americna Guild Organists. Avocations: movies, reading, travel. Office: Fairlawn Presbyterian Ch 2611 Fairlawn Dr Columbus IN 47203 Office Phone: 812-372-3882.

LIM, YOUN-KYUNG, design educator; BS, Korea Advanced Inst. Sci. and Tech., Daejon, Republic of Korea, 1997; M in Design, Ill. Inst. Tech., Chgo., 1999, PhD, 2003. Rschr., instr. Ill. Inst. Tech., 2000—03; lectr. Ill. Inst.Tech., 2003; post doctoral fellow Ind. U., Bloomington, Ind., 2004, asst. prof., 2004—. Designer Communicable Story Building Toy, 1999 (Hon. Mention award Inst. Design Mag., 1999), MusicCleaner, 1999 (Spl. prize LG Electronics Internat. Design Competition, 1999). Cantor St. Paul Cath. Ctr., Bloomington, 2005. Fellow, IBM, 1999, Tangible Knowledge Consortium, 2000—03; scholar, Inst. Design, Ill. Inst. Tech., 1998; Rado Watch Design scholarship, Worldstudio, 1999. Mem.: IEEE (Best Paper award 2000), Design Rsch. Soc., Assn. Computing Machinery. Achievements include development of frameworks, methods, and tools for various design activities in interactive system development processes; research in analyzing effects and characteristics of different prototyping approaches used in interactiv system design activities; proposing a new notion of interaction between human and technologies for designing interactive systems. Office: Indiana Univ 901 E 10th St Bloomington IN 47408 Home Phone: 812-336-5066. Business E-Mail: younlim@indiana.edu.

LIMA, ADRIANA FRANCESCA, model; b. Salvador, Brazil, June 12, 1982; Signed with Elite Model Mgmt., NYC; appeared on covers of Vogue (Italy), 1997, Vogue (UK), 1998, Marie Claire (Brazil), 1998, Vogue (US), 1999, Marie Claire (Italy), 1999, Harper's Bazaar, Elle; appeared in Victoria's Secret Catalogues, 2000—; modeled for Anna Sui Jeans, Bebe, Gasoline, Mossimo, BCBG, Keds, XOXO. Actor: (films) The Hire: The Follow, 2001; appearances include The Victoria's Secret Fashion Show, 2001, 2002, 2003. Named Winner Ford Supermodel of Brazil Contest, 1996. Office: Elite Model Mgmt 111 E 22nd St New York NY 10010

LIMA, ROBERT, language educator; b. Havana, Cuba, Nov. 7, 1935; came to U.S., 1945; BA in English and Philosophy, Villanova U., 1957, MA in Theatre Arts and Drama, 1961; PhD in Romance Lit., NYU, 1968. Prof. Spanish and comparative lit. Pa. State U., Univ. Pk., Pa., 1965—2002, prof. emeritus, 2002—. Fellow Inst. for Arts and Humanistic Studies Pa. State U., 1986-2002, fellow emeritus, 2002-; vis. prof. comparative lit. Pontificia U. Cath., Peru; poet-in-residence U. Nat. Mayor de San Marcos, Peru, 1976-77; lectr. Romance langs. and lits. Hunter Coll. CUNY, 1962-65, USIA lectr., Peru, Cameroon, Equatorial Guinea. Author: The Theatre of Garcia Lorca, 1963, An Annotated Bibliography of Ramon del Valle-Inclan, 1972, (poetry) Fathoms, 1981, The Olde Ground, 1985, Mayaland, 1992, Dark Prisms Occultism in Hispanic Drama, 1995, Valle-Inclan. El Teatro de su Vida, 1995, Ramon del Valle-Inclan: An Annotated Bibliography, 1999, (poetry) Sardinia/Sardegna, 2000, Tracking The Minotaur, 2003, The Dramatic World of Valle-Inclan, 2003, Stages of Evil Occultism in Western Theatre and Drama, 2005; co-author: Dos Ensayos Sobre Teatro Español de los Veinte, 1984; editor, translator: Borges the Labyrinth Maker (A.M. Barrenechea), 1965, Valle-Inclan: Autobiography, Aesthetics, Aphorism, 1966; editor, contbr. Borges and the Esoteric, 1993, Cauda Pavonis issue on Leonora Carrington, 2000; translator: The Lamp of Marvels, Aesthetic Meditations (Ramon del Valle-Inclan), 1986, Savage Acts: Four Plays (Valle-Inclan), 1993, Santa Rosalia A Cantata, 2007; co-editor Readers Ency. Am. Lit., 1962, Homenaje A--Tribute to Martha T. Halsey, 1995, Texts and Contexts: A Tribute to Beno Weiss, 2001; contbr. articles to profl. jours.; prodr., cons., TV and radio programs Centro de Estudios TV la U. Cath., Lima, Peru, 1976-77, Voice of Am., NYC, 1961-62, Pendulum Prodns., 1960-61. Bd. dirs. Pa. Ctr. for Book. Decorated Knight Comdr. Order Queen Isabel Spain, 2003; recipient Founders Day award NYU, 1968, Play Translation prize Modern Internat. Drama, cert. of merit Writer's Digest Mag., 1982, Disting. Alumnus medal Villanova Univ., 1999; Rsch. grant Fund for Rsch. Pa. State U., Inst. for Arts and Humanistic Studies; Cintas Found. fellow in poetry Inst. Internat. Edn., 1971-72, fellow Commonwealth Speakers Program Pa. Humanities Coun., Sr. Fulbright fellow Coun. Internat. Exch. Scholars, 1976-77; others. Fellow Inst. for Arts and Humanistic Studies, Phi Kappa Phi (hon.), Phi Sigma Iota (hon.); mem. Internat. PEN, Poetry Soc. Am., Am. Assn. Tchrs. Spanish and Portuguese, Archaeol. Inst. Am., Am. Comparative Lit. Assn., Internat. Comparative Lit. Assn., Galician Studies Assn., Internat. Assn. Valleinclanistas, Am. Name Soc., Am. Soc. Sephardic Studies, Poets and Writers, Hermetic Text Soc., Beast Fable Soc., Pa. Humanities Coun. (academician), N.Am. Acad. Spanish Lang., Fulbright Alumni Assn., Enxebre Orden da Vieira, Real Academia Española (corr.), Alpha Psi Omega. Home: 485 Orlando Ave State College PA 16803-3477 Office: Pa State U 211 Burrowes Bldg University Park PA 16802 Business E-Mail: rxl2@psu.edu.

LIMAN, LEWIS JEFFREY, lawyer; b. NYC, Dec. 3, 1960; s. Arthur Lawrence and Ellen Liman; m. Lisa Cohen Liman, Jan. 16, 1999; children: Abigail Goodman, Gillian Cohen. AB, Harvard U., Cambridge, Mass., 1983; MSc in Econ., London Sch. Econs., 1984; JD, Yale U., New Haven, 1987. Law clk. US Dist. Ct., NYC, 1987—89, US Supreme Ct., Washington, 1989—91, assoc. NYC, 1991—94; asst. US atty. US Attys. Office, NYC, 1994—99; ptnr. Wilmer Cutler, NYC, 2000—03, Cleary Gottlieb, NYC, 2003—. Office: Cleary Gottlieb 1 Liberty Plz New York NY 10023 Home Phone: 212-875-8073; Office Phone: 212-225-2550. Business E-Mail: lliman@cgsh.com.

LIMATO, EDWARD FRANK, talent agent; b. Mt. Vernon, NY, July 10, 1936; s. Frank and Angelina (Lacerra) L. Grad. high sch., Mt. Vernon. With IFA (formerly Ashley Famous Agency), NYC, 1966—78; sr. exec. William Morris Agy. Inc., LA, 1978—88; with Internat. Creative Mgmt., 1988—2007, talent agt. NYC, LA, co-pres., 1999—2007; talent agt. William Morris Agy. Inc., Beverly Hills, 2007—. Bd. dirs. Abercrombie & Fitch Co., 2003—, Motion Picture and TV Fund, L.A. Conservancy, Am. Cinematheque. Mem. Acad. Motion Picture Arts & Scis. (assoc.). Republican. Roman Catholic. Office: William Morris Agy Inc One William Morris Pl Beverly Hills CA 90212*

LIMBACHER, RANDY L., energy executive; B in Petroleum Engring., La. State U., 1980. V.p. Burlington Resources Oil & Gas Co., Gulf Coast Divsn., Houston, 1996—98, pres., CEO, 1998—2000, BROG GP Inc., 2000—01; sr. v.p., prod. Burlington Resources, Inc., 2001—02, exec. v.p., COO, 2002; exec. v.p., exploration & production Am. Conoco-Phillips, Houston, 2002—, bd. dir., 2004—. Mem.: La. State U. Engring. Industry Adv. Bd., Am. Petroleum Inst., Indep. Petroleum Assoc. Am., Soc. Petroleum Engrs., Houston Area Jr. Achievement. Mailing: Conoco Phillips PO Box 2197 Houston TX 77252-2197*

LIMBAUGH, RONALD HADLEY, retired historian, cultural organization administrator; b. Emmett, Idaho, Jan. 22, 1938; s. John Hadley and Evelyn E. (Mortimore) L.; m. Marilyn Kay Rice, June 16, 1963; 1 child, Sally Ann. BA, Coll. Idaho, Caldwell, 1960; MA, U. Idaho, Moscow, 1962, PhD, 1967. Hist. libr. Idaho State Hist. Soc., Boise, 1963-66; instr. Boise Coll., 1964-66; asst. prof. history U. of the Pacific, Stockton, Calif., 1966-71, archivist, curator, 1968-87, prof. history, 1977-2000, Rockwell Hunt chair of Calif. history, 1989-2000; dir. Holt-Atherton Ctr., U. of the Pacific, Stockton, 1984-87. Exec. dir. Conf. of Calif. Hist. Socs., Stockton, 1973-76, 77-78, 82-86, 90-97, bd. trustees, 2006—; dir. John Muir Ctr. for Regional Studies, U. of Pacific, Stockton, 1989-2000; cons., evaluator NEH, 1983-86. Author: Rocky Mountain Carpetbaggers, 1982, John Muir's Stickeen and the Lessons of Nature, 1996; co-author: Calaveras Gold, 2003; co-editor: (microform) John Muir Papers, 1986, (book) Guide to Muir Papers, 1986; contbr. articles to profl. jours. With U.S. Army, 1955-56. NDEA fellow, 1960; grantee Calif. Coun. Humanities, 1976, Nat. Hist. Publs. and Records Commn., 1980-82, NEH, 1983, Inst. European Studies, 1989, Hoover Libr. Assn., 1997. Mem. Western History Assn., Mining History Assn. Christian Humanist. Avocations: hiking, birdwatching. Office: U Pacific 3601 Pacific Ave Stockton CA 95211-0197 Home Phone: 707-785-3814; Office Phone: 209-946-2145. Business E-Mail: limbaugh@mcn.org.

LIMBAUGH, RUSH HUDSON, III, radio talk show host; b. Cape Girardeau, Mo., Jan. 12, 1951; s. Rush Hudson Jr. and Millie Limbaugh; m. Roxy Maxine McNeely, Sept. 24, 1977 (div. July 10, 1980) m. Marries Michelle Sixta, 1983 (div. 1990), m. Marta Fitzgerald, May 27, 1994 (div. Dec. 21, 2004). Student Southeast Mo. State U.; Grad., Elkins Inst. Radio & Tech. Disc jockey KQV radio, Pitts., 1971, WHB radio, Kansas City, 1975—78; dir, group sales Kansas City Royals, 1979—83, dir. sales & spl. events; political commentator KMBZ radio, Kansas City, 1983—84; radio talk show host KFBK-AM radio, Sacramento, 1984—88, The Rush Limbaugh Show, NYC, 1988—. Author: The Way Things Ought To Be, 1992, See, I Told You So, 1993; TV syndicated show The Rush Limbaugh Show, 1992-1996, commentator, NFL Countdown, ESPN, 2003; publisher, monthly newsletter, The Limbaugh Letter, 1995—; film appearances: Forget Paris, 1995; TV appearance: Hearts Afire, 1994, The Drew Carey Show, 1998. Named to, Broadcasting Hall of Fame, 1993, Nat. Assn.

Broadcasters Hall of Fame, 1998; recipient Marconi Radio award for Syndicated Radio Personality of the Year, Nat. Assn. Broadcasters, 1992, 1995, 2000, 2005. Republican. Office: The Rush Limbaugh Show 1270 Ave Americas New York NY 10020 Office Phone: 212-563-9166. E-mail: rush@eibnet.com.

LIMBAUGH, STEPHEN NATHANIEL, federal judge; b. Cape Girardeau, Mo., Nov. 17, 1927; s. Rush Hudson and Bea (Seabaugh) L.; m. DeVaughn Anne Mesplay, Dec. 27, 1950; children— Stephen Nathaniel Jr., James Pennington, Andrew Thomas. BA, S.E. Mo. State U., Cape Girardeau, 1950; JD, U. Mo., Columbia, 1951. Bar: Mo. 1951. Prosecuting atty. Cape Girardeau County, Mo., 1954-58; judge U.S. Dist. Ct. (ea. and we. dists.) Mo., St. Louis, 1983—. With USN, 1945-46. Recipient Citation of Merit for Outstanding Achievement and Meritorious Service in Law, U. Mo., 1982 Fellow Am. Coll. Probate Counsel, Am. Bar Found.; mem. ABA (ho. of dels. 1987-90), Mo. Bar Assn. (pres. 1982-83). Republican. Methodist. Office: US Dist Ct Thomas F Eagleton Courthouse 111 S 10th St Ste 3 125 Saint Louis MO 63102 Office Phone: 314-244-7400. Business E-Mail: stephen_limbaugh@moed.uscourts.gov. E-mail: limbaugh@moed.uscourts.gov.

LIMBAUGH, STEPHEN NATHANIEL, JR., state supreme court judge; b. Cape Girardeau, Mo., Jan. 25, 1952; s. Stephen N. and Anne (Mesplay) L.; m. Marsha Dee Moore, July 21, 1973; children: Stephen III, Christopher K. BA, So. Meth. U., 1973, JD, 1976; LLM, U. Va., 1998. Bar: Tex. 1977, Mo. 1977. Assoc. Limbaugh, Limbaugh & Russell, Cape Girardeau, 1977-78; pros. atty. Cape Girardeau County, Cape Girardeau, 1979-82; shareholder, ptnr. Limbaugh, Limbaugh, Russell & Syler, Cape Girardeau, 1983-87; cir. judge 32d Jud. Cir., Cape Girardeau, 1987-92; judge Mo. Supreme Ct., Jefferson City, 1992—. Mem. ABA, State Bar Tex., Mo. Bar. Office: Supreme Ct Mo 207 W High St Jefferson City MO 65101-1516 Office Phone: 573-751-4375.

LIMBURG-SANTISTEVAN, ELLEN H., retired geologist, artist; b. Bedford, NY, Nov. 24, 1964; d. Peter R. and Margareta F. (Fischerström) Limburg; m. Mark A. Santistevan; children: Margareta, Dorothe, Mark stepchildren: Lauren, Janis, John. BA with honors, Wesleyan U., Middletown, Conn., 1986; postgrad., SUNY, Purchase, 1986-88; MS, N.Mex. Inst. Mining and Tech., Socorro, 1990. Vet. asst. Dr. Pierre Thouin, Banksville, N.Y., 1983; stable mgr. Quarrytown Stables, Portland, Conn., 1984-86; land surveyor, geologist R.H. Gorr & Assocs., Mahopac, N.Y., 1986-88; teaching asst. N.Mex. Inst. Mining and Tech., Socorro, 1988-90; rsch. asst. N.Mex. Bur. Mines, Socorro, 1989; geologist US Geol. Survey, Reston, Va., 1990—92; owner Santistevan Enterprises, Los Lunas, N.Mex., 1992—; owner, ptnr. Santos de Santistevan, Los Lunas, 1995—. Contbr. abstracts and article on volcanoes to profl. jours. Mem.: NOW, Nat. Wildlife Fedn. Avocations: horseback riding, motorcycling, gardening, reading, cooking.

LIMEHOUSE, HARRY BANCROFT, JR., real estate developer, transportation consultant; b. Charleston, SC, Dec. 3, 1938; m. Frankie Fennell, Jan. 18, 1961; children: Chip, Brien, Barry, Brad. BA in English, The Citadel, 1960, LLD (hon.), 1997, D (hon.) in Bus., 1997; D in Hospitality (hon.), Johnson & Wales U., 1995. Lic. real estate broker S.C. Mgmt. trainee Deering-Millikin, 1960-61; agt. Prudential Ins. Co., Charleston, 1962-67, mgr. W. Palm Beach, Fla., 1967-69; dir. campaign mgmt. divsn. Rep. Nat. Com., Washington, 1967-69; pres., founder Limehouse Properties, Charleston, 1970—. Bankruptcy trustee U.S. Trustee's Office, Columbia, SC, 1988—. Chmn. Pub. Rys. Commn. S.C., 1989—93, 1992—93; past pres. Carolina chpt. Real Estate Securities Inst.; charter pres. Charleston chpt. Comml. Income Properties Coun.; founding pres. Palmetto State Games; chmn. So. Govs. Conf., 1992, S.C. Dept. Transp. Commn., 1994—99; cons. Ga. Dept. Transp., 2000—02; Citadel bd. visitors, 2004. Named Hotelier of the Yr., S.C. Hospitality Assn., 1994, Man of the Yr., 1996, S.F. Taxpayers Assn., Conservationist of the Yr., S.C. Wildlife Fedn., 1996—; named to, Order of the Palmetto, 1995, 1998. Mem.: Nat. Assn. Realtors, Hibernian Soc., Aircraft Owners and Pilots Assn., Downtown Athletic Club. Avocation: flying. Office: Sec Transportation 955 Park No 309 Columbia SC 29201 Office Phone: 803-737-1302. Business E-Mail: limehousehb@scdot.org.

LIMERICK, DIANNE A., mathematics educator, athletic trainer; b. Yokohama, Japan, Sept. 14, 1954; d. Thomas and Louise Limerick. BA in Elem. Edn., Christopher Newport Coll., Coll. William and Mary, Newport News, Va., 1976; MA in Secondary Edn., Christopher Newport Coll., Coll. William and Mary, Williamsburg, Va., 1981. Lic. athletic trainer Va. Tchr. Williamsburg James City Pub. Sch., 1976—; h.s. athleic trainer Newport News/Hampton Pub. Schs., 1978—2000; nat. team trainer US Swimming Nat. Governing Body, Colorado Springs, Colo., 1985—; athletic trainer, strength coach Williamsburg Aquatic Club, 2000—. Water safety instr., sports safety instr. ARC, Williamsburg, Va., 1970—; sholastic all Am. com. USA Swimming, Colorado Springs, 1999—. Mission dir. King of Glory Luth. Ch., Williamsburg, 2000—06; storybook connection prison ministry coord. King of Glory Luth. Ch. and Va. Peninsula Regional Jail, Williamsburg, 2000—06; safety coord. Va. Swimming Local Swimming Com., Williamsburg. Named to Hall of Fame, ARC, 2005; recipient Glenn Hummer award, USA Swimming, 1988, Phillips 66 Performance award, Va. Swimming, 2004. Mem.: Nat. Athletic Trainers Assn., Va. HS Coaches Assn. (life Dr. Frank McCue award 1988), USA Swimming (life; sec. sports medicine soc., coun. 1979—99). Independent. Lutheran. Avocations: travel, hockey. Home Phone: 757-565-4621. Personal E-mail: dlime@aol.com.

LIMERICK, PATRICIA NELSON, history professor; b. Banning, Calif., May 17, 1951; BA, U. Calif., Santa Cruz, 1972; PhD, Yale, 1980. Prof. history dept. U. Colo., Boulder. Chmn. bd. dirs. Ctr. Am. West. Author: (books) Desert Passages: Encounters With the American Deserts, 1985, The Legacy of Conquest: The Unbroken Past of the American West, 1987, Something in the Soil: Legacies and Reckonings in the New West, 2000. MacArthur fellow, 1995. Office: U Colo Ctr Am West MAcky 229 282 UCB Boulder CO 80309 E-mail: patricia.limerick@colorado.edu.

LIMOGES, RICHARD FREDERICK, psychiatrist; b. Detroit, Apr. 27, 1938; s. Joseph Frederick and Corrine Limoges. AB, Princeton U., NJ, 1960; MD, Temple Sch. Medicine, Phila., 1964. Diplomate Am. Bd. Psychiatry and Neurology, cert. group therapist, lic. medicine and surgery Pa., N.J., N.Y. Attending psychiatrist Pa. Hosp., Phila., 1971—; sr. attending psychiatrist Inst. Pa., 1975—97; attending psychiatrist Grad. Hosp., Phila., 1979—94; cons. Phila. prisons, ', 1977—79; pvt. practice Phila., 1971—. Lt. USN, 1965—68. Fellow: Am. Soc. Addiction Medicine, Am. Psychiat. Assn. (disting. life), Am. Acad. Forensic Scis., Coll. Physicians Phila., N.Y. Acad. Medicine; mem.: Am. Acad. Psychiatry. Avocations: travel, opera, photography. Office: 822 Pine St 1-B Philadelphia PA 19107 Office Phone: 215-627-5650.

LIMPERT, JOHN H., JR., fund raising executive; b. Bklyn., May 14, 1933; s. John H. and Sophia (Douropoulos) L.; children: Alexandra Michelle, John Harold III. AB, Harvard U., 1955, postgrad., 1955-56. Cert. fund raising exec. Pub. rels. mgr. Frankfort Distillers Co. div. Seagram, NYC, 1959-63; account exec. McCann-Erickson, Inc., NYC, 1963-65, account dir., 1965-68; v.p. Ted Bates & Co., Inc., NYC, 1968-71; mgr. lectrs., speakers Keedick Lecture Bur., Inc., NYC, 1971-73; dir. membership and devel. Mus. Modern Art, NYC, 1973-83, dir. devel., 1983-86; v.p. for devel. and mktg. NY Bot. Garden, 1986-88; v.p. devel. Lincoln Ctr. for Performing Arts Inc., 1988-89; assoc. fund counsel Charles H. Bentz Assocs., Inc., NYC, 1990—; trustee Children's Aid Soc., 1966-74, Festival Orch. and Chorus, 1967-69, Schola Cantorum, 1963-65; bd. dirs. Assoc. Harvard Alumni, 1967-69, 73-74, Bronx C. of C., 1988-91, NY chpt., Nat. Soc. Fund Raising Execs., 1989-93; vestryman Grace Episcopal Ch., Plainfield, 1992-95. With US Army, 1956-58. Office: 950 Hillside Ave Plainfield NJ 07060-3150 Office Phone: 908-753-7289. Office Fax: 908-753-0550.

LIMPITLAW, JOHN DONALD, publishing executive, priest; b. NYC, Jan. 4, 1935; s. Robert and Olga (Lang) L.; m. Susan Elizabeth Glover, May 21, 1960; children: Alison, Amy Elizabeth. BA, Trinity Coll., Hartford, Conn., 1956; MA in Religion, Yale U., 1992. With Marine Midland Bank Trust Co. N.Y., NYC, 1956-61, Celanese Corp., NYC, 1961-63; mgr. personnel Westvaco Corp., NYC, 1963-69; v.p. Warnaco Inc., Bridgeport, Conn., 1969-77, Macmillan Inc., NYC, 1977-89; vicar Parish of Christ's Ch., Easton, Conn., 1992-97; bd. dirs. St. Mark's Day Care Ctr., Bridgeport, 1995—. Seminarian Yale Divinity Sch., New Haven, Conn., 1989-92; trustee Episcopal Investment Funds; bd. dirs. Inter-Ch. Residences, Inc., 3030 Park, Inc.; dir. Operation Hope; bd. dirs. Habitat, Easton, Conn., bd. ops., Fairfield, Conn., 1998—. Democrat. Episcopalian. Avocations: sailing, skiing. Home: 140 Whidah Way Wellfleet MA 02667-7735 also: 6825 Grenadier Blvd Naples FL 34108-7218 Home Phone: 508-349-1190. Personal E-mail: jlimpitlaw@aol.com.

LIMPUS, CHARLES EVERETT, III, non-commissioned officer; b. Fuka oka, Japan, Oct. 29, 1948; s. Charles Everett Limpus Jr. and Dorothy Pierce Limpus. Svc. officer VFW, Orlando, 1995, legis. officer, 1995—97, svc. officer, 1997, surgeon, 1999, svc. officer, 1997—. With US Army, 1967—70, Vietnam. Mem.: 173rd ABN. BDE Soc., 82nd ABN. Div. Assn., VFW. Republican. Avocations: fishing, art, painting, drawing.

LIMTIACO, ALICIA GARRIDO, attorney general, former prosecutor; b. Agaba, Guam, Aug. 7, 1963; d. Francisco Perez and Julia Garrido Limtiaco; m. Vincent Untalan Muñoz; 1 child, Julia Faye Limtiaco Muñoz. BSBA, U. So. Calif., 1985; JD, UCLA Sch. Law, 1990. Law clk. Superior Ct. Guam; assoc. Arriola, Cowan & Arriola; ptnr. Torres, Limtiaco, Cruz & Sison, P.L.L.C., Limtiaco, Cruz & Sison, P.L.L.C.; lawyer rep. US Dist. Ct. Guam (9th cir.); asst. atty. gen. prosecution divsn., lead atty. criminal sexual conduct and family violence unit Guam Atty. Gen.'s Office, 1991—96, acting chief prosecutor, 1994—95; atty. gen. Territory of Guam, 2007—. Chair Gov.'s Family Violence Task Force; adj. faculty, asst. prof. pub. adminstrn. and legal studies prog. Sch. Bus. and Pub. Adminstrn. U. Guam Coll. Profl. Studies; adj. faculty basic law enforcement acad. and criminal justice prog. Guam Cmty. Coll.; mem. Family Violence Info. Network, Com. Family Violence, Sex Offender Registry Steering Com.; mem. crisis ctr. steering com. Healing Hearts. Bd. dirs. Make a Wish Found. Guam, Guam Coun. of Arts and Humanities Agy. Named Outstanding Woman of Yr., 1999. Office: Office of Atty Gen Justice Bldg 287 W O'Brien Dr Hagatna GU 96910*

LIN, ALICE LEE LAN, physicist, researcher, educator; b. Shanghai, Oct. 28, 1937; came to U.S., 1960, naturalized, 1974; m. A. Marcus, Dec. 19, 1962 (div. Feb. 1972); 1 child, Peter A. AB in Physics, U. Calif., Berkeley, 1963; MA in Physics, George Washington U., Washington, 1974. Statis. asst. dept. math. U. Calif., Berkeley, Calif., 1961-63; rsch. asst. in radiation damage Cavendish Lab. Cambridge U., England, 1965-66; info. analysis specialist Nat. Acad. Sci., Washington, 1970-71; tchng. fellow, rsch. asst. George Washington U., Cath. U. Am., Washington, 1971-75; physicist NASA /Goddard Space Flight Ctr., Greenbelt, Md., 1975-80, Army Materials Tech. Lab., Watertown, Mass., 1980—. Contbr. articles to profl. jours. Mencius Ednl. Found. grantee, 1959-60. Mem. AAAS, N.Y. Acad. Scis., Am. Phys. Soc., Am. Ceramics Soc., Am. Acoustical Soc., Am. Men and Women of Sci., Optical Soc. Am. Democrat. Avocations: computers, opera, ballet, gardening, coin collecting/numismatics. Home: 28 Hallett Hill Rd Weston MA 02493-1753 Office Phone: 781-899-6751. Business E-Mail: plinmarcus@alumni.tufts.edu.

LIN, CHUEN-SEN, mechanical engineer, educator; b. TsingTao, Taiwan, Dec. 22, 1948; arrived in U.S., 1976; s. Chi-Chi and Yu-Ming Yao Lin; m. Hsueh-Fen Chao, May 27, 1976; children: Chery, Jennifer. MS, U. Hawaii, Manoa, 1978; PhD, U. Minn., 1988. Cert. marine engr., Taiwan. Marine engr. China Transport Co., Taipei, Taiwan, 1973—75; lectr. Calif. State U., Fullerton, 1988—90; assoc. prof. U. Alaska, Fairbanks, 1990—; project engr. ICRC, Madison Heights, Mich., 1998—99. Contbr. articles to profl. publs. Recipient awards, Tank-Automotive and Armaments Command Dept. Def., 1998—99, Integrated Concepts and Rsch. Corp. Dept. Energy, 2000—05, Exptl. Program to stimulate Competitive Rsch. NSF, 2001; grantee, Alaska Space, 1993, MAPCO Corp., 1997, ASHRAE, 1997. Mem.: ASME, Am. Soc. Engring. Edn., Nat. Assn. Mental Illness, Pi Tau Sigma. Avocations: swimming, tai chi. Office: U Alaska Fairbanks 337 DU PO Box 755905 Fairbanks AK 99775 Office Phone: 907-474-5126. E-mail: ffcl@uaf.edu.

LIN, CHUN CHIA, research physicist, educator; b. Canton, China, Mar. 7, 1930; s. Yue Hang Lam and Kin Ng. BS, U. Calif., Berkeley, 1951, MA, 1952; PhD, Harvard U., 1955. Asst. prof. physics U. Okla., Norman, 1955-59, assoc. prof. physics, 1959-63, prof. physics, 1963-68, U. Wis., Madison, 1968—. Cons., univ. retainee Tex. Instruments Inc., 1960-68; cons. Sandia Labs., 1976-81; sec. Gaseous Electronics Conf., 1972-73, chmn., 1990-92. Contbr. articles ot profl. jours. Sloan Found. fellow, 1962-66; rsch. grantee NSF and Air Force Office Sci. Rsch. Fellow Am. Phys. Soc. (sec. divsn. electron and atomic physics 1974-77, chair divsn. atomic molecular and optical physics 1994-95, Will Allis prize 1996). Home: 1652 Monroe St Apt C Madison WI 53711-2046 Office: U Wis Dept Physics Madison WI 53706 Office Phone: 608-262-0697.

LIN, DAHANG, medical physicist; arrived in U.S., 1985; s. Meitan Lin and Wenzhen Zhang; m. Qixian Zhang; children: Gang, Xia. Diploma, Tsing Hua U., 1967, MS Physics, 1982; MA Physics, Bklyn. Coll., 1989; PhD Physics, CUNY, 1992. Lic. med. physicist N.Y. Instr. Hubei Coll. Traditional Chinese Medicine, Wuhan, 1974—78, Wuhan Poly. Inst., China, 1981—85; tchg. asst. Bklyn. Coll., 1985—92; med. physicist, assoc. dir. Elmhurst Hosp. Ctr., NY, 1992—. Contbr. articles to profl. jours. Bd. dirs. N.Y. Chinese Am. Assn., Flushing, 1998—. Mem.: Am. Assn. Physicists in Medicine, Soc. Nuc. Medicine. Avocations: travel, photography, fishing, sports. Home: 40-11 Murray St Flushing NY 11354 Office: Elmhurst Hosp Ctr 79-01 Broadway Elmhurst NY 11373 Business E-Mail: lind@nychhc.org.

LIN, EDWARD C., engineering educator; b. Chgo., Sept. 25, 1979; s. Bao-Shih (Paul) and Lingfen (Cecilia) Lin. BS, U. Ill., Urbana-Champaign, 2001; MS, PhD, Carnegie Mellon U., Pitts., 2003. Intern Philips Innovation Ctr., Taipei, Taiwan, 1999; rsch. U. Ill. Elec. and Computer Engring. Dept., Urbana, 2000—01; rsch. asst. Carnegie Mellon U. Elec. and Computer Engring. Dept., 2001—; intern Intel Corp., Santa Clara, Calif., 2003—03, Apple Corp., Cupertino, Calif., 2004—04. Mem.: IEEE, Phi Eta Sigma, Eta Kappa Nu. Achievements include research in high performance speech recognition systems using custom hardware. Avocations: basketball, poker, rock climbing. Home Phone: 412-972-0218.

LIN, FRANK C., computer company executive; Chmn. bd. dirs., pres., CEO Trident Microsys. Inc., Mountain View, Calif. Office: Trident Microsystems 1090 E Arques Ave Sunnyvale CA 94085-4601

LIN, GEORGE, research and development company executive, biomedical researcher; s. Tsyh-Shyong and Sie-Mei Lin. AB, Harvard U., Cambridge, Mass., 1995; MD, PhD, U. Pa., Phila., 2003. Rsch. asst. Nat. Cancer Inst., Frederick, Md., 1992—95, Brigham and Women's Hosp., Boston, 1993—94, Procept, Inc., Cambridge, Mass., 1994—95, Stellar-Chance Lab., Phila., 1996; rsch. biologist So. Rsch. Inst., Frederick, Md., 1997—98; rsch. asst. Wistar Inst., Phila., 1998—99, U. Pa. Sch. Medicine, Phila., 1999—2003; COO, CFO Biol. Mimetics, Inc., Frederick, 2003—. Founder, bd. dirs. Biol. Mimetics, Inc., Frederick, 1996—. Contbr. articles to profl. jours. Bd. dirs. Friends of Harvard U. Cycling Assn., Cambridge, 2006; alumni interviewer Harvard U. Schools Com., Voorhees, NJ, 2000—06. Recipient First Pl. Physics, Del. Valley Sci. Fair, 1991, First Pl. Physics and Best of Fair, Thomas Edison Sci. Fair, 1991, 50th Westinghouse Sci. Talent Search, 1991, USA Today All-USA Coll. Academic Team, 1995, Balduin Lucke Meml. prize, U. Pa., 2001, Stuart Mudd award, 2003; scholar Nat. Sci. Scholar, NSF, 1991, Harvard U., 1991—93, Keystone Symposia, 2002, 50th Westinghouse Sci. Talent Search, 1991, USA Today All-USA Coll. Academic Team, 1995; NJ Gov.'s Sch. in the Sciences fellow, Drew U., 1990, Superconductivity and Materials Sci. fellow, Argonne Nat. Lab., 1991, Nat. Merit scholar, 1991, Tng. grant, Nat. Rsch. Svc. Award, 2000—01, Travel grant, Conf. on Retroviruses and Opportunistic Infections, 2001—03, NIH Med. Scientist Tng. Program scholar. Mem.: Assn. Biosci. Fin. Officers, Chinese Biopharm. Assn., Harvardwood, Trump Nat. Golf Club, Westchester, NY, Harvard Club. Achievements include patents pending for HIVs useful in vaccine devel. and HIV drug design. Avocations: bicycling, tennis, running, coin collecting/numismatics, futures trading. Office: Biological Mimetics Inc 124 Byte Dr Frederick MD 21702 Home Phone: 856-768-1262; Office Phone: 301-620-7565. Personal E-mail: george.lin.1@gmail.com. Business E-Mail: lin@bmi-md.com.

LIN, HAI, physicist; b. Hangzhou, Zhejiang, China, 1979; arrived in U.S., 2001; Attended, Hangzhou Fgn. Lang. Sch., 1991—97; BS, Peking U., 2001; MA, Princeton U., 2003, PhD, 2006. Asst. instr. Princeton U., NJ, 2002—05. Mem.: London Math. Soc., Soc. Indsl. and Applied Math., Am. Chem. Soc., Biophysical Soc., Am. Math. Soc., Am. Phys. Soc., Sigma Xi, N.Y. Acad. Scis. Achievements include research works in quark distribution in nucleons; research in black hole thermodynamics quantum gravity and string theory; bacterial cell communication and chemotaxis; duality between string theory and gauge theory. Office: Dept Physics U Mich Ann Arbor 450 Church St Ann Arbor MI 48109-1040 Home Phone: 609-240-2678. Business E-Mail: hailin@umich.edu.

LIN, HENRY C., physician, researcher; b. Taiwan, China, Mar. 10, 1958; MD, SUNY Upstate Med. U., 1982. Diplomate Am. Bd. Internal Medicine, 1985, Gastroenterology Am. Bd. Internal Medicine, 1987. Asst. to assoc. prof. medicine UCLA Geffen Sch. Medicine, LA, 1990—2003; assoc. prof. medicine U. So. Calif. Keck Sch. Medicine, LA, 2003—07; prof. internal medicine N. Mex. VA Health Care Sys., U. N. Mex., Albuquerque, 2007—, chief gastroenterology sect., 2007—. Dir. gi motility program & nutrition Cedars-Sinai Med. Ctr., LA, 1990—2003. Mem.: Am. Motility Soc., Am. Gastroent. Assn. Achievements include patents in field.

LIN, JAMES CHIH-I, biomedical and electrical engineer, educator; b. Dec. 29, 1942; m. Mei Fei, Mar. 21, 1970; children: Janet, Theodore, Erik. BS, U. Wash., 1966, MS, 1968, PhD, 1971. Engr. Crown Zellerbach Corp., Seattle, 1966-67; asst. prof. U. Wash., Seattle, 1971-74; prof. Wayne State U., Detroit, 1974-80, U. Ill., Chgo., 1980—, head dept. bioengring., 1980-92, dir. robotics and automation lab., 1982-89, dir. spl. projects Coll. Engring., 1992-94, rsch. chair NSC, 1993-97. Vis. prof., Beijing, Rome, Shan Dong, Taiwan Univs.; lectr. short courses, 1974—; cons. Battelle Meml. Inst., Columbus, Ohio, 1973-75, SRI Internat., palo Alto, Calif., 1978-79, Arthur D. Little Inc., Cambridge, Mass., 1980-83, Ga. Tech. Rsch. Inst., Atlanta, 1984-86, Walter Reed Army Inst. Rsch., 1973, 87, 88, Naval Aerospace Med. Rsch. Labs., Pensacola, 1982-83, U.R.S. Corp., San Francisco, 1985-87, CBS Inc., N.Y., 1988, U. Va., 1991-92, ACS Inc., Santa Clara Calif., 1989-90, Luxtron Corp., Mountainview, Calif., 1991-92, Commonwealth Edison, Chgo., 1991-95, Lucent Tech./Bell Labs., 1998-2000; program chmn. Frontiers of Engring. and Computing Conf., Chgo., 1985; chmn., convener URSI Jt. Symposium Electromagnetic Waves in Biol. Sys., Tel Aviv, 1987, Internat. Conf. on Sci. and Tech., 1989-91; chmn. Chinese-Am. Acad. and Profl. Conv., 1993; mem. Congrl. Health Care Adv. Coun., 13th dist., Ill., 1987-99; panelist NSF Presdl. Young Investigator award com., Washington, 1984, 89; mem. NIH diagnostic radiology, 1981-85, chmn. spl. study sect., 1986—2004; mem. U.S. Nat. Commn. for URSI, NAS, 1980-82, 90-99, chair Commn. K., 1990-99, Extremely Low Frequency Field monitoring com., 1995-97; mem. Internat. Commn. on Nonionizing Radiation Protection, 2004—; mem. Pres. Com. Nat. Medal of Sci., 1992-93; mem. Nat. Coun. Radiation Protection and Measurement, 1992—, chmn. radio frequency sci. com., 1995—, v.p. 2005-07; chmn. Internat. Union of Radio Scis. Commn., Electromagnetics in Biology and Medicine, 1996-99; chmn. Internat. Sci. Meeting on Electromagnetics in Medicine, 1997; mem. citizens adv. coun. Hinsdale Ctrl. H.S., 1988-93 Author: Microwave Auditory Effects and Applications, 1978, Biological Effects and Health Implications of Radiofrequency Radiation, 1987, Electromagnetic Interaction with Biological Systems, 1989, Mobile Comm. Safety, 1996; editor: Advances in Electromagnetic Fields in Living Systems, 1994—, EMB Mag., 1997—99, Wireless Networks, 1996—97; editor in chief: Bioelectromagnetics, 2006—; contbr. articles to profl. jours., columns to mags. Recipient Nat. Rsch. Svcs. award 1982, Disting. Svc. award, Outstanding Leadership award Chinese Am. Acad. and Profl. Assn. MidAm., 1989. Fellow AAAS, AIMBE, IEEE (tech. policy coun. 1990-91, chmn. com. on man and radiation, 1990-91, assoc. and guest editor transactions on biomed. engring., guest editor transaction on microwave theory and techniques, disting. lectr. engring. in medicine and biology 1991—, com. chair 2007-, Transaction Best Paper award 1975); mem. Biomed. Engring. Soc. (sr. mem.), Robotics Internat. (sr. mem.), Am. Soc. Engring. Edn., Bioelectromagnetics Soc. (charter, pres.-elect 1993-94, pres. 1994-95, chmn. ann. meeting 1994, d'Arsonval medal 2003), Marconi Found. (sci. com. 1996—), Golden Key, Sigma Xi, Phi Tau Phi (v.p.), Tau Beta Pi. Office: U Ill Coll Engring 1030 SEO MC/154 851 S Morgan St Chicago IL 60607-7042 Office Phone: 312-413-1052. Business E-Mail: lin@uic.edu.

LIN, JAMES K., communications executive, educator; b. Shanghai, Sept. 22, 1941; s. Hua Kun Lin and Sho Cheng Chiang; m. Ellen Lin; children: Vincent, Geoffrey, Charles. BS, Nat. Taiwan U., Taipei, 1965; MS, Pratt Inst., 1969; postgrad., U. Pa.; PhD, U. Southwestern La., 1977; DSc, U. Am., 1977. Sr. analyst, engr. mgr. RCA Global Comms., NYC, 1975-77; mgr. timesharing ctr. CDC Taiwan, Taipei, 1977-81, sales mgr. country mktg., 1981-85; country mgr. CDC China/Hong Kong, Beijing, 1985-89; dep. gen. mgr. WANG Labs., Taipei, 1989-92; regional dir. EDS Asia, Hong Kong, 1992-94; gen. mgr. ABB China Ltd., Hong Kong, 1994—. Prof. (part time) CUNY, 1973-74; spkr. in field. Mem. Chinese Academic and Profl. Assn. in Am. (pres. 1975-77), Chinese-Am. Assn. China (exec. dir. 1995-97), Am. C. of C. in China, Am. High Tech. Forum in China (treas. 1987-89), Comm. Network Assn. (exec. dir. 1992-94), Open Sys. Assn. Taiwan (mng. supr. 1989-91, Excellent Performances 1990). Avocations: swimming, basketball, music, travel. Home: 5257 Purdue Ave Culver City CA 90230-5349 Office: ABB China Ltd South Tower 14 East Third Ring Rd N 100026 Beijing China

LIN, JIIN-HUEY CHERN, engineering educator; b. Kaoshung, Taiwan, Republic of China, Feb. 19, 1949; d. Fen-Fu and Chung-Lin Lin Chen; m. Luh-Yuan Lin, July 5, 1973; children: Albert Isaac, Alice, Seraphina. BS in Physics, Chung Yuan Christian U., Taiwan, 1970; MS in Physics, N.E. La.

U., 1974; PhD in Biomaterials, Northwestern U., 1983. Vis. specialist Nat. Yang-Ming U., Taipei, Tawian, 1984-85; asst. prof. Northwestern U., Chgo., 1985-89, vis. prof., 1996-97, Nat. Cheng-Kung U., Tainan, Taiwan, 1987-88, assoc. prof., 1989-95, prof., 1995—, dir. Ctr. for Biomaterials Rsch., 2002—05, dir. Ctr. for Biomaterials and Heart Sci. Rsch., 2005—. Strategic com. Nat. Sci. Coun., Taipei, 1997-99. Jour. reviewer Dental Materials, Liverpool, U.K., 1995—, Jour. of Materials Chemistry and Physics, Liverpool, 1997—, Biomaterials, 2004—; contbr. numerous articles to profl. jours.; inventor in field Grantee Nat. Sci. Coun. of Republic of China, Nat. Health Rsch. Inst., 1994—. Fellow The Acad. of Denal Materials; mem. Soc. of Biomaterials, Soc. of Dental Materials, Chinese Bioengring. Soc., Am. Ceramic Soc. Home: 911 Tower Rd Winnetka IL 60093-1935 Office: Nat Cheng-Kung U Tainan Taiwan Office Phone: 886-6-274-8086. Business E-Mail: chernlin@mail.ncku.edu.tw.

LIN, KAI, research scientist; m. Betty Tang; 1 child, Brian. PhD, U. Pa., Phila., 1999. Investigator Vertex Pharmaceuticals, Inc., Cambridge, Mass.; group leader virology Novartis, Cambridge, Mass., 2004—. Office: Novartis 500 Technology Sq Cambridge MA 02139

LIN, KANT, plastic surgeon, educator; b. NYC, Feb. 9, 1959; s. Samuel Pao-Hsi and Joanna Tu Lin; children: Samantha, Michelle. BA, U. Pa., 1980; MD, Mt. Sinai Sch. Medicine, 1984. Diplomate Am. Bd. Plastic Surgery. Itern Hosp. U. Pa., 1984—85, resident, 1985—91; fellow Hosp. Sick Children U. Toronto, 1991—92; asst. prof. U. Va., Charlottesville, 1992—98, assoc. prof., 1998—. Author, editor: Craniofacial Surgery: Science and Surgical Technique, 2001. Named one of Am.'s Top Physicians, Consumers Rsch. Coun. Am. Fellow: ACS, Am. Assn. Plastic Surgeons, Am. Soc. Plastic Surgeons (bd. dirs.); mem.: Alpha Omega Alpha, Phi Beta Kappa. Office: Univ VA Box 800376 Charlottesville VA 22908 Business E-Mail: kyl5s@virginia.edu.

LIN, KWEI-JAY, education educator, researcher; s. Chin-Fa and Shuan Chiao (Hsieh) Lin; m. Fuchye Doong, Jan. 8, 1983; children: Shannon D., Christine G. PhD, U. Md., College Park, 1985. Assoc. prof. U. Ill., Urbana-Champaign, 1985—93; prof. U. Calif., Irvine, 1993—. Mem.: IEEE (co-chair CS TC on e-commerce 2003—). Office: U Calif Dept EECS Irvine CA 92697-2625 Office Phone: 949-824-7839. Business E-Mail: klin@uci.edu.

LIN, LIANLIAN, management educator; b. Liaoning, China, Aug. 22, 1956; d. Jiang Lin and Jianhua Sun; 1 child, Nika Qiao. BA in Econs., Liaoning U., China, 1982; MA in Internat. Fin., Fudan U., Shanghai, China, 1985; LLM, U. Pa., Phila., 1988; PhD in Bus. Adminstrn., U. Tex., Austin, 1992. Mem. law faculty Fudan U., China, 1985—87; prof. mgmt. Calif. State Poly. U., Pomona, 1992—. Vis. prof. Peking U., Beijing, 2000; pres. Asian Pacific faculty staff and student assn. Calif. State Poly U., Pomona, 2001—02. Contbr. articles to profl. jours, also books. Mem.: Chinese Am. Faculty Assn. Scholarship Found. So. Calif. (pres. 2005—07), Chinese Am. Faculty Assn. So. Calif. (pres. 2003—04), Chinese Scholars Assn. So. Calif. (pres. 2004—05). Office: Calif State Poly U 3801 W Temple Ave MHR Pomona CA 91768

LIN, LIHUI, business educator; d. Xiuqing Lin and Shulan Wang; m. Wei Liu, July 29, 1997. PhD, U. Tex., Austin, 2002. Asst. prof. Boston U., 2002—. Contbr. articles to profl. jours. Office: Boston U 595 Commonwealth Ave Boston MA 02215 Office Phone: 617-353-6145.

LIN, MARIA C.H., lawyer; b. Kunming, Yunnan, China, Jan. 27, 1942; BSc, Coll. Mount St. Vincent, 1966; MSc, U. Kans., 1970; JD, Fordham U., 1978. Bar: N.Y. 1979, U.S. Dist. Ct. (so. and ea. dists.) N.Y. 1979, U.S. Ct. Appeals (Fed. cir.) 1982, U.S. Patent and Trademark Office, 1979, U.S Supreme Ct. 1985. Ptnr. Morgan & Finnegan LLP, NYC. Bd. mem. HBV Found. Mem. ABA, Internat. Intellectual Propery Soc. (chair 2000—02). Office: Morgan & Finnegan LLP Shanghai Rep Off Aetna Tower Ste 408 107 Zunzi Rd Shanghai 200051 China Office Phone: 86 21 6237 5322. E-mail: mclin@morganfinnegan.com.

LIN, MAYA, architect, sculptor; b. Athens, Ohio, Oct. 5, 1959; d. Henry H. and Julia (Chang) L. m. Daniel Wolf; 2 children. BA, Yale U., 1981, MA, 1986, PhD in Fine Arts, 1987. Architectural designer Peter Forbes & Assocs., NYC, 1986-87; pvt. practice NYC, 1987—. Bd. dir. So. Poverty Law Ctr.'s Teaching Tolerance project, Kennedy Mus. Art at Ohio Univ. Prin. work include Vietnam Veterans Meml., Washington, 1981 (Twenty-five Yr. award, AIA, 2007), Civil Rights Meml., Montgomery, Ala., 1986. Author: Boundaries, 2000. Bd. mem. Yale Corp., Natural Resources Def. Fund. Mem.: AAAL. Achievements include submitting the winning design for the Vietnam Veterans Memorial at the age of 21.

LIN, MING-CHANG, physical chemistry professor, researcher; b. Hsinpu, Hsinchu, Taiwan, Oct. 24, 1936; came to U.S., 1967, naturalized, 1975; s. Fushin and Tao May (Hsu) L.; m. Juh-Huey Chern, June 26, 1965; children: Karen, Linus H., Ellena J. BSc, Taiwan Normal U., Taipei, 1959; PhD, U. Ottawa, Ont., Can., 1966. Postdoctoral rsch. felloww U. Ottawa, 1965-67; postdoctoral rsch. assoc. Cornell U., Ithaca, NY, 1967-69; rsch. chemist Naval Rsch. Lab., Washington, 1970-74, supervisory rsch. chemist, head chem. kinetics sect., 1974-82, sr. scientist for chem. kinetics, 1982-88; Robert W. Woodruff prof. phys. chemistry Emory U., Atlanta, 1988—2005, Robert W. Woodruff emeritus prof., 2005—, Woodruff sr. rsch. asst., 2005—. Mem. adv. bd. Internat. Jour. Chem. Kinetics, 1990-93, Inst. Atomic and Molecular Sci., Taipei, 1991-2003, Chemistry, Inst. Physics, Taiwan, 2000—, Nat. Ctr. for High-performance Computing, Taiwan, 2002—, Nat. Synchrotron Radiation Ctr., Taiwan, 2002—; mem. young presdl. award com. NSF, Washington, 1990; Nat. Sci. Coun. disting. vis. prof. Nat. Chiao Tung U., Taiwan, 2002-04; Taiwan Semicond. Comp. disting. prof., 2005—; Taiwan Nat. Rsch. Coun. disting. vis. prof., 2005—. Contbr. over 450 articles to profl. jours. 2d lt. Taiwan ROTC, 1960-62. Recipient Civilian Meritorious award USN, 1979, Humboldt award Humboldt Found., 1982, prize in sci. tech. Taiwanese-Am. Found., 1989, The Capt. Robert Dexter Conrad award U.S. Navy, 1998; Guggenheim fellow, 1982. Mem. Am. Chem. Soc. (Hillebrand prize 1975), Combustion Inst., Am. Vacuum Soc., Materials Rsch. Soc., N.Am. Taiwanese Profs. Assn., Sigma Xi (Pure Sci. award 1976 Naval Rsch. Lab. chpt.), Academia Sinica (Taiwan). Achievements include discovery of numerous chemical lasers, use of lasers to elucidate mechanisms of combustion, propulsion and gas-surface reactions; first use of lasers to ionize nonfluorescing radicals and to probe for radicals formed in heterogeneous catalytic reactions. Office: Emory Univ Dept Chemistry 1515 Pierce Dr NE Atlanta GA 30322-1003 Business E-Mail: chemmcl@emory.edu.

LIN, PEN-MIN, electrical engineer, educator; b. Liaoning, China, Oct. 17, 1928; arrived in US, 1954; s. Tai-sui and Tse-san (Tang) Lin; m. Louise Shou Yuen Lee, Dec. 29, 1962; children: Marian, Margaret, Janice. BSEE, Taiwan U., 1950; MSEE, N.C. State U., 1956; PhD in Elec. Engring., Purdue U., 1960. Asst. prof. Purdue U., West Lafayette, Ind., 1961-66, assoc. prof., 1966-74, prof. elec. engring., 1974-94, prof. emeritus, 1994—. Author: (with L.O. Chua) Computer Aided Analysis of Electronic Circuits, 1975, Symbolic Network Analysis, 1991, (with R.A. DeCarlo) Linear Circuit Analysis, 1995, 2d edit., 2001. Fellow: IEEE (life). Home: 3029 Covington St West Lafayette IN 47906-1107 Office: Purdue Univ Sch Of Elec Engring West Lafayette IN 47907

LIN, QIUYUN, education educator; b. Fuqing, China, Aug. 17, 1964; arrived in US, 2000; d. Lin Shengxian and Weng Deying; m. Dongfu Su, Dec. 25, 1990; 1 child, Wanling Su. BA in English, Fujian Tchrs. U., China, 1985; EdD, Indiana U., Pa., 2003. Assoc. prof. Fuzhou U., China, 1992—99; asst. prof. Mt. Aloysius Coll., Cresson, Pa., 2003—. Contbr. over 30 articles to profl. jours. Fellow, Nat. Ctr. Edn. Stats., 2001, 2006. Mem.: Am. Ednl. Rsch. Orgn. (assoc.).

LIN, RAY-QING, physicist, researcher; d. Pa-Yan Lin and Dou-Cheng Young; m. David Gary Sibeck. PhD, UCLA, 1988. Assoc. scientist Johns Hopkins U., Balt., 1995—96; civil servant David Taylor Model Basin, West Bethesda, Md., 1996—. Contbr. articles to profl. jours. Democrat. Achievements include patents for numerical prediction model for ship wave interaction. Home Phone: 301-776-5999; Office Phone: 301-227-3945.

LIN, ROBERT PEICHUNG, physicist, educator, researcher; b. Kwangsi, People's Republic of China, Jan. 24, 1942; s. Tung Hua and Susan Lin; m. Lily Wong, Aug. 14, 1983; 1 stepson, Linus Sun. BS, Calif. Inst. Tech., 1962; PhD, U. Calif., Berkeley, 1967. Asst. rsch. physicist Space Sci. Lab., U. Calif., Berkeley, 1967-74, assoc. rsch. physicist, 1974-79, rsch. physicist, 1979-88, sr. fellow, 1980-88; adj. prof. astronomy dept. U. Calif., Berkeley, 1988-91, prof. physics dept., 1991—, assoc. dir. space scis. lab., 1992—98, dir. space scis. lab., 1998—. Vis. prof. geophysics program U. Wash., Seattle, 1987; mem. solar physics panel Astronomy and Astrophysics Survey, Nat. Acad. Sci., 1989-91; mem. working groups for astrophysics, solar physics, space plasma, cosmic and heliospheric physics, balloons, space and applications adv. com. NASA, 1977—, mem. various rev. panels, 1977—. Contbr. articles to Jour. Geophys. Rsch., Solar Physics, Phys. Rev. Letters, Rev. Sci. Instruments, Astrophys. Jour., Geophys. Rsch. Letters. Grantee NASA, 1980—, NSF, 1981—. Mem. Am. Geophys. Union, Am. Astron. Soc., NAS; fellow Am. Acad. Arts & Sciences Achievements include research on solar and interplanetary physics, high energy astrophysics, lunar and planetary science, and physics of the earth's magnetosphere. Office: U Calif Space Scis Lab Berkeley CA 94720-0001

LIN, RONGHUI, chemist, researcher; arrived in US, 1992; s. Liangyue Lin and Qianliang Qiu; m. Liya Chen, Jan. 24, 1987; children: Xinyue, Cindy. BS in Chemistry, Sichuan U., Chengdu, China, 1983; MS in Organic Chemistry, Hangzhou U., China, 1986; PhD in Chemistry, So. Ill. U., Carbondale, Ill., 1996. Lectr. chemistry Hangzhou (China) U., 1986—92; postdoctoral fellow, vis. scholar U. Calif., Berkeley, Calif., 1996—98; prin. scientist Johnson & Johnson Pharm. Rsch. & Devel., LLC, Raritan, NJ, 1998—. Contbr. articles to profl. jours. Mem.: Internat. Isotope Soc., Internat. Union Pure and Applied Chemistry, Am. Chem. Soc., Sino-American Pharm. Assn. (life). Achievements include patents for over ten issued patents and patent applications. Home Phone: 732-432-0294; Office Phone: 908-704-5268.

LIN, STEPHEN HOUNG TZE, music educator; b. Louisville, May 20, 1953; s. Richard and Julia (Lam) L.; m. Sharon Elaine Brown, Aug. 20, 1977; 1 child, Stephen Wang Jr. B in Music Edn., Morehead State U., 1975; MEd, U. Louisville, 1980. Cert. tchr., Ky. Choral, gen. music tchr. Jefferson County Pub. Schs., 1975—; head music dept. Atherton H.S., Louisville, 1976—. Chair All Jefferson County Sr. High Chorus, Louisville, 1979; guest conductor All-Dist. Jr. H.S. Chorus, Ctrl. Ky. Music Educators Assn., Danville, 1986; mem. Ednl. Profl. Standards Bd, Ky. 2004. Mem. So. Bapt. Theol. Sem. Oratorio Chorus, Louisville, 1975-76; deacon Broadway Bapt. Ch., Louisville, 1981-85; pres. bd. dirs. Louisville Youth Choir, 1982-83. Named Ky. H.S. Tchr. of Yr., 2002, Ky. Tchr. of Yr., 2002; recipient Ashland Oil Inc. Tchr. Achievement award, 2002, Tchr. award winner, WHAS-TV, 2003, LG & E ExCEL, 2003. Mem. NEA, Ky. Educators Assn., Jefferson County Tchrs. Assn., Am. Choral Dirs. Assn. (co-chair nat. conv. 1987—), Ky. Music Educators Assn. (state choral chair 1985-87), Jefferson Dist. Music Educators Assn. (dist. choral chair 1981-85, pres.-elect 1988-89), Louisville Bach Soc. Republican. Office: Atherton High Sch 3000 Dundee Rd Louisville KY 40205*

LIN, YUKWENG M., engineer, educator; b. Fuzhou, Fujian, China, Oct. 30, 1923; arrived in U.S., 1954, naturalized, 1964; s. Fa Been and Chi Ying (Cheng) Lin; m. Ying-yuh June Wang, Mar. 29, 1952; children: Jane, Della, Lucia, Winifred. BS, Xiamen U., 1946; MS, Stanford U., 1955, PhD, 1957; D of Engring. (hon.), U. Waterloo, Can., 1994. Tchr. Xiamen U., China, 1946-48, Imperial Coll. Engring., Ethiopia, 1957-58; engr. Vertol Aircraft Corp., Morton, Pa., 1956-57; rsch. engr. Boeing Co., Renton, Wash., 1958-60; asst. prof. U. Ill., Urbana, 1960-62, assoc. prof., 1962-65, prof. aero. and astron. engring., 1965-83; Charles E. Schmidt Eminent scholar chair Coll. Engring., dir. Ctr. for Applied Stochastics Rsch. Fla. Atlantic U., Boca Raton, 1984—. Vis. prof. mech. engring. MIT, 1967-68; sr. vis. fellow Inst. Sound and Vibration Research, U. Southampton, Eng., 1976; cons. Gen. Motors Corp., Boeing Co., Gen. Dynamics Corp., TRW Corp., Brookhaven Nat. Lab. Author: Probabilistic Theory of Structural Dynamics, 1967, Probabilistic Structural Dynamics: Advanced Theory and Applications, 1995, Probabilistic Structural Dynamics, 2004; editor: Stochastic Structural Mechanics, 1987, Stochastic Approaches in Earthquake Engineering, 1987, Stochastic Structural Dynamics, 1990, Stochastic Dynamics and Reliability of Nonlinear Ocean Systems, 1994; contbr. articles to profl. jours. Recipient sr. postdoctoral fellowship, NSF, 1967—68, Alexander von Humboldt Sr. US Scientist award, 2000, J.P. Den Hartog award, ASME, 2001. Fellow: ASCE (Alfred M. Freudenthal medal 1984, Theodore von Karman medal 1998), Am. Acad. Mechs.; mem.: Am. Assn. Wind Engring., Internat. Assn. Structural Safety and Reliability (Sr. Rsch. award 1993, Spl. prize for numerous landmark contbns. 2005), Russian Acad. Engring. (fgn. mem.), Nat. Acad. Engring., Sigma Xi. Home: 2684 NW 27th Ter Boca Raton FL 33434-6001 Office: Fla Atlantic U Coll Engring Boca Raton FL 33431 Office Phone: 561-297-3449. Business E-Mail: linyk@fau.edu.

LIN, YUSEN EASON, microbiologist, educator; m. Mei-ying Shang. PhD, MBA, U. Pitts., 1999. Rsch. asst. prof. U. Pitts., 2000—01; assoc. prof. Nat. Kaohsiung Normal U., Taiwan, 2001—. Mem.: Am. Soc. Microbiology. Office: Nat Kaohsiung Normal U 62 Shen Chong Rd Yanchao Kaohsiung Hsien 824 Taiwan Office Phone: 8867-6051036.

LINAWEAVER, WALTER ELLSWORTH, JR., physician; b. San Pedro, Calif., Oct. 16, 1928; s. Walter Ellsworth and Catherine Breathed (Bridges) L.; m. Lydia Anne Whitlock, Oct. 5, 1957 (dec. 2005); children: Catherine Ann, Nancy Alyn, Walter E. III; m. Vicki Beckham, July 30, 2005. BA cum laude, Pomona Coll., 1952; MD, Rochester U., NY, 1956. Diplomate Am. Bd. Allergy and Immunology, Am. Bd. Pediat., Am. Bd. Pediatric Allergy. Intern pediat. Med. Ctr. U. Rochester, 1956-57, resident pediat. Med. Ctr., 1958-59; asst. resident pediat. Med. Ctr. UCLA, 1957-58; fellow allergy and immunology Med. Ctr. U. Colo., Denver, 1959-61, instr. pediat. Sch. Medicine, 1961; pvt. practice Riverside (Calif.) Med. Clinic, 1962—. Asst. clin. prof. pediat. Loma Linda U. Med. Sch., 1965—. Elder Presbyn. Ch. Staff sgt. U.S. Army, 1946-48. Inducted into Athletic Hall of Fame Pomona Coll., Claremont, Calif., 1979. Fellow: L.A. Acad. Medicine, Am. Acad. Pediat., Am. Acad. Allergy, Asthma and Immunology; mem.: AMA, Calif. Med. Assn., Riverside County Heart Assn. (pres. 1965—66), Riverside County Med. Soc. (councilor 1964—66). Dfl. Avocations: American and British military history, gardening. Home: 1296 Tiger Tail Dr Riverside CA 92506-5475 Office Phone: 951-782-3681.

LINBERGER, PETER, school librarian; b. Barberton, Ohio, May 17, 1957; s. John Linberger and Eva Puhl. BS in secoundary edn., U. Akron, 1980, MS in Geography, 1988; MLS in Libr. Sci., Kent State U., 1988. Ref. asst. U. Akron Librs., Ohio, 1983—90, ref. libr., 1990—92, asst. prof. bibliography, libr., 1993—2000, asoc. prof. bibliography, libr., 2000—. Contbr. bibliography, articles to profl. jours. Geography and Map Divsn. summer internship, Libr. of Congress, 1996. Mem.: ALA (map and geography roundtable, publs. com., edn. com. 1994—2002). Achievements include grant to preserve, electronically, historic atlases of Akron and Summit County, Ohio. Office: Univ of Akron Bierce Libr 179B Akron OH 44325-1707 Business E-Mail: pl@uakron.edu.

LIN CHIEN, CHESTER, electronics executive; BSEE, Taipei Inst. Tech., Taiwan. Mem. prodn., quality and engring. staff, ops. mgr. Gen. Instruments of Taiwan; products mgr. GE, 1984; with SCI Systems; CEO NatSteel Electronics, 1993—2001; exec. v.p. Solectron Corp., Milpitas, Calif., 2001—, pres. Asia/Pacific region, 2001—. Recipient Stars of Asia award, Bus. Week mag., 1999. Office: Solectron Corp 777 Gibraltar Dr Milpitas CA 95035

LINCICOME, BRITTANY, professional golfer; b. St. Petersburg, Fla., Sept. 19, 1985; d. Tom and Angie Lincicome. Profl. golfer, 2004—; mem. LPGA Tour, 2005—. Achievements include winning the HSBC Women's World Match Play Championship, 2006, and Ginn Open, 2007, on the LPGA Tour. Avocations: poker, fishing. Mailing: LPGA 100 Internat Golf Dr Daytona Beach FL 32124-1092*

LINCICOME, DAVID RICHARD, biomedical scientist, animal scientist; b. Champaign, Ill., Jan. 17, 1914; s. David Rosebery and Olive Iola (Casper) L.; m. Dorothy Lucile Van Cleave, Sept. 1, 1941 (dec. Nov. 1952); children: David Van Cleave, Judith Ann; m. Margaret Stirewalt, Dec. 29, 1953 (dec. Apr. 2003). BS, U. Ill., 1937, MS with high honors, 1937, PhD in Tropical Medicine, Tulane U., 1941. Diplomate (emeritus) Am. Bd. Microbiology; diplomate Am. Coll. Animal Physiology; cert. animal scientist Am. Registry Profl. Animal Scientists. Asst. instr. U. Ill., 1937; instr. tropical medicine Tulane U. Med. Sch., 1937-41; asst. prof. parasitology U. Ky., 1941-47, U. Wis. Med. Sch., 1947-49; sr. rsch. parasitologist Du Pont Co., 1949-53; from asst. prof. to full prof. biol. scis. Howard U., 1953-70. Vis. sci. NIH, 1965-66; founder, registrar, Jacob Sheep Conservancy, 1988-96, bd. dirs., 1990-97, pres., 1996; vis. scholar Nat. Agrl. Libr., USDA, 1990-92; guest scientist USDA Exp. Sta., Beltsville, Md., 1978-2007, Naval Med. Rsch. Inst., 1954-62. Founder, editor Exptl. Parasitology, 1949-76; editor Transactions of the Ky. Acad. Sci., 1946-49, Transactions of the Am. Microscopical Soc., 1970-71, Internat. Rev. Tropical Medicine, 1953-63; founder Virology, 1950, Advances in Vet. Sci., 1952. Lt. col. Med. Svc. Corps, U.S. Army, WWII, PTO. Named Eminent Fellow, Wisdom Hall of Fame, 2001; recipient Anniversary award, Helminthological Soc., 1975, Sir Winston Churchill medal, Wisdom Soc. Advancement of Knowledge, Learning and Rsch. in Edn., 2001, 25th anniversary Genetic Conservation award, Am. Livestock Breeds Conservancy, 2002; grantee, NIH, 1958—68. Fellow: AAAS, Explorers Club; mem.: Am. Soc. Tropical Medicine (emeritus), Va. State Dairy Goat Assn. (founder), Ut Prosim Soc. (Va. Poly. Inst. and State U.), Soc. Exptl. Biology and Medicine (sec. D.C. chpt. 1976, emeritus), Midwestern Conf. Parasitologists (1st sec. 1949, founder), Va. State Dairy Goat Assn. (pres. 1976, founder, Friend of VSDGA award 1999), Am. Livestock Breeds Conservancy (bd. dirs. 1994—97, 25th Anniversary award 2002), Nat. Tunis Sheep Registry (sec. 1991—92, bd. dirs. 1991—93), Jacob Sheep Breeders Assn., Natural Colored Wool Growers Assn. (bd. dirs. 1988—94), Nat. Pygmy Goat Assn. (bd. dirs. 1976—92, pres. 1979, founder), Am. Dairy Goat Assn. (bd. dirs. 1972—87, 1st sec. rsch. found. 1979, founder), Am. Goat Soc. (bd. dirs. 1990—96), Royal Soc. Tropical Medicine (emeritus), Am. Microscopical Soc. (emeritus), Am. Soc. Cell Biology, Am. Soc. Parasitologists, Am. Soc. Zoologists (emeritus), Soc. Invertebrate Zoology (emeritus), Am. Physiol. Soc. (emeritus), Helminthological Soc. (pres. 1958, emeritus), President's Coun., U. Ill., Soft-Coated Wheaten Terrier Club Am., Greater Washington DC Area Soft Coated Wheaten Terrier Club (pres. 1991—92, bd. dirs. 1999—2001, founder), President's Coun., Va. Polytechnic Inst. and State U., U. Ill., Univ. Ill. Found., Sigma Xi (pres. Howard chpt. 1962), Phi Beta Kappa. Achievements include breeding of two rare and endangered breeds of sheep, Jacob and Tunis, early breeder of West African Pygmy Goats and a rare dog, the Soft-coated Wheaten Terrier; founder and first sec. The Rsch. Found. of the Am. Dairy Goat Assn.; founder Midwestern Conf. of Parasitologists; founder four sci. jours. Exptl. Parasitology, Internat. Rev. Tropical Medicine, Virology, and Advances in Vet. Sci. Office Phone: 860-355-1031. Personal E-mail: wheatens@sbcglobal.net, sheepman@frogmoor.org.

LINCK, CHARLES EDWARD, JR., English language educator; b. Lowemont, Kans., June 6, 1923; s. Charles Edward and Grace Elizabeth (Miller) L.; m. Alice Eugenie Meyer (div. Feb. 1964); m. Ernestine Marie Porcher Sewell, Aug. 23, 1970. AB magna cum laude, St. Benedict's Coll., Atchison, Kans., 1951; MS, Kans. State Coll., 1953; PhD in English, U. Kans., 1962. Prof. English East Tex. State U., Commerce, 1958-91, prof. emeritus, 1991—. Owner, pub. Cow Hill Press. Author, editor: Edgar Rye: North Central Texas Cartoonist and Journalist, 1972; co-editor: Bibliography of Evelyn Waugh, 1984; editor, pub. Evelyn Waugh in Letters by Terence Greeniage, 1994; editor, pub. Colleen, The Mountain Maid - A Story of War and Feud in Kentucky, 1994; editor: Bokay of Biscuits, 3 vols., 1997. With USN, 1943-46, PTO. Mem. MLA, Tex. Coll. English Assn. (pres. 1972), Am. Studies Assn., Tex. Folklore Soc. (pres. 1984), Evelyn Waugh Soc. Democrat. Roman Catholic. Avocations: antique printing, Native American Indian arts and crafts, photography. Home: Tex A&M U PO Box 3002 Commerce TX 75429-3002 E-mail: linck@tamu-commerce.edu.

LINCKE, ERIC THEODORE, retired surgeon; b. Rochester, NY, Feb. 26, 1932; s. Eric Theodore Lincke and Helen Crabtree; m. Constance M. Sprague; children: Eric, Yvonne, Keith, Lorelei. BA, U. Rochester, NY, 1954, MD, 1957; BA, No. Mich. U., Marquette, 1998. Diplomate Am. Bd. Gen. and Thoracic Surgery. Staff surgeon Marquette Gen. Hosp., 1964—93; ret., 1993. Lt. comdr. USN, 1962—64. Fellow, Baylor Sch. Medicine, Houston, 1973, Bowman Gray Med. Sch., Winston-Salem, N.C., 1974—75. Fellow: ACS; mem.: Kiwanis. Avocation: clock and watch repair. Home: 410 E Ohio St Marquette MI 49855

LINCOLN, ALEXANDER, III, financial analyst, lawyer, private investor; b. Boston, Dec. 1, 1943; s. Alexander Jr. and Elizabeth (Kitchel) L.; m. Isabel Fawcett Ross, Dec. 27, 1969. BA, Denver U., 1967; JD, Boston U., 1971. Bar: Colo. 1972, U.S. Ct. Appeals (10th cir.) 1972, U.S. Supreme Ct. 1979. Atty. Dist. Ct. Denver, 1973-78, Colo. Ct. Appeals, Denver, 1978-80; mng. ptnr. Alexander Lincoln & Co., Denver, 1980—. Mem. Colo. Bar Assn. (fin. com. 1975-76), Colo. Soc. Mayflower Descendants (life, bd. dirs. 1975—), Order of Founders and Patriots (life). Republican. Avocations: skiing, mountain climbing, horticulture. Home and Office: 121 S Dexter St Denver CO 80246-1052

LINCOLN, ANNA, publishing executive, language educator; b. Warsaw, Dec. 13, 1932; came to U.S., 1948; d. Wigdor Aron and Genia Szpiro; m. Adrian Courtney Lincoln Jr., Sept. 22, 1951; children: Irene Anne, Sally Linda, Allen, Kirk. Student, U. Calif., Berkeley, 1949-50; BA in French and Russian with honors, NYU, 1965; student, Columbia Tchrs. Coll., 1966-67. Tchr. Waldwick (N.J.) H.S., 1966-69; chmn. Tuxedo Park (N.Y.) Red Cross, 1969-71; pres. Red Cross divsn. Vets. Hosp.; pres. China Pictures U.S.A. Inc., Princeton, NJ, 1994—; prof. fgn. rels. Fudan U., Shanghai, 1994—, prof. English and humanitarian studies, 1996—. Adv. bd. guidance dept. Waldwick (N.J.) H.S., 1966-69; hon. bd. dirs. Shanghai Fgn. Lang. Assn., 1994; hon. prof. Fudan U., Shanghai, 1994; leader seminars, China at top univs., 1996—; pub. spkr., human rels., China, 2003—. Author: Escape to China, 1940-48, 1985, Chinese transl., 1985,

The Art of Peace, 1995, Anna Lincoln Views China, 2000; publ.: China Beyond the Year 2000 and the Nature of Love, 1997, Anna Lincoln Views China, 1999; co-dir. (TV docudrama) Escape to China 1941-48, 1998. Hon. U.S. Goodwill amb. for peace and friendship, China, 1984, 85, 86, 88; founder Princeton-Lincoln Found., Inc., 1985—. Named Woman of Yr. Am. Biog. Soc., 1993; recipient Peace Through the Arts prize Assn. Internat. Mujeres en las Artes, Madrid, 1993. Mem. AAUW, Women's Coll. Club (publicity chmn. 1991-96), Lit. Coll. Princeton, Present Day Club. Avocations: reading, swimming, bridge, seminars, ballroom dancing. Home and Office: China Pictures USA Inc 550 Rosedale Rd Princeton NJ 08540-2315

LINCOLN, BLANCHE LAMBERT, senator; b. Helena, Ark., Sept. 30, 1960; m. Stephen R. Lincoln; 2 children. BS in Biology, Randolph-Macon Woman's Coll., 1982. Intern Sotheby's, NYC; sr. assoc. The Pagonis & Donnelly Group, Inc., 1989-91; mem. US Congress from 1st Ark. dist., 1992-96; US Senator from Ark., 1999—. Chair minority outreach team US Senate, mem. com. agr., nutrition, and forestry, com. fin., spl. com. aging. Author (with Catherine Whitney): Nine and Counting: The Women of the Senate, 2000. Bd. dirs. Ark. Delta Coun., U. Ark. Med. Sci. Found.; mem. Lower Miss. Delta Develop. Coun., Am. Red Cross. Named Woman of Yr., Nat. Sportfishing Assn., 1996; named one of Outstanding Young Americans, Jr. C. of C., 1999; recipient Congressional Leadership award, Nat. Telephone Coop. Assn., 2001, Humanitarian of Yr., Ark. Rice Depot, 2002, Humanitarian award, Alzheimer's Assn., 2003, Nat. Energy Leadership award, Nat. Bio-Diesel Bd., 2003, Leg. of Yr. award, Biotechnology Industry Orgn., 2005. Democrat. Episcopalian. Office: US Senate 355 Dirksen Senate Office Bldg Washington DC 20510-0001 also: District Office 912 W Fourth St Little Rock AR 72201 Office Phone: 202-224-4843, 501-375-2993. Office Fax: 202-228-1371, 501-375-7064.*

LINCOLN, EDMOND LYNCH, investment banker; b. Wilmington, Del., Aug. 3, 1949; s. Edmond Earl and Mary Margaret (Lynch) Lincoln; m. Pamela Wick, Sept. 3, 1977; children: Lucy Arms, Emily Lord. BA magna cum laude, Harvard U., 1971, MBA with distinction, 1974. Rare book libr. Henry Francis duPont Winterthur Mus., Del., 1971—72; with Kidder Peabody & Co., Inc., NYC, 1974—94, asst. v.p., 1977—79, v.p., 1979—91, sr. v.p., 1991—94, mgr. govt. agy. fin., 1984—86, transp. group, 1986—94; mng. dir. PaineWebber Inc., NYC, 1994—2000; cons. UBS Warburg LLC, NYC, 2000—03; mng. dir. Hilltower Group, NYC, 2003—05; instr. faculty program NYU, 2004—. Pub. interest dir. Fed. Home Loan Bank of NY, 1987—89. Treas. Fed. Hall Meml. Assocs., 1981—87; mem. vis. com. Harvard Coll. Libr., 1981—86, 1988—94; mem. exec. com. Friends of Harvard U. Track, 1972—, sec., 1976—87; dir. U. Del. Libr. Assocs., 2006—. Recipient Washburn History prize, Harvard U., 1971; fellow, Pierpont Morgan Libr., 1998—2002. Mem.: Investment Assn. NY, Soc. Naval Architects and Marine Engrs. (assoc.), Assn. Internat. de Bibliophilie, Friends of Winterthur (trustee 1976—81, sec. 1978—81, trustee 1987—93, Winterthur Mus. acad. affairs com. 1993—, Cert. Recognition 2004), Wilmington Country Club, India House, Grolier Club (coun. 1982—84, 2001—07, treas. 2002—06), Club of Odd Volumes, Bond Club NY, Harvard Club (NYC), Wilmington Club, Phi Beta Kappa. Republican. Roman Catholic. Home: 161 E 79th St New York NY 10075

LINCOLN, HOWARD, manufacturing company and sports team executive; b. Oakland, Calif., Feb. 14, 1940; m. Grace; c. Brad BA in Polit. Sci., U. Calif., Berkeley, 1962; JD, U. Calif. Sch. Law, 1965. Practiced law, Seattle, 1970—83; legal work Nintendo Am. Inc., 1981—83, sr. v.p., gen. counsel, 1983—94, chmn., 1994—2000, chmn. emeritus, 2000—; chmn., CEO Seattle Mariners, 1999—. Bd. dirs. Nintendo of Am., Nintendo Co. Ltd. of Kyoto, Japan; chmn. Interactive Digital Software Assn. Instrumental in creating Nintendo's charitable contbns. program, including Starlight Found.; major initiator in Club Mario/after-sch. program with Bellevue, Wash. Boys & Girls Club; trustee Seattle Children's Hosp. Found., Western Washington U.; chmn., Washington Roundtable; hi-tech chmn. United Way of King County, Wash., 1999, campaign chair, 2003-2004; bd. dirs. Boalt Hall Alumni Assn., U. Calif., Berkeley, ArtsFund, Bellevue Boys & Girls Club, The Baseball Club of Seattle, LP, Seattle Mariners, Pacific Sci. Ctr., Corp. Coun. for the Arts, chief Seattle coun. Boys Scouts Am., others; supports Mariners Care Found. Naval officer Judge Advocate Gen. Corps USN, 1966—70. Recipient Lifetime Achievement award, Acad. of Interactive Arts & Sci., 2007. Office: c/o Seattle Mariners Safeco Field PO Box 4100 Seattle WA 98104*

LINCOLN, MARGARET, library media specialist; b. NYC, May 22, 1949; d. Irving Herman and Ann Ruth (Silver) Goldin; m. Gary Samuel Lincoln, June 5, 1971; children: Geoffrey, Benjamin, Ruth. AB in French, U. Mich., 1970, AMLS, 1973; Edn. Tech. Specialist, Mich. State U., East Lansing, 1996; PhD in Info. Sci., U. North Tex., Denton, 2006. Libr. media specialist Lakeview HS, Battle Creek, Mich., 1973—. Computer skills, internet rsch. tchr. Battle Creek Area Pub. Schs., 1997—; chair, sec. REMC 12 Media Coun., Marshall, Mich., 1996—. Contbr. articles to profl. jours. Vol. libr. Temple Beth El, Battle Creek, 1984—, Sunday sch. tchr., 1984—. Recipient AASL Sch. Libr. Collaboration award, 2004, Info. Literacy award, Mich. Libr. Assn., 2005; grantee Excellence in Edn., Kellogg Found., 1994, 1999; Am. Memory fellow, Libr. of Congress, 2000, Mandel fellow, US Holocaust Meml. Mus., 2002. Mem.: Phi Beta Kappa, Beta Phi Mu. Home: 13166 11 Mile Rd Ceresco MI 49033-9769 Office: Lakeview HS 15060 S Helmer Rd Battle Creek MI 49015

LINCOLN, STEPHEN, publishing executive; Pub. Nat. Law Jour., NY Law Jour. Office: Nat Law Jour 8th Fl 105 Madison Ave New York NY 10016

LINCOLN, THOMAS L., pathologist, educator; b. Pitts., Jan. 4, 1929; s. John J. and Jean Gregg Lincoln; m. Nancy, Apr. 15, 1956 (dec. Feb. 1971); children: Elizabeth, John; m. Catherine Delaprée, May 30, 1972; 1 child, Iris. BS, Yale U., 1955, MD, 1960. Diplomate Nat. Bd. Med. Examiners, Am. Bd. Anat. Pathology. Intern in pathology Yale U., New Haven, 1960-61, resident, 1961-63; rsch. asst. prof. Inst. for Fluid Dynamics and Applied Math., U. Md., 1963-66; assoc. clin. prof., dept. pathology U. So. Calif. Cancer Ctr., LA, 1975-77, assoc. prof., 1977-87, prof. rsch. pathology, 1987-96; prof. emeritus U. So. Calif.; sr. scientist Sunquest Info. Sys., Tucson, 1995-96, Rand Corp., Santa Monica, Calif., 1967—; prof. Coll. Health and Human Devel. Scis., U. Ill., Chgo., 1997—2000. Vis. prof. dept. clin. epidemiology and social medicine, St. Thomas's Hosp. Med. Sch., London, 1972; cons., rschr. in field. Contbr. articles to profl. jours. Fellow Pathology, Johns Hopkins, 1963—65. Mem. AMA, IEEE, Johns Hopkins Med. Soc., Leukemia Soc. Am. (patient advisor, L.A., 1970-82), Cosmos Club (Washington), Coll. of Am. Pathologists, Am. Informatics Asn., Am. Coll. Med. Informatics, others. Episcopalian. Avocations: history, politics, calendar algorithms, computers, psychology. Home: 802 Franklin St Santa Monica CA 90403-2318 Office: Rand Corp 1776 Main St Santa Monica CA 90401-3297

LIND, ERIC HAWTHORN, sales executive; b. Montgomery, Ala., Aug. 30, 1956; s. Peter Malcom and Georgette (Davis) Lind; m. Deborah Ann Jermstad; 1 child, Rachel. BS, Wash. State U., Pullman, 1978; JD, U.Puget Sound Sch. of Law, Tacoma, Washington, 1981; ThM, Andersonville Bapt.Sem., Carmilla, Ga., 1999. Gen. mgr./recreational vehicle sales Family Fun RV, Fife, Wash., 1994—99; sales Great Am. RV, Fife, Wash., 1999—2002. Bd. dirs. Spafford Children's Ctr., Bellevue, Wash., 1984—2001. Avocations: fly fishing, travel. Office: Great American RV 5800 Pacific Hwy E Tacoma WA 98424 Office Fax: 253-926-3079. Personal E-mail: rvconsultant@integrity.com.

LIND, NIELS CHRISTIAN, civil engineering educator; b. Copenhagen, Mar. 10, 1930; s. Axel Holger and Karen (Larsen) L.; m. Veronica Claire Hummel, Nov. 29, 1957 (div. 1979); children: Julie Wilhelmina, Peter Christian, Adam Conrad; m. Viriginia Patricia Cano Reynoso, Jan. 26, 1985 (div. 1996); 1 child, Andreas. MSc, Tech. U. Denmark, 1953; PhD, U. Ill., 1959. Design engr. Dominia Ltd., Copenhagen, 1953—54; engr. I Bell Telephone Co., Montreal, 1954—55; field engr. Drake-Merritt, Labrador, Nfld., 1955; asst. prof. U. Ill., Urbana, 1959—60; assoc. prof. civil engring. U. Waterloo, Ont., 1960—62, prof., 1962—91, disting. prof. emeritus, 1992, dir. Inst. Risk Research, 1982—88. Adj. prof. U. Victoria, B.C., 1993-95. Recipient Ostenfeld gold medal, 1978; recipient Cancam award Can. Congress Applied Mechanics, 1981, CERRA award Civil Engring. Reliability and Risk Assn., 1999. Fellow Royal Soc. Can., Am. Acad. Mechanics (pres. 1972-73). Office Phone: 250-598-5914. E-mail: nlind@telus.net.

LIND, THOMAS OTTO, barge transportation company executive; b. New Orleans, Apr. 24, 1937; s. Henry Carl Lind and Elinor (Rooney) Messersmith; m. Eugenia Niehaus, June 8, 1963; children: Elinor Ashley, Elizabeth Kelly. BSME, Tulane U., 1959, LLB, 1965. Cert. mech. engr., 1959. Assoc. Jones, Walker, Waechter, Poitevent, Carrere and Denegre, New Orleans, 1965-66; v.p., sec., counsel Ingram Corp., New Orleans, 1966-84; v.p. Gulf Fleet Marine Corp., New Orleans, 1984-85; v.p., regulatory counsel, sec. and asst. treas. New Orleans Pub. Svc., Inc. and La. Power and Light Co., 1985-92; regional counsel for La. Entergy Svcs., Inc., 1993-94; risk mgr. Canal Barge Co., Inc., New Orleans, 1994-97, sec., 1995—, gen. counsel, 1997—. Trustee Metairie Park Country Day Sch., 1991-95; mem. bd. govs. Trinity Sch., New Orleans, 1982-85; vestryman Trinity Ch., New Orleans, 1987-91; active Family of Cmty. and Utility Supporters, New Orleans, 1987-94; bd. dirs. Greater New Orleans (La.) Coun. Navy League U.S., 2004—. Lt. (j.g.) USN, 1959-62; comdr. USNR, 1962-79. Mem. ABA (ho. of dels. 1996-97), Fed. Energy Bar Assn. (bd. dirs. New Orleans chpt. 1988-92, pres. 1992), La. Bar Assn. (bd. dirs. corp. law sect. 1973-75), La. Assn. Waterways Operators and Shipyards (bd. dirs. 1999—), New Orleans Bar Assn. (bd. dir. 1989-97, 2d v.p. 1989-90, sec. 1992-93, 1st v.p. 1993-94, pres.-elect 1994-95, pres. 1995-96, bd. dirs. New Orleans Pro Bono project 1994-96), Assn. Corp. Counsel (bd. dirs. La. chpt. 2006—), La. Orgn. for Jud. Excellence (bd. dirs., sec. 1998-2000, v.p. 2000—), New Orleans Lawn Tennis Club (pres. 1986-88). Republican. Episcopalian. Avocation: tennis. Home: 5423 Perrier New Orleans LA 70115-3130 Office: Canal Barge Co Inc 835 Union St Ste 300 New Orleans LA 70112-1469 Home Phone: 504-895-3893; Office Phone: 504-584-1531. Business E-Mail: tlind@canalbarge.com.

LINDA, GERALD, advertising and marketing executive; b. Boston, Nov. 25, 1946; s. Edward Linda and Anne Beatrice (Lipofsky) Coburn; m. Claudia Wollack, Sept. 24, 1978; children— Jonathan Daniel Rezny, Jessica Simone. BS in Bus. Adminstrn., Northeastern U., 1969, MBA, 1971; postgrad., U. Mich., 1971-75. Faculty U. Ky., Lexington, 1975-77; ptnr. Tatham-Laird & Kudner, Chgo., 1977-80; v.p. Marsteller, Chgo., 1980-84; sr. v.p. HCM, Chgo., 1984-86; pres. Gerald Linda & Assocs., Chgo., 1986-89; prin. Kurtzman/Slavin/Linda, Inc., Chgo., 1990-93, Kapuler Mkgt. Rsch., Chgo., 1993-94; pres. Gerald Linda & Assocs., Glenview, Ill., 1994—. Mem. editorial review bd. Jour. Current Issues and Rsch. in Advt., 1984—. Named scientific lectr., Inst. Food Technologists. Mem.: Am. Mgmt. Assn. (mktg. faculty mem.). Office Phone: 847-729-3403. Personal E-mail: glinda@gla-mktg.com.

LINDAHL, SHEENA, entrepreneur; b. 1982; m. Michael Simmons. Grad. in Communication Studies, NYU Steinhardt Sch. Edn., 2005. Pres., co-founder Extreme Entrepreneurship Edn. Corp., NYC, 2003—. Mgr. due diligence process GreenHills Ventures, NYC. Co-author: The Student Success Manifesto, 2003, All or Nothing, Now or Never. Lead tchr. Project R.E.A.D. Named one of Best Entrepreneurs Under 25, BusinessWeek, 2006. Achievements include launching a nationwide speaking tour called the Extreme Entrepreneur Tour in 2005. Office: Extreme Entrepreneurship Edn Corp 120 Wall St 29th Fl New York NY 10005 Office Phone: 800-930-8021. E-mail: sheena@extremee.org.

LINDALL, TERRANCE, artist; b. Mpls., Oct. 13, 1944; s. Arnold Walfred and Jessie May Lindall. BA, Hunter Coll., NYC, 1970. Mag. cover illustrator Warren Mag, NYC, 1978—81; story illustrator Marvel's Epic Mag., NYC, 1981. Twilght zone mag. TZ Publ., NYC, 1980; story illustrator Heavy Metal Mag., NYC, 1979—80; pres. Williamsburg Art & Hist. Ctr., Bklyn., 1996—; founder Greenwood Mus., Smyrna, NY, 1986—96; writer 11211 Mag., Bklyn., 2003—, Art and Antiques Mag., 2006. Illus. book, Paradise Lost Illustrated (Soc. of Illustrators Award of Merit, 1981); contbr. articles pub. to profl. jour.; creator (TV series) Brave Destiny. Home: 385 Clinton Ave #2-S Brooklyn NY 11238 Office: Williamsburg Art & Historical Center 135 Broadway Brooklyn NY 11211 Home Phone: 718-789-6008; Office Phone: 719-486-7372. Personal E-mail: wahcenter@earthlink.net.

LINDARS, LAURENCE EDWARD, retired health care products executive; b. NYC, Oct. 14, 1922; s. Arthur John and Florence Vera (Cunard) L.; m. Mary Gibson Grandy, Jan. 22, 1972; children— John L., William A., Nancy E. Student, Dartmouth Coll., 1943-44; BS, Columbia U., 1947. Sr. auditor Arthur Young & Co., NYC, 1947-51; chief acct. Deering, Milliken & Co., 1951-53; treas., dir. Poloron Products, Inc., New Rochelle, NY, 1953-58; controller Atlas Gen., Inc., NYC, 1958-59; controller, treas., dir. fin. planning Pepperidge Farm, Inc., Norwalk, Conn., 1959-67; with C.R. Bard, Inc., Murray Hill, NJ, 1967-88, dir., 1972-92, vice chmn., 1983-88. Mem. adv. bd. of Summit Trust Co., 1970-84 Trustee Overlook Hosp., 1973-79, Found., 1988-91, treas., 1989-90; trustee Epilepsy Found. N.J., 1985-90, pres., 1986-87, chmn., 1988-90. Lt. (j.g.) USNR, 1943-46. Mem. Fin. Execs. Inst., Canoe Brook Country Club, Delta Upsilon. Presbyterian. Home: 199 Woodland Ave Summit NJ 07901

LINDAUER, ERIK D., lawyer; b. Bklyn., Oct. 1, 1956; s. Albert and Dinah (Epner) L.; m. Lisa Diamond, Aug. 16, 1981; children: Jacob, Samuel. BA, SUNY, Albany, 1978; JD, SUNY, Buffalo, 1981. Bar: NY 1982, US Dist. Ct. (ea. dist.) NY 1982, US Dist. Ct. (so. dist.) NY 1982. Assoc. Sullivan & Cromwell, NYC, 1981-89, ptnr. project fin., 1989—, and coord. corp. reorganization/bankruptcy practice area. Mem.: ABA. Office: Sullivan & Cromwell 125 Broad St New York NY 10004-2489 Office Phone: 212-558-3548. Business E-Mail: lindauere@sullcrom.com.

LINDBERG, CHARLES DAVID, lawyer; b. Moline, Ill., Sept. 11, 1928; s. Victor Samuel and Alice Christine (Johnson) L.; m. Marian J. Wagner, June 14, 1953; children: Christine, Breta (dec.), John, Eric. AB, Augustana Coll., Rock Island, Ill., 1950, DHL, 2000; JD, Yale U., New Haven, Conn., 1953. Bar: Ohio 1954. Assoc. Taft, Stettinius & Hollister, Cin., 1953-61, ptnr., 1961-85, mng. ptnr., 1985-98, of counsel, 1999—. Bd. dirs. Cin. Bengals Profl. Football Team, 1982—2003; chmn. bd. dirs. Schonstedt Instrument Co., 1994—97. Editor: Nat. Law Jour., 1979—90. Bd. dirs. Taft Broadcasting Co., Cin., 1973-87, Dayton Walther Corp., 1986-87, Gibson Greeting, Inc., 1991-2000; bd. dirs. Augustana Coll., 1978-87, 91-99, 2000—, sec., 1981-82, vice-chmn., 1982-83, chmn., 1983-86; pres. Cin. Bd. Edn., 1971, 74, Zion Luth. Ch., Cin., 1966-69; chmn. policy com. Hamilton County Rep. Com., 1981-90; mem. exec. com. Ohio Rep. Fin. Com., 1989-90; chmn. Tyler Davidson Com., 1999-2000; trustee Greater Cin. Ctr. Econ. Edn., 1976-91, pres., 1987-89, chmn., 1989-91; chmn. law firm divsn. Fine Arts Fund, 1985; trustee Pub. Libr. Cin. and Hamilton County, 1982—, pres., 1989, 96, 2001, 07. Mem. Cin. Bar Assn., Greater Cin. C. of C. (trustee 1985, exec. com., vice chmn. govt. and cmty. affairs com. 1989-91), Ohio Libr. Trustees Assn. (bd. dirs. 1986-87), Ohio C. of C. (bd. dirs. 1988-89), Queen City Club (sec. 1989-91), Commonwealth Club, Comml. Club (sec. 1994-96), Optimists. Office: 1800 US Bank Tower 425 Walnut St Cincinnati OH 45202-3923 Office Phone: 513-357-9300. Business E-Mail: lindberg@taftlaw.com.

LINDBERG, DONALD ALLAN BROR, library director, pathologist, educator; b. NYC, Sept. 21, 1933; s. Harry B. and Frances Seeley (Little) L.; m. Mary Musick, June 8, 1957; children: Donald Allan Bror, Christopher Charles Seeley, Jonathan Edward Moyer. AB, Amherst Coll., 1954, ScD (hon.), 1979; MD, Coll. Physicians and Surgeons, Columbia U., 1958; ScD (hon.), SUNY, 1987, U. Health Sci. Med. Informatics and Tech., Austria, 2004; LLD (hon.), U. Mo., Columbia, 1990. Diplomate Am. Bd. Pathology, Am. Bd. Med. Examiners (exec. bd. 1987-91). Rsch. asst. Amherst Coll., 1954-55; intern in pathology Columbia-Presbyn. Med. Ctr., 1958-59, asst. resident in pathology, 1959-60; asst. in pathology Coll. Physician and Surgeons Columbia U., NYC, 1958-60; instr. pathology Sch. of Medicine U. Mo., 1962-63, asst. prof. Sch. of Medicine, 1963-66, assoc. prof. Sch. of Medicine, 1966-69, prof. Sch. of Medicine, 1969-84, dir. Diagnostic Microbiology Lab. Sch. of Medicine, 1960-63, dir. Med. Ctr. Computer Program Sch. of Medicine, 1962-70, staff, exec. dir. for health affairs Sch. of Medicine, 1968-70, prof., chmn. dept. info. sci. Sch. of Medicine, 1969-71; dir. Nat. Libr. of Medicine, Bethesda, Md., 1984—. Adj. prof. pathology U. Md. Sch. Medicine, 1988—, clin. prof. pathology U. Va., 1992—; dir. Nat. Coord. Office for High Performance Computing and Comms., exec. office of Pres., Office Sci. & Tech. Policy, 1992-95; mem. computer sci./engring. bd. Nat. Acad. Sci., 1971-74, chmn. Nat. Adv. Com. Artificial Intelligence in Medicine, Stanford U., 1975-84; U.S. rep. to Internat. Med. Info. Assn./Internat. Fedn. Info. Processing, 1975-84; bd. dirs. Am. Med. Info. Assn., 1992—, Health on the Net Found.; adv. coun. Inst. Medicine, 1992—. Author: The Computer and Medical Care, 1968; The Growth of Medical Information Systems in the United States, 1979; editor: (with W. Siler) Computers in Life Science Research, 1975; (with others) Computer Applications in Medical Care, 1982; editor Methods of Info. in Medicine, 1970-83, assoc. editor, 1983—; editor Jour. Med. Systems, 1976—, Med. Informatics Jour., 1976—; chief editor procs. 3d World Conf. on Med. Informatics, 1980; editorial bd. Jour. of AMA, 1991—; contbr. articles to jours. Simpson fellow Amherst Coll., 1954-55, Markle scholar in acad. medicine, 1964-69; recipient Silver Cord award Internat. Fedn. for Info. Processing, 1980, Walter C. Alvarez award Am. Med. Writers Assn. 1989, PHS Surgeon Gen.'s medallion, 1989, Nathan Davis award AMA, 1989, Presdl. Disting. Exec. Rank award, Sr. Exec. Svc., Outstanding Svc. medal Uniformed Svcs. U. Health Scis., 1992, Computers in Healthcare Pioneer award, 1993, recognition award High Performance Computing Industry, 1995, silver award U.S. Nat. Commn. on Librs. and Info. Scis., 1996, meritorious award Coun. Biol. Editors, 1996, pres.'s award Med. Libr. Assn., 1997, Morris F. Collen, M.D. award of excellence Am. Coll. Med. Informatics, 1997, Info. Frontier award N.Y. Acad. Medicine, 1999, Ranice W. Crosby Disting. Achievement award Johns Hopkins U. Sch. Medicine, 1998, Spl. Recognition award Coll. P&S Columbia U. Alumni, 2001, Lila A. Wallis Women's Health award, Am. Med. Women's Assn., 2005, U.S. Medicine Frank Brown Berry award, 2005. Fellow: AAAS, Am. Acad. Arts & Sciences; mem.: Am. Med. Informatics Assn. (pres. 1988—91), Gorgas Meml. Inst. Tropical and Preventive Medicine (bd. dirs. 1987—), Am. Assn. Med. Systems and Informatics (internat. com. 1982—89, bd. dirs. 1982, editor conf. procs. 1983, 1984), Salutis Initas (Am. v.p. 1981—91), Assn. for Computing Machines, Mo. Med. Assn., Coll. Am. Pathologists (commn. on computer policy and coordination 1981—84), Inst. Medicine of NAS, Cosmos Club (38th Cosmos Club award 2001), Sigma Xi. Democrat. Avocations: photography, riding. Home: 13601 Esworthy Rd Germantown MD 20874-3319 Office: Nat Libr Medicine Bldg 38 Rm 2E-17B 8600 Rockville Pike Bethesda MD 20894-0002 Office Phone: 301-496-6308, 301-496-6221. Business E-Mail: mehnert@nim.nih.gov, lindberg@nlm.nih.gov.*

LINDBERG, DUANE R., bishop, historian; b. Thief River Falls, Minn., Apr. 16, 1933; s. Edgar and Alice (Amundson) L.; m. E. Mardell Kvitne, June 6, 1954; children: Erik Duane, Karen Kristin Kelle, Karl Stephen, Martha Alice Stone, Kristian John. BS in Chemistry, U. N.D., 1954; MDiv in Theology, Luther Sem., St. Paul, 1961; MA in Am. Studies, U. Minn., 1969, PhD in Am. Studies, 1975. Rsch. chemist DuPont Co., 1954; asst. ops. and tng. office Army Chem. Corps Sch., Ft. McClelland, Ala., 1955—56; tchg. asst. chemistry dept. U. Wis., Madison, 1956-57; chemist Minn. Farm Bur. Lab., St. Paul, 1957-59; pastor Epping and Wheelock (N.D.) Luth. Chs., 1961-68; rsch. historian Minn. State Hist. Soc., St. Paul, 1969-71; pastor Zion Luth. Ch., West Union, Iowa, 1971-78; sr. pastor Trinity Luth. Ch., Waterloo, Iowa, 1978-87, Acension Luth. Ch., Waterloo, 1987—98, sr. pastor emeritus, 1998—; nat. ch. body founder, presiding pastor Am. Assn. Luth. Chs., Mpls., 1987-99, presiding pastor emeritus, 1999—; interim pastor St. Luke Luth. Ch., Traer, Iowa, 2003—05. Vis. prof. Upper Iowa U., Fayette, 1976-77; adj. prof. Am. Luth. Theol. Sem., St. Paul, 1996—; chemistry instr. Valley Luth. HS, Cedar Falls, Iowa, 2005—. Author: Uniting Word, 1969, Men of the Cloth, 1980; contbr. articles to profl. jours. Bd. dirs. Palmer Meml. Hosp., West Union, Iowa, 1972-78, Allen Meml. Hosp., Waterloo, 1979-05, Northeast Iowa Med. Edn. Found., Waterloo, 1983-02; founder, bd. mem. Buffalo Trails Mus., Epping, N.D., 1964-68; founder, bd. mem. Fayette County Hist. Soc., West Union, 1975-78; dean Decorah Conf. Am. Luth. Ch., 1976-78, exec. com. Iowa Dist., 1976-78; bd. dirs. Great Plains Inst. Theology, 1965-68; pres. Eastern Iowa Luth. H.S. Assn., 1997-04, major gifts dir., 2006—. 1st lt. U.S. Army, 1954-56. Recipient award of commendation Concordia Hist. Inst., St. Louis, 1980, Nehemiah award Abiding Word Ministries, Mpls., 1990, award of excellence Allen Meml. Hosp., Waterloo, 1995. Mem. numerous profl. ministerial groups and ch. bds., Rotary, Sons of Norway. Lutheran. Office: Valley Luth HS 4520 Rownd St Cedar Falls IA 50613

LINDBERG, FRANCIS LAURENCE, JR., management consultant; b. Jacksonville, Fla., Mar. 13, 1948; s. Francis Laurence and Mildred Hortense (Parrish) L.; m. Anne Louise Stearns, Dec. 29, 1972 (div.); 1 child: Kristen Anne; m. Alexis Jean Parker, Nov. 12, 1983 (dec. May 1996); m. Carol Annette Freeman, Jan. 6, 2001; 1 child, Robert Laurence. Student, Eckerd Coll., 1965-66; BA, Jacksonville U., 1969; MBA, U. North Fla., 1976. CPA, Ga. Actuarial asst. Gulf Life Ins. Co., Jacksonville, 1967-73; asst. actuary Am. Heritage Life, Jacksonville, 1973-77; asst. sec.-treas., prin. acctg. officer Atlantic Am. Corp., Atlanta, 1977-84; assoc. v.p. fin. Security Benefit Group, Topeka, 1985-86; exec. v.p., chief fin. officer Am. Way Group of Cos., Southfield, Mich., 1986-87; prin. Lindberg Consulting Group, Inc. (formerly Lindberg Group), Atlanta, 1987-98, pres., 1998—. V.p. fin Carson-Brooks, Inc., Atlanta, 1991-93; treas., bd. adv. Good News Comm., Inc., 1986-94; dep. receiver USEC Ga., Atlanta, 1995—; asst. dep. receiver Star Group Assurance, Atlanta, 1998-2005, Renaissance Mutual Captive Ins. Co., Atlanta, 2005—, Dalton Fl. Coverings Mkt. Workers Comp. Fund, Ga., 2005—, AACA Workers Compensation Fund, Atlanta, 2005—. Recipient Membership Achievement award, Inst. Mgmt. Accts., 1983, George E. Wilson award Inst. Mgmt. Accts., 1991. Mem. AICPA, Soc. Fin. Examiners, Ga. Soc. CPAs. Republican. Methodist. Business E-Mail: lindberg_group@bellsouth.net.

LINDBERGH, REEVE, writer, poet; d. Charles A. Lindbergh and Anne Morrow L.; m. Nathaniel Tripp. Graduate, Radcliffe Coll., 1968. Bd. dir. Charles A. and Anne Morrow Lindbergh Found., 1977—, v.p., 1986—95, pres, 1995—2004, hon. chairwoman, 2004—. Author: (memoirs) Under a Wing, 1998, No More Words: A Journal of My Mother, Anne Morrow Lindbergh, 2001, (novels) Moving to the Country, 1983, The Names of the Mountains, 1992, (book of essays) View from the Kingdom, 1987, (children's books) The Midnight Farm, 1987, Benjamin's Barn, 1990, There's a COW in the Road, 1993, What Is The Sun?, 1994, Grandfather's

Lovesong, 1995, The Day the Goose Got Loose, 1995, If I'd Known Then What I Know Now, 1996, Awful Aardvarks Shop for School, 2000, The Circle of Days, 2002, On Morning Wings, 2002, My Hippie Grandmother, 2003, Our Nest, 2004, The Visit, 2005. Office: Charles A and Ann Morrow Lindbergh Foundation Ste 310 2150 Third Ave N Anoka MN 55303-2200

LINDBLOM, MARJORIE PRESS, lawyer; b. Chgo., Mar. 17, 1950; d. John E. and Betty (Grace) P.; m. Lance E. Lindblom, June 13, 1971; children: Derek, Ian. AB cum laude, Radcliffe Coll., 1971; JD with honors, U. Chgo., 1978. Bar: Ill. 1978, U.S. Dist. Ct. (no. dist.) Ill. 1978, U.S. Ct. Appeals (7th cir.) 1978, U.S. Ct. Appeals (10th cir.) 1983, U.S. Supreme Ct. 1983, U.S. Ct. Appeals (5th cir.) 1984, N.Y. 1995, U.S. Dist. Ct. (so. and ea. dist.) N.Y. 1995, U.S. Ct. Appeals (2d cir.) 1995. Assoc. Kirkland & Ellis, Chgo., 1978-84, ptnr., 1984-94; NYC, 1994—. Asst. dir. fiscal affairs Ill. Bd. Higher Edn., 1973-75; budget analyst Ill. Bur. Budget, Office of Gov., 1972-73; admissions officer Princeton U., 1971-72; adj. prof. Northwestern U., Evanston, Ill., 1994. Comment editor U. Chgo. Law Rev., 1977-78. Bd. dirs. Chgo. Lawyers Com. for Civil Rights Under Law, 1989-94, Pub. Interest Law Initiative, 1989-94. Mem. ABA, Chgo. Coun. Lawyers (bd. govs. 1987-91, legal counsel 1986-87), 7th Cir. Bar Assn., Women's Bar Assn. of Ill., Lawyers Com. for Civil Rights Under Law (co-chair, 2004-2005). Office: Kirkland & Ellis Citicorp Ctr 153 E 53rd St New York NY 10022-4611 Office Phone: 212-446-4868. Office Fax: 212-446-4900. Business E-Mail: mlindblom@kirkland.com.

LINDBLOOM, CHAD M., transportation executive; BS, MBA, Univ. Minn. Staff acct. CH Robinson Worldwide Inc., Eden Prairie, Minn., 1990—98, corp. contr., 1998—99, v.p., CFO, 1999—. Office: CH Robinson Worldwide 8100 Mitchell Rd Eden Prairie MN 55344-2248*

LINDE, ARMANDO STEVEN, economist; arrived in US, 1960; children: Steven Felipe, Nikki Rene. BS, U. Md., College Park, 1970, M, 1974. Dep. sec. IMF, Washington, 1976—. Mem.: Assn. Study Cuban Economy (pres. 2006—), Rose Bank Rd. Citizens Assn. (vice-president 1996—2000), Omicron Delta Epsilon. Home Phone: 301-365-0322.

LINDE, DAVID, film company executive; b. 1960; Grad., Swarthmore Coll. With Paramount Pictures Corp., 1985—88; v.p. Fox/Lorber Associates, 1990—91; v.p. acquisitions Miramax Films, 1991—92, sr. v.p., 1992—97; exec. v.p., head of sales Miramax Internat., 1992—97; ptnr. GOOD Machine (bought by Universal Pictures and merged into new studio, Focus), NYC, 1997—2006; co-pres. Focus Features, NYC, 2002—06; pres. Rogue Pictures, 2002—06; co-chmn. Universal Pictures, Universal City, Calif., 2006—. Bd. dirs. Am. Film Mktg. Assn. Exec. prodr.: (films) The Who's Tommy, the Amazing Journey, 1993, Wonderland, 1997, Happiness, 1998, Ride with the Devil, 1999, The King is Alive, 2000, Crouching Tiger, Hidden Dragon, 2000, Storytelling, 2001, And Your Mother Too, 2001, They, 2002, How to Deal, 2003; prodr.: The Hitcher, 2007. Bd. dirs. Bklyn. Woods. Named one of 50 Most Powerful People in Hollywood, Premiere mag., 2006. Office: Universal Pictures 100 Universal City Plz Universal City CA 91608*

LINDE, EDWARD H., real estate manager; BS in Civil Engring., MIT, 1962; MBA, Harvard Bus. Sch. V.p., sr. project mgr. Cabot, Cabot & Forbes; co-founder Boston Properties, 1970, pres., CEO, 1997—. Dir. Jobs State Mass.; exec. com. Nat. Assn. Real Estate Investment Trusts. Vice-chmn., chmn. elect Boston Symphony Orchestra; former chmn. Board Beth-Israel Hospital. Mem.: Real Estate Round Table (mem. bd. dir.). Office: Boston Properties 111 Huntington Ave Boston MA 02199-7610 Office Phone: 617-236-3300. Office Fax: 617-536-5087.

LINDE, HANS ARTHUR, state supreme court justice; b. Berlin, Apr. 15, 1924; came to US, 1939, naturalized, 1943; s. Bruno C. and Luise (Rosenhain) L.; m. Helen Tucker, Aug. 13, 1945; children: Lisa, David Tucker. BA, Reed Coll., 1947; JD, U. Calif., Berkeley, 1950. Bar: Oreg. 1951. Law clk. U.S. Supreme Ct. Justice William O. Douglas, 1950-51; atty. Office of Legal Adviser, Dept. State, 1951-53; pvt. practice Portland, Oreg., 1953-54; legis. asst. U.S. Sen. Richard L. Neuberger, 1955-58; from assoc. prof. to prof. U. Oreg. Law Sch., 1959-76; justice Oreg. Supreme Ct., Salem, 1977-90, sr. judge, 1990—. Fulbright lectr. Freiburg U., 1967-68, Hamburg U., 1975-76; cons. U.S. ACDA, Dept. Def., 1962-76; mem. Adminstrv. Conf. U.S., 1978-82, Oreg. Law Commn., 1997—; pub. commr. Oreg. Legislature, 2005-06; disting. scholar in residence Willamette U. Coll. Law, Salem, Oreg., 1994—. Author: (with George Bunn) Legislative and Administrative Processes, 1976. Mem. Oreg. Constl. Revision Commn., 1961-62, Oreg. Law Commn., 1997—, Oreg. Commn. on Pub. Broadcasting, 1990-93, Pub. Commn. Oreg. Legislative, 2005-06; bd. dirs. Oreg. Pub. Broadcasting, 1993-99. With U.S. Army, 1943-46. Fellow Am. Acad. Arts and Scis.; mem. Am. Law Inst. (council), Order of Coif, Phi Beta Kappa. Office: Willamette U Coll Law Salem OR 97301 Business E-Mail: hlinde@willamette.edu.

LINDE, LUCILLE MAE (LUCILLE JACOBSON), motor-perceptual specialist; b. Greeley, Colo., May 5, 1919; d. John Alfred and Anna Julia (Anderson) Jacobson; m. Ernest Emil Linde, July 5, 1946 (dec. Jan. 27, 1959). BA, Colo. State Coll. of Edn., 1941, MA, 1947; EdD, U. No. Colo., 1974. Cert. tchr. Calif., Colo., Iowa, N.Y.; cert. ednl. psychologist; guidance counselor. Dean of women, dir. residence C.W. Post Coll. of L.I. Univ., 1965-66; asst. dean of students SUNY, Farmingdale, 1966-67; counselor, tchr. West High Sch., Davenport, Iowa, 1967-68; instr. grad. tchrs. and counselors, univ. counselor, researcher No. Ariz. U., Flagstaff, 1968-69; vocat. edn. and counseling coord. Fed. Exemplary Project, Council Bluffs, Iowa, 1970-71; sch. psychologist, counselor Oakdale Sch. Dist., Calif., 1971-73; sch. psychologist, intern Learning and Counseling Ctr., Stockton, Calif., 1972-74; pvt. practice rsch. in motor-perceptual tng. Greeley, 1975—. Rschr. ocumeter survey Lincoln Unified Sch. Dist., Stockton, 1980, 81, 82, Manteca (Calif.) H.S., 1981; spkr. Social Sci. Edn. Consortium, U. Colo., Boulder, 1993; mem. Monday Morning steering com. House Spkr. Newt Gingrich, 1997-98; mem. Attention Disorder Advocacy Group, 1997-2001; instr. seminars for ADD and ADHD, alleviating lag/dysfunction in neural system noted, 1997-98, 1998-99, presenter seminars in field. Author: Psychological Services and Motor Perceptual Training, 1974, Guidebook for Psychological Services and Motor Perceptual Training (How One May Improve in Ten Easy Lessons!), 1992, Manual for the Lucille Linde Ocumeter: Ocular Pursuit Measuring Instrument, 1992, Motor-Perceptual Training and Visual Perceptual Research (How Students Improved in Seven Lessons!), 1992, Effects of Motor Perceptual Training on Academic Achievement and Ocular Pursuit Ability, 1992, Teaching University of Northern Colorado Laboratory Students and Greeley District 6 Students Motor-Perceptual Training Seminar, 2001; inventor ocumeter, instrument for measuring ocular tracking ability, 1989, ocutarget for use, 1991, cure for oculomotor dysfunction noted; patentee in field. Mem. Rep. Presdl. Task Force, 1989-96, trustee, 1991-92, charter mem., 1994—, life mem., 1994-95; mem. Rep. Nat. Com., 1990, 93-2007, Rep. Nat. Com. on Am. Agenda, 1993, Nat. Rep. Congl. Com., 1990, 92, 93, 95-2007, Nat. Fedn. Rep. Women, Greeley Rep. Women, 1996-2007; advisor Senator Bob Dole for Pres.; charter mem. Rep. Newt Gingrich's Speaker's Task Force, Senator Phil Gramm's Presdl. Steering Com.; at-large del. Rep. Platform Planning Com.; team leader Nat. Rep. Rapid Response Network, Campaign America, 1996; active Heritage Found. (certificate as honored mem. leadership adv. bd., 1998-2000), Christian Bus. Men's Assn., Friends U. N.C. Librs., Citizens Against Govt. Waste, 1996-2007, Concerns of Police Survivors, 1996-98, Nat. Assn. of Police Orgn., elected to Libr. of Congress Nat. membership, 1997-2001; mem. WW II Vets. Com., 2000-03, Rep. Gov.'s Assn., 2001; mem. Rep. Gov.'s Policy Commn. Recipient Presdl. medal of merit and lapel insignia, 1990, Nat. Rep. Senatorial Com., 1991-2007, cert. of appreciation Nat. Rep. Congl. Com., 1992, 95, lapel pin Rep. Senatorial Inner Circle, 1990-96, Rep. Presdl. commemorative honor roll, 1993, Rep. Senatorial Freedom medal, 1994, Rep. Legion of Merit award, 1994, 96, Rep. Congl. Order of Freedom award, 1995, Senatorial Inner Cir. Lapel Pin, 1998, Lapel Pin award RNC, 1996, Leadership citation Rep. Senatorial Inner Cir./ Rep. Nat. Conv., 1996, Legion of Merit Rep. Presdl. exec. com., 1996, Honor cert. House Spkr. Newt Gingrich, 1996, Rep. Presdl. Legion of Merit medallion and matching lapel pin, 1994, Order of Merit, 1996, Conservative Leadership award Young Am.'s Found., 1999, Nat. Rep. Congl. Com. Rep. of the Yr. from Colo. award, 2000, Majority Leader's Commn. Cert., 2001, 2001 Conservative Patriot award The Pres., Ron Robinson and Bd. of Dirs. of The Young America's Found., Congl. Order Merit, Nat. Rep. Congressman Senancintheny, 2006; named to Rep. Nat. Hall of Honor, 1992. Mem. AAUP, NAFE, Nat. Assn. Sch. Psychologists and Psychometrists (spkr. conf. 1976), Rep. Senatorial Inner Cir. (name engraved on Ronald Wilson Reagan Eternal Flame of Freedom, 1995, on the Nat. Rep. Victory Monument, Washington, 1996, Rep. Sen. Inner Cir. (Conv. Medallion 1996, RNC Mems. Only pin 1996), 20th Century Rep. Leader, Rep. Sen. Inner Cir., 1998, The Smithsonian Assocs., Ronald Reagan Presdl. Libr. and Mus., Bush Presdl. Libr. and Mus., Nat. Trust for Hist. Preservation, Physicians Adv. Bd. to Pres. Bush (Pioneer Healthcare award, 2004), Internat. Platform Assn., Friends of Newt Gingrich, 1998-99, Independence Inst., Assn. Children Learning Disabilities (spkr. internat. conv. 1976), Libr. of Congress Assn., 1999, Children and Adults with Attention Deficit Disorder, Learning Disabilities Assn. Colo., Nat. Fragile X Found., Fraxa Rsch. Found., Pi Omega Pi, Pi Lambda Theta. Avocations: music, architecture. Home: 1954 18th Ave Greeley CO 80631-5208 Office Phone: 970-353-0592. Personal E-mail: dlcinclimlinde@cs.com.

LINDE, MAXINE HELEN, lawyer, corporate financial executive, investor; b. Chgo., Sept. 2, 1939; d. Jack and Lottie (Kroll) Stern; m. Ronald K. Linde, June 12, 1960. BA summa cum laude, UCLA, 1961; JD, Stanford U., 1967. Bar: Calif. 1968. Applied mathematician, rsch. engr Jet Propulsion Lab., Pasadena, Calif., 1961—64; law clk. U.S. Dist. Ct. No. Calif., 1967—68; mem. firm Long & Levit, San Francisco, 1968—69, Swerdlow, Glikbarg & Shimer, Beverly Hills, Calif., 1969—72; sec., gen. counsel Envirodyne Industries, Inc., Chgo., 1972—89; pres. The Ronald and Maxine Linde Found., 1989—; vice chmn. bd., gen. counsel Titan Fin. Group, LLC, Chgo., 1994—98. Mem. bd. visitors Stanford Law Sch., 1989—92, law and bus. adv. coun., 1991—94, dean's adv. coun., 1992—94. Mem.: Alpha Lambda Delta, Pi Mu Epsilon, Phi Beta Kappa, Order of Coif.

LINDE, RONALD KEITH, investor; b. LA, Jan. 31, 1940; s. Morris and Sonia Doreen (Hayman) L.; m. Maxine Helen Stern, June 12, 1960. BS with honors, UCLA, 1961; MS (Inst. scholar), Calif. Inst. Tech., 1962, PhD (ARCS scholar, Rutherford scholar), 1964. Cons. Litton Industries, LA, 1961-63, engr., 1961; materials scientist Poulter Labs., Stanford Rsch. Inst., Menlo Park, Calif., 1964; head solid state rsch. Stanford Rsch. Inst., Menlo Park, Calif., 1965-67; chmn. shock wave physics dept., mgr. tech. svcs. Poulter Labs., 1967, dir. shock and high pressure physics div., 1967-68, chief exec. labs., 1968-69; dir. phys. scis. Stanford Rsch. Inst., 1968-69; chmn. bd., CEO Envirodyne Industries, Inc., Chgo., 1969-89; chmn. bd. The Ronald and Maxine Linde Found., Phoenix, 1989—. Co-chmn. bd. Titan Fin. Group, LLC, Chgo., 1994-98; law and bus. adv. coun. Stanford Law Sch., 1991-94, dean's adv. coun. 1992-94. Contbr. articles to various publs.; patentee in field. Mem. adv. bd. ARCS Found., Chgo., 1993-98; mem. Northwestern U. Assocs., 1978-2005; trustee Calif. Inst. Tech., 1989—, chmn. alumni rels. com., 1997-2002, chmn. audit and compliance com., 2002—, Harvey Mudd Coll., 1989-98, vice chmn., bd. trustees, 1993-98, vice chmn. emeritus, 1998—. Mem. Sigma Xi, Tau Beta Pi, Phi Eta Sigma.

LINDEGREN, CECILE KEYSER, music educator; b. DeFuniak Springs, Fla., July 1, 1946; d. Charles Renshaw and Ouida (Higdon) Keyser; m. John Emory Lindegren, Feb. 14, 1981; children: Erica Kristen. AA, Pensacola Jr. Coll., Fla.; B in Mus. Edn., Fla. State U.; M in Mus. Edn., U. South Miss. Cert. elem. and secondary music tchr., Fla. Choral dir. Pryor Jr. High Sch. (now Pryor Mid. Sch.), Ft. Walton Beach, Fla.; adult choir dir. Hurlburt Field AFB Chapel, 1982—84; choral dir. Pryor Jr. High Sch. (now Pryor Mid. Sch.), Ft. Walton Beach, Fla., Walton Mid. Sch., 1996—; dir. music and youth Mary Esther (Fla.) United Meth. Ch.; owner, instr. Lindegren Music Studio, Ft. Walton Beach; chorus and band dir. Walton Mid. Sch., 2001—. Children's choir dir. Trinity United Meth. Ch. Dir. Ft. Walton Beach Cmty. Chorus; bd. dirs. Mattie Kelly Fine Arts Ctr. Coun. Mem. Okaloosa County Music Tchrs. Assn (pres. 1981-83), Fla. Vocal Assn. (chmn. local dist. 2 terms, music performance assessment adjudicator 1976—), Fla. State Music Tchrs. Assn., Emerald Coast Concert Assn. (sec. 1984-86, 88-89, bd. dirs. 1984-89), Music Educators Nat. Conf., Fla. League of Arts (state pres. 2003—), Fla. Music Educators Assn., Fla. Vocal Assn., Ft. Walton Beach Woman's Club (music dir. 1984-87, 2d v.p. 1984-86), Choctaw Bay Music Club (pres. 1985-86). Democrat. Unitarian.

LINDELL, ANDREA REGINA, dean, nurse; b. Warren, Pa., Aug., 21, 1943; d. Andrew D. and Irene M. (Fabry) Lefik; m. Warner E. Lindell, May 7, 1966; children: Jennifer I., Jason M. B.S., Villa Maria Coll., 1970; M.S.N. Catholic U., 1975, D.N.Sc., 1976; diploma R.N., St. Vincent's Hosp., Erie, Pa. Instr. St. Vincent Hosp. Sch. Nursing, 1964-66; dir. Rouse Hosp., Youngsville, Pa., 1966-69; supr. Vis. Nurses Assn., Warren, Pa., 1969-70; dir. grad. program Cath. U., Washington, 1975-77; chmn., assoc. dean U. N.H., Durham, 1977-81; dean, prof. Oakland U., Rochester, Mich., 1981-90, dean, Schmidlapp prof. nursing U. Cin., 1990—; bd. dirs. CHEMED Corp.; cons. Moorehead U., Ky., 1983. Editor; Jour. Profl. Nursing, 1985; contbr. articles to profl. jours. Mem. sch. bd. Strafford Sch. Dist., N.H., 1977-80; Gov.'s Blue Ribbon Commn. Direct Health Policies, Concord, N.H., 1979-81; vice chmn. New England Commn. Higher Edn. in Nursing, 1977-81; mem. Mich. Assn. Colls. Nursing, 1981—. Named Outstanding Young Woman Am., 1980. Mem. Nat. League Nursing, Am. Assn. Colls. Nursing (pres. 1996—), Sigma Theta Tau. Democrat. Roman Catholic. Avocations: water skiing, roller skating, reading, fishing, camping. Office: College of Nursing & Health 3110 Vine St Cincinnati OH 45221-0001

LINDELL, EDWARD ALBERT, academic and religious organization administrator; b. Denver, Nov. 30, 1928; s. Edward Gustaf and Estelle (Lundin) L.; m. Patricia Clare Eckert, Sept. 2, 1965; children: Edward Paul, Erik Adam. BA, U. Denver, 1950, MA, 1956, Ed.D., 1960, L.H.D. (hon.), 1975; Litt.D. (hon.), Tusculum Coll., 1979; D.H.L. (hon.), Roanoke Coll., 1981; Litt.D (hon.), Christ Coll., Irvine, 1992. Tchr. North Denver High Sch., 1952-61; asst. dean Coll. Arts and Scis., U. Denver, 1961-65, dean, 1965-75; pres. Gustavus Adolphus Coll., St. Peter, Minn., 1975-80, Luth. Brotherhood Mut. Funds, Mpls., 1980—. V.p. Luth. Brotherhood Found., 1980—, also exec. dir. Mem. exec. bd. Rocky Mountain Synod Luth. Ch. Am., 1968—, Luth. Coun. U.S.A., v.p., 1975—; also pres. bd. coll. edn. and ch. vocations; trustee Midland Luth. Coll., Fremont, Nebr., Kans. Wesleyan U., Colo. Assn. Ind. Colls. and Univs., Luth. Med. Center, Wheatridge, Colo., Luth. Sch. Theology, Chgo., 1975—, St. John's U., Minn., 1978—; bd. dirs. Swedish Coun. in Am., 1978—, pres., chmn.-elect, 2001, pres., 2002; adv. bd. Royal Swedish Acad. Scis., 1980; v.p. Am.-Swedish Inst., 1980; exec. v.p. external affairs Luth. Brotherhood, 1981—; pres. Nat. Fraternal Congress Am., 1988—; bd. dirs. Pacific Luth. Theol. Sem., 1978-80, Loretto Heights Coll., Colo., 1978-86, Gettysburg Theol. Sem., 1981-83, Wittenberg U., 1988, Bethany Coll., 1991—, Minn. Orch., 1983—, Am. Scandinavian Found., 1982—, Fairview Hosp., 1982—, Luth. Internat. Congress, 1996-2000; bd. dirs. U.S. Swedish Found. Internat. Sci. Rsch., 1981—, v.p. 1986—; bd. dirs. Habitat for Humanity Internat., 1992—, mem. global leadership com., 2003—; pres. U.S. Wittenberg Found., 1996—. Named Outstanding Faculty Mem. Coll. Arts and Scis., U. Denver, 1964; decorated knight King of Sweden, 1976; recipient Suomi Disting. Svc. award, 1989. Mem. Good Samaritan Soc. (bd. dirs. 1997—, vice-chmn. 98-99, chmn.-elect 1999, chmn. 2000—), Swedish Pioneer Hist. Soc. (dir. 1979—), U. Denver Alumni Assn. (Career Alumni Achievement award 1994), Phi Beta Kappa. Office: Swedish Coun Am 2600 Park Ave S Minneapolis MN 55407 E-mail: 2swedes@outtech.com.

LINDELOF, DAMON, television producer, scriptwriter; Script writer (TV series) Nash Bridges, 1996, Undressed, 1999, Wasteland, 1999, script writer & co-prodr. Crossing Jordan, 2001, script writer & exec. prodr. Lost, 2004 (best TV series, drama, Producers Guild Am., 2006). Mailing: c/o Lost ABC Inc 500 South Buena Vista St Burbank CA 91521-4562

LINDEMAN, BARRY JAMES, internal auditor, nurse, minister; b. Cheverly, Md., July 31, 1952; s. Robert Carlton and Eva Mae Lindeman; m. Hilda Alfreda Edelstein, Sept. 8, 2000. ADN, Calhoun CC, 1974; BS in Org. Mgmt., Tusculum Coll., 2003, MBA in Org. Mgmt. Cert. Managed Healthcare Profl. Health Ins. Assn., 1998; RN; cert. Compliance Profl. Healthcare Fraud & Abuse Compliance Inst., Case Mgr. Various nursing positions, Knoxville, Birmingham, Charleston, Huntsville; adminstr. govt. programs John Deere Healthcare, Moline, Ill., sr. regional auditor, 1994—2001; sr. auditor Covenant Health, Knoxville, Tenn., 2001—. Founding mem. MCO fraud roundtable Tenn. Bur. Investigation, Nashville, 1995—; founding mem. working group OIG East Tenn. Healthcare Fraud, Knoxville, 2000—; mem. Coun. Ethical Orgs., 2003—. Sec. Kiwanis, South Knoxville, 1993; organizer Out of the Box, Knoxville, 2003—; bd. dirs. Kiwanis, South Knoxville, 1990—92. Named Outstanding Citizen, City of Knoxville, 2001. Fellow: Am. Coll. Healthcare Execs.; mem.: Inst. Internal Auditors, Assn. Cert. Fraud Examiners, Omicron Pi. Personal E-mail: blindema@couhlth.com.

LINDEMAN, JANET CLAIRE, psychologist, educator; b. Dumaguette City, The Philippines, Dec. 8, 1941; (parents Am. citizens); d. Paul Raymond and Clara (Malbon) Lindholm; m. Michael John Lindeman, Dec. 27, 1966; 1 child, Christopher Paul. BA in History, Oberlin Coll., Ohio, 1963; MA in Teaching, Harvard U., 1964; MS in Psychology, U. Alaska, 1973; PhD in Guidance and Counseling, Wash. State U., 1977. Lic. psychologist, Alaska. Tchr. Episcopal Deanery Day Sch., San Francisco, 1965-66; social worker, tchr. Alaska Div. Social Svcs. and Dept. Edn., Bethel, 1966-68; vol. U.S. Peace Corps, Manila, 1968-69; social worker Head Start Program, Anchorage and Chugiak, Alaska, 1970-73; counselor intern Wash. State U. Student Counseling Ctr., Pullman, 1974-77; family therapist Alaska Clinic, Anchorage, 1977-79; psychologist Langdon Psychiat. Clinic, Anchorage, 1979-81; pvt. practice Anchorage, 1981—. Adj. instr. U. Alaska, 1979—, Alaska Pacific U., 2003—. Foster parent Dept. Corrections, Anchorage, 1982-86. Mem. Am. Psychol. Assn., Alaska Psychol. Assn. (sec. 1978-80). Avocations: teaching yoga, meditation. Office: 4050 Lake Otis Ste 201 Anchorage AK 99508 Office Phone: 907-276-8740. E-mail: janetlphd@netscape.net.

LINDEMAN, RICHARD RUSSELL, electronics engineer; b. Salt Lake City, Aug. 31, 1978; s. Russell Leroy and Linda Keding Lindeman; m. Conny Goodman Lindeman, June 24, 2000; children: Enoch, Spencer. BS Electronics and Engring. Tech., DeVry U., Phoenix, 2001. Cert. in data processing Utah, bus. edn. Utah, in word processing Utah. Electronics, device tech. Phoenix Semiconductor, 2000; head test equipment engr. ParJit Internat., 2000—06; device characterization engr. ON Semiconductor, Phoenix, 2006—. Adj. tchr. DeVry U., Phoenix, 2004. Mem.: Mensa. Lds Ch. Avocations: home improvement, reading, web design. Home: 11202 W Holly St Avondale AZ 85323-5073 Office: ON Semiconductor 5005 E McDowell Rd Phoenix AZ 85008 Office Phone: 602-244-6416.

LINDEMANN, ADAM, communications executive; b. 1962; BA in Spanish Lit., Amherst Coll., Mass.; JD, Yale Univ. Law Sch., New Haven, Conn. Founder, pres., CEO Mega Comm. Co., NYC, 1998—; appointed Bush-Cheney FCC Adv. Com., 2001. Named one of Top 200 Art Collectors, ARTnews, 2006. Office: Mega Communications 701 Dahlia St NW Washington DC 20012

LINDEMANN, GEORGE L., gas industry executive; b. NYC, 1936; BS in Econ., Univ. Pa. Pres. Smith, Miller and Patch pharmaceuticals, 1962—72, Vision Cable Comm., 1972—81; founder, chmn., CEO Metrol Mobile CTS Inc. (merged with Bell Atlantic), 1983—92; chmn., CEO Activated Comm. Inc., NYC, Southern Union Co., Wilkes Barre, Pa., 1990—2005, chmn., pres., CEO, 2005—. Bd. dir. Met. Club, NYC, New Orleans Mus. Art, Internat Class A Yacht Assn., Perto Cervo, Sardinia, Italy. Named one of Forbes' Richest Americans, 2006. Office: Southern Union Co 1 PEI Ctr Wilkes Barre PA 18711 Office Phone: 570-820-2400.*

LINDEMULDER, LAURIE, piano educator, concert pianist; b. Detroit, Jan. 22, 1938; d. Ralph Leslie and Wilmine (Vanderveen) Lindemulder; m. Charles Thomas Harris, Jan. 15, 1966; children: Leslie Law Harris, Charles Jason Harris. MusB, U. Mich., 1959, MusM, 1961. Mem. faculty Kingswood Sch. Cranbrook, Bloomfield Hills, Mich., 1959—61, Detroit Inst. Musical Art, 1961—65, Detroit Cmty. Music Sch., 1962—65, Tuesday Musical, Detroit, 1963—81; self-employed, 1966—81; mem. faculty Wayne County C.C., Detroit, 1969—71; pianist Theater on Wheels, Houston, 1981—83; mgr., tchr. Loftis Music Studios, Houston, 1987—91; tchr. Houston Conservatory Music, 1990—92; self-employed pvt. studio, Houston, 1989—; tchg. artist Tex. Inst. Arts in Edn., Houston, 1996—2003. Founding mem. Music for a While Concert series, Grosse Pointe Woods, Mich., 1978—81; originator Arts Always, Houston, 1984—86; musician piano duet team with Alice Ellison, Detroit, 1963—94, with Norman Schack, Houston, 1994—2000; coord. Am. field svc. fgn. student's com. St. John's Sch., Houston, 1989—92. Founding sec. Cy-Fair Assn. Edn. Academically Talented, 1984; chmn. cultural arts com. Post Elem. Sch., Cypress-Fairbanks Ind. Sch. Dist., Houston, 1984—86; bd. dirs. Houston Chamber Orch., 2001—05; vol. video dir., cameraman First Presbyn. Ch., Houston, 1987—2004. Travel grantee, Cultural Arts Coun. Houston, 1999. Mem.: Houston Music Tchrs. Assn. Edn. Found. (pres. 2000—02, bd. dirs. 2002—04), Houston Music Tchrs. Assn. (v.p., program chmn. 1994—97, pres.-elect 1997—98, pres. 1998—2000), Tex. Music Tchrs. Assn., Nat. Piano Tchrs. Guild, Music Tchrs. Nat. Assn. (life cert. piano tchr.), Tues. Musical Club (Houston), Bayou City Federated Music Club (founding pres. 1995—96). Studio: 4507 Richmond Ave Houston TX 77027-6709 Personal E-mail: laurie_lindemulder@yahoo.com.

LINDEN, HENRY ROBERT, chemical engineer, researcher; b. Vienna, Feb. 21, 1922; arrived in US, 1939, naturalized, 1945; s. Fred and Edith (Lermer) Linden; m. Natalie Govedarica, 1967; children from previous marriage: Robert, Debra. BS, Ga. Inst. Tech., Atlanta, 1944; MChemE, Poly. U., 1947; PhD, Ill. Inst. Tech., Chgo., 1952. Chem. engr. Socony Vacuum Labs., 1944-47; with Inst. Gas Tech., 1947-78, various rsch. mgmt. positions, 1947-61, dir., 1961-69, exec. v.p., dir., 1969-74, pres., trustee, 1974-78; various acad. appointments Ill. Inst. Tech., Chgo., 1954-86, Frank W. Gunsaulus Disting. Prof. chem. engring., 1987-90, McGraw prof. energy and power engring. and mgmt., 1990—, interim pres., CEO, 1989-90, interim chmn., CEO Ill. Inst. Tech. Rsch. Inst., 1989-90; COO GDC, Inc., Chgo., 1965-73; CEO Gas Devel. Corp. subs. Inst. Gas Tech., Chgo., 1973-78, also bd. dirs.; pres., dir. Gas Rsch. Inst.,

Chgo., 1976-87, exec. advisor, 1987-2000. Contbr. articles to profl. jours. Named to Hall of Fame, Ill. Inst. Tech., 1982, Engring. Hall of Fame, Ga. Tech., 1996; recipient award of merit oper. sect., Am. Gas Assn., 1956, Disting. Svc. award, 1974, Gas. Industry Rsch. award, 1982, R & D award, Nat. Energy Resources Orgn., 1986, Homer H. Lowry award for excellence in fossil energy rsch., U.S. Dept. Energy, 1991, award, U.S. Energy Assn., 1993, Walton Clark medal, Franklin Inst., 1972, Bunsen-Pettenkofer-Ehrentafel medal, Deutscher Verein des Gas und Wasserfaches, 1978, Lifetime Achievement award, Energy Daily Jour., 1996, Alumni medal, Ill. Inst. Tech., 1995. Fellow: AAAS, AIChE (Ernest W. Thiele award 2000), Inst. Energy; mem.: Am. Chem. Soc. (chmn. divsn. fuel chemistry 1967, councilor 1969—77, H.H. Storch award), So. Gas Assn. (hon.), NAE. Achievements include patents for fuel technology. Office: Ill Inst Tech PH 135 10 W 33rd St Chicago IL 60616-3730 Office Phone: 312-567-3095. Business E-Mail: linden@iit.edu.

LINDEN, PAUL FREDRICK, environmental engineer, educator; b. London, Jan. 29, 1947; s. Frederick H. and Muriel C. (Blackwell) L.; m. Carolyn A. Webber, Oct. 16, 1968 (div. 1979); m. Diana M. Readman, June 16, 1979; children: Rebecca, Charlotte. BSc, U. Adelaide, Australia, 1966; BSc with hons., U. Adelaide, 1967; MSc in Math., Flinders U. So. Australia, 1968; PhD in Applied Math., U. Cambridge, Eng., 1972. Rsch. asst. dept. applied math. and theoretical physics U. Cambridge, 1972-76, asst. dir. rsch., 1976-91, dir. Fluid Dynamics Lab., 1976—98, reader geophys. fluid dynamics, 1991—98; fellow, dir. studies math. Downing Coll., 1977—98; Blasker prof. environ. sci. and engring. dept. mech. and aerospace engring. U. Calif., San Diego, 1998—, chair dept. mech. and aerospace engring., 2004—, interim dir. environment and sustainability initiative, 2007—. Dir. Cambridge Environ. Rsch. Cons. Contbr. over 120 articles to profl. jours. Fellow Royal Meteorol. Soc., Am. Phys. Soc., Royal Soc. UK. Office: Dept Mech and Aerospace Engring U Calif San Diego 9500 Gilman Dr La Jolla CA 92093-0411 Office Phone: 858-822-2274. Office Fax: 858-534-7720. E-mail: pflinden@ucsd.edu.*

LINDEN, PEPPY G., museum director; b. Louisville, Dec. 19, 1949; d. Bernard Sylvan and Helen Novitsky Goldstein; m. Russell Mathew Linden, May 9, 1971 (div. May 1979). BEd, U. Mich., 1971. Cert. elem. tchr. Va. Program coord. Project Cmty., Ann Arbor, Mich., 1971-72; sr. rsch. asst. Inst. for Social Rsch., Ann Arbor, 1972-74; infant educator dept. pediats. U. Va., Charlottesville, 1975-76; pediat. admissions and adolescent coord. Kluge Children's Rehab. Ctr., U. Va. Med. Ctr., Charlottesville, 1976-89; exec. dir. Va. Discovery Mus., Charlottesville, 1990—. Mem. Cable TV Citizens' Adv. Com., Charlottesville, 1992-98; mem. Social Svcs. Adv. Bd., Charlottesville, 1996-2005. Judge Nat. History Day, Charlottesville, 1993-96; bd. dirs. Piedmont Coun. of Arts, Charlottesville, 1989-92, Charlottesville Regional Tourism Coun., 2001-04, Charlottesville Regional Tourism Bd., 2007—; regional bd. dirs. Sorensen Inst. for Polit. Leadership, 2001—; sec., chair Charlottesville Electoral Bd., 1993-96; election ofcl. City of Chalottesville, 1991-93; pres., v.p. North Downtown Residents' Assn., Charlottesville, 1986-89; treas. Nat. Host Program, Charlottesville, 1993-94; mem. adv. bd. Piedmont Va. C.C. Dickinson Theater; mem. program com. Paramount Theatre, 2002-04; founding bd. Va./N.C. Nat. Soc. for Arts and Letters, 2003—; mem. state social svc. bd., 2005—, sec., 2006, 07—. Named Woman of Distinction, Va. Skyline coun., Girl Scouts U.S., 1993, Artist of Yr., Piedmont Coun. of Arts, 2001; named one of Area's Disting. Dozen, 2004. Fellow Sorensen Inst. Polit. Leadership; mem. Leadership Charlottesville Jewish. Avocations: theater, water sports, politics, films. Office: Va Discovery Mus 524 E Main St Charlottesville VA 22902-5336 Office Phone: 434-977-1025.

LINDENBAUM, S(EYMOUR) J(OSEPH), physicist; b. NYC, Feb. 3, 1925; s. Morris and Anne Lindenbaum; m. Leda Isaacs, June 29, 1958. AB, Princeton U., 1945; MA, Columbia U., 1949, PhD, 1951. With Brookhaven Nat. Lab., Upton, NY, 1951-96, sr. physicist, 1963-96, sr. physicist emeritus, 1996—, group leader high energy physics research group, 1954-89; vis. prof. U. Rochester, 1958-59; Mark W. Zemansky chair in physics CCNY, 1970-95, Mark Zemansky prof. emeritus of physics, 1995—. Cons. Centre de Etudes Nucleaire de Saclay, France, 1957, CERN, Geneva, 1962; head CCNY Experimental High Energy and Nuclear Physics Rsch. Group, 1970—; dep. for sci. affairs ERDA, 1976-77 Author: Particle Interaction Physics at High Energies, 1973; scriptwriter, narrator, sci. prodr. (multi-screen, audio-visual slide show) Atom Smashing, Atom Smashers: Fifty Years, Smithsonian Instn. Exhibit, 1977; contbr. articles to profl. jours. Fellow Am. Phys. Soc.; mem. NY Acad. Scis., AAAS. Achievements include discovering nucleon isobars dominated high energy particles interactions, isobar model; inventor on line computer technique in scientific experiments; proved experimentally that Einstein's special theory of relativity was correct down to subnuclear distances one hundredth the radius of a proton; discovered the glueball states predicted by quantum chromodynamics. Office: Brookhaven Nat Lab Dept Physics Bldg 510A Upton NY 11973 *I was always fascinated by the orderly and powerful laws of nature. Thus I decided to concentrate on one of mankind's greatest intellectual endeavours—scientific inquiry into the physical laws which govern our universe.*

LINDENBERGER, HERBERT SAMUEL, writer, literature educator; b. LA, Apr. 4, 1929; s. Hermann and Celia (Weinkrantz) L.; m. Claire Flaherty, June 14, 1961; children: Michael James, Elizabeth Celia. BA, Antioch Coll., Yellow Springs, Ohio, 1951; PhD, U. Wash., Seattle, 1955. From instr. to prof. English and comparative lit. U. Calif., Riverside, 1954-66; prof. German and English, chmn. program comparative lit. Washington U., St. Louis, 1966-69; Avalon prof. humanities Stanford (Calif.) U., 1969—2001, Avalon prof. emeritus, 2001—, chmn. program comparative lit., 1969-82; dir. Stanford Humanities Ctr., 1991-92. Author: On Wordsworth's Prelude, 1963, Georg Büchner, 1964, (play) Lear and Cordelia at Home, 1968, Georg Trakl, 1971, Historical Drama: The Relation of Literature and Reality, 1975, Saul's Fall: A Critical Fiction, 1979, Opera: The Extravagant Art, 1984, The History in Literature: On Value, Genre, Institutions, 1990, Opera in History: From Monteverdi to Cage, 1998, Dogstory: A Memoir in Hypertext, 1999; contbr. chpts. to books, articles to profl. jours. Fulbright scholar Austria, 1952-53; Guggenheim fellow, 1968-69; Nat. Endowment Humanities fellow, 1975-76, 82-83; Stanford U. Humanities Ctr. Fellow, 1982-83 Mem.: MLA (pres. 1997). E-mail: lindenberger@stanford.edu.

LINDENFELD, JOANN, physician, educator; b. Benton Harbor, Mich., Feb. 11, 1948; d. Nelson Albert and Viola C. Lindenfield. MD, U. MIch., 1973. Diplomate in internal medicine, cardiology and critical care medicine Am. Bd. Internal Medicine. Asst. prof. medicine U. Colo., Denver, 1980-85, assoc. prof. medicine, 1985-90, prof. medicine, 1990—. Mem. cardiovenal adv. panel FDA, Washington, 1995—; cons. for pharm. firms. Author: Geriatric Internal Medicine, 1995, 99; contbr. articles to profl. jours. Recipient numerous awards U. Colo., Denver. Fellow Am. Coll. Cardiology, Am. Heart Assn. (clin. coun. rep.); mem. Internat. Soc. Heart and Lung Transplant, Am. Soc. Transplant Physicians. Avocations: hiking, poetry, gardening, writing. Office: U Colo Health Scis Ctr 4200 E 9th Ave B130 Denver CO 80262-0001 Home Phone: 303-733-4352; Office Phone: 303-315-4410. Business E-Mail: joAnn.lindenfeld@uchsc.edu.*

LINDENFELD, PETER, physics professor; b. Vienna, Mar. 10, 1925; came to U.S., 1948, naturalized, 1957; s. Bela and Elda (Lachs) L.; m. Lore Kadden, May 31,1953; children: Thomas, Naomi. Student, U. Man., Can., 1942-43; BASc., U.B.C., Can., 1946, MA Sc., 1948; PhD, Columbia U., 1954. Vis. lectr. Drew U., Madison, NJ, 1952-53; instr. Rutgers U., 1953-55, asst. prof. physics, 1955-61, asso. prof., 1961-66, prof., 1966-99, prof. emeritus, 1999—. Cons. summer inst. AID, Tirupati, India, 1965; regional counselor N.J. Am. Inst. Physics, 1963-71; dir. NSF In-svc. Insts. High Sch. Tchrs., 1964-66; Rutgers Rsch. Coun. fellow and guest scientist Faculte de Scis., U. Paris-Sud, Orsay, France, 1970-71; vis. scholar Kyoto U., Japan, 1982. Contbr. articles to profl. jours. Recipient Warren I. Susman award for excellence in teaching, 1988, Robert A. Millikan Lecture award and medal Am. Assn. Physics Tchrs., 1989. Fellow Am. Phys. Soc.; mem. AAUP, Am. Assn. Physics Tchrs. (hon. mem. N.J. sect., N.J. sect. award for lifetime contbns. to physics tchg. 2004). Home: 121 Harris Rd Princeton NJ 08540-3375 Office: Rutgers U Dept Physics and Astronomy Piscataway NJ 08854-8019 E-mail: lindenf@physics.rutgers.edu.

LINDENMAYER, ELISABETH, international organization administrator; married; 2 children. Degree, U. Paris-Sorbonne, U. Geneva, NYU. Various positions with Office of Human Resources Mgmt., UN, 1977, spl. asst. to the then asst. sec.-gen. for personnel svcs.; provided polit. back-up and support Iraq-Kuwait UN Observation Mission (UNIKOM), UN Hdqs., 1992, UN Ops. in Somalia (UNOSOM I, UNITAF Task Force and UNOSOM II), UN Hdqs., 1992—94, UN Mission in Rwanda (UNAMIR), UN Hdqs., 1994—96, Great Lakes Region, Burundi and Zaire (now the Dem. Rep. of Congo); budget officer Office of Programme Planning, Budget, and Fin.; spl. asst. to the controller UN Hdqs., exec. asst. to sec.-gen., 1997—2004, asst. sec.-gen. to the post of dep. chef de cabinet in the exec. office of the sec.-gen., 2004—05. Adj. prof. Columbia U., NYC, 2005—. Office Phone: 212-963-1234, 718-625-0597. Office Fax: 212-963-4879, 718-852-5816. Business E-Mail: elindenmayer2@aol.com.

LINDENMEYER, PETER W., retail executive; Grad., De La Salle Inst., Chgo., 1971. Evansville distbn. dir. T.J. Maxx TJX Cos., Inc., 1986—88, asst. v.p. T.J. Maxx, 1988—91, v.p. distbn. ctr. ops. T.J. Maxx, 1991—96, v.p. distbn. svcs. Marmaxx Group, 1996—98, sr. v.p., dir. distbn. svcs. Marmaxx Group, 1998, exec. v.p., chief logistics officer, 2005—. Office: TJX Cos Inc 770 Cochituate Rd Framingham MA 01701 Office Phone: 508-390-1000. Office Fax: 508-390-2091.*

LINDER, FANNIE RUTH, psychotherapist, concert soprano; b. Hartwell, Ga., Mar. 14, 1934; d. Marion Taylor and Nobie (Gaines) Barnes; m. Raymond Linder, Jan. 30, 1953; children: Raymond T., Michael C. BA, Empire State Coll., SUNY, 1986; MA, Liberty U., 1990; D in Psychology, Hamilton U., 2002. Tchr. Romulus (N.Y.) Ctrl. Sch., 1969-70; owner, prodr. ISHI Rec. Studio, Apalachin, N.Y., 1981—; pvt. psychologist Apalachin, 1984—. Bd. dirs. The Stewart W. and Willma C. Hoyt Found., Binghamton; bd. mem. So. Tier Inst. for Arts in Edn., Binghamton, 1993—, Eckelberger Towers, Binghamton, 1993—; mem. ethics com. United Health Hosps., Binghamton, 1993—; lectr. in field. Concert soprano worldwide, 1968—. Spokesperson, chair Police/Community Group, Binghamton, 1987-93. Named Outstanding Young Women of Am., 1965; recipient Appreciation award Gen. Commn. on Chaplains and Armed Forces Pers., Romulus, 1970, Lucia Humanitarian award, Cmty. Activism award, Broome County Coun. Churches. Mem. Assn. for Psychol. Type (Merit award), Personality Inst. (bd. chmn., founder, Recognition award). Avocations: reading, research, music. Home: 21 W Glann Rd Apalachin NY 13732-4026

LINDER, HARVEY RONALD, lawyer, arbitrator, mediator; b. Pitts., July 23, 1949; s. Charles Joseph and Rose (Ruben) Linder; m. Reva Rebecca Vertman, Aug. 14, 1971 (div.); children: Zalman F., Seth A.; m. Gail Lynne Silberman, May 26, 2002; children: Aaron B., Leah M. BA, Duquesne U., 1971, JD, 1975. Bar: Pa. 1975, Ga. 2003, U.S. Dist. Ct. (we. dist.) Pa. 1975, U.S. Supreme Ct. 1979. Legal intern Dist. Atty.'s Office, Pitts., 1974-75; asst. mgr. arbitration U.S. Steel, Pitts., 1975-80, mgr. labor rels., 1980-81, supt. employee rels. Clairton, Pa., 1981-83; corp. dir. employee rels. U.S. Steel Agri-Chemicals, Atlanta, 1984-86; corp. dir. law and human resources LaRoche Industries Inc., Atlanta, 1986-88, v.p., gen. counsel, 1988-96, Orion Mgmt. Svcs. Inc., 1996-97, SED Internat., Inc., 1997-99; interim rabbi B'Nai Torah, 2000—01. Arbitrator, mediator, 1996—; pres. A.C.I.R.A., 1987-90; gen. counsel Marcus Jewish Cmty. Ctr. of Atlanta, Inc., 2004—. Contbr. poetry and photography to Duquesne Literary Mag., 1968-74. Exec. cons. Jr. Achievement, Pitts., 1978—83; head coach Atlanta Jewish Cmty. Ctr., Dunwoody, Ga., 1984—, bd. dirs., 1991—, v.p., 2001—; pres. Hunter's Woods Homeowners' Assn., Dunwoody, 1986—87; commr. Baseball & Soccer Leagues; bd. dirs. Atlanta Jewish Fedn., 1995—96, Hillels of Ga., 2000—03; pres. B'nai Torah Synagogue, 1995—97, interim rabbi, 2000—01. Steel fellow Am. Iron and Steel Inst., 1977-85. Mem. ABA, Allegheny County Bar Assn., Indsl. Rels. Rsch. Assn., Duquesne U. Law Sch. Alumni Assn. (bd. dirs. 1980-84), B'nai B'rith (local v.p. 1975-80), Amer-Israel C. of C. (bd. dirs. 1993-2001). Avocations: coaching, collecting books and sports memorabilia. Home and Office: 5342 Tilly Mill Rd Atlanta GA 30338 Office Phone: 770-395-2510. Business E-Mail: hrlaw1@aol.com.

LINDER, JOHN E., congressman, dentist; b. Deer River, Minn., Sept. 9, 1942; s. Henry and Vera Elizabeth Davis L.; m. Lynne Leslee Peterson, 1963; children: Kristine Kerry, Matthew John. BS, U. Minn., 1964, DDS, 1967. Pvt. practice, Atlanta, 1969—82; mem. Ga. Ho. Reps., 1975-80, 82-90; pres. Linder Fin. Corp., 1977-92; mem. US Congress from 7th Ga. dist., 1993—; mem. homeland sec. com., house admin. com. House rules com., subcom. on legis. process, steering com., former mem. Nat. Rep. Congl. Com. exec. com. US Ho. Reps., chmn. Founder I Care, 1970. Capt. USAF, 1967-69. Mem. ADA, Ga. Dental Assn., No. Dist. Dental Soc., Rotary. Republican. Presbyterian. Office: US Ho Reps 1026 Longworth Ho Office Bldg Washington DC 20515-1007*

LINDER, MARY CARROLL, air transportation executive; b. NYC, Dec. 8, 1947; d. John Kennedy and Ruth (McNally) C.; m. Frederick Martin Linder, III, Nov. 28, 1980. BA in English Lit., Boston Coll., 1969. Editl. asst. Famous Artists Sch. Internat., NYC, 1974-75; pub. rels. dir. Dominican Republic Tourist Office, NYC, 1975-79; mgr. pub. rels., investor Hemisphere Hilton Internat., NYC, 1979-83; dir. pub. rels. Hilton Internat., NYC, 1983-87; v.p. external affairs US ops. Grand Met. PLC, Montvale, NJ, 1987-89, v.p. pub. affairs food sector Mpls., 1989-91, v.p. pub. affairs US ops., 1991-92, corp. comm. dir. London, 1992; sr. v.p. global comm. Estee Lauder Cos., NYC; sr. v.p. corp. comm. NW Airlines Corp., Minn., 2001, sr. v.p. corp. and brand comm., 2001—. Mem. Nat. Investors Rels. Inst., Internat. Pub. Rels. Assn. Office: NW Airlines Corp 2700 Lone Oak Pky Eagan MN 55121 Office Phone: 612-726-2111.*

LINDER, VIRGINIA LYNN, state supreme court justice; b. Cañon City, Colo., Apr. 20, 1953; d. Irene D. Linder. BS in Polit. Sci., So. Oreg. State U., 1975; JD, Willamette U., 1980. Bar: Oreg., U.S. Dist. Ct. Oreg. 1981, U.S. Ct. Appeals (9th cir.) 1981, U.S. Supreme Ct. 1983. Asst. atty. gen. Oreg. Dept. Justice, Salem, 1980-83, atty. in charge edn. sect., gen. counsel, 1983-84, asst. solicitor gen., 1984-86, solicitor general, 1986-97; judge Oreg. Ct. Appeals, Salem, 1997—2007; assoc. justice Ore. Supreme Ct., 2007—. Presenter, spkr., panelist in fields of women's law, constnl. law, family and juvenile law, capital cases, other topics; adj. law prof. Willamette U., 1998—, U. Oreg. Law Sch., 1988; mem. Oreg. Judicial Dept. exec. com.; mem. appellate ct. tech. com., 1997—; mem. Coun. on Ct. Procedures, 1997—; mem. Appellate Cts. Settlement Conf. com., 1994; mem. Ho. Task Force on Oreg. Appellate Ct. Sys;., 1993-94; apptd. Oreg. Appellate Ct. rules com., 1990, 92-93; mem. 9th Cir. Death Penalty Task Force, 1988-91. Prin. author minority report Videotape Ct. Reporting Evaluation com., trial level, 1990, appellate level, 1991. Judge Nat. We the People (Bill of Rights) H.S. Competition, Washington, 1993; judge state-wide h.s. We the People Competition, Oreg. Law Related Edn. Program, 1992, 93; trial practice instr./judge, Willamette U., 1983—. Recipient Outstanding Alumna award, So. Oreg. State Coll., 1987; recipient Cmty. award YWCA Tribute to Outstanding Women, 1991; recipeint merit award Oreg. Gay and Lesbian Lawyers Assn., 1996. Mem. Nat. Assn. Attys. Gen. (state specialist group providing amicus support and expertise on 8th amendment issues), Oreg. State Bar (exec. com. constnl. law sect., chair appellate practice sect. 1994-95, vice chair 1993-94, chair-elect 1994-95), Oreg. Women Lawyers (bd. mem. 1997—, exec. com. mem.), Marion County Bar Assn. (Law Practices Career Day host 1991, 92), Willamette Inns of Ct. Office: Ore Supreme Ct 1163 State St Salem OR 97301-2563 Office Phone: 503-986-5555. Office Fax: 503-986-5730. E-mail: ojd.info@ojd.state.or.us.*

LINDERMAN, ERIC GRAHAM, librarian; b. Euclid, Ohio, Oct. 21, 1970; s. Frederick George and Ora Jeanne Linderman; m. Amy Martha Guillaume, Aug. 29, 1998; children: Brennan Kenneth children: Broderick Hugh. BA in Art History, Kent State U., Ohio, 1989—93, MLS, 1996—98. Cert. pub. libr. The Ohio Libr. Coun., 2002. Adult svcs. libr. Ida Rupp Pub. Libr., Port Clinton, Ohio, 1998—99, supr., adult svcs., 1999—2000, East Cleve. Pub. Libr., Ohio, 2000—06; adult svcs. mgr. Euclid Pub. Libr., 2006—. Author: (jour.) Librs. & Culture, Libr. Instruction Round Table News, (book reviews) Libr. Jour. Literacy tutor Project Read, Port Clinton, Ohio, 1999—2000. Grantee, Ohio Humanities Coun., 2002. Mem.: ALA (mem. Libr. Instrn. Round Table, mem., Ethnic and Multicultural Info. Exch. Round Table), Clevnet Pub. Svc. Spl. Interest Group, Kent State U. Sch. of Libr. and Info. Sci. Alumni Adv. Bd., Ohio Libr. Assn. Intellectual Freedom Com., Beta Phi Mu. Avocations: painting, bread baking. Home: 29126 Fuller Ave Wickliffe OH 44092 Office: Euclid Public Library 631 East 222nd Street Euclid OH 44123 Office Phone: 216-541-4128. Business E-Mail: elinderman@ecpl.lib.oh.us.

LINDERMAN, JEANNE HERRON, priest; b. Erie, Pa., Nov. 14, 1931; d. Robert Leslie and Ella Marie (Stearns) Herron; m. James Stephens Linderman; children: Mary Susan, John Randolph, Richard Webster, Craig Stephens, Mark Herron, Elizabeth Stewart. BS in Indsl. and Labor Rels., Cornell U., 1953; MDiv magna cum laude, Lancaster Theol. Sem., 1981; postgrad., clin. pastoral edn., Del. State Hosp., New Castle, 1981. Ordained priest Episcopal Ch. Mem. pers. staff Hengerer Co., Buffalo, 1953-55; chaplain Cathedral Ch. St. John, Wilmington, Del., 1981-82; priest-in-charge Christ Episcopal Ch., Delaware City, Del., 1982-87, vicar, 1987-91; assoc. rector St. Andrew's Episcopal Ch., Wilmington, 1992—94, priest in charge, 1995-96; assoc. priest for pastoral care The Episc. Ch. of Sts. Andrew and Matthew, 1998—. Chair human sexuality task force Diocese of Del., 1981—82, mem. clergy compensation com., mem. diocesan coun., 1982—86, mem. com. constitution and canons, 1989, pres. standing com., 1991—95, designer, leader religious/spiritual retreats, chaplain to the ret. clergy, 1999—, bishop's chaplain to ret. clergy, 2004. Author, editor: hist. study papers. Bd. dirs. St. Michael's Day Nursery, Wilmington, 1985—88; bd. dirs., chmn. pers. com. Geriatric Svcs. Del., 1989—96, sec. bd. dirs., 1993—96; mem. secondary schs. com. Cornell U. Recipient award for excellence in ministry, Lancaster Theol. Sem., 2005. Mem.: Nat. Assn. Episcopal Clergy, Del. Episcopal Clergy Assn., Women's Witnessing Cmty. at Lambeth, Episcopal Women's Caucus, Cornell Women's Club (pres. Del. chpt. 1966), Patriotic Soc. Del. (sec.-treas. conv. 1965—68), Dutch Colonial Soc., Mayflower Soc. (elder Del. chpt. 2000—, surgeon 1983—95, elder gen. 2005—), DAR (vice-regent Ceasar Rodney chpt. 1996—), Nat. Soc. Colonial Dames Am., Stoney Run Questers (pres.), Women St. James the Less (pres. 1972—73), Chi Omega. Republican. Avocations: history, genealogy, travel. Home: 307 Springhouse Ln Hockessin DE 19707-9691 Office: The Episcopal Ch of Sts Andrew and Matthews Eighth And Shipley St Wilmington DE 19801 E-mail: linderjs@verizon.com.

LINDERT, ERIC ALTON, operations research specialist, small business owner; b. Milw., May 11, 1950; s. Homer Henry Lindert and Ollie Idalia Alton. BS in Physics, U. Wis., Madison, 1992; MSc in Physics, Ind. U., Bloomington, 2003. Propr. Allegheny Audio, Lockport, Ill., 1983—; accelerator ops. specialist Argonne Nat. Lab., Ill., 1997—. Brigade ops. officer US Army Tng. Brigade, Ft. McClellan, Ala., 1997—98; info. mgmt. officer 416th Engring. Command, Darien, Ill., 1999—2001. Maj. inf. US Army, 1972—2001. Decorated Army Commendation medal US Army, Meritorious Svc. medal. Mem.: Mensa, Argonne Club (v.p. 2003—). Home: 360 RiverEdge Dr Lockport IL 60441 Office: Argonne Nat Lab 9700 S Cass Ave Argonne IL 60439 Home Phone: 815-886-4504; Office Phone: 630-252-4115. Office Fax: 630-252-4118. E-mail: eric.lindert@us.army.mil, lindert@phy.anl.gov.

LINDGREN, CHARLOTTE HOLT, language educator; b. Ipswich, Mass., Jan. 5, 1924; d. Hilmer Harold and Edith Grace (Whittier) L.; m. Donald James Winslow, Aug. 11, 1978. AB, Boston U., 1945, AM, 1947, PhD, 1961; MA (hon.), Emerson Coll., 1967. Tchr. Pinkerton Acad., Derry, NH, 1945-46, Medfield (Mass.) H.S., 1947-49; adminstrv. asst. Boston Univ., 1949-60; prof. Emerson Coll., Boston, 1960-89, chmn. english dept., 1965-80, prof. emerita, 1989—. Co-leader Emerson Abroad Program, 1966-78; corporator Lasell Coll., Auburndale, Mass., 1997—. Co-author: William Barnes Dorset Engravings, 1986 (Mansell-Pleydell award 1986), Gerald Warner Brace: Writer, Sailor, Teacher, 1998; editor: The Love Poems and Letters of William Barnes, 1986; contbr. articles to History Today, Dorset Yr. Book, T. Hardy Jour. Mem. Thomas Hardy Soc., William Barnes Soc., Herman Melville Soc., Winthrop Soc. (trustee), Women in Arts, Phi Beta Kappa. Avocations: photography, book reviewing. Home: 23 Maple St Auburndale MA 02466-2404 E-mail: lindwin24@aol.com.

LINDGREN, D(ERBIN) KENNETH, JR., retired lawyer; b. Mpls., Aug. 25, 1932; s. Derbin Kenneth and Margaret (Anderson) Lindgren; m. Patricia Ann Ransier, Dec. 17, 1955; children: Christian Kenneth, Carol Ann, Charles Derbin. BS, U. Minn., 1954, JD, 1958. Bar: Minn. 1958, U.S. Tax Ct. 1959, U.S. Supreme Ct. 1968, U.S. Ct. Appeals (DC cir.) 1981. Pvt. practice law, Mpls., 1958-99; mem. Larkin, Hoffman, Daly & Lindgren, Ltd., Mpls., 1960-95, of counsel, 1995; ret., 1995. Contbr. articles to profl. jours. Active Ind. Sch. Dist. 274 Bd. Edn., Hopkins, Minn., 1970—76, chmn., 1972—76; active Ind. Sch. Dist. 287 Bd. Edn., 1979—83; trustee Mpls. Soc. Fine Arts, 1982—88, Minn. Landscape Arboretum Found., 1989—99, pres., 1992—95, hon. trustee, 2000; mem. Gov.'s Commn. Reform Govt., 1983; bd. overseers Mpls. Coll. Art and Design, 1980—86, vice-chmn., 1982—83, chmn., 1983—86, trustee, 1988—96; bd. overseers Mpls. Inst. Art, 1986—88. Lt. USAF, 1955—57. Fellow: Am. Coll. Trust and Estate Counsel; mem.: ABA, Hennepin County Bar Assn., Minn. Bar Assn., Troon Country Club (bd. dirs. 2000—03), Interlachen Country Club (bd. dirs. 1981—89, pres. 1987), Phi Delta Phi, Alpha Delta Phi. Presbyterian. Home: 11003 E Desert Vista Dr Scottsdale AZ 85255-8061 Personal E-mail: dklindgren@cox.net.

LINDGREN, ROBERT R., academic administrator; m. Cheryl Lindgren; children: Jim, Greg, Andrea. BA, U. Fla., 1976, JD, 1981; PhD, Oxford U., 1978. Asst. to Pres. U. Fla., asst. dean Coll. Law, v.p., chief devel. officer; chief exec. U. Fla. Found.; joined Johns Hopkins U., Balt., 1994; v.p. devel. and alumni rels. The Johns Hopkins Insts., Balt.; pres. Randolph-Macon Coll., Ashland, Va., 2006—. Editl. bd. Internat. Jour. Ednl. Advancement. Sr. dir. Brasenose Coll. Charitable Found. Grantee Rotary Fellowship. Office: Randolph-Macon Coll PO Box 5005 Ashland VA 23005-5505*

LINDGREN, WILLIAM DALE, librarian; b. Peoria, Ill., Mar. 8, 1936; s. Hugh Gottfried and Olive Kathryn (Myer) L. BA, Bradley U., 1958, MA, 1959; MSLS, U. Ill., 1967. Tchr. Limestone High Sch., Bartonville, Ill., 1960-68; asst. dir. Learning Resources Ctr. Ill. Cen. Coll., East Peoria, 1968-73, dir., 1973—. Mem. transition bd. merger of four systems, 1993-94; bd. dirs. Alliance Libr. Sys.; mem. Ill. State Libr. Com. on

Resolving the Unserved Problem, 1996—. Singer Ephphetha Schola Cantorum Gregoriana, 1996—; singer Carnegie Hall concerts, 2001, 03, European concert tours, 2002, 03. Chmn. East Peoria Oral History Com., 1983-84, Resource Sharing Alliance West Ctrl. Ill. Adv. Coun., 1985—; v.p. Ill. Valley Libr. Sys., pres. bd., 1988, 90—, treas., 1989, bd. dirs., 1990—; regional chair recruitment com. Am. Heart Assn., 1996—; election judge, 2002—. Mem. ALA, Ill. Libr. Assn. (co-chair cracker barrels program ann. conf. 1989, 90, 91), Assn. Ednl. Media Tech., Assn. Ednl. Media and Tech. Ill., Coun. Libr. Tech., Creve Coeur Club (Peoria).

LINDHEIM, RICHARD DAVID, broadcast executive, director; b. NYC, May 28, 1939; s. Gilbert R. and Pearl (Gruskin) L.; m. Elaine Lavis, Dec. 22, 1963; children: Susan Patricia, David Howard. BS, U. Redlands, 1961; postgrad, U. So. Calif., 1963. Adminstrv. asst. story dept. CBS, LA, 1962-64; project dir. entertainment testing ASI Market Rsch., LA, 1964-69; v.p. program research NBC, LA, 1969-78, v.p. dramatic programs, 1978-79; producer Universal TV, LA, 1979-81, v.p. current programs, 1981-85, sr. v.p. series programming, 1986-87, exec. v.p. creative affairs, 1987-91; exec. v.p. program strategy MCA TV Group, 1991-92; exec. v.p. Paramount TV Group, 1992-99; exec. dir. Inst. for Creative Techs., U. So. Calif., LA, 1999—; with ICT, Marina Del Rey, Calif. Asst. prof. Calif. State U.; sr. lectr. U. So. Calif.; lectr. UCLA; reviewer NEH; bd. dirs. Am. Fgn. Svc. Intercultural Program-USA. Author: (with Richard Blum) Primetime: Network Television Programming, 1987, Inside Television Producing, 1991; contbr. articles to profl. jours. Mem. Acad. TV Arts and Scis., Producers Guild Am., Writers Guild Am. Democrat. Jewish. Avocations: model building, photography, music, travel. Office: ICT 4676 Admiralty Way Ste 1001 Marina Del Rey CA 90292 Office Phone: 310-574-5706. E-mail: lindheim@ict.usc.edu. *In this sophisticated society there are fewer and fewer opportunities for the individual. Technology has made most tasks too complex for one man. As a result the ability to work with other people and to provide leadership and management to groups of people has become vital. The key ingredients are communication, respect for others, and a feeling of belonging, while working in a relaxed, casual environment, where the leader is responsible and receptive.*

LINDHOLM, CLIFFORD FALSTROM, II, engineering executive, mayor; b. Passaic, NJ, Dec. 8, 1930; s. Albert William and Edith (Neandross) L.; m. Margery Nye (div.); children: Clifford, Elizabeth, John; m. Karen Cooper, Oct. 7, 1989. BS in Engring., Princeton U., 1953; M in Engring., Stevens Inst. Tech., 1957. Supr. prodn. GM, Linden, N.J., 1953-56; chmn. bd. Falstrom Co., Passaic, N.J., 1956—. Bd. dirs. N.J. Mfg. Ins. Co., Trenton, N.J. Reins. Co., Trenton, 1977-2003, Employers Assn. N.J., Albert Payson Terhune Found., N.J., pres. 2001-05. Mayor Twp. Montclair, N.J., 1988-92; pres. Montclair Bd. Edn., 1968-72. Mem. NJ Bus. and Industry Assn. (bd. dirs. 1977—03), Montclair Soc. Engrs. (pres. 1998-2000), Landings Assn. (bd. dirs. 2007—), Mantoloking Yacht Club, Nassau Club, Landings Club. Republican. Mem. Ch. Of Christ. Office: Falstrom Co 3 Falstrom Ct Passaic NJ 07055 Home: 7 Woodbrook Ct Savannah GA 31411 Personal E-mail: lindholmcfii@comcast.net.

LINDHOLM, DWIGHT HENRY, lawyer; b. Blackduck, Minn., May 27, 1930; s. Henry Nathanial and Viola Eudora (Gummert) L.; m. Loretta Catherine Brown, Aug. 29, 1958; children: Douglas Dwight, Dionne Louise, Jeanne Marie, Philip Clayton, Kathleen Anne. Student, Macalester Coll., 1948-49; BBA, U. Minn., 1951, LLB, 1954; postgrad., Mexico City Coll. (now U. of Ams.), 1956-57. Bar: Minn. 1954, Calif. 1958. Sole practice, Los Angeles, 1958-65, 72-81, 84—; ptnr. Lindholm & Johnson, Los Angeles, 1965-69, Cotter, Lindholm & Johnson, Los Angeles, 1969-72; sole practice Los Angeles, 1972-81; of counsel Bolton, Dunn & Moore, Los Angeles, 1981-84. Mem. Calif. Rep. Ctrl. Com., 1962-63, L.A. Republican County Ctrl. Com., 1962-66; bd. dirs. Family Service L.A., 1964-70, v.p., 1968-70; bd. dirs. Wilshire YMCA, 1976-77; trustee Westlake Girls Sch., 1978-81; hon. presenter Nat. Charity League Coronet Debutante Ball, 1984; bd. dirs. Calif. State U.-Northridge Trust Fund, 1989-93; bd. dirs. Queen of Angeles/Hollywood Presbyn. Med. Ctr., 1990-98; chmn., CEO Queen of Angels, Hollywood Presbyn. Found., 1997-2000; bd. dirs., corp. sec. QueensCare, 1998-2002. Served as capt. JAG Corps USAF, 1954-56. Recipient Presdl. award LA Jr. C. of C., 1959 Mem. Calif. Bar Assn., L.A. County Bar Assn., Wilshire Bar Assn. (bd. govs. 1989-91), Internat. Genealogy Fellowship of Rotarians (founding pres. 1979-86), Calif. Club, Ocean Cruising Club Eng. (Newport Harbor port officer), Rotary (dir. 1975-78), Delta Sigma Pi, Delta Sigma Rho, Delta Theta Phi (state chancellor 1972-73). Presbyterian. Avocations: sailing, offshore cruising. Office: 3580 Wilshire Blvd Fl 17 Los Angeles CA 90010-2501

LINDHOLM, RICHARD THEODORE, economics and finance educator; b. Eugene, Oreg., Oct. 5, 1960; s. Richard Wadsworth and Mary Marjorie (Trunko) L. m. Valaya Nivasananda, May 8, 1987. BA, U. Chgo., 1982, MA, 1983, PhD, 1993. Ptnr. Lindholm and Osanka, Eugene, 1986-89, Lindholm Rsch., Eugene, 1995—2001, owner, 1995—, The Lindholm Co., 1995—; ptnr. DBA Lindholm Rsch., Eugene, 2001—. Guest lectr. Nat. Inst. Devel. Adminstrn., Bangkok, Thailand, 1989; pres. Rubicon Inst., Eugene, 1988—; adj. asst. prof. U. Oreg., Eugene, 1988—. Campaign co-chmn. Lane C.C. Advocates, Eugene, 1988; coord., planner numerous state Rep. Campaigns, Oreg., 1988—; campaign mgr. Jack Roberts for Oreg. State Labor Commn., 1994; mem. staff Oreg. Senate Rep. Office, 1989-90; precinct committeeperson Oreg. Rep. Party, 1987-92, 94—; bd. dirs. Rubicon Soc., Eugene, 1987—, pres., 1993-98. Republican. Lutheran. Home: 3335 Bardell Ave Eugene OR 97401-8021

LINDLEY, CHARLES ALEXANDER, aerospace engineer, consultant; b. Union City, Ind., May 12, 1924; s. Charley Alexander and Thursetta (Hall) Lindley; m. Agnes Stucker, Jan. 17, 1946 (dec. July 1997); children: Susan Marie, Charles A.(dec.). BS and MS in Aero. Engring., Ohio State U., 1949; PhD in Aeronautics, Calif. Inst. Tech., 1956. Instr. Ohio State U., Columbus, 1947—49; compressor aerodynamicist Thompson Aircraft Products, Euclid, Ohio, 1949—52, turbomachinery cons., 1952—55; rsch. cons. The Marquardt Corp., Van Nuys, Calif., 1955—63; vehicle tech. The Aerospace Corp., El Segundo, Calif., 1963—85, sr. scientist threat analysis, 1985—92, cons., 1992—. Guest lectr., cons. UCLA and U. Calif.-Santa Barbara, 1961—78. Contbr. articles to profl. jours. Chmn. bd. dirs. Premier Chorale and San Fernando Valley Master Chorale, LA, 2001—. 2nd lt. Signal Corps US Army, 1943—46., Guggenheim Fellow, 1952—55. Achievements include over 100 inventions including liquid air cycle, air collection systems, reuseable boosters, scramjets, external burning ramjets, artificial gravity systems, wind & solar energy, space reconnaissance. Avocations: singing, vocal music, model aircraft. Home: 18900 Pasadero Dr Tarzana CA 91356 Office Phone: 818-342-8589. Personal E-mail: 74537.3706@compuserve.com.

LINDLEY, DAVID, mechanical engineer; b. June 26, 1939; s. William and Millicent (Caine) Lindley; m. Dorothy Tumock, July 14, 1962; children: Simon David(dec.), Nicolas Rhys, Jonathan Peter, Sarah Jane. BSc, U. Salford, 1962; PhD, U. Wales, 1966; cert. advanced engring. design, U. Cambridge, 1967. Apprentice, mgr. Pump Exptl. Dept. Mather & Platt Ltd., Manchester, England, 1955-63; head Turbo Machinery Aerothermodynamics Dept. CEGB, 1967-70; sr. lectr. mech. engring. U. Canterbury, New Zealand, 1970-78; mgr. Energy Sys. Group Jet Propulsion Lab. Calif. Inst. Tech., 1975-76; mng. dir. Wind Energy Group Ltd., 1979-91; dir. Taylor Woodrow plc Group Cos., 1984-91; mng. dir. Nat. Wind Power Ltd., Buckinghamshire, England, 1991-96, Lindley Assocs. Ltd., Buckinghamshire, 1996—; chmn. Ocean Power Delivery Ltd., 2002—; dir. KP Renewables plc, London, 2004—. Chmn. Brit. Wind Energy Assn., 1982, 94; mem. Adv. Coun. for R&D for Fuel and Power, 1986—92, Adv. Coun. SAM Private Equity Sustainability Fund II, Switzerland, 2006—; dir., pres. European Wind Energy Assn., 1986—89; mem. Renewable Energy Adv. Group, London, 1991—92; vis. prof. Loughborough U. Tech., 1994—2003, U. Nottingham, 1997—2003; Royal Acad. Engring. vis. prof. De Montfort U., 1994—; academician The Russian Internat. Higher Edn. Acad. Scis., 1994; mem. edn. program exec. bd. The Royal Acad. Engring., 2000—. Mem. adv. council SAM Private Equity Sustainability Fund II, Switzerland, 2006—. Decorated officer Brit. Empire, 1997; recipient James Watt medal Inst. Civil Engrs., 1987, Stephenson medal U. Newcastle, 1989, Melchett medal Inst. Energy, 1990, BWEA Industry award, 1995, BWEA Pres. award, 1996. Fellow: Royal Meteorol. Soc., Royal Acad. Engring., Instn. Mech. Engrs., Royal Soc. Arts, Manufacture and Commerce; mem.: ASME, AIAA. Avocations: walking, skiing, sailing, photography, reading. Office: Lindley Assocs Ltd Woodfield Farm Ln Jordans Beaconsfield Bucks HP9 2UP England Office Phone: 44-1494-676570. Personal E-mail: DavidLindleyOBE@aol.com.

LINDLEY, DAVID MORRISON, lawyer; b. Montclair, NJ, June 17, 1949; s. Dwight Newton and Janie (Morrison) L.; m. Jane Cowan von der Heyde, June 12, 1971; children: Camilla von der Heyde, Carolyn Field. AB, Columbia Coll., 1971; JD, Harvard U., 1974. Bar: N.J. 1974, U.S. Dist. Ct. N.J. 1974, N.Y. 1976,U.S. Dist. Ct. (so. and ea. dists.) N.Y. 1977, U.S. Ct. Appeals (1st cir.) 1983, U.S. Ct. Appeals (2d cir.) 1991. Assoc. McCarter & English, Newark, 1974-77, Hale Russell & Gray, NYC, 1977-82, ptnr., 1983-85, Winthrop Stimson Putnam & Roberts, NYC, 1985—, Pillsbury Winthrop Shaw Pittman LLP, NYC. Contbr. Mem. ABA (co-chair internat. law and practice sect. litig. com.), Assn. Bar NYC, NY State Bar Assn., Fellows Am. Bar Found. Episcopalian. Office: Pillsbury Winthrop Shaw Pittman LLP 1540 Broadway New York NY 10036-4039 Office Fax: 212-858-1500. Business E-Mail: david.lindley@pillsburylaw.com.

LINDLEY, F(RANCIS) HAYNES, JR., foundation executive, lawyer; b. LA, Oct. 15, 1945; s. Francis Haynes and Grace Nelson (McCanne) L.; 1 child, Anne Hollinger Lindley. BA, Claremont Men's Coll., Calif., 1967; MFA, Claremont Grad. Sch., Calif., 1972; JD, Southwestern U., L.A., 1976. Bar: Calif. 1976, U.S. Supreme Ct. 1980. Deputy pub. defender Office of Pub. Defender, LA, 1977-79; staff atty., Dept. Trial Counsel The State Bar of Calif., LA, 1979-81; pvt. practice, 1981-90; pres. John Randolph Haynes and Dora Haynes Found., LA, 1987-97, pres. emeritus, 1997—. Trustee John Randolph Haynes and Dora Haynes Found., L.A., 1978—. Bd. dirs. TreePeople, L.A., 1985-87, So. Calif. Assn. Philanthropy, L.A., 1985-89; mem. bd. fellows Claremont (Calif.) U. Ctr. and Grad. Sch., 1987—2006; bd. dirs. Marin Agrl. Land Trust, 1995-2005, Family and Children Law Ctr., Marin County, 2006—. Recipient Disting. Svc. award The Claremont (Calif.) Grad. Sch., 1994. Avocations: sailing, art history, guitar. Home: PO Box 3058 Sausalito CA 94966-3058 Office: John Randolph Haynes & Dora Haynes Found 888 W 6th St Ste 1150 Los Angeles CA 90017-2737 Office Phone: 213-623-9151.

LINDLEY, HAMILTON P., lawyer; s. Philip E. and Maroline H. Lindley; m. Bonnie Houghtaling, June 19, 2004. BBA, Baylor U., Waco, Tex., 1996—2000, JD, 2000—04. Bar: Supreme Ct. Tex. 2004. Atty. Provost Umphrey, Dallas, 2004—. State chmn. Assn. Trial Lawyers Am. Recipient Am. Registry of Outstanding Profls. Mem.: ABA, Dallas Assn. Young Lawyers, Am. Trial Lawyers (assoc.), Dallas Bar Assn. (assoc.). Office: Provost Umphrey 3232 McKinney Ste 700 Dallas TX 75204 Home Phone: 214-827-0450; Office Phone: 214-744-3000. Office Fax: 214-744-3015. Business E-Mail: hlindley@provostumphrey.com.

LINDLEY, JAMES GUNN, JR., neurosurgeon; b. Key West, Fla., Jan. 23, 1956; s. James Gunn Lindley Sr. and Jane Kennedy Lindley; m. Stephanie Curl, July 3, 1999; children: Jennifer Anne, James Gunn III. BS in Chemistry, East Carolina U., Greenville, NC, 1979; MD, Med. U. SC, Charleston, 1984. Diplomate Am. Bd. of Neurol. Surgeons, 1993. Intern in gen. surgery Wake Forest U. Med. Ctr., 1984, resident in neurol. surgery, 1985—90; neurosurgeon Neurol. Inst. of Savannah, Ga., 1990—. Chief of surgery St. Joseph's Hosp., Savannah, Ga., 2003—05, vice chief of staff, 2005—07, chief of staff, 2007—. Fellow: Am. Coll. Surgeons; mem.: AMA, N.Am. Spine Soc., Spine Arthroplasty Soc., Am. Acad. of Spine Physicians, Ga. Med. Soc., Med. Assn. of Ga., Ga. Neurosurgical Soc. (sci. program chmn. 1998—99), So. Neurosurgical Soc. (v.p. 2001—02), Congress of Neurol. Surgeons, Am. Assn. of Neurol. Surgeons. Republican. Episcopalian. Office: Neurol Inst Savannah 4 Jackson Blvd Savannah GA 31405 Home Phone: 912-356-0183.

LINDNER, CARL H., III, insurance company executive; s. Carl H. Lindner, Jr. and Edith Lindner. With Great Am. Ins. Co. (subs. Am. Fin. Group Inc.), 1975—, various ins. ops. positions, 1987—, now vice chmn., pres.; co-pres. Am. Fin. Group, 1996—2005, co-CEO, co-pres., 2005—. Office: Am Fin Group Inc 1 E 4th St Cincinnati OH 45202

LINDNER, CARL HENRY, JR., insurance company executive, professional sports team owner; b. Dayton, Ohio, Apr. 22, 1919; s. Carl Henry and Clara (Serrer) Lindner; m. Edyth Bailey, Dec. 31, 1953; children: Carl Henry III, Stephen Craig, Keith Edward. HHD (hon.), Xavier U., 1991. Co-founder United Dairy Farmers, 1940; pres. Am. Fin. Group, Cin., 1959—84, chmn., 1959—, CEO, 1984—2005; owner, CEO Cin. Reds, 1999—. Chmn. Great Am. Fin. Resources, Inc., Great Am. Ins. Group. Bd. advisors Bus. Adminstrn. Coll., U. Cin. Named one of Forbes' Richest Americans, 2006; recipient Heritage award, Urban League of Greater Cin., 1997. Republican. Baptist. Office: Am Fin Group 1 E 4th St Cincinnati OH 45202-3717*

LINDNER, RICHARD G., telecommunications industry executive; b. St. Louis; BSBA, U. Mo., St. Louis; grad. advanced mgmt. prog. in telecom., UCLA. Audit supr. Peat, Marwick, Mitchell & Co.; sr. v.p., CFO Turco Devel. Co.; contr. Southwestern Bell Telecom., 1986—90; dir. investor rels. SBC, 1990—91; dir. fin. SBC Internat., 1991—92; contr. SBC Comm., 1992—96; v.p., CFO Southwestern Bell Tel., San Antonio, 1996—99; pres., CEO Southwestern Bell Wireless, 1999; sr. v.p., COO SBC Wireless Inc., 1999—2000; CFO Cingular Wireless, Atlanta, 2000—04; sr. exec. v.p., CFO SBC Comm., San Antonio, 2004—05, AT&T Inc. (merger of SBC Comm. & AT&T Corp.), San Antonio, 2005—. Bd. mem. Sabre Holdings Corp., 2002—. Mailing: AT&T Inc 175 E Houston St PO Box 2933 San Antonio TX 78299-2933*

LINDNER, S(TEPHEN) CRAIG, insurance company executive; s. Carl H. Lindner Jr. and Edith Lindner. BBA, U. Cinn., 1977. With Am. Fin. Group Inc., Cin., 1977—, co-pres., 1996, co-CEO, 2005—. Pres., CEO Great Am. Fin. Resources; pres. Am. Money Mgmt. Corp. Office: Am Fin Group Inc 1 E 4th St Cincinnati OH 45202-3717*

LINDO, ALLEN PINEDA (APL.DE.AP), rap artist; b. Angeles City, Philippines, Nov. 28, 1974; arrived in U.S.A., 1988; Founding mem. band Atban Klann, 1992—95, band Black Eyed Peas, 1998—. Singer: (albums) Behind the Front, 1998, Bridging the Gap, 2000, Elephunk, 2003, Monkey Business, 2005 (Favorite Rap/Hip-Hop Album, Am. Music Awards, 2006), (songs) Joints & Jams, 1998, Where is the Love? (feat. Justin Timberlake), 2003, Shut Up, 2003, Hey Mama, 2004 (MTV Music Video award), The Apl Song, 2004, Let's Get It Started, 2004 (Grammy, Best Rap Performance, 2005), Don't Lie, 2005, Don't Phunk with My Heart, 2005 (Grammy award, Best Rap Group Performance, 2006), My Humps, 2005 (MTV Video Music award for Best Hip-Hop Video, 2006). Recipient MTV Europe award for Best Pop Act (with Black Eyed Peas), 2004, 2005, Favorite Pop Group & Rap Group, Am. Music Awards, 2005, Favorite Soul/Rhythm & Blues Grp., 2006, Favorite Rap/Hip-Hop Grp., 2006.*

LINDO, DELROY, actor; b. London, Nov. 18, 1952; m. Neshormeh Lindo; 1 child, Damiri. Actor (films) Find the Lady, 1976, Voice of the Fugitive, 1978, More American Graffiti, 1979, The Blood of Heroes, 1988, Mountains of the Moon, 1990, Bright Angel, 1991, The Hard Way, 1991, Malcolm X, 1992, Bound by Honor, 1993, Mr. Jones, 1993, Crooklyn, 1994, Congo, 1995, Clockers, 1995, Get Shorty, 1995, Broken Arrow, 1996, Feeling Minnesota, 1996, The Winner, 1996, L'Exil du roi Behanzin, 1996, Ransom, 1996, The Devil's Advocate, 1997, A Life Less Ordinary, 1997, Glory and Honor, 1998, Strange Justice, 1999, Romeo Must Die, 1999, Book of Stars, 1999, Pros & Cons, 1999, Cider House Rules, 1999, Gone in Sixty Seconds, 2000, Last Castle, 2001, Heist, 2001, The One, 2001, The Core, 2003, Wondrous Oblivion, 2003, Sahara, 2005, Domino, 2005; (TV movies) Perfect Witness, 1989, Soul of the Game, 1996 First-Time Felon, 1997, Glory & Honor, 1998, Strange Justice, 1999, Profoundly Normal, 2003, Lackawanna Blues, 2005, The Exonerated, 2005; (TV series) Kidnapped, 2006-; (TV appearances) Beauty and the Beast, 1987, A Man Called Hawk, 1989, (voice only) The Simpsons, 2002 Office: William Morris Agy One William Morris Pl Beverly Hills CA 90212

LINDO, STEPHEN T., lawyer; b. Watertown, NY, July 30, 1947; AB, Princeton U., 1969; JD, Boston U., 1974; LLM in Taxation, NYU, 1980. Bar: NY 1975. Ptnr., chair Exec. Compensation and Employee Benefits Dept. Willkie Farr & Gallagher LLP, NYC. Mem. N.Y. State Bar Assn. (co-chmn. nonqualified employee benefits com. tax sect. 1991-94). Office: Willkie Farr & Gallagher 787 Seventh Ave New York NY 10019-6099 Office Phone: 212-728-8242. Business E-Mail: slindo@willkie.com.

LINDQUIST, LEE A., geriatrician, educator; BS, Loyola U., Chicago, 1996; MD, Northwestern U. Med. Sch., 2000; MPH, Northwestern U., 2005. Diplomate Am. Bd. Internal Medicine, 2000, cert. Geriatric Medicine Am. Bd. Internal Medicine, 2004. Instr. medicine Northwestern U. Med. Sch., Chgo., 2003—05, asst. prof. medicine, 2005—. Founding mem. Northwestern Ctr. Patient Safety; assoc. clin. program dir. Northwestern Geriatrics; media spokesperson Am. Geriatrics Soc. Grantee, Nat. Inst. Health Rsch.:, Augusta Webster Fellowship. Mem.: ACP (assoc.), Soc. Gen. Internal Medicine (assoc.), Am. Geriat. Soc. (assoc.). Achievements include development of cruise ships as alternatives to assisted living facilities; research in geriatric medicine, assisted living alternative, patient safety and transitional care of the elderly. Office: Northwestern Univ Med Sch 675 N St Clair Ste 14-200 Chicago IL 60611 Office Phone: 312-695-4525. Office Fax: 312-695-6060. E-mail: lal425@md.northwestern.edu.

LINDQUIST, LOUIS WILLIAM, artist, researcher, writer; b. Boise, Idaho, June 26, 1944; s. Louis William and Bessie (Newman) L.; divorced; children: Jessica Ann Alexandra, Jason Ryan Louis. BS in Anthropology, U. Oreg., 1968; postgrad., Portland State U., 1974-78. Researcher, co-writer with Asher Lee, Portland, Oreg., 1977-80; freelance artist, painter, sculptor Oreg., 1980-91, 98-99. Sgt. U.S. Army, 1968-71, Vietnam. Mem.: NRA, AAAS, Am. Anthropol. Assn. Republican. Avocations: reading, beachcombing, listening to classical, jazz and native North American music. Home and Office: PO Box 991 Bandon OR 97411-0991

LINDQUIST, MICHAEL ADRIAN, career military officer; b. Cheyenne, Wyo., Nov. 12, 1946; s. Swen George and Beryl Esme (Edwards) L.; m. Frances Eleanor Arnold, Apr. 14, 1968 (div. Aug. 20, 2003); children: Michella, Michael, Patricia. BS in Econs., U. Tampa, 1975; MS in Logistics Mgmt., Fla. Inst. Technology, Melbourne, 1985; EdD in Orgnl. Leadership, U. Sarasota, 2002. Enlisted U.S. Army, 1966, advanced through grades to col., staff officer 3d Support Command Frankfurt, West Germany, 1980-83, exec. officer 8th Maintenance Group Hanau, West Germany, 1983-85, cmdr. 601st Ord BN Aberdeen Proving Ground, Md., 1986-88, dep. dir. tests Test & Evaluation Command, 1988-89, action officer The Joint Staff Pentagon, 1990-93, comdr. Tobyhanna (Pa.) Army Depot, 1993-95, comdr. Combat Equipment Group Asia Charleston, SC, 1995-97; cons. Adrian Cons., Charleston, 1998—; prof. U. Phoenix, 2002—, lead faculty, area chair, 2003—; former exec. dir. Congl. Medal of Honor Soc. Decorated Legion of Merit (three awards), Bronze Star Medal, Defense Meritorious Svc. Medal, Meritorious Svc.Medal with three oak leaf clusters, seven awards of Air Medal, Army Commendation Medal with two oak leaf clusters. Mem. Assn. U.S. Army, VFW, Ret. Officers Assn., Ordnance Assn., Mil. Order of World Wars. Avocations: golf, coin collecting/numismatics, stamp collecting/philately. Personal E-mail: dr_col_mal@earthlink.net. Business E-Mail: adrianconsulting@earthlink.net.

LINDQUIST, SUSAN LEE, biology and microbiology professor; b. June 5, 1949; BA in Microbiology with honors, U. Ill., 1971; PhD in Biology, Harvard U., 1976. Asst. prof. dept. molecular biology U. Chgo., 1978-84, assoc. prof., 1984—99, full prof., 1988, Albert D. Lasker prof. med. sciences, 1999—2001, investigator Howard Hughes Med. Inst., 1988—2001; dir. Whitehead Inst. Biomedical Rsch., Cambridge, Mass., 2001—04, mem., 2001—; prof. biology MIT, Cambridge, Mass., 2001—; investigator Howard Hughes Med. Inst., 2006—. Mem. com. genetics, com. devel. biology U. Chgo., 1999—; cons. Mus. Sci. & Industry, Chgo., 1983-87; vis. scholar Cambridge U., 1983; cons., prin. in film Lights Breaking, 1985; mem. sci. adv. com. Helen Hay Whitney Found., 1997—; bd. dirs. Johnson & Johnson, 2004-; lectr. in field. Co-editor: The Stress Induced Proteins, 1988, Heat Shock, 1990; assoc. editor The New Biologist, 1991-93; mem. editl. bd. Cell Regulation, 1989—, Molecular and Cell Biology, 1984—, Gene Expression, 1994-95, Cell Stress and Chaperones, 1995—, Current Biology, 1996—, Molecular Biology of the Cell, 1996—; monitoring editor Jour. Cell Biology, 1993—; contbr. articles to profl. jours. Teaching fellow Harvard U., 1973-74, Postdoctoral fellow Am. Cancer Soc., 1976-78, U. Chgo.; recipient Novartis Drew award in Biomedical Rsch., 2000, Dickson prize in Medicine, 2003, Sigma Xi William Procter prize for Scientific Achievement, 2006, Emil Christian Hansen Gold medal, 2006, U. Ill. Alumni Achievement award, 2006; named one of Top 50 Women Scientists, Discover Mag., 2002. Fellow Am. Acad. Microbiology, AAAS, NAS, Am. Acad. Arts and Sci.; mem. Am. Soc. Cell Biology, Am. Soc. Microbiology, Fedn. Am. Scientists for Exptl. Biology, Genetics Soc. Am. (former sec.), Molecular Medicine Soc., Inst. Medicine. Achievements include research in the impact of protein-conformational changes on diverse processes in cellular and organismal biology. Office: Whitehead Inst Nine Cambridge Ctr Cambridge MA 02142-1479 Office Phone: 617-258-5184. E-mail: lindquist_admin@wi.mit.edu.*

LINDQVIST, GUNNAR JAN, management consultant, international trade consultant; b. Stockholm, July 12, 1950; s. Bengt Olof Sigfrid and Greta (Nyberg) L.; m. Mary Grady, 1984; children: Greta Louise, Mary Kerstin. Grad. with honors, Stockholm Sch. Econs., 1974. Lic. realtor, Ga. Asst. acctg. mgr. Granges Shipping, Stockholm, 1975-77; asst. budget mgr. Dynapac AB, Stockholm, 1978-79; asst. treas., contr. Peeples Industries, Savannah, Ga., 1980-83; owner, pres. Cash Mgmt., Inc., Savannah, Ga., 1983—; owner iTech for Bus., LLC, Savannah, Ga., 2002—. Mem. The Carpenter's Order, Stockholm, 1978—. Served with Swedish Army. Mem. Scandinavian-Am. Found. Ga. (bd. govs. 1988-2002), Savannah Area C. of C. (chmn. subcom. Small Bus. Coun. 1984-89), Swedish-Am. C. of C., Savannah Yacht Club. Home and Office: 6800 Sandnettles Dr Savannah GA 31410-2317

LINDROS, ERIC, professional hockey player; b. London, Ont., Can., Feb. 28, 1973; s. Carl and Bonnie Lindros. Student, York U., Toronto. Center Oshawa Generals, 1989—92, Phila. Flyers, 1992—2000, NY Rangers, 2001—04, Toronto Maple Leafs, 2005—06, Dallas Stars, 2006—. Player NHL All-Star Game, 1994, 1997—2000, 2002; mem. Team Can., Olympic Games, Albertville, France, 1992, Nagano, Japan, 98, Salt Lake City, 2002. Named MVP, World Jr. Hockey Championships, 1990, Ont. Jr. Hockey Assn., 1991, Player of Yr., Can. Hockey League, 1991; named to All-Rookie Team, NHL, 1993, Second All-Star Team, 1996; recipient Plus/Minus award, Can. Hockey League, 1991, Red Tilson Trophy, 1991, Eddie Powers Meml. Trophy, 1991, Hart Trophy, 1995, Lester B. Pearson Award, NHL, 1995. Achievements include being a member of silver medal Canadian Hockey team, Albertville Olympic Games, 1992, gold medal Canadian Hockey team, Salt Lake City Olympic Games, 2002. Office: Dallas Stars 2601 Avenue of the Stars Frisco TX 75034

LINDROTH, LINDA (LINDA HAMMER), artist, writer, curator; b. Miami, Sept. 4, 1946; d. Mark Roger and Mae Lang Hammer; m. David George Lindroth, May 26, 1968 (div. Mar. 1985); m. Craig David Newick, June 6, 1987; 1 child, Zachary Eran Newick. BA in Art, Douglass Coll., 1968; studied with Gordon Matta-Clark, Rutgers U., 1975; studied with Garry Winogrand, NYC, 1976; MFA in Art, Rutgers U., 1979; master class in non-fiction writing, Yale U., 1997. Adj. asst. prof. liberal arts Quinnipiac Coll., Hamden, Conn., 1998—. editor: Co-author, Virtual Vintage: The Insider's Guide to Buyin and Selling Fashion Online. Exhibitions include Aetna Gallery, 1987, 1989, 1991, Franklin Furnace, N.Y.C., 1977, Conn. Commn. Arts, Hartford, 1985, 1996, Aldrich Mus. Contemporary Art, Ridgefield, Conn., 1987, 1987, Downey Mus. Art, Calif., 1989, Zimmerlo Art Mus. Rutgers U., 1989, Wesleyan U. Ctr. for Arts, 1990, Boston Pub. Libr., 1991, John Michael Kohler Art Ctr., Sheboygan, Wis., 1992, Joseloff Gallery U., Hartford, 1994, Artspace, New Haven, 1991, 1992, 1993, 1994, 1995, DeCordova Mus., Lincoln, Mass., 1995, Urban Glass, Bklyn., 1996, U. Conn. Atrium Gallery, 1999, Creative Arts Workship, 1999, New Haven Hist. Soc., 1999, Stedman Gallery, 1999, Rutgers U., 1999, others, Represented in permanent collections The Mus. Modern Art, N.Y.C., The Met. Mus. Art, The Mus. City of N.Y., Internat. Polaroid Collection/Artist Program, N.J. State Mus., Trenton, The Bibliotheque Nationale, Paris, Ctr. Creative Photography, Tucson, The Newark Mus., The Jane Voorhees Zimmerli Art Mus., New Brunswick, N.J., High Mus. Art, Atlanta, Yale U., Mus. d'art et d'histoire, Fribourg, Switzerland; co-author: Out of Bounds, 1994 (1st prize), Virtual Vintage, 2002. Dir. Artspace, Inc., New Haven; mem. Mayor's Task Force on Pub. Art, New Haven. Recipient Ann. Design Rev. award ID Mag., 1990, 91, 93, Honorable Mention, Nat. Peace Garden Design Competition, 1989, Pitts. Corning Archtl. Design Competition, 1988, Individual Artist fellow N.J. State Coun. on Arts, 1974-75, 83-84, Wilmer Shields Rich award Coun. Founds., 1995, Printing Industry Am. award, 1995; grantee Found. Contemporary Performance Arts, Inc., 1989, 90, Fission Fusion NEA InterArts, 1989, New Eng. Found. for Arts, 1992, Fairfield U., 1995, Ruth Chenven Found., NYC, 1997, Ruth Chevnen Found., 1997, fellowship grantee in sculpture Conn. Commn. on the Arts, 2000, Te Found. Grant, 2002, Photography grantee Conn. Commn. on Culture and Tourism, 2006; Conn. Commn. Arts fellow, 1995, New Eng. Found. Arts/NEA Regional Photography fellow, 1995-96; Emerging Voices lectr. Arch. League of NY, 1996. Studio: 219 Livingston St New Haven CT 06511-2209

LINDSAY, DIANNA MARIE, educational administrator; b. Boston, Dec. 7, 1948; d. Albert Joseph and June Hazelton Raggi; m. James William Lindsay III, Feb. 14, 1981. BA in Anthropology, Ea. Nazarene Coll., 1971; MEd in Curriculum and Instrn., Wright State U., 1973, MA in Social Studies Edn., 1974, MEd in Edn. Adminstrn., 1977; EdD in Urban History, Ball State U., 1976; MA in Counseling, U. Dayton, 2000. Supr. social edn. Ohio Dept. Edn., Columbus, 1976-77; asst. prin. Orange City Schs., Pepper Pike, Ohio, 1977-79; prin. North Olmsted (Ohio) Jr. High Sch., 1979-81; dir. secondary edn. North Olmsted City Schs., 1981-82; supt. Copley (Ohio)-Fairlawn City Schs., 1982-85; prin. North Olmsted High Sch., 1985-89, New Trier High Sch., Winnetka, Ill., 1989-96, Worthington Kilbourne H.S., Columbus, Ohio, 1996-2001; headmaster Columbus Jewish Day Sch., New Albany, Ohio, 2001—03; prin. Ridgefield H.S., Ridgefield, Conn., 2003—. Bd. dirs. Harvard Prins. Ctr., Cambridge, Mass., adj. prof. ednl. adminstrn., Grad. Sch. Edn., U. Dayton, Bexley, OH Contbr. articles to profl. jours. Bd. dirs. Nat. PTA, Chgo., 1987-89 (Educator of Yr. 1989), Found. Human Potential, Chgo.,; bd. trustee Columbus Jewish Country Day Sch. Named Prin. of Yr. Ohio Art Tchrs., 1989, one of 100 Up and Coming Educators, Exec. Educator Mag., 1988, Milken Educator of the Yr. Ohio, 1999; recipient John Vaughn Achievements in Edn. North Cen. Assn., 1988; named Ohio Prin. of Yr, 2000. Mem. AAUW, Ill. Tchrs. Fgn. Lang., Rotary Internat., Phi Delta Kappa. Methodist. Avocations: stained glass, reading, travel, biking, harpist. Office: Ridgefield HS 700 N Salem Rd Ridgefield CT 06877 E-mail: dlindsay@ridgefield.org.

LINDSAY, GEORGE CARROLL, former museum director; b. Cochranville, Pa., Sept. 28, 1928; s. J. George and M. Elizabeth (Copeland) L.; m. Mary-Edythe Shelley, June 27, 1953. BA, Franklin and Marshall Coll., 1950; student, Dickinson Sch. Law, 1950-53; MA (Wintherthur fellow early Am. culture 1953-55), U. Del., 1955. Asst. to dir. Henry Francis du Pont Wintherthur Mus., Del., 1955-56; asst. curator ethnology Smithsonian Instn., 1956-57, asso. curator cultural history, 1957-58, curator mus. service, 1958-66; dir. mus. services N.Y. State Mus., 1966-81, dir., 1981-83, dir. planning and program devel., 1983-86; exec. dir. Vanderbilt Mus., 1986-89, ret., 1989. Lectr. early Am. decorative arts and architecture; cons. in field; v.p. Alexandria Assn., Va., 1961-62, pres., 1962-63; programming com. Greater Washington Ednl. TV Assn., 1965-66; com. furnishing ofcl. reception room State Dept., 1960-75 Bd. dirs. Menands Pub. Libr., NY, 1970-86, Albany Symphony Orch., 1969-72, ARC, Albany, 1977-86; active Strasburg Borough Coun., Pa., 1992-96, pres., 1994-95; planning commn. Strasburg Boro, 1995—2003; trustee Octoraro Covenanter Presbyn. Ch., 1993—, Strasburg Heritage Soc., 1997—. Mem. Am. Assn. Mus. (coun. 1969-72, v.p. 1970-71, chmn. profl. rels. com. 1974-80), N.Y. State Assn. Mus. (sec. 1968-77, pres. 1977-79, coun. 1985-89), N.E. Mus. Conf. (bd. govs. 1982-85, chmn. long range planning com. 1983-85), St. Andrew's Soc. (pres. Albany 1983-85), St. Andrew's Soc. Phila. Mem. Soc. Of Friends. Address: 255 Wallingford Rd Strasburg PA 17579-1448

LINDSAY, GEORGE PETER, lawyer; b. Bklyn., Feb. 22, 1948; s. Charles Joseph and Marie Antionette (Faraone) Lindsay; m. Sharon Winnett, Sept. 8, 1973; children: William Charles, Kimberly Michelle. BA, Columbia U., 1969; JD, Harvard U., 1973. Bar: N.Y. 1974, Mass. 1985, U.S. Dist. Ct. (so. dist.) N.Y. 1974, U.S. Ct. Appeals (2d cir.) 1975. Assoc. White & Case, NYC, 1973-82; ptnr. Miller, Wrubel & Dubroff, NYC, 1982-83, Sullivan & Worcester LLP, NYC, 1983—. Mem. ABA, Assn. Bar City of N.Y., N.Y. State Bar Assn., Internat. Bar Assn. Office: Sullivan & Worcester LLP 1290 Avenue of Americas 29th Fl New York NY 10104 Business E-Mail: glindsay@sandw.com.

LINDSAY, LESLIE, packaging engineer; b. Amsterdam, NY, Oct. 30, 1960; d. R. Gardner and Dorothy (Loucks) Lindsay. BA in Advt., Mich. State U., 1981, BS in Package Engring., 1982. Registered profl. engr. in packaging. Constrn. insp. NY State Dept. Transp., Albany, 1983; sr. package design engr. Wang Labs., Inc., Lowell, Mass., 1983—90; sr. packaging engr. Apple Computer, Inc., Cupertino, Calif., 1990—97, Bose Corp., Framingham, Mass., 1997—2002, Dell, Inc., Austin, Tex., 2006—; dir. packaging Syratech Corp., East Boston, Mass., 2003—05; mgr. tech. bus. Markson Rosenthal & Co., Maynard, Mass., 2005—06; sr. packaging engr. Dell, Inc., 2006—. Conf. spkr. Internat. Safe Transit Assn., 1994; judge AmeriStar, 1999, 2000. Staff editor: Packaging Horizons Mag. Recipient Silver Ameristar award for Electronics Packaging, 1993, 2000, ID Mag. Packaging award, 1993, Ameristar Judges award for Merit, 1995; N.Y. State Regents scholar, 1977. Mem.: Molded Pulp Environ. Packaging Assn. (seminar spkr. 1997, founding bd. dirs.), Inst. Packaging Profls. (mem. reduction, reuse, and recycling protective packaging task group, cert.), Women in Packaging, Wang Ultimate Frisbee (social chmn. 1986—89), Am. Contract Bridge League, Boston Women's Rugby Club (tour chmn. 1985). Home: 15708 Belfin Dr Austin TX 78717-3977 Office Phone: 512-723-9745. Personal E-mail: leslie.lindsay@rcn.com.

LINDSAY, MICHAEL ANTHONY, lawyer; b. Omaha, Nebr., May 9, 1958; s. William J. and Mary F. Lindsay. BA summa cum laude, Marquette U., 1980; degree in Gen. Studies with first class honors, London Sch. Econ., 1980; JD cum laude, U. Chgo., 1983. Bar: Minn. 1985, U.S. Dist. Ct. Minn. 1985. Law clk. to judge Richard Posner U.S. Ct. Appeals, Chgo., 1983-84; assoc. Dorsey & Whitney, Mpls., 1985-90, ptnr., trial practice group, 1991—, and co-chmn., anti-trust group. Adj. prof. Law Sch. Hamline U., St. Paul, 1988-99, U. St. Thomas, Mpls., Minn., 2002—. Pres. Prevention Alliance, Mpls., 1991-96. Mem.: Phi Beta Kappa, Order of Coif. Office: Dorsey & Whitney Ste 1500 50 S Sixth St Minneapolis MN 55402-1498 Office Phone: 612-340-7819. Office Fax: 612-340-2868. Business E-Mail: lindsay.michael@dorsey.com.

LINDSAY, REGINALD CARL, judge; b. Birmingham, Ala., Mar. 19, 1945; s. Richard and Louise L.; m. Cheryl E. Hartgrove, Aug. 15, 1970. Cert., U. Valencia, 1966; AB in Polit. Sci. cum laude, Morehouse Coll., 1967; JD, Harvard U., 1970; LLD (hon.), New Eng. Sch. Law, 2003. Bar: Mass. 1971, US Ct. Appeals (1st cir.) 1971. Assoc. Hill & Barlow, 1970-75, 78-79, ptnr., 1979-93; judge US Dist. Ct. Mass., Boston, 1994—. Arbitrator, mem. comml. arbitration panel Am. Arbitration Assn., 1994—; commr. Mass. Dept. Pub. Utilities, Boston, 1975-77; pres. adv. bd. Mus. of Nat. Center of Afro-Am. Artists, 1975-81, v.p., 1981—; trustee Thompson Islands Edn. Center, Boston, 1975-81; bd. dirs. United Way of Mass. Bay, 1981-84, Morgan Meml. Goodwill Industries, Boston, 1992—. Ptnrs. for Youth with Disabilities, Boston; mem. Nat. Consumer Law Ctr. (bd. dirs.), Mass. Commn. on Jud. Conduct, 1982-88; trustee Newton (Mass.)-Wellesley Hosp. Recipient Ruffin-Fenwick Trailblazer award Harvard Black Law Students Assn., 1994, Amanda V. Houston cmty. svc. award Boston Coll., 1998, Frederick E. Berry Expanding Ind. award Easter Seals, 1999, Heroes Among Us award Boston Celtics, 2001, Leadership award New Eng. Black Law Students Assn., 2001, N. Neal Pike prize N. Neal Pike Inst. Boston U. Sch. Law, 2005. Mem. ABA, Nat. Bar Found., Mass. Bar Assn., Boston Bar Assn. (coun. 1977—, citation jud. excellence 1999), Pi Sigma Alpha, Phi Beta Kappa. Office: 1 Courthouse Way Ste 5130 Boston MA 02210-3007

LINDSAY, ROGER ALEXANDER (BARON OF CRAIGHALL), investment executive; b. Dundee, Scotland, Feb. 18, 1941; s. Archibald Carswell Lindsay and Edith Paterson Bissett. Student, The Morgan Acad., Dundee, U. St. Andrews, Scotland. Asst. acct., office mgr. Andrew G. Kidd Ltd., Dundee, 1964-66; head office acct. Associated British Foods Ltd., London, 1966-71; sec., treas. Wittington Investments, Ltd., Toronto, 1971-95; exec. v.p. Wittington Investments Ltd., Toronto, 1991-95; pres. Fort House Investments, Toronto, 1989. Bd. dirs. United World Coll. Internat. Can., Inc., The W. Garfield Weston Found., Benedictine Heritage Ltd.; past chair St. John Coun. Ont. Past moderator Presbytery of East Toronto; aide-de camp Lt. Gov. of Ont.; past chair bd. govs. Knox Coll. U. Toronto; chief of protocol Priory Coun. of Can. Venerable Order of St. John. Decorated comdr. Venerable Order Hosp. St. John. Fellow Chartered Inst. Mgmt., Inst. Dirs., Soc. Antiquaries Scotland; mem. Inst. Chartered Accts. Scotland, Royal Overseas League, The Nat. Club (Toronto). Avocations: heraldry, antique silver, genealogy. Office: Fort House Investments 150 Heath St W Ste 1302 Toronto ON Canada M4V 2Y4 Office Phone: 416-487-9291. E-mail: fhilral@aol.com.

LINDSAY, RONALD THOMAS, lawyer, paper company executive; b. 1950; BS in Chemical Engring., N.C. State, 1972; JD, U. N.C., 1975. Bar: N.C. 1975. Law clerk es. dist. N.C. US Dist. Judge, 1976; assoc. Beaman, Kellum, Mills & Kafer, 1977; ptnr. Bell, Seltzer, Park & Gibson, 1978-86; v.p., gen. coun., sec. Collins Aikman Corp., Charlotte, NC, 1988—99, sr. v.p., gen. coun., sec., 1999—2002, sr. v.p. law, 2003; v.p., gen. counsel, sec. Bowater, Inc., Greenville, SC, 2004—. Office: Bowater Inc 55 E Camperdown Way Greenville SC 29602

LINDSAY, SHARON WINNETT, lawyer, consultant; b. NYC, Apr. 10, 1949; d. William Richardson and Rosemary (Walton) Winnett; m. George Peter Lindsay, Sept. 8, 1973; children: William Charles, Kimberly Michelle. BA, MA, Fordham U., 1970; JD, Harvard U., 1973. Bar: N.Y. 1974, U.S. Dist. Ct. (fed. dist.), U.S. Ct. Appeals 1974. Atty. Milbank, Tweed, Hadley & McCloy, NYC, 1973-83; v.p., asst. gen. counsel J.P. Morgan & Co., Inc., NYC, 1983-95; pvt. practice, 1996—. Trustee Fordham U., Bronx, N.Y., 1994—; pres. bd. dirs., Westchester Symphony Orch., 1998—, Greenacres Assn. 1998; mem. bd. Appeals, Village of Scarsdale. Mem. ABA, N.Y. State Bar Assn., Bar Assn. City of N.Y., Scarsdale Golf Club, Stockbridge Golf Club, Phi Beta Kappa. Roman Catholic. Avocations: tennis, golf, cooking. Home and Office: 25 Mamaroneck Rd Scarsdale NY 10583-2847 Office Phone: 914-472-9568.

LINDSAY, WILLIAM KERR, surgeon; b. Vancouver, BC, Can., Sept. 3, 1920; s. James Arthur and Lottie Mary (Early) L.; m. Frances Beatrice Ferris, Feb. 15, 1945; children— William Arthur, Barbara Susanne, Katherine Mary, Anne Louise. MD, U. Toronto, 1945, BS in Medicine, 1949, MS, 1959. Intern Toronto Gen. Hosp., 1945-46; resident Toronto Gen. Hosp. and Hosp. Sick Children, 1948-51, Montreal Gen. Hosp., 1951-52, Baylor U. Hosp., 1952-53; practice medicine, specializing in plastic surgery Toronto, 1953—; staff surgeon to head divsn. plastic surgery Hosp. for Sick Children, 1953-86, cons., 1965-86; project dir. Research Inst., 1954-85; faculty dept. surgery U. Toronto Faculty of Medicine, 1953-86, prof., 1968-86, chmn. interhospital com. for plastic surgery, 1965-86, prof. emeritus, 1986—. Chmn. med. dental staff com. Bloorview MacMillan Treatment Ctr. (formerly Hugh MacMillan Treatment Ctr. and Ont. Crippled Childrens Treatment Ctr.), 1958-63, cons., 1963—. Trustee McLaughlin Found., 1986-2002. With M.C., Royal Can. Army, 1943-46; surg. lt. Royal Can. Navy, 1946-47. Named Hon Head burn and plastic surgery dept. Gansu Provincial Peoples' Hosp., Lanzhou City, China, 1994—; recipient Arbor award, 1994. Fellow ACS, Royal Coll. Surgeons Can.; mem. Am. Assn. Plastic Surgeons (pres. 1970-71, Hon. award 1995), Can. Soc. Plastic Surgeons (pres. 1963), Easter Seal Soc. Ont. (chmn. med. adv. com. 1957-65, cons. 1952-95, mem. rsch. inst. 1979-95, Gold award 1995, Lifetime Achievement award, 2004), Order of Ontario, Am. Soc. Plastic and Reconstructive Surgeons (Spl. Achievement award 1979), Am. Soc. Surgery of Hand, Am. Cleft Palate Assn., Brit. Soc. Surgery of Hand. Home and Office: 77 Clarendon Ave Apt 202 Toronto ON Canada M4V 1J2

LINDSAY-ABAIRE, DAVID, playwright; BA, Sarah Lawrence Coll., NY; MFA, Lila Acheson Wallace American Playwrights Program Juliard Sch. Playwright: plays A Devil Inside, 1997, The Li'l Plays, 1997, The Snow Angel, 1999, Fuddy Meers, 1999, Dotting and Dashing, 2000, Wonder of the World, 2000, Kimberly Akimbo, 2000, Rabbit Hole, 2006 (Pulitzer Prize for Drama, 2007), screenwriter: films Robots, 2005. Recipient Commisions from South Coast Repertory, Dance Theatre Workshop, Jerome Found. Office: c/o Biltmore Theater 261 W 47th St New York NY 10011*

LINDSETH, ERIK LARS, humanities educator; b. Syracuse, NY, Aug. 13, 1961; s. Richard Emil and Marilyn Miller Lindseth. BA, Wabash Coll., Crawfordsville, Ind., 1983; PhD, Edinburgh U., Scotland, 1992; MLS, Ind. U., Indpls., 1999. Sr. lectr. Ind. U., Indpls., 1990—; v.p. Nat. Libr. Bindery Co. Ind., Indpls., 2001—. Mem. bd. vis. Jordan Coll. Fine Arts, Butler U., Indpls., 2007—. Recipient Outstanding Lectr. award, Ind. U. Sch. Liberal Arts, 2006, Trustees Tchg. award, Ind. U., 2007. Mem.: Columbia Club. R-Liberal. Office: Ind Univ Purdue Univ Ind 425 University Blvd CA 505 Indianapolis IN 46202 Business E-Mail: elindset@iupui.edu.

LINDSEY, CASIMIR CHARLES, zoologist, educator; b. Toronto, Ont., Can., Mar. 22, 1923; s. Charles Bethune and Wanda Casimira (Gzowski) L.; m. Shelagh Pauline Lindsey, May 29, 1948. BA, U. Toronto, 1948; MA, U. B.C., Vancouver, 1950; PhD, Cambridge U., Eng., 1952. Div. biologist B.C. Game Dept., 1952-57; with Inst. Fisheries, also dept. zoology U. B.C., 1953-66; prof. zoology U. Man., Winnipeg, 1966-79; dir. Inst. Animal Resource Ecology, U. B.C., 1980-85; mem. Fisheries and Oceans Adv. Council, 1981-86; prof. emeritus U. B.C., 1988—. Bd. govs. Vancouver Pub. Aquarium, 1956—66, 1980—95, patron, 1996—2004; external assessor univs., Singapore and Nanyang, 1979—81; cons. in field. Author papers in field. Served with Can. Army, 1943-45. Recipient Publ. award Wildlife Soc., 1972; Saunderson award for excellence in teaching U. Man., 1977; Rh Inst. award, 1979; Nuffield Found. grantee, 1973; Killam sr. fellow, 1985-86. Fellow Royal Soc. Can.; mem. Can. Soc. Zoologists (pres. 1977-78), Can. Soc. Environ. Biologists (v.p. 1974-75), Am. Soc. Ichthyologists and Herpetologists (gov.), Fedn. Can. Artists. Office: U BC Dept of Zoology 6270 University Blvd Vancouver BC Canada V6T 1Z4

LINDSEY, DAVID HOSFORD, lawyer; b. Kingsville, Tex., July 25, 1950; s. Ernest Truman and Helen Elizabeth (Hosford) L.; m. Marilyn Kay Williams, June 8, 1974; children: Seth Williams, Brooks Daniel. BS in Bus. Adminstrn., U. Mo., 1972; JD, Washburn U., 1975. Bar: Mo. 1975. With trust dept. Commerce Bank, Kansas City, Mo., 1974—75, from asst. v.p. to sr. v.p., 1979—94, chief credit officer, 1989—, exec. v.p., 2000—; mgr., sales dept. Pioneer Pallet, Inc., North Kansas City, Mo., 1976; from asst. cashier to v.p. Nat. Bank, North Kansas City, 1977—79. Vice-chmn. planning and zoning com. City of Liberty, Mo., 1981-93, tax increment fin. commr., 2002—; bd. dirs. Kansas City Met. YMCA. Mem. Mo. Bar Assn., Lawyers Assn. Kansas City, Kansas City Met. Bar Assn., Robert Morris Assn. (bd. dirs. Kansas City chpt.), Kansas City C. of C., Kansas City Alumni Assn. (bd. dirs.), Clayview Country Club, Phi Gamma Delta, Omicron Delta Kappa. Baptist. Home: 602 Camelot Dr Liberty MO 64068-1176 Office: Commerce Bank 1000 Walnut St Ste 1800 Kansas City MO 64106-2123

LINDSEY, JOANNE M., flight attendant, poet; b. Peoria, Ill., Aug. 27, 1936; d. George Edward and Elsie Rosetta (Mann) Lindsey; AA, El Camino Coll., Torrance, Calif., 1958. Exec. adminstrv. sec. Space Tech. Labs. (formerly Ramo-Woolridge), Hawthorne, Calif., 1958-64; flight attendant Am. Airlines, LA, 1964—, Civil Res. Air Fleet Mil. Missions, 2003. Mem. acad. coun. Diplomatic Acad., London; vice consul Internat. Biog. Ctr.; with Airlift Svcs. Solicitation, 2003—. Contbr. poems to anthologies, including Internat. Libr. Poetry, Noble House. Attended People to People Amb. Program's S. African Tour of Women Writers, 1998; active Civil Res. Air Fleet Mil. Missions, 2003; with Airlift Svcs. Solicitation, 2003—. Decorated Congl. medal; named to Internat. Libr. Poetry, 1996, 1997, 1998, 2002, 2004, 2005; recipient 7 Poetry Editor's Choice awards in anthologies. Mem.: Internat. Soc. Poets, Audie Murphy Rsch. Found., Acad. Am. Poets. Avocations: gardening, writing, skiing, mountain biking, home refurbishing. Home: 846 American Oaks Ave Newbury Park CA 91320-5572

LINDSEY, JOHN H., former insurance agency executive; b. Waxahachie, Tex., July 28, 1922; s. Harry E. and Marie (Smith) L.; m. Sara Houstoun, Aug. 30, 1946; children: Edwin (dec.), David C. BA, Tex. A&M U., 1944. Cons. Lindsey Ins. Agy., Houston, 1953—2002. Past bd. regents Texas A&M U. Sys. Former v.p. Houston Mus. Fine Arts; former pres. Alley Theatre; former bd. dirs. South Tex. Coll. Law, Tex. A&M Rsch. Found., College Station; bd. dirs. George Bush Presdl. Libr. Found.; pres. Tex. A&M U. Alumni, 1964; former vice chmn. bd. visitors U.S. Mil. Acad.; former mem. bd. visitors Tex. A&M at Galveston. 1st lt. US Army, WWII. Recipient Disting. Alumni award Tex. A&M U. Home: 3640 Willowick Houston TX 77019-1114 Office: Ste 1100 2001 Kirby Dr Houston TX 77019-6081

LINDSEY, JONATHAN ASMEL, academic administrator, school librarian, educator; b. Bulloch County, Ga., June 9, 1937; s. Joel Wesley and Ethel Iora (Stickland) L.; m. Edythe Annette Loewer, Apr. 3, 1965; children: Julianna Elizabeth, Jonathan Edward. AB, George Washington U., 1961; BD, So. Bapt. Sem., Louisville, 1964; PhD, So. Bapt. Sem., 1968; MSLS, U. Ala., 1975. Assoc. prof., libr. Judson Coll., Marion, Ala., 1967-77; assoc. dean, libr. Meredith Coll., Raleigh, NC, 1977-83; libr. Baylor U., Waco, Tex., 1983-89, dir. found. devel., 1989-95, dir. donor info. and recognition, 1995-2001, asst. v.p. donor and info. svcs., 2001—07. Author librarianship and profl. fund raising, 1988—. Author: (monographs) Free To Be, 1975, Change and Challenge, 1978, Professional Ethics and Librarians, 1985, Performance Evaluation: A Management Basic, 1986; editor: N.C. Libraries (H.W. Wilson award 1981), 1979-83, contbr. articles and book revs. to profl. publs. Mem. Waco Peace Alliance, PTA. Mem. ALA, Assn. Profl. Rschrs. in Advancement, Assn. Fundraising Profls., Coun. for Advancement and Support of Edn., Tex. Libr. Assn. Home: 8265 Mosswood Dr Waco TX 76712-2407 Office Phone: 254-710-3801. Business E-Mail: jonathan_lindsey@baylor.edu.

LINDSEY, LAWRENCE BENJAMIN, economist; b. Peekskill, NY, July 18, 1954; s. Merritt Hunt and Helen Ruth (Hissam) Lindsey; m. Susan Ann McGrath, Aug. 28, 1982; 3 children. AB magna cum laude, Bowdoin Coll., Brunswick, Maine, 1976; MA, Harvard U., 1981, PhD, 1985; JD (hon.), Bowdoin Coll., 1993. Economist Coun. Econ. Advisers, Washington, 1981—84; from asst. prof. to assoc. prof. Harvard U., Cambridge, Mass., 1984—90; faculty rsch. fellow Nat. Bur. Econ. Rsch., Mass., 1984—89; from assoc. dir. to spl. asst. to Pres., Office of Policy Devel., The White House, Washington, 1989—91; gov. Fed. Res. Bd., 1991—97; resident scholar Am. Enterprise Inst., 1997—2001; mng. dir. Econ. Strategies, Inc., 1997—2001; asst. to Pres. for econ. policy The White House, Washington, 2001—02, dir. Nat. Econ. Coun., 2001—02; pres., CEO Lindsey Group, 2003—. Author: The Growth Experiment, 1990, Economic Puppetmasters: Lessons From the Halls of Power, 1999; contbr. articles to profl. jours. Recipient Walter Wriston award, Manhattan Inst., 1988, Disting. Pub. Svc. award, Boston Bar Assn., 1994.

LINDSEY, ROBERTA LEWISE, music researcher, historian, educator; b. Munich, Apr. 23, 1958; d. Fred S. and Elsie E. (White) L. BMus, Butler U., 1980, MMus, 1987; PhD, Ohio State U., 1996. Pres., owner Profl. Typing Svcs., Indpls., 1980-84; mktg. specialist Merchants Mortgage Corp., Indpls., 1985-87; exec. asst. Ind. Arts Commn., Indpls., 1988-90; GTA Ohio State U., Columbus, 1990-94, music libr. asst., 1991-93, student coord. music in Ohio festival, 1993, vol. tutor coord., 1994-95, lectr. Marion, 1995; rsch. editor Ind. High Tech. Directory, 1995-97; lectr. Ind. U. Sch. Music, 1998, vis. asst. prof. Indianapolis, 1999—2001, asst. prof. Indpls., 2001—, advisor music minor program, 2000—, reader IU Press, 2004. Rep. Susan Porter Meml. symposium Ohio State U., Columbus, 1995; program com. AMS Midwest, 2001—02; vis. rsch. fellow Am. Music Rsch. Ctr., 1997; tchr. of record Digital Music Libr. Grant project Ind. U., 2000—05; presenter and spkr. nat. and internat. confs. Book reviewer Ohioana Jour., 1997—2002, contbg. editor Lenten Devotional,

2000—01; contbr. articles to profl. jours. Reader Ctrl. Ind. Radio Reading, Inc., Indpls., 1985-90; co-founder, Grad. Music Students Assn., Ohio State U., Columbus; multicultural diversity com. Coun. of Grad. Students, Columbus, 1992, orgns. and elections com., 1992, co-chair orientation com., 1993; pre-concert lectr. Carmel Symphony Orch., 1998; active Inst. Rep. for the Arts, 1999—, IUPUI/Eiteljorg; adv. bd. Eiteljorg Mus., 1999—, docent, 2004—. Recipient Grad. Student Alumni Rsch. award, Ohio State U., 1993, Innovative Teaching Recognition award, Ind. U. Sch. Music, 2002, Trustee Tchg. award, Ind. U. Purdue U. Indpls., 2006, 2007; grantee Dena Epstein grantee, 2001, Ind. U. Purdue U. Indpls., 2001. Mem. Soc. Am. Music, Am. Musicol. Soc. (prof. com. 2001—, program com. midwest chpt. 2001-02), Coll. Music Soc. (Gt. Lakes chpt. conv. 2001-02), Soc. Ethnomusicology, Am. Music Rsch. Ctr. Office Phone: 317-278-7868. Business E-Mail: rlindsey@iupui.edu.

LINDSEY, SARA ANN, sociologist, educator; b. Huntington, W.Va., Feb. 20, 1925; d. Alexis Brenier and Iris Neville (Smith) McMullen; m. Douglas Griffith Lindsey, Sept. 12, 1924; children: Douglas McMullen, Bruce McRee, Ann Griffith(dec.), Robert Warfield. AB, Sweetbriar Coll., Amherst, Va., 1947; MA, George Washington U., 1965. Caseworker Dept. Pub. Welfare, Alexandria, Va., 1947—49; journalist Alexandria Gazette, 1951—54; instr. sociology U. Va. Sch. Continuing Edn., 1965—75; ret. Democrat. Episcopalian. Avocations: gardening, travel, collecting antique furniture. Home: 6104 Woodmont Rd Alexandria VA 22307

LINDSEY, SETH MARK, lawyer; b. LA, Oct. 18, 1947; s. Seth Rankin and Lela Belle L.; m. Susan Adelaide Badger, June 29, 1968; 1 child, Samantha. BA, U. So. Calif., LA, 1968; JD, Yale U., 1971. Bar: Calif. 1972, U.S. Supreme Ct. 1984. Honors atty. Housing and Urban Devel., Washington, 1971-72, atty., 1972-76; asst. chief counsel Fed. Railroad Adminstrn., Washington, 1976-86, chief counsel, 1986—, acting adminstr., 1993, 2001. Spl. counsel for Conrail and Union Sta. Redevel. Fed. Railroad Adminstrn., 1984-86. Recipient Silver medal Dept. Transp., 1977, 83, Gold medal, 1984, Presdl. Rank award 2003. Baptist. Office: Dept Transp Fed RR Adminstrn 1120 Vermont Ave NW Ms 10 Washington DC 20590-0001 Home Phone: 703-860-9136; Office Phone: 202-493-6052. E-mail: mark.lindsey@fra.dot.gov.

LINDSEY, STEVEN W., astronaut, military officer; b. Arcadia, Calif., Aug. 24, 1960; s. Arden and Louise Lindsey; m. Diane Renee Trujillo; 3 children. BS in Engring. Scis., USAF Acad., Colo. Springs, Colo., 1982; MS in Aeronautical Engring., USAF Inst. Tech., Wright Field, Dayton, Ohio, 1990. Commd. 2d lt. USAF, Colo. Springs, 1982, advanced through grades to lt. col., student pilot Reese AFB, Tex., 1982—83; pilot USAF 12th Reconnaissance Squadron, Bergstrom AFB, Tex., 1984—87; grad. student USAF Inst. Tech., Wright AFB, Dayton, Ohio, 1987; test pilot student USAF Test Pilot Sch., Edwards AFB, Calif., 1989—90; test pilot USAF, Eglin AFB, Fla., 1990—93; grad. student USAF Air Command and Staff Coll., Maxwell AFB, Ala., 1993—94; team leader integrated product USAF, Eglin AFB, 1994—95; astronaut NASA Johnson Space Flight Ctr., Houston, 1996—. Dep. Shuttle Ops.; co-chmn. Space Shuttle Cockpit Coun.; chief Internat. Space Station Ops.; pilot STS-87, 1997, STS-95, 1998, STS-104, 2001; commdg. pilot STS-121 (Discovery), a return-to-flight test mission and assembly flight to the Internat. Space Station, 2006. Named Disting. Grad. Undergrad. Pilot Tng., USAF, 1983; recipient Leithen-Tittle award, USAF Test Pilot Sch. Class 89A, 1989, 3 Space Flight medals, NASA, Disting. Flying Cross, Def. Superior Svc. medal, Def. Meritorious Svc. medal, NASA Outstanding Leadership medal, NASA Exceptional Svc. medal, Air Force Meritorious Svc. medal, Air Force Commendation medal, Air Force Achievement medal, Aerial Achievement medal. Mem.: Soc. Exptl. Pilots, USAF Acad. Assn. Grads., Assn. Space Explorers. Achievements include 4500 flying hours using 50 different types of aircraft; 3 space flights, mission commander on 1, 896 hours in space. Avocations: camping, skiing, scuba diving, windsurfing, mountain and dirt biking. Office: Astronaut Office/CB Johnson Space Ctr Houston TX 77058

LINDSEY, SUSAN LYNDAKER, zoologist; b. Valley Forge, Pa., Aug. 23, 1956; d. Howard Paul and Lillian Irene (Whitman) Lyndaker; m. Kevin Arthur Lindsey, July 17, 1982; children: Ryan Howard, Shannon Marie. BS in Biology, St. Lawrence U., 1978; MA in Zoology, So. Ill. U., Carbondale, 1980; PhD in Zoology, Colo. State U., 1987. Rschr. St. Lawrence U., Kenya, East Africa, 1978; tchr. Beth Jacob H.S., Denver, 1986-87; rschr. mammal dept. Dallas Zoo, 1988-93; exec. dir. Wild Canid Survival and Rsch. Ctr., Eureka, Mo., 1993—. Adj. prof. Cedar Valley Coll., 1992-93, So. Ill. U., Carbondale, 1996—; mgmt. group mem. Red Wolf Species Survival Plan, Tacoma, Wash., 1994—, Mexican Gray Wolf Species Survival Plan, Albuquerque, 1993—, Maned Wolf Species Survival Plan, Washington, 1999—, African Wild Dog Species Survival Plan, 2005—, Swift Fox Species Survival Plan, 2006—; advisor Mex. Gray Wolf Species Survival Plan Behavioral. Author: (with others) The Okapi: Mysterious Animal of Congo-Zaire, 1999; contbr. articles to profl. jours. Docent Denver Zool. Found., Denver Zoo, 1985-88. Recipient Disting. Alumni citation, St. Lawrence U., 2003. Mem. Acad. Sci. St. Louis, Assn. Zoos and Aquariums, Am. Behavior Soc., Am. Soc. of Mammalogists, Beta Beta Beta, Phi Beta Kappa, Psi Chi. Avocations: horseback riding, canoeing, gardening, photography, travel. Office: Wild Canid Survival Rsch Ctr Wash U PO Box 760 Eureka MO 63025-0760 Home Phone: 636-742-4956; Office Phone: 636-938-5900.

LINDSEY, TOMMIE, secondary school educator; BA, U. San Francisco, 1973, BS, 1976. Cert. secondary tchg. U. San Francisco, 1976. Tchr. Alameda County Ct. Schs., 1975—80, El Rancho Verde H.S., 1980—88; tchr., head coach speech and debate team James Logan H.S., Union City, Calif., 1988—. Named MacArthur Fellow, John D. and Catherine T. MacArthur Found., 2004; named to KEY Coch Soc., Nat. Forensic League, 2004. Office: James Logan HS 1800 H St Union City CA 94587

LINDSKOG, DAVID RICHARD, lawyer; b. Aug. 4, 1936; s. Gustaf Elmer and Charlotte (Birely) L.; m. Elisabeth Lagg, Jan. 28, 1978; 1 child, Stefanie. BA, Yale U., 1958; LLB, U. Va., 1965. Bar: N.Y. 1966, conseil juridique France 1978, avocat 1992. Assoc. Curtis, Mallet-Prevost, Colt & Mosle, NYC, 1965-72, ptnr., 1973-99; sr. v.p., gen. counsel Leach Holding Corp., Westport, Conn., 1999—. Lt. USNR, 1958-62. Mem. Internat. Bar Assn. Episcopalian. Home: 22 Shore Acre Dr Old Greenwich CT 06870-2130 Office: Leach Holding Corporation PO Box 272 Monroe CT 06468-0272

LINDSLEY, JOYCE LILLIAN, music educator; b. Brewerton, NY, Nov. 2, 1948; d. Lee Harry and Florence Imogene Wickham; children: Janice, Michael. AA in Music, Onodaga CC, Syracuse, NY; MusB, SUNY, Potsdam, NY; postgrad., Syracuse U. Music tchr. Ctrl. Sq. Schs., NY. Mem. Hist. Preservation Am., NY, Hist. Preservations NY, Syracuse, Humane Soc., Town Brewerton Presevation Expansion Program; mem Rep. Coun. Mem.: Am. RR Soc. Republican. Ch. Of Christ. Avocations: travel, hurling, historic homes.

LINDSTROM, ERIC EVERETT, ophthalmologist; b. Helena, Mont., Nov. 28, 1936; s. Everett Harry and Nan Augusta (Johnson) L.; m. Nancy Jo Alexander, July 24, 1960; children: Laura Ann, Eric Everett. BS, Wheaton Coll., 1958; MD, U. Md., 1963; MPH, Harvard U., 1966. Diplomate Am. Bd. Preventive Medicine, Am. Bd. Ophthalmology. Intern Madigan Army Med. Ctr., Tacoma, 1963-64; resident in aerospace medicine Sch. Aerospace Medicine, Brooks AFB, Tex., 1966-68; resident in ophthalmology Brooke Army Med. Ctr., Ft. Sam Houston, Tex., 1972-75; surgeon 12th combat aviation group U.S. Army, Vietnam, 1968-69; chief profl. svcs. and aviation medicine Beach Army Hosp., Ft. Wolters, Tex., 1969-72; asst. chief ophthalmology clinic Madigan Army Med. Ctr., Tacoma, 1975-76; with Lindstrom Eye Clinic, 1987—; med. dir. Palo Pinto County (Tex.) Mental Health Clinic, 1970-72; ret. Cons. Tex. State Rehab. Com., 1971-72; chmn. bd. trustees South Ctrl. Regional Med. Ctr., 1982-2001; sr. aviation med. examiner, FAA; flight surgeon Miss. Air N.G. (ret.). Deacon First Bapt. Ch., Laurel, Miss., 1978—; bd. dirs. Laurel Salvation Army, Good Shepherd Clin., Laurel. Decorated Bronze Star, Air medal with 2 oak leaf clusters, Meritorious Svc. medal. Fellow ACS, Am. Coll. Physician Execs., Am. Coll. Preventive Medicine (assoc.), Aerospace Med. Assn. (assoc.), Am. Acad. Ophthalmology; mem. AMA, Am. Acad. Cataract and Refractive Surgery, New Orleans Acad. Ophthalmology, Miss. Med. Assn. (pres.), South Miss. Med. Soc., So. Med. Assn. (councilor), Flying Physicians Assn., Soc. Mil. Ophthalmologists, Soc. USAF and US Army Flight Surgeons, Alliance Air N.G. Flight Surgeons, Mil. Officers Assn. Am., Aircraft Owners and Pilots Assn., Kiwanis, Nu Sigma Nu. Home: 809 Cherry Ln Laurel MS 39440-1651 Office: Lindstrom Eye Clinic PO Box 407 Laurel MS 39441-0407 Office Phone: 601-426-9454. Business E-Mail: drelindstrom@c-gate.net.

LINDSTROM, GREGORY P., lawyer; b. Hollywood, Calif., Aug. 4, 1953; AB summa cum laude, UCLA, 1975; JD, U. Chgo., 1978. Bar: Calif. 1978. With Latham & Watkins, 1978—, former mng. ptnr., Orange County office, now mng. ptnr., San Francisco office. Fellow Am. Coll. Trial Lawyers; mem. Phi Beta Kappa. Office: Latham & Watkins 505 Montgomery St Ste 2000 San Francisco CA 94111-2552 Office Phone: 415-391-0600. Business E-Mail: gregory.lindstrom@lw.com.

LINDSTROM, ROSETTA ARLINE, retired medical technician; b. Fay, Okla., Aug. 30, 1943; d. Paul George and Gladys Arline Prickett; m. Richard Jacobsen, 1962 (div. 1980); children: Richard P. Jacobsen, Ronald J. Jacobsen, Christine Jacobsen Carroll; m. John Lindstrom, 1988 (div. 1996). Degree Med. Assistance, Lawton Coll. Med. Technologies, 1975. Registered Diagnostic Cardiac Sonographer 1988. Sr. technician EKG and Echo Dept. Kaiser-Permanante Hosp., Redwood City, Calif., 1977—87; supr. Echocardiography Lab. VA Med. Ctr. Stanford, Palo Alto, Calif., 1989—2002; ret., 2002. Instr. Echocardiography Stanford U. Fellows Program, 1989—2002; site instr. Dept. Med. Ultrasound Foothill Coll., 1995—2001. Author (editor): El Toro Yearbook, Shovel Bull., 1968. Named Sr. Divsn. Winner, N. Am. Sailing Championship, 1968, Season Champion El Toro Sr. Divsn., Small Boat Racing Assn. No. Calif., 1969; recipient Tchg. award in Echocardiography, Stanford U. Sch. Medicine, Graduating Fellows, 2000. Avocations: writing, childrens literature.

LINDZEN, RICHARD SIEGMUND, meteorologist, educator; b. Webster, Mass., Feb. 8, 1940; s. Abe and Sara (Blachman) L.; m. Nadine Lucie Kalougine, Apr. 7, 1965; children: Eric, Nathaniel. AB, Harvard U., 1960, SM, 1961, PhD, 1964. Research assoc. U. Wash., Seattle, 1964-65; Research asso. U. Oslo, 1965-66; with Nat. Center Atmospheric Research, Boulder, Colo., 1966-68; mem. faculty U. Chgo., 1968-72; prof. meteorology Harvard U., 1972-83, dir. Center for Earth and Planetary Physics, 1980-83; Alfred P. Sloan prof. meteorology MIT, 1983—. Lady Davis vis. prof. Hebrew U., 1979; Sackler prof. Tel Aviv U., 1992; Vikram Sarabhai prof. Phys. Rsch. Lab., Ahmendabad, India, 1985; Lansdowne lectr. U. Victoria, 1993; Haurwitz lectr. Am. Meteorol. Soc., 1997; cons. NASA, Jet Propulsion Lab., others; corr. mem. com. on human rights NAS. Author: Dynamics in Atmospheric Physics; co-author: Atmospheric Tides; contbr. to profl. jours. Recipient Macelwane award Am. Geophys. Union, 1968 Fellow NAS, AAAS, Am. Geophys. Union, Am. Meteorol. Soc. (Meisinger award 1969, councillor 1972-75, Charney award 1985, Haurwitz lectr. 1997), Am. Acad. Arts and Scis., Norwegian Acad. Scis. and Letters; mem. Internat. Commn. Dynamic Meteorology, Institut Mondial des Scis. (founding mem.). Jewish. Office: MIT 54 1720 Cambridge MA 02139

LINEEN, EDWARD M., lawyer, information technology executive; b. Feb. 28, 1941; BS, JD, Fordham U. Bar: N.Y. 1971. Atty. IBM, Armonk, NY, 1970—83, counsel sales & distbn., 1983—85, counsel comm. & tech. group, 1985—89, gen. counsel personal computer group, 1989—94, v.p. & assist. gen. counsel products, intellectual property, 1995—2002, sr. v.p., gen. counsel, 2002—06. Exec. leader People with Disabilities Exec. Task Force, IBM. Office Phone: 914-499-4836. E-mail: lineen@us.ibm.com.*

LINEHAN, JOHN H., engineering educator, biomedical engineer; BS, Marquette U., 1960; MS, Rensselaer Polytechnic Inst., 1962; PhD, U. Wis., Madison, 1968. Founding chmn. Biomedical Engring. Dept. Marquette U., 1989, Bagozzi prof.; joined Whitaker Found., Arlington, Va., 1998, v.p. biomed. engring. programs, 2001—; consulting prof. dept. bioengring., mem. exec. faculty program in biodesign James H. Clark Ctr. Stanford U., Calif., 2007—. Fellow: American Soc. of Mech. Engring.; mem.: NAE, Biomedical Engring. Soc. (pres. 1992—93), Am. Inst. for Med. and Biological Engring. (pres. 1999—2000). Office: Stanford U Dept Bioengring James H Clark Ctr 318 Campus Dr Rm E-125 Stanford CA 94305-5428 Business E-Mail: linehan@stanford.edu.

LINEHAN, SCOTT, professional football coach; b. Sunnyside, Wash., Sept. 17, 1963; m. Kristen Linehan; 3 children. Grad., U. ID, 1982—86. Quarterbacks coach U. Nev., Las Vegas, 1991—92; wide receivers coach U. Idaho, 1989—91, offensive coord., quarterbacks coach, 1992—94; wide receivers coach U. Nebr., 1994—96, offensive coord., 1996—98; offensive coord., quarterbacks coach U. Louisville, 1999—2001, Minn. Vikings, 2002—05; offensive coord. Miami Dolphins, 2005—06; head coach St. Louis Rams, 2006—. Office: c/o St Louis Rams 1 Rams Way Saint Louis MO 63045

LINEHAN, WILLIAM MARSTON, urologic surgeon, cancer researcher; b. Tulsa, Okla., June 25, 1947; s. John Marston and Ella Marie (Bourg) L.; m. Tracey Ann Rouault, Sept. 29, 1979; children: Erin Louise, Emily Pauline. AB, Brown U., 1969; MD, U. Okla., Okla. City, 1973. Diplomate Am. Bd. Urology. Intern medicine U. Okla., 1973-74; intern and resident surgery Duke U., 1974-76, fellow cancer rsch., 1976-78, resident urologic surgery, 1978-82; chief urologic oncology br. Nat. Cancer Inst., Bethesda, Md., 1982—. Mem. urology interag. coord. com. NIH, Bethesda, 1987—. Mem. editl. bd. Jour. Urology, 1990—; assoc. editor Jour. Nat. Cancer Inst., 1992—; contbr. articles to Nature Science, P.N.A.S., New Eng. Jour. Medicine, Jour. Nat. Cancer Inst. Recipient Gold Cystoscope award Am. Urological Assn., 1992. Fellow ACS; mem. Am. Urol. Assn., Am. Assn. Cancer Rsch., Am. Assn. Genitourinary Surgeons. Achievements include co-discovery of kidney cancer disease gene in sporadic renal cell carcinoma as well as in the familial renal cell carcinoma associated with von Hippel Lindau syndrome; co-discovery of hereditary papillary renal carcinoma gene; co-discovery of the BHD kidney cancer gene; detailing of molecular genetic changes associated with initiation and progression of kidney cancer; evaluation of new anti-neoplastic agents for patients with advanced prostate carcinoma. Office: Nat Cancer Inst Urologic Oncology Br 9000 Rockville Pike Bethesda MD 20892-1107

LINEN, JONATHAN S., diversified financial services company executive; With Am. Express, 1969—; pres., CEO, dir. mktg. group and travelers cheque group Am. Express Co. Travel Related Svcs., 1988-90; pres., CEO Shearson Lehman Bros., 1990—92; pres., COO Am. Express Travel Related Svcs., 1992—93; vice chmn. Am. Express, NYC, 1993—2005, adv. to chmn., 2006—. Bd. dir. Yum! Brands Inc., Bausch & Lomb, Intercontinental Hotels Group. Mailing: Yum! Brands Bd Directors 1900 Col Sanders Lane Louisville KY 40213*

LINETT, DAVID, retired lawyer; b. Perth Amboy, NJ, Apr. 9, 1934; s. Jack K. and Anne L.; children: Jon, Peter, Maren. BA, Yale U., 1956; JD, Harvard U., 1959. Bar: D.C. 1959, N.J. 1960. Law sec. to assignment judge Superior Ct. NJ, 1959—60; assoc. Gross, Weissberger & Linett, New Brunswick, N.J., 1960-62, ptnr., 1962-77; prosecutor Somerset County, N.J., 1977-82; of counsel Lowenstein, Sandler, Brochin, Kohl et al and predecessor, Roseland and Somerville, N.J., 1982-85; ptnr. Gindin & Linett, Bridgewater, NJ, 1985—2004. Chmn. N.J. State Bar Com. on Programs for Law Enforcement Personnel, 1978-80; mem. com. on county dist. cts. N.J. Supreme Ct., 1980-82, mem. Post-Indictment Delay Task Force, 1980, dist. XIII ethics com., 1986-90, chair N.J. Supreme Ct., 1989-90, ethics fin. com., 1990-94, treas., 1992-94; gen. counsel United Heritage Bank, 1997-2004. Mem. N.J. Dem. State Com., 1973-77; bd. dirs. Somerset County Resource Ctr. for Women and Their Families, 1982-83; chmn. bd. trustees, Assn. for Advancement of Mentally Handicapped, 1987-89; commr. N.J. Election Law Enforcement Commn., 1987-2000, vice chair, 1996-2000; mem. Ct. House study com., Somerset County Bd. Freeholders, 1979-82; gen.chmn. Rotary Internat. Task Force on Edn. and Tng., 2001-02. Mem. ABA (corp., real property law sect.), Nat. Dist. Attys. Assn. (nat. treas., exec. com. 1981-82, Pres.'s award for outstanding svc. as chmn. fin. com. 1982), New Brunswick Bar Assn. (pres. 1974), N.J. Bar Assn. (land use sect., real property sect.), Somerset County Bar Assn., Somerset County C. of C. (bd. dirs. 1984-90, Outstanding Citizen of Yr. 1989), Rotary (pres. 1986-87, dist. gov. 1991-92, internat. bd. dirs. 2004-06). Personal E-mail: ginlin@aol.com.

LINFORD, RULON KESLER, physicist, electrical engineer; b. Cambridge, Mass., Jan. 31, 1943; s. Leon Blood and Imogene (Kesler) L.; m. Cecile Tadje, Apr. 2, 1965; children: Rulon Scott, Laura Linford Williams, Hilary Linford Henderson, Philip Leon. BSEE, U. Utah, 1966; MSEE, MIT, 1969, PhD in Elec. Engring., 1973. Staff CTR-7 Los Alamos (N.Mex) Nat. Lab., 1973-75, asst. group leader CTR-7, 1975-77, group leader CTR-11, 1977-79, program mgr., group leader compact toroid CTR-11, 1979-80, program mgr., asst. divsn. leader compact toroid CTR divsn., 1980-81, assoc. CTR divsn. leader, 1981-86, program dir. magnetic fusion energy, 1986-89, program dir., divsn. leader CTR divsn. office, 1989-91, program dir. nuc. sys., 1991-93, staff LER, 1993-94; coord. sci. and tech. U. Calif., 1994-97; assoc. vice provost lab. programs Office of the Pres., U. Calif., Oakland, 1997—2001, assoc. vice provost, 2001—03, asst. v.p. lab. programs, 2003—04; ret., 2004. Contbr. articles to profl. jours. Recipient E. O. Lawrence award Dept. of Energy, Washington, 1991. Fellow Am. Phys. Soc. (exec. com. 1982, 90-91, program com. 1982, 85, award selection com. 1983, 84, fellowship com. 1986); mem. AAAS, Sigma Xi. Home: 1055 Aquarius Way Oakland CA 94611-1939 E-mail: cecile.rulon@comcast.net.

LING, BAI, actor; b. Chengdu, China, Oct. 10, 1970; Grad., Lee Strasberg Instit. Vis. scholar, Dept. Film NYU, 1991. Actor: (films) Huguan, 1989, Homicide: Life on the Street - And the Rockets Dead Glare, 1993, The Crow, 1994, Dead Funny, 1995, Nixon, 1995, Somewhere in the City, 1997, Red Corner, 1997 (Best Breakthrough Performer, Nat. Board of Review, 1997), Wild Wild West, 1999, Anna and the King, 1999, Row Your Boat, 2000, Angel: She, 2000, The Breed, 2001, Face, 2001, The Lost Empire, 2001, My Baby's Daddy, 2003, Paris, 2003, Taxi 3, 2003, Sky Captain and the World of Tomorrow, 2004, Dumplings, 2004 (Best Supporting Actress award, Golden Horse Awards, 2004); actor, actor: (films) The Beautiful Country, 2004, She Hates Me, 2004, Three...Extremes, 2004, Lords of Dogtown, 2005, Man About Town, 2005, Star Wars: Episode III - Revenge of the Sith, 2005, Edmond, 2005, Entourage: Chinatown, 2005, Southland Tales, 2006, (appearances): (TV series) Touched By an Angel, 1998; guest appearances The Tonight Show with Jay Leno. Entertainer, singer, dancer People's Liberation Army, 1984, Tibet. Named one of 50 Most Beautiful People in the World, People Mag., 1998; recipient Female Discovery of the Yr. award, Golden Apple Found., 1997.

LING, CHUNG-MEI, b. Wen-Ling, Zhejiang, China, May 5, 1931; came to U.S., 1960; s. Hsin-Sao Ling and San-Mei Juan; m. Jeanine Wu; children: Dori Shawn, Ellen Katelin. BS, Nat. Taiwan U., 1958; MS, Ill. Inst. Tech., 1962, PhD, 1965. Head virology lab. Abbott Labs., North Chicago, Ill., 1968-81, rsch. fellow, 1978-84, mgr. rsch. and devel., 1981-84; founder, chmn. bd. dirs., chief sci. officer Gen. Biologicals Corp., Hsinchu, Taiwan, 1984-88, hon. chmn. bd., 1991—; prof. Nat. Tsing-Hua U., Hsinchu, 1991-93. Asst. prof. Ill. Inst. Tech., Chgo., 1965-68; sci. specialist Nat. Inst. Preventative Medicine, Taipei, Taiwan, 1984-85; dir. biosci. rsch. ctr. KangLing Biotech. Corp., Hsinchu, 1988—. Contbr. articles to profl. jours. Fellow Am. Acad. Microbiology; mem. Am. Soc. Biol. Chemists, Am. Clin. Chem., Sigma Xi. Achievements include invention of hepatitis B diagnostics; therapeutics and various health products; patents in field. Avocations: sight-seeing, singing, interior design. Office: 5 Debill Ct Vernon Hills IL 60061

LING, HUPING, history professor; PhD, Miami U., Oxford, Ohio, 1991. Prof. history Truman State U., Kirksville, Mo., 1991—. Author: Surviving on the Gold Mountain: A History of Chinese American Women and Their Lives, 1998, Jinshan Yao: A History of Chinese American Women, 1999, Ping Piao Mei Guo: New Immigrants in America, 2003, Chinese St. Louis: From Enclave to Cultural Community, 2004, Chinese in St. Louis 1857-2007, 2007, Voices of the Heart: Asian Amercian Women on Immigration, Work and Family, 2007; contbr. articles to profl. jours. Named Allan fellow, Truman State U., 2005—06. Mem.: Assn. Asian Am. Studies (life; bd. dirs. 2001—03). Office: Truman State U 100 E Normal Kirksville MO 63501 Office Phone: 660-785-4654.

LING, JAHJA WANG-CHIEH, conductor; b. Jakarta, Indonesia, Oct. 25, 1951; came to U.S., 1970; s. Bok-Som and Eng-Nio (Kwee) L.; m. Jane Yuan, May 8, 1976 (div.), Jessie Chang, Jan. 1, 2001; children: Gabriel En-Wei, Daniel En-Hao, Priscilla, Stephanie. BMus, Julliard Sch., 1974, MMus, 1975; DMus Arts, Yale U., 1980. Asst. conductor San Francisco Symphony, 1981-83, assoc. conductor, 1983-84, Cleve. Orch., 1984-85, resident conductor, 1985—2003; music dir. Fla. Orch., Tampa, 1988—2002, San Diego Symphony Orch., 2004—. Founding music dir. San Francisco Symphony Youth Orch., 1981-84, Cleve. Orch. Youth Orch., 1986-96; music dir. San Francisco Conservatory Orch., 1981-84; co-dir. Tanglewood (Mass.) Young Artists Orch., 1983-84; guest conductor Boston Symphony, Phila. Orch., Minn. Orch., Nat. Symphony in D.C. Recipient Bronze medal Artur Rubinstein Internat. Piano Competition, 1977, Seaver/NEA Conductors award, 1988; Leonard Bernstein fellow Tanglewood Music Ctr., 1980, Exxon/Arts Endowment conductor Affiliate Artists, 1981-84. Home: 1458 Woodglen Ter Bonita CA 91902-4283 E-mail: jahjaling@yahoo.com.

LING, PEI-RA, medical educator; b. Shanghai, May 18, 1946; arrived in US, 1984; d. Yi-Ming Ling and Xu-Yin Yiao; m. Yong-Ming You, Sept. 4, 1971; 1 child, Yi-Qian Nancy You. BS in Biology, Beijing U., China, 1967; MD, Peking Union Med. Coll., China, 1970; MS in Med. Sci., Peking Union Med. Coll., 1981. Diplomate ob-gyn China. Resident Minghe County Hosp., China, 1970—78; clin. fellow Qinghai Province Gen. Hosp., China, 1972—73; sr. resident Peking Union Med. Sch. Hosp., Beijing, 1978—82, chief resident, 1982—83, attending physician, 1983—84; lectr. Peking Union Med. Coll., Nursing Sch., Beijing, 1982—84; instr. Peking Union Med. Coll., 1983—84; rsch. fellow New England Deaconess Hosp., Nutrition Metabolism Lab., Boston, 1984—87; sr. rsch. assoc. New England Deaconess Hosp. Nutrition Infection Lab., 1987—89, assoc. scientist, 1989—93; scientist Beth Israel Deaconess Med. Ctr., Nutrition Infection Lab., Boston, 1993—; instr. Harvard Med. Sch., Boston, 1989—93, asst. prof., 1993—. Clin. fellow supr. Peking Union

Med. Coll. Hosp., 1982—84; presenter, speaker various profl. confs., seminars; reviewer various profl. jours., 1999—2005. Contbr. articles various profl. jours., scientific papers. Recipient Physician award, Nutrition Week ASPEN, 2005; various nutritional grants. Mem.: European Soc. Parenteral and Enteral nutrition, Am. Soc. Parenteral And Enteral Nutrition, Chinese Soc. Medicine. Home: 173 Pleasant St 208 Cambridge MA 02139 Office: Beth Israel Deaconess Med Ctr 330 Brookline Ave Boston MA 02215 Office Phone: 617-632-8523. Business E-Mail: pling@BIDMC.harvard.edu.

LING, ROBERT M., JR., lawyer, consumer products company executive; b. Marquette, MI, 1957; Grad., Tufts U., 1979; JD, U. Michigan Law Sch., 1982. Bar: Wis. 1982. V.p., gen. counsel Unified Western Grocers (formerly Certified Grocers of Calif.), LA, 1996—97, sr. v.p., gen. counsel, sec., 1997—98, exec. v.p., gen. counsel, 1998—. Office: Unified Western Grocers Inc PO Box 513396 5200 Sheila St Los Angeles CA 90051-1396

LING, ROBERT MALCOLM, banker, publishing executive; b. Akron, Ohio, July 6, 1931; s. Howard George and Catherine Zola (Smith) L.; m. Lois Claire Fisher Ling, Nov. 1, 1992; children: Shelly, Robert Jr., Amy, Beth, Patricia. BA in Journalism, Mich. State U., 1952. Asst. pres. Dike-O-Seal, Inc., Chgo., 1955-56; gen. mgr. Vollwerth Marquette (Mich.) Co., 1956-58, pres., 1958-75, Vandco Incorp., Marquette, 1975-85, Cable Americal Corp., Rancho Cordova, Calif., 1985-89, Romali Holdings, Inc., Rancho Cordova, Calif., 1989—. Chmn. Gold River Bank, Fair Oaks, Calif., 1990-92, Sacramento Safety Ctr., Inc., 1996—; publisher Grapevine-Independent newspaper, Rancho Cordova, Calif. Mayor City of Marquette, 1980-83, City of Rancho Cordova, Calif., 1986-87. Capt. U.S. Army, 1952-55. Republican. Home: 6032 Puerto Dr Rancho Murieta CA 95683-9313 Office: Romali Holdings Inc 3338 Mather Field Rd Rancho Cordova CA 95670-5966 Office Phone: 916-361-1234.

LING, TA-YUNG, physicist; b. Shanghai, Feb. 2, 1943; married, 1969; 3 children. BS, Tunghai U., Taiwan, 1964; MS, U. Waterloo, Ont., Can., 1966; PhD in Physics, U. Wis., 1971. Rsch. asst. U. Wis., 1967-71; rsch. assoc. physics U. Pa., Phila., 1972-75, asst. prof., 1975-77; from asst. prof. to assoc. prof. Ohio State U., Columbus, 1977-83, prof. physics, 1983—. Recipient Outstanding Jr. Investigator award Dept. of Energy, 1977. Mem. Am. Phys. Soc. Achievements include research in experimental high energy physics; deep inelastic neutrino-nucleon scattering, neutrino masses and mixing, neutrino oscillations, deep inelastic electron-proton scattering, high energy proton-proton collisions. Office: Dept Physics 191 W Woodruff Ave Columbus OH 43210-1117 E-mail: ling@mps.ohio-state.edu.

LING, VICTOR, oncologist, educator; b. Mar. 16, 1943; BS in Biochemistry, U. Toronto, 1966; PhD in Biochemistry, U. BC, 1971. Staff scientist Ont. Cancer Inst., Toronto, 1971-98, head divsn. molecular and structural biology, 1989-98; asst. dean, prof., dept. biochemistry & molecular biology U. BC, Vancouver, 1998—, prof., dept. of pathology & lab. medicine, 1998—; v.p., rsch., assoc. vice chair BC Cancer Rsch Ctr., Vancouver, Canada, 1995—. Prof. med. biophysics U. Toronto, 1983-95, mem. coun. sch. grad. studies, 1984-90, mem. faculty of medicine rsch. com., 1985-95, vice-chmn., 1988—; mem. study sect. of experimental therapeutics Nat. Insts. of Health, USA, 1986—; bd. govs. Wellesly Hosp. Rsch. Inst., 1988-90; mem. MRC scholarship com. Med. Rsch. Coun. of Can., 1988—, bd. sci. advisors Hong Kong Inst. Biotech., 1989—, adv. bd. Internat. Jour. Anti-cancer Drugs, 1990—, external adv. com. U. Wis. Clin. Cancer Ctr., 1990—, bd. sci. counselors divsn. cancer treatment Nat. Insts. of Health, 1990—; bd. dirs. Hosp. for Sick Children Found., 1992—. Assoc. editor Cancer Rsch., 1986—, Jour. Cellular Physiology, 1989—, Jour. Cellular Pharmacology, 1989—, Jour. Molecular Pharmacology, 1992—, Jour. Biomed. Sci., 1992-; contbr. to 180 peer-reviewed publs. Victoria U. Alumni scholar in Life Scis., 1965, Centennial fellow MRC of Can., 1969-71; recipient C. Chester Stock award Meml. Sloan-Kettering Cancer Ctr., 1988, Cancer Rsch. award The Milken Family Med. Found., 1988, Merit award The FCCP (Ont.) Edn. Found., 1989, Internat. award Gairdner Found., 1990, Charles F. Kettering prize GM Cancer Rsch. Found., 1991, Joseph Steiner Cancer Rsch. award, 1991 Fellow Royal Soc. Can.; mem. Am. Assn. Cancer Rsch. (bd. dirs. 1992—, Bruce F. Cain Meml. award 1993), Am. Soc. Cell Biology, Can. Cancer Soc. (bd. dirs. 1992—), Can. Soc. Cell Biology, Can. Biochem. Soc., Genetics Soc. Can., Can. Breast Cancer Rsch. Initiative, Nat. Cancer Inst., Hosp. for Sick Children Found., Toronto; mem. GM Adv. Council, Cancer Rsch. Found. Achievements include revolutionizing cancer therapy and research into chemotherapy resistance with his discovery of the membrane transport protein P-glycoprotein, a protein the resists anti-cancer drugs in 1974. Office: BC Cancer Rsch Ctr 601 West 10th Ave Vancouver BC V5Z 4E6 Canada Address: Dept Biochemistry and Molecular Biology Faculty of Medicine Univ of BC 2010-2146 Health Sciences Mall Vancouver BC V6T 1Z3 Canada Office Phone: 604-877-6010, 604-822-3178, 607-877-6000 2524, 604-877-6151. Office Fax: 604-822-5227, 604-877-6150. Business E-Mail: vling@bccancer.bc.ca.

LINGEMAN, RICHARD ROBERTS, editor-in-chief, writer; b. Crawfordsville, Ind., Jan. 2, 1931; s. Byron Newton and Vera Frances (Spencer) L.; m. Anthea Judy Nicholson, Apr. 3, 1965; 1 child, Jenifer Kate. BA, Haverford Coll., 1953; postgrad., Yale U. Law Sch., 1956-58, Columbia U. Grad. Sch. Comparative Lit., 1958-60. Exec. editor Monocle mag., NYC, 1960-69; assoc. editor, columnist N.Y. Times Book Review, 1969-78; exec. editor The Nation, NYC, 1978-95, sr. editor, 1995—. Author: Drugs from A to Z, 1969, Don't you Know There's A War On?, 1971, reissued, 2003, Small Town America, 1980, Theodore Dreiser: At the Gates of the City 1871-1907, 1986, Theodore Dreiser: An American Journey, 1908-1945, 1990 (Chgo. Sun-times Book of Yr.), paperback, 1993, Sinclair Lewis: Rebel from Main Street, 2002, paperback, 2005, Double Lives, 2006; co-author: (play) Starr's Last Tape, 1999; mem. editl. bd. Dreiser Studies. Pres. 12 W. 96th Street Corp. With U.S. Army, 1953-56. NEH fellow. Mem. PEN, Authors Guild, Soc. Am. Historians, N.Y. Hist. Soc., Phi Beta Kappa. Office: Nation 33 Irving Pl New York NY 10003-2332

LINGENFELTER, SHERWOOD GALEN, academic administrator, retired anthropologist; b. Hollidaysburg, Pa., Nov. 18, 1941; s. Galen Miller and Kathern Margaretta (Rogers) L.; m. Judith Elaine Beaumont, Aug. 10, 1962; children: Jennifer Elaine, Joel Sherwood. BA, Wheaton Coll., 1963; PhD, U. Pitts., 1971. Dir. acad. advising U. Pitts., 1964-66; instr. SUNY, Brockport, 1966-67, asst. prof, 1969-74, assoc. prof., 1974-82, prof. anthropology, 1982-83; NIH predoctoral fellow U. Pitts., 1967-69; prof. Biola U., La Mirada, Calif., 1983-88, provost, sr. v.p., 1988-99; dean Sch. of World Mission Fuller Theol. Sem., Pasadena, Calif., 1999—2002, provost, sr. v.p., 2001—. Cons. in anthropology Summer Inst. Linguistics, Dallas, 1977-2003; tng. cons. Liebenzell Mission Am., Schooleys Mountain, NJ, 1981-89; evaluating cons. Trust Ter. of the Pacific Islands, Saipan, Mariana Islands, 1969-74. Author: Yap: Political Leadership, 1975, The Deni of Western Brazil, 1980, Ministering Cross-Culturally, 1986, Transforming Culture, 1992, 2d edit., 1998, Agents of Transformation, 1996, Teaching Cross-Culturally, 2003, Breaking Tradition to Accomplish Vision, 2006; editor: Political Development in Micronesia, 1974, Social Organization of Sabah Societies, 1990. Bd. dirs. Christian Scholars Rev., 1989-95, Grace Brethren Internat. Missions, 1994—; mem. Sr. Accrediting Commn. Western Assn. Schs. and Colls., 2000-06, pres., 2002-, chair, 2007-. Recipient Disting. Tchg. award Biola U., 1987-88; grantee NSF, 1967-69, 79-81, SUNY Rsch. Found., 1970. Fellow Am. Anthrop. Assn., Soc. for Applied Anthropology, Am. Ethnol. Soc.; mem. Assn. Social Anthropology Oceania, Am. Conf. Acad. Deans. Democrat. Mem. Grace Brethern Ch. Office: Fuller Theol Sem Provost and Sr VP 135 N Oakland Ave Pasadena CA 91182-0001 Office Phone: 626-584-5205. Business E-Mail: provost@fuller.edu.

LINGERFELT, B. EUGENE, JR., minister; b. Highland Park, Mich., Dec. 18, 1955; s. Beecher Eugene and Nellie Beatrice (Sampson) L.; m. Suzanne Marie Martin, Aug. 7, 1976; children: Austin Stuart, Krystina Marie. BA, Ctrl. Bible Coll., Springfield, Mo., 1976; MDiv, Tex. Christian U., 1980; D of Ministry, Southwestern Bapt. Theol., 1984. Ordained min. Cathedral of Praise Ch., 1984. Assoc. pastor Bethel Temple, Ft. Worth, 1978—82; missionary, guest lectr. East Africa Sch. of Theology, Nairobi, Kenya, 1982—83; marriage enrichment seminar spkr., 1983; founder, sr. pastor Cathedral of Praise, Arlington, Tex., 1984—. Founder Cathedral Christian Acad., 1988—; founder Overcoming Faith TV, 1994—. Author: The Spirit of Excellence, 1994, Compromise in the Modern Church, 1995, God's Very Own Child, 2000; co-author: Money: A Spiritual Force, 1985, You, Me & God, 1999, The God Touch, 2006; contbr. articles to religious jours. Named to Outstanding Young Men of Am., 1980. Republican. Office: Cathedral of Praise PO Box 121234 Arlington TX 76012-1234 Office Phone: 817-561-3400.

LINGL, FRIEDRICH ALBERT, psychiatrist; b. Munich, Apr. 4, 1927; came to U.S., 1957, naturalized, 1962; s. Friedrich Hugo and Marie Luise (Lindner) L.; m. Leonore E. Trautner, Nov. 15, 1955; children— Herbert F., Angelika M. MD, Ludwig-Maxim U., Munich, 1952. Diplomate Am. Bd. Psychiatry and Neurology); cert. mental health adminstr. Intern Edward W. Sparrow Hosp., 1957-58; resident internal medicine City Hosp., Augsburg, Germany, 1953-54; resident psychiatry Columbus (Ohio) State Hosp., 1958-61; supt. Hawthornden State Hosp., Northfield, Ohio, 1963-66; dir. Cleve. Psychiat. Inst., 1966-72; pvt. practice, 1972-92; med. dir. Windsor Hosp., 1976-92, med. dir. emeritus, 1992—. Asst. clin. prof. Case Western Res. U., Cleve., 1970-97. Contbr. articles to med. jours. Fellow Am. Psychiat. Assn. (disting. life); mem. AMA, Ohio Med. Assn., Ohio Psychiat. Assn., Cleve. Psychiat. Soc. Address: 40 Farwood Dr Chagrin Falls OH 44022-6848

LINGLE, CRAIG STANLEY, glaciologist, educator; b. Carlsbad, N.Mex., Sept. 11, 1945; s. Stanley Orland and Margaret Pearl (Ewart) L.; m. Diana Lynn Duncan, Aug. 21, 1972; 1 son, Eric Glenn. BS, U. Wash., 1967; MS, U. Maine, 1978; PhD, U. Wis., 1983. Nat. rsch. coun. resident rsch. assoc. Coop. Inst. for Rsch. in Environ. Scis., U. Colo., Boulder, 1983-84, rsch. assoc., 1984-86; program mgr. polar glaciology divsn. polar programs NSF, Washington, 1986-87; cons. Jet Propulsion Lab., Pasadena, Calif., 1987-88; nat. rsch. coun. resident rsch. assoc. NASA Goddard Space Flight Ctr., Oceans and Ice Branch, Greenbelt, Md., 1988-90; rsch. assoc. prof. Geophys. Inst. U. Alaska, Fairbanks, 1990-2000, acting dir. Alaska synthetic aperture radar facility Geophys. Inst., 1997-98, rsch. prof. geophysics Geophys. Inst., 2000—, group leader snow, ice and permafrost Geophys. Inst., 2003—. Contbr. articles to profl. jours. Recipient Antarctic Svc. medal of U.S., NSF, 1987, Rsch. Project of Month award Office of Health and Environ. Rsch., U.S. Dept. Energy, 1990, Group Achievement award NASA, 1992. Mem. AAAS, Internat. Glaciological Soc., Am. Geophys. Union, Sigma Xi. Avocations: downhill and cross-country skiing, canoeing. Office: U Alaska Geophys Inst PO Box 757320 Fairbanks AK 99775-7320 Office Phone: 907-474-7679. E-mail: craig.lingle@gi.alaska.edu.

LINGLE, LINDA, governor; b. St. Louis, June 4, 1953; BJ, Calif. State U., Northridge, 1975. Mayor County of Maui, Hawaii; chair. Democratic Party of Hawaii; mem. Maui County Coun., 1980—90; mayor Maui County, 1990—98; chmn. Hawaii Republican Party, 1999—2001; gov. State of Hawaii, Honolulu, 2002—. Recipient Evelyn McPhail award, 2000. Republican. Jewish. Office: Off of the Gov State Capitol Executive Chambers Honolulu HI 96813 Address: PO Box 25111 Honolulu HI 96825 Office Phone: 808-586-0034. Office Fax: 808-586-0006.*

LINGLE, MARILYN FELKEL, journalist, columnist, writer; b. Hillsboro, Ill., Aug. 16, 1932; d. Clarence Frederick and Anna Cecelia (Stank) Felkel; m. Ivan L. Lingle, Oct. 4, 1950 (dec. Aug. 2001); children: Ivan Dale, Aimee Lee, Clarence Craig. Sec. Ill. State Police, 1950; with welfare dept. Ill. Pub. Aid, Hillsboro, 1951-52; rschr. Small Homes Coun., Champaign, 1952-53; sec. Hillsboro Schs., 1954; office, payroll clk. Eagle Picher Zinc, Hillsboro, 1955—56; continuity dir. Sta. WSMI, Litchfield, 1966—87. Adv. bd. Am. Savs. Bank/Citizens Savs. Bank, vice chmn., 1986-93; founder Dunsford Books, 2004. Author: Configurations, 2004, numerous poems; columnist: Here's Looking at You, 2006—. Cmty. edn. bridge instr. Lincoln Land C.C.; fin. chmn. Hillsboro Hosp. Aux., 1972; lit. vol. Graham Correctional Ctr., Hillsboro, 1986-97; pres., bd. dirs. Montgomery Players and Encore Play Theatre, 1954-70. Recipient Vol. of Yr. award Graham Correction Ctr., 1995, award of Merit Ill. State Bd. Edn., 1994-95. Mem. Cousteau Soc., Internat. Wildlife Fedn., Nat. Wildlife Fedn., Natural Resources Def. Coun., Phi Theta Kappa Internat., Hillsboro Country Club, Hillsboro Book Club, Red Hat Soc. Democrat. Lutheran. Avocations: bridge, golf, gardening, travel, reading.

LINHARDT, ROBERT JOHN, chemistry professor; b. Passaic, NJ, Oct. 18, 1953; s. Robert J. and Barbara A. (Kelley) L.; m. Kathryn F. Burns, May 31, 1975; children: Kelley, Barbara. BS in Chemistry, Marquette U., 1975; MA in Chemistry, Johns Hopkins U., 1977, PhD in Organic Chemistry, 1979; postgrad., Mass. Inst. Tech., 1979-82. Rsch. assoc. Mass. Inst. Tech., Cambridge, 1979-82; asst. prof. U. Iowa, Iowa City, 1982-86, assoc. prof., 1986-90, prof. medicinal and natural products chemistry, 1990—2003, prof. chem. and biochem. engring., 1996—2003, F. Wendell Miller Disting. prof., 1996—2003, prof. chemistry, 1999—; constellation chair in biocatalysis and metabolic engring. Rensselaer Poly. Inst., Troy, NY. Cons. in field.; interacad. exchange scientist to USSR NAS, 1988. Mem. editl. bd. Applied Biochemistry and Biotech., 1985—, Carbohydrate Rsch., 1990—, Jour. Carbohydrate Chemistry, 1995—, Jour. Biol. Chem., 1995-2000, Analytical Biochemistry, 1991-97, 2001—; contbr. numerous articles to profl. jours. Johnson and Johnson fellow MIT, 1981; NIH grantee, 1982—. Mem. AAAS, AACP (Volwiler award 1999), Am. Chem. Soc. (Horace S. Isbell award Carbohydrate Chemistry 1994, Claude S. Hudson award in carbohydrate chemistry 2003), Soc. Glycobiology. Office: Rensselaerp Poly Inst 110 8th St Troy NY 12180 Home: 214 Lancaster St Albany NY 12210-1132 E-mail: linhar@rpi.edu.

LINHART, JOSEPH WAYLAND, retired cardiologist, educational administrator; b. NYC, Feb. 7, 1933; s. Joseph and Myrla Watson (Wayland) L.; m. Marilyn Adele Voight, Sept. 1, 1956; children: Joseph, Mary-Ellen, Richard, Jennifer, Donna-Lisa, Daria. BS, George Washington U., 1954, MD, 1958. Diplomate Am. Bd. Internal Medicine with subspecialty in cardiovascular diseases. Intern Washington Hosp. Ctr., 1958-59; resident George Washington U. Hosp., Washington, 1959-60, Duke U. Hosp., Durham, NC, 1961, fellow, 1960, 62-63, Nat. Heart Inst./Johns Hopkins Hosp., Bethesda/Balt., Md., 1963-64; asst. prof. medicine U. Fla., Gainesville, 1964-67; clin. assoc. prof. U. Miami, Fla., 1967-68; assoc. prof. medicine U. Tex., San Antonio, 1968-71; prof., dir. cardiology Hahnemann Med. Coll., Phila., 1971-75; prof., chmn. dept. medicine Chgo. Med. Sch., 1975-79, Oral Roberts U., Tulsa, 1979-83; prof. medicine U. South Fla., Tampa, 1983-92; prof., regional chmn. medicine Tex. Tech. U., Odessa, 1992-93; prof. medicine La. State U., Shreveport, 1993-97; chief med. svc. VA Med. Ctr., Shreveport, 1993-97, acting chief of staff, 1996-97; ret., 1997. Cons. in cardiology and med./legal questions. Contbr. articles to profl. jours.; author 4 books. Mem. med. adv. com. YMCA, Niles, Ill., 1976-79; bd. govs. Phila. Heart Assn., 1972-75; mem. rsch. coun. Okla. Heart Assn., Tulsa, 1980-83. Fellow ACP, Am. Coll. Cardiology; mem. AAAS, Planetary Soc., Nat. Space Soc., Astron. Soc. of Pacific, Alpha Omega Alpha. Republican. Avocations: astronomy, history, model building, organ playing, music. Home: 625 Red Cedar Ct NE Saint Petersburg FL 33703-6203

LINICK, ANDREW S., direct marketing expert; b. 1945; PhD in Indsl. Psychology, NYU, 1972. Chmn. bd. dirs. Linick Group Inc., Middle Island, NY. Office: Linick Group Inc The Linick Bldg 7 Putter Lane PO Box 102 Middle Island NY 11953-0102 Office Phone: 631-924-8855. Business E-Mail: LinickGrp@att.net.

LINK, DONALD, chef; Attended, Calif. Culinary Inst., San Francisco. Chef Flying Saucer, San Francisco, Cha, Cha, Cha, San Francisco, Scala's Bistro, San Francisco, Zazie, San Francisco, Bayona, New Orleans, 1995, sous chef; opening chef Jardinière, San Francisco, 1997; exec. chef Elite Café, Mojo, Palo Alto, Calif., Cochon; ptnr., exec. chef Herbsaint Restuarant, New Orleans, 2000—. Named a Top Ten Chef to Watch, Forbes Mag.; named Chef of Yr., New Orleans Mag., 2002, Best Chef: South, James Beard Found., 2007; named to Top 40 Under 40 Power Generation, New Orleans City Bus. Office: Herbsaint 701 St Charles Ave New Orleans LA 70130 Office Phone: 504-524-4114.*

LINK, GEORGE HAMILTON, retired lawyer; b. Sacramento, Calif., Mar. 26, 1939; s. Hoyle and Corrie Elizabeth (Evans) L.; m. Betsy Leland; children— Thomas Hamilton, Christopher Leland. AB, U. Calif., Berkeley, 1961; LLB, Harvard U., 1964. Bar: Calif. 1965, U.S. Dist. Ct. (no., ea., ctrl. and so dists.) Calif. 1965, U.S. Ct. Appeals (9th cir.) 1965. Assoc. Brobeck, Phleger & Harrison, San Francisco, 1964-69, ptnr., 1970—2001, mng. ptnr. LA, 1973-93, mng. ptnr firmwide, 1993-96; ret., 2001. Chmn. Pacific Rim Adv. Coun., 1992-95. Bd. regents U. Calif., 1971-74; trustee Berkeley Found., Jr. Statesmen Am.; bd. govs. United Way, 1979-81; trustee, v.p. Calif. Hist. Soc., 1987—; bd. dirs. Ancient Egypt Rsch. Assocs. Fellow Am. Bar Found.; mem. ABA, Calif. Bar Assn., L.A. Bar Assn., U. Calif. Alumni Assn. (pres. 1972-75), Calif. Club, Bohemian Club, Jonathan Club. Republican. Methodist. Office Phone: 310-476-1836. Personal E-mail: georgehlink@msn.com.

LINK, PHOEBE FORREST, education educator, writer, social worker, poet; b. Palmerton, Pa., Feb. 20, 1926; d. John Nevins and Phoebe Eleanor (Lewis) Forrest; m. Robert H. Link, July 13, 1962; children: David Forrest, Anne Harris. BA in Psychology, Pa. State U., State Coll., 1947, MS in Child Devel. and Family Relationships, 1952; postgrad., U. Rochester, NYC, 1957—59, Harvard U., 1958. Dir. teen age program YWCA, Lansing, Mich., 1947—50, Rochester, NY, 1952—56; rsch. asst. Pa. State U., State College, 1950—52; tchr. Rochester, 1956—60; demonstration tchr. William Antheil Sch., Trenton, NJ, 1960—63; mem. faculty Trenton State Coll., 1960—63; tchr. State College Area Schs., 1971—93. Lectr. Am. Home Econs. Assn. Conf.; cons. family studies, leader continuing edn. workshops Pa. State U., 1977, others; mem. staff dean women Harvard U., Cambridge, Mass., 1958; dir. Children's Program for Pa. Dist. Attys.; featured author TV series The Writing Life; reader-editor WPSX-TV. Author: Small? Tall? Not At All, 1973, Passionate Realist, 1994; staff writer: Horizon, 1985—87, author, creator: Heartthrob series, 1987; contbr. articles to profl. jours. Trustee Schlow Pub. Libr., State College, 1980—83; founder, 1st chmn. poetry com. Ctrl. Pa. Festival Arts; featured spkr. 50th class reunion Pa. State U.; mentor Women's Leadership Initiative, Pa. State U., 2004; dir. youth choir Univ. Bapt. Ch.; vis. deacon spiritual ministry team State College Presbyn. Ch., 2002; mem. aux. com. Centre Vols. in Medicine, 2004. Recipient Excellence in Edn. award with highest distinction, Pa. State U., 1993, merit award, William Antheil Sch., 1958; AAUW Simmons grantee, 1984. Mem.: NEA, AAUW, State College Area Edn. Assn. (scholarship com.), Peterson Soc., Mortar Bd. Alumni (founder, 1st pres., pres.), Pa. State U. Coll. Human Devel. Alumni (bd. dirs.), Tau Phi Sigma, Omicron Nu Alumni, Phi Delta Kappa.

LINK, PHYLLIDA KORMAN, artist, educator; b. Bronx, NY, May 2, 1949; d. Charles and Minette Rose (Roschelle) Korman. BA, City Coll., NY, 1970; MA, CUNY, 1987. Cert. Art Sorbonne, Paris, 1980, lic. tchg. NY State Bd. of Edn. Tchr. NYC Bd. Edn., 1971—79; English tchr. Gardiner's Acad., Paris, 1980—85; adj. prof. Hudson County Cmty. Coll., Jersey City, 1988—93, St. Peter's Coll., Jersey City, 1986—. Exhibitions include SI Mus., NY, 1983, Nabisco Gallery, 1988, Milburn Playhouse Gallery, NJ, 1990, Internet, 2000—02, Riverdale Gallery, NY, 2007. Grantee Dept. of Comp Lit., Grad. Ctr. CUNY, 1985; scholar found. scholar, Helena Rubinstein Found., 1986—87. Fellow: NOW; mem.: La Maison Française, Columbia U., Pen and Brush Club. Avocations: films, excursions, museums.

LINK, ROBERT JAMES, lawyer, educator; b. Washington, May 25, 1950; s. Robert Wendell and Barbara Ann (Bullock) L.; children: Robert Edward, Holden James. BA, U. Miami, 1972, JD, 1975. Bar: Fla. 1975, U.S. Dist. Ct. (mid. dist.) Fla. 1980, U.S. Ct. Appeals (5th cir.) 1980, U.S. Ct. Appeals (11th cir.) 1981, U.S. Supreme Ct. 1984, U.S. Dist. Ct. (no. dist.) Fla. 1989. Asst. pub. defender City of Miami, Fla., 1975-78, City of Jacksonville, Fla., 1978-82; ptnr. Greenspan, Goodstein & Link, Jacksonville, 1982-84, Goodstein & Link, Jacksonville, 1984-85; pvt. practice, Jacksonville, 1985-88; assoc. Howell, Liles & Milton, Jacksonville, 1988-89; ptnr. Pajcic & Pajcic P.A., 1990—. Guest instr. U. Miami, 1976, U. Fla., 1979-88, Stetson U. Law Sch., 1984, Jacksonville U., 1987-88, U. North Fla., 1991, Fla. Coastal Sch. Law, 2007. Atty. legal panel ACLU, Jacksonville, 1982-88; bd. dirs. Jackson Area Legal Aid, 1992-94. Mem. Fla. Bar Assn. (chmn. com. representation of indigents criminal law sect. 1980, cert. criminal trial lawyer 1989), Nat. Assn. Criminal Def. Lawyers (vice-chmn. post conviction com. 1990), Fla. Pub. Defender Assn. (death penalty steering com. 1980-82, instr. 1979-00, guest spkr. 2006), Assn. Fla. Trial Lawyers (seminar spkr. 2000), Attys. Info. Exchange Group (guest spkr. 2005). Democrat. Methodist. Avocations: sailing, fishing, diving, softball. Home: 1797 San Marco Blvd 3 Jacksonville FL 32207-5836 Office: 1900 Independent Dr Jacksonville FL 32202-5023 Office Phone: 904-358-8881. Business E-Mail: bob@pajcic.com.

LINK, ROBERT O., JR., lawyer; b. Ottumwa, Iowa, Dec. 4, 1954; BS with highest honors, U. Tenn., 1977, MBA, JD, 1980. Bar: Tenn. 1980, Ga. 1982, NY 1985. Assoc. Cadwalader, Wickersham & Taft, NYC, 1987—90, ptnr., 1990—, chmn., mng. ptnr., mem. mgmt. com. & chmn. Capital Markets Dept. Mem. N.Y.C. Olympic 2012 Legal Adv. Com.; mem. adv. council Dean of Coll. Bus. Adminstrn., Univ. Tenn.; bd. dir. Wall St. Rising. Recipient Am. Jurisprudence awards. Mem.: Mortgage Bankers Assn., N.Y. State Bar Assn., Order of Coif. Office: Cadwalader Wickersham & Taft LLP 1 World Fin Ctr New York NY 10281 Office Phone: 212-504-6172. Office Fax: 212-504-6666. Business E-Mail: robert.link@cwt.com.

LINK, SCOTT J., lawyer; b. Kankakee, Ill., Oct. 16, 1961; BS with honors, Ea. Ill. U., 1983; JD magna cum laude, No. Ill. U., 1986. Bar: Fla. 1986, US Dist. Ct. (no., so., middle dist. Fla.), US Ct. Appeals (11th cir.). Ptnr. Gunster Yoakley & Stewart, 1986—96; founding ptnr., bus. & securities litigation Ackerman Link & Sartory LLP, West Palm Beach, Del., 1996—. Mem. NASD Nat. Arbitration & Mediation Com. Named one of Fla. Legal Elite, Fla. Trend mag., 2004, 2005; named to Best Lawyers in Am., 2003—06, Top Lawyers List, South Fla. Legal Guide mag., 2003,

2004, 2005, 2006. Mem.: ABA, Fla. Bar, Palm Beach County Bar Assn. Office: Ackerman Link & Sartory LLP 222 Lakeview Ave West Palm Beach FL 33401 Office Phone: 561-838-4100. Office Fax: 561-838-5305. Business E-Mail: slink@alslaw.com.

LINK, WILLIAM ALLEN, history educator; b. Evanston, Ill., Aug. 18, 1954; s. Arthur Stanley and Margaret McDowell (Douglas) L.; m. Susannah Hopkins Jones, June 21, 1980; children: Percy Anne, Margaret Dorothy, Josephine McDowell. BA, Davidson Coll., 1976; MA, U. Va., 1979, PhD, 1981. Asst. prof. history U. N.C., Greensboro, 1981-86, assoc. prof. history, 1986-92, prof. history, 1992—2004, assoc. dean, Coll. Arts and Scis., 1995—98, head history dept., 1998—2004; Richard J. Milbauer prof. history U. Fla., 2004—. Mem. editl. bd. History of Edn. Quar., 1994-96, Jour. So. History, 2006—. Author: A Hard Country and a Lonely Place: Schooling, Society, and Reform in Rural Virginia, 1870-1920, 1986, The Paradox of Southern Progressivism, 1880-1930, 1992, William Friday: Power, Purpose, and American Higher Education, 1995, Roots of Secession: Slavery and Politics in Antelellum Viginia, 2003. Elder, Starmount Presbyn. Ch., Greensboro, 1996—99. Recipient Mayflower prize, N.C. Lit. and Hist. Assn., 1993, 95. Mem. Am. Hist. Assn., Hist. Edn. Soc., So. Hist. Assn., Hist. Soc. N.C., Organ. Am. Historians, Phi Beta Kappa. Presbyterian. Home: 5727 NW 43rd Rd Gainesville FL 32606-4380 Office: U Fla 231 Keene Flint Hall PO Box 117320 Gainesville FL 32611-7320 E-mail: linkwa@ufl.edu.

LINKE, RICHARD A., optical engineer; b. Plainfield, NJ, Feb. 15, 1946; married; 2 children. BA, Columbia U., 1968, MS, 1970, PhD in Physics, 1972. Tech. staff radio physics rsch. Bell Telephone Labs., 1972-86, head lightwave comm. rsch. dept., 1986-89; sr. rsch. scientist NEC Rsch. Inst.; dir., sci. policy Optical Soc. Am., 2003—06; exec. dir. Inst. Electrical & Electronics Engineers Lasers & Electro-Optics Soc., Piscataway, 2006—. Fellow IEEE, Optical Soc. Am. Office: 445 Hoes Ln Piscataway NJ 08854

LINKER, ARTHUR S., lawyer; b. NYC, May 20, 1947; s. Jack and Gertrude (Reibeisen) L.; m. Diane Spanier, June 4, 1973; children: Beth, Jennifer, Michael, Anne. AB summa cum laude, Columbia U., 1968, MA, 1970; JD cum laude, Harvard U., 1974. Bar: NY, US Dist. Ct. (so. and ea. dists.) NY, US Ct. Appeals (2d cir.) 1975, (4th cir.) 1989, (8th cir.) 1990, (9th cir.) 2000; US Supreme Ct. 1979. Ptnr. Rosenman & Colin LLP, NYC, 1974—2002, Katten Muchin Rosenman LLP, NYC, 2002—. Mem. ABA, N.Y. State Bar Assn., Assn. Bar City N.Y. Avocations: computers, astronomy. Office: Katten Muchin Rosenman LLP 575 Madison Ave Fl 26 New York NY 10022-2585 Home Phone: 914-725-2350; Office Phone: 212-940-7007. Business E-Mail: arthur.linker@kattenlaw.com.

LINKLATER, WILLIAM J., lawyer; b. Chgo., June 3, 1942; s. William John and Jean (Connell) L.; m. Dorothea D. Ash, Apr. 4, 1986; children: Erin, Emily. BA, U. Notre Dame, 1964; JD, Loyola U., 1968. Bar: Ill. 1968, U.S. Dist. Ct. (no. dist.) Ill. 1968, U.S. Ct. Appeals (7th cir.) 1971, U.S. Supreme Ct. 1971, U.S. Ct. Appeals Wash. 1978, Calif. 1981, U.S. Dist. Ct. (cen. dist.) Calif. 1981, U.S. Tax Ct. 1982, U.S. Dist. Ct. (no. dist.) Calif. 1983, U.S. Dist. Ct. (ea. dist.) Mich. 1989, Colo., 1990, U.S. Ct. Appeals (6th cir.) 1990, U.S. Dist. Ct. Hawaii 1992, U.S. Ct. Appeals (11th cir.), 1999, U.S. Ct. Appeals (5th cir.), 1999, Wyo. 2005. Atty. Fed. Defender Project, Chgo.; assoc. Baker & McKenzie, Chgo., 1968-75, ptnr., 1975—, dir. profl. responsibility. Contbr. articles to profl. jours. Named one of World's Leading White Collar Crime Lawyers, Euromoney, World's Leading Competition and Antitrust Lawyers. Mem.: FBA, ABA (past co-chmn. com. on internat. criminal law criminal justice sect., mem. criminal practice and procedure com. antitrust sect., others), Wyo. Bar Assn., Nat. Assn. Criminal Def. Lawyers, Am. Bd. Criminal Lawyers, Am. Coll. Trial Lawyers, Colo. Bar Assn., Calif. Bar Assn., Chgo. Bar Assn. (pres. 2000—01, bd. mgrs. 1997—2002, past v.p. jud. candidates evaluation com., chmn. large law firm com.), 7th Cir. Bar Assn., Ill. Bar Assn., Wong Sun Soc. San Francisco (internat. proctor), Chgo. Inn of Ct., Alpha Sigma Nu. Office: Baker & McKenzie LLP 130 E Randolph Dr Ste 2500 Chicago IL 60601 Office Phone: 312-861-2794.

LINKLETTER, ARTHUR GORDON, radio and television broadcaster; b. Moose Jaw, Sask., Can., July 17, 1912; s. Fulton John and Mary (Metzler) L.; m. Lois Foerster, Nov. 25, 1935; children: Jack, Dawn, Robert (dec.), Sharon, Diane (dec.). AB, San Diego State Coll., 1934. Program dir. Sta. KGB, San Diego, 1934; program dir. Calif. Internat. Expn., San Diego, 1935; radio dir. Tex. Centennial Expn., Dallas, 1936; San Francisco World's Fair, 1937-39; pres. Linkletter Prodns.; ptnr., co-owner John Guedel Radio Prodns. Chmn. bd. Linkletter Enterprises; owner Art Linkletter Oil Enterprises. Author: theme spectacle Cavalcade of Golden West, 1940; author and co-producer: theme spectacle Cavalcade of Am, 1941; writer, producer, star in West Coast radio shows, 1940-55; former star, writer: People Are Funny, NBC-TV and radio, Art Linkletter's House Party, CBS-TV and radio; Author: People Are Funny, 1953, Kids Say The Darndest Things, 1957, The Secret World of Kids, 1959, Confessions of a Happy Man, 1961, Kids Still Say The Darndest Things, 1961, A Child's Garden of Misinformation, 1965, I Wish I'd Said That, 1968, Linkletter Down Under, 1969, Oops, 1969, Drugs at My Door Step, 1973, Women Are My Favorite People, 1974, How to be a Super Salesman, 1974, Yes, You Can!, 1979, I Didn't Do It Alone, 1979, Public Speaking for Private People, 1980, Linkletter on Dynamic Selling, 1982, Old Age is not for Sissies, 1988; co-host (with Bill Cosby) series Kids Say the Darnedest Things, 1998—; lectr. convs. and univs. Nat. bd. dirs. Goodwill Industries; commr. gen. to U.S. Exhibit at Brisbane Expo 88, Australia, 1987; commr. gen. to rank of U.S. amb. to The 200th Anniversary Celebration, Australia, 1987—; bd. regents Pepperdine U.; chmn. bd. Ctr. on Aging, UCLA; chmn. bd. French Found. for Alzheimers Rsch., Solargenix; pres. USA-Next (sr.). Recipient numerous awards. Mem.: United Srs. Assn. (pres.). Address: 11601 Wilshire Blvd Ste 500 Los Angeles CA 90025

LINKONIS, SUZANNE NEWBOLD, retired probation officer, retired counselor; b. Phila., Aug. 24, 1945; d. William Bartram and Kathryn (Taylor) Newbold; m. Bertram Lawrence Linkonis, May 29, 1966; children: Robert William, Deborah Anne, Richard Anthony. AA in Psychology, Albany Jr. Coll., Ga., 1979; BA in Psychology, Albany State U., Ga., 1981; MS in Indsl. Psychology, Va. Commonwealth U., 1986. Office mgr., media buyer Long Advt. Agy., Richmond, Va., 1981-84; media mgr. Clarke & Assocs., Richmond, 1984-85; human resources asst. Continental Ins., Richmond, 1985; rsch. assoc. Signet Bank, N.A., Richmond, 1986-87; program coord. Med. Coll. Va., Richmond, 1988; personnel mgr. Bur. Microbiology, Richmond, 1988-89; pers. specialist Va. State Dept. Corrections, Richmond, 1989-90; human rights adv. Va. State Dept. Youth and Family Svcs., Richmond, 1990-92, rehab. counselor, 1992-94, sr. rehab. counselor, 1994; pre-trial case mgr./counselor Henrico County Govt., Richmond, 1994-97, cmty. corrections case mgr., counselor, 1997-2000, sr. county probation officer, counselor, 2001—06. Future dir., cons. Mary Kay Cosmetics, Springfield, Va., 1975-77. Republican. Roman Catholic. Avocations: walking, reading, boating, fishing, genealogy. Home: 281 Shoreline Dr New Bern NC 28562 E-mail: slinkonis@cs.com.

LINKOUS, WILLIAM JOSEPH, JR., lawyer; b. Roanoke, Va., July 17, 1929; s. William Joseph and Mary Virginia (Lester) L.; m. Anita Marie Stedronsky, Oct. 15, 1960; children: William Joseph III, Brian Keith BA, Roanoke Coll., Salem, Va., 1951; MA in Econs., U. Va., 1954, JD, 1956. Bar: Va. 1956, Ga. 1957. Assoc. Powell, Goldstein, Frazer & Murphy, Atlanta, 1956-62, ptnr., 1962-79, 85—, mng. ptnr., 1979-85. Trustee Holy Innocents Episcopal Sch., Atlanta, 1974-80, Roanoke Coll., 1980-95, emeritus 1995—. Fellow Am. Coll. Trust and Estate Counsel, Am. Bar Found.; mem. State Bar Ga. (past chmn. fiduciary sect., chmn. Ga. trust law revision com. 1988-91, 2003—, chmn. Ga. probate code revision com. 1991-97, chmn. Ga. guardianship code revision com.1997-2003), Va. State Bar, Am. Law Inst., Internat. Acad. Estate and Trust Law, Atlanta Estate Planning Coun. (pres. 1983-84). Avocation: tennis. Office: Powell Goldstein LLP One Atlantic Ctr Fourteenth Fl 1201 West Peachtree St NW Atlanta GA 30309-3488 Office Phone: 404-572-6610. Business E-Mail: wlinkous@pogolaw.com.

LINN, DALE E., secondary school educator; s. Loren Eugene and Emma June Linn; m. Christine Anne Haskal, Aug. 5, 1995; 1 child, Meredith Anne. BA, Mo. Bapt. U., St. Louis, 1982; MA, Webster U., St. Louis, 1990. Tchr. Hazelwood Sch. Dist., Florissant, 1987—. Adult basic edn. instr., Florissant, 1982—95. Mem.: NEA, Mo. Edn. Assn., Nat. Coun. Social Studies. Home: 924 Zohmer Ct Florissant MO 63031 E-mail: dlinn@hazelwood.k12.mo.us.

LINN, DIANA PATRICIA, retired elementary school educator; b. Perth, Australia, Dec. 31, 1943; arrived in US, 1948; d. Evan Andrew and Grace Henrietta (Springhall) Jarboe; m. Jim F. Erlandsen, July 9, 1966 (div. Mar. 1989); children: Rebecca Erlandsen, Tim Erlandsen, Jenny Erlandsen; m. Richard George Linn, Mar. 31, 1990; 1 stepchild, Cristal. AA, Olympic Coll., 1963; BA in Elem. Edn., Western Wash. U., 1965; MA, U. Ariz., 1969. Cert. tchr. Wash. Tchr. Neomi B. Willmore Elem., Westminster, Calif., 1965-66; tchr. English and sci. Sunnyside Jr. H.S., Tucson, 1966-70; tchr. kindergarten All Seasons Sch., Tucson, 1972-74; tchr. St. Cyril's Sch., Tucson, 1974-77; elem. tchr. Grace Christian Sch., Tucson, 1977-80; kindergarten and elem. tchr. Ridgeview Christian Ctr., Spokane, Wash., 1983-85, Spokane Christian Schs., 1985-87; dir. Ridgeview Christian Learning Ctr., Spokane, 1987-88; tchr. kindergarten Arlington Elem. Sch., Spokane, 1988-96, Grant Elem. Sch., Spokane, 1996—2005; ret. Spokane Sch. Dist. #81, 2006. Mem. curriculum study com. Sunnyside Sch. Dist., Tucson, 1967—68; chmn. accreditation and sch. bd. St. Cyril's Sch., Tucson, 1976—77; chair faculty involvement group, chair staff devel, chair wellness com. Arlington Elem., Spokane, 1992—93, sch. reporter, 1994—95, chair faculty involvement group, mem. strategic plan equity com., 1995—96; instr. reading readiness Family Learning Fair, Home Schooling Seminar, Spokane Falls CC, Spokane, 1968; chair, coord. pre-sch. coop. Arlington Elem. with Spokane Falls CC, 1992—93; chair faculty involvement group Grant Elem. Sch., 1996—97, wellness chair, 1992—2001, site coun. faculty rep., 2001—05, primary team faculty rep., 2002—05, pres. site coun., 2003—04. Brownie troop leader Willmore Elem., Westminster, 1965—66; ednl. restructuring rep. Spokane Sch. Dist. 81 Arlington Elem., 1992—93, mem. equity com., 1996—99, mem. early childhood com., 1996—2004, mem. strategic planning com., 1998—2003, wellness chmn., 1998—2000, mem. instrnl. team, 1999—2003; primary rep. site coun. Grant Elem., 2002, pres. site coun., 2003—04; coord. Christian edn. Valley Foursquare Ch., Spokane, 1982—87; coord. children's ch. Victory Faith Fellowship, Spokane, 1993—2003. Scholar, Naval Officer's Wives Club, 1961—62; Eisenhower grantee, 1990, 1994, 1996—97. Mem.: NEA, ASCD, Spokane Edn. Assn. (Arlington Elem. rep. 1991—93), Wash. Edn. Assn., CPA Wives Club (sec., ball chair 1983—84), Alpha Delta Kappa (membership chair 1994—95, corr. sec. 1996—99). Republican. Avocations: doll collecting, plate collecting, swimming, quilting. Home: 1324 S Perry St Spokane WA 99202-3572 E-mail: d2linn@yahoo.com, diane.linn@gmail.com.

LINN, MARCIA CYROG, education educator; b. Milw., May 27, 1943; d. George W. and Frances (Vanderhoof) Cyrog; m. Stuart Michael Linn, 1967 (div. 1979); children: Matthew, Allison; m. Curtis Bruce Tarter, 1987 (div. 2003). BA in Psychology and Stats., Stanford U., 1965, MA in Ednl. Psychology, 1967, PhD in Ednl. Psychology, 1970. Prin. investigator Lawrence Hall Sci. U. Calif., 1970-87, prin. investigator Sch. Edn., 1985—, asst. dean Sch. Edn., 1983-85, prof., 1989—; prin. investigator NSF Funded Ctr.- Tech.-Enhanced Learning in Sci. (TELS), 2003—08; chancellor's prof., 2003—. Fulbright prof. Weizmann Inst., Israel, 1983; exec. dir. seminars U. Calif., 1985-86, dir. instnl. tech. program, 1988-96, chair cognition and devel., 1996—98; cons. Apple Computer, 1983—90; mem. adv. com. on sci. edn. NSF, 1978—85, Ednl. Testing Svc., 1986—90, Smithsonian Instn., 1986—, Fulbright Program, 1983-86, Grad. Record Exam. Bd., 1990-94, adv. com. edn. and human resources directorate, NSF, 2002—; chair Cognitive Studes Bd. McDonell Found., 1994-97; mem. computing svcs. adv. bd. Carnegie Mellon U., 1991-99; mem. steering com. 3d Internat. Math. and Sci. Study, U.S., 1991-2002. Author: Education and the Challenge of Technology, 1987; co-author: The Psychology of Gender--Advances Through Meta Analysis, 1986—, Designing Pascal Solutions, 1992—, Designing Pascal Solutions with Data Structures, 1996, Computers, Teachers, Peers-Science Learning Partners, 2000, Internet Environments for Science Education, 2004; contbr. articles to profl. jours. Sci. advisor Parents Club, Lafayette, Calif., 1984-87; mem. Internat. Women's Forum, Women's Forum West, 1992—, membership com., 1995-98; bd. dirs. Nat. Ctr. for Sci. Edn., 1997—, GIS and edn. com., 2000—; mem. bd. on behavioral, cognitive and sensory scis. Nat. Rsch. Coun., 1997-2005, mem. com. on info. tech. literacy, computer sci. and telecomms., 1997-2000; mem. nat. adv. bd. Nat. Ctr. for Improving Student Learning and Achievement in Math. and Sci., 1997—; mem. com. on info. tech. fluency and H.S. grad. outcomes NRC, 2004-05. Recipient fellow Ctr. for Adv. Study in Behavior. Scis. 1995-96, 2001-02, Excellence Ednl. Rsch. award Coun. Sci. Soc. Pres., 1998. Fellow AAAS (bd. dirs. 1996-2001, chair-elect edn. sect. 2005—), APA, AAUW (mem. commn. tech. and gender 1998-2001), Am. Psychol. Soc.; mem. Nat. Assn. Rsch. in Sci. and Teaching (bd. dirs. 1983-86, assoc. editor jour., Outstanding Paper award 1978, Outstanding Jour. Article award 1975, 83, Disting. Contbns. to Sci. Edn. Through Rsch. award 1994), Am. Ednl. Rsch. Assn. (chmn. rsch. on women and edn. 1983-85, Women Educators Rsch. award 1982, 88, edn. in sci. and tech. 1989-90, ann. mtg. program com. 1996, Willystine Goodsell award 1991), Internat. Soc. Learning Svcs. (bd. dirs. 2005—), Nat. Sci. Tchrs. Assn. (mem. rsch. agenda com. 1987-90, task force 1993-94), Soc. Rsch. in Child Devel. (editl. bd. 1984-89), Soc. Rsch. Adolescence, Nat. Acad. Edn., Sierra Club. Avocations: skiing, hiking. Office: U Calif Grad Sch Edn 4611 Tolman Hl Berkeley CA 94720-0001

LINN, RICHARD, federal judge; b. Bklyn., Apr. 13, 1944; BEE, Rensselaer Poly. Inst., 1965; JD, Georgetown U., 1969. Bar: Va., DC 1970, NY 1994. Patent examiner US Patent Office, 1965—68; patent agent US Naval Rsch. Lab., 1968—69; assoc. Brenner, O'Brien, Guay, Connors, 1970—71; patent advisor US Naval Air Systems Command, 1971—72; assoc. Stepno & Neilan, 1972—73; partner Stepno, Schwabb & Linn, 1973—74, Imirie, Smiley & Linn, 1974—77, Marks & Murase, L.L.P., 1977—97, exec. comm., 1987—97; partner, pract. group leader intellectual prop. dept Foley & Lardner, 1997—99; judge US Ct. Appeals (Fed. cir.), Washington, 1999—. Lecturer Geo. Washington Sch. of Law, 2001—; mem. Intellectual Property Adv. Bd., GWU Sch. of Law. Recipient Rensselaer Alumni Assn Fellows award, 2000.*

LINN, STUART MICHAEL, biochemist, educator; b. Chgo., Dec. 16, 1940; s. Maurice S. and Pauline Linn; children: Matthew S., Allison D., Meagan S. BS in Chemistry with honors, Calif. Inst. Tech., 1962; PhD in Biochemistry, Stanford U., 1967. Asst. prof. biochemistry U. Calif., Berkeley, 1968-72, assoc. prof., 1972-75, prof., 1975-87, head divsn. biochemistry and molecular biology, 1987-90, 1995-2000. Mem. editl. bd. Nucleic Acids Rsch., 1974—, Jour. Biol. Chemistry. 1975—80, Molecular and Cellular Biology, 1987—91; contbr. articles to profl. jours., chapters to books. Helen Hay Whitney fellow, 1966—68, John Simon Guggenheim fellow, 1974—75, Merit grantee, USPHS, 1988—97. Mem.: AAAS, Am. Soc. Microbiologists, Am. Soc. Biol. Chem. Molecular Biol., Am. Acad. Arts and Scis. Office: U Calif Divsn Biochem & Molec Bio Barker Hall Berkeley CA 94720-3202 Business E-Mail: slinn@berkeley.edu.

LINNÉA, SHARON, writer, playwright; d. William Diderichsen and Marilynn Joyce Webber; m. Robert Owens Scott; children: Jonathan Brendan Scott, Linnéa Juliet Scott. Student, Wheaton Coll., 1974-76; BA, NYU, 1978. With editl. dept. various titles William Morrow and Co., NYC, 1977-78, Taplinger and Assocs., NYC, 1978-80, Flying Magazine, NYC, 1982-83; features editor Scholastic Voice, NYC, 1983-85; staff writer Guideposts Mag., NYC, 1985-91; contbg. editor, 1991—99, Angels on Earth, 1995—99; prodr. Inspiration Beliefnet.com, 1999—2002; head writer New Morning Show Hallmark Network, 2002. V.p. Imagining Things Enterprises, NYC; spkr. in field. Prodr. (film) Knowing Lisa, 1991 (Silver award Worldfest/Houston film festival); author: (study guide) Romeo and Juliet by William Shakespeare, 1984, Hedda Gabbler and A Doll's House by Henrik Ibsen, 1985, (book) Raoul Wallenberg: The Man Who Stopped Death, 1993 (Best Book of 1993 Jewish World, Dayton Jewish Chronicle, The Speaker), Princess Ka'iulani: Hope of A Nation, Heart of A People, 1999 (Carter G. Woodson award), (with Jeff Meyer) America's Famous and Historic Trees, 2001, Chicken Soup from the Soul of Hawaii, 2003, (plays), Clown of God, 1977, The Singer, 1978, A Matter of Time, 1981, Tales from the Vermont Woods, 1982, Chasing Eden, 2007, Beyond Eden, 2007, (screenplays) Missouri, Ma Cheri, Tomorrow Is My Dancing Day; ghostwriter articles in Reader's Digest and Guideposts Mag.; profile biographer World of Heroes Sch. Curriculum; psychology columnist, film reviewer Beliefnet.com; freelancer Marvel Comics, Children's TV Workshop, Hallmark Hall of Fame; freelance editor Chicken Soup for the Soul; contbr. to book pubs. including From the Ashes, 2001, Big Book of Angels, 2002; contbr. articles to popular publs. Recipient Storytelling World award, 2004. Mem.: Authors Guild. Avocations: latching rugs, public speaking. Office: PO Box 377 Warwick NY 10990 E-mail: sharon@sharonlinnea.com.

LINNERT, TERRENCE GREGORY, lawyer; b. Cleve., Oct. 16, 1946; s. Ralph Marshall and Mary Gertrude (Gessner) L.; m. Susan Kay Chesnes, Jan 25, 1969; children: Michael, Patrick, Terrence, Timothy. BSEE, U. Notre Dame, 1968; JD, Cleve. State U., 1975. Bar: Ohio 1975. Engr. Cleve. Electric Illuminating, 1968-77, corp. counsel, 1977-84, sr. corp. counsel, 1984-86, Centerior Energy Corp., Independence, Ohio, 1986-87; prin. counsel Centerior Service Co., Independence, Ohio, 1987; asst. gen. counsel Centerior Svc. Co., Independence, Ohio, 1988-89; gen. counsel Centerior Energy Corp., Independence, 1989-92, v.p., legal & govtl. affairs, 1992-95; sr. v.p. adminstrn. & gen. counsel Goodrich Corp., Charlotte, NC, 1995—2002, exec. v.p. adminstrn., gen. counsel, 2004—. Mem. Citizens' League, Cleve; pres. St. Gabriel's Parents' Assn., Concord, Ohio, 1984-85, v.p. parish coun., 1986-87; pres. Lake Cath. Edn. Commn., Mentor, Ohio, 1991-92. Mem.: ARC, Econ. Am., Leadership Cleve. & Akron. Roman Catholic. Home: 14521 Nolen Ln Charlotte NC 28277-1576 Office: Goodrich Corp Four Coliseum Center 2730 W Tyvola Rd Charlotte NC 28217-4578 Office Phone: 704-423-5520, 704-423-7000. Office Fax: 704-423-5540. Business E-Mail: terry.linnert@goodrich.com.*

LINNEY, BEVERLY See HALLAM, BEVERLY

LINNEY, LAURA, actress; b. NYC, Feb. 5, 1964; d. Romulus Linney and Ann Leggett Perse; m. David Adkins, Sept. 1995 (div. 2000). BFA, Brown U., 1986; grad., Juilliard Sch., 1989. Motion picture and T.V. actress. Films include Lonrenzo's Oil, 1992, Searching for Bobby Fischer, 1993, Blind Spot, 1993, Dave, 1993, A Simple Twist of Fate, 1994, Congo, 1995, Primal Fear, 1996, The Truman Show, 1998, Absolute Power, 1998, Lush, 1999, You Can Count on Me, 2000, The House of Mirth, 2000, Running Mates, 2000, Maze, 2000, The Laramie Project, 2002, The Mothman Prophecies, 2002, The Life of David Gale, 2003, Mystic River, 2003, Love Actually, 2003, P.S., 2004, Kinsey, 2004, The Squid and the Whale, 2005, The Exorcism of Emily Rose, 2005, Driving Lessons, 2006, Jindabyne, 2006, The Hottest State, 2006, Man of the Year, 2006, The Savages, 2007, Breach, 2007, The Nanny Diaries, 2007(TV films) Tales of the City, 1993, More Tales of the City, 1998, Love Letters, 1999, Wild Iris, 2001; theatre prodn.: The Crucible, 2002 (Tony nominee). Office: c/o Creative Artists Agy 9830 Wilshire Blvd Beverly Hills CA 90212-1804*

LINOWES, DAVID FRANCIS, finance educator, corporate financial executive; b. NJ, Mar. 16, 1917; m. Dorothy Lee Wolf, Mar. 24, 1946; children: Joanne Linowes Alinsky, Richard Gary, Susan Linowes Allen (dec.), Jonathan Scott. Founder, ptnr. Leopold & Linowes (now BDO Siedman), Washington, 1946-62; cons. sr. ptnr. Leopold & Linowes, Washington, 1962-82; nat. founding ptnr. Laventhol & Horwath, 1965-76; chmn. bd, CEO Mickleberry Comm. Corp., 1970-73; chmn., CEO Perpetual Investment Co., Inc., 1950-88; dir. Horn & Hardart Co., 1971-77, Piper Aircraft, 1972-77, Saturday Rev./World Mag., Inc., 1972-77, Chris Craft Industries, Inc., 1958—2004; prof. polit. economy, pub. policy, bus. adminstrn. U. Ill., Urbana, 1976—2000, Boeschenstein prof. emeritus, 1987—. Cons. DATA Internat. Assistance Corps., 1962-68, U.S. Dept. State, UN, Sec. HEW, Dept. Interior; chmn. Fed. Privacy Protection Commn., Washington, 1975-77, U.S. Commn. Fair Market Value Policy for Fed. Coal Leasing, 1983-84, Pres.'s Commn. on Fiscal Accountability of Nation's Energy Resources, 1981-82; chmn. Pres.' Commn. on Privatization, 1987-88; mem. Council on Fgn. Relations; cons. panel GAO; adj. prof. mgmt. NYU, 1965-73; Disting. Arthur Young Prof. U. Ill., 1973-74; emeritus chmn. internat. adv. com. Tel Aviv U.; headed U.S. State Dept. Mission to Turkey, 1967, to India, 1970, to Pakistan, 1968, to Greece, 1971; U.S. rep. on privacy to Orgn. Econ. Devel. Intergovtl. Bur. for Informati cs, 1977-81, cons., N.Y.C., 1977-81; U.S. State Dept. mission to Chile, Argentina and Uruguay, July, 1988, Yugoslavia, May, 1991. Author: Managing Growth Through Acquistion, Strategies for Survival, Corporate Conscience; commn. report Personal Privacy in Information Society, Fiscal Accountablility of Nation's Energy Resources; editor: The Impact of the Communication and Computer Revolution on Society, Privacy in America, 1989, Creating Public Policy, 1998, Living Through 50 Years of Economic Progress with 10 Presidents-The Most Productive Generation in History 1946-1996, 2000; contbr. articles to profl. jours. Trustee Boy's Club Greater Washington, 1955-62, Am. Inst. Found., 1962-68; assoc. YM-YWHA's Greater N.Y., 1970-76; chmn. Charities Adv. Com. of D.C., 1958-62; emeritus bd. dirs. Religion in Am. Life, Inc.; former chmn. U.S. People for UN; chmn. citizens com. Combat Charity Rackets, 1953-58. 1st lt. Signal Corps, AUS, 1942-46. Recipient 1970 Human Relations award Am. Jewish Com., U.S. Pub. Service award, 1982, Alumni Achievement award U. Ill., 1989, CPA Distinguished Pub. Svc. award, Washington, 1989. Mem. AICPA (v.p. 1962-63), U. Ill. Found. (emeritus bd. dirs.), Coun. Fgn. Rels., Cosmos Club, Univ. Club, Phi Kappa Phi (nat. bd. dirs.), Beta Gamma Sigma. Home: 5630 Wisconsin Ave 801 Chevy Chase MD 20815

LINSCOTT, ROSS EDWARD, school psychologist; b. Columbus, Ohio, July 24, 1981; s. Howard R. Linscott and Linda S. Perkins; m. Ashley Lynn Wagner, Mar. 31, 2007. BA (hon.), Ohio Wesleyan U., Delaware, 2003; MS, Miami U., Oxford, Ohio, 2006. Grad. asst. ednl. psychology dept. Miami U., 2003—05; intern sch. psychologist Clermont County Ednl. Svc. Ctr., Batavia, Ohio, 2005—06; sch. psychologist Cardington-Lincoln Local Schs., Cardington, Ohio, 2006—. Mem.: NASP (assoc.), Phi Gamma Delta (mem. bd. chpt. advisors 2004—06). Republican. Methodist. Avocations: travel, sports, music, guitar. Home: 347 Prairie Run Dr Sunbury OH 43074 Office: Cardington-Lincoln Local Schs 121 Nichols St Cardington OH 43315 Home Phone: 740-965-1303; Office Phone: 419-864-3691 5008. Personal E-mail: ross.linscott@cardingtonschools.org.

LINSENMEIER, CAROL VINCENT, music educator; b. Manchester, Conn., Feb. 5, 1952; d. Donald Scott and Alys (Campbell) Vincent; m. John Andrew Linsenmeier, Dec. 28, 1979; children: Andrew, Thomas. B Music Edn., Coll. of Wooster, Ohio, 1974; M Music Edn., U. Ga., Athens, 1978; PhD in Spl. Edn., Kent State U., Ohio, 2004. Strings specialist Greenville County Schs., SC, 1974—76; Suzuki coord. U. Ga., Athens, 1977—80; violin/viola tchr. Sch. of Fine Arts, Willoughby, Ohio, 1980—, chair music dept., 1988—2005. Violin and viola tchr. Rabbit Run Cmty. Arts Assn., Madison, Ohio, 2005—, Ashtabula Arts Ctr., Ohio, 2005—. Arranger: children's musical How Big Is Your Circle, 2000. Rschr., bd. trustees No. Ireland Cmty. Cooperation Initiative, Mentor, Ohio, 1999—2003; sec., bd, trustees Svcs. for Ind. Living, Cleve., 1998—; treas., trustee Suzuki Assn. No. Ohio, Stow, Ohio, 2001—. Mem.: Suzuki Assn. of the Americas. Avocations: Irish fiddling, Traditional Am. fiddling, needlepoint. Office: The Fine Arts Assn 38660 Mentor Ave Willoughby OH 44094 Office Phone: 440-951-7500. Personal E-mail: carollinsenmeier@mac.com.

LINSENMEYER, TODD ALAN, urologist, physician, educator; Student, Whittier Coll., Calif., 1971-72; BS with honors, Stanford U, 1975; MD, U. Hawaii, 1979. Diplomate Am. Bd. Spinal Cord Medicine, Am. Bd. Urology, Am. Bd. Phys. Medicine and Rehab. Surg. intern Queen's Hosp., Honolulu, 1979-80; resident urology Tripler Amy Med. Ctr., Honolulu, 1980-84; resident physical medicine and rehab. Stanford (Calif.) Med. Ctr., 1986-89; clin. asst. prof. surgery U. Medicine and Dentistry/N.J. Sch. Medicine, Newark, 1989-95, asst. prof. rehab. medicine, 1989-97, asst. prof. surgery, 1995—, assoc. prof. rehab. medicine, 1996—, assoc. prof. surgery, 1997—; asst. chief urology 98th Gen. U.S. Army Hosp., Nuremberg, Germany, 1984-86; dir. urology Kessler Inst. Rehab. Medicine, West Orange, N.J., 1989—. Cons. urodynamics Dept. Vets. Affairs Med. Ctr., East Orange, 1991—; vis. prof. phys. medicine and rehab. Stanford U., 1992; reviewer Male Spinal Cord Injury Fertility Program: Miami Project for Cure of Paralysis, 1994; mem. sci. adv. bd. Paralyzed Vets. Am., 1995—; mem. grant rev. com. NIH, 1991, 92; mem. adv. com. Spinal Cord Injury Practice Consortium, 1995—, mem. steering com., 1995—; chmn. autonomic dysreflexia practice parameter guideline com. SCI Practice Parameter Consortium, 1995—; presenter various meetings, orgns., confs. Contbr. articles to profl. jours., chpts. to books. Maj. M.C. U.S. Army, 1980-87. Recipient 2nd pl. award paper competition ACS, Honolulu, 1984; grantee Sprague Dawley Rat Eastern Paralyzed VA, 1992-93, NIH, 1992-95, VA, 1995-98, Am. Paraplegia Soc., 1995-96. Mem. AMA, Am. Paraplegia Soc. (bd. dirs. 1993—, membership com. 1990, chmn. membership com. 1992-94, chmn. clin. practice parameter com. 1995—, pres. 2003—), Am. Spinal Cord Injury Assn. (mem. urology com. sexuality and disability 1991—, mem. program com., publs. com. 1994-99), Am. Acad. Phys. Medicine and Rehab., Am. Congress Rehab. Medicine (mem. nat. task force on sexuality and disability 1988—), Am. Urodynamics Soc. (assoc.), Assn. Acad. Physiatrists, Am. Urol. Assn. Office: Kessler Inst Rehab 1199 Pleasant Valley Way West Orange NJ 07052-1499

LINSHAW, ANDREW ROSS, mathematician; b. Kansas City, Dec. 20, 1976; s. Michael Abram and Diane Drusin Linshaw. PhD in Math., Brandeis U., Waltham, Mass., 2005. S. E. Warschawski asst. prof. U. Calif., San Diego, 2006—. Fellow, Nat. U. Singapore, 2006. Mem.: Am. Math. Soc. (corr.), Phi Beta Kappa. Achievements include research in theory of vertex algebras. Avocations: painting, piano, tennis, hiking, numismatics. Home: 3435 Lebon Dr Apt 1131 San Diego CA 92122 Office: University of California San Diego 9500 Gilman Dr La Jolla CA 92093-0112 Office Phone: 858-534-2627. Office Fax: 858-534-5273. E-mail: alinshaw@math.ucsd.edu.

LINSK, MICHAEL STEPHEN, real estate company executive; b. LA, Apr. 20, 1940; s. Abe P. and Helen Linsk; m. Wilma M. Stahl, Aug. 11, 1979; children from previous marriage: Cari E., Steven D. BSBA, U. So. Calif., 1965, MBA, 1969. CFO Larwin Group, Inc., Encino, Calif., 1970-75; v.p. fin., dir. Donald L. Bren Co., LA, 1976-78; v.p., CFO, treas., dir. Wilshire Mortgage/Wilshire Diversified, Burbank, Calif., 1980-81; pres., dir. subs. Wilshire Mortgage Corp., Burbank, 1981-84; pres., dir. Wilshire Realty Investments, Burbank, 1981-84, Glenfed Investments Inc., subs. Glendale Fed. Savs., 1982-84; pres. Eastern Pacific Fin. Group, LA, 1984-85; sr. v.p. Leisure Tech., Inc., LA, 1985-87; CEO Investec Realty Group, Inc., Encino, 1987-88; sr. v.p. LA Land Co., 1988-91; mng. dir. FTI Consulting (formerly Price Waterhouse Coopers), 1992—. Bd. dirs. Savs. Bank, Jewel City Ins., Verdugo Svcs., Inc. Treas., bd. dirs. Am. Theater Arts; bd. dirs. North Hollywood Cultural Ctr., Inc., Cmty. Friends, Inc., 1998—; trustee Temple Judea, Tarzana, Calif., 1981—83, treas., 1982—83. Mem.: AICPA, Urban Land Inst., Calif. Soc. CPAs, Bldg. Industry Assn. (bd. dirs. LA chpt. 1981—88), Beta Gamma Sigma. Office: FTI Consulting Inc 633 W 5Th St Ste 1600 Los Angeles CA 90071-2030 Office Phone: 213-452-6009. Business E-Mail: michael.linsk@fticonsulting.com.

LINSKY, JEFFREY LAWRENCE, astrophysicist; b. Buffalo, June 27, 1941; s. Max and Rose Linsky; m. Lois F. Linsky, June 25, 1967; children: Joel, Samara. BS in Physics, MIT, 1963; MS in Astronomy, Harvard U., 1965, PhD in Astronomy, 1968. Postdoctoral rsch. assoc. U. Colo., Boulder, 1968-69, fellow Joint Inst. Lab. Astrophysics, 1971—, adj. prof. dept. astrophysy., planetary and atmospheric scis., 1979-95, fellow Ctr. Astrophysics and Space Astronomy, 1986—, rsch. prof. dept. astrophysy., planetary and atmospheric scis., 1996—; astronomer quantum physics divsn. Nat. Inst. Standards and Tech., 1969-95. Mem. solar physics working grp. NASA, 1978—80, mem. com. space astronomy and astrophysics, 1979—82, mem. astrophysy. coun., 1985—87, chmn. infrared astronomy projects panel, 1985—86, chmn. space ops. br., 1988—91, chmn. sr. rev. com. astrophysics mission ops. and data analysis progs., 1988, mem. panel on computing and data analysis, 1989—90, mem. panel on ultraviolet and optical astronomy from space, 1989—90, mem. panel on status of profession of astronomy, 1989—90; mem. astronomy rsch. sect. oversight com. NSF, 1981; mem. sci. adv. com. Internat. Space Sci. Inst., Bern, Switzerland, 1997—2001; mem. sci. teams, Internat. Ultraviolet Explorer and Far Ultraviolet Spectrograph Explorer satellites; interdisciplinary scientist for Chandra x-ray observatory; mem. sci. teals for Goddard High Resolution Spectrograph, Space Telescope Imaging Spectrograph; mem. sci. teals Cosmic Origins Spectrograph instruments on Hubble Space Telescope. Contbr. articles to profl. jours.; mem. editl. bd.: Solar Physics. Recipient Medal for Exceptional Sci. Achievement, NASA, 1988, Grp. Achievement award, 1991, Goddard Exceptional Achievement award, 1994. Mem.: Internat. Astron. Union, Am. Astron. Soc. (mem. coun. 1995—98). Office: JILA U Colo Campus Box 440 Boulder CO 80309-0440 Office Phone: 303-492-7838. Business E-Mail: jlinsky@jila.colorado.edu.

LINSKY, MARTY, education educator; b. Brookline, Mass., Aug. 28, 1940; s. Harold Max and Ruth Doran L.; m. Helen Roberts Strieder, Dec. 10, 1964 (div. Jan. 1979); children: Alison, Sam; m. Lynn H. Staley, July 7, 1979; 1 child, Max. BA, Williams Coll., Williamstown, Mass., 1961; JD, Harvard U., 1964. Asst. atty. gen. Commonwealth of Mass., Boston, 1967, chief sec. to the gov., 1992-95; mem. and asst. minority leader Mass. Ho. of Reps., Boston, 1967-72; editorial writer and reporter The Boston Globe, 1973-75; editor-in-chief The Real Paper, Cambridge, Mass., 1975-79; asst. dir. Inst. of Politics, John F. Kennedy Sch., Cambridge, 1981-85; instr. in law Boston Coll., Newton, Mass., 1973-85; lectr. in pub. policy John F. Kennedy Sch. of Govt. at Harvard, Cambridge, 1985-92, 95—; co-founder, prin. Cambridge Leadership Assocs., 2002—. Coord. seminars Ethics Ctr., Poynter Inst. for Media Studies, St. Petersburg, Fla., 1987-88, dir. ownership and leadership project, 1995-97; project dir. Revson Found., N.Y.C., 1982-85. Author: Impact: How the Press Affects Federal Policy Making, 1986, How the Press Affects Federal Policy Making: 6 Case Studies, 1986, (with Ed Grefe) The New Corporate Activism, 1995, (and Ronald Heifetz) Leadership on the Line: Staying Alive Through the Dangers of Leading, 2002; consulting editor: (books) Getting to Yes, 1981, Beyond the Hotline, 1985. Bd. dirs., selection com. Cavallo Found., Cambridge, 1988-96; bd. dirs. Ford Hall Forum, Boston, 1989-92; regular polit. commentator Monitor Network, Boston, 1992, WHDH-TV, CBS affiliate, Boston, 1990; trustee Gaudino Meml. Fund, Williams Coll., 1992-2002, chair, 1999-2002; chair selection com. William Bulger Excellence in Legis. Leadership award, 1999—. Recipient cash prize, second place essay competition, Woodrow Wilson Ctr. for Media Studies, Washington, 1990. Mem. Inst. for Alternative Journalism (bd. dirs. 1983-95, chair 1992-95), Poynter Inst. for Media Studies (bd. advisors 1981-97). Avocations: running, mexican food, collecting baseball cards. Home: 333 Central Park W Apt 26 New York NY 10025-7104 Office: Cambridge Leadership Assocs 124 Mt Auburn St Ste 200N Cambridge MA 02138 Home Phone: 212-316-9892; Office Phone: 617-576-5766. Personal E-mail: mahty@pipeline.com. Business E-Mail: marty@cambridge-leadership.com.

LINSTER, MICHELLE LYNN, education educator, consultant; d. John Bufer, Sr. and Susie Graves Linster; m. George Thalma Glenn, Oct. 19, 1985 (div. Dec. 16, 2001); children: George Thalma Glenn III, Mari-Michele Linster Glenn, Jonathan Maxwell Linster Glenn. Masters, U. of N.C., 1981, PhD, 1985. Practicing Psychologist N.C. Psychology Bd., 1990. Adj. faculty Ctr. for Creative Leadership, Greensboro, NC, 1994—; asst. prof. Winston-Salem State U., NC, 1997—. Asst. prof. Bennett Coll., Greensboro, NC, 1986—91, chair psychology dept., 1990—91; practicing psychologist Pvt. Practice, Greensboro, NC, 1992—98. Mem. Jr. League, Greensboro, NC, 1989—2003; steering com. mem. Com. of 100, Greensboro, NC, 1994—99; bd. mem. Greensboro Montesorri Sch., Greensboro, NC, 1996—99; mem. APA, Washington, 1994—2000; co-chair outreach Super Computing Conf. 2003, 2002—03; evaluation specialists Super Computing Global 2003, 2002—03; mem. N.C. Psychol. Assn., Greensboro, NC, 1994—98. Scholar Fulbright Hayes Short Term Scholarship, Fulbright Found., 1990. Mem.: Southeastern Psychol. Assn., Am. Psychol. Soc., Jr. League, Jack and Jill, Inc. (sec. 2001—04), Psi Chi (advisor wssu chpt. 2001—03), Delta Sigma Theta Sorority. Conservative. Baptist. Avocations: reading, writing, volunteering. Personal E-mail: linsterglenn1@msn.com.

LINSTONE, HAROLD ADRIAN, management consultant, educator; b. Hamburg, Germany, June 15, 1924; came to U.S., 1936; s. Frederic and Ellen (Seligmann) L.; m. Hedy Schubach, June 16, 1946; children: Fred A., Clark R. BS, CCNY, 1944; MA, Columbia U., 1947; PhD, U. So. Calif., 1954. Sr. scientist Hughes Aircraft Co., Culver City, Calif., 1949—61, The Rand Corp., Santa Monica, Calif., 1961—63; assoc. dir. planning Lockheed Corp., Burbank, Calif., 1963—71; prof. Portland State U., Oreg., 1970—. Pres. Systems Forecasting, Inc., Santa Monica, 1971-98; cons. 1973—. Author: Multiple Perspectives for Decision Making, 1984, Decision Making for Technology Executives, 1999; co-author: The Unbounded Mind, 1993, The Challenge of the 21st Century, 1994; co-editor The Delphi Method, 1975, Technological Substitution, 1976, Futures Research, 1977; editor-in-chief Technol. Forecasting Social Change, 1969—. Recipient Disting. Svc. award World Future Soc., 2003, Leadership Tech. Mgmt. award, PICMET, 2007; NSF grantee, Washington, 1976, 79, 85. Mem. Inst. Mgmt. Scis., Ops. Rsch. Soc., Internat. Soc. Systems Scis. (pres. 1993-94). Avocation: photography. Office: Portland State U PO Box 751 Portland OR 97207-0751 Home: 76400 Sweet Pea Way Palm Desert CA 92211 Personal E-mail: linstoneh@aol.com.

LINSTROTH, TOD BRIAN, lawyer; b. Racine, Wis., Feb. 19, 1947; s. Eugene and Gloria Linstroth; m. Jane Kathryn Zedler, June 23, 1972; children: Kathryn, Krista, Kassandre, Kyle. BBA in Acctg., U. Wis., 1970, JD, 1973. Bar: Wis. Assoc. Michael, Best & Friedrich, Madison, Wis., 1973-79, ptnr., 1980—, past chmn., mem. firm mgmt. com., 1997—2005. Chmn. Wis. Tech. Coun., Inc., 2001—. Mem. Wis. Gov.'s Sci. and Tech. Coun., Madison, 1993—95; pres. Madison Repertory Theatre; bd. visitors U. Wis. Sch. Bus., 1991—94. Mem.: Wis. Venture Fair (chair steering com. 1997—), Greater Madison Area C. of C. Avocations: skiing, sailing, reading. Office: Michael Best & Friedrich 1 S Pinckney St Ste 700 Madison WI 53703-4236 Office Phone: 608-283-2242. Business E-Mail: TBLinstroth@michaelbest.com.

LINTON, FRED ERNEST JULIUS, mathematics professor, publishing executive; b. Genova, Italy, 1938; arrived in US, 1940; s. Martin and Melitta L.; m. Barbara Mikolajewska, Dec. 18, 1990. BA, Yale U., 1958; MA, Columbia U., 1959, PhD, 1963; MA (hon.), Wesleyan U., Middletown, Conn., 1972. Asst. prof. Wesleyan U., Middletown, 1963-68, assoc. prof., 1968-72, prof. math., 1972—2006, chmn. math. dept., 1975, prof. emeritus, 2006. Co-founder Lintons' Video Press, 1979. Mem.: Math Assn. Am., Am. Math Soc. Home: 36 Everit St New Haven CT 06511-2208 Office: Wesleyan U Dept Math Middletown CT 06459-0001

LINTON, JACK ARTHUR, lawyer; b. NYC, May 29, 1936; s. Paul Phillip and Helen (Feller) L.; div.; children: Ann Deborah Linton Wilmot, James Paul, John Michael. BA, Albright Coll., 1958; JD, NYU, 1961, LLM in Taxation, 1966. Bar: Pa. 1962, N.Y. 1963, U.S. Tax Ct. 1966, U.S. Dist. Ct. (ea. dist.) Pa. 1978, U.S. Ct. Appeals, 1984. Assoc. DeLong, Dry & Binder, Reading, Pa., 1961-63; asst. house counsel Bob Banner Assocs., Inc., NYC, 1963-66; ptnr. DeLong, Dry, Cianci & Linton, Reading, 1967-70, Williamson, Miller, Murray & Linton, Reading, 1970-72, Gerber & Linton, P.C., Reading, 1972-88, Linton, Giannascoli, Barrett & Distasio, P.C., Reading, 1989-97, Linton, Giannascoli, Distasio & Adams, PC, Reading, 1997-98, Linton, Distasio, Adam & Kauffman, PC, Reading, 1998—2001, Linton, Distasio, Adams & Palanga, P.C., Reading, 2001—04, Linton, Distasio, Adams & Edwards, P.C., Reading, 2004—. Solicitor Reading Parking Authority, 1967-76, City of Reading, 1980-96, City of Reading Officers and Employees Retirement Bd., 1996—; solicitor, contr. County of Berks, 2002—; bd. dirs. The Group, Inc., Small Bus. Coun. Am., Inc., chmn. polit. action com., 1988—, others; co-founder, mem. Estate Planning Coun. Berks County, 1978—; lectr. in field. Editor Tax Law Rev., 1965-67; contbr. articles to profl. jours. Pres. Berks County Mental Health Assn., 1968-69, Reading Jewish Community Ctr., 1980-82; mem. Mental Health/Mental Retardation Bd. Berks County, 1974-80; treas., bd. dirs. Reading-Berks Youth Soccer League, 1982-85; bd. dirs. Gov. Mifflin Sch. Dist., Shillington, 1985-93, Exeter Township Sch. Dist., 1999-, v.p., 2000-. Kenneson fellow, NYU Sch. Law, 1965—67. Mem. ABA (mem. personal svc. orgn. com., tax sect. 1981—, chairperson task force for repeal top-heavy rules 1987-89, vice chmn. personal svc. orgn. com. 1990-92, chmn. personal svc. orgn. com. 1992-94), Pa. Bar Assn., Berks County Bar Assn. (treas. 1969-72), Berks County C. of C. (mem. govt. affairs com.). Democrat. Jewish. Avocations: sports, reading. Office: Linton Distasio Adams Edwards PO Box 461 Reading PA 19603-0461 Home Phone: 610-779-9399. Business E-Mail: linton@ldaklaw.com.

LINTON, MICHAEL ALAN, food products executive; b. East Cleveland, Ohio, Dec. 7, 1956; s. Ralph Edwin and Katherine (Vodanoff) L. BSBA, Bowling Green State U., 1978; MBA, Duke U., 1980. Brand asst. Proctor & Gamble, Cin., 1980-81, asst. brand mgr., 1982-83, brand mgr., 1983-87; mktg. mgr. Progressive Ins., Cleve., 1987-88, ops. adn ins. svcs. mgr., 1988-89, gen. mgr., asst. v.p., 1989-93; v.p. James River Corp., 1993-97; sr. v.p., strategic mktg. Best Buy Co., Inc., Eden Praire, Minn., 1999—2002, chief mktg. officer, EVP, consumer and brand marketing Richfield, Minn., 2002—06; sr. v.p. marketplaces eBay, 2006—. Bd. dirs. The Walker Mus. Contemp. Art, 2004—06, Peet's Coffee & Tea, 2005—. Avocations: sports, travel, current events, biking. Office Phone: 403-376-3443.

LINVILL, JOHN GRIMES, engineering educator; b. Kansas City, Mo., Aug. 8, 1919; s. Thomas G. and Emma (Crayne) L.; m. Marjorie Webber, Dec. 28, 1943; children: Gregory Thomas, Candace Sue. AB, William Jewell Coll., 1941; SB, Mass. Inst. Tech., 1943, SM, 1945, ScD, 1949; D of Applied Sci., U. Louvain, Belgium, 1966; DSc, William Jewell Coll., 1992. Asst. prof. elec. engring. Mass. Inst. Tech., 1949-51; tech. staff Bell Telephone Labs., 1951-55; assoc. prof. elec. engring. Stanford U., 1955-57, prof., dir. solid-state electronics lab., 1957-64, prof., chmn. dept. elec. engring., 1964-80, prof., dir. Center for Integrated Systems, 1980-90—, Canon USA prof. engring., 1988-89, prof. emeritus, 1989—; co-founder, dir. Tele Sensory Corp., 1971-2000; dir. Read-Rite Corp., 1992-2000. Author: Transistors and Active Circuits, 1961, Models of Transistors and Diodes, 1963; inventor Optacon reading aid for the blind. Recipient citation for achievement William Jewell Coll., 1963, John Scott award for devel. of Optacon, City of Phila., 1980, Medal of Achievement Am. Electronics Assn., 1983, Louis Braille Prize Deutscher Blindenverband, 1984. Fellow IEEE (Edn. medal 1976), AAAS; mem. Nat. Acad. of Engring., Am. Acad. of Arts and Scis. Office: Stanford U Dept Elec Engring Stanford CA 94305 Home: 620 Sand Hill Rd Apt 122 F Palo Alto CA 94304 Business E-Mail: linvill@ee.stanford.edu.

LINVILLE, RANDAL L., agricultural company executive; married; 1 child. BS in Bus. Finance and Agrl. Economics, Kans. State U., 1976, MS in Agrl. Economics, 1977. Merchandise mgr. The Scoular Co., 1984, v.p., gen. mgr. grain divsn., 1992, CEO, 1999—.

LINVILLE, RAY PATE, English educator, retired military officer, editor, writer; b. Winston-Salem, NC, Feb. 27, 1946; s. Clyde Burton and Nellie Pearl (Helm) L.; m. Mary Ann Slordal, July 30, 1970; children: Russell Pate, Rachel Ann. BA in Journalism, U. N.C., 1967; MS in Logistics Mgmt. with distinction, Air Force Inst. Tech., 1973. Commd. 2d lt. USAF, 1967, advanced through grades to col., 1989, materials mgr. Madrid, 1973-76, staff analyst Washington, 1981-85; mem. staff Tactical Air Command, Hampton, Va., 1976-79; plans officer UN Command, Seoul, Korea, 1980-81; rsch. fellow Harvard U., Cambridge, Mass., 1985-86; chief combat support analysis Joint Chiefs of Staff, Washington, 1986-89; dir. logistics plans Strat. Air Command, Omaha, 1989-92; chief logistics plans and programs Air Combat Command, Hampton, 1992-93; ret. USAF, 1994; rsch. fellow Logistics Mgmt. Inst., McLean, Va., 1993-2000. Adj. grad. prof. U. So. Calif., LA, 1981; adj. prof. U. Va., Falls Church, 1986—88; grad. prof. Webster U., Washington, 1988—2000; mgr. alumni edn. U. NC Gen. Alumni Assn., 2000—07; English instr. Wake Tech. CC, Raleigh, 2003, Sandhills CC, Pinehurst, NC, 2004—. Author: (monograph) Command and Control of Forces..., 1987; editor, asst. editor, mem. rev. bd. Logistics Spectrum, 1990-2000; contbr. articles to profl. jours. Dir., v.p., treas. Danbury Forest Com. Assn., Springfield, Va., 1982-84; youth group advisor, deacon Presbyn. Ch., Omaha and Fairfax, Va., 1986-99. Decorated Legion of Merit; recipient Outstanding Young Man of Am. award U.S. Jaycees, 1978. Mem. Internat. Soc. Logistics (sr., life, cert. profl. logistician, chpt. chmn. 1990-91, Bronze award 1991, Pres.'s award for Merit 1996, 97, 99), Air Force Assn. (life), U. N.C. Gen. Alumni Assn. (life), U.S. Chess Fedn. (life), Sigma Iota Epsilon. Avocations: writing, golf, music, chess. Home: 845 St Andrews Dr Pinehurst NC 28374-9621 Office: Sandhills CC 3395 Airport Rd Pinehurst NC 28374 Business E-Mail: linville@carolina.net.

LINXWILER, JAMES DAVID, lawyer; b. Fresno, Calif., Apr. 9, 1949; s. George Edwin and Stella Ruth (Schmidt) L.; m. Robyn Kenning, July 12, 1986; children: Elizabeth Ann, John Edwin, Jeffrey David. BA, U. Calif., Berkeley, 1971; JD, UCLA, 1974. Bar: DC 1976, US Dist. Ct. Alaska 1976, US Dist. Ct. (DC cir.) 1976, Alaska 1977, US Ct. Appeals (9th cir.) 1977, US Supreme Ct. 1988. Lawyer US Dept. Interior, Washington, 1974-76, Cook Inlet Region, Inc., Anchorage, 1976-78, Sohio Petroleum Co., 1978-81; shareholder Guess & Rudd, 1981—2007, mng. shareholder, 2000—03. Spkr. seminars on environ. and natural resources law. Contbr. chpts. to book, articles to profl. jours. Chmn. Alaska Coalition Am. Energy Security, 1986-87, Alliance Arctic Nat. Wildlife Refuge Com., 1986-87; bd. dirs. Commonwealth North, 1993-2002, pres., 1999-2000. Mem. ABA, Fed. Bar Assn., Alaska Bar Assn. (chmn., exec. com. nat. resources sect. 1988-93), DC Bar Assn. Democrat. Home: 2407 Loussac Dr Anchorage AK 99517-1272 Office: Guess & Rudd 510 L St Ste 700 Anchorage AK 99501-1959 Office Phone: 907-793-2200.

LINXWILER, LOUIS MAJOR, JR., retired finance company executive; b. Blackwell, Okla., Mar. 7, 1931; s. Louis Major and Flora Mae (Horton) Linxwiler; m. Susan Buchanan, July 27, 1963 (dec.); children: Louis Major III, Robert William. BS, Okla. State U., 1953. Mgr. credit dept. Valley Nat. Bank, Tucson, 1957-60; sales rep. Vega Industries, Syracuse, NY, 1960-62; program dir. Am. Cancer Soc., Phoenix, 1962-67; v.p., mgr. credit dept. United Bank Ariz., Phoenix, 1967-76; dean edn. Am. Inst. Banking, Phoenix, 1976-80; cons. United Student Aid Funds Inc., Phoenix, 1980—81, U. Phoenix, 1981; founder, pres., CEO, bd. dirs. Ariz. Student Loan Fin. Corp., 1981—88; founder, chmn., CEO Western Loan Mktg. Assn., Phoenix, 1984-90; pres. Precision Design and Engring., Inc., Phoenix, 1993—; organizer, mng. ptnr. Energy Transition Products, L.L.C., 1998—. Organizer, chmn. bd. dirs. Pollution Free Planet Found. Editor: Money and Banking, 1978, The Solar Hydrogen Civilization, 2003. Pres. bd. dirs. Phoenix YMCA, 1974—75; v.p. N. Mountain Behavioral Inst., Phoenix, 1975—77; pres. City Commn. Sister Cities, Phoenix, 1986—87, Am. Inst. Banking, Phoenix, 1973—74. Served to 1st lt. US Army, 1954—56. Mem.: Rotary (bd. dirs. 1982—83, 1993—94, 1996—97, 2003—04, 2005—), Shriners, Beta Theta Pi. Republican. Presbyterian. Avocations: auto restoration, WWII history. Home: 222 S 54th Pl Mesa AZ 85206-1406 Personal E-mail: loulinx@cox.net.

LINZ, ANTHONY JAMES, osteopathic physician, consultant, educator; b. Sandusky, Ohio, June 16, 1948; s. Anthony Joseph and Margaret Jane (Ballah) Linz; m. Kathleen Ann Kovach, Aug. 18, 1973; children: Anthony Scott, Sara Elizabeth. BS, Bowling Green State U., 1971; D.O., Des Moines U., 1974; MPH, NW Ohio Consortium for Pub. Health, 2006. Diplomate Nat. Bd. Osteo. Examiners; bd. cert., diplomate Am. Osteo. Bd. Internal Medicine, Internal Medicine, Med. Diseases of Chest and Critical Care Medicine. Intern South Pointe Hosp. Brentwood Hosp., Cleve., 1974-75; resident in internal medicine South Pointe Hosp. Cleve. Clinic Sys., 1975-78; chief resident Brentwood Hosp., 1977-78; subsplty. fellow in pulmonary diseases Riverside Meth. Hosp., Columbus, Ohio, 1978-80; med. dir. pulmonary svcs. Sandusky Meml. Hosp., Ohio, 1980-85; med. dir. cardio-pulmonary svcs. Firelands Cmty. Hosp., Sandusky, 1985—. Cons. staff dept. medicine Good Samaritan Hosp., 1982—85, sect. internal medicine specializing pulmonary diseases; cons. pulmonary, critical care and internal medicine Firelands Regional Med. Ctr., 1985—, active staff sect. internal medicine, chmn. dept. medicine, head div. pulmonary medicine, 1985—; cons. pulmonary, critical care, and internal medicine Providence Hosp., Sandusky, Mercy Hosp., Willard, Ohio; clin. prof. pulmonary and critical care med.,internal med. Ohio U. Coll. Osteo. Medicine; clin. prof. medicine Univ. Health Scis. Coll. Osteo. Medicine, Kansas City, Mo.; clin. asst. prof. med. Med. Coll. of Ohio at Toledo; adj. prof. applied scis. Bowling Green State U., mem. respiratory tech. adv. bd. Firelands Campus, pub. health faculty, 1983—, med. dir. respiratory care tech. program, 1984—; clin. prof. pulmonary and critical care med. Des Moines U.; rep. Pub. Health Adminstrn., 2001—; exec. bd. pub. health student orgn. N.W. Ohio Consortium for Pub. Health; med. dir., cons. physician O.E. Meyer Corp., 2003—; adj. asst. prof. pub. health Bowling Green State U., Ky. Contbr. articles and abstracts to profl. jours. Water safety instr. ARC, 1965—; med. dir., clin. rsch. investigator Camp Superkid Asthma Camp, 1984-97; trustee Stein Hospice, 1986-90, chmn., 2000-;

mem. adv. bd. Ams. with Disabilities Act, City of Sandusky, Ohio, chmn., 2001-; mem. LPN adv. bd. Sandusky Career Ctr., 2005-; med. dir. in residence Camp Superkids Asthma Camp, 1984-97; practical nursing adv. bd. Sandusky Career Ctr., Sandusky Pub. Schs. Recipient Edward Ruff Cmty. Svc. award Am. Lung. Assn., 1985, Master Clinician award Ohio U. Coll. Osteopathic Medicine, 1987, Golden Rule award J.C. Penney, 1990, Disting. Alumna/Alumnus award Firelands Coll., Bowling Green State U., 1995. Fellow: ACP-Am. Soc. Internal Medicine (Ohio chpt.), Am. Coll. Osteo. Internists (master) (Grover Gillum Soc. Master Fellows), Am. Coll. Critical Care Medicine, Am. Coll. Chest Physicians; mem.: AAAS, Ohio Lung Assn. (N.W. regional adv. bd.), Found. Critical Care (mem. Founder's Cir.), Ohio Pub. Health Assn., Am. Soc. Internal Medicine, So. Critical Care Medicine, Ohio Soc. Respiratory Care (med. adviser/dir. 1982—), Nat. Assn. Med. Dirs. Respiratory Care, Sandusky Yacht Club (corr.), Am. Lung Assn. (bd. dirs. Ohio's So. Shore sect. 1984—, pres., 1st v.p., exec. bd. dirs., med. adv. bd. chmn., bd. dirs. Ohio Norwest Region), Ohio Thoracic Soc., Am. Thoracic Soc., Am. Heart Assn., Ohio Osteo. Assn. (past pres., past v.p., past sec.-treas., acad. trustees 5th dist. acad.), Am. Osteo. Assn., European Thoracic Soc., Phi Kappa Phi, Atlas Med. Fraternity, Pi Kappa Alpha, Beta Beta Beta, Alpha Epsilon Delta. Roman Catholic. Office Fax: 419-621-0642. Personal E-mail: doclinz@aol.com.

LINZER, MARK, medical educator, internist; b. Phila., Feb. 4, 1952; s. Morton and Lila Linzer; children: Ben, Elizabeth. BA, Oberlin Coll., Ohio, 1973; MD, Johns Hopkins Sch. Medicine, Balt., 1977. Asst. prof. Montefiore Hosp., Bronx, NY, 1980—85, Duke U., Durham, NC, 1985—89, Tufts U., Mass., 1989—93, New Eng. Med. Ctr., Boston, 1989—93; prof. and chief sect. gen. internal medicine U. Wis., Madison, Wis., 1993—2007, chief internal medicine, 2007—. Pres. Assn. Chiefs in Gen. Internal Medicine, Washington, 2002—03; co-chair workforce com. Assn. Specialty Profs., 2004—05, chair part time task force, 2006—; chair equity and diversity com. sect. gen. internal medicine U. Wis., Madison, 2004—. Contbr. articles to profl. jours. Recipient professionalism award, U. Wis., 1998, Spinoza Professorship, U. Amsterdam, Netherlands, 1999, Rhodes award, Soc. Gen. Medicine, 2001, Bedside Tchg. award, U. Wis., Sch. Medicine, 2004. Mem.: Am. Coll. Physicians, Soc. Gen. Internal Medicine, Assn. Gen. Internal Medicine. Avocations: guitar, songwriting, running. Office: UW Gen Internal Medicine MC 9054 Ste 100 2828 Marshall Ct Madison WI 53705

LINZEY, DONALD WAYNE, biologist, educator, researcher; b. Balt., Md., Sept. 4, 1939; s. Charles Herbert and Dorothy Katherine Linzey; m. Juanita Bird Linzey, May 18, 1985; m. Alicia Terry Vogt, June 2, 1963 (div. Oct. 19, 1982); children: David Wayne, Thomas Alan. BA, Western Md. Coll. (now McDaniel Coll.), Westminster, Md., 1961; MS, Cornell U., Ithaca, NY, 1963, PhD, 1966. Instr. biology Cornell U., Ithaca, 1966—67; assoc. prof. biology U. South Ala., Mobile, 1967—77; instr., rsch. assoc. Va. Tech, Blacksburg, 1977—82; prof. biology Wytheville CC, Va., 1989—. Chmn. Va. Cougar Investigation, Blacksburg, 1978—; rsch. assoc. Va. Mus. Natural History, Martinsville, 1988—90; dir. Blue Ridge Highlands Regional Sci. Fair, Dublin, 1992—; chmn. mammal taxonomic working group All Taxa Biodiversity Inventory, Gt. Smoky Mountains Nat. Pk., Gatlinburg, Tenn., 1996—; lectr. Wilderness Wildlife Week, Pigeon Forge, Tenn., 1996—; rsch. assoc. Bermuda Zool. Soc., Flatts, Hamilton, Bermuda, 1997—; cons. in field. Author: Mammals of Great Smoky Mountains National Park, 1971, 1995, Alabama Wildlife, Vols. 1 and 2, 1972—73, Snakes of Alabama, 1979, Snakes of Virginia, 1981, The Mammals of Virginia, 1998, Vertebrate Biology, 2001;: rev. edit., 1995;; editor: Endangered and Threatened Plants and Animals of Virginia, 1979. Active Ea. Cougar Found., North Springs, W.Va., 2000—07, Va. Mus. Natural History, Martinsville, 1988—90. Named Va. Prof. of Yr., Carnegie Found. for the Advancement Sci., 1999—2000; recipient Disting. Alumni award, Western Md. Coll. (now McDaniel Coll.), 2003, Outstanding Faculty award, Commonwealth of Va. State Coun. of Higher Edn., 1996, C.C. Leadership Program award, Nat. Orgn. for Staff and Orgnl. Devel. Austin, Tex., 1996, 1998, 2001, Chancellor's Professorship award, Va. CC Sys., 1998, Disting. Svc. award, Wytheville CC, 1998. Mem.: Yellowstone Assn. for Natural Sci., History, and Edn. (assoc.), Va. Natural History Soc. (assoc.), Va. Herpetological Soc. (assoc.), Gt. Smoky Mountains Assn. (assoc.), Friends of the Gt. Smoky Mountains (assoc.), Human Anatomy and Physiology Soc. (assoc.), Nature Conservancy (assoc.), Am. Soc. Mammalogists (life), Sigma Xi. Democrat. Methodist. Avocations: travel, hiking, wildlife observation, collecting mechanical banks. Home: 1418 Nellies Cave Rd Blacksburg VA 24060 Office: Wytheville Cmty Coll 1000 E Main St Wytheville VA 24382 Office Phone: 276-223-4824. Office Fax: 276-223-4778. Business E-Mail: wclinzd@wcc.vccs.edu.

LINZEY, JUANITA BIRD, biology professor; d. Ignacio Acosta and Lucy Jennette Bird; m. Donald Wayne Linzey, May 19, 1985; children: Robert Laurence Holton, David Judson Holton. BS, Marymount Coll., Tarrytown, NY, 1963; MS, U. NC, Chapel Hill, 1965, Va. Tech, Blacksburg, 1993. Rsch. asst./assoc. Fla. State U., Tallahassee, 1968—71; lab. specialist Va. Tech, Blacksburg, 1980—85, med. technologist, 1985—89; asst. prof. New River C.C., Dublin, Va., 1989—99, assoc. prof., 1999—. Textbook reviewer West Pub. Co., Amesbury, Mass., Harper Collins Publishers, NYC; exam. writer for nursing's standardized human anatomy and physiology exam. Nat. League Nursing, NYC, 1991. Author: (sci. rsch.) Jour. Immunology, Biochimica et Biophysica Acta, Jour. of the Elisha Mitchell Sci. Soc., Jour. of the Helminthological Soc. Washington, (abstract) Sixty-third Con. Rsch. Workers on Animal Diseases, (paper presentation) Fourteenth World Congress on Diseases of Cattle, Am. Soc. Immunology. Dir. Blue Ridge Highlands Regional Sci. Fair, Dublin, Va., 1991—. Grantee An Evaluation of Declining Amphibian Populations in Bermuda, Va. C.C. Sys., 1995, A Microbiol. Investigation of Declining Amphibian Populations, New River C.C., 1995, A Microbiol. Evaluation of Declining Amphibian Populations, Va. C.C. Sys., 1996, The Incorporation of Multimedia and Interactive Physiology Software into Human Anatomy and Physiology Lab. Courses, 1997, Devel. of Multimedia Presentations for Integration into Human Anatomy and Physiology Lectures, 1998, Devel. of an Asynchronous Distant Learning Course for Human Anatomy and Physiology, 1999, Devel. of an On-line Course: Intro. to Human Systems, 2000, Devel. of Human Anatomy/Physiology Lab. to a Digitally Produced Experience Comparable to On-Campus Lab. Sessions, 2001. Mem.: Va. Assn. Biol. Edn., Va. C.C. Assn., Human Anatomy Physiology Soc., Nature Conservancy, Phi Kappa Phi. Avocations: bicycling, swimming, scuba diving, hiking, photography. Office: New River CC PO Box 1127 Dublin VA 24084 Office Phone: 540-674-3600. Business E-Mail: nrlinzj@nr.edu.

LINZEY, VERNA MAY, minister, writer; b. Coffeyville, Kans., May 17, 1919; d. Carey Franklin Hall Jr. and Alice May (Hart) Hall-Doyle; m. Stanford Eugene Linzey Jr., July 13, 1941; children: Gena May English, Janice Ellen Mathis, Stanford Eugene III, Virginia Darnelle Lemons(dec.), Sharon Faye, George William, Vera Evelyn Clark, Paul Edward, David Leon, James Franklin. Student, Southwestern Assembly of God U., Waxahachie, Tex., 1938—39, Fuller Theol. Sem., Pasadena, Calif., 1980—. Lic. Minister Assembly of God, 1945. Asst. minister First Assembly of God, Baldwin Park, Calif., 1953—54; co-founder Holy Spirit Evangelism, Escondido, Calif., 1976—. Cons. Holy Spirit Evangelism, Escondido, Calif., 1976—; leader Pentecostal Movement Worldwide, 1976; TV interviews/appearances PBS, 2004, Prime Time Christian Broadcasting Networkk, 2004. Author: The Baptism with the Holy Spirit, 2004, Spirit Baptism, 2007; prodr.: (video) The Baptism with the Holy Spirit, 2004; songwriter: O Blessed Jesus, 2007; radio broadcaster Lectures on Pneumatology, 2007, host (TV program) Holy Spirit Today, 2007; contbr. articles to religious publs., 2001—02. Mem. adv. bd. Operation Freedom, 2003—; mem. nat. com. Dem. orgn., 1943—45, Republican Orgn., 1946—. Recipient Cert. of Recognition, Mayor of Escondido, Calif., 2001, Congressional Proclamation Rev. Dr. Verna May Linzey Day April 29th, 2001. Avocations: gardening, piano, photography, genealogy, singing. Office: Verna M Linzey 354 E Washington Ave Ste A Escondido CA 92025 Home Phone: 760-743-3913; Office Phone: 760-735-8961. Personal E-mail: vlinzey@aol.com.

LINZNER, JOEL, lawyer; b. Phila., May 11, 1952; BA, Brandeis U., 1974; JD, U. Calif., Berkeley, 1977. Bar: Calif. 1977, U.S. Ct. Appeals (9th cir.) 1979, U.S. Supreme Ct. 1987. Former ptnr. Crosby, Heafey, Roach & May P.C., Oakland, Calif.; v.p. worldwide bus. affairs Electronic Arts, Calif., 1999—2002, sr. v.p. worldwide bus. affairs, 2002—04, sr. v.p. legal & bus. affairs, 2004—. Adj. prof. Sch. Law Santa Clara U., 1990, 92-93. Contbr. articles to profl. jours. Mem. ABA, State Bar Calif., Bar Assn. San Francisco. Office: Electronic Arts Inc 209 Redwood Shores Pky Redwood City CA 94065*

LIOI, SARA ELIZABETH, judge; b. Canton, Ohio, Dec. 17, 1960; BA summa cum laude, Bowling Green State U., 1983; JD, Ohio State U., 1987. Bar: Ohio 1987. Assoc. Day, Ketterer, Raley, Wright & Rybolt, Ltd., 1987—93, ptnr., 1993—97; judge Stark County Ct. Pub. Pleas, 1997—2007, US Dist. Ct. (no. dist.) Ohio, 2007—. Mem. Leadership Stark County, Cmty. Svcs. Stark County, Walsh U. Adv. Bd., Plain Local Schools Found., Stark County Humane Soc.*

LION, LINDA N., retired federal agency administrator; b. Brookline, Mass., Feb. 18, 1949; m. Donor M. Lion, Sept. 29, 1978; 2 children. BA in Biology, Wheaton Coll., 1970; PhD, MIT, 1975; grad., Nat. Def. U., Ft. Lesley J. McNair, Washington, 1990. Instr. human nutrition MIT, Cambridge, 1975-76; ind. nutrition cons. Haiti, Dominican Republic, Ghana, Bolivia, 1976-77; regional health and nutrition adviser Health & Nutrition Divsn. Office Devel. Resources Bur. Latin Am. and Caribbean USAID, Washington, 1977-78; dir. Office Health, Population & Nutrition USAID, Jamaica, 1978-79; health devel. officer, officer policy devel. & program rev. Bur. Policy and Program Coord. USAID, Washington, 1979; dir. Office Health Population & Nutrition USAID, Guyana, 1979-81, dir. Office Project Devel. & Monitoring Pakistan, 1981-85; chief Mid. East Divsn. Office Project Devel. Bur. Asia and Near East USAID, Washington, 1985-86; chief Capital Devel. Project Divsn. USAID, Peru, 1986-87, dir. Office Human Resources, 1987-89, dep. dir. Office Info. Resources Mgmt. Bur. Mgmt. Washington, 1990-94, mission dir. regional support mission for East Asia Bangkok, 1994-96, dep. asst. adminstr. human resources Bur. Mgmt. Washington, 1996—2000, dep. asst. adminstr. global programs, 2000—02. Avocations: golf, bridge. Office: 6600 Baymeadow Ct Mc Lean VA 22101

LIONAKIS, GEORGE, architect; b. West Hiawatha, Utah, Sept. 5, 1924; s. Pete and Andriani (Protopapadakis) L.; student Carbon Jr. Coll., 1942-43, 46-47; BArch., U. Oreg., 1951; m. Iva Oree Braddock, Dec. 30, 1951; 1 dau., Deborah Jo. With Corps Engrs., Walla Walla, Wash., 1951-54; architect Liske, Lionakis, Beaumont & Engberg, Sacramento, 1954-86, Lionakis-Beaumont Design Group, 1986—. Mem. Sacramento County Bd. Appeals, 1967—, chmn., 1969, 75, 76; pres. Sacramento Builders Exchange, 1976. Served with USAAF, 1943-46. Mem. AIA (pres. Central Valley chpt., 1972—), Constrn. Specifications Inst. (pres. Sacramento chpt., 1962; nat. awards, 1962, 63, 65), Sacramento C. of C. (code com., 1970—). Club: North Ridge Country (pres. 1987). Lodge: Rotarian (pres. East Sacramento 1978-79). Prin. works include Stockton (Calif.) Telephone Bldg., 1968, Chico (Calif.) Main Telephone Bldg., 1970, Mather AFB Exchange Complex Sacramento, 1970, Base Chapel Mather AFB, Sacramento, 1970, Woodridge Elementary Sch., Sacramento, 1970, Pacific Telephone Co. Operating Center Modesto, Calif., 1968, Sacramento, 1969, Marysville, Calif., 1970, Red Bluff, Calif., 1971, Wells Fargo Banks, Sacramento, 1968, Corning, Calif., 1969, Anderson, 1970, Beale AFB Exchange Complex, Marysville, 1971, Cosumnes River Coll., Sacramento, 1971, base exchanges at Bergstrom AFB, Austin, Tex., Sheppard AFB, Wichita Falls, Tex., Chanute AFB, Rantoul, Ill., McChord AFB, Tacoma, Wash., health center Chico State U., Sacramento County Adminstrn. Center, Sacramento Bee Newspaper Plant. Home: 160 Breckenwood Way Sacramento CA 95864-6968 Office: Lionakis Beaumont Design Group 1919 19th St Sacramento CA 95814-6714

LIONE, GAIL ANN, lawyer; b. NYC, Oct. 22, 1949; d. James G. and Dorothy Ann (Marsino) L.; 1 child, Margo A. Peyton. BA magna cum laude in Polit. Sci., U. Rochester, 1971; JD, U. Pa., 1974. Bar: Pa. 1974, Ga. 1975, DC 1990, NC 1998. Atty. Morgan, Lewis & Bockius, Phila., 1974-75, Hansell & Post, Atlanta, 1975-80; v.p. 1st Nat. Bank Atlanta, 1980-86; sr. v.p., corp. sec., gen. counsel Sun Life Group of Am., Inc., Atlanta, 1986-89; v.p. Md. Nat. Bank, Balt., 1989-90; gen. counsel, sec. US News & World Report, LP, Applied Graphics Technologies, Atlantic Monthly Co., Washington, 1990—97; v.p., gen. counsel, sec. Harley-Davidson, Inc., Milw., 1997—. Sec., dir., com. chair State Bar Ga. (Young Lawyers Sect.), 1976-84; Chmn. bd. Spl. Audiences, Inc., 1983-85, bd. dirs., 1975-89; trustee Client Security Fund State Bar Ga., 1985-89; vice chmn. Metro Atlanta United Way Campaign, 1986-87; chmn. bd. Atlanta Ballet, 1985-86, bd. dirs., 1975-89; mem. Atlanta Legal Aid Soc., 1981-89; bd. mgrs. U. Pa. Law Sch., 1982-85; mem. U. Rochester Trustee Coun., 1994—; bd. dirs. YMCA Balt., 1989-90; past bd. dirs. Metro YMCA, Atlanta, Sudden Infant Death Syndrome Inst., Atlanta Cmty. Food Bank; mem. Leadership Atlanta, 1988; mem. fin. com. Nat. Symphony Ball, 1995; adv. bd. Cardiovascular Ctr. Medical Coll. Wis., 1999-2002; mem., bd. dirs. Bradley Ctr. Sports & Entertainment Corp., 2003-; Milw. Art Mus., 2004-, Outstanding Atlanta award, TOYPA, 1982, outstanding Vol. Golden Rule award, 1984; named one of Top 40 Under 40 Atlanta Mag., 1984, Top 20 Women in Atlanta by Atlanta Bus. Chronicle, 1987; teaching fellow Salzburg Inst., 1989. Mem. ABA (mem. ho. dels., 1980-84, chmn. standing com. comm. on assn. comm., 1993-96, co-chair. litig. sect. com. fed. legis. 1994—96, regional co-chair forum on comm. law, 1996—98, standing com. on pub. oversight and strategic comm., 1996-2000), Copywright Soc. USA (trustee 1996-99), Mfg. Inst., 2002-, Nat. Assn. Mfrs., Phi Beta Kappa. Office: Harley Davidson 3700 W Juneau Ave PO Box 653 Milwaukee WI 53201-0653 Office Phone: 414-343-4044. Office Fax: 414-343-4189.*

LIOTA, VINCENT, television producer; Student, Pratt Inst., NY; BFA in Film Prodn., NYU, 1983. Local news cameraman, editor, reporter WTNH-TV, New Haven, 1983—93; editor, World New Tonight, 20/20, PrimeTime ABC News, 1993—2000, editor, sci., bus. segments, 2000—04; prodr., NOVA ScienceNow WGBH Found., Boston, 2004—. Recipient Science Journalism award for TV reporting, AAAS, 2006. Office: NOVA Science-NOW 125 Western Ave Allston MA 02134

LIOTTA, JEANNE, film director, educator; b. NYC, 1960; Film instructor Sch. Mus. Fine Arts, Boston; vis. artist Bard, San Francisco Art Inst. Dir.: (films) Blue Moon, 1988, Soma Sema, 1988, Open Sesame, 1989, Fungus Eroticus, 1990, Dervish Machine, 1992, Cici N'est Pas, 1997, What Makes Day and Night, 1998, Muktikara, 1999, Struck by the Hand, 2001, Window, 2001, L'air du Temps, 2003, One Day This May No Longer Exist, 2005; Exhibited in group shows at Whitney Biennial, Whitney Mus. Art, 2006, Internat. Film Festival, Rotterdam, Pacific Film Archives, Berkeley, Calif., Anthology Film Archives, NYC, Mus. Modern Art, NYC. Fellow MacDowell Colony, 2002; grantee Jerome Found., NY State Coun. Arts, Experimental Television Ctr. Office: SMFA Boston 230 The Fenway Boston MA 02115

LIOTTA, LANCE ALLEN, pathologist; b. Cleve., July 12, 1947; married; 2 children. BA in Gen. Sci. and Biology, Hiram Coll., 1969; PhD in Biomed. Engring. and Biomath., Case Western U., 1974, MD, 1976. Cert. basic life support Am. Heart Assn., advanced life support Am. Heart Assn. Instr. pathology for inhalation therapists dept. pathology St. Luke's Hosp., Cleve., 1972-74; sr. instr. pulmonary pathology Phase I and Phase II, Sch. Medicine Case Western Reserve U., 1973-74; USPHS resident physician Lab. Pathology, Nat. Cancer Inst. NIH, Bethesda, Md., 1976-78, pathologist, expert/cons. Lab. Pathophysiology, Nat. Cancer Inst., 1978-80, sr. investigator, pub. health svc. officer Lab. Pathophysiology and Pathology, Nat. Cancer Inst., 1980-82, chief tumor invasion and metastases sect. Lab. Pathology and Lab. Pathology, Nat. Cancer Inst., 1982—, dir. anatomic pathology residency program Lab. Pathology, Nat. Cancer Inst., 1982—, dep. dir. intramural rsch., 1992-93. Adj. clin. prof. pathology Sch. Medicine George Wash. U.; mem. adj. faculty Sch. Medicine Georgetown U.; invited faculty mem. Rockefeller U., 1979; speaker in field. Author: (with others) Cancer Invasion and Metastasis, 1977, Pulmonary Metastasis, 1978, Metastatic Tumor Growth, 1980, Bone Metastasis, 1981, Cell Biology of Breast Cancer, 1980, New Trends in Basement Membrane Research, 1982, Tumor Invasion and Metastasis, 1982, Progress in Clinical and Biological Research, 1982, Growth of Cells in Hormonally Defined Media, 1982, Understanding Breast Cancer: Clinical and Laboratory Concepts, 1983, The Role of Extracellular Matrix in Development, 1984, Basic Mechanisms and Clinical Treatment of Tumor Metastasis, 1985, Hemostatic Mechanisms and Metastasis, 1984, Biological Responses in Cancer, vol. 4, 1985, The Cell in Contact: Adhesions and Junctions as Morphogenetic Determinants, 1985, Rheumatology, vol. 10, 1986, Progress in Neuropathology, vol. 6, 1986, Cancer Metastasis: Experimental and Clinical Strategies, 1986, Biochemistry and Molecular Genetics of Cancer Metastasis, 1986, Basement Membranes, 1985, 1986 Year Book of Cancer, New Concepts in Neoplasia as Applied to Diagnostic Pathology, 1986, Head and Neck Management of the Cancer Patient, 1986, Cancer Metastasis: Biological and Biochemical Mechanisms and Clinical Aspects, 1988, Important Advances in Oncology, 1988, Breast Cancer: Cellular and Molecular Biology, 1988, Cancer: Principles and Practice of Oncology, vol. 1, 3d edit., 1989, Molecular Mechanisms in Cellular Growth and Differentiation, 1991, Peptide Growth Factors and Their Receptors, 1990, Molecuar Genetics in Cancer Diagnosis, 1990, Cancer Surveys-Advances & Prospects in Clinical, Epidemiological and Laboratory Oncology, vol. 7, no. 4, 1988, Genetic Mechanisms in Carcinogenesis and Tumor Progression, 1990, Molecular and Cellular Biology, Host Immune Responses and Perspectives for Treatment, 1989, Origins of Human Cancer: A Comprehensive Review, 1991, Cancer and Metastasis Reviews, vol. 9, 1990, Comprehensive Textbook of Oncology, 1991, Textbook of Internal Medicine, 2d edit., vol. 2, 1992, Molecular Foundations in Oncology, 1991, Genes, Oncogenes, and Hormones: Advances in Cellular and Molecular Biology of Breast Cancer, 1991, Cell Motility Factors, 1991, Oncogenes and Tumor Suppressor Genes in Human Malignancies, 1993, Principles and Practice of Gnecologic Oncology, 1992, Cancer Medicine, 3d edit., 1993; contbr. articles to profl. jours. NIH Pre-doctoral fellow; recipient Arthur S. Flemming award, 1983, Flow award lectureship Soc. Cell Biology, 1983, Nat. award and lectureship Am. Assn. Clin. Chemistry, 1987, Rsch. award Susan G. Komen Found., 1987, Disting. Lectr. award Rush Cancer Ctr., 1987, George Hoyt Whipple award and lectureship Sch. Medicine U. Rochester, 1988, Karen Grunebaum Symposium award lectureship Hubert H. Humphrey Cancer Rsch. Ctr., 1988, Cancer Rsch. award Milken Family Med. Found., 1988, William M. Shelly Meml. award and lectureship Centennial Johns Hopkins Med. Inst., 1989, Josef Steiner Cancer Found. prize, 1989, Basic Rsch. award Am. Soc. Cytology, 1989, Officer's Recognition award Equal Employment Opportunity, 1990, John W. Cline Cancer Rsch. award and lectureship U. Calif., 1990, Herman Pinkus award lectureship Am. Soc. Dermatology, 1990, Simon M. Shubitz award U. Chgo. Cancer Ctr., 1991, Stanley Gore Rsch. award, 1991, Lila Gruber Cancer Rsch. award Am. Acad. Dermatology, 1991, Am.-Italian Found. Cancer Rsch. award, 1992, Scie. Achievement medal U.S. Surgeon Gen., 1994. Mem. Am. Assn. Cancer Rsch. (bd. dirs., 6th Ann. Rhoads Meml. award 1985), Am. Assn. Pathologists (Warner-Lambert/Parke-Davis award 1984), Am. Soc. Cell Biology, Am. Soc. Clin. Investigation, Internat. Acad. Pathology, Internat. Assn. Metastasis Rsch. (pres. 1990-93), Sigma Xi, Phi Beta Kappa. Achievements include patents for method and device for determining the concentration of a material in a liquid, method for isolating bacterial colonies, test method for separating and/or isolating bacteria and tissue cells, device and method for detecting phenothiazine-type drugs in uring, in vitro assay for cell invasiveness, enzyme immunoassay with two-zoned device having bound antigens, metalloproteinase peptides, matrix receptors role in diagnosis and therapy of cancer, genetic method for predicting tumor aggressiveness, therapeutic application of an anti-invasive compound; patents for role of tumor motility factors in cancer diagnosis, role of tumor metalloproteinases in cancer diagnosis, peptide inhibitor of metalloproteinases, protein inhibitors of metalloproteinases, autotaxin motility stimulating proteins diagnosis and therapy, motility receptor protein and gene diagnosis and therapy.

LIOTTA, RAY, actor; b. Newark, Dec. 18, 1954; s. Alfred and Mary Liotta; m. Michelle Grace Liotta, Feb. 15, 1997 (div. 2004); 1 child. Grad., U. Miami. Actor: (films) The Lonely Lady, 1983, Something Wild, 1986, Arena Brains, 1987, Dominick and Eugene, 1988, Field of Dreams, 1989, Goodfellas, 1990, Article 99, 1992, Unlawful Entry, 1992, No Escape, 1994, Corrina, Corrina, 1994, Operation Dumbo Drop, 1995, Unforgettable, 1996, Turbulence, 1997, Copland, 1997, Phoenix, 1998, Forever Mine, 1999, Muppets From Space, 1999, Pilgram, 2000, A Rumor of Angels, 2000, Hannibal, 2001, Heartbreakers, 2001, Blow, 2001, Narc, 2002 (also prodr.), John Q, 2002, Identity, 2003, The Last Shot, 2004, Control, 2004, Revolver, 2005, Slow Burn, 2005, Take the Lead, 2006 (also exec. prodr.), Even Money, 2006, Comeback Season, 2006, Smokin' Aces, 2006, Wild Hogs, 2007; actor, prodr. (films) Narc, 2002; actor (TV movies) Hardhat & Legs, 1980, Crazy Times, 1981, Women and Men 2: In Love There Are no Rules, The Rat Pack, 1998, Point of Origin, 2002; (TV series) Another World, 1978-81, Casablanca, 1983, Our Family Honor, 1985-86, Smith, 2006; (TV appearances) St. Elsewhere, 1983, Mike Hammer, 1984, Frasier, 1995, Family Guy (voice), 2001, Just Shoot Me!, 2001, 2002, ER, 2004 (Creative Arts Primetime Emmy awards for guest actor in a drama, 2005). Mem. SAG, AFTRA. Office: Endeavor Talent Agency 9601 Wilshire Blvd Ste 300 Beverly Hills CA 90210-5200*

LIOTTA, WILLIAM A., theater educator; b. NYC, July 26, 1964; s. Thomas and Paula Marie Liotta, Marty Pefley (Stepfather); m. Kierstin Andrea Eaton, Dec. 26, 1992 (div. Mar. 1, 1996); m. Missy Fabian Ledbetter, May 29, 2001; 1 child, Sydney Alessandra. BA, Calif. State U., Fullerton, 1982—86; MFA, Calif. Inst. Arts, Valencia, 1997—98. Faculty Calif. Inst. Arts, 1990—97; prof. U. Wis., Milw., 1998—99, Tulane U., New Orleans, 1999—2003, U. N.Mex, Albuquerque, 2003—. Designer, cons., owner Liotta Designs, Albuquerque, 1986—; film grip, electrician Internat. Alliance Theatrical Stage Employees, Local 480 Motion Picture Studio Mechanics, Santa Fe; mem. US contingent Prague Quadrennial, Praque, Czech Republic, 2007. Lighting designer (profl. theatrical prodn.) In Walks Ed (Big Easy award for best lighting design for New Orleans, 2003), lighting & sound designer (internat. theatrical prodn.) A Dream Play, Ctrl. Academy Drama, Beijing. Voting mem. High Desert Homeowners Assn., Albuquerque, 2006—. Mem.: United Scenic Artists Local 829, US Inst. Theatre Tech. (assoc.; vice-commr. 2000—06, co-commr. 2006, sound commn. 2000—). Democrat. Catholic. Achievements include patents for Gamchek entertainment industry lighting testing device. Avocations: skiing, golf, travel. Home: 12819 Northern Sky Ave Albuquerque

NM 87111 Office: Univ New Mexico Coll Fine Arts Albuquerque NM 87131 Home Phone: 505-250-7355. Office Fax: 505-277-8921; Home Fax: 505-277-8921. Business E-Mail: wliotta@unm.edu.

LIOY, PAUL JAMES, environmental health scientist; b. Passaic, NJ, May 27, 1947; s. Nicholas Paul and Jean Elizabeth (Licurse) L.; m. Mary Jean Yonone, June 13, 1971; 1 child, Jason. BA in Physics and Edn., Montclair State Coll., 1969; MS in Physics and Applied Math., Auburn U., 1971; MS in Environ. Sci., Rutgers U., 1973, PhD in Environ. Sci., 1975. Sr. engr. air pollution Interstate Sanitation Commn., NYC, 1975-78; asst. to assoc. prof. Inst. Environ. Medicine/NYU Med. Ctr., NYC, 1978-85, dep. dir. lab. of aerosol rsch., 1982-85; assoc. prof. to prof. Robert Wood Johnson Med. Sch. U. Medicine and dentistry of N.J., Piscataway, N.J., 1985—; dir. exposure measurement and assessment divsn. Environ. and Occupational Health Scis. Inst. (EOHSI), Piscataway, 1986—, dep. dir., 1995—, assoc. dir., 2001—; mem. grad. faculty Rutgers U., 1986—, admissions chair in environ. scis., 1993—; prof. N.J. Sch. Pub. Health, U. Medicine and Dentistry N.J., 2000—, dir. Ctr. for Exposure and Risk Modeling, 2001—. Dir. joint grad. program in human exposure access Rutgers U./U. Medicine and Dentistry N.J., 1994-96; mem. Cancer Inst. N.J., 1997—; cons. bd. environ. studies and toxicology NRC, NAS, Washington, 1989-92, mem. numerous coms., 1984—; chmn. Com. on Exposure Analysis for Air Pollution, 1987-90, Clean Air Coun., N.J. Dept. Environ. Protection, Trenton, 1981-94; mem. Internat. Air Quality Bd., Internat. Joint Commn. U.S.-Can., 1992—; mem. sci. adv. bd. U.S. EPA, 1991—, chair subcom. on health and ecol. evaluation for Clean Air Act; mem. European com. European Exposure Study-EXPOLIS, 1996—; acad. advisor State Legislature, N.J., 1998—; mem. dean's adv. bd. Coll. Sci. and Math. Auburn U., Ala., 1996—; adj. asst. prof. Bklyn. Coll., 1977-78; adj. prof. Med. U. S.C., 1996—; mem. sci. adv. com. Harvard U.; sci. and litigation cons. on environ. health, indoor air pollution, human exposure, and hazardous waste investigations and remediations. Author 182 sci. publs., 1975—, chpts. in 70 books; author: Toxic Air Pollution, 1987, co-editor: (with M.J. Yonone-Lioy) Air Sampling Instruments, 1985; exec. editor: Atmospheric Environment jour., 1989-94; assoc. editor: Environ. Rsch., 1995—, Aerosol Rsch. and Tech., 1990-93; editl. bd. Jour. Applied Environ. and Occupl. Hygiene, Internat., 1999—. Chair Cranford (N.J.) Environ. Commn., 1978; treas. Cranford Little League, 1984-85. Rsch. grantee EPA, NIH, CDC, ATSDR, N.J. Dept. Environ. Protection, API, DOE, HUD Indsl., 1978—. Fellow Collegium Ramazzini (Italy); mem. Air Waste Mgmt. Assn. (chmn. editorial bd. 1978-80), Am. Conf. Gov. Indsl. Hygiene (chmn. air sample inst. com. 1984-87), Am. Assn. Aerosol. Rsch. (editorial bd. 1988-90), Internat. Soc. Environ. Epidemiology (bd. councilors 1988-89), Internat. Soc. Exposure Analysis (founder, pres. 1993-94, treas. 1990-91, exec. com. 1989-95, Wesolowski Lifetime Achievement award 1998), Soc. of Risk Analysis, Assn. Profl. Indsl. Hygienists, Cranford C. of C. (bd. dirs. 2000—). Avocations: restoration of houses, tennis, automobiles. Office: Environ/Occup Hlth Scis Inst 170 Frelinghuysen Rd Piscataway NJ 08854-8020

LIPCON, CHARLES ROY, lawyer; b. NYC, Mar. 20, 1946; s. Harry H. and Rose Lipcon; m. Irmgard Adels, Dec. 1, 1974; children: Lauren, Claudia. BA, U. Miami, 1968, JD, 1971. Bar: Fla. 1971, U.S. Dist. Ct. (so. dist.) Fla. 1971, U.S. Ct. Appeals (5th cir.) 1972, U.S. Supreme Ct. 1976, U.S. Ct. Appeals (D.C. cir.) 1980, U.S. Dist. Ct. (so. dist.) Tex. 1982, U.S. Dist. Ct. (mid. dist.) Fla. 2000, U.S. Ct. Appeals (11th cir.) 1994, U.S. Dist. Ct. Colo. 1999, U.S. Dist. Ct. (no. dist.) Fla. 2003, Ct. of Fed. Claims, 2003. Pvt. practice, Miami, Fla., 1971—. Lectr. U. Miami Sch. Law. Author: Help for the Auto Accident Victim, 1984, Seaman's Rights in the United States When Involved in An Accident, 1989; pub., editor The Cruise Line Law Reporter; contbr. articles to profl. jours. Named Commodore of High Seas, Internat. Seaman's Union. Mem. ABA, ATLA, Fla. Bar Assn., Fla. Trial Lawyers Assn., Dade County Bar Assn., Dade County Trial Lawyers, Fla. Admiralty Trial Lawyers Assn., Mensa. Office: 2 S Biscayne Blvd Ste 2480 Miami FL 33131-1803 Office Phone: 305-373-3016. E-mail: sealaw@aol.com.

LIPELES, MAXINE INA, lawyer, law educator; b. NYC, Sept. 26, 1953; d. David Arthur and Pauline (Cooper) L.; m. Joel Kramer Goldstein, Aug. 31, 1980; children: Rachel, Joshua. AB, Princeton U., 1975; JD, Harvard U., 1979. Bar: Mass. 1980, Mo. 1982, U.S. Dist. Ct. (ea. dist.) Mo. 1982, U.S. Dist. Ct. Mass., U.S. Ct. Appeals (1st cir.) 1980, U.S. Ct. Appeals (8th cir.) 1982. Law clk. U.S. Dist. Ct. (no. dist.) Calif., San Francisco, 1979-80; asst. atty. gen. State of Mass., Boston, 1980-82; assoc. Husch & Eppenberger, St. Louis, 1982-86, ptnr., 1986-94, of counsel, 1995—99; dir. (interdisciplinary environ. clinic), sr. lectr. in law Wash. U. Sch. of Law, St. Louis. Part-time prof. environ. regulation and policy sch. engring. Wash. U., St. Louis, 1990—; dir. environ. engring. program Wash. U., St. Louis, 1994-99. Co-author: Hazardous Waste, 3rd edit., 1997, Water Pollution, 1993, Environmental Law Anthology, 1996. Mem. ABA, Mo. Bar Assn., Bar Assn. Met. St. Louis (chmn. environ. law com. 1986-88). Office: Wash U Sch of Law Anheuser Busch Hall Rm 102A 1 Brookings Dr Campus Box 1120 Saint Louis MO 63130-4899 Office Phone: 314-935-5837. Office Fax: 314-935-6493. Business E-Mail: milipele@wulaw.wustl.edu.

LIPEZ, KERMIT V., federal judge, former state supreme court justice; b. Phila., 1941; BA, Haverford Coll., 1963; LLB, Yale Law Sch., 1967; LLM, Univ. Va. Law Sch., 1990. Staff atty., civil rights divsn. US Dept. of Justice, 1967—68; spec. asst. & legal counsel Gov. Kenneth M. Curtis, Maine, 1968—71; legis aide US Sen. Edmund Muskie, 1971—72; ptnr. Curtis, Thaxter, Lipez, Stevens, Broder & Micoleau, 1975—85; judge Maine Superior Ct., 1985—94; assoc. justice Supreme Jud. Ct. of Maine, Portland, 1994—98; judge US Ct. Appeals (1st cir.) Maine, Portland, 1998—. Mem. fed.-state jurisdiction com. Jud. Conf. Mem.: Justice Action Group (chair), Am. Law Inst., Cumberland County Bar Assn., Maine Bar Assn. Office: 156 Federal St Portland ME 04101-4152*

LIPFORD, ROCQUE EDWARD, lawyer; b. Monroe, Mich., Aug. 16, 1938; s. Frank G. and Mary A. (Mastromarco) L.; m. Marcia A. Griffin, Aug. 5, 1966; children: Lisa, Rocque Edward, Jennifer, Katherine. BS, U. Mich., 1960, MS, 1961, JD with distinction, 1964. Bar: Mich. 1964, Ohio 1964. Instr. mech. engring. U. Mich., 1961—63; atty. Miller, Canfield, Paddock & Stone, Detroit, 1965—66; asst. gen. counsel Monroe Auto Equipment Co., 1966—70, gen. counsel, 1970—72, v.p., gen. counsel, 1973—77, Tenneco Automotive, 1977—78; ptnr. firm Miller, Canfield, Paddock & Stone, Detroit, 1978—, mng. ptnr., 1988—91. Bd. dirs. La-Z-Boy Inc., MBT Fin. Mem.: Knights of Malta, Legatus, Mich. Bar Assn., Mariner Sands Golf and Country Club, Monroe Golf and Country Club, North Cape Yacht Club, Otsego Ski Club, Pi Tau Sigma, Tau Beta Pi. Home: 1065 Hollywood Dr Monroe MI 48162-3045 Office: Miller Canfield Paddock & Stone 214 E Elm Ave Ste 100 Monroe MI 48162-2682 Office Phone: 734-243-2000. Business E-Mail: lipford@mcps.com.

LIPINSKI, ANN MARIE, publishing executive; b. Trenton, Mich. m. Steve Kagan; 1 child, Caroline. B in Am. Studies, U. Mich. Joined Chgo. Tribune, 1978, named head investigative team, 1990, assoc. mng. editor met. news., 1991—93, dep. mng. editor, 1994—95, mng. editor, 1995—2000, v.p. & exec. editor, 2000—01, sr. v.p. & exec. editor, 2001—. Juror Pulitzer Prize, 2001, 02; mem. Pulitzer Prize Bd., 2003—. Bd. visitors Poynter Inst., U. Mich. Journalism Fellows program, Stanford U. Journalism Fellows program. Recipient Pulitzer Prize for investigative reporting, 1988; Nieman Fellowship Harvard U., 1989-90. Office: Chgo Tribune 435 N Michigan Ave Chicago IL 60611-4066*

LIPINSKI, DANIEL, congressman; b. Chgo., July 15, 1966; s. William and Marie Lipinski; m. Judy Lipinski. BS, Northwestern Univ., 1988; MA, Stanford Univ., 1989; PhD in polit. sci., Duke Univ., 1998. Assoc. prof. Notre Dame Univ., 2000—01, Univ. Tenn., 2001—04; mem. U.S. Congress from 3d Dist Ill., 2005—; mem. sci. com., small bus. com. U.S. Ho. of Reps. Democrat. Roman Catholic. Office: US House Reps 1217 Longworth House Office Bldg Washington DC 20515-1303 Office Phone: 202-225-5701. Office Fax: 202-225-1012.*

LIPINSKI, TARA KRISTEN, retired professional figure skater; b. Phila., June 10, 1982; Prof. figure skater Stars On Ice, 1998—. Nat. spokesperson Campaign for Tobacco-Free Kids. Tara Lipinski's A Night of Skating Champions, Houston, 2003; actor(TV appearance): 7th Heaven, 2003, The Wayne Brady Show, 2003. Recipient Mary Lou Retton award, U.S. Olympic Festival, 1994, 2nd Place, Skate Can., 1996, 1st (team), Postal Svc. Challenge, 1996, 2nd Place, Nations Cup, 1996, 3rd Place, Trophy Lalique, 1996, 1st Place, Hershey's Kisses Challenge, 1997, World Championships, 1997, Champion Series Final, 1997, 1998, 1st Nat. Sr., 1997, 2nd Place, Nat. Championship, 1998, 1st Place, Rattle and Roll, 1998, Gold Medal, Winter Olympic Games, 1998. Achievements include youngest Olympic Festival gold medalist at age 12. Avocations: reading, cooking, tennis.

LIPINSKI, WILLIAM OLIVER, former congressman; b. Chgo., Dec. 22, 1937; s. Oliver and Madeline (Collins) L.; m. Rose Marie Lapinski, Aug. 29, 1962; children: Laura, Daniel. Student, Loras Coll., Dubuque, Iowa, 1957-58. Various positions to area supr. Chgo. Parks, 1958-75; alderman Chgo. City Coun., 1975-83; mem. 98th-108th Congresses from 5th (now 3rd) Dist. Ill., 1983—2005, mem. transp. and infrastructure com. Dem. ward committeeman, Chgo., 1975—; del. Dem. Nat. Midterm Conv., 1974, Dem. Nat. Conv., 1976, 84, 88; pres. Greater Midway Econ. and Community Devel. Com.; mem. Chgo. Hist. Soc., Art Inst., Chgo., pres.'s coun. St. Xavier Coll.; mem. Congl. Competitive Caucus, Congl. Caucus for Women's Issues, Congl. Hispanic Caucus, Congl. Human Rights Caucus, Congl. Populist Caucus, Dem. Study Group, Export Task Force, Inst. for Ill., Maritime Caucus, N.E.-Midwest Congl. Coalition, Urban Caucus. Named Man of Yr. Chgo. Park Dist. 4, 1983; recipient Archer Heights Civic Assn. award 1979, 23d Ward Businessmen and Mchts. award Chgo., 1977, Garfield Ridge Hebrew Congregation award Chgo., 1975-77, Installing Officer award Vittum Park Civic Assn., 23d Ward Minuteman award, Friends of Vittum Park Polish award, Nathan Hale Grand award from S.W. Liberty Soc., S.W. Am. Edn. and Recreation program award, Sentry of Yr. award Stars & Stripes Soc., Ill. State Minuteman award 1991. Mem. Polish Nat. Alliance, Kiwanis (Disting. Svc. award, pres., Peace Through Strength Leadership award 1991). Democrat. Roman Catholic.

LIPKIN, ALAN F., otolaryngologist; b. NYC, Apr. 2, 1956; s. Nathan J. and Gladys B. Lipkin; m. Barbara L. Shapiro, Apr. 5, 1981; children: Richard, Sam, Molly. BA magna cum laude, U. Rochester, NY, 1976; MD, Columbia U., NYC, 1980. Cert. Am. Bd. Otolaryngology. Resident, fellow Baylor Coll. Medicine, Houston, 1980—86; ptnr. Assocs. Otolaryngology, Denver, 1986—. Recipient Coakley Meml. prize, Columbia U., 1980. Fellow: Am. Acad. Otolaryngology/Head and Neck Surgery; mem.: Am. Neurotology Soc., Phi Beta Kappa. Achievements include patents for method of inserting transtracheal catheter. Avocations: photography, hiking, snowshoeing, skiing. Office: Assocs Otolaryngology 950 E Harvard #500 Denver CO 80210

LIPKIN, DAVID LAWRENCE, physician; b. Bklyn., Mar. 9, 1938; s. Herman and Celia (Granate) Lipkin; m. Nicole Van Laere, Sept. 23, 1962; children: Lawrence, Elline, Diane. AB in Biology, Clark U., Worcester, Mass., 1957; MD, Catholic U. Louvain, Belgium, 1964. Diplomate Am. Bd. Phys. Medicine and Rehab. Intern Lutheran Med. Ctr., Bklyn., 1963—64; resident in pediat. N.J. Coll. Medicine, Jersey City, 1964—66; resident rehab. medicine Albert Einstein Coll. Medicine, Bronx, NY, 1966—68, chief resident, 1968—69; clin. instr. U. Miami, 1974—80, clin. asst. prof. dept. rheumatology, 1980—84, clin. assoc. prof. dept. orthopedics and rehab., 1992—96. Med. dir. rehab. Pkwy. Regional Med. Ctr. Humana Hosp., Biscayne, Fla., 1974—88; med. dir. Bon Secours Hosp., North Miami, Fla., 1984—88; chief dept. rehab. medicine Sinai Med. Ctr.; cons. in field. Chmn. stroke com. Am. Heart Assn., Monroe and Dade Counties, Fla., 1980—82; bd. dirs. Multiple Sclerosis Soc., Dade, 1987, Villa Maria Nursing Ctr., 1986. Named one of Best Lawyers in Am. Comml. Litigation White Collar Criminal Defense, 2005—06; NIH fellow, 1966—69. Mem.: So. Soc. Phys. Medicine and Rehab., Am. Acad. Phys. Medicine and Rehab. Fla. Rheumatology Soc., Am. Rheumatism Assn., Fla. Soc. Phys. Medicine and Rehab. (pres. 1976—78, 1989—91), Fla. Med. Assn., Dade County Med. Assn.

LIPKIN, MARTIN, medical educator, researcher; b. NYC, Apr. 30, 1926; s. Samuel S. and Celia (Greenfield) Lipkin; m. Joan Schulein, Feb. 16, 1958; children: Richard Martin, Steven Monroe. AB, NYU, 1946, MD, 1950. Diplomate Nat. Bd. Med. Examiners. Mem. staff NY Hosp., Meml. Hosp. for Cancer and Allied Diseases, 1972-96; prof. medicine Cornell U. Med. Coll., 1978—, prof. Grad. Sch. Med. Scis., 1978—; mem. and attending physician Meml. Sloan-Kettering Cancer Ctr., 1985-96; dir. clin. rsch. Strang Cancer Prevention Ctr., NYC, 1996—. Vis. physician Rockefeller U. Hosp., 1981—2006; nominator Nobel Prize for Physiology and Medicine, 1982; Chao disting. lectr. U. Calif., 2000. Mem. editl. bd. Internat. Jour. Oncology, World Jour. Gastroenterology; editor: Gastrointestinal Tract Cancer, 1978, Inhibition of Tumor Induction and Development, 1981, Gastrointestinal Cancer: Endogenous Factors, 1981, Calcium, Vitamin D and Prevention of Colon Cancer, 1991, Cancer Chemoprevention, 1992; contbr. articles to profl. jours. Bd. dirs., officer Med. Ednl. and Sci. Found. NY; bd. dirs. Internat. Soc. Cancer Chemoprevention; chmn. bd. dirs. Weinstein Found. Officer USN, 1953—55. Recipient NIH Career Devel. award, 1962—71, Albert F. R. Andresen award, NY State Med. Soc., 1971, medallion, Nat. Cancer Ctr. Rsch. Inst., Tokyo, 1976, U. Padua, Italy, 1978, Elise Strang L'Esperance Leadership award, NY, 2005. Fellow: ACP, Am. Coll. Gastroenterology; mem.: Am. Gastroenterol. Assn., Am. Assn. Cancer Rsch., Am. Physiol. Soc., Am. Soc. Clin. Investigation, Med. Soc. State of NY (chmn. sci. program com. 1990—91, chmn. edn. com. 1991—99). Achievements include introducing computers into medicine; first identification of cell cycle in humans, the first human intervention study of dietary calcium as a chemopreventive agent against colon cancer. Office: 428 E 72d St New York NY 10021-6307 Business E-Mail: lipkin@rockefeller.edu.

LIPKIN, SEYMOUR, musician, conductor, educator; b. Detroit, May 14, 1927; s. Ezra and Leah (Vidaver) L.; m. Catherine Lee Bing, Dec. 27, 1961 (div. 1983); 1 son, Jonathan Michael; m. Ellen Werner, 2003. MusB, Curtis Inst. Music, 1947; studied piano with, David Saperton, 1938-41, Rudolf Serkin, Mieczyslaw Horszowski, 1941-47; conducting with, Serge Koussevitzky, Berkshire Music Center, 1946, 48-49. Piano tchr. Juilliard Sch. Music, NYC, 1986—. Faculty Manhattan Sch. Music, 1965-70, 72-86, NYU, 1980-86; piano faculty Curtis Inst. Music, 1969—, New Eng. Conservatory, 1984-86, faculty music dept. Marymount Coll., Tarrytown, N.Y., 1963-72, chmn. music dept., 1968-71. Condr. Bklyn. Coll. Orch., 1973-74; Ford Found. commn. to perform concerto by Harold Shapero, 1959; debut with Detroit Civic Orch., 1937; apprentice condr. to George Szell, Cleve. Orch., 1947-48; appearances as pianist other U.S. orchs. including Boston Symphony in Tanglewood; ann. tours including soloist, Buffalo and Nat. Symphony, soloist, asst. condr. N.Y. Philharm. tour, Europe and Russia, 1959; conducting debut Detroit Symphony, 1944; recitalist, 92d St YMHA, N.Y.C., 1981, 83, soloist N.Y. Philharm., N.Y.C., 1983, participant in chamber music, Spoleto Festivals, 1982, 83, co-condr. Curtis Inst. Orch., 1952-53, asst. condr. Goldovsky Opera Co. on tour, 1953, condr. N.Y.C. Opera Co., 1958, 1 of 3 asst. condrs. New York Philharm., 1959-60; mus. dir. Teaneck Symphony, N.J., 1961-70, L.I. Symphony, 1963-79, Scarboro Chamber Orch., N.Y., 1964-65, Joffrey Ballet, N.Y. City Center, 1966-68, 1972-79, prin. guest condr., 1968-72; artistic dir. Kneisel Hall Summer Chamber Music Sch. and Festival, 1987— (performed cycle of 32 Beethoven Sonatas 1988-90, Gardner Mus., Boston, 1996-99, Beethoven Soc., N.Y., 1997—, 10 Beethoven Violin Sonatas with Andrew Dawes 1995, Uto Ughi, Santa Cecilia, Rome, 1995, 5 cello sonatas with David Soyer 1989, Laurence Lesser, 1996, 5 piano concertos with Santa Fe Symphony 1993, complete sonatas of Schubert at Kneisel Hall, Gardner Mus., Boston, Kaye Playhouse, N.Y.C.); appearances as opera condr. Curtis Inst., Teatro Petruzzelli, Bari, Italy, 1986-87; participant in chamber music Norfolk Fest., 1984-85, Marlboro Fest., 1986; recorded Stravinsky Piano Concerto and Capriccio with N.Y. Philharm., Bernstein, Grieg, Saint-Saens, Strauss sonatas with Aaron Rosand (violin), Grieg, Dohnanyi, Weiner sonatas with Oscar Shumsky (violin), Franck Sonata, Chausson Concerto with Rosand, Beethoven Sonatas op. 106 and 109, complete Schubert violin and piano works with Arnold Steinhardt (violin), 32 Beethoven piano sonatas; tour of China, recitals and master classes, 2004; artistic dir. internat. piano festival and William Kapell competition U. Md., 1988-92. Recipient 1st prize Rachmaninoff Piano Competition, 1948. Home: 420 West End Ave New York NY 10024-5708 Office: Perform Artist Internat 4417 Dunwick Ln Ste 300 Fort Worth TX 76109-2508

LIPMAN, DAVID, retired journalist, multi-media consultant; b. Springfield, Mo., Feb. 13, 1931; s. Benjamin and Rose (Mack) L.; m. Marilyn Lee Vittert, Dec. 10, 1961; children: Gay Ilene, Benjamin Alan. BJ, U. Mo., 1953, LHD (hon.), 1997. Sports editor Jefferson City (Mo.) Post-Tribune, 1953, Springfield Daily News, 1953-54; gen. assignment reporter Springfield Leader and Press, 1956-57; reporter, copy editor Kansas City (Mo.) Star, 1957-60; sports reporter St. Louis Post-Dispatch, 1960-66, asst. sports editor, 1966-68, news editor, 1968-71, asst. mng. editor, 1971-78, mng. editor, 1979-92; chmn. Pulitzer 2000 Pulitzer Pub. Co., St. Louis, 1992-96, multimedia cons., 1997-2000. Guest lectr. Am. Press Inst., Columbia U. Journalism Sch., 1967-70; chmn. bd. advisors U. Mo. Sch. Journalism, 1989-2001, chmn. bd. dirs. multi-cultural mgmt. program, 1995-97; bd. dirs. Columbia Missourian; chmn. U. Mo. Jounalism Sch. task force, 2001-02; 1st v.p. Mo. Press Found., 2003—. Author: Maybe I'll Pitch Forever, The Autobiography of LeRoy (Satchel) Paige, 1962, reissued, 1993, Mr. Baseball, The Story of Branch Rickey, 1966, Ken Boyer, 1967, Joe Namath, 1968; co-author: The Speed King, The Story of Bob Hayes, 1971, Bob Gibson Pitching Ace, 1975, Jim Hart Underrated Quarterback, 1977. Bd. dirs. Mid-Am. Press Inst., 1973-97, chmn., 1975-77; mem.-at-large nat. coun., bd. dirs. Am. Jewish Com. St. Louis, 1997—, life time adv. bd. mem., 2005—; bd. dirs. Rabbi Samuel Thurman Ednl. Found., 1997—; trustee United Hebrew Congregation, 1975-77; bd. dirs. Parkview Housing Corp., 1999-2004; chmn. com. 21st Century, U. Mo., 1993-94; vice chair Mo. Gov.'s Commn. on Info. Tech., 1994-95; chmn. ethics commn. City of Creve Coeur, 2001-02, chair new tech. com., 1997-2001; mem. Creve Coeur Charter Commn., 2000-2001; cons. Mo. Press-Bar Commn., 1995-2002; mem. adv. bd. Jewish Light, 2001—. 1st lt. USAF, 1954-56. Named a St. Louis Media Hall Fame, 2007; named to Writers Hall of Fame of Am., Springfield, Mo., 2002, Mo. Newspapers Hall of Fame, 2002; recipient Univ. Mo. Faculty and Alumni award, 1988, Univ. Mo. Disting. Svc. in Journalism medal, 1989, St. Louis Jermiah award, 1991. Mem. Am. Soc. Newspaper Editors, Newspaper Assn. Am. (mem. industry devel. com. 1993-96), Mo. Editors and Pubs. Assn. (pres. 1990-91), Mo. Soc. Newspaper Editors (bd. dirs. 1990-97, vice chmn. 1992-93, chmn. 1993), Mo. Press Assn. (1st v.p. 1994-95, pres. 1997, bd. dirs. 1998-2002), Mo. AP Mng. Editors Assn. (pres. 1990), U. Mo. Sch. Journalism Nat. Alumni Assn. (chmn. 1980-83), Press Club of St. Louis (chmn. 1987-94), Soc. Profl. Journalists (pres. St. Louis chpt. 1976-77), Kappa Tau Alpha, Omicron Delta Kappa. Jewish.

LIPMAN, DAVID J., medical association administrator, researcher; BA with honors, Brown U., Providence, RI, 1976; MD, SUNY, Buffalo, 1980. Rsch. fellow math. rsch. br. Nat. Inst. Diabetes, Digestive & Kidney Diseases; dir. Nat. Ctr. Biotechnology Info., Bethesda, Md., 1989—, exec. sec. Bd. Sci. Counselors; editor-in-chief Biology Direct. Contbr. articles to profl. publs. Recipient 3 Pub. Health Svc. Outstanding Svc. medals, Dir.'s award, NIH, Sr. Scientist Accomplishment award, Internat. Soc. Computational Biology (ISCB), 2004. Fellow: Am. Coll. Med. Informatics; mem.: NAS Inst. Medicine. Achievements include development of FASTA biol. sequence comparison prog., 1985; Basic Local Alignment Search Tool (BLAST), 1990; contributed to some of the most important tools in gene sequence analysis. Office: Nat Ctr Biotechnology Info Bldg 38A Rm 8N807 8600 Rockville Pike Bethesda MD 20894 Office Phone: 301-496-2475. Office Fax: 301-480-9241. E-mail: lipman@ncbi.nlm.nih.gov.*

LIPMAN, FREDERICK D., lawyer, educator, writer; b. Phila., Nov. 16, 1935; s. Charles S. and Beatrice (Sanderow) Lipman; m. Gail Heller, July 25, 1965; children: L. Keith, Darren A. AB, Temple U.; LLB, Harvard Law Sch. Bar: Pa. 1960, N.Y. Practitioner, Phila., 1960-62; corp. counsel AEL Industries, Inc., Colmar, Pa., 1962-69; ptnr. Blank Rome LLP, Phila., 1970—. Lectr. U. Pa. Law Sch., 1989—98, Temple U. Law Sch., 1989—94, Wharton Sch. Bus., 1998—2003. Author: Going Public, 1994, How Much is Your Business Worth, 1996, Venture Capital and Junk Bond Financing, 1998, Financing Your Business with Venture Capital, 1998, Complete Going Public Handbook, 2000, Audit Committees, 2001, The Complete Guide to Employee Stock Options, 2001, The Complete Guide to Valuing and Selling Your Business, 2001, Valuing Your Business, 2005, Corporate Goverance Best Practices, 2006. Bd. dirs. Walnut St. Theatre, 1997—99, Phila. Geriatric Ctr., Penjerdel, Phila. Ch. Bezalel, 1989—91; bd. trustees Jewish Fedn. Greater Phila., 2006—, tristee, 2006—. Scholar, Temple U., 1953, Harvard Law Sch., 1957. Mem.: Harvard Law Sch. Assn. Greater Phila. (pres. 1988—89), Greater Phila. C. of C. (bd. dirs., mem. exec. com. 1980—90, chmn. tech. coun. 1983—85), Masons. Democrat. Jewish. Avocation: tennis. Office: Blank Rome LLP 1 Logan Sq Fl Three Philadelphia PA 19103-6998 Business E-Mail: lipman@blankrome.com.

LIPMAN, HANNAH ILENE, medical educator; b. NY, Sept. 28, 1971; BA, Northwestern U., Evanston, Ill., 1993; MD, Columbia U., NY, 1998. Diplomate Am. Bd. Internal Medicine, 2001. Asst. prof. medicine Montefiore med. ctr. Albert Einstein Coll. Medicine, Bronx, NY, 2006—. Home Phone: 212-865-2635.

LIPMAN, IRA ACKERMAN, security service company executive; b. Little Rock, Nov. 15, 1940; s. Mark and Belle (Ackerman) L.; m. Barbara Ellen Kelly Couch, July 5, 1970; children: Gustave K., Joshua S, M Benjamin. Student, Ohio Wesleyan U., 1958-60; LLD (hon.), John Marshall U., Atlanta, 1970; LLD (Hon.), Northeastern U., Boston, 1996. Salesman, exec. Mark Lipman Svc. Inc., Memphis, 1960-63; v.p. Guardsmark, Inc., Memphis, 1963-66, pres., 1966—, CEO, 1968—, chmn. bd., 1968—. Bd. dirs. Nat. Coun. on Crime and Delinquency, 1975—, exec. com., 1976-2004, chmn. fin. com., treas., 1978-79, vice chmn. bd. dirs., 1982-86, chmn. exec. com., 1986-93, chmn. bd. dirs., 1993-94, chmn. emeritus, 1993—, hon. chmn. 1997—; bd. dirs. Greater Memphis Coun. Crime and Delinquency, 1976-78, entrepreneurial fellow U. Memphis., 1976; mem. environ. security com., pvt. security adv. coun. Law Enforcement Assistance Adminstrn., 1975-76; mem. conf. planning com. 2d Nat. Law Enforcement Explorer Conf., 1980. Author: How to Protect Yourself From Crime, 1975, 4th edit., 1997; contbr. numerous articles to profl. jours., mags. and newspapers. Bd. dirs. Memphis Jewish Cmty. Center, 1974, Memphis Shelby County unit Am. Cancer Soc., 1980-81, Memphis Orchestral Soc., 1980-81, Memphis Jewish Fedn., 1974-83; chmn. Shelby County. U.S. Savs. Bonds, 1976; mem. pres.'s coun. U. Memphis.,

1975-79; mem. visual arts coun., 1980-82; Memphis met. chmn. Nat. Alliance Businessmen, 1970-71; mem. task force Reform Jewish Outreach, Union Am. Hebrew Congregations, 1979-83; mem. young leadership cabinet United Jewish Appeal, 1973-78, mem. S.E. regional campaign cabinet, 1980; exec. bd. Chickasaw council Boy Scouts Am., 1978-81; bd. dirs., exec. com. Tenn. Ind. Coll. Fund, 1979; trustee Memphis Acad. Arts, 1977-81; mem. president's club Christian Bros. U., 1979-89; bd. dirs. Future Memphis, 1980-83, 83-86; nat. trustee NCCJ, 1980-92, exec. com., 1981-92, nat. Jewish co-chmn., 1985-88, nat. chmn., 1988-92, life hon. chmn., past nat. chmn. Nat. Conf. Christians and Jews, 1992—; bd. dirs. Memphis chpt., 1980-85, life bd. dirs. Memphis chpt. 1985—; group II chmn. for 1982 campaign United Way Memphis, 1984-1985, founder, chmn. Alexis de Tocqueville chpt., 1984-85, chmn., 1985; campaign bd. trustees United Way Greater Memphis, 1986—; exec. adv. coun. United Way Mid-South, 1988—; v.p. exec. com. Internat. Coun. Christians and Jews, 1992-94; bd. govs. United Way of Am., 1992-99, bd. gov.'s liaison, 1991-92, chmn. ethics com., 1992-97, mem. exec. com., 1992-97, co-chmn. vol. involvement com., 1992—, mem. strategic planning com., 1994-96, diversity com., 1997-99; chmn. UWLC steering com. 1995-96; mem. Alexis de Tocqueville Soc. Nat. Leadership Coun., 1992-97, mem. emeritus, 1998—, mem. Second Century Initiative Vol. Involvement com., 1987-91; chair Task Force on Critical Markets, 1987-91, mem. exec. cabinet, 1990-91; trustee Memphis Brooks Mus. Art, 1980-83, Yeshiva U. of L.A., 1982-; trustee Simon Wiesenthal Ctr., 1982—, chmn. nominating com., 2004-05, chmn. governance com., 2005—, chmn. campaign com., 1983-92, mem. fin. and audit com., 1993-04, exec. com., 1994—, co-chmn. budget and fin. com. Jerusalem Project, 1999-04; bd. dirs. Nat. Alliance against Violence, 1983-85, Nat. Ctr. Learning Disabilities, 1989-94; founder, bd. overseers B'nai B'rith, 1980; bd. dirs. Tenn. Gov.'s Jobs for High Sch. Grads. Program, 1980-83; trustee Ohio Wesleyan U., 1988-97; vice chmn. spl. task force on endowment growth Ohio Wesleyan U., 1990-97; mem. bd. overseers Wharton Sch., U. Pa., 1991-2004, 05—, devel. com., 1995-04, exec. adv. bd. Zicklin Ctr. Bus. Ethics Rsch., 1997-2005; mem. Northeastern U. Corp., 1997-2005; bd. dirs. The Sherry-Netherland, Inc., 2002—; mem. Dean's Coun., Mt. Sinai Sch. Medicine, 2004—; mem. exec. com. Am. Israel Pub. Affairs Com., 1991-01, 02-05; bd. trustees Com. Econ. Devel., 1999—; adv. bd. dirs., Tenn. Titans, 1999-2000; mem. Hillel Internat. Bd. Govs., 2001-03; bd. trustees, Fifth Ave. Synagogue, 2001—; trustee The Jewish Mus., NY, 2003-07, Am. Jewish Hist. Soc., 1986-, v.p., 1993—; founding bd. mem. Nat. Campaign Against Youth Violence, 1999-02; mem. Coun. on Fgn. Rels., 2002, chmn.'s adv. coun., 2004—, corp. affairs com., 2003—; founding mem. Homeland Security Project, 2004—; bd. dirs. Ligue Internationale des Sociétés de Surveillance, 2004—; adv. bd. Ctr. Values Based Leadership Sacred Heart U., 2002-03, Ctr. Bus. Ethics Bentley Coll., 1996—, Libr. of Congress, James Madison Coun., 2004—; bd. trustees NY Hist. Soc., 2007—. Named one of Best Corp. Chief Exec. of Achievement, Gallagher Pres.'s Report, 1974; recipient Humanitarian of Yr. award, NCCJ, 1985, Outstanding Cmty. Sales award, Sales and Mktg. Execs. Memphis, 1987, Jr. Achievement Master Free Enterprise award, 1987, Alexis de Tocqueville Soc. award, 1995, Corp. Citizenship award, Com. for Econ. Devel., 2002, Stanley C. Pace award leadership in ethics, Ethics Resource Ctr., 2002, Dean's Medal, Wharton Sch., U. Pa., 2004. Mem. Internat. Assn. Chiefs Police, Am. Soc. Criminology, Internat. Soc. Criminology, Am. Soc. Indsl. Security (cert. protection profl.), Memphis 100 Club, Memphis Econ. Club (bd. dirs. 1980-86, v.p. 1983-84, pres. 1984-85, chmn. exec. com. 1984-85), The Grolier Club, Bus. Execs. Nat. Security. Republican. Founded The John Chancellor Award for Excellence in Journalism, 1995. Office: Guardsmark LLC 10 Rockefeller Plz 12th Fl New York NY 10020-1903

LIPMAN, MARVIN MATTHEW, physician, medical educator, medical editor, writer; b. NYC, Nov. 6, 1928; s. Louis B. and Bertha L.; m. Naomi L. Lipman, June 17, 1951; children: Barry D., Amy F., Mark A., Harry W. AB, Columbia Coll., 1949; MD, Columbia Coll. of Phys. & Surg., 1954. Intern, asst. resident Columbia-Presbyn. Med. Ctr., 1954-56; sr. resident Mass. Gen. Hosp., 1959-61; chief of endocrinology N.Y. Med. Coll., Valhalla, 1967—81, White Plains (N.Y.) Hosp. Ctr., 1980—85, chief of medicine, 1985—90; prof. clin. medicine N.Y. Med. Coll., Valhalla, 1986—. Bd. trustees U.S. Pharmacopeia, 2000-05; chief med. adviser Consumers Union, Yonkers, N.Y., 1967—. Author: The Medicine Show, 1972, The Best of Health, 1998, Guide to a Healthy Heart, 2003; med. editor: Consumer Reports Mag., 1967—, Consumer Reports on Health, 1989—. Capt. US Army, 1956—58. Fellow: Am. Coll. Endocrinology, ACP; mem.: Physicians for Social Responsibility, Physicians for a Nat. Health Program, Am. Assn. Clin. Endocrinologists, Endocrine Soc., Am. Fedn. Med. Rsch., Am. Diabetes Assn., Alpha Omega Alpha. Avocations: theater, opera, chamber music, squash. Office: Scarsdale Med Group 259 Heathcote Rd Scarsdale NY 10583 Office Phone: 914-723-8100. Business E-Mail: mml83@columbia.edu.

LIPMAN, PETER W., research scientist; b. NYC, Apr. 21, 1935; s. Howard W. and Jean H. Lipman; m. Beverly S. Showalter, June 17, 1962; children: Ben H., Tim E. BS, Yale U., New Haven, Conn., 1957; MS, Stanford U., Palo Alto, Calif., 1958—62, PhD, 1962. Br. chief, program coord. US Geol. Survey, Menlo Park, Calif., sr. rsch. geologist, 1994—2002, sr. rsch. geologist emeritus, 2002—. Contbr. articles to profl. jours. Exec. com. San Jose Mus. Art, Calif., 2000—07, pres. bd. trustees, 2007—. Recipient Disting. Svc. award, Geol. Soc. Am., 2004. Fellow: Am. Geophys. Union (life); mem.: Internat. Assn. Volcanology and Chemistry Earth's Interior (corr.; v.p. 1986—90). Achievements include research in volcanic hazards. Office: US Geological Survey 345 Middlefield Rd Menlo Park CA 94025 Office Phone: 650-329-5295. Office Fax: 650-329-5203. E-mail: plipman@usgs.gov.

LIPMAN, RICHARD PAUL, pediatrician; b. Cambridge, Mass., Aug. 1, 1935; s. Hyman Zelig and Betty (Likovsky) L.; m. Mary Alice Wilcox, Aug. 25, 1963; children: Gregory, Susan; m. Lora H. Higgins, July 6, 1996; children: Sarad, Michael Tomlinson. AB magna cum laude, Harvard U., 1957; MD cum laude, Tufts U., 1961. Diplomate Am. Bd. Pediatrics. Intern Boston Floating Hosp., 1961-62, jr. resident, 1962-63, sr. resident, 1963-64, chief resident, 1964; rsch. fellow infectious disease Med. Sch. U. N.C., Chapel Hill, 1967-69; practice pediatrics Peabody and Salem, Mass., 1969—. Mem. staff North Shore Children's Hosp., Salem, Mass., assoc. chief of staff, 1974-76, pres., chief of staff, 1976-79, chief of medicine, 1979-83, trustee, 1980-84, corporator, 1985-86; mem. staff Tufts-New Eng. Med. Ctr., Boston, Boston Children's Hosp., North Shore Children's Hosp., Beverly Hosp., Melrose-Wakefield Hosp., Salem Hosp.; clin. instr. pediatrics Tufts U. Sch. Medicine, Boston, 1969-74, asst. clin. prof., 1974-78, assoc. clin. prof., 1978—; bd. dirs. Tufts Assoc. Health Maintenance Orgn., 1988-95, North Shore Health Systems, Inc., 1995-96. Contbr. articles to profl. jours. Capt. M.C., AUS, 1964-66. Fellow Am. Acad. Pediatrics; mem. AMA, Am. Soc. Microbiology, Mass. Med. Soc., Tufts Alumni Assn., Nat. Assn. Watch and Clock Collectors. Office: 10 Centennial Dr Peabody MA 01960 Office Phone: 978-535-1110.

LIPMAN-BLUMEN, JEAN, public policy and organizational behavior educator; b. Brookline, Mass., Apr. 28, 1933; AB, Wellesley Coll., 1954, AM, 1956; PhD, Harvard U., 1970; postgrad., Carnegie-Mellon U., 1970-71, Stanford U., 1971-72; LHD (hon.), U. La Verne, 2005. Asst. dir., Nat. Inst. Edn., dir women's rsch. program, 1973-78; spl. asst., mem. domestic policy staff The White House, Office of Asst. Sec. Edn.; pres. LBS Internat., Ltd., 1979-84; prof. orgnl. behavior Claremont Grad. U., Calif., Thornton F. Bradshaw prof. pub. policy Peter F. Drucker and Masatoshi Ito Grad. Sch. Mgmt., 1983—. Vis. prof. sociology and orgnl. behavior U. Conn., 1978—80, U. Md., 1980—82; spkr. in field; cons. Exec. Office of Pres., Dept. State, Dept. Labor, Dept. HHS, Dept. Agr., Dept. Edn., Bell Labs., Singapore Airlines, MarketIndex, Finland, various fgn. govts.; tchr. exec. mgmt. and MBA programs. Author, editor (with Jessie Bernard): Sex Roles and Social Policy, 1978; author: The Paradox of Success: The Impact of Priority Setting in Agricultural Research and Extension, 1984, Metaphor for Change: The USDA Competitive Grants Program, 1978-84, 1985, Gender Roles and Power, 1984, Women in Corporate Leadership: Reviewing a Decade's Research, 1996, The Connective Edge: Leading in an Independent World, 1996 (Pulitzer prize nomination); author: (with Harold J. Leavitt) Hot Groups: Seeding, Feeding, and Using Them to Ignite Your Organization, 1999 (Best Book award Assn. Am. Pubs., 1999); author: Connective Leadership: Managing in a Changing World, 2000; author: (with Grace Gabe) Step Wars: Overcoming the Perils and Making Peace in Adult Stepfamilies, 2004, Making Adult Stepfamilies Work-Strategies for the Whole Family When a Parent Marries Later in Life, 2005; author: The Allure of Toxic Leaders: Why We Follow Destructive and Corrupt Politicians-and How We Can Survive Them, 2005. Fellow, Ctr. Advanced Study Behavioral Sci., 1978, 1979. Fellow: AAAS. Office: Claremont Grad U 1021 N Dartmouth Ave Claremont CA 91711 Office Phone: 909-621-8083. Personal E-mail: jeanlipman@earthlink.net.

LIPNICK, ANNE RUTH, advocate; b. Cambridge, Mass., Aug. 9, 1943; d. Henry and Celia Florence (Weinberg) Goldberg; m. Robert Louis Lipnick, June 11, 1967; children: Deborah Ellen Lipnick Bort, David Henry. BA, Brandeis U., 1965; MSW, U. Minn., 1972. Rsch. asst. Brandeis U., Waltham, Mass., 1965—66; social worker Divsn. Child Guardianship, Boston, 1966—68, Jewish Family Svc., St. Paul, 1968—70, Family and Children's Svcs., Stamford, Conn., 1974—78; coord. spl. edn. parent resource ctr. Alexandria (Va.) City Pub. Schs., 1989—. Study group chair Children Together, Alexandria, 1999—; mem. Early Intervention Interagency Coordinating Coun., Alexandria. Exec. com. Brookville-Seminary Valley Civic Assn., Alexandria, 2002—03; v.p. for youth svcs. Agudas Achim Congregation, Alexandria, 1999—2001. Recipient Riggs-ARC Ednl. Leadership award, Assn. for Retarded Citizens No. Va., 1991, John Duty Collins III Outstanding Adv. for Persons with Disabilities award, Alexandria Commn. on Persons with Disabilities, 1996. Mem.: NASW (cert. 2005). Home: 5308 Pender Ct Alexandria VA 22304 Office Phone: 703-706-4552. Business E-Mail: alipnick@acps.k12.va.us.

LIPNICK, ROBERT LOUIS, chemist, toxicologist; b. Balt., Sept. 9, 1941; s. David Aaron and Dorothy (Moss) L.; m. Anne Ruth Goldberg, June 11, 1967; children: Deborah Ellen Lipnick, David Henry. BS in Chemistry, U. Md., 1963; PhD in Organic Chemistry, Brandeis U., 1969. Postdoctoral fellow dept. chemistry U. Minn., Mpls., 1968-72; rsch. assoc. Sloan-Kettering Inst. Cancer Rsch., Rye, NY, 1974-79; leader, structure activity group US EPA, Washington, 1980—85, sr. chemist, 1985—; com. sci. fellow US Dept. of State, Washington, 1993—94. Vis. lectr. various African univs., 1973-74, 125th anniversary of Pharmacological Inst. U. Marburg, Germany, 1992; Crafoord Found. vis. scientist Pharm. Inst., U. Lund, Sweden, summer 1989; Umweltbundesamt vis. scientist Borstel Rsch. Inst., Fed. Republic of Germany, summer 1986; co-organizer EPA workshop on structural properties determining mechanisms of toxic action, 1988; invited lectr. on quantitative structure-activity relationships in environ. chemistry and toxicology Commn. of European Communities, Ispra, Italy, 1990; invited feature lectr. Duke U. Med. Ctr. Libr., 2004; invited sci. specialist, 1992; mem. internat. sci. com. 4th Internat. Workshop on Quantitative Structure-Activity Relationships Environ. Toxicology, Netherlands, 1990, 5th, Duluth, Minn., 1991; invited speaker Rekker Symposium, Netherlands, 1993; organizer Am. Chem. Soc. Symposium, San Francisco, 2006; mem. EPA Agy.-wide Risk Assessment Forum project on guidance and tools for modeling metals bioaccumulation, 2005—. Author: (with others) Probing Bioactive Mechanisms, 1989, Comprehensive Medicinal Chemistry, 1990; editor: C.E. Overton's Studies of Narcosis, 1991; mem. editorial bd. Xenobiotica, Quantitative Structure Activity Relationships; co-editor Persistent Bioaccumulative and Toxic Chemicals, 2000, Chemicals in the Environment: Fate, Transport, and Remediation, 2002; assoc. editor Spl. Publs., Soc. Environ. Toxicology and Chemistry; manuscript reviewer; contbr. 72 sci. pubs., articles to profl. jours., chapters to books. Bd. dirs., v.p. Friends of Marshlands, Rye, 1977-79; bd. dirs. Dowden Terr. Recreation Assn., Alexandria, Va., 1984-85; mem. publs. com. Wood Libr.-Mus. of Anesthesiology, 1993—94; mem. validation and tech. transfer com. Johns Hopkins U. Ctr. for Alternatives to Animal Testing; mem. Interagency Regulatory Alternatives Group; US rep. sound mgmt. chem. group working group, Trilateral CEC. Mem. Am. Chem. Soc. (mem. environ. chem. divsn. exec. com.), Soc. Environ. Toxicology and Chemistry (charter), QSAR Soc. Jewish. Home: 5308 Pender Ct Alexandria VA 22304-1937 Office Phone: 202-564-7632. Personal E-mail: rllipnick@verizon.net. Business E-Mail: lipnick.robert@epa.gov.

LIPNIKOV, KONSTANTIN, mathematician; b. Yaroslavl, Russia, July 8, 1967; arrived in U.S., 1999; s. Nikolay Lipnikov and Zinaida Lipnikova. MS in Applied Math., Moscow Inst. Physics & Tech., 1990; PhD in Math., U. Houston, 2002. Postdoc Los Alamos Nat. Lab., N.Mex., 2002—04, staff mem., 2005—. Contbr. articles to profl. jour. Mem.: Soc. Indsl. and Applied Math. (assoc.). Achievements include research in theory of mimetic finite difference methods on polyhedral meshes; theory of error estimates on anisotropic adaptive meshes. Office: Los Alamos Nat Lab Ms B284 Los Alamos NM 87545 Home Phone: 505-662-0892; Office Phone: 505-667-1719. Office Fax: 505-665-5757. E-mail: lipnikov@lanl.gov.

LIPOVETSKY, STAN(ISLAV), statistician, mathematician; b. Moscow, Jan. 13, 1947; s. Simeon Eliezer Lipovetsky and Rebecca Abraham Sandalova; m. Natalia J. Smoliannikova, Oct. 24, 1994; 1 child, Steven J.; m. Olga N. Tarasova, Dec. 19, 1970 (div. May 1, 1990); children: Lena, Daniel. MSc in Theoretical Physics, Moscow U., 1971, PhD in Math. Methods in Econs., 1989. Prof. faculty mgmt. Tel Aviv U., 1990—95; rsch. mgr. GFK Custom Rsch. Inc., Mpls., 1998—. Mem. adv. bds.: internat. jours. on ops. rsch.; contbr. articles to profl. jours. Mem.: Internat. Soc. on Multiple Criteria Decision Making, Inst. Ops. Rsch. and Mgmt. Scis., Math. Assn. Am., Am. Statis. Assn. Office: GFK Custom Rsch Inc 8401 Golden Valley Rd Minneapolis MN 55427 Office Phone: 763-417-4509. Business E-Mail: stan.lipovetsky@gfk.com.

LIPOVSKY, ROBERT P., marketing executive; b. Chgo., Apr. 15, 1950; s. Rudoplh John and Anna Mary (Nemec) L.; m. Sharon Sue Zelienka, July 1, 1972; children: Katherine Michelle, Robert Paul. BS, Western Ill. U., 1972. Dist. mgr. W.R. Grace and Co., Peoria, Ill., 1972-78; mktg. mgr. Doane Agrl. Svc., St. Louis, 1978-82; v.p., div. mgr. Maritz Mktg. Rsch. Inc., St. Louis, 1982—, pres., Maritz Performance Improvement Co., Fenton, Mo. Mem. Nat. Agrl. Mktg. Assn. Republican. Lutheran. Avocations: golf, hunting, sports, skeet shooting. Office: Maritz Performance Improvement Co 14 S Hwy Dr Fenton MO 63099-0001

LIPP, ROBERT I., insurance company executive; b. 1938; m. Martha Berman; 5 children. Grad., Williams Coll.; grad. in bus., Harvard U.; JD, NYU, 1969. With Chem. Bank, NYC, 1963-86, sr. trainee, 1963-65, office asst. control div., 1965-66, asst. controller, 1966-67, asst. v.p. corp. planning, 1967-69, corp. sr. v.p., dep. head ops., 1972-74, exec. v.p., head ops. div., 1974-77, exec. v.p., head met. div., 1977-79, corp. sr. exec. v.p., head met. div., 1979, sr. exec. v.p., 1979-83, pres., 1983-86; v.p. corp. planning, treas. Chem. NY Corp., 1969-70, dep. mgr. ops. div., 1970-72; exec. v.p. for consumer fin. services group Comml. Credit Co., Balt., 1986-89, chmn. consumer fin. svcs., 1999; exec. v.p. consumer fin. svcs. Primerica Corp. (parent co.), NYC, 1988; exec. v.p., chmn., CEO Travelers Aetna Property, Hartford, Conn., 2001—04; exec. chmn. St. Paul Travelers Cos., Inc., Minn., 2004—05, also bd. dirs. Bd. dirs. J.P. Morgan Chase & Co., 2003—, sr. advisor, 2005—; bd. dirs. Accenture Ltd. Dir. NYC Ballet; trustee Jackie Robinson Found., Carnegie Hall Society; chmn. exec. com. Williams Coll. Office: St Paul Travelers 385 Washington St Saint Paul MN 55102 also: JP Morgan Chase 270 Park Ave 39th Fl New York NY 10017

LIPPA, CAROL FRANCES, neurologist; b. Erie, Pa., Aug. 19, 1955; d. John Winn and Dorothy Marie (Zarembski) Ryan; m. Robert Leo Lippa, July 1982; children: Sara Marie, Alex Mitchell, Adam Lee. BA, McGill U., 1978; MD, U. Mass., 1983. Diplomate Am. Bd. Psychiatry and Neurology, Am. Bd. Neurorehab. Intern St. Vincent Hosp., Worcester, Mass., 1983—84; resident in neurology U. Mass. Med. Ctr., Worcester, 1984—86, chief resident, 1986—87, resident in neuropathology, 1987—88, fellow neurobiology of aging, 1988—89, asst. prof. neurology, 1989—95, dir. brain donation program, 1993—, investigator clin. drug trials, 1992—; physician neurorehab. svc. Fairlawn Rehab. Hosp., 1992—96; prof. neurology Drexel U. Coll. Medicine, Phila., 1996—; chief neurology svc. Med. Coll. Pa.-Hahnemann U., Phila., 2000—03, dir. Memory Disorders Ctr., 1996—. Contbr. more than 150 abstracts and articles to profl. jours. Recipient 2d prize residents and fellows presentation, Boston Soc. Neurology and Psychiatry, 1985. Mem.: Phila. Neurol. Soc. (pres. 2004—05), Am. Neurol. Assn., Am. Soc. Neurorehab., Soc. Neurosci., Am. Acad. Neurology, Alpha Omega Alpha. Home: 16 Radcliff Rd Bala Cynwyd PA 19004-2631 Office: Hahnemann Hosp Mailstop 423 245 N 15th St Philadelphia PA 19102 Business E-Mail: clippa@drexelmed.edu.

LIPPARD, LUCY ROWLAND, writer, educator, critic, curator; b. NYC, Apr. 14, 1937; d. Vernon William and Margaret Isham (Cross) L.; m. Robert Tracy Ryman, Aug. 19, 1961 (div. 1968); 1 child, Ethan Isham Ryman. BA, Smith Coll., 1958; MA in Art History, NY Inst. Fine Arts, 1962; DFA (hon.), Moore Coll. Art, 1972, San Francisco Art Inst., 1984, Maine Coll. Art, 1994, Mass. Coll. Art, 1998, Art Inst. Chgo., 2003, Nova Scotia Coll. Art and Design, 2007. Freelance writer, lectr., curator, 1964—; rsch. assoc. Mus. N.Mex., Santa Fe. Prof. Sch. Visual Arts, NYC, Williams Coll., Queensland U., Brisbane, Australia, U. Colo., Boulder; mem. adv. bd. Franklin Furnace, NYC, 1979—; co-founder, bd. dirs. Printed Matter, NYC; bd. dirs. Ctr. Study Polit. Graphics, LA, Time & Space Ltd., Hudson, NY, Sustainable Settings, Woody Creek, Colo., Earth Works Inst., Santa Fe, Ctr. Am. Pls., Stanton, Va.; co-founder W.E.B., Ad Hoc Women Artist's Com., Artists Meeting for Cultural Change, Heresies Collective and Jour., Artists Call Against US Intervention in Ctrl. Am., Polit. Art Documentation/Distbn.; lectr. in field. Author: Pop Art, 1966, The Graphic work of Philip Evergood, 1966, Changing: Essays in Art Criticism, 1971, Tony Smith, 1972, Six Years: The Dematerialization of the Art Object, 1973, From the Center: Feminist Essays on Women's Art, 1976, Eva Hesse, 1976, (with Charles Simonds) Cracking (Brüchig Werden), 1979, Issue: Social Strategies by Women Artists, 1980, Ad Reinhardt, 1981, Overlay: Contemporary Art and the Art of Prehistory, 1983, Get the Message? A Decade of Art for Social Change, 1984, Mixed Blessings: New Art in a Multicultural America, 1990, A Different War: Vietnam in Art, 1990, The Pink Glass Swan: Selected Feminist Essays on Art, 1995, The Lure of the Local: Senses of Place in a Multicentered Society, 1997, Florence Pierce: In Touch With Light, 1998, On the Beaten Track: Tourism, Art and Place, 1999, (with Alfred Barr and James Thrall Soby) The School of Paris, 1965, (novel) I See/You Mean, 1979; author, editor: Partial Recall: Photographs of Native North Americans, 1992; editor: Surrealists on Art, 1970, Dadas on Art, 1971; contbg. editor: Art in Am.; founding editor El Puente de Galisteo, 1997—; contbr. monthly columns Village Voice, 1981-85, In These Times, Z Mag.; contbr. articles to profl. jours., popular mags.; curator 50 exhbns.; performer in guerrilla and st. theater. Mem. Santa Fe County Open Lands and Trails Planning and Adv. Com. (COLTPAC), 1999. Recipient Frederick Douglass award North Star Fund, 1994, Frank Jewett Mather award Coll. Art Assn., 1974, Claude Fuess award Phillips Andover Acad., 1975, Curating award Penny McCall Found., 1989, citation NYC mayor David Dinkins, 1990, Smith Coll. medal, 1992, Athena award RISD, 2004, Lifetime Achievement award Coll. Art Assn., 2007, Womens Caucus for Art, 2007; Guggenheim fellow, 1968, ArtTable award, 1999; grantee Lannan Found., 2000. Avocations: hiking, rock art, local history. Home Phone: 505-466-1276; Office Phone: 505-466-1276.

LIPPE, PHILIPP MARIA, neurosurgeon, educator, academic administrator; b. Vienna, May 17, 1929; came to U.S., 1938, naturalized, 1945; s. Philipp and Maria (Goth) L.; m. Virginia M. Wiltgen, 1953 (div. 1977); children: Patricia Ann Marie, Philip Eric Andrew, Laura Lynne Elizabeth, Kenneth Anthony Ernst; m. Gail B. Busch, Nov. 26, 1977. Student, Loyola U., Chgo., 1947-50; BS in Medicine, U. Ill. Coll. Medicine, 1952, MD with high honors, 1954. Diplomate Am. Bd. Neurol. Surgery, 1965, Nat. Bd. Med. Examiners, 1955, Am. Bd. Pain Medicine, 1992. Rotating intern St. Francis Hosp., Evanston, Ill., 1954-55; asst. resident gen. surgery VA Hosp., Hines, Ill., 1955, 58-59; asst. resident neurology and neurol. surgery Neuropsychiat. Inst., U. Ill. Rsch. and Ednl. Hosps., Chgo., 1959-60, chief resident, 1962-63, resident in neuropathology, 1962, postgrad. trainee in electroencephalography, 1963; resident in neurology and neurol. surgery Presbyn.-St. Luke's Hosp., Chgo., 1960-61; practice medicine, specializing in neurol. surgery/pain medicine San Jose, Calif., 1963—93; clin. prof. neurosurgery Stanford U., Calif., 1996—; exec. v.p. Am. Bd. of Pain Medicine, 1994—; exec. med. dir. Am. Acad. of Pain Medicine, 1996—. Instr. neurology and neurol. surgery U. Ill,. 1962-63; clin. instr. surgery and neurosurgery Stanford U., 1965-69, clin. asst. prof., 1969-74, clin. assoc. prof., 1974-96, clin. prof., 1996—; staff cons. in neurosurgery O'Connor Hosp., Santa Clara Valley Med. Ctr., San Jose Hosp., Los Gatos Cmty. Hosp., El Camino Hosp. (all San Jose area); chmn. divsn. neurosurgery Good Samaritan Hosp., 1989-97, chmn. dept. clin. neuroscis., 1997-99; founder, exec. dir. Bay Area Pain Rehab. Ctr., San Jose, 1979—; clin. adviser to Joint Commn. on Accreditation of Hosps.; mem. dist. med. quality rev. com. Calif. Bd. Med. Quality Assurance, 1976-87, chmn., 1976-77; cons., med. expert Med. Bd. Calif., 1996—; participant, moderator of numerous profl. seminars and sessions. Assoc. editor Clin. Jour. Pain; contbr. articles to profl. jours. Fellow ACS, Am. Coll. Pain Medicine (bd. dirs. 1991-94, v.p. 1991-92, pres. 1992-93, exec. med. dir.); mem. AMA (ho. of dels. 1981-, CPT editl. panel 1995-99, sr. adv. panel Guides to the Evaluation of Permanent Impairment 1997—, chair pain and palliative medicine splty. sect. coun. 2006-), Am. Coll. Physician Execs., Calif. Med. Assn. (ho. of dels. 1976-80, sci. bd., coun. 1979-87, sec. 1981-87, Outstanding Svc. award 1987), Santa Clara County Med. Soc. (coun. 1974-81, pres. 1978-79, Outstanding Contbn. award 1984, Benjamin J. Cory award 1987), Chgo. Med. Soc., Congress Neurol. Surgeons, Calif. Assn. Neurol. Surgeons (dir. 1974-82, v.p. 1975-76, pres. 1977-79, Pevehouse Disting. Svc. award 1997), San Jose Surg. Soc., Am. Assn. Neurol. Surgeons (chmn. sect. on pain 1987-90, dir. 1983-86, 87-90, Disting. Svc. award 1986, 90), Western Neurol. Soc., San Francisco Neurol. Soc., Santa Clara Valley Profl. Stds. Rev. Orgn. (dir., v.p., dir. quality assurance 1975-83), Fedn. Western Socs. Neurol. Sci., Internat. Assn. for Study Pain, Am. Pain Soc. (founding mem.), Am. Acad. Pain Medicine (sec. 1983-86, pres. 1987-88, Philipp M. Lippe Disting. Svc. award 1995, exec. med. dir. 1996—), Am. Bd. Pain Medicine (pres. 1992-93, exec. v.p. 1994—), Am. Soc. Law, Medicine, and Ethics, Alpha Omega Alpha, Phi Kappa Phi. Achievements include pioneer in medical application of centrifugal force using flight simulator; pioneer in the developing medical specialty of pain medicine. Avocations: photography, travel, computers, raising animals. Office: PO Box 41217 San Jose CA 95160-1217 Address: Am Acad Pain Medicine 4700 W Lake Glenview IL 60025 Personal E-mail: pmlippe@att.net.

LIPPER, KENNETH, investment banker, film producer, writer; b. NYC, June 19, 1941; s. George and Sally L.; m. Evelyn Rebecca Gruss, June 12, 1966 (div. 2000); children: Joanna Helene, Daniella, Tamara, Julie BA,

Columbia U., 1962; JD, Harvard U., 1965; LLM, NYU, 1966; postgrad., Faculté de Droit et Economique, Paris, 1967. Bar: NY 1965. Assoc. Fried, Frank, Harris, Shriver & Jacobson, NYC, 1967-68; dir. industry policy Office Fgn. Direct Investment, Washington, 1968-69; assoc., ptnr. Lehman Bros., NYC, 1969-75; mng. dir., ptnr. Salomon Bros., NYC, 1976-82; dep. mayor City of NY, 1983-85; chmn. Lipper & Co., 1986—2004; exec. v.p. Cushman & Wakefield, NYC, 2004—. Adj. prof. internat. affairs Sch. Internat. and Pub. Affairs, Columbia U., NYC, 1976-83; mem. adv. bd. Fed. Res. Bank NY, 1994-2003, J.P. Morgan Chase Manhattan Bank, 1994-2003. Author: (novel) Wall Street, 1987 and chief tech. advisor movie, 1987; author, screenwriter, prodr. City Hall, 1996; prodr. film and play The Winter Guest, 1997; prodr. The Last Days, 1998 (Acad. award 1999); pub. Lipper Viking Penguin Biograph. Series, 1997—. Mem. exec. com. Harvard U. Resources, 1994—; bd. dirs. Case New Holland N.V., 1997—, Sundance Inst., 1997-2005; hematologic oncology vis. com. Dana Farber Cancer Inst., 2005—. Recipient medal of distinction City of NY, 1985; John Harvard fellow, 2001. Mem. Internat. Inst. Strategic Studies, Coun. Fgn. Rels., Econ. Club NY, Century Assn., Phi Beta Kappa Office: Cushman & Wakefield 51 W 52nd St 12th Fl New York NY 10019 Office Phone: 212-841-5906. E-mail: ken.lipper@cushwake.com.

LIPPERT, NELS T., lawyer; b. Plainfield, NJ, Oct. 21, 1943; BS, Bethany Coll., 1965; JD, Case-Western Reserve U., 1968. Bar: N.Y. 1970, U.S. Patent & Trademark Office. Atty. White & Case, NYC; ptnr., vice chmn. Intellectual Property dept., mem. exec. com. Wilmer Cutler Pickering Hale & Dorr, NYC, 2000—. Adj. prof. Banjamin N. Cardozo Sch. Law, NYC. Contbr. articles to profl. jours. Mem. ABA, Am. Intellectual Property Law Assn., Internat. Trademark Assn., WIPO Domain Name Panel of Neutrals. Office: Wilmer Cutler Pickering Hale & Dorr 399 Park Ave New York NY 10022 Office Phone: 212-937-7201. Office Fax: 212-230-8888. Business E-Mail: nels.lippert@wilmerhale.com.

LIPPES, GERALD SANFORD, lawyer; b. Buffalo, Mar. 23, 1940; s. Thomas and Ruth (Landsman) Lippes; children: Tracy E, David S, Adam F. Student, U. Mich., 1958-61; JD, U. Buffalo, 1964. Bar: NY 1964. Sr. ptnr. Lippes, Mathias, Wexler Friedman LLP, Buffalo, 1964—; sec., dir., gen. counsel Mark IV, Industries, Inc., Amherst, NY, 1969-2000. Chmn. Del. Photographic Products, Buffalo, 1970—88, Ingram Micro-D, Buffalo, 1982—86, Abels Bagels, Inc., Buffalo, 1972—75; bd. dirs. Gilbraltar Industries, Inc., Hamister Group Cos., Tisports LLC, Adampluseve Inc. Bd dirs. Buffalo Fine Arts Acad., U. Buffalo Found., U. Buffalo Coun., N.Y. State Arts Coun.; chmn. bd dirs. Kaleida Health Sys., 2001—02. Named Entrepreneur of the Yr, 1993; recipient Distinguished Alumni Award, Univ Buffalo Law Sch, Citation Award, Nat Conf Christians and Jews, 1997, Jaeckle Award, SUNY, Bufflo. Mem.: Am Soc Corp Secys, Erie County Bar Asn, NY State Bar Asn. Office: Lippes Mathias Wexler Friedman 665 Main St Ste 300 Buffalo NY 14203

LIPPES, RICHARD JAMES, lawyer; b. Buffalo, Mar. 18, 1944; s. Thomas and Ruth (Landsman) L.; m. Sharon Richmond, June 4, 1972; children: Amity, Joshua, Kevin. BA, U. Mich., 1966; JD cum laude, SUNY, Buffalo, 1969. Bar: NY 1970, US Dist. Ct. Md. 1970, US Dist. Ct. (we. dist.) NY 1971, US Dist. Ct. (no. dist.) NY 1973, US Dist. Ct. (so. dist.) NY 1985, US Ct. Appeals (2d and 4th cirs.) 1970. Clk. to presiding justice U.S. Ct. Appeals (4th cir.), Balt., 1970; exec. dir. Ctr. for Justice Through Law, Buffalo, 1971; pvt. practice, Buffalo, 1971-77; ptnr. Moriarity, Allen, Lippes & Hoffman, Buffalo, 1977-79, Allen & Lippes, Buffalo, 1979—. Adj. prof. SUNY, Buffalo, 1978, 79, 2004; lead counsel and spl. environ. counsel for hazardous waste, mass toxic tort cases. Contbr. articles to profl. jours. Chmn. Atlantic chpt. Sierra Club, 1978-82; chmn. Buffalo chpt. Am. Jewish Com., 1986-88; chmn. lawyers com. Niagara Frontier chpt. N.Y. Civil Liberties Union, 1971, chpt. chmn., 1972-74; chmn. Buffalo Environ. Mgmt. Commn., 1987-96; bd. dirs. N.Y. State Preservation League; chmn. Buffalo Task Force, 1986-87; pres. Erie County Preservation Coalition, 1998—. Urban and Environ. Law fellow, 1969. Mem. Erie County Bar Assn (former chmn. pub. interest law com. and prepaid legal svcs. com.). Democrat. Office Phone: 716-884-4800. E-mail: rlippes@concentric.net.

LIPPINCOTT, JAMES ANDREW, retired biochemistry and biological sciences educator; b. Cumberland County, Ill., Sept. 13, 1930; s. Marion Andrew and Esther Oral (Meeker) L.; m. Barbara Sue Barnes, June 2, 1956; children— Jeanne Marie, Lisa Ellen, John James. AB, Earlham Coll., 1954; A.M., Washington U., St. Louis, 1956, PhD, 1958. Lectr. botany Washington U., 1958-59; Jane Coffin Childs Meml. fellow Centre Nat. de la Recherche Scientifique, France, 1959-60; asst. prof. biol. scis. Northwestern U., Evanston, Ill., 1960-66, assoc. prof., 1966-73, prof., 1973-81, prof. biochemistry, molecular biology and cell biology, 1981-94, prof. emeritus Evanston, Ill., 1994—, assoc. dean biol. scis., 1980-83; ret., 1994. Vis. assoc. prof. U. Calif., Berkeley, 1970-71; vis. prof. Inst. Botany U. Heidelberg (Germany), 1974. Contbr. articles to profl. jours. Grantee NIH, NSF, Am. Cancer Soc., USDA Mem. Am. Soc. Biol. Chemists, Am. Soc. Plant Physiologists, Bot. Soc. Am., Am. Soc. Microbiology

LIPPINCOTT, JOAN K., library director; AB with honors, Vassar Coll.; MLS, SUNY Geneseo; postgraduate studies, Cornell Univ., George Washington Univ.; PhD edn. policy planning & adminstrn., Univ. Md. Reference & instruction libr. SUNY Brockport; instruction libr. Georgetown Univ.; head of reference George Washington Univ.; head pub. services. Albert R. Mann Libr., Cornell Univ.; positions with Nat. Ctr. for Postsecondary Governance & Fin., Am. Council on Edn.; with Coalition for Networked Information, Washington, 1990—, interim exec. dir., 1996—97, assoc. exec. dir. Mem. steering com. Networked Digital Libr. of Theses & Dissertations; mem., founding chair, New Directions in Teaching & Learning Discussion Group Assn. Coll. & Rsch. Libraries; bd. mem. Nat. Initiative for a Networked Cultural heritage. Contbr. chapters to books, articles to profl. jours. Mem.: ALA. Office: Coalition for Networked Information 21 Dupont Cir Washington DC 20036 Office Phone: 202-296-5098. Office Fax: 202-872-0884. Business E-Mail: joan@cni.org.

LIPPINCOTT, JOHN, educational association administrator; m. Joan Lippincott; 2 children. BA with high honors, Wesleyan U., MA in Tchg. Asst. prof. English Genesee CC, 1972—78; instr. English Clatsop CC, 1978—79; pub. info. specialist NEH, 1979—82; dir. coll. rels. Ithaca Coll., 1982—88; assoc. vice chancellor for advancement U. Sys. Md., 1988—99; v.p. comm. and mktg. Coun. for Advancement and Support of Edn., Washington, 1999—2004, interim pres., 2003—04, pres., 2004—. Avocations: golf, woodworking, reading. Office: Coun for Advancement and Support of Edn 1307 New York Ave NW Ste 1000 Washington DC 20005-4701 Office Phone: 202-478-5655. E-mail: lippincott@case.org.*

LIPPINCOTT, JOSEPH P., photojournalist, educator; b. Somerset, Pa., Mar. 12, 1940; s. Joseph Britton and Louise Frances (Picking) L.; widowed; children: Douglas B., David S.; m. Karen L. Krause, 1999. BA in Journalism, U. Iowa, 1968. Staff photographer The Miami (Fla.) Herald, 1964-67; pub. rels. dir. Lock Haven (Pa.) State Coll., 1967-68; mag. editor Caterpillar Tractor Co., Peoria, Ill., 1968-69; photo editor, photographer The Detroit Free Press, 1969-75; photo advisor The State News Mich. State U., East Lansing, 1975-84; instr. Lansing C.C., 1977-84; photo editor The Detroit News, 1984-87, The Patriot Ledger, Quincy, Mass., 1988-95; lectr. Boston U., 1990—. Author: An Introduction to Camera Maintenance, 1980, Care and Repair of Classic Cameras for Photographers and Collectors, 1999. Mem. Nat. Press Photographers Assn. (chmn. nat. portfolio critique 1994-96, Pictures of the Yr. awards). Avocation: unique photographic equipment. Home: 95 Old Colony Ave # 291 Quincy MA 02170-2629

LIPPINCOTT, PHILIP EDWARD, retired paper company executive; b. Camden, NJ, Nov. 28, 1935; s. J. Edward and Marjorie Nix (Spooner) L.; m. Naomi Catherine Prindle, Aug. 22, 1959; children: Grant, Kevin, Kerry. BA, Dartmouth Coll., 1957; MBA with distinction, Mich. State U., 1964. With Scott Paper Co., Phila., 1959-94, staff v.p. corp. planning, 1971, div. v.p., consumer products mktg., 1971-72, corp. v.p., mktg., 1972-75, sr. v.p., mktg., 1975-77, v.p., group exec. packaged products div., 1977—79, dir., 1978-94, pres., COO, 1980-94, chief exec. officer, 1982-94, chmn., 1983-94; ret., 1994. Chmn. bd. Campbell Soup Co., 1999-2001; bd. dirs. Campbell Soup Co., Exxon Mobil Corp., Oryon Tech., LLC; trustee Penn Mut. Life Ins. Co. Lifetime trustee Fox Chase Cancer Ctr., Phila., 1981—, chmn. bd. trustees, 1995-2003. Capt. U.S. Army, 1957-59. Mem. Pine Valley Golf Club, Quail West Golf and Country Club, Park Meadows Country Club, Kappa Kappa Kappa, Pi Sigma Epsilon, Beta Gamma Sigma. Mem. Society Of Friends. E-mail: lipper66@msn.com.

LIPPINCOTT, WALTER EDWARD, law educator; b. Bronxville, NY, Aug. 15, 1959; s. Walter Edwin and Helen (Patterson) L.; m. Andrea Pratt, July 30, 1983; children: Brittany Marie, Matthew, Anna. BS, Roger Williams Coll., 1981; JD, Western New Eng. Coll., 1984; MS, Fla. Inst. Tech., 1995. Bar: Conn. 1984, D.C. 1985. Prosecutor State of Conn. Judicial Dept., Hartford, 1990-93; prof. Naugatuck Valley Cmty. Coll., Waterbury, Conn., 1993—, U. Conn., Storrs, 1996-97. Col. U.S. Army, 1985-90, USAR, 1990—. Mem. ABA, Conn. Bar Assn., D.C. Bar Assn. Home: 1167Highland Ave Torrington CT 06790-4410

LIPPINCOTT, WALTER HEULINGS, JR., retired publishing executive; b. Phila., Jan. 16, 1939; s. Walter Heulings and Helen B. (Howe) L.; m. Caroline Seebohm, June 8, 1974 (div. June 1993); children: Sophie, Hugh. AB, Princeton U., 1960. With Morgan Guaranty Trust Co., NYC, 1960-63; coll. traveler Harper & Row Pubs., 1963-65, editor, 1965-70, editor-in-chief, coll. dept., 1970-74; editorial dir. Cambridge Univ. Press, NYC, 1974-81; assoc. dir. Cornell Univ. Press, 1982, dir., 1983-86, Princeton U. Press, NJ, 1986—2005; ret., 2005. Mem.: Knickerbocker (N.Y.C.), Century (N.Y.C.). Home: 1 River Knoll Dr Titusville NJ 08560-1308 Office: Princeton U Press 41 William St Princeton NJ 08540-5237

LIPPMAN, JONATHAN, judge; BA in Govt. & Internat. Rels., NYU, 1965; JD, NYU Sch. Law, 1968. Bar: NY 1968. Law sec. Justice Samuel Spiegel, 1974; dep. chief Law Dept., 1977; chief clk. State Supreme Ct. Manhattan, 1983—89, dep. chief adminstr. mgmt. support, 1989—95; judge NY Ct. Claims, 1995; chief adminstrv. judge NY State Unified Ct. System, 1996—2007; judge NY State Supreme Ct., 2006—, presiding judge Appellate divsn., First Jud. Dept. NYC, 2007—. Chair NY State Ct. Facilities Cap. Review Bd.; mem. NY State Probation Commn.; pres. State Ct. Administrators Conf.; mem. bd. dirs. Nat. Conf. State Courts. Recipient Hispanic Heritage Recognition award, Cervantes Soc., 2002, Benjamin N. Cardozo award, Jewish Lawyers Guild, Pub. Svc. award, Law Alumni Assn., NYU Sch. Law, 2003. Mem.: NY State Trial Lawyers Assn. (Jud. Recognition award 2002), Trial Lawyers Assn. of City of NY (Harlan Fiske award), Bar of City of NY (Bernard Botein Medal), NY State Bar Assn. (Millennium 2000 award, Robert L. Haig award for Disting. Pub. Svc., 2006 Award for Excellence in Pub. Svc.). Office: NY State Supreme Court Appellate Divsn 1st Dept 27 Madison Ave New York NY 10010 Office Phone: 212-340-0400.*

LIPPMAN, LAURA, writer; BS in Journalism, Northwestern Univ. Reporter Waco Tribune-Herald, Tex., 1981—83, San Antonio Light, 1983—89, Balt. Evening Sun, 1989—91, Balt. Sun, 1991—2001. Author: (novels) Baltimore Blues, 1997, Charm City, 1997 (Edgar award, Shamus award, Anthony award nominee), Butchers Hill, 1998 (Agatha award, Anthony award, Edgar, Shamus, Macavity awards nominee), In Big Trouble, 1999 (Anthony award, Shamus award, Edgar, Agatha awards nominee), The Sugar House, 2000 (Best PI Novel of Yr. nominee, Romantic Times), In a Strange City, 2001 (NY Times Notable Book), The Last Place, 2002, Every Secret Thing, 2003 (Anthony award, Barry award, Nero Wolfe award), By a Spider's Thread, 2004 (Edgar Award nominee for best novel, 2005), To the Power of Three, 2005, No Good Deeds, 2006. Recipient Mayor's award for lit. excellence, Balt. Mailing: c/o Author Mail William Morrow 10 E 53rd St New York NY 10022

LIPPMAN, MARC ESTES, oncologist, educator, medical researcher; b. Bklyn., Jan. 15, 1945; BA magna cum laude, Cornell U., 1964; MD, Yale U., 1968. Intern Osler med. svc. Johns Hopkins Hosp., Balt., 1968-69, asst. resident, oncology, 1969-70; clin. assoc. leukemia svc. Nat. Cancer Inst., NIH, Washington, 1970-71, clin. assoc. lab. biochemistry, 1971-73, sr. investigator med. br., 1974-88, head med. breast cancer sect., 1976-88; clin. prof. medicine and pharmacology Uniformed Svcs. U. Health Scis., 1978-88; dir. Vincent T. Lombardi Cancer Rsch. Ctr. Georgetown U., Washington, 1988—2001, prof. medicine and oncology, 1988—2001, also chair, dept. oncology, chief, divsn. hematology/oncology; John G. Searle prof. and chair, dept. internal medicine U. Mich. Health Sys., 2001—07; Kathleen & Stanley Glaser prof., chmn., dept. medicine Leonard M. Miller Sch. Medicine, U. Miami, 2007—. Mem. merit rev. bd. oncology Vet. Adminstrn. Med. Rsch. Svc., 1977-81, endocrine treatment com. Nat. Surg. Adjuvant Breast Project, 1977-86; cons. dept. pharmacology George Washington Sch. Medicine, 1978-89; co-chmn. Gordon Rsch. Conf. on Hormone Action, 1984, chmn., 1985; treas. Internat. Congress Hormones & Cancer, 1984—; mem. med. adv. bd. Nat. Alliance Breast Cancer Orgn., 1986—; mem. stage III monitoring com. Nat. Surg. Adjuvant Project Breast & Bowel Cancers, 1987-89; bd. trustees Am. Cancer Soc., Washington, 1989-92; mem. sci. adv. bd. Coordinated Coun. Cancer Rsch., 1989—; hon. dir. Y-ME, Nat. Orgn. Breast Cancer Info. & Support, 1990—; Woodward vis. prof., mem. Sloan-Kettering, 1990; Sidney Sachs Meml. lectr. Case Western Reserve, 1985, D.R. Edwards lectr. Tenovus Inst., Wales, 1985, Gosse lectr. Dalhousie U., Halifax, N.S., 1987, Transatlantic lectr. Brit. Endocrine Socs., 1989, Barofsky lectr. Howard U., 1990, Rose Kushner Meml. lectr. Long Beach Meml. Med. Ctr., 1990, Constance Wood Meml. lectr. Hammersmith Hosp., Eng., 1991; adj. prof. internal medicine, U. Mich. Med. Sch., Ann Arbor, Mich., 2007-; mem. clin. adv. bd., Raven Biotechnologies, Inc.; mem. scientific adv. bd., Seattle Genetics, 2000-, Perseus-Soros Fund; bd. dir. Ascenta Therapeutics; co-founder Oncologix (sold to Aronex), Peregrine Biotechnology (sold to Techniclone); invited spkr. in field. Contbr. articles to profl. jours., chapters to books. Endocrinology fellow Yale Med. Sch., 1973-74; recipient Mallinckrodt award Clin. Radioassay Soc., 1978, D.R. Edwards medal Tenovus Inst., 1985, Transatlantic medal Brit. Endocrine Socs., 1989, Tiffany award of Distinction, Komen Found., 1989, Brinker Internat. prize for Basic Rsch. in Breast Cancer. Fellow ACP, Am. Fedn. Clin. Rsch.(Clin. Investigator prize), Am. Soc. Cell Biology, Am. Assn. Cancer Rsch. (program com. 1986, Richard and Hinda Rosenthal Found. award, 1994), Am. Soc. Clin. Oncology (program com. 1987-89, chmn. local organizing com. 1989-90), Endocrine Soc. (pub. affairs com. 1980-81, Edward B. Astwood Lecture award, 1991), Metastasis Rsch. Soc.; mem. Assn. Am. Physicians, Am. Soc. Clin. Investigators (program com. 1988), Am. Soc. Biol. Chemists, Alpha Omega Alpha. Achievements include research in growth regulation of cancer, breast cancer, cancer endocrinology, growth factor receptors. Office: U Miami Dept Medicine Room 1001 MSTL 1430 NW 11th Ave Miami FL 33101 Office Phone: 305-243-9120. Business E-Mail: m.lippman@miami.edu.*

LIPPMAN, SHARON ROCHELLE, art historian and therapist, filmmaker; b. NYC, Apr. 9, 1950; d. Emanuel and Sara (Goldberg) L. Student, Mills Coll., Columbia U., 1968; BFA, New Sch. Social Rsch., 1970, CCNY, 1972; MA in Cinema Studies, NYU, 1976, postgrad., 1987. Cert. secondary tchr., N.Y.; cert. in nonprofit orgn. mgmt. Instr., dir., founder Sara Sch. of Creative Art, Sayville, NY, 1976-85; founder, exec. dir., tchr. Art Without Walls, Inc., Sayville and NYC, 1985—; curator art exhbn. Mus. Without Walls Heckscher State Park, East Islip, NY, 1985-87; exec. dir., curator Profl. Artist Network for Artists Internationally, 1991—; founder Art Without Walls, Inc., 1985—, Mus. Without Walls, Ctrl. Park, NYC, 2005. Organizer Profl. Artist Network for Nat./Internat. Artists, 1994; curator Pub. Art in Pub. Spaces,Scott Landoll Art Exhbn., West Islip; instr. art therapy sessions Maryhaven Ctr. Pub. Libr., Port Jefferson, N.Y., 2004, Mus. Without Walls - Rhapsody in Art, 2006; head art therapy project Mary Haven Ctr., Port Jefferson, N.Y., 2004; origami zoo art therapist Southside Hosp., Bayshore, N.Y., 2005. Author: Patterns, 1968, College Poetry Press Anthology, 1970, America at the Millennium, 2000; exhibited in group shows at LI Children's Mus., Garden City, NY, 1995-97, Suffolk County Legislature, Hauppauge, NY, 1997, Bayport-Bluepoint Libr., 1997, East Islip Libr., 1997-98, U.S. Dept. Interior, Ft. Wadsworth, NY, 2001, Ellis Island Immigration Mus., NY, 2002, West Islip Libr., 2000-01, 07, Battery Park, NYC, 2002, Central Park, NYC, 2003, Spirit Walk Gallery, Sayville, NY, 2003, Within These Walls, Nassau County Detetion Ctr., Westbury, NY, 2003, South St. Seaport, NYC, 2004, 06, Southside Hosp., Bayshore, NY, 2005, West Islip Libr., 2005, 07, South Country Libr., Bellport, NY, 2005, Mus. Without Walls-Ctr. Pk., NYC, 2005-06, 07, South County Libr., Bellport, 2005, Nassau County Detention Ctr., 2005, Nassau Denention Ctr., Westbury, 2006, West Sayville Firehouse, NY, 2007; pub. art mural History of LI Baymen, 1987, Immigration on the NYS Waterways, 2001, Leadership Tng. Inst., Hempstead, NY, 2003, Nassau County Detention Ctr., 2003, Southside Hosp., Bay Shore, 2004, Mary Haven Ctr., Port Jefferson Station, NY, 2004, Miko Mus. Art Therapy, 2006, West Islip Pub. Libr., NY, 2006-07; represented in permanent collection Devel. Disabilities Inst., Suffolk County Legis. Bldg., Polish Consulate, NY, West Islip Pub. Libr., East Islip Pub. Libr., Ctrl. Park Zoo, Coll. Art Assn. Bull. Conv. NY, Robert Moses State Park, NY, Smith Haven Mall Lake Grove, Garden City Mall, NY, Southside Hosp., Bayshore, Rhapsody in Art, Nassau Detention Ctr., Westbury, 2006, West Islip Public Libr., NY, 2007, West Sayville Firehouse, NY, 2007, Bryant Park, NYC, 2007. Vol. Good Samaritan Hosp., 1984, Southside Hosp., 1983, U. Stony Brook Hosp., 1985, Schneider Children's Hosp., New Hyde Park, N.Y., 1992, New Light-AIDS Patients, Smithtown, N.Y., 1993, Helen Keller Svcs. for the Blind, Hempstead, N.Y., 1993-94, St. Charles Hosp. and Rehab. Ctr., 1996, Nat. Health Bill Pub. Forum, Sayville Mid. Sch., 1996, Art Puzzles-Art Therapy Geriatrics Ward, Brookhaven (N.Y.) Meml. Hosp., 1990, Art Therapy Program Original Dept. Disabilities, Suffolk County, N.Y., 1988, Din-o-Soar Art Therapy Southside Hosp.-Pediatrics Ward, Bayshore, N.Y., 1999, Art Box-Art Therapy, Pediat. Ward Southside Hosp., Bayshore, 2000, It Takes Two Art Therapy, St. Charles Hosp., Port Jefferson, N.Y., 2000; mem. Whitney Mus., Guggenheim Mus., Mus. Modern Art, Met. Mus. Art, Jewish Mus., Mus. of the City of N.Y., Art in Am., Art News, Am. Artist; trustee Sayville Libr. Bd., 1996; bd. dirs. Friends of the Arts St. Joseph's Coll., N.Y., 1997. Recipient Suffolk County New Inspiration award, 1990, 2006, Am. Artist Art Svc. award Am. Artists mag., 1993, Suffolk County Legis. proclamation, 1993, Newsday Leadership Vol. award Newsday newspaper, 1994, Nat. Women's Month award Town of Islip, 1996, Disting. Women's award Town of Islip, 1996, Nat. Poetry Press award, 1996, Cmty. Action award Suffolk County Ret./Sr. Vol. Program, 2002; named to L.I. Vol. Hall of Fame for Cultural Arts, 2004; Inspiration award Suffolk County News, 2005. Mem. Orgn. Through Rehab. and Tng., Coll. Art Assn., Met. Mus. Art, Mus. Modern Art Univ. Film Assn., Sayville C. of C. Avocations: fine art, books, cinema, political science, inventions. Office: Art Without Walls Inc PO Box 2066 New York NY 10185-2066 also: Art Without Walls Inc PO Box 341 Sayville NY 11782 Office Phone: 631-567-9418. Business E-Mail: artwithoutwalls@webtv.net.

LIPPMAN, WILLIAM JENNINGS, investment company executive; b. NYC, Feb. 13, 1925; s. Henry J. and Fanny (Schapira) L.; m. Doris Kaplan, July 11, 1948; children— Howard Mark, Deborah Ellen. BBA cum laude, CCNY, 1947; MBA, N.Y.U., 1957. Marketing mgr. Pavelle Color, Inc., NYC, 1947-50; sales mgr. Terminal Home Sales Corp., NYC, 1950-55; div. mgr. King Merritt & Co., Inc., Englewood, N.J., 1955-60; pres., dir. Pilgrim Distbrs. Inc., Ft. Lee, N.J., 1960-86; pres. L.F. Rothschild Managed Trust L.F. Rothschild Fund Mgmt. Inc., NYC, 1986-88, also dir.; pres. Franklin Managed Trust, New York, 1988—. Mem. faculty Fairleigh Dickinson U. Sch. Bus. Adminstrn., 1957-69; bd. govs. Investment Co. Inst. Contbg. author: Investment Dealer Digest. Mem. Nat. Assn. Securities Dealers (investment cos. com.) Office: Franklin Managed Trust 1 Parker Plz Fort Lee NJ 07024-2937 Home: 1500 Palisade Ave Fort Lee NJ 07024 Office Phone: 201-592-6700.

LIPPOLD, ROLAND WILL, retired surgeon; b. Staunton, Ill., May 1, 1916; s. Frank Carl and Ella (Immenroth) L.; m. Margaret Cookson, June 1, 1947; children: Mary Ellen Lippold Elvick, Catherine Anne Lippold Rolf, Carol Sue Lippold Webber. BS, U. Ill., 1940, MD, 1941. Diplomate Am. Bd. Surgery. Intern Grant Hosp., Chgo., 1941-42, resident in surgery, 1942-43, 47-48, St. Francis Hosp., Evanston, Ill., 1946-47; fellow in pathology Cook County Hosp., Chgo., 1947-48, resident in surgery, 1949-50; practice medicine specializing in surgery Chgo., 1950-53; also asst. in anatomy U. Ill., Chgo., 1950-53; practice medicine specializing in surgery Sacramento, 1953-68; chief med. officer No. Reception Ctr.-Clinic, Calif. Youth Authority, Sacramento, 1954-68, chief med. services, 1968-79; ret. Cons. in med. care in correctional instns.; cons. Calif. State Personnel Bd. Contbr. articles to med. publs. Chmn. Calif. Expn. Hall of Health, 1971-72. Comdr. M.C., USNR, 1943-73, PTO. Mem. Sacramento Surg. Soc., Sacramento County Med. Soc., Calif. Med. Assn., AMA, Sacramento Hist. Soc. (life). Republican. Lutheran. Home: 1811 Eastern Ave Sacramento CA 95864-1724

LIPPOLDT, VAUGHN ARTHUR, retired music educator; b. Dodge City, Kans., Mar. 15, 1936; s. Dennis Victor and Lois De Selms Lippoldt; m. Velma Lee Miller; children: Valerie Lippoldt Mack, Scott. AA, Dodge City CC, Kans., 1956; MusB in Edn., Bethany Coll., 1959; MusM in Edn., U. Colo., 1963. Instr. music Holyrood Pub. Schs., Kans., 1956—58, Moundridge Pub. Schs., 1959—62, Garden City Pub. Schs., 1963—67, Colby CC, 1967—87, Coffeyville CC, 1987—96; chmn. music Iowa We. CC, Coun. Bluffs, Iowa, 1996—2004; ret., 2004. Dir. choir various chs., 1997—. Mem.: Kans. Music Educators Assn. (pres. 1987—89), Music Educators Nat. Conv. (pres. southwestern divsn. 1991—93), Am. Choral Dir.'s Assn. (life). Home: 125 Bonham Cir Council Bluffs IA 51503

LIPPS, JERE HENRY, biology and geology professor; b. LA, Aug. 28, 1939; s. Henry John and Margaret (Rosaltha) L.; m. Karen Elizabeth Loeblich, June 25, 1964 (div. 1971); m. Susannah McClintock, Sept. 28, 1973; children: Jeremy Christian, Jamison William. BA, UCLA, 1962, PhD, 1966. Asst. prof. U. Calif., Davis, 1967-70, assoc. prof., 1970-75, prof., 1975-88, Berkeley, 1988—, prof. paleontology, 1988-89, prof. integrative biology, 1989—; dir. Mus. Paleontology, Berkeley, 1989-97. Dir. Inst. Ecology U. Calif., Davis, 1972-73, chmn. dept. geology, 1971-72, 79-84, chmn. dept. integrative biology, Berkeley, 1991-94. Contbr. articles to sci. publs. Dir. Micropaleontology Project, Inc. Cushman Found., NYC, pres., 1983—84, 2002—03. Recipient U.S. Antarctic medal NSF, 1975, Darwin award NCSE, 2002, Joseph A. Cushman award, 2006; Lipps Island, Antarctica named in his honor, 1979. Fellow: Com. for the Sci. Investigation of Claims of the Paranormal, AAAS, Paleontol. Soc. (pres. 1996—97), Cushman Found. (pres. 1983—84, 2001—02), Geol. Soc. Am.,

Calif. Acad. Scis.; mem.: Coun. for Media Integrity. Avocation: scuba diving. Office: U Calif Mus Paleontology #4780 1101 Valley Life Sciences Bldg Berkeley CA 94720-4780 Home Phone: 510-531-4269. Business E-Mail: jlipps@berkeley.edu.

LIPPY, KAREN DOROTHY FETHE, nurse psychotherapist; b. Balt., July 2, 1946; d. Vernon Harold and Dorothy Margaret (Wirth) Fethe; m. Robert Eugene Lippy, July 29, 1972; 1 child, Jarrod Blaire. BS in Nursing, U. Md., Balt, 1972, MS in Nursing, 1975. Cert. clin. specialist in adult psychiat./mental health nursing, master addictions counselor, critical incident stress mgmt., eye movement desensitization and reprocessing, diplomate Am. Coll. Profl. Mental Health Practitioners; cert. nursing adminstrn.-advanced. Clin. nurse specialist Springfield Hosp. Ctr., Sykesville, Md., 1975-79, asst. dir. nursing, 1979-86, dir. nursing, 1986-97; nurse psychotherapist Reentry Mental Health Svcs., Westminster, Md., 1983—; mem. Carroll County Criticial Incident Stress Mgmt. Team, 1999—. Task force on RN stds. practice Md. State Bd. Nursing; patient rights, classification, RN job specification, and credentialing/privileging task forces Md. Mental Hygiene Adminstrn. Recipient Gov.'s Citation for Excellence, State of Md., Achievement in Nursing Adminstrn., Md. Dept. Mental Hygiene. Mem. ANA, Md. Nurses Assn. (dist. bd. dirs.), Internat. Critical Incident Stress Found., EMDR Internat. Assn., Sigma Theta Tau, Phi Kappa Phi. Home: 2519 Bird View Rd Westminster MD 21157-8309 Office: 40 S Church St Ste 105 Westminster MD 21157-5414 Office Phone: 410-848-9244.

LIPSCHUTZ, MICHAEL ELAZAR, chemistry professor, consultant, researcher; b. Phila., May 24, 1937; s. Maurice and Anna (Kaplan) L.; m. Linda Jane Lowenthal, June 21, 1959; children: Joshua Henry, Mark David, Jonathan Mayer. BS, Pa. State U., 1958; S.M., U. Chgo., 1960, PhD, 1962. Gastdocent U. Bern, Switzerland, 1964-65; from asst. prof. chemistry to assoc. head dept. Purdue U., West Lafayette, Ind., 1965—93, prof. chemistry, 1973—2007, prof. emeritus, 2007—, assoc. head dept. of chemistry, 1993—2001; dir. chemistry ops. Purdue Rare Isotope Measurement Lab. (PRIME), 1990—2002. Vis. assoc. prof. Tel Aviv U., 1971-72; vis. prof. Max-Planck Inst. fuer Chemie, Mainz, Fed. Republic Germany, 1987; mem. panel space sci. experts Com. on Space Rsch., Space Agy. Forum of the Internat. Space Yr., Internat. Coun. Sci. Unions, 1990-92; cons. in field. Assoc. editor 11th Lunar and Planetary Sci. Conf., 3 vols., 1980; fin. editor Meteoritics and Planetary Sci., 1992-2000; contbr. numerous articles to profl. jours. Served to 1st lt. USAR, 1958-64. Recipient Cert. of Recognition, NASA, 1979, Cert. of Spl. Recognition, 1979, Group Achievement award, 1983, Cert. Appreciation, Nat. Commn. on Space, 1986; postdoctoral fellow NSF, 1964-65, NATO, 1964-65; Fulbright fellow, 1971-72 Fellow Meteoritical Soc. (treas. 1978-84, mem. joint com. on pubs. of Geochem. and Meteoritical Socs. 1985-93, fin. officer 1985-93, chmn. 1988-90); mem. AAAS, Am. Chem. Soc., Am. Geophys. Union, Planetary Soc., Internat. Astron. Union (US rep. 1988—), Sigma Xi. Achievements include having minor planet named in honor of Lipschutz by Internat. Astron. Union, 1987, Cert. of Recognition, Dept. Def., 1999. Office: Purdue U Dept Chemistry West Lafayette IN 47907 Home Phone: 765-463-2895; Office Phone: 765-494-5326. Business E-Mail: rnaapuml@purdue.edu.

LIPSCHUTZ, NEAL S., editor; b. Brooklyn; BA in Journalism, NYU. Editor Dow Jones Capital Market Report Dow Jones & Co., 1982; asst. mng. editor Dow Jones News Svc., 1989, deputy mng. editor, 1990—97, mng. editor, 1997—99, sr. editor Americas Jersey City, 1999—2005, v.p., mng. editor, 2005—. Office: 800 Plaza Two 8th Fl Harborside Financial Center Jersey City NJ 07311

LIPSCOMB, JAMES LOUIS, lawyer, insurance company executive; b. Albany, NY, Feb. 14, 1947; s. Eric and Vinel Lee (Motley) Lipscomb; m. Nancy Angela Moore; children: Kathryn, Julie, Angela. AAS, Hudson Valley Cmty.Coll., Troy, NY, 1967; BA, Howard U., 1969; JD, Columbia U., 1972; LLM, NYU, 1977. Bar: NY 1973, Calif. 1980, US Dist. Ct. (so. dist.) NY 1975, US Dist. Ct. (no. dist.) Calif. 1980, US Ct. Appeals (2nd cir.) 1975. Atty. Met. Life Ins. Co., NYC, 1972-79, asst. gen. counsel San Mateo, Calif., 1979-81, assoc. gen. counsel Foster City, Calif., 1981-88, v.p., assoc. gen. counsel, 1988, head mortgage portfolio real estate investments dept., 1992—98, head corp. planning and strategy, 1998—2000; pres., CEO Conning Corp. (former MetLife subs.), 2000—01; sr. v.p., dep. gen. counsel Met. Life Ins. Co., NYC, 2001—03, exec. v.p., gen. counsel, 2003—. Dir. MetLife Found., Life Ins. Coun. NY. Author: Structuring Complex Real Estate Transactions, 1988. Treas. Emmanuel Bapt. Ch., San Jose, Calif., 1984—, stewardship chmn., 1987—; vice chair Citizens Budget Commn.; bd. dirs. NY Citizens Crime Commn. Mem. Am. Coll. Real Estate Lawyers (mem. bd. govs., editor ACREL papers), Calif. State Bar Assn. (real property law sect. 1981—), ABA (mem. real property, probate and corp. law sects.), Assn. of Life Ins. Counsel, Am. Council Life Ins., City of NY Bar Assn. (treas., mem. exec. com.), NY Bar Assn. Avocations: racquetball, painting. Office: MetLife Inc 200 Park Ave New York NY 10166*

LIPSCOMB, LEWIS D., obstetrician, gynecologist; s. Lewis D. and Gertrude W. Lipscomb; m. Leslie Antici, June 5, 1999; children: John Webster, Mary Grace. B of Engring., Vanderbilt U., Nashville, 1994; MD, U. Miss., Jackson, 1999. Cert. clin. densitometrist Internat. Soc. of Clin. Densitometry. Resident physician Wake Forest U. Sch. Medicine, Winston-Salem, NC, 1999—2003; physician Pinehurst Surg. Clinic, NC, 2003—05, Winston-Salem Womancare, NC, 2005—. Fellow: ACS, ACOG. Roman Catholic. Office: Winston-Salem Womancare PA 114 Charlois Blvd Winston Salem NC 27103 Home Phone: 336-760-3431; Office Phone: 336-765-5470.

LIPSCOMB, OSCAR HUGH, archbishop; b. Mobile, Ala., Sept. 21, 1931; s. Oscar Hugh and Margaret (Saunders) Lipscomb. STL, Gregorian U., Rome, 1957; PhD, Cath. U. Am., 1963. Ordained priest Roman Cath. Ch., 1956, consecrated bishop 1980. Asst. pastor, Mobile, 1959—65; tchr. McGill Inst., Mobile, 1959—62; vice chancellor Diocese of Mobile-Birmingham, 1963—66, chancellor, 1966—80; pastor St. Patrick Parish, Mobile, 1966—71; lectr. history Spring Hill Coll., Mobile, 1971—72; asst. pastor St. Matthew Parish, Mobile, 1971—79, Cathedral Immaculate Conception, Mobile, 1979—80; adminstr. sede vacante Archdiocese of Mobile, 1980, archbishop, 1980—. Pres. Cath. Housing Mobile, Mobile Senate Priests, 1978—80; chmn. com. on doctrine Nat. Conf. Cath. Bishops, 1988—91. Contbr. articles to profl. jours. Chmn. NCCB Com. on Ecumenical and Interreligious Affairs, 1993—96, Cath. Common Ground Initiative, 1996—, chmn. com. on the liturgy, 1999—; mem. Mixed Internat. Commn. for Theol. Dialogue Between the Cath. Ch. and the Orthodox Ch., 1999—2002, Vox Clara commn. Congregation for Divine Worship, Rome, 2002—; Chmn. bd. dirs. Mobile Mus., 1966—88, Ala. Dept. Archives and History, 1979—, chmn., 1999—; chmn. bd. dirs. Cath. U. Am., Washington, 1983—98, Spring Hill Coll., Mobile, 1982—; chmn. bd. govs. N.Am. Coll., Rome, 1982—85. Mem.: Am. Cath. Hist. Assn., Ala. Hist. Assn., So. Hist. Assn. (pres. 1971—72, exec. com. 1981—88), Hist. Mobile Preservation Soc., Lions. Roman Catholic. Address: 36633 400 Government St PO Box 1966 Mobile AL 36633-1966

LIPSCOMB, STEVEN, sports association executive; BA, Dartmouth Coll.; JD, U. Chgo. Atty. Gibson, Dunn, & Crutcher; prodr. Lipscomb Entertainment; founder, CEO World Poker Tour, LLC, 2002—04; CEO WPT Enterprises Inc. (formerly World Poker Tour, LLC), 2005—. Prodr., dir. On the Inside of The World Series of Poker, 1999, Tournament of Champions of Poker, 2001, exec. prodr. Cruisin' to a Million, creator, exec. prodr. (TV series) World Poker Tour. Office: WPT Enterprises, Inc Ste 350 5700 Wilshire Blvd Los Angeles CA 90036 Office Phone: 323-330-9900. Office Fax: 323-330-9901.*

LIPSCOMB, THOMAS HEBER, III, media company executive; b. Washington, Sept. 12, 1938; s. Thomas Heber and Louise Buchanan (Heiss) L.; children: Peter Scott, Adrienne Clare. BA, Coll. William and Mary, 1961; MA, Ind. U., 1965. Editor Bobbs-Merrill Co., 1965-67, Stein & Day Pubs., 1967-69; sr. editor Prentice-Hall, Inc., 1969-70; exec. editor, editor-in-chief Dodd, Mead & Co., 1970-73; pres. Mason & Lipscomb Pubs., 1973-74; ptnr. Hamilton Assocs., 1974-76; pres., CEO Times Books (N.Y. Times Book Co.), 1976-81; chmn. bd. New Capital Publs., Inc., 1981-85; pres. Delphi Assocs., NYC, 1985-87; pres., CEO Cryptologics Internat., 1988-91, Infosafe Sys., Inc., NYC, 1992-96, chmn., 1996-97, Ctr. for the Digital Future, 1997—. Chmn. bd. Atlantech Aquaculture Ltd., chmn. Cardiact, Inc., 1999-2004. Contbr. articles to profl. jours. including N.Y. Times, Wall St. Jour., Washington Post, Chgo. Sun-Times, others; patents in digital tech. Mem. exec. bd. Am. Ctr. PEN, 1973-79; trustee Internat. Ctr. for Econ. Growth, Robert Coll., Istanbul, Turkey, 1973-81; panel of advisors George Polk Award, 1977—, Mus. Digital Licensing Collection; chmn. NY Vietnam Vet.'s Leadership Program, 1985-88; dir. Giraffe Project, 1989—, NYU Ctr. Copyright in New Media. Lt. U.S. Army, 1961-64. Fellow Digital Copyright Forum; mem. Coun. on Fgn. Relations, Internat. Broadcast Inst., East-West Inst. Security Studies, Gibraltar-Am. Coun., St. Nicholas Soc., N.Y. Acad. Scis., Holland Lodge, Mid-Atlantic Club, Nat. Press Club. Office: 1360 York Ave Ste 3D New York NY 10021 E-mail: tom@digitalfuture.org.

LIPSCOMB, WILLIAM NUNN, JR., retired chemistry professor; b. Cleve., Dec. 9, 1919; s. William Nunn and Edna Patterson (Porter) Lipscomb; m. Mary Adele Sargent, May 20, 1944; children: Dorothy Jean, James Sargent; m. Jean Craig Evans, 1983; 1 child, Jenna. BS, U. Ky., 1941, DSc (hon.), 1963; PhD, Calif. Inst. Tech., 1946; DSc (hon.), U. Munich, 1976, L.I. U., 1977, Rutgers U., 1979, Gustavus Adolphus Coll., 1980, Marietta Coll., 1981, Miami U., 1983, U. Denver, 1985, Ohio State U., 1991, Transylvania U., 1992; DSc h.c. (hon.), Mahidol U., Bangkok, Thailand, 2003. Phys. chemist Office of Sci. R&D, 1942—46; faculty U. Minn., Mpls., 1946—59, asst. prof., 1946—50, assoc. prof., 1950—54, acting chief phys. chemistry divsn., 1952—54, prof. and chief phys. chemistry divsn., 1954—59; prof. chemistry Harvard U., Cambridge, Mass., 1959—71, Abbott and James Lawrence prof., 1971—90, prof. emeritus, 1990—. Mem. U.S. Nat. Commn. for Crystallography, 1954—59, 1960—63, 1965—67; chmn. program com. 4th Internat. Congress of Crystallography, Montreal, 1957; mem. sci. adv. bd. Robert A. Welch Found.; mem. adv. bd. Mich. Molecular Biology Inst.; mem. adv. com. Inst. Amorphous Studies; mem. sci. adv. com. Nova Pharms., Daltex Med. Svc., Gensia Pharms., Binary Therapeutics. Author: The Boron Hydrides, 1963; author: (with G.R. Eaton) NMR Studies of Boron Hydrides and Related Compounds, 1969; assoc. editor: Jour. Chem. Physics, 1955—57; contbr. articles to profl. jours. Clarinetist, mem. Amateur Chamber Music Players. Named Robert Welch Found. lectr., 1966, 1971, Howard U. disting. lecture series, 1966, George Fisher Baker lectr., Cornell U., 1969, centenary lectr., Chem. Soc., London, 1972, lectr., Weizmann Inst., Rehovoth, Israel, 1974, Evans award lectr., Ohio State U., 1974, Gilbert Newton Lewis Meml. lectr., U. Calif., Berkeley, 1974, lectr., Mich. State U., 1975, U. Iowa, 1975, Ill. Inst. Tech., 1976; recipient Harrison Howe award in chemistry, 1958, Disting. Alumni Centennial award, U. Ky., 1965, Disting. Svc. in advancement inorganic chemistry, Am. Chem. Soc., 1968, George Ledlie prize, Harvard, 1971, Nobel prize in chemistry, 1976, Disting. Alumni award, Calif. Inst. Tech., 1977, First Outstanding Alumni award, U. Ky., 1999, Sr. U.S. Scientist award, Alexander von Humboldt-Stiftung, 1979, award lecture, Internat. Acad. Quantum Molecular Sci., 1980; fellow Guggenheim, Oxford U., Eng., 1954—55, Cambridge U., Eng., 1972—73, NSF sr. postdoctoral fellow, 1965—66, Overseas fellow, Churchill Coll., Cambridge, Eng., 1966, 1973. Fellow: Am. Acad. Arts and Scis.; mem.: NAS, Academie Europeenne des Scis., des Arts et des Lettres, The Netherlands Acad. Arts and Scis. (fgn.), Royal Soc. Chemistry (hon.), Assn. Bioinorganic Scientists (hon.), Am. Crystallographic Assn. (pres. 1955), Am. Chem. Soc. (chmn. Minn. sect. 1949—50, Peter Debye award phys. chemistry 1973), Phi Mu Epsilon, Sigma Pi Sigma, Phi Lambda Upsilon, Alpha Chi Sigma, Sigma Xi, Phi Beta Kappa. Office: Harvard U Dept Chemistry & Chem Biol 12 Oxford St Cambridge MA 02138-2902 Business E-Mail: lipscomb@chemistry.harvard.edu.

LIPSEY, CHARLES E., lawyer; b. Pensacola, Fla., Nov. 27, 1950; BChE, Ga. Inst. Tech., 1972; JD with high honors, George Washington U., 1977, LLM in Patent and Trade Regulation Law with highest honors, 1981. Bar: Va. 1977, D.C. 1979, U.S. Ct. Appeals (fed. cir.) 1979, U.S. Patent and Trademark Office. Ptnr. Finnegan, Henderson, Farabow, Garrett & Dunner, Washington. Tech. advisor to Assoc. Judge Giles S. Rich, U.S. Ct. Customs and Patent Appeals, 1976-78; profl. lectr. law George Washington U., 1984-89; cons. U.N. Indsl. Devel. Orgn.; expert cons. Implications Advances in Genetic Engring. for Developing Countries, Vienna, 1981. Co-author: Patent Law Perspectives, 1982-88. Recipient Joseph Rossman Meml. award, 1979; named one of best lawyers in intellectual property law, Best Lawyers in Am., 2005. Mem. ABA, Am. Intellectual Property Law Assn., Va. State Bar, D.C. Bar, Bar Assn. D.C., Tau Beta Pi, Order of Coif. Office: Finnegan Henderson Farabow Garrett & Dunner LLP Two Freedom Sq 11955 Freedom Dr Reston VA 20190-5675 Office Phone: 571-203-2700. Office Fax: 202-408-4400. Business E-Mail: charles.lipsey@finnegan.com.

LIPSEY, HOWARD IRWIN, lawyer, educator; b. Providence, Jan. 24, 1936; s. Harry David and Anna (Gershman) L.; children: Lewis Robert, Bruce Stephen. BA (hon.), Providence Coll., 1957; JD, Georgetown U., 1960. Bar: R.I., 1960; U.S. Dist. Ct. R.I., 1961; U.S. Supreme Ct., 1972. Assoc. Edward I. Friedman, 1963-67, Kirshenbaum and Kirshenbaum, 1967-72; ptnr. Abedon, Michaelson, Stanzler, Biener, Skolnik, and Lipsey, 1972-83, Lipsey and Skolnik Esquires, Ltd., Providence, 1983-93; assoc. justice R.I. Family Ct., Providence, 1993—. Lectr. trial tactics Nat. Coll. Adv., 1986, U. Bridgeport, Yale U., U. Denver, Suffolk U.,1987—; adj. prof. U. Houston., 1994-98; adj. prof. family law Roger Williams U., 1996-2000; co-chair R.I. Supreme Ct. Future of the Courts Com., 2004; chair R.I. Supreme Ct. Permanent com. Women and Minorities in the Courts, 2005—. Contbg. author: Valuation and Distribution of Marital Property, 1984; bd. editors Georgetown U. Law Jour. Capt. JAGC, USAR, 1960-71. Fellow: Am. Acad. Matrimonial Lawyers, Am. Coll. Trial Lawyers; mem.: ATLA, ABA (chair trial advocacy inst. 1994—97, coun. 1995—2001, sec. family law sect. 2002—03, vice chair 2003—04, chair 2005—06, bd. edit. Family Advocate), Family Law Inn of Ct. (founder, counselor), R.I. Bar Assn., B'nai B'rith. Office: RI Family Ct 1 Dorrance Plz Providence RI 02903-3922 Office Phone: 401-458-5310.

LIPSEY, JOSEPH, JR., wholesale distribution executive; b. Selma, Ala., Sept. 12, 1934; s. Joseph and Anna (Bendersky) L.; m. Betty Fay Wellan, June 5, 1960; children: Debora, Joseph III, Elizabeth, Tami. BA, La. State U., 1955, LLB, 1957; grad. Owner/Pres. Mgmt. Program, Harvard Grad. Sch. Bus., 1985. Bar: La. 1957, U.S. Dist. Ct. La. 1957, Korea 1959, Ryukyu Islands 1958. Ptnr. Howell & Lipsey, Baton Rouge, 1960—65; v.p. Wellan's, Inc., 1965—81, Lipsey's Wholesale, Baton Rouge, 1965—81; pres. Palais Royal, Inc., Shreveport, La., 1986—89. Pres. Wellan's, Inc., Alexandria, La., 1981-89, 2005—, So. Media Rsch. Co., Monroe, La., 1984-92, mng. ptnr. Rapides Interests, Inc., Alexandria, 2003—; chmn. Composite Analysis Group, Inc., Alexandria, 1989—; chmn. Lipsey Mountain Spring Water, Atlanta, 1990—, Nantahalla Spring Water Bottling Co., Highlands, NC, 1994—; chmn., sec.-treas. EAS Pub. Co., Inc., 1994—; bd. dir., ind. dir. Weingarten Golden State, Inc., Houston, Tex., 2001—; spkr. OPM 10 Harvard U., 1985; lectr. La. State U. Law Sch. Baton Rouge, 1961-63, Freeman Sch. Bus., Tulane U.; mem. chancellor's bd. Paul M. Hebert Law Ctr., La. State U., 2001-04, bd. trustees, 2002-05; chmn. Fashion Mcht. Conf., NYC, 1977-81. Mem. exec. com. Com. for a Better La., Baton Rouge, 1971-86; mem. La. State U. Found., 1975—, pres., 1980-81. Capt. USAF, 1957-60. Inducted into La. State U. Law Sch. Hall Fame, 1987. Mem. La. State C. of C. (pres. 1973-75), Alexandria C. of C. (pres. 1971-72), Bus. Exec. for Nat. Security, Rotary. Democrat. Jewish. Office Phone: 770-449-0001. Business E-Mail: lipsey@lipseywater.com.

LIPSEY, RICHARD GEORGE, economist, educator; b. Victoria, BC, Can., Aug. 28, 1928; s. Richard Andrew and Faith Thirell (Ledingham) L.; m. Diana Louise Smart, Mar. 17, 1960; children: Mark Alexander (stepson), Mathew Richard, Joanna Louise, Claudia Amanda. BA with honours, U. BC, 1950; MA, U. Toronto, 1953; PhD, London Sch. Econs., 1955; LLD (hon.), McMaster U., 1983, Victoria U., 1985, U. Carleton, 1987, Queens U., 1990, Toronto U., 1992; DLitt (hon.), U. Guelph, 1993; LLD (hon.), U. Essex, Eng., 1996, U. BC, 1999, Simon Fraser U., 2007. Rsch. asst. B.C. Dept. Trade and Industry, 1950-53; from asst. lectr. to prof. econs. London Sch. Econs., 1955-63; prof. econs., chmn. dept., dean Sch. Social Studies, U. Essex, England, 1965-69; vis. prof. U. B.C., 1969-70, U. Colo., 1973-74; Irving Fisher vis. prof. Yale U., 1979-80; Sir Edward Peacock prof. econs. Queens U., Kingston, Ont., 1970-87; prof. Simon Fraser U., Vancouver, B.C., 1989-97, prof. emeritus, 1997—. Sr. rsch. advisor C.D. Howe Inst., 1983-89; dir. rsch. into growth in U.K. Nat. Econ. Devel. Coun. U.K., 1961-63; mem. coun. and planning com. Nat. Inst. Econ. and Social Rsch. U.K., 1962-69; mem. bd. Social Sci. Rsch. Coun. U.K., 1966-69. Author: An Introduction to Positive Economics, 11th edit, 2007, The Theory of Customs Unions: A General Equilibrium Analysis, 1971; co-author: An Introduction to a Mathematical Treatment of Economics, 3d edit, 1977, Economics, 13th edit., 2007, Mathematical Economics, 1976, An Introduction to the U.K. Economy, 1983, 4th edit., 1993, Common Ground for the Canadian Common Market, 1984, Canada's Trade Options in a Turbulent World, 1985, Global Imbalances, 1987, First Principles of Economics, 1988, 3d edit., 1996, Evaluating the Free Trade Deal, 1988, The NAFTA, What's In, What Next, 1994, Business Economics, 1997, A Structuralist Assessment of Innovation Policies, 1998, Economic Transformations: General Purpose Technologies and Long Term Economic Growth, 2005; editor: Rev. Econ. Studies, 1962-64. Decorated officer Order of Can.; Can. Inst. for Advanced Rsch. fellow, 1989—2002. Fellow Econometric Soc., Royal Soc. Can., IC2 Soc. (Austin, Tex.); mem. Royal Econ. Soc. (coun. 1967-71), Econ. Study Soc. (chmn. 1965-69), Am. Econ. Assn., Can. Econ. Assn. (pres. 1980-81), Atlantic Econ. Soc. (chmn. 1986-87). Personal E-mail: rlipsey@sfu.ca.

LIPSEY, ROBERT EDWARD, economist, educator; b. NYC, Aug. 14, 1926; s. Meyer Aaron and Anna (Weinstein) L.; m. Sally Irene Rothstein, Nov. 24, 1948; children: Marion (Mrs. William Greenlee), Carol (Mrs. William Hersh), Eleanor (Mrs. William Ho). BA, Columbia U., 1944, MA, 1946, PhD, 1961. Rsch. asst. Nat. Bur. Econ. Rsch., NYC, 1945-53, rsch. assoc., 1953-60, sr. rsch. staff, 1960—, v.p. rsch., 1970-75, dir. internat. studies, 1975-78, dir. NY Office, 1978—. Lectr. econs. Columbia U., 1961-64; prof. econs. Queens Coll. and Grad. Ctr., CUNY, 1967-95, prof. emeritus, 1995—; cons. Dept. Commerce, Deutsche Bundesbank, Fed. Res. Bd., UN, World Bank; mem. Pres. Adv. Bd. on Internat. Investment, 1977-78; bd. dirs. Rsch. Found. CUNY, 1994-95, NYC Census Rsch. Data Ctr.; adv. com. European Union Studies Ctr., CUNY, 1994—. Author: Price and Quantity Trends in the Foreign Trade of the U.S, 1963, (with Raymond W. Goldsmith) Studies in the National Balance Sheet of the U.S, 1963, (with Doris Preston) Source Book of Statistics Relating to Construction, 1966, (with Irving B. Kravis) Price Competitiveness in World Trade, 1971, (with Phillip Cagan) Financial Effects of Inflation, 1978, (with Irving B. Kravis) Saving and Economic Growth: Is the U.S. Really Falling Behind, 1987, (with Magnus Blomström and Lennart Ohlsson) Economic Relations Between the U.S. and Sweden, 1989, Measures of the Transnationalization of Economic Activity, United Nations, New York and Geneva, 2001; editor: (with Helen Stone Tice) The Measurement of Saving, Investment and Wealth, 1989, (with Robert E. Baldwin and J. David Richardson) Geography and Ownership as Bases for Economic Accounting, 1998, (with Alan Heston) International and Interarea Comparisons of Income, Output, and Prices, 1999, (with Jean-Louis Mucchielli) Multinational Firms and Impacts on Employment, Trade, and Technology, 2002, (with Heinz Herrmann) Foreign Direct Investment in the Real and Financial Sector of Industrial Countries, 2003; assoc. editor Rev. of Econs. and Stats., 1989-92; mem. editl. bd. Rev. of Income and Wealth, 1992—, Internat. Trade Jour., 1998—, Contemporary Econ. Policy, 2000—; contbr. articles to profl. jours. Fellow Am. Statis. Assn., NY Acad. Scis.; mem. Acad. Internat. Bus., Nat. Assn. for Bus. Econs., Am. Econ. Assn., Internat. Assn. for Rsch. in Income and Wealth, Conf. on Rsch. in Income and Wealth, Econometric Soc., Internat. Trade and Fin. Assn. (pres. 1997), Western Econ. Assn. (bd. dirs. 1996-99), European Econ. Assn. Office: National Bureau Of Economic Research 365 5th Ave Fl 5 New York NY 10016-4309 Home Phone: 212-260-8221; Office Phone: 212-817-7961. E-mail: rlipsey@gc.cuny.edu.

LIPSEY, STANFORD, newspaper publisher; b. Omaha, Oct. 8, 1927; s. Jacob and Molly (Brick) L.; m. Jeanne Blacker, June 15, 1949 (div. 1981); children: Janet Gail, Daniel Jacob; m. Judith C. Hojnacki, May, 2002. AB in Econs., U. Mich., 1948. Sales rep., pub. relations rep. Libby, McNeil & Libby, Los Angeles, 1948-50; reporter, advt. mgr., editor, pub. owner Sun Newspapers Omaha, 1952-80; vice-chmn. Buffalo News, 1980-83, pres. & pub., 1983—. Pres., founder Nebr. chpt. Multiple Sclerosis Soc., Omaha, 1951; bd. dirs., founder Strategic Aerospace Mus., Nebr., 1972; The Buffalo News Inc., Inc., Bus. Coun. of N.Y. State, Roswell Park Inst.; mem. Jr. League; Greater Buffalo Partnership; Darwin Martin House Restoration Corp.; Newspaper Assn. of Am. With USAF, 1950-52. Pub. 1st weekly group to receive Pulitzer prize for investigative reporting Sun. Newspapers, Omaha; recipient Gov.'s Pks. and Preservation award, 1998. Office: Buffalo News PO Box 100 Buffalo NY 14240-0100*

LIPSHUTZ, LAUREL SPRUNG, psychiatrist; b. Easton, Pa., Dec. 11, 1946; d. Joseph A. and Helen A. (Rochlin) S.; m. Robert M. Lipshutz, June 15, 1975; 1 child, Jonathan. BA, U. Pa., 1968; MD, Albany Med. Coll. of Union U., 1972. Diplomate Am. Bd. Psychiatry and Neurology. Resident in psychiatry Johns Hopkins Hosp., Balt., 1972-75; unit chief psychiat. inpatient unit Phila. Gen. Hosp., 1975-77; dir. psychiat. inpatient svc. Pa. Hosp., Phila., 1977-96; assoc. dir. residency tng. Inst. of Pa. Hosp., Phila., 1983-96; coord. psychiat. clerkship for U. Pa. med. students Pa. Hosp., Phila., 1982-95; psychiatrist, 1995—. Sr. examiner Am. Bd. Psychiatry and Neurology, 1979—; sr. attending psychiatrist Inst. Pa. Hosp., Phila., 1989-97, psychiatrist, 1984—; clin. assoc. prof. psychiatry U. Pa. Sch. Medicine, Phila., 1997—, Thomas Jefferson Med. Coll., Phila. 1994-97. Fellow Am. Psychiat. Assn. (disting.); mem. Am. Soc. Psychoanalytic Physicians, Pa. Psychiat. Assn. (com. on women), Phila. Psychiatry Soc., Assn. Acad. Psychiatry (region III Excellence in Tchg. award 1995). Office: The Curtis Ctr 601 Walnut St Ste 960W Philadelphia PA 19106 Office Phone: 215-923-7851. Office Fax: 215-592-7853.

LIPSHUTZ, ROBERT JEROME, lawyer, former government official; b. Atlanta, Dec. 27, 1921; s. Allen A. and Edith (Gavronski) L.; m. Barbara Sorelle Levin, Feb. 16, 1950 (dec.); children: Randall M., Judith Ann, Wendy Jean, Debbie Sue; m. Betty Beck Rosenberg, Feb. 10, 1973;

stepchildren: Robert, Nancy Fay. JD, LLB, U. Ga., 1943. Bar: Ga. 1943, D.C. 1980. Practice in, Atlanta, 1947-77, 79—; ptnr. firm Lipshutz, Greenblatt & King, 1979—. Counsel to Pres. U.S., Washington, 1977-79 Past vice chmn. Ga. Bd. Human Resources; treas., legal counsel Jimmy Carter Presdl. campaign com., 1976; trustee The Carter Ctr.; adv. com. Jimmy Carter Libr. Lt. AUS, 1943-46. Mem. ABA, Ga. Bar Assn., Atlanta Bar Assn., Atlanta Lawyers Club, Atlanta., B'nai B'rith (past pres., Disting. Svc. award). Jewish (past pres. The Temple). Office: Lipshutz Greenblatt & King Harris Tower 233 Peachtree St Ste 2400 Atlanta GA 30303-1504 Home Phone: 404-252-7100; Office Phone: 404-688-2300.

LIPSIG, ETHAN, lawyer; b. NYC, Dec. 11, 1948; s. Daniel Allen and Haddassah (Adler) L. BA, Pomona Coll., 1969; postgrad., Oxford U., 1969-70; JD, UCLA, 1974. Bar: US Dist. Ct. (cen. dist.) Calif. 1974, US Ct. Appeals (9th cir.) 1974, US Tax Ct. 1978. Ptnr. Paul, Hastings, Janofsky & Walker LLP, LA, 1982—. Author: Individual Retirement Arrangements, 1980, Downsizing, 1996. Mem.: ABA (subcom. fed. preemption 1978—79, subcom. investments and funding 1981, employee benefits com., labor and employment law and tax sects.), European Labor Network (mem. adv. bd.), US C. of C., Nat. Assn. Pub. Pension Attys., State Bar Calif. (chmn. employee benefits com. 1981—84, tax. sect.), Am. Coll. Employee Benefits Counsel (charter mem.), LA Men's Garden Club, Soc. Fellows of Huntington Libr., Order Coif. Avocations: travel, horticulture, wine, music, art. Office: Paul Hastings Janofsky & Walker LLP 515 S Flower St Fl 25 Los Angeles CA 90071-2280 Office Phone: 213-683-6304. Office Fax: 213-627-0705. Business E-Mail: ethanlipsig@paulhastings.com.

LIPSITT, LEWIS PAEFF, psychology professor; b. New Bedford, Mass., June 28, 1929; s. Joseph and Anna Naomi (Paeff) L.; m. Edna Brill Duchin, June 8, 1952; children: Mark, Ann. BA, U. Chgo., 1950; MS, U. Mass., 1952; PhD, U. Iowa, 1957; Doctorate (hon.), U. Athens, Greece, 2006. Lic. Psychologist RI, 1965. Instr. dept. psychology Brown U., Providence, 1957, asst. prof., 1958-61, assoc. prof., 1961-66, prof., 1966-96, dir. Child Study Ctr., 1967-92, Wriston lectr., 1993—, prof. emeritus psychology, med. sci. and human devel., 1996—, rsch. prof. psychology, 1996—. Mem. Gov.'s Adv. Commn. on Mental Retardation, 1963-66; cons. Nat. Inst. Health; edn. task force Model Cities Program, Providence, 1969-71; fellow Stanford Ctr. for Advanced Study in Behavioral Scis., 1979-80; vis. scientist Nat. Inst. Mental Health, 1986-87; chair steering com. nat. child care project Nat. Inst. Child Health and Human Devel., 1994-99, adv. com., 1999-2001. Co-author: Child Development, 1979; founder, editor: Infant Behavior and Devel., 1978-82; founding co-editor: Advances in Child Development and Behavior, 1963-70, 78-82; co-editor: Research Readings in Child Psychology, 1963, Experimental Child Psychology, 1971, Advances in Infancy Research, 1981-99, Self-regulatory Behavior and Risk Taking, 1991, Progress in Infancy Research, 1991-99; contbr. articles to profl. jours. Bd. dirs. Providence Child Guidance Clinic, 1960-63, RI Kids Count, 2003-04, chmn., 2004-07; trustee Butler Hosp., Providence, 1965-84, 2006—; mem. bd. sci. counselors Nat. Ins. Child Health and Human Devel., 1984-88; nat. co-dir. Lee Salk Family Ctr., Kidspeace, Allentown, Pa., 1993—; participant White House Conf. on Child Care, 1998. With USAF, 1952—54, clin. psychologist USAF, 1952—54, Lackland AFB. Recipient Mentor Lifetime Achievement award, AAAS, 1995, Profl. Achievement citation, U. Chgo., 1995, James McKeen Cattell award, 1979, Lifetime Achievement Child Studies award, Internat. Soc. Infant Studies, Japan Soc. Baby Studies, 2006; USPHS Spl. Rsch. fellow, 1966, Guggenheim fellow, 1972—73, USPHS fellow, 1973. Fellow AAAS (Lifetime Mentor award 1994), APA (exec. com. divsn. devel. psychology 1967-70, pres. divsn. devel. psychology 1980-81, bd. sci. affairs 1985-88, exec. dir. for sci. 1990-91, sci. officer 1991-92, Nicholas Hobbs award 1990, exec. com. divsn. gen. psychology 1997-01, coun. of reps. 1997-00, pres. divsn. gen. psychology 1999-00, exptl. psychology coun. of reps. 2001-, Ernest R. Hilgard award for life achievement in gen. psychology 2004, Urie Bronfenbrenner award for studies in child devel. 2004), Internat. Soc. Infant Studies (founding mem. 1978-, citation lifetime achievement studies on babies 2006); mem. AAUP, Soc. Rsch. in Child Devel., Internat. Soc. Study Behavioral Devel. (membership sec. 1981-83, exec. com. 1984-89), Am. Psychol. Soc. (founding mem., charter fellow, bd. dirs. 1989-90), Can. Inst. for Advanced Rsch. (chair adv. com. human devel. group 1995-03, mem. adv. com. human devel. and population health 2000-04), RI Psychol. Assn. (bd. dirs. 1995-98, Mental Health Svc. award 1998). Jewish. Office Phone: 401-863-2332. Business E-Mail: Lewis_Lipsitt@brown.edu.

LIPSKY, BURTON G., lawyer; b. Syracuse, NY, May 29, 1937; s. Abraham and Pauline (Leichtner); m. Elaine B. Mannheimer, July 27, 1967; 1 child, Erika S., m. Carol S. Samberg, Feb. 4, 1973; 1 child, Andrew H. BBA, U. Mich., 1959; JD summa cum laude, Syracuse U., 1962. Bar: N.Y. 1962, U.S. Supreme Ct. 1967. Trial atty. U.S. Dept. Justice, Washington, 1962-67; assoc. Kaye, Scholer, Fierman, Hays & Handler, NYC, 1967-72; ptnr. Delson & Gordon, NYC, 1972-87, Lipsky & Stout, NYC, 1991-96; pvt. practice, NYC, 1996—. Mem. bd. visitors Syracuse U. Coll. of Law, 1989—; sec.-treas., dir. Robert Mapplethorpe Found., Inc., 1988—. Mem. ABA, N.Y. Bar Assn., Order of Coif, Justinian Soc., Am. Contract Bridge League (life master). Office Phone: 212-452-3449. Personal E-mail: BurtLip@aol.com.

LIPSKY, IAN DAVID, biochemical manufacturing executive, director; b. Bklyn., May 26, 1957; s. Eugene Herman and Janet Dorothy (Heller) Lipsky; m. Cheryl Joy Weinberg; 1 child, Ethan Maxwell. BS in Marine Engrng., Maine Maritime Acad., 1979; MBA, U. San Francisco, 2000. Lic. eng contractor, Calif; US Coast Guard, Merchant Mariners Document steam & motor vessels. Third asst. engr. Interlake Steamship Co., Cleve., 1979-81; port engr. Exxon Internat. Co., Florham Park, NJ, 1981-84; prodn. supr. Alfred Conhagen Inc. Calif., Hercules, 1984-87, gen. mgr., 1987-89, v.p., 1989-2000; sr. mgr. facilities svcs. dept. Genentech, Inc., South San Francisco, 2001—, assoc. dir., head of facilities biochem. mfg., 2003—. Pres. No. Calif. alumni chpt. Maine Maritime Acad., 2003—. Mem.: ASME, NSPE, Port Engrs. San Francisco, Inst. Marine Engrs. (London), Marine Port Engrs. NY, Soc. Naval Architects and Marine Engrs., U. San Francisco MBA Alumni Soc. (bd. dirs. 2003—). Democrat. Jewish. Avocations: golf, running, bicycling, drums. Office: Genentech Inc 1 DNA Way South San Francisco CA 94080-4990 Home: 34 Madera Del Presidio Dr Corte Madera CA 94925-2068 Personal E-mail: idlipsky@yahoo.com.

LIPSKY, JACK BENDER, insurance company executive; b. NY, Apr. 29, 1951; m. Rhonda E. Forman, Nov. 26, 1975. BS, SUNY, Albany; MBA, Hofstra U., Uniondale, NY. CLU The Am. Coll., 1980, chartered fin. cons. The Am. Coll., 1984. Prin., owner Lipsky Fin. Group, Inc., Great Neck, NY. Founder Gt. Neck Baseball League, 1993—. Mem.: Million Dollar Round Table. Home: 6 Shore Park Rd Great Neck NY 11023 Office: Lipsky Financial Group Inc 98 Cutter Mill Rd Great Neck NY 11021 Home Phone: 516-829-6187; Office Phone: 516-829-1890. Office Fax: 516-829-1844.

LIPSKY, JOHN PHILLIP, international banking official; b. Cedar Rapids, Iowa, Feb. 19, 1947; s. Abbott Bennett and Joan Emily (Miller) L.; m. Zsuzsanna Sylvia Karasz, Sept. 6, 1974; children: Elisa, Daniel, Andrea Lipsky-Karasz. BA in Econs., Wesleyan U., 1968; MA in Econs., Stanford U., 1974, PhD in Econs., 1980. Asst. chief IMF, Washington, 1974-84, resident rep. Chile, 1978—80, first dep. mng. dir., 2006—; with Salomon Bros., 1984—97, dir. European Econ. and Market Analysis Group London, 1989—92, chief economist NYC, 1992—97, JPMorgan Investment Bank, vice chmn.; chief economist, dir. rsch. Chase Manhattan Bank. Bd. dirs. Nat. Bur. Econ. Rsch. Office: IMF 700 19th St NW Washington DC 20431 Office Phone: 202-623-7000. Office Fax: 202-623-4661.

LIPSKY, PAT, artist; b. NYC, Sept. 21, 1941; d. Bernard G. and Bernice D. (Brown) Sutton; children: David Lipsky, Jonathan Lipsky. BFA, Cornell U., 1963; postgrad., Bklyn. Mus. Art Sch., 1960-61, Art Student's League, 1963; MA, Hunter Coll., 1968. Faculty Fairleigh Dickinson U., 1968-69, Hunter Coll., 1972, San Francisco Art Inst., 1974; assoc. prof. U. Hartford, 1983—2002. Guest lectr. Hirshhorn Mus., 1975, Va. Commonwealth U., Bennington Coll., 1977, U. Pitts., 1974, NYU, 1983, SACI, Florence, 1986, Springfield Mus., 1987-88, U. Miami, 1992, Pollock-Krasner House and Study Ctr., East Hampton, L.I., N.Y., 1995, Am. U., 1997, Muhlenberg Coll., 1999; guest lectr. Parsons Sch. Design, 1990, lectr., 1982-83, 90; instr. SUNY, Purchase, 1980-81; adv. coun. Cornell U. Coll. Art and Architecture, 1988—. One-woman shows include Andre Emmerich Gallery, N.Y.C., 1970, 72, 74, 75, Deichter O'Reilly Gallery, 1976, Medici-Berenson Gallery, 1976, Everson Mus., 1970, Gloria Luria Gallery, Miami, 1988, Slater-Price Gallery, NYC, 1986, Hartell Gallery Cornell U., 1989, Andre Zarre Gallery, 1991, Virginia Miller Gallery, Coral Gables, Fla., 1994, Bookstein Fine Arts, N.Y.C., 1997, The Kitchen, 1999, Elizabeth Harris Gallery, 1999, 2001, 03, 04, Piltzer Gallery, Barbizon, France, 2002, L.I.C.K. Ltd. Fine Art, Long Island City, NY, 2003, Elizabeth Harris Gallery, 2004, New Monotypes, Aurobora Press Gallery, San Francisco, 2005, Cathedral of St. John the Divine, NY, 2006, Elizabeth Harris Gallery, NY, 2006, others; exhibited in group shows at Whitney Mus. Am. Art, 1971, Hirshhorn Mus. and Sculture Garden, 1975, Promenade Gallery, Hartford, 1984, U. Mass. Art Gallery, Amherst, 1987, Gloria Luria Gallery, 1988, 92, Andre Zarre Gallery, 1990, 95, Denise Renè Gallery, Paris, 1993, Gallery One, Toronto, 1996, Snyder Fine Art, NYC, 1996, Lori Bookstein/Fine Arts, 1997, Am. Acad. Arts & Letters, 2001, DC Moore Gallery, 2004, Am. Embassy, Sarajevo, Bosnia, 2005; represented in permanent collections Herbert Johnson Mus., Ithaca, NY, Witney Mus., Hirshhorn Mus., Walker Art Ctr., Hunter Coll., Fogg Art Mus., Harvard U., San Francisco Mus. Art, Bklyn. Mus., Blanton Mus. Art, U. Tex., Austin, Wadsworth Atheneum, Hartford, Portland Mus. Art, Mus. Fine Arts, Houston, State Dept. U.S.; stage designer (play) Custody, Westbeth Theatre, N.Y.C., 1991; works include silkscreen and poster edit. Lincoln Ctr./List Great Performers Series, 2004. Recipient Childe Hassam Purchase prize AAAL, 2001; grantee N.Y. State Coun., 1972, NY Found. Arts, 1992, 99, 2007, Jerome Found., 1999, Adolph & Esther Gottlieb Found., 1999, Pollock-Krasner Found., 2000; sponsorship from Winsor and Newton Paint Co., 1992; fellow Va. Ctr. for Creative Arts, 1986, 93, Tyrone Guthurie Centre, Co., Moneghan, Ireland, 1996. Home: 410 W 24th St New York NY 10011-1303 Studio: 526 W 26th St Rm 1011 New York NY 10001-5541 Personal E-mail: patlipsky@patlipsky.com.

LIPSMAN, RICHARD MARC, lawyer, educator; b. Bklyn., Aug. 17, 1946; s. Abraham W. and Ruth (Weinstein) L.; m. Geri A. Russo, 1979; children: Eric, Dara Briana. BBA, CCNY, 1968; JD, St. John's U., Jamaica, NY, 1972; LLM in Taxation, Boston U., 1976. Bar: NY 1973, Mass. 1975, US Dist. Ct. (ea. and so. dists.) NY 1977, US Supreme Ct. 1978, US Tax Ct. 1979; CPA, NY, Mass. Tax atty. Arthur Young & Co., NYC, 1972-74; assoc. Gilman, McLaughlin & Hanrahan, Boston, 1974-76, Lefrak, Fischer & Meyerson, NYC, 1976-77; ptnr. Tarnow, Landsman & Lipsman, NYC, 1978; pvt. practice NYC, 1979—. Adj. faculty Baruch Coll. CUNY, 1984-86, curriculum specialist Rsch. Found. CUNY, 1977-78; adj. faculty Pratt Inst., Bklyn., 1974, Queensboro Coll., Bayside, NY, 1978-80. Author, producer book/cassette program Learning Income Taxes, 1978—. Mem. ABA, AICPA, NY State Bar Assn., Assn. Bar City NY, NY State Soc. CPA's. Jewish. Office Phone: 212-532-7700. Personal E-mail: rmlny@pipeline.com.

LIPSON, ABIGAIL, psychologist; b. Washington, Mar. 6, 1956; d. Leon Samuel and Dorothy Ann (Rapoport) L.; m. Craig Nicholson, 1996. BA, Hampshire Coll., 1977; PhD, Duke U., 1981. Lic. clin. psychologist. Clin. psychology intern Harvard U., Cambridge, Mass., 1981—82; sr. counselor Harvard U. Bur. Study Counsel, Cambridge, Mass., 1982—97; pvt. practice Cambridge, Mass., 1983—97; dir. psychol. svcs. Am. U., Washington, 1997—2005; dir. Bur. of Study Counsel Harvard U., 2005—. Vis. faculty Cambridge Coll., 1984, Kennedy Sch. Govt., Cambridge, 1985, 91; NIMH rsch. assoc. U. Mass., Amherst, 1989-91. Co-author: BLOCK, 1990; contbr. articles to psychology and edn. jours. Mem. APA, Am. Ednl. Rsch. Assn., Mass. Psychol. Assn. Office Phone: 617-495-2581.

LIPSON, ALLEN S., former entertainment company executive, lawyer; b. NYC, Dec. 15, 1942; BS, U. Wis., 1964; JD, Columbia U., 1967. Bar: N.Y. 1968, U.S. Dist. Ct. (so. dist.) N.Y. 1968, Conn. 1989. Assoc. Casey, Lane & Mittendorf, NYC, 1967-72; asst. gen. counsel Textron, Inc., Providence, 1972-77; corp. counsel BIC Corp., Milford, Conn., 1977-88; gen. counsel, v.p. adminstrn., sec. Remington Products, Inc., Bridgeport, Conn., 1988—96, v.p. adminstrn., gen. counsel, sec., 1996—99; exec. v.p. bus. & legal affairs, sec. Marvel Enterprises, Inc., NYC, 1999—2003, pres., CEO, 2003—05.

LIPSON, STEVEN MARK, virologist, microbiologist, environmental scientist, educator; b. Bklyn., May 25, 1948; s. Jonas and Ana (Rogers) L.; m. Heleen P. Bleiweiss, Apr. 25, 1971; children: Tracy J., Jennifer B. BS in Biology, L.I. U., 1967; MS in Microbiology and Marine Sci., C.W. Post Coll., 1972; PhD in Cell Biology and Microbiology, NYU, 1981. Cert. dir. in virology and immunology N.Y. State Dept. Health, in virology Am. Soc. Clin. Pathologists, lic. in biology and health edn. N.Y. State Dept. Edn.; cert. radioactive materials N.Y. State Dept. Health. Tchr. biology NYC HS Sys., 1967—74; rsch. assoc. hematology/oncology Bklyn. Hosp.-Caledonian Hosp., 1980-82; rsch. assoc. immunology lab. dept. neoplastic diseases Mt. Sinai Sch. Medicine, NYC, 1982-84; chief virology lab., assoc. dir. divsn. microbiology Nassau County Med. Ctr., East Meadow, NY, 1984-90; dir. virology lab., rsch. asst. prof. microbiology/medicine North Shore U. Hosp.-NYU Sch. Medicine, Manhasset, NY, 1990-00; acting dir. Flow Cytometry/Cellular Immunology Lab. North Shore U. Hosp.-NYC Sch. Medicine, Manhasset, NY, 1995-97; chief Virology Lab., Columbia-Presbyn. Med. Ctr., NYC, 2000; asst. prof. pathology Columbia U. Coll. Physicians and Surgeons, NYC, 2000; with Virology Cons., Inc., Bklyn., NYC, 2000—; prof. biology dept. St. Francis Coll., Bklyn. Heights, NY, 2002—. Adj. prof., L.I. U., NY, 1987—2001; asst. prof. dept. biology NYC Tech. Coll, CUNY, 2001—02; profl. adv. panel Med. Lab. Advisor, 1994—; tchg. hosp. edn. specialist clin. microbiology lab. dept. pathology SUNY, Stony Brook, 2001—05; rsch. scientist DVA, Northport, NY, 2001—02; cons. in clin. and applied virology and environ. sci., 1995—; invited reviewer grants rsch. profl. staff congress CUNY, 2004—; presenter, lectr. in field. Contbr.: Clinical Microbiology Procedures Manual (Virology), 1993, guest editl. bd. Clin. Rev. in Microbiology, 1995, Manual of Clin. Microbiology, 1995, Jour. Infectious Disease, Arch. Path. Lab. Med., European Jour. Epidemiology, mem. editl. bd.: Med. Sci. Monitor, assoc. editor: Diagnostic Microbiol. Infectious Disease; contbr. articles to profl. jours. Vol. lectr. Kiwanis Club, Long Island, 1985-90; vol. N.Y. Hall of Sci., Queens, 1996. Grantee, Am. Cranberry Inst., 2005. Mem.: Met. Assn. Col. Univ. Biology, Long Island Infectious Disease Soc., N.Y. Infectious Diseases Soc., Am. Soc. for Microbiology (nat. and N.Y. City br.), Ind. Order Odd Fellows (noble grand 2006—), Borough Park Lodge. Achievements include research in anti-viral compounds in plants, rapid viral diagnostics, mechanism of virus survival in soil and water. Avocations: fine dining, stamp collecting/philately, travel, motorcycling, scuba diving. Office: Biology Dept St Francis College 180 Remsen St Brooklyn NY 11201 Office Phone: 718-489-5210. Personal E-mail: montmor@aol.com.

LIPSTEIN, ROBERT A., lawyer; b. Wilmington, Del., Dec. 6, 1954; s. Eugene Joseph and Leona (Feld) L.; m. Cheryl A. Artibee-Wedlake, July 30, 1978; children: Rebecca Lynn, Matthew Wedlake. BA in Econs., Stanford U., 1975; JD, Stanford Law Sch., 1978. Bar: D.C. 1978, U.S. Dist. Ct. D.C., 1979, U.S. Ct. Appeals (D.C. cir.) 1980, U.S. Ct. Internat. Trade, 1984, U.S. Ct. Appeals (fed. cir.), U.S. Supreme Ct. 1990. Assoc. Morgan, Lewis & Bockius, Washington, 1978-84, Coudert Bros., Washington, 1984-86, ptnr., 1987-94; mng. ptnr. Lipstein, Jaffe & Lawson, L.L.P., 1994—2003; ptnr. Crowell & Moring LLP, 2003—. Mem. ABA (antitrust sect., law practice mgmt. sect.), D.C. Bar Assn., Phi Beta Kappa. Avocations: golf, tae kwon do (4th degree black belt). Home: 511 Stonington Rd Silver Spring MD 20902-1545 Office Phone: 202-624-2630. E-mail: rlipstein@crowell.com.

LIPTAK, ADAM, lawyer, reporter; b. Stamford, Conn., Sept. 2, 1960; s. Bela G. and Martha (Szacsvay) L.; m. Jennifer L. Bitman, June 7, 1986. Student, Columbia Coll., 1978-80, Eotvos Lorand, Budapest, 1980; BA, Yale U., 1984, JD, 1988. Bar: N.Y. 1988, U.S. Ct. Appeals (2d cir.) 1991, U.S. Ct. Appeals (11th cir.) 1995, U.S. Supreme Ct. 1992. Assoc. Cahill Gordon & Reindel, NYC, 1988-92; sr. counsel The New York Times Co., NYC, 1992—2002; nat. legal affairs reporter New York Times, 2002—. Contbr. articles to New Yorker, Vanity Fair, Rolling Stone, New York Observer, American Lawyer, Brill's Content, Annual Survey of American Law, Journal of Law & Policy. Home: 606 W 113th St Apt 2C New York NY 10025-7910 Office: The New York Times Co 229 W 43rd St New York NY 10036-3959 Office Phone: 212-556-1882. Business E-Mail: liptaka@nytimes.com.

LIPTON, BOB, music educator, composer; b. Montclair, NJ, July 7, 1954; s. Martin and Natalie Lipton; m. Hisayo Okano, July 28, 1991. MusB, San Francisco State U., 1991. Music educator Kennedy Mid. Sch., Cupertino, Calif., 1991—. Composer: (music for school orchs.) Tudo Bem, Novo Cetvorno. Named Outstanding Musical Grad., San Francisco State U., 1991. Mem.: Calif. Band Dirs. Assn., Am. String Tchrs. Assn., Music Educators Nat. Conf. Home Phone: 408-248-5221. Personal E-mail: bliptontuba@yahoo.com.

LIPTON, BRONNA JANE, marketing communications executive; b. Newark, May 10, 1951; d. Julius and Arlene (Davis) L.; m. Sheldon Robert Lipton, Sept. 23, 1984. BA in Spanish, Northwestern U., 1973. Cert. Zumba Instructor. Tchr. Spanish Livingston (N.J.) H.S., 1973-78; profl. dancer Broadway theater, film, TV, NYC, 1978-82; v.p., mgr. Hispanic mktg. svcs. Burson-Marsteller Pub. Rels., NYC, 1982-89; exec. v.p. Lipton Comm. Group, Inc., NYC, 1989-99, Latin Reports, 1996-99; v.p. Bienestar LCG Comm., Inc., 1999—2003; prin. Cmty. Direct, NYC, 2003—. Minority initiatives task force Am. Diabetes Assn., Alexandria, Va., 1987-90, pub. rels. com., 1990-91, visibility and image task force, 1991-92, bd. dirs. NY Downstate affiliate, chmn. visibility and image com., 1992-93. Mem. rev. panel Hispanic Designers, Inc. Recipient Pinnacle award Am. Women in Radio and TV (NY Chpt.), 1984, Value Added award Burson-Marsteller, NYC, 1982-84. Avocations: ballet, jazz dance, tennis, foreign travel, birding. Home: 1402 Chapel Hill Rd Mountainside NJ 07092-1405 Office Phone: 212-966-8222. Business E-Mail: blipton@gocommunitydirect.com.

LIPTON, CHARLES, public relations executive; b. NYC, May 11, 1928; s. Jack B. and Bertha (Lesser) Lipton; m. Audrey Williams, Nov. 11, 1951; children: Susan, Jack. AB, Harvard U., 1948. Market rschr. Cecil & Presbury, Inc., NYC, 1948—49; spl. events dir. 20th Century Fox Film Corp., NYC, 1949—52; account exec. Ruder & Finn, Inc., NYC, 1953—58, v.p., 1958—63, sr. v.p., 1963—69, vice-chmn., 1969—95; sr. counsel, bd. dirs., 1995—. Guest lectr. Boston U., 1967—68. Mem. coun. Ctr. for Vocat. Arts, Norwalk, Conn., 1966—74; treas., mem. exec. com. Norwalk Symphony Soc., 1972—85; chmn. parents coun. Washington U., St. Louis, 1976—77, trustee, 1977—; chmn. Wycliffe Charities Found., 1998—; trustee Norwalk Jewish Ctr., 1966—70. Mem.: Nat. Investor Rels. Inst., Nat. Emphysema Soc. (trustee), USIA (pub. rels., pvt. sector com. 1988—93), Internat. Pub. Rels. Assn., Am. Soc. Colon and Rectal Surgeons (trustee), Harvard Varsity Club, Harvard Club. Home: 4542 Hazleton Ln Wellington FL 33449-8633 Office: Ruder Finn Inc 301 E 57th St Fl 3 New York NY 10022-2900 Personal E-mail: audles@aol.com.

LIPTON, GLENN E., orthopaedic surgeon; b. Syracuse, NY, Apr. 26, 1970; BA in Biology, Temple U., 1993; MD, Temple U. Sch. Med., 2001. Lic. Pa., 2001. Resident Drexel U. Sch. Medicine, Phila.; clin. rschr. Dept. Orthop. Surgery Alfred I. duPont Inst., Wilmington, Del., 1993—97. Founder, dir. Ann. Student Orthop. Rsch. Fellowship, 2001; founder, pres. Brandywine Inst. Orthops., 2006. Contbr. chapters to books, articles to profl. jours. Mem.: AMA, Pa. Orthop. Soc., Phila. Orthop. Soc., Am. Acad. Orthop. Surgeons, Temple U. Surg. Soc., Temple Ambler Philanthropist Soc.

LIPTON, JOAN ELAINE, advertising executive; b. NYC, July 12, 1927; 1 child, David Dean. BA, Barnard Coll., 1948. With Young & Rubicam, Inc., NYC, 1948-52, Robert W. Orr & Assocs., NYC, 1952-57, Benton & Bowles, Inc., NYC, 1957-64; asso. dir. Benton & Bowles, Ltd., London, 1964-68; with McCann-Erickson, Inc. (advt. agy.), NYC, 1968-85, v.p., 1970-79, sr. v.p., creative dir., 1979-85; pres. Martin & Lipton Advt. Inc., 1985—. Mem. Bus. Coun. UN Decade Women, 1977-78; bd. vis. PhD program bus. CUNY, 1986—. Recipient Honors award Ohio U. Sch. Journalism, 1976, Matrix award, 1979, YWCA award women achievers, 1979, Clio Classic award; named Woman Yr., Am. Advt. Fedn., 1974, Advt. Woman Yr., 1984; named Matrix Hall Fame, 1998. Mem. Advt. Women NY (1st v.p. 1975-76, v.p. Found. 1977-78), Women's Forum (bd. dirs. 1988-90), Women Comm. (pres. NY chpt. 1974-76, named Nat. Headliner 1976). Office: 163 E 62nd St New York NY 10065 Office Phone: 212-832-3049.

LIPTON, LESTER, ophthalmologist, entrepreneur; b. NYC, Mar. 14, 1936; s. George and Rita (von Steinbaum) L.; m. Harriet Arfa, June 25, 1960; children: Sherri, Brandi, Shawn BA, NYU, 1959; MD, Chgo. Med. Sch, 1964. Rsch. fellow Chgo. Med. Sch., 1959-60; intern Brookdale Hosp. Ctr., Bklyn., 1964-65; resident Harlem Eye and Ear Hosp., NYC, 1965-68; assoc. attending Polyclinic French hosps., NYC, 1968-75; asst. attending physician, ophthalmologist, surg. instr. St. Clare's Hosp., NYC, 1975—; attending ophthalmologist Cabrini Med. Ctr., NYC, 1982—, St. Vincent's Hosp., NYC, 1995—. Founder Lipton Eye Clinic, N.Y.C., 1981—; v.p. Van Arfa Realty, N.Y.C., 1984-88; pres. H&L Realty, Suffern, N.Y., 1981—; mem. bd. dirs. Salisbury (Conn.) Pub. Health Nursing Assn. Mem. U.S. Congl. Adv. Bd.; mem. bd. deacons Congregationalist Ch. With AUS, 1956-58. Named Internat. Amigo, OAS; recipient Presdl. Citation for outstanding community svc., 1991 Mem. N.Y. Med. Soc., Am. Assn. Individual Investors, Bronx High Sch. Sci. Alumni Assn., Sharon Country Club, United Shareholders Assn., Internat. Platform Assn., Wider Quaker Fellowship, Vanderbilt U. Cabinet Club. Republican. Home: 55 Interlaken Estates Box 1923 Lakeville CT 06039 Mailing: PO Box 1923 Lakeville CT 06039 Office: Lipton Eye Clinic PO Box 1923 Lakeville CT 06039 Personal E-mail: hslipton@sbcglobal.net.

LIPTON, LOIS JEAN, lawyer; b. Chgo., Jan. 14, 1946; d. Harold and Bernice (Reiter) Farber L.; m. Peter Carey, May 30, 1978; children: Rachel, Sara. BA, U. Mich., 1966; JD summa cum laude, DePaul Coll. Law, Chgo., 1974; postgrad., Sheffield U., Eng., 1966. Bar: Ky. 1974, U.S. Dist. Ct. (we. dist.) Ky. 1974, U.S. Ct. Appeals (6th cir.) 1974, Ill. 1975, U.S. Dist. Ct. (no. dist.) Ill. 1975, U.S. Ct. Appeals (7th cir.) 1976. Staff counsel Roger Baldwin Found. of ACLU, Inc., Chgo., 1975-79, dir. reproductive rights project, 1979-83; atty. McDermott, Will & Emergy, Chgo., 1984-86, G.D. Searle, Skokie, Ill., 1988-90; sr. atty. AT&T, Chgo., 1990—. Del. White

House Conf. on Families, Mpls., 1980; chmn. elect Chgo. Found. for Women. Recipient Durfee award, 1984, Roger Baldwin Lifetime Achievement award 2004. Mem. ACLU (v.p.), ABA, Chgo. Coun. Lawyers. Office: AT&T # R15 222 W Adams St Chicago IL 60606-5017 Home Phone: 847-491-1850; Office Phone: 312-230-2667. Personal E-mail: llipton@att.com.

LIPTON, MARTIN, lawyer; b. Jersey City, June 22, 1931; s. Samuel D. and Fannie L.; m. Susan Lytle, Feb. 17, 1982; children: James, Margaret, Katherine, Samantha BS in Econs., U. Pa., 1952; LLB, NYU, 1955. Bar: N.Y. 1956. Founding ptnr., corp. dept. Wachtell Lipton Rosen & Katz, NYC, 1965—. Spl. counsel NYC, 1975—78, US Dept. Energy, 1979—80; acting gen. counsel US Synthetic Fuels Corp., 1980; counsel NY Stoc Exch. Com. on Mkt. Structure, Governance & Ownership, 1999—2000. Chmn. bd. trustees NYU 1998-; trustee NYU Sch. Law 1972-, chmn. 1988-98; mem. exec. com. Partnership for N.Y.C.; chmn. Legal Adv. Com., NYSE, 2002-04; bd. dirs. Inst. Jud. Adminstrn. Named one of 100 Most Influential Lawyers, Nat. Law Jour., 2006. Mem.: ABA, Assn. Bar City of N.Y., N.Y.C. Lawyers Assn., Am. Law Inst. (council mem.), Am. Acad. Arts and Scis. Office: Wachtell Lipton Rosen & Katz 51 W 52nd St Fl 29 New York NY 10019-6150 Office Phone: 212-403-1200. Office Fax: 212-403-2200. Business E-Mail: mlipton@wlrk.com.

LIPTON, ROBERT STEVEN, lawyer; b. NYC, May 12, 1946; s. Max and Mildred (Goodman) Lipton; m. Stephanie F. Kass, Aug. 8, 1971. BA, NYU, 1967, JD, 1971. Bar: NY 1972, US Ct. Appeals (2d cir.) 1972, US Dist. Ct. (so. dist.) NY 1973, US Supreme Ct. 1975. Assoc. Curtis, Mallet-Prevost, Colt, and Mosle, NYC, 1971—80, ptnr., 1980—2001, of counsel, 2001—05. Editor: NYU Law Rev., 1969—71. Mem.: ABA, NYC Bar Assn., NY State Bar Assn., Fed. Bar Coun., Phi Beta Kappa. Home Phone: 212-691-6962.

LIPTZIN, BENJAMIN, psychiatrist; b. NYC, Sept. 17, 1945; s. David Murray and Mollie (Brody) L.; m. Sharon Leslie Rothstein, June 10, 1968; children: Shoshanna, Daniel, Deborah. BA, Yale U., 1966; MD, U. Rochester, NYC, 1971. Diplomate Am. Bd. Psychiatry and Neurology. Resident in psychiatry U. Va. Hosp., Charlottesville, 1971-74; med. officer NIMH, Rockville, Md., 1974-78; dir. geriatric psychiatry McLean Hosp., Belmont, Mass., 1978-89, asst. gen. dir., 1989-90; chief dept. psychiatry Baystate Med. Ctr., Springfield, Mass., 1990—; prof., dep. chmn. dept. psychiatry Tufts U. Sch. Medicine, 1990—. Contbr. articles to profl. jours. With USPHS, 1972-78. Recipient Acad. award NIMH, 1983. Fellow Am. Psychiat. Assn. (trustee-at-large 1992-95); mem. AMA, Am. Coll. Psychiatrists, Am. Assn. Geriatric Psychiatry (sec., treas. 2007—), Group Advancement Psychiatry (chmn. com. aging). Democrat. Jewish. Office: Baystate Med Ctr Dept Psychiatry 759 Chestnut St Springfield MA 01199-1001 Office Phone: 413-794-4235. E-mail: benjamin.liptzin@bhs.org.

LIRO, JOSEPH R., diversified financial services company executive; BA in Monetary Econs., MA in Monetary Econs., Am. U.; PhD in Econs., Syracuse U., NY. Staff rschr. Fed. Res. Sys.; prof. Sch. Mgmt. U. Mass.; sr. economist Fin. Control Bd., 1984—86; chief economist S.G. Warburg & Co., 1986—95, CIBC Oppenheimer Corp., 1995—98; v.p. Stone & McCarthy Rsch. Assocs., Skillman, NJ, 1998—, equity strategist, 1998—. Office: Stone & McCarthy Rsch Assocs 101 Business Park Dr Skillman NJ 08558

LIS, DANIEL T., lawyer; b. Toledo, Aug. 20, 1946; s. John J. and Stella Lis; m. Nancy J. Wilson, May 17, 1974; children: Daniel, Jennifer, John. BS in Econs., John Carroll U., 1968; MBA in Fin., U. Toledo, 1971; JD, U. Detroit Mercy, 1976. Bar: Mich. 1976. Assoc. Douglas V. Austin & Assocs., Toledo, 1970-71; sr. v.p., sec., gen. counsel NBD Bank, Detroit, 1971; gen. counsel Bank One, Mich., 1987—2000; sr. v.p., gen. counsel, corp. sec. Kelly Services, Inc., Troy, Mich., 2004—. With U.S. Army, 1968-70, Vietnam. Mem. Mich. Bar Assn., Am. Corp. Counsel Assn. (regional dir. 1998—), Am. Soc. Corp. Secs. (regional pres. 1976). Home: 28953 King William Farmington Hills MI 48331 Office: Kelly Svcs 999 W Big Beaver Rd Troy MI 48084-4782

LIS, DAVID JOSEPH, priest; b. Toledo, Ohio, Sept. 18, 1950; s. Stanley Joseph and Helen Marie Lis. BA in Theology, St. Mary's Coll., Orchard Lake, 1972; MA in Religious Studies, U. Detroit, Mich., 1979; MDiv, St. John's Prov. Seminary, Plymouth, 1980. Roman Cath. priest Archdiocese of Detroit, 1980—86; warehouse supr. Directel, Columbus, 1986—93; traffic-distribution mgr. Internat. Computer Net, Newington, Va., 1993—95, Edwards Bros., Inc., Ann Arbor, Mich., 1995—98; rector St. John The Baptist Ch., Black Lick, Pa., 2000—02, St. Nicholas Ch., Burton, Mich., 2002—04, Holy Assumption Ch., Marblehead, Ohio, 2005—. Recipient Eagle Scout, Boys Scouts Am., 1996. Mem.: Danbury Clergy Assn. Orthodox. Avocations: sailing, reading, jogging, travel. Office: Holy Assumption Orthodox Ch 114 E Main St Marblehead OH 43440 Office Phone: 419-798-4591. Business E-Mail: holyassumptionmarblehead@verizon.net.

LISAK, ROBERT PHILIP, neurologist, researcher, educator; b. Bklyn., Mar. 17, 1941; s. Irving Arthur and Sylvia Lillian (Kadish) L.; m. Deena Freda Penchansky, Aug. 2, 1964; children: Ilene Ann, Michael Loren. BA, NYU, 1961; MD, Columbia U., 1965; MA (hon.), U. Pa., 1976. Diplomate Am. Bd. Neurology. Intern in medicine Montefiore Hosp. and Med. Ctr., Bronx, 1965-66; rsch. assoc. NIMH, Bethesda, Md., 1966-68; resident in medicine Bronx Mcpl. Med. Ctr., 1968-69; resident in neurology Hosp. of the U. of Pa., Phila., 1969-72; with Sch. of Medicine U. Pa., Phila., 1972-87, prof. neurology Sch. of Medicine, 1980-87, vice chmn. dept. neurology Sch. of Medicine, 1985-87; prof., chmn. dept. neurology Sch. of Medicine Wayne State U., Detroit, 1987—. Mem. adv. bd. Guillain-Barre Syndrome Internat., Wynnewood, Pa., 1985—; mem. med. adv. bd. Myasthenia Gravis Found., Mpls., 1988—, Nat. Multiple Sclerosis Soc., N.Y.C., 1988—. Co-author: Myasthenia Gravis, 1982; mem. editl. bd. Jour. Neuroimmunology, 1984-98, Muscle and Nerve Jour., 1981-86, 92-95, 98-2002, Neurology, 1981-86, Annals of Neurology, 1990-95, Jour. Peripheral Nervous Sys., 1995-2006, Clin. Neuropharm., 1997—; editor-in-chief Jour. Neurol. Sci., 1998—; contbr. articles to profl. jours. With USPHS, 1966-68. Fulbright rsch. scholar, London, 1978-79; recipient Disting. Teaching award U. Pa., 1985, Drs. award Myasthenia Gravis Found., 1991. Fellow Am. Acad. Neurology (sci. issues com. 1987-93); mem. Am. Neurol. Assn. (membership com. 1989-91, chmn. 1990-91, sci. program com. 1994-96, councillor 2002—), Internat. Soc. Neuroimmunology (exec. com. 1987-91, 95-2001, sec.-treas. 1991-95), Am. Assn. Immunologists, Soc. for Neurosci., Norwegian Neurol. Assn., Royal Soc. Medicine. Office: Wayne State U Sch Medicine 8DE-UHC 4201 St Antoine Detroit MI 48201 Home Phone: 248-646-2974. Business E-Mail: rlisak@med.wayne.edu.

LISANTI, MARK V., blogger, writer; b. Yonkers, NY, May 1974; BA, Georgetown Univ.; MFA, Emerson Coll., Boston. Blog host BunsenTV; blog editor Defamer.com, LA. Named Most Influential and Intimidating Gossip in Hollywood, LA mag., 2005; named one of Top 25 Web Celebs, Forbes mag., 2007. Address: care of Gawker Media 76 Crosby St New York NY 10012 E-mail: mark@defamer.com.*

LISBAKKEN, JAMES ROBERT, lawyer; b. Washington, June 25, 1945; s. Robert Benjamin and Genevieve Louise (Roberts) L.; m. Linda Jean Alvey, Jan. 2, 1982; children: Kelly, Benjamin. BS, Oreg. State U., 1967; JD, U. Oreg., 1975. Bar: Wash. 1975, U.S. Dist. Ct. Wash. 1975. Engr. Westinghouse Electric Nuclear Power Div., Monroeville, Pa., 1967-70; assoc. Perkins Coie, Seattle, 1975-81, ptnr., 1981-83; dir., exec. v.p., sec., gen. counsel Genetic Systems Corp., Seattle, 1983-85; ptnr., Bus. Law Practice Area Perkins Coie, Seattle, 1985—. Mem. Mcpl. League, Seattle, 1976-80; organizing com. Northwest Biotech. Series. Mem. ABA, Wash. Bar Assn., Seattle King County Bar Assn., Phi Delta Phi, Tau Beta Pi, Wash. Athletic Club. Republican. Presbyterian. Avocations: tennis, skiing, mountain climbing, sailing. Office: Perkins Coie 1201 Third Ave Ste 4800 Seattle WA 98101-3099 Office Phone: 206-359-8660. Office Fax: 206-359-9000. Business E-Mail: jlisbakken@perkinscoie.com.

LISBOA-FARROW, ELIZABETH OLIVER, public and government relations consultant; b. NYC, Nov. 25, 1947; d. Eleuterio and Esperanza Oliver; m. Jeffrey Lloyd Farrow, Dec. 31, 1980; 1 child, Hamilton Oliver Farrow; 1 stepchild, Maximillian Robbins Farrow. Student pvt. schs., N.Y.C. With Harold Rand & Co. and various other pub. rels. firms, NYC, 1966—75; dir. pub. rels. N.Y. Playboy Club and Playboy Clubs Internat., 1975—79; pres., CEO Lisboa Assocs., Inc., NYC, 1979—. Chmn., CEO The Oliver Group, Inc., 2006; chair svc. and quality oversight com. Carefirst Holding Co., 2007. Counselor Am. Woman's Devel. Corp. Sec. Nat. Acad. Concert and Cabaret Arts; mem. nat. adv. coun. SBA, 1980-81, apptd., 1994—; exec. dir. Variety Club of Greater Washington Children's Charity, Inc., 1985-90; bd. dirs. Variety Myoelectric Limb Bank Found., 1990-91, Comcast, 2001, Hispanic Radio Network, 2001, Group Hosp. and Med. Svcs., Inc. d/b/a Carefirst Blue Cross Blue Shield, 2005; mem. Hispanic Coll. Fund, 1995—, vice chair, 1996—, co-chair, 2005, chmn., 2006; chair bd. trustees Southeastern U., 1997-2004; mem. adv. bd. Indsl. Bank, N.A., 1996. Named Pub. Rels. Woman of Yr., Women in Pub. Rels., 1992, Empresaria del Milenio, Duodecimo Encuentro Empresarian, P.R., 2001, Hispanic Bus. Woman of Yr., Nat. Hispanic Bus. Coun., 1996, Hispanic of Yr. in Bus., La Nacion Newspaper, 1997, Entrepreneur of Yr., Hispanic Mag., 1999, Bus Woman of Yr., N.Y. State Hispanic Chambers Commerce; recipient Disting. award of Excellence, SBA, 1992, Women Bus. Enterprise award, U.S. Transp. Nat. Hwy. Transp. Safety Adminstrn., 1994, Civic Cmty. Achievement, Black Bus. and Profls. Network, 1999, Excellence in Entrepreneurship award, Dialogue on Diversity, Inc., 1995, Women of Distinction award, Nat. Conf. Coll. Women Student Leaders, 2000, Applause award, Women's Bus. Enterprise Nat. Coun., 2000, Imagen award, San Juan, P.R., 2001, Presdl. medal, Sistema U. Ana G. Mendez, U. Metropolitana, San Juan, 1999, Internat. Leadership award, Mex. Am. C. of C., 2001. Mem. U.S. Hispanic C. of C. (bd. dirs. 1998-2004, Nat. Hispanic Businesswoman of Yr. 1996, vice chair 1999, chair 2000-02), D.C. C. of C. (pres. 2000), Small Bus. Adv. Coun., U.S. C. of C. (Blue Chip Enterprise award 1993), Advt. Coun., Am. Heart Assn., Hispanic Bus. and Profl. Women's Assn., Ibero-Am. C. of C. (bd. dirs. 1993, v.p. 1995, pres. 1997, 1998, adv. chair 1999, Small Bus. award 1993, Corp. of Yr. award 2000), Nat. Edn. Assn. Found. (bd. dirs. 2004). Office: 5335 Wisconsin Ave NW Washington DC 20015 Home Phone: 301-718-4774; Office Phone: 202-293-2541. E-mail: elisboa@lisboa.com.

LISBON, ALAN, anesthesiologist, critical care physician; BS, Cornell U., Ithaca, NY, 1972; MD, NYU, NYC, 1976. Vice chmn. critical care Beth Israel Deaconess Med. Ctr., Boston, 2000—; assoc. prof. anaesthesia Harvard Med. Sch., Boston. Office: Beth Israel Deaconess Med Ctr 1 Deaconess Rd CC 470 Boston MA 02215 Office Phone: 617-754-2702.

LISENBY, DORRECE EDENFIELD, realtor; b. Sneads, Fla., Dec. 2, 1942; d. Neal McLendon and Linnie (McCroan) Edenfield; m. Wallace Lamar Lisenby, Nov. 18, 1961; children: Pamela Ann, Wallace Neal. BS in Tech. Bus. magna cum laude, Athens U., Ala., 1991. Stenographer State of Fla., Tallahassee and Miami, Fla., 1960-62, Gulf Oil Corp., Coral Gables, Fla., 1962-64, Gulf Power Co., Pensacola, Fla., 1965-68; loan svc. asst. First Fed. Savs. and Loan Assn., Greenville, SC, 1969-70; various real estate positions Greenville, 1978-85; adminstrv. asst. Charter Retreat Hosp., Decatur, Ala., 1986-91; broker/salesperson Ferrell Realty Plus, Inc., Tallahassee, 1995-2001; broker, owner Lisenby Realty, Inc., 2001—. Mem.: P.E.O. Sisterhood, Tallahasee C. of C., Econ. Club Fla., Tallahassee Symphony Soc., Killearn Ladies Club (pres.), Taylor's Garden Club (prs. Taylor's chpt. 1975—76), Avondale Forest Cmty. Club (pres. Taylors, S.C. chpt. 1969), Am. Legion (Citizenship award 1957). Republican. Baptist. Avocations: reading, music, bridge, gardening. Home: 2925 Shamrock St S Tallahassee FL 32309-3226 Office Phone: 850-383-7567. Business E-Mail: dorrece@lisenbyrealty.com.

LISENBY, TERRY S., manufacturing executive; BS, U. NC, 1976. Mgr. fin. acctg. Nucor Corp., Charlotte, NC, 1985—91, v.p., corp. contr., 1991-2000, exec. v.p., treas., CFO, 2000—. Office: Nucor Corp 1915 Rexford Rd Charlotte NC 28211 Office Phone: 704-366-7000. Office Fax: 704-362-4208.*

LISHER, JAMES RICHARD, lawyer; b. Aug. 28, 1947; s. Leonard B. and Mary Jane (Rafferty) L. AB, Ind. U., 1969, JD, 1975. Bar: Ind. 1975, US Dist. Ct. (so. dist.) Ind. 1975, US Supreme Ct. 2000. Assoc. Rafferty & Wood, Shelbyville, Ind., 1975, Rafferty & Lisher, Shelbyville, Ind., 1976-77; dep. prosecutor Shelby County Prosecutor's Office, Shelbyville, 1976-78; ptnr. Yeager, Lisher & Baldwin, Shelbyville, 1977-96; pvt. practice Shelbyville, 1996—. Pros. atty. Shelby County, Shelbyville, 1983-95, pub. defender, 1995—, chief pub. defender, 2000—. Speaker, faculty advisor Ind. Pros. Sch., 1986. Editor: (manual) Traffic Case Defenses, 1982, First Law Office, 1998. Bd. dirs. Girls Club of Shelbyville, 1979-84, Bears of Blue River Festival, Shelbyville, 1982-2002; pres. Shelby County Internat. Rels. Coun., 1997-2003. With USNR, 1969—75. Recipient Citation of Merit, Young Lawyers Assn. Mem. ITLA, VFW, Nat. Assn. Criminal Def. Lawyers, Ind. Pub. Defender Assn., Ind. State Bar Assn. (bd. dirs. young lawyer sect. 1979-83, bd. dirs. gen. practice sect. 1996-98, treas. 1997-98, vice-chmn. 1998-99, chmn. 2000-01), Shelby County Bar Assn. (sec.-treas. 1986, v.p. 1987, pres. 1988), Ind. Prosecuting Attys. Assn. (bd. dirs. 1985-95, sec.-treas. 1987, v.p. 1988, pres. 1987-90), Masons, Lions. Home: 106 Western Trce Shelbyville IN 46176-9765 Office: 406S Harrison St Shelbyville IN 46176-2170 Office Phone: 317-392-2500. Personal E-mail: vettelaw@sbcglobal.net.

LISHER, JOHN LEONARD, lawyer; b. Indpls., Sept. 19, 1950; s. Leonard Boyd and Mary Jane (Rafferty) L.; m. Mary Katherine Sturmon, Aug. 17, 1974. BA in History with honors, Ind. U., 1975, JD, 1975. Bar: (Ind.) 1975. Dep. atty. gen. State of Ind., Indpls., 1975-78; asst. corp. counsel City of Indpls., 1978-81; assoc. Osborn & Hiner, Indpls., 1981-86; ptnr. Osborn, Hiner & Lisher, P.C., 1986—. Pres. Brendonwood Common Inc.; asst. vol. coord. Marion County Rep. Com., Indpls., 1979-80; vol. Don. Bogard for Atty. Gen., Indpls., 1980, Steve Goldsmith for Prosecutor, Indpls., 1979-83, Mayflower Classic, Indpls., 1981-86. Recipient Outstanding Young Man of Am. award Jaycees, 1979, 85, Indpls. Jaycees, 1980. Mem. ABA, Ind. Bar Assn., Indpls. Bar Assn. (membership com.), Assn. Trial Lawyers Am., Ind. U. Alumni Assn., Hoosier Alumni Assn. (charter, founder, pres.), Ind. Trial Lawyers Assn., Ind. Def. Lawyers Assn., Ind. U. Coll. Arts and Scis. (bd. dirs. 1983-92, pres. 1986-87), Wabash Valley Alumni Assn. (charter), Founders Club, Pres. Club, Phi Beta Kappa, Eta Sigma Phi, Phi Eta Sigma, Delta Xi Alumni Assn. (Outstanding Alumnus award 1975, 76, 79, 83), Delta Xi Housing Corp. (pres.), Pi Kappa Alpha (midwest regional pres. 1977-86, parliamentarian nat. conv. 1982, del. convs. 1978-80, 82, 84, 86, trustee Meml. Found. 1986-91, 2004—). Presbyterian. Avocations: reading, golf, jogging, roman coin collecting. Home: 5725 Hunterglen Rd Indianapolis IN 46226-1019 Office: Osborn Hiner & Lisher PC 8500 Keystone Xing Ste 480 Indianapolis IN 46240-2460 Office Phone: 317-257-2400. Business E-Mail: jlisher@ohllaw.com.

LISI, MARY M., federal judge; BA, U. RI, 1972; JD, Temple U., 1977. Tchr. history Prout Meml. High Sch., Wakefield, RI, 1975—76; law clk. US Atty., Providence, 1976, U.S. Atty., Phila., 1976—77; asst. pub. defender RI Office Pub. Defender, 1977—81; asst. child adv. Office Child Adv., 1981—82; pvt. practice atty. Providence, 1981—82; dir. office ct. apptd. spl. adv. RI Family Ct., 1982—87; dep. counsel office disciplinary counsel RI Supreme Ct., 1988—90, chief disciplinary counsel, 1990—94; U.S. Dist. judge Dist. Ct., Providence; US Dist. judge Dist. RI (1st cir.), Providence, 1994—. Mem. Select Com. to Investigate Failure of R.I. Share and Deposit Indemnity Corp., 1991-92. Recipient Providence 350 award, 1986, Meritorious Svc. to Children of Am. award, 1987. Office: Fed Bldg and US Courthouse 1 Exchange Ter Providence RI 02903-1744

LISIO, DONALD JOHN, historian, educator; b. Oak Park, Ill., May 27, 1934; s. Anthony and Dorothy (LoCelso) Lisio; m. Suzanne Marie Swanson, Apr. 22, 1958; children: Denise Anne, Stephen Anthony. BA, Knox Coll., 1956; MA, Ohio U., 1958; PhD, U. Wis., 1965. Mem. faculty overseas div. U. Md., 1958-60; from asst. prof. history to prof. emeritus Coe Coll., Cedar Rapids, Iowa, 1964—2002, prof. emeritus, 2002—. Author: (book) The President and Protest: Hoover, Conspiracy, and the Bonus Riot, 1974, Hoover, Blacks, and Lily-Whites: A Study of Southern Strategies, 1985; contbg. author: book The War Generation, 1975; contbr. articles to hist. jours. Mem. exec. com. Cedar Rapids Com. Hist. Preservation, 1975—77. With US Army, 1958—60. Fellow William F. Vilas Rsch., U. Wis., 1963—64, NEH, 1969—70, Rsch., 1984—85, Am. Coun. Learned Socs., 1977—78; grantee, 1971—72, Rsch., U.S. Inst. Peace, 1990. Mem.: AAUP, Am. Hist. Assn., Orgn. Am. Historians, Rancho Bernardo Rotary Club. Roman Catholic. Home Phone: 858-676-1226.

LISKO (DOZER), BONNIE LEE, education educator; b. Zanesville, Ohio, Dec. 15, 1924; d. Carl Raymond Dozer and Luanna Faye Swingle; m. Andrew Lisko, Aug. 1, 1953; children: Karen Luann, Daniel Andrew, Margaret Lee. BA, Capital U., Columbus, Ohio, 1946; MA in Sch. Langs., Middlebury Coll., Vt., 1952. Cert. tchr. Ohio, 1946. Tchr. French I, II, English I, II, Sci., drama Bryan HS, Yellow Springs, Ohio, 1946—47; tchr. French, Spanish, ESL, dean of women Concordia Jr. Coll., Bronxville, NY, 1947—51; tchr. French and Spanish, head resident Berea (Ky.) Coll., 1951—52; asst. dean of women, tchr. modern lang. dept. Capital Univ., Columbus, Ohio, 1952—87; pvt. French tchr. Interpreter Gov. Richard Celeste, Country Club, Cols. and Pres. of Senegal, 1987. Recipient award, Am. Luth. Ch., 1942, French Govt. to Middlebury Sch. French, 1948, Fulbright award, 1952. Mem.: AAUP (state pre.), Am. Assn. Tchrs. French (pres.). Presbyterian. Avocations: reading, swimming, fishing. Home: 805 Pleasant Ridge Ave Columbus OH 43209 Office: Campus Learning Ctr Modern Lang Dept Columbus OH 43209 Home (Summer): RR #1 Peterborough ON Canada K9J 6X2

LISKOW, FREDERIC CULLEN (RIC), printing company executive; b. Apr. 26, 1960; m. Beth Liskow; 5 children. B in Polit. sci., Rice U., 1982; JD, So. Meth. U. With Jenkens & Gilchrist, PC, Ins. Group, Ft. Worth; sr. v.p., gen. counsel Citigroup's Am. Health and Life, Citigroup, Inc./Assocs. First Capital Corp., 1993—2002; with Kinko's, Dallas, 2002—, sr. v.p., gen. counsel, sec., 2003—. Office: Kinkos 13155 Noel Rd Ste 1600 Dallas TX 75240

LISLE, LAURIE, author; b. Providence, Sept. 11, 1942; d. Laurence Lisle and Adeline Cole Simonds; m. Robert I. Kipniss, Dec. 17, 1994. BA in English, Ohio Wesleyan U., 1965. Rschr. Newsweek mag., NYC, 1970-78; assoc. prof. Southampton Coll. of L.I. U., 1981-82; ind. scholar So. Conn. Libr. Coun., Hamden, 1989—2002; spkr. N.Y. Coun. for the Humanities, NYC, 2000—02. Author: Portrait of an Artist: A Biography of Georgia O'Keeffe, 1980, Louise Nevelson: A Passionate Life, 1990, Without Child: Challenging the Stigma of Childlessness, 1996, Four Tenths of an Acre: Reflections on a Gardening Life, 2005. Mem.: The Authors Guild, The Century Assn., Am. Pen Ctr. Democrat. Unitarian Universalist. Mailing: PO Box 1067 Sharon CT 06069 Personal E-mail: llisle@ix.netcom.com.

LISOVICZ, NEDRA FORD, director; d. George Tarleton and Marguerite Slade Ford; m. Robert Paul Lisovicz, Sept. 9, 1972; children: Jason Paul, Loren Nichole. BA in Pers. Mgmt., U. So. Miss., Hattiesburg, 1986, MPH, 1986, PhD, 2004. Cert. Nat. Commn. Health Edn. Credentialing, Inc., 1995. Billing specialist So. Miss. Elec. Power Assn., 1974—95; program coord. Cmty. Health Advisor Network, Hattiesburg, 1996—97; dir. regional cancer control Am. Cancer Soc., Hattiesburg, 1997—99; dir. tng. Ctr. Sustainable Health Outreach, Hattiesburg, 1999—2005; program mgr. Morehouse Sch. Medicine Comprehensive Cancer Ctr. Partnership U. Ala., Birmingham, Ala., 2006—. Site dir. working well project M.D. Anderson Cancer Ctr., Hattiesburg, 1993—95. Contbr. articles to profl. jours. Mem. spkrs. bur. Susan B. Komen Cancer Found. Recipient, Com. Resources & Svcs. Women, U. So. Miss., 1999, Disting. Alumni award, Coll. Health & Human Scis., U. So Miss., 2002; fellow, M.D. Anderson Cancer Ctr., 1995; grantee, NIH, 2005. Mem.: Gamma Beta Phi. Republican. Office: U Alabama at Birmingham 1717 11th Ave South Birmingham AL 35294 Office Phone: 205-996-2850. Office Fax: 205-996-2974. Business E-Mail: lisovicz@uab.edu.

LISS, NORMAN, lawyer; b. NYC, May 7, 1932; m. Sandra Hirsch, Feb. 28, 1959. BS, NYU, 1952, LLB, 1955. Bar: N.Y. 1955, U.S. Dist. Ct. (so. dist.) N.Y. 1961, U.S. Supreme Ct. 1961, U.S. Dist. Ct (ea. dist.) N.Y. 1962. Assoc. Booth, Lipton & Lipton, New York, 1956-57, Seymour Detsky, New York, 1957-58; pvt. practice New York, 1958—. Cons. to Portugal Re-Cultural Events in U.S.; jour. chair UJA Trial Lawyers USCG Acad. Law Day, 1987, 89, 94, 98. Contbr. articles to profl. jours. Chmn. Bronx County Bar divsn. United Jewish Appeal, Hist. Documents Exhbn., Operation Sail, 1986, USCG Acad. Law Day, 1987, 89; chmn. devel. Ellis Island Restoration Commn.; counsel N.Y. State Statue of Liberty Centennial Com., Mayor's Handicapped Citizens Adv. Bd., N.Y.C., Coun. on Arts; mem. Bronx County 350 Commn., N.Y.C. Commn. for Presdl. Conv.; rep., counsel N.Y.C. Com. on Bicentennial of U.S. Constitution; cons. Soc. Congl. Medal of Honor; commd. lt. col. N.Y. Guard Judge Advocate Gen. Unit; exec. com. Am. Jewish Congress; trustee Am. Jewish Hist. Soc.; Def. of Liberty 9/11, N.Y. Recipient Disting. Humanitarian award Inst. Applied Human Dynamics, Meritorious Pub. Svc. award USCG, 1989, 9/11 Def. of Liberty medal NY Guard; named Man of Yr. Am. Jewish Congress, Man of Yr. Kinneret Sch., 1985. Mem. ABA, N.Y. Bar Assn., Bronx County Bar Assn., Am. Arbitration Assn. (panel arbitrators), Assn. Trial Lawyers Am., Law Day Outreach Com., NYU Alumni Assn. (adv. coun.). Home: 2727 Palisade Ave Bronx NY 10463-1018 Office: 200 W 57th St New York NY 10019-3211 Office Phone: 212-586-6165. Business E-Mail: lisslaw@earthlink.net.

LISS, WILLIAM J., lawyer; b. LA, Jan. 29, 1971; BA in English, Ohio U., 1993; JD, U. Cin., 1997; LLM in Taxation, U. Fla., 1999. Bar: Ohio 1997, Nev. 1998, US Dist. Ct. Southern Dist. Ohio 1998, Fla. 1999, US Tax Ct. Assoc. Santen & Hughes, Cin. Named one of Ohio's Rising Stars, Super Lawyers, 2006. Mem.: Ohio State Bar Assn., Cin. Bar Assn., Phi Beta Kappa. Office: Santen & Hughes Ste 3100 312 Walnut St Cincinnati OH 45202 Office Phone: 513-721-4450. Office Fax: 513-721-0109.

LISSAUER, JACK JONATHAN, astronomy educator; b. San Francisco, Mar. 25, 1957; s. Alexander Lissauer and Ruth Spector. SB in Math., MIT, Cambridge, 1978; PhD in Applied Math., U. Calif., Berkeley, 1982. NAS-NRC resident rsch. assoc. NASA-Ames Rsch. Ctr., Moffett Field, Calif., 1983-85; asst. rsch. astronomer U. Calif., Berkeley, Calif., 1985, vis. rschr. dept. physics Inst. for Theoretical Physics Santa Barbara, Calif.,

1985-87; asst. prof. astronomy program dept. earth and space sci. SUNY, Stony Brook, 1987-93, assoc. prof., 1993-96; space scientist NASA Ames Rsch. Ctr., 1996—. Rep. Univs. Space Rsch. Assn., SUNY, Stony Brook, 1987-96; vis. scholar dept. planetary sci. and lunar and planetary lab. U. Ariz., Tucson, 1990; guest prof. dept. physics U. Paris VII et Observatoire Paris, Meudon, France, 1990; mem. Lunar and Planetary Geoscis. Rev. Panel, 1989, 91, 99, mem. outer planets rsch. program rev. panel, 2005-06; vis. asst. rsch. physicist Inst. for Theoretical Physics, U. Calif., Santa Barbara, 1992, organizer Program on Plant Formation, 1992; rsch. assoc. Inst. d'Astrophysique, Paris, 1993; vis. scholar dept. astronomy U. Calif., Berkeley, 1994-95; adj. assoc. prof. SUNY, Stony Brook, 1996-2002; Yuval Ne'eman Disting. lectr. geophysics, atmosphere and space sci. Tel Aviv U., 2001, cons. prof. dept. geology and environ. sci. Stanford U., 2002—. Textbook author "Planetary Sciences" Cambridge Univ. Press; Planetary sci. editor New Astronomy Reviews; contbr. numerous articles on planet and star formation, extrasolar planets, spiral density wave theory, rotation of planets and comets to profl. jour. including Nature, Astron. Jour., Icarus, Sci., Astrophys. Jour. Letters, Astrophys. Jour., Jour. Geophys. Rsch., Astron. Astrophysics, Ann. Rev. Astron. Astrophysics, Revs. of Modern Physics. Recipient Spot Beam award Calif. Space Authority, 2006; NASA Grad. student fellow, 1981-82, Alfred P. Sloan Found. fellow, 1987-91, NASA Ames Assoc. fellow, 2007. Mem. Am. Astronomical Assn. (divsn. planetary sci., divsn. dynamical astronomy, Harold C. Urey prize divsn. planetary sci. 1992), Internat. Astronomical Union, Am. Geophys. Union. Achievements include research in planetary accretion, extrasolar planets, dynamics of planetary rings, cratering, binary and multiple star systems, circumstellar disks, resonances and chaos. Office: NASA Ames Rsch Ctr Space Sci Astrobiology Divsn 245-3 Moffett Field CA 94035 Business E-Mail: lissauer@galileo.arc.nasa.gov.

LISSKA, ANTHONY JOSEPH, humanities educator, philosopher; b. Columbus, Ohio, July 23, 1940; s. Joseph Anthony and Florence (Wolfel) L.; m. Marianne Hedstrom, Mar. 16, 1968; children: Megan Catherine, Elin Elizabeth. BA in Philosophy cum laude, Providence Coll., 1963; AM in Philosophy, St. Stephen's Coll., Dover, Mass., 1967; PhD in Philosophy, Ohio State U., 1971; Cert., Harvard U., Cambridge, 1979. Asst. prof. Denison U., Granville, Ohio, 1969—76, assoc. prof., 1976—81, dean of coll., 1978—83, prof. philosophy, 1981—, dir. honors program, 1987—2002, Charles and Nancy Brickman disting. svc. chair, 1998—2001, Maria Theresa Barney chair in philosophy, 2004—. Project reviewer NEH, Washington, 1979-90, evaluator; adv. bd. Midwest Faculty Seminar, Chgo., 1981-90; vis. scholar U. Oxford, Eng., 1984; mem. scholarship com. Sherex Chem. Co., Dublin, Ohio, 1984-92; cons. Franklin Pierce Coll., Ringe, N.H., 1991, Hampden-Sydney Coll., Va., 1998, Luther Coll., 2005; referee various philosophy jours.; lectr. in field. Author: Philosophy Matters, 1977, Aquinas's Theory of Natural Law, 1996, paperback edit. 1997, 2002, Illustrated History of Buckeye Lake Yacht Club, 2007; co-editor: The Historical Times, 1988—, Bi-centennial History of Granville, 2004; contbr. numerous articles to profl. jours., chpts. to books. Bd. mgmt. Granville Hist. Soc., 1987-2002; precinct rep. Dem. Party, Granville, 1994—; convener Civil War Roundtable, Granville, 1989-95; v.p. The Granville Found., 2003-, pres. 2004; mem. Granville Bicentennial Commn., 1996-2006. Named Carnegie Prof. of Yr., Carnegie Found., 1994; recipient Sears Found. Teaching award, 1990, Historian of Yr. award, 2005; NEH grantee, 1973, 77, 85; R.C. Good fellow, 1990, 96, 02. Mem. Am. Philos. Assn. (program com. 2003, Tchg. award 1994), Am. Cath. Philos. Assn. v.p., 2004-05, pres., 2005-06), Nat. Collegiate Honors Coun., Soc. for Ancient Greek Philosophy, Soc. for Medieval and Renaissance Philosophy, Internat. Thomas Aquinas Soc., Phi Beta Kappa. Democrat. Roman Catholic. Avocations: history, photography. Home: 285 Burtridge Rd Granville OH 43023-1214 Office: Denison U Dept Philos Knapp Hall Granville OH 43023 Office Phone: 740-587-5616. Business E-Mail: lisska@denison.edu.

LIST, ERICSON JOHN, environmental engineering science educator, consultant; b. Whakatane, New Zealand, Mar. 27, 1939; came to U.S., 1962; s. Ericson Bayliss and Freda Helen (Sunkel) L.; m. Olive Amoore, Feb. 3, 1962; children: Brooke Meredith, Antonia Michael. B.E. with honors, U. Auckland, New Zealand, 1961, B.Sc., M.E., U. Auckland, New Zealand, 1962; PhD, Calif. Inst. Tech., 1965. Registered profl. engr., Calif., S.C., N.C., Ga., Fla., Nev. Sr. lectr. U. Auckland, 1966-69; asst. prof. Calif. Inst. Tech., Pasadena, 1969-72, assoc. prof., 1972-78, prof. environ. engring. sci., 1978-97, exec. officer, 1980-85, prof. emeritus, 1997; with Flow Sci. Inc., Pasadena, 1997—. Bd. dirs. Environ. Def. Scis., Pasadena; bd. chmn. Flow Sci. Inc., Pasadena, 1983-; cons. So. Calif. Edison, Rosemead, Calif., 1973-, City and County of San Francisco, 1974-. Author: (with Hugo B. Fischer et al), Mixing in Inland and Coastal Waters, 1979, (with W. Rodi) Turbulent Jets and Plumes, 1982, (with Roscoe Moss Co.) Handbook of Ground Water Development, 1990. Mem. Blue Ribbon Commn. City of Pasadena, 1976-78. Recipient Spl. Creativity award NSF, 1982 Fellow ASCE (life, editor Jour. Hydraulic Engring. 1984-89, Athenaeum (Pasadena) (chmn. wine com. 1981-83). Office: Flow Sci Inc 723 E Green St Pasadena CA 91101-2111 Home: 196 Wandolea Dr Mount Pleasant SC 29464-2524 Home Phone: 843-388-8044; Office Phone: 843-856-8925. Business E-Mail: ejlist@flowscience.com.

LISTENGART, JOSEPH, lawyer, energy executive; b. June 2, 1968; BA in Econs., Stanford U., 1990; JD magna cum laude, Boston U., 1994, MBA, 1995. Atty. Hitchens, Wheeler & Dittmar, 1995—98; v.p., gen. counsel Kinder Morgan Energy Ptnrs., Houston, 1999—2001, v.p., gen. counsel, sec., 2001—. Office: Kinder Morgan Energy Ptnrs 500 Dallas St Houston TX 77002*

LISTER, EARLE EDWARD, retired research executive; b. Harvey, NB, Can., Apr. 14, 1934; s. Earle Edward and Elizabeth Hazel (Coburn) L.; m. Teresa Ann Moore, June 4, 1983. BSc in Agriculture, McGill U., Montreal, Can., 1955, MSc in Animal Nutrition, 1957; PhD in Animal Nutrition, Cornell U., 1960. Feed nutritionist Ogilvie Flour Mills, Montreal, 1960—65; rsch. scientist rsch. br. Animal Rsch. Ctr. Agriculture Can., Ottawa, 1965—74, dep. dir. rsch. br. Animal Rsch. Ctr., 1974—78, program specialist ctrl. region rsch. br., 1978—80, dir. gen. Atlantic region rsch. br. Halifax, N.S., Canada, 1980—85, dir. gen. plant health and plant products and pesticides, food prodn. and inspection br. Ottawa, 1985—87, dir. rsch. br. Animal Rsch. Ctr., 1987—91; dir. Ctr. Food and Animal Rsch., 1991—92; cons., 1992—2001; chmn. Can. Found. for Conservation Farm Animal Genetic Resources, 1996—; hon. dir. Can. Farm Animal Genetic Resource Found. Presenter seminars in India, Hong Kong, Taiwan; mem. Can. del. to gen. FAO meetings. Co-chmn. United Way/Health Ptnrs. for Agriculture Can., Ottawa, 1991; former dir. N.S. Inst. Agrologists. McGill U. scholar, 1953-55; recipient Nat. Rsch. Coun. Post Grad. Spl. scholarship Cornell U., 1957-59. Fellow: Agrl. Inst. Can.; mem.: Ont. Inst. Agrologists, Can. Soc. Animal Sci. (life; former dir.). Achievements include research in the determination of nutrient requirements of beef cattle, determination of protein and energy levels and appropriate sources of nutrients for dairy calves; development of intensive feeding system for raising high quality beef from Holstein male calves. Home: 6929 Lakes Pk Dr Greely ON Canada K4 P1M6 E-mail: elister@rogers.com.

LISTER, GEORGE, pediatrician; b. Miami, May 8, 1947; BA in psychology/religious studies, Brown U., 1969; MD, Yale U. Sch. Medicine, 1973. Intern Yale-New Haven Hosp., 1973—74, resident in pediat., 1974—75; fellow in pediat. cardiology and neonatology U. Calif., 1975—78; asst. to full prof. pediat. and anesthesiology Yale U. Sch. Medicine, 1978—2003, section chief pediat. critical care medicine, 1978—2003, dir. pediat. intensive care unit, 1978—2003; Robert L. Moore chair pediat. and prof. pediat. Southwestern Med. Sch., Dallas, 2003—. Former editor-in-chief Pediat. Rsch.; sr. editor Rudolph's Pediat.; editor Rudolph's Pediat. Online. Named one of Best Doctors Am., 1992; recipient Established Investigator award, Am. Heart Assn., 1985; fellow, Fulbright. Mem.: Am. Bd. Pediat. (past chair), Soc. Pediat. Rsch. (past pres., Maureen Andrew Mentor award 2004), Internat. Pediat. Rsch. Found., Am. Pediat. Soc., Am. Acad. Pediat. (Disting. Career award, section on critical care 1999). Office: UT Southwestern Med Ctr Dallas Pediat 5323 Harry Hines Blvd Dallas TX 75390-9063 Office Phone: 214-648-3563.

LISTER, GRAEME GEORGE, physicist, journalist; b. Melbourne, Victoria, Australia, Jan. 30, 1945; s. Leslie Charles and Betty Margaret Lister; m. Ilse Margarete Weikmann, June 22, 1990; 1 child, Elisabeth Tonia. BS, U. Melbourne, Australia, 1965, MS, 1967; PhD, Flinders U., Adelaide, Australia, 1970. Sr. scientist Thorn EMI, London, 1990—95; staff scientist Osram Sylvania Inc., Beverly, Mass., 1995—. Vis. prof. U. Salford, 1995—2000; industry rep. physics Edn. and Tng. Com., Sci. Edn. and Tng. Com., Sci. and Materials Bd., SERC, London, 1991—94; sec. Plasma and Ion Surface Engring., 1993—94; vice chmn. Plasma Sci. and Technique Divsn., Inernat. Union for Vacuum Sci., Technique and Applications, 1995—98. Mem.: Inst. Physics (group com. mem. 1990—95). Office: Osram Sylvania Inc 71 Cherry Hill Dr Beverly MA 01915 Home Phone: 978-468-6192; Office Phone: 978-750-1514. E-mail: graeme.lister@sylvania.com.

LISTER, HARRY JOSEPH, financial company consultant; b. Teaneck, NJ, Jan. 27, 1936; s. Harry and Arline L.; m. Erika Anna Maria Englisch, Sept. 3, 1960; children: Harry Joseph Jr., Karen P. Lister Lawson, Leslie M. Lister Fidler, Andrea A. Lister Lytle, Michael P. BS in Fin. and Econs., Lehigh U., 1958. Rsch. analyst Hugh W. Long and Co., 1958, Calvin Bullock, Ltd., NYC, 1959-61, assoc. dir. estate planning, 1961-65, dir. estate planning, 1965—72, asst. v.p., 1969-72; v.p. N.Y. Venture Fund, Inc., NYC, 1970-72; registered rep. Johnston, Lemon & Co., Inc., Washington, 1972—2004, from v.p. to sr. v.p., 1978—90; from v.p. to pres., CEO Wash. Mgmt. Corp., 1972—2004, also bd. dirs.; pres., dir. JL Fin. Svcs., Inc., Washington, 1975-90; from v.p. to pres., CEO to vice chmn. Washington Mut. Investors Fund, Inc., Washington, 1972—2004; pres., vice chmn. Growth Fund of Washington, Inc. (now JP Morgan Value Opportunities Fund), 1985—2005; vice chmn., pres., CEO Washington Funds Distbrs., Inc., 1985—93. Former pres., vice chmn. bd. trustees Tax Exempt Fund Md. and Tax Exempt Fund Va., 1986-2005; vice chmn., bd. dirs. Washington Investment Advisers, Inc., 1991-2001; cons. Johnston, Lemon Group, Inc., 2004—, Capital Group, Inc., L.A., 1972-2002; regent Coll. for Fin. Planning, Denver, 1979-84, exec. com., 1980-84, chmn. bd. regents, 1981-83. Author: Your Guide to IRAs and 14 Other Retirement Plans, 1985. Bd. dirs. ctrl. Bergen chpt. ARC, Hackensack, N.J., 1968-72, chmn. exec. com., 1970-72; bd. dirs. Westwood (N.J.) Planning Bd., 1969-72, vice chmn., 1970-72; bd. dirs. Westwood Zoning Bd. Adjustment, 1970-72; bd. dirs. ICI Edn. Found., 1996-2006, chmn., 1997-2006. Mem.: Nat. Assn. Securities Dealers, Inc. (investment cos. com. 1984—87, bd. arbitrators 1987—98), Investment Co. Inst. (pension com., chmn. 1976—81, tax com., rsch. com., dirs. svc. com.), Mt. Vernon Ladies Assn. (mem. adv. com. 2001—), Lowes Island Club, Univ. Club, Met. Club.

LISTER, THOMAS EDWARD, lawyer; b. Columbus, Ohio, Apr. 19, 1948; s. Richard Elwyn and Jean (Nelson) L.; m. Sarah Gray Robinson, July 25, 1970; children: Matthew Thomas, Joshua Capps. BA, DePauw U., 1970; JD, U. Wis., 1973. Bar: Wis. 1973, U.S. Dist. Ct. (we. dist.) Wis. 1973. V.p. Coll. Mktg. and Rsch. Corp., Indpls., 1969-70; staff criminal appeals unit Wis. Dept. Justice, 1971-73; ptnr. Sherman, Stutz & Lister, Black River Falls, Wis., 1973-83; dist. atty. Jackson County, Wis., Black River Falls, 1975-80, corp. counsel, 1975-78; mem. firm Stutz & Lister, S.C., Black River Falls, 1983—. Guest lectr. U. Wis., Madison, 1988; pres. Wis. Global Tech. Ltd., 1992—; chmn. ThermoSense Co., LLC, 1998—; vice chmn., dir., v.p. legal affairs Hyperformance Materials, Inc., Greensboro, N.C.; corp. dir. Lunda Constrn. Co., Black River Falls, Wis., 2000—; apptd. ct. commr., Jackson County, Wis., 2006. Chmn. S.W. Coun. on Criminal Justice, 1979-82; mem. Wis. Coun. on Criminal Justice, 1982-83, Wis. County Forest Adv. Coun., 1982-84; bd. dirs. Tri-County Cmty. Mental Health, Alcohol and Drug Abuse Bd, 1976-82, Black River Falls Youth Hockey, 1983-84; co-founder, dir. Black River Falls Area Found., 1986-88; chmn. Mayor's Commn. Golf Course Expansion Fundraising, 1988-90, Wazee Lake Recreation Commn., 1991-96; commencement spkr. Black River Falls H.S., 1992; mem. com., presenter All-Am. City Finalist Competition, Charlotte, N.C., 1992; chmn. adminstrv. coun. United Meth. Ch., Black River Falls, 1992-93, bldg. commn., co-chair fundraising, 1992-94; mem. cmty. rels. com. Wis. Dept. Corrections, 1993—. Named elected fellow, Wis. Law Found., 2005. Fellow Wis. Bar Found.; mem. ABA, ATLA, Wis. Acad. Trial Lawyers (bd. dirs. 1984-90), Wis. Bar Assn., Tri-County Bar Assn. (pres. 1991-92), Black River Falls C. of C. (bd. dirs.), Rotary (bd. dirs., past pres. youth exch. officer), Black River Recreation Assn., Skyline Golf Club (bd. dirs., pres. 1993). Achievements include patents pending for phase change technology. Home: N6570 Riverview Dr Black River Falls WI 54615-9207 Office: Stutz & Lister SC PO Box 370 Black River Falls WI 54615-0370 Office Phone: 715-284-7453. Business E-Mail: tom@tlister.com.

LISTON, JEFFERSON EDWARD, lawyer; b. Troy, Ohio, Apr. 11, 1954; s. George Edward and Jane Britannia Liston; m. Teresa L. Liston, Mar. 20, 1983; 1 child, Jane Elizabeth. BA in Govt., Otterbein Coll., Westerville, Ohio, 1975; JD, Case Western Res. U., Cleve., 1978. Bar: Ohio 1978, US Dist. Ct. (so. dist.) Ohio 1987, US Supreme Ct. 1987. Pvt. practice, Columbus, 1978—84; atty. bur. of support Franklin County Domestic Ct., Columbus, 1984—85; ct. magistrate Franklin County Juvenile Ct., Columbus, 1985—90; assoc. Tyack & Blackmore, Columbus, 1990—93; ptnr. Tyack, Blackmore & Liston, Columbus, 1993—. Founding pres. Ohio Magistrates Assn., 1989—90, Ctrl. Ohio Assn. Juvenile Lawyers, 1997; mem. gov.'s task force Investigation and Prosecution of Child Abuse, 2001—03, MR/DD Victims of Crime, 2002—03; mem. juvenile justice adv. com. Franklin County, 2001—; mem. adv. bd. Franklin County Juvenile Ct., 2001—; bd. trustees Juvenile Justice Coalition, 1994—; mem. Ohio Pub. Defender Commn., 2006—; spkr. in field. Co-author: Justice Cut Short: An Assessment of Access to Counsel and Quality of Representation in Delinquency Proceedings in Ohio, 2003. Mem. adv. bd. Ctrl. Juvenile Defender Ctr.; bd. trustees St. Joseph Montessori Sch., 1990—97; past mem. Juvenile Justice Advocacy Group; past mem. cmty. adv. bd. League Against Child Abuse; past founding mem. chem. assessment referral, evaluation svcs. adv. bd. Children's Hosp. Recipient award of distinction, Nat. Juvenile Defender Ctr., 2004. Mem.: ATLA, ABA, Ohio Assn. Criminal Def. Lawyers (bd. dirs., pres. 2001—02), Columbus Bar Assn. (cmty. svc. award 1988), Ohio State Bar Assn., Ohio Acad. Trial Lawyers, Franklin County Trial Lawyers, Nat. Assn. Criminal Def. Lawyers. Office: Tyack Blackmore & Liston Co LPA 536 S High St Columbus OH 43215 Home Phone: 614-890-5160; Office Phone: 614-221-1341. Office Fax: 614-228-0253.

LISTROM, LINDA L., lawyer; b. Topeka, Mar. 17, 1952; BA magna cum laude, U. Houston, 1974; JD, Harvard U., 1977. Bar: Ill. 1977. Ptnr. Jenner & Block, Chgo., sr. ptnr. Adj. prof. Northwestern U. Sch. Law; adv. coun. Corp. Legal Times SuperConf., 2002—; lead trial counsel Gen. Dynamics Corp. Contbr. articles to various profl. journs. Bd. dirs. Cook County Court Watching Project, Inc., 1983-92. Recipient Top 20 women litigators US Minority Corp. Counsel Assn., 2004, Top 50 Female Ill. Super Lawyers, Law & Politics, 2005—06, Top 100 Ill. Super Lawyers, 2005—06, 500 leading lawyers US, LawDragon Mag., 2005—06, 500 leading litigators US, 2006. Mem. ABA, fellow Am. Coll. Trial Lawyers, 2000-, Nat. Inst. Trial Advocacy. Office: Jenner & Block 330 N Wabash Ave Chicago IL 60611 Office Phone: 312-923-2761. Office Fax: 312-840-7761. Business E-Mail: llistrom@jenner.com.

LIT, MARK ALAN, recreational facility executive; b. Northampden, Mass., May 16, 1949; s. Joseph Benjamin and Shana Lit; m. Joyce Knight, June 16, 1974; children: Ari Benjamin, Noah Joseph, Joshua Izaac, Gabriel Seth. BA, Rockford Coll., Ill., 1971; student, Ariz. State U., Tempe, 1972—74. Exec. dir. Jewish Cmty. Ctr., San Antonio, 1989—99; CEO Jewish Cmty. Assn. Austin, Tex., 1999—2005; exec. dir. Jewish Cmty. Ctr. Detroit, West Bloomfield, Mich., 2005—. Dir.: (plays) (named Best Dir., Best Musical, Globe Awards, 1995); author: (plays) Grandma's PeachTree, Refusenik (Best New Musical Composition award, 1992). Home: 8573 Immensee Dr Commerce Township MI 48382 Office: Jewish Cmty Ctr Detroit 6600 West Maple West Bloomfield MI 48322 Home Phone: 248-363-1796; Office Phone: 248-432-5421.

LITAN, ROBERT ELI, lawyer, economist; b. Wichita, Kans., May 16, 1950; s. David and Shirley Hermine (Krischer) Litan. BS in Econs., U. Pa., 1972; MPhil in Econs., Yale U., 1976, JD, 1977, PhD in Econs., 1987. Bar: (DC) 1980. Rsch. asst. Brookings Instn., 1972-73; instr. to lectr. econs. Yale U., 1975-76; energy cons. NAS, 1975-77; regulation and energy specialist Pres.'s Coun. Econ. Advs., 1977-79; assoc. Arnold & Porter, Washington, 1979-82; assoc., then ptnr. and counsel Powell, Goldstein, Frazer & Murphy, Washington, 1982-90; sr. fellow Brookings Instn., Washington, 1984-92, 2003—, dir. Ctr. for Econ. Progress, 1987-93, v.p., dir. econ. studies, Cabot family chair in econs., 1996—2003; dep. asst. atty. gen. Dept. Justice, Washington, 1993-95; assoc. dir. Office of Mgmt. and Budget, Washington, 1995-96. Cons. Inst. Liberty and Democracy, Lima, Peru, 1985—88; vis. lectr. Yale U. Law Sch., 1985—86; mem. Presdl. Congl. Commn. Causes of Savs. and Loan Crisis, 1991—92; cons. U.S. Dept. Treasury, 1996—97, 1999—2000; v.p. rsch. and policy The Kauffman Found., 2003—; sr. fellow The Brookings Inst., 2003—. Author: What Should Banks Do?, 1987, Blueprint for Restructuring America's Financial Institutions, 1989; co-author: Energy Modeling for an Uncertain Future, 1978, Reforming Federal Regulation, 1983, Saving Free Trade: A Pragmatic Approach, 1986; author: Banking Industry in Turmoil, 1990, The Revolution in U.S. Finance, 1991, The Liability Maze, 1991; co-author: Liability: Perspectives and Policy, 1988, American Living Standards: Threats and Challenges, 1988, Down in the Dumps: Administration of the Unfair Trade Laws, 1991, The Future of American Banking, 1992, Growth With Equity, 1993, Assessing Bank Reform, 1993, Verdict, 1993, Financial Regulation in a Global Economy, 1994, Footing the Bill for Superfund Cleanups, 1995, American Finance for the 21st Century, 1997, Globaphobia: Confronting Fears of Open Trade, 1998, None of Your Business: World Data Flows and the European Privacy Directive, 1998, The GAAP Gap, 2000, Beyond the Dot.Coms, 2001, Sticking Together: The Israeli Experiment in Pluralism, 2002, Protecting the American Homeland, 2002, Following the Money: Corporate Disclosure After Enron, 2003, Financial Statecraft, 2005, Worldwide Financial Reporting, 2006, Good Capitalism, Bad Capitalism and the Economics of Growth and Prosperity, 2007, Competitive Equity: An Alternative Model for Mutual Funds, 2007; contbr. articles to profl. jours. Recipient Class of 1964 award, U. Pa., W. Gordon award, 1972, Albert A. Berg award, 1971, 1972, Felix S. Cohen award, Yale U., 1976, Silver medal, Royal Soc. Arts, 1972; fellow Thouron, Eng., 1972. Mem.: ABA, Coun. on Fgn. Rels., Am. Econs. Assn. Democrat. Home: 5437 Mohawk St Fairway KS 66205-2732 Office: The Kauffman Found 4801 Rockhill Rd Kansas City MO 64110 Home Phone: 913-262-0731; Office Phone: 816-932-1179. Business E-Mail: rlitan@brookings.edu, rlitan@kauffman.org.

LITES, JAMES R., professional hockey team executive; b. Pentwater, Mich. m. Denise Lites; children: Brooke, Samuel. BA with highest honors, U. Mich., 1975; JD cum laude, Wayne State U., 1978. Exec. v.p. Detroit Red Wings, 1982—93; COO Olympia Arenas, Inc; v.p. Little Caesar's Internat., Inc.; pres. Dallas Stars, 1993—2002, 2002—, Phoenix Coyotes, 2002, Texas Rangers, Arlington, 1999—2002. Team rep. bd. govs. NHL. Office: Dallas Stars 2601 Ave Of The Stars Ste 100 Frisco TX 75034-9016

LITEWKA, ALBERT BERNARD, entertainment executive; s. Joel and Leah L. BA summa cum laude, UCLA, 1964; postgrad., U. Calif., Berkeley, 1964-65. Mgr. purchasing McGraw-Hill Book Co., NYC, 1965-67; pres. Mktg. Innovations, Inc., NYC, 1967-69; v.p. Westinghouse Leisure Time Industries, NYC, 1972-75; exec. v.p. mktg. The Baker & Taylor Co. (W.R. Grace & Co.), NYC, 1975-77; pres. Pix of Am. (W. R. Grace & Co.), NYC, 1978; v.p. consumer services group W.R. Grace & Co., NYC, 1977-79; pres. Macmillan Gen. Books div., NYC, 1980-82; sr. v.p. Macmillan Pub. Co., Inc., 1980-82; pres. Warner Software, Inc., 1982-85; chmn., CEO Air Creative Group, L.A. and NYC, 1986-98, Creative Domain, Inc., LA, 1991—2005, Winning Entertainment, LA, 2005—. Author: Warsaw: A Novel of Resistance, 1989. Chmn. bd. trustees Oakwood Sch., 2003—06. Internat. Ladies Garment Workers Union Nat. scholar, 1959-64, U. Calif. Regents scholar, 1959-64; Woodrow Wilson Nat. Grad. fellow, 1964-65; recipient 1st prize Acad. Am. Poets, 1964. Mem. Am. Film Inst., Authors Guild, Authors League Am., Acad. TV Arts & Scis. Office: Winning Entertainment 9000 Sunset Blvd Ste 915 Los Angeles CA 90069-5801 Home Phone: 323-850-5651.

LITFIN, A. DUANE, academic administrator; b. Mich. m. Sherri Litfin; 3 children. B in Bibl. Studies, Phila. Coll. of the Bible, 1966; ThM, Dallas Theol. Seminary; PhD in Interpersonal Comm., Purdue U.; DPhil in N.T. Studies, Oxford U. Tchr. Purdue U., Ind. U.; pastor Metea Bapt. Ch., Lucern, Ind.; assoc. prof. pastoral ministries Dallas Theol. Sem., 1974—84; sr. pastor First Evang. Ch., Memphis, 1984—93; pres. Wheaton Coll., Ill., 1993—. Author: Public Speaking: A Handbook for Christians, 1992, St. Paul's Theology of Proclamation, 1994. Office: Wheaton Coll 501 College Ave Wheaton IL 60187-5593 Office Phone: 630-752-5002. E-mail: Duane.Litfin@wheaton.edu.*

LITHERLAND, ALBERT EDWARD, physics professor; b. Wallasey, Eng., Mar. 12, 1928; emigrated to Can., 1953, naturalized, 1964; s. Albert and Ethel (Clement) L.; m. Anne Allen, May 12, 1956; children: Jane Elizabeth, Rosamund Mary. B.Sc., U. Liverpool, Eng., 1949, PhD, 1955; DSc (hon.), U. Toronto, 1998. Rutherford scholar Atomic Energy of Can., Chalk River, Ont., 1953-55, sci. officer, 1955-66; prof. physics U. Toronto, 1966-79, Univ. prof., 1979-93, Univ. prof. emeritus, 1993—. Contbr. articles to profl. jours. Recipient Rutherford medal Inst. Physics, London, 1974, Silver medal for accelerator-based dating techniques Jour. Applied Radiation and Isotopes, 1980; Guggenheim fellow, 1986-87. Fellow Royal Soc. Can. (Henry Marshall Tory medal 1993), Royal Soc. London, AAAS, Am. Phys. Soc.; mem. Can. Assn. Physicists (Gold medal for achievement in physics 1971) Home: Apt 801 120 Rosedale Valley Rd Toronto ON Canada M4W 1P8 Office: 60 St George St Toronto ON Canada M5S 1A7

LITHGOW, JOHN ARTHUR, actor, film director; b. Rochester, NY, Oct. 19, 1945; s. Arthur and Sarah L.; m. Jean Taynton, Sept. 10, 1966 (div.); 1 child, Ian; m. Mary Yeager, 1981; children: Phoebe, Nathan. Grad. magna cum laude, Harvard U., 1967; postgrad., London Acad. Music and Dramatic Art, 1967-69; ArtsD (hon.), Harvard U., 2005. Printmaker, founder Lithgow Graphics. Actor (movies) Obsession, 1976, The Big Fix, 1978, Rich Kids, 1979, All That Jazz, 1979, Blow Out, 1981, I'm Dancing as Fast as I Can, 1982, The World According to Garp, 1982, Twilight Zone: TheMovie, 1983, Terms of Endearment, 1983, 2010: The Year We Make Contact, 1984, Footloose, 1984, Adventures of Buckaroo Banzai Across the 8th Dimension, 1984, Santa Claus, 1985, Mesmerized, 1986, The

Manhattan Project, 1986, Harry and the Hendersons, 1987, Distant Thunder, 1988, Out Cold, 1989, Memphis Belle, 1990, At Play in the Fields of the Lord, 1991, Richochet, 1991, Raising Cain, 1992, Cliffhanger, 1993, The Pelican Brief, 1993, Good Man in Africa, 1994, Silent Fall, 1994, Princess Caraboo, 1994, Hollow Point, 1995, Special Effects: Anything Can Happen (voice), 1996, Officer Buckle and Gloria, 1998, Johhny Skidmarks, 1998, Homegrown, 1998, A Civil Action, 1998, Portofino, 1999, (voice) Rugrats in Paris: The Movie-Rugrats II, 2000, C-Scam, 2000, (voice) Shrek, 2001, Orange County, 2002, The Life and Death of Peter Sellers, 2004, Kinsey, 2004; (Broadway plays) Sweet Smell of Success, 2000-03 (Tony for Best Male Actor 2002), The Retreat from Moscow, 2004, Dirty Rotten Scoundrels, 2005; (TV series and movies) Mom, the Wolfman and Me, 1983, Not in Front of the Children, 1982, The Day After, 1983, The Glitter Dome, 1984, Resting Place, 1986, Baby Girl Scott, 1987, Traveling Man, 1989, Ivory Hunters, 1990, The Boys, 1991, The Wrong Man, 1993, Love, Cheat and Steal, 1993, Then There Were Giants, 1994, American Cinema, 1994, World War II: When Lions Roared, 1994, The Tuskegee Airmen, 1995, My Brother's Keeper, 1995, Redwood Curtain, 1995, Christmas in Washington, 1996, 3rd Rock from the Sun, 1996-2001 (Emmy for Outstanding Lead Actor in a Comedy Series 1996, 97, 99, Golden Globe award for Best Actor in a TV Series Musical and Comedy 1996), Don Quixote (miniseries), 1999; TV guest appearances include Amazing Stories, 1985 (Emmy for Outstanding Guest Performer in a Drama Series 1986), Tales from the Crypt, 1989, Cosby, 1996; singer (song) Singing in the Bathtub, 1999; author (children's books) The Remarkable Farkle McBride, 2000, Marsupial Sue, 2001, I'm a Manatee, 2003, Carnival of the Animals, 2004. Named to Theater Hall of Fame, 2005.

LITKE, DONALD PAUL, acquisition executive, retired military officer; b. Denver, Nov. 7, 1934; s. Walter Monroe and Alice Vivian (Fowler) L.; m. Myrna Kay McDonald, July 1, 1956; children— Bradley, Susan, Lisa BS in Econs., Colo. A&M U., 1956; MS in Internat. Affairs, George Washington U., 1966. Ops. and staff positions U.S. Air Force, 1956-79; vice comdr. Oklahoma City Air Logistics Ctr., 1979-81; dep. dir. logistics and security assistance U.S. European Command, Stuttgart, Germany, 1981-83; comdr. U.S. Logistics Group, Ankara, Turkey, 1983-85; dep. dir. Def. Logistics Agy., Alexandria, Va., 1985-86; pres. Bus. Devel. Internat., Alexandria and Niceville, Fla., 1986—2004. Contbr. articles to profl. jours. Mem. Air Force Assn. (Middle Mgr. of Yr. 1970, award of excellence 1977), Alpha Tau Omega Methodist. Avocations: auto restoration, racquetball. Home and Office: 2422 Edgewater Dr Niceville FL 32578-2305 Personal E-mail: dnklitke@cox.net.

LITKO, KENNETH R., aerospace engineer, researcher; b. Harvey, Ill., Oct. 9, 1976; s. Robert Thomas and Barbara Marie Litko; m. Amber Rae Gress, Apr. 8, 2005. BS in Aerospace Engring., Ill. Inst. Tech., Chgo., 2001, MS in Metall. and Materials Engring., 2001. Lic. Profl. Engr., Ind. Profl. Licensing Agy., 2003. Asst. engr. IIT Rsch. Inst., Chgo., 1999—2002. Office: Litko Aerosys Inc 1453 Brandywine Rd Crown Point IN 46307 Home Phone: 219-988-2594; Office Phone: 219-310-4280. Office Fax: 708-575-0721. Business E-Mail: ken@litkoaero.com.

LITMAN, BERNARD, electrical engineer, consultant; b. NYC, Oct. 26, 1920; s. Nathan and Gussie (Friedman) L.; m. Ellen Ann Kaufman, Feb. 27, 1949; children— Barbara, Richard. BS in Elec. Engring, Columbia U., 1941, PhD, 1949; MS, U. Pitts., 1943. Design engr. energy equipment Westinghouse Electric Co., Pitts., 1941-47; with AMBAC Industries div. United Tech. Corp., Garden City, N.Y., 1949-83, tech. dir. guidance equipment Atlas inter-continental missile, 1962-63, chief engr. systems devel. and research, 1964-83; dir. advanced tech. Gull Electronics Systems Div., Parker Hannifin Corp., 1983-93; tech. cons., 1994-96; ret., 1996. Westinghouse lectr. U. Pitts., 1944; lectr. Adelphi U., Garden City. Co-author: Gyroscopics, 1961; patentee rotary amplifiers, axial motors, gravity pendulums, inductors, 2 axis accellerometers, ballistic missile safety devices, gyro attenuators, thrust retainers. William Petit Trobridge fellow, 1948 Asso. fellow Am. Inst. Aeros. and Astronautics (Achievement award L.I. sect. 1966); mem. IEEE (sr.), Am. Automatic Control Council, N.Y.-N.J. Trail Conf., Sigma Xi. Jewish. Home: 1114 Laurel Oak Rd Apt 313 Voorhees NJ 08043

LITMAN, HARRY PETER, lawyer, educator; b. Pitts., May 4, 1958; s. S. David and Roslyn M. (Margolis) L.; m. Julie Roskies, Sept. 21, 2003; children: David, Lila. BA, Harvard U., 1981; JD, U. Calif., Berkeley, 1986. Bar: Calif. 1987, U.S. Ct. Appeals (D.C. cir.) 1987, Pa. 1988, D.C. 1989, U.S. Ct. Appeals (9th cir.) 1990, U.S. Dist. Ct. (so. dist.) Tex. 1992, U.S. Supreme Ct. 1992, U.S. Dist. Ct. (ea. and we. dists.) Pa. 1993, U.S. Ct. Appeals (7th cir.) 1994, U.S. Dist. Ct. (ea. dist.) Va. 1997. Prodn. asst. feature films, NYC, 1980-82; newsman, clk. baseball desk AP, NYC, 1982-83, sports reporter, 1983-86; law clk. to Hon. Abner J. Mikva U.S. Ct. Appeals (D.C. cir.), 1986-87; law clk. to Hon. Thurgood Marshall U.S. Supreme Ct., Washington, 1987-88, law clk. to Hon. Anthony M. Kennedy, 1989; asst. U.S. atty., dep. chief appellate sect. Dept. Justice, San Francisco, 1990-92, dep. assoc. atty. gen. Washington, 1992-93, dep. asst. atty. gen., 1993-98; U.S. atty. Western Dist. of Pa., 1998—2001; of counsel Phillips & Cohen, Washington, 2001—, San Francisco, 2001—. Adj. prof. Boalt Hall Sch. Law U. Calif., Berkeley, 1990-92, Georgetown U. Law Ctr., 1996-99, U. Pitts. Law Sch., 1999—, Rutgers Law Sch., 2003-, Princeton U., 2005-; disting. visitor, fellow law and pub. affairs Princeton U., 2001-03; gen. counsel for Pa., Kerry-Edwards Campaign, 2004. Editor-in-chief Calif. Law Rev., Vol. 73; writer (TV show) Without a Trace; contbr. articles to profl. jours. Presdl. scholar, 1976. Mem. Pa. Bar Assn., State Bar Calif., D.C. Bar, Order of Coif. Office Phone: 412-456-2000.

LITMAN, JACK THEODORE, lawyer; b. NYC, July 26, 1943; s. Charles Louis and Sarah G. (Hornblas) L.; m. Helena Dunica, Aug. 25, 1968; children: Sacha F., Benjamin S. BA, Cornell U., 1964; LLB, Harvard U., 1967; diploma, Inst. Criminology, Paris, 1968. Bar: NY 1968, US Dist. Ct. (so. and ea. dists. NY) 1973, US Ct. Appeals (2nd cir.) 1973, US Supreme Ct. 1975. Asst. dist. atty. NY County, NYC, 1968-74; sr. trial asst., dep. chief Homicide Bur., 1968—74; sr. ptnr. Litman, Asche, & Gioiella, LLP, NYC, 1974—. Adj. prof. law NYU, 1970-93. Editor: Criminal Trial Advocacy, 1975; contbr. articles to profl. jours. Fulbright scholar, 1967-68. Mem. NY State Bar Assn. (mem. exec. com. criminal justice sect. 1983—, named Outstanding Practitioner of Yr. 1986), Assn. of Bar of City of NY (mem. com. criminal courts and law procedure 1975-78), NY Criminal Bar Assn. (pres. 1987-89, bd. dirs.), NACDL (bd. dirs.), NY State Assn. Criminal Def. Lawyers (bd. dirs., pres. 1990-91) Democrat. Jewish. Avocations: chess, movies, sports, number theory. Office: Litman Asche & Gioiella 45 Broadway Atrium New York NY 10006-3007

LITMAN, ROBERT BARRY, physician, writer, television and radio commentator; b. Phila., Nov. 17, 1947; s. Benjamin Norman and Bette Etta (Saunders) L.; m. Niki Thomas, Apr. 21, 1985; children: Riva Belle, Nadya Beth, Caila Tess, Benjamin David. BS, Yale U., New Haven, Conn., 1968, MD, 1970, MS, MPhil in Anatomy, 1972. Diplomate Am. Bd. Family Practice, cert. Am. Bd. Family Medicine. Postdoct. rsch. fellow Am. Cancer Soc. Yale U., New Haven, 1970-73, USPHS fellow, 1974-75; resident in gen. surgery Bryn Mawr Hosp., Pa., 1973-74; pvt. practice in medicine and surgery Ogdensburg, NY, 1977-93, San Ramon, Calif., 1993—; mem. staff A. Barton Hepburn Hosp., 1977-93, John Muir Med. Ctr., 1993—, San Ramon Regional Med. Ctr., 1993—, also chmn. med. edn., chmn. dept. family practice, 1998-99, chmn. med. edn., 2004—06. Commentator Family Medicine Stas. WWNY-TV and WTNY-Radio, TCI Cablevision, Contra Costa T.V.; moderator Ask the Dr.; clin. preceptor dept. family medicine State U. Health Sci. Ctr., Syracuse, 1978—. Author: Wynnefield and Limer, 1983, The Treblinka Virus, 1991, Allergy Shots, 1993; contbr. articles to numerous profl. jours. Pres. No. NY chpt. AHA. Fellow Life Ins. Med. Rsch. Fund, U. Coll. Hosp., U. London, 1969-70; recipient We. Access Video Excellence award, 1998, 2001, Bay Area Cable Excellence award, 1999, Telly award, 1999-2005, 06-07. Fellow Am. Coll. Allergy, Asthma, and Immunology, Am. Acad. Family Physicians; mem. AMA (Physicians Recognition award 1970—), Calif. State Med. Assn., Alameda-Contra Costa County Med. Assn., Joint Coun. Allergy and Immunology, Nat. Assn. Physician Broadcasters (charter), Acad. Radio and TV Health Communicators, Book and Snake Soc., Gibbs Soc. Yale U. (founder), Sigma Xi, Nu Sigma Nu, Alpha Chi Sigma. Home and Office: PO Box 1857 San Ramon CA 94583-6857 Office Phone: 925-866-7007.

LITMAN, ROSLYN MARGOLIS, lawyer; b. NYC, Sept. 30, 1928; d. Harry and Dorothy (Perlow) Margolis; m. S. David Litman, Nov. 22, 1950; children: Jessica, Hannah, Harry. BA, U. Pitts., 1949, JD, 1952. Bar: Pa. 1952; approved arbitrator for complex comml. litigation and employment law, Am. Assn. Arbitrators. Practiced in Pitts., 1952—; ptnr. firm Litman Law Firm, 1952—; adj. prof. U. Pitts. Law Sch., 1958—. Permanent del. Conf. U.S. Circuit Ct. Appeals for 3d Circuit; past chair dist. adv. group U.S. Dist. Ct. (we. dist.) Pa., 1991-94, mem. steering com. for dist. adv. group, 1991—; chmn. Pitts. Pub. Parking Authority, 1970-74; mem. curriculum com. Pa. Bar Inst., 1986—, bd. dirs., 1972-82; bd. visitors sch. law U. Pitts. Bd. dirs. United Jewish Fedn., 1999—, cmty. rels. com., co-chair ch./state com.; bd. dirs. City Theatre, 1999—; bd. visitors U. Pitts. Sch. Law. Recipient Roscoe Pound Found. award for Excellence in Tchg. Trial Advocacy, 1996, Disting. Alumnus award U. Pitts. Sch. Law, 1996, Disting. Svc. award Acad. Trial Lawyers, 2004; named Fed. Lawyer of Yr., We. Pa. Chpt. FBA, 1999. Mem. ABA (del., litigation sect., anti-trust health care com.), ACLU (nat. bd. dirs., Marjorie H. Matson Civil Libertarian award Greater Pitts. chpt. 1999), Pa. Bar Assn. (bd. govs. 1976-79), Allegheny County Bar Assn. (bd. govs. 1972-74, pres. 1975, Woman of Yr. 2001), Allegheny County Acad. Trial Lawyers (charter), Order of Coif. Home: 5023 Frew St Pittsburgh PA 15213-3829 Office: One Oxford Centre 34th Fl Pittsburgh PA 15219 Home Phone: 412-621-6777; Office Phone: 412-456-2000. Business E-Mail: rlitman@litman-law.com.

LITOFF, JUDY BARRETT, history professor; b. Atlanta, Dec. 23, 1944; d. John and Dorothy (Woodall) Barrett; children: Nadja Barrett, Alyssa Barrett. BA, Emory U., Atlanta, 1967; MA, Emory U., 1968; PhD, U. Maine, 1975. Asst. prof. history Bryant U., Smithfield, RI, 1975-81, assoc. prof. history, 1981-87, prof. history, 1987—. Scholarly reader U. Ga. Press, Greenwood Press, U. Ill. Press, Prentice Hall, Univ. Press of Ky., Univ. Press of Colo.; project dir. U.S. Info. Agy. Grant, Minsk, Belarus, 1997-2000, higher edn. support program, Grant, Minsk, 1999. Author: American Midwives, 1978, American Midwife Debate, 1986; co-author: Miss You, 1990, Since Your Went Away, 1991, Dear Boys, 1991, We're In This War, Too, 1994, European Immigrant Women, 1994, American Women in a World at War, 1997, Dear Poppa, 1997, What Kind of World Do We Want?, 2000, Fighting Fascism in Europe, 2003, An American Heroine in the French Resistance, 2006; contbr. articles to profl. jours.; book reviewer many profl. jours. Bd. dirs. RI Hist. Soc., RI Com. for Humanities, 1982-86, RI Black Heritage Soc., 2005-, Festival Ballet, Providence, 2007-; bd. dirs., chair Goff Inst. for Ingenuity and Enterprise, 1998—2003; bd. overseers The Lincoln Sch., Providence, 1982-88, The Moses Brown Sch., Providence, 1984-93; leader Girl Scouts RI, 1978-87. Recipient Disting. Faculty award Bryant Faculty Fedn., 1988, Bryant Alumni Assn., 1989, James Madison prize Soc. for History in Fed. Govt., 1994, Bryant U. Rsch. and Pub. award, 1997, 2005; Ford Career scholar Emory U., 1965-67. Mem. Orgn. Am. Historians, Am. Hist. Assn., So. Hist. Assn., R.I. Hist. Soc., R.I. Black Heritage Soc. (bd. dirs. 2004—), Humanities Forum R.I. (bd. dirs. 2000—), Coordinating Com. on Women in the Hist. Profession, So. Assn. Women Historians, Phi Kappa Phi, Phi Alpha Theta. Avocations: skiing, hiking, yoga. Home: 248 Morris Ave Providence RI 02906-2424 Office: Bryant Univ 1150 Douglas Pike Smithfield RI 02917-1291 Home Phone: 401-272-5942; Office Phone: 401-232-6248. E-mail: jlitoff@bryant.edu.

LITOW, MARK I., lawyer; b. 1947; AB, JD, Washington U., St. Louis. Bar: Mo. 1973. V.p., gen. counsel Enterprise Rent-A-Car, St. Louis. Office: Enterprise Rent-A-Car 600 Corporate Park Dr Saint Louis MO 63105-4211 Office Phone: 314-512-5000. Office Fax: 314-512-4706.

LITRENTA, FRANCES MARIE, psychiatrist; b. Balt., June 25, 1928; d. Frank P. and Josephine (DeLuca) L. AB, Coll. Notre Dame Md., 1950; MD, Georgetown U., 1954. Diplomate Am. Bd. Psychiatry and Neurology. Intern St. Agnes Hosp., Balt., 1954-55, asst. resident in psychiatry, 1955-56; fellow psychiatry Univ. Hosp., Balt., 1956-57; fellow child psychiatry Georgetown U. Hosp., Washington, 1957-59; clin. instr. psychiatry Med. Ctr. Georgetown U., Washington, 1959-63, clin. asst. prof. Med. Ctr., 1963-72, clin. assoc. prof. psychiatry Med. Ctr., 1972-87; pvt. practice Balt., 1959—. Cons. St. Vincent's Infant Home, Balt., 1965-75; mem. coun. to dean Georgetown U. Sch. Medicine, 1977-93. Recipient Georgetown U. Alumni Assn. John Carroll award, 1998. Fellow Am. Acad. Child and Adolescent Psychiatry, Am. Orthopsychiat. Assn. (life); mem. Am. Psychiat. Assn. (life), Md. Psychiat. Soc. (life), Georgetown Med. Alumni Assn. (nat. comm. chair 1987-90, class co-chair 1974-87, class comm. chair 1987—, bd. dirs. 1989—, gov. 1989-95, senator 1995—), Georgetown U. Alumni Assn. (Founder's award 1994, John Carroll award 1998). Office: 6110 York Rd Baltimore MD 21212-2697 Office Phone: 410-435-6340.

LITROWNIK, ALAN JAY, psychologist, educator; b. Los Angeles, June 25, 1945; s. Irving and Mildred Mae (Rosin) L.; m. Hollis Merle, Aug. 20, 1967; children: Allison Brook, Jordan Michael BA, UCLA, 1967; MA, U. Ill., Champaign-Urbana, 1969, PhD, 1971. Psychologist Ill. Dept. Mental Health, Decatur, 1970-71; asst. prof. psychology San Diego State U., 1971-75, assoc. prof., 1975-78, prof., 1978—, chmn. dept. psychology, 1981-87, assoc. dean for curriculum and acad. planning, North County Campus, 1987-88; co-dir. Ctr. for Behavioral and Community Health Studies, San Diego, 1989—2004. Cons. San Diego County Dept. Edn. Program Evaluation, 1975-81; project dir. Self-Concept and Self-Regulatory Processes in Developmentally Disabled Children and Adolescents, 1975-78; co-dir. Child Abuse Interdisciplinary Tng. Program, 1987-2002; project dir. tobacco use prevention in youth orgns., 1989-92. Research, publs. in field. Contbr. chpts. to books Mem. San Diego County Juvenile Justice Commn., 1989-92; mem. juvenile systems adv. group San Diego County Bd. Suprs., 1989-91. Grantee U.S. Office Edn., 1975-78, 80-81, Nat. Ctr. Child Abuse, 1987—, Calif. Dept. Health, 1989-92, U. Calif. Tobacco-Related Disease Rsch. Program, 1992-94. Office Phone: 858-966-7703 7146.

LITSCHGI, RICHARD JOHN, computer manufacturing company executive; b. St. Louis, July 1, 1937; s. William J. and Mary F. (Eynatten) L.; m. Christine Ewert, Aug. 21, 1968. BS, St. Louis U., 1959; MS, U. Okla., 1964. Cert. meteorology St. Louis U./USAF, 1960. Rsch. asst. U. Okla. Rsch. Inst., 1962—63; rsch. assoc. MIT, 1963—64; supr. Bellcomm, Inc., Washington, 1964-67; mgr. Computer Scis., Brussels, 1967-68, Intranet Computing Co., LA, 1968-71, Xerox Corp., El Segundo, Calif., 1971-76; dir. Honeywell Info. Sys. Inc., LA, 1976-80, v.p. Phoenix, 1980-85, Mpls., 1985-87, Honeywell Bull, Inc., 1987-88, Bull HN, Inc., Boston, 1988-89, Groupe Bull, Boston and Paris, 1990-93, Vanguard Automation, Inc., Tucson, 1993-94; ret., 1994. Bd. dirs. Arizonians for Cultural Devel., 1981-85; trustee Phoenix Art Mus., 1982-85. Capt. USAF, 1959-62. Mem.: Assn. Computing Machinery, Am. Geophys. Union, Am. Meteorology Soc., Pi Mu Epsilon. Home: 24 Tupelo Rd Falmouth MA 02540-1945

LITT, MITCHELL, chemical engineer, bioengineer, educator; b. Bklyn., Oct. 11, 1932; s. Saul and Mollie (Steinbaum) L.; m. Zelda Sheila Levine, Sept. 6, 1955; children: Ellen Beth, Steven Eric. AB, Columbia U., 1953, BS in Engring, 1954, MS, 1956; D.Engring. Sci., Columbia, 1961. Research engr. Esso Research and Engring. Co., 1958-61; faculty U. Pa., 1961—, assoc. prof. chem. engring., 1965-72, prof., 1972—, prof. bioengring., 1977—2001, chmn. dept. bioengring., 1981-90, prof. bioengring. emeritus, 2001—. Vis. prof. environ. medicine Duke, 1971-72; vis. prof. Weizmann Inst., Israel, 1979; v.p. research and devel. KDL Med. Techs. Inc., 1984-95; v.p. rsch. & devel. BioFlo Systems, Inc., 1995—. Co-editor: Rheology of Biological Systems, 1973; asso. editor: Biorheology; contbr. articles to profl. engrs. Mem. IEEE (engring. in medicine and biology soc.), Am. Inst. Chem. Engrs., Am. Soc. Engring. Edn., Am. Chem. Soc., Biomed. Engring. Soc., Internat. Soc. Biorheology, N.Am. Soc. Biorheology, Am. Inst. Med. Biol. Engring., Phi Beta Kappa, Sigma Xi, Tau Beta Pi, Phi Lambda Upsilon, Theta Tau. Achievements include spl. research biorheology transp. processes, chemically reacting systems, med. aspects engring. Home: 2420 Spruce St Philadelphia PA 19103-6423 Office: Univ Pa Dept Bio Engring Philadelphia PA 19104 Office Phone: 215-898-7249. Personal E-mail: mitchlitt@comcast.net. Business E-Mail: litt@seas.upenn.edu.

LITT, ROBERT S., lawyer; b. Dec. 29, 1949; BA, Harvard Univ., 1971; MA, Yale Univ., 1973, JD, 1976. Bar: N.Y. 1978, D.C. 1980, Md. 1998. Law clk. Judge Edward Weinfeld, US Dist. Ct., So. N.Y. Dist., 1976—77, Justice Potter Stewart, US Supreme Ct., 1977—78; asst. U.S. atty., So. Dist. N.Y. U.S. Dept. Justice, 1978—84; spec. adv. U.S. Dept. of State, Washington, 1993—94; dep. asst. atty. gen. U.S. Dept. Justice, Washington, 1994—97, prin. assoc. dep. atty. gen., 1997—99; ptnr., White Collar Practice Group Arnold & Porter, Washington, 1999—. Mem.: ABA (past chmn. White Collar Crime Com., Criminal Justice Sect.). Office: Arnold & Porter 555 Twelfth St NW Washington DC 20004-1260 Office Phone: 202-942-6380. Office Fax: 202-942-5999. Business E-Mail: robert.litt@aporter.com.

LITTELL, JONATHAN, writer; b. NYC, Oct. 10, 1967; s. Robert Littell; married; 2 children. BA, Yale U., 1989. Former internat. humanitarian aid organizer Action Against Hunger, 1994—2001. Author: (novels) Bad Voltage, 1989, Les Bienveillantes, 2006 (Gran Priz du Roman, l'Acedemie Francaise, 2006, Prix Goncourt, 2006). Office: Editions Gallimard 5 rue Sebastien-Bottin 75328 Paris France*

LITTELL, MARCIA SACHS, Holocaust and genocide studies professor; b. Phila., 1937; d. Leon Harry Sobel and Selma Lipson; children: Jonathan R., Robert L. Jr., Jennifer; m. Franklin H. Littell, Mar. 23, 1980. BS in Edn., Temple U., 1971, MS in Edn., 1975, EdD, 1990. Internat. exec. dir. Anne Frank Inst., Phla., 1981-89; exec. dir. Ann. Scholars' Conf. on the Holocaust & the Chs., Merion, Pa., 1980—; prof. Holocaust and genocide studies, founding dir. MA program Holocaust & genocide studies The Richard Stockton Coll. N.J., 1997—. Adj. prof. Temple U., Phila., 1990-97; vis. prof. Phila. C.C., 1974-76; dir. Phila. Ctr. on the Holocaust, Genocide and Human Rights, 1989—; exec. com. Remembering for the Future, Oxford, Eng. and Berlin, 1986—; mem. edn. com. U.S. Holocaust Meml. Mus., Washington, 1987-89, chmn.'s adv. com., 1985. Mem. editl. bd. Holocaust & Genocide Studies, Oxford U. Press, 1987—, Bridges: An Interdisciplinary Journal of Theology, Philosophy, History and Science, 1995—; editor: Holocaust Education: A Resource for Teachers and Professional Leaders, 1985, Liturgies on the Holocaust: An Interfaith Anthology, 1986, rev. edit., 1996 (Merit of Distinction award), The Holocaust: Forty Years After, 1989, The Netherlands and Nazi Genocide, 1992, From Prejudice to Destruction: Western Civilization in the Shadow of Auschwitz, 1995, Remembrance and Recollection: Essays on the Centennial Year of Martin Niemoeller and Reinhold Niebuhr, 1995, The Uses and Abuses of Knowledge: The Holocaust and the German Church Struggle, 1997, The Holocaust: Lessons For the Third Generation, 1997, Holocaust and Church Struggle: Religion, Power and the Politics of Resistance, 1996, Confronting the Holocaust: A Mandate for the 21st Century, part 1, 1997, part 2, 1998, A Modern Prophet, 1998, Hearing the Voices: Teaching the Holocaust to Future Generations, 1999, Women in the Holocaust, 2001, The Century of Genocide, 2002, The Genocidal Mind, 2005. Exec. com. YM/YWHA Arts Coun., Phila., 1980—; adv. bd. Child Welfare, Montgomery County, 1975-80, Am. Friends the Ghetto Fighters House; bd. govs. Lower Merion Scholarship Fund, 1972-80. Named Woman of the Yr., Brith Sholom Women, Phila., 1993; recipient Eternal Flame award Anne Frank Inst., 1988; named to Hall of Fame Sch. Dist. of Phila., 1988. Fellow Nat. Assn. Holocaust Educators, Assn. of Holocaust Orgns. (founding sec. 1985-88), Nat. Coun. for the Social Studies. Democrat. Jewish. Avocations: walking, travel, reading. Office: PO Box 10 Merion Station PA 19066-0010 Office Phone: 609-652-4418. Business E-Mail: drlittell@comcast.net.

LITTLE, ALAN BRIAN, gynecologist, educator; b. Montreal, Que., Canada, Mar. 11, 1925; emigrated to U.S., 1951, naturalized, 1959; s. Herbert Melville and Mary Lizette (Campbell) L.; m. Nancy Alison Campbell, Aug. 20, 1949 (div.); children: Michael C. (dec.), Susan MacF. and Deborah MacF. (twins), Catherine E., Jane A., Mary L.; m. Bitten Stripp, Mar. 31, 1983 BA, McGill U., 1948, MD, CM, 1950. Intern Montreal Gen. Hosp., 1950-51; resident Boston Lying-in and Free Hosp. for Women, 1951-55, asst. obstetrician, asso. obstetrician and gynecologist, 1955-65; teaching fellow, asst. prof. Harvard Med. Sch., 1952-65; prof. ob-gyn, then Arthur H. Bill prof. ob-gyn Case Western Res. U. Sch. Medicine, Cleve., 1965-82, chmn. dept. reproductive biology, 1972-82; prof. gynecology McGill U., Montreal, 1983—, chmn. dept. ob-gyn., 1983-94; clin. prof. ob-gyn. U. Medicine and Dentistry N.J., Newark, 1994—. Dir. dept. ob-gyn. Univ. Hosps., Cleve., to 1982, Royal Victoria Hosp., Montreal, 1983-94; mem. nat. adv. com. Nat. Inst. Child Health and Human Devel. Author: (with B. Tenney) Clinical Obstetrics, 1962; editor: (with others) Gynecology and Obstetrics-Health Care for Women, 1975, 2d edit., 1982; (with D. Tulchinsky) Maternal Fetal Endocrinology, 2d edit., 1994; contbr. articles to profl. jours. Served with RCAF, 1943-45. Fellow: ACS, Am. Coll. Obstetricians and Gynecologists, Royal Coll. Surgeons Can.; mem.: Soc. Ob-Gyn. Can., Soc. Gynecol. Investigation, Assn. Profls. Ob-Gyn., Am. Gynecol. and Obstet. Soc. Office: UMDNJ MSB E506 185 S Orange Ave Newark NJ 07103-2757 Business E-Mail: littleb1@umdnj.edu.

LITTLE, ARTHUR DEHON, investor; b. Providence, Feb. 13, 1944; s. Royal and Augusta Willoughby (Ellis) L.; m. Jann E. Leeming, Sept. 6, 1974; children: Cameron Royal, Kimberley Murray. BA in History, Stanford U., 1966. With Narragansett Capital Corp., Providence, 1967—86, asst. to pres., 1968-69, v.p., 1969-73, exec. v.p., treas., 1975-76, pres., treas., chief operating officer, dir., 1976-77, pres., treas., chief exec. officer, dir., 1977-80, pres., chief exec. officer, dir., 1980, chmn. bd., chief exec. officer, 1980-86; mng. dir. Narragansett Capital, Inc., Providence, 1986—92; prin. The Little Investment Co., Boston, 1992—2000, A&J Acquisition, 1996—. Bd. dirs. R.I. Zool. Soc., Lyford Cay Found., Jr. Achievement No. New Eng., Jr. Achievement Internat. Adv. Bd., Capital Resource Ptnrs.; dir., chair governance commn. Iron Mountain. Mem. Lyford Cay Club, Kittansett Club, Lake Winnepesaukee Golf Club, Bayonne Golf Club.

LITTLE, BERTIS BRITT, medical research scientist, obstetrician educator, university administrator; b. Whiteville, NC, Feb. 22, 1957; s. Gardner Burris and Mildred Eleanor (Denton) L.; m. Beverly A. DelHomme; 1 child, Bertis Britt II. BA, Appalachian State U., Boone, NC, 1976; MA, Ball State U., Muncie, Ind., 1979; PhD, U. Tex., Austin, 1983.

Instr. Cape Fear Tech. Inst., Wilmington, NC, 1977—78; lectr. U. Tex., Austin, 1982—84, rsch. scientist, 1984—85, asst. prof. Southwestern Med. Ctr. Dallas, 1985—92, assoc. prof. Southwestern Med. Ctr., 1992—99; asst. v.p. rsch. Tarleton State U.-Tex. A&M U. Sys., 1998—99, assoc. v.p. rsch., prof. dept. math., physics, engring. and academic affairs, 2000—. Internat. sci. adv. com. Data Mining and Info. Engring. Wessex Inst. Tech., England, 2005—. Author: Drugs and Pregnancy, 1992, 2d edit., 1998, Treatment of Psychiatric Disorders During Pregnancy, 2001, Handbook of Drugs and Pregnancy, 2006; reviewer profl. jours. including Obstetrics and Gynecology, Am. Jour. Ob-Gyn., Human Biology, Early Human Devel., Am. Jour. Med. Genetics; mem. editl. bd. Am. Jour. Human Biology, 1991-02, Ann. Human Biology, London, 2004-; contbr. numerous articles to profl. jours. Mem. com. Mayor's Lead Task Force, Dallas, 1985-89; vol. drug educator, cons., talented and gifted HS mentor, Dallas Ind. Sch. Dist., 1990—; scoutmaster troop 1 Boy Scouts Am., 1994-00; expert reviewer Dept. Homeland Security, 2002-; provider testimony US Senate, 2005, US House of Reps., 2006. Acad. scholar Appalachian State U., 1975-76; Doctoral fellow U. Tex. Grad. Sch., Austin, 1979-83; grantee Am. Heart Assn., Austin, 1990-94, Hogg Found. Mental Health, 1994-98, Tex. Commn. Alcoholism and Drug Abuse, 1990-91, 94-98, Ont. Student Assistance Program US Pub. Health Svc., Washington, 1991-96, NIH Nat. Inst. Drug Abuse, 1996-98, US Dept. Edn., 1999-04, USDA Risk Mgmt. Agy., 2000-07, US Dept. Justice, 2006-; named one of the Top 100 Reviewers in Ob-gyn., 2003; recognized as having one of the Best Papers in Econs., 2004. Fellow AAAS, Human Biology Coun., Royal Anthrop. Inst., Am. Soc. Human Genetics, Am. Assn. Phys. Anthropologists, Soc. Study Human Biology, Assn. Computing Machinery, Soc. Indsl. and Applied Math., Sigma Xi. Achievements include research in association of genetic zygosity with human physical growth; metabolism of cocaine by human placentae; effects of cocaine, alcohol and other drug abuse on the human embryo, fetus and pregnancy; placental transfer of anti-HIV drugs; effects of medically administered drugs on embryofetal development; inbreeding and genetic evolution in a Zapotec Indian genetic isolate; pharmacokinetics during pregnancy; pharmaco-epidemiology; applied data mining and data warehousing; risk analysis and fraud detection; childhood obesity in the US, Mexico and The United Arab Emirates; lead exposure during fetal development and childhood. Office: Tarleton State U Tex A&M U Sys Dept Math Physics Engring and Academic A Stephenville TX 76402-0010

LITTLE, BRUCE WASHINGTON, professional society administrator; b. Feb. 22, 1936; m. Nancy J. Mains; children: Elizabeth, Thomas, David. BS, Kans. State U., 1963, DVM, 1965. Pvt. practice assoc., Normal, Ill., 1965-69; pvt. practice Americana Animal Hosp., Bloomington, Ill., 1969-85; asst. exec. v.p. AVMA, Schaumburg, Ill., 1986-96, exec. v.p., 1996—. Rabies control officer McLean County, Ill., 1968-72; instr. U. Ill. Extension Svc., 1974, adv. Mclean County Bd. of Health, 1980-85; pres., ops. mgr. Blooming Grove Farm, Inc., Bloomington, 1983—; bd. dirs. Assn. Forum Chicagoland, 2003—, Am. Vet. Med. Found., 1996-, Nat. Commn. of Vet. Econ. Issues, 1998-; spkr. in field. Contbr. articles to profl. jours. Coach, Ill. 4-H Equine Judging Teams, 1974-76; bd. dirs. Mclean County Assn. Commerce Industry, 1983-85, Assn. Forum Chicagoland, 2003—, Am. Vet. Med. Found., 1996—, Nat. Commn. on Vet. Econ. Issues, 1999—; v.p. Ill. State U. Athletic Booster Club, 1980-82, pres., 1982-84. With U.S. Army, 1955-57. Named an alumni fellow, Kans. State U., 1998. Mem. AVMA, Ill. State Vet. Med. Assn., Chgo. Vet. Med. Assn., (hon.) Brit. Vet. Assn., Rotary (Paul Harris Fellow), Alpha Zeta. Avocations: sports, golf, reading, horse breeding. Office: Am Vet Med Assn 1931 N Meacham Rd Schaumburg IL 60173-4364

LITTLE, CHARLOTTE LOUISE, poet, writer; b. Scotia, Calif., May 9, 1948; d. Henry Author East and Melva Berniece Clifford; m. Stanley Lee Little, July 30, 1966; 1 child, Stan Lee; 1 child, Rhonda Meichelle. Diploma, John A. Rowland, Rowland Heights, Calif., 1966. Poet, writer, Riverside, Calif. Author: numerous poems; contbr. poetry to poethunter-.com, poetry to internet website. Deacon Solid Rock Ch. Internat. Named to Internat. Poetry Hall of Fame, 1996; recipient Diamon Homer trophy, Famous Poet Soc., 1996, Shakespeare Trophy of Excellence award, 2003, Poet of Yr. Medallion, 2003. Mem.: Internat. Soc. Poets (disting. mem., Internat. Poet of Merit award 1996). Avocations: writing, guitar, crafts, Bible reading, gardening.

LITTLE, DALLAS, minister; s. Chester and June Little. BA in English, Auburn U., Montgomery, 1993; MDiv, Emory U., Atlanta, 1996. Ordained elder United Meth. Ch., 1999, endorsed chaplain Bd. Higher Edn. & Ministry, United Meth. Ch., 2001. Chaplain internship Northside Hosp., Atlanta, 1996; assoc. pastor United Meth. Ch., Ft. Walton Beach, Fla., 1996—2001; active duty chaplain USAF, 2001—. Counselor Rape Crisis Ctr. DeKalb County, Ga., Atlanta, 1995—96; crisis counselor Bridgeway Ctr. Crisis Line, Ft. Walton Beach, 1998—2001; counselor St. Luke's Homeless Ministry, Atlanta, 1996—97; bd. mem. Cath. Charities Okaloosa County, Fla., Ft. Walton Beach, 1999—2001, Emerald Coast Marine Inst., Ft. Walton Beach, 2000—01. Capt. USAF, 2001—07, Miss., Turkey, Florida. Decorated Nat. Def. Svc. medal USAF, Global War on Terror Expeditionary medal, Global War Terror Svc. medal, Air Force Commendation medal with two oak leaf clusters, Humanitarian Svc. medal, Air Force Outstanding Unit award with v device for valor, Air Force Expeditionary Svc. ribbon with combat border, Air Force Overseas Short Tour ribbon. Mem.: VFW, Am. Assn. Pastoral Counselors, Am. Legion. Achievements include being one of the first air force chaplains in Iraq when Operation Iraqi Freedom began.

LITTLE, DANIEL EASTMAN, philosopher, educator, director; b. Rock Island, Ill., Apr. 7, 1949; s. William Charles and Emma Lou (Eastman) L.; m. Ronnie Alice Friedland, Sept. 12, 1976 (div. May 1995); children: Joshua Friedland-Little, Rebecca Friedland-Little. BS in Math. with highest honors, AB in Philosophy with high honors, U. Ill., 1971; PhD in Philosophy, Harvard U., 1977. Asst. prof. U. Wis.-Parkside, Kenosha, 1976-79; vis. assoc. prof. Wellesley (Mass.) Coll., 1985-87; vis. scholar Ctr. Internat. Affairs Harvard U., 1989-91, assoc. Ctr. Internat. Affairs, 1991-95; asst. prof. Colgate U., Hamilton, NY, 1979-85, assoc. prof., 1985-92, prof., 1992-96, chmn. dept. philosophy and religion, 1992-93, assoc. dean faculty, 1993-96; v.p. academic affairs Bucknell U., Lewisburg, Pa., 1996-2000, prof. philosophy, 1996-2000; chancellor U. Mich., Dearborn, 2000—, prof. philosophy, 2000—; faculty assoc. Inter-U. Consortium for Social and Political Rsch., 2000—. Teaching fellow Harvard U., 1973-76; participant internat. confs. Ctr. Asian and Pacific Studies, U. Oreg., 1992, Social Sci. Rsch. Coun./McArthur Found., U. Calif., San Diego, 1991, Budapest, Hungary, 1990, Morelos, Mex., 1989, Rockefeller Found., Bellagio, Italy, 1990, U. Manchester, Eng., 1986; mem. screening com. on internat. peace and security Social Sci. Rsch. Coun./MacArthur Found., 1991-94; manuscript reviewer Yale U. Press, Cambridge U. Press, Princeton U. Press, Oxford U. Press, Westview Press, Harvard U. Press, Can. Jour. Philosophy, Philosophy Social Scis., Synthese, Am. Polit. Sci. Rev.; grant proposal reviewer NSF, Social Sci. Rsch. Coun., Nat. Endowment for Humanities; tenure and promotion reviewer U. Tenn., Bowdoin Coll., Duke U., U. Wis.; faculty assoc. Inter-Univ. Consortium for Social and Polit. Rsch., 2000—. Author: The Scientific Marx, 1986, Understanding Peasant China: Case Studies in the Philosophy of Social Science, 1989, Varieties of Social Explanation: An Introduction to the Philosophy of Social Science, 1991 (Outstanding Book award Choice 1992), On the Reliability of Economic Models, 1995, Microfoundations Method and Causation: On the Philosophy of the Social Sciences, 1998, The Paradox of Wealth and Poverty: Mapping the Ethical Dilemmas of Global Development, 2003; contbr. articles to profl. jours., books. Social Sci. Rsch. Postdoctoral fellow MacArthur Found., 1989-91, Rsch. grantee NSF, 1987, Woodrow Wilson Grad. fellow, 1971-72. Mem. Am. Philos. Assn., Assn. Asian Studies, Internat. Devel. Ethics Assn., Social Sci. History Assn., Soc. for the History of Tech., Phi Beta Kappa. Office: Chancellor U Mich Dearborn 4901 Evergreen Rd Dearborn MI 48128 E-mail: delittle@umich.edu.

LITTLE, GEORGE DANIEL, clergyman; b. St. Louis, Dec. 18, 1929; s. Henry and Agathe Cox (Daniel) L.; m. Joan Phillips McCafferty, Aug. 22, 1953; children: Deborah Philips, Cynthia McCafferty (dec.), Alice Annette, Daniel Ross, Benjamin Henry. AB, Princeton U., 1951; MDiv, McCormick Theol. Sem., Chgo., 1954; LLD (hon.), Huron Coll., 1977. Ordained to ministry Presbyn. Ch., 1954; pastor East London Group Ministry, Presbyn. Ch. Eng., 1954-56, Friendship Presbyn. Ch., Pitts., 1956-62; assoc. dir. dept. urban ch., planning assoc. Bd. Nat. Missions, United Presbyterian Ch. U.S.A., NYC, 1962-72; assoc. for budgeting Gen. Assembly Mission Council, 1973-76, exec. dir. council, 1976-84; pastor First Presbyn. Ch., Ithaca, NY, 1984-93; interim pres. McCormick Theol. Sem., Chgo., 1993-94; pastor-in-residence Village Presbyn. Ch., Prairie Village, Kans., 1995-96, Westminster Presbyn. Ch., Mpls., 1997-99, 2002; ret., 1999. Presbyterian. Home: 6205 Mineral Point Rd Apt 103 Madison WI 53705-4577 E-mail: danglittle@aol.com.

LITTLE, GEORGE L., lawyer; b. Winston-Salem, NC, Sept. 14, 1942; s. George Lester and Jean (Misenheimer) L.; m. Susan Pollard, June 19, 1965; children: George L., Sara Lee. BA, Davidson Coll., NC, 1964; JD with hons., U. N.C., 1967. Bar: N.C. 1967, U.S. Supreme Ct., U.S. Ct. Appeals (4th, 9th, 11th and Fed. cir.), U.S. Dist. Ct. (ea., middle, we. dist.) N.C. Assoc. Petree Stockton & Robinson, Winston-Salem, 1971-75; ptnr. Kilpatrick Stockton LLP, Winston-Salem, 1976—. Author: The Antitrust Health Care Handbook, 1988. Mem. Winston-Salem Forsyth County Util. Commn.; bd. dirs., exec. com. Piedmont Opera Theatre; past pres. St. Andrew's Soc. NC, Inc., Pinehurst; bd. dirs. Winston-Salem Alliance, Idealliance; past chmn. Greater Winston-Salem C. of C., Winston-Salem Bus. Inc.; past exec. com. Piedmont Triad Partnership; v.p., dir. Winston-Salem Symphony Assn., 1987-89, United Way of Forsyth County, Winston-Salem, 1976-82. Capt. U.S. Army, 1967-71. Mem. ABA, Internat. Trademark Assn. (mem. disting. panel neutrals), NC Bar Assn., Oldtown Club, Rotary Democrat. Lutheran. Avocations: wine, gardening, opera, sailing, scottish heritage. Office: Kilpatrick Stockton LLP 1001 W 4th St Winston Salem NC 27101-2400 Office Phone: 336-607-7300. Office Fax: 336-734-2620. Business E-Mail: glittle@kilpatrickstockton.com.

LITTLE, GLEN GORDON, retired circus clown, educator; b. Genoa, Nebr., Dec. 5, 1925; s. Glenn Arthur and Elsie Viola L.; m. Shirley Mae-Moss, Oct. 12, 1950 (div. Oct. 1970); 1 child, Tawnya René Little Wiseman; m. Patricia Margaret Cosgrove, Oct. 12, 1971; stepchildren: Roxanne Kay Cosgrove Webster, Deborah Rene Wagner. Pvt. practice, Denver, 1963-67; from circus clown to dir. clowns Ringling Brothers-Barnum and Bailey Circus, Venice, Fla., 1968-80, dir. clowns, 1980-90, ret., 1990. Author: Circus Stories, 1997. With USN, 1943-44. Achieved Master Clown status Irving Feld pres. Ringling Brothers-Barnum and Bailey Circus, Washington, 1983; inducted to Clown Hall of Fame, Delavin, Wis., 1991; face on collector plate Danbury (Conn.) Mint, 1994. Mem. DAV. Avocations: building clown gags, reading history books. Home: 222 E 8th St Burley ID 83318-1337

LITTLE, (WILLIAM) GRADY, professional baseball coach; b. Abilene, Tex., Mar. 30, 1950; m. Debi Little. Player-coach Yankee orgn., 1971—73; coach Ea. League, West Haven, Conn., 1974; minor league coach Balt., 1980, FSL, Miami; mgr. Appalachian League Oriole's Blufield rookieclub; mgr. minor league Atlanta, 1980—95, mgr., 1986, Richmond, 1993—95; coach bullpen Nat. League West Divsn. Championships, San Diego, 1996; bench coach Indians; bench coach, instr. Boston Red Sox, 1997—99, mgr., 2002—03; asst. gen. mgr. Chicago Cubs, 2004—05; mgr. LA Dodgers, 2005—. Named Mgr. of Yr., Richmond, 1994; recipient Mgr. of Yr. awards, Baseball Am., Sporting News, 1992. Office: Dodgers Stadium 1000 Elysian Park Ave Los Angeles CA 90012

LITTLE, JAN NIELSEN, lawyer; b. Oakland, Calif., Jan. 20, 1958; d. Jack Harry and Patricia Ann (Holzknecht) N.; m. Rory K. Little, Mar. 19, 1983. AB in English Lit. (hon.), U Calif., Berkeley, 1978; JD, Yale U., 1981. Bar: Calif. 1981, DC 1984. Law clk. to judge William W Schwarzer US Dist. Ct. (no. dist.) Calif., San Francisco, 1981-82; trial atty. Dept. Justice, Washington, 1982-86; assoc. Keker & Brockett, San Francisco, 1986-88, ptnr., 1989, Keker & Van Nest LLP, San Francisco. Spkr. in field. Contbr. articles to profl. jour. Recipient Spl. Commendation award Dept. Justice, Wash., 1984, Criminal Justice award, Calif. Atty for Criminal Justice 1995, Wayland Prize, named Calif. Top 75 Women Litig., LA Daily Jour. 2005-06, Best Lawyers In Am. 2006, Internat. Who's Who of Bus. Lawyers 2006, Top 500 Litig. in US 2006, Top 100 Lawyers in no. Calif., Lawdragon magazine, Top 50 Women Lawyers in no. Calif., San Francisco mag./Law and Politics 2005-06. Mem. ABA (co-chair litig. sect. complex crimes com. & no. calif. white collar crime com.), Calif. Bar Assn. DC Bar Assn. Home: 148 Bret Harte Rd San Rafael CA 94901-5249 Office: Keker & Van Nest LLP 710 Sansome St San Francisco CA 94111-1704 Office Phone: 415-391-5400. Office Fax: 415-397-7188. Business E-Mail: jlittle@kvn.com.

LITTLE, JOHN BERTRAM, radiologist, educator, researcher; b. Boston, Oct. 5, 1929; s. Bertram Kimball and Nina (Fletcher) L.; m. Francoise Cottereau, Aug. 4, 1960; children: John Bertram, Frederic Fletcher AB in Physics, Harvard U., 1951; MD, Boston U., 1955. Diplomate Diplomate Am. Bd. Radiology. Intern Johns Hopkins Hosp., Balt., 1955—56; resident in radiology Mass. Gen. Hosp., Boston, 1958-61; fellow Harvard U., Cambridge, Mass., 1961-63; from instr. to assoc. prof. radiobiology Harvard Sch. Pub. Health, Boston, 1963-75, prof., 1975—, chmn. dept. physiology, 1980-83, James Stevens Simmons prof. radiobiology, 1987—, chmn. dept. cancer cell biology, 1997—2002, dir. Ctr. Radiation Scis. and Environ. Health, 1998—2006; dir. Kresge Ctr. Environ. Health, Boston, 1982-98. Cons. radiology Mass. Gen. Hosp., Boston, 1965—, Brigham and Women's Hosp., Boston, 1968—2000; chmn. bd. sci. counsellors Nat. Inst. Environ. Health Sci., 1982—84; bd. sci. counsellors Nat. Toxicology Program, 1988—92; mem. sci. coun. Radiation Effects Rsch. Found., Hiroshima, Japan, 1992—98, chmn., 1996—98; bd. dirs. on radiation effects rsch. NAS, 1992—98, chmn., 1996—98; mem. Coun. Internat. Assn. for Radiation Rsch. Mem. editorial bd. numerous nat. and internat. jours.; contbr. chpts. to books and articles to profl. jours. Mem. coun. Nat. Coun. on Radiation Protection and Measurements, 1993—; trustee various hist. and cultural orgns. Capt. U.S. Army, 1956-58. Named one of Outstanding Investigator grantee, Nat. Cancer Inst., 1988—; recipient numerous rsch. and tng. grants, NIH, 1968—; grantee, Am. Cancer Soc., 1965—68. Mem. AAAS (coun. in med. scis. 1988-91), Radiation Rsch. Soc. N.Am. (pres.-elect 1985, pres. 1986-87), Am. Assn. Cancer Rsch., Am. Physiol. Soc., Health Physics Soc., Am. Soc. Photobiology, Internat. Assn. Radiation Rsch. (coun.). Natl. Assoc. mem., Natl. Acad. of Sci. Avocations: music, architecture. Office: Harvard U Dept Cancer Cell Biology 665 Huntington Ave Boston MA 02115-6021

LITTLE, JOHN DUTTON CONANT, management scientist, educator; b. Boston, Feb. 1, 1928; s. John Dutton and Margaret (Jones) L.; m. Elizabeth Davenport Alden, Sept. 12, 1953; children: John Norris, Sarah Alden, Thomas Dunham Conant, Ruel Davenport. SB in Physics, MIT, 1948, PhD, 1955; PhD (hon.), U. Liege, Belgium, 1992, Cath. U. of Mons, 1997; PhD (hon.), U. London, 2002. Engr. Gen. Electric Co., Schenectady, 1949-50; asst. prof. ops. research Case-Western Res. U., 1957-60, assoc. prof., 1960-62; research asst. MIT, 1951-54, assoc. prof. mgmt., 1962-67, prof., 1967-78, George M. Bunker prof. mgmt., 1978-89, Inst. prof., 1989—, dir. Ops. Research Ctr., 1969-76, head mgmt. sci. group Sloan Sch. Mgmt., 1972-82, head behavioral and policy scis. area, 1982-88, chmn. undergrad. program, 1990—; pres. Mgmt. Decision Systems, Inc., 1967-80, chmn. bd. dirs., 1967-85; dir., advisor to bd. dirs. Info. Resources, Inc., 1985—2003. Cons. ops. rsch. indsl. govtl. orgns., 1958—; vis. prof. mktg. European Inst. Bus. Adminstrn., Fontainebleau, France, fall 1988; researcher math. programming, queuing theory, mktg., traffic control, decision support systems, e-commerce; bd. dirs. InSite Mktg. Technology, Inc., 1997-99. Assoc. editor: Mgmt. Sci, 1967-71; contbr. articles to profl. jours. Trustee Mktg. Sci. Inst., 1983-89. Served with AUS, 1955-56. Fellow AAAS (mem. coun. 2000—03); mem. NAE, Ops. Rsch. Soc. Am. (coun. 1970-73, pres. 1979-80), Inst. Mgmt. Scis. (v.p. 1976-79, pres. 1984-85), Fellow Inst. for Ops. Rsch. and the Mgmt. Scis. (pres. 1995), Am. Mktg. Assn., Sigma Xi. Home: 37 Conant Rd Lincoln MA 01773-3912 Office: MIT Sloan Sch Mgmt Cambridge MA 02142-1347 Office Phone: 617-253-3738.

LITTLE, JOHN WILLIAM, plastic surgeon, educator; b. Indpls., Mar. 12, 1944; s. John William Jr. and Naida (Jones) L.; m. Patricia Padgett Lea, May 26, 1969 (div. 1974); m. Teri Ann Tyson, Feb. 28, 1981 (div. 1982). AB, Dartmouth Coll., 1966, B in Med. Scis., 1967; MD, Harvard U., 1969. Diplomate Am. Bd. Med. Examiners, Am. Bd. Surgery, Am. Bd. Plastic Surgery. Intern Case Western Res. U., Cleve., 1969-70, resident in surgery, 1970-74, resident in plastic surgery, 1973-75; fellow in plastic surgery U. Miami, 1975-77; asst. prof. Georgetown U., Washington, 1977-82, assoc. prof., 1982-87, prof., 1987-92, clin. prof., 1992—, dir. div. plastic surgery, residency tng. program, plastic surgeon-in-chief univ. hosp., 1979-92; dir. Nat. Capital Tng. Program in Plastic Surgery affiliated hosps. Georgetown U. and Howard U., 1988-92; dir. Georgetown Plastic Surgery Fellowship in Breast and Aesthetic Surgery, 1990-92; pvt. practice Washington, 1992—. Prof. postgrad. edn. in plastic surgery Internat. Soc. Aesthetic Plastic Surgery, 1999—; chief plastic surgery Medlantic Ctr. for Ambulatory Surgery, Inc., 1993—, mem. med. adv. bd., 1993—; cons. Nat. Cancer Inst., NIH, Bethesda, Md., 1977-92, Washington VA Med. Ctr., 1981-92, Reach to Recovery program Nat. Capital chpt. Am. Cancer Soc., 1981—, RENU program in breast reconstrn., 1982; specialist site visitor plastic surgery residency rev. com. Accreditation Coun. for Grad. Med. Edn., 1982-95; vis. lect. various insts.; bd. govs. Nat. Endowment for Plastic Surgery, 1995—. Adv. editor Plastic and Reconstructive Surgery, 1997—, manuscript reviewer Plastic and Reconstructive Surgery, Annals of Plastic Surgery; assoc. editor Surgery of the Breast: Principles and Art, 1998; contbr. numerous articles to med. jours., numerous chpts. to books. Bd. dirs. Triann reconstructive surgery teams to Caribbean and S.Am., Georgetown Tissue Bank, 1986-88, Operation Luz del Sol; founder, pres., med. dir. Reconstructive Surgeons Vol. Program; bd. dirs. Washington Summer Opera Theater; trustee Washington Opera, 1993—, artistic com., 1994—; Domingo Circle, 1995—, Laureates' medal, 1999. Recipient Laureate medallion Domingo Cir., 1999, Mem. AMA, ACS (coord. plastic surgery audiovisual program Ann. Clin. Congress 1988-90, 92-93, bd. govs., Met. Washington chpt. councillor 1985-94, chmn. sci. program com. 1990-91, v.p. 1991-92, pres. 1992-93, bd. govs. 1998—), Nat. Capital Soc. Plastic Surgeons (sec. treas. 1982-83, pres. 1984-85), Am. Soc. Plastic Surgeons (audiovisual program dir. ann. meeting 1984-86, strategic planning com. 1987-96, fin. com. 1989-94, conv. policy com. 1993-96, ops. com. 1993-96, chmn. 1994-95, spokesperson network steering com. 1994-96, bd. dirs. 1994-96, exec. com. 1995-96, spokesperson 1998—, rep. to IPRAS 1999—), Am. Assn. Plastic Surgeons (co-chmn. various coms.), Plastic Surgery Ednl. Found. (bd. dirs. 1985-97, devel. com. 1991—, chmn. 1997-2000, chmn. various coms., rep. to Coun. Plastic Surg. Orgns. 1989-95, parliamentarian 1992-93, v.p. 1993-94, pres. adv. coun. 1993-96, commr. various commns., pres.-elect, 1995, pres. 1995-96, Maliniac fellow 1998—, Disting. Svc. award, 2000), Med. Soc. D.C. (chmn. plastic surgery sect. 1985), D.R. Millard Surg. Soc. and Ednl. Found. (pres. 1985-87), Am. Cleft Palate Assn., Am. Soc. Maxillofacial Surgeons, Washington Acad. Surgeons (coun. 1988-90), Am. Soc. Aesthetic Plastic Surgery (In Chun Sung award philanthropic svc. 2000), NE Soc. Plastic Surgeons (chmn. various coms., v.p. 1991-92, pres. 1992-93, historian 1994-99), Internat. Soc. Aesthetic Plastic Surgery (chmn. bylaws com. 1990-93, 95-97, parliamentarian 1990-93, mem. membership com. 1993-97, chmn. 1993-95, sec. gen. 1997-2000, rep. to IPRAS 1997-2000, prof. postgrad. edn. in aesthetic plastic surgery, others), Am. Alpine Workshop in Plastic Surgery (founder, pres. 1991-92, historian 1995—), Internat. Confedn. Plastic Reconstructive and Aesthetic Surgery (mem. exec. com. 1997-2000, coun. dels. 1999—), Nat. Endowment Plastic Surgeons (bd. govs. 1995—), Internat. Plastic, Reconstructive and Aesthetic Surgery Found. (bd. dirs. 1999—, ednl. program com. chmn. 1999—, vice chmn. devel. com. 1999—, publs. and videotape com.), European Assn. Plastic Surgeons (corr.), Turkish Soc. Plastic Surgeons (hon.), Argentine Soc. Plastic, Reconstructive and Aesthetic Surgeons (assoc.), Atlantic Soc. Plastic Surgeons (hon.), Soc. Am. and Italian Plastic Surgeons (founding mem. 1988—), Turkish Soc. Plastic Surgeons (hon. mem. 1996—), Argentina Soc. Esthetic Plastic Surgery and Repair (corr. mem. 1999—), European Assn. Plastic Surgeons (corr. mem 2000—), Atlantic Soc. Palstic Surgeons (hon. mem. 2000—), Mediterranean Soc. Plastic and Aesthetic Surgery (active mem. 2001—); fellow Am. Israeli Plastic Surgeons (charter mem. 1997—), Republican. Presbyterian. Home: 3030 K St NW Ph 212 Washington DC 20007-5107 Office: 1145 19th St NW Ste 802 Washington DC 20036-3700

LITTLE, KAREN J., counselor; b. Santa Fe, N.Mex., Aug. 13, 1960; children: Andrew R., Jenna K. MA in Sociology, N.Mex State U., Las Cruces, 1997; MA in Counseling and Ednl. Psychology, N.Mex State U., Las Cruces, N. Mex., 2004. Lic. Baccalaureate Social Worker N.Mex Regulation and Licensing Dept., 1990; Profl. Mental Health Counselor N.Mex Regulation and Licensing Dept., 1994, cert. Criminal Justice Specialist Nat. Assn. of Forensic Counselors, 2004, Domestic Violence Counselor III Nat. Assn. of Forensic Counselors, 2004, clinical mental health counselor N. Mex. Regulation and Licensing Dept., 2005. Outreach specialist/job developer Alternative Ho., Inc., Las Cruces, N.Mex., 1985—87; case mgmt. supr. SW Counseling Ctr., Inc, Las Cruces, N.Mex., 1987—97; non-resident program coord. La Casa, Inc., Las Cruces, N.Mex., 1997—2002; program mgr. N.Mex Commn. on the Status of Women, Las Cruces, N.Mex., 2002—. Contbr. paper presented to conf. Recipient Counseling Student of the Yr., Counseling Masters Student Assn., 2003. Mem.: ACA (assoc.), Phi Kappa Phi (licentiate). Avocations: reading, bowling. Office: TeamWorks 2205 S Main Suite A Las Cruces NM 88005 Home Phone: 505-524-3190; Office Phone: 505-524-6290. Business E-Mail: kjlittle2003@yahoo.com.

LITTLE, KEVIN GERARD, lawyer; b. NYC, Feb. 25, 1966; s. Henry Leroy Little, Jr. and Bertha Marie Little; m. Virna Liza Santos, Aug. 18, 1990; 1 child, Enrique Raymond Santos. BA cum laude, Harvard U., 1987, JD cum laude, 1990. Bar: Calif. 1990, U.S. Supreme Ct. 1994, U.S. Ct. Appeals (all circuits) 1994, U.S. Ct. Fed. Claims 1994, U.S. Dist. Ct. (cen. dist.) Calif. 1990, U.S. Dist. Ct. (ea. dist.) Calif. 1995, U.S. Dist. Ct. (no. dist.) Calif. 1998, U.S. Dist. Ct. P.R., U.S. Dist. Ct. (we. dist.) Tex. Assoc. O'Melveny & Myers, LA, 1991—92; law clk. Hon. Consuelo B. Marshall, LA, 1991—92, Hon. Cecil F. Poole, San Francisco, 1992—93; solo practitioner San Juan, 1993—95; atty. Frampton, Williams & Little, Fresno, Calif., 1995—2001; solo practitioner Fresno, Calif., 2001—. Vis. atty. Boalt Hall Sch. Law, Berkeley, Calif., 2001; guest spkr. Ea. Dist. Calif. Law Enforcement Summit, Squaw Valley, 2002, Bay Area Police Watch, San Francisco, 1999—2000. Sponsor Big Bros./Big Sisters, Fresno, 1996—; participant Campaign Against Prop 209, Fresno, 1997. Named one of most tenacious litigators in Calif., Calif. Lawyers Mag.; recipient Svc.

award, Helping Our Own Destiny, Fresno, 1997, San Joaquin Coll. Law, 1998—. Democrat. Office: 1275 E Province Fresno CA 93780 Office Phone: 559-486-5730. E-mail: fwllaw@aol.com.

LITTLE, LAURA ANN, elementary school educator, art educator; b. Lincoln Pk., Mich., Feb. 4, 1960; d. John Elliott Little and Patricia Ann Peckham; m. Jeffrey Hart Genthner (div.). Degree in Interior Design, Alma Coll., Mich., 1979; BA in Interior Design, Mich. State U., East Lansing, Mich., 1982. Tchr. elem. art Curriculum Svcs., Elkhart, Ind., 2002—; freelance photographer Detroit News, 2003—. Tchr. art and music Detroit Symphony Orch., 2005. Greeting cards, Detroit Opera House, 2005—, Cranbrook Art Mus., Bloomfield Hills, Mich., 2006—. Recipient Best of Photography award, Photographer's Forum, 1996, 1997, 1998, Photo of Day award, Detroit News, 2004; grantee Kodak Camera award for use by 60 children, Nat. Geographic Soc., 1998. Mem.: Mich. Press Photographers Assn., Nat. Press Photographers Assn., Nat. Mus. Women in Arts (Wash., DC), Detroit Inst. Arts, The Scarab Club. Republican. Presbyn. Avocations: painting, travel, movies, photography. Home: 100 Riverfront Dr 1010 Detroit MI 48226 Office Phone: 313-610-6837. E-mail: littleimages@comcast.net.

LITTLE, R. DONALD, real estate entrepreneur; b. Gastonia, NC, Mar. 18, 1937; s. Coy Marshall and Stella May (Pruett) L.; m. Jacqueline Beatrice Mandel, June 10, 1967 (dec. Mar. 1995); Linda Lee Stoner; Sept. 7, 1999; children by previous marriage: Tina June Whitman, Diana Dawn Little, Laura Marie Van Meel; stepchildren: Keith, Don. BA, U. Md., 1972; BS in Architecture, Cath. U. Am., 1981, MArch, 1983. Ordained, chartered non-denominational minister, 1998. Blood bank and med. technologist Dr. Oscar B. Hunter Meml. Lab., Washington, 1961-66; biol. lab. technologist Naval Med. Rsch. Inst., Bethesda, Md., 1966-68; blood bank and med. technologist, supr. Ctrl. Lab. Doctor's Hosp., Washington, 1959-79; jr. architect VVKR Inc., University Park, Md., supr. architect; br. head design divsn. Naval Surface Weapons Ctr., Silver Spring, Md., 1981-87; supr. architect, chief facility engring. br. Agrl. Rsch. Svc., USDA, 1987-96; area adminstrv. officer BARC Rsch. Svc., USDA, Beltsville, Md., 1996—2002; ret., 2002; real estate entrepreneur, 2002—. With USN, 1956—61. Mem. Am. Assn. Blood Banks, Am. Soc. Med. Technologists. Home: 148 Williams Way Lewes DE 19958-4376 Office: Long and Foster Realtors 720 Rehoboth Ave Rehoboth Beach DE 19971 Office Phone: 302-236-1373. E-mail: coolsummerbreeze@aol.com.

LITTLE, RICHARD ALLEN, mathematics professor, computer science educator; b. Cochocton, Ohio, Jan. 12, 1939; s. Charles M. and Elsie Leanna (Smith) L.; children from previous marriage: Eric, J. Alice, Stephanie; m. Laura Ann Novosel, June 15, 1991. BS in Math. cum laude, Wittenberg U., 1960; MA in tchg., Johns Hopkins U., 1961; EdM in Math., Harvard U., 1965; PhD in Math. Edn., Kent State U., 1971. Tchr. Culver Acad., Ind., 1961-65; instr., curriculum cons. Harvard U., Cambridge, Mass. and Aiyetoro, Nigeria, 1965-67; from instr. to assoc. prof. Kent State U., Canton, Ohio, 1967-75; from assoc. prof. to prof. Baldwin-Wallace Coll., Berea, Ohio, 1975—, dept. chair, 1978-83. Mathematician/educator Project Discovery Ohio Bd. Regents, 1992-96; vis. prof., math. Ohio State U., Columbus, 1987-88, 92-95; pres. Cleve. Collaborative on Math. Edn., 1986-87; policy bd. Ohio Resource Ctr. for Math. Sci. and Reading, 2000—, exec. com. policy bd., 2001—, chair exec. com., 2002-03; vis. prof., dept. math. and stats. Bowling Green State U., 2004-05; lectr. in field. Contbr. articles to profl. jours. Bd. dirs. Canton Symphony Orch., 1973-75; Sunday sch. tchr. Bethany English Luth. Ch., Cleve., 1991—; bd. deacons Holy Cross Luth. Ch., Canton, 1968-74, chmn., 1971-74. Recipient Strosacker Excellence in Tchg. award and Student Senate Faculty Excellence award Baldwin-Wallace Coll., 1999. Mem. Nat. Coun. Tchrs. Math. (profl. devel. and status adv. com. 1987-90, program com. ann. meeting 1997), Ohio Coun. Tchrs. Math. (pres. 1974-76, v.p. 1970-73, sec. 1982-84, dir. state math. contest 1983-92, Christofferson-Fawcett award 1990), Ohio Math. Educators Leadership Coun. (pres. 1990-91, bd. dirs. 1988-92), Greater Canton Coun. Tchrs. Math. (pres. 1969-70), Math. Assn. Am. (pres. Ohio sect. 1983-84, editor 1977-83). Avocations: hiking, tennis, handball. Office: Baldwin-Wallace Coll Dept Math & Computer Sci 275 Eastland Rd Berea OH 44017-2005 Home Phone: 216-529-0775; Office Phone: 440-826-2006. Business E-Mail: rlittle@bw.edu.

LITTLE, ROBERT, reporter; B, Towson U., Md.; M, Columbia U. Politics and govt. reporter Virginian-Pilot, Norfolk, Va., Carroll County Times, Westminster, Md.; bus. reporter The Baltimore Sun, 1998—2003, nat. corr., 2003—. Author: (three-part series) Dangerous Remedy, The Baltimore Sun, 2006 (George Polk award for Med. Reporting, 2006). Achievements include featuring stories about the shortages of medical supplies for troops fighting in Iraq. This led to immediate policy changes and corrective measures by the US Army. Office: Baltimore Sun Nat Desk 501 N Calvert St Baltimore MD 21278-0001 Office Phone: 410-332-6409. Office Fax: 410-783-2517. Business E-Mail: Robert.little@baltsun.com.*

LITTLE, ROBERT DAVID, library science professor; b. Milw., July 11, 1937; s. Kenneth Edwin and Grace Elizabeth (Terwileger) L. BA, U. Wis., Milw., 1959; MA, U. Wis., 1964, PhD, 1972. Tchr., sch. librarian Sevastapol Pub. Schs., Sturgeon Bay, Wis., 1959-62; sch. librarian Highland Park (Ill.) High Sch., 1962-63; supr. sch. libraries Sevastapol/Gilbraltor Pub. Sch., Sturgeon Bay, 1963-65; state sch. library supr. Wis. Dept. Pub. Instrn., Madison, 1965-69, program adminstr., 1969-70; asst. prof. libr. sci. U. Wis., Milw., 1970-71, acting dir. Sch. Libr. Sci., 1971; assoc. prof. libr. sci. Ind. State U., Terre Haute, 1971-77, prof., 1977-97, chmn. dept., 1971-93. Cons. Ind. Nat. Network Study, Terre Haute, 1978-79; cons., researcher Nat. Ctr. Edn. Stats., Washington, 1978-79; mem. Ind. State Libr. Adv. Coun., Indpls., 1981-91. Co-author: Public Library Users and Uses, 1988; editor: Cataloging, Processing, Administering AV Materials, 1972; contbr. articles to profl. jours. Pres. West Cen. Ind. chpt. Ind. Civil Liberties Union, 1988-92. Edn. Act fellow U. Wis., Madison, 1967, 68. Mem. ALA, Am. Assn. Sch. Librs., Assn. Ind. Media Educators (pres. 1981-82, Peggy Leach Pfeiffer Svc. award 1987). Methodist. Avocations: reading, travel. Home: 500 W 43rd St Apt 22H New York NY 10036-4335

LITTLE, ROBERT EUGENE, engineering educator; b. Enfield, Ill., May 24, 1933; s. John Henry and Mary (Stephens) L.; m. Barbara Louina Farrell, Feb. 4, 1961; children: Susan Elizabeth, James Robert, Richard Roy, John William. BSME, U. Mich., 1959; MSME, Ohio State U., 1960; PhDME, U. Mich., 1963. Asst. prof. mech. engring. Okla. State U., Stillwater, 1963-65; assoc. prof. U. Mich., Dearborn, 1965-68, prof., 1968—. Author: Statistical Design of Fatigue Experiments, 1975, Probability and Statistics for Engineers, 1978, Mechanical Reliability Improvement, 2003. Mem. ASTM, Am. Statis. Assn. Home: 3230 Pine Lake Rd West Bloomfield MI 48324-1951 Office: U Mich 4901 Evergreen Rd Dearborn MI 48128-1491 Office Phone: 313-593-5122.

LITTLE, THOMAS M., public relations executive; b. Columbus, Ohio, Dec. 21, 1935; s. John William and Eulalia Josephine (Mayer) L.; m. Susan Mulford, Sept. 29, 1959; children: Carin Andrea, Debora Mayer, Sharon Mulford, Patricia Anne. BS in Journalism, Northwestern U., 1958; post-grad., Bradley U., 1958. Account supr. Philip Lesly Co., Chgo., 1962—65; v.p., account supr. Burson-Marsteller, NYC, 1966—76; v.p. Foote Cone & Belding, Inc., NYC, 1977-78; pres. FCB Pub. Rels., NYC, 1978-81, Bus. Orgn., Inc. divsn. Carl Byoir & Assocs., NYC, 1982, Tracy-Locke/BBDO Pub. Rels., Dallas, 1983-85; exec. v.p., gen. mgr. Manning, Selvage & Lee, NYC, 1986; pres. T.J. Ross & Assocs., NYC, 1986-87; pres., gen. mgr. Golin/Harris Communication, NYC, 1987-91; pub. rels. cons., 1992—. Bd. dirs. Damon Runyon-Walter Winchell Cancer Fund, NYC Lt. (j.g.) USN, 1959-62. Mem. Am. Mktg. Assn., Pub. Rels. Soc. Am. (SC and Ga. chpts.), Hilton Head Island C. of C., Publicity Club NYC, Mt. Kisco Country Club (NY), Sea Pines Country Club (Hilton Head Island), Lotos Club (NYC), Sigma Alpha Epsilon. Roman Catholic. Home and Office: PO Box 1959 43 Village E Rd Wilmington VT 05363-1959 Personal E-mail: littlevthh@aol.com.

LITTLE, WILLIAM ARTHUR, physicist, researcher; b. South Africa, Nov. 17, 1930; came to U.S., 1958, naturalized, 1964; s. William Henry and Margaret (Macleod) L.; m. Annie W. Smith, July 15, 1955; children—Lucy Claire, Linda Susan, Jonathan William. PhD, Rhodes U., S. Africa, 1953, Glasgow U., Scotland, 1957. Faculty Stanford, 1958—, prof. physics, 1965-94; prof. emeritus, 1994—. Cons. to industry, 1960—; co-founder, chmn. MMR Techs. Inc., 1980—, 3L&T, Inc., 1999—. Recipient Deans award disting. tchg. Stanford U., 1975-76, Walter J. Gores award for excellence in tchg., Stanford U., 1979, IR-100 award Indsl. R&D, 1981, R&D 100 award, 2006, Samuel C. Collins award, 2007; NRC Can. postdoctoral fellow Vancouver, Can., 1956-58, Sloan Found. fellow, 1959-63, John Simon Guggenheim fellow, 1964-65, NSF sr. postdoctoral fellow, 1970-71. Fellow Am. Phys. Soc.; mem. Am. Chem. Soc. Achievements include spl. research low temperature physics, superconductivity, neural network theory, cryogenics; holder 15 patents in area of cryogenics and med. instrumentation. Home: 15 Crescent Dr Palo Alto CA 94301-3106 Office: Stanford U Dept Physics Stanford CA 94305 Business E-Mail: bill@mmr.com.

LITTLE, WM. A. (WILLIAM ALFRED LITTLE), language educator, researcher, musicologist; b. Boston, July 28, 1929; s. Wm. A. and Myrle A. (Holmes) L. BA, Tufts U., 1951; LTCL, Trinity Coll., London, 1952; MA, Harvard U., 1953; PhD, U Mich., 1961. Asst. prof. Williams Coll., Williamstown, Mass., 1957-63; assoc. prof., chair Tufts U., Medford, Mass., 1963-66; chair U. Va., Charlottesville, 1966-72, prof., 1966-95, prof. German and music emeritus, 1995—. Vis. prof. musicology U. Rochester, N.Y., 1996. Author: G.A. Bürger, 1974; editor: Mendelssohn-Complete Organ Works, 5 vols., 1987-90; editor The German Quarterly, 1970-78; contbr. articles to profl. jours. Cpl. U.S. Army, 1953-55. Sesquicentennial fellow U. Va., 1972-73, 78-79, 88-89. Mem. MLA (chair comp. lit. 1970-72), Am. Assn. Tchrs. German (nat. exec. coun. 1968-78), Am. Guild Organists (registrar Mass. chpt. 1949-53, dean Charlottesville chpt. 1977-78, registrar, archivist Ctrl. Fla. chpt. 1995-99, nat. com. profl. edn. 1990-2002), Am. Mus. Soc., Orgn. Hist. Soc., Am. Bach Soc., Am. Brahms Soc., Neue Bachgesellschaft (Leipzig). Home: 245 Terrell Rd West Charlottesville VA 22901 E-mail: wal@virginia.edu.

LITTLEDOG, PAT, writer; b. College Station, Tex., June 23, 1941; d. Ollie McLaurin and Nina Lucille Ellis; m. Robert Joseph Guidry (div.); children: Morgan Guidry, Morris Guidry, Brook Guidry; m. Charles Bruce Taylor Jr. (div.). BA in English, U. Tex., El Paso, 1969, MA in Creative Writing, 1976. Writer, 1959—; instr. English U. Tex., El Paso, 1974—76, 1993, Austin CC, Tex., 1983, 1989—93; instr. creative writing U. Utah, Salt Lake City, 1976—78; mgr. Paperbacks Plus, Dallas and Austin, 1980—88; reader Tex. Assessment of Skills Placement Test Nat. Evaluations Sys., Austin, 1990—2002; banquet server Hospitality Pers., Miles Frost, Austin, 1996—2002. Poet in residence Tex. Commn. Arts, 1978—80; clown Balloon Boutique, Austin, 1982—93. Author: Border Healing Woman - The Story of Jewel Babb, 1981 (SW Book award, 81), Tonics, Teas, Roots & Remedies, 1982, Afoot in a Field of Men, 1983 (Austin Book award, 83), The God-Chaser, 1986, In Search of the Mother of Jobs, 1991, (poetry) When the Sky Splits, 1995, Out of This World, 2004; contbr. various pieces to anthologies, short stories, articles to mags., newspapers, lit. publs.; editor, pub.: Goat Lore, 1980, Night of the Luminarias, 1984, Breathing, 1990, Dancing, 1993 (Austin Book award, 93). Mem. So. Poverty Law Ctr., Montgomery, Ala., 1996—, United Negro Coll. Fund, Fairfax, Va., 2004—, Cal Farley Boys Ranch, Amarillo, Tex., 2004—. Writing fellow, U. Tex., El Paso, 1974—76, U. Utah, Salt Lake City, 1976—78, Nat. Endowment Arts, Washington, 1978, Dobie-Paisano fellow, U. Tex., 1986. Mem.: Tex. Inst. Letters. Avocation: walking. Home: 9952 FM 1854 Dale TX 78616

LITTLEFIELD, JOHN WALLEY, geneticist, cell biologist, pediatrician; b. Providence, Dec. 3, 1925; s. Ivory and Mary Russell (Walley) Littlefield; m. Elizabeth Lascelles Legge, Nov. 11, 1950; children: Peter P., John W., Elizabeth I. MD, Harvard U., 1947; MHS, Johns Hopkins U, 1992. Diplomate Am. Bd. Internal Medicine. Intern Mass. Gen. Hosp., Boston, 1947-48, resident in medicine, 1948-50, staff, 1956-74, chief genetics unit children's service, 1966-73; assoc. in medicine Harvard U. Med. Sch., 1956-62, asst. prof. medicine, 1962-66, asst. prof. pediatrics, 1966-69, prof. pediatrics, 1970-73; prof., chmn. dept. pediatrics Johns Hopkins U. Sch. Medicine, Balt., 1974-85; pediatrician-in-chief Johns Hopkins U. Hosp., 1974-85; prof., chmn. dept. physiology Johns Hopkins U. Sch. Medicine, Balt., 1985-92. Author: Variation, Senescence and Neoplasia in Cultured Somatic Cells, 1976. With USNR, 1952—54. Fellow Guggenheim, 1965—66, Josiah Macy Jr. Found., Oxford U., 1979. Mem.: NAS, Assn. Am. Physicians, Am. Pediatric Soc., Am. Soc. Human Genetics, Soc. Pediatric Rsch., Tissue Culture Assn., Am. Soc. Clin. Investigation, Am. Soc. Biol. Chemists, Am. Acad. Arts and Scis., Phi Beta Kappa, Delta Omega, Alpha Omega Alpha. Home: 304 Golf Course Rd Owings Mills MD 21117-4114 Office: Johns Hopkins U Sch Medicine Dept Physiology Baltimore MD 21205 E-mail: jlittlef@jhmi.edu.

LITTLEFIELD, PAUL DAMON, retired management consultant; b. Cambridge, Mass., June 8, 1920; s. W. Joseph and Sally Pastorius (Damon) L.; m. Emmy Farnsworth Neiley, June 19, 1943 (dec. Apr. 9, 1982); children: Diane Neiley Littlefield Ritsher, Elizabeth Damon Littlefield Lehman, Paul Damon Jr.; m. Lucy Jean Boyd, Dec. 30, 1983. AB, Harvard U., 1942, MBA with distinction, 1948. Assoc. Freeport Minerals Co., NYC, 1948-50, 52-62, treas., 1956-62; v.p. fin., treas. Arthur D. Little, Inc., Cambridge, 1962-73, sr. v.p., CFO, 1973-85, cons., 1985—. Asst. to pres. Coty, Inc., 1951-52; bd. mem. Cambridge Trust Co., 1965-2000. Hon. trustee, past chmn. Old Sturbridge Village, mem. investment com. With destroyers and submarines to Lt. cmdr., 1942, USNR, 1945. Baker scholar, Harvard U., 1948. Mem. Fin. Execs. Inst., Harvard Bus. Sch. Assn. Boston (past pres.), Cape Ann Hist. Assn. (bd. mgrs.). Home: 15 Norwood Heights Annisquam Gloucester MA 01930

LITTLEFIELD, ROBERT STEPHEN, communications educator, training consultant; b. Moorhead, Minn., June 21, 1952; s. Harry Jr. and LeVoyne Irene (Berg) L.; m. Kathy Mae Soleim, May 24, 1974; children: Lindsay Jane, Brady Robert. BS in Edn., Moorhead State U., 1974; MA, N.D. State U., 1979; PhD, U. Minn., 1983. Tchr. Barnesville (Minn.) Pub. Schs., 1974-78; teaching asst. N.D. State U., Fargo, 1978-79, lectr., 1979-81; teaching assoc. U. Minn., Mpls., 1981-82; instr. N.D. State U., Fargo, 1982-83, asst. prof., chmn., 1983-89, assoc. prof., chmn., 1989-90, interim dean, 1990-92, assoc. prof., chmn., 1992-94, prof., 1994—; dir. Inst. for Study of Cultural Diversity, 1992-97. Owner KIDSPEAK Co., Moorhead, 1987-97. Author/co-author: (series) KIDSPEAK, 1989-92; lyricist (centennial hymn) Built on a Triangle with Faith in the Triune, 1989; contbr. more than 50 articles to profl. jours. Vol. forensic coach Fargo Cath. Schs. Network, 1992—; mem. N.D. dist. com. Nat. Forensic League, 1995—; advisor to exec. coun. Nat. Jr. Forensic League, 1995—. Recipient Burlington No. award N.D. State U., 1988-89; named Outstanding Speech Educator, Nat. Fedn. High Sch. Activities Assn., 1990-91. Mem. Am. Forensic Assn. (sec. 1990-92), N.D. Speech and Theatre Assn. (historian 1989—, pres. 1985-87, Hall of Fame 1989, Scholar of Yr. 1989), N.D. Multicultural Assn., Speech Comm. Assn., Pi Kappa Delta (nat. coun. 1983—, nat. pres. 1991-93, nat. sec.-treas. 1993—), Fargo Lions Club (pres. 1990-91). Democrat. Lutheran. Office: ND State U 321G Minard Hall Fargo ND 58105

LITTLEFIELD, ROY EVERETT, III, association executive, law educator; b. Nashua, NH, Dec. 6, 1952; s. Roy Everett and Mary Ann (Prestipino) L.; m. Amy Root; children: Leah Marie, Roy Everett IV, Christy Louise. BA, Dickinson Coll., 1975; MA, Catholic U. Am., 1976, PhD, 1979. Aide US Senator Thomas McIntyre, Democrat, NH, 1975-78, Nordy Hoffman, U.S. Senate Sergeant-at-arms, NH, 1979; dir. govt. rels. Nat. Tire Dealers and Retreaders Assn., Washington, NH, 1979-84; exec. dir. Svc. Sta. and Automotive Repair Assn., Washington, NH, 1984—2003; exec. v.p. Svc. Sta. Dealers of Am., 1994—2003, Tire Industry Assn., 2003—. Faculty Cath. U. Am., Washington, 1980—; cons. Internat. Tire and Rubber Assn., 1984-2003; exec. v.p. Tire Industry Assn., 2003-. Author: William Randolph Hearst: His Role in American Progressivism, 1980, The Economic Recovery Act, 1982, The Surface: Transportation Assistance Act, 1984; editor Nozzle mag.; contbr. over 3300 articles to acad., profl. and legal jours. Mem. Nat. Dem. Club, 1978—. Mem. Am. Soc. Legal History, Md. Hwy. User's Fedn. (pres.), Am. Hwy. User's Alliance (treas., sec.), Nat. Capitol Area Transp. Fedn. (v.p.), NH Hist. Soc., Kansas City C. of C., Capitol Hill Club, Phi Alpha Theta. Roman Catholic. Home: 1707 Pepper Tree Ct Bowie MD 20721-3021 Office: 1532 Pointer Ridge Pl Ste G Bowie MD 20716-1883 Office Phone: 301-430-7280, 301-430-7280, 800-876-8372. Personal E-mail: royel3@aol.com.

LITTLEFIELD, WARREN, television executive; b. Lincoln, Neb. m. Theresa Littlefield; 2 children. Student, Am. U., Washington; grad. in psychology, Hobart Coll., Geneva, NY. With Westfall Prodns., NYC; dir. comedy devel. Warner Bros. TV, 1979; mgr. comedy devel. NBC, 1979—81, v.p. current comedy programs, 1981—85; sr. v.p series, spls. and variety programming NBC Entertainment, 1985—87, exec. v.p. prime time programs, 1987—90, pres., 1990—98; founder, prodr. Littlefield Co., 1999—; head programming Sony Pictures Entertainment, Inc., Culver City, Calif.; with Paramount Network TV, 2001—05, Touchstone TV, 2005—. Bd. dirs. Lauch Media, Inc. Prodr.: (TV films) The Last Giraffe, 1979; exec. prodr.: (TV series) Do Over, 2002, Like Family, 2003—04, Keen Eddie, 2003—04, Repo Cohen, 2004, Harry Green and Eugene, 2004, Foody Call, 2005—, Love, Inc., 2005—, others. Address: Launch Media Inc 2700 Pennsylvania Ave Santa Monica CA 90404-4066

LITTLEFORD, WILLIAM DONALDSON, retired publishing executive; b. Ft. Thomas, Ky., Aug. 4, 1914; s. Roger Seiter and Marjorie (Donaldson) L.; m. Mariana Weber, May 8, 1936 (dec. Feb. 1958); children: Anne, Michael; m. Marian Hastings Towne, Aug. 20, 1958; children: Joseph M. Towne, Marian Towne. Student, U. Cin.; grad. advanced mgmt. program, Harvard U., 1951. With Billboard Pub., Inc., Cin., 1934-85, gen. mgr., 1943-58, pres., 1958-76, chmn. bd., 1976-85, chmn. emeritus, 1985-99. Chmn. bd. Am. Bus. Press, 1960-61. McAllister fellow Northwestern U., Chgo., 1987; named to Pub. Hall of Fame, 1989; established William D. Littleford Found. for Corp. Cmty. Svc., 1998. Mem. Beta Theta Pi, Harvard Club (N.Y.C.). Episcopalian.

LITTLE GURLEY BRADY O'LITTLE, CASSANDRA ONEDA, education educator; d. Rodger William Little and Norma Lucille Newberg Little; m. John Thomas Gurley, Oct. 30, 1971 (div. Jan. 8, 1978); m. John Steven Brady, June 18, 1988 (div. Dec. 31, 1996). Student, Fla. Presbyn. Coll., St. Petersburg, 1969—71; BA magna cum laude, Ga. State U., Atlanta, 1978, MA, 1978. Cert. WSI & lifeguard ARC, 1993, ARC, 1969, scuba instr. Nat. Assn. Underwater Instrs., 2000. Instr. Info. Mapping, Inc., Waltham, Mass., 1992—2002, Ga. Perimeter Coll., Lawrenceville, Ga., 2002—. Active Siddha Yoga, Atlanta, 2004—07. With USAF. Named one of Outstanding Women, Ga. Perimeter Coll., 2006. Democrat. Buddhist. Avocations: scuba diving, bicycling, camping, kayaking, history. Home Phone: 770-934-5646. Personal E-mail: casscool1@yahoo.com.

LITTLEJOHN, DAVID, writer; b. San Francisco, May 8, 1937; s. George Thomas and Josephine Mildred (Cullen) Littlejohn; m. Sheila Beatrice Hageman, June 10, 1963; children: Victoria, Gregory David. BA, U. Calif., Berkeley, 1959; MA, Harvard U., 1961, PhD, 1963. Asst. prof. English, U. Calif., Berkeley, 1963-69, assoc. prof. journalism, 1969-76, prof., 1976-97, vice chmn. acad. senate, chmn. senate policy com., 1984-86, assoc. dean Grad. Sch. Journalism, 1974-78, 85-86, 87-89, prof. emeritus, 1997—. Arts critic Sta. KQED-TV, San Francisco, 1965-75, PBS nationwide, 1971-72; critic and corr. London Times, 1975-89, Architecture mag., 1984-89, Wall Street Jour., 1990—. Author: Architect: The Life and Work of Charles W. Moore, 1984, The Ultimate Art: Essays Around and About Opera, 1992, The Fate of the English Country House, 1997, The Real Las Vegas, 1999, 11 other books; contbr. over 350 articles and 200 TV programs. Fulbright lectr., Montpellier, France, 1966-67; Am. Coun. Learned Socs. rsch. fellow, London, 1972-73, Berkeley fellow, 2004; NEH grantee 1976-77. Mem.: Am. Inst. Arch. (hon.), Arts Club Berkeley (sec.). Democrat. Roman Catholic. Home and Office: 719 Coventry Rd Kensington CA 94707-1403 Home Phone: 510-527-1554; Office Phone: 510-527-1554. E-mail: dtl@berkeley.edu.

LITTLEJOHN, JAMES R., lawyer; b. Hartford, Conn., Mar. 27, 1951; BBA with highest honors, So. Meth. U., Dallas, 1973, JD, 1976. Bar: Tex. 1976. Shareholder Winstead, Sechrest & Minick, P.C., Dallas. Vestry and sr. warden Episcopal Ch. of Ascension, Tex.; bd. dirs. Dallas Leukemia Soc. Named one of Best Lawyers in Dallas, D Mag., 2001, 2003, 2005. Mem.: Tex. Assn. Bank Counsel (past bd. dir.), Dallas Bar Assn., Phi Delta Phi. Office: Winstead Sechrest & Minick PC 5400 Renaissance Tower 1201 Elm St Dallas TX 75270-2199 Office Phone: 214-745-5197. Office Fax: 214-745-5390. E-mail: jlittlejohn@winstead.com.*

LITTLEJOHN, JOHN JOSEPH, petroleum engineer; b. Waco, Tex., Sept. 6, 1948; s. Lacy Welborn and Winfred Rachael (Young) L.; m. Susan Louise Ilse, 1972; children: Hillary, Elizabeth, Neal, Nathan. BS, Baylor U., 1971; MA, Harvard U., 1972, PhD, 1975. Explorationist Shell Oil Co, Houston, 1975-78; cons. various cos., Houston, 1978-81; pres. Rubicon Petroleum Inc., Houston, 1981-91, chmn., pres., Colorado Springs, Colo., 1978—99; ptnr. Virtual Capital Corp., 2001—05. Vice-chmn. Advocates Internat., Annandale, Va., 1993—98; chmn. Internat. Tchg. Ministry, Dallas, 1994—. Mem. Am. Assn. Petroleum Geologists, Soc. Exploration Geophysics, Soc. Petroleum Engring. Baptist. Office: Rubicon Companies LLC PO Box 82 Beeville TX 78104 Office Phone: 361-358-0492. E-mail: drjjl@worldnet.att.net.

LITTLER, GENE ALEC, professional golfer; b. San Diego, July 21, 1930; s. Stanley Fred and Dorothy (Paul) L.; m. Shirley Mae Warren, Jan. 5, 1951; children: Curt Michael, Suzanne. Student, San Diego State Coll. Mem. U.S. Ryder Cup Team, 61, 63, 65, 67, 69, 71, 75. Served with USN, 1951-54. Achievements include winning Nat. Jr. Championship, 1948, Calif. State Open, 1953, Calif. State Amateur, 1953, Nat. Amateur Championship, 1953, also winning 29 PGA tour events including San Diego Open (as an amateur), 1954, U.S. Open, 1961, Canadian Open, 1965, Tournament of Champions, 1955, 56, 57, World Series of Golf, 1966, Taheiyo Masters, Japan, 1974, 75, Australian Masters, 1980, 15 sr. tour titles and Coca Cola Grand Slam, Japan, 1983, Fuji Elec. Grand Slam, Tokyo, Japan, 1987.

LITTLE RICHARD, (RICHARD WAYNE PENNIMAN), musician, lyricist, minister; b. Macon, Ga., Dec. 5, 1932; s. Bud and Leva Mae Penniman; m. Ernestine Campbell, 1957 (div.). BA, Oakwood Coll. Sem., Huntsville, Ala., 1961. Ordained to ministry Seventh Day Adventist Ch., 1961 (performed marriage of Bruce Willis and Demi Moore, Las Vegas). Began singing and dancing on streets of Macon, Ga., 1942; won talent shows in Atlanta, 1943 and 1951; toured with Dr. Hudson's Medicine Show and other shows, 1949-51; worked with own band doing dances and clubs, 1951-52, with Tempo Toppers in New Orleans, 1953-54; recording artist Peacock Records, Houston, 1953-54, Splty. Records, 1955-58, 64; toured in Big 10 Package shows, U.S., Australia and Gt. Brit., 1957-58; recording artist Veejay Records, 1964-65. Songs include Long Tall Sally, Tutti Frutti, Slippin' and Slidin', Rip it Up, Ready Teddy, Lucille, Send Me Some Lovin', Jenny, Jenny, Miss Ann, Keep A-Knockin', Good Golly Miss Molly, Baby Face, True Fine Mama, Kansas City, Bama Lama Bama Loo, Freedom Blues, Greenwood Mississippi; albums include Here's Little Richard, 1958, Little Richard 2, 1958, The Fabulous, 1959, Well Alright, 1959, Sings Gospel, 1964, Coming Home, 1964, Sings Freedom Songs, 1964, King of Gospel Songs, 1965, Wild & Frantic, 1965, The Explosive, 1967, The Explosive & Roy Orbison, 1970, The Rill Thing, 1971, King of Rock N Roll, 1971, Second Coming, 1971, All Time Hits, 1972, Rock Hard Rock Heavy, 1972, The Very Best Of, 1975, Georgia Peach, 1980, Get Down With It, 1982, Ooh! My Soul, 1983, Lucile, 1984, Shut Up, 1988, The Specialty Sessions, 1990, Greatest Songs, 1995, Mega-Mix, 1995; film appearances include The Girl Can't Help It, 1956, Don't Knock the Rock, 1957, She's Got It, 1957, Mr. Rock and Roll, 1957, Jimi Plays Berkeley, 1970, Let the Good Times Roll, 1973, Jimi Hendrix, 1973, Down and Out in Beverly Hills, 1985 Chuck Berry Hail! Hail! Rock 'n' Roll, 1987, Purple People Eater, 1988, Scenes from the Class Struggle in Beverly Hills, 1989, Magic Years, Vols. 1-3, 1989, Sunset Heat, 1991, The Naked Truth, 1992, The Last Action Hero, 1993, The Pickle, 1993, The History of Rock 'n' Roll, Vol. 1, 1995, Why Do Fools Fall in Love, 1998, Mystery, Alaska, 1999; TV appearances include Tonight Show, Merv Griffin Show, Mike Douglas Show, Smothers Brothers Show, American Bandstand, Glen Campbell Good Time Hour, Tom Jones Show, Midnight Special, Donny & Marie Show, The Godess of Love, 1988, Mother Goose Rock 'n' Rhyme, 1990, Happy Birthday Bugs!: 50 Looney Years, 1990, Columbo: Columbo & the Murder of a Rock Star, Sinatra: 80 Years My Way, 1995, The Late Shift, 1996, The Fifties, 1997, Motown 40: The Music is Forever, 1998, Hollywood Squares, 1998; stage appearances include Paramount Theatre, The Felt Forum, Wembley Stadium, Hollywood Paladium. Inducted Rock & Roll Hall of Fame, 1986. Achievements include being referred to as the Architect of Rock 'n Roll.

LITTLETON, CHRISTINE A., law educator; b. 1952; BS, Pa. State U., 1974; JD, Harvard U., 1982. Bar: Calif. 1982. Law clk. to Hon. Warren J. Ferguson U.S. Ct. Appeals, LA, 1982-83; acting prof. UCLA, 1983-89, prof. LA, 1989—, prof. law and women's studies, 1983—. Dir. Women's Studies Prog., 1993-96; chaired Women's Studies Prog., 1999-. Contbr. articles to profl. journs. Bd. dirs. Calif. Women's Law Ctr., 1989—; mem. Feminist Critical Legal Scholars. Office: UCLA Box 951476 Los Angeles CA 90095 Office Phone: 310-825-4841. Business E-Mail: littletn@law.ucla.edu.

LITTLETON, HARVEY KLINE, artist; b. Corning, NY, June 14, 1922; s. Jesse Talbot and Bessie (Cook) L.; m. Bess Toyo Tamura, Sept. 6, 1947; children: Carol Louise Littleton Shay, Thomas Harvey, Kathryn Tamra (dec.), Maurine Bess, John Christopher. Student, U. Mich., 1939-42, B in Design, 1947; MFA, Cranbrook Acad. Art, 1951; DFA (hon.), Phila. U. of the Arts, 1982, RISD, 1996, U. Wis., 2000; Docorate (hon.), N.C. State U., Raleigh, 2004. Instr. ceramics Toledo Mus. Art, 1949-51; prof. art U. Wis., Madison, 1951-77, chmn. dept., 1964-67, 69-71, prof. emeritus, 1977—; curator Littleton Studios. Author: Glass Blowing - A Search for Form, 1971; one- and two-man exhbns. include Lee Nordness Galleries, N.Y.C., 1969-70, Maison de Culture, Liege, Belgium, 1974, J & L Lobmeyr, Vienna, 1974, Brooks Meml. Art Gallery, Memphis, 1975, Contemporary Art Glass Gallery, N.Y.C., 1977, 78, 79, Habatat Gallery, Detroit, 1980, 81, Heller Gallery, N.Y.C., 1980, 81, 82, 83, 84, 85, Glasmuseum Ebeltoft, Sweden, 1989, Royal Copenhagen Gallery, 1989, Finnish Glasmuseum, Riihimaki, Finland, 1989, Kunsthaus am Mus., Cologne, Germany, 1990, Immenhausen, Germany, 1990, Glasmuseum, Frauenau, Germany, 1992, Yokohama (Japan) Mus. Art, 1995, retrospective exhbn. originated by High Mus. Art, Atlanta, 1984, traveling to the Renwick Gallery, Am. Craft Mus., Iowa State U., Milw. Art Mus. and Portland Mus. Art, Maine, originated at Mint Mus. Craft & Design, Charlotte, N.C., 1999-2000, traveling to Ark. Art Ctr. Decorative Arts Mus., Little Rock, St. John's Mus. Art, Wilmington, N.C., Hunter Mus. Art, Chattanooga, Elvehjem Art Ctr., Madison, Wis.; represented in permanent collections, Victoria and Albert Mus., London, museums in, Germany, Holland, Switzerland, Belgium, Austria and, Czechoslovakia, also, Met. Mus. Art, N.Y.C., Mus. Modern Art, N.Y.C., Am. Craft Mus., N.Y.C., L.A. County Mus. Art., L.A., Corning Mus. of Glass, Toledo Mus. Art, Detroit Art Inst., Milw. Art Center, Smithsonian Instn., Washington, High Mus. Art, Atlanta, Chrysler Mus., Norfolk, Va., U. Mich., U. Ill., Ohio State U., Phila. Mus. Art, The White House, Washington, numerous other pub. and pvt. collections. Bd. dirs. Penland Sch., NC, pres. bd. dirs., 1986-88; pres., chmn. Littleton Co., Inc., Spruce Pine, NC, 1981—. With Signal Corps U.S. Army, 1942-45, ETO. Recipient diploma of honor Glass Mus. Frauenau, Germany, Fine Arts award Gov. N.C., 1987, Master of Medium award James Renwick Alliance, 1997, Disting. Alumnus award U. Mich. Sch. Art, Wis. Visual Art Lifetime Achievement award, 2004, honor for contbn. and leadership to Studio Glass Movement Nat. Am. Glass Club, 2005; named Living Treasure, State N.C.; Rsch. grantee U. Wis., 1954, 57, 62, 73, 75, Toledo Mus. Art, 1962, grantee Louis Comfort Tiffany Found. grantee, 1970-71, Corning Glass Works, 1974, Nat. Endowment for Arts, 1978-79. Fellow Wis. Acad. Arts and Scis., Am. Crafts Coun. (trustee 1957, 61-64, trustee emeritus, gold medal 1983), Corning Mus. Glass (Rakow award for excellence in art of glass); mem. Nat. Coun. for Edn. in Ceramic Arts (hon.), Glass Art Soc. (hon. life, lifetime achievement award 1993), Am. Ceramic Soc. (hon. life), Nat. Assn. Schs. Art and Designs (Disting. Svc. in Visual Arts citation 1996, Urbanglass award for Lifetime Achievement in Glass 1998). Office Phone: 772-595-9845. E-mail: glassman@vol.com, hklittle@bellsouth.net.

LITTLETON, ISAAC THOMAS, III, retired library director; b. Hartsville, Tenn., Jan. 28, 1921; s. Isaac Thomas Jr. and Bessie (Lowe) L.; m. Dorothy Etta Young, Aug. 12, 1949; children— Sally Lowe Littleton Phillips, Thomas Young, Elizabeth Ann BA, U. N.C., 1943; MA, U. Tenn., Knoxville, 1950; MSLS, U. Ill., Champaign-Urbana, 1951, PhD, 1968. Circulation librarian, asst. librarian U. N.C., Chapel Hill, 1951-58; asst. dir. then dir. libraries N.C. State U., Raleigh, 1959-87, emeritus dir. libraries, 1987—. Mem. N.C. Libr. Networking Steering Com., Raleigh, 1982-85; bd. dirs. Southeastern Libr. Network, Atlanta, 1973-74, 83-86, chmn., 1985-86; chmn. Assn. Southeastern Rsch. Librs., 1969-71; mem. com. Gov.'s Conf. on Libr. and Info. Svcs., 1990. Author: The Literature of Agricultural Economics, 1969, State Systems of Higher Education and Libraries, 1977, D.H. Hill Library: An Informal History, 1993; editor: N.C. Union List of Scientific Serials, 1967. Bd. dirs., treas. Theater in Park, Raleigh, 1982-85, Friends of Wake County Pub. Librs.; sec. N.C. State U. Friends of Libr., Raleigh, 1964-87, bd. dirs., 1990-94, life mem. 1988; pres. Friends of N.C. Libr. for Blind and Physically Handicapped, 1989-93, bd. dirs. 1993-94; v.p. Wake County UN Assn., 1994-95, sec., 1999-2000, pres., 2001-04. Lt. (j.g.) USN, 1943-46, PTO. Council on Library Resources fellow, Washington, 1975-76 Mem. Southeastern Libr. Assn. (exec. bd. 1974-78), N.C. Libr. Assn. (exec. bd. 1969-71, hon. life), Torch Club (pres. Raleigh 1974-75), Raleigh Golden K Kiwanis Club (pres. 2001-02). Mem. Community United Ch. of Christ. Avocations: theater, reading. Home: 4813 Brookhaven Dr Raleigh NC 27612-5706 E-mail: littletons@mindspring.com.

LITTLETON, JESSE TALBOT, III, radiology educator; b. Corning, NY, Apr. 27, 1917; s. Jesse Talbot and Bessie (Cook) L.; m. Martha Louise Morrow, Apr. 17, 1943 (dec. 1994); children: Christine, Joanne, James, Robert, Denise; m. Mary Lou Durizch, Mar. 25, 1995. Student, Emory and Henry Coll., 1934-35, Johns Hopkins U., 1935-39; MD, Syracuse U., 1943. Diplomate Am. Bd. Radiology. Intern Buffalo Gen. Hosp., 1943; resident in medicine, surgery and radiology Robert Packer Hosp., Sayre, Pa., 1946-51, assoc. radiologist, 1951-53, chmn. dept. radiology, 1953-76; prof. radiology U. South Ala., Mobile, 1976-87, prof. emeritus, 1987—. Cons. in field. Author 4 textbooks; contbr. chpts. to books and articles to profl. jours., sci. exhibits to profl. confs. Served with M.C., U.S. Army, 1944-46, PTO. Fellow Am. Coll. Radiology; mem. AMA, Radiol. Soc. N.Am., Am. Roentgen Ray Soc., Ala. Acad. Radiology, Med. Assn. Ala., French Soc. Neuroradiology, Country Club of Mobile, Sigma Xi, Alpha Omega Alpha. Republican. Methodist. Achievements include research on conventional tomography, physical principles, equipment development and testing and clinical applications; transportation and radiology of acutely ill and traumatized patient; development of patient litter with removable top leading to placement of backboards in ambulances; development of dedicated trauma x-ray machine; angiography, development of first sheet film serialograph; development of equipment for sectional radiographic anatomy with Durizch. Home: 5504 Churchill Downs Ave Theodore AL 36582-9601 Office: U South Ala Med Ctr 2451 Fillingim St Mobile AL 36617-2238 Office Phone: 251-471-7674. E-mail: littletonjtandml@aol.com.

LITTLETON, TAYLOR DOWE, humanities educator; b. Birmingham, Ala., Mar. 14, 1930; s. M. Taylor and Florence (Longcrier) L.; m. Lucy Williams, Aug. 7, 1954; children: Dowe, George, Franklin, Mary Wood. BS, Fla. State U., 1951, MA, 1952, PhD, 1960. Tchg. fellow Fla. State U., Tallahassee, 1954-57; from instr. to prof. dept. English Auburn U., Ala., 1957—, dean undergrad. studies Ala., 1968-71, v.p. for acad. affairs Ala., 1972-83, W. Kelly Mosley prof. sci. and humanities Ala., 1983—. Author: Advancing American Art: Painting, Politics, and Cultural Confrontation at Mid-century, 1989, 2d edit., 2005, Athletics and Academe: An Anatomy of Abuses and a Prescription for Reform, 1991, The Color of Silver: William Spratling, His Life and Art, 2000; author, editor: To Prove A Villain: The Case of King Richard III, 1964, The Idea of Tragedy, 1965; editor: multi-vol. series The Franklin Lectures in Sci. and Humanities: Approaching the Benign Environment, 1970; The Shape of Likelihood, 1974, A Time To Hear and Answer, 1977, The Rights of Memory, 1985; assoc. editor So. Humanities Rev., 1967-70. With US Army, 1952—54. Mem. So. Atlantic MLA, Phi Kappa Phi, Omicron Delta Kappa, Phi Beta Kappa. Democrat. Episc. Home: 415 Norman Cir Auburn AL 36830-6307 Office: Auburn U Dept English & Humanities Haley 9030 Auburn AL 36830

LITTLEWOOD, DOUGLAS BURDEN, brokerage house executive; b. Buffalo, Sept. 24, 1922; s. Frank and G. Joan (Burden) L.; m. Jevene Hope Baker, July 2, 1949; children— Douglas Baker, Dean Houston, Laurie Littlewood Vogelsang BS in Mech. Engring, Rensselaer Poly. Inst., 1945; MBA, Harvard, 1947. Sales engr. Otis Elevator Co., 1948-49; asst. to sec. Nat Gypsum Co., Buffalo, 1949-52, sec., 1952-67; investment banker Hornblower & Weeks, 1967-68; pres. Littlewood Assocs., Inc., 1968-95, chmn. bd., 1995—. Past pres. Greater Niagara Frontier coun. Boy Scouts Am.; active Buffalo YMCA, United Fund; bd. dirs. Presbyn. Homes of Western N.Y.; bd. dirs., chmn. emeritus Salvation Army; v.p. N.E. region Boy Scouts Am. Served to lt. (j.g.) USNR, 1943-46. Recipient Silver Beaver, 1965; recipient Silver Antelope, 1978, Disting. Eagle, 1979 Mem. Country Club of Sebring, Buffalo Jr. C. of C. (past dir., chmn. bd.), Am. Soc. Corp. Secs., Buffalo Canoe Club (past commodore), Buffalo Country Club. Home (Winter): 1121 Lakeview Dr Sebring FL 33870-4938 Office: 22 Dawnbrook Ln Buffalo NY 14221 E-mail: lotawood22@aol.com. *If you truly believe you are happy and successful then, and only then, you truly are.*

LITTMAN, BRETT, museum director, art critic; BA in Philosophy, U. Calif., San Diego. Assoc. dir. UrbanGlass, Brooklyn, 1995—2001; co-exec. dir. Dieu Donné Papermill, SoHo, NY, 2001—03; dep. dir. P.S.1 Contemporary Art Ctr., Long Island City, 2003—07; mng. dir. P.S.1 Radio Station, 2003—04; exec. dir. Drawing Ctr., 2007—. Mem. Brooklyn Arts Council Adv. Bd.; chair Brooklyn Arts Council Visual Arts Panel, 1995—98. Author: (numerous articles) Glass Quarterly, Am. Ceramics, Craft Arts, Object, Sculpture, Art on Paper, East Hampton Star; co-dir., co-prodr. (films) Puro Party: Celebrating a Genocide, 1992, Pretty Vacant. Mem.: Glass Art Soc. (co-char Bridge to the Future Conf. 2000), Internat. Art Critics Assn. Office: Drawing Ctr 35 Wooster St New York NY 10013*

LITTMAN, DAN R., microbiologist; MD, PhD, U. Wash., 1980. Helen L. and Martin S. Kimmel prof. molecular immunology, prof. pathology and microbiology NYU Sch. Medicine; dir. molecular pathogenesis program, Skirball Inst. NYU; investigator Howard Hughes Med. Rsch. Inst. Fellow: Am. Acad. Arts and Sciences; mem.: NAS. Office: Skirball Inst Biomolecular Medicine 2nd Fl Lab 17 540 First Ave New York NY 10016 Business E-Mail: dan.littman@med.nyu.edu.

LITTMAN, EARL, advertising and public relations executive; b. Jan. 29, 1927; s. David and Cele Littman; m. Natalie Carol Jacobson, Dec. 21, 1948; children: Erica Humphrey, Bonnie Likover, Michael L. Littman. BS, NYU, 1948. With George N. Khan, NYC, 1948-50, Jones & Brown, Pitts., 1950-52; chmn., CEO Goodwin, Dannenbaum, Littman & Wingfield Inc., Houston, 1952-92; pres. The Advertizing Firm, Inc., 1992, Two Nerds and a Suit, Inc., 1994; chmn., CEO Point of Product Broadcasting Co. Founder, inventor new wireless advt. in-store P.O.P. Broadcasting Co. Inc., 2003—. Bd. dir. Ctr. Am. History, U. Tex., mem. Chancellor's Coun.; chmn. Anti-Defamation League, Tex., 1984; bd. dir. Am. Heart Assn., Houston, Glassell Sch, Houston chpt. World Pres. Orgn.; active End Hunger Network, Houston, 1984; active NCCJ; founder, exec. dir. Drugs Kill Prevention/Edn. Program, 1997; exec. dir. Drugs Kill. With USN, 1944-45. Recipient Silver medal Am. Advt. Fedn., 1989, Outstanding Vol. award Savvy, 1990, Anti-Defamation League Popkin award, 1990, End Hunger Network award, 1992; Am. Heart Assn. honoree, 1988, John McMahon award Am. Heart Assn., 1996; Heritage award Am. Women in Radio and TV, 1992, Cmty. Champion award Tex. Commn. Alcohol and Drug Abuse, 2000; named Mktg. Man of Yr., Am. Mktg. Assn., 1999. Mem.: Am. Advt. Agy. Assn. (gov. Houston chpt. 1990, Paul Dudley White award 1991), Marathon Assn., Winedale Hist. Assn. (former pres.), Houston Advt. Fedn. (Living Legend award 1993, Heritage award), Affiliated Advt. Agys. Internat. (pres. 1979—80). Home Phone: 713-621-7678; Office Phone: 832-476-9249. E-mail: earl@popbroadcasting.com.

LITTMAN, HOWARD, chemical engineer, educator; b. Bklyn., Apr. 22, 1927; s. Morris and Gertrude (Goldberg) L.; m. Arline F. Caruso, July 3, 1955; children— Susan Joy, Vicki Kim, Paul William. BChemE, Cornell U., 1951; PhD, Yale U., 1956. Asst., then assoc. prof. Syracuse U., 1955-65; on leave to Brookhaven Nat. Lab., summer 1957, Argonne Nat. Lab., 1957-59; faculty Rensselaer Poly. Inst., Troy, NY, 1965—, prof. chem. engring., 1967—2001, chmn. faculty coun., 1975—76, rsch. prof. emeritus, 2001—. Vis. prof. Imperial Coll., London, 1971—72, Chonn'am Nat. U., Kwangju, Republic of Korea, 1988; Fulbright lectr. U. Belgrade, Yugoslavia, 1972. Patentee in field; contbr. articles to profl. jours. A founder Onondaga Hill Free Library, 1961, trustee, 1961-65, pres., 1965; a founder Onondaga Library System, 1962, trustee, 1962-65, v.p., 1965; trustee Capital Dist. Library Council, 1969-75, pres., 1970, 73. Served with USN, 1945-46. IREX grantee U. Belgrade, summer 1973; recipient Disting. Faculty award Rensselaer Poly. Inst., 1988. Mem. Am. Inst. Chem. Engrs., Am. Chem. Soc., Sigma Xi. Home: 7 Tulip Tree Ln Schenectady NY 12309-1837 Office: Rensselaer Poly Inst Troy NY 12180-3590 Office Phone: 518-276-6039. Business E-Mail: littmh@rpi.edu.

LITTMAN, MARLYN KEMPER, information scientist, educator; b. Mar. 26, 1943; d. Louis and Augusta (Jacobs) Janofsky; m. Bennett I. Kemper, Aug. 1, 1965 (dec. June 1987); children: Alex Randall, Gari Hament, Jason Myles; m. Lewis Littman, Apr. 22, 1990. BA, Finch Coll., 1964; MA in Anthropology, Temple U., 1970; MA in Info. Sci., U. South Fla., 1983; PhD in Info. Sci., Nova Southeastern U., 1986. Dir. Hist. Broward County Preservation Bd., Hollywood, Fla., 1979—87; automated systems libr. Broward County Main Libr., Ft. Lauderdale, Fla., 1984—86; assoc. prof. info. sci. Nova U., Ft. Lauderdale, Fla., 1987—94, dir. info. sci. doctoral program, 1987—94; prof. info. sci. Nova Southeastern U., Ft. Lauderdale, Fla., 1995—. Weekly columnist Ft. Lauderdale News, 1975—79; contbg. editor Hyper Nexus-Jour. Hypermedia and Multimedia Studies, 1996—2000; assoc. editor Jour. On-Line Learning, 1997—2002. Author: A Comprehensive Documented History of the City of Pompano Beach, 1982, A Comprehensive History of Dania, 1983, A Comprehensive History of Hallandale, 1984, A Comprehensive History of Deerfield Beach, 1985, A Comprehensive History of Plantation, 1986, A Comprehensive History of Davie, 1987, Networking: Choosing a LAN Path to Interconnection, 1987, Building Broadband Networks, 2002; author: (with others) Mosaics of Meaning, New Ways of Learning, 1996; contbr. articles to profl. jours., chapters to books. Pub. info. officer Broward County Hist. Commn., 1975—79; vice chmn. Broward County Adv. Bd., 1987—92; bd. dirs. Ctrl. Agy. Jewish Edn., 1992—94. Recipient Judge L. Clayton Nance award, 1977, Broward County Hist. Commn. award, 1979. Mem.: IEEE, Assn. Computing Machinery, Info. Resources Mgmt. Assn. Internat., Phi Kappa Phi, Beta Phi Mu, Upsilon Pi Epsilon. Home: 2845 NE 35th St Fort Lauderdale FL 33306-2007 Office: Nova Southeastern U Grad Sch Computer and Info Sci 3301 College Ave Fort Lauderdale FL 33314 Office Phone: 954-262-2078. Business E-Mail: marlyn@nova.edu.

LITTMAN, RICHARD ANTON, psychologist, educator; b. NYC, May 8, 1919; s. Joseph and Sarah (Feinberg) L.; m. Isabelle Cohen, Mar. 17, 1941; children— David, Barbara, Daniel, Rebecca. AB, George Washington U., 1943; postgrad., Ind. U., 1943-44; PhD, Ohio State U., 1948. Faculty U. Oreg., 1948—, prof. psychology, 1959—, chmn. dept., 1963-68, vice provost acad. planning and resources, 1971-73, prof. emeritus, 1990. Vis. scientist Nat. Inst. Mental Health, 1958-59 Contbr. articles to profl. jours. Sr. postdoctoral fellow NSF, U. Paris, 1966-67; sr. fellow Nat. Endowment for Humanities, U. London, 1973-74; Ford Found. fellow, 1952-53; recipient U. Oreg. Charles H. Johnson Meml. award, 1980. Mem. APA, Western Psychol. Assn., Am. Psychol. Soc., Soc. Research and Child Devel., Psychonomics Soc., Animal Behavior Soc., Soc. Psychol. Study of Social Issues, Internat. Soc. Developmental Psychobiology, History of Sci. Soc., Am. Philos. Assn., AAUP, Sigma Xi. Home: 3625 Glen Oak Dr Eugene OR 97405-4736 Office: U Oreg Dept Psychology Eugene OR 97403 Business E-Mail: rlittman@uoregon.edu.

LITTO, JUDITH CHERYL, art educator; b. Amsterdam, NY, June 16, 1945; d. Forrest Whitlock and Gladys Orcelia Van Zandt; m. Leo Litto (div.); 1 child, Teo Matthew. BA, SUNY, Potsdam, 1967; MS, Coll. St. Rose, Albany, 1969. Cert. tchr. NY. Art tchr. Shenendahowa C. Schs., Clifton Park, NY, 1967—70, Schalmont (NY) Ctrl. Schs., 1970—71; art specialist Guilderlund (NY) Ctrl. Schs., 1971—2003; visual arts coord., project arts coord. Web Dubois HS, Bklyn., 2003—. Visual, performing arts tchr. Rochester (NY) City Schs., 1977—78; owner Litto Design Co., Albany, NY, Parisian Flea, Albany. Editor: Transitions Mag. Pres. NE chpt. NY State Art Tchrs.; v.p. Hudson Mohawk Consortium Coll. and Univ., Albany; pres. Suburban Coun. Art Supervisors Bd., Albany. Grantee, NY State Hist. Assn., 1972, Donors Choose, NYC, 2004—06. Mem.: Am. Mus. Folk Art, Mus. Modern Art. Avocations: antiques, reading, painting, drawing. Home: 378 Greene Ave Brooklyn NY 11216 Office Phone: 518-253-0397.

LITTON, ANDREW, conductor, music director; b. NYC, May 16, 1959; BS, MBA, Juilliard Sch. Music; Doctorate (hon.), Univ. Bournemouth. Asst. condr. Teatro alla Scala, Nat. Symphony; music dir. Dallas Symphony, 1994—2007, music dir. emeritus, 2007—; music dir. Bergen Philharm. Orch.; condr. Bournemouth Symphony, 1988—94, condr. laureate. Artistic dir. Sommerfest, Minn. Orch.; guest condr. St. Louis Symphony Orch., Dresden Philharm., NHK Orch., Scottish Chamber Orch., Bergen Philharm., Phila. Orch., Dallas Symphony Orch., Eng. Nat. Opera, Welsh Nat. Opera, Moscow Orch., Israel Orch., LA Opera House. Named winner BBC Internat. Conductors Competition; recipient Sanford Medal for musical achievement, Yale Univ. Office: Morton H Meyerson Symphonic Ctr 2301 Flora St Ste 300 Dallas TX 75201-2404*

LITUCHY, GREGG, dentist; b. NYC, Mar. 31, 1959; BA in Biology, SUNY, Binghamton, 1980; DDS, Columbia U., 1984. Gen. practice intern L.I. Coll. Hosp., 1984—85; pvt. practice cosmetic dentistry Lowenberg and Lituchy, NYC, 1985—. Cons. ABC's Extreme Makeover; guest Oprah Winfrey Show, Good Morning Am., The View; former spokesman Listerine mouthwash; formerspokesman Crest toothpaste. Mem.: ADA, Dental Soc. State of N.Y., Am. Acad. Implant Dentistry, Internat. Congress of Oral Implantologists, Am. Acad. Cosmetic Dentistry, Acad. Gen. Dentistry. Office: Lowenberg and Lituchy 230 Central Park S New York NY 10019 Office Phone: 212-586-2890. Office Fax: 212-586-2889.

LITVACK, MARK D., lawyer; b. 1958; BA, Hamilton Coll., 1980; JD, Northwestern U. Sch. Law, 1995. Bar: Conn. 1983, NY 1984, Calif. 1995. Sr. atty. Texaco Inc.; v.p., dir., legal affairs, world-wide anti-piracy Motion Picture Assn. Am.; ptnr. Mitchell Silberberg & Knupp, Manatt, Phelps & Phillips, LA, 2006—. Mem.: Fed. Bar Assn., NY Bar Assn., Conn. Bar Assn., ABA (counsel mem., Sci. and Tech. com.). Office: Manatt Phelps & Phillips LLP Trident Ctr East Tower 11355 W Olympic Blvd Los Angeles CA 90064 Office Phone: 310-312-4121. Office Fax: 310-312-4224.*

LITVACK, SANFORD MARTIN, lawyer; b. Bklyn., Apr. 29, 1936; s. Murray and Lee M. (Korman) L.; m. Joanna R. Swomley, Apr. 2, 2006; children: Mark, Jonathan, Sharon, Daniel. BA, U. Conn., 1956; LLB, Georgetown U., 1959. Bar: Va. 1959, NY 1964, DC 1981, Calif. 1995. Trial atty. antitrust div. Dept. Justice, Washington, 1959-61, asst. atty. gen., 1980-81; assoc. firm Donovan, Leisure, Newton & Irvine, NYC, 1961-69, ptnr., 1969—80, chmn., 1981—86; ptnr., head litig. dept. Dewey, Ballantine, Bushby, Palmer & Wood, NYC, 1987-91; gen. counsel The Walt Disney Co., Burbank, Calif., 1991—94, chief corp. ops., 1994—99, vice chmn., 1999—2001, ptnr., 2001—02, also bd. dirs.; ptnr. Quinn, Emanuel, Urquhart, Oliver & Hedges, 2002—04, Hogan & Hartson, 2004—. Bd. dirs. Bet Tzedek. Fellow Am. Coll. Trial Lawyers; mem. ABA, Fed. Bar Coun., NY State Bar Assn. (sec. antitrust sect. 1974-77, chmn. antitrust sect. 1985-86), Va. Bar Assn., Calif. Inst. of Arts (bd. trustees), Am. Arbitration Assn. (bd. dirs.), Antitrust Modernization Commn. (commr.), Sesame Workshop (bd. trustees), Lawyers' Com. for Civil Rights Under Law (bd. trustees). Office: Hogan & Hartson LLP 875 Third Ave New York NY 10022 Office Phone: 212-918-8271. Business E-Mail: slitvack@hhlaw.com.

LITVAK, DAVID A., surgeon; b. Cambridge, Mass., May 28, 1967; s. Marvin Litvak and Marilyn Latvik; m. Kathleen Kennedy, Oct. 15, 1993; children: Emmett, Audrey, Lillian. BA in Biology, U. Calif. San Diego, La Jolla, 1989; MD, U. Chgo., 1993. Diplomate Am. Bd. Surgery, 2001. Fellow surg. oncology John Wayne Cancer Inst., Santa Monica, Calif., 2000—02; surg. oncologist Mich. State U., Lansing, 2002—04, Kaiser Permanente, Anaheim, Calif., 2004—. Reviewer Archives Surgery, Oakland, Calif., 2000—05; presenter in field. Recipient award, AAES, 1998; grantee, Ingham Found., 2001—02. Fellow: ACS; mem.: Soc. Surgery Alimentary Tract (assoc.), Soc. Surg. Oncology (assoc.), Golden Key Honor Soc. (life), Phi Beta Kappa (life). Achievements include research in stem cell origin of pancreatic tumors. Office: Kaiser Permanente 411 N Lakeview Ave Anaheim CA 92807 Office Phone: 714-279-5645.

LITVIN, JOEL M., sports association executive, lawyer; m. Lisa Litvin; children: Jesse, Jane. Grad., U. Pa. Wharton Sch., 1981; JD, NYU, 1985. Atty. Willkie, Farr & Gallagher, NYC; staff atty. NBA, NYC, 1988, asst. gen. counsel, v.p., dep. gen. counsel, sr. v.p., gen. counsel, 1999—2000, exec. v.p. legal and bus. affairs, 2000—06, pres. league and basketball ops., 2006—. Sec. sports law com. NY City Bar Assn. Office: NBA Olympic Tower 645 5th Ave Fl 10 New York NY 10022-5986*

LITVINOFF, SAUL, lawyer, educator; b. Buenos Aires, Mar. 15, 1925; widowed; 1 child. AB, U. Buenos Aires, 1944, LLB, 1949, SJD, SCD, U. Buenos Aires, 1956; LLM, Yale U., 1964. Assoc. Ibero Berenguer & Assoc., Buenos Aires, 1949—54, ptnr., 1954—59; sr. ptnr. Merlino Litvinoff & Rodriguez, Buenos Aires; vis. prof. U. Puerto Rico, 1963—65, La. State U., 1965—67, assoc. prof., 1967, prof., 1970—85, Boyd prof., 1985—93, Boyd prof. & Stockwell prof., 1993—, dir. Ctr. Civil Law Studies, 1977—2005. Vis. prof. Universite Catholique de Louvain, Belgium, 1986—94. Author: The Law of Obligations, 1996, Damages and Putting in Default, 1999, The Law of Obligations in the Louisiana Jurisprudence, 2000, of 17 books on banking & finance laws; contbr. articles to profl. jour. Recipient Medaille Henri Capilant, France, Order Jose Cecilio del Valle, Honduras, Sauberan medal, Argentina, James William Rivers award, Univ. Southwestern La., Year 2000 Prof. Law award, La. Bar Found. Mem.: Argentine Bar, La. State Bar Inst., Honduras Bar (hon.), Costa Rica Bar (hon.), Argentine Nat. Acad. Legal Sci., Order of the Coif. Office: La State U Hebert Law Ctr Rm W326D Baton Rouge LA 70803-1000 Home Phone: 225-383-3976; Office Phone: 225-578-1126. Business E-Mail: saul.litvinoff@lsu.edu.

LITWACK, LEON FRANK, historian, educator; b. Santa Barbara, Calif., Dec. 2, 1929; s. Julius and Minnie (Nitkin) L.; m. Rhoda Lee Goldberg, July 5, 1952; children: John Michael, Ann Katherine. BA, U. Calif., Berkeley, 1951, MA, 1952, PhD, 1958. Asst. prof., then assoc. prof. history U. Wis., Madison, 1958-65; mem. faculty U. Calif., Berkeley, 1965—, prof. history, 1971—, Alexander F. and May T. Morrison prof. history, 1987—; dir. NDEA Inst. Am. History, summer 1965. Vis. prof. U. S.C., 1975, Colo. Coll., Sept. 1974, 79, La. State U., 1985; Fulbright prof. Am. history U. Sydney, Australia, 1991, Moscow (USSR) State U., 1980; Wentworth scholar-in-residence U. Fla., Spring 1983; mem. Nat. Afro-Am. History and Culture Commn., 1981-83; mem. screening com. Fulbright Sr. Scholar Awards, 1983-86; bd. acad. advisors The American Experience Sta. WGBH-TV, 1986—, Africans in America, WGBH-TV, 1990-98; Ford Found. prof. So. studies U. Miss., 1989; mem. exec. com. of dels. Am. Coun. of Learned Socs., 1993-96; lectr. in field. Author: North of Slavery: The Negro in the Free States, 1790-1860, 1961, Been in the Storm So Long: The Aftermath of Slavery, 1979, Trouble in Mind: Black Southerners in the Age of Jim Crow, 1998; (film) To Look for America, 1971; co-author: The United States, 1981, rev. edit., 1991, Without Sanctuary: Lynching Photography in America, 2000; editor: American Labor Movement, 1962; co-editor: Reconstruction, 1969, Black Leaders in the Nineteenth Century, 1988, Harvard Guide to African American History, 2001. Mem. Bradley Commn. on History in Schs., 1987-90, Schomburg Commn. for the Preservation of Black Culture; trustee Nat. Coun. for History Edn., 1990-96, mem. steering com. 1994 NAEP History Consensus Project; chair U. Calif. Acad. Senate Libr. Com. 1995-97. Served with AUS, 1953-55. Recipient Excellence in Teaching award U. Calif., Berkeley, 1967, 95, Disting. Tchg. award, 1971, 95 Mem. Orgn. Am. Historians (chmn. nominations bd. 1975-76, exec. bd. 1983-85, pres. 1986-87), Am. Hist. Assn. (chmn. program com. 1980-81), So. Hist. Assn. (bd. dirs. 2003-05, pres. 2007—), So. Historian Assn. (pres. 2007—), Soc. Am. Historians, Am. Acad. Arts and Scis., Am. Antiquarian Soc., U. Calif. Alumni Assn., Assn. for the Study African Am. Life and History, PEN Am. Ctr. Office: U Calif Dept History 3229 Dwinelle Hall Berkeley CA 94720-2550 Business E-Mail: llitwack@berkeley.edu.

LITWIN, BURTON HOWARD, lawyer; b. Chgo., July 26, 1944; s. Manuel and Rose (Boehm) L.; m. Nancy I. Stein, Aug. 25, 1968; children: Robin Litwin Levine, Keith Harris, Jill Stacy. BS with honors, BA with honors, Roosevelt U., Chgo., 1966; JD cum laude, Northwestern U., 1970. Bar: Ill. 1970, U.S. Dist. Ct. (no. dist.) Ill. 1970, U.S. Tax Ct. 1971, U.S. Ct. Fed. Claims 1983; CPA, Ill. Sr. counsel Neal, Gerber & Eisenberg, Chgo., 2002—. Author chpts. of books; contbr. articles to profl. jours. Recipient Gold Watch award Fin. Execs. Inst., Chgo., 1965. Mem. ABA (chmn. nonfiler task force for No. Ill. 1992-94), Chgo. Bar Assn. (chmn. adminstrv. practice subcom., fed. taxation subcom. 1982-83) Avocations: painting, photography. Office: Neal Gerber & Eisenberg LLP Two N LaSalle St Ste 2200 Chicago IL 60602-3801 Home Phone: 847-398-5377; Office Phone: 312-269-5986. Business E-Mail: blitwin@ngelaw.com. E-mail: gosox13@aol.com.

LITWIN, ETHAN, lawyer; m. Lisa Rimmeli. BA, Duke U., 1992; JD, Georgetown U., 1998. Bar: NY 1999, solicitor: Law Soc. Eng. and Wales 2003. Assoc. Simpson Thacher & Bartlett LLP, New York, NY, 1998—2007; ptnr. Howrey LLP, NYC, 2007—. Contbr. articles to profl. jours. Mem. Apollo Cir., Met. Mus. of Art, NYC, 2005—, Young Assocs., Met. Opera, NYC, 2005—. Mem.: Delta Kappa Epsilon (life). Office: Howrey LLP Citigroup Ctr 153 E 53rd St Fl 54 New York NY 10022 Home Phone: 212-737-2149; Office Phone: 212-896-6591. Office Fax: 212-896-6501. Business E-Mail: litwine@howrey.com.

LITWIN, LEONARD, real estate company executive; s. Harry Litwin; married; 2 children. Prin. Glenwood Mgmt., NYC. Named one of 400 Richest Ams., Forbes mag., 1985, 1991, 1995, 1998, 2006. Office: Glenwood Mgmt Corp 10 Liberty St New York NY 10005

LITWIN, PAUL JEFFREY, lawyer; b. Boston, May 4, 1955; s. Robert I. and Tamara D. L.; m. Robin Gile, June 28, 1986; children: Peter Hill, Alexander James. BA with honors, U. Wis., 1977; JD cum laude, Suffolk U., 1983. Paralegal Hale and Dorr, Boston, 1979-80; clk. to presiding justice Mass. Superior Ct., Boston, 1983-84; staff atty. Mass. Supreme Ct., Boston, 1984-85; sports, entertainment atty. Bob Woolf Assocs., Boston, 1985-86; ptnr. entertainment law practice Shames & Litwin, Boston, 1986—; asst. prof. entertainment law Berklee Coll. Music, Boston, 1990-97, Emerson Coll., Boston, 1995-96. Comml. arbitrator Am. Arbitration Assn., Boston, 1991-97. Co-chmn. Brookline, Mass. Dem. Com., 1984-86; mem. Concord, Mass. Dem. Com., 1986—; del. Mass. State Dem. Conv., 2004. Mem. ABA, Mass. Bar Assn., Boston Bar Assn. (founder, chmn. sports and entertainment com. 1987-89, del. to Mass. State Democratic Convention, 2004). Democrat. Avocations: skiing, sailing, tennis, travel. Home: 23 Wright Farm Concord MA 01742-1528 Office: Shames & Litwin 535 Boylston St 8th Fl Boston MA 02116 Office Phone: 617-236-0175. Business E-Mail: plitwin@shames-litwin.com.

LITWIN, TODD, software engineer; s. Larry and Evelyn Litwin; m. Karen Codman; children: Oren, Asher. BS in Applied Physics, Harvey Mudd Coll., Claremont, Calif., 1979. Sr. tech. staff Jet Propulsion Lab., Pasadena, Calif., 1979—. Jewish. Home Phone: 562-868-5673; Office Phone: 818-354-5028.

LITWINOWICZ, ANTHONY, information scientist, researcher; b. Jelenia Gora, Poland, July 29, 1952; came to U.S., 1978; s. Anthony and Anna (Zdrojewski) L.; m. Catherine Veronica Gajdos, June 30, 1979; children: Catherine, Anthony, John Paul, Peter. MA in History and Philosophy, Lodz U., Poland, 1976; MS in Info. Studies, Drexel U., 1984, postgrad., 1985-90. Cert. in info. mgmt. Sr. info. specialist Laventhol & Horwath CPAs, Phila., 1984-89; instr. info. sci. Delaware Valley Coll., Doylestown, Pa., 1989-91; dir. Info. Ctr. Samsung Electronics, Ridgefield Park, N.J., 1992—. Author: Nazi Occupation of Poland, 1978; contbr. articles to profl. jours. Mem.: Soc. Competitive Intelligence Profls., Assn. Independent Info. Profls., Spl. Librs. Assn., Nat. Assn. Investigative Specialists. Republican. Roman Catholic. Avocations: collecting antiques, reading, martial arts. Personal E-mail: elcidpa@yahoo.com.

LITYNSKI, DANIEL MITCHELL, optical engineer, educator, physicist, retired military officer; b. Amsterdam, NY, Mar. 13, 1943; s. Mitchell Peter and Stella Agnes Litynski; m. Dianne Helene Miller, Dec. 28, 1963; children: Laura Ann Ropelis, James Mitchell, John Thomas. BS in Physics, Rensselaer Poly. Inst., 1965; MS in Optics, U. Rochester, 1971; PhD in Physics, Rensselaer Poly. Inst., 1978. National Defense University, Industrial College of the Armed Forces US Dept. of Def., 1989, US Army Command & General Staff College US Army, 1974, US Army Ordnance Officer Advanced Course US Army, 1969, US Army Mechanical Maintenance Officer Course US Army, 1967, US Army Airborne School US Army, 1965, US Army Armor Officers Course US Army, 1965. Commd. officer US Army, 1965, advanced through grades to brig. gen., exec. officer and adjutant HHC USA Armor & Engr. Bd. Ft. Knox, Ky., 1965—66, platoon leader & exec. officer B Co. 2nd Bn. 34th Armor Ft. Irwin, Calif., Vietnam, 1966—67, commdg. officer 551st Light Maintenance Co., 1967, commdg. officer HHC USA Ordnance Ctr. and Sch. Aberdeen Proving Ground, Md., 1967—68, rsch. physicist Ballistic Rsch. Labs., 1969—69, materiel officer 19th Maintenance Bn. Vietnam, 1971—72, optical physicist Ballistic Rsch. Labs. Aberdeen Proving Ground, Md., 1972—73, exec. officer 79th Maintenance Bn. Germany, 1978—80; rsch. officer, instr., asst. prof. physics US Mil. Acad., West Point, NY, 1974—78, assoc. prof., prof., deputy head, elec. engring., 1980—89, prof. and head, elec. engring. and computer sci., 1990—99; ret., 1999; dean engring. and applied scis., provost and v.p. for academic affairs, interim pres. Western Mich. U., Kalamazoo, 1999—2004, prof. elec. and computer engring., 1999—; program dir., acting divsn. dir., Divsn. Undergraduate Edn. Nat. Sci. Found., Washington, 2004—07. Mem. internat. adv. com. internat. faculty engring. Tech. U. Lodz, Poland, 1992—93; rev. panel chair and mem. NSF, Washington, 1993—97; conf. co-chair FIE 2001 Frontiers in Edn. Conf., Reno, 2000—02; presenter in field. Contbr. chapters to books, articles to profl. jours. Vol. Chapel Parish, Stewart Field, Newburgh, NY, 1974—78, Most Holy Trinity Chapel, West Point, NY, 1980—99, St. Thomas More Student Parish, Kalamazoo, 1999—. Commd. second lt. (2LT), 1965, advanced to brig. gen. (BG), 1999. Decorated two Commendation medals US Army, three Bronze Stars, DSM; named US Mil. Acad. fellow to Nat. Def. U. Indsl. Coll. of Armed Forces, 1988—89; recipient Order Merit, 1994, 10th Anniversary medal, Internat. Faculty Engring., Tech. U. Lodz, 2003, Cavalier Cross of Merit, Pres. of the Republic of Poland, 2002, GCETE Excellence award, 2005; scholar, Rensselaer Poly. Inst., 1960—63; NY State Regents Engring. scholar, NY State, 1960—64. Mem.: IEEE (sr.; v.p. 2002—03, pres. IEEE Edn. Soc. 2004—06), NY Acad Sci., Assn. Computing Machinery, Armed Forces Comm. and Electronics Assn., Soc. Photo-Optical Instrumentation Engrs., Am. Assn. Physics Tchrs., Am. Physical Soc., Optical Soc. Am., Am. Soc. for Engring. Edn. (Meritorious Svc. award for Academic Leadership 2003), Computer, Edn., Lasers and Electro-Optics Soc. (sr.), Rotary Internat., Tau Beta Pi, Upsilon Pi Epsilon, Sigma Pi Sigma, Eta Kappa Nu, Phi Kappa Phi, Sigma Xi, Sigma Phi Epsilon (life; pres. NY Delta 1963, Citation award for Success and Stature in Professions 2003). Roman Catholic. Achievements include patents for Photonic Analog-to-Digital Converter Based on Temporal and Spatial Oversampling Techniques. Avocations: sailing, golf, skiing, travel, genealogy. Home: 1430 Long Rd Kalamazoo MI 49008-1320 Office: Western Mich Univ Coll Engring Applied Sci Dept Elec and Computer Engring Kalamazoo MI 49008-5204 Office Phone: 269-276-3932. Office Fax: 269-276-3151. Personal E-mail: ddlitynski@msn.com. Business E-Mail: dan.litynski@wmich.edu.

LITZSINGER, RICHARD MARK, retail executive; b. Houston, Sept. 7, 1955; s. Paul Richard and Dona Lucy (Follett) L. BFA, Tex. Christian U., 1978. Mgmt. trainee Saddleback C.C. Bookstore, Mission Viejo, Calif., 1978, Follett Coll. Stores, Elmhurst, Ill., 1978-79; bookstore mgr. U. Ill., Champaign, 1979-81, Northwestern U., Evanston, Ill., 1981-83; dir. of mktg. Follett Coll. Stores, Elmhurst, Ill., 1983-85, spl. asst. to pres., 1985-88; dir. of devel. Follett Corp., Chgo., 1989—91, also bd. dirs., pres. Custom Acad. Pub. Co., 1991—98, vice chmn., 1998—2001, chmn., 2001—. Trustee Follett Ednl. Found. Republican. Presbyterian. Avocations: tennis, skiing, running, paddle tennis, golf. Office: Follett Corp 2233 N West St River Grove IL 60171-1895

LIU, BEDE, electrical engineering educator; b. Shanghai, Sept. 25, 1934; arrived in U.S., 1954, naturalized, 1960; s. Henry and Shan (Yao) L.; m. Maria Agatha Sang, Jan. 31, 1959; 1 child, Beatrice Agatha. BS in Elec. Engring., Nat. Taiwan U., 1954; MEE, Poly. Inst. Bklyn., 1956, DEE, 1960. Equipment engr. Western Electric Co., NYC, 1954-56; intermediate engr. A.B. DuMont Lab., Clifton, NJ, summer 1956; mem. tech. staff Bell Telephone Labs., Murray Hill, NJ, 1959-62, summers 1957, 58, 66; mem. faculty Princeton U., 1962—, prof. elec. engring., 1969—; dept. chmn., 1994-97. Vis. prof. Nat. Taiwan U., 1970—71, U. Calif., Berkeley, 1971, Shanghai Jiao Tong U., 1979; hon. prof. Acad. Sinica, Beijing, 1988, Chinese U. Electronics, Sci. and Tech., Chengdu, 1997. Co-author: (Book) Digital Signal Processing, 1976, Multamedia Data Hiding, 2002; editor: Digital Filters and the Fast Fourier Transform, 1975. Mem.: IEEE (pres. Cir. and Systems Soc. 1982, bd. dirs. 1984—85, Centennial medal 1984, Achievement award Signal Processing Soc. 1985, Edn. award Cir. and Systems Soc. 1988, Soc. award Signal Processing Soc. 1997, Mac Van Valkenburd award Cir. and Systems Soc. 1997, Millenium medal 2000), Nat. Acad. Engring. Achievements include patents in field. Office: Princeton Univ Dept Elec Engring Princeton NJ 08540 E-mail: liu@princeton.edu.

LIU, BEN-CHIEH, economist; b. Chungking, China, Nov. 17, 1938; came to U.S., 1965, naturalized, 1973; s. Pei-juang and Chung-su L.; m. Jill Jyh-huey, Oct. 2, 1965; children— Tina Won-ting, Roger Won-jung, Milton Won-ming. BA, Nat. Taiwan U., 1961; MA, Meml. U. Nfld., 1965, Washington U., St. Louis, 1968, PhD, 1971. Economist Chinese Air Force and Central Customs, Taiwan, 1961-63; resource economist Canadian Land Inventory and Forest Services, Nfld., 1963-65; research project dir. St. Louis Regional Indsl. Devel. Corp., 1968-72; prin. econs. Midwest Research Inst., Kansas City, Mo., 1972-80; mgr. Energy and Environ. Systems Div., Argonne (Ill.) Nat. Lab., 1980-81. Prof. econs., assoc. dir. rsch. Oklahoma City U., 1981-82; prof. mgmt., mktg. and info. systems Chgo. State U., 1982—; pres. Liu & Assocs., Inc., 1982—; vis. prof. econs. U. Mo., 1970-78, Nat. Taiwan U., 1991-92; Fulbright prof., dir. Internat. Enterprises Inst., Nat. Dong-Hwa U., Taiwan, 1997-98; dean Coll. Bus., Chung-Yuan Christian U., Taiwan, 2000-01; cons. UN, NSF; mem. Gov. Thompson's Adv. Com. on Agrl. Export, 1985-87, Congressman Fawell's Adv. Com. on Sci. and Tech., 1985-98; commr. Nat. Commn. on Librs. and Info. Svcs., 1991-94. Author: Interindustrial Structure Analysis: An Input-Output Study for St. Louis Region, 1968, The Quality of Life in the United States, 1970, Rating, Index and Statistics, 1973, Quality of Life Indicators in U.S. Metropolitan Areas, 1975, Physical and Economic Damage Functions for Air Pollutants by Receptors, 1976, Earthquake Risk and Damage Functions, An Integrated Model, 1981, Income, Energy and Quality of Life: An Information Systems Approach to Decisions, 1988; mem. editl. bd.: Internat. Jour. Math. Social Sci, Am. Jour. Econs. and Sociology, 1978—, Hong Kong Jour. Bus. Mgmt., Internat. Jour. of Bus.; Internat. Jour. Mgmt.; contbr. articles to profl. jours. Recipient rsch. study award, Am. Indsl. Devel. Coun., 1969—, Fulbright scholar awards, 1992, 1996, Faculty Meritorious awards, Chgo. State U., 1983, 1986, 1989, 1990, 2002, Disting. Prof. Advancement Increase awards, 1990, 1996, 2003, Outstanding Rsch. award, Nat. Sci. Coun., 1997—98; U.S. Econ. Devel. Adminstrn. fellow, 1967—68, Korean Govt. scholar, 1963—65, Fulbright scholar, Mgmt. Devel. Inst., Delhi U., 1992. Fellow Am. Statis. Assn. (com. mem.); mem. Am. Econ. Assn. (com. mem.), Econometric Soc., Royal Econ. Soc., Internat. Statis. Instn., Assn. for Social Econs. (com. mem.), Tax Inst. Am., Chinese Acad. and Profl. Assn. (pres. 1984-85), Chinese Econ. Assn. in N.Am. (pres. 1988-90), Chinese Am. Profs. Assn. (pres. 1996—). Home: 5360 Pennywood Dr Lisle IL 60532-2032 Office: Chgo State U Chicago IL 60628 Home Phone: 630-964-0236. Personal E-mail: liuasso1982@yahoo.com. E-mail: bencliu678@hotmail.com. *The joy of living may temporarily rest on present or past glory, but it is the immersion in planning for the future— the living ahead of one's time— which ensures permanently the flourishing of the joy of life. In a commonwealth society, happiness does not come from doing what we like to do, but from liking what we have to do for the less-well-to-do-ones.*

LIU, C. Q., engineer; s. Xiuesu Liu and Tiensu Zhang; m. Zefeng Ma, Aug. 1968; children: Xiaobo, Xiaofeng. BS, Tsinghua U., Beijing, 1968; MS, Chongqing U., China, 1980, U. Cin., 1982; PhD, U. Cin., Ohio, 1991. Postdoctoral assoc. U. Cin., 1991—93; nvh engr. Ford Motor Co., Dearborn, Mich., 1991—; sr. technical specialist DaimlerChrysler Corp., Auburn Hills, 2005—. Author: (text books) Formulas for Dynamic Analysis; contbr. over 46 articles to profl. pubs. Recipient Recognition award, Chrysler Corp., 1999. Office: DaimlerChrysler Corp 800 Chrysler Dr Auburn Hills MI 48326-2757 Office Fax: 248-576-2244. Business E-Mail: cl31@dcx.com.

LIU, CEJUN, science educator, researcher, program analyst; s. Chengxong Liu and Suqiu Li; m. Qun Wang, July 28, 1992; 1 child, Kun. Diploma in Physics, Xiangtan Normal U., 1982; BS in Physics, Hunan Ednl. Inst., 1987; MS in Statis. Physics, Shanghai Jiaotong U., 1991; MS in Applied Stats., U. Ga., 2002, PhD in Computational Statis. Physics, 2002. Physics instr. Xiangtan Tech. Sch., China, 1982—85; lectr. physics divsn. physics South China Agrl. U., Guangzhou, China, 1991—95, assoc. prof. physics, head divsn. physics, 1996—97; grad. tchg. asst. dept. physics and astronomy U. Ga., Athens, 1997—99, grad. rsch. asst. ctr. simulational physics, 1999—2002, post-doctoral rsch. assoc. ctr. simulational physics, 2002—03; program analyst Rainbow Tech., Inc., Divsn. Math. and Analysis, Nat. Ctr. Stats. and Analysis, Nat. Hwy. Traffic Safety Adminstrn., Dept. Transp., 2003—. Author: (book) General Physics, 1985, General Physics Experiment, 1986; contbr. over 30 sci. papers to profl. jours. and govt. publs. Named Excellent Grad. Student, Ministry of ShangHai Higher Edn., 1991, Excellent Young Tchr., GuangDong People's Govt., 1996. Mem.: Am. Phys. Soc., Am. Statis. Assn. Home: 2325 Riviera Dr Vienna VA 22181 Office Phone: 202-366-5354. Business E-Mail: cejun.liu@nhtsa.dot.gov.

LIU, C(HAIN)-T(SUAN), materials scientist, researcher; b. Chung King, Szechuan, China, Oct. 12, 1937; came to U.S., 1962; s. Chung-Hsu and Chao-Hwang (Ren) L.; m. Ta-chang Ching, June 10, 1967; children: Evelyn, Kent. MS, Brown U., 1964, PhD, 1967. Rsch. asst. Brown U., Providence, 1962-66; rsch. staff mem. Oak Ridge Nat. Lab., Tenn., 1967-82, group leader Tenn., 1983—, sr. corp. fellow Tenn.; corp. fellow Martin Marietta Energy System, Oak Ridge, 1985—. Mem. rev. panel NASA/U.S. Dept. of Energy/USN and NSF, Washington, 1986—. Prin. editor Jour. of Material Rsch.; contbr. over 200 articles to profl. jours. V.p. Orgn. Chinese Am., Oak Ridge, 1983-85. Recipient Henry J. Albert award Internat. Precious Metals Inst., 1980, E.O. Lawrence award, Presdl. award U.S. Dept. of Energy, 1988. Fellow Am. Soc. for Metals; mem. NAE, Metall. Soc. (sec. alloy phases com. 1989), Internat. Precious Metals Inst. (hon.), Materials Rsch. Soc. (co-organizer 1984, 86, 88, 91). Achievements include contributions to understanding ductility and fracture in ordered intermetallics and improving their mechanical properties by alloy design; patents for new high temperature structural materials. Home: 122 Newell Ln Oak Ridge TN 37830-8110 Office: Oak Ridge Nat Lab PO Box 2008 Oak Ridge TN 37831-2008

LIU, CHAO-MIN, biochemist, biotechnologist, researcher; b. Minhsiung, Taiwan, Aug. 9, 1936; arrived in US, 1963; s. Shin-ruh and She-O (Yu) Liu; m. Sharon Shih, Aug. 10, 1969; children: Franklin, Daniel. BS, Nat. Taiwan U., 1958, MS in Phytopathology, 1960; MS in Biochemistry, U. Wis., 1967, PhD in Biochemistry, 1969. Rsch. asst. Nat. Taiwan U., Taipei, 1961-62; instr. biochemistry Taipei Med. Coll., 1962-63; rsch. asst. U. Wis., Madison, 1963-69; rsch. assoc. Waksman Inst., New Brunswick, NJ, 1970-72; sr. scientist Hoffmann-La Roche Inc., Nutley, NJ, 1972-79, rsch. fellow, 1979-85, rsch. investigator, 1985-91, rsch. leader, 1991-2001, sr. rsch. leader, 2001—, disting. rsch. leader, 2003—. Contbr. articles to profl. jours. Mem. Arts Students League NY. Fellow: Am. Acad. Microbiology; mem.: Am. Soc. Microbiology, European Soc. Animal Cell Tech., Soc. Indsl. Microbiology, Am. Chem. Soc. Achievements include patents for antibiotics and processes for their production; discovery of ionomycin as a Ca++ ionophore, antibiotic X-14868A as an anti-coccidial agt. trade name Cygro. Avocation: painting. Home: 36 Rockledge Pl Cedar Grove NJ 07009-1627 Office: Hoffmann-La Roche Inc 340 Kingsland St Nutley NJ 07110-1199 Office Phone: 973-235-4253. Business E-Mail: chao-min.liu@roche.com.

LIU, DAVID RUCHIEN, biochemist, educator; b. Riverside, Calif., June 12, 1973; BA summa cum laude in Chemistry, Harvard Coll., 1994; PhD in Organic Chemistry, U. Calif., Berkeley, 1999. Asst. prof. chemistry and chem. biology Harvard U., 1999—2003, John L. Loeb assoc. prof. natural scis., assoc. prof. chemistry and chem. biology, 2003—04, prof. chemistry and chem. biology, 2005—; investigator Howard Hughes Med. Ctr., 2005—. Contbr. articles to profl. jours.; mem. editl. bd.: Current Opinion in Chem. Biology, mem. editl. adv. bd.: Chem. Revs., ChemBioChem. Named Rsch. Scholar, Am. Cancer Soc., 2001, Rschr. of Yr., Small Times Mag., 2004; named one of Brilliant 10, Popular Sci. mag., 2004, Top 100 Young Innovators, MIT Tech. Rev., 2004; recipient CAREER award, NSF, 2001, Genome-related Pilot Rsch. award, Merck, 2003, Excellence in Chemistry award, AstraZeneca, 2003, Arthur C. Cope Young Scholar award, Am. Chem. Soc., 2004, Chemistry Scholarship award, Glaxo-Smith-Kline, 2004, Camille Dreyfus Tchr.-Scholar award, 2004, Pure Chemistry award, Am. Chem. Soc., 2006; Rsch. Fellow, Alfred P. Sloan Found., 2002. Achievements include patents in field. Office: Harvard U Dept Chemistry and Chem Biology 12 Oxford St Cambridge MA 02138 Office Phone: 617-496-1067. Office Fax: 617-496-5688. E-mail: liu@chemistry.harvard.edu.

LIU, DAVID SHIAO-KUNG, research scientist, consultant; b. Chung King, China, Aug. 27, 1940; s. Chen and Betty Shih Liu; m. Emily Tsai; children: John, Jeffrey, Joanne. BSc, Nat. Cheng Kung U., Taiwan, 1962; MS, U. Calif., Berkeley, 1965; PhD, NYU, 1972. Registered profl. engr.,

NY, civil engr., Calif. Sr. scientist RAND Corp., Santa Monica, Calif., 1971—91; pres. Gen. Sys., Malibu, Calif., 1990—. Sr. adv. sci. adv. bd. Office Prime Min., Taipei, Taiwan, 1987—2000; sr. cons. RAND Corp., Santa Monica, 1995—2000; prof. oceanographic engring. Nat. Cheng-Kung U., Tainan, Taiwan, 1980—87; adj. assoc. prof. U. So. Calif., LA, 1977—85; sr. cons. Ministry of Econ. Affairs, Taipei, Taiwan, 1989—2000; sr. advisor Cen. Weather Bur., Taipei, Taiwan, 1986—2000; sr. cons. Coun. Econ. Devel., Taiwan, 1994—97, Naval Hydrographic Bur., Taiwan, 1981—96. 2d lt. mil. police, 1962—63, Taiwan. Achievements include development of 3-dimensional numerical model, water quality of NY Harbor. Home: 3706 Oceanhill Way Malibu CA 90265-5640

LIU, DEREK C., military officer; b. La Mirada, Calif., Jan. 15, 1982; s. Chih and Kim Hsu Liu; m. Nicola Yunyee Jim. MA in Intelligence and Internat. Security, King's Coll., London, 2004. Signals intelligence officer 3rd Radio Bn., USMC, 2003—06; counter terrorism officer NSA/CSS Hawaii, Kunia, 2006—. 1st lt. USMC, 2003—06. Mem.: Royal United Svcs. Inst. (assoc.). Home: 157 Ulupa St Kailua HI 96734 Office: USMC Mcbh M C B H Kaneohe Bay HI 96863 Home Phone: 503-929-0191. Personal E-mail: dliu115@hotmail.com. E-mail: derek.liu@usmc.mil.

LIU, DERONG, electrical and computer engineer, educator; b. Baicheng, Jilin, China, Jan. 3, 1963; arrived in US, 1990; s. Yucheng Liu and Guizhi Chen; m. Connie C. Zhang, July 20, 1987; 1 child, Emilie C. BSME, East China Inst. Tech., (now Nanjing U. Sci. and Tech.), 1982; MSEE, Chinese Acad. Scis., Beijing, 1987; PhD, U. Notre Dame, 1994. Product design engr. China North Industries Corp., Jilin, 1982-84; instr. Chinese Acad. Scis. Grad. Sch., Beijing, 1987-90; staff fellow GM R&D Ctr., Warren, Mich., 1993-95; asst. prof. Stevens Inst. Tech., Hoboken, N.J., 1995-99, U. Ill., Chgo., 1999—2002, assoc. prof., 2002—06, prof., 2006—. Co-author: Dynamical Systems with Saturation Nonlinearities, 1994, Qualitative Analysis and Synthesis of Recurrent Neural Networks, 2002, Stability and Control with Applications, 2003, Fuzzy Modeling an dFuzzy Control, 2006, Advances in Computational Intelligence, 2006; contbr. articles to profl. jours. Recipient H.N. Davis Disting. Tchg. award Stevens Inst. Tech., 1997, Faculty Early Career Devel. award NSF, 1999; Michael J. Birck Fellowship, 1990. Fellow IEEE; mem. Assn. for Computing Machinery, Internat. Neural Networks Soc. Office: ECE Dept (MC154) U Ill 851 S Morgan St Chicago IL 60607-7042 Home Phone: 708-366-6009. E-mail: dliu@ece.uic.edu.

LIU, DON H., lawyer, printing company executive; b. Seoul, Korea, 1961; BA magna cum laude, Haverford Coll., Pa.; JD, Columbia U., NYC. Bar: Pa. 1986. Law clk. NJ Supreme Ct.; atty. Richards & O'Neil, NYC, Simpson, Thacher & Bartlett, NYC; v.p., dep. chief legal officer Aetna US Healthcare, 1992—99; sr. v.p., gen. counsel Ikon Office Solutions Inc., Malvern, Pa., 1999—2005; sr. v.p., gen. counsel, chief compliance officer Toll Bros. Inc., Horsham, Pa., 2005—07; sr. v.p., gen. counsel, sec. Xerox Corp., Stamford, Conn., 2007—. Bd. mem. Mercy Health Systems. Mem. ABA, Nat. Asian Pacific Am. Bar Assn., Assn. Corp. Counsel (bd. mem.), Minority Corp. Counsel Assn. (bd. mem.) Office: Xerox Corp 800 Long Ridge Rd Stamford CT 06904 Office Phone: 203-968-3000.*

LIU, GANG, education educator, researcher; s. Gui Zhu Liu and Shu Ling Zhang; m. Ping Men, Feb. 15, 1985; 1 child, Yang. BS, Beijing U., China, 1982; MS, Nankai U., Tianjin, China, 1985; PhD, Heidelberg U., Germany, 1990. Lectr. Nankai U., 1985—87; guest scientist German Cancer Rsch. Ctr., Heidelberg, 1990; postdoctoral fellow Fla. State U., Tallahassee, 1991; rsch. assoc. U. Utah, Salt Lake City, 1992—99, rsch. instr., 2000—04, rsch. asst. prof., 2004—. Ad-hoc grant reviewer Alzheimer Assn., Chgo., 2004—; ad-hoc jour. reviewer Expert Opinion, 2006—, Brain Rsch., 2006—, Neuroscience Letters, 2006—. Author: (book chpt.) Nanoparticles for the treatment of Alzheimer's disease: the theoretical rationale, present status and future perspectives. Grantee, NIH, 2003—. Mem.: Am. Soc. Bone and Mineral Rsch., Am. Chem. Soc. Achievements include patents for nano-particle technology to separate and identify bio-molecules that can serve as biomarkers for disease diagnosis; patents pending for using this technology to deliver drugs to specific organs, thus investigating disease pathologies and treating diseases. Avocations: ping pong/table tennis, soccer, basketball, travel, reading. Office: Univ Utah 729 Arapeen Dr #2334 Salt Lake City UT 84108 Office Phone: 801-581-3429. Office Fax: 801-581-7008. Business E-Mail: gang.liu@m.cc.utah.edu.

LIU, HANLI, biomedical engineer, educator; b. Beijing, Mar. 6, 1960; d. Li-ya Wang and Zhongcheng Liu; m. Anqi Wu, July 6, 1957; children: Eric Wu, Rodney Wu. PhD in Physics, Wake Forest U., Winston-Salem, NC, 1994. Rsch. assoc. U. City Sci. Ctr., Phila., 1992—96; post-doctoral fellow U. of Pa, Phila., 1994—96; from asst. prof. to prof. biomed. engring. U. of Tex., Arlington, 1996—2006, prof. biomedical engring., 2006—. Adj. faculty mem. joint program in biomed. engring. U. Tex. Southwestern Med. Ctr., Dallas, 1996—. Recipient Outstanding Young Scientist award, Houston Soc. for Engring. in Medicine and Biology, 1998, Outstanding Young Faculty Award, Coll. of Engring., U. of Tex., Arlington, 1999, Univ. Outstanding Rsch. Achievement award, U. Tex. Arlington, 2004. Mem.: IEEE, Internat. Soc. for Optical Engring., Optical Soc. of Am. Home: 1211 Hillary Ln Arlington TX 76012 Office: U Tex Arlington PO Box 19138 Arlington TX 76019 Office Phone: 817-272-2054. Business E-Mail: hanli@uta.edu.

LIU, HANS HAMILTON, infectious disease physician, educator; m. Gwendolyn Joan Liang; children: Christina, Michelle. AB, Johns Hopkins U., Balt., 1974; MD, Harvard U., Boston, 1978. Diplomate Am. Bd. Internal Medicine, Am. Bd. Infectious Diseases. Asst. prof. medicine Thomas Jefferson U., Phila., 1985—91, prof. medicine, 1998—; clin. asst. prof. medicine U. Pa., Phila., 1991—95, clin. assoc. prof. medicine, 1995—97; assoc. prof. medicine Allegheny U. Health Scis., Phila., 1997—98. Infectious diseases cons. Bryn Mawr (Pa.) Med. Specialists, 1998—. Named Outstanding Tchg. Attending, Presbyn. Med. Ctr., Phila., 1992, 1993, 1997. Fellow: ACP. Office: Bryn Mawr Med Specialists 933 Haverford Rd Bryn Mawr PA 19010 Office Phone: 610-527-8118.

LIU, HUNG-WEN (BEN), science educator, researcher; b. Taiwan, Republic of China; BS in Chemistry, Tunghai U., 1974; MA, Columbia U., 1978, PPhil, PhD, Columbia U., 1981. Nat. Inst. of Environ. Health Sciences postdoctoral fellow MIT, 1981—84; asst. prof., dept. chemistry U. Minn., 1984—90, assoc. prof., dept. chemistry, 1990—94, full prof., dept. chemistry, 1994—99, Disting. McKnight Univ. Prof., 1999—2000; George H. Hitchings Regents Chair in Drug Design, Coll. Pharmacy U. Tex., Austin, 2000—, prof., medicinal chemistry, 2000—, prof. chemistry and biochemistry, 2000—. Vis. prof. ICSN-CNRS (Ctr. Nat. Scientific Rsch.), Gif-sur-Yvette, France, 1996, Technion-Israel Inst. Tech., Haifa, Israel; hon. prof. chemistry U. Hong Kong, 2001—. Contbr. several articles to profl. jours. Two years of mil. svc. Recipient Camille & Henry Dreyfus Grant for Disting. New Faculty in Chemistry, 1984, Am. Cancer Soc. Jr. Faculty Rsch. award, 1985, Eli Lily Life Sci. Young Investigator award, 1985, NIH Rsch. Career Develop. award, 1990—95, MERIT award, Nat. Inst. Gen. Med. Sciences, 1999. Fellow: Japan Soc. for the Promotion of Sci., Am. Soc. Microbiology, AAAS; mem.: Soc. of Chinese Bioscientists in Am., Chinese Am. Chem. Soc., Am. Soc. for Biochemistry and Molecular Biology, Am. Chem. Soc. (assoc. editor, Organic Letters, Horace S. Isbell award, Carbohydrate Divsn. 1993, Nakanishi prize 2007). Office: Univ Texas Austin Chemistry and Biochemistry 1 University Station PHR 3206B WEL 5 235 Austin TX 78712 Office Phone: 512-232-7811. Office Fax: 512-471-2746. Business E-Mail: h.w.liu@mail.utexas.edu.*

LIU, JING, pathologist, educator; b. Beijing, Sept. 28, 1957; d. Songtao and Suru Liu; m. David Youdong Tong, July 9, 1983; children: Lawrence Guoxin Tong, Brian Alexander Tong. MD, Capital U. Med. Sci., Beijing, 1982; PhD, Tex. A&M U., College Station, 1992. Diplomate Am. Bd. Pathology, 1999. Pediatric cardiologist Beijing Childrens' Hosp., Beijing, 1985—87; asst. prof. U. Tex., S.W. Med. Sch., Dallas, 1999—2000, U. Tex. Med. Sch., Houston, 2000—05, dir. cytopathology, 2004—, assoc. prof., 2005—. Contbr. articles to profl. jours. Recipient Sci. and Technol. Advance award, Beijing Pub. Health Bur., 1986, Travel award, Fifth World Congress for Microcirculation, 1991, Am. Soc. Investigative Pathology, 1995. Fellow: Am. Soc. Clin. Pathology, Coll. Am. Pathologists; mem.: Tex. Soc. Cytology, US and Can. Acad. Pathology, Am. Soc. Cytopathology, Phi Kappa Phi. Achievements include research in immunocytochemistry, mechanisms of myogenic enhancement by norepinephrine research, utility of doppler echocardiography. Office: Univ Tex 6431 Fannin St Rm 2136 Houston TX 77030 Office Phone: 713-500-5327. Office Fax: 713-500-0732. Business E-Mail: jing.liu.1@uth.tmc.edu.

LIU, JINSONG, pathologist; b. Taxin County, Jiangsu Province, China, Jan. 20, 1962; s. Xinzhong Liu and Zhifang Yu; m. Bijun Yang, July 27, 1986; children: Terrence T., T Benjamin. MD, Shanghai Med. U., 1983; PhD, Case Western Res. U., Cleve., 1991. Diplomate Am. Bd. Pathology, 2002. Resident NYU, NYC, 1994—98; assoc. prof. U. Tex. MD Anderson Cancer Ctr., Houston, 1999—; mem. U. Tex. Health Sci. Ctr., Grad. Sch. Biomedical Sci., 2003—. Contbr. articles to profl. jours. Recipient 5-yr. Svc. award, MD Anderson Cancer Ctr., 2004; fellow, NYU, 1998—99; grantee Career Devel. awards, NIH, 2001—02; scholar, Chinese Govt. Ednl. Commn., 1984. Mem.: Internat. Assn. Gynecologic Cancer, Am. Assn. Cancer Rsch., US and Can. Acad. Pathology. Achievements include research in ovarian cancer model. Home: 4144 Ruskin St Houston TX 77005 Office: UT MD Anderson Cancer Center 1515 Holcombe Boulevard Houston TX 77030-4095 Home Phone: 713-838-9189; Office Phone: 713-745-1102. Office Fax: 713-792-5529. Personal E-mail: jinsongliu1962@yahoo.com. E-mail: jliu@mdanderson.org.

LIU, JUN O., pharmacologist, educator; s. Shiqing Liu and Lunying Chang; m. Alice Zou. PhD, MIT, Cambridge, Mass., 1990. From asst. to assoc. prof. MIT, 1993—2000; prof. Johns Hopkins Sch. Medicine, Balt., 2001—. Dir. grad. program in pharmacology Johns Hopkins Sch. Medicine, Balt., 2006—. Achievements include invention of a three-hybrid system for detecting small molecule-protein interactions; discovery of two novel signaling proteins named Cabin1 and Carabin; invention of a number of lead compounds with potential as anticancer, anti-angiogenic, immunosuppressive, antimalarial and antibiotic activities. Office: Johns Hopkins Sch Medicine 725 N Wolfe St Baltimore MD 21205 Office Phone: 410-955-4619.

LIU, KAI, physics professor; b. Changzhou, Jiangsu, China; PhD, Johns Hopkins U., Balt., 1998. Asst. prof. U. Calif., Davis, 2001—05, assoc. prof., 2005—. Presenter in field. Contbr. articles to profl. jours. Fellow, Alfred P. Sloan Found., 2005—; grantee, Lawrence Livermore Nat. Lab., 2002—03, 2003—04, 2003—05, NSF, 2002—05, 2005—06, U. Calif., 2003—06, 2004—06, Am. Chem. Soc., Petroleum Rsch. Fund, 2003—05, 2005—07; Jr. Faculty Rsch. fellow, U. Calif., 2003. Mem.: IEEE, Neutron Scattering Soc. Am., Materials Rsch. Soc., Am. Phys. Soc. Achievements include patents in field; patents pending for. Office: UC Davis Physics Dept One Shields Ave Davis CA 95616 Office Phone: 530-752-4109. Office Fax: 530-752-4717. E-mail: kailiu@ucdavis.edu.

LIU, KAI-LIH, epidemiologist; b. Hualien, Taiwan, Apr. 24, 1964; arrived in US, 1990, naturalized, 2005; s. Bao-Chong Liu and Eng-Lian Chen. MPH in Epidemiology, Nat. Taiwan U., Taipei, 1988; PhD in Epidemiology, Yale U., New Haven, 1996. Rsch. asst. Nat. Taiwan U., Taipei, 1986—88; epidemiologist RI Dept. Health, Providence, 1996—98; rsch. fellow/scientist Columbia U., NYC, 1998—99; city rsch. scientist NYC Dept. Health and Mental Hygiene, 2000—, NIMH postdoc. fellow, 1998—99. Mem.: Internat. AIDS Soc. Buddhist. Achievements include evaluation the Rhode Island Syringe Exchange Program for HIV prevention research, data analyses for various CDC-funded HIV research projects on perinatally infected children/adolescents, HIV patients, gay men, transgenders and injection drug users in New York City; preparation of presentations, conference abstracts, and peer-reviewed manuscripts to disseminate important HIV research findings. Office: NYC Dept Health and Mental Hygiene 346 Broadway Rm 701 Box 44 New York NY 10013 Business E-Mail: kliu@health.nyc.gov.

LIU, KATHERINE CHANG, artist, art educator; b. Kiang-si, China; came to U.S., 1963; d. Ming-fan and Ying (Yuan) Chang; m. Yet-zen Liu; children: Alan S., Laura Y. MS, U. Calif., Berkeley, 1965. Instr. U. Va. Ext., Longwood Coll.; tchg. staff Intensive Studies Seminar, Santa Fe, 1995-2000, 02-07; invited mem. LA Artcore Reviewing and Curatorial Bd., 1993; invited curator Contemplation, Lew Allen Contemporary Gallery, Santa Fe, 2003; curator Introspection, Jenkins Johnson Gallery, San Francisco, 2006; curator Addition/Reduction, Gail Harvey Gallery, Santa Monica, 2007; curatory Duality, Lew Allen Contemporary Gallery, Santa Fe, 2004; sole juror Taos (N.Mex.) Exhbn. Am. Watercolor, 2000, Va. Watercolor Soc. Ann., Richmond, 2001, Rocky Mountain Nat. Competition, 2001, Collage/Assemblage/USA I, Ventura (Calif.) Coll. 2001, Collage/Assemblage/USA II, 2002, La. Watercolor Soc.-Internat. Competition, New Orleans, 2003, Aqueous Open Nat. Show, Tubac Art Ctr., Ariz. 2004, Pikes Peak Watercolor Competition, Colo. Springs Coll., Colo., 2005; chmn. jury selection Nat. Watercolor Soc. 80th Annual Competition Exhbn., 2000; juror, lectr. in field. One-woman shows include Harrison Mus., Utah State U., Riverside (Calif.) Art Mus., Ventura (Calif.) Coll., Fla. A&M U., Gail Harvey Gallery, Santa Monica, 1998, J.J. Brookings Gallery, San Francisco, 1998, Louis Newman Galleries, LA, LA Artcore, Lung-Men Gallery, Taipei, Republic of China, Lew Allen Contemporary, Golden West College Gallery, 1999, Rosaline Koener Gallery, Westhampton, NY, 2000, AMA Gallery, Turku, Finland, 2001, Gail Harvey Gallery, Santa Monica, Calif., 2001, Rosaline Koener Gallery, LI, NY, 2002, Galerie Egelund, Copenhagen, 2002, 04, Le Cercle Optique, Lyon, France, 2003, Galerie Parsi Parla, Lyon, France, 2005, Galarie Cour de Louges, Lyon, 2005; invitational shows include Crossing Cultures, Lewallen Contemporary, 1998, Parkland Coll. Ill., 1989, 91, 97, Treasures for the Community: The Chrysler Mus. Collects, 1989-96, 97, Watercolor U.S.A. Hon. Soc. Invitational, 1989, 91, 93, 95, 97, Hunter Mus. Art, Tenn., 1993, Bakersfield Art Mus., 1994, Sandra Walters Gallery, Hong Kong, 1994, Horwitch-Newman Gallery, Scottsdale, Ariz., 1995, Hong Kong U. Sci. and Tech. Libr. Art Gallery, 1996, J.J. Brookings Gallery, San Francisco, 1996-98, John N Joe Gallery, LA, 1996, Bill Armstrong Gallery, Springfield, Mo., 1996, Chrysler Mus. Fine Art, Norfolk, Va., 1997, U. B.C. Art Gallery, 1992, U. Sydney Art Mus., 1992, Ruhr-West Art Mus., Wise, 1992, Macau Art Mus., 1992, Rosenfeld Gallery, Phila., 1994, Mandarin Oriental Fine Arts, Hong Kong, 1994, Hampton U. Mus., 2000, Fukuoka Asian Art Mus., 2001, Lew Allen Contemporary Gallery, N.Mex., 2001, Asian Am. Artists, Calif. State Channel Islands, Calif., 2002, Foothills Art Ctr., Golden, Colo., 2002, Jenkins Johnson Gallery, 2005-07, Lew Allen Contemporary Gallery, Santa Fe, N.Mex., 2005, Christel Dahlen Gallery, Copenhagen, 2006; exhibited in group shows at Lew Allen Contemporay, 2003; contbr. chpts. to books, articles to profl. jours. Co-curator Taiwan-USA-Australia Watermedia Survey Exhbn., Nat. Taiwan Art Inst., 1994; sole juror San Diego Watermedia Internat., 1993, Triton Mus. Open Competition, 1994, Northern Nat. Art Competition, 1994, Watercolor West Nat., 1993, Tenn., Utah, Hawaii, N.C. Watercolor Socs., North Am. Open, others; co-juror Rocky Mountain Nat., San Diego Internat. and West Fedn. Exhibits. Recipient Rex Brandt award San Diego Watercolor Internat., 1985, Purchase Selection award Watercolor USA and Springfield (Mo.) Art Mus., 1981, Gold medal, 1986, Mary Lou Fitzgerald meml. award Allied Arts Am. Nat. Arts Club, N.Y.C., 1987, Achievement award of Artists Painting in Acrylic Am. Artists Mag., 1993; NEA grantee, 1979-80. Mem. Nat. Watercolor Soc. (life, chmn. jury 1985, pres. 1983, Top award 1984, cash awards 1979, 87; chmn. jury selection 80th ann. open competition exhibit 2000), Watercolor U.S.A. Honor Soc., Nat. Soc. Painters in Casein and Acrylic (2nd award 1985), Rocky Mountain Nat. Watermedia Soc. (juror 1984, awards 1978, 80, 86). Personal E-mail: kchangliu@verizon.net.

LIU, KELLY H., geophysicist, educator; b. China; Doctoral, U. Calif., 1998. Post doctoral Carnegie Instn. of Wash.; asst. prof. Kans. State U., Manhattan, Kans., 2000—. Mem.: Soc. of Exploration Geophysicists, Seismol. Soc. of Am., Am. Geophys. Union. Office: Kans State U 108 Thompson Hall Manhattan KS 66503 Office Phone: 785-532-2249. Office Fax: 785-532-5159. E-mail: liu@ksu.edu.

LIU, LEONARD, software services company executive; b. 1941; Grad., Taiwan Univ.; PhD, Princeton Univ., NJ, 1968. Mgr. CICS, SNA, and AIX IBM, 1969—85, mgr. world-wide database, 1985—89; pres. ACER Group; COO Cadence Design Sys.; CEO Walker Interactive Sys.; pres. ASE Group; currently chmn., CEO Augmentum, Shanghai and Calif. Spkr. in field; former professor comp. sci. Univ. Mich. Office: Augmentum Co Ste 400 1065 E Hillsdale Blvd Foster City CA 94404 Office Fax: 650-240-2295.

LIU, LEWIS-GUODO, information scientist, educator; s. Bao Hang Liu and Rui Qin Chou; 1 child, Cathy. BS Beijing Tchr. Coll.; MBA, Niagara U., NY, 1993; MS in Info. Sci., U. Ill., Urbana-Champaign, 1994; PhD in Econ. of Edn., SUNY, Buffalo, 1993. Asst. prof. Beijing Tchr. Coll., 1984—86; tchg. and rsch. fellow SUNY, Buffalo, 1986—93; adj. prof., bus. info. specialist Wright State U.; assoc. prof. Baruch Coll., CUNY, NYC, 1999—2005, prof., 2005—. Author: (books) The Internet and Library and Information: Issues and Trends, 1996, Internet Resources and Service for International Business, 1998, Global Economic Growth, 2000, Internet Resources and Services for International Finace and Investment, 2001; editor: The Role and Impact of the Internet on Library and Information Services, 2001; series editor (book series) Global Guides to Internet Business Resources including the following books: Internet Resources and Services for Real Estate, for Marketing, for Finance and Investment, and for International Business, 2002; contbr. articles to profl. jours. Recipient Faculty Scholarships & Achievement awards, CUNY, 2003—05; Tchg. & Rsch. fellowships, SUNY, 1986—90. Achievements include research in economic theory of academic research libraries and developing quantitative research methodologies for measuring multiple-product and multi-services of academic research libraries. Home: PO Box 1383 New York NY 10159 Office: Baruch Coll CUNY E 151 25th St New York NY 10010 Business E-Mail: lewis_liu@baruch.cuny.edu.

LIU, LUCY, actress; b. Queens, NY, Dec. 2, 1968; Student, NYU; BA in Chinese Lang. and Culture, U. Mich., 1990. Actor: (TV series) Beverly Hills, 90210, 1991, L.A. Law, 1993, Coach, 1994, Home Improvement, 1995, Hercules: The Legendary Journeys, 1995, ER, 1995, The X-Files, 1996, Nash Bridges, 1996, High Incident, 1996, The Real Adventures of Johnny Quest, 1997, NYPD Blue, 1997, Michael Hayes, 1997, Sex and the City, 2001, (voice only) King of the Hill, 2002, Jackie Chan Adventures, 2004, Game Over, 2004, Maya & Miguel, 2004, Pearl, 1996—97, Ally McBeal, 1998—2002; (TV films) Riot, 1997; (films) Ban wo zong heng, 1992, Protozoa, 1993, Bang, 1995, Jerry Maguire, 1996, Gridlock'd, 1997, City of Industry, 1997, Guy, 1997, Flypaper, 1997, Love Kills, 1998, Payback, 1999, True Crime, 1999, Molly, 1999, The Mating Habits of the Earthbound Human, 1999, Play It to the Bone, 1999, Shanghai Noon, 2000, Charlie's Angels, 2001, Hotel, 2001, Ballistics: Ecks vs. Sever, 2002, Cypher, 2002, Chicago, 2002, Charlie's Angels: Full Throttle, 2003, Kill Bill: Vol. 1, 2003, Domino, 2005, Lucky Number Slevin, 2006; exec. prodr.: Freedom's Fury, 2006; exec. prodr., actor: Code Name: The Cleaner, 2007. Apptd. U.S. Fund for UNICEF amb., 2005. Recipient Visibility award, Asian Excellence Awards, 2006. Office: William Morris Agy One William Morris Pl Beverly Hills CA 90212*

LIU, MINETTA CHUNG-SUI, oncologist, educator; b. Dec. 6, 0199; AB, Princeton U.; MD, Jefferson Med. Coll. Phila., 1995. Cert. Internal Medicine, Med. Oncology. Intern Georgetown U. Hosp., 1995, 1996, fellow, 2001, resident, internal medicine, 1998; joined breast cancer program Lombardi Comprehensive Cancer Ctr., Georgetown U., Washington, 2001—, chief fellow, asst. prof. medicine and oncology. Office: Lombardi Comprehensive Cancer Ctr Podium B Georgetown U 3800 Reservoir Rd NW Washington DC 20057 Office Phone: 202-444-3677, 202-444-2988. Business E-Mail: liumc@georgetown.edu.*

LIU, PETER, bank executive; Former sr. v.p. Credit Suisse First Boston; former v.p. Chase Manhattan Bank; former regional COO UBS Investment Bank; former sector head, bus. consulting svc. IBM China/Hong Kong Limited; former chief info. officer Bank of China Hong Kong; founder, vice chmn. New Resource Bank, 2006—. Adv. bd. Clean Tech. Investment Advisory Calif. Public Employees Retirement System; adv. bd. Calif. Teachers' Retirement System; co-founder, vice-chair China-U.S. Energy Efficiency Alliance. Office: New Resource Bank 405 Howard St Ste 110 San Francisco CA 94105

LIU, QINGMIN, software engineer, materials engineer; s. Cai Liu and Xiufang Cao; m. Huiman Wu, Mar. 11, 1989; children: Jenny, Rena. BS, Northeastern U., Shenyang, China, 1985; MS, Chinese Acad. Scis., Shenyang, 1988, U. Wis., Milw., 2002. Engr. Inst. Metal Rsch., Chinese Acad. Scis., Shenyang, 1988—98; sr. software engr. Jackson Graphics, Inc., Milw., 2003—04; analyst and engr. Motor Techs. Group, Milw., 2004—05; software engr. Voting Techs. Internat., Milw., 2005—. Contbr. articles to profl. jours. Mem.: Am. Foundry Soc. (assoc.). Achievements include patents for apparatus for preparing metal matrix composite by electromagnetic centrifugal casting; apparatus for preparing single crystal materials in electromagnetic field by floating zone method; a new apparatus for electromagnetic centrifugal casting; research in SiC particle reinforced metal matrix composites; gradient composites; Hi-Tc superconductors; development of simulation of solidification. Home: 9623 W Hunt Club Dr Mequon WI 53097 Office: Voting Techs Internat 757 N Broadway Ave Milwaukee WI 53202 Home Phone: 262-238-1376. Personal E-mail: qingmin.liu@gmail.com.

LIU, QINGYUN, thermal and mechanical research engineer; b. DaTong, ShanXi, China, Nov. 12, 1968; m. Dongmei An, Oct. 25, 1993; children: Anqi, Anna. BS in Aerospace Engring., Beijing Inst. Tech., 1989, MS in Aerospace Engring., 1992; PhD in Computational Engring., Miss. State U., Starkville, 2000—03. Asst. prof. aerospace engring. Beijing Inst. Tech., 1992—99, assoc. prof. aerospace engring., 1999—2000; grad. rsch. asst. Miss. State U., 2000—03, postdoctoral rsch. assoc., 2004—. Finalist One of 3 finalists for The FuelCellSouth Crystal Flame Innovation award, FuelCellSouth Partners Forum, Inc, 2006; recipient Sci. & Tech. Achievement award, Ministry Machinery Industry, 1993. Mem.: ASME (assoc.). Home: 36J Wallace Cir Starkville MS 39759 Office: Miss State Univ HPC Bldg 2 Rsch Blvd Starkville MS 39759 Home Phone: 662-325-5093. Personal E-mail: liuqingyun@gmail.com. Business E-Mail: liuqy@hpc.msstate.edu.

LIU, SHUMO, molecular biologist; b. Shanghai, Oct. 2, 1954; s. Yumin Liu and Jia-xiu Pan. BS, U. Oreg., Eugene, 1981—84; MS, MIT, Cambridge, 1986—90. Rsch. asst. Rockefeller U., NYC, 1994—98; sr. rsch. assoc. NEC Rsch. Inst., Princeton, NJ, 1998—2003; specialist U. Calif. San Diego, La Jolla, Calif., 2003—06; cons. Allele Biotech., San Diego, 2006—. Cons. NEC Rsch. Inst., 1995—98. Office: UCSD 9500 Gilman Dr MC0379 La Jolla CA 92093 Home Phone: 609-638-3644. Office Fax: 858-534-5819. Business E-Mail: sliu@physics.ucsd.edu.

LIU, SONGTAO, medical researcher; s. Wanjin Liu and Fuling Sun; m. Jing Han, June 18, 1998. MD, Shandong Med. U., Jinan, China, 1997. Lic. Ministry of Health, China, 1997. Asst. prof. radiology Qilu Hosp. Shandong U., Jinan, 1999—2002; rsch. scientist NYU Sch. Medicine, 2002—. Author: Heart and Thrombus Disease, 2000, Liver Cancer, 2000; contbr. articles to profl. jours. Recipient Sci. & Tech. Progress award, Shandong Province Govt., China, 1999—2001. Mem.: Am. Soc. Neuroradiology, Radiol. Soc. N.Am., Internat. Soc. for Magnetic Resonance in Medicine. Achievements include development of advanced magnetic resonance spectroscopy (MRS) localization methods and MRS pulse sequence for high field MRI imager; post-processing software to visualize the MRS information and to facilitate its absolute quantification; research in neurological deficits in brain disorders, such as multiple sclerosis, Alzheimer's disease, and brain tumors, using MRS and MRI techniques. Office Phone: 212-263-3329. Office Fax: 212-263-7541.

LIU, TA-CHIANG, research scientist, physician, consultant; s. Di Liu and Ming-Chu Liu Cheng; m. Ju-Fang Chang, Nov. 9, 2003. MD, Nat. Yang Ming U., Taipei, Taiwan, 1997; PhD, U. London, Eng., 2003. Lic. Dept. of Health, Taiwan, 1997. House officer Nat. Cheng Kung U. Hosp., Taiwan, 1999—2000; rsch. fellow Mass. Gen. Hosp. and Harvard Med. Sch., Boston, 2004—. Cons. Ella Cheong (intellectual property consulting), Hong Kong, 2005—. Contbr. articles to profl. jour. Lt. Taiwanese Army, 1997—99. Recipient Overseas Rsch. Student award, Brit. Coun., 2002—03; Overseas Grad. Student scholar, Ministry of Edn., Taiwan, 2000-2003. Mem.: Am. Soc. Gene Therapy (assoc.), Am. Assn. for Cancer Rsch. (assoc.). Achievements include first to propose and demonstrate that viruses with deletions in antiapoptotic genes can be used as oncolytic agents. Office: Mass Gen Hosp 185 Cambridge St CPZN-3800 Boston MA 02114 Office Fax: 617-643-3422. E-mail: tliu2@partners.org.

LIU, TONY, chef; b. Oahu, Hawaii, 1975; Degree in Culinary Arts and Patisserie, Kapiolani Cmty. Coll., Hawaii; attended, Culinary Inst. Am., NYC. Intern Lespinasse; cook Daniel, NYC, Tabla, NYC, Restaurante Martin Berasategui, Spain, 2001; sous chef Babbo, NYC; exec. chef August, NYC, 2004—. Named one of NYC's Rising Stars, StarChefs.com, 2006. Office: August 359 Bleecker St New York NY 10014 Office Phone: 212-929-4774.

LIU, WEI, telecommunications industry executive, researcher; b. Ganzhou, Jiangxi, China; BA, Huazhong U. Sci. and Tech., Wuhan, China, 1998, MA, 2001; PhD, U. Fla., Gainesville, 2005. Rsch. assoc. U. Fla., 2001—05; sr. mem. tech. staff Scalable Network Techns., LA, 2005—. Contbr. articles to profl. jours., chapters to books. Mem.: IEEE (grantee 2003—04, 2007). Achievements include research in network and communication algorithms and protocols, model and simulate and performance study of large-scale communication networks. Office Phone: 310-338-3318.

LIU, XIAOFAN SOPHIE, engineering educator; d. Dapeng Liu and Caixia Huang; m. Chunbiao Guo; children: Bing Ju Guo, Bing Zhuo Guo, Bing Chen Guo. BS, Sichuan U., China; M Engring., Xidian U., China, 1992; PhD (hon.), Nat. U. Singapore, 1996. Lectr. Temesek Poly., Singapore, 1996—2001; asst. prof. Nanyang Technol. U., Singapore, 2002—04; assoc. prof. Oral Roberts U., Tulsa, Okla., 2004—. Contbr. articles to profl. jours. Trustee, com. mem. Agape Chinese Bapt. Ch., Tulsa. Grantee, Singapore Nat. Sci. and Tech. Bd., 1999—2000; Sch. Computer Engring. Start-up grantee, Nanyang Technol. U., Singapore, 2003. Mem.: IEEE (hon.). Office: Oral Roberts University 7777 S Lewis Ave Tulsa OK 74171 Office Phone: 918-495-6929.

LIU, XINSHENG, chemist; b. Jilin, China, Dec. 24, 1953; came to U.S., 1990; s. Hongru Liu and Gaoqin Wei; m. Xianying Meng, Feb. 2, 1978; children: Lei, Dan. MS, Jilin U., 1981; PhD, U. Cambridge, Eng., 1986. Lectr., assoc. prof. Jilin U., Changchun, China, 1977-90; vis. scholar U. Cambridge, 1990; rsch. assoc., rsch. prof. U. Notre Dame, Ind., 1990-96; sr. chemist, sr. rsch. assoc. BASF Catalysts LLC (formerly Engelhard Corp.), Iselin, NJ, 1996—. Contbr. articles to profl. jours. Grantee Chinese Nat. Sci. and Tech. Com., 1988. Mem. Am. Chem. Soc., Chinese Chem. Soc. (Solid State Chemistry divsn. com.). Achievements include discovering a galliation method for introducing gallium into structures of zeolites; synthesizing for the first time gallosilicate zeolite, and titanosilicate molecular sieves using solid TiO_2, new insights in surface structure of alumina and electron transfer and trapping sites in zeolites, developing SCR catalysts for NOx and SCO catalysts for ammonia slip, in stationary source applications. Home: 6 Ventnor Dr Edison NJ 08820-2734 Office: BASF Catalysts LLC 25 Middlesex Essex Turnpike Iselin NJ 08830-2703 Office Phone: 732-205-7038. Business E-Mail: xinsheng_@basf.com.

LIU, XIONG, atmospheric physicist; s. Qiqi and Wanzhen (Xiao) Liu; m. Dan Liu, July 9, 1998; children: Jesse Enoch, Joanna Peony. BS in Environ. Sci., Nankai U., Tianjin, China, 1995; MS in Atmospheric Chemistry, Chinese Acad. Sciences, Beijing, 1998; PhD in Atmospheric Sci. with honors, U. Ala., Huntsville, 2002, MS in Computer Sci. with honors, 2002. Vis. scientist Harvard-Smithsonian Ctr. for Astrophysics, Cambridge, Mass., 2003, physicist, 2004—. Vis. Scientist fellow, Smithsonian Instn., 2003, NASA New Investigator Program awardee, 2006—. Mem.: Am. Geophys. Union (corr.). Achievements include first to directly retrieve the global distribution of tropospheric column ozone from space; development of two novel techniques to retrieve troposhpheric ozone profiles from airborne and ground-based spectrometers; demonstration of the need to homogenize available ozonesonde observations and standardize furture operational procedures for reliable satellite validation and ozone trend analysis; development of multi-year global dataset of tropospheric ozone; contribute first satellite observation of I.O. Home: 289 Highland Ave Apt 105 Somerville MA 02144 Office: Harvard-Smithsonian Ctr For Astrophysics 60 Garden St Cambridge MA 02138 Home Phone: 857-928-3758; Office Phone: 617-496-2136. Office Fax: 617-496-2136. Business E-Mail: xliu@cfa.harvard.edu.

LIU, YONG, engineering educator; s. Yaoming Liu and Qiying Wen. BS in Engring., U. Sci. and Tech., China, 1994; PhD, U. Mass., Amherst, 2002. Sr. postdoctoral rsch. assoc. U. Mass., Amherst, 2002—05; asst. prof. Poly. U., Bklyn., 2005—. Mem.: IEEE. Achievements include research in computer networking. Office: Poly U 5 MetroTech Ctr LC 258 Brooklyn NY 11201 Office Phone: 718-260-3959. Office Fax: 718-260-3906. Business E-Mail: yongliu@poly.edu.

LIU, YONG CHENG, chemist, educator; b. Ningbo, Zhejiang, China, Apr. 22, 1963; s. Xiqing and Caihua (Ou) L.; m. Jianghong Qian. PhD in Chemistry, Fudan U., Shanghai, 1996. Asst. prof., dir. Ningbo U., 1991-93; asst. prof. chemistry Fudan U., Shanghai, 1993—. Dir. Ningbo Membrane Rsch. Ctr., 1989-93. Contbr. articles to profl. jours.; patentee in field. Recipient 1st prize of sci. and tech. Ningbo U., 1991-93, 3d prize of sci. and tech. Zhejiang Province, 1994-96, Ministry Edn., China, 1999, Unilevel prize Fudan U., 1996. Mem. AAAS, Am. Chem. Soc., Internat. Union Pure and Applied Chemistry, Shanghai Chem. Soc. Avocations: music, sports, novels.

LIU, ZHENG, economist, educator; s. Fenchuan Liu and Yuqing Li; m. Ping Wu, May 24, 2002; 1 child, Alan Emory. BA, Renmin U., Beijing, 1988, MA, 1991, U. Minn., Mpls., 1994, PhD, 1997. Instr. U. Minn., Mpls., 1994—97; asst. prof. Clark U., Worcester, Mass., 1997—2001, Emory U., Atlanta, 2001—06, assoc. prof., 2006—. Vis. scholar Boston U., 2000—01; rsch. visitor European Ctrl. Bank, Frankfurt, Germany, 2001—03; vis. scholar Fed. Res. Bank of Atlanta, Atlanta, 2001—, Fed. Res. Bank of Mpls., Mpls., 2005—06, U. Minn., Mpls., 2005—06. Contbr. articles to profl. jours. Named Disting. Instr., U. Minn., 1994, 1995, 1996. Mem.: Friendship Assn. Chinese Students and Scholars (pres. 1996—97), Chinese Fin. Assn. (dir. 1995—96), Econometric Soc., Am. Econ. Assn., Chinese Economist Soc. Avocations: travel, tennis, volleyball, ping pong/table tennis. Office: Department of Economics Emory University Atlanta GA 30322 Office Phone: 404-727-1128. Office Fax: 404-727-4639. Business E-Mail: zheng.liu@emory.edu.

LIU, ZI-KUI, materials engineer, educator; b. Xiang Dong Tungsten Mine, Cha-Ling Hunan, China, Jan. 21, 1963; arrived in U.S., 1996; s. Kecal Liu and You Lin Song; m. Weiming Huang; children: Erik, David. BS, Ctrl. South U. Tech., Changsha, China, 1982; MS, U. Sci. and Tech., Beijing, 1985; PhD, Royal Inst. Tech., Stockholm, 1992, docent, 1996. Tchg. staff U. Sci. and Tech., Beijing, 1985—87; rschr. Royal Inst. Tech., Stockholm, 1992—96; rsch. assoc. U. Wis., Madison, 1996—98; sr. rsch. scientist Questek Innovations LLC, Evanston, Ill., 1998; asst. prof. Pa. State U., University Park, 1999—2003, assoc. prof., 2003—06, prof., 2006—. Dir. NSF Ctr. Computational Materials Design, 2005—. Editor-in-chief CALPHAD, 2001—; contbr. articles to profl. jours. Recipient 3d prize, China Nat. Key Projects, Ministry Metallurgy, China, 1988, Career award, NSF, 1999. Fellow: Am. Soc. Metals; mem.: Materials Rsch. Soc., Mineral Metals and Materials Soc. (TMS Young Leader 1998), Sigma Xi. Avocations: tennis, skiing, golf. Office: Pa State Univ 209 Steidle Bldg University Park PA 16802-5006 Business E-Mail: zikui@psu.edu.

LIVA, EDWARD LOUIS, eye surgeon; b. Lyndhurst, NJ, Aug. 30, 1925; s. Paul Francis and Lucy Agnes (Andreozzi) L.; m. Dorothea Lucille Carter, Aug. 29, 1946; children: Edward Jr., Bradford, Douglas, Jeffrey, Elaine. SB, Harvard U., 1946, MD, 1950. Diplomate Am. Bd. Ophthalmology. Intern Med. Coll. Va., Richmond, 1950-51; fellow in eye pathology Mass. Eye and Ear, Boston, 1951; resident Brooklyn Eye and Ear, NY, 1952-53; chief ophthalmic examiner Workman's Compensation Bd., NYC, 1957-63; sr. ophthalmic surgeon Hackensack (N.J.) Med. Ctr., 1957—, Valley Hosp., Ridgewood, NJ, 1963-99; sr. ophthalmic surgeon, resident instr. oculoplastics Manhatten Eye, Ear and Throat, NYC, 1957-96, emeritus, 1996—. Pres. Bergen Surg. Ctr., Paramus, N.J., 1991—, Eye Inst. of Paramus, 1987—. Author: Advances in Ophthalmic Plastic, 1983. Active Rep. Club, Ridgewood, 1960—. Capt. USAF, 1955-57. Fellow AMA, Am. Acad. Ophthalmology, Internat. Coll. of Surgeons, Am. Soc. of Ophtalmic Plastic and Reconstructive Surgery (chartered). Republican. Roman Catholic. Achievements include development of new lid flaps oculoplastics, prototype of lid canal laceration repair, major modification of ptosis surgical procedures widely used, disproved Trichromatic theory of color vision in 1952. Office: Liva Eye Ctr One West Ridgewood Ave Paramus NJ 07652 Personal E-mail: eliva@mac.com.

LIVAUDAIS, MARCEL, JR., federal judge; b. New Orleans, Mar. 3, 1925; m. Carol Black (dec.); children: Julie, Marc, Durel. BA, Tulane U., 1945, JD, 1949. Bar: La. 1949. Assoc. Boswell & Loeb, New Orleans, 1949-50, 52-56; ptnr. Boswell Loeb & Livaudais, New Orleans, 1956-60, Loeb & Livaudais, 1960-67, 71-77, Loeb Dillon & Livaudais, 1967-71; U.S. magistrate, 1977-84; judge U.S. Dist. Ct. (ea. dist.) La., New Orleans, 1984-96, sr. judge, 1996—. Mem. Am. Judicature Soc. Office: US Dist Ct C-405 US Courthouse 500 Camp St New Orleans LA 70130-3313

LIVENGOOD, SCOTT A., former food products executive; b. Salisbury, NC, Aug. 11, 1952; BS, U. N.C., 1974. With Krispy Kreme Doughnuts Inc., 1977—2005, COO, 1992—98, pres., 1992—2005, CEO, 1998—2005, chmn., 1999—2005, dir., 1994—2005. Mem. exec. com. U. N.C. Chapel Hill Ednl. Found.; advisor Carolina First Campaign Com., Winston-Salem, NC.

LIVERIS, ANDREW N., chemical company executive; b. Darwin, Australia; married; 3 children. BS in Chemical Engring., U. Queensland, 1976. Joined Dow Chem. Co., 1976, gen. mgr. all ops. Thailand, 1989—92, group bus. dir. Midland, Mich., 1992—93, gen. mgr., 1993—94, v.p., 1994—95, pres., Dow chem. pacific Hong Kong, 1995—98, v.p. splty. chems. Midland, 1998—2000, bus. group pres., 2000—04, pres., 2003—, COO, 2003—04, CEO, 2004—, chmn., 2006—. Bd. mem., exec. com. OPTIMAL Group, Malaysia; bd. dirs. Dow Corning Corp., Dow Chemical Co., 2004—, Citigroup, 2005—; bd. trustees Herbert H. and Grace A. Dow Found. Bd. mem. Lake Huron Area Coun., Boy Scouts Am. Mem.: Am. Chemistry Coun., Soap and Detergent Assn., Comerica Bank (Midland advisory bd. mem.), Inst. Chem. Engrs. (UK) (corp. mem.), Midland Ctr. for the Arts (bd. mem.). Office: The Dow Chem Co 47 Building Midland MI 48667*

LIVERMAN, BETTY JEAN, elementary school educator; b. Murfreesboro, NC, Sept. 14, 1965; d. Ealone and Minnie Pearl Liverman; 1 child, Grybrielle Micheal. BS, East Carolina U., Greenville, NC, 1987; MEd, Elon U., NC, 2006. Cert. tchr. N.C., 1992. Tchr. Wake County Pub. Sch. Sys., Raleigh, NC, 1988—; ptnr. Paper Creations, Durham, NC, 2000—. Co-dir. Saturday Dance Acad., Raleigh, NC, 1990—91; founder/dir. Drama Mama Prodn., Fuquay Varina, NC, 1990—, Team Spirit, Durham, NC, 2000—. (exhibition) A Touch of C.L.A.S.S (1st pl. Most Talented award, 2005); dir.: (conducted over 300 dramatic perfomances) Drama Mama Productions, (gospel dramatic performances) Mt. Zion Children Drama and Dance ministry; prodn. dir.: (TV series) Beyond Gifted. Mem. NAACP, Greenville, North Carolina, NC, 1984—85; tchr. Mt. Zion Missionary Bapt. Ch. Children Ministry, Cary, NC, 1996—2006; pres. Head Start Tchr. Parent Student Orgn., Holly Springs, NC, 1995—96. Recipient scholarship, N.C. Bus. Women Orgn., 2004; grantee, Wake Edn. Partnership, 1990, 2005 and 2006. Mem.: N.C. Assn. of Educators (corr.), Apex Arts Coun. (corr.). Avocations: theatre arts, dance, being a mommy, church activities, reading /quiet time. Home Phone: 919-740-6304; Office Phone: 919-850-8700. Office Fax: 919-850-8709. Personal E-mail: bliverman@wcpss.net.

LIVERMORE, ANN MARTINELLI, computer company executive; b. Greensboro, NC, Aug. 23, 1958; m. Tom Livermore. BA in Econs., U. NC, Chapel Hill, 1980; MBA, Stanford U., 1982. Various mgmt. positions Hewlett-Packard Co., Palo Alto, Calif., 1982-1995, corp. v.p., 1995—2002, pres., CEO enterprise computing divsn., 1998—2003, exec. v.p., 2002—, exec. v.p. tech. solutions, 2004—. Bd. dirs. United Parcel Svc., 1997—; bd. advs. Stanford Bus. Sch.; bd. visitors Kenan-Flagler Bus. Sch. Named one of 100 Most Powerful Women in Bus., Forbes mag., 2005—06, 50 Most Powerful Women in Bus., Fortune mag., 2006, 50 Women to Watch, Wall St. Jour., 2006.*

LIVERMORE, SAMUEL MORGAN, lawyer; s. Norman Banks Livermore, Jr. and Virginia Pennoyer Livermore; m. Cynthia Saranec Livermore, Jan. 11, 1975; children: Sealy, Morgan. AB summa cum laude, Dartmouth Coll., Hanover, NH, 1973; MSc, London U., 1974; JD, Stanford U., Palo Alto, Calif., 1978. Bar: Calif. 1978, U.S. Dist. Ct. (no. dist.) Calif. 1978. Assoc. Thelen Marrin Johnson & Bridges, San Francisco, 1978—85, ptnr., 1986—92, Sheppard Mullin Richter & Hampton LLP, San Francisco, 1992—96, Cooley Godward Kronish, LLP, San Francisco, 1996—. Mem. mgmt. com. Cooley Godward Kronish, LLP, San Francisco, 2003—, head San Francisco bus. and tech., 2003—. Bd. mem., chmn. Marin County Day Sch., Corte Madera, Calif., 1979—86; founder, bd. mem., chmn. The Yosemite Fund, San Francisco, 1988—; bd. mem. Save-the-Redwoods League, San Francisco, 1998—. Recipient Barrett Cup, Dartmouth Coll., 1973. Mem.: ABA, Lagunitas Country Club, Pacific-Union Club. Avocations: outdoor recreation, camping, hunting, fishing. Office: Cooley Godward Kronish LLP 5th Fl 101 California St San Francisco CA 94111

LIVERS, THOMAS HENRY, not-for-profit fundraiser, consultant; b. Louisville, Sept. 15, 1946; s. Henry Edgar and Katherine (Ellison) Livers; m. Karen Culter, June 13, 1970 (div. June 1988); children: Zehra Livers Hudson, Floyd Forrest; m. Beverly Morgan Dennis, June 1996; children: Eric Dennis, Jarrett Dennis. BA, U. Louisville, 1970; postgrad., Butler U., Indpls., U. Conn., Bridgeport. Cert. fund raising exec. Elephant zookeeper Louisville Zoo, 1968-70; curator Indpls. Zoo, 1970-72; zoo dir. Breadsley Park Zoo, Bridgeport, 1972-75; exec. dir. East Bay Zool. Soc., Oakland, Calif., 1975-77; zoo supt. Lafayette Zool. Park, Norfolk, Va., 1977-82; exec. dir. Nature Ctr. of Charlestown, Devault, Pa., 1982-85, Cmty. Health Task Force, Phila., 1985-86; regional dir. Nat. Soc. to Prevent Blindness, Harrisburg, Pa., 1986-89; exec. dir. Nat. Kidney Found., Ind., 1990-92; mortgage broker, loan officer Louisville, 1992-94; dir. devel. Holy Rosary Acad., Louisville, 1994-96, Presbyn. Cmty. Ctr., Louisville, 1996-98, Cedar Lake Found., LaGrange, Ky., 1998-2000, Bridgehaven, Inc., Louisville, 2000-01; assoc. dir. Cmty. Found. of South Ala., Mobile, 2001—05; cons., 2005—; dir. devel. Wilmer Hall Children's Home, 2006; resource devel. dir. Trover Health Sys., Madisonville, Ky., 2006—. Cons. Conn. Gen. Assembly, Hartford, Conn., 1973—75; co-chair Non-Profit Summit, 2003. Writer newspaper column Phoenixville News, 1983-85; contbr. articles to mags. Active Leadership Mobile, 2003; fin. chair Envision Ala. Transit Summit, 2005; bd. dir. Ind. Organ Donors Adv. Bd., Indpls., 1990—92, Earth Day Louisville Zoo, Louisville Audubon Soc., Louisville Nature Ctr., Kentuckiana Children's Ctr., Fair Housing Ctr.; mem. adv. bd. Gulf Coast Zoo. Recipient Outstanding Exec. Fundraiser of Yr. award, Gulf Coast chpt. Assn. Fundraising Profls., 2004. Mem.: Assn. Fundraising Profl. (pres. Gulf Coast Chpt. 2005—, cert. bd. chair Greater Metro Louisville chpt., v.p. bd. Gulf Coast AFP chpt., cert. chair Gulf Coast chpt., Outstanding Fundraising Exec. 2004), Univ. Club Louisville, Focus Louisville, Exch. Club of U.S. (life hon.). Avocations: painting, gardening, reading, writing, travel. Office: Trover Health Sys 435 N Kentucky Ave Ste A Rm 122 Madisonville KY 42431 Home: 1805 Tartan Dr Madisonville KY 42431 Office Phone: 270-824-3786. Personal E-mail: liverst@bellsouth.net.

LIVERSAGE, RICHARD ALBERT, cell biologist, educator; b. Fitchburg, Mass., July 8, 1925; s. Rodney Marcellus and Hazel Mildred (Huntting) L.; m. June Patricia Krebs, June 19, 1954; children: John Walter, Robert Richard, James Keith, Ross Andrew. BA, Marlboro Coll., 1951; A.M., Amherst Coll., 1953; A. M., Princeton U., 1957, PhD, 1958. Fellow Bowdoin Coll., Brunswick, Maine, 1953-54; instr. Amherst Coll., 1954-55, Princeton, 1958-60; mem. faculty U. Toronto, 1960—, prof. zoology, 1969—, grad. sec. dept., 1975-77, assoc. chmn. grad. affairs dept., 1978-84, acting chmn., 1980-81. Investigator Huntsman Marine Lab., St. Andrews, N.B., Can., 1968-71; vis. prof. Strangeways Rsch. Lab., Cambridge, Eng., 1972. Contbr. numerous articles on role of nerves and endocrine secretions and the genetic basis of vertebrate appendage regeneration to sci. jours. Served as flight engr. USAAF, 1943-45. Recipient 5 decorations. Mem. Royal Can. Inst., Sigma Xi (exec. com., v.p., pres. U. Toronto chpt.). Home: PO Box 651 RR 3 Bobcaygeon ON Canada K0M 1A0 Office: Univ Toronto Dept Cell and Sys Biology Ramsay Wright Labs Toronto ON Canada M5S 3G5 Office Phone: 416-978-3476. Business E-Mail: rliversage@nexicom.net.

LIVESAY, JACQUELINE RYDER, elementary school educator, music educator, director; b. Charlottesville, Va., Feb. 13, 1949; d. Eldridge G. and Elizabeth Row Ryder; m. Charles Jackson Livesay, June 30, 1973; children: Jennifer Livesay Pereira, Jean, Ellen(dec.). MusB, Westminster Choir Coll., Princeton, NJ, 1973; MusM, U. Mich., Ann Arbor, 1977; MA in Edn., Spring Arbor U., Mich., 2001. Organist, min. music Trinity United Meth. Ch., Jackson, Mich., 1977—2003; tchr. elem. music Vandercook Lake Pub. Schs., 1989—98, Jackson Pub. Schs., 1998—; dir. children's music, organist First United Meth. Ch., Jackson, 2003—; dir. Orff music First Presbyn. Ch., Jackson, 2005—. Adj. instr. music Albion Coll., Mich., 2003—; planning com. mem. Jackson Symphony Orch. Family Concert, 2003—06; mem. human resources com. Jackson Pub. Schs., 2003—05, mem. magnet com., 2007. Mem. Western HS Acad. Boosters, Jackson, 1995—2004, Tuesday Musical Assn., 1998—, Jackson Symphony Guild, 1999—. Named Outstanding Elem. Educator, Jackson Pub. Schs., 2001. Avocations: reading, travel, walking, gardening. Home: 4897Indian Creek Dr Jackson MI 49201 Office: Frost Elem Sch S Wisner St Jackson MI 49203 Personal E-mail: jlivesay@jpsmail.org.

LIVESAY, THOMAS ANDREW, museum director, educator; b. Dallas, Feb. 1, 1945; s. Melvin Ewing Clay and Madge Almeda (Hall) L.; m. Jennifer Clark, June 15, 1985 (div.); 1 child, Russell; m. Amanda Haralson, Nov. 12, 1994; children: Heather Marie, Seth Stover. BFA, U. Tex., Austin, 1968, MFA, 1972; postgrad., Harvard U. Inst. Arts Adminstrn., 1978. Curator Elisabet Ney Mus., Austin, 1971-73; dir. Longview (Tex.) Mus. and Arts Ctr., 1973-75; curator Amarillo (Tex.) Art Ctr., 1975-77, dir., 1977-80; asst. dir. for adminstrn. Dallas Mus. Fine Arts, 1980-85; dir. Mus. of N.Mex., Santa Fe, 1985-2000, Whatcom Mus. History and Art, Bellingham, Wash., 2000—; exec. dir. La. State U. Mus. Art, Baton Rouge, 2007—. Mem. touring panel Tex. Commn. Arts; mem. panel Nat. Endowment Arts, Inst. Mus. Svcs.; adj. prof. U. Okla., Coll. Liberal Studies, 1992—, U. N.Mex., 1992—; chmn. N.Mex. State Records and Archives Commn., 1986—. Author: Young Texas Artists Series, 1978, Made in Texas, 1979; editor: video tape American Images, 1979, Ruth Abrams, Paintings, 1940-85, NYU Press. Served with U.S. Army, 1969-71. Named to Centennial Honor Roll, Am. Assn. Museums, 2006. Mem. Am. Assn. Mus. (coun. 1986-89, commn. on ethics 1992—, accreditation commn. 1994—, chmn. accreditation commn. 1997-2003, bd. dirs. 2004—, chmn. governance com. 2006, named to Centennial Honor Roll 2006), Tex. Assn. Mus. (v.p. 1981, pres. 1983), Rotary. Presbyterian. Office: 100 Lafayette St Baton Rouge LA 70801 Office Phone: 225-389-7200. Business E-Mail: tlivesay@lsu.edu.

LIVINGOOD, WILSON S., protective services official; b. Phila., Oct. 1, 1936; s. Clarence S. and Louise S. L.; stepchildren; Sarah, Elizabeth, Anne. BS in Police Adminstrn., Mich. State U., 1961. Spl. agt. U.S. Secret Svc., Dallas, 1961-69, spl. agt. in charge, 1969-86, deputy asst. dir., 1986-89, exec. asst. to dir., 1989-95; sgt. at arms U.S. Ho. of Reps., Washington, 1995—. Bd. dirs. Fed. Law Enforcement Tng. Ctr., Glynco, Ga. Bd. dirs. Make A Wish Mid. Atlantic Region. With USN, 1954—57. Mem. Nat. Sheriffs Assn., Internat. Assn. Chiefs of Police (exec. com. 1993—), Belle Haven Country Club (past bd. dirs.). Epsicopalian. Avocations: tennis, running, skiing, sailing, golf. Office: US House of Reps H-124 The Capitol Washington DC 20515-0001

LIVINGSTON, BOB (ROBERT LINLITHGOW LIVINGSTON JR.), lawyer, retired congressman; b. Colorado Springs, Colo., Apr. 30, 1943; s. Robert L. and Dorothy (Godwin) Livingston; m. Bonnie Robichaux, Sept.

13, 1965; children: Robert Linlithgow III, Richard Godwin, David Barkley, SuShan Alida. BA in Econs., Tulane U., 1967, JD, 1968; postgrad., Loyola Inst. Politics, 1973. Bar: La. 1968. Ptnr. Livingston & Powers, New Orleans, 1976—77; asst. U.S. atty., dep. chief criminals divsn. U.S. Attys. Office, 1970—73; chief spl. prosecutor, chief armed robbery divsn. Orleans Parish Dist. Atty.'s Office, 1974—75; chief prosecutor organized crime unit La. Atty. Gen.'s Office, 1975—76; mem. 95th-106th Congresses from 1st La. Dist., 1977—99; chair appropriations com., 1996—98; founder The Livingston Group, Washington, 1999—. Bd. dirs. Holcim, Inc. Bd. suprs. Smithsonian Inst., 1995—98; trustee Tulanne Health Sci. Ctr., 2005—; bd. dirs. Internat. Rep. Inst., 1993—2003, Ctr. for Democracy, 1996—2003, Medal of Honor Found., Shakespeare Theatre, Washington, 2004—, Internat. Found. for Election Security, 2003—; bd. trustees Am. U. Central Asia, Kyrgyzstan, 2001—06. Named Outstanding Asst. U.S. Atty., 1973. Mem.: ABA, New Orleans Bar Assn., La. Bar Assn., Fed. Bar Assn., Am. Legion, Navy League. Roman Catholic. Office: The Livingston Group 499 S Capitol St SW Ste 600 Washington DC 20003 Home: 7703 Northdown Rd Alexandria VA 22308-1333 Home Phone: 703-765-0681; Office Phone: 202-289-9881.

LIVINGSTON, BRADFORD LEE, lawyer; b. Detroit, Apr. 15, 1954; s. L. Clayton and Helen Barbara (Grudzien) L.; m. Kathleen Ann Holuj, Mar. 9, 1980; children: Clayton Thomas, Amy Catherine. BA, U. Mich., 1976, JD, 1979. Bar: Ill. 1979, Wis. 1988, U.S. Dist. Ct. (no. dist.) Ill. 1980, U.S. Dist. Ct. (ea. dist.) Wis. 1980, U.S. Ct. Appeals (7th cir.) 1983, U.S. Dist. Ct. (cen. dist.) Ill. 1987, U.S. Dist. Ct. (ea. dist.) Mich. 1987, U.S. Ct. Appeals (3d cir.) 1994, U.S. Supreme Ct. 1998. Assoc. Seyfarth Shaw LLP, Chgo., 1979-87, ptnr., 1987—. Assoc. editor: Practice and Procedure in Labor Arbitration, 1991; contbg. author Global Counsel Handbooks Labour and Employee Benefits, 2004-05. Mem. ABA (labor and employment law and litigation sect.), Ill. State Bar Assn., Wis. Bar Assn., Chgo. Bar Assn., Internat. Bar Assn. (employment and indsl. rels. com.), Phi Delta Phi. Roman Catholic. Home: 408 Fuller Rd Hinsdale IL 60521-3621 Office: Seyfarth Shaw LLP 131 S Dearborn St Chicago IL 60603 Home Phone: 630-920-0941; Office Phone: 312-296-8880. E-mail: blivingston@seyfarth.com.

LIVINGSTON, CAROLYN HARRIS, music educator; b. Cookeville, Tenn., Jan. 7, 1936; d. Frazier and Myrtle (Lee) H.; m. Frank W. Medley, Jr., June 28, 1955 (dec. Dec. 1967); children: Frank, Jane, Jennifer Medley Martin; m. Jesse B. Livingston, Sept. 1, 1969 (dec. Jan. 1993); stepchildren: Jeffrey, Patrick, Laura Livingston Nuttle; m. Burton Zitkin, May 29, 2000. Student, U. Md., 1958—59; BS, Tenn. Tech. U., 1959; MEd, U. Fla., 1981, PhD, 1986. Tchr. music pvt. practice, Bowie, Md., 1960-68; music specialist Prince Georges County Schs., Bowie, Md., 1968—69; tchr. music pvt. practice, Gainesville, Fla., 1970-80; dir. choirs 1st Luth. Ch., Gainesville, Fla., 1976-83; music specialist Putnam County Schs., Cookeville, Tenn., 1984-86, Memphis City Schs., 1986-87; asst. prof. U. R.I., Kingston, 1987-93, coord. music edn., 1989—97, assoc. prof., 1993-99, dir. grad. studies in music, 1997—2006, prof., 1999—. Author: Charles Faulkner Bryan: His Life and Music, 2003; mem. editl. bd. Bulletin Hist. Rsch. Music Edn., 1990—; mem. editl. com. Jour. Hist. Rsch. Music Edn., 2004—; contbr. articles to profl. jours. Founder, dir. U. R.I. Childrens Chorus, 1993-2000. U. RI Humanities fellow, 2004. Mem. Music Educators Nat. Conf., History Spl. Rsch. Interest Group (vice-chair 1997-99, chair 1999-01, Svc. award 2006), Music Tchrs. Nat. Assn., R.I. Music Tchrs. Assn. (pres. 1992-94), Sigma Alpha Iota, Pi Kappa Lambda, Kappa Delta Pi, Phi Kappa Phi. Lutheran. Avocations: gardening, travel. Home: 31 Rosemary St Cranston RI 02920-8157 Home Phone: 401-467-4049; Office Phone: 401-874-2763. Business E-Mail: musiced@uri.edu.

LIVINGSTON, DAVID MORSE, internist, biomedical researcher; b. Cambridge, Mass., Mar. 29, 1941; s. Arthur Joshua and Phyllis Freda (Kanters) Livingston; m. Jacqueline Gutman, June 23, 1963 (div. 1983); m. Emily Rabb, Jan. 25, 1986; children: Catherine Ellen, Julie. AB cum laude, Harvard U., Cambridge, Mass., 1961; MD magna cum laude, Tufts U., Medford, Mass., 1965. Diplomate Am. Bd. Internal Medicine. Intern, resident Peter Bent Brigham Hosp., Boston, 1965—67; rsch. assoc., sr. staff fellow, sr. investigator NCI-NIH, Bethesda, Md., 1967—69, 1971—73; rsch. fellow in biol. chemistry Harvard Med. Sch., Boston, 1969—71, asst. prof. medicine, 1973—76, assoc. prof. medicine, 1976—82, prof. medicine, 1982—92, Emil Frei prof. medicine, 1992—, chmn. exec. com. rsch., 1995—2000, 2005—; v.p. Dana-Farber Cancer Inst./Harvard Med. Sch., Boston, 1989—91, dir., physician-in-chief, 1991—95, dep. dir., mem. exec. com., 1999—. Mem. editl. bd. Virology, 1989—97, MOI & Cell Biology, 1998—2000; editor: BBA Revs. on Cancer, 1988—2001; contbr. articles to profl. jours. Vice chmn. sci. adv. com. Pezcoller Found., Trento, Italy, 1994—; mem. sci. adv. bd. Inst. Cancer Rsch., Fox Chase, Pa., 1991—96, Lineburger Comprehensive Cancer Ctr., U. N.C., Chapel Hill, 1993—95, MIT Cancer Ctr., 1994—; mem. ext. adv. com. Fred Hutchinson Cancer Rsch. Ctr., 1992—96, Ctr. Cancer Rsch. MIT, 1994—; chmn. bd. sci. advisers, mem. exec. com. NCI/NIH, 1995—99; mem. sci. adv. com. Damon Runyan-Walter Winchell Cancer Fund, NYC, 1988—92, chmn. sci. adv. com., 1989—92, bd. dirs., 1992—97, bd. dirs., vice-chmn. sci. programs; pres. bd. Cancer Rsch. Fund, 1997—. Comdr. USPHS, 1967—73. Recipient Claire & Richard Morse award for Rsch., Dana-Farber Cancer Inst., 1991, Baxter award, AAMC, 1997, Brinker award, Susan Komen Found., 1997, Lila Gruber award, 2001, Clowes Meml. award, Am. Assn. Cancer Rsch., 2005, Boveri award for molecular cancer genetics, German Cancer Soc., 2005. Fellow: Am. Acad. Arts and Scis.; mem.: NAS, Am. Acad. Microbiology, Inst. Medicine of NAS, Am. Soc. Virology, Am. Soc. Biol. Chemistry and Molecular Biology, Assn. Am. Physicians, Am. Soc. for Clin. Investigation, Harvard Club (NYC, Boston), St. Botolph Club, Met. Club Washington, Alpha Omega Alpha. Achievements include discovery of important aspects of the neoplastic transforming process and of the mechanisms governing control of the mammalian cell cycle. Office: Dana-Farber Cancer Inst 44 Binney St Smith Bldg Rm 870 Boston MA 02115-6084 Office Phone: 617-632-3074. Office Fax: 617-632-4381. Business E-Mail: david_livingston@dfci.harvard.edu.

LIVINGSTON, DEBRA ANN, federal judge, educator; b. Waycross, GA, Apr. 15, 1959; d. Robert Livingston; m. Stephen J. Massey, Oct. 18, 1986 (div.). BA magna cum laude, Princeton U., 1980; JD magna cum laude, Harvard U., 1984. Law clk. to Hon. J. Edward Lumbard US Ct. Appeals (2nd Cir.), 1984—85; assoc. Paul, Weiss, Rifkind, Wharton & Garrison, 1985—86, 1991—92; asst. US atty. (so. dist.) NY US Dept. Justice, 1986—91, dep. chief of appeals, 1990—91; asst. prof. law U. Mich. Law Sch., 1992—94; assoc. prof. law Columbia Law Sch., NYC, 1994—2000, prof. law, 2000—07, Paul J. Kellner prof. law, 2004—07, vice dean, 2005—06; judge US Ct. Appeals (2nd. Cir.), 2007—. Legal cons. UN High Commr. for Refugees, Bangkok, 1982—83; commr. NYC Civilian Complaint Review Bd., 1994—2003. Co-author: Comprehensive Criminal Procedure, 2001. Office: US Ct Appeals 500 Pearl St New York NY 10007

LIVINGSTON, DONALD RAY, lawyer; b. Oak Ridge, Tenn., Jan. 11, 1952; s. Tally R. and Pansy L. (Heiskell) L.; m. Anne Davis, May 2, 1992; children: John Tally, Elizabeth Davis. AB in Econs., U. Ga., 1974, JD, 1977. Bar: Ga. 1977, U.S. Dist. Ct. (no. dist.) Ga. 1977, U.S. Dist. Ct. (mid. dist.) Ga. 1978, U.S. Dist. Ct. (no. dist.) Calif. 1984, U.S. Dist. Ct. (no. dist.) N.Y. 1994, U.S. Ct. Appeals (5th cir.) 1978, U.S. Ct. Appeals (4th and 11th cirs.) 1981, U.S. Ct. Appeals (6th cir.) 1984, U.S. Supreme Ct. 1983. Assoc. Adair, Goldthwaite, Stanford & Daniel, Atlanta, 1977-79; ptnr. Adair, Goldthwaite & Daniel, Atlanta, 1979-87; exec. asst. to gen. counsel EEOC, Washington, 1987-90, acting gen. counsel, 1990-91, gen. counsel, 1991-93; ptnr., head labor and employment practice group Akin, Gump, Strauss, Hauer & Feld, Washington, 1993—. Lectr. seminars on employment law, 1987—. Author: EEOC Litigation & Change Resolution, 2005; contbr. articles to profl. jours. Mem. ABA, Ga. Bar Assn. (chair labor law sect. 1985-86), D.C. Bar Assn., Coll. Labor and Employment Lawyers. Office: Akin Gump Strauss Hauer & Feld Ste 400 1333 New Hampshire Ave NW Washington DC 20036-1564 Office Fax: 202-955-7806. Business E-Mail: dlivingston@akingump.com.

LIVINGSTON, FREDERIC HOLLEYMAN, mechanical engineer; b. Bryn Mawr, Pa., Feb. 17, 1948; s. William Henry and Joan Holleyman Livingston; m. Christine Ann Dalrymple, Sept. 15, 1979; children: Jason Matthew, Corey Bradford. BSME, Pa. State U., State College, 1970. Registered profl. engr., Pa., 1978, Mass., 1981, Nev., 2005. HVAC engr. Kling Lindquist, Phila., 1972—81, Charles T, Main, Boston, 1981—84; assoc. prin., project mgr. R. G. Vanderweil Engrs., Boston, 1984—. Mem.: ASHRAE, Am. Soc. Plumbing Engrs. Episcopalian. Office: R G Vanderweil Engrs 274 Summer St Boston MA 02210 Office Phone: 617-423-7423. Office Fax: 617-423-7401. Business E-Mail: flivingston@vanderweil.com.

LIVINGSTON, JAMES DUANE, physicist, researcher; b. Bklyn., June 23, 1930; s. James Duane and Florence (Boullee) L.; m. Nancy Lee Clark, June 27, 1953 (div. 1976); children: Joan, Susan, Barbara; m. Sharon Hood Penney, Mar. 30, 1985. B in Engring. Physics, Cornell U., 1952; PhD in Applied Physics, Harvard U., 1956. Physicist R & D GE, Schenectady, NY, 1956-89; sr. lectr. dept. material sci. and engring. MIT, Cambridge, 1989—. Author: Driving Force: The Natural Magic of Magnets, 1996, Electronic Properties of Engineering Materials, 1999; co-author: A Very Dangerous Woman: Martha Wright and Women's Rights, 2004; author, co-author over 100 publs. in field. Coolidge Fellow Gen. Electric Corp. R & D, 1987; recipient Disting. Career award Hudson-Mohawk chpt. AIME, 1986. Fellow Am. Soc. Metals, Am. Phys. Soc.; mem. Nat. Acad. Engring., IEEE, AAAS, Materials Rsch. Soc., The Minerals, Metals and Materials Soc. Democrat. Unitarian Universalist. Achievements include 7 patents; advanced research in superconducting, ferromagnetic, and mechanical properties of materials. Home: 90 Albee Dr Braintree MA 02184-8252 Office: MIT 16-206 Cambridge MA 02139 Business E-Mail: jdliv@mit.edu.

LIVINGSTON, JO ELLEN BROOKS, music educator; b. Beckley, W.Va., Dec. 4, 1953; d. Henry Edward and Ramona Ann Brooks; m. James M Livingston, Oct. 3, 1981. BS in music edn., Concord Coll., 1971—77; MusM, U. of So. Miss., 1977—80. Music educator St. Francis de Sales Sch., Beckley, 1980—81; music dir. Theatre W.Va., Beckley, 1981—90, Curtain Callers, Mt. Hope, W.Va., 1981—94; music educator Raleigh County Pub. Schools, Beckley, W.Va., 1981—94, Prince William County Pub. Schools, Manassas, Va., 1995—; music dir. Ctr. for the Arts, Manassas, 1995—, Rooftop Players, Manassas, 2003—. Music curriculum com. Prince William County Pub. Schools, Manassas, 2001; min. of music Meml. Bapt. Ch., Beckley, 1992—94; performer Gary Matheny Trio, Athens, W.Va., 1971—77, Commanders Big Band, Athens, 1972—77; percussionist Hattiesburg Light Opera Co., Hattiesburg, Miss., Opera South, Jackson, Miss., Miss. Ballet Orch., Jackson, Jackson Symphony Orch., Tupelo (Miss.) Symphony Orch., Meridian (Miss.) Symphony Orch., Miss. Opera Co., Jackson; string solo and ensmble chair Prince William County Schools, Manassas, 2002—; percussionist W.Va. Symphony Orch., Charleston; mid. sch. honor choir chair Prince William County, Manassas; Prince William County Mid. Sch. honors orch. chair Prince William County Schools, Manassas; dist. mid. sch. honor choir chair Va. Music Educators Assn., Manassas; dist. 9 honor bands audition chair VBODA, District 9, Va.; region i chair W.Va. Music Educators Assn., Region I, all-state h.s. honors chorus chair, Charleston; auditorium mgr. Woodrow Wilson H.S., Beckley, 1988—90. Musician: Nova/Manassas Symphony Orch., 2006—. Mem. Curtain Callers, Mt. Hope, W.Va. Recipient Gilbert award, U. of So. Miss. Theater, Governor's Citation for Musical Contributions, State Of W.Va. Mem.: Nat. Educators Assn. (assoc.; state del. and sch. rep.), Va. Music Educators Assn. (assoc.), Omicron Delta Kappa (assoc.), Mu Phi Epsilon (assoc.; v.p. 1978). Avocation: painting. Home: 9301 Battle St Manassas VA 20110 Office: Parkside Middle School 8602 Mathis Ave Manassas VA 20110 Office Phone: 703-361-3106. Personal E-mail: jbldiva@comcast.net. E-mail: livingjb@pwcs.edu.

LIVINGSTON, JOHNSTON REDMOND, manufacturing executive; b. Foochow, China, Dec. 18, 1923; s. Henry Walter V and Alice (Moorehead) Livingston; m. Caroline Johnson, Aug. 17, 1946 (dec.); children: Henry, Ann, Jane, David; m. Patricia Karolchuck, Sept. 4, 1965. BS in Engring. with honors, Yale U., 1947; MBA with distinction, Harvard U., 1949. With Mpls.-Honeywell Regulator Co., 1949-55; with Whirlpool Corp., 1956-66, v.p., until 1966, Redman Industries, Dallas, 1966-67; dir. Constrn. Tech., Inc., Dallas, 1967—, pres., chmn. bd. dirs. Denver, 1974-89; chmn. bd. dirs. Enmark Corp., Denver, 1979-90. Pres. Marcor Housing Sys., Inc., Denver, 1971-74. Past mem. industry adv. com. Nat. Housing Ctr.; bd. dirs., past pres. Nat. Home Improvement Coun.; pres., chmn. bd. dirs. Denver Symphony Assn., 1977-81; bd. dirs., past chmn. bd. dirs. Rocky Mountain Regional Inst. Internat. Edn.; trustee, chmn. emeritus, bd. dirs. Bonfils-Stanton Found., Denver, 1979—; hon. trustee Inst. Internat. Edn., N.Y. Recipient Internat. Leadership award Rocky Mountain Regional Inst. Internat. Edn., 2003; Baker scholar, Harvard U., 1949. Mem. Rocky Mountain World Trade Assn. (bd. dirs., past chmn. bd. dirs.), Denver Country Club, Yale Club N.Y., Sigma Xi, Tau Beta Pi. Home: 2800 S University Blvd No 27 Denver CO 80210 Office: 5070 Oakland St Denver CO 80239-2724 Personal E-mail: johnston.livingston@comcast.net.

LIVINGSTON, KIMBERLY R., elementary school educator; b. Columbia, SC, June 9, 1968; d. Larry L. and Angeline R. Rankin; m. James P. Livingston, May 20, 1990; children: Taylor K., James P. Jr., Samuel H. III. BA in Psychology, U. S.C., Aiken, 2000; MEd, U. S.C., 2005. Cert. tchr. elem. edn. S.C. Tchr. Aiken County Pub. Schs., Ridge Spring, SC, 1995—. Team capt. Relay for Life, Samoa, 2005; bd. dirs. 1st Steps S.C., Samoa, 2000—01. Mem.: Nat. Coun. Tchrs. English, Internat. Reading Assn., Alpha Tau. Republican. Baptist. Avocations: horses, Japanese gardening, mosaics. Home: 429 Murphy Farm Rd Ridge Spring SC 29129 Office: Ridge Spring Elem 422 Hazzard Cir Ridge Spring SC 29129 Office Phone: 803-685-2000. Office Fax: 803-685-2008. E-mail: klivingston@aiken.k12.sc.us.

LIVINGSTON, LORI WINDER, lawyer; d. George M. and Virginia M. Winder; children: Jeffrey Michael, Matthew James. BS, U.C., Irvine, 1971—75; JD, Pepperdine U., Malibu, Calif., 1979; LLM in Taxation, U. Miami, Fla., 1980. Bar: US Tax Ct. 1981. Pres. Lori Winder, Inc., Newport Beach, Calif., 1985—; of counsel Voss, Cook and Thel, Newport Beach. Mem. endowment coun. Orange County Performing Arts Ctr., Costa Mesa, Calif., Am. Cancer Soc., Santa Ana, Calif., Hoag Hosp., Newport Beach; promotion of conservation easements and granting of same. Mem.: Orange County Bar Tax Assn. (past pres.). Office: Voss Cook & Thel 895 Dove St Ste 450 Newport Beach CA 92660 Home Phone: 949-644-7215. Business E-Mail: livingston@vctlaw.com.

LIVINGSTON, LOUIS BAYER, lawyer; b. NYC, Dec. 12, 1941; s. Norman and Helen (Bayer) L.; m. Mari Livingston, Apr. 6, 1968; children: Diana, Alex, Ann. BA, Yale U., 1963; LLB, Harvard U., 1966. Bar: N.Y. 1967, Oreg. 1971. Atty. NLRB, Memphis, 1967-68, Poletti, Freidin et al., NYC, 1968-71; ptnr. Miller Nash LLP, Portland, Oreg., 1971—. Office: Miller Nash LLP 111 SW 5th Ave Ste 3400 Portland OR 97204-3699

LIVINGSTON, MYRAN JAY, author, film writer, director and producer; b. NYC, Mar. 19, 1934; s. Myran Jabez and Anne Josephine (White) L.; m. Elizabeth Rasmussen, July 28, 1956 (div. May 1971); 1 child, Lisa Browning; m. Bernice Helen Beck, Nov. 8, 1971; children: Simon Jabez, Sarah Gustine. Student, Kenyon Coll., 1952-56, U.C.L.A., 1957-58. Writer/dir. CBS TV Network, LA, 1956-64, McCann-Erickson, San Francisco, 1965-71, Eastman Kodak, Rochester, N.Y., 1980-83; owner, operator Promethean Prodns., LA, 1983-96. Guest lectr. Coll. of Marin, San Franciso, 1972-73, Loyola Marymount U., L.A., 1979, Rochester Inst. of Tech., 1982. Author: (novels) The Prodigy, 1979, The Synapse Function, 1985, Tchr. in comml. prodn. San Francisco Women in Advertising, 1976, The Del Monte Corp., San Francisco, 1970, Van Nuys (Calif.) H.S., 1980, Mira Catalina Sch., Palos Verdes, Calif., 1986. Recipient 7 Golden Eagle awards Coun. on Internat. Theatrical Events, 1982-84, 1st place Gold Camera award U.S. Indsl. Film Festival, 1984, CLIO for "Most Beautiful Spot" award Bullocks, 1978, 4 Telly Silver and Bronze awards 14th and 17th Ann. Competition, 1993,96. Mem. Writer's Guild of Am., The Author's Guild. Episcopalian. Avocations: classical piano, songwriting. Home and Office: 12475 Centerville Rd Chico CA 95928 Personal E-mail: mjayliv@hughes.net.

LIVINGSTON, PAMELA A., corporate image and marketing management consultant; b. Richmond Hill, NY, Nov. 21, 1930; d. Paul Yount and Anna Margaret (Altland) L. BA, Adelphi U., 1951; postgrad., NYU, 1952, Columbia U., 1959, Am. Acad. Dramatic Art, 1954, IBM Sys. and Mktg. Schs., 1967-70, Brandon Sch. Electronic Data, 1973, Pa. State U., 1993. Pers. and pub. rels. depts. Am. Can Co., NYC, 1951-60; exec. sec. to pres. York divsn. Borg-Warner Corp., Pa., 1962-65; freelance writer, 1965-67; mktg. ofcl. IBM Corp., 1967-70; rsch. analyst, dir. new EDP bus. Ins. Co. N.Am., 1971-74; asst. to v.p. corp. affairs IU Internat., Phila., 1974-75; comm. and mktg. mgmt. cons. specializing in corp. identity, 1975—. Corp. image cons., 1984—; freelance writer, spkr. on identity, 1994—. Contbr. articles to tech jours. Recipient various journalism awards, award in mktg. and sales IBM, 1969-70, award for innovative product application, 1969. Mem. AAUW, Sales/Mktg. Execs. Internat., Art Alliance, Pub. Rels. Soc. Am., Econs. Club of York C. of C., Phila. Club Advt. Women, Phila. Acad. Fine Arts, World Affairs Coun., English-Speaking Union, Kappa Kappa Gamma. Home and Office: 108 S Rockburn St York PA 17402-3467

LIVINGSTON, ROBERT GERALD, historian, journalist; b. NYC, Nov. 17, 1927; s. Robert Teviot and Geraldine (Gray) L.; m. Jeanne Andrée Nettel, May 12, 1955; children: Catherine Schuyler Livingston Fernandez, Robert Eric. AB, AM, Harvard U., 1953, PhD, 1959. Fgn. svc. officer U.S. Dept. State, Washington, 1956-74; v.p. German Marshall Fund U.S., Washington, 1974-77, pres., 1977-81; writer Washington, 1981-83; acting dir. Am. Inst. for Contemporary German Studies, Johns Hopkins U., Washington, 1983-87, dir. Am. Inst. for Contemporary German Studies, 1987-94, chief devel. officer, 1995-96; sr. vis. fellow German Hist. Inst., Washington, 1997—. Commentator "Deutsche Welle" and other German radio stas., 2004—, The Atlantic Times, Berlin, 2005—. Co-author, editor The Federal Republic in the 1980s, 1983, West German Political Parties, 1986; contbr. over 300 articles to polit. jours. and newspapers. Sgt. U.S. Army, 1946-49. Mem. German Studies Assn. U.S., Coun. on Fgn. Rels., N.Y. Soc. Sons of the Cincinnati, Cosmos Club, Chevy Chase Club, Barnstable Yacht Club (Mass.), Phi Beta Kappa. Democrat. Episcopalian. Avocations: hiking, swimming. Office: German Historical Inst 1607 New Hampshire Ave NW Washington DC 20009-2562 Personal E-mail: jliving844@aol.com.

LIVINGSTON, VERNON, retired health facility administrator; b. Phila., Oct. 29, 1942; s. Lee and Orietta (Lawton) Livingston; m. Shirley Livingston, Jan. 25, 1965; 1 child, Crystal. Student, Temple U. Hosp., 1964—65. Map maker U.S. Govt.: Aero. Corp., Phila., 1962—63; dir. respiratory therapy Meth. Holistic Hosp., Phila.; supr. Temple U., 1965—66; dept. supr. U. Pa. Hosp., 1966—67, health facility adminstr., 1967—90; ret., 1990. Achievements include invention of standardly-used oxygen mask.

LIVINGSTON, WILLIAM SAMUEL, retired academic administrator, political scientist, educator; b. Ironton, Ohio, July 1, 1920; s. Samuel G. and Bata (Elkins) L.; m. Lana Sanor, July 10, 1943; children: Stephen Sanor, David Duncan. BA, MA, Ohio State U., 1943; PhD, Yale U., 1950. Asst. prof. U. Tex., Austin, 1949-54, assoc. prof., 1954-61, prof. govt., 1961—, chmn. dept. govt., 1965-69, Jo Anne Christian centennial prof. Brit. studies, 1982-95, asst. dean Grad. Sch., 1954-58, chmn. Grad. Assembly, 1965-68, vice chancellor acad. programs, 1969—71, chmn. faculty senate, 1973-79, chmn. comparative studies program, 1978-79; v.p., dean grad. studies U Tex., Austin, 1979-95, acting pres., 1992-93, sr. v.p., 1995—2007. Vis. prof. Yale U., 1955-56, Duke U., 1960-61; sec.-treas. Assn. Grad. Schs., 1982-85; bd. dirs. Coun. Grad. Schs. in U.S., 1983-86. Author: Federalism and Constitutional Change, 1956; contbg. author: World Pressures on American Foreign Policy, 1962, Teaching Political Science, 1965, Federalism: Infinite Variety in Theory and Practice, 1968, Britain at the Polls 1979, 1981; editor: The Presidency and Congress: A Shifting Balance of Power, 1979; co-editor: Australia, New Zealand and the Pacific Islands Since the First World War, 1979; editor, contbr. author: Federalism in the Commonwealth, 1963, A Prospect of Liberal Democracy, 1979, The Legacy of the Constitution: An Assessment for the Third Century, 1987; book rev. editor: Jour. Politics, 1965-68, editor-in-chief, 1968-72; mem. editl. bd. Publius: Jour. of Federalism, 1971-95; mem. bd. editors: P.S, 1976-82, chmn., 1978-82. Served to 1st lt. FA AUS, 1943-45. Decorated Bronze Star, Purple Heart.; Recipient Tchg. Excellence award, 1959; Ford Found. fellow, 1952-53; Guggenheim fellow, 1959-60; USIS lectr. in U.K. and India, 1977; ProBene Meritis award U. Tex., 1995, Disting. Svc. award Ex-Students Assn., 2003, Presdl. Citation, 2005. Mem.: Southwestern Social Sci. Assn. (pres. 1977—78), Austin Soc. for Pub. Adminstrn. (pres. 1973—74), Tex. Coun. for the Humanities (bd. dirs. 1999—, treas. 2002—05), Philos. Soc. Tex., Hansard Soc. (London), Southwestern Polit. Sci. Assn. (pres. 1973—74), So. Polit. Sci. Assn. (exec. coun. 1964—67, pres. 1974—75, Daniel Elazar award for contbn. to study of federalism 2006), Am. Polit. Sci. Assn. (exec. coun. and adminstrv. com. 1972—74, chmn. nominating com. 1973—74, 1978—79), Pi Sigma Alpha (nat. coun. 1976—84, nat. pres. 1980—82), Phi Gamma Delta, Omicron Delta Kappa, Phi Beta Kappa (bd. dirs. alumni assn. 2000—06). Home: 3203 Greenlee Dr Austin TX 78703-1621 Office: U Tex Office Sr VP Austin TX 78712 Office Phone: 512-471-3266. Business E-Mail: wsl@po.utexas.edu.

LIVINGSTONE, E. FRANKLIN, rehabilitation physician, director; b. Seattle, Mar. 29, 1949; s. Edgar Alan Livingstone and Dangy Lorraine Tungseth; 1 child, Jason Franklin. BS in Microbiology with distinction, U. Wash., Seattle, 1968—76; MS in Rehab. Medicine, U. Wash., 1981—83, MD, 1976—80. Cert. ABPM&R, 1985. Rehab. dir. St. Elizabeth Med. Ctr., Yakima, Wash., 1983—87, St. Mary Corwin Hosp., Yakima, 1987—91, Ea. Idaho Regional Med. Ctr., Yakima, 1991—95, Havasu Regional Med. Ctr., Lake Havasu City, Ariz., 2001—; ind. rehab. dir. Shreveport, La., 1995—2001. Protestant. Avocations: skeet shooting, billiards. Office: Havasu Regional Med Ctr 101 Civic Center Ln Lake Havasu City AZ 86403

LIVINGSTONE, JOHN LESLIE, accountant, economist, management consultant, educator; b. Johannesburg, Aug. 29, 1932; m. Trudy Dorothy Zweig, Aug. 7, 1977; children: Roger Miles, Adrienne Jill, Graham Ross, Robert Edward. B of Commerce, U. Witwatersrand, South Africa, 1956; MBA, Stanford U., 1963, PhD, 1966. CPA, N.Y., Tex.; cert. in bus. valuation. Budget dir. Edgars Stores Ltd., South Africa, 1958-61; asso. prof. Ohio State U., Columbus, 1966-69, Arthur Young Disting. prof., 1970-73; Fuller E. Callaway prof. Ga. Inst. Tech., Atlanta, 1973-78, mem. exec. bd., 1976-78; ptnr. Coopers & Lybrand, NYC, 1978-81; prin., v.p.

Mgmt. Analysis Center, Inc., Cambridge, Mass., 1975-90; prof., chmn. div. acctg. and law Babson Coll., 1985-89, adj. prof., 1990-99; ret., 1999. Cons. FPC, SEC, HEW, also maj. corps. Author: Accounting for Changing Prices: Replacement Cost and General Price Level Adjustments, 1976, Management Planning and Control, 1987, The Portable MBA: Finance and Accounting, 1992, 3d edit., 2002, Economics Made Easy, 2007, Guide to Bus. Valuation, 2007; assoc. editor: Decision Scis., 1973-78; mem. editl. bd. The Acctg. Rev., 1969-72, 76-78, Acctg., Orgns. and Socs., 1975-78, Jour. Acctg. and Pub. Policy, 1983-95; contbr. numerous articles to profl. jours. Mem. AICPA, Fla. Inst. CPAs, N.Y. Soc. CPAs, Inst. Bus. Appraisers, Nat. Assn. for Forensic Econs., Nat. Assn. Bus. Economists, Am. Arbitration Assn. (arbitrator comml. panel), Tex. Soc. CPAs, Pres. Country Club (West Palm Beach). Office: 2300 Palm Beach Lakes Blvd Ste 312 West Palm Beach FL 33409-3303

LIVINGSTONE, SUSAN MORRISEY, management consultant, former federal agency administrator; b. Carthage, Mo., Jan. 13, 1946; d. Richard John II and Catherine Newell (Carmean) Morrisey; m. Neil C. Livingstone III, Aug. 30, 1968. AB, Coll. William and Mary, 1968; MA, U. Mont., 1973; postgrad., Tufts U., 1972—73, Fletcher Sch. Law and Diplomacy, 1973—. Rschr. Senator Mark O. Hatfield, Washington, 1969-70; chief legis. and press asst. Congressman Richard H. Ichord, Washington, 1973-75, adminstrv. asst., 1975-81; cons. Congressman Wendell Bailey, Washington, 1981; exec. asst. VA, Washington, 1981-85, assoc. dep. adminstr. logistics and mgmt., 1985-86, sr. procurement exec., 1985-89, assoc. dep. adminstr. logistics, 1985—89; asst. sec. Army U.S. Dept. of Def., Washington, 1989-93; v.p. health and safety svcs. ARC, Washington, 1993-97; cons. mgmt., 1997-2001; under sec. of Navy U.S. Dept. Navy, Washington, 2001—03; mem. return-to-flight task group NASA, 2003—05. Mem interagy. com. on women's bus. enterprise The White House, 1985-89, mem. commn. future Am.'s Vets., 2006—; mem. Pres.'s Coun. on Mgmt. Improvement, 1985-86; cons. Def. Sci. Bd., 1998, 00; mem. adv. bd. Martin Inst. U. Idaho, 2000-01; mem. nat. security studies bd. advs., Maxwell Sch. Syracuse U., 2003—06; bd. dirs. The Atlantic Coun., 2004; mem. adv. subcom. on naval history Sec. of Navy, 2004-06. Vice chair White House Commn. on Nat. Moment of Remembrance, 2002—03; mem. Commn. on th Future for Am.'s Vets., 2006—; bd. dirs. The Army Hist. Found. Inc., 2005—. Mem. Procurement Round Table (bd. dirs. 1994-03, 05—), Assn. U.S. Army (bd. dirs. 1994-, coun. trustees 1996-01, CEO, dep. chmn. 2000-01), Women in Internat. Security (mem. adv. bd. 1994-97). Episcopalian.

LIVINGSTONE, TRUDY DOROTHY ZWEIG, dancer, educator; b. NYC, June 9, 1946; d. Joseph and Anna (Feinberg) Zweig; m. John Leslie Livingstone, Aug. 7, 1977; 1 child, Robert Edward. Student, Charles Lowe Studios, NYC, 1950-53, Nina Tinova Studio, 1953-56, Ballet Russe de Monte Carlo, 1956-57, Bklyn. Coll., 1964-66; BA in Psychology cum laude, Boston U., 1968, MEd, 1969; postgrad., Serena Studios, Carnegie Hall Ballet Arts, NYC, 1973-74. Tchr. Millis (Mass.) Pub. Schs., 1969-72, Hebrew Acad. Atlanta, 1974-76, Palm Beach County Pub. Sch., 2002—; profl. dancer various orgns. including Rivermont Country Club, Jewish Community Ctr., Callanwolde Performing Arts Ctr., Atlanta, 1974-84; founder, owner, instr. dance Sasha Studios, Atlanta, 1974-77; owner Trudy Zweig Livingstone Studios, Wellesley, Needham, Mass., 1987-88, Palm Beach, Fla., 1989—. Judge dance competition Atlanta Council Run-Offs, 1976. Vol. League Sch., Bklyn., 1965, Kennedy Meml. Hosp., Brighton, Mass., 1969, Nat. Affiliation for Literacy Advances, Santa Monica, Calif., 1982. Mem. Am. Alliance for Health, Phys. Edn., Recreation and Dance, Poets of the Palm Beaches, L.A. Athletic Club, Wellesley Coll. Club, Governor's Club (West Palm Beach). Avocation: poetry.

LIVNE, NAVA LEVIA, psychologist, researcher; b. Haifa, Israel, Aug. 12, 1952; arrived in US, 2002; d. Moshe Yitzchak and Guta Tova Meiri; m. Giora Livne, Jan. 2, 1978; children: Oren, Nilly. Student, U. Ill., Chgo., 1972—73; BA in Advanced Studies in Psychology (disting. scholar), Hebrew U., Jerusalem, 1977; MSc in Social Psychology (disting. scholar), Bar Ilan U., Ramat Gan, Israel, 1996; PhD in Ednl. Psychology (Excellence in Rsch. scholar), Tel Aviv U., 2002. Lic. psychologist Israel. Mentor Hebrew U., Jerusalem, 1974—75; mentor, advisor to highly gifted children Israel, 1978—95; dir. extended learning program City of Kiryat Motzkin, Israel, 1982—89, City of Kiryat Yam, Israel, 1989—91; dir. unit rsch. and assessment Sch. Edn. Bar Ilan U., Ramat Gan, 1996—98; dir. workshops Ctr. Advancement Tchg. Tel Aviv U., 1998—2002; rsch. specialist U. Calif., Irvine, 2002—04; postdoctoral fellow U. N.Mex, Albuquerque, 2004; ednl. rschr. and program dir. U. Utah, Salt Lake City, 2005—06. Contbr. scientific papers to profl. jours. Vol. tchr. Jewish Sch. Congregation Kol Ami, Salt Lake City, 2005. With Isreali Def. Force, 1970—72. Recipient Excellence in Rsch. award, Am. Mensa, 1999; Jr. Faculty fellow, NSF, 2004. Mem.: APA, Internat. Soc. Learning Scis., World Coun. Gifted and Talented, Am. Ednl. Rsch. Assn., Alpha Delta Lambda (life). Avocations: hiking, symphonic concert, opera, lectures, reading. Office: U Utah 1901 S Central Campus Dr Rm 3490 Salt Lake City UT 84112 Office Phone: 801-587-5835. Business E-Mail: nlivne@aoce.utah.edu.

LIVNE, OREN ELIEZER, mathematician, educator; b. Ramat Gan, Israel, Dec. 7, 1978; s. Giora and Nava L. Livne. Rsch. prof. applied math. U. Utah, Salt Lake City. Contbr. articles to profl. jours. Lt. Israel Def. Forces, 1999—2002. Achievements include patents in field. Office: 227 H St #106 Salt Lake City UT 84103 Office Phone: 801-631-6831. Business E-Mail: olivne@aoce.utah.edu.

LIVSEY, ROBERT CALLISTER, lawyer; s. Robert Frances and Rosezella Ann (Callister) L.; m. Renate Karla Guertler, Sept. 10, 1962; children: Scott, Rachel, Daniel, Benjamin. BS, U. Utah, 1962, JD, 1965; LLM, NYU, 1967. Bar: Utah 1965, Calif. 1967. Prof. Haile Selassie U., Addis Abbaba, Ethiopia, 1965-66; spl. asst. to chief counsel IRS, Washington, 1977-79; assoc., then ptnr. Brobeck, Phleger & Harrison, San Francisco, 1967—2003; of counsel Morgan, Lewis & Bockius, San Francisco, 2003—. Adj. prof. U. San Francisco Law Sch., 1970-77; mem. adv. com. IRS Dist. Dirs., 1986-89; mem. western region liason com IRS (chmn. 1989). Research editor U. Utah Law Rev., 1964-65; editor Tax Law Rev., 1966-67; contbr. articles to profl. jours. Bd. dirs. Gilead Group, 1986-88, East Bay Habitat for Humanity, 1987-88, Morning Song, 1992-94. Mem. ABA (chmn. subcom. real estate syndications 1981-84), State Bar Calif. (chmn. taxation sect. 1984-85), San Francisco Bar Assn. (chmn. taxation sect. 1982), Am. Coll. Tax Counsel, Am. Law Inst., Tax Litigation Club (pres. 1986-87), Order of Coif, Beta Gamma Sigma. Democrat. Mem. Evangelical Covenant Ch. Club: Commonwealth (San Francisco). Home: 128 La Salle Ave Piedmont CA 94610-1233 Office: Morgan Lewis & Bockius 1 Market Plz Fl 31 San Francisco CA 94105-1100 Office Phone: 415-442-1230. Business E-Mail: rlivsey@morganlewis.com.

LIXEY, ELIZABETH VOULGARAKIS, secondary school educator; b. Erie, Pa., Jan. 28, 1952; d. Paul Thomas Voulgarakis and Irene Elizabeth Gourgonis-Voulgarakis; m. William Henry Lixey, Dec. 16, 1978; children: Heather Elizabeth, Jennifer Laura. AA in Theatre Arts, Am. River Coll., 1971; BA in Drama, Calif. State U., 1973; MEd, Jacksonville State U., Ala., 1991. Cert. tchr. Ala., 1991, Dept. of Def. Dependents Schs., 1992, profl. cert. Pa., 1995, provisional edn. cert. Mich., 1998, cert. profl. educator Mich., 2004. Social Security Adminstrn. benefit authorizer HHS, San Francisco, 1974—79, Social Security Adminstrn. tech. advisor Richmond, Calif., 1979—81, Social Security Adminstrn. svc. rep. Roseville, Mich., 1981—82; mid. and secondary lang. arts educator Taegu Am. H.S., Camp George, Republic of Korea, 1992—93; adj. English prof. Keimyung U., Taegu, Republic of Korea, 1993, Hyosung U., Hayang, Republic of Korea, 1993—94; liturgy and chapel comm. coord. Holy Family Parish, Maxwell AFB, Ala., 1995—96; outreach program coord. U.S. Army Cmty. Svcs., Ft. McClellan, Ala., 1996; secondary lang. arts educator Hale (Mich.) Area H.S., 1998—. Advisor drama club Hale H.S., 1998—, co-advisor English club, 1999—, co-chair sch. improvement team, 2000—, advisor Nat. Honor Soc., 2001—05. Sta. chmn. ARC, Ft. McClellan, 1997—98, teen program dir., 1997; chem. spouses sr. leader Chem. Sch., Ft. McClellan, 1996—98; catechist, lector, eucharistic min. Holy Family Parish, East Tawas, Mich., 1999—. Decorated Outstanding Civilian Svc. medal Dept. of the Army; recipient Comdr.'s award for pub. svc., 1994, 1998; fellow Nat. Writing Project, Jacksonville State U., 1997. Mem.: Nat. Collegiate Players Honorary Dramatic Soc., Hale Fedn. Tchrs. (HS Tchr. of Yr. 2005), Quota Club Internat., Kappa Delta Pi, Delta Kappa Gamma Soc. Internat. (v.p. 2006). Republican. Roman Catholic. Avocations: photography, creating computer media, boating, golf, reading. Home: 2706 Lixey Beach Rd East Tawas MI 48730 Office: Hale Area HS 415 E Main Hale MI 48739 Home Phone: 989-362-4662. Personal E-mail: eagleteacher98@hotmail.com.

LIZARRAGA, DAVID C., non-profit community development corporation administrator; b. LA, Apr. 25, 1941; m. Priscilla Lizarraga; 1 child, Michael. LHD (hon.), UCLA, 2006. Founder The Maravilla Found., LA; dir. social svcs. TELACU (The East LA Cmty. Union), 1971—74, pres., CEO, chmn., 1974—; chmn. Cmty. Commerce Bank, 1976—; chmn. founder LINC TELACU Edn. Found., 1983—. Apptd. to Nat. Commn. on Neighborhoods, US Pres. Jimmy Carter, 1977—81; minority bus. adv. (regional and local) Minority Bus. Devel. Agy., 2002. Mem. Calif. Arts Coun., 1991—99, Calif. World Trade Commn., 1992—98; trustee Whittier Coll., 1991—; bd. dirs. Rurul Devel. and Fin. Corp., 2003—, Calif. New Motor Vehicle Bd., 2003—; mem. Nat. Cmty. Adv. Coun. Bank of Am., 2005—; mem. adv. bd. SBLI USA Mutual Life Ins. Co., 2006—. Named Internat. Citizen of Yr., Internat. Visitor's Coun. of LA, 1992, Entrepreneur of Yr., Entrepreneur Mag., 1992, Ernst & Young/Merrill Lynch, 1992, Philanthropist of Yr., Latin Bus. Assn., 1999, 2003, Nat. Minority Small Bus. Advocate of Yr., US Small Bus. Adminstrn., 2002; recipient Spirit of Life award, City of Hope, 1992, Am. Eagle award, Nat. Hispanic Heritage Presdl. Tribute, 1992, Leadership award, Jewish Inst. for Nat. Security Affairs, 1993, Thurgood Marshall award, NAACP, 2001, Lifetime Achievement award, Nat. Assn. Minority Automobile Dealers, 2002, Nat. Director's Appreciation award for Access to Capital, Minority Bus. Devel. Agy., 2002, Chairwoman's award, Calif. Hispanic C. of C., 2003, LA36, LA Area Emmy, The Cris Franco Show, 2004. Mem.: Congl. Hispanic Caucus Inst. (mem. bd. dirs.), US Hispanic C. of C. (chmn. 2004—05, 2006—, mem. bd. dirs., Hispanic Bus. Man of Yr. 1991). Office: TELACU Millenium LLC Ste 300 5400 E Olympic Blvd Los Angeles CA 90022 Office Phone: 323-721-1655. Office Fax: 323-724-3372. Business E-Mail: dlizarraga@telacu.com.

LJUBIMOV, ALEXANDER V., molecular biologist, cell biologist, researcher; b. Moscow, Oct. 27, 1952; s. Vladimir V. Ljubimov and Margarita S. Ljubimova; m. Julia Y. Savchenko, Apr. 1, 1989; children: Anna A., Vladimir A. PhD, Russian Cancer Rsch. Ctr., Moscow, 1977. Staff scientist Russian Cancer Rsch. Ctr., 1979—93; rsch. scientist Cedars Sinai Med. Ctr., LA, 1993—2002, dir. Ophthalmology Rsch. Labs., 2002—; prof. UCLA Sch. Medicine, 2003—. Mem. editl. bd.: Frontiers in Biosci., Exptl. Eye Rsch., Investigative Ophthalmology and Visual Science, Brain Rsch. Bull.; contbr. articles to profl. jours. Grantee, NIH, 1998—. Mem.: Internat. Soc. Eye Rsch., Am. Diabetes Assn., Assn. Rsch. in Vision and Ophthalmology, Assn. UICC Fellows. Achievements include patents for cancer research and angiogenesis. Office: Cedars Sinai Med Ctr Ste D2025 8700 Beverly Blvd Los Angeles CA 90048 E-mail: ljubimov@cshs.org.

LJUNGREN, WENDY, engineering executive; m. Terence Mulkern; children: James, Ciaran. BSEE, ND State Universary; MSEE, Ariz. State U. Cert. Six Sigma Green Belt, Honeywell, Ariz. Engring. & mgmt. Honeywell Bus., Regional & Gen. Aviation, Glendale, Ariz., 1984—2004; v.p. engring. L-3 Comm. Avionics Systems, Grand Rapids, Mich., 2004—. Designated engring. rep. FAA, Long Beach, Calif., 1990—99. Office: L-3 Communications Avionics Systems 5353 52nd St SE Grand Rapids MI 49512 Office Phone: 616-285-4343. Personal E-mail: ljungren@ieee.org.

LLAURADO, JOSEP G., nuclear medicine physician, researcher; b. Barcelona, Catalonia, Spain, Feb. 6, 1927; s. José and Rosa (Llaurado) Garcia; m. Catherine D. Entwistle, June 28, 1958 (dec.); children: Thadd, Oleg, Montserrat; m. Deirdre Mooney, Nov. 9, 1966; children: Raymund, Wilfred, Mireya. BS, BA, Balmes Inst., Barcelona, 1944; MD, Barcelona U., 1950, PhD in Pharmacology, 1960; MSc in Biomed. Engring., Drexel U., 1963. Diplomate Am. Bd. Nuclear Medicine. Resident Royal Postgrad. Sch. Medicine, Hammersmith Hosp., London, 1952-54; fellow M.D. Anderson Hosp. and Tumor Inst., Houston, 1957-58, U. Utah Med. Coll., Salt Lake City, 1958-59; asst. prof. U. Otago, Dunedin, New Zealand, 1954-57; sr. endocrinologist Prizer Med. Rsch. Lab., Groton, Conn., 1959-60; assoc. prof. U. Pa., Phila., 1963-67; prof. Med. Coll. Wis., Milw., 1970-82, Marquette U., Milw., 1967-82; clin. dir. nuc. medicine svc. VA Med. Ctr., Milw., 1977—82; chief nuc. medicine svc. VA Hosp., Loma Linda, Calif., 1983—; prof. dept. radiation scis. Loma Linda U. Sch. Medicine, 1983—. U.s. rep. symposium dynamic studies with radioisotopes clin. medicine and rsch. IAEA, Rotterdam, Netherlands, 1970, Knoxville, Tenn., 74. Hon. editor: Internat. Jour. Biomed. Computing, dep. editor: Mgmt. Environ. Quality (now Mgmt. Environ. Quality: an Internat. Jour.); contbr. articles to profl. jours. Merit badge counselor Boy Scouts Am., 1972—; pres. Hales Corners (Wis.) Hist. Soc., 1981—83. Recipient Commendation cert., Boy Scouts Am., 1980, Joan d'Alos prize, Cardiovasc. Ctr. St. Jordi, Barcelona, 1999, XII Batista-Roca prize, Inst. Exterior Projection Catalan Culture, 2000. Fellow: Am. Coll. Nutrition; mem.: IEEE (life), Calif. Med. Assn. (mem. sci. adv. panel nuc. medicine 1993—), Soc. Catalana Biologia, Am. Soc. Nuc. Cardiology, Endocrine Soc., Soc. Math. Biology (founding), Am. Soc. Pharmacology and Exptl. Therapeutics, Am. Physiol. Soc., Biomed. Engring. Soc. (charter), IEEE Medicine and Biology Soc. (mem. nat. adminstrv. com. 1986—89), Soc. Nuc. Medicine (computer and acad. couns.), Royal Acad. Medicine Catalonia/Barcelona, Casal dels Catalans Calif. (pres. 1989—91). Roman Catholic. Office: VA Hosp Nuclear Med Svc Rm 115 11201 Benton St Loma Linda CA 92357-0001 Office Phone: 909-583-6102.

LLERANDI PHIPPS, CARMEN GUILLERMINA, nutritionist and dietitian; b. Aguadilla, PR., Jan. 6, 1958; came to U.S., 1979; d. Pablo Manuel Llerandi Alum and Carmen Estela (Santana Phipps) Llerandi; m. June 21, 1981 (div. 1990); 1 child, Paul Gabriel Vallejo Llerandi. BA, Glasboro Coll., NJ, 1984; postgrad., Loma Linda U., Calif., 1994—. Lic. and registered dietitian. Pub. health nutritionist Sa Lantic Health Svc., Hammonton, N.J., 1989-90; clin. mgmt. dietitian Clifton T. Perkins Psychiat. Hosp., Jessup, Md., 1990-91; adminstrv. clin. dietitian Brownsville (Tex.) Med. Ctr., 1991-93; clin. dietictan, pediatric outpatient clin. dietitian Loma Linda U. Childrens Hosp., 1993-95; nutrition cons. Rio Grande Valley Midway House, Inc., Harlingen, Tex., 1993—; chief adminstrv. sect. Jerry L. Pettis VA Med. Ctr., Loma Linda, 1995—. Mem. bd. dietetic and nutrition depts. U. Tex., 1991-93. Mem. Am. Dietetic Assn., Am. Assn. Diabetes Educators, Seventh Day Adventist Dietetic Assn., Nutrition Edn. Assn. Office: Jerry L Pettis Meml Vets Med Ctr 11201 Benton St Loma Linda CA 92357-1000 Home Phone: 909-796-2271; Office Phone: 909-825-7084 x 2104. E-mail: llerandic1@aol.com.

LLEWELLYN, JOHN SCHOFIELD, JR., former food company executive; b. Amsterdam, NY, Jan. 10, 1935; s. John S. and Dorothea (Breedon) L.; m. Mary Martha Pallotta, June 9, 1962; children: Mary M., John S. III, Robert J., James P., Timothy J. AB, Holy Cross Coll., 1956; MBA, Harvard U., 1961. With mktg. Gen. Foods Corp., White Plains, NY, 1961-69, Sunshine Biscuit div. Am. Brands, NYC, 1973-77; exec. v.p. Morton Frozen Foods div. ITT Continental Baking Co., Charlottesville, Va., 1977-79; gen. mgr. Continental Kitchens ITT Continental Baking Co., Rye, 1980-81; sr. v.p. Ocean Spray Cranberries Inc., Plymouth, Mass., 1982-86, exec. v.p., chief operating officer, 1986-87, pres., chief exec. officer, 1988-97; ret., 1997. Bd. dirs. Dean Foods Co., 1994-2007. Trustee St. Sebastian's Country Day Sch., Needham, Mass., 1991-2006; bd. dirs. Mass. Environ. Trust, 1991—; counselor Sr. Corps Ret. Execs. Capt. USMC, 1957-63. Roman Catholic. Home: Steamboat Ln Hingham MA 02043 E-mail: jsllewe@comcast.net.

LLEWELLYN, LEONARD FRANK, real estate broker, investment company executive; b. Harlowton, Mont., Oct. 31, 1933; s. Ralph Emory and Frances Louise (Ewing) L.; m. Patricia Lockrom, Aug. 16, 1951 (div. 1955); m. Corrie J. Spruit, Apr. 21, 1974 (div. 1995); m. Anna N. McKinney, 1997. BSEE, Eastern Mont. Coll. Edn., 1955. Enlisted USMC, 1957, advanced through grades to capt., 1960, ret., 1967; owner Capitol Fla. Assn., Inc., Alexandra, Va., 1966-74; pres., owner Fla. Properties, Inc., Balt., 1968-74; chmn. Marco Beach Realty, Inc., Marco Island, Fla., 1975-82, 82—, Cons., Inc. of S.W. Fla., Marco Island, 1982—2001; mng. dir., founding ptnr. Capital Mgmt. Co., 1999—. Served as presdl. pilot for presidents Kennedy and Johnson, 1963-66; bd. dirs. Founders Nat. Bank and Trust Co.; mem. adv. bd. Founding Ptnrs. Capital Mgmt. Co., co-mng. dir., 1999—. Author: (manual) Aero-Gunnery Tactics, 1958. Bd. dirs. Collier County Conservancy, 1978-83; trustee Naples (Fla.) Cmty. Hosp., 1980-83, Cmty. Found. Collier County, 1990-94; sheriff's commr., Collier County, Fla., 1990-2001. Named Top Gun, USN, USMC, 1958, Citizen of Yr. Marco Island N.Y. Times and Marco Island Eagle, 1982. Mem.: Nat. Assn. Sales Masters, Marco Island C. of C. (pres. 1981—82, pres. emeritus 1984), Marco Island Bd. Realtors (pres. 1982), Naples Forum (pres. 1985—86), Nat. Cutting Horse Assn., Am. Quarter Horse Assn., Rotary, Nat. Aviation Club. Republican. Office: Newgate Ctr Ste 119 5100 N Tamiami Trail Naples FL 34103 Home: 5251 FM 2946 Emory TX 75440 Home Phone: 903-473-3937; Office Phone: 239-514-2900. Personal E-mail: lenllew@yahoo.com.

LLEWELLYN, LINDA J., motivational speaker, consultant, writer; d. Floris and Eva Copier; m. Lee N. Llewellyn, Sept. 18, 1973; children: Jeremy Lee, Jason Lyn, Jenny Marie Llewellyn Boren. Cert. med. asst., Utah Tech. Coll., Salt Lake City, 1972. Lic. med. asst. Utah, 1972. Owner, CEO Llewellyn HVAC, Inc., Riverton, Utah, 1978—83; med. adminstr. Mountain View Pediat., Sandy, Utah, 1986—91; med. adminstr., med. asst. The Ctr. for Advanced Plastic Surgery, St. George, Utah, 1991—94, SW Internal Medicine, St. George, 1994—99; med. adminstr., med. asst., x-ray tech. Zion Pain Mgmt., St. George, 2000—02; owner, CEO Dixie Comm. Svc., St. George, 2002—04; owner, CEO, profl. spkr., cons. Finding Your New Normal, Inc., St. George, 2004—. Author: It's Time To Fly; prodr.: (CD) It's Time To Fly; author: Finding Your New Normal. Tchr., music dir., youth leader LDS Ch., St. George, 1973—. Named Outstanding Woman in the Cmty., Zion Bank/GrapeVine Radio Sta., 2004. Mem.: MADD (assoc.), Muscular Dystrophy Assn. (hon.; poster child mother, treas. 1981—83). Republican. Avocations: travel, camping, singing, reading, spending time with the elderly. Office: Finding Your New Normal Inc PO Box 219 Santa Clara UT 84765-0219 Home Phone: 435-688-8465; Office Phone: 800-573-7066. Personal E-mail: linda.llewellyn@gmail.com. Business E-Mail: linda@findingyournewnormal.com.

LLEWELLYN, RALPH ALVIN, physics professor; b. Detroit, June 27, 1933; s. Ralph A. and Mary (Green) L.; m. Laura Diane Alsop, June 12, 1955; children: Mark Jeffrey, Rita Annette, Lisa Suzanne, Eric Matthew. BS in Chem. Engring. with high honors, Rose-Hulman Inst. Tech., 1955; PhD in Physics, Purdue U., 1962. Mem. faculty Rose-Hulman Inst. Tech., Terre Haute, Ind., 1961-70, assoc. prof. physics, 1964-68, prof., 1968-70, chmn. dept. physics, 1969-70; prof., chmn. dept. Ind. State U., Terre Haute, 1970-72, 74-80; dean Coll. of Arts and Scis. U. Ctrl. Fla., Orlando, 1980-84, prof., 1980—, chmn. dept. physics, 2003—06. Exec. sec. Energy Bd., staff officer environmental Studies Bd. NAS/NRC, Washington, 1972-74; vis. prof. Rensselaer Poly. Inst., Troy, N.Y., 1964; cons. Commn. on Coll. Physics, 1987-89, NSF, 1965-66; mem. Ind. Lt. Gov.'s Sci. Adv. Coun., 1974-80; adv. bd. Ind. Gov.'s Energy Extension Svc., Fla. Solar Energy Ctr., policy coun. Fla. Inst. Govt., Fla. Radon Adv. Coun., 1988-96; mem. environ. adv. com. Fla. Inst. Phosphate Rsch.; mem. grievance com. Fla. Bar, nat. adv. coun. Nat. Commn. on Higher Edn. Issues, 1982. Author: (with others) Physics 3E, 1991, Elementary Modern Physics, 1992, Modern Physics 3E, 1999, Modern Physics 4E, 2003; contbr. articles to profl. jours.; producer instructional films and TV. Trustee Merom (Ind.) Inst. Recipient Tchg. Incentive award Fla. State Univ. Sys., 1994, 97; NSF Coop. fellow, 1959-60, Am. Coun. Edn. Acad. Adminstrn. Internship Program fellow. Fellow Ind. Acad. Sci. (chmn. physics divsn. 1969-70, Spkr. of Yr. award 1975, pres.-elect 1980); mem. AAAS, AAUP, Am. Phys. Soc., Am. Assn. Physics Tchrs. (pres. Ind.), N.Y. Acad. Scis., Fla. Acad. Scis. (endowment com.), Internat. Oceanographic Found., Ind. Acad. Sci., Sigma Xi, Tau Beta Pi. Home: 1463 Palomino Way Oviedo FL 32765-9304 Office: U Cen Fla Dept Physics Orlando FL 32816-0001 Business E-Mail: ral@physics.ucf.edu.

LLINÁS, RODOLFO RIASCOS, neuroscientist, researcher; b. Bogota, Colombia, Dec. 16, 1934; came to U.S., 1959, naturalized, 1973; s. Jorge Enrique (Llinas) and Bertha (Riascos) L.; m. Gillian Kimber, Dec. 24, 1965; children: Rafael Hugo, Alexander Jorge. BS, Gimnasio Moderno, Bogota, 1952; MD, U. Javeriana, Bogota, 1959; PhD, Australian Nat. U., 1965; MD (hon.), U. Salamanca, Spain, 1985; PhD (hon.), U. Barcelona, Spain, 1993, U. Nacional Bogota, Colombia, 1994; D, Univ. Complutense, Madrid, 1997. Research fellow Mass. Gen. Hosp.-Harvard U., 1960-61; NIH research fellow in physiology U. Minn., Mpls., 1961-63, assoc. prof., 1965-66; assoc. mem. AMA Inst. Biomed. Research, Chgo., 1966-68, mem., 1970, head neurobiology unit, 1967-70; assoc. prof. neurology and psychiatry Northwestern U., 1967-71; guest prof. physiology Wayne State U., 1967-74; professorial lectr. pharmacology U. Ill.-Chgo., 1967-68, clin. prof., 1968-72; prof. physiology, head neurobiology div. U. Iowa, 1970-76; prof., chmn. physiology and biophysics NYU, NYC, 1976—, Thomas and Suzanne Murphy prof. neurosci., 1985—. Mem. neurol. sci. research tng. com. Nat. Inst. Neurol. Diseases and Stroke, NIH, 1971-73; mem. neurology A study sect. div. research grants NIH, 1974-78; assoc. neurosci. research program MIT, 1974-83; mem. U.S. Nat. Com. for IBRO, 1978-81; acting chmn. U.S. Nat. Com. For IBRO, 1982, chmn., 1983-89, exec. com., 1985—; mem. sci. adv. bd. Max-Planck Inst. for Psychiatry, Munich, 1979-83; professorial lectr. Coll. de France, Paris, 1979, Nat. Poly. Inst., Mexico City, 1981; IBRO internat. lectr., S.Am., 1982; McDowall lectr. King's Coll., London, 1984 Author: (with Hubbard and Quastel) Electrophysiological Analysis of Synaptic Transmission, 1969; editor: Neurobiology of Cerebellar Evolution and Development, 1969, (with W. Precht) Frog Neurobiology: A Handbook, 1976; chief editor: Neurosci., 1974—1999; mem. editorial bd.: Jour. Neurobiology, 1980—; mem.: Pfluegers Archives, 1981—, Jour. Theoretical Neurobiology, 1981—. Recipient John C. Krantz award U. Md., 1976, Einstein Gold medal UNESCO, 1991, Signoret award in cognition, Fondation Ipsen La Salpêtrière, Paris, 1994. Mem. NAS, Soc. For Neurosci. (council 1974-78), Am. Physiol. Soc. (Bowditch Lectr. 1973), Am. Soc. Cell Biology, Biophys. Soc., Harvey Soc., Internat. Brain Research Orgn., N.Y. Acad. Scis., Am. Acad. Arts & Scis., Am. Philosophical Soc., Real Academia Nacional de Medicina, Nat. Deafness and Other Communication Disorders, Nat. Inst. of Health (adv. coun.), Alpha Omega Alpha (hon.), French Acad. Scis. Office: NYC Sch Med 550 1st Ave New York NY 10016-6402

LLORENS, MERNA GEE, elementary school educator, retired music educator; b. Ofahoma, Miss., Oct. 4, 1939; d. Junior McKinley and Birdie Rose Smith; m. Ramon James Llorens Sr., Oct. 1, 1960; children: Regina Llorens Shamburger, Ramon James Llorens Jr. BS, Western Mich. U., Kalamazoo, 1971. Sec. Follet Pub. Co., Chgo., 1960-62, Mohawk Tablet Co., Chicago Heights, Ill., 1963-65; elem. tchr. St. Basil Cath. Sch., South Haven, Mich., 1965-79, South Haven Pub. Schs., 1979—2004, ret., 2004. Pres. St. Basil WSG, 2007; chair Jubilee 100th Ann. St. Basil Ch., Faith and Vision campaign com. Mem.: South Haven Edn. Assn. (chair courtesy com. 1985—2000), Black History Leadership Soc. (charter, treas., publicity/program chair, Spl. Tribute Role Model of Yr. award 2001), St. Basil Altar Rosary Women's Svc. Guild (treas. 2002—, Woman of Yr. 1990, 2005), Lions Club (sgt.-at-arms 2004, dist. 11-B2 Region 1 Zone chmn. 2005—, 1st v.p., region chmn. region 1 2006—, named Lion of Yr. Covert Township Club 2003, pres. Covert Township Club 2004—05), Delta Sigma Theta (pres. 1999—2001, sgt.-at-arms 2002, Benton Harbor/St. Joseph Alumnae chpt.). Democrat. Roman Catholic. Avocations: crafts, camping, gardening, Minnie Pearl impersonation. Home: 67556 County Rd 338 South Haven MI 49090-8372 Personal E-mail: mergee@aol.com.

LLORENTE, MARIA DORTA, psychiatrist, geriatrician, educator; b. Havana, Cuba, Jan. 10, 1960; arrived in US, 1961; d. Jorge E. and Maria L. Dorta-Duque; m. Carlos M. Llorente, Aug. 31, 1985; children: Carlos Jorge, Kasey Michelle, Bryan Anthony. BA in Psychology, English Lit., U. Miami, 1982; MD, U. Fla., Gainseville, Fla., 1986. Diplomate Am. Bd. of Psychiatry and Neurology, 1993, qualifications in geriatric psychiatry Am. Bd. of Psychiatry and Neurology, 2004. Intern to resident Jackson Meml. Hosp., Miami, Fla., 1986—90, chief resident in psychiatry, 1989—90; staff physician Miami VA Healthcare Sys., 1990—91, 1995—, chief psychiatry, 2004—; pvt. practice Fla., 1991—92; faculty mem. U. Miami, Mt. Sinai Med. Ctr., Miami Jewish Home & Hosp., Jackson Meml. Hosp., 1992—95; prof. psychiatry Miller Sch. Medicine U. Miami, 2005—. Mem. geriatric psychiatry certification com. Am. Bd. Psychiatry and Neurology, Deerfield, Ill. Sec. Am. Psychiat. Found., Arlington, Va., 2002; mem. Geriatric Mental Health Found., Washington, 2006. Named one of Best Doctors in Am., 2005. Mem.: Am. Assn. Geriatric Psychiatry, Am. Psychiat. Assn. Roman Cath. Office: Dept of Veterans Affairs 1201 Nw 16 St 116a Miami FL 33125 Office Phone: 954-873-6108. Business E-Mail: maria.llorente@va.gov.

LLOYD, ALEX, lawyer; b. Atlantic, Iowa, Aug. 13, 1942; s. Norman and Ruth (R.) L.; m. Jacqueline Roe, Aug. 24, 1963 (dec.); children: Erin, Andrea, John, Peter. BA in Econs., Colby Coll., 1964; LLB, Yale U., 1967. Bar: Conn., U.S. Dist. Ct. Conn., U.S. Ct. Appeals (2d cir.), U.S. Tax Ct., U.S. Supreme Ct. Assoc. Shipman & Goodwin, 1967-72, ptnr., 1972—, chmn. mgmt. com., 1985-96. Bd. dirs. Hartford Hosp., Conn. Health Sys., Inc. Recipient Dist. Svc. award, Conn. Legal Svcs. Fellow Am. Bar Found., Conn. Bar Found. (bd. dirs.); mem. ABA, Am. Soc. of Hosp. Attys., Conn. Bar Assn. (Charles J. Parker award). Avocations: golf, boating, fishing, raquet sports, piano. Office: Shipman & Goodwin One Constitution Plz Hartford CT 06103-1919 Office Phone: 860-251-5102. Business E-Mail: alloyd@goodwin.com.

LLOYD, BOARDMAN, investment company executive; b. Concord, NH, Jan. 8, 1942; s. Francis Vernon and Elisabeth (Boardman) L.; m. Barbara Horwich, Mar. 20, 1966 (div. 1999); children: Pamela, Amy, Emily; m. Lyn C., May 21, 2005. BA, Yale U., 1964; JD, U. Chgo., 1967. Bar: N.Y. 1968, Mass. 1971. Assoc. Casey, Lane & Mittendorf, NYC, 1967-69, Choate, Hall & Stewart, Boston, 1969-76, ptnr., 1976-90; pres. Harris & Lloyd Inc., Belmont, Mass., 1991—. Chmn. Cambridge United Way, 1975-82, Yale U. Parents Com., 1986-90, com. mem., 1986-90, chmn., 1989-90; bd. dirs. Greater Boston Legal Svcs., 1986—; trustee First Night, Boston, 1987-90, Shady Hill Sch., Cambridge, 1980-84; trustee Coydog Found., 1996—. Mem. N.Y. Bar Assn., Boston Bar Assn. Office: Harris & Lloyd Inc 2 Brighton St 2d Fl Belmont MA 02478

LLOYD, CHRISTOPHER, actor; b. Stamford, Conn., Oct. 22, 1938; Actor, Neighborhood Playhouse, N.Y.C.; actor: summer stock and off-Broadway, including title roles in Kaspar, 1973 (Obie award, Drama Desk award), Trumbo, 2003; Broadway appearances include Red, White and Maddox, Macbeth, Twelfth Night, Mornings at Seven, N.Y. Shakespeare in the Park; film appearances include Butch Cassidy and the Sundance Kid, 1969, Three Warriors, One Flew Over the Cuckoo's Nest, 1975, Goin South, 1978, The Onion Field, 1979, The Black Marble, 1980, The Legend of the Lone Ranger, 1981, Mr. Mom, 1983, To Be or Not to Be, 1983, Star Trek III, 1984, Adventures of Buckaroo Banzai, 1984, Joy of Sex, 1984, Back to the Future, 1985, Clue, 1985, Who Framed Roger Rabbit, 1988, Walk Like a Man, 1987, Eight Men Out, 1988, Track 29, 1988, Why Me, The Dream Team, 1989, Back to the Future, Part II, 1989, Back to the Future, Part III, 1990, The Addams Family, 1991, Suburban Commando, 1991, Dennis the Menace, 1993, Twenty Bucks, 1993, Addams Family Values, 1993, Angels in the Outfield, 1994, The Pagemaster, 1994, Camp Nowhere, 1994, The Radioland Murders, 1994, Things To Do in Denver When You're Dead, 1995, Changing Habits, 1996, Cadillac Ranch, 1996, Quicksilver Highway, 1997, Real Blonde, 1997, Anastasia, 1997, My Favorite Martian, 1999, Man on the Moon, 1999, Baby Geniuses, 1999, Wit, 2001, Interstate 60, 2002; dependent film appearance: Flakes; TV films: Lacy and the Mississippi Queen, 1978, The Word, 1978, Stunt Seven, 1979, Money on the Side, 1982, September Gun, 1983, Avonlea, 1991 (Emmy award, Best Actor in a Drama Series, 1992), Dead Ahead: Exxon Valdez, 1992, T-Bone N Weasel, 1992, Rent-A-Kid, 1995, The Ransom of Red Chief, 1996, The Right to Remain Silent, 1996, Alice in Wonderland, 1999; TV appearances as a regular in Taxi, 1978-83 (Best Supporting Actor Emmy award 1982, 83), Stacked; guest spots: Cheers, 1982, Road to Avonlea, 1992 (Best Actor Emmy), Back to the Future, 1991-92, Deadly Games, 1995, Spin City, 1996, Ed, 2000, Malcolm in the Middle, 2000, The Tick, 2002, Tremors, 2003, The West Wing; TV movie Amazing Stories, 1985; TV series: Clubhouse, 2004-. Office: The Gersh Agency c/o Bob Gersh 252 N Canon Dr Beverly Hills CA 90210-5302 also: Andy Freedman, Mgr 20 Ironsides St Venice CA 90292

LLOYD, CHRISTOPHER, television writer and producer; m. Arleen Sorkin. Writer: (films) Flushed Away, 2006, (TV series) The Golden Girls, 1986-89, Wings, 1992-93; writer, exec. prodr.: (TV series) Frasier, 1992—2004 (Emmy award for outstanding comedy series 1995); exec. prodr.: (films) Dream for an Insomniac, 1996, (TV series) Down Home, 1990-91, Bram and Alice, 2002, Out of Practice, 2005-. Office: care Broder Kurland Webb Offner Agy 9242 Beverly Blvd Ste 200 Beverly Hills CA 90210-3731*

LLOYD, DAVID LIVINGSTONE, JR., lawyer; b. Butler, Pa., Aug. 28, 1952; s. David Livingstone and Jean Marie (Basher) L.; m. Dana L. Kadison, June 26, 1983; children: John Gabriel, Margaret Kadison. BS, AB, U. Pa., 1974, JD, 1977. Bar: NY 1977. Assoc. Dewey Ballantine, NYC, 1977-85, ptnr., 1986-93; sr. counsel financing and transactions GE Aircraft Engines, Cin., 1993—97, v.p. & gen. counsel, 1997—. Bd. dirs. Greater Cin. Conv. & Visitors Bur., Cin. Playhouse in the Park, NYC Musical Theatre Works; bd. trustees Berkshire Theatre Festival, Mass. Recipient Scott Paper Leadership award, Wharton Sch. Bus. Mem.: ABA, NY State Bar Assn.

LLOYD, DOUGLAS SEWARD, physician, public health administrator; b. Bklyn., Oct. 16, 1939; s. Heber Hughes and Virginia Seward (Chamberlin) L. AB in Chemistry, Duke U., 1961, MD, 1971; postgrad., Old Dominion U., 1965-67; MPH in Health Planning, U. N.C., 1971. Diplomate Am. Bd. Preventive Medicine. Intern Duke U., Durham, NC, 1971-72, clin. scholar, 1972, resident in family practice, 1972-73; commr. health Conn. Dept. Health Services, 1973-87; assoc. med. dir. Nat. Med. Rsch. Corp., Hartford, Conn., 1987-89; pres. Doug Lloyd Assocs., Farmington, Conn., 1989-92; dir. Ctr. Pub. Health Practice Health Resources and Svcs. Adminstrn., Rockville, Md., 1992-98; with Assn. Schs. Pub. Health, Washington, 1999—2001. Lectr. Yale U., Conn., 1973-87; chmn. bd. Pub. Health Found., 1984-87. Contbr. articles to profl. jours. Capt. USNR, ret. Recipient Lange Publ. award, 1971, McCormick award for excellence in pub. health, 1987, Ervin award for creative vision, The Pub. Health Found., 2001. Fellow Am. Coll. Preventive Medicine; mem. AMA, Am. Pub. Health Assn., Assn. State and Territorial Health Ofcls. (past pres.). Home: 10804 Bird Song Path Columbia MD 21044-3693 Office: Ctr for Pub Health HRSA Parklawn 8a17 5600 Fishers Ln Rockville MD 20857 Home Phone: 301-854-3646. Business E-Mail: dLloyd@hrsa.gov.

LLOYD, ELISABETH ANNE, philosophy educator; b. Morristown, NJ, Sept. 3, 1956; d. Stuart Phinney and Ruth Elisabeth (Sorensen) L. BA in Gen. Studies summa cum laude, U. Colo., 1980; PhD in Philosophy, Princeton U., 1984. Asst. in instrn. philosophy dept. Princeton (N.J.) U., 1983; vis. scholar dept. genetics Harvard U., Cambridge, Mass., 1983-84; vis. lectr. dept. philosophy U. Calif.-San Diego, La Jolla, 1984-85, asst. prof. dept. philosophy, 1985-88, U. Calif., Berkeley, 1988-90; rsch. assoc. Mus. Comparative Zoology Harvard U., Cambridge, 1989; vis. sr. lectr. philosophy dept. U. Auckland, New Zealand, 1990; affiliated faculty history & philosphy of sci. program U. Calif., Davis, 1990—, assoc. prof. dept. philosophy Berkeley, 1990—. Mem. panel oversight rev. com. NSF, Washington, 1988, 89, 92. Author: The Structure and Confirmation of Evolutionary Theory, 1988, 94; editor: Keywords in Evolutionary Biology, 1992 (Newbridge Book Club 1993); contbr. articles to profl. jours.; cons. referee NSF jours., 1985-94; mem. editl. bd. Biology and Philosophy jour., Dordrecht, The Netherlands, 1989—; assoc. Behavioral and Brain Scis. jour., 1994—; contbr. photographic portraits to The Economist, MIT Press, Oxford U. Press, Blacknell, Penguin Press, Routledge, 1984—. Campaign writer, contbr. Calif. and Nat. Dem. Party, Sacramento, 1984—; mem., contbr. Nature Conservancy, Washington, 1985—, Fairness & Accuracy in Reporting, N.Y.C., 1993—; mem., activist NOW, Washington, 1980-92. Grad. fellow NSF, 1980-83, fellow U. Calif. Humanities Rsch. Inst., 1989, 91; scholarly rsch. grantee NSF, 1986, 87, 88. Mem. Internat. Soc. for History, Philosophy, and Social Studies of Biology (bd. dirs. 1991-95), Soc. for Social Studies of Sci. (program com. 1989), Philosophy of Sci. Assn. (nominating com. 1990-91, program com. 1991-92), Am. Philos. Assn. (program com. 1988-91, award referee for Matchette prize 1992-94), Bay Area Philosophy of Sci. Reading Group (founder 1988—), Phi Beta Kappa. Unitarian Universalist. Avocations: gardening, Aikido, knitting, swimming, acoustic and electric guitar. Office: U Calif Philosophy Dept 314 Moses Hall Berkeley CA 94720-2390

LLOYD, EUGENE WALTER, retired construction company executive; b. Bklyn., Apr. 9, 1943; s. Walter Vincent and Mary Regina L.; m. Julia Ann Bain Menzies, May 6, 1967; children: Deborah Ann, Doreen Marie. AA in Constrn., N.Y. Tech. Coll., 1960-63. With Stephen H. Falk & Assocs., Great Neck, N.Y., 1962-65, Builder's Estimating Service, NYC, 1965-67; estimator Humphreys & Harding, Inc., NYC, 1967-68; chief estimator, corp. sec. Conforti & Eisele, Inc., NYC, 1968-76; exec. v.p. Torcon, Inc., Westfield, N.J., 1976-93; v.p., dir. The Henderson Corp., Raritan, N.J., 1994-98; contract mgr. Huber, Hunt & Nichols, Inc., Indpls., 1998; ret., 1998. Served with U.S. Army, 1963-69. Republican. Roman Catholic. Home: 6910 E Bobwhite Way Scottsdale AZ 85266-8526 Personal E-mail: eugenewlloydaz@aol.com.

LLOYD, FRANCIS LEON, JR., lawyer; b. Winchester, Va., Dec. 1, 1955; s. Francis Leon Sr. and Jeannette Marie (Dove) L.; m. Myra Denise DuBose, Sept. 18, 1982. BA in English and French, U. Richmond, 1978; JD, U. Va., 1981. Bar: Va. 1981, Tenn. 1982, U.S. Dist. Ct. (ea. dist.) Tenn. 1982, U.S. Ct. Appeals (6th cir.) 1984. Assoc. Herndon, Coleman, Brading & McKee, Johnson City, Tenn., 1981-86, ptnr., 1987-88; of counsel The Taylor Group, Ltd., Johnson City, 1983; law clk. to judge U.S. Dist. Ct. (ea. dist.) Tenn., Knoxville, 1988-98; assoc. London & Amburn, PC, Knoxville, 1998-99, mem., 1999—2002, London, Amburn & Lloyd, PC, Knoxville, 2003—04; spl. counsel Kramer, Rayson, Leake, Rodgers & Morgan LLP, Knoxville, 2004, ptnr., 2005—06, Kramer Rayson LLP, 2006—. Avocations: literature, music, hiking. Home: 817 Dorset Dr Knoxville TN 37923-1640 Office: Kramer Rayson LLP PO Box 629 Knoxville TN 37901-0629 Home Phone: 865-694-8322; Office Phone: 865-525-5134. Business E-Mail: fllloyd@kramer-rayson.com.

LLOYD, HUGH ADAMS, lawyer; b. Pine Apple, Ala., Oct. 5, 1918; s. James Adams and Kate (Compton) L.; m. Lydia Douglas, Sept. 18, 1942; children: Kathryn Lloyd Allen, Sally Douglas (Mrs. Charles Proctor), Elizabeth Anne (Mrs. Thomas Goodman), Hugh Adams Jr. Student, Oglethorpe U., 1936-37; AB, U. Ala., 1941, LL.B., 1942. Bar: Ala. 1942, U.S. Supreme Ct 1958. Adjudicator VA, Montgomery, Ala., 1946-47; ptnr. Lloyd, Dinning, Boggs & Dinning, Demopolis, Ala., 1947—2000; mem. Lloyd & Dinning LLC, Demopolis, 2001—. Active Boy Scouts Am.; chmn. Demopolis Indsl. Devel. Com., 1970; mem. Regional Com. Juvenile Delinquency, 1970; chmn. Marengo County Devel. Bd., 1972-73; mem. Demopolis City Coun., 1974; chmn. Indsl. Devel. Bd. Marengo County, 1980; pres. Marengo County Port Authority, 1987—2006, Demopolis City Schs. Found., 1995—; trustee Judson Coll., Marion, Ala., 1981, vice-chmn. bd., 1989, chmn., 1991; bd. dirs. Judson Coll.-Marion Inst. Joint Found.; Sunday sch. tchr. First Bapt. Ch., Demopolis, 1950—; past chmn. ch. bd. deacons bylaws com. Ala. State Bapt. Conv., 1997. With AUS, 1943-45. Decorated Bronze Star; recipient Silver Beaver award Boy Scouts Am., 1972, Paul Harris Fellow award Rotary Found., 1998, award for cmty. svc. West Ala. Mental Health Bd., 1998, Demopolis Citizen of Yr. award, 1998. Mem. ABA, Am. Judicature Soc., Ala. Bar Assn., 17th Jud. Circuit Bar Assn. (pres.), Marengo County Hist. Soc. (v.p. 1980), Demopolis C. of C. (pres., Citizen of Yr. 1998, Lifetime Achievement award 2002), Ala. Law Inst. (coun.), Bus. Coun. Ala. (dir. 1995), Ala. Safety Coun. (past bd. dirs.), Demopolis Country Club (pres. 1967-68), Kiwanis (dist. gov. 1967, chmn. internat. com. Key clubs 1969, internat. com. on boys and girls work 1972, dist. chmn. laws and regulations com. Ala. dist. 1979). Home: 1408 Colony Dr Demopolis AL 36732-3443 Office: PO Drawer 740 501 N Walnut Ave Demopolis AL 36732-2037 Office Phone: 334-289-0556. Business E-Mail: hlloyd@westal.net.

LLOYD, JAMES D., federal agency administrator; b. Granville, NY, Oct. 5, 1947; BSME with honors, Union Coll., 1969; M Indsl. Engring., Tex. A&M U., 1970. Safety engr. US Army Aviation Sys. Command, St. Louis; prin. safety engr., chief program evaluation US Army Materiel Command, Alexandria, Va., dir. field safety activity, 1979—87; dir. product assurance Space Sta. Program NASA Hdqrs., Washington, 1987—93, dir. safety and risk mgmt. divsn. Office of Safety and Mission Assurance, 1993—2003, deputy chief office of safety and mission assurance, 2003—. With Material Command US Army. Office: NASA Hdqrs Mail Ste 5U39 300 E St SW Washington DC 20546 Office Phone: 202-358-1930. Business E-Mail: james.d.lloyd@nasa.gov.

LLOYD, JEAN, retired early childhood educator; b. Montgomery, Ala., Mar. 3, 1935; d. James Jack and Dorothy Gladys (Brown) L.; 1 child, Jamie Angelica. BA, Queens Coll., 1957; MA, NYU, 1960, PhD, 1976. Tchr. jr. HS NYC Bd. of Edn., 1961, dir. head start ctr., 1966, 67 summer, tchr. early childhood, 1961-69, tchr. kindergarten, 1984—2004; instr., asst. prof. U. Coll. Rutgers U., Newark, 1969-83; ret., 2004. Cons. Bd. Examiners, N.Y.C., 1982, Dept. of Pers., N.Y.C., 1985; rsch. cons. Seymour Laskow CPA, 1983; chmn. bd. dirs. Your Family Inc., N.Y.C., 1989-2004; prodr. New Ventures cable TV show (Manhattan), 1987-2004. Author: Sociology and Social Life, 1979; contbr. over 10 articles to profl. jours. Recipient Ed Press award Ednl. Press Assn., 1968; Project Synergy fellow Tchrs. Coll., Columbia, 1991-93. Mem. ASCD, United Fedn. of Tchrs., Delta Kappa Gamma. Democrat. Methodist. Avocations: writing poetry and feature articles, singing in church choir. Home: 180 W End Ave New York NY 10023-4902 Personal E-mail: jlpoetry3@verizon.net.

LLOYD, JOHN RAYMOND, mechanical engineering educator; b. Mpls., Aug. 1, 1942; s. Raymond Joseph and Wilma Mable (Epple) L.; m. Mary Jane Whiteside, Dec. 20, 1963; children: Jay William, Stephanie Christine. BS in Engring., U. Minn., 1964, MSME, 1966, PhDME, 1971; D in Tech. Sci. (hon.), Russian Acad. Scis., 2000. Devel. engr. Procter & Gamble Co., Cin., 1966-67; prof. mech. engring. U. Notre Dame, South Bend, Ind., 1970-83; disting. prof. Mich. State U., East Lansing, 1983—, chmn. dept. mech. engring., 1983-91, dir. Inst. Global Engring. Edn., 1997—2001. Cons. LeRoy Troyer & Assocs., Mishawaka, Ind., 1980—90, Azdel Inc., Shelby, NC, 1987—90; advisor NSF, Washington, 1987—90; Nat. Bur. Stds. assessment panel NRC, Washington, 1987—93; mem. exec. com. Internat. Ctr. Heat and Mass Transfer, 2003—; chmn. Midwest Energy Consortium, 1993—2000; adv. editor McGraw Hill, Inc., 1990—. Adv. editor Internat. Jour. Heat and Fluid Flow, 1985—, Jour. Engring. Physics and Thermodynamics, 1993—; contbr. over 100 articles to profl. jours., chpts. to books. Recipient Outstanding Faculty award U. Notre Dame, 1975, 82, Ralph R. Teetor Ednl. award Soc. Automotive Engrs., 1986. Fellow: ASME (nat. bd. comm. 1983—90, rsch. and tech. devel. bd. 1985—99, editor Jour. Heat Transfer 1989—95, coun. on edn., critical techs. com. 1991—93, v.p. rsch. 1995—98, sr. v.p. engring. 1999—2002, gov. 2002—05, Outstanding Paper award 1977, Melville medal 1978, Heat Transfer Meml. award 1995, Dedicated Svc. award 1999); mem.: European Acad. Scis. Office: Mich State U Dept Mech Engring 2242 Engring Bldg East Lansing MI 48824 E-mail: lloyd@egr.msu.edu.

LLOYD, JOHNNY KEITH, biology professor; b. Louisville, Dec. 20, 1952; s. Robert Lee and Mary Lorrete Lloyd; children: Chelsea Lynn, Andrew Jonathan. BS, Ky. State U., Frankfort, 1975; MS, Wright State U., Dayton, Ohio, 1980; PhD, No. Ill. U., DeKalb, 1997. Cert. secondary edn. tchr. sci. Ky., 1975, electron microscopy technologist in biological sci. Electron Microscopy Soc. Am., 1982, multi-disciplinary program in geriatrics for non-physicians U. Ill., Urbana-Champaign, 2003. Sci. tchr. Woodford County HS, Versailles, Ky., 1975—77; tchg. asst. biology Wright State U., 1977—79; electron microscopy technologist Children's Hosp. Med. Ctr., Arkon, Ohio, 1979—83; electron microscopist Toledo Hosp., 1983—86; rsch. assoc. Baxter Healthcare Corp., Round Lake, Ill., 1986—90; tchg. asst. biology No. Ill. U., 1990—92; health professions coord., asst. prof. Wheaton Coll., Ill., 1992—99; assoc. prof. biology Aurora U., Ill., 1999—. Recipient Endowment Fund Trustee Investigator award, Toledo Hosp., 1985, 2d prize, Kodak/ASCP, 1985, Pro-Medical Health Care Found. Investigator award, Toledo Hosp., 1986, Mem. of Yr. award, Midwest Soc. Electron Microscopists, 1989, Student Rsch. award, 1991, President's award for dedication & loyalty, 1993, Advisor of Yr. award, Aurora U., 2005; grantee Animal Support grant, Nat. Instn. Aging, 1992, Faculty Devel. grant, Wheaton Coll., 1994. Mem.: Associated Colls. Chgo. Area (assoc.; biology divsn. chair 2005—06), Human Anatomy and Physiology Soc. (assoc.). Office: Aurora Univ Biology Dept 347 S Gladstone Ave Aurora IL 60506 Business E-Mail: jlloyd@aurora.edu.

LLOYD, KENNETH L., columnist; PhD Mgmt., UCLA Anderson, 1972. Syndicated columnist NY Times Syndicated Sales Corp. Vis. lectr. UCLA Anderson Sch. Mgmt.; orgnl. devel. cons. Writer (syndicated column) On the Job; author: Sexual Harassment: How to Keep Your Company Out of Court, 1995, Jerks at Work, 1999, Be the Boss Your Employees Deserve, 2002; co-author: Unlimited Selling Power: How to Master Hypnotic Selling Skills, 1990, KISS Guide to Selling, 2001, Ultimate Selling Power: How to Create & Enjoy a Multimillion Dollar Sales Career, 2002. Mem.: Soc. Indsl. & Orgnl. Psychology, Am. Psychol. Assn. Office: NY Times Syndication Sales Corp 14th Fl 122 E 42nd St New York NY 10168 also: UCLA Anderson Sch Mgmt Human Resources & Orgnl Behavior A-416 Box 951481 Los Angeles CA 90095-1481 Office Phone: 212-499-3300. Office Fax: 212-499-3382, 310-825-8358, 310-825-0218. E-mail: ken.lloyd@anderson.ucla.edu.

LLOYD, MARGARET ANN, psychologist, educator; b. Weiser, Idaho, Sept. 14, 1942; d. Laurance Henry and Margaret Jane (Patch) L. BA, U. Denver, 1964; MS in Edn., Ind. U., 1966; MA in Psychology, U. Ariz., 1972, PhD in Psychology, 1973. Asst. prof. psychology Suffolk U., Boston, 1973-76, assoc. prof., 1976-79, prof., 1979-88, chair dept., 1981-88; prof. Ga. So. U., Statesboro, 1988—2004, head dept., 1988—93, prof. emerita and chair, 2004—. Author: Adolescence, 1985; author: (with others) Psychology Applied to Modern Life, 1991, 1994, 1997, 2000, 2003, 2006; contbr. articles to profl. jours. Mem. AAUP, APA (bd. ednl. affairs 2000-2002, sec.-treas. divsn. 2, 1990-93, pres. 1994-95, coun. rep. 2003—), New Eng. Psychol. Assn. (steering com. 1984-86), Mass. Psychol. Assn. (sec. 1979-81, chair bd. acad. and. sci. affairs 1981-82), Coun. Undergrad. Psychology Programs (chmn. 1990-91). Home: 805 Shelter Pointe Rd Statesboro GA 30458-9113 Home Phone: 912-764-2915. Personal E-mail: mlloyd@georgiasouthern.edu.

LLOYD, PATRICK M., dean, dental educator; B in Mathematics, Marquette U., 1974; DDS, Marquette U. Sch. Dentistry, 1978; MS, Marquette U. Grad. Sch., 1989. Cert. in Prosthodontics Vet. Adminstrn. Med. Ctr., 1981, diplomate Am. Bd. Prosthodontics. Chief dental geriatrics VA Med. Ctr., Milwaukee, 1981—85; nat. coord. geriatric dental programs Dept. Vet. Affairs, 1985—92; head, Special Patient Care Clinic Marquette U. Sch. Dentistry-, 1992—96; head dept. family dentistry U. Iowa Coll. Dentistry, 1996—2003; dean U. Minn. Sch. Dentistry, 2004—. Editor-in-chief: Journal of Prosthodontics, 1993—. Fellow: Gerontological Soc. Am., Clin. Med. Sect. (mem. fellowship com. 1998—), Am. Coll. Prosthodontics (pres. elect); mem.: Publs. Com., Greater NY Acad. of Prosthodontics, Scientific Investigation Com., Greater NY Acad. of Prosthodontics, Internat. Coll. Prosthodontics (co-pres. 2001—03). Office: U Minn Sch Dentistry Room 15-209 MoosT 1291 515 Deleware St SE Minneapolis MN 55455 Office Phone: 612-624-2424. Business E-Mail: plloyd@umn.edu.

LLOYD, RAY DIX, retired health physicist; b. Mar. 10, 1930; s. Ray Ernest and Dixie (Penrose) L.; m. Louise Mortensen, July 10, 1954; children: Thomas R., Janna L. Brady, Alan T., Christopher R., Heather L. Smith. BS, U. Utah, 1954, MS, 1956, PhD, 1974; postgrad., U. Southwestern La., 1959, La. State U., 1960. Diplomate Am. Bd. Health Physics. From rsch. asst. radiobiology divsn. to rshc. prof. U. Utah, 1961—84, rsch. prof. dept. pharmacology, radiobiology divsn., 1984-92; part-time rsch. prof. U. Utah Sch. Medicine, 1992—2007, ret., 2007. Adj. asst. prof. dept. mech. engring. U. Utah, 1975-90; adj. prof. engring. U. Utah, 1997—, rsch. prof. radiology, 1998—; cons. in field; mem. Nat. Coun. Radiation Protection and Measurements, 1980-92, consociate mem., 1992—; mem. radiol. health adv. com. Utah State Divsn. Health. Assoc. editor: (jour.) Health Physics, 1990-92; (book) Delayed Effects of Bone Seeking Radionuclides; reviewer: Radiation Rsch., Health Physics, Radiat. Protection, Internat. Jour. Radiation Biology, others; contbr. articles to profl. jours., chpts. to books; patentee radiation detector. Master sgt. US Army, 1951—52, Korea. Fellow Health Physics Soc.; mem. Am. Acad. Health Physics, Radiation Rsch. Soc., Health Physics Soc. (Great Salt Lake chpt.), Utah br. Am. Assn. for Lab. Anim. Sci., Internat. Radiation Protection Assn., Sigma Xi, Phi Kappa Phi, Gamma Theta Upsilon. Home Phone: 801-982-0741; Office Phone: 801-581-6810. Business E-Mail: ray.lloyd@hsc.utah.edu.

LLOYD, REGINALD IVAN, prosecutor, former judge; b. Camden, SC, Feb. 16, 1967; m. Melissa Lloyd; 1 child, Will. Student, U. Miami, 1985—86; BA, Winthrop Coll., 1989; JD, U. SC Sch. Law, 1993. Atty. Nexsen, Pruit, Jacobs, & Pollard, 1993—95; with Office Atty. Gen. State of SC, 1995—98; chief counsel, dir. rsch. to jud. com. SC Ho. Reps., 1998—2000; atty. Nelson, Mullins, Riley & Scarborough, Willoughby & Hoefer; judge-at large SC Cir. Ct. Seat No. 9, 2003—06; US atty. Dist. SC US Dept. Justice, Columbia, 2006—. Recipient Compleat Lawyer award, U. SC Sch. Law. Achievements include being the first African American to become the US Attorney. of South Carolina. Office: US Attys Office First Union Bldg 1441 Main St Ste 500 Columbia SC 29201*

LLOYD, ROBERT BLACKWELL, JR., lawyer; b. York, Pa., July 20, 1926; s. Robert Blackwell and Grace Irene (Dunkelberger) L.; m. Mary Ruth Hall, May 29, 1951; children: Lisa, Robert Bradford. AB, Harvard Coll., 1947; LLB., Duke U., 1950, JD, 1971. Bar: NC 1950. Assoc. Norman Block, Greensboro, NC, 1950-52; ptnr. Block, Meyland & Lloyd, Greensboro, 1952-80; sec. treas. Block, Meyland & Lloyd, P.A., Greensboro, 1981—91; with Turner Enochs & Lloyd, Greensboro, 1991-2002, Lloyd Miller & Assoc., Greensboro, 2002—. Bd. dirs. Eastern Music Festival, Greensboro, 1976—80; bd. dirs. NC Symphony Soc., 1974-76; dist. chmn. Gen. Greene council Boy Scouts Am., 1962-65; deacon, elder, chmn. bd. deacons, clk. session Starmount Presbyterian Ch. Served with USNR, 1944-61. Fellow Am. Coll. Trust and Estate Counsel (NC state chmn, 1985-86, practice com., editl. bd. 1996—); mem. ABA, NC Bar Assn. (chmn. sect. probate and fiduciary law 1980-81), Greensboro Bar Assn., NC State Bar (vice chmn. splty. com. on estate planning and fiduciary law of bd. of specialization 1984—94), 4th Fed. Cir. Jud. Conf. (mem. legal elite). Democrat. Clubs: Lions, Starmount Forest Country, 100 Club. Office: Lloyd Miller & Assoc PA PO Box 29247 Greensboro NC 27429-9247 Office Phone: 336-373-5991. Business E-Mail: rbl@lloydmillerlaw.com.

LLOYD, SETH, physicist; b. Boston, Aug. 2, 1960; s. Robert Andrew and Susan Margaret (McIntosh) L. AB, Harvard U., 1982; M.Phil, Cambridge U., 1984; PhD, Rockefeller U., 1988. Rsch. fellow Calif. Inst. Tech., Pasadena, 1988-91, Los Alamos (N.Mex.) Nat. Lab., 1991—94; prof. mech. engring. and engring systems Mass. Inst. Tech., Cambridge, Mass., 1994—, prin. investigator rsch. lab. electronics. Adj. faculty Santa Fe Inst., 1988—. Mem. ASME, Am. Phys. Soc. Achievements include research in complex systems and foundations of quantum mechanics. Office: Mass Inst Tech 77 Massachusetts Ave Bldg 3-160 Cambridge MA 02139-4307 Office Phone: 617-252-1803. Business E-Mail: slloyd@mit.edu.

LLOYD, WILLIAM FREDERICK, lawyer; b. Youngstown, Ohio, Dec. 27, 1947; AB magna cum laude, Brown U., 1969; JD cum laude, U. Chgo., 1975. Bar: Ill. 1975, U.S. Supreme Ct. 1980, US Dist. Ct. (no. dist.) Ill. 1975, (no. dist.) Calif. 1986, US Ct. of Appeals, 7th cir. 1978, DC cir., 1980, 3rd cir. 1988, 10th cir. 1988, 8th cir. 1993, 5th cir. 2004. Assoc. Sidley & Austin, Chgo., 1975—82; ptnr. and head, securities and fin. litig. group Sidley Austin Brown & Wood LLP, Chgo., 1982—2005; gen. counsel Deloitte & Touche USA LLP, NYC, 2005—. Mem. ABA (mem. litigation and bus. sects.), Chgo. Bar Assn. Office: Deloitte & Touche USA LLP 1633 Broadway New York NY 10019 Office Phone: 212-492-3826. Office Fax: 212-492-4288. Business E-Mail: wlloyd@deloitte.com.

LLOYD, WILLIAM J., imaging company executive; BSEE, UCLA; MSEE, Stanford U., Calif. Various positions including group v.p. & chief tech. officer consumer imaging & printing Hewlett-Packard Co.; co-CEO Phogenix Imaging, 2000; exec. v.p., chief tech. officer Gemplus Internat., 2000—02; pres. Inwit, Inc., 2002—03; dir. portfolio planning & analysis Eastman Kodak Co., Rochester, NY, 2003, v.p., dir. inkjet systems program, 2003—05, sr. v.p., 2005—, chief tech. officer, 2005—. Contbr. articles to profl. jours. Bd. mem. Infotonics Tech. Ctr.; mem. Dean's Council Golisano Coll., Rochester Inst. Tech. Achievements include patents in field. Office: Eastman Kodak Co 343 State St Rochester NY 14650 Office Phone: 585-724-4000.*

LLOYD-JONES, SIR (PETER) HUGH (JEFFERD), writer; b. St. Peter Port, Guernsey, Sept. 21, 1922; s. William and Norah Leila (Jefferd) Lloyd-J.; m. Frances E. Hedley, 1953 (div. 1981); children: Edmund Stephen, Ralph Alexander, Antonia; m. Mary R. Lefkowitz, 1982. MA, Oxford U., Eng., 1947; DHL (hon.), U. Chgo., 1970; PhD (hon.), U. Tel Aviv, 1984, Thessalonica U., 1999, U. Göttingen, 2002. Author: The Justice of Zeus, 1971, 2d edit., 1983, Blood for the Ghosts, 1982, Classical Survivals, 1982, (with P.J. Parsons) Supplementum Hellenisticum, 1983, (with N.G. Wilson) Sophoclis Fabulae, 1990, (with N.G. Wilson) Sophoclea, 1990, Academic Papers, 2 vols., 1990, 3 vols., 2005, Greek in a Cold Climate, 1991, Sophocles, 3 vols., 1994-96, (with N.G. Wilson) Sophocles: Second Thoughts, 1997, Supplementum Supplementi Hellenistici, 2005; others; translator Oresteia (Aeschylus), 1970. With Brit. Army, 1942—46. Fellow Jesus Coll., Cambridge (Eng.) U., 1948-54; fellow and E.P. Warren praelector in classics Corpus Christi Coll., Oxford, 1954-60; Regius prof. Greek, Oxford U., 1960-89; vis. prof. Yale U., 1964, 67, U. Chgo., 1972, Harvard U., 1976; Sather prof. U. Calif., Berkeley, 1969. Fellow: Acad. Athens, Brit. Acad.; mem.: Am. Philos. Soc., Bayerische Acad., Lettere e Belle Arti, Accademia di Archeologia Naples, Nordrhein-Westfälische Acad., Am. Acad. Arts and Scis. Address: 15 W Riding St Wellesley MA 02482-6914 also: Christ Ch Oxford OX1 1DP England E-mail: mlefkowitz@wellesley.edu.

LLOYD-LEE, BEVERLY, interior designer; d. Clifford Raymond and Ruth Elisabeth (Anderson) Bettinger; children: Amy Borner, Timothy Lloyd. Student, Lindenwood Coll., St. Charles, Mo., 1944—45, Monmouth Coll., Ill., 1945—46. Interior design practice, Denver, 1963—89, Vero Beach, Fla., 1989—94; interior designer Robb & Sticky, Ft. Myers, Fla., 1994—2000, Scottsdale, Ariz., 2000—; interior designer, owner Lloyd-Lee, LLC, Scottsdale, 2000—. Bd. dirs. St. Charles, Inc., Denver, 1984—89; adv. bd. Indian River CC, Ft. Pierce, Fla., 1992—94; lectr. in field. Chair ski ball US Ski Team, Denver, 1976; founder Indian River Ct. Watch.; chair antiques show Rep. Roundtable, Denver, 1961—64; precinct com. man Rep. Party, Denver, 1961—67; bd. dirs. Vero Heritage Hist. Soc., Vero Beach, 1990—94. Mem.: Am. Inst. Interior Designers (pub. rels. chair 1972—74), Am. Soc. Interior Designers (chair Vero Beach designers showhouse). Republican. Anglican. Avocations: classical music, jazz, backgammon, skiing, art. Office: Lloyd-Lee LLC 23013 N 87th St Scottsdale AZ 85255

LLOYD WEBBER, LORD ANDREW (BARON OF SYDMONTON), composer; b. London, Eng., Mar. 22, 1948; s. William Southcombe and Jean Hermione (Johnstone) Lloyd-Webber; m. Sarah Jane Tudor Hugill, July 24, 1971 (div. 1983); children: Imogen Lloyd-Webber, Nicholas Lloyd-Webber; m. Sarah Brightman, Mar. 1984 (div. 1990); m. Madeleine Astrid Gurdon, Feb. 1, 1991; children: Alastair Adam Lloyd-Webber, William Richard Lloyd-Webber, Isabella Aurora Lloyd-Webber. Student, Westminster Sch., Magdalen Coll., Oxford U.; FRCM, Royal Coll. Music, 1988. Theatre owner Palace Theatre, 1983—, Theatre Royal Drury Ln., London Palladium, The Adelphi, The Cambridge, Her Majesty's, The New London. Composer: (Broadway plays) Joseph and the Amazing Technicolor Dreamcoat, 1968, 1973, 1991 (Tony nomination best original score, 1982), 2003, The Likes of Us, The Beautiful Game; prodr.: (Broadway plays) Joseph and the Amazing Technicolor Dreamcoat, 1973, 1974, 1978, 1980, 1991; composer, orchestrator (Broadway plays) Jesus Christ Superstar, 1970 (Tony nomination best original score, 1972), composer, prodr., 1996, 1998; composer: (Broadway plays) Jeeves, 1975; composer, prodr. (Broadway plays) By Jeeves (revision of Jeeves), 1996; prodr.: Jeeves Takes Charge, 1975; composer, orchestrator (Broadway plays) Evita, 1976, (stage version Broadway plays), 1978; composer: Tell Me on a Sunday, 1980, 2003; composer, prodr. (Broadway plays) Cats, 1981 (Tony award best original score, 1983), Song and Dance, 1982 (Tony nomination best musical, 1986, Tony nomination best original score, 1986), Starlight Express, 1984 (Tony nomination best original score, 1987), The Phantom of the Opera, 1986 (Tony nomination best book of a musical, 1988, Tony nomination best original score, 1988), Aspects of Love, 1989 (Tony nomination best book of a musical, 1990, Tony nomination best original score, 1990), Sunset Boulevard, 1993 (Tony award best book of a musical, 1995, Tony award best original score, 1995), Whistle Down the Wind, 1996, 1998; composer: The Beautiful Game, 2000 (First London Critic's Circle award), The Woman in White, 2004 (Tony nomination best original score, 2006); prodr., orchestrator (films) Jesus Christ Superstar, 1973, Evita, 1996 (Tony award best original score, 1980); prodr.: (films) The Phantom of the Opera, 2004; prodr.: (Broadway plays) The Phantom of the Opera, 2006; composer: (films) Gumshoe, 1971, The Odessa File, 1974, Starlight Express 3D, 2003, (other musical works) The Toy Theatre Suite, 1959, Variations, 1977, Requiem, 1985 (Three Grammy awards best classical composition, Six Oliviers, a Golden Globe, One Oscar award, Internat. Emmy award, The Praemium Imperiale and the Richard Rodgers award excellence in musical theatre), (TV series) The South Bank Show, 1978, Watership Down, 1999; prodr.: (Broadway plays) Bombay Dreams, 2002, Daisy Pulls It Off, 1983, The Hired Man, 1984, On Your Toes, 1984, Café Puccini, 1986, The Resistable Rise of Arturo Ui, 1987, Lend Me a Tenor, 1988; prodr.: The Sound of Music; prodr.: (Broadway plays) Shirley Valentine, 1989, La Bête, 1992, Evita, 2006; author (with Timothy Rice): Evita, 1978; author: Cats: the book of the musical, 1981; author: (with Timothy Rice) Joseph and the Amazing Technicolor Dreamcoat, 1982, 2007; author: The Complete Phantom of the Opera, 1987, The Complete Aspects of Love, 1989, Sunset Boulevard: from movie to musical, 1993. Decorated knight Her Majesty the Queen; named a Living Legend Grammy, 1989, Created an Hon. Life Peer, 1997; named one of The Top 200 Collectors, ARTnews Mag., 2004; recipient Grammy awards, 1980, 1983, 1985, Triple Play award, ASCAP, 1988, City and Music Ctr. of L.A., 1991, Praemium Imperiale award for music, 1995, Richard Rodgers award for Excellence in Musical Theatre, 1996, Bernard Delfont award for contbn. to show bus., 1997, Acad. award, 1997, Internat. Emmy award, Golden Globe award, Six Olivier awards, Oscar award, Kennedy Ctr. award achievement in arts, 2006. Fellow: Royal Coll. Music. Avocations: architecture, Collector of 18th to 20th century paintings, especially the Pre-Raphaelites. Office: 22 Tower St London WC2H 9TW England

LNENICKA, WADE SHERIDAN, purchasing agent, councilman; b. Kansas City, Mo., Nov. 1, 1951; s. William Joseph and Georgia Marie (Ericksen) L.; m. Robin Ann Brown, June 22, 1985. BS in Mgmt., Ga. Inst. Tech., 1973; MBA, U. Mich., 1978; grad. with honors, U.S. Army Command and Gen. Staff Coll., 1983; grad., Nat. Def. U., 1991. Cert. purchasing mgr. Inst. for Supply Mgmt. Bus. mgr. Wink Davis Equipment Co., Inc., Atlanta, 1978-79; order control supr. Printpack Inc., Atlanta, 1980-82, purchasing supr., 1982-87, purchasing mgr., 1987-2000; mem. Smyrna City Coun., Ga., 1988—2003; v.p. purchasing CPG-Pepsi Bottlers, Inc., Atlanta, 2000—04; mayor pro tem City of Smyrna, 2003—; prin. BuyWell Inc., 2006—. Civic adv. com. Emory-Adventist Hosp. Home Health, 1997—2003; mem. Emory-Adventist Hosp. Sr. Oasis, 1998—2000; adv. bd. Small Cities newsletter, 1998—; bd. dir. Woodland Assisted Living, Inc., 1998—. 1st lt. US Army, 1973—76, maj. USAR, 1976—95. Mem. Am. Legion, Vets. Meml. Assn. of Smyrna, Ga., Inc., US Lacrosse, Cobb Mcpl. Assn. (sec. 1992, treas. 1993, v.p. 1994, pres. 1995), Cobb County C. of C. (vice-chmn. Smyrna Area coun. 2005, chmn. 2006, bd. dirs. 2005—, past chmn., 2007—), US Army Ranger Assn., Ga. Lacrosse Ofls. Assn. Avocations: bridge, lacrosse, military history, politics. Home: 3950 Glenhurst Dr SE Smyrna GA 30080-5896

LO, ANITA, chef; b. Mich. Graduate, Columbia Univ.; studied, Riz-Escoffier Sch., Paris. Garde-manger chef Bouley Restaurant; with Chanterelle Restaurant; chef Can Restaurant, SoHo, NY, Maxim's Restaurant, Mirezi Restaurant, Annisa Restaurant. Several TV appearances. Office: Annisa 13 Barrow St New York NY 10014 Office Phone: 212-741-6699.

LO, BERNARD, medical educator; BA summa cum laude, Harvard Univ., 1966; MA, Univ. Sussex, England, 1968; AM, Harvard Univ., 1970; MD, Stanford Univ., 1975, postdoctoral fellow, 1978—80. Internship, residency UCLA, 1975—77; residency Stanford Univ., 1977—78; asst. prof. Univ. Calif., San Francisco, 1980—87, assoc. prof., 1987—93, co-dir. UCSF-Stanford Robert Wood Johnson Clinical Scholars prog., 1989—96, dir. prog. in Medical Ethics, 1989—, prof. medicine, 1993—. Author: Resolving Ethical Dilemmas: A Guide for Clinicians; contbr. articles to profl. jours. Mem.: Am. Soc. of Law Medicine & Ethics (bd. dir.), Inst. Medicine (mem., bd. of health sci. policy, coun. mem. 2006—), Am. Assoc. Physicians, We. Soc. for Clinical Investigation, Phi Beta Kappa. Office: U Calif Dept Medicine PO Box Cc-126 San Francisco CA 94143-0001*

LO, CHESTER C.H., research scientist; b. Hong Kong, 1970; arrived in U.S., 1998; s. Hin W. Lo and Shun S. Leung. BSc, Chinese U. Hong Kong, 1992, MPhil, 1994; PhD, U. Oxford, Eng., 1998. Post doctoral rsch. fellow Ames lab. Iowa State U., Ames, 1998—2000, assoc. scientist Ctr. Nondestructive Evaluation, 2000—. Presenter at internat. profl. confs.; cons. Gillette Advances Tech., USA. Contbr. scientific papers to profl. jours., chapters to books. Recipient Hetherington prize, U. Oxford, 1996; fellow, NSF-NATO, 2000; grantee, NSF, 2000, 2001, 2004, Midwest Forensics Rsch. Resource Ctr., 2002, Roy J. Carver Charitable Trust, 2002, 2004, U.S. Dept. Edn., 2005; scholar, Croucher Found., Hong Kong, 1994—97. Achievements include patents pending in field. Office: Iowa State Univ Rm 285 ASCII Ames IA 50010 Office Phone: 515-294-6802. Business E-Mail: clo@iastate.edu.

LO, CHIENKUO, engineering educator; b. Nanjing, China, July 9, 1946; arrived in US, 1976; s. ShuYen Lo and HuaYin Chiang; m. ChunYao Lee; 1 child, LiYen. PhD, U. Iowa, Iowa City, 1981. Prof. Calif. Polytechnic State U., San Luis Obispo, 1983—. Recipient Excellence in Tchg. award, Nat. Civil Engrs. Honor Soc. Pacific Dist., 1995. Mem.: Chi Epsilon (hon.). Office: Cal Poly State U 1 Grand Ave San Luis Obispo CA 93407 Home Phone: 805-546-8580; Office Phone: 805-756-1442. Business E-Mail: klo@calpoly.edu.

LO, KWOK-YUNG, astronomer, educator, researcher, administrator; b. Nanking, Jiangsu, China, Oct. 19, 1947; arrived in US, 1965, naturalized, 1977; s. Pao-Chi and Ju-Hwa (Hsu) Lu; m. Helen Bo Kwan Chen Lo, Jan. 1, 1973; children: Jan Hsin, Derek. BS in Physics, MIT, 1969, PhD in Physics, 1974. Rsch. fellow Calif. Inst. Tech., Pasadena, 1974-76, sr. rsch. fellow, 1978-80, asst. prof., 1980-86; prof. U. Ill., Urbana, 1986-2000, assoc. Ctr. for Advanced Study, 1991-92, chmn. astronomy dept., 1995-97; dir., disting. fellow Inst. Astronomy and Astrophysics, Academia Sinica, Taipei, Taiwan, 1997—2002, elected academician, 1998; prof. physics Nat. Taiwan U., 1998—2002; disting. astronomer, dir. Nat. Radio Astronomy Obs., Charlottesville, Va., 2002—; rsch. prof. U. Va., Charlottesville, 2003—. Chmn. vis. com. to Haystack Obs., Westford, Mass., 1991—92; chmn. adv. panel Academic Sinica Inst. Astronomy and Astrophysics, Taipei, Taiwan, 2002—; mem. AUI vis. com. for Nat. Radio Astronomy Obs., 1993—97; mem. steering com. Australia Telescope Nat. Facility, 1999—2001; mem. ALMA Bd., 2004, assessor, 2004—; mem. NASA Astrophysics Subcom., 2006—. Contbr. articles to profl. jours.; mem. editl. bd.: Chinese Jour. Astronomy & Astrophysics, 2001—. Recipient Alexander von Humboldt award, 1995; grantee NSF, 1977-96; Miller fellow U. Calif., Berkeley, 1976-78, James Clerk Maxwell telescope fellow U. Hawaii, 1991. Fellow Am. Assn. Advancement of Sci.; mem. Am. Astron. Soc., Internat. Astron. Union, Acad. Sinica, Internat. Union Radio Sci. Achievements include identification of accretion of ionized gas in center of Galaxy, size measurement of compact radio source at Galactic Center, first suggestion of circumnuclear H2O masers in active galaxies, and conditions of star formation in galaxies; observation of cosmic microwave background; megamaser distance determination of hubble constant. Office: Nat Radio Astronomy Observatory 520 Edgemont Rd Charlottesville VA 22903-2475 Business E-Mail: flo@nrao.edu.

LO, YEE ON, composer; b. Chong Qing, Si Chuan, China, Sept. 29, 1945; came to U.S., 1966; p. Kei-Pak and Bih-Tang Lo. AB, U. Calif., Berkeley, 1972, MS, 1979; PhD, Stanford U., 1987. Composer Wings II: Portrait, aka Portrait of Timbre as a Wild Wooddove, performed worldwide, 1994—, Greece, 1997, France, 1998, Chile, 2000, Spain, 2001, Can. 2002, Switzerland 2005; Dream I - Shattered (La Maquinta de Escribir), performed worldwide, When That Call Shudders 'cross..., Duo Concertant - Le Conte du Troubador, The Interrupted Serenade, Three Postludes, Dreams-Sequence, River Through Time, Night Space, 1998, Mobile, 2002; solo cd Shapes of Color, Selected Works, 2002. Recipient Program Music prize Bourges Concours Internat., Bourges, France, 1997. Mem. ASCAP (awards 1997, 98, 99), Avocation: photography. Home and Office: PO Box 62 Palo Alto CA 94302-0062 Personal E-mail: acoustic@panix.com.

LOACKER, LYNN J., lawyer; AB, Stanford U., 1974; JD, Hastings College Law, 1979. Bar: Wash., New York. Atty., shareholder Heller, Ehrman, White, & McAuliffe, New York, NY, 1999—, Co-Chair, Corp. Finance. Trustee Henry Art Gallery, 1997—; dir. Resources for Children with Spl. Needs, 2003—. Mem.: Seattle Opera Assn. (trustee 1986—2005, mem. bd. advisors 2005—), NYC Opera Assn. (dir., co-chair strategic planning com. 2005—), NY State Bar Assn., Wash. State Bar Assn., Order of the Coif. Office: Heller Ehrman 120 West 45th St New York NY 10036 Office Phone: 212-847-8647. Office Fax: 212-763-7600. E-mail: lynn.loacker@hellerehrman.com.*

LOAR, PEGGY ANN, foundation administrator, museum administrator; b. Cin., May 14, 1948; d. Jerome Vincent and Elizabeth (Ranz) Wahl; m. Bartholomew Voorsanger, 2004. BA in History of Art, U. Cin., 1970, MA in History of Art, 1971; postgrad., Stanford U., 2003. Summer intern Met. Mus. Art, NYC, 1968; curator edn. Indpls. Mus. Art, 1971-76, asst. to the dir., 1974-75, asst. dir., 1975-77; asst. dir. programs and policy Inst. Mus. Svcs., 1977-80; dir. Smithsonian Inst. Traveling Exhbn. Svc., Washington, 1980-87; founding dir. Wolfsonian Found., Miami, Fla., 1987—96, Genoa, Italy, 1987—96; founding dir., pres. Copia: The American Center for Wine, Food and the Arts, Napa, Calif., 1997—2005, pres. emerita; dir. mus. studio Voorsanger Architects, NYC, 1997—2005; planning cons. Van Alen Inst., NYC, 2006—. Lectr. art history U. Cin., 1970-71; lectr. art appreciation and criticism Ind. U., Purdue U., 1975-77; mem. women's health adv. com. Stanford U., 2002—; guest lectr. in field. Project dir.: The Art of Cameroon Exhibition and Catalog, 1984, Treasures from the Smithsonian Inst. Exhibition and Catalog, 1984, Paris Style 1900: Art Noveau Bing, 1986, Hollywood: Legend & Reality Exhibition Catalog, 1988. Bd. dirs. Jean Louis Palladin Found., 2005—, Aspen Design Summit, 2005—. Travel grantee Japan Found., 1984; Swedish Inst. grantee; Aspen Inst. Humanistic Studies fellow, 1986-87, recipient Smithsonian Gold Medal for Disting. Service, 1987. Mem. Am. Assn. Museums (mus. ethics com. 1980-98), Internat. Coun. Museums (pres. U.S. nat. com., 1996-2002), Com. Internat. Musees d'Art Moderne. Avocations: bicycling, hiking, dogs, gardening, wine. Address: 845 UN Plaza 11H New York NY 10017 Office: Voorsanger Architects 246 W 38th St New York NY 10018

LOARIE, THOMAS MERRITT, healthcare executive; b. Deerfield, Ill., June 12, 1946; s. Willard John and Lucile Veronica (Finnegan) L.; m. Stephanie Lane Fitts, Aug. 11, 1968 (div. Nov. 1987); children: Thomas M., Kristin Leigh Soule. BSME, U. Notre Dame, 1968; Student, U. Minn., 1969-70, U. Chgo., 1970-71, Columbia U., 1978. Registered profl. engr., Calif. Prodn. engr. Honeywell, Inc., Evanston, Ill., 1968-70; with Am. Hosp. Supply Co., 1970—83, pres. Heyer-Schulte divsn., 1979—83; pres. and COO Novacor Med. Corp., Oakland, Calif., 1984—85, bd. dir.; pres. ABA Bio Mgmt., Danville, 1985—87; chmn. and CEO Keravision, Inc., Fremont, 1987—2001; founder, chmn. and med. device CEO Roundtable, 1993—2002; founder, chmn. and CEO Learnings, Danville, Calif., 2001—; co-founder and chmn. CardioProfile, Inc., Berkeley, 2002—05, Adams Merritt, Inc., Danville, 2003—; chmn. and CEO Mercator MedSystems, Inc., San Leandro, 2005—. Asst. prof. surgery Creighton U. Med. Sch., Omaha, 1986-94; guest lectr. Anderson Sch. Mgmt., UCLA, 2001-2003, Haas Sch. Bus., U. Calif., Berkeley, 2002-03; trustee Grad. Theol. Union, Berkeley, Calif., 2003—; mem. adv. bd. Occulogix, Inc., Tampa, 2001-03, Uptake Med. Inc., Seattle, 2003-2006, Promed Capital Ptnr., N.Y.C., 2006—, Sch. Mech. Engring., U. Calif., Berkeley, 2007-; program dir. Catholics at Work, 2005-; bd. dirs. Clarity Med. Sys., Inc., Pleasanton, Calif.; mem. adv. bd. Sch. Mech. Engring., U. Calif., Berkeley, 2007—; spkr. in field. Contbr. articles on med. tech. and pub. policy to Wall St. Jour., Jour. Retractive Surgery, others. Bd. dir. Marymount Sch. Bd., 1981-84; bd. dir. United Way Santa Barbara, 1981-84, assoc. chair, 1982-83, treas., 1983. Named One of 50 Rising Stars: Exec. Leaders for the 80's Industry Week mag., 1983. Mem. Assn. for Rsch. in Vision and Ophthalmology, Contact Lens Assn. Ophthalmology, Health Industry Mfrs. Assn. (spl. rep. bd. dirs. 1993-96, 2006—, bd. dirs. 1997-2001, exec. com. 1997-2001, treas. 1998-2000, chmn.-elect 2000-01), Am. Entrepreneurs for Econ. Growth, Med. Tech. Leadership Forum, Calif. Healthcare Inst. (bd. dirs. 1998-2001, exec. com. 1999-2001), Diablo Venture Alliance. Roman Catholic. Achievements include leading development of Intacs corneal ring segments for treatment of nearsightedness (named One of Top 10 Medical Advances by Health Magazine/CNN 1999). Personal E-mail: tloarie@mercatormed.com.

LOBANOV-ROSTOVSKY, OLEG, management consultant; b. San Francisco, July 12, 1934; s. Andrei and Grace S. (Pope) L-R.; m. Susan Waters, Sept. 8, 1979; 1 child, Alexandra; children by previous marriage: Christopher, Nicholas. BA, U. Mich., 1956. Cmty. concert rep. Columbia Artists Mgmt. Inc., 1958-59; mgr. Columbus (Ohio) Symphony Orch., 1959-62, Hartford (Conn.) Symphony Orch., 1962-65, Balt. Symphony, 1965-69; program officer div. humanities and arts Ford Found., 1969-75; exec. dir. Denver Symphony Orch., 1975-76; mng. dir. Nat. Symphony Orch., Washington, 1977-80; cons. Fed. Coun. on Arts, 1980-81; exec. dir. Del. Ctr. for Performing Arts, 1981-82; from exec. v.p., mng. dir. to pres. Detroit Symphony Orch., 1982-89; ind. cons., 1989-90; mng. ptnr. Middle Am. divsn. Jerold, Panas, Young & Ptnrs. Inc., Chgo., 1990-91; pres. Calif. Ctr. for the Arts, Escondido, Calif., 1991-96; sr. ptnr. Jerold Panas, Linzy & Ptnrs., Inc., Chgo., 1996—2004; v.p. found. and leadership giving Cath. Relief Svcs., Balt., 2004—. Address: 12 Ayr St SW Leesburg VA 20175

LOBAY, IVAN, mechanical engineering educator; b. Koltuny, Ukraine, Oct. 4, 1911; came to U.S., 1961, naturalized, 1968; s. Stephan and Clementina (Maret) Lobay; m. Halyna Makarenko, Apr. 25, 1943; children: Maria Ivanna, Halyna Blahoslava. Mech. Engr., Inst. Tech., Brno, Czechoslovakia, 1940, Cen. U. Venezuela, Caracas, 1956. Registered profl. engr., Conn., 1965. Engr., designer Erste Bruenner Maschinenfabriksgesellschaft, Brno, 1940-41; asst. prof. dept. mech. engring. Inst. Tech., Lviv, Ukraine, 1942-43, sci. asst. dept. mech. engring. Brno, 1943-45; engr. san. and civil engring. Ministry San. Affairs, Caracas, Venezuela, 1948-59; prof. dept. civil engring. U. Santa Maria, Caracas, 1957-60; prof., chmn. divsn. tech. machines & prodn Cen. U. Venezuela Mech. Engring. Sch., Caracas, 1956-62; prof. dept. mech. engring. U. New Haven, West Haven, 1963-77, 83-84, prof. emeritus, 1984—; prof. gas sect. Inst. Algerien du Petrole,

Boumerdes, Algeria, 1977-82. Cons. Ministry of Edn., Ukraine, Kyiv, 1993. Author: Lecciones de Elementos de Maquinas, No. 3, 1960, No. 2, 1961, Estudio Sobre Descarga de Aguas de Lluvia, 1962, Free Lateral Discharge from an Open Triangular Channel, 1993, Education of Engineering Squads in USA, 1996, Workload of University Professors in USA, 1996, Faculty in Higher Education in USA, 1997, Governance in Higher Education in USA, 1999, Memoirs, 1999. With U.S. Army, 1945-47. Decorated Hramota and Cross of Merit Bukovynian Battalion, 1995; recipient Hramota award Govt. in Exile of Ukrainian Nat. Republic, 1992. Mem. AAUP, AAAS, ASME, NSPE, Conn. Soc. Profl. Engrs., N.Y. Acad. Scis., Ukrainian AAUP, Ukrainian Engrs. Soc. Am., Coll. Engrs. Venezuela, Assn. Profs. U. Ctrl. Venezuela, Acad. Engrng. Scis. Ukraine. Home: 873 Orange Center Rd Orange CT 06477-1712

LOBB, WILLIAM ATKINSON, financial services executive; b. Arlington, Pa., Apr. 21, 1951; s. Anthony William and Annamarie (Hilpert) L.; m. Maureen Veronique O'Hagan, July 7, 1977; children: William Atkinson III, Anthony Hagan. BS, Georgetown U., 1977. Account exec. Johnston Lemon, Washington, 1977-78; sr. account exec. Merrill Lynch, Alexandria, Va., 1979-83; asst. v.p. E.F. Hutton, Washington, 1983-85; mng. dir., ptnr.-in-charge Oppenheimer, Inc., Atlanta, 1985—. Bd. dirs. Atlanta Charity Clays, Ferst Books Found. Mem. Nat. Securities Traders Assn., Ga. Securities Assn., Univ. Club, Burge Plantation Hunt Club, Piedmont Driving Club, Nairn Golf Club (Scotland). Avocation: squash. Office: Oppenheimer Inc 1200 Monach Plz 3414 Peachtree Rd NE Atlanta GA 30326-1153 Office Phone: 404-262-5355. Business E-Mail: will.lobb@opco.com.

LOBB, WILLIAM K., dean, dental educator; Student, Notre Dame U., Nelson, BC, U. Calgary, 1970—72; DDS, U. Alberta, Edmonton, 1977; MS in orthodontics, U. Mich., Ann Arbor, 1981. Resident in dentistry U. Alberta Hosp., Edmonton, Canada; pvt. orthodontics practice Edmonton; mem. faculty U. Alberta, Edmonton, 1981—89; chair dept. orthodontics Dalhousie U., Halifax, 1989—94; assoc. dean acad. affairs Sch. Dentistry Marquette U., 1994—97, dean, 1997—. Recipient W.W. Wood award for excellence in dental edn., Assn. Can. Faculties Dentistry, Disting. Service Award, Marquette Sch. of Dentistry. Fellow: Internat. Coll. Dentists, Pierre Fachard Acad., Am. Coll. Dentists; mem.: ADA, Wis. Dental Assn., Omicron Kappa Upsilon. Office: Marquette Univ Sch Dentistry 1801 W Wisconsin Ave Milwaukee WI 53233 Office Phone: 414-288-7485. Office Fax: 414-288-3586. Business E-Mail: william.lobb@marquette.edu.

LOBDELL, DAVID HILL, pathologist; b. Erie, Pa., July 9, 1930; s. Webster Alexander Lobdell, Christine (Kern) Lobdell. AB, Kenyon Coll., 1952; MD, U. Mich., 1956. Diplomate Am. Bd. Pathology 1961. Resident Pathology Bellevue-NYU Med. Ctr., 1956—60; pathologist St. Vincent's Med. Ctr., Bridgeport, Conn., 1960—63, chair Dept. Lab. Medicine, 1963—95, sr. pathologist, 1996—. Asst. clin. prof. Pathology NYU Sch. Medicine, 1961—69; assoc. clin. prof. Allied Health U. Conn., Storrs, 1984—95. Sec., bd. dirs. St. Vincent's Med. Found., Bridgeport. Fellow: Am. Soc. Clin. Pathology, Coll. Am. Pathologists (del. House of Dels. 1991—97); mem.: Conn. Soc. Pathologists (pres. 1982—83), Alpha Omega Alpha, Phi Beta Kappa. Avocation: stamp collecting/philately. Office: St Vincent Med Ctr 2800 Main St Bridgeport CT 06606

LOBDELL, FRANK, artist; b. Kansas City, Mo., 1921; m. Dorothy Taffinder, 1946; 1 child, Frank Saxton; m. Ann Morency, 1952; 1 child, Judson Earle; m. Jinx Rowan, 1996. Studied, St. Paul Sch. Art, 1938-39, Calif. Sch. Fine Arts, 1947-50, Academie de la Grande Chaumiere, Paris, France, 1950-51. Tchr. Calif. Sch. Fine Arts, 1957-65; prof. art, Stanford, 1965—. One man shows, Lucien Labaudt Gallery, 1949, Martha Jackson Gallery, 1958, 60, 63, 72, 74, de Young Meml. Mus., San Francisco, 1959, Ferus Gallery, 1962, Pasadena Art Mus., 1961, San Francisco Mus. Art, 1969, Benador Gallerie, Geneva, Switzerland, 1964, Gallerie Anderson-Mayer, Paris, 1965, Smith-Anderson Gallery, San Francisco, 1982, Oscarsson Hood Gallery, N.Y.C., 1983, 84, 85, John Berggruen Gallery, San Francisco, 1987, Campbell-Thiebaud Gallery, San Francisco, 1988, 90, 92, 95, Printworks Gallery, Chgo., 1988-96, Stanford Mus. Art, 1988, Hackett Freedman Gallery, 2002, Charles Cowles Gallery, N.Y.C., 2002, The Palace of the Legion of Honor, San Francisco, 2003, Hackett-Freedman Gallery, San Francisco, 2003, 04, Portland Art Mus., 2004, Fresno Art Mus., 2004, San Jose Mus. Contemporary Art, 2005, retrospective show, Pasadena Art Mus. and Stanford Mus., 1966, San Francisco Mus. Modern Art, 1983, Stanford Mus., 1993, Saint Mary's Coll., 1998, Western Mich. U. Art Gallery; exhibited group Shows, Salon du Mai, Paris, 1950, III Sao Paulo Biennial, 1955, Whitney Mus. Am. Art, 1962-63, 72, Guggenheim Mus., N.Y.C., 1964, Van Abbemuseum, Eindhoven, Holland, 1970, Corcoran Gallery Art, Washington, 1971, U. Ill., 1974, 15 Calif. Modernists, Fresno Art Mus., 1995; represented in permanent collections, San Francisco Mus. Art, Oakland Mus. Art, L.A. County Mus., Nat. Gallery Washington, others. Served with AUS, 1942-46. Recipient Nealie Sullivan award San Francisco Art Inst., 1960, award of merit AAAL, 1988.

LOBEL, MARTIN, lawyer; b. Cambridge, Mass., June 19, 1941; s. I. Alan and Dorothy W. l.; m. Geralyn Krupp, Mar. 15, 1981; children: Devra Sarah, Rachel Melissa, Hannah Krupp. AB, Boston U., 1962; JD, 1965; LLM, Harvard U., 1966. Bar: Mass. 1965, D.C. 1968, U.S. Supreme Ct. 1968. Ptnr. Lobel & Lobel, Boston, 1965-66; asst. prof. law U. Okla., Norman, 1967; congl. fellow Washington, 1968; legis. asst. to Senator William Proxmire, 1968-72; ptnr. Lobel, Novins & Lamont, LLP, Washington, 1972—. Lectr. Law Sch. Am. U., Washington, 1972—; resellers referee, U.S. Dist. Ct., Wichita; chmn. Tax Analysts, 1972—. Contbr. artticles to legal jours. Chmn. tax notes/tax analysis. Mem. ABA, Mass. Bar Assn., D.C. Bar Assn. (ch,m. consumer affairs com. 1976-77, chmn. steering com. on antitrust and consumer affairs sect.), Order of Coif, Harvard Club (Washington), Boston U. Club (Washington). Home: 4525 31st St NW Washington DC 20008-2130 Office: Lobel Novins & Lamont LLP 888 17th St NW #810 Washington DC 20006 Home Phone: 202-362-8818; Office Phone: 202-371-6626. Business E-Mail: lobel@lnllaw.com.

LO BELLO, JOSEPH DAVID, bank executive; b. Northampton, Mass., Feb. 5, 1940; s. Joseph Vincenzo and Marie (Mandella) Lo B.; m. Karen Suzanne Martin, June 21, 1969; children: Mark, Kara, Kimberly. BS, Babson Coll., 1961; MBA, U. Mass., 1963; postgrad., Harvard Bus. Sch., 1987. Loan officer Third Nat. Bank Hampden County, Springfield, Mass., 1963-65, v.p., 1965-75, sr. v.p., 1975-81; exec. v.p. Bank of New Eng. West, N.A., Springfield, 1981-90; regional pres. Bank of New Eng. N.A., Springfield, 1990-92; pres., chief exec. officer Peoples Savs. Bank, Holyoke, Mass., 1992—. Dir. Mass. Indsl. Fin. Agy., Boston, 1987, Conn. Online Computer, 1994, Credit Data Svcs., Inc., 1993; treas., trustee Basketball Hall of Fame, Springfield, 1985; trustee Springfield Coll., 1984; chmn. Baystate Health System, Springfield, 1983. Mem. Rotary Club. Avocations: golf, hiking, theater, travel. Home: 152 Meadowbrook Rd Longmeadow MA 01106-1341

LOBENFELD, ERIC JAY, lawyer; b. Bklyn., Aug. 18, 1950; s. Samuel J. and Ruth E. (Rifkin) L.; m. Patricia L. McCarron, May 3, 1981; children: Claire A., Margot R. BA, SUNY, Binghamton, 1971; JD, Bklyn. Law Sch., 1975. Bar: N.Y. 1976. Assoc. Donovan, Leisure, Newton and Irvine, NYC, 1975-84, ptnr., 1984-86, Dewey Ballantine, NYC, 1987-91, 92-94; v.p., chief litigation counsel Reliance Group Holdings, Inc., NYC, 1991-92; ptnr. Chadbourne & Parke, NYC, 1994—2001, Clifford Chance, NYC, 2001—03, Hogan & Hartson LLP, NYC, 2003—, dir. litig. practice group. Adj. assoc. prof. Bklyn. Law Sch., 1984-90; lectr. Practising Law Inst., N.Y.C., 1987-90, 2001—. Mem. ABA, N.Y. State Bar Assn., Fed. Bar Coun., Internat. Intellectual Property Assn., N.Y. Intellectual Property Assn., Nat. Inst. for Trial Advocacy (faculty mem.). Republican. Avocations: stamp collecting/philately, music, sports. Home: 174 Clarence Rd Scarsdale NY 10583-6318 Office: Hogan & Hartson LLP 875 Third Ave New York NY 10022 Office Phone: 212-918-8202. Office Fax: 212-918-3100. Business E-Mail: ejlobenfeld@hhlaw.com.

LOBENHERZ, WILLIAM ERNEST, consumer products company executive, trade association administrator, lawyer; b. Muskegon, Mich., June 22, 1949; s. Ernest Pomeroy and Emajean (Krautheim) L.; m. Carla Rae Krieger; children: Heidi, Jessica Anne, Rebecca Jean, Christopher William, Andrew William. BBA, U. Mich., 1971; JD cum laude, Wayne State U., 1974. Bar: Mich. 1974. Legal counsel Mich. Legis. Svcs. Bur., Lansing, Mich., 1974-77; legal legis. cons. Mich. Assn. of Sch. Bds., Lansing, 1977, asst. exec. dir. for legal legis. affairs, 1977-79; asst. v.p. state and congl. rels. Wayne State U., Detroit, 1979-81, assoc. v.p. state rels., 1981-82, v.p. govtl. affairs, 1982-87; assoc. Dykema Gossett, Lansing, Mich., 1987-89; pres., CEO Mich. Soft Drink Assn., Lansing, 1989—, MSDA Svc. Corp., Lansing, 1997—. Guest lectr. in govtl. affairs, Wayne State U., U. Mich., U. Detroit; referee Mich. Tax Tribunal, 1993-97. Contbr. chpt. Mich. Handbook for School Business Officials, 1979, 2nd edit., 1980; also articles to profl. jours. and mags. Mem. govtl. affairs com. New Detroit Inc., 1984-87, chmn. state subcom. of govtl. affairs com., 1986-87; chmn. ind. schs. campaign Greater Metro Detroit United Fund Torch Dr., 1979, chmn. Colls. and Univs. campaign, 1980; bd. dirs. Mich. Epilepsy Ctr., 1991-97, Coun. for Mich. Pub. Univs., 1991—, Tourism Industry Coalition of Mich., vice-chair, 1998—; mem. 2d bd. dir. Mich. Recycling Partnership, 1997—. Recipient Book award Lawyer's Coop. Pub. Co., 1973, Outstanding Svc. award Mich. Assn. for Marriage and Family Therapy, 1992, 95, Silver scholar key Wayne State U. Law Sch., 1974; named among Top 10 Single Interest Lobbyists, Inside Mich. Politics, 2001, 05. Mem. Mich. Bar Assn., NAACP, Coun. for Advancement and Support of Edn. (Mindpower citation 1982), Mich. Delta Found. (bd. dirs. 1977-97, sec. 1981-84, v.p. 1987-88), Greater Metro Detroit C. of C. (contact interviewer bus. attraction and expansion coun. 1984-86). Home: 430 Leland Pl Lansing MI 48917 Office: Mich Soft Drink Assn 124 W Allegan Ste 634 Lansing MI 48933-1707 Office Phone: 517-371-4499. E-mail: msda@voyager.net.

LOBER, IRENE MOSS, educational consultant; b. NYC, Aug. 1, 1927; d. David and Beckie Moss; m. Solomon William Lober, Oct. 25, 1947; children: Clifford Warren, Richard Wayne, Lori Ann. BS in Edn., CCNY, 1948; MA, George Washington U., 1967; EdD, Va. Poly. Inst. and State U., 1974. Registered sch. bus. adminstr. Formerly tchr., libr.; prin. staff devel. Fairfax County Pub. Schs., Va., 1965—77; supt. University City (Mo.) Pub. Schs., 1977—81, Danbury (Conn.) Pub. Schs., 1981—85; prof. SUNY, New Paltz, 1985—98, chmn. dept. ednl. adminstrn., 1990—98, dir. EdD program, 1993—95, coord. distance learning programs, 1995—98, cons. ednl. adminstrn., 1998—. Guest lectr. Washington U., George Washington U., Va. Poly. Inst. and State U., U. Va., Fordham U., C.W. Post Coll., L.I. U.; mem. bus. adv. coun. Datahr, Inc., 1982—85; pres. N.Y. State Coun. for Advancement of Depts. of Ednl. Adminstrn., 1994; cons. in field; founding incorporator Sci. Horizons, Inc., Danbury, 1984—85, COMPUtourney, Inc., 1990—98; designated disting. expert and peer reviewer Asst. Sec. Edn. Chester Finn, 1987—89; spkr./presenter various internat., nat. and state confs. and convs.; book reviewer Tchrs. Coll. Press, Columbia U., 2004. Author: Promoting Your School, 1993; contbr. articles to profl. jours.; book reviewer: Teacher's Coll. Press, 2004. Mem. legal and govt. studies group Nat. Inst. Edn. Dept. HEW; nat. adv. bd. U. Wis. R & D Ctr., 1978—80; chairperson Mo. Instrnl. TV Coun., 1981; lay adv. bd. St. Louis Met. Med. Soc., 1980—81; bd. advisors St. Joseph's Inst. Deaf, 1980—81; apptd. supt. in residence Western Conn. State U., 1984; divsn. chairperson United Way Campaign, 1982—86; mem. bd. edn. Poughkeepsie City Sch. Dist., 1993—96; mem. instl. rev. bd. M.D. Anderson Cancer Ctr., Orlando, 2002—04; pres. Lake Mary chpt. AARP, 2001—03; pres. Rishona-Chavaret group, Orlando chpt. Hadassah, 2005—, co-pres., 2004—05; bd. dirs. Temple Israel, Longwood, Fla., 2005—, v.p. edn., 2006—, adminstrv. v.p., 2005—07; pres. Temple Israel Sisterhood, Longwood, 2007—, bd. dirs.; pres. adv. cabinet Greater St. Louis coun. Girl Scouts U.S., 1980—81, bd. dirs. Southwestern Conn. Coun., 1981—85; bd. dirs. Fairfield coun. Boy Scouts Am.; bd. dirs. Danbury region Jr. Achievement, 1981—86, Regional Hospice, Danbury, 1984—86, Danbury Coun. Am. Heart Assn., 1985—86; exec. bd., trustee United Way No. Fairfield County; trustee, bd. dirs. United Way, Danbury, 1982—85; bd. dirs. TRIAD Seminole County, Fla., 2001—, Meals on Wheels Inc. Seminole County, Fla., 2000—04. Recipient Townsend Harris medal, CCNY Alumni Assn., Nat. Leadership award, Hadassah, 2005;, IDEA fellow, Ford Found. grantee, 1977—78. Mem.: NEA, ASCD, Authors League, Authors Guild, Nat. Assn. Secondary Sch. Prins. (chair profs. secondary sch. adminstrn. com.), Assn. Sch. Bus. Ofcls. Internat. (nat. chmn. maintenance and ops. rsch. com. 1985—89), N.Y. State Assn. Sch. Bus. Ofcls., N.Y. State Coun. Sch. Supts., Ednl. Rsch. Svc., Sch. Adminstrs. Assn. N.Y. State, Am. Assn. Sch. Adminstrs. (nat. chmn. higher edn. com. 1987—89, chmn. membership svcs. com. 1995—96), Pi Lambda Theta (publs. adv. bd. 1981—84), Phi Kappa Phi, Phi Delta Kappa (pres. New Paltz chpt. 1991—93). Personal E-mail: loberim@bellsouth.net.

LOBER, LIONEL M., scriptwriter, film producer; b. Alexandria, Egypt, Nov. 13, 1933; s. Louis and Eva (Horowitz) L.; m. Mati Elpern, June 20, 1961 (dec. Nov. 1983); children: Sharon Nadine, Alma Nora. BA in Theater, English, Brandeis U., 1955. Assoc. prodn. mgr., asst. to Otto Preminger Exodus, 1960; exec. asst. to exec. v.p. United Artists Corp., NYC, 1961-63; v.p. European prodn. Metro-Goldwyn-Mayer, 1963-65; exec. in charge of prodn. D.E.A.R. Studios, Rome, 1965-70; v.p. Prodigal Prodns., Paris, 1970-75; writer, producer Warner Bros. TV, United Artists Corp., Cannon Films, NYC, Los Angeles, London, 1975-78. Lectr. on film writing and prodn. Calif. State U., Northridge. Screenwriter: A Candle for the Dead, 1969, Black Madonna, 1972, Who Stole Irving, 1975, The Second Coming, 1979, He and She, 1983, Slit Throat, 1987, The Corsican Brothers, 1987, Final Scream, 1988, Danger Girl, 1989, Cop Out, 1990, Checkmate, 1991, Double Impact, 1992, Turnabout, 1994, An Ideal Husband, 1995, (play) Shadow of Guilt, 1996, Lost Soul, 1998, With A Bang!, 1999, Kiss and Run, 2004, Away From Home, 2005. Capt. USMC, 1956-60. Mem. Writers Guild Am. West, Brit. Acad. Film and TV Arts (L.A.). Democrat. E-mail: loberlionel@hotmail.com.

LOBES, MARK ROBERT, graphic design educator, coach; b. Downers Grove, Ill., Mar. 17, 1978; s. Robert Allan and Kathleen Geraldine (Koss) L. BA in History, Ea. Ill. U., Charleston, 2001, BS in Tech. Edn., 2001; MA in Ednl. Leadership, Aurora U., Ill., 2005. History and drafting/design educator Downers Grove North HS, Ill., 2001—03; tech. edn. educator Lockport Twp. HS, Ill., 2003—05; graphic design educator, CTE coord. Victor J. Andrew HS, Tinley Park, Ill., 2005—. Asst. boys bowling coach Victor J. Andrew HS, Tinley Park, 2005—, Skills USA advisor, 2005—, asst. boys tennis coach, 2006—. Mem.: Internat. Tech. Edn. Assn. (assoc.), Nat. Trust for Hist. Preservation (assoc.), Frank Lloyd Wright Preservation Trust (assoc.), Chgo. Arch. Found. (assoc.), BMW Car Club of Am. (assoc.). Republican. Roman Catholic. Avocations: tennis, bowling, Jimmy Buffett concerts, architecture, Chicago Cubs baseball. Home: 15056 W Sagebrush Ln Lockport IL 60441 Office: Victor J Andrew H S 9001 W 171st St Tinley Park IL 60487 Office Phone: 708-342-4527.

LOBIG, JANIE HOWELL, retired special education educator; b. Peoria, Ill., June 10, 1945; d. Thomas Edwin and Elizabeth Jane (Higdon) Howell; m. James Frederick Lobig, Aug. 16, 1970 (dec. Dec. 2001); 1 child, Jill Christina. BS in Elem. Edn., So. Ill. U., 1969; MA in Spl. Edn. Severely Handicapped, San Jose State U., 1989. Cert. elem. tchr., Calif., Mo., Ill., handicapped edn., Calif., Mo.; ordained to ministry Presbyn. Ch. as deacon, 1984. Tchr. trainable mentally retarded children Spl. Luth. Sch., St. Louis, 1967—68; tchr. trainable mentally retarded and severly handicapped children Spl. Sch. Dist. St. Louis, 1969—80, head tchr., 1980—83; tchr. severely handicapped children San Jose Unified Sch. Dist., Calif., 1983—86; tchr. autistic students Santa Clara County Office Edn., San Jose, 1986—2007; tchr. Suzanne Dancers, 1991—92; ret., 2007. Vol. Am. Cancer Soc., San Jose, 1986—89, 1992, Am. Heart Assn., 1985—, Multiple Sclerosis Soc., 1990—, Wildlife Ctr. Silicon Valley, 1998—; moderator bd. deacons Evergreen Presbyn. Ch., 1986—89. Avocations: golf, motor home travel, bridge, needlecrafts. Home: 3211 Bracciano Ct San Jose CA 95135 Personal E-mail: JanieAngel@aol.com.

LOBIONDO, FRANK A., congressman; b. Bridgeton, NJ, May 12, 1946; m. Tina Ercole; children: Adina, Amy. BA in Bus. Adminstrn., St. Joseph's U., Pa., 1968. Ops. mgr. LoBiondo Bros. Motor Express, Inc., Rosenhayn, NJ, 1968-94; mem. Cumberland County Bd. Freeholders, NJ, 1985-88, NJ Gen. Assembly from Dist. 1, 1988-94, US Congress from 2nd NJ dist., 1995—, mem. transp. and infrastructure com., armed svcs. com. Pres. Cumberland County Guidance Ctr., 1982—84; mem. Cumberland County Econ. Devel. Bd., 1985—88; liaison Cumberland County Health and Welfare Dept., 1985—88; founder Cumberland County Environ. Health Task Force, 1987; chmn. Cumberland County chpt. Am. Heart Assn., 1989—90; hon. chmn. ann. fund raising drive Cumberland County Hospice, 1992; mem. bd. Vineland Young Men's Christian Assn., 1986—, bd. dirs., 1978—94, YMCA, trustee, 1981—84, 1990—94; bd. dirs. Literacy Vols. Am., Cape May County chpt., 1991—. Recipient Guardian of Small Bus. award, Nat. Fedn. Independent Bus., Friend of Nat. Pks. award, Nat. Pks. Conservation Assn., 2005, South Jersey Breast Cancer Coalition award, 2005. Mem.: Vineland, NJ Rotary. Republican. Roman Cath. Office: 5914 Main St Mays Landing NJ 08330 Office Phone: 202-225-6572, 609-625-5008. Office Fax: 609-625-5071.*

LOBL, HERBERT MAX, lawyer, writer; b. Vienna, Jan. 10, 1932; s. Walter Leo and Minnie (Neumann) L.; m. Dorothy Fullerton Hubbard, Sept. 12, 1960; children: Peter Walter, Michelle Alexandra. AB magna cum laude, Harvard U., 1953, LLB cum laude, 1959, Avocat honoraire, 1993. Bar: N.Y. 1960, U.S. Tax Ct. 1963, French Conseil Juridique 1973; French avocat. mem. Paris bar, 1992, avocat hon., 1993. Assoc. Davis, Polk & Wardwell, NYC, 1959-90, NYC and Paris, 1963-69, ptnr., 1969-92, sr. counsel, 1993—; assoc. counsel to Gov. Nelson Rockefeller Albany, NY, 1960-62. Lectr. law Columbia U., NYC, 1993—95; mem. supervisory bd. CII-HB Internationale, Amsterdam, 1977—82. Author: Welcome to West Berlin, 2002, A Tender Offer, 2004. Gov. Am. Hosp. Paris, 1981-83, 88-93; bd. trustees Am. Libr., Paris, 1969-81, Nantucket (Mass.) Cottage Hosp., 1996-99, dir. Nantucket Arts Coun., 2000-02. Served to 1st lt. USAF, 1954—56. Fulbright scholar, U. Bonn, Germany, 1954. Mem.: Am. C. of C. (bd. dirs. France 1988—90), Harvard Club, Univ. Club. Office: Davis Polk & Wardwell 450 Lexington Ave New York NY 10017-3911 Office Phone: 212-450-4665. Personal E-mail: d-h-lobl@earthlink.net.

LOBLEY, ALAN HAIGH, retired lawyer; b. Elkhart, Ind., Aug. 26, 1927; s. Frederick Askew and Eva May (Haigh) L.; m. Kathleen Covert Nolan, Mar. 2, 1957; children: James, Sarah. BSChemE, Purdue U., 1949; JD, Ind. U., 1952. Bar: Ind. 1952, US Dist. Ct. (so. dist.) Ind. 1955, US Ct. Appeals (7th cir.) 1963, US Supreme Ct. 1971, US Ct. Appeals (6th cir.) 1979. From assoc. to ptnr. Ice, Miller, Donadio & Ryan (formerly Ross, McCord, Ice & Miller), Indpls., 1955-97; ret., 1997. Commr. Indpls. Hist. Preservation Comm., 2001-; 1st lt. USAF, 1952-54. Mem. ABA, Am. Arbitration Assn. Panel of Arbitrators, Ind. Bar Assn., Indpls. Bar Assn., Indpls. Rowing Ctr. (bd. dirs.). Democrat. Avocations: photography, music, sculling. Home: 4535 N Park Ave Indianapolis IN 46205-1836 Office Phone: 317-283-1928. Personal E-mail: a-klobley@att.net.

LOBO, REBECCA, professional basketball player; b. Hartford, Conn., Oct. 6, 1973; BA in Polit. Sci., U. Conn., 1995. Basketball player USA Women's Nat. Team, N.Y. Liberty, 1997—2001, Houston Comets, 2001—02, Conn. Sun, Uncasville, 2003—. Mem. U.S. Olympic Festival East Team, 1992, Jr. World Championship Qualifying Team, 1992, USA Jr. World Championship Team, 1993. Co-author: The Home Team, 1996. Founder Ruth Ann & Rebecca Lobo scholarship in allied health U. Conn., 2001. Named Big East Conf. Player of Yr., Nat. Player of Yr., Naismith, U.S. Basketball Writers Assn., 1995, Big East Tournament Most Outstanding Player, 1994, Big East Conf. Women's Basketball Scholar Athlete of Yr., 1995, Female Athlete of Yr., AP, 1995; named to All-Am. 1st team, Kodak, 1994, 1995; recipient Wade trophy. Office: c/o Conn Sun 1 Mohegan Sun Blvd Uncasville CT 06382

LOBO, ROGERIO ARNALDO, obstetrician, gynecologist; b. Hong Kong, 1949; MD, Georgetown U., 1974. Diplomate Am. Bd. Ob-Gyn. Intern U. Chgo. Hosps., 1974-75, resident in obstetrics, 1975-78; fellow in reproductive endocrinology L.A. County-U. So. Calif. Med. Ctr., 1980; physician Presbyn. Hosp., NYC, 1995—; dir. Sloane Hosp. for Women, Columbia Univ. Med. Ctr., NYC, 1995—2002; Willard C. Rappleye prof. and chmn. ob-gyn. Columbia Coll. Physicians and Surgeons, NYC, 1995—2002. Editor Jour. Soc. for Gynecol. Investigation, 1993-06. Mem. ACOG, Am. Soc. Reproductive Medicine, Endocrine Soc., Soc. Gynecol. Investigation (past pres.). Office: Columbia Univ Med Ctr 622 W 168th St Rm 16 69 New York NY 10032-3720 Office Phone: 212-305-6337.

LOBOA, ELIZABETH GRACE, biomedical engineer, educator; d. Letha Loboa and Ron Mertens (Stepfather); m. Rama O. Polefka, June 21, 1998; children: Auria Loboa Polefka, Lachlan David Polefka. BS, U. Calif., Davis, 1995; MS, Stanford U., Calif., 1997, PhD, 2002. Acting asst. prof. Dept. Mech. Engrng. Stanford (Calif.) U., 2002; asst. prof. Joint Dept. Biomedical Engrng. U. N.C. and N.C. State U., Raleigh, NC, 2003—. Dir. Cell Mechanics Lab., NC State U., Raleigh, NC, 2003—; adj. asst. prof. Dept. Orthopaedics U. N.C., Chapel Hill, NC, 2005—. Contbr. articles to profl. jours. Recipient Ralph E. Powe Jr. Faculty Enhancement award; grantee, NIH, 2003 - present, N.C. Biotechnology Ctr., Nat. Textile Ctr., Nonwovens Coop. Rsch. Ctr. Mem.: ASME, Am. Soc. Engrng. Edn., Assn. Women in Sci., Biomedical Engrng. Soc., Orthopaedic Rsch. Soc. Office: Biomedical Engineering UNC-CH & NCSU 2142 Burlington Labs Campus Box 7115 Raleigh NC 27562 Office Phone: 919-513-4015. Business E-Mail: egloboa@ncsu.edu, egloboa@unc.edu.

LOBRANO, JOHN D., lawyer; b. Norwalk, Conn., Feb. 18, 1957; BA magna cum laude, Amherst Coll., 1979; JD, NYU, 1983. Bar: NY 1984. Assoc. Simpson Thacher & Bartlett LLP, 1983—91, ptnr., 1991—, mem. corp. dept. Mem.: ABA, Assn. of Bar of City of NY, NY State Bar Assn., Internat. Bar Assn. Office: Simpson Thacher & Bartlett LLP 425 Lexington Ave New York NY 10017-3954 Office Phone: 212-455-2890. Office Fax: 212-455-2502. E-mail: jlobrano@stblaw.com.

LOBRANO, MARY ELIZABETH, radiologist, director; b. Ft. Worth, Feb. 5, 1969; d. Leo Monte and Betty Lou Burden; m. Jerry Joseph Lobrano, Oct. 9, 1993; children: Robert Leo, Charles Allen. MD, Tulane U., New Orleans, 1994. Cert. Am. Bd. Radiology, 1998. Asst. prof. La. State U. Med. Sch., New Orleans, 1998—2000; asst. med. dir. radiology East Jefferson Gen Hosp., Metairie, La., 2000—01; med. dir. radiology East Jefferson Gen. Hosp., 2001—; med. dir. Pet Fusion Ctr., 2002—; CEO Radiology and Interventional Assocs. of Metairie, 2001—. Physician adv. bd. mem. East Jefferson Gen. Hosp. Found., 2005—. Vol. Med. Alumni Assn.; pianist, choir dir. Assumption Our Lady Ch., Braithwaite, La.,

2000—05; choir mem. St. Andrew the Apostle Ch., Algiers, La., 2005—06. Named Vol. Yr., Tulane Young Alumni, 2005; recipient Janet Glasgow Meml. award, Am. Med. Women's Assn., 1994, Plaque Recognition for Outstanding Svc. to Ch. and Cmty., St. Thoma/Assumption Parish, 2001. Mem.: Am. Roentgen Ray Soc., Am. Coll. Radiology, Radiol. Soc. N.Am. (Resident Rsch. award 1998). Roman Catholic. Avocations: piano, hunting.

LOBRON, BARBARA L., speech educator, editor, photographer, writer; b. Phila., Mar. 19, 1944; d. Martin Aaron and Elizabeth (Gots) L. Student, Pa. State U., 1962—63; BA cum laude, Temple U., Phila., 1966; student art therapy, Erika Steinberger, NYC, 1994—2003; MS, Coll. Mt. St. Vincent, 2001. Reporter, writer Camden (N.J.) Courier-Post, 1966-68; editl. asst. Med. Insight mag., NYC, 1970-71; mng. editor Camera 35 mag., NYC, 1971-75; also assoc. editor photog. anns. U.S. Camera/Camera 35, 1972, 73; freelance editor as Word Woman NYC, 1975-77, 79-99; acct. exec. Bozell & Jacobs, NYC, 1977-79; copy editor Camera Arts mag., NYC, 1981-83; editl. coord. Ctr. mag. Nat. Ctr. Health Edn., 1985; editl. coord. Popular Photography mag., 1986-95; assoc. editor Sony Style, 1995; tchr. speech improvement N.Y.C. Bd. Edn., 1995—. Contbg. editor: Photograph; participant 3M Editor's Conf. (1st woman), 1972; photography group exhbns. include Internat. Women's Art Festival, N.Y.C., 1975, Rockefeller Ctr., N.Y.C., 1976, Photograph Gallery, N.Y.C., 1981; acrylic painting exhbns. Tchrs. Coll., N.Y.C., 1994, Warwick Hotel, N.Y.C., 1995; represented in collection Libr. Calif Inst. Arts, Valencia; copy editor: The Complete Guide to Cibachrome Printing, 1980, The Popular Photography Question and Answer Book, 1979, The Photography Catalog, 1976, Strand: Sixty Years of Photography, 1976, You and Your Lens, 1975; contbr. articles to comml. publs., chpts. to books. Tchr. Sch. Vol. Program, N.Y.C. Recipient 1st pl. honors Dist. 1, Internat. Assn. Bus. Communicators, 1977. Mem. Soka Gakkai Internat. Buddhist. Avocations: dance, reading, photography, origami, walking. Home: 85 Hicks St Apt 7 Brooklyn NY 11201-6825 E-mail: barbaralobron@hotmail.com.

LOBUE, ANGE, psychiatrist, author; s. Joseph Vincent Lobue and Augustine Lobue Palmintier; m. Chantal Madeleine Giebert, Dec. 24, 2000; children: Robert Kent Jr., Sandrine Kent. BS in Pharmacy, U. Miss., 1960; MD, La. State U., 1964; MPH, UCLA, 1968. Diplomate Am. Bd. Psychiatry and Neurology. Med.-surg. intern So. Pacific Meml. Hosp., San Francisco, 1964-65; resident in psychiatry Dept. Preventive and Social Medicine UCLA Sch. Medicine, 1968-71, resident in psychiatry Dept. Psychiatry, 1969-72, asst. clin. prof., 1972-92; instr. Sch. Cinema-TV U. So. Calif., LA, 1987—89; pvt. practice Santa Rosa, Calif., 1988—97, Mendocino, Calif. Vis. fellow U. Belgrade (Yugoslavia) and the Fed. Inst. Pub. Health, U. Edinburgh (Scotland) and the Ministry of Health, 1969, St. Thomas Hosp. and the Ministry of Health, London, 1969; vis. scholar, spl. asst. to adminstr. Health Svcs. and Mental Health Adminstrn., HEW, Washington, 1970; vis. scholar, asst. to pres. N.Y.C. Health and Hosps. Corp., 1970-71; registered pharmacist, mgr. Briargrove Pharmacy, Houston, Tex., 1960; writer, spkr., lectr., numerous workshops, hosps., colls., univs., TV, assns.; apptd. staff Santa Rosa Meml. Hosp., UCLA Ctr. Health Scis., Warrack Hosp., Santa Rosa. Editor: Psychiatry and the Media, 1983; contbr. articles to profl. jours. Sr. pub. health physician Venice Youth Clinic, L.A., 1969. Capt. U.S. Army Med. Corps, 1965-67. Fellow Acad. Psychosomatic Medicine, Am. Coll. Preventive Medicine (assoc.), Am. Geriatrics Soc. (founding), Royal Soc. Health; mem. NATAS, MENSA (life), Am. Film Inst. Alumni Assn., Am. Med. Writers Assn., Biofeedback Cert. Inst. Am., Mendocino-Lake County Med. Soc., Nat. Thespian Soc., Physicians Coun. on Drug Dependence, Sonoma County Med. Assn., UCLA Alumni Assn., Delta Omega. Avocations: music, literature, art, theater, gardening. Office Phone: 707-444-1616. Personal E-mail: trinidadca@gmail.com.

LOCASCIO, JOSEPH A., surgeon, educator; b. May 8, 1949; Asst. prof. U. SC, Columbia; surgeon, dir. Ctr. Sight, Wilmington, W.Va. Office: 5170 US Rte 60 E Huntington WV 25755

LOCATELLI, PAUL LEO, academic administrator; b. Santa Cruz, Calif., Sept. 16, 1938; s. Vincent Dino and Marie Josephine (Piccone) L. BS in Acctg., Santa Clara U., 1961; MDiv, Jesuit Sch. Theology, 1974; DBA, U. So. Calif., 1971. CPA, Calif.; ordained priest Roman Cath. Ch., 1974. Prof. acctg. Santa Clara (Calif.) U., 1974-86, assoc. dean Bus. Sch., 1976—78, acad. v.p., 1978—86, pres., 1988—. Mem. Silicon Valley Leadership Group, Cath. Relief Svcs.; trustee Jesuit Sch. Theology, Berkeley. Mem. acad. adv. bd. Panetta Inst.; mem. internat. com. Jesuit Higher Edn.; sec. higher edn. Soc. Jesus. Mem. Calif. Soc. CPAs (Disting. Prof. of the Yr. award 1994), Assn. Jesuit Colls. and Univs., Commonwealth Club Silicon Valley. Democrat. Office: Santa Clara U 500 El Camino Real Santa Clara CA 95053-0015

LOCHBIHLER, FREDERICK VINCENT, lawyer; b. Chgo., Jan. 30, 1951; s. Frederick Louis and Marion Helen (Rutkauskas) L.; m. Darlene Gotfryde Wantuch; 1 child, Frederick Karlman. AB in Govt. summa cum laude, U. Notre Dame, 1973; JD with honors, U. Chgo., 1976. Bar: Ill. 1976, U.S. Dist. Ct. (no. dist.) Ill. 1977, U.S. Ct. Appeals (7th cir.) 1980, U.S. Ct. Appeals (8th cir.) 1981, U.S. Supreme Ct. 1982, U.S. Dist. Ct. (ctrl. dist.) Ill. 1983, U.S. Dist. Ct. Ariz. 1991, U.S. Ct. Appeals (Fed. cir.) 2001, U. S. Dist. Ct. (so. dist.) Ind. 2002. Assoc. Chapman and Cutler, Chgo., 1976-84, ptnr., 1984—. Mem. Phi Beta Kappa, Order of Coif. Avocations: military history, literature, travel. Office: Chapman and Cutler 111 W Monroe St Ste 1700 Chicago IL 60603-4006 Office Phone: 312-845-3705. E-mail: lochbihl@chapman.com.

LOCHNER, PHILIP RAYMOND, retired communications executive, former commissioner; b. New Rochelle, NY, Mar. 3, 1943; s. Philip Raymond and Maryl (Browning) L.; m. Sally Soth, July 23, 1973; children: Lauren Soth, John Philip. BA, Yale U., 1964, LLB, 1967; PhD, Stanford U., 1971. Bar: N.Y. 1972, D.C. 1992. Assoc. dean, asst. prof. law SUNY, 1971-73; assoc. Cravath Swaine & Moore, NYC, 1973-78; various legal staff positions, including gen. counsel Time Inc., NYC, 1978-90; commr. SEC, Washington, 1990-91; sr. v.p., chief adminstrv. officer Time Warner, Inc., NYC, 1991-98. Bd. dirs. Apria Healthcare Group, Inc., Lake Forrest, Calif., Clarcor, Inc., Nashville, Gtech Holdings Inc., West Greenwich, R.I., Solutia Inc., St. Louis, Adelphia Comm. Corp, Denver, Monster Worldwide, Inc., 2006-; bd. advs. Republic N.Y. Corp., N.Y.C., 1997—; bd. govs. Am. Stock Exch., N.Y.C., 2002-04; past mem. bd. advs. Investment Mgmt. Advs., Inc.; adj. faculty Law Sch. Columbia U. Contbr. articles to profl. jours., newspapers. Bd. dirs. Canterbury Sch., Investor Responsibility Rsch. Ctr. Fulbright fellow U. London, 1968. Mem. Nat. Assn. Securities Dealers (former gov.), Phi Beta Kappa. Avocations: kayaking, sailing, hiking.

LOCHRIDGE, JULIE DEANE, retired communications executive; b. NYC, Feb. 27, 1935; d. Albert William and Dorothea Margaret (Stewart) Deane; m. Edward Evans (dec.); children: Michelle Evans, Deanne Evans; m. Benjamin Sturges Lochridge, Feb. 26, 1991 (dec. Jan. 2005); children: Benjamin Jr., Willard, Laurie, Daryl, Roger. AS, Averett U., Danville, Va., 1955. Exec. sec. to v.p. Dept. Censorship and Editing CBS, NYC, 1955—57, exec. sec. to gen. sales mgr. Radio Network Sales, 1957—60, exec. sec. to v.p. Radio Network Sales, 1960—61; sec. to mgr. Dist. Agy. Prudential Ins. Co. Am., Newark, 1961—63; ret., 1963. Recipient Alumni Svc. award, Averett U., 1990. Avocations: theater, travel. Home: 1611 Village Crossing Dr Chapel Hill NC 27517-7577

LOCHRIDGE, LLOYD PAMPELL, JR., lawyer; b. Austin, Tex., Feb. 3, 1918; s. Lloyd Pampell and Franklyn (Blocker) Lochridge; m. Frances Potter, Jan. 23, 1943; children: Anne, Georgia, Lloyd P. III, Patton G., Hope N., Frances P. AB, Princeton U., 1938; LLB, Harvard U., 1941. Bar: DC 1942, Tex. 1945, U.S. Ct. Appeals (5th cir.), U.S. Supreme Ct. Assoc. Law Office Vernon Hill, Mission, Tex., 1945-46; ptnr. Hill & Lochridge, Mission, 1946-49, Hill, Lochridge & King, Mission, 1949-59, McGinnis, Lochridge & Kilgore, Austin, 1959—. Mem. adv. bd. Salvation Army, Austin, 1962—; trustee Austin Lyric Opera, 1986—; mem. vestry Ch. Good Shepherd, Austin, 1968—73. Comdr. USNR, 1941—46, ETO. Mem.: ABA (bd. govs. 1989—92), Hidalgo County Bar Assn. (pres. 1954—55), Travis County Bar Assn. (pres. 1970—71), State Bar Tex. (pres. 1974—75). Episcopalian. Avocations: tennis, squash, sailing. Office: McGinnis Lochridge and Kilgore 600 Congress Ave Ste 2100 Austin TX 78701-2499 Office Phone: 512-495-6002. Business E-Mail: llochridge@mcginnislaw.com.

LOCHRIDGE, PATTON G., lawyer; b. McAllen, Tex., Dec. 30, 1949; s. Lloyd and Frances (Potter) L.; m. Candy Lundgren, June 28, 1975; children: Eleanor, Patton, Joe, Lloyd. BA, U. Tex., 1972, JD, 1976. Bar: Tex. 1976, Okla. 2005, US Dist. Ct. (no., so., ea. and we. dists.) Tex., US Ct. Appeals (5th cir.), US Supreme Ct. Law clk. to Hon. Joseph T. Sneed US Ct. Appeals (9th cir.), San Francisco, 1976-77; assoc. to ptnr., comml. litig. McGinnis Lochridge & Kilgore LLP, Austin, Tex., 1977—, mng. ptnr., 2000—. Chmn. com. ct. adminstrn. US Dist Ct. we. dist. Tex., 1986—97, chmn. admissions com., 1995—. Trustee Salvation Army, Austin, St. Andrews Episc. Sch. Austin. Fellow: Am. Coll. Trial Lawyers; mem.: ABA, Am. Bd. Trial Advocates, Travis County Bar Assn., Phi Delta Phi, Order of the Coif. Avocations: rugby, skiing, ranching. Office: McGinnis Lochridge & Kilgore 600 Congress Ave Ste 2100 Austin TX 78701 Office Phone: 512-495-6044. Office Fax: 512-505-6344. Business E-Mail: plochridge@mcginnislaw.com.

LOCIGNO, PAUL ROBERT, public relations executive; b. Cleve., Sept. 17, 1948; s. Paul Robert and Anna Mae (Zingale) L.; m. Ki Cho Rim; children: Paul III, Tammy, Robert. AA, Cuyahoga C.C., Parma, Ohio, 1974; BA, Case We. Res. U., 1976; postgrad., Cleve. State U., 1977—78. Part-time faculty Cuyahoga C.C., 1979—83; vice-chmn. Presdl. Inaugural Labor Com., Washington, 1980—81; vice-chmn. labor com. Presdl. Inaugural Com., Washington, 1984—85; legis. agt. Internat. Brotherhood of Teamsters, Washington, 1977—90, dir. govt. internat. affairs, 1983—89, dir. Asian/Pacific br. Taipei, Taiwan, 1985—88; spl. rep. of chmn. Hill & Knowlton Pub. Affairs Worldwide, Washington, 1989—92; founding ptnr. Capitoline Internat., Inc., 1992—96; pres., founding ptnr. Rollins Internat. Ltd., Alexandria, Va., 1997—2004; CEO Ganeden Biotech Inc., San Diego, 2004—; pres. Locigno Internat. Inc., 2004—. Mem. budget com., Prince William County, 2002, 05. Mem. Pres.'s Export Coun., 1988-89; mem. Asia adv. com. Bicentennial of U.S. Constitution, 1990; bd. govs. Am. League for Exports and Security Assistance, 1989; mem. Nat. Commn. for Employment Policy, Washington, 1981-86; mem. zoning ordinance rev. com. Prince William County, Va., budget com., 2001, 04. Mem.: Marine Corps. Assn. Home: 3650 Secret Grove Ct Dumfries VA 22025-3600 Home Phone: 703-583-7904; Office Phone: 703-583-7273. Personal E-mail: locigno@comcast.net.

LOCK, ALBERT LARRY, JR., finance company executive; b. St. Louis, Nov. 20, 1947; s. Albert Larry and Bernadine Helen (Syron) L.; m. Barbara Ann Harding, Feb. 13, 1971; children: Brian C., Sean M. Student, U. Mo., St. Louis, 1966-68; AA, Northwest Mo. State U., 1975; MS in Fin. Svcs., The Am. Coll., 1998. CLU, 1979, ChFC, 1983. Ins. agt. Western and So. Life, St. Louis, 1970-74; field underwriter Home Life of N.Y., St. Louis, 1975—84; owner, fin. advisor Universal Fin. Group Inc., St. Louis, 1984—. Cons. fin. planning workshop St. Louis C.C., 1983-90; mem. broker/dealer Pres.'s Coun. Mutual Svc. Corp., 1992--; bd. dirs., legis. chmn. St. Louis Assn. Ins. and Fin. Advisors, mem. Top-of-the-Table Million Dollar Round Table. Pres. St. Paul Sch. Bd., 1990-91; bd. dirs. Bishop DuBourg H.S., 1997-2000, Marianist Retreat Ctr., St. Louis, 1997-2002. Sgt. U.S. Army, 1968-70, Vietnam. Decorated Bronze star, Air medals. Mem. St. Louis Soc. Fin. Svcs. Profls. (pres. 1988-89. chair fin. counseling sects.), Nat. Assn. Securities Dealers (registered prin.), Million Dollar Round Table. Roman Catholic. Avocation: racquetball. Office: Universal Fin Group Inc 7751 Carondelet Ave Saint Louis MO 63105-3316

LOCK, EDOUARD, performing company executive; b. Casablanca, Morocco, Mar. 3, 1954; Founder Lock-Danseurs now La La La Human Steps, 1980. Mem. Can. Coun. Arts. Artistic dir. performances include those at N.Y.'s Dance Theatre Workshop (Bessie award for choreography, 1986), dir., co-conceived David Bowie's Sound and Vision world tour; also dir. films. associated with prodn., 1989, showcased in the documentary Inspirations by Michael Apted, photographer (exhibitions) included in cities such as Stockholm, Los Angeles and Amsterdam, (private collections) Universite du Quebec a Montreal and Air Canada. Named Officer of the Order of Can., 2002; named one of Quebec's 10 most influential personalities; named to Chevalier de l'Ordre National du Quebec; recipient Chalmers Nat. Dance prize, 2001, Nat. Arts Ctr. prize. Office: La La La Human Steps 5655 ave du Parc Ste 206 Montreal PQ H2V 4H2 Canada*

LOCK, GERALD SEYMOUR HUNTER, retired mechanical engineering educator; b. London, June 30, 1935; arrived in Can., 1962, naturalized, 1973; s. George and Mary (Hunter) L.; m. Edna Burness, Sept. 19, 1959; children: Graeme, Gareth, Grenville. B.Sc. with honors, U. Durham, Eng., 1959, PhD, 1962. Asst. prof. mech. engring. U. Alta. (Can.), Edmonton, 1962-64, assoc. prof., 1964-70, prof., 1970-93, dean interdisciplinary studies, 1976-81; cons. mech. engr., Edmonton, 1993—. Chmn. Internat. Arctic Sci. Commn. Regional Bd., 1993-96. Vice chmn. Alta. Manpower Adv. Coun., 1979-84, chmn., 1984-89; chmn. Salvation Army Red Shield Appeal, 1980-82; bd. govs. Alta. Coll., chmn., 1982-85; founding pres. Alta. Poetry Festival Soc., 1981. Recipient Queen Elizabeth II Silver Jubilee medal, 1977 Fellow Engring. Inst. Can, Can. Soc. Mech. Engring. (pres. 1977-78), ASME; mem. Sci. Coun. Can., Can. Polar Commn. Mem. Progressive Conservative Party. Anglican. Home: 11711 83rd Ave Edmonton AB Canada T6G 0V2 Office: U Alta Edmonton AB Canada T6G 2G3

LOCKARD, KATHLEEN ANN, educational association administrator; d. John Paul and Marjorie Ellen Kunch; m. Herbert Wayne Lockard, July 19, 1969; children: Angela Kaye Reed, David Scott, John Steven, Christopher Brett. BEd, N.W. Mo. State U., 1976; MEd, Drake U., Des Moines, Iowa, 1988. Instr. elem. edn. East Union Cmty. Sch., Afton, Iowa, 1984—2000; coord. profl. devel. Green Valley Area Edn. Agy., Creston, Iowa, 2000—. Adj. prof. Buena Vista U., Creston, Iowa, 1999—. Sec. adminstrv. bd. United Meth. Ch., Afton, 2006—. Mem.: Iowa Cmty. Edn. Assn., Nat. Staff Devel. Coun., Sch. Adminstrs. Iowa, Iowa Sci. Tchrs. Assn. (sec. 2004—06, dir. region 1996—2006). Home: 409 South Browning Afton IA 50830 Office: Green Valley Area Edn Agy 1405 North Lincoln St Creston IA 50801 Home Phone: 641-347-5544; Office Phone: 641-782-8443. Office Fax: 641-782-4298. Personal E-mail: lockard@mddc.com. Business E-Mail: klockard@aea14.k12.ia.us.

LOCKE, CARL EDWIN, JR., academic administrator, engineer, educator; b. Palo Pinto County, Tex., Jan. 11, 1936; s. Carl Edwin Sr. and Caroline Jane (Brown) L.; m. Sammie Rhae Batchelor, Aug. 25, 1956; children: Stephen Curtis, Carlene Rhae. BSChemE, U. Tex., 1958, MSChemE, 1960, PhDChemE, 1972. Rsch. engr. Continental Oil Co., Ponca City, Okla., 1959-65; prodn. engr. R.L. Stone Co., Austin, Tex., 1965-66; prodn. rsch. engr. Tracor Inc., Austin, 1966-71; vis. assoc. prof. U. Tex., Austin, 1971-73; from asst. prof. to prof., dir. chem. engring. U. Okla., Norman, 1973-86; dean engring. U. Kans., Lawrence, 1986—2002, prof. chem. and petroleum engring., 1986—2005, prof. emeritus, 2005—. Co-author: Anodic Protection, 1981; contbr. articles to profl. jours. Recipient Disting. Engring. Svc. award U. Kans. Sch. Engring., 2002; named Disting. Engring. grad. U. Tex., 1993, Kansas Engr. of Yr. Kansas Engring. Soc., 1996. Fellow AIChE, NSPE; mem. ASTM, Nat. Assn. Corrosion Engrs. (regional chair 1988-89, Eben Junkin award South Cen. region 1990), Am. Soc. Engring. Edn. (vice-chair engring. deans coun. 1999-2001, chair 2001-02), Lawrence C. of C., Rotary (pres. 2001-02). Democrat. Presbyterian. Office: U Kans Sch Engring 4132D Learned Hall 1530 W 15th St Lawrence KS 66045-7526 Office Phone: 785-864-2929. Office Fax: 785-864-4967. E-mail: lok@ku.edu.

LOCKE, EDWIN ALLEN, III, retired psychologist, educator; b. NYC, May 15, 1938; s. Edwin Allen and Dorothy (Clark) Locke; m. Cathy Durham, Apr. 13, 2001. BA, Harvard U., 1960; MA, Cornell U., 1962, PhD, 1964. Assoc. research scientist Am. Inst. Research, 1964-66, research scientist, 1966-70; asst. prof. psychology U. Md., College Park, 1967-69, assoc. prof., 1969-70, assoc. prof. bus., mgmt. and psychology, 1998—2001, dean's prof. of leadership & motivation, 1984—96; chmn. faculty mgt. and orgn. Coll. Bus. and Mgmt. U. Md., College Park, 1984-96, prof. emeritus, 2001. Author: A Guide to Effective Study, 1975, The Prime Movers: Traits of the Great Wealth Creators, 2000; co-author: Goal Setting: A Motivational Technique That works, 1984, A Theory of Goal Setting and Task Performance, 1990, The Essence of Leadership, 1991; editor: Generalizing from Laboratory to Field Settings, 1986, Handbook of Principles of Organizational Behavior, 2000, Postmodernism in Management: Pros Cons and the Alternative, 2003; contbr. articles to profl. jours. Office Naval Research grantee, 1964, 79; NIMH grantee, 1967; Army Rsch. Inst. grantee, 1993. Fellow APA, Acad. Mgmt. (Lifetime Achievement award, Disting. Sch. Contbn. award), Am. Psychol. Soc., Soc. Indsl. and Orgnl. Psychology (Disting. Sci. Contbn. award 1993, Career Contbn. award 2005), Assn. Psychol. Sci. (J.M. Cattell award). E-mail: elocke@rhsmith.umd.edu. *The most important literary/philosophical influence in my life has been Ayn Rand. Her philosophy of Objectivism demonstrates that man's highest moral purpose is the achievement of his own happiness and that reason is his only means to achieve it. Her novels, which portray man as an heroic being, are an inspiration to every man to achieve the best within him.*

LOCKE, ELIZABETH HUGHES, retired foundation administrator; b. Norfolk, Va., June 30, 1939; d. George Morris and Sallie Epps (Moss) Hughes; m. John Rae Locke, Jr., Sept. 13, 1958 (div. 1981); children: John Rae III, Sallie Curtis. BA magna cum laude, Duke U., 1964, PhD, 1972; MA, U. N.C., 1966; DHum (hon.), Furman U., 2004. Instr. English U. N.C., Chapel Hill, 1970-72; dir. univ. pubs. Duke U., Durham, NC, 1973-79; corp. contbns. officer Bethlehem Steel Corp., Pa., 1979-82; dir. edn. divsn. & comm. Duke Endowment, Charlotte, NC, 1982-96, exec. dir., 1996-97, pres., 1997—2004; ret., 2004. Vis. prof. English Duke U., 1972—73. Editor: Duke Encounters, 1977, prospectus for Change: American Private Higher Education, 1985, (mag) Issues, 1985-96. Pres. Angier B. Duke Meml., Inc., 1997-2005, Duke Endowment, 1997-2005, Nanaline H. Duke Fund, 1997-2005, Doris Duke Trust, 1998, Jr. League, Durham, 1976, Hist. Preservation Soc., Durham, 1977, Charlotte Area Donors Forum; past pres. Comm. Philanthropy, Washington, Sch. of Arts, Charlotte; mem. legis. com. Coun. on Founds., 1997-, Washington, 1995; trustee Southeastern Coun. of Founds., 1997—, Wing Haven Found.; commr. So. Assn. Colls. & Schs., 1998—; bd. vis. Davidson Coll., Charlotte Country Day Sch., Duke U., Johnson C. Smith U.; trustee Winghaven Found. Recipient Leadership award Charlotte C. of C., 1984; Danforth fellow, 1972. Mem. Nat. Task Force, English Speaking Union, The Most Venerable Order of St. John of Jerusalem (officer sister), Colonial Dames Am., Charlotte City Club (bd. govs.), Phi Beta Kappa. Democrat. Episcopalian. Office: 100 N Tryon St Ste 3500 Charlotte NC 28202-4001 Personal E-mail: betsL@earthlink.net.

LOCKE, GARY F., lawyer, former governor; b. Wash., Jan. 21, 1950; s. James and Julie Locke; m. Mona Lee, Oct. 15, 1994; children: Emily Nicole, Dylan James, Madeline Lee. BA in Polit. Sci., Yale U., 1972; JD, Boston U., 1975. Dep. prosecuting atty. State of Wash., King County; mem. Wash. State Ho. of Reps., Olympia, 1983—94; gov. State of Wash., Olympia, 1996—2005; ptnr. Davis Wright Tremaine LLP, Seattle, 2005—. Cmty. rels. mgr. U.S. West; chief exec. King County, 1994—97; bd. dirs. Safeco Corp., Seattle, 2005—. Named First in effectiveness among Puget Sound area lawmakers Seattle Times, 1990. Democrat. Became first Chinese-Am. gov. in US history when elected gov. of Washington in 1996. Office: Davis Wright Tremaine LLP 2600 Century Sq 1501 4th Ave Seattle WA 98101

LOCKE, GENE L., lawyer; b. Conroe, Tex., 1947; BA, U. Houston, 1965; JD, South Tex. Coll. Law, 1981. Bar: Tex. 1981, US Dist. Ct. (So. Dist.) Tex., US Dist. Ct. (No. Dist.) Tex., US Dist. Ct. (Ea. Dist.) Tex., US Dist. Ct. (We. Dist.) Tex., US Ct. Appeals (5th Cir.), US Supreme Ct. Adminstrv. asst., legal counsel US Congressman Mickey Leland, 1983-85; assoc. mcpl. judge City Houston, 1986-89, city atty., 1995—; mng. ptnr. Nelson & Locke PC, Houston, 1985-95; ptnr. Mayor, Day, Caldwell & Keeton, Houston, 1995—; ptnr., Pub. Law Practice Andrew Kurth LLP, Houston, mem. mgmt. com. Adj. prof. govt. U. Houston, 1981-83; presenter in field. Fellow Am. Leadersip forum, 1991—; bd. trustees Houston Cmty. Coll. Sys., 1989-95, chmn. 1989-90; bd. dirs. U. Houston Alumni Assn., 1989-92; chmn. bd. dirs. SHAPE Cmty. Ctr., 1985-88. Recipient Freedom award outstanding svc. NAACP, 1993, Outstanding Alumnus award U. Houston Black Alumni Assn., 1995, Disting. Alumnus award South Tex. Law Sch., 1996. Mem. ABA, Nat. Bar Assn., State Bar Tex. (govt. sect.), Tex. Bar Found., Assn. Trial Lawyers Am., Houston Bar Assn. (bd. dirs. 1993—), Houston Bar Found., Houston Lawyers Assn. Office: Andrews Kurth LLP 600 Travis St Ste 4200 Houston TX 77002-3090 Office Phone: 713-220-3956. Office Fax: 713-238-7294. Business E-Mail: genelocke@andrewskurth.com.

LOCKE, GREGORY DUANE, evangelist; b. Donelson, Tenn., May 18, 1976; s. Judy Lynelle Sumner; m. Melissa Kay Biggers, Apr. 24, 1971; 1 child, Hudson-Taylor Kemle. Grad. in Theology, Amb. Bapt. Coll., Lattimore, NC, 1998; B in Bibl. Studies, Bapt. Theol. Sch. New Eng., Pascoag, RI, 2000, M in Bibl. Studies, 2001, DD, 2004. Ordained Somerville Bapt. Ch., AL., 1998, lic. Somerville Bapt. Ch., AL., 1998. Pres. and evangelist Greg Locke Ministries, Murfreesboro, Tenn., 1996—. Chaplain Rutherford County Sheriffs Dept., Murfeesboro, 2004—; founder and pres. Hudson Bible Coll., Benin City, Nigeria, 2004—; founder and pastor Global Vision Baptist Ch., Nashville, 2006—. Author: Revival: Then Fire Of The Lord Fell, 2002, Blinded By Benny, 2005, The Trap Of Christian Rap, 2005; host: Windows of Heaven. Coop. bd. mem. Good Shepherd Children's Home, Murfreesboro, Tenn., 2003—06; bd. dirs. Reaching World's Families For Christ, Inc., 2006—. Recipient Pastors award, Franklin Rd. Bapt. Ch., 1995, Outstanding Preacherboy award, Franklin Rd. Christian Sch., 1995, Golden Web award, Internet Assn. Webmasters and Designers, 2003, Innovative Contbn. award, Earle C. Job Corps, 2003; scholarship, Chick fil a Restaurant, 1997. Achievements include crusades in forty three states and a dozen foreign countries. Avocation: travel. Home: 212 Woodcraft Rd Murfreesboro TN 37127 Office: Greg Locke Ministries PO Box 1099 Murfreesboro TN 37133 Home Phone: 615-494-4698; Office Phone: 615-405-1665. Personal E-mail: greg@greglockministries.com.

LOCKE, JOHN R., music educator, director; b. Charleston, W.Va., Nov. 18, 1952; s. James R. Locke and Eunice S. Krebs; m. Susanne H. Hall, May 25, 1974; children: John Philip, Matthew Ryan. MusB in Edn., W.Va. U., Morgantown, W.Va., 1974, MusM in Music Edn., 1975; EdD in Music Edn., U. Ill., Urbana-Champaign, Ill., 1982. Grad. tchg. asst. band W.Va. U., Morgantown, 1974—75, asst. dir. band, 1975—76; dir. bands S.E. Mo. State U., Cape Girardeau, Mo., 1976—80; doctoral tchg. asst. U. Ill., Urbana-Champaign, Ill., 1980—82; prof. music U. N.C., Greensboro, NC, 1982—, dir. bands, 1982—. Founder, dir. summer music camp U. N.C.; founder, dir. The Carolina Band Festival and Conductors Conf. Contbr. articles to profl. jours. Solicitor state employees combined campaign United Way & Related Agys., Greensboro, 1990. Recipient Outstanding Tchr. of Yr. award, U. N.C. Sch. Music, 2004. Mem.: Am. Sch. Band Dirs. Assn., Nat. Band Assn. (Excellence citation 1988, 1993, 1998), Music Educators Nat. Conf. (pres. N.C. chpt. 1991—93), Am. Bandmasters Assn. (pres. 2005—06), Coll. Band Dirs. Nat. Assn. (pres. So. Divsn. 1999—2001), Phi Beta Mu (named Bandmaster of Yr. 1993), Phi Mu Alpha Sinfonia (Orpheus Award 1980, Orpheus award 1980). Home: 3803 Friendly Acres Drive Greensboro NC 27410 Office: University of North Carolina at Greensbo PO Box 26170 Greensboro NC 27402-6170 Home Phone: 336-282-2177; Office Phone: 336-334-5299. Business E-Mail: lockej@uncg.edu.

LOCKE, L. MURIEL, mathematician, educator; b. Phila., Nov. 25, 1950; d. Moses Farrar and Vivian Farrar Burton; m. Ezra Levi Locke, July 23, 1977; children: Jonathan Levi, Ezra Nathaniel. BS in Math. Edn., Temple U., Phila., 1972; MA in Math. Edn., U. NC, Charlotte, 1982; postgrad., Old Dominion U., Norfolk, Va., 1997. H.s. math tchr. Camden Pub. Schs., Camden, NJ, 1972—74; asst. systems engr. IBM, Phila., 1974—76; h.s. math tchr. Phila. Pub. Schools, 1976—77, Charlotte-Mecklenburg Pub. Schs., Charlotte, NC, 1977—85; life ins. agt. Life of Va., Charlotte, NC, 1985—86; math instr. Ctrl. Piedmont C.C., Charlotte, 1986—87, Tidewater C.C., Chesapeake Campus, Va., 1987—93, asst. prof., 1993—97, assoc. prof., 1997—. President's adv. and planning com. Tidewater C.C., Norfolk, Va., 2002—03, sci., tech., engrng. and math adv. com. (stem), 2005—. Assoc. choir dir. Temple Beth El, Suffolk, Va., 1983—; mem. Belleville Sr. Housing, Inc., Suffolk, Va., 2002—; sec. Levi Solomon Plummer Learning Ctr., Suffolk, Va., 2004—. Mem.: Am. Math. Assn. of Two-Yr. Colls., Va. Math. Assn. of Two-Yr. Colls., Math. Assn. of Am. Avocations: choir singing, reading, composing songs. Home: 2905 Sir Walter Crescent Chesapeake VA 23321 Office: Tidewater Community College 1428 Cedar Rd Chesapeake VA 23322 Home Phone: 757-483-9396; Office Phone: 757-822-5188. E-mail: mlocke@tcc.edu.

LOCKE, MICHELLE IVY, curator; BFA, U. Tex., Austin, 1967—71. Curator Art Mus. S.Tex., Corpus Christi, Tex., 1999—. Office: Art Mus S Texas 1902 N Shoreline Blvd Corpus Christi TX 78401 Office Fax: 361-825-3520. Business E-Mail: michelle.locke@tamucc.edu.

LOCKE, NORTON, hotel and construction executive; b. Mpls., May 22, 1927; s. Ben and Harriet (Markus) L.; m. Peggy Jane Smith, Nov. 6, 1959; children: Alexandria, Jonina, Elizabeth, Victoria. BS, U. Wis., 1951; MBA, Mich. State U., 1957, cert. food and beverage exec., 1984, cert. hotel adminstr., 1986, cert. food service profl., 1988. Corp. dir. food and beverage Kahler Corp., Rochester, Minn., 1970; gen. mgr., chief exec. officer Carolando Corp., Orlando, Fla., 1971-74; also dir.; gen. mgr. Radisson Muehlebach Hotel, Kansas City, Radisson Cadillac Hotel, Detroit, 1974-79; v.p., gen. mgr. White Co. Hospitality Div., Merrillville, Ind., 1979-80; dist. dir. I.D.M. Mgmt. Co., Chgo., 1980-83; v.p., gen. mgr. Skirvin Plaza Hotel, Oklahoma City, 1983-87; v.p., dir. ops. SBI Mgmt. Co., Oklahoma City, 1987-91; v.p., gen. mgr. Anaheim (Calif.) Plz. Hotel, 1991-93; corp. dir. Midwest Hospitality Mgmt., Anaheim, Calif., 1993-99. Faculty Vallencia Coll., 1971-74; adj. prof. Oklahoma City C.C., 1983-89, Century Coll., San Diego, 1996-98, ITT Tech. Coll., San Diego, 1997-99 Author: Hard Times Cook Book, World Without Milk Cookbook, Land of Milk and Honey, Heritage, A Taste of Tradition. Bd. dirs. U. Minn. Tech. Coll., 1970-75, Am. Hotel and Motel Assn. Sch., 1975-79, Detroit Conv. and Visitors Bur. Served with inf. AUS, 1944-46. Mem. Internat. Food Service Execs. Assn. (dir. 1971-74), Am. Hotel and Motel Assn. (cert.), Am. Chefs Assn., Mich. and Ind. Hotel Assn., Nat. Restaurant Assn., Hotel Sales Mgrs. Assn., Am. Fisheries Inst. (dir. 1970-71), Okla. State Hotel Assn. (Innkeeper of Yr. 1985, Bd. Mem. of Yr. 1986) Clubs: Masons (Scottish Rite 32 degree), Shriners, Rotary, SKAL Internat, Toastmasters Internat. Republican.

LOCKE, THOMAS EDWARD, JR., retired industrial engineer; s. Thomas Edward and Josephine Driskill Locke; m. Penny Ann Reich, July 27, 1980; children: Joseph Edward, Katherine Elizabeth. Student, U. Va., Charlottesville, 1963—65. Indsl. engr. Burlington Industries, Drakes Branch and Brookneal, Va., 1967—86; plant indsl. engr. J.P. Stevens, Brookneal, 1986—88; indsl. engr. mgr. The Bibb Co., Brookneal, 1988—98; indsl. engrng. mgr. Dan River, Inc., Brookneal, 1998—2006; ret., 2006. Mem. adv. bd. River Cmty. Bank, Drakes Branch, 2006—. Bd. mem. Charlotte County Indsl. Authority, Charlotte Court House, Va., 1981—87; vice chmn. Charlotte County Sch. Bd., Charlotte Court House, 1986—; deacon Drakes Branch Bapt. Ch., 1975—. With US Army, 1965—66. Mem.: Am. Mensa, U. Va. Alumni Assn. Republican. Baptist. Avocations: woodworking, automotive work, gardening, reading. Home: 3055 Tollhouse Hwy Drakes Branch VA 23937

LOCKE, VIRGINIA OTIS, writer; b. Tiffin, Ohio, Sept. 4, 1930; d. Charles Otis and Frances Virginia (Sherer) L. BA, Barnard Coll., NYC, 1952; MA in Psychology, Duke U., Durham, NC, 1972, postgrad. Program officer, asst. corp. sec. Agrl. Devel. Coun., NYC, 1954-66; staff psychologist St. Luke's-Roosevelt Med. Ctr., NYC, 1973-75; freelance writer and editor NYC, 1976-85; writer-editor Cornell U. Med. Coll./N.Y. Hosp. Med. Ctr., NYC, 1986-89; sr. editor humanities and social scis. coll. divsn. Prentice Hall, Upper Saddle River, NJ, 1989-96; profl. writer behavioral scis., 1996—. Co-author: (coll. textbook) Introduction to Theories of Personality, 1985, (book) The Agricultural Development Council: A History, 1989, (coll. textbook) Child Psychology: A Contemporary Viewpoint, 6th edit., 2006; co-editor: The Life and Work of Arthur T. Mosher, 2001. Founder Help Our Neighbors Eat Yearround (H.O.N.E.Y.), Inc., N.Y.C., chmn., 1983-87, vol., 1987-99, newsletter editor, 1992-97; reader Recording for the Blind, N.Y.C., 1978-84; vol. Reach to Recovery program Am. Cancer Soc., Bergen County, N.J., 1990-96. Recipient Our Town Thanks You award, N.Y.C., 1984, Mayor's Vol. Svc. award, N.Y.C., 1986, Cert. of Appreciation for Community Svc. Manhattan Borough, 1986, Jefferson award Am. Ins. Pub. Svc., Washington, 1986. Home and Office: 9316 Bocina Ln # G Atascadero CA 93422 Personal E-mail: volwriter@mindspring.com.

LOCKE, WILLIAM, retired endocrinologist; b. Morden, Man., Can., Mar. 16, 1916; s. Corbet and Ruby Louise (Brown) L.; m. Katherine Elizabeth Acer Russell, Sept. 29, 1945 (dec.). MD, U. Man., Winnipeg, 1938; MS in Medicine, U. Minn., Rochester, 1947. Diplomate Am. Bd. Internal Medicine. Intern Winnipeg Gen. Hosp., Manitoba, Canada, 1937-38; fellow in medicine Mayo Found., Rochester, Minn., 1938-40, 46-48; rsch. fellow Harvard U., Boston, 1948-50; staff Ochsner Clinic, New Orleans, 1950-2000, sr. cons., 1987-2000, head sect. of endocrinology, 1968—76, 1986—89; clin. prof. medicine Tulane U., New Orleans, 1968-86, prof. emeritus, 1986—, ret., 2000. Sec. Alton Ochsner Med. Found., New Orleans, 1976—81; pres. med. staff Ochsner Found. Hosp., New Orleans, 1954—55, trustee, 1978—2003, councillor, 2003—, cons. in endocrinology, 1998—. Author, co-editor: Hypothalmus and Pituitary in Health and Disease, 1972; contbr. chpts. to books and articles to profl. jours. Lt. comdr. RCNVR, 1940-46. NIH grant, 1958-62. Fellow ACP; mem. Am. Diabetes Assn., Endocrine Soc., Sigma Xi. Republican. Episcopalian. Home: 150 Broadway St Apt 1104 New Orleans LA 70118-7612 Personal E-mail: williamlocke1@cox.net.

LOCKE, WILLIAM HENRY, lawyer; b. Eagle Pass, Tex., Nov. 14, 1947; s. William Henry and Genevieve (Moss) L.; children: William Henry III, Elizabeth Madeleine. AA with honors, Del Mar Coll., Corpus Christi, Tex., 1967; BA, U. Tex., 1969, JD with honors, 1972. Bar: Tex. 1972; cert. in real estate law. Exec. dir. The Kleberg Law Firm, Corpus Christi, Tex., 1972-99, Graves, Dougherty, Hearon & Moody, Austin, Tex., 2000—. Co-dir. advanced real estate law course State Bar of Tex., 1986-87. Author: Seizure of Lender's Collateral Under Drug Enforcement Laws, 1990, Contractual Indemnity in Texas, 1991, Civil Forfeiture Actions, 1993, Shifting of Risk: Contractual Provisions for Indemnity, Additional Insureds, Wavier of Subrogation and Exculpation, 1995, Texas Foreclosure Manual, 2006, Risk Management: Through Contractual Provisions for Indemnity, Additional Insureds Waiver of Subrogation, Releases and Exculpation, 1997, 2002, Sales Contracts: A Framework for Risk Allocation, 1998, Due Diligence in the Acquisition of Income Producing Properties, 2000, Annotated Risk Management Forms, 2003, Landlord and Tenant: Risk Management Issues, 2003, Protecting Landlords, Tenants and Contractors as Additional Isureds and Indemnified Parties, 2004, Papering the Deal-Real Estate Acquisition to Development, 2004, Documenting the Office Condominium, 2005, Risk Allocation in the AIA A201 General Conditions: An Examination of the AIA in Light of Texas Law, Allocating Risk in Leases-Indemnity Insurance Release and Exculpations Condemnation, 2006, Annotated Risk Management Provisions: Indemnity and Insurance, 2007; contbg. author: Texas Construction Law, 1988. Chmn. Corpus Christi Planning Commn., 1984-85, Corpus Christi Airport Zoning Commn., 1985; bd. dirs., sec. Leadership Corpus Christi, 1984-85, Leadership Austin, 2002-06; pres. Palmer Drug Abuse Program, Corpus Christi, 1985-87, pres., 2002; treas. St. James Episcopal Elem. Sch., 1987-91. Named one of Best Lawyers in Am. Real Estate, Martindale-Hubbell, 2006—07. Fellow Tex. Bar Found. (life), Tex. Coll. Real Estate Law (dir. 1990-2001), Coll. Law of State Bar Tex.; mem. ABA, Am. Coll. Real Estate Lawyers, Corpus Christi Bar Assn. (pres. 1987-88), Rotary (bd. dirs. Corpus Christi 1987-88, sec. 1989, Disting. Svc. Above Self award 1985, Corpus Christi merit award 1987), Beta Theta Pi. Democrat. Episcopalian. Office Phone: 512-480-5736. Fax: 512-480-5837. Business E-Mail: blocke@gdhm.com.

LOCKER, RAYMOND DUNCAN, editor; b. Dunkirk, NY, Apr. 15, 1960; s. Robert Smith and Margaret Ellen (Duncan) L.; m. Debbie Elizabeth Long, July 2, 1988 (div. Oct. 9, 1997); 1 child Margaret Katherine L.; m. Margaret Ellen Talev, May 12, 2001; 1 child Abbey Quinn (Talev) L. BA in Political Sci., U. Cin., 1982; MS in Journalism, Ohio U., 1984. Reporter Lake Wales Highlander, Lake Wales, Fla., 1982-83, The Montgomery Advertiser, Montgomery, Ala., 1985-87; political reporter The Tampa Tribune, Tampa, Fla., 1987-89, Washington corr., 1989-91, polit. columnist, 1991-93, night metro editor, 1993-94, polit. editor, 1994-97, sr. editor, 1997-2000; asst. city editor LA Times, Los Angeles, Calif., 2000—01; Sacramento bur. chief The Assoc. Press, Sacramento, 2001—05; editor nat. security, intelligence USA Today, Washington, 2005—. Panelist Tampa Bay Week, WEDU-TV, 1993-2000, Bayside, WTOG-TV, 1994-2000. Roman Catholic. Home: 5832 Edson Lane Rockville MD 20852 Office: USA Today 1100 New York Ave NW Washington DC 20005 Personal E-mail: rlocker@earthlink.net.

LOCKEY, JAMES PETER, public health service officer; b. Huntington, NY, May 6, 1965; s. Robert Edwin Lockey and Nancy Helen Dion. Cert. in culinary arts, The New Sch., 1983; student, Marlboro Coll., 1983—84, Evergreen State Coll., 1984—86; BA in Social Ecology cum laude, Franklin Pierce Coll., 1989. Registered environ. health specialist Nat. Environ. Health Assn. Pub. health sanitarian technician Dept. Environ. Health, Nashua, NH, 1988—89; mgr. Office Fin. Antioch New Eng. Grad. Sch., Keene, NH, 1990; analytical chemist Amtest Labs., Redmond, Wash., 1991—92; environ. health specialist Seattle-King County Dept. Pub. Health, 1992—2002. Dir. illegal methamphetamine lab. program Pub. Health Seattle & King County, 1992—2002; air quality expert SEACAMP Program to Reduce Asthma, Seattle, 1994—2002; charter founding mem. Inter-Agy. Resource Com., Seattle, 1994—2002; dir. pub. health grand rounds sch. medicine U. Wash., 1993—2001; cons. in field, 2002—. Actor: (films) Celebrity, 1995, The Graffiti Artist, 2003; contbr. articles to profl. jours. Vol. Marlboro Music Festival, Vt., 1985; mem. conservation commn. Town of Rindge, NH, 1990; fundraiser, cmty. educator Wash. Death With Dignity, Seattle, 1990; active Chicken Soup Brigade, Seattle, 1994—96; mem. Cold Spring Harbor Whaling Mus. Soc., NY, Eagle Dock, Cold Spring Harbor; mem. guild Met. Opera, NY, 2005—. Mem.: Nat. Environ. Health Assn., Libr. Gen. Soc. Mechanics and Tradesmen NY, Vershire Sch. Alumni Orgn., Montauk Club. Avocations: sailing, mountain climbing, acting. Home: Apt 14K 225 Adams St Brooklyn NY 11201 Office: 225 Adams St Apt 14K Brooklyn NY 11201 Office Phone: 347-693-4754.

LOCKEY, RICHARD FUNK, allergist, immunologist, educator; b. Lancaster, Pa., Jan. 15, 1940; s. Stephen Daniel and Anna (Funk) L.; m. Carol Lee Madill, July 3, 1982; children: Brian Christopher, Keith Edward. BS, Haverford Coll., 1961; MD, Temple U., 1965; MS, U. Mich., 1972. Diplomate Am. Bd. Internal Medicine, Am. Bd. Allergy and Immunology. Intern Temple U. Med. Sch., Phila., 1965-66; asst. resident internal medicine Univ. Hosp. U. Mich., Ann Arbor, 1966-67, resident, 1966-68, fellow in allergy and immunology, 1969-70; asst. prof. medicine U. South Fla. Coll. Medicine, Tampa, 1973-77, assoc. prof. medicine, 1977-83, asst. dir. divsn. allergy and immunology, 1979-82, dir. allergy and immunology, 1982—, prof. medicine, 1983—, prof. pediat., 1983—, prof. pub. health, 1987—; asst. chief sect. allergy and immunology VA Hosp., Tampa, 1973-82, chief sect. allergy and immunology, 1983—, Joy McCann Culverhouse endowed chair allergy and immunology, 1997. Mem. allergenic adv. com. FDA, 1985-89. Editor: Allergy and Clinical Immunology, 1980, World Allergy Orgn. website, 2005—; co-editor: (with S.C. Bukantz) Fundamentals of Immunology and Allergy, 1987, (with S.C. Bukantz) Principles of Immunology and Allergy, 1987, JAMA Primer on Allergic and Immunologic Diseases, 1987, (with S. C. Bukantz) Allergen Immunotherapy, 1991, (with M. Levine) Monograph on Insect Allergy, 1995, (with S. Bukantz) Allergens and Allergen Immunotherapy, 1999, (with D. Ledford) Immunotherapy: A Practical Review and Guide, 2000, (with S. Kemp) Diagnostic Testing of Allergic Disease, 2000, (with S. Bukantz) Allergens and Allergen Immunotherapy Allergic Diseases, 4th edit., 2004, (with M. Levine) Insect Allergy, 4th edit., 2004; mem. editl. bd. Jour. on Allergy and Immunology, 1999-04; contbr. more than 500 articles to profl. jours. and chpts. to books; author monographs. Hon. chmn. R.I. chpt. Asthma and Allergy Found., 2004. Served to maj. USAF, 1971-73. Rrecpient Alumni Achievement award Temple U. Sch. of Medicine Alumni Assn., 1990, Outstanding Leadership in Chpt. Devel. and Patient Support, Nat. Asthma and Allergy Found. of Am. award, 1992, Cert. of Appreciation Fla. Med. Assn., 1992, medalist Fla. Acad. Scis., 2000, Disting. Svc. award Univ. S. Fla., 2001, Alumni award McCaskey HS, 2007; Named Outstanding Med. Specialist, Town and Country Mag., 1989, Claude P. Brown Meml. lectr. Assn. Clin. Scientists, ADA, 1981, Disting. Visitor Ann. Meeting of Coll. of Medicine, Republic of Costa Rica, 1979, spl. mem. Internat. Sci. Bd. Pharmacia Allergy Rsch. Found., 1992—. Fellow ACP, AAAS, AMA, Am. Coll. Chest Physicians, Am. Acad. Allergy and Immunology (chmn. com. on insects 1978-81, chmn. undergrad. and grad. edn. com. 1982-88, com. on occupl. lung disease 1982—, chmn. com. on standardization of allergenic extracts 1983-86, exec. com. mem. at large 1986-88, historian 1988-89, sec. 1989-90, treas. 1990-91, pres.-elect 1991-92, pres. 1992-93, Am. Bd. Allergy and Immunology (bd. dirs. 1993-98), World Allergy Assn. (bd. dirs. 1997—, editor web page, 2004, treas. 2006—), Soc. Allergy and Immunology of Cordoba, Argentina (hon.), John M. Sheldon U. of Mich. Allergy Soc. (councilor 1977-80, pres. 1980-82), Fla. Allergy and Immunology Soc. (sec.-treas. 1979-80, pres. 1981-82, Disting. Svc. award 2002), Southeastern Allergy Assn., Hillsborough County Med. Assn., Joint Coun. Allergy and Immunology, Clin. Immunology Soc., Fla. Thoracic Soc., Univ. Club, Tampa Yacht Club. Avocations: antique cut glass, antique tools, hunting, fishing. Home: 2708 W Marlin Ave Tampa FL 33611 Office: U So Fla VA Hosp 13000 Bruce B Downs Blvd Tampa FL 33613 Office Phone: 813-972-7631.

LOCKHART, DENNIS P., bank executive; b. Bakersfield, Calif., Feb. 1, 1947; BA in Polit. Sci. and Economics, Stanford U., 1968; MA in Internat. Economics and Am. Fgn. Policy, Johns Hopkins U. Sch. Adv. Internat. Studies, 1971. Head, infrastructure project financing Citicorp/Citibank (now Citigroup), Saudi Arabia, tng. dir. Greece, COO, comml. and consumer banking joint venture Iran, sr. corp. officer, southeast office, 1978—86, head, Latin-Am. debt-to-equity swap investment prog., 1987—88; pres. Heller Internat. Grp., 1988—2001; mng. ptnr. Zephyr Mgmt., L.P., NY, 2001—03; adj. prof. Nitze Sch. Adv. Internat. Studies, Johns Hopkins U., 2001; faculty Walsh Sch. Fgn. Svc., Georgetown U., 2003—; pres., CEO Fed. Res. Bank Atlanta, 2007—. Mem. adv. coun. Export-Import Bank; mem. bd. dirs. CapitalSource Inc., Tri-Valley Corp., Greenfield Holdings Credit Ltd., Bunge Corp., Brazil; chmn. Small Enterprise Assistance Funds. Lt. USMC, 1968—74. Mem.: Emerging Markets Pvt. Equity Assn. (mem. adv. com.). Office: Fed Res Bank Atlanta 100 Peachtree St NE Atlanta GA 30309-4470 Office Phone: 404-498-8500.*

LOCKHART, GREGORY GORDON, prosecutor; b. Dayton, Ohio, Sept. 2, 1946; s. Lloyd Douglas and Evelyn (Gordon) L.; m. Paula Louise Jewett, May 20, 1978; children: David H., Sarah L. BS, Wright State U., 1973; JD, Ohio State U., 1976. Bar: Ohio 1976, US Dist. Ct. (so. dist.) Ohio 1977, US Ct. Appeals (6th cir.) 1988, US Supreme Ct. 1993. Legal advisor Xenia and Fairborn (Ohio) Police Dept., 1977-78; asst. pros. atty. Greene County Prosecutor, Xenia, 1978-87; ptnr. DeWine & Schenck, Xenia, 1978-82, Schenck, Schmidt & Lockhart, Xenia, 1982-85, Ried & Lockhart, Beavercreek, Ohio, 1985-87; asst. US atty. (so. dist.) OH US Dept. Justice, Columbus, 1987-2001, US atty. (so. dist.) Ohio, 2001—. Adj. prof. Coll. Law U. Dayton, 1990—, Wright State U., Dayton, 1979—. Co-author: Federal Grand Jury Practice, 1996. Pres. Greene County Young reps., Xenia, 1977-79. With USAF, 1966-70; Vietnam. Named Outstanding Alumni, Wright State U., 2005; named to Xenia H.S. Hall of Honor, 2006; recipient Outstanding Contributions in Field of Drug Law Enforcement, 1989. Mem. Fed. Bar Assn. (chpt. pres. 1994-95), Dayton Bar Assn., Kiwanis (pres. 1983-84, lt. gov. 1986-87), Jaycees (pres. 1976-79), Am. Inns of Ct. (master of bench emeritus), Dayton Lawyer's Club. Methodist. Avocations: golf, tennis, hiking. Office: US Attys Office Federal Bldg 200 W 2d St Rm 602 Dayton OH 45402 Office Phone: 937-225-2910. E-mail: gregory.lockhart@usdoj.gov.

LOCKHART, JAMES BICKNELL, III, federal agency administrator; b. White Plains, NY, May 13, 1946; s. James Bicknell Jr. and Mary Ann (Riegel) L.; m. Carolyn Strahan Zoephel, June 17, 1972; children: James Bicknell IV, Grace Strahan. BA, Yale U., 1968; MBA, Harvard U., 1974. Asst. treas. Gulf Oil (E.H.), London, 1979-80; fin. dir. Gulf Oil Belgium, Brussels, 1980-81; sr. mgr. Gulf Oil Corp., Pitts., 1981-82, asst. treas., 1982-83; v.p., treas. Alexander and Alexander Services, NYC, 1983-89; exec. dir. Pension Benefit Guaranty Corp., Washington, 1989-93; mng. dir., head pvt. fin. group Smith Barney, Inc., NYC, 1993-95; sr. v.p. fin. Nat. Reins. Corp., 1996; mng. dir., CFO NetRisk, Greenwich, Conn., 1997—2001; dep. commr., COO Social Security Adminstrn., Washington, Balt., 2002—06; dir. Office Fed. Housing Enterprise Oversight, Washington, 2006—. Contbr. articles to profl. jours. Served to lt. (j.g.) USNR, 1969-72. Fellow Assn. Corp. Treas. (Eng.); mem. Assn. Pvt. Pension and Welfare Plans (bd. dirs. 1993-95). Office: Office Fed Housing Enterprise Oversight 1700 G St NW Washington DC 20552

LOCKHART, KEITH ALAN, conductor, music director; b. Poughkeepsie, NY, Nov. 7, 1959; s. Newton Frederick and Marilyn Jean (Woodyard) Lockhart. BA summa cum laude in German, Furman U., 1981, MusB summa cum laude Piano Performance, 1981; MFA in Orch. Conducting, Carnegie-Mellon U., 1983; D, Boston Conservatory, 1996; D (hon.), Northeastern U., 1998, Furman U., 2000; Doctorate (hon.), Boston Conservatory. Mem. condrs. faculty Carnegie-Mellon U., 1983-89; music dir. Pitts. Civic Orch., 1987-90; asst. condr. Akron Symphony Orch., 1988-90, Cin. Symphony Orch., Cin. Pops Orch., 1990-92, assoc. condr., 1992-95; music dir. Cin. Chamber Orch., 1992-99, Boston Pops Orch., 1995—, Utah Symphony Orch., 1998—. Guest condr. Chgo. Symphony Orch., Cleve. Orch., L.A. Philharm., L.A. Chamber Orch., Toronto Symphony, Mont. Symphony Orch., Indpls. Symphony, N.Y. Philharm., Phila. Orch., Houston Symphony, Milw. Symphony, Dallas Symphony, Orch. Sinfonica de Tucuman, Argentina, New Japan Philharm.; condr. Utah Symphony, Olympic Winter Games, 2002, Olympic Arts Festival, 2002; mem. adv. bd. Music Educators Nat. Conf.; pres. nat. adv. bd. Brevard Music Ctr., 1996—. Co-editor (arranger performance edit. opera): John Gay: The Beggar's Opera, 1985; rec. artist Christmas Songs with Mel Torme, Telarc, 1992, works by Galbraith, Alonso-Crespo, 1995, New Energy from the Americas, Cin. Chamber Orch., 1996, Runnin Wild: The Boston Pops Play Glenn Miller, 1996, American Visions, 1997, The Celtic Album, 1998, Holiday Pops, 1998, Splash, 1999, The Latin Album, 2000, My Favorite Things: A Richard Rodgers Celebration, 2000, condr. (TV specials) Salute to the Symphony, 4Utah/ABC (Emmy award). Mem.: Condr.'s Guild Am., Symphony Orch. League, Am. Fedn. Musicians. Avocations: reading, cooking, skiing, racquetball, outdoor sports. Office: The Boston Pops Orchestra 301 Massachusetts Ave Symphony Hall Boston MA 02115 E-mail: klockhart@bso.org.*

LOCKHART, MICHAEL D., manufacturing executive; b. Muncie, Ind., Mar. 25, 1949; s. Roy Eugene and Marjorie Ilene (Thornburg) L.; children: Jennifer, Jessica, Kathleen Coleman. MBA, U. Chgo., 1975. Systems analyst Needham Harper & Steers, Chgo., 1969-74; v.p. Boston Consulting Group, 1975-81, GE Credit Corp., 1981-83, GE Corp. Exec. Office, Fairfield, Conn., 1984-85, GE Turbine Bus. Ops., Schenectady, NY, 1985-87, GE Aircraft Engines, Cin., 1987-88, GE Transp. Systems, Erie, Pa., 1989-91; v.p., gen. mgr. GE Aircraft Engines, Cin., 1992-94; pres. Gen. Signal Corp., Stamford, Conn., 1994-99, chmn., CEO, Armstrong World Industries Inc., Lancaster, Pa., 2000—. Mem. Beta Gamma Sigma. Office: Armstrong World Industries 2500 Columbia Ave Lancaster PA 17603-4117*

LOCKHEAD, GREGORY ROGER, retired psychology professor; b. Boston, Aug. 8, 1931; s. John Roger and Ester Mae (Bixby) L.; m. Jeanne Marie Hutchinson, June 9, 1957; children: Diane, Elaine, John. BS, Tufts U., 1958; PhD, Johns Hopkins, 1965. Psychologist rsch. staff IBM Research, Yorktown Heights, NY, 1958-61; rsch. assoc., instr. Johns Hopkins U., Balt., 1961-65; asst. prof. psychology Duke U., Durham, NC, 1965-68, assoc. prof., 1968-71, prof., 1971-2001, chmn. dept. exptl. psychology, 1991-97, prof. dept. psychol. and brain scis., 2001—06; prof. emeritus, 2006—. Scholar Stanford U.; rsch. assoc. U. Calif., Berkeley, 1971-72; fellow Wolfson Coll., Oxford (Eng.) U., 1980-81; scholar Fla. Atlantic U., 1981; cons. in human engrng. Cons. editor: Perception and Psychophysics, 1972-92; contbr. articles to profl. jours., co-author, editor chpts. in books. With USN, 1951-55. NSF grantee, 1966-69, 79-84, USPHS grantee, 1963-69, 70-79, Air Force Office Sci. Rsch., 1983-91.

Fellow APA, Am. Psychol. Soc., Soc. Exptl. Psychologists; mem. Psychonomic Soc., Internat. Soc. Psychophysics, Sigma Xi, Phi Beta Kappa (hon.). Home: 2900 Montgomery St Durham NC 27705-5638 Office: Duke U Dept Psychology and Brain Scis Durham NC 27708

LOCKLEAR, ARLINDA FAYE, lawyer; b. Ft. Bragg, NC, Sept. 9, 1951; d. Edsel Locklear and Mary Elizabeth (Revels) Joyce; m. Gilbert Leon Hall, June 12, 1983; children: Garret, Rachel. BA, Coll. of Charleston, 1973; JD, Duke U., 1976; DHL (hon.), SUNY, 1990. Bar: N.C. 1976, D.C. 1978, Md., U.S. Supreme Ct. 1982. Staff atty. Native Am. Rights Fund, Boulder, Colo., 1976-77, Washington, 1977—87; atty., private practice Jefferson, Md., 1987—; of counsel, Native Am. Affairs, Public Policy practices Patton Boggs LLP, Washington. Guest lectr. Harvard Inst. Politics, Boston, 1983, NYU Law Sch., 1986, Colgate U., Hamilton, N.Y., 1986. Contbr. articles to profl. jours. Bd. dirs. ACLU, N.Y.C., 1984-88; Inst. for Development of Indian Law; trustee Univ. N.C. Pembroke; mem. bd. adv. Ency. of Native Am. in the 20th Century; mem. adv. panel, Winds of Change (PBS series); mem. Lumbee tribe, Cheraw Indians. Recipient Am. Heroine award Ladies Home Jour., 1984; named one of Young Women of Promise Good Housekeeping Mag., 1985; Outstanding Woman of Color award, Nat. Inst. for Women of Color, 1987; Julian T. Pierce award, Pembroke State Univ. 1994; Carpathian Award for Speaking Out, N.C. Equity, 1995. Democrat. Office: Patton Boggs LLP 2550 M St NW Washington DC 20037-1350 Office Fax: 202-457-6000, 202-457-6315. Business E-Mail: alocklear@pattonboggs.com.

LOCKLEAR, HEATHER, actress; b. Westwood, Calif., Sept. 25, 1961; d. Bill and Diane L.; m. Tommy Lee, May 10, 1986 (div. Aug. 16, 1993); m. Richie Sambora, Dec. 17, 1994 (div. Apr. 11, 2007), 1 child, Eva Elizabeth. Student, UCLA. Appeared in (TV series) Dynasty, 1981-89, T.J. Hooker, 1982-87, Going Places, 1990, Melrose Place, 1993-99, Spin City, 1999-2002, LAX, 2004, Boston Legal, 2005; (films) Firestarter, 1986, Return of the Swamp Thing, 1990, The Big Slice, 1991, Wayne's World 2, 1993, A Dangerous Woman, 1993, The First Wives Club, 1996, Double Tap, 1997, Money Talks, 1997, Uptown Girls, 2003, Looney Toons: Back in Action, 2003, The Perfect Man, 2005; (TV movies) Twil, 1981, City Killer, 1984, Blood Sport, 1986, Rock 'n' Roll Mom, 1988, Rich Men, Single Women, 1990, Her Wicked Ways, 1991, Dynasty: The Reunion, 1991, Highway Heartbreaker, 1992, Body Language, 1992, Fade to Black, 1993, Texas Justice, 1995, Shattered Mind, 1996, Too Many Lovers, 2003, Once Around the Park, 2003.

LOCKLEDGE, JACK E., retired principal; b. West Pittston, Pa., Oct. 6, 1928; s. Louis Frank Lockledge and Edna Mae Curnow; m. Mary Anne Potter, Aug. 10, 1957 (div. June 1984); children: David Evans, Jeffrey Carleton, Scott Potter. BA in Psychology, U. Ariz., 1954; BA in Fgn. Trade, Am. Inst. Fgn. Mgmt., 1955; MS in Edn., Hofstra U., 1960; student, Lehigh U., 1962-63; EdD, Nova U., 1982. Fgn. trade salesperson E.I. Dupont de Nemours, Wilmington, Del., 1955-56; tchr. Porterville (Calif.) Union H.S., 1956-57, Newbridge Rd. Sch., East Meadow, N.Y., 1958-61, Linden Sch., Doylestown, Pa., 1961-62, Hancock Elem. Sch., Norristown, Pa., 1962-63; prin. Ichabod Crane Ctrl. Schs., Kinderhook, N.Y., 1963-65, Highland (N.Y.) Ctrl. Sch., 1965-67, Canton (Pa.) Area Sch. Dist., 1967-86; headmaster St. Andrew's Elem. and Middle Sch., Annapolis, Md., 1986-91; ret., 1992. Founder Open Space Sch., 1968; bd. dirs. Laurel Hollow Condominium. Assn., 2005, 06. With USN, 1946-49. NDEA Inst. Fgn. Langs. scholar Pa. State U., U. Kans., 1962, 63. Mem. Md. Child Care Assn. (legis. com.), Wyo. Camp Meeting Assn. (bd. dirs. 2002—), Masons, Rotary (past pres.), Venice Opera Guild (grant officer), Laurel Hollow Condo Assn. (bd. dirs. 2006—, v.p.), Phi Delta Epsilon (past pres.), Gamma Epsilon, Kappa Alpha (past pres.). Republican. Episcopalian. Avocations: hiking, swimming, opera, sculpting, painting. Home: 225 Laurel Hollow Dr Nokomis FL 34275-4014 Personal E-mail: jack@lockledge.com, jelockledge@comcast.net.

LOCKMAN, STUART M., lawyer; b. Jersey City, July 18, 1949; s. Albert Korey and Edna Sally (Easton) Lockman; m. Deena Laurel Young, Dec. 27, 1970; children: Jeffrey, Alison Susan, Stephen, Karen. BA, U. Mich., 1971, JD, 1974. Bar: Mich. 1974, Fla. 1991; bd. cert. health law specialist, Fla. Ptnr. Honigman Miller Schwartz and Cohn LLP, Detroit, 1974—. Office: Honigman Miller Schwartz & Cohn 2290 1st National Bldg Detroit MI 48226 Office Phone: 313-465-7500. E-mail: sml@honigman.com.

LOCKMON, NANCY, mathematics educator; m. Bob Lockmon, May 24, 1986; children: Jenny, Lisa, Kady. BS in Edn., U. Nebr., Kearney. Math. tchr. Stuart Pub. Sch., Nebr., 1988—2005, Giltner Pub. Sch., Nebr., 2005—, Keya Paha County H.S., Springview, Nebr. Home: 2107 Tipperary Rd Aurora NE 68818 Home Phone: 402-694-6787.

LOCKNER, VERA JOANNE, farmer, rancher, state legislator; b. St. Lawrence, SD, May 19, 1937; d. Leonard and Zona R. (Ford) Verdugt; m. Frank O. Lockner, Aug. 7, 1955; children: Dean M., Clifford A. Grad., St. Lawrence (S.D.) High Sch., 1955. Bank teller/bookkeeper First Nat. Bank, Miller, SD, 1963-66, Bank of Wessington, SD, 1968-74; farmer/rancher Wessington, 1955-2000. Sunday sch. tchr. Trinity Luth. Ch., Miller, 1968-72; treas. Trinity Luth. Ch. Women, 2005—; treas. PTO, Wessington, 1969-70; treas., vice chmn., chmn., state com. woman Hand County Dems., Miller, 1978-2003, state com. woman, 2007-; SD state legislator, 1992-2000; mem. SD Dem. Exec. Bd., 1997-2000. Named one of Outstanding Young Women of Am., Women's Study Club, Wessington, 1970. Mem. Order of Ea. Star (warder, marshall, chaplain 1970-2002). Democrat. Avocations: painting, crafts, gardening, photography. Home and Office: 301 3rd St NW Saint Lawrence SD 57373-2324

LOCKRIDGE, DEBORAH ANN, minister, educator, small business owner; b. Dallas, Sept. 12, 1962; d. Lee Odis Fantroy and Georgia M. Smith; children: Shancorey Demond, Verelandria Lametris, Robert Lamond. Cert. profl. developmental lang. So. Meth. U., 2005, presch. tchr., level 1 So. Meth. U., 2005. Head start tchr. Head Start Greater Dallas, 2000—; youth min. God's Holy Ch. Christ, Dallas, 2003—; co-owner L&D Janitorial Svcs., Dallas, 2006—, Praise Tea Parties & Blessed Body Oils, Dallas, 2007—. Vol. youth program MAAS Inc., Galveston, Tex., 1997—; vol. homelss feeding program God's Holy Ch. Christ, Dallas, 1999, prison ministry, 2000, distributor healing pillows for children. Mem.: Nat. Head Start Assn. Home: 1632 Owega Dallas TX 72216 Personal E-mail: dlockjesus@yahoo.com.

LOCKSHIN, MICHAEL DAN, rheumatologist; b. Columbus, Ohio, Dec. 9, 1937; s. Samuel Dan and Florence (Levin) L.; m. Jane Toby Roberts, Sept. 2, 1965; 1 child, Amanda. AB, Harvard U., 1959, MD, 1963. Cert. in Internal Medicine, 1969, Rheumatology, 1972; Diplomate Am. Bd. Internal Medicine. Resident in internal medicine Bellevue Hosp., NYC, 1966—68; fellow in rheumatology Columbia-Presbyn. Hosp., NYC, 1968—70; from asst. prof. to prof. Cornell U. Weill Med. Coll., NYC, 1970-89; attending physician Hosp. for Spl. Surgery and N.Y. Hosp., NYC, 1970-89; dir. extramural program Nat. Inst. Arthritis & Musculoskeletal Skin Diseases/NIH, Bethesda, Md., 1989-97, acting dir., 1994-95; dir. Barbara Volcker Ctr. Hosp. for Spl. Surgery, NYC, 1997—. Prof. Cornell U. Med. Coll., N.Y.C., 1997—. Editor: Arthritis & Rheumatism, 2005-; contbr. over 150 articles to jours., chpts. to books. Mem. Am. Rheumatism Assn. (2d v.p. 1984-85), La Sociedad Chilena de Reumatologica (hon.), Alpha Omega Alpha. Achievements include research in Lupus/SLE; Antiphospholipid Syndrome; Pregnancy-Rheumatic Disease. Office: 535 E 70th St New York NY 10021-4872 Home Phone: 212-588-0028; Office Phone: 212-606-1461. Business E-Mail: volckerctr@hss.edu.

LOCKWOOD, BERT BERKLEY, JR., law educator; b. Utica, NY, Feb. 12, 1944; s. Bert Berkley and Mildred (Dowling) L.; m. Lynn Grigoli, Dec. 23, 1979; children: Matthew, Dylan, Courtney, Meredith. BA, St. Lawrence U., 1966; JD, Syracuse U., 1969; LLM, U. Va., 1971. Bar: Ohio 1981. Exec. dir. Procedural Aspects of Internat. Law Inst., NYC, 1980-89; asst. dir., sr. fellow Ctr. for Internat. Studies NYU, NYC, 1971-74; program dir. World Peace Through Law Ctr., Washington, 1974-76; assoc. dean Am. U. Law Sch., Washington, 1976-79; assoc. prof. U. Cin. Law Sch., 1979-86, prof., 1986—, dir. Urban Morgan Inst. for Human Rights, 1979—; vis. scholar U. Essex, Colchester, U.K., 1994. Adv. bd. Internat. Human Rights Law Group, Washington, 1978—, Can. Found. on Human Rights, Montreal, Quebec, Can., 1984—. Editor in chief Human Rights Quar., 1982—, Amnesty Internat. USA Legal Support Network Newsletter, 1990-93; series editor Pennsylvania Studies in Human Rights, 1988—. Coord. Group 86 Amnesty Internat., Cin., 1984—; adv. bd. Diana Project, 1994—. Recipient Sol Feinstein Alumni award St. Lawrence U., 1990; honoree Cin. chpt. ACLU, 1991. Mem. ABA, Cin. Bar Assn., Am. Soc. Mag. Editors, Internat. Law Assn. (human rights com. 1982—). Office: U Cincinnati Coll of Law Urban Morgan Institute PO Box 210040 Cincinnati OH 45221-0040 Office Phone: 513-556-6805. Office Fax: 513-556-2391.*

LOCKWOOD, GARY LEE, lawyer; b. Woodstock, Ill., Dec. 3, 1946; s. Howard and Luella Mae (Behrens) L.; m. Cheryl Lynn Wittrock, Jan. 5, 1967; children: Jennifer, Lee, Cynthia. BA magna cum laude, Iowa Wesleyan Coll., 1969; student, Albert Ludwig U., Freiburg in Breisgau, Fed. Republic Germany, 1968-69; JD, Northwestern U., 1976. Bar: Ill. 1976, U.S. Dist. Ct. (no. dist.) Ill. 1976, U.S. Ct. Appeals (7th cir.) 2000, U.S. Ct. Appeals (9th cir.) 2002. Assoc. Lord, Bissell & Brook, Chgo., 1976-85, ptnr., 1985—2005; ptnr., founder Walker, Wilcox, Matousek LLP, 2005—. Bd. dirs. McHenry Sch. Dist. 15, Ill., 1974-85, pres., 1979-80. Served to sgt. U.S. Army, 1970-72. Mem. ABA. Methodist. Avocation: sports. Home: 333 N Canal St Chicago IL 60606 Office: Walker Wilcox Matousek LLP 225 West Washington St Ste 2400 Chicago IL 60606 Office Phone: 313-244-6701. Business E-Mail: glockwood@wwmlawyers.com.

LOCKWOOD, ROBERT W., management consultant; b. Boise, Idaho, June 11, 1924; s. Walter Thomas and Elizabeth C. (Chamberlain) L.; m. Lois M. Minely, Feb. 19, 1945; children— Linda Kay Lockwood Johnson, Craig H. BS, U. Calif., Berkeley, 1949, MBA, 1950; LL.D. (hon.), Northrop U., 1971. Civilian chief mgmt. Los Angeles procurement dist. U.S. Army, 1955-56; cons. Booz Allen and Hamilton, Los Angeles, 1956-58; v.p. United Calif. Bank, Los Angeles, 1958-75; v.p. acad. affairs Northrop U., 1975-76; asst. to pres. Bradston Hurricane, 1979-80; pres. Diversified Baby Products Internat., West Covina, Calif., 1980—. Grad. prof. mgmt. Northrop U., Nat. U., San Diego. 1st lt. USAR, 1942—45. Fellow Am. Inst. Indsl. Engrs. (pres. 1971-72) Clubs: Masons.

LOCKWOOD, THEODORE DAVIDGE, retired academic administrator; b. Hanover, NH, Dec. 5, 1924; s. Harold John and Elizabeth (Van Campen) L.; m. Elizabeth Anne White, Apr. 13, 1944 (dec. Feb. 1980); children: Tamara Jane Lockwood Quinn, Richard Davidge, Mavis Ferens Borak, Serena Katherine; m. Lucille LaRose Abbot, Sept. 7, 1980. BA, Trinity Coll., 1948, LittD (hon.), 1981; MA, Princeton, 1950, PhD, 1952; LHD, Concord Coll., 1968; LLD, Union Coll., 1968, U. Hartford, 1969; LHD, Wesleyan U., Middletown, Conn., 1970. Instr. great issues Dartmouth, 1952-53; asst. prof. history Juniata Coll., Huntingdon, Pa., 1953-55, MIT, 1955-60; dean faculty Concord Coll., Athens, W.Va., 1960-64; provost, dean faculty Union Coll., Schenectady, 1964-68; pres. Trinity Coll., Hartford, Conn., 1968-81, Armand Hammer United World Coll. of Am. West, Montezuma, N.Mex., 1981-93. Chmn. Greater Hartford Consortium for Higher Edn., 1972-81. Author: Mountaineers, 1945, Studies in European Socialism, 1960, Our Mutual Concern: The Role of the Independent College, 1968, Dreams and Promises: The Story of the Armand Hammer United World College, 1997. Bd. dirs. Vols. Internat. Tech. Assistance, 1965-85, chmn., 1966-71; Bd. fellows Trinity Coll., 1962-64, trustee, 1964-81; corporator Hartford Hosp., 1978-81, Hartford Pub. Libr., 1969-81; bd. dirs. Inst. for Living, 1969-81, Edn. Commn. of States, 1969-71, Am. Coun. on Edn., 1977-81; trustee Northwood Sch., Lake Placid, N.Y., 1969-78; dir. adv. coun. Audubon Soc. Expdn. Inst., 1978-90; bd. dirs. Harry Frank Guggenheim Found., 1979—, Nepal adv. com. World Wildlife Fund, 1985-95; dir. Ars Publica, 1989-95. With U.S. Army, 1943-45. Belgian-Am. Fellow, 1959 Mem. Assn. Am. Colls. (dir. 1973-78, chmn. 1976-77, mem. project on undergrad. edn. 1981-85), Greater Hartford C. of C. (dir. 1977-81), Phi Beta Kappa, Pi Gamma Mu. Unitarian Universalist.

LOCKWOOD-BENET, MILDRED M., language educator; b. Mo., Dec. 24, 1962; d. William Lockwood and Ilia Irma Benet; m. Juan Fernandez-Gonzalez, Feb. 13, 1988; children: Camila, Guillermo, Marilia. BA in Elem. Edn., Boston Coll., 1984; M, Columbia U., 1987; EdD, U. P.R., 2003. Prof. English U. P.R., Guaynabo, PR, 1988—. Cons. Coll Bd., PR, Santillana Docentes, PR, First Hosp. Corp. Health Svcs., PR. Mem.: TESOL, Am. Ednl. Rsch. Assn. Avocations: reading, pilates, sewing. Home: S-21 California St Urb Mallorca Guaynabo PR 00969 Office: Univ PR Coll Gen Studies English Dept PO Box 23323 San Juan PR 00931 Office Phone: 787-764-0000 2186. Business E-Mail: mlockwood@uprrp.edu.

LOCKYER, BILL (WILLIAM LOCKYER), state official, former state attorney general; b. Oakland, Calif., May 8, 1941; children: Lisa, Diego. BA in Polit. Sci., U. Calif., Berkeley; cert. in sec. tchg., Calif. State U., Hayward; JD, U. of the Pacific. Past tchr., San Leandro, Calif.; Mem. Calif. State Assembly, 1973; state senator State of Calif., 1982; pres. pro tem, chmn. senate rules com., chmn. senate jud. com. Calif. State Senate, 1994—98; atty. gen. State of Calif., 1999—2007, state treas., 2007—. Active San Leandro Sch. Bd., 1968—73. Past chair Alameda County Dem. Ctrl. Com. Named Legislator of Yr., Planning and Conservation League, 1996, Calif. Jour., 1997. Democrat. Office: Calif State Treas Office PO Box 942809 915 Capitol Mall C-15 Sacramento CA 94209-0001 Office Phone: 916-322-3360. Business E-Mail: piu@doj.ca.gov.*

LOCNISKAR, DANA MICHAEL, financial consultant; b. Detroit, Dec. 10, 1944; s. John F. Locniskar and Mary Elizabeth (Mero) Caspers; m. Jacqueline A. Schroeder, Oct. 9, 1965 (div. Mar. 1978); children: Dawn Louise, Robin Anne. BS in Mortuary Sci., Wayne State U., Detroit, 1965. Fin. cons. Merrill Lynch, Detroit, 1970—, 1st v.p. to sr. v.p. pvt. banking and investment group, 1989—. Trustee Detroit Sci. Ctr.; pres. SE Mich. Planned Giving, Detroit, 1991—; bd. dirs. Alliance for Greater and Safer Detroit, 1992—; bd. trustees Detroit Pub. TV. Named one of Top 100 Wealth Advisors, Worth, 2005, Top 100 Brokers, Barron's, 2005, Top 100 Fin. Advisors, 2007. Mem. Fin. Analysts Soc., Bar-Levav Ednl. Assn., Mus. Trustees Assn., Detroit Athletic Club, Renaissance Club, Detroit Curling Club. Republican. Office: Merrill Lynch 500 Woodward Ave Ste 3000 Detroit MI 48226-5400 Office Phone: 313-446-1000. E-mail: dana_locniskar@ml.com.*

LOCRICCHIO, MATTHEW, actor, writer; s. Paul P. and Virginia Mary Locricchio; life ptnr. Richard Keohane Farley. Student, Ea. Mich. U., Ypsilanti, 1967—69, No. Mich. U., Marquette, 1966—67, Macomb County C.C., Warren, Mich., 1965—66. Theater/film/TV actor, San Francisco, 1971—81; actor/playwright NYC, 1982—99; author Marshall Cavendish Corp., Tarrytown, NY, 1998—2004. Nominating com. SAG, NYC, 2002—03; lectr. in field. Author: (book) Internat. Cookbook for Kids, 2004, (plays) Fabric of a Vision, 1993, The Legend of Sleepy Hollow, 1993; actor: (plays) Largo Desolato, 1986, Ghetto, 1992, When You Comin' Back, Red Ryder?, 1976, Of Mice and Men, 1987, (TV movie) Stone Pillow, 1985. Fund raiser Nat. AIDS Meml. Grove, San Francisco, 1996—97. Named Best Actor, San Francisco Chronicle, 1977; recipient The Yr. of Thomas Cole award, Gov. of N.Y., 1993, Gourmand World Cookbook award best book children's families, 2005, Disney Adventures Book award, Best Book Children and Family; MD Ednl. Commn. scholar, Am. Conservatory Theatre, 1972. Mem.: AFTRA, SAG, Actors Equity, Slow Food USA (assoc.). Avocations: carpentry, New York history, gardening, interior decorating.

LODDE, GORDON MAYNARD, health physics consultant; b. Lafayette, Ind., Aug. 19, 1933; s. Herman Morris and Eva Grace (Robinson) Lodde; m. Nancy Jean Caldwell, Aug. 21, 1955 (dec. Aug. 2006); children: Gordon A., Bruce C., Melissa J. BS, Purdue Univ., 1958; MS, Univ. Rochester, 1964. Health physist U.S. Army, 1959-79; health physics cons. Porter Cons., Ardmore, Pa., 1979-84; cons. engr. GPU Nuclear, Middletown, Pa., 1984-94; health physics cons. Mt. Joy, Pa., 1994—. Contbr. Handbook for Management of Radiation Protection Programs, 1992; contbg. author Ency. Occupl. Health and Safety, 1997. Scoutmaster Boy Scouts Am., White Sands, N.Mex., 1967—70, Edgewood, Md., 1975—79, post adv., 1976—80. With Med. Svc. Corp US Army, 1959—79. Decorated Commendation medal with two oak leaf clusters,,, Legion of Merit; recipient Merit award, Boy Scouts Am., 1976, Silver Beaver award, 1978. Fellow: Health Physics Soc.; mem.: N.Y. Acad. Scis., Am. Assn. Physicists in Medicine, Am. Indsl. Hygiene Assn., Am. Conf. of Gov. Hygienists, Am. Nuc. Soc. Home and Office: 742 Ferndale Rd Mount Joy PA 17552-9384 Personal E-mail: gml-hpc@msn.com.

LODDENKEMPER, TOBIAS, neurologist; b. Paderborn, Germany, Oct. 31, 1972; s. Hermann and Maria Charlotte Loddenkemper. MD, Westfalische Wilhelms U., Munster, Germany, 1992—99. MD Ednl. Commn. for Fgn. Med. Grads., 2003. Resident Westfalische Wilhelms U., 1999—2000; rsch. fellow in clin. neurophysiology Cleve. Clinic, 2000—03; fellow in pediatric neurology Cleve. Clinic Found., 2003—. Achievements include research in epilepsy. Office Phone: 216-444-2200.

LODE, TRYGVE TENNYSON, entrepreneur, actor; b. Mankato, Minn., Feb. 3, 1963; s. Tenny Dahlin and Jane (Bosch) Lode. Student, U. Denver, 1981. Owner Lode Data Corp., Denver, 1982—; pres., bd. dirs. Nyx Net, Littleton, Colo., 1997—; owner The Midgard Corp., Littleton, 1998—, Warriorquest Internat., Denver, 2000—, Valkyrie Illumination, Littleton, 2000—, Asgard Entertainment, Denver, 2001—. Exec. prodr. Inferno Film Prodns., Littleton, 1999—. Actor: (films) Dragon and the Hawk, The Shadow Walkers. Achievements include writing The Design Assistant which became the industry standard for broadband communication systems design. Avocations: weightlifting, bicycling, humor writing. Home: 6529 Lakeside Cir Littleton CO 80125-9615 Home Phone: 303-470-3200. Home Fax: 303-470-1011. Personal E-mail: trygve@trygve.com.

LODER, JOHN MARK, lawyer; b. Minot, ND, Sept. 22, 1958; s. LeRoy Albert and Ann Louise (Hennes) L.; m. Elizabeth Janet Wentz, June 1, 1985; children: Thomas A., Stephen A.C. AB, Harvard U., 1980, JD, 1983. Bar: Mass. 1985. Law clk. Judge Myron H. Bright U.S. Ct. Appeals (8th Cir.), Fargo, ND, 1983-84; assoc. Ropes & Gray LLP, Boston, 1984-92, ptnr., 1992—. Bd. dirs. New Eng. Philharm. Orch., 2003—; bd. overseers Boston Symphony Orch., 2005—. Avocations: mountain biking, music. Home: 36 Marsh St Dedham MA 02026-4306 Office: Ropes & Gray LLP 1 International Pl Boston MA 02110-2624 also: Ropes & Gray LLP 1 Embarcadero Ctr San Francisco CA 94111 Office Phone: 617-951-7405. Business E-Mail: john.loder@ropesgray.com.

LODEWICK, PHILIP HUGHES, equipment leasing company executive; b. Bklyn., Dec. 31, 1944; s. Robert John and Louise Mary (Bockhold) L.; m. Christine Helen Lobeck, July 5, 1969; children: Alyssa Erin, Kendra Blythe. BS, U. Conn., 1966, MBA, 1967. With sales dept. IBM Corp., NYC, 1969-71; officer Boothe Fin. Corp., San Francisco, 1971-80; pres. The Tradewell Corp., equipment leasing co., Ridgefield, Conn., 1980—. Gen. ptnr. Sierra Assoc. IV, San Francisco, 1981-88; CFO Wicklo's Maple Hill Farm, Ridgefield, 1983-; bd. dirs. Ancora Coffee Roasters Inc., U. Conn. Found.; chmn., bd. dirs. Project Graphics, Inc.; bd. overseers U. Conn. Bus. Sch.; chmn. bd. trustees U. Conn. Found. Trustee U. Conn. Found.; bd. dirs. St. Andrew's Luth. Ch., Ridgefield, 1979—; mem. Conn. Refugee Resettlement Commn., 1985-88; bd. dirs., treas. Family Y in Ridgefield, 1985-89; founder, dir. Discovery Ctr., 1986—; founder, pres. A Better Chance in Ridgefield, 1987—; founding dir. Internat. Forgiveness Inst., Madison, Wis. With AUS, 1967-69, Korea. Mem. Computer Lessors and Dealers Assn., Golden Bridge Hounds, L.I. Golden Retreiver Club (pres. 1979-80), Golf Club on the Internet (bd. dirs.). Republican. Lutheran. Avocations: golf, tennis, basketball, travel, reading. Home and Office: Tradewell Corp 201 Spring Valley Rd Ridgefield CT 06877-1229

LODGE, GEORGE C(ABOT), business administration educator; b. Boston, July 7, 1927; s. Henry Cabot Jr. and Emily (Sears) L.; m. Nancy Kunhardt, Apr. 23, 1949 (dec. Feb. 1997); children: Nancy Lodge Burmeister, Emily Lodge Pingeon, Dorothy Lodge Peabody, Henry, George Jr., David; m. Susan Alexander Powers, Aug. 2, 1997. AB cum laude, Harvard U., 1950; doctorate (hon.), INCAE, 1994. Polit. reporter, columnist Boston Herald, 1950-54; dir. info. U.S. Dept. Labor, Washington, 1954-58, asst. sec. labor for internat. affairs, 1958-61, U.S. del. to ILO, chmn. governing body, 1960-61; lectr. Grad. Sch. Bus. Adminstr., Harvard U., Boston, 1961-68, assoc. prof., 1968-72, prof. bus. adminstrn., 1972-91, Jaime and Josefina Chua Tiampo prof. bus. adminstrn., 1991-98, prof. emeritus, 98—. Author: Spearheads of Democracy: Labor in the Developing Countries, 1962, Engines of Change: United States Interests and Revolution in Latin America, 1970, The New American Ideology, 1975 (Ann. Book award Am. Acad. Mgmt. 1995), The American Disease, 1984, Perestroika for America, 1990, Comparative Business-Government Relations, 1990, Managing Globalization in the Age of Interdependence, 1995; co-author: Ideology and National Competitiveness, 1987, A Corporate Solution to Global Poverty, 2006; editor: U.S. Competitiveness in the World Economy, 1984. Rep. candidate U.S. Senate, Mass., 1962; vice-chmn. Inter-Am. Found., 1970-77. With USN, 1945-46. Named one of 10 Outstanding Youn Men in U.S., U.S. Jr. C. of C., 1961; recipient Arthur S. Fleming award, 1961, McKinsey award Harvard Bus. Rev., 1970, 74, Disting. Svc. award Harvard Bus. Sch., 2001; Lee Kuan Yew fellow Gov. of Singapore, 1991. Mem. Coun. Fgn. Rels., Carnegie Endowment for Internat. Peace (emeritus trustee). Office: Harvard U Bus Sch Soldiers Fld Boston MA 02163-1317 Office Phone: 617-495-6589. Business E-Mail: glodge@hbs.edu.

LODGE, HENRY SEARS, physician; b. Oct. 20, 1958; BA, U. Pa., 1981; MD, Columbia U., 1985. Diplomate Am. Bd. Internal Medicine. Intern Columbia U. Presbyterian Med. Ctr., NYC, residency; attending physician N.Y. Presbyterian Hosp., 1988—; asst. clin. prof. Coll. Physicians and Surgeons Columbia U., NYC, 1989—; pvt. practice specializing internal medicine and prevention NYC. Chmn., CEO N.Y. Physicians LLP; past pres. Presbyn. Hosp. Alumni Assn., N.Y. Clin. Soc., Soc. Practitioners of Columbia Presbyn. Med. Ctr. Mem. Am. Coll. Physicians. Office: 635 Madison Ave New York NY 10022-1009

LODGE, J. RICHARD, lawyer; b. Franklin County, Tenn., June 16, 1949; BA cum laude, U. of the South, 1971; JD, Vanderbilt U., 1974. Bar: Tenn. 1974. Asst. atty. gen. State of Tenn., 1974-76; legis. dir. U.S. Senator Jim Sasser, 1977-78; mem. Willis & Knight, Nashville, 1977—85; mem., litig. practice Bass, Berry & Sims, Nashville, 1985—. Chmn. Tenn. Dem. Party, 1983—88, Sports Authority Nashville-Davidson County, Tenn.,

1995—2000. Chmn. Nashville Legal Aid, 1981—82; mem. bd. regents U. of South at Sewanee. Named one of Power 100, Nashville Post, 2002—03. Fellow Nashville Bar Found.; mem. ABA, Tenn. Bar Assn, Nashville Bar Assn. Office: Bass Berry & Sims Suite 2700 AmSouth Ctr 315 Deaderick St Nashville TN 37238-3001 Office Phone: 615-742-6254. Office Fax: 615-742-2754. Business E-Mail: dlodge@bassberry.com.

LODGE, PATTI ANNE, state senator; b. Pitts., July 29, 1942; m. Edward J. Lodge; children: Mary Jeanne, Edward, Anne Marie. BA, Maryhurst U., 1964. Edn. media specialist Caldwell Sch. Dist., 1968-99, edn. media coord., 1980-97; pres. Windridge Vineyards, 1987—; mem. Idaho State Senate, Idaho, 2000—. Vice chair health and welfare com., jud. and rules com.; mem. commerce and human resources com., e-commerce interim com., tech. interim com., drug court coord. interim com.; del. Nat. Rep. Platform Com., 1996; cons. St. Paul's Sch., Our Lady of the Valley, 1999—. Nat. Fedn. GOP Women Resolutions, 1997—99; chair Miss Rodeo Caldwell Com., 1964—80, Canyon County Reps., 1986—88; bd. dirs. Day at the Legislature, 2000; dir. Idaho H.S. Rodeo Dist. 3, 1970—78; precinct chair Canyon County Rep. Com. 22, 1980—2000; pres. Idaho Fedn. Rep. Women, 1991—96; chair Idaho Rep. Gala Celebration, 2000; vol. Latino Voter Registration, 2000; chair bd. dirs. West Valley Med. Ctr., 1986; bd. dirs. Idaho Cath. Found., 1992—. Roman Catholic. Office: Idaho State Senate State Capitol 700 W Jefferson Boise ID 83720-0081 also: PO Box 83720 Boise ID 83720-0003 Fax: 208 459-7199.

LODICO, CHERYL MADELINE, secondary school educator; b. Bklyn., Aug. 24, 1944; d. Philip and Helen (Kutner) Miller; m. Nicholas Joseph Micucci, Feb. 13, 1969 (dec. Aug. 1987); m. Emanuel Joseph Lodico, Jan. 15, 1989; stepchildren: Diana Lynn, William Maurice. BA, Cortland State Coll., 1966; MS in Edn. in English, Queens Coll., 1971. Permanent cert. to teach English grades 7-12. English tchr. grade 9 Jerusalem Ave. Jr. H.S. North Bellmore, LI, N.Y., 1966; English tchr. grades 7, 8, 9, also grade 6 gifted Lawrence Middle Sch., LI, 1966-96; ret., 1996; tchr. ECC Acad., Bayside, N.Y., 1997-98; writer, 1998—. Sponsor, editor Creative Writing Club. Author: Counter-Attack, 2006, poetry; contbr. articles to profl. jours. Mem. Nat. Coun. Tchrs. English. Home: 14712 15th Dr Whitestone NY 11357-2509 Personal E-mail: le2345567@aol.com.

LODISH, LEONARD MELVIN, marketing educator, entrepreneur; b. Cleve., Aug. 1, 1943; s. Nathan H. and Sylvia (Friedman) Lodish; m. Susan Joyce Fischer, July 11, 1965; children: Max, Jacob, Chaim. AB magna cum laude, Kenyon Coll., 1965, LLD (hon.), 1999; PhD, MIT, 1968. Asst. prof. mktg. U. Pa., Phila., 1968-71, assoc. prof., 1971-75, prof. mktg., 1975-87, chmn. mktg. dept., 1984-88, Samuel R. Harrell prof., 1988—, vice dean Wharton West, 2001—; founding dir. Evergreen Health Group, Inc., 1984-91; founder, chmn. The Wharton Global Cons. Practicum, 1995—. Co-founder, prin. Mgmt. Decisions Sys., Inc., Waltham, Mass., 1967—85; co-founder, dir. Shadow Broadcast Svcs., Bela Cynwyd, Pa., 1991—98; bd. dirs. DVTEL, First Flavor, 1800DIAPERS, J&J Snack Foods, Franklin Elec. Pubs. Author: The Advertising and Promotion Challenge: Vaguely Right or Precisely Wrong?, 1986, Entrepreneurial Marketing: Lessons from Wharton's Pioneering MBA Course, 2001, Marketing That Works: How Entrepreneurial Marketing Can Add Substance Value To Any Sized Company, 2007; mem. editl. bd. Mgmt. Sci., Jour. Mktg. Sci., Jour. Advt. Rsch., Jour. Personal Selling and Sales Mgmt.; contbr. articles to profl. jours. Pres. Temple Beth Hillel/Beth El, Wynnewood, Pa., 1983—85, bd. dirs., 1975—98, 1999, trustee, 1995—. Recipient Odell award for Best Impact Article, 2000. Mem.: Am. Mktg. Assn. (winner 1st Paul E. Green award 1996), Ops. Rsch. Soc. Am., Inst. Mgmt. Scis. (Franz Edelman award 1987), Phi Beta Kappa. Jewish. Home: 301 Kent Rd Wynnewood PA 19096-1814 Office: U Pa Wharton Sch Dept Mktg Philadelphia PA 19104

LODOR, MARCI ANN, dietitian; b. Pitts., Pa., Aug. 2, 1965; d. Anthony Nicola Mincucci and Julia Anna Renac; m. John Anthony Lodor Jr., June 1, 2002. BS in Clin. Dietetics, Univ. Pitts., 1988. Registered dietitian Am. Dietetic Assn. Asst. food svc. dir. Morrisons & Wightman, Squirrel Hill, Pa., 1988—91; clin. dietitian Mc Keesport (Pa.) Hosp., 1991—95; cons. dietitian Pvt. Practice, Pitts., 1996—97; food svc. dir. various long term care facilities, Pitts., 1997—2000; regional dietitian Extendicare, We. & Ctrl. Pa., 2000—02; registered dietitian HCR Manorcare, North Hills, Pa., 2003; nutritionist Greater Pitts. Cmty. Food Bank, Duquesne, 2004—05; cmty. connections program coord., nutrition specialist Luth. Svc. Soc., Bellevue, 2005. Dietitian cons. Three Rivers Family Hosp., White Oak, Pa., 1996—. Bd. dir. White Oak Animal Safe Haven, 2002—. Avocations: skating, dance, flea markets, reading, theater. Home: 612 Park St Mc Keesport PA 15132 E-mail: mlodor@aol.com.

LODOWSKI, CHARLES ALAN, trade association administrator, lobbyist; b. Dallas, May 10, 1945; s. Charles Harry and Genevieve (Gowaty) L.; m. Patricia Anne Snead, May 27, 1967; children: Charles, Tracy, Amy. BBA in Fin., U. Tex., 1968. Pres. East Tex. Citizens Credit Union, Palestine, Tex., 1978-86; dist. rep. Nat. Fedn. Ind. Bus., Nashville, 1987-88, regional tng. mgr., 1991-93, div. mgr., 1989-90, 94-96, dir. sales ops., 1996—2002; pres. BLTN, Inc., Brentwood, Tenn., 2002—. Republican. Avocations: woodworking, gardening. Office: BLTN Inc PO Box 1164 Brentwood TN 37024-1164 Home: 6132 Brentwood Chase Dr Brentwood TN 37027-4443 Office Phone: 615-641-3450. Business E-Mail: cl@bltngroup.com.

LODWICK, GWILYM SAVAGE, radiologist, educator; b. Mystic, Iowa, Aug. 30, 1917; s. Gwylim S. and Lucy A. (Fuller) Lodwick; m. Maria Antonia De Brito Barata; children from previous marriage: Gwilym Savage III, Philip Galligan, Malcolm Kerr, Terry Ann. Student, Drake U., 1934—35; BS, State U. Iowa, 1942, MD, 1943. Resident in pathology State U. Iowa, 1947—48, resident in radiology, 1948—50; fellow, sr. fellow radiologic and orthop. pathology Armed Forces Inst. Pathology, 1951; asst., then assoc. prof. State U. Iowa Med. Sch., 1951—56; prof. radiology, chmn. dept. U. Mo. at Columbia Med. Sch., 1956—78, rsch. prof. radiology, 1978—83, interim chmn. dept. radiology, 1980—81, chmn. dept. radiology, 1981—83, prof. bioengring., 1969—83, acting dean, 1959, assoc. dean, 1959—64; assoc. radiologist Mass. Gen. Hosp., 1983—88, radiologist, 1988—91, hon. radiologist Boston, 1991—; vis. prof. dept. radiology Harvard Med. Sch., 1983—93. Vis. prof. Keio U. Sch. Medicine, Tokyo, 1974; chmn. sci. program com. Internat. Conf. on Med. Info., Amsterdam, 1983; trustee Am. Registry Radiologic Technologists, 1961—69, pres., 1964—65, 1968—69; mem. radiology tng. com. Nat. Inst. Gen. Med. Scis., NIH, 1966—70; com. radiology NAS-NRC, 1970—75; chmn. com. computers Am. Coll. Radiology, 1965, Internat. Commn. Radiol. Edn. and Info., 1969—73; cons. to health care tech. divsn. Nat. Ctr. for Health Svcs., Rsch. and Devel., 1971—76; dir. Mid-Am. Bond Tumor Diagnostic Ctr. and Registry, 1971—83; adv. com. mem. NIH Biomed. Image Processing Grant Jet Propulsion Lab., 1969—73; nat. chmn. MUMPS Users Group, 1973—75; mem. radiation study sect. divsn. rsch. grants NIH, 1976—79, mem. study sect. on diagnostic radiology and nuc. medicine divsn. rsch. grants, 1979—82, chmn., 1980—82; mem. bd. sci. counselors Nat. Libr. Medicine, 1985, chmn., 1987—89; dir. radiology Spaulding Rehab. Hosp., 1986—92; cons. in field. Adv. editl. bd.: Radiology, 1965—86, cons. to editor:, 1986—91, adv. editl. bd.: Current/Clin. Practice, 1972—88, mem. editl. bd.: Jour. Med. Systems, 1976—, Radiol. Sci. Update divsn. Biomedia, Inc., 1975—83, Critical Revs. in Linguistic Imaging, 1990, mem. cons. editl. bd.: Skeletal Radiology, 1977—92, Contemporary Diagnostic Radiology, 1978—80, assoc. editor: Jour. Med. Imaging, 1988—. Served to maj. US Army, 1943—46, ETO. Decorated Sakari Mustakallio medal Finland; named Most Disting. Alumnus in Radiology, State U. Iowa Centennial, 1970; recipient Sigma Xi Rsch. award, U. Mo., Columbia, 1972, Gold medal, XIII Internat. Conf. Radiology, Madrid, 1973, Founder's Gold medal, Internat. Skeletal Soc., 1990, Disting. Alumni Achievement award, U. Iowa, 2002. Fellow: AMA (radiology rev. bd. coun. med. edn., coun. rep. on residency rev. com. for radiology 1969—74), Am. Coll. Radiology (co-chmn. ACR-NEMA standardization com. 1983—90, NEMA Med. Tech. Leadership award 1995); mem.: Phila. Roentgen Ray Soc., Ind. Roentgen Soc., Tex. Radiol. Soc., Salutis Unitas, Mo. Radiol. Soc. (1st pres. 1961—62), Finnish Radiol. Soc. (hon.), Portuguese Soc. Radiology and Nuc. Medicine (hon.), Assn. Univ. Radiologists, Radiol. Soc. N.Am. (3d v.p. 1974—75, chmn. ad hoc com. representing assoc. scis. 1979—87, chmn. assoc. scis. com. 1981—87), Nat. Acad. Practice in Medicine, Am. Coll. Med. Informatics (founding), NAS Inst. Medicine, Cosmos, Harvard of Boston Club, Rotary, Alpha Omega Alpha. Home: 3900 Galt Ocean Dr Apt 307 Fort Lauderdale FL 33308-6622 Personal E-mail: lodwickmd@aol.com.

LÖE, HARALD, retired dentist, educator, researcher; b. Steinkjer, Norway, July 19, 1926; s. Haakon and Anna (Bruem) Löe; m. Inga Johansen, July 3, 1948; children: Haakon, Marianne. DDS, U. Oslo, 1952; D in Odontology, 1961; degree (hon.), U. Gothenburg, 1973, Royal Dental Coll., Aarhus, 1980, U. Athens, 1980, Cath. U., Leuven, 1980, U. Lund, 1983, Georgetown U., 1983, U. Bergen, 1985, U. Md., 1986, Med. U. NJ, 1987, Royal Dental Coll., Copenhagen, 1988, U. Toronto, 1989, U. Detroit, 1990, SC Med. U., 1990, U. Helsinki, Finland, 1992, Pacific U., 1993, U. Milan, Italy, 1994. Instr. Sch. Dentistry, Oslo U., 1952-55; rsch. assoc. Norwegian Inst. Dental Rsch., 1956-62; Fulbright rsch. fellow, rsch. assoc. dept. oral pathology U. Ill., Chgo., 1957-58; Univ. rsch. fellow Oslo U., 1959-62, asso. prof. dept. periodontology, 1960-61; prof. dentistry, chmn. dept. periodontology Royal Dental Coll., Aarhus, Denmark, 1962-72, asso. dean, dean-elect, 1971-72; prof., dir. Dental Rsch. Inst., U. Mich., Ann Arbor, 1972-74; dir. Nat. Inst. Dental Rsch. Nat. Inst. Dental Rsch., Bethesda, Md., 1983-96; dean, prof. periodontology U. Conn. Health Ctr. Sch. Dental Medicine, Farmington, 1974-82, univ. prof., 1994-97; vis. prof. U. Bern, Switzerland, 1997—2006. Vis. prof. periodontics Hebrew U., Jerusalem, 1966—67; hon. prof. Med. Scis. U. Beijing, 1987; cons. FDA, WHO, NIH; lectr. in field. Contbr. over 350 articles to sci. publs. With Norwegian Army, 1944—48. Decorated knight of Danebrog, comdr. Royal Norwegian Order of Merit; recipient War medal, 1940—45, 75th Anniversary award, Norwegian Dental Assn., 1958, prize, Aalborg Dental Soc., 1965, William J. Gies Periodontology award, 1978, Alfred C. Fones medal, U.S. Surgeon Gen.'s medal and Exemplary award, 1988, Internat. award, Swedish Dental Assn., 1989, Harvard medal, 1992, Scandinavian Pub. Health award, 1994. Mem.: ADA (Gold medal 1994, Callahan medal 1995, Spenadel medal 1995, U. Conn. medal 2003, Pierre Fauchard medal 2003), AAAS, Mass. Dental Soc. (Internat. award), Am. Soc. Preventive Dentistry (Internat. award), Scandinavian Assn. Dental Rsch., Danish Dental Assn., Am. Acad. Periodontology, Am. Coll. Dentists, Inst. Medicine NAS, Internat. Assn. Dental Rsch. (pres. 1980, Basic Rsch. in Periodontology award 1969), Internat. Coll. Dentists, Am. Assn. Dental Rsch. (hon.).

LOEB, ABRAHAM (AVI LOEB), astrophysics educator, researcher; b. Beit Hanan, Israel, Feb. 26, 1962; came to US, 1988; s. David and Sarah (Ben-Bassat) Loeb; m. Ofrit Liviatan; 2 children. BSc in Physics and Math., Hebrew U., Jerusalem, 1983, MSc in Physics, 1985, PhD in Physics, 1986. Head theoretical grp. Electromagnetic Propulsion Lab. Soreq NRC, Yavne, Israel, 1985—88; long-term mem. Princeton U. Inst. Advanced Study, NJ, 1988-93; asst. prof. astronomy dept. Harvard U., Cambridge, Mass., 1993-95, assoc. prof., 1995-96, prof. astronomy, 1997—. Mem. cosmology panel and ADP rev. com. for proposals NASA, 1993; Einstein Minerva Ctr. fellow Weizmann Inst. Sci., 2003, vis. prof. physics Einstein Ctr. Theoretical Physics, 2004—. Contbr. articles to sci. jours. Recipient Kennedy prize, Hebrew U. Jerusalem, 1987, Hoopes prize, 1996, Bergmann Meml. award, US-Israel Binational Sci. Found., 1999; grantee fellowship, John Simon Guggenheim Meml. Found., 2002. Jewish. Achievements include development of theory for origin of the first galaxies and quasars in the early universe; patent for method and apparatus for accelerating masses to high velocities; development of method to accelerate electrons to high energies with lasers; patent in field. Office: Harvard-Smithsonian Ctr Astrophysics 60 Garden St MS-51 Cambridge MA 02138 E-mail: aloeb@cfa.harvard.edu.*

LOEB, BEN FOHL, JR., retired law educator; b. Nashville, May 15, 1932; s. Ben Fohl and Frances (Paysinger) L.; m. Anne Nelson, Sept. 23, 1961 (div. 1982); children: Charles Nelson, William Nelson. BA, Vanderbilt U., 1955, JD, 1960. Bar: Tenn. 1960, NC 1975, US Supreme Ct. 1966. Law clk. Office of Sec. of Navy, 1959; assoc. Crownover, Branstetter & Folk, Nashville, 1960-64; asst. dir. Inst. Govt. U. N.C., Chapel Hill, 1964—2004, prof. pub. law and govt. Sch. Govt., 1972—2004, prof. emeritus, 2004—. Counsel to N.C. legis. coms. on motor vehicle law and transp., Raleigh, 1973-83; cons. on alcohol beverage control, 1985-89; cons. on wildlife, natural and scenic areas, 1989-93; mem. U. N.C. Faculty Coun., 1994-97. Author: Traffic Law and Highway Safety, 1970, Alcohol Beverage Control Law, 1971, Motor Vehicle Law, 1975, Legal Aspects of Dental Practice, 1977, Eminent Domain Procedure, 1984, Punishments for Crimes and Motor Vehicle Offenses, 1999; assoc. editor Vanderbilt Law Rev., 1959-60. 1st lt. US Army, 1955—57. Mem. ABA, Tenn. Bar Assn., Phi Beta Kappa, Phi Delta Phi, Pi Kappa Alpha (chpt. pres. 1954-55), Carolina Club (Chapel Hill). Democrat. Baptist. Home: 17 Bluff Trail Chapel Hill NC 27516-1603 Personal E-mail: benloeb@bellsouth.net.

LOEB, DANIEL SETH, investment company executive; b. 1962; m. Margaret Loeb. AB in Economics, Columbia U., 1984. Assoc. E.M. Warburg Pincus & Co., 1984; sr. v.p. distressed debt dept. Jefferies & Co., 1991—93; v.p. high-yield sales Citigroup Inc., 1994; founder, CEO Third Point LLC, NYC, 1995—. Chmn. Am. Restaurant Group; dir. Ligand Pharmaceuticals, Ception Therapeutics, Massey Energy Co., Fulcrum Pharmaceuticals. Trustee Prep for Prep, NYC. Named one of Top 200 Collectors, ARTnews mag., 2006. Office: Third Point LLC 390 Park Ave New York NY 10017 Office Phone: 212-907-6800. Office Fax: 212-224-7401.*

LOEB, G. HAMILTON, lawyer; s. Ferdinand M. and Margaret (Gibbs) L.; m. Bonnie Schlitz, June 9, 1973; children: Miller Anne, Maxwell Lazard. BA with high distinction, U. Va., 1973; JD magna cum laude, Harvard U., 1978. Bar: Calif. 1979, DC 1980, US Ct. Appeals (9th cir.) 1979, US Ct. Appeals (DC cir.) 1980, US Dist. Ct. DC 1981. Legis. asst. to Hon. Robert Steele U.S. Ho. Reps., Washington, 1973-74; law clerk to Hon. James Browning U.S. Ct. Appeals, San Francisco, 1978-79; assoc. Wald, Harkrader & Ross, Washington, 1981-82; ptnr. Paul, Hastings, Janofsky & Walker, LLP, Washington, 1982—, mng. ptnr. Washington Office, 1997—, vice chairperson litig. dept. Author, editor: North American Free Trade Agreement, 1993; articles editor Harvard Law Review., 1977-78. Chair, pres. Washington Area Lawyers for the Arts, 1986-92; mem. exec. com. Netherlands Am. Amity Trust, 1987—. Echols scholar U. Va., 1973. Jewish. Home: 3802 Gramercy St NW Washington DC 20016-4226 Office: Paul Hastings Janofsky & Walker LLP 875 15th St NW 10th Fl Washington DC 20005 Office Phone: 202-551-1711. Business E-Mail: hamiltonloeb@paulhastings.com.

LOEB, JANE RUPLEY, academic administrator, educator; b. Chgo., Feb. 22, 1938; d. John Edwards and Virginia Pentland (Marthens) Watkins; m. Peter Albert Loeb, June 14, 1958; children: Eric Peter, Gwendolyn Lisl, Aaron John. BA, Rider Coll., 1961; PhD, U. So. Calif., 1969. Clin. psychology intern Univ. Hosp., Seattle, 1966-67; asst. prof. ednl. psychology U. Ill., Urbana, 1968-69, asst. coord. rsch. and testing, 1968-69, coord. rsch. and testing, 1969-72, asst. to vice chancellor acad. affairs, 1971-72, dir. admissions and records, 1972-81, assoc. prof. ednl. psychology, 1973-82, assoc. vice chancellor acad. affairs, 1981-94, prof. edn. psychology, 1982—. Author: College Board Project: the Future of College Admissions, 1989; co-editor: Academic Couples: Problems and Promises, 1997. Chmn. Coll. Bd. Coun. on Entrance Svcs., 1977-82; bd. govs. Alliance for Undergrad. Edn., 1988-93; active charter com. Coll. Bd. Acad. Assembly, 1992-93. HEW grantee, 1975-76. Mem. APA, Am. Ednl. Rsch. Assn., Nat. Coun. Measurement in Edn., Harvard Inst. Ednl. Mgmt. Avocation: french horn. Home: 1405 N Coler Ave Urbana IL 61801-1625 Office: U Ill 1310 S 6th St Champaign IL 61820-6925

LOEB, JOHN LANGELOTH, JR., investment counselor, consultant; b. NYC, May 2, 1930; s. John Langeloth and Frances (Lehman) L.; children: Nicholas, Alexandra. Grad., Hotchkiss Sch., 1948; AB cum laude, Harvard, 1952, MBA, 1954; LL.D. (hon.), Georgetown U. With Loeb, Rhoades & Co., NYC, from 1956, gen. ptnr., mem. mgmt. com., 1964-73, mng. ptnr., pres., 1971-73, ltd. ptnr., 1973-84; chmn. bd. Holly Sugar Co., Colo., 1969-71; amb. to Denmark Copenhagen, 1981-83; chmn. John L. Loeb, Jr. Assocs., NYC, 1984—. U.S. del. to 38th session Gen. Assembly of UN; spl. advisor environ. matters to Gov. Nelson A. Rockefeller, 1967-73; chmn. Gov. N.Y. Coun. Environ. Advisors, 1970-75, Langeloth Found. 1996-2001, trustee 1978-; trustee Winston Churchill Found., 1975—, pres. 1981-2003, chmn. 2003—; trustee Ednl. Testing Svc., Princeton, N.J., 1986-93. Bd. trustee Monefiore Hosp. and Med. Ctr., Mus. City, NY, 1962—94; bd. trustees John and Frances L. Loeb Found., 1957—98; mem. vis. com. Harvard Bus. Sch., 1968—79; mem. Harvard Vis. Com. Loeb Drama Ctr., 1988—94, N.Y. State Coun. on the Arts, 1996—; pres. John L. Loeb Jr. Found., 1963—; bd. dirs. Am.-Scandinavian Found., 2002—. Lt. USAF, 1954—56. Lord of the Manor of Brinsley; Decorated Grand Cross of the Order of Dannebrog (Denmark); recipient Lee Max Friedman award Am. Jewish Hist. Soc., Disting. Patriot award SAR; Hon. Comdr. of the Most Excellent Order of the Brit. Empire. Mem. Downtown Assn. (N.Y.C.), Harvard Club, Century Country Club, Sleepy Hollow Club (Westchester, N.Y.), Buck's Club, Brooks's Club, Hurlingham Club (London), Royal Danish Yacht Club (Copenhagen), Royal Swedish Yacht Club (Stockholm), Lyford Cay Club (Nassau, Bahamas), Soc. Colonial Wars, NY. Home: Ridgeleigh 194 Anderson Hill Rd Purchase NY 10577-2101 Office: John L Loeb Jr Assocs Inc 50 Broad St Rm 1137 New York NY 10004-2307 Office Phone: 212-509-1500. E-mail: johnloeb@aol.com.

LOEB, JOHN NICHOLS, physician, educator; b. NYC, Dec. 17, 1935; s. Robert Frederick and Emily Guild (Nichols) L. AB summa cum laude, Harvard Coll., 1957; MD summa cum laude, Harvard Med. Sch., 1961. Intern in medicine Mass. Gen. Hosp., Boston, 1961-62; asst. resident in medicine Presbyn. Hosp., NYC, 1962-63, chief resident in medicine, 1965-66, asst. physician, 1966—67, asst. attending physician, 1967-73, assoc. attending physician, 1973-79, attending physician, 1979—98, secy. medical bd., 1976—77; attending physician NY-Presbyn. Hosp., 1998—; rsch. assoc. lab. of molecular biology Nat. Inst. Arthritis and Metabolic Diseases, NIH, Bethesda, Md., 1963-65; NIH trainee in metabolism Columbia U. Coll. Phys. and Surg., 1966—67; instr. medicine Columbia U., NYC, 1965—66, asst. prof. medicine, 1967—73, assoc. prof. medicine, 1973-79, prof. medicine, 1979—2004, prof. emeritus medicine, 2005—, spl. lectr. in medicine, 2005—, assoc. chmn. rsch. dept. medicine, 1997—2003, vice chmn. for acad. affairs, 2003—04. Vis. chief resident Mass. Gen. Hosp., Boston, Mass., 1966; asst. vis. physician Harlem Hosp., NYC, 1968-73; adj. asst. prof. Rockefeller U., NYC, 1970-75, adj. assoc. prof., 1975-83; vis. prof. dept. internal medicine Pahlavi U., Shiraz, Iran, 1974, 77; vis. prof. dept. medicine U. Cape Town, 1982; sec. med. bd. Presbyn. Hosp., 1976-1977; mem. Med. Coun. of the Iran Found., 1974-75; councillor Harvard Med. Alumni Assn., 1982-85; dir. Royal Soc. Medicine Found., NY, 1984-95; praktikant Friedrich Miescher Inst., Basel, Switzerland, 1986. Contbr. articles to profl. jours. Elder Presbyn. Ch., 1982—; ruling elder Madison Ave. Presbyn. Ch., NYC, 1983-88; mem., bd. dirs. Amateur Chamber Music Players, Inc., 1984-99, vice chmn., 1985-99, mem. adv. coun., 1999-2006. Lt. comdr. grade surgeon USPHS, 1963-65 Recipient Boylston medal Harvard U., 1961, P&S Club Tchg. award, 1969, Career Scientist award Irma T. Hirschl Charitable Trust, 1973-77, Disting. Tchr. award Coll. of Physicians and Surgeons, Columbia U., 1974, Tchg. award citation, 1975, House Staff Recognition award Presbyn. Hosp., 2004, Disting. Svc. award, Coll. Physicians and Surgeons, Columbia U., 2007; grantee NIH, 1967-99, MERIT award, 1988-99. Fellow AAAS, ACP, NY Acad. Medicine, Royal Soc. Medicine; diplomate Am. Bd. Internal Medicine; mem. Assn. Am. Physicians, Practitioners' Soc. NY (sec. 1973, 74, pres. 1985, 86), Am. Soc. Clin. Investigation, Am. Fedn. Clin. Rsch., Harvey Soc., Am. Clin. and Climatological Assn., Century Assn., Soc. for Exptl. Biology and Medicine, Endocrine Soc., Soc. Gen. Physiologists, Peripatetic Club (councillor 1987-94), Interurban Clin. Club, Charaka Club (pres. 1984-85), Am. Philos. Soc. (councillor 2006—), Phi Beta Kappa, Alpha Omega Alpha. Presbyterian. Achievements include research in mechanisms of hormone action, physical chemistry of receptor-ligand interactions and their quantitative relationship to biological response, and regulation of glucose and monovalent cation transport. Home: 80 Haven Ave New York NY 10032-2617 Office: Columbia Univ Dept Medicine 630 W 168th St New York NY 10032-3702

LOEB, LARRY MORRIS, communications company executive; b. Morgan City, La., Oct. 13, 1940; s. Richard Levy and Pauline Endler (Forgotston) L.; m. Maria-Luisa Elvira Achino, Apr. 5, 1968; children: Maddalena, Leonora. BA, Tulane U., 1962; postgrad., Columbia U., 1962-63, JD, 1966. Bar: NY 1967. Staff atty. ABC, Inc., NYC, 1966—68, gen. atty., 1968—80; v.p., dir. bus. affairs ABC Video Enterprises Inc., NYC, 1980—86; v.p. legal and bus. affairs Video Enterprises and Pub. Capital Cities/ABC, Inc., NYC, 1986—93; v.p. cable and internat. devel., legal ABC, Inc., NYC, 1993-97; sr. counsel, asst. sec. The Hearst Corp., NYC, 1998—. Mgmt. com. A & E Networks, NYC, 1981-96, Lifetime, 1983-85; adv. coun. TMM (RTL2), 1996-97; mng. dir. Hearst Enterprises, B.V., 2000-2003; bd. dirs. SCMP Hearst Pubs., Hong Kong, Edimar Ltd., Cyprus, Hearst Entertainment Latin Am., Inc. Bd. dirs. Theater for a New Audience, N.Y.C., 1981—. Woodrow Wilson fellow, 1962-63. Mem. N.Am. Nat. Broadcasters Assn. (pres. 1996-97), European Broadcasting Union (legal com. 1973-97). Democrat. Jewish. Avocations: piano, theater, reading, travel, languages. Home: 164 W 94th St New York NY 10025-7015 Office: 300 W 57th St New York NY 10019 Office Phone: 212-649-2027. Business E-Mail: lmloeb@hearst.com.

LOEB, LISA, singer, lyricist; b. Bethesda, Md., 1968; BA in Comparative Lit., Brown U., 1990; student, Berklee Sch. Music. Founder Lisa Loeb and Nine Stories, 1990. Singer, musician: (albums) Tails, 1995, Firecracker, 1997 (Grammy nomination), Cake and Pie, 2002, Hello Lisa, 2002; (single): Stay (Reality Bites soundtrack), 1994 (Grammy nomination, 1994, Critic's Choice award, 1995), (children's albums): Catch the Moon (with Elizabeth Mitchell), 2004; co-host: (TV series) Dweezil & Lisa, 2004. Office: Artemis Records 130 5th Ave 7th Fl New York NY 10011

LOEB, MARSHALL ROBERT, journalist; b. Chgo., May 30, 1929; s. Monroe Harrison and Henrietta (Benjamin) L.; m. Elizabeth Peggy Loewe, Aug. 14, 1954; children: Michael, Margaret. BJ, U. Mo., 1950; postgrad., U. Goettingen, Germany, 1950-51. Reporter Garfield News and Austinite, Chgo., 1944-45; reporter, columnist Garfieldian and Austin News, Chgo., 1946-47, 49-51; reporter Columbia Missourian, 1948-50; staff corr. UP, Frankfurt, Germany, 1952-54; reporter St. Louis Globe-Democrat, 1955-56; contbg. editor Time mag., 1956-61, assoc. editor, 1961-65, sr. editor, 1965-80, econs. editor and columnist, 1978-80; mng. editor Money Mag., 1980-84; editor Time Inc. Mag. Devel., 1984-86; mng. editor Fortune,

1986-94, editor-at-large, 1994-95, columnist, 1996; editor Columbia Journalism Rev., 1997-99; columnist, adv. bd. mem. Marketwatch website, 1999—. Daily commentator CBS Radio Network; assoc. fellow Yale U., Berkeley Coll., 1977—; bd. dirs. priceline.com. Author (with William Safire): Plunging Into Politics, 1962; author: Marshall Loeb's Money Guide, 1983, ann. edits., 1985—94, Money Minutes, 1986, Lifetime Financial Strategies, 1996, 52 Weeks to Financial Fitness, 2001; editor (with Andrew Leckey): Best Business Stories of the Year, 2001. Bd. dirs. Nat. Neurofibromatosis Found., Recording for the Blind and Dyslexic; bd. advisors Knight-Bagehot Fellowship. Recipient Gerald M. Loeb award UCLA Sch. Mgmt., 1974, Lifetime Achievement award, 1996, Journalism medal U. Mo., 1988, TJFR Bus. Journalism Luminaries award 1990, 2000, Disting. Achievement award Soc. Am. Bus. Editors and Writers, 1998. Mem. Econ. Club of N.Y., Coun. Fgn. Rels., Am. Soc. Mag. Editors (pres. 1988-90), Overseas Press Club Am. (v.p.). Jewish. Home: 31 Montrose Rd Scarsdale NY 10583-1129 Office: MarketWatch dot com 1697 Broadway New York NY 10019-2925 Office Phone: 212-975-8694. Business E-Mail: mloeb@marketwatch.com.

LOEB, SUSANNA, education educator; BSCE, Stanford U., 1988, BA in Polit. sci., 1988; MPP in Pub. Policy studies, U. Mich., 1994, PhD in Econs., 1998. Rsch. asst. U. Mich. Sch. Edn., 1991—93; rsch. asst. dept. econs. U. Mich., 1993—96; rsch. fellow Population Studies Ctr., U. Mich., 1995—; rsch. asst. U. Mich. Sch. Edn., 1996—; asst. prof. U. Calif., Davis, 1998—99; asst. prof. edn. Stanford (Calif.) U., Calif., 1999—. Rsch. cons. Inst. for Rsch. on Women and Gender, U. Mich., 1997—. Office: Stanford U Sch Edn 485 Lasuen Mall Stanford CA 94305-3096

LOEB, THOMAS WOLF, plastic surgeon; b. June 20, 1954; MD, Wash. U., St. Louis, 1980. Cert. Plastic Surgery. Intern, gen. surgery NYU, 1980—81, resident, 1981—82; resident, plastic surgery Booth Meml. Hosp./NYU, Flushing, 1982—84; resident Baylor Coll. Medicine, Houston, 1984—86; private practice NYC. Quoted in numerous magazines including, Vogue, Allure, Elle, Mirabella and Glamour., regular gueat appearances on CBS Evening News NBC, MSNBC, Fox News, Good Day NY, American Journal, Inside Edition, Extra and The View. Named Top Doctor, NY Mags. Mem.: Am. Soc. Plastic Surgeons. Achievements include being a world renowned plastic surgeon. Highly sought after by celebrities and non-celebrities; created a revolution in rhinoplasty in 1998, transformed Paula Jones' nose; named among the ten best eye surgeons in the world. Office: 994 Fifth Ave #1C New York NY 10028 Office Phone: 212-327-3700. Office Fax: 212-327-4506.*

LOEBSACK, DAVE, congressman, former political science professor; b. Mount Vernon, Iowa, Dec. 23, 1952; m. Terry Loebsack; children: Jennifer, Sarah stepchildren: Marcos Melendez, Madeleine Melendez. BS in Polit. Sci., Iowa State U., 1974, MA in Polit. Sci., 1976; PhD in Polit. Sci., U. Calif. Davis, 1985. Prof. polit. sci. Cornell Coll., 1982—2006; mem. US Congress from 2nd Iowa dist., 2007—, mem. armed svcs. com., edn. & labor com. Former chair Cornell Coll. Politics Dept.; former pres. Iowa Conf. Polit. Scientists; bd. mem. UN Am. Linn County coord. Howard Dean for Pres., 2000; local leader Bill Bradley Presdl. Campaign, 2000; chair Linn Phoenix Club, 2002—05. Mem.: Humanities Iowa Speakers Bur. Democrat. Methodist. Office: 1513 Longworth House Office Bldg Washington DC 20515 also: 125 S Dubuque St Iowa City IA 52240*

LOEFFLER, FRANK JOSEPH, physicist, educator; b. Ballston Spa, NY, Sept. 5, 1928; s. Frank Joseph and Florence (Farrell) Loeffler; m. Eleanor Jane Chisholm, Sept. 8, 1951; children: Peter, James, Margaret, Anne Marie. BS in Engring. Physics, Cornell U., 1951, PhD in Physics, 1957. Rsch. assoc. Princeton U., 1957-58; mem. faculty Purdue U., Lafayette, Ind., 1958-97, prof. physics, 1962-97, prof. emeritus, 1997—. Vis. prof. Hamburg U., Germany, 1963—64, Heidelberg U., Germany, CERN, Switzerland, 1971, Stanford U. Linear Accelerator Ctr., 1980—83, U. Hawaii, 1985—86; trustee, mem. exec. com., chmn. high energy com. Argonne Univs. Assn., 1972—76, 1978—79, mem. com. fusion program, 1979—80. Contbr. articles to profl. jours. Recipient Antarctic Svc. medal, NSF/USN, 1990, Ruth and Joel Spira award for Outstanding Tchg., 1992. Fellow: Am. Phys. Soc., Sigma Xi, Tau Beta Pi. Achievements include development of undergraduate physics laboratory experiements and lecture demonstration apparatus; research in astophysics; high energy gamma ray astronomy; high energy particle interactions and on-line data acquisitions-processing systems; established gamma ray astronomy lab at South Pole, Antarctica. Home: 341 Hokulani St Makawao HI 96768-8612 Office: Purdue U Dept Physics Lafayette IN 47907 Home Phone: 808-572-8804; Office Phone: 808-572-8804. Personal E-mail: fjloef@aol.com.

LOEFFLER, MARTIN H., electronics executive; Pres. Amphenol Corp., Wallingford, Conn., 1987—, CEO, 1997—, chmn., 1997—. Office: Amphenol 358 Hall Ave Wallingford CT 06492 Office Phone: 203-265-8900. Fax: 203-265-8516.*

LOEFFLER, TOM (THOMAS GILBERT LOEFFLER), lobbyist, former congressman; b. Fredericksburg, Tex., Aug. 1, 1946; s. Gilbert and Marie L.; m. Nancy, 1987, children: Lance, Cullen, Lauren. BBA, U. Tex., 1968, JD, 1971. Bar: Tex. 1971. Lawyer, rancher, Tex.; legal counsel US Dept. Commerce, 1971-72; chief legis. counsel to Senator John Tower US Senate, 1972-74; dep. for congl. affairs Fed. Energy Adminstrn., 1974-75; spl. asst. to Pres. for legis. affairs The White House, Washington, 1975-77; counsel Tenneco, Inc., Washington, 1977; mem. Banister & Loeffler, Kerrville, Tex., 1977-78, US Congress from 21st Tex. Dist., 1979—87; mem. com. on appropriations, com. on energy & commerce, com. on budget, chief dep. whip; founder, chmn., sr. ptnr. The Loeffler Group, San Antonio, 1987—. Prin. coord. for Ctrl. Am. The White House, 1987. Bd. regents U. Tex. System, 1989—2001. Named Outstanding Alumnus, U. Tex. Law Sch., 2002, U. Tex., 2003. Mem. Am. Bar Assn., Tex. Bar Assn. Republican. Lutheran. Office: The Loeffler Group 755 E Mulberry Ste 200 San Antonio TX 78212 E-mail: tloeffler@loefflerlp.com.

LOEHLIN, JOHN CLINTON, psychologist, educator; b. Ferozepore, India, Jan. 13, 1926; s. Clinton Herbert and Eunice (Cleland) L.; m. Marjorie Leafdale, Jan. 2, 1962; children: Jennifer Ann, James Norris. AB, Harvard U., 1947; PhD, U. Calif., Berkeley, 1957. With rsch. dept. McCann-Erickson, Inc., Cleve., 1947-49; instr. to asst. prof. psychology U. Nebr., Lincoln, 1957-64; faculty U. Tex., Austin, 1964—69, prof. psychology and computer scis., 1969-92, prof. emeritus, 1992—. Author: Computer Models of Personality, 1968, Latent Variable Models, 1987, Genes and Environment in Personality Development, 1992; co-author: Race Differences in Intelligence, 1975, Heredity, Environment and Personality, 1976, Introduction to Theories of Personality, 1985. With USNR, 1945-47, 51-53. Fellow Ctr. Advanced Study Behavioral Scis., 1971-72. Fellow Am. Psychol. Soc.; mem. Behavior Genetics Assn., Soc. Multivariate Exptl. Psychology. Home: 304 Almarion Dr Austin TX 78746-5644 Office: U Tex Dept Psychology 1 U Station A8000 Austin TX 78712-0187 Home Phone: 512-327-2159; Office Phone: 512-475-7008. E-mail: loehlin@psy.utexas.edu.

LOEHWING, LORD RUDI CHARLES, publicist, radio broadcasting executive, journalist; b. Newark, July 26, 1957; s. Rudy Charles Sr. and Joan Marie (Bell) L.; m. Lady Claire Popham, Sept. 4, 1987; children: Aspasia Joyce, Tesia Victoria, Rudi Douglas, Anna Marie, Samantha Diane, Ian Ryan. Student, Biscayne U., 1975, Seton Hall U., 1977, Hubbard U., 1980. Announcer radio stas. WNEW-FM, WHBI-FM, NYC, 1970—72; producer Am. Culture Entertainment, Belleville, N.J., 1973-74, exec. producer Hollywood, Calif., 1988-94; CEO Broadcaster's Network Internat., La Crescenta, Calif., 1989—, U.K., 1989—. Co-founder BNI Comms., L.A., 1989; bd. dirs. First Break, Hollywood, also U.K., 1988—; founder, pres. World Inst. Natural Health Scis., 2006. Author: Growing Pains, 1970; dir. exec. producer TV documentaries and comml. advertisements, 1983; patentee in field. Bd. dirs. Civic Light Opera of South Bay Cities, 1998—, L.A. Civic Light Opera, Tax Edn. Assn., Just Say No to Drugs, L.A., 1989, Hands Across the Atlantic, Internat. Country Top 10, The Rock of Russia, Job Search, Hollywood, U.K. and Russia, Strategic Bus. Alliances Network. Named Youngest Comml. Radio Producer and Announcer for State of N.Y., Broadcaster's Network Internat., 1972 Mem. Nat. Press Club, Broadcasters Network Assn. (bd. dirs. 1977—), Profl. Bus. Comms. Assn. (founder 1989), BNI News Bur. (chmn. 1991—), Civic Light Opera of South Bay Cities (bd. dirs. 1996—), Friars Club. Avocations: music, writing, photography, martial arts (recipient awards). Home: Leicester House 11487 Mt Gleason Ave Los Angeles CA 91042-1229 Office: Broadcasters Network Internat Ltd Leicester House 11417 Mt Gleason Ave Tujunga CA 91042 Business E-Mail: rudi@loehwing.com.

LOENGARD, JOHN BORG, photographer, editor; b. NYC, Sept. 5, 1934; s. Richard Otto and Margery (Borg) L.; m. Eleanor Sturgis, Aug. 25, 1963 (div. 1987); children: Charles, Jennifer, Anna BA, Harvard Coll., Cambridge, Mass., 1956. Staff photographer Life mag., NYC, 1961-72, picture editor, 1973-87; freelance photographer, 1987—; columnist Popular Photography mag., NYC, 1987, Am. Photographer, NYC, 1988—. Author: Pictures Under Discussion, 1987, Life Classic Photographs: A Personal Interpretation by John Loengard, 1988, Life Faces: Commentary by John Loengard, 1991, Celebrating the Negative, 1994, Georgia O'Keeffe at Ghost Ranch, 1995, Life Photographers: What They Saw, 1998, As I See It, 2005, Georgia O'Keeffe Paintings/John Loengard Photographs, 2006, Images and Imagination, Georgia O'Keefe, 2007; cons. editor: The Great Life Photographers, 2004; essays in Life mag., The Shakers, 1967, Georgia O'Keeffe, 1968, Vanishing Cowboys, 1970, Photographers Over 80, 1982, Henry Moore, 1983, Interstate 80, 1989. Recipient Ansel Adams award Am. Soc. Mag. Photographers, 1987, Lifetime Achievement award Photog. Adminstrs., Inc., 1996, Henry Luce Lifetime Achievement award Time Inc., 2004; named one of Most Influential People in Photography, Am. Photo Mag., 2005. Home: 20 W 86th St New York NY 10024-3604 Personal E-mail: loenpics@aol.com.

LOENGARD, RICHARD OTTO, JR., lawyer; b. NYC, Jan. 28, 1932; s. Richard Otto and Margery (Borg) L.; m. Janet Sara Senderowitz, Apr. 11, 1964; children: Maranda C., Philippa S.M. AB, Harvard U., 1953, LLB, 1956. Bar: N.Y. 1956, U.S. Dist. Ct. (so. dist.) N.Y. 1958. Assoc. Fried, Frank, Harris, Shriver & Jacobson, predecessor firms, NYC, 1956-64, ptnr., 1967-97; of counsel Fried, Frank, Harris, Shriver & Jacobson, NYC, 1997—; dep. tax legis. counsel, spl. asst. internat. tax affairs U.S. Dept. Treasury, Washington, 1964-67. Mem. Commerce Clearing House, Riverwoods, Ill. Editl. bd. Tax Transaction Libr., 1982-94; contbr. articles to profl. publs. Fellow Am. Coll. Tax Counsel; mem. ABA, N.Y. State Bar Assn. (exec. com. tax sect. 1984—, sec. 1994-95, vice chair 1995-97, chair 1997-98), Assn. Bar City N.Y. Office: Fried Frank Harris Shriver & Jacobson 1 New York Plz New York NY 10004-1980 Business E-Mail: loengri@ffhsj.com.

LOEPERE, CAROL COLBORN, lawyer; b. Mpls., Oct. 6, 1959; BA in History, Radcliffe Coll., Harvard U., 1981; JD, NYU, 1984. Bar: Md. 1985, DC 1985, US Ct. Appeals 7th Cir. 1986. Assoc. Reed Smith LLP, Washington, 1984—92, ptnr., 1992—, also head health care group. Mem.: Women's Bar Assn. of DC, Am. Health Lawyers Assn., DC Bar Assn. Office: Reed Smith LLP 1301 K St NW, Ste 1100 - East Tower Washington DC 20005 Office Phone: 202-414-9216. Office Fax: 202-414-9299. Business E-Mail: cloepere@reedsmith.com.

LOERKE, WILLIAM CARL, art historian, educator; b. Toledo, Aug. 13, 1920; s. William Carl and Anna Louisa (Stallbaum) L.; m. Helen Trautmann, 1944; children— Anna Hurd, Timothy, Eric, Alison, Lisa Huff, Ellen, Martha. BA, Oberlin Coll., 1942; M.F.A., Princeton U., 1948, PhD, 1957. Acad. positions history of art Brown U., 1949-59; assoc. prof. Bryn Mawr Coll., 1959-64; prof. art history U. Pitts., 1964-71, chmn. fine arts dept., 1964-69; prof. Byzantine art Harvard U., Dumbarton Oaks Research Library, 1971-88, prof. emeritus, 1988—; dir. studies Ctr. Byzantine Studies, 1971-77; vis. prof. Cath. U. Am., 1978-88. Vis. prof. U. Md., 1988-92; mem. adv. bd. Ctr. for Advanced Study in Visual Arts, Nat. Gallery Art, Washington, 1979-82, 89-92, 97-2000. Co-author: The Place of Book Illumination in Byzantine Art, Princeton, 1975, Monasticism and the Arts, 1984, Codex Rossanensis, Commentarium, Rome, 1987, Architecture: Fundamental Issues, N.Y., 1990; contbr. Byzantine East, Latin West: Art Historical Studies in Honor of Kurt Weitzman, 1995; contbr. articles to profl. jours.; contbr. to Oxford Dictionary of Byzantium, 1991. Served with USNR, 1943-46. Jr. fellow Princeton U., 1946-48, Dumbarton Oaks Harvard U., 1948-49, Danforth Tchr. fellow, 1956-57; Fulbright Rsch. scholar Am. Acad. Rome, 1952-53; recipient A.K. Porter prize Coll. Art Assn., 1961. Mem. Coll. Art Assn., Medieval Acad. Am., Soc. Fellows, Am. Acad. at Rome, Internat. Ctr. Med. Art. Home: 3010 N Ridge Rd C504 Ellicott City MD 21043

LOESCH, ARTHUR Z., environmental scientist, educator; b. Lvov, Ukraine, June 29, 1942; s. Casimir Loesch and Irene Zlobnicki; m. Carolyn Rovelli, Nov. 18, 1948; children: Eric Casimir, Gregory M. PhD, U. Chgo., 1972. Prof. SUNY, Albany, 1973—2007. Vis. prof. Fla. State U., Tallahassee, 1980—85. Contbr. articles to profl. jours. Fellow, NDEA, 1968—71, Nat. Ctr. Atmospheric Rsch., Boulder, Colo., 1972—73; grantee, NSF, 1973—95. Mem.: Am. Meteorol. Soc. (assoc.). Liberal. Roman Catholic. Achievements include research in nonlinear atmospheric dynamics. Avocations: skiing, bicycling, hiking, music. Home Phone: 518-456-0717; Office Phone: 518-442-4560. Personal E-mail: azl@atms.albany.edu. E-mail: azl@atmos.albany.edu.

LOESCH, KATHARINE TAYLOR, communications educator, theater educator; b. Berkeley, Calif., Apr. 13, 1922; d. Paul Schuster and Katharine (Whiteside) Taylor; m. John George Loesch, Aug. 28, 1948; 1 child, William Ross. Student, Swarthmore Coll., 1939-41, U. Wash., 1942; BS, Columbia U., 1944, MA, 1949; grad., Neighborhood Playhouse Sch., 1946; postgrad., Ind. U., 1953; PhD, Northwestern U., 1961. Instr. speech Wellesley (Mass.) Coll., 1949-52, Loyola U., Chgo., 1956; asst. prof. English and speech Roosevelt U., Chgo., 1957, 62-65; assoc. prof. comm. and theatre U. Ill., Chgo., 1968-87, assoc. prof. emeritus, 1987—. Contbr. articles to profl. jours.; author numerous poems; performer of poetry. Active ERA, Ill., 1975-76. Grantee, Am. Philos. Soc., 1970, U. Ill., Chgo., 1970; Fgn. Travel grantee, 1983, Dylan Thomas scholar. Mem. MLA, Am. Soc. for Aesthetics, Linguistic Soc. Am., Chgo. Linguistic Soc. (co-chmn. 1954-56), Nat. Comm. Assn. (chair interpretation divsn. 1979-80, Golden Ann. award 1969), Celtic Studies Assn. N.Am., Pi Beta Phi. Episcopalian. Office: Univ Ill Dept Performing Arts M/C 255 1040 W Harrison St Chicago IL 60607-7130 Home: 2400 Lakeview 1901 Chicago IL 60614 Personal E-mail: dpa@uic.edu. Business E-Mail: william.loesch@goldberg.kohn.com.

LOESCHER, PETER HANS, electronics executive; b. Sept. 17, 1957; MBA Vienna Sch. Economics, Vienna U., 1985; Fellowship, Chinese U. of Hong Kong, 1985; cert. Advanced Mgmt. Program, Harvard Bus. Sch., 1997. Sr. mgmt. cons. Kienbaum Consulting Group, Germany, 1985—87; mgr. corp. strategic planning Hoechst AG, Germany, 1988—89; dir. bus. develop. Hoechst Celanese Corp., 1989—91; mng. dir. Hoechst Roussel Veterinaria AIE, Spain, 1991—94; v.p., gen. mgr. Hoechst Roussel Agri-Vet Co., 1994—95; project leader NYSE listing Hoechst shares Hoechst AG, Germany, 1996—97; pres., CEO Hoechst Marion Roussel Ltd. United Kingdom, Hoechst Marion Roussel Ltd. Japan, 1999; chmn., pres., CEO Aventis Pharma Ltd., Japan, 2000—02; pres. Amersham Health, bd. dirs. Amersham PLC, 2002—04; COO Amersham PLC (acquired by GE), 2004; pres., CEO GE Healthcare Bio-Sciences, mem. corp. exec. coun. GE, 2004—05; pres. global human health Merck & Co., Inc., 2006—07; pres., CEO Siemens AG, Munich, 2007—. Bd. dir. Nokia Siemens Networks B.V., 2007—. Trustee Glyndebourne Arts Trust. Office: Siemens AG Wittelsbacherplatz 2 Munich 80333 Germany*

LOESCHER, RICHARD ALVIN, retired gastroenterologist; b. Brockton, Mass., Feb. 6, 1940; s. Vernon Alvin and Anna Marie (Good) Loescher; m. Linda Rockwell Clifford, June 5, 1955 (div. Jan. 1982); children: Steven Clifford, Laura May. BA, DePauw U., Greencastle, Ind., 1961; MD cum laude, Harvard U., Cambridge, Mass., 1965. Diplomate Am. Bd. Internal Medicine, 1972, Am. Bd. Gastroenterology, 1973. Chief med. svc. USPHS Hosp., Lawton, Okla., 1967-69, chief med. staff, 1968-69, svc. unit dir., 1969, attending physician Seattle, 1970-71, Univ. Hosp., Seattle, 1970-71; active staff Sacred Heart Med. Ctr., Eugene, Oreg., 1973—2005, Eugene Hosp., Oreg., 1972—88; courtesy staff McKenzie-Willamette Hosp., Springfield, Oreg., 1982—2004. Recipient Rector scholarship DePauw U., 1957-61, Maimonides award Harvard Med. Sch., 1965. Mem. AMA, ACP-Am. Soc. Internal Medicine, Lane County Med. Soc., Oreg. Med. Assn., Am. Soc. for Gastrointestinal Endoscopy, Am. Acad. Med. Acupuncture, Alpha Omega Alpha, Phi Beta Kappa. Democrat. Unitarian Universalist. Avocations: physical fitness, personal growth, magic, outdoor activities. Home: 2345 Patterson St Apt 34 Eugene OR 97405-2974

LOESCHKE, MARAVENE S., academic administrator, theater educator; m. C. Richard Gillespie. BS, Towson U., 1969, MEd, 1972; PhD, The Union Inst., 1976. Prodn. asst., actress Md. Pub. TV; instr. theatre arts Towson U., 1970—74, asst. prof., 1974—83, assoc. prof., 1983—90, prof., 1990—96, acting dean Coll. Fine Arts and Comm., 1996—97, dean, 1997—2002; provost Wilkes U., 2002—06; pres. Mansfield U. of Pa., 2006—. Contbr. articles to profl. jours. Office: Office of Pres Mansfield Coll 500 North Hall Mansfield PA 16933 Office Phone: 570-662-4046, 570-662-4045.

LOESER, HANS FERDINAND, lawyer; b. Kassel, Germany, Sept. 28, 1920; s. Max and Cecilia H. (Erlanger) Loeser; m. Herta Lewent, Dec. 14, 1944; children: Helen, Harris M., H. Thomas. Student, CCNY, 1940—42, U. Pa., 1942—43; LLB magna cum laude, Harvard U., 1950. Bar: Mass. 1950, U.S. Supreme Ct. 1968. Assoc. Foley, Hoag & Eliot, Boston, 1950—55, ptnr., 1956—. Hon. consul-gen. Republic of Senegal, 1970—85; former mem. Mass. Bd. Bar Overseers; trustee Vineyard Open Land Found., Martha's Vineyard, Mass.; mem. exec. com., nat. bd. Lawyers' Com. for Civil Rights Under Law; steering com., past chmn. Lawyers Com. for Civil Rights Under Law of Boston Bar Assn.; founder, dir., treas. Lawyers Alliance for World Security, Washington. Corporator Mt. Auburn Hosp., Cambridge, Mass. Capt. US Army, 1942—46. Decorated Bronze Star, Purple Heart; hon. fellow, U. Pa. Law Sch., 1978—79. Fellow: Mass. Bar Found., Am. Bar Found.; mem.: ABA, Boston Bar Assn., Mass. Bar Assn., Cambridge Club. Office: Foley Hoag LLP 155 Seaport Blvd Boston MA 02210-2600 Home Phone: 617-354-3959; Office Phone: 617-832-1139. Personal E-mail: hloeser@comcast.net. Business E-Mail: hloeser@fhe.com.

LOETE, STEVEN DONALD, pilot; b. Tacoma, Aug. 21, 1959; s. Donald Kenneth and Ida Lorraine (Buck) L.; m. Jodi Christine Barnett, 1998; children: Samantha, Tiffani, Joshua, Taylor. BA, Pacific Luth. U., 1984. Pilot contracting office USAF, Williams AFB, Ariz., 1985; flight instr. Clover Park Tech. Coll., Tacoma, 1986, 99; charter pilot Stellar Exec., Chandler, Ariz., 1986-87; pilot, airline capt. Maui Airlines, Guam, 1987; airline capt., checkairman Westair Airlines, Fresno, Calif., 1987-98; airline pilot Air Wis., 1998—; owner Northwestern Properties; corp. pilot Exec. Jet Mgmt., Cin., 1999—2004; pilot Aerodynamics, Inc., 2004—. Contbr. Save the Children, 1988-90; mem. Angel Flight, U. Puget Sound, 1981-83; bd. dirs. aviation adv. com. Clover Park Tech. Coll., 1991—. 1st lt. USAF, 1983-93. Mem. Airline Pilots Assn. (chmn. organizing com. 1989, chmn. coun. 1989-91). Republican. Methodist. Avocations: racquetball, fishing. Office: Box 760 Spanaway WA 98387 Home: 17012 12th Ave Ct E Spanaway WA 98387 Office Phone: 253-906-2000. E-mail: northwesternproperties@comcast.net.

LOEW, BRENDA, publisher; b. Boston, Apr. 1, 1951; d. Kenneth F. and Florence (Rosoff) L.; m. Ira R. Tatelbaum, Aug. 1970 (div. May 1983); children: Laura Rani, Max Loew. BA, Boston U., 1971, postgrad., 1980—83; MA, Brown U., 1973; PhD in Internat. Comm. (hon.), World U., 1992; cert. paralegal profl., Northeastern U., 2000; grad., Newton Civilian Police Acad., 2000, Bojack Acad., 2001. Cert. manicurist Mass., English, speech tchr. Mass., Reiki Master Tchr. Usui Shiki Ryoho, 2003, Seichim Reiki Master Ctr. Seichim-Reiki Tng., 2003, Ordained minister Universal Ministries, Ill., 2003, Universal Life Ch., Calif., 2003, Ordained clergy Ch. Spiritual Humanism, Pa., 2003. Libr. asst. John D. Rockefeller Libr., Providence, 1973; speech therapist (Mass.) Pub. Sch., Dartmouth, Mass., 1974-79; pub., editor Eidos mag., Boston, 1984—; pres., treas., bd. dir. Brush Hill Press, Inc., Boston, 1984-88; founder and pub. Tatelbaum Assn. Pub. Rels. & Fund Raising, Boston, 1987; recruiter Newbury Coll., Brookline, Mass., 1998; circulation sales Cmty. Newspapers, Needham, Mass., 1998-99; team leader Smarter Kids.Com, Needham, Mass., 1999; customer care Toysmart.com, Waltham, Mass., 1999; prodr. Newton (Mass.) Talk, Newton, Mass., 2000—; owner Brenda Loew & Assocs., Newton, Mass. Active fundraising and pub. rels., Bill Baird AIDS Awareness Fund., 1987; mem. ad hoc com. reproductive freedom Boston U., 1987; chair Bill Baird Pro-Choice Def. League, Boston, 1989—99; cons., reflexology demonstrator Bojack Acad., West Roxbury, Mass., 2000—; owner 4 Paws Dog Walking Svc., Newton, Mass.; instr. Boston Learning Soc., Needham, Mass., Cambridge Ctr. for Adult Edn., Mass., Open Doors, Braintree, Mass.; pres. dir. New England Vintage Film Soc., Inc., 2006—. Author: Eden Poems, 1982, Life Evolves From Living, 1983; short stories; editor: Boston Collection of Women's Poetry, 1983; editor (mag.) Eidos; contbg. articles to profl. jour., mag.; contbr. Cmty. Adv., Marlborough, Mass. Vol. instr. citizenship program ARC, Boston; vol. med. massage team Boston Marathon, 2002; media coord. Emerson Coll. Polit. Awareness Orgn.-Safer Sex March, Boston, 1987; candidate Newton (Mass.) Sch. Com., 1999, 2003; bd. dir. Nat. AIDS Telethon, Boston, 1987. Recipient Lifestyle award, 1993, Golden Phallus award, 1996, Patriotic Citizen award, VFW, Vol. of Yr., New TV Red Carpet Awards, 2005; named Saint, Universal Life Ch., Inc., 1997; named to Playboy Online Hall of Fame; appointed Mass.Goodwilll Ambasssador, Pet Sitters Internat., 2003; winner New TV Red Carpet award, 2005, Vol. of Yr. award New TV, 2005. Fellow: World Lit. Acad.; mem.: New England Vintage Film Soc. (pres., dir.), Nat. Assn. Profl. Petsitters, Nat. Kidney Found. (life), Mass. Fully Informed Jury Assn. (contact 1997—2004), Pet Sitters Internat., Hadassah (life). Avocations: politics, law, writing, canoeing, golf. Office Phone: 617-965-3512. E-mail: brendaloew@yahoo.com.

LOEWENBERG, GERHARD, political science professor; b. Berlin, Oct. 2, 1928; came to U.S., 1936, naturalized, 1943; s. Walter and Anne Marie (Cassirer) L.; m. Ina Perlstein, Aug. 22, 1950; children: Deborah, Michael. AB, Cornell U., 1949, A.M., 1950, PhD, 1955. Mem. faculty Mount Holyoke Coll., 1953-69, chmn. dept. polit. sci., 1963-69, acting academic dean, 1968-69; prof. polit. sci. U. Iowa, Iowa City, 1970—2003, U. Iowa Found. Disting. prof. emeritus, 2003—, chmn. dept., 1982-84, dean Coll. Liberal Arts, 1984-92, dir. Comparative Legis. Research Center, 1971-82, 92—; vice chair East-West Parliamentary Practice Project, 1990-2000. Vis.

assoc. prof. Columbia, UCLA, 1966, U. Mass. summer session at Bologna, Italy, 1967, Cornell U., 1968; mem. council Inter-Univ. Consortium for Polit. Research, 1971-74, chmn., 1973-74 Author: Parliament in the German Political System, 1967, Parlamentarismus im politischen System der Bundesrepublik Deutschland, 1969, Modern Parliaments: Change or Decline, 1971; co-author: Comparing Legislatures, 1979; co-editor: Handbook of Legislative Research, 1985, Legislatures: Comparative Perspectives on Representative Assemblies, 2002; contbr. articles to profl. jours. Trustee Mt. Holyoke Coll., 1971-84, chmn., 1979-84. Fulbright fellow, 1957-58, Rockefeller fellow, 1961-62, Social Sci. Rsch. Coun. Faculty Rsch. fellow, 1964-65, Guggenheim fellow, 1969-70. Fellow Am. Acad. Arts and Scis.; mem. Am. Polit. Sci. Assn. (coun. 1971-73, v.p. 1990-91, Frank J. Goodnow award 2001), Midwest Polit. Sci. Assn., Phi Beta Kappa, Phi Kappa Phi, Pi Sigma Alpha. Office: U Iowa 336 Schaeffer Hall Iowa City IA 52242-1409 Business E-Mail: g-loewenberg@uiowa.edu.

LOEWENSTEIN, ANDREW B., lawyer; AB in Polit. Sci. magna cum laude, Brown U., 1996; MS, London Sch. Econs., 1997; JD cum laude, Georgetown U., 2000. Bar: Mass. 2001, US Dist. Ct. (Dist. Mass.), US Ct. Appeals (1st Cir.), US Ct. Appeals (10th Cir.). Law clk. to Hon. William J. Holloway, Jr. US Ct. Appeals (10th Cir.); assoc. Foley Hoag LLP, Boston. Mem. Mass. Supreme Judicial Ct. Historical Soc. Mem.: Internat. Bar Assn. (litig. com., arbitration com.), ABA, Boston Bar Assn. (internat. dispute resolution), Internat. Inst. Strategic Studies. Office: Foley Hoag LLP Seaport World Trade Center West 155 Seaport Blvd Boston MA 02210-2600 Office Phone: 617-832-3015. E-mail: aloewenstein@foleyhoag.com.

LOEWENSTEIN, WALTER BERNARD, nuclear energy industry executive; b. Gensungen, Hesse, Germany, Dec. 23, 1926; arrived in U.S., 1938; m. Lenore C. Pearlman, June 21, 1959; children: Mark Victor, Marcia Beth. BS, U. Puget Sound, Tacoma, Wash., 1949; postgrad., U. Wash., Seattle, 1949-50; PhD, Ohio State U., Columbus, Ohio, 1954. Registered profl. engr., Calif. Rsch. asst., fellow Ohio State U., Columbus, 1951-54; rsch. asst. Los Alamos Nat. Lab., 1952-54; sr. physicist, divsn. dir. Argonne (Ill.) Nat. Lab., 1954-73; dept. dir., dep. divsn. dir. Electric Power Rsch. Inst., Palo Alto, Calif., 1973-89, profl. cons., 1989—, mem. large aerosol containment experiment project bd., 1983-87. Mem. Marviken project bd. Studsvik Rsch. Ctr., Stockholm, 1978-85; mem. LOFT project bd. Nuc. Energy Agy., Paris, 1982-89; mem. tech. adv. com. nuc. safety Ontario Hydro Corp., 1990-98; mem. nuc. engring. dept. adv. com. Brookhaven Nat. Lab., 1992-96; mem. advanced tech. divsn. adv. com. Los Alamos Nat. Lab., 1994-99; mem. nuc. engring. dept. adv. com. U. Calif., Berkeley, 1994-2003. With USNR, 1945-46. Recipient Alumnus Cum Laude award U. Puget Sound, 1976. Fellow Am. Phys. Soc., Am. Nuc. Soc. (v.p., pres. 1988-90); mem. Am. Assn. Engring. Socs. (sec., treas. 1990), Nat. Acad. Engring. Jewish. Avocations: history, golf. Home and Office: 515 Jefferson Dr Palo Alto CA 94303

LOEWY, ROBERT GUSTAV, aerospace executive, engineering educator; b. Phila., Feb. 12, 1926; s. Samuel N. and Esther (Silverstein) L.; m. Lila Myrna Spinner, Jan. 16, 1955; children: David G., Esther Elizabeth, Joanne Victoria, Raymond Matthew. B in Aero. Engring., Rensselaer Poly. Inst., 1947; MS, MIT, 1948; PhD, U. Pa., 1962. Sr. vibrations engr. Martin Co., Balt., 1948-49; assoc. rsch. engr. Cornell Aero. Lab., Buffalo, 1949-52, prin. engr., 1953-55; staff stress engr. Piasecki Helicopter Co., Morton, Pa., 1952-53; chief dynamics engr., then chief tech. engr. Vertol divsn. Boeing Co., Essington, Pa., 1955-62; from assoc. prof. to prof. mech. and aerospace scis. U. Rochester, 1962-73, dean Coll. Engring. and Applied Sci., 1967—73; dir. Space Sci. Ctr., 1966—71; v.p., provost Rensselaer Poly. Inst., Troy, NY, 1973—78, inst. prof., 1978-93; dir. Rotorcraft Tech. Ctr., 1982-93; chmn. sch. aerospace engring. Ga. Inst. Tech., 1993—, Wm. R.T. Oakes prof., 2000—. Chief scientist USAF, 1965-66; cons. govt. and industry, 1959—; mem. aircraft panel Pres.'s Sci. Adv. Coun., 1968-72; mem. Air Force Sci. Adv. Bd., 1966-75, 1978-85, vice chmn., 1971, chmn., 1972-75, chmn. aero. systems div. adv. group, 1978-84; mem. Post Office Rsch. and Engring. Adv. Coun., 1966-68; mem. rsch. and tech. adv. com. on aeros. NASA, 1970-71, mem. rsch. and tech. adv. coun., 1976-77, chmn. aero. adv. com., 1978-83; mem. aerospace engring. bd. NRC, 1972-78, 1988-93, mem. bd. on army sci. and tech., 1986-90; mem. naval studies bd. NAS, 1979-82; chmn. tech. adv. com. FAA, 1976-77; bd. dirs. Vertical Flight Found. Contbr. articles to profl. jours. Served with USNR, 1944-46. Recipient NASA Disting. Pub. Svc. award, 1983; Gotshall-Powell scholar Rensselaer Poly. Inst., 1946; USAF Exceptional Civilian Svc. awards, 1966, 75, 85, Spirit of St. Louis medal ASME, 1996, Guggenheim medal, 2007. Fellow AAAS; hon. fellow AIAA (Lawrence Sperry award 1958, Dryden lectr. 1999), Am. Helicopter Soc. (pres. 2002-03, tech. dir. 1963-64, chmn. bd. 2003-04, Nikolsky lectr. 1984); mem. Am. Soc. Engring. Edn., Nat. Acad. Engring., Sigma Xi, Sigma Gamma Tau, Tau Beta Pi. Achievements include research on unsteady rotor aerodynamics first showing it to be fundamentally different from fixed wing. Home: 3420 Wood Valley Rd NW Atlanta GA 30327-1518 Office: Ga Inst Tech Sch Aerospace Engring Atlanta GA 30332-0001 Office Phone: 404-894-3002. Business E-Mail: robert.loewy@ae.gatech.edu. *Looking back, I was fortunate to have known somehow, from an early age, that I would be an aeronautical engineer. That profession, through positions in industry, research and education, has provided challenge, satisfaction and valued associations.*

LOFGREN, CHARLES AUGUSTIN, historian, educator; b. Missoula, Mont., Sept. 8, 1939; s. Cornelius Willard and Helen Mary (Augustin) L.; m. Jennifer Jenkins Wood, Aug. 6, 1986. AB with great distinction, Stanford U., 1961; AM, 1962, PhD, 1966. Instr. history San Jose State Coll., 1965-66; asst. prof. Claremont McKenna Coll., 1966-71; assoc. prof., 1971-76; prof., 1976—; prof. Am. history and politics, 1976—. Author: Government from Reflection and Choice, 1986, The Plessy Case, 1988, Claremont Pioneers, 1996; contbr. articles to profl. jours. Served with USAR, 1957-63. Mem. Am. Soc. Legal History, Orgn. Am. Historians, Am. Hist. Assn. Republican. Roman Catholic. Office: Claremont McKenna Coll Dept History 850 Columbia Ave Claremont CA 91711-6420 Home Phone: 909-626-6731. Business E-Mail: clofgren@cmc.edu.

LOFGREN, CHRISTOPHER B., trucking executive; BS in Indsl. and Mgmt. Engring., MS in Indsl. and Mgmt. Engring., Mont. State U.; PhD in Indsl. and Systems Engring., Georgia U. Tech. With Symantec Corp., Motorola Inc., CAPS Logistics; v.p. Schneider Nat., Inc., Green Bay, Wis., 1994—96, chief tech. officer, 1996—99, chief info. officer, 1999—2000, COO, 2000—02, pres., CEO, 2002—, also bd. dir. Bd. dir. Computer Assocs. Internat., Inc. (now called CA), Islandia, NY, 2005—. Bd. dir. Green Bay Chpt. of the Boys and Girls Club Am.; bd. advisors Sch. Indsl. and Sys. Engring., Ga. Inst. Tech. Office: Schneider Nat Inc PO Box 2545 3101 S Packerland Dr Green Bay WI 54306-2545

LOFGREN, ZOE, congresswoman; b. Palo Alto, Calif., Dec. 21, 1947; d. Milton R. and Mary Violet Lofgren; m. John Marshall Collins, Oct. 22, 1978; children: Sheila Zoe Lofgren Collins, John Charles Lofgren Collins. BA in Polit. Sci., Stanford U., 1970; JD cum laude, U. Santa Clara, 1975. Bar: Calif. 1975, D.C. Adminstrv. asst. to Congressman Don Edwards, San Jose, Calif., 1970-79; ptnr. Webber and Lofgren, San Jose, 1979-81; mem. Santa Clara County Bd. Suprs., 1981-94, U.S. Congress from 16th Calif. dist., 1995—, Homeland Security com., House Adminstrn. com. and Judiciary com., Joint com. on Libr. Mem. com. on stds. of ofcl. conduct, jud. com., sci. com.; part-time prof. law U. Santa Clara, 1978-80. Exec. dir. Cmty. Housing Developers, Inc., 1979-80; trustee San Jose C.C. Dist., 1979-81; bd. dirs. Cmty. Legal Svcs., 1978-81, San Jose Housing Svc. Ctr., 1978-79; mem. steering com. sr. citizens housing referendum, 1978; del. Calif. State Bar Conv., 1979-82, Dem. Nat. Conv., 1976; active Assn. Immigration and Nationality Lawyers, 1976-82, Calif. State Dem. Ctrl. Com., 1975-78, Santa Clara County Dem. Ctrl. Com., 1974-78, Notre Dame H.S. Blue Ribbon Com., 1981-84, Victim-Witness Adv. Bd., 1981-94. Recipient Bancroft-Whitney award for Excellence in Criminal Procedure, 1973. Mem. Santa Clara County Bar Assn. (trustee 1979—), Santa Clara County Women Lawyers Com. (exec. bd. 1979-80), Santa Clara Law Sch. Alumni Assn. (v.p. 1977, pres. 1978), Nat. Women's Polit. Caucus, Assn. of Bay Area Govts. (exec. bd. 1981-86). Democrat. Office: US Ho Reps 102 Cannon Ho Office Bldg Washington DC 20515-0516 also: Dist Office Ste B 635 N 1st St San Jose CA 95112-5110*

LOFINK, GLENDA JEAN, science educator; b. Easley, SC, Nov. 20, 1963; d. Arthur Glen and Emily Jean Stewart; m. Robert William Lofink, Jr., Feb. 1, 1991; children: Robert W. III, Alexandra Leigh; 1 child, Brandy Nicole Simmons. BSc, Clemson U., SC, 2000, MEd, 2004. Pharmacy technician Revco (now CVS), Easley, 1986—89; hair stylist self-employed, Pickens, SC, 1989—94; cert. pharmacy technician Revco/CVS, Pickens, 1994—97; tchr. sci. Pickens County Sch. Dist., 2000—. Mem. bd. Behavioral Health Svcs. Mem., holder several offices Jr. C. of C. (Jaycees), 1989—2004. Mem.: Nat. Assn. Biology Tchrs., NSTA. Wesleyan. Avocations: hiking, wildlife advocacy, coaching girls soccer. Home: 590 Allgood Bridge Rd Pickens SC 29671 Office: Pickens HS 111 Blue Flame Dr Pickens SC 29671 Business E-Mail: lofinkgj@pickens.k12.sc.us.

LOFLAND, GARY KENNETH, cardiac surgeon; b. Milford, Del., Mar. 5, 1951; s. Joseph Sudler and Doris Louise (Peters) L.; m. Janice Marie Show, Feb. 3, 1979; children: Kiernan Sudler, Glennis Kathleen. BA cum laude, Boston U., 1969, MD cum laude, 1975. Diplomate Am. Bd. Surgery, Am. Bd. Thoracic Surgery; lic. physician, Va., N.Y., Mont., N.C. Intern, jr. asst. resident in surgery Duke U. Med. Ctr., Durham, NC, 1975-81, rsch. fellow dept. surgery, 1979-81, sr. asst. resident in surgery, 1981-84, chief resident in surgery, 1984-85, teaching scholar in cardiac surgery, 1985-86; sr. registrar in cardiothoracic surgery Hosp. for Sick Children, London, 1986-87; dir. cardiovascular surgery Children's Hosp. of Buffalo, 1987-88; asst. prof. surgery SUNY, Buffalo, 1987-88; assoc. prof. surgery/pediatrics, Med. Coll. Va., Richmond, 1988-94, dir. pediatric cardiac surgery/med. dir. cardiac surgery ICU, 1988-94; clin. prof. surgery Georgetown U., Washington, 1994-97; dir. Columbia/HCA Ctr. Congenital Heart Disease, Richmond, 1994-97; dir. cardiovascular surgery Children's Mercy Hosp., Kansas City, Mo., 1997—; prof. surgery U. Mo. Kansas City Sch. Medicine, 1997—, Joseph Boon Gregg chair sect. cardiac surgery. Editor (in chief): Progress in Pediat. Cardiology, 2002—; mem. editl. rev. bd.:, —, Year Book of Thoracic Surgery, —; contbr. articles to profl. jours. Pres. Am. Heart Assn., Richmond; mem. bd. trustees Transplant Found. Lt. comdr. USPHS, 1977-79. Recipient Univ. Hosp. Trustees award, Boston, 1975; HEW/USPHS commendation medal, 1979. Mem. AMA, Am. Heart Assn., Am. Assn. Thoracic Surgery, Assn. for Acad. Surgery, Internat. Soc. for Heart Transplantation, Med. Soc. Va., Richmond Acad. Medicine, Richmond Surg. Soc., So. Thoracic Surg. Assn., Soc. for Thoracic Surgeons, Congenital Heart Surgeons Soc., Alpha Omega Alpha. Home: PO Box 126 Crozier VA 23039-0126 Office: Children's Mercy Hosp Divsn Cardiovascular Surgery 2406 Gillham Rd Kansas City MO 64108 Office Phone: 816-234-3580. Business E-Mail: glofland@cmh.edu.

LOFQUIST, VICKI L., journalist; b. Des Moines, Aug. 2, 1949; d. Edgar William and Gwendolyn Marjorie Lofquist; m. Craig Peter Thiesen, May 23, 1997. Student, St. Andrews U., Scotland, 1969—70; BA, Grinnell Coll., 1971; MA, U. Minn., 1976. Cert. fund raising exec. 2004. Prodr. Sta. KUOM Radio U. Minn., Mpls., 1974—85, 1989—91; cons., ind. radio prodr. Mpls., 1992—96; devel. dir. Minn. Internat. Ctr., Mpls., 1997—2000, Books for Africa, St. Paul, 2000—; devel. officer Children's Home Soc. and Family Svcs., St. Paul, 2001—04; alumni rels., ann. fund coord. Metro. State U., St. Paul, 2004—. Prodr.(writer): (radio documentaries) Leading to Beijing: Voices of Global Women (Clarion Award, Women In Communication, 1996, Hon. Mention, Internat. Assn. of Women in Radio & T.V., 1997), Science Lives: Women & Minorities in the Sciences, Sound Studies in Psychology, a CPB/Annenberg Project. Bd. dirs. St. Paul LWV, 2002—07. Grantee Bicentennial Swedish-Am. Exch. Fund, Swedish Inst., Stockholm, Sweden, 1991. Office: Metro State Univ 700 E 7th St Saint Paul MN 55106 Office Phone: 651-793-1810. Business E-Mail: vicki.lofquist@metrostate.edu.

LOFT, LLOYD MARK, otolaryngologist; b. NYC, Aug. 5, 1960; MD, N.Y. Med. Coll., 1986. Diplomate Am. Bd. Otolaryngology. Intern St. Vincent's Hosp. Med. Ctr., NYC, 1986-88; resident in otolaryngology Manhattan Eye Ear & Throat Hosp., NYC, 1988-91, attending surgeon; mem. staff Lenox Hill Hosp., NYC, St. Vincent's Hosp., NYC; pvt. practice. Asst. prof. otolaryngology Weill med. coll. Cornell U. Fellow ACS, Am. Acad. Otolaryngology-Head and Neck Surgery; mem. Am. Rhinol. Soc., MSSNY/NYCMS. Office: 115 East 57th St Ste 600 New York NY 10022

LOFTFIELD, ROBERT BERNER, biochemistry professor; b. Detroit, Dec. 15, 1919; s. Sigurd and Katherine (Roller) L.; m. Ella Bradford, Aug. 24, 1946 (dec. Dec. 1990); children: Lore Loftfield DeBower, Eric, Linda, Norman, Bjorn, Curtis, Katherine, Earl, Allison Dinsdale, Ella-Kari. BS, Harvard U., 1941, MA, 1942, PhD, 1946. Research assoc. MIT, Cambridge, 1946-48; research assoc. to sr. research assoc. Mass. Gen. Hosp., Boston, 1948-64; asst. to assoc. prof. biochemistry Harvard U. Sch. Medicine, Boston, 1948-64; prof. biochemistry Sch. Medicine U. N.Mex., Albuquerque, 1964-90, chmn. dept. biochemistry, 1964-71, 78-90, prof. emeritus, 1990—. Contbr. articles on protein biosynthesis and enzymology to profl. jours. Served as corp. U.S. Army, 1945-46. Fellow Damon Runyon Fund, 1952-53, Guggenheim Found., 1961-62; Fulbright fellow, 1977, 83; sr. fellow NIH, 1971-72. Mem. AAAS, Am. Soc. Biol. Chemists, Am. Chem. Soc., Am. Assn. Cancer Rsch., Biophys. Soc., Marine Biol. Lab. Lutheran. Avocations: sailing, hiking, camping, skiing. Home: 707 Fairway Rd NW Albuquerque NM 87107-5718 Office: U NMex Sch Medicine Dept Biochemis & Molecular Biology Albuquerque NM 87131-0001

LOFTHUS, LEE J., federal agency administrator; MBA, Am. U., 1982. With US Dept. Justice, Washington, 1982—; fin. br. chief Fed. Bur. Prisons, Washington, 1995—99; dir. fin. staff Justice Mgmt. Divsn., US Dept. Justice, Washington, 1999—2003, dep. CFO, 2003, prin. dep. asst. atty. gen., contr., 2003—06, acting asst. atty. gen. adminstrn., 2006, asst. atty. gen. adminstrn., 2006—. Office: US Dept Justice Justice Mgmt Divsn 950 Pennsylvania Ave NW Rm 1111 Washington DC 20530 Office Phone: 202-514-3101. Office Fax: 202-616-6695. E-mail: lee.j.lofthus@usdoj.gov.

LOFTIN, NANCY CAROL, lawyer, utilities executive; b. Phoenix, 1954; BA, Ariz. State U., 1976; JD, U. Ariz. Sch. of Law, 1979. Bar: Ariz. 1979. Special counsel & dir. enforcement Ariz. Corp. Commn.; staff atty. Ariz. Public Service, 1985—87; v.p., gen. counsel, sec. Pinnacle West Capital Corp. & Ariz. Pub. Svc. Co., 1987—. Mem. Edison Electric Inst. Bd. mem. Phoenix Children's Hospital, former bd. chair. Mem.: ABA, Am. Soc. of Corporate Secretaries, Ethics Officer Assn. Office: Pinnacle West Capital Corp PO Box 53999 Phoenix AZ 85072-3999*

LOFTIS, JOHN (CLYDE), JR., language educator; b. Atlanta, May 16, 1919; s. John Clyde and Marbeth (Brown) L.; m. Anne Nevins, June 29, 1946; children: Mary, Laura, Lucy. BA, Emory U., 1940; MA, Princeton U., 1942, PhD, 1948. Instr. English Princeton, 1946-48; instr., then asst. prof. English UCLA, 1948-52; faculty Stanford U., 1952-81, prof. English, 1958-81, Bailey prof. English, 1977-81, Bailey prof. emeritus, 1981—, chmn. dept., 1973-76. Author: Steele at Drury Lane, 1952, Comedy and Society from Congreve to Fielding, 1959, La Independencia de la Literatura Norteamericana, 1961, The Politics of Drama in Augustan England, 1963, The Spanish Plays of Neoclassical England, 1973, (with others) The Revels History of Drama in English, Vol. V, 1976, Sheridan and the Drama of Georgian England, 1977, Renaissance Drama in England and Spain: Topical Allusion and History Plays, 1987; editor: (Steele) The Theatre, 1962, Restoration Drama: Modern Essays in Criticism, 1966, (with V.A. Dearing) The Works of John Dryden, Vol. IX, 1966, (Sheridan) The School for Scandal, 1966, (Nathaniel Lee) Lucius Junius Brutus, 1967, (Addison) Essays in Criticism and Literary Theory, 1975, The Memoirs of Anne, Lady Halkett and Ann, Lady Fanshawe, 1979, (with D.S. Rodes and V.A. Dearing) The Works of John Dryden, Vol. XI, 1978, (with P.H. Hardacre) Colonel Bampfield's Apology, 1993; co-editor Augustan Reprint Society, 1949-1952, English Literature, 1660-1800: A Current Bibliography, 1951-56; gen. editor: Regents Restoration Drama Series, 35 vols, 1962-81; mem. editorial bd.: Studies in English Literature, 1966-76, Huntington Library Quar., 1968-76, Wesleyan Edit. Works Henry Fielding, 1970-83, Augustan Reprint Soc., 1985-90. Served with USNR, 1942-46, PTO. Fellow Fund Advancement Edn., 1955-56; Fulbright lectr. Am. studies Peru, 1959-60; Guggenheim fellow, 1966-67; fellow Folger Shakespeare Library, 1967; NEH fellow, 1978-79 Mem. MLA, Phi Beta Kappa, Kappa Alpha. Home: 7 Arastradero Rd Portola Valley CA 94028-8012 Office: Stanford Univ Dept English Stanford CA 94305 Personal E-mail: jaloftis@comcast.net.

LOFTON, BRENDA M., secondary school educator; b. Alexandria, La., July 10, 1959; d. Bobbie Frank and Bobbiline McLemore; m. Terry Lee Lofton, June 3, 1978; children: Janna Michelle Young, Jennifer Leigh. BA, N.E. La. U., Monroe, 1980; MA, La. Tech U., Ruston, 1986. Cert. early adolescence math. Nat. Bd. Profl. Tchg. Standards, 2002. Tchr. Glen View Elem. Sch., Ruston, 1986—92, A.E. Phillips Lab. Sch., Ruston, 1992—2006, Dubach H.S., La., 2006—. Children's choir dir. Calvary Bapt. Ch., Ruston, 2003—06, worship leader praise band, keyboard; accompanist Masterworks Young Singers, Ruston, 2000—05. Named Tchr. of Yr., A.E. Phillips Lab. Sch., 2003, 2006, Lincoln Parish Sch. Bd., 2003, 2006, Tchr. of Yr., La. Dept. of Edn., 2006; named one of Finalist Mid. Sch. Tchr. of Yr., 2003. Mem.: Associated Profl. Educators La., Nat. Coun. Tchrs. Math. Baptist. Avocations: piano, hiking, camping, travel, gardening. Home: 5785 Hwy 33 Choudrant LA 71227 Home Phone: 318-255-5467; Office Phone: 318-777-3479. E-mail: blofton@lincolnschools.org.*

LOFTON, KEVIN EUGENE, medical facility administrator; b. Beaumont, Tex., Sept. 29, 1954; BS, Boston U., 1976; M Health Care Adminstrn., Ga. State U., 1979. Adminstrv. resident Meml. Med. Ctr., Corpus Christi, Tex., 1978-79; adminstr. emergency svcs. Univ. Hosp., Jacksonville, Fla., 1979-80, adminstr. material mgmt., 1980-81, asst. exec. dir. ambulatory care, 1981-82, asst. v.p. ambulatory svcs., 1982-83, v.p. profl. svcs., 1983-86; exec. v.p. Univ. Med. Ctr., Jacksonville, 1986-90; exec. dir. Howard Univ. Hosp., Washington, 1990-93, U. Ala. Hosp., Birmingham, 1993-98; group pres. Cath. Health Initiative, Louisville, 1998-99, COO Denver, 1999—. Contbr. articles to profl. publs. Fellow Am. Coll. Health Care Execs. (R.S. Hudgens award 1993); mem. Am. Hosp. Assn. (bd. dirs.), Nat. Assn. Health Svcs. Execs. (past pres., bd. dirs.).

LOFTON, THOMAS MILTON, lawyer; b. Indpls., May 12, 1929; s. Milton Alexander and Jane (Routzong) L.; m. Betty Louise Blades, June 20, 1954; children: Stephanie Louise, Melissa Jane. BS, Ind. U., 1951, JD, 1954, LLD (hon.), 2000, Wabash Coll., 2001. Bar: Ind. 1954, U.S. Ct. Appeals (7th cir.) 1959, U.S. Supreme Ct. 1958. Law clk. to justice U.S. Supreme Ct., Washington, 1954-55; ptnr. Baker & Daniels, Indpls., 1958-91. Dir. Ind. U. Found., Bloomington, 1978-91, Clowes Fund, 1980-2001; chmn. bd. Lilly Endowment, Indpls., 1991—; mem. bd. visitors Ind. U. Law, Bloomington, 1976—. Editor-in-chief Ind. Law Jour., 1953. Trustee Earlham Coll., 1988—91; dir. Allen Whitehill Clowes Charitable Found., 1990—. 1st lt. US Army, 1955—58. Recipient Peck award Wabash Coll., 1982, Disting. Alumni Svc. award Ind. U., 1997. Mem.: Ind. Acad., Masons, Order of Coif, Sigma Nu, Beta Gamma Sigma. Republican. Presbyterian. Home: 9060 Pickwick Dr Indianapolis IN 46260-1714 Office: Lilly Endowment 2800 N Meridian St Indianapolis IN 46208-4713

LOFTUS, CARROLL MICHAEL (MICHAEL LOFTUS), lawyer; b. Cheverly, Md., Oct. 9, 1946; s. Joseph P. and Margaret M. (Boland) L.; m. Claire E. Barbour, Oct. 12, 1968; children: Kevin M., Christopher D., James B., Elizabeth A. BS in Acctg., Wheeling Coll., W.Va., 1968; JD, Cath. U., 1973. Bar: Md. 1973, DC 1975, admitted to practice: US Dist. Ct. Md. 1974, US Supreme Ct. 1978, US Dist. Ct. (DC) 1984. Law clk. to Judge Joseph H. Young US Dist. Ct. Md., Balt., 1973-74; assoc. Venable, Baetjer & Howard, Balt., 1974-75; from assoc. to ptnr. Slover & Loftus, Washington, 1975—. Contbr. articles to profl. jour. Mem.: ABA, DC Bar Assn., Md. Bar Assn. Republican. Roman Catholic. Avocations: golf, skiing, boating, fishing, hiking. Office: Slover & Loftus 1224 17th St NW Washington DC 20036-3081 Office Phone: 202-347-7170. Business E-Mail: cml@sloverandloftus.com.

LOFTUS, ELIZABETH F., psychology professor; b. LA; d. Sidney and Rebecca Fishman; m. Geoffrey Loftus, June 30, 1968 (div. Jan. 1991). BA, UCLA; MA, PhD, Stanford U.; DSc (hon.), Miami U.; D (hon.), Leiden U.; D (hon.), U. Haifa, Israel; LLD (hon.), John Jay Coll. Criminal Justice; DSc (hon.), U. Portsmouth, Eng. Prof. U. Wash., Seattle, 1973—2002; Disting. Univ. prof. U. Calif., Irvine, 2002—. Author: Eyewitness Testimony, 1979, 2d. edit., 1996, Witness for the Defense, 1991, Myth of Repressed Memory, 1994. Recipient The Grawemeyer award for Psychology, U. Louisville, 2005. Fellow: Royal Soc. Edinburgh (corr.); mem.: Am. Philosophical Soc., NAS. Office Phone: 949-824-3285. Business E-Mail: eloftus@uci.edu.

LOFTUS, JEAN M., plastic surgeon; b. Milw., Sept. 9, 1963; MD, U. Wis., 1988. Cert. Am. Bd. Plastic Surgery, Am. Bd. Otolaryngology. Internship U. Calif.-Davis, Sacramento, 1988—89; residency U. Wis., Madison, 1989—93; residency plastic surgery U. Cin., 1993—95; pvt. practice Cin., 1995—. Author: The Smart Woman's Guide to Plastic Surgery: Essential Information from a Female Plastic Surgeon, 2000; contbr. articles to profl. jours.; appeared on MSNBC, CNN, The Today Show, The View. Fellow: Am. Coll. Surgeons; mem.: Am. Soc. Plastic Surgeons. Office: 10506 Montgomery Rd Cincinnati OH 45242*

LOFTUS, STEPHEN EDWARD, elementary art educator; b. Stoughton, Wis., Sept. 17, 1949; s. Edward Henry and Gladys Lillian (Lange) L. BS, U. Wis., Platteville; M in Art Edn., U. Wis., 1995. Cert. tchr., Wis. Art tchr. Wausau (Wis.) Pub. Schs., 1981—. Sculpture judge State Visual Arts Classic Competition, Madison; presenter in field. Contbr. Jour. on Japan's Edn. in Art, 1991; sculptor; songwriter; contbr. articles to profl. jours. Vol. tchr. Ctr. for the Visual Arts; sculpture judge State Visual Arts Classic Competition MATC, Madison; citizen amb. Japan art educators, People to People Program, Wausau, summer 1991; soapbox derby judge, art advisor Boy Scouts Am.; vol. Meals on Wheels; counselor, choir mem. United Meth. Ch.; representer WAEA Cranbrook Estate western region state's ann. meeting art edn. issues, Mich.; del. NAEA Conf., Boston, 2005; planning com. mem. We. Region Leadership Conf. Meeting, Madison, 2004-05. Recipient Award of Excellence for mixed media painting, State Wis. Art. Edn. Assn. Conf., 2000, Award of Excellence for sculpture, Ctr. Visual Arts Wausau, Resolution of Commendation, Pres. Philip R. Albert, MD, Wausau Pub. Schs. Sch. Bd., 2000, 2d Resolution Commendation bringing recognition to Wausau Pub. Schs., Christine A. Bremer Pres. Bd. Edn., Wausau, Wis. Mem. NEA, Nat. Art Edn. Assn. (v.p. North Ctrl. region bd. 1993-95, pres.-elect del. at dels. assembly nat. spring conf. 2002, 03), State Edn. Assn., Wis. Art Edn. Assn. (pres. 2003-05, Art Educator of Yr. 2000), Wis. Alliance Arts Edn. (Disting. Svc. award within the arts edn. profession 2000). Home: 1243 Sunset Dr Wausau WI 54401-4256 Office: 2701 Robin Ln Wausau WI 54401 Office Phone: 715-261-2350. E-mail: stephen.loftus@charter.net.

LOFTUS, THOMAS DANIEL, lawyer; b. Nov. 8, 1930; s. Glendon Francis and Martha Helen (Wall) L. BA, U. Wash., Seattle, 1952, JD, 1957. Bar: Wash. 1958, US Ct. Appeals (9th cir.) 1958, US Dist. Ct. Wash. 1958, US Ct. Mil. Appeals 1964, US Supreme Ct. 1964. Trial atty. Northwestern Mut. Ins. Co., Seattle, 1958—62; sr. trial atty. Unigard Security Ins. Co., Seattle, 1962—68, asst. gen. counsel, 1969—83, govt. rels. counsel, 1983—89; of counsel Groshong, LeHet & Thornton, 1990—98; spkrs. counsel, parlimentarian Wash. House of Reps., 1969—72; mem. Wash. Commn. on Jud. Conduct (formerly Jud. Qualifications), 1982—88, vice-chmn., 1987—88; self-employed arbitrator, mediator, 1998—; judge pro tem Seattle Mcpl. Ct., 1973—81; mem. nat. panel of mediators Arbitration Forums, Inc., 1990—; pvt. practice arbitrator, mediator, 1998—. Nat. committeeman Wash. Young Rep. Fedn., 1961-63, vice-chmn., 1963-65; pres. Young Reps. King County, 1962-63; bd. dirs. Seattle Seafair, Inc., 1975; v.p. Salvation Army Adult Rehab. Ctr., 1979-86; pres., bd. dirs. Vis. Nurse Svcs., 1979-88; Sec., trustee Seattle Opera Assn., 1980-91; pres., bd. dirs., gen. counsel Wash. Ins. Coun., 1984-86, sec., 1986-88, v.p., 1988-90; bd. dirs. Arson Alarm Found., 1987-90; Am. Mediation Panel Mediators, 1990-96; bd. visitors Law Sch. U. Wash., 1993-98; counsel to spkr., 1969-72; parliamentarian Washington House of Reps., 1969-72. 1st lt. US Army, 1952—54, col. USAR, 1954—85. Fellow Am. Bar Found.; mem. Am. Arbitration Assn. (nat. panel arbitrators 1965—, nat. panel mediators 2000—), Am. Arbitration Forums, Inc. (nat. panel arbitrators 1992), Nat. Assn. Security Dealers (bd. arbitrators 1997—), Am. Mediation Panel, Wash. Bar Assn. (gov. 1981-84), Seattle King County Bar Assn. (sec., trustee 1977-82), ABA (ho. of dels. 1984-90), Internat. Assn. Ins. Counsel, U.S. People to People (del. NATO conf. of young polit.leaders, Oxford, 1965, del. Moscow internat. law-econ. conf. 1990), Def. Rsch. Inst., Wash. Def. Trial Lawyers Assn., Wash. State Trial Lawyers Assn., Am. Judicature Soc., Res. Officers Assn., Judge Advocate Gen.'s Assn., Assn. Wash. Gens., U. Wash. Alumni Assn., Coll. Club Seattle, Wash. Athletic Club, Masons, Shriners, English Spkg. Union, Ranier Club, Pi Sigma Alpha, Delta Sigma Rho, Phi Delta Phi, Theta Delta Chi. Republican. Presbyterian. Home: 3515 Magnolia Blvd W Seattle WA 98199-1841 Office: Coll Club Bldg 505 Madison St Ste 300 Seattle WA 98104-1123 Office Phone: 206-622-1264.

LOGA, SANDA, physicist, researcher; b. Bucharest, Romania, June 13, 1932; came to U.S., 1968; d. Stelian and Georgeta (Popescu) L.; m. Karl Heinz Werther, Mar. 1968 (div. 1970); m. Radu Zaciu, 1996. MS in Physics, U. Bucharest, 1955; PhD in Biophysics, U. Pitts., 1978. Asst. prof. faculty medicine and pharmacy, Bucharest, 1963-67; rsch. asst. Presbyn./St. Luke's Hosp., Chgo., 1968-69; assoc. rsch. scientist Miles Labs., Elkhart, Ind., 1969-70; rsch. asst. U. Pitts., 1971-78; rsch. assoc. Carnegie-Mellon U., Pitts., 1978-80; health physicist VA Med. Ctr., Westside, Chgo., 1980; med. physicist, VA Med. Ctr. N. Chgo, 1980-97. Assoc. prof. Chgo. Med. Sch., N. Chgo., 1985-2004. Mem. Am. Assn. Physicists in Medicine, Health Physics Soc. Office: Chgo Med Sch U Health Scis 3333 Green Bay Rd North Chicago IL 60064-3037 Business E-Mail: sanda.loga@rosalindfranklin.edu.

LOGAN, BEN H., III, lawyer; b. Medina, Ohio, 1951; BA magna cum laude, Duke U., 1973; JD, Stanford, 1976. Bar: Calif. 1976, US Dist. Ct. (Ctrl. Dist. Calif.) 1978, DC 1984, US Dist. Ct. (No. and So. Dists. Calif.) 1986, US Dist. Ct. (Dist. Ariz) 1990, US Dist. Ct. (Ea. Dist. Calif.) 1991, US Ct. Appeals (2nd Cir.) 1991, US Ct. Appeals (9th Cir.) 1994. Ptnr. O'Melveny & Myers LLP, Los Angeles. Mem. Stanford Law Review, 1974—76; editor: Stanford Law Review, 1975—76. Mem. ABA, State Bar Calif. (mem., debtor/creditor rels. and bankruptcy subcommittee, comml. law and bankruptcy sect.1986-91), LA County Bar Assn. (mem. bankruptcy com. 1989-92), Phi Beta Kappa; fellow Am. Coll. Bankruptcy. Office: O'Melveny & Myers 400 S Hope St Los Angeles CA 90071-2899 Office Phone: 213-430-7704. Office Fax: 213-430-6407. Business E-Mail: blogan@omm.com.

LOGAN, DAVID BRUCE, health facility administrator, nurse; b. Grand Rapids, Mich., Jan. 30, 1942; s. Wesley Goldsmith and Ernestine (Sovereen) L.; m. Joann Fern Jordan, Nov. 5, 1961; children: Jennifer, Julie, Jeanine, David II, Douglas, Dean. MusB, U. Mich., 1964; B Zoology with honors, Mich. State U., 1970; MBA, U. Ill., 1978. Tchr. sci. Flint (Mich.) Pub. Schs., 1970-71; health care adminstr. USAF, Mpls., 1971-75; asst. chief, med. adminstrn. svc. trainee VA, Mpls., 1975-76, asst. chief med. adminstrn. svc. Danville, Ill., 1976-78; asst. med. dist. coord. VA Med. Dist. 15, Indpls., 1978-80; med. dist. coord. VA Med. Dist. 8, Durham, NC, 1980-87; nat. disaster med. system mgr. VA, Salisbury, NC, 1987-99, ret. Dir. choir Kirk of Kildaire Presbyn. Ch., 1981-85; asst. scoutmaster, scoutmaster Boy Scouts Am., 1978-94. Capt. USAF, 1964-68, lt. col. Res. ret. Fellow Am. Coll. Healthcare Execs., Soc. Air Force Res. Med. Officers, Air Force Assn., Res. Officers Assn. (bd. dirs. Minn. 1973-74, jr. v.p. for air 1974-75).

LOGAN, FRANCIS DUMMER, retired lawyer; b. Evanston, Ill., May 23, 1931; s. Simon Rae and Frances (Dummer) Logan; m. Claude Riviere, Apr. 13, 1957; children: Carolyn Gisele, Francis Dummer. BA, U. Chgo., 1950; BA Juris, Oxford U., 1954; LLB, Harvard U., 1955. Bar: N.Y. 1956, Calif. 1989. Assoc. Milbank, Tweed, Hadley & McCloy, NYC, 1955-64, ptnr. NYC and L.A., 1965-96, chmn., 1992-96. Commr. Burbank-Glendale-Pasadena Airport Authority, Calif., 2005—. Overseer Huntington Libr., Art Collections and Bot. Gardens, Calif., 2006—. Mem.: N.Y. State Bar, Pacific Coun. Internat. Policy, Am. Law Inst., Coun. Fgn. Rels., Calif. State Bar. Home: 1726 Linda Vista Ave Pasadena CA 91103-1132

LOGAN, JAMES KENNETH, lawyer, retired judge; b. Quenemo, Kans., Aug. 21, 1929; s. John Lysle and Esther Maurine (Price) Logan; m. Beverly Jo Jennings, June 8, 1952; children: Daniel Jennings, Amy Logan Sliva, Sarah Logan Sherard, Samuel Price. AB, U. Kans., 1952; LLB magna cum laude, Harvard U., 1955. Bar: Kans. 1955, Calif. 1956. Law clk. U.S. Cir. Judge Huxman, 1955—56; with firm Gibson, Dunn & Crutcher, LA, 1956—57; asst. prof. law U. Kans., 1957—61, prof., dean Law Sch., 1961—68; ptnr. Payne and Jones, Olathe, Kans., 1968—77; judge U.S. Ct. Appeals (10th cir.), 1977—98; pvt. practice Logan Law Firm LLC, Olathe, 1998—2001, Foulston Siefkin LLP, Overland Park, Kans., 2002—. Ezra Ripley Thayer tchg. fellow Harvard Law Sch., 1961—62; vis. prof. U. Tex., 1964, Stanford U., 1969, U. Mich., 1976; sr. lectr. Duke U., 1987, 91, 93; commr. U.S. Dist. Ct., 1964—67; mem. U.S. Jud. Conf. Adv. Com. Fed. Rules of Appellate Procedure, 1990—97, chair, 1993—97. Author (with W.B. Leach): Future Interests and Estate Planning, 1961; author: Kansas Estate Administration, 5th edit., 1986; author (with A.R. Martin) Kansas Corporate Law and Practice, 2d edit., 1979; author: The Federal Courts of the Tenth Circuit: A History, 1992, also articles. Candidate for U.S. Senate, 1968. With US Army, 1947—48. Recipient Disting. Svc. citation, U. Kans., 1986, Francis Rawle award, ABA-ALI, 1990; scholar Rhodes Scholarship, 1952. Mem.: ABA, Kans. Bar Assn., Order of Coif, Phi Delta Phi, Alpha Kappa Psi, Pi Sigma Alpha, Omicron Delta Kappa, Beta Gamma Sigma, Phi Beta Kappa. Democrat. Presbyterian. Office Phone: 913-498-2100. Business E-Mail: jlogan@foulston.com.

LOGAN, JOHN ARTHUR, JR., retired foundation executive; b. Chgo., Dec. 8, 1923; s. John Arthur and Dorothea (Halstead) L.; m. Ann Orr deForest, Aug. 30, 1960. Grad., Taft Sch., Watertown, Conn., 1942; BA, Yale, 1949, MA, 1951, PhD, 1954; LL.D., Western Md. Coll.; L.H.D., Hollins Coll. Faculty Yale, 1949-61, asst. prof. history, 1958-61; pres. Hollins Coll., 1961-75, Ind. Coll. Funds Am., NYC, 1975-86. Vis. lectr. Salzburg Seminar in Am. Studies, 1961. Author: No Transfer: An American Security Principle, 1961. Served to capt. AUS, 1942-46. Fellow Saybrook Coll., Yale, 1950— Mem. Phi Beta Kappa. Clubs: Elizabethan (New Haven); Century Assn. (N.Y.C.), Yale (N.Y.C.). Home: 88 Notch Hill Rd Apt 353 North Branford CT 06471-1853

LOGAN, KENNETH RICHARD, lawyer; b. NYC, Dec. 26, 1944; s. John S. and Hazel (Mathias) L.; m. Grace Winter-Durennel, Aug. 12, 1967; children: Finlay, Emily. BA, Princeton U., 1967; JD, U. Pa., 1972. Bar: N.Y., U.S. Dist. Ct. (so. dist.) N.Y., U.S. Ct. Appeals (2nd cir.). Assoc. Simpson Thacher & Bartlett, NYC, 1972-79, ptnr., 1979—. Served with US Army, 1969—70. Office: Simpson Thacher & Bartlett 425 Lexington Ave Fl 15 New York NY 10017-3954 Office Phone: 212-455-2650. Office Fax: 212-455-2502. Business E-Mail: klogan@stblaw.com.

LOGAN, KENT, retired securities industry executive; b. 1944; m. Vicki Logan, 1985. Grad., Wharton Sch. Bus. With Barclays de Zoete Wedd Inc., Paine Webber Inc., Rotan Mosle Inc., Goldman Sachs; sr. ptnr. Montgomery Securities, San Francisco, 1990—99. Bd. dirs. Clyfford Still Mus., Denver, Aspen Art Mus., Aspen, Colo. Mem. town coun., Vail, Colo., 2003—. Named one of Top 200 Collectors, ARTNews Mag., 2000—. Avocation: art collection.

LOGAN, LARA, news correspondent; b. Durban, South Africa, Mar. 29, 1971; m. Jason Siemon. B in Commerce, Univ. Natal, Durban, 1992; diploma French language, culture, history, Universite de L'Alliance Francaise, Paris. Former swimsuit model; hostess Water Club, NYC; reporter Sunday Tribune, Durban, South Africa, 1988—89, Daily News, Durban, 1990—92; prodr. Reuters, London; freelance corr., assignment editor, prodr. several news orgn. including ITN, Fox/SKY, CBS, NBC, European Broadcast Union, London, 1996—99; freelance corr. CNN, London, 1998—99; corr. GMTV, ITV, London, 2000—02, CBS News Radio; war corr., Mideast CBS News, 2002—, chief fgn. corr., 2006—. Contbr. 60 Minutes II, 2002—04, reporter 60 Minutes, 2005—. Recipient Gracie Allen award Best News Story, Am. Women in Radio & TV, 2000, 2002, 2003, Gracie Allen Award Individual Achievement for Best Reporter/Corr., 2004, David Kaplan award, Overseas Press Club Am., 2007. Office: CBS News 530 West 57th St New York NY 10019*

LOGAN, LEE ROBERT, orthodontist, department chairman; b. LA, June 24, 1932; s. Melvin Duncan and Margaret (Seltzer) L.; m. Maxine Nadler, June 20, 1975; children: Chad, Casey. BS, UCLA, 1952; DDS, Northwestern U., Evanston, Ill., 1956, MS, 1961. Diplomate Am. Bd. Orthodontics. Gen. practice dentistry, Reseda, Calif., 1958—59; pvt. practice Northridge, Calif., 1961—, 2000—; vice chair dental dept., 2006—. Med. staff Northridge Hosp., 2000—, vice chair med. staff dental dept.; owner Maxine's Prodn. Co., Maxine's Talent Agy.; guest lectr. dept. orthodontics UCLA, U. So. Calif. Contbr. articles to profl. jours. Achievements include patent and licensing agreement with 3M for a device to attach braces, 2001, Can. patent, 2004, patents U.K., Germany, France, Japan. Served to lt. USNR, 1956-58. Named 1st Pl. winner, Autistic Jogathon, 1981—2001, (with wife) Couple of Yr., Autistic Children Assn., 1986, in his honor Logan's Run, Walk for Autism; named to Best Dentist's in Am., 2004—07; recipient Nat. Philanthropy award, 1987, winner, Logan's Run, 2005—06, Founder's award, Autistic Assn., 2007. Mem. ADA, San Fernando Valley Dental Assn. (pres. 1998), Am. Assn. Orthodontists, Pacific Coast Soc. Orthodontists (dir., pres. so. sect. 1974-75, chmn. membership 1981-83), Foudn. Orthodontic Rsch. (charter mem.), Calif. Soc. Orthodontists (chmn. peer rev. 1982-93), G.V. Black Soc. (charter) Angle Soc. Orthodontists (pres. 1981-82, bd. dirs. 1982—, nat. pres. 1985-87), U.S.C. Century Club Fraternity, Xi Psi Phi, Chi Phi. Achievements include patents in field. Home: 4830 Encino Ave Encino CA 91316-3813 Office: 18250 Roscoe Blvd Northridge CA 91325-4226 Home Phone: 818-788-2361. Personal E-mail: orthologan@aol.com.

LOGAN, MATHEW KUYKENDALL, journalist; b. Norman, Okla., Aug. 19, 1933; s. Leonard Marion and Floy-Elise (Duke) L.; m. Linda Dianne Elderkin, Dec. 31, 1964. BA in Journalism, U. Okla., 1955. Reporter UPI, 1957—58; city editor Daily Oklahoman, 1958—69; asst. mng. editor Houston Post, 1969—76, mng. editor, 1976—83, Sta. KHOU-TV, 1984—87; asst. dean for community affairs Med. Sch. U. Tex., 1987—92; v.p. pub. affairs and mktg. Hermann Hosp., 1992—97; v.p. corp. comm. Meml. Hermann Healthcare Sys., 1997—2002; vis. prof. journalism Sam Houston State U., Huntsville, 2002—05. Served with AUS, 1957. Mem. UPI Editors Tex. (pres. 1977), Tex. AP Mng. Editors Assn. (pres. 1983), Sigma Chi. Methodist. Home: 24 Sunlit Forest Dr The Woodlands TX 77381-2986 Fax: 281-367-2686. E-mail: kuyklogan@houston.rr.com.

LOGAN, SANDRA JEAN, retired economics and business professor; b. Dayton, Ohio, Jan. 3, 1940; d. Max B. and Edna E. (Sanderson) Parrish; m. John E. Logan, Apr. 25, 1964. BA, Drew U., 1962; MBA, Columbia U., NYC, 1964; PhD, U. S.C., 1976. Piano tchr., Whippany, N.J., 1957-64; lab. analyst Bear Creek Mining Co., Morristown, N.J., summer 1957, 58; rsch. asst. Drew U., Madison, N.J., summer 1962; staff asst. N.J. Bell Telephone Co., Newark, summer 1963, 64-67; instr. bus. U. Toledo, 1967-69; asst. prof. econs. and bus. S.C. State Univ., Orangeburg, 1970-76; prof. econs. and bus. Newberry (S.C.) Coll., 1976—2002, emeritus, 2002—, acting v.p. acad. affairs, 1993-95. Cons. econs., Ohio and S.C., 1967—, N.J. Bell Telephone Co., Newark, 1968; lectr. bus. Ea. Mich. U., Ypsilanti, spring 1969. Active Coldstream Home Owners Assn., Columbia, S.C., 1972-80; officer St. Andrews Woman's Club, Columbia, 1969-76. Rsch. grantee, U. SC and SC State U., 1974—75. Mem. Am. Econs. Assn., So. Econs. Assn. Republican. Presbyterian. Home: 112 Smiths Market Ct Columbia SC 29212-1923

LOGAN, SHARON BROOKS, lawyer; b. Nov. 19, 1945; d. Blake Elmer and Esther N. (Statum) Brooks; children: John W. III, Troy Blake. BS Econs., U. Md., 1967, MBA Mktg., 1969; JD, U. Fla., 1979. Bar: Fla. 1979. Prin. Raymond Wilson, Esq., Ormond Beach, Fla., 1980; atty. Landis, Graham & French, Daytona Beach, Fla., 1981, Watson & Assocs., Daytona Beach, 1982—84, Sharon B. Logan, PA, Ormond Beach, 1984—. Legal adv. to paralegal program Daytona Beach CC, 1984—. Sponsor Ea. Surfing Assn., Daytona Beach, 1983—, Nat. Scholastic Surfing Assn., 1987—; bd. dir. Ctr. for Visually Impaired, 1991—. Recipient Citizenship award, Rotary Club, 1962—63; fellow Woodrow Wilson, U. Md., 1967. Mem.: Daytona Beach Area Bd. Realtors, Volusia County Estate Planning Coun., Fla. Supreme Ct. Hist. Soc., Volusia County Real Property Coun., Inc. (sec. 1987—88, bd. dirs., v.p. 1988—89, pres. 1989—90, sec. 1990—91, 1991—97, pres. 1997—98, 1998—), Volusia County Bar Assn. (bd. dir.), Fla. Bar Assn. (cert. real estate atty. 1996, real property and probate sect.), Halifax River Yacht Club, Beech Mountain Country Club, Gator Club, Ducks Unlimited, Mus. Arts and Scis., Md. Club, Sigma Alpha Epsilon, Delta Delta Delta (Scholarship award 1964), Omicron Delta Epsilon, Phi Kappa Phi, Alpha Lamba Delta, Beta Gamma Sigma. Democrat. Episcopalian. Avocations: interior decorating, cooking, sewing, tennis, aerobics. Office: Sharon B Logan PA 180 Vining Ct PO Box 4258 Ormond Beach FL 32175-4258 Office Phone: 386-673-5787. E-mail: sharonbloganpa@clearwire.net.

LOGAN, WILLIAM, poetry critic, literature and language professor, poet; BA, Yale Univ., 1972; MFA, Univ. Iowa, 1975. Dir., creative writing Univ. Fla., Gainesville, 1983—2000, prof., English dept., 2000—. Author: (poetry collections) Sad-faced Men, 1982, Difficulty, 1985, Sullen Weedy Lakes, 1988, Vain Empires, 1998, Night Battle, 1999, Macbeth in Venice, 2003, The Whispering Gallery, 2005, (poetry criticism) All the Rage, 1998, Reputations of the Tongue, 1999 (Nat. Book Critics Cir. award in criticism finalist), Desperate Measures, 2002, Undiscovered Country, 2005 (Nat. Book Critics Cir. award for criticism, 2005); co-editor: Certain Solitudes, 1997. Recipient Citation for Excellence in Reviewing, Nat. Book Critics Cir., Peter I.B. Lavan award, Acad. Am. Poets, John Masefield and Celia B. Wagner awards, Poetry Soc. Am., J. Howard and Barbar M.J. Wood prize, Poetry, Corrington award for lit. excellence, 2004, Amy Lowell Poetry Traveling Scholarship. Office: Dept English Univ Fla-Turlington Hall 4211H PO Box 117310 Gainesville FL 32611-7310 Office Phone: 352-392-6650 ext. 239. Office Fax: 352-392-0860. Business E-Mail: wlogan@english.ufl.edu.

LOGEMANN, JERILYN ANN, speech pathologist, educator; b. Berwyn, Ill., May 21, 1942; d. Warren F. and Natalie M. (Killmer) L. BS, Northwestern U., 1963; MA, 1964, PhD, 1968. Grad. asst. dept. communicative disorders Northwestern U., 1963-68; instr. speech and audiology DePaul U., 1964-65; instr. dept. communicative disorders Mundelein Coll., 1967-71; rsch. assoc. dept. neurology and otolaryngology and maxillo, 1970-74; asst. prof., 1974-78; dir. clin. and rsch. activities of speech and lang., 1975—; assoc. prof. depts. neurology, otolaryngology and comm. scis, 1978-83; prof., 1983; chmn. dept. comm. scis. and disorders, 1982-96; Ralph and Jean Sundin Prof. of Comm. Scis. and Disorders, 1995—; mem. assoc. staff Northwestern meml. Hosp., 1976—; Evanston (Ill.) Hosp., 1988—. Cons. in field; assoc. dir. cancer control Ill. Comprehensive Cancer Coun., Chgo., 1980-82; mem. rehab. com. Ill. divsn. Am. CAncer Soc., 1975-79, chmn., 1979—; mem. upper aerodigestive tract organ site com. Nat. Cancer Inst., 1986-89; postdoct. fellow Nat. Inst. Neurologic Disease, Communicative Disorders and Stroke,Northwestern U., 1968-70. Author: The Fisher-Logeman Test of Articulation Competence, 1971, Evaluation and Treatment of Swallowing Disorders, 1983, 2nd edit., 1998, Manual for the Videofluorographic Evaluation of Swallowing, 1985, 93; assoc. editor: Jour. Speech and Hearing Disorders, Dysphagia Jour., 1978—. Fellow Inst. Medicine Chgo., 1981—; grantee Nat Cancer Inst., 1975—, Am. Cancer Soc., 1981-82, Nat. Inst. Dental Rsch., 1996-2000, Nat. Inst. Deafness and Other Comm. Disorders, 1997—; recipient Honors award Conn. Speech Lang. Hearing Assn., 1995, Am. Acad. Otolaryngology-Head Neck Surgery, 1997, Appreciation award Coun. Grad. Prgrams in Comms. Scis. and Disorders, 1995, Cellular One award Vanderbilt U., Am. Special Lang. Hearing Assn., 2003. Fellow Speech, Lang. and Hearing Assn. (pres. 1994, 2000, Honors award 2003), Inst. Medicine, Ill. Speech- Lang. Hearing Assn.(Honors 2003); mem. Internat. Assn. Logopedics and Phoniatrics, AAUP, Acoustic Soc. Am. (program com. Chgo. regional chpt.), Linguistic Soc. Am., Speech Comm. Assn., Am. Cleft Palate Assn., Ill. Speech and Hearing Assn. (DiCarlo award 1988), Chgo. Heart Assn., Chgo. Speech Therapy and Auditory Soc. Office: Northwestern U Feinberg Sch Medicine 10-205 Galter Pavilion 201 E Huron Chicago IL 60611 also: Northwestern U Dept Comm Sci and Disorder 2240 Campus Dr Evanston IL 60208-0001 Home Phone: 847-492-9527; Office Phone: 847-491-2490.

LOGGIE, JENNIFER MARY HILDRETH, retired physician, educator; b. Lusaka, Zambia, Feb. 4, 1936; arrived in U.S., 1964, naturalized, 1972; d. John and Jenny (Beattie). M.B., B.Ch., U. Witwatersrand, Johannesburg, South Africa, 1959. Intern Harare Hosp., Salisbury, Rhodesia, 1960-61; gen. practice medicine Lusaka, 1961-62; sr. pediatric house officer Derby Children's Hosp., also St. John's Hosp., Chelmsford, England, 1962-64; resident in pediatrics Children's Hosp., Louisville, 1964, Cin. Children's Hosp., 1964-65; fellow clin. pharmacology Cin. Coll. Medicine, 1965-67; mem. faculty U. Cin. Med. Sch., 1967—, prof. pediatrics, 1975-98, assoc. prof. pharmacology, 1972-77, prof. emeritus pediatrics, 1998—; ret., 1998. Contbr. articles to med. publs.; editor Pediatric and Adolescent Hypertension, 1991. Grantee, Am. Heart Assn., 1970—72, 1989—90. Mem. Am. Pediatric Soc. (Founder's award 1996), Midwest Soc. Pediatric Rsch. Episcopalian. Home: 1133 Herschel Ave Cincinnati OH 45208-3112 Personal E-mail: jennlog@webtv.net.

LOGIE, JOHN HOULT, former mayor, lawyer; b. Ann Arbor, Mich., Aug. 11, 1939; s. James Wallace and Elizabeth (Hoult) Logie; m. Susan G. Duerr, Aug. 15, 1964; children: John Hoult Jr., Susannah, Margaret Elizabeth. Student, Williams Coll., 1957-59; BA, U. Mich., 1961, JD, 1968; MS, George Washington U., 1966; D of Pub. Svc. (hon.), Ferris State U., 2004. Bar: Mich. 1969, U.S. Dist. Ct. (we. and ea. dists.) Mich. 1969, U.S. Ct. Appeals (6th cir.) 1987. Assoc. Warner, Norcross & Judd, Grand Rapids, Mich., 1969-74, ptnr., 1974—2001, of counsel, 2002—; mayor City of Grand Rapids, 1991—2003. Instr. U.S. Naval Acad., 1964—66; chmn. civil justice adv. group U.S. Dist. Ct. (we. dist.) Mich., 1995—99; bd. vis. Sch. Bus. and Pub. Mgmt. George Washington U., 1995—2004; program coord. condemnation law sect. Inst. CLE; guest lectr. Grand Rapids CC, Grand Valley State U., Western Mich. U., Mich. State U. V.p., bd. dirs. Am. Cancer Soc., Grand Rapids, 1970—81; pres. Grand Rapids PTA Coun., 1971—73; pres., trustee Heritage Hill Assn., 1971—84, pres., 1976; v.p., bd. dirs. Goodwill Industries, Grand Rapids, 1973—79; chmn. Grand Rapids Urban Homesteading Commn., 1975—80, Grand Rapids Hist. Commn., 1985—90, Grand Rapids/Kent County Sesquicentennial Com., 1986—88, Clarke Hist. Libr., Ctrl. Mich. U., 2000—; pres., trustee Hist. Soc. Mich., 1984—90; mem. Headlee Blue Ribbon Commn., 1993—94, Mich. Workforce Devel. Bd., 2002—04; trustee Grand Valley State U. Found., 1998—; bd., sec. Mich. Land Use Inst., 2004. Lt. USN, 1961—66. Recipient Media Access Leadership award, Cmty. Media Ctr., 2000, Lifetime Achievement award, Mich. Hist. Preservation Network, 2000, Econ. Club, 2004, Emeritus award, Aquinas Coll., 2002, Disting. Trustee award, Leadership Grand Rapids, 2005, Disting. Cmty. Trustee award, Grand Rapids C. of C., 2005, Cmty. Leadership award, Convention/Arena Authority, 2006, Baxter History award, Grand Rapids Hist. Soc., 2007. Mem.: ABA (mem. forum com. healthlaw 1980—), Mich. Soc. Hosp. Attys. (pres. 1976—77), Grand Rapids Bar Assn. (dir. young lawyers sect. 1970, Worsfold Lifetime Svc. award 2004), Mich. Bar Assn. (chmn. condemnation com. real property sect. 1985—88), Am. Health Lawyers Assn., Univ. Club (dir. 1979—82, pres. 1980—82). Avocations: motor cruising, hunting, fishing. Home: 601 Cherry St SE Grand Rapids MI 49503-4726 Office: Warner Norcross and Judd 111 Lyon St NW Ste 900 Grand Rapids MI 49503-2487 Home Phone: 616-458-0951; Office Phone: 616-752-2111. Business E-Mail: jlogie@wnj.com.

LOGUE, DENNIS EMHARDT, finance educator, writer, banker, consultant; b. Bklyn., Mar. 28, 1944; s. Joseph Paul and Helen Rose (Emhardt) L.; m. Marcella Julia Watson, June 11, 1966; children: Dennis E. Jr., Patrick G. AB, Fordham U., 1964; MBA, Rutgers U., 1966; PhD, Cornell U., 1971. Asst. prof. Ind. U., Bloomington, 1971-73; sr. economist U.S. Treasury, Washington, 1973-74; prof. bus. Tuck Sch., Dartmouth Coll., Hanover, 1974—2001, Steven Roth prof. mgmt., former assoc. dean; dean Michael F. Price Coll. Bus. U. Okla., 2001—05, Fred E. Brown chair Price Coll. Bus., 2001—05. Chmn. bd. dirs., founding dir. Ledyard Nat. Bank, 2005—; bd. dirs. Waddell and Reed Fin. Inc., Abraxas Petroleum Corp., Duckwell ALCO Stores, Hypotherm. Author: Legislative Influence on Corporate Pension Plans, 1979, The Investment Performance of Corporate Pension Plans, 1988, Managing Retirement Plans, 2004, Managing Pension and Retirement Plans, 2005; editor: Handbook of Modern Finance, 1998; co-editor Fin. Mgmt., 1978-81 Former pres. bd. trustees Crossroads Acad.; founding mem. Josiah Bartlett Ctr. for Pub. Policy Rsch.; bd. trustees Montshire Mus. Sci. 1st lt. U.S. Army, 1966-68. Fellow Fin. Mgmt. Assn.

(bd. dirs., pres. 1995-96); mem. Am. Econ. Assn., Am. Fin. Assn. (bd. dirs. 1981-84), Knights of Malta, Equestrian Order Holy Sepulchre, Fin. Econ. Roundtable, Beta Gamma Sigma Republican. Roman Catholic. Home: 116 Shaker Blvd Enfield NH 03748 Office: Ledyard Nat Bank 38 S Main St Hanover NH 03755 Office Phone: 603-640-2664. Business E-Mail: dennis.logue@ledyardbank.com.

LOGUE, JAMES NICHOLAS, epidemiologist; b. Duryea, Pa., June 18, 1946; s. James and Lucille (Polen) L.; m. Mary Frances Carey, Nov. 25, 1972; children: Melissa, Jimmy, Jeffrey. BS, Kings Coll., 1968; MPH, U. Mich., 1971; DrPH, Columbia U., 1978. Statistician Warner Lambert Co, Morris Plains, NJ, 1969-70, 71-73; sr. med. biostatistician Ciba-Geigy Co., Summit, NJ, 1973-78; epidemiologist GEOMET Technologies, Inc., Rockville, Md., 1978-80; supervisory epidemiologist US FDA, Rockville, 1980-82; dir. divsn. environ. health epidemiology Pa. Dept. Health, Harrisburg, 1982—; acting dir. Bur. Epidemiology, 2004—07. Office: Pa Dept Health PO Box 90 Harrisburg PA 17108-0090

LOGUE, JEAN EVELYN, music educator; b. Chgo., Mar. 14, 1918; d. John Philip and Annaline Hazel Jeffrey; m. Osby Russell Logue, Mar. 12, 1938; children: Eleanor Jean Evans, Jeffrey, Don, Anne. Student, Cornell Coll., 1935-38; BS in History, Ea. Ill. U., 1968, MA in Music, 1977. Pvt. practice piano and organ tchr., Springfield, Ill., 1977—96, Chesterfield, Mo., 2001—, Ballwin, Mo., 2002—05, Farmington, N.Mex., 2005—. Asst. organist, pianist New Convenant United Meth. Ch., Farmington. Historian Genealog. Assn.; dir. ch. camps; dir. bell choir and children's choir. Mem.: Decatur Music Tchrs. Assn. (past v.p., sec.), Cooking Club Am. Democrat. Methodist. Avocations: organ, quilting. Office Phone: 505-330-3994. Personal E-mail: jelogue@advantss.net.

LOGUE, JOSEPH CARL, electronics engineer, consultant; b. Phila., Dec. 20, 1920; s. Percival J. and Mathilda (Moser) L.; m. Jeanne Martha Neubecker, Mar. 31, 1943; children: Raymond, Marilyn, Paul. BEE, Cornell U., 1944, MEE, 1949. Instr. Cornell U., Ithaca, NY, 1944-49, asst. prof., 1949-51; engr. IBM, Poughkeepsie, NY, 1951-86, dir. rsch. divsn. Yorktown Heights, NY, 1986; CEO Lorex Industries Inc., Poughkeepsie, 1986—. 30 patents in field; contbr. papers to profl. publs. IBM fellow. Fellow IEEE, AAAS; mem. NAE, Rsch. Soc. Am. Avocations: scuba diving, photography. Home: 52 Boardman Rd Poughkeepsie NY 12603-4228

LOGUE, JUDITH FELTON, psychoanalyst, educator; b. Phila., Aug. 21, 1942; d. Martin and Laura (Goldman) Kirshenbaum; m. Stephen Felton, Feb. 8, 1966 (div. Aug. 1989); 1 child, Jane Jennifer; m. A. Douglas Logue, Feb. 14, 1990. AB in Govt., Wheaton Coll., Mass., 1963; MSW, Rutgers U., 1966, PhD, 1983; grad., NY Ctr. Psychoanalytic Tng., 1978. Diplomate Am. Bd. Psychotherapy, Am. Bd. Forensic Medicine, Am. Bd. Examiners Clin. Social Worker, Am. Bd. Forensic Examiners, Am. Bd. Psychol. Specialties, cert. profl. coach, mentor coach. Clin. social worker VA, Newark, 1967; psychotherapist Santa Barbara (Calif.) Mental Health Svcs., 1967-69; supr. Santa Barbara Counselling Ctr., 1967-69; pvt. practice psychoanalysis, 1969—; pres. Goldilox Co. Inc., 1997—, Shairing Co., 2001—. Psychoanalyst, therapist Fifth Ave. Ctr. for Psychotherapy, NYC, 1969-72; instr. Marymount Manhattan Coll., 1971; psychotherapy supr. clin. faculty, dept. psychiatry Rutgers Med. Sch., New Brunswick, NJ, 1972-75, tchg. asst. Grad. Sch. Social Work, 1974-76; vis. lectr. Bryn Mawr Coll. Sch. Social Work and Social Rsch., 1980; faculty NY Ctr. for Psychoanalytic Tng., 1980—, NJ Inst. Psychoanalysis and Psychotherapy, 1982—; adv. bd. Am. Bd. Forensic Social Workers, 1999—, chair adv. bd., 2000; pres. Goldilox Co., Inc., 1997, ShAIRing, Inc., 2000; faculty So. NJ Psychoanalytic Inst., Brigantine, 2004—, bd. dirs. Mem. editl. bd. jour Current Issues in Psychoanalytic Practice, 1983-93; contbr. articles to profl. jours. Bd. dirs. N.Y. Ctr. for Psychoanalytic Tng., Inst. for Psychoanalysis and Psychotherapy N.J. Faculty, 1982—. Recipient Disting. Faculty award Atlantic County Psychoanalytic Soc., 1987; NIMH fellow, 1965. Fellow N.J. Soc. for Clin. Social Work; mem. AAUP, NASW, APA (pres. divsn. 39 2003-04, bd. dirs. 2005—, com. psychoanalytic psychotherapists, bd. dirs. divsn. 39 2006—), Nat. Assn. for Advancement of Psychoanalysis, Acad. Cert. Social Workers, Soc. for Psychoanalytic Tng. (bd. dirs. 1983-90, dir. social sci. program 1983-86), Am. Coll. Forensic Examiners Internat. (mem. editl. bd. jours. 1999—, Outstanding Svc. award 2000), Internat. Coach Fedn.; mem. APA (pres. div. 39 sec. III, 2003-04), Am. Psychoanalytic Assn. (psychotherapy task force, psychoanalysis and undergrad. edn. task force, com. on psychotherapist assocs. 2003—), Am. Coll. Forensic Social Workers (chair 2000-01), Women in Aviation Internat, 99's Internat. Orgn. Women Pilots, Nat. Bus. Aviation Assn, Rutgers U. Alumni Assn. (bd. dirs. 2003-05), So. NJ Psychoanalytic Inst. (faculty mem. 2004-06, bd. dirs. 2004-06). Home and Office: 159 Valley Rd Princeton NJ 08540-3442 Home Phone: 609-921-0828; Office Phone: 609-921-0828. Personal E-mail: judith@judithlogue.com.

LOGUE, RONALD E., investment company executive; BS, Boston Coll., 1967, MBA, 1974. Head mutual fund custody divsn. State Street Corp., Boston, 1990—92, head global investor svcs. group, 1992—99, vice chmn., 1999—2001, COO, pres., 2001—04, chmn., CEO, 2004—. Bd. dir. Fed. Reserve Bank, Boston. Bd. dir. Metro. Boston Housing Project. Office: State Street Corp 225 Franklin St Boston MA 02110*

LOGUE-KINDER, JOAN, public relations consultant; b. Richmond, Va., Oct. 26, 1943; d. John T. and Helen (Harvey) Logue; m. Lowell A. Henry Jr., Oct. 6, 1963 (div. Sept. 1981); children: Lowell A. Henry III, Catherine D. Henry, Christopher Logue Henry; m. Randolph S. Kinder, Dec. 13, 1986 (div. Nov. 1995). Student, Wheaton Coll., 1959-62; BA in Sociology, Adelphi U., 1964; cert. in edn., Mercy Coll., Dobbs Ferry, NY, 1971; postgrad., NYU, 1973; cert. in edn., St. John's U., 1974. Asst. to dist. mgr. U.S. Census Bur., NYC, 1970; tchr. and adminstr. social studies Yonkers (N.Y.) Bd. Edn., 1971-75; dir. pub. rels. Nat. Black Network, NYC, 1976-83; corp. v.p. NBN Broadcasting (formerly Nat. Black Network), NYC, 1984-90; sr. v.p. The Mingo Group/Plus, NYC, 1990-91; v.p. Edelman Pub. Rels. Worldwide, NYC, 1991-93; dep. asst. sec. pub. affairs U.S. Dept. Treasury, Washington, 1993-94, asst. sec. pub. affairs, 1994-95; dir. corp. comm. programs The Seagram Co., NYC, 1995-96; v.p. Save the Children, Westport, Conn., 1997-98; sr. v.p., dir. mktg. and comm. Lynch, Jones & Ryan, NYC, 1998—99; v.p. investment devel. Overseas Pvt. Investment Corp., Washington, 1999—2001; dir. comm. Office of the Mayor of D.C., 2001; cons. Phila. Acad. Fine Arts, 2001—, Sari Katz for Mayor, 2001—, Greater Jamaica Devel. Corp., 2001—. Mem. alumnae recruitment coun. Wheaton Coll.; mem. Nigerian-Am. Friendship Soc., 1978-81; bd. dirs. Westchester Civil Liberties Union, 1974-77, Greater N.Y. coun. Girl Scouts U.S.A., 1985-93, Operation PUSH, 1985-93; del. White House Conf. on Small Bus.; active polit. campaigns, including Morris Udall for U.S. Pres., Howard Samuels for Gov.; sr. black media advisor Dukakis/Bentsen presdl. campaign, 1988; conv. del. N.Y. State Women's Polit. Caucus, 1975, pres. black caucus, 1976-77. Recipient Excellence in Media award Inst. New Cinema Artists, 1984. Mem. World Inst. Black Comm. (bd. dirs. 1983-91). Address: 5703 Woodcrest Ave Philadelphia PA 19131-2224 Home Phone: 215-878-1001, 610-457-8077; Office Phone: 718-291-0282 129. E-mail: jlk45plus@msn.com.

LOH, ARTHUR TSUNG YUAN, finance company executive; b. Shanghai, People's Republic of China, Dec. 2, 1923; came to U.S., 1948; s. Chengor and Kwei N. (Wang) L.; m. Monica K.L. Chen, Apr. 16, 1955; children: Stephanie T.L., Pamela T.K. BA, St. John's U., Shanghai, 1945; MS, U. Ill., 1949, PhD, 1952. V.p., co-owner R.W. Pressprich & Co., NYC, 1952-69; exec. v.p. fin. GAC Corp., Allentown, Pa., 1970-71; v.p., co-owner N.Y. Securities Co., NYC, 1972-74; sr. v.p., chief fin. officer Govt. Employees Ins. Co., Criterion Ins. Co., Washington, 1974-80; chief fin. officer Rotary Internat., Evanston, Ill., 1981-88; founder, chmn. Loh Assocs., Greenwich, Conn., 1988—. Chmn. bd. GAC Securities Co., Ft. Lauderdale, Fla., 1973-74. Chmn. devel. com. Travelers Aid Soc., N.Y.C.; active Rep. Nat. Com., Washington, Heritage Found.; dir. Mid. Patent Rural Cemetery. Mem. Assn. for Investment Mgmt. and Rsch., Internat. Soc. Security Analysts, Am. Econ. Assn., Fin. Execs. Inst., Inst. Chartered Fin. Analysts (chartered), N.Y. Soc. Security Analysts, Wall Street Club, Bankers Club Am., Windmill Club, Greenwich Polo Club, Rotary, Downtown Assn. (N.Y.C.), City Midday Club (N.Y.C.). Methodist. Avocations: tennis, swimming, skiing, travel. Home: 9 North Ln Armonk NY 10504-2238 also: East of Rte 7 Danby VT 05739 Office: Loh Assocs 2001 W Main St Stamford CT 06902-4501 E-mail: atyloh@aol.com.

LOH, HORACE H., pharmacology educator; b. Canton, Republic of China, May 28, 1936; BS, Nat. Taiwan U., Taipei, Republic China, 1958; PhD, U. Iowa, 1965. Lectr. dept. pharmacology U. Calif. Sch. Medicine, San Francisco, 1967; assoc. prof. biochem. Wayne State U., Detroit, 1968-70; lectr., rsch. assoc. depts. psychiatry, pharmacology Langley Porter Neuropsychiatric Inst. U. Calif. Sch. Medicine, San Francisco, 1970-72, assoc. prof. depts. psychiatry, pharmacology Langley Porter Neuropsychiatric Inst., 1972-75, prof. depts. psychiatry, pharmacology Langley Porter Neuropsychiatric Inst., 1975-88; prof., head dept. pharmacology U. Minn. Med. Sch., Mpls., 1989—, Frederick and Alice Stark prof., head dept. pharmacology, 1990—. Chmn. ann. meeting theme com. on receptors Fedn. Am. Socs. for Exptl. Biology, 1984; mem. exec. com. Internat. Narcotic Rsch. Conf., 1984—87, chair sci. program ann. meeting, 1986; mem. adv. com. Nat. Tsing Hua U. Inst. Life Scis., Taiwan, China, 1985—89; mem. exec. com. Com. on Problems of Drug Dependence, Inc., 1985—88; mem. sci. adv. coun. Nat. Found. for Addictive Diseases, 1987—; cons. U.S. Army R & D Dept. Def., 1980—84. Mem. editl. adv. bd. Life Scis., 1978—, Substance and Alcohol Abuse, 1980—, Neurochemistry Internat., 1980—88, Neuropharmacology, 1992—, Neurosci. Series, 1982—83, Ann. rev. Pharmacology and Toxicology, 1984—89, Jour. Pharmacology and Exptl. Therapeutics, 1987—, assoc. editor CRC Critical Rev. in Pharmacol. Scis., 1987—88, Ann. Rev. Pharmacology and Toxicology, 1990—95; contbr. 56 chpts. in books, 300 articles to profl. jours. Recipient Career Devel. award, USPHS, 1973—78, 1978—83, Rsch. Scientist award, 1983—88, 1989—94, Humboldt award for sr. U.S. scientists, 1977. Mem.: We. Pharmacology Soc. (councilor 1980—83, pres. 1984—85), Soc. Chinese Bioscientists in Am. (pres. 1985—86), Am. Soc. Pharmacology and Exptl. Therapeutics (program com. 1976—86, trustee bd. publs. 1987—93, com. on confs. 1990—93), Am. Coll. Neuropsychopharmacology (honorific awards com. 1988—). Office: U Minn Med Sch Dept Pharmacology 6-120 Jackson 321 Church St SE Minneapolis MN 55455-0217 Office Phone: 612-625-9997. Business E-Mail: lohxx001@umn.edu.

LOH, ROBERT N. K., engineering educator; b. Lumut, Malaysia; arrived in Can., 1962, came to U.S., 1968; m. Annie Loh; children: John, Peter, Jennifer. BSc in Engring., Nat. Taiwan U., Taipei, 1961; MSc in Engring., U. Waterloo, Ont., Can., 1964, PhD, 1968. Asst. prof. U. Iowa, Iowa City, 1968-72, assoc. prof., 1973-78; prof. Oakland U., Rochester, Mich., 1978—, John F. Dodge prof., 1984—, assoc. dean, 1985-98, dir. Ctr. for Robotics and Advanced Automation, 1984—. Mem. editorial bd. Info. Systems, 1975—, Jour. of Intelligent and Robotic Systems, 1987—, Asia-Pacific Engring. Jour., 1990—; contbr. over 190 jour. publs. and tech. reports. Recipient numerous research grants and contracts from Dept. Def., NSF and pvt. industry. Mem. IEEE, Soc. Machine Intelligence (bd. dirs. 1985—), Assn. Unmanned Vehicle Systems, 1987—, Sigma Xi, Tau Beta Pi. Office: Oakland U Ctr for Robotics and Advanced Automation Dodge Hall Engring Rochester MI 48309-4401

LOH, SHAUN, radiologist; b. Bklyn., Feb. 17, 1976; s. Nicholas and Emily Loh; m. Karen S. Ko, June 2, 2006. BS, Stanford U., Palo Alto, Calif., 1998; MD, MBA, Tufts U. Sch. Medicine, Boston, 2006. Transitional intern Caritas Carney Hosp., Dorchester, Mass.; resident radiology U. Calif. Med. Ctr., Sacramento; sr. assoc. Triage Cons. Group, San Francisco, Mass.; bus. analyst Broadlane, Inc., Oakland, Mass., 2001—02; rsch. fellow Beth Israel Deaconess Med. Ctr., Boston, 2003—. Contbr. articles to profl. jours. Recipient Most Valuable Employee award, Broadlane, Inc, 2002. Mem.: Radiol. Soc. N.Am. (assoc.), Am. Roentgen Ray Soc. (assoc.). Office: Caritas Carney Hos 2100 Dorchester Ave Dorchester MA 02124 Home Phone: 617-524-8212; Office Phone: 617-296-4000.

LOHAN, LINDSAY DEE, actress; b. NYC, July 2, 1986; d. Michael and Dina Lohan. Former model. Actor: (TV series) Another World, 1996—97, Bette, 2000; (TV films) Life-Size, 2000, Get A Clue, 2002; (films) The Parent Trap, 1998 (Best Performance in Feature Film - Leading young Actress, Young Artist Awards, 1999), Freaky Friday, 2003 (Breakthrough Female Performance, MTV Movies Awards, 2004), Confessions of a Teenage Drama Queen, 2004, Mean Girls, 2004 (Teen Choice award, 2004, Best Female Performance, MTV Awards, 2005), Herbie: Fully Loaded, 2005, Just My Luck, 2006, A Prairie Home Companion, 2006, Bobby, 2006, Chapter 27, 2007, Georgia Rule, 2007, I Know Who Killed Me, 2007; singer: (albums) Speak, 2004, A Little More Personal (Raw), 2005. Named Superstar of Tomorrow, Young Hollywood Awards, 2005; recipient Breakthrough Actress of the Yr. award, Hollywood Awards, 2006, Blimp award, Kids' Choice Awards, 2006. Office: Creative Artists Agy 9830 Wilshire Blvd Beverly Hills CA 90212*

LOHMAN, ARTHUR GROVER, civilian military employee; b. Barksdale AFB, La., Dec. 6, 1950; s. Paul Oswald and Julia Alice (Rider) L.; m. Julie Rae Bohn, July 25, 1975 (div. Dec. 5, 1986; dec. Feb. 1998); children: Arthur G. Jr., Timothy E.; m. Terry Ann Hess, Jan. 10, 1988 (div. Nov. 19, 1990). Student logistics, C.C. of the Air Force, Maxwell AFB, 1974, 77-78; student, Weber State U., 1969, 74, 83-85. Enlisted USAF, 1970, advanced through the grades to sgt., ret., 1982, electronics tech. LN-12 navigation sect. Hill AFB, Utah, 1984-88, electronics tech. cir. bd. mfg. sect., 1988-92, electronics tech. aim 9 sidewinder missile sect., 1992-95, electronics tech. F16/B1 aircraft microwave sect., 1995—; mail clk., date transcriber IRS, Ogden, Utah, 1983-84. Mem. hazardous waste process action team, safety monitor working group Air Craft Avionics Divsn., Hill AFB, Utah, 1989-90; hazardous waste site mgr. Cir. Card Mfg., Hill AFB, Utah, 1988-90, mem. quality com., 1989-90; participant Peace Autograph Project Display, Mus. Peace and Solidarity, Samarkand, Uzbekistan, 1993—. Creator: Cartoon Bug, 1982. Pub. affairs cmty. escort Ogden Air Logistics Ctr., Hill AFB, Utah, 1988-90; judge sci. fair Bonneville H.S., Weber State Univ., Ogden, Utah, 1989, speech contest judge, 12th Annual Health Occupation Students Am. Nat. Leadership Conf., Utah, 1989; master of ceremonies Hill AFB Talent Competition, 1993; jr. olympic bowling coach Young Am. Bowling Alliance, Layton, 1996—. Mem. Utah State Poetry Soc. (affil. Acad. Am. Poets and Nat. Fedn. State Poetry Socs.), Learning Disabilities Assn. Utah, Toastmasters Internat. (gov.'s award 1990), Order of Internat. Fellowship. Avocations: poetry, chess, bowling, acting in community theater, collecting rare books. Office: OO-ALC/LARPJ 7274 Wardleigh Rd Hill AFB UT 84056-5137 Home: 620 W 1800 N Layton UT 84041-1622

LOHMAN, GORDON RUSSELL, retired manufacturing executive; b. 1934; BS, MIT, 1955. Rsch. metallurgist, project engr. Amsted Industries, Inc., Chgo., 1958-61; project engr. Amsted Rsch. Labs., Chgo., 1961-67; dir. rsch. Amsted Industries, Inc., Chgo., 1967-68, pres. rsch., 1968-76, pres. MacWhyte divsn., 1976-78, v.p., 1978-87, exec. v.p., then pres., 1987-88, pres., COO, 1988-90, pres., CEO, 1990-1999; ret., 1999. Trustee Ill. Inst. Tech.; bd. dirs. Fortune Brands Inc., Ameren, ACCO Brands. Lt. USAF, 1955—58.

LOHMANN, CHRISTOPH HUBERTUS, orthopaedic surgeon, researcher; b. Goettingen, Germany, Sept. 25, 1967; s. Ernst August and Sigrun Lohmann. MD, U. Goettingen, 1994. Prof. orthopaedics, dep. chmn. U. Hamburg-Eppendorf, 2006—. Recipient award Assn. for Basic Sci., German Soc. for Orthopaedics and Traumatology, 1999. Mem. Am. Soc. for Bone and Mineral Rsch., German Soc. for Orthopaedics and Traumatology, European Orthopaedic Rsch. Soc. Achievements include research on regulation of osteobalsts and chondrocytes. Office Fax: 49 551 392651. E-mail: lohmannch@t-online.de.

LOHMANN, GEORGE YOUNG, JR., neurosurgeon, health facility administrator, artist; b. Scranton, Pa., Aug. 9, 1947; s. George Young Lohmann and Elizabeth (Nichols) Frantzen; m. Joette Calabrese, May 15, 1973 (div. 1981); m. Rosemary Ei-Ling Ma, Sept. 24, 1988 (div. 1998); 1 child, Norelle Christa Victoria. AB in Chemistry with honors, Hobart Coll., 1968; MD, SUNY, Buffalo, 1972. Diplomate Am. Bd. Neurol. Surgeons, Am. Acad. Pain Specialists, Am. Bd. Forensic Medicine, Am. Acad. Disability Analysts. Resident gen. surgery Wesley Meml. Hosp., Chgo., 1972-73; asst. med. dir. West Side Orgn., Chgo., 1973-74; emergency physician St. James Hosp., Chicago Heights, Ill., 1973-74; from jr. resident to chief resident neurosurgery Georgetown U. Hosp., Washington, 1975-79; chief resident neurosurgery Washington Vets. Hosp., 1978; pvt. practice Baton Rouge, 1979-81, 81-84; dir. dept. neurosurgery Brookdale Hosp. Med. Ctr., Bklyn., 1984-93; pres. Bklyn. Neurosurg. Svcs., Inc., 1985—; pvt. practice Midland, Tex., 1994-96; founding pres. Dragongate Adoption Cons., Inc., 1999—. Mem. Med. Dir. Com., Risk Mgmt. Com., Exec. Quality Assurance Com., 1987-93; mem. Med. Bd. Com., 1985-93, Exec. Bd. Com., 1984-93, Pain Mgmt. Com., 1988-91; regional dir. Tex. Physicians Resource Coun., 1996-97. Editl. bd. Computerized Radiology, 1975—85, assoc. editor, 1975—85; contbr. articles to profl. jours.; actor: (in amatur theatre). Mem. adv. bd. Ctr. Latin Affairs, Baton Rouge, 1982-84; mem. Senatorial Inner Cir., 1988, mem. presdl. roundtable, 1991; mem. Presdl. Roundtable, 1992; trustee Christian Victory Ctr., Hempstead, N.Y., 1986-88; vol. Appalachian Project, 1970; mem. transition team for Pres. Ronald Reagan, 1980-81. Named to Compton-Connolly Guide to Best Physicians in the N.Y. Met. Area; selected by peers as one of Best Doctors in America Ctrl. Region, 1996-97. Fellow ACS, Am. Coll. Pain Mgmt., Am. Coll. Forensic Examiners, Am. Coll. Disability Analysts; mem. AMA, Am. Assn. Neurol. Surgeons (sect. intensive care), Christian Med. and Dental Soc., Am. Assn. Neurologic Surgeons, N.Y. State Neurosurg. Soc., N.Y. Soc. Neurosurgery, Congress Neurologic Surgeons (spine sect., sect. on trauma, sect. on intensive care), Tex. State Med. Soc., So. Med. Soc. Presdl. Roundtable (presdl. transition team 1980-81), NRA (life), West Tex. Cigar Soc., Physicians Resource Coun. (Tex. regional dir., mem. cmty. resource coun. troubled youth West Tex., 2005, mem. mission bd. China 2005), Argentier Honoraire Confrerie de la Chaine des Rotisseurs, Bailli Fondateur de Midland-Confrerie de la Chaine des Rotisseurs, Midland Confrerie de la Chaine des Rotisseurs (Bailli Honoraire), Chaine des Rotisseurs (comdr.), Consul de L'Ordre Mondial des Gourmets Degustateurs, Brilliat-Savarin Soc., Shanhai Tiffin Club, Donyin Sister City Assn., Midland Arts Assn., Midland C. of C., Midland-Odessa Symphony and Choral Soc. Achievements include patents in field. Avocations: skiing, painting, poetry, music, cooking.

LOHMULLER, MARTIN NICHOLAS, retired bishop; b. Phila., Aug. 21, 1919; s. Martin Nicholas and Mary Frances (Doser) L. BA, St. Charles Borromeo Sem., Phila., 1942; D.Canon Law, Cath. U. Am., 1947. Ordained priest Roman Cath. Ch., 1944. Officialis Diocese Harrisburg, Pa., 1948—63; vicar for religious Diocese of Harrisburg, 1958—70; pastor Our Lady of Good Counsel Parish, Marysville, Pa., 1954—64, St. Catherine Laboure Parish, Harrisburg, 1964—68; consecrated Bishop of Ramsbury, 1970; vicar gen. Archdiocese Phila., 1970—94; aux. bishop of Phila., 1970—94; pastor Old St. Mary's Parish, Phila., 1976—89, Holy Trinity Parish, Phila., 1976—89; ret., 1994. Roman Catholic. Office Phone: 215-343-3684. E-mail: bishiplo@adphila.org.

LOHNER, HENNING, composer, filmmaker; b. Bremen, Germany, July 17, 1961; s. Edgar Lohner and Marlene Clewing; m. Ariane Rieckër. MA, Johann Wolfgang Goethe U., Germany, 1987. Artist in residence Inst. for New Media, Frankfurt, Germany, 1994—96; composer in residence Remote Control Prodns., Santa Monica, Calif., 1996—. Guest lectr. Film Akademie Baden-Württemberg, Ludwigsburg, Germany, 2003—; guest prof. HMT Acad. Music and Theater, Zurich, Switzerland, 2005—. Exhibition, audio & video installation, Raw Material, Vol. 1 - 11; dir.: (film) The Revenge of the Dead Indians (Input TV Conf., 1993), Peefeeyatko (1st Internat. Music Film awards, Cannes, 1991), One11 And 103 (Silver Apple, Nat. Edn. awards, 1993); composer: (concert for prepared piano & orchestra) Orlac's Hands, (orchestral suite) Catching the Stars for World Expo, 2000, (orchestral soundtrack) Der Große Bagarozy, (orchestral soundtracks) Hellraiser: Deader, 2003, Incident at Loch Ness, 2003, Santa's Slay, 2004, Ring 2, 2005 (BMI Film Music award, 2006), Bloodrayne, 2005, 10.5 Apocalypse, 2006, In the Name of the King, 2006. Office: Remote Control Prodns / Lohneranger 1547 14th St Santa Monica CA 90404

LOHR, HAROLD RUSSELL, retired bishop; b. Gary, SD, Aug. 31, 1922; s. Lester Albert and Nora Helena (Fossum) L.; m. Theola Marie Kottke, June 21, 1947 (div. Dec. 1973); children: Philip Kyle, David Scott, Michael John; m. Edith Mary Morgan, Dec. 31, 1973. BS summa cum laude, S.D. State U., 1947; PhD, U. Calif.-Berkeley, 1950; MDiv summa cum laude, Augustana Theol. Sem., Rock Island, Ill., 1958. Ordained to ministry Augustana Luth. Ch., 1958; installed as bishop, 1980. Research chemist Argonne Nat. lab., Lemont, Ill., 1950-54; pastor Luth. Ch. of Ascension, Northfield, Ill., 1958-70; assoc. exec. Bd. Coll. Edn., NYC, 1970-73; dir. research Div. Profl. Leadership, Phila., 1973-77, assoc. exec., 1977-80; synodical bishop Luth. Ch. in Am., Fargo, N.D., 1980-87, Evang. Luth. Ch. in Am., Moorhead, Minn., 1988-91, ret., 1991. Mem. exec. council Luth. Ch. in Am., N.Y.C., 1982-87; mem. commn. of peace and war, 1983-85. Contbg. author: Growth in Ministry, 1980; also articles to sci. jours. Bd. dirs. Gustavus Adolphus Coll., 1980-87, Luther Northwestern Sem., St. Paul, 1980-87, Concordia Coll., Moorhead, Minn., 1988-91; mem. ch. coun. Evang. Luth. Ch. in Am., Chgo., 1990-91, disciplinary hearing officer, 1992-97, interim dir. synodical rels., 1993-94; mem. bd. govs. Chgo. Ctr. Religion and Sci., 1987-99, Zygon Ctr. Religion and Sci., Chgo., 1999-2003; mem. Summit on Environ., Joint Appeal in Religion and Sci., Washington, 1992; mem. adv. bd. Ctr. for Faith and Sci. Exch., Concord, Mass., 1995-99, mem. exec. bd., 1999-2001; mem. diocesan rev. com. Roman Cath. Diocese of Worcester, Mass., 2003—. Recipient Suomi award Suomi Coll., 1983. Mem. Phi Kappa Phi. Democrat. Home: 47 Brook Ln Berlin MA 01503-1671 Personal E-mail: hrlohrs@juno.com.

LOHR, JACOB ANDREW, pediatrician, educator; b. Lexington, NC, Aug. 15, 1940; s. Dermot and Blanche (Grimes) L.; m. Elizabeth Waite, June 19, 1967 (div. 1978); m. Lura Galloway, Nov. 27, 1993; children: Jason Merrill, Lara Jane Parker (dec.), Jonathan Waite, Elizabeth Brice. AB, U. N.C., 1962, MD, 1967. Diplomate Am. Bd. Pediats. Chief resident dept. pediat. U. Va., Charlottesville, 1969-70, prof., 1984-90, divsn. chief, assoc. chair, 1976-90; prof. dept. pediat. U. N.C., Chapel Hill, 1990—, divsn. chief, assoc. chair, 1990-98, vice chair dept. pediat., 1998-2000; pediatrician-in-chief N.C. Children's Hosp., Chapel Hill, 1999-2000, sr. clinician, 2000—; exec. dir. Gov.'s Inst. Alcohol and Substance Abuse,

1998—. Cons. to task force on urinary tract infections Am. Acad. Pediats., 1992-99, WHO Com. on Hospitalized Children at Risk, Geneva, 1999-2000; McLemore Birdsong disting. prof. U.Va., 1984-90. Editor: Pediatric Outpatient Proceedings, 1992, Guidelines for Nurse Practitioners, 1994, 5th edit., 1999, Essence of Pediatrics, 2000; med. editor Am. Bd. pediats., 1996—; contbr. articles to profl. jours. Bd. dirs. Head Start, Charlottesville, 1973-76, Ronald McDonald House, 1980-82, Orange County Ptnrship. for young Children, Chapel Hill, 1994-96; trustee Bowman Fund, U. Va., 1972—. Lt. comdr. USN, 1970-72. Recipient H. Fleming Fuller award, U. NC Healthcare Sys. Fellow Am. Acad. Pediats.; mem. Am. Soc. for Microbiology, Ambulatory Pediat. Assn., Pediat. Infectious Disease Soc., Infectious Disease Soc. Lutheran. Avocations: golf, boating. Office: U NC Dept Pediat 5041 Bioinformatics Bldg Chapel Hill NC 27599-0001 Business E-Mail: jlohr@med.unc.edu.

LOHR, MICHAEL F., lawyer; BA cum laude, U. Md., 1974, JD cum laude, 1977; LLM summa cum laude, George Wash. U., 1984. With office gen. coun. USN; clk. State Dist. Ct. Md.; def. counsel, sr. trial counsel, adminstrv. atty. Naval Legal Svc. Office, San Francisco; staff judge advocate USS Coral Sea USN, 1981, with internat. law divsn. office judge advocate gen., 1984—87, asst. spl. counsel to chief naval ops., 1987, sr. def. counsel Naval Legal Svc. Office Washington, 1987—88, internat. law atty., comdr.-in-chief U.S. Pacific Fleet, staff judge advocate to comdr. U.S. Naval Forces Ctrl. Command Pearl Harbor, 1988—89, fleet judge advocate U.S. Second Fleet Norfolk, 1989—91, with U.S. Seventh Fleet Yokosuka, Japan, 1991—93; dep. legal counsel to chmn. Joint Chiefs of Staff Pentagon, 1993—96, legal counsel to chmn., 1997—2000; comdr. Mid-Atlantic USN, Norfolk, 1996—97, dep. JAG, comdr. U.S. Legal Svc. Command, 2000—02, JAG, 2002—04; counsel The Boeing Co., Arlington, Va., 2005—. Rep. ocean policy affairs Dept. Def. Decorated Def. Superior Svc. Medal with oak leaf cluster, Legion of Merit, Meritorious Svc. Medal (three awards), others; recipient DSM, 2004. Office: The Boeing Co 1200 Wilson Blvd Arlington VA 22209

LOHR, STEVE, reporter; Grad, Columbia Univ. Sch. Journalism, 1975. Reporter Binghamtom Press, Bus. Week; fgn. correspondent NY Times, Tokyo, Manila, London, 1979—90, tech. reporter NYC, 1990—. Author: Go To: The Story of the Math Majors, Bridge Players, Engineers, Chess Wizards, Maverick Scientists and Iconoclasts - the Programmers who Created the Software Revolution, 2001; co-author (with Joel Brinkley): U.S. v Microsoft, 2000. Recipient Gerald Loeb award, UCLA Anderson Sch. Mgmt., 2005. Office: New York Times 229 W 43d St New York NY 10036 Office Phone: 212-556-3814. Office Fax: 212-556-1448. Business E-Mail: lohr@nytimes.com.

LOIACONO, JOHN P., information technology executive; BA in Comm., Fresno State U. With Sun Microsystems, Santa Clara, Calif., 1987—2006, chief mktg. officer, sr. v.p. operating platforms group, exec. v.p. software group; sr. v.p., creative solutions. Adobe Systems, Inc., San Jose, Calif., 2006—. Office: Adobe Systems Inc 345 Park Ave San Jose CA 95110-2704 Office Phone: 650-960-1300, 800-555-9786. Office Fax: 408-276-3804.

LOIELLO, JOHN PETER, diplomat, international consultant; b. Oceanside, NY, Aug. 16, 1943; s. Rosario Paul and Mary Agnes (Butler) L.; m. Elaine Margaret Robinson, June 14, 1944. BA in History, Fordham U., 1965; MA in History, SUNY, Buffalo, 1973; PhD in African History, U. London, 1980. Tchr. history The Gow Sch., South Wales, 1967-71; instr. U. Md., London, 1976-78; exec. dir. Dem. Party Com. Abroad, Washington and London, 1978-80; sr. cons. Assn. Am. Chambers of Commerce in Latin Am., Washington, 1980; spl. asst. to chmn. NEH, Washington, 1978-82; assoc. dir. Democracy Prog., Washington, 1982-83; founding exec. dir. Nat. Dem. Inst. for Internat. Affairs, Washington, 1983-85; pres. Gowran Internat., Washington, 1985-93, 2000—; assoc. dir. ednl. and cultural affairs US Info. Agy., Washington, 1994-98, sr. advisor to dir., 1999-2000. Pres. Alcide de Gaspari Found. (US), Washington, 1987-89. Contbr. articles to profl. jours. Commr. Commn. on Platform Accountability, Dem. Nat. Com., Washington, 1981-85, chmn. fgn. policy subcom., 1980, platform com., 1980; sec. Tax Equity for Ams. Abroad, London, 1977-79; sec. Dems. Abroad, London, 1976-79. Recipient Commdr. of Order of Lion Senegal, 1999; African Studies scholar, U. London, 1974-78, grantee, 1975. Mem. Nat. Italian Am. Found., Royal African Soc. Democrat. Roman Catholic. Avocations: travel, reading, swimming.

LOISELLE, JOAN BRENDA, elementary school educator, art educator; b. Huntington, W.Va., Aug. 22, 1947; d. Irvin Thomas and Anne (Questel) Sowards. BA, U. South Fla., 1969, MA, 1974. Cert. tchr. Fla. Dept. Edn., 1969, assoc. master tchr. cert. Fla. Dept. Edn., 1984. Tchr. Thonatosassa Elem. Sch., Tampa, Fla., 1969—70, Lorah Pk. Elem. Sch., Miami, Fla., 1970—73; head tchr. Day Care Ctr. U. South Fla., Tampa, 1974; tchr. Mabry Elem. Sch., Tampa, 1974—89; specialist art Carrollwood Elem. Sch., Tampa, 1989—92, Hunter's Green Elem. Sch., Tampa, 1992—. Mem. sch. leadership team Hunter's Green Elem. Sch., 1992—; adj. prof. U. Tampa, 2001—; rep. area 1 visual arts Hillsborough County Sch. Dist., Tampa, 1990—, resource tchr. gifted program, 1993—98; presenter in field. Exhibitions include Teco Plaza Art Gallery, Tampa, Fla., 2000—05. Coord. Neighborhood Involvement Kids Edn. Art Lab., Tampa, 1988; coord. multicultural art box project Tampa Arts Coun., 1989—90; sch. facilitator empty bowls project Second Harvest, Tampa, 1994—2006; rep. area visual arts Friends Offering Children Unlimited Success, Tampa, 1995; tchr. participant Tim Rollins mural project U. South Fla., 1996; facilitator Canstruction Tampa (Fla.) Archs., 1997; facilitator Tampa Mus. Art Grant: Arts Connect All, Tampa, 2005—06; mem. com. tchr. certification Fla. Dept. Edn., 2002—04, mem. com. Fla. Blueprint 2000 Assessment Design Project, 1994. Finalist County Tchr. of Yr. award, Hillsborough County Sch. Dist., 1994; recipient Tchr. of Yr. award, Hunter's Green Elem. Sch., 1994, Performance Pay award, Fla. Dept. Edn., 2003—06, Gold Star Tchr. award, Binnie & Smith, Inc. and Wal-Mart, 2003—05, Maj.'s Outstanding Tchr. award, Tampa Water Conservation Initiative, 2003—06; grantee, Hillsborough Edn. Found., 1993—94, 1996, State of Fla. Artful Truth, 1999. Mem.: Hillsborough Art Edn. Assn. (pres. 2000—01, chmn. profl. devel. com. 2002—, parliamentarian 2002—, Disting. Svc. award 2002—05), Fla. Art Edn. Assn. (presenter confs.), Nat. Art Edn. Assn., Tampa Mus. Art (edn. adv. com. 2000—03, edn.adv. com. 2006—), PTA (co-chmn. reflections/cultural arts com. 2000—05), Phi Delta Kappa (Fifteen Yr. Member cert. 2003), Phi Kappa Phi (life), Delta Kappa Gamma (pres. chi chpt. 1990—92, chmn. starwalk com. 1994—, parliamentarian 2002—). Office: Hunters Green Elementary 9202 Highland Oak Dr Tampa FL 33647-2541 Home: 3712 W Santiago St Tampa FL 33629 Home Phone: 813-839-9272; Office Phone: 813-973-7394. Business E-Mail: joan.loiselle@sdhc.k12.fl.us.

LOIZOS, DIMITRIOS, electrical engineer, researcher; b. Athens, Greece, July 4, 1980; arrived in US, 2003; s. Nikolaos Loizos and Maria Malikiosi-Loizos. Diploma in Elec. and Computer Engring., Nat. Tech. U. Athens, 2003; MS in Elec. and Computer Engring., Johns Hopkins U., Balt., 2005, PhD in Elec. Engring., 2007. Cert. elec. and computer engr., Tech. Chamber Greece, 2003. Jr. rschr. Inst. Lang. and Speech Processing, Athens, 2001—03; cons. guidance and support, go-online program Greek Ministry Devel., Athens, 2003; grad. rschr. Johns Hopkins U., 2004—. Fellow, Chertkof Found., 2003—04. Mem.: IEEE, Tech. Chamber Greece. Achievements include patents pending for prime-rational frequency synthesis method and frequency synthesizers. Business E-Mail: dloizos@jhu.edu.

LØJ, ELLEN MARGRETHE, ambassador; b. Gedesby, Denmark, Oct. 17, 1948; Grad. econs., Copenhagen U., 1973. Joined Ministry Fgn. Affairs, 1973; first sec. Permanent Mission to the UN Ministry Fgn. Affairs, NYC, 1977—80, counsellor Permanent Representation of Denmark to the European Cmty. Brussels, 1982—85, head dept., 1986—89; amb. to Israel Ministry Fgn. Affairs, 1989—92; under-sec. multilateral affairs South Group Ministry Fgn. Affairs, 1992—94, under-sec. bilateral affairs South Group, 1994—96, state sec. South Group, 1996—2001, permanent rep. of Denmark to the UN, amb., 2001—. Mem. supervisory bd. The Investment Fund Ctrl. and Ea. Europe, 1994—96, The Industrialization Fund for Developing Countries, 1994—96, Scandlines AG and Scandlines A/S, 1998—2001; participant Danish dels. to several internat. meetings and U.N. confs. Office: Permanent Rep of Denmark to the UN One Dag Hammarskjöld Plaza 885 Second Ave 18th Fl New York NY 10017-2201 Office Phone: 212-705-4968.

LOKEN, BARBARA, marketing educator, social psychologist; b. Owatonna, Minn., Aug. 22, 1951; d. Gordon Keith and June Rosaline (Iverson) Anderson; 1 child, Elizabeth Loken Diebel. BA in Psychology magna cum laude, U. Minn., 1973; MA, NYU, 1976; PhD in Social Psychology, U. Ill., 1981. Rsch. and statis. asst. Nat. Soc. Prevention Blindness, NYC, 1974-76; rsch. asst. dept. psychology U. Ill., 1976, 78-80, instr., 1977-78; NIMH trainee in measurement, 1979-80; asst. prof. dept. mktg. U. Minn., 1980-86, assoc. prof., 1986-92, prof., 1992—. Co-dir. edn. evaluation Minn. heart health project Sch. Pub. Health, 1982-88, adj. assoc. prof. dept. psychology, 1987-92, adj. prof., 1992—; vis. assoc. prof. mktg. UCLA, 1988. Assoc. editor: Jour. Consumer Rsch., 1996-99; contbr. articles to profl. jours. Rsch. grantee Sch. Mgmt., U. Minn., 1981-84, 86, 88-2005. Mem. Am. Psychol. Assn., Am. Mktg. Assn., Assn. Consumer Rsch., Assn. for Consumer Rsch. 2000 (treas.).

LOKEN, JAMES BURTON, federal judge; b. Madison, Wis., May 21, 1940; s. Burton Dwight and Anita (Nelson) Loken; m. Caroline Brevard Hester, July 30, 1966; children: Kathryn Brevard, Kristina Ayres. BS, U. Wis., 1962; LLB magna cum laude, Harvard U., 1965. Law clk. to Hon. J. Edward Lumbard US Ct. Appeals (2d Cir.), NYC, 1965—66; law clk. to assoc. justice Byron White US Supreme Ct., Washington, 1966—67; assoc. atty. Faegre & Benson, Mpls., 1967—70, ptnr., 1973—90; gen. counsel Pres.'s Com. on Consumer Interests, Office of Pres. of U.S., Washington, 1970; staff asst. Office of Pres. of U.S., Washington, 1970—72; judge US Ct. Appeals (8th cir.), St. Paul, 1990—2003, chief judge, 2003—. Editor: Harvard Law Rev., 1964—65. Mem.: Am. Law Inst., Phi Beta Kappa, Phi Kappa Phi. Avocations: golf, running. Office: US Courthouse 300 S 4th St Ste 11W Minneapolis MN 55415-0848 also: US Ct Appeals 8th Cir 111S 10th St Rm 24-32 Saint Louis MO 63102*

LOKHNAUTH, JOHN, chemist, researcher; m. Sharada Singh, Apr. 19, 2001. PhD, Seton Hall U., NJ, 2005. Sr. chemist Eon Labs., Laurelton, NY, 1997—99; scientist Altana Inc., Melville, NY, 1999—2001; prin. rsch. scientist Wyeth Rsch., Pearl River, NY, 2001—. Contbr. articles to profl. jours. Mem.: Am. Chem. Soc. (assoc.). Achievements include research in solid phase microextraction coupled to ion mobility spectrometry. Office: Wyeth Research 401 N Middletown Rd Pearl River NY 10965 Home Phone: 201-794-9730; Office Phone: 845-602-4034. Personal E-mail: jkl30@msn.com.

LOKMER, STEPHANIE ANN, international business development consultant; b. Wheeling, W.Va., Nov. 14, 1957; d. Joseph Steven and Mary Ann (Mozney) Lokmer. BA in Comm., Bethany Coll., 1980; cert., U. Tübingen, Germany, 1980, Sprach Inst., Tübingen, 1980; MGC in Negotiation, Georgetown U., 2003; degree in nat. security telecom., George Washington U., 2003. V.p. Wheeling Coffee and Spice, W.Va., 1981—; pres. Lokmer & Assocs., Inc., McLean, W.Va., 1986-2000; v.p. strategic devel. Telia Internat. Carrier, Inc., 2000—04; cons. internat. bus. Lokmer & Assocs., 2004—. Bd. dirs. Am. Found. of Ivory Coast. Mem.: Internat. Assn. Tech. of No. Va., Counselors Acad., World Affairs Coun., Pub. Rels. Soc. Am., Fed. City Club, Zeta Tau Alpha. Republican. Avocations: reading, tennis. Office Phone: 202-744-4740. Personal E-mail: slokmer@attglobal.net.

LOLLEY, WILLIAM RANDALL, minister; b. Troy, Ala., June 2, 1931; s. Roscoe Lee and Mary Sara (Nunnelee) L.; m. Clara Lou Jacobs, Aug. 28, 1952; children: Charlotte, Pam. AB, Samford U., 1952, DD (hon.), 1980; BD, Southeastern Sem., 1957, ThM, 1958; ThD, Southwestern Sem., 1962; DD (hon.), Wake Forest U., 1971, U. Richmond, 1984; LLD (hon.), Campbell U., 1986; LittD (hon.), Mercer U., 1988. Ordained to ministry So. Bapt. Conv., 1951. Pastor First Bapt. Ch., Winston-Salem, NC, 1962-74; pres. Southeastern Bapt. Theol. Sem., Wake Forest, NC, 1974-88; pastor First Bapt. Ch., Raleigh, NC, 1988-90, Greensboro, NC, 1990-96, ret., 1996. Author: Crises in Morality, 1963, Bold Preaching of Christ, 1979, Servant Songs, 1994. Mem. Coop. Bapt. Fellowship, Rotary. Democrat. Baptist.

LOLLIS, BLAKE DAVID, physician, military officer; b. Oklahoma City, Dec. 24, 1962; s. David Wayne and Sue Evelyn Lollis; m. Lori Anne Connally, Dec. 17, 1988; children: Brian David, Bridget Connally. AA in Music, Rose State Coll., Midwest City, Okla., 1983; BS in Zoology, U. Okla., Norman, 1987; MD, U. Okla., Oklahoma City, 1991; postgrad., U. Tex., Galveston, 2006—. Commd. officer USAF, 1995, advanced through grades to lt. col.; intern psychiatry program Portsmouth Naval Hosp., Va., 1991—92; sr. med. officer Br. Naval Clinic, Idaho Falls, Idaho, 1992—95; resident family practice U. Okla., Tulsa, 1995—97; chief family practice 341st Med. Group, Great Falls, Mont., 1997—2000; pvt. practice physician, chief profl. staff 189th Med. Squadron, Little Rock, 2000—03; flight comdr. USAF 92d Med. Group, Spokane, Wash., 2003—06. Author: Travelling: A Collection of Stories, 2002. Troop physician Boy Scouts Am. Troop 362, Beebe, Ark., 2000—03, Boy Scouts Am. Troop 117, Spokane, 2003—06. Named Flight Surgeon of Yr., 92d Air Refueling Wing USAF, 2005. Fellow: Am. Acad. Family Practice. Republican. Methodist. Avocation: fly fishing. Home: 7112 N Winston Dr Spokane WA 99208

LOLLIS, STUART SCOTT, neurosurgeon; b. NY, NY, Dec. 19, 1975; s. Stuart Holman and Mary Fearey Lollis; m. Frederique Anne Thibault, June 25, 2005; 1 child, William Stuart. AB, Dartmouth Coll., Hanover, NH, 1998; MD, Columbia U., NYC, 2003. Resident in neurosurgery Dartmouth-Hitchcock Med. Ctr., Lebanon, NH, 2003—. Mem.: Am. Assn. Neurol. Surgeons, Alpha Omega Alpha. Episcopalian. Achievements include research in ventriculoperitoneal shunting, perilymphatic fistula, Chiari malformation, magnetic resonance elastography, glioma vaccination. Avocations: skiing, mountain climbing, running, carpentry. Home Phone: 802-295-5609; Office Phone: 603-650-5109.

LOMAN, MARY LAVERNE, retired mathematics professor; b. Stratford, Okla., June 10, 1928; d. Thomas D. and Mary Ellen (Goodwin) Glass; m. Coy E. Loman, Dec. 23, 1944; 1 child, Sandra Leigh Loman Easton. BS, U. Okla., 1956, MA, 1957, PhD, 1961. Grad. asst., then instr. U. Okla., Norman, 1956-61; asst. prof. math. U. Ctrl. Okla., Edmond, 1961-62, assoc. prof., 1962-66, prof., 1966-93, prof. emeritus, 1993—. NSF fellow, 1965-67. Mem. Math. Assn. Am., Nat. Coun. Tchrs. Math., Okla. Coun. Tchrs. Math. (v.p. 1972-76), Higher Edn Alumni Coun. Okla., VFW Aux., Delta Kappa Gamma. Home: 2201 Tall Oaks Trl Edmond OK 73052-2325 *Strive to do each task to the best of your ability. Then don't look back, saying "If only I had...", but look forward to the next, knowing you gave your very best effort.*

LOMAS, LYLE WAYNE, agricultural research administrator, educator; b. Monett, Mo., June 8, 1953; s. John Junior and Helen Irene Lomas; m. Connie Gail Frey, Sept. 4, 1976; children: Amy Lynn, Eric Wayne. BS, U. Mo., 1975, MS, 1976; PhD, Mich. State U., 1979. Asst. prof., animal scientist S.E. Agrl. Rsch. Ctr., Kans. State U., Parsons, 1979-85, assoc. prof., 1985-92, prof., 1992—, head, 1985—. Contbr. articles to refereed sci. jours. Mem. Am. Soc. Animal Sci., Am. Registry Profl. Animal Scientists, Am. Forage and Grassland Coun., Rsch. Ctr. Adminstrs. Soc. (bd. dirs. 1993—, sec. 1999-2000, 2d v.p. 2000-01, v.p. 2001-02, pres. 2002-03), Rotary (bd. dirs. Parsons 1992—96 v.p. 1994-95, pres. 1995-96), Phi Kappa Phi, Gamma Sigma Delta. Presbyterian. Achievements include research in ruminant nutrition, forage utilization by grazing stocker cattle. Home: 24052 Douglas Rd Dennis KS 67341-9014 Office: Kans State U SE Agrl Rsch Ctr PO Box 316 Parsons KS 67357-0316 Home Phone: 620-421-0033; Office Phone: 620-421-4826. Business E-Mail: llomas@oznet.ksu.edu.

LOMAX, MICHAEL LUCIUS, non-profit association administrator; b. LA, Oct. 2, 1947; m. Pearl Cleage, 1969 (div. 1979); 1 child, Deignan; m. Cheryl Ferguson Lomax, 1986; children: Michele, Rachel. BA in English, Morehouse Coll., 1968; MA in English lit., Columbia U.; PhD in Am. and Afro-Am. Lit., Emory U., 1984. Faculty mem. Morehouse Coll., Spelman Coll.; dir. pks., librs., and cultural and internat. affairs Atlanta, 1975—78; bd. commrs. Fulton County, Ga., 1978—93, bd. chair Ga., 1981—93; pres., CEO Nat. Faculty, Atlanta, 1994—97; pres. Dillard U., New Orleans, 1997—2004; pres., CEO United Negro Coll. Fund, Inc., Fairfax, Va., 2004—. Vis. prof. Emory U., Ga. Inst. Tech., U. Ga. Founding chmn. Nat. Black Arts Festival, 1988; bd. dirs. Studio Mus. in Harlem, Emory U. Carter Ctr., United Way of Am., Teach for Am.; mem. Presdl. Adv. Bd. on Historically Black Colls. and Univs., 2002-; mem. Nat. Mus. African Am. Hist. and Cultural Plan for Action Presdl. Commn. Named one of Most Influential Black Ams., Ebony mag., 2006; named to The Ebony Power 150, 2007. Office: United Negro Coll Fund PO Box 10444 8260 Willow Oaks Corporate Dr Fairfax VA 22031-8044*

LOMBARD, JOHN JAMES, JR., lawyer, writer; b. Phila., Dec. 27, 1934; s. John James and Mary R. (O'Donnell) L.; m. Barbara Mallon, May 9, 1964; children: John James, William M., James G., Laura K., Barbara E. BA cum laude, LaSalle Coll., 1956; JD, U. Pa., 1959. Bar: Pa. 1960. Ptnr. Obermayer, Rebmann, Maxwell & Hippel, Phila., 1959-84; mgr. personal law sect. Morgan Lewis & Bockius LLP, Phila., 1985-90, vice-chair personal law sect., 1990-92, chair, 1992-99; spl. counsel McCarter & English LLP, Phila., 2000—. Sec., dir. Airline Hydraulics Corp., Phila., 1969-2000; adv. com. on decedents estates laws Joint State Govt. Commn., 1992—, mem. subcom. on powers of atty., 1993—; co-chair So. Jersey Ethics Alliance, 1993-97. Co-author: Durable Powers of Attorney and Health Care Directives, 1984, 3d edit. 1994; contbr. articles to profl. jours. Bd. dirs. Redevel. Authority Montgomery County, Pa., 1980-87, Gwynedd-Mercy Coll., Gwynedd Valley, Pa., 1980-89, LaSalle Coll. H.S., Wyndmoor, Pa., 1991-97. Recipient Treat award Nat. Coll. Probate Judges, 1992, Disting. Estate Planner award Phila. Estate Planning Coun., 2002. Mem. ABA (chmn. com. simplification security transfers 1972-76, chmn. mem. com. 1972-82, mem. coun. real property, probate and trust law sect. 1979-85, sec. 1985-87, divsn. dir. probate div. 1987-89, chair elect 1989-90, chair 1990-91, co-chair Nat. Conf. Lawyers & Corp. Fiduciaries), Pa. Bar Assn. (ho. of dels. 1979-81), Phila. Bar Assn. (chmn. probate sect. 1972), Am. Coll. Trust and Estate Counsel (editor Probate Notes 1983, bd. regents 1986-91, mem. exec. com. 1988-91, elder law com. 1993—, pres. found., 2005-07), Internat. Acad. Estate and Trust Law (exec. com. 1984-88, 90-94, v.p. 2006—), Am. Bar Found., Internat. Fish and Game Assn., Union League Club (Phila.), Ocean City Club (N.J.), Marlin and Tuna Club, Ocean City Yacht Club. Office: McCarter & English LLP Mellon Bank Ctr Ste 700 1735 Market St Philadelphia PA 19103

LOMBARD, KENNETH T., beverage and music company executive; Pres. Johnson Develop. Corp., Magic Johnson Theatres, 1992—2004; sr. v.p., pres. Starbucks Entertainment Starbucks Corp., Seattle, 2004—; chief mgr. Hear Music label, LA, 2007—. Office: Starbucks Corp 2401 Utah St Seattle WA 98134

LOMBARD, RICHARD SPENCER, lawyer; b. Panama Canal Zone, Jan. 28, 1928; s. Eugene C. and Alice R. (Quinn) L.; m. Arlene Olson, Dec. 27, 1952; children: Anne, James. AB, Harvard U., 1949, JD, 1952. Bar: N.Y. 1953, Tex. 1971. Assoc. Haight, Gardner, Poor & Havens, NYC, 1952-55; mem. law dept. Creole Petroleum Corp., Caracas, Venezuela, 1955-65, mgr., 1963-65; gen. counsel Esso Chem. Co., NYC, 1966-69; assoc. gen. counsel Humble Oil & Refining Co., Houston, 1969-71; asst. gen. counsel Exxon Corp., NYC, 1971-72, assoc. gen. counsel, 1972-73, gen. counsel, 1973-93, v.p., 1980-93; counsel Baker & Botts, Dallas, 1993-96. Trustee Parker Sch. Fgn. and Comparative Law, Columbia U., 1977—, chmn. bd. trustees, 1985-2003. Author: American-Venezuelan Private International Law, 1965. Served with USAAF, 1946-47. Fellow Am. Bar Found.; mem. Am. Law Inst., Am. Arbitration Assn. (bd. dirs., chmn. bd. 1983-86), Assn. Bar City of N.Y., State Bar of Tex., Univ. Club (N.Y.C.).

LOMBARDI, DEAN, professional sports team executive; b. Holyoke, Mass. Grad., U. New Haven; JD with honors, Tulane U. Player agent; asst. gen. mgr. Minn. North Stars, San Jose Sharks, 1990—92, pres., dir. hockey ops., 1992—96, exec. v.p., gen. mgr., 1996—2003; pro scout Phila. Flyers, 2003—06; pres., gen. mgr. LA Kings, 2006—. Office: LA Kings Ste 3100 1111 S Figueroa St Los Angeles CA 90015

LOMBARDI, DENNIS M., lawyer; b. LA, May 15, 1951; s. Peter Joseph and Jean (Nelson) L.; m. Suan Choo Lim, Jan. 9, 1993; children: Alexis Jeanne, Erin Kalani. BA, U. Hawaii, 1974; JD summa cum laude, U. Santa Clara, 1977. Bar: Calif. 1977, U.S. Dist. Ct. Hawaii, 1981, D.C. 2004. Assoc. Frandzel & Share, Beverly Hills, Calif., 1977-79; pvt. practice Capistrano Beach, Calif., 1979-81; ptnr. Case Lombardi & Pettit, Honolulu, 1982—. Named one of Leaders in Their Field, Chambers and Ptnrs. USA, 2005—07, Best Lawyers in Am., Woodward and White, 2005—07. Office: Case Lombardi & Pettit 737 Bishop St Fl 26 Honolulu HI 96813-3201 Home Phone: 808-373-9300; Office Phone: 808-547-5446. Business E-Mail: dlombardi@caselombardi.com.

LOMBARDI, EUGENE PATSY, retired conductor, musician, educator; b. North Braddock, Pa., July 7, 1923; s. Nunzio C. and Mary (Roberto) L.; m. Jacqueline Sue Davis, Mar. 1955; children: Robert, Genanne. BA, Westminster Coll., 1948; MA, Columbia U., 1948; Edn. Specialist, George Peabody Coll., 1972; MusD, Westminster Coll., 1981. Band dir. Lincoln H.S., Midland, Pa., 1948-49; orch. dir. Du Pont Manual H.S., Louisville, 1949—50, Male H.S., Louisville, 1949-50, Phoenix Union H.S., 1950-57; orch. dir., prof. Ariz. State U., Tempe, 1957-89; ret., 1989. Condr. Phoenix Symphonete, 1954-61, 70-73, Phoenix Symphony Youth Orch., 1956-66, Phoenix Pops Orch., 1971-83, Fine Arts String Orch., Phoenix, 1995-97 With USAAF, 1943-46. Decorated Bronze Star; recipient Alumni Achievement award Westminster Coll., 1976, gold medal Nat. Soc. Arts and Letters, 1973, Disting. Tchr. award Ariz. State U. Alumni, 1974, Phoenix appreciation award, 1983 Mem. Music Educators Nat. Conf., Am. String Tchrs. Assn. (pres. Ariz. unit 1965-67), Am. Fedn. Musicians, Ariz. Music Educators Assn. (pres. higher edn. sect. 1973-75, Excellence in Teaching Music award 1989), Ind. Order Foresters, Phi Delta Kappa, Phi Mu Alpha, Alpha Sigma Phi. Republican. Methodist. Home: 2625 E Southern C-164 Tempe AZ 85282-7635 Personal E-mail: lomsemiquaver@peoplepc.com.

LOMBARDI, FREDERICK MCKEAN, lawyer; b. Akron, Ohio, Apr. 1, 1937; s. Leonard Anthony and Dorothy (McKean) L.; m. Margaret J. Gessler, Mar. 31, 1962; children: Marcus M., David G., John A., Joseph F.

BA, U. Akron, 1960; LLB, Case Western Res., 1962. Bar: Ohio 1962, U.S. Dist. Ct. (no. and so. dists.) Ohio 1964, U.S. Ct. Appeals (6th cir.) 1966. Prin., shareholder Buckingham, Doolittle & Burroughs, Akron, 1962—, chmn. comml. law and litigation dept., 1989-99. Bd. editors Western Res. Law Rev., 1961-62. Trustee, mem. exec. com., v.p. Ohio Ballet, 1985-93; trustee Walsh Jesuit H.S., 1987-90; life trustee Akron Golf Charities, NEC World Series of Golf; bd. mem. Summa Health Sys. Found., Downtown Akron Partnership, St. Hilary Parish Found. Mem. Ohio Bar Assn. (coun. of dels. 1995-97), Akron Bar Assn. (trustee 1991-94, 97-2000, v.p., pres.-elect 1997-98, pres. 1998-99), Case Western Res. U. Law Alumni Assn. (bd. mem. 1995-98, 2003—06), Case Western Res. Soc. Benchers, Fairlawn Swim and Tennis Club (past pres.), Portage Country Club, Pi Sigma Alpha Democrat. Roman Catholic. Office: Buckingham Doolittle & Burroughs 3800 Embassy Pkwy Ste 300 Akron OH 44333 Office Phone: 330-376-5300. Business E-Mail: flombardi@bdblaw.com.

LOMBARDI, JOHN V., academic administrator, historian; b. LA, Aug. 19, 1942; s. John and Janice P. Lombardi; m. Cathryn Lee; children: John Lee, Mary Ann. BA, Pomona Coll., 1963; MA, Columbia U., 1964, PhD, 1968. Prof. contratado Escuela de Historia, Universidad Central de Venezuela, Caracas, 1967; lectr. history Ind. U. S.E., Jeffersonville, 1967-68, asst. prof., 1968-69; vis. asst. prof. Ind. U., Bloomington, 1968-69, from asst. prof. history to dean, 1969—85, dean Coll. Arts and Scis., 1985—87; provost, vp. for acad. affairs, 1987-89; pres. U. Fla., Gainesville, 1989-99, prof. history, dir. The Ctr., 1999; prof. history, chancellor U. Mass., Amherst, Mass., 2002—07; pres. La. State U. Sys., 2007—. Author: (with others) Venezuelan History: A Comprehensive Working Bibliography, 1977, People and Places in Colonial Venezuela, 1976, Venezuela: Search for Order, Dream of Progress, 1982, The Top American Research Universities, 2000-; Mem. editorial bd.: (with others) UCLA Statis. Abstracts Latin Am, 1977—; contbr. (with others) articles to profl. jours. Fulbright-Hayes research fellow, 1965-66 Mem. Am. Hist. Assn., Latin Am. Studies Assn., Pan Am. Inst. Geography and History, Academia Nacional de la Historia (corr. mem.) Office: La State U Sys 3810 W Lakeshore Dr Baton Rouge LA 70808*

LOMBARDI, JOSEPH J., retail executive; BA, U. Notre Dame; MBA, NYU. CPA. V.p., controller Toys 'R' Us, Inc.; ptnr. Ernst & Young Consumer Products Practice; CFO The Mus. Co. Inc.; v.p., controller Barnes & Noble, NYC, 2002—03, CFO, 2003—. Office: Barnes & Noble 122 Fifth Ave New York NY 10011 Office Phone: 212-633-3215. Business E-Mail: jlombardi@bn.com.

LOMBARDI, MARK OWEN, academic administrator, international relations educator; b. Providence, Dec. 14, 1960; s. Martin Thomas and Betty Natalie (Owen) L.; m. Judy Rollins Downs, Dec. 31, 1993; stepchild, Richie Downs. BA, Purdue U., 1982; MA, Ohio State U., 1986, PhD, 1989. Asst. Consortium for Internat. Edn., Columbus, Ohio, 1983-85; grad. asst. Ohio State U., Columbus, 1983-86; vis. instr. Wittenberg U., Springfield, Ohio, 1987-88; asst. prof. to prof., chmn., Dept. Govt., History & Sociol. U. Tampa, Fla., 1988—2001, dir. Baccalaureate Experience, Office Internat. Programs & Develop. Fla., 1992—2001; v.p. academic & student affairs Coll. of Santa Fe, N.Mex., 2001—04, provost N.Mex., 2004—05, pres. N.Mex., 2005—07, Maryville U., St. Louis, 2007—. Polit. cons. WTOG News, Tampa, 1989-95; advisor Vision Quest, Tampa, 1994-95. Author: The Unfolding Legacy of 9/11, 2004; editor: Perspectives on Third World Sovereignty, 1995; contbr. chpt. to book and articles to profl. jours. Umpire S.E. Umpires Assn., Tampa, 1991-93. Dana Found. grantee U. Tampa, 1989, 91, 93, 95; Social Sci. grantee U. Toledo, 1992. Mem. Internat. Studies Assn., African Studies Assn., Acad. Polit. Sci., Pi Gamma Mu (advisor), Pi Sigma Alpha. Avocations: golf, reading, walking, jogging. Office: Maryville U Office of Pres 650 Maryville University Dr Saint Louis MO 63141*

LOMBARDI, MARY LUCIANA, musician, historian; d. John and Maryellen Lombardi, Janice May Lombardi (Stepmother). BA, Occidental Coll., LA, 1961; MA, Ind. U., Bloomington, 1971; MLS, UCLA, 1965, PhD, 1977. Reference libr. N.Y. Pub. Libr., 1965—66; indexer H. W. Wilson Co., Bronx, 1967—69; bibliographer Ind. U. Librs., Bloomington, Ind., 1969—71, U. Calif., LA, 1971—74; indexer Lombardi Indexing Svcs., L.A., Davis, Santa Cruz, 1973—92; musician various, Calif. and Ind., 1976—; instr. U. Calif., Santa Cruz, 1977—80, Cabrillo Coll., Aptos, Calif., 2002—03. Classical music DJ Pub. Radio KUSP-FM, Santa Cruz, 1977—2004; founding festival player, concert mgmt. Santa Cruz Baroque Festival, 1977—87; founder/dir./performer, concert mgmt. Santa Cruz Festival Viols, 1978—94; musician, prodr./dir.: performance demonstrations for children Santa Cruz County Schs., Watsonville, Capitola, Santa Cruz, 1984—2001; artistic dir., performer, concert mgmt. Santa Cruz Chamber Players, 1990—97; founder/dir./performer, concert mgmt. Calif. Gamba Consort, Santa Cruz, 1994—98. Editor: (book online) Cantar e Viver/To Sing Is To Live: Music by Lucilia Guimaraes Villa-Lobos, 2002; author: (rev.) The Frontier in Brazilian History; contbr. articles to profl.jour. Mem. planning, ednl. coms. Cultural Coun. Santa Cruz County, 1978—94; area rep., Viola da Gamba Soc. Am., Monterey Bay, Calif., 1984—. Recipient Pataphysician of Yr., Pub. Radio KUSP-FM, 1989; fellow Fgn. Area Fellowship Program, Social Sci. Rsch. Coun./Ford Found., 1970—73; grantee, UCLA, 1972—77; scholar Summer Viol program, Cornell U., 1982, 1983, 1985. Mem.: Early Music Am., Inst. for Hist. Study, Am. Fedn. Musicians (Local 153). Achievements include creation of concerts featuring women composers, 1987, 94-96, 98, 2006; creation of classical music radio broadcasts for 27 yrs., including special programs featuring women composers. Home Phone: 831-476-1131. Personal E-mail: mll621@aol.com.

LOMBARDI, MICHAEL, application developer; b. Montclair, NJ, Sept. 4, 1958; s. Michael C. and Rose (Zarro) Lombardi. BA, Trenton State Coll., Ewing, NJ, 1981. Data processing programmer II, III State N.J., Trenton, 1984—87, data processing analyst II, 1987—97, software devel. specialist, 1997—. Adj. faculty instr. Mercer County C.C., West Windsor, NJ, 1998—2000. Br. recording sec. CWA Local 1032, Ewing, 1997—99, exec. bd. mem., 2000—, br. pres., 2000—. Avocations: running, exercise, swimming, canoeing, tubing. Home: 19 Morning Glory Lane Levittown PA 19054

LOMBARDO, ANN MARIE, special education educator, writer, artist; b. Melrose, Mass., Jan. 10, 1955; d. James William Pike, II and Mary Ann (Duncan) Pike; m. Steven Edward Lombardo, Sept. 11, 1982; children: Nicholas Michael, Kali Ann. Student, Plymouth State Coll., 1973; BA, Rivier Coll., 1978. Freelance tchr. arts and crafts, Hollis, NH, 1972—73, 1975; art tchr. Hollis (N.H.) Elem. and Secondary Schs., Hollis, NH, 1978; proprietor, asst. Jameson Fine Arts Gallery, La Jolla, Calif., 1978—79; graphic artist, tech. writer J.M. Yurick Assocs., Smersworth, NH, 1980—87; spl. needs educator Winthrop Elem. Sch., Ipswich, Mass., 1995—. Freelance artist, writer, 1983—92; presenter, cons. in field. Author (artist & correspondent): (column) The Portsmouth (N.H.) Herald, 1988—93; Yonder Mountain (A Cherokee Legend), 1999, one-woman shows include Link Art Gallery, Rowley, Mass., 2002; columnist: Annadotes; radio commentary WERZ talk radio. Tchr. arts and crafts Nashua (N.H.) Orphanage, 1970; cook, distributor The Food Kitchen Shelter, San Diego, 1988; rschr., artist Ea. Bank Cherokees, Qualla Bouundary, NC, 1999—2001. Recipient Outstanding Regional Art award, 1973. Mem.: Newburyport Art Assn., San Diego (Calif.) Art Assn. Avocations: painting furniture, cross country skiing, hiking, camping. Home: 101 Leslie Rd Rowley MA 01969 Mailing: PO Box 124 Ipswich MA 01938 Office Phone: 978-376-1856. E-mail: artnannie@yahoo.com.

LOMBARDO, FREDRIC ALAN, pharmacist, educator; b. New Castle, Pa., May 11, 1948; s. Valentine Frank and Clara Eleanor (Cugini) Lombardo; m. Loretta D. Patts, May 22, 1971; children: Alan John, Lauren Beth, Leslie Anne. BS in Pharmacy, Duquesne U., Pitts., 1971, PharmD, 1974; MS, Fla. Inst. Tech., Melbourne, 1979. Lic. pharmacist Pa., Va., D.C., Tex., cert. Am. Coll. Clin. Pharmacists. Resident in hosp. pharmacy Mercy Hosp., Pitts., 1973; commd. 2nd lt. US Army, 1974, advanced through grades to lt. col., 1993; chief clin. pharmacy support svc. Brooke Army Med. Ctr., Ft. Sam Houston, Tex., 1980-85; chief outpatient pharmacy svc. Walter Reed Army Med. Ctr., Washington, 1985-86, chief cancer treatment sect., chief hematol.-oncol. pharmacy, 1986-92; resigned active duty entered US Army reserve, 1993; sr. clin. pharmacy supr. Nat. Heart, Lung and Blood Inst., NIH, Bethesda, Md., 1992-95; assoc. prof. clin. and adminstrv. pharmacy sci. Howard U., Washington, 1995—, assoc. prof. psychiatry Coll. Medicine, assoc. prof. cmty. medicine and family practice; asoc. prof. U. Md. Adj. ordinary prof. pharmacology Cath. U., Washington, 1995—; assoc. prof. pharmacology H. Lee Med. Sch., USPHS, Bethesda, Md., 1995—; assoc. prof. pharmacology Cancer Ctr., Ctr. Sickle Cell Disease Howard U., 1995—, asst. dir. Cancer Ctr., 1997; adj. assoc. prof. neurology Howard U., Coll. Medicine; prof. Found. Advancement Edn. Sci., Grad. Sch. NIH, 1996—; mem. Mid-Atlantic Oncology Adv. Group, Washington, 1997; mem. coun. experts com. Oncologic Diseases USP; mem. faculty, cons. Comprehensive AIDS Tng. Initiative and Nat. Minority AIDS Edn. and Tng. Ctr.; cons. faculty Nat. Minority AIDS Edn. and Tng. Ctr. Faculty Comprehensive AIDS Tng. Inst.; mem. DC Medicare Pharmacy and Therapeutics Com., Washington, 2007. Co-host Ask the Pharmacy Doctor program Sta. WRC-980, Washington, 1997—, guest various TV and radio programs; editor: Jour. of Hosp. Ethics. Active Urban Health U., Urban Family Inst., Washington, 1996—97. Lt. col. USAR, 1993—. Named Pharmacist of Yr., Washington Met. Health Sys. Pharmacists, 2006; Rsch. grant, Ortho-McNeil Pharm., Washington, 1996—97. Fellow: Am. Soc. Cons. Pharmacists; mem.: Nat. Pharm. Assn., Am. Soc. Health Professions, Am. Pharm. Assn. (bd. cert. in pharmacotherapy nutrition support, oncology, psychopharmacology, and geriatrics), KC, Am. Legion. Democrat. Roman Catholic. Avocations: military history, mathematics. Home: 13503 Apple Barrel Ct Herndon VA 20171-4006 Office: Howard U Sch Pharmacy and Coll Medicine 2300 4th St NE Washington DC 20002 Business E-Mail: flombardo@howard.edu.

LOMBARDO, JOSEPH T., aerospace transportation executive; B in Sociology, San Diego State U., 1971; MBA, Long Beach State U., Calif., 1984. With Douglas Aircraft, 1975, various leadership roles in prodn. and material control, planning and mfg., gen. mgr. prodn. for twin-jets; v.p. co-prodn. Gulfstream Aerospace (subs. of Gen. Dynamics), 1996—98, sr. v.p., 1998—2001, COO, 2001—07, pres., 2007—; v.p. Gen. Dynamics, 2001—07, exec. v.p. aerospace, 2007—. Recipient Silver Knight award, Nat. Mgmt. Assn. Office: Gulfstream Aerospace Gen Dynamics 500 Gulfstream Rd Savannah GA 31408 Office Phone: 912-965-3000. Office Fax: 912-965-3775.*

LOMBARDO, PHILIP JOSEPH, broadcasting company executive; b. Chgo., June 13, 1935; s. Joseph Pete and Josephine (Franco) L.; m. Marilyn Ann Tellefsen, June 22, 1963; children: Dean, Jeffrey. Student, U. Ill., 1953-55; BA in Speech, Journalism and Radio/TV, U. Mo., 1958, postgrad. speech, 1958; grad. advanced mgmt. program, Harvard U., 1976. Account exec. Sta. WWCA, Ind., 1959-60; producer-dir. Sta. WBBM-TV, Chgo., 1960-65; program mgr., acting gen. mgr. Sta. WLWT, Cin., 1965-67; v.p., gen. mgr. Sta. WGHP-TV, NC, 1968-73; pres., chief exec. officer Corinthian Broadcasting Corp., NYC, 1973-82; chmn., pres., chief exec. officer Champlain Communications Corp., NYC, 1982-84; mng. gen. ptnr. Citadel Communications Co. Ltd., NYC, 1982—; chmn., pres., chief exec. officer Citadel Communications, Co. Ltd., C.C.C. Communications Corp., Lombardo Communications II, Inc., P.J.L. Investments, Inc., NYC, 1984—; mng. gen. ptnr., nat. sales rep. U.S. and Can. TV stas. Can. Communications Co., Toronto, 1985—; mng. gen. ptnr. Coronet Communications Co., NYC, 1985—, Capital Comm. Co., Inc., 1994—, Citadel Comm., LLC, 1995—. Bd. dirs. The Gabelli Group, The Lynch Corp., N.Y.C., ABC-TV Affiliate Assn.; chmn. Nat. Assn. Broadcasters, Broadcasters' Found. Am. Mem. adv. bd. Salvation Army; com. budget, bd. dirs. United Fund; mem. com. High Point (N.C.) United Schs.; 1st vice chmn. Central Carolina chpt. Nat. Multiple Sclerosis Soc., 1968-73; bd. dirs. High Point Arts Council, 1968-73; mem. Columbus Citizens Found., Inc. Served with AUS, 1959, 62. Recipient Disting. Svc. award Freedom Found., Am. Legion, High Point (N.C.) Youth Coun. Mem. Dirs. Guild Am., Internat. Radio and TV Soc. (bd. govs.). Clubs: Winged Foot Golf, Marco Polo, Board Room, Bronxville Field, Chgo. Press, Broadcasters Found. Am. (chmn.), Rotary, Kiwanis, Siwanoy Country Club, Longboat Key Club. Home: 24 Masterton Rd Bronxville NY 10708-4804 Office: Citadel Comm Co 99 Pondfield Rd Bronxville NY 10708-3902 Home Phone: 914-793-2672; Office Phone: 914-793-3400, 914-793-3400. Personal E-mail: citnyltd@aol.com.

LOMBARDO, ROBERT, composer, educator; b. Hartford, Conn., Mar. 5, 1932; s. Michele and Rosalie Lombardo; m. Kathleen Kristine Knudsen, Mar. 27, 1965; children: Rosalia, Adreana. MusB, Hartt Sch. Music, Hartford, 1954, MusM, 1955; PhD in Composition, U. Iowa, Iowa City, 1961. Theory tchr. U. Iowa, Iowa City, 1959—61, Hartt Sch. Music, Hartford, 1963—64; prof. theory and composition Chgo. Musical Coll., Roosevelt U., 1964—99, composer-in-residence, 1964—99. Vis. prof. theory and composition Oberlin Conservatory, Ohio, 1985—86. Composer: (over two hundred compositions) including Last Letters Home (meditations on war), Against Forgetting (a cantata), and Largo Doloroso (for string orch.). Fellow, Ill. Arts Coun., Chgo., 1983, 1984, 1985, 1992, 2002. Mem.: BMI. Avocation: painting. Home: 1040 W Wellington Ave Chicago IL 60657

LOMBARDO APPLEBY, LINDA ROSE, music educator; b. Jamestown, NY, Dec. 6, 1951; d. Philip Patrick and Jacqueline Beatrice Lombardo; children: Venezia Monique Appleby, Zuri Elise Appleby. BS in Music Edn., Daemen Coll., 1974; MA in Student Pers. Adminstrn., SUNY, Buffalo, 1978, postgrad., 2005. Vocal/gen. music tchr. Buffalo Bd. Edn., 1974—. Min. music St. Mary of Sorrows Ch., Buffalo, 1986—; mus. dir. numerous theater groups and orgns., 1974—; home sch. instr., tudor, 2004; facilitator Tchr. Ctr., Buffalo, 2004—, course instr., 2005; performances include Mayor's Inauguration, Buffalo, 1993, Broadway mus., 1995, Supreme Ct. Justice Sandra Day O'Connor, 2000, Gov. of NY, Albany, 2002. Named Tchr. of Yr., Iota Phi Lambda, 2001; recipient Keep the Dream Alive award, City Honors H.S., Buffalo, 2002. Mem.: Nat. Choral Dirs. Assn., NY State Music Educators, Erie County Music Assn., Music Educators Nat. Conf. Democrat. Roman Catholic. Avocations: gardening, bicycling, walking, stained glass, crafts. Home: 60 Winston Rd Buffalo NY 14216 Office Phone: 716-816-3350. E-mail: blusky678@aol.com.

LOMET, DAVID BRUCE, computer scientist; b. Neptune, NJ, Aug. 2, 1939; s. Pierre and Helen (Foster) L.; m. Charlotte Jean Vandermark, Aug. 15, 1964; children: Bruce, Kevin. BS in Physics, Lafayette Coll., Easton, Pa., 1961; MS in Math., George Washington U., Washington, DC, 1966; PhD in Computer Sci., U. Pa., Phila., 1969. Mem. rsch. staff IBM Corp., Yorktown Heights, NY, 1969—85; vis. rschr. U. Newcastle (UK upon Tyne), 1975—76; prof. computer sci. Wang Inst. Grad. Studies, Tyngsboro, Mass., 1985—87; sr. info. cons. Digital Equipment Corp., Nashua, NH, 1987—89, sr. cons. engr. and mem. rsch. staff Cambridge, Mass., 1989—94; prin. rschr., mgr. database rsch. group Microsoft Corp., Redmond, Wash., 1995—. Chmn. program com. FODO93; vice-chmn. program com. ICDE, 1995, 96, 98, co-chmn. program com., 2000, conf. co-chmn., 01, mem. conf. steering com., 2001—, vice chmn. program com., 2002, 03, 04, Very Large Databases (VLDB) program core. track chair, mem. bd., 06, mem. tech. com. data dnegrs. exec. com. Editor IEEE Data Engring. Bull., Parallel and Distributed Database Sys. Jour., ACM SIGMOD Digital Revs; contbr. over 85 articles to profl. publs. Mem., v.p. Bd. Edn., Yorktown Heights, NY, 1980-85. Recipient 2 Best Paper awards SIGMOD Conf.; IBM resident grad. fellow, 1966. Fellow IEEE (life, Outstanding Contbn. award, Golden Core, Meritorious Svc. award), ACM (past editor Transactions on Database Sys., assoc. editor ACM SIGMOD Anthology, SIGMOD Digital Reviews); mem. AAAS, Phi Beta Kappa. Democrat. Achievements include 32 patents; research in database systems, programming languages, computer architecture and distributed systems. Office: Microsoft Rsch One Microsoft Way Redmond WA 98052

LOMICKA, WILLIAM HENRY, investor; b. Irwin, Pa., Mar. 9, 1937; s. William and Carabel Lomicka; m. Carol L. Williams, Feb. 14, 1979; 1 child, Edward W. BA, Coll. Wooster, Ohio, 1959; MBA, U. Pa., 1962. Sr. securities analyst Guardian Life Ins. Co., NYC, 1962-65; treasury svcs. mgr. L. B. Foster Co., Pitts., 1966-68, Welch Foods Co., Westfield, NY, 1969-70; asst. treas. Ashland Oil, Inc., Ky., 1970-75; sr. v.p. fin. Humana Inc., Louisville, 1975-85; pres., fin. cons. Old South Life Ins. Co., Louisville, 1985-87; sec. econ. devel. Commonwealth of Ky., 1987-88; acting pres. Citizens Security Life Ins. Co., Louisville, 1988-89; pres. Mayfair Capital, Inc., Louisville, 1988-99; chmn. Coulter Ridge Capital, Tucson, 1999—. Bd. dirs. Pomeroy IT Solutions, Inc., Counsel Corp. Chair Heuser Hearing Inst.; bd. trustees Ariz.-Sonora Desert Mus., chair. With USAR, 1962—63. Home and Office: 7406 N Secret Canyon Dr Tucson AZ 85718-1435

LOMIO, J. PAUL, law librarian, researcher; B in Psychology, St. Bonaventure U., 1972; JD, Gonzaga U., 1978; LLM, U. Wash., 1979; MLS, Cath. U. Am., 1982. Bar: Wash. 1978. Law clk. for Judge T. Patrick Corbett King County Superior Ct., Seattle, 1980; reference and documents libr. Robert J. White Law Libr., Columbus Sch. Law, Cath. U. Am., Washington; reference libr. Robert Crown Law Libr., Stanford U. Law Sch., Calif., 1982, assoc. pub. svcs. libr. Calif., 1983, asst. dir. info. svcs. Calif., 1994, acting dir. Calif., 2004—05, dir. Calif., 2005—. Chair Stanford U. Pub. Svcs. Coordinating Coun., 1989; mem. Law Librarians' Adv. Com., Calif. Office of Adminstrv. Law., Electronic Ct. Filing Task Force, US Dist. Ct. (no. dist.) Calif. Mem. editl. bd. DATABASE; contbr. articles to law jours. Recipient Marshall D. O'Neill Award. Office: Robert Crown Law Libr Stanford Law Sch 559 Nathan Abbott Way Stanford CA 94305 Office Phone: 650-725-0804. E-mail: plomio@stanford.edu.*

LOMON, EARLE LEONARD, physicist, educator, consultant; b. Montreal, Nov. 15, 1930; came to U.S., 1951, naturalized, 1965; s. Harry and Etta (Rappaport) L.; m. Ruth Margaret Jones, Aug. 4, 1951; children: Martha Glynis, Christopher Dylan, Deirdre Naomi. B.Sc., McGill U., Montreal, 1951; PhD, MIT, 1954. NRC Can. overseas research fellow Inst. Theoretical Physics, Copenhagen, 1954-55; fellow Weizmann Inst., Rehovoth, Israel, 1955-56; research assoc. lab. nuclear studies Cornell U., Ithaca, NY, 1956-57; assoc. prof. theoretical physics McGill U., Montreal, 1957-60; assoc. prof. physics MIT, Cambridge, 1960-70, prof., 1970-99, prof. emeritus, 1999—; program dir. NSF, 2002—. Vis. staff mem. Los Alamos Nat. Lab., 1968—; project dir. Unified Scis. and Math. for Elem. Schs., Cambridge, 1970-77; adj. prof. U. Louvain-la-Neuve, Belgium, 1980; vis. prof. U. Paris, 1979-80, 86-87, UCLA, 1983, U. Wash., 1985, Nanjing U., 2002; vis. rschr. Kernforschungsanlage Jülich, 1986-92, U. Geneva, 1993, CERN, Geneva, 1994, IPN, Orsay, 1994, U. Perugia, 1988, 2006; Lady Davis vis. prof. Hebrew U., Jerusalem, 1993-94; vis. rschr. U. Tübingen, 1997; vis. fgn. scientist KEK (Tanashi br.), Tokyo, 1999-2000, vis. rschr. and lectr. Nanjing U., 2002. Contbr. articles to profl. jours. Guggenheim Meml. Found. fellow CERN, Geneva, 1965-66; Dupont fellow, 1952-53; Ossabaw Island Project fellow (Ga.), 1978; Sci. Research Council fellow U. London, 1980 Fellow Am. Phys. Soc.; mem. Can. Assn. Physicists Office: MIT NE25-4047 77 Mass Ave Cambridge MA 02139-4307 Office Phone: 617-253-4877. Business E-Mail: lomon@lns.mit.edu.

LOMONACO, JOHN JOSEPH, JR., plastic surgeon; b. San Francisco, Jan. 10, 1963; MD, U. Tex., Houston, 1990. Cert. Am. Bd. Surgery, 1999, Am. Bd. Plastic Surgery, 2001. Intern plastic surgery Hermann Hosp., Houston, 1990—91; resident U. Tex. Med. Sch., Houston, 1991—97, fellow, 1997—99; asst. prof. U. Tex., Houston, 1999; dir. plastic surgery Lyndon B. Johnson Gen. Hosp.; pvt. practice surgeon Houston. Achievements include traveling to El Salvador as part of a medical relief mission to perform surgery on children with facial deformities in 1999. Office: 1009 Missouri St Houston TX 77006 Office Phone: 713-526-5550. Office Fax: 713-526-5563. E-mail: jlmd@peoplepc.com.*

LOMONOSOFF, JAMES MARC, marketing professional; b. Van Nuys, Calif., Apr. 29, 1951; s. Boris Marc and Eileen Fairfax (Thomson) Lomonosoff; m. Elisabeth Maas, June 12, 1982; children: Marc Frederik, James Forrest. BA in Econs., Colgate U., 1973; MBA in Gen. Mgmt., U. Va., 1975. With Saatchi and Saatchi Advt., NYC, 1975-93, v.p., account supr., 1975-85, sr. v.p., mgmt. supr., 1986-87, exec. v.p., mgmt. dir., 1987-93, pres. Collateral Plus divsn., 1987-90; CEO, pres. Saatchi & Saatchi Specialized Comm., 1991-92; account dir. VDB/Compton B.V., Amsterdam, Netherlands, 1980-83; acct. dir. Saatchi and Saatchi Compton S.A., Madrid, 1983-84; regional acct. dir. Saatchi and Saatchi Compton Worldwide, London, 1984-86; mng. dir., CEO BSB/Saatchi and Saatchi, Prague, 1992-93; v.p. internat. mktg. Walt Disney Attractions Inc., Lake Buena Vista, Fla., 1994-98, v.p. internat. mktg. and sales L.Am. Coral Gables, Fla., 1999; sr. v.p. mktg. Celebrity Cruises Inc., Miami, Fla., 1999—2001; pres. Lomonosoff Ptnrs., Inc., Miami, Fla., 2001—. Mem.: Beta Theta Pi. Republican. Home: 4211 Monserrate St Coral Gables FL 33146-1207 Office Phone: 305-666-7019. Personal E-mail: jamesmlomonosoff@netscape.net.

LONA, MARIE A., lawyer; b. St. Louis, June 21, 1966; d. Marco A. and MaryAnn Lona; m. Bradley S. Coolidge, Nov. 6, 1993. BA with distinction, Northwestern U., 1998; JD, Stanford U., 1991. Bar: Ill. 1991, US Dist. Ct. (no. dist.) Ill. 1991, US Ct. Appeals (7th cir.) 1994, US Ct. Appeals (6th cir.) 1996. Ptnr. Winston & Strawn, Chgo., 1991—; chair E-discovery Practice Group. Head Winston & Strawn's e-discovery practice group. Author: Why eBay Heightens Risk for Share-Dealing Directors, 2004; singer: (performance) Christmas Spirits; mng. editor: Stanford Law Rev. Bd. dirs. Chgo. Abused Women's Coalition, 2002—, sec. of bd., 2006—07; bd. dirs. Ravinia Assocs., 2005—, Redmoon Theater, 2006—, Hubbard St. Dance Co., 2006—; dir. Chgo. Humanities Festival, 2006—. Named to 40 Under 40 Lawyers to Watch in Ill., Chgo. Lawyer Mag., 2005. Mem.: ABA, Profl. Women's Club Chgo., Nat. Assn. Women Execs., Latino Giving Cir., Chgo. Bar Assn. Avocations: performance (singing, dancing, acting), theater, horseback riding, wine, photography. Office: Winston & Strawn 35 W Wacker Chicago IL 60601 Office Phone: 312-558-5692. Business E-Mail: mlona@winston.com.

LONBORG, JAMES REYNOLD, dentist, former professional baseball player; b. Santa Maria, Calif., Apr. 16, 1942; s. Reynold H. and Ada (Ryan) L.; m. Rosemary Irene Feeney, Nov. 21, 1970; children: Phoebe Lea, Claire Elizabeth, Nicholas James, Nora Kathleen, John Bartholomew, Jordon Michael. BA, Stanford U., 1964; D.MD, Tufts U. Dental Sch., 1983. Baseball player Boston Red Sox, 1965-71, Milw. Brewers, 1972; pitcher Phila. Phillies, 1973-79; gen. dentist, 1979—. Asst. to adminstr. New Eng. Rehab. Clinic, Woburn, Mass., 1972-74 Mem. sports medicine com. U.S. Olympic Com., 1997. Recipient Cy Young award, 1967 Achievements include recording 1000th maj. league strikeout, Aug. 19, 1973; career record 157 wins, 137 losses. Home: 498 First Parish Rd Scituate MA 02066-3201 Office: 105 Webster St Hanover MA 02339-1227 Office Phone: 781-871-4039.

LONCHYNA, VASSYL A., thoracic surgeon; b. Steubenville, Ohio, Oct. 6, 1949; s. Bohdan Ivan and Irene Lonchyna; m. Rosksolana M. Tymiak, Aug. 7, 1976; children: Melania, Inna. BS, U. Detroit, 1971; MD, Wayne State U., Detroit, 1975. Diplomate Am. Bd. Surgery, Am. Bd. Thoracic Surgery. Assoc. prof. Loyola U. Med. Ctr., Maywood, Ill., 1987—98; prof. Tulane U. Med. Ctr., New Orleans, 1998—99; surgeon Chgo. Cardiac Surgeons, 2000—01, Cardio-Thoracic Surgeons Chgo., 2001—05, Surg. Critical Care, Cook County Hosp., 2006—07. Humanitarian med. mission, Lviv, 2001, 2002, 2003, 2004, 2005, 2006. Maj. USAF, 1980—84. Alley-Sheridan scholar, Thoracic Surgery Found., 1998. Fellow: Am. Coll. Surgeons; mem.: Soc. Thoracic Surgeons, Am. Coll. Cardiology. Home: 828 S Washington St Hinsdale IL 60521 Office Phone: 630-215-3687. Personal E-mail: vassyl@aol.com.

LONCHYNA-LISOWSKY, MARIA, music educator; b. Munich, Sept. 26, 1945; d. Bohdan Ivan and Irene Lonchyna; m. Bohdan Lisowsky, May 31, 1969; children: Mykola Lisowsky, Danylo Lisowsky, Taras Lisowsky, Petro Lisowsky. Diploma of Artistic Merit, Ukrainian Music Inst. Am., Detroit, 1967; BA, U. Detroit, 1967; MMus, Wayne State U., 1969. Cert. tchr. piano Mich. Music Tchrs. Assn., 2001, nat. cert. piano tchr. Music Tchrs. Nat. Assn., 2005. Piano soloist, accompanist various venues, 1960—99; piano tchr. Ukrainian Music Inst. Am., Detroit, 1967—, dir., 2001—. Accompanist Suzuki workshops, Troy, Mich., 1984—98, Mich. Sch. Band and Orch. Assn. Solo and Ensemble Festivals, Troy, 1984—98, 2004—06, Trembita Chorus, Detroit, 1975—77, others, 2004—; music dir. Luna Ensemble, Warren, Mich., 1977—83; pianist Ukrainian Music Inst. Trio, Detroit, 1965—67; accompanist Immaculate Conception Ukrainian Cath. H.S. Chorus and Orch., Hamtramck, Mich., 1959—63; accompanist for nat. edn. com. Ukrainian Nat. Women's League Am., Inc. Musician: (recordings) Listen and Sing Along - Ukrainian Christmas Carols, 1981, Ukrainian Stories for Children, 1976, Listen and Sing Along, 1979. Librarian Detroit Symphony Civic Orch., Detroit, 1996—98. Recipient Alumna of Yr. award, Parents Club of Immaculate Conception Ukrainian Cath. H.S., 1991. Mem.: Mich. Music Tchrs. Assn., Music Tchrs. Nat. Assn., Ukrainian Arts Soc. (pres. 1996—), Ukrainian Ednl. Assn. (treas. 1985—86, pres. 1986—92, treas. 1992—97), Plast, Inc. (corr. sec. Detroit region 1964—69, subscription chair, sr. divsn. 1984—92, dues, sr. divsn. 1984—92, subscriptions 1992—96, Recognition award 1999), Met. Detroit Musicians League (sec. 2001—04, pres. 2005—07, Tchr. of the Yr. 2003—04), Tuesday Musicale of Detroit, Ukrainian Nat. Women's League of Am. (ednl. com. chair chpt. 53 1976—78, rec. sec. chpt. 53 1978—80, corr. sec. 1980—84, pres. chpt. 53 1995—97, corr. sec. regional coun. 1997—99, press sec. Ukranian lang. 2003—05, corr. sec. 2004, corr. sec. regional coun. 2004—05, mem. audit com. 2005—, Recognition award 1998).

LOND, HARLEY WELDON, editor, publishing executive; b. Chgo., Feb. 5, 1946; s. Henry and Dorothy L.; m. Marilyn Moss, Aug. 20, 1981; 1 child Elizabeth. BA in Journalism, Calif. State U., LA, 1972. Adminstrv. dir. Century City Ednl. Arts Project, LA, 1972-76, hon. dir., 1982—; founder, editor Intermedia mag., LA, 1974-80; prodn. mgr. FilmRow Publs., LA, 1981; assoc. editor Box Office mag., Hollywood, Calif., 1981-84, editor, assoc. pub., 1984-94; dir. publs. Entertainment Data, Inc., 1994-95; pres. CyberPod Prodns., 1995—; webmaster OnVideo.org, 1996—, Dreamsville.com, 2007—; asst. news editor The Hollywood Reporter, 1995-2000, news editor, 2000—07, mng. editor, 2007—. Syndicated columnist Continental Features, Washington, Tel-Aire Publs., Dallas, 1986—; hon dir. Monterey (Calif.) Film Festival, 1987; mem. media adv. bd. Cinetex Internat. Film Festival, 1988; cons. Take 3 Info. Svc.; web architect-master, OnVideo website, 1995—. Editor: Entertainment Media Electronic Info. Svc.; contbg. editor: (video) Family Style Mag.; contbr. articles to profl. publs. Calif. Arts Council grantee, 1975, Nat. Endowment for Arts grantee, 1976-77. Mem. MLA, Soc. Profl. Journalists, Assn. for Edn. in Journalism and Mass Communication, Speech Communication Assn., Soc. for Cinema Studies. Home and Office: PO Box 17377 Beverly Hills CA 90209-3377 Home Phone: 310-277-0778. Personal E-mail: harleyl@earthlink.net.

LONDEN, JACK W., lawyer; b. Boulder, Colo., Feb. 11, 1953; married; 3 children. BA magna cum laude, Harvard U., 1975; JD, Yale U., 1978. Bar: Calif. 1979, Ariz. 1979. Law clerk to Hon. William W. Schwarzer U.S. Dist. Ct. (no. dist.) Calif., 1979-80; assoc. Morrison & Foerster, San Francisco, 1980—84, ptnr., 1984—. Chmn. Californians for Legal Aid; vice-chmn. Calif. Commissn. on Access to Justice. Named one of Top Ten Lawyers in Bay Area, San Francisco Chronicle, 2003, 100 Most Influential Lawyers, Nat. Law Jour., 2006; recipient Loren Miller Legal Services Award, State Bar of Calif, 1996. Mem.: Legal Aid Soc. of San Francisco (bd. dirs.). Office: Morrison & Foerster 425 Market St San Francisco CA 94105-2482 Office Phone: 415-268-7415. Business E-Mail: jlonden@mofo.com.*

LONDON, ANDREW BARRY, film editor; b. Bronx, NY, Jan. 1, 1949; s. Max Edward and Nellie (Steiner) L. BA in Cinema magna cum laude, U. So. Calif., 1970. Prin. works include: (features) Big Eden, 2000, The Meteor Man, 1993, F/X 2, 1991, Rambo III, 1988, Planes, Trains and Automobiles, 1987, Link, 1986, Cloak & Dagger, 1984, Psycho II, 1983, The True Story of Eskimo Nell, 1975; (TV shows) The Soul Collector, 1999, A Memory in My Heart, 1999, Murder at 75 Birch, 1999, Before He Wakes, 1997, Perfect Crime, 1997, Divided By Hate, 1997, The Crying Child, 1996, Evil Has a Face, 1996, Don't Talk to Strangers, 1994, Day of Reckoning, 1993, Mortal Sins, 1992, Running Delilah, 1992, True Tales, 1992, Sweet Poison, 1991, Tales from the Crypt, 1989-90, Beauty and the Beast Pilot, 1987, The Christmas Star, 1986; sound editor: Wolfen (MPSE Golden Reel award 1982), Hammett, Roadgames, Psycho II, I'm Dancing As Fast As I Can, Perfect, Protocol, Coal Miner's Daughter, The Long Riders, others. Recipient Golden Reel award, Motion Picture Sound Editors, 1982, Best Feature Sound Editing, WOLFEN. Mem. Acad. Motion Picture Arts and Sci., Phi Beta Kappa. Office: 3085 St George St #5 Los Angeles CA 90027-2532

LONDON, CHARLOTTE ISABELLA, secondary school educator; b. Guyana, S.Am., June 11, 1946; came to U.S., 1966, naturalized, 1980; d. Samuel Alphonso and Diana Dallett (Daniels) Edwards; m. David Timothy London, May 26, 1968 (div. May 1983); children: David Tshombe, Douglas Tshaka. BS, Fort Hays State U., 1971; MS, Pa. State U., 1974, PhD, 1977. Elem. sch. tchr., Guyana, 1962-66; secondary sch. tchr., 1971-72; instr. lang. arts Pa. State U., University Park, 1973-74; reading specialist/ednl. cons. N.Y.C. C.C., 1975; dir. Skills Acquisition and Devel. Ctr. Stockton (N.J.) State Coll., 1975-77; reading specialist Pleasantville (N.J.) Pub. Schs., 1977—, supr. English dept., supr. gifted and talented program, 1999—, supr. world langs., 2002—. Ind. specialist United Nations Devel. Programme, Guyana, 1988—; v.p. Atlantic County PTA, 1980-82; del. N.J. Gov.'s Conf. Future Edn. N.J., 1981; founder, pres. Guyana Assn. Reading and Lang. Devel., 1987. Sec. Atlantic County Minority Polit. Women's Caucus. Mem. Internat. Reading Assn., Nat. Coun. Tchrs. English, ASCD, AAUW, Pi Lambda Theta, Phi Delta Kappa (sec.). Mem. African Meth. Episcopal Ch. Home: 6319 Crocus St Mays Landing NJ 08330-1107 Office: Pleasantville Pub Schs W Decatur Ave Pleasantville NJ 08232

LONDON, CRAIG, electronics executive; BS in Physics, U. Calif., Berkeley, Calif.; MBA, Pepperdine U. With AT&T, Pacific Telephone, Electronic Sys. Assocs., Rockwell Internat. Telecomms., Nortel Networks; pres., CEO Diva Comms., Inc.; exec. officer, mng. dir. tech. products Safeguard Scientifics, Inc.; exec. v.p. to pres. Tech. Solutions Solectron Corp., 2002, exec. v.p., strategy, mktg., global svcs., corp. devel., 2002—. Bd. dirs. Boy Scouts Am.-Am.-Pacific Skyline Coun., The San Francisco (Calif.) Zool. Soc. Office: Solectron Corp 777 Gibraltar Dr Milpitas CA 95035

LONDON, HERBERT IRA, humanities educator, academic administrator; b. NYC, Mar. 6, 1939; s. Jack and Esta (Epstein) L.; m. Joy Weinman, Oct. 13, 1942 (div. 1974); children: Staci, Nancy; m. Vicki Pops, Nov. 18, 1950; 1 child, Jaclyn. BA, Columbia U., 1960, MA, 1961; PhD, N.Y. U., 1966; DL, U. Aix.-Marseille, Aix-en-Province, France, 1982, Grove City Coll., 1993. Teaching fellow N.Y. U., NYC, 1963-64, instr., 1964-65, asst. prof., 1967-68, univ. ombudsman, 1968-69, assoc. prof., 1969-73, prof., 1973—2005, dean Gallatin div., 1972-92, John M. Olin U. Prof. Humanities, 1992—2005, prof. emeritus, 2005—; instr. New Sch. for Social Research, NYC, 1964-65; rsch. scholar Australian Nat. U., Canberra, Australia, 1966—67; pres. Hudson Inst., 1997—. Bd. overseers Ctr. for Naval Analysis, Washington, 1983-93; trustee Hudson Inst., Indpls., 1979—, research fellow 1974—; sr. fellow Nat. Strategy Info. Ctr. Created TV programs: Myths That Rule America, The American Character; contbr. numerous articles to profl. jours. Bd. dirs., former chmn. Nat. Assn. Scholars, N.Y.C., 1986; bd. advisors Coalition for Strategic Def. Initiative, Washington, 1986; candidate for mayor of N.Y.C., 1989; conservative candidate for gov., N.Y., 1990, 94; candidate for comptroller of N.Y. State, 1994. Named Danford Assoc., Danford Found., 1971; recipient Anderson award, NYU, 1965, Fulbright award, U.S. Govt., 1966—67, Def. Sci. award, Def. Sci. Jour., 1985, Martin Luther King award, Congress of Racial Equality, 1995, Peter Shaw Meml. award, Exemplary Writing Nat. Assn. Scholars, 1996, Jacques Maritain Humanitarian award, Am. Maritain Assn., 1996, Ellis Island Medal of Honor, 2000, Am. Jewish Congress award, 2001, Libery and Media award, 2002. Mem. Freedom House, Am. Hist. Assn., Edn. Excellence Network, Heritage Found (assoc. scholar 1983—), Ethics and Pub. Policy Ctr. (assoc. scholar 1985—), Nat. Strategy Info. Ctr., Coun. Fgn. Rels. Republican. Jewish. Avocations: writing, tennis. Home: 10 West St New York NY 10004 Office Phone: 212-232-8722. Business E-Mail: herb@hudson.org.

LONDON, IRVING MYER, physician, educator; b. Malden, Mass., July 24, 1918; s. Jacob A. and Rose (Goldstein) London; m. Huguette Piedzicki, Feb. 27, 1955; children: Robert L.J., David T. B in Jewish Edn., Hebrew Coll., 1938; AB summa cum laude, Harvard U., 1939, MD, 1943; DSc (hon.), U. Chgo., 1966. Sheldon Traveling fellow Harvard U., 1939—41, Delamar research fellow med. sch., 1940—41; intern Presbyn. Hosp., NYC, 1943, asst. resident, 1946—47, asst. physician, 1946—52, assoc. attending physician, 1954—55; Rockefeller fellow in medicine Coll. Physicians and Surgeons, Columbia U., 1946—47; instr. Columbia U., 1947—49; asso. in medicine Coll. Phys. and Surg., Columbia U., 1949—51; asst. prof. Coll. Phys. and Surg., Columbia, 1951—54, assoc. prof., 1954—55; prof., chmn. dept. medicine Albert Einstein Coll. Medicine, NYC, 1955—70, vis. prof. medicine, 1970—; dir. med. svc. Bronx Mcpl. Ctr., 1955—70; prof. biology MIT, 1969—89, prof. emeritus, 1989—; vis. prof. medicine Harvard Med. Sch., 1969—72, prof. medicine, 1972—89, prof. emeritus, 1989—; founding dir. divsn. health scis. and tech. Harvard and MIT, 1969—85, prof. medicine, 1972—, Grover M. Hermann prof. health scis. and tech., 1977—89, prof. emeritus, 1989—; dir. Whitaker Coll. Health Scis., Tech. and Mgmt., MIT, 1978—83. Delta Epsilon lectr. U. Colo., 1962, Harvey lectr., 61; Jacobaeus lectr., Stockholm, 64; vis. scientist Pasteur Inst., Paris, 1962—63; Commonwealth Fund fellow, 1962—63; Alpha Omega Alpha lectr. Yale, Boston U., Columbia, SUNY Downstate Med. Ctr., U. Chgo.; Harry L. Alexander vis. prof. Washington U., St. Louis, 1968; Alpha Omega Alpha vis. prof. Johns Hopkins U., 1970; Eugene A. Stead Jr. vis. lectr. Duke Med. Ctr., 1970; cons. to Surgeon Gen. AUS, 1957—60; chmn. metabolism study sect. USPHS, 1961—63; Med. fellowship bd. NAS, NRC, 1955—64; mem. bd. sci. cons. Sloan Kettering Inst., 1960—72; bd. sci. counselors Nat. Heart Inst., 1964—68; exec. com. Health Rsch. Coun., City N.Y., 1958—63; mem. sci. adv. coun. Pub. Health Rsch. Inst., NYC, 1958—63; mem. adv. com. to dir. NIH, 1966—70, nat. cancer adv. bd., 1972—76; physician Brigham and Women's Hosp., 1972—83, sr. physician, 1983—; chmn. rsch. group Nat. Commn. on Arthritis, 1975—76; chmn. adv. com. Divsn. Health Scis., Inst. Medicine, 1979—82; mem. Bd. Sci. Counselors, NIH and NIADDK, 1979—83; bd. dirs., cons. Johnson and Johnson, 1982—89; founder Genetix Pharms., 1996. Assoc. editor: Jour. Clin. Investigation, 1952—57, mem. editl. bd.: Am. Jour. Medicine, 1965—79. Bd. overseers Hebrew Coll., 2000—; bd. dirs. Philippe Found. Capt. US Army, 1944—46. Recipient Bloomfield medal and lectr., Lady Davis Inst., 1986. Fellow: Am. Acad. Arts and Scis., Am. Assn. Advancement Scis. (Theobald Smith award in med. scis. 1953); mem.: NAS (med. bd. medicine 1967—70, founding mem. Inst. Medicine 1970), Assn. Am. Physicians, Internat. Soc. Hematology, Am. Soc. Hematology, Am.-Soc. Clin. Investigation (pres. 1963—64), Am. Soc. Biol. Chemists, Alpha Omega Alpha, Phi Beta Kappa. Office: Harvard U-MIT Div Health Scis and Tech 77 Massachusetts Ave Cambridge MA 02139-4301 E-mail: imlondon@mit.edu.

LONDON, J. PHILLIP (JACK LONDON), information technology executive; b. Oklahoma City, Apr. 30, 1937; s. Harry Riles and Laura Evalyn (Phillips) L.; children: J. Phillip Jr., Laura McLain. BSc, U.S. Naval Acad., 1959; MSc, U.S. Naval Postgrad. Sch., 1967; D in Bus. Adminstrn., George Washington U., 1971. Commd. ensign USN, 1959, advanced through grades to capt., resigned, 1971; program mgr. Challenger Research Inc., 1971-72; mgr. CACI Internat. Inc., Arlington, Va., 1972-76, v.p., 1976-77, sr. v.p., 1977-79, exec. v.p., 1979-82, pres. operating div., 1982-84, pres., chief exec. officer, 1984-90, chmn., pres., CEO, 1990—2007, exec. chmn., 2007—. Recipient Alumni of Yr. award George Washington U. Sch. Govt. & Bus. Adminstrn., Washington, 1987, High Tech Entrepreneur award KPMG Peat Marwick, 1995. Mem. George Town Club (Washington), Cosmos Club (Washington). Episcopalian. Office: CACI Internat Inc 1100 N Glebe Rd Ste 200 Arlington VA 22201-4797*

LONDON, MARTIN, lawyer; b. Glen Cove, NY, Apr. 4, 1934; children: Jesse, Lizbeth; m. Doris Wilke, July 28, 1983. AB, Cornell U., 1955; LLB, NYU, 1957. Bar: N.Y. 1958, U.S. Dist. Ct. (so. dist.) N.Y. 1962, U.S. Tax Ct. 1968, U.S. Dist. Ct. (ea. dist.) N.Y. 1969, U.S. Ct. Appeals (2d cir.) 1969, U.S. Dist. Ct. D.C. 1970, U.S. Supreme Ct. 1971, U.S. Ct. Appeals (6th and 7th cirs.) 1982, U.S. Ct. Appeals (4th cir.) 1990. Assoc. Gallop, Climenko & Gould, NYC, 1958-61, Paul, Weiss, Rifkind, Wharton & Garrison, NYC, 1962-68, ptnr., 1969—. Spl. counsel judiciary relations com. First Judicial Dept., 1973-74, counsel gov.'s judicial nomination com., 1975-82, chmn. deptl. disciplinary com., 1980-85; spl. trial counsel Ct. on the Judiciary, 1977. Served as sgt. U.S. Army, 1957-58, 61-62. Mem. Am. Coll. Trial Lawyers, Assn. of Bar of City of N.Y., Fed. Bar Council, Am. Arbitration Assn. (nat. panel arbitrators). Avocations: deep sea fishing, skiing. Office: Paul Weiss Rifkind Wharton & Garrison LLP Ste 2613 1285 Avenue Of The Americas New York NY 10019-6064 Office Phone: 212-373-3197. E-mail: mlondon@paulweiss.com.

LONDON, NORA ELEONOR, foundation administrator; arrived in U.S., 1941; d. Jacob Schapiro and Jeanne Begagon; m. George London (dec. 1985); children: Andrew Garvin, Philip Garvin, Marina, Marc. Student, Barnard Coll., NYC, 1941—43. Founder, hon. pres. George London Stiftung, Vienna, 1988—; pres. George London Found. for Singers, NYC, 1991—. Author: Aria for George, 1986, George London, of Gods and Demons, 2005. Home: 1 Lincoln Plz Apt 36P New York NY 10023-7159

LONDRÉ, FELICIA MAE HARDISON, theater educator; b. Ft. Lewis, Wash., Apr. 1, 1941; d. Felix M. and Priscilla Mae (Graham) Hardison; m. Venne-Richard Londré, Dec. 16, 1967; children: Tristan Graham, Georgianna Rose. BA with high honors, U. Mont., Missoula, 1962; MA, U. Wash., Seattle, 1964; PhD, U. Wis., Madison, 1969. Asst. prof. U. Wis. at Rock County, Janesville, 1969-75; asst. prof., head theatre program U. Tex. at Dallas, Richardson, 1975-78; assoc. prof. U. Mo., Kansas City, 1978-82, prof. theatre, 1982-87, curators' prof., 1987—; women's chair in humanistic studies Marquette U., 1995. Dramaturg Mo. Repertory Theatre, Kansas City, 1978-2001, Nebr. Shakespeare Festival, 1990—; guest dramaturg Gt. Lakes Theater Festival, 1988; mem. archives task force Folly Theatre, 1982-83; artistic advisor New Directions Theatre Co., 1983-90; hon. lectr. Mid.-Am. State Univs. Assn., 1986-87; mem. U.S.-U.S.S.R. Joint Commn. on Theatre Historiography, 1989; mem.adv. bd. Contemporary World Writers, 1991—; lectr. univs. Budapest, Pecs, Debrecen, Hungary, 1992; vis. prof. Hosei U., Tokyo, 1993; vis. scholar Wabash Coll., 2003, lectr. U. Rouen, Caen, Paris, 2003; Geske lectr. U. Nebr., Lincoln, 2005. Author: Tennessee Williams, 1979, Tom Stoppard, 1981, Federico Garcia Lorca, 1984, Love's Labour's Lost: Critical Essays, 1997; The History of World Theater: From the English Restoration to the Present, 1991 (Choice Outstanding Acad. Book award 1991); (play) Miss Millay Was Right, 1982 (John Gassner Meml. Playwriting award 1982), Chow Chow Pizza, 1995 (Kansas City Gorilla Theatre First Prize, Stages '95 Competition, Dallas); (opera libretto) Duse and D'Annunzio, 1987; (with Daniel J. Watermeier) The History of North American Theater: The United States, Canada, and Mexico from Pre-Columbian Times to the Present, 1998, Words at Play: Creative Writing and Dramaturgy, 2005, The Enchanted Years of the Stage: Kansas City at the Crossroads of American Theater 1870-1930, 2007; co-editor: Shakespeare Companies and Festivals: An International Guide, 1995; book rev. editor: Theatre Jour., 1984-86; assoc. editor: Shakespeare Around the Globe: A Guide to Notable Postwar Revivals, 1986; mem. editl. bd. Theatre History Studies, 1981-87, 89—, Studies in Am. Drama, 1945 to the present, 1984-93, 19th Century Theatre Jour., 1984-95, Bookmark Press, Tennessee Williams Rev., 1985-87, Jour. Dramatic Theory and Criticism, 1986—, On-Stage Studies, Elizabethan Rev., 1992-99, Theatre Symposium, 1994—, Oxfordian, 1998—, Estreno Contemporary Spanish Plays, 1998—, So. Ill. U. Press Theater in the Americas series, 2000—, Eugene O'Neill Rev., 2005—; contbr. articles to profl. jours. Hon. co-founder Heart of Am. Shakespeare Festival, bd. dirs., 1991-2004, v.p., 2000-04; bd. dirs. Edgar Snow Meml. Fund, 1993-2002; active UMKC Grad. Coun., 2001-04, acad. stds. com. Coll. Arts and Scis., 2001-04; elected Nat. Theatre Conf., 2001, trustee, 2004-05, sec., 2005—; sec. Coll. Fellows Am. Theatre, 2001-03. Fulbright grantee U. Caen, Normandy, France, 1962-63, NEH grantee, 1971, 80, Faculty Rsch. grantee U. Mo., 1985-86, 90-91, tchr. seminar grantee Mo. Humanities Coun., 1993, 96; recipient Disting. Alumni award U. Mont., 1998, winner Amy and Eric Burger Essay on Theatre Competition, U. Wyo., 2003, Inspirational Faculty award, U. Mo. Kansas City, 2006; grad. fellow U. Wis., 1966-67, Trustees fellow U. Kansas City, 1987-88; inductee Coll. Fellows Am. Theatre. Fellow Mid-Am. Theatre Conf. (chair grad. rsch. paper competition 1985); mem. Assn. Francaise des Studes Americaines, Am. Soc. Theatre Rsch. (exec. com. 1984-90, program chair 1995), Shakespeare Theatre Assn. Am. (sec. 1991-93), Internat. Fedn. for Theatre Rsch. (del. gen. assembly 1985), Am. Theatre Assn. (commn. on theatre rsch. 1981-87, chmn. 1984-86), Theatre Libr. Assn., Dramatists Guild, Literary Mgrs. and Dramaturgs Am., Shakespeare Oxford Soc., Am. Theatre and Drama Soc. (v.p. 1995-97, pres. 1997-99), Nat. League of Am. PEN Women (v.p. 2002-04, pres. 2004—06, bd. dirs. Kansas City-Westport br.), Assn. for Theatre in Higher Edn. (v.p. for awards 2001-03, Outstanding Tchr. award 2001), Internat. Al Jolson Soc., Lewis and Clark Heritage Found. Roman Catholic. Avocations: travel, theater, history. Home: 528 E 56th St Kansas City MO 64110-2769 Office: Dept Theatre 4949 Cherry St Kansas City MO 64110-2499 Office Phone: 816-235-2781. Business E-Mail: londref@umkc.edu.

LONDRIGAN, THOMAS FOSTER, lawyer; b. Springfield, Ill., May 10, 1937; s. Joseph Aloysius and Bridgett Loretta (Foster) L.; m. Carol Ann Fish, Aug. 31, 1963; children: Joseph, Patrick, Thomas Jr., Genevieve. AB, U. Notre Dame, 1959; LLB, U. Ill., 1962. Bar: Ill. 1962. Asst. U.S. Atty., Springfield, 1963-65; law clerk 4th Dist. Appellate Ct., Springfield, 1965-66; sr. ptnr. Londrigan, Potter & Randle, Springfield, 1966—. Contbr. articles to profl. jours. Activities chmn. Illini for Kennedy, Champaign, Ill., 1960; pres. U. of Ill. Young Dems., Champaign, 1961; co-chair Ill. Dems. for Reagan, Springfield, 1980. Mem. ABA, Internat. Acad. Trial Lawyers, Ill. Bar Assn. (co-chair Com. on Uniform Circuit Ct. Rules 1974-75), Sangamon County Bar Assn., Assn. of Trial Lawyers of Am. (bd. mem. 1988-90). Am. Coll. of Trial Lawyers, Ill. Trial Lawyers Assn. (pres. 1983-84), Soc. of Trial LAwyers, 7th Cir. Ct. of Appeals Bar Assn. Democrat. Roman Catholic. Avocation: competitive sailing. Office: Londrigan Potter & Randle PO Box 399 Springfield IL 62705-0399 Office Phone: 217-544-9823. Business E-Mail: tom@lprpc.com.

LONEGAN, THOMAS LEE, retired restaurant corporation executive; b. Kansas City, Mo., July 4, 1932; s. Thomas F. and Edna L. (Payton) L.; m. Donna F. Ednie, Apr. 11, 1958; children: Timothy L., John M. BSME, Gen. Motors Inst., 1955; MS in Mgmt., USN Post Grad Sch., 1963; grad., Indsl. Coll. Armed Forces, Washington, 1970; postgrad., Calif. State U., Long Beach, 1979-83; grad., Coll. for Fin. Planning, Denver, 1984. Registered profl. engr., Mass.; CFP. Commd. ensign USN, 1956, advanced through grades to comdr., 1978; dir. pub. works, officer in charge of constrn. Naval Weapons Sta., Seal Beach, Calif., 1974-78; ret., 1978; dir. cen. staff McAthco Enterprises, Inc., Camarillo, Calif., 1985, exec. v.p., CFO, 1986-90, pres., CEO, 1991-93, exec. v.p., CFO, 1994-95; ret. Bd. dirs. McAthco Enterprises; exec. v.p. engring. Orange County Engring. Coun., 1977-78. Author: Analysis and Attenuation of Air Borne Noise in Industrial Plants, 1955, Formalized Training of Maintenance Personnel, 1963. Vol. various couns. Boy Scouts Am., 1968-76. Decorated Bronze Star with combat device, Meritorious Svc. medal, Jt. Svcs. Commendation medal, Navy Achievement medal; decorated Order of Chamoro (Guam); recipient Silver medal Boy Scouts Am., 1974. Fellow Soc. Am. Mil. Engrs., Mil. Officers Assn. Am., GM Inst. Robots Honor Soc.; mem. Beta Gamma Sigma. Avocations: reading, music. E-mail: tomlonegan@socal.rr.com.

LONERGAN, EDWARD F., manufacturing executive; BA, Union Coll., 1981. Mgmt. positions through gen. mgr. Ahold customer team Procter & Gamble, 1981—2002; pres. comml. ops. Europe Gillette Co., 2002—06; pres., CEO JohnsonDiversey Inc., Sturtevant, Wis., 2006—. Office: JohnsonDiversey Inc 8310 16th St Sturtevant WI 53177-1964*

LONERGAN, ROBERT A., lawyer, chemicals executive; m. Marsha Lonergan. AB in English Lit., Fordham Coll., 1972; JD, Forham U., 1975; grad., Harvard U., 1997. With Cadwalader, Wickersham & Taft, NYC; counsel Bethlehem (Pa.) Steel Corp.; v.p., gen. counsel, sec. Kusan, Inc., Brentwood, Tenn.; v.p., gen. counsel, sec., bd. mem. Kennecott Corp., Salt Lake City; sr. v.p., gen. counsel, sec. Pegasus Gold, Inc., Spokane, Wash., 1995—99; v.p., gen. counsel Rohm and Haas Co., Phila., 1999—2002, v.p., corp. sec., gen. counsel, 2002—07, exec. v.p., corp. sec., gen. counsel, 2007—. Mem. bd. trustees Inst. for Law and Econs., U. Pa.; bd. dirs. Phila. Mus. Art, Nat. Assn. Mfrs., Walnut St. Theatre, Com. of Seventy, Atlantic Legal Found. With US Army, Vietnam. Mem.: Greater Phila. C. of C. (bd. dirs.). Office: Rohm and Haas Co 100 Independence Mall West Philadelphia PA 19106-2399*

LONEY, GLENN MEREDITH, theater educator; b. Sacramento, Dec. 24, 1928; s. David Merton and Marion Gladys (Busher) L. BA, U. Calif., Berkeley, 1950; MA, U. Wis., 1951; PhD, Stanford U., 1953. Teaching asst. U. Calif., Berkeley, 1949-50, Stanford U., Calif., 1952-53; instr. San Francisco State U., 1955-56, U. Nev., Las Vegas, 1956; prof. U. Md., Europe, N. Africa, Middle East, 1956-59; instr. Hofstra U., Hempstead, NY, 1959-61, Adelphi U., Garden City, NY, 1959-61; prof. speech and theater Bklyn. Coll. and City U. Grad. Ctr., 1961-71, prof. theater, 1971—. Author: Briefing and Conference Techniques, 1959, Peter Brook Midsummer Night's Dream, 1974, The Shakespeare Complex, 1974, Young Vic Scapino, 1980, The House of Mirth-The Play of the Novel, 1981, Twentieth Century Theatre, 1983, California Gold Rush Drama, Musical Theatre in America, 1984, Unsung Genius, 1984, Creating Careers in Music Theatre, 1988, Staging Shakespeare, 1990, Peter Brook: Oxford to Orghast, 1997; editor: The Modernist; founding editor, project dir. various online publications Served with AUS, 1953-55. Fellow Am. Scandinavian Found.; mem. AAUP, Am. Theatre Critics Assn., Am. Dance Critics, Outer Critics Circle (sec.), Am. Music Critics Assn., Am. Soc. Theatre Research, Internat. Fedn. Theatre Research, Theatre Library Assn., Theatre Hist. Soc., Internat. Assn. Theatre Critics, Phi Beta Kappa, Alpha Mu Gamma, Phi Eta Sigma, Phi Delta Phi. Democrat. Office: 3 E 71st St New York NY 10021-4154 Home Phone: 212-879-5386; Office Phone: 212-879-5386.

LONEY, MARY ROSE, former airport administrator, aviation industry consultant; b. Ohio, 1952; B in Sociology and Philosophy, U. Pitts., 1973; MPA, U. Nev., Las Vegas, 1983. Ticket sales staff Grand Canyon Airlines, 1973—75; mgr. Lucky's Grocery Stores, 1976—78; planning svcs. mgr. McCarran Internat. Airport, Las Vegas, Nev., 1979-84; asst. aviation dir. Albuquerque Internat. Airport, 1984-86; asst. dir. aviation San Jose (Calif.) Internat. Airport, 1986-89; first dep. commr. aviation Chgo. Airport Sys., 1989-92; dep. exec. dir. fin. and adminstrn. Dallas/Ft. Worth Internat. Airport, 1992-93; dir. aviation Phila. Internat. Airport, 1993-96; commr. aviation Chgo. Airport Sys., 1996—99; pres. Travelways, Inc., NJ, 1999—2000; pres., CEO The Loney Group, Satellite Beach, Fla., 2000—. Bd. dirs. Chgo. Tourism and Visitors Bur., 1993—2000, Phila. Conv. and Visitors Bur., 1993—2000, Chgo.-Gary Airport Authority, 1996—2000; bd. mem. Chgo. Econ. Devel. Commn., 1996—2000. Trustee St. Joseph's U., Phila., 1994—97; bd. dirs. Chgo. Pub. Art Commn., 1996—2000. Named Santa Clara County Woman of Achievement, 1988, Woman of Yr., Phila. Customs Brokers and Freight Forwarders Assn., 1994, one of State Pa. Honor Roll of Women, 1996; recipient YWCA's Tribute to Women in Industry award, 1989, Bus. Woman of Yr. award Great Valley Regional C. of C., 1994, Transp. award March of Dimes, 1995. Mem. FAA (appointed rsch. engring. and devel. adv. com.), Am. Assn. Airport Execs. (accredited airport exec., nat. bd. dirs. 1995-97, chmns. award 1994), St. Joseph's U. (bd. trustees). Home: 1290 Highway A1A Ste 102 Satellite Beach FL 32937-2477

LONG, ALAN K., research administrator; b. Burlington, Vt., June 19, 1950; married; 2 children. BS, Yale U., 1971; MA, Harvard U., 1976, PhD, 1979. From rsch. assoc. to lab. dir. depts. chem. and earth sci. Harvard U., Cambridge, Mass., 1979—, asst. dean for rsch. fins. and sys. Faculty Arts and Scis., 2002—. Mem. Am. Chem. Soc. Office: Harvard U Faculty Arts and Scis 1414 Massachusetts Ave # 430 Cambridge MA 02138

LONG, ANGUS QUENTIN, lawyer, art association administrator; s. Benjamin Franklin Long and Mary Diane Griffin. BA, Davidson Coll., NC, 1997; MBA, JD, Carolina U., 2001. Bar: NC 2001; lic. real estate broker SC, 2005. Pvt. practice law, 2001—; pres. Internat. Fine Arts Soc., 2001—. Atty. ACLU SC, 2003—06. Office: Internat Fine Arts Soc 189 Broad St Charleston SC 29401

LONG, ANTHONY ARTHUR, classics educator; b. Manchester, Eng., Aug. 17, 1937; came to U.S. 1983; s. Tom Arthur and Phyllis Joan (LeGrice) L.; m. Janice Calloway, Dec. 30, 1960 (div. 1969); 1 child, Stephen Arthur; m. Mary Kay Flavell, May 25, 1970 (div. 1990); 1 child, Rebecca Jane; m. Monique Marie-Jeanne Elias, Mar. 22, 1997. BA, U. Coll. London, 1960; PhD, U. London, 1964. Lectr. classics U. Otago, Dunedin, New Zealand, 1961-64, U. Nottingham, England, 1964-66; lectr. Greek and Latin U. Coll. London, 1966-71; reader in Greek and Latin U. London, 1971-73; Gladstone prof. Greek U. Liverpool, England, 1973-83, pub. orator, 1981-83; prof. classics U. Calif., Berkeley, 1982—, chmn. dept. classics, 1986-90, Irving Stone prof. lit., 1991—. Mem. Inst. Advanced Study, Princeton, NJ, 1970, 79; vis. prof. U. Munich, 1973, Ecole Normale Supérieure, Paris, 1993, 2001; Cardinal Mercier prof. philosophy U. Louvain, Belgium, 1991; Belle van Zuylen prof. philosophy, U. Utrecht, Netherlands, 2003; mem. selection com. Mellon Fellowships, 1984-90, Stanford U. Humanities Coun., 1985-86; Corbett lectr. U. Cambridge, 1998-99; faculty rsch. lectr. U. Calif., Berkeley, 1999-2000, affiliated prof. philosophy, 2005-; Brackenridge lectr., U. Tex., San Antonio, 2003. Author: Language and Thought in Sophocles, 1968 (Cromer Greek prize 1968), Problems in Stoicism, 1971, 96, Hellenistic Philosophy, 1974, 2d edit., 1986, (with Fortenbaugh and Huby) Theophrastus of Eresus, 1985, (with Sedley) The Hellenistic Philosophers, 1987, (with Dillon) The Question of Eclecticism, 1988, 96, (with Bastianini) Hierocles, 1992, (with others) Images and Ideologies, 1993, Stoic Studies, 1996, 2d edit., 2001, Cambridge Companion to Early Greek Philosophy, 1999, Epictetus, 2002-04, From Epicurus to Epictetus: Studies in Hellenistic and Roman Philosophy, 2006; editor: Classical Quar., 1975-81, Classical Antiquity, 1987-90; gen. editor: (with Barnes) Clarendon Later Ancient Philosophers, 1987—. Served to lt. Royal Arty., Eng., 1955-57 Named hon. citizen City of Rhodes, Greece; sr. fellow humanities coun. Princeton U., 1978, short-term fellow, 2002, Bye fellow Robinson Coll., Cambridge, 1982, Guggenheim fellow, 1986-87, sr. fellow Ctr. for Hellenic Studies, 1988-93, Wissenschaftskolleg fellow, Berlin, 1991-92, William Evans fellow U. Otago, New Zealand, 1995; fellow NEH, 1990-91, Ctr. Advanced Study in Behavioral Scis., Stanford, 2007-. Fellow Am. Acad. Arts and Scis., Brit. Acad. (corr.); mem. Classical Assn., Aristotelian Soc., Am. Philol. Assn., Phi Beta Kappa (hon.). Avocations: music, walking, travel, bridge. Home: 32 Sunset Dr Kensington CA 94707-1139 Office: U Calif Dept Classics Berkeley CA 94720-0001 E-mail: aalong@berkeley.edu.

LONG, CEDRIC WILLIAM, health facility administrator; b. Mpls., Mar. 4, 1937; s. Tracy Steven and Clarice Cecilia (Robertson) L. BA, UCLA, 1960, MA, 1962; PhD, Princeton U., 1966. Postdoctoral fellow U. Calif., Berkeley, 1966-68; instr. NYU Med. Sch., NYC, 1968-70; lab. chief Flow Labs., Rockville, Md., 1970-76, Litton Industries, Frederick, Md., 1976-80; preclin. chief NIH, Nat. Cancer Inst., DCT, Bethesda, Md., 1980-86; gen. mgr. Nat. Cancer Inst.- Frederick Cancer R & D Ctr., 1986-97; spl. asst. to dir. Nat. Cancer Inst. - Divsn. Extramural Activities, 1997-2000, asst. dir., 2000—. Home: 2 Basildon Cir Rockville MD 20850-2724

LONG, CHARLES FARRELL, insurance company executive; b. Charlottesville, Va., Nov. 19, 1933; s. Cicel Early and Ruth Elizabeth (Shifflett) L.; m. Ann Tilley, May 28, 1960; children: C. Farrell, Linda. CLU; chartered fin. analyst. Founder, pres. Casualty Underwriters, Inc., Charlottesville, 1959-72, Group Underwriters, Inc., Charlottesville, 1959—. Mem. Assay Commn. of U.S., 1975; bd. dirs. Am. Heart Assn.; mem. U. Va. Student Aid Found. With USN, 1954-58. Mem. Am. Soc. CLUs, Ctrl. Va. CLUs Assn. (dir.), Va. Press Assn., Inland Press Assn. Chgo., Million Dollar Round Table. Creator Queen's medal for Queen Elizabeth, 1976. Home: 1400 W Leigh Dr Charlottesville VA 22901-7719 Office: Madison Park Charlottesville VA 22903

LONG, CHARLES FRANKLIN, retired corporate communications executive; b. Norman, Okla., Jan. 19, 1938; s. James Franklin and Mary Katherine (Nemecek) L.; m. Joan Hampton, Sept. 16, 1961; children: Charles Franklin, David Hampton, Stephen Andrew. BA, U. Okla., 1961. Sports writer San Angelo (Tex.) Standard-Times, 1961-62; news reporter Norman Transcript, 1962-63; asso. editor Sooner mag., U. Okla., 1963-66; news editor Quill mag., Chgo., 1967-71, editor, 1971-80; sr. editor Cahners Pub. Co., Des Plaines, Ill., 1981-83; mgr. internal communications Beatrice Cos., Inc., Chgo., 1983-86, dir. communications, 1986-88; dir. corp. communications Tellabs, Inc., Lisle, Ill., 1989-99. Author: With Optimism for the Morrow, 1965. Bd. dirs. Wheaton (Ill.) Youth Outreach, 1988-94, Western DuPage Spl. Recreation Assn. Found., 1994-98; chmn. exec. com. Wheaton Grand Theatre, 1999-2000, 05-06; mem. Fine Arts and Cultural Commn., Wheaton, 2005—. Named to Okla. Journalism Hall of Fame, 1979, We. DuPage Spl. Recreation Assn. Found. Hall of Fame, 2003. Mem. Internat. Assn. Bus. Communicators (Spectra Excellence award Chgo.), Soc. Profl. Journalists-Sigma Delta Chi, Beta Theta Pi. United Methodist. Home: 1106 N Washington St Wheaton IL 60187-3860 Home Phone: 630-653-0789; Office Phone: 630-212-0972. Personal E-mail: clsooner@hotmail.com. *My parents, through gentle persuasion and by their own example, taught their sons to be curious and conscientious. I suppose it was those principles which eventually led me into a career in journalism and to come to realize that the supreme test of any good journalism is the measure of its public service— to serve the truth; to subscribe to ethical standards; to enlighten the public as to the nature and meaning of journalistic pursuits, especially in how those efforts support the American people's stake in their First Amendment to the Constitution.*

LONG, CHARLES THOMAS, lawyer, history professor; b. Denver, Dec. 19, 1942; s. Charles Joseph and Jessie Elizabeth (Squire) L.; m. Susan Rae Kircheis, Aug. 9, 1967; children: Brian Christopher, Lara Elizabeth, Kevin Charles. BA, Dartmouth Coll., Hanover, NH, 1965; JD cum laude, Harvard U., Cambridge, Mass., 1970; PhD in History, George Wash. U., Washington, DC, 2005. Bar: Calif. 1971, US Dist. Ct. (cen. dist.) Calif. 1971, US Ct. Appeals (9th cir.) 1975, DC 1980, US Dist. Ct. DC 1981, US Ct. Claims 1995. Assoc. Gibson, Dunn & Crutcher, Los Angeles, 1970-77, ptnr., 1977-79, Washington, 1979-83; dep. gen. counsel Fed. Home Loan Bank Bd., Washington, 1984-85; ptnr. Jones, Day, Reavis & Pogue, Washington, 1985-98; grad. tchg. asst. hist. dept. George Washington U., 1998—2002, tchg. fellow, asst. professorial lectr., 2003—06, lectr. history and internat. affairs, 2007—. Adj. instr. history dept. St. Mary's Coll. Md., 2005-06. Contbr. articles to profl. jours. Mem. Chesapeake Bay Maritime Mus., Friends of the Nat. Maritime Mus., Greenwich, Eng.; pres. Leigh Mill Meadows Assn., Great Falls, Va., 1980, 2007. Served to lt. USNR, 1965-67. Mem. ABA, Calif. Bar Assn., DC Bar Assn., Coun. for Excellence in Govt., Women in Housing and Fin., Dartmouth Lawyers Assn., Herrington Harbour Sailing Assn. (sec.-treas. 1996), Soc. for Mil. History, N.Am. Conf. on Brit. Studies, Navy Records Soc. (London), US Naval Inst., Am. Hist. Assn., Orgn. Am. Historians, Omohundro Inst. Early Am. History and Culture, Chesapeake Bay Maritime Mus., Friends of the Nat. Maritime Mus. (Greenwich, Eng.), Westwood Country Club (Vienna, Va.). Republican. Methodist. Avocations: sailing, photography, computers, naval history.

LONG, CLARENCE DICKINSON, III, lawyer; b. Princeton, NJ, Feb. 7, 1943; s. Clarence Dickinson and Susanna Eckings (Larter) L.; children: Clarence IV, Andrew, Amanda, Victoria, Stephen. BA, Johns Hopkins U., 1965; JD, U. Md., 1971; postgrad., Judge Adv. Gen.'s Sch., 1979-80. Bar: Ct. Appeals Md. 1972, U.S. Dist. Ct. D.C. 1972, U.S. Ct. Mil. Appeals 1975, U.S. Supreme Ct. 1976, N.C. 1978, U.S. Ct. Claims 1982, U.S. Ct. Appeals (fed. cir.) 1990. Asst. state's atty., Balt., 1973-74; trial atty., trial team chief Office Chief Trial Atty. Contract Appeals Divsn., U.S. Army, Washington, 1980-84; chief atty. Def. Supply Svc., Washington, 1984-87; trial team chief contract appeals divsn. U.S. Army, Washington, 1987-92; sr. atty. USAF, Washington, 1992—. Contbr. articles on Am. Civil War to various periodicals. Lt. col. U.S. Army. Decorated Silver Star, Soldier's medal, Bronze Star, Purple Heart (2), Meritorious Svc. medal (2), Army Commendation medal (2), Cross of Gallantry with gold star, Combat Infantryman's badge, Legion of Merit. Mem. D.C. Bar Assn., N.C. Bar Assn., BCA Bar Assn. (editor), Federalist Soc., Grant Monument Assn. (trustee).

LONG, DAVID W., lawyer; b. Punxsutawney, Pa., Feb. 18, 1942; AB, Duke U., 1964; JD, U. N.C., 1967. Bar: N.C. 1967, U.S. Ct. Appeals (4th cir.) 1970, U.S. Tax. Ct. 1972, U.S. Supreme Ct. 1979. Asst. U.S. atty. U.S. Dist. Ct. (ea. dist.) N.C., 1969-71; mem., litig. practice Poyner & Spruill, Raleigh, NC. Mem. com. on local rules practice and procedure U.S. Dist. Ct. (ea. dist) N.C., mem. magistrate merit selection panel, 1985; mem. Fed. Bar Adv. Coun., 1988-93, chmn., 1991-92; mem. merit screening com. Fed. Pub. Defender, 1991; chmn. Ea. Dist. N.C. Adv. Group under Civil Justice Reform Act 1990. Fellow Internat. Soc. Barristers; assoc. Am. Bd. Trial Advocates; mem. ABA, Nat. Assn. Criminal Def. Lawyers, NC Bar Assn., NC Acad. Trial Lawyers, Wake County Bar Assn. (bd. dirs. 1979-80, 88-89), 10th Jud. Dist. Bar Assn. (pres. 1997). Office: Poyner & Spruill PO Box 10096 3600 Glenwood Ave Raleigh NC 27605-0096 Office Phone: 919-783-2808. Office Fax: 919-783-1075. Business E-Mail: dwlong@poynerspruill.com.

LONG, DEBORAH JOYCE, lawyer; b. Oct. 26, 1953; d. Thomas C. and Margaret N. (Falks) Long; m. William Daniel Sockwell, May 26, 1979; 1 child, Daniel Long Sockwell. BA, Auburn U., 1975; JD, U. Ala., 1980. Bar: Ala. 1980, US Ct. Appeals (5th cir.) 1980, US Ct. Appeals (11th cir.) 1981, US Dist. Ct. (no. dist.) Ala. 1981. Law clk. U.S. Ct. Appeals for 5th Cir., Montgomery, Ala., 1980-81; assoc. Cabaniss, Johnston, Gardner, Dumas & O'Neal, Birmingham, Ala., 1981-84, Maynard, Cooper & Gale, P.C., Birmingham, 1984—94; exec. v.p., gen. counsel Protective Life Corp., Birmingham, Ala., 1994—. Recipient Cert. of Appreciation, Ala. Bar Assn., Montgomery. Mem. Farrah Soc., Ala. State Bar (bd. bar examiners 1987-92, bd. editors 1991-94), Birmingham Bar Assn. (bd. editors 1989-90), Assn. Life Ins. Counsel (pres. 2005) Office: Protective Life Corp 2801 Highway 280 S Birmingham AL 35223-2488

LONG, DON SCOTT, physiatrist; s. Donald Melvin and Wealthia Stevens Long; m. Jacintha Lorene Watkins-Long, June 13, 1992; children: Donai O., Jailah N., Mahalle I. BA, Ohio State U., Columbus, 1990; MD, Ohio State U., 2000. Diplomate Am. Bd. Phys. Medicine and Rehab. Libr. asst. State Libr. Ohio, Columbus; med. claims adjuster Bur. Disability Determination, Columbus, 1992—94; resident Ohio State Med. Ctr., Columbus, 2000—04; staff physician Group Health Assoc., Cin., 2004—. Mng. ptnr., pres. Functional Specialist Ohio, Cin., 2003—; med. cons. Riverview SNU, Cin., 2005—, Shawnee Springs SNU, Harrison, Ohio, 2005—. Fellow: Am. Acad. Phys. Medicine and Rehab.; mem.: Ohio Sickle Cell and Health Assn., Am. Acad. Neuromuscular Electrodiagnostic Medicine (diplomate), Kappa Alpha Psi (bd. dirs. guide right program 2005—). Baptist. Avocations: fishing, reading, coaching basketball, golf. Office: Group Health Assoc Physicians & Surgeons 2001 Anderson Ferry Rd Cincinnati OH 45238 Personal E-mail: functional3@hotmail.com.

LONG, DONLIN MARTIN, surgeon, educator; b. Rolla, Mo., Apr. 14, 1934; s. Donlin M. and Davene E. (Johnson) L.; m. Harriett Page, June 13, 1959; children: Kimberley Page, Elisabeth Merchant, David Bradford. Student, Jefferson City Jr. Coll., 1951-52; MD, U. Mo., 1959; PhD in Neuroanatomy, U. Minn., 1964. Diplomate Am. Bd. Neurol. Surgery. Intern U. Minn. Hosps., Mpls., 1959-60; resident in neurol. surgery U. Minn. Health Sci. Ctr., Mpls., 1960-64, Peter Bent Brigham and Children's Hosp. Med. Center, Boston, 1965; practice medicine specializing in neurosurgery Balt., 1973—; asst. prof. dept. neurosurgery U. Minn. Hosps., 1967-70, neurosurgeon, 1967-73, assoc. prof., 1970-73; neurosurgeon-in-chief dept. neurosurgery Johns Hopkins Hosp., 1973-2000; prof. and chmn. dept. neurosurgery Johns Hopkins U., 1973—, mem. prin. staff Applied Physics Lab., 1976—. Cons. neurosurgery Mpls. VA Hosp., 1967-73, John F. Kennedy Inst., 1977, Balt. City Hosp., 1973— Contbr. numerous articles on neuropathology and surgery to profl. jours.; contbr. to book chpts. in field. Served with USPHS, 1965-67. Mem. Soc. Neurosci., Am. Assn. Neuropathologists, Soc. Neurol. Surgeons, AAAS, AMA, Balt. Neurol. Soc., Internat. Assn. Study of Pain, Internat. Soc. Pediatric Neurosurgery, William T. Peyton Soc., Congress Neurol. Surgeons, Johns Hopkins Med. and Surg. Assn., Electron Microscopy Soc. Am., Md. Neurosurg. Soc., Am. Acad. Neurosurgery, Am. Assn. Neurol. Surgery, Neurol. Soc. Am., Cajal Club, Sigma Xi, Omicron Delta Kappa, Alpha Omega Alpha, Phi Eta Sigma, Pi Mu Epsilon, Mystical 7. Home: 9 Blythewood Rd Baltimore MD 21210-2401 Office: Johns Hopkins Hosp Dept Neurosurgery 600 N Wolfe St Carnegie 466 Baltimore MD 21287-7709 Office Phone: 410-614-3536. Fax: 410-955-6407. Business E-Mail: dmlong@jhmi.edu.

LONG, EDWARD ARLO, management consultant, retired manufacturing executive; b. Detroit, May 5, 1927; s. Arlo Russell and Florence Viola (Magown) L.; m. Lorraine Ruth Nordin, May 21, 1947; children: Karin Louise Long Schelke, Marian Elizabeth Long Benton. BS, Wayne State U., 1956, MBA, 1964. Mfg. mgr. Ex-Cell-O Corp., Detroit, 1950-68; v.p. mktg. Colonial Broach & Machine, Warren, Mich., 1968-70; group v.p. Blue Bird Body Co., Fort Valley, Ga., 1970-75; pres. tool equipment div. Chgo. Pneumatic Tool, Franklin, Pa., 1975-77; group v.p. Joy Mfg. Co., Pine Bluff, Ark., 1977-87; v.p., gen. mgr. Wheeling Machine Products Co./Cooper Industries, Pine Bluff, 1987-94; ret., 1994. Dir. Security Nat. Bank, Wheeling, W.Va.; elected scorer Counselors to Am.'s Small Bus., 2007. Bd. dirs. Franklin Hosp., 1976-76, Oglebay Inst., Wheeling, 1981-83, Ohio Valley Hosp. Trust, Wheeling, 1982-83, Ark. Ind. Colls., 1984, Jefferson County Indsl. Found., 1985; pres. Pine Bluff Fifty for the Future, 1985, Pine Bluff Symphony Orch., 1987, Leadership Pine Bluff, 1990; apptd. zoning commr., Pine Bluff, 1995. Served with USCG, 1945-46. Scholar Nat. Office Mgmt. Assn., 1952, Beta Gamma, Detroit, 1953 Mem. AIME, Am. Petroleum Inst., Duquesne (Pitts.) Club, Rotary, Alpha Kappa Psi, Psi Chi, Sigma Iota Epsilon. Democrat. Roman Catholic. Home and Office: 7409 S Laurel St Pine Bluff AR 71603-8121 Home Phone: 870-534-3321. E-mail: longtrapper2@sbcglobal.net.

LONG, EDWIN TUTT, surgeon; b. St. Louis, July 23, 1925; s. Forrest Edwin and Hazel (Tutt) L.; m. Mary M. Hull, Apr. 16, 1955; children: Jennifer Ann, Laura Ann, Peter Edwin. AB, Columbia U., 1944, MD, 1947. Diplomate Am. Bd. Surgery, Am. Bd. Thoracic Surgery. Rotating intern Meth. Hosp., Bklyn., 1947—48; surg. intern U. Chgo. Clinics, 1948-49, resident in gen. surgery, 1952-55, resident in thoracic surgery, 1955-57; asst. prof. surgery U. Chgo., 1957-59; thoracic and cardiovasc. surgeon Watson Clinic, Lakeland, Fla., 1960-69, chief surgery dept., 1969; dir. Watson Clinic Rsch. Found., 1965—69; assoc. prof. surgery U. Pa., Phila., 1970-73; attending thoracic and cardiovasc. surgeon Allegheny Cardiovasc. Surg. Assocs., Pitts., 1973-88; exec. v.p. Mailings Clearing House and Roxbury Press, Inc., 1988-90, pres., 1990-96, chmn. bd. dirs., 1991—; regent Rockhust U., 2002—. Disting. lectr., curriculum advisor Healthcare Leadership Program, Helzberg Sch. Mgmt., Rockhurst U., 2001—, mem. dean's adv. com., 2004—; nat. adv. panel Ctr. for Practical Health Reform, 2003—, regional co-chair Kansas City chpt., 2003—. Capt. USAF, 1950—52. Pressure Vectorography Rsch. grant Alfred P. Sloan Found., 1963; Nelson-Atkins Mus. fellow, 1997—. Fellow Heart Rhythm Soc.; mem. AMA, ACS, Am. Coll. Cardiology, Soc. for Vascular Surgery, Allegheny Vascular Soc. (pres. 1987), Ea. Vascular Soc., Soc. Thoracic Surgery, Ctr. for Practical Bioethics, Kansas City Consensus, Woodside Club, Rotary, Sigma Xi, Beta Theta Pi. Achievements include patents for gas sterilizer. Home: 4550 Warwick Blvd # 1204 Kansas City MO 64111-7725 Office: 4550 Warwick Blvd # 1209 Kansas City MO 64111 also: Roxbury Press Inc 601 E Marshall St Sweet Springs MO 65351-0295 Office Phone: 816-753-0089. E-mail: elongmd@kc.rr.com.

LONG, ELAINE, writer, editor; b. Sterling, Colo., Jan. 12, 1935; d. Guy William and Evelyn Irene (Simpson) Mullenax; m. Thomas John O'Rourke, Aug. 17, 1963 (dec. Feb. 1965); 1 child, Mary Kendall; m. Arthur Warren Long, Oct. 4, 1969 (dec. Jan., 2003). BA, U. Colo., 1955. Tchr. Portland (Oreg.) Pub. Schs., 1955-57, Denver Pub. Schs., 1957-58, U.S. Civil Svc., Upper Heyford, Eng., 1958-59; copywriter KBOL Radio, Boulder, Colo., 1959-61; ranch hand Guy Mullenax, Gillette, Wyo., 1961-62; copy and feature writer, traffic mgr. KKAR Radio, Pomona, Calif., 1962-63; freelance writer Denver, 1966—. Editor Boulder, Buena Vista, Colo., 1974—. Author: Jenny's Mountain, 1987, Bittersweet Country, 1991, Bear Ridge-A Novel, 2006; cons. editor: Separate Lives: The Story of Mary Rippon, 1999, Dancing with Principle: Hanya Holm in Colorado, 1941-1983, 2001, A Texas Tragedy: Orphaned by Bootleggers, 2001, Behind the Badge: 125 Years of the Boulder Police Department, 2003, Out of the Shadows, 2004, author short stories; contbr. articles to profl. jours. Mem. Western Writers Am. (Spur awards chmn. 1993, 2005, Svc. award 1994-95, 2005, bd. dirs. 1994-95), Aircraft Owners and Pilots Assn., Women Writing the West, Author's Guild NY, Colo. Authors' League (bd. dirs. 1987-88). Avocations: flying, songwriting, singing, hiking, reading. E-mail: elainelong@chaffee.net.

LONG, EUGENE THOMAS, III, philosophy educator, academic administrator; b. Richmond, Va., Mar. 16, 1935; s. Eugene Thomas and Emily Joyce (Barker) L.; m. Carolyn Macleod, June 25, 1960; children: Scott, Kathryn. BA, Randolph-Macon Coll., 1957; BD, Duke U., 1960; PhD, U. Glasgow, Scotland, 1964. Asst. prof. philosophy Randolph-Macon Coll., 1964-67, assoc. prof., 1967-70, U. S.C., Columbia, 1970-73, prof., 1973—2002, prof. emeritus, 2002—, chmn. dept., 1972-87. Author: Jaspers and Bultmann, 1968, Existence, Being and God, 1985, Twentieth Century Western Philosophy of Religion, 1900-2000, 2000; contbr., editor: God, Secularization & History, 1974, Experience, Reason and God, 1980, Prospects for Natural Theology, 1992, God, Reason and Religions, 1995; editor: Handbook of Contemporary Philosophy of Religion, 1995—; editor-in-chief Internat. Jour. for Philosophy of Religion, 1990—; assoc. editor Internat. Jour. Philosophy of Religion, 1975-90, So. Jour. Philosophy, 1978-83; contbr., co-editor: God and Temporality, 1984, Being and Truth, 1986; mem. editl. bd. The Works of William James, 1974-88, Correspondence of William James, 1988—; editor, contbr. Issues in Contemporary Philosophy of Religion, 2001, Selt and Others: Essays in Continental Philosophy of Religion, 2007; contbr. articles to profl. jours. Mem. S.C. Com. for Humanities, 1980-85; mem. adv. bd. The Franklin J. Matchette Found., 1992—. Recipient Rsch. award NEH, 1968, Duke U./U. N.C. Coop. Program in Humanities, 1968-69. Mem. Soc. Philosophy in Religion (pres. 1980-81), Metaphys. Soc. Am. (sec. treas. 1977-81, exec. coun. 1991-94, v.p./pres.-elect 1996-97, pres. 1997-98), So. Soc. Philosophy and Psychology (exec. coun. 1976-79), Am. Philos. Assn. (sec. treas. eastern divsn. 1985-94). Office: U SC Dept Philosophy Columbia SC 29208-0001 Office Phone: 803-777-4166. Business E-Mail: longq@sc.edu.

LONG, FRANK WESLEY, JR., chemist; b. Springfield, Ill., Aug. 26, 1925; s. Frank Wesley and Elizabeth Margaret (Franke) L.; m. Thelma Elizabeth Keil Long, Nov. 17, 1951; children: Stephen Wesley, William Douglas, Valerie Elizabeth Long Feiss. BS, U. Ill., 1946; PhD in Organic Chemistry, State U. Iowa, 1950. Grad. asst. State U. Iowa, Iowa City, 1946-50; lab. chemist 3M Co., Mpls., summer 1948, Ethyl Corp., Ferndale, Mich., summer 1949, GAF Corp., Easton, Pa., 1950-52; project mgr. textile dyeing and finishing U.S. Army Quartermaster, Phila., 1952-53; sec. mgr. sales devel. Hooker Electrochem. Co., Niagara Falls, NY, 1953-64; dir.

product devel. Princeton (N.J.) Chem. Rsch. Inc., 1964-67; product dir. ARCO Chem. Co. (subsidiary of Atlantic Richfield Co.), Phila., 1967-83; owner Riverside Assocs., Princeton, 1983—; dir. bus. devel. Princeton Advanced Tech., Princeton, 1991—. Expert witness in field. Contbr. chpts. to books: Chemicals in Plastics, 1967, U.S. Petrochemical Industry, 1974, Fundamentals of the U.S. Petroleum Industry, 1980. Pres. elem. sch. PTA, Niagara Falls, 1963. Mem. Comml. Devel. Assn. (bd. dirs. 1976-78, Golden C award 1991), Am. Chem. Soc. (bd. dirs. chem. mktg. divsn. 1974-76), Am. Assn. Textile Chemists and Colorists, Chem. Cons. Network, John Priestley Soc. of Chem. Heritage Found., Princeton Ind. Cons., Chemist's Club, Old Guard of Princeton. Achievements include development of flame retardant chemicals and plastics, heat resistant plastics, petrochemicals. Home and Office: Riverside Assocs 292 Riverside Dr Princeton NJ 08540-5432

LONG, GREGORY ALAN, lawyer; b. San Francisco, Aug. 28, 1948; s. William F. and Ellen L. (Webber) L.; m. Jane H. Barrett, Sept. 30, 1983; children: Matthew, Brian, Michael, Gregory. BA magna cum laude, Claremont Men's Coll., Calif., 1970; JD cum laude, Harvard U., 1973. Bar: Calif. 1973, U.S. Dist. Ct. (ctrl. dist.) Calif. 1973, U.S. Ct. Appeals (9th cir.) 1976, U.S. Supreme Ct. 1977, U.S. Ct. Appeals (fed. cir.) 1984. Assoc. Overton, Lyman & Prince, LA, 1973-78, ptnr., 1978-87, Sheppard, Mullin, Richter & Hampton, LA, 1987—. Arbitrator L.A. Superior Ct. Fellow Am. Bar Found.; mem. ABA (young lawyers divsn. exec. coun. 1974-88, chmn. 1984-85, ho. of dels. 1983-89, exec. coun. litigation sect. 1981-83), Calif. Bar Assn. (del. 1976-82, 87-88), L.A. County Bar Assn. (exec. com. 1979-82, trustee 1979-82, barristers sect. exc. coun. 1976-82, pres. 1981-82, exec. coun. trial lawyers sect. 1984-88, chair amicus briefs com. 1989-92). Office: Sheppard Mullin Richter & Hampton 333 S Hope St Los Angeles CA 90071-1406 Office Phone: 213-617-5443. Business E-Mail: glong@smrh.com.

LONG, GREGORY R., botanic garden administrator; LHD (hon.), CUNY. Staff mem. Met. Mus. Art, Am. Mus. Natural Hist., NY Zoological Soc.; v.p. pub. affairs NY Pub. Libr.; CEO and pres. NY Bot. Garden, Bronx, NY, 1989—. Author: Historic Houses of the Hudson River Valley, 2004; editor: The NY Botanical Garden. Mem. Mayor's Adv. Commn. on Cultural Affairs; bd. dirs. Bronx Overall Econ. Devel. Corp.; mem. adv. com. Getty Leadership Inst. for Mus. Mgmt.; bd. dirs. Jerome Pk. Conservancy, Trees NY; mem. steering com. Cultural Institutions Group of NYC, chmn., 1992—95; bd. dirs. Ancram Preservation Group, Natural Sci. Collections Alliance, Preservation League of NY State, 1991—. Named to Centennial Honor Roll, Am. Assn. Museums, 2006. Mem.: Assn. of Sci. Mus. Directors. Office: NY Botanical Garden 200th St & Kazimiroff Blvd Bronx NY 10458-5126*

LONG, HOWARD CHARLES, retired physics professor; b. Seizholtzville, Pa., Dec. 12, 1918; s. Howard William and Isabella Geneva (Reese) L.; m. Frances Monroe Hoke, Apr. 16, 1945; children— Howard Charles, David William, Carol Joyce. BA, Northwestern U., Evanston, Ill., 1941, postgrad., 1941-42; PhD, Ohio State U., Columbus, 1948. Asst. prof. physics Washington and Jefferson Coll., 1948-51; head Electromagnetism Influence Fields sec., U.S. Naval Ordnance Lab., 1951-52; assoc. prof., dept. chmn. physics Am. U., 1952-53; prof. physics, chmn. dept. Gettysburg Coll., 1953-59; prof. physics Dickinson Coll., 1959-81, chmn. dept., 1963-75, Joseph Priestley Chair of Natural Philosophy, 1973, prof. emeritus, 1981—. Cons. physicist Naval Ordnance Lab., White Oak, Md., 1952-73, McCoy Electronics Co., Mt. Holly Springs, Pa., 1958-59 Contbr. articles to ednl. jours. Active Boy Scouts Am. With USNR, 1944-45. Mem. Am. Assn. Physics Tchrs. (sec.-treas. Central Pa. sect. 1958-59, v.p. 1959-60, pres. 1960-61), A.A.U.P. (sec.-treas. Dickinson chpt. 1963-64, v.p. 1964-65, pres. 1965-66), A.A.A.S., Am. Phys. Soc., Cumberland Conservancy. Methodist (chmn. adminstrn. bd. 1961-62, chmn. ofcl. bd. 1957-59, mem. conf. bd. edn. 1971-73). Home: 240 Belvedere St Carlisle PA 17013-3501

LONG, J. GRAHAME, curator; b. Charlotte, Sept. 10, 1972; s. John Harleigh and Margaret Simmons Long; m. Melissa Carolyn Sumner, Nov. 16, 2002; 1 child, Macie Reynolds. BA, Presbyn. Coll., Clinton, SC, 1996. Dir. edn. The Old Exch. Bldg., Charleston, SC, 1998—2000; curator The Charleston Mus., 2000—. Prodr.: (exhibition) Charleston At Play: Sports and Games of the Carolina Lowcountry, 2002, (exhibition) From Clay to Kiln: Traditional Pottery of the American South, 2002, (exhibition) Pages of History: The Post and Courier's First 200 Years, 2003, Sterling Faith: 300 Years of Charleston's Sacred Silver, 2004; contbr. articles to profl. jours. Mem.: SC Silver Soc. Avocation: hunting. Office: The Charleston Mus 360 Meeting St Charleston SC 29403 Office Phone: 843-722-2996. Business E-Mail: glong@charlestonmuseum.org.

LONG, JAMES JAY, lawyer; b. Pitts., Jan. 23, 1959; s. James E. and Barbara E. (Holsberg) L.; m. Tamara Rae Beer, Sept. 7, 1985. AB, U. Chgo., 1981; JD magna cum laude, U. Minn., 1984. Bar: Ill. 1984, U.S. Dist. Ct. (no. dist.) Ill. 1984, Minn. 1988, U.S. Dist. Ct. Minn. 1989. Atty. Winston & Strawn, Chgo., 1984-87; assoc. Briggs & Morgan, St. Paul, 1987-91, shareholder, mem., bd. dir., 1991—. Contbr. articles to profl. jours. Mem. St. Paul Jaycees (v.p. 1989-90, pres. 1993-94), Order of Coif. Democrat. Avocations: travel, sports, coaching youth sports. Home Phone: 651-779-9179; Office Phone: 612-977-8582. Business E-Mail: jlong@briggs.com.

LONG, JEANINE HUNDLEY, retired state legislator; b. Provo, Utah, Sept. 21, 1928; d. Ralph Conrad and Hazel Laurine (Snow) Hundley; m. McKay W. Christensen, Oct. 28, 1949 (div. 1967); children: Cathy Schuyler, Julie Schulleri, Kelly M. Christensen, C. Brett Christensen, Harold A. Christensen; m. Kenneth D. Long, Sept. 6, 1968. AA, Shoreline C.C., Seattle, 1975; BA in Psychology, U. Wash., 1977. Mem. Wash. Ho. of Reps., 1983-87, 93-94, mem. Inst. Pub. Policy; mem. Wash. Senate, Dist. 44, Olympia, 1995—2003. Ranking mem. Human Svcs. and Corr. com. Wash. Senate, 1995-96, 99-2002, chair, 1997-98; vice-chair Rep. Caucus, 1997-98; mem. Braam panel to monitor Dept. Social and Health Svcs., 2005—. Mayor protem, mem. city coun. City of Brier, Wash., 1977-80. Republican. Office: PO Box 40482 Olympia WA 98504-0482 E-mail: long_je@leg.wa.gov.

LONG, JOHN BROADDUS, JR., economist, educator; b. Bklyn., Feb. 28, 1944; s. John Broaddus and Katharine Lumpkin (Wicker) L.; m. Carol Elaine Stephens, Aug. 6, 1966; children: Jennifer Tipton, Owen Rosser, John McCauley BA, Rice U., 1966; PhD, Carnegie-Mellon U., 1971. Asst. prof. U. Rochester, NY, 1969-74, assoc. prof. NY, 1974-84, prof. NY, 1984—. Editor Jour. Fin. Econs., 1982-96, adv. editor, 1996-98; contbr. articles to profl. jours. Office: U Rochester William E Simon Grad Sch Bus Adminstrn Wilson Blvd Rochester NY 14627 Business E-Mail: long@simon.rochester.edu.

LONG, LARRY, state attorney general; b. Brookings, SD, Sept. 30, 1947; m. Jan Anderson; children: Claire, Craig. BA, SD State U., 1969; JD, U. SD, 1972. Pvt. practice, Martin, 1972—73; state's atty. Bennett County, 1973—90; chief dep. atty. gen. SD, 1991—2002; atty. gen. State of SD, 2003—. With US Army. Republican. Office: Office of Atty Gen Ste 1 1302 East Highway 14 Pierre SD 57501-8501 Office Phone: 605-773-3215.*

LONG, LELAND TIMOTHY, retired geophysics educator, seismologist; b. Auburn, NY, Sept. 6, 1940; s. Walter K. and Carmalita Rose Long; m. Sarah Alice Blackard, Mar. 1970; children: Sarah Alice, Katherine Rose, Amy Virginia. BS in Geology, U. Rochester, 1962; MS in Geophysics, N.Mex. Inst. Mining and Tech., 1964; PhD in Geophysics, Oreg. State U., 1968. Registered profl. geologist, Ga. From asst. to assoc. prof. Sch. Earth and Atmosphere Scis. Ga. Inst. Tech., Atlanta, 1968-81, prof., 1981—2005, ret., 2005. Cons. in seismology, near-surface seismic imaging, seismic road vibrations, blast vibrations and gravity data analysis. Contbr. articles to profl. jours. Recipient award, Jesuit Seismology Assn., 2006. Office: Ga Inst Tech Earth And Atmospheric Scis Atlanta GA 30332-0340 Business E-Mail: tim.long@eas.gatech.edu.

LONG, LYDIA ANN, literature and composition professor; b. St. Louis; d. Isaac Adelbert and Lydia Kimbrough (Allen) Long; m. Roland Charles Baer Jr. (div.); children: Roland Charles Baer III, Claxton Allen Baer, Alexander Beckers Baer; m. Samuel Tribble Crews, Nov. 26, 1994. Student, Vassar Coll., Poughkeepsie, NY, 1959—61; BA, Washington U., St. Louis, 1964, MA, 1982. Lectr. Washington U., 1980—82; adj. faculty mem. St. Louis CC Forest Park, 1982—88, St. Louis CC Meramec, 1984—88; prof. St. Charles CC, St. Peters, Mo., 1988—. Recipient Golden Apple award for excellence in tchg., St. Peters C. of C., Mo., 2007. Mem.: Acad. Am. Poets, Nat. Coun. Tchrs. English, Mo. CC Assn., Mo. Bot. Barden, Eliot Soc. Washington U., St. Louis Art Mus., Mo. History Mus., Phi Beta Kappa. Episcopalian. Avocations: poetry, travel. Home: 6904 Washington Ave Saint Louis MO 63130 Office: St Charles CC 4601 Mid Rivers Dr Saint Peters MO 63376

LONG, MAXINE MASTER, lawyer; b. Pensacola, Fla., Oct. 20, 1943; d. Maxwell L. and Claudine E. (Smith) M.; m. Anthony Byrd Long, Aug. 27, 1966; children: Deborah E., David M. AB, Bryn Mawr Coll., 1965; MS, Georgetown U., 1971; JD, U. Miami, 1979. Bar: Fla. 1979, U.S. Ct. Appeals (5th cir.) 1980, U.S. Dist. Ct. (so. dist.) Fla. 1980, U.S. Ct. Appeals (11th cir.) 1981, U.S. Dist. Ct. (mid. and no. dists.) Fla. 1987. Law clk. to U.S. dist. judge U.S. Dist. Ct. (so. dist.) Fla., Miami, 1979-80; assoc. Shutts & Bowen, Miami, 1980-90, of counsel, 1990-92, ptnr., 1992—. Mem. Fla. Bar Assn. (cert. bus. litigator, mem. bus. litigation cert. com. 1995-99, vice chair, 1996-97, past chair bus. litigation com., chair bus. law sect. 2004-05) Dade County Bar Assn. (mem. fed. cts. com., recipient pro bono award/Vol. Lawyers for the Arts 1989). Office: Shutts & Bowen 201 S Biscayne Blvd Ste 1500 Miami FL 33131-4308 Office Phone: 305-358-6300. Business E-Mail: mlong@shutts-law.com.

LONG, MEREDITH J., art dealer; b. Joplin, Mo., Sept. 14, 1928; s. Emery Meredith and Martha M. (Attebury) L.; m. Cornelia Cullen, June 23, 1967; children: Meredith, Jenny, Gretchen, Martha Katherine. BA, U. Tex., 1950, postgrad. Law Sch., 1950-51, 53-54. Exec. Curtis Mathes Corp., Houston, 1953-57; owner Meredith Long & Co., Houston, 1957—, Meredith Long Contemporary, NYC, 1977-80; prin. Davis & Long, NYC, 1974-80, Watson-de Nagy and Co., Houston, 1974-80; mem. cultural property adv. com. U.S. State Dept., 2003—. Dir. Bank S.W., 1975-84, S.W. Bancshares, 1984; bd. dirs. MCorp, Quintana Petroleum Corp., 1984-94, dir. 1983-2003. Editor: Americans at Home and Abroad Catalogue, 1971, Tradition and Innovation-American Paintings 1860-1870 Catalogue, 1974, Americans at Work and Play, 1845-1944 Catalogue, 1980. Chmn. mcpl. arts, City of Houston, 1976-78; bd. dirs., exec. com., trustee Mus. Fine Arts, 1974-78; bd. dirs., mem. exec. com. Houston, Alley Theatre, Houston, 1975—, chmn. emeritus, 1989-93; trustee Houston Ballet Found., 1974-76, exec. com., 1976-77, adv. com., 1979-80; bd. dirs. Contemporary Arts Mus., 1970-76, mem. exec. com., 1971-76, v.p., 1971; mem. pres.'s adv. bd. John F. Kennedy Center of Performing Arts, until 1980; v.p. devel. Houston Symphony Soc., dir., 1986, adv. bd., 1987—, past bd. dirs., pres.'s counc. Houston Grand Opera; mem. adv. council U. Tex. Coll. Fine Arts, Austin, 1979—; trustee Houston chpt. Multiple Sclerosis Soc., 1981, Archives of Am. Art, 1989-95, Cultural Arts Coun. City of Houston, 1991—; chmn. Tex. Heart Inst., 1991—97; mem. U.S. State Dept. Cultural Property Adv. Com., 2003—. Mem. Am. Assn. Museums, Am. Fedn. Arts, Visual Artists and Galleries Assn. (dir. 1977-78), Art Dealers Assn. Am., Art Dealers Assn. Houston (past pres.), Ducks Unlimited Inc. (nat. trustee 1969-80, sponsor of yr. 1979), River Oaks Country Club, Bayou Club, Coronado (bd. dirs., past pres.), The Houstonian Club, Doubles Club (N.Y.C.), Knickerbocker Club (N.Y.C.). Home: 3722 Knollwood St Houston TX 77019-1110 Office: 2323 San Felipe St Houston TX 77019-3494

LONG, MICHAEL ALAN, musician, writer; b. Chgo., Oct. 14, 1945; s. Irving Robert and Libby (Zasser) L.; m. Nokuthula Ende Ngwenyama. BA in English, Ariz. State U., 1967; MusM, Phila. Inst. Music, Kharkov Ukraine, 1993; Mus D, Philharm. State Inst. Music, Kharkov, Ukraine, 1997. Artist in residence Ariz. State U., Tempe, 1968-73; investment banker Bancom Fin. Corp., Phoenix, 1972-83; pres. Michael Long Violins, 1993—; v.p. EDI Records, 2005—. Edn. dir. U.S. Office Econ. Opportunity, Phoenix, 1969-72; fed. program writer, Migrant Opportunity Program, 1973; pres. Solaris Classics, Phoenix, 1997—; internat. mgr. Russian Fed. Orch., Moscow, 1995-00; artist adv. U.S. Commn. of the Arts, Phoenix, 1970-75; cons. Ministry of Culture of Republic of Ukraine; vis. prof. Philharm. Inst., Kharkov, 1997-00; internat. mgr. Russian Nat. Orch.; cons. concerts in field, worldwide. Classical recordings include Hovhaness Symphony for Guitar, Music of the Royal Courts, Hovhaness Mystery of the Holy Martyrs, Tristeza de Amor, Partitas of J.S. Bach, Che, 2005, Il Principe, 2006, On the 8th Day, 2006; writer, prodr., performer Mr. Cobb's Corner, 1978, PBS TV series In Concert, CBS series Perimeter; dramatist: Il Valentino, 1996, Don Carlos, 1997. Recipient Best Documentary Sound Track, U.S. Commn. of the Arts, 1969, Internat. Gold medal Swedish Arabian Horse Assn., Stockholm, 1982, Gold Medal Premio Roma, 5 Grammy award nominations. Jewish. Avocations: weightlifting, collecting books and art, ancient numismatics, breeding horses, collecting fine musical instruments. Office: 3550 N Central Ave Ste 1110 Phoenix AZ 85012-2109

LONG, MICHAEL ELDON, government and history educator; b. Charleston, W.Va., Aug. 15, 1950; s. Roy Eldon and Alice Mae (Leonard) Long; m. Marilyn Sue Branscome, May 25, 1970 (div. Sept. 1997); children: Lisa Michelle, Michael Brent. BA, U. Charleston, 1973; postgrad., George Washington U., 1974—75, U. Hawaii-Manoa, 1983; MS, Cen. Mich. U., 1985; postgrad., Marshall U., 1999, U. S. Fla., 2002. Enlisted U.S. Army, 1977, commd. officer, 1978—97; maj. (ret.) USAR, 1997; asst. prof. history and polit. sci. Pasco-Hernando C.C., 2001—. Adj. prof. govt. and history Southside Va. C.C., 1992—93, St. Petersburg Jr. Coll., Fla., 1999—2001, U. Charleston, W.Va., 1999, Pasco-Hernando C.C., Fla., 2000—01, Fla. Met. U., Tampa, 2000—01; cons. Discussant Southwestern Polit. Sci. Assn., 2001. Manuscript/book reviewer: Jour. Politics, White Ho. Studies, Fla. Hist. Qur., W.Va. History, Richmond Times-Dispatch, Mil. Rev. Dir. Ft. Scammon Hist. Assn., South Charleston, W.Va., 1964—65; seasonal ranger-historian Nat. Pk. Svc., Petersburg Nat. Battlefield, Va., 1972; curator divsn.hist. preservation Fairfax County Pk. Authority, Annandale, Va., 1973—75; participant Woodlawn Conf. Hist. Site Adminstrn., Mt. Vernon, Va., 1974; curator collection and exhibits Hist. Bethlehem, Inc., Pa., 1975—76; exec. dir. Parkersburg (W.Va.) Arts Ctr., 1976—77; bd. dirs. Meherrin River Arts Coun., Emporia, Va., 1990—91, South Charleston Mus. Found., 1998—99. Mem.: So. Polit. Sci. Assn. (panel chair 2001), Am. Polit. Sci. Assn., Acad. Polit. Sci., Am. Hist. Assn., Assn. U.S. Army Club (Suncoast chpt.), Am. Legion. Republican. Roman Catholic. Avocation: historic preservation. Home: 9222 Foremast Ave #3812 Port Richey FL 34668 Office Phone: 727-816-3255. Business E-Mail: longm@phcc.edu.

LONG, MICHAEL J., electronics executive; BBA, U. Wis.; student, Milw. Sch. Engring. Various leadership positions Schweber Electronics, 1983—90; with Arrow Electronics, Inc., 1991—, pres. Capstone Electronics, 1994, pres. Gates/Arrow Distbg., 1995—99, pres., COO Arrow North Am. Computer Products (now Arrow Enterprise Computing Solutions), 1998—2005, pres. N.Am. and Asia/Pacific components, 2006, sr. v.p., pres. Global Components, 2006—. Bd. dirs. AmerisourceBergen. Bd. dirs. Denver Zoo. Named one of Top 25 Execs., Computer Reseller News, 2002, 2004. Office: Arrow Electronics Inc 50 Marcus Dr Melville NY 11747-4210 Office Phone: 631-847-2000.*

LONG, MICHAEL THOMAS, lawyer, manufacturing executive; b. Hartford, Conn., Feb. 22, 1942; s. Michael Joseph and Mary Fagan (Maguire) L.; m. Ann Marie O'Connell, Sept. 9, 1967; children: Michael, Maura, Deirdre. BBA, U. Notre Dame, Ind., 1964; JD, U. Conn., Storrs, 1967, postgrad., 1968. Bar: Conn. 1967. Law clk. US Bankruptcy Ct., US Dist. Ct., Hartford, 1966-68; supr. indsl. rels. Ensign-Bickford Industries, Inc., Simsbury, Conn., 1968-72, contract adminstr., 1972-74, div. controller, 1974-79, mgr. govt. and legal affairs, 1978-81, gen. counsel, sec., 1981-83, v.p., gen. counsel, sec., 1983—2002, sr. v.p., chief legal officer, 2002—04, interim pres., COO, 2004—05, exec. v.p., 2005—06, mng. dir., 2006—, Ensign-Bickford Realty Corp., 2006—07, chmn. bd., 2007—. Bd. dirs. Ensign-Bickford Co., 1981-, Dyno Nobel, Inc., 2003-05; pres., chief exec. officer Ensign-Bickford Haz-Pros Inc., 1989-99; U. Notre Dame Alumni Clubs of Greater Hartford scholarship chmn., 1990—; deputy sheriff Hartford Co., 1988-2000. Chmn. Dem. Town Com., Simsbury, 1971-81, Dem. State Ctrl. Com. of Conn., 1992-96, 02-, Bradley Internat. Airport Com., Windsor Locks, Conn., 1983-91; mem. pub. bldg. com. Town of Simsbury, 1981-85, mem. cultural, parks and recreation com., 1986-87; mem. Simsbury Police Comm., 1999-, chmn., 2004—; mem. Simsbury Jr. Achievement, 1970-74; pres. parish council St. Mary's Ch., Simsbury, 1982-85; bd. dirs. Bradley Internat. Airport, 2001-, vice chmn., 2001—, town moderator, Town of Simsbury, Conn., 2005-. Named Home Town Hero Town of Simsbury, 1987, Simsbury C. of C. Bus. Leader of Yr., 2007; recipient Man of Yr. award U. Notre Dame Alumni Clubs of Greater Hartford, 1995. Mem. ABA, Conn. Bar Assn., Hartford Bar Assn., Inst. Makers of Explosives (bd. govs. 1987—, chmn. legal affairs com. 1986-93, 95—), Am. Corp. Counsel Assn. (bd. dirs. Hartford chpt. 1988-94), Greater Hartford C. of C. (bd. dirs. 1991-94), Internat. Soc. Explosive Engrs., Simsbury Farms Men's Club (founder 1972), Hop Meadow Country Club, Friendly Sons St. Patrick Greater Hartford (named Irishman of Yr. 2005). Democrat. Roman Catholic. Office: Ensign-Bickford Industries Inc 100 Gristmill Rd PO Box 7 Simsbury CT 06070-0007 Office Phone: 860-843-2843. Business E-Mail: mtlong@E-bsnd.com.

LONG, PATRICIA N., academic administrator; m. Dennis Long. BA, Southwest Baptist U., 1973; MSE, Ctrl. Mo. State U., 1978; EdD, U. Kans., 1993. Dir. admissions and records Johnson County C. of C., 1987—95, asst. dean student enrollment svcs. and fin. aid, dean student svcs., 1995—2000; vice chancellor student affairs and enrollment mgmt. U. Mo.-Kansas City, 2000—03, dep. chancellor Univ. Comm., 2003—06, acting exec. vice chancellor, 2005—06; pres. Baker U., Baldwin City, Kans., 2006—. Office: Baker U Office of Pres PO Box 65 Baldwin City KS 66006-0065 Office Phone: 816-235-1141. E-mail: longp@umkc.edu.

LONG, PETER AVARD CHIPMAN, retired military officer; b. Montreal, Que., Can., Feb. 19, 1944; m. Janet Hall. BS, U.S. Naval Acad., 1967; MS in Pers. Mgmt., Naval Postgrad. Sch., Monterey, Calif., 1972; PhD in Learning Tech., Nova Southeastern U., Ft. Lauderdale, 1991. Commd. ensign U.S. Navy, 1967, advanced through grades to rear adm., 1994; main propulsion asst., damage control asst. USS Dennis J. Buckley, 1967-69; engr. officer USS Hepburn, 1972-75; comdg. officer USS Moctobi, Pearl Harbor, Hawaii, 1975-76; exec. officer USS Albert David, 1980-81; comdg. officer USS David R. Ray, 1985-87, USS Reeves, 1991-93; rear adm. Cruiser-Destroyer Group 5, Kitty Hawk Battle Group, 1994—. Exec. officer Navy Recruiting Dist., San Diego; placement officer, detailer Naval Mil. Pers. Command, Washington; CNO chair Indsl. Coll. Armed Forces; commdg. officer Naval Sta., Mayport, Fla., Naval Sta., Pearl Harbor, Hawaii; comdr. Logistics Group We. Pacific, Singapore; dep. chief of staff for shore installation mgmt., US Pacific Fleet; provost Naval War Coll., 1998-2000; pres. Valley Forge Mil. Acad. and Coll., 2000-04. Decorated Navy DSM, Legion of Merit with 4 gold stars, Navy Commendation medal with gold star; recipient Navy Achievement medal.

LONG, PHILLIP CLIFFORD, retired museum director; b. Tucson, Oct. 11, 1942; s. Hugh-Blair Grigsby and Phyllis Margaret (Clay) L.; m. Martha Whitney Rowe, Aug. 26, 1972; children— Elisha Whitney, Charlotte Clay, Elliot Sherlock BA, Tulane U., 1965. Sec. Fifth Third Bancorp, Cin., 1974-94; sr. v.p., sec. Fifth Third Bank, Cin., 1974—94; dir. Taft Mus. Art, Cin., 1994—2006; ret., 2007. Trustee Contemporary Arts Ctr., 1974-84, Art Acad. Cin., 1980-94, Cin. Symphony Orch., 1981-87, Cin. Nature Ctr., 1982-88, Taft Mus., 1987-94, Cin. Country Day Sch., 1991-97; trustee, treas. Cin. Music Hall, 1981-92, Convalescent Hosp. for Children, 1989—, Spring Grove Cemetery, 1989—, Cin. Assn. for Arts, 1992—. Mem. The Camargo Club, Queen City Club. Home: 4795 Burley Hills Dr Cincinnati OH 45243-4007

LONG, RALPH STEWART, clinical psychologist; b. Pitts., Feb. 23, 1926; s. Ralph S. and Virginia (Hawk) L.; m. Vera Lazorchak, June 16, 1951; children: Karen Virginia, Brian Reed, Lauri Michelle. BS, Lock Haven U., 1950; MEd, Pa. State U., 1951; PhD, Washington U., St. Louis, 1965. Lic. psychologist, Tex. Commd. 2d lt. med. svc. corp USAF, 1951, clin. psychologist to chief clin. psychology svcs. hosp. Sampson AFB, NY, 1951—55; chief psychology svc. hosp. Warren AFB, Wyo., 1955—57; Inst. Tech. scholar, Wash. U. USAF, St. Louis, 1957—61, chief psychology dept. med. ctr. Andrews AFB, DC, 1961—62, dir. psychol. svcs. Scott AFB, Ill., 1962—65, dir. psychol. svcs. regional med. ctr. Sheppard AFB, Tex., 1965—67, dir. psychol. svcs. hosp. Wiesbaden, Germany, 1967—70, dir. psychol. svcs. regional med. ctr. Sheppard AFB, Tex., 1970—71, advanced through grades to lt. col., 1968; ret., 1971; dir. psychol. svcs. Cmty. Ctr. Mental Health, Mental Retardation, Wichita Falls, Tex., 1971-72; psychol. cons. Family Counseling Ctr., Wichita Falls, 1972-74; dir. psychol. svcs. Nueces County Mental Health-Mental Retardation Cmty. Ctr., 1974-77; dir. Corpus Christi Counseling Ctr./Physicians-Surgeons Hosp., Tex., 1977-79, Psychol. Cons., Corpus Christi, 1979-82; exec. dir. Personal Dynamics Inst., Corpus Christi, 1982—, dir., 1988—2005, emeritus, 2005—. Instr. dept. psychology McKendree Coll., Lebanon, Ill., 1962-63; instr. So. Ill. U., 1962-64; adj. prof. human rels. Webster U., Webster Groves, Mo., 1976-79, 88-93; adj. prof. psychology Del Mar Coll., Corpus Christi, 1977-83, adj. prof. bus. adminstrn., 1991-93; cons. Tex. Dept. Corrections, 1988-90; bd. dir. Ctr. Creative Living; cons., trainer Crisis Svc., 1980-2005; profl. adv. bd. North Tex. Regional Coun. Alcoholism, 1971-74, Mental Health Assn. Coastal Bend, 1974-83, Wichita Mental Health Assn., 1965-67, 70-74; adj. prof. Embry-Riddle U., Corpus Christi, 1991-93; clin. dir. Shoreline Chem. Dependency Treatment Ctr., 1989-92; consulting psychologist Nueces County Juvenile Justice Ctr., Corpus Christi, 1992-2005, Warm Springs Rehab. Ctr., Corpus Christi, 1992-2005, MCC Managed Behavioral Care, Inc., Eden Prairie, Minn., 1992—2005, Champus Provider, 1972-2005; presenter in field. Active Tex. chpt. ARC; founding mem. Nat. Campaign for Tolerance; charter sponsor Air Force Meml. Found., Statue of Liberty-Ellis Island Found.; mem. Nat. Com. to Preserve Social Security and Medicine; charter mem. Citizens Against Govt. Waste. With USN, 1944—51, Pacific Theater WWII. Named Am. Man Sci., 1962. Fellow: Soc. Air Force Clin. Psychologists; mem.: DAV, APA, VFW (life), Air Force Meml. Found. (charter sponsor), Military Officers Assn. of Am., Anti-Defamation League, Prescribing Psychologists Register, Nat. Air and Space Soc. (founding), US Naval Inst., Air Force Assn. (life), Nat. Register Health Svc. Providers in Psychology, Tex. Assn. Mental Health, Tex. Assn. Mental Health (exec. com. 1980—83), Libr. of

Congress (charter), Am. Inst. Hypnosis, U.S. Navy Meml. (charter mem.), Nat. D-Day Mus. (charter), Mil. Officers Assn. Am., Am. Air Mus. in Britain (charter), US Holocaust Meml. Mus. (charter), Am. Assn. Ret. Persons, Ret. Officers Assn., Am. Mil. Soc., Common Cause, Citizens Against Govt. Waste (charter), WWII Meml. Soc. (charter), Earth Justice Legal Def. Fund., Nat. Arbor Day Found., United Srs. Assn., Theosophical Soc. Am., Nat. Wildlife Fedn., Nat. Mus. Am. Indian (charter), F.D. Roosevelt Meml. (founding), Nat. Trust Hist. Preservation, National Audubon Soc., Smithsonian, Sierra Club, Shriners, Masons, Am. Legion, Sigma Xi (life). Avocations: painting, writing, travel, camping, fishing.

LONG, ROBERT C., retired military officer, management consultant; b. Phila., June 12, 1945; s. Claude Adam Long and Teresa Masgai; m. Janet V. Long, Dec. 7, 1963; children: Tracy, Robert, Gina. AS in Electronics, Chulo Vista CC, Calif., 1973; BS in Bus., U. N.Y., 1985; MS in Bus. Adminstrn., Ctrl. Mich. U., 1995. Commd. ensign USN, 1963, advanced through grades to commdr., 1991, ret., 2003, electronics officer USS Kitty Hawk, 1987—89, ops. officer USS Constellation, 1989—93, comdg. officer Naval Brig. Phila., 1993—95, comms. officer New Orleans, 1995—97, chief staff Norfolk, Va., 1997—98; prin. cons. PriceWaterHouseCoopers, Fairfax, Va., 1998—2000; mgr. smart ship Nausses Phila., 2000—. Decorated 3 Meritorious Svc. awards USN, 5 Commendation medals, 2 Achievement awards, 3 Gold Conduct awards; recipient Outstanding Civil Svc. award, 1996. Mem.: Naval Inst., Navy League, Shriners. Avocation: auto restoration. Home: 2575 Gallaway Rd Bensalem PA 19020

LONG, ROBERT EMMET, author; b. Oswego, NY, June 7, 1934; s. Robert Emmet and Verda (Lindsley) L. BA, Columbia Coll., 1956; MA, Syracuse U., 1964; PhD, Columbia U., 1968. Instr. SUNY, Cortland, 1962-64; asst. prof. Queens Coll., CUNY, NYC, 1968-71; writer, 1971—. Author: The Great Succession: Henry James and the Legacy of Hawthorne, 1979, The Achieving of the Great Gatsby, 1979, Henry James: The Early Years, 1983, John O'Hara, 1983, Nathanael West, 1985, Barbara Pym, 1986, James Thurber, 1988, James Fenimore Cooper, 1990, The Films of Merchant Ivory, 1991, 2d revised edit., 1997, Ingmar Bergman: Film and Stage, 1994, Broadway, the Golden Years: Jerome Robbins and the Great Choreographer-Directors, 2001, First Impressions: Observations on Theater and Books, 2003, An Enlarging Vision: Early Essays and Stories, 2004, James Ivory in Conversation: How Merchant Ivory Makes Its Movies, 2005, Gallagher House, 2005, Acting, American Theatre Wing: Working in the Theatre, 2006, Producing & the Theatre Business, American Theatre Wing: Working in the Theatre, 2007, Writing, American Theatre Wing: Working in the Theatre, 2007; editor numerous books, including John Huston: Interviews, 2001, George Cukor: Interviews, 2001, Liv Ullmann: Interviews, 2006; contbr. articles to profl. jours. and popular mags. Democrat. Episcopalian. Avocations: films, theater, ballet, jazz, travel. Address: 254 S 3rd St Fulton NY 13069-2356 Personal E-mail: rlong@twcny.rr.com.

LONG, ROBERT LEROY, retired utilities executive, consultant; b. Renovo, Pa., Sept. 9, 1936; s. John Leroy and Mary Geraldine (Olmstead) L.; m. Ann Gullborg, Sept. 2, 1957; children: Beth, Jeff, Mark. BSEE, Bucknell U., 1958; MS in Engring., Purdue U., 1959, PhD in Nuclear Engring., 1962. Rsch. assoc. exp. reactor physics Argonne Nat. Lab., 1960-62; reactor specialist nuclear effects br. White Sands (N.Mex.) Missile Range, 1962-65; from asst. prof. to prof. nuclear engring. U. N.Mex., Albuquerque, 1965-78, asst. dean., 1972-74, chmn. chem. and nuc. engring. dept., 1974-78; with GPU Service Corp. (name now GPU Nuc. Corp.), Parsippany, NJ, 1978-96, mgr. generation productivity dept., 1978-79, dir. reliability engring. dept., 1979-80, dir. tng. and edn., 1980-82, v.p. nuclear assurance Parsippany, NJ, 1982-87, v.p. planning and nuclear safety, 1987-89; v.p. corp. svcs. GPU Nuc. Corp., Parsippany, 1989-93, v.p. svcs., 1993-95, v.p. nuclear svcs., 1995-96; recovery officer, v.p. human resources N.E. Nuc. Energy Co., 1998—. With rsch. partic. Sandia Corp., 1965-78; cons. White Sands Missile Range Fast Burst Reactor Facility, 1965-78, Sandia Lab., Albuquerque, 1965-70, Con Edison, N.Y.C., 1970-73, Electric Power Rsch. Inst., Palo Alto, Calif., 1976-78, NSF, U.S. Dept. Energy, others; rsch. assoc. nuc. rsch. divsn. Atomic Weapons Rsch. Estab., Eng., 1966-67; mem. Nuc. Stewardship, LLC. Contbr. articles to profl. jours. Served to capt. U.S. Army, 1962-64. AEC fellow, 1958-59; recipient Disting. Engring. Alumnus award Purdue U., 1993. Fellow Am. Nuc. Soc. (chmn. edn. divsn. 1974-75, chmn. nuc. engring. dept. heads com. 1975-76, chmn. No. N.J. chpt. 1986-87, 88-89, v.p., pres.-elect 1990-91, pres. 1991-92, Pioneer in Nuc. Tng. award 1999); mem. Nuc. Energy Inst., Profl. Reactor Operators Soc. Presbyterian. Avocations: church school teaching, woodworking, reading, choir, model garden railroading. Home: 9615 Elena Dr NE Albuquerque NM 87122-3866

LONG, ROBERT RADCLIFFE, fluid mechanics engineer, educator; b. Glen Ridge, NJ, Oct. 24, 1919; s. Clarence D. and Gertrude (Cooper) L.; m. Cristina Nersing, 1962; children: John Radcliffe, Robert William. AB in Econs, Princeton, 1941; MS in Meteorology, U. Chgo., 1949, PhD, 1950. Meteorologist U.S. Weather Bur., Paris, France, 1946-47; asst. prof. Johns Hopkins U., Balt., 1951-56, assoc. prof., 1956-59, prof. fluid mechanics, 1959-88, prof. emeritus, 1988—, dir. hydrodynamics lab., 1951-88. Assoc. dept. aero. and mech. engring. Ariz. State U. Author: Mechanics of Solids and Fluids, 1960, Engineering Science Mechanics, 1964; contbr. articles to profl. jours. Home: 3989 Myrtle St Sarasota FL 34235-5157 Personal E-mail: rrlong4@comcast.net.

LONG, ROBERT RICHARD, banker; b. Atmore, Ala., Mar. 4, 1937; s. Robert Richard and Vivian (Crook) L.; m. Jane Hamilton Hancock, June 22, 1968; children: Robert Richard, Caroline Tison. BS, Auburn U., 1959; MBA, Harvard U., 1967. With Merchants Nat. Bank, Mobile, Ala., 1961-65, Sun Trust Bank, Atlanta, 1967—; controller Trust Co. Bank, Atlanta, 1972-73, group v.p., 1973-74, exec. v.p. Savannah, Ga., 1974-77, sr. v.p. Atlanta, 1977-78, exec. v.p., 1978-85, pres., 1985—, pres., chmn. and CEO, 1995—, also bd. dirs. Vice pres. Am. Cancer Soc., Atlanta City unit, 1983, pres., 1985; treas. Atlanta Arts Alliance, 1984-87; trustee Morris Brown Coll., 1984—, bd. dirs. 1998—; bd. Atlanta C. of C., 1997—; bd. dirs. C. of C., 1996—; Served to 1st lt. U.S. Army, 1959-61, Korea. Clubs: Piedmont Driving (Atlanta); Oglethorpe (Savannah). Home: 119 Brighton Rd NE Atlanta GA 30309-1539 Office: SunTrust Bank, Atlanta 25 Park Pl NE Atlanta GA 30303-2900

LONG, ROGER LEONARD, artist; b. Jackson, Tenn., Oct. 26, 1978; s. Roger Long, Linda Marie Long; m. Athena Adele Wilson, May 22, 1999. Owner, artist Portrait Phenomena, Ridgeland, Miss., 1998—; art, dance instr. Smarty Pants Ednl. Svcs., Jackson, Miss., 2000; art, dance instr./asst. mgr. Basic Skills Learning Ctr., Madison, Miss., 2001. Owner, choreographer Go Long Prodns., Ridgeland, Miss., 2001—; instr., choreographer Choreorobics, Jackson, Miss., 2001—; dir., cons. Artual Minds, Jackson, 2001—; choreorobics instr. prime-of-life program City of Ridgeland, 2001—. Uncle, 1993 (Scholastic award, 1994), Elvis, 1993 (Clarion Ledger Elvis Drawing Contest award, 1993); choreographer performer Tribute to a Young Man, 2001. Min. Christian Congregation Jehovah's Witness, Jackson, 1995—. Avocation: Avocations: dancing, drawing, writing, music. Office Phone: 601-853-7480.

LONG, RUSSELL CHARLES, retired academic administrator; b. Alpine, Tex., Oct. 9, 1942; s. Roy Joel and Lovis Lorene (Graham) L.; m. Elaine Gresham, May 8, 1964 (div. Jan. 1986); 1 child, Mark Roy; m. Natrelle Hedrick, Mar. 28, 1986. BS, Sul Ross State U., Alpine, 1965; MA, N.Mex. State U., 1967; PhD, Tex. A&M U., 1977. Assoc. prof. Schreiner Coll., Kerrville, Tex., 1967-69; instr. Tarleton State U., Stephenville, Tex., 1969-72, asst. prof., 1972-77, assoc. prof., 1977-85, prof., 1985-92, asst. v.p. acad. adminstrn., 1987-90, chair dept. English and Lang., 1990-92; provost and v.p. acad. adminstrn. West Tex. A&M U., Canyon, 1992-94, interim pres., 1994-95, pres., 1995—2005; pres. emeritus, 2005—. Office: West Texas A&M Univ Wt Sta 2501 4th Ave Canyon TX 79016-0001 Business E-Mail: rlong@mail.wtamu.edu.

LONG, SARAH ANN, librarian; b. Atlanta, May 20, 1943; d. Jones Lloyd and Lelia Maria (Mitchell) Sanders; m. James Allen Long, 1961 (div. 1985); children: Andrew C., James Allen IV; m. Donald J. Sager, May 23, 1987. BA, Oglethorpe U., 1966; M in Librarianship, Emory U., 1969. Asst. libr. Coll. of St. Matthias, Bristol, England, 1970-74; cons. State Libr. Ohio, Columbus, 1975-77; coord. Pub. Libr. of Columbus and Franklin County, Columbus, 1977-79; dir. Fairfield County Dist. Libr., Lancaster, Ohio, 1979-82, Dauphin County Libr. Sys., Harrisburg, Pa., 1982-85, Multnomah County Libr., Portland, Oreg., 1985-89; sys. dir. North Suburban Libr. Sys., Wheeling, Ill., 1989—. Chmn. Portland State U. Libr. Adv. Coun., 1987-89, bd. dirs. Am. Libr., Paris, 2000-02. Contbr. to weekly column in Daily Herald; monthly cable show Whats New in Libraries; contbr. articles to profl. jours. Bd. dirs. Dauphin County Hist. Soc., Harrisburg, 1983-85, ARC, Harrisburg, 1984-85; pres. Lancaster-Fairfield County YWCA, Lancaster, 1981-82; vice chmn. govt. and ednl. divsn. Lancaster-Fairfield County United Way, Lancaster, 1981-82; sec. Fairfield County Arts Coun., 1981-82; adv. bd. Portland State U., 1987-89; mentor Ohio Libr. Leadership Inst., 1993, 95; mentor Synergy. Leadership Inst. Ill. State Libr., 2006; moderator Congl. Ch., Deerfield Ill., 2006—. Recipient Dir.'s award Ohio Program in Humanities, Columbus, 1982, Emory medal Emory U., 2006, Ken Haycock award, 2005; Sarah Long Day established in her honor Fairfield County, Lancaster, Bd. Commrs., 1982. Mem. ALA (pres. 1999-2000, elected coun. 1993-97, chair Spectrum fund raising com. 2001-02), Pub. Libr. Assn. (pres. 1989-90, chair legis. com. 1991-95, chair 1998, nat. conf. com. 1995-98), Ill. Libr. Assn. (pub. policy com. 1991-97, Librarian of Yr. award 1999), Ill. Libr. Sys. Dirs. Orgn. (pres. 2000-05), Libr. Cmty. Found. (bd. dirs. 1995-2005) Office: N Suburban Libr Systems 200 W Dundee Rd Wheeling IL 60090-4750 Business E-Mail: slong@nsls.info.

LONG, SARAH ELIZABETH BRACKNEY, physician; b. Sidney, Ohio, Dec. 5, 1926; d. Robert LeRoy and Caroline Josephine (Shue) Brackney; m. John Frederick Long, June 15, 1948; children: George Lynas, Helen Lucille Corcoran, Harold Roy, Clara Alice Lawrence, Nancy Carol Sieber. BA, Ohio State U., 1948, MD, 1952. Intern Grant Hosp., Columbus, Ohio, 1952—53; resident internal medicine Mt. Carmel Med. Ctr., Columbus, 1966—69, chief resident internal medicine, 1968—69; med. cons. Ohio Bur. Disability Determination, Columbus, 1970—. Physician student health Ohio State U., Columbus, 1970-73; sch. physician Bexley City Schs., Ohio, 1973-83; physician advisor to peer rev. Mt. Carmel East Hosp., Columbus, 1979-86, med. dir. employee health, 1981-96; physician cons. Fed. Black Lung program U.S. Dept. Labor, Columbus, 1979-98. Mem.: AMA, Gerontol. Soc. Am., Columbus Med. Assn., Ohio State Med. Assn., Ohio Hist. Soc., Phi Beta Kappa, Alpha Epsilon Delta. Home: 2765 Bexley Park Rd Columbus OH 43209-2231

LONG, SARAH HOLLEY, lawyer; b. Ft. Worth, Aug. 12, 1977; BS in Corp. Comm., U. Tex., Austin; JD, Baylor U. Bar: Tex. 2002, US Dist. Ct. (no. so. and ea. dists. Tex.). Assoc. atty. Biggers, Beasley, Earle & Hightower, P.C., 2002—03, Touchstone, Bernays, Johnston, Beall, Smith & Stollenwerck, L.L.P., 2003—06; assoc. trial divsn. Walters, Balido & Crain, Dallas. Named a Rising Star, Tex. Super Lawyers mag., 2006. Mem.: ABA (mem. litig. divsn.), Dallas Women Lawyers Assn., Dallas Bar Assn., Dallas Assn. Young Lawyers. Office: Walters Balido & Crain 900 Jackson St Founders Sq Ste 600 Dallas TX 75202 Office Phone: 214-347-8342. E-mail: sarah.long@wbclawfirm.com.*

LONG, SARAH SUNDBORG, pediatrician, educator; b. Portland, Oreg., Oct. 31, 1944; MD, Jefferson Med. Coll., 1970. Diplomate Am. Bd. Pediat. Intern St. Christopher Hosp. for Children, Phila., 1970-71, resident, 1971-73, fellow pediat. and infectious diseases, 1973-75, staff, 1975—2002; prof. pediat. Drexel U. Coll. Medicine, 2002—. Chief editor: Principles and Practice of Pediatric Infectious Diseases, 1997; assoc. editor Jour. Pediatrics, 1997—; contbr. over 100 articles to med. jours. Mem. Am. Acad. Pediat., Soc. for Pediat. Rsch., Am. Pediat. Soc., Pediatric Diseases Soc. (pres. 1999-2001). Office: St Christopher Child Hosp Sect Infectious Diseases Erie Ave at Front St Philadelphia PA 19134 Office Phone: 215-427-5204.

LONG, SHARON RUGEL, dean, molecular biologist, educator; b. Mar. 2, 1951; d. Harold Eugene and Florence Jean (Rugel) Long; m. Harold James McGee, July 7, 1979 (div. 2004); 2 children BS, Calif. Inst. Tech., 1973; PhD, Yale U., 1979. Rsch. fellow Harvard U., Cambridge, Mass., 1979-81; from asst. prof. molecular biology to prof. Stanford U., Palo Alto, Calif., 1982-92, prof. biol. scis., 1992—, William C. Steere, Jr.-Pfizer Inc. prof. biological scis., dean Sch. Humanities and Scis., 2001—07. Investigator Howard Hughes Med. Inst., 1994-2001; adv. bd. Jane Coffin Childs Meml. Fund; bd. dirs. Ann. Revs. Inc., Monsanto Co. Recipient award NSF, 1979, NIH, 1980, Shell Rsch. Found. award 1985, Presdl. Young Investigator award NSF, 1984-89; grantee NIH, Dept. Energy, NSF; MacArthur fellow, 1992-97, Georges Morel fellow I.N.R.A., France, 1998; fellow Noble Found. Fellow Assn. Women in Sci.; mem. NAS (elected coun. 2007—), Genetics Soc. Am., Am. Soc. Plant Physiology (Charles Albert Shull award 1989), Am. Soc. Microbiology, Soc. Devel. Biology. Office: Stanford U Dept Biol Scis 371 Serra Mall Stanford CA 94305-5020 Office Fax: 650-725-8309. E-mail: srl@stanford.edu.

LONG, SHEILA JOAN, academic administrator; b. Durant, Okla., Sept. 6, 1962; d. Troy E. and Beulah M. Phillips; m. William Donnie Long, May 12, 1984; 1 child, Mitchell R. BA in Edn., Southeastern Okla. U., Durant, 1985; MEd, Southeastern Okla. State U., 1994. Cert. tchr. Okla. Social studies tchr. Bokchito Pub. Schs., Bokchito, Okla., 1986—87; fin. aid svcs. profl. Southeastern Okla. State U., 1988—94; dir. Power I Carl Albert State U., Poteau, Okla., 2001—. Mem. policy coun. Kibois Head Start, 2005—06. Mem.: Okla. Assn. Career and Tech. Edn. (admntrn. policy coun. 2006—), Assn. Career and Tech. Edn. (chair profl. devel. 2006—), OKCTEEC (pres.-elect 2004—06, Outstanding Leadership award 2005), Career and Tech. Educators Equity Coun. (conf. co-chair 2004—05). Baptist. Avocations: reading, travel. Home: PO Box 681 Poteau OK 74953 Office: POWER I Carl Albert State Coll 1507 S McKenna St Poteau OK 74953-5207 Office Phone: 918-647-1291.

LONG, SHELLEY (SHELLEY LEE LONG), actress; b. Fort Wayne, Ind., Aug. 23, 1949; d. Evandine and Leland L. m. Bruce Tyson Oct., 1981 (filed for div.); 1 child, Juliana. Student, Northwestern U. Writer, assoc. prodr., co-host Chgo. TV program Sorting It Out, 1970s (3 local Emmys 1970); mem. Second City, Chgo.; guest TV appearances various shows including Love Boat, 1978, Family, 1979, Trapper John, MD, 1979, M.A.S.H., 1980, Lois & Clark, 1995, Suzie Q, 1996, Murphy Brown, 1995, 96, Boston Common, 1996, Sabrina, The Teenage Witch, 1998, Diagnosis Murder, 1998, Chicken Soup for the Soul, 1999, Beggars and Choosers, 2000, Frasier, 1994, 1996, 2001, 8 Simple Rules...for Dating My Teenage Daugther, 2003, Strong Medicine, 2003, Joan of Arcadia, 2004, Boston Lega;, 2005, Yes, Dear, 2005, Complete Savages, 2005; regular TV series Cheers, 1982-87, Good Advice, 1993-94, Kelly Kelly, 1998; motion pictures include The Key, 1977, A Small Circle of Friends, 1980, Caveman, 1981, Night Shift, 1982, Losin' It, 1983, Irreconcilible Differences, 1984, The Money Pit, 1986, Outrageous Fortune, 1987, Hello Again, 1987, Comicitis, 1989, Troop Beverly Hills, 1989, Don't Tell Her It's Me, 1990, Frozen Assets, 1992, The Brady Bunch Movie, 1995, A Very Brady Sequel, 1996, The Adventures of Ragtime, 1998, Dr T and the Women, 2000, Trust Me, 2005, Honeymoon with Mom, 2006; TV films include The Dooley Brothers, 1979, The Cracker Factory, 1979, The Promise of Love, 1980, Ghost of a Chance, 1981, The Princess and the Cabbie, 1981, Fatal Memories, 1992, Memory of a Murder, 1992, A Message from Holly, 1992, The Women of Spring Break, 1995, Freaky Friday, 1995, A Different Kind of Christmas, 1996, Melinda: First Lady of Magic, 1997, The Adventures of Ragtime, 1998, Vanished Without a Trace, 1999, Comic Relief Jukebox, 1999, The Brady Bunch in the White House, 2002, The Santa Trap, 2002, Falling in Love with the Girl Next Door, 2006; TV mini-series, Voices Within: The Lives of Trudy Chase, 1990; voice Jingle Bells, 1999. Recipient Emmy award Outstanding Actress in a Comedy Series for Cheers, 1983.

LONG, STEPHEN R., lawyer; b. Hackensack, NJ, 1951; BA, Seton Hall U., 1973, JD, 1980. Bar: NJ 1980. Assoc. Drinker Biddle & Reath LLP, 1980—88, ptnr., litig., 1988—, and vice chair, litig. dept., mem. labor, employment practice group Florham Park, NJ. Arbitrator US Dist. Ct., Dist. NJ. Frequent writer, lectr. in field. Mem.: ABA, NJ Bar Assn., Trial Attys. NJ, Assn. Fed. Bar NJ. Office: Drinker Biddle & Reath LLP 500 Campus Dr Florham Park NJ 07932-1047 Office Phone: 973-549-7280. Office Fax: 973-360-9831. Business E-Mail: stephen.long@dbr.com.

LONG, TERESA C., city health department administrator; m. Tom Denune; 1 child, Katherine. MD, U. Calif., San Francisco; MPH, U. Calif., Berkeley. Med. dir., asst. health commr Columbus Health Dept., Ohio, 1986—2002, commr., 2002—; clin. assoc. prof. Ohio State U., Coll. Medicine and Pub. Health. Chair Ctrl. Ohio Med. Dirs. Coalition, Columbus Area Asthma Coalition; co-chair Healthy Columbus Adv. Bd. Recipient Elizabeth Blackwell award for Pioneering Efforts to Improve Women's and Cmty. Health. Mem.: Columbus Med. Assn. (past pres., past pres., bd. trustees found.). Office: Columbus Health Dept 240 Parsons Ave Columbus OH 43215

LONG, THAD GLADDEN, lawyer; b. Dothan, Ala., Mar. 9, 1938; s. Lindon Alexander and Della Gladys (Pilcher) L.; m. Carolyn Frances Wilson, Aug. 13, 1966; children: Louisa Frances Stockman, Wilson Alexander. AB, Columbia U., 1960; JD, U. Va., 1963. Bar: Ala. 1963, U.S. Dist. Ct. (no. dist., so. dist., mid. dist.) Ala., U.S. Ct. Appeals (11th cir., 5th cir.), U.S. Supreme Ct. Assoc. atty. Bradley, Arant, Rose & White, Birmingham, Ala., 1963-70, ptnr., 1970—. Adj. prof. U. Ala., Tuscaloosa, 1988—2002, Samford U., Birmingham, Cumberland Law Sch., 1999—2002. Co-author: Unfair Competition Under Alabama Law, 1990, Protecting Intellectual Property, 1990; mem. editl. bd. The Trademark Reporter; contbr. articles to profl. jours. Chmn. Columbia U. Secondary Schs. Com. Ala. Area, 1975—, pres., chmn., Greater Birmingham Arts Alliance, 1977-79; trustee, pres. Birmingham Music Club, 2000-03; trustee Oscar Wells Trust for Mus. Art, Birmingham, 1983—, Canterbury Meth. Found., 1993-2002, sec., 1993—; chmn. Entrepreneurship Inst. Birmingham, 1989; vice chmn., trustee Sons Revolution Found., Ala., 1994-2002; pres. Birmingham-Jefferson Hist. Soc., 1995-97; trustee Birmingham Music Club Endowment, 1995—, Birmingham-Jefferson History Mus., 2004-06; mem. Birmingham Com. Fgn. Rels. Fellow: Ala. Bar Found.; mem.: U.S. Patent Bar, Internat. Trademark Assn., Am. Law Inst., Ala. Law Inst., Birmingham Legal Aid Soc., Ala. Bar Assn. (chmn., founder bus. torts and antitrust sect.), Biotechnology Assn. of Ala., Inc. (sec. 1998—2001), Am. Arbitration Assn., St. Andrew's Soc. of Middle South, S.R. (pres. 1994—95), U. Va. Law Alumni (chmn. Birmingham chpt. 1984—89), Soc. Colonial Wars (gov. Ala. chpt.), Gen. Soc. S.R. (gen. solicitor 1994—2000), Order of the Coif, Omicron Delta Kappa. Republican. Methodist. Avocations: travel, writing, ping pong/table tennis. Home: 2880 Balmoral Rd Birmingham AL 35223-1236 Office: One Federal Place Birmingham AL 35203 Office Phone: 205-521-8259. Business E-Mail: tlong@bradleyarant.com.

LONG, THOMAS LESLIE, lawyer; b. Mansfield, Ohio, May 30, 1951; s. Ralph Waldo and Rose Ann (Cloud) L.; m. Peggy L. Bryant, Apr. 24, 1982. AB in Govt., U. Notre Dame, 1973; JD, Ohio State U., 1976. Bar: Ohio 1976, U.S. Dist. Ct. (so. dist.) Ohio 1976, U.S. Dist. Ct. (no. dist.) Ohio 1977, U.S. Ct. Appeals (6th cir.) 1978. Assoc. Alexander, Ebinger, Fisher, McAlister & Lawrence, Columbus, Ohio, 1976-82, ptnr., 1982-85, Baker & Hostetler, Columbus, 1985—. Mem. ABA, Ohio Bar Assn., Columbus Bar Assn., Fed. Bar Assn., Assn. Trial Lawyer Am. Clubs: Capitol (Columbus). Democrat. Roman Catholic. Home: 2565 Leeds Rd Columbus OH 43221-3613 Office: Baker & Hostetler 65 E State St Ste 2100 Columbus OH 43215-4260 Office Phone: 614-228-1541.

LONG, TIMOTHY EDWARD, philosopher, research scientist; b. Anderson, Ind., Sept. 17, 1946; s. Andrew Edward and Bonnie Jeanne (Scott) Long; m. Juana Maria Busot, May 15, 1967 (div. Jan. 1973); children: Katae Jeanne, Mary Antaña Long Martinez. BA in Philosophy, U. N.Mex., Albuquerque, 1969, MA in Philosophy of Sci., 1985; AAS in Laser Electronics, U. N.Mex., Los Alamos, 1985. Optical technician Los Alamos Nat. Lab., 1985-87; electronics technician Amtech Sys. Corp. (TransCore Inc.), Santa Fe/Albuquerque, 1992—; rsch. scientist Libre Arts, Santa Fe, 1978—. Contbr. articles to profl. jours. Mem., v.p., pres. Los Alamos Mobile Emergency Svcs. Assn., 1974-91. Mem. AAAS, AIAA, N.Y. Acad. Sci., Soc. Photo-Optical Instrumentation Engring., Optical Soc. Am., Phi Sigma Tau, Tau Alpha Pi. Democrat. Mem. League for Spiritual Discovery. Buddhist. Achievements include patent application for Photon Structure: resolution of the wave-particle duality. Avocations: drums, guitar, songwriting, search and rescue. Home: PO Box 2001 Santa Fe NM 87504-2001 Office: Libre Arts PO Box 2001 Santa Fe NM 87504-2001 Office Phone: 505-603-2783.

LONG, TIMOTHY SCOTT, chemist, consultant; b. Racine, Wis., Dec. 20, 1937; s. Leslie Alexander and Esther (Sand) L.; m. Karen M. Koniarski, July 13, 1985; children by previous marriage: Corinne, Christine. BS in Chemistry, Winona State U., 1975. Staff chemist IBM, Rochester, Minn., 1962-77, adv. chemist Harrison, NY, 1977-80, IBM Instruments, Inc., Danbury, Conn., 1980-81, mgr. Midwest Instrument Ctr. Chgo., 1981-85; mgr. corp. environ. engring. IBM, Stamford, Conn., 1985-89, industry cons. White Plains, NY, 1989-92; environ. cons. Geraghty & Miller, Inc., Rochelle Park, NJ, 1992-94, Indpls., 1994-97. Mem. World Environ. Ctr., N.Y.C., 1985-89; adv. bd. Coop. Ctr. Rsch. in Hazardous and Toxic Substances, Newark, 1985-89. Author: Testing for Prediction of Material Performance, 1972, Methods for Emissions Spectrochemical Analysis, 1977, 2d edit., 1982; contbr. articles to Applied Spectroscopy, Plating, Polymer Engring. and Sci. Mem. ASTM (com. emission spectroscopy), Soc. Applied Spectroscopy (chmn. Minn. sect. 1976-77), Soc. Plastics Engrs. (bd. reviewers 1975-76). Achievements include demonstration of world's first application using ion chromatography in the analysis of indsl. waste water. Home: 2 Calle Final Placitas NM 87043-9214

LONG, TOM, brewery executive; BA, U. NC, Chapel Hill; MBA, Harvard U. With Gulf & Western, McCann Erickson, Goldman Sachs; mktg. exec. Coco-Cola Co., 1988—2005, mgr. market planning Atlanta, v.p. 7-Eleven account, 1993, v.p. Wal-Mart global account, 1995, v.p. nat. sales, dir. rsch. and trends, dir. global strategic mktg., pres. Great Britain & Ireland, pres. N.W. Europe Div. London; chief mktg. officer Miller Brewing Co., Milw., 2005—06, pres., CEO, 2006—. Office: Miller Brewing Co 3939 W Highland Blvd Milwaukee WI 53208*

LONG, VIRGINIA, state supreme court justice; b. Mar. 1, 1942; m. Jonathan D. Weiner; 3 children. Grad., Dunbarton Coll. of Holy Cross, 1963; JD, Rutgers U., 1966. Dep. atty. gen. State of NJ; assoc. Pitney, Hardin, Kipp and Szuch; dir. NJ Divsn. Consumer Affairs, 1975; commr. NJ Dept. Banking, 1977-78; judge NJ Superior Ct., 1978-84, Appellate Divsn. NJ Superior Ct., 1984-95, presiding judge, 1995-99; assoc. justice NJ Supreme Ct., 1999—. Office: Supreme Ct NJ PO Box 970 Trenton NJ 08625-0970*

LONG, WILLIAM D., grocery store executive; b. Watertown, Wis., Nov. 30, 1937; s. William D. and Olive (Piper) L.; m. Doreen Loveall, Sept. 23, 1967; children: Angela, Scott, Irene, Jeffrey, William, Jennifer. Student, U. Wis., Madison. Store mgr. Safeway, Salt Lake City, 1961-68; pres., CEO WinCo Foods, Inc, Boise, Idaho, 1968—. Cpl. U.S. Army, 1957-60. Office: Winco Foods 650 N Armstrong Pl Boise ID 83704

LONG, WILLIAM MCMURRAY, physiology educator; b. Greenville, SC, Nov. 9, 1948; s. William McMurray and Cecile Mae (Ariail) L.; m. Kathleen Webb, Mar. 18, 1971 (dec. Oct. 1990); m. Marianne Castrén, July 22, 1992. BA, Tulane U., 1970, BS, 1974; PhD, La. State U., 1980. Rsch. assoc. Med. Ctr. La. State U., New Orleans, 1974-75; pathology extern Charity Hosp. of La., New Orleans, 1975-80; Nat. Rsch. Svc. Award fellow Pa. State Med. Ctr., Hershey, 1980-82; rsch. assoc. Mt. Sinai Med. Ctr., Miami Beach, Fla., 1983-89; rsch. physiologist VA Med. Ctr., Miami, Fla., 1982-89; asst. prof. medicine U. Miami, 1982-89; asst. prof. physiology U. N.D., Grand Forks, 1989-94; CFO OBI Lab. Co., 1994-2000, dir., 2000—. Cons. VA Med. Ctr., Miami, 1991; ad hoc reviewer Am. Jour. Physiology, Bethesda, Md., 1990-91, Va. Ctrl. Office, 1987-90; dir. Minority Access to Rsch. Careers, U. N.D., Ah'jo'gun to the Baccalaureate. Author: Non-Steriodal Agents in Sepsis Syndrom, 1989, (with others) Airways: Asthma, Bronchietasis and Emphysema, 1992; contbr. articles to profl. jours. Chmn. Nat. Letter-In Com., New Orleans, 1968, Cliff Solar Fund, New Orleans, 1973; cood. Spring Jazz Festival, New Orleans, 1970. Recipient Rsch. award Bush Found., 1990, Nat. Rsch. Svc. award NIH, 1980-82; grantee NIH, 1986-89, Fla. Lung Assn., 1984-85, VA, 1986-90, Am. Heart Assn. Dakota affiliate, 1991-93, Nat. Inst. Gen. Med. Scis., 1992—. Mem.: Am. Physiol. Soc., Am. Thoracic Soc., N.Y. Acad. Scis., Da Vinci Soc. (sec. 1987—88). Achievements include research in modification of cardiac proteolysis with amino acid methyl esters, in inefficacy of steroids in treatment of septic shock syndrome, in differentiation of histamine effects on bronchial flow and bronchomotor tone, on protein profiles in differentiating mechanisms of pulmonary edema, in role of bronchial blood flow in allergic airway disease and pharmacologic modification of that response; establishment of research and science education program for minorities and statewide tribal colleges; differential accumulation in brain of radon daughters in Alzheimer's Disease and Parkinson Disease. Office: OBI Labs 1339A Clara Brown Rd PO Box 718 Prosperity SC 29127-0718

LONGABERGER, TAMI, home decor accessories company executive; BSBA in Mktg., Ohio State U., 1984. Joined Longaberger Co., Newark, Ohio, 1984, pres., 1994, CEO, 1998. Mem. 60th commn. human rights United Nation; bd. dirs. Woodrow Wilson Internat. Ctr. Scholars; chair Nat. Women's Bus. Coun.

LONGAKER, RICHARD P., II, lawyer; b. Madison, Wis., Feb. 21, 1950; s. Richard Longaker; children: Andrew, Hannah. BA magna cum laude, U. Calif., Santa Barbara, 1973; JD, Loyola U., LA, 1977. Bar: US Dist Ct. (no. dist.) Calif., US Dist Ct. (so. dist.) Calif., US Dist Ct. (ctrl. dist.) Calif., US Dist Ct. (ea. dist.) Calif., US Cir. Ct. Appeals (9th cir.), US Ct. Internat. Trade, US Supreme Ct. Pvt. practice, LA, 1979—; assoc. Kirtland & Packard, LA, 1985-87; gen. counsel Pacific Triangle Mgmt. Corp., LA, 1987-92. Judge pro tem LA Superior Ct., 1989—, Beverly Hills Mcpl. Ct.; spkr. in field. Contbr. articles to profl. pubs., jours. Mem. ABA (litig. sect., trial practice com., study complex litig., trial complex trials subcom.), Calif. Bar Assn. (statewide bench/bar coalition), Beverly Hills Bar Assn. (exec. com. bus. law sect.), Santa Monica Bar Assn. (pres. 2005-06), LA County Bar Assn. (real estate litig. subcom., corp. law sect.), U. Calif. Alumni Assn. (bd. dirs. LA chpt.), Calif. Bar Conf. Dels., Am. Corp. Counsel Assn. So. Calif. (bd. dirs.), Assn. Bus. Trial Lawyers, Profl. Liability Underwriters Soc., Congress of Fellows Ctr. Internat. Studies. Avocations: skiing, fishing. Office: 612 Sepulveda Blvd Los Angeles CA 90049 Office Phone: 310-476-0576. Business E-Mail: rpl@longakerlaw.com.

LONGAKER, RICHARD PANCOAST, retired political science professor, academic administrator; b. Phila., July 1, 1924; s. Edwin P. and Emily (Downs) L.; m. Mollie M. Katz, Jan. 25, 1964; children— Richard Pancoast II, Stephen Edwin, Sarah Ellen, Rachel Elise. BA in Polit. Sci, Swarthmore Coll., 1949; MA in Am. History, U. Wis., 1950; PhD in Govt, Cornell U., 1953. Teaching asst. Cornell U., 1950-53, vis. asso. prof., 1960-61; asst. prof. Kenyon Coll., 1953-54, asso. prof., 1955-60; asst. prof. U. Calif., Riverside, 1954-55, faculty Los Angeles, 1961-76, chmn. dept. polit. sci., 1963-67, prof., 1975—76, dean acad. affairs grad. div., 1970-71; prof. Johns Hopkins U., Balt., 1976-87, provost and v.p. for acad. affairs, 1976-87, prof. emeritus, cons. western states office Santa Monica, Calif., 1987—; prof. in residence UCLA, 2001—. Author: The Presidency and Individual Liberties, 1961; co-author: The Supreme Court and the Commander in Chief, 1976, also articles, revs. Served with AUS, 1943-45. Mem.: Am. Polit. Sci. Assn. Office: 16550 Chalet Ter Pacific Palisades CA 90272-2344

LONGAN, GEORGE BAKER, III, real estate company executive; b. Kansas City, Mo., Apr. 20, 1934; s. Benjamin Hyde and Georgette Longan O'Brien; divorced; 1 child, Nancy Ann Longan LaPoff. BSBA, U. Ariz., 1956; postgrad., U. Kans., 1956-57. Cert. real estate broker. Sr. v.p., gen. mgr. Paul Hamilton Co., Kansas City, 1963-84; pres. Eugene D. Brown Co., Kansas City, 1984-93; v.p. J.C. Nichols Real Estate, 1993-94, Long Realty Co., Tucson, 1994—2007, pres., 2007—. Bd. dirs. Genesis Relocation Network, N.J. Served to staff sgt. USAF, 1958-62. Mem. Nat. Real Estate Assn. (bd. dirs. 1991-94, 99, 2000), Mo. Real Estate Assn. (bd. dirs. 1987-90), Ariz. Real Estate Assn. (bd. dirs. 1999, 2000), Real Estate Bd. Kansas City (bd. dirs. 1987-90), Met. Kansas City Real Estate Bd. (pres. 1992), Beta Sigma Psi, Sigma Chi. Episcopal. Avocations: antique collecting, swimming. Office: Long Realty Co 900 E River Tucson AZ 85718

LONGBRAKE, WILLIAM ARTHUR, bank executive; b. Hershey, Pa., Mar. 15, 1943; s. William Van Fleet and Margaret Jane (Barr) L.; m. Martha Ann Curtis, Aug. 23, 1970; children: Derek Curtis, Mark William, David Robert, Dorothy Eleanor Lois. BA, Coll. of Wooster, 1965; MA, U. Wis., 1968, MBA, 1969; D. Bus. Adminstrn., U. Md., 1976. Jr. asst. planner Northeastern Ill. Planning Commn., Chgo., 1966; instr. Coll. Bus. and Mgmt. U. Md., 1969-71, lectr., 1976, 79-81; fin. economist FDIC, Washington, 1971-75, sr. planning specialist Office Corp. Planning, 1975-76, spl. asst. to chmn., acting contr., 1977-78; assoc. dir. div. banking rsch. Office Compt. of Currency, Treas. Dept., Washington, 1976, dep. dir. econ. rsch. and analysis div., 1976-77, dep. compt. for rsch. and econ. programs, 1978-81, acting sr. dep. compt. for policy, 1981-82, sr. dep. compt. for resource mgmt., 1982; exec. v.p., CFO Wash. Mut. Savs. Bank, Seattle, 1982—95; CFO, dep. to chmn. FDIC, Washington, 1995—96; exec. v.p., CFO Wash. Mut. Inc., Seattle, 1996—99, mem. exec. com., 1996—, vice chmn., CFO, 1999—2002, vice chmn., 2002—. Bd. dir. Fed. Home Loan Bank Seattle, Wash. Fin. League, America's Cmty. bankers. Assoc. editor Fin. Mgmt., 1974-78; mem. editorial adv. bd. Issues in Bank Regulation, 1977-84, Jour. Econs. and Bus., 1980-83; contbr. articles to profl. jours. Mem. College park (Md.) Citizen's Adv. Com. on Code Enforcement, 1973-74, cons., 1975; lectr. Albers Sch. Bus. Seattle U., 1985, student mentor, 1994; bd. dirs. Pget Sound Coun. Fin. Insts., Seattle, dir., 1986-90, v.p., 1988, pres., 1989-90; mem. Seattle Mcpl. League, 1986—, treas., 1988-90, pres., 1990-93; past chmn. Capitol Hill Housing Improvement Program, Seattle; mem. The King County Housing Partnership, Seattle exec. com., chmn. outreach and tech. assistance com., 1990-92; bd. visitors Sch. Nursing U. Wash., Seattle, 1983-92, chmn., 1986-90; mem. of local initiative support corp. Seattle/Tacoma Adv. Bd., 1989-91; bd. dirs. Diabetes Rsch. Coun., Seattle, 1984-89, v.p., 1987-88; bd. dirs. N.W. Symphony Orch., Seattle, 1987-89, treas., 1988-89, adv. bd.; trustee Kenney presbyn. Home, West Seattle, exec. com., chmn. fin. com.; trustee Intiman Theatre Co., Seattle, 1988-92; past chmn. tax com. Wash. Savs. league; mem. Seattle Comprehensive Plan Implement Task Force, 1993-94; past chmn. adv. bd. Wash. State Affordable Housing; dir. Nat. Assn. Housing partnerships; mem. King County Growth Mgmt., planning coun. affordable housing task force, 1992-93; co-chair Gov.'s Task force on Affordable Housing, Washington, 1992-93, chmn. bd. dirs. Threshold Housing, 1992—; mem. Impact Fees commn., 1992-92, Coun. Washington's Future, arrangement's chair, 1988-91; mem. Governor's Council Econ. Adv., Wash.; mem. adv. bd. Univ. Wsh. Bus. Sch. Recipient Kenneth E. Trefftz prize Western Fin. Assn., 1971, certo of recognition William A. Jump Meml. Found., 1978. Mem. Am. Econs. Assn., Am. Fin. Assn., Fin. Mgmt. Assn. (dir. 1978-80), Fin. Execs. Inst. (Puget Sound chpt., bd. dirs. 1988—, chmn. acad. rels. com. 1988-89, chmn. tec. com. 1989-90, treas. 1990-91, v.p. 1991-93, pres. 1993-94, chmn. nominating com. 1994—), Coll. of Wooster Alumni Assn. (pres. Washington Alumni Assn. 1976, pres. Seattle Alumni Assn. 1983—, trustee 1988—, mem. fin., audit, religious dimension, student rels. com. alumni bd. 1988—), Nat. Coun. Savings Instns. (mortgage fin. com. 1989), Columbia Tower Club. Presbyn. (trustee 1973-75, chmn. 1975, elder 1979-82, clk. 1980-82, deacon 1985-88, tras. 1993—). Avocations: jogging, painting, singing, piano. Office: Wshington Mutual Inc 1201 3d Ave Seattle WA 98101*

LONGENECKER, MARK HERSHEY, JR., lawyer; b. Akron, Ohio, Feb. 16, 1951; s. Mark Hershey and Katrina (Hetzner) L.; children: Emily Irene, Mark Hershey III; m. Marcie Garrison, June. 5, 2004. BA, Denison U., 1973; JD, Harvard U., 1976. Bar: Ill. 1976, Ohio 1979. Atty. Lord, Bissell & Brook, Chgo., 1976-79; ptnr. Frost Brown Todd LLC (and predecessor firms), Cin., 1979—2002, chmn. bus.-corp. dept., 1996—2002; mem. Greenebaum, Doll & McDonald, PLLC, 2002—06; ptnr. Porter Wright Morris & Arthur LLP, Cin., 2006—. Dir. ST Media Group Internat., HealthPro Brands, Inc. Bd. govs. Ohio Fair Plan Underwriting Assn., Columbus, 1989-92; bd. dirs. Salvation Army, Cin., 2000—, Cin. Union Bethel, 2006—. Mem. Cin. Country Club, Harvard Club (Cin. pres. 1993-94). Home: 7708 Chumani Ln Cincinnati OH 45243 Office: Porter Wright Morris & Arthur lLP Ste 2200 250 E Fifth St Cincinnati OH 45202 Business E-Mail: mlongenecker@porterwright.com.

LONGENECKER, MARTHA W., museum director; BA in Art, UCLA; MFA, Claremont Grad. Sch.; studied with Millard Sheets, Shoji Hamada, Tatsuzo Shimaoka. Owner ceramics studio, Claremont, Calif.; prof. art, now prof. emerita San Diego State U.; founder, dir. Mingei Internat. Mus., San Diego. Coord. editing, design and prodn. of exhbn. documentary publs.; condr. tours. Contbr. chpts. to books; developer videotapes; exhibited at Dalzell Hatfield Galleries. San Diego State U. Found. grantee, 1967, Calif. State U. Rsch. grantee, 1978; recipient Disting. Alumna award Claremont Grad. Sch., 1980, Essence of Life award ElderHelp of San Diego, 1993, Living Legacy award Women's Internat. Ctr., 1994, Women of Distinction award Soroptimist Internat. of La Jolla, 1994, Headliner of Yr. Art, San Diego Press Club, 1998, Disting. Svc. medal, San Diego State U., 1998, Reischauer Internat. Edn. award, Japan Soc. San Diego and Tijuana, 1999, San Diego Women Who Mean Bus. award, Foley Vardner Attys. at Law, San Diego Bus. Jour., 2000, Gold Rays with Rosette, Order of Rising Sun, Emperor of Japan, 2003, Golden Hanger Spl. award, Fashion Careers of Calif. Coll., 2004. Office: Mingei Internat Mus Balboa Park 1439 El Prado San Diego CA 92101-1617 also: Mingei International Museum 1439 El Prado San Diego CA 92101-1617

LONGFIELD, WILLIAM HERMAN, health products executive; b. Chgo., Aug. 8, 1938; s. William A. and Elizabeth (Beringer) L.; m. Nancy Shofstall, June 10, 1961; children: William, Scott. BS, Drake U., 1960; grad. bus. mgmt. program, Northwestern U., 1972. Pres. Convertors divsn. Am. Hosp. Supply, Evanston, Ill., 1961-82; exec. v.p., dir. Lifemark, Inc., Houston, 1982-83; pres., CEO Cambridge Group, Inc., Dallas, 1983-89; chmn., CEO C.R. Bard, Inc., Murray Hill, NJ, 1989—2003, also bd. dirs.; ret., 2003. Bd. dirs. Atlantic Health Sys., Manor Care, Inc., Toledo, West Pharm. Svcs., Pa., Horizon Health Corp., Dallas; bd. dirs. Internat. Non-Wovens Assn., N.Y.C., 1975-82; chmn. AdvaMed; bd. dirs. Applera. Chmn., bd. dirs. Deerfield (Ill.) Youth Orgn., 1975-80. Recipient Pres.' award Nat. Nurse Cons. Assn., 1980. Mem. Baltrusol Golf Club, Metedeconk Country Club, Hamilton Farm Golf Club, Bull Bay Golf Club. Republican. Presbyterian. Avocations: golf, tennis.

LONGHOFER, RONALD STEPHEN, financial consultant; b. Junction City, Kans., Aug. 30, 1946; s. Oscar William and Anna Mathilda (Krause) L.; m. Elizabeth Norma McKenna; children: Adam, Nathan, Stefanie. BMus, U. Mich., 1968, JD magna cum laude, 1975, MBA with distinction, 2004. CPA Ill., accredited in bus. valuation; bar: Mich. 1975, U.S. Dist. Ct. (ea. dist.) Mich., U.S. Ct. Appeals (6th cir.), U.S. Supreme Ct.; cert. chartered fin. analyst, fraud examiner. Law clk. to judge U.S. Dist. Ct. (ea. dist.) Mich., Detroit, 1975-76; ptnr. Honigman, Miller, Schwartz & Cohn, Detroit, 1976—2003, chmn. litigation dept., 1993-96; dir. Stout, Risius, Ross, Inc., 2004—06; prin. RSL Financial Cons., LLC, Plymouth, Mich., 2003—. Co-author: Courtroom Handbook on Michigan Evidence, 2007, Michigan Court Rules Practice, 1998, Michigan Court Rules Practice-Evidence, 2002, Introducing Evidence at Trial, 2007; author: Courtroom Handbook on Michigan Civil Procedure, 2007, Michigan Court Rules Practice, 2004; editor Mich. Law Rev., 1974-75. Bd. dir. Plymouth Canton Symphony Soc. With US Army, 1968—72. Mem. Acad. Ct. Appointed Masters, FBA, Am. Inst. CPAs, Oakland County Bar Assn., CFA Soc. Detroit, CFA Inst., Assn. Cert. Fraud Examiners, Ill. CPA Soc., Mich. Assn. Cert. Pub. Accts., Inst. Bus. Appraisers, U. Mich. Pres.' Club, Order of Coif, Phi Beta Kappa, Phi Kappa Phi, Pi Kappa Lambda, Beta Gamma Sigma. Home: 974 Penniman Ave Plymouth MI 48170 Office: RSL Fin Cons LLC 249 S Main St Plymouth MI 48170 Home Phone: 248-252-5459; Office Phone: 734-207-1004. Business E-Mail: rlonghofer@rslfinancialconsulting.com.

LONGHURST, ROBERT RUSSELL, retired secondary school educator; b. Montgomery, Ala., Feb. 28, 1921; s. Lawrence Alston and Margaret Earlene (King) L.; m. Anne McMahon, Nov. 26, 1952 (div. 1982). Student, Vanderbilt U., 1942; BA in Econs., Peabody Coll., 1949, MA, 1950. Cert. tchr., Tenn. Various positions Stinson Aviation & Consol.-Vultee Aircraft Corp., 1940-43; tech. rep. Lockheed Overseas Corp., British Isles, 1943-44; tchr. Nashville Bd. Edn., 1950-77, coordinator vocat. edn., 1977-87; ret., 1987. Nat. defense course in aeronautics, Vanderbilt U., 1942. Served as petty officer USNR, 1944-46, PTO. Mem. NEA, Tenn. Edn. Assn., Met. Nashville Edn. Assn., Am. Vocat. Assn., Am. Legion, Pi Gamma Mu. Mem. Ch. of Christ. Avocations: woodworking, music, financial planning, investing. Home: 2421 Eastland Ave Nashville TN 37206-1101

LONGIN, THOMAS CHARLES, retired academic administrator; b. Lewistown, Mont., Nov. 17, 1939; s. Charles Otto and Anne Dorothy (Vavrovsky) L.; m. Nancy Tillinghast; children: Kevin C., Teresa L., Karl T., Anne M. BA in History, Carroll Coll., 1962; MA in History, Creighton U., 1965; PhD in Am. History, U. Nebr., 1970. Instr. Carroll Coll., Helena, Mont., 1965-67; asst. prof. Va. Poly. Inst. and State U., Blacksburg, 1970-73; asst. prof., then assoc. prof. Ithaca (N.Y.) Coll., 1973-82, dean humanities and scis., 1976-82, provost, 1985-96; v.p. acad. affairs Seattle U., 1982-85; v.p. programs and rsch. Assn. of Governing Bds., Washington, 1997—2002, ret., 2002. Workshop facilitator, cons. AGB, 2002—. Exec. editor Planning in Higher Education, 2004—. Home: 10452 Courtney Dr Fairfax VA 22030 Personal E-mail: tom-longin@cox.net.

LONGLEY, MARJORIE WATTERS, newspaper executive; b. Lockport, NY, Nov. 2, 1925; d. J. Randolph and Florence Lucille (Craine) Watters; m. Ralph R. Longley, Oct. 1, 1949 (dec.). BA in English with highest honors cum laude, St. Lawrence U., 1947. Sports editor, feature writer Lockport Union Sun and Jour., 1945; with N.Y. Times, NYC, 1948-88, asst. to v.p. consumer mktg., 1975-78, circulation sales mgr., 1978-79, sales dir., 1979-81, dir. pub. affairs, 1981-88; pres. Gramercy Internat., Inc (mktg. and pub. rels.), NYC, 1988—; assoc. pub. The Earth Times, NYC, 1996—. Dir. pub. affairs and pub. info., N.Y.C. Off-Track Betting Corp., 1990-94; mem. Nat. Newspapers' Readership Coun., 1979-82; mem. adv. coun. API, 1980-85. Author: America's Taste, 1960. Trustee St. Lawrence U., 1969-75, 77—; chmn. bd. dirs. Am. Forum for Global Edn., 1977-98, chmn. emerita, 1999—; pres. N.Y. City Adult Edn. Coun., 1974-77, Grmercy Pk. Lot Owners Assn., Inc., 1995—; mem. N.Y. State Adv. Coun. for Vocat. Edn, 1976-81, postsecondary edn., 1978-81, Mayor's Coun. Environment of N.Y.C., 1983-96; bd. dirs. Nat. Charities Info. Bur., 1983-96, Literacy Ptnrs., Inc., 1996—; chmn. 42d St. Edn., Theatre, Culture, 1984-88, chmn. emeritus, 1988—. Mem. Nat. Inst. Social Scis., Am. Mgmt. Assn. (nat. mktg. coun. 1972-89, bd. dirs. 1986-88), Nat. Arts Club, Overseas Press Club, Phi Beta Kappa. Democrat. Baptist. Office: Gramercy Internat Inc 34 Gramercy Park E New York NY 10003-1731

LONGMAN, ANNE STRICKLAND, special education educator, consultant; b. Metuchen, NJ, Sept. 17, 1924; d. Charles Hodges and Grace Anna (Moss) Eldridge; m. Henry Richard Strickland, June 22, 1946 (dec. 1960); m. Donald Rufus Longman, Jan. 20, 1979 (dec. 1987); children: James C., Robert H. BA in Bus. Adminstrn., Mich. State U., 1945; teaching credentials, U. Calif., Berkeley, 1959; postgrad., Stanford U., 1959-60; MA in Learning Hand, Santa Clara U., 1974. Lic. educator. Exptl. test engr. Pratt & Whitney Aircraft, East Hartford, Conn., 1945-47; indsl. engr. Marchant Calculators, Emeryville, Calif., 1957-58; with pub. rels. Homesmith, Palo Alto, Calif., 1959-62; cons. Right to Read Program, Calif., 1978-79; monitor, reviewer State of Calif., Sacramento, 1976-79; tchr. diagnosis edn. Cabrillo Coll., Aptos, Calif., 1970-79; lectr. edn. U. Calif., Santa Cruz, 1970-79; cons. Santa Cruz Bd. Edn., 1970-79; reading rschr. Gorilla Found., Woodside, Calif., 1982—. Bd. mem. Western Inst. Alcoholic Studies, L.A., 1972-73; chmn. Evaluation Com., Tri-County, Calif., 1974; speaker Internat. Congress Learning Disabilities, Seattle, 1974; ednl. cons. rsch. on allergies, 1993—; artist-in-residence Yosemite, 1998-2004 Author: Word Patterns in English, 1974-92, Cramming 3D Kids, 1975—, 50 books for migrant students, 1970-79; artist Watsonville Pajaronian; contbr. articles on stress and alcoholism and TV crime prevention for police, 1960-79. Founder Literacy Ctr., Santa Cruz, 1968-092; leader Girl Scouts U.S.A., San Francisco, 1947-50; vol. Thursday's Child, Santa Cruz, 1976-79, Golden Gate Kindergarten, San Francisco, 1947-57; vol. Yosemite Nat. Pk.; judge art Santa Cruz County Fair, Calif. Recipient Fellowships Pratt & Whitney Aircraft, 1944, Stanford U., 1959 Mem. Internat. Reading Assn. (pres. Santa Cruz 1975), Santa Clara Valley Watercolor Soc., Artists Equity, Arts Habitat, Los Altos Art Club (v.p. 1992), Eichler Swim and Tennis Club. Republican. Episcopalian. Avocations: drawing, watercolor, watercolor painting, travel, drama. Home and Office: 651 Sinex Ave #J211 Pacific Grove CA 93950

LONGNECKER, DAVID EUGENE, anesthesiologist, educator; b. Kendallville, Ind., 1939; MD, Ind. U., 1964, MA in Anesthesiology, 1968. Diplomate Am. Bd. Anesthesiology. Intern Blodgett Meml. Hosp., Grand Rapids, Mich., 1964—65; resident in anesthesiology U. Ind., 1965—69; asst. prof. dept. anesthesiology U. Mo., 1970—73; assoc. prof. dept. anesthesiology U. Va., Charlottesville, 1974—78, prof., 1978—88; Robert D. Dripps prof., chmn. dept. anesthesia U. Pa., Phila., 1999—2002, sr. v.p., corp. chief med. officer, 2002—04, Robert D. Dripps prof. anesthesia emeritus, 2005—; dir. Assn. Am. Med. Coll., 2005—. With USPHS, 1968—70. Mem.: Inst. Medicine, Am. Soc. Anesthesiologists. Office: AAMC 2450 N St NW Washington DC 20037-1127 Office Phone: 202-862-6113. Business E-Mail: dlongnecker@aamc.org.

LONGO, DAN LOUIS, internist, researcher, oncologist; b. St. Louis, Apr. 25, 1949; s. Dominic L. and Alene V. (Bratcher) L.; m. Nancy Kay Schiffman, May 29, 1971; children: Jennifer Alene, Adam Daniel, Paul Anthony. AB, Washington U., St. Louis, 1970; MD cum laude, U. Mo., 1975. Diplomate Am. Bd. Internal Medicine, Am. Bd. Oncology, Nat. Bd. Med. Examiners. Resident in medicine Peter Bent Brigham Hosp., Boston, 1975-77; fellow in oncology Nat. Cancer Inst., Bethesda, Md., 1977-78; postdoctoral fellow in immunology Nat. Inst. Allergy and Infectious Diseases, Bethesda, 1978-80; sr. investigator Medicine Br. Nat. Cancer Inst., Bethesda, 1980—85; assoc. dir. Biolog. Response Modifiers Program Nat. Cancer Inst., Frederick, Md., 1985-95; sci. dir. Nat. Inst. on Aging, Balt., 1995—. Mem. editl. bd. Critical Reviews in Oncology/Hematology; editor: Clin. Oncology Alert, 1985—2000, Cancer Chemotherapy and Biol. Response Modifiers Annual, 1987—2000, Harrison's Principles of Internal Medicine, 1995—; asst. editor Am. Jour. Clin. Nutrition, 1981—91, assoc. editor Jour. Nat. Cancer Inst., Clin. Cancer Rsch., Jour. Immunology, Clin. Immunology, Blood, Jour. Gerontology, Med. Sci.; contbr. chpts. to textbooks, over 700 articles to profl. jours. Rear adm. USPHS, 1977—2006. Recipient Harvard Book award, 1965, Young Physician award U. Mo. Alumni Assn., Citation of Merit, 1997, Tovi Comet-Walerstein award Bar-Ilan Univ., Israel, 1992. USPHS Commendation mMedal, 1987, Outstanding Svc. medal, 1992 and 2005. NIH Merit sward, 1993, NIH Dir. award 1996. Fellow: AAAS, ACP (MKSAP IX Oncology Subsplty. Com. 1989—91, MKSAP 12 1999—2001, MKSAP 13 2002—04), Molecular Medicine Soc.; mem.: Am. Soc. Blood and Marrow Transplantation, Am. Soc. Clin. Pharm. and Theraputics, Am. Soc. Cell Bio., Am. Geriatrics Soc., Internat. Cytokine Soc., Soc. Leukocyte Bio., N.Y. Acad. Scis., Assn. Am. Physicians, Clin. Immunology Soc. (councilor 1987—90), Am. Soc. Cell Biology, Am. Soc. Clin. Investigation, Am. Soc. Hematology (subcom. on Neoplasia 1989—91, chmn. 1990, program com. 1994), Am. Assn. Cancer Rsch. (program com. 1986), Am. Assn. Immunologists, Am. Soc. Clin. Oncology (edn. com. 1992—94), Am. Soc. Clin. Nutrition (award com. 1989—91, program com. 1990), Am. Inst. Nutrition, Am. Soc. Microbiology, Am. Fedn. Clin. Rsch., Alpha Omega Alpha, Phi Kappa Phi, Sigma Xi. Achievements include 11 patents in field. Office: Nat Inst Aging GRC 5600 Nathan Shock Dr Baltimore MD 21224-6825 Home Phone: 301-942-7176; Office Phone: 410-558-8110. Business E-Mail: longod@grc.nia.nih.gov.

LONGO, LAWRENCE DANIEL, physiologist, obstetrician, gynecologist, educator; b. LA, Oct. 11, 1926; s. Frank Albert and Florine Azelia (Hall) L.; m. Betty Jeanne Mundall, Sept. 9, 1948; children: April Celeste, Lawrence Anthony, Elisabeth Lynn, Camilla Giselle. BA, Pacific Union Coll., 1949; MD, Coll. Med. Evangelists, Loma Linda, Calif., 1954. Diplomate Am. Bd. Ob-Gyn. Intern L.A. County Gen. Hosp., 1954-55, resident in ob-gyn., 1955-58; asst. prof. ob-gyn UCLA, 1962-64; asst. prof. physiology and ob-gyn U. Pa., 1964-68; prof. physiology and ob-gyn Loma Linda U., 1968—; dir. ctr. for perinatal biology Loma Linda U. Sch. Medicine, 1974—. Perinatal biology com. Nat. Inst. Child Health, NIH, 1973-77; co-chmn. reprodn. scientist devel. program NIH; NATO prof. Consiglio Nat. delle Rsch., Italian Govt. Editor: Respiratory Gas Exchange and Blood Flow in the Placenta, 1972, Fetal and Newborn Cardiovascular

Physiology, 1978, Charles White and A Treatise on the Management of Pregnant and Lying-in Women, 1987; co-editor: Landmarks in Perinatology, 1975-76, Classics in Obstetrics Gynecology, 1993, Dearest G..., Yours W.O., William Osler's Letters from Egypt to Grace Revere Osler, 2003, William Osler's Man's Redemption of Man, 2003, Our Lords the Sick..., 2004; editor classic pages in ob-gyn. Am. Jour. Ob-Gyn.; contbr. articles to profl. jours. Served with AUS, 1945-47. Founder Frank A. and Florine A. Longo lectureship in faith, knowledge, and human values Pacific Union Coll., 1993. Fellow Royal Coll. Ob-Gyns., Am. Coll. Ob-Gyns.; mem. Am. Assn. History Medicine (coun.), Am. Osler Soc. (bd. govs., sec.-treas., pres.), Am. Physiol. Soc., Assn. Profs. Ob-Gyn., Perinatal Rsch. Soc., Soc. Gynecologic Investigation (past pres.), Neurosci. Soc., Royal Soc. Medicine. Adventist. Office: Loma Linda U Sch Medicine Ctr Perinatal Biology Loma Linda CA 92350-0001 Business E-Mail: llongo@llu.edu.

LONGO, RONALD ANTHONY, lawyer; b. Schenectady, NY, Nov. 17, 1952; s. Vito Frank and Frances (Scardamaglia) L.; m. Susan Fraioli, Nov. 15, 1980; children: Kristen, John Michael. BS, Cornell U., 1974; JD, Pace U., 1980. Bar: N.Y. 1981, U.S. Dist. Ct. (so. dist.) N.Y. 1984, U.S. Supreme Ct. 1984. Asst. dir. labor rels. Onondaga County, Syracuse, N.Y., 1974-75; dir. employee rels. Ardsley (N.Y.) Sch. Dist., 1975-80; assoc. Plunkett & Jaffe, White Plains, N.Y., 1980-86, ptnr., 1986-93, Keane & Beane, P.C., White Plains, N.Y., 1993—. Dep. town atty. Town of Clarkstown, New City, N.Y., 1985—; adj. assoc. prof. Iona Coll., New Rochelle, N.Y., 1982-90; adj. prof. L.I. U., Brookville, N.Y., 1986-88; instr. labor rels. studies program Cornell U., 1991-92. Author: (with others) Public Sector Labor and Employment Law, 1988, 98. Mem. ABA, N.Y. State Bar Assn., N.Y. State Pub. Employer Labor Rels. Assn. (sec., treas. 1979-81, pres. 1982-83, Disting. Svc. award 1983). Office: Keane & Beane PC 445 Hamilton Ave White Plains NY 10601-2319 Office Phone: 914-946-4777.

LONGO, WALTER E., colon and rectal surgeon, educator, director; b. NY, Dec. 22, 1955; BS in Chemistry, Syracuse U., 1978; MS in Chemistry, Fordham U., 1980; MD, NY Med. Coll., 1984; MBA in Internat. Bus., St. Louis U., 2001; MA (hon.), Yale U., 2004. Cert. in gen. surgery, in colon and rectal surgery, Nat. Bd. Med. Examiners, lic. Conn. Surg. intern Yale U. Med. Ctr., 1984—85, jr. surg. resident, 1985—87, gastrointestinal rsch. fellow, 1987—88, sr. surg. resident, 1988—89, chief surg. resident, 1989—90; colon/rectal fellow Cleve. Clinic Found., 1990—91; asst. prof. surgery St. Louis U. Sch. Medicine, 1991—96; chief gen. surgery St. Louis VA Med. Ctr., 1997—2003; prof., chief gastrointestinal surgery, dir. colorectal surgery, program dir. gen. surg. residency program Yale Sch. Medicine, 2003—. Vis. prof. surgery Fairfax Hosp., Va., 1993, SUNY, Stony Brook, 1995, U. Conn., 2000; assoc. prof. surgery St. Louis U. Sch. Medicine, 1996—2001, program dir. colon and rectal surgery fellowship, 1998—2003, prof. surgery, 2001—03. Editor: (books) Minimally Invasive Surgery: Principles and Technique, 1998, Intestinal Disorders, 1998, Modern Management of Rectal Cancer, 2001, Reoperative Colon and Rectal Surgery, 2003; regional editor: Surg. Rsch. Comm., 1994—97, editor-in-chief: Internat. Jour. Surg. Investigation, 1997—2002, mem. editl. bd.: Jour. Joint Ctr. for Rsch., 1996—2003, Colorectal Cancer, 2003—, World Jour. Gastroenterology, 2004—; contbr. articles to profl. jours., chapters to books. Recipient Vallee Willman Excellence award in surg. edn., 2001. Fellow: ACS, Am. Soc. Colon and Rectal Surgeons; mem.: Assn. VA Surgeons (mem. by-laws com. 1995—98, program com. chmn. 1995—2001, treas. 2000—03, v.p. 2003—04, pres.-elect 2004—05), Yale Surg. Soc., Soc. Univ. Surgeons, Soc. Surg. Oncology, Soc. Surgery of Alimentary Tract, Soc. Am. Gastrointestinal Endoscopic Surgeons, New Eng. Surg. Soc., Nat. Found. Ileitis and Colitis, Internat. Soc. Univ. Colon and Rectal Surgeons, Ctrl. Surg. Assn., Am. Surg. Assn., Assn. Acad. Surgeons, Am. Paraplegic Soc., Am. Gastrointestinal Assn., Surg. Biology Club III, Alpha Epsilon Delta, Sigma Xi, Phi Kappa Psi. Office: Yale Sch Medicine 330 Cedar St LH118 PO Box 208062 New Haven CT 06520-8062 Office Phone: 203-785-2616. Office Fax: 203-785-2615. Business E-Mail: walter.longo@yale.edu.*

LONGOBARDI, DAVID, editor-in-chief; b. 1962; AB, Harvard U., 1984; M in Journalism and Mass Comm., NYU. Editl. dir. Water's Info. Svs., 1990—96; pub., editl. dir. Securities Industry News, 1996—99; editor-in-chief Am. Banker Mag., 1999—. Office: Am Banker Mag 1 State St Plz 27th Fl New York NY 10004*

LONGOBARDO, ANNA KAZANJIAN, engineering executive; b. NYC; d. Aram Michael and Zarouhy (Yazejian) Kazanjian; m. Guy S. Longobardo, July 12, 1952; children: Guy A., Alicia. Student, Barnard Coll., 1947; BSME, Columbia U., 1949, MSME, 1952. Sr. systems engr. Am. Bosch Arma Corp., Garden City, NY, 1950-65; rsch. sect. head Sperry Rand Corp., Gt. Neck, NY, 1965-68, rsch. sect. head systems mgmt., 1968-73; mgr. engring. personnel utilization Sperry Corp., Gt. Neck, 1973-77, mgr. systems mgmt. program planning, 1977-81, mgr. planning systems mgmt. group, 1981-82, dir. tech. svc. sys. devel., 1982-89, dir. field engring., 1989-93; dir. strategic initiatives Unysis Corp., Gt. Neck, 1993-95; bd. dirs. Engring. Found. Gateway Engring. Edn. Coalition, 1998—, also bd. dirs.; vice chmn. Engring. Conf. Found. Bd., 2001—04. Chmn. exec. compensation com. Woodward-Clyde Group, Denver, 1989-97. Contbr. articles to profl. publs. Trustee Columbia U., N.Y.C., 1990-96, trustee emerita, 1996—; mem. Columbia Engring. Coun., 1987—, chmn., 1987-91; vice chmn. Bronxville (N.Y.) Planning Bd.; chmn. Bronxville Design Rev. Com., 1993—; pres. Soc. Columbia Grads., 1998-2000. Recipient hon. citation Wilson Coll. Centennial, 1970, Alumni medal for conspicuous svc. Columbia U., 1980, Egleston medal for disting. engring. achievement Columbia U., 1997; named One of 100 N.Y. Women of Influence, New York Woman mag., 1986. Fellow Soc. Women Engrs. (founder, pioneer); mem. AIAA (sr.), ASME (sr.), Columbia U. Engring. Alumni Assn. (pres. 1977-81), Columbia U. Alumni Fedn. (pres. 1981-85), Bronxville Field Club.

LONGOBARDO, GUY ALFRED, lawyer, department chairman; b. NYC, May 9, 1961; s. Guy S. and Anna Grace (Kazanjian) L.; children: Alice Elisabeth, Anne Abigail. BA cum laude, Williams Coll., 1982; JD, Columbia U., 1985. Bar: N.Y. 1986. Assoc. Milbank, Tweed, Hadley & McCloy, NYC, 1985-95; mng. dir., chief adminstrv. officer, orgn. and adv. HSBC Securities, Inc., 1995-97, mng. dir., head of corp. fin., 1997-98; gen. counsel, v.p. bus. devel. AMNEX, Inc., New Rochelle, NY, 1998—2001; chmn., CEO ETS Payphones, Inc., Lithia Springs, Ga., 2001—. Dep. village counsel Village of Bronxville, 1991-96. Mem. long range planning com. Village of Bronxville; mem. com. for non-partisan nomination and election of sch. trustees Bronxville, N.Y., 1995-96, coach Eastchester Youth Soccer Assn., 1995-98; gov. Bronxville Field Club, 2000-06; pres. Bronxville Field Club, 2003-06; dir. Am. Pub. Comm. Coun., 2001-06. Harlan Fiske Stone scholar Columbia U., 1983. Mem. Bronxville Field Club (gov. 2000-06, pres. 2003-06). Christian Scientist. Avocations: tennis, skiing, platform tennis. Personal E-mail: glongbard@aol.com.

LONGORIA, EVA (EVA JACQUELINE LONGORIA, EVA LONGORIA CHRISTOPHER), actress; b. Corpus Christi, Tex., Mar. 15, 1975; m. Tyler Christopher, Jan. 20, 2002 (div. Jan. 19, 2005); m. Tony Parker, July 7, 2007. BS in Kinesiology, Tex. A&M-Kingsville. Actress (TV series) The Young and the Restless, 2001—03 (ALMA award for Outstanding Actress in a Daytime Drama), L.A. Dragnet, 2003, Desperate Housewives, 2004— (co-recipient, Outstanding Performance by an Ensemble in a Comedy Series, Screen Actors Guild award, 2005, 2006), (video) Snitch'd, 2003, Señorita Justice, 2004, (TV films) The Dead Will tell, 2004, (films) Hustler's Instinct, 2005, The Sentinel, 2006, Harsh Times, 2006, actress, co-prodr. Carlita's Secret, 2004, co-prodr., performer (variety show, video) Hot Tamales Live: Spicy, Hot and Hilarious, 2003; performer: (Broadway plays) What the Rabbi Saw; guest appearances Beverly Hills, 90210, 2000, George Lopez, 2006, host Nat. Coun. La Raza ALMA awards, 2006. Named Miss Corpus Christi, 1998, Favorite Female Star-TV, People's Choice Awards, 2007; named one of Ten New Faces to Watch, Variety, 2004, Fall's TV's Hot 11, USA Today, 2004, New Faces of Fall, TV Guide, 2004, Hot 100 for 2004, Maxim Mag., 2004, 25 Most Beautiful People, People en Espanol's; recipient Person of Yr., Nat. Coun. La Raza ALMA award (Am. Latin Media Arts), 2006. Address: Desperate Housewives Touchstone Televison 100 University City Plaza Bldg 2128 Ste Universal City CA 91608*

LONGSTAFF, RONALD EARL, federal judge; b. Pittsburg, Kans., Feb. 14, 1941; m. Norma Jeanne Miller, July 25, 1970. BA, Kans. State Coll., 1962; JD with distinction, U. Iowa, 1965. Assoc. McWilliams, Gross and Kirtley, Des Moines, 1967-68; law clk. to Hon. Roy L. Stephenson US Dist. Ct. (so. dist.) Iowa, 1965-67, ct. clk., 1968-76, magistrate judge, 1976-91, judge Des Moines, 1991—2001, chief judge, 2001—06, sr. judge, 2006—. Adj. prof. law Drake U., 1973-76. Mem. Iowa State Bar Assn. (chmn. spl. commn. to revise Iowa exemption law 1968-70, mem. adv. com. 8th cir. ct. appeals 1988—). Office: US Dist Ct 422 US Courthouse 123 E Walnut St PO Box 9344 Des Moines IA 50306-9344

LONGSTREET, JOHN CHARLES, retired computer scientist; s. John Henry and Erkle Mae Longstreet; m. Deborah S. Longstreet, June 17, 1944; children: Jennifer Tressler, Jeannette. BA, U. Chgo., 1960; MBA, Roosevelt U., 1974. Engr. computer sys. Internat. Minerals and Chem. Corp., Libertyville, Ill., 1969—72; pvt. practice computer sys. analyst Chgo., 1972—78; from assoc. prof. Harold Washington Coll. to prof. City Colls. Chgo., 1978—2002, disting. prof., 1988—89, prof. emeritus, 2002—. Cons. in field. Recipient Outstanding Profl. Employee award, City Colls. Chgo., 1978, Outstanding Tchr. award, U. Tex., Austin, 1989. Avocations: chess, music, internet. Personal E-mail: jclongstreet@yahoo.com.

LONGSTRETH, BEVIS, lawyer; b. NYC, Jan. 29, 1934; s. Alfred Bevis and Mary Agnes (Shiras) L.; m. Clara Seymour St. John, Aug. 10, 1963; children: Katherine Shiras, Thomas Day, Benjamin Hoyt. BS cum laude, Princeton U., 1956; LL.M., Harvard U., 1961. Bar: NY 1962. Assoc. Debevoise & Plimpton, NYC, 1962-70, ptnr., 1970-81; commr. SEC, Washington, 1981-84; ptnr. Debevoise & Plimpton, 1984-97, of counsel, 1997—2000. Lectr. Columbia U. Law Sch., NYC, 1975-81, adj. prof., 1994-99; cons. Ford Found., 1971-72; cons. to Comptroller Gen. of US; mem. pension fin. com. World Bank, 1987-95; bd. govs. Am. Stock Exch., 1992-98; bd. dirs. AMVESCAP, plc, Coll. Ret. Equities Fund, Grantham, Mayo and Von Otterloo. Author: Spindle and Bow, 2005; author other books, numerous articles on investment, securities and law. Trustee Nathan Cummings Found., 1991-97, 1999-2005, The Textile Mus., New Sch. U.; mem. fin. com. Rockefeller Family Fund; chmn. Fund for Independence in Journalism, 2004-. Lt. USMC, 1956-58. Mem. Am. Law Inst., Coun. Fgn. Rels. Democrat. Home: 322 Central Park W New York NY 10025-7629 Office: Debevoise & Plimpton 919 3rd Ave New York NY 10022-6225 Home Phone: 212-663-0576; Office Phone: 212-909-6651. Personal E-mail: blongstreth@mindspring.com. E-mail: blongstreth@debevoise.com.

LONGSTRETH, ROBERT MAYNE, lawyer; b. Nov. 8, 1925; BA in Polit. Sci., U. Wash., Seattle, 1951, JD, 1954. Bar: Calif. 1955, Hawaii 1987, Calif. (specialist family law) 1980. Pvt. practice law, Menlo Park, Calif., 1955—63, Honolulu, 1989—; ptnr. Longstreth & Siegel, Menlo Park, 1963—73, Longstreth & Russell, Menlo Park, 1973—89. Mem.: Hawaii Yacht Club, Shriners, Masons. Home: 239 Halemaumau St Honolulu HI 96821-2055

LONGSWORTH, ROBERT MORROW, language educator; b. Canton, Ohio, Feb. 15, 1937; s. Robert H. and Margaret Elizabeth (Morrow) L.; m. Carol Herndon, Aug. 16, 1958; children: Eric D., Margaret W., Ann E. AB, Duke U., 1958; MA, Harvard U., 1960, PhD, 1965. Asst. prof. Oberlin Coll., 1964-70, assoc. prof., 1970-75, prof. English, 1975—, emeritus prof., 2001—, dean Coll. Arts and Scis., 1974-84. Author: The Cornish Ordinalia, 1967, The Design of Drama, 1972 A Decade of Campus Language at Oberlin College, 2003; contbr. articles to profl. jours. Danforth Found. fellow Fellow Am. Coun. Learned Socs., Nat. Humanities Ctr.; mem. MLA, Medieval Acad. Am., Cornwall Archaeol. Soc., Phi Beta Kappa.

LONGWELL, HARRY J., retired oil industry executive; b. Bunkie, La., July 20, 1941; BS in Petroleum Engring., La. State U., 1963. Joined Exxon, 1963; engr. drilling Exxon Co., U.S.A., New Orleans, mgr. ops. Corpus Christi, 1974, LA, 1974—77, divsn. mgr., 1977—80, mgr. ops. dept. prodn. Houston, 1980—83, v.p. dept. prodn., 1983—86; v.p. exploration and prodn. in Europe Exxon, London, 1986; exec. asst. to chmn. Exxon Corp., NYC, 1986; v.p. exploration and prodn. Exxon Co., Internat., Florham Park, NJ, 1987—88, sr. v.p., 1988—90, exec. v.p., 1990—92; pres. Exxon Co., U.S.A., 1992—95; sr. v.p., dir. Exxon Corp. (now Exxon Mobil Corp.), Irving, Tex., 1995—2001; exec. v.p., dir. Exxon Mobil Corp., Irving, Tex., 2001—05. Chmn. bd. trustees U. Dallas; mem. bd. visitors U. Tex. M.D. Anderson Cancer Ctr.; mem. adv. bd. Dallas Area Habitat for Humanity. Office: Exxon Mobil Corp 5959 Las Colinas Blvd Irving TX 75039-4202 Office Phone: 972-444-1976. E-mail: hl5223@comcast.net.

LONGWORTH, RICHARD COLE, journalist; b. Des Moines, Mar. 13, 1935; s. Wallace Harlan and Helen (Cole) L.; m. Barbara Bem, July 19, 1958; children: Peter, Susan. BJ, Northwestern U., 1957; postgrad., Harvard U., 1968-69. Reporter UPI, Chgo., 1958-60, parliamentary corr. London, 1960-65, corr. Moscow, 1965-68, Vienna, 1969-72, diplomatic corr. Brussels, 1972-76; econ. and internat. affairs reporter Chgo. Tribune, 1976-86, bus. editor, econ. columnist, 1987-88, chief European corr., 1988-91, sr. writer, 1991—2002, sr. corr., 2002—03; internat. affairs commentator Sta. WBEZ-FM, Chgo., 1984—; exec. dir. Global Chgo. Ctr. of Chgo., Coun. on Fgn. Rels., 2003—06; sr. fellow Chgo. Coun. Global Affairs, 2006—. Adj. prof. Northwestern U., 1998—, guest scholar, 2001. Author: Global Squeeze: The Coming Crisis for First-World Nations, 1998, Global Chicago, 2000. With U.S. Army, 1957-58. Nieman fellow, 1968-69; recipient award for econ. reporting U. Mo., 1978, 80, John Hancock, 1978, 79, 82, Gerald Loeb award for econ. reporting, 1979, Media award for econ. understanding Dartmouth Coll., 1979, award Inter-Am. Press Assn., 1979, Peter Lisagor award Sigma Delta Chi, 1979, Sidney Hillman award, 1985, Lowell Thomas award for travel writing, 1985, Beck award for fgn. corr., 1986, Domestic Reporting award, 1987, Overseas Press Club award, 1994, 97, Alumni Merit award Northwestern U., 2000, finalist, Pulitzer prize, 1979, 2003 Mem. Coun. Fgn. Rels. N.Y., Assn. Am. Corrs. in London, Internat. Music Found. (dir.), Ednl. Found. for Nuclear Sci. (dir.). Office: Chgo Coun Global Affairs 332 South Michigan Ave 11th Fl Chicago IL 60604 Office Phone: 312-821-7508. Business E-Mail: rlongworth@thechicagocouncil.org.

LONSBERG, JOHN V., lawyer; BA summa cum laude, U. Notre Dame, 1976; JD cum laude, U. Mich., 1979. Bar: Mo. 1979. Ptnr. Fulbright & Jaworski LLP, St. Louis, leader Mid. East practice. Mem.: Pi Sigma Alpha, Phi Beta Kappa. Office: Fulbright & Jaworski LLP 8000 Maryland Ave Ste 1190 Saint Louis MO 63105 Office Phone: 314-505-8800. Business E-Mail: jlonsberg@fulbright.com.

LOO, BEVERLY JANE, publishing executive; b. LA; d. Richard Y. and Bessie E. Sue Loo. BA, U. Calif., Berkeley. Dir. subs. rights Prentice-Hall, Inc., NYC, 1957—59; fiction editor McCall's mag., 1959—62; exec. editor and dir. subs. rights, gen. books div. McGraw-Hill Book Co., NYC, 1962—82; pres. Beverly Jane Loo Assocs., Inc., NYC, 1982—85; sr. editor, dir. subs. rights World Almanac Pharos Books, NYC, 1985—88; dir. mktg. and subs. rights Paragon House, NYC, 1988—91; dir. mktg. and sales Thomasson-Grant, Charlottesville, Va., 1991—93; dir. pub. and comm. inst. U. Va. Sch. Continuing Edn. and Profl. Studies, Charlottesville, 1993—2004; asst. prof., dir. Masters of Profl. Studies in Pub. George Washington U., Coll. Profl. Studies, Washington, 2005—. Mem.: U. Va. Faculty Club, Va. Writers Club, Overseas Press Club (N.Y.C.), Arts Club (London). Home: Lewis & Clark Sq # 701 250 W Main St Charlottesville VA 22902-5072 Office: George Washington U Coll Profl Studies 805 21st St NW Ste 301 Washington DC 20052 Office Phone: 202-994-3004. Business E-Mail: bevloo@gwu.edu.

LOO, LYNN (YUEH-LIN), chemical engineer; BSE in materials sci. and engring., U. Pa., 1996, BSE in chemical engring., 1996; MA in chemical engring., Princeton U., 1998, PhD in chemical engring., 2001. Asst. prof. dept. chemical engring. U. Tex., Austin, Ctr. Nano-and Molecular Sci. and Tech., Tex. Materials Inst. Contbr. articles to profl. jour. Named one of Top 100 Young Innovators, MIT Tech. Review, 2004; recipient Frank J. Padden award for excellence in polymer rsch., APS, 2000, Camille & Henry Dreyfus New Faculty award, 2002, DuPont Young Prof. award, 2003, Career award, NSF, 2004; Porter Ogden Jacobus fellow, Princeton U., 2000. Office: U Tex Dept Chemical Engring CPE 4422 1 University Station C0400 Austin TX 78712-1062 Business E-Mail: lloo@che.utexas.edu.

LOO, MARCUS HSIEU-HONG, urologist, physician, educator; b. NYC, Aug. 12, 1955; s. David Wei and Patricia (Pai) L.; m. Donna C. Wingshee, Oct. 3, 1987; children: Christopher, Courtney. BSEE with distinction, Cornell U., 1977, MD, 1981. Diplomate Am. Bd. Urology. Attending urologist NY Hosp. Presbyn. Hosp., NYC, 1988—; clin. asst. prof. urology Cornell U. Med. Coll., NYC, 1994-2000, clin. assoc. prof. urology, 2000—05, clin. prof. urology, 2005—. Admissions com. Cornell U. Med. Coll.; mem. univ. coun. Cornell U.; mem. operating bd. Columbia Cornell Care, LLC.; cons. Chinatown Health Cilnic; clin. dir. Asian Am. Cancer Awareness Rsch. and Tng. grant. Author: The Prostate Cancer Source Book, 1998. Mem. Univ. Coun. Cornell U., 2002—, trustee, 2003—. Fellow: ACS; mem.: IEEE, AMA, Fedn. Chinese Am. and Chinese Can. Med. Socs. (bd. dirs., v.p.), Chinese Am. Med. Soc. (pres., bd. dirs. 1990—97), Soc. Internat. d'Urologie, Am. Urological Assn., Am. Assn. Clin. Urologists, Cornell U. Med. Coll. Alumni Assn. (bd. dirs.), Tau Beta Pi, Phi Tau Phi, Eta Kappa Nu. Office: 449 E 68th St New York NY 10021-4941 Office Phone: 212-925-8388.

LOOBY, BRIAN WILLIAM, lawyer, lobbyist; b. Albany, NY, May 9, 1971; s. William Hill and Pauline Elizabeth Looby. BS in Polit. Sci., Kennesaw State U., Ga., 2000; JD, U. Ga., Athens, 2004. Bar: Ga. 2004. Legal and legis. asst. Med. Assn. Ga., Atlanta, 1998—2001, assoc. gen. counsel, 2004—. With govt. rels. Med. Assn. Ga., 2004—. Contbr. articles to profl. jours. Recipient Appreciation cert., Gov.'s Office Hwy. Safety, DUI Task Force, 2005. Mem.: Am. Soc. Med. Assn. Counsel. Avocations: travel, music. Office: Medical Assn Georgia 1849 The Exchange Ste 200 Atlanta GA 30339 Home Phone: 404-797-0488; Office Phone: 404-881-5045.

LOOCKERMAN, WILLIAM DELMER, retired educational administrator; b. Phila., Feb. 24, 1939; s. William Delmer and Kathleen (Cullen) L.; m. Alice Clara Winnemore, June 9, 1962; 1 child, Alice B. BS in Health and Phys. Edn., West Chester U., Pa., 1962, MS in Health and Phys. Edn., 1967; EdD in Phys. Edn., Temple U., 1970; cert. sch. dist. adminstr., Niagara U., 1974. Tchr. Upper Darby (Pa.) Schs., 1965-68; tchg. assoc. Temple U., Phila., 1968-70; asst. prof. SUNY, Buffalo, 1970-73; dir. health, phys. edn. and recreation Orchard Park (NY) Ctrl. Schs., 1973-81; registered sch. bus. adminstr. Springville (NY) Griffith Inst. Ctrl. Sch. Dist., 1981-2001, ret., 2001, adminstr. emeritus, 2001—. Adj. asst. prof. Niagara U., Niagara Falls, NY, 1975—77; adj. prof. Canisius Coll., Buffalo, 1979—81; statewide rep. Group 491 Ins. Safety Program, Albany, NY, 1983—2001, trustee, 1991—2001, mem. exec. com., 1991—2001, chair, 1996—2001; spkr. local, state, nat. and internat. meetings. Contbr. articles to profl. jours. Mem. Springville Cmty. Choir, 1997. Capt. USN ret. Recipient spl. honor award NY State Coaches Assn., 1980, honor award NY State Assn. Health, Phys. Edn. and Recreation, 1979, conf. dedication, 1980; Colden Sch. gymnasium named in his honor, 2001. Mem. Internat. Assn. Sch. Bus. Ofcls. (mem. choir 1989—, song leader Opening Gen. Session 1997, appreciation award 1990, 94), NY State Sch. Bus. Ofcls. (chpt. exec. com. 1983-85), AMVETS, Naval Order U.S. (chpt. comdr. 1987-96, 2000-01, companion to gen. coun. 1997-99, Naval Res. Assn. (chpt. pres., nat. budget/fin. com. 1995—, nat. v.p. 1997-99, 2001-03, nat. treas. 1999-2001, 2005—, mem. nat. adv. com. 1987—, mem. nat. investment oversight com. 1995—, chmn., 2003-2005, chair 50th ann. com. 2004, Nat. award of Merit 2001, Nat. Pres.'s award 2004), Am. Legion (WNY Armed Forces Week com. 1980—, post 1st vice comdr. 2003-2005, bd. dirs. 2002-05, 06—, chmn. 2003-04), Navy League of U.S. (exec. v.p. coun. 2004, pres. coun. 2005). Republican. Episcopalian. Avocation: woodworking. Home: 7643 Lewis Rd Holland NY 14080-9625 Personal E-mail: wloockerman@aol.com.

LOOKADOO, REGAN, psychology professor; b. Paducah, Ky., Apr. 29, 1975; d. Ronnie and Wanda Mott; m. Eric Lookadoo, Dec. 18, 1999; 1 child, Camryn. PhD, U. Ala., Tuscaloosa, 2002. Asst. prof. psychology Georgetown Coll., Ky., 2001—. Mem.: Alpha Delta Kappa. Office: Georgetown Coll 400 East College St Georgetown KY 40324 Office Phone: 502-863-8165.

LOOMAN, JAMES R., lawyer; b. Vallejo, Calif., June 5, 1952; s. Alfred R. and Jane M. (Halter) L.; m. Donna G. Craven, Dec. 18, 1976; children: Alison Marie, Mark Andrew, Zachary Michael. BA, Valparaiso U., Ind., 1974; JD, U. Chgo., 1978. Bar: Ill. 1978, U.S. Dist. Ct. (no dist.) Ill. 1978, U.S. Claims Ct. 1979. Assoc. Isham, Lincoln & Beale, Chgo., 1978—83, Sidley & Austin, Chgo., 1983—86; ptnr. Sidley Austin LLP, 1986—. Assoc. gen. counsel Comml. Fin. Assn., 2002—. Bd. dirs. Valparaiso U., Ind., 2006—. Fellow Am. Coll. Comml. Fin. Lawyers; mem. ABA, Chgo. Bar Assn. (chmn. comml. and fin. transactions com. 1996-97, 2002-03), Chgo. Athletic Assn., Skokie Country Club, Mid-Day Club, Univ. Club Chgo. Lutheran. Office: Sidley Austin LLP One South Dearborn St Chicago IL 60603-2003 Home Phone: 847-835-2457; Office Phone: 312-853-7133. Business E-Mail: jlooman@sidley.com.

LOOMIS, CAROL J., journalist; b. Marshfield, Mo., June 25, 1929; d. Harold and Mildred (Case) Junge; m. John R. Loomis, Mar. 19, 1960; children: Barbara, Mark. Student, Drury Coll., 1947-49; B in Journalism, U. Mo., 1951. Editor Maytag News, Maytag Co., Newton, Iowa, 1951-54; rsch. assoc. Fortune Mag., NYC, 1954-58, assoc. editor, 1958-68, mem. bd. editors, 1968—2002, editor-at-large, 2003—. Office: Fortune Mag 1271 Avenue Of The Americas New York NY 10020-1300

LOOMIS, HOWARD KREY, banker, director; b. Omaha, Apr. 9, 1927; s. Arthur L. and Genevieve (Krey) L.; m. Florence Porter, Apr. 24, 1954; children: Arthur L. II, Frederick S., Howard Krey, John Porter. AB, Cornell U., 1949, MBA, 1950. Mgmt. trainee Hallmark Cards Inc., Kansas City, Mo., 1953-56; sec., contr., dir. Mine Svc. Co. Inc., Ft. Smith, Ark., 1956-59; contr., dir. Electra Mfg. Co., Independence, Kans., 1959-63; v.p., dir. The Peoples Bank, Pratt, Kans., 1963-65, pres., 1966-2001, chmn., dir., 1998—. Pres., dir. Gt. Plains Leasing Inc., Pratt, 1966-80, Ctrl. States Inc., Pratt, 1970-76; pres. Krey Co. Ltd., Pratt, 1978-99, chmn., dir. 1999—; fin. chmn. Econ. Lifelines, Topeka; chmn. bd. dir. All Ins. Inc., Pratt. Past pres. Pratt County United Fund, Kanza coun. Boy Scouts Am.; past chmn. Cannonball Trail chpt. ARC; bd. dir., past comdg. gen. Kans. Cavalry; past dir. Kans. Wildscape Found. With U.S. Army, 1950-52. Mem. Kans. C. of C. and Industry (past transp. chmn., dir., v.p.), Pratt Area C. of C. (past pres., bd. dir.), Kans. Bankers Assn. (past bd. dir.), Fin. Execs. Inst., Park Hills Country Club (past pres.), Elks, Rotary, Sigma Delta Chi, Chi Psi. Republican. Presbyterian. Home: 502 Welton St Pratt KS 67124-0928 Office: Krey Co Ltd 118 E Third St Pratt KS 67124-0928

LOOMIS, JAMES COOK, mathematician, cyberneticist, writer, educator, navigator; b. Long Beach, Calif., Sept. 22, 1935; s. Joseph Gray and Elizabeth Cook L.; children: Gannon Joseph, Megan Leslie Loomis Powers. BS, U. Calif., 1958, MA, 1961; postgrad., U. Mich., 1962. Dept. head math. Culver City (Calif.) H.S., 1962-70; dir. Cetacean Rels. Soc., Maui, Hawaii, 1976-98, Planetary Healing Pageants, Maui, Hawaii, 1976—2005. PhD fellow Mental Health Rsch. Inst., Prisoner's Dilemma, under Dr. Merril Flood, Genetic Algorithms, under John Holland and dir. J.G. Miller, Living Systems; spkr., U Hawaii Matsunaga Peace Inst., 1st Global Peace Rsch. Conf., 1994, SHE PEACE: A World Peace Beadgame; Creating Future Friendly ECO-GEO-CEO's; capt., Proj. Jonah Grant, 1976, Deep Breathold diving Dolphin Entertainer; creator, Y2Kaper FOANA-TUNUP-HAS Flags of All Nations and The United Nations Underwater Parade Honoring All Species for the Global Millenium Television network 2001, 24 hr. Broadcast. Author: Saving the Cosmos ('Til Tuesday), 1995, Strange Fluke, 1990 (1st prize Maui Writers Conf., 1994); creator US-UP-UC? United Species Underwater Parade Uniting Civilizations, 2007. Address: PO Box 790958 Paia HI 96779-0958 Office Phone: 808-573-8622. E-mail: loomis@unitedspecies.net.

LOOMIS, KENAN GREGG, lawyer; b. Apr. 11, 1961; BA, Tulane U., 1983; JD, Emory U. Sch. Law, 1986. Bar: Ga. 1986, NC 2005, Ga. Ct. Appeals, Ga. Supreme Ct., US Ct. Appeals (8th cir.), US Ct. Appeals (11th cir.), US Dist. Ct. (ea. dist.) NC, US Dist. Ct. (mid. dist.) Ga., US Dist. Ct. (mid. dist.) NC, US Dist. Ct. (no. dist.) Ga., US Dist. Ct. (so. dist.) Ga., US Dist. Ct. (we. dist.) NC. Mng. ptnr. Smith Helms Mulliss & Moore, Atlanta, 1998—2002; mng. ptnr., assoc. Smith Moore LLP, Atlanta, 2002—06; ptnr. Cozen O'Connor, Atlanta, 2006—. Named Ga. Super Lawyer, Law & Politics, 2005—06, Atlanta mag., 2005—06. Mem.: Moot Ct. Soc., State Bar Ga., Atlanta Bar Assn., Def. Rsch. Inst., ABA. Office: Cozen O'Connor Ste 2200 SunTrust Plz 303 Peachtree St NE Atlanta GA 30308 Office Phone: 404-572-2028. Office Fax: 866-591-9127.*

LOOMIS, MICKEY, professional sports team executive; children: Alex, Katherine. Grad. in Acctg., U. Oreg., Eugene; M in Sports Adminstrn., Wichita State U., Kans. With NFL Seattle Seahawks, 1983—98, v.p. fin., 1990—92, exec. v.p., 1992—98; dir. football adminstrn. NFL New Orleans Saints, 2000—02, exec. v.p., gen. mgr., 2002—; gen. mgr. Arena Football League New Orleans VooDoo. Named Sporting News George Young NFL Exec. of Yr., 2007. Office: New Orleans Saints 5800 Airline Dr Metairie LA 70003 Office Phone: 504-733-0255.*

LOOMIS, NORMA IRENE, marriage and family therapist; b. Dunlap, Ind., May 6, 1941; d. Edwin Clifford and Lucille DeVere (Hall) Dick; m. Edwin Dale Loomis; children: William Dale, James Vernon. BS in Edn., Western Mich. U., 1973, MA in Edn., 1976; PhD in Christian Counseling, Rocky Mountin Inc., 1990. Cert. marriage and family therapist, forensic therapist Nat. Assn. Forensic Therapists, Internat. Bd. Christian Counselors, 2007. Tchr. Cassopolis (Mich.) Schs., 1973—; counseling Christian Counseling Svcs., Goshen, Ind., 1985—. Presenter Elkhart (Ind.) Pub. Schs., 1992—95, Middlebury (Ind.) Pub. Schs., 1992—94, Elkhart Ct., 1995—97; pres. Champion Reality Inc., Elkhart, 1983—; founder, pres. Soaring As Women of Value, 2001, Abundant Life, 2004. Contbr. articles to profl. publs.; author tchg. materials Hot Shots Prodns. Mem. Cmty. Corrections Adv. Bd., Elkhart County, 1994—; pres. Juniper Beach Assn., Mears, Mich., 1985-96, Women in Action, Elkhart, 1985-94. Mem. ACA, Am. Mental Health Counselors Assn., Ind. Counselors Assn. for Alcohol and Drug Abuse, Am. Assn. Christian Counselors, Christian Assn. Psychol. Studies, Oceana County Hist. and Geneal. Soc. (bd. dirs. 2006—). Republican. Mem. Bretheran Ch. Avocations: swimming, boating, bowling, crafts. Office: Christian Counseling Svcs 3095 N Lakeshore Dr Mears MI 49436 E-mail: nl641@gtlakes.com.

LOOMIS, REBECCA C., psychologist; b. New London, Conn., Nov. 9, 1959; d. Aubrey Kingsley and Marillyn Louise (Dirks) Loomis; m. DeWitt Montgomery Smith, Nov. 24, 1984 (div. Sept. 1997); children: Adrienne Kingsley Smith, Walker Loomis Smith; m. Jack G. Gental, July 9, 2005; stepchildren: Alexander Gentul, Robert Gentul. BA in Sociology and Polit. Sci., Vanderbilt U., 1981; MEd, U. Houston, 1990, PhD in Counseling Psychology, 2004. Lic. psychologist NY. Group rep. Home Life Ins., Houston, 1981—83; sr. account exec. CNA Ins. Co., Houston, 1983—87; rsch. asst. dept. ednl. psychology U. Houston, 1988—90, 1991—93, tchg. asst., 1993, rsch. asst. Clearwater, Tex., 1993; acad. advisor Montclair (N.J.) State U., 2001—02; psychology intern Assn. Help of Retarded Children, NYC, 2002—03; prin. investigator St. Luke's-Roosevelt Hosp. Manhattan Ctr. for Pain Mgmt., 1999—2004; clinician Assn. for Help of Retarded Children, NYC, 2003—07; psychologist Manhattan Ctr. Pain Mgmt., St. Luke's-Roosevelt Hosp., NYC, 2007—. Group facilitator children div. parents, counselor Houston Child Guidance, 1990; counselor learning support svcs. U. Houston, 1990, counselor counseling and testing svcs., 1994—95; facilitator mentorship program Wildwood Elem. Sch., Mountain Lakes, NJ, 1996. Contbr. articles to various profl. jours. Hospice aid Casa de Ninos Hospice, Houston, 1986—87; vol. Houston Area Women's Ctr., 1992—93, 1994—95; cmty. aid Mountain Lakes, 1999—; vol. organizer grief workshop for September 11, 2001 attacks Cmty. Ch. Mem.: APA, N.J. Psychol. Assn. Democrat. Home and Office: 249 Morris Ave Mountain Lakes NJ 07046 Personal E-mail: beckyloomis@earthlink.net.

LOOMIS, RICHARD MORGAN, literature and language educator; b. Denver, Dec. 29, 1926; s. Arthur Kirkwood and Ethel Morgan Loomis; m. Mary Josephine Guerriere, Aug. 21, 1954; children: Leonard, Mario. BA, John Carroll U., Cleve., 1949; MA, Cornell U., Ithaca, NY, 1954, PhD, 1959. Prof. English King's Coll., Wilkes-Barre, Pa., 1956—70, Nazareth Coll., Rochester, NY, 1970—92, prof. English emeritus, 1992—. Author: Dafydd ap Gwilym: The Poems, 1982; editor: Life of Hugh of Avalon by Gerald of Wales, 1985; co-editor: Medieval Welsh Poems, 1992. Min. communion St. John Bapt. Ch., Wilkes-Barre, 2000—. With USNR, 1944—46. Rsch. grantee, Nazareth Coll., 1972—86. Mem.: Nat. Assn. Scholars, St. David's Soc. Rochester and Genesee Region (founding mem.), Alumni Deep Springs and Telluride Assn. Republican. Roman Catholic. Avocations: writing, performing traditional songs. Home: 25 Wyndwood Dr Wilkes Barre PA 18705

LOOMIS, RICK, photographer; b. Raleigh, NC, Mar. 22, 1969; Student, Palm Beach Cmty. Coll., 1987—88; BA, Western Ky. U., Bowling Green, 1993. HS intern Palm Beach Post, 1987, lab technician, 1987—89; summer intern Ft. Wayne News Sentinel, 1990, Colo. Springs Gazette Telegraph, 1991, Seattle Times, 1992, Syracuse (NY) Newspapers, 1993; staff photographer Coll. Heights Herald, Western Ky. U., 1991—92; photographer LA Times, 1994—. Co-recipient Pulitzer Prize for Explanatory Reporting, 2007; recipient Sigma Delta Chi award, Soc. Profl. Journalists, 2003, Journalist of Yr. award, LA Press Club, 2004, Sidney Hillman Found. award for Overall Excellence in Photojournalism, 2005. Mem.: Nat. Press Photographers Assn. (Photographer of Yr. 2003), Calif. Press Photographers Assn. (Photographer of Yr. 2002, 2004). Office: LA Times 202 W 1st St Los Angeles CA 90012*

LOOMIS, SALORA DALE, psychiatrist; b. Peru, Ind., Oct. 21, 1930; s. S. Dale Sr. and Rhea Pearl (Davis) L.; m. Carol Marie Davis, Jan 3, 1959; children: Stephen Dale, Patricia Marie. AB in Zoology, Ind. U., 1953, MS in Human Anatomy, 1955, MD, 1958. Diplomate Am. Bd. Psychiatry and Neurology. Intern Cook County Hosp., Chgo., 1958-59; resident in psychiatry Logansport (Ind.) State Hosp., 1959-60, Ill. State Psychiat. Inst., Chgo., 1960-62; staff psychiatrist Katharine Wright Psychiat. Clinic, Chgo., 1962-65, dir., 1965-92. Cons. Ill. Youth Commn. 1962-64; instr. psychiatry Northwestern U. Med. Sch., Chgo., 1962-64, assoc. 1964-67; asst. dir. Northwestern U. Psychiat. Clinics, Chgo., 1963-65; attending psychiatrist St. Joseph Hosp., Chgo., 1964—; lectr. psychiatry and neurology Loyola U. Med. Sch. Chgo., 1964-65, assoc. 1965, asst. prof. 1965-73, lectr. 1980-89, clin. assoc. prof., 1989-2002, clin. prof., 2002—; psychiat. cons. Ill. Dept. Pub. Health, 1967-92; sr. attending psychiatrist, chmn. dept. psychiatry Ill. Masonic Med. Ctr., Chgo. 1970-92, chmn. emeritus, 1992—; clin. assoc. prof. psychiatry U. Ill. Coll. Medicine, Chgo., 1973—. Fellow Am. Coll. Psychiatrists, Am. Psychiat. Assn. (disting. life), Acad. Psychosomatic Medicine; mem. AMA, Ill. State Med. Soc. (chmn. council on mental health and addiction 1974-75, chmn. joint peer rev. com. 1975-76), Ill. Psychiat. Soc. (chmn. ethics com. 1974-75, chmn. peer rev. com. 1976-78), Chgo. Med. Socs. Office Phone: 312-343-7313. Personal E-mail: sdaleloomis@mac.com.

LOONEY, CLAUDIA ARLENE, health facility administrator; b. Fullerton, Calif., June 13, 1946; d. Donald F. and Mildred B. Schneider; m. James K. Looney, Oct. 8, 1967; 1 child, Christopher K. BA, Calif. State U., 1969. Dir. youth YWCA No. Orange County, Fullerton, Calif., 1967-70; dir. dist. Camp Fire Girls, San Francisco, 1971-73, asst. exec. dir. LA, 1973-77; asst. dir. cmty. resources Childrens Hosp., LA, 1977-80; dir. cmty. devel. Orthopaedic Hosp., LA, 1980-82; sr. v.p. Saddleback Meml. Found./Saddleback Meml. Med. Ctr., Laguna Hills, Calif., 1982-92; v.p. planning and advancement Calif. Inst. Arts, Santa Clarita, Calif., 1992-96; pres. Northwestern Meml. Found., Chgo., 1996-99; sr. v.p. Childrens Hosp., LA, 1999—. Instr. U. Calif., Irvine, Univ. Irvine; mem. steering com. U. Irvine. Steering com. United Way, LA, 1984-86, bd. mem. Woodmark Forum, 2004-, sec., 2005-. Recipient Orange County Woman of Achievement award, YWCA, 2004. Fellow Assn. Healthcare Philanthropy (nat. chair-elect, chmn. program Nat. Edn. Conf. 1986, regional dir. 1985-89, 98, fin. com. 1988—, pres., com. chn. 1987—, Give To Life com. chmn. 1987-91, mid-west regional conf. chmn. 1998, Orange County Fund Raiser of Yr. 1992, LA County Fund Raiser of Yr. 1996); mem. Nat. Soc. Fund Raising Execs. Found. (cert., vice chmn. 1985-90, chair 1993—, mem. Chgo. conf. com. 1997, 98), So. Calif. Assn. Hosp. Devel. (past pres., bd. dirs.), Profl. Ptnrs. (chmn. 1986, instr. 1988—), Philanthropic Ednl. Orgn. (past pres.), Assn. for Healthcare Profls. (regional conf. co-chmn. 2003), Assn. Fundraising Profls. (mem. internat. ethics com. 2003—), Orange County Women of Achievement. Avocations: swimming, sailing, photography. Office: Children's Hosp LA 4650 Sunset Blvd Ste 29 Los Angeles CA 90027 Office Phone: 323-671-3856.

LOONEY, GERALD LEE, medical educator, administrator; b. Bradshaw, W.Va., Nov. 22, 1937; s. Noah Webster and Anna Belle (Burris) L.; m. Linda Louise Pluebell, Oct. 19, 1962 (div. Apr. 1975); children: Deborah Lynn, Catherine Ann, Karen Marie, Kelli Rachelle. AB, Johns Hopkins U., 1959, MD, 1963; MPH, Harvard U., 1968. Diplomate Am. Bd. Preventive Medicine, Am. Bd. Pediatrics. Resident pediatrics Tufts-New Eng. Med. Ctr., Boston, 1965-67; physician-in-chief Kennedy Meml. Hosp., Boston, 1969-71; asst. prof. family and cmty. medicine U. Ariz. Coll. Medicine, Tucson, 1971-72; asst. prof. emergency medicine U. So. Calif. Sch. Medicine, LA, 1972-77; assoc. clin. prof. medicine U. Calif., Irvine, 1991—; emergency dept. dir. Glendale (Calif.) Adventist Med. Ctr., 1978-84, Orthopaedic Hosp., LA, 1985-88; urgent care dir. Bay Shore Med. Group, Torrance, Calif., 1988-93; med. dir. Surecare and LAX Clinics Centinela Hosp., Inglewood, Calif., 1993-95; dir. med. svc. Boeing Co. Mil. Aircraft, Long Beach, Calif., 1996—. Bd. dirs. Beach Cities Health Dist., Redondo Beach, Calif., 1992-93. Avocation: history. Home Phone: 702-240-1637; Office Phone: 310-962-6616. E-mail: docger@hotmail.com.

LOONEY, JOSEPH W., lawyer; b. Shreveport, La., May 10, 1948; BA cum laude, Loyola U., 1970; JD, Tulane U., 1976. Bar: La. 1976, U.S. Dist. Ct. (ea. dist.) La. 1976, U.S. Ct. Appeals (5th cir.) 1977, U.S. Supreme Ct. 1980, U.S. Ct. Appeals (11th cir.) 1982. Ptnr. Adams and Reese, New Orleans, 1991—. Adj. prof. Tulane Law Sch. Mem. ABA, Fed. Bar Assn., Def. Rsch. Inst., Maritime Law Assn. U.S., La. State Bar Assn., Internat. Trademark Assn., Am. Intellectual Property Lawyers Assn. Office: Adams & Reese 701 Poydras Str Suite 4500 New Orleans LA 70139-4501

LOONEY, WILLIAM FRANCIS, JR., lawyer; b. Boston, Sept. 20, 1931; s. William Francis Sr. and Ursula Mary (Ryan) L.; m. Constance Mary O'Callaghan, Dec. 28, 1957; children: Willam F. III, Thomas M., Karen D., Martha A. AB, JD, Harvard U. Bar: Mass. 1958, D.C. 1972, U.S. Supreme Ct. 1972, U.S. Dist. Ct. (ea. dist.) Mich. 1986. Law clk. to presiding justice Mass. Supreme Jud. Ct., 1958-59; assoc. Goodwin, Procter & Hoar, Boston, 1959-62; chief civil divsn. US Attys. Office, 1964-65; ptnr. Looney & Grossman, Boston, 1965-94, sr. counsel, 1995—. Asst. US atty. Dist. Mass., 1962-65; spl. hearing officer US Dept. Justice, 1965-68; mem. Mass. Bd. Bar Overseers, 1985-91, vice-chmn., 1990-91; corp. mem. Greater Boston Legal Svcs., Inc., 1994—; spl. asst. Atty. Gen., Commonwealth of Mass., 2002—. Mem. Zoning Bd. of Appeals, Dedham, Mass., 1971-74; bd. dirs. Boston Latin Sch. Found., 1981-85, pres. 1981-84, chmn. bd. dirs., 1984-86; trustee Social Law Libr., 1994-97; chmn. ADR adv. com. US Dist. Ct., 1998—; spl. asst. atty. gen. Commonwealth of Mass., 2003— Fellow Am. Coll. Trial Lawyers (state com. 1996-2001); mem. Mass. Bar Assn. (co-chmn. standing com. lawyers responsibility for pub. svc. 1987-88, chmn. fed. ct. adv. com. alternative dispute resolution 1998-2006), Boston Bar Assn. (pres. 1984-85, coun. 1985-90, chmn. sr. lawyers sect. 1992-94, Maguire award for professionalism 1995), Nat. Assn. Bar Pres.'s, Boston Latin Sch. Assn. (pres. 1980-82, life trustee 1982—, Man of Yr. 1985), USCG Found. (bd. dirs. 1987-2000, dir. emeritus 2000—), Norfolk Golf Club, Harvard Club, Harvard U. Alumni Assn. (bd. dirs. 2001-04). Democrat. Roman Catholic. Home: 43 Coronation Dr Dedham MA 02026-6230 Office: 101 Arch St Fl 9 Boston MA 02110-1112 Office Phone: 617-951-2800. Business E-Mail: wloon@lgllp.com.

LOONEY, WILLIAM R., III, career military officer; b. Norman, Okla., Mar. 5, 1949; BS, USAF Acad., 1972; student, Squadron Officer Sch., 1977; M in Mgmt., Ctrl. Mich. U., 1979; student, Armed Forces Staff Coll., 1983, Nat. War Coll., 1990, Exec. Warfare Course, 1993, Joint Flag Officer Warfighting Course, 1997, Joint Force Air Component Comdr. Course, 1997, Undergraduate Space & Missile Training Staff Course, 1998, Nat. & Internat. Security Seminar, 1999. Commd. 2d lt. USAF, 1972, advanced through grades to gen., 2005, AC-130 gunship pilot Ubon Royal Thai AFB, Thailand, 1973-74; instr. pilot 50th Flying Tng. Squadron, Columbus AFB, Miss., 1975-78; air staff tng. program Directorate of Pers. Plans, The Pentagon, Washington, 1978-79; instr. pilot, flight comdr. and asst. ops. officer 94th Tactical Fighter Squadron, Langley AFB, Va., 1980-83; aide-de-camp to dep. comdr. in chief U.S. European Command, Stuttgart, West Germany, 1983-85; chief of wing plans 36th Tactical Fighter Wing, Bitburg AB, West Germany, 1985-86; ops. officer to comdr. 22nd Tactical Fighter Squadron, Bitburg AB, 1986-89; conventional negotiations br. chief Directorate of Strategic Plans and Policy, The Pentagon, Washington, 1990-92; vice comdr. Air Forces Iceland, Keflavik Naval Air Sta., Iceland, 1992-93; comdr. 33rd Fighter Wing, Eglin AFB, Fla., 1993-95, 1st Fighter Wing, Langley AFB, Va., 1995-96; comdt. Armed Forces Staff Coll., Norfolk, Va., 1996—98; comdr. Space Warfare Ctr., Schriever AFB, Colo., 1998-99; dir. ops. USAF, Peterson AFB, Colo., 1999—2000; comdr. 14th Air Force & Component Comdr. US Space Command, Vandenberg AFB, Calif., 2000—02; comdr. Aero. Systems Ctr. Air Force Material Command, Hanscom AFB, Mass., 2002—03, Wright Patterson AFB, Ohio, 2003—05; comdr. Air Edn. & Training Command, Randolph AFB, Tex., 2005—. Decorated DSM with oak leaf cluster, Def. Superior Svc. medal, Def. Meritorious Svc. medal with oak leaf cluster, Legion of Merit with oak leaf cluster, Air medal, Aerial Achievement medal, Air Force Commendation medal with oak leaf cluster, Air Force Achievement medal, Combat Readiness medal with oak leaf cluster, Global War on Terrorism medal with oak leaf cluster, Humanitarian Svc. medal, Air and Space Campaign medal. Office: Air Edn & Training Command 12FTW/PA Randolph Afb TX 78150

LOOPER, MARCIA LYNN, elementary school educator, consultant; b. Texarkana, Ark., May 6, 1954; d. Charles Benjamin and Nancy Nichols Graves; children: Scott Aaron, Cory Michael, Jonathan Reed. BS in Elem. Edn., U. Tex., Austin, 1976. Cert. tchr. gifted/talented Tex., tchr. Tex. Tchr. Spring Br. Ind. Sch. Dist., Houston, 1992—; trainer, first grade reading acad. Region IV Edn. Ctr., Houston, 1999—2004. Curriculum writer social studies, trainer social studies curriculum overview Spring Br. Ind. Sch. Dist., Houston, 1994—, trainer new tchr. inst., 1998—; adv. bd. Valley Oaks Elem. Sch. PTA, Houston, 1997—; trainer, first grade reading acad. Region IV Edn. Ctr., Houston, 1999—2004; trainer Steven Covey's Seven Habits for Highly Effective People, Houston, 1999—2000; cons., writer, reading specialist Classroom Connect, El Segundo, Calif., 2003—05; sponsor, trip leader to DC WorldStride, Charlottesville, Va., 2004—; presenter in field. Sponsor cmty. svc. projects Valley Oaks Elem. Student Coun., Houston, 2000—06; Houston Ambassador to Saudi Arabia; sunday sch. tchr., bible study leader, choir dir. Houston's First Bapt. Ch., 1981—92. Named Marcia Looper Day in her honor, Robert Eckels County Judge of Harris County, Tex., 2005, Elem. Tchr. of Yr., Spring Br. Ind. Sch. Dist., 2004—05; recipient Christa McAuliffe Excellence in Tchg. award, Houston West C. of C., 2005, Lifetime Mem. award, Valley Oaks PTA, 1999, Tchr. of Yr., Valley Oaks Elem. Sch., 2000—01, 2004—05, History Tchr. Yr. award, Preserve Am., 2007. Mem.: Spring Br. Social Studies Coun. (corr.; v.p. 2006—), Tex. Gifted and Talented (corr.), Friends of Geography (corr.), Nat. Coun. Social Studies (corr.), Tex. Coun. of Social Studies (corr.). Avocations: reading, travel. Home: 1461 Woodhollow Dr #29203 Houston TX 77057 Office: Valley Oaks Elem Sch 8390 Westview Houston TX 77055 Home Phone: 281-787-2590; Office Phone: 713-365-4080. Office Fax: 713-365-4086. Personal E-mail: mlooper@aol.com. Business E-Mail: marcia.looper@springbranchisd.com.

LOORY, STUART HUGH, journalist; b. Wilson, Pa., May 22, 1932; s. Harry and Eva (Holland) L.; m. Marjorie Helene Dretel, June 19, 1955 (div. July 1995); children: Joshua Alan, Adam Edward, Miriam Beth; m. Nina Nikolaevna Kudriavtseva, Aug. 17, 1995. BA, Cornell U., 1954; MS with honors, Columbia U., 1958; postgrad., U. Vienna, Austria, 1958. Reporter Newark News, 1955-58, N.Y. Herald Tribune, 1959-61, sci. writer, 1961-63, Washington corr., 1963-64, fgn. corr. Moscow, 1964-66; sci. editor Metromedia Radio Stas., 1962-64, Moscow corr., 1964-66; sci. writer N.Y. Times, 1966; White House corr. Los Angeles Times, 1967-71; fellow Woodrow Wilson Internat. Center for Scholars, Washington, 1971-72; exec. editor WNBC-TV News, 1973; Kiplinger prof. pub. affairs reporting Ohio State U., Columbus, 1973-75; assoc. editor Chgo. Sun-Times, 1975-76, mng. editor, 1976-80; v.p., mng. editor Washington bur. Cable News Network, 1980-82, Moscow bur. chief, 1983-86, sr. correspondent, 1986, exec. producer, 1987-90; exec. dir. internat. rels. Turner Broadcasting System, Inc., Atlanta, 1988—; editor-in-chief CNN World Report, 1990-91; v.p. CNN, 1990-95; exec. v.p. Turner Internat. Broadcasting, Russia, 1993-97; v.p., supervising prodr. Turner Original Prodns., 1995. Lee Hills chair in free press studies U. Mo., Columbia, 1997—; lectr. in field. Author: (with David Kraslow) The Secret Search for Peace in Vietnam, 1968, Defeated: Inside America's Military Machine, 1973, (with Ann Imse) Seven Days That Shook the World: The Collapse of Soviet Communism, 1991; Editor IPI Report (Internat. Press Inst.), 1998-1999, IPI Global Journalist, 1999-2005, Global Journalist, 2005; contbr. articles mags. and encys. Recipient citation Overseas Press Club, 1966; Raymond Clapper award Congl. Press Gallery, 1968; George Polk award L.I.U., 1968; Du Mont award U. Calif. at Los Angeles, 1968; Distinguished Alumni award Columbia, 1969; 50th Anniversary medal Columbia Sch. Journalism, 1963; Edwin Hood award for diplomatic corr. Nat. Press Club, 1987; Pulitzer traveling scholar, 1958. Jewish. Office: U Mo Sch Journalism 132A Neff Annex Columbia MO 65211-1200 Office Phone: 573-884-1599. Business E-Mail: loorys@missouri.edu.

LOOS, JOHN THOMPSON, business owner; b. West Palm Beach, Fla. s. John T. and Margaret (Browning) L.; children: Amy, John, Melissa. BSBA, U. Fla. Co-founder, v.p., bd. dirs. Am. Mktg. and Mgmt., Inc., Ft. Lauderdale, Fla., 1970-78; pvt. practice real estate investor Ft. Lauderdale, 1978—. Pres. First Lauderdale Investments-Di-Mar Properties. Active Ft. Lauderdale Riverwalk Com., 1987-91, Jud. Nominating Commn., Broward County, Fla., 1988-92; bd. dirs. Broward County YMCA, 1982—, past pres.; bd. dirs., vice-chmn., chmn. North Broward Hosp. Dist., 1989-93; bd. dirs., vice chmn. Downtown Devel. Authority, Ft. Lauderdale, 1990, 93, 96, 03, chmn., 1990-94, active, 1988-2000, 2001-2005; chmn. Cmty. Svcs. Bd., Ft. Lauderdale, 1986-90; bd. dirs. North Lauderdale-Progreso Devel. Dist., 1990-91, Broward County Planning Coun., 1993-95, Broward County Charter Rev. Com., 1994-96, Broward County Partnership for the Homeless, 1997-98; bd. dirs. Downtown Coun., Fort Lauderdale Transp. Mgmt. Authority. Named Downtowner of Yr., Ft. Lauderdale, 1997, Person of Yr., Ft. Lauderdale Riverwalk, 2002. Mem.: Lauderdale Yacht Club. Republican. Home: 1815 Cordova Rd Ste 210 Fort Lauderdale FL 33316-2199

LOOS, WILLIAM H(ENRY), librarian, consultant; b. North Tonawanda, NY, Feb. 26, 1937; s. William R. and Hildegarde Ida (Nickel) Loos; m. Judylee Rita Matesick, Feb. 17, 1979. BA in History, SUNY, Buffalo, 1965; MA in Libr. Sci., Syracuse U., 1968. Cert. pub. libr. Libr. trainee City of Tonawanda, 1965—67; reference libr. Buffalo and Erie County Pub. Libr., 1968—70, cataloger, 1970—72, curator Grosvenor Rare Book Rm., founder, 1972—2002; ret., 2002; pres., trustee Western N.Y. Heritage Press, Cheektawoga, NY, 2001—. Cons. Western N.Y. Libr. Resources Coun., Buffalo, 1969—77; mem. N.Y. State Libr. Adv. Coun. on Preservation and Conservation, 1985—88; lectr. in field. Author: Negro Exhibit at the Pan American Exposition 1901, 2001; co-editor: Western New York Union List of Serials, 1970; contbr. libr. periodicals. Pres. Salisbury Club, Buffalo, 1975—77. Pub. Libr. Tng. grantee, N.Y. State, 1967. Mem.: ALA (rare books and manuscripts sect.), Bibliographical Soc. Am., Manuscript Soc., Am. Printing Hist. Assn., Beta Phi Mu. Republican. Mem. United Ch. Of Christ. Achievements include playing a leading role in the recovery of the first half of the manuscript of Mark Twain's Adventures of Huckleberry Finn missing for 105 years. Avocation: collecting fine books, prints and maps. Home: 119 Colvinhurst Dr Tonawanda NY 14223-1469

LOOSER, DEVONEY KAY, English literature educator; b. St. Paul, Apr. 11, 1967; d. LeRoy Joseph and Sharon Lee Ann (Sarslow) Looser; m. George Lewis Justice, 1996; children: Carl Anchor Justice, Lowell Williamson Justice. BA, Augsburg Coll., 1989; PhD, SUNY, Stony Brook, 1993. Instr. English SUNY, Stony Brook, 1989-93; asst. prof. English Ind.

State U., Terre Haute, 1993-98, acting dir. women's studies, 1997-98; asst. prof. women's studies U. Wis., Whitewater, 1998-2000; vis. asst. prof. English Ariz. State U., 2000-2001; asst. prof. English La. State U., 2001—02, U. Mo., Columbia, 2002—, assoc. prof. English, 2004—. Author: British Women Writers and the Writing of History, 1670-1820, 2000 (Choice Outstanding Acad. Title award 2001); editor: Jane Austen and Discourses of Feminism, 1995; co-editor: (with E. Ann Kaplan) Generations: Academic Feminists in Dialogue, 1997, Jour. for Early Modern Cultural Studies, 2004—; contbr. articles to profl. jours. Fellow, NEH, 1994, Nat. Humanities Ctr. Inst., 2003, Huntington Libr., 2004, King's Coll., London, 2004, Spencer Libr., U. Kans., 2004, Newberry Libr., 2005; Big 12 fellow, 2006. Mem. MLA (exec. com. late eighteenth century divsn. 2004—, exec. com. Midwest sect. 2004-07, v.p. Midwest sect. 2007—), Am. Soc. Eighteenth Century Studies, Jane Austen Soc. N.Am. (bd. dirs. 2000-02), Nat. Women's Studies Assn., N.Am. Soc. Study of Romanticism, Soc. for Study of Early Modern Women. Office: U Mo Columbia Dept English Columbia MO 65211 Office Phone: 573-884-7791. Business E-Mail: looserd@missouri.edu.

LOOSER, DONALD WILLIAM, academic administrator; b. Lufkin, Tex., June 14, 1939; s. William E. and Mildred H. (Wageneck) L.; m. Elsa Jean Albritton, Aug. 20, 1966; 1 child, William Gregory. MusB, Baylor U., 1962; MusM, Northwestern U., 1963; PhD, Fla. State U., 1972. Instr. Miss. Coll., Clinton, 1963-64; asst. prof. Houston Bapt. U., 1964-68, asst. to pres., 1968-72, dean gen. edn., 1972-77, v.p. adminstrv. affairs, 1977-83, v.p. acad. affairs, 1983—2007, v.p. emeritus, 2007. Pres. Conf. Deans Faculties and Acad. V.P.s, 1985-86; mem Harvard U. Inst. Edn. Mgmt., 1985; pres. Nat. Conf. Acad. Deans, 1990-91. Contbr. articles to profl. jours.; rec. artist A Jubilant Song, 1983. Mem. adv. bd. Houston Symphony Orch., Houston Grand Opera, pianist Tallowood Bapt. Ch., 1965-88; pianist Second Bapt. Ch., Houston, 1988-98. Mem. Am. Assn. Higher Edn., Houston Philos. Soc., Rotary, Phi Delta Kappa, Omicron Delta Kappa, Pi Kappa Lambda, Kappa Delta Pi. Office Phone: 281-649-3232. E-mail: dlooser@hbu.edu.

LOOSER, WILLIAM GREGORY, lawyer; b. Houston, July 24, 1969; BA, JD, Baylor U., 1991. Bar: Tex. 1994, U.S. Dist. Ct. Tex. (No. dist.) 1995, U.S. Dist. Ct. Tex. (So. dist.) 1996. Atty. Bracewell & Guiliani, LLP, Houston; asst. gen. counsel Pride Internat., Inc., Houston, 1999—2003, v.p., gen. counsel, sec., 2003—05, sr. v.p., gen. counsel, sec., 2005—. Mem.: ABA, Am. Corp. Counsel Assn., Internat. Assn. Def. Counsel, Houston Young Lawyers Assn. (co-chair profl. devel. com. 1997), State Bar Tex., Houston Bar Assn., Nat. Order Barristers, Phi Delta Phi. Office: Pride Internat Inc 5847 San Felipe Ste 3300 Houston TX 77057*

LOOTS, JAMES MASON, lawyer; b. Iowa City, May 24, 1958; s. Robert James and Mary (Ladd) L.; children: Mason S., Karl R. BSJ, Northwestern U., Evanston, Ill., 1980; JD cum laude, Mich. Law Sch., 1984. Bar: D.C. 1984, U.S. Dist. Ct. D.C. 1985, U.S. Dist. Ct. Md., 1992, U.S. Ct. Appeals (D.C. cir.) 1985, U.S. Tax Ct. 1990, U.S. Ct. Fed. Claims 1998, U.S. Ct. Appeals (4th cir.) 2000, U.S. Supreme Ct. 2006. Assoc. Skadden, Arps, Slate, Meagher & Flom, Washington, 1984-89, Jones, Day, Reavis & Pogue, Washington, 1989-92; ptnr. Barrymore & Loots, Washington, 1992-95, Perry, Simmons & Loots, Washington, 1995-99, Goldstein & Loots, Washington, 1999—2002, Ford & Harrison LLP, Washington, 2002—05, James M. Loots PC, 2005—. Treas. Worldly Goods, Inc., Washington, 1988-94; adj. prof. Am. U. Wash. Coll. Law, 1990-96. Editorial Bd. Mich. Law Rev., 1982-84. Vol. VISTA, Baton Rouge, 1980-81; v.p. Bedford Springs (Pa.) Festival, 1987-89; adv. bd. Washington Legal Counsel for the Elderly, 1988-97; mem. D.C. Small Bus. Adv. Bd., 1990-99; chmn. D.C. Commn. Human Rights, 1991-2001; bd. dirs. Capitol Hill Assn. Merchants & Profls., 1994-97. Mem. D.C. Bar Assn. (Pro Bono Lawyer of Year, 1988), Washington Coun. Lawyers, Phi Alpha Delta Legal Frat. Mailing: PO Box 76852 Washington DC 20013 Office: 236 Massachusetts Ave NE # 204 Washington DC 20002 Home Phone: 202-544-1552; Office Phone: 202-536-5650. Business E-Mail: jloots@lootslaw.com.

LOOYENGA, ROGER L., insurance company executive; BS, Minot State Coll. CLU, CPCU. Exec. v.p. Auto-Owners Ins. Co., Lansing, Mich., 1999—2004, chmn., CEO, 2004—. Trustee Am. Inst. for CPCU, 2004—, Ins. Inst. Am., 2004—. Office: Auto Owners Insurance Co 6101 Anacapri Blvd Lansing MI 48917

LOPACH, JAMES JOSEPH, political science professor; b. Great Falls, Mont., June 23, 1942; s. John Ernest and Alma Marie (Schapman) L.; div. Dec. 10, 1991; children: Christine, Paul. AB in Philosophy, Carroll Coll., 1964; MA in Am. Studies, U. Notre Dame, 1967, MAT in English Edn., 1968, PhD in Govt., 1973. Mgr. Pacific Telephone, Palo Alto, Calif., 1968-69; adminstr. City of South Bend, Ind., 1971-73; prof. U. Mont., Missoula, 1973—, chmn. dept. polit. sci., 1977-87, 2006—07, assoc. dean Coll. Arts and Scis., 1987-88, acting dir. Mansfield Ctr., 1984-85, spl. asst. to the univ. pres., 1988-92, assoc. provost, 1992-95, spl. asst. to provost, 1995-96. Cons. local govts., state agys., tribal govts., law firms, 1973—; expert witness. Author, editor: We the People of Montana, 1983, Tribal Government Today, 1990, 98, Planning Small Town America, 1990, Jeannette Rankin: A Political Woman, 2005; contbr. articles to profl. jours. Roman Catholic. Office: U Mont Dept Polit Sci Missoula MT 59812-0001 Office Phone: 406-243-5202. E-mail: james.lopach@umontana.edu.

LOPACKI, EDWARD JOSEPH, JR., lawyer; b. Bklyn., June 4, 1947; s. Edward Joseph and Lillian Jane (Wallace) L.; m. Crystal May Miller, June 21, 1969; children: Edward Joseph III, Elizabeth Jane BA in Sociology, Villanova U., Pa., 1971; JD, Vt. Law Sch., 1980. Bar: Fla. 1981, US Dist. Ct. (mid. dist.) Fla. 1983, US Ct. Appeals (11th cir.) 1986. Mgmt. trainee Bankers Trust Co., NYC, 1968—72; counselor NJ State Employment Svcs., Red Bank, 1972—77; pvt. practice Bradenton, Fla., 1981—. Adj. prof. law Nova U., Ft. Lauderdale, Fla., 1981, Manatee C.C., Bradenton, Fla., 1994-96; mem.Suncoast Ctr. for Ind. Living, 1995-99, cons. 1999-2001 Mem. Fla. Ind. Living Coun., 1996-00, dist. VI adv. coun. Fla. Dept. Health and Rehabilitative Svcs., 1988-92, Manatee County Health Care Adv. Bd., 1993-05, Manatee County Coun. on Access for Disabled, 1994-04, Manatee Coun. Aging, 1986-87, De Soto Boys Club, 1982-87, sec.; bd. dirs. Disability Independence Group, Inc. Mem. Nat. Orgn. Social Security Claimants Reps., Nat. Coun. Ind. Living, Manatee County Bar Assn, KC, Lions. Democrat. Roman Catholic. Avocations: reading, advocacy for civil rights of people with disabilities. Home: 6612 27th Avenue Dr W Bradenton FL 34209-7405 Office: PO Box 14604 Bradenton FL 34280 Office Phone: 941-792-8244. Business E-Mail: LopackiLaw@aol.com.

LOPATE, PHILLIP, language educator, writer; b. NYC, Nov. 16, 1943; s. Albert and Frances (Berlow) L.; m. Carol Ascher, Jan. 15, 1964 (div. 1968); m. Cheryl Cipriani, Dec. 31, 1990; 1 child. BA, Columbia U., 1964; PhD, Union Grad. Sch., 1979. Edn. dir. Tchrs. & Writers Collaborative, NYC, 1968-80; assoc. prof. English U. Houston, 1980-88; adj. prof. English Columbia U., 1988-92; prof. English Bennington (Vt.) Coll., 1992-93, Hofstra U., Hempstead, NY, 1993—. Author: The Eyes Don't Always Want to Stay Open, 1972, Being With Children, 1975, The Daily Round, 1976, Confessions of Summer, 1979, Bachelorhood, 1981, The Rug Merchant, 1987, Against Joie de Vivre, 1989, Portrait of My Body, 1996, Getting Personal, 2003, Waterfront, 2004, Rudy Burkhardt Photographer, 2004; editor (anthology) The Art of the Personal Essay, 1994, Writing New York, 1998, American Movie Critics, 2006. Juror Pulitzer Prize, N.Y.C., 1984, Nat. Book Award, N.Y.C., 1990, Associated Writing Programs, 1993; various coms. Mcpl. Arts Soc., N.Y.C., 1989—. Recipient Best Non-Fiction Book award Tex. Inst. Letters, 1981; grantee NEA, 1978, 85; fellow John Simon Guggenheim Found., 1988, NY Pub. Libr. Ctr. for Scholars and Writers fellow, 2000-01. Mem. Authors Guild, Tchrs. & Writers Collaborative (bd. dirs. 1980—), PEN; fellow Am. Acad. Arts & Sciences Home and Office: 402 Sackett St Brooklyn NY 11231-4704 Personal E-mail: plopate@aol.com.

LOPATIN, ALAN G., lawyer; b. New Haven, May 25, 1956; s. Paul and Ruth (Rosen) L.; m. Debra Jo Engler, May 17, 1981; children: Jonah Adam, Asa Louis. BA, Yale U., 1978; JD, Am. U., 1981. Bar: D.C. 1981, U.S. Supreme Ct. 1985. Law clk. FMC, Washington, 1980-81; counsel com. on post office and civil svc. U.S. Ho. of Reps., Washington, 1981-82, counsel com. on budget, 1982-86, dep. chief counsel, 1986-87, counsel temp. joint com. on deficit reduction, 1986, dep. gen. counsel com. on post office and civil svc., 1987-90, gen. counsel com. on edn. and labor, 1991-94; pres. Ledge Counsel, Inc., Washington, 1995—; exec. dir. Nat. and Cmty. Svc. Coalition, 1995-99; ptnr. Valente Lopatin & Schulze, Washington, 1998—2002; of counsel Valente and Assoc., Washington, 2003—. Mem. presdl. task force Health Care Reform, Washington, 1993. Mem. ABA, D.C. Bar Assn., Nat. Assn. Thrift Savs. Plan Participants (pres. 1999—), Nat. Dem. Club, Yale Club (Washington). Democratic. Jewish. Home: 4958 Butterworth Pl NW Washington DC 20016-4354 Office: Ledge Counsel Inc 4958 Butterworth Pl NW Washington DC 20016-4354 Home Phone: 202-362-0447. Business E-Mail: alan@ledgecounsel.com.

LOPER, CARL RICHARD, JR., metallurgical engineer, educator; b. Wauwatosa, Wis., July 3, 1932; s. Carl Richard S. and Valberg (Sundby) Loper; m. Jane Louise Loehning, June 30, 1956; children: Cynthia Louise Loper Koch, Anne Elizabeth. BS in Metall. Engring., U. Wis., 1955, MS in Metall. Engring., 1958, PhD in Metall. Engring., 1961; postgrad., U. Mich., 1960. Metall. engr. Pelton Steel Casting Co., Milw., 1955-56; instr., rsch. assoc. U. Wis., Madison, 1956-61, asst. prof., 1961-64, assoc. prof., 1964-68, prof. metall. engring., 1968-88, prof. materials sci. and engring., 1988-2001, ret. prof. materials sci. and engring., 2001, assoc. chmn. dept. metall. and mineral engring., 1979-82; pres. CRL Corp., 1979—. Rsch. metallurgist Allis Chalmers, Milw., 1961; adj. prof. materials U. Wis., Milw., 2002—; cons., lectr. in field. Author: (book) Principles of Metal Casting, 1965; contbr. articles to profl. jours. Chmn. 25 Anniversary Ductile Iron Symposium, Montreal, Canada, 1973; pres. Ygdrasil Lit. Soc., 1989—90. Recipient Adams Meml. award, Am. Welding Soc., 1963, Howard F. Taylor award, 1967, Svc. citation, 1969, 1972, others, Silver medal award, Sci. Merit Portuguese Foundry Assn., 1978, medal, Chinese Foundrymen's Assn., 1989, E.J. Walsh Award, 2002, Merton Flemings award, Materials Processing Inst., 2006; fellow Foundry Ednl. Found., 1953—55, Wheelbrator Corp., 1960, Ford Found., 1960. Fellow: Am. Soc. Metals (chmn. 1969—70), Am. Inst. Mgmt.; mem.: Yedrasil-Norwegian-Am. Lit. Soc., Tau Beta Pi, Korean Inst. Metals and Materials (hon.), Foundry Ednl. Found. (E.J. Walsh award 2002), Am. Welding Soc., Am. Foundry Soc. (Wis. bd. dirs. 1967-70, 76-79, Foundry Ednl. Found. dirs. award 1994, Cast Iron Hon. Lecture 2006, Best Paper award 1966, 67, 85, John A. Penton gold medal 1972, Hoyt Meml. lectr. 1992, Aluminum Divsn. award sci. merit 1995), Blackhawk Country Club, Torske Klubben (bd. dirs., co-founder 1978—, Foundry Hall of Honor 2001), Gamma Alpha, Alpha Sigma Mu, Sigma Xi. Lutheran. Achievements include research in understanding the solidifcation and metallurgy of ferrous and non-ferrous alloys; solidification and cast iron metallurgy, education in metallurgy and materials science. Office Phone: 608-836-1296. Business E-Mail: loper@engr.wisc.edu.

LOPER, JAMES LEADERS, broadcasting executive; b. Phoenix, Sept. 4, 1931; s. John D. and Ellen Helen (Leaders) L.; m. Mary Louise Brion, Sept. 1, 1955; children: Elizabeth Margaret Sehran (Mrs. Michael K. Sehran), James Leaders Jr. BA, Ariz. State U., 1953; MA, U. Denver, 1957; PhD, U. So. Calif., 1967; DHL (hon.), Columbia Coll., 1973; LLD (hon.), Pepperdine U., 1978. Asst. dir. bur. broadcasting Ariz. State U., Tempe, 1953-59; news editor, announcer Sta. KTAR, Phoenix, 1955-56; dir. ednl. TV Calif. State U., LA, 1960-64; v.p. Cmty. TV So. Calif., LA, 1962-63; asst. to pres. Sta. KCET-Pub. TV, LA, 1963-65, sec., 1965-66, dir. ednl. svcs., 1964-65, asst. gen. mgr., 1965-66, v.p., gen. mgr., 1966-69, exec. v.p., gen. mgr., 1969-71, pres., gen. mgr., 1971-76, pres., CEO, 1976-82; exec. dir. Acad. TV Arts and Scis., 1983—99. Vis. exec. and adj. prof. Annenberg Sch. Comm., U. So. Calif., 1999—; bd. dirs., chmn. audit com. Western Fed. Savs. and Loan Assn., L.A., 1979-93; bd. dirs. Tenn. Ernie Ford Ent.; chmn. bd. Pub. Broadcasting Svcs., Washington, 1969-72; dir. Calif. Arts Coun., 1991-99, chmn., 1999; adj. prof. sch. Cinema and TV, U. So. Calif., 1984-99, sr. lectr., 1969-70; vis. exec., adj. prof. U. So. Calif., 1999—; pres. Western Ednl. Network, 1968-70; mem. Gov.'s Ednl. TV and Radio adv. Com., Calif., 1968-74; U.S. rep. CENTO Conf. Radio and TV, Turkey, 1978; trustee Internat. Coun. Nat. Acad. TV Arts and Scis., 1988-98. Contbr. articles to profl. jours.; contbr. to ETV: The Farther Vision, 1967, Broadcasting and Bargaining: Labor Relations in Radio and Television, 1970. Mem. adv. bd. Jr. League of L.A., 1970-76, Jr. League of Pasadena, 1972-75, L.A. Jr. Arts Ctr., 1968-72; exec. v.p. Assocs. of Otis Art Inst., 1971-77, pres., 1975-77; chmn., dir. The Performing Tree, L.A.; bd. dirs. Sears-Roebuck Found., 1976-79; chmn. bd. visitors Annenburg Sch. Comm., U. So. Calif., 1975-80; trustee Poly. Sch., Pasadena. Recipient Disting. Alumnus award Ariz. State U., 1972, Alumni Award of Merit, U. So. Calif., 1975, Gov.'s award Hollywood chpt. Nat. Acad. TV Arts and Scis., 1975, Alumni Achievement award Phi Sigma Kappa, 1975; named Centennial Alumnus Nat. Assn. of State Univs. and Land Grant Colls., 1988; named to Hall of Fame Walter Cronkite Sch. Comms., Ariz. State U., 1994. Mem. Acad. TV Arts and Scis. (past gov., v.p. Hollywood chpt., trustee nat. acad.), TV Acad. Found., Hollywood Radio and TV Soc. (treas., dir.), Western Ednl. Soc. Telecom. (past pres.), Assn. Calif. Pub. TV Stas. (past pres.), Young Pres.'s Orgn., Valley Hunt Club (Pasadena), Calif Club (L.A.), Sunset Club (past pres.), 100 of L.A., Twilight Pasadena, Lincoln Club (L.A.). Presbyterian (chmn. Mass Media Task Force So. Calif. Synod 1969-75).

LOPER, JOHNNY M., lawyer; b. Forest, Miss., July 25, 1952; BS with highest distinction, Miss. State U., 1974, MBA, 1975; JD magna cum laude, U. Miss. Sch. Law, 1983. Bar: Miss. 1983, admitted to practice: US Ct. Appeals (4th Cir.), US Dist. Cts. (Ea., Mid. and Western Dists., NC), No. and So. Dists. Miss. Summer assoc. Brunini, Grantham, Grower & Hewes, Jackson, Miss., 1981—82, assoc., 1983—87; ptnr. bus. litig. dept. Womble Carlyle Sandridge & Rice PLLC, Raleigh, NC, mem. mgmt. com., recruiting com., budget com., tech. com., personal resources com., office pro bono coord. Lectr. in field. Mng. editor Miss. Law Jour., 1983. Mem., pub. info. com. Adminstrn. of justice Task Force; mem. Pub. Speakers Bur. Mem.: 10th Jud. Dist. Bar Assn., NC State Bar Assn., NC Bar Assn. (mem., litig. sect.). Office: Womble Carlyle Sandridge & Rice PLLC 150 Fayetteville St Ste 2100 Raleigh NC 27601 Mailing: Womble Carlyle Sandridge & Rice PLLC PO Box 831 Raleigh NC 27602 Office Phone: 919-755-2116. Office Fax: 919-755-6056. Business E-Mail: jloper@wcsr.com.

LOPER, JOYCE E., plant pathologist, educator; BS in Biol. Scis., U. Calif., Davis, 1974, MS in Plant Pathology, 1978; PhD in Plant Pathology, U. Calif., Berkeley, 1983. Prof. dept. botany and plant pathology Oreg. State U., 1987—; rsch. plant pathologist USDA-Agrl. Rsch. Svc., 1985—, rsch. leader Hort. Crops Rsch. Lab., 2000—04. Mem. agr. bd. NRC, ecologically-based pest mgmt.: new solutions for a new century panel NAS, Washington, 1992-95, sci. adv. panel NSF Ctr. Microbial Ecology Mich. State U., 1992-96; councilor-at-large Am. Phytopathol. Soc., 1997-2000. Sr. editor Am. Phytopathol. Soc. Press, 1990-93; assoc. editor Molecular Plant-Microbe Interactions, 1996-99; mem. editl. com. Ann. Revs. of Phytopathology, 1996—2005; mem. editl. bd. European Jour. Plant Pathology, 1995—2005. Recipient CIBA GEIGY award Am. Phytopathological Soc., 1995. Fellow Am. Phytopathol. Soc. Office: USDA ARS Hort Crops Lab 3420 NW Orchard Ave Corvallis OR 97330-5014

LOPER, LINDA SUE, librarian; b. Wakefield, RI, Jan. 28, 1945; d. Delmas Field and Dora Belle (Hanna) Sneed; children: Matthew Lee Mathany, Amanda Virginia Mathany Van DerHeyden, Morgan Lynnclare Loper. BA, Peabody Coll., Nashville, 1966, MLS, 1979; EdD in Ednl. Adminstrn., Vanderbilt U., Nashville, 1988. Tchr. Parkway Sch., Chesterfield, Mo., 1966-68, Charlotte Mecklenburg Schs., Charlotte, N.C., 1968-71; dir. city libr. Jackson George Regional Libr. System, Pascagoula, Miss., 1979-82; media ctr. specialist Pascagoula Mcpl. Sch. Dist., 1982-83, Moore County Sch. System, Lynchburg, Tenn., 1983-91; ref. libr. Motlow State C.C., Tullahoma, Tenn., 1983-85; dir. learning resource ctr. Columbia (Tenn.) State C.C., 1991-99; CEO Grant Seekers, Inc., 1996-99, Loper Literary Agy., 1999—2001; accounts svcs. mgr. E.B. Stephens Co., 1999—2001; spl. collections divsn. mgr. Nashville Pub. Libr., 2001—05; libr. dir. Germantown (Tenn.) Cmty. Libr., 2005—07; dir. opns. Wolf River Libr. Consortium, Germantown, 2005—07; dir. devel. Libr. Sys. and Svcs. LLC, 2007—. Presenter TLA Ann. Conv., Knoxville, 1998, 2005, 2006, Am. Assn. Women in C.C.s Regional Conf., 1997, LEAP State Dept. Edn. Conf. for Libr., Chattanooga; career ladder participant Tenn. Edn. Dept. Level II; TIM trainer Dept. Edn., Nashville; exec. dir. Tenn. Bd. of Regents Media Consortium, 1993-96; chair profl. staff orgn. Columbia State C.C., 1998-99; presenter, judge 6th Ann. Cumberland Writers Conf., Cookeville, Tenn. Author: Bibliography for Tennessee Commission on Status of Women, 1979; contbr. article to profl jour. Pres. Moore County Friends of Libr., Lynchburg, Tenn., 1991; bd. dirs. Moore County Hist. and Geneal. Soc., Lynchburg, 1991; mem. Tenn. Bicentennial Com., Giles County, 1996; co-dir. So. Tapestry, a Bicentennial oral history project; sec., mem. exec. bd. Hope Ho. Domestic Violence Shelter, 1993—96, mem. adv. bd., 1996—99; mem. steering com. Bus., Industry, Edn. Partnership, 1994—99; mem. adv. bd. Nashville Pub. TV Cmty., 2003—05; Emmy judging panel Cultural Programming Mid-East Divsn., 2004. Recipient Gov.'s Acad. award State Dept. of Edn., U. Tenn., 1988, Inst. for Writing Tenn. History, U. Tenn., 1990, Gov.'s Conf. on Info. Sci., Nashville, 1990. Mem. ASCD, Am. Info. Assn. (Mid. Tenn. chapter), S.E. Libr. Assn., Tenn. Libr. Assn. (co-chair strategic planning com. 1996-99), TENNSHARE (chair collection devel. com. 1996-99), Moore County Edn. Assn. (treas., chair tchrs. study coun., chair polit. action commn. 1989-91), Giles County Edn. Found. UDC, DAR, Tenn. Acad. Libr. Collaborative (exec. coun. 1996-99), Soc. of Tenn. Archivists, Phi Delta Kappa, Beta Phi Mu, Delta Kappa Gamma. Democrat. Episcopalian. Avocations: cross stitch, sewing, reading, gardening. Office: Germantown Cmty Libr 1925 Exeter Rd Germantown TN 38138

LOPERA, GUSTAVO ADOLFO, cardiologist, electrophysiologist; s. Bernardo Lopera and Rosa Guevara de Lopera. MD, Pontificia Bolivariana U., 1998. Fellow in clin. cardiac electrophysiology U. Miami Sch. Medicine, Jackson Meml. Hosp., 1998—2001; post doctoral work Harvard Med. Sch., Brigham and Women's Hosp., 2001—02; cardiologist, electrophysiologist Cedar Valley Med. Specialist, Waterloo, Iowa, 2003—05, VA Med. Ctr., St. Petersburg, 2005; fellow in cardiovasc. disease U. Miami Jackson Meml. Hosp.; fellow in electrophysiology Brigham and Women's Hosp. Harvard Med. Sch.; cardiologist, physiologist Vets. Med. Affairs, St. Petersburg, Fla., Tampa Gen. Hosp. U. South Fla. Home Phone: 727-595-4015.

LOPES, JAMES LOUIS, lawyer; b. Watsonville, Calif., Feb. 1, 1947; s. Allen M. and Norma Maxine (McElroy) L.; m. Gail R. Lopes, Mar. 24, 1979; children: Elizabeth, Jane. BS, U.Calif., Davis, 1969; JD, U. Pacific, 1974; LLM, Harvard U., 1975. Bar: Calif. 1974, U.S. Ct. Appeals (9th cir.), U.S. Dist. Ct. (no., ea., ctrl. dists.) Calif. Assoc. Gendel, Raskoff, Shapiro & Quittner, LA, 1975-78; ptnr. Gordon, Peitzman & Lopes, San Francisco, 1978-81, Howard, Rice & Nemerovski, San Francisco, 1982—. Adv. com. bankruptcy/creditors' rights Practicing Law Inst., 1992—. Fellow Am. Coll. Bankruptcy, Calif.; mem. Bankruptcy Forum (bd. dirs. 1990-93), Calif. State Bar Assn. Avocations: flying, contract bridge. Office: Howard Rice & Nemerovski 3 Embarcadero Ctr Ste 7 San Francisco CA 94111-4074 Office Phone: 415-434-1600. E-mail: jlopes@howardrice.com.

LOPES, JERRY, broadcast executive; b. Providence; m. Rhonda Wade. Attended, Boston U. With Armed Forces Radio & Television service, 1970—73; news dir. WILD, Boston, 1974—75; with WHDH/ WCOZ, Boston, 1975—80; news dir. Sheridan Broadcasting Network, Washington, 1980—90, v.p. programming & ops. Pitts., 1990—92; exec. v.p. programming Am. Urban Radio, Pitts., 1992—93, pres., 1993—. Office: Am Urban Radio Networks 960 Penn Ave Ste 200 Pittsburgh PA 15222-3811

LOPES, ROSALY MUTEL CROCCE, astronomer, planetary geologist; b. Rio de Janeiro, Jan. 8, 1957; came to U.S., 1989; d. Walmir Crocce and Atir (Mutel) Lopes; m. Thomas Nicholas Gautier, III, Nov. 17, 1990 (div.); 1 child, Thomas N. Gautier. BSc in Astronomy, U. London, 1978, PhD in Physics, 1986. Curator Old Royal Obs., Greenwich, Eng., 1985-88; rsch. assoc. Vesuvius Obs., Naples, Italy, 1989; NRC rsch. assoc. Jet Propulsion Lab., Pasadena, Calif., 1989-91, rsch. scientist Galileo Project, 1991—2002, rsch. scientist Cassini Project, 2002—04, prin. scientist Cassini Project, 2004—. Mem. Volcanic Eruption Surveillance Team, U.K., 1981. Author: Volcanic Worlds, 2004, The Volcano Adventure Guide, 2005, Io After Galileo, 2006, numerous other works in sci. field. Recipient Latinas in Sci. award Commn. Feminil Mexicana Nat., L.A., 1990, NASA Exceptional Svc. medal, 2007; named Woman of the Yr. in Sci., Gems TV, 1997. Fellow AAAS, Explorers Club; mem. Internat. Astron. Union, Am. Astron. Soc. (Carl Sagan medal 2005), Am. Geophys. Union. Office: Jet Propulsion Lab Mail Stop 183-601 4800 Oak Grove Dr Pasadena CA 91109-8001 Home Phone: 626-304-0688; Office Phone: 818-393-4584. Business E-Mail: rosaly.m.lopes@jpl.nasa.gov.

LOPEZ, BARRY HOLSTUN, writer; b. Port Chester, NY, Jan. 6, 1945; s. Adrian Bernard and Mary Frances (Holstun) L.; m. Sandra Jean Landers, June 10, 1967 (div. Jan. 16, 1999). BA cum laude, U. Notre Dame, 1966, MA in Teaching, 1968; postgrad., U. Oreg., 1968-69; LHD (hon.), Whittier Coll., 1988, U. Portland, 1994, Tex. Tech. U., 2000; LHD in Environ. Studies (hon.), Utah State U., 2002. Free-lance writer, 1970—. Assoc. Media Studies Ctr. at Columbia Univ., N.Y.C., 1985—; mem. U.S. Cultural Delegation to China, 1988. Author: Desert Notes, 1976, Giving Birth to Thunder, 1978, Of Wolves and Men, 1978 (John Burroughs Soc. medal 1979, Christophers of N.Y. medal 1979, Pacific Northwest Booksellers award in nonfiction 1979), River Notes, 1979, Winter Count, 1981 (Disting. Recognition award Friends Am. Writers in Chgo. 1982), Arctic Dreams, 1986 (Nat. Book award in nonfiction Nat. Book Found. 1986, Christopher medal 1987, Pacific Northwest Booksellers award 1987, Frances Fuller Victor award in nonfiction Oreg. Inst. Literary Arts 1987), Crossing Open Ground, 1988, Crow and Weasel, 1990 (Parents Choice Found. award), The Rediscovery of North America, 1991, Field Notes, 1994 (Pacific Northwest Booksellers award in fiction 1995, Critics' Choice award 1996), Lessons From the Wolverine, 1997, About This Life, 1998, Apologia, 1998, Light Action in the Caribbean, 2000, Vintage Lopez, 2004, Resistance, 2004 (H.L. Davis Short Fiction Lit. Arts award, Oreg., 2005); also numerous articles, essays and short stories; editor: Home Ground, 2006; contbg. editor Harper's mag., 1981-82, 1984-2004, N.Am. Rev., 1977—, Ga. Rev., 2000—, Manoa, 2006—; works translated into Japanese, Swedish, German, Dutch, Italian, French, Norwegian, Chinese, Finnish, Slovak, Spanish, Arabic. Recipient award in Lit., Am. Acad. Arts and Letters, 1986, Antarctic Svc. medal U.S. Congress, 1989, Gov.'s award for

Arts, 1990, Lannan Found. award, 1990, Internat. Environ. award Prescott Coll., 1992, John Hay award, The Orion Soc., 2002, St. Francis of Assisi award DePaul U., 2002, Denise Levertov award Image mag., 2002, Robert F. Griffin award U. Notre Dame, 2007; Title V fellow HEA, 1967, fellow John Simon Guggenheim Found., 1987; residency fellow Lannan Found., 1999; Bernadine Kielty Scherman Residency fellow The Macdowell Colony in Vt., 2004; grantee NSF, 1987, 88, 91, 92, 99, vis. disting. scholar Tex. Tech U., 2003—. Fellow Explorers Club; mem. PEN Am. Ctr., PEN Ctr. USA West, Authors Guild, Poets and Writers, Amnesty Internat., Nature Conservancy (hon. life), Arctic Inst. N.Am. (life). Achievements include archive purchased for The James Sowell Family Collection in Literature, Community and the Natural World, Tex. Tech. U., 2000.

LOPEZ, CAROL SUE, artist; b. McCook, Nebr., Jan. 7, 1945; d. Norma Lee Wessell and Felix M. Rivera; m. Stanley Roland Lopez, May 6, 1962; children: Philip Eugene, Bryan Stanley, Eric Roland, Thea Katharine Hand. Dir. Atsugi Child Care Ctr., Atsugi, Japan, 1978—80; owner/dir. Galeria de Suenos Art Gallery, Mesilla/Las Cruces, N.Mex., 1999—. Display chairperson Mesilla Valley Fine Arts Gallery, 2004—. Encaustic painting (beeswax medium), Stained Glass (Best of Show, Southern N.M. State Fair, 1998), Light Show (Best of Show, Black Range Artists Assn., Deming, N.M., 2005), encaustic (beeswax) miniature painting, Just a Dream (2d pl., Black Mountain Ctr. for Arts, N.C., 2002), Day Dream (2d pl., Miniature Arts Soc. Fla., 2004), Camouflage (award of Merit, Artist's Guild Inc., Casper, Wyo., 2005). Recipient 2d Pl., Miniature Arts Bardean-Albuquerque, N.M., 2003, Hon. Mention, Roswell Fine Arts League, Roswell, N.M., 2003. Mem.: Las Cruces City of Artists Promotional Assn. (v.p., pres. 2005—06), Nat. Mus. Women in Arts, Miniature Art Soc. Fla., Mesilla Valley Fine Arts Gallery (governing bd., display chairperson 2004—06), Black Range Artists, Inc. Independent. Baptist. Avocations: travel, reading, museums & art galleries. Home: 1625 Country Club Cir Las Cruces NM 88001 Office: Galeria de Suenos Gallery and Studio 1625 Country Club Cir Las Cruces NM 88001 Home Phone: 505-523-0731; Office Phone: 505-523-0731.

LOPEZ, CAROLYN CATHERINE, physician; b. Chgo., Oct. 13, 1951; d. Joseph Compean and Angela (Silva) L. BS, Loyola U., Chgo., 1973; MD, U. Ill., 1978. Diplomate Am. Bd. Family Practice. Intern, resident Rush/Christ Hosp., Chgo., 1978-81; med. dir. Wholistic Health Ctr., Oak Lawn, Ill., 1981-82; clin. dir. Anchor HMO, Oak Brook, Ill., 1982-84, assoc. med. dir., 1984-87; med. dir. Chgo. Pk. Dist., 1987-91; v.p. Rush Access HMO, Chgo., 1992-93; asst. dean Rush Med. Coll., 1990-93; med. dir. Rush Access HMO, Chgo., 1991-93, v.p., 1992-93; v.p. for profl. affairs Rush Anchor HMO, 1993; sr. v.p. and chief med. officer Rush-Prudential Health Plans, 1993-95; chair dept. family practice Cook County Hosp., 1996—. Pres. Inst. Medicine, Chgo., 2006—; interim co-chief Cook County Bur. Health, 2006. Mem. Chgo. Bd. Health, 2004—; bd. govs. Inst. Medicine, Chgo., 2003—. Primary Care Policy fellow USPHS, 1993. Fellow: Inst. Medicine Chgo. (bd. govs. 2003—, pres. 2006—, 2006—); mem.: AMA, Am. Med. Women's Assn., Ill. Acad. Family Physicians (bd. dirs. 1987—89, spkr. 1990—91, bd. chair 1990—91, pres.-elect 1991—92, pres. 1992—93), Am. Acad. Family Physicians (alt. del. 1992—95, del. 1996—99, vice-spkr. 1999—2002, spkr. 2002—04). Roman Catholic. Avocations: swimming, cooking. Office: Cook County Hosp Dept Family Practice 1900 W Polk St Chicago IL 60612-3736

LOPEZ, DAVID, lawyer; b. NYC, May 9, 1942; s. Damaso and Carmen (Gonzalez) L.; m. Nancy Mary Cea, Aug. 29, 1964; children: David, Jonathan. AB, Cornell U., 1963; JD, Columbia U., 1966. Bar: N.Y. 1966. Assoc. firm Leon, Weill & Mahoney, NYC, 1966-67, Bressler & Meislen, 1967-70; pvt. practice NYC, 1970—. Chmn. bd. A.T.I. Adv. Svcs., Inc., 1979—; dir. Nancy Lopez, Inc., Southampton, N.Y. Mem. ABA, N.Y. State Bar Assn., Suffolk County Bar Assn., Barrel Hill Conservancy, Inc. Office: 171 Edge of Woods Rd PO Box 323 Southampton NY 11969-0323 Home Phone: 631-287-5520; Office Phone: 631-287-5520. Personal E-mail: davidlopezesq@aol.com.

LOPEZ, DAVID TIBURCIO, lawyer, arbitrator, mediator, educator; b. Laredo, Tex., July 17, 1939; s. Tiburcio and Dora (Davila) L.; m. Romelia G. Guerra, Nov. 20, 1965; 1 child, Vianei López Robinson. Student, Laredo Jr. Coll., 1956-58; BJ, U. Tex., 1962; JD summa cum laude, South Tex. Coll. Law, 1971. Bar: Tex. 1971, US Dist. Ct. (so. dist.) Tex. 1972, US Ct. Appeals (5th cir.) 1973, US Dist. Ct. (we. dist.) Tex. 1975, US Ct. Claims 1975, US Ct. Appeals (fed. cir.) 1975, US Supreme Ct. 1976, US Dist. Ct. (ea. dist.) Tex. 1978, US Dist. Ct. N.Mex. 2000, US Ct. Appeals (11th cir.) 1981, US Ct. Appeals (9th cir.) 1984; cert. internat. com. arbitrator Internat. Ctr. for Arbitration; mediator tng. Atty.-Mediator Inst. Reporter Laredo Times, 1958-59; cons. Mexican Nat. Coll. Mag., Mexico City, 1961-62; reporter Corpus Christi Caller-Times, Tex., 1962-64; state capitol corr. Long News Svc., Austin, Tex., 1964-65; publs. dir. Interam. Regional Orgn. of Workers, Mexico City, 1965-67; nat. field rep. AFL-CIO, Washington, 1967-71, publs. dir. Tex. chpt. Austin, 1971-72; pvt. practice Houston, 1971—. Adj. prof. U. Houston, 1972-74, Thurgood Marshall Sch. Law, Houston, 1975-76; mem. adv. bd. Inst. Transnat. Arbitration; charter mem. Resolution Forum Inc.; mem. adv. bd. Frank Evans Ctr. for Conflict Resolution; mem. nat. panel of neutrals Am. Arbitration Assn. Mem. bd. edn. Houston Ind. Sch. Dist., 1972—75; bd. dirs. Pacifica Found., NYC, 1970—72, Houston CC, 1972—75, FM Radio Sta., 2000—02. With US Army. Recipient Outstanding Trial Lawyer award, Tex. Bar Found., 2007. Mem.: FBA, ABA (steering group Internat. Comml. Dispute Resolution), Indsl. Rels. Rsch. Assn., Am. Judicature Soc., World Assn. Lawyers (chair internat. lab. sect.), Hispanic Bar Assn., US-Mex. Bar Assn., Inter-Pacific Bar Assn., Mex.-Am. Bar Assn., Bar of US Fed. Cir., Interam. Bar Assn., Internat. Bar Assn., Houston Bar Assn., Tex. Bar Assn. (bd. editors bar jour.), Am. Arbitration Assn. (neutral), Phi Alpha Delta, Sigma Delta Chi. Democrat. Roman Catholic. Home: 28 Farnham Ct Houston TX 77024 Office: 3900 Montrose Blvd Houston TX 77006-4959 Office Phone: 713-523-3900. Business E-Mail: dtlopez@lopezlawfirm.com.

LOPEZ, DONALD ROBERT, parochial school educator, writer; b. Glendale, Calif., Aug. 23, 1956; s. Daniel Ruben and Mary Felix Lopez. BA in Econs., UCLA, 1979; tchg. credential, Calif. State U., LA, 2003. Ins. rep. United-Pacific/Reliance Ins., LA, 1980—82; ins. analyst Alexsis Risk Mgmt. Svcs., West Covina, Calif., 1983—97; educator Montebello Christian Sch., Calif., 1997—. Fellow: Nat. Coun. Social Studies, Nat. Coun. Tchrs. Math. Republican. Baptist. Office: Montebello Christian Sch 136 S 7th St Montebello CA 90640 Office Phone: 323-728-4119. Personal E-mail: ddrline@aol.com.

LOPEZ, FILEMON, broadcast executive; b. San Luis Potosi, Mexico; married; 3 children. BA in Radio, TV, Film, Valdosta State Univ., Ga.; MA in Mass Comm., Ea. Ill. Univ.; student TV, Film, Univ. Madrid, Spain. With Cox Cable, Storer Cable Comm.; dir. advt. sales, SE region Comcast Corp., 1990—91, corp. v.p. advt. sales, 1992—95, sr. v.p. corp. advt. sales, 1996—2000, pres., Comcast Univ. Phila., 2000—03, sr. v.p., S. Fla. region Miami, 2003—. Named one of 50 Most Important Hispanics in Tech. & Bus., Hispanic Engr. & Info. Tech. mag., 2005. Office: Comcast 2501 SW 145th Ave Hollywood FL 33027 Office Phone: 954-534-7433.

LOPEZ, GEORGE, actor, comedian; b. Mission Hills, Calif., Apr. 23, 1961; m. Ann Serrano, 1993. Radio show host MEGA 92.3 (KCMG), Los Angeles, 2001; co-founder The George & Ann Lopez-Richie Alarcon Care Found. Actor: (films) Fist of Fear, Tough of Death, 1980, Ski Patrol, 1990, Fatal Instinct, 1993, Bread and Roses, 2000, Real Women Have Curves, 2002, Outta Time, 2002, Ali G In Da House, 2002, Balls of Fury, 2007; appearances (TV specials) Latino Laugh Festival, 1997, 2nd Annual Latino Laugh Festival, 1998, host Loco Comedy Jam, 4th Annual Latin Grammy Awards, 2003, 5th Annual Latin Grammy Awards, 2004, correspondent (TV series) Inside the NFL, HBO, 2003—; actor: (TV miniseries) Fidel, 2002; actor, co-creator, writer, prodr. George Lopez, 2002—07, comedian (headliner) ARCO Arena, Sacramento, Shoreline Amphitheater, San Francisco, Majestic Theatre, Dallas, San Antonio, Wiltern Theatre, Los Angeles, HBO US Comedy Arts Festival, Aspen; performer: (live comedy albums) Team Leader, 2003 (Grammy nom. best comedy album, 2003), Right Now Right Now, 2004; author: Why You Crying?: My Long, Hard Look at Life, Love, and Laughter, 2004. Spokesperson Stop the Violence program, Los Angeles Police Dept. Named one of 25 Most Influential Hispanics, Time Mag., 2005; recipient Nat. Hispanic Media Coalition Impact award, Community Spirit award, Manny Mota Found., Artist of the Yr. award, Harvard Found. for Intercultural & Race Relations, 2004. Achievements include first Latino to headline a morning radio show on an English-language station in Los Angeles. Office: c/o Ron DeBlasio SDM Inc 740 N La Brea Ave Los Angeles CA 90039

LOPEZ, JAVIER, psychiatrist; b. Jackson Heights, NY, June 17, 1978; s. Joaquin and Maria Isabel Lopez. BA in Chemistry summa cum laude, NYU, NYC, 2000, MD, 2004. Resident in psychiatry Yale U. Sch. Medicine, New Haven, 2004—. Mem. exec. bd. Dean's Svc. Honor Corps. Recipient Hema Sakhrani Meml. award in chemistry, NYU, Harold Seidenstein award in chemistry, George Granger Brown scholarship, Hossein Jafari Meml. award, Sherborne Vernon Damerel Meml. award, N.Y. U.; Baird MacCracken scholar, Stanley Rsch. fellowship. Mem.: Yale Psychiatry Residents Assn. (co-pres. 2005—06), Am. Psychiat. Assn., Lesbian, Gay, Bisexual, Transgender People in Medicine (v.p. NYU chpt. 2001—02), Gay and Lesbian Med. Assn., Phi Beta Kappa, Phi Lambda Upsilon (pres. 1999—2000). Avocations: swimming, travel, skiing, theater, art. Home: 44 Orange St # 718 New Haven CT 06510

LOPEZ, JENNIFER, actress, singer, dancer; b. Bronx, NY, July 24, 1970; d. David and Guadalupe Lopez; m. Ojani Noa, Feb. 22, 1997 (div. Jan. 1, 1998); m. Cris Judd, Sept. 29, 2001 (div. Jan. 26, 2003); m. Marc Anthony, June 5, 2004. Launched clothing line J-Lo by Jennifer Lopez, 2001, lingerie line, 2004; released signature fragrance Glow, 2002, Still, 2004, Miami Glow, 2005, Live Jennifer Lopez, 2005, Love at First Glow, 2006; owner Madre's restaurant, Pasedena, 2002-. Won dance competition and was hired as dancer for TV series In Living Color, 1991-93; actress (TV series) Second Chances, 1993-94, South Central, 1994, Hotel Malibu, 1994; actress (films) Money Train, 1995, Jack, 1996, Blood and Wine, 1996, Anaconda, 1997 (ALMA award 1998), Selena, 1997 (ALMA award 1998), My Family, 1995, U-Turn, 1997, Antz (voice only), 1998, Out of Sight, 1998 (ALMA award 1999), Thieves, 1999, Pluto Nash, 1999, The Cell, 2000 (Blockbuster Entertainment award for Favorite Actress, MTV Movie award for Best Dressed), The Wedding Planner, 2001, Angel Eyes, 2001, Enough, 2002, Maid in Manhattan, 2002, Gigli, 2003, Jersey Girl, 2004, Shall We Dance?, 2004, Monster-in-Law, 2005, An Unfinished Life, 2005, El Cantante, 2006; (TV appearances) Will & Grace, 2004; singer (albums) On the 6, 1999, J.Lo, 2001, J to Tha L-O!: The Remixes, 2002, This Is Me...Then, 2002, Rebirth, 2005, Como Ama Una Mujer (How a Women Loves), 2007, Brave, 2007. Recipient ALMA Female Entertainer Yr. award 2000, Lasting Image award 1998, Lone Star Film and TV award 1998, Artists for Amnesty award Amnesty Internat., 2007; named one of 50 Most Beautiful People in the World, People mag., 1997; voted #1 in 100 Sexiest Women list, FHM, 2000, 2001; named one of 25 Most Influential Hispanics, Time Mag., 2005, 100 Most Influential Hispanics, People en Espanol, 2007 Office: c/o Simon Fields Nyuorican Prodns 1100 Glendon Ave Ste 920 Los Angeles CA 90024 also: Internat Creative Mgmt c/o Jeff Berg or Ed Limato 10250 Constellation Blvd Los Angeles CA 90067

LOPEZ, LINDA CAROL, social sciences educator; b. NYC, Dec. 26, 1949; d. Ralph B. and M. Lopez. BA, U. Wis., Madison, 1972; MA, Ohio State U., Columbus, 1974, PhD, 1976. Vis. asst. prof. U. Wis., Eau Claire, 1976-77; from instr. to asst. prof. SUNY, Oneonta, 1977-83; assoc. prof. Rockford (Ill.) Coll., 1983—89; prof. dept. social scis. Western N.Mex U., Silver City, 1989—, dir. field experience, 1989—91. Contbr. (to profl. jours. articles) including Psychol. Reports, Internat. Jour. Addiction, Hispanic Jour. Behavioral Scis., Jour. Genetic Psychology, Jour. Employment Counseling, Perceptual and Motor Skills, Reading Improvement, Counseling and Values, Social Studies. Recipient Best Paper award, New Eng. Ednl. Rsch. Orgn., 1979; Postdoctoral Faculty fellow, Northeastern U., Boston, 1980—81. Mem.: Ill. Psychol. Assn., Nat. Assn. Hispanic and Latino Studies. Avocations: walking, reading, travel. Home: PO Box 1479 Bayard NM 88023 Office: Western NMex U Dept Social Scis 1000 W College Ave Silver City NM 88062 Business E-Mail: lopezl@wnmu.edu.

LOPEZ, MANDI J., veterinarian, scientist; BS magna cum laude, Humboldt State U., Arcata, Calif., 1988; DVM, U. Calif., Davis, 1993; MS, U. of Wis., Madison, 1997; PhD, U. Wis., Madison, 2001. Diplomate Am. Coll. of Vet. Surgeons, 1999. Rsch. asst. Amgen, Thousand Oaks, Calif., 1988—89, rsch. assoc., 1989; large animal technician U. Calif., Davis, 1990—92; food animal medicine and surgery intern Kans. State U., Manhattan, Kans., 1993—94; large animal surgery resident U. Wis., Madison, 1994—97, rsch. assoc., 1997—98, clin. instr., 1998—99, grad. rsch. asst., 1998—2001, asst. scientist, post-doctoral fellow, 2001—04; asst. prof., dir. lab. for equine and comparative orthop. rsch. La. State U., Baton Rouge, 1994—; adj. faculty Madison Area Tech. Coll., Madison, 2002. Equine cons. Madison Area Tech. Coll., Madison, Wis., 1999—2002. Charitable donator La. Art. Sci. Mus., Recreation and Park Commn. Parish East Baton Rouge, USS Kidd Vets. Meml. Mus., Baton Rouge Zoo, Baton Rouge Recreation; vol. Trinity Epsic. Day Sch., Baton Rouge, 2004—06; vol. veterinarian for Hurricane Katrina animal shelter La. State U., Baton Rouge, 2005. Recipient Travel award, Arthritis Found., 2001, 2003, Achievement awards for Coll. Scientists, U. Calif. Davis, 1991, Achievement Award for Coll. Scientists, U. Calif., Davis, 1990, Marsh Outstanding Grad. Student award, U. Wis. Madison, 2001; fellow, Morris Animal Found., 2002; grantee Basic Rsch. award, 2001—03, Mentored Rsch. Scientist award, NIH, 2001—06, Vet. Clin. Sci. Corp grantee, Dept. of Vet. Clin. Sci., LSU Sch. of Vet. Medicine, 2004—05; Resident in Tng. Rsch. grantee, Am. Coll. Vet. Surgeons, 1996—97, Am. Assn. Equine Practitioners, 1996—97, Companion Animal grantee, U. Wis. Sch. Vet. Medicine, 1996—2000, Individual Nat. grantee, NIH, 1998—2001, Orthop. Rsch. grantee, Vet. Orthop. Soc., 2000—01, Companion Animal grantee, U. Wis. Sch. Vet. Medicine, 2003—04, Diplomate Rsch. grantee, Am. Coll. Vet. Surgeons, 2003—05, Acad. Staff Profl. Devel. grantee, U. of Wis. Madison, 2003, ACORN grantee, Am. Kennel Club, 2004—05, Vet. Clin. Sci. Corp grantee, Dept. of Vet. Clin. Sci. LSU Sch. of Vet. Medicine, 2004—05, La. State U. Equine Health Studies Program, 2005—06, Faculty Travel grantee, La. State U., 2005, Small Bus. Tech. Transfer Program grantee, NIH, 2005—06, Vilas Travel fellow, U. Wis., 2001, George B. Hart scholar, U. Calif. Davis, 1991. Mem.: Am. Coll. Vet. Surgeons (pubs. com. mem. 2000—03, editl. rev. bd. 2000—06, rsch. com. mem. 2003—06), Vet. Orthop. Soc., Orthop. Rsch. Soc., AVMA (editl. rev. bd. 2004—06), Phi Zeta. Achievements include patents pending for DGY2000 - Device to measure stability of dog knee. Avocations: horseback riding, gardening. Office: LSU School of Veterinary Medicine Skip Bertman Dr Baton Rouge LA 70803

LOPEZ, MANUEL, immunology and allergy educator; b. Bucaramanga, Colombia, Sept. 30, 1939; came to U.S., 1964. married; 4 children. BS, Colegio San Pedro Claver, Bucaramanga, 1956; MD, Univ. Javeriana, Bogota, Colombia, 1963. Diplomate Am. Bd. Allergy and Immunology, Am. Bd. Diagnostic Lab. Immunology. Intern Hosp. San Juan De Dios, Bucaramanga, 1962-63, resident, 1963-64, med. dir., 1969-71; clin. and rsch. fellow dept. medicine allergy unit Harvard U. and Harvard Med. Sch. at Mass. Gen. Hosp., Boston, 1964-68; dir. med. rsch. Univ. Indsl. De Santander, Bucaramanga, 1968-69; dir. immunology svc. lab. La. State Med. Ctr., New Orleans, 1971-74; asst. prof. medicine med. ctr. La. State U., New Orleans, 1971-74; from clin. asst. prof. to assoc. prof. med. sch. Tulane U., New Orleans, 1974-89, prof., 1989—, dir. immunology diagnostic lab. med. sch., 1974-83, dir. clin. immunology labs., 1983—99, program dir. allergy and immunology tng. program, 1990—98, acting chief sect. allergy and clin. immunology, 1990-91, chief sect. clin. immunology, allergy & rheumatology, 1991—. Mem. med.-sci. adv. com. Asthma and Allergy Found. Am., 1986-89; ad hoc mem. immunological sci. study sect. NIH, 1987, allergy and clin. immunology spl. reviewer immunology and transplantation rsch. com., 1988, mem. gen. clin. rsch. ctrs. com., 1993-94; reviewer merit rev. grants VA, 1988, 89, 90; grant program reviewer Ctrs. of Excellence, Dept. Health and Human Svcs., 1991; mem. allergic products adv. com. FDA, 1993-96; mem. spl. rev. com. Nat. Inst. Allergy and Infectious Diseases, 1993; presenter in field. Mem. editl. bd. Jour. Allergy and Clin. Immunology, 1986-94, reviewer, 1987—; mem. editl. bd. Annals of Allergy, 1998—2003; contbr. articles to profl. jours. and chpts. to books. Fellow John Simmon Guggenheim Meml. Found., 1964-66. Fellow Am. Acad. Allergy and Clin. Immunology (mem. internat. com. 1986-89, mem. immunotherapy of asthma com. 1987-88, mem. Latin Ctrl. and South Am. com. 1987—, chmn. internat. grant aids 1988-89, mem. continuing med. edn. com. 1992-94, chmn. EOD interest sect. 1999-01); mem. Am. Assn. Immunologists, Am. Fedn. Clin. Rsch., Am. Thoracic Soc., U.S.-Colombian Med. Assn. (pres. IX Congress 1989), La. Allergy Soc. (pres. 2003-04), N.Y. Acad. Scis., Southeastern Allergy Assn., Internat. Assn. Aerobiology, Cordoba Allergy Soc. (hon.), Hispanic Am. Med. Assn. La. (pres. 2001-03). Office: Tulane U Med Sch Clin Immunology Sect 1700 Perdido St SL-57 New Orleans LA 70112-1210

LOPEZ, MARTIN, III, lawyer; b. Las Cruces, N.Mex., June 20, 1954; s. Abenicio Rafael and Angelina Cordelia (Griego) L.; m. Elizabeth Crawford, Aug. 5, 1978; children: Alisa Angelina Maria, Martin IV. BA, U. N.Mex., 1976; JD, George Washington U., 1979; MPA, U. N.Mex., 1982, MBA, 1989. Bar: N.Mex. 1979, U.S. Dist. Ct. N.Mex. 1980, U.S. Ct. Appeals (10th cir.) 1981, U.S. Supreme Ct. 1982, U.S. Ct. Claims 1983, U.S. Tax Ct. 1984, D.C. 1985, U.S. Ct. Appeals (4th and 9th cirs.) 1996. Legal intern property tax dept. State of N.Mex., Santa Fe, 1977; legal intern Pub. Defender Svc., Washington, 1977-78, EEOC, Washington, 1978-79; asst. pub. defender State of N.Mex., Albuquerque, 1979-82, asst. atty. gen., 1982-84; ptnr., dir. firm Lopez & Lopez, P.C., Albuquerque, 1984-86; ptnr. Lopez, Lopez & Jaffe, P.C., Albuquerque, 1986-87; pvt. practice Albuquerque, 1988—. Mem. N.Mex. Bar Examiners, 1998—. Past pres. Alternative House, Inc.; past pres., St. Mary's Sch. Bd., 1990-97; v.p., pres. St. Pius X H.S. adv. sch. bd., 1999—; mem. coun. Holy Rosary Parish, 1991-98; mem. citizens' adv. group City of Albuquerque, 1992-94; grad. Leadership Albuquerque, 1994. Recipient Alumni award U. N.Mex., 1972. Mem. ABA, ATLA, N.Mex. Criminal Def. Lawyer's Assn., N.Mex. State Bar Assn., N.Mex. Hispanic Bar Assn., N.Mex. Trial Lawyers Assn., Albuquerque Hispano C. of C., Greater Albuquerque C. of C., Albuquerque Jaycees, Socorro County C. of C., Phi Alpha Theta, Pi Alpha Alpha, Phi Alpha Delta. Democrat. Roman Catholic. Home: 6124 Carousal Ave NW Albuquerque NM 87120-2171 Office: 1500 Mountain Rd NW Albuquerque NM 87104-1359 Office Phone: 505-243-2900. Personal E-mail: ML3law@aol.com.

LOPEZ, NANCY, retired professional golfer; b. Torrance, Calif., Jan. 6, 1957; d. Domingo and Marina (Griego) Lopez; m. Ray Knight, Oct. 25, 1982; children: Ashley Marie Knight, Erinn Shea Knight, Torri Heather Knight. Student, U. Tulsa, 1976-78. Founder, prin. Nancy Lopez Golf Co., 1997—. Player U.S.A. Solheim Cup, 1990. Author: The Education of a Woman Golfer, 1979. Named first victory winner, Bent Tree Classic, Sarasota, Fla., 1978, AP Athlete, 1978, Rolex Rookie of the Yr., 1978, Rolex Player of the Yr., 1978, 1979, 1985, winner, LPGA Championship, 1978, 1985, Mazda LPGA Championship, 1989, others; named to LPGA Hall of Fame, 1987, PGA World Golf Hall of Fame, 1989; recipient Vare Trophy, 1978. Mem.: LPGA (Player and Rookie of the Yr. 1978). Republican. Achievements include winning 48 LPGA Tour events, 3 maj. championships. Office: care Internat Mgmt Group 1360 E 9th St Ste 100 Cleveland OH 44114-1715

LOPEZ, PERNILLE See SPIERS-LOPEZ, PERNILLE

LOPEZ, PLACIDA RAMOS, elementary school educator; b. Stafford, Tex., Oct. 11, 1944; d. Urbano Zapata Ramos and Josefina (Saldaña) Arias; m. Jose Jesus Lopez Sr., Aug. 26, 1969 (dec.); 1 child, Gabriel Elizalde. Student, Victoria Coll., Tex., 1964—66, Our Lady of Lake U., San Antonio, 1967—68; BA Elem. Edn., Dominican Coll., Houston, 1975; postgrad., U. St. Thomas, 1987. Tchr. 3d grade, coach volleyball Our Lady of Guadalupe Parochial Sch., Houston, 1966—73; bilingual tchr. Pasadena Ind. Sch. Dist., Tex., 1972—82; tchr. 1st grade Alvin Ind. Sch. Dist., Tex., 1984—89, tchr. 5th grade, 1989—94, bilingual tchr., 1994—2004; ret., 2004. Bilingual cons. Alvin Ind. Sch. Dist., 2005—06. Mem. Tex. Bilingual Textbook com. Pasadena Ind. Sch. Dist.; transl. Cmty. and Parish Members; coun. La Raza Southern Poverty Law Ctr. Recipient Tchr. of Year, 1990. Mem.: PTA, NEA, Houston Assn. Bilingual Edn., Alvin Tchrs. Assn., Pasadena Tchrs. Assn., Classroom Tchrs. Assn., Bay Area Reading Coun., Tex. Assn. Bilingual Edn., Tex. State Tchrs. Assn., Nat. Assn. Bilingual Edn., Parent Tchr. Orgn., Tex. Ret. Tchrs. Assn. Avocations: singing, writing. Home: 9540 Ruth Rd Rosharon TX 77583

LOPEZ, RALPH IVAN, pediatrics educator; b. San Juan, Jan. 3, 1942; s. Ralph and Aida (Miranda) L.; m. Paula, July 30, 1964; 1 child, Abigail AB cum laude, Fordham Coll., 1963; MD, NYU, 1967. Intern pediatrics NYU Bellevue Hosp., NYC, 1967-68, resident pediatrics, 1968-69, Boston Children's Hosp., Harvard Med. Ctr., 1969-70; asst. prof. pediatrics N.Y. Hosp., NYC, 1973-79, assoc. prof. pediatrics, 1979-83, clin. assoc. prof. pediatrics, 1983—2007; clin. prof. pediatrics O'Neill Med. Coll., Cornell U., 2007—. Cons. physician Dalton Sch., NYC, 1973-86, Nightingale Bamford, NYC, 1986-90. Editor: Adolescent Medicine Topics, 1976, 2d edit. 1980; author: The Teen Health Book, 2002; contbr. articles to profl. jours. Bd. dirs. Louis August Jones Found., Rhinebeck, NJ, 1973-91, chmn. bd. dirs., 1990—; bd. dirs. Covenant House, NYC, 1990-92; chmn. Ind. Doctors of NY; nominating com. Girl Scouts U.S., NYC, 1991. Lt. comdr. USNR, 1971-73 Mem. Phi Beta Kappa. Office: 418 E 71st St New York NY 10021-4894 Office Phone: 212-772-8989.

LOPEZ, SOLEDAD, actress; d. Primitivo Lopez and Mariana Hernandez; m. Angel Gil Orrios, Feb. 22, 1980; children: Sebastian Gil-Lopez, Mariana Gil-Lopez. Cert. acting The Real Stage, Ny, 1985. Actor: (plays) Jaime Salom's Almost a Goddess (Best Actress award, ACE, 2005), Renaldo Ferradas' La Visionaria, Alegre Cudos' Verde Doncella Asalta Un Cine, Don Juan Por Los Siglos De Los Siglos (Best Actress award, Golden Age Festival, El Paso, 1989), Alegre Cudos' La Madre Que Te Pario, Calderon de la Barca's The Purgatory of Saint Patrick, Garcia Lorca's The Audience & Play Without A Title, Almodovar/Cabal's Dark Habits, Sartre's No Exit, Espriu's Piel de Toro, La Pasion De Cristo, Ramos Perea's We Women Do It Better (Best Actress award, ACE and Hola, 2004), Tiempo Del 98, Santiago Moncada's Caprichos, Carlos Fuentes' The One-eyed Man Is King, Jardiel Poncela's Brake Four Hearts, Picasso's Guernica, Calderon de la Barca's The Great Theatre of the World (Best Actress award, Hola, 2001), Miguel Sierra's Palomas Intrepidas (Best Actress award, ACE, 1996), Santiago Moncada's Entre Mujeres (Best Actress award, ACE, 1995), Martin Descalzo's Las Prostitutas Os Precederan en el Reino de los Cielos (Best Actress award, ACE, 1994). Recipient

Vermeil medal, French Acad. Arts, Scis. and Letters, Paris, 2005. Mem.: Hispanic Orgn. Latin Actors (Best Actress award 2001, 2003). Home Phone: 718-786-5632. Personal E-mail: soledad@thaliatheatre.org.

LOPEZ, STEVE, journalist; married; 2 children. With Oakland (Calif.) Tribune, San Jose (Calif.) Mercury News; reporter, columnist Phila. Inquirer, 1986—98, Time Inc., 1998—2001; reporter, Points West columnist LA Times, 2001—. Author: Land of Giants: Where No Good Deed Goes Unpunished, 1995, (novels) Third & Indiana, 1994, The Sunday Macaroni Club, 1997, In the Clear, 2002. Recipient Ernie Pyle Lifetime Achievement award, Nat. Soc. Newspaper Columnists, 2004, Media award, Nat. Alliance on Mental Illness, 2006, Nat. Journalism award for commentary, Scripps Howard Found., 2006, Ernie Pyle award for human interest writing, Nat. Headliner award for column writing, H.L. Mencken Writing award. Office: LA Times 202 W 1st St Los Angeles CA 90012 Office Phone: 213-237-7847. Office Fax: 213-237-4712. E-mail: steve.lopez@latimes.com.

LOPEZ-ALEGRIA, MICHAEL ELADIO, astronaut; b. Madrid, May 30, 1958; s. Eladio and Louise Lopez-Alegria; m. Daria Robinson; 1 child. BS in Systems Engring., U.S. Naval Acad., 1980; MS in Aeronautical Engring., U.S. Naval Postgrad. Sch., 1988; grad. Sr. Execs. in Nat. and Internat. Security Program, Harvard U. Commd. ensign USN, 1980, advanced through grades to capt.; flight instr. Pensacola, Fla., 1981—83; pilot, mission comdr.; engring. test pilot, program mgr. Naval Air Test Ctr., Patuxent River, Md.; astronaut NASA, Houston, 1992—, with Astronaut Office, crew rep. Kennedy Space Ctr., dir. ops. Yuri Gagarin Cosmonaut Tng. Ctr., Star City, Russia, head ISS Crew Ops. br. of Astronaut Office. Capt. astronaut USAAF, NASA Johnson Space Ctr/ Houston, TX. Mem.: Assn. Naval Aviation and Assn. of Space Explorers, Soc. Exptl. Test Pilots. logged over 4,500 flight hours in over 30 different types of aircraft; logged over 42 days in space; flight engr. STS-73 Columbia (1995); crew STS-92 Discovery (2000); crew STS-113 Endeavour, 2002; assigned to command Expedition-14 and will serve as the NASA station science officer and spacewalker aboard the International Space Station. Expedition-14 is scheduled for launch aboard a Russian Soyuz TMA-9 spacecraft in September 2006; In February, 2007, sets U.S. record of most time walking in space (61 hours and 22 minutes) and also marked the first time three spacewalks have been conducted in such a short period without a space shuttle docked to it on Expedition-14 mission; performed spacewalk to repair antenna on Russian cargo ship, 2007; set U.S. record for most time living and working in space, breaking the previous record of 196 days, 2007. Office: Astronaut Office/CB NASA Johnson Space Ctr Houston TX 77058*

LOPEZ-BAUTISTA, JUAN MANUEL, biology professor, research scientist; arrived in US, 1992; s. Manuel Lopez-Tamez and Esther Bautista-Ortega. Degree, U. Nuevo Leon, Monterey, Mex., 1980; PhD, La. State U., BAton Rouge, 2000. Prof. U. NE, Tampico, Mexico, 1981—86, Tech. Inst., Victoria City, Mexico, 1986—92; postdoctoral rschr. U. Ala., Lafayette, 2000—03, asst. prof. Tuscaloosa, 2003—. Dir. biology dept. U. NE, 1981—86, Tech. Inst., 1989—92; algal curator U. Ala., 2003—, marine sci. co-advisor, 2003—; faculty ad honorem U. PR, Mayaguez, 2003—. Contbr. articles to profl. jours. Named Edn. Fellow Mentor in Life Sciences, Nat. Academies, 2005—06; grantee, Miss.-Ala. Sea Grant Program, 2004—05, Mobile Bay Nat. Estuary Program, 2004—05, NSF, 2004, 2006—. Mem.: Phycological Soc. Mex. (founding mem.), Internat. Phycological Soc., Phycological Soc. Am. Achievements include discovery of new species; expeditionary work in Africa and the Amazonian rainforests; research in molecular systematics, phylogeny, and biodiversity of algae; development of courses in introductory biology and biology of algae. Office: U Ala 500 Hackberry Ln 425 SCF Tuscaloosa AL 35487 Office Phone: 205-348-1791. Office Fax: 205-348-6460. Business E-Mail: jlopez@ua.edu.

LÓPEZ-MORILLAS, FRANCES (MAPES), translator; b. Fulton, Mo., Sept. 3, 1918; d. Erwin Kempton and Laura (Hinkhouse) Mapes; m. Juan López-Morillas, Aug. 12, 1937; children: Martin Morell, Consuelo, Julian. BA, U. Iowa, 1939, MA, 1940. Translator Collins Radio Co., Cedar Rapids, Iowa, 1940-43; tchr. Spanish Lincoln Sch., Providence, 1943-44; tchr. French and Spanish Mary C. Wheeler Sch., Providence, 1951-64; tchr. ESL Internat. Inst., Madrid, 1957-58; freelance translator, 1964—. Editor (with E. K. Mapes): J. J. Fernandez de Lizardi, El Periquillo Sarmiento, 1952; translator: 25 books and numerous articles, Journey to the Alcarria: Travels through the Spanish Countryside, 1964, Miguel de Unamuno, 1966, An Economic History of Spain, 1969, Spain in the Fifteenth Century, 1971, Tales of Potosí, 1975, The Krausist Movement and Ideological Change in Spain, 1981, Torquemada, 1986, Understanding Spain, 1990, The Medieval Heritage of Mexico, 1992, Castaways: The Narrative of Álvar Núñez Cabeza de Vaca, 1993, Selected Writings of Andrés Bello, 1997, Natural and Moral History of the Indies, 2002. Recipient Transl. prize, Tex. Inst. Letters, 1991; grantee, NEH, 1984, NEA, 1986. Mem.: Am. Lit. Translators Assn., Internat. Assn. Hispanists, Phi Beta Kappa. Home: 355 Blackstone Blvd Providence RI 02906-4946 Personal E-mail: fmorillas@aol.com.

LOPEZ-MURPHY, RICARDO HIPOLITO, economist; b. Buenos Aires, Aug. 10, 1951; s. Juan Jose Lopez-Aguirre and Brigida Murphy; m. Norma Ruiz Huidobro; children: Pablo, Analia, Ezequiel. MA, U. Chgo., 1980. Prof. U. La. Plata (Argentina), 1975—; cons. IMF, Buenos Aires, 1984-88; chief economist, rsch. economist FIEL, Buenos Aires, 1990—; min. of defense Govt. of Argentina, Buenos Aires, 2000-01, min. of economy, 2001—; Presdl. candidate, 2003. Mem. Assn. Argentina Economics. (sec. 1995). Roman Catholic. Office: FIEL Cordoba 637 Fl 40 1054 Buenos Aires Argentina Office Phone: 5411 4314 1990. E-mail: ricardo@fiel.org.ar.

LOPEZ NEGRETE, KARIANN MAY, psychologist; b. Reed City, Mich., Apr. 10, 1978; d. Nolan Dwayne Pritchard and Gloria May VanBurgel, adopted d. William John VanBurgel; m. Carlos Manuel Lopez Negrete, May 24, 2003; 1 child, Esperanza Maya. BA in Psychology, Albion Coll., Mich., 2000. Cert. ednl. specialist in sch. psychology Mich. State U., 2004. Sch. psychologist Calhoun Intermediate Sch. Dist., Marshall, Mich., 2004—05, Flushing Cmty. Schs., Mich., 2005—. Mem.: Mich. Assn. Sch. Psychologists, Nat. Assn. Sch. Psychologists. Avocations: travel, gardening, golf. Office: Flushing Cmty Schs 522 N McKinley Rd Flushing MI 48433 Home Phone: 517-303-1378; Office Phone: 810-591-2323. Business E-Mail: kariann.lopeznegrete@flushing.k12.mi.us.

LOPICCOLO, JOSEPH, psychologist, educator, author; b. LA, Sept. 13, 1943; s. Joseph E. and Adeline C. (Russo) Lo P.; m. Leslie Joan Matlen, June 20, 1964 (div. 1978); 1 child, Joseph Townsend; m. Cathryn Gail Pridal, Dec. 20, 1980; 1 child, Michael James. BA with highest honors, UCLA, 1965; MS, Yale U., 1968, PhD, 1969. Lic. psychologist, Mo. Asst. prof. U. Oreg., Eugene, 1969-73; assoc. prof. U. Houston, 1973-74; prof. SUNY, Stony Brook, 1974-84, Tex. A&M U., College Station, 1984-87; prof. psychology U. Mo., Columbia, 1987—, chmn. dept., 1987-90. Vis. scholar Cambridge (Eng.) U., 1991. Author: Becoming Orgasmic, 1976, 2d edit., 1988, also book chpts.; editor: Handbook of Sex Therapy, 1978; contbr. numerous articles to profl. jours. Woodrow Wilson Found. fellow; NIH rsch. grantee, 1973-84 Fellow Am. Psychol. Assn.; mem. Internat. Acad. Sex Rsch., Soc. for Sci. Study of Sex (pres. 1983-84, Alfred Kinsey Meml. Rsch. award), Soc. for Sex Therapy and Rsch. (Masters and Johnson Rsch. award 1997), Phi Beta Kappa, Sigma Xi. Office: U Mo Dept Psychology 210 McAlester Hall Columbia MO 65211-2500 Office Phone: 573-882-7752. Business E-Mail: LoPiccoloJ@missouri.edu.

LOPPNOW, MILO ALVIN, clergyman, former church official; b. St. Charles, Minn., Jan. 13, 1914; s. William and Doretta (Penz) L.; m. Gertrude Stoltz, Feb. 6, 1942; children— Donald, Bruce, David. BA, Moravian Coll., 1937; M.Div., Moravian Theol. Sem., 1940, D.D., 1970. Ordained to ministry Moravian Ch. in Am., 1940; pastor congregations nr. Wisconsin Rapids, Wis., 1940-41, Waconia, Minn., 1941-53, Lakeview Ch., Madison, Wis., 1953-64; dist. pres. Western Dist. Moravian Ch., Madison, 1965-78; elected bishop, 1970. Chmn. Youth Commn., Madison, 1957-63; Trustee Moravian Coll., 1954-78, Moravian Theol. Sem., Bethlehem, Pa.; former chaplain, dir. devel. Marquardt Meml. Manor, Watertown, Wis. Mem. Moravian Ch. E-mail: malopp@gdinet.com.

LOPREATO, JOSEPH, evolutionary sociologist, writer; b. Stefanaconi, Italy, July 13, 1928; arrived in US, 1951; s. Frank and Marianna (Pavone) L.; m. Carolyn H. Prestopino, July 18, 1954; (div. 1971); children: Gregory F., Marisa S. Schmidt; m. Sally A. Cook, Aug. 24, 1972 (div. 1978). BA in Sociology and Anthropology, U. Conn., Storrs, 1956; MA in Sociology, Yale U., New Haven, Conn., 1957, PhD in Sociology, 1960. Asst. prof. sociology U. Mass., Amherst, 1960-62; vis. lectr. U. Rome, 1962-64; assoc. prof. U. Conn., Storrs, 1964-66; prof. sociology U. Tex., Austin, 1966-98, chmn. dept. sociology, 1969-72. Vis. prof. U. Catania, Italy, 1974, U. Calabria, Italy, 1980; steering com. Council European Studies, Columbia U., 1977-80; chmn. sociology com. Council for Internat. Exchange Scholars, 1977-79; mem. Internat. Com. Mezzogiorno, 1986-88; Calabria Internat. Com., 1988-90. Author: Italian Made Simple, 1959, Vilfredo Pareto, 1965, Peasants No More, 1967, Italian Americans, 1970, Class, Conflict and Mobility, 1972, Social Stratification, 1974, The Sociology of Vilfredo Pareto, 1975, La Stratificazione Sociale negli Stati Uniti, 1945-1975, 1977, Human Nature and Biocultural Evolution, 1984, Evoluzione e Natura Umana, 1990, Mai Più Contadini, 1990, Crisis in Sociology: The Need for Darwin, 1999; contbr. articles to profl. jours. Mem. Nat. Italian-Am. Com. for U.S.A. Bicentennial; mem. exec. com. Congress Italian Politics, 1977-80. Served to cpl. U.S. Army, 1952-54. Fulbright faculty research fellow, 1962-64, 73-74; Social Sci. Research Council faculty research fellow, 1963-64; NSF faculty research fellow, 1965-68; U. Tex. Austin research fellow, 1973-74, spring 1985, spring 1993; Guido Dorso award for U.S.A., Italy, 1992. Mem.: AAAS (behavioral sci. rsch. prize com. 1992—94), Internat. Soc. Human Ethology, Evolution and Behavior Soc., Internat. Sociol. Assn. Catholic-Episcopalian. Home and Office: 115 Yellowstone Rd Georgetown TX 78633 Office Phone: 512-869-8479. Personal E-mail: jlopreato@suddenlink.net.

LOPRETE, JAMES HUGH, lawyer; b. Detroit, Sept. 17, 1929; s. James Victor and Effie Hannah (Brown) LoP.; m. Marion Ann Garrison, Sept. 11, 1952; children: James Scott, Kimberly Anne, Kent Garrison, Robert Drew. AB, U. Mich., 1951, JD with distinction, 1953. Bar: Mich. 1954. Practiced law, Detroit, 1954—; atty. Chrysler Corp., Detroit, 1953; assoc. Monaghan, LoPrete, McDonald, Yakima, Grenke & McCarthy, P.C. and predecessor firms, Detroit, 1954, mem. firm, 1966—2001, pres., 1979—2001. Bd. dirs. Drake's Batter Mix Co.; instr. legal writing Wayne State U., Detroit, 1955-57. Trustee scholarship fund U. Mich. Club of Detroit, 1961, pres., 1982—; trustee Samuel Westerman Found., 1971—, pres., 1984; trustee John R. and M. Margrite Davis Found.; pres., dir. Louis and Nellie Sieg Found., 2000—, Frank G. and Gertrude Dunlap Found., 2001— Named Disting. Alumnus, U. Mich. Club, Detroit. Fellow Am. Coll. Trust and Estate Counsel (litig. com. 1997-, state chair 2006-), Internat. Acad. Estate and Trust Law; mem. ABA, Oakland County Bar Assn., State Bar Mich. (chmn. probate and estate planning sect. 1977), Detroit Athletic Club (dir. 1983-88, sec. 1986-88), Orchard Lake Country Club, U. Mich. of Greater Detroit (pres. 1966). Avocations: travel, sailing, swimming. Home: 2829 Warner Dr Orchard Lake MI 48324-2449 Office: Monaghan LoPrete McDonald et al 40700 Woodward Ave Ste A Bloomfield Hills MI 48304-5110 Office Phone: 248-642-5770. Business E-Mail: bqasawa@monaghanpc.com.

LOPRIORE, RICHARD P., utilities executive; BS, So. Vt. Coll., Bennington. Electrician New Eng. Power Svc. Co.; maintenance mgr. Vt. Yankee; various mgmt. positions including plant mgr. Brunswick Nuc. Plant, NC; various sr. leadership positions Ont. Hydro Nuc.; plant mgr. Byron Sta. Exelon, 1999—2001, v.p. Byron Sta., 2001—03, corp. v.p. ops. support, 2003—04, v.p. ops. Midwest boiling water reactors, 2004; sr. v.p. Mid-Atlantic ops. Exelon Nuc.; pres. PSEG Fossil, 2007—. Mem.: Am. Nuc. Soc. Office: PSEG PO Box 570 Newark NJ 07101 Office Phone: 973-430-7000.*

LORANGER, STEVEN R., industrial manufacturing company executive; BA, MA, Colo. U. Sales mgr. mil. power sys. Garret Turbine Engine Co., 1984—87; v.p. comml. aux. power AlliedSignal Inc., pres. Bendix Truck Brake Group, pres., CEO AlliedSignal Engines; pres., CEO engines, systems and svcs. Honeywell Internat. Inc., 1999—2002; exec. v.p., COO Textron, Inc., 2002—04; chmn., pres., CEO ITT Corp., White Plains, NY, 2004—. Bd. dir. Nat. Air and Space Mus. With USN, 1975—81. Mem.: Congl. Medal of Honor Bd., Nat. Assn. Mfrs., Aerospace Industries Assn., Phi Beta Kappa. Office: ITT Corp Four West Red Oak Ln White Plains NY 10604*

LORBER, BARBARA HEYMAN, communications executive, event producer; b. NYC; d. David Benjamin and Gertrude (Meyer) Heyman. AB in Polit. Sci., Skidmore Coll.; MA, postgrad., Columbia U. Asst. dir. young citizens divsn. Dem. Party; exec. asst. to dean Albert Einstein Coll. Medicine, Bronx, NY; exec. asst. to v.p. devel. Vanderbilt U., Nashville; spl. projects dir. Am. Acad. in Rome, NYC, Met. Opera, NYC; sr. v.p. Hill and Knowlton, NYC; pres. Lorber Group, Ltd., NYC; v.p. comms. and planning NYC Partnership and C. of C.; sr. v.p. major events and promotions NYC & Co.; exec. v.p. NYC & Co. Found., NYC. Guest lectr. Arts and Bus. Coun., NYC, Internat. Soc. Performing Arts Adminstrs., Columbia U. Tchrs. Coll., NYC, 1988; event prodr. Broadway Under the Stars, 2002—; team leader Salt Lake Olympic Torch Relay NYC, 2002, 2004 Athens Olympic Torch Relay in NYC, 2004; spl. projects cons. NYC 2012 Olympic Games Bid Com. Contbr. chapters to books, articles to profl. jours. Office: NYC & Company/Major Events 810 7th Ave 3d Fl New York NY 10019-5818

LORBER, HOWARD MARK, investments executive; b. Bronx, NY, Sept. 8, 1948; s. Charles and Celia (Benrubi) L.; m. Thea Janet Hallman, Feb. 6, 1971; children: Brian, Michael. BA, L.I. U., 1970, MS in Taxation. Cert. chartered life underwriter, chartered fin. cons. Chmn. of bd. Hallman & Lorber Assocs., Inc., Valley Stream, NY, 1975—; chmn. Aegis Capital Corp., Valley Stream, NY, 1984—; chmn., CEO Nathans Famous, Inc., Westbury, NY, 1987—; pres., COO New Valley Corp., Miami, Fla., Vector Group Ltd., Miami, Fla., 1994—; co-owner, chmn. Prudential Douglas Elliman, 2003—. Bd. trustees Long Island U., N.Y. Bd. dirs. Peninsula Counseling Ctr., Woodmere, N.Y., Five Towns United Way, Woodmere, Nat. Victim Ctr., Prime Hospitality Corp., Fairfield, N.J. Mem. Friars Club, Mid. Bay Country Club (pres. 1989—). Jewish. Avocations: boating, fishing, golf. Office: Nathans Famous Inc 1400 Old Country Rd Ste 400 Westbury NY 11590 also: Vector Group 100 SE 2nd St Miami FL 33131

LORBER, JEFFREY H., jazz musician, composer; b. Phila., Nov. 4, 1952; s. Stan H. and Selma Anita (Rosen) L.; children: Jessica, Nica Martha. Student, Berkeley Coll. Music, 1971, Boston U., 1972-73. Ind. musician and composer, 1973—; Rec. artist for Arista, Inner City and Warner Bros. labels. Musician: (albums) The Jeff Lorber Fusion, 1977, Soft Space, 1978, Water Sign, 1979, Wizard Island, Galaxian, 1981, It's a Fact, 1982, In the Heat of the Night, 1984, Lift Off, 1984, Step by Step, 1984, Private Passion, 1990, Worth Waiting For, 1991, West Side Stories, 1994, State of Grace, 1996, Midnight, 1998, Kickin' It, 2001, Philly Style, 2003, Flipside, 2005, He Had a Hat, 2007. Mem. Nat. Assn. Rec. Arts and Scis. Office: c/o Bud Harner Chapman & Co Mgmt 14011 Ventura Blvd Ste 405 Sherman Oaks CA 91423*

LORBER, MORTIMER, retired physiology educator; b. NYC, Aug. 30, 1926; s. Albert and Frieda (Levin) L.; m. Eileen Segal, May 20, 1956; children: Kenneth, Stephanie. BS, NYU, 1945; DMD cum laude, Harvard U., 1950, MD cum laude, 1952. Diplomate Nat. Bd. Med. Examiners. Rotating intern A.M. Billings Hosp., 1952-53; resident in hematology Mt. Sinai Hosp., NYC, 1953-54, asst. resident in medicine, 1957; asst. resident medicine Georgetown U. Hosp., Washington, 1958; instr., asst. prof. dept. physiology and biophysics Georgetown U., Washington, 1959-68, assoc. prof., 1968-97; ret., 1997. Lectr. physiology U.S. Naval Dental Sch., Bethesda, Md., 1962-70, Walter Reed Army Inst. Dental Rsch., Washington, 1963-70; guest scientist Naval Med. Rsch. Inst., Bethesda, 1978-83. Contbr.: The Merck Manual, 14th-17th edits., 1982, 87, 92, 99; contbr. articles to profl. jours. Lt. USNR, 1954-56. Recipient Lederle Med. Faculty award Lederle Co., Pearl River, N.Y., 1960-63, USPHS Rsch. Career Devel. award Nat. Inst. Dental Rsch., Bethesda, 1963-70; grantee Am. Cancer Soc., USPHS. Mem. Am. Physiol. Soc., Am. Soc. Hematology, Assn. Rsch. in Vision and Ophthalmology, Internat. Assn. Dental Rsch. Jewish. Achievements include discovery that the ground substance is masked but not lost in calcification, removal of spleen is followed by a reticulocytosis that is permanent in dogs, dogs have many more young reticulocytes in their blood than man, stretching of skin increases mitoses in the rat showing physical factors can modulate DNA and cell division, adult Gaucher cells contain iron secondary to erythrophagocytosis, the spleen protects against insecticide-induced hematoxicity, biological armature provides internal stability to exocrine glands, rat lacrimal glands are stretched by their attachments and contain somatostatin, mastication reflexly increases gastroduodenal motility. Home: 5823 Osceola Rd Bethesda MD 20816-2032 Personal E-mail: melorber@aol.com.

LORBERBAUM, JEFFREY S., textiles executive; With Aladdin Mills, Inc., Calhoun, Ga., 1976-86, v.p. ops., 1986-94; pres., CEO Mohawk Industries, Inc., Calhoun, Ga., 1994—2004, chmn., pres., CEO, 2004—. Office: Mohawk Industries Inc 160 S Indsl Blvd Calhoun GA 30701*

LORCH, KENNETH F., lawyer; b. Indpls., July 24, 1951; BSBA, Washington U., 1973; JD, John Marshall Sch. Law, 1976. Bar: Ill. 1976, U.S. Dist. Ct. (no. dist.) Ill. 1977; CPA, Ill. Ptnr. Hamilton Thies Lorch & Hagnell LLP, Chgo. Mem. planned giving adv. coun. Chgo. Symphony Orch.; mem. Chgo. bd. Am. Technion Soc.; mem. Chgo. Coun. on Planned Giving; v.p. Coun. for Jewish Elderly; mem. profl. adv. com. Chgo. Cmty. Trust; mem. planned giving adv. coun. Lincoln Park Zoo, Chgo. Mem. Chgo. Bar Assn. (exec. com., Cook County Probate Ct. rules and forms com., mem. legis. com., mem. probate practice com. 1991, mem. trust law com., chmn. estate planning com., mem. young lawyers sect. 1983-85), Chgo. Estate Planning Coun., Jewish Fedn. Chgo. (past chair profl. adv. com.). Office: Hamilton Thies Lorch & Hagnell LLP 200 S Wacker Dr Ste 3800 Chicago IL 60606 Home Phone: 847-251-3027; Office Phone: 312-650-8640. Business E-Mail: lorch@htlhlaw.com.

LORCH, MARISTELLA DE PANIZZA, writer, educator; b. Bolzano, Italy, Dec. 8, 1919; came to U.S., 1947, naturalized, 1951; d. Gino and Giuseppina (Cristoforetti) de Panizza Inama von Brunnenwald; m. Claude Bové, Feb. 10, 1944 (div. 1955); 1 child, Claudia; m. Edgar R. Lorch, Mar. 25, 1956; children: Lavinia Edgarda, Donatella Livia. Student, Liceo Classico, Merano, 1929-37; Dott. in Lettere e Filosofia, U. Rome, 1942; DHL (hon.), Lehman Coll., CUNY, 1993. Prof. Latin and Greek Liceo Virgilio, Rome, 1941-44; assoc. prof. Italian and German Coll. St. Elizabeth, Convent Station, NJ, 1947-51; faculty Barnard Coll. and Columbia U., 1951-90; prof. Barnard Coll., 1967—, chmn. dept., 1951-90, co-founder, chmn. medieval and renaissance program, 1972-90; vice chmn. emeritus prof. Columbia U., 2005—, v.p. emerita, 2005—. Founder, dir. Ctr. Internat. Scholarly Exch., Barnard Coll., 1980-90; dir. Casa Italiana, Columbia U., 1969-76, chmn. exec. com. Italian studies, 1980-90, founding dir. Italian Acad. Advanced Studies in Am., 1991-96, founding dir. emerita and dir. external rels., 1996—. Author: Critical edit. L. Valla, De vero falsoque bono, Bari, 1970, (critical edit.) Michaelida (with W. Ludwig), 1976, On Pleasure (with A. K. Hieatt), 1981, A Defense of Life: L. Valla's Theory of Pleasure, 1985, Folly and Insanity in Renaissance Literature, 1986, (with E. Grassi) All' America, 1990, Italy at the Millennium, 2001, (novel) Mamma in Her Village, 2005; editor: Il Teatro Italiano del Renascimento, 1981, Humanism in Rome, 1983, La Scuola, New York, 1987; mem. editorial bd. Italian jour. Romanic Review; also articles on Renaissance lit., philosophy and theater. Chmn. Am. Ariosto Centennial Celebration, 1974; trustee Lyceé Française NY, 1986—2004, mem. adv. bd., 2004—; adv. bd. Marconi Found., 1998; chmn. bd. trustees La Scuola NY, 1986—92. Decorated cavaliere della Repubblica Italiana, commendatore della Repubblica Italiana, grande ufficiale della Republica Italiana; recipient AMITA award for Woman of Yr. in Italian Lit., 1973, Columbus '92 Countdown prize of excellence in humanities, 1990, Elen Cornaro award Sons of Italy Woman of Yr., 1990, Father Ford award, 1994, hon. mem. Legendary Women, 1997, founding dir. emeritus Italian Acad. in Advance Studies in Am., Columbia U. Mem. Medieval Acad. Am., Renaissance Soc. Am., Am. Assn. Tchrs. Italian, Am. Assn. Italian Studies (hon. pres. 1990-91), Internat. Assn. for Study of Italian Lit. (Am. rep., assoc. pres. 8th Congress 1973), Acad. Polit. Sci. (life), Pirandello Soc. (pres. 1972-78), Arcadia Acad. (Asteria Aretusa 1976). Home: 445 Riverside Dr New York NY 10027-6801 Office: Columbia Univ Italian Acad Adv Study Casa Italiana New York NY 10027 Office Phone: 212-854-2306. Business E-Mail: ml4r6@columbia.edu.

LORCH, ROBERT K., corporate financial executive; V.p. global picture tube bus. Thomson Multimedia; sr. v.p., CFO Marmon Group, 2002—. Exec. positions GE, RCA Corp.; with mgmt., fin., global gen. mgmt., sales and mktg., and strat. planning. Office: Marmon Group 225 Washington St Ste 1900 Chicago IL 60606*

LORD, ALBERT L., finance company executive; BS in Bus., Pa. State U., 1967. With Student Loan Mktg. Assn., 1981—90, exec. v.p., COO, 1990—94; pres., founder LCL, Ltd., 1994—97; vice chmn., CEO SLM Corp. (Sallie Mae), Reston, Va., 1997—2005, chmn., 2005—. Bd. dirs. SLM Corp., 1995—, SS&C Technologies, Inc, 2001—, BearingPoint, Inc., 2003—, Nat. Acad. Found., Student Loan Mktg. Assn, Va Found. Ind. Coll., Va Ballet Theatre; mem. advisory bd. Abington Coll-Pa. State U. Office: Sallie Mae 12061 Bluemont Way Reston VA 20190

LORD, BARBARA JOANNI, lawyer; b. Bay Shore, NY, Aug. 7, 1939; d. Theodore and Doris Aileen (Smith) Joanni; m. Robert Wilder Lord, June 24, 1967. BA, U. Miami, 1961; JD, NYU, 1966. Bar: N.Y. 1967, Fla. 1978, U.S. Supreme Ct. 1991. Asst. editor A.M. Best Co., NYC, 1961-64; contract analyst Guardian Life Ins. Co., NYC, 1964-66; legal trainee N.Y. State Liquor Authority, NYC, 1966-67, atty., 1967-70, sr. atty., 1970-80, assoc. atty., 1980—. Mem.: ABA, Fla. Bar Assn., N.Y. State Bar Assn., Order of Ea. Star. Office: NY State Liquor Auth 317 Lenox Ave New York NY 10027

LORD, EVELYN MARLIN, mayor; b. Melrose, Mass., Dec. 8, 1926; d. John Joseph and Mary Janette (Nourse) Marlin; m. Samuel Smith Lord Jr., Feb. 28, 1948; children: Steven Arthur, Jonathan Peter, Nathaniel Edward, Victoria Marlin, William Kenneth. BA, Boston U., 1948; MA, U. Del., 1956; JD, U. Louisville, 1969. Bar: Ky. 1969, U.S. Supreme Ct. 1973.

Exec. dir. Block Blight Inc., Wilmington, Del., 1956—60; mem. Del. Senate, Dover, 1960—62; administrv. asst. county judge Jefferson County, Louisville, 1968—71; corr. No. Ireland News Jour. Co., Wilmington, 1972—74; legal adminstr. Orgain, Bell & Tucker, Beaumont, Tex., 1978—83; v.p. Tex. Commerce Bank, Beaumont, 1983—84; councilman City of Beaumont, 1980—82, mayor pro tem, 1982—84, mayor, 1990—94, 2002—05. Tourism chmn. U.S. Conf. Mayors, 1994, adv. bd., chmn. arts, culture and recreation, 1992—94; sr. counselor Ky. Bar, 2002—; adv. bd. U.S. Com. Mayors, 1992—94, 2002—05. Pres. United Way, 1994, 1997; adv. bd. Boy Scouts Am., Three Rivers, 1978—84, 1989—94, exec. bd., 2000—05, 2007—; life mem. Girl Scouts U.S.A., pres. Kentuckiana coun., 1966—70, governing bd. San Jacinto coun., 2006—07; trustee Lamar U. Found., 1999—2003; pres. Tex. Energy Mus., 1995—2001; trustee United Way, Beaumont, 1990—; mem. Southwest Tex. Adv. Bd., 2007—; bd. dirs. Evelyn M. Lord Teen Ct., 1993—, Found. S.E. Tex., 1990—, Lincoln Inst., 1994—2001, Beaumont Pub. Schs. Found., 1993—99, 2006—, Ptnrs. for Children, Child Protective Svcs.; chmn. Spindletop 2001 Com. Named Citizen of Yr., Sales and Mktg. Assn., 1990, Beaumont Man of the Yr., 1993, Woman with Heart, Am. Heart Assn., 2000, Free Ent. Person of the Yr., Assn. Bldg. Contrs., 2000, Newsmaker of the Yr., Press Club Jefferson County, 2001, Hurricane Evelyn, ARC, 2001, Disting. Law Alumni, U. Louisville, 2002, Woman of Yr., Quota Club Internat., 2002; recipient Silver Beaver award, Boy Scouts Am., Beaumont, 1979, Disting. Alumni award, Boston U., 1983, Disting. Leadership award, Nat. Assn. Leadership Orgns., Indpls., 1991, Labor-Mgmt. Pub. Sector award, 1991, Cmty. Builder award, Grand Masonic Lodge of Tex., 1991, 2003, Disting. Grad. award, Leadership Beaumont, 1993, Rotary Svc. Above Self award, 1994, Excellency award, Tex. State Hist. Commn., 2001, Athena award, Beaumont C of C, 2003, Mrs. S.E. Tex. award, Dogwood Festival, 2004, Regional Leadership award, S.E. Tex. Regional Planning Commn., 2005. Mem.: DAR, LWV (Del. state pres. 1960—62, bd. dirs. Tex. 1978—80), Bus. and Profl. Women Assn. (Woman of Yr. 1983), Colonial Dames (Citizenship award 2004), Symphony Soc. S.E. Tex. (hon.; bd. dirs. 1990—98, 2002—), Soc. Mayflower Descs., Rotary, 100 Club (pres. 1995—97). Avocations: writing, reading, african violets, genealogy. Home: 1240 Nottingham Ln Beaumont TX 77706-4316 Personal E-mail: evelynlord@aol.com. *Basically - I believe in "blooming where you're planted". Life with my husband has taken me all over the world but we've always managed to be "at home" wherever we've been able to give a bit of ourselves.*

LORD, GEOFFREY CRAIG (G. CRAIG LORD), lawyer; b. Boston, Apr. 12, 1946; s. Charles A. and Shirley (Ellice) L.; m. Rosemary Crumlish, May 29, 1970; children: Patrick C., Frances C., Irene R. BA magna cum laude, Gettysburg Coll., 1968; JD magna cum laude, U. Pa., 1971. Bar: Pa. 1972, Fla. 1977. Law clk. to presiding justice Supreme Ct. Pa., 1971-72; assoc., then ptnr. Blank, Rome, Comisky & McCauley, Phila., 1972-86; gen. counsel Core Group, Phila., 1986-88; judge Phila. Ct. Common Pleas, 1988-97; atty. Raynes, McCarty, Binder, Ross & Mundy, Phila., 1997—99; ptnr., Blank Rome LLP, Phila., 1999—, head fin. svcs. and real estate dept., 2003—06. Active Fairmount Park Commn., 1986-88, Phila. City Planning Commn., 1983; trustee Friend's Cen. Sch., 1987—. Capt. USAR, 1972. Mem. ABA, Pa. Bar Assn., Phila. Bar Assn., U. Pa. Law Sch. Alumni Assn. (treas. 1977-79), Order of Coif, Phi Beta Kappa. Office: Blank Rome LLP One Logan Sq Philadelphia PA 19103-6998 Office Phone: 215-569-5496. Office Fax: 215-832-5496. Business E-Mail: lord@BlankRome.com.

LORD, GEORGE FRANK, educational director; s. George F. and Maryanne Flanagan Lord; m. Sarah Hurley, Jan. 16, 1984; children: Zachary Hurley, Austin Hurley, Meg Hurley. BA in Sociology, Coll. William & Mary, Newport News, Va., 1977; MA in Sociology, La. State U., Baton Rouge, 1979, PhD in Sociology, 1982. Prof. sociology U. Mich., Flint, 1987—98; social scis. dept. head Pitts. State U., 1998—2000; criminology, sociology, social work & geography dept. head Ark. State U., 2000—03; dean Coll. Liberal Arts Grambling State U., 2003—05; dean Sch. Pub. & Environ. Affairs Ind. U. NW, Gary, 2005—06; dir. rsch. Partners In Pub. Edn., Memphis, 2006—. Contbr. articles to profl. jours. Mgr., rsch. clearinghouse Nat. Home-Sch. Assn., 1997—2000; dir. Memphis Regional P-16 Coun., 2006—; dir., pres. Flint & ACLU, Mich., 1990—95; mem. Shiawassee County Cmty. Mental Health Bd., Owosso, Mich., 1989—93; pres. Horses of Hope, Inc., Baxter Springs, Kans., 1999—2002; mem. NW Ind. Quality Life Coun., Lake County, Ind., 2006, Lake County Workforce Investment Bd., Ind., 2006. 1st lt. US Army, 1966—69. Grantee Rsch. Excellence Fund, State Mich., 1996; Rsch. grant, NIMH, 1990, U. Mich., 1994, 1996, Ark. Dept. Edn., 2000—03, Children's Def. Fund/W. K. Kellog Found., 2001—02, Pub. Edn. Network, 2006. Mem.: Am. Edn. Rsch. Assn., So. Sociol. Soc. Avocation: travel. Office Phone: 901-766-9444.

LORD, HEAVEN, consciousness studies educator, minister, translator; b. Paget, Bermuda, May 1, 1963; arrived in U.S., 1975; d. Percival Whaley and Sylvia (Keller) Baynard. BA in Spanish, Coll. of Charleston, 1984, BA in Polit. Sci., 1985, BA in Bus., 1986; MA in Spanish, U. No. Iowa, 1991; MA in Humanistic Psychology, State U. West Ga., 1992; PhD in Consciousness Studies and Theology of Miracles, Union Inst. and U., Cin., 1999. Instr. Spanish State U. West Ga., Carrollton, 1991—92, Duke U., Durham, NC, 1993; rsch. asst. Inst. Parapsychology, Durham, NC, 1993; instr. Spanish U. Mo., Kansas City, 1999; min. of prayer Silent Unity, Unity Village, Mo., 1996—; Spanish translator Traducciones Espirituales, Lee's Summit, Mo., 2000—. Cons. in field, Lee's Summit, 2001—. Avocations: travel, writing, reading, singing, dance. Home: 511 NE Tudor Rd Apt 1 Lees Summit MO 64086 Personal E-mail: professor_lord@prodigy.net.

LORD, JACQUELINE WARD, retired accountant, photographer, artist; b. Andalusia, Ala., May 16, 1936; d. Marron J. and Minnie V. (Owen) Ward; m. Curtis Gaynor, Nov. 23, 1968. Student U. Ala., Montgomery, 1966, Auburn U., Ala., 1977, Huntingdon Coll., Montgomery, 1980, Troy State U., Ala., 1980; BA in Bus. Adminstrn., Dallas Bapt. U., 1985. News photographer corr. Andalusia Star-News, Ala., 1954-59, Sta. WSFA-TV, Montgomery, 1954-60; acct., bus. mgr. Reihardt Motors, Inc., Montgomery, 1962-69; office mgr., acct. Cen. Ala. Supply, Montgomery, 1969-71; acct. Chambers Constrn. Co., Montgomery, 1972-75; pres. Foxy Lady Apparel, Inc., Montgomery, 1973-76; acct. Rushton, Stakely, Johnston & Garrett, attys., Montgomery, 1975-81; acctg. supr. Arthur Andersen & Co., Dallas, 1981-82; staff acct. Burgess Co., CPAs, Dallas, 1983; owner Lord & Assocs. Acctg. Svc., Dallas, 1983—2006; tax acct. John Hasse, CPA, Dallas, 1984-86, Dallas Bapt. Assn., 1986-2006, ret., 2006. Vol. election law commr. Sec. of State of Ala. Don Siegelman, Montgomery, 1979-80; active Montgomery Art Guild, 1964-65, Ala. Art League, 1964-65, Montgomery Little Theatre, 1963-65, Montgomery Choral Soc., 1965. Recipient Outstanding Achievement Bus. Mgmt. award Am. Motors, 1968. Mem. Am. Soc. Women Accts. (del. ann. meeting 1975-78, pres. Montgomery chpt. 1976-77, area day chmn. 1978), Soroptimists Internat. (pres. elect Montgomery chpt. 1975-76), Nat. Assn. Ch. Bus. Adminstrn. Home: 3806 Heatherbrook Pl Dothan AL 36303

LORD, JAMES GREGORY, organizational, community and philanthropic counsel; b. Cleve., Aug. 23, 1947; s. James Nelson and Esther Lord; m. Wendy Franklin, July 10, 1977; children: Michael Richard, Rebecca Esther. Student, U. Md., Far East Campus, 1966—68, Cleve. State U./, 1968—72. TV news prodr. Far East Network, Tokyo, 1965—68; wire editor News-Herald, Willoughby, Ohio, 1968—69; pub. rels. assoc. United Way, Cleve., 1969—70; free-lance pub. rels. person Cleve., 1970—72; dir. pub. rels. Ketchum, Inc., Pitts., 1972—77; cons. devel. philanthropic instns. Cleve., 1977—. Cons. White House Endowment Fund, Washington, 1983—94, Vatican Info. Svc., Vatican City, 1993, Nat. 4-H, Chevy Chase, Md., 1994—95, United Religions, San Francisco, 1996; assoc. Cambridge (Eng.) Partnership for Orgnl. Transformation, Cambridge U., 1995—, Taos (N.Mex.) Inst., 2003—; co-founder Appreciative Inquiry Cons., LLC, 2001—; chief devel. officer Cleve. Mus. Art, 1984—85; vis. fellow St. Mary's Coll., 1993; chair Mgmt. of Change Think Tank; fellow Mt. Vernon Inst., 1995; developer The Philanthropic Quest Methodology, 1995—97; del. United Religions Charter Writing Summit, 1996; developer one-man photography exhbns., 15 worldwide sites, 1968—72; frequent keynote spkr. Author: Philanthropy and Marketing, 1981, The Raising of Money, 1983, Building Your Case, 1984, The Campaign Manuals, 1985, The Development Consultant, 1985, Guide for the Professional, 1986, Philanthropic Quest series of 9, 1996, The Practice of the Quest series of 5 books, 1998, Translating the Quest to Volunteers Monograph, 1996, The Age of Possibility, 2002, What Kind of World Do You Want?: Here's How We Can Get It, 2007; editor: Results: Time Management System, 1986, Market Smart, 1988, The Campaign Letter, Non-Profit Mgmt. Report; contbr. articles to profl. jours. Home: 28050 S Woodland Rd Cleveland OH 44124-5638 Home Phone: 216-464-3351; Office Phone: 216-831-3727. E-mail: quest@lord.org.

LORD, JEROME EDMUND, education administrator, writer; b. Waterbury, Conn., Dec. 24, 1935; s. James Andrew and Mary Frances (Hayes) L.; m. Eleanor Louise Collins, Apr. 22, 1967; children: Hayes Alexander FitzWarin, Stavely Hampston deHodnet, Savile Collins de Montenay, Dorian Warfield d'Amours, Wallis Jennings dePantulf. BA, Georgetown U., 1957; MA, Boston Coll., 1962, Columbia U., 1963, PhD, 1969; diploma (hon.), U. Madrid, 1962. Tchr. The Taft Sch. Peekskill Mil. Acad., 1957—60; editor, lang. recs. supr. Allyn and Bacon Inc., Boston, 1961—62; administrv. assoc. internat. programs and services Tchrs. Coll. Columbia U., NYC, 1963—65, assoc. in higher edn., 1965—66; asst. prof. edn., exec. asst. to dean acad. devel. CUNY, 1965—67, assoc. prof. edn., exec. asst. to vice chancellor exec. office, 1967—69; dir. rsch. Ford and Carnegie Study of Fed. Politics of Edn. Brookings Instn., Washington, 1969—70; program officer Nat. Ctr. for Ednl. Tech., US Dept. Edn., Washington, 1971—73; sr. assoc. Nat. Inst. Edn., Washington, 1973—86, Office Ednl. Rsch. and Improvement, Washington, 1986—2002, Office Inst. Edn. Scis., Dept. Edn., Washington, 2002—06. Pres. Jerome Lord Enterprises, Inc., Palm Beach, Fla.; advisor to vol. edn. policy group Office Dir. Def. Edn., US Dept. Def., 1975-76; chmn. Fed. Interagy. Panel for Rsch. on Adulthood; founder Nat. Soc. Aesthetics and Competitive Garglers Am., 2005; mem. World Affairs Coun., Washington; cons. and lectr. in field. Playwright: Teresa, 1971, The Election, 1972, Audition!, 1973, Decent Exposure, 1979, Amazing Grace, 1987, Heads You Win, 1991, Making Believe, 1996, My One and Only, 1997, Susie of Chicago, 2005; author: Perfectly Proper, 1993, Teacher Training Abroad: New Realities, 1993, Adult Literacy Programs: Guidelines for Effectiveness, 1995, (collection of letters) Letters To Minerva, 2007, The Greatest French Food Book in the World, 2007; contbr. articles to profl. jours. Trustee St. John's Child Devel. Ctr., Washington, 1978-83; mem. nat. bd. sponsors Protestant and Orthodox Ctr., NY World's Fair, 1964; mem. adv. bd. NYC Urban Corps, 1965-69, others; mem. coun. of friends Folger Shakespeare Libr.; sponsor Nat. Symphony Orch.; mem., donor reception rooms Dept. State. Named Coakley scholar, 1953-57, M.T. Runyan scholar, 1967-68; fellow W.T. Kellogg Found., 1968-69, Rinehart Found., 1970-71, others. Mem. Nat. Soc. Aesthetic and Competitve Garglers Am. (founder, grand-garglemaster pro-tem 2005), Soc. Friends St. George's and Desc. Knights of Garter, Acad. Am. Poets, Pilgrims of the US, World Affairs Coun., The Lansdowne Club (London), Met. Club, Kappa Delta Pi, Phi Delta Pi, Eta Sigma Phi. Episc. Avocations: historic preservation, music, art history, architecture, antiques. Personal E-mail: jeromeelord@aol.com.

LORD, MARJORIE, actress; b. San Francisco, July 26; d. George Charles and Lillian Rosalie (Edgar) Wollenberg; m. John Archer, Dec. 30, 1941 (div. 1954); children: Gregg, Anne; m. Randolph M. Hale, May 26, 1958 (dec. Aug. 1974); m. Harry Joseph Volk, Aug. 14, 1976 (dec. 2000). Student high sch., San Francisco. Bd. dirs. The Joffrey Ballet, The Friends of the Library, U. So. Calif. Appeared in theater prodns. including The Old Maid, Anniversary Waltz on Broadway, Springtime for Henry; more than 30 feature films including Johnny Come Lately; starred in Make Room for Daddy, 1957-64; countless TV shows including Love American Style, Sweet Surrender, 1987; TV film Side by Side, 1987; dir. and actress theater prodns.; dir. Sunday in New York, Black Comedy, The Tiger at Claremont College, Ginger in the Morning; author (memoir) A Dance & Hug, 2005. Bd. dirs. Hollywood Entertainment Mus., Friends of Libr. Home: 1110 Maytor Pl Beverly Hills CA 90210-2600 Personal E-mail: maggielord@adelphia.net.

LORD, MARVIN, apparel executive; b. NYC, Sept. 22, 1937; s. Harry and Irene (Taub) L.; m. Joan Simon, Aug. 5, 1961; children— Elisa Anne, Michael Harris BS, Long Island U., Bklyn., 1959. Mdse. mgr. Oxford Industries, Inc., NYC, 1964-66, gen. mdse. mgr., 1966-70, v.p., gen. mgr., 1970-73; pres. Holbrook Co., Inc. Div Oxford Industries, Inc., NYC, 1970-85; pres., chief exec. officer Crystal Brands, Inc.-Youthwear Group, NYC, 1985—; pres. Cluett Shirtmakers, NYC, 1988—, M.L. Enterprises, Roslyn Heights, NY, 1990—; pres., chief oper. officer Sanyo Fashion House, NYC, 1991—; pres., CEO MAternity Resources Inc., NYC, 1994—; exec. v.p. E.A. Hughes & Co., NYC, 1996—. Chmn. Fathers Day Coun., N.Y.C., 1984—; bd. dirs. Nat. Conf. Cmty. and Justice, 1997, Fashion Inst. of Tech., 1997. Recipient Disting. Alumni award L.I. U., 1987. Mem. Mens Fashion Assn., Young Menswear Assn. Jewish. Avocation: tennis. Home: 53 Parkway Dr Roslyn Heights NY 11577-2705 Office: E A Hughes & Co 245 Fifth Ave New York NY 10016-3108 Office Phone: 212-689-4600. Business E-Mail: mlord@eahughes.com.

LORD, RICHARD DENNIS, photographer; b. Cleve., June 22, 1951; s. James Nelson and Esther (Pollock) L.; m. Patricia L. Michelsen, July 14, 1974 (div. Apr. 1987); children: Tanya, Michele, Arthur. BA, Boston U., 1973, MA, 1975; postgrad., U. Copenhagen, 1974-75, NYU, 1983—85; BA (hon.), Africa U., 2006. Pres. The Mgmt. Group, NYC, 1987-91; pvt. practice photographer NYC, 1991—. Lectr. NYU, N.Y.C., 1989, Seton Hall U., West Orange, N.J., 1989-90, Pace U., White Plains, N.Y., 1990-91; cons. in field, 1986-90. Author: The Management Reports, 1987, The Non Profit Problem Solver, 1989; photo exhibits at UN Gen. Assembly, 17 U.S. embassies, Photo District Gallery, N.Y.C., Parsons Gallery, N.Y.C., Boston Ctr. for the Arts, Otis Art Inst., L.A, Bklyn. Coll.; featured in documentary "Photographers" (Alan Weiss prod.), 2001. Trustee City and County Sch., N.Y.C., 1986-88; mem. Hells Kitchen Neighborhood Assn., N.Y.C. Recipient Photography awards Religious Communicators Coun., UMAC. Mem. Advt. Photographers of Am., Am. Soc. Media Photographers, Rotary Internat., United Meth. Assn. Comm., Phi Beta Kappa. Office: PO Box 173 Ivy VA 22945 Address: 652 W 163 St 28 New York NY 10032 E-mail: rlord@rlordphoto.com.

LORD, RUTH, retired researcher, philanthropist, writer; b. NYC, Jan. 14, 1922; d. Henry Francis duPont and Ruth Wales; m. George deForest Lord (div.); children: Pauline, George de Forest Jr., Edith S.(dec.), Henry; m. John Grier Holmes, Mar. 3, 1990 (dec. 1997). BA, Vassar Coll., 1943; MA, Yale U., 1950. Rsch. affiliate Yale Child Study Ctr., New Haven, 1967—85, rsch. assoc., 1986—98; ret., 1998. Spkr. in field. Co-author: When Home is No Haven, 1992; author: Henry F. du Pont and Winterthur, 1999; contbr. numerous articles to psychol. jours. Vol. Pub. Edn. Assn., NYC, 1943—47; intermittent team capt. United Fund, New Haven, 1948—53; trustee Winterthur Mus., 1952—74; pres. Long Wharf Theatre, New Haven, 1967—90, bd. dirs., 1980—, Vassar Coll., 1956—57, Austen Riggs Found., Stockbridge, Mass., 1975—; dir. Cornerstone Inc., New Haven, 1968—75. Recipient Foxcroft Disting. Alumna award, 1994, Nat. Arts Club award, 1989; fellow, Saybrook Coll., 1980—. Mem.: Family Svc. Assn. Am. (bd. dirs. 1954—57), Public Edn. Assn. (trustee 1947—51), Colonial Dams Am., Century Assn., Colony Club, Phi Beta Kappa. Democrat. Avocations: theater, writing, bridge, gardening. Home: 190 St Ronan St New Haven CT 06511

LORD, VICTORIA LYNN, artist; b. Danville, Ill., May 29, 1956; d. Delno and Merlyn LaDonna (Gillis) Gilliland; m. Maurice Powers Lord II, Dec. 1, 1987. Student, Purdue U., 1974-77. Host, instr. painting series PBS, Learning Channel, U.S., Can., Mexico, 1990—; instr. various orgns. Author: Techniques in Acrylics, Alkyds, Oils, 1987, Painting with Alkyds and Oils, 1989, First Steps in Acrylics, 1996. Named one of Top 100 Wildlife Artists, Artist Mag., 1990, Sponsor Artist, Ducks Unltd., Ind., 1991, Featured Ad Artist, Winsor & Newton, 1990-91. Mem. Soc. of Layerists in Multimedia, Soc. Exptl. Artists, Soc. Decorative Painters, Am. Craft Coun., Soc. of Painters in Casein and Acrylic, Tippecanoe Arts Fedn. (bd. dirs. 1992-95). Office: PO Box 2195 West Lafayette IN 47996-2195 Office Phone: 765-463-6425.

LORDI, KATHERINE MARY, lawyer; b. Jersey City, Mar. 24, 1949; d. Peter G. and Hilde E. (Illy) Lordi. AB, Trinity Coll., Washington, 1971; JD, Fordham U., 1975. Bar: N.J. 1975, U.S. Dist. Ct. N.J. 1975, U.S. Supreme Ct. 1983, U.S. Ct. Appeals (3d cir.) 1989. Clk. Friedman & D'Allessandro, East Orange, NJ, 1974-75, assoc., 1975-76; pvt. practice Bloomfield, NJ, 1976—. Adj. instr. Coll. St. Elizabeth, Convent Station, NJ, 1978—86, adj. prof., 1986—; legal adviser Mcpl. Ct. Clks. Assn., 1977—84. Notes editor: Fordham Urban Law Jour., 1974—75. Trustee Cath. Family and Cmty. Svcs., 1980—, v.p., 1986—; mem. adv. bd. Acad. St. Elizabeth, Convent Station, 1980—84; mem. Essex County Adv. Bd. Status Women, 1983—92, chmn., 1985—88, co-chair, 1990—92; trustee New Sch. Arts, 1988—89, Family Svc. League, Inc., 1986—2000, pres., 1991—94; trustee Bloomfield C. of C., 1986—94, v.p. legis., 1990—94. Fellow: Royal Soc. Encouragement Arts, Manufactures and Commerce; mem.: ABA, Essex County Bar Assn., N.J. Bar Assn., Bloomfield Lawyers Club. Roman Catholic. Office: 54 Fremont St Bloomfield NJ 07003-3428 Office Phone: 973-743-0050. E-mail: k.lordi@worldnet.att.net.

LORD OF CURSONS, See RAWL, ARTHUR

LORDS, TRACI ELIZABETH (NORA LOUISE KUZMA), actress, singer; b. Steubenville, Ohio, May 7, 1968; d. Louis and Patricia Kuzma; m. Brook Yeaton, 1990 (div. 1995); m. Ryan Riel Grainger, 1999 (div. 2000); m. Jeffrey Lee, 2002. Film appearances include Not of This Earth, 1988, Fast Food, 1989, Shock 'Em Dead, 1990, Cry-Baby, 1990, Raw Nerve, 1991, A Time to Die, 1991, Laser Moon, 1992, The Nutty House, 1992, Season Two, 1993, Skinner, 1993, Desperate Crimes, 1993, Intent to Kill, 1993, Dragstrip Girl, 1994, Ice, 1994, Serial Mom, 1994, Circuitry Man II-Plughead Rewired, 1994, The Nutty Nut, 1995, Vertuosity, 1995, As Good as Dead, 1995, Dead Man's Island, 1996, Underworld, 1996, Nowhere, 1997, Extramarital, 1997 (also exec. prodr.), Blade, 1998, Boogie Boy, 1998, Stir/Highway Hitcher, 1998, Epicenter, 2000, Certain Guys, 2000, Chump Change, 2000 (Best Actress, US Comedy Arts Festival, Aspen), The Killing Club, 2001, D.R.E.A.M. Team, 2001, Black Mask 2: City of Masks, 2002, Frostbite, 2004, Farewell to Raskolnikov's, 2005 and others, (TV film) Bandit, 1994, Dragstrip Girl, 1994, As Good As Dead, 1995, Dead Man's Island, 1996, Deathlands, 2003,; writer, dir. Sweet Pea, 2005; TV appearances in Wiseguy, 1988, Married...With Children, 1989, 1991, MacGyver, 1990, Highlander, 1993, Tales From the Crypt, 1993, Roseanne, 1993, 1995, Melrose Place, 1995, Nash Bridges, 1997, Hercules: The Legendary Journeys, 1999, Gilmore Girls, 2003, Wanted, 2005, Will & Grace, 2005, (miniseries) The Tommyknockers, 1993; voice The Chosen One, 2006; series regular Profiler, 1997-98, First Wave, 2000-01; (voice-video game) True Crime: New York City, 2005(Best Supporting Female Performance, Spike TV Video Game awards, 2005); singer, songwriter 1000 Fires; composer (video game-song) Virtuosity, 1995, Mortal Kombat, 1995. Avocations: baking, running, kayaking, studying Ninjitsu. Office: c/o TIMEcom 2109 S Wilbur Ave Walla Walla WA 99362

LORE, JOHN S., health facility administrator; s. Raymond and Lillian (Malanfant) Lore; m. Judith Lynne Bell, July 25, 1964; children: Christopher John, Matthew Scott. Mgmt. trainee Ford Motor Co., Dearborn, Mich., 1965—66; dir. alumni and devel. Western Mich. U., Kalamazoo, 1966—72; pres., v.p. devel. and planning Nazareth Coll., Kalamazoo, 1972—80; pres., CEO Mich. Coll. Found., 1980—86; from sr. v.p. to pres., CEO Sisters of St. Joseph Health Sys./Ascension Health, Ann Arbor, Mich., 1986—2000, St. Louis, 1986—2000; pres., CEO ConnectMich. Alliance, Lansing, 2001—04; interim pres., CEO Bay Econ. Devel. Corp./Bay Future, Inc., Bay City, 2004—05; sr. v.p. corp. devel. Detroit Med. Ctr., 2004—06, cons. corp. devel., 2006—. Adj. prof. Mich. State U. Coll. Comm. Arts and Scis., Lansing, 2006—, Saginaw State U. Coll. Arts and Behavioral Scis., University Center, Mich., 2007—. Home: 253 Jennison Pl Bay City MI 48708

LO RE, VINCENT, JR., retired academic administrator, municipal official; b. Bayonne, NJ, Feb. 16, 1947; s. Vincent Sr. and Josephine Rose Lo R.; m. Janice Kapec, Nov. 15, 1969; 1 child, Vincent Lo Re III. BA, N.J. City U., 1969; MBA, Rutgers U., 1974. Assoc. contr. NJ City U., Jersey City, 1969—2002; ret., 2002. Adj. prof. Jersey City State U., Hudson County C.C., Stevens Inst. Tech. V.p. Bayonne Hosp. Found.; bd. trustees Hudson County C.C.; city chmn. Bayonne Columbus Comm.; pres. Jersey City State Coll. Alumni Assoc.; bd. dirs. Bayonne coun. Boy Scouts Am.; mem. coun. City of Bayonne, 1990-94, 1994-98, 1998-2002, 2002-06, 2006-, pres. and coun. mem., 1998-2002, 2002-06, 2006-, mem. mcpl. planning bd., sch. bd., commr. local redevel. bd.; bd. mem. Bayonne Town Ctr. Recipient Civic award Bayonne br. Nat. Assoc. Advancement Colored People, 1993; named Man of Yr. Sicilian Citizens Club, 1993, named Man of Yr. Circolo Italiano Club, 2003; Support Fund award Bayonne Youth Ctr., 1994. Mem. Sicilian Citzens Club-Bayonne, Nat. Conf., Order Sons Italy Am., Rotary (pres., mem. Bayonne Holocaust Remembrance commn., Rotarian of Yr. 1980, 84, 2004). Democrat. Roman Catholic. Avocations: reading, travel, history. Home: 835 Avenue A Bayonne NJ 07002-1959 Office Phone: 201-858-6019. Personal E-mail: v.re@att.net.

LOREE, JAMES M., consumer products company executive; BA in Econ., Union Coll. With fin. mgmt. staff Stanley Works, New Britain, Conn., 1980—99, exec. v.p. fin. and strategic planning, CFO, 1999—. Office: Stanley Works 1000 Stanley Dr New Britain CT 06053

LOREFICE, LAURENCE SANTO, psychiatrist; b. NYC, May 11, 1950; s. Lawrence Salvatore and Gemma (Patrone) L.; m. Mary Ellen Foulds; children: Jeanne, Kristine, Luke. BA, Johns Hopkins U., 1971; MD, U. Pa., 1975; MPH, Harvard U., 1979. Diplomate Am. Bd. Psychiatry and Neurology; cert. psychopharmacology. Internship and resident in psychiatry Mass. Gen. Hosp., Boston, 1975-78, fellow in social and community psychiatry, 1978-79; chief resident Outpatient Clinic Erich Lindemann Mental Health Ctr., Boston, 1977-78; clin. fellow psychiatry Med. Sch. Harvard U., 1975-79; chief psychiatrist Day Treatment Program, mem. staff Mt. Sinai Med. Ctr., NYC, 1979-80; dir. Intermediate Care Treatment Unit Westchester County (N.Y.) Med. Ctr., 1980-82; dir. Washington Heights Outpatient Clinic N.Y. State Psychiat. Inst., 1982-84; assoc. chief dept. psychiatry Stamford (Conn.) Hosp., 1986-96; instr. N.Y. Med. Coll., Valhalla, 1980-82, clin. asst. prof. psychiatry, 1985-96; asst. clin. prof.

psychiatry Coll. Physicians and Surgeons Columbia U., NYC, 1982-95; pvt. practice Old Greenwich, Conn., 1978—. Contbr. articles to profl. jours. Fellow Am. Psychiat. Assn. (disting., Tchg. award). Office: 39 Ballwood Rd Old Greenwich CT 06870

LORELL, BEVERLY H., medical products executive; BA with distinction, Stanford U., 1971; MD, Stanford Sch. Medicine, 1975. Intern to resident physician Stanford U. Hosp.; clin. rsch. fellowship, cardiology Mass. Gen. Hosp., Harvard Med. Sch.; dir., program in heart failure, also mem. interventional cardiology team Besth Israel Deaconess Med. Ctr.; prof., medicine Harvard U. Med. Sch.; v.p., chief med. tech. officer Guidant Corp., Indpls., 2003—. Served as an advisor to the fed. govt., including svc. on study sect. of the NIH and Cardiovascular and Renal Drugs Adv. Com. of the FDA; lectr. at various heart conf. and symposiums around the world. Contbr. articles to profl. jours. Mem.: Besth Israel Intervention Cardiology Team, Am. Coll. Cardiology, Heart Failure Soc. of Am., Am. Heart Assn., Guidant Compass Bd. Office: Guidant Corp 111 Monument Cl 2900 Indianapolis IN 46204-5129

LORELL, JEFFREY W., lawyer; b. 1947; BA, CCNY, 1968; JD, NYU, 1973, LLM Trade Regulation, 1986. Bar: NJ 1973, NY 1984, US Dist. Ct., Dist. NJ, So. and Ea. Dist. NY, US Ct. Appeals, Second and Third Circuits, US Tax Ct., US Supreme Ct. With Clapp & Eisenberg P.C., Atlantic City; atty. Saiber Schlesinger Satz & Goldstein, LLC, Newark. Mem.: John C. Lifland Am. Inn. Ct., Essex County Bar Assn., Morris County Bar Assn., NJ State Bar Assn., NY State Bar Assn., ABA. Office: Saiber Schlesinger Satz & Goldstein LLC One Gateway Ctr 13th Fl Newark NJ 07102-5311

LORELLI, ELVIRA MAE, artist, art educator; d. Clement Vladimir Svoboda and Sylvia Georgiana Nikl; m. Pasqualino Geovani Lorelli, Nov. 22, 1955 (dec.); children: Patrick Eugene, Rhonda Mae Gilbert, Nancy Diane Yomogida. BA, Pomona Coll., 1950; MA in Art Edn., Claremont Grad. U., 1961, MA in Edn., 1969. Cert. elem. edn. Calif., 1960, secondary edn. Calif., 1960, tchg., jr. coll. specialization Calif., 1968. Art tchr. Trona Jr.-Sr. HS, Calif., 1952—54; art tchr., art coord. Barstow Unified Sch. Dist., Calif., 1954—59; art tchr. Barstow HS, 1959—62; art dept. head Barstow CC, 1962—82; art instr. U. Calif., Riverside, 1978—87, Chapman Coll., Barstow, 1979—84, Calif. Veteran's Home, Barstow, 1996—; artist, art instr. Elmae Studio, Barstow, 1976—. Coord. instructor's guide Stamp & Stencil, 1965; organizer faculty art workshops Barstow Sch. Dist., 1960—64. Author: (book) Art With And Without Music, 1960; murals, Barstow Bapt. Ch., 1969, Barstow Meth. Ch., 1984, sculptures, Centennial Park, Barstow, Calif., 1990, sculpture, St. Philip Neri Ch., Lenwood, Calif., 1996, exhibitions include Calico Ann. Fine Arts Festival, Yermo, Calif., 1980—95, Lorain's Coffee Shop, Barstow, 2004—, Idle Spurs Restaurant, Barstow, Calif., 2005—, Barstow C. of C., Calif., 2005—, Art on the Lake, Big Bear, Calif., 2005—. Judge Ann. Art Exhibition Newberry Art Guild, Newberry Springs, Calif., 1985; judge Ann. Art Show Officer's Wives, Fort Irwin, Calif., 1987; judge, parade floats Kiwanis Club, Barstow, 1989, 1995; designer parade float Veteran's Home, Barstow, 1997; literacy tutor Barstow Libr., 1999—; bd. mem. Projects for Achieving Creativity in Edn. in San Bernadino, 1976—84. Recipient Cert. Appreciation, Skyline North Sch. PTA, 1984, Kederka award, Barstow Veteran's Home Calif., 2004. Mem.: Calif. Retired Tchrs. Assn., Barstow Artists' Guild (pres. 1966—68), Barstow Emblem Club (trustee 2003—, historian 1994—96, 1998—99, Sister of Yr. 1998—99). Republican. Roman Catholic. Avocations: photography, camping, swimming, bowling, golf, line dancing. Office Phone: 760-256-6636.

LORELLI, MICHAEL KEVIN, consumer products company executive; b. NYC, Apr. 17, 1951; s. Domenic and Effie (Stankevich) L.; m. Nancy Buck; children: Karen, Elizabeth. BE, NYU, 1972, MBA in Mktg., 1973. Dir. mktg. Clairol Co., NYC, 1973-81, v.p., gen. mgr. divsn. Almay cosmetics, 1983-84; v.p., gen. mgr. internat. div. Playtex, Stamford, Conn., 1981-84; v.p. mktg. Apple Computer, Cupertino, Calif., 1984-85; exec. v.p. Pepsi-Cola Co., Somers, NY, 1985-88; pres. Pepsi-Cola East, Somers, NY, 1989-92, Pizza Hut Internat., 1993-95; pres. America's divsn. Tambrands, Inc., White Plains, NY, 1995-96; ptnr. Bryant Ptnrs. L.L.C., 1997-99; v.p., chief devel. officer Air Express Internat., Darien, Conn., 1999-2001; pres., CEO Lens Express, Inc., Yonkers, NY, 2001—02; pres. Latex Internat., Shelton, 2003—, CEO, 2003—. Bd. dirs. Trident Internat., Inc., Closure, Inc., Rosenbluth Travel. Author: Traveling Again, Dad?. Avocations: flying, golf, running. Office Phone: 203-655-2444. Personal E-mail: miklorelli@aol.com.

LOREN, ALLAN Z., former financial services company executive; Grad., Queens Coll., NYC, Stanford U. Various positions including chief info. officer, chief adminstrv. officer Cigna Corp., 1971-87; chief info. officer, then pres. Apple Computer, 1987-91; pres., CEO Galileo Internat., 1991-94; exec. v.p., chief info. officer Am. Express Co., 1994-2000; chmn. Dun & Bradstreet, Short Hills, NJ, 2000—05, CEO, 2000—05. Bd. dirs. Dun & Bradstreet Corp., U.S. Cellular Corp., Hershey Foods Corp., Reynolds & Reynolds Co., Venator Group, Inc., First Knowledge Ptnrs. Inc.; mem. adv. bd. eCustomers.com.*

LOREN, DONALD PATRICK, federal official, retired military officer; b. NYC, Mar. 17, 1952; s. Nicholas A. and Helen T. (Carrado) L.; m. Maureen M. Lynch, Jan. 12, 1991. BS in Ops. Analysis, U.S. Naval Acad., 1974; MS in Edn., Old Dominion U., 1983; postgrad., Harvard U., 1993-94, MIT, 1994-95. Commd. ens. USN, 1974, advanced through grades to rear adm., combat sys. officer, Destroyer Squadron Thirty-One, 1978; ops. officer USS Peterson, 1979-80; ops. and readiness officer Destroyer Squadron Two Staff, 1981-82; asst. chief of staff for comms. Cruiser Destroyer Group Eight Staff, 1983-85; exec. officer USS John Hancock, 1985-86; flag sec. to comdr. in chief U.S. Naval Forces, Europe, 1986-88; NATO policy officer Strategic Plans and Policy Directory, Joint Staff, 1989-91; comdg. officer USS Elrod FFG-55, 1991-93; doctrine devel. officer Naval Doctrine Command, 1993; fed. exec. fellow Ctr. for Internat. Affairs Harvard U., Cambridge, Mass., 1993-94; profl. staff mem. Ind. Commn. on Roles and Missions of Armed Forces, 1993-94; comdr. Destroyer Squadron Twenty-eight, Norfolk, Va., 1995-97; dep. dir. strategy and policy divsn. Office the the Chief of Naval Ops., 1997-98; exec. asst. to comdr. in chief U.S. Naval Forces Europe, 1998—2001; and comdr. in chief Allied Forces So. Europe, 1998—2001; exec. asst., prin. advisor to operational comdr. NATO Combat Forces, 1999—2001; dep. dir. surface ships Office of the Chief of Naval Ops., 2001—03; dep. dir. politico-mil. affairs Europe, NATO,Russia and Africa, The Joint Staff, 2003—05; dep. dir. ops. support Nat. Counterterrorism Ctr., Washington, 2006—07; dep. asst. sec. def. homeland security integration Dept. Def., Washington, 2007—. Fellow MIT, Seminar XXI, fgn. politics, internat. rels. and the nat. interest, 1994-95; fellow nat. security studies Maxwell Sch., Syracuse U., 2003; fellow NATO Def. Coll., Rome, 2004; fellow sr. execs. in nat. and internat. security program Harvard U. JFK Sch. Govt., 2004, Northwestern U. Kellogg Sch. Mgmt., 2006, U. Md. Sch. Pub. Policy, 2006. Author: Shape Up! A Shipboard Program for Physical Fitness, 1981; contbr. articles to profl. publs. Decorated Def. Superior Svc. medal U.S. Army, Bronze star, Order Merit Italian Republic, Conspicuous Svc. Star and Cross N.Y. State. Mem. Phi Kappa Phi, Sigma Iota Epsilon. Avocations: jogging, weight training, classical music, ballet, opera. Office: 6504 John Thomas Dr Alexandria VA 22315

LOREN, NORMAN JAMES, lawyer; s. Jefford George and Carrol Adina (Nesbitt) Loren; m. Myrna Marlene Mullenix, Dec. 23, 1967; children: Linnea Kristina, Bradley Norman, Aaron Jefferson, Eric Justin, Bethany Jo. BA, U. Minn., Mpls., 1964; JD, U. Minn., 1969. Bar: Minn. 1969. Atty. Kanabec County, Minn., 1972—.

LOREN, SOPHIA, actress; b. Rome, Sept. 20, 1934; d. Riccardo Scicolone and Romilda Villani; m. Carlo Ponti, Apr. 12, 1967 (dec. Jan. 9, 2007); children: Carlo Jr., Edoardo. Student, Scuole Magistrali Superiori. Films include E Arrivato l'Accordatore, 1951, Africa sotto i Mari, La Favorita, La Tratta Delle Bianche, 1952, Aida, Tempi Nostri, Ci Troviamo in Gellera, La Domenica Della Buona Genti, Il Paese dei Campanelli, Un Giorno in Pretura, Due Notti con Cleopatra, Pelegrini d'Amore, Attila, Carosello Napoletano, 1953, Miseria e Nobilta, Gold of Naples, Woman of the River, Too Bad She's Bad (Best Actress award Buenos Aires Festival), 1954, Lucky To Be A Woman, Sign of Venus, The Millers Wife, Scandal in Sorrento, 1955, Pride and Passion, Boy on a Dolphin, Legend of The Lost, 1957, Desire Under the Elms, Houseboat, The Key (Best Actress award Japan), 1958, That Kind of Woman, Black Orchid, 1959 (Best Actress Venice Festival, David Di Donatello award Italy, Victoire Popularity award France), Heller in Pink Tights (Best Actress Rapallo Festival Italy), It Started in Naples, A Breath of Scandal, The Millionaires, 1960, Two Women, (11 Best Actress awards including Oscar, Hollywood, Di Donatello award, Cannes Film Festival, N.Y. Critics, Golden Globe, Brit. Film Acad., others from Ireland, Japan, Belgium, Spain, France, W. Ger., also other awards), El Cid, Madame, Bocaccio 70, 1961, The Condemned of Altona, Five Miles to Midnight, 1962, Yesterday, Today and Tomorrow, (Best Actress Di Donatello award, Golden Globe award), 1963, The Fall of the Roman Empire, Marriage Italian Style, 1964 (Best Actress Di Donatello award, Golden Globe award, Alexander Korda award Brit. Film Inst., others), Operation Crossbow, Lady L, Judith, 1965, Arabesque, A Countess From Hong Kong, 1966, Happily Ever After, Ghosts, Italian Style (Best Fgn. Actress Diploma USSR), 1967, More Than A Miracle, (Ramo d'Oro award Italy, other awards), 1968, Sunflower (Best Actress Di Donatello award), 1969, The Priest's Wife, 1970, Lady Liberty, White Sister, 1971, Man of La Mancha, 1972, The Voyage (Di Donatello award), 1973, Brief Encounter, The Verdict, 1974, The Cassandra Crossing, A Special Day, 1977, Firepower, 1978, Brass Target, 1979, Blood Feud, 1981, Ready to Wear (Prêt-à-Porter), 1994, Grumpier Old Men, 1995, Messages, 1996, Soleil, 1997, Destinazione Verna, 1999, Between Strangers, 2002, Too Much Romance.It's Time for Stuffed Peppers, 2004; TV film appearances include Sophia Loren: Her Own Story, 1980, Angela, 1982, Aurora, 1985, Mother Courage, 1986, The Fortunate Pilgrim (Best Actress of Yr. for TV mini-series), 1987, La Ciociara, 1989. Recipient numerous awards including Nastro d'Argento, Italy, 14 Bambi and Bravo Popularity awards, Fed. Republic Germany, 3 Prix Uilenspigoel Fiamingo award, Belgium, Popularity awards Am. Legion, Tex. Cinema Exhibitors, 4 Snosiki Popularity awards, Finland, 2 Best Actress awards Bengal Film Journalists Assn., India, Box-Office Favourite Medal, Italy, Helene Curtis award, U.S.A., Simpatia Popularity award, Italy, Rudolph Valentino Screen Svcs. award, Italy, Best Actress award Moscow Film Festival, Hon. Acad. award, 1990; named Most Popular Actress in Italy. Address: c/o La Concordia Ranch 1151 Hidden Valley Ranch Rd Thousand Oaks CA 91361

LORENO, NINA LOUISE, elementary school educator; b. Mpls., Sept. 16, 1972; d. Francis and Roberta Kay Loreno; m. Eric Andrew Cook, June 19, 2004. BA in Speech and Comms., U. Minn., 1995, BA in English, 1999; cert. tchr., U. St. Thomas, 2000, MA in Edn., 2001. Ednl. asst. Mpls. Pub. Schs., 1998—2000, mid. sch. tchr., 2001—. Avocations: running, reading. Office: Cityview Cmty Sch 3350 4th St N Minneapolis MN 55412 Personal E-mail: ninalouise2003@yahoo.com.

LORENSEN, FREDERICK HAMILTON, educational administrator, consultant; b. Bridgeport, Conn., Nov. 12, 1943; s. Frederick Irving and Virginia Francis (Hamilton) L.; m. Ruth Ann Hogan, July 8, 1967; children: Lisa, Erik, Kevin. BA, Fairfield U., Conn., 1965, MEd, 1966; PhD, U. Conn., 1979. Tchr. social studies Masuk H.S., Monroe, Conn., 1966-67; admissions counselor Fairfield U., 1967-69, assoc. dir. admissions, 1969-79; dir. admissions Duquesne U., Pitts., 1979-91, dir. freshman devel. and spl. student svcs., 1991—. Cons. scholarships Ednl. Testing Svc., Princeton, N.J., 1986—, Alcoa, Pitts., 1991-99; ednl. cons. Northwood Realty, Pitts., 1986-96; presenter numerous workshops. Mem. acad. excellence com. North Allegheny H.S., Wexford, Pa., 1986; Cub Scout pack leader Boy Scouts Am., Wexford, 1980-82. Recipient Loyola award Fairfield (Conn.) U., 1965, Svc. award Nat. Assn. Coll. Admissions Counselors, 1985, Presdl. Staff Excellence award, Duquesne U., 2000; Glee Club scholar Fairfield U., 1964-65, Dissertation fellow U. Conn., 1978. Mem. Nat. Orientation Dirs. Assn., Middle States Assn. Registrars and Officers of Admissions (pres. 1990-91, named hon. mem. 1999), Assn. on Higher Edn. and Disability. Roman Catholic. Avocations: reading, swimming. Office: Duquesne U 309 Duquesne Un Pittsburgh PA 15282-0001 Home Phone: 412-369-3781; Office Phone: 412-396-6657. Business E-Mail: lorensen@duq.edu.

LORENTZ, JOSHUA A., lawyer; b. Orlando, Fla., Feb. 12, 1975; BA in Polit. Sci., Ohio U., 1998, BS in Bio., 1997; JD, U. Dayton Sch. Law, 2001. Bar: Ohio 2001, US Dist. Ct. Southern Dist. Ohio 2001, US Ct. of Appeals Sixth Cir. 2001, US Ct. of Appeals Fed. Cir. 2001, US Patent and Trademark Office. Assoc. Dinsmore & Shohl LLP, Cin. Named one of Ohio's Rising Stars, Super Lawyers, 2006. Mem.: Licensing Exec. Soc., Am. Intellectual Property Law Assn., Ohio State Bar Assn., Cin. Bar Assn. Office: Dinsmore & Shohl LLP 255 E Fifth St Ste 1900 Cincinnati OH 45202-4700 Office Phone: 513-977-8564. Office Fax: 513-977-8141.

LORENZ, HANS ERNEST, photographer; b. Karlsbad, Czechoslovakia, Sept. 11, 1940; came to U.S., 1950; naturalized, 1954; s. Hugo and Maria (Gareis) L.; m. Pamela Marie Carswell, May 27, 1978; 1 child, April Nicole BA, Okla. Bapt. U., 1962. Tchr. pub. schs., Prince George County, Va., 1964—65; sr. curatorial photographer Colonial Williamsburg Found., Va., 1965—. Writer, lectr. 19th Century photographic history Contbr. photographs to numerous books on 18th Century antiques Mem. Nat. Stereoscopic Assn., Am. Numismatic Assn Baptist. Home: 116 Walnut Hills Dr Williamsburg VA 23185-3433 Office: PO Box 1776 Williamsburg VA 23187-1776 E-mail: hlorenz@cwf.org.

LORENZ, HUGO ALBERT, retired insurance executive, consultant; b. Elmhurst, Ill., July 5, 1926; s. Hugo E. and Linda T. (Trampel) L. BS, Northwestern U., 1949; LL.B., Harvard U., 1952. Bar: Ill. 1954. Mem. patent staff Bell Telephone Labs., Murray Hill, NJ, 1952-53; atty. First Nat. Bank Chgo., 1954-58; gen. counsel N.Am. Life Ins. Co. of Chgo., 1958-73; dir., v.p., gen. counsel, sec. Globe Life Ins. Co., Chgo., 1973-95; v.p. Union Fidelity Life Ins. Co., Chgo., 1993-96; sec. Gt. Equity Life Ins. Co., Chgo., 1977-80, Pat Ryan & Assos. Inc., Va. Surety Co., Chgo., 1977-96. Bd. dirs. Sr. Ctrs. Met. Chgo., 1977-93, pres., 1983-85; trustee Hull House Assn., 1983-88. With USNR, 1944-46. Mem. Assn. Life Ins. Counsel, Connoisseurs Internat (bd. dirs. 1972—2004, pres. 1980-95), Internat. Wine and Food Soc. Chgo. (gov. and oenologist 1980—2006). Unitarian Universalist. Home: 950 N Clark St # A Chicago IL 60610-8701

LORENZ, JOHN GEORGE, librarian, consultant; b. NYC, Sept. 28, 1915; s. John W. and Theresa T. (Wurtz) L.; m. Josephine R. Trumbull, Oct. 1, 1944; children: Laurence T., Janice R. BS (Library fellow), CCNY, 1939; BS in L.S, Columbia U., 1940; MS in Pub. Adminstrn., Mich. State U., 1952. With Queens Borough (N.Y.) Library, then Schenectady Pub. Library, 1940-44; chief reference div. Grand Rapids Pub. Library, 1944-46; asst. librarian Mich. State Library, 1946-56; with U.S. Office Edn., 1957-65, dir. div. library services and ednl. facilities, 1964-65; dep. librarian of congress Library of Congress, Washington, 1965-76; exec. dir. Assn. Research Libraries, 1976-80; library cons., 1980—; interim dir. libraries Cath. U. Am., 1982-83; liaison mem. com. sci. and tech. info. exec. office, 1966-73; interim dir. CAPCON, 1985; spl. asst. to librarian Georgetown U. Library, 1985-87; interim dir. Washington Research Library Consortium, 1987-88; coord. libr. stats. program Nat. Commn. on Librs. and Inf. Sci., 1988-97. Exec. com. Nat. Book Com., 1968-74 Contbr. articles to profl. jours., chapters to books. Presdl. appointee Nat. Hist. Publs. and Records Commn., 1979-83; bd. dirs. Pitts. Lifetime Care Cmty. Recipient Superior Svc. award HEW. Mem. ALA (coun. 1960-64, 69-73, chmn. panel UNESCO 1965-70, exec. bd. 1970-75, Lippincott award 1993), D.C. Libr. Assn., Internat. Fedn. Libr. Assn. (mem. program devel. group 1974-78), Am. Nat. Stds. Inst. (treas. libr. stds. com. 1980-88), Cosmos Club. Home: 100 Norman Dr Apt 311 Cranberry Township PA 16066-4229

LORENZ, KATHERINE MARY, bank executive; b. Barrington, Ill., May 1, 1946; d. David George and Mary (Hogan) L. BA cum laude, Trinity Coll., 1968; MBA, Northwestern U., 1971; grad., Grad. Sch. for Bank Adminstrn., 1977. Ops. analyst Continental Bank, Chgo., 1968, supr. ops. analysis, 1969—71, asst. mgr. customer profitability analysis, 1971—73, acctg. officer, mgr. customer profitability analysis, 1973—77, 2d v.p., 1976, asst. gen. mgr. contr.'s dept., 1977—80, v.p., 1980, contr. ops. and mgmt. svcs. dept., 1981—84, v.p., sector contr. retail banking, corp. staff and ops. depts., 1984—88, v.p., sr. sector contr. pvt. banking, centralized ops. and corp. staff, 1988—90, v.p., sr. sector contr. bus. analysis group/mgmt. acctg., 1990—94, mgr. contrs. dept. adminstrn. and tng., 1990—94; v.p., chief of staff to chief adminstrv. officer Bank Am. Ill., Chgo., 1994—96, sr. v.p., mgr. adminstrv. svcs., 1996—97, mng. dir., mgr. adminstrv. svcs., 1998—99; sr. v.p., Chgo. adminstrn. exec. Bank Am., 1999—. Mem.: Execs. Club Chgo. Office: Bank of Am ILI-231-13-20 231 S La Salle St Chicago IL 60697 Office Phone: 312-828-4756.

LORENZ, LEE SHARP, cartoonist; b. Hackensack, NJ, Oct. 17, 1932; s. Alfred Lloyd and Martha (Castagnetta) L.; children: Matthew, Martha, Ava. Student, Carnegie Inst. Tech., 1950-51; BFA, Pratt Inst., 1954. Staff cartoonist New Yorker mag., 1958—, art editor, 1973—97. Author: The Art of the New Yorker, 1995, The World of William Steig, 1998, The Essential George Booth, 1999, The Essential Charles Barsott, 1999, The Essential Jack Ziegler, 2001. Trustee Swann Coll. of Cartoon and Caricature, 1978—; dir. Mus. for African Art. Mem. Century Club. Home: PO Box 117 Easton CT 06612-0117

LORENZ, MATHIAS, art director; b. Hamburg, Germany, Oct. 1, 1961; arrived in US, 1996; s. Karl-Heinz and Marianne Lorenz; m. Michaela Albrecht, Nov. 7, 1972; children: Rachel Melody, Joshua Benjamin. Student, U. Hamburg, Germany, 1984—86. Creative dir. SSP Advt., Hamburg, 1989—95; tech. dir. Walt Disney Feature Animation, Orlando, Fla., 1992—2003; creative dir. Scholz & Friends, Hamburg, 1996; tech. dir. Walt Disney Feature Animation, Burbank, Calif., 1997—2001, Warner Bros. Feature Animation, Sherman Oaks, Calif., 2001—02; art dir. Electronic Arts, Orlando, 2004—. Online artist and publ. Exhibitions include Siggraph 1996 Video Review and Computer Animation Festival Electronic Theater, Walt Disney Feature Animation, Fla., le festival du Dessin Anime, 1997, Computer Illusions 1997, PBS, 1997, ISEA96, 1996, Represented in permanent collections online exhibit, pluginz.com, anthologies including, Art of Fiction; dir.: (animated short film) Paris 1999 (First place Morpheus Forge Entertainment), 2d place Morpheus Forge Entertainment); Superman Returns-The Videogame, Digital Webbing Presents #8 Anthology; contbr. chapters to books. With German Army, 1981—82. Home: 5020 Olde Kerry Dr Orlando FL 32837 Office: Electronic Arts 1950 Summit Park Dr Orlando FL 32810 Office Phone: 407-232-4942. Office Fax: 407-386-4001. Personal E-mail: mlorenz1@cfl.rr.com. Business E-Mail: mlorenz@ea.com.

LORENZ, NANCY, artist; BFA in Painting and Printmaking, U. Mich., 1985; MFA in Painting, Tyler Sch. Art, Phila. and Rome, 1988. Instr. R.I. Sch. Design, 1996; lectr. in field. One-woman shows include Temple U., Rome, 1988, Willoughby Sharp Gallery, NY, 1990, Genovese Gallery, Boston, 1990, 1991, 1994, others, exhibited in group shows at Helander Gallery, NY, 1989—93, JG Contemporary, NYC, 2006, Helander Gallery, Palm Beach, 1989—91, NY Pub. Libr., 1994, Austin Ackles Studio, NY, 1995, PDX, Portland, 1996, 1998, 2000, Galerie Verneil des Saints-Péres, Paris, Galerie Xippas, numerous others, Represented in permanent collections Senayan Hotel, Jakarta, Yokahama Hotel, Japan, Soho Grand Hotel, NY, MIA Ins., Pan Am. Bldg., San Francisco, Muscat Hilton, Oman, David Barton Gym, NY Pub. Libr., Champion Paper, Ohio, Shinwa Med. Inc., Nagoya, Japan, Aero Studios, NY, The Boston Co., numerous others. Guggenheim fellow, 1998. Office: Pdx Gallery 925 NW Flanders St Portland OR 97209-3123 E-mail: pdxgallery@aol.com.

LORENZ, TED R., lawyer; m. Lesley Howe Lorenz. BA, U. Tex., Austin; JD, U. Houston, 2000. Bar: Tex. Trial atty., Dallas; founding ptnr. Lorenz & Lorenz, L.L.P., Austin, Tex., 2001—. Named a Rising Star, Tex. Super Lawyers mag., 2006. Mem.: Assn. Trial Lawyers of Am., Capital Area Trial Lawyers Assn., Austin Bar Assn. Office: Lorenz & Lorenz LLP 2224 Walsh Tarlton Ste 225 Austin TX 78746 Office Phone: 512-477-7333. E-mail: TedLorenz@AustinAccidentAttorney.com.*

LORENZE, MARK DAVID, orthopedist, surgeon; b. Richmond, Va., July 20, 1966; BS, Yale U., 1988; MD, Tufts U., 1992. Cert. Orthop. Surgeon. Intern gen. surgery Yale-New Haven Hosp., Conn., resident orthop. surgery Conn.; fellowship hand and upper extremity surgery Tufts U., Boston, 1997; orthop. surgeon Shoreline Orthops. and Sports Medicine LLC, Essex, Conn.; staff mem. Middlesex Hosp., Middletown, Conn. Named one of Top 250 Golfer Doctors in Am., Golf Digest, 2006. Mem.: AMA, Middlesex County Med. Soc., Ct. State Med. Soc., Am. Acad. Orthopaedic Surgeons, Ea. Orthopaedic Assn., Alpha Omega Alpha. Office: Shoreline Orthops and Sports Medicine LLC 12 Bokum Rd Essex CT 06426 also: 1353 Boston Post Rd Madison CT 06443 Office Phone: 860-767-9053. Office Fax: 860-767-1146.*

LORENZEN, ROBERT FREDERICK, ophthalmologist; b. Toledo, Mar. 20, 1924; s. Martin Robert and Pearl Adeline (Bush) L.; m. Lucy Logdson, Feb. 14, 1970; children: Roberta Jo, Richard Martin, Elizabeth Anne. BS, MD, Duke U., 1948; MS, Tulane U., 1953. Intern Presbyn. Hosp., Chgo., 1948-49; resident Duke U. Med. Ctr., 1949-51, Tulane Grad. Sch., 1951-53; practice medicine specializing in ophthalmology Phoenix, 1953—. Bd. dirs. St. Vincent de Paul Eye Clinic; mem. staff St. Joseph's Hosp., St. Luke's Hosp., Good Samaritan Hosp., Surg. Eye Ctr. of Ariz. Pres. Ophthalmic Scis. Found., 1970-73; chmn. bd. trustees Rockefeller and Abbe Prentice Eye Inst. of St. Luke's Hosp., 1975—. Editor in chief Ariz. Medicine, 1963-66, 69-70. Named to Honorable Order of Ky. Colls.; recipient Gold Headed Cane award, 1974. Fellow ACS, Internat. Coll. Surgeons, Am. Acad. Ophthalmology and Otolaryngology, Pan Am. Assn. Ophthalmology; mem. Am. Assn. Ophthalmology (sec. of ho. of dels. 1972-73, trustee 1973-76), Ariz. Ophthal. Soc. (pres. 1966-67), Ariz. Med. Assn. (bd. dirs. 1963-66, 69-70), Royal Soc. Medicine, Rotary (pres. Phoenix 1984-850). Republican. Office: 3333 E Camino Sin Nombre Paradise Valley AZ 85253

LORENZO, MICHAEL, engineer, real estate broker, government official; b. Newton, NJ, 1920; m. Anastasia Hackett; 5 children. BS in Chemistry and Physics, Pa. State U., 1947; MEA, George Washington U., 1956, postgrad., 1975-78, USDA Grad. Sch. Registered profl. engr., D.C., Md.; cert. Internat. Property Specialist, FIPC; lic. real estate broker, Md., Va., D.C. Field instrumentation engr. Fischer and Porter Co., Harboro, Pa., 1947-52; aerospace engr. Dept. Def., 1952-65; with Westinghouse Electric Corp., Friendship, Md., 1965-81; mgr. Air Resources Westinghouse Mgmt. Services, Inc., 1966-70, dir. environ. quality control, 1970-73; founder, pres. Tech. Protection Engring. Co., 1982—; dep. under-sec. def. Washington, 1981-82; founder, prin. broker First Lady Realty Corp., Falls Church, Va., 1986—, Best Real Estate Corp., Falls Church, 2007—. Author: (with others) Chemical Equipment Costs, 1950; assoc. editor: Missile and Rockets, 1958-61; contbr. articles to profl. jours.; patentee stall surge sonic sensor. Rear Adm. AC USN, World War II, Korea. Decorated D.S.M., D.F.C. (2), Air medals (7) Mem.: Profl. Tennis Registry. Office: Best Real Estate Corp 3126 Shadeland Dr Falls Church VA 22044-1726 Office Phone: 703-534-7920. *Healthy mind requires healthy body and vice versa. Per Winston Churchill "A Democracy is one of the worst forms of Government invented, except for all the others." It's my time in life to give back. You don't get a second chance to make a good first impression.*

LORETTA, MARK, professional baseball player; b. Santa Monica, Calif., Aug. 14, 1971; Infielder Mil. Brewers, 1995—2002, Houston Astros, 2002, San Diego Padres, 2003—05. Achievements include starting second baseman AL team MLB All-Star Game, 2006. Office: Boston Red Sox 4 Yawkey Way Boston MA 02215-3496

LORI, WILLIAM E., bishop; b. Louisville, May 6, 1951; BA, St. Pius X Sem., Covington, Ky., 1973; MA, Mount St. Mary's Sem., Emmitsburg, Md., 1977; STD, Cath. U. Washington, 1982. Ordained priest Roman Cath. Ch. 1977. Sec. to James Cardinal Hickey, 1983-94; chancellor/vicar gen., moderator of Curia, 1994-95; titular bishop Diocese of Bulla, 1995-2001; aux. bishop, vicar gen./moderator of Curia, Archdiocese of Washington, 1995-2001; bishop of Bridgeport, Conn., 2001—. Chmn. Archdiocesan Commn. for Ecumenical and Interreligious, 1982—86; theol. advisor to Archbishop, 1982—94; mem. com. in edn. USCC, 1996, mem. com. on human values, 96; trustee Cath. U. Am., 1997—, chmn. bd. trustees, 2003—, chair acad. affairs com., 1998—; mem. USCCB Commn. on Doctrine, 2001, USCCB Com. on Pro Life Activities; chmn. bd. trustees Sacred Heart U., Fairfield, Conn., 2001—. Mem.: KC (supreme chaplain 2005—). Roman Catholic. Office: 238 Jewett Ave Bridgeport CT 06606

LORIA, JEFFREY H., sports team executive; b. NYC; 3 children. Grad., Yale U., New Haven, Conn., 1962; MBA, Columbia U., NYC. Owner Oklahoma City 89ers, 1989-93; chmn., CEO Montreal Expos, 1999—2002; owner Florida Marlins, 2002—; internat. art dealer. Author: Collecting Original Art, What's It All About Charlie Brown. Former bd. dirs. Art Dealers Assn. Am. Named Am. Assn. 1992 Exec. of Yr. Office: Pro Player Stadium 2267 Dan Marino Blvd Miami FL 33028

LORIA, MARTIN A., lawyer; b. NYC, Apr. 11, 1951; s. Daniel Bernard and Estelle Miriam (Barasch) L.; m. Carol Berkowitz, June 3, 1973; children: Alyson, Marissa. BA, SUNY, Albany, 1972; JD, Suffolk U., 1975. Bar: Mass. 1975, U.S. Dist. Ct. Mass. 1976, U.S. Supreme Ct. 1979. Atty. New Eng. states counsel Lawyers Title Ins. Corp., Boston, 1979—82; ptnr. Adelson, Golden & Loria, P.C., Boston, 1983—2000, Cherwin Theise Adelson & Loria LLP, Boston, 2001—02, Adelson Loria & Weisman PC, Boston, 2003—. Lectr. Mass Conveyances Assn. Contbg. author Massachusetts Continuing Legal Education Crocker's Notes. Named Best Real Estate Lawyer in Boston, Boston Mag., 2002; named one of Top Boston Lawyers, 2004, 2005. Mem. ABA, Mass. Bar Assn., Boston Bar Assn., Mass. Conveyancers Assn. (pres. 1991, bd. dirs. 1988-2000), Abstract Club (bd. dirs., pres.). Office: Adelson Loria & Weisman PC One Internat Place Boston MA 02110 Office Phone: 617-330-1625. Business E-Mail: mloria@alwfirm.com.

LORIMER, LINDA KOCH, university educator; children: Katharine Elizabeth, Peter Brailler. AB, Hollins Coll., 1974; JD, Yale U., 1977; DHL (hon.), Green Mountain Coll., 1991, Washington Coll., 1992, Randolph-Macon Coll., 1992. Bar: N.Y. 1978, Conn. 1982. Assoc. Davis Polk and Wardwell, NYC, 1977-78; asst. gen. counsel Yale U., New Haven, 1978-79, assoc. gen. counsel, 1979-84, assoc. provost, 1983-87, acting assoc. v.p. human resources, 1984-85; prof. law, pres. Randolph-Macon Woman's Coll., Lynchburg, Va., 1987-93; v.p., sec. Yale Univ., New Haven, 1993—. Lectr. Yale Coll. Undergrad. Seminars, 1980, 83; bd. dirs. Sprint, McGraw Hill, Yale-New Haven Hosp.; mem. corp. Yale U., 1990-93, chair Virginia Rhodes scholarship com., 1991-93; trustee HollinsU., Berkeley Divinity Sch. Chair editorial bd. Jour. Coll. and Univ. Law, 1983-87. Former trustee Hollins Coll., Berkeley Div. Sch.; mem. com. on responsible conduct rsch. Inst. Medicine, NAS, 1988; bd. dirs. Norfolk Acad.; cabinet mem. United Way of Greater New Haven. Mem. Nat. Assn. Coll. and Univ. Attys. (exec. bd. 1981-84), Nat. Assn. Schs. and Colls. United Meth. Ch. (1st v.p.), Am. Assn. Colls. and Univs. (pres. bd.), Assn. Am. Colls.,(pres. bd. dirs., chmn. bd.), Am. Assn. Theol. Schs. (bd. dirs.), Mory's Assn., Phi Beta Kappa. Episcopalian. Office: Woodbridge Hall PO Box 208230 Yale Univ New Haven CT 06520-8230

LORIMER, THOMAS HAROLD, minister; b. Elmhurst, Ill., Dec. 5, 1955; s. Dr. Frank Martin and Linda Leone (Lautzenhiser) L.; m. Rebekah Ann Mathes, Aug. 13, 1976; children: Amy Beth, Stephen Andrew, David Wesley, Daniel Paul. BA summa cum laude, Olivet Nazarene U., Kankakee, Ill., 1977, MA, 1981, M in Ch. Mgmt., 1988. Assoc. pastor First Ch. Nazarene, Ottawa, Ill., 1977-79; pastor Kempton (Ill.) Ch. Nazarene, 1979-83, First CH. Nazarene, Waukesha, Wis., 1983-84, Clarion (Iowa) Ch. Nazarene, 1984-90, First Ch. Nazarene, Fort Madison, Iowa, 1990—. Abstractor Religous and Theol. Abstracts, Myerstown, Pa., 1983—; dir. lay training Iowa Dist. Sunday Sch. Ministries Bd., 1989—; sec. treas. Clarion (Iowa) Ministerial Assn., 1988-90; treas. Iowa Dist. Nazarene World Missionary Soc., 1991—. Author: Why Not? Why is Premarital Sex Wrong?, 1989, An Index to Money, 1987. Dir. Wright County Right to Life, Iowa, 1985-90; active mem. North Lee County Right to Life, 1990—. Benner Scholar Olivet Nazarene U., 1978-79. Mem. Am. Mensa, Ltd., Tri-State Homeschool Assn. (newsletter editor 1990—). Home: 511 22nd St Fort Madison IA 52627-2311 Office: Church of the Nazarene 503 22nd St Fort Madison IA 52627-2311 *All around are open doors of opportunites and relationships. Walking through one open door does not mean I must close the others. I chose to leave open all the doors I can. Someday, I may need to walk through the others.*

LORING, ARTHUR, lawyer, diversified financial services company executive; b. NYC, Oct. 13, 1947; s. Murray and Mildred (Rogers) Loring; m. Vicki Hootstein, June 4, 1978. BS in Commerce, Washington and Lee U., 1969; JD cum laude, Boston U., 1972. Bar: Mass. 1972. Atty. Fidelity Mgmt. & Rsch. Co., Boston, 1972-98, sr. legal counsel, 1980-82, v.p., gen. counsel, 1983—93, sr. v.p., gen. counsel, 1993-98; v.p.-legal FMR Corp., Boston, 1982-98; sec. Fidelity Group of Funds, Boston, 1982-98; dir. Fidelity Capital Publs. Inc., 1991-98; v.p. Fidelity Distbr. Corp., Boston, 1984-98; sr. v.p., gen. counsel Fidelity Investments Instnl. Svcs., Inc., 1994-98; mng. dir. Cypress Holding Co., 1998-2000; mng. dir., mem. exec. com. Spyglass Investments LLC, Boston, 2000—04. Bd. govs. Investment Co. Inst., 1988—90; chmn. ICI SEC Rules Com., 1990—95; mem. adv. bd. Fund Directions, 1993—98; bd. dirs., chmn. audit com. New River, Inc., 1998—; dir. Global Alliance Value Investors, Ltd., 1999—2000, Advantage Bank, bd. dirs., chmn. investment com., 2000—03; bd. dirs. 1st United Bank, 2005—. Case editor: Boston U. Law Rev., 1971—72. Bd. dirs. Tradition of the Palm Beaches, 2004—, pres., 2004—; bd. dirs. Jewish Fedn. Palm Beach, 2001—, chmn. found. com., 2001—03, exec. com., 2002—, v.p., 2004—06, chmn. adminstrv. com., 2005—, pres.-elect, 2006—; adv. bd. Sch. Commerce, Washington and Lee U., 1996—; bd. dirs. Kramer Sr. Svc. Agy., 2000—, Morse Geriatric Ctr., 2001—, pres., 2004—06, Morse Life Found., 2002—, Morse Life, Inc., 2001—, bd. dirs., 2005—, pres. bd. dirs., 2005—07, chmn. bd. dirs., 2007—. Mem.: Palm Beach Country Club (bd. dirs. 2002—, treas. 2005—06, sec. 2006—), Pine Brook Country Club (bd. gov. 1996—, v.p. 2000—02, pres. 2002—04), Cavendish Club (bd. dirs. 1981—84), Boston Chess Club (pres. Brookline, Mass. 1981—83). Republican. Jewish. Avocations: golf, bridge, exercise, poker. Home: 622 N Flagler Dr 1001 West Palm Beach FL 33401

LORING, GLORIA JEAN, vocalist, actress, writer; b. NYC, Dec. 10, 1946; d. Gerald Louis and Dorothy Ann (Tobin) Goff; m. Alan Willis Thicke, Aug. 22, 1970 (div. 1986); children: Brennan Todd, Robin Alan; m. Christopher Beaumont, June 18, 1988 (div. 1993); m. René Lagler, Dec. 20, 1994. Grad. high sch. Owner Glitz Records, LA, 1984—; pres. Only Silk Prodns., LA, 1985-90; owner Silk Purse Prodns., 1992—. Began profl. singing, Miami Beach, 1965; appeared in numerous TV shows; featured singer: Bob Hope's Ann. Armed Forces Christmas Tour, 1970; featured several record albums; featured actress: Days of Our Lives, 1980-86; composer: TV themes Facts of Life, 1979, Diff'rent Strokes, 1978; author: Days of Our Lives Celebrity Cookbook, 1981, Vol. II, 1983, Living the Days of Our Lives, 1984, Kids, Food and Diabetes, 1986, Parenting a Diabetic Child, 1991, The Kids Food and Diabetes Family Cookbook, 1991, Parenting a Child with Diabetes, 1999, Living With Type 2 Diabetes: Moving Past the Fear, 2006. Celebrity chmn. Juvenile Diabetes Rsch. Found. Recipient Humanitarian of Yr. award Juvenile Diabetes Rsch. Found., 1982, 88, Lifetime Commitment award Juvenile Diabetes Rsch. Found., 1999, Woman of Achievement award Miss Am. Orgn., 1999. Office Phone: 310-274-8111. E-mail: gloria@glorialoring.com. *Life is a constant amazement!.*

LORING, JOHN ROBBINS, artist, writer; b. Chgo., Nov. 23, 1939; s. Edward D'Arcy and China Robbins (Logeman) L. BA, Yale U., 1960; postgrad., Ecole Beaux Arts, Paris, 1960-63; D in Arts (hon.), Pratt Inst., 1996. Disting. vis. prof. U. Calif., Davis, 1977; bur. chief Archtl. Digest mag., NYC, 1977—78; mem. acquisitions com. dept. prints and illustrated books Mus. Modern Art, NYC, 1990—99. Contbg. editor: Arts mag., 1973-79, Archtl. Digest mag., 2000—; books include: The New Tiffany Tablesettings, 1981, Tiffany Taste, 1986, Tiffany's 150 Years, 1987, The Tiffany Wedding, 1988, Tiffany Parties, 1989, The Tiffany Gourmet, 1992, A Tiffany Christmas, 1996, Tiffany's 20th Century, 1997, Tiffany Jewels, 1999, Paulding Farnham, Tiffany's Lost Genius, 2000, Magnificent Tiffany Silver, 2001, Louis Comfort Tiffany at Tiffany & Co., 2002, Tiffany Flora/Tiffany Fauna, 2003, Tiffany in Fashion, 2003, Tiffany Timepieces, 2004, Greetings from Andy, 2004, Tiffany Diamonds, 2005, Tiffany's Palm Beach, 2005, Tiffany Pearls, 2006, Tiffany Colored Gems, 2007; one-man exhbns. include Balt. Mus. Art, 1972, Hundred Acres Gallery, N.Y., 1972, Pace Edits., 1973, 77, Long Beach Mus. Art, 1975, A.D.I. Gallery, San Francisco, 1976; group exhbns. include Phila. Mus. Art, 1971, N.Y. Cultural Ctr., 1972, Biennale graphic Art, Ljubljana, Yugoslavia, 1973, 77, Intergrafia 74, Cracow, Poland, 1974, Bklyn. Mus. Nat. Print Exhbn., 1974, Art Inst. Chgo., 1975, R.I. Sch. Design, 1976; represented in permanent collections Mus. Modern Art, N.Y.C., Whitney Mus. Am. Art, Chgo. Art Inst., Boston Mus. Fine Arts, R.I. Sch. Design, Balt. Mus. Art, Yale U. Art Gallery; commd. by U.S. Customhouse, N.Y.C., Prudential Ins. Co. Am. Eastern Home Office, Woodbridge, N.J., City of Scranton, Pa., Western Savs., Phila., Tivoli Garden, Copenhagen. Recipient Edith Wharton award Design & Art Soc., 1988, Distinction in Design award Fashion Group Internat., 1996, Legends award Pratt Inst., 2002, Dallas Fashion award, 2004, Lifetime Achievement award Mus. Art and Design, NYC, 2005. Office: Tiffany & Co 600 Madison Ave New York NY 10022-2580 Address: 115 W 18th St New York NY 10011 Office Phone: 212-230-5339. *I look on whatever talents I may have as natural resources to be given freely wherever needed. A lot has been given out; a lot has come in.*

LORMAN, BARBARA K., retired state senator; b. Madison, Wis., July 31, 1932; 3 children. Student, U. Wis., Whitewater and Madison. Pres. Lorman Iron and Metal Recycling Co., Ft. Atkinson, Wis., 1979—87; mem. Wis. Senate, Madison, 1980—94. Formerly chair edn. com.; mem. health, human svc. and aging com., mem. fin. insts. and cultural affairs com., mem. select com. on healthcare reform; sec. Legis. Coun., also chmn. spl. com. on farm safety, mem. spl. com. on women offenders in correctional system; mem. spl. com. study sch. aid formula; commr. Edn. Commn. of States. bd. mem. Ft Atkinson Health Svcs., Auril; bd. mem. Ft. Healthcare Ptnrs. Bd. dirs. Rainbow Hospice Care, Inc., Ft. Atkinson (Wis.) Devel. Coun., Ft. Atkinson Meml. Hosp., Madison Area Tech. Coll., Wis. Pub. Radio Assn., past pres.; bd. dirs., past pres. Ft. Atkinson Hist. Soc., Ft. Atkinson Cmty. Found.; mem. exec. bd. Sinissippi coun. Boy Scouts Am.; mem. Wis. Gov.'s Commn. USS Wisconsin; mem. bd. visitors U. Wis. Extension; active Wis. Rep. Com.; chmn. spl. projects com. City of Ft. Atkinson. Mem.: Rotary. Address: 1245 Janette St Fort Atkinson WI 53538-1526

LORNE, SIMON MICHAEL, lawyer; b. Hampton, Eng., Feb. 1, 1946; arrived in US, 1952, naturalized, 1961; s. Henry Thomas and Daphne Mary (Brough) Lorne; children: Christopher, Michele, Allison, Nathan James, Katrina. AB cum laude, Occidental Coll., 1967; JD magna cum laude, U. Mich., 1970. Bar: Calif. 1971. Assoc. firm Munger, Tolles & Olson, LA, 1970—72, ptnr., 1972—93; gen. counsel U.S. SEC, 1993—96; mng. dir. Salomon Bros. Inc., 1996—. Vis. assoc. prof. law U. Pa., 1977—78; acting dir. Ctr. Study of Fin. Instns., 1977—78; lectr. in law, corp. fin. U. So. Calif., 1986—88. Author: (book) Acquisitions and Mergers: Negotiated and Contested Transactions, 1985. With USMCR, 1967—68. Mem.: ABA, L.A. County Bar Assn., Calif. (exec. com. bus. and corps. law sect., chmn. 1984—85), L.A. Area C. of C. (leadership mission to People's Republic of China 1980, exec. com., internat. commerce com.), Jonathan Club. Republican. Roman Catholic.

LOS, CORNELIS ALBERTUS, economist, finance educator, risk analyst; b. Purmerend, Netherlands, Dec. 14, 1951; arrived in U.S., 1977, naturalized, 1994; s. Klaas and Adriaantje (Nieuwland) Los; m. Diane Nichols, June 10, 1979 (div. 1984); 1 child, Francesca R. E.; m. Elizabeth M. Ten Houten, June 18, 1986 (div. 1991); 1 child, Marguerita E. A.; m. Rose Lee Haubenstock, May 5, 1994 (div. 2006); m. Elvira R. Kelgenbayeva, Aug. 25, 2006. Candidatus cum laude (BA Hon), U. Groningen, 1974, Doctorandus (MPhil), 1976; diploma, Inst. Social Studies, The Hague, 1977; MPhil, Columbia U., 1980, PhD, 1984. Tchg. asst. Columbia U., NYC, 1978-80, preceptor, 1979, instr., 1980-81; economist Fed. Res. Bank NY, NYC, 1981-85, sr. economist, 1985-87, Nomura Rsch. Inst. (America) Inc., 1987—90; chief U.S. economist NMB Postbank Group/ING Bank/ING Capital, NYC, 1991-93; assoc. prof. banking and fin. Nanyang Tech. U., Singapore, 1995-99; assoc. prof. fin. U. Adelaide, Australia, 2000; vis. assoc. prof. fin. Deakin U., 2001; assoc. prof. fin. Kent State U., 2001—05; prof. fin. and acctg. Kazakh-British Tech. U., 2005—06. Adj. lectr. Hunter Coll., NYC, 1980, CCNY, 1980—81; adj. prof. Baruch Coll., NYC, 1985—86; rsch. assoc. Ctr. Math. Sys. Theory U. Fla., Gainesville, 1986—92; CEO EMEPS Assocs. Inc., 1986—; cons. Worldbank, 1994—96, Inter-Am. Devel. Bank, 1994—96, Asian Devel. Bank, 1996—98; vis. prof. fin. Peter F. Drucker and Masatoshi Ito Grad. Sch. Mgmt., Claremont Grad. U., 2007—; vis. prof. fin. mgmt. Claremont Grad. U.; lectr. in field. Author: Computational Fin.-A Sci. Perspective, 2001, Financial Market Risk: Measurement & Analysis, 2003, Solutions Manual to Accompany Computational Finance, 2004, Solutions Manual to Accompany Financial Market Risk, 2004; contbr. articles to profl. jours., chapters to books. Mem. acad. bd. Nanyang Tech. U., 1997—99; bd. dirs. The Netherland-Am. Found., Inc., 1991—95. Recipient Lady Van Renswoude of The Hague Found. awards, 1974—75, MAOC Countess Van Bylandt Found. award, 1976, Scholten Cordès Found. awards, 1976—77; Fulbright-Hays scholar, 1977. Fellow: Soc. Columbia Scholars, Australasian Inst. Banking and Fin., Am. Coll. Forensic Examiners (life); mem.: CFA Inst., IEEE (sr.), European Fin. Mgmt. Assn., Bachelier Fin. Soc., NY Acad. Sci., Am. Math. Soc., Am. Fin. Assn., Am. Econ. Assn., Am. Statis. Assn., Internat. Assn. Math. and Computer Modeling, Internat. Assn. Fin. Engrs., Econometric Soc., Math. Assn. Am., Friends of New Netherland, London Goodenough Trust, World Coun. Alumni Internat. Ho. (NYC), Grad. Faculties Alumni Columbia U., Contemporary Long Rifle Assn., Co. Mil. Historians, Nat. Rifle Assn. (life), Nat. Muzzle Loading Rifle Assn., Columbia U. Club (Singapore) (found. treas.), Nat. Econ. Club. Republican. Avocations: history, travel, target shooting with flintlocks, photography. Home: 2122 W Arrow Rte 716 Upland CA 91786 Office: Peter F Drucker and Masatoshi Ho Grad Sch Mgmt 1021 N Dartmouth Ave Claremont CA 91711-3933 Office Phone: 909-607-9062. Personal E-mail: cal149@columbia.edu. Business E-Mail: cornelis.los@cgu.edu.

LOS, MARINUS, retired agrochemical researcher; b. Ridderkerk, The Netherlands, Sept. 18, 1933; arrived in U.S., 1960; s. Cornelis and Neeltje (Zoutewelle) Los; m. Lorraine Betty Lowe, May 11, 1957; children: Simon, Sija, Michael, Martin(dec.). BS, Edinburgh U., Scotland, 1955, PhD, 1957. Sr. rsch. chemist Am. Cyanamid Co., Princeton, NJ, 1960—71, group leader, 1971—84, sr. group leader, 1984—86, mgr. crop protection chems., 1986—88, assoc. dir. crop scis., 1988-92, rsch. dir. crop scis., 1992—96; ret., 1996. Recipient Disting. Inventor of 1990 award, Intellectual Property Owners, Inc., Washington, 1990, Thomas Alva Edison Patent award, R&D Coun. of N.J., 1991, Nat. Medal of Tech., NSF, 1993, Achievement award, Indsl. Rsch. Inst. Inc., 1994. Mem.: AAAS, Plant Growth Regulator Soc., Am. Chem. Soc. (Perkin medal 1994, Creative Invention award 1995, Heroes of Chemistry 1999, Internat. award for rsch. in agrochemicals 2002). Achievements include patents in field. Personal E-mail: mar6lor2000@yahoo.com.

LOSADA-ZARATE, GLORIA, psychologist; b. Havana, Cuba, Apr. 20, 1957; came to U.S., 1962; m. Juan Zarate. BA, Fla. Internat. U., 1980; D Psychology, Nova U., 1984. Lic. psychologist, Conn. Pre-doctoral pyschology fellow Yale U., New Haven, 1983-84; dir. treatment program for mentally retarded offenders Southbury Tng. Sch., Stat of Conn., 1984—86; clin. psychologist State of Conn. Dept. Mental Retardation New Haven Ctr., New Haven, 1986-88; dir. psychol. svcs. State of Conn. Dept. Mental Retardation Region 6, Waterford, Conn., 1988-92; clin. psychologist State of Conn. Dept. of Mental Health and Addiction Svcs., Middletown, 1997—2002; supervising psychologist Conn. Dept. Children and Families, Middletown, 2002—. Pvt. practice psychology, 1986—. Mem. APA. Democrat. Roman Catholic. Avocations: ballet, classical music, jazz, contemporary dance. Office: 95 E Main St Ste B-15 Meriden CT 06450

LOSANOFF, JULIAN EMIL, surgeon, educator; b. Sofia, Bulgaria, June 26, 1961; arrived in US, 2000, naturalized, 2004; s. Emil Krumov and Margarita Hristova L.; m. Krassimira Sabina Losanoff, Nov. 12, 1987; 1 child, Kristian Julian. MD, Med. U., Sofia, 1987; MSc in Econ., U. Economy, 1996. Diplomate Bulgarian Bd. Gen. Surgery. Chief physician Med. Ctr., Drenovets, Bulgaria, 1987—91; asst. prof. surgery Mil. Med. Acad., Sofia, 1991—2000; rsch. instr. U. Mo., Columbia, 2000—03, SICU burn fellow, 2003—04; fellow divsn. transplantation U. Chgo., 2004—06; staff surgeon John D. Dingell VAMC, Detroit, 2006—. Assoc. prof. surgery Harper Hosp., Wayne State U., Detroit. Contbr. articles to profl. jours. Lt. Bulgarian Army, 1976—78. Mem.: Am. Soc.Transplantation. Avocations: painting, graphics. Office: John D Dingell VAMC Surgery 11S 4646 John R Detroit MI 48201 Personal E-mail: jelosanoff@yahoo.com.

LOSCALZO, ANTHONY JOSEPH, lawyer; b. Bklyn., May 13, 1946; s. Frank Anthony and Frances (Puliatti) L.; m. Kathryn Mary Pica, Aug. 4, 1973. BBA, St. John's U., 1967, JD, 1969. Bar: N.Y. 1969, Fla. 1971, U.S. Dist. Ct. (so. and ea. dists.) N.Y. 1973, U.S. Ct. Appeals (2d cir.) 1975, U.S. Supreme Ct. 1975. Ptnr. Loscalzo & Loscalzo, P.C., NYC, 1981—. Mem. ABA, Assn. Trial Lawyers Am., Fla. Bar Assn., N.Y. State Trial Lawyers Assn., N.Y. State Bar Assn. Office Phone: 212-505-9080. E-mail: aloscalzo@loscalzolaw.com.

LOSCALZO, JOSEPH, cardiologist, biochemist; b. Camden, NJ, Oct. 26, 1951; s. Joseph and Dolores Rita (Ventura) L.; m. Anita Beth Sendrow, Mar. 10, 1974; children: Julia, Alexander. AB summa cum laude, U. Pa., 1972, MD and PhD, 1978. Diplomate in internal medicine and cardiovasc. disease Am. Bd. Internal Medicine. Postdoctoral fellow U. Pa., Phila., 1978; resident in internal medicine Brigham and Women's Hosp., Boston, 1978-81, clin. fellow cardiology, 1981-83, chief med. resident, 1983-84, instr. medicine, 1983-85, chair, dept med., 2005—, physician-in-chief, 2005—; clin. fellow medicine Harvard Med. Sch., Boston, 1978-81, asst. prof. medicine, 1985-88, assoc. prof., 1989-93, Hersey prof., 2005—; chief cardiol. sect. Brockton West Roxbury VA Med. Ctr., Boston, 1989-93; prof. biochemistry Boston U., 1994—2005, disting. prof. medicine, 1994—97, dir. Whitaker Cardiovasc. Inst., Sch. Medicine, 1994—2005, vice chmn. dept. medicine, chief cardiovasc. medicine, 1994-96, Wade prof., chmn. dept. medicine, 1997—2005; Hersey prof. theory and practice medicine Med. Sch. Harvard U., 2005—; chmn. dept. medicine Brigham and Women's Hosp., 2005—. Mem. rsch. rev. com. Am. Heart Assn., 1988—, chmn., 2000—02; rsch. rev. coms. Nat. Heart, Lung and Blood Inst., Bethesda, Md., 1990—, mem. bd. sci. counselors, 2000—04, chair, 2001—04, mem. adv. coun., 2005—; dir. NIH Specialized Ctr. Rsch. in Ischemic Heart Disease, 1995—2005; chair cardiovsac. disease bd. Am. Bd. Internal Medicine, 1999—2003. Author, or editor 23 books on vascular biology, medicine, thrombosis and hemostasis; editor-in-chief Circulation, 2004—; assoc. editor New Eng. Jour. Medicine, 1995-2004; contb. mem. editl. bd. Circulation, Circulation Rsch., Jour. Am. Coll. Cardiology, Jour. Thrombosis and Thrombolysis, Vascular Medicine, Am. Jour. Cardiology, Jour. Am. Coll. Cardiology; contbr. over 500 articles to profl. jours. Recipient Med. Scientist Tng. award NIH, 1972-77, Rsch. Career Devel. award, 1989-94, Clin. Scientist award Am. Heart Assn., 1983-88, Disting. Scientist award Am. Heart Assn., 2004, Rsch. Achievement award Am. Heart Assn., 2006, Outstanding Investigator award Internat. Soc. Heart Rsch., 2006. Fellow ACP, Am. Coll. Cardiology; mem. Am. Fedn. Clin. Rsch., Am. Soc. Clin. Investigation, Assn. Am. Physicians, Assn. Univ. Cardiologists, Am. Soc. Biol. Chemistry, Inst. Medicine of Nat. Acads., Phi Beta Kappa, Alpha Omega Alpha. Achievements include 26 patents related to nitric oxide congeners. Office: Brigham and Womens Hosp 75 Francis St Boston MA 02115

LOSCHEN, EARL LEE, psychiatrist, educator; b. Minden, Nebr., Jan. 10, 1944; s. Herman George and Agnes Anna (Garrelts) L.; m. Marilyn Jean Reinhardt, June 15, 1974; children: Rebecca, Elizabeth. BS, Midland Luth. Coll., 1966; MD, U. Nebr., Omaha, 1970; MS in Edn., So. Ill. U., 1988. Diplomate Am. Bd. Psychiatry and Neurology. Asst. prof. U. Nebr., Omaha, 1973-74, So. Ill. U., Springfield, 1974-80, assoc. prof., 1980-95; prof., 1995—2002; prof. emeritus So. Ill. U., 2002—, asst. chmn. dept. psychiatry Springfield, 1980-92, chmn. dept. psychiatry, 1992—2002. Cons. Ill. Dept. Pub. Health, Springfield, 1976-88, Ill. Dept. Rehab. Services, Springfield, 1977-88, Aid to Retarded Citizens, Springfield, 1981-95, Macoupin County Mental Health, Carlinville, Ill., 1974-95; mem. psychiat. panel Health Care Financing Adminstrn., 1986—. Contbr. chpts. to books. Mem. com. rights of minors Ill. Commn. Children, 1974-77, com. youth and law, 1977-79; del. 1980 Ill. White House Conf. on Children, 1980, Ill. Conf. Children's Priorities of 1980's, 1981; bd. dirs. ARC-IL, 2002—, treas., 2003—; mem. Ill. Task Force on Autism, 2004—. Fellow Am. Psychiat. Assn. (disting. life); mem. AMA, NADD (bd. dirs. 2000-01), ARC (bd. dirs. Ill. chpt. 2002—), Nat. Assn. Rural Mental Health (bd. dirs. 1985-91, pres. 1988-89), Ill. State Med. Soc. (coun. mental health and addiction 1985-88, com. on drugs and therapeutics 1995-2005), Ill. Psychiat. Soc. (downstate counselor 1996-2001, pres.-elect 2001-02, pres. 2002-2003), Am. Assn. Intellectual and Developmental Disabilities. Avocations: photography, gardening.

LOSCHER, TRICIA DIANE, curator, director; b. Peoria, Ill., Dec. 23, 1969; d. Walter Ray Loscher and Kathleen Gronewold Loscher. BA with honors in Art History, Ariz. State U., Tempe, 1994, cert. Museum Studies, 1996, MA in Art History, 2000, PhD in History and Theory of Art, 2004. Curatorial intern West Valley Art Mus., Surprise, Ariz., 1990; curatorial intern Nelson Fine Art Ctr. Ariz. State U., Tempe, 1993—94, rsch. asst., 1993—96; curatorial intern Heard Mus., Phoenix, 1996, curatorial technician, 1997, coord. ednl. tour and outreach, 1998—2000, prospect rschr., 2000—01, curator Heard Mus. North, 2001—, dir. program Heard Mus. North, 2001—. Interpreter Ariz. Capitol Mus., Phoenix, 1997; rschr. Manitou Wordworks, Inc., Gross Pointe, Mich., 1997; guest curator Ariz. State Capitol Mus., Phoenix, 2000—01; asst. Corinne Cain Ltd., Appraiser Fine Arts and Native Am. Arts, Phoenix. Author: Tentative Title: The Norman L. Sandfield Collection of Silver Seed Pots at the Heard Museum; contbr. articles to profl. jours. and mags. Judge guild's Indian fair and market Heard Mus., 2003—05, judge native Am. student art show and sale, 2004—05. Recipient Rudy Turk award, Coll. Fine Arts, Ariz. State U., Tempe, 1994, Sonnichsen Article of Yr. award, 2003; scholar, Ariz. State U., Tempe, 1992—93. Mem.: We. Art Assocs. Phoenix Art Mus., Native Am. Art Studies Assn. (mem. local planning com. 2004—05). Avocations: writing, yoga, painting. Office: Heard Museum 2301 North Ctrl Ave Phoenix AZ 85004 Home Phone: 602-616-7522; Office Phone: 602-251-0285. Office Fax: 602-252-9757. Business E-Mail: tloscher@extremezone.com.

LOSCHIAVO, LINDA BOSCO, library director; b. Rockville Ctr., NY, Aug. 31, 1950; d. Joseph and Jennie (DelRegno) Bosco; m. Joseph A. LoSchiavo, Sept. 7, 1974. BA, Fordham U., 1972, MA, 1990; MLS, Pratt Inst., 1974. Picture cataloguer Frick Art Reference Libr., NYC, 1972-75; sr. cataloguer Fordham U. Libr., Bronx, NY, 1975-87, head of retrospective conversion, 1987-90, systems libr., 1990-91, dir. libr. at Lincoln Ctr., 1991—. Libr. cons. Mus. Am. Folk Art Libr., N.Y.C., 1985-90; indexer Arco Books, N.Y.C., 1974. Editor: Macbeth, 1990, Julius Ceasar, 1990, Romeo and Juliet, 1990. Mng. producer Vineyard Opera, N.Y.C., 1981-88. Mem. ALA, N.Y. Tech. Svcs. Librs., Beta Phi Mu, Alpha Sigma Nu. Home: 317 Collins Ave Mount Vernon NY 10552-1601 Office: Fordham Univ Library 113 W 60th St New York NY 10023-7404

LOSEE, JOHN FREDERICK, JR., manufacturing executive; b. Milw., Apr. 27, 1951; s. John Frederick and Helen (Joslyn) L.; m. Jane Agnes Trawicki, Aug. 25, 1973; children: Nicole Marie, John Michael. BSME, Marquette U., 1973, MS in Indsl. Engring., 1982. Registered profl. engr., Wis.; cert. numerical control mgr., Wis. Mfg. engr. OMC-Evinrude div. Outboard Marine Corp., Milw., 1975-78, mfg. engr. supr., 1978-80, mgr. tool engring., 1980-85, mgr. process and tool engring., 1985-86, dir. mfg. engring., 1986-88; v.p. ops. Rytec Corp., Jackson, Wis., 1988-90; v.p. adminstrn. Custom Products Corp., 1990-91; part-owner Nat. Mfg. Co, Inc., Milw., 1991-96; owner JFL Mfg., Inc., Sussex, Wis., 1996—. Mem. Numerical Control Soc., Soc. Mfg. Engrs., Computer and Automated Systems Assn. Republican. Roman Catholic. Home: W264 N6565 Hillview Dr Sussex WI 53089-3452 Office Phone: 262-820-9090. Personal E-mail: jflmfg27@aol.com.

LOSEK, DARREN THOMAS, property manager, sales manager; b. Cranston, RI, May 25, 1966; s. Thomas Micheal and Alice Rose Losek; m. Caryl Ann Ruth Hussey, Aug. 27, 1993; 1 child, John. BA in Psychology, RI U., 1991; M in Vocat. Rehablitation & Counseling, Assumption Coll., 2000. Cert. in crisis prevention intervention 1986, in workplace law and safety Inst. Labor Studies & Rsch., in personal mgmt. of aggresive behaviors 1990, open water I scuba diver Nat. Assn. Underwater Instructors, 1991, tchrs. asst. RI Dept. Edn., 1992, lic. capt. US Power Squadron, 1995. Behavior specialist No. RI Collaborative, Cumberland, 1986—90; vocat. facilitation specialist Regional Vocat. Transition & Devel. Ctr., Cumberland, 1990—95; clin. unit supr. The Groden Ctr., Providence, 1997—2001, transp. coord., 1997—2001, cmty. vocat. dir., 1998—2001; salesman RI Home Improvement, Warwick, regional sales mgr., 2004—. Mem. jacho accreditation com., health & safety com., tech. commitee, & bldg. fire warden The Groden Ctr., Providence, 1998—2001. Mem.: RI Rehab. Assn., Vocat. Evaluation & Work Adjustment Assn., Nat. Rehab. Assn., Town Coun. CRC, Nat. Assn. Underwater Instructors, Nat. Geog. Soc., New Eng. Aquarium, Mensa. Avocations: underwater photography, scuba diving, travel. Office: Rhode Island Home Improvement/RBA 1815 Post Rd Warwick RI 02886 Home Phone: 401-295-8805; Office Phone: 401-739-1000. Office Fax: 401-739-1003.

LOSER, JOSEPH CARLTON, JR., dean, retired judge; b. Nashville, June 16, 1932; s. Joseph Carlton and Pearl Dean (Gupton) L.; m. Mildred Louise Nichols, May 25, 1972; 1 child, Joseph Carlton III. Student, U. Tenn., 1950-51, Vanderbilt U., 1952-55; LLB, Nashville YMCA Night Law Sch., 1959. Bar: Tenn. 1959. Pvt. practice, 1959-66; judge Gen. Sessions Ct., Davidson County, Tenn., 1966-69, Cir. Ct. 20th Jud. Dist. Tenn., 1969-86; dean Nashville Sch. Law, 1986—. Mem. ABA, Tenn. Bar Assn., Nashville Bar Assn., Am. Legion, Masons, Shriners, Sigma Delta Kappa, Kappa Sigma. E-mail: jcloser@comcast.net.

LOSI, MAXIM JOHN, medical communications executive; b. Jersey City, Dec. 27, 1939; s. Maxim Fortune and Carrie (Rivoli) Losi; m. Mary Ann De Grandis, May 30, 1968; children: Christopher, Benjamin. AB, Princeton U., 1960; postgrad., N.Y. Med. Coll., 1960-61, Albert Einstein Coll. Medicine, 1961-62; PhD in English, NYU, 1972. Lectr. English C.W. Post Coll., Greenvale, NY, 1965-67; instr. English, Centenary Coll. for Women, Hackettstown, NJ, 1967-71, chmn. dept., 1970-71; med. abstractor, indexer Coun. for Tobacco Rsch., NYC, 1972-73; freelance med. writer, 1973-74; sr. clin. info. scientist Squibb Inst. Med. Rsch., Princeton, NJ, 1974-77, project team leader, 1975-77; chief med. writer ICI Ams., Wilmington, Del., 1977-79; dir. biomed. comm. Revlon Health Care Group, Tuckahoe, NY, 1979-86; exec. dir. documentation mgmt. and regulatory submissions Covance Clin. and Peri-Approval Svcs. Inc., Princeton, 1987-97; v.p. regulatory affairs Scirex Corp., Blue Bell, Pa., 1997-98; pres. Max Losi Assocs. Pharm. Regulatory Cons. & Comm., Trenton, NJ, 1998—; cons. med. writer Rsch. Pharm. Svcs. Inc., 2002—. FDA cons. Microbiol. Assocs., Bethesda, Md., 1973; mgmt. cons. Robert S. First Assocs., N.Y.C., 1974; vis. lectr. med. writing techniques St. George U. Med. Sch., Grenada, W.I., 1977; adj. asst. prof. English, Rider U., Lawrenceville, N.J., 1999—. Mem.: Drug Info. Assn., Am. Med. Writers Assn. (pres. N.Y. chpt. 1984—85, nat. pres. 1987—88). Roman Catholic. Office Phone: 609-477-4322.

LOSICK, RICHARD M., biology professor; BA in Chem., Princeton Univ.; PhD in Biochem., MIT. Past. chmn. dept. molecular and cellular biology Harvard Coll., Maria Moors Cabot prof. biology. Former vis. scholar Phi Beta Kappa Soc.; sci. adv. bd. Tularik Tex. Corp., 1995—; chair, sci. adv. bd. Cumbre; rsch. prof. Howard Hughes Med. Inst., 2002—. Contbr. articles to sci. jours.; mem. editl. bd.: Science, Cell. Recipient Howard Hughes Med. Inst. grant, 2002. Fellow: Am. Acad. Microbiol., AAAS, Am. Acad. Arts and Scis.; mem.: NAS (Selman A. Waksman award in Microbiol. 2007). Office: Biology Dept Harvard Coll Rm 3023 16 Divinity Ave Cambridge MA 02138 Office Phone: 617-495-4905. E-mail: losick@mcb.harvard.edu.*

LOSIER, MARIE, film director; b. Boulogne, France, 1972; Film programmer French Institute / Alliance Francaise, NYC, 2000—. Exhibited in group shows at Tribecca Film Festival, Internat. Film Festival, Rotterdam, Seoul Film Festival, Lausagne Film Festival, York Underground Film Festival, Lake Placid Film Festival, Whitney Biennial, Whitney Mus. Art, 2006; dir.: (films) Chick-chick, 2000, The Touch Retouched, 2001, Loula Meets Charlie, 2002, Marie-Onette, 2002, Broken Blossoms, 2002, The Passion of Joan of Arc, 2002, Sanitarium Cinema, 2002, Mike Kuchar is on My Roof, 2003, Lunch Break on the Xerox Machine, 2003, Bird, Bath, and Beyond, 2003, Electrocute Your Stars, 2004, Eat Your Makeup!, 2005, The Ontological Cowboy, 2005, Flying Saucey!, 2006. Grantee Nat. Art Studio Club Grant, 1997, NY State Coun. Arts, 2004. Office: French Inst 22 E 60th St New York NY 10022

LOSINSKI, PATRICK A., library director; m. Vicky Losinski; 2 children. Exec. dir. Pikes Peak Libr. Dist., Colorado Springs, 1997—2002, Columbus Met. Libr., Ohio, 2002—. Chair Charlie Robinson Award jury Pub. Libr. Assn. Recipient Excellence in Customer Svc. award, BBB, 2000. Office: Columbus Met Libr 96 S Grant Ave Columbus OH 43215 Office Phone: 614-849-1005. E-mail: plosinski@columbuslibrary.org.*

LOSS, JOHN C., architect, retired educator; b. Muskegon, Mich., Mar. 6, 1931; s. Alton A. and Dorothy Ann (DeMars) Forward; m. LaMyma Lois Draggoo, June 7, 1958. BArch, U. Mich., 1954, MArch, 1960. Registered arch., Md., Mich. Architect Eero Saarinen & Assocs., Bloomfield Hills, Mich., 1956-57; owner John Loss & Assocs., Detroit, 1960-75; prof., acting dean Sch. Architecture, U. Detroit, 1960-75; prof., head dept. architecture NC State U., Raleigh, 1975—79; assoc. dean. Sch. Architecture U. Md., College Park, 1981-83, prof. architecture, 1979-93, prof. emeritus architecture, 1993—; dir. architecture and engring. Performance Info. Ctr., 1982—93; pvt. practice, Annapolis, College Park, 1979-93, Whitehall, Mich., 1993—. Mem. com. NRC-NAS, 1982—93; mem. bldg. diagnostics com. Adv. Bd. Build Environ., 1983—93; mem. com. earthquake engring. NRC, 1983—93; leader survey team tornado damage in Pa. and Ohio, 1985; mem. acad. adv. bd. Baker Coll., Muskegon, Mich., 2004—. Author: Building Design for Natural Hazards in Eastern United States, 1981, Identification of Performance Failures in Large Structures and Buildings, 1987, Analysis of Performance Failures in Civil Structures and Large Buildings, 1990, Performance Failures in Buildings and Civil Works, 1991; prin. works include med. clinic, NC, Aldersgate Multi Family Housing, Oscoda, Mich. Advisor Interfaith Housing, Inc., Detroit, 1966—74, Detroit Mayor's Office, 1967—69, Interim Housing Com. Mich. State Housing Devel. Authority, Lansing, 1969—71, Takoma Park Citizens Schs., Md., 1981—82; advisor, cons. Hist. Preservation Commn., Prince George's County, Md.; mem. planning commn. Blue Lake Twp., Mich., 1994—2006; mem. art and environ. commn. Grand Rapids Diocese of Cath. Ch., 1996—2002; vol. tchr. St. James Sch., Montague, Mich., 2001—06; mem. design com. City Whitehall, Mich., 2007—; mem. acad. adv. bd. Baker Coll., Muskegon, Mich., 2004—. With US Army, 1954—56. Named one of Men of Yr., Engring. News Record, 1984; NSF grantee, 1978—84, 1986—90. Fellow: AIA; mem.: KC (charter Grand Knight 2001—). Democrat. Roman Catholic. *To participate, as an architect, in the continuing saga of the creation of the built environment and, as a teacher, in the continuing rebirth of our intellectual and spiritual lives remains a very special honor. I feel a sincere debt of gratitude to my mother who read to me when I was a very small child and who launched me on a life of reading and service. Happiness is a spiritual thing - not a physical thing! Success (our happiness) begins with what we aspire to be - not what we have or want.*

LOSS, MARGARET RUTH, lawyer; b. Phila., June 17, 1946; d. Louis and Bernice Rose (Segaloff) L.; 1 child, Elizabeth Loss Johnson. BA, Radcliffe Coll., 1967; LLB, Yale U., 1970. Bar: Conn. 1970, N.Y. 1973. Assoc. Sullivan & Cromwell, NYC, 1971-77; with Equitable Life Assurance Soc. U.S., NYC, 1977-88, asst. gen. counsel, 1979-85, v.p. and counsel, 1985-88; counsel LeBoeuf, Lamb, Greene & MacRae, NYC, 1988-98. Mem. com. Yale Law Sch. Fund. Mem. ABA, Am. Law Inst., Conn. Bar Assn., Assn. of Bar of City N.Y. Home and Office: 201 E 80th St # 12A New York NY 10021-0516 Home Phone: 212-717-6132; Office Phone: 212-717-6132. E-mail: margaretloss@cs.com.

LOTAN, RACHEL, education educator; BA in English Lit. and French Lang., Lit. and Civilization, Tel Aviv U., 1971; MA in Edn., Stanford U., 1981, MA in Sociology, 1983, PhD in Edn., 1985. Tchr. jr. and sr. h.s., 1969—80; rsch. asst. Ctr. for Ednl. Rsch., Stanford U., Calif., 1982—85; assoc. prof. edn. Stanford (Calif.) U., 1999—, and dir., tchr. edn. program. Vis. asst./assoc. prof. Inst. for Advancement of Social Integration in Schs., Bar-Ilan U., Israel, 1986—91. Mem. editl. bd.: European Jour. for Intercultural Edn. Office: Stanford U Sch Edn 485 Lasuen Mall Stanford CA 94305-3096

LOTAN, YAIR, urologist; b. Tel Aviv, Mar. 18, 1972; m. Sandra Lotan. BA in Biology, U. Tex., Austin; MD, Baylor Coll., Houston, 1997. Diplomate Am. Bd. Urology, 2005. Asst. prof. U. Tex. Southwestern Med. Ctr., Dallas, 2003—. Mem.: Am. Urologic Assn. Achievements include research in decision analyses, molecular markers and cancer screening. Office: U Tex Southwestern Med Ctr 5323 Harry Hines Blvd J8112 Dallas TX 75390-9110 Office Phone: 214-648-0389. Office Fax: 214-648-8786. Business E-Mail: yair.lotan@utsouthwestern.edu.

LOTAS, JUDITH PATTON, advertising executive; b. Iowa City, Apr. 23, 1942; d. John Henry and Jane (Vandike) Patton; children: Amanda Bell, Alexandra Vandike. BA, Fla. State U., 1964. Copywriter Liller, Neal, Battle and Lindsey Advt., Atlanta, 1964-67, Grey Advt., NYC, 1967-72; creative group head SSC&B Advt., NYC, 1972-74, assoc. creative dir., 1974-79, v.p., 1975-79, sr. v.p., 1979-82, exec. creative dir., 1982-86; founding ptnr. Lotas Minard Patton McIver, Inc., NYC, 1986—. Fundraiser Nat. Coalition Homeless, NYC, 1986—; mem. creative rev. bd. Partnership Drug-Free Am.; rep. Afghan Am. Peace Corp., Kabul and Talalabad; bd. dirs. Samuel Wasman Cancer Rsch. Found., NYC, 1981—88, Women's Venture Fund, 1995—; active scholarship fund raising, 2004. Named Woman of Achievement, YWCA; named one of Advt.'s 100 Best Women, Ad Age, 1989; recipient Clio award, Venice Film Festival award, Graphics award, Am. Inst. Graphic Artists, 1970, Effie award, Grad. of Distinction award, Fla. State U., 1993. Mem.: Ad. Coun. (mem. creative rev. bd. 1994—, bd. dirs. 1995—), Advt. Women N.Y. (bd. dirs. 1981—87, 1st v.p. 1984—87, Advt. Woman of the Yr. 1993), Kappa Alpha Theta. Democrat. Office Phone: 212-288-5676. E-mail: jlotas@earthlink.net, jlotas@lpny.com.

LOTCHIN, ROGER WILLIAMS, history professor, writer; b. Shelbyville, Ill., Jan. 31, 1935; s. Theodore and Lucille Williams Lotchin; m. Phyllis Jo Morris, June 1, 1958; 1 child, Theodore Roger. BA in History, Millikin U., Decatur, Ill., 1957; MA in History, U. Chgo., PhD in History, 1969. Prof. history U. NC, Chapel Hill, 1966—. Author: San Francisco: 1846-56, Fortress California, The Bad City in the Good War; editor: The Way We Really Were, The MArtial Metropolis; contbr. articles to profl. jours. Named to, Ill. Basketball Hall Fame; recipient Medallion award, Millikin U., 2003. Mem.: Urban History Assn. (pres. 2004—05). Avocations: tennis, travel, gardening, reading.

LOTEMPIO, JULIA MATILD, retired accountant; b. Budapest, Hungary, Oct. 14, 1934; came to U.S., 1958, naturalized 1962; d. Istvan and Irma (Sandor) Fejos; m. Anthony Joseph LoTempio, Mar. 11, 1958. AAS in Lab. Tech. summa cum laude, Niagara County C.C., Sanborn, NY, 1967; BS in Tech. and Vocat. Edn. summa cum laude, SUNY, Buffalo, 1970; MEd in Guidance and Counseling, Niagara U., 1973, BBA in Acctg. summa cum laude, 1983, MBA in Mgmt., 1998. Sr. analyst, rschr. Gt. Lakes Carbon Co., Niagara Falls, N.Y., 1967-71; tchr. sci. Niagara Falls Schs., 1973-75; tchr. sci. and English Starpoint Sch. System, Lockport, N.Y., 1975-77; club adminstr., acct. Twinlo Racquetball, Inc., Niagara Falls, 1979-81; bus. cons. Twinlo Beverage, Inc., Niagara Falls, 1981-85; staff acct. J.D. Elliott & Co. PC, CPAs, Buffalo, 1986-87; acct. Lewiston, NY, 1988—2001; instr. applied chemistry Niagara County C.C., Sanborn, NY, 1979, instr. acctg. principles, 1989—2001; ret., 2001. Bd. dirs. Niagara Frontier Meth. Home Inc., Niagara Frontier Nursing Home Inc., The Blocher Homes Inc., Buffalo. Mem. faculty continuing edn., speaker, chairperson fin. and community rels. coms. United Meth. Ch., Dickersonville, N.Y., 1985-90; guest speaker, counselor, tchr. Beechwood Svc. Guild, Buffalo, 1987-91; bd. dirs. Niagara Frontier Meth. Home, Inc., Getzville, N.Y., 1988-2001; bd. dirs., mem. fin., investment, pension, ins., and community rels. coms. Niagara Frontier Nursing Home Co., Inc., Getzville, 1988-2001, Blocher Homes, Inc., Williamsville, N.Y., 1988-2001; asst. sec., bd. dirs., mem. exec., quality and assurance coms., chmn. community rels. com. Beechwood/Blocher Community, Buffalo, 1990-2001; mem. Coop. Parish Coun., Sanborn, N.Y., 1991-94; mem. adminstrv. bd., chmn. outreach com. Pekin (N.Y.) United Meth. Ch., 1992-2000; sec. to bd. dirs. Beechwood/Blocher Found., Amherst, N.Y., 1992-93, asst. treas., 1993-94, treas., 1994, vice chmn., 1994-2001. Mem. NAFE, Nat. Soc. Pub. Accts., Nat. Assn. Accts., Nat. Fedn. Bus. and Profl. Women's Club, Internat. Platform Assn., Niagara U. Alumni Assn., SUNY Coll. Buffalo Alumni Assn., Niagara County C.C. Alumni Assn. Avocations: public speaking, walking, travel, reading, computers. Home and Office: 1026 Ridge Rd Lewiston NY 14092-9704 Personal E-mail: ajlotempio@juno.com.

LOTEYRO, CORAZON BIGATA, physician; b. Manila, Apr. 9, 1951; arrived in U.S., 1979; d. Victor G. Loteyro and Emilia Bigata; 1 child, Elizabeth. BS, Mindanao State U., Marawi City, Philippines, 1972; MD, U. East Med. Ctr., Manila, 1976. Bd. cert. Am. Bd. Family Physicians, Diplomate Fellow Am. Acad. Family Physicians. Physician Humana Medfirst, Peoria, Ill., 1984-85, Family Health Plan, Elm Grove, Wis., 1985-96, Covenant Health, Pewaukee, Wis., 1996—. Vol. Salvation Army, Milw., 1993. Fellow Am. Acad. Family Physicians; mem. Filipino-Am. Med. Assn. (pres. 1994-95), U. of East Alumni Assn. Midwest (treas. 1990-94). Republican. Roman Catholic. Avocations: skiing, travel, movies, reading, music. Home: 4285 Windsong Pl Plover WI 54467 Office: 2401 Plover Rd Plover WI 54467 Office Phone: 715-295-3800. Personal E-mail: cbloteyromd@yahoo.com.

LOTH, RENÉE, editor; b. Port Chester, NY, Dec. 26, 1952; d. Howard and Irene (Maio) L. BS, Boston U., 1974. Editor East Boston (Mass.) Community News, 1977-79; staff writer Boston Phoenix, 1979-84; assoc. editor New Eng. Monthly, Haydenville, Mass., 1984-85; became staff writer Boston Globe, 1985, deputy editor Editorial Page, 1994—2000, editor Editorial Page, 2000—. Mem. emeritus East Boston Community Communications, Inc., 1979—. Contbr. articles to profl. jours. Recipient Excellence in Media award Nat. Women's Polit. Caucus, 1986. Office: Boston Globe 135 Morrissey Blvd Boston MA 02107-3338

LOTHIAN, JAMES ROBERT, economist, educator; b. Queens, NY, Apr. 23, 1945; s. James Robert and Margaret Virginia Lothian; m. Judith Ann McLaughlin, June 21, 1969; children: James Robert, Mary Nora Gibbons, John Andrew, Ann Ruth McCartney, Elizabeth Julia. BA magna cum laude, Cath. U. Am., Washington, DC, 1967; MA, U. Chgo., 1969, PhD, 1973. Economist Citibank, NYC, 1972—76, asst. v.p., 1976—78, v.p., 1978—87; vis. prof. NYU, NYC, 1988—90; prof. Fordham U., NYC, 1990—97, disting. prof. fin., 1997—. Cons. Nat. Bur. Econ. Rsch., NYC, 1976—78, rsch assoc., 1978—82; vis. scholar Fed. Res. Bank. Atlanta, Fed. Res. Bank Atlanta, 2003, 04, 06, Internat. Monetary Fund, Washington, 1978—82, Maastricht U., Netherlands, 1998, 2006; mem. editl. bd. Jour. Internat. Money and Fin., 1982—86; editor Jour. of Internat. Money and Fin., 1986—; North Am. corr. Brandsma Rev., Dun Laoghiro, Ireland, 1996—; sci. com. Internat. Tor Vergata Conf. on Banking and Fin., Rome, 2001—; mem. editl. bd. Jour. Fin. Stability, 2004—; vis. lectr. U. Coll. Dublin, 2004, 05. Author: The Internat. Trnsmission of Inflation; contbr. articles to profl. jours. Recipient mem., Phi Beta Kappa, 1966, Gladys and Henry Crown Faculty Excellence award, Fordham U. Grad. Sch. Bus., 1998; fellow Richard Weaver, Intercollegiate Studies Inst., 1968, 1969. Fellow: European Soc. Computational Methods in Sci. and Engring. (hon.; fin. forecasting sect. 2005); mem.: Mont Pelerin Soc., Cliometric Soc., Fin. Mgmt. Assn., Am. Econ. Assn. Office: Fordham U Sch Bus 113 West 60th St New York NY 10023 Office Phone: 212-636-6147. Business E-Mail: lothian@fordham.edu.

LOTKO, WILLIAM, engineering educator; m. Mary K. Hudson; 2 children. B in engring. physics, U. Kans.; M in engring. physics, U. Mo.; PhD in plasma physics, UCLA, 1981. Mem. faculty Dartmouth Coll. Thayer Sch. Engring., 1984—, prin. investigator Sun-Earth Connection Theory program, co-investigator Ctr. for Integrated Space Weather Modeling, sr. assoc. dean, 1999—2004, interim dean, 2004—05. Mem. bd. NH Space Grant Consortium, 1991—; vis. scientist Max Planck Institut for Extraterrestrische Physik, Germany, Space Sciences Lab., U. Calif., Berkeley, Los Alamos Nat. Lab. Author: numerous articles and papers; contbg. author (book) Auroral Plasma Physics, 2003. Mem.: IEEE, Am. Soc. Engring. Edn., Am. Geophys. Union, AAAS. Office: Thayer Sch Engring Dartmouth Coll 8000 Cummings Hall Hanover NH 03755-8000

LOTMAN, HERBERT, food processing executive; b. Phila., Oct. 9, 1933; s. Samuel Meyer and Gertrude Lotman; m. Karen Levin, Apr. 6, 1957; children: Shelly Hope, Jeffrey Mark. Pres., chmn. bd. Keystone Foods Corp., Bryn Mawr, Pa., 1951, pres., 1960, chmn. bd., CEO, 1960—. Bd. dirs. Nat. Juvenile Diabetes Found. Served US Army, 1952—54. Mem.: Young Pres. Orgn. Office: Keystone Foods Corp Ste 600 300 Barr Harbor Dr Conshohocken PA 19428

LOTSCH, ALEXANDER, scientist; b. Singen, Germany, Oct. 3, 1971; s. Gernot and Gertrud Lotsch; m. Yi Chung Lung, Sept. 18, 2004. BS in Geography, Agr. Sci., Chemistry, Free U. Berlin, 1997; MA in Geography, Boston U., 1999, PhD in Geo-Info. Sci., 2004. IT cons. ESRI Inc., Boston, 1997—99; rschr. Boston U., 2001—03, NASA, Mountain View, Calif., 2003; scientist The World Bank, Washington, 2004—. Fulbright fellow, 1997. Mem.: Am. Geophysical Union. Avocations: jazz, bicycling. Home Phone: 202-244-7227; Office Phone: 202-458-7801. Business E-Mail: alotsch@worldbank.org.

LOTSHAW, DAVID PAUL, physiologist, educator; b. Iowa City, Oct. 19, 1950; s. Elmer Paul and Ann Lotshaw; 1 child, Thomas Paul. BSc, Ohio U., 1972; MA, Miami U., 1975; PhD, SUNY, Albany, 1983. Vis. asst. prof. U. Ky., Lexington, 1990—93; assoc. prof. No. Ill. U., DeKalb, 1993—. Mem.: Am. Heart Assn. (Grant-In-Aid award 1994—98), Am. Physiol. Soc. Achievements include research in ion channel physiology. Office: Dept Biol Sci No Ill Univ Dekalb IL 60115 Home Phone: 815-758-3530; Office Phone: 815-753-7835. Office Fax: 815-753-0461. Business E-Mail: dlotshaw@niu.edu.

LOTSPIECH, JEFFREY, computer scientist, consultant; b. LA, July 7, 1949; s. John Lotspiech and Jacqueline Carrau; m. Karen Mary Samson, July 1, 1972. BS, MIT, Cambridge, Mass., 1970, MS, 1972. Rsch. staff mem. IBM Almaden Rsch. Ctr., San Jose, Calif., 1972—2005. Dir., webmaster Menlo-Atherton HS Alumni Assn., Calif., 1997—2006. Achievements include more than 50 patents in the area of content protection; invention of latest content protection schemes used to protect movies and music. Home Phone: 702-263-2347; Office Phone: 702-263-2450. Business E-Mail: jeff@lotspiech.com.

LOTSTEIN, JAMES IRVING, lawyer; b. Steubenville, Ohio, Jan. 27, 1944; s. Jack and Dorothy (Nach) L.; m. Paulette L. Gutcheon, June 25, 1972; children: Melissa A., Amanda J. BSBA, Northwestern U., 1965; JD, U. Conn., 1968. Bar: Conn. 1969, U.S. Ct. Appeals (2d cir.) 1971, U.S. Supreme Ct. 1972. From assoc. to ptnr. Hoppin, Carey & Powell, Hartford, Conn., 1969-86; ptnr. Cummings & Lockwood, Hartford, 1986—96, ptnr.-in-charge, 1988-95, chmn. dept. Mergers and Acquisitions Practice Group, 2001—03; ptnr. Edwards Angell Palmer & Dodge, LLP, Hartford, Conn., 2003—. Adv. bd. Conn. chpt. Nat. Assn. Corp. Dirs.; adv. com. Hartford (Conn.) chpt. Am. Soc. Corp. Secs. Author: An Introduction to the Connecticut Business Corporation Act, 1994, Ten Things You Can Do Now to Prepare for the New Connecticut Business Corporation Act, Connecticut Business Corporation Act Sourcebook, New Indemnification Provisions of the Connecticut Business Corporation Act, 1997, Why Choose Connecticut? Advantages of the Connecticut Business Corporation Act Over the Delaware General Corporation Law, 2000, Update on Connecticut Corporation Law, Corporate Governance of Connecticut Nonprofit Corporations, 2002, Amendments to the Connecticut Business Corporation Act, 2003, Commonly Negotiated Provisions in Business Acquisitions, 2005. Mem. adv. bd. Conn. chpt. Nat. Assn. Corp. Dirs.; mem. adv. com. Hartford chpt. Am. Soc. Corp. Secs.; mem. Sec. of State's bus. adv. com. State of Conn.; active Am. Coll. Investment Counsel; mem. Econ. Devel. Agy., Canton, Conn., 2001— 1st lt. JAGC, USAR, 1968-74. Mem. ABA (chmn. dirs. and officers task force 1996-2002, mem. corp. laws com. 1992), Conn. Bar Assn. (chmn. mcpl. law and govtl. svc. com. 1981-82, chmn. bus. law sect. 1990-92, co-chmn. Conn. bus. corp. act task force 1993-98). Office: Edwards Angell Palmer & Dodge LLP 90 State House Sq 9th Fl Hartford CT 06103

LOTT, HAMILTON, JR., manufacturing executive; Design engr. Vulcraft, Florence, SC, 1975, engring. mgr. St. Joe, Ind., 1982—86, sales mgr., 1987, gen. mgr. Grapeland, Tex., 1987—93, Florence, 1993—99; v.p. Nucor Corp., Charlotte, NC, 1988—99, exec. v.p., 1999—. Office: Nucor Corp 1915 Rexford Rd Charlotte NC 28211 Office Phone: 704-366-7000. Office Fax: 704-362-4208.*

LOTT, IRA TOTZ, pediatric neurologist; b. Cin., Apr. 15, 1941; s. Maxwell and Jeneda (Totz) L.; m. Ruth J. Weiss, June 21, 1964; children: Lisa, David I. BA cum laude, Brandeis U., 1963; MD cum laude, Ohio State U., 1967. Intern Mass. Gen. Hosp., Boston, 1967, resident in pediatrics, 1967-69, resident in child neurology, 1971-74; clin. assoc. NIH, Bethesda, Md., 1969-71; from clin. rsch. fellow to asst. prof. Harvard Med. Sch., Boston, 1971-82; clin. dir. Eunice Kennedy Shriver Ctr. for Mental Retardation, Waltham, Mass., 1974-82; assoc. prof. U. Calif., Irvine, 1983-91, prof., 1992—, chmn. dept. pediat., 1990-2000, dir. clin. neurosci. devel., 2000—03; assoc. dean for clin. neuroscis. U. Calif. Irvine Health Sys., 2003—. Chmn. dept. pediat. U. Calif., Irvine, 1990-2000, dir. pediat. neurology, 1983—, clin. neuroscience devel., 2000-01, assoc. dean clin. neurosciences, 2002—; pres. Prof. Child Neurology, Mpls., 1992—. Editor: Down Syndrome-Medical Advances, 1991; contbr. articles to profl. jours. Sec., treas. Child Neurology Soc., Mpls., 1987-90. Lt. comdr. USPHS, 1969-71. Recipient Career Devel. award Kennedy Found., 1976, Spotlight award Outstanding Svc. People with Devel. Disabilities as Health Care Provider, Regional Ctr. Orange County, 2005; NIH grantee, 1974—. Fellow Am. Acad. Neurology; mem. Am. Pediatric Soc., Am. Neurol. Assn., Nat. Down Syndrome Soc. (sci. acad. bd. 1985—, chmn. sci. adv. bd., 2005—, dir. sci. adv. bd. 2005, Rsch. award, 2004, Christian Puschel Meml. Rsch. award, 2005), Western Soc. for Pediatric Rsch. (councillor 1989-91). Achievements include research in relationship of Down Syndrome to Alzheimer's disease, neurometabolic disease. Office: U Calif Irvine Med Ctr Dept Pediatrics 101 The City Dr S # 2 Orange CA 92868-3201

LOTT, JOHNNYE JO, elementary school educator, writer; b. Natchitoches, LA, Dec. 6, 1935; d. John Adams and Mildred (Slaughter) Foshee; m. Stanley George Lott, Sept. 2, 1956; children: Philip, Jo Lynn Chesser, Brantley. B of Music Edn., Northwestern State U., 1957. Cert. Tchg. La. Tchr. music Orleans Parish Bd. Edn., New Orleans, 1958—59; tchr. first grade Ferncrest Pvt. Sch., 1962; tchr. lang. arts, gifted cirriculum Monroe County Schs., Forsyth, Ga., 1969—80; tchr. gifted curriculum Rapides Parish Schs., Alexandria, La., 1980—85; dir., bus. owner Sylvan Learning Ctr., 1987—96; freelance writer Murfreesboro, NC, 1996—. Author: In The Cold Of The Sun: Children In Crisis, 2002. Vol. Habitat Humanity, Murfreesboro, NC, 2002; bd. dirs. Hist. Assn.; leader Dulcimer Ensemble sponsored by Emmanuel Bapt. Ch., Alexandria, La., 2005—; vol. tchr. Mountain Dulcimer, Alexandria, La., 2005. Mem.: Friends Whitaker Libr. (bd. dirs. 2000—02), La. Coll. Faculty Women (pres. 1994—95), Phi Kappa Phi, Sigma Alpha Iota. Democrat. Baptist. Avocations: piano, reading, travel, gardening, writing. Home: 157 Adams Path Pineville LA 71360-7905

LOTT, MARLEY, lawyer; b. Greenwood, Miss., Aug. 27, 1947; BA with honors, Hollings Coll., 1969; JD cum laude, Harvard U., 1977. Bar: Tex. 1978. Ptnr., global projects & mem. exec. com. Baker & Botts L.L.P., Houston. Bd. dir. Contemporary Arts Mus., Houston; mem. exec. com. & vice-chmn. projects Friends of Herman Park, Houston. Named a Texas Super Lawyer, Texas Monthly mag. & Law & Politics mag., 2003—04. Mem. ABA, State Bar Tex., Houston Bar Assn., Phi Beta Kappa. Office: Baker Botts LLP One Shell Plz 910 Louisiana St Houston TX 77002-4995 Office Phone: 713-229-1666. Office Fax: 713-229-7766. Business E-Mail: marley.lott@bakerbotts.com.

LOTT, RONNIE (RONALD MANDEL LOTT), retired professional football player, television broadcaster; b. Albuquerque, May 8, 1959; BS in Pub. Adminstrn., U. So. Calif., 1981. With San Francisco 49ers, 1981—90, L.A. Raiders, 1991—93, N.Y. Jets, 1993—94, Kansas City Chiefs, 1994—95; analyst NFL Fox Broadcasting Co., Beverly Hills, Calif., 1996—. Founder All Stars Helping Kids, 1989. Named to Sporting News Coll. All-Am. team, 1980, Pro Bowl team, 1981—84, 1986—91, Sporting News All-Pro team, 1981, 1987, 1990.

LOTT, (CHESTER) TRENT, senator; b. Grenada, Miss., Oct. 9, 1941; s. Chester P. and Iona (Watson) L.; m. Patricia E. Thompson, Dec. 27, 1964; children: Chester T., Jr., Tyler Elizabeth. BA in Public Adminstrn., U. Miss., 1963, JD, 1967. Bar: Miss. 1967. Assoc. Bryan & Gordon, Pascagoula, Miss., 1967; adminstrv. asst. to Congressman William M. Colmer, 1968-72; mem. US Congresses from 5th Miss. dist., 1973-89; US Senator from Miss., 1989—; majority whip, 1995—96; majority leader, 1996—2002; minority whip, 2007—; mem. armed svcs. com., budget com., energy, natural resource. Field rep. for U. Miss., 1963-65; acting alumni sec. Ole Miss Alumni Assn., 1966-67; named as observer from House to Geneva Arms Control talks; chmn. Commerce, Sci. & Transp.; mem. Senate Republican Policy Com., Commerce, Fin. Com., 1996, Rules Com., 1996. Author: (autobiography) Herding Cats, A Lifetime in Politics, 2005. Recipient Golden Bulldog award Watchdogs of Treasury, Guardian of Small Bus. award Nat. Fedn. Independent Bus., Bryce Harlow award Bryce Harlow Found., 1995, Disting. Legis. award Animal Health Inst., 1998, Imperial Potentate's award merit, Shrine N.Am., 1999-2000, William Wallace award Am. Scottish Found., 2000, Hartranft award govt. svc. Aircraft Owners and Pilots Assn., 2000, George E. Brown Jr. Congressional Honor award Imaging and Geospatial Info. Soc., 2003, Disting. Svc. Congressional award Nat. Assn. State Directors Career Technical Edn. Consortium, 2004. Mem. ABA, Jackson County Bar Assn., Sigma Nu, Phi Alpha Delta. Lodges: Mason. Republican. Baptist. Office: US Senate 487 Russell Senate Office Bldg Washington DC 20510-0001 also: Federal Bldg Ste 127 911 Jackson Ave Oxford MS 38655 Office Phone: 202-224-6253, 601-965-4644, 601-965-4007. Office Fax: 202-224-2262.*

LOTTER, CHARLES ROBERT, retired lawyer; b. 1937; married. BA in Math., St. Johns U., 1959, JD, 1962; LLM, NYU, 1969. With anti-trust div. U.S. Dept. Justice, 1962-65; with Revere Copper & Brass, Inc., 1965-69, Del E. Webb Corp., 1969-70, Louis O. Kelso, 1970-71; joined J.C. Penney Co. Inc., LA, 1971, gen. atty. Washington, 1974—84, NYC, 1984—85, assoc. gen. counsel Plano, Tex., 1985—87, sr. v.p., sec., gen. counsel, 1987—93, exec. v.p., sec., gen. counsel, 1993—2005. Mem. legal affairs coun. U.S. C. of C.; bd. dirs. Legal Svcs. of No. Tex. Inc.; mem. adv. bd. Inst. Internat. and Comparative Law Ctr. Am. and Internat. Law; bd. dirs. Eckerd Corp., 1996—, J.C. Penney Corp. Inc., 2002—. Mem. adv. bd. Corp. Counsel Law Review Symposium So. Methodist U., Corp. Counsel Inst. Georgetown U. Law Ctr.; with USAFR, 1962—64, USNR, 1964—70. Mem.: Texas Bar Assn., State Bar of Tex., State Bar of Calif., State Bar of Ariz., NY State Bar, DC Bar, Am. Corp. Counsel. Assn. (corp. governance com.), ABA.

LOTTI, MICHAEL, marketing professional; MA in Statistics, Western Mich. U.; MBA in Mktg. and Fin., U. Rochester. Mem. applied mat. group Eastman Kodak Co., market rsch. coord. Asia, Africa & Australia Region, 1980, dir. bus. rsch., v.p. corp. mktg.; founding mem. In4mation Insights. Chair Adv. Com. of Profl. Assns. Census Bureau. Mem.: Mktg. Sci. Inst., Am. Mktg. Assn. (chmn. bd. 2007—, v.p. mktg. rsch. divsn. 1998—99). Office: Am Mktg Assn 311 S Wacker Dr Ste 5800 Chicago IL 60606-2266 Office Phone: 312-542-9000. Office Fax: 312-832-2266.*

LOTTIE, ADRIAN JEROME, writer, educator, consultant; s. Arthur Julius and Lou Willie Lottie. BA in Psychology, Wayne State U., Detroit, 1985, BA in Econs., 1985, MA in Econs., 1988, PhD, 1996. Asst. prof. Ea. Mich. U., Ypsilanti, 1992—2002; pres. Adrian J. Lottie & Assocs. Bus. & Econ. Consultants, Detroit, 1996—; assoc. dir. Inst. Diversity and Bus. Ea. Mich. U., Ypsilanti, 1996—2002, assoc. dir. African Am. Ctr. for applied rsch. and svcs., 2000—, assoc. prof., 2002—. Cons. New Detroit Inc., 1995—2001, Alliance for Fair Banking, 1996—2003, Assoc. Gen. Contractors of Am. Greater Detroit Br. Workforce Devel./Edn. Com., Southfield, Mich., 1997—, U.S. SBA, 1997, New Detroit, 1997—2001, Booker T. Washington Bus. Assn., 1997, U.S. Small Bus. Adminstrn., Office of Civic Rights Compliance, 1997, Gt. Lakes Constrn. Alliance, Detroit, 1999—, Mich. Econ. Devel. Corp. Office of Econ. Independence and Entrepreneurship, Detroit, 2000—02, Mich. Minority Bus. Devel. Coun., 2002, Nat. Action Network, Detroit, 2006—, Pete Trish PC, 2007—; evaluation cons. Mich. Inst. for Nonviolence Edn., Detroit, 2002—. Contbr. articles to profl. jours. Bd. dirs. Internat. Inst. of Met., Detroit, 1997—, pres., 2001—02; judge Ctr. for Civic Edn., 1998—99; pres. Erma Henderson Found., Detroit, 2001—02. With US Army, 1966—68. Grantee Project Start, New Detroit Inc., 1996-1999, Project Connect, Bank One, 1996-2001, Rsch. Excellence Fund, Ea. Mich. U., 1996-2003; Minority Grad. fellow, Skillman Found., 1985- 1988. Mem.: Am. Soc. Pub. Administrators, Acad. Polit. Sci., Am. Econ. Assn., Am. Polit. Sci. Assn. Independent. Protestant. Avocations: travel, swimming, hiking, golf, reading. Office: Eastern Michigan Univ 601-R Pray-Harrold Ypsilanti MI 48197 Office Phone: 313-231-4114. Personal E-mail: AdrianLottie@aol.com. E-mail: adrian.lottie@emich.edu.

LOTVEN, HOWARD LEE, lawyer; b. Springfield, Mo., Apr. 8, 1959; s. Isadore and Gytel (Tuchmeier) L. BA, Drake U., Des Moines, 1981; JD, U. Mo., Kansas City, 1984. Bar: Mo. 1984, US Dist. Ct. (we. dist.) Mo. 1984. Pvt. practice, Kansas City, 1984—; asst. prosecutor Kansas City, 1985; prosecutor, atty. City of Harrisonville, Mo., 1989—91; prosecutor City of Lake Lafayette, Mo., 2001—07; judge City Napoleon, Mo., 2007—. Commr. Jackson County Human Rels. and Citizens Complaints Com., Mo., 2006—; prosecutor City of Napoleon, Mo., 2001-07, judge 2007-. Mem. Hyde Park Crime Patrol, 1985—91, Hyde Park Assn. Zoning and Planning Commn., 1993—97; vol. Heartland United Way, 1995; trustee Pilgrim Svc., Inc., 2001—05, Heart of Am. Stand Down, 1995—2007; bd. dirs. We. Mo. Coalition Abolish Death Penalty, Mo., 2003—, Kans. City Ctr. Urban Agr., 2006—; bd. dir. Turner Men's Baseball League, 2007—; judge Mo. Sta H.S. Moot Ct. Competition, 1992. Named CASA Vol. Atty. of Yr., 2002. Mem. ABA, Mo. Bar Assn. (young lawyers coun. 1986-88, lectr. 1987-90, criminal law com. 1989—, gen. practice law com. 1990—, co-chair criminal law com. 1991-92, exec. coun. gen. practice law com. 1993-99, Law Day spkr. 1986, 96, lectr. 1987-90, 92, 97), Kansas City Metro. Bar Assn. (chmn. mcpl. cts. com. 2002, Vol. Atty. Project, 1992—, Vol. Atty. Project award winner 1994, continuing edn. spkr. 2000—), House Rabbit Soc., We. Mo. Coalition to Abolish the Death Penalty, Delta Theta Phi, Omicron Delta Kappa, others. Democrat. Jewish. Avocation: sports. Office: 1125 Grand Blvd Ste 1200 Kansas City MO 64106 Office Phone: 816-471-0070.

LOTWIN, STANFORD GERALD, lawyer; b. NYC, June 23, 1930; s. Herman and Rita (Saltzman) L.; m. Judy Scott, Oct. 15, 1994; children: Lori Hope, David. BS, Bklyn. Coll., 1951, LLB, 1954, LLM, 1957. Bar: N.Y. 1954, U.S. Supreme Ct. 1961, Pa. 1986. Ptnr. Blank Rome LLP, NYC, 1987—. Served with U.S. Army, 1954-56. Fellow Am. Acad. Matrimonial Lawyers (bd. of mgrs. 1984—); mem. NY State Bar Assn. (family law sect.), NY County Trial Lawyers (lectr. 1980—), Internat. Acad. Matrimonial Attys. (referee Commn. on Judicial Conduct). Office: 405 Lexington Ave New York NY 10174-0002 Office Phone: 212-885-5560. E-mail: slotwin@blankrome.com.

LOTZE, BARBARA, retired physicist; b. Jan. 4, 1924; came to U.S., 1961, naturalized, 1967. d. Matyas and Borbala (Toth) Kalo; m. Dieter P. Lotze, Oct. 6, 1958 (dec. Dec. 1987); m. Herbert L. Retcofsky, July 1998. Applied Math. Diploma with honors, Eotvos Lorand U. Scis., Budapest, Hungary, 1956; PhD, Innsbruck U., Austria, 1961. Mathematician Hungarian Cen. Statis. Bur., Budapest, 1955-56; tchr. math. Iselsberg, Austria, 1959-60; from asst. prof. physics to assoc. prof. to prof. Allegheny Coll., 1963-90, prof. emeritus, 1990—, chmn. dept., 1981-84. Lectr. in history of physics; spkr. to civic groups. Editor: Making Contributions: An Historical Overview of Women's Role in Physics, 1984; co-editor: The First War Between Socialist States: The Hungarian Revolution of 1956 and Its Impact, 1984; contbr. articles to profl. jours. Mem. AAUW, Am. Phys. Soc. (mem. com. internat. freedom of scientists 1993-95), Am. Inst. Physics (mem. adv. com. history of physics 1994-97), Am. Assn. Physics Tchrs. (coun., sect. rep. Western Pa. 1978-86, chmn. com. on women in physics 1983-84, com. internat. physics edn. 1991-93, com. history and philosophy of physics 1996-98, Disting. Svc. award 1986, cert. of appreciation 1988), Am. Hungarian Educators Assn. (pres. 1980-82). Home: 2269 Watchfield Dr South Park PA 15129-8977

LOTZENHISER, GEORGE WILLIAM, musician, educator, academic administrator, composer; b. Spokane, Wash., May 16, 1923; m. Kathryn Tuttle, 1944 (dec. 2006); children: William (dec.), Jon. BA cum laude, Ea. Wash. U., 1946, BEd in Social Sci., 1947; MusM, U. Mich., 1948; EdD, U. Oreg., 1956. Prof. music U. Ariz., Tucson, 1948-60; prof. Ea. Wash. U., Cheney, 1960-83, dir. H.S. creative arts summer series, 1960-83; dean Ea. Wash. U. Sch. Fine Arts, Cheney, 1960-83, dean emeritus, 1983—. Cons. and lectr. in field; tchg. fellow U. Mich., 1947-48, U. Oreg., 1955-56. Author: A Study of Faculty Loads in Member Schools of the National Association of Schools of Music, 1963, A Study of the Selection Process of Administrators of the Fine Arts in Colleges and Universities in the U.S., 1970, Music 200: A Programmed Music Theory Text; numerous solo and ensemble compositions; contbr. articles to profl. jours.; profl. condr./trombonist symphony, opera, musical theatre, ballet, circus, etc. Mem. Wash. State Music Adv. Com., 1967-83, exec. com. Alliance for Arts Edn., 1972-83; mem. Spokane Riverfront Festival of the Arts, 1976-78, Allied Arts of Wash. State, 1977-83. Served to rear adm. USNR, 1942-82. Decorated Legion of Merit; recipient Silver Antelope, named Disting. Eagle Scout, Boy Scouts Am. Mem. ASCAP, Nat. Assn. Schs. Music (accreditation com. chmn. 1960—), Nat. Music Educators Research Council, N.W. Assn. Accreditation Com., Western Assn. Schs. and Colls. Com. Congregationalist. Home: PO Box 1528 Coupeville WA 98239-1528 E-mail: glotz@whidbey.net.

LOU, JIANZHONG, chemical engineer, educator; arrived in U.S., 1987; s. Zongshi Liu and Huixin Lou; m. Hong Yin, Apr. 21, 1991; children: Bob, Lily. BS in Chem. Engring., Zhejiang U. Tech., 1982; PhD in Chem. Engring., U. Utah, 1994. Sr. rsch. staff Clopay Plastics Co., Cin., 1999—2001; supr. staff engr. Tate & Lyle N.Am., Arabi, La., 1994—99; assoc. prof. mech. and chem. engring. N.C. Agrl. and Tech. State U., Greensboro, NC, 2001—. Recipient Excellence in Mentoring award, NASA SHARP Program, 2003—04; grantee, NSF, 2003, USDA, 2003; scholar, Am. Soc. for Engring. Edn., 2002. Mem.: AIChE (pres. 2002—03, John J. McKetta grants 2002—03, Planning grant 2002—03), Piedmont Coun. Engring. and Tech. Socs. (treas. 2003—05), Soc. Plastics Engrs. (founder and advisor 2003—04), Greensboro (N.C.) Chinese Assn. (v.p. 2004—05). Achievements include invention of ultrahigh selectivity filled polymer membranes; discovery of rheological percolation in filled polymers. Home: 2802 Norwell Ct Oak Ridge NC 27310 Office: 1601 E Market St Greensboro NC 27411 Home Phone: 336-549-9089; Office Phone: 336-334-7620. Personal E-mail: jlou888@yahoo.com. E-mail: lou@ncat.edu.

LOU, LIZA, artist; Student, San Francisco Art Inst. One-woman shows include Santa Monica Mus. Art, Bass Mus. Art, Miami, Kemper Mus. Contmporary Art, Kansas City, Ctr. Estudis Art Contemporani, Barcelona, exhibited in group shows at New Mus., NYC, Heinie Onstad Kunstenter, Norway, Victoria and Albert Mus., London, Fondation Cartier, Paris. Fellow MacArthur Found. fellow, 2002; grantee MacArtur Found. Office: c/o Elizabeth Schwartz/Deitch Projects 76 Grand St New York NY 10013

LOU, MANZA, psychology professor; s. Jerry and Diane Manza; m. Lisa M. Geier, Dec. 2, 1989; children: Johnathan Manza, Nicholas Manza, Louie Manza. BA, SUNY, Binghamton, 1988; MA, Bklyn Coll., 1992; PhD, CUNY, 1992. Vis. asst. prof. Gettysburg Coll., Pa., 1992—95; chair & assoc. prof. psychology Lebanon Valley Coll., Annville, Pa., 1995—. Avocation: marathon running. Office: Lebanon Valley Coll 101 N College Ave Annville PA 17003 Office Phone: 717-867-6193. Office Fax: 717-867-6894. Business E-Mail: manza@lvc.edu.

LOU, YIMING, chemical engineer; B in Engring., Zhejiang U., 1997, M in Engring., 2000; PhD, UCLA, 2004. Rsch. assoc. dept. chem. engring. UCLA, 2000—04; sr. engr. Advanced Projects Rsch. Inc., 2004—. Presenter in field. Contbr. scientific papers. Recipient O. Hugo Shuck Best Paper award, Am. Automatic Control Coun., 2004; Univ. fellow, UCLA, 2000, Rockwell scholar, 1997. Mem.: IEEE, AIChE, Sigma Xi. Home: 1140 Golden Springs Dr Unit A Diamond Bar CA 91765 Office: Advanced Projects Rsch Inc 1925 McKinley Ave Ste B La Verne CA 91750 Home Phone: 909-860-5373; Office Phone: 909-392-1103. Personal E-mail: ylou@ieee.org.

LOU, ZHENG (DAVID), technical specialist; b. Changshu, Jiangsu, Peoples Republic China; came to U.S., 1982; s. Gui-Xin and Pei-Ling Lou; m. Min Yu, 1984; children: Katherine, Paul, Craig. BE, Zhejiang U., Hangzhou, China, 1982; PhD, U. Mich., 1990. Asst. rsch. scientist Transp. Rsch. Inst. U. Mich., Ann Arbor, 1990-93; tech. specialist Ford Motor Co., Ypsilanti, Mich., 1993-2000; tech. fellow Visteon Corp., Plymouth, Mich., 2000—04; pres. LGD Tech., LLC, Plymouth, 2004—. Contbr. articles to Jour. Rheology, Jour. Biomechanics, others, tech. papers in field. Grantee NASA, 1992-94, U.S. Army, 1992-94. Mem. ASME, SAE. Achievements include first to research in nonlinear dynamic interaction between an electrorheological fluid and a viscometer, study of electrorheological valves and dampers, heat transfer model in hyperthermia as a tumor therapy; major publications in biofluid study, active engine valve control for fuel economy, hydraulic pressure regulators, powertrain thermal systems, a fully-dynamic two-phase A/C model; patents in field. Home: 11200 Fellows Creek Dr Plymouth MI 48170-6382 Office: LGD Tech LLC 11200 Fellows Creek Dr Plymouth MI 48170 Home Phone: 734-459-3556; Office Phone: 734-693-4818. E-mail: zlou@comcast.net.

LOUARGAND, MARC ANDREW, real estate executive, financial consultant; b. San Francisco, July 3, 1945; s. Andrew Louargand and Edna Antoinette McNeil (dec.); m. Elizabeth A. Warner, June 18, 1966 (div. Oct. 1978); m. J. R. McDaniel, Feb. 14, 1986. BA, U. Calif., Santa Barbara, 1967; MBA, UCLA, 1974, PhD, 1982. Asst. prof. Calif. State Polytech. U., Pomona, 1975-77; assoc. prof. Calif. State U., Northridge, 1977-83, U. Mass., Boston, 1983-88; sr. lectr. Ctr. for Real Estate Devel. MIT, Cambridge, 1986-93; 2d v.p., sr. officer Mass. Mut. Life Ins. Co., Springfield, Mass., 1993-94; mng. dir., co-founder Cornerstone Real Estate Advisors, 1993—. Chmn. Mile Square Farm Inc., Vt. Only of Mile Square Farm; cons. in field. Author: CRE2000: Managing the Fifth Strategic Resource, Study Guide to Financial Management, 1986, (with others) Principles and Techniques of Appraisal Review, 1980, Handbook of Real Estate Portfolio Management; co-editor Jour. Real Estate, Portfolio Mgmt.; assoc. editor Jour. Real Estate Lit., Jour. Corp. Real Estate (UL), Briefings in Real Estate Fin., (UK); contbr. articles to profl. jours. Bd. dirs. Beverly Glen Assn., Bel Air, Calif., 1973-77, Citronia Homeowners Assn., Northridge, Calif., 1978-83; chmn. Carlisle (Mass.) Bd. Assessors, 1985-93. Fellow, Homer Hoyt Inst. Fellow Am. Real Estate Soc. (pres.-elect, bd. dirs.), Counselor Real Estate; mem. Nat. Coun. Real Estate Investment Fiduciaries (chair portfolio strategy com.). Republican. Avocations: tree farming, skiing, building restoration.

LOUCKS, ALLEN FRAZIER, prosecutor, lawyer; b. Huntington Park, Calif., Oct. 31, 1957; married; 1 child. BA, U. Rochester, 1979; MA, Columbia U., 1980; JD, George Washington U., 1985. Bar: Md. 1985, D.C. 1986, U.S. Ct. Appeals (4th cir.) 1986. Assoc. Venable, Baetter & Howard, Balt., 1985-87, Murphy & McDaniel, Balt., 1987, Smith Somerville & Case, Balt.; asst. US atty. chief civil divsn. (dist. Md.) US Dept. Justice, 2001—, interim US atty., 2005. Adj. prof. law U. Balt., 1989—. Office: United States Attorney Office 36 S Charles St Ste 400 Baltimore MD 21201-3119

LOUCKS, DANIEL PETER, environmental systems engineer; b. Chambersburg, Pa., June 4, 1932; s. Emerson Hunsberger and Eleanor Wright (Johnson) L.; m. Marjorie Ann Grant, June 24, 1967; children: Jennifer Lee, Susan Louise. BS, Pa. State U., 1954; MS, Yale U., 1955; PhD, Cornell U., 1965. Asst. prof. environ. engring. Cornell U., Ithaca, NY, 1965-70, assoc. prof., 1970-74, prof., 1974—, chmn. dept., 1974-80, assoc. dean research and grad. studies Coll. Engring., 1980-81. Rsch. fellow Harvard U., Cambridge, Mass., 1968; economist IBRD, Washington, 1972-73; vis. prof. MIT, Cambridge, 1977-78; rsch. scholar Internat. Inst. for Applied Sys. Analysis, 1981-82; vis. disting. prof. U. Colo., 1992, U. Adelaide, 1992, Tech. U. Aachen, Germany, 1993, U. Tech., Delft, The Netherlands, 1995; Maass/White fellow U.S. Army C.E. Inst. for Water Resurces, 2002; cons. NATO, UN, WHO, FAO, UNESCO, IRBD on water resources and regional devel. projects in Asia, Western and Eastern Europe, Africa and L.Am., 1970—, EPA on water quality planning USSR, 1975-77;

vis. prof. Internat. Inst. Hydraulic and Environ. Engring., Delft, 1976-80, 86—; environ. adv. bd. U.S. Army Corps Engrs., 1994-98, chmn. 1996-98; dir. NATO Advanced Rsch. Workshops, 1990, 95. Contbr. articles to jours. and books on math. models. for mng. water resources systems and environ. quality. Bd. dirs. Wilderness Corp., Plymouth, Vt., 1968-96, treas., 1987-96; pres. Cmty. Improvement Assn., Ithaca, 1976-77, 99-2000. Capt. USNR, 1956—81. Recipient U.S. Sr. Rsch. award Alexander von Humboldt Found., 1992, Joy Wyatt Challenge (EDUCOM) award, 1991, Disting. Lecture award Nat. Rsch. Coun. Taiwan, 1990, 99, Warren A. Hall medal Univs. Coun. Water Resources, 2000, Cannes Internat. grand prize Network Rsch. Founds., 2005; Fulbright-Hayes fellow Yugoslavia, 1975. Fellow Am. Geophys. Union; mem. ASCE (hon., Walter Huber rsch. award 1970, Julian Hinds award 1986), NAE, Internat. Water Resources Assn., Am. Water Resources Assn., Internat. Assn. Hydraulic Rsch., Internat. Assn. Hydrologic Scis., Sigma Xi. Home: 116 Crest Ln Ithaca NY 14850-2704 Office: Cornell U Hollister Hall Ithaca NY 14853 Home Phone: 607-257-3529; Office Phone: 607-255-4896. Business E-Mail: DPL3@cornell.edu.

LOUCKS, KATHLEEN MARGARET, lawyer; b. Milw., 1971; Student, Bethel Coll., 1989—92; BA, U. Minn., Mpls., 1995; JD, William Mitchell Coll. Law, 1999. Bar: Minn. 1999, US Dist. Ct. (dist. Minn.), Iowa 2005. Assoc. Gislason & Hunter, L.L.P., Minnetonka. Named a Rising Star, Minn. Super Lawyers mag., 2006. Mem.: Minn. Trial Lawyers Assn., Minn. State Bar Assn., ABA, Minn. Women Lawyers, Hennepin County Bar Assn., Minn. Def. Lawyers Assn. Office: Gislason & Hunter LLP 701 Xenia Ave S Ste 500 Minneapolis MN 55416 Office Phone: 763-225-6000. E-mail: kloucks@gislason.com.*

LOUDA, J. WILLIAM, chemist, biochemist, educator; b. Cin., Apr. 20, 1947; s. Joseph John and Jeanne Helen (Haeufle) Louda; m. Deborah Ann Wernander, May 1, 1993. BS in Biology, Wright State U., 1971; MS in Biology, Fla. Atlantic U., 1978; PhD in Marine Sci., U. South Fla., 1993. Rsch. assoc. Wright State U., Dayton, Ohio, 1970—71; rsch. asst. Fla. Atlantic U., Boca Raton, 1971, tchg. asst. in marine biology, invertebrate zoology, animal physiology, 1972—74, from rsch. assoc. to sr. lab. specialist, 1978—99, asst. scientist, 1999—2003, assoc. scientist, 2003—; rsch. asst. Aquatic Scis., Boca Raton, 1972. Vis. instr. dept. chemistry Fla. Atlantic U., Boca Raton, 1987—88, adj. faculty dept. chemistry and biochemistry, 1995—99; presenter in field. Contbr. articles to profl. jours. Grantee, South Fla. Water Mgmt. Dist., 1995—98, 2002—05, US Dept. Commerce Nat. Marine Fisheries Divsn., 2001—02, U. Miami, 2003. Mem.: AIChE, Coastal Edn. and Rsch. Found., Estuarine Rsch. Fedn., Am. Soc. Limnology and Oceanography, Latin-Am. Assn. Organic Geochemistry, Fla. Acad. Scis. (chmn. environ. and chem. scis. sect. 2000—01), European Assn. Organic Geochemists, Am. Chem. Soc., Ocean Conservancy, Nature Conservancy, Nat. Geographic Soc., Audubon of the Everglades, Loxahatchee Groves Landowners Assn. (pres. 1996—2004, bd. dirs., planning com.), Audubon Soc., Sierra Club, Phi Eta Tau. Avocations: fishing, skeet shooting, canoeing. Home: PO Box 1238 Loxahatchee FL 33470 Office: Fla Atlantic Univ 777 Glades Rd Boca Raton FL 33431 Office Phone: 561-297-3309. Business E-Mail: blouda@fau.edu.

LOUDEN, WM. BRUCE, lawyer; b. Fairfield, Iowa, May 14, 1938; s. Robert and Martha Hunnel Louden; m. Molly O'Neill, Aug. 11, 1962; children: Shannon O'Neill, David Andrew, Gregory Bruce. BA, U. Fla., 1961, JD, 1963. Ptnr. Holland & Knight, Lakeland, Fla., 1967—69, Ribicoff & Kotkin, Hartford, Conn., 1971—78, Louden, Byrne, Shechtman, Slater & Rose, Hartford, 1978—81, Steinberg & Louden, Hartford, 1981—87, Louden & Forzani, Hartford, 1989—2000; prin. Louden Legal Group LLC, Hartford, 2000—. Mem. standing com. profl. discipline ABA, 1973—79; pres. Swift's Inn, Hartford, 1977—78; adj. faculty U. Conn. Law Sch., 1979—84; chmn. profl. discipline com. Conn. Bar Assn., 1979—83; pres. Hartford chpt. Lawyers' Alliance for Nuc. Arms Control, 1981—86, nat. bd. dirs., 1982—84; pres. Conn. chpt. Am. Acad. Matrimonial Lawyers, 1991—92. Author: articles in profl. law jours. Pres. Rotary Club, Lakeland, Fla., 1968—69; sr. warden St. David's Episcopal Ch., Lakeland, 1968—69; trustee Webber Coll., Babson Park, Fla., 1968—71. Named one of Best Lawyers in Am., 1983—2007. Fellow: Am. Bar Found. D-Liberal. Episcopalian. Home: 37 Gin Still Lane West Hartford CT 06107 Office: Louden Legal Group LLC 638 Prospect Ave Hartford CT 06105

LOUDERBACK, JIM, broadcast executive; BS in Math., U. Vt., 1983; MBA in Computer Applications and Info. Sys., NYU, 1986. Asst. dir. stas. Air Vt., 1982—83; sr. analyst Chase Manhattan, NY, 1984—86; sr. cons. Mgmt. Dynamics, NY, 1986—87, Am. Mgmt. Sys., NJ, 1987—91; exec. lab. dir. PCWeek Ziff Davis Media Inc., Boston, 1991—95, v.p., editl. dir. PC Week, 1996—97, editor-in-chief Windows Sources NY, 1995—96, v.p., editl. dir. ZDTV San Francisco, 1997—2000, editor-in-chief Internet Properties, 2002—05, editor-in-chief, PC Magazine, 2005—07, and editl. dir., consumer tech. group, 2005; v.p. products, news and editl. dir. TechTV, San Francisco, 2000—02; CEO Revision3, 2007—. Contbg. editor, TechSmart columnist USA Weekend, 2000; founder Louderback Consulting, Pacifica, Calif. Mem.: Phi Beta Kappa. Office: Revision3 Corp 3255 Sawtelle Blvd Number 107 Los Angeles CA 90066*

LOUDERMILK, JOEY M., lawyer, insurance company executive; b. Warner Robins, Ga., Apr. 4, 1953; BS cum laude, Ga. State U., 1975; JD, U. Ga., 1978. Bar: Ga. 1978, US Dist. Ct. (mid. and no. dists. Ga.) 1978, US Ct. Appeals (11th cir.) 1981. Assoc. Moore & Worthington, Columbus, Ga., 1981—83; dir. legal dept. AFLAC Inc., Columbus, Ga., 1983—2000, dir. govt. rels., 1988—2000, sr. v.p., corp. counsel, 1989—91, sr. v.p., gen. counsel, 1991—2000, exec. v.p. legal and govt. affairs, gen. counsel, 2000—, corp. sec. Bd. dirs. Ga. Pub. Policy Found. Pres. Rotary Club, Columbus, Ga.; elder Edgewood Bapt. Ch.; bd. dirs. Ga. State U. Law Sch., Columbus Regional Med. Found., Ga. Humanities Coun., Ga. Mil. Affairs Coordinating Com. Mem.: Am. Soc. Corp. Secs., Am. Corp. Counsel Assn., State Bar Ga. Office: AFLAC Inc 1932 Wynnton Rd Columbus GA 31999 Office Phone: 706-323-3431.*

LOUDON, CRAIG MICHAEL, video specialist; b. Chgo., June 23, 1950; s. Howard Edgar and Laverne Anne (McKeeta) L. BS in Broadcast Prodn., So. Ill. U., Carbondale, 1976. Lic. radiotelephone operator, FCC. Announcer, engr. Sta. WGSB, St. Charles, Ill., 1976-77, Sta. WVVX-AM-FM, Highland Park, Ill., 1977; video tape operator, editor, cameraman ABC-TV, Chgo., 1977-84; video tape operator, editor Sta. KABC-TV, Hollywood, Calif., 1984, The Video Tape Co., North Hollywood, Calif., 1985-86, Bluth Video Systems, Burbank, Calif., 1986-87; video tape operator NBC-TV, 1987-89, Paramount Pictures, Hollywood, 1989—2002, Prime Post, LA, 2002—03; video tape quality control oper Studio Svcs. Internat., Burbank, 2003—05; mastering coord. The Walt Disney Co., 2004; with CBS-TV, Hollywood, 2005—. Avocations: volleyball, coin collecting/numismatics. Home: 18543 Devonshire St # 137 Northridge CA 91324 E-mail: winwoodie@aol.com.

LOUGANIS, GREG E(FTHIMIOS), retired Olympic athlete, actor; b. San Diego, Jan. 29, 1960; s. Peter E. and Frances I. (Scott) Louganis. Student, U. Miami, 1978—80; BA in Drama, U. Calif., 1983. Former mem. US Nat. Diving Team; ret., 1989. Color commentary US Olympic Festival, 1985, US Diving Championships, 1985, Circus of the Stars, 1986, US Diving Nats., 1990; coach Hill-Nickleodeon Sport Theater, 1997. Author: Breaking the Surface, 1995, For the Life of Your Dog, 1999; prodr.: (video diary) Breaking the Surface; actor: (plays) Working, 1978, (plays, Camelot), 1978; (plays) Carousel, 1978, Equus, 1980, Dance Kaliedescope, 1987, Cinderella, 1989, The Boyfriend, 1990, Jeffrey, 1994, The Only Thing Worse You Could Have Told Me..., 1995, Just Say No, 1999, Nunsense A-Men, 1999; (TV series) Battle of the Sexes, 1979, 1981, The Brain, 1985, NBC Superstars, 1985, Battle of the Network Stars, 1985, Circus of the Stars, 1986, Hollywood Sqs., 1986, 2000, 1987; host (TV series) Where Are They Now?, 1997; actor: (films) 16 Days of Glory, 1985, 1989, Dirty Laundry, 1985, Object of Desire, 1990, Mighty Ducks II, 1992, It's My Party, 1995, Touch Me, 1997. Named winner 47 U.S. Nat. Diving Titles, winner 5 World Diving Championships (platform and springboard), 1986; named to Olympic Hall of Fame, 1985; recipient Silver medal, Olympic Games, 1976, 2 Gold medals, 1984, 1988, James E. Sullivan award, 1984, Jesse Owens award, 1987, Gold medal, Pan Am. Games, 1979, 1983, 1987, Gold medal (platform and springboard), Seoul Olympic Games, 1988, Maxwell House/US Olympic Com. Spirit award, Olympic Games, 1988. Home: PO Box 4130 Malibu CA 90264-4130 Office: Img Artists Llc 152 W 57th St # 5 New York NY 10019-3310 Office Phone: 212-774-6735. Business E-Mail: greg@louganis.com.

LOUGEAY, DENRUTH COLLEEN, clinical psychologist, educator; b. Chgo., Nov. 7, 1943; d. Denzil Gordon Barre and Ruth Marion (Bergstrom) Larsen; m. Denis Howard Lougeay, Aug. 14, 1965; children: Stace Michael, Gregg Christopher. BS, U. Ill., Urbana, 1965; MEd, U. Ill., 1968; PhD, U.S. Internat. U., San Diego, 1986. Lic. clin. psychologist, Calif. Tchr. spl. edn. Urbana (Ill.) Pub. Schs., 1965-68; ednl. diagnostician Clin. Classroom Joliet (Ill.) Pub. Schs., 1968-69; counselor Women's Resource Ctr., San Luis Rey, Calif., 1980-82; psychologist Delmont Prt. Hosp., Victoria, Australia, 1982-83; group therapist Parents United East and North San Diego County, 1982-84; psychologist Palomar Coll., San Marcos, Calif., 1984-87; pvt. practice, Encinitas, Calif., 1988—. Disaster mental health officer ARC, San Diego, 1994—. Recipient State ARC Leadership award, 1991—97. Fellow San Diego Psychol. Assn. (pres. 1998); mem. APA (Calif. state coord. disaster response 1995—, nat. adv. bd. disaster response 1998-2001, Presdl. Citation 2000), Calif. Disaster Mental Health Coalition (charter), Calif. Psychol. Assn. (state chair disaster response 1995—, Silver Psi award 1998, Disting. Humanitarian award, 2006), Soc. Mental Health Profls. (pres. 1989-90, bd. dirs.), Assn. Psychol. Type (sec. San Diego chpt. 1988-90, bd. dirs.), Mensa, Illini Club San Diego County (bd. dirs. 1987—). Avocations: hot air ballooning, genealogy, travel. Office: Arrow Psychol Svc 404 Alviso Way Encinitas CA 92024-2616 Office Phone: 760-436-5620.

LOUGEE, DAVID LOUIS, lawyer; b. Worcester, Mass., Mar. 20, 1940; s. Laurence H. and Erma Virginia (MacAllister) L.; m. Mary Anne Strebb, July 15, 1979; children: Adam, Sara, Barbara, Laurence. AB, Bates Coll., Lewiston, Maine, 1962; LLB, Duke U., Durham, NC, 1965. Bar: Mass. 1965. Ptnr. Mirick O'Connell, DeMallie & Lougee, Worcester, 1965—2006, of counsel, 2006—, mng. ptnr., 1985—2001. Bd. dirs. The Protector Group, Inc., Quirk Wire Co., Inc. Named Woodward White, The Best Lawyers in Am. Mem.: Tatnuck Country Club (bd. govs., pres.). Office: 100 Front St Worcester MA 01608-1425 Office Phone: 508-791-8500. Business E-Mail: dllougee@modl.com.

LOUGEE, WENDY PRADT, university librarian, educator; b. Rhinelander, Wis., Aug. 9, 1950; d. Alan Emmons Pradt and Marie Elizabeth Wendland; m. Michael Durand Lougee, Aug. 25, 1973; 1 child, Mariel. BA, Lawrence U., 1972; MS, U. Wis., 1973; MA, U. Minn., 1977. Head grad. libr. U. Mich. Libr., Ann Arbor, Mich., 1984—93, assoc. dir., 1993—2002; univ. libr., McKnight presdl. prof. U. Minn., Mpls., 2002—. Contbr. articles to profl. jours. JSTOR Project grantee Mellon Found., 1996. Mem. ALA (life), Am. Soc. Info. Sci. Office: U Minn 499 O Meredith Wilson Libr 309 19th Ave S Minneapolis MN 55455 Office Phone: 612-624-1807. Fax: 612-626-9353. E-mail: wlougee@umn.edu.*

LOUGHEED, PETER, lawyer, former Canadian premier; b. Calgary, Alta., Can., July 26, 1928; s. Edgar Donald and Edna (Bauld) L.; m. Jeanne Estelle Rogers, June 21, 1952; children— Stephen, Andrea, Pamela, Joseph. BA, U. Alta., 1950, LL.B., 1952; MBA, Harvard U., 1954. Bar: Alta 1955. With firm Fenerty, Fenerty, McGillivray & Robertson, Calgary, 1955-56; sec. Mannix Co., Ltd., 1956-58, gen. counsel, 1958-62, v.p., 1959-62, dir., 1960-62; individual practice law, from 1962; formerly mem. Alta. Legislature for Calgary West; formerly leader Progressive Conservative Party of Alta., 1965-85; premier of Alta., 1971-85; ptnr. Bennett Jones, Calgary, 1986-99, counsel, 1999—. Named an inductee, Canadian Med. Hall of Fame, 2001. Office: Bennett Jones LLP 855 2nd St SW 4500 Bankers Hall Calgary AB Canada T2P 4K7

LOUGHLIN, MICHAEL J., bank executive; BA, Univ. Calif., Berkeley, 1978. Mgmt. positions Wells Fargo & Co., San Francisco, 1986—, regional v.p. comml. banking, head U.S. corp. banking; exec. v.p. Wells Fargo Bank, 2000—06; sr. credit officer comml. banking Wells Fargo & Co., San Francisco, 2000—03, head credit officer wholesale banking, 2003—06, dep. chief credit officer, 2006, exec. v.p. chief credit officer, 2006—. Office: Wells Fargo & Co 420 Montgomery St San Francisco CA 94163*

LOUGHLIN, WALTER P., lawyer; b. 1950; BA, U. Calif. LA, 1972; MA, JD, Yale U., 1976. Bar: Conn. 1977, NY 1999. Lectr. Columbia Law Sch.; law clk. US Dist. Judge (dist. Conn.), 1976—77, US Ct. Appeals (2nd cir.), 1977—78; chief appellate atty., asst. US Atty. US Atty. (so. dist.) NY, 1979—83; dir. Vera Inst. Justice, London, 1985—86; assoc. ind. counsel Iran-Contra prosecutions, 1986—89, White House Dep. Chief of Staff Michael K. Deaver prosecution, 1986—89; pvt. practice, 1990—; ptnr. Kirkpatrick & Lockhart Preston Gates Ellis LLP, NYC, 2006—. Author: Modern Federal Jury Instructions, 1984, and semi-annual updates. Mem.: ABA. Office: Kirkpatrick & Lockhart Preston Gates Ellis LLP 599 Lexington Ave New York NY 10022-6030 Office Phone: 212-536-4065. Office Fax: 212-536-3901.

LOUGHRAN, PETER J., lawyer; b. Feb. 22, 1964; BA, Georgetown U., 1986; JD, Columbia U., 1989. Bar: NY 1990, Conn. 1990. With Debevoise & Plimpton LLP, NYC, 1989—, ptnr., mem Securities Practice Group. Mem.: Assn. Bar of City NY. Office: Debevoise & Plimpton LLP 919 Third Ave New York NY 10022 Office Phone: 212-909-6375. Office Fax: 212-909-6836. E-mail: pjloughran@debevoise.com.

LOUGHREY, F. JOSEPH, manufacturing executive; b. Holyoke, Mass., Oct. 27, 1949; s. F. Joseph and Helen T. (Barrett) Loughrey; m. Deborah Jane Welsh, July 23, 1988; 1 stepchild, Blair Edward Boehmer. BA in Econs., African Studies, U. Notre Dame, 1971. Pres. AIESEC-U.S. Inc., NYC, 1971-73; mgr. corp. employment Cummins Engine Co., Columbus, Ind., 1974-75, mgr. internat. personnel, 1975-79, dir. personnel (mktg.), 1979-81, dir. personnel (mktg. and subs.), 1981-83, dir. internal mgmt., 1983-84; mng. dir. Holset Engring. Co. Ltd., Huddersfield, Eng., 1984-86; v.p. employee rels. Cummins Engine Co., Columbus, Ind., 1986-87, from. v.p. So. Ind. ops. to v.p. heavy duty engines, 1988-90, group v.p. worldwide ops., 1990-95, exec. v.p., group pres. indsl. and chief tech. officer, 1996-99, pres.-engine bus., 1999—2005, pres., COO, 2005—. Sr. mem. nat. adv. bd. Tauber Mfg. Inst. U. Mich.; mem. adv. coun. coll. arts and letters U. Notre Dame; pres. bd. disr. Developmental Svcs., Inc.; bd. dirs. Sauer-Danfoss, Inc., Cummins Found., Columbus Learning Ctr., 2003—, Cummins Inc.; chmn. Mfg. Inst., 2005—, Conexus Ind. Mem.: NAM (bd. dirs. 2002—), AIESEC Interna. (sr.), Conexus Ind. (chmn.). Democrat. Roman Catholic. Office: Cummins Inc PO Box 3005 Columbus IN 47202-3005 Office Phone: 812-377-5123. Business E-Mail: joe.loughrey@cummins.com.

LOUGHRIDGE, JOHN HALSTED, JR., lawyer; b. Chestnut Hill, Pa., Oct. 30, 1945; s. John Halsted Sr. and Martha Margaret (Boyd) L.; m. Amy Claire Booe, Aug. 3, 1980 (div. Apr. 1995); 1 child, Emily Halsted. AB, Davidson Coll., 1967; JD, Wake Forest U., 1970. Bar: N.C. 1970, U.S. Dist. Ct. 1970, U.S. Ct. Mil. Appeals 1986, U.S. Supreme Ct. 2002. Divsn. head, v.p., counsel Wachovia Mortgage Co., Winston-Salem, N.C., 1971-79; sr. v.p., counsel Wachovia Corp. and Bank, Charlotte and Winston-Salem, NC, 1980—. UCC Article 5 drafting com. NC Gen. Statues Commn., 1999. Mem. cabinet, chair profl. divsn. United Way Forsyth County, 1994; mem. Rep. Nat. Com.; mem. Presdl. Bus. Commn., 2005—; Rep. Presdl. Victory Team leader, 2004; hon. chmn. bus. adv. coun. Nat. Rep. Congl. Com., 2004—; GOP Attys. Com.-Help Am. Vote Act, 2004—; founding sponsor Nat. Mus. U.S. Army, 2005. Col. JAGC, USAR, 1970-00. Named Businessman Yr., Nat. Rep. Congrl. Com., 2005—06; recipient Ronald Reagan Rep. Gold Medal award, 2004, 2005, Congl. Medal of Distinction, Nat. Rep. Congl. Com., 2006, Pres. Vol. Svc. award, 2006. Mem.: ABA (corp. banking and bus. law sects. 1970—, internat. law and practice sects. 1999—2002, comml. fin. svcs. com. 2006—, real estate financing subcom. 2006—, adv. panel 2006—), Dept. Def. NC Com. Employer Support Guard and Res. (area chair 2005, ombudsman 2006—, dir. mil. liaison 2006—), NC Bar Found. (CLE program planner 2000, 2001, 2007), Mortgage Bankers Assn. Am. (legal issues com. 1982—92, fin. affiliates com. 1988—92), Assn. Corp. Counsel (bd. dirs. and v.p. NC chpt. 1988—98, 2001—04, fin. svcs. com. 2006—), Forsyth County Bar Assn., NC Coll. Advocacy, NC State Bar (bar examination candidate interviewer 2001—02), NC Bar Assn. (real property sect. 1971—, bus. law sect. 1971—, internat. law sect. 1984—, fin. instns. com. 1985—, governing coun. real property sect. 1988—91, corp. counsel sect. 1989—, real property curriculum com. 1990—93, governing coun. corp. coun. sect. 1992—98, treas. 1999—2000, bus. law curriculum com. 1999—2001, corp. coun. sect. sec. 2000—01, vice chair 2001—02, chmn. 2002—03, nominating com. 2003—05, vice chair 2006—07), Res. Officers Assn. (chpt. pres. 1996—97, sec. 1997—, named to Nat. Brigade Vols. 2005), Davidson Coll. Alumni Assn. (bd. dirs. 2001—03, Fideles Soc. 2004—, Alumni Svc. award 2007), Rotary Club, Forsyth Country Club, Twin City Club (sec. 1990—97, gov. 1994—2005, pres. 1997—2001), Union League Phila., Phi Delta Theta, Phi Delta Phi. Republican. Presbyterian. Avocations: golf, tennis. Home: 615 Arbor Rd Winston Salem NC 27104 Office: Wachovia Corp 301 S College St Charlotte NC 28288-0630 Office Phone: 704-374-3191. Business E-Mail: john.loughridge@wachovia.com.

LOUGHRIDGE, MARK, computer company executive; b. Leadville, Colo., 1953; BSME, Stanford U.; MBA, U. Chgo. Joined IBM Corp., Armonk, NY, 1977, various key fin. positions, 1988—91, v.p., contr., 1998—2002, sr. v.p., gen. mgr. personal systems group, 2002—04, CFO, sr. v.p., 2004—. Designer (video games) devel. by various companies. Office: IBM Corp 1 New Orchard Rd Armonk NY 10504*

LOUI, MICHAEL CONRAD, engineering educator; b. Phila., June 1, 1955; m. Cynthia Margaret Wood, May 29, 1983; children: Eric, Jeremy. BS, Yale U., 1975; MS, MIT, 1977, PhD, 1980. Prof. elec. and computer engring.,Univ. Disting. Tchr./Scholar U. Ill., Urbana, 1981—; program dir. NSF, Washington, 1990-91; assoc. dean grad. coll. U. Ill., Urbana, 1996—2000; Carnegie scholar Carnegie Found. for Advancement of Tchg., 2003. Exec. editor: Coll. Tchg., 2006; mem. editl. bd. Info. and Computation, 1997—, Accountability in Rsch., 1999—, Tchg. Ethics, 2002—. Recipient Luckman Disting. Undergrad. Tchg. award, U. Ill., Urbana, 1995. Fellow IEEE; mem. Assn. Computing Machinery, Am. Soc. Engring. Edn. (Dow Outstanding Young Faculty award 1985), Assn. for Practical and Profl. Ethics. Office: Coord Sci Lab 1308 W Main St Urbana IL 61801-2307 Office Phone: 217-333-2595.

LOUIE, DAVID MARK, lawyer; b. Oakland, Calif., Oct. 8, 1951; s. Paul and Emma (Woo) L.; m. Johanna C. Chuan, Sept. 6, 1986; children: Ryan David, Jenna Rachel. AB cum laude, Occidental Coll., 1973; JD, U. Calif., Berkeley, 1977. Bar: Calif. 1977, U.S. Dist. Ct. (no. Dist.) Calif. 1977, U.S. Ct. Appeals (9th cir.) 1977, Hawaii 1978, U.S. Dist. Ct. Hawaii 1978. Ptnr. Case & Lynch, Honolulu, 1977-88; sr. ptnr. Roeca, Louie & Hiraoka, Honolulu, 1988—. Faculty mem. Profl. Edn. Systems, Inc. (PESI) Seminars: Hawaii Ins. & Tort Update, 1995, 1996, Depositions (Strategies, Tactics & Mechanics), 1990, Nat. Bus. Inst. (NBI) Seminars: Arbitrating and Trying the Automobile Injury Case in Hawaii, 1993, Ins. Litigation in Hawaii, 1992, Pacific Law Inst. (PLI) Seminars: Premises Liability, 1995, Hawaii State Bar Assn. Depositions, 1997, Mediation Techniques, 2001, miscellaneous seminars: Hawaiian Bitumuls & Paving Co., Job Site Accidents, 1994, Hawaiian Dredging Construction Co., Job Site Accidents, 1993; mem. Def. Rsch. Inst., 1990—. Contbg. author: Going Back, 1972, Hawaii Tort Liability Issues in Work Site Accident Cases, 1989, Trying the Automobile Accident Case, 1991, Hawaii Tort Law Update, 1992, 94. Bd. dirs. Jr. Achievement Hawaii, Honolulu, Aloha Tower Devel. Corp., 1998—2006, chmn., 1999—2006; sec., v.p., dir. Ohana Ins. Co. Hawaii, Inc., 1994-95. Mem. ABA (sects. on tort and ins. practice litigation 1978—, minority couns. demonstration program 1994), Hawaii State Bar Assn. (bd. dirs. 1994-98, v.p. 2000, pres. 2001), Calif. State Bar Assn., Hawaii Def. Lawyers Assn. (bd. dirs. 1990—, sec.-treas. 1994-99), Nat. Asian Pacific ABA (Hawaii chpt. pres. 1992-95, bd. dirs. 1996—), Mensa, Pacific Club. Home: 4122 Pakolu Pl Honolulu HI 96816-3930 Office: Roeca Louie & Hiraoka 841 Bishop St Ste 900 Honolulu HI 96813-3917

LOUIE, JANIS, chemistry professor; b. 1971; BS, Univ. Calif., 1993; PhD, Yale Univ., 1998; postdoctoral studies, NIH, Calif. Inst. Tech., 1998—2001. Henry Eyring asst. prof. chemistry Univ. Utah, Salt Lake City. Mem.: Am. Chem. Soc. (Arthur C. Cope Scholar award 2007). Office: Dept Chemistry Univ Utah 315 South 1400 East Salt Lake City UT 84112 Office Phone: 801-581-7309. Office Fax: 801-581-8433. Business E-Mail: louie@chem.utah.edu.*

LOUIE, STEVEN GWON SHENG, physics professor, researcher; b. Canton, China, Mar. 26, 1949; came to U.S., 1961; s. Art and Kam Shui (Lau) L.; m. Jane Yuk Wong, Aug. 3, 1975; children: Jonathan S., Jennifer Y., Sarah W. AB in Math. and Physics, U. Calif., Berkeley, 1972, PhD in Physics, 1976. IBM postdoctoral fellow IBM Watson Rsch. Ctr., Yorktown Heights, NY, 1977-79; mem. vis. tech. staff AT&T Bell Labs., Murray Hill, NJ, 1979; asst. prof. U. Pa., Phila., 1979-80; NSF postdoctoral fellow physics dept. U. Calif., Berkeley, 1976-77, assoc. prof., 1980-84, prof., 1984—, Miller rsch. prof., 1986, 95. Faculty scientist Lawrence Berkeley Lab., 1980-93, sr. faculty scientist, 1993—; cons. Exxon Rsch. & Engring. Co., Annandale, N.J., 1981-87; Closs lectr. U. Chgo., 2006. Editor Solid State Comm., 1994—; contbr. over 380 articles to sci. jours. Recipient sustained outstanding rsch. in solid state physics award Dept. Energy, 1993, Feynman prize Foresight Inst., 2003, Outstanding Overseas Chinese award Chinese Consol. Benevolent Assn., 2005; fellow A.P. Sloan Found., 1980, Guggenheim fellow, 1989. Fellow AAAS, Am. Phys. Soc. (Aneesur Rahman prize 1996, Davisson-Germer prize 1999); mem. NAS, Materials Rsch. Soc. Baptist. Achievements include patents in field. Avocations: gardening, skiing, tennis. Home Phone: 510-527-2921.

LOUIS, GLEN, music educator; b. Bklyn., May 3, 1951; B, Juilliard Sch., 1973. Lic. tchr. N.Y. Clk. IRS, Holtsville, NY, 1976; music tchr., 1973—. Mem.: Am. Fedn. Musician. Avocations: golf, tennis. Home: 2928 Ruddell Rd #123 Lacey WA 98503-7829 Office Phone: 360-455-1786. E-mail: studio123@hotmail.com.

LOUIS, LESTER See BROWN, LES

LOUIS, PAUL ADOLPH, lawyer; b. Key West, Fla., Oct. 22, 1922; s. Louis and Rose Leah (Weinstein) L.; m. Nancy Ann Edgeworth Lapof, Dec. 28, 1971; children: Louis Benson, IV, Connor Cristina and Marshall Dore (twins). BA, Va. Mil. Inst., Lexington, 1947; LL.B., U. Miami, Fla., 1950, JD, 1967. Bar: Fla. 1950, U.S. Dist. Ct. (so. dist.) Fla. Asst. state atty., 1955-57; atty. Beverage Dept. Fla., 1957-60; spl. asst. atty. gen. State of Fla., 1970-71; partner firm Sinclair, Louis, Heath, Nussbaum & Zavertnik (P.A.), Miami, 1960—; mem. Fed. Jud. Nominating Commn., 1977-80; mem. peer rev. com. U.S. Dist. Ct. for So. Dist. Fla., 1983-85. Author: Defamation, How Far Can You Go, Trial and Tort Trends, 1969; contbr.: chpts. to Fla. Family Law, 1967, 72. Founder mem. Palm Springs Gen. Hosp. Scholarship Com., 1968; mem. Dade County Health Facilities Authority, 1979-82; trustee Fla. Supreme Ct. Hist. Soc., 1994—. Served to 1st lt. USAAF, 1943-45, ETO, maj. USAF Res., 1962. Decorated Air medal with three oak leaf clusters, Bronze Star (7), Purple Heart. Mem. ABA, Fla. Bar (bd. govs. 1970-74), Dade County Bar Assn. (dir. 1954-55, 66-69), Am. Judicature Soc., Va. Mil. Inst. Alumni Assn. Clubs: Miami, Bath. Democrat. Jewish. Home: 4411 Palm Ln Miami FL 33137-3346 Office: 1125 A I duPont Bldg 169 E Flagler St Miami FL 33131-1210

LOUIS, VIRGIE LEE, retired secondary school educator; b. New Orleans, May 27, 1945; d. John Reddick and Marguerite (LaFrance) Reddick-Ragas; m. Alfred James Louis I, Dec. 24, 1966; children: Alfred, Tyra BS, Grambling State U., 1969; postgrad., Creighton U., 1972—73, U. Nebr., 1973—75, postgrad., 1982, U. Calif.; MS Classroom Tech., Lesley U., 2000. Instr. Omaha Pub. Schs., 1969—2003; operator Northwestern Bell Tel., Omaha, 1970; educator Ceta Youth Program, Omaha, 1982—84, asst. dir., 1985; tchr. gen. ednl. devel. Omaha Pub. Schs., 2003—, intergenerational mentor program for edn. majs., 2004—. Mem. Citizens Mature Leadership, Omaha, 1985—; curriculum devel. Career Edn. Workshop, Omaha; host family to fgn. exch. students, 1988-99; sponsor Golden Viking's Vikettes Pom Pons, 1986-91; del. 1992 Dem. Nat. Conv., 1996 Dem. Nat. Conv.; rep. dist. 2 Nebr. Dem. Women's Caucus; mem. exec. bd. Douglas County Dem.; mem. Nebr. State Pers. Bd., 1993-05; dist. 11 legis. co-chair, 1992; dist. II legis. chair, 2007-; Family Svcs. mentor, 1992; mem. met. dist. bd. Pub. Affairs, chair, 1997—; bd. dirs., chair Charles Drew Health Ctr., 1996-00. Recipient Nebr.'s Favorite Tchr's award Nebr. State PTA, 1988 Mem. NEA, ASCD, Omaha Edn. Assn. (v.p. ret. group 2007-), Nebr. Edn. Assn., Nebr. Bus. Edn. Assn., Nat. Bus. Edn. Assn., Assn. Mary Immaculate (missionary). Democrat. Roman Catholic. Avocations: reading, travel, workshops. Office: Omaha Pub Schs Skinner Magnet Ctr 4410 N 33d St Omaha NE 68111-2207 Personal E-mail: agent30zill@yahoo.com.

LOUIS, WILLIAM ROGER, historian; b. Detroit, May 8, 1936; s. Henry Edward and Bena May (Flood) L.; m. Dagmar Cecilia Friedrich; children: Antony Andrew, Catherine Ann. BA, U. Okla., 1959; MA, Harvard U., 1960; DPhil, Oxford U., 1962, DLitt, 1979; DLitt (hon.), Westminster Coll., 1998. Asst. prof., then assoc. prof. history Yale U., 1962-70; prof. history U. Tex., Austin, 1970-85, dir. Brit. Studies, 1975—, Kerr chair English history and culture, 1985—, disting. teaching prof., 1998—. Supernumerary fellow St. Antony's Coll., U. Oxford, Eng., 1986-96, hon. fellow, 1996—; fellow Brit. Acad., 1993—; Chichele lectr. All Souls Coll., U. Oxford, Eng., 1990, 2002, 03, 06; Disting. lectr. London Sch. Econs., 1992; Cust lectr. Nottingham U., 1995; Elie Kedourie Meml. lectr. Brit. Acad., 1996; Churchill Meml. lectr., 1998; history faculty lectr. U. Oxford, Eng., 2001; disting. vis. prof. Am. U. in Cairo, 2001; Kalb lectr. Rice U., 2001; Fusco lectr. U. Conn., 2001, Costa lectr. U. Ohio, 2002; dir. summer seminars NEH, 1985, 88, 90, 91, 96, 2000; Antonius lectr. Oxford U., 2002, Leonard Stein lectr., 2005; founding dir. Nat. History Ctr.; chmn. US State Dept. Hist. Adv. Com.; scholars coun., Libr. Congress. Author: Ruanda-Urundi, 1963, Germany's Lost Colonies, 1967, (with Jean Stengers) The Congo Reform Movement, 1968, British Strategy in the Far East, 1919-1939, 1971, Imperialism at Bay, 1977 (History Book Club), British Empire in the Middle East, 1984 (George Louis Beer prize Am. Hist. Assn. and Tex. Inst. Letters award), In The Name of the God Go! Leo Amery and the British Empire in the Age of Churchill, 1992; editor British Documents on the End of the Empire, 1988—; editor-in-chief Oxford History of the British Empire, 1992—; editor: (with P. Gifford) Britain and Germany in Africa, 1967, France and Britain in Africa, 1971, The Origins of the Second World War: A.J.P. Taylor and His Critics, 1972, National Security and International Trusteeship in the Pacific, 1972, Imperialism: The Robinson and Gallagher Controversy, 1976, (with William S. Livingston) Australia, New Zealand and the Pacific Islands Since the First World War, 1979, (with P. Gifford) The Transfer of Power in Africa, 1982, (with R. Stookey) End of the Palestine Mandate, 1986, (with H. Bull) The Special Relationship: Anglo-American Relations Since 1245, 1986, (with P. Gifford) Decolonization and African Independence, 1988, (with James Bill) Musaddiq, Iranian Nationalism and Oil, 1988, (with Roger Owen) Suez 1956: The Crisis and Its Consequences, 1989, (with Robert A. Fernea) The Iraqi Revolution of 1958, 1991, (with Robert Blake) Churchill, 1993, Adventures with Britannia, 1995, More Adventures with Britannia, 1998, Still More Adventures with Britannia, 2003, Yet More Adventures with Britannia, 2005, Burnt Orange Britannia, 2006, Penultimate Adventures with Britannia, 2007, Ends of British Imperialism, 2006, (with Michael Howard) The Oxford History of the Twentieth Century, 1998, (with Judith Brown) The Oxford History of the British Empire: The Twentieth Century, 1999, (with Ronald Hyam) The Conservative Government and the End of Empire, 1957-64, 2000, Festschrift: The Statecraft of British Imperialism: Essays in Honor of William Roger Louis, 1999, (with Roger Owen) A Revolutionary Year: The Middle East in 1958, 2002. Trustee Brit. Empire Mus., Bristol, England. Decorated comdr. Brit. Empire; Woodrow Wilson fellow Harvard U., 1959-60, Marshall scholar Oxford U., 1960-62, NEH fellow, Am. Inst. Indian Studies fellow, Guggenheim fellow, vis. fellow All Souls Coll., U. Oxford, Balliol Coll., Oxford U., overseas fellow Churchill Coll., U. Cambridge, Eng., fellow Woodrow Wilson Internat. Ctr.; guest scholar Brookings Instn.; disting. visitor hist. dept. Peking U., Beijing, 1999. Fellow Royal Hist. Soc.; mem. Am. Hist. Assn. (pres. 2001), Coun. on Fgn. Rels. (N.Y.C.), Tex. Inst. Letters, Reform Club (London), Century (N.Y.C.), Met. Club (Washington). Democrat. Office: U Texas Dept History Austin TX 78712

LOUISA, ANGELO JOSEPH, social studies educator, researcher; b. Bridgeville, Pa., Oct. 12, 1951; s. Joseph Peter and Anna Maria Louisa; m. Pamela Lynn Acre, June 19, 1976. BA magna cum laude, St. Vincent Coll., Latrobe, Pa., 1973; MA, Duquesne U., Pitts., 1975; PhD, U. Minn., Mpls., 1985. Cert. temp. tchr. social studies Pa., 1973. Tchg. asst. dept. history Duquesne U., Pitts., 1973—75, U. Minn., Mpls., 1975—79, reader-grader dept. history, 1978—79, instr., 1979; cmty. faculty mem. Met. State U., St. Paul, 1982—87; instr. dept. history Concordia Coll., Moorhead, Minn., 1983, Lakewood C.C., White Bear Lake, Minn., 1985; asst. prof. Met. State U., St. Paul, 1987—88; lectr. dept. history U. Nebr., Omaha, 1994—96, asst. prof., 1996—97, lectr., 1997—99, asst. prof., 1999—2000; lectr. dept. history Creighton U., Omaha, 1999—2002, asst. prof., 2002—03, lectr., 2003—04, asst. prof., 2004, lectr., 2005—06; self-employed rschr., writer, 2006—. Editl. assoc. Historicus, Lawrence, Kans., 1979—81; asst. to the Minn. state dir. Nat. History Day program, Mpls., 1979—83; exec. and fin. dir. The Coll. Football Stats. Quar., Omaha, 1989—94; judge Omaha metro area competition Nat. History Day program, Omaha, 1997—, judge Nebr. state competition, Lincoln, 1999, 2001, 07; co-founder and mem. steering com. Rose and Thistle Soc. U. Minn.; co-founder and mem. steering com. Medieval/Renaissance Studies minor program U. Nebr., Omaha; coord., chair, lectr. academic confs. Co-creator Maj. League Brief 'n' Brisk Baseball Game; contbr. articles to ency., to profl. jours. Mem. Nebr. State Hist. Records Adv. Bd., Lincoln, 2001—07. Named Outstanding Faculty, Order of Omega, Creighton U., 2003; recipient Student Assn. award, St. Vincent Coll., 1973, Grad. Student Assn. award in History, Duquesne U., 1975; McMillan Travel grant, U. of Minn., 1979. Mem.: Soc. for Am. Baseball Rsch., Am. Hist. Assn., The Robert W. Maxwell Football Club, Pi Gamma Mu, Omicron Delta Kappa, Phi Kappa Phi, Phi Alpha Theta (scholarship 1979). Avocations: music, reading, walking, baseball history, movies. Home: 10327 Fieldcrest Ct #311 Omaha NE 68114

LOUIS-DREYFUS, JULIA, actress; b. NYC, Jan. 13, 1961; d. William and Judith Louis-Dreyfus; m. Brad Hall, 1987; children: Henry, Charles. Attended, Northwestern U. Former mem. Second City and the Practical Theatre Company, Chicago, Ill. Actor (TV series) Saturday Night Live, 1982-85, Day by Day, 1986-89, The Art of Being Nick, 1986, Seinfeld, 1989-98 (Emmy award supp. actress, 1996, Emmy nom., 1992, 93, 94, 95, 97, 98, Amer. Comedy award best supp. actress, 1993, 94, 95, 97, 98, Golden Globe award supp. actress, 1994, SAG award, 1997, 98), The New Adventures of Old Christine, 2006-(Emmy award for outstanding lead actress in a comedy series, 2006); actor, prodr. Watching Ellie, 2002-2003; (TV appearances) Family Ties, 1988, Dinosaurs, 1991, The Single Guy, 1995, Hey Arnold, 1997, Curb Your Enthusiasm, 2000, 01, The Simpsons (voice), 2001, Arrested Development, 2002, 2004, 2005; (films) Soul Man, 1986, Troll, 1986, Hannah and Her Sisters, 1986, National Lampoon's Christmas Vacation, 1989, Jack the Bear, 1993, North, 1994, Father's Day, 1997, Deconstructing Harry, 1997, A Bug's Life (voice) 1998, Gilligan's Island, 1999, Speak Truth to Power, 2000; (TV movies) London Suite, 1996, Animal Farm (voice), 1999, Gepetto, 2000 Office: Jonas PR 240 26th St Ste 3 Santa Monica CA 90402 also: Hofflund/Polone 9465 Wilshire Blvd Beverly Hills CA 90212*

LOUM, ANTHONY WEBSTER, librarian; MEd; MLS, U. Wash., 1997. Asst. br. libr. Cypress Hills Bklyn. Pub. Libr., mgr. adult libr. svcs. cluster 1, coord. adult svcs., 2004—. Recipient NY Times Libr. award, 2006. Mem.: ALA (past mem. com. on diversity, mem. internat. rels. com. of black caucus), Pub. Libr. Assn. (mem. membership com.), NY Black Librs. Caucus (v.p./pres.-elect). Office: Central Libr Grand Army Plz Brooklyn NY 11238 Office Phone: 718-230-2173. E-mail: a.loum@brooklynpubliclibrary.org.

LOUNSBURY, DAVE EDMOND, medical editor, retired medical educator, military officer; b. Stoneham, Mass., Mar. 23, 1950; s. Robert Stewart and G. Laurette (Gauthier) Lounsbury. MD, U. Vt., 1979. Commd. 2d lt. U.S. Army, 1979, advanced through grades to col.; dir. Borden Inst. at Walter Reed Army Med. Ctr., Washington, 2001—05; asst. prof. medicine Uniformed Svcs. U., Bethesda, Md., 2002—05; dep. comdr. clin. svcs. 10th Combat Hosp., Kuwait and Iraq; ret., 2005. Med. liaison to UK, 1999—2001. Editor: Emergency War Surgery, 2004; editor-in-chief: textbooks on mil. medicine. Decorated Legion of Merit (2), Bronze Star, Meritorious Svc. medal (4); named Tchr. of Yr., Walter Reed Med. Ctr., 1993. Fellow: ACP; mem.: Worshipful Soc. Apothecaries (yeoman), Royal Soc. Medicine, Explorers Club, Alpha Omega Alpha. Avocation: hiking. Home: PO Box 875 Farmington ME 04938 Personal E-mail: davelounsbury@gmail.com.

LOUNSBURY, DAVID ARTHUR, protective services official, educator; b. Mt. Kisco, NY, Dec. 5, 1952; s. George Stephan and Janette May (Conner) Lounsbury; m. Evelyn Ruth Downey, Apr. 28, 1973; children: Jennifer Leigh, Heather Lynn Lounsbury Mogg. BS, U. New Haven, West Haven, Conn., 1974, MS, 1977; PhD, Capella U., Mpls., 2003. Diplomate Am. Bd. Medico-Legal; cert. cert. fraud examiner Assn. Certified Fraud Examiners. Police officer VA Police Dept., West Haven, 1973—75; enlisted U.S. Army, 1975, ret., 1996; patrolman Naples Police Dept., Fla., 1996—97; detective sgt. Police Dept. Fla. Gulf Coast U., Ft. Myers, 1997—2002, asst. prof., 2002—. Mem. Criminal Justice Adv. Bd., Ft. Myers, 2002—; dir. Inst. for Forensic Excellence, Ft. Myers, 2004—; cons. in field. Contbr. articles to profl. jours. Former spl. agent US Army Criminal Investigation Command. Recipient The XX Award for Recognition of Excellence, Fla. Gulf Coast U., 2000—01, Drug Abuse Prevention award, Lee County Coalition for Drug Free SW Fla., 2000, recognition of svc. award, Fla. Gulf Coast U. Police Dept., 2002; grantee, Nat. Inst. Justice, 2003, 2004, Office Sponsored Rsch., 2006. Mem.: NRA (life), Assn. Certified Fraud Examiners, Military Police Corp Assn., CID Agents Assn., SW Fla. Crime Prevention Assn., Fla. Crime Prevention Assn., Internat. Narcotics Officers Assn., Internat. Soc. Crime Prevention Practicioners, Am. Bd. Medico-Legal Death Investigators, Toxicology Hist. Soc., Internat. Narcotics Officer Assn., CID Agents Assn., Fla. Divsn. Internat. Assn. for Identification, Internat. Assn. for Identification, Assn. Cert. Fraud Examiners (cert. fraud examiners), Am. Acad. Forensic Sci. (assoc.), John E. Reid Inst., Audobon Fla., Am. Legion. Republican. Episcopalian. Avocations: firearms, fly fishing, music. Office: Fla Gulf Coast Univ 10501 FGCU Blvd S Fort Myers FL 33965-6565 Office Phone: 239-590-7831. Office Fax: 239-590-7842. Business E-Mail: dlounsbu@fgcu.edu.

LOUNSBURY, STEVEN RICHARD, lawyer; b. Evanston, Ill., July 26, 1950; s. James Richard and Reba Jeanette (Smith) L.; m. Dianne Louise Daley, Apr. 16, 1983; children: Jimson, Cody Summer, Richard. BA, U. Calif., Santa Barbara, 1973; JD, U. West LA, 1977. Bar: Calif. 1979, Oreg. 1997, US Dist. Ct. (cen. dist.) Calif. 1979, US Dist. Ct. Oreg. 1999. Pvt. practice, LA, 1979-83; contract atty. FAA, LA, 1981; trial atty. Hertz Corp., LA, 1983-86; mng. counsel 20th Century Ins. Co., Woodland Hills, Calif., 1986-94; mng. atty. Lounsbury and Assocs., Brea, Calif., 1986-94; sr. trial atty. Bollington, Lounsbury and Chase, Brea, 1994-99; asst. Coos County counsel, Coquille, Oreg., 1999—2002; county counsel Coos County, 2002—04, Clackamas County, Oregon City, Oreg., 2004—. Arbitrator Orange County Superior Ct., Santa Ana, Calif., 1992-99. Chmn. Westside com. LA Jr. C. of C., 1980—81, bd. dirs., 1981—82. Mem. Calif. Bar Assn., Oreg. Bar Assn., Oreg. County Counsel Assn. (legis. com. 2005, 2007, v.p. 2006, pres. 2007), Oreg. State Bar (mem. govt. law sect. 2000—, exec. com. 2006, 2007), Oreg. Dist. Attys. Assn. (exec. com. 2007), Clackamas County Bar Assn. Avocations: music, flute, saxophone. Home: PO Box 217 Camas Valley OR 97416 Office: Office of County Counsel Clackamas County Pub Svcs Bldg 2051 Kaen Rd Oregon City OR 97045 Business E-Mail: stevenlou@co.clackamas.or.us.

LOURIA, DONALD BRUCE, medical educator; b. Bklyn., July 11, 1928; s. Milton and Lucy (Littauer) Louria; m. Barbara Watson, May 21, 1955; children: Dana, Charles, Anne Ludes. BS cum laude, Harvard U., Cambridge, Mass., 1949; MD cum laude, Harvard Med. Sch., Boston, 1953. Cert. internal medicine, epidemiology, Am. Bd. Internal Medicine, 1959, Am. Coll. Epidemiology, 1982. Resident The N.Y. Hosp., 1953—55; asst. surgeon NIH, Bethesda, Md., 1955—57; instr. Cornell U. Med. Sch., NYC, 1958—60, assoc. prof., 1964—69, asst. prof., 1960—64; chmn. dept. preventive medicine N.J. Med. Sch., Newark, 1969—99, prof., 1999—. Bd. mem. Poly Prep County Day Sch., Bklyn., 1973—76, Nuc. Policy Rsch. Inst., Washington, 2003—; mem. adv. bd. Quantia Comm., Cambridge, Mass., 2006—. Author: (books) The Drug Scene, 1968, Overcoming Drugs, A Program for Action, 1971, Your Healthy Body, Your Healthy Life. How to Take Control of Your Medical Destiny, 1989; author: (and co-author) 350 articles in med. jours. 90 chpts. in monographs or books, and 2 short stories. Pres. N.Y. State Coun. on Drug Addiction, 1965—72, World Future Soc., NJ, 1984—94, N.Y. Young Rep. Club, 1969; pres. N.J. chpt. Physicians Social Responsibility, Newark, 1982—85. Recipient Golden Apple Tchg. award, N.J. Med. Sch., 1972, 1980, 1981, 1982, Gov.'s Clara Barton, N.J., 1991, Med. Svc. award. Master: Am. Coll. Physicians (Rosenthal Found. award 1991); fellow: Infectious Diseases Soc. Am., Am. Coll. Epidemiology; mem.: Am. Coll. Preventive Medicine, World Future Soc., Am. Soc. Clin. Investigation. D-Liberal. Mem. Soc. Of Friends. Achievements include creating Healthful Life Program now law in New Jersey as the Health Wellness Promotion Act. Avocations: squash, photography. Home: 61 Overleigh Rd Bernardsville NJ 07924-1509 Office: UMDNJ Med Sch 30 Bergen St Ste 1605 Newark NJ 07107-3000 Home Phone: 908-766-2184; Office Phone: 973-972-0125. Office Fax: 973-972-0025. Business E-Mail: louriado@umdnj.edu.

LOURIE, ALAN DAVID, federal judge; b. Boston, Jan. 13, 1935; AB, Harvard U., 1956; MS, U. Wis., 1958; PhD, U. Pa., 1965; JD, Temple U., 1970. Bar: Pa. 1970. Chemist Monsanto Co., St. Louis, 1957-59; lit. scientist, chemist, patent agt. Wyeth Labs., Radnor, Pa., 1959-64; counsel Smith Kline Beecham Corp., Phila., 1964-90, successively as patent agt., atty., dir. corp. patents, asst. gen. counsel, v.p. corp. patents; judge US Ct. Appeals (Fed. cir.), Washington, 1990—. Mem. Judicial Conf. Com. on Financial Disclosure, 1990-98, Com. on Codes of Conduct, 2005-; mem. US del. to Diplomatic Conf. on Revision of Paris Conv. for Protection of Indsl. Property, 1982, 84; vice chmn. industry functional adv. com. to US Trade Rep. and Dept. Commerce, 1987-90; chmn. US group of US-Japan Bus. Coun. Task Force on Patents. Bd. visitors Law Sch., Temple U. Mem. Phila. Patent Law Assn. (pres. 1984-85), Am. Intellectual Property Law Assn. (bd. dirs. 1982-85), Assn. Corp. Patent Counsel (treas. 1987-89), Pharm. Mfrs. Assn. (chmn. patent com. 1981-86), Am. Chem. Soc., Cosmos Club, Harvard Club Washington. Office: US Ct Appeals Fed Cir 717 Madison Pl NW Washington DC 20439-0002*

LOUX, GORDON DALE, philanthropic consultant; b. Souderton, Pa., June 21, 1938; s. Curtis L. and Ruth (Derstine) L.; m. Elizabeth Ann Nordland, June 18, 1960; children: Mark, Alan, Jonathan. Diploma, Moody Bible Inst., Chgo., 1960; BA, Gordon Coll., Wenham, Mass., 1962; BD, No. Bapt. Sem., Oak Brook, Ill., 1965, MDiv, 1971; MS, Nat. Coll. Edn., Evanston,Ill., 1984; LHD (hon.), Sioux Falls Coll., 1985. Ordained to ministry, Bapt. Ch., 1965. Assoc. pastor Forest Park (Ill.) Bapt. Ch., 1962-65; alumni field dir. Moody Bible Inst., Chgo., 1965-66, dir. pub. rels., 1972-76; dir. devel. Phila. Coll. Bible, 1966-69; pres. Stewardship Svcs., Wheaton, Ill., 1969-72; exec. v.p. Prison Fellowship Ministries, Washington, 1976-84, pres., CEO, 1984-88, Prison Fellowship Internat., Washington, 1979-87; pres. Internat. Students, Inc., Colorado Springs, Colo., 1988-93, Gordon D. Loux & Co., LLC, Colorado Springs, 1994—, Trinity Cmty. Found., 1996—. Author: Uncommon Courage, 1987, You Can Be a Point of Light, 1991; contbg. author: Money for Ministries, 1989, Dictionary of Christianity in America, 1989. Bd. dirs. Evang. Coun. for Fin. Accountability, Washington, 1979-92, vice chmn., 1981-84, 86-87, chmn., 1987-89; vice chmn. Billy Graham Greater Washington Crusade, 1985-85; bd. dirs. Evang. Fellowship of Mission Agys., 1991-94, Ctr. for Christian Jewish Dialogue, Colorado Springs, 1996—, Hope and Home, Colorado Springs, 1998—, C2ure, Mechanicsburg, Pa., 1999—, Global Leaders Initiative. Named Alumnus of Yr., Gordon Coll., 1986. Mem. Broadmoor Golf Club (Colo. Springs). Republican. Home: 740 Bear Paw Ln N Colorado Springs CO 80906-3215 Office: PO Box 38898 Colorado Springs CO 80937-8898 Personal E-mail: louxco@aol.com.

LOUX, JONATHAN DALE, business development consultant, director; b. Oak Park, Ill., Mar. 23, 1966; s. Gordon Dale and Elizabeth (Nordland) L.; m. Jan Mary Peters, July 22, 1989; children: Kara Leigh, Kurtis Dale, Kenton Stanley, Kourtney Grayce. BS, Eastern Coll., St. Davids, Pa., 1988. CPA, Ill. Acctg. supr. Capin, Crouse, LLP, Wheaton, Ill., 1989-93; supr. internal audit Select Beverages, Ind., Darien, Ill., 1993-94; pres. Gordon D. Loux Co., LLC, Colorado Springs, Colo., 1994—, Loux Group, LLC, Colorado Springs, 1996—2005; v.p. Cure Internat., Lemoyne, Pa., 2002—05; program dir. RDV Corp., Grand Rapids, Mich., 2005—. Trustee Eastern Coll., St. Davids, Pa., 2000—. Republican. Presbyterian. Home: 5381 Royale Ct Ne Rockford MI 49341-8646 Business E-Mail: jonl@rdvcorp.com.

LOUX, P. OGDEN, distribution company executive; Grad., Drexel Univ. Mgmt. positions GE; fin. mgmt. positions W.W. Grainger, Inc., Lake Forest, Ill., 1987—94, v.p. fin., 1994—96, sr. v.p. fin., CFO, 1997—. Past bd. dir. Condell Med. Ctr. Office: WW Grainger Inc 100 Grainger Pkwy Lake Forest IL 60045-5201*

LOVE, ANGEL See CHESNUT, NONDIS

LOVE, BEN HOWARD, retired organization executive; b. Trenton, Tenn., Sept. 26, 1930; s. Ben Drane and (Whitehead) Virginia; m. Ann Claire Hugo, Mar. 4, 1933; children: Ben H. Jr., Phillip H.(dec.), Leigh Anne, Mark E. BS, Lambuth Coll., 1955, HHD (hon.), 1986; Dr. Philanthropy (hon.), Pepperdine U., 1987; LHD (hon.), Montclair State U., 1991. With Boy Scouts Am., 1955—, dist. exec. Jackson, Tenn., 1955-60, scout exec. Delta area council, Clarksdale, Miss., 1960-64, dir. Nat. coun. North Brunswick, NJ, 1964—68, scout exec. Longhorn coun. Ft. Worth, 1968—71, scout exec. Sam Houston coun. Houston, 1971—73, dir. Northeast region Dayton, NJ, 1973—85, chief scout exec. Nat. coun. Irving, Tex., 1985—93. Bd. dirs. AIG Valic I, Valic II. Served with U.S. Army, 1951-52. Recipient Gold medal SAR, Bronze Wolf award World Scout Orgn. Republican. Presbyterian. Avocations: tennis, golf, swimming, reading, spectator sports. Office: 1327 Anna Ct Cedar Park TX 78613

LOVE, CHARLES MARION, III, lawyer; b. Charleston, W.Va., Mar. 23, 1939; s. Charles Marion Jr. and Naomi (Nale) L.; m. Sally Biddle McCue, Oct. 21, 1965; children: Charles M. IV, John Lewis Biddle, Peter Stuart McKinley. AB, W.Va. U., 1963, LLB, 1965. Bar: W.Va. 1965, U.S. Supreme Ct. 1969, U.S. Tax Ct. 1980. Assoc. Dayton, Campbell & Love, Charleston, W.Va., 1965-66; asst. U.S. atty. U.S. Atty.'s Office, Charleston, W.Va., 1966-69; assoc. Stone Bowles Kauffelt & McDavid, Charleston, W.Va., 1969-71; ptnr. Bowles Rice McDavid Graff & Love LLP, Charleston, W.Va., 1971—. Mem. jud. conf. for U.S. Ct. Appeals, 4th cir. Chmn., CEO W.Va. Housing Devel. Fund, Charleston, 1981—2003; past mem. former officer bd. trustees Herbert J. Thomas Meml. Hosp. Fellow ABA, W.Va. State Bar Assn. (chmn. legal ethics com. 1991-94, mem. ethics com. 1988-94, mem. bd. trustees, pres. 2004-); mem. W.Va. Bar Assn. (mem. exec. coun., pres.) Kanawha County Bar Assn., Am. Bd. Trial Advocates, W.Va. State Bar (pres., 2004-05), W.Va. Bar Assn. (pres., 2004-2005), Phi Delta Phi. Democrat. Office: Bowles Rice McDavid Graff & Love PLLC 600 Quarrier St Charleston WV 25301-2121 Office Phone: 304-347-1104. Office Fax: 304-347-1746. Business E-Mail: clove@bowlesrice.com.*

LOVE, COURTNEY, singer, actress; b. San Francisco, July 9, 1964; d. Hank Harrison and Linda Carroll; m. James Moreland, 1989 (div. 1989), m. Kurt Cobain, Feb. 24, 1992 (dec. April 5, 1994); 1 child, Frances Bean. Singer, writer, musician Hole, 1989—2002. Albums (with Hole) Pretty on the Inside, 1991, Live Through This, 1994, Celebrity Skin, 1998; (Solo albums) America's Sweeteart, 2004; actress (films) Sid and Nancy, 1986, Straight to Hell, 1987, Tapeheads, 1988, Basquiat, 1996, Feeling Minnesota, 1996, The People vs. Larry Flynt (Best Supporting Actress award, NY Film Critics Cir., Boston Soc. of Film Critics), 1996, Not Bad For a Girl, 1996 (also co-prodr.), Man on the Moon, 1999, 200 Cigarettes, 1999, Beat, 2000, Julie Johnson, 2001, Trapped, 2002; author (books) Dirty Blonde, 2006.*

LOVE, DANA FRANCIS IGNATIUS, telecommunications industry executive; b. Hartford, Conn., Dec. 1, 1969; d. Francis Henry and Alice Love; m. Faith Ellen Moser, Sept. 25, 1968. BS, U. Richmond, 1988; MBA, Harvard U., 1992; PhD in Econs., Chelsea U., 2004. V.p. Radnet, Inc., Cambridge, Mass., 1995—98; prin. investigator, internet protocol comm. GTE, Waltham, Mass., 1998—99; exec. v.p. Metacloud Comm., Vienna, Va., 1999—2000; v.p., gen. mgr. ADC Telecom., Washington,

2000—01; exec. v.p., sales and mktg. Prosodie Interactive, Washington, 2001—03; cons. Radnet Sys., Boyds, Md., 2003; pres. Astyra Corp., Richmond, Va., 2003—07; sr. v.p. C4i, INc., Herndon, Va., 2007—. Adv. bd. Sonim Tech., Inc., Redwood City, Calif., 2002—, Gerson Lehrman Group, NYC, 2003—. Editor: Connecting to the Internet: A Practical Guide about LAN-Internet Connectivity, 1998, Frame Relay: Technology and Practice, 1999. Mem.: Conferie Chaine Rotisseurs, Bailliage des Etats-Unis (chevalier 2002). Republican. Roman Catholic. Achievements include patented development of system and method for monitoring packet telephony network with in-band custom quality of service; enhanced telephone service system with packet telophony system and out-of-band routing tools; apparatus and method for determining quality of service on an arbitrary packet telephony network using in-band signaling. Home: 11413 Braidstone Ln Chesterfield VA 23838 Office Phone: 703-673-4130. Personal E-mail: me@danalove.com.

LOVE, DANIEL JOSEPH, consulting engineer; b. Fall River, Mass., Sept. 27, 1926; s. Henry Aloysius and Mary Ellen (Harrington) L.; m. Henrietta Maurisse Popper, June 10, 1950 (dec. Mar. 1986); children: Amy, Timothy (dec.), Terence, Kevin; m. Adeline Aponte Esquivel, Feb. 11, 1989; stepchildren: Eric, Brian, Jason. BSEE, Ill. Inst. Tech., 1951, MSEE, 1956; MBA, Calif. State U., Long Beach, 1973. Registered profl. engr., Calif.; cert. fire protection Calif. Test engr. Internat. Harvester Co., Chgo., 1951-52; designer Pioneer Svc. & Engrng. Co., Chgo., 1952-53; project engr., ops. mgr. Panellit Co., Skokie, Ill., 1953-60; mktg. mgr. Control Data Co., Mpls., 1961-62; mktg. mgr., asst. to pres. Emerson Electric Co., Pasadena, Calif., 1963-65; pres., gen. mgr. McKee Automation Co., North Hollywood, Calif., 1965-68; engrng. specialist Bechtel Co., Vernon and Norwalk, Calif., 1968-80, chief elec. engr. Madrid, 1980-83, engrng. specialist Norwalk, Calif., 1983-87; cons. engr. Hacienda Heights, Calif., 1987—. Contbr. articles to jours. in field. Pres. Wilson High Sch. Band Boosters, Hacienda Heights, 1971-73. With USN, 1944-46. Named Outstanding Engr., Inst. for Advancement Engrng., 1986; recipient 3d place prize paper award Industry Application Soc., 1995. Fellow IEEE (disting. lectr., chmn. Met. L.A. sect. 1973-74, chmn. L.A. coun. 1977-78, chmn. protection com. 1990-91, Richard Harold Kaufmann award 1994, Ralph H. Lee prize paper award 1995); mem. NSPE, Instrument Soc. Am. (sr.), Soc. Fire Protection Engrs. Republican. Roman Catholic. Avocations: duplicate bridge, travel, walking, writing. Home: 16300 Soriano Dr Hacienda Heights CA 91745 E-mail: dan.love@ieee.org.

LOVE, EDITH HOLMES, theater producer; b. Boston, Oct. 17, 1950; d. Theodore Rufus and Mary (Holmes) L. Student, Denison U., 1968-72; BFA, U. Colo., 1973. Freelance designer various orgns., Atlanta, 1974-75; costumer Atlanta Children's Theatre, 1975-77; prodn. acct. David Gerber Co., LA, 1980-81; bus. mgr. Alliance Theatre/Atlanta Children's Theatre, 1977-79, adminstrv. dir., 1981-83, gen. mgr., 1983-85, mng. dir., 1985-96, Dallas Theater Ctrn., 1997—2003, Portland (Oreg.) Ctr. Stage, 2003—. Adv. bd. Stage Hands, Inc., Atlanta, 1983-89; mem. exec. com. Prodn. Values, Inc., Atlanta, 1985-89; mem. adv. com. arts mgmt. program Carnegie Mellon U.; panelist Nat. Endowment for Arts, 1994-96; mem. Nat. Theatre Conf., 2005—; vis. prof. Yale Sch. Drama, 1997. Active Cultural Olympiad Task Force, 1996 Summer Olympic Games, 1992-96, Met. Atlanta Arts Fund Bd., 1992-97; bd. dirs. Atlanta Convention and Vistor's Bur., 1993-95, Arts Dist. Friends, Theatre Comm. Group; exec. com. Dallas Theatre League, 1999—2003. Recipient Deca award for Outstanding Bus. Women in Atlanta, 1992. Mem. League Resident Theatres (treas. 1987-97, v.p. 1997-2000), Atlanta Theatre Coalition (exec. com. 1987-91, pres. 1989), Atlanta C. of C. (bd. dirs. bus. coun. for arts 1988-97), Leadership Atlanta, Charter 100 Dallas, Bd. Arts Dist. Found. Home: 4109 NE Thompson St Portland OR 97212-5432 Office: Portland Center Stage 1111 SW Broadway Portland OR 97212

LOVE, GAY MCLAWHORN, manufacturing executive; m. J. Erskine Love (dec. 1987); children: Dennis, Jimmy, Bill, Keith, David; 1 child, Carol Anne Love Jennison. Grad., Duke U. Chair PrintPack Inc., Atlanta, 1987—. Co-founder The Gay and Erskine Love Found., 1976. Named an honorary alumnus, Georgia Tech., 1989. Office: PrintPack Inc PO Box 43687 Atlanta GA 30336-0687

LOVE, GEORGE H., JR., lawyer; b. Latrobe, Pa., Dec. 30, 1943; m. Joann A. Love, Aug. 16, 1969; children: George H. III, Jennifer A. BA, Wabash Coll., 1966; JD, Duquesne U., 1973. Bar: Pa. 1973, U.S. Dist. Ct. (we. dist.) Pa. 1973, U.S. Supreme Ct. 1976. Various positions VA, Pitts., 1970-76, atty. Dist. Counsel's Office, 1977-81, asst. dist. counsel, 1981-95, prin. sr. atty. Regional Counsel's Office, 1995-98, asst. regional counsel, 1998-2001; ret.; mng. ptnr. Love Law Firm, LLC, Youngstown, Pa., 2002—. Bd. dirs. Lincoln Hwy. Heritage Corridor, 2004-05; Latrobe Vets. Home Assn., 2002—; chmn. labor law sect. Westmoreland Bar Assn., 2003-04; mem. Youngstown Mcpl. Authority, 2002—. Lance cpl. USMC, 1967-68, Viet Nam; lt. JAG, U.S. Navy. Home: 847 Youngstown Ridge Rd Latrobe PA 15650-3709 Office: PO Box 594 310 Main St Youngstown PA 15696-0594 Office Phone: 724-537-0654. E-mail: glovelaw@adelphia.net.

LOVE, JAMES SANFORD, III, communications executive; b. Jackson, Miss., Aug. 4, 1944; s. James Sanford Jr. and Jo Ellis (Buie) L.; m. Barbara Ann Harris, June 11, 1966 (div. Oct. 1981); children: James S. IV, Caroline E., Gillian M. BBA in Bus. and Govt., U. Miss., 1966; MBA, U. Va., 1968. Acct. exec. J. Walter Thompson, NYC, 1968-70; rsch. analyst, asst. v.p. Dean Witter Co., NYC, 1970-73; chmn., CEO Love Broadcasting Co., Biloxi, Miss., 1972-91, Lakewood Meml. Pk., Jackson, Miss., 1972-91; rsch. analyst Baker Weeks & Co., NYC, 1973-75; rsch. analyst, v.p. Paine Webber & Co., NYC, 1975-77; chmn., CEO Love Comm. Co., Jackson, 1991—. Cosn. Norberg Capital, N.Y.C., 1979-97; co-founder Millsaps Buie House Bed and Breakfast Inn, 1987—; owner White House Hotel, Biloxi, Miss., 1989—. Exec. prodr.: Miss. News Tonight, 1991-92. Trustee Millsaps Coll., Jackson, 1989—, Land Trust for the Miss. Coastal Plain, Miss. chpt. Nature Conservancy, 1990—, chmn. bd. trustees, 1996—97; chmn. leadership bd. Boys and Girls Club of Miss. Gulf Coast, 1994—96; mem. adv. bd. Salvation Army, 1997—2001. Named to All-Am. Rsch. Team, Instl. Investor Mag., 1974-75; recipient George Foster Peabody award U. Ga., 1989, regional Emmy award, 1990, 50th Anniversary Hero award The Nature Conservancy Miss. Chpt. Mem. Boston Club (New Orleans), Windance Country Club (Gulfport, Miss.), Univ. Club (Jackson), Biloxi Yacht Club. Episcopalian. Avocations: gardening, photography, salt water fishing, history. Home: 12137 Hickman Rd Biloxi MS 39532-9429 Office: Love Comm 979 Howard Ave Biloxi MS 39530 also: PO Box 4997 Biloxi MS 39535

LOVE, JOSEPH LEROY, history professor, former cultural studies center administrator; b. Austin, Tex., Feb. 28, 1938; s. Joseph L., Sr. and Virginia (Ellis) Love; m. Laurie Reynolds, Dec. 23, 1978; children: Catherine R., David A.;children from previous marriage: James A., Stephen N. AB in Econs. with honors, Harvard U., 1960; MA in History, Stanford U., 1963; PhD in History with distinction, Columbia U., 1967. From instr. to prof. U. Ill., Urbana-Champaign, 1966—, dir. ctr. Latin Am. and Caribbean studies, 1993-99. Rsch. assoc. St. Anthony's Coll. Oxford U.; vis. prof. Pontifical Cath. U., Rio de Janeiro; presenter in field. Author: Rio Grande do Sul and Brazilian Regionalism, 1882-1930, 1971, SAo Paulo in the Brazilian Federation, 1889-1937, 1980, Crafting the Third World: Theorizing Underdevelopment in Rumania and Brazil, 1996; editor (with Robert S. Byars): Quantitative Social Science Research on Latin America, 1973; editor: (with Nils Jacobsen) Guiding the Invisible Hand: Economic Liberalism and the State in Latin American History, 1988; editor: (with Werener Baer) Liberalization and Its Consequences: A Comparative Perspective on Latin America and Eastern Europe, 2000; bd. editors Latin AM. Rsch. Rev., 1974—78, Hispanic Am. Hist. Rev., 1984—89, The Americas, 1995—99; contbr. articles to profl. jours. Fellow, Social Sci. Rsch. Coun., IREX, Guggenheim; vis. scholar, U. Sao Paulo, Inst. Ortega y Gasset, Madrid, U. Nova, Lisbon; Fulbright-Hays Rsch. grantee, Sr. Rsch. fellow, NEH, others, Sr. Univ. scholar, U. Ill., 1993—96. Mem.: Latin Am. Studies Assn., Conf. Latin Am. History (chair Brazilian studies com. 1973, mem. gen. com. 1983, Conf. prize 1971), Am. Hist. Assn. Unitarian Universalist. Office: U Ill Dept History 309 Gregory Hall 810 S Wright St Urbana IL 61801-3644 Office Phone: 217-333-3182. Business E-Mail: j-love2@uiuc.edu.

LOVE, KEITH SINCLAIR, communications executive; b. Apr. 26, 1947; s. James and Ruth L. BA, NYU, 1980. Editor N.Y. Times, NYC, 1973-79; editor, polit. writer L.A. Times, 1979-90; asst. to v.p. ops. McClatchy Newspapers, Inc., 1990-92; pub. Ellensburg (Wash.) Daily Record, 1992-98; comm. dir. Gov. State of Washington, Olympia, 1998-99; v.p. comm. St. Michelle Wine Estates, Woodinville, Wash., 1999—. Office: Stimson Lane Vineyards State Wash PO Box 1976 Woodinville WA 98072-1976

LOVE, LISA A., lawyer; b. 1959; BS, U. Tenn., Knoxville; JD, Salmon P. Chase Coll. of Law. Assoc. counsel, mgr. insurance ops. Cincinnati Insurance Co., 2000—03, sr. counsel, 2003—. Office: Cincinnati Insurance Co PO Box 145496 6200 S Gilmore Rd Cincinnati OH 45250

LOVE, MARY ANN E., state legislator; b. West Pittston, Pa., Feb. 21, 1940; married; 2 children. Grad., Wilkes-Barre (Pa.) Bus. Sch., 1959. State legis. dist.32 Md. Ho. Reps., Annapolis, 1993—, mem. econ. matters com. Chmn. Anne Arundel County Delegation, 1999—. Bd. dirs. Providence Ctr., Hospice of the Chesapeake, North Arundel Hosp. Recipient County Achievement award Nat. Assn. Counties, 1986-89, Anne Arundel Trade Coun. Legis. of Yr. award, 1997. Mem. No. Anne Arundel County C. of C. (Pres.'s award 1996). Office: Md House Reps 165 Lowe House Office Bldg Annapolis MD 21401 Office Phone: 410-841-6511. Business E-Mail: maryann_love@house.state.md.us.

LOVE, MICHAEL JOSEPH, lawyer; b. Chicopee, Mass., Mar. 1, 1958; BA, U. Mass., 1984; student, Vanderbilt U., 1991-92; JD, U. Denver, 1992. Bar: Tenn., U.S. Dist. Ct. (mid. dist.) Tenn. 1992. Ptnr. Zellar, Cartwright & Love, PLLC, Clarksville, Tenn., 1994-96, Cartwright & Love, PLLC, Clarksville, 1996—. Gen. editor U. Denver Law Rev. Mem. legal com. Nat. Orgn. for Reform of Marijuana Laws. With U.S. Army, 1975-78. Mem. Nat. Assn. Criminal Def. Lawyers (life). Office Fax: 931-647-3610. E-mail: MichaelJLove@msn.com.

LOVE, ROBERT LYMAN, retired education educator, consultant; b. Oswego, NY, July 28, 1925; s. Robert Barnum and Marion Alberta (Peavy) L.; m. Janet May Fuller, June 26, 1948 (dec. Aug. 2006); children: Robert H., Andrew L., Charles D., Cynthia S. Student, U. Rochester, 1943-44; AB, Syracuse U., 1945, postgrad., 1946-48, MEd, 1949; postgrad., Cornell U., 1963-64. Sci. tchr. Middlesex Valley Central Sch., Rushville, N.Y., 1949-53; mem. faculty Agrl. and Tech. Coll., SUNY-Alfred, 1953-81; prof., dean Agrl. and Tech. Coll., SUNY (Sch. Allied Health Techs.), until 1981, dean emeritus, 1981—; pres. Edn. Cons. Services, Alfred Station, NY, 1981—. Former mem. bd. dirs. Nat. Tech. Inst. Deaf Med. Records program; program evaluation steering com. AMA; allied health reviewer HEW; mem. health sub-com. 39th Congl. Dist. Author: He and She, An Introduction to Human Sexuality and Birth Control, 1970; editor: Upward Mobility for Lab Personnel, 1970. Literacy vol.; pres., bd. dirs. Genesee Valley Habitat for Humanity, Inc., 1993—95, treas., 1995—96, Allegany County Office for Aging Handyman's Svc.; fin. sec., mem. adminstrv. bd. Alfred United Meth. Ch., bd. dirs. presch. and day care ctr., 1992—2003, pres., 1998—2003; mem. Roving Vols. in Christ's Svc., 1982—91, bd. dirs., 1984—86, 1989—91, chmn. bd. dirs., 1989—90; mem. Selected Vols. in Christ's Svc., 1987—88; chaplain vol. Thompson Meml. Hosp., Canandaigua, NY, 2004—, M.M. Ewing Continuing Care Ctr., Canandaigua, 2004—. Fellow Sci. Tchrs. Assn. N.Y. State, Am. Soc. Allied Health Professions; mem. Gideons Internat. (past pres. Hornell Camp), Literacy Vols. Am. (bd. dirs. Allegany County chpt. 1990-93), Masons, Order Eastern Star. Republican. Personal E-mail: rlove4@rochester.rr.com. *Having had the opportunity to work with young people has kept me young and knowing the Lord has saved me.*

LOVE, SCOTT ANTHONY, lawyer; b. Houston, Dec. 30, 1969; BA in Hist. with honors, U. Houston, 1993, JD, 1997. Bar: Tex. 1997, US Dist. Ct. (so. dist. Tex.) 1998, US Dist. Ct. (ea., we., and no. dists. Tex.) 1999. Law clk. Abraham, Watkins, Nichols & Friend, Houston, 1995-97; assoc. Duckett, Bouligny & Collins, L.L.P., El Campo, Tex., 1997-99, Wojciechowski & Assocs., P.C., Houston, 1999, Fleming & Assocs., L.L.P., Houston. Lectr. in field. Named a Rising Star, Tex. Super Lawyers mag., 2006. Mem. Assn. Trial Lawyers Am., Tex. Young Lawyers Assn., Tex. Trial Lawyers Assn., Houston Young Lawyers Assn., Houston Bar Assn., Houston Trial Lawyers Assn. Office: Fleming & Assocs LLP 1330 Post Oak Blvd Ste 3030 Houston TX 77056-3019 Office Phone: 713-621-7944. Office Fax: 713-621-9638. Business E-Mail: scott_love@fleming-law.com.

LOVE, SHIRLEY, mezzo-soprano; b. Detroit, Jan. 6, 1940; Student, Avery Crew, Marinka Gurewich, Margaret Harshaw., Armen Boyajian. Prof. voice Music Conservatory Westchester, White Plains, NY, 2002—, Internat. Acad. Music, Lucca, Italy, 2002—; pvt. voice studio Hartsdale, NY; artist in residence Music Conservatory of Westchester, NY, Internat. Acad. Music, Castelnuovo di Garfagnona, Italy. Operatic debut in Die Zauberflote, Met. Opera Assn., 1963; appeared with maj. opera cos. including De Nederlanse Operastichting, Amsterdam, Netherlands, Teatro Communale, Bologna and Florence, Italy, Balt. Opera Co., Lyric Opera Chgo., Cin. Opera Assn., Lake George Opera Festival, Greater Miami (Fla.) Opera Assn., Opera Co. Phila.; now resident mem. Met. Opera Assn., N.Y.C.; founding mem. Met. Opera Madrigal Singers; appeared with Phila. Orch., Boston, Balt., Detroit, Chgo., Tuscon, Wichita, Nat. orchs., and at Carmel (Calif.) Bach, Kalamazoo, Winter Park, Robin Hood Dell, Saratoga, Ravenwood, Tanglewood, Wolf Trap, Mostly Mozart, Basically Bach, Chatauqua festivals; featured artist for the Cunard Line Music Festival at Sea, 1991—. Recipient Arts Achievement award Wayne State U., 1990.

LOVE, SUSAN MARGARET, surgeon, educator, writer; b. NJ, Feb. 9, 1948; d. James Arthur and Margaret Connick (Schwab) L.; life ptnr. Helen Sperry Cooksey, Sept. 8, 1982; 1 child, Katherine Mary Love-Cooksey. BS, Fordham U., 1970; MD, SUNY, NYC, 1974, DSc (hon.), 1998; MBA, UCLA, 1998; DSc (hon.), Northeastern U., 1991, Trinity Coll., 1999; D of Humane Sci. (hon.), Simmons Coll., 1992; LHD (hon.), U. R.I., 1997. Surgery intern Beth Israel Hosp., Boston, 1974—75, surgical resident, 1975—79, chief resident, 1979, clin. fellow in pathology, 1980, asst. in surgery, 1980—87, dir. breast clinic, 1980-88, assoc. surgeon, 1987—92; clin. fellow in surgery Harvard Med. Sch., Boston, 1977-78, clin. instr. in surgery, 1980-87, asst. clin. prof. surgery, 1987-92; clin. assoc. in surg. oncology Dana Farber Cancer Inst., Boston, 1981-92; dir. Faulkner Breast Ctr. Faulkner Hosp., Boston, 1988-92; assoc. prof. clin. surgery UCLA Med. Sch., 1992-96, adj. prof. divsn. gen. surgery, 1996—2002; dir. Revlon/UCLA Breast Ctr., 1992-96; clin. prof. divsn. gen. surgery David Geffen Sch. Medicine, UCLA, 2002—; founder, chief med. officer Windy Hill Med., 2006—. Prin. investigator Nat. Surg. Adjuvant Breast and Bowel Project, 1985—96; adv. com. Women's Health Initiative Program, Washington, 1993—95; adv. coun. Breast and Cervical Cancer Program and Breast Cancer Early Detection Program, State of Calif. DHS, 1994—98; mem. Pres.'s Nat. Action Plan on Breast Cancer, DHHS, 1994—2000; co-chair Biol. Resources Working Group, 1994—98; mem. Nat. Cancer Adv. Bd., 1998—2004; nat. adv. environ. health sci. coun. NIH, 2003—04; med. dir. Dr. Susan Love Rsch. Found. (formerly Santa Barbara Breast Cancer Inst., 1983-2000, The Susan Love MD Breast Cancer Research Foundation, 2000-04), 1995—; pres. bd. dirs. Dr. Susan Love Rsch. Found.; founder, sr. ptnr., dir. LLuminari, Inc., 2000—; bd. dirs. Sanarus Med.; cons. Cytyc Health Corp., 2002. Author: Dr. Susan Love's Breast Book, 1990, 4th edit., 2005, Dr. Susan Love's Menopause and Hormone Book, 1997, 2nd edit., 2003; Atlas of Techniques in Breast Surgery, 1996; contbr. chpts. to books, articles to profl. jours. Founder, bd. dirs. Nat. Breast Cancer Coalition, 1991—; bd. dirs. Lesbian Health Found., 1992—, Soc. Menstrual Cycle Rsch., 2000—, Y-ME Nat. Breast Cancer Orgn., 2001—. Recipient Rose Kushner award, Am. Med. Writers Assn., 1991, Achievement award, Am. Assn. Physicians for Human Rights, 1992, Women Making History award, U.S. Senator Barbara Boxer, 1993, Woman of Yr. award, YWCA, 1994, Frontrunner award, Sara Lee Corp., 1994, Spirit of Achievement award, Albert Einstein Coll. of Yeshiva U., 1995, Abram L. Sachar medallion, Brandeis U., 1996, Bicentennial honoree, U. Louisville, 1997, Walker prize, Boston Mus. Sci., 1998, Radcliffe medal, 2000, Humanitarian of Yr. award, Western U. Health Sci., Pomona, Calif., 2001, Excellence in Cancer Awareness award, Cancer Rsch. Found. Am., 2002, Dir.'s award, Nat. Cancer Inst., 2004;, Dept. Def. grantee, 1994, 1996, others. Mem. Am. Med. Women's Assn. (pres. br. 39 1987, Lila Wallis Women's Health award 2004), Soc. for Study of Breast Disease, Am. Soc. Preventive Oncology, Southwestern Oncology Group (women's health and breast com. 1992-96, surg. rep. 1992-96), L.A. Med. Soc., Boston Surg. Soc., N.Am. Menopause Soc., Am. Assn. Cancer Rsch., Am. Coll. Women's Health Physicians, Assn. Women Surgeons. Office: Dr Susan Love Rsch Found PO Box 846 Pacific Palisades CA 90272-0846 Office Phone: 310-230-1712. Business E-Mail: slove@earthlink.net.

LOVE, WILLIAM ALLAN, lawyer, educator; b. Phila., June 19, 1959; s. Norman and Arlene (Basiches) L.; m. Sari Rose Perlman, Aug. 28, 1988; children: Meranda Beth, Gary Isaac. BA in Criminal Justice, Temple U., 1982; JD, Thomas M. Cooley, 1987. Bar: Pa. 1988, N.J. 1989, U.S. Dist. Ct. (ea. dist.) Pa. 1988, U.S. Dist. Ct. N.J. 1989. Clk. Shop N Bag Market, Phila., 1977-83; police officer U.S. Dept. Def., Phila., 1983-84; admissions counselor Thomas Cooley Law Sch., Lansing, Mich., 1985-87; assoc. Mark Koral Assocs., Phila., 1988-90; pvt. practice Phila., 1990—. Instr. C.C. Phila., 1992—; panel arbitrator Phila. Ct. Common Pleas, 1990—. Fundraiser Gary Love Cancer Rsch. Fund, Phila., 1985—. Mem. Am. Soc. Criminology, Phila. bar Assn. (faculty, planner continuing edn. 1995), Pa. Bar Assn. Republican. Jewish. Avocations: music, reading, cars. Office: 1218 Chestnut St Ste 600 Philadelphia PA 19107-4814

LOVE, WILLIAM EDWARD, lawyer; b. Eugene, Oreg., Mar. 13, 1926; s. William Stewart and Ola A. (Kingsbury) L.; m. Sylvia Kathryn Jaureguy, Aug. 6, 1955; children: Kathryn Love Petersen, Jeffrey, Douglas, Gregory. BS, U. Notre Dame, 1946; MA in Journalism, U. Oreg., 1950, JD, 1952. Bar: Oreg. 1952. Newspaper reporter Eugene Register Guard, 1943-44, 47-52; asst. prof. law, asst. dean Sch. Law U. Wash., Seattle, 1952-56; ptnr. Cake, Jaureguy, Hardy, Buttler & McEwen, Portland, Oreg., 1956-69; pres., chmn., CEO Equitable Savs. & Loan, Portland, 1969-82; sr. ptnr. Schwabe, Williamson & Wyatt, Portland, 1983—. Chmn. Oreg. Savs. League, 1976; dir. Portland Gen. Electric, 1976-83, Fed. Home Loan Bank of Seattle, 1976-79, 85-96, adv. coun. Fed. Nat. Mortgage Assn., Washington, 1978-80; exec. dir. Oreg. Facilities Authority, 1990-2006. Author (with Jaureguy): Oregon Probate Law and Practice, 2 vols., 1958; contbr. articles to profl. jours. Commr., past chmn. Oreg. Racing Commn., 1963-79; pres. Nat. Assn. State Racing Commrs., 1977-78; commr. Port of Portland, 1979-86, pres. 1983; referee Pac-10 football, 1960-81, Rose Bowl, 1981; active United Way, Boy Scouts Am., Portland Rose Festival, polit. campaigns; mem. adv. coun. Jockey's Guild, Inc., 1990-2001. Served to lt. (j.g.) USN, 1944-47. Mem. Oreg. Bar Assn., Multnomah County Bar Assn., Multnomah Athletic Club, Golf Club (Portland). Republican. Home: 421 SW 70th Terr Portland OR 97225-4356 Office: Schwabe Williamson & Wyatt 1211 SW 5th Ave Ste 1800 Portland OR 97204-3713 Office Phone: 503-222-9981.

LOVE-HASSELL, ESTHER BOYER, special education educator, consultant; b. Raleigh, NC, July 18, 1950; d. James Alexander and Emma Perry Boyer; m. Cedric Ricardo Hassell, Aug. 9, 1991; children: Jaimye Love Hassell, Sheryl Love Hassell, Emily Skinner, Elizabeth Camille Hassell. BA in English Edn., St. Augustine's Coll., Raliegh, NC, 1972; MA in Edn. English, U. Rochester, NYC, 1974; cert. in spl. edn., LI U., Bklyn., 1991. Substitute tchr. Peekskill and Rockland County, NY, 1980—81, N.Y.C. Schs., 1981—83; tchr. choral music Schimer Jr. HS, Queens, NY, 1983; reading & critical thinking instr. Malcolm/King Coll., NYC, 1983—87; spl. edn. tchr. Pub. Sch. 76, NYC, 1984—88, Jr. HS 88 Wadleigh, NYC, 1988—89; resource rm. tchr. Pub. Sch. 180, NYC, 1989—. Reading specialist Rochester City Schs., 1974—78; head reading dept. Culbreth Jr. HS, Chapel Hill, NY, 1979—80; tutorial instr. Mercy Coll., Peekskill, NY, 1980—81. Dir. ARC, Rochester, 1972. Recipient Humanitarian award, Harlem Cmty. Harlem Week, 1989. Mem.: Sigma Tau Delta (pres. 1974), Delta Sigma Theta. Democrat. Episcopalian. Avocations: singing, travel, running, reading, writing. Home: 350 W 115th St Apt 2B New York NY 10026 Office: PS 180 Hugo Newman Coll Prep 370 W 120th St New York NY 10026

LOVEJOY, CLAUDE OWEN, anthropologist, educator; b. Puducah, Ky., Feb. 11, 1943; s. Claude Kildow and Barbara S. Lovejoy; m. Melanie A. McCollum, Mar. 30, 1965. MS, Case Inst. Tech., Cleve., 1967; PhD, U. Mass., 1970. Univ. prof. anthropology dept. sociology and anthropology Kent State U., Ohio, 1968—. Tech. adv. Cuyahoga County Coroner's Office, Cleve., 1985—; prof. NE Ohio Coll. Medicine, Rootstown, 1985—2001. Contbr. articles to profl. jours. Recipient Gov. cert., 2000. Mem.: NAS. Office: Kent State U Hilltop Dr Kent OH 44242 Office Phone: 330-672-4748. Office Fax: 330-672-2999. Personal E-mail: olovejoy@aol.com. E-mail: olovejoy@kent.edu.*

LOVEJOY, GEORGE MONTGOMERY, JR., real estate company executive; b. Newton, Mass., Apr. 15, 1930; s. George Montgomery and Margaret (King) L.; m. Ellen West Childs, June 30, 1956; children: George Montgomery III, Edward R., Philip W., Henry W. BA, Harvard U., Cambridge, Mass., 1951. V.p. Minot, DeBlois & Maddison, Boston, 1955-72; from exec. v.p. to chmn. Meredith & Grew, Inc., Boston, 1972—95; chmn. Fifty Assoc., Boston, 1988-94, pres., 1994—2001. Active Weston Planning Bd., Mass., 1961-68, chmn., 1965-67; active Bd. Selectmen, 1968-71, chmn., 1970-71; bd. dirs. Boston Mcpl. Rsch. Bur., 1966—, chmn., 1982-84; com. mem. Fund for Preservation Wildlife and Natural Areas, 1985-94, chmn., 1992-94; trustee New Eng. Aquarium, 1969-2002, overseer, 2002—, pres. 1992-94, chmn. 1994; trustee Radcliffe Coll., 1987-95, trustee Scudder Kemper Inc. Mut. Funds, 1975-2000; mem. Corp. Northeastern U., 1983-2002; bd. dirs. Pioneer Inst. for Pub. Policy Rsch., 2002-06. Mem. Counselors of Real Estate (past pres., bd. dir.), Greater Boston Bldg. Owners and Mgr. Assn. (past pres.), Inst. Real Estate Mgmt. (past pres. New Eng. chpt.), Greater Boston Real Estate Bd. (past pres.), Mass. Assn. Realtors, Nat. Assn. Realtors, Nature Conservancy (mem. Mass. adv. bd., chmn. 1994-97, emeritus trustee, 2006-), Harvard Club Boston (past pres.). Avocation: outdoor activities. Home: 54 Beacon St Boston MA 02108-3531 Office: 50 Congress St Ste 543 Boston MA 02109-4002

LOVEJOY, PAUL ROBERT, lawyer, air transportation executive; b. Rochester, NY, Jan. 30, 1955; s. V. Paul and Jean M. Lovejoy; m. Susan Seyfarth, Dec. 30, 1978; 1 child, Kate Hightower. BA summa cum laude,

New Eng. Coll., 1977; JD, Case Western Res. U., 1981. Bar: Ohio 1981, NY 1988, Ill. 2005. Assoc. Squire, Sanders & Dempsey, Cleve., 1981—89, ptnr., 1989—90; asst. gen. counsel Texaco Inc., White Plains, NY, 1990—99; ptnr. Weil, Gotshal & Manges, NYC, 1999—2003; sr. v.p., gen. counsel, sec. UAL Corp., Chgo., 2003—. Trustee New Eng. Coll., Henniker, NH, 1993—2002. Office: UAL Corp 77 W Wacker Dr Chicago IL 60601

LOVEJOY, THOMAS EUGENE, tropical and conservation biologist, association executive; b. NYC, Aug. 22, 1941; s. Thomas Eugene and Audrey Helen (Paige) L.; m. Charlotte Seymour, 1966 (div. 1978); children: Elizabeth Paige and Katherine Seymour (twins), Anne Williams. BS, Yale U., 1964, PhD in Biology, 1971; DSc (hon.), Colo. State U., 1989, Williams Coll., 1990; LHD (hon.), Lynn U., 1991. Co-chmn. premed. adv. bd. U. Pa., 1971-72; exec. asst. to sci. dir. Acad. Natural Scis., Phila., 1972-73, asst. to v.p. for resources and planning, 1972-73; program dir. World Wildlife Fund-U.S., Washington, 1973-78, v.p. for sci., 1978-85, exec. v.p., 1985-87; asst. sec. environ. & external affairs Smithsonian Instn., Washington, 1987-94, counselor to sec. for biodiversity and environ. affairs, 1995; chief biodiversity adv. World Bank, lead specialist environ. Latin Am. and Caribbean; spl. adv. to pres. UN Found.; pres. The Heinz Ctr., Washington, 2002—. Sci. advisor to Sec. Interior, 1993; bd. dirs. Manhattan Life Ins. Co., N.Y.C., chmn. exec. com., 1982-87, dir., 1986—; rsch. assoc. in ornithology Acad. Natural Scis., 1971—; bd. dirs. Wildlife Preservation Trust Internat., 1974—; bd. dirs. Henry Fdn. for Botanical Rsch., 1975—; prin. advisor Minimum Critical Size of Ecosys. Project, 1979—; mem. commn. ecology IUCN, 1980—; founder, advisor Nature series Sta. WNET, 1980—; vis. lectr. on tropical ecology Yale U. Sch. Forestry and Environ. Studies, 1982. Co-author: Nearctic Avian Migrants in the Neotropics, 1983; co-editor: Key Environments: Amazonia, 1985, Conservation of Tropical Forest Birds, 1985, Global Warming and Biological Diversity, 1992; contbr. articles, chpts. to profl. publs. Mem. Smithsonian Coun., 1982-87; trustee Millbrook Sch., N.Y., 1971—, Rocky Mountain Biol. Lab., 1983—, Acad. Natural Scis. Phila., 1987—, The Ozone Soc., 1990—; mem. U.S.-Brazil panel White House Office of Sci. and Tech., Washington, 1986-87; past chmn. U.S. Man and Biosphere Com., 1987—; treas., mem. exec. com. Sci. Com. on Problems of the Environ., 1988-91; sec. J. Paul Getty Wildlife Conservation prize, Washington, 1974-87, jury mem. 1988—; mem. adv. & tech. bd. Fundacion Neotropica and de Parques Nacional, Costa Rica, 1987—; mem. White House Sci. Coun., exec. office Pres., 1988-90; mem. Pres.'s Coun. Advisors in Sci. & Tech., 1990-92; dir. Rainforest Alliance, 1988—; mem. sci. coun. FPCN (Conservation Found., Peru), 1988—; mem. adv. bd. Am. Soc. Protection Nature Israel, 1988—; co-prin. investigator World Wildlife Fund/INPA, North Manaus, Brazil, 1979—; bd. govs. N.Y. Botanical Garden, N.Y.C., 1986—; dir. Ctr. for Plant Conservation, 1987—; bd. dirs. Fundacion Maquipucuna, Ecuador, 1988—, Resources for the Future, 1989—, World Resources Inst., 1989—, Peruvian Cultural Ctr., 1989—. Grantee Nat. Geog. Soc., NIH, NSF, Mellon Found., Rockefeller Found.; recipient Ibero-Am. award II Ibero Am. Ornithological Congress, 1983, Cert. of Merit, Goeldi Mus., 1985, 50th Anniversary medal Brazilian Nat. Parks, 1987, Carr medal Fla. Mus. Natural History, 1990; named comdr. Order of Merit of Mato Grosso, 1987, comdr. Order of Rio Branco, Brazil, 1988, UN Environment Programme Global 500 Roll of Honour, 1992. Fellow AAAS (wildlife panel 1981), N.Y. Zool. Soc., Linnean Soc. London, Am. Ornithologists Union; mem. Am. Inst. Biol. Scis. (bd. dirs. 1989—, pres. 1991-92), Ecol. Soc. Am., Brit. Ecol. Soc., Brit. Ornithologists Union, Cooper Ornithol. Soc., Soc. Study of Evolution, Internat. Union for Conservation of Nature (species survival commn.), Soc. for Conservation Biology (gov. 1986-89, pres. 1989-91), Century Club, Cosmos Club, Knickerbocker Club, New Haven Lawn Club. Office: The Heinz Ctr Ste 700 900 17th St NW Washington DC 20006

LOVELACE, ELDRIDGE HIRST, retired landscape architect, city planner, civil engineer; b. Kansas City, Kans., Mar. 16, 1913; s. Charles Wilson and Eva (Hirst) L.; m. Marjorie Van Evera, May 15, 1937; children: Jean (Mrs. William C. Stinchcombe), Richard. B.F.A. in Landscape Architecture, U. Ill., 1935. Registered profl. engr., Mo. With Harland Bartholomew & Assocs., Inc., St. Louis, 1935— 81, mem., 1943-79, chmn. bd., 1979— 81. V.p. Internat. Fedn. Landscape Architects, 1975-77, sec. gen., 1980—81. Author: Harland Bartholomew: His Contributions to American Urban Planning. Mem. bd. commrs. Tower Grove Park, 1971—, pres. 1986-94. Fellow Am. Soc. Landscape Architects (past sec.), ASCE; mem. Am. Inst. Cert. Planners. Achievements include development of comprehensive plans for 100 American cities; master plans for military bases in US, Pacific, Hawaii and P.I; final design plans for Jefferson National Expansion Memorial (The Arch), St. Louis. Home: 8600 Delmar Blvd Saint Louis MO 63124-1973 Personal E-mail: eldridgelovelace@yahoo.com.

LOVELACE, GAIL T., human resources specialist; married. Various positions Gen. Svcs. Adminstrn., Washington, 1979—98, chief people officer, 1998—. Chief Human Capital Officers Coun. Recipient Presdl. Rank award, 2002, Sr. Exec. Svc. Disting. Exec. award, 2001. Mem.: Internat. Personnel Mgmt. Assn. Office: 1800 F St NW Washington DC 20405

LOVELACE, JON (JONATHAN BELL LOVELACE), investment management company executive; b. Detroit, Feb. 6, 1927; s. Jonathan Bell and Marie (Andersen) L.; m. Lillian Pierson, Dec. 29, 1950; children: Carey, James, Jeffrey, Robert. AB cum laude, Princeton U., 1950. Personnel asst. Pacific Finance Co., 1950-51; with Capital Research & Mgmt. Co., LA, 1951—, treas., 1955-62, v.p., 1957-62, exec. v.p., 1962-64, pres., 1964-75, 82-83, chmn. bd., 1975—82, 1983, chmn. emeritus, also dir. Chmn. bd. Investment Co. Am., 1982—, Capital Income Builder, 1987—, Am. Mut. Fund Inc., 1971—; bd. dirs. Capital Research Co., 1967—, Am. Pub. Radio; pres., dir. New Perspective Fund. Trustee Claremont McKenna Coll.; mem. bd. fellows Claremont U. Ctr.; mem. adv. bd. Stanford U. N.E. Asia/U.S. Forum on Internat. Policy; trustee Calif. Inst. Arts, chmn., 1983-88; trustee Santa Barbara Med. Found. Clinic, J. Paul Getty Mus., chmn. 1988—. Named one of Forbes' Richest Americans, 2006. Mem. Council on Fgn. Relations, Sierra Club. Clubs: Princeton (N.Y.C.), University (N.Y.C.); Calif. (Los Angeles). also: 780 El Bosque Rd Santa Barbara CA 93108-1310 Address: 333 S Hope St Fl 47 Los Angeles CA 90071-1406

LOVELACE, JULIANNE, former library director; b. Jackson, Miss., July 30, 1941; d. Benjamin Travis and Julia Elizabeth (Knight) Robinson; m. William Frank Lovelace, July 6, 1963 (div. Mar. 17, 1972); 1 child, Julie Lynn. BA in History, So. Meth. U., 1963; MLS, U. North Tex., 1970. Clk. Dallas Pub. Libr., 1963-64, children's libr. asst., 1964-66, children's libr., 1966-69; libr. Richardson (Tex.) Pub. Libr., 1971-72, supr. pub. svcs., 1972-87, dir., 1987-2001; CFO 4womenShopping, Inc., 2000—. Active Richardson Adult Literacy Ctr., Altrusa Internat., Inc. Richardson, Leadership Richardson Alumni Assn., Friends of the Richardson Pub. Libr., Richardson Regional Med. Ctr., Women's Adv. Coun.; mem. exec. steering com. Wildflower Arts & Music Festival. Named one of 21 for the 21st Century, Collin County Bus., 2000. Mem.: Rotary (vocat. svcs. chair Richardson chpt.). Avocation: blackjack. Personal E-mail: jl3430@verizon.net.

LOVELACE, RICHARD VAN EVERA, education educator, research scientist; s. Eldridge Hirst and Marjorie Van Evera Lovelace; m. Marina M. Romanova, Oct. 11, 1997; children: Jennifer B., Evera U., Alisa Blinova, Alena Blinova. BS, Wash. U., 1961—64; PhD, Cornell U., 1964—70. Rsch. assoc. Cornell U. Lab. of Plasma Studies, 1970—73; asst. prof. Cornell U. Dept. of Applied and Engring. Physics, 1974—80, assoc. prof., 1980—86; prof. Cornell U., Dept. of Applied and Engring. Physics and Dept. of Astronomy, 1986—. Guggenheim fellowship, Guggenheim Found., 1989, Churchill Coll. Overseas fellow, Churchill Coll., Cambridge U., 1994, Orsan Anderson fellow, Los Alamos Nat. Lab., 2000. Fellow: Am. Phys. Soc.; mem.: Internat. Astron. Union. Office: Cornell Univ Dept Astronomy 410 Space Science Building Ithaca NY 14853-6801

LOVELACE, ROSE MARIE SNIEGON, federal space agency administrator; b. Sweet Hall, Va., Feb. 19, 1937; d. Adolph and Annie (Mickel) Sniegon; m. William Wayne Lovelace, Aug. 11, 1962. Degree in bus., Longwood Coll., 1957. Adminstrv. aide Dept. of Navy, Washington, 1957-60; adminstrv. asst. Joint Blood Coun.-Pvt., Washington, 1960-63; exec. staff NASA, Washington, 1963-73, program analyst-specialist, 1973-80, chief adminstrv. ops. and Congl. affairs br., 1980-92; ret., 1992. Cons. NASA, 1992—. Editor, author: (pamphlet) Space Operations, 1989, (video) Space Communications, 1991. Pres. Jr. Achievement Co., 1953-55, Kettering Recreation Coun., Largo, Md., 1974-76; league coord. U.S. Tennis Assn., Anne Arundel County, Md., 1989-91, team capt., 1984-99, 2001, 04-07; active Hospice Cup Regatta, sponsor 2000-, Hospice Beacon Hope Gala Com. Fundraiser, 2004-07, Hospice Circle of Care Soc., 2005-, LWV, Hospice Planned Giving Coun. Recipient Jr. Achievement Exec. award and Nat. Speakers award, 1954, Gold medal Parks and Planning, Prince Georges County, Md., 1976, Exceptional Svc. award NASA, 1983, Exceptional Svc. medal NASA, 1992. Mem.: Nat. Women's Hist. Mus. (charter mem.), Hospice Cir. of Care Soc., Heritage Soc. Anne Arundel Med. Ctr., Historic Annapolis Found., Anne Arundel County Tennis Assn., Am. Heart Assn. (Heart Ball com. fundraiser 2000), Annapolis Opera, Inc., Sportfit Racquet and Fitness Club, Severn Town Club (pres. 1996—98, chair Holly Ball fundraiser 1998—99). Republican. Methodist. Avocations: tennis, gardening, flower arranging, organizing social and tennis events, designing and painting wearable art.

LOVELAND, EUGENE FRANKLIN, retired gas industry executive; b. Anderson, Ind., Sept. 11, 1920; s. Irving Eugene and Clare (Macfarlane) L.; m. Joan King, Aug. 4, 1944; children: Jeffrey, David C. and Peter F. (twins), Mark, Laurie E. BA, Wesleyan U., Middletown, Conn. With Shell Oil Co., 1946-80, v.p. central mktg. region, 1968-71, v.p. oil products Houston, 1972-80; pres. Transworld Oil USA, Inc. (formerly T.W. Oil Inc.), Houston, 1981—; chmn., chief exec. officer T.W. Oil Inc., 1983-89, ret., 1989. Bd. dirs. Transworld Oil Ltd., Bermuda. Bd. dirs. Lyric Theatre, Houston, Am. Dance Cos.; chmn. Houston Ballet Found., Combined Arts Corp., Campaign, Houston, Greater Houston Skating Coun., vice chmn. Better Bus. Bur., Houston; hon. counsul gen. Republic of Malta in Tex.; dir. Cultural Arts Coun. Houston, 1989-93; chmn. Greater Houston Ice Skating Coun., 1989—; mem. exec. com. Houston Internat. Festival, 1992; chmn. devel. commn. Fay Sch., 1992. With USNR, 1943-45. Decorated D.F.C., Air medal (2); recipient Disting. Alumnus award Wesleyan U., 1993, Nat. Order of Merit, Country of Malta, 2003. Mem. Mil. and Hospitaller Order St. Lazarus Jerusalem.

LOVELAND, JOHN BIGELOW, editor, writer; b. NYC, Apr. 17, 1934; s. John Howland Gibbs and Daphne Tilton Pell; m. Ellen Pell (dec.); children: John D. Pell, William B. Pell, Daphne C. Pell; m. Bara H. Fischer, July 2, 2001. BA in philosophy, SUNY, 1991. Securities analyst John H.G. Pell & Co., NYC, 1957—60; workshop investigator NYC, 1960—62; gen. assoc. Pell Gallery, NYC, 1963—75; freelance writer, 1975—78; reg. rep. First Investors Corp., NYC, 1978—79; v.p. Wall St. Mgmt. Corp., NYC, 1980—84; compliance assoc. Morse, Williams & Co., NYC, 1984; ins. agt. Equitable Fin. Svcs., NYC, 1985; proofreader Fact Typographers, NYC, 1986; typesetter Cardinal Type Svc., NYC, 1987, Cosmos Commn., NYC, 1987—88; editor Beauty Fashion, Inc., NYC, 1988—89; pres., founder New Earth Found., Sedona, Ariz., 1997—; founder, pres., CEO Earth Cmty. Rsch. Corp., Beaver Creek, Ariz., 2000—. Pres., trustee Ft. Ticonderogo Assn., Ticonderoga, NY, 1988—94. With US Army, 1954—56, Germany. Mem.: Am. Assn. Ret. Persons, Coop Am., Ft. Ticonderoga Assn. Independent. Episcopalian. Avocations: hiking, squash, gardening, opera, piano, reading, plays. Home and Office: Earth Cmty Rsch PO Box 5214 Lake Montezuma AZ 86342 Personal E-mail: john@earthcommunityresearch.net.

LOVELAND, L. JOSEPH, JR., lawyer; b. Richmond, Va., July 27, 1951; BA with highest honors, U. NC, 1973; JD cum laude, Harvard U., 1976. Bar: Ga. 1976, Tex. 1994. Ptnr. King & Spalding. Contbr. articles to profl. jours. Named Best Lawyers Am., one of Ga's. Top 100 Super Lawyers, Am's. Leading Bus. Lawyers, by Chambers USA, 2006. Mem. ABA, State Bar Ga., State Bar Tex., Atlanta Bar Assn., Houston Bar Assn., Phi Beta Kappa, fellow Am. Coll. Trial Lawyers. Office: King & Spalding 1180 Peachtree St NE Atlanta GA 30309 Office Phone: 404-572-4783. Office Fax: 404-572-5100. Business E-Mail: jloveland@kslaw.com.

LOVELAND, SYLVIA MARIE, translator; d. Trafton Joseph and Liliane Jane Loveland. Lic. in translation, Inst. Superior l'Etat, Brussels. Freelance translator, Granada Hills, Calif., 1987—2009; editor Psychiatry, Van Nuys, Calif., 1999—2002, abstractor, 2002—. Mem.: Internat. High IQ Soc., Mensa, Nat. Honor Soc. Avocations: logic puzzles, music, computers, reading.

LOVELESS, GEORGE GROUP, retired lawyer; b. Baldwinsville, NY, Sept. 16, 1940; s. Frank Donald and Mayme (Lont) L.; m. Shirley Morrison, Nov. 27, 1965; children: Michael, Peter. BS, Cornell U., 1962, MBA, 1963; JD, U. Md., 1968. Bar: Pa. 1969, U.S. Dist. Ct. (ea. dist.) Pa., U.S. Ct. Appeals (3d cir.). Ptnr. Morgan, Lewis & Bockius LLP, Phila., 1968-2000; ret., 2000. With USAFR, 1963-68. Republican. Presbyterian. Home: 11 Rose Valley Rd Media PA 19063-4217 Office: Morgan Lewis & Bockius LLP 1701 Market St Philadelphia PA 19103-2921 Office Phone: 610-566-1132. E-mail: GGL1@cornell.edu.

LOVELESS, KEITH, lawyer, air transportation executive; b. Chgo., 1956; BA, Vanderbilt U., 1979, JD, 1983. Bar: Wash. 1983, US Dist. Ct. (ea. dist) Wash. 1983, US Dist. Ct. (we. dist.) Wash. 1983. Corp. sec., asst. gen. counsel Alaska Air Group, Inc., 1996—99, v.p. legal & corp. affairs, gen. counsel, corp. sec., 1999—. Mem.: ABA. Office: Alaska Air Group Inc 19300 Internat Blvd Seattle WA 98188

LOVELESS, PEGGY ANN, social work administrator; b. Decatur, Ill., June 9, 1952; d. William Walter and Rose Marie (Sheppard) L. Student, Ill. State U., 1970-72; BA, U. Ill., 1974, MSW, 1976. Cert. lic. clin. social worker; cert. in health care ethics; diplomate Am. Bd. Examiners in Clin. Social Work. Social worker Met.-Police Social Svcs., Urbana, Ill., 1976-80; clin. supr. Ctr. Children's Svcs., Danville, Ill., 1980-84; med. social worker Sarah Bush Lincoln Health Ctr., Mattoon, Ill., 1984-86, Portland (Oreg.) Adventist Med. Ctr., 1986-88; dept. supr., social worker Oreg. Health Scis. U., Portland, 1988-92, interim dir. social work, 1992-93, asst. dir. social work Ctr. Ethics, 1993-96, mem. ethics consulting svc., 1991-96; behavioral health case mgr. PacifiCare Behavioral Health, 1996-98; case mgr. Pacific Gateway Hosp., Portland, Oreg., 1998-99; clin. supr. Multnomah County, Behavioral Health Divsn. Managed Care Program, Portland, Oreg., 1999—. Vol. Goose Hollow Family Homeless Shelter, Portland, 1993-94, vol. supr., 1994-95, bd. dirs., 1996-97. Mem. Soc. Social Work Adminstrs. Health Care (com. nominations 1995-96, chair, pres. meeting planning com. 1994, com. mem. devel. 1997), Oreg. Soc. Social Work Adminstrs. Health Care (pres. elect 1993, pres. 1994, chair/conf. com. 1995). Avocations: reading, walking, skiing, travel. Office: Multnomah County Behavioral Health Divsn Managed Care Program 421 SW Sixth Ave 166/5 Portland OR 97204

LOVELL, CARL ERWIN, JR., lawyer; b. Riverside, Calif., Apr. 12, 1945; s. Carl Erwin and Hazel (Brown) L.; mchildren: Carl Erwin III, Timothy C., Tishia R., Ashley P., Garrett T., Christopher C. BA, Vanderbilt U., 1966, JD, 1969. Bar: Nev. 1969, D.C. 1971, U.S. Supreme Ct. 1973. Jr. editor Land and Water Law Rev., 1973-89; instr. bus. law U. Nev., Las Vegas, Clark County C.C.; city atty. City of N. Las Vegas, 1970-73; elected city atty. City of Las Vegas, 1973-77; v.p., sec.-treas., legal counsel Circus Circus Hotels, Inc., Las Vegas, 1977-83; sr. ptnr. Lovell, Bilbray & Potter, Las Vegas, 1984-89; pvt. practice Las Vegas, 1989—; ptnr. Lovell & Lovell, 2000—03, Mitchelson & Lovell, Calif., 2001—03; v.p., dir. Air Nev. Airlines, Inc. U.S. rep. to China-U.S. Internat. Trade and Law Talks, Beijing, 1987; arbitrator, AAA, 1989—. Bd. dirs., v.p. BBB, 1983-91; chmn. NCCJ; pres., trustee Nev. Donor Network, Inc., 1992-96. Mem. ABA, ATLA, Nev. State Bar, Nev. Trial Lawyers Assn. Office Phone: 702-362-7922. Business E-Mail: carl@lovell-lovell.com.

LOVELL, EDWARD GEORGE, mechanical engineering educator; b. Windsor, Ont., Can., May 25, 1939; s. George Andrew and Julia Anne (Kopacz) Lovell; m. Roxann Engelstad; children: Elise, Ethan. BS, Wayne State U., 1960, MS, 1961; PhD, U. Mich., 1967. Registered profl. engr., Wis. Project engr. Bur. Naval Weapons, Washington, 1959, Boeing Co., Seattle, 1962; test engr.-Ford Motor Co., Troy, Mich., 1960; instr. U. Mich., Ann Arbor, 1963-67; design engr. United Tech., Hartford, Conn., 1970; prof. engring. U. Wis., Madison, 1968—, chmn. dept. engring. mechanics and astronautics, 1992-95, assoc. chmn. dept. of mech. engring., 1999—. Cons. structural engring. to govt. labs., indsl. orgns., maj. textbook pubs., 1968— Contbr. numerous articles to profl. jours. Postdoctoral research fellow Nat. Acad. Sci., 1967; NATO Sci. fellow, 1973; NSF fellow, 1961 Mem. Wis. Fusion Tech. Inst., Wis. Ctr. for Applied Microelectronics, Sigma Xi, Tau Beta Pi, Phi Kappa Phi Office: U Wis Dept Mech Engring 1513 University Ave Madison WI 53706-1572

LOVELL, FRANCIS JOSEPH, retired investment company executive; b. Mar. 21, 1949; s. Frank J. and Patricia Anna (Donnellan) L. BBA, Nichols Coll., 1971. With Brown Bros. Harriman & Co., Boston, 1971—2005, v.p., 1971—2005, ret., 2005. Trustee Nichols Coll., 2003—06; pres. Nichols Coll. Alumni, 2003—06. Mem. New Eng. Hist. Gen. Soc., Union Club of Boston. Democrat. Home: 25 Pomfret St West Roxbury MA 02132-1809 also: 48 Hidden Village Rd West Falmouth MA 02574

LOVELL, LISA INEZ, special education educator; b. Hobbs, N.Mex., June 13, 1968; d. Earnest Clay and Betty Dell Cox; m. Stacy Monroe Lovell, Feb. 24, 1995; children: Kyle, John. AA, Ranger Jr. Coll., Tex., 1994; BS, Midwestern State U., Wichita Falls, Tex., 1996, studied. Spl. edn. tchr. Graham Ind. Sch. Dist., Tex., 1996—. Mem.: Assn. Tex. Profl. Educators, Coun. for Exceptional Children, Delta Kappa Gamma. Baptist. Avocations: reading, water-skiing, cooking, travel. Office: Graham Ind Sch Dist 1317 Old Jacksboro Rd Graham TX 76450 Business E-Mail: lisa.lovell@grahamisd.com.

LOVELL, MALCOLM READ, JR., public information officer, educator, retired trade association administrator, federal official; b. Greenwich, Conn., Jan. 1, 1921; s. Malcolm Read and Emily (Monihan) L.; m. Celia Coghlan, 1978; children by previous marriage: Lucie, Sara. Annette, Caroline. Student, Brown U., 1939-42; I.A., Harvard U., 1943; MBA, Harvard, 1946. With Ford Motor Co., Dearborn, Mich., 1946-58; mgr. employee services Am. Motors Corp., Detroit, 1958-61; chmn. State Labor Mediation Bd., Detroit, 1963; dir. Mich. Office Econ. Opportunity, 1964, Mich. Employment Security Commn., Detroit, 1965-69; exec. asso. Manpower, Urban Coalition, 1969; dep. asst. sec. of labor and manpower adminstr., 1969-70; asst. sec. of labor for manpower, 1970-73; pres. Rubber Mfrs. Assn., 1973-81; asst. dir. Office Policy Coordination and Econ. Affairs, Office Pres.-Elect, 1980; undersec. Dept. Labor, Washington, 1981-83; vis. scholar Brookings Instn., Washington, 1983-85; disting. vis. prof. govt. and dir. Labor Mgmt. Inst., George Washington U., 1985-92, 99—; pres. Nat. Policy Assn., 1992-99; sr. fellow Hudson Inst., 1985-88; exec. Exec. Coaching Network, 1999—; exec. in residence George Washington U. Sch. Bus. and Pub. Mgmt., 1999—. Mem. Nat. Adv. Coun. on Vocat. Edn., 1975-79, Nat. Commn. for Manpower Policy, 1977-79; chmn. sec. labor Task Force on Econ. Adjustment and Worker Dislocation, 1985-86; mediator Collective Bargaining Forum, 1983-2000; adj. prof. Sch. Bus., George Washington U. V.p. Birmingham (Mich.) Sch. Bd., 1956-60; bd. dirs. Nat. Alliance Bus., 1984—; bd. dirs. Travelers Aid of Washington, 1983-86, pres., 1985-86. Lt. USNR, 1943-46. Sr. fellow Hudson Inst., 1985-88. Mem. Clean Plate (Washington), Cosmos Club (Washington), Alpha Delta Phi. Personal E-mail: maclovell@worldnet.att.net. Business E-Mail: maclovell@gwu.edu.

LOVELL, MICHAEL C., retired economics professor; b. Cambridge, Mass., Apr. 11, 1930; s. Reginald Ivan and Rose Mary (Chittenden) L.; m. Adrienne Goolkasian, June 21, 1959; children: Leslie Rosemary, Stacie Alice, George Ivan, Martin Benjamin BA, Reed Coll., 1952; MA, Stanford U., 1954; PhD, Harvard U., 1959. Instr. Yale, 1958-59, asst. prof., 1959-63; mem. staff Cowles Found., 1958-63; assoc. prof. Grad. Sch. Indsl. Adminstrn., Carnegie-Mellon U., 1963-66, prof., 1966-69; prof. econ. Wesleyan U., Middletown, Conn., 1969—, chmn. dept., 1973—75, 1994—96; prof. Chester D. Hubbard/ Soc. Sci., 1996—2002; ret., 2002. Vis. prof. Sch. Mgmt. Yale U., 1981-82, 86, 88; cons. Pres.'s Coun. Econ. Advisors, 1964, 67; sr. adviser Brookings Panel on Econ. Activity, 1974-90. Author: (with Albert Hirsch) Sales Anticipations and Inventory Behavior, 1969, Macroeconomics: Measurement, Theory and Policy, 1975, (with Attila Chikan) The Economics of Inventory Management, 1988, Economics With Calculus, 2004; assoc. editor Econometrica, 1965-68, Jour. Econs. and Bus., 1983-86, Jour. Econ. Behavior and Orgn., 1987-98, Rev. Econs. and Stats., 1991-92, Social Sci. Computer Rev., 1993-99; fgn. editor Rev. Econ. Studies, 1968-70. With U.S. Army, 1953-55. Recipient 1st prize Joint Council Econ. Edn., Kazanjian Found. awards program for teaching econs., 1973-74; Ford Found. Faculty Research fellow, 1964-65; Social Sci. Research Council Tng. fellow, 1957-58; Earhart Found. fellow, 1956-57; Harvard Grad. Sch. fellowship, 1955-56; W.H. Robinson fellowship, 1952-53; NSF research grantee, 1962-64, 66-68, 70-72 Fellow Econometric Soc.; mem. Am. Econ. Assn. (chmn. publs. com. 1975-78), Am. Statist. Assn. (assoc. editor Jour. 1975-78), Internat. Soc. Inventory Rsch. (exec. com., chmn. inventories and nat. economy sect. 1982—, pres. 1992-94) Home: 121 Paterson Dr Middletown CT 06457 E-mail: mlovell@wesleyan.edu.

LOVELL, THEODORE, electrical engineer, consultant; b. Paterson, NJ, May 10, 1928; s. George Whiting and Ethel Carol (Berner) L.; m. Wilma Syperda, May 8, 1948 (div. Oct. 1961); m. Joyce Smelik, July 15, 1962; children: Laurie, Dorothy Jane, Valerie, Cynthia, Karen, Barbara. BEE, Newark Coll. Engring., NJ, 1948; postgrad., Canadian Inst. Tech., 1950. Exec. dir. Lovell Electric Co., Franklin Lakes, N.J., 1955-82; ptnr., exec. dir. Lovell Design Services, Swedesboro, N.J., 1982—. Author engring. computer software, 1982. Bd. dirs., treas. Contact "Help" of Salem County, 1991-93; pres. Bloomingdale Bd. Edn., N.J., 1970-82; mem. Mcpl. Planning Bd., Bloomingdale, 1980-82, Swedesboro/Woolwich Bd. Edn., 1987-94, v.p., 1990-92, pres. 1993-94; mayoral candidate Borough of Bloomingdale, 1982; v.p. Woolwich Twp. Rep. Club, 1996—; chmn. Woolwich Twp. Bus. Adv. Com., 1997—; mem. Gloucester County Econ. Devel. Coun., 1998-2002, chmn., Woolwich Township Nike Base Com.,

2004-. Recipient Outstanding Service award Lake Iosco Co., Bloomingdale, 1985, 20 Yr. Svc. award N.J. Sch. Bd. Assn., 1994. Fellow Radio Club Am.; mem. Soc. Engring. Technicians, Dickinson Theater Organ Soc. (corp. sec., bd. dirs.), Am. Theatre Organ Soc., Theatre Organ Soc. S. Jersey. Presbyterian. Avocations: history, organ music. Home: 16 Liberty Ct Woolwich Township NJ 08085-3010 Office: Lovell Design Svcs PO Box 366 Swedesboro NJ 08085-0366 Home Phone: 856-467-0959. Personal E-mail: tedlovell@verizon.net. *It has become apparent to me, slowly perhaps that as I progress through life, the things that bring lasting joy and satisfaction are not personal achievements, but those things that help others.*

LOVELL, WHITFIELD, artist; b. NYC, 1959; BFA, Cooper Union Sch. Art, 1981. Artist-in-residence Mousem D'Asilah, Morocco, 1988, Art Awareness, Lexington, NY, 1991, Warhol Mus., Pitts., 1998, U. North Tex., 1999, Hand Workshop Art Ctr., Richmond, Va., 2000, Ctr. for Documentary Studies, Duke U., Durham, NC, 2001, Contemporary Art Ctr. Va., 2002; Diebenkorn fellow San Francisco Art Inst., 2003. One-man shows include Interchurch Ctr., N.Y., 1982, Galeria Morivivi, 1984, John Jay Coll., 1985, Harlem Sch. Arts, 1987, Jersey City Mus., 1988, Lehman Coll. Art Gallery, N.Y., 1993, Southeastern Ctr. Contemporary Art, Winston-Salem, 1997, D.C. Moore Gallery, N.Y., 1997—2000, 2002, The Andy Warhol Mus., Pitts., 1998, U. North Tex. Art Gallery, Denton, 1999, Studio Mus., Harlem, N.Y., 2000, Neuberger Mus. Art, N.Y., 2000, Montclair (N.J.) Art Mus., 2001, Tubman African Am. Mus., Ga., 2001, Jones Ctr. Contemporary Art, Tex., 2000, Knoxville Mus., Tenn., 2001, Boston U. Art Gallery, 2001, Hand Workshop, Richmond, Va., 2001, Evansville (Ind.) Mus., 2002, U. Wyo. Art Mus., Laramie, 2002, Columbus (Ga.) Mus., 2002, Thomasville Cult Ctr., Ga., 2002, Black History Mus., Va., 2002, Cont. Art Ctr., 2002, Hurston Nat. Mus., Fla, 2003, Art Mus. S.E. Tex., 2003, Bronx Mus., N.Y., 2003, Flint (Mich.) Inst. Arts, 2003, Mus. Contemporary Art, Sydney, 2004, others, exhibited in group shows at AIR Gallery, N.Y., 1981—82, ABC No Rio, 1982, Cayman Gallery, 1983, one-man shows include Flint Inst., Mich., 2003, exhibited in group shows at Kenkeleba Gallery, N.Y.C., 1984—85, Howard U. Gallery of Art, Washington, 1985, Bronx River Art Gallery, N.Y.C., 1985, Longwood Arts Gallery, 1986, Met. Life Gallery N.Y., 1987, Alijira Gallery, Newark, 1988, Cinque Gallery, N.Y., 1989, Snug Harbor Cultural Ctr., 1990, Pepsico Gallery, 1991, Boston Mus. Fine Arts, 1991, Allen Meml. Art Mus., Miami, Fla., 1992, Intar Gallery, N.Y., 1993, Agustin Barrios Gallery, Asuncion, Paraguay, 1994, 450 Broadway Gallery, N.Y., 1994, Puffin Found., N.Y.C., 1994, Exit Art, 1995, Ark. Arts Ctr., Little Rock, 1995, DC Moore Gallery, N.Y., 1995, 1996, 1998, Round 3 Inst. Project Row Houses, Houston, 1996, Atrium Gallery, Morristown, N.J., 1997, David Klein Gallery, Birmingham, Mich., 1997, Sexta Biennial, Havana, Cuba, 1997, Craven Gallery, West Tisbury, Mass., 1998, Bronx Mus. Art, 1999—2000, Nat. Mus. Am. Art, Washington, 1999, Seattle Art Mus., 2000, Yale U. Art Gallery, New Haven, 2000, Megura Mus., Tokyo, 2001, Hunter Coll., N.Y., 2000, Bronx Mus., 2000, Colby Coll., Maine, 2001, Met. Mus. Art, N.Y.C., 2003, Corcoran Gallery, Washington, 2003, others, Represented in permanent collections The Libr. of Congress, Washington, Met. Mus. Art, N.Y.C., New Sch. Social Rsch., Seattle Art Mus., Yale U. Art Gallery, Neuberger Mus. Art, N.Y.C., Nat. Mus. Am. Art, Washington, Hunter Mus. Art, Tenn., The Promise of Learnings Collection, N.Y.C., Ark. Arts Ctr., Bronx Mus., Chrysler Mus., Va., Flint Inst. Arts, Mich., Greenville Co. Mus., S.C., Harvard Bus. Sch., MA, Montclair Mus., N.J., Whitney Mus., N.Y., Corcoran Gallery, Washington, Met. Mus. Art, NY, Montclair (NJ) Art Mus., Ark. Arts Ctr., Little Rock. Fellow Jerome Found. fellow, Robert Blackburn Printmaking Workshop, 1982, Regional fellow, Mid-Atlantic Nat. Endowment Arts, 1992; scholar Eastman scholar, Skowhegan Sch. Painting and Sculpture, 1985; Joan Mitchell Found. grantee, 1996, Robert Blackburn Printmaking Workshop fellow, 1985, N.Y. Found. Arts fellow, 1997, N.Y. State Coun. Arts grantee, 1986—87, Penny McCall Found. grantee, 1990, Artists Homeless Shelter Collaborative grantee, 1991, N.Y. Found. Arts grantee, 1991. Office: care DC Moore Gallery 724 5th Ave New York NY 10019-4106

LOVEMAN, GARY W., gaming company executive; BA in Econs., Wesleyan U., 1982; PhD in Econs., MIT, 1989. Assoc. prof. bus. adminstrn. Harvard U., 1989—98; cons. Harrah's Entertainment, Inc., exec. v.p., 1998—2001, COO, 1998—2003, pres., 2001—, CEO, 2003—, chmn., 2005—. Bd. dirs. Coach, 2002—. Co-author: The Evolving Role of Small Business and Some Implications for Employment and Training Policy, 1990; author: An Assessment of the Productivity Impact of Information Technologies, 1994; co-author: Starting Over in Eastern Europe: Entrepreneurship and Economic Renewal, 1995. Recipient Apgar award for Excellence and Innovation in Tchg., Harvard Bus. Sch.; Alfred Sloan Doctoral Dissertation fellow. Mem.: Phi Beta Kappa. Office: One Harrahs Ct Las Vegas NV 89119 Office Phone: 702-407-6316.*

LOVEN, ANDREW WITHERSPOON, environmental engineering company executive; s. Andrew Witherspoon Loven and Annie Laura (Crowell) Stewart; m. Elizabeth Joann DeGroot, June 20, 1959 (dec.); children: Laura Elizabeth, James Edward. BS, Maryville Coll., 1957; PhD in Chemistry, U. N.C., 1962. Registered profl. engr., Colo., Ga., La., Md., N.C., S.C., D.C., Ohio, Fla., Mich., Va. Rsch. assoc. U. N.C., Chapel Hill, 1962-63; sr. rsch. chemist Westvaco Corp., Charleston, SC, 1963-66, mgr. carbon devel., 1966-71, mgr. wastewater cons. svc., 1967-71; mgr. engring. concepts Engring.-Sci. Inc., McLean, Va., 1971-74, v.p., regional mgr. Atlanta, 1974-80, group v.p., 1980-86; pres., CEO Engring. Sci. Inc., Pasadena, Calif., 1986-95, also chmn. bd. dirs.; exec. v.p. Parsons Engring. Sci. Inc., Pasadena, Calif., 1995; pres., CEO Millennium Sci. & Engring., Inc., McLean, Va., 1995—. Contbr. articles to profl. jours. NSF grantee, 1958-59; recipient Maryville Coll. Alumni Citation award, 1992. Mem. AIChE, NSPE, Am. Acad. Environ. Engrs. (diplomate, membership com. 1985—), Water Environment Fedn., Am. Water Works Assn., Am. Pub. Works Assn., Constrn. Industry Pres. Forum, Country Club Roswell, Sigma Xi, Alpha Gamma Sigma. Avocations: golf, hiking. Home: 1512 Barksdale Ct Kennesaw GA 30152 Office: Millennium Sci & Engring Inc 6145 Barfield Rd Ste 110 Atlanta GA 30328 Home Phone: 678-354-2134.

LOVENTHAL, MILTON, writer, playwright, lyricist; b. Atlantic City; s. Harry and Clara (Feldman) L.; m. Jennifer McDowell, July 2, 1973. BA, U. Calif., Berkeley, 1950, MLS, 1958; MA in Sociology, San Jose State U., 1969. Researcher Hoover Instn., Stanford, Calif., 1952-53, spl. asst. to Slavic Curator, 1955—58; librarian San Diego Pub. Library, 1957-59; librarian, bibliographer San Jose State U., Calif., 1959-92. Tchr. writing workshops, poetry readings, 1969-73; co-producer lit. and culture radio show Sta. KALX, Berkeley, 1971-72; editor, pub. Merlin Press, San Jose, 1973—, Lipstick & Toy Balloons Publ. Co., 1978—, Abbie & Dolley Records, 2003—. Author: Books on the USSR, 1951-57, 57, Black Politics, 1971 (featured at Smithsonian Inst. Special Event, 1992), A Bibliography of Material Relating to the Chicano, 1971, Autobiographies of Women, 1946-70, 72, Blacks in America, 1972, The Survivors, 1972, Contemporary Women Poets an Anthology, 1977, Ronnie Goose Rhymes for Grown-Ups, 1984; co-author: (Off-Off-Broadway plays) The Estrogen Party to End War, 1986, Mack the Knife, Your Friendly Dentist, 1986, Betsy & Phyllis, 1986, The Oatmeal Party Comes to Order, 1986, (plays) Betsy Meets the Wacky Iraqi, 1991, Bella and Phyllis, 1994; co-writer (mus. comedy) Russia's Secret Plot to Take Back Alaska, 1988; lyricist Intern Girl, 1998, Smithsonian, 2002; (musical revs., CD) She, A Tapestry of Women's Lives (Found. award Calif. State U. ERFA, 2004). Recipient Bill Casey Award in Letters (Soviet Studies), 1980; grantee, San Jose State U., 1962—63, 1984. Mem. Assn. Calif. State Profs., Calif. Alumni Assn., Calif. Theatre Coun., Am. Assn. for Advancement of Slavic Studies, Soc. for Sci. Study of Religion. Office: PO Box 5602 San Jose CA 95150-5602 Office Phone: 800-889-8305. Personal E-mail: jeditorphd@earthlink.net.

LOVETT, CHRISTOPHER C., history professor, consultant; b. Glen Ridge, NJ, Feb. 15, 1947; s. Harold C. and Kathleen M. (Hoey) Lovett; m. Cherylene Grace Nail, July 30, 1973; 1 child, Elizabeth Catherine. BA, Coll. Emporia, 1966; MA, Kans. State Tchrs. Coll., 1975; MLS, Emporia State U., 1978; PhD, Kans. State U., 1989. Tchr. Topeka (Kans.) Pub. Schs., 1974—80, Shawnee Heights Pub. Schs., Tecumseh, 1981—84; grad. asst. Kans. State U., Manhattan, 1985—87; asst. prof. U. Iowa, Iowa City, 1988—92, Fort Hays State U., Hays, Kans., 1992—96; prof. Emporia State U., 2006—. V.p. Kans. Coun. History Edn., Topeka, 2000—; analyst Kans. Army National Guard, Leavenworth, Kans., 1988—2001, RDA Logigon, Leavenworth, 1992—92; book reviewer Choice; senator Faculty Senate Emporia (Kans.) State U., 1998—2002; cons. Sunflower Journeys, Topeka, 1996—98; dir. pubs. Tchg. History, Kans., 2002—; asst. historian Kans. Army Nat. Guard, 2002—05. Contbr. chapters to books, articles to profl. jours. With US Army, 1971—2005, Vietnam, chief warrant officer nat. guard US Army, 1985, ret. nat. Guard US Army, 2005. Recipient Anne Steward Higham prize, Kans. State U., 1987, Innovation in Tchg. award, Emporia State U., 1999, Outstanding Prof. award, Phi Eta Sigma, 2000, 2001; grantee Am. History tchg., Chanute Pub, Schs., 2002—05, Asst. Dir. Tchr. as Scholars, Kansas, 2002—06. Mem.: Nat. Coun. History Edn., Orgn. Am. Historians, Am. Hist. Assn., Phi Kappa Phi (sec. 2000—02). Democrat. Roman Catholic. Home: 3508 SW Kent Ct Topeka KS 66614 Office: Emporia State Univ 1200 Commercial St Emporia KS 66801 Office Phone: 620-341-5571.

LOVETT, CLARA MARIA, retired academic administrator, historian; b. Trieste, Italy, Aug. 4, 1939; came to U.S., 1962; m. Benjamin F. Brown. BA equivalent, U. Trieste, 1962; MA, U. Tex., Austin, 1967; PhD, U. Tex., 1970. Prof. history Baruch Coll. CUNY, NYC, 1971-82, asst. provost, 1980-82; chief European divsn. Libr. of Congress, Washington, 1982-84; provost, v.p. acad. affairs George Mason U., Fairfax, Va., 1988-93; on leave, dir. Forum on Faculty Roles and Rewards Am. Assn. for Higher Edn., 1993-94; pres. No. Ariz. U., Flagstaff, 1994-2001, pres. emerita, 2001—; sr. fellow, dir. Ctr. for Competency-Measured Edn. The Oquirrh Inst., 2002—03; pres., CEO Am. Assn. for Higher Ed., 2003—05; ret., 2005. Vis. lectr. Fgn. Svc. Inst., Washington, 1979-85. Author: Democratic Movement in Italy 1830-1876, 1982 (H.R. Marraro prize, Soc. Italian Hist. Studies); Giuseppe Ferrari and the Italian Revolution, 1979 (Phi Alpha Theta book award); Carlo Cattaneo and the Politics of Risorgimento, 1972 (Soc. for Italian Hist. Studies Dissertation award), (bibliography) Contemporary Italy, 1985; co-editor: Women, War, and Revolution, 1980, (essays) State of Western European Studies, 1984; contbr. sects. to publs., U.S., Italy. Organizer Dem. clubs Bklyn., 1972-76; mem. exec. com. Palisades Citizens Assn., Washington, 1985-87; vestry mem. St. David's Episc. Ch., Washington, 1986-89; bd. dirs. Blue Cross Blue Shield Ariz., 1995-2004, Nat. Coun. Tchr. Quality, 2005-, Ariz. Women's Edn. Employment Inc., 2001-; trustee Western Govs. U., 1996-2007, Thunderbird, The Grad. Sch. of Internat. Mgmt., 2006—, Scottsdale Cultural Coun., 2006-; mem. Ariz. State Bd. Edn., 1999-2001; advisory bd. Project Ariz. Future, 2005-, Channel 8 PBS Station, 2005-. Fellow Guggenheim Found., 1978-79, Woodrow Wilson Internat. Ctr. for Scholars, 1979 (adv. bd. West European program), Am. Coun. Learned Socs., 1976, Bunting Inst. of Radcliffe Coll., 1975-76, others; named Educator of Yr. Va. Fedn. of Bus. and Profl. Women, 1992. Mem. Am. Assn. Higher Edn. (cons. 1979—), Soc. for Italian Hist. Studies, Assn. Am. Coll. and Univs. (bd. dirs. 1990-93). Avocations: choral singing, swimming. Office Phone: 602-728-9505. Business E-Mail: clara.lovett@nau.edu.

LOVETT, JOHN ROBERT, retired chemical company executive; b. Norristown, Pa., June 17, 1931; s. James and Margaret (Creighton) L.; m. Sandra Miller, May 26, 1956; children: Judy, Jackie, John Robert Jr. BS, Ursinus Coll., 1953; MS, U. Del., 1955, PhD, 1957. Rsch. chemist Exxon Rsch., Linden, NJ, 1957-64; lab. dir. Exxon Rsch./Exxon Chem., Linden, 1964-70; v.p. Paramins Exxon Chem., Houston, 1970-74, tech. mgr. Linden, 1974-76; v.p. rsch. Air Products and Chems., Inc., Allentown, Pa., 1976-81; pres. Europe Air Products and Chems., Inc., Hersham, England, 1981-88; group v.p. chems. Air Products and Chems., Inc., Allentown, 1988-92, exec. v.p. gases & equipment, 1992-93, exec. v.p. strategic planning and tech., 1993-96. Mem. AICE, Chem. Mfrs. Assn. (bd. dirs. 1990-95), Am. Chem. Soc., Soc. Chem. Industry. Home: 2830 W Liberty St Allentown PA 18104-4748

LOVETT, JUANITA PELLETIER, clinical psychologist; b. Youngstown, Ohio, Mar. 9, 1937; d. Joseph Arcadia and Alice Beatrice (Davis) Pelletier; children: Laura Ann, James Emmett. BA summa cum laude with honors in Psychology, Fairleigh Dickinson U., 1975; MPhil, Columbia U., 1978, MA, 1979, PhD, 1980. Freelance fashion cons., 1958-70; psychology fellow Westchester divsn. NY Hosp.-Cornell Med. Ctr., White Plains, 1977-80; program dir. inpatient svc. Fair Oaks Hosp., Summit, NJ, 1980-82; pvt. practice Summit, 1980—; asst. dir. med. rsch. CIBA-GEIGY Pharms., Summit, 1982-83; cons. AT&T Bell Labs., Murray Hill, NJ, 1983, Lucent Techs., 1996—. Adj. asst. prof. psychology and edn., Dept. Psychology, Tchrs. Coll., Columbia U., NYC, 1980-84; field supr. grad. sch. applied profession psychology Rutgers U., 1981-83; assoc. prof. Polytechnic, NY, 1988—. Union County Mental Health Bd. mem., 1974-76; bd. dirs. Wye River Group on Healthcare, Am. Found. for Healthcare Policy. Author: (book) Solutions for Adults With Aspergers Syndrome; contbr. articles to profl. jours. Recipient Laurie Shavel award, 1975; Mennen scholar, 1975. Mem. APA, NY Acad. Scis., NJ Psychol. Assn., Sigma Xi, Phi Omega Epsilon. Office: 86 Summit Ave Summit NJ 07901-3647 Home Phone: 908-277-9596; Office Phone: 908-273-5147. E-mail: jplovett@comcast.net.

LOVETT, KEITH W., retail executive; B in Polit. Sci., Willamette U., 1965; JD, Coll. of Law, Willamette U., 1968. Labor rels. mgr. Alberton's Inc., Boise, Idaho, 1974—84; sr. v.p. human resources Eagle Food Centers Inc., Milan, Ill., 1988—92; sr. v.p., human resources Fred Meyer, Inc., 1992—2000; sr. v.p. human resources Rite Aid Corp., Camp Hill, Pa., 2000—. Office: Rite Aid Corporation 30 Hunter Lane Camp Hill PA 17011

LOVETT, LAURENCE DOW, retired real estate and steamship executive; b. Jacksonville, Fla., Apr. 13, 1930; s. William Radford and Agnes Nisbet (Dow) L. BA, Harvard U., 1951, LL.B., 1954. Vice pres. Eric Boulton, Inc., NYC, 1958-60; vice pres. Eastern Steamship Lines, Miami, Fla., 1960-65, Suwanee Steamship Co., NYC, Jacksonville, 1965-78; pres. Burgoyne Properties, 1978-85; v.p. Piggly Wiggly Corp., 1965-82. Chmn. bd. dirs. Met. Opera Guild, 1979-86, Chamber Music Soc. of Lincoln Ctr., 1989-93; bd. dirs. Met. Oprea Assn., 1979-93; chmn. Save Venice Inc., 1987-98, Venetian Heritage, Inc., 1998—. With AUS, 1955-57. Mem.: Knickerbocker. Address: 11 Ave Princess Grace Monte Carlo 98000 Monaco

LOVETT, MELENDY, electronics executive; BS in Mgmt. and Mgmt. Info. Systems, Tex. A&M U., College Station; MS in Acctg., U. Tex., Dallas. CPA. Sr. mgr. Coopers & Lybrand; v.p. human resources Tex. Instruments Inc., sr. v.p. Dallas, 2004—, pres. ednl. tech., 2004—. Named to Hall of Fame, Women in Tech. Internat., 2005. Office: Tex Instruments Inc PO Box 660199 Dallas TX 75266-0199 Office Phone: 972-995-2011. Office Fax: 972-995-4360.*

LOVETT, RADFORD DOW, marine terminal real estate and investment company executive; b. Jacksonville, Fla., Sept. 6, 1933; s. William Radford And Agnes (Dow) L.; m. Katharine R. Howe, June 25, 1955 (dec. Jan. 1991); children: Katharine, William Radford, Philip, Lauren; m. Susan Wylie Rogers, June 16, 1995; children: Nick, Peter, Teddy Rogers. With Merrill Lynch, Pierce, Fenner & Smith Inc., NYC, 1958-78; mng. dir. Capital Markets Group, 1975-78; pres. Piggly Wiggly Corp., Jacksonville, Fla., 1978-82; chmn. bd. Commodores Pt. Terminal Corp., Jacksonville, 1978—. Chmn. Southcoast Capital Mgmt. Corp., Jacksonville, 1995—; bd. dirs. Wachovia Corp., Fla. Rock Industries Inc., Patriot Transp., Inc., Winn-Dixie Stores, Inc. Trustee Drew U., 1976-79, St. Vincent's Found., Jacksonville Zool. Soc. Lt. F.A. U.S. Army, 1955-57. Mem. Coastal Conservation Assn. Fla. (bd. dirs.). Episcopalian. Office: Ste 1600 One Independent Dr Jacksonville FL 32202-5009

LOVETT, RICHARD, talent agency executive; b. Wis. m. Brittany Lovett. Attended, U. Wis.-Madison. Began as mailroom employee and advanced from agent trainee to agent Creative Artists Agy., pres., 1995—. Tchr. Venice H.S., 1994—; co-founder Creative Artists Agency Found., 1996; bd. dirs. Artists Rights Found. Named one of 50 Most Powerful People in Hollywood, Premiere mag., 2004—06; recipient City of Angels Helen Bernstein award, David Niven award, 2000, Champion of Children award, Fulfillment Fund, 2002, Amb. for Humanity award, Shoah Found., 2004. Avocations: sports, yoga. Office: Creative Artists Agency 9830 Wilshire Blvd Beverly Hills CA 90212-1825

LOVETT, RICHARD A., writer, photographer; b. Dixon, Ill., 1953; s. Richard E. and Patricia H. Lovett. BS in Astrophysics, Mich. State U., E. Lansing, 1975; JD summa cum laude, U. Mich., Ann Arbor, 1978; PhD in Economics, U. Mich., 1981. Vis. prof. law U. Minn. Law Sch., Mpls., 1982—83; sr. econ. policy analyst Pope-Reid Assocs., St. Paul, 1983—85; instr. environ. studies & economics Calif. State U., Sacramento, 1986—88; vis. asst. prof. agrl. & resource economics Oreg. State U., Corvallis, 1988—89; freelance writer, photographer Portland, Oreg., 1989—. Author: (books) The Essential Touring Cyclist, 2nd edit., The Essential Cross-Country Skier; co-author: Alberto Salazar's Guide To Running, Alberto Salazar's Guide to Road Racing; contbr. more than 2, 700 mag. & newspaper articles, articles to profl. jours. Coach Team Red Lizard Running Club, Portland, Oreg., 2005—07; elder Westminster Presbyn. Ch., Portland, 1999—2007. Recipient Analytical Lab. award, 2002, 2003, 2005, 2006, Reader's Choice award, Analog Scis. Fact and Fiction Mag. Mem.: Sci. Fiction and Fantasy Writers Am., Nat. Assn. Sci. Writers. Home and Office: Richard A Lovett 10325 NE Hancock #42 Portland OR 97220 Home Fax: 503-257-6899. Business E-Mail: ralovett@aol.com.

LOVETT, ROBERT G., lawyer; b. York, Pa., Aug. 17, 1944; BA, U. Pitts., 1966; JD, Duquesne U., 1969. Bar: Pa. 1970. Ptnr. Lovett Bookman Harmon Marks, LLP, Pitts. Past chmn. real property, probate and trust law Penn. Bar Assn.; past mem. Estate Planning Coun. Pitts.; trustee Univ. Pitts., Bellefield Ednl. Trust, Pressley Ridge Schools; dir. U. Pitts. Med. Ctr. Contbr. articles to numerous legal jours. Office: Lovett Bookman Harmon Marks LLP Fifth Ave Pl Suite 2900 120 Fifth Ave Pittsburgh PA 15222

LOVETT, WAYNE J., air transportation executive, lawyer; b. 1950; m. Margaret A. Lovett, 1969; 1 child, David. BA in Mgmt., Northeastern U., 1972; JD, South Tex. Coll. Law, Houston, 1977. Bar: Tex. 1977. Trial lawyer pvt. practice; in-house counsel Centurion Petroleum Corp., 1982; corp. counsel, sec. Comm. Transmission Inc. (now Broadwing Corp.); presiding judge Lakeway Mcpl. Ct., Tex., 1993—97; gen. counsel Mercury Air Grp. Inc., LA, 1997—, corp. sec., 1999—, exec. v.p., 2001—. Avocations: history, reading. Office: Mercury Air Group Inc 5456 McConnell Ave Los Angeles CA 90066

LOVETT, WENDELL HARPER, architect, educator; b. Seattle, Apr. 2, 1922; s. Wallace Herman and Pearl (Harper) L.; m. Eileen (Whitson), Sept. 3, 1947; children: Corrie, Clare. Attended, Pasadena Jr. Coll., 1943-44; BArch, U. Wash., 1947; MArch, M.I.T., 1948. Arch., designer Naramore, Bain, Brady, and Johanson, Seattle, 1948; arch. assoc. Bassetti and Morse, Seattle, 1948-51; instr. architecture U. Wash., 1948-51; pvt. practice, arch. Seattle, 1951—; asst. prof. U. Wash., 1951-60, assoc. prof., 1960-65, prof., 1965-83, prof. emeritus, 1983—. Lectr. Technische Hochschule, Stuttgart, 1959-60. Prin. works include nuclear reactor bldg., U. Wash., 1960; Villa Simonyi Medina, Wash., 1989; patentee in field. Pres. Citizen's Planning Coun., Seattle, 1968-71; bd. dir. Seattle Baroque Orch., 1998-2002. Served in AUS, 1943-46. Recipient 2d prize Progressive Architecture U.S. Jr. C. of C., 1949; Internat. design award Decima Triennale di Milano, 1954; Arch. Record Homes awards, 1969, 72, 74; Interiors award, 1973; Sunset-AIA awards, 1959, 62, 69, 71; Fulbright grantee, 1959; AIA fellow, 1978 Mem. AIA (sec. Wash. chpt. 1953-54, bd. dirs. Found. Seattle chpt. 1991-92, Seattle chpt. medal 1993, pres. sr. coun. 1991-92, Plestcheeff Inst. bd. dir. 1992; bd.dir., Soc. of Architectural Historians, MDRC, 2002-05. Home and Office: 420 34th Ave Seattle WA 98122-6408 Home Phone: 206-329-5211.

LOVETT, WILLIAM LEE, surgeon; b. Natchez, Miss., June 12, 1941; s. Frank Lee and Lucille (Mullen) L.; m. Martha Lynn Gray, Aug. 15, 1964; children: Shelby Elizabeth Lovett Cuevas, Heather Lee Lovett Dunn, Michael Gray. BA, U. Miss., Oxford, 1963; MD, U. Miss., Jackson, 1967. Diplomate Am. Bd. Surgery, Am. Bd. Hand Surgery. Intern in surgery U. Va. Med. Ctr., Charlottesville, 1967-68, jr. asst. resident in surgery, 1968-69, sr. asst. resident in surgery, 1970-72, co-chief resident in surgery, 1972-73; fellow surg. rsch. dept. surgery U. Va., Charlottesville, 1969-70; physician S.W. Hand Surgeons Ltd., Phoenix, 1983—; vice chief of staff St. Joseph's Hosp., Phoenix, 1990-93, rep. orthopedic surgery com., 1990—, vice chair dept. orthopedics, 1991-92, chief of staff, 1996-98; physician S.W. Hand Surgeons Ltd., Phoenix; med. dir., med. staff adminstrn. St. Joseph's Hosp. and Med. Ctr., Phoenix, 2002—. Mem. sports medicine adv. team Ariz. State U., 1991-95; presenter in field. Contbr. articles to profl. jours. Mem. Sch. Bd. Xavier High Sch., 1983-87, v.p., 1985-86, pres., 1986-87; chief Webelos den Roosevelt coun. Boy Scouts Am., Phoenix, 1992-93, asst. scoutmaster, 1993—. Comdr. USN, 1974-76. Fellow ACS (pres. Ariz. chpt. 1983-84); mem. AMA, Am. Soc. for Surgery of the Hand, Ariz. Med. Assn. (del. 1985), Phoenix Surg. Soc. (pres. 1985-86), Muller Surg. Soc., Scottsdale Mounted Posse. Avocations: horseback riding, fly fishing, quail hunting, canoeing. Home: 6049 N 5th Pl Phoenix AZ 85012-1219 Home Phone: 602-266-0630; Office Phone: 602-406-4095. Personal E-mail: L5hand@cox.net.

LOVICK, NORMA MCGINNIS, social studies educator; b. Norfolk, Va., June 20, 1964; d. Harry Ralph McGinnis and Jenny Cavender Michel; children: Sarah Louise, Allen James. MEd, Cambridge Coll., Chesapeake, Va., 2004; BS in secondary edn., social studies, Old Dominion U., 1985. Cert. advanced grad. studies Cambridge Coll., 2005. Tchr. social sci. St. Matthews Sch., Virginia Beach, Va., 1985—86, Norfolk Pub. Sch., Va., 1987—. Master tchr. WHRO-Pub. TV, Norfolk, Va., 1998—2001. Eucharistic min. St. Pius X Ch., Norfolk, Va., 2003—; mem. PTA - St. Pius X Sch., Norfolk, Va., 1998—, Va. Living Mus., Newport News, Va., 1998—, Va. Marine Aquarium, Virginia Beach, Va., 1999—, PTA- Norview Mid. Sch., Norfolk, Va., 2001—; supporter Sta. WHRO-Pub. TV, Norfolk, Va., 1988—. Recipient Nat. Tchr. Tng. Inst. Tchr. of the Yr., Sta. WHRO-Pub. TV, 2000, Sch. Bell award, Norfolk Pub. Schs., 2001, 2004, 2005. Mem.: ASCD, Nat. Wildlife Fedn., Am. Fedn. Tchrs., Nat. Coun. for the Social Studies, Mil. Order of World Wars (life; historian 1989—90). Independent. Roman Catholic. Avocations: historical reenacting, garden design/landscaping, reading, genealogy. Home Phone: 757-587-0613; Office Phone: 757-852-4600. Personal E-mail: normalovick@aol.com. E-mail: nlovick@nps.k12.va.us.

LOVICK, NORMAN, accountant; b. Wilson, NC, July 10, 1942; s. Henry J. and Ella (Lovick) Webb; children: Norman Lovick Jr., Michael D. BS, Durham Coll., NC, 1963; AA, N.C. Cen. Coll., Durham, 1961; MS, Am.

U., 1964; Adv. Deg., USDA Grad. Sch., Washington, 1971. Acctg. analyst U.S. Dept. Treasury, Washington, 1967-76; fin. analyst Midland Nat. Corp., Wheaton, Md., 1976-78; tax cert. fin. planner Lovick's Fin. Assocs., Hyattsville, Md., 1978-88, chief exec. officer, pres., 1985—. Gen. agt. Bankers United, Cedar Rapids, Iowa, 1977-79; notary pub. With US Army, 1965—67. Mem. Nat. Assn. Accts., D.C. Life Underwriters Assn., Nat. Assn. Life Underwriters, Nat. Soc. Pub. Accts., Am. Inst. Profl. Bookkeepers, D.C. Soc. Ind. Accts., Am. Mgmt. Assn., Masons (32 deg., chaplain). Democrat. Pentecostal Ch. Avocations: fishing, boating, reading, dance. Office: Lovick's Fin Assoc Inc 3601 Hamilton St Ste 201 Hyattsville MD 20782-3946 Office Phone: 301-927-5630. Personal E-mail: nlovick@aol.com, nlovick@verizon.net.

LOVIN, KEITH HAROLD, retired academic administrator, philosopher, educator; b. Clayton, N.Mex., Apr. 1, 1943; s. Buddie and Wanda (Smith) L.; m. Marsha Kay Gunn, June 11, 1966; children: Camille Jenay, Lauren Kay BA, Baylor U., 1965; postgrad., Yale U., 1965-66; PhD, Rice U., 1971. Prof. philosophy Southwest Tex. State U., San Marcos, 1970-77, chmn. dept. philosophy, 1977-78, dean liberal arts, 1978-81; provost, v.p. acad. affairs Millersville U., Pa., 1981-86; provost, v.p. acad. and student affairs U. So. Colo., Pueblo, 1986-92; pres. Maryville U. St. Louis, 1992—2005, pres. emeritus, 2005—. Adv. bd. Southwest Studies in Philosophy, 1981—90. Contbr. articles to profl. jours. Bd. dirs. St. Louis Symphony Orch., 1995-2001, United Way Greater St. Louis, 1992-99, Boys Hope, Jr. Achievement Mississippi Valley, Inc., 1992-2001, Nat. Coun. Alcohol and Drug Abuse Adv. Bd., St. Louis Intercollegiate Athletic Conf., Higher Edn. Coun., St. Luke's Hosp., vice-chmn., 2001-03, chmn., 2003—; bd. dirs., pres. Ind. Colls. and Univs. Mo., 1999-2002, vice chair, 2002-03; mem. pres.'s adv. com. Mo. Coordinating for Bd. Higher Edn., 2002-05; trustee KETC Channel 9, 2003—05. Mem.: Chesterfield C. of C., Gov. Bus. Edn. Roundtable, St. Louis Club. Avocation: fly fishing. Home: 3006 Hawthorne Cove Georgetown TX 78628 Office Phone: 512-869-2053. Personal E-mail: klovin@yahoo.com.

LOVING, SUSAN BRIMER, lawyer, former state official; m. Dan Loving; children: Lindsay, Andrew, Kendall. BA with distinction, U. Okla., 1972, JD, 1979. Asst. atty. gen. Office of Atty. Gen., 1983-87, 1st asst. atty. gen., 1987-91; atty. gen. State of Okla., Oklahoma City, 1991-94; ptnr. Lester, Loving & Davies, Edmond, Okla., 1995—. Master Ruth Bader Ginsburg Inn of Ct., 1995-97. Mem. Pardon and Parole Bd., 1995—96, 2003—, vice-chmn., 1995, chmn., 2004; mem. Gov.'s Commn. on Tobacco and Youth, 1995—97; mem. med. steering com. Partnership for Drug Free Okla., Inst. for Child Advocacy, 1996—97; bd. dirs. Bd. for Freedom of Info., Okla. Inc., 1995—2001, Legal Aid Svcs. of Okla., 2002—03, Legal Aid of West Okla., 1995—2001. Recipient Nat. Red Ribbon Leadership award Nat. Fedn. Parents, Headliner award, By-liner award Okla. City and Tulsa Women in Comm., First Friend of Freedom award, Freedom of Info., Okla., Dir. award Okla. Dist. Attys. Assn. Mem.: Oklahoma County Bar Assn. (bd. dirs. 2001—), Okla. Bar Assn. (mem. ho. dels. 1996—97, 2001—04, past chmn. adminstrv. law sect., chmn. adminstrn. of justice com., chmn. profl. responsibility commn., Spotlight award 1997), Phi Beta Kappa. Office: Lester Loving & Davis PC 1701 S Kelly Ave Edmond OK 73013-3623 Office Phone: 405-844-9900. Business E-Mail: sloving@lldlaw.com.

LOVINGER, ANDREW JOSEPH, polymer scientist; b. Athens, Greece, May 15, 1948; s. Joseph and Berta (Gross) L.; m. Eleanor Saul, Feb. 29, 1976; children: Michael Joseph, Daniel Abraham. BSChemE and Applied Chemistry, Columbia U., 1970, MSChemE and Applied Chemistry, 1971, ScDChemE and Applied Chemistry, 1977. Mem. tech. staff Bell Labs. Lucent Tech. (formerly AT&T Bell Labs.), Murray Hill, NJ, 1977—85, disting. mem. tech. staff, 1985—2001, head polymer chemistry rsch. dept., 1985-94; dir. polymers program divsn. materials rsch. NSF, Arlington, Va., 1995—. Adj. assoc. prof. dept. chem. engring. Columbia U., N.Y.C., 1980-83; lectr. in field. Assoc. editor Macromolecules, 1988—; contbr. over 160 articles to profl. publs., chpts. to books. Recipient Frazer Price award U. Mass., 1993. Fellow AAAS, Am. Phys. Soc. (Dillon medal 1985, Polymer Physics prize 2003); mem. NAE, Am. Chem. Soc., Materials Rsch. Soc. Achievements include research on structures and properties of polymeric materials, morphology and phase transitions, ferroelectric polymers, high-performance polymers, silicon-based polymers, organic and polymeric thin-film transistors.

LOVINS, AMORY BLOCH, physicist, energy consultant; b. Washington, Nov. 13, 1947; s. Gerald Hershel and Miriam (Bloch) L.; m. L. Hunter Sheldon, 1979 (div. 1999). Student, Harvard U., 1966—67, student, 1964—65, Magdalen Coll., Oxford, Eng., 1967—69; MA, Oxford U., Oxford, 1971; DSc (hon.), Bates Coll., 1979; DSc (hon.), Williams Coll., 1981, Kalamazoo Coll., 1983; DSc (hon.), U. Maine, 1985; LLD (hon.), Ball State U., 1983; D of Environ. Sci. (hon.), Unity Coll., 1992; D of Pub. Serv. (hon.), Northfield Coll., 2001. Jr. research fellow Merton Coll., Oxford, England, 1969-71; Brit. rep., policy advisor Friends of the Earth, San Francisco, 1971-84; regent's lectr. U. Calif., Berkeley and Riverside, 1978, 81; CEO, CFO and dir. Rocky Mountain Inst., Old Snowmass, Colo., 1982—. Govt. and indsl. energy cons., 1971—; vis. prof. Dartmouth Coll., 1982; disting. vis. prof. U. Colo., 1982, U. St. Gallen, Switzerland, 1999; prin. tech. cons. E Source, 1989-99; prin. The Lovins Group, 1994-99; mem. Def. Sci. Bd. panel U.S. Sec. Def., 1999-2001; chmn., dir. Hypercar Inc., Basalt, Colo., 1998—. Author (also layout artist and co-photographer): Eryri, The Mountains of Longing, 1971; author: The Stockholm Conference: Only One Earth, 1972, Openpit Mining, 1973, World Energy Strategies: Facts, Issues, and Options, 1975, Soft Energy Paths: Toward a Durable Peace, 1977; co-author (with J. Price): Non-Nuclear Futures: The Case: The Case for an Ethical Energy Strategy, 1975; co-author: (with L.H. Lovins) Energy/War: Breaking the Nuclear Link, 1980; co-author: Brittle Power: Energy Strategy for National Security, 1982; co-author: (with L.H. Lovins, F. Krasue and W. Bach) Least-Cost Energy: Solving the CO2 Problem, 1982; co-author: (with L.H. Lovins, F. Krause and W. Bach), 1989; co-author: (with L.H. Lovins, sr. author and S. Zuckerman) Energy Unbound: A Fable for America's Future, 1986; co-author: (hardware reports) The State of the Art: Lighting, 1988, The State of the Art: Drivepower, 1989; co-author: The State of the Art: Appliances, 1990, The State of the Art: Water Heating, 1991, The State of the Art: Space Cooling and Air Handling, 1992; co-author: (with Paul Hawkena and L.H. Lovins) Natural Capitalism, 1999; co-photographer (book) At Home in the Wild: New England's White Mountains, 1978;, author numerous poems; contbr. articles to profl. jours., reports to tech. jours. Co-founder, treas. Windstar Land Conservancy, Colo., 1996-2000. Recipient Right Livelihood award Right Livelihood Found., 1983, Sprout award Internat. Studies Assn., 1977, Pub. Edn. award Nat. Energy Resources Orgn., 1978, Pub. Svc. award Nat. Assn. Environ. Edn., 1980; Mitchell prize Mitchell Energy Found., 1982, Delphi prize Onassis Found., 1989, Nissan prize Internat. Symposium Automotive Tech. and Automation, 1993, Award of Distinction, Rocky Mountain chpt. AIA, 1994, Heinz award 1997, Lindbergh award 1999, World Tech. award 1999, Happold medal U.K. Construction Industries Coun., 2000, Heroes for the Planet award Time, 2000; MacArthur fellow John D. and Catherine T. MacArthur Found., Chgo., 1993. Fellow: AAAS, Lindisfarne Assn., World Acad. Art and Sci.; mem.: Internat. Orgn. Found., World Bus. Acad., Internat. Assn. Energy Econs., Am. Solar Energy Soc., Soc. Automotive Engring., Am. Phys. Soc., Fedn. Am. Scientists. Achievements include patents in field. *Personal philosophy: Devotion to efficient and sustainable use of resources as a path to global security, with emphasis on how advanced technologies, market economics, and Jeffersonian politics can provide new solutions to old problems, or better still, avoid them altogether.*

LOVINS, L. HUNTER, public policy institute executive, consultant, educator; b. Middlebury, Vt., Feb. 26, 1950; d. Paul Millard and Farley (Hunter) Sheldon; m. Amory Bloch Lovins, Sept. 6, 1979 (div. 1999). BA in Sociology, Pitzer Coll., 1972, BA in Polit. Sci., 1972; JD, Loyola U., LA, 1975; LHD, U. Maine, 1982. Bar: Calif. 1975. Asst. dir. Calif. Conservation Project, LA, 1973-79; policy advisor Friends of the Earth, 1979—81; co-CEO, co-founder Rocky Mountain Inst., Snowmass, Colo., 1982—2002; co-chair Natural Capitalism Group, Snowmass, 2000—; pres. Natural Capitalism Solutions, 2004—. Vis. prof. U. Colo., Boulder, 1982; Henry R. Luce vis. prof. Dartmouth Coll., Hanover, N.H., 1982; prof. sustainable mgmt. Presidio World Coll., 2003—; pres. Nighthawk Horse Co., 1993; bd. dirs. EcoStructure Fin. Co-author: Brittle Power, 1982, Energy Unbound, 1986, Least-Cost Energy Solving the CO2 Problem, 2d edit., 1989, Factor Four, 1997, Green Development, 1998, Natural Capitalism, 1999, The Natural Advantage of Nations, 2005. Bd. dirs. Basalt and Rural Fire Protection Dist., 1987-2000, Nighthawk Horse Co., Rocky Mountain Inst., 1982-2002, Windstar Land Conservancy, 1996-2002, Internat. Ctr. Sustainable Devel., 2004-; vol. EMT and firefighter, Engrs. Without Borders, 2003, bd. dirs., 2003-; advisor Energy Ministry Afghanistan, 2004—. Recipient Mitchell prize Woodlands Inst., 1982, Right Livelihood Found. award, 1983, Best of the New Generation award Esquire Mag., 1984, Nissan prize, 1995, Lindbergh award, 1999, Bd. Govs.' award Loyola Law Sch., 2000, LOHAS award for svc. to bus., 2001, Shingo Prize for Excellence in Mfg. Rsch., 2001, Leadership in Bus. award, 2001; named Hero of Planet, Time Mag., 2000. Mem. Calif. Bar Assn., Am. Quarter Horse Assn., Am. Polocrosse Assn. Avocations: rodeo, fire rescue, polocrosse. Office: Natural Capitalism Solutions PO Box 3125 Eldorado Springs CO 80025 Office Phone: 303-554-6550.

LOVITCH, JOAN, science educator, coach; b. NYC, Oct. 14, 1950; d. Isidore and Bella Weider; m. Jeffrey D. Lovitch, Mar. 25, 1972; children: Scott Benjamin, Gina Jennifer. BA, MA, CCNY, NYC. Cert. tchr. sci. N.Y. and N.J., 1973. Tchr. sci. No. Valley Regional H.S., Old Tappan, NJ, 1996—; coach US Academic Decathlon, 1993—. Regional dir. Academic Decathlon NJ, 2005—. Recipient Decade of Championships, Academic Decathlon, 2004; grantee, Bergen County Sch. Boards Assn., 1999, No. Valley Edn. Found., 1999. Mem.: Phi Beta Kappa (life). Achievements include 12 consecutive Academic Decathlon state championships. Home: 27 Amelia Dr Old Tappan NJ 07675 Office: Northern Valley Regional HS Central Ave Old Tappan NJ 07675 Home Phone: 201-666-4915; Office Phone: 201-666-7655. Business E-Mail: lovitch@nvnet.org.

LOW, ANDREW M., lawyer; b. NYC, Jan. 1, 1952; s. Martin Laurent and Alice Elizabeth (Bernstein) L.; m. Margaret Mary Stroock, Mar. 31, 1979; children: Roger, Ann. BA, Swarthmore Coll., 1973; JD, Cornell U., 1976. Bar: Colo. 1981, U.S. Dist. Ct. Colo. 1981, U.S. Ct. Appeals (10th cir.) 1986. Assoc. Rogers & Wells, NYC, 1977-81, Davis Graham & Stubbs LLP, Denver, 1981-83, ptnr., 1984—. Editor: Colorado Appellate Handbook, 1984, 94. Pres. Colo. Freedom of Info. Coun., Denver, 1990-92, Colo. Bar Press Com., 1989, appellate practice subcom. Colo. Bar Assn. Litig. Coun., 1994—; bd. dirs. CLE in Colo., Inc., 1993-96; trustee 9 Health Fair, Denver, 1988—; mem. Colo. Supreme Ct. Joint Com. on Appellate Rules, 1993—. Avocations: skiing, golf, fly fishing. Office: Davis Graham & Stubbs LLP Ste 500 1550 17th St Denver CO 80202 E-mail: andrew.low@dgslaw.com.

LOW, ANTHONY, language educator; b. San Francisco, May 31, 1935; s. Emerson and Clio (Caroli) L.; m. Pauline Iselin Mills, Dec. 28, 1961; children: Louise, Christopher, Georgianna, Elizabeth, Peter, Catherine, Nicholas, Alexandra, Michael, Frances, Jessica, Edward, Charlotte. AB, Harvard U., 1957, MA, 1959, PhD, 1965. Mem. faculty Seattle U., 1965—68, NYU, NYC, 1968—2006, prof. English lit., 1978—2006, chmn. dept. English, 1989—95, prof. emeritus, 2006—. Vis. scholar Jesus Coll., Cambridge, Eng., 1974-75. Author: Augustine Baker, 1970, The Blaze of Noon, 1974, Love's Architecture, 1978, The Georgic Revolution, 1985, The Reinvention of Love, 1993, Aspects of Subjectivity, 2003; editor: Urbane Milton, 1984. Pres. Conf. on Christianity and Lit., 1996-99. Pew Evangelical fellow, 1995; Milton scholar, 1996. Mem. Milton Soc., Donne Soc., MLA, Renaissance Soc., Phi Beta Kappa. Home: 748 Kent Hill Rd East Calais VT 05650 E-mail: low@compuserve.com.

LOW, ARNOLD KINMAN, systems executive; b. San Francisco, Feb. 22, 1942; s. Howard Y. and Patricia M. (Lee) L.; m. Junko Nerio; 1 child, Sara. AB, Dartmouth Coll., 1963; MBA, San Francisco State U., 1976; Mng. Info. Svcs. Resource, Harvard Bus. Sch., 1984. Sys. assoc. So. Pacific Co., San Francisco, 1965-67; sys. analyst Applied Data Sys. Inc., San Francisco, 1967-68; mgr. data processing I. Magnin & Co., San Francisco, 1968-77; sr. v.p. 1st Nationwide Bank, San Francisco, 1977-86; pres. Low & Assocs., San Francisco, 1986—. Pres. Data Processing Mgmt. Assn., 1973-74; mem. internat. bd. advisors U.S. China Ednl. Inst., San Francisco, 1989-2002. Mem. adv. bd. San Francisco C.C. Dist., 1974-78; pres. Urban Crossroads Sch., San Francisco, 1975-89; pres. Big Bros.-Big Sisters, San Francisco, 1989-90; foreman San Francisco Civil Grand Jury, 1993-94; trustee Ft. Mason Found., San Francisco, 1996-99. Mem. Olympic Club. Office: 2915 Baker St San Francisco CA 94123-3209

LOW, BOON CHYE, physicist; b. Singapore, Feb. 13, 1946; came to U.S., 1968; s. Kuei Huat and Ah Tow (Tee) Lau; m. Daphne Nai-Ling Yip, Mar. 31, 1971; 1 child, Yi-Kai. BSc, U. London, Eng., 1968; PhD, U. Chgo., 1972. Scientist High Altitude Observatory Nat. Ctr. for Atmospheric Rsch., Boulder, Colo., 1981-87, sect. head, 1987—90, 1997—2004, acting dir., 1989-90, sr. scientist, 1987—. Mem. mission operation working group for solar physics NASA, 1992-94; vis. sr. scientist Princeton Plasma Physics Lab., 1998-99; mem. Living With a Star steering com. for targeted rsch. and tech. NASA, 2004; mem. Theoretical Inst. for Advanced Rsch. in Astrophysics, Taiwan, 2004—; mem. rev. panel Nat. Rsch. Coun. Associateship Program, 2005—. Mem. editl. bd. Solar Physics, 1991—. Named Fellow Japan Soc. for Promotion of Sci., U. Tokyo, 1978, Sr. Rsch. Assoc., NASA Marshall Space Flight Ctr., 1980. Mem. Am. Physical Soc., Am. Astron. Soc., Am. Geophysical Union. Office: Nat Ctr for Atmosph Rsch PO Box 3000 Boulder CO 80307-3000 Home Phone: 303-554-0049; Office Phone: 303-497-1553. Business E-Mail: low@hao.ucar.edu.

LOW, EUGENE JENSEN, pathologist; b. Ames, Iowa, Sept. 25, 1940; s. Jessop Budge Low and June Jensen; m. Patricia Louise Pickering, Sept. 14, 1966; children: Jennifer, Leslie, Deborah, Rebecca, Jeffrey, Rachel. BS, Utah State U., Logan, 1964; MD, U. Utah, Salt Lake City, 1968. Diplomate Am. Bd. Pathology, 1972. Resident South Bend Med. Found., Ind., 1968—72; pathologist Martin Army US Hosp., Ft. Benning, Ga., 1972—74, McKay-Dee Hosp., Ogden, Utah, 1974—2003; ret. Dir. pathology svc. US Army Martin Army Hosp., Ft. Benning, 1972—74; dir. pathology lab. McKay-Dee Hosp., Ogden, 1985, 88. Scout master Boy Scouts Am., Ogden, 1999—2003. Maj. US Army, 1972—74, Ga. Mem.: Am. Med. Assn., Am. Soc. Clin. Pathologist, Am. Coll. Pathologist. Ch. Jesus Christ Of Latter Dy Saints. Avocations: hiking, reading, golf, skiing.

LOW, FREDERICK EMERSON, language educator; b. Oct. 25, 1943; AA, Am. Coll., Paris, France, 1967; BA, Queens Coll., 1969, MLS, 1976; MA, CUNY, 1972. Prof. La Guardia Comm. Coll., CUNY, Long Island City, N.Y., 1978-95; dir. Asia World Learning Ctr., Inc., Flushing, NY, 1996—2001, Asian-Am. Ctr. for Edn. of N.Y., Inc., Flushing, 1998—2001; pvt. tchr., rschr., 2001—. Home: 15 Croyden St New Hyde Park NY 11040 Personal E-mail: fredelow@yahoo.com.

LOW, HARRY WILLIAM, judge; b. Oakdale, Calif., Mar. 12, 1931; m. May Ling, Aug. 24, 1952; children: Larry, Kathy, Allan. AA, Modesto Jr. Coll., 1950; AB Polit. Sci. with honors, U. Calif., Berkeley, 1952, JD, 1955. Bar: Calif. 1955, U.S. Ct. Appeals (9th cir.) 1955. Commr. Worker's Compensation Commn., 1966; teaching assoc. Boalt Hall, 1955-56; dep. atty. gen. Calif. Dept. Justice, 1956-66; judge Mcpl. Ct., San Francisco, 1966-74, presiding judge, 1972-73; judge Superior Ct., San Francisco, 1974-82; presiding justice Calif. Ct. Appeals, 1st dist., 1982-92; commr. Calif. Ins. Dept., San Francisco, 2000—03; arbitrator/mediator JAMS, 2003—. Pres. San Francisco Police Commn., 1992-96; pres. San Francisco Human Rights Commn., 1999-2000, 2003; mem. Jud. Arbitration and Mediation Svcs., 1992-2000, 2003-, Commn. on Future of Cts., 1991-94; Calif. Ins. Commr., 2000-03, BAJI-Jury Instrn. Com. Contbr. articles to profl. jours. Chmn. bd. Chinese-Am. Internat. Sch., 1979-99; bd. visitors U.S. Mil. Acad., 1980-83; bd. dirs. Friends of Recreation and Parks, Salesian Boys Club, World Affairs Coun., 1979-85, NCCJ, San Francisco chpt. St. Vincent's Boys Home, Coro Found., 1970-76, San Francisco Zool. Trust, 1987, Union Bank Calif., 1993-2000, Calif. Health Plan Found., 2003—; pres. San Francisco City Coll. Found., 1977-87, Inst. Chinese Western History U. San Francisco, 1987-89. Mem. ABA (chmn. appellate judges conf. 1990-91, commr. on minorities, Spirit of Excellence award, 2002), San Francisco Bar Assn., Chinese Am. Citizens Alliance (pres. San Francisco chpt. 1976-77, nat. pres. 1989-93), Calif. Judges Assn. (pres. 1978-79), Calif. Jud. Coun., State Bar Calif. (rsch. editor publs. 1958-76, pub. affairs com. 1987-90, exec. bd. 1992-94), Calif. Conf. Judges (editor jour. cts. commentary 1973-76), Calif. Judges Assn. (exec. bd. 1976-79), Asian Bus. League (dir. 1986-93), Nat. Ctr. State Cts. (bd. dirs. 1986-91), San Francisco Bench Bar Media Commn. (chmn. bd. dirs. 1987-92), Boalt Hall Alumni Assn. (Distinguished Svc. award 1992, Judge Lowell Jensen award 2000), Phi Alpha Delta. Office Phone: 415-982-5267. *Try to enjoy whatever task you are doing and enjoy the good company of those with whom you associate. Be an active part of the community and try to improve it. Keep busy and try to understand and respect others.*

LOW, JAMES A., physician; b. Toronto, Ont., Can., Sept. 22, 1925; s. Donald M. and Doris V. (Van Duzer) L.; m. Margery Una, Oct. 5, 1952; children: Donald E., Margeret P., Norman I. MD, U. Toronto, 1949. Intern Toronto Gen. Hosp., 1949-50; resident in ob-gyn U. Toronto, 1950-54; fellow ob/gyn Duke U., 1955; clin. instr. dept ob-gyn U. Toronto, 1955-65; prof. and chmn. dept. ob-gyn Queens U., Kingston, Ont., Canada, 1965-85, prof., 1985—2003. Exéc. dir. Mus. Health Care at Kingston, 1995—. Mem. editl. bd. Ob-Gyn., 1986-89, Am. Jour. Ob-Gyn., 1995-99. Served with Can. Navy, 1943-45. Recipient Disting. Svc. award, Queen's U., 2007. Fellow: Royal Coll. Obstetricians and Gynecologists, Royal Coll. Physicians and Surgeons Can. (chmn. splty. com. 1976—82, chmn. manpower com. 1984—92); mem.: Am. Acad. Cerebral Palsy, Can. Soc. Clin. Investigation, Soc. Obstetricians and Gynecologists Can., Soc. Gynecol. Investigation, Am. Gynecol. and Obstet. Soc., Assn. Profs. Ob-Gyn. Can. (sec.-treas. 1972—80, pres. 1983—84). Home: 185 Fairway Hills Kingston ON Canada K7M 2B5 Office: Queens U Dept Ob Gyn Kingston ON Canada K7L 3N6 Home Phone: 613-548-8381; Office Phone: 613-549-6666 ext 4094. Business E-Mail: lowj@kgh.kari.net.

LOW, JAMES WILLIAM, lawyer; b. Ann Arbor, Mich., Dec. 3, 1974; s. James Thomas and Louise Anderson Low. BS, Mich. State U., East Lansing, 1997; JD, Mich. State U. Coll. Law, East Lansing, 0201. Bar: Mich. 2001, US Dist. Ct., (we. dist.), Mich. 2002, US Dist. Ct., (ea. dist.), Mich. 2004, US Dist. Ct. (ea. dist.), Wis. 2006, US Ct. Appeals (6th cir.) 2004. Atty. Collins, Einhorn, Farrell & Ulanoff, PC, Southfield, Mich., 2004—. Steering com., web page chair, profl. liability com. Def. Rsch. Inst., Chgo., 2006—. Mem.: ABA, State Bar Mich (exec. coun. 2006—), Oakland County Bar Assn. (bd. dirs. 2005—, Lawyer of Month 2005), Detroit Met. Bar Assn., Mich. Def. Trial Counsel, Def. Rsch. Inst., Assn. Def. Trial Counsel (edn. chair), Am. Inns of Ct. (assoc.), Mensa, Sigma Pi (pres. 1995—96). Avocations: tennis, golf, hockey. Office: Collins Einhorn Farrell and Ulanoff PC 4000 Town Ctr Ste 909 Southfield MI 48075 Home Phone: 734-276-1591; Office Phone: 248-355-4141.

LOW, JOHN WAYLAND, lawyer; b. Denver, Aug. 7, 1923; s. Oscar Wayland and Rachel E. (Stander) L.; m. Merry C. Mullan, July 8, 1979; children: Lucinda A., Jan W. BA, Nebr. Wesleyan U., 1947; JD cum laude, U. Denver, 1951. Bar: Colo. 1951, U.S. Dist. Ct. (Colo. dist.) 1951, U.S. Ct. Appeals (10th cir.), U.S. Supreme Ct. 1960. Ptnr. Sherman & Howard LLC, Denver, 1951-93, counsel, 1993—. Trustee U. Denver, 1987—; chmn. bd. Denver Symphony Assn., 1989-90; vice chmn. Colo. Symphony Assn., 1990-96; pres. Colo. Symphony Found., 1995—, Mesa Verde Found., 1997-2003; chmn. Colo. Alliance of Bus., Denver, 1983-87; pres. First Plymouth Found, 1982—; dir. Public Edn. and Bus. Coalition, 1995—; dir. Inst. Internat. Edn., 2005—. 1st lt. U.S. Army, 1942-46, CBI. Recipient Learned Hand award Am. Jewish Com., 1989, Outstanding Law Alumni award U. Denver, 1994, Evans Disting. Svc. award U. Denver, 2001. Mem. ABA, Colo. Bar Assn., Denver Bar Assn., University Club of Denver, Garden of Gods Club (Colorado Springs). Republican. Mem. United Ch. of Christ. Office: Sherman & Howard 633 17th St Ste 3000 Denver CO 80202-3665 Home Phone: 303-777-2541; Office Phone: 303-299-8148. Business E-Mail: jlow@sah.com.

LOW, MARY LOUISE (MOLLY), documentary photographer; b. Quakertown, Pa., Jan. 3, 1926; d. James Harry and Dorothy Collyer (Krewson) Thomas; m. Antoine Francois Gagné, Nov. 3, 1945 (div.); children: James L., David W., Stephen J., Jeannie Wolff-Gagné; m. Paul Low, July 11, 1969 (dec. July 1991). Student, Oberlin Conservatory of Music, 1943-44, Oberlin Coll., 1944; cert., Katharine Gibbs Sec. Sch., 1945; degree in psychiat. rehab. work, Einstein Coll. Medicine, 1968-70. Sec. Dept. Store, NYC, 1945; sec., treas. Gagné Assocs., Consulting Engrs., Binghamton, NY, 1951-66; psychiat. rsch. asst. Jacobi Hosp., Bronx, 1969-70; asst. to head of sch. Brearley Sch., NYC, 1976-78; pvt. practice San Diego, 1984—. Contbr. articles to profl. jours. Pres., bd. trustees Unitarian-Universalist Ch., 2005—. Recipient Dir.'s award for excellence Area Agy. on Aging, San Diego, 1993, Citizen Recognition award County of San Diego, Calif., 1993. Avocations: singing, documentary photography, writing, travel. Office: Molly Low Photography 5576 Caminito Herminia La Jolla CA 92037-7222 Personal E-mail: molly@mollylow.com.

LOW, MERRY COOK, civic worker; b. Uniontown, Pa., Sept. 3, 1925; d. Howard Vance and Eleanora (Lynch) Mullan; m. William R. Cook, 1947 (div. 1979); m. John Wayland Low, July 8, 1979; children: Karen, Cindy, Bob, Jan. Diploma in nursing, Allegheny Gen. Hosp., Pitts., 1946; BS summa cum laude, Colo. Women's Coll., 1976. RN Colo. Dir. patient edn. Med. Care and Rsch. Found., Denver, 1976-78. Contbr. chpt. to Pattern for Distribution of Patient Education, 1981. DuArt bd. dirs. U. Denver, 1998—2004; docent Denver Art Mus., 1979—99, vol. exec. bd., 1988—94, nat. docent symposium com., 1991, chair collectors' choice benefits, 1988, pres. vols., 1988—90; co-chair art auction Colo. Alliance Bus., 1992—93, com., 1994—97; founding chair Rocky Mountain Conservation Ctr., 1989; chair Living Libr. Fund, 1994—; trustee ch. coun., chair invitational art show 1st Plymouth Congl. Ch., Englewood, Colo., 1981—84; bd. dirs. women's libr. assn. U. Denver, 1982—, vice chmn., 1985—86, chair, 1986—87, co-chair spl. event, 1992; bd. dirs. Humanities Inst., 1993—, pres., 1999; bd. dirs. Rocky Mountain Conservation Ctr., 1999—2000, co-chair Founder's Day com., 1994—, awards com., 1994—, chair Culturefest, 1995—96; bd. dirs. Lamont Sch. Music Assocs., 1990—96. Recipient Disting. Svc. award U. Denver Coll. Law, 1988, King Soopers Vol. of Week award, 1989, Citizen of Arts award Fine Arts Found., 1993, Outstanding Vol. Colo. Alliance of Bus., 1994, U. Denver Cmty. Svc. award, 1996. Mem. Am. Assn. Mus. (vol. meeting coord. 1990-91), P.E.O.

(pres. Colo. chpt. DX 1982-84), U. Denver Alumni Assn. (bd. dirs. 1994-2000, sec. 1996-98), Welcome to Colo. (sec. 2004-06), Women for Profit Investment Club (sec. 1999-2002, co-presiding ptnr. 2003-05). Republican. Congregationalist. Home: 2552 E Alameda Ave Apt 11 Denver CO 80209-3324 Personal E-mail: merrylow@aol.com.

LOW, MORTON DAVID, retired neuroscientist, healthcare educator; b. Lethbridge, Alta., Can., Mar. 25, 1935; s. Solon Earl and Alice Fern (Litchfield) L.; m. Cecilia Margaret Comba, Aug. 22, 1959 (div. 1983); children— Cecilia Alice, Sarah Elizabeth, Peter Jon Eric; m. Barbara Joan McLeod, Aug. 25, 1984; 1 child, Kelsey Alexandra MD, C.M., Queen's U., 1960, M.Sc. in Medicine, 1962; PhD with honors, Baylor U., 1966. From instr. to asst. prof. Baylor Coll. Medicine, Houston, 1965-68; assoc. prof. medicine U. B.C., Vancouver, Can., 1968-78, prof. medicine, 1978-89, clin. assoc. dean, 1974-76, assoc. dean rsch. and grad. studies, 1977-78, coord. health scis., 1985-89, creator Health Policy Rsch. Unit, 1987; Alkek-Williams Disting. Prof. and pres. U. Tex. Health Sci. Ctr., Houston, 1989-2000, disting. mem. faculty Grad. Sch. Biomed. Scis., 1989—2004, dir. Health Policy Inst., 1990—2000; Rockwell chair in soc. and health, dir. Ctr. Soc./Population Health U. Tex., Houston, 2000—04; prof. neurology U. Tex. Med. Sch., Houston, 1989—2001; prof. health policy and mgmt. Sch. Pub. Health U. Tex., 1989—2004, prof. emeritus, 2005—. Cons. in neurology U. Hosp. Shaughnessy site, Vancouver, 1971—89, U. B.C. site, Vancouver, 1970—89; dir. dept. diagnostic neurophysiology Vancouver Gen. Hosp., 1986—87; cons. in EEG, 1987—89; exec. dir. Rsch. Inst., 1981—86; med. sci. adv. com. USIA, 1991—93; adj. prof. Health Informatics Sch. Allied Health Scis.; adj. prof. psychology Simon Fraser U., 2004—; adj. prof. health scis. U. Calgary, 2005—; mem. Premier's Adv. Coun. on Health, Alta., Canada, 2000—02; strategic adv. Calgary Regional Health Auth., 2002—; spl. advisor to the pres. on pub. health program devel. U. Calgary, 2005—07. Mem. editorial bd. numerous jours.; contbr. articles to profl. jours Bd. dirs. Tex. Inst. for Rehab. and Rsch. Found., Greater Houston Ptnrship., 1994-2000, Episcopal Health Charities Found., 1997-2004, Houston Ind. Sch. Dist. Found., 2002-04; governing bd. Houston Mus. Natural Sci., 1991-97; trustee Kinkaid Sch., Houston, 1991-2004, Meml.-Herman Hosp. Sys., 1997-2000 Med. Rsch. Coun. Can. grantee, 1968-80; recipient Tree of Life award Jewish Nat. Fund, 1995, Caring Spirit award Inst. Religion, 1995 Fellow Am. EEG Soc., Royal Coll. Physicians (Can.), Royal Soc. Medicine (London); mem. AMA, Tex. Med. Assn. (coun. on med. edn. 1990-2000), Tex. Found. Soc. & Health (founding chmn. 1999), Can. Soc. Clin. Neurophysiology, Internat. Fedn. Socs. for EEG and Clin. Neurophysiology (rules com. 1977-81, sec. 1981-85), Assn. Acad. Health Ctrs. (task force on access to care and orgn. health svcs. 1988-95, chmn. 1992, task force on instnl. values 1989-95), Harris County Med. Soc., Am. Coun. Edn., Forum Club of Houston Avocations: sailing, photography, soccer, skiing, flying. Office Phone: 205-468-1825. E-mail: mdlow@shaw.ca.

LOW, PHILIP STEVEN, research scientist, entrepreneur; b. Vienna, Aug. 16, 1979; arrived in U.S., 1996; s. Steven Low and Sonja Evelyn Toth. BSc. in Math., U. Chgo., 2000; PhD in Computational Neurobiology, U. Calif., San Diego, 2007. Rschr. in oncology Harvard Med. Sch., Boston, 1999; rschr. in neurobiology U. of Chgo., 2000—01; rschr. in computational neurobiology Salk Inst., La Jolla, Calif., 2001—; founder, CEO Neurovigil, Inc., La Jolla, 2007—. Spl. projects advisor Sci. Network, La Jolla, 2003—; founder, CEO NeuroVigil, Inc., 2007—. Fellow, NSF, 2001; Merck fellowship, Merck Co., 2001, Sloan-Swartz fellowship, Alfred P. Sloan Swartz Founds., 2002—06, Kavli fellowship, Kavli Inst. for Brain and Mind, 2007—. Mem.: AAAS, Soc. for Neurosci., Math. Assn. of Am. Achievements include discovery of anti-fibrotic drug halofuginone inhibits proliferation and collagen production by leiomyoma smooth muscle cells; Mammalian-like Features of Sleep Structure in a Songbird; Fine Structure of Human Sleep; patents pending for Sleep Parametric EEG Automated Recognition System (SPEARS). Office: Salk Inst 10010 N Torrey Pines Rd La Jolla CA 92037 Home Phone: 858-531-4490; Office Phone: 858-453-4100. Office Fax: 858-587-0417. E-mail: philip@salk.edu.

LOW, RANDALL, internist, cardiologist; b. San Francisco, June 24, 1949; s. Huet Hee and Betty Tai (Quan) L.; m. Dorothy Fung, May 4, 1975; children: Audrey, Madeleine, Jennifer. AA, City Coll., San Francisco, 1969; BA, U. Calif., Berkeley, 1971; MD, U. Calif., Davis, 1975. Diplomate Am. Bd. Internal Medicine, Nat. Bd. Med. Examiners, Am. Bd. Cardiovascular Diseases. Intern Hosp. of Good Samaritan, LA, 1975-76, resident, 1976-77, chief med. resident, 1977-78, fellow in cardiology, 1979-81; mem. staff St. Francis Meml. Hosp., San Francisco, 1981—, chmn. dept. cardiology, 1995—; pvt. practice internal medicine and cardiology San Francisco, 1981—; mem. staff Chinese Hosp., San Francisco, 1981—, chief of medicine, 1991-92; asst. clin. prof. U. Calif., San Francisco, 1994-2000. Courtesy staff St. Mary's Hosp., San Francisco, 1981—, Calif. Pacific Med. Ctr., San Francisco, 1990—; cardiology cons. Laguna Honda Hosp., San Francisco, 1981—. Home health quality assurance com. Self Help for Elderly, San Francisco, 1991—; bd. trustees San Francisco Health Authority, 2000—; bd. dirs. Youth Advocates, San Francisco, 1992-99. Recipient Hearst Pub. Svc. award U. Calif.-Berkeley, 1970, Homecare Recognition award Self Help for Elderly, 1993. Mem, ACP, Am. Soc. Internal Medicine, Am. Coll. Cardiology, Am. Heart Assn. (bd. govs. 1983-90), Calif. Acad. Medicine, Calif. Med. Soc., San Francisco Med. Soc. (bd. dirs. 1999-2005), Assn. Chinese Cmty. Physicians (sec.-treas. 1986-89), Chinese Cmty. Health Care Assn. (pres. 1991-96, 99-2002), Fedn. Chinese Am. and Canadia Med. Soc. (pres. 2005-06, chmn. bd.). Office: 909 Hyde St Ste 501 San Francisco CA 94109-4853

LOWDEN, CHRISTINE C., school system administrator; d. Ralph and Christine Scheffert; m. Dean Lowden, July 13, 1986; children: Michael, Alex. B, Boston Coll., Chestnut Hill, 1982—86; M, Pace U., White Plains, NY, 1986—90; PhD, Seton Hall U., S.Orange, NJ, 2000—03. Cert. sch. dist. adminstr. NY, 1999. Dir. tech., asst. supt. Fallsburg Ctrl. Sch. Dist., NY, 1999—2004; asst. supt. curriculum & instrn. Arlington Ctrl. Sch. Dist., Poughkeepsie, NY, 2004—. Contbr. articles to profl. jours. Mem.: ASCD (assoc.), AASA, NSDC (nat. presenter), NY Staff Devel. Coun. (assoc.; state bd. mem. 2005—06), Kappa Delta Pi (assoc.). Home: 27 Wintergreen Pl Hopewell Junction NY 12533 Office: Arlington Ctrl Sch Dist 696 Dutchess Turnpike Poughkeepsie NY 12603 Personal E-mail: lowdenchristine@netscape.net.

LOWDEN, JOHN L., retired manufacturing executive; b. Yakima, Wash., Oct. 29, 1921; s. Roy Ruben and Hildegarde Annie (Grommesch) L.; m. Janet Katherine Langan, Jan. 21, 1961; children: Susan Elizabeth, Jonathan Roy, Andrew Matthias. BA, U. Nev., 1949. Account supr. Campbell-Ewald Advt., 1951-57, Erwin, Wasey Advt., 1957-59; advt. dir. Gen. Dynamics Corp., 1959-61; account supr. Foote, Cone & Belding, 1961-63; with ITT Corp., 1963-84, v.p. corp. rels. and advt., 1977-84. Author: Silent Wings at War, 1992. Served with USAAF, 1941-45. Decorated Air medal with oak leaf cluster, Presdl. Unit Citation, Bronze Arrowhead of initial assault troops, 4th degree Knight Order of William Netherlands. Catholic.

LOWDER, ROBERT E., bank executive; BS, Auburn Univ., 1966. Chmn., CEO Colonial Banc Group, Inc., Montgomery, Ala., 1990—. Trustee Auburn Univ. Office: Colonial Banc Group Inc PO Box 1108 Montgomery AL 36101-1108*

LOWDERMILK, JOHN LLOYD, special education educator, special education services professional; b. Denton, Tex., Oct. 18, 1969; s. John Lloyd and Deirdre Lowdermilk; m. Carey Ann McKee. PhD in Emotional and Behavioral Disorders, U. N. Tex., Denton, 2004. Postdoctoral rschr. U. Ky., Lexington, 2004—06; asst. prof. spl. edn. U. Tex. Pan Am., Edinburg, 2006—. Assistive tech. cons. L-Group Consulting, McAllen, Tex., 2004—. Mem.: Coun. Exceptional Children (profl. devel. chair tech. and media divsn. 2007). Democrat. Episcopal. Avocations: travel, comic book collecting. Home: 2019 N 44th Ln Mcallen TX 78501 Office: U Tex Pan America 1201 W University Dr Edinburg TX 78541 Home Phone: 859-536-9857; Office Phone: 956-381-3466. Office Fax: 956-381-2395. Personal E-mail: jlowdermilk@utpa.edu.

LOWE, ALAN CONNER, library director; b. Paris, Ky., Feb. 21, 1964; s. Frances Delia Otte and Roy Allen Lowe, Harry Clifford Otte (Stepfather); m. Kathy Ecton, June 25, 1988; 1 child, Carolyn Marie. BA in History, U. Ky., 1986, MA in History, 1988. Archivist Ronald Reagan Presdl. Libr., Simi Valley, Calif., 1989—92; mgmt. and program analyst Office of Presdl. Libraries, Washington, 1992—2003; acting dir. Roosevelt Presdl. Libr., Hyde Park, NY, 1998—99; exec. dir. Howard Baker Ctr. for Pub. Policy Hoskins Libr., Knoxville, Tenn. Majority leader's appointee Adv. Com. on the Records of Congress, Washington, 2003—; adv. bd. mem. Inst. for Rural Journalism and Cmty. Issues, Lexington, Ky., 2005—, 91.9 Inc., Knoxville, Tenn. Mem. leadership Knoxville Class 2007. Recipient Ky. Col., The Gov. of Ky., 1989; scholar Internat. Grad. Summer Sch. at Oxford U., The English Speaking Union, 1986. Mem.: Blount Mansion Assn. (bd. dirs. 2006—), Rotary Club of Knoxville. Conservative. Presbyterian. Avocations: reading, music, writing. Home: 943 Andover View Ln Knoxville TN 37922 Office: Howard Baker Ctr for Pub Policy 217 Hoskins Library Knoxville TN 37996 Home Phone: 865-671-2585; Office Phone: 865-974-0931. Office Fax: 865-974-8777. Personal E-mail: alowe4@utk.edu. Business E-Mail: bakercenter@utk.edu.

LOWE, CALVIN W., university president; B in Physics, N.C. A&T; M in Physics, M in Physics, PhD in Physics, MIT. Former asst. prof. physics U. Ky.; former asst. and assoc. prof., chair dept. physics Hampton U., former v.p. for rsch., dean grad. coll.; former chair dept. physics Ala. A&M; pres. Bowie (Md.) State U. Office: Bowie State U Office of Pres 14000 Jericho Park Rd Henry Admin Bldg Rm 206 Bowie MD 20715-9465

LOWE, CAMERON ANDERSON, dentist, endodontist, educator; b. Alcester, SD, Dec. 19, 1932; s. Richard Barrett and Emma Louise Lowe; m. Doris Teresita Franquez, Dec. 23, 1957; children: Barrett, Steven, Leslie. Student, George Washington U., 1951-53, U. Va., 1955-56; DDS, Georgetown U., 1956-60; cert. residency in endodontics, U.S. Naval Dental Sch., 1967-69. Commd. lt. (j.g.) U.S. Navy Dental Corps, 1960, advanced through grades to capt., 1976, ret., 1978; pvt. practice endodontist Newport News, Va., 1978-81; assoc. prof. dentistry emeritus Old Dominion U., Norfolk, Va., 1991, asst. chair Sch. Dental Hygiene, 1985-89. Adj. asst. prof. Med. Coll. Va.-Va. Commonwealth U. Sch. Dentistry, Richmond, 1979-81. Contbr. articles to profl. jours. and to book: Oral Pathology, 3d edit., 1989. Tutor adult literacy, 1994-99; coord. Neighborhood Watch, 1994-98; pack and troop chmn. Boy Scouts Am., Guam, 1969-72, Virginia Beach, Va., 1972-78. With USN, 1953-55. Mem. Assn. Mil. Surgeons of U.S., Am. Assn. Endodontists, Am. Acad. Oral Medicine, Am. Dental Assn., Va. Acad. Endodontics, USN Assn. Endodontists, Peninsula Dental Soc., Sigma Alpha Epsilon, Delta Sigma Delta, Sigma Phi Alpha (Dental Hygiene Honor Soc.). Methodist. Avocations: tennis, drawing, carving, reading, sculpting. Home: 1497 Wakefield Dr Virginia Beach VA 23455-4541

LOWE, CLAYTON KENT, radio film critic, educator; b. Endicott, NY, July 10, 1936; s. Clayton Edwin and Loretta Arlene (Terry) L.; m. Janet E. Snider, 1957 (div. 1977); children: Steven Scott, Kim Ann Parker, David William, Rebecca Michelle Sobel; m. Robin S. McKell, 1980 (div. 1993). BA, Bethany Coll., 1958; MS, Butler U., 1967; PhD, Ohio State U., 1970; BD, Christian Theol. Sem., Indpls., 1962. Pastor Bellaire (Ohio) Christian Ch., 1957-58, Beallsville (Ohio) Christian Ch., 1958, Russellville (Ind.) Christian Ch., 1958-60, Montclair (Ind.) Christian Ch., 1960-61; youth dir. St. Paul United Ch. of Christ, Columbus, 1967-70; asst. prof. journalism U. Ga., 1970-72; asst. prof. comm. Ohio State U., Columbus, 1972-73, asst. prof. photography and cinema, 1973-74, assoc. prof., 1974—, chairperson photography and cinema, 1974-78, assoc. prof. emeritus, 1992—. Comml. TV prodr., dir., writer Sta. WISH-TV, 1960—66, Sta. WLWI-TV, 1966—67, Sta. WOSU-TV, 1967—70; moderator World Film Classics, Educable TV-25, 1991—97, also bd. dirs.; part-time faculty Franklin U., 2000—; film critic It's Movie Time WCBE FM, 2001—; part-time faculty Denison U., 2003. Editor: The Movies on Media Catalog, 1995, 2000, Movies on Media Video Collection. Bd. dirs. Columbus Friends of the Libr.; trustee Met. Libr., 1997—2002. Nominee Regional Emmy award, Lucasville, 1970, High Street, 1975; recipient Casper award for A Thing Called Hope, WISH-TV, 1966, Regional Emmy award for A Tribute to Dr. King, 1968, Leadership award, Ohio State U. Outstanding Alumni Soc., 1997, Communicator award of excellence for It's Movie Time New Yr.'s Spl., Sta WCBE-FM, 2002, Silver Microphone award, It's Movie Time, 2002, 2003, 2004, 2005; grantee, Eli Lilly Found., 1961—63, Ohio State U. Devel. of media on media Study Collection, 1985, Ohio Humanities Coun., 1996—97, 1999. Mem.: Ohio State U. Dept. Photography and Cinema Alumni Assn. (pres. 1994—95, 2001—02, bd. dirs. 1994—), Kiwanis. Home: 68 Walhalla Rd Columbus OH 43202-1441 Office Phone: 614-262-3284. Personal E-mail: claytonlowe@hotmail.com. *If these were my last words, I would write of the beauty that has filled me and that I in turn have filled. I would look past the darkness and pain, toward those radiant spots of light when family and friends were most open and life was at its wondrous best.*

LOWE, DAVID WAYNE, elementary school and education educator; b. Galax, Va., Jan. 21, 1957; s. Charles Raymond and Mary Harmon Lowe; m. Sharon Farmer Lowe, Dec. 16, 1989; children: Whitley, Rose, Hui. BA in Econ., Emory and Henry Coll., Emory, Va., 1979; EdM in Reading, U. NC, Charlotte, 1993. Lic. local pastor United Meth. Ch., 2001; tchr. State of NC, 1989. Grad. asst. U. NC, Charlotte, 1987—88; mid. sch. tchr. Rowan County Schs., Salisbury, 1988—92, Stanly County Schs., Albermarle, 1992—2000, literacy facilitator, 2002—05; tchr. academically gifted Union County Schs., Monroe, 2000—01; pastor United Meth. Ch., Charlotte, 2001—02; tchr. grade 6 Anson County Schs., Wadesboro, 2005—. Adj. instr. reading and edn. Pfeiffer U., Misenheimer, NC, 1997—; presenter best ednl. practices fair Southwest Edn. Alliance, Charlotte, NC, 1999; reading curriculum specialist Montgomery County Schs.-East Mid. Sch., Biscoe, NC. Contbr. articles to profl. jours. Sunday sch. supt. Cedar Grove United Meth. Ch., 2004—; minister Mt. Zion United Meth. Ch., Norwood. Named Citizenship Tchr. of Yr., VFW, 1999—2000. Mem.: NEA, NC Edn. Assn., Internat. Reading Assn., Phi Kappa Phi. Democrat. Achievements include development of local history program for Town of Norwood, NC. Avocations: reading, computers, writing, local history. Home: 466 Doody Ave Norwood NC 28128 Office: Anson County Schs Morven Elem Sch US Hwy 523 Morven NC 28119 Office Phone: 704-851-9306. Office Fax: 704-851-3074. Personal E-mail: dlowe4@alltel.net.

LOWE, EDWIN NOBLES, retired lawyer; b. Minturn, Ark., Oct. 4, 1912; s. James A. and Ether (Nobles) L.; m. Catherine McDonald, June 9, 1934 (div. 1959); children: Nancy, Edwin N.; m. Margaret Breece, Dec. 1, 1961; 1 son, James W. AB, U. Ark., 1932, JD, 1934; postgrad., Harvard U. Bus. Sch. Advanced Mgmt. Program, 1950. Bar: Ark. 1934, N.Y. 1936, U.S. Ct. Appeals (2d cir.) 1938, D.C. 1975, U.S. Ct. Internat. Trade 1979, U.S. Supreme Ct. 1944. Mem. staff Ark. Bond Refunding Bd., 1934; with legal dept. Electric Bond & Share Co., NYC, 1934-35; assoc. mng. atty., ptnr. Reid & Priest, 1935-43; gen. counsel Westvaco Corp. (formerly W.Va. Pulp & Paper), NYC, 1943-77; dir. pub. rels. Westvaco Corp., 1944-48, dir. govt. affairs, 1947-76, sec., 1947-66, v.p., 1966-77; spl. ptnr. Gadsby & Hannah, NYC, 1978-79; mem. firm Lowe & Knapp, NYC, 1979-84; sole practice NYC, 1985-86, Carmel, NY, 1986—2007; ret., 2007. Gen. counsel Photography in the Fine Arts, 1957-68; sec., 1974-00, dir. Fund for Modern Cts., NY, 1974—; counsel, dir. Photographic Adminstrs., Inc., 1995-02. Asst. editor Haynesville (La.) News, 1929-30. Dir. and counsel Putnam County Alliance, 1990-99; dir. Putnam County Arts Coun., 1992—2002, organizer ann. exhibit, 1993—; bd. dirs. Putnam Hosp. Ctr., 1986-98, Putnam Hosp. Found., 1990—; trustee Emma Willard Sch., Troy, NY, 1956-64, chmn. Schs. Second Century Fund, 1964-68; chmn. Bronxville Adult Edn., 1957-60, hon. dir., 1961-88, Mercantil Libr. Bd., 1946-72, Clinton Hall Assn., 1962-. Fellow Inst. Jud. Administrn., 1974-85; recipient Disting. Alumni cert. U. Ark., 1972, 50 Yr. Outstanding Law Practice award Fellows of Am. Bar Found., 1985, CLE Spl. award Am. Law Inst.-ABA, 1985, Practice Law Inst. Seligson CLE award, 1986, Disting. Svc. awards U. Maine, Pulp and Paper Found., 1990, 2003, Honor award, 2003, Disting. Svc. award N.Y. chpt. Am. Corp. Counsel Assn., 1990, Order of the Arrow award Boy Scouts, 1926; Eagle Scout, 1928. Mem. ABA (bus. law sect., coun. mem. 1955—, founder, chmn. corp. law dept. com. 1955, sr. lawyers divsn. coun. 1992-2003, founder, chmn. 1st corp. law dept., 1955-74, founder, chmn. 2d corp. law dept.), Inst. for NY City Bar and ABA, Am. Arbitration Assn. (exec. com. 1969—, hon. mem. 1977—, chmn. 1972-74, chmn. bd. 1974-77, Whitney North Seymour medal 2003), Am. Law Inst. (life mem.), N.Y. State Bar Assn., 1995-00, Practicing Law Inst. (trustee 1966-86, pres. 1972-79, chmn. 1979-86, chmn. emeritus 1986—, mem. exec. com. 1974—, fin. com. 1974—), Gen. Counsel Assn., Dutch Treat Club (gov., sec. 1993-00, chmn. 2000-05, hon. chmn. 2005—), Assn. Bar City NY (past v.p., exec. chmn., mem. several coms. 1945-86), Am. Soc. of Corp. Sec., Inc. (nat. dir. 1956-59), World Soc. Ekistics (v.p., exec. com. UN rep. NGO, chmn. & dir. NY chpt. 1980-2003), Merc. Libr. (pres., dir. 1953-74), Univ. Club NY (past v.p. coun., club activities chmn., charter revision com. 1973-2003), Gipsy Trail Club, Nat. Arts Club, Sigma Nu. Methodist. Home and Office: The Knoll 554 Gypsy Trail Rd Carmel NY 10512 Personal E-mail: enlowe@comcast.net.

LOWE, ERIC JEFFREY, hematologist, oncologist, director; b. Olney, Md., Mar. 14, 1972; s. Dale and Becky Lowe; m. Susan Frank, Apr. 1, 2000; children: Anna, William. BS in Biomedical Engring., Johns Hopkins U., Balt., 1994; MD, Emory U., Atlanta, 1998; MS, U. Tenn., Memphis, 2004. Cert. in pediatrics Am. Bd. Pediat., 2001, in pediatric hematology & oncology Am. Bd. Pediat., 2004. Med. dir. for pediatric oncology CHKD, Norfolk, Va., 2006—; nhl steering grp. mem. Children's Oncology Grp., primary investigator CHKD. Contbr. articles to profl. jours. Med. adv. bd. Victory Junction Gang Camp, NC, 2005—07. Recipient Zollinger award, 1998. Mem.: Am. Soc. Oncology, Am. Soc. Hematology, Am. Soc. Pediatric Hematology/Oncology, Am. Acad. Pediat. Office: CHKD 601 Children's Ln Norfolk VA 23507

LOWE, GREGG A., electronics executive; b. Cleve. BSEE, Rose Hulman Inst. Tech., Terre Haute, Ind., 1984; grad. from Stanford Exec. Program, Stanford U., Calif. Field sales Tex. Instruments, Inc., 1984—89, dir. European automotive sales teams (led teams in Germany, Italy, Eng. and Spain), 1989—94, mgr. microcontroller orgn., 1994—98, mgr. ASIC orgn., 1998—2001, mgr. high speed comm. and controls, High Performance Analog Unit Dallas, 2001, sr. v.p., mgr. High Performance Analog bus. unit, 2001—06, sr. v.p., mgr. total analog bus. unit, 2006—. Office: Tex Instruments Inc PO Box 660199 Dallas TX 75266-0199 Office Phone: 972-995-2011. Office Fax: 972-995-4360.*

LOWE, J. ALLEN, minister; b. Midland, Tex., Dec. 20, 1945; s. Homer Allen and Theresa (Lowry) L.; m. Shirley Christy, Apr. 9, 1965; children: Robert Allen, John David, Steven Scott. BS, Howard Payne U., 1968; MDiv, Tex. Christian U., 1976; postgrad, Princeton Theol., 1990, postgrad., 2002. Cert. secondary tchr.; ordained to the ministry Christian Ch., 1976. Instr. Biblical history Midland Ind. Sch. Dist., Tex., 1968-74; assoc. min. First Christian Ch., Denison, Tex., 1974-76, sr. min. Richardson, Tex., 2000—07; campus min. United Campus Ministries, Ctrl. Mo. State U., Warrensburg, 1976-78; nurture min. Meml. Christian Ch., Midland, Tex., 1978-84; assoc. min. 1st Christian Ch., Corpus Christi, Tex., 1984-91; sr. min. South Shore Christian Ch., Corpus Christi, 1991-2000; sr. minister Creekwood Christian Ch., 2007—. Chmn. Cen. Area Youth Coun., Tex., 1980-84; moderator Youth Ministry Coun. S.W., 1984-87, Bluebonnet Area Youth Coun., 1986-93; advisor Internat. Youth Coun. Christian Ch. (Discoples of Christ), 1985-87; vice moderator Bluebonnet Area of Christian Ch. in S.W., 1994-95. Mem. IMPACT, 1974-82; charter mem. Nat. Peace Acad., 1973-78; coach YMCA basketball, 1980-81, Little League, Youth Flag Football teams, Denison and Midland, 1967-68, 70, 74; mem. ethics commn. City of Corpus Christi, 1994-2000; active City League Youth Basketball, Corpus Christi, 1995-97; mem. com. on the ministry Christian Ch. in the S.W., 1997-2000, 2002-2006; mem. North Tex. Area Youth Min. Coun., 2001-2004; spkr. Christian Youth Confs., 1980-2004. Recipient Friend of Youth City award, 1989, Friend of Youth City award, 1989; O.H. Karr Ministerial scholar Tex. Christian U., 1975-76. Home: 2722 Laurel Oaks Dr Garland TX 75044 Office: Creekwood Chirstian Ch 2660 Forest Vista Dr Flower Mound TX 75028 Business E-Mail: office@fccrichardson.org. *My guiding principle is that Christianity is a relationship. Therefore, it must be lived as a relationship-we experience the love of God only in relationship to another (others) and thus only in relationship can we teach Christianity. In short, the slogan "Preach the Gospel, use words if necessary.".*

LOWE, JAMES ALLISON, lawyer, educator; b. Cleve., July 15, 1945; s. Allison S. and Betty B. (Bernstein) L.; m. Jacalyn S. Scholss, June 24, 1967 (div.); children: David, Joseph, Jeremiah; m. Teresa L. DiPuccio, Aug. 13, 1989; 1 child, Alison. BA, U. Pa., 1967; JD cum laude, Cleve. State U., 1972. Bar: Ohio 1972, U.S. Dist. Ct. (no. dist.) Ohio 1973, U.S. Ct. Appeals (6th cir.) 1981, U.S. Supreme Ct. 1979; cert. civic trial adv. Nat. Bd. Trial Advocacy. Assoc. Berkman, Gordon & Kancelbaum, Cleve., 1972—74; sole practice Cleve., 1974—76; ptnr. Sindell, Lowe & Guidubaldi Co., L.P.A., Cleve., 1976—96, Lowe Eklund Wakefield Co., LPA, Cleve., 1996—, Lowe Eklund Wakefield & Mulvihill Co., LPA, Cleve., 2000—. Instr. law Cleve. State U., 1974-77, Case Western Res. U., 1979-92. Author: Products Liability Litigation: Pretrial Practice, 1988, Product Liability in Ohio After Tort Reform, 1988. Active Jewish Cmty. Fedn.; fellow Roscoe Pound Found. Named one of Best Lawyers in Am., 1993—2007, Top 100 Lawyers, Ohio Super Lawyers, 2007. Fellow Internat. Soc. Barristers, Am. Bd. Trial Advs. (v.p.), Am. Coll. Trial Lawyers; mem. ABA, ATLA (chmn. products liability adv. com., chmn. products liability sect., dir. products liability sect.), Ohio Acad. Trial Attys. (chmn. products liability sect. 1987-89, trustee 1990—), Ohio Bar Assn., Cleve. Acad. Trial Attys. (bd. dirs. 1988—, v.p. 1996, pres. 1991-92), Greater Cleve. Bar Assn., Attys. Info. Exch. Group (v.p. 2005-06, pres. elect 2007-), Am. Bd. Trial Advocates (treas. Ohio). Office: Lowe Eklund Wakefield & Mulvihill Co LPA 610 Skylight Office Tower 1660 W 2nd St #610 Cleveland OH 44113-1454 Office Phone: 216-781-2600. Business E-Mail: Jlowe@lewm.com.

LOWE, JAMES EDWARD, JR., plastic and reconstructive surgeon; b. Warsaw, NC, Dec. 5, 1950; s. James Edward and Alice Mae (Gavin) L.; m. Philamina Lucy Lozado, Oct. 7, 1989; children: James III, Jesse, Joseph. BS, Livingstone Coll., 1971; MD, Meharry Med. Coll., 1975. Diplomate Am. Bd. Plastic Surgery. Intern Downstate Med. Ctr., Bklyn., 1975—76, resident in surgery, 1975—78, 1978—82; resident in plastic surgery Lenox Hill Hosp., NYC, 1982—84; pvt. practice NYC, 1984—; assoc. attending surgeon Lenox Hill Hosp., 1984—99, Good Hope Hosp., Erwin, NC,

1999—. Student mentor Purchase (N.Y.) Coll., 1996—; elder Presbyn. Ch., Scarborough, N.Y., 1999—; student tutor Highland Presbyn. Ch., Fayetteville, N.C., 2003. Health Career scholar Harvard U. Med. Sch., Boston, 1970. Mem.: NAACP, AMA (Physicians Recognition award 2006—), NC Med. Soc., Cumberland County Med. Soc., Nat. Med. Soc., Lenox Hill Plastic Surgery Soc., The Morestin Soc., Phi Beta Sigma. Office: 4155 Ferncreek Dr Ste 102 Fayetteville NC 28314 E-mail: jameselowe@msn.com.

LOWE, JOHN, III, consulting civil engineer; b. NYC, Mar. 14, 1916; s. John and Rose Marie (Jahoda) L.; m. Jeanne Wright, June 19, 1943; children: Jonathan Alan, Barbara Jean, Heather Ellen. BS in Engring., CCNY; MSC.E., MIT. Registered profl. engr., N.Y., La., PR., Calif. Instr. U. Md., College Park, 1937-40, MIT, Cambridge, Mass., 1942—44; physicist David Taylor Model Basin, Carderock, Md., 1945; chief soils engr. Tippetts-Abbett-McCarthy-Stratton, NYC, 1945-55, assoc. ptnr., 1956-62, ptnr., 1962-83; pvt. practice geotech. and dam engring., 1984—99. Adj. assoc. prof. NYU, 1949-51; lectr. soil mechanics CCNY, 1953-60; 8th Terzaghi lectr., 1971, 4th Nabor Carrillo lectr., 1978, 2d U.S. Com. on Large Dams lectr., 1982, Marty Kapp lectr., 1986; keynote address Roller Compacted Concrete II, 1988, Mueser/Rutledge lectr., 1997; cons. Corps. Engrs., Washington, 1962-80; dam constrn. projects in many countries including U.S., Turkey, Taiwan, Morocco, Pakistan, Brazil, Greece. Contbr. chpts. to 4 books, 38 articles in field to profl. jours. Decorated comdr. Order of Alouites (Morocco); recipient Townsend Harris medal Alumni CCNY, 1982. Fellow ASCE; mem. NAE, U.S. Com. Large Dam (chmn. 1977-78), Nat. Com. Soil Mechanics and Found. Engring., Moles, Univ. Club, Bronxville Field Club. Achievements include first to place concrete in a dam by roller compacted concrete methods; perform consolidation tests under back pressure to ensure saturation; development of undisturbed soil samplers with liners; in charge of soil and foundation engineering of the largest dam in the world, Tarbela DAM, from reconnaissance studies through design, supervisor of construction until intitial filling, 1960-74; in charge of additions and repairs 1974-87. Personal E-mail: jloweiii@aol.com.

LOWE, JOHN BURTON, medical association administrator, molecular biologist, educator, pathologist; b. Sheridan, Wyo., June 13, 1953; s. Burton G. and Eunice D. Lowe. BA, U. Wyo., 1976; MD, U. Utah, 1980. Diplomate Am. Bd. Pathology. Asst. med. dir. Barnes Hosp. Blood Bank, St. Louis, 1985-86; instr. Sch. of Medicine Washington U., St. Louis, 1985, asst. prof. Sch. of Medicine, 1985-86; asst. investigator Howard Hughes Med. Inst., Ann Arbor, Mich., 1986-92, assoc. investigator, 1992-96, investigator, 1997—2005; asst. prof. Med. Sch. U. Mich., Ann Arbor, 1986-91, assoc. prof. Med. Sch., 1991-95, prof. Med. Sch., 1995—2005; Henry Willson Payne prof. and chair dept. pathology Case Western Res. U. Sch. Medicine, Cleve., 2005—, prof., chmn. dept. pathology, 2005. Dep. editor Jour. Clin. Investigation, 1997—2002, mem. editl. bd. FEBS Jour., 2001—; contbr. articles to profl. jours. including Jour. Biol. Chemistry, Genes and Devel., Nature, Cell, Sci. Fellow: AAAS; mem.: Am. Assn. Physicians, Am. Soc. Clin. Investigation. Office: Dept Pathology Case We Reserve Univ Sch Medicine 10900 Euclid Ave Cleveland OH 44106-7288

LOWE, JOHN C., medical researcher, director; b. Carrabelle, Fla., Jan. 22, 1946; s. Evelyn Edna and Harvey Monroe Lowe; m. Tammy Lewis Lowe; 1 child, Michele Nicole Carter. BA, MA, U. West Fla., Pensacola, 1973; BS, DC, LA Coll. Chiropractic, Glendale, 1977. Bd. cert. pain mgmt. Am. Acad. Pain Mgmt., 1993. Dir. rsch. Fibromyalgia Rsch. Found., Boulder, 1993—; bd. med. advisors Thyroid UK, London, 2002—; mem. internat. reviewers' panel Med. Sci. Monitor, NYC, 2004—. Author: (scientific and clinical book) The Metabolic Treatment of Fibromyalgia (Study Sphere award Excellence, 2006), (book) Your Guide to Metabolic Health. Mem.: Nat. Assn. Myofacial Trigger Point Therapists (life; hon. mem.). Independent. Achievements include research in Proved that fibromyalgia is a disorder of abnormally low metabolism caused mainly by hypothyroidism and/or thyroid hormone resistance, and developed an effective treatment for the disorder. Avocation: philosophy. Home Phone: 303-947-0009; Office Phone: 603-931-6061. Office Fax: 303-604-0771; Home Fax: 303-604-0773.

LOWE, JOHN E., oil industry executive, accountant; b. Oskaloosa, Iowa, 1959; BS, Pitts. State Univ., Kanas, 1981. Dir. fin. ConocoPhillips, Houston, 1993—97, supply chain mgr. for refining, mktg. & transport., 1997—99, mgr., strategic growth projects, 1999, v.p. planning and strategic growth, 1999—2000, sr. v.p. planning and strategic trans., 2000—01, sr. v.p. planning and devel., 2001—02, dir., exec. v.p. planning and strategic trans., 2002—06, exec. v.p. comml., 2006—07, exec. v.p. exploration & production, 2007—. Bd. dirs. ChervonPhillips Chem. Co., Duke Energy Field Svcs., Houston Mus. Natural Sci., DCP Midstream Ptnrs. Office: ConocoPhillips 600 N Dairy Ashford Rd Houston TX 77079*

LOWE, JOHN STANLEY, law educator; b. Marion, Ohio, May 11, 1941; s. John Floyd and Florence (Andrews) L.; m. Jacquelyn Taft, Jan. 15, 1968; children: Sarah Staley, John Taft. BA, Denison U., 1963; LLB, Harvard U., 1966. Bar: Ohio 1966, Okla. 1980, U.S. Supreme Ct. 1972, Tex. 1989. Adminstrv. officer Govt. of Malawi, Limbe, 1966-69; assoc. Emens, Hurd, Kegler & Ritter, Columbus, Ohio, 1970-75; asst. and assoc. prof. law U. Toledo, Ohio, 1975—78; prof. law U. Tulsa, 1978-87, So. Meth. U., Dallas, 1987—. Vis. prof. U. Tex., Austin, 1983; disting. vis. prof. natural resources law U. Denver, 1987; disting. vis. prof. U. N.Mex., 1996; vis. lectr. U. Dundee, Scotland, 2001-; sr. fellow U. Melbourne, Australia, 2006-. Author: Oil and Gas Law in a Nutshell, 1983, 4th edit., 2003, Hemingway on Oil and Gas Law, 4th edit., 2004; editor: Cases and Materials on Oil and Gas Law, 1986, 4th edit., 2002; editor Internat. Petroleum Transactions, 1993, 2d edit., 2000, others. Pres., trustee Rocky Mtn. Mineral Law Found., 2003-04. Recipient Outstanding Law Rev. Article award Tex. Bar Found., 1988, 96. Mem. ABA (chair natural resources, energy and environ. law sects. 1992-93), Ctr. Am. and Internat. Law (former vice chair, mem. exec. com. adv. bd. Energy Law Inst. 1998-04), Am. Arbitration Assn., CPR Inst. Dispute Resolution. Episcopalian. Avocation: sailing. Office: So Meth U 3315 Daniel Ave Dallas TX 75275-0116 Home: 12014 Lueders Ln Dallas TX 75230-2373 Office Phone: 214-768-2595. Business E-Mail: jlowe@mail.smu.edu.

LOWE, JOHN THOMAS, JR., church and concert musician; b. Lynchburg, Va., Sept. 1, 1970; s. John Thomas Lowe and Evelyn G. Lowe-Woody. BS in Organ Performance, Liberty U., 1993; MusM, U. Ala., 1996; MusD, Ind. U., 2005. Organist United Meth. Ch. World Conf. Ctr., Lake Junaluska, NC, 1993; organist, choirmaster Canterbury Chapel Episcopal Ch. and Student Ctr., Tuscaloosa, Ala., 1993—96; full-time music intern West End United Meth. Ch., Nashville, 1996—98; dir. music, organist Congregation Micah, Nashville, 1996—98; music dir., organist The Ch. of the Nativity (Episcopal), Indpls., 1998—2003, First United Meth. Ch., Ocala, Fla., 2003—07; condr., artistic dir. Ctrl. Fla. Master Choir, Ocala, 2004—07; dir. music, organist Holy Trinity Episc. Ch., Gainesville, Fla., 2007—. Organist: CD Singing Hymns and Spiritual Songs, 1998. Finalist organ performance competition, Deerfield, Ill., 1991, undergrad. competition in organ performance, Ottumwa, Iowa, 1991, 1992; recipient 1st prize nat. student auditions, Nat. Fedn. Music Clubs, 1995, 2d prize organ performance competition, San Marino, Calif., 1996. Mem.: Fellowship of United Methodists in Music and Worship Arts, Choristers Guild (Ruth Kriebhel Jacobs Meml. scholar 1999—2000), Am. Choral Dirs. Assn., Am. Guild English Handbell Ringers, Am. Guild Organists (Ocala chpt. dean 2004—07, 1st prize regional competition for young organists 1991, 2d prize 1993), Organ Hist. Soc., Phi Mu Alpha (life). Home: 320 SE 3rd St C11 Gainesville FL 32601 Office: Holy Trinity Episc Ch 100 NE 1st St Gainesville FL 32601 Office Phone: 352-372-4721. Personal E-mail: johntlowejr@aol.com. Business E-Mail: lowe@holytrinitygnv.org.

LOWE, JONATHAN WAYNE, lawyer; b. Miami, Dec. 15, 1947; BS, U. Pa., 1970; JD, Harvard U., 1975. Bar: U.S. Dist. Ct. (no. dist.) Ga. 1975. Assoc. Alston & Bird, Atlanta, 1975-82, ptnr., corp. health care & technology group, 1982—. Trustee Paideia Sch., Atlanta, 1986—; mem. Leadership Atlanta, 1989. 1st lt. U.S. Army QMC, 1970-72. Recipient Spl. Vol. award Gov. of State Ga., 1985. Mem. Ansley Golf Club. Office: Alston & Bird One Atlantic Ctr 1201 W Peachtree St NW Ste 4200 Atlanta GA 30309-3449 Office Phone: 404-881-7555. Office Fax: 404-881-7777. Business E-Mail: jlowe@alston.com.

LOWE, KATHLENE WINN, lawyer; b. San Diego, Dec. 1, 1949; d. Ralph and Grace (Rodes) Winn; m. Russell Howells Lowe, Oct. 3, 1977; 1 child, Taylor Rhodes. BA in English magna cum laude, U. Utah, 1971, MA in English, 1973, JD, 1976. Bar: Utah 1976, US Dist. Ct. Utah 1976, US Ct. Appeals (10th cir.) 1980, Calif. 1989, US Ct. Appeals (9th cir.), US Dist. Ct. Calif. Assoc. Parsons, Behle & Latimer, Salt Lake City, 1976-80, ptnr., 1980-84; v.p. law, asst. gen. counsel Am. Stores Co., Salt Lake City, 1984—89; office mng. ptnr. Brobeck, Phleger & Harrison, Newport Beach, Calif., 1999—2003; ptnr.-in-charge, So. Calif. Dorsey & Whitney LLP, Irvine, Calif. Comment editor Utah Law Rev., 1975-76. Mem. ABA, Calif. Bar Assn., Utah Bar Assn. Avocations: fly fishing, reading, skiing, golf, travel. Office: Dorsey & Whitney LLP 38 Technology Dr Irvine CA 92618-5310 Office Phone: 949-932-3600. Office Fax: 949-932-3601. Business E-Mail: lowe.kathlene@dorsey.com.

LOWE, KENNETH W., multimedia executive; BA radio, television, motion pictures, UNC. With Southern Broadcasting, 1969, Harte-Hanks Broadcasting, 1970—80; gen. mgr., Radio Properties E.W. Scripps Co., 1980—88, v.p., programming, promotion, marketing, 1988—94; CEO Scripps Network, 1994—2000; pres., CEO E.W. Scripps Co., 2000—. Bd. dir. Greater Cincinnati Chamber of Commerce; chmn. Cincinnati USA Partnership; bd. dir. Cincinnati Center City Development Center; trustee Fine Arts Fund; bd. of advisors U.N.C. Dept. of Communication. Office: c/o EW Scripps 312 Walnut Street 2800 Scripps Center Cincinnati OH 45202*

LOWE, KEVIN HUGH, professional sports team executive, former hockey player and coach; b. Lachute, Que., Can., Apr. 15, 1959; m. Karen Percy. Defenseman Edmonton Oilers, 1979-92, 98-99, capt., 1991-92; defenseman NY Rangers, 1992-98; head coach Edmonton Oilers, 1999—2000, gen. mgr., exec. v.p., 2000—. Player NHL All-Star Game, 1984—86, 1988—90, 1993. Named Budweiser/NHL Man of Yr., 1990; recipient King Clancy Meml. Trophy, 1990. Achievements include being a member of Stanely Cup Champion Edmonton Oilers, 1984, 1985, 1987, 1988, 1989, NY Rangers, 1994. Office: Edmonton Oilers 11230 110th St Edmonton AB Canada T5G 3H7

LOWE, KRISTIN, film company executive; b. Dec. 9, 1971; With Michael Bay Films, Metro-Goldwyn-Mayer, Inc.; creative exec. to dir. devel. Warner Bros. Pictures, 2002—04; dir. devel. Universal Pictures, 2004—06, v.p. prodn., 2006—. Prodn. asst.: Armageddon, 1998. Achievements include overseeing day-to-day production of the films Inside Man, The Break-Up and You, Me and Dupree. Office: Universal Pictures 100 Universal City Plz Ste 3200 Universal City CA 91608*

LOWE, LOUIS ROBERT, JR., lawyer; b. Indpls., May 30, 1937; BSCE, Purdue U., 1959; LLD, Ind. U., 1967. Bar: U.S. Dist. Ct. (so. dist.) Ind. 1967, U.S. Tax Ct. 1977; lic. profl. engr. Engr. various cons. engring. cos., Indpls., 1960-64, Ind. Hwy Needs Study, Indpls., 1966-67; ptnr. Lowe, Gray, Steele & Darko, Indpls., 1967—2002, Bose McKinney & Evans, LLP, Indpls., 2003—. Contbr. articles to profl. jours. Sec. English Speaking Union, Indpls., 1967—; trustee Hanover Coll.; elder and trustee Second Presbyn. Ch., Indpls. Fellow Indpls. Bar Found.; mem. Ind. Bar Assn., Purdue U. Alumni Assn., Indpls. Purdue Assn. (pres. 1968-69), Contemporary Club (pres. 1986-87), Columbia Club (bd. dirs. 1993-96), Columbia Club Found. (pres. 1995-97, trustee 1998-), Gyro Club (pres. 2006—). Office: 2700 First Ind Plz 135 N Pennsylvania St Indianapolis IN 46204 Home: 6471 Oxbow Way Indianapolis IN 46220-7108 Home Phone: 317-846-5845; Office Phone: 317-684-5351. Business E-Mail: rlowe@boselaw.com.

LOWE, LYLE JUSTIN, lawyer; b. Oklahoma City, Feb. 22, 1973; s. Lyle Don and Cheri Lyn Lowe. BA, BS in Criminal Justice, Oklahoma City U., 1995, JD, 2000. Atty. Dellvono & Crow, Oklahoma City; owner, atty. Justin Lowe P.C., Oklahoma City. Mem.: ABA, ATLA, Okla. Bar Assn., Okla. Trail Lawyers Assn. Office: 3133 NW 63 Oklahoma City OK 73116

LOWE, MARK J., physicist; m. Julia B. Lowe; children: Donovan J., Brendon M. Sims, Morgan C. Sims. BS, Mich. State U., East Lansing, 1986; PhD, U. Minn., Mpls., 1991. Rsch. asst. Mich. State U., 1982—86; tchg. asst. U. Minn., 1986—88, rsch. asst., 1988—91; postdoctoral fellow Rice U., Houston, 1991—94, U. Wis., Madison, 1994—96; asst. prof. Ind. U., Indpls., 1997—2003; staff Cleve. Clinic, 2003—. Polarimeter coord. CERN, Geneve, Switzerland, 1995—96; dir. rsch. MRI facility Ind. U., Indpls., 1997—2003; dir. high field MRI Cleve. Clinic, 2003—. Mem. editl. bd. NeuroImage, 2006—. Tutor Boys Club Am., Cleve., 2006. Mem.: AAAS, Orgn. Human Brain Mapping, Internat. Soc. Magnetic Resonance in Medicine, Am. Assn. Physicists in Medicine, Am. Phys. Soc., Sigma Pi Sigma, Phi Beta Kappa. Achievements include research in investigate and develop novel methods for measuring functional connectivity in the human brain using MRI; patents for direct thermal monitoring for MRI safety of implanted devices. Avocations: amateur radio, bicycling. Office: Cleve Clinic 9500 Euclid Ave Cleveland OH 44195 Home Phone: 317-887-3362; Office Phone: 216-445-2661. E-mail: mjlowe@sbcglobal.net.

LOWE, MARY FRANCES, federal official; b. Ft. Meade, Md., Apr. 15, 1952; d. Benno Powers and Peggy Catherine (Moore) L. BA, Coll. William and Mary, 1972; MA, Fletcher Sch. Law and Diplomacy, 1974, MA Law and Diplomacy in, 1975; diplome, Grad. Inst. Internat. Studies U. Geneva, Switzerland, 1975; M.P.H. in epidemiology, Johns Hopkins Sch. Hygiene and Pub. Health, 1986. External collaborator ILO, Geneva, 1974; legis. asst. to U.S. Senator Richard S. Schweiker Washington, 1975-76; profl. staff mem. health and sci. rsch. subcom. U.S. Senate Com. Labor and Human Resources, Washington, 1976-81; exec. sec. U.S. Dept. HHS, Washington, 1981-85; sr. asst. to commr. program policy FDA, 1985-89; sr. asst. pesticide programs EPA, 1989-96; asst. Office Environ. Policy U.S. Dept. State, Washington, 1997-99; program advisor pesticide program govt. and internat. svcs. EPA, Washington, 1999—. Rep. U.S. delegations World Health Assemblies, Geneva, NAFTA and WTO Coms., 1995-98, Codex Alimentarius, UN Sub-Com. Experts on the Globally Harmonized System of Classification and Labelling Chems.; alt. trustee Woodrow Wilson Internat. Ctr. Scholars. Mem. Soc. for Epidemiologic Rsch., Am. Assn. World Health, Exec. Women in Govt., Soc. for Chem. Hazard Comm., Soc. Risk Analysis, Washington World Affairs Coun., Delta Omega. Home: 7920 Spotswood Dr Alexandria VA 22308-1125 Office: US EPA 1200 Pennsylvania Ave NW Washington DC 20460-0001 Home Phone: 703-765-3530; Office Phone: 703-305-5689. Business E-Mail: lowe.maryfrances@epa.gov.

LOWE, NICK, vocalist, musician, producer; b. Woolridge, Suffolk, Eng., Mar. 24, 1949; m. Carlene Carter, 1979. Bassist, vocalist Brinsley Schwarz band, 1972-75, solo career, 1975—, Rockpile band, 1977-80, Noise To Go band, 1982-83. Albums include Pure Pop for Now People, 1978, Labor of Lust, 1979, Nick the Knife, 1982, The Abominable Showman, 1983, Rose of England, 1985, (with Brinsley Schwarz) Nervous on the Road, 1972, (with Rockpile) Seconds, Party of One, 1990, At My Age, 2007; singles: I Love the Sound of Breaking Glass, 1978, Cruel to Be Kind, 1979; producer various artists including Graham Parker, The Rumour, Wreckless Eric, Elvis Costello, Carlene Carter, Dr. Feelgood, Paul Carrack, Fabulous Thunderbirds, John Hiatt. Office: ICM 40 W 57th St Fl 16 New York NY 10019-4098*

LOWE, PATRICIA A., psychologist, educator; b. Landstuhl, Germany, July 31, 1957; (parents Am. citizens); d. Gerald H. and Hazel C. Lowe. BS magna cum laude, Boise State U., 1980; PhD, Tex. A&M U., 2000. Lic. psychologist Idaho, cert. sch. psychologist Idaho, Kans. Grad. rsch./tchg. asst. Tex. A&M U., College Station, 1995—99; psychology intern Warm Springs Counseling Ctr. and Tng. Inst., Boise, Idaho, 1999—2000, post-doctoral resident, 2000—01; prof. U. Kans., Lawrence, 2001—. Cons. for tech. initiative grant The Ind. Sch. Dist. of Boise City, 1999—2000; cons./tech. advisor to Nat. Ctr. on Learning Disabilities U. Kans., Lawrence, 2002—, clin. supr. Assoc. editor: book Encyclopedia of School Psychology; co-author: (test manual) Adult Manifest Anxiety Scale, (test) Adult Manifest Anxiety Scale-Elderly Version, Adult Manifest Anxiety Scale-Adult Version, Adult Manifest Anxiety Scale-College Version, (book) Clinical Applications of Continuous Performance Tests: Measuring Attention and Impulsive Responding in Children and Adults, Encyclopedia of School Psychology, (test) Test Anxiety Inventory for Children and Adolescents; contbr. chapters to books, articles to profl. jours.; mem. editl. bd. profl. jours. Faculty rep. U. Kans. Cir. K Svc. Orgn., Lawrence, 2001—03; univ. trainer Kans. Assn. Sch. Psychologists, 2001—02. Recipient Alumni award, Boise State U., 1980, cert. of achievement, Kans. Assn. Sch. Psychologists; Lechner Grad. Merit fellow, Tex. A&M U., 1995—96, Rsch. grantee, U. Kans., 2002, 2003. Mem.: APA, NASP, Psi Chi, Kappa Delta Phi, Phi Kappa Phi. Achievements include test development. Avocations: skiing, tennis, racquetball, swimming, running. E-mail: tlowe@ku.edu.

LOWE, RALPH EDWARD, lawyer; b. Hinsdale, Ill., Nov. 24, 1931; s. Charles Russell and Eva Eleanor (Schroeder) L.; m. Patricia E. Eichhorst, Aug. 23, 1952; children: John Stuart, Michael Kevin, Timothy Edward. BA, Depauw U., 1953; LLB, U. Ill., 1956. Bar: Ill. 1956, U.S. Dist. Ct. (no. dist.) Ill. 1957, Ga. 1974, U.S. Dist. Ct. (no. dist.) Ga. 1980, S.C. 1990. Assoc. Ruddy & Brown, Aurora, Ill., 1956-58; ptnr. Lowe & Richards, Aurora, 1959-62, Vincent, Lowe & Richards, Aurora, 1963-71; pvt. practice, Aurora and Atlanta, 1974-85; prin. Lowe & Steinmetz, Ltd., Aurora and Atlanta, 1985-91; pvt. practice, Aurora, Ill., 1972-74, 92—. Chmn. Inter-Am. Devel. Corp., Ill., 1965-67. Office: 407 W Galena Blvd Aurora IL 60506-3946 Home Phone: 630-879-7702; Office Phone: 630-897-0900.

LOWE, RANDALL B., lawyer; b. Englewood, NJ, Nov. 20, 1948; BA, U. R.I., 1970; JD, Washington U., 1973. Bar: Ill. 1973, Conn. 1975, D.C. 1976, U.S. Ct. Appeals (2d and D.C. cirs.) 1976, N.J. 1977, U.S. Dist. Ct. N.J. 1977, U.S. Ct. Appeals (3d cir.) 1977, U.S. Ct. Appeals (9th cir.) 1979, N.Y. 1980, U.S. Dist. Ct. (ea. and so. dists.) N.Y. 1980. Atty. Callis & Filcoff, Granite City, Ill., 1973-75, AT&T, Washington and NYC, 1975-78, ITT Corp, 1978-83, Surrey & Morse, Washington, 1983-86; ptnr. Jones, Day, Reavis & Pogue, Washington, 1986-94, Piper & Marbury, Washington, 1994-99, 1999-2000; exec. v.p./chief legal officer Prism Comms. Svcs., 1999-2001; ptnr. Davis Wright Tremaine, Washington, 2001—. Office: 1919 Pennsylvania Ave NW Washington DC 20006-3402 Office Phone: 202-973-4221. Business E-Mail: randylowe@dwt.com.

LOWE, ROB, actor; b. Charlottesville, Va., Mar. 17, 1964; m. Sheryl Berkoff, July 22, 1991; 2 children. Appeared in films including The Outsiders, 1983, Class, 1983, The Hotel New Hampshire, 1984, Oxford Blues, 1984, St. Elmo's Fire, 1985, Youngblood, About Last Night..., 1986, Square Dance, 1987, Illegally Yours, Masquerade, 1988, Bad Influence, 1991, The Dark Backward, 1991, Wayne's World, 1992, Frank and Jesse (also prodr.), 1994, Billy the Third, 1995, First Degree, 1995, Eye of the Storm, 1995, Tommy Boy, 1995, Mullholland Falls, 1996, Crazy Six, 1997, Austin Powers: International Man of Mystery, 1997, Living in Peril, 1997, Contact, 1997, Hostile Intent, 1997, One Hell of a Guy, 1998, Crazy Six, 1998, Under Pressure, 1999, Statistics, 1999, Dead Silent, 1999, Austin Powers: The Spy Who Shagged Me, 1999, Proximity, 2001, Austin Powers in Goldmember, 2002, View from the Top, 2003, Thank You for Smoking, 2006; appearances include (TV series) A New Kind of Family, The West Wing, 1999-2003, The Lyon's Den, 2003-04, Dr. Vegas, 2004 (also prodr.); (mini-series) Atomic Train, 1998, Beach Girls, 2005, (TV films) Thursday's Child, A Matter of Time, Schoolboy Father, Stephen King's The Stand, On Dangerous Ground, 1995, Midnight Man, 1995, Outrage, 1998; (stage) A Few Good Men, London, 2005; writer, dir. (TV films) Desert's Edge, 1997, Jane Doe, 2001, Framed, 2002, Salem's Lot, 2004, Perfect Strangers, 2004, The Christmas Blessing, 2005; TV guest appearances include The Larry Sanders Show, 1992, The Naked Truth, 1995. Office: Brillstein Grey 9150 Wilshire Blvd Ste 350 Beverly Hills CA 90212-3453

LOWE, ROBERT CHARLES, lawyer; b. New Orleans, July 3, 1949; s. Carl Randall and Antonia (Morgan) L.; m. Theresa Louise Acree, Feb. 4, 1978; 1 child, Nicholas Strafford. BA, U. New Orleans, 1971; JD, La. State U., 1975. Bar: La. 1975, U.S. Dist. Ct. (ea. dist.) La. 1975, U.S. Ct. Appeals (5th cir.) 1980, U.S. Dist. Ct. (we. dist.) La. 1978, U.S. Supreme Ct. 1982. Assoc. Sessions, Fishman, Rosenson, Boisfontaine, and Nathan, New Orleans, 1975—80, ptnr., 1980—87, Lowe, Stein, Hoffman, Allweiss and Hauver, New Orleans, 1987—. Author: Louisiana Divorce, West Pub. Co., 1984; mem. La. Law Rev., 1974-75; contbr. articles to profl. jours. Named one of Best Lawyers in Am., 1983—2007, Top Fifty La. SuperLawyers, 2007; named to La. State U. Law Ctr. Hall of Fame, 1987. Mem. ABA, La. State Bar Assn. (chmn. family law sect. 1984-85), La. Assn. Def. Counsel, New Orleans Bar Assn. (chmn. family law sect. 1991-92), La. State Law Inst., La. Trial Lawyers Assn. (chmn. family law sect. 2006-07), Order of Coif, Phi Kappa Phi. Republican. Home: 9625 Garden Oak Ln New Orleans LA 70123-2005 Office: 701 Poydras St Ste 3600 New Orleans LA 70139-7735 Office Phone: 504-581-2450.

LOWE, ROBERT STANLEY, lawyer; b. Herman, Nebr., Apr. 23, 1923; s. Stanley Robert and Ann Marguerite (Feese) L.; m. Anne Kirtland Selden, Dec. 19, 1959; children: Robert James, Margaret Anne. AB, U. Nebr., 1947, JD, 1949. Bar: Wyo. 1949, Nebr. 1949, Ill. 1967, DC 1983, Colo. 1989. Ptnr. McAvoy & Lowe, Newcastle, 1949—51, Hickey & Lowe, Rawlins, 1951—55; county and pros. atty. Rawlins, 1955—59; pvt. practice, 1959—67; assoc. dir. Am. Judicature Soc., Chgo., 1967—74; gen. counsel True Oil Co. and affiliates, 1974—98, of counsel, 1998—99. Bd. dirs. Hilltop Nat. Bank, Casper, sec., 1981—; legal adv. divsn. Nat. Ski Patrol Sys., 1975-88; city atty. City of Rawlins, 1963-65; atty., asst. sec. Casper Mountain Ski Patrol, 1988—. Author: Wyoming's Greatest Admiral: Emory S. Land; columnist: Vets Hotline, 1994— (hon. mention award, Wyo. Press Assn., 2004); editor (and contbr.): WY-VETS News, 1997—2003. Chmn. mil. affairs com. Casper C. of C., 1995-2000; mem. Wyo. Ho. of Reps., 1952-54; bd. dirs. Vols. in Probation, 1969-82; leader lawyer del. to China, People to People, 1986; mem. Wyo. Vets. Affairs Commn., 1994-2003, chmn., 1996-2003; mem. legis. com. United Vets. Coun. Wyo., 1993—; trustee Troopers Found., Inc., 1994—, pres., 1994-99, 2005 -; pres. Casper WWII Commemorative Assn., 1995-96; dir. Vets.'

History Project, 2003—; mem. adv. bd. Wyo. Meml. Mus., 2002-. Recipient Dedicated Cmty. Worker award Rawlins Jr. C. of C., 1967, Yellow merit star award Nat. Ski Patrol System, 1982, 85, 87, 88, Small Bus. Administrate Vet. Adv. award, 1998, Disting. Svc. award Disabled Am. Vets. Dept., 1994, Commendation award Joint Resolution Wyo. Legis., 2003, 07, Medal of Excellence award N.G. Assn., 2003, R. Stanley Lowe Adminstrv. award, 2004; proclaimed R. Stanley Lowe Day, City of Casper, Oct. 11, 2003. Fellow Am. Bar Found. (life); mem. VFW (post adv. 1991-96, nat. aide-de-camp 1993-94, 98-99, judge adv. dist. 3 Dept. Wyo., 1994-01, mil. order of cootie grand judge adv. 1994-01), ABA (sec. jud. adminstrn. divsn. lawyers conf., exec. com. 1975-76, chmn. 1977-78, chmn. judicial qualification and selection com. 1986-93, coun. jud. adminstrn. divsn. 1977-78, mem. com. to implement jud. adminstrn. stds. 1978-83, Ho. of Dels. state bar del. 1978-80, 86-87, state del. 1987-93, Assembly del. 1980-83, mem. standing com. on the fed. judiciary 1997-99, ad hoc com. state justice initiatives 1997-99), Am. Judicature Soc. (dir. 1961-67, 85-89, bd. editors 1975-77, Herbert Harley award 1974), Wyo. State Bar (chmn. com. on cts. 1961-67, 77-87), Nebr. State Bar Assn., Ill. State Bar Assn., D.C. Bar, Selden Soc., Navy League (Wyo. coun. pres. 1997-00, state pres. 2000-03, pres. Rocky Mountain North Area. 2003-04, nat. dir. 2003—, nat. merchant marine and legis. coms., 2005—), Rocky Mountain Oil and Gas Assn. (legal com. 1976-99, chmn. 1979-82, 90-91), Rocky Mountain Mineral Law Found. (trustee 1980-94), Am. Law Inst. (life), Order of Coif, Delta Theta Phi (dist. chancellor 1982-83, chief justice 1983-93, assoc. justice 1993—; Percy J. Power Meml. award 1983, Gold Medallion award 1990), Am. Legion (chmn. Americanism com. 1993-03, post 2d vice comdr. 2003-04, post comdr. 2004—, nat. merchant marine and legis. coms.), Casper Rotary Club (pres. 1985-86, first recipient Craig Thomas Leadership award), Casper Rotary Found. (dir. 1990—, sec. 1990-00), Internat. Skiing Fellowship of Rotarians (sec., bd. dirs. 1994-98, bd. dirs. 1998-2001, Appreciation plaque 2004), Davis Boyd Meml. Found. (bd. trustees 1999-). Mem. Ch. Of Christ. Avocations: skiing, hiking, reading, writing. Home and Office: 97 Primrose Casper WY 82604-4018 Office Phone: 307-265-1585. Business E-Mail: rolowe@tribcsp.com.

LOWE, SANDRA ELVETA, psychologist; b. Petersburg, Va., Sept. 27, 1946; d. James Elwood and Senora Stith Lowe. BA, Davis and Elkins Coll., Elkins, W. Va., 1968; MS, Ill. Inst. Tech., Chgo., 1970; MA, PhD, Loyola U. Chgo., 1980. Lic. Clin. Psychologist Ill., 1982. Rehab. counselor J.J. Madden Mental Health Ctr., Hines, Ill., 1970—72; instr. psychology Luther Coll., Decorah, Iowa, 1972—74; resident in clin. psychology Northwestern Meml. Hosp., Inst. Psychiatry, Chgo., 1976—77; clin. psychology intern Ravenswood Hosp. Med. Ctr., Chgo., 1977—78; counselor Ctrl. Austin Counseling Ctr., Chgo., 1979—80; staff psychologist Loyola U. Chgo., 1980—2002; clin. psychologist Sandra E. Lowe, Ph.D., Chgo., 1981—. Bd. dirs. Cathedral Counseling Ctr., Chgo., 1994—2000. Voter registrant City of Chgo., 49th Ward, 1992—96; mem., co-chair Peace and Social Justice Commn., St. James Cathedral, Chgo., 1994—2002; presbyterate discernment weekend listening team mem. Episcopal Diocese of Chgo., 1999—; mem. Commn. on Ordained Ministry, Episcopal Diocese of Chgo., 2002—06; vol. Deborah's Pl., Chgo., 1992—. Mem.: APA, Assn. Black Psychologists (pres. 1997—98, co-chair, social action com. 1992—96, bd. dirs. 1988—99, treas. 1989—96), Episcopal Peace Fellowship, Nat. Alliance against Racist and Polit. Repression (life). Episcopalian. Avocations: reading, travel, photography, politics. Office: Sandra E Lowe PhD 737 N Mich Ave Chicago IL 60611 Home Phone: 773-465-5090; Office Phone: 312-440-1709, 312-771-5090. Personal E-mail: elveta@aol.com.

LOWE, SIDNEY, men's college and former professional basketball coach; b. Wash., DC, Jan. 21, 1960; m. Melanie Lowe; children: Sidney Jr., Lindsey, Lantzen. Attended, N.C. State, 1980—83. Guard Ind. Pacers, 1983—84, Detroit Pistons, 1984—85, Atlanta Hawks, 1985, Charlotte Hornets, 1988—89, Minn. Timberwolves, 1989—90, asst. coach, 1991—93, head coach, 1993—94, Vancouver Grizzlies (later Memphis Grizzlies), 2001—03; asst. coach Detroit Pistons, 2004—06; head coach NC State U., 2006—. TV analyst Minn. Timberwolves, 1990—91. Office: NC State U Box 8502 Raleigh NC 27695-8501*

LOWELL, ABBE DAVID, lawyer; b. NYC, Apr. 28, 1952; s. Armand A. and Sylvia (Newman) L.; M. Rhonda F. Kleiner; children: Alizah, Elana. BA magna cum laude, Columbia U., 1974, JD, 1977. Bar: NY 1978, Md. Fed. 1981, US Supreme Ct. 1981, US Ct. Appeals (DC cir.) 1981, US Ct. Appeals (4th cir.) 1981, US Dist. Ct. (dist. Md.) 1981, US Dist. Ct. (DC cir.) 1981, DC 1981, Md. 1984, US Ct. Appeals (2nd cir.) 1986, Conn. Fed. 2001, US Dist. Ct. (so. dist. NY) 2001. Trial atty. US Dept. Justice, Washington, 1977-78, spl. asst. US atty., 1978-79, spl. asst. to atty. gen., 1979—81; assoc. Venable, Baetjes, Houdl & Ciulletti, Washington, 1982-83; founding and mng. ptnr. Brand & Lowell, Washington, 1983—99; DC mng. ptnr., head white collar and spl. investigations practice group Manatt Phelps & Phillips, LLP, Washington, 1999—2003; ptnr. Chadbourne & Parke, Washington, 2003—07, McDermott Will & Emery LLP, 2007—. Mem. nat. adv. bd. Ctr. Nat. Policy, Washington; adj. prof. law Georgetown U., Washington, 1984; counselor to UN High Commr. for Human Rights 1994-95, spl. counselor 1995-96; chief minority counsel of Pres. Clinton to US Ho. Reps. 1998-99. Editor, Columbia Law Rev.; contbr. articles to profl. jours. Mem. Dem. Ctrl. Com. Montgomery County, Kensington, Md., 1982; bd. dirs. Jewish Cmty. Ctr., Rockville, Md., 1982 (gen. counsel 1986); bd. trustee, The Shakespeare Theatre at the Landsburgh. Named one of Top Lawyers in Washington, Washingtonian Mag., 1989, 1992, 1997, 2002, 2004, 75 Best Lawyers in Washington, 2002, Top 10 Most Successful Trial Lawyers, Nat. Law Jour., 2002, 100 Most Influential Lawyers, 2006; Harlan Fiske Stone Scholar. Mem. ABA (former chair, com. on rules, white collar crime sect.), NACDL, Phi Beta Kappa. Avocations: writing, tennis, jogging. Office: McDermott Will & Emery LLP 600 13th St NW Washington DC 20005-3096 Office Phone: 202-974-5600. E-mail: adlowell@chadbourne.com.*

LOWELL, BRET, lawyer; b. NY, Aug. 5, 1953; s. Stanley and Elaine Lowell; 1 child, Michael Stuart. BS in Econs., SUNY, Buffalo, 1975; JD, Georgetown U., 1978. Bar: D.C. 1978, U.S. Dist. Ct. D.C. 1979, U.S. Ct. Appeals (D.C. cir.) 1979, U.S. Supreme Ct. 1997, Va. 2003. Assoc. Brownstein Zeidman and Lore, Washington, 1978-85; ptnr. Brownstein & Zeidman, Washington, 1985-96, Rudnick & Wolfe, Washington, 1996-99, Piper Rudnick LLP, Washington, 1999—2004; ptnr., co-chmn. Franchise & Distribution practice group DLA Piper LLP (formerly known as DLA Piper Rudnick Gray Cary), Reston, Va., 2005—. Author: Regulation of Buying and Selling a Franchise, 1983, 1997, Franchising, 1989, Franchise Sales and Full Agreement Compliance, 1990, Multiple-Unit Franchising: The Key to Rapid System Growth, 1991; coord. (book) Survey of Foreign Laws Affecting International Franchising, 1982; editor Franchise Law Jour., 1984-88, Franchise Law Compliance Manual, 2000. Mem. ABA (forum on franchising, governing com. 1988-97, chair 1992-95, gen. practice sect., co-chair franchise law com. 1989-92), Internat. Bar Assn., N.Am. Securities Adminstrs. Assn. (franchise advisor 1989—), Internat. Franchise Assn., DC Bar Assn., Am. Intellectual Property Law Assn., Licensing Exec. Soc. Office: DLA Piper LLP 1775 Wiehle Ave Ste 400 Reston VA 20190-5159 Office Phone: 703-773-4242. Office Fax: 703-773-5053. Business E-Mail: bret.lowell@dlapiper.com.

LOWELL, FREDERICK K., lawyer; b. NYC, Aug. 9, 1948; BA, Columbia U., 1971; JD, U. Va., 1975. Bar: Va. 1975, Calif. 1975. Assoc. then ptnr. Pillsbury, Madison & Sutro, San Francisco, 1975—2001; (Pillsbury Madison & Sutro merged with Winthrop, Stimson, Putnam and Roberts, 2001); ptnr., govt. relations & polit. law Pillsbury Winthrop LLP, San Francisco, 2001—05; (Pillsbury Winthrop LLP merged with Shaw Pittman LLP, 2005); ptnr., govt. relations & polit. law, chair polit. law group Pillsbury Winthrop Shaw Pittman LLP, San Francisco, 2005—. Author: The Regulation of Politics in Calif. Immediate past chair Lincoln Club of No. Calif.; Calif. delegate Nat. Rep. Convention, 1992, 1996, 2000, 2004; volunteer counsel Bush 2000 Campaign, Bush-Cheney 2004 Campaign. Mem.: ABA, San Francisco Bar Assn., Va. State Bar Assn., Calif. State Bar Assn., Calif. Polit. Atty. Assn. (former pres.). Office: Pillsbury Winthrop Shaw Pittman LLP 50 Fremont St San Francisco CA 94105 Office Phone: 415-983-1585. Office Fax: 415-983-1200. Business E-Mail: frederick.lowell@pillsburylaw.com.

LOWELL, HOWARD PARSONS, archivist, federal agency administrator; b. Rockland, Maine, May 10, 1945; s. Chauncey Vernon Lowell and Delia Coffin (Parsons) Morey; m. Marica Barrell, Feb. 15, 1969 (div. 1980); m. Charlesa Ann Gatson, July 27, 1985 (dec. Oct. 2003); 1 stepchild, Garrett Timmons; m. Mary Harjula, May 5, 2007. BA, U. Maine, Orono, 1967; MS, Simmons Coll., 1974. Adminstrn. svcs. officer Maine State Archives, Augusta, 1968-72; ednl. specialist Mass. Bur. Libr. Ext., Boston, 1974-75; dir. Revere (Mass.) Pub. Libr., 1975-76; freelance cons. Salem, Oreg., 1976-81, Denver, 1976-81; adminstr. resources br. Okla. Dept. Librs., Oklahoma City, 1981-89; archivist, records adminstr. State of Del., 1990-2000; dep. asst. archivist records svcs. Washington Nat. Archives and Records Adminstrn., College Park, Md., 2000—. Acting dir. N.E. Document Conservation Ctr., Andover, Mass., 1978. Commr. Nat. Hist. Publs. and Records Commn., 1997—2000. Mem.: Nat. Assn. Govt. Archives and Records Adminstrs. (bd. dirs. 1985—87, 1995—96, pres. 1992—94), Acad. Cert. Archivists, Phi Beta Kappa, Beta Phi Mu, Phi Alpha Theta, Phi Kappa Phi. Democrat. Unitarian. Office: Nat Archives for Records Adminstrn 8601 Adelphi Rd College Park MD 20740-6001 E-mail: hplowell@aol.com.

LOWELL, J(AMES) DAVID, geological consultant, cattle rancher; b. Nogales, Ariz., Feb. 28, 1928; s. Arthur Currier and Lavina (Cumming) L.; m. Edith Walmisly Sykes, Mar. 30, 1948; children: Susan, William, Douglas. BS in Mining Engring., U. Ariz., 1949, E.Geol., 1959; MS in Geology, Stanford U., 1957; D. Hon. Causa, U. N at. Mayor de San Marcos, Peru, 1998; Dsc (hon.), U. Ariz, 2000. Registered profl. engr., Ariz. Mining engr. to mine foreman Asarco, Chihuahua City, Mex., 1949-51; field geologist to dist. geologist AEC, Grand Junction, Colo., 1951-54; chief geologist to v.p. S.W. ventures Ventures Ltd. and subs., Denver, Tucson, 1955-59; dist. geologist Utah Internat., San Francisco, Tucson, 1959-61; geol. cons. Lowell Mineral Exploration, Tucson, 1961—, pres. Chile, 1985—, Acuarios Mineral, Peru, 1991-96; chmn. Areguipa Resources Ltd., Can., 1993-96; pres. Exploraciones Mineras Lowell SA de CV, Mex., 1998—, Lowell Mineral Exploration LLC, Ariz., 1998—; chmn. Bear Creek Mining Co., 2002—05, exec. chmn., Peru Copper Inc., 2004—07. Mem. bd. dirs. Soc. Econ. Geologists Found., 1986-91; Thayer Lindsley disting. lectr. Soc. Econ. Geologists, 1978; disting. exch. lectr. Soc. Econ. Geologists, 2000-02; cons. to 120 other oil and mining cos., U.S. and fgn. countries, 1961—, to nat. govt. orgn., US; dir. Nat. Mining Hall of Fame, 2000-. Assoc. editor Econ. Geology, New Haven, 1970-75. Recipient Disting. Citizen award U. Ariz., 1974, Soc. Econ. Geol. Thayer Lindsley Dist. Lectr., 1977, Silver Medal Soc. Econ. Geologists, 1983, Medal of Merit Am. Mineral Hall of Fame, 1994; named Can. Mining Man of Yr., No. Miner, 1999; inductee Am. Mining Hall of Fame, 2002. Mem. Ariz. Geol. Soc. (pres. 1965-66), Soc. Econ. Geologists (Silver medal 1983), Am. Inst. Mining Engrs. (pres. Yavapai sect. 1957, Daniel Jackling award 1970, Robert Dreyer award 2000, Earll McConnell award 2000), Can. Inst. Mining and Metall. Engrs. (disting. lectr. 1972), Internat. Assn. on Genesis of Ore Deposits, Mining and Metallurgy Soc. Am. (gold medal award 2001, Soc. Econ. Geologists Penrose medal 2004), Mining Club S.W. (dir. 1969-70), Prescott Country Club. Republican. Episcopalian. Home: 789 Avenida Beatriz Rio Rico AZ 85648-2200 Office: Lowell Mineral Exploration 789 Avenida Beatriz Rio Rico AZ 85648-2200 Home Phone: 520-281-1911; Office Phone: 520-281-8271. Business E-Mail: davidlowell@jdlcopper.com.

LOWELL, MIKE, professional baseball player; b. San Juan, Feb. 24, 1974; m. Bertica Lowell; 1 child, Alexis Ileana. Grad. in Fin., Fla. Internat. U., Miami. Draft pick NY Yankees, 1995, third baseman, 1998—99, Fla. Marlins, 1999—2005, Boston Red Sox, 2005—. Pres. Mike Lowell Found. Named Person of Yr., Boys and Girls Club of Miami, 2003; named to Nat. League All-Star Team, 2002—04, Am. League All-Star Team, 2007; recipient Silver Slugger award, 2003, Nat. League Gold Glove award, 2005. Achievements include being a member of the World Series Champions, 2003. Office: Boston Red Sox 4 Yawkey Way Boston MA 02215-3496*

LOWELL, RICHARD LEE, music educator, musician; b. Dover, NH, Sept. 3, 1944; s. George Earl and Dorothy Lowell; m. Mary Jane Dwyer, May 18, 1968; children: Elizabeth Anne Spingler, Timothy Aaron. B, Berklee Coll. Of Music, 1966. Assoc. prof. jazz composition Berklee Coll. Of Music, Boston, 1970—. Author: (method book) Arranging For Large Jazz Ensemble (Excellence in Tchg. award, 2000). Coach Wakefield (Mass.) Youth Hockey, 1992—96. With US Army, 1967—70. Home: 352 Salem St Wakefield MA 01880 Office: Berklee Coll of Music 1140 Boylston St Boston MA Personal E-mail: richardlowellt@aol.com.

LOWELL, SCOTT, restaurant manager, real estate developer; b. 1967; m. Carolyn Howard. Degree in Bus., Wayne State U., 1993. Pres. Traffic Jam & Snug, Detroit, 1998—, Pied A Terre Inc., Detroit; ptnr. Bronx Bar, Detroit, Cliff Bell's, Detroit, 2006—. Named one of 40 Under 40, Crain's Detroit Bus., 2006. Mem.: U. Cultural Ctr. Assn. (bd. mem.). Office: Traffic Jam & Snug 511 W Canfield Detroit MI 48201 Office Phone: 313-831-9470.

LOWELL, VIRGINIA LEE, retired librarian; b. San Jose, Calif., Nov. 21, 1940; d. Earnest S. and Dorothy (Givens) Greene; children: Michael Edward, Christopher Scott. Student, Reed Coll, 1958-61; BA, U. Calif., Berkeley, 1963; MSLS, Western Res. U., 1964. Cataloger Wittenberg U., Springfield, Ohio, 1965-66, John Carroll U., Cleve., 1966-68, Cuyahoga Community Coll., Cleve., 1968-70, cons., instr., 1970; head catalog dept. Cuyahoga County Pub. Library, Cleve., 1976-78; dir. tech. svcs. Cuyahoga County Pub. Libr., Cleve., 1979-89; dir. Jackson (Mich.) Dist. Libr., 1989—98; state libr. State of Hawaii, 1998—2003. Chmn. bd. trustees Ohionet, Columbus, 1987-89. Mem. ALA, Ohio Libr. Assn. (coord. automation and tech. div. 1988—), No. Ohio Tech. Svc. Librs. (chmn. 1988-89), Ohio Women Librs. (treas. 1987-89), Am. Mgmt. Assn., Mich. Libr. Assn. Democrat. Roman Catholic. Avocation: choral singing.

LOWENBERG, DAVID A., pharmaceutical executive; Pres. Healthcare Devel. Consulting; sr. v.p., dir. site ops. Express Scripts, Inc., Md. Heights, Mo., 1993—99, exec. v.p., COO, 1999—2006, CEO CuraScript, Inc., 2006—; dep. dir. Ariz. Health Care Cost Containment Sys. Bd. dirs. Logos Sch. Office: Express Scripts Inc 13900 Riverport Dr Maryland Heights MO 63043*

LOWENBERG, MARC GREGORY, dentist; b. NYC, Mar. 2, 1946; m. Joan Levy. BA in psychology, Am. U., Washington, DC, 1968; DDS, NYU, 1972. Gen. practice intern Met. Hosp., NYC, 1972—73; pvt. practice cosmetic dentistry Lowenberg and Lituchy, NYC, 1973—. Cons. ABC's Extreme Makeover; adv. bd. cancerandcareers.org; guest Oprah Winfrey Show, Good Morning Am., The View. Mem.: ADA, Dental Soc. State NY, Am. Acad. Implant Dentistry, Internat. Congress Oral Implantologists, Am. Acad. Cosmetic Dentistry, Acad. Gen. Dentistry. Office: Lowenberg and Lituchy 230 Central Park S New York NY 10019 Office Phone: 212-586-2890. Office Fax: 212-586-2889.

LOWENBERG, MICHAEL J., lawyer; s. Carlos Herman Lowenberg and Lupe Casillas-Lowenberg; m. Katherine Amanda Lowenberg, May 11, 2002. BBA in Engring. Route to Bus., U. Tex., Austin, 1995; JD, South Tex. Coll. Law, Houston, 1997. Bar: Tex., US Dist. Ct. (so. and no. dists.) Tex., US Ct. Appeals (5th cir.), US Supreme Ct. Assoc. O'Quinn Law Firm, Houston, 1998—. Mem.: ATLA, Am. Inns Ct., Tex. Trial Lawyers Assn., Houston Trial Lawyers Assn., Houston Young Lawyers Assn., Houston Bar Assn. Office: O'Quinn Law Firm 440 Louisiana St Ste 2300 Houston TX 77002 Office Phone: 713-223-1000. Office Fax: 713-222-6903. Business E-Mail: mikel@oqlaw.com.

LOWENFELD, ANDREAS FRANK, law educator; b. Berlin, May 30, 1930; s. Henry and Yela (Herschkowitsch) L.; m. Elena Machado, Aug. 11, 1962; children: Julian, Marianna. AB magna cum laude, Harvard U., 1951, LLB magna cum laude, 1955. Bar: NY 1955, US Supreme Ct. 1961. Assoc. Hyde and de Vries, NYC, 1957-61; spl. asst. legal adv. US State Dept., 1961-63, asst. legal adviser econ. affairs, 1963-65, dep. legal adviser, 1965-66; fellow John F. Kennedy Inst. Politics Harvard U., Cambridge, Mass., 1966-67; prof. law Sch. Law NYU, NYC, 1967—, Charles L. Denison prof. law, 1981-94, Herbert and Rose Rubin prof. internat. law, 1994—. Arbitrator internat. comml. panels Internat. C. of C., Am. Arbitration Assn., Internat. Ctr. Settlement Investment Disputes. Author (with Abram Chayes and Thomas Ehrlich): Internat. Legal Process, 1968—69; author: Aviation Law, Cases and Materials, 1972, 2d edit., 1981, Internat. Economic Law, vol.I, 1975, 3d edit., 1997, vol. II, 1976, 2d edit., 1982, vol. III, 1977, vol. IV, 1977, 2d edit., 1984, vol. VI, 1979;: 2d edit., 1983, Conflict of Laws, Fed., State and Internat. Perspectives, 1986, 2002, Internat. Litig. and Arbitration, 1993, 2d edit., 2002, 3d edit, 2006, Internat. Litig.: The Quest for Reasonableness, 1996, The Role of Govt. in Internat. Trade: Essays Over Three Decades, 2000, Internat. Econ. Law, 2002, Lowenfeld on International Arbitration, 2005; editor, co-author Expropriation in the Americas: A Comparative Law Study, 1971; assoc. reporter: Am. Law Inst. Restatement on Foreign Relations Law, 1987; co-reporter Am. Law Inst. Project on Internat. Jurisdiction and Judgments, 2006; contbr. articles to profl. jours. Mem.: ABA, Internat. Acad. Comparative Law, Inst. de Droit Internat., Coun. Fgn. Rels., Am. Law Inst., Am. Arbitration Assn. (arbitrator), Am. Soc. Internat. Law (Manley O. Hudson medal 2007), Assn. Bar City NY, Gray's Inn (assoc.). Home: 5776 Palisade Ave Bronx NY 10471-1212 Office: NYU Sch Law Sch Law 40 Washington Sq S New York NY 10012-1005 Office Phone: 212-998-6208. E-mail: andreas.lowenfeld@nyu.edu.

LOWENFELS, FRED M., lawyer; b. Richmond, Va., Mar. 22, 1944; s. Fred C. and Joan (Weber) L.; m. Joan Roberta Brafman, June 10, 1974; children: Erica Anne, Helene Beth. AB, Harvard U., 1965, JD, 1968; postgrad., Univ. Libre de Bruxelles, 1968—69. Bar: N.Y. 1969. Assoc. Wolf, Haldenstein, Adler, Freeman & Herz, NYC, 1970-74; exec. v.p., gen. counsel Transammonia Inc., NYC, 1974—. Trustee Jewish Home & Hosp. Lifecare Sys., NYC, 1974—, chmn. bd. trustees, 2001—05. Mem. Assn. Bar. City of N.Y., Am. Corp. Counsel Assn., Harvard Club N.Y.C. Office: Transammonia Inc 320 Park Ave New York NY 10022-6815 Office Phone: 212-223-3200.*

LOWENFELS, LEWIS DAVID, lawyer; b. NYC, June 9, 1935; s. Seymour and Jane (Phillips) L.; m. Fern Gelford, Aug. 15, 1965; children: Joshua, Jacqueline. BA magna cum laude, Harvard U., 1957, LLB, 1961. Bar: N.Y. 1961, (lic. corp. and securities atty.). Ptnr. Tolins & Lowenfels, NYC, 1967—. Adj. prof. Seton Hall U. Law Sch; lectr. Practicing Law Inst., Southwestern Legal Found., U. Minn. Fed. Bar Assn., 1972; pub. gov. Am. Stock Exch., 1993-96. Co-author: Bromberg and Lowenfels on Securities Fraud and Commodities Fraud, 7 vols., 2004; contbr. articles to profl. jours. With USAR, 1957—63. Mem. ABA (fed. regulation of securities com. 1978—, lectr.), NY County Lawyers Assn. (securities and exchanges com. 1974—), Phi Beta Kappa, Harvard Club. Avocations: reading, writing, athletics. Office: Tolins & Lowenfels 747 3d Ave 19th Fl New York NY 10017-1028 Home Phone: 845-357-1557; Office Phone: 212-421-1965. Business E-Mail: lew@tolinslowenfels.com.

LOWENHAUPT, CHARLES ABRAHAM, lawyer; b. St. Louis, May 19, 1947; s. Henry Cronbach and Cecile (Koven) L.; m. Rosalyn Lee Sussman, Dec. 28, 1969; children: Elizabeth Anne, Rebecca Jane. BA cum laude, Harvard U., 1969; JD magna cum laude, U. Mich., 1973. Bar: Mo. 1973, NY 2006, U.S. Dist. Ct. (ea. dist.) Mo. 1975, U.S. Ct. Appeals (8th cir.) 1975, U.S. Tax Ct. 1975, U.S. Ct. Claims 1975, U.S. Supreme Ct. 1987. Law clk. to presiding justice U.S. Tax Ct., Washington, 1973-75; ptnr. Lowenhaupt & Chasnoff, St. Louis, 1977-94, mem., 1994—; mng. mem. Lowenhaupt & Chasnoff LLC, 2004—; CEO Lowenhaupt Global Advisors LLC, 2006. Spkr. Nat. Assn. Ind. Schs., St. Louis Assn. Legal Assts., Washington U. Bus. Sch., Inst. for Pvt. Investors, numerous others; mem. adv. bd. dirs. Textile Mus., Washington; mem. adv. faculty Inst. for Pvt. Investors 1991-93, emeritus mem. adv. faculty, 1995-; cmty. outreach adv. coun. St. Louis Coll. Pharmacy, 1998—; nat. coun. mem. Washington U., 2004—; lectr. law dept. Fudan U., Shanghai, 1999; spkr. Beijing U. Law Sch. Contbg. author: The Deal, 2003; co-author: Estate Planning, 2001, Wealthy and Wise, 2002. Bd. dirs. Ctrl. West End Assn., Inc., St. Louis, 1976-80, Temple Emanuel, St. Louis, 1982-89, Butterfly Ho., St. Louis, sec., 1995-, Craft Alliance St. Louis, 1987-90, Helicon Found., San Diego, St. Louis Met. Assn. for Philanthropy, St. Louis Regional Med. Ctr. Found., 1993-98 chmn. 1995-98, Crown Ctr. St. Louis sect., St. Louis Zoo Found., 1993-99, sec., 1995-98, Nat. Coun. Jewish Women, 1994-96, Found. for Fiduciary Studies, Pitts., 2000-, Forest Park Forever, 2005-, Barnes Jewish Hosp. Found., 2006-; mem. St. Louis Zool. Subdist. commn., 1989-92, St. Louis Cmty. Sch. Assn., 1981-89, George W. Warren Brown Sch. Social Work nat. coun. Washington U., 2000—; mem. bd. govs. Clements Libr. Assocs., U. Mich., 1997—; mem. exec. com. U.S.-China C. of C. Midwestern Regional Office; pres. Assn. St. Louis U. Librs., Inc., 1982-83; com. chair, Alliance for Bldg. Capacity, Washington U., 2002-; mem. campaign cabinet Cath. Cmty. Svcs. and Archbishops Commn. on Cmty. Health, 2001; bd. trustees St. Louis Art Mus., 2004—. Recipient St. Louis Argus Disting. Citizen award, 2001, Cmty. Svc. award, Young Dems. of St. Louis, 1996. Mem. ABA (tax section, estate and gift section, real property section, probate and trust law, task force legal financial planning, chmn. generation-skipping transfer tax subcom., estate and gift tax com. tax sect. 1995-2004), Mo. Bar Assn. (tax section, probate and trust section), Bar Assn. of Met. St. Louis (tax section, real property and development sect.), Order of the Coif, St. Louis Estate Planning Coun., Order of the Coif. Home: 801 S Skinker Blvd Saint Louis MO 63105-3269 Office: Lowenhaupt And Chasnoff Llc 10 S Broadway Ste 550 Saint Louis MO 63102-1740

LOWENKRON, BARRY FREDERICK, federal agency administrator; BS, Northeastern U.; MS, John Hopkins U. Dir. European security affairs Nat. Security Coun., 1988—89, 1991—93; dir. analytic staff Nat. Intelligence Coun.; spl. asst. to dir. CIA; prin. dep. dir. policy planning staff U.S. Dept. State, asst. sec. democracy, human rights and labor, 2005—. Adj. lectr. Am. fgn. policy John Hopkins U., 1979—; vis. fellow Rand Corp.; mem. Coun. on Fgn. Rels.; spkr. in field. Office: US Dept of State Harry S Truman Bldg 2201 C St NW Rm 7802 Washington DC 20520 Office Phone: 202-647-2590. Office Fax: 202-647-5283.

LOWENSTEIN, ARLENE JANE, nursing educator, health facility administrator; b. Phila., Oct. 10, 1936; d. Nathan Morris and Rae (Greenburg) Needleman; m. Manfred Lowenstein, June 9, 1957; children: Jay David, Russell Scott. Diploma in nursing, Hosp. of U. Pa., Phila., 1957; BSN, Fairleigh Dickinson U., 1969; MA, NYU, 1974; PhD, U. Pitts., 1985. Staff and tchg. nurse Albert Einstein Med. Ctr., Hosp. U. Pa., 1957-59; instr. Middlesex County Coll., Edison, NJ, 1969-71; staff nurse Vis. Nurse Svc., NYC, 1970-72; supr. obstet. and pediat. Middlesex Gen. Hosp., New Brunswick, NJ, 1972-74; dir. ambulatory & cmty. health Peter Bent Brigham Hosp., 1974-79, dir. nurse practitioner program, 1974-81; dir. surg. nursing Brigham and Women's Hosp., Boston, 1980—81; acting dir. nursing Peter Bent Brigham Hosp., Boston, 1978-80; assoc hosp. dir., dir nursing svc. U. Ky. Med. Ctr., Lexington, 1981-83; asst. prof. U. Pitts., 1983-85; prof. nursing, dept. chair. Med. Coll. Ga., Augusta, 1985-95; prof., dir. grad. program in nursing Mass. Gen. Hosp. Inst. of Health Professions, Boston, 1995—2003, prof. emeritus, 2003—. Dir. health professions edn. post masters program, Simmons Coll., 2005—. Author textbooks; contbr. articles to profl. jours. Bd. dirs. Sr. Citizens Coun. of Ctrl. Savannah River Area, Augusta, 1982-95; coord. vols. Opera Boston. Mem. ANA, Coun. Grad. Edn. for Nursing Adminstrs. (chair 1990-92), Sigma Xi, Sigma Theta Tau. Avocations: opera, music, art. Home: 312 Lewis Wharf Boston MA 02110-3905 Business E-Mail: alowenstein@mghihp.edu.

LOWENSTEIN, DEREK IRVING, physicist; b. Hampton Court, Eng., Apr. 26, 1943; came to U.S., 1946; s. Siegfried and Ilse Lowenstein; m. Elaine Hartmann, July 6, 1968; children: Jessica R. Lowenstein-Leif, Peter D. BS, CCNY, 1964; MS, U. Pa., 1965, PhD, 1969. Postdoctoral fellow U. Pa., Phila., 1969-70; research assoc. U. Pitts., 1970-73; asst. physicist Brookhaven Nat. Lab., Upton, NY, 1973-75, assoc. physicist, 1975-77, physicist, 1977-83, sr. physicist, 1983—, head Exptl. Planning and Support div., 1977-84, dep. chmn. accelerator dept., 1981-84, chmn. Alternating Gradient Synchrotron dept., 1984-99, chmn. collider accelerator dept., 1999—; prin. investigator NASA Space Radiation Lab., 2003—; chmn. bd. govs. U.S. Particle Accelerator Sch., 2005—. Assoc. mem. U.S.-Russia Joint Coordinating Commn. on Fundamental Properties of Matter, 1983—, U.S.-Japan Commn. on High Energy Physics, 1984—; mem. Dept. of Energy High Energy Physics Adv. Panel, 1993-96. Contbr. articles on particle and accelerator physics to profl. jours. Fellow AAAS, Am. Phys. Soc.; mem. N.Y. Acad. Scis., Sigma Xi. Office: Brookhaven Nat Lab Collider-Accelerator Dept Upton NY 11973 E-mail: lowenstein@bnl.gov.

LOWENSTEIN, JAMES GORDON, former diplomat, international consultant; b. Long Branch, NJ, Aug. 6, 1927; s. Melvyn Gordon and Katherine Price (Goldsmith) L.; children: Laurinda Vinson (Douglas), Price Gordon. Grad., Loomis Sch., 1945; BA, Yale U., 1949; postgrad., Harvard Law Sch., 1955—56. With Office Spl. Rep. in Europe, Econ. Cooperation Adminstrn., Paris, 1950—51; mem. US Spl. Mission to Yugoslavia, Sarajevo, 1951; fgn. svc. officer Bur. European Affairs Dept. State, 1957—58; fgn. svc. officer Am. Embassy, Colombo, 1959—61, Belgrade, 1961—64; cons. Fgn. Rels. Com., US Senate, Washington, 1965—74; prin. dep. asst. sec. state for European affairs Washington, 1974—77; amb. to Luxembourg, 1977—81; with Bur. European Affairs, Dept. State, 1981—82; ptnr. IRC Group, Washington, 1982—87; sr. cons. APCO Assoc., Washington, 1988—99; sr. advisor Heller and Rosenblatt, Washington, 2000—. Mem. internat. observer group Sri Lanka elections, 1993, 94, sr. elections adv. Osce Mission to Bosnia, 1996, 97; past chmn. bd. dir. The Ukraine Fund; past trustee Lafarge (U.S.) Holdings Trust; past sec. bd. Emerging Eastern European Fund; past chmn. Baltic Investments; past dir. AIS Worldwide Fund; co-founder, bd. dir. French-Am. Found.; past bd. dir. Refugees Internat.; past mem. adv. coun. Sch. Advanced Internat. Studies and Bologna (Italy) Ctr. Johns Hopkins U.; trustee Am. Libr. Paris. Lt. (j.g.) USNR, 1952-55, staff Naval War Coll., 1954-55. Decorated officer Légion d'Honneur (France); Grand Croix de la Couronne de Chene (Luxembourg). Mem. Coun. Fgn. Rels., Internat. Inst. Strategic Studies, French Inst. Internat. Rels., Met. Club, Century Assn., Knickerbocker Club, Explorers Club, River Club, Travellers Club of Paris, Polo de Paris. Home: 3139 O St NW Washington DC 20007-3117 also: 52 Rue de Varenne 75007 Paris France Office: Heller & Rosenblatt Ste 205 1101 15th St NW Washington DC 20005-5002 Office Phone: 202-466-4700. Personal E-mail: jamesglowen@aol.com.

LOWENSTEIN, LOUIS, law educator; b. NYC, June 13, 1925; s. Louis and Ralphina (Steinhardt) L.; m. Helen Libby Udell, Feb. 12, 1953; children: Roger Spector, Jane Ruth, Barbara Ann. BS, Columbia, 1947, LL.B., 1953; M.F.S., U. Md., 1951. Bar: N.Y. 1953. Pvt. practice law, NYC, 1954-78; Assoc. Judge Stanley H. Fuld, N.Y. Ct. Appeals, 1953-54; assoc., then partner Hays, Sklar & Herzberg, 1954-68; partner Nickerson, Kramer, Lowenstein, Nessen, Kamin & Soll, 1968-78; Simon H. Rifkind prof. emeritus law and fin. Columbia U. Law Sch., 1980—, project dir. Instl. Investor Project, 1988-94; pres. Supermarkets Gen. Corp., Woodbridge, NJ, 1978-79. Bd. dirs. Liz Claiborne, Inc. 1988-96; mem. pub. oversight bd. Panel on Audit Effectiveness, 1998-2000. Author: What's Wrong with Wall Street, 1988, Sense and Nonsense in Corporate Finance, 1991; contbr., co-editor: Knights, Raiders and Targets, 1988; editor in chief Columbia Law Rev., 1951-53. V.p., mem. exec. com. Fedn. Jewish Philanthropies N.Y.; pres. Jewish Bd. Family and Children's Svcs. N.Y., 1974—78; trustee Beth Israel Med. Ctr., NYC, 1975—81; dir. Goddard-Riverside Cmty. Ctr., 1996—2002; mem. Citizens Budget Commn., 2003—, NY State Commn. Pub. Authority Reform, 2005—06; chmn. bd. dirs. Coalition for the Homeless, 1997—2004, chmn. emeritus, 2004—. Mem.: ABA, Am. Law Inst., Assn. Bar City of NY. Office: Columbia U Law Sch 435 W 116th St New York NY 10027-7297

LOWENSTEIN, RALPH LYNN, university dean emeritus; b. Danville, Va., Mar. 8, 1930; s. Henry and Rachel (Berman) L.; m. Bronia Grace Levenson, Feb. 6, 1955; children: Joan, Henry. BA, Columbia U., 1951, MS in Journalism, 1952; PhD in Journalism, U. Mo., 1967. Reporter Danville Register, Va., 1952, El Paso Times, 1954-57; asst. prof. journalism U. Tex. at El Paso, 1956-62, assoc. prof., 1962-65; publs. editor Freedom of Info. Ctr., Columbia, Mo., 1965-67; vis. prof., head journalistic studies Tel Aviv U., 1967-68; assoc. prof. Sch. Journalism, U. Mo., Columbia, 1968-70, prof., 1970-76, chmn. news-editorial dept., 1975-76; press critic CBS Morning News, 1975-76; dean Coll. Journalism and Communications, U. Fla., Gainesville, 1976-94. Bd. dirs. Aliyah Bet & Machal Archives U. Fla. Librs. Author: Bring My Sons from Far, 1966, Pragmatic Fund-Raising, 1997; author: (with John C. Merrill) Media, Messages and Men, 2d edit., 1979, Macromedia, 1990; editor (with Paul Fisher): Race and the News Media, 1967. Dir. Mus. Am. and Can. Vols., Israel's War of Independence, 2004-. Served with Israeli Army, 1948; AUS, 1952-54. Named to Fla. Freedom of Info. Hall of Fame, 1997; recipient Disting. Svc. award, Columbia Journalism Alumni, 1957, 30th Anniversary award, State of Israel, 1978, Freedom Forum Journalism Adminstr. of Yr. award, 1994. Mem.: Soc. Profl. Journalists (Rsch. in Journalism award 1971), Assn. Edn. in Journalism and Mass Comm. (pres. 1990—91). Home: 1705 NW 22nd Dr Gainesville FL 32605-3953 Office Phone: 352-392-6525. Business E-Mail: rlowenstein@jou.ufl.edu.

LOWENTHAL, ABRAHAM FREDERIC, international relations educator; b. Hyannis, Mass., Apr. 6, 1941; s. Eric Isaac and Suzanne (Moos) L.; m. Janet Wyzanski, June 24, 1962 (div. 1983); children: Linda Claudina, Michael Francis; m. Jane S. Jaquette, Jan. 20, 1991. AB, Harvard U., 1961, MPA, 1964, PhD, 1971; postgrad., Harvard Law Sch., 1961—62. Tng. assoc. Ford Found., Dominican Republic, 1962-64, asst. rep. Lima, Peru, 1969-72; asst. dir., then dir. of studies Coun. Fgn. Rels., NYC, 1974-76; dir. Latin Am. program Woodrow Wilson Internat. Ctr. for Scholars, Washington, 1977-83; exec. dir. Inter-Am. Dialogue, Washington, 1982-92; prof. Sch. Internat. Rels., U. So. Calif., LA, 1984—; dir., ctr. internat. studies U. So. Calif., 1992-97; pres. Pacific Coun. Internat. Policy, LA, 1995—2005; v.p. Coun. Fgn. Rels., 1995—2005. Vis. fellow, rsch. assoc. Ctr. Internat. Studies, Princeton U., 1972-74, lectr., 1974; vis. lectr. polit. sci. Cath. U. Santiago, Dominican Republic, 1966; spl. cons. Commn. U.S.-L.Am. rels., N.Y.C., 1974-76; mem. internat. adv. bd. Ctr. U.S.-Mex. Rels., U. Calif.-San Diego, 1981-94; mem. internat. adv. bd. Helen Kellogg Inst., 1984-95; cons. Ford Found., 1974-90. Author: The Dominican Intervention, 1972, 2nd edit., 1995, Partners in Conflict: The United States and Latin America in 1990s, 1991; editor, contbg. author: The Peruvian Experiment: Continuity and Change Under Military Rule, 1975, Armies and Politics in Latin America, 1976, Exporting Democracy: The United States and Latin America, 1991; co-editor, contbg. author: The Peruvian Experiment Reconsidered, 1983, The California-Mexico Connection, 1993; editor Latin Am. and Caribbean Record, vol. IV, 1985-86, vol. V, 1986-87, Latin America in a New World, 1994, Constructing Democratic Governance: Latin America, 1996; mem. editl. bd. Jour. Inter-Am. Studies and World Affairs, 1980-97, New Perspectives Quarterly, 1984—, Hemisphere, Internat. Security, 1977-85, Wilson Quar., 1977-83; contbr. articles to profl. jours. Mem. nat. adv. coun. Amnesty Internat., 1977-83, Ctr. for Nat. Policy, 1986—. Mem. Internat. Inst. Strategic Studies, Am. Polit. Sci. Assn. (coun. 1979-81), Latin Am. Studies (exec. coun. 1979-81), Coun. Fgn. Rels. Democrat. Jewish. Office: U So Calif Los Angeles CA 90089-0035 Office Phone: 213-740-0793. Business E-Mail: afl@usc.edu.

LOWENTHAL, CONSTANCE, art historian, consultant; b. NYC, Aug. 29, 1945; d. Jesse and Helen (Oberstein) L. BA cum laude, Brandeis U., 1967; AM, Inst. Fine Arts, NYU, 1969; PhD, Inst. Fine Arts, NYU, NYC, 1976. Mem. faculty Sarah Lawrence Coll., Bronxville, NY, 1975-78; asst. mus. educator Met. Mus. Art, NYC, 1978-85; exec. dir. Internat. Found. Art Research, NYC, 1985-98; dir. Commn. for Art Recovery World Jewish Congress, NYC, 1998-2001; cons. art ownership disputes NYC, 2001—. Bd. dirs. Ctr. for Edn. Studies, Inc. Regular contbr. Art Crime Update column Wall Street Jour., 1988-97; mem. editl. bd.: The Spoils of War, World War II and Its Aftermath: The Loss, Reappearance and Recovery of Cultural Property, 1997; contbr. articles to Mus. News and other profl. publs. Business E-Mail: cl@lowenthal-inc.com.

LOWENTHAL, DAVID, historian, geographer; b. NYC, Apr. 26, 1923; s. Max and Eleanor (Mack) L.; m. Mary A. Lamberty, Oct. 16, 1970. BA, Harvard U., 1943; MA, U. Calif., Berkeley, 1950; PhD, U. Wis., 1953. Rsch. analyst U.S. State Dept., Washington, 1945-46; asst. prof. history Vassar Coll., Poughkeepsie, NY, 1952-56; rsch. assoc. Am. Geog. Soc., NYC, 1958-72; with U. of the West Indies, Jamaica, 1956-70, history lectr., rsch. assoc., cons. to vice chancellor; with Inst. of Race Rels., London, 1961-72; prof. geography U. Coll., London, 1972-85, hon. rsch. fellow, 1986—; vis. prof. heritage studies St. Mary's U. Coll. Strawberry Hill, England, 1995-2000. Mem. bd., contbg. editor Internat. Ency. Social Scis., 1964-68; U.S., U.K. del. Internat. Coun. on Monuments and Sites, mem. gen. assembly, 1981, 87, cons. hist. landscapes and site authenticity, 1994—. Author: George Perkins Marsh: Versatile Vermonter, 1958, West Indian Societies, 1972, The Past is a Foreign Country, 1985 (Univ. and Profl. Pub. award 1986), The Heritage Crusade and the Spoils of History, 1996, George Perkins Marsh, Prophet of Conservation, 2000 (J.B. Jackson award, finalist Brit. Acad. prize). Georgian Group del. Harrow Conservation Area Adv. Com., 1987—97; sec., dir. Crown St. and Area Residents Assn., Harrow, 1974—2001. With US Army, 1943—45. Recipient Victoria medal, Royal Geog. Soc., 1997, Cullum Geog. medal, Am. Geog. Soc., 1999, medal, Royal Scottish Geog. Soc., 2004; fellow, Leverhulme emeritus, 1992—93, John Simon Guggenheim Found., 1965—66, Brit. Acad., 2001; Landes Sr. fellow, Rsch. Inst. the Study of Man, 1992—93. Mem. AAAS (councilor 1964-71), Soc. for Caribbean Studies (founding chair 1977-79), Landscape Rsch. Group (vice chair 1979-84, chair 1984-89), Internat. Cultural Property Soc. (editl. bd. 1989—). Office: Univ Coll London London England Home: 22 Heron Place 9 Thayer St London W1U 3JL England also: 1401 LeRoy Ave Berkeley CA 94708 Business E-Mail: d.lowenthal@ucl.ac.uk.

LOWENTHAL, STEVEN R., lawyer; BS, U. Calif., Berkeley, 1979; JD, Stanford U., 1982. Bar: Calif. 1982, admitted to practice: US Ct. Appeals (9th Cir.), US Dist. Ct. (No. and Ctrl. Dists. Calif.), Ct. Fed. Claims, Washington, DC. Ptnr. Farella Braun & Martel LLP, San Francisco, mng. ptnr., 2005—. Faculty, trial advocacy program Stanford Law Sch. Advocacy Skills Workshop. Mem.: Assn. Bus. Trial Lawyers (v.p.). Office: Farella Braun & Martel LLP Russ Bldg 235 Montgomery St San Francisco CA 94104-3105 Office Phone: 415-954-4405. Office Fax: 415-954-4480. Business E-Mail: slowenthal@fbm.com.

LOWER, ELYSE E., physician, educator; b. Salem, Ohio, Mar. 28, 1953; d. John E. and Joyce E Lower; m. Robert P. Baughman, May 26, 1984. BS, Baylor U., Waco, Tex., 1975; MA, Baylor U., 1977; MD, U. Cin., 1981. Fellow in hematology-medical oncology U. Cin., 1984—87, asst. prof. internal medicine, 1987—92, assoc. prof., 1992—99, prof. internal medicine, 1999—; ptnr. Oncology-Hematology Care, Inc., Cin., 1999—. Named Health Care Hero, Cin. Bus. Courier, 1999; recipient award of hope, Greater Cin. Breast Cancer Alliance, 1996, honoree, Speaking of Women's Health, 2000, Leading Women Honoree, Cin. Bus. Courier, 2001. Fellow: ACP (fellow 1999); mem.: Am. Soc. Clin. Oncology (life). Office: U Cin Holmes Rm 1001 Eden and Bethesda Cincinnati OH 45267-0565 Home Phone: 513-221-0067.

LOWER, JOSEPH, air transportation executive; b. 1967; BS, Northwestern Univ., Chgo. Investment banker Credit Suisse First, Boston, 1990; v.p. corp., strategic. devel. Boeing Co., Chgo., 2002—. Named one of 40 Under Forty, Crain's Chgo. Bus., 2005. Avocation: bicycling. Office: Boeing Co 100 North Riverside Chicago IL 60606*

LOWER, ROBERT CASSEL, lawyer, educator; b. Oak Park, Ill., Jan. 8, 1947; s. Paul Elton and Doris Thatcher (Heaton) L.; m. Jean Louise Lower, Aug. 24, 1968 (dec. Aug. 1985); children: David Elton, Andrew Bennett, James Philip Thatcher; m. Cheryl Bray, July 26, 1986. AB magna cum laude with highest honors, Harvard U., 1969, JD, 1972. Bar: Ga. 1972. Assoc. Alston & Bird, Atlanta, 1972-78; ptnr., e-commerce, healthcare, privacy area Alston & Bird LLP, Atlanta, 1978—. Adj. prof. Emory U., 1978-85, 92. Contbr. articles to profl. jours. Co-founder, pres. Ga. Lawyers for the Arts, Inc., 1975—79; chmn. Fulton County (Ga.) Arts Coun., 1979—87; trustee Woodruff Arts Ctr., 1988—95, Piedmont Coll., Ga. Found. Ind. Colls. Mem. Ga. Bar Assn., Atlanta Bar Assn., Midtown Bus. Assn. (bd. dirs. 1988-90), Author's Ct. Harvard Club (Ga.), Phi Beta Kappa. Presbyterian. Avocations: running, music, bonsai. Office: Alston & Bird LLP 1 Atlantic Ctr 1201 W Peachtree St NW Atlanta GA 30309-3400 Office Phone: 404-881-7455. Business E-Mail: bob.lower@alston.com.

LOWERY, CHARLES DOUGLAS, historian, dean, educator; b. Greenville, Ala., May 8, 1937; s. Reuben F. and Frances Louise (Jordan) L.; m. Sara Bradford, June 24, 1961; children: Thomas Bradford, Douglas Trenton, Charles Daniel. BA, Huntingdon Coll., 1959; MA, Fla. State U., 1961; PhD, U. Va., 1966. Asst. prof. history Ball State U., Muncie, Ind., 1964-66; from asst. prof. to prof. Miss. State U., Starkville, 1966—, head dept. history, 1985—, asst. dean Coll. Arts and Scis., 1971-74, assoc. dean, 1974-81, dir. Inst. for Humanities, 1981-85. Author: James Barbour: The Biography of A Jeffersonian Republican, 1984, (with others) America: The Middle Period, 1973, Encyclopedia of African-American Civil Rights: From Emancipation to the Present, 1992, The Greenwood Encyclopedia of African-American Civil Rights, 2004; contbr. articles to profl. jours. Mem. Miss. Com. for Humanities, Jackson, 1986-88; vice chmn. Miss. Humanities Coun., Jackson, 1988-89; active Habitat for Humanity. Grantee NEH, 1980, 81, 84, Miss. Humanities Coun., 1983, 84, 88. Mem. Orgn. Am. Historians, Soc. Historians of Early Am. Rep., So. Hist. Soc., Miss. Hist. Soc. (com. chmn. 1989-90). Democrat. Presbyterian. Avocations: camping, travel, fishing, historical preservation, woodworking. Home: 609 Sherwood Rd Starkville MS 39759-4009 Office: Miss State U Dept History Drawer H Mississippi State MS 39762 Personal E-mail: charsue36@excite.com.

LOWERY, CHRISTOPHER M., men's college basketball coach; b. Evansville, Ind., July 7, 1972; m. Erika Lowery. B in Phys. Edn., So. Ill. U., 1995. Asst. coach Rend Lake CC, Ina, Ill.; head coach Mo. So. State Coll.; asst. coach S.E. Mo. State, U. Ill., 2003, So. Ill. U., Carbondale, head coach, 2004—. Named a Divsn. I All-Dist. Coach (Dist. 11), Nat. Assn. Basketball Coaches, 2007; named Mo. Valley Conf. Coach of Yr., 2005, 2007. Office: Intercollegiate Athletics So Ill U Mailcode 6620 Carbondale IL 62901 Office Phone: 618-453-4667. E-mail: cmlowery@siu.edu.*

LOWERY, CLAY, federal agency administrator; BA, U. Va.; MS, London Sch. Econs. Dir. internat. fin. NSC, Exec. Office of Pres., Washington; dep. asst. sec. internat. debt. devel. & quantitative analysis US Dept. Treasury, asst. sec. internat. affairs, 2005—; v.p. markets & sector assessments Millennium Challenge Corp., 2002—05. Office: US Dept Treasury Rm 4460 1500 Pennsylvania Ave NW Washington DC 20220 Office Phone: 202-622-1270. Office Fax: 202-622-0417.

LOWERY, DANIEL LOUIS, publishing executive; b. Geneva, Ill., July 4, 1963; s. Martin Bernard Lowery and Rita Louise Kunka; m. Claudia Gomez, Apr. 14, 2001; 1 child, Ryan Alexander. BS, Ill. State U., Normal, 1986. Pres. Lowery Books, Santa Barbara, Calif., 2006—. Author: Battling The Corporate Giants: The Ultimate David and Goliath Story, 2006 (Selected as a book of note by Jewish Book World, 2007). Mem.: Lambda Chi Alpha (assoc.). Democrat. Avocations: chess, swimming, travel, literature, history. Home Phone: 805-637-9857; Office Phone: 805-882-9201. Personal E-mail: lowerybooks@netscape.com. Business E-Mail: dlowery@lowerybooks.com.

LOWERY, DAVID J., lawyer; b. Belleville, Ill., Dec. 3, 1953; BBA cum laude, So. Meth. U., 1975, JD, 1978. Bar: Tex. 1978. Mem. Jones, Day, Reavis & Pogue, Dallas; now ptnr., co-chair real estate practice worldwide Jones Day, Dallas. Editorial bd. Briefings in Real Estate Fin. Mem.: Nat. Assn. Real Estate Investment Trusts, State Bar of Tex. Office: Jones Day 2727 N Harwood St Dallas TX 75201-1515 Office Phone: 214-969-3710. Office Fax: 214-969-5100. Business E-Mail: djlowery@jonesday.com.

LOWERY, KATHLEEN ANN, elementary school educator; b. Oswego, NY, Aug. 28, 1949; d. Joseph Harold and Mary Agnes (Mulcahey) Lowery. BS, SUNY, Oswego, 1971. Art tchr. Little Falls City Sch. Dist., NY, 1971—73, kindergarten tchr., 1973—2006; ret., 2006. Mem. early childhood adv. com. Herkimer County C.C., NY, 1993—2006. Mem.: NY State United Teachers, Little Falls Tchrs. Assn. Avocations: art, sports, crafts. Home: 305 Lansing St Herkimer NY 13350

LOWERY, ROBERT CHESLEY, thoracic surgeon, educator; b. Columbus, Ohio, Oct. 7, 1949; s. Robert Lowery and Rutha Mae Whiteside; m. Nancy Lowery, July 19, 1986 (div. Dec. 9, 2002); 1 child, Jason. At, State U. of Calif. at LA, 1969—72; MD, U. Calif., San Francisco, 1976. Cert. Nat. Bd. of Med. Examiners, 1978, Am. Bd. of Surgery, 1984, Am. Bd. of Thoracic Surgery, 1986. Dir. sickle cell screening and testing, student nat. med. ctr. U. Calif., San Francisco, 1974—75; acting chief divsn. of cardiothoracic surgery Howard U., Washington, 1987—88; chmn. med. adv. com. Washington Regional Transplant Consortium, 1987—89; co-founder Cardiovasc. and Thoracic Surgery Assoc., Washington, 1994; prof. surgery SUNY Downstate Sch. of Medicine, Bklyn., 2002—06; chief divsn. of cardiothoracic surgery, Downstate Sch. of Medicine SUNY, Bklyn., 2002—06; pvt. practice Washington, 1989—2002. Pres. Stillwild Photography, Washington, 1995—; mem. bd. med. dirs. Life Link MD, Washington, 2000—05. Contbr. articles to profl. jours. Fundraiser DC Pub. Sch., Washington, 2002. Recipient commendation, NY Health and Hosp. Corp., 1979, Patient Choice award, Washington Hosp. Ctr., 1997—2001, Top Dr., Washingtonian mag., 1999. Mem.: Cosmos Club, Sigma Alpha, Epsilon Boulé chpt. Roman Catholic. Achievements include development of new vascular procedure. Avocations: skiing, scuba diving, photography, hiking, wine collecting. Office: SUNY Downstate Med Ctr 450 Clarkson Ave Brooklyn NY 11203 Office Phone: 718-270-1981. Business E-Mail: rlowery@downstate.edu.

LOWERY, WILLIAM HERBERT, lawyer; b. Toledo, June 8, 1925; s. Kenneth Alden and Drusilla (Pfanner) L.; m. Carolyn Broadwell, June 27, 1947; children: Kenneth Latham, Marcia Mitchell; m. Janice Gamble Gerrie, Dec. 28, 2002. PhB, U. Chgo., 1947; JD, U. Mich., 1950. Bar: Pa. 1951, U.S. Supreme Ct. 1955. Assoc. Dechert Price & Rhoads, Phila., 1950-58, ptnr., 1958-89, mng. ptnr., 1970-72; mem. policy com., chmn. litigation dept., 1962-68, 81-84; of counsel Dechert, Phila., 1989—; counsel S.S. Huebner Found. Ins. Edn., Phila., 1970-89. Faculty Am. Conf. of Legal Execs., Pa. Bar Inst.; permanent mem. com. of visitors U. Mich. Law Sch. Author: Insurance Litigation Problems, 1972, Insurance Litigation Disputes, 1977. Pres. Strafford Civic Assn., 1958; chmn. Tredyffrin Twp. Zoning Bd., Chester County, Pa., 1959—75; bd. dirs. Paoli Meml. Hosp., 1964—89, chmn., 1972—75; bd. dirs. Main Line Health, Radnor, 1984—89; permanent mem. Jud. Conf. 3d Cir. Ct. 2n lt. USAF, 1943—46. Mem. ABA (chmn. life ins. com. 1984-85, chmn. Nat. Conf. Lawyers and Life Ins. Cos. 1984-88), Order of the Coif, Royal Poinciana Golf Club (bd. dirs. 1997-2003, sec. 1997-2000, v.p. 2000-03), Phi Gamma Delta, Phi Delta Phi. Home: 160 Moorings Pk Dr Apt 301 Naples FL 34105

LOWES, ALBERT CHARLES, lawyer; b. Oak Ridge, Mo., Dec. 1, 1932; s. Guy Everett and Lillian Bertina (Tuschhoff) L.; m. Peggy Rae Watson, Aug. 27, 1960; children: Danita Rae, Albert Charles II, Kurt Brandon. Student, Cape State Coll., 1954-56; JD, U. Mo., 1959. Bar: Mo. 1959, U.S. Dist. Ct. (ea. dist.) Mo. 1959, U.S. Ct. Appeals (8th cir.) 1971. With Buerkle, Lowes, Beeson & Ludwig, Jackson, Mo., 1959-84; ptnr. Lowes & Drusch, Cape Girardeau, 1984—. Atty. City of Jackson, 1960-62. Staff sgt. USMC, 1950-54, Korea. Mem. Mo. Bar Assn., VFW (judge adv. dept. Mo.1962-64, 67-68, 97-98), Masons, Shriners, Elks. Democrat. Lutheran. Avocations: reading, history, legal fields. Office: Lowes & Drusch 2913 Independence St Cape Girardeau MO 63703-8320

LOWEY, NITA MELNIKOFF, congresswoman; b. NYC, July 5, 1937; m. Stephen Lowey, 1961; children: Dona, Jacqueline, Douglas. BA in Mktg., Mt. Holyoke Coll., Mass., 1959. Cmty. activist, prior to 1975; asst. to NY sec. state for econ. devel. and neighborhood preservation, dir. divsn. econ. oppurtunity NY State, 1975—85, asst. sec. state, 1985—87; mem. US Congress from 20th NY dist., 1989-92, US Congress from 18th NY dist., 1993—. Mem. homeland security com. US Congress, mem. appropriations com., chairwoman state and fgn. ops. subcommittee, co-chair Congl. anti-terrorism financing task force, co-founder Hudson River Caucus. Bd. dirs. Close-Up Found., Effective Parenting Info. for Children, Windward Sch. Named Legislator of Yr., MADD; named one of 10 Women's Health Heroes, Reader's Digest, 1999; recipient Herbert Tenzer award, Pub. Svc., Five Towns Jewish Coun., 1999, Excellence in Nat. Pub. Leadership award, Nat. Assembly Health and Human Svc. Orgns., 1999, Congl. Leadership award, Coalition to Stop Gun Violence, 2001, Responsible Choices award, Planned Parenthood Fedn. Am. Mem.: Women's

Network of YWCA. Democrat. Jewish. Office: Dist Office 97-45 Queens Blvd Rego Park NY 11374 also: US House Reps 2329 Rayburn House Office Bldg Washington DC 20515 Office Phone: 202-225-6506. Office Fax: 202-225-0546.*

LOWI, THEODORE JAY, political science professor; b. Gadsden, Ala., July 9, 1931; s. Alvin R. and Janice (Haas) L.; m. Angele M. Daniel, May 11, 1963; children: Anna Amelie, Jason Daniel. BA, Mich. State U., 1954; MA, Yale U., 1955, PhD, 1961; HLD (hon.), Oakland U., 1972; LittD (hon.), SUNY, Stony Brook, 1988; Doctorate (hon.), Nat. Found. Polit. Scis., Paris, 1992. Mem. faculty dept. govt. Cornell U., Ithaca, NY, 1959—65, 1972—, asst. prof., 1961-65, John L. Senior prof. Am. instns., 1972—; assoc. prof. U. Chgo., 1965—69, prof., 1969—72. Fellow Ctr. Advanced Study in Behavioral Scis., 1977-78; chair Am. civilization U. Paris, 1981-82. Author: At the Pleasure of the Mayor, 1964, The End of Liberalism, 1969, 2d edit., 1979, Japanese edit., 1981, French edit., 1987, The Politics of Disorder, 1971, Incomplete Conquest: Governing America, 1981, The Personal President: Power Invested, Promise Unfulfilled, 1985, Spanish edit., 1993, The End of the Republican Era, 1995, 2d edit., 2006, La Scienza del Politiche, 1999; author: (with others) Poliscide - Big Government, Big Science, Lilliputian Politics, 1976, 1991, Nationalizing Government: Public Policies in America, 1981; author: (with B. Ginsberg and Kenneth Shepsle) American Government: Power and Purpose, 1990, 9th edit., 2006; author: (with B. Ginsberg) Embattled Democracy, 1995; author: (with B. Ginsberg and M. Weir) We the People, 1997, 6th edit., 2007; author: (with J. Romance) A Republic of Parties? Debating the Two-Party System, 1998; author: (with Robert Kennedy) The Pursuit of Justice, 1964. Recipient Richard Neustadt award for Best Book on Presidency, 1986; Social Sci. Rsch. Coun. fellow, 1963-64; Guggenheim Found. fellow, 1967-68; fellow NEH, 1977-78, Ford Found., 1977-78; Fulbright 40th Anniversary Disting. fellow, 1987; Stephen H. Weiss Presdl. fellowship, 2006. Mem. Am. Polit. Sci. Assn. (v.p. 1985-86, pres. 1991), Am. Acad. Arts and Scis., Policy Studies Orgn. (pres. 1977), Internat. Polit. Sci. Assn. (1st v.p. 1994-97, pres. 1997-2000). Home: 101 Delaware Ave Ithaca NY 14850-4707 Office Phone: 607-255-6766. E-mail: TJL7@cornell.edu. *If there is a how-to of success it is this: a passion for work, an ethic of workmanship, and an idea of what, in the end, is a good product.*

LOWINGER, FREDERICK CHARLES, lawyer; b. Chgo., July 18, 1955; s. Alexander I. and Muriel (Rosencranz) L.; m. Lynn T. Wollins, July 12, 1981; Lauren, Daniel, Stephen. BS in Acctg., MS in Acctg., U. Pa., 1977; JD, U. Chgo., 1980. CPA. Bar: Ill. 1982. Law clk. to Judge J. Skelly Wright US Ct. Appeals (DC cir.), Washington, 1980-81; clk. to Justice William J. Brennan Jr. US Supreme Ct., Washington, 1981-82; assoc. Sidley & Austin, Chgo., 1982—88; ptnr. Sidley Austin LLP, Chgo., 1988—, mem. exec. com., 1996—, head, Chgo. office corp. group, 1999—. Dir. Jewish Vocat. Svc., Chgo., 1993-98. Mem. ABA, Chgo. Bar Assn., Lawyers Club Chgo. Avocations: golf, skiing. Office: Sidley Austin LLP One S Dearborn St Chicago IL 60603 Office Phone: 312-853-7238. Office Fax: 312-853-7036. Business E-Mail: flowinger@sidley.com.

LOWITT, IAN T., investment company executive; BSc in Elec. Engring., U. Witwatersrand, Johannesburg, MSc in Digital Electronics; BA in Philosophy, Politics and Econs., U. Oxford, Eng., MSc in Econs. Engagement mgr. McKinsey and Co.; with Lehman Bros. Holdings, 1994—, chmn. Lehman Bros. Bank FSB, head strategy and corp. devel., global treas., global head of tax, exec. v.p., chief adminstrv. officer Lehman Bros. Europe, co-chief adminstrv. officer, 2006—. Named a Rhodes Scholar. Office: Lehman Bros Holdings 745 Seventh Ave New York NY 10019 Office Phone: 212-526-7000.*

LOWITT, RICHARD, history professor; b. NYC, Feb. 25, 1922; s. Eugene and Eleanor (Lebowitz) L.; m. Suzanne Catharine Carson, Sept., 1953; children: Peter Carson, Pamela Carson Bennett. BSS., CCNY, 1943; MA, Columbia U., NYC, 1945, PhD, 1950. Instr. U. Md., College Park, 1948-52; asst. prof. U. RI, Kingston, 1952-53; faculty mem. Conn. Coll., New London, 1953-66, prof. history, 1966, Fla. State U., Tallahassee, 1966-68, U. Ky., Lexington, 1968-77; prof., chmn. dept. history Iowa State U., Ames, 1977-87, prof., 1987-89, U. Okla., Norman, 1990-97; Regents prof. Univ. Sci. and Arts, Okla., Chickasha, 1998—. Mem. Iowa Humanities Bd., 1987-89; mem. Okla. Humanities Bd., 1995-2001; vis. prof. U. Colo., summer 1953, Yale U., 1961-62, Brown U., 1965-66, U. Chattanooga, summer 1965, Emory U., Atlanta; Sutton prof. U. Okla., 1989-90; Regents prof. U. Sci. and Arts of Okla., Chickasha, 1998—. Author: A Merchant Prince of the 19th Century, 1954, George W. Norris, 3 vols., 1963, 71, 78; editor: Nils Olsen and the Bureau of Agricultural Economics, 1980; co-editor: One Third of a Nation-Lorena Hickok Reports on the Great Depression, 1981, The New Deal and the West, 1984, Letters From An American Farmer: The Eastern European and Russian Correspondence by Roswell Garst, 1987, Henry A. Wallace's Irrigation Frontier: On the Trail of the Cornbelt Farmer, 1990, Bronson M. Cutting, Progressive Politican, 1992, Politics in the Postwar American West, 1995, Fred Harris: His Journey From Liberalism to Populism, 2002 (Outstanding Book Okla. History award Hist. Soc. Okla., 2002), The Standing Bear Controversy: Prelude to Indian Reform, 2003, American Outback: The Oklahoma Panhandle in the Twentieth Century, 2006, Elmer Thomas: Forty Years as Legislator, 2007 Trustee Pub. Libr., Lexington, 1973-77. NEH sr. fellow, 1974, John Simon Guggenheim Found. fellow, 1957; grantee Social Sci. Rsch. Coun., 1958, Am. Coun. Learned Socs., 1962, Am. Philos. Soc., 1964, Huntington Libr., 1986; recipient Gaspar Perez de Villagra award Hist. Soc. N.Mex., 1993, Muriel H. Wright award Hist. Soc. Okla., 1995, 2006. Fellow Agrl. History Soc. (exec. com. 1973-75, pres. 1991-92); mem. Am. Hist. Assn., So. Hist. Assn. (membership com. 1973, Ramsdell prize com. 1975, program com. 1983, nominating com. 1990), Western History Assn. (bd. editors 1986-88, program com. 1995, merit award 1992), Orgn. Am. Historians (nominating com. 1970, Turner prize com. 1972-76, bd. editors 1985-87). Democrat. Office: Univ Okla Dept History Norman OK 73019-0001 Business E-Mail: richard.lowitt-1@ou.edu.

LOWMAN, DAVID, mortgage company executive; b. 1957; married; 2 children. Grad., U. Md. CPA. Auditor KPMG Peat Marwick; CFO Prudential Home Mortgage; mng. dir., Servicing CitiMortgage, 1996—98, pres., COO, 1998—2000; chief servicing and tech. officer Citigroup's US Mortgage Bus., 2000—03; CEO CitiFinancial Internat., 2004—06; CEO, Global Mortgage, mem. exec. com. JPMorgan Chase & Co., NYC, 2006—. Former pres. Consumer Mortgage Coalition. Former bd. mem. Habitat for Humanity, St. Louis; mem., Devel. Bd. Family Support Network. Office: JPMorgan Chase & Co 270 Park Ave New York NY 10017 Office Phone: 212-270-6000. Office Fax: 212-270-1648.*

LOWMAN, JOHN D., JR., physical therapist, researcher; s. John D. Lowman Sr. and Carol W. Smith, Sandra S. Lowman (Stepmother) and Bobby M. Canode (Stepfather), Robert A. Smith (Stepfather); m. Mary (Beth) E. Lindsay, Aug. 17, 1996. BS in Edn., Va. Poly. Inst. and State U., 1993; MS, Duke U., 1995; PhD, Va. Commonwealth U., 2004. Lic. phys. therapist N.C. Bd. Phys. Therapy Examiners, 1995, Ala. State Bd. Phys. Therapists, 2005, cert. cardiovasc. and pulmonary phys. therapy clin. specialist Am. Bd. Phys. Therapy Specialties, 1999. Phys. therapist Vencor Hosp., Greensboro, NC, 1995—96, Interim Healthcare, Durham, 1996—97, Duke U. Med. Ctr., 1996—2005; grad. rsch. and tchg. asst. Va. Commonwealth U., Richmond, 2000—04; postdoctoral assoc. Va. Commonwealth U. Med. Ctr., Richmond, 2005; asst. prof. dept. phys. therapy U. Ala., Birmingham, 2005—. Phys. therapist asst. exam. devel. com. Fedn. State Bds. Phys. Therapy, Alexandria, Va., 2004—06, chair, 2007—; cardiovasc. and pulmonary specialization acad. content experts and specialty coun. Am. Bd. Phys. Therapy Spltys., 2003; adj. instr. New River C.C., Dublin, 1993. Asst scoutmaster Boy Scouts Am. Troop 45, Dublin, 1989—93, Boy Scouts Am. Troop 430, Richmond, 2001—02; asst. scoutmaster Boy Scouts Am. Troop 736, Glen Allen, Va., 2003—05. Recipient Disting. Svc. award, Va. Tech., Cardiac Therapy and Intervention Ctr., 1992, Outstanding Sr. of Yr., Va. Tech Coll. Edn., 1992—93, Paul Gunsten Leadership award, Va. Tech., Health and Phys. Edn. Dept., 1993, Outstanding Acad. Achievement award, Va. Tech., Coll. Edn., 1993, U. Outstanding Svc. award, Va. Commonwealth U., 2004, U. Outstanding Leadership award, 2004; scholar, Va. Tech., Health and Phys. Edn. Dept., 1993, Found. Phys. Therapy, 2003—04; Andrea Walnes Meml. scholar, Va. Tech., Coll. Edn., 1992—93. Mem.: Am. Assn. Cardiovasc. and Pulmonary Rehab., Am. Physiol. Soc., Am. Phys. Therapy Assn. Avocations: bicycling, hiking, backpacking, rock climbing. Office: U Ala Dept Phys Therapy Sch Health Related Pro RMSB 344 1530 3d Ave S Birmingham AL 35294-1212 Home Phone: 205-909-3991; Office Phone: 205-934-5892. Personal E-mail: jdlowman@charter.net. Business E-Mail: jlowman@uab.edu.

LOWMAN, ROBERT PAUL, psychology professor, academic administrator; b. Lynwood, Calif., Jan. 23, 1947; s. Hubert Alden and Martha Guynn (Howard) L.; m. Kathleen Marie Drew, June 25, 1972; children: Sarah Guynn, Amy Katherine. AB, U. So. Calif., 1967; MA, Claremont U., 1969, PhD, 1973. Asst. prof. U. Wis., Milw., 1972-76; adminstrv. officer APA, Washington, 1976-81; asst. dean Kans. State U., Manhattan, 1981-86, assoc. dean grad. sch., 1986-90, assoc. vice provost, 1990-91; dir. rsch. svcs. U. N.C., Chapel Hill, 1991—2002, adj. assoc. prof. psychology, 1991—, assoc. vice chancellor for rsch., 1994-96, 2001—, assoc. vice provost for rsch., 1996-2001. Editor: APA's Guide to Rsch. Support, 1981; contbr. over 30 articles to profl. jours. Recipient numerous grants. Mem. AAAS, APA (sec. bd. sci. affairs 1976-81, sec. com. on internat. rels. in psychology 1978-81), Soc. Psychologists in Mgmt. (newsletter editor 1994-96, bd. dirs. 1996-01, pres. 2000), Nat. Coun. U. Rsch. Adminstrs. (newsletter co-editor 2006—, profl. devel. com. 2006—), Phi Beta Kappa (exec. sec. Alpha NC chpt. 2005—), Phi Kappa Phi, Phi Eta Sigma, Psi Chi. Democrat. Methodist. Home: 104 Chesley Ln Chapel Hill NC 27514-1459 Office: Univ NC Office Vice Chancellor Rsch & Econ Devel CB # 4100 Chapel Hill NC 27599-4100 E-mail: lowman@unc.edu.

LOWMAN, SARA ALLISON, library director; b. Iowa City, Dec. 26, 1961; d. George Willard and Eileen Audrey Sudenga; m. Christopher Jon Lowman; children: Abigail, Kathryn. BA, Carleton Coll., 1984; MLS, U. Iowa, 1985. Sci. and engring. reference libr. Rice U., Houston, 1985—90, head reference dept., 1990—95, asst. univ. libr. pub. svcs., 1995—98, assoc. univ. libr., 1998—2000, dir. Fondren Libr., 2001—, acting vice provost, univ. libr., 2007—. Mem.: ALA (multiple coms. 1985—2001), Jr. League Houston, Beta Phi Mu. Presbyterian. Avocations: travel, aerobics, gardening. Home: 6608 Mercer St Houston TX 77005 Office: Fondren Libr Rice U 6100 S Main St Houston TX 77251-1892 Office Phone: 713-348-2457. Personal E-mail: lowman@rice.edu.*

LOWRANCE, MURIEL EDWARDS, retired educational specialist; b. Ada, Okla., Dec. 28, 1922; d. Warren E. and Mayme E. (Barrick) Edwards; B.S. in Edn., E. Ctrl. State U., Ada, 1954; 1 child: Kathy Lynn Lowrance Gutierrez. Acct., adminstrv. asst. to bus. mgr. E. Ctrl. State U., 1950-68; grants and contracts specialist U. N.Mex. Sch. Medicine, Albuquerque, 1968-72, program specialist IV, dept. orthopaedics, 1975-86; asst. adminstrv. officer N.Mex. Regional Med. Program, 1972-75. Bd. dirs. Vocat. Rehab. Center, 1980-84. Cert. profl. contract mgr. Nat. Contract Assn. Mem. Am. Bus. Women's Assn. (past pres. El Segundo chpt., Woman of Yr. 1974), AAUW, Amigos de las Americas (dir.). Democrat. Methodist. Club: Pilot (Albuquerque) (pres. 1979-80, dir. 1983-84, dist. treas. 1984-86, treas. S.W. dist., 1984-86, gov.-elect S.W. dist. 1986-87, gov. S.W. dist. 1987-88). Home: 4333 Berwick Dr Wichita Falls TX 76309

LOWREY, ALEX ANDRE, biology professor; b. Chgo., Aug. 13, 1955; s. Richard Columbus and Ollie Ruth Lowrey. BS, Ill. State U., Normal, 1976; MS, U. Ill., Chgo., 1980; PhD, U. Ill., Urbana-Champaign, 1989. Rsch. chemist Stepan Chem. Co., Northfield, Ill., 1978—79; post-doctoral rsch. fellow Howard Hughes Med. Inst., U. Chgo., 1989—91, Argonne Nat. Lab., Ill., 1991—93; asst. prof. biology Gainesville Coll., Ga., 1995—2000, assoc. prof. biology, 2000—05; prof. biology Gainesville State Coll., Ga., 2005—. Event supr. Regional Sci. Olympiad, Gainesville, 1998—2006; mem. NE Ga. Med. Ctr. Adv. Bd., Gainesville, 2006—07. Recipient Nat. Rsch. Svc. award, USPHS, 1990—92. Mem.: Project Kaleidoscope Faculty for the 21st Century Network, Assn. Coll. and U. Biology Educators. Avocations: astronomy, container gardening, hiking, comic book collecting. Office: Gainesville State College PO Box 1358 Gainesville GA 30503-1358 Home Phone: 770-925-4143; Office Phone: 770-718-3772. Business E-Mail: alowrey@gsc.edu.

LOWRIE, WILLIAM G., former oil company executive; b. Painesville, Ohio, Nov. 17, 1943; s. Kenneth W. and Florence H. (Strickler) L.; m. Ernestine R. Rogers, Feb. 1, 1969; children: Kristen, Kimberly. BChemE, Ohio State U., 1966. Engr. Amoco Prodn. Co. subs. Standard Oil Co. (Ind.), New Orleans, 1966-74, area supt., Lake Charles, La., 1974-75, div. engr., Denver, 1975-78, div. prodn. mgr., Denver, 1978-79, v.p. prodn., Chgo., 1979-83; v.p. supply and marine transp. Standard Oil Co. (Ind.), Chgo., 1983-85; pres., Amoco Can., 1985-86; sr. v.p. prodn., Amoco Prodn. Co., 1986-87, exec. v.p. USA, 1987-88; exec. v.p. Amoco Oil Co., Chgo., 1989-90, pres., 1990-92; pres. Amoco Prodn. Co., 1992-94; exec. v.p. E&P sector Amoco Corp., 1994-95, pres. 1996-98, dep. CEO BP Amoco. Bd. dirs. Jr. Achievement, Northwestern Meml. Corp.; trustee, bd. dirs. Nat. 4-H Coun. Named Outstanding Engring. Alumnus, Ohio State U., 1979, Disting. Alumnis Ohio State U., 1985. Mem. Am. Petroleum Inst., Soc. Petroleum Engrs., Mid-Am. Club (Chgo.). Republican. Presbyterian.

LOWRY, ALAIRE HOWARD, psychologist; b. Phila., June 4, 1943; d. Lorn Lambier and Etha Johannaber Howard; m. Thomas Wells Lowry, Apr. 20, 1963; children: Michael Andrew, Thomas Ethan. BA in Music with high honors, So. Meth. U., Dallas, 1965; MusM in Conducting, U. Tex., Austin, 1969, Dr.Mus.Arts, 1972, PhD in Psychology, 1988. Diplomate in group psychology Am. Bd. Profl. Psychology; lic. psychologist Tex., 1990. Harpist Dallas Symphony Orch., 1962—65, 1967; tchr. 2d grade St. Mary's Cathedral Sch., Austin, 1965—66; tchr. Ursuline Acad., Dallas, 1966—67; tchg. asst. U. Tex., Austin, 1967—72; instr. Southwestern U., Georgetown, Tex., 1972—79; from asst. to assoc. prof. U. Tex., Austin, 1973—82; psychologist in pvt. practice Austin, 1988—. Asst. scoutmaster, Philmont Trek leader Boy Scouts Am., Austin, 1988—90; chair Psy-Pac, Tex., 1993—94; adminstrv. bd. chair Univ. United. Meth. Ch., Austin, 2001—03; v.p. bd. dirs. Capital Area Mental Health Ctr., Austin, 1992—94; bd. dirs. Am. Group Psychotherapy Found., 2000—01. Mem.: Am. Group Psychotherapy Assn. (ann. meeting mktg. chair 2006), Southwestern Group Psychotherapy Soc. (sec., inst. chair, tng. chair, newsletter editor, mem. chair), Austin Mental Health Ind. Practice Assn. (sec. bd. dirs. 1996—97), Tex. Psychol. Assn. (bd. trustees 1998—2001), Phi Beta Kappa. Democrat. Methodist. Avocations: travel, reading, photography, hiking, skiing. Office: 8140 N Mopac Bldg 2 Ste 200 Austin TX 78759 Office Phone: 512-346-2332. Business E-Mail: dr_lowry@mac.com.

LOWRY, CHARLES BRYAN, librarian, dean; b. Pensacola, Fla., Nov. 9, 1942; s. Charles Wade and Susie (Kinney) L.; m. Marcia Duncan, Nov. 2, 1985; children: Bryan W., Druhan S. BS in History, Spring Hill Coll., Mobile, Ala., 1964; MA in History, U. Ala., 1965; MS in Libr. Sci., U. N.C., 1974; PhD in History, U. Fla., 1979. Chair social scis. Faulkner State Coll., Bay Minette, Ala., 1965-69; head reference Charlotte Libr., U. NC, 1974-78; dir. libr. and learning resources Elon Coll., NC, 1978-80; dir. librs. U. South Ala., Mobile, 1980-85, U. Tex., Arlington, 1985-92; univ. libr. Carnegie Mellon U., Pitts., 1992; dean librs., prof. U. Md., College Park. Ind. libr. cons. mgmt. and info. technologies; vice chair, bd. dirs. So. Libr. Network, Atlanta, 1983-85; users coun. rep. Ctr. Rsch. Librs., Chgo., Online Computer Libr. Ctr., Dublin, Ohio, 1986-88, mem. adv. com. on coll. and U. librs., 1991—; treas., bd. dirs. AMIGOS Bibliog. Coun., Dallas, 1988-92, chmn. bd. dirs., 1991-92, treas., 1990-91, mem. budget and fin. com., 1989-90; chair libr. com. Assn. for Higher Edn. in North Tex., 1987-89; mem. U. Tex. Bd. Regents Com. on Libr. Automation Standards, 1986-87; mem. Tex. Coun. state Univ. Librs., 1985—, access adv. panel Ctr. Rsch. Librs., 1994—. Editor, assoc. editor Assn. Jour. Libr. Adminstrn. and Mgmt., 1987-91; editor Mng. Tech. column Jour. Acad. Librarianship, 1993—; manuscript reviewer U. Ala. Press Com., 1981-85; contbr. articles to profl. jours. Presenter Tex. Voices Sesquicentennial, Ft. Worth, 1986; mem. Forum Ft. Worth, 1987-92, Leadership Ft. Worth, 1986-87, Mayor's Com., 1989-90, Leadership Pitts., 1992—. NDEA fellow U. Fla., Gainesville, 1970-72, UCLA sr. fellow Grad. Sch. Libr. and Info. Sci., Coun. Libr. Resources, 1985; Libr. Tech. Demonstration grantee U.S. Dept. Edn., U. Tex., 1989-91; recipient G.K. Sauer award for best article in Coll. and Rsch. Librs., 1993. Mem. ALA (bd. dirs. libr. adminstrn. and mgmt. assn. 1989-91), Rotary. Democrat. Roman Catholic. Office: U Md Rm 4121 McKeldin Libr College Park MD 20742-7011 Office Phone: 301-405-9127. Office Fax: 301-314-9408. E-mail: clowry@umd.edu.*

LOWRY, EDWARD FRANCIS, JR., lawyer; b. LA, Aug. 13, 1930; s. Edward Francis and Mary Anita (Woodcock) L.; m. Patricia Ann Palmer, Feb. 16, 1963; children: Edward Palmer, Rachael Louise. Student, Ohio State U., 1948—50; AB, Stanford U., 1952, JD, 1954. Bar: Ariz. 1955, D.C. 1970, U.S. Supreme Ct. 1969. Camp dir. Quarter Circle V Bar Ranch, 1954; tchr. Orme Sch., Mayer, Ariz., 1954—56; trust rep. Valley Nat. Bank Ariz., 1958—60; pvt. practice Phoenix, 1960—; assoc. atty. Cunningham, Carson & Messinger, 1960—64; ptnr. Carson, Messinger, Elliott, Laughlin & Ragan, 1964—69, 1970—80, Gray, Plant, Mooty, Mooty & Bennett, 1981—84, Eaton, Lazarus, Dodge & Lowry Ltd., 1985—86; exec. v.p., gen. counsel Bus. Realty Ariz., 1986—93; pvt. practice, Scottsdale, Ariz., 1986—88; ptnr. Lowry & Froeb, Scottsdale, 1988—89, Lowry, Froeb & Clements, P.C., Scottsdale, 1989—90, Lowry & Clements P.C., Scottsdale, 1990, Lowry, Clements & Powell, P.C., Scottsdale, 1991—. Asst. legis. counsel Dept. Interior, Washington, 1969-70; mem. Ariz. Commn. Uniform Laws, 1972—, chmn., 1976-88; judge pro tem Ariz. Ct. Appeals, 1986, 92-94. Chmn. Coun. Stanford Law Socs., 1968; bd. dirs. Scottsdale Prevention Inst., 1999-2003, Cox Comms. Charities, 2006—; vice chmn. bd. trustees Orme Sch., 1972-74, treas., 1981-83; trustee Heard Mus., 1965-91, life trustee, 1991—, pres., 1974-75; ops. bd. dirs. Rio Salado Found., 2006—; bd. visitors Stanford Sch. Law, dir. operational bd. dirs. Rio Salado Town Lake Found., 2003-2006; magistrate Town of Paradise Valley, Ariz., 1976-83, town councilman, 1998-2004, mayor, 1998-2004; juvenile ct. referee Maricopa County, 1978-83. Capt. USAF, 1956-58. Fellow Ariz. Bar Found. (founder); mem. ABA, Maricopa County Bar Assn., Scottsdale Bar Assn., State Bar Ariz. (chmn. com. uniform laws 1979-85), Stanford Law Soc. Ariz. (past pres.), Scottsdale Bar Assn. (bd. dirs. 1991—2001, v.p. 1991, pres. 1992-95), Ariz. State U. Law Soc. (bd. dirs.), Nat. Conf. Commrs. on Uniform State Laws (life), Delta Sigma Rho, Alpha Tau Omega, Phi Delta Phi. Home: 7600 N Moonlight Ln Paradise Valley AZ 85253-2938 Office: Edward F Lowry Jr PC 4200 N 82d St Ste 2001 Scottsdale AZ 85251-2771 Office Phone: 480-423-1200.

LOWRY, GLENN DAVID, art museum director; b. NYC, 1954; s. Warren and Laure (Lynn) L.; m. Susan Chambers, Aug. 24, 1974; children: Nicholas, Alexis, William. BA, Williams Coll., 1976; MA, Harvard U., 1978, PhD, 1982; PhD (hon.), Penn. Acad. Fine Arts, 2000. Asst. curator Fogg Art Mus., Harvard U., Cambridge, Mass., 1978-80; rsch. asst. Archeol. Survey of Mediterranean Town of Amalfi, Italy, 1980; curator Oriental art Mus. Art, R.I. Sch. Design, Providence, 1981-82; dir. Joseph and Margaret Muscarelle Mus. Art, Williamsburg, Va., 1982-84; curator Nr. Ea. art Arthur M. Sackler and the Freer Gallery Art, Smithsonian Instn., Washington, 1984-90, curatorial coord., 1987-89; dir. Art Gallery Ont., Toronto, Can., 1990-95, MoMA, NYC, 1995—. Mem. adv. coun. dept. art history and archaeology Columbia U., Smithsonian Coun.; steering com. Aga Kahn Arch. award. Co-author: Fatehpur-Sikri: A Source Book, 1985, From Concept to Context: Approaches to Asian and Islamic Calligraphy, 1986, An Annotated Checklist of the Vever Collection, 1988, A Jeweler's Eye: Art of the Book from the Vever Collection, 1988, Timur and the Princely Vision: Persian Art and Culture in the Fifteenth Century, 1989, Europe and the Arts of Islam: The Politics of Taste, 1991. Trustee Metro Toronto Conv. and Visitors Assn. Recipient Inst. Turkish Studies Travel award Smithsonian Instn., 1980, Spl. Exhbns. award, 1987, Scholarly Studies award, 1990., Officer of Order Arts & Letters award, 2004, Govt. France. Mem. Assn. Am. Art Mus. Dirs., Coll. Art Assn., Am. Acad. Arts & Scis. Mailing: Mus Modern Art 11 W 53rd St New York NY 10019-5498 Office Phone: 212-708-9773. E-mail: glenn_lowry@moma.org.

LOWRY, HOUSTON PUTNAM, lawyer; b. NYC, Apr. 1, 1955; s. Thomas Clinton Falls and Jean Allen (Day) L.; m. Kathryn Santoro Curtiss. BA, Pitzer Coll., 1976; MBA, U. Conn., 1980; JD cum laude, Gonzaga U., 1980; LLM in Internat. Law, U. Cambridge, Eng., 1981. Bar: Conn. 1980, U.S. Dist. Ct. Conn. 1981, U.S. Tax Ct. 1982, U.S. Ct. Mil. Appeals 1982, U.S. Ct. Appeals (1st, 2d, 5th, 11th cirs.) 1982, U.S. Ct. Claims 1984, D.C. 1985, U.S. Ct. Appeals (4th, 6th, 7th, 9th, fed., D.C. cirs.) 1985, U.S. Ct. Appeals (3d, 8th, 10th cirs.) 1986, U.S. Supreme Ct., N.Y. 1989. Law clk. to Judge William M. Acker, Jr. U.S. Dist. Ct., Birmingham, Ala., 1982-83; assoc. Tarlow, Levy & Droney, Farmington, Conn., 1983-88; prin. Tarlow, Levy & Droney, P.C., Farmington, Conn., 1989-93, Brown & Welsh P.C., Meriden, Conn., 1993—. Mem. adj. faculty internat. trade law and internat. comml. arbitration U. Conn. Law Sch., 1990-95, 99—. Mem. adv. com. on pvt. internat. law Sec. of State, 1996—. Fellow Chartered Inst. Arbitrators, Worshipful Co. Arbitrators (Liveryman, London); mem. ABA (various coms.), Conn. Bar Assn. (various coms.), Am. Soc. Internat. Law, Internat. Law Assn., Am. Law Inst., Hon. Soc. Gray's Inn, Hartford Club. Office: Brown & Welsh PC PO Box 183 530 Preston Ave Meriden CT 06450-4893 Office Phone: 203-235-1651. Business E-Mail: hplowry@brownwelsh.com.

LOWRY, JAMES HAMILTON, management consultant; b. Chgo., May 28, 1939; s. William E. and Camille C. Lowry; m. Doris Davenport; 1 child, Aisha. BA, Grinnell Coll., 1961; M in Polit. and Instnl. Adminstrn., U. Pitts., 1965; diploma in mgmt., Harvard U., 1973. Assoc. dir. Peace Corps, Lima, Peru, 1965-67; spl. asst. to pres., project mgr. Bedford-Stuyvesant Restoration Corp., Bklyn., 1967-68; sr. assoc. McKinsey & Co., Chgo., 1968-75; pres. James H. Lowry & Assocs., Chgo., 1975-2000; v.p. Boston Consulting Group, 2000—05, sr. v.p., 2005—07, sr. advisor, 2007—. Mem. Small Bus. Adv. Com.; bd. dirs. Ill. Coalition, Holland Trust Fund. Mem. vis. com. Harvard U.; adv. bd. J.L. Kellogg Grad. Sch. Mgmt., Northwestern U., also adj. prof.; trustee Grinnell Coll.; bd. dirs. Northwestern Hosp., Chgo. Pub. Libr.; chmn. City of Chgo. Durban/Chgo. Sister City Program; chmn. bd. trustees Sengstacke Enterprises; chmn. Entrepreneur Ctr., Howard U., mem. Sch. Mgmt.; active Exec. Leadership Coun. Named to Minority Bus. Hall of Fame, 2005; John Hay Whitney fellow, 1963—65. Mem. Harvard Alumni Assn. (dir., vis. com.), Inst. Mgmt. Cons., Econ. Club, Univ. Club, Comml. Club Chgo. Home: 3100 N Sheridan Rd Chicago IL 60657-4954 Office: 200 S Wacker Dr 27th Fl Chicago IL 60606 Office Phone: 312-993-3300.

LOWRY, JULIE ROYAL, music educator; b. Aug. 21, 1971; MusB, Shorter Coll., Rome, Ga., 1994; MusM, U. Ala., Tuscaloosa, 1997. Adj. prof. music Shorter Coll., 1998—2003, U. West Ga., Carrollton, 2002—. Mem.: Nat. Assn. Tchrs. Singing. Personal E-mail: julielowry@earthlink.net.

LOWRY, LARRY, engineering company executive; s. Frank William and Viola L.; m. Jean Carroll Greenbaum, June 23, 1973; 1 child, Alexandra Kristin BSEE, MIT, 1969, MSEE, 1970; MBA, Harvard U., 1972. Mgr. Boston Consulting Group, Menlo Park, Calif., 1972—80; sr. v.p., mng. ptnr. Booz, Allen & Hamilton Inc, San Francisco, 1980—2000, McKinsey & Co., 2001—03; chmn. Demand Tec Inc., 2004—. Western Electric fellow, 1969, NASA fellow, 1970 Mem. Sigma Xi, Tau Beta Pi, Eta Kappa Nu Home: 137 Stockbridge Ave Atherton CA 94027-3942

LOWRY, LOIS (LOIS HAMMERSBERG), writer; b. 1937; Author: A Summer to Die, 1977, Find A Stranger, Say Goodbye, 1978, Anastasia Krupnik, 1979, Autumn Street, 1980, Anastasia Again, 1981, Anastasia at Your Service, 1982, The One Hundredth Thing About Caroline, 1983, Taking Care of Terrific, 1983, Anastasia, Ask Your Analyst, 1984, Us and Uncle Fraud, 1984, Anastasia on Her Own, 1985, Switcharound, 1985, Anastasia Has the Answers, 1986, Anastasia's Chosen Career, 1987, Rabbie Starkey, 1987, All About Sam, 1988, Number the Stars, 1989 (John Newbery medal 1990), Your Move, J.P.!, 1990, Anastasia at This Address, 1991, Attaboy, Sam!, 1992, The Giver, 1993 (John Newbery medal 1994), Anastasia Absolutely, 1995, See You Around, Sam!, 1996, Stay! Keeper's Story, 1997, Looking Back, 1998, Zooman Sam, 1999, Gathering Blue, 2000, Gooney Bird Greene, 2002, The Silent Boy, 2003, Messenger, 2004, Gooney Bird and the Room Mother, 2005, Gossamer, 2006. Recipient Chgo. Tribune Young Adult Book prize, 2003, Margaret A. Edwards award for lifetime achievement, 2007. Address: 205 Brattle St Cambridge MA 02138-3345 Office: care Houghton Mifflin 222 Berkeley St Boston MA 02116-3748

LOWRY, MONTECUE JUDSON, military historian; b. Ft. Worth, Tex., Feb. 23, 1930; s. Mark and Susan Olivia (Hall) Lowry; m. Jo Gail Tuttle, June 4, 1955 (div. Mar. 1985); 1 child, Mary; m. Jennifer Lynn Gunlock, Dec. 27, 1985; children: Jeremy, Montecue J. II. BS, U.S. Mil. Acad., West Point, NY, 1953; BA, U. So. Miss., 1958; MS, U.S. Naval Postgrad. Sch., Monterey, Calif., 1965; MA, U. So. Miss., 1967; PhD in Physics, Tex. Christian U., 1977; PhD in History, U. North Tex., 1988. Officer U.S. Army, 1953-73; chief quality control Vinnell Corp., Riyadh, Saudi Arabia, 1982-83; instr. history U. North Tex., Denton, 1983-86; mil. analyst CIA, Washington, 1986-88; assoc. prof. history Liberty U., Lynchburg, Va., 1988-89; assoc. prof. physics Houston Bapt. U., 1990-96; mil. historian, 1996—. Author: Forge of West German Rearmament, 1990, Glasnost, 1991, Great Captains of the Faith, 2002, Pioneers, Patriots, and Preachers, 2006; contbr. articles to profl. jours. Neighborhood commr. Boy Scouts Am., Fulda, Germany, 1960—62; pres. PTA, Fulda, 1961—62. Mem.: Soc. Mil. History. Avocations: bicycling, weightlifting, classical music, reading. Home: 7402 Redding Rd Houston TX 77036-5542

LOWRY, NICHOLAS D., art appraiser; b. NYC, 1968; s. George S. Lowry. BA in Art Hist., Cornell Univ., 1990. Tchr. English, Prague; journalist; dir., poster dept. Swann Galleries, NYC, 1995—, pres., prin. auctioneer, 2001—. Appraiser Antiques Roadshow, WGBH-PBS. Named one of 100 Most Eligible Bachelors, Gotham Mag., 2004. Office: Swann Galleries 104 E 25th St New York NY 10010 Office Phone: 212-254-4710. Office Fax: 212-979-1017. Business E-Mail: nlowry@swanngalleries.com.

LOWSETH, LISA ANNE, veterinarian; b. Rock Springs, Wyo., May 6, 1958; d. Ernest James and Frances Margaret Lowseth. BS with honors, U. Wyo., 1980; DVM, Kans. State U., 1985. Assoc. veterinarian Good Shepherd Animal Clin., Albuquerque, 1986-87; rsch. fellow Lovelace Inhalation Toxicology Rsch. Inst., Albuquerque, 1987-89; relief veterinarian, 1990-92; study dir. Internat. Rsch. and Devel. Corp., Mattawan, Mich., 1992-98; sr. toxicologist Alcon Rsch. Ltd., Ft. Worth, 1998—2006. Contbr. articles and abstracts to profl. jours. Mem. adv. bd. Rock Springs (Wyo.) Humane Soc., 1990-92. Mem. Am. Vet. Med. Assn., Wyo. Vet. Med. Assn., Am. Coll. Toxicology, Phi Zeta, Gamma Sigma Delta, Alpha Zeta. Achievements include discovery that serum alpha fetoprotein can be used as a diagnostic tool for canine hepatic tumors. Home: 3720 Lawndale Ave Fort Worth TX 76133-2938

LOWTHER, EDWARD GLENN, school system administrator, educator; b. Buckhannon, W.Va., Feb. 12, 1967; s. Steven Dale and Sharon Ann Marteny; m. Angela Marie Dittamo; children: Rachel Noel, Joshua Alexander, Emily Cooleen, Aaron Patrick, Madeline Kate. BSc in Therapeutic Recreation, George Mason U., 1998; MA in Edn. and Human Devel., George Wash. U., Washington, 2001, degree in Edn., 2004; EdD, Nova Southeastern U., Ft. Lauderdale, Fla., 2007. Cert. tchr., adminstr. Va. Dept. Edn., 2005. Tchr. spl. edn. Alexandria City Pub. Schs., Va., 1998—2004; coord. transition coord. Prince William County Pub. Schs., Manassas, Va., 2004—. Adj. prof. spl. edn. George Mason U., 2000—04. Mem.: Nat. Alternative Edn. Assn. (bd. dirs. 2007, bd. dirs. Va. chpt. 2007). Avocations: travel, tennis, singing, trumpet, piano. Home: 2898 Cedar Crest Ct Woodbridge VA 22192 Office: Prince William County Pub Schs 8886 Rixlew Ln Manassas VA 20109 Home Phone: 703-491-5164; Office Phone: 703-393-0163.

LOWTHER, FRANK EUGENE, research physicist; b. Orrville, Ohio, Feb. 3, 1929; s. John Finger and Mary Elizabeth (Mackey) Lowther; m. Elizabeth E Koons, Apr. 21, 1951; children: Cynthia E, Victoria J, James A, Frank Eugene. BS Engring. Physics, Ohio State U., Columbus, 1952; postgrad., Boston U., 1952-54. Scientist missile divsn. Raytheon Corp., Boston, 1952-57, GE, Syracuse, NY, 1957—65, Daytona Beach, Fla., 1957—65; adv. to pres. Gen. Railway Signal, Rochester, NY, 1965-67; chief sci. Purification Sci., Inc., 1967-72; mgr. ozone R & D W.R. Grace Co., Curtis Bay, Md., 1972-75; sr. engring. assoc. Linde divsn. Union Carbide Corp., Tonawanda, NY, 1975-80; scientist Atlantic Richfield-Energy Conversion and Materials Lab., LA, 1980—83; prin. scientist Atlantic Richfield-Corp. Tech., LA, 1983-85, sci. advisor, 1985-88, rsch. advisor Plano, Tex., 1988-93, cons. tech. advisor, 1993—2001. Advisor Energy Sci Inc, Canandaigua, NY, 1993—, Custom Technology Creations Inc, Canandaigua, NY, 1993—, World Ecol Inc, Geneva, 1999—. Named to Wall of Honor, Nat Aviation and Space Exploration, 2001; recipient Inventor of the Yr Award, Patent Law Assn and Tech Socs Coun, 1976. Fellow: AIAA; mem.: AAAS, IEEE (life), NY Acad Scis, Masons. Achievements include patents for ozone technology, plasma generators, solid state power devices, internal combustion engines, electro-desorption, oil field technology, chemical and physical reactors, weapons, others. Home and Office: 4965 Adams Dr Canandaigua NY 14424-4200 Home Phone: 585-394-1099.

LOWTHER, FREDERICK M., lawyer; b. Sewickly, Pa., Dec. 28, 1943; AB magna cum laude, Brown U., 1965; JD with honors, Yale U., 1968. Bar: NY 1969, Pa. 1970, DC 1973, US Supreme Ct. 1977. Law clk. to Hon. Caleb M. Wright US Dist. Ct., Dist. Del., Wilmington, 1968—69; assoc. Pepper Hamilton & Scheetz, Phila., 1969—71; atty. U.S. Maritime Adminstrn., 1971-72; dir. Office of Energy Programs U.S. Dept. Commerce, 1972-73; atty. Dickstein, Shapiro & Morin, Washington, 1973—82; ptnr. Dickstein, Shapiro Morin & Oshinsky LLP, Washington, 1982—, mng. ptnr., 1982—89, group leader, Corp. & Fin. Practice Group. Bd. dirs. Northeast Gas Markets. Mem.: US-Russian Coun., Pa. Bar Assn., NY State Bar Assn., DC Bar, Fed. Energy Bar Assn., ABA, Phi Beta Kappa, Phi Kappa Psi. Office: Dickstein Shapiro Morin & Oshinsky LLP 2101 L St NW Washington DC 20037-1526 Home Phone: 703-684-4075; Office Phone: 202-828-2208. Office Fax: 202-887-0689. Business E-Mail: lowtherf@dsmo.com.

LOWTHER, GERALD HALBERT, lawyer; b. Slagle, La., Feb. 18, 1924; s. Fred B. and Beatrice (Halbert) L.; children by previous marriage: Teresa, Craig, Natalie, Lisa. AB, Pepperdine Coll., 1951; JD, U. Mo., 1951. Bar: Mo. 1951. Since practiced in, Springfield; ptnr. firm Lowther, Johnson, Joyner, Lowther, Cully & Housley. Mem. Savs. and Loan Commn. Mo., 1965-68, Commerce and Indsl. Commn. Mo., 1967-73; lectr. U. Tex., 1955-57, Crested Butte, Colo., 1958-59 Contbr. articles law jours. Past pres. Ozarks Regional Heart Assn.; Del., mem. rules com. Democratic Nat. Conv., 1968; treas. Dem. Party Mo., 1968-72, mem. platform com., 1965, 67, mem. bi-partisan commn. to reapportion Mo. senate, 1966; Bd. dirs. Greene County Guidance Clinic, Ozark Christian Counseling Service, Greene County, Mo.; past pres. Cox Med. Center. Served with AUS, 1946-47; Col. staff of Gov. Hearnes 1964, 68, Mo. Mem. ABA, Mo. Bar Assn., Greene County Bar Assn., Def. Orientation Conf. Assn., Internat. Assn. Ins. Counsel, Def. Rsch. Inst., Springfield C. of C. Clubs: Kiwanian (pres. 1962), Quarterback (pres. 1958), Tip Off (pres. 1960). Office: 540 Foggy River Rd Hollister MO 65672

LOWTHER, THOMAS EDWARD, lawyer; b. St. Louis, Aug. 14, 1936; s. Noel Edward and Catherine Virginia (Polliham) L.; m. Lois Duggins, Dec. 28, 1963 (dec. 2003); children: Nancy, Sandra, Patricia, Susan LLB, Washington U., St. Louis, 1962, MLA, 1999. Bar: Mo. 1962. Assoc. The Stolar Partnership LLP, St. Louis, 1962, ptnr., 1967—, mem. exec. com., 1985—. Mem. nat. coun. Washington U. Sch. Law, 1994—, nat. vice chair campaign cabinet 2001, co-chair 125th Anniversary Com; mem alumni bd. govs. Washington U., 1995-, vice chair, 1999, chair, 2000, trustee; bd. dirs., pres. St. Joseph's Home for Boys, 1997-2001; bd. dirs. St. Joseph's Home and Family Svcs., 2001-06, Catholic Services for Children and Youth, 2006-, pres., Marion Hall for Girls, 1997-2002, sec., 2002; co-trustee Suzanne Feld Zalk Charitable Trust; bd. dirs., treas. St. Louis Mardi Gras Found., 2004—; bd. dirs. Shakespeare Festival St. Louis Recipient Disting. Alumnus award Washington U. Sch. Law, 1997, Washington U., 2002; named one of the Best Lawyers in Am., 1996-. Mem.: ABA, Nat. Assn. Bond Lawyers, St. Louis Bar Assn., Mo. Bar Assn. Avocations: archaeology, travel, trout fishing. Office: The Stolar Partnership LLP 911 Washington Ave Ste 7 Saint Louis MO 63101-1243 Office Phone: 314-231-2800. Business E-Mail: tel@stolarlaw.com.

LOWTHIAN, PETRENA, academic administrator; b. Feb. 10, 1931; d. Leslie Irton and Petrena Lowthian; m. Clyde Hennies (div.); children: David L. Hennies, Geoffrey L. Hennies; m. Nisson Mandel. Grad., Royal Acad. Dramatic Art, London, 1952. Retail career with various orgns., London and Paris, 1949-57; founder, pres. Lowthian Coll. divsn. Lowthian Inc., Mpls., 1964-97. Mem. adv. coun. Minn. State Dept. Edn., St. Paul 1974-82; mem. adv. bd. Mpls. Comty. Devel. Agy., Mpls., 1983-85; mem. Downtown Coun. St. Paul, 1972, chmn. retail bd., 1984-92; mem. Bd. Bus. Indsl. Advisors U. Wis.-Stout, Menomonie, 1983-89. Mem. Fashion Group, Inc. (regional bd. dirs. 1980), Rotary (mem. career and econ. edn. 1988—). Address: 10 Creekside Dr Long Lake MN 55356-9431

LOWY, DOUGLAS RONALD, oncologist, researcher; b. NYC, 1942; MD, NYU, 1968. Intern Stanford Med. Ctr., Calif., 1968—69, resident in internal medicine, 1969—70; rsch. assoc. lab. viral diseases Nat. Inst. Allergy and Infectious Diseases, NIH, 1970—73; resident in dermatology Yale-New Haven Med. Ctr., 1973—75; with Lab. Cellular Oncology Nat. Cancer Inst., Bethesda, Md., 1975—, chief Lab. Cellular Oncology, 1983—, dep. dir. Ctr. Cancer Rsch., 1996—, also chief Basic Rsch. Lab. Recipient Wallace Rowe award for virus rsch. Mem.: Inst. of Medicine. Office: Nat Cancer Inst Lab Cellular Oncology 37 Convent Dr Bldg 37 Rm 4106C Bethesda MD 20892 Office Phone: 301-496-9513. Office Fax: 301-480-5322. E-mail: dl60z@nih.gov.

LOWY, FREDERICK HANS, academic administrator, psychiatrist; b. Grosspetersdorf, Austria, Jan. 1, 1933; arrived in Can., 1944; s. Eugen and Maria (Braun) Lowy; m. Anne Louise Cloudsley, June 25, 1965 (dec. 1973); children: David, Eric, Adam; m. Mary Kathleen O'Neil, June 1, 1975; 1 child, Sarah. BA, McGill U., Montreal, Can., 1955, MD, 1959, LLD, 2001, U. Toronto, Can., 1998. Intern, resident in internal medicine Royal Victoria Hosp., Montreal, Que., Canada; resident in psychiatry U. Cin. Hosp., Cin. VA Hosp.; psychoanalytic tng. Montreal Psychoanalytic Inst.; psychiatrist Allan Meml. Inst.-Royal Victoria Hosp., Montreal-McGill U. Faculty Medicine, 1965-70; psychiatrist-in-chief Ottawa Civic Hosp., Canada; prof. dept. psychiatry U. Ottawa, 1971-74; prof. psychiatry, chmn. dept. U. Toronto, dir. Clarke Inst. Psychiatry, 1974-80, dean Sch. Medicine, 1980-87, dir. Ctr. for Bioethics, 1989-95; pres., vice chancellor Concordia U., Montreal, 1995—2005. Co-editor: (book) A Method of Psychiatry, 1980, Alzheimer's Disease Research, 1991; contbr. articles to profl. jours. Decorated officer Order of Can. Fellow: Am. Coll. Psychiatrists, Royal Coll. Physicians and Surgeons; mem.: Am. Psychiat. Assn., Can. Psychiat. Assn. (editor jour. 1972—76), Internat. Psychoanalytic Assn. Office: Penthouse 1005 1515 Dr Penfield Ave Montreal QC Canada H3G 2R8 Office Phone: 514-848-8653. Business E-Mail: frederick.lowy@concordia.ca.

LOWY, GEORGE THEODORE, lawyer; b. NYC, Oct. 6, 1931; s. Eugene and Elizabeth Lowy; m. Pier M. Foucault, Sept. 7, 1957. BA cum laude, LLB cum laude, NYU. Bar: NY 1955, US Dist. Ct. (so. dist.) NY 1958, US Supreme Ct. 1972, US Ct Appeals (2d cir.) 1975. Assoc. Cravath, Swaine and Moore, NYC, 1957-65, ptnr., 1965—81, sr. coun., 1982—. Trustee NYU Law Ctr. Found.; bd. dirs. Equitable Life Assurance Soc. U.S., Eramet, Paris, Axa Fin., U.S.; adj. prof. NYU Law Sch., 1983—88; bd. overseers Brandeis U. Internat. Bus. Sch. Fellow ABA; mem. Am. Law Inst., Assn. of Bar of City of NY (chmn. com. on corp. law), Internat. Bar Assn., Union Internat. des Avocats, Cercle Interallie Paris. Home: 580 Park Ave New York NY 10021-7313 Office: Cravath Swaine & Moore World Wide Pla 825 8th Ave Fl 38 New York NY 10019-7416 E-mail: glowy@cravath.com.

LOWY, PETER, corporate financial executive; Exec. dir. Westfield Mgmt. Ltd., 1986, Westfield Holdings Ltd., 1987, Westfield Am. Mgmt. Ltd., 1996, mng. dir. LA, 1997—, bd. dir. Bd. gov. Nat. Assn. of Real Estate Investment Trusts; bd. dir. Lowy Inst. for Internat. Policy. Office: Westfield Corp Inc 11601 Wilshire Blvd 11th Fl Los Angeles CA 90025-1748 Office Phone: 310-478-4456. Office Fax: 310-478-1267.

LOY, FRANK ERNEST, retired federal agency administrator; b. Nuremberg, Germany, Dec. 25, 1928; arrived in U.S., 1939; s. Alfred Loewi and Elizabeth (Loeffler) L.; m. Dale Haven, 1963; children: Lisel, Eric Anthony. BA, UCLA, 1950; LLB, Harvard U., 1953. Bar: DC 1953, Calif. 1954. With O'Melveny & Myers, LA, 1954-65; spl. asst. to adminstr. FAA, 1961-63; spl. cons. to adminstr. AID, 1963-64; dep. asst. sec. state for econ. affairs, 1965-70; sr. v.p. Pan Am. World Airways, Inc., NYC, 1970-73; pres. Pennsylvania Co., Washington, 1974-79, Penn Ctrl. Corp., 1978-79; dir. Bur. Refugee Programs, Dept. State, Washington, 1980-81; pres. German Marshall Fund of U.S., 1981-95; chmn. League Conservation Voters, Washington, 1993-98, pres., 1995-96; chmn. Found. Civil Soc., 1997-98; under sec. of state for Global Affairs US Govt., Washington, 1998—2001. Chmn. U.S. delegation to Climate Change Conf., The Hague, The Netherlands, 2000; dir. Nat. Gallery of Art, 1998—2001; vis. lectr. Yale Law Sch., 1996; dir. Pharm. Product Devel., Inc., 1995—98. Chmn. bd. trustees Goddard Coll., Vt., 1976-78, Environ. Def. Fund, 1983-90, Washington Ballet, 1991-94, PSI, 2004—, Resources for the Future, 2005-07; bd. mem. Regional Environ. Ctr. for Ctrl. and Ea. Europe, Budapest, Hungary, 1990-97, Pew Ctr. for Global Climate Change, 2003—, The Nature Conservancy, 2006—. With US Army, 1953-55. Personal E-mail: loyfrank@aol.com.

LOY, JAMES MILTON, former federal agency administrator, retired coast guard officer; b. Altoona, Pa., 1942; m. Kay McGirk; children: Kelly Loy Morf, Michael. BS in Gen. Engring., USCG Acad., 1964; MS in History/Govt. and Pub. Adminstrn., U. R.I., Kingston; postgrad., Indsl. Coll. Armed Forces, Washington, Harvard U. Commd. ensign USCG, 1964, advanced through grades to adm.; comdr. 4 coast guard cutters, various locations, Eight Coast Guard Dist., New Orleans; chief ops. divsn. Atlantic Area; instr. Coast Guard Acad.; chief officer of pers. and tng. Coast Guard Hdqrs.; comdr. Atlantic Area and U.S. Maritime Def. Zone Atlantic, 1994—96; chief of staff, comdg. officer USCG Hdqrs., Washington, 1996-98; comdt. USCG, 1998—2002; dep. under sec. for transport. security, COO Transp. Security Adminstrn., 2002; under sec. for security US Dept. Transp., 2002—03; acting dep. sec. US Dept. Homeland Security, 2003, dep. sec., 2003—05, acting sec., 2005; sr. counselor Cohen Group, Washington, 2005—; nat. co-chmn. ProtectingAmerica.org, Washington, 2006—. Bd. dirs. Lockheed Martin Corp., Bethesda, Md., 2005—. Decorated Coast Guard Disting. Svc. medal (4), Legion of Merit (2), Def. Superior Svc. medal, Bronze Star with combat V, Meritorious Svc. medal, others. Office: ProtectingAmerica 1200 Nineteenth St NW Ste 400 Washington DC 20036 also: The Cohen Group 1200 19th St NW Ste 400 Washington DC 20036 E-mail: jloy@cohengroup.net.

LOY, RICHARD FRANKLIN, civil engineer; b. Dubuque, Iowa, July 6, 1950; s. Wayne Richard and Evelyn Mae (Dikeman) L.; m. Monica Lou Roberts, Sept. 2, 1972 (div.); children: Taneha Eve, Spencer Charles. BSCE, U. Wis., Platteville, 1973. Registered profl. engr., Wis., Ohio. Engr. aid Wis. Dept. of Transp., Superior, 1969; asst. assayer Am. Lead & Zinc Co., Shullsburg, Wis., 1970; asst. grade foreman Radandt Construction Co., Eau Claire, Wis., 1970; air quality technician U. Wis., Platteville, 1972-73; asst. city engr. City of Kaukauna, Wis., 1973-77, City of Fairborn, Ohio, 1977—89, city engr. Ohio, 1989—93, pub. works dir. Ohio, 1993—2001, city engr. Ohio, 2001—. Bd. dirs. YMCA Fairborn, 1990-95; mem. coun. Trinity United Ch. of Christ, Fairborn, 1989-98; chmn. Chillicothe dist. Tecumseh coun. Boy Scouts Am., 1991-93. Recipient Blue Coat award, 1983; named to Exec. Hall of Fame, N.Y., 1990. Mem.: NSPE, ASCE, Pub. Works Hist. Soc., Street Maintenance and Sanitation Ofcls., Inst. Transp. Engrs., Am. Water Works Assn., Am. Pub. Works Assn.

LOYD, WARD EUGENE, lawyer; b. Henderson, Ky., Feb. 8, 1943; s. Ward Beecher Loyd and Maxine Watkins; m. Suzanne Keeler, Dec. 29, 1966; children: Katherine Marie, Keele Suzanne. BA, Southwestern Coll., 1965; JD with honors, Washburn U., Kans., 1968. Bar: Kans. 1968, US Dist. Ct. Kans. 1968, US Ct. Appeals (10th cir.) 1969. Pvt. practice, Garden City, Kans., 1968—; mem. Kans. Ho. of Reps., 1998—2006. Gen. counsel Garden City Urban Renewal Agy., 1969-75, Garden City Pub. Sch. Sys., 1972-91, Garden City C.C., 1971-, S.W. Kans. Area Coop., Ensign, 1995—; mem. Kans. Supreme Ct. Stds. Com., Topeka, 1980, Kans. Supreme Ct. Client Protection Fund Commn., 2000-06, Kans. Supreme Ct. child support guidelines adv. commn., 2002-06, bd. dirs. Western State Bank, Garden City; chmn. Kans. Criminal Justice Recodification, Rehab. and Restoration Commn., 2004-07, Kans. Reentry Policy Coun., 2006-07, Kans. Adv. Group Juvenile Justice and Delinquency Prevention, 2006—; co-chmn. Pub. Safety and Justice Task Force, 2005-06; mem. governing body/exec. bd. Coun. State Govts., 2004-06; mem. Interstate Migrant Edn. Coun., 2005-2007. Comments editor Washburn Law Jour., 1967-68. City commr. City of Garden City, 1985-89, 90-94, 97, mayor, 1986, 88; mem. First United Meth. Ch., Garden City; past bd. mem., past pres. Cmty. Day Care Ctr.; past mem. Kans. League Municipalities. Recipient Award of Merit, Garden City Area C. of C., 1992, Outstanding Pub. Ofcl. of Yr., Kans. Assn. Addition Profls., 2003, Intergovtl. Leadership award League of Kans. Municipalities, 2006. Fellow Kans. Bar Found.; mem. Nat. Assn. Sch. Bds. (coun. sch. attys.), Kans. Bar Assn. (mem. ethics com. 1978-82), S.W. Kans. Bar Assn. (pres. 1986-88, sec. 1992-93, dir.), Kans. Sch. Attys. Assn. (regional dir. 1980-84), Kanš. Assn. Def. Counsel, Finney County Bar Assn., Garden City C. of C. (bd. dirs. 1990-92), Phi Alpha Delta (justice 1968). Republican. Home: 2203 Center Garden City KS 67846-3525 Office: Ward Loyd Law Office LLC PO Box 834 118 W Pine St Garden City KS 67846-5444 Office Phone: 620-275-1415. Business E-Mail: loyd@gcnet.com.

LOYE, ESTELLE C., contractor, travel consultant; b. Medford, Oreg., Nov. 10, 1968; d. Judd John Greenman and Yvonne C. Huston; m. Jeffrey Treadwell (div.); children: Jeremiah Treadwell, Benjamin Treadwell; m. Todd P. Loye, May 25, 2002. Student, Rogue C.C., Medford, Oreg., 1986—87, So. Oreg. State U., Ashland, 1986—88; A of Elec. Tech., DeVry Inst. Tech., Phoenix, 1991; student, So. Oreg. State U., Ashland, 2001—05. Elec. tech. Microtest, Inc., Scottsdala, Ariz., 1988—91; data processor NW Mail Svcs., Medford, 1994—98; splty. constrn. contractor Drywall Concepts, Medford, 1998—; travel cons. Rogue Travel, Medford, 2003—05, Jackson Travel, Medford, 2006—. Mem. Medford Leads, 2005—, Success Cir., Medford, 2006—; mem. bus. planning, mktg. roundtable So. Oreg. Women's Access to Credit, Medford, 2006—; table capt. Living Opportunities, Medford, 2005, co-chair table capt., 2006—07; coord. blood dr. ARC, Central Point, Oreg., 2004—05. Mem.: Medford Jackson County Chamber, Women Entrepreneurs So. Oreg. (pres. 2006—), Mensa. Avocations: reading, languages.

LOYER NELSON, EDITH MERILYNN, retired social worker; b. Seattle, June 19, 1944; d. Clark Laurence and Dorothy Jessie Loyer; children: Monica Lynne Robbins, Paul Eddy Nelson. BA, We. Wash. State Coll., 1966. Tchr. Seattle Sch. Dist., 1966—72; social worker Indian Child Welfare Unit Divsn. Children and Family Svcs. State of Wash., Seattle, 1984—91, rsch. program mgr., 1991—97, social worker supr., 1997—2003, ret., 2003. Vol. King County Children and Family Svcs. Commn., Seattle, 1992—96; adv. Shoreline (Wash.) Governance Com., 1991—92; grant reader Shoreline (Wash.) Health and Human Svcs. Allocation Comm., 2000—05; precinct committeeperson Wash. State Democrats, Shoreline, 1972—91; adv. bd. Local Indian Child Welfare Adv. Com., Seattle, 2003—06; as a mem. of the bd. of trustees, hire the coll. pres., develop and guide the long term strategic plan of the coll. Shoreline C.C., Shoreline, Wash., 1996—2006; adv. Ctr. Human Svcs., Shoreline; coun. mem. Duwamish Indian Tribe, Seattle, 1989—96. Avocations: tribal activites, beach walks, reading. Home: 19544 15th Ave NW Seattle WA 98177-2730 Personal E-mail: edieloyernelson@msn.com.

LOZANČIĆ, NIKO, President of Federation of Bosnia and Herzegovina; b. Kakanj, Bosnia, 1957; Mem. Croatian Dem. Union Party, head, 2001, v.p., 2001—; former dep. pres. Croatian Dem. Union of Bosnia and Herzegovina; former mem. House of Peoples; pres. Fedn. of Bosnia and Herzegovina, 2003—. Office: Office of Pres 7100 Sarajevo Bosnia-Herzegovina Office Phone: (33) 472618.*

LOZANO, JOSE, nephrologist; b. San Vicente, El Salvador, Feb. 11, 1941; came to U.S., 1968; s. Jose E. and Transito Maria (Mendez) L.; m. Hilda Berganza, Jan. 27, 1965; children: Jose E., Claudia Maria. MD, U. El Salvador, 1965. Diplomate Am. Bd. Internal Medicine, Am. Bd. Nephrology. Rotating intern Nat. Med. Ctr., San Salvador, El Salvador, 1963-64; asst. resident in internal medicine Rosales Hosp., San Salvador, 1965-66, resident in internal medicine, 1966-67, chief resident in internal medicine,

1967-68; resident in internal medicine Baylor U. Affiliated Hosps., Houston, 1968-70, fellow in nephrology, 1970-71, 73-74; asst. prof. medicine U. El Salvador, 1971-72; internist and nephrologist Social Security Hosp., San Salvador, 1971-72; instr. in medicine Baylor Coll. Medicine, Houston, 1974-75, asst. prof. medicine in nephrology, 1975-76, clin. asst. prof. medicine, 1976-80; mem. staff internal medicine St. Elizabeth Hosp., Beaumont Med./Surg. Hosp., Bapt. Hosp., Beaumont, Tex., 1976; med. dir. Golden Triangle Dialysis Ctr., Beaumont, 1977-98, BMA Jasper, Jasper, Tex., 1986-98, BMA Orange, Orange, Tex., 1987-90, Kidney Ctr., Beaumont, Tex., 2001—, Jasper, 2001—. Med. dir. Jasper Dialysis Ctr., 1986-98, Kidney Ctr. of Jasper, 2001-, Beaumont Kidney Ctr., 2001-; mem. Kidney Health Care Adv. Com., 1981-82; pesenter in field. Contbr. articles to profl. publs. Fellow ACP, Am. Soc. Nephrology; mem. AMA, Internat. Soc. Nephrology, Tex. Med. Assn., Harris County Med. Soc., Jefferson County Med. Soc., Physicians for A Nat. Health Plan. Office: 2955 Harrison Ste 100 Beaumont TX 77702 E-mail: bmtnp410@aol.com. *In terms of health care we need a system that provides easy, uncomplicated access to primary care services. We urgently need a health care system that provides universal and comprehensive access to health care without considerations given to the ability to pay, race, gender, religion or sexual orientation. We need a system that is independent of employment, in which people with existing conditions are not restricted from free and adequate access to health care. The creation of a universal health care system is in the best interests of all citizens of this country.*

LOZANO, KAREN, engineering educator; BSME, U. Monterrey, Mex.; M, Rice U., 1996, D, 1999. Postdoctoral rsch. assoc. Rice U., Houston, 2000; asst. prof. U. Tex. Pan Am., Edinburg, 2000—03, assoc. prof., 2003—. Named Most Promising Scientist, Hispanic Engring. Nat. Achievement Awards Coop., 2002, Power Hitter in Bus. and Tech., Hispanic Engring. and Info. Tech., 2003; recipient Career award, NSF, 2000, Pres.'s award, U. Tex. Pan Am., 2002, U. Excellence Rsch. award, 2004. Achievements include patents for oriented nanofibers. Office: U Tex Pan Am 1201 W University Dr Edinburg TX 78541 Office Phone: 956-381-2394. Office Fax: 956-381-3527.

LOZANO, MONICA CECILIA, publishing executive; b. LA, July 21, 1956; d. Ignacio Eugenio and Marta Eloisa (Navarro) Lozano; m. Marcelo Centanino, Sept. 27, 1987 (div.); c. Santiago Alberto and Gabriela. Student, U. Oreg., 1974—76; student San Francisco City Coll.; LHD (hon.), Occidental Coll., 1999. Mgr. Copy-Copia, Inc., San Francisco, 1980—85; mng. editor La Opinion, LA, 1985—89, assoc. pub., 1989—91, assoc. pub., exec. editor, 1991—2000, pres., COO, 2000—04, pub., CEO, 2004—; pub. El Eco del Valle, San Fernando, Calif., 1990—91; v.p. Lozano Comm., 2000—04; sr. v.p. ImpreMedia LLC, 2004—. Bd. dirs. The Walt Disney Co., Union Bank Calif., Calif. Health Care Found., Tenet Healthcare Corp., Nat. Coun. La Raza; trustee SunAm. Asset Mgmt. Corp. Trustee U. So. Calif.; mem. bd. regents U. Calif., 2000—; bd. dirs. L.A. County Mus. Art, Venice Family Clinic, Ctrl. Am. Resource Ctr. Co-recipient José Ortega y Gasset award, Madrid, 2006; recipient Humanitarian award, Cen. Am. Refugee Ctr., L.A., 1989, Outstanding Achievement, Mex. Am. Opportunities Found., L.A., 1989. Mem. Nat. Assn. Hispanic Pubs., Nat. Assn. Hispanic Journalists, Calif. Hispanic Pubs., Am. Soc. Newspaper Editors, Calif. Chicano News Assn., Nat. Network Hispanic Women. Avocations: photography, reading, water sports.

LOZANO, RUDOLPHO, federal judge; b. East Chgo., Ind., 1942; BS in Bus., Ind. U., 1963, LLB, 1966. Mem. firm Spangler, Jennings, Spangler & Dougherty, P.C., Merrillville, Ind., 1966-88; judge U.S. Dist. Ct. (no. dist.) Ind., Hammond, 1988—2007; sr. judge US Dist. Ct. (no. dist.) Ind., 2007—. With USAR, 1966-73. Mem. ABA, Ind. State Bar Assn., Def. Rsch. Inst. Office: US Dist Ct 205 Fed Bldg 507 State St Hammond IN 46320-1533

LOZANSKY, EDWARD DMITRY, physicist, consultant, writer; b. Kiev, Ukraine, Feb. 10, 1941; arrived in U.S., 1977; s. Dmitry R. and Dina M. (Chizhik) Lozansky; m. Tatiana I. Yershov, Feb. 27, 1971; 1 child, Tania. MS, Moscow Phys. Engring. Inst., 1966; PhD, Inst. Atomic Energy, Moscow, 1969; LHD, Waynesburg Coll., 1995. Asst. prof. Moscow State U., 1969-71; assoc. prof. Mil. Tank Acad., Moscow, 1971-75; prof. U. Rochester, NY, 1977-80, Am. U., Washington, 1981-83, L.I. U., Bklyn., 1983-87; pres. Independent U., Washington, 1987-91, Russia House, Inc., 1991—, Am. U. Moscow, 1992—, Am. Univs. in Russia, Ukraine and New Independent States, 1994—. Author: Theory of the Spark, 1976, Mathematics, 1976, For Tatiana, 1984, Andrei Sakharov, 1986, Winning Solutions, 1988, Democracy: USA-Russia, 1994, Winning Solutions, 1996, Russia: Experience in Democracy, 1997, Foundations of Free Society, 1998, Sociology of Politics: Comparative Study of the American and Russian Realities, 2001, Society, Power, Politics, 2003, Russian Lobby in America, 2004, Russia Between China and America, 2007. Mem.: Russian Acad. Soc. Scis. Avocations: skiing, chess. Office: Russia House 1800 Connecticut Ave NW Washington DC 20009-5731 Office Phone: 202-986-6010. Personal E-mail: lozansky@gmail.com.

LOZOFF, BETSY, pediatrician, educator; b. Milw., Dec. 19, 1943; d. Milton and Marjorie (Morse) L.; 1 child, Claudia Brittenham. BA, Radcliffe Coll., 1965; MD, Case Western Res. U., 1971, MS, 1981. Diplomate Am. Bd. Pediat. From asst. prof. to prof. pediatrics Case Western Res. U., Cleve., 1974-93; prof. pediat. U. Mich., Ann Arbor, 1993—, dir. Ctr. Human Growth and Devel., 1993—2004, rsch. prof. Ctr. Human Growth and Devel., 2004—. Recipient Rsch. Career Devel. award Nat. Inst. Child Health and Human Devel., 1984-88. Fellow Am. Acad. Pediatrics; mem. Soc. for Pediatric Rsch., Soc. Rsch. in Child Devel. (program com. 1991-97), Soc. Behavioral Pediatrics (exec. com. 1985-88), Ambulatory Pediatric Soc. Office: Univ Mich Ctr Human Growth and Devel 300 N Ingalls St Ann Arbor MI 48109-2007 Office Phone: 734-764-2443. E-mail: blozoff@umich.edu.

LU, BAO-LIANG, computer scientist, educator; b. Qingdao, Shandong, China, Nov. 22, 1960; s. Jimei Lu and Aiyan Liu; m. Jing Li, Aug. 14, 1987; 1 child, Qianshu. BS, Qingdao U. of Sci. & Tech., Qingdao, China, 1982; MS, Northwestern Poly. U., Xi'an, China, 1989; PhD, Kyoto U., Japan, 1994. Rsch. asst. Qingdao U. of Sci. & Tech., Qingdao, Shandong, China, 1982—86, 1989—91; rschr. The Inst. of Phys. and Chem. Rsch., Wako, Saidama, Japan, 1994—2002; prof. Shanghai Jiao Tong U., China, 2002—. Contbr. articles to profl. jours. Mem.: IEEE (sr.). Achievements include research in new algorithm for inverting trained feedforward neural networks using linear and nonlinear programming; new modular neural network model for pattern classification; an emergent learning theory that can be used to explain some learning mechanism of the brain; patents for a method for constructing pattern classifiers that is capable of incremental learning; a method for automatic detecting data errors in large-scale corpus or other databases. Home: 19-23A No 99 Ln Nan Dan Dong Rd Shanghai 200030 China Office: Dept Computer Science SJTU 800 Dong Chuan Shanghai 200240 China Home Phone: 86-21-6438-6126; Office Phone: 86-21-3420-5422. Office Fax: 86-21-3420-5422. Business E-Mail: bllu@sjtu.edu.cn.

LU, CHANG, engineering professor; b. Heilongjiang, China; arrived in US, 1998; s. Delin Lu; m. Danfeng Yao. BS in Chemistry, Peking U., 1998; MS in Chem. Engring., U. Ill., Urban-Champaign, 2001; PhD, U. Ill., Urbana, 2002. Postdoctoral assoc. Cornell U., Ithaca, NY, 2002—04; asst. prof. biol. and chem. engring. Purdue U., West Lafayette, Ind., 2004—. Contbr. articles to profl. jours. Mem.: AIChE, Am. Chem. Soc., Am. Soc. Agrl. and Biol. Engrs., Am. Engring. Soc., Soc. Biol. Engrs. Achievements include patents in field. Office: Purdue Univ 225 S Univ St West Lafayette IN 47907 Home Phone: 765-494-1188; Office Phone: 765-494-1188. E-mail: changlu@purdue.edu.

LU, DAVID JOHN, historian, writer; b. Keelung, Taiwan, Sept. 28, 1928; arrived in U.S., 1950, naturalized, 1960; s. Ming and Yeh (Lai) Lu; m. Annabelle Compton, May 29, 1954; children: David John, Daniel Mark, Cynthia King, Stephen Paul. BA in Econs, Nat. Taiwan U., 1950; postgrad., Westminster Theol. Sem., Phila., 1950-52; M. Internat. Affairs, Columbia, 1954; certificate, East Asian Inst., 1954, PhD, 1960. Editor Prentice-Hall, Inc., 1956-60; instr. Rutgers U., 1959; asst. prof. history Bucknell U., Lewisburg, Pa., 1960-64, assoc. prof., 1964-69, prof., 1969-94, prof. emeritus, 1994—, dir. Ctr. for Japanese Studies, 1965-94. Cons. on global edn. Pa. Dept. Edn., 1961—62, 1978, U.S. Dept. Edn., 1973—85; resident dir. associated Kyoto program Doshisha U., 1987—88. Author: From the Marco Polo Bridge to Pearl Harbor, 1961; author: (Japanese edit.) Taiheiyo Senso e no Dotei, 1967; author: Sources of Japanese History, 1974, Bicentennial History of the United States, 1976, The Life and Times of Matsuoka Yosuke, 1880-1946, 1981, Inside Corporate Japan: The Art of Fumble-Free Management, 1987, Japan: A Documentary History, 1997, Agony of Choice, Matsuoka Yosuke and the Rise and Fall of the Japanses Empire, 2002; translator: The China Quagmire, 1983, What is Total Quality Control? The Japanese Way, 1985, Kanban, Just-in-Time at Toyota, 1986, Total Quality Control for Management: Strategies and Techniques from Toyota and Toyoda Gosei, 1987, TQC (Total Quality Control), The Wisdom of Japan, 1988; contbr. Sekai to Nippon, (The World and Japan) weekly, Tokyo. Fulbright-Hays scholar Japan, 1966—67. Presbyterian. Home: 1303 Mazeland Dr Bel Air MD 21015-6358 Personal E-mail: david.lu@verizon.net.

LU, EDWARD TSANG, astronaut; b. Springfield, Mass., July 1, 1963; s. Charlie and Snowlily Lu. BSEE, Cornell U., 1984; PhD in Applied Physics, Stanford U., 1989. Vis. scientist High Altitude Observatory, Boulder, Colo., 1989—92; postdoctoral fellow Inst. Astronomy, Honolulu, 1992—95; mission specialist NASA, Houston, 1995—. Astronaut Space Shuttle Atlantis, 1997, 2000, International Space Station, 2003. Fellow, Hughes Aircraft Co.; scholar Presdl. scholar, Cornell U. Mem.: Am. Astronomical Soc., Exptl. Aircraft Assn., Aircraft Owners & Pilots Assn. Avocations: aerobatic flying, coaching wrestling, piano, tennis, surfing. Office: Astronaut Office CB NASA Johnson Space Center Houston TX 77058

LU, ERDONG, research scientist; s. Shouzhu Lu and Liqun Zhou; m. Guangping Zhao, Mar. 25, 1987; children: Daniel Yuyi, Andrew Hongjian. PhD, U. Sci. and Tech. China, Hefei, 1998. Sci. rsch. staff Ohio U., Athens, 2004—. Mem.: Am. Phys. Soc. (assoc.). Achievements include patents for novel wet passivation method for GaAs and related III-V semiconductors; development of reconstruction control of magnetic properties during epitaxial growth of ferromagnetic MnGa thin films on wurtzite GaN. Office Phone: 740-593-1757. Business E-Mail: lue@ohio.edu.

LU, GUIYANG, electrical engineer, executive; b. Guiyang, China, May 10, 1946; arrived in U.S., 1982; s. Wen and Yunqiu Deng; m. Jing Du; 1 child, Jia. Degree in elec. engring., Tsing Hua U., Beijing, 1970; postgrad., South China U. Tech., Guangzhou, 1980-81; MA in Math., Calif. State U., Fresno, 1984; MSEE, Poly. U., NYC, 1986. Instr. in elec. engring. South China U. Tech., Guangzhou, 1973-80; v.p. engring. Kawahara Corp., NYC, 1986-88; H.S. math. tchr. N.Y.C. Bd. Edn., 1988-90; engring. cons. Measurement and Control Sys., NYC, 1989-90; sr. R&D engr. Avid Inc., Norco, Calif., 1991-98; sr. RF engr. Securay Key, Chatsworth, Calif., 1998—2002; rsch. assoc. Avery Dennison, Irwindale, Calif., 2002—04; dir. R&D Avid Identification Sys., Norco, Calif., 2004—. U.S. patentee in field. Mem.: IEEE. Home: 1718 Eastgate Ave Upland CA 91784-9210 Office: Avid Identification Sys 3185 Hamner Ave Norco CA 92860 Personal E-mail: gylu@aol.com.

LU, HANCHAO, humanities educator, writer; PhD, UCLA. Prof., dir. grad. studies Sch. of History, Tech. and Soc., Ga. Inst. Tech., Atlanta. Author: (monograph) Beyond the Neon Lights: Everyday Shanghai in the Early Twentieth Century (Best Book award Urban History Assn., 2001), Street Criers: A Cultural History of Chinese Beggars, Hede Zhuan: A Biography of Sir Robert Hart; editor: (anthology) Modernity and Cultural Identity in Taiwan, (book series) Culture and Customs of Asia, (jour.) Chinese Historical Rev. Office: Ga Inst Tech 685 Cherry St Atlanta GA 30332-0345 Home Phone: 404-668-0622; Office Phone: 404-894-6844. Office Fax: 404-894-0535.

LU, HONG LIANG, telecommunications industry executive; b. Taiwan; BS civil engring., Univ. Calif., Berkeley. COO Unison World Inc., pres., CEO, 1983—86, Kyocera Unison, 1986—91, Unitech Telecom, 1991—95; chmn. pres., CEO UTStarcom, Alameda, Calif., 1995—. Mem. strategic adv. bd. Pacrim Venture Partners. Office: UTStarcom 1275 Harbor Bay Pkwy Alameda CA 94502

LU, LUCIA Y., education educator; b. Taipei, Taiwan, Dec. 29, 1952; arrived in US, 1991; d. John Lu and Lisa Chi-Lu; m. Peter Sheim; 1 child, Josephine Sheim. BA, Nat. Taiwan U., Taipei, 1975; MEd, Okla. U., Oklahoma City, 1987; PhD in Reading, Ind. U., Bloomington, 1997. Prof. Fu-Jen Cath. U., Taipei, 1987—91, Clark Atlanta U., 1998—2005, Longwood U., Farmville, Va., 2005—. Translator life study Livign Stream Ministry, Anaheim, Calif., 1975—2005; book and jour. reviewer Hacolm Heathwing Pub., Ariz., 2003—06. Editor: Jour. Balanced Reading, 2006. Grantee, NSF, 2003, NOES, 2004. Mem.: Nat. Coun. Tchrs. English (Svc. award 1998), Internat. Reading Assn. (Svc. award 1998). Avocation: swimming. Home: PO Box E Farmville VA 23901 Office: Longwood U Farmville VA 23909

LU, MI, computer engineer, educator; b. Chongqing, Sichuan, China, July 22, 1949; d. Chong Pu Lu and Shu Sheng Fan. MS, Rice U., Houston, 1984, PhD, 1987. Registered profl. engr. From asst. prof. to assoc. prof. Tex. A&M U., Coll. Sta., 1987-98, prof., 1998—. Conf. chmn. Internat. Conf. Computer Sci. and Informatics, 2000, 02, 03. Assoc. editor Jour. Computing and Info., 1995-97, Info. Sci., 1996-97. 2002-03; contbr. articles to profl. jours. Mem. Computer Soc. of IEEE (sr.). Office: Tex A&M U Dept Elec Engring College Station TX 77843 Office Phone: 979-845-3749. Business E-Mail: mlu@ece.tamu.edu.

LU, NATALIE, federal agency administrator; PhD, U. Md., 1995. Rsch. assoc. Johns Hopkins U., Balt., 1995—98; program mgr. Dept. Justice, Washington, 1998—. Achievements include patents pending for Monoclonal antibody specific for crack cocaine metabolites, a cell line producing the same, and crack cocaine conjugates. Home Phone: 202-616-5209. Personal E-mail: nat518@yahoo.com.

LU, SHU JIANG, literature and language professor; MA, U. Western Ontario, London, 1992, PhD, 2001. Assoc. prof. U. Piits., Greensburg, Pa., 2001—. Recipient Tchg. Excellence award, U. Pitts., Greensburg, 2006. Home: 3233 Ridgeway Rd Greensburg PA 15601 Office: Univ Pitts 136 Finoli Dr Greensburg PA 15601-5804

LU, YEN-WEN, adult education educator; PhD, UCLA, 2004. Rschr. UCLA, 1998—2004; asst. prof. Rutgers U., Piscataway, NJ, 2004—. Achievements include development of Microscopic Hand. Office: Rutgers University 98 Brett Road Piscataway NJ 08854 Office Phone: 732-445-3282. Business E-Mail: ywlu@jove.rutgers.edu.

LU, YI, chemistry professor; BS, Beijing Univ.; PhD, UCLA; postdoctoral rsch., Calif. Inst. Tech. Assoc. prof., dept. chem., dept. biochem. and computational biology Univ. Ill. Urbana-Champaign. Faculty Environ. Coun., Ctr. for Nanoscale Sci., Tech., Univ. Ill. Urbana-Champaign; rsch. prof. Howard Hughes Med. Inst., 2002—. Adv. bd. Jour. of Biological Inorganic Chemistry; contbr. articles to profl. journals. Recipient Nat. Sci. Found. Career award, Arnold and Mabel Beckman Young Investigator award, 1996, Rsch. Corp. Cottrell Scholars award, 1997, Alfred P. Sloan Rsch. Fellowship, 1998, Camille Dreyfus Teacher-Scholar award, 1999, Howard Hughes Med. Inst. grant, 2002. Office: Dept Chem A322 Chem & Life Sci Univ Ill 600 S Mathews Ave Urbana IL 61801 Office Phone: 217-333-2619. Office Fax: 217-333-2685. Business E-Mail: yi-lu@uiuc.edu.

LUBAR, JEFFREY STUART, journalist, trade association executive; b. Rockville Centre, NY, Apr. 15, 1947; s. Sidney and Rose (Grupsmith) L.; m. Barbara Ruth Bigelman; children— Debra, Adam, Rachel. BA, Am. U., 1969. Dir. Washington News Bur., Susquehanna Broadcasting Co., 1969-86; v.p. pub. affairs Nat. Assn. Realtors, Washington, 1987-99; dir. comms. Mortgage Ins. Cos. of Am., 2000—. Mem. exec. com. of corrs. Radio-TV Assn. (U.S. Congress), 1974-75 Served with AUS, 1969-75. Mem.: Nat. Press Club. Jewish. Home: 6307 Karmich St Fairfax Station VA 22039-1622 Office: 1425 K St NW Washington DC 20005 Office Phone: 202-682-2683. E-mail: jeff@micadc.org.

LUBARS, DAVID, advertising executive; b. Bklyn. s. Walter Lubars; m. Cindy Bost; children: Alex, Michael. BA in comm., Boston U., 1980. With Leonard Monahan Saabye (name changed to Leonard, Moniker, Lubars, and Kelly), Providence, 1982—85, Chiat/Day, Calif., 1985—87; ptnr., exec. v.p., creative dir. Leonard, Moniker, Lubars, and Kelly, Providence, 1988—93; exec. v.p., exec. creative dir. BBDO West, LA, 1993—94, pres., exec. creative dir., 1994—98; creative dir. Mpls. office Fallon Worldwide, 1998—99, co-pres., exec. creative dir. Mpls. office, 1999—2004, pres., exec. creative dir. N. Am., 2002—04; chmn., chief creative officer BBDO N. Am., NYC, 2004—. Named Creative Dir. Yr., Adweek, 2000. Office: BBDO Worldwide 1285 Ave Am New York NY 10019 Office Phone: 212-459-5000.

LUBARSKY, DAVID ALAN, anesthesiologist, educator; Prof., chair dept. anesthesiology U. Miami, 2002—06. Office: U Miami Dept Anesthesia 1611 NW 12th St C300 Miami FL 33136 Office Phone: 305-585-7037 1. Office Fax: 305-545-6501. Business E-Mail: lubarsky@miami.edu.

LUBATTI, HENRY JOSEPH, physicist, researcher; b. Oakland, Calif., Mar. 16, 1937; s. John and Pauline (Massimino) L.; m. Catherine Jeanne Berthe Ledoux, June 29, 1968; children: Karen E., Henry J., Stephen J.C. AA, U. Calif., Berkeley, 1957, AB, 1960; PhD, U. Calif., 1966; MS, U. Ill., 1963. Research assoc. Faculty Scis. U. Paris, Orsay, France, 1966-68; asst. prof. physics MIT, 1968-69; assoc. prof., sci. dir. visual techniques lab. U. Wash., 1969-74, prof., sci. dir. visual Techniques lab., 1974-98. Vis. lectr. Internat. Sch. Physics, Erice, Sicily, 1968, Herceg-Novi, Yugoslavia Internat. Sch., 1969, XII Cracow Sch. Theoretical Physics, Zapokane, Poland, 1972; vis. scientist CERN, Geneva, 1980-81; vis. staff Los Alamos Nat. Lab., 1983-86; guest scientist SSC Lab., 1991-93; mem. physics editl. adv. com. World Sci. Pub. Co. Ltd., 1982-93; guest scientist Fermilab, 1999-2000; vis. scientist U. Rome, summers 2001-06. Editor: Physics at Fermilab in the 1990's, 1990; contbr. numerous articles on high energy physics to profl. jours. Alfred P. Sloan Rsch. fellow, 1971-75. Fellow AAAS, Am. Phys. Soc.; mem. Sigma Xi, Tau Beta Pi. Office: Elem Particle Experiment Group U Wash PO Box 351560 Seattle WA 98195-1560 Home Phone: 206-524-2496; Office Phone: 206-543-8964. E-mail: lubatti@u.washington.edu.

LUBAWSKI, JAMES LAWRENCE, healthcare consultant; b. Chgo., June 4, 1946; s. Harry James and Stella Agnes (Pokorny) L.; m. Kathleen Felicity Donnellan, June 1, 1974; children: Kathleen N., James Lawrence, Kevin D., Edward H. BA, Northwestern U., 1968, MBA, 1969, MA, 1980. Asst. prof. U. Northern Iowa, Cedar Falls, 1969-72; instr. Loyola U., Chgo., 1974-76; dir., market planning Midwest Stock Exchange, Chgo., 1976-77; dir. mktg. Gambro Inc., Barrington, Ill., 1977-79; mktg. mgr. Travenol Labs., Deerfield, Ill., 1979-82; dir. mktg. Hollister Inc., Libertyville, Ill., 1982-84; pres., chief exec. officer Neomedica Inc., Chgo., 1984-86; v.p. bus. devel. Evangl. Health Svcs., Oak Brook, Ill., 1986-87; pres., chief exec. officer Cath. Health Alliance Met. Chgo., 1987-95; mng. dir. Ward Howell Internat., Chgo., 1995-98; v.p. A.T. Kearney, Chgo., 1998-2000; pres. Zwell Internat., Chgo., 2000—02; founder Lubawski & Assocs., Northfield, 2002—. Author: Food and Man, 1974, Food and People, 1979; co-editor: Consumer Behavior in Theory and in Action, 1970. Mem. Evanston Golf Club (pres. 2000-02). Avocations: golf, fishing. Office: 1765 Maple St Ste 15 Northfield IL 60093 Office Phone: 847-441-7300. Personal E-mail: Jim@Lubawski.com.

LUBBERS, ALICE DIANNE, operating room nurse; b. Spokane, Wash., Nov. 10, 1956; d. Donald Lee and Dianne B. (Engstrom) L. BS, U. Idaho, 1979; BSN, Ctr. for Nursing Edn., 1985; grad, U.S. Army Command and Gen. Staff Coll., 1999; MS in Bus. Orgn., U. La Verne, Calif., 2002. RN, Wash.; cert. oper. rm. nurse. Commd. U.S. Army, 1988, advanced through grades to lt. col.; oper. rm. nurse Kootenai Med. Ctr., Coeur d'Alene, Idaho; psychiatric nurse Sacred Heart Med. Ctr., Spokane; neurosurg. head nurse operating room Madigan Med. Ctr., U.S. Army Nurse Corps., Ft. Lewis, Wash., 1988—90; head nurse dept. urology Madigan Army Med. Ctr., 1990—91; head nurse oper. rm. and ctrl. supply Bassett Army Cmty. Hosp., Ft. Wainwright, Alaska, 2000—04; head nurse ctrl. supply 47th Combat Support Hosp., Operation Iraqi Freedom, 2003; chief oper. room and ctrl. supply Bayne Jones Army Cmty. Hosp., Ft. Polk, La., 2004—06; head nurse oper. rm. Madigan Army Med. Ctr., Ft. Lewis, Wash., 2006—. Clin. staff perioperative nurse 47th Combat Support Hosp., Operation Desert Shield/Desert Storm, 1991; head nurse OR/CMS 18th MASH, 1991-92; head nurse same day surgery/OR, Bayne-Jones Army Cmty. Hosp., Ft. Polk, La., 1993-96; OR edn. coord./laser safety officer Madigan Army Med. Ctr., Ft. Lewis, Wash., 1997-2000. Decorated Meritorious Svc. medal (3), Army Achievement medal (5), Army Commendation medal (5), Southwest Asia medal with 3 combat stars, Kuwait Liberation medal, Saudi Arabia liberation medal, Nat. Defense medal (2), Meritorious Unit Citation medal (2), Global War on Terrorism Epiditionary medal with one combat star, Global War on Terrorism Svc. medal, Overseas medal, Humanitarian Svc. medal, Iraqui Freedom medal. Mem. Assn. Oper. Rm. Nurses, Am. Soc. Laser Medicine and Surgery, Laser Inst. Am. Office: Oper Rm Madigan Army Med Ctr Fort Lewis WA Office Phone: 253-968-2235.

LUBBERS, AREND DONSELAAR, retired academic administrator; b. Milw., July 23, 1931; s. Irwin Jacob and Margaret (Van Donselaar) L.; m. Eunice L. Mayo, June 19, 1953 (div.); children— Arend Donselaar, John Irwin Darrow, Mary Elizabeth; m. Nancy Vanderpol, Dec. 21, 1968; children— Robert Andrew, Caroline Jayne. AB, Hope Coll., 1953; AM, Rutgers U., 1956; LittD, Central Coll., 1977; DSc, U. Sarajevo, Yugoslavia, 1987; LHD, Hope Coll., 1988; DSc, Akademia Ekonomiczna, Krakow, Poland, 1989, U. Kingston Univ., Eng., 1995. Rsch. asst. Rutgers U., 1954-55; rsch. fellow Reformed Ch. in Am., 1955-56; instr. history and polit. sci. Wittenberg U., 1956-58; v.p. devel. Central Coll., Iowa, 1959-60, pres., 1960-69, Grand Valley State U., Allendale, Mich., 1969-2001; ret., 2001. Mem. Am. Assn. State Colls. and Univs. seminar in India, 1971. Fed. Commn. Orgn. Govt. Conduct Fgn. Policy, 1972; USIA insp., Netherlands, 1976; mem. pres.'s commn. NCAA, 1984-87, 89—, chmn. pres.'s commn., 1998-2002; bd. dirs. Grand Bank, Grand Rapids, Mich., Macatawa Bank; cons. Grand Valley State U., Hackley Hosp., Olivet Coll., Pierce Cedar

Creek Inst. Environ. Rsch. and Edn. Student Cmty. amb. from Holland (Mich.) to Yugoslavia, 1951; bd. dirs. Grand Rapids Symphony, 1976-82, 99, Butterworth Hosp., 1988; chmn. divsn. II NCAA Pres.'s Commn., 1992-95, 98-99, mem. pres.'s coun., 1997; mem. Michigan Cmty. Svc. Commn., 2001-; mem. exec. com. West Mich. Sports Commn., 2007. Recipient Golden Plate award San Diego Acad. Achievement, 1962, Golden-Emblem Order of Merit Polish Peoples Republic, 1988, trustee's award cmty. leadership Aquinas Coll., 1998, Lifetime Achievement award Econ. Club Grand Rapids, 2001; named 1 of top 100 young men in U.S. Life mag., 1962. Mem. Mich. Coun. State Univs. Pres. (chmn. 1988, 2000—), Grand Rapids World Affairs Council (pres. 1971-73), Phi Alpha Theta, Pi Kappa Delta, Pi Kappa Phi. Home: 4195 N Oak Pointe Ct Grand Rapids MI 49525 Office Phone: 616-331-6607. Business E-Mail: lubbers@gvsu.edu.

LUBBOCK, JAMES EDWARD, retired writer, photographer, media consultant; b. St. Louis, Sept. 12, 1924; s. Winans Fowler and Hildegard Beauregard (Whittemore) Lubbock; m. Charlotte Frances Ferguson, Aug. 24, 1947; children: Daniel Lawrason(dec.), Brian Wade, Kathleen Harper. BA in English, U. Mo., 1949. Asst. editor St. Louis County Observer, 1949-51; staff writer St. Louis Globe-Dem., 1951-53, state editor, 1954-56; mng. editor Food Merchandising mag., 1956-57; freelance indsl. writer-photographer, cons. St. Louis, 1958-89. Pres. James E. Lubbock, Inc., 1981—89. With Signal Corps US Army, 1943—46. Mem.: ACLU, Mo. Citizens for Arts, Common Cause, St. Louis Press Club. Democrat. Home and Office: 10734 Clearwater Dr Saint Louis MO 63123-4911 Personal E-mail: anonynony@peoplepc.com.

LUBCHENCO, JANE, environmental scientist, marine ecologist, science association director; b. Denver, Dec. 4, 1947; married; 2 children. BA in Biology, Colo. Coll., 1969; MS in Zoology, U. Wash., 1971; PhD in Ecology, Harvard U., 1975; DSc (hon.), Drexel U., 1992, Colo. Coll., 1993, Bates Coll., 1997, Unity Coll., 1998, Southampton Coll., 1999, LI Univ., 1999, Princeton U., 2001, Plymotuh State Coll., 2002, Mich. State U., 2003. Asst. prof. ecology Harvard U., Cambridge, Mass., 1975—77; rsch. assoc. Smithsonian Inst., 1978—84; asst. prof. Oreg. State U., Corvallis, 1977—82, assoc. prof., 1982—88, prof. zoology, 1988—, chair, dept. zoology, 1989—92, disting. prof. zoology, 1993—, Wayne and Gladys Valley prof. marine biology, 1995—. Vis. prof. U. West Indies, Kingston, Jamaica, 1976, Universidad Catolica, Santiago, Chile, 1986, Inst. Oceanography, Academica Sinica, Qingdao, P.R. China, 1987, U. Canterbury, Christchurch, New Zealand, 1995—96, Christchurch, 1999—2000, Christchurch, 2002—03; prin. investigator NSF, 1976—, Marine Ecosystem Dynamics Consortium, 1992—2007; exec. com. SCOPE, 1992—95; mem. roster of experts UN Environment Programme Scientific & Tech. Advisory Panel, 1993—2000; sect. co-coordinator UN Environ. Programme, Biodiversity and Ecosystem Functioning, Global Diversity Assessment, 1993—95; co-founder, chair Aldo Leopold Leadership program, 1993—2002, co-chair, 2003—08; nat. sci. and tech. council's Nat. forum on Environment & Natural Resources, chair, biodiversity and ecosystem dynamics group White House Office of Sci. & Tech. Policy, 1994; mem. adv. com. Pew Fellows Program in Conservation and the Environ., 1995—98; trustee, mem. program com. Monterey Bay Aquarium, 1995—; trustee. sci. adv. com. Environ. Defense, 1995—, co-chair, oceans com., 1997—, mem. develop. com., 2002—, v.p., 2005—; mem. scientific adv. bd. UN Educational, Scientific and Cultural Orgn., 1996—99; mem. com. on edn. and human resources Nat. Sci. Bd., 1996—97, mem. com. on programs and plans, 1997—, mem. task force on the environ., 1998—2000, mem. internat. task force, 2000—02, 2005—, mem. task force on sci. and engring. infrastructure, 2001—03, mem. com. on strategy and budget, 2001—, mem. nominating com., 2002, mem. subcommittee on polar issues, 2002—; US Delegate, Unions XXV Gen. Assembly Internat. Coun. for Sci., Washington, 1996, US Delegate to First World Conf. Sci., Budapest, 99, NAS Delegate to the ICSU, XXXVI gen. assembly, Cario, 99, mem. com. on scientific programs and review, 2000—02, mem. exec. bd., 2002—07, pres., 2002—05, mem. XXXVII gen. assembly as pres. elect and chair of forum on sustainability sci., 2002, pres. elect, 1999—2002; exec. chair of scientific and religious steering com. Religion, Sci. and the Environ. II: The Balck Sea as a Paradigm, 1996—98; scientific and religious steering com. Religion, Sci., and the Environ. III: The Danube, 1998—2000; hon. com. Religion, Sci., and the Environ. IV: The Adriatic, 2001—03, Religion, Sci., and the Environ. V; The Baltic, 2002—03, Religion, Sci., and the Environ. VI: The Caspian Sea, 2004—05, Religion, Sci., and the Environ. VII: The Amazon Basin, 2005—06; mem. adv. bd. Sea Studios Found. The Shape of Life Prodn., 1997—2001; mem. scientific adv. com. Pacific Ocean Conservation Network, 1997—98; mem. Ecosystem Principles Advisory Panel Nat. Marine Fisheries Service, 1997—2000; mem., com. on biodiversity and ecosystems President's Council of Advisors on Sci. & Tech., 1997—98; mem. sci. panel Oreg. State Environ. Report, 1998—99; mem. adv. forum Consultative Group on Biol. Diversity, 1998; mem. adv. bd. Sci. and Tech. News Network, 1998—; mem. tech. adv. com. Nat. Geographic Soc. Sustainable Seas Expeditions, 1998—2001; mem. World Econ. Forum, Davos, Switzerland, 1998—2001, Davos, 2004—05; mem. nat. coun. Earth Day 2000, 1999—2000; lead prin. investigator Partnership for Interdisciplinary Studies of Coastal Oceans, 1999—2009; mem. Ecotrust Coun., 1999—; principal Communication Partnership for Sci. and the Sea (COMPASS), 1999—2004; mem. adv. bd. Forum on Religion and Ecology, 1999—, Internat. Biodiversity Observation Yr., 2000—02; mem. antarctic rsch. program Nat. Sci. Bd. Review Team, 2000; commr., mem. Pew Oceans Commn., 2000—03; dir. SeaWeb, 2000—; mem. adv. bd. Sea Studios Found., Strange Days on Planet Earth prodn., 2001—; mem. Ctr. for Informal Learning and Schools, 2001—; invited presenter in field, 2002—05; ex-officio mem. Inter-Acad. Panel, 2002—05; mem. systheis team, South Africa Science in Kruger Nat. Park, 2002; mem. vis. com. Environ. Def. Marine Protected Area, Cuba, 2002; mem. Mng. for Resilience in Coastal Marine Ecosystems, 2004; co-chair Governor's Adv. Group on Global Warming, 2004; task force mem. Joint Oceans Commn. Initiative. Mem. editl. bd. American Naturalist, 1978-81, Oecologia, 1985-88, Journal of Phycology, 1987-90, Ecological Applications, 1989-93, The Northwest Environmental Journal, 1991-93, Trends in Ecology & Evolution, 1991-, Conservation Ecology, 1995-2001, Issues in Ecology, 1995-2002, 2003-, Ecosystems, 1997-99, Environmental Conservation, 1998-99; advisory editor, Ecological Studies, Springer-Verlag, 1993-2000; assoc. editor, Encyclopedia of Biodiversity, Academic Press, 1997-2000; mem. internat. adv. bd., Encyclopedia of Global Environmental Change, Wiley, 1998-2001; editor for Special Issue on Marine Reserves, Ecological Applications, 1999-2002; Ad-hoc editor, Proceedings of the NAS, 1998-present; mem. adv. bd. Frontiers in Ecology, 2001-, Human-Environment Interactions (U. Michigan book series), 2003-, Faculty of 1000, 1 of 3 Heads of Faculty for Ecology and Evolution, 2003-; mem. scientific adv. bd., PBS Radio Show, Living On Earth, 1997-2000; convening lead author, Synthesis Chapter for Business and Industry and lead author, Millennium Development Goals Chapter, 2002-2005; contbr. articles to profl. jours. Trustee David and Lucile Packard Found., 2001—04, trustee emeritus, 2004, mem. selection com., interdisciplinary sci. program, 1998—2001; mem. adv. commn. on open space Corvallis City Coun., 1995—98; mem. adv. com. Doris Duke Charitable Found., 2002; advisor Vulcan, 2000—02; mem. ten yr. review com. U. Washington, Friday Harbor Lab., 2002; bd. visitors U. Washington, Dept. Biology, 2002—, mem. external review adv. bd., 2003—; chair U. Washington, Friday Harbor Lab. Centennial Symposium Com., 2003—04; co-chair Gov. Oregon's Global Warming Adv. Group, 2003—; mem. selection com. Pew Fellows in Marine Conservation, 1995—98, Aldo Leopold Leadership program, 1998—2002, John B. Oakes award for Disting. Environ. Journalism, 1999—2004; mem. selection com. for global and complex systems fellows James S. McDonnell Centennial Fellowships, 1997—99. Co-recipient Golden Eagle award, Coun. for Internat. Nontheatrical Events, Washington, DC (for Nat. Geographic film Diversity of Life), 1994; named Oreg. Scientist of Yr., Oreg. Acad. Scis., 1994, Highly Cited Rscher. in Ecology/Environment, Info. Sci. Inst., 2002; named one of 50 Outstanding Women Scientist, Discover Mag., 2002; recipient Nat. Conservation award, Daughters of the Am. Revolution, 1998, Founder's Edn. award, 1998, Sustained Achievement award, Renewable Natural Resources Found., 1998, David B. Stone award, New England Aquarium, 1999, Howard Vollun award, Reed Coll., 1999, Gold Plate award, Am. Acad. Achievement, 2001, Heinz Environmental award, Heinz Family Found., 2002, Ed Ricketts Meml. award, Monterey Bay Nat. Marine Sanctuary, 2002, Leadership Citation, Coun. for Scientific Soc. Presidents, 2002, Disting. Svc. award, Soc. for Conservation Biology, 2003, Nierenberg prize for Science in Pub. Interest, Scripps Institution of Oceanography, 2003, Disting. Scientist award, Am. Inst. Biol. Sciences, 2004, Environ. Law Inst. award, 2004; Pew Scholar in conservation and environment, 1992—95, John D. and Katherine T. MacArthur Found. Fellow, 1993—98, MacArthur fellow, 1993—98. Fellow: AAAS (pres.-elect, pres., chair bd. dirs. 1995—98, mem. Millennium Symposium 1998—2000, Science, editor-in-chief 1999—2000, 2005 AAAS Pub. Understanding of Sci. and Tech. award 2006), Assn. for Women in Sci.; mem.: NAS (mem. panel on adaption, policy implications of greenhouse warming 1989—91, mem. temporary nominating group on global change 1996, mem. com. on creationism 1996, mem. robertson meml. lecture selection com. 1998, coun. 1999—2002, mem. develop. com. 1999—2002, mem. coun. 1999—2002, mem. coun. com. on budget and internal affairs 1999—2002, mem. coun. com. on scientific programs 1999—2002, mem. com. on class and sect. structure 1999—, first chair of newly created sect. environ. sciences and ecology 2000—01, exec. com. 2001—02, mem. com. sustainability sci. 2002—03), Nat. Rsch. Coun. (mem. bd. environ. studies and toxicology (BEST) 1989—92, mem. com. to review Dept. Interior's mineral mgmt. svc. study liaison 1989—92, BEST, chair of natural resources & applied ecology working group II 1990—92, mem. ecol. effects of human activity, planning mtg. 1991, mem. com. on environ. rsch. 1991—93, mem. bd. environ. studies and toxicology (BEST) 1992—95, mem. ocean studies bd., workshop on biodiversity in marine systems 1994, mem. com. on ecosystem mgmt. and sustainable fisheries 1995—97, mem. com. on biodiversity forum 1995—97, mem. delegate to class membership com. 1997, mem. ecosystem panel 1997—, mem. biol. systems & dynamics of global change working group 1998, mem. delegate to class membership com. 1998), Western Soc. Naturalists, Internat. Congress Ecology, Am. Soc. Limnology and Oceanography, Am. Acad. Arts and Sciences, Royal Swedish Acad. Sciences' Beijer Inst. Environ. Economics (bd. dir. 1999—2004), Royal Soc. London (fgn. mem.), British Ecological Soc. (hon.), Third World Acad. Sciences (assoc.), European Acad. Sciences, Am. Philosophical Soc., Am. Inst. Biol. Sci. (mem. sub-committee, earth, environ., agriculture and resources 1999—), Am. Soc. Zoologists, Am. Soc. Naturalists, Phycological Soc. Am. (nat. lectr. 1987—89, Nat. Lectr. 1987—89), Ecol. Soc. Am. (mem. coun. 1982—84, chair awards com. 1983—86, nominating com. 1986, pres. 1992—94, nominating com. 2001—02, George Mercer award 1979, Disting. Svc. award 1997), Golden Key Nat. Honor Soc. (hon.). Achievements include research in population and community ecology, plant-herbivore and predator-prey interactions, competition, marine ecology, algal ecology, agal life histories, biogeography and chemical ecology. Office: Oreg State U Dept Zoology 3029 Cordley Hall Corvallis OR 97331-2914 also: Internat Council Sci 51 Bd de Montmorency 75016 Paris France Office Phone: 541-737-5337. Office Fax: 541-737-3360. Business E-Mail: lubchenj@bcc.oregonstate.edu.

LUBECK, MARVIN JAY, ophthalmologist; b. Cleve., Mar. 20, 1929; s. Charles D. and Lillian (Jay) L. A.B., U. Mich., 1951, M.D., 1955, M.S., 1959. Diplomate Am. Bd. Opthamology; m. Arlene Sue Bitman, Dec. 28, 1955; children: David Mark, Daniel Jay, Robert Charles. Intern, U. Mich. Med. Ctr., 1955-56, resident ophthalmology, 1956-58, jr. clin. instr. ophthalmology, 1958-59; pvt. practice medicine, specializing in ophthalmology, Denver, 1961—; mem. staff Rose Hosp., Porter Hosp., Presbyn. Hosp., St. Luke's Hosp. With U.S. Army, 1959-61. Fellow ACS; mem. Am. Acad. Ophthalmology, Denver Med. Soc., Colo. Ophthalmol. Soc. Home: 590 S Harrison Ln Denver CO 80209-3517

LUBELL, ELLEN, writer; b. Bklyn., Apr. 7, 1950; d. Edward and Sonia Lubell. BA in Fine Arts, SUNY, Stony Brook, 1971. Contbg. editor Arts Mag., NYC, 1972-79; founder, editor Womanart Mag., Bklyn., 1976-78; columnist Soho Weekly News, NYC, 1977-79; contbr. Art in Am., NYC, 1981-85; dir. pub. rels. Gerstman & Meyers Inc., NYC, 1984-89; freelancer, columnist, publicist The Village Voice, NYC, 1984-91; columnist, freelancer N.Y. Newsday, 1988—89; dir. comm. Inform, Inc., NYC, 1991-95; comm. dir. Child Care Action Campaign, NYC, 1995-99; freelance writer Star-Ledger, Newark, 1996-97; dir. pub. rels. The Childrens Aid Soc., NYC, 1999—. Art Critics fellow, Nat. Endowment for the Arts, 1978.

LUBELL, MICHAEL STEPHEN, physicist, educator; b. NYC, Mar. 25, 1943; s. Richard M. and Lillian (Aronoff) L.; 1 child, Karina B. BA, Columbia U., 1963; MS, Yale U., 1965, PhD, 1969. Postdoctoral fellow Yale U., New Haven, 1970, instr., 1971—72, asst. prof., 1972—77, assoc. prof., 1977—80, CUNY, 1980—82, prof., 1983—, chmn. dept. physics, 1999—2005, 2006—07. Advisor basic rsch. U.S. Army, 1980-84; mem. exec. com. Internat. Conf. on Physics of Elec. and Atomic Collisions, 1983-91, co-chmn. local organizing com., 1989; vis. scientist Brookhaven Nat. Lab., 1986-87; chmn. com. on atomic and molecular sci. NRC, 1988-90; mem. adv. com. on pub. info. Am. Inst. Physics, 1988-90, adv. com. on media and govt. relations, 2003; mem. steering com. Sci. Coalition, 2003-; vis. lectr. Inst. Theoretical Physics, U. Calif., Santa Barbara, 1990; vis. prof. U. Tex., Austin, 1990, U. Bielefeld, 1993; cons. in field; sci. and tech. policy columnist APS News. Sci. and sci. policy spokesman, radio and TV and print media; contbr. articles to profl. jours. and books. Sci., tech. adv. U.S. Sen. Christopher J. Dodd, Washington, 1980—; chmn. Dem. Town com., Westport, Conn., 1986-91; del. Dem. Nat. Conv., 1984. Rsch. grantee and contracts NSF, Dept. Energy, Dept. Def., 1974—; fellow AEC, 1970, Alfred P. Sloan Found., 1980-84 Fellow AAAS, Am. Phys. Soc. (panel on pub. affairs 1983-84, co-organizer Congl. Day 1991-92, dir. pub. affairs 1995—); mem. Sigma Xi. Home: PO Box 188 Westport CT 06881-0188 Office: CUNY City Coll Dept Physics Convent Ave New York NY 10031 Office Phone: 202-662-8705. E-mail: lubell@aps.org.

LUBENSKY, EARL HENRY, diplomat, anthropologist; b. Marshall, Mo., Mar. 31, 1921; s. Henry Carl and Adele Gertrud (Biesemeyer) L.; m. Anita Ruth Price, June 27, 1942 (dec. July 1992); children: Tom, Gerald, John Christopher; m. Margot Truman Patterson, Mar. 26, 1994. BA, Mo. Valley Coll., 1948, LLD (hon.), 1968; BS, Georgetown U., 1949; MS, George Washington U., 1967; diploma, Nat. War Coll., 1967; MA, U. Mo., 1983, PhD, 1991. Mgr. Tavern Supply Co., Marshall, Mo., 1938—42; real estate salesman Mitchell Quick Realtor, Silver Spring, Md., 1948; analyst rsch. Georgetown U., Washington, 1949; reference asst. Libr. Congress, Washington, 1949; fgn. svc. officer Dept. of State, Washington, 1949—79, inter-Am. reg. polit. affairs officer, 1956—61, served in Germany, Philippines, Spain, Ecuador, Colombia and El Salvador, 1950—78, officer-in-charge Antarctic affairs Washington, 1958—59. Diplomat-in-residence, Olivet, Albion and Adrian Colls., Mich., 1973-74; sr. staff mem. internat. affairs Coun. on Environ. Quality, Washington, 1974-76; spl. amb. to inauguration Pres. Romero, El Salvador, 1977; adj. rsch. assoc. anthropology U. Mo., 1992—. Contbr. articles to profl. jours. Mem. bd. dirs. Columbia Entertainment Co., 1993-99. With Mo. N.G. 1937-40, 48, 2d lt. AUS, 1944, U.S. Army, 1942-45, lt. col. USAR, 1948-81. Eagle Scout Boy Scouts Am., 1939. Mem. Mo. Archaeol. Soc. (charter, treas. 1981-90, chmn. bd. trustees 2001-2003, trustee 1991—, Appreciation award 1991, 2002, disting. svc. award, 2003), Soc. for Am. Archaeology (Presdl. Recognition award 1991), Inst. Andean Studies, Fgn. Svc. Assn., Diplomatic and Consular Officrs Retired, Boone County Hist. Soc., The Theatre Soc. (treas. 1993-99). Democrat. Avocations: genealogy, gardening, music, amateur radio, stamp collecting/philately. Home: 1408 Bradford Dr Columbia MO 65203-2302 Office: Dept Anthropology Univ Mo Columbia MO 65211-0001 E-mail: lubenskye@missouri.edu.

LUBENSKY, TOM CARL, physics professor; b. Kansas City, Mo., May 7, 1943; s. Earl Henry and Anita Ruth (Price) L.; m. Amy Ruth Waldstreicher, Sept. 21, 1968; children: David K., Ellen P. BS, Calif. Inst. Tech., 1964; MA, Harvard U., 1965, PhD, 1969. NSF postdoctoral fellow U. Paris, Orsay, France, 1969-70; postdoctoral fellow Brown U., Providence, 1970-71; asst. prof. physics U. Pa., Phila., 1971-75, assoc. prof., 1975-80, prof., 1980—, Mary Amanda Wood Chair, Dept. Physics, 1998, chmn., Dept. Physics, 2001—. Vis. prof. Ecole Nomale Supérieur, Paris, 1981-82; cons. Exxon Rsch. and Engring., Annandale, N.J., 1990-95; assoc. dir. Lab. Rsch. Structure of Matter at UPenn, 1998-2001; editl. bd. Physical Review E, 1997-2004. Contbr. over 200 articles to profl. jours. Fellow Alfred P. Sloan Found., 1975-77, Guggenheim Found., 1981. Fellow Am. Phys. Soc. (mem. exec. com. Condensed Matter Physics, 1998-2001, Oliver E. Buckley prize, 2004), Am. Liquid Crystal Soc. (hon. mem., 2004, chmn. Gordon Conf., 2001), Nat. Acad. Sci. Office: U Pa Dept Physics Philadelphia PA 19104 Office Phone: 215-898-7002. Office Fax: 215-573-3897. E-mail: tom@physics.upenn.edu.

LUBER, THOMAS J(ULIAN), lawyer; b. Louisville, Feb. 16, 1949; s. John J. and Martha E. (Cotton) L.; m. Dorothy Ann Carter, Dec. 19, 1975; children: Katharine Ann, Allison Julia. BS in Acctg., U. Louisville, 1972, JD with honors, 1976; LLM in Taxation, NYU, 1977. Bar: Ky. 1976. Agt. IRS, Louisville, 1972-73; assoc. Fahey & Gray, Louisville, 1977-79; from assoc. to ptnr. Wyatt, Tarrant & Combs and predecessor firms, Louisville, 1979—, chmn. tax sect., 1983—. Lectr. U. Louisville, 1978-80; speaker in field; bd. advisors Jour. Multistate Taxation. Contbr. articles to profl. jours. Bd. dirs. Univ. Pediatrics Found., Louisville, Univ. Ob-gyn. Found., Louisville, Assumption High Sch., Louisville. With USAF, 1967-69. Mem. ABA, Ky. Bar Assn. (chmn. tax sect. 1983-84), Louisville Bar Assn., Ky. Inst. Fed. Taxation (mem. planning com. 1981—, chmn. 1984—), Jefferson Club, Big Spring Country Club. Democrat. Roman Catholic. Avocations: hiking, working out. Office: Wyatt Tarrant & Combs PNC Plz 500 W Jefferson St Louisville KY 40202-2898 E-mail: tluber@wyattfirm.com.

LUBERDA, GEORGE JOSEPH, lawyer, educator; b. NYC, Apr. 27, 1930; s. Joseph George and Mary Loretta (Koslowski) L. BS, Georgetown U., 1951, LLB, 1959. Bar: D.C. 1959, U.S. Ct. Appeals (D.C. cir.) 1959, Mich. 1970, Mo. 1973. Washington rep. Ford Motor Co., Washington, 1955-59; atty. FTC, Washington, 1960-64; trial atty. Antitrust Divsn. Dept. Justice, Washington, 1965-69; sr. atty. Bendix Corp., Mich., 1970-71; assoc. Butzel, Long, Gust, Klein & Van Zile, Detroit, 1972; antitrust counsel Monsanto Co., St. Louis, 1973-88; assoc. Herzog, Crebs and McGhee, 1988-93; ptnr. Luberda & Carp, St. Louis, 1993—2002, Luberda, Gusdorf & Weir, LLC, St. Louis, 2002—06; sr. counselor Mo. Bar, 2006—. Adj. prof. St. Louis U., 1985-96. Mem. Mo. Bar Assn., Bar Assn. Met. St. Louis. Republican. Roman Catholic. Home and Office: 716 Ridgeview Circle Ln Ballwin MO 63021-7810 Office Phone: 636-230-0727.

LUBETSKI, EDITH ESTHER, librarian; b. Bklyn., July 16, 1940; m. Meir Lubetski, Dec. 23, 1968; children: Shaul, Uriel, Leah. BA, Bklyn. Coll., 1962; MLS, Columbia U., 1965; MA in Jewish Studies, Yeshiva U., 1968. Judaica libr. Stern Coll. Yeshiva U., NYC, 1965-66, acquisitions libr., 1966-69, head libr., 1969—. Author (with Meir Lubetski): (book) Building a Judaica Library Collection, 1983; author: The Jewish Woman: Recent Books, 1995; contbr. articles to profl. jours. Mem. exec. bd. Jewish Book Coun., 1998—. Mem.: ACRL, ALA, N.Y. Libr. Assn., Assn. Jewish Librs. (corr. sec. 1980—84, pres. N.Y. chpt. 1984—86, nat. v.p. 1984—86, nat. pres. 1986—88, Fanny Goldstein Merit award 1993, Life Membership award 2003). Office: Yeshiva U Hedi Steinberg Libr 245 Lexington Ave New York NY 10016-4605 Office Phone: 212-340-7720. E-mail: Lubetski@ymail.yu.edu.

LUBEZKI, EMMANUEL, cinematographer; b. Mexico City; Attended, Nat. Univ., Mexico. Cinematographer: (films) Sera por eso que la quiero tanto, 1985, Los Buzos diamantistas, 1988, La Muchacha, 1990, Bandidos, 1991, Solo con tu pareja, 1991, Like Water for Chocolate, 1992 (Ariel Best Cinematography, 1992), Twenty Bucks, 1993, Miroslava, 1993 (Ariel Best Cinematography, 1993), The Harvest, 1993, Reality Bites, 1994, Amber, 1994 (Ariel Best Cinematography, 1994), A Little Princess, 1995, A Walk in the Clouds, 1995, The Birdcage, 1996, Great Expectations, 1998, Meet Joe Black, 1998, Sleepy Hollow, 1999 (Boston Film Critics Best Cinematography, 1999, Golden Satellite Best Cinematography, 1999, Online Film Critics Soc. Best Cinematography, 1999), Things You Can Tell Just by Looking at Her, 2000, Y tu mama tambien, 2001, De Mesmer, con amor o Te para dos, 2002, The Cat in the Hat, 2003, Lemony Snicket's A Series of Unfortunate Events, 2004, The New World, 2005, Children of Men, 2006 (BAFTA Best Cinematography, 2007, Nat. Soc. Film Critics Best Cinematography, 2007, LA Film Critics Best Cinematography, 2006); cinematographer, cinematographer: (TV series) Hora Marcada, 2004, Fallen Angels, 1993 (CableAce award Best Cinematography, 1994); prodr., prodr.: (films) Caifanes, 2004, Camino largo a Tijuana, 1991; dir.: (films) Ejercicio de 20 ano, 1985, Marlena en la pared, 1986; prodr., dir.: (films) Caifanes, 1986; (TV series) Hora Marcada, 1989; editor: (films) Ejercicio de 20 ano, 1985, Caifanes, 1990.*

LUBIC, BENITA JOAN ALK, travel company executive; b. Green Bay, Wis., May 18, 1936; d. Isadore George and Marion (Segal) A.; m. Robert Bennett Lubic, May 31, 1959; children: Wendie Alison, Bret David, Robin Kimberly Lubic Bliss. BBA, U. Wis., 1958. Cert. travel cons. Pres., owner Transeair Travel, LLC, Washington, 1959—. Instr. Internat. Travel Tng. Sch., 1982-91; lic. Cuba Travel Svc. Provider, 2000—. Contbr. articles on incentive travel to mags. Mem. SKAL, Washington; mem. adv. bd. Braniff Airlines, Republic Airlines, Sonesta Hotel Corp. Mem. Am. Soc. Travel Agts. (pres. Washington subchpt. 1985-88, bd. dirs. 1979-96), Wash. Exec. Women in Travel (v.p. 1982-83, treas. 1984-85, bd. dirs. 1985-05), Internat. Fedn. Women's Travel Orgns. (dir. 1993-94, 99-05), SKAL Internat. Democrat. Jewish. Avocations: golf, tennis, swimming, bicycling, travel. Home: 2813 McKinley Pl NW Washington DC 20015-1104 Office: Transeair Travel LLC 2813 McKinley Pl NW Washington DC 20015-1104 Office Phone: 202-362-6100. Personal E-mail: blubic@aol.com.

LUBIC, RUTH WATSON, health facility administrator, nurse midwife; b. Bucks County, Pa., Jan. 18, 1927; d. John Russell and Lillian (Kraft) Watson; m. William James Lubic, May 28, 1955; 1 child, Douglas Watson. Diploma, Sch. Nursing Hosp. U. Pa., 1955; BS, Columbia U., 1959, MA, 1961, EdD in Applied Anthropology, 1979; cert. in nurse midwifery, SUNY, Bklyn., 1962, DSc (hon.), 1993; LLD (hon.), U. Pa., 1985; DSc (hon.), U. Medicine and Dentistry, NJ, 1986; LHD (hon.), Coll. New Rochelle, 1992, Pace U., 1994. Staff nurse through head nurse Meml. Hosp. for Cancer and Allied Disease, NYC, 1955-58; clin. assoc. Grad. Sch. Nursing NY Med. Coll., NYC, 1962-63; parent educator, cons. Maternity Ctr. Assn., NYC, 1963-67, gen. dir., 1970-95, dir. clin. projects, 1995-97; project dir. Nat. Assn. of Childbearing Ctrs., Washington, 1997-99; pres., CEO DC Developing Families Ctr., 1998—2002, founder, pres. emeritus, 2003—; pres., CEO DC Birth Ctr., Washington, 1998—2007, founder, chair emeritus, 2007—. Cons. in midwifery, nursing and maternal and child health Office Pub. Health and Sci. HHS, 1995—97; adj. prof. divsn. nursing NYU, 1995—; bd. dirs., v.p. Am. Assn. World Health U.S. Com. WHO, 1975—94, pres. Am. Assn. World Health U.S. Com., 1980—81; mem. bd. maternal child and family health NRC, 1974—80; mem. Commn. Grads. Fgn. Nursing Schs., 1979—83, v.p., 1980—81, treas., 1982—83; bd. govs. Frontier Nursing Svc., 1982—92; bd. dirs. Pan Am. Health Edn. Found., pres., 1987—88; vis. prof. King Edward Meml. Hosp., Perth, Australia, 1991; Kate Hanna Harvey vis. prof. cmty. health nursing Frances Payne Bolton Sch. Nursing Case Western Res., 1991; Lansdowne lectr. U. Victoria, B.C., Canada, 1992; adj. prof. Sch. Nursing, Georgetown U., 1997—; Therese Dondero lectr. Am. Coll. Nurse-Midwives Found., 1995; Andrea Printy Meml. lectr. U. Minn., 1998; Kemble lectr. Sch. Nursing, U. NC, Chapel Hill, 2000; Hugh P. Davis lectr. Emory U. Sch. Nursing, 2004. Author (with Gene Hawes): (book) childbearing: A Book of Choices, 1987; contbr. articles to profl. jours. Named Maternal-Child Health Nurse of the Yr., ANA, 1985, Disting. Alumna, U. Pa., 1992; named to Nursing Hall of Fame, 1999; recipient Letitia White award, Florence Nightingale medal, 1955, Nursing Practice award, U. Pa., 1980, Rockefeller Pub. Svc. award, 1981, Hattie Hemschemeyer award, 1983, Alumnae award, Sch. Nursing U. Pa., 1986, McManus medal, Tchrs. Coll. Columbia U., 1992, Disting. Svc. award, Francis Payne Bolton Sch. Nursing, 1993, Hon. Recognition, NY State Nurses Assn., 1993, Nurse-Midwifery Faculty award, Columbia U., 1993, Spirit of Nursing award, Vis. Nurses Svc. NY, 1994, Maes-Macinnes award, Divsn. Nursing NYU, 1994, Hon. Recognition, ANA, 1994, Carola Warburg Rothschild award, Maternity Ctr. Assn., 1997, Healthy Babies Project award, 1998, Woman of Distinction award, Nat. Assn. Women in Edn., 1999, Never Say Die award, DC Primary Care Assn., 2001; Irving Harris vis. scholar, Coll. Nursing U. Ill., 1999, MacArthur fellow, 1993. Fellow: AAAS, Soc. for Applied Anthropology, Am. Acad. Nursing (Living Legend award 2001); mem.: APHA (mem. com. on internat. health, sec. maternal and child health coun. 1982, mem. governing coun. 1986—89, mem. nominating com. 1987, mem. action bd. 1988—90), Vis. Nurse Svc. of NY (Lillian Wald award 2003), Herman Biggs Soc. (sec.-treas. 1989—90), Am. Assn. Colls. Nursing (McGovern lectr. 1997), Nat. Assn. Childbearing Ctrs. (pres. 1983—91, Lifetime Achievement award 2005), Inst. of Medicine of NAS (Lienhard award 2001), Am. Coll. Nurse Midwives (v.p. 1964—66, pres.-elect 1969—70), NY Acad. Medicine, Alpha Omega Alpha (hon.). Home Phone: 212-749-8590; Office Phone: 202-484-6289. Personal E-mail: Rlubic@aol.com. *As a professional nurse-midwife and public health scientist, the guiding principles of my professional life are to listen carefully to the families to be served and to combine their needs with proven scientific knowledge in constructing models for care. It is my belief that the primary purpose of maternal and child health programs is to assist families to achieve a sense of self-confidence about their ability to bring forth and rear offspring in conjunction with, but not dependent upon, professional guidance.*

LUBICK, DONALD CYRIL, lawyer; b. Buffalo, Apr. 29, 1926; s. Louis and Minna D. (Nabith) L.; m. Susan F. Cohen, June 5, 1960; children: Jonathan, Caroline, Lisa. BA summa cum laude, U. Buffalo, 1945; JD magna cum laude, Harvard U., 1949. Bar: N.Y. 1950, Fla. 1974, D.C. 1981; lic. fgn. law cons. Ont., 1989. Teaching fellow Harvard U. Law Sch., 1949-50; lectr. law U. Buffalo, 1950-61; assoc., then ptnr. Hodgson, Russ, Andrews, Woods & Goodyear, Buffalo and Washington, 1950-61, 64-77, 81-94; tax legis. counsel Treasury Dept., Washington, 1961-64, asst. sec. for tax policy, 1977-81, dir. tax adv. program for countries of Ctrl. and Ea. Europe and former Soviet Union Paris, 1994-96, from acting to asst. sec. for tax policy, 1996-99. Adj. prof. law Washington Coll. Law, Am. U., 2002—05. Author: (with Hussey) Basic World Tax Code and Commentary, 1992, 95. Chmn. Tax Revision Com., City of Buffalo, 1958; mem. adv. com. to select Com. on Election Reform, N.Y. State Legislature, 1974, mem. adv. group to commr. internal revenue, 1976. Served with USAAF, 1945-46. Harvard Internat. Tax Program sr. fellow, 1991—. Mem. ABA, Am. Law Inst., Am. Bar Found., N.Y. State Bar Assn., Fla. Bar Assn., Erie County Bar Assn. Democrat. Jewish. Office Phone: 301-951-0127. Personal E-mail: donaldlubick@msn.com.

LUBIN, DONALD G., lawyer; b. NYC, Jan. 10, 1934; s. Harry and Edith (Tannenbaum) L.; m. Amy Schwartz, Feb. 2, 1956; children: Peter, Richard, Thomas, Alice Lubin Spahr. BS in Econs., U. Pa., 1954; LLB, Harvard U., 1957. Bar: Ill. 1957. Ptnr. Sonnenschein Nath & Rosenthal LLP, Chgo., 1957—, chmn. exec. com., 1991-96. Past exec. com., fin. com., chmn. nominating and corp. governance com. McDonald's Corp.; bd. dirs. Molex, Inc., Daubert Industries Inc., Charles Levy Co.; founding bd. dirs. Lake County Cmty. Trust; former bd. dirs., First Nat. Bank Highland Park. Former mem. Navy Pier Redevel. Corp., Highland Park Cultural Arts Commn., Chgo. Bicentennial Commn.; life trustee, former chmn. bd. Highland Park Hosp., Ravinia Festival Assn.; chmn. Chgo. Metropolis 2020, Renaissance Schs. Fund; trustee, exec. com. Rush U. Med. Ctr.; life trustee Chgo. Symphony Orch.; bd. dirs., v.p. Ronald McDonald House Charities, Inc., Chgo. Found. for Edn.; mem. Evanston Northwestern Healthcare Found.; pres., bd. dir. Barr Fund; former bd. dirs., v.p., sec. Ragdale Found.; bd. govs. Art Inst. Chgo.; former bd. overseers Coll. Arts and Sci., U. Pa.; former dir. Smithsonian Inst., Washington, Nat. Mus. Am. History, Washington. Woodrow Wilson vis. fellow Fellow Am. Bar Found., Ill. Bar Found., Chgo. Bar Found.; mem. Chgo. Bar Assn., Civic Com. (mem. steering com.), Lawyers Club Chgo., Chgo. Hort. Soc. (past bd. dirs.), Comml. Club, Std. Club, Lakeshore Club, Beta Gamma Sigma. Home: 2269 Egandale Rd Highland Park IL 60035-2501 Office: Sonnenschein Nath & Rosenthal LLP 233 S Wacker Dr Ste 7800 Chicago IL 60606-6491 Office Phone: 312-876-8007. Personal E-mail: dlubin@sonnenschein.com.

LUBIN, MICHAEL FREDERICK, physician, educator; b. Phila., Mar. 20, 1947; BA, Johns Hopkins U., 1969, MD, 1973. Resident Emory U. Affiliated Hosp., Atlanta, 1973-76; asst. prof. medicine Emory U. Sch. Medicine, Atlanta, 1976-82, assoc. prof. medicine, 1982—2001, dir. div. gen. medicine, 1989-95; dir. preoperative clinic Grady Hosp., Atlanta, 1995—; chmn. housestaff evaluation com. dept. medicine Emory U. Sch. Medicine, 1985—2001, dir. geriatrics assessment clinic, 1998—, prof. medicine, 2001—. Chmn. univ. adv. coun. tchg. Emory U., 2004—. Editor: Medical Management of the Surgical Patient, 1982; editor: (3d rev. edit.), 1995; editor: Med. Rounds, 1988—90; mem. editl. bd. I-M: Internal Medicine, 1992—95; contbr. to Med. Knowledge Self Assessment Program X, 1994. Chmn. univ. adv. coun. on tchg. Emory U.; mem. alumni coun. Johns Hopkins U., 1995—2001; mem. Cmty. Supporters of Atlanta Symphony Orch., 1996—98, bd. dirs., 1996—97. Scholar Hartford scholar in Geriatrics, UCLA, 1984—85, Ctr. for Medicare & Medicaid Svcs. Health Policy scholar, 2003. Fellow: ACP, Phi Beta Kappa (bd. dirs. Met. Atlanta chpt. 1996—2000, v.p. 2000—05, bd. dirs. 2005—); mem.: Soc. Gen. Internal Medicine (edn. com. 2003—), Am. Geriat. Soc., Alpha Omega Alpha, Fellows of Phi Beta Kappa (bd. dirs. 2002—), Phi Lambda Upsilon. Office: Emory U Sch Medicine 49 Jesse Hill Jr Dr Atlanta GA 30303 Office Phone: 404-778-1607.

LUBIN, STANLEY, lawyer; b. May 7, 1941; children: David Christopher, Jessica Nicole; m. Barbara Ann Lubin. AB, U. Mich., 1963, JD with honors, 1966. Bar: D.C. 1967, U.S. Ct. Appeals (D.C. cir.) 1967, U.S. Ct. Appeals (4th cir.) 1967, Mich. 1968, U.S. Ct. Appeals (6th cir.) 1968, U.S. Supreme Ct. 1970, Ariz. 1972, U.S. Ct. Appeals (9th cir.) 1976, U.S. Ct. Appeals (fed. cir.) 1985, Tex. 2005, U.S. Ct. Appeals (5th cir.) 2002, U.S. Dist. Ct. (ctrl. and so. dist.) Tex. 2005. Atty. NLRB, Washington, 1966-68; asst. gen. counsel UAW, Detroit, 1968-72; assoc. Harrison, Myers & Singer, Phoenix, 1972-74, McKendree & Tountas, Phoenix, 1975; ptnr. McKendree & Lubin, Phoenix and Denver, 1975-84; shareholder Treon, Warnicke & Roush, P.A., 1984-86; pvt. practice Law Offices Stanley Lubin, Phoenix, 1986-95, The Law Offices of Stanley Lubin, P.C., 1996-98, Lubin & Enoch, P.C., Phoenix and Dallas, 1999—. Mem. Ariz. Employment Security Adv. Coun., 1975—77. Co-author: Union Fines and Union Discipline Under the National Labor Relations Act, 1971. Active ACLU, dir. Ariz. chpt., 1974-81; vice chair Ariz. State Cen. Com. Dem. Party, 1986-91, 93-2004, sec., 1991-92, mem. state exec. com., 1986-2004, Ariz. Dem. Coun., 1987-99, chmn., 1988-93, Thomas Jefferson Forum, 1987-99, chmn., 1988-93. Mem.: Ariz. Indsl. Rels. Assn. (exec. bd. 1973—, pres. 1979—80, 1984), Indsl. Rels. Rsch. Assn. Home: 7520 N 9th Pl Phoenix AZ 85020-4138 Office: 349 N 4th Ave Phoenix AZ 85003 also: 1450 Empire Ctrl Ste 170 Dallas TX 75247 Office Phone: 602-234-0008, 214-951-9666. Business E-Mail: stan@lubinandenoch.com.

LUBIN, STEVEN, concert pianist, musicologist; b. NYC, Feb. 22, 1942; s. Jack and Sophie Lubin; m. Wendy Lubin, June 2, 1974; children: Benjamin, Nathaniel. AB in Philosophy, Harvard U., 1963; MS in Piano, Juilliard Sch. Music, 1965; PhD in Musicology, NYU, 1974. Mem. faculty Juilliard Sch. Music, NYC, 1964-65, Aspen (Colo.) Music Sch., 1965; Mem. faculty Vassar Coll., Poughkeepsie, NY, 1970-71; coordinator grad. music theory program Cornell U., Ithaca, NY, 1971-75; prof. Conservatory of Music, SUNY, Purchase, 1975—; founding mem. The Mozartean Players, 1978—. Mem., NYU Electronic Composers Workshop, 1967-68; concert pianist tours in U.S. and Europe, 1976—; appeared as fortepiano soloist and condr. in Authentic-Instrument concert series, N.Y.C., 1981—; rec. artist Decca, Arabesque Records, Harmonia Mundi; filmed solo performances for Brit. documentary TV in London and Vienna, 1986; soloist in complete Beethoven piano concertos for London/Decca Records, 1987; performed complete cycle Beethoven concertos, London, 1987; solo recordings (new series) Decca including Beethoven Sonatas, 1991; contbr. articles to N.Y. Times, Keyboard Classics, others. Martha Baird Rockefeller grantee, 1968. Mem. Am. Mus. Soc., Soc. Music Theory.

LUBINIECKI, GREGORY MICHAEL, physician; b. Pitts., Nov. 18, 1972; s. Anthony Stanley and Robin Lea Lubiniecki; m. Min Lubiniecki, Aug. 30, 2003. SB, MIT, 1994; MD, Johns Hopkins U., 1998. Diplomate in internal medicine and oncology Am. Bd. Internal Medicine. Resident physician Mayo Clinic, Rochester, Minn., 1998-2001; fellow hematology, oncology U. Pa., Phila., 2001—04, clin. asst. prof. medicine, 2004—. Lector Roman Cath. Ch., 1988-2003. Mem.: ACP, AMA, Am. Soc. Hematology, Am. Soc. Clin. Oncology, Sigma Xi, Phi Beta Kappa, Alpha Chi Sigma. Avocations: bicycling, literature. Office: Presbyn Med Ctr Univ Pa Med Arts Bldg Rm 103 Presbyn Med Ctr 39th and Market Sts Philadelphia PA 19104 Home: 10 Benjamin West Way Marlton NJ 08053 Office Phone: 215-662-8947. Business E-Mail: luber@alum.mit.edu.

LUBKIN, GLORIA BECKER, physicist; b. Phila., May 16, 1933; d. Samuel Albert and Anne (Gorrin) B.; m. Yale Jay Lubkin, June 14, 1953 (div. Apr. 1968); children: David Craig, Sharon Rebecca. AB, Temple U., 1953; MA, Boston U., 1957; postgrad., Harvard U., 1974—75. Mathematician Fairchild Stratos Co., Hagerstown, Md., 1954, Letterkenny Ordnance Depot, Chambersburg, Pa., 1955-56; physicist TRG Inc., NYC, 1956-58; acting chmn. dept. physics Sarah Lawrence Coll., Bronxville, NY, 1961-62; v.p. Lubkin Assocs., electronic cons., Port Washington, NY, 1962-68; assoc. editor Physics Today Am. Inst. Physics, NYC, 1963-69, sr. editor, 1970-84, editor, 1985-94, editl. dir., 1994-00, editor-at-large, 2001—03, editor emerita, 2004—. Cons. in field; mem. Nieman adv. com. Harvard U., 1978-82; co-chmn. search/adv. com. Theoretical Physics Inst., U. Minn., 1987-89, co-chmn. oversight com. 1989—; mem. mng. com. Westinghouse Sci. Writing Prizes, 1988-91; mem. selection com. Knight Fellowships, 1990. Contbr. articles to profl. publs. Gloria Becker Lubkin Professorship of Theoretical Physics established in her honor U. Minn., 1990; Nieman fellow, 1974-75. Fellow: AAAS (chmn. nominating com. for sect. B physics 1989, nominating com. sect. B physics 2003—06, chmn. 2005—06), Am. Phys. Soc. (founding mem. com. status of women in physics 1971—72, exec. com. forum physics and soc. 1977—78, exec. com. history physics divsn. 1983—86, 1992—95, 1998—2005, coun. mem. 1998—2005, mem. Lilienfeld prize com. 1999—2002, exec. bd. 2000—01, com. on coms. 2000—02, chair Lilienfeld prize com. 2002, audit com. 2004, com. on coms. 2004—06, vice chair history physics divsn. 2007); mem.: Com. Concerned Journalists, DC Sci. Writers Assn., Nat. Assn. Sci. Writers, NY Acad. Scis. (mem. The Scis. pub. com. 1992—93), Sigma Pi Sigma. Jewish. Office: Am Inst Physics One Physics Ellipse College Park MD 20740 Office Phone: 301-209-3050. Business E-Mail: glubkin@aip.org.

LUBLINSKI, MICHAEL, lawyer; b. Eskilstuna, Sweden, Sept. 11, 1951; came to U.S., 1956; s. Walter and Dora L. BA magna cum laude, CCNY, 1972; JD, Georgetown U., 1975. Bar: N.Y. 1976, Calif. 1980, D.C. 2001, Ct. Internat. Trade 1981, U.S. Dist. Ct. (cen. dist.) Calif. 1981, U.S. Dist. Ct. (so. dist.) N.Y. 1981, U.S. Ct. Appeals (D.C. cir.) 1982. Atty. U.S. Customs Service, Washington, 1975-79, U.S. Dept. Commerce, Washington, 1980; assoc. Mori & Ota, LA, 1980-84, Kelley Drye & Warren LLP, LA, 1984-85, ptnr., mem. intellectual property practice group, 1986—2003. Panel moderator Calif. continuing edn. of bar Competitive Bus. Practices Inst., L.A. and San Francisco, 1984. Mem. ABA, Calif. Bar Assn., Los Angeles County Bar Assn., NY State Bar Assn., DC Bar Assn., Phi Beta Kappa. Avocations: travel, movies. Office: 300 Three Islands Blvd Ste 119 Hallandale FL 33009 E-mail: mlublinski@bellnet.ca.

LUBNAU, THOMAS EDWIN, II, lawyer; b. Laramie, Wyo., Dec. 12, 1958; s. Thomas Edwin and Cynthia L'Vere (Kirkland) L. BS in Fin., U. Wyo., 1981, JD, 1984. Bar: Wyo. 1984, U.S. Dist. Ct. Wyo. 1984, U.S. Ct. Appeals (10th cir.) 1984, U.S. Supreme Ct. 1995. Mem. Lubnau, Bailey & Dumbrill, P.C., Gillette, Wyo., 2000—. Chmn. Wyo. Bd. CLE, Cheyenne, 1990-92; trustee Rocky Mountain Mineral Law, Denver, 1992-95; legal counsel Wyo. Jaycees, Gillette, 1986-94, Campbell County Rep. Party, Gillette, 1989-96 Contbr. to Land and Water Law rev., 1984. Rep. Wyo. State Legis., 2004—; bd. dirs. Campbell County Libr. Found.; chalice bearer, lay reader Holy Trinity Episcopal Ch., Campbell County Rep. Party (state committeeman 1988-89), Campbell County C. of C. (chmn. 1993-94). Mem. ABA, Assn. Trial Lawyers Am., Campbell County C. of C. (bd. dirs.), Gillette Rotary (bd. dirs.), Wyo. State Bar (commnr. 1998-2001, v.p. 2001-02, pres.-elect 2002-03, pres. 2003-04), Campbell County Bar Assn. (pres. 2000-01), Gov.'s Probate Com. (1984-90), Bd. Continuing Ed. (chmn. 1988-91), Rocky Mtn. Mineral Law Found. (trustee 1992-95), Atty.'s Assistance Com. (co-chair, 1995-96), Jackrabbit Bar Assn. (chancellor 2004-05) Republican. Avocations: woodworking, photography, writing. Office: Lubnau Bailey & Dumbrill PC PO Box 1028 Gillette WY 82717-1028

LUBNER, MARY F., retired elementary school educator; adopted d. Maryadelle Tornowske (Kearney) and Louie A Tornowske; m. Donald C Lubner, Jan. 5, 1979; children: Charles G, Andrew E, Sigrid M, Erich S. BS, U. Wis., LaCrosse, 1969. Cert. phys. edn. tchr. K-12 Wis., 1969. Elem. phys. edn. tchr. Grafton Pub. Schools, Grafton, Wis., 1969—2004, team mgr. Destination Imagination, 2004—; instr. Acad. of Marial Arts, Grafton, Wis., 1991—. Contbr. articles to profl. jours. Co-orgnl. leader Towna nd Country 4-H Club, 2003—; mem. Oz County Leaders Bd. Assn., Port Washington, Wis., 4-H Dos Project, Port Washington, 2004—. Mem.: NEA, Am. Assn. Health, Physical Edn., Recreation and Dance, Wis. Edn. Assn., North Shore United Educaors, Ozaukee County Ret. Tchrs. (v.p. 2005—06), U.S. Tae Kwon Do Fedn. (assoc. 4th deg. black belt), Wis. Assn. of Health, Phys. Edn., Recreation and Dance. Home Phone: 262-377-1258.

LUBOVITCH, LAR, dancer, choreographer; b. Chgo. Student, Art Inst. Chgo., U. Iowa, Juilliard Sch. Music, Am. Ballet Theatre Sch., Martha Graham, Anthony Tudor. Dancer debut with Pearl Lang Dance Co., 1962, with modern cos. Glen Tetley, John Butler, Sophie Maslow and Donald McKayle, Manhattan Festival Ballet, Santa Fe Opera, Harkness Ballet, formed Lar Lubovitch Dance Co., 1968; guest choreographer Bat-Dor Dance Co., Gulbenkian Ballet, Dutch Nat. Ballet, Ballet Rambert, Pa. Ballet, Am. Ballet Theatre, Royal Danish Ballet, Bejart Ballet XX Century, Alvin Alley Am. Dance Theater, John Curry Ice Dancing Co., Les Grandes Ballets Canadiens, Stuttgart Ballet, N.Y.C. Ballet, Pacific N.W. Ballet, Paris Opera Ballet, White Oak Dance Project, ballets choreographed include Blue, 1968, Freddie's Bag, 1968, Journey Back, 1968, Greeting Sampler, 1969, Whirligogs, 1969, Unremembered Time-Forgotton Place, 1969, Variations and Theme, 1970, Ecstasy, 1970, Sam Nearlydeadman, 1970, The Teaching, 1970, Some of the Reactions, 1970, The Time Before, 1971, Clear Lake, 1971, Air, 1972, Joy of Man's Desiring, 1972, Chariot Light Night, 1973, Scherzo for Massah Jack, 1973, Three Essays, 1974, Zig Zag, 1974, Avalanche, 1975, Rapid Transit, 1975, Session, 1975, Eight Easy Pieces, 1975, Girl on Fire, 1975, Marimba, 1976, Les Noches, 1976, Scriabin Dances, 1977, Exultate Jubilate, 1977, North Star, 1978, Valley, 1978, Tiltawhirl, 1979, Up Jump, 1979, Mistral, 1980, Cavalcade, 1980, American Gesture, 1981, Beau Danube, 1981, Big Shoulders, 1983, Tabernacle, 1983, Adagio and Rondo, 1984, A Brahms Symphony, 1985, Concerto Six Twenty-Two, 1986, Blood, 1986, Of My Soul, 1987, Musette, 1988, Rhapsody in Blue, 1988, Fandango, 1989, Just Before Jupiter, 1990, Hautbois, 1990, Sinfonia Concertante, 1991, Waiting for the Sunrise, 1991, American Gesture, 1992, So In Love, 1994, Touch Me, 1996, Bach Adagio, 1996, Gershwin Variations, 1996, I'll Be Seeing You, 1996, Othello, 1997, Thus is All, 1998, Yiddish Songs of Love and Wonder, 1999, Meadow, 1999, All Ye Need to Know, 2000, Men's Stories, 2000, My Funny Valentine, 2001, Smile with my Heart, 2002, Artemis, 2003; choreographer Pentimento, 2004, Do You Be, 2004, Love Stories, 2005, Elemental Brubeck, 2005, Recordare, 2005, Little Rhapsodies (solo), 2006, Little Rhapsodies (trio), 2007, Dvorak Serenade, 2007, (TV films) Sleeping Beauty (WGBH-TV), 1987, (TV series) The Planets, A&E-TV, 1994, (TV films) Othello, WNET-TV, 2003, (Broadway plays) Into the Woods, 1987, Salome, 1992, The Red Shoes, 1993, The King and I, 1998, High Society, 1998, The Hunchback of Notre Dame, Berlin, 1999. Recipient Tony award nominee, 1988, Astaire award, 1993—94, Elan award, 2004; Guggenheim fellow, CAPS grantee, NEA grantee. Address: care Lubovitch Dance Co 229 W 42d St 8th Fl New York NY 10036 Office Phone: 212-221-7909. Personal E-mail: Lubovitch@aol.com.

LUBS, HERBERT AUGUSTUS, retired genetics educator, administrator; b. Jan. 7, 1929; BA, Washington and Lee U., 1950; MD, Yale U., 1954. Diplomate Am. Bd. Internal Medicine, Am. Bd. Med. Genetics. Intern Yale-New Haven Hosp., 1954-55, resident in medicine, 1957-59, chief resident Conn., 1959-60; clin. assoc., endocrinology br. Nat. Cancer Inst., USPHS, Bethesda, Md., 1955-57; spl. trainee in rsch. and genetics NIH, Dept. of Human Genetics, U. Mich. and Dept. Biology, Yale U., 1957-63; instr. in Medicine Yale Sch. Medicine, New Haven, 1959-63, asst. prof. Medicine, chief sect. medicine genetics, 1963-67; clin. investigator VA Hosp., West Haven, Conn., 1960-63; dir. Yale Pvt. Diagnostic Clinic, New Haven, 1964-66; assoc. prof. dept. pediatrics U. Colo. Med. Ctr., Denver, 1968-79, assoc. prof. dept. biophysics and genetics, 1973-79; prof. dept. pediatrics, dir. genetics div., Mailman Ctr. for Child Devel. U. Miami Sch. Medicine, Fla., 1979—2004, prof. emeritus, 2004—; prof. genetics U. Tromsø, Norway, 1992-99. Lectr. numerous med. schs. and meetings; sci. presentations at nat. and internat. meetings; mem. human subjects rev. com., 1980-83, U. Miami Sch. Medicine, dean's task force on genetics, 1982-84, human subjects exec. rev. com., 1984—. Editor: Computers in Biology and Medicine; editor Am. Jour. Med. Genetics, BioEssays (corr.), Birth Defects Ency. Chmn. Com. on Environ. Hazards, Am. Soc. of Human Genetics, NICHD sponsored meeting genetic counseling, 1979; cons. Standing Com. on Chromosome Nomenclature; mem. Med. Adv. Com. to Indor Radon Study, Grand Junction, Colo., 1975-79, Gov.'s Adv. Coun. on Radiation, Colo., 1979; co-chmn. NIH mtg. on Marker X, 1983; chmn. Am. Soc. of Human Genetics Genetic Svcs. subcom. on Cytogeneticvs Lab. Proficiency Testing and Quality Assurance; steering com. NICHD Collaborative Study on Chorionic Villus Sampling and Amniocentesis, 1984—; mem. various NIH site visit coms. and ad hoc rev. coms., 1979—. Recipient VA clin. investigatorship, 1960-63, USPHS Career Devel. award, 1963-73, Joseph P. Kennedy Jr. Internat. award for rsch. in mental retardation, 1986. Mem. Am. Soc. of Human Genetics (bd. dirs., Genetic Svcs. Com. 1985—, Travel Com. 1986, Tissue Culture Soc.), Am. Fed. for Clin. Rsch., Soc. for Study of Social Biology, So. Soc. for Pediatric Rsch., Alpha Omega Alpha, Phi Beta Kappa. Home: 31374 Nandua DR Painter VA 23420-3113 Home Phone: 757-442-9374; Office Phone: 757-442-9374. E-mail: hlubs@verizon.net.

LUBY, MICHAEL A., insurance company executive; BS in Math., USAF Acad., Colo.; MBA in Fin. and Mktg., Pepperdine U., Malibu, Calif. With Computer Svcs. Corp., Atlantic Richfield Co., First Interstate Bank; sr. v.p. ops. CoBank; COO iVesta Fin. Solutions; sr. v.p. ops. Fed. Savs. Bank USAA (United Svcs. Automobile Assn.), pres. Fed. Savs. Bank. Capt., flight examiner, inst. pilot USAF. Office: USAA 9800 Fredericksburg Rd San Antonio TX 78288 Office Phone: 210-498-8222.*

LUBY, MICHAEL J., research and development company executive; BA, Dartmouth Coll.; MBA, U. Pa. With Merck-Medco Managed Care Merck & Co., Inc., mktg. rsch. analyst for Vasotec and Prilosec, sr. mktg. mgr. for Fosamax, dir. new product mktg., sr. dir. mktg. Worldwide for New Products; co-founder, pres., CEO, bd. mem. TargetRx. Named one of 40 Under 40, Phila. Bus. Jour., 2006. Office: TargetRx, Inc Ste 200 220 Gibraltar Rd Horsham PA 19044 Office Phone: 215-444-8700. Office Fax: 215-444-8701.

LUCÀ-MORETTI, MAURIZIO, research scientist, nutritionist; b. Rome, June 2, 1945; came to U.S., 1995; s. Giuseppe and Elena (Moretti) L.; m. Anna Grandi, Jan. 2, 1974; 1 child, Elena. BS, Ministry of Edn., Caracas, Venezuela, 1969; PhD in Allied Health Scis., Pacific Western U., 1990, DSc in Human Nutrition, 1990; MD (hon.), Universidad Santo Tomas, La Paz, Bolivia, 1994; MPH (hon.), Inst. Superiore di Studi Sanitari, Rome, 1995. Rschr. Inst. Italiano di Terapia Fisica e Medicina Interna, Rome, 1974-76, sr. rschr., 1976-78, dir. rsch., 1978-80, Caracas, Venezuela, 1980-88; dir. human nutrition rsch. program and AIDS rsch. program InterAm. Med. and Health Assn., Boca Raton, Fla., 1989—, pres., 1989—; gen. sec. World Acad. Medicine, 1992—; prof. emeritus Pacific Western U., New Orleans, 1992; dir. rsch. Internat. Nutrition Rsch. Ctr., 1995—. Invited prof. Univ. di Chiete, Italy, 1991, Univ. de Asuncion, Paraguay, 1992, Univ. di Roma, Rome, 1995; hon. prof. Univ. de Granada, Spain, 1994, Univ. Nacional Pedro Enrique Ureña, Santo Domingo, Dominican Rep., 1994, Inst. Superiore di Studi Sanitari, 1996, Univ. Catolica Santo Domingo, Dominican Rep., 1996, St. Thomas U., Miami, 1998. Recipient medal Univ. Asuncion, Paraguay, 1992, medal Univ. Granada, Spain, 1993; decorated Cruz de Alfonso X el Sabio, Spani, 1997. Fellow NAS (Dominican Rep.), Royal Nat. Acad. Medicine Spain, Royal Acad. Scis. Spain, Royal Acad. Medicine Salamanca, Royal Acad. Medicine Granada, Royal Acad. Medicine Valencia, Royal Acad. Medicine of Zaragoza, Nat. Acad. Medicine Bolivia, Nat. Acad. Medicine Ecuador, Nat. Acad. Medicine Paraguay, Nat. Acad. Medicine Dominican Rep., Acad. Medicine Maracaibo, Reial Acad. Medicina Catalunya. Achievements: discovery of the Master Amino Pattern (MAP); discovery of the Dietary Protein Engring. (DPE); also patents in nutritional amino acids formulations with extremely high human Net Nitrogen Utilization (NNU). Home:

3025 Saint James Dr Boca Raton FL 33434-3370 Office: Internat Nutrition Rsch Ctr 7900 Los Pinos Cir Coral Gables FL 33143 Office Phone: 305-740-7480. E-mail: inrc@msn.com.

LUCANDER, HENRY, investment banker; b. Helsingfors, Finland, Dec. 21, 1940; came to U.S., 1965, naturalized, 1974; m. Karen-Jean Olson, Aug. 22, 1981. Student, Gronesche Handelsschule, Hamburg, W.Ger., 1961-62, Pontificia U. Catolica, Rio de Janeiro, 1963-64; diploma, Brazilian Coffee Inst., Rio de Janeiro, 1965; MBA, Columbia U., 1968. With Schenkers Internat. Forwarders, Inc., NYC, 1965-66; coffee merchandizer Anderson Clayton & Co., Inc., NYC, 1966-68; with Smith Barney & Co., Inc., NYC, 1968-69, Kidder Peabody & Co., Inc., NYC, 1969-70, LCI Management.com Investment Bankers, NYC, 1970—; pres. LCI Management, Investment Bankers, Cheyenne, Wyo., 1972—. Served to lt. Finnish Army, 1960-61.

LUCAS, ALEXANDER RALPH, child psychiatrist, educator, writer; b. Vienna, July 30, 1931; came to U.S., 1940, naturalized, 1945; s. Eugene Hans and Margaret Ann (Weiss) L.; m. Margaret Alice Thompson, July 6, 1956; children: Thomas Alexander, Nancy Elizabeth Watson, Alexander Eugene, Peter Clayton. BS, Mich. State U., 1953; MD, U. Mich., 1957. Diplomate Am. Bd. Psychiatry and Neurology (psychiatry and child and adolescent psychiatry), Am. Bd. of Med. Specialties. Intern U. Mich. Hosp., 1957-58; resident in child psychiatry Hawthorn Ctr., Northville, Mich., 1958-59, 61-62, staff psychiatrist, 1963-65, sr. psychiatrist, 1965-67; resident in psychiatry Lafayette Clinic, Detroit, 1959-61, rsch. child psychiatrist, 1967-71, rsch. coord., 1969-71; asst. prof. psychiatry Wayne State U., 1967-69, assoc. prof., 1969-71; cons. child and adolescent psychiatry Mayo Clinic, 1971-97; assoc. prof. Mayo Med Sch., 1973-76, prof., 1976-97; emeritus prof., 1998—; head sect. child and adolescent psychiatry Mayo Clinic, Rochester, Minn., 1971-80, emeritus cons., 1998—. Dir. com. on certification in child and adolescent psychiatry Am. Bd. Psychiatry and Neurology, 1997-2001; residency rev. com. Accreditation Coun. for Grad. Med. Edn., 1999-2001. Author (with C. R. Shaw): The Psychiatric Disorders of Childhood, 1970; author: Demystifying Anorexia Nervosa, 2004. Recipient Eating Disorders Scientific Achievement award, 1998. Fellow Am. Acad. Child and Adolescent Psychiatry (life, editl. bd. jour. 1976-82), Am. Orthopsychiat. Assn. (life), Am. Psychiat. Assn. (life); mem. Minn. Soc. Child and Adolescent Psychiatry (pres. 1993-95), Soc. Profs. Child and Adolescent Psychiatry (pres. 2000-02), Sigma Xi Achievements include research in biol. aspects of child psychiatry, psychopathology, psychopharmacology, eating disorders, psychiat. treatment of children, adolescents, and young adults. Office: Mayo Clinic 200 1st St SW Rochester MN 55905-0002 Home Phone: 507-288-9641.

LUCAS, AUBREY KEITH, retired university president; b. State Line, Miss., July 12, 1934; s. Keith Caldwell and Audelle Margaret (Robertson) L.; m. Ella Frances Ginn, Dec. 18, 1955; children: Margaret Frances, Keith Godbold (dec.), Martha Carol Pittman, Alan Douglas, Mark Christopher. BS, U. So. Miss., 1955, MA, 1956; PhD, Fla. State U., 1966; DHL, Miss. Coll., 1997. Instr. Hinds Jr. Coll., Raymond, Miss., 1956-57; pres. Delta State U., Cleveland, Miss., 1971-75; asst. dir. reading clinic U. So. Miss., Hattiesburg, 1955-56, dir. admissions, 1957-61, registrar, 1963-69, dean Grad. Sch., 1969-71, pres., 1975-96, pres. emeritus and prof. higher edn., 1997—. Author: The Mississippi Legislature and Mississippi Public Higher Education, 1890-1960; contbg. author: A History of Mississippi, 1973. State chmn. Am. Cancer Soc., 1978; campaign chmn. Forrest United Way, 1979, So. U. Conf., 1995-96; mem. Commn. on Nat. Devel. Postsecondary Edn., 97th Congress; pres. Miss. Econ. Coun., 1982-83; lay bd. dir. Africa U., 1997-, treas., 1999—; bd. dir. Miss. Assn. Coll., 1979-80, pres., 1979-80; bd. dir. Miss. Inst. Tech. Devel., 1984-96, Miss. Arts Commn., 1977-87,chmn., 1983-85; bd. dir.Pine Burr Area coun. Boy Scouts Am., 1990-2003; exec. bd. Commn. on Colls. So. Assn. Colls. and Schs., 1990-93; bd. visitors Air U., 1990-94, chmn., 1991-92; bd. dir. Salvation Army, chmn., 2000-02; gen. bd. Global Ministries, United Meth. Ch., 1984-92, gen. bd. higher edn. and ministry, 1992-2000, investment com., 2002—; lay leader Miss. Meth. Conf., 1980-88, 2004—. Mem. Hattiesburg C. of C., Miss. Forestry Assn., Newcomen Soc. N.Am., Am. Assn. State Colls. and Univs. (bd. dirs. 1982-86, chmn. 1984-85), Am. Coun. Edn. (bd. dirs. 1984-86), Miss. Inst. Arts and Letters (pres. 1999-2000), Miss. Assn. Coll. (pres. 1979-80), Hattiesburg Cmty. Found., Hattiesburg Conv. Ctr. Commn., Lauren Rogers Mus. Art (bd. trustees, chmn. 2001-04), Red Red Rose Club, Sigma Phi Epsilon, Omicron Delta Kappa, Phi Kappa Phi, Pi Gamma Mu, Pi Tau Chi, Kappa Delta Pi, Phi Delta Kappa, Kappa Pi. Home: 3200 Jamestown Rd Hattiesburg MS 39402-2333 Office: U So Miss 118 College Dr # 5164 Hattiesburg MS 39406-0001 Office Phone: 601-266-4351. Business E-Mail: aubrey.lucas@usm.edu.

LUCAS, C. PAYNE, development organization executive; b. Spring Hope, NC, Sept. 14, 1933; s. James Russell and Minnie (Hendricks) L; m. Freddie Emily Myra Hill, Aug. 29, 1964; children: Therese Raymonde, C. Payne Jr., Hillary Hendricks. BA in History, U. Md.; LLD (hon.), U. Md., 1975; MA in Govt., Am. U. Asst. dir. Peace Corps, Togo, 1964, dir. Niger, 1965-67, dir. Africare region, 1967-71; co-founder, pres. Africare, Washington, 1971—2002; sr. adv. Pan-African Health Found., 2002—, allAfrica.com, 2002—. Lectr. in field. Author: (with Kevin Lowther) Keeping Kennedy's Promise--The Peace Corps: Unmet Promise of the New Frontier, 1978; contbr. articles to profl. publs. Bd. dirs. Coun. Fgn. Rels., Overseas Devel. Coun. World Resources Inst., InterAction, Population Action Internat., Kagiso Trust USA, Nat. Planning Assn.; bd. dirs., chmn. Reach & Teach USA; bd. dirs., founding mem. Corp. Coun. on Africa. Recipient Disting. Fed. Svc. award Pres. Lyndon B. Johnson, Presdl. Hunger award for Outstanding Achievement, Pres. Ronald Reagan, 1984, Aggrey medal Phelps-Stokes Fund, 1986, Order of Disting. Svc. award Pres. Kenneth Kaunda of Zambia, 1986, Recognition awards Nat. Order of Rep. Niger, 1988, Zambia, Cote D'Iroire, Senegal, Benin, Disting. Bicentennial award Land Grant Coll., 1990, Hubert H. Humphrey Pub. Svc. award APSA, 1991, Ronald H. Brown Internat. Community Svc. award, Great Washington Urban League, 2001 Mem. Cosmos Club, Omega Psi Phi., D.C. Bd. Teenage Pregnancy Office: allAfrica com 920 M St SE Washington DC 20003 E-mail: cplucas@africare.org.

LUCAS, DONALD LEO, investor; b. Upland, Calif., Mar. 18, 1930; s. Leo J. and Mary G. (Schwamm) L.; m. Lygia de Soto Harrison, July 15, 1961; children: Nancy Maria Lucas Thibodeau, Alexandra Maria Lucas Ertola, Donald Alexander Lucas. BA, Stanford U., 1951, MBA, 1953. Assoc. corp. fin. dept. Smith, Barney & Co., NYC, 1956-59; gen., ltd. ptnr. Draper, Gaither & Anderson, Palo Alto, Calif., 1959-66; pvt. investor Menlo Park, Calif., 1966—. Bd. dir. Cadence Design Systems, San Jose, Calif., Oracle Corp., Redwood Shores, Calif., Vimicro Corp., Beijing, 51job Inc., Shanghai, Dexcom, Inc., San Diego. Mem. bd. regents Bellarmine Coll. Prep., 1977-2002; regent emeritus U. Santa Clara, 1980—. 1st lt. AUS, 1953-55. Mem. Am. Coun. Capital Formation (dir.), Stanford U. Alumni Assn., Stanford Grad. Sch. Bus. Alumni Assn., Order of Malta, Stanford Buck Club, Menlo Circus Club (Atherton, Calif.), Bighorn Country Club, Calif., Zeta Psi. Office: 3000 Sand Hill Rd Ste 3-210 Menlo Park CA 94025-7119 Home: 449 Selby Ln Atherton CA 94027-5411 Office Phone: 650-854-4223.

LUCAS, FRANCES, academic administrator; MA, Miss. State U.; PhD in Higher Edn., U. Ala. With student affairs dept. Miss. State U.; v.p. student affairs, v.p. Baldwin-Wallace Coll., Ohio; sr. v.p. campus life Emory U.; pres. Millsaps Coll., Jackson, Miss., 2000—. Pres. Miss. Found. of Independent Colls., So. Univ. Conf., Nat. Assn. Schs. and Colls. of United Meth. Church, Jackson Med. Edn. Dist. Bd.; bd. dirs. Nat. Assn. Independent Colls. and Univs.; mem. Annapolis Group; spkr. in field. Bd. dirs. Trustmark Nat. Bank; bd. visitors U. Miss. Dental Sch. Named Miss. Bus. Woman of Yr., Miss. Bus. Jour., 2003, Outstanding Miss. Woman of Yr., Miss. State U. Women's Commn., 2004. Mem.: Newcomen Soc. (exec. bd. mem.). Office: Millsaps Coll 1701 N State St Jackson MS 39210-0001*

LUCAS, FRANK D., congressman; b. Cheyenne, Okla., Jan. 6, 1960; m. Lynda L. Bradshaw, 1988; 3 children. BS in Agrl. Econs., Okla. State U., 1982. County coord. Staff of US Senator Don Nickles of Okla.; mem. Okla. State Ho. Reps., 1989-94, US Congress from 3rd (formerly 6th) Okla. dist., 1994—, mem. fin. svcs. com., mem. sci. & tech. com., mem. agr. com., chmn. conservation, credit, rural devel. and rsch. subcommittee. Named a Congl. Conservation Champion, 2001, Property Rights Champion, League of Property Voters, 2002, Hero of the Taxpayer, Ams. for Tax Reform; recipient Wheat Champion award, Nat. Assn. Wheat Growers, Friend of the Farm Bur. award, Am. Farm Bur. Fedn., Staff of Life award, Okla. Wheat Commn., Guardian of Small Bus. award, Nat. Fedn. Ind. Bus., Champion of Small Bus. award, Small Bus. Survival Com. Mem.: Okla. Cattlemen's Assn., Okla. Farmer's Union, Okla. Farm Bur. Republican. Baptist. Office: 720 South Husband Ste 7 Stillwater OK 74075 Office Phone: 202-225-5565, 405-624-6407. Office Fax: 405-624-6467.*

LUCAS, GENE, academic administrator; BS, U. Calif., Santa Barbara, 1973; MS, MIT, 1975, ScD, 1978. Joined faculty U. Calif., Santa Barbara, 1978, exec. vice chancellor, 2003—. Office: Exec Vice Chancellor 5105 Cheadle Hall Univ Calif Santa Barbara CA 93106 Office Phone: 805-893-2126. Business E-Mail: gene.lucas@evc.ucsb.edu.

LUCAS, GEORGE RAMSDELL, JR., philosophy educator; b. San Angelo, Tex., Sept. 8, 1949; s. George Ramsdell and Clare Elizabeth (Baldwin) L.; m. Patricia Cook; children: Jessica, Kimberly, Theresa. BS summa cum laude, Coll. William and Mary, 1971; PhD, Northwestern U., 1978. Asst. prof., chmn. dept. philosophy Randolph-Macon Coll., Ashland, Va., 1978-82; assoc. prof., chmn. dept. philosophy Santa Clara U., Calif., 1982-86; assoc. prof. Emory U., Atlanta, 1986-87; prof. philosophy Clemson U., SC, 1987-91; asst. dir. rsch. divsn. NEH, Washington, 1991-95; prof. bus. Georgetown U., Washington, 1996—98; assoc. dept. chmn., prof. ethics US Naval Acad., 1996—2006, prof. philosophy, dir. navy & nat. programs, Stockdale Ctr. for Ethical Leadership, 2006—. Exec. dir. Am. Acad. for Liberal Edn., 1998—99. Author: The Genesis of Modern Process Thought, 1983, The Rehabilitation of Whitehead, 1989, Perspectives on Humanitarian Military Intervention, 2001, Ethics and the Military Profession: The Moral Foundations of Leadership, 2005; editor: Lifeboat Ethics: Moral Dilemmas of World Hunger, 1976, Poverty, Justice and the Law, 1986; philosophy editor SUNY Press, Albany, 1990—, Ency. Americana; contbr. articles to profl. jours. Am. Coun. Learned Socs. fellow, 1982; Fulbright rsch. fellow, 1989. Mem. Am. Philos. Assn., Metaphys. Soc. Am., Hegel Soc. Am., Omicron Delta Kappa, Phi Beta Kappa. Office: Dept Leadership Ethics & Law MS 7-B US Naval Acad Annapolis MD 21402 Office Phone: 410-293-6142. Business E-Mail: grlucas@usna.edu.

LUCAS, GEORGE WALTON, JR., film director, producer, scriptwriter; b. Modesto, Calif., May 14, 1944; Student, Modesto Jr. Coll.; BA, U. So. Calif., 1966. Chmn. Lucasfilm Ltd., San Rafael, Calif., 1971—. Mem. TV bd. councilors U. So. Calif.; chmn. George Lucas Ednl. Found., Artists Rights Found., Joseph Campbell Found., Film Found. Asst. to Francis Ford Coppola The Rain People, 1969, creator short film, dir., co-writer THX-1138:4EB, 1970, THX-1138, 1971, dir., co-writer American Graffiti, 1973, dir., author screenplay Star Wars, 1977 (earned seven Acad. awards); exec. prodr.: More American Graffiti, 1979, The Empire Strikes Back, 1980, Raiders of the Lost Ark, 1981, Indiana Jones and the Temple of Doom, 1984, Labyrinth, 1986, Howard the Duck, 1986, Willow, 1988, Tucker, 1988, Radioland Murders, 1994, (co-author screenplay): Return of the Jedi, 1983; co-exec. prodr. Mishima, 1985; co-author (co-exec. prodr.): Indiana Jones and the Last Crusade, 1989; exec. prodr.(TV series): The Young Indiana Jones Chronicles, 1992—93; author (dir., exec. prodr.): Star Wars: Episode I The Phantom Menace, 1999, Star Wars: Episode II Attack of the Clones, 2002, Star Wars: Episode III Revenge of the Sith, 2005 (Favorite Movie and Favorite Movie Drama, People's Choice award, 2006). Mem. adv. bd. Sci. Fiction Mus. and Hall of Fame. Recipient Irving G. Thalberg Meml. award, Academy of Motion Picture Arts and Sciences, 1991, Lifetime Achievement award, Am. Film Inst., 2005. Office: Lucasfilm Ltd PO Box 2009 San Rafael CA 94912-2009 Office Phone: 415-662-1800.

LUCAS, HENRY CAMERON, JR., information scientist, educator, writer; b. Omaha, Sept. 4, 1944; s. Henry Cameron and Lois (Himes) L.; m. Ellen Kuhbach, June 8, 1968; children: Scott C., Jonathan G. BS in Indsl. Adminstrn. magna cum laude, Yale U., 1966; MS, MIT, 1968, PhD, 1970. Cons. Arthur D. Little, Inc., Cambridge, Mass., 1966-70; asst. prof. computer and info. systems Stanford (Calif.) U., 1970-74; assoc. prof. computer applications and info. systems NYU, 1974-78, prof., chmn. dept. info. systems, 1978-84; on leave IBM European Systems Rsch. Inst., Belgium, 1981; INSEAD Fontainebleau, France, 1985; prof. info. systems NYU, 1985-2000; Shaw Found. Prof. Nat. Tech. U., Singapore, 1997-98; Robert H. Smith prof. info. sys. Robert H. Smith Sch. Bus. U. Md., 2000—; co-dir. Ctr. for Electronic Markets and Enterprises, 2001—04. Author: The T-Form Organization, 1996 Computer-Based Information Systems in Organizations, 1973, The Information Systems Environment, 1980 (with F. Land, T. Lincoln and K. Supper) Casebook for Management Information Systems, 3d edit., 1985, The Analysis, Design and Implementation of Information Systems, 4th edit., 1992, Information Technology for Management 7th edit., 2000, Coping with Computers: A Manager's Guide to Controlling Information Processing, 1982, Introduction to Computers and Information Systems, 1986, Managing Information Services, 1989, Information Technology and Productivity Paradox: Assessing the Value of Investing in IT, 1999, Strategies for Electronic Commerce and the Internet, 2002, (with G. Anandalingam) Beware the Winner's Curse: Victories that can Sink You and Your Company, 2004, Information Technology: Strategic Decision Making for Managers, 2005; editor Indsl. Mgmt., 1967-68; mem. editl. bd. Sloan Mgmt., Rev., 1975-91; assoc. editor MIS Quar., 1977-83; editor-in-chief Systems, Objectives, Solutions, 1980—, v.p. publs. Assn. for Info. Systems, 1996-98; editor-in-chief Jour. and Comms. of AIS, 1998-2001; contbr. articles to profl. jours. Recipient award for excellence in tchg. NYU Sch. Bus., 1982. Fellow Assn. Info. Sys.; mem. IEEE, Publs. Assn. (v.p. 1995—), Assn. Computing Machinery, Phi Beta Kappa, Tau Beta Pi. Home: 871 Coach Way Annapolis MD 21401-6481 Office: Smith Sch Bus U Md 4351 Van Munching Hall College Park MD 20742-1106 Home Phone: 410-849-3493; Office Phone: 301-405-0100. Business E-Mail: hlucas@rhsmith.umd.edu.

LUCAS, JAMES E(VANS), operatic director; b. San Antonio, Mar. 15, 1933; s. Mason Harley and Nora Norton (Evans) L. BA, Hiram Coll., 1951; postgrad., Stanford U., 1951-52, Juilliard Sch. Music, 1952-53. Faculty Temple U., 1965-71, Mannes Coll. Music, 1964-70, Manhattan Sch. Music, 1970-78, Carnegie-Mellon U., 1977-79; prof. music, stage dir. Ind. U., 1987-94; vis. prof. Seoul Nat. U., 1996, Dartmouth Coll., 1997. Free-lance operatic stage dir.; worked for opera cos. in U.S., Can. including, Met. Opera, San Francisco Opera, N.Y.C. Opera, Can. Opera Co.; dir. for various summer festivals. Mem. Am. Guild Musical Artists, Am. Fedn. Musicians, Can. Actors Equity. Home and Office: 201 W 85th St New York NY 10024-3907 Personal E-mail: jameselucas@verizon.net.

LUCAS, JAMES RAYMOND, company executive, writer, consultant, speaker; b. St. Louis, Mar. 9, 1950; s. James Earl and Anna LaVerne (Ryan) L.; m. Pamela Kay Petersen, June 10, 1972; children: Laura Christine, Peter Barrett, David Christopher, Bethany Gayle. BS in Engring. Mgmt., U. Mo., 1972, postgrad., 1978, postgrad., 1999, Regent Coll. Vancouver, 1999; profl. degree in sci. and tech., Mo. U., 2007. Registered profl. engr., Mo., Kans. Product analyst The Lee Co., Westwood, Kans., 1971—73; mgr. planning Black & Veatch, Kansas City, Mo., 1973—79; dir. constrn. Hallmark Cards, Kansas City, Mo., 1979—81; project mgr. The Pritchard Corp., Kansas City, Mo., 1981—83; gen. mgr., pres., CEO EMCI Mfg., Kansas City, Mo., 1984—86; pres. and CEO Luman Cons. Internat., Overland Park, Kans., 1983—; exec. dir. Relationship Devel. Ctr., 1992—. Prof. Rockhurst U., 2000-02; sr. mem. seminar faculty, faculty adv. coun. Am. Mgmt. Assn., 1994—; pub., pres. Quintessential Books, 1993—. Author: The Parenting of Champions, 1989, Voyage to a New Earth, 1991, Proactive Parenting, 1993, Walking Through Fire, 1996, Fatal Illusions: Shredding a Dozen Unrealities That Can Keep Your Organization From Success, 1997, 2001, Balance of Power: Fueling Employee Power Without Relinquishing Your Own, 1998, 2002, The Passionate Organization: Igniting the Fire of Employee Commitment, 1999, 1001 Ways to Connect With Your Kids, 2000, 03, Broaden the Vision and Narrow the Focus: Managing in a World of Paradox, 2005, High-Performance Ethics, Ten Timeless Principles for Next-Generation Leadership, 2007, Passionate Lives and Leaders, 2007. Mem. ASTD, Soc. Mfg. Engrs. (sr.), Am. Soc. for Engring. Mgmt., Acad. Engring Mgmt. (pres.), Am. Assn. Christian Counselors (charter), Am. Mgmt. Assn., Christian Leaders and Spkrs. Soc. Avocations: piano, music, reading, travel. Home: 7303 Rosewood Shawnee Mission KS 66208-2458 Office: Luman Cons Internat 6320 Lamar Ste 230 Overland Park KS 66202 Office Phone: 913-248-1733. E-mail: jlucas@lumanconsultants.com.

LUCAS, JAMES WALTER, federal official; b. Frankfort, Ind., Oct. 20, 1940; s. Walter Kenneth and Hester (Kesterson); m. Sara Sue Stewart, Feb. 17, 1962; 1 child, Catherine Anne Lucas Fulkerson. BS, Ball State U., 1963, MA, 1964; postgrad., Am. U., 1977, Harvard U., 1990; DA, George Mason U., 1995. Asst. dir. intelligence coordination Nat. Security Council, Washington, 1975-76; exec. asst. to dep. dir. CIA, Washington, 1976-77, dep. exec. sec., 1977-79; CIA program budget officer Intelligence Community Staff, 1979-81; dep. asst. sec. U.S. Dept. Air Force, 1981-82, prin. dep. asst. sec., 1982-83; dir. crisis mgmt. planning staff Nat. Security Council, 1983-85; Disting. prof., dean Def. Intelligence Coll., Washington, 1985-93; assoc. dir. liaison Def. Intelligence Agy., 1993-96; dep. dir. Open Source Info., CIA, 1996-97; prof. Nat. Def. U., Washington, 1997—2003. Adj. prof. U. Md.-Far East divsn., 1970-71, Def. Intelligence Coll., 1974-83; guest lectr. Am. U., Washington, 1971-77; cons. Pres.'s Fgn. Intelligence Adv. Bd. 1981-85. Author: Intelligence and National Security in the Nixon Administration, 1972, Simulation and Strategic Intelligence Analysis, 1973, Information Needs of Presidents, 1989, Organizing the Presidency: The Role of the Director of Central Intelligence, 1995. Pres. Muncie Young Republican's Club, Ind., 1959-64; pres. Students for Goldwater, 1964; mem. Reston Rep. Assn. With USAF, 1965-77, brig. gen. USAF Res., 1977-96. Decorated Legion of Merit, Bronze Star medal, Meritorious Svc. medal, Republic of Vietnam Gallantry Cross with palm. Mem. Am. Polit. Sci. Assn., Air Force Assn., Nat. Mil. Intelligence Assn., Assn. Former Intelligence Officers, Res. Officers Assn., Pi Sigma Alpha, Phi Gamma Mu, Sigma Chi Lodges: Masons. Office: Nat Def Univ Washington DC 20319-0001 E-mail: jwlucas@erols.com.

LUCAS, JANET MARIE, language educator; b. May 20, 1962; AA, Peninsula Coll., Port Angeles, Wash., 1998; BA summa cum laude, Ea. Wash. U., Cheney, Wash., 2001, MA, 2003; postgrad., Ind. U. Pa. English instr., dir. writing ctr. Peninsula Coll., 2003—. Recipient Exceptional Faculty award, Peninsula Coll. Found., 2006. Mem.: Two-Yr. Coll. Assn., Nat. Coun. Tchrs. English.

LUCAS, JOE N., biophysicist, researcher; b. Calif. PhD, U. Calif., Berkeley, 1977. Sr. scientists U. of Calif., Lawrence Livermore Nat. Lab., Livermore, Calif., 2000—07; chief scientist officer ChromoTrax, Inc., Frederick, Md., 2007—. Contbr. articles to profl. jours. Chair or bd. Lucas Ednl. Found., Inc., San Ramon, Calif., 1978—. Achievements include patents for solutin hybridization. Office: Chromotrax Inc 401 Rosemont Ave Frederick MD 21701 Office Fax: 925-361-4660. Personal E-mail: lcjoe@aol.com.

LUCAS, JOSH (JOSH MAURER), actor; b. Little Rock, Ark., June 20, 1971; Actor: (films) Alive, 1993, Father Hood, 1993, McGregor, 1993, Thinner, 1996, True Blue, 1996, Minotaur, 1997, The Definite Maybe, 1997, Harvest, 1998, Restless, 1998, You Can Count on Me, 2000, American Psycho, 2000, Drop Back Ten, 2000, The Dancer, 2000, The Weight of Water, 2000, The Deep End, 2001, When Strangers Appear, 2001, Session 9, 2001, A Beautiful Mind, 2001, Coastlines, 2002, Sweet Home Alabama, 2002, Four Reasons, 2002, Hulk, 2003, Secondhand Lions, 2003, Wonderland, 2003, Around the Bend, 2004, Stealth, 2005, An Unfinished Life, 2005, Glory Road, 2006; (TV films) Child of Darkness, Child of Light, 1991, Class of '61, 1993, In the Heat of the Night: A Matter of Justice, 1994; (TV series) Snowy River: The McGregor Saga, 1993; (TV miniseries) Empire Falls, 2005, (TV appearances) True Colors, 1990, Life Goes On, 1990, Parker Lewis Can't Lose, 1991, Jake and the Fatman, 1991, (off-Broadway play) Corpus Christi, 1998, Spalding Gray: Stories Left to Tell, 2007.

LUCAS, KATHERINE E., epidemiologist; d. William C. and Patricia A. Lucas. BS in Econs., Villanova U., Pa., 1982; PhD, Johns Hopkins U., Balt., 2004. Asst. contr. Valley Forge Labs., Inc., Devon, Pa., 1982—84; mgr. acctg. Diversified Imaging, King of Prussia, Pa., 1984—88; mgr. fin. planning BMG Distbn., NY, 1988—91; co-prin. investigator Gulf war illnesses study sch. medicine Johns Hopkins U., Balt., 2000—03, post-doctoral fellow sch. pub. health, 2004—07; health ins. specialist Ctrs. for Medicare and Medicaid Svc., Balt., 2007—. Patient adv. Faith in Action, Balt., 2002—04; coord. ministry healing prayer cirs. Grace Fellowship Ch., Timonium, Md., 2004—. Recipient Hon. Mention award, Nat. Def. Sci. & Engring. Fellowship, 1998—99, Career Devel. award, AAUW, 1997. Mem.: Order St. Luke the Physician (assoc.), Hopkins Toastmasters Club (pres. 1999—2001), Johns Hopkins Club, Beta Gamma Sigma, Phi Kappa Phi. Avocations: cooking, reading, walking. Office Phone: 410-786-7723.

LUCAS, KURT JOHN, health facility director; b. Derby, Conn., Mar. 1, 1951; s. John Paul and Anna Pauline Lucas; m. Karen Elizabeth Woodford, Nov. 28, 1975; 1 child, Adam Woodford. BA, So. Conn. State U., New Haven, 1973. Emergency med. svcs. instr. Conn. Dir. cmty. health access Littleton Regional Hosp., NH, 1992—. Exec. dir. NH Emergency Med. Svcs. Conf., Littleton, 1992—; charter mem. and past pres. Seymour Ambulance Corps, Conn., 1969—76; program founder, dir. Littleton Regional Hosp. Paramedic Program, 2001—; part-time dir. Littleton Area Health Consortium, 1997—. Recipient Declaration of Kurt J. Lucas Day for Meritorious Svc., City of Stamford, 1982, Meritorious Svc. award, So. Maine Emergency Med. Svcs. Coun., 1987, NW Conn. Emergency Svcs. Coun., 1979, SW Conn. Emergency Med. Svcs. Coun., 1986, Recognition award, State of NH, Divsn. of Emergency Med. Svc., 2001. Mem.: Am. Mensa (assoc.), NH Pub. Health Assn. (assoc.; bd. dirs.), New Eng. Coun. for EMS (assoc.; past sec.), Seymour Ambulance Corps (assoc.; charter mem., past pres. 1969—76), No. NH Emergency Med. Svcs. Coun. (assoc.; chmn. 2001—, Leadership award 1999, 2001). Lutheran. Avocations: gardening, travel. Home: 249 Old County Rd Franconia NH 03580 Office: Littleton Regional Hosp 600 St Johnsbury Rd Littleton NH 03561

LUCAS, MICHELE ANGELYN, learning consultant, special education educator; d. Robert Stephen Burrows and Mary Elizabeth Carvin-Burrows; m. Joseph William Lucas, Oct. 17, 1970; 1 child, Danielle Angelyn. BA, Ricker Coll., 1969; MS in Edn., Monmouth U., 1979, MSEd, 1988. Cert. learning disability tchr. cons., reading specialist, tchr. of handicapped, elem. tchr. Various positions Freehold Twp. (NJ) Bd. Edn., 1973—; learning cons. Jersey Shore U. Med. Ctr., Neptune, NJ, 1994—. Sec. Manasquan (NJ) PTA, 1983; mem. Manasquan Tchr. Advisory, 1991, Manasquan Hist. Assn., 1997. Fellow: Learning Disability Assn., Coun. Exceptional Children (Edn. Diagnosis Spl. Education recognition 2004—); mem.: NEA, NJ Edn. Assn. Avocations: collecting vintage jewelry, walking, theater, reading, antiques.

LUCAS, PATRICIA LATOURETTE, writer; b. June 27, 1925; m. William Erich Lucas; children: Kathleen Lucas-Roberts, Nancy Williams, Karen Johnson, Suzanne Watson, Elizabeth Atkinson. BA, Whitman Coll., 1947. Author: Overlake, 1979, Historical Highlights of Seattle Tennis Club, 1982, Seattle Children's Home, 1984, Branching Out, History of Laird Norton Families, 1989, Percy, 1990, Sequim Bay Point, 1993, Story of St. Thomas Episcopal Church, 1994, Growing with Seattle, The Story of Sellen Construction Company, 1996, Bridging the Generations, the History of Manson Construction, 2000, Overlake Golf and Country Club, 2nd edit., 2005. Home and Office: PO Box 376 Medina WA 98039-0376 Office Phone: 425-455-4667.

LUCAS, ROBERT EMERSON, JR., economist, educator; b. Yakima, Wash., Sept. 15, 1937; BA, U. Chgo., 1959, PhD, 1964; PhD (hon.), U. Paris-Dauphine, 1992, Athens U. Econ. and Bus., 1994; DSc (hon.), Technion-Israel Inst. Tech., 1996; PhD (hon.), U. Montréal, 1998. Lectr. U. Chgo., 1962-63; asst. prof., economics Carnegie-Mellon U., Pittsburgh, 1963-67; assoc. prof., 1967-70; prof., 1970-75; prof., economics U. Chgo., 1975—, vice chmn. Dept. Econs., 1975—83, named John Dewey Disting. Svc. prof., 1980, chmn. Dept. Econs., 1986—88. Ford Found. vis. rsch. prof. U. Chgo., 1974-75; vis. prof. econ. Northwestern U., Chgo., 1981-82. Author: Studies in Business-Cycle Theory, 1981, Models of Business Cycles, 1987, Lectures on Economic Growth, 2001; co-author: Recursive Methods in Economic Dynamics, 1989; co-editor: Rational Expectations and Econometric Practice, 1981; assoc. editor Jour. Econ. Theory, 1972-78, Jour. Monetary Econs., 1977—; editor Jour. Polit. Theory, 1978-81, 1988-; contbr. articles to profl. jours. Woodrow Wilson fellow, 1959-60, Brookings fellow, 1961-62, Woodrow Wilson Dissertation fellow, 1963, Ford Found. Faculty fellow, 1966-67, Guggenheim Found. fellow, 1981-82; Proctor and Gamble scholar, 1955-59; recipient Nobel Prize in Econ., 1995. Fellow AAAS, Econometric Soc. (2nd v.p. 1995, pres. 1997), Am. Acad. Arts and Scis.; mem. NAS, Econometric Soc. (2nd v.p., v.p. 1995, pres. 1997), Am. Econ. Assn. (v.p. 1987, pres. 2001), European Acad. Arts, Scis. and Humanities, Am. Philosophical Soc., Phi Beta Kappa. Achievements include developing and applying the hypothesis of rational expectations, and thereby having transformed macroeconomic analysis and deepened out understanding of economic policy. Office: U Chgo Dept Econs 1126 E 59th St Chicago IL 60637-1580*

LUCAS, ROBERT FRANK, lawyer; b. Beacon Falls, Conn., Nov. 11, 1935; s. Otto F. and A. Helen (Schuster) L.; m. Regina Abbiati, July 16, 1960; children: Robert Frank Jr., David R., Jennifer J. AB, Bates Coll., Lewiston, Maine, 1956; JD, Boston U., 1959. Bar: Mass. 1960, US Dist. Ct. Mass. 1962, US Supreme Ct. 1973. Trial atty. Boston Legal Aid Soc., 1960-63; prin. Nigro, Pettepit & Lucas, Wakefield, Mass., 1963—. Mem. standing list of masters Mass. Superior Ct., Cambridge, 1979—. Chmn. bd. appeals City of Melrose, Mass., 1982—2003, city solicitor, 2003—05; trustee Melrose H.S. Permanent Scholarship Fund, 1979—; mem. Rep. City Com., Melrose, 1980—84; lay leader 1st United Meth. Ch., Melrose, 1979—82. With USAR, 1959—65. Mem.: ABA, 1st Dist. Ea. Middlesex Bar Assn. (pres. 1987—88), Middlesex County Bar Assn. (bd. dirs. 1986—99), Mass. Bar Assn. (bd. dels. 1980—83, chmn. fee arbitration bd. 1983—84, 20th Century Club 1985, exec. com. 1993, bd. dels. 2004—, treas. 2006—07, Cert. of Appreciation 1988, Cmty. Svc. award 1989), Bellevue Golf Club, Masons (dist. dep. grand master 1982—83). Avocations: music, choral singing, youth sports. Home: 20 Pilgrim Rd Melrose MA 02176-3019 Office: Nigro Pettepit & Lucas 649 Main St Wakefield MA 01880-5216 Office Phone: 781-245-4545.

LUCAS, STEVEN MITCHELL, lawyer; b. Ada, Okla., Jan. 19, 1948; s. John Dalton and Cherrye (Smith) Lucas; m. Lori E. Seeberger (dissolved); children: Steven Turner, Brooke Elizabeth, Sarah Grace. BA, Yale U., 1970; JD, Vanderbilt U., 1973. Bar: DC 1973, US Ct. Mil. Appeals 1974, US Dist. Ct. DC 1979, US Ct. Appeals (DC cir.) 1979, US Supreme Ct. 1979. Assoc. Shaw, Pittman, Potts & Trowbridge, Washington, 1978-82, ptnr., 1983-92; ptnr., head fin. instns. practice Wiley, Rein & Fielding, Washington, 1992-93, Winston & Strawn, Washington, 1993-97; pvt. practice Washington, 1997—. Cons. internat. rels. Rockefeller Found., NYC, 1978; mem. negotiating team Panama Canal Treaty, Washington, 1975—77; legal advisor Dept. Def. Panama Canal negotiations working group; presdl. apptd. U.S. panelist Internat. Ctr. Settlement Investment Disputes, ICSID-World Bank, 2002—; mem. panel of arbitrators Nat. Arbitration Forum, 2004—; sr. cons. Iraq Reconstrn. Mgmt. Office, Dept. of State, 2004—05. Editor-in-chief: Vanderbilt U. Jour. Transnational Law, 1972—73. Capt. JAGC US Army, 1974—77. Republican. Episcopalian. Home and Office: 1001 Jigger Ct Annapolis MD 21401 E-mail: smlucas@comcast.net.

LUCAS, TERI KATHLEEN, secondary school educator; d. Donald Paul and Joan McKee; m. Martin Vince Lucas, Dec. 23, 1970; children: Shawn Martin, Brian Donald, Kevin Michael, Heather Kathleen. BA, Francis Marion U., SC, 1987. Cert. Edn. in English, Speech, Drama, Health Tex. Edn. Agy., 1988. Tchr. Pflugerville Mid. Sch., Tex., 1989—. Author: (non-fiction novel) Spontaneous Beats (Second Pl.- Golden Triangle Writer's Guild, 1997). Vol. EMT Pflugerville Vol. Fire Dept., Tex., 1997—2006; pres. Unity Ctr., Austin, 2006; spkr. Am. Heart Assn., Austin, 2003—06. Decorated USAR Europe Helping Hand award VII Army; recipient Cert. of Appreciation, ARC, 1981, Honored Hero award, 2004, Pres.'s award, Pflugerville Vol. Fire Dept., 1999, Humanitarian of Yr., Pflugerville Mid. Sch., 2002; scholar, Women of Francis Marion U., 1986. Avocations: sign language classes, swimming, reading, travel, needlepoint. Business E-Mail: teri.lucas@pflugervilleisd.net.

LUCAS, TRUETT LAVAN, retired communications technician; b. Esto, Fla., Dec. 13, 1935; s. Willie Fay Lucas and Bertie Vonceil Kirkland; m. Mona Anita Gleitsmann, Mar. 29, 1942; 1 child, Ramona Gayle Lucas Gilliland. Grad high sch., Panama City, Fla. Non commd. officer US Army, 1953, advanced through ranks to sgt. first calss, 1968, ret., 1974; park supr. Bay County, Panama City, Fla., 1974—80; elec. tech. USN, Panama City, 1980—98; ret., 1998. Author: From Cotton Patch to the White House in 16 Years. Mem.: VFW, Vietnam Vets. Am., 1600 Comm. Assn. Republican. Presbyterian. Avocations: woodworking, fishing. Home: 3235 E Orlando Rd Panama City FL 32405

LUCAS, WILLIAM RAY, aerospace scientist, consultant; b. Newbern, Tenn., Mar. 1, 1922; married 1948; 3 children. BS, Memphis State U., 1943; MS, Vanderbilt U., 1950, PhD in Chem. Metallurgy, 1952; L.H.D. (hon.), Mobile Coll., 1977; D.Sc. (hon.), Southeastern Inst. Tech., 1980, U. Ala., Huntsville, 1981. Instr. chemistry Memphis State U., 1946-48; chemist guided missile devel. div. Redstone Arsenal, 1952-54, chief chem. sect., 1954-55; chief engr. material sect. Army Ballistic Missile Agy., 1955-56, chief engr. material br., 1956-60; with Marshall Space Flight Center, NASA, 1960—, chief engring. materials br., 1960-63, material div., 1963-66, dir. propulsion and vehicle engring. lab., 1966-68, dir. program devel., 1968-71, dep. dir., 1971-74, dir., 1974-86; pvt. practice aerospace cons. Hunstville, Ala., 1986—2002; ret. Served as lt. USNR, 1943-46. Recipient Exceptional Sci. Achievement medal NASA, 1964, 2 Exceptional Service medals, 1969, Disting. Service medal, 1972, Disting. Service award, 1981, 86; Presdl. rank Disting. Exec., 1980; Roger W. Jones award for outstanding exec. leadership Am. U., 1981; Space award for outstanding contbns. in field of space VFW, 1983; Disting. Alumni award Memphis State U., 1984; Aubrey D. Green award Lions Club Ala., 1986; named one of Tenn. Outstanding Scientists and Engrs., Tenn. Tech. Found., 1986; named to Ala. Engring. Hall of Fame, 1990. Fellow Am. Soc. Metals, Am. Astronautical Soc. (Space Flight award 1982), AIAA (Oberth award 1965, Holger N. Toftoy award 1976, Elmer A. Sperry group award 1986); mem. Nat. Acad. Engring., Am. Chem. Soc., Sigma Xi, Tau Beta Pi Achievements include research in materials engring. metallurgy, inorganic chemistry, environ. effects on materials, especially space environ. effects.

LUCCA, DAVID ALAN, money manager; b. Vineland, NJ, Apr. 6, 1957; s. Joseph A. and Harriet M. Lucca; m. Janette Seaton, Feb. 26, 1994; children: John Russell, Carol Joy, Sveta Lucca. BS, Pa. State U., 1980; dipl., Internat. Christian Grad. U., San Bernardino, 1983; MA, Dallas Theol. Sem., 1986; postgrad., Coll. Fin. Planning, Denver. Sr. fellow Campus Crusade for Christ, Bozeman, Mont., 1980-83; pres. ICSCN Glass, Garland, Tex., 1984-86; investment analyst Gary C. Smith, CPA, PC, Dallas, 1986-88; mng. ptnr. east coast Rhoads Lucca Capital Mgmt., Dallas, 1988—. Adj. faculty Coll. for Fin. Planning, Denver, 1990; instr. Brookhaven CC, Farmers Branch, Tex., 1990, Richland CC, Richardson, Tex., 1993-96; co-mgr. Autopilot Managed Growth Fund. Del. Republican Party, Garland, 1986—. Republican. Avocations: gardening, reading, genealogy.

LUCCA, LOUIS ANTHONY, academic administrator; s. Louis and Freda Habib Lucca. BA in Modern Langs., Seton Hall U., 1987; MA in TESOL, NYU, 1992, PhD in Applied Linguistics, 2002. Internat. acct. rep. McGraw Hill, Inc., NYC, 1980—86, asst. mgr. Std. and Poor's ratings group, cash sys., 1986—91; tutor MAC Testing and Cons., Inc., Red Bank, NJ, 1980—92; instr. CUNY, NYC, 1992—95, instr. English Lang. Inst., 1992—95, coord. speech. comm. Media Studies and The Speech Ctr. and Lang. Acquisition Lab., 2000—, assoc. prof. Seminar leader Virtual Interest Groups, ePortfolio, eChoose, Digital Storytelling, Oral Comm. across Curriculum; presenter in field. Contbr. articles on virtual interest groups. Mem.: TESL, MLA, Assn. Advancement Computing in Edn., Nat. Comm. Assn., Internat. Comm. Assn. Home: 9728 Third Ave # 341 Brooklyn NY 11209-7742 Office: FH Iaguardia C C 31-10 Thomson Ave Long Island City NY 11101 Office Phone: 718-482-5692. E-mail: luccalo@lagcc.cuny.edu.

LUCCHESI, LIONEL LOUIS, lawyer; b. St. Louis, Sept. 17, 1939; s. Lionel Louis and Theresa Lucchesi; m. Mary Ann Wheeler, July 30, 1966; children: Lionel Louis III, Marisa Pilar. BSEE, Ill. Inst. Tech., 1961; JD, St. Louis U., 1969. Bar: Mo. 1969. With Emerson Electric Co., 1965-69; assoc. Polster, Polster & Lucchesi, St. Louis, 1969-74, ptnr., 1974—. City atty. City of Ballwin, Mo., 1979—85, 1992—2007. Mem. Zoning Commn., 1971—77; alderman City of Ballwin, 1977—79. Recipient Am. Jurisprudence award, St. Louis U., 1968—69; scholar NROTC, 1957—61. Mem.: ATLA, ABA, Newcomen Soc. N.Am., St. Louis Met. Bar Assn. (exec. com., pres.-elect 1984, pres. 1985—86), Am. Patent Law Assn., Superstition Mountain Club, Forest Hills Club, Rotary (pres.-elect St. Louis 1991—92, pres. 1992—93). Republican. Roman Catholic. Office: 12412 Powers Ct Dr Saint Louis MO 63131 Home Phone: 636-391-8443; Office Phone: 314-238-2400. E-mail: llucchesi@patpro.com.

LUCCHINO, LAWRENCE, sports team executive, lawyer; b. Pitts., Sept. 6, 1945; s. Dominic A. and Rose (Rizzo) L. AB cum laude, Princeton U., 1967; JD, Yale U., 1972. Bar: Calif. 1973, Pa. 1973, DC 1975. Counsel Impeachment Inquiry, House Judiciary Commn., Washington, 1974; assoc. Williams & Connolly, Washington, 1975-79, ptnr., 1979—; pres., CEO Balt. Orioles, 1988-93, San Diego Padres, 1995; vice chmn. Boston Red Sox, Boston. Sec., bd. dirs., gen. counsel Wash. Redskins Football Club, 1978-85; bd. dirs., gen. counsel Balt. Orioles Baseball Club, from 1979, v.p., 1982-88, pres., CEO, 1988-93; CEO San Diego Padres Baseball Club, 1994—; bd. dirs. Army Times, Springfield, Va. Trustee Nat. Found. on Counseling, Princeton, N.J., 1984—; bd. dirs. Nat. Aquarium Natl., Balt. Symphony, Princeton Electronic Bd., Babe Ruth Mus. Mem. ABA Democrat. Roman Catholic. also: Williams & Connolly 725 12th St NW Washington DC 20005-3901 Office: Boston Red Sox 4 Yawkey Way Boston MA 02215*

LUCCO, JAMES PERRY, writer; b. Jamestown, NY, Nov. 2, 1946; s. James Perry and Josephine Helen Lucco; m. Gail Catherine Frazier, July 14, 1986. BA, Columbia U., NYC, 1971; MALS, post grad., Kean U., NJ, 2007—. Asst. to pres. P&A Ent., Miami, Fla., 1972—74; sr. hearing officer State of N.J., Trenton, 1975—77; comptroller Tiger Mgmt., NYC, 1985—97; asst. to pres. Empire Rubbish & Ash, NYC, 1993—96, Moyer Plating, Newark, 1992—95; bus. assoc. T.W. Alexander Esq., Elizabeth, NJ, 1995—. Founder The Urban Triangle Enterprise, 2002; golf staff mem. Union County, NJ; founder, exec. dir. Jacob Haberman Meml. Libr. and Found., 2005. Author: (play) A Pagans Wine, 1968, (novels) New York City Garbage Wars, 2000, Old Soldiers, 2003, The Last Tiger, 2004, Luca, 2005, La Cosa Nova, 2005, There Were Battleships, 2007. Bd. dirs. South Orange Sr. Citizens, NJ, 1992—2004. Mem.: Lions (dir. pub. rels. 1998—2004). Roman Catholic. Avocation: golf. Home: 376 Williamson St #8 Elizabeth NJ 07202 Home Phone: 908-469-8359; Office Phone: 908-469-8359.

LUCCOCK, THOMAS NELSON, auditor, director; s. Randolph Naphthali and Jewel Norene (Nelson) Luccock; m. Catherine Marcella Orr, Aug. 2, 1986. At, Southwestern U., Georgetown, Tex., 1966—67; BS, U. Okla., Norman, 1970; MBA, U. Tex., Austin, 1972; grad. Exec. Mgmt. Program, Ind. U., Bloomington, 1983. CPA Tex., 1975, Okla., 1978, Mich., 2000, cert. internal auditor, 2000. Staff acct. Arthur Andersen LLP, Dallas, 1973—75; mgr. auditing Cities Svc. Co., Tulsa, 1976—83; corp. mgr. internal audit Occidental Petroleum Corp., 1983—99; dir. internal audit Mich. State U., East Lansing, 2000—. Bd. Inst. Internal Auditors, Okla., 1983—99, pres. Tulsa chpt., 1988—89, bd., Lansing, Mich., 2000—, pres. Lansing chpt., 2003—04; bd. mem. U. Okla., Norman, 1995—, chmn. acctg. adv. bd., 2002—05. Established Catherine and Thomas Luccock Libr. Endowment U. Okla.; mem. Tulsa Opera Bd., Okla., 1989—90; bd. mem. Bizzell Libr. U. Okla, Norman, 1999—; chmn. bd. Am. Heart Assn., Tulsa, 2001—02, revenue generation com. mem. Heartland affiliate St. Louis, 2002—06; established Jewel Luccock Piano scholarships, Randolph Luccock Petroleum Engring. scholarships. Capt. USAR, 1971—79. Recipient Paragon award, Leadership Tulsa, 2002. Mem.: AICPA, Inst. Internal auditors (bd. mem. Tulsa chpt. 1983—99, bd. mem. Lansing chpt. 2000—, pres Lansing chpt. 2003—04, pres Tulsa chpt. 1988—89), Phi Beta Kappa. Avocations: golf, art, travel. Home: 7216 E 65th Pl Tulsa OK 74133 Office: Mich State U 309 Olds Hall East Lansing MI 48824 Personal E-mail: tnlucky@worldnet.att.net.

LUCE, CHARLES FRANKLIN, retired utilities executive, lawyer; b. Platteville, Wis., Aug. 29, 1917; s. James Oliver and Wilma Fisher (Grindell) L.; m. Helen G. Oden, Oct. 24, 1942; children: James O., Christine Mary, Barbara Anne, Charles Franklin; m. Margaret E. Richmond, Nov. 9, 2001. BA, LL.B., U. Wis., 1941; Sterling fellow, Yale U., 1941-42. Bar: Wis. 1941, Wash. 1946, Oreg. 1945, N.Y. 1981. Law clk. Justice Hugo L. Black, U.S. Supreme Ct., 1943-44; gen. practice law Walla Walla, Wash., 1946-61; adminstr. Bonneville Power Adminstrn., Dept. Interior, Portland, Oreg., 1961-66; under sec. interior Washington, 1966-67; chmn. bd. Consol. Edison Co. of N.Y., Inc., 1967-82, chief exec. officer, 1967-81, chmn. emeritus, 1982—; ptnr. Preston, Thorgrimson, Ellis & Holman, Portland, Oreg., 1982-86; spl. counsel Met. Life Ins. Co., 1987-94. Dir. emeritus UAL and Met. Life Ins. Co.; trustee Henry M. Jackson Found.; trustee emeritus Columbia U., N.Y.C. Mem. Wis. Bar Assn., Phi Beta Kappa, Order of Coif. Episcopalian. Office: Consol Edison 4 Irving Pl New York NY 10003-3502

LUCE, DONALD SANDERS, social worker; b. East Calais, Vt., Sept. 20, 1934; s. Collins Andrew and Margaret Sanders L. BS, U. Vt., 1957; MS, Cornell U., 1959. Vol. Internat. Vol. Svcs., Vietnam, 1958—59, dir., 1960—67; rsch. assoc. Cornell U., Ithaca, NY, 1967—68; rsch. dir. World Coun. Chs., Vietnam, 1969—71; dir. Asia Resource Ctr., Washington, 1971—90; pres., CEO Internat. Vol. Svcs., Washington, 1991—96, AIDS prevention coord., 1997—98; dir. devel. Cmty. Missions, Niagara Falls, NY, 1998—. Co-author: Viet Nam: The Unheard Voices, 1968, Hostages of War, 1972. Bd. dirs. Am. Friends Svc. Com., Phila., 1971-91; AIDS prevention activist Western NY Peace Ctr., Buffalo, 1985—. Recipient Peace award War Resistors League, NYC, 1990, Gold medal NY Film Festival, NYC, 1985, Medal of Honor, Govt. Vietnam, 2004. Mem. United Ch. of Christ. Avocation: poetry. Office Phone: 716-285-3403 x 2226.

LUCE, EDWARD ANDREW, plastic surgeon; b. Syracuse, NY, Mar. 5, 1940; s. Edward Andrew and Constance Faith (Jones) L.; m. Rebecca Sue Wall (div.); children: Darcie, Michael, Caitlin. BS, U. Dayton, 1961; MD, U. Ky., 1965. Diplomate Am. Bd. Surgery, Am. Bd. Plastic Surgery (chmn. 1990-91). Resident in surgery Barnes Hosp., St. Louis, 1965-71; resident in plastic surgery Johns Hopkins Hosp., Balt., 1971-73, asst. prof. plastic surgery, 1973-75; assoc. prof. plastic surgery U. Ky., Lexington, 1975-87, prof. plastic surgery, 1987-95, chief plastic surgery, 1975-95, VA Hosp., 1975-95; Kiehn-DesPrez prof. surgery Case Western Reserve U., Cleve., 1995—2004; chief plastic surgery U. Hosps. of Cleve., 1995—2004, VA Hosp., Cleve., 1995—2004; prof. plastic surgery U. Tenn., Memphis, 2004—; pvt. practice Plastic Surgery Group of Memphis, 2004—. Attending plastic surgeon St. Joseph Hosp., Lexington, 1975-95, Good Samaritan Hosp., Lexington, 1978-95, Humana Hosp., Lexington, 1982-95; Kiehn-DesPrez Prof. and Chief of Plastic Surgery, Case Western Reserve U. and Univ. Hosps. of Cleveland; pres. Assn. Acad. Chmn. of Plastic Surgery, 1989-90, Am. Soc. Maxillofacial Surgeons (pres. 1990-91), Southeastern Soc. Plastic and Reconstructive Surgeons (pres. 1992-93) Pres. U. Ky. Med. Alumni Assn., 1977-78; pres. John Hoopes Plastic Surgery Found., 1993. Recipient Clinician of Yr., Am. Assn. Plastic Surgeons, 1990, Prejidential citation Am. Soc. Head and Neck Surgeons, 2000, Dist. Svc. award Am. Soc. Plastic Surgeons, 2000 Mem. Plastic Surgery Ednl. Found. (pres. 1993-94), Am Coll. Surgeons, Am. Surg. Assn., So. Surg. Assn., Am. Assn. Plastic Surgeons (pres. 2000-2001), Am. Soc. Plastic and Reconstructive Surgeons (pres. 2001-2002), Soc. Head and Neck Surgeons. Avocations: clinical photography, military history of small, obscure wars, collecting old and rare medical books. Home Phone: 216-921-7863, 901-374-9184; Office Phone: 901-761-9030. Personal E-mail: edluce@yahoo.com.

LUCE, Mrs. HENRY See HADLEY, LEILA

LUCE, PRISCILLA MARK, public relations executive; b. NYC, Feb. 4, 1947; d. S. Carl and Patricia (Greenfield) Mark; m. Robert Warren Luce, July 19, 1969; children: James Warren, David Mark. BA, U. Pa., 1968. Adminstrv. asst. Phila. Mus. Art, 1968-69; asst. dir. pub. info. Mt. Holyoke Coll., South Hadley, Mass., 1969-71; v.p. Barnes & Roche, Inc., Phila., 1971-82; mgr. civic programs TRW Inc., Cleve., 1982-85, mgr. cmty. rels., 1985-88, mgr. external comm., 1988-90, dir. pub. affairs and advt., 1990-92, v.p. TRW info. sys. and svcs. comms., 1992-94, v.p. mktg. and orgn. comm., 1994—2001, v.p. corp. comm., 2001—03. Trustee New Orgn. Visual Arts, Cleve., 1983—97, pres., 1984—86; trustee Cmty. Info. Vol. Action Ctr., Cleve., 1984—86, Albert M. Greenfield Found., Phila., 1989—, pres., 1999—; trustee Cleve. State U. Found., 1996—, chmn. devel. com., 1998—, vice-chmn., 1999—2004, chmn., 2004—; trustee Bus. Vols. Unltd., Cleve., 1998—2003, WVIZ/PBS, WCPN Radio, 1997—2005, chmn. pub. rels. com., 1998—2001; chmn. media and mktg. com. Cleve. Today, 1999—2001; trustee Ohio Chamber Orch., Cleve., 1986—92, chmn. devel. com., 1987—88, chmn., trustee, 1991—92, exec. v.p., 1990—91; mem. steering com. Cleve. Art Festival, 1983—84, Mayor's Cultural Arts Planning Task Force, 1985—87; trustee Ret. Sr. Vol. Prog., 1991, Western Res. Hist. Soc., 1999—2002; leadership devel. prog. participant United Way Svcs., Cleve., 1983, cons., 1983—85; steering com. Bus. Volunteerism Coun. of Cleve., 1984—92; comm. adv. com. Work in NE Ohio Coun., 1991—94. Recipient Woman of Profl. Excellence award, YWCA of Cleve., 1990.

LUCE, R. DUNCAN (ROBERT DUNCAN LUCE), psychology professor; b. Scranton, Pa., May 16, 1925; s. Robert Rennselaer and Ruth Lillian (Downer) L.; m. Gay Gaer, June 6, 1950 (div.); m. Cynthia Newby, Oct. 5, 1968 (div.); m. Carolyn A. Scheer, Feb. 27, 1988; 1 child, Aurora Newby. BS, MIT, Cambridge, Mass, 1945, PhD, 1950; MA (hon.), Harvard U., Cambridge, Mass, 1976; D of Math. (hon.), U. Waterloo, Calif., 2007. Mem. staff research lab electronics MIT, 1950-53; asst. prof. Columbia U., 1953-57; lectr. social relations Harvard U., 1957-59; prof. psychology U. Pa., Phila., 1959-69; vis. prof. Inst. Advanced Study, Princeton, 1969-72; prof. Sch. Social Scis., U. Calif., Irvine, 1972-75; Alfred North Whitehead prof. psychology Harvard U., Cambridge, Mass., 1976-81, prof., 1981-83, Victor S. Thomas prof. psychology, 1983-88, Victor S. Thomas prof. emeritus, 1988, chmn., 1988-94; disting. prof. cognitive sci. U. Calif., Irvine, 1988-94, dir. Irvine Rsch. Unit in math. behavioral sci., 1988-92, disting. rsch. prof. cognitive sci. and rsch. prof. econs., 1994—; dir. Inst. for Math. Behavioral Sci., 1992-98. Chmn. assembly behavioral and social scis. NRC, 1976-79 Author: (with H. Raiffa) Games and Decisions, 1957, Individual Choice Behavior, 1959, (with others) Foundations of Measurement, I, 1971, II, 1989, III, 1990, Response Times, 1986, (with others) Stevens Handbook of Experimental Psychology, I and II, 1988, Sound & Hearing, 1993, Utility of Gains and Losses, 2000. Served with USNR, 1943-46. Recipient Disting. award Rsch. U. Calif., Irvine, 1994, medal, 2001, Extraordinarius award, 2006, Gold medal Am. Psychol. Found., 2001, Daniel G. Aldrich, Jr. Disting. Svc. award U. Calif., Irvine, 2003, Ramsey medal Soc. Decision Analysis, 2003, Norman Anderson award Soc. Exptl. Psychologists, 2004, Nat. medal of Sci., 2003; Ctr. Advanced Study in Behavioral Scis. fellow, 1954-55, 66-67, 87-88, NSF Sr. Postdoctoral fellow, 1966-67, Guggenheim fellow, 1980-81. Fellow: Am. Psychol. Soc. (bd. dirs. 1989—91), APA (bd. sci. affairs 1993—95, exec. com. divsn. I 2000, disting. sci. contbn. award 1970), AAAS (chair elect psychology sect. 1998—99, chair 1999); mem.: Soc. Math. Psychology (pres. 1979), Psychonomic Soc., Psychometric Soc. (pres. 1976—77), Fedn. Behavioral Psychol. and Cognitive Scis. (pres. 1988—90), Math. Assn. Am., Am. Math. Soc., Nat. Acad. Scis. (chmn. sect. psychology 1980—83, class behavioral and social scis. 1983—86, mem. dbasse bd. 2005—), Am. Philos. Soc., Am. Acad. Arts and Sci., Tau Beta Pi, Phi Beta Kappa, Sigma Xi. Home: 20 Whitman Ct Irvine CA 92617-4057 Office: U Calif Social Sci Plz Irvine CA 92697-5100 Office Phone: 949-824-6239. Business E-Mail: rdluce@uci.edu.

LUCE, RICHARD, university librarian; BA in Polit. Sci., Univ. San Diego; MPA, San Diego State Univ.; MS in Libr. Info. Sci., Univ. S. Fla. Network dir. Irving Libr. Network, Boulder, Colo., 1985—88; exec. dir. SE Fla. Libr. Info. Network, 1988—91; rsch. libr. dir. Los Alamos Nat. Lab., N.Mex., 1991—2006; vice provost, dir. libr. Emory Univ., Atlanta, 2006—. Exec. bd. Nat. Info. Standards Orgn., 1998—2004; sr. adv., Ctr. for Info. Mgmt. Max Planck Soc., 2000—06; co-founder Open Archives Initiative. Office: Emory Univ Library 540 Asbury Cir Atlanta GA 30322 Office Phone: 404-727-6861.*

LUCE, THOMAS WARREN, III, former federal agency administrator; b. Dallas, June 18, 1940; s. Thomas Warren and Ruth (Hardy) L.; m. Phoebe Ann McCain; children: Ken, Ellen Luce Tucker, Susan. Student, Va. Mil. Inst.; BBA in Acctg., So. Meth. U., 1963, LLB, 1966. Bar: Tex. 1966, U.S. Dist. Ct. (no. dist.) Tex. 1966, U.S. Supreme Ct. 1971, U.S. Ct. Appeals (2d cir.) N.Y. 1976, U.S. Ct. Appeals (5th cir.) La. 1981, U.S. Ct. Appeals (11th cir.) Ga. 1981. Assoc. McKenzie & Baer, Dallas, 1966-67; assoc. then ptnr. Jenkens, Spradley & Gilchrist, Dallas, 1968-73; founding ptnr. Hughes & Luce, LLP, Dallas, 1973—97, of counsel, 1997—2005; chief justice pro tempore Tex. Supreme Ct., Dallas, 1988; asst. sec., Office Planning Evaluation & Policy Devel. US Dept. Edn., Washington, 2005—06. Bd. dirs. Dell Inc., 1991—2005, 2006—. Chmn. Nat. Ctr. for Ednl. Accountability; chief of staff Tex. Select Com. of Pub. Edn.; delegate Edn. Commn. of the States 1995-98; dir. Libr. Congress Trust Fund; chmn. & founder Just for the Kids 1995-; trustee So. Meth. U., Dallas; bd. dirs., founding mem. Episcopal Sch. Dallas; bd. dirs. Dallas Citizen Council; chmn. Tex. Nat. Rsch. Lab. Commn., 1987-89. Mem. ABA, Tex. Bar Assn., Dallas Bar Assn. Clubs: Salesmanship of Dallas.

LUCE, WILLARD RAY, historian, director; b. Blanding, Utah, Mar. 2, 1942; s. Willard Ray and Celia Geneva (Larson) Luce; m. Mary Kay Rogers, Feb. 9, 1968; children: Mary Katurah Wheeler, David Ray, Rachel Ann Pena, Amy Rebecca Cisneros, Thomas Jay. BS, Brigham Young U., Provo, Utah, 1966, MS, 1968; PhD, U. Va., Charlottesville, 1978. Historian Nat. Register Hist. Places Nat. Pk. Svc., Washington, 1974—79; hist. preservation officer Ohio Hist. Soc., Columbus, Ohio, 1980—95; mgr. Hist. Preservation Divsn. Ga. Dept. Natural Resources, Atlanta, 1996—99, dir. Hist. Preservation Divsn., 1999—. Guide Nauvoo Restoration, Ill., 1966; adj. instr. Hist. Preservation Program Ga. State U., Atlanta, 1998—. Author: Cohens v Virginai (1821) The Supreme Court and State Rights, a Reevaluation of Influences and Impacts, 1990; co-author: National Register Bulletin #22, Guidelines for Evaluating and Nominating Properties that Have Achieved Significance within the Last Fifty Years., Orson Squire Fowler, in Master Builders, A Guide to Famous American Architects (National Trust for Historic Preservation), 1985; contbr. articles to profl. jours. Mem. Cambell Task Force Orgn. of Preservation Movement, Washington, 1995—96; mem. adv. com. Ga. Cities Found., Atlanta, 2001—07; mem. adv. coun. hist. preservation Washington, 1994—95; mem. gov.'s commn. Ga. History and Hist. Tourism, Atlanta, 2001—02; mem. Ga. Capitol Commn., Atlanta, 1999—2007. Recipient Spl. Commendation award, Nat. Pk. Svc., 1996. Mem.: Nat. Conf. State Hist. Preservation Officers (pres. 1994—95), Ga. Trust Hist. Preservation (assoc.; hon. trustee 1999—2006), Phi Eta Sigma, Phi Alpha Theta, Blue Key, Phi Kappa Phi. Mem. Lds Ch. Avocations: travel, birdwatching, photography. Office: Historic Preservation Division 34 Peachtree Street NW Suite 1600 Atlanta GA 30303 Office Phone: 404-656-2840. Office Fax: 404-657-1046. Business E-Mail: rluce@dnr.state.ga.us.

LUCENTE, SAM, industrial designer; m. Cynthia Lucente; 2 children. Grad. (magna cum laude), Coll. Design, Architecture and Art, Univ. Cin. With IBM; dir., user experience, tech. grp. Netscape Comm. Corp.; led own design co., 1999—2003; v.p., design Hewlett-Packard Co., 2003—. Spkr. and lectr. at numerous universities, museums and design symposiums; advisor Big Tribe. Represented in permanent collections MoMA, San Francisco, NYC, Smithsonian Nat. Design Mus. Numerous awards for design excellence from Indsl. Designers Soc. Am., I.D. Mag., Industrie Forum, Germany, Compasso d'Oro, Italy, Ministry Internat. Trade and Industry, Japan; named one of 25 Masters of Innovation, BusinessWeek. Co-designer of IBM's Leapfrog Computer with Richard Sapper in 1993; lead design teams for IBM ThinkPad 701 and 560; several patents in field. Office: Hewlett Packard Co 3000 Hanover St Palo Alto CA 94304

LUCERO, CARLOS, federal judge; b. Antonito, Colo., Nov. 23, 1940; m. Dorothy Stuart; 1 child, Carla. BA, Adams State Coll.; JD, George Washington U., 1964. Law clk. to Judge William E. Doyle US Dist. Ct., Colo., 1964—65; pvt. practice Alamosa, Colo., 1966—95; sr. ptnr. Lucero, Lester & Sigmund, Alamosa, Colo.; judge US Ct. Appeals (10th cir.), 1995—. Mem. Pres. Carter's Presdl. Panel on Western State Water Policy. Bd. dirs. Colo. Hist. Soc., Sante Fe Opera Assn. of N.Mex. Recipient Outstanding Young Man of Colo. award, Colo. Jaycees, Disting. Alumnus award, George Washington U.; fellow Paul Harris, Rotary Found. Fellow: Internat. Soc. Barristers, Internat. Acad. Trial Lawyers, Colo. Bar Found. (pres.), Am. Coll. Trial Lawyers, Am. Bar Found.; mem.: ABA (mem. action com. to reduce ct. cost and delay, mem. adv. bd. ABA jour., mem. com. on the availability of legal svcs.), Colo. Rural Legal Svcs. (bd. dirs.), Colo. Hispanic Bar Assn. (Profl. Svc. award), Nat. Hispanic Bar Assn., San Luis Valley Bar Assn. (pres.), Colo. Bar Assn. (pres. 1977—78, mem. ethics com.), Order of the Coif. Office: US Ct Appeals 1823 Stout St Denver CO 80257*

LUCEY, JEROLD FRANCIS, pediatrician; b. Holyoke, Mass., Mar. 26, 1926; s. Jeremiah F. and Pauline A. (Lally) L.; m. Ingela Barth, Oct. 7, 1972; 1 child, Patrick; children by previous marriage: Colleen, Cathy, David. AB, Dartmouth Coll., 1948; MD, NYU, 1952. Intern Bellevue Hosp., NYC, 1952-53; resident in pediat. Columbia-Presbyn. Med. Ctr., 1953-55; rsch. fellow Harvard-Children's Hosp., 1955-56; rsch. fellow in biochemistry U. Vt., 1956-60, from asst. prof. to prof. pediat., 1961-74, prof., 1974—95, Harry Wallace prof. of neonatology, 1995—. Rsch. fellow in biol. chemistry Harvard Coll., 1960—61; cons. NIH; vis. prof. Royal Soc. Medicine, England, 1980; mem. senate U. Vt., 2000—. Editor-in-chief Pediatrics, 1974—; contbr. articles on neonatology, phototherapy and transcutaneous oxygen to profl. jours. With USN, 1944—46. Recipient Humbolt Sr. Scientist award, 1978, United Cerebral Palsy Rsch. award, 1984, McDonald prize, 1991, Apgar award, 1993; Markel scholar, 1960-65, Humbolt scholar, 1978, Univ. scholar, 1991, Columbia Alumnus of Yr. award, 1995, Vt. Physician of Yr., 2005. Fellow Am. Acad. Pediat. (Grulee award 1988, Lifetime Achievement award 1997), Royal Soc. Pediatrics (hon.); mem. Royal Soc. Medicine, World Congress on Perinatal Medicine (pres. 1993), Indian Pediat. Soc. (hon., Gold medal 1994, Perinatal Edn. award 1997), Inst. Medicine, Finnish Pediat. Soc. (hon.), Vt. Acad. Sci., Brit. Pediatric and Child Health Assn (hon.). Home: 52 Overlake Park Burlington VT 05401 Office: Given Bldg D201 89 Beaumont Ave Burlington VT 05405-0068 Office Phone: 802-656-5248.

LUCHAK, FRANK ALEXANDER, lawyer; b. Alta., Can., Feb. 19, 1950; came to US, 1956; s. George and Elizabeth (Szilagyi) Luchak. BA in Econs., Princeton U., 1972; JD, SUNY, Buffalo, 1978. Bar: Pa. 1978, NJ 1979, US Dist. Ct. NJ 1979, US Dist. Ct. Ea. Dist. Pa. 1980, US Ct Appeals 3rd Cir., US Supreme Ct. 1986. With internat. divsn. Bank of Montreal, Quebec, Canada, 1972—75; assoc. Harvey, Pennington, Herting & Renneisen, Ltd., Phila., 1977-81, Duane, Morris & Heckscher (now Duane Morris LLP), 1981-86, ptnr., 1986—, mng. ptnr. Marlton/Cherry Hill office NJ, 1992—2004, mng. ptnr. Princeton office, 2004—, team member partners bd., 1998—. Mem. life, health, accident and disability ins. com. Def. Rsch. Inst. Mem. ABA, NJ State Bar Assn., Camden County Bar Assn., Burlington County Bar Assn. Office: Duane Morris LLP PO Box 5203 Princeton NJ 08543-5203 Office Phone: 609-631-2444. Office Fax: 609-631-2401. Business E-Mail: luchak@duanemorris.com.

LUCHINI, JOSEPH S., lawyer; b. 1948; BS in Aerospace Engring. with high honors, W.Va. U., 1970; JD, Georgetown U., 1973. Bar: Va. 1973, DC 1990, US Ct. Appeals for Armed Forces 1974. Served in Judge Adv. Gen.'s Office USAF, 1973—79; with Hazel & Thomas, PC (combined with Reed Smith in 1999), 1979—99; ptnr. Reed Smith LLP, Falls Church, Va., 1999—. Va. practice group leader litig. group. Office: Reed Smith LLP 3110 Fairview Park Dr, Ste 1400 Falls Church VA 22042 Office Phone: 703-641-4274. Office Fax: 703-641-4340. Business E-Mail: jluchini@reedsmith.com.

LUCHINS, DANIEL JONATHAN, psychiatrist; b. NYC, July 1, 1948; s. Abraham Samuel and Edith (Hirsch) L.; children: Kerith, Matthew. BSc, McGill U., Montreal, Que., Can., 1971, MD, 1973. Diplomate in psychiatry and geriatric psychiatry Am. Bd. Psychiatry and Neurology. Vis. scientist NIMH, Washington, 1977-81; assoc. prof. U. Chgo., 1981—; med. coord. mental health Ill. Dept. Mental Health, Chgo., 1989-91; chief of adult psychiatry U. Chgo., 1991-93; chief clin. svcs. Office Mental Health, Ill. Dept. Human Svcs., Chgo., 1995—2005; chief pub. psychiatry U. Chgo., 1996. Dir. SGA Youth and Family Svcs., 2001—. Contbr. articles to profl. publs. Recipient A.E. Bennett award Soc. Biol. Psychiatry, Geriatric Mental Health acad. award NIMH, 1984-87, Exemplary Psychiatrist award NAMI, 1998. Fellow Am. Psychiat. Assn. (disting.); mem. Ill. Psychiat. Assn. (councillor 1989-91, pres. 1995, Am. Psychiat. Assn. rep.). Jewish. Achievements include development of criteria for hospice care for demented patients. Office: U Chgo Dept Psychiatry 5841 S Maryland Ave Chicago IL 60637-1463 Home Phone: 773-667-5947; Office Phone: 773-702-9716. Business E-Mail: danl@yoda.bsd.uchicago.edu.

LUCHOK, JOSEPH ALAN, communications executive, consultant; b. Morgantown, W.Va., May 5, 1947; s. John and Anna Luchok; m. Florence Dorsey Carver, Feb. 24, 1979. BA, W.Va. U., 1969, MA, 1971-73. Dir. debate U. Ga., 1976-83; dir. forensics Mo. Western State Coll., St. Joseph, 1983-94; program instr. CloseUp Found., Alexandria, Va., 1994-97; comm. specialist Am. Accreditation Health Care Commn., Washington, 1998-2000; comms. mgr. Health Ins. Assn. Am., Washington, 2000—02; mgr. pub. affairs comm. March of Dimes, 2004—. Keynote spkr. CloseUp Found., 2000—; pub. spkr. Mem.: Nat. Press. Club, Pub. Rels. Soc. Am., Am. Forensic Assn. Avocations: reading, travel. Home: 2924 S Buchanan St C-1 Arlington VA 22206 Office: March of Dimes 1146 19th St NW 6th Fl Washington DC 20036 Office Phone: 202-261-7582, 202-659-1800. Personal E-mail: joseph.luchok@verizon.net.

LUCHS, ALISON, curator, art historian; b. Washington, Oct. 5, 1948; d. Wallace Jr. and Barbara Ann (Baer) Luchs; m. Richard Albin Best Jr., Apr. 1, 1989; 1 child, Benjamin A. Best. BA, Vassar Coll., Poughkeepsie, NY, 1970; PhD, Johns Hopkins U., Balt., 1976. Asst. prof. Swarthmore Coll., Pa., 1976—77, Syracuse U., NY, 1977—80; rsch. asst. Ctr. Advanced Study in Visual Arts, Washington, 1980—83; asst. curator sculpture Nat. Gallery Art, Washington, 1982—89, assoc. curator early European sculpture, 1989—96, curator early European sculpture, 1996—. Author: Cestello: A Cistercian Church of the Florentine Renaissance, 1977, Tullio Lombardo and Ideal Portrait Sculpture in Renaissance Venice, 1490-1530, 1995; translator: The World of the Florentine Renaissance Artist, 1981; author: (guidebook) The Convent of Santa Maria Maddalena de' Pazzi and its Works of Art, 1990; contbr. articles to profl. publs.; co-curator (sculpture) Desiderio da Settignano, 2006—07. Grantee, Samuel H. Kress Found., 1994—95; Robert H. Smith Rsch. Leave grantee, Nat. Gallery Art, 1988, 1998, Ailsa Mellon Bruce Curatorial Sabbatical fellow, Ctr. Advanced Study Visual Arts, 1992—93, 2003. Mem.: Renaissance Soc., Coll. Art Assn. (Millard Meiss grantee 1994—95), Italian Art Soc. Avocation: historic preservation research. Office: Nat Gallery Art Sculpture Dept 2000 B South Club Dr Landover MD 20785

LUCHS, JODI IAN, ophthalmologist; b. NYC, May 26, 1965; s. Saul Myron and Marjorie Ellen Luchs; children: Ethan, Evan, Elana. BA, U. Pa., Phila., 1987; JD, Albert Einstein Coll. Medicine, Bronx, NY, 1991. Diplomate Am. Bd. Ophthalmology. Intern Mt. Sinai Med. Ctr., NYC, 1991—92; resident LI Jewish Med. Ctr., New Hyde Park, NY, 1992—95; Cornea fellow Wills Eye Hosp., Phila., 1995—96; ophthalmologist South Shore Eye Care, Wantagh, NY, 1996—; dir. dept. refractive surgery LI Jewish/North Shore U. Health Sys, Great Neck, NY, 2006—. Clin. instr. cornea svc. LI Jewish Med. Ctr.; adj. clin. asst. prof. surgery NY Coll. Osteo. Medicine; clin. trials in field; presenter, lectr. in field; mem. staff North Shore U. Hosp., Manhasset, Syosset, Plainview, LE Jewish Med. Ctr., New Island Hosp, Queens Hosp. Author (with C.J. Rapuano and T. Kim): The Requisites in Ophthalmology: Anterior Segment, 2000; contbr. articles to profl. jours. Mem. med. adv. bd. Eye Bank for Sight Restoration, NYC. Fellow: ACS, Nassau County Med. Soc., Am. Acad. Ophthalmology; mem.: LI Ophthalmol. Soc. (asst. sec./treas. 2006, sec./treas. 2007), Nassau Acad. Medicine (trustee), Am. Soc. Cataract and Refractive Surgeons, Med. Soc. State NY, NY State Ophthalmol. Soc., Internat. Soc. Refractive Surgery, Alpha Omega Alpha. Office: South Shore Eye Care 2185 Wantagh Ave Wantagh NY 11793 Office Phone: 516-785-3900. Personal E-mail: jluchs@aol.com.

LUCHSINGER, JOHN FRANCIS, JR., lawyer; b. Pensacola, Fla., Mar. 3, 1944; s. John and Marion (Bex) L.; m. Pamela I. Baumgartner, Aug. 19, 1967; children: Heather Leigh, Todd James, James Bradley. AB, Syracuse U., 1966; JD, Bklyn. Law Sch. 1971. Law clk. NY State Supreme Ct., Mineola, 1969; law intern Nassau County Dist. Atty.'s Office, Mineola, 1970; admitted to NY bar, 1971; assoc. firm Pelletreau & Pelletreau, Patchogue, NY, 1971-73; trial atty. Hiscock, Lee, Rogers, Henley & Barclay, Syracuse, NY, 1973-79; v.p., gen. counsel, sec. Farmers and Traders Life Ins. Co., Syracuse, 1987—, also bd. dirs.; adj. prof. Syracuse U. Sch. Mgmt.; guest lectr. Syracuse U. Sch. Law. V.p. Jamesville-Dewitt Bd. Edn., 1977-82; pres. Canal Ctr., Inc., 1976-77, Dewitt Cmty. Libr., 1976-77; v.p. Citizens Found., 1987-88, pres., 1989—; trustee Onondaga CC Found., 1990—, pres. bd. trustees 1996-98, chair bd. trustees 2001-03, WCNY-PBS, 2000-03; referee NY State Commn.; bd. dirs. Syracuse Symphony Orch., 2004, Crouse Health Found., 2005; pres. bd. dirs. Everson Art Mus., 1995-97, Erie Canal Mus., 2001-02. Jud. Conduct. 2d lt. Armored Corps US Army, 1967-70. Mem. Syracuse Def. Trial Lawyers Assn. (pres. 1980-81), Am. Bar Assn. (pres. Upstate NY, 1984-85), NY State Bar Assn., Onondaga County Bar Assn. (chmn. corp. sect. 1985-86), Assn. Life Ins. Counsel, Assn. Life Ins. Cos. NY, Jaycees (Jaycee of Yr. 1971-72). Clubs: Rotary (pres. 1978-79; dist. gov. 1983-84), Onondaga Golf and Country, Century (bd. govs. 1986-89), Limestone Tennis. Republican. Home: 7935 Halite Crse Fayetteville NY 13066-9687 Office: 960 James St Syracuse NY 13203-2503 Home Phone: 315-637-4235; Office Phone: 315-471-5656 233. Personal E-mail: luchsinger@prodigy.net.

LUCHT, JOHN CHARLES, management consultant, writer; b. Reedsburg, Wis., June 1, 1933; s. Carl H. and Ruth A. (Shultis) L.; m. Catherine Ann Seyler, Dec. 11, 1965 (div. 1982). BS, U. Wis., 1955, LLB, 1960. News dir. Sta. WISC-AM/FM, Madison, Wis., 1952-55; merchandising dir. The Bartell Group (radio and TV stas.), Milw., 1955-56; instr. U. Wis. Law Sch., 1959-60; TV contracts exec., account exec. J. Walter Thompson Co., NYC, 1960-64; product mgr., new products supr., dir. new product mktg. Bristol-Myers Co., NYC, 1964-69; dir. mktg. W.A. Sheaffer Pen Co., Ft. Madison, Iowa, 1969-70; gen. mgr. Tetley Tea div. Squibb Beech-Nut Inc., NYC, 1970-71; v.p. Heidrick & Struggles, NYC, 1971-77; pres. The John Lucht Consultancy, Inc., NYC, 1977—, The Viceroy Press Inc., 1987—, RiteSite.com, 1998—. Lectr. in field. Author: Rites of Passage at $100,000 to $1 Million Plus, The Insiders's Guide to Executive Job-Changing, Executive Job-Changing Workbook, Insights for the Journey—Navigating to Thrive, Enjoy and Prosper in Senior Management. Mem. Soc. Am. Bus. Editors and Writers, Internat. Assn. Corp. and Profl. Recruiters, State Bar Wis., N.Y. Bd. Trade, Assn. Exec. Search Cons., N.Y. Acad. Scis., Overseas Press Club, Met. Club, Can. Club, Phi Beta Kappa, Phi Eta Sigma, Phi Kappa Phi, Phi Delta Phi, Sigma Alpha Epsilon. Office: Worldwide Plaza West Ste 8-B 350 W 50th St New York NY 10019 Office Phone: 212-259-9211.

LUCHT, ORREN JESSE, retired mechanical engineer; b. Mora, Minn., May 2, 1927; s. Albert Adolph and Alice Marion Lucht; m. Margarete Berta Breuckner; children: Jean Amy McKeague, Jo Ann Nelson, Erich Albert, Charles Roscoe, Alane Gay. Owner Lucht Studio, Mora, 1955—68; pres. Lucht Color Lab. Inc., Mora, 1966—70, Lucht Engring. Inc., Bloomington, Minn., 1973—87, Castle Rock Mfg. Inc., Mpls., 1988—90; v.p. Internat. Precision Optics Inc., Blaine, Minn., 1988—2003; ret. Pres. East Ctrl. Minn. Photographers, 1962—64. Active Castle Rock Twp. Planning Commn., Farmington, Minn., 2006—; mem. Farmington Luth. Ch., 1997—2007. With US Army, 1946—48, WWII. Named Accredited Photographer, Minn. Profl. Photographers Assn., 1966. Mem.: Bloomington C. of C. (finalist Small Bus. Person of Yr. 1984). Achievements include 7 patents on photo finishing machines; patents in field. Avocations: photography, machine shop, machine design, woodworking, flying. Home Phone: 651-463-4540.

LUCHTERHAND, RALPH EDWARD, financial advisor; b. Portland, Oreg., Feb. 9, 1952; s. Otto Charles II and Evelyn Alice (Isaac) L.; children: Anne Michelle, Eric Alexander, Nicholas Andrew, Mistie Rose Beaudoin; m. Victoria Marie Schiffbauer, Nov. 8, 1997. BS, Portland State U., 1974, MBA, 1986. Cert. fin. planner; gen. securities broker NYSE/NSAD, registered investment prin. Mech. engr. Hyster Co., Portland, 1971-75, svc. engr., 1975-76; project engr. Lumber Systems Inc., Portland, 1976-79; prin. engr. Moore Internat., Portland, 1979-81, chief product engr., 1981-83; project engr. Irvington-Moore, Portland, 1983, chief engr., 1983-86; ind. cons. engr., 1986; engring. program mgr. Precision Castparts Corp., Portland, 1986-87; personal fin. advisor Ameriprise Fin., West Linn, Oreg., 1987—94, sr. fin. advisor, 1994—; prin. Ralph Luchterhand & Assocs. (a fin. adv. br. of Am. Express Fin. Advisors), West Linn, 2001—05; pres. Ralph Luchterhand & Co., Mulino, Oreg., 2001—. Ptnr. Bacon, Luchterhand Wilmot & Assocs. (a fin. adv. br. of Am. Express Fin. Advisors), Clackamas, Oreg., 1996-2001, br. mgr., 1999-2000; apptd. to Silver Team, 1991, Gold Team, 1994; bd. dirs. Whiskey Hill Jazz Assn., treas., 2002-05. Treas., Village Bapt. Ch., Beaverton, Oreg., 1988-91; bd. dirs. Carus Cmty. Planning Orgn., Oregon City, Oreg., 1993-99; active Rolling Hills Cmty. Ch., Tualatin, Oreg., 1995—. Mem.: Christian Fin. Profl. Network, Fin. Planning Assn. Republican. Office: Ameriprise Fin 1800 Blankenship Rd Ste 300 West Linn OR 97068 Mailing: PO Box 1216 Mulino OR 97042 E-mail: hilltop650@yahoo.com.

LUCIA, MARILYN REED, physician; b. Boston; m. Walter M. Dickie Jr., 1951 (div. 1958); m. Salvatore P. Lucia, 1959, (dec. 1984); m. C. Robert Russell, 1985 (dec. 2000); children: Elizabeth, Walter, Salvatore, Darryl. AB with highest honors, U. Calif., Berkeley, 1951; MD, U. Calif., San Francisco, 1956. Cert. in psychiatry and child psychiatry Am. Bd. Psychiatry and Neurology. Intern Stanford U. Hosp., 1956-57; NIMH fellow, resident in psychiatry Langley Porter, U. Calif., San Francisco, 1957-60; NIMH fellow, resident in child psychiatry Mt. Zion Hosp., San Francisco, 1964-66; NIMH fellow, in cmty. psychiatry U. Calif., San Francisco, 1966—68, clin. prof. psychiatry, 1982—. Founder, cons. Marilyn Reed Lucia Child Care Study Ctr., U. Calif., San Francisco; cons. Cranio-facial Ctr., U. Calif., San Francisco; No. Calif. Diagnostic Sch. for Neurologically Handicapped Children; dir. children's psychiat. svc. Contra Costa County Hosp., Martinez. Fellow Am. Psychiat. Assn. (disting. life), Am. Acad. Child Psychiatry; mem. Am. Cleft Palate Assn., San Francisco Med. Soc., Phi Beta Kappa. Office: 350 Parnassus Ave Ste 602 San Francisco CA 94117-3608

LUCID, SHANNON W., biochemist, astronaut; b. Shanghai, Jan. 14, 1943; d. Joseph Oscar and Mary Wells; m. Michael F. Lucid, 1968; children: Kawai Dawn, Shandara Michelle, Michael Kermit. BS in Chemistry, U. Okla., 1963, MS in Biochemistry, 1970, PhD in Biochemistry, 1973. Sr. lab. technician Okla. Med. Rsch. Found., 1964-66, rsch. assoc., from 1974; chemist Kerr-McGee, Oklahoma City, 1966-68; astronaut NASA Lyndon B. Johnson Space Ctr., Houston, 1979—, mission specialist flights STS-51G (Discovery), 1985, mission specialist flights STS-34 (Atlantis), 1989, mission specialist on STS-43 (Atlantis), 1991, mission specialist flight STS-58 (Columbia), 1993, mission specialist flight STS 76 & 79, 1996, mgmt., astronaut office Houston, 2003—; mission specialist stationed on Space Station Mir, 1996; chief scientist NASA Hdqs., Washington, 2003—03. Recipient Space award Aviation Week and Space Tech., 1997, Congl. Space Medal of Honor, President Bill Clinton, Order of Friendship Medal, Russian President Boris Yeltsin. Achievements include first woman to fly on the shuttle three times; remained aloft 188 days in shuttle Mir; holds the US single mission space flight endurance record on the Russian Space Station; has the most flight hours on orbit by any women and the most flight hours in orbit by any non-Russian. Avocations: flying, camping, hiking, hiking. Address: NASA Johnson Space Ctr CB-Astronaut Office Houston TX 77058*

LUCIER, P. JEFFREY, publishing executive; b. Manchester, NH, June 20, 1941; s. Paul A. and Elaine (Wilson) Fraser L.; m. Judith Margaret Akers, Dec. 21, 1963 (div. 1975); children: Kathryn Elizabeth, Amy Wilson; m. Velma Lee Frye, Nov. 27, 1976 (div. 1981); m. Susan Elizabeth Hess, May 25, 1985; children: Madalyn Antonette, Caitlin Elaine. BA, Union Coll., NY, 1963; MA, U. Chgo., 1964. Instr. English, Northwestern U., Evanston and Chgo., 1967-69; registered rep. Paine Webber, Akron, Ohio, 1969-71; asst. to pres. Banks-Baldwin Law Pub., Cleve., 1971-74, v.p. editorial, 1974-76, exec. v.p., 1977-78, pres., editor-in-chief, 1978-96; CEO, Pegasus Techs. Ld., Painesville, Ohio, 1996-98, All-Stater Pub. LLC, Columbus, Ohio, 1997-2000; chmn. STACK LLC, 2005—. Pres. The Banks-Baldwin Found. Bd. dirs. Hawken Sch., Cleve. Music Sch. Settlement, Cleve. Bot. Garden, Mus. Contemporary Art Cleve., ECity, Cleve. affiliate of Nat. Found. for Tchg. Entrepreneurship. Mem.: Cleve. Playhouse Club, Cleve. City Club. Democrat. Roman Catholic. Home Phone: 216-321-0137; Office Phone: 216-570-4863. E-mail: pjl@en.com.

LUCK, DENNIS NOEL, retired biologist, educator, researcher; b. Durban, Natal, South Africa, Dec. 8, 1939; s. Peter Burvill and Eva Annie (Taylor) L.; m. Joan Burchall, Jan. 18, 1969; 1 child, Roy Burvil. BSc, U. Natal, South Africa, 1961, MSc, 1963; DPhil, Oxford U., Oxford, Eng., 1966. Lectr. in biochemistry U. Natal, South Africa, 1966-69; vis. asst. prof. Baylor Coll. Medicine, Houston, 1969-70; asst. prof. zoology U. Tex., Austin, 1970-72; asst. prof., assoc. prof. biology Oberlin Coll., Ohio, 1972-82, prof., 1982—2006, chmn., 1995-98, prof. emeritus, 2006—. Cons. Gilford Instrument Labs., Oberlin, 1980-82, The Oberlin Sci. Co., 1989-90; fgn. expert Shanxi Agrl. U., Taigu, China, summer, 1982. Contbr. more than 20 articles to profl. jours. including Nature, Molecular Endocrinology, DNA, Procs. NAS, Biochimica et Biophysica Acta, Protein Engring.; speaker at maj. sci. meetings, 1988, 90, 94. Eleanor Roosevelt Internat. Cancer fellow Internat. Union Against Cancer, Geneva, Switzerland, 1978-79; grantee NSF, 1975-80, 1984-98. Fellow Ohio Acad. Sci.; mem. Biochem. Soc. London. Achievements include research in structure-function analysis of bovine prolactin. Home: 240 Oak St Oberlin OH 44074-1518 Office: Dept Biology Science Ctr 119 Woodland St Oberlin OH 44074 Office Phone: 440-775-8315. Business E-Mail: dennis.n.luck@oberlin.edu.

LUCK, JAMES I., foundation executive; b. Akron, Ohio, Aug. 28, 1945; s. Milton William and Gertrude (Winer) L.; children: Andrew Brewer,

Edward Aldrich, L. BA, Ohio State U., 1967; MA, U. Ga., 1970. Caseworker Franklin County Welfare Dept., Columbus, Ohio, 1967-69; dir. forensics Tex. Christian U., Ft. Worth, 1970-74; assoc. dir. Bicentennial Youth Debates, Washington, 1974-76; exec. dir. Nat. Congress on Volunteerism and Citizenship, Washington, 1976-77; fellow Acad. Contemporary Problems, Columbus, Ohio, 1977-79; exec. dir. Battelle Meml. Inst. Found., Columbus, 1980-82; pres. Columbus Found., 1981—2001, pres. emeritus, 2001—; exec. dir. Columbus Youth Found. and Ingram-White Castle Funds, 1981—2001; chmn. Am Resource Devel., LLC, Columbus, 2002—; pres., CEO Global 3E, 2003—. Co-chmn. Task Force on Citizen Edn., Washington, 1977; mediator Negotiated Investment Strategy, Columbus, 1979; chmn. Ohio Founds. Conf., 1985; cons. HEW, Peace Corps., U. Va. Author: Ohio-The Next 25 Years, 1978, Bicentennial Issue Analysis, 1975; editor: Proceedings of the Nat. Conf. on Argumentation, 1973; contbr. articles to profl. jours. Trustee Godman Guild Settlement House, Columbus, 1979-81, Am. Diabetes Assn., Ohio, 1984-88; chmn. spl. com. on displacement Columbus City Coun., 1978-80; bd. dirs. Commn. on the Future of the Professions in Soc., 1979. Mem. Donors Forum Ohio. Clubs: Capital, Columbus Club, Columbus Met., Kit-Kat. Lodges: Rotary. Avocations: travel, reading. Home: 799 Pinecliff Pl Worthington OH 43085-1906 Home Phone: 614-846-3303; Office Phone: 614-364-7111. E-mail: jluck@ard501.cm.

LUCKE, ROBERT VITO, investment company executive; b. Kingston, Pa., July 26, 1930; s. Vito Frank and Edith Ann (Adders) L.; m. Jane Ann Rushin, Aug. 16, 1952; children: Thomas, Mark, Carl. BS in Chemistry, Pa. State U., 1952; MS in Mgmt., Rensselaer Polytech Inst., 1960. Polymer chemist Uniroyal Naugatuck Chem. Div., Conn., 1954-60; comml. devel. engr. Exxon Enjay Div., Elizabeth, NJ, 1960-66; group gen. mgr. Celanese Advanced Composites, Summit, NJ, 1966-70; bus. mgr. polymer div. Hooker Chem., Burlington, NJ, 1970-74; gen. mgr. Oxy Metal Industries Environ. Equipment. Divs., Warren, Mich., 1974-79; corp. v.p., group gen. mgr. Hoover Universal Plastic Machinery Divs., Manchester, Mich., 1979-84; pres. Egan Machinery, Somerville, NJ, Bone Markem UK, Bone Cravens, England, 1984—87; pres., chief exec. officer Krauss Maffei Corp., Cin., 1987—90; pres. Adventa Global LLC, 1990—2007. Instr., Chem. Market Rsch. Assn., 1974. Author: (with others) Plastics Handbook, 1972. 1st lt. corp. engrs., 1952—54, Korea. Senatorial scholar, Pa. State U., 1948-52. Mem. Am. Chem. Soc., Soc. Plastics Engrs. (sect. engr. STDS com. 1969), Tech. Assn. Pulp Paper Industry, Comml. Devel. Assn., Assn. Corp. Growth (pres. So. Ohio Chpt, 1998). Achievements include 6 patents in field. Avocations: golf, skiing, travel, gardening. Office: Arvel LLC subs Adevnta Global LLC 2260 Heather Hill Blvd Cincinnati OH 45244-2664 Home Phone: 513-474-2999; Office Phone: 513-474-2999. Personal E-mail: wiseowl726@aol.com.

LUCKE, STEPHEN P., lawyer; b. 1957; AB in Econ. magna cum laude, Coll. Holy Cross, 1980; JD magna cum laude, Georgetown Univ., 1983. Bar: Minn. 1984, Wis. 1990. Law clerk, Hon. Myron H. Bright US Ct. Appeals (8th cir.), 1983—84; assoc. Dorsey & Whitney, Mpls., 1984—90, ptnr., trial group, co-head, ERISA litig., 1991. Mng. editor Georgetown Law Jour., 1982—83. Mem.: ABA, Hennepin County Bar Assn., Minn. State Bar Assn., Alpha Sigma Nu, Phi Beta Kappa. Office: Dorsey & Whitney LLP Ste 1500 50 S Sixth St Minneapolis MN 55402-1498 Office Phone: 612-340-2600. Office Fax: 612-340-8800. Business E-Mail: lucke.steve@dorsey.com.

LUCKER, JAY K., library consultant; b. NYC, Feb. 23, 1930; s. Joseph Jerome and Ella (Schwartz) L.; m. Marjorie Stern, Aug. 17, 1952 (dec. Aug. 1997); children— Amy Ellen, Nancy Judith. AB, Bklyn. Coll., City U. N.Y., 1951; MS, Columbia, 1952; postgrad., N.Y. U., 1955-57. Head procurement br., acquisition div. New York Pub. Library, 1954-57, first asst., acting chief, sci. and tech. div., 1957-59; asst. univ. librarian for sci. and tech., assoc. prof. Princeton U. Library, 1959-68, assoc. univ. librarian, prof., 1968-75; dir. librs. MIT, Cambridge, 1975-95; vis. prof. Grad. Sch. Libr. and Info. Sci. Simmons Coll., Boston, 1995-2001. Chmn. bd. dirs. Captain Libr. Svcs. Corp., 1972-75; vis. lectr. Drexel U. Grad. Sch. Libr. Svc., 1962-67; vice chmn. New Eng. Libr. Info. Network, 1978-79, chmn., 1980-82. Bd. dirs. Boston Libr. Consortium; mem. adv. coms. Brown U., Tufts U., Washington U., St. Louis, Libr. Congress, Engring. Info. Inc. Served with Signal Corps U.S. Army, 1952-54. Council on Library Resources fellow, 1970-71 Fellow AAAS; mem. ALA (council 1978-82), Am. Soc. Info. Sci., N.J. Library Assn. (Distinguished Service award coll. and univ. sect. 1975), Assn. Research Libraries (chmn. interlibrary loan com. 1976-80, dir. 1977-80, pres. 1980-81), Spl. Libraries Assn., Phi Beta Kappa, Alpha Phi Omega, Beta Phi Mu. Personal E-mail: jklucker@mit.edu.

LUCKERT, MARLA JO, state supreme court justice; b. Goodland, Kans., July 20, 1955; d. William Gottleib and Gladys Iona (Rohr) L.; m. Steven. K. Morse, May 25, 1980; children: Sarah, Alisa. BA, Washburn U., 1977, JD, 1980. Bar: Kans. 1980, U.S. Dist. Ct. Kans. 1980, U.S. Ct. Appeals (10th cir.) 1980. Assoc. Goodell, Stratoon, Edmond & Palmer, Topeka, 1980—92; judge Third Jud. Dist., Kans. Supreme Ct., Kans., 1992—2000, chief judge Kans., 2000—03; justice Kans. Supreme Ct., Kans., 2003—. Adj. prof. Washburn Univ. Sch. Law, Topeka, 1980-81, 1990—. Author: Kansas Consent Manual, 1988, Record Relations Guide, 1988, Kansas Law for Physicians, 1989. Pres. Mobile Meals of Topeka (Kans.), Inc., 1987-89, Mobile Meals of Topeka (Kans.) Found., 1989—; co-chair YWCA Nominating Com., Topeka, 1988-89. Recipient Woman of Excellence Award, YWCA, Topeka, Kans. Mem. ABA (co-chair young lawyers health law com. 1988-90), Am. Acad. Hosp. Attys., Kans. Assn. Hosp. Attys., Kans. Assn. Def. Counsel (bd. dirs. 1988—, disting. svc. award 1990), Kans. Bar Assn. (pres. young lawyers 1989-90, outstanding svc. award 1990), Topeka Bar Assn. (chair law day pubs. com.), Women Attys. Assn. Kans., Topeka (pres. 1988-89), Sam A. Crow Inn of Ct., Am. Judges Assn., Nat. Assn. Women Judges, Nat. Ctr. State Courts, Supreme Ct. Historical Soc., Am. Judicature Soc.; fellow Am. Bar Found., Kans. Bar Found. Office: Kansas Judicial Ctr 301 SW 10th Ave Topeka KS 66612-1507*

LUCKETT, BYRON EDWARD, JR., chaplain, retired military officer; b. Mineral Wells, Tex., Feb. 2, 1951; s. Byron Edward and Helen Alma (Hart) L.; m. Kathryn Louise Lambertson, Dec. 30, 1979; children: Florence Louise, Byron Edward III, Barbara Elizabeth, Stephanie Hart. BS, U.S. Mil. Acad., 1973; MDiv, Princeton Theol. Sem., 1982; MA, Claremont Grad. Sch., 1987. Commd. 2d lt. U.S. Army, 1973, advanced through grades to lt. col.; stationed at Camp Edwards E., Korea, 1974-75; bn. supply officer 563rd Engr. Bn., Kornwestheim, Germany, 1975-76; platoon leader, exec. officer 275th Engr. Co., Ludwigsburg, Germany, 1976-77; boy scout project officer Hdqrs., VII Corps, Stuttgart, Germany, 1977-78; student intern Moshannon Valley Larger Parish, Winburne, Pa., 1980-81; Protestant chaplain Philmont Scout Ranch, Cimarron, N.Mex., 1982; asst. pastor Immanuel Presbyn. Ch., Albuquerque, 1982-83, assoc. pastor, 1983-84; tchr. Claremont High Sch., 1985-86; Protestant chaplain 92nd Combat Support Group, Fairchild AFB, Wash., 1986-90; installation staff chaplain Pirinclik Air Station, Turkey, 1990-91; Protestant chaplain Davis-Monthan AFB, Ariz., 1991-95; dir. readiness ministries Offutt AFB, Nebr., 1995-96, sr. Protestant chaplain Nebr., 1996-98, Elmendorf AFB, Alaska, 1998-2000; wing chaplain Minot AFB, ND, 2000—01; sr. career advisor Bernard Haldane Assocs., Las Vegas, 2001—02; on-call chaplain St. Rose Dominican Hosp., Henderson, Nev., 2002—; sr. cons. IDC, Henderson, Nev., 2003—04, account exec., 2004—05; pres. Luckett Capital Group, Las Vegas, 2005—. Mem. intern program coun. Claremont (Calif.) Grad. Sch.; affiliate faculty Regis U., Las Vegas, 2003—. Contbr. articles to profl. jours. Bd. dirs. Parentcraft, Inc., Albuquerque, 1984, United Campus Ministries, Albuquerque, 1984, Proclaim Liberty, Inc., Spokane, 1987-90, Amazing Grace Ministry, Las Vegas, 2005—; bd. dirs. western region Nat. Assn. Presbyn. Scouters, Irving, Tex., 1986-89, chaplain, 1991-93; mem. N.Mex. Employer Co. in Support of the Guard and Reserve, Albuquerque, 1984, Old Baldy coun. Boy Scouts Am., 1986; chmn. Fairchild Parent Coop., Fairchild AFB, 1986-87; pres. Co. Grade Officers Coun., Fairchild AFB, 1987-88; pres. Luckett Family Found. Capt. U.S. Army Reserve; chaplain USAF Res., 1983-86; lt. col. 1998; campaign dir. combined fed. campaign, So. Nev., 2007—. Recipient Dist. Award of Merit for Disting. Svc. Boy Scouts Am., 1977, Aubrey Douglas award, Claremont Grad. U., 1986, Excellence Tchg. award, Regis U., 2007. Mem. Soc. Cin. Md., Mil. Order Fgn. Wars U.S., Civil Affairs Assn., Huguenot Soc. Tex. Presbyterian. Office: Luckett Capital Group 604 Napatree St Las Vegas NV 89144 Home Phone: 702-360-3342. Personal E-mail: ekluckett@cox.net. Business E-Mail: luckettcapital@mac.com.

LUCKEY, ALWYN HALL, lawyer; b. Biloxi, Miss., Oct. 3, 1960; s. Toxie Hall and Joy Evelyn (Smith) L.; m. Jeanne Elaine Carter, Aug. 4, 1984; children: Laurel McKay, Taylor Leah. BA in Zoology, U. Miss., 1982, JD, 1985. Bar: Miss. 1985, U.S. Dist. Ct. (so. and no. dist.) Miss. 1985, U.S. Ct. Appeals (5th cir.) 1985. Assoc. Richard F. Scruggs, Pascagoula, Miss., 1985-88, shareholder, 1988—, Asbestos Group PA, 1988-93; prin. Alwyn H. Luckey, Atty. at Law, Ocean Springs, Miss., 1993—2005, Luckey & Mullins PLLC, 2005—. V.p., bd. dirs. Marine Mgmt., Inc., Ocean Springs, Miss., 1987—. Author: Mississippi Landlord Tenant Law, 1985. Deacon First Presbyn. Ch., Ocean Springs, 1989; chmn. Dole for Pres. com., Jackson County, 1988. Mem. Am. Trial Lawyers Assn., Miss. Bar Assn., Miss. Trial Lawyers Assn., Jackson County Bar Assn., Jackson County Young Lawyers Assn. (v.p.), Ocean Springs Yacht Club, Bienville Club, Treasure Oak Country Club. Avocations: tennis, boating, travel. Office: PO Box 724 Ocean Springs MS 39566-0724

LUCKEY, DORIS WARING, civic volunteer; b. Union City, NJ, Sept. 17, 1929; d. Jay Deloss and Edna May (Ware) Waring; m. George William Luckey, Mar. 29, 1958; children: G. Robert, Jana Elizabeth, John Andrew. AB, U. Rochester, 1950; CLU, Am. Coll., Bryn Mawr, Pa., 1957. With pers. dept., supr. life dept. Travelers Ins. Co., Rochester, NY, 1952-58; agt. asst. life underwriting Mass. Mut. Ins. Co., Rochester, NY, 1958. Chair, various past offices Bd. Coop. Ednl. Svc. and State Edn. Dept. Vocat. Tech. Adv. Com., Rochester and Albany, NY, 1975—2003, pres. Rochester, 1975—85, Monroe County Sch. Bd. Assn., Rochester, 1980—81; v.p. Penfield (N.Y.) Sch., 1978—81; mem., past pres. William Warfield Scholarship Fund Bd.; coord. Young Artist Competition Penfield Symphony Orch; former adv. to bd. St. John's Home for Aging Bd., former mem. fin., pension and pers. com., former bd. dir., former exec. com.; pres. Leslie Norwood Carter Music Scholarship Fund; vol. numerous other civic, cultural, ch. and artistic orgn.; former pres. new investments United Ch. Christ, Genesee Valley, trustee ch. coun., former pres. ch. coun., former chair ch. and min. com.; property trustee Brighton United Ch. Christ, chair pastoral search com., 2001—02, co-chair investment com., co-chair long-range planning com; mem. program and mission com. Genesee Valley Assn. United Ch. Christ. Mem.: LWV (co-chmn. nominating com. Rochester Metro chpt., chair spkrs. bur. Rochester Metro chpt.), AAUW (past pres. Greater Rochester br., past bd. dirs., dist. 1 state rep.). Republican.

LUCKEY, GEORGE WILLIAM, chemist, researcher; b. Dayton, Apr. 17, 1925; s. George Paul and Olive (Lehmer) L.; m. Doris Waring, Mar. 29, 1958; children: Robert, Jana, John. BA in Chemistry, Oberlin Coll., 1947; PhD in Chemistry, U. Rochester, 1950. Rsch. and staff asst. Eastman Kodak Co., Rochester, NY, 1950-59, rsch. assoc., 1959-69, lab. mgr., rsch. fellow, 1969-86. Contbr. articles to profl. jours. Mem. Am. Chem. Soc., Am. Phys. Soc., The Electrochem. Soc., Royal Soc. Chemistry, Sigma Xi, Phi Beta Kappa. Achievements include U.S. and fgn. patents; rsch. in diagnostic imaging with x-rays by improvements in intensifying screens, films and processing systems; performance of systems for mammography, other diagnostic uses. Home: 240 Weymouth Dr Rochester NY 14625-1917

LUCKEY, ROBERT REUEL RAPHAEL, retired academic administrator; b. Houghton, NY, Nov. 19, 1917; s. James Seymour and Edith Bedell (Curtis) L.; m. Ruth Ida Brooks, Aug. 25, 1945; children: James, John, Linda, Peter, Daniel (dec.), Thomas. BS, BA, Houghton Coll., 1937; MA, N.Y. U., 1939; PhD, Cornell U., 1942; LittD, Houghton Coll., 1980; LLD, Marion Coll., 1987. Secondary tchr. Wilson (N.Y.) Cen. Sch., 1937-39; math. & physics instr. Houghton Coll., 1942, assoc. prof., prof. math. and physics, alumni dir., 1954, dir. devel., v.p. in devel.; pres. Ind. Wesleyan U. (formerly Marion (Ind.) Coll.), 1976-84, 1986-87. Pres. Seneca Council Boy Scouts Am., Olean, N.Y., 1964-65; assessor Township of Caneadea, N.Y., 1951-76. Recipient Silver Beaver award Boy Scouts Am., 1965; named Alumnus of Yr. Houghton Coll., 1976, Disting. Alumnus Houghton Coll., 1984, Sagamore of the Wabash by Gov. of Ind., 1980. Mem. Grant County C. of C. (bd. dirs. 1981-84). Republican. Wesleyan. Avocation: spectator sports. Home: PO Box 24 Houghton NY 14744-8719

LUCKMAN, SHARON GERSTEN, arts administrator; b. Sioux City, Iowa, Oct. 10, 1945; d. Robert S. and Libbie (Izen) Gersten; m. Peter Luckman, Nov. 22, 1968 (div. 1979); children: Melissa, Gregory; m. Paul Shapiro, Dec. 13, 1981. BS, U. Wis., 1967; cert. Inst. Not-For-Profit Mgmt., Columbia U., 1982. Dir. 92d St YM/YHA Dance Ctr., NYC, 1978-86; dir. devel. & new ventures Twyla Tharp Dance Found., NYC, 1986-87, exec. dir., 1988; dir. Vol. Lawyers for Arts, NYC, 1988-92; dir. devel. Alvin Ailey Dance Found., NYC, 1992—95, exec. dir., 1995—. Dance tchr. 92nd St. Y, N.Y.C., 1963-78, Nassau C.C., Garden City, N.Y., 1963-78, Long Beach (N.Y.) Pub. Schs., 1963-78; dir. Brant Lake (N.Y.) Dance and Sports Ctr., 1980-86; bd. dirs. Dance USA. Chairperson Laban/Bartenieff Inst. Movement Studies, N.Y.C., 1984-87. Democrat. Jewish. Office: Alvin Ailey Dance Foundation 405 W 55th St New York NY 10019-4402

LUCKNER, BRIAN WILLIAM, choir director, organist, composer; b. Massillon, Ohio, Apr. 22, 1959; s. William Joseph and Dorothy Margaret Luckner; m. Danielle Leanne Lang, Aug. 25, 2001; children: George William, Henry John. MusB, Oberlin Coll., 1981; MusM, U. Cin., 1983, MusD, 1992. Asst. organist Ch. of St. Joseph, Massillon, 1971—77, St. John the Baptist Cath. Ch., Canton, Ohio, 1974—75; organist, choirmaster Christ Episcopal Ch., Oberlin, 1978—81, Holy Trinity Episcopal Ch., Cin., 1981—82; dir. music, organist Ch. Guardian Angels, Cin., 1983—87; asst. liturgical music Basilica Nat. Shrine Immaculate Conception, Washington, 1987—88; dir. music, organist Cathedral St. Joseph the Workman, La Crosse, Wis., 1988—. Dir. Diocese La Crosse Choir & Chorale, La Crosse, Wis., 1995—; instr. sacred music Holy Cross Sem. House of Formation, La Crosse, Wis., 1996—2004; adj. faculty in organ, ch. music Viterbo U., Wis., 1995—97, 2005—; chmn. of conf. Roman Cath. Cathedral Musicians, 1997—2002. Composer: choral music Welcome All Wonders, 1995, If I Have Washed your Feet, 1996, O Redeemer, 1997, Hosanna to the Son of David, 1998, The Spirit of the Lord Is upon Me, 2000, Easter Gospel Acclamation, 2000, Five Psalms for the Communion Procession, 2002, May We Abide in Union, 2003, Intercessions for the Elect and the Candidates, 2004, Dominus Dixit Ad Me, 2005. Mem.: Conf. Roman Cath. Cathedral Musicians, Ch. Music Assn. Am., Soc. Cath. Liturgy, Am. Guild Organists. Avocations: carpentry, bicycling. Office: Cathedral St Joseph The Workman 530 Main St La Crosse WI 54601 Office Phone: 608-782-0322 ext. 232.

LUCKNER, HERMAN RICHARD, III, interior designer; b. Newark, Ohio, Mar. 14, 1933; s. Herman Richard and Helen (Friednour) L. BS, U. Cin., 1957. Cert. interior designer and appraiser. Interior designer Greiwe Inc., Cin., 1957-64; owner, internat. designer Designers Loft Interiors, Cin., 1964—; owner Designer Accents, Cin., 1991—. Mem. bd. adv. Ohio Valley Organ Procurement Ctr., Cin., 1987—, U. Cin. Fine Arts Collection and Hist. Southwest Ohio, 1987-97; bd. dirs. Cin. Club Travelers, 1997-2000. Mem.: Appraisers Assn. Am., Am. Soc. Interior Designers, Met. Club. Republican. Avocations: needlepoint, collecting 18th century chinese porcelain. Home and Office: 555 Compton Rd Cincinnati OH 45231-5005 Home Phone: 513-521-5434; Office Phone: 513-521-5434.

LUCKOVICH, MIKE, cartoonist; b. Seattle, 1960; BS, U. Wash., 1982. Cartoonist Greenville News, Greenville, SC; editorial cartoonist New Orleans Times-Picayune, 1984—89, Atlanta Constitution, 1989—. Cartoonist (books) Lots of Luckovich, 1996, Four More Wars, 2006, illustrator Take Them at Their Words: Startling Quotations from the G. O. P., Their Friends and a Few Others, 1994-2004, 2004. Nominee Pulitzer prize, 1986; recipient Overseas Press Club award, 1989, 1994, Nat. Headliner award, Press Club, Atlantic City, 1991, Robert F. Kennedy award, 1994, Pulitzer prize for editl. cartooning, 1995, 2006, Thomas Nast award, Overseas Press Club, 2006, Reuben award, Nat. Cartoonist Soc., 2006. Office: Atlanta Journal-Constitution PO Box 4689 Atlanta GA 30302

LUCY, DENNIS DURWOOD, JR., neurologist, educator; b. Little Rock, July 3, 1934; s. Dennis Durwood and Ann Louise (Besiegel) L.; m. Patricia Wilch, Nov. 26, 1958; children: Stephen H., Vincent A., Denise D., David D. BS, MD, U. Ark., 1959. Diplomate: Am. Bd. Psychiatry and Neurology. Intern U. Ark. Med. Scis., 1959-60, resident in internal medicine, 1960-62, resident in psychiatry, 1962-63; resident in neurology U. Iowa Hosp., 1963-64, 65-66; from instr., acting head dept. neurology to prof. U. Ark., 1964—74, prof., 1974—; chmn. Coun. Departmental Chmn., 1980—81; chief of staff Univ. Hosp., 1973—76; chmn. acad. senate U. Ark. for Med. Scis., 2002—03. Bd. dirs. Ark. chpt. Multiple Sclerosis Soc., 1965-78; mem. Ark. Council Devel. Disabilities, 1971-74; bd. dirs. Ark. chpt. Epilepsy Soc., 1972-76; bd. dirs. Holy Souls Cath. Sch., 1974-77, pres. bd., 1976-77. Recipient Golden Apple award U. Ark., 1968-69 Mem. Am. Acad. Neurology, Alpha Omega Alpha. Roman Catholic. Home: 17 Robinwood Dr Little Rock AR 72227-2241 Office: 4301 W Markham St Little Rock AR 72205-7101 Office Phone: 501-686-5135.

LUCY, WILLIAM (BILL LUCY), labor union administrator; BS engring., Univ. Calif. Berkeley. Engr. Contra Costa Co.; pres. AFSCME Local 1675; exec asst. pres. AFSCME; founder, pres. Coalition Black Trade Unionists. Named one of Most Influential Black Americans, Ebony mag., 2006. Mem.: TransAfrica (mem. bd. dir.), NAACP (mem. bd. dir.). Office: Caolition Black Trade Unionists 628 Desoto Ave Clarksdale MS 38614 Office Phone: 662-627-6340.

LUCZO, STEPHEN J., computer equipment company executive; Sr. mng. dir. fin., co-head Bear Stearns Global Tech. Group, 1993; exec. v.p. corp. devel. Seagate Software; sr. mng. dir. fin. Bear Stearns; exec. v.p. corp. devel. Seagate Tech., Inc., Scotts Valley, Calif., 1993—97, pres., 1997—98, pres., CEO, 1998—2002, chmn., pres., CEO, 2002—04, chmn., 2004—. Bd. dir. Crystal Decisions Inc., e2open. Office: Seagate Tech Inc 920 Disc Dr Scotts Valley CA 95066-4542

LUDACRIS, (CHRIS BRIDGES), musician, actor; b. Champaign, Ill., Sept. 11, 1977; CEO Disturbing Tha Peace Records; DJ & radio personality Hot 97.5-FM, Atlanta. Musician: (albums) Incognegro, 1999, Back for the First Time, 2000, Word of Mouf, 2001, Chicken-N-Beer, 2003, Red Light District, 2004, Disturbing tha Peace, 2006, Release Therapy, 2006 (Grammy award for Best Rap Album, 2007), (with Disturbing Tha Peace) Golden Grain, 2002, Disturbing tha Peace, 2005, (songs) Money Maker, 2006 (Grammy award for Best Rap Song, 2007); actor: (films) The Wash, 2001, 2 Fast 2 Furios, 2003, Crash, 2004, Hustle and Flow, 2005; (TV series) Chappelle's Show, 2004, Saturday Night Live, 2005; composer: (films) The Fast and the Furious, 2001, Rush Hour 2, 2001, How High, 2001. Co-founder, chmn. & CEO The Ludacris Found., Atlanta, 2001. Co-recipient Best Rap/Sung Collaboration award for Yeah, Grammy Awards, 2005, (with Mary J. Blige) Best Collaboration for Runaway Love, Black Entertainment TV (BET) Awards, 2007; recipient Rap Song of the Year, Billboard Awards, 2005, Outstanding Performance by a Cast in a Motion Picture, Screen Actors Guild, 2006. Office: The Ludacris Foundation PO Box 768511 Roswell GA 30076*

LUDDEN, JOHN FRANKLIN, retired economist; b. Michigan City, Ind., May 6, 1930; BS in Econs., U. Wis., 1952, MS in Econs., 1955; postgrad., U. Mich., 1955-59. Wage and hour investigator U.S. Dept. Labor, 1960, mgmt. intern, 1960-61, labor economist, 1963; economist, instr. U.S. Bur. of Labor Statis., 1961-63; economist Office of Internat. Ops. IRS, 1963-68, fin. economist Audit div., 1968-86, fin. economist Office of the Asst. Commr. Internat., 1986-95; ret., 1995. With US Army, 1952—54. Recipient Spl. Svc. award US Dept. Treasury, 1967-68, 87, Spl. Achievement award, 1984, Spl. Act award, 1990, Albert Gallatin award, 1995.

LUDDINGTON, BETTY WALLES, retired multi-media specialist; b. Tampa, Fla., May 11, 1936; d. Edward Alvin and Ruby Mae (Hiott) L.; m. Robert Morris Schmidt, Sept. 20, 1957 (div. Dec. 1981); children: Irene Schmidt-Losat, Daniel Carl Schmidt. *Betty Luddington, school librarian media specialist, lives her dream of being surrounded by books which were scarce during her childhood. After twenty three years, she returned to college to earn BA, MA, and Eds degrees. In 1987, Betty had the good fortune to visit Luddington, England, to see the land where her ancestors may have lived. This special trip included climbing the Wallace Monument and having tea in the Dylan Thomas' Boathouse. Betty's life continues to be enriched with daughter Irene Losat's twin sons, Nicholas and Ryan, and son U.S. Army Capt. Daniel Schmidt's daughters, Kristen and Kayla, and son, Colin, while her quaint bungalow, "Luddington Cottage," reflects her eclectic style. Dreams are Wonderful!* AA, U. South Fla., 1979, BA in Am. Studies and History, 1980, MA in Libr., Media and Info. Studies, 1982, EdS in Gifted Edn., 1986. Cert. tchr. media and gifted edn., Fla. Media intern Witter Elem. Sch., spring 1982; media specialist Twin Lakes Elem. Sch., 1982-84, Just Elem. Sch., 1984-87, Blake Jr. H.S., 1987-88, Dowdell Jr. H.S. (now Dowdell Mid. Sch.), 1988—2005; ret., 2005. Educator Saturday enrichment program for gifted children U. South Fla., springs 1980, 84, 85; participant pilot summer program in reading and visual arts Just Elem. Sch., 1987; educator gifted edn. program in visual and performing arts Kingswood Elem. Sch., summers 1985, 86, gifted edn. program in video camera Apollo Beach Elem. Sch., summer 1989, Gifted Enrichment Prog. Imagi-lympics 2012, Maniscalco Elem. Sch., 1998, others. Author: (poetry) Aaron Tippin: A Hillbilly Knight, 1993, numerous poems; composer Luddington Cottage, 2004; contbr. articles to profl. jours. Parent vol. media ctr. Witter Elem. Sch., 1976-78; tchr. sponsor Storytelling Club, Dowdell Jr. H.S., 1994-95; news media liaison, tchr. vol. Dowdell Jr. H.S., 1993-96. Recipient Student Affairs Golden Signet award U. South Fla., 1980, Parent award for continuing support of Fla. chpt. # 39 Am. Indsl. Arts Student Assn., 1987-88, Editor's Choice award Nat. Libr. of Poetry, 1996; nominee Tchr. of Month, Sta. WTSP-TV, 1994; recognized for contbn. of motivational activity for Sunshine State Young Reader's Award program Fla. Assn. for Media in Edn., Inc., 1985; named to Internat. Poetry Hall of Fame, 1996. Mem. Internat. Soc. Poets (Disting. mem. 1995), Hillsborough Classrm. Tchrs. Assn. (grantee 1988, 90), Hillsborough Assn. Sch. Libr. Media Specialists, Clan Wallace Soc. (life), Phi Kappa Phi, Kappa Delta Pi, Phi Alpha Theta (pres., v.p., rep. to honors coun. 1980, 81, Outstanding Student award), Omicron Delta Kappa (treas., chairperson, del., mem. selection com. 1981, Leslie Lynn Walbolt book award), Pi Gamma Mu. Episcopalian. Avocations: poetry, books, cats, country music. Home: 1032 E Robson St Tampa FL 33604-4344

LUDES, JACOB, III, educational association administrator; B, SUNY, Fredonia, 1964; MA, State U. Buffalo, 1966; student, SUNY, Fredonia, 1966, U. Conn., 1974, SUNY, Fredonia, 1975—77, U. NH, 1984; LHD (hon.), Endicott Coll., 2004. Coord. social sci. K-12 Westfield Acad. and Ctrl. Sch., 1966—76; asst. HS prin. Fredonia, NY, 1976—78; prin. Manchester HS, Conn., 1978—89; supt. Montville Pub. Schs., Conn., 1989—99; exec. dir., CEO New Eng. Assn. Schs. and Colls., Inc., 1999—. Lectr. higher edn., faculty mem. Jamestown CC, 1969—73, State U. Coll., Fredonia, NY, 1975—78, Fredonia, 1995, So. Conn. State U., 1992—94. Bd. dirs. Savings Bank Manchester, Conn., 1984. Recipient Outstanding Young Educator award, NY State, 1969, Conn. Prin. of Yr., 1984—85; Kettering Found. Fellowship, U. NH, 1984. Mem.: Con. Assn. Pub. Sch. Supt. (bd. mem. 1996—97), New Eng. Assn. Schs. and Colls. (chmn., com. on internat./am. sch. abroad 1994—95), Conn. Assn. Secondary Sch. (treas. 1988—89), Southeastern Conn. Assn. Sch. Adminstr. (sec. 1993, pres. 1996), The Headmasters Assn. (mem. 1985—), Conn. Interscholastic Athletic Conf. (mem. 1980—, chmn. 1985—89), NY Social Studies Supervisory Assn. (pres. 1977, 1978), Phi Delta Kappa. Office: New Eng Assn Schs and Colls 209 Burlington Rd Ste 201 Bedford MA 01730-1433 Office Phone: 781-271-0022. Office Fax: 781-271-0950.*

LUDINGTON, THOMAS LAMSON, federal judge; b. Midland, Mich., Dec. 28, 1953; s. John S. and Dorothy (Lamson) L.; m. Katrina McGuire, Sept. 20, 1986. BA, Albion Coll., Mich., 1976; JD, U. San Diego, 1979. Bar: Calif. 1980, Mich. 1981. Assoc. Currie & Kendall, P.C., Midland, 1979-2000; cir. ct. judge Midland County Ct. House, Mich., 2000—06; dist. judge US Dist. Ct. (Ea. dist.) Mich., Bay City, 2006—. Mem. hearing panel Atty. Discipline Bd., Detroit, 1987—. Bd. dirs. Jr. Achievement of Midland County, Gerstacker Found.; mem. Midland Found.; bd. trustees Saginaw Valley State U. Found., Albion Coll. Mem. ABA, State Bar Mich., State Bar Calif., Midland County Bar Assn., Assn. Trial Lawyers Am., Nat. Order Barristers. Methodist. Office: US Dist Ct PO Box 913 Bay City MI 48707 Office Phone: 989-894-8810.

LUDMERER, KENNETH MARC, medical educator; b. Long Beach, Calif., Jan. 13, 1947; s. Sol and Norma (Helfer) L.; m. Loren Rae Starobin, Aug. 9, 1987. AB, Harvard U., 1968; MA, Johns Hopkins U., 1971, MD, 1973. Med. resident, fellow Washington U., St. Louis, 1973-78; chief resident internal medicine Barnes Hosp., St. Louis, 1978-79; asst. prof. medicine, asst. prof. history Faculty Arts and Scis. Washington U., St. Louis, 1979-86, assoc. prof. medicine, assoc. prof. history, 1986-92, prof. medicine, prof. history, 1992—. Clin. scholars adv. com. mem. Robert Wood Johnson Found., Princeton, N.J., 1988-92; new pathway program evaluation com. mem. Assn. Am. Med. Colls., 1986-88; mem. nat. adv. com. Robert Wood Johnson Found. Clin. Scholars Program, Princeton, N.J., 1988-92; mem. adv. bd. Culpeper Found. Program in Med. Humanities, Stanford, Conn., 1992-93; mem. task force on med. edn. Acadia Inst.-Med. Coll. Pa., Phila., 1992-96; mem. vis. com. Harvard Med. Sch., Boston, 2000-2002, North Shore-L.I. Jewish Health Sys., Manhasset, N.Y., 2003—; med. edn. cons. numerous schs., hosps., profl. orgns., state govts., 2000—. Author: Genetics and American Society: A Historical Appraisal, 1972, Learning to Heal: The Development of American Medical Education, 1985, Time to Heal: American Medical Education from the Turn of the Century to the Era of Managed Care, 1999 (William Welch medal 2004); mem. editl. bd. Am. Jour. Medicine, 1981-96, Jour. History Medicine, 1981-83, 88-90, The Pharos, 1986—, History Edn. Quar., 1993-96, Annals Internal Medicine, 1993—. Med. adv. com. St. Louis Sci. Ctr., 1985-87; trustee Mo. Hist. Soc., St. Louis, 1987-93, St. Louis History Mus., 1987-93, Jewish Fedn. St. Louis, 2002—, Sommers Children's Welfare Bur., St. Louis, 2000—; chair cmty. rsch. peer rev. com. St. Louis Heart Assn., 1988-89. Faculty scholar gen. internal medicine Henry J. Kaiser Family Found., 1981-86; recipient Rsch. award Joseph Macy Jr. Found., 1989-96. Master ACP (com. on publ. policy 1988-93, Tchg. and Rsch. scholar 1980-83); fellow AAAS, Am. Acad. Arts and Scis. (Midwest coun.); mem. Assn. Am. Physicians, Am. Clin. and Climatol. Assn., Am. Assn. History Medicine (coun. 1984-87, 2000—, v.p. 2000-02, pres. 2002-04), Am. Fedn. for Clin. Rsch., History Sci. Soc., Am. Osler Soc. (bd. govs. 1988-96, v.p. 1992-94, pres. 1994-95), Phi Beta Kappa, Alpha Omega Alpha, Sigma Xi. Avocations: music, running, travel. Home: 42 Rio Vista Dr Saint Louis MO 63124-1745 Office: Washington U Sch Medicine Dept Medicine Box 8066 660 S Euclid Ave Saint Louis MO 63110 Business E-Mail: kludmere@im.wustl.edu.

LUDOLF, MARILYN MARIE KEATON, lay worker; b. Morganton, NC, July 19, 1932; d. Charles Jefferson and Dora Esther (Whitener) Keaton; m. Edwin Forrest Ludolf, Dec. 22, 1957; children: David Forrest, Jonathan Charles. BA, Lenoir Rhyne, 1954. Youth worker Cen. Bapt. Ch., Greenville, SC, 1964-71, Park Bapt. Ch., Rock Hill, SC, 1958-64; with coll. students Becks Bapt. Ch., Winston Salem, NC, 1971-89; lay worker singles Calvary Bapt. Ch., Winston Salem, 1989—. Youth seminar leader youth activities Park Bapt., Rock Hill, S.C.; youth-Sunday sch. Tng. Union-All areas of Ch. Work, Greenville, S.C. and Winston Salem, N.C.; pub. spkr., sem. leader, Women's Conf. Keynoter. Author: Freed by Faith, 1995; contbr. articles to profl. jours. Chmn. Christian Women's Club Luncheon, Winston Salem, 2000-2002. Mem. Old Town Woman's Club (pres. 1975-77, Woman of Yr. 1977). Republican. Home: 3745 Whitehaven Rd Winston Salem NC 27106-2530 Personal E-mail: eludolf@prodigy.net. *Enjoy life. This is Not a Dress Rehearsal. It is a temporary assignment. We each choose our behavior daily. Choose life! The greatest decision I ever made was to let go and let God lead in my life!.*

LUDROF, JEFFREY A., insurance company executive; b. Allentown, Pa. BSBA, Bloomsburg U. CPCU. From claims adjuster to dist. sales mgr. Erie Ins. Group, Allentown, 1981—89, asst. v.p., mgr. Erie, 1989—93, from regional v.p. to exec. v.p. ins. ops., 1993—2002, pres., CEO, 2002—. Bd. dirs. Ins. Inst. for Hwy. Safety. Bd. dirs. Erie Regional Chamber and Growth Partnership. Mem.: Nat. Assn. Ind. Insurers (bd. dirs., bd. govs.), Soc. Cert. Ins. Counselors, Soc. Chartered Property Casualty Underwriters. Office: Erie Ins Group 100 Erie Insurance Pl Erie PA 16530*

LUDWIG, CHRISTA, retired mezzo soprano; b. Berlin; d. Anton and Eugenie (Besalla) L.; m. Walter Berry, Sept. 29, 1957 (div. 1970); 1 son, Wolfgang; m. Paul-Emile Deiber, Mar. 3, 1972. Student German schs. Prof. H.C. Senat, Berlin, 1995. Hon. mem. Vienna Philharm., 1995. Appeared at Staedtische Buehnenm, Frankfurt, W. Ger., 1946-52, Landestheatre, Darmstadt, W. Ger., 1952-54, Hannover, W. Ger., 1954-55, Vienna (Austria) State Opera, 1955—, Medaille, Ville de Paris, 1993, Shibuya-Price, Japan, 1993, others, U.S. appearances include Avery Fisher Hall, N.Y.C., 1978, Lyric Opera, Chgo., 1959-60, 70-71, 73-74, Philharmonic Hall, N.Y.C., 1968, 69, 72, 74, Goldene Ehrennadel Landstadt, Vienna, 1997, others; guest artist London, Buenos Aires, Munich, Berlin, Tokyo, Salzburg Festival, Athens Festival, Saratoga Festival, Hunter Coll., Met. Mus., Scala Milano, Expo 67, Montreal, and others; rec. artist; author: (biography) In My Own Voice. Decorated Commdr. des Arts et des Lettres, France, 1988, Goldenes Ehren Zeichen Stadt, Salzburg, 1988, Goldene Ehrennadel Stadt und Land, Wien, Austria, 1988, Ordre Pour le Merit, France, 1997, France Officier Légion d'Honneur, 2004, Grosses Bundesverdienst Krewz, 2004; chevalier Legion d'Honneur, France, 1989; recipient Mozart medal, Mahler medal, Hugo Wolf medal, Fidelio medal Opera Wien, 1991, Shibuya prize Japan, 1993, Medaille ville Paris, 1993, Medaille Ville de Dijon, 1993, Echo Deutscher Preis, 1994, Karajan preis, Berliner Bär, 1994, Grosses Ehrenzeichen Osterreich, 1994, Ehrenmitglied der Wiener Philharm., Silver Rose, Vienna Philharm., Golden Ring, Vienna Staatsoper, Musician of Yr. award Musical Am., 1994, Cordandeur Pour le Merit France, 1997, Grosses Bundesverdienstivirez, Germany, 2004; named Kammersaengerin, Govt. of Austria, 1962. Mem. NARAS, Legion D'Honneur (officer 2003-).

LUDWIG, DAVID S., endocrinologist; b. LA, Calif., Dec. 24, 1957; PhD, Stanford U. Sch. Medicine, Calif., 1988, MD, 1990. Cert. Pediatrics, Endocrinology. Intern, pediatrics Children's Hosp. Boston, Mass., 1990—91, resident, pediatrics Mass., 1991—93, fellow, pediatric endocrinology Mass., 1993—95, attending physician Mass., 1995—, dir. obesity program Mass., 1998—, assoc. prof. pediatrics Mass., 2003—. Developed Optimal Weight for Life Program; serves as prin. or co-investigator of several epidemiological and clin. studies to identify dietary factors that contribute to obesity. Contbr. articles to profl. jours. Office: Childrens Hosp Boston Divsn Endocrinology LO-624 300 Longwood Ave Boston MA 02115 Office Phone: 617-355-5159, 617-355-4878. Office Fax: 617-730-0505.

LUDWIG, EDMUND VINCENT, federal judge; b. Phila., May 20, 1928; s. Henry and Ruth (Viner) L.; children: Edmund Jr., John, Sarah, David. AB, Harvard U., Cambridge, Mass., 1949, LLB, 1952. Assoc. Duane, Morris & Heckscher, Phila., 1956-59; ptnr. Barnes, Biester & Ludwig, Doylestown, Pa., 1959-68; judge Common Pleas Ct., Bucks County, Pa., 1968-85, US Dist. Ct. (ea. dist.), Phila., 1985—. Faculty Pa. Coll. of the Judiciary, 1974-85; presenter Villanova U. Law Sch., Pa., 1975-80, lectr., 1984-97; vis. lectr. Temple Law Sch., 1977-80; clin. assoc. prof. Hahnemann U., Phila., 1977-85; mem. Pa. Juvenile Ct. Judge's Commn., 1978-85; chmn. Pa. Chief Justice's Ednl. Com., 1984-85; pres. Pa. Conf. State Trial Judges, 1981-82; co-chmn. 3d cir. task force on counsel for ind. litigants in civil cases, 1998; jurist in residence, Drexel U., Coll. of Law, 2006-. Contbr. articles to profl. jours. Chmn. Children and Youth Adv. Com., Bucks County, 1978-83; mem. Pa. Adv. Com. on Mental Health and Mental Retardation, 1980-85; founder, bd. dirs. Today, Inc., Newtown, Pa., 1971-85, Probation Vols., Bucks County, 1971-81; bd. dirs. New Directions for Women, Del. Valley, 1988—; mem. Pa. Joint Coun. Criminal Justice, Inc., 1979-80; mem. Joint Family Law Coun. Pa., 1979-85; vice chmn. Human Services Council Bucks County, 1979-81; mem. Com. to Study Unified Jud. System Pa., 1980-82, Pa. Legislative Task Force on Mental Health Laws, 1986-87; chmn. Juvenile Justice Alliance, Phila., 1992—; co-chmn. Doylestown Revitalization Bd., Pa., 1993-96; mem. 3d cir. task force on equal treatment in the cts., 1995-97; chmn. Doylestown (Pa.) Hist. Soc., 1995—. Recipient Disting. Svc. award Bucks County Corrections Assn., 1978, Spl. Svc. award Big. Bros., 1989, Humanitarian award United Way Bucks County, 1980, Founder's award Vol. Svcs., 1982, Spl. award Bucks County Juvenile Ct., 1985, Humanitarian award Ctrl. Bucks County C. of C., 1994, Disting. Jurist award John Peter Zenger Soc., 2000; Wasserstein Pub. Interest fellow Harvard Law Sch., 1996-97. Mem. ABA, Pa. Bar Assn. (chmn. com. legal svcs. to disabled 1990-92), Phila. Bar Assn. (pro bono pub. award 1998, Pub. Interest Disting. Svc. award 1998, Justice Brennan Disting. Jurist award 2005), Fed. Bar Assn. (hon.), Harvard Club (NYC and Phila., v.p. 1979-80), Harvard Law Sch. Assn. (exec. com. 1993—), Fed. Judges Assn. (bd. dirs. 1998—, v.p., mem. chmn. 1999—), US Jud. Conf. (com. on ct. adminstrn. and case mgmt.), Am. Law Inst., Pa. Task Force on Medical Malpractice. Office: US Dist E Dist PA US Cthse 601 Market St # 12614 Philadelphia PA 19106-1775 Office Phone: 215-580-2030. Personal E-mail: evl164@aol.com. Business E-Mail: Chambers_of_Judge__Edmund_V._Ludwig@paed.uscourts.gov.

LUDWIG, EDWARD J., medical technology executive; Grad., Holy Cross Coll., Columbia U. Bus. Sch. In mgmt. Becton, Dickinson and Co., Franklin Lakes, NJ, 1979—87, corp. planning & devel. mgr., 1987—89, pres. diagnostics divsn. Balt., 1989—94, sr. v.p. fin., CFO Franklin Lakes, NJ, 1995—99, exec. v.p., 1998—99, pres., 1999—, CEO, 2000—, chmn. bd., 2002—. Bd. dirs. Aetna; chmn. HealthCare Inst. of NJ. Trustee Johns Hopkins U.; mem. adv. bd. Johns Hopkins Bloomberg Sch. of Public Health; trustee Hackensack U. Medical Ctr., Coll. of Holy Cross; bd. dirs. US Fund for UNICEF. Mem.: Advanced Medical Tech. Assn. (chmn.-elect, chair bd. comt. tech. and regulation). Office: BD 1 Becton Dr Franklin Lakes NJ 07417-1815*

LUDWIG, EUGENE ALLAN, financial consultant, lawyer, former US Comptroller of the Currency; b. Bklyn., Apr. 11, 1946; s. Jacob and Louise (Rabiner) L.; m. Carol Lynn Friedman, Mar. 11, 1978; children: Abigail Sarah, Elizabeth Madelaine Cathleen, David Maxwell. BA magna cum laude, Haverford Coll., 1968; BA, MA, Oxford U., Eng., 1970; LLB, Yale U., 1973. Bar: D.C. 1973. Assoc. Covington & Burling, Washington, 1973-81, ptnr., 1981-93; comptr. of the currency Dept. of the Treasury, Washington, 1993-98; vice chmn. Bankers Trust, New York, 1998—; founder, CEO Promontory Fin. Group, Washington, 2000—. Pres. Yale Legis. Svcs., 1972-73; guest lectr. Harvard U., Georgetown U., 1974-77, 79, Yale U., 1989. Editor Yale Law Jour., 1972-73; mem. editorial bd., Jour. Internat. Banking Law, 1989; contbr. articles to profl. jours. Office: Promontory Fin Group 1201 Pennsylvania Ave NW Washington DC 20004 Office Phone: 202-662-6980. Business E-Mail: eludwig@promontory.com.

LUDWIG, GEORGE HARRY, retired physicist, electrical engineer; b. Johnson County, Iowa, Nov. 13, 1927; s. George McKinley and Alice (Helm) Ludwig; m. Rosalie F. Vickers, July 21, 1950; children: Barbara Rose, Sharon Lee Taylor, George Vickers, Kathy Ann Ramsay. BA in Physics cum laude, U. Iowa, 1956, MS, 1959, PhD in Elec. Engring., 1960. Head fields and particles instrumentation sect. Goddard Space Flight Center, NASA, 1960-65, chief info. processing div., 1965-71, assoc. dir. for data ops., 1971-72; dir. systems integration Nat. Environ. Satellite Service, NOAA, 1972-75, dir. ops., 1975-80, tech. dir., 1980; sr. scientist Environ. Rsch. Labs., NOAA, Boulder, Colo., 1980-81, dir. Environ. Rsch. Labs., 1981-83; asst. to chief scientist NASA Hdqrs., 1983-84; ind. cons. data mgmt. and space sta. design, 1983-92; sr. rsch. assoc. Lab. for Atmospheric and Space Physics, U. Colo., 1985-91; ret., 1991. Vis. sr. scientist NASA hdqrs. Calif. Inst. Tech., 1989—91; prin. designer radiation detection instrumentation for numerous sci. spacecraft including Explorer I, 1956—65; co-discoverer Van Allen radiation belts; expert on NASA sci. and applications rsch. data processing; overseer devel. and operation U.S. Nat. Environ. Satellite Sys. with its GOES and Tiros-N Spacecraft, 1972—80; dir. atmospheric and oceanic rsch. programs NOAA, 1981—83. Served from pvt to capt. USAF, 1946—52, pilot USAF, 1948—52. Named Van Allen scholar, 1958, rsch. fellow, U.S. Steel Found., 1958—60; recipient Exceptional Svc. medal, NASA, 1969, Program Adminstrn. and Mgmt. award, NOAA, 1977, Exceptional Sci. Achievement medal, NASA, 1984. Mem.: Am. Geophys. Union (life), IEEE (sr., life), Torch Club, Eta Kappa Nu, Phi Eta Sigma, Sigma Xi, Phi Beta Kappa. Home: 215 Aspen Trl Winchester VA 22602-1404 Personal E-mail: ludwiggh@visuallink.com.

LUDWIG, LAURA LONSHEIN, poet; b. Bklyn., July 26, 1955; d. Howard Lonshein, Gloria Lonshein; m. Ray Ludwig. Student, Franconia Coll., 1975—77. Writer Self-Employed, New York, NY, 1991—. Resident poet Joe Franklin Memory Lane Radio Show, WOR-AM, New York City, 1999—; screenwriter Joe Franklin Prodns., Inc., New York City, 1999—. Author (poetry, satires): Robo-Sapiens, 2001; author: (screenplays) Sounds Like a Plot, 2001, (novels) Reflections for the Renaissance, 2004, The Haunted House and the Stolen Gold. Gulliver of New York, 2006, (plays) The Stolen Gold, 2006; co-author (with Richard Ornstein and Jerome C. Smollen): Of the Desk; prodr.(actress): classical concerts, ballet, opera, stage, short screenplays and T.V. programs,: (TV series) Earth is not on Tape. Recipient Guardian Angel award, Hope for Children Found., 1999; grantee, N.Y. State Coun. for the Arts. Home: 71 Joel M Austin Rd N Cairo NY 12413 Office Phone: 518-622-9747.

LUDWIG, L(OWELL) MARK, social studies educator; b. Estevan, Can., Jan. 2, 1933; s. Daniel Robert and Minette Louise (Baue) L.; m. Elizabeth Ann Maimone, Nov. 25, 1968 (div. Oct. 1979); 1 child, Lara Elizabeth; m. Marlyn Ginsburg Josselson, Jan. 6, 1991. AB in Govt., Valparaiso U., 1959; BS in Edn., Kent State U., 1962, MA in History, 1967, PhD in Edn., 1976. Cert. tchr., Ohio. Tchr. social studies Nordonia H.S., Northfield, Ohio, 1959-69; prof. social scis. Cuyahoga Cmty. Coll., Cleve., 1970-86; adj. prof. Cleve. State U., 1987-89; program mgr. U.S. Dept. of Navy, Cleve., 1989-91; quality improvement advisor U.S. Dept. Def., Cleve., 1991-95; emeritus prof. Cuyahoga Cmty. Coll., 1989—, adj. prof., 1996—, assoc. dean, liberal arts, 2004—. Author: Introduction to Social Science, A Personalized course, Vols. I & II, 1977-78, The Urban Mix: Cultural Groups in American Cities, 2004; contbr. articles to sci. and profl. jours. Fulbright fellow U.S. Dept. Edn., 1963, 72, 74. Democrat. Lutheran. Avocations: reading, highpointing, golf, hiking, travel. Home: 3675 Traynham Rd Shaker Heights OH 44122

LUDWIG, RICHARD JOSEPH, small business owner; b. Lakewood, Ohio, July 28, 1937; s. Mathew Joseph and Catherine Elizabeth (Sepich) L.; m. Erleen Catherine Halambeck Ramus, July 22, 1977; children: Charleen, Tracey, Charles, Cassandra. Student, Ohio State U., 1955-59; BBA Fenn Coll., Cleve. State U, 1963. C.P.A., Ohio. Sr. acct. Ernst & Whinney, Cleve., 1964-66; supervising acct. Ernst & Young, 1966-70; asst. treas. Midland Ross Corp., Cleve., 1970-71, treas., 1971-76; v.p. fin., treas. U.S. Realty Investments, 1976-78, v.p.-fin., chief fin. officer, 1978-79; owner Boston Mills Ski Resort, Inc., Peninsula, Ohio, 1979—2002; ptnr. White Oak Winery, Healdsburg, Calif., 1988—; owner Brandywine Ski Resort, Inc., Sagamore Hills, Ohio, 1990—2002; ptnr. Honor Mansion, Healdsburg, 2003—. Mem. Firestone Country Club (Akron, Ohio), Black Diamond Ranch Club (Lecanto, Fla.), Mayacama Golf Club (Santa Rosa, Calif.), The Club at Mediterra (Naples), Stonewater Golf Club (Highland Heights, Ohio). Home: 15911 Roseto Way Naples FL 34110

LUDWIG, STEPHEN, pediatrics and emergency medicine educator; b. Phila., Nov. 12, 1945; m. Zella Wolgin, 1968; children: Susannah, Elisa, Aubrey. BA with honors, Pa. State U., 1966, BS, 1967; MD, Temple U., 1971. Diplomate Am. Bd. Pediat., Nat. Bd. Med. Examiners; cert. pediat. emergency medicine, CPR advanced life support, ATLS instr., PALS. Intern and resident pediat. Children's Hosp. Nat. Med. Ctr., Washington, 1971-74, chief resident, 1973-74; assoc. pediat. U. Pa. Sch. Medicine, Phila. Gen. Hosp., 1974-76; asst. prof. pediat. U. Pa. Sch. Medicine, Children's Hosp. Phila., 1976-83, assoc. prof. pediat., 1983-89; prof. pediat. U. Pa. Sch. Medicine, 1989—, prof. emergency medicine, 1994—. Asst. physician The Children's Hosp. Phila., 1974-76, sr. physician, 1979—, divsn. chief gen. pediat., 1988-95, assoc. physician-in-chief for med. edn. dept. pediat., 1995—, sec. med./dental staff, 1986-88, v.p. med./dental staff, 1988-90, exec. com. dept. pediat., 1993—,; attending physician, dir. in-patient svcs. Phila. Gen. Hosp., 1974-76, asst. chief svc. pediat. dept., 1989—; lectr. in field. Editor-in-chief Children's Doctors, 1995—; co-editor-in-chief Pediat. Emergency Care, 1985—; mem. editl. bd. Pediat. Emergency and Critical Care, 1987—, Jour. Ambulatory Pediat. Assn., 1998—; adv. editl. bd. Pediat. Emergency Trends, 1986—; contbg. editor Yearbook of Emergency Medicine, 1988-93; reviewer Clin. Pediat., 1979-93, Pediat., 1980—, Jour. AMA, 1986—, Yearbook Pediat., 1990—, Annals Emergency Medicine, 1990—, Archives Pediat. and Adolescent Medicine, 1992—; contbr. chpts. to books and articles to profl. jours. Grantee Robert Wood Johnson Found., 1982-83, 82-84, 85-87. Mem. Internat. Soc. Child Abuse and Neglect, Am. Acad. Pediat. (chmn. emergency medicine sect. 1984-86, chmn. com. on pediat. emergency medicine 1988-92, exec. bd. sect. on child abuse, membership chmn. 1988-90, Career Achievement award sect. pediat. emergency medicine 1992), Am. Pediat. Soc., Am. Pediat. Assn. (exec. bd. 1989-92, founding mem. pediat. emergency medicine interest group 1989—), Am. Bd. Pediat. (program dirs. com.), Am. Profl. Soc. Against Child Abuse, Am. Coll. Emergency Physician (co-chmn. edn. com. Pa. chpt. 1980-88, treas., co-chmn. edn. com. Pa. chpt. 1986-89), Ambulatory Pediat. Assn. (Nat. Tchg. award 1988), Phila. Emergency Physicians Soc. (steering com.), Phila. Pediat. Soc., Univ. Assn. for Emergency Medicine, Soc. Tchrs. Emergency Medicine, Phila. Trauma Consortium, Pediat. Emergency Medicine Fellowship Dirs. (chmn. 1984-87), Soc. for Pediat. Trauma (charter), Soc. for Pediat. Emergency Medicine (charter), Assn. Pediat. Program Dirs., Helfer Soc. (founder). Office Phone: 215-590-2162. Business E-Mail: ludwig@email.chop.edu.

LUDZIK, STEVE, professional hockey coach; m. Mary Ann Ludzik; children: Stephen, Ryan. Hockey player Niagara Falls Flyers, Ont. Hockey League, 1981-82, Chgo. Blackhaws, NHL, 1982-88, Buffalo Sabres, NHL, 1988-89, Am. Hockey League's Rochester Americans, 1989-92; coach Muskegon Fury, Colonial Hockey League, 1993-94; head coach Detroit Vipers, Internat. Hockey League, 1994-99, Tampa Bay Lightning, NHL, 1999—2001, Mississauga Ice Dogs, Ontario Hockey League, 2002, San Antonio Rampage, 2003; asst coach. Fl. Panthers, 2003—04; head coach San Antonio Rampage, 2004—. Office: San Antonio Rampage One SBC Center San Antonio TX 78219

LUEBBERT, TERRY LYNNE, elementary school educator; b. Kans. City, Mo., Aug. 5, 1963; d. Esten E. and Beverly Lea Gray; m. David Luebbert, Oct. 26, 1989; 1 child, Kelsey Lynne. B in edn., William Woods U., 1999; M in edn., Lesley U., 2002. Art tchr. Williamsburg Elem., Williamsburg, Mo., 1999—2000, New Bloomfield R III, New Bloomfield, Mo., 2000—. Author: (poem) Nature's Gentle Kiss, 2003, The Best Poems and Poets, 2003. Cath. Avocations: painting, photography, horse shows. Home: 1113 Ashton Cir W Fulton MO 65251 Office: New Bloomfield Elem 307 Redwood New Bloomfield MO 65063 Office Phone: 573-491-3352. E-mail: tlbbrt@sbcglobal.net.

LUEBKE, MARTIN FREDERICK, retired curator, retired private school educator; b. Concord, Wis., Oct. 2, 1917; s. Frederick John and Martha (Kretzmann) L.; m. Dorothy Lorraine Kutschinski, July 5, 1947 (dec. Mar. 2001); children: Judith, Charles. BS, Concordia Coll., 1941; MA, U. Mich., 1952; PhD, U. Ill., 1966; postdoctoral, Cambridge U., 1974. Tchr. Our Savior Luth. Sch., Chgo., 1938-45; prin. Immanuel Luth. Sch., Grand Rapids, Mich., 1945-58; prof., dean Concordia Theol. Sem., Springfield, Ill., 1958-76, Ft. Wayne, Ind., 1976-80; curator Saxon Luth. Meml., Frohna, Mo., 1980-86; asst. to pastor Chapel of the Cross Luth., St. Louis, 1987—2001. Editor: Curriculum in Process, 1963; contbr. articles to profl. jours. Bd. dirs. Mich. Dist. Luth. Ch., Mo. Synod, 1962-75; commr., sec. Perry County Tourism Commn., Perryville, Mo., 1983-86; bd. dirs. River Heritage Assn., Cape Girardeau, Mo., 1984-86. Faculty fellow Aid Assn. Luths., 1963, 73; recipient Outstanding Educators Am. award, 1972, Commendation award Concordia Hist. Inst., St. Louis, 1987; Kramer-Luebke Visitor Ctr. at Saxon Luth. Meml. named in his honor, 2001. Avocations: music, tour hosting. Home: 4505 Parker Rd Apt 302 Florissant MO 63033-4271 E-mail: mfluebke@aol.com.

LUEBKE, NEIL ROBERT, philosophy educator; b. Pierce, Nebr., Sept. 15, 1936; s. Robert Carl and Cinderetta Amelia (Guthmann) L.; m. Phyllis Jean Madsen, June 15, 1957; children: Anne Elizabeth, Karen Marie. BA, Midland Coll., Nebr., 1958; MA, Johns Hopkins U., Balt., 1962, PhD, 1968. Asst., assoc. then prof. philosophy Okla. State U., Stillwater, 1961-98, head philosophy dept., 1979-85, 89-96, Regents Svc. prof., 1997-98, prof. emeritus, 1998—. Dir. Exxon Critical Thinking Project,

1971-74 Contbr. articles to profl. jours. Woodrow Wilson nat. fellow, 1958-59 Mem. Am. Philos. Assn., Soc. Bus. Ethics, Mountain-Plains Philos. Conf. (chmn. 1971-72, 80-81), Southwestern Philos. Soc. (pres. 1981-82), Phi Kappa Phi (nat. pres. 1998-2001). Democrat. Lutheran. Home: 616 W Harned Ave Stillwater OK 74075-1303 Personal E-mail: nluebke_osu@brightok.net. E-mail: nluebke@okstate.edu.

LUECHTEFELD, MONICA, consumer products company executive; b. LA, Jan. 23, 1949; 1 child. BS, Mt. St. Mary's Coll., LA, 1971. With recruiting office Mt. St. Mary's Coll., LA; sales rep. Maloney's Office Supply, LA, 1979—93; gen. mgr. So. Calif. Region Office Depot, Inc., Delray Beach, Fla., 1993, exec. v.p. E-Commerce, 2000—05, exec. v.p. strategy and devel., 2005, exec. v.p. bus. devel., supply chain and info. tech., 2005—. Office: Office Depot Inc 2200 Old Germantown Rd Delray Beach FL 33445 Office Phone: 561-438-4800.*

LUECK, MARTIN R., lawyer; b. St. Paul, Sept. 25, 1956; BS, Winona State U., 1978; JD cum laude, William Mitchell Coll. Law, 1984. Bar: Minn. 1984, US Dist. Ct. (dist. Minn.) 1984, US Dist. Ct. (no. dist. Calif.) 1987, US Supreme Ct. 1997, US Dist. Ct. (dist. Ariz.) 1998, US Ct. Appeals (11th and fed. cirs.) 1998, NY Supreme Ct. Appellate (3rd jud. dist.) 2003, NY 2003, US Dist. Ct. (dist. Colo.). Law clk. Sahr Kunert & Tamornino, Mpls., 1981—83; ptnr. Robins, Kaplan, Miller & Ciresi LLP, Mpls., 1983—, mem. exec. bd., 1996—, chmn. bus. litigation group, 1999—. Spkr, lectr. in field, 1992—. Contbr. articles to profl. jour. Named one of Minn. Lawyer's 15 Attys. of Yr., 2003, Top 10 Trial Lawyers in Am., Nat. Law Jour., 2004, Best Lawyers in Am., 2006—07. Fellow: Am. Coll. Trial Lawyers; mem.: ABA (mem. tng. the trial lawyer task force), Am. Assn. Justice, Internat. Bar Assn., Fed. Cir. Bar Assn., Hennepin County Bar Assn., Minn. Intellectual Property Law Assn., Am. Intellectual Property Law Assn. Office: Robins Kaplan Miller & Ciresi LLP 2800 LaSalle Plz 800 LaSalle Ave Minneapolis MN 55402-2015 Office Phone: 612-349-8500. Office Fax: 612-339-4181. E-mail: mrlueck@rkmc.com.

LUECKE, ELEANOR VIRGINIA ROHRBACHER, civic volunteer; b. St. Paul, Mar. 10, 1918; d. Adolph and Bertha (Lehman) Rohrbacher; m. Richard William Luecke, Nov. 1, 1941; children: Glenn Richard, Joan Eleanor Ratliff, Ruth Ann (dec.). Student, Macalester Coll., St. Paul, 1936-38, St. Paul Bus. U., 1938-40. Author lit. candidate and ballot issues, 1970-2003; producer TV local issues, 1981—; contbr. articles to profl. jours. Founder, officer, dir., pres. Liaison for Inter-Neighborhood Coop., Okemos, Mich., 1972—; chair countrywide special edn. millage proposals, 1958, 1969; trustee, v.p., pres. Ingham Intermediate Bd. Edn., 1959-83; sec., dir. Tri-County Cmty. Mental Health Bd., Lansing, 1964-72; founder, treas., pres. Concerned Citizens for Meridian Twp., Okemos, 1970-86; mental health rep. Partners of the Americas, Belize, Brit. Honduras, 1971; trustee Capital Area Comprehensive Health Planning, 1973-76; v.p., dir. Assn. Retarded Citizens Greater Lansing, 1973-83; chair, mem. Cmty. Svcs. for Developmentally Disabled Adv. Coun., 1973-87; dir., founder, treas. Tacoma Hills Homeowners Assn. Bd., 1985-97; facilitator of mergers Lansing Child Guidance Clinic, Clinton and Eaton counties Tri-County Cmty. Mental Health Bd., Lansing Adult Mental Health Clinic, founder; founder, treas., officer Mid-Mich. Land Conservancy, 2002—. Recipient Greater Lansing Cmty. Svcs. Coun. "Oscar," United Way, 1955, state grant Mich. Devel. Disabilities Coun., Lansing, 1983, Disting. award Mich. Assn. Sch. Bds., Lansing, 1983, Pub. Svc. award C.A.R.E.ing, Okemos, 1988, Earth Angel award WKAR-TV 23, Mich. State U., East Lansing, 1990, Cert. for Cmty. Betterment People for Meridian, Okemos, 1990, 2nd pl. video competition East Lansing/Meridian Twp. Cable Comm. Commn., 1990, 1st pl. award video competition, 1992, Outstanding Sr. Citizen award Charter Twp. of Meridian, Okemos, Mich., 2001; Ingham Med. Hosp. Commons Area named in her honor, Lansing, 1971. Mem. Advocacy Orgn. for Patients and Providers (dir. 1994-99). Avocations: reading, interior design, landscaping, gardening. Home: 2700 Burcham Dr Rm 230 East Lansing MI 48823-3891

LUECKE, PAMELA, editor, educator; BA in Philosophy, Carleton Coll., 1974; MA in Journalism, Northwestern U., 1975; MBA, U. Hartford, 1979. Features reporter Hartford Courant, Hartford, Conn., 1975—79; bus. editor The Louisville Times, Louisville, 1981—84; various positions The Courier-Journal, Louisville, 1981—89; asst. mng. editor/metro Hartford Courant, Hartford, Conn., 1989—95, deputy mng. editor, 1995; editorial page editor Lexington (Ky.) Herald-Leader, 1995—96, editor, v.p., 1996—2000, editor, sr. v.p., 2000—01; prof., Reynolds Chair Dept. Journalism and Mass Comm., Washington and Lee Univ., Va., 2001—. Office: Washington & Lee Univ Lexington VA 24450

LUECKE, ROBERT KENNETH, social studies educator, department chairman; b. Sheboygan, Wis., Apr. 15, 1948; s. Kenneth Robert and Erna Else Luecke; m. Rita Verona Timm, June 17, 1971; children: Daryl, Darla, Donna. BA, Concordia Coll., St. Paul, 1971; MA, Saginaw Valley Coll., Mich., 1976; BS, Minn. State U., Mankato, 1981. Tchr. 1st Luth. Elem. Sch., Glencoe, Minn., 1971—72, Trinity Luth. Elem. Sch., Warren, Mich., 1972—77; tchr. social studies Mayer Luth H.S., Minn., 1977—. Dept. head humanities Mayer Luth. H.S., Mayer, Minn., 1977—. Contbr. to social studies curricula. Campaign vol. Rep. Party, Young America, Minn., 1978, 1980. Mem.: Minn. Coun. Social Studies. Lutheran. Avocations: bicycling, reading. Home: 410 4th Ave SW Young America MN 55397-9235 Office Phone: 952-657-2251 x 310. Personal E-mail: rluecke@hotmail.com.

LUEDDERS, JERRY DUANE, music educator, academic administrator; b. Sturgis, Mich., June 27, 1943; life ptnr. Joseph Douglas Gilbert, Feb. 21, 2002. MusB, U. Mich., Ann Arbor, 1965; MusM, Ind. U., Bloomington, 1967; cert., Paris Conservatory, France, 1971. Asst. prof. St. Cloud State U., Minn., 1967—72; dean fine arts Coll. St Benedict, St. Joseph, Minn., 1972—77; dir. sch. music Lewis & Clark Coll., Portland, Oreg., 1977—86; chmn. dept. music Calif. State U., Northridge, 1986—2003, prof., 2003—, asst. provost, 2003—. Bd. dirs. Muriel Pollia Found., LA, pres., 2005—07. Musician over 1000 concerts. Named Knight, St. Catherine Sinai, 2005; recipient Freidheim award, 1987, Wang Family Excellence award, Calif. State U., Northridge, 2002. Mem.: Nat. Assn. Schs. Music (regional pres. 1993—95), Mil. and Hospitaller Order St. Lazarus (chevalier 2001—07). Democrat. Avocations: travel, kayaking. Office: Calif State Univ Northridge 18111 Nordhoff St Northridge CA 91330-8200 Home Phone: 323-851-6987; Office Phone: 818-677-2757. Business E-Mail: jerry.luedders@csun.edu.

LUEDEMAN, GERALD WARREN, radiologist; b. Kansas City, Mo., Jan. 17, 1941; s. Clarence Henry and Hazel McClure Luedeman; m. Brenda Jane Kvamme, Sept. 1, 1984; children: Robert Warren, Richard Brandt. AB cum laude, Harvard Coll., Cambridge, Mass., 1962; MD, George Washington U., Washington, 1966. Diplomate Am. Bd. Radiology, 1974, Am. Bd. Nuc. Medicine, 1976. Intern Grady Meml. Hosp., Atlanta, 1966—67; resident radiology Med. Coll. Va., Richmond, 1970—73; radiologist Ventura County Cmty. Hosp., Calif., 1973—75; pvt. practice Radiology Cons. PA, Winter Haven, Fla., 1975—. Capt. US Army, 1967—69. Mem.: Radiol. Soc. N.Am., Am. Inst. of Ultrasound in Medicine, Soc. of Nuc. Medicine, Roentgen Ray Soc., Masons Lake Region Yacht and Country Club. Avocations: travel, reading, golf.

LUEDER, DIANNE CAROL, library director; b. Racine, Wis., Aug. 5, 1944; d. James Richard and Margaret Ann Helland; m. Roland Herman Lueder, Aug. 29, 1981 (dec. July 1993); children: Daniel Lee Bertelsen, Barbara Marie Lantz. BA, U. Wis.-Parkside, Kenosha, 1972; MLS, U. Wis., Milw., 1979. Ref./outreach libr. Elk Grove Village Libr., Ill., 1979-80; dir. Bartlett Pub. Libr., Ill., 1980-84; asst. exec. dir. DuPage Libr. Sys., Geneva, Ill., 1984-88; pres. Lueder Enterprises, Inc., Wauconda, Ill., 1988—2003; exec. dir. Roselle Pub. Libr., Ill., 1990—2001; libr. dir. Menomonie Pub. Libr., Wis., 2001—07. Author: Administrator's Guide to Library Building Maintenance, 1992. V.p. Roselle Pub. Libr. Found., 1994-2001. Mem.: ALA, Wis. Libr. Assn., Menomonie Woman's Club, Optimist Club (pres. 2004—05). Lutheran. Avocations: travel, learning Norwegian language. Home: 343 Red Cedar St Menomonie WI 54751 Home Phone: 715-231-6075. E-mail: dclueder@wwt.net.

LUEDERS, WAYNE RICHARD, lawyer; b. Milw., Sept. 23, 1947; s. Warren E. and Marjorie L. (Schramek) L.; m. Patricia L. Rasmus, Aug. 1, 1970 (div. Nov. 1990); children: Laurel, Daniel, Kristin; m. Kristine Harbrecht, May 22, 2004. BBA with honors, U. Wis., 1969; JD, Yale U., 1973, Yale Law Sch. Bar: Wis. 1973. Acct. Arthur Andersen & Co., Milw., 1969-70; atty. Foley & Lardner, Milw., 1973-80, ptnr., 1980—. Bd. dirs. numerous cos. Bd. dirs. Riveredge Nature Ctr., Milw., 1983-92, 96-99, Wis. Pro Soccer, 1986-2003, Milw. Art Mus., 1992-2001, Child Abuse Prevention Fund, Milw., 1989-2003, Michael Fields Agrl. Inst., 1991—, Florentine Opera Co., 1992—; class agt. Yale Law Sch., 1978—. With U.S. Army, 1969-75. Mem. ABA, AICPA (Wisc.), Wis. Bar Assn., Milw. Bar Assn., Estate Counselors Forum, Univ. Club (Milw.), Phi Kappa Phi. Avocations: theater, racquetball, violin. Office: Foley & Lardner LLP 777 E Wisconsin Ave Ste 3500 Milwaukee WI 53202-5306 Home Phone: 414-271-6452; Office Phone: 414-297-5786. Business E-Mail: wlueders@foley.com.

LUEDKE, FREDERICK LEE, manufacturing executive; b. Milw., Jan. 19, 1938; s. Frederick William and Martha Marie (Widiger) L.; m. Wilma Jeanne Seacat, July 3, 1960; children; Tracy Jeanne, Frederick William II. BSIE, Wichita State U., Kans., 1960; MBA, Harvard U., Cambridge, Mass., 1966. Mfg. tng. program GE, 1960-64; prodn. gen. supr. Polaroid Corp., Waltham, Mass., 1966-70; mgr. mfg. Millipore Corp., Bedford, Mass., 1970-76; dir. mfg. Berol Corp., Danbury, Conn., 1976-87; exec. v.p. Neoperl Inc., Waterbury, Conn., 1987-92; pres. Neoperl, Inc., Waterbury, Conn., 1992—. Bd. dirs. Naugatuck Valley Devel. Corp., 1994—, v.p., 1996—98; bd. dirs. Platt Bros. and Co., 1996—, Waterbury Partnership 2000, 1999—2001, Greater Waterbury Workforce Devel. Bd., 2001—; mem. Gov.'s coun. for Econ. Competitiveness and Tech., 1999—, Waterbury City Champion, Inner City Bus. Strategy Initiative, 1999. Founder Waterbury Neighborhood Coun., 1994; bd. dir. Waterbury Devel. Corp., 2004—; mem. Waterbury Planning and Fin. Assistance Bd., 2004—; pres. Luth. Ch. of Newtons, Mass., 1974—75, 1st Luth. Ch., Waterbury, 1988—89; bd. dirs. Danbury ARC, 1982—84, Easter Seals, 1993—2000, vice chmn., 1994—96, chmn., 1996—98; pres. bd. trustees East Hill Woods Retirement Ctr., Southbury, Conn., 1989—97; mem. Waterbury Found., 1991—; chmn. Incorporators of Waterbury Hosp., 1995—97; trustee Waterbury Hosp., 1997—2006, chmn., 2003—06; bd. dirs. Greater Waterbury Health Network, 1999—, vice chmn., 2006—; bd. dirs. Waterbury Partnership for Growth, 2001—04. Mem. ASME, Am. Soc. Plumbing Engrs., Plumbing Mfrs. Inst. (pres. 1999-2000, bd. dirs. 1995-2000), Am. Soc. Sanitary Engring., Greater Waterbury C. of C. (bd. dirs. 2000—, Mfr. of Yr. 2003), Rotary (bd. dirs.), Waterbury Club (pres. 1996-98). Republican. Lutheran. Avocations: tennis, mountain hiking. Home: 98 Woodlawn Ter Waterbury CT 06710-1929 Office: Neoperl Inc 171 Mattatuck Heights Rd Waterbury CT 06705-3832

LUENING, ROBERT ADAMI, retired agricultural studies educator; b. Milw., Apr. 20, 1924; s. Edwin Garfield and Irma Barbara (Adami) L.; m. Dorothy Ellen Hodgskiss, Aug. 27, 1966. BS, U. Wis., 1961, MS, 1968. Dairy farmer, Hartland, Wis., 1942-58; fieldman Waukesha County Dairy Herd Improvement Assn., Waukesha, Wis., 1958; adult agr. instr. Blair Sch. Dist., Wis., 1961-63; extension farm mgmt. agt. U. Wis.-Racine, 1963-69; extension farm record specialist dept. agrl. and applied econs. U. Wis.-Madison, 1969-88; free-lance work, 1988—. Author: (with others) The Farm Management Handbook, 1972, 7th edit., 1991, Teacher's Manual, 1991, Managing Your Financial Future Farm Record Book Series, 1980, 4th edit., 1987, USDA Yearbook of Agriculture, 1989, Beef, Sheep and Forage Production in Northern Wisconsin, 1992, Dairy Farm Business Management, 1996, Poultry Farm Business Management, 1999, 2d edit., 2000, revised, 2004; writer mag. column: Agri-Vision, 1970-88. Founder, exec. pres. Lüning Family Orgns. U.S.A., Inc.; bd. dirs. Friends of the Max Kade Inst. for German-Am. Studies. Recipient John S. Donald Excellence in Teaching award U. Wis.-Madison, 1980; recipient Wis. State Farmer award Vocat. Agr. Inst. Wis., 1980, Second Mile award Wis. County Agts. Assn., 1980, Outstanding Svc. to Wis. Agr. award Farm and Industry Short Course, 1989. Mem. Wis. Soc. Farm Mgrs. and Rural Appraisers (hon., coll. v.p. 1976, chmn. editl. com. 1978-80, sec.-treas. 1968-80, pres. 1982, Silver Plow award 1988), Wis. State Geneal. Soc. (pres. S.C. chpt. 1995-96, pres. PAF Users group 1995), Epsilon Sigma Phi (Disting. Service award 1988), Alpha Gamma Rho, Kiwanis. Lodges: Masons. Presbyterian. Personal E-mail: rluening@wisc.edu.

LUEPKER, RUSSELL VINCENT, epidemiology educator; b. Chgo., Oct. 1, 1942; s. Fred Joseph and Anita Louise (Thornton) L.; m. Ellen Louise Thompson, Dec. 22, 1966; children: Ian, Carl. BA, Grinnell Coll., 1964; MD with distinction, U. Rochester, 1969; MS, Harvard U., 1976; PhD (hon.), U. Lund, Sweden, 1996. Intern U. Calif., San Diego, 1969-70; resident Peter Bent Brigham Hosp., Boston, 1973-74; cardiology fellow Peter Bent Brigham Hosp./Med., Boston, 1974-76; asst. prof. divsn. epidemiology med. lab. physiol. hygiene U. Minn., Mpls., 1976-80, assoc. prof., 1980-87, prof. divsn. epidemiology and medicine, 1987—, dir. divsn. epidemiology, 1991—2004, Mayo prof. pub. health, 2000—. Cons. NIH, Bethesda, Md., 1980—, U. So. Calif., L.A., 1985—, Armed Forces Epidemiology Bd., 1993-97; vis. prof. U. Goteborg, Sweden, 1986, Ninewells Med. Sch., Dundee, Scotland, 1995. With USPHS, 1970—73. Harvard U. fellow, 1974-76, Bush Leadership fellow, 1990; recipient Prize for Med. Rsch. Am. Coll. Chest Physicians, 1970, Nat. Rsch. Svc. award Nat. Heart, Lung and Blood Inst., Bethesda, 1975-77, Disting. Alumni award Grinnell Coll., 1989. Fellow ACP, Am. Coll. Cardiology, Am. Heart Assn. (chmn. coun. on epidemiology 1992-94, chair program com. sci. sessions 1995-97, award of merit 1997), Am. Coll. Epidemiology; mem. Am. Epidemiol. Soc., Am. Soc. Preventive Cardiology (Joseph Stokes award 1999), Delta Omega Soc. (Nat. Merit award 1988). Office: Univ Minn Sch Pub Health Div Epidemiology 1300 S 2nd St Minneapolis MN 55454-1087 Home Phone: 612-729-2659; Office Phone: 612-624-6362. Business E-Mail: luepker@epi.umn.edu.

LUETKEHOELTER, GOTTLIEB WERNER (LEE LUETKEHOELTER), retired bishop, clergyman; b. Wheatwyn, Sask., Can., Nov. 16, 1929; s. Henry William and Marie Louise (Schlepper) L.; m. Betty Edwards, July 25, 1959; children— David Lee, Jonathan Richard. BA, U. Sask., 1952; B.D., Lutheran Coll. and Sem., Saskatoon, Sask., 1955; S.T.M., Vancouver Sch. Theology, 1975; DD, St. John's Coll., U. Manitoba, 1990, Luth. Theol. Sem., Saskatoon, 2000. Ordained to ministry United Luth. Ch. in Am., 1955. Pastor Markinch-Wheatwyn-Cupar Parish, 1955-57; pastor St. Mark's Luth. Ch., Regina, Sask., 1957-61, Erloeser Luth. Ch., Phila., 1961-63, Faith Luth. Ch., Burnaby, B.C., Canada, 1963-69, Trinity Luth. Ch., Edmonton, Alta., Canada, 1969-76; bishop Central Can. Synod, Luth. Ch. in Am., Winnipeg, Man., Canada, 1976-85; bishop Man./Northwestern Ont. Synod, Evang. Luth. Ch. in Can., Winnipeg, Man., Canada, 1985-94; ret., 1994. Mem. exec. coun. Luth. Ch. in Am., N.Y.C., 1978-85, Anglican-Luth. Dialogue, Can., 1983-95; dir. Can. Luth. World Relief, 1989-98; lectr. Univ. Winnipeg, 1997-98. Bd. govs. Luth. Theol. Sem., Saskatoon, 1976-94, Schmieder resident, 1994-95, lectr. Luth. Theol. Sem., 1995-96. With Royal Can. Navy, 1952-54. Lutheran. Avocations: golf, swimming, writing. Home Phone: 204-837-3312. E-mail: lee7lue@shaw.ca.

LUETSCHWAGER, MARY SUSAN, educational consultant; b. Bloomingdale, Ind., Nov. 19, 1937; d. William Blaine Shade and Goldina VandaVeer (Newlin) Brown; children: Roger, Tisa, Julia, Angela, Robert, William; m. Bruce E. Luetschwager, Sept. 9, 2000. Grad. high sch., Rockville, Ind. Sec., treas. Tri-State Transport, Inc., 1968-73; road driver Roadway Express, Chicago Heights, Ill., 1977—2006, safety team capt., 1991-92, 94; program mgr., instr. Rider's Edge New Rider Tng., Calumet Harley-Davidson, Munster, Ind., 2006—. Completed Passport Tour (Abate), 1990, 94, 2000; mem. Roadway Express Dist. Road Team Dist. 12, 1995-97. Past mem. newsletter com. focus group Roadway Express; mem. focus group Kenworth Driver's Bd., 1992—; active Motorcycle Safety Found., Basic Rider Course; Rider coach 1999—, ABATE of Ind., Ind. Dept. Edn.; instr. motorcycle training Rider's Edge, 2006—. Recipient truck driving competition awards and motorcycle rally trophies, 3d place 8/48 rally Motorcycle Endurance Rider's Assn., 1996; 1st woman to finish on a Harley-Davidson motorcycle World Famous Iron Butt Rally, 1995, finished 6th place out of 78 starts and 61 finishers in 8th Iron Butt Rally, 1997, placed 3d in twin-trailer truck driving championships in Ill., 2000; placed 2nd in competition at Delta Nu Alpha truck driving fraternity in Rockford Ill, 2001, 1st pl. award (grand champion overall) in twin-trailer divsn. of truck driving championships, Ill., 2001; named Ill. TDC Sportsman of the Yr., 1995. Mem.: Chgo. Area BMW Owner's Assn., Chgo. Region BMW Owners Assn., Ladies of Harley, Harley Owners Group (newsletter editor Calumet region chpt. 1994—96, Munster, Ind. asst. dir. Calumet region chpt. 1996—99, historian 2000—06, sec. 2004, newsletter editor Calumet region chpt. 2005), Am. Radio Relay League, Am. Bikers Aim Toward Edn., Am. Motorcycle Assn. Avocations: motorcycling, amateur radio. Home and Office: PO Box 316 Griffith IN 46319-0316 Office Phone: 219-934-6366.

LUFFSEY, WALTER STITH, air transportation executive, consultant; b. Richmond, Va., Mar. 15, 1934; s. Roland Emmit and Bernice Irene (Hall) L.; m. Louise Arlington Hicks, Dec. 19, 1956; children: Dennis Glenn, Melinda Denise. Student, U. Richmond, 1952—55, Agrl. Dept. Grad. Sch., 1963—65. With FAA, 1957—, supervisory air traffic control specialist Atlantic City, 1960-63, air traffic control specialist rsch., 1963-65, sr. air traffic control analyst systems rsch. and devel. svc., 1965-71, chief program analysis and reports br. Washington, 1971-72, asst. chief program mgmt. staff, 1972-73, spl. asst., assoc. adminstr. for engring. and devel., 1973-74, chief program mgmt. staff system rsch. and devel. svc., 1974-75, tech. asst., assoc. adminstr. policy devel. and rev., 1975-78, tech. asst., assoc. adminstr. policy and internat. aviation affairs, tech. asst. to the assoc. adminstr. for aviation stds., 1978-79, dep. assoc. adminstr. for aviation stds., 1979-80, assoc. adminstr. for aviation stds., 1980-85, assoc. adminstr. for air traffic, 1985-86, dir. advanced aviation sys. design team, 1986-89; sr. v.p. ops. and planning Tech. and Mgmt. Assistance, Washington, 1989-90, exec. v.p., 1990-97; pres. WSL Enterprises, Arlington, Va., 1989—. Author: Air Traffic Control: How to Become an FAA Air Traffic Controller, 1990; contbr. articles to profl. jours. Served with USAF/Va. Air N.G., 1955-58. Recipient Spl. Achievement award FAA, 1970, 78, 85, Disting. Svc. award Aviation Week and Space Tech.-Flight Safety Found., 1982, Laurel award, 2000, Sec.'s award, 1982, Meritorious Exec. award-Presdl. Rank, 1983, Adminstr.'s Superior Achievement award, 1985, others. Mem. AIAA (aero. policy com.), Soc. Sr. Aerospace Execs., Nat. Aero. Assn., Exptl. Aircraft Assn., Aircraft Owners and Pilots Assn., Profl. Women Contrs. Assn., Air Traffic Control Assn. (hon., past chair publs. com., Meritorious Achievement award 1965, Tech. Writing 1st pl. award), John Marshall Cadet Alumni Assn., Soc. Airway Pioneers, Va. Aero. Hist. Soc., Order of Quiet Birdmen, Silver Wings Fraternity, Aero Club, Nat. Aviation Club (past pres., gov. emeritus), Kiwanis (past pres. Crystal City). Home and Office: WSL Enterprises 9115 Alexandria Dr Weeki Wachee FL 34613 Personal E-mail: waltluffsey@prodigy.net.

LUFRANO, MICHAEL RICHARD, lawyer; b. Chgo., July 8, 1965; s. Ned Nathan and Joan Audrey (Gold) L. BA, U. Ill., 1987; JD, Harvard U., 1992. Bar: Ill. 1992, D.C. 1993, U.S. Dist. Ct. (no. dist.) Ill. 1995. Assoc. city atty. City of Atlanta, 1992-93; spl. asst. to pres., dep. dir. advance White House, Washington, 1993-95; media/intellectual property atty. Sonnenschein, Nath & Rosenthal, Chgo., 1995—; with Chgo. Nat. League Ball Club Inc., Chgo. Issues dir., speechwriter Dukakis for Pres., Boston, 1987-88. Rotary Internat. scholar, 1987. Office: Chgo Nat League Ball Club Inc 1060 W Addison St Chicago IL 60613 Office Phone: 773-404-2827. Office Fax: 773-404-4111. Business E-Mail: mlufrano@cubs.com.

LUFT, ERIC V.D., writer, educator, publisher; b. Woodbury, NJ, Dec. 5, 1952; s. Alexander v.d. and Barbara Elaine (Meeker) L.; m. Jennifer Hamlin, June 23, 1979 (div. Nov. 1993); children: Sarah, Mary Grace; m. Diane Kathryn Davis, June 13, 2002. AB magna cum laude, Bowdoin Coll., 1974; MA, Bryn Mawr Coll., 1977, PhD, 1985; student, Columbia U. Rare Book Sch., 1988-89; MLS, Syracuse U., 1993; student, U. Va. Rare Book Sch., 1997. Cataloging asst., libr. asst. Bryn Mawr (Pa.) Coll., 1976-80, 81-82; hist. collections asst. Coll. Physicians Phila., 1980-81; instr. philosophy Villanova (Pa.) U., 1983-85; curator hist. collections SUNY Upstate Med. U. Health Scis. Libr., Syracuse, 1987—2006; manuscript cataloger, Coll. Environ. Science & Forestry SUNY, 1993; prin., owner Gergensatz Press, North Syracuse, NY, 1996—; list owner ALHHS-L (online listserve), 1999—2006. Adj. instr. Humanistic Studies Ctr., Syracuse U., 1986-96, 2002-04, adj. instr. Sch. of Information Studies, Syracuse U., 2002-03; lectr. Ctr. for Bioethics and Humanities, SUNY Upstate Med. U., 2002—; cons. rare book cataloging Syracuse U., 1994-96; proprietor Gegensatz Press, North Syracuse, N.Y., 1996—; participant internat. confs., Australia, Eng., Belgium, Can., Germany, Iceland; vis. lectr. U. Iceland, U. Copenhagen; freelance photographer specializing in rare books, 1981-90; facilities planning cons. St. Lawrence County Hist. Assn., N.Y., 1999-2000; co-founder Upstate N.Y. Colloquium for History of Sci. and Medicine, 2003. Author: Hegel, Hinrichs and Schleiermacher on Feeling and Reason in Religion, 1987, God, Evil and Ethics: A Primer in the Philosophy of Religion, 2004, SUNY Upstate Medical University: A Pictorial History, 2005, How I Became a Life Master Playing the Weak No Trump, 2006, A Socialist Manifesto, 2007; editor: Schopenhauer: New Essays, 1988, Thirty-Five Treasures of Special Collections, 1993, Synapse, 1995-2006, The Watermark, 2004—; contbg. editor: Biographical Dictionary of Literary Influences, the Nineteenth Century, 1800-1914, 2004; assoc. editor: The Owl of Minerva, 1983-96; pronunciation editor: Biographical Ency. of 20th Century World Leaders, 1998-99; contbr. Young Hegelians, 1983, History and System, 1984, Hegel's Philosophy of Spirit, 1987, Existence of God, 1988, Hegel and his Critics, 1989, Dictionary Am. Biography, 1992-96, Scribner Ency. Am. Lives, 1997—, Science and Its Times, 1999-2001, International Dictionary of Library Histories, 1999-2001, Magill's Guide to Military History, 2000, Land Warfare Ency., 2000, World of Genetics, 2002, Ency. of the Ancient World, 2002, Ground Warfare, 2002, Science in Dispute, 2002-03, Great Cultural Ends of the Western World, 2002, World of Microbiology and Immunology, 2003, World of Earth Science, 2003, Ency. of Espionage, Intelligence and Security, 2004, Dictionary of Literary Influences, the Twentieth Century, 1914-2006, 2004, Oxford Dictionary of National Biography, 2004, Ency. of NJ, 2004, Ency. of NY State, 2005, Ency. of 20th Century Technology, 2005, Dictionary of Modern American Philosophers, 2005, World of Forensic Science, 2005, Great Lives from History, 2005, Great Events from History, 2006, The New Hegelians, 2006, Terrorism: Essential Primary Sources, 2006; contbr. articles to profl. jours., chpts. to books. Vol. tutor Ethical, Legal and Social Issues in Medicine. Recipient Prologue prize, 1972, Brown Composition prize, 1974, Adèle Mellen prize for excellence in scholarship, 1985, Pres.'s award for excellence in L.S., SUNY Health Sci. Ctr., Syracuse, 1997, Murray Gottlieb prize Med. Libr. Assn., 1999, Links2Go Key Resource award, 2000, award of distinction for spl. alumni projects Assn. Am. Med. Colls., 2001; Surdna Rsch. fellow, 1973, Whiting fellow in humanities, 1982-83, Francis C. Wood Inst. for History of Medicine fellow, 1984, 99, U.S. Dept. Edn. fellow, 1992-93. Mem. Am. Philos. Assn., Friedrich Nietzsche Soc., N. Am. Nietzsche Soc., Hume Soc., Am. Philos. Assn. (life mem., non-acad. careers com., 2002-), Metaphysical Soc. Am., Hist. Soc. (charter), Hegel Soc. Am. (councillor 1988-92, sec. 1992-94), N.Y. State Assn. European Historians, Interdisciplinary 19th Century Studies, Friends of Rare Book Sch., Documentary Heritage Com. Ctrl. N.Y., Internat. Soc. Intellectual History, Soc. for Bioethics and Classical Philosophy, Archivists and Librs. in History of Health Scis. (steering com. 2003-), Bowdoin Alumni Club Ctrl. N.Y. (pres. 1985-92). Democrat. Avocations: bridge, chess, genealogy, fishing, carpentry. Home: 108 Deborah Ln North Syracuse NY 13212-1931 Office: Gegensatz Press 108 Deborah Ln Syracuse NY 13212-1931 Office Phone: 315-464-4585. E-mail: gegensatz@alumni.bowdoin.edu.

LUFTGLASS, MURRAY ARNOLD, corporate financial executive; b. Bklyn., Jan. 2, 1931; s. Harry and Pauline (Yaged) L.; children by previous marriage: Paula Jean, Bryan Keith, Robert Andrew, Richard Eric; 1 child from 2d marriage: Andrew William. BS, Ill. Inst. Tech., 1952; MS, U. So. Calif., 1959; MBA, U. Conn., 1972. With Shell Chem. Co., Torrance, Calif., 1955-60, 64-66, NYC, 1960-61, 66-69, Wallingford, Conn., 1961-64; asst. gen. mgr. Westchester Plastics div. Ametek, Inc., Mamaroneck, NY, 1969-75, dir. corp. devel. NYC, 1975-76, v.p., 1976-83, sr. v.p. corp. devel., 1984-96; mng. dir. M&A London, LLC, 1996—. Contbr. articles to profl. jours., publs.; patentee in field. Lt. (j.g.) USN, 1952—55. Mem. NAM, Soc. Plastics Industry, Assn. Corp. Growth, Soc. Plastics Engrs., Tau Beta Pi, Beta Gamma Sigma, Phi Lambda Upsilon, Univ. Club (N.Y.C.). Office: M&A London LLC PO Box 150 Montclair NJ 07042-0150 Home Phone: 973-783-2910; Office Phone: 973-783-2266. Business E-Mail: murray@mandalondon.com.

LUFTY, JOYBETH, minister; d. Pat Apple. BSc, Steven F. Austin State U., 1975; MSW, Western Mich. U., 1979; Dr. of Ministry, U. Creation Spirituality (now Wisdom U.), 2003. Head counselor, asst. dir. Otero Jr. Coll., LaJunto, Colo., 1976—77, instr. psychology, 1977; adolescent and family specialist Cmty. Health Counseling Svcs., Bangor, Maine, 1979—81; cons.-in-charge Crawford Health Rehab. Svcs., Bangor, 1983—85; counselor/educator Med. Care Devel., Bucksport, Maine, 1985—88; counselor Mystic Pines, East Orland, Maine, 1981—99; dir./internat. presenter Soul Integrators, East Orland, 1999—. Cons./sys. analyst WERU Cmty. Radio, East Orland, 1990—2000; vis. faculty Sch. of Holistic Spirituality, Buenos Aires, 2004—. Author: (book) Beyond Belief Into Knowing, 2001, A Soul's Delight, 2001, The We That Is Me, 2004. Vol. The Grand Theatre, Ellsworth, Maine; mem. campaign mgmt., trails com. Great Pond Mountain Conservation Trust, 2005—. Mem.: Sacred Dance Guild (ea. regional dir. 2005—). Avocations: singing, painting, hiking, swimming, dance. Personal E-mail: souldelite@aol.com.

LUGAR, DICK (RICHARD GREEN LUGAR), senator; b. Indpls., Apr. 4, 1932; s. Marvin L. and Bertha (Green) L.; m. Charlene Smeltzer, Sept. 8, 1956; children: Mark, Robert, John, David. BA, Denison U., 1954; BA, MA (Rhodes scholar), Oxford U., Eng., 1956. Mayor, Indpls., 1968-75; vis. prof. polit. sci. U. Indpls., 1976; US Senator from Ind., 1977—; chmn. com. fgn. rels. US Senate, 1985-86, 2003—06, chmn. com. on agr., nutrition and forestry, 1995-2001; chmn. Nat. Rep. Senatorial Com., 1983-84. Pres. Lugar Stock Farm, Inc.; mem. Indpls. Sch. Bd., 1964-67, v.p., 1965-66; vice chmn. Adv. Commn. on Intergovtl. Relations, 1969-75; pres. Nat. League of Cities, 1970-71; mem. Nat. Commn. Standards and Goals of Criminal Justice System, 1971-73; Del., mem. resolutions com. Republican Nat. Conv., 1968, del., mem. resolutions com., 1992, Keynote speaker, 1972, del., speaker, 1980., 88, 92, 96. Author: Letters to the Next President, 1988. Trustee Denison U., 1966—, U. Indpls., 1970-2002; bd. dirs. Nat. Endowment for Democracy, 1992-2000, Nuclear Threat Initiative, 2000—. Served to lt. (j.g.) USNR, 1957-60. Pembroke Coll., Oxford U. hon. fellow Mem. Rotary, Blue Key, Phi Beta Kappa, Omicron Delta Kappa, Pi Delta Epsilon, Pi Sigma Alpha, Beta Theta Pi. Republican. Methodist. Office: US Senate 306 Hart Senate Bldg Washington DC 20510-0001

LUGAR, THOMAS R., manufacturing executive; BS mech. engring., Purdue Univ. With Allison Div. Gen. Motors Co., Indpls., 1955-57; pres. Thomas L. Green & Co., Indpls., 1957—2001; chmn. Reading Bakery Systems. Served US Army. Mem.: Cookie and Snack Bakers Assn., Biscuit & Cracker Manufacturers Assn. Office: Thomas L Green Co Inc 7802 Moller Rd Indianapolis IN 46268-2117

LUGENBEEL, EDWARD ELMER, publisher; b. Balt., June 6, 1932; s. Nimrod Augustus and Victoria Elizabeth (Shilling) L.; m. Alice Marie Smith, June 12, 1953; children: Craig Edward, Susan Elizabeth, Douglas Paul, Leslie Jean. BS, U. Md., 1954. With Prentice-Hall, Inc., NJ, 1957-76, exec. editor, asst. v.p., 1972-76; pres. D. Van Nostrand Co., div. Litton Ednl. Pub., Inc. (pubs. coll. textbooks), NYC, 1976-81; v.p. Lynne Palmer Exec. Recruitment, Inc., NYC, 1981-83; v.p., edit. dir. W.B. Saunders Med. Pubs., Phila., 1983-85; exec. editor Columbia U. Press, NYC, 1985-98, ret., 1998-99. Cons. Columbia U. Earth Inst. Tchr. Tai Chi Chuan, Rockland County, N.Y., 1999—, SUNY-Rockland Cmty. Coll., 2000-01, Ramapo, Clarkstown and Nyack Sr. ctrs., Fountainview Sr. Residence, Pomona YM/YWHA. Served as 1st lt. USAF, 1954-57. Mem. AAAS, Am. Inst. Biol. Scis., Am. Geophys. Union, Soc. Vertebrate Paleontology, Internat. Assn. Landscape Ecology, Soc. Conservation Biology, Nyack Tai Chi Acad. (Black Sash Third degree 2007; cert. tchr. 2007), Shukokai World Karate Union (Brown Belt), Delta Sigma Pi.

LUGER, DONALD R., engineering company executive; b. May 12, 1938; s. George A. and Elizabeth M. Luger; m. Pat Sanders, Feb. 17, 1968 (dec. 1982); m. Sharon L. Luger, May 14, 1983; children: Christopher Daniel, Morgan Kathleen. BCE, Auburn U., 1962, MSCE, 1964; exec. program, Stanford U., 1979. Registered profl. engr., N.C., Ga., Mich., Va., N.Y. Structural engr. NASA, Huntsville, Ala., summer 1962; area engr. E.I. DuPont Co., Nashville, 1964; structural engr. Hayes Internat. Corp., Huntsville, 1964-65; resident engr. Fibers Industries, Inc., Shelby, N.C. and, Greenville, S.C., 1965-66; project mgr. Lockwood Greene Engrs., Inc., Atlanta, 1967-71, 1971-74, v.p., corp. dir., 1974-78, sr. v.p., corp. dir., 1978-82, pres., 1982-99, CEO, 1983-99, chmn., 1989; pres. D.R. Luger Enterprises, Atlanta, 1999—. Adv. bd. N.Am. br. AMEC, 2001—04; chmn. bd. Morrison Hershfield; bd. dirs. Qore, Inc., Syncroflo, Kliklok, Inc. Mem. ASCE, NSPE, Ga. Soc. Profl. Engrs., Auburn U. Alumni Assn., Auburn Alumni Engring. Coun., Commerce Club.

LUGER, RICHARD, economics professor; b. Montreal, Que., Canada, Nov. 16, 1968; arrived in US, 2004; m. Nancy Davin, July 16, 2004; children: Maxim, Sarah. BSc in Computer Sci., U. Montreal, 1990, PhD, 2001; BSc in Math., Concordia U., Montreal, 1993; MA in Econs., McGill U., Montreal, 1995. Economist Bank of Can., Ottawa, Ont., 2000—04; asst. prof. econs. Emory U., Atlanta, 2004—. Contbr. articles to profl. jours. Office: Dept Econs Emory Univ Atlanta GA 30322-2240 Office Phone: 404-727-0328. Office Fax: 404-727-4639. Business E-Mail: rluger@emory.edu.

LUGER, SELINA, medical educator; BA, Harvard U., Cambridge, Mass.; MD, McGill U., Montreal. Assoc. prof. medicine U. Pa., Phila., 1994—; dir. leukemia program Abramson Cancer Ctr. of U. Pa., Phila. Trustee Leukemia Lymphoma Soc., Phila. Office: U Pa 3400 Spruce St Philadelphia PA 19106 Office Phone: 215-662-6348. Office Fax: 215-662-4064.

LUGG, MARLENE MARTHA, immunization coordinator, health information systems specialist, health planner; b. Wauwatosa, Wis., Mar. 6, 1938; d. Armand Werner and Elise (Kuehni) Heinrich; m. Richard S.W. Lugg, June 11, 1966 (div. Dec. 1976); children: Jennifer Elsie, William Thomas Armand. BS in Gen. Sci., U. Wis., Milw., 1960; MPH in Med. and Hosp. Adminstrn., U. Pitts., 1966, DrPH in Health Svcs. Rsch. and Planning, 1981. Dep. chair Nat. Com. on Health and Vital Stats., Canberra, Australia, 1973-83; dir. State Ctr. for Health Stats. and Planning Health Dept. Western Australia, Perth, 1966-83; dir. health info. systems program UCLA, 1983-88; vis. prof. pub. health Calif. State U., Northridge, 1987—; health info. systems specialist Kaiser-Permanente-So. Calif., Pasadena, 1988-98; immunization coord., sr. rschr. Panorama City Med. Ctr. Kaiser Permanente, Calif., 1998—; prof., chair curriculum com. West Coast U., 2003—. Co-founder Australian and New Zealand Soc. for Epidemiology and Cmty. Health, Sydney, 1966-68, Pub. Health Assn. Australia, Canberra, 1968-83; examiner LA Civil Svc. Commn., 1986-88; vis. prof. Pasadena City Coll., 1992-98; mem. Calif. State Health Info. Policy Interagy. Com., 1992-94; mem. Calif. Health Data Coordinating Coun., 1995-2000; bd. dirs. Pub. Health Found. Enterprises, LA, 1994-2006, sec., 1995-97; co-chmn. LA Immunization Coalition, 2000-2001, chmn., 2002—; steering com. Calif. Adult Immunization Coalition, 2001—; mem. adv. bd. Calif. Coalition for Childhood Immunization, 2000—, Nat. Network Immunization Nurses and Assocs., 2001—; apptd. CDC Vaccine VAERS Reporting Group, 2003-2005, CDC/AIRA Immunization Practice Com., 2005—; CDC/AIRA Immunization Data Workgroup, 2006—; cons. in field. Author: Medical Manpower in Western Australia, 1978; contbg. editor Australian Health Rev., 1998-2004; contbr. articles on injury, health data systems, immunization, air quality and illness, injury control and Pub. Health Conf. stats./records to profl. jours. Leave No Trace Master Educator, 1998—; leader, trainer Girl Scouts USA, Milw., Pitts., LA, 1956—, Australian Girl Guides, Perth, Australia, 1966-82; instr., trainer ARC, Milw., Pitts., LA, 1959-, Girl Scouts USA, 1995—; explorer leader, trainer Boy Scouts Am., Western LA and Verdugo Hills, 1983-99; venturer leader, trnr. Boy Scouts Am., Verdugo Hills, 1999—; del. Girl Scouts Nat. Coun., 1996-2002. Recipient Broughton award Izaak Walton League Am., Wis., 1966, Fisher award Am. Med. Technologists, 1971, Outstanding Young Person award Western Australian Jaycees, Perth, Australia, 1977, Take Pride in Am. award US Govt., Washington, 1990, 2007, Wm. T. Hornaday Gold medal Boy Scouts Am., 1991, Silver Beaver Boy Scouts Am., 1999, Venturer Adult Leadership award, 1999, Thanks Badge Girl Scouts USA, 1990, Thanks Badge II, 2000, Outstanding Family award Girl Scouts San Fernando Valley, 1992, UN Environ. Conservation award, 1992, Wm. Spurgeon award, 1995, Nat. Vohs Quality award Kaiser Permanente, 1995, Outstanding Cmty. Svc. Alumni award U. Wis., Milw., 1997, Spotlight on Leadership award Kaiser Permanente, 1999, Innovations in Immunization award Am. Assn. Health Plans, 2001, Margaret Gloninger Alumni Cmty. Svc. award U. Pitts., 2004, Venturer Leader Merit award, 2005, Disting. Alumni award U. Pitts., 2006, Natalie J. Smith M.D. Meml. Immunization Champion award Calif. Coalition for Childhood Immunization, 2006; named Woman of Yr. Western Australia, 1976, Career Woman of Yr., Daily News, 1983, Woman of the Year San Fernando Valley Girl Scouts, 1995; Nat. Health and Med. Rsch. Coun. pub. health fellow, Australia, 1978. Fellow APHA, Australian Coll. Health Execs. (state bd. dirs. 1977-82), Royal Soc. Health, London; mem. Internat. Epidmiological Assn., Am. Coll. Forensic Examiners (cert. level III homeland security), So. Calif. Pub. Health Assn. (bd. dirs. 1987-95), NY Acad. Scis., Wilderness Med. Soc., Delta Omega. Lutheran. Achievements include research in serial section microcinematography, large linked databases, and vaccine safety studies. Office: Kaiser-Permanente So Calif 13652 Cantara St Panorama City CA 91402-5423 Business E-Mail: marlene.m.lugg@kp.org.

LUGINBUEHL, MARSHA LEE, psychologist; d. Harley W. and Betty Marie Knapp; m. Peter Luginbuehl, Dec. 28, 1973; children: Nicole Sitter, Matthew, Kellie Goode. BA in Psychology, U. Kans., 1974; PhD, U. South Fla., 2003. Cert. Nat. Assn. Sch. Psychologists, 1992, lic. sch. psychologist Dept. Health, Fla., 1996. Sch. psychologist Pasco County Sch. Dist., Land 'O Lakes, Fla., 1987—; pres. Child Uplift, Inc., Clearwater, Fla., 1997—2007, Fairview, Wyo., 2007—. Counselor, Sunday sch. and youth leader LDS Ch., Dunedin and Clearwater, Fla., 1984—2006; sec., chmn. Action Youth Care Fla., 1993—98. Named Fla. Student Svcs. Person of Yr., Pasco County, 2004. Mem.: APA (Oustanding Dissertation of Yr. award 2003), So. Sleep Soc., Am. Assn. Sleep Medicine, Fla. Assn. Sch. Psychologists, Nat. Assn. Sch. Psychologists. Achievements include invention of sleep disorders inventory for students. Mailing: PO Box 146 Fairview WY 83119 Home and Office: Child Uplift Inc 92 Moose Manor Dr Fairview WY 83119 Office Phone: 307-886-9096. Office Fax: 307-886-9093. Personal E-mail: mllugin@aol.com. Business E-Mail: childuplift@aol.com.

LUGO, EMIL J., retired secondary school educator; b. NYC, Sept. 7, 1946; s. Abraham and Margaret Lugo; m. Yvette Corsino-Lugo, July 19, 1980; children: Karl P., Cynthia M. BA, St. John's U., NYC, 1968; MA, Fordham U., Bronx, 1976. Cert. tchr. secondary edn. N.Y. Tchr. social studies Automotive H.S., Bklyn., 1971—72, Washington Irving H.S., NYC, 1973—76; tchr. social studies and Japanese lang. Stuyvesant H.S., NYC, 1968—72, 1972—73, 1976—2000; ret., 2000. Del. United Fedn. Tchrs., NYC, 1973—75; N.C. English/Spanish interpreter, 2004—. Bd. dirs. Watauga, Avery, Mitchell, Yancey Counties Cmty. Action, Inc., 2005—, vice-chmn., 2006—07. Recipient Tchr. Who Made a Difference award, N.Y. Times, 2001; Summer Study grantee, N.Y. State, 1969, Fulbright scholar, Fulbright/Japan Found., 1985. Mem.: High Country Amigos (English instr. 2000—06). Republican. Roman Catholic. Avocation: home repair, remodeling, and japanese rock gardening. Home: 661 Hopewell Church Rd Boone NC 28607 Personal E-mail: corsino-lugo@aol.com.

LUGO-PAOLI, LUZ MINERVA, counselor, educator; b. Mayaguez, PR, Aug. 7, 1976; d. Julio Cesar Lugo and Luz Minerva Rivera; m. Omar Ismael Paoli Breban, July 29, 2001. BSN, U. P.R., 2000; MA in Edn. with honors, U. Interamericana, 2005. Asst. social and cultural activities dept. U. P.R., Mayaguez, PR, 1994—99; assoc. prof. Sistema U. Ana G. Mendez-U. del Este, Santa Isabel, PR, 2003—04, profl. counselor, 2002—. Activities bd. Sistema U. Ana G. Mendez, 2005—; mem. adv. bd. U. del Este Santa Isabel, Santa Isabel, PR, 2006—. Vol. Lance Armstrong Found., 2005; mem. Livestrong Survivor Found., 2006; dir. Sabbath sch. Seventh Day Adventist Ch., Salinas, PR, 2004—. Recipient Gonzalez Excellence award, U. Interamericana at Aguadilla Campus, 1998, P.R. Youth medal, Gov. P.R., Anibal Acevedo Vila, 2005. Fellow: Am. Cancer Assn. (corr.); mem.: Nat. Acad. Advising Assn. (assoc.), Assn. Puertorriquena de Consejeros Profls. (assoc.), Am. Counselor Assn. (assoc.), UPR-RUM-CAAM Fadu Alumi (dir. comm.), Student Nurses Assn. (del pres. P.R. chpt. 1998—99, nat. pres. 1999—2000, cons. 1999—2004, nat. constituent, nominee Isabbel Hampton Robb Leadership award 2000), U. Students Assn. (activities planner 2003—), P.R. Epilepsy Soc. (assoc.). Seven Day Adventist. Achievements include design of. Avocations: travel, scrapbooks, wedding planner, interior decorating, cultivate orchids. Office: Sistema Universitario Ana G Mendez-UNE PO Box 756 Santa Isabel PR 00757-9998 Home Phone: 787-923-6464; Office Phone: 787-845-3080. Office Fax: 787-845-3660. Personal E-mail: luz_lugo@hotmail.com. Business E-Mail: llugo@suagm.edu.

LUHMAN, WILLIAM SIMON, community development administrator; b. Belvidere, Ill., May 15, 1934; s. Donald R. and H. Elizabeth (Rudberg) L. AB, Park Coll., 1956; MA, Fla. State U., 1957. City planner City of Moline, Ill., 1959-64; planning dir. Rock Island County, Ill., 1964-66; exec. dir. Bi-State Met. Planning Commn., Rock Island, 1966-71; dir. regional devel. Northeastern Ill. Planning Commn., Chgo., 1971-74, assoc. dir., 1975-76, dep. dir., 1977-79, acting exec. dir., 1979-80, asst. dir., 1980-81; v.p. Pub. Mgmt. Info. Svc., Chgo., 1981; asst. dir. No. Ill. U. Ctr. Govt. Studies, DeKalb, 1981-91, program coord., 1991; exec. dir. Growth Dimensions for Belvidere-Boone County, Ill., 1991—2001, pres., 1982-86, asst. dir., 2002—04. Vis. instr. Augustana Coll., Rock Island, 1967, 69. Bd. dirs. Rockford Area Coun. of 100, 1983-86; Boone County Regional Planning Commn., 1986—, chmn., 1986-90, 2002—; mem. Belvidere-Boone County Regional Planning Commn., 1986—, chmn., 1990-92; bd. dirs. Sch. Dist. 100 Found. for Excellence in Edn., 1992-99; mem. Sch. Dist. 100 Citizens Adv. Coun., 1999-2000, Sch. Dist. 100 Com. Strat. Planning, 1999; bd. dirs. Boone County United Way, 1999-2004; trustee Cmty. Found. of No. Ill., 2002-2004; active Boone County Arts Coun., Friends of Ida Pub. Libr., Ill. Regional Pub. Libr. Svc. Planning Panelist, 1996. Mem.: Am. Soc. Pub. Adminstrn., Am. Planning Assn. Home: 1538 Fremont St Belvidere IL 61008-5939 Personal E-mail: bluhman@aol.com.

LUI, ANTHONY TAT YIN, physicist; b. Hong Kong, Dec. 29, 1945; s. Siu Wai and Choi Dai (Chow) L.; m. Theresa Susan Szabo, Nov. 10, 1973; children: Jennifer, Michael, Victoria. BS, Hong Kong U., 1969; MS, U. Calgary, 1971, PhD, 1974. Postdoctoral fellow U. Calgary, 1974-75, U. Alaska, Fairbanks, 1975-76; rsch. assoc. NRC of Can., Ottawa, Ont., 1977-79, The Johns Hopkins U./Applied Physics Lab., Laurel, Md., 1979-83, sr. staff, 1984-85, prin. profl. staff, 1986—. Mem. steering com. of CDAW, NASA, Greenbelt, Md., 1984-90; mem. Grand Tour Cluster SDT, NASA Hdqts., Washington, D.C., 1990-92, mem. Mercury Orbiter SDT, 1996-99; mem. inter-agy. cons. group, NASA, 1993—; cons. Los Alamos Nat. Lab., N.Mex., 1990-95; external examiner for PhD degree, U. Calgary, Can., 1992. Editor: Magnetotail Physics, 1987 (JHU/APL Outstanding Publ. 1987); assoc. editor Geophys. Rsch. Letters, 1997-2000; contbg. author: Amazing Mysteries of the World, 1983; contbr. articles to profl. jours. Linkage grantee, NATO, 1993—96. Mem.: Am. Geophys. Union (chair student awards com. 1996—98). Home: 10809 Beech Creek Way Columbia MD 21044-1031 Office: Johns Hopkins U/Applied Phy 11100 Johns Hopkins Rd Laurel MD 20723-6005 Business E-Mail: tony.lui@jhuapl.edu.

LUI, ELWOOD, lawyer; b. LA, Feb. 4, 1941; BS, UCLA, 1962, MBA, 1964, JD, 1969. Bar: Calif. 1970, D.C. 1990; CPA, Calif. Dep. atty. gen. State of Calif., 1969-71; judge mcpl. ct. LA Judicial Dist., 1975-79, LA County Superior Ct., 1980-81; assoc. justice 2nd appellate dist. Calif. Ct. Appeals, 1981-87; mem. Jones, Day, LA; ptnr.-in-charge San Francisco office Jones Day. Mem. Judicial Coun. Calif., 1983-87; adj. prof. law U. So. Calif., 1977-87, Loyola U., LA, 1984. Recipient Bernard Witkin medal, State Bar Calif., 2006. Fellow: Am. Acad. Appellate Lawyers; mem.: Calif. Acad. Appellate Lawyers. Office: Jones Day Ste 4600 555 S Flower St Los Angeles CA 90050 also: Jones Day 26th Fl 555 California St San Francisco CA 94104 Office Phone: 213-489-3939, 415-626-3939. Office Fax: 415-875-5700. Business E-Mail: elui@jonesday.com.

LUING, GARY ALAN, financial management educator; b. Collins, Iowa, Apr. 24, 1937; s. Dwight Orn and Marjorie Mae (Clemons) L.; m. Sherry Lea Gates, Dec. 19, 1954; 1 child, Heather Sherry-Anne. BS cum laude, Stetson U., 1960; MA, U. Ill., 1961; Dr. Adminstrn. (hon.), Canadian Sch. Mgmt. Auditor Arthur Andersen & Co., Chgo., 1963; prof. Fla. Atlantic U., Boca Raton, 1965—, dean Sch. Bus., 1970-87. Cons. U.S. Treasury; expert witness on valuing closely held corps., 1972—; lectr., U.S., various fgn. countries; dir. Fla. Liquid Assets, Templeton Trust Co., Stewart Pvt. Found., 1999—; mem. faculty Internat. Assn. Fin. Planners. Editor Fla. C.P.A., 1974; assoc. editor Intellect, 1975-79; tax editor Quick Print, 1988—; contbr. articles to profl. jours. Chmn. Palm Beach County Transp. Com., 1972-75; treas. Ridge Audubon Soc., 1997-98. Served to 1st lt. U.S. Army, 1961-63. Recipient Disting. Svc., Fla. Accountants Assn., 1991, Alumni Assn. award for Outstanding Svcs., Fla. Atlantic Univ., 1997. Hon. fellow Internat. Soc. Preventive Medicine, Canadian Sch. Mgmt.; mem. AICPA, Am. Acctg. Assn., Acctg. Rsch. Assn., Beta Gamma Sigma, Beta Alpha Psi, Phi Beta Phi (pres. 1974), Phi Kappa Phi. Baptist. Home: 2612 Lake Front Dr Lake Wales FL 33898-7206 Home Phone: 863-696-4804. Personal E-mail: luing@msn.com. *In the professions, as in life, so much is owed to those who have gone before.*

LUJAN, MANUEL, JR., think-tank executive, former secretary of the interior, retired congressman; b. San Idlefonso, N.Mex., May 12, 1928; s. Manuel and Lorenzita (Romero) L.; m. Jean Kay Couchman, Nov. 18, 1948; children: Terra Kay Everett, James Manuel, Barbara Frae, Robert Jeffrey. BA, Coll. Santa Fe, 1950; postgrad., St. Mary's Coll., Calif., 1946-47. Engaged in ins. bus., Santa Fe and Albuquerque, 1948; mem. US Congress from 1st N.Mex. Dist., 1969-89; mem. interior and insular affairs com., energy and environ. subcom., sci. and tech. com.; sec. US Dept. Interior, Washington, 1989-93; founder Hispanic Alliance for Progress Inst., 2004—; founder, chmn. Hispanic Alliance for Progress Ins., Washington, 2004—. Office: Hispanic Alliance for Progress Inst 1101 Pennsylvania Ave NW Ste 600 Washington DC 20004

LUJAN, ROSA EMMA, bilingual specialist, trainer, consultant, assistant principal; b. El Paso, Tex., May 17, 1949; d. Rosendo G. and Petra (Rubalcava) López; m. Daniel Lujan, Feb. 21, 1976; children: Lorena Janel, Daniel Omar, Carina Viani, Crystal Rose. BA in Elem. Edn., U. Tex. El Paso, 1972, MS in Edn., 1978, postgrad., 1988, N.Mex. State U. Tchr. Ysleta Ind. Sch. Dist., El Paso, 1972-74, bilingual tchr., 1974-90, immigrant tchr., 1990—, now bilingual program supr. project mariposa. Cons. Internat. Acad. Coop. Learning, 1994; mem. Tex. Task Force on Profl. Preparation and Profl. Devel.; nat. bd. dirs. profl. tchg. stds. com. English as a New Lang., 1994; cooperating tchr. U. Tex. El Paso, 1978—; tchr. tnr. Ysleta Ind. Sch. Dist., 1980—; rschr. tnr. Johns Hopkins, U. Tex. El Paso, Haifa U., Israel, 1988—; mentor tchr. U. Tex. El Paso, El Salvador C.A., Boise, Idaho, 1990—; bd. dirs. Nat. Bd. for Profl. Tchg. Stds. Editor: (bilingual newsletter) El Chisme Bilingüe, 1986—. Pres. Ysleta Assn. Bilingual Edn., 1975-76, SW Assn. Bilingual Edn., El Paso, 1990-91; mem. Mt. Carmel Sch. Bd., El Paso, 1991-94, Tex. Com. Student Learning, Austin, 1992—. Named Tex. Tchr. of Yr., Tex. Edn. Agy., 1991-92, Tex. Elem. Tchr. of Yr., 1991-92. Mem. Nat. Assn. Bilingual Edn., Tex. Assn. Bilingual Edn., Phi Kappa Phi, Delta Kappa Gamma, Kappa Delta Pi. Democrat. Roman Catholic. Avocations: reading, sewing, travel, dance. Office: Ysleta Ind Sch Dist 9600 Sims Dr El Paso TX 79925-7200

LUKA, BISHOY, pharmacologist, educator; PharmD, LI U., 2002. Residency in pharmacy SUNY Upstate U. Hosp., Syracuse, NY, 2002—03; residency in critical care pharmacy Kingsbrook Jewish Med. Ctr., Bklyn., 2003—04, clin. pharmacist, 2004—; asst. prof. pharmacy Arnold & Marie Schwartz Coll. Pharmacy, LI U., Bklyn., 2004—; adj. prof. pharmacology SUNY Downstate Coll. Nursing, 2005—. Mem. critical care com. Kingsbrook Jewish Med. Ctr., 2004—, co-chair nutrition com., 2005—. Author: (abstracts) Propofol-Induced Torsades, Tenofovir-Induced Fanconi Syndrome; contbr. chpt. to book, articles to profl. jours. Recipient Merck award, NY State Coun. Health-Sys. Pharmacists, 2003, Pfizer Mentorship award, Kingsbrook Jewish Med. Ctr., 2005. Mem.: Am. Soc. Parenteral & Enteral Nutrition, Soc. Critical Care Medicine, NY State Coun. Health-Sys. Pharmacists, Am. Soc. Health-Sys. Pharmacists, Am. Coll. Clin. Pharmacists. Office: Kingsbrook Jewish Med Ctr 585 Schenectady Ave Brooklyn NY 11203

LUKACH, ARTHUR S., JR., manufacturing executive; b. NYC, Feb. 14, 1935; s. Arthur S. and Marion (Long) L.; 1 child, Justin A. C. BSME, Rensselaer Poly. Inst., 1956; MBA, Harvard U., 1964. V.p. Systemation Inc., Boston, 1967-70; prin. Lukach & Assocs., Cambridge, Mass., 1970-74; mgr. McKinsey & Co. Inc., NYC, 1975-81; pres. Micromold Products Inc., Yonkers, NY, 1982—. Guest lectr. Harvard U., Stanford U., Rensselaer Poly. Inst., Columbia U., Tulane U. Bd. dirs., treas. Vis. Nurse Svc., N.Y.C. Mem. ASME, ASCE, Soc. Plastics Engrs., Harvard Bus. Sch. Club (N.Y.C.), Harvard Club. Avocations: sailing, windsurfing, skiing, tennis. Home: 36 Northwest Rd East Hampton NY 11937 Office: Micromold Products Inc 200 Corporate Blvd S Yonkers NY 10701-6806 also: 50 W 70th St New York NY 10023-4624

LUKACS, JOHN ADALBERT, historian, retired educator; b. Budapest, Hungary, Jan. 31, 1924; came to US, 1946, naturalized, 1953; s. Paul and Magdalena Maria L.; m. Helen Schofield, May 29, 1953 (dec. 1970); children: Paul, Annemarie; m. Stephanie Harvey, May 18, 1974 (dec. 2003); m. Pamela Grant Hall, Apr. 30, 2005. PhD, Palatine Joseph U., Budapest, 1946; fed. doctorate (hon.). Prof. history Chestnut Hill Coll., 1947-94, Chmn. dept. history, 1947-74, ret., 1994; vis. prof. history La Salle Coll., 1949-82, Columbia U., 1954-55, U. Toulouse, France, 1964-65, U. Pa., 1964, 67, 68, Johns Hopkins U., 1970-71, Fletcher Sch. Law, Diplomacy, 1971-72, Princeton U., 1988; vis. prof. U. Budapest, 1991, U. Pa., 1995-97. Author: The Great Powers and Eastern Europe, 1953, A History of the Cold War, 1961, Decline and Rise of Europe, 1965, The Passing of the Modern Age, 1970, Historical Consciousness, 1968, 2d edit., 1985, The Last European War, 1939-41, 1976; 1945, Year Zero, 1978, Philadelphia: Patricians and Philistines, 1900-1950, 1981, Outgrowing Democracy: A historical interpretation of the U.S. in the 20th Century, 1984, Budapest 1900, 1988, Confessions of an Original Sinner, 1990, The Duel (Hitler vs. Churchill 10 May-31 August 1940), 1991, the End of the 20th Century (and the End of the Modern Age), 1993, Destinations Past, 1994, The Hitler of History, 1997, George F. Kennan and the Origins of Containment 1944-46, 1997, A Thread of Years, 1998, Five Days in London, 1999, At the End of an Age, 2002, Churchill, Visionary, Statesman, Historian, 2002, Democracy and Populism, 2005, A John Lukacs Reader: The Remembered Past, 2005, June 1941, Hitler and Stalin, 2006, George Kennan. A Study of Character, 2007, others; contbr. articles to profl. jours. Mem. Schuylkill Twp. (Pa.) Planning Commn. Recipient Ingersoll prize, 1991, Order of Merit, Republic Of Hungary, 1994, Matthias Corvinus chain, 2001. Fellow Soc. Am. Historians; mem. Am. Cath. Hist. Assn. (pres. 1977), Royal Hist. Soc., Am. Philos. Soc. (First Disting. Citizen award 2006). Home: Pickering Close 129 Valley Park Rd Phoenixville PA 19460

LUKACS, MICHAEL EDWARD, electro-optics researcher; b. NYC, Mar. 25, 1946; s. William and Hannah (LeWitter-Wolf) L.; m. Diane Harriet Katz, Oct. 29, 1967. Student, CUNY, Queens, 1965-68; T-3, Radio Corp. Am. Inst. now Tech Careers Inst., NYC, 1968-69. Tech. aide Bell Telephone Labs., Holmdel, NJ, 1969-72, sr. tech. aide, 1972-77, assoc. mem. tech. staff, 1977-81, mem. tech. staff, 1981-83, Bell Comm. Rsch., Red Bank, NJ, 1983-94, rsch. scientist, 1994-99, Telcordia Techs. (formerly Bell Comms. Rsch.), Red Bank, NJ, 1999—2002; prin. scientist Innovative Tech. Solutions-NovaSol, Honolulu, 2002—. Patentee cathode ray tube dynamic focus apparatus, cathode ray tube electro-optic linearization device, infinitely expandable video conferencing sys., video conf. sys. with multilayer keying of multi video images; (co-inventor) pel recursive motion compensated video coder; (inventor) "Lukacs" coding, disparity corrected predictive coding for 3-D video, "Personal Presence System" advanced multimedia video bridge, multilayer priority video keying, infinitely extensible video conferencing. Recipient Notable Achievement award Bell Labs Research Lab. 113, 1983; R&D 100 award, 1996. Mem. IEEE, Assn. Computing Machinery (Best Paper award 1994), Soc. Motion Picture TV Engrs., Lasers & Electro Optical Soc. (LEOS). Avocations: reading, autocross, antiques. Office Phone: 352-205-8136. Personal E-mail: whoswho@mikelukacs.com. Business E-Mail: michael.lukacs@nova-sol.com.

LUKASZEWSKI, JAMES EDMUND, communications executive; b. Kewaunee, Wis., Aug. 27, 1942; s. Edmund Ignatius and Virginia Francis Lukaszewski; m. Barbara Ann Bray, Dec. 18, 1964; children: Charles Todd Lukaszewksi, James Moir Lukaszewksi. BA, Met. State U., 1974. Asst., press sec. State of Minn., Office of Governor Wendell R. Anderson, St. Paul, 1974-76; deputy commr. Dept. of Econ. Devel., State of Minn., St. Paul, 1976-78; pres. Media Info. Systems Corp., New Brighton, Minn., 1978-83, Brum & Anderson Exec. Tng., Inc., Mpls., 1984-86; ptnr. Chester Burger Co., NYC, 1986-87; sr. v.p., dir. exec. communication programs Georgeson & Co., Inc., 1987-89; pres., chmn. bd. The Lukaszewski Group Inc., White Plains, N.Y., 1989—. Civillian advisor to internat. disaster adv. com. USMC, 1986—, US Dept. State, 1990—94; adj. assoc. prof. mgmt. and comm. divsn. degree studies, mktg. & mgmt. NYU Sch. Continuing and Profl. Studies, 1991—; mem. dean's adv. bd. Ancell Sch. Bus., We. Conn. Sch. Bus., 2005; mem. pres. cabinet future of univ. Minn. Met. Sate U., 2006; lectr., spkr. in field. Author: Executive Television Training Handbook, 1983, The Publicity Handbook, 1984;: Having Effective Media Interviews, 1984, The Tactical Ingenuity Pyramid, 1989, Executive Action Crisis Management Anthology, 1992, Executive Action Crisis Management Workbook, 1992, 1993, Executive Action Emergency Media Relations Guide, 1992, 1993, Influencing Public Attitudes: Strategies that Reduce the Media's Power, 1992, War Stories and Crisis Communication Strategies, An Anthology, 2000, Crisis Communication Planning Strategies, A Workbook, 2000, Media Relations Strategies During Emergencies, A Guide, 2000, (video) Executive Action Crisis Management System; co-author: Executive Action Crisis Communication Plan Compoenets and Models, 2005, Crisis Response: Inside Stories on Managing Image Under Siege, 1993, Disaster Recovery Testing: Exercising Your Contingency Plan, 1994, Environmental Health and Safety Auditing Handbook, 1994, Practical Public Affairs in an Era of Change: A Cutting Edge Guide for Government, Business and College, 1995; contbg. editor: Pub. Rels. Quar., 1997—; author: Strategy Quar. supplement to P.R. Reporter, 1998—2003; guest columnist, mem. editl. bd.: PR News, 2000—01; editor: TRUST newsletter, 2001—02; mem. adv. bd. Media Rels. Insider, 2001—; contbg. columnist: O'Dwyer's PR Svcs. Report, 2003—; contbr. articles to profl. jours. Chmn. Brooklyn Pk. Tater Daze Celebration, Minn., 1972; trustee, v.p. Met. State U. Found., St. Paul, 1976—86; chmn. Met. State U. Alumni Assn., St. Paul, 1974; chmn. venture fund drive Minn. Met. State U., 1990—91, mem. pres. cabinet of future of univ., 2005—06; mem. dean's adv. bd. Ancell Sch. Bus., Western Conn. State U. Sch. Bus., 2005—06. Named Alumnus of Yr., Minn. Met. State U., 2007, Sound Citizen of Yr., Park Jaycees, 1972; named one of 28 Experts to Call When All Hell Breaks Loose, Corp. Legal Times, 2003, 22 Crunch-Time Counselors Who Should Be on the Speed Dial in a Crisis, PR Week, 2004; recipient Silver Key award, Brooklyn Pk. Jaycees, 1973, Drew Middleton award for Disting. Svc. in Support of USMC E. Coast Comdrs., Media Tng. Symposium, 1992, Outstanding Svc. award, Choice in Dying, 1996, Nat. Pub. Rels. Achievement award, Ball State U., 2004, Lifetime Achievement award, PR News, 2005. Fellow: Soc. Am., Pub. Rels. Soc. Am. (bd. ethics and profl. stds. 1990—, past mem. Counselors Acad., corp., employee rels. and pub. affairs/govt. sects., Pres.'s Citation award 1991, 2000, Patrick Jackson Disting. Svc. award 2004, Pres.'s Citation award 2006, Lloyd B. Dennis award for disting. leadership in pub. affairs 2006, Pres.'s Citation award 2006, Lloyd B. Dennis award for Disting. Leadership in Pub. Affairs 2006, accredited); mem.: Fairfield County Pub. Rels. Assn., Issue Mgmt. Coun., Internat. Churchill Soc., Ctr. Study Presidency, Soc. Corp. Compliance and Ethics (cert.), Pub. Rels. Soc. NY, Intenrat. Assn. Bus. Communicators. Avocation: writing. Home: 16 Sunset Dr Snug Harbor Danbury CT 06811-3132 Office: Ten Bank St Ste 530 White Plains NY 10606 Office Phone: 914-681-0000.

LUKE, DAVID LINCOLN, III, retired paper company executive; b. Tyrone, Pa., July 25, 1923; s. David Lincoln and Priscilla Warren Luke; m. Fanny R. Curtis, June 11, 1955. AB, Yale U., 1945; LLD (hon.), Juniata Coll., 1967, Lawrence U., 1976, Salem Coll., 1983, W. Va. U., 1984; DSc. (hon.), Cold Spring Harbor Lab., 2001. V.p., dir. Westvaco Corp., NYC, 1953-57, exec. v.p., dir., 1957-62, pres., bd. dirs., 1962-80, chief exec. officer, 1963-88, chmn. bd. dirs., 1980-96. Trustee emeritus, past chmn. Cold Spring Harbor Lab.; hon. bd. dirs., former bd. dirs. Josiah Macy Jr. Found.; past chmn., trustee emeritus Hotchkiss Sch. Served from aviation cadet to combat pilot. USMCR., 1942-45. Mem. The River Club, Piping Rock Club, John's Island Club.

LUKE, DAVID RUSSELL, mathematician, educator; b. Clifton Forge, Va., Apr. 20, 1969; s. Anne (Nina) Roosevelt and Nicholas James Gibson (Stepfather), Douglas Siglar and Sarah Mullen Luke (Stepmother); m. Anja Karin Sturm, June 15, 2001. BA cum laude, U. Calif., Berkeley, Calif., 1991; MSc, U. Wash., 1997, PhD, 2001. Wissenchaftliche assistent U. Goettingen, Lower Saxony, Germany, 2001—03; postdoctoral fellow Pacific Inst. Math. Scis., Vancouver, British Columbia, Canada, 2003—04; asst. prof. U. Del., Newark, Del., 2004—. Assistant editor (films) The Ride to Wounded Knee, 1992; dir.(prodr., editor): (films) 29 and 7 Strong, 1995. Vol. VISTA Okanogan (Wash.) Cmty. Action Coun., 1994—95. Fellow, NASA, 1998—2001, Pacific Inst. Math. Scis., 2002—04. Mem.: IEEE, Soc. Indsl. and Applied Math., Am. Math. Soc. Independent. Office: University of Delaware Department of Mathematics Newark DE 19716-2553 Home Phone: 302-234-2923.

LUKE, DOUGLAS SIGLER, investment company executive; b. Middletown, NY, Oct. 1, 1941; s. Douglas Sigler Luke and Joanne (Benton) Cowles; m. Anne Sturgis Roosevelt, June 20, 1964 (div. Sept. 1976); m. Sarah Chappell Mullen, Mar. 23, 1991; children: Haven Roosevelt, David Russell, Lindsay Hall. Student, Mexico City Coll., 1961; BA Fgn. Affairs, U. Va., 1964; MBA, The Darden Sch., Charlottesville, Va., 1966. Mem. staff chem. divsn. WestVaco Corp., Covington, Va., 1966-69; dir. corp. planning SCOA Industries, Columbus, Ohio, 1969-71; v.p. fin. Multicon Prop. divsn. Bethlehem Steel Corp., Columbus, 1971-72; gen. ptnr., CEO, Personal Investments, Columbus, 1972-79; v.p. Rothschild, Inc. (formerly New Court Securities), NYC, 1979-83, sr. v.p., 1984-87, mng. dir., 1987-90; pres, CEO, WLD Enterprises, Inc., Ft. Lauderdale, Fla., 1991-98; pres., CEO HL Capital, Inc., NYC, 1999—. Bd. dirs. MeadWestraco Corp., N.Y.C., Regency Ctrs. Corp., Jacksonville, Fla.; mem. adv. bd. Nat. Outdoor Leadership Sch., 1994-99, trustee, 2000-06, 2006—. Founding donor Adopt-a-Class, N.Y.C., 1988;mem. space adv. bd. U. Colo., 1985-89; bd. dirs. condrs. com. Columbus Symphony Orch., 1972-75; trustee The Columbus Acad., Gahanna, Ohio, 1973-77, Girl Scouts U.S., Piedmont Region, Roanoke, Va., 1967-69, Adirondack Coun., 2001—, Adirondack Nature Conservancy, Adirondack Land Trust, 2004—; high tech. com. working group N.Y.C. Partnership Inc., 1988-90. Mem. Ausable Club (St. Huberts, NY), Adirondack Mountain Reserve (St. Huberts, trustee 1985-94, pres. 1988-91, chmn. 1991-94), Va. Club/Yale Club (NYC), Mashomack Fish and Game Preserve (Pine Plains, NY). Avocations: skiing, fly fishing, horsepacking, fox hunting. Office: HL Capital Inc The Chrysler Bldg 48th Fl 405 Lexington Ave New York NY 10174 Office Phone: 212-983-3170. Business E-Mail: dluke@hlcapital.com.

LUKE, JOHN ANDERSON, JR., paper, packaging and chemical company executive; b. Nov. 24, 1948; s. John Anderson Luke Sr. and Joy (Carter) Luke; m. Kathleen Allen, June 30, 1984; children: Lindsay Allen, Elizabeth Carter, John A. III. BA, Lawrence U., 1971; MBA, U. Pa., 1979. Unit sales mgr. Procter & Gamble, 1974—77; corp. assoc. Westvaco Corp., NYC, 1979—81, sr. fin. analyst, 1981—82, asst. treas., 1982, treas., 1983—86, v.p., treas., 1986, sr. v.p. mktg., internat. and Brazilian subsidiary, 1987—90, exec. v.p., 1990—92, pres., 1992—2002, chmn., 1996—2002; CEO Westvaco (now MeadWestvaco), Stamford, Conn., 1992—; chmn. MeadWestvaco, Stamford, Conn., 2002—. Dir. FM Global, The Timken Co.; trustee Am. Enterprise Inst. for Pub. Policy Rsch.; chmn. Am. Forest Found., Nat. Assn. Mfr.; vice chmn. Sustainable Forestry Bd.; bd. dirs. Bank of N.Y., The Tinker Found., Ams. Soc., Bank of N.Y.; bd. trustees Lawrence U.; mem. President's Export Coun. Bd. govs. NCASI; dir. United Negro Coll. Fund. Officer USAF, 1971—74, S.E. Asia, Vietnam conflict. Mem.: Am. Forest and Paper Assn. (dir., exec. com.), The Commonwealth Club, The Links, Univ. Club. Office: MeadWestvaco Corp 1 High Ridge Park Stamford CT 06905*

LUKE, KAREN, chemist, researcher; arrived in Can., 1989, naturalized, 1999; d. Reginald George and Ruth Lynn Ogilvie Luke. BSc with honors, Aberdeen U., 1977, PhD, 1982. Sr. rsch. scientist Dowell, Divsn. Dow Chems., Tulsa, Okla., 1983—84; rsch. fellow U. of Aberdeen, 1985—87; project leader/rschr. U. of Sherbrooke, Sherbrooke, Que., Canada, 1987—91; sr. devel. engr. Dowell Schlumberger, St. Ettienne, France, 1991—93; rsch. scientist Schlumberger Cambridge Rsch., Cambridge, England, 1993—94; rsch. asst./cons. U. of Toronto, Ont., Canada, 1995; project leader/rsch. scientist Can. Fracmaster, Calgary, Alta., Canada, 1995—98; tech. project mgr./cons. Dalriada, Calgary, Alberta, Canada, 1998—2000; sci. advisor - chemist Halliburton Energy Svcs., Duncan, Okla., 2000—. Contbr. articles to profl. jours., chapters to books. Fellow: Royal Microscopical Soc.; mem.: Am. Concrete Inst., Soc. of Petroleum Engrs. (membership com. mem. 2000—03). Achievements include 6 patents for method and compositions for sealing subterranean zones; for generating gas in well fluids; for generating gas in well treating fluids; for methods of generating gas in and foaming well cement compositions and for use of zeolites in oil and gas wells; patents pending for 10 other compositions and methods. Home Phone: 580-251-3353; Office Phone: 580-251-3353. Office Fax: 580-251-4745; Home Fax: 580-251-4745. Business E-Mail: karen.luke@halliburton.com.

LUKE, RANDALL DAN, retired manufacturing executive, lawyer; b. New Castle, Pa., June 4, 1935; s. Randall Beamer and Blanche Wilhelmina (Fisher) L.; m. Patricia Arlene Moody, Aug. 4, 1962 (div. Jan. 1977); children: Lisa Elin, Randall Sargent; m. Saralee Frances Krow, Mar. 1, 1979; 1 stepchild, Stephanie Sogg. BA in Econs. with honors, U. Pa., 1957, JD, 1960. Bar: Ohio 1960, Calif. 1962, Ill. 1989. Assoc., ptnr. Daus, Schwenger & Kottler, Cleve., 1965-70; ptnr. Kottler & Danzig, Cleve., 1970-75, Hahn, Loeser, Freedheim, Dean & Wellman, Cleve., 1975-81; assoc. gen. counsel The Firestone Tire & Rubber Co., Akron, Ohio, 1981-82, v.p., assoc. gen. counsel and sec., 1982-88, Bridgestone/Firestone, Inc., Akron, 1988-91, ret., 1991; of counsel Hahn Loeser & Parks, Cleve., 1991-2000; ret., 2000. Trustee, Akron Art Mus., 1982-87, Akron Symphony Orch., 1986-87, Cleve. Opera League, 1992-98. Served to Capt. USNR, 1960-81; ret. 1981. Mem.: Ohio Bar Assn., Ill. Bar Assn., Calif. Bar Assn., Union Club, Mayfield Country Club, Cleve. Skating Club. Republican. Avocations: tennis, golf, skiing, swimming, exercise. Home: 13901 Shaker Blvd Cleveland OH 44120-1582

LUKE, ROBERT GEORGE, nephrologist, medical educator; b. Sept. 4, 1935; s. Henry and Jemima (McCracken) L.; m. Catriona Mary MacDonald, Mar. 10, 1964; children: Colin Henry, Margaret Ann M.B., Ch.B., U. Glasgow, Scotland, 1959. Intern, then resident Univ. Hosps., U. Glasgow, 1959-63; Dir. renal div. U. Ky. Med. Ctr., Lexington, 1968-79; dir nephrology rsch. and tng. ctr. U. Ala., Birmingham, 1979-88; chmn. dept. medicine U. Cin. Med. Ctr., 1988—2004. Contbr. articles to profl. jours. Grantee NIH, 1972-91; fellow Yale U. Med. Ctr., 1964-65. Master ACP (bd. regents 2004—); mem. Assn. Am. Physicians, Am. Soc. Clin. Investigation, Nat. Kidney Found., Am. Soc. Nephrology (past pres.), Clin. and Climatol. Assn. (past pres.). Presbyterian. Avocation: tennis. Business E-Mail: robert.luke@uc.edu.

LUKEHART, CHARLES MARTIN, chemistry professor; b. DuBois, Pa., Dec. 21, 1946; s. David Blair and Grace Dorothy L.; m. Marilyn Orleana McKinney, Aug. 4, 1973; children: Mark, Brian, Laura. BS in Chemistry, Pa. State U., 1968; PhD in Inorganic Chemistry, MIT, 1972. Postdoctoral assoc. Tex. A&M U., College Station, 1972-73; asst. prof. chemistry Vanderbilt U., Nashville, 1973-77, assoc. prof. chemistry, 1977-82, prof., 1982—. Author: Fundamental Transition Metal Organometallic Chemistry, 1985. Rsch. fellow Alfred P. Sloan Found., 1979-81. Mem. Am. Chem. Soc. (chmn. Nashville sect. 1979, 92), Materials Rsch. Soc. Office: Vanderbilt U Dept Chemistry VU Station B 351822 Nashville TN 37235 Home Phone: 615-352-6783; Office Phone: 615-322-2935. Business E-Mail: charles.m.lukehart@vanderbilt.edu.

LUKENS, MAX L., manufacturing executive; b. Wash., May 6, 1948; m. Chris Lukens; children: K.C., Nick, Reid, Patrick, Steven. BS, Miami U., Oxford, Ohio, 1970, MBA, 1971. With Deloitte Haskins & Sells, Washington and Dayton, Ohio, 1970-81; v.p. fin. Reed Tubular Products, Baker Hughes Inc. (formerly Baker Internat.), Houston, 1982-84, v.p. fin. Milpark, 1984-89, v.p., CFO, 1984-89, pres. Hughes Tool Co., 1989-93, pres. Baker Hughes Prodn. Tools, 1989-93, pres., COO, 1995-96, pres., CEO, 1996-98; chmn., CEO Baker Hughes Inc., Houston, 1998-99; pres., CEO Stewart & Stevenson Svcs., Houston, 2002—. Bd. dir. NCI Building Systems, Inc., Stewart & Stevenson Svcs. Office: Stewart & Stevenson Svcs 2707 North Loop West Houston TX 77008

LUKKEN, WALTER L., commissioner; b. 1967; s. Wayne and Carol Lukken; m. Dana Bostic Lukken; children: William, Genevieve. BS with honors, Ind. U. Kelley Sch. Bus., 1989; JD, Lewis & Clark Law Sch., 1992. Bar: Ill. Legis. asst. in fin. and tax matters to Senator Richard Lugar US Senate, Washington, 1992—97, profl. staff agr. com., 1998—2002; commr. Commodity Futures Trading Commn., Washington, 2002—, acting chmn., 2007—, chmn., Global Markets Adv. Comm., 2003—04. Mem.: Ill. State Bar Assn. Office: CFTC Three Lafayette Ctr 1155 21st St NW Washington DC 20581 Office Phone: 202-418-5014. Office Fax: 202-418-5550.*

LUKOWSKY, GERHARD HANS, internist; b. Berlin, Aug. 20, 1926; arrived in U.S., 1957; s. Georg and Dorothea Lukowsky; m. Martha Maria Tills, Nov. 9, 1957; children: Andrea Longo, Maria, Tania Bruno. Diploma, Christian Albrecht U., Kiel, Germany, 1949, MD, 1952. Diplomate Am. Bd. Internal Medicine. Internship Meml. Hosp., Worcester, Mass., 1953—54, resident, 1954—55, St. Vincent Hosp., 1957—58, Georgetown U. Hosp., Washington, 1958—60; pvt. practice internist Alexandria, Va., 1960—96; chief medicine Mt. Vernon Hosp., Alexandria, 1976; vice chief med. dept. Alexandria Hosp.; instr. medicine Georgetown U. Hosp., Washington, 1960—65. Contbr. articles to med. jours. Bd. dirs. Alexandria Vis. Nurses Assn., 1964—68; co-founder recital series Alexandria. Mem.: AMA, ACP, Am. Soc. Internal Medicine, Va. Med. Soc. Avocations: philosophy, music, gardening. Home: 15822 Spyglass Hill Loop Gainesville VA 20155

LUKS, ALLAN BARRY, executive director; b. NYC, June 27, 1941; s. Joseph Moses and Evelyn (Gropper) L.; m. Karen Greenbaum, Feb. 22, 1969; children: Rachel, David. BA, U. N.C., 1963; JD, Georgetown Law Sch., 1966. Bar: N.Y. Vol. U.S. Peace Corps, Maracay, Venezuela, 1967-69; legal dir. Children's Aid Soc. East Harlem, NYC, 1970-72; asst. dir. Life Ins. Industry Urban Investment Program, NYC, 1972-75; sec.-treas. N.Y.C. Rand Inst., 1975-78; exec. dir. Alcoholism Coun. of Greater N.Y., NYC, 1978-88, Inst. for the Advancement of Health, NYC, 1988-90, Big Bros./Big Sisters of N.Y., NYC, 1990—. Author N.Y.C. law, warning posters on drinking during pregnancy, 1983; adj. prof. Fordham U. Grad. Sch. Social Svc., N.Y.C., 1979-88; chmn. legal sect. Internat. Coun. on Alcohol and Addictions, Lausanne, Switzerland, 1980-88; mem. NGO-Crime Prevention and Criminal Justice, UN, N.Y.C., 1982-90. Author: Will America Sober Up?, 1983, The Healing Power of Doing Good, 1991; co-author: You Are What You Drink, 1989; editor Having Been There, 1979. Pres. Cadman Towers Housing, Bklyn., 1971-75; sch. bd. mem. N.Y.C. Sch. Bd. #13, Bklyn., 1975-80; v.p. Brooklyn Heights Assn., N.Y.C., 1982-86; adv. coun. mem. Jr. League N.Y., N.Y.C., 1984-88. Recipient Vol. Leadership award Mayor of N.Y., N.Y.C., 1987, Pub. Svc. award Crains N.Y. Bus. Mag., N.Y.C., 1994, Nat. Lewis Hine award for leadership on behalf of children and families, 2007. Office: Big Bros/Big Sisters NYC 223 E 30th St New York NY 10016-8203 Office Phone: 212-686-2042. E-mail: aluks@bigsnyc.org.

LULL, WILLIAM PAUL, engineering consultant; b. Indpls., Nov. 5, 1954; s. William Roger and Florence Elizabeth (Morris) L.; m. Mary Ann Garrison, Dec. 22, 1989. Student, Ind. State U., 1973-75; BS in Arts & Design, MIT, 1978. Systems designer James Assocs., Architects, Engrs., Indpls., 1978-79; architect TVA, Knoxville, Tenn., 1980; mgr. energy mgmt. div. Dubin-Bloome, Engrs., NYC, 1981; asst. chief of design Syska & Hennessy, Engrs., NYC, 1982-83; prin. Garrison/Lull Inc., Princeton Junction, N.J., 1984—. Adj. assoc. prof. NYU, 1983—; lectr., presenter cons. environ. field. Author: Conservation Environment Guidelines for Libraries and Archives, 1990; co-author: Criteria for Storage of Paper-Based Archival Records, 1984, Humidity Control Design Guide, 2001; contbr. articles to profl. publs. Mem. ASHRAE (conf. presenter), Illuminating Engring. Soc. N.Am., Am. Inst. Conservation of Historic and Artistic Works (assoc.), Sigma Pi Sigma. Achievements include pioneering discipline of consulting on conservation environments for preservation of museum library and archival collections. Home: 7 High St Allentown NJ 08501-1914 Office: Garrison/Lull Inc PO Box 459 Princeton Junction NJ 08550-0459

LUM, GREGORY, high school librarian; m. JoAnn Lum; 4 children. MLS, George Peabody Coll., Vanderbilt U., 1985. Libr. Jesuit High School, Portland, Oreg. Mem. selection com., Best Young Adult Fiction Am. Libr. Assn., 2007. Named one of the Movers & Shakers, Libr. Jour., 2007; recipient Oreg. Secondary Library Media Tchr. of Yr. award, 2002, AECT National Sch. Media Specialist of Yr. award, 2003. Mem.: Oreg. Ednl. Media Assn. (current pres.-elect). Office: Jesuit HS 9000 SW Beaverton Hillsdale Hwy Portland OR 97225 E-mail: glum@jesuitportland.org.

LUM, JEAN LOUI JIN, nursing educator; b. Honolulu, Sept. 5, 1938; d. Yee Nung and Pui Ki (Young) L. BS, U. Hawaii, Manoa, 1960; MS in Nursing, U. Calif., San Francisco, 1961; MA, U. Wash., 1969, PhD in Sociology, 1972. Registered nurse, Hawaii. From instr. to prof. Sch. Nursing U. Hawaii Manoa, Honolulu, 1961-95, acting dean, 1982, dean, 1982-89, prof. emeritus, 1995—. Project coordinator Analysis and Planning Personnel Svcs., Western Interstate Commn. Higher Edn., 1977; extramural assoc. div. Rsch. Grants NIH, 1978-79; mem. mgmt. adv. com. Honolulu County Hosp., 1982-96; mem. exec. bd. Pacific Health Rsch. Inst., 1980-88; mem. health planning com. East Honolulu, 1978-81; mem. rsch. grants adv. coun. Hawaii Med. Svcs. Assn. Found., Nat. Adv. Coun. for Nursing Rsch., 1990-93. Contbr. articles to profl. jours. Trustee Straub Pacific Health Found., Honolulu; bd. dirs. Friends of the Nat. Inst. of Nursing Rsch., 1994-97. Recipient Nurse of Yr. award Hawaii Nurses Assn., 1982, Gov.'s commendation State of Hawaii, 2006; named Disting. Practitioner in Nursing, Nat. Acads. Practice, 1986; USPHS grantee, 1967-72. Fellow Am. Acad. Nursing; mem. Am. Nurses Assn., Am. Pacific

Nursing Leaders Conf. (pres. 1983-87), Council Nurse Researchers, Nat. League for Nursing (bd. rev. 1981-87), Western Council Higher Edn. for Nurses (chmn. 1984-85), Western Soc. for Research in Nursing, Am. Sociol. Assn., Pacific Sociol. Assn., Assn. for Women in Sci., Hawaii Pub. Health Assn., Hawaii Med. Services Assn. (bd. dirs. 1985-92), Western Inst. Nursing, Mortar Bd., Phi Kappa Phi, Sigma Theta Tau (Kupuna award 2003), Alpha Kappa Delta, Delta Kappa Gamma. Episcopalian. Office: U Hawaii Manoa Sch Nursing Webster Hall 2528 The Mall Honolulu HI 96822

LUM, LARRY, lawyer; b. Hong Kong, Dec. 25, 1960; BA, SUNY, Stony Brook, 1983; JD, Albany Law Sch., Union U., 1986. Bar: NY 1987, US Dist. Ct. So., We. & Ea. Districts NY. Ptnr. Wilson, Elser, Moskowitz, Edelman & Dicker LLP, NYC. Mem.: ABA, Nat. Asian Am. Bar Assn., Assn. of the Bar of the City of NY. Office: Wilson Elser Moskowitz Edelman & Dicker LLP 23rd Fl 150 E 42nd St New York NY 10017-5639 Office Phone: 212-490-3000 ext. 2292. Office Fax: 212-490-3038. Business E-Mail: luml@wemed.com.

LUM, MARY, artist, educator; BFA, U Mich.; MFA, Rochester Inst. Tech. Mem. faculty Sch. Art & Design, Albert U., NY, 1984—2004, prof. painting NY, co-chair MFA program in electronic integrated arts NY; mem. faculty painting and drawing Bennington Coll., Vt., 2005—. Work exhibited at, Hallwalls, Buffalo, NY, INTAR Gallery, NYC, Washington Project for the Arts, Washington, DC, So. Exposure, San Francisco, Art in General, NYC, Burchfield Art Ctr. and State Mus. of NY, Buffalo, Kean Coll., Union, NJ, Printed Matter, NYC, Ernest Rubenstein Gallery, U. Wis., Bernard Toale Gallery, Boston, Paris Project Room, 2002, Aldrich Contemporary Mus. Art, Ridgefield, CT, 2004. Grantee, Nat. Endowment for the Arts, NY Found. for the Arts, Constance Saltonstall Found. for the Arts, NY State Coun. on the Arts; Radcliffe Inst. Fellow, Harvard U., 2004—05, residency, Cite Internationale des Arts, Paris, Internat. Studio/Curatorial Program, NY, MacDowell Colony, Petersborough, NH, 2003. Office: Bennington Coll 1 Coll Dr Bennington VT 05201-6003

LUMAN, RICHARD GORDON, retired religious studies educator; b. Ottumwa, Iowa, June 20, 1930; s. David Edward and Metta Lee Luman. BA, State U. Iowa, Iowa City, 1952, MA, 1956, PhD, 1965. Grad. asst. State U. Iowa, 1956—57; history instr. State U. SD, Vermillion, 1959—61; instr. ancient medieval and reformation ch. history U. Chgo. Div. Sch., 1961—65; asst. prof. dept. history U. Chgo., 1965—68; assoc. editor Encyclopedia Britannica, 1968—69; assoc. prof. religion Haverford Coll., 1969—92, prof., 1992—95, prof. emeritus, 1995—, chair dept. religion, 1976—77, 1982—83, 1984—87, 1994. Vis. prof. Princeton Theol. Seminary, 1971; vis. prof. dept. theology St. Joseph's Coll., Phila., 1976; adj. assoc. prof. religion dept. Columbia U., NYC, 1983—84, vis. assoc. prof. dept. religion, dept. history, 1987—88; vis. prof. exptl. seminar program Elizabethtown Coll., Pa., 1990—91, rsch. fellow Young Ctr. for the Study of Pietist Groups, 1990—91. Contbr. articles to profl. jours. Recipient Disting. Tchg. award; grantee, NEH. Avocations: stamp collecting/philately, historical autographs, coin collecting/numismatics, railroads. Home: 7 Schwartz Dr Ottumwa IA 52501-1133

LUMB, WILLIAM VALJEAN, veterinarian; b. Sioux City, Iowa, Nov. 26, 1921; m. Lilly Carlson, 1949; 1 child, John W. DVM, Kans. State U., 1943; MS, Tex. A&M U., 1953; PhD in Vet. Medicine, U. Minn., 1957; DSc (hon.), Ohio State U., 1999. Intern, resident Angell Meml. Animal Hosp., Boston, 1946—48; from instr. to assoc. prof. medicine and surgery Tex. A&M U., 1949—52; asst. prof. clin. surgery Colo. State U., 1954—58; assoc. prof. surgery and medicine Mich. State U., 1958—60; assoc. prof. medicine Coll. Vet. Medicine, Colo. State U., Ft. Collins, 1960—63, dir. surg. lab., 1963—79, prof. surgery, 1963—81, emeritus prof., 1981—; prof. Ross U., St. Kitts, West Indies, 1986. Pres., CEO The Lubra Co., 1972—99. Author: Small Animal Anesthesia, 1963; author: (with E.W. Jones) Veterinary Anesthesia, 1973, 1984, Veterinary Anesthesia, Japanese and Spanish translations, 1979; editor: Vet Surgery, 1982; contbr. over 150 articles to profl. jours.; patentee in field. With Vet. Corps US Army, 1943—46. Named Colo. Vet. of Yr., 1981; recipient Gaines medal, 1965, Ralston Purina Rsch. award, 1980, Disting. Svc. award, Kans. State U., 1982, Jacob Markowitz award, 1986, Glover Disting. Faculty award, Colo. State U., 2004. Mem.: NAS, AAAS, AVMA, Nat. Acads. of Practice, Am. Assn. Vet. Clinicians, N.Y. Acad. Sci., Am. Coll. Vet. Surgeons (founding diplomate, pres., chmn. bd. 1974—75), Am. Coll. Vet. Anesthesiologists (founding diplomate, Svc. award 1982). Address: 1905 Mohawk St Fort Collins CO 80525-1501

LUMBARD, ELIOT HOWLAND, lawyer, educator; b. Fairhaven, Mass., May 6, 1925; s. Ralph E. and Constance Y. Lumbard; m. Jean Ashmore, June 21, 1947 (div.); m. Kristen Dehner, June 28, 1981 (div.); children: Susan, John, Ann, Joshua Abel, Marah Abel. BS in Marine Transp., US Mcht. Marine Acad., 1945, DSc (hon.), 2005; BS in Econs., U. Pa., Wharton, 1949; JD, Columbia U., NYC, 1952. Bar: NY 1953, US Supreme Ct. 1959, Pa. 1983. Assoc. Breed, Abbott and Morgan, NYC, 1952-53; asst. U.S. atty. So. Dist. NY, 1953-56; assoc. Chadbourne, Parke, Whiteside & Wolff, NYC, 1956-58; ptnr. Townsend & Lewis, NYC, 1961-70, Spear and Hill, NYC, 1970-75, Lumbard and Phelan, P.C., NYC, 1977-82, Saul, Ewing, Remick & Saul, NYC, 1982-84; pvt. practice law NYC, 1984-86; ptnr. Haight, Gardner, Poor & Havens, NYC, 1986-88; pvt. practice law NYC, 1988-92; ret. Chief counsel NY State Commn. Investigation, 1958-61; spl. asst. counsel for law enforcement to Gov. NY, 1961-67; organizer NY State Identification and Intelligence Sys., 1963-67; chair Oyster Bay Conf. on Organized Crime, 1962-67; criminal justice cons. to Gov. Fla. and other states, 1967; chief criminal justice cons. to NJ Legis., 1968-69; chmn. com. on organized crime NYC Criminal Justice Coordinating Coun., 1971-74; organizer schs. of criminal justice at SUNY Albany and Rutgers, Newark; mem. departmental disciplinary com. First Dept., NY Supreme Ct., 1982-88; trustee bankruptcy Universal Money Order Co., Inc., 1977-82, Meritum Corp., 1983-89; spl. master in admiralty Hellenic Lines Ltd., 1984-86; chmn. Palisades Life Ins. Co. (former Equity Funding subs. 1974-75); bd. dir. RMC Industries Corp.; chair Am. Maritime History Project, Inc., Kings Point, NY, 1996—; lectr. trial practice NYU Law Sch., 1963-65; mem. vis. com. Sch. Criminal Justice, SUNY-Albany, 1968-75; adj. prof. law and criminal justice John Jay Coll. Criminal Justice, CUNY, 1975-86; arbitrator Am. Arbitration Assn. and NY Civil Ct.-Small Claims Part, NY County; mem. Vol. Master Program US Dist. Ct. (so. dist.) NY Contbr. articles to profl. jours. Bd. dirs. Citizens Crime Commn. NYC, Inc., Big Bros. Movement, Citizens Union; trustee Trinity Sch., 1964-78, NYC Police Found., Inc., 1971-92, chmn., 1971-74, emeritus. Lt. j.g. USNR, 1943-52. Recipient Disting. Svc. award SUNY, Albany, 1985, US Merchant Marine Acad., 2005. Mem. Assn. Bar City NY, NY County Lawyers Assn., ABA, NY State Bar Assn., Maritime Law Assn., Down Town Assn. Club. Republican. Home: 10 Allds St No 357 Nashua NH 03060

LUMENG, LAWRENCE, physician, educator; b. Manila, Aug. 10, 1939; came to US, 1958; s. Ming and Lucia (Lim) Lu; m. Pauline Lumeng, Nov. 26, 1966; children: Carey, Emily. AB, Ind. U., 1960, MD, 1964, MS, 1969. Intern U. Chgo., 1964-65; resident Ind. U. Hosps., Indpls., 1965-67, fellow, 1967-69, asst. prof. Sch. of Medicine, 1971-73, assoc. prof. Sch. of Medicine, 1974-79, prof. Sch. of Medicine, 1979—2003, dir. div. gastroenterology and hepatology Sch. of Medieine, 1984—; chief gastroenterology sect. VA Med. Ctr., Indpls., 1979—2003. Merit rev. bd. VA. Cen. Office, Washington, 1981-84; alcohol biomed. res. rev. com. NIAAA, Washington, 1982-86; grant rev. panel USDA, Washington, 1985-2003. Contbr. over 290 articles to profl. jours. Maj. U.S. Army, 1969-71. Fellow ACP; mem. Am. Soc. Clin. Investigation, Am. Soc. Biol. Chemists, Rsch. Soc. on Alcoholism (treas. 1985-87, sec. 1987-89), Am. Gastroenterological Assn., Am. Assn. Study Liver Diseases, Am. Assn. Physicians, Cen. Soc. Clin. Rsch., Am. Liver Found. (vet. hepatitis C liver disease coun.), Am. Coll. Gastroenterology. Avocations: painting, music, gardening. Office: Ind U Med Ctr 975 W Walnut St Indianapolis IN 46202-5181 Home Phone: 317-873-6679; Office Phone: 317-274-3505. Business E-Mail: llmning@iupui.edu.

LUMLEY, JOHN LEASK, physicist, researcher; b. Detroit, Nov. 4, 1930; s. Charles S. and Jane Anderson Campbell (Leask) L.; m. Jane French, June 20, 1953; children: Katherine Leask, Jennifer French, John Christopher. BA, Harvard, 1952; MS in Engring., Johns Hopkins, 1954, PhD, 1957; Doctorate honoris causa, U. de Poitiers, France, 2004; Haute distinction honoris causa, Ecole Central de Lyon, France, 1987. Postdoctoral fellow Johns Hopkins, 1957-59; mem. faculty Pa. State U., 1959-77, prof. aerospace engring., 1963-74, Evan Pugh prof. aerospace engring., 1974-77; Willis H. Carrier prof. engring. Cornell U., 1977-2001, prof. emeritus, 2001—. Prof. d'echange U. d'Aix-Marseille, France, 1966-67; Fulbright sr. lectr. U. Liege; vis. prof. U. Louvain-La-Neuve, Belgium; Guggenheim fellow U. Provence and Ecole Centrale de Lyon, France, 1973-74. Author: (with H.A. Panofsky) Structure of Atmospheric Turbulence, 1964, Stochastic Tools for Turbulence, 1970, (with H. Tennekes) A First Course in Turbulence, 1971, (with P. Holmes and G. Berkooz) Turbulence, Coherent Structures, Dynamical Systems and Symmetry, 1996, Engines: An Introduction, 1999, Still Life with Cars: An Automotive Memoir, 2005; also articles; editor: (with A. Acrivos, L.G. Leal and S. Leibovich) Research Trends in Fluid Dynamics, 1996; tech. editor: Statistical Fluid Mechanics, 1971, 75, Variability of the Oceans, 1977; assoc. editor: Physics of Fluids, 1971-73; assoc. editor Ann. Rev. of Fluid Mechanics, 1976-85, co-editor, 1986-99, 03—, editor, 1999-03; chmn. tech. editl. bd. Izvestiya: Atmospheric and Oceanic Physics, 1971-96; editorial bd.: Fluid Mechanics: Soviet Research, 1972-94; editor Theoretical and Computational Fluid Dynamics, 1989-98; prin.: films Deformation of Continuous Media, 1963, Eulerian and Lagrangian Frames in Fluid Mechanics, 1968. Recipient medallion U. Liege, Belgium, 1971, Timoshenko medal ASME, 1993. Fellow Am. Acad. Arts and Scis., Am. Acad. Mechanics, Am. Phys. Soc. (exec. com. divsn. fluid dynamics 1972-75, 81-84, chmn. exec. com. divsn. fluid dynamics 1982, 87-89, Fluid Dynamics prize 1990), AIAA (fluid and plasma dynamics award 1982, Hugh L. Dryden rsch. lectureship 1996); mem. NAE, AAAS, N.Y. Acad. Sci., Soc. Natural Philosophy, Am. Geophys. Union, Johns Hopkins Soc. Scholars (charter), Sigma Xi. Home: 743 Snyder Hill Rd Ithaca NY 14850-8708 Office: Cornell U 256 Upson Hall Ithaca NY 14853-7501 Office Phone: 607-255-0992. Business E-Mail: jll4@cornell.edu.

LUMMIS, CYNTHIA MARIE, former state official, lawyer; b. Cheyenne, Wyo., Sept. 10, 1954; d. Doran Arp and Enid (Bennett) L.; m. Alvin L. Wiederspahn, May 28, 1983; children: Annaliese Alex. BS, U. Wyo., 1976, BS, 1978, JD, 1985. Bar: Wyo. 1985, U.S. Dist Ct. of Wyo. 1985, U.S. Ct. of Appeals (10th cir.) 1986. Rancher Lummis Livestock Co., Cheyenne, 1972—; law clk. Wyo. Supreme Ct., Cheyenne, 1985-86; assoc. to ptnr. Wiederspahn, Lummis & Liepas (now called Wiederspahn & Reese, P.C.), Cheyenne, 1986—; treas. State of Wyo., 1999—2006. Mem. Wyo. Ho. Judiciary Com., 1979-86, Ho. Agriculture, Pub. Lands & Water Resources Com., 1985-86, Wyo. State Senate, 1993-94, Senate Judiciary Com., 1993-94, Senate Mines, Minerals, Econ. Devel. Com., 1993-94, U. Wyo. Inst. for Environment and Natural Resource Policy and Rsch.; chmn. County Ct. Planning Com., Wyo., 1986-88, Ho. Rev. Com., 1987-92, Joint Revenue Interim Com., 1988-89, 91-92; mem. adv. bd. U. Mont. Ctr. for the Rocky Mountain West, 1998—. Sec. Meals on Wheels, Cheyenne, 1985-87; mem. Agrl. Crisis Support Group, Laramie County, Wyo., 1985-87; mem. adv. com. U. Wyo. Sch. Nursing, 1988-90; mem. steering com. Wyo. Heritage Soc., 1986-89. Mem.: Rep. Women's (Cheyenne) (legis. chmn. 1982). Republican. Lutheran. Office: Wiederspahn & Reese PC 211 W 18th St Ste 400 Cheyenne WY 82001*

LUMPKIN, JOHN O., news organization executive; b. Nashville, Tenn. BA, Univ. Va. Reporter Richmond (Va.) Times-Dispatch, Fort Worth (Tex.) Star-Telegram; joined AP, 1971, bur. chief Dallas, 1982—2003, regional v.p., south, 2003—05, v.p., bus. ops, 2005—. Recipient Katie award for specialty reporting, 2002. Address: 4851 LBJ Fwy Ste 300 Dallas TX 75244-6047

LUMPKIN, JOHN ROBERT, public health physician, state official; b. Chgo., July 28, 1951; s. Frank and Beatrice (Shapiro) L.; m. Mary S. Blanks, Jan. 28, 1984; children: Alia, John R. Jr. BS, Northwestern U., Evanston, Ill., 1973; MD, Northwestern U., Chgo., 1974; MPH, U. Ill., Chgo., 1985. Diplomate Am. Bd. Emergency Medicine. Intern U. Chgo. Hosps., 1975, resident in anesthesiology, 1976-78, vice-chmn. emergency medicine, 1981-84; asst. prof. U. Chgo., 1978-84; asst. dir. emergency medicine South Chgo. Hosp., 1984-85; staff physician St. Mary of Nazareth Hosp., Chgo., 1985; assoc. dir. Ill. Dept. Pub. Health, Springfield and Chgo., 1985-90, dir., 1990—2003; sr. v.p. Robert Wood Johnson Found., Princeton, NJ, 2003—, dir. Health Care Group, 2003—. Cons. Egyptian Ministry Health, Cairo, 1986-90; chmn. Nat. Com. on Vital & Health Stats., 1996-, mem. sec.'s adv. com. on injury control Ctrs. for Dis. Control, Atlanta, 1989-93. Recipient Arthur MacCormack Excellence & Dedication in Pub. Health award, Assn. State & Territorial Health Officials, Jonas Salk Health Leadership award, Ill. Pub. Health Assn., Leadership in Pub. Health. Fellow Am. Coll. Med. Informatics, Am. Coll. Emergency Physicians (bd. dirs. 1987-93); mem. Soc. Tchrs. Emergency Medicine (pres. 1981-82), Ill. Coll. Emergency Physicians (pres. 1982-83, Bill B. Smiley award 1986), Assn. State and Territorial Health Ofcls. (pres. 1995-96), Inst. Medicine. Avocations: racquetball, model trains, football, computers. Office: Robert Wood Johnson Found PO Box 2316 College Rd E & Rt 1 Princeton NJ 08543

LUMPKIN, MURRAY M., federal agency administrator; m. Janet Lucille Rose, Dec. 22, 1978; 2 children. BA in German, Davidson Coll., 1975; MD, Wake Forest U., 1979; MSc in Med. Parasitology, U. London, 1984. Resident in pediats., fellow pediatric infectious disease Mayo Clinic, Rochester, Minn., 1979—84; chief pediatric infectious diseases E. Tenn. Children's Hosp., Knoxville, 1984—87; med. dir. Abbott Labs., Abbott Park, Ill., 1987—89; dir. divsn. anti-infective drug products FDA, Rockville, Md., 1989-93, dep. dir. Ctr. for Drug Evaluation and Rsch., 1993—2000, prin. assoc. commr., 2000—03, acting dep. commr. internat. and spl. programs, 2003—05, dep. commr. internat. and spl. programs, 2005—. Fulbright scholar. Mem.: Am. Acad. Pediats. Avocations: history, geography, biking, organ, hiking. Office: FDA HF 3 5600 Fishers Ln Rockville MD 20852

LUMPKINS, ROBERT L., food products executive; b. Lawrenceburg, Tenn., Jan. 25, 1944; s. Robert L. and Maude (Holthouse) L.; m. Sara Jane O'Connell, Dec. 29, 1966; 1 child, Christine Jane. BS in Math. magna cum laude, U. Notre Dame, 1966; MBA, Stanford U., 1968. Fin. analyst Cargill Inc., Mpls., 1968-70, mgr. fin. info. svcs. dept., 1970-73, gen. mgr. Cargill Leasing corp., 1973-75, group contr., 1975-82, sec., fin. com., 1975-82, pres. fin. svcs. divsn., 1983-88, chief fin. officer Cargill Europe London, 1988-89, CFO, 1989—2005, vice chmn., 1995—. Chmn. Mosaic Co.; bd. dir. Ecolab Inc., Wherenet Corp. Mem. sci. adv. coun. U. Notre Dame, 1994--; bd. dirs. Minn. Orch. Assn., Mpls., 1993-2000; trustee Minn. Med. Found., Mpls., 1992-2000; bd. dirs. Greater Mpls. Met. Housing Corp., 1996-99, Technoserve Inc., 1997—; trustee Howard U., 1998—; mem. adv. coun. Stanford Bus. Sch., 2000—. Mem. Minikahda Club. Roman Catholic. Office: Cargill Inc PO Box 9300 Minneapolis MN 55440-9300*

LUMSDEN, RACHEL LEE, musician; b. Richmond, Va., Dec. 14, 1977; d. David Clarke and Deborah LaBonté Lumsden. MusB in Performance, Va. Commonwealth U., Richmond, 1999; MA in Music Performance, CUNY-Queen's Coll., 2005; MA in Music Theory, CUNY-Quenn's Coll., 2007. Pvt. flute instr., 1998—; piano program instr. Poppenhusen Inst., College Point, NY, 2005—. Recipient Grosser award for woodwind performance, CUNY-Queens Coll., 2002, 2004, Discimus ut Serviamus award, 2002, 2003, 2004; Provost scholar, Va. Commonwealth U. Mem.: Music Theory Soc. of NY State, Soc. Music Theory, Phi Eta Sigma, Golden Key.

LUNA, BARBARA CAROLE, financial analyst, accountant; b. NYC, July 23, 1950; d. Edwin A. and Irma S. (Schub) Schlang; m. Dennis Rex Luna, Sept. 1, 1974; children: John S., Katherine E. BA, Wellesley Coll., Mass., 1971; MS in Applied Math., Harvard U., Cambridge, Mass., 1973, PhD in Applied Math., 1975. CPA; cert. gen. real estate appraiser Calif. Office Real Estate Appraisers; cert. valuation analyst and forensic fin. analyst Assn. Cert. Valuation Analysts; cert. fraud examiner Assn. Cert. Fraud Examiners, mgmt. cons. Inst. Mgmt. Consultants; accredited sr. appraiser Am. Soc. Appraisers; accredited bus. valuation Am. Inst. CPAs. Investment banker Warburg Paribas Becker, LA, 1975-77; cons., sr. mgr. Price Waterhouse, LA, 1977-83; sr. mgr. litigation Pannell Kerr Forster, LA, 1983-86; nat. dir. litigation cons. Kenneth Leventhal & Co., LA, 1986-88; ptnr. litigation svcs. Coopers & Lybrand, LA, 1988-93; sr. ptnr. litigation svcs. White, Zuckerman, Warsavsky, Luna, Wolf & Hunt, Sherman Oaks, Calif., 1993—. Expert witness. Wellesley scholar, 1971. Mem. AICPA, Assn. Bus. Trial Lawyers, Am. Soc. Appraisers, Assn. Cert. Valuation Analysts, Calif. Office Real Estate Appraisers, Assn. Cert. Real Estate Appraisers, Appraisal Inst., Assn. Cert. Fraud Examiners, Inst. Mgmt. Cons., Calif. Soc. CPAs (econ. damages common interest mem. svcs. com., fraud common interest mem. svcs. com., bus. valuation common interest mem. svcs. com.), Am. Bd. Forensic Accts. and Examiners. Avocations: golf, swimming. Home: 18026 Rodarte Way Encino CA 91316-4370 Office Phone: 818-981-4226. Personal E-mail: bluna@wzwlw.com.

LUNA, PATRICIA ADELE, marketing executive; b. Charleston, SC, July 22, 1956; d. Benjamin Curtis and Clara Elizabeth (McCrory) L. BS in History, Auburn U., 1978, MEd in History, 1980; MA in Adminstrn., U. Ala., 1981, EdS in Adminstrn., 1984, postgrad. in Adminstrn. Cert. tchr., Ga., Ala. History tchr. Harris County Mid. Sch., Ga., 1978-79, head dept. Ga., 1979-81; residence hall dir. univ. housing U. Ala., 1981-83, asst. dir. residence life, 1983-85; intern Cornell U., Ithaca, NY, 1983; dir. mktg. Golden Flake Snack Foods, Inc., Birmingham, Ala., 1985-89; sr. v.p. Quest U.S.A., Inc., Atlanta, 1989-90; pres. Promotion Mgmt. Group, Inc., Montgomery, Ala., 1990—. Cons. Capital Campaigns; lectr. in field. Author: Specialization: A Learning Module, 1979, Grantsmanship, 1981, Alcohol Awareness Programs, 1984, University Programming, 1984, Marketing Residential Life, 1985, The History of Golden Flake Snack Foods, 1986, Golden Flake Snack Foods, Inc., A Case Study, 1987, Cases in Strategic Marketing, 1989, Cases in Strategic Management, 1990, Frequency Marketing, 1992. Fundraiser U. Ala. Alumni Scholarship Fund, Tuscaloosa, 1983, Am. Diabetes Assn., Tuscaloosa, 1984, Urban Ministries, Birmingham, 1985-88; fundraiser, com. chmn. Spl. Olympics, Tuscaloosa, 1985; chmn. Greene County Relief Project, 1982-89; bd. dirs. Cerebral Palsy Found., Tuscaloosa, 1985-86; lay rector and com. chmn. Kairos Prison Ministry, Tutwiler State Prison, Ala., 1986-92; lobbyist, com. chmn. task force Justice Fellowship, 1988-91; bd. dirs. Internat. Found. Ewha U., Seoul, Korea, 1988-91; chmn. bd. dirs. Epiphany Ministries, 1991-98; bd. dirs. Hunting Coll. Fine Arts, chair Coll. Ministries, Whitfield Meml. United Meth. Ch., 1999-2000, chmn. capital fund campaign, 2000, chmn. stewardship bd. discipleship, 2000-02; chair Ala.-West. Fla. conf. United Meth. Ch., 2002; chair bd. discipleship Ala. UMC Conf., 2002—; retreat leader Upper Room, Acad. for Spiritual Formation, 2005—; com. chmn. Emmaus Ministry, 1985—; chmn. Chrysalis steering com., 1995-97; mem. bd. devel. Upper Rm. Ministries. Recipient Nat. award Joint Coun. Econ. Edn., 1979, Rsch. award NSF, 1979, Harry Denman Evangelism award, 2001; named to Hon. Order Ky. Cols. Commonwealth of Ky., 1985. Mem. Sales and Mktg. Execs. (chmn. com. 1985-86), Leadership Ala. (pres. 1982-83), Am. Mktg. Assn. (Disting. Leadership award 1987, Commemorative Medal of Honor 1988), Assn. Coll. and Univ. Housing Officers (com. chmn. 1983-85), Nat. Assn. Student Pers. Officers, Snack Food Assn. (mem. mktg. com. and conf. presenter), Internat. Coun. Shopping Ctrs. (Merit award 1991, program com.), Commerce Exec. Soc., Omega Rho Sigma (pres. 1983-84), Omicron Delta Kappa, Phi Delta Kappa, Kappa Delta Pi, Phi Alpha Theta. Mem. United Methodist Ch. Avocations: skiing, tennis, kayaking, community/church work, public speaking. Home and Office: 1327 Woodward AVE Montgomery AL 36106-2023 Office Phone: 334-262-9440. E-mail: patluna@charter.net.

LUNA, PEDRO P., academic administrator; s. Florentino Luna and Carmen E. Aleman; m. Pedro Luna; children: Peter A., Shyla R. BA, Hobart Coll., Geneva, NY, 1994—98; MS with honors, Syracuse U., NY, 2001—06. Phys. & health edn. coord. Boys & Girls Clubs, Geneva, 1997—98; oppty. program counselor Hobart & William Smith; academic counselor Syracuse U., 2000—. Recipient Prof. Larry Young prize in sociology, Hobart & William Smith Colls., 1998, Nat. Youth Svc. award, 1998, Elizabeth Eaton White award, 1998, Leadership, Collaboration, Caring Svc. award, Divsn. Support & Retention, Syracuse U., 2005. Mem.: Higher Edn. Oppty. Program Profl. Orgn., Am. Ednl. Rsch. Assn., Nat. Academic Advising Assn., Ann. Nat. Conf. Race & Ethnicity in Am. Higher Edn., Profl. & Orgnl. Devel. Network Higher Edn. (chair of the diversity commn. 2002—03, chair diversity commn. 2002—03).

LUNA, THOMAS, school system administrator; m. Cindy Luna; 6 children. Grad., Thomas Edison State Coll. Former mem., chmn. Nampa Sch. Bd., Idaho; spl. asst. Office of Under Sec. of Edn., US Dept. Edn., Washington, dir. Rural Edn. Task Force; mem. Idaho Assessment and Accountability Commn.; supt. pub. instrn. Idaho Dept. Edn., Boise, 2007—. Pres. Scales Unlimited Inc., 1985. Mem.: Western Weights and Measures Assn., Nat. Conf. on Weights and Measures, Nampa Exchange Club. Republican. Office: Idaho Dept Edn 650 W State St PO Box 83720 Boise ID 83720-0027 Office Phone: 208-332-6815. E-mail: Trluna@sde.idaho.gov.*

LUND, DARYL BERT, retired food science educator; b. San Bernardino, Calif., Nov. 4, 1941; married June 15, 1963; children: Kristine, Eric. BS in Math., U. Wis., 1963, MS in food Sci., 1965, PhD in Food Sci., 1968. Rsch. asst. in food sci. U. Wis., Madison, 1963-67, instr., 1967-68, asst. prof., 1968-72, assoc. prof., 1972-77, prof. food sci., 1977-87, chmn. dept. food sci., 1984-87; chmn. dept. food sci., assoc. dir. agrl. experiment sta. Rutgers, the State U., New Brunswick, 1988-89, interim exec. dean agr. and natural resources, 1989-91, exec. dean agr./natural resources, 1991-95, exec. dir. N.J. Agrl. Experiment Sta., dean Cook Coll., 1991-95; Ronald P. Lynch dean of agr. and life scis. Cornell U., Ithaca, NY, 1995-2000; exec. dir. North Ctrl. Regional Assn. U. Wis., Madison, 2001—06; emeritus prof food sci. U. Wis., Madison, 2007—. Vis. engr. Western Regional Rsch. Lab., Berkeley, Calif., 1970-71; advisor for evaluation of food tech. dept. Inst. Agr., Bogor, Indonesia, 1973; mem. four-man evaluation team to review grad. edn. programs Brazilian univs., 1976; vis. prof. food process engring. Agrl. U., Wageningen, The Netherlands, 1979; invited vis. prof. food process engring. Univ. Coll., Dublin, 1982; invited advisor Inter-Univ. Ctr. on Food Sci. and Nutrition, Bogor, 1991; advisor Agrl. U., Bogor, 1992; Woodroof lectr. U. Ga., 2003; lectr. in field Contbr. over 200 articles to profl. jours.; editor 5 books; co-author text book. Fellow Inst. Food Sci. and Tech., UK, 2000; recipient Food Engring. award Dairy and Food

Industries Supply Assn. and Am. Soc. Agrl. Engring., 1987, Internat. award Inst. Food Technologists, 2001, Irving award Svc., Am. Distance Edn. Consortium 2001, Carl Fellers award IFT, 2003, Harris award Ohio State U., 2006. Fellow Inst. Food Technologists (Wis. sect. 1968-87, N.Y. sect. 1988-95, ctrl. N.Y. 1995-2000), Internat. Union Food Sci. and Tech.; mem. AIChE, Am. Inst. Nutrition, Internat. Acad. Food Sci. and Tech., 1999 (charter mem.), Sigma Xi, Gamma Sigma Delta, Phi Tau Sigma. Avocations: golf, travel, woodworking. Home: 151 E Reynolds St Cottage Grove WI 53527

LUND, FREDERICK HENRY, aerospace and electrical engineer; b. Seattle, June 2, 1929; s. Henry George and Minnie (Wilbern) L.; m. Joyce Pauline Mon Pleasure, Sept. 8, 1950; children: Frederick Bradley, Christopher Michael, Peter Andrew, Andrea Leslie. BSEE, U. Wash., Seattle, 1951; postgrad., U. Calif., LA, 1954-56, 57-59; MS in Aeros., MIT, 1957. Registered profl. engr., Fla. Electronics engr. U.S. Naval Air Missile Test Ctr., Point Mugu, Calif., 1951, 53-56; head systems employment br., aero. rsch. engr. U.S. Naval Missile Ctr., Point Mugu, 1957-61, head plans and analysis group, gen. engr., 1961-65; sr. rsch. engr. Stanford Rsch. Inst., Menlo Park, Calif., 1965-69; mem. profl. staff Martin Marietta Missile Systems, Orlando, Fla., 1969-93; P.E. cons., 1994—95; electronics engr. Naval Air Depot, Jacksonville, Fla., 1995—. Chmn. com. Ventura area Coun. Boy Scouts Am., Camarillo, Calif., 1962-65, asst. dist. commr., Stanford area coun., Los Altos, Calif., 1967-69, instnl. rep. Cen. Fla. counc., Orlando, 1972-74; mem. pres.'s coun. U. Fla., Gainesville, 1987—. 1st lt. C.E., USAR, 1951-53. USN Bur. Aeros. scholar, 1956-57. Mem. AIAA (sr., missile sys. tech. com. 1987-91), IEEE (life, sect. chmn. 1962-63), Aerospace and Electronics Systems Soc. of IEEE (chpt. chmn. 1972-73), Mil. Ops. Rsch. Soc. (dir. 1962-66), Assn. Old crows (sec. 1973, club dir. 1986-90), Adelphi (sub-chpt. pres. 1948-51), Wesley, Kiwanis, Sigma Xi. Home and Office: 28 Montrano Ave Saint Augustine FL 32080-3819 E-mail: lund@ieee.org, lund@computer.org.

LUND, JAMES LOUIS, lawyer; b. Long Beach, Calif., Oct. 4, 1926; s. G. Louis and Hazel Eunice (Cochran) L.; m. Jo Alvarez, Aug. 5, 1950; 1 son, Eric James. Student, Stanford U., 1943; BA in Math., U. So. Calif., 1946; postgrad., Grad. Sch. U.S. Naval Acad., Annapolis, MD, 1949; JD, Southwestern U., 1955; postgrad., U. So. Calif., 1956. Bar: Calif. 1955, U.S. Dist. Ct. (cen. dist.) Calif. 1955, U.S. Ct. Appeals (9th cir.) 1955, U.S. Tax Ct. 1955, U.S. Supreme Ct. Spl. agt. U.S. Govt., 1950-52; gen. mgr. Pacific ops., gen. counsel Holmes & Narver, Inc., LA, 1952-66; exec. v.p. Calif. Fabricators, Oakland and Honolulu, 1966-67; sr. ptnr. James Lund Law Firm, Beverly Hills, 1967-83; pres., founder Fortres Mgmt. Co.; sr. ptnr. James Lund Law Firm, Tehran, 1967—83, Tokyo, 1967—83, London, 1967—83; ptnr. Lund & Lund, 1983—. Chmn. bd. Envirotire, 1998—; dir. Superior Vision Svcs., Inc. Lt. comdr. USNR, 1943—46, lt. comdr. USNR, 1948—50. Mem. ABA, SAR, L.A. County Bar Assn., Internat. Bar Assn., Inter-Am. Bar Assn., Asia Pacific Lawyers Assn., Les Ambassadeurs Club (London). Office: Ste 1555 1901 Avenue Of The Stars Los Angeles CA 90067-6052 Office Phone: 310-286-2861. Business E-Mail: jlundesq@sbcglobal.net.

LUND, JOHN RICHARD, entertainment company executive; b. Phila., Mar. 30, 1960; s. Robert Lee and Catherine Mary (Walsh) L.; m. Yolande Simon, July 3, 1987; children: Eleonore, Eugenie. BA summa cum laude, St. Joseph's U., Phila., 1982; MA, Columbia U., 1984; PhD with gen. distinction, RAND Grad. Sch. Policy Studies, 1987. Def. analyst Maltese Mission to UN, NYC, 1984; grad. fellow, policy analyst RAND Corp., Santa Monica, Calif., 1984-87, internat. policy analyst, 1988-92; mgr. transport devel. Euro Disney SCA, Marne-La-Vallee, 1992-93, mgr. telecom., transp., 1993-95, dir. telecom. and multimedia, 1995-96, dir. process re-engring., 1996—97, dir. exec. adminstrn., 1997-99, dir. operational labor mgmt., 1999—2000, v.p., chief of staff, 2001—03; v.p. process improvement Walt Disney Imagineering, Glendale, Calif., 2003—04; sr. v.p. strategic asset mgmt. Walt Disney Parks and Resorts, Glendale, Calif., 2004—06, sr. v.p. supply chain mgmt., 2006—. Dep. dir. RAND/Project AIR FORCE Hdqrs. USAF Europe, Ramstein AFB, Germany, 1988. Author: Don't Rock the Boat: Reinforcing Norway in Crisis and War, 1989; co-author: The New Calculus: Analyzing Airpower's Changing Role in Joint Theater Campaigns, 1993; contbr.: (with others) Transition and Turmoil in the Atlantic Alliance, 1991. Mem. bd. advisors Coll. Arts and Scis. St. Joseph U., 2007—. Mem.: Internat. Assn. Amusement Pks. and Attractions (bd. dirs.), Internat. Inst. for Strategic Studies. Roman Catholic. Office: Walt Disney Parks and Resorts 1401 Flower St Glendale CA 91221 Home: 2887 Bottlebrush Dr Los Angeles CA 90077-2011 Home Phone: 310-470-2243; Office Phone: 818-544-2700. Personal E-mail: john@john-lund.com. Business E-Mail: john.lund@disney.com.

LUND, RITA POLLARD, aerospace engineer, consultant; b. Vallscreek, W.Va., Aug. 28, 1950; d. Willard Garfield and Faye Ethel (Perry) Pollard. Student, Alexandria Hosp. Sch. Nursing, 1969-70, Columbia Pacific U., 1989-91. Notary pub. Va. Confidential asst. U.S. Ho. of Reps., Washington, 1975-76; exec. asst. White Ho. Domestic Policy Staff, Washington, 1977-82; exec. asst. to dep. sci. advisor to pres. White Ho. Sci. Office, Washington, 1982-83; asst. to pres. Telecom Futures Inc., Washington, 1983-84, v.p. for adminstrn., 1985-86; internat. accounts mgr. TFI Ltd., McLean, Va., 1987-89; ind. cons. telecom. Washington, 1989-90; aerospace cons., 1990—98; rep. Scott Sci. & Tech., Washington, 1992—2000; cons. Vanguard Space Corp., Washington, 1992—2000. Exec. dir. Puckett Bros. Corp., 1995—. Marriage commr. State of Va., 2000—; pres. Fairvew Beach Residents Assn., 1997—2001. Mem.: AIAA, Competitive Alliance Space Enterprise, Am. Space Transp. Assn., Women in Aerospace, NAFE. Republican. Methodist. Avocations: travel, genealogy, reading.

LUND, VICTOR L., healthcare company executive; b. Salt Lake City, 1947; married BA, U. Utah, 1969, MBA, 1972. Audit mgr. Ernst and Whinney, Salt Lake City, 1972-77; sr. v.p. Skaggs Cos. Inc., from 1977; v.p., contr. Am. Stores Co., 1980-83, sr. v.p., contr., from 1983, exec. v.p., co-chief exec. officer, vice-chmn., chief fin. and adminstrv. officer, pres., CEO, dir., 1992-95, chmn., CEO, dir., 1995-99; vice chmn. bd. dirs. Albertsons Inc., Boise, 1999—2002; non-exec. chmn. bd. Mariner Health Care, Inc., Atlanta, 2002—. Bd. mem. Borders Group, Inc., Svc. Corp. Internat. NCR, State Bd. Regents, Utah. Office: Mariner Health Care Off of Non-Exec Chairman One Ravinia Drive Ste 1500 Atlanta GA 30346

LUNDBACK, STAFFAN BENGT GUNNAR, lawyer; b. Stockholm, Mar. 23, 1947; arrived in US, 1965; s. B. Holger and Ingrid (Fjellstrom) L.; m. Lee Craig, June 14,1969; children: Hadley Elizabeth, Erik Burchfield. Student, U. Stockholm, 1966-67; BA, U. Rochester, 1970; JD, Boston U., 1974. Bar: N.Y. 1975, Fla. 1983. Assoc. Nixon Peabody, LLP, Rochester, NY, 1974—83, ptnr., 1983—. Bd. dirs. Scandinavian Seminar, Amherst, Mass., 1986-92; chmn. Scanamerican Properties, Inc., Atlanta, 1989-99. Mem. Swedish-Am. C. of C. (sec., bd. dirs. 1994—), Country Club of Rochester, Phi Beta Kappa. Avocations: music, literature, sports, current events, photography, golf. Office: Nixon Peabody LLP 1100 Clinton Sq Rochester NY 14604-1792 Office Phone: 585-263-1212. Personal E-mail: slundback@aol.com. Business E-Mail: slundback@nixonpeabody.com.

LUNDBERG, CARL-ERIK WILHELM, telecommunications executive, researcher; b. Karlskrona, Sweden, July 7, 1943; arrived in US, 1984; s. Erik Wilhelm and Martha Maria (Snaar) S. MEE, U. Lund, Sweden, 1966, PhD, 1975. Tchr., rsch. asst., lectr. U. Lund, 1966-75, rsch. prof. (docent), 1977-84; rsch. fellow European Space Agy., Nordwijk, The Netherlands, 1975-76; disting. mem. tech. staff AT&T Bell Labs., Murray Hill, NJ, 1984-96, Lucent Technologies, Bell Labs., 1997-2000; with media signal processing rsch. dept. Agere Sys., 2000—01, iBiquity Digital, Warren, NJ, 2002—03; prin., owner SundComm, Chatham, NJ, 2003—. Cons. L.M. Ericsson, Gothenburg, Sweden, 1976-77, Bell Labs., Crawford Hill, NJ, 1981-82; instr. Carl Cranz Gesellschaft, Oberpfaffenhofen, Fed. Republic Germany, 1990-93; vis. prof Korea U., Seoul, 2003-04 Co-author: Digital Phase Modulation, 1986, Source-Matched Mobile Communications, 1995; contbr. articles to profl. jours.; patentee in field. Served in Swedish Navy, 1968. Fellow IEEE (Best Paper award 1986, guest editor Jour. on Selected Areas in Comm. 1988-89, 2005—, 2 papers named among 50 most influential 2002), IEE Marconi Premium (Best Paper award 1989); mem. Swedish Union Radio-Scientifique Internat Lutheran. Avocations: travel, history, photography. Home and Office: SundComm 395 Ano Nuevo Ave Apt 1107 Sunnyvale CA 94085 Business E-Mail: cews@ieee.org.

LUNDBERG, GEORGE DAVID, II, medical editor-in-chief, pathologist; b. Pensacola, Fla., Mar. 21, 1933; s. George David and Esther Louise (Johnson) Lundberg; m. Nancy Ware Sharp, Aug. 18, 1956 (div.); children: George David III, Charles William, Jean Carol; m. Patricia Blacklidge Lorimer, Mar. 6, 1983; children: Christopher Leif, Melinda Suzanne. AA, North Park Coll., Chgo., 1950; BS, U. Ala., Tuscaloosa, 1952; MS, Baylor U., Waco, Tex., 1963; MD, Med. Coll. Ala., Birmingham, 1957; ScD (hon.), SUNY, Syracuse, 1988, Thomas Jefferson U., 1993, U. Ala., Birmingham, 1994, Med. Coll. Ohio, 1995. Cert. anatomic, clinical Am. Bd. Pathology, 1962. Intern Tripler Hosp., Hawaii; resident Brooke Hosp., San Antonio; assoc. prof. pathology U. So. Calif., LA, 1967—72, prof., 1972—77; assoc. dir. labs. L.A. County-U. So. Calif. Med. Ctr., 1968—77; prof., chmn. dept. pathology U. Calif.-Davis, Sacramento, 1977—82; v.p. scientific info., editor Jour. AMA, Chgo., 1982—99, editor in chief scientific publ., 1991—95; editor-in-chief AMA Sci. Info. and Multimedia, Chgo., 1995—99, Medscape, 1999—2001, editor-in-chief emeritus, 2001—03; editor Medscape Gen. Medicine, 1999—; editor-in-chief and exec. v.p. Medicalogic/Medscape, 2000—02; spl. healthcare advisor to CEO WebMD, 2002—03; editor-in-chief Medscape Core, 2005—, eMedicine, 2006—. Vis. prof. U. London, 1976, Lund U., Sweden, 1976; prof. clin. pathology Northwestern U., Chgo., 1982—; adj. prof. health policy Harvard U., Boston, 1993—, vis. prof. pathology, 1994—96; sr. fellow Northwestern U., 1999—; cons. prof. health policy Stanford U., Palo Alto, Calif., 2005—. Author, editor Managing the Patient Focused Laboratory, 1975, Using the Clinical Laboratory in Medical Decision Making, 1983, 1951, Landmark Articles in Medicine, 1984, AIDS From the Beginning, 1986, Caring for the Uninsured and Underinsured, 1991, Violence, 1992, 100 Years of JAMA Landmark Articles, 1997, Severed Trust: Why American Medicine Hasn't Been Fixed, 2001, paperback edit., 2002; contbr. articles to profl. jours. Lt. col. M.C. US Army, 1956—67. Fellow: Am. Soc. Clin. Pathologists (past pres.); mem.: Inst. Med., N.Y. Acad. Scis., Am. Acad. Forensic Sci., Alpha Omega Alpha. Democrat. Episcopalian. Office: Medscape 76 9th Ave New York NY 10001 Office Phone: 212-301-6697. Business E-Mail: glundberg@medscape.net.

LUNDBERG, SUSAN ONA, musical organization administrator; b. Mandan, ND, Mar. 15, 1947; d. Robert Henry and Evelyn (Olson) L.; m. Paul R. Wick, July 2, 1972 (div. May 1976); 1 child, Melissa. BA, Stephens Coll., 1969; MLS, Western Mich. U., 1970; MPA, Calif. State U., Fullerton, 1980. Children's and reference libr. Bismarck (N.D.) Pub. Libr., 1970-71; reference libr. U. Tenn., Knoxville, 1971-72; coord. children's svcs. Orange County (Calif.) Pub. Libr., 1972-75; exec. dir. Bismarck-Manda Orch. Assn., 1992—. Exec. dir., founder Sleepy Hollow Summer Theatre, Bismarck, 1990—; trustee Gabriel J. Brown Trust, Bismarck, 1989—. Exhibitions include of paintings Scandinavian Threads of Inheritance, 2002. Chair Nat. Music Week N.D., 1990—, Friends of the Belle, 1997—; chair small budget orchs. Am. Symphony Orch. League, 2000-03; mem. civic chorus Bismarck-Mandary. Named Outstanding Leaders of Yr. Bismarck Tribune, 1995; recipient hon. portrait, Belle Mehus City Auditorium, Vol. award, DAR, 2004, Family Vol. award, Folk Fest, 2004. Mem. DAR (Vol. award 2004), Calif. Libr. Assn. (pres. children's svcs. 1971-72), Bismarck Art Assn. (pres. 1982-84), Bismarck Art and Galleries Assn. (bd. dirs. 1985-2000, pres. 1986-88, Honor Citation award 1992), Jr. Svc. League. Lutheran. Avocations: painting, singing. Home: 112 Ave E W Bismarck ND 58501 Office Phone: 701-258-8345.

LUNDBLAD, ROGER LAUREN, biotechnology consultant; b. San Francisco, Oct. 31, 1939; s. Lauren Alfred and Doris Ruth (Peterson) L.; m. Susan Hawly Taylor, Oct. 15, 1966 (div. 1985); children: Christina Susan, Cynthia Karin. BSc, Pacific Luth. U., 1961; PhD, U. Wash., 1965. Rsch. assoc. U. Wash., Seattle, 1965-66, Rockefeller U., NYC, 1966-68; asst. prof. U. NC, Chapel Hill, 1968-71, assoc. prof., 1971-77, prof. pathology and biochemistry, 1977-91, adj. prof., 1991—; dir. sci. tech. devel. Baxter-Hyland/Immuno, Duarte, Calif., 1991-99; biotech. cons., 2000—. Vis. scientist Hyland divsn. Baxter Healthcare, Glendale, Calif., 1988-89. Author: Chemical Reagents for Protein Modification, 1984, 2d edit., 1990, 3d edit., 2004, Techniques in Protein Chemistry, 2994, The Evolution of Protein Chemistry to Proteomics, 2005, Compendium for Biochemistry and Molecular Biology, 2007; editor: Chemistry and Biology of Thrombin, 1977, Chemistry and Biology of Heparin, 1980, Techniques in Protein Modification, 1994; editor-in-chief: Biotechnology and Applied Biochemistry, 1996-2003, Internet Jour. Genomics and Proteomics; contbr. articles to profl. jours. Mem. Am. Soc. Biochem. Molecular Biology, Sigma Xi. Office: PO Box 16695 Chapel Hill NC 27516-6695 Home Phone: 919-929-5082; Office Phone: 919-929-5082. Personal E-mail: lundbladr@bellsouth.net.

LUNDE, ASBJORN RUDOLPH, lawyer; b. S.I., NY, July 17, 1927; s. Karl and Elisa (Andenes) L. AB, Columbia U., 1947, LLB, 1949. Bar: N.Y. 1949. Pvt. practice, NYC, 1950-91; with Kramer, Marx, Greenlee & Backus and predecessors, 1950-68, mem., 1958-68; pvt. practice Columbia County, NY, 1991—. Bd. dirs., v.p. Orch. da Camera, Inc., 1964—, Sara Roby Found., 1971—; bd. dirs. Clarion Concerts in Columbia County, 1999—; mem. vis. com. dept. European paintings Met. Mus. Art. Fellow Met. Mus. Art (life, benefactor); mem. ABA, N.Y. State Bar Assn., Assn. Bar City N.Y., Met. Opera Club, East India Club (London). Avocation: art collecting. Home and Office: 135 LaBranche Rd Hillsdale NY 12529-5713 Office Phone: 518-392-4430.

LUNDE, DOLORES BENITEZ, retired secondary school educator; b. Honolulu, Apr. 12, 1929; d. Frank Molero and Matilda (Francisco) Benitez; m. Nuell Carlton Lunde, July 6, 1957; 1 child, Laurelle. BA, U. Oreg., 1951, postgrad., 1951-52, U. So. Calif., LA, 1953-54, Colo. State U., 1957-58, Calif. State U., Fullerton, 1967-68. Cert. gen. secondary tchr., Calif.; cert. lang. devel. specialist. Tchr. Brawley (Calif.) Union High Sch., 1952-55; tchr. Fullerton (Calif.) Union High Sch. Dist., 1955-73; tchrs. aide Placentia (Calif.) Unified Sch. Dist., 1983-85; tchr. continuing edn. Fullerton Union High Sch. Dist., 1985-91; tchr. Fullerton Sch. Dist., 1988, Fullerton Union H.S. Dist., 1989-94. Presenter regional and state convs., so. Calif., 1986-88. Innovator tests, teaching tools, audio-visual aids. Vol. Luth. Social Svcs., Fullerton, 1981-82, Messiah Luth., Yorba Linda, Calif., 1981-88, 91-2001. Recipient Tchr. of Yr. award Fullerton Union High Sch. Dist., 1989. Mem. NEA, AAUW (life, bull. editor 1979-80, corr. sec. 1981-83, program v.p. 1983-84, gift honoree Fullerton br. 1985), Calif. State Tchrs. Assn., Fullerton Secondary Tchrs. Assn., Internat. Club/Spanish Club (advisor La Habra, Calif. 1965-72), Tchrs. English to Speakers Other Langs., Calif. Assn. Tchrs. English to Speakers Other Langs. Avocations: singing, folk and interpretive dance, guitar, reading, travel. Home: 4872 Ohio St Yorba Linda CA 92886-2713

LUNDE, HAROLD IRVING, retired management educator; b. Austin, Minn., Apr. 18, 1929; s. Peter Oliver and Emma (Stoa) L.; m. Sarah Jeanette Lysne, June 25, 1955; children: Paul, James, John, Thomas. BA, St. Olaf Coll., 1952; MA, U. Minn., 1954, PhD, 1966. Assoc. prof. econs. Macalester Coll., St. Paul, 1957-64; fin. staff economist Gen. Motors Corp., NYC, 1965-67; corp. sec. Dayton Hudson Corp., Mpls., 1967-70; mgr. planning and gen. research May Dept. Stores Co., St. Louis, 1970-72, v.p. planning and rsch., 1972—78; exec. v.p. adminstrn. Kobacker Stores, Inc., Columbus, Ohio, 1979; prof. mgmt. Bowling Green (Ohio) State U., 1980-98, emeritus, 1998—. Bd. dir. and trustee AgCredit, Fostoria, Ohio, Goodwill Industries N.W. Ohio, U.S. Naval War Coll. Found., Newport, RI. Mem. Acad. Mgmt., Am. Econ. Assn., Nat. Assn. Bus. Economists, Decision Scis. Inst., Phi Beta Kappa, Phi Kappa Phi, Omicron Delta Kappa, Beta Gamma Sigma. Home: 880 Country Club Dr Bowling Green OH 43402-1602 Personal E-mail: hlunde@bgsu.edu.

LUNDEBERG, PHILIP KARL BORAAS, curator, historian; b. Mpls., June 14, 1923; s. Olav Knutson and Vivian Juliet (Boraas) L.; m. Eleanore Lillian Berntson, July 18, 1953; 1 son, Karl Fredrik. BA summa cum laude, Duke U., 1944, MA, 1947; PhD, Harvard U., 1954. Asst. to historian U.S. Naval Ops. in World War II, Navy Dept., 1950-53; asst. prof. history St. Olaf Coll., 1953-55, U.S. Naval Acad., 1955-59; assoc. curator naval history Nat. Mus. History and Tech., Smithsonian Instn., 1959-61, curator of naval history, 1961-84, curator emeritus, 1984—. V.p. Am. Mil. Inst., 1968-71, pres., 1971-73; chmn. Internat. Congress Maritime Museums, 1972-75; v.p. U.S. Commn. on Mil. History, 1975-79, pres., 1980-83; sec. Internat. Com. Mus. Security, 1975-79; pres. Coun. Am. Maritime Museums, 1976-78. Author: The Continental Gunboat Philadelphia, 1966, 2d edit., 1995, Samuel Colt's Submarine Battery, 1974, American Anti-submarine Operations in the Atlantic, 1943-1945, 1997; co-author: Sea Power: A Naval History, 1960, 81; contbg. author: Guide to the Sources of U.S. Military History, 1975, 93, Seafaring and Society, 1987, To Die Gallantly, 1994, The Battle of the Atlantic (1939-1945), 1994; editor: Bibliographie de L'Histoire des Grandes Routes Maritimes: États-Unis d'Amèrique, 1970; exhibits: Armed Forces of U.S., 1961-2004, By Sea and by Land, 1981, The Continental Gonndola, Phila., 1963-2006. With USNR, 1943-83, 89, comdr. Res. ret., 1992. Decorated Bronze Star, Purple Heart; recipient Bronze medal Internat. Commn. Mil. History, 1975; Austin fellow Harvard U., 1949. Fellow Am. Mil. Inst. (Moncado prize 1964); mem. Coun. Am. Maritime Mus. (hon.), N.Am. Soc. for Oceanic History (K. Jack Bauer award 1998), Naval Hist. Found. (life), Internat. Congress Maritime Mus. (life), Soc. for Mil. History, Phi Beta Kappa. Home: 1107 Croton Dr Alexandria VA 22308-2009 Office Phone: 202-633-3924.

LUNDEEN, BRADLEY CURTIS, lawyer; b. Karlstad, Minn, Nov. 16, 1958; s. Curtis W. and LaVonne M. (Oistad) L.; m. Kristina Ogland, May 18, 1984 (div. Dec. 1991); 1 child, Jonathan B. BA, Moorhead State U, 1980; JD cum laude, William Mitchell Coll. Law, 1984. Bar: Minn. 1984, Wis. 1984, Ariz., 2002. Assoc. Gwin, Gilbert, Gwin, Mudge & Porter, Hudson, Wis., 1984, Gilbert, Mudge & Porter, Hudson, 1985; ptnr. Gilbert, Mudge, Porter & Lundeen, Hudson, 1986-92; lawyer, shareholder Mudge, Porter & Lundeen S.C., Hudson, 1992-94, Mudge, Porter, Lundeen & Seguin S.C., Hudson, 1995-99, Lundeen Law Ltd., 2000—02, Bell O'Connor & Campbell, Phoenix, 2002—04, Goldwater Law Firm, LLC, Scottsdale, Ariz., 2004—. Bd. dirs. Hudson Rotary, 1990-91; chmn. bd. dirs. Bank St. Croix, Hudson, Wis., 1987-94; bd. dirs. St. Croix Valley Employers Assn., 1996-2002, pres., 1999-2001. Mem. ATLA (nursing home litigation group), Ariz. Trial Lawyers Assn., State Bar Assn. Ariz., State Bar Assn. Wis., Desert Wind Homeowners Assn. (bd. dirs., v.p. 2004—), Masons, Shriners. Lutheran. Avocations: golf, skiing, travel, computers and cooking. Home: 5342 E Gloria Lane Cave Creek AZ 85331-5554 Office: Goldwater Law Firm 15333 N Pima Rd Ste 225 Scottsdale AZ 85260 Home Phone: 480-513-1229; Office Phone: 480-203-2000. Business E-Mail: blundeen@goldwaterlaw.com.

LUNDEN, JOAN, television personality; b. Fair Oaks, CA, Sept. 19, 1950; d. Erle Murray and Gladyce Lorraine (Somervill) Blunden; m. Michael Krauss, 1978 (div. 1992); children: Jamie Beryl, Lindsay Leigh, Sarah Emily; m. Jeff Konigsberg, 2000; children: Kate Elizabeth, Max Aaron, Kimberly, Jack. Student, Universidad de Las Americas, Mexico City, U. Calif., Calif. State U., Am. River Coll., Sacramento, Calif. Began broadcasting career as co-anchor and prodr. at Sta. KCRA-TV and Radio, Sacramento, 1973-75; with Sta. WABC-TV, N.Y.C., 1975—97, co-anchor, 1976-80; co-host Good Morning America, ABC-TV, 1980-97; host spl. report TV for Whittle Comm.; host Everyday with Joan Lunden, 1989, Behind Closed Doors With Joan Lunden, 1994-2000 (ABC), 2000- (A&E); pres., host Women's Supermarket Network; film appearances include: Macho Callahan, 1970, What About Bob?, 1991, Free Willy 2, 1995, Conspiracy Theory, 1997; film appearances include Thank You for Smoking, 2006; spl. appearances: (TV series) Murphy Brown, 1992, 93, LateLine, 1998; Author: Good Morning, I'm Joan Lunden, 1986, Joan Lunden's Mother's Minutes, 1986, Your Newborn Baby: Everything You Need to Know, 1988, Joan Lunden's Healthy Cooking, 1996, Joan Lunden's Healthy Living, 1997, Joan Lunden's A Bend in the Road Is Not the End of the Road, 1998, Wake-Up Calls: Making the Most Out of Every Day, 2000; syndicated columnist: Parent's Notes. Recipient Outstanding Mother of Yr. award, Nat. Mother's Day Com., 1982; Albert Einstein Coll. of Yeshiva U. Spirit of Achievement award; Nat. Women's Polit. Caucus award; NJ Divsn. of Civil Rights award; Baylor U. Outstanding Woman of the Year award; Decoration for Disting. Civilian Svc., US Army. Office: LMNO Prodns PO Box 4361 Los Angeles CA 90028 also: Creative Artists Agy c/o Debra Goldfarb 9830 Wilshire Blvd Beverly Hills CA 90212-1825 also: Rm 4332 1271 Avenue Of The Americas New York NY 10020-1401

LUNDERGAN, BARBARA KEOUGH, lawyer; b. Chgo., Nov. 6, 1938; d. Edward E. and Eleanor A. (Erickson) Keough; children: Matthew K., Mary Alice. BA, U. Ill., Urbana, 1960; JD, Loyola U., Chgo., 1964. Bar: Ill. 1964, Ga. 1997, Minn. 2004, U.S. Dist. Ct. (no. dist.) Ill. 1964, U.S. Tax Ct. 1974. Ptnr. Seyfarth Shaw LLP, Chgo., 1971—98, of counsel, 1998—2004, Hristendahl Moersch and Dorsey PA, Northfield, Minn., 2004—. Fellow Am. Coll. Trust and Estate Counsel; mem. ABA (com. on fed. taxation), Ill. Bar Assn. (coun. sect. on fed. taxation 1983-91, chair 1989, coun. sect. on trusts and estates sect. coun. 1992-97, sec. 1996-97, editl. bd. Ill. Bar Jour. 1993-96), Chgo. Bar Assn. (chmn. trust law com. 1982-83, com. on fed. taxation). Office: Hristendahl Moersch and Dorsey PA 311 Water St Northfield MN 55057 Home Phone: 507-645-6713; Office Phone: 507-645-9358. Business E-Mail: bkl@hvmd.com.

LUNDGREN, CARL WILLIAM, JR., physicist; b. Columbus, Sept. 17, 1933; s. Carl William and Anne Katherine (Kuntz) Lundgren; m. Virginia Anne Cullis, Dec. 7, 1963; children: David John, Janet Marie. BEE, U. Cin., 1957, MS, 1959, PhD, 1961. Coop undergrad. engr. govt. products divsn. Avco Corp., Cin., Evendale, Ohio, 1953-56; asst. supr., rsch. fellow U. Cin. Basic Sci. Rsch. Lab., 1959-61; tech. staff Bell Tel. Labs., Murray Hill, NJ, 1961-66, Holmdel and Middletown, NJ, 1966-84; dist. mgr. advanced fiber optics planning Bell Comm. Rsch., Inc., Red Bank, NJ, 1984-92; dir. transmission sys. engring. Bellcore, Morristown and Red Bank, 1992-95; dist. mgr., tech. cons. local access architecture AT&T, Holmdel, 1996-98, Middletown, 1998—. Contbr. articles to profl. jours. Capt. signal corps US Army, 1961—63. Mem.: IEEE, AAAS, Nat. Spectrum Mgrs. Assn., Sierra Club, Gideons Internat., Omicron Delta Kappa, Phi Eta Sigma, Eta Kapa Nu, Tau Beta Pi, Delta Tau Delta. Republican. Episcopalian. Achievements include patents in field. Home: 60 Woodhollow Rd Colts Neck NJ 07722-1323 Office: AT&T R&D South 200 S Laurel Ave Middletown NJ 07748-1998 Office Phone: 732-420-2611. E-mail: cwlxxvcl@optonline.net.

LUNDGREN, COLLEEN BOWLING, elementary school educator, consultant; b. Frankfort, Mich., Sept. 25, 1949; d. Steven Bowling and Vera Opal Grossnickle; m. Dennis David Lundgren, Dec. 18, 1971; 1 child, David Steven. BA, Western Mich. U., 1971, MA, 1976. Cert. tchr. K-8 Mich., 1976. Tchr. Seely-McCord Elem. Sch., Benton Harbor, Mich., 1971—80; adult reading tchr. Lakeshore Pub. Schs., Stevensville, 1978—78; reading curriculum specialist Benton Harbor Area Schs., 1979, English lang. arts presenter, 1991—, Mich. literacy progress profile trainer, 2001—, title I reading tchr., 1980—2006; Reading First facilitator Mich. Dept. Edn., 2006—. Grantee AT&T. Mem.: Internat. Reading Assn., Mich. Reading Assn., Phi Delta Kappa. Lutheran. Avocations: reading, singing, gardening. Home Phone: 269-429-4974. Personal E-mail: colleen.lundgren@sbcglobal.net.

LUNDGREN, DENNIS DAVID, elementary school educator, secondary school educator; b. Benton Harbor, Mich., May 9, 1950; s. Walter O. and Helen F. Lundgren; m. Colleen K. Bowling, Dec. 18, 1971; 1 child, David S. MusB, Western Mich. U., Kalamazoo, 1975, EdS, 1982; MusM, Andrews U., Berrien Springs, Mich., 1979. Cert. adminstr. Mich., continuing tchr. cert. Mich. Tchr. and prin. Lakeshore Pub. Schs., Stevensville, Mich., 1975—94; dir. math. and sci. ctr. Berrien County Intermediate Sch. Dist., Mich., 1995—2004, dir. tech. and media svcs., 2004—. Assoc. The Cambridge Group, Montgomery, Ala., 1993—96. Congregation pres. Saron Luth. Ch., St. Joseph, Mich., 1998—2003. Finalist Tchr. of Yr., State of Mich., 1993. Mem.: ASCD, Computer Sci. Tchrs. Assn., Mich. Assn. Computer Users in Learning, Nat. Assn. Secondary Sch. Principals, Nat. Assn. Specialized Secondary Schs. of Math., Sci. and Tech. (pres. 2003—04), Am. Choral Dirs. Assn. (life), Phi Delta Kappa. Office: Berrien County Intermediate Sch Dist 711 St Joseph Ave Berrien Springs MI 49103 Office Phone: 269-471-7725. Business E-Mail: dlundgre@remc11.k12.mi.us.

LUNDGREN, GAIL M., lawyer; b. Tacoma, Wash., June 14, 1955; d. Arthur Dean and Vera Martha (Grimm) L. AB cum laude, Vassar Coll., 1977; JD cum laude, Seattle U., 1980. Bar: Wash. 1981, Oreg. 2003. Legal intern Reed, McClure, Moceri & Thonn, Seattle, 1979, Burges & Kennedy, Tacoma, 1979-80, Lee, Smart, Cook, Martin & Patterson, P.S., Inc., Seattle, 1980-81, assoc., 1981-92; prin. Law Offices Gail L. Weber, Bothell, Wash., 1992-95, Tom Chambers & Assocs., 1995-99; lawyer Law Offices of Kirk Bernard, Seattle, 1999; ptnr. Bernard & Lundgren PLLC, Seattle, 1999—2005. Vestry com. Queen Anne Luth. Ch., 1983-86, v.p. congregation, 1988, 89, mem. worship and music com., 1982-83, 84-86, parish edn. com., 1983-84. Recipient Am. Jurisprudence Book award in Criminal Procedure, Corps. and Bus. Planning, 1980. Mem.: ABA, Order of Barristers, Wash. State Trial Lawyers Assn., Fed. Bar Assn., Wash. State Vassar Club (chmn. alumni admissions 1983—85, rep. 1986—92, 2001—, chmn. alumni admissions 2001—). Democrat. Avocations: tennis, classical music, needlepoint, stitchery, snorkeling.

LUNDGREN, JOHN F., consumer products company executive; b. Braintree, Mass., Sept. 3, 1951; BA cum laude, Dartmouth Coll., Hanover, NH, 1973; MBA, Stanford U., Calif., 1975. Product mgr. Gillette, Boston, 1975—76; product mgr., group product mgr., mktg. dir. Am. Can, Greenwich, Conn., 1976—82; mktg. dir., strategic planning, mfg. planning James River Corp., Norwalk, Conn., 1982—88, v.p., corp. devel. Richmond, Va., 1988—90, v.p., strategic planning, mktg. & bus. devel. Brussels, 1990—95, pres., European consumer products, 1995—2001, Ga.-Pacific Corp., 2001—03; chmn., CEO The Stanley Works, New Britain, Conn., 2003—. Office: The Stanley Works 1000 Stanley Dr New Britain CT 06053*

LUNDGREN, LENA MARGARETA, social sciences educator, researcher; d. Oskar and Lilly Lundgren; children: Eleni Margareta Gaveras, Lee George William Gaveras. BA, Umea U., Sweden, 1982; MA, U. Chgo., 1984, PhD, 1991. Asst. prof. Boston U. Sch. Social Work, 1994—2001, dir. ctr. work and family, 1996—2006, assoc. prof., 2001—, dir. ctr. for addictions rsch. and svc., 2007—. Consulting editor social work; manuscript reviewer Jour. Substance Abuse Treatment, Jour. of Ethnic and Racial Studies, AIDS Edn. and Prevention: Ctrs. Disease Control, Journal Evaluation and Program Planning; grant reviewer Ctr. for Substance Abuse Treatment, Alfred P. Sloan Found., Swedish Nat. Rsch. Bd. Grantee, Centers for Disease Control, 1995—97, Alfred P. Sloan Found., 1996—2001, Ctr. for Substance Abuse Treatment, Mass. Dept. Pub. Health, 2000—04, Ctr. for Substance Abuse Treatment, SAMHSA, 2002—;, Robert Wood Johnson Found., 2000—04, Rsch grants, Ctr. for Substance Abuse Treatment, 2002—. Mem.: Am. Evaluation Assn., Nat. Coun. on Social Work Rsch., Am. Pub. Health Assn., Nat. Assn. Social Work. Office: Boston U Sch Social Work 264 Bay State Rd Boston MA 02215 Home Phone: 781-862-5077; Office Phone: 617-353-1634. Business E-Mail: llundgre@bu.edu.

LUNDGREN, RICHARD JOHN, real estate executive, city planner, preservationist; b. NYC, Dec. 13, 1940; s. John H. and Helen C. (Vetter) Lundgren; m. Nancy Whitin Truslow, Apr. 1, 1972 (dec. 2000); children: Andrew Auchincloss, Elizabeth Whitin. BS, Rensselaer Poly. Inst., 1964; MS, Pratt Inst., 1968; MPA, Harvard U., 1990. Sr. planner Herr Assocs., Boston, 1968-69; project dir. Boston Redevel. Authority, 1969-72; dir. planning Hilgenhurst & Assocs., Boston, 1972-77; v.p. Hunneman Comml. Co., Boston, 1977-82, sr. v.p., 1982—94, 2003—, pres., 1994—2003. Trustee The Trustees of Reservations, 1985—, Emerald Necklace Conservancy, 1997-2004, Mass. Farm and Conservation Lands Trust, 1985-92, Boston Local Devel. Corp., 1986-91; dir. Preservation Mass., 2002-2005, Initiative for a Competitive Inner City, Boston, 1999-2003, Vis. Nurse Assn. of Boston, 1972-82; mem. Met. Area Planning Coun., 1978-80, Boston Coord. Com., 1983, Mass. Gov.'s Com. on Pvt. Rental Housing Prodn., 1983-84, Boston Mayor's Com. on Linkage, 1983-84, Center City Task Force, 1983-87, Boston Mayor's Jobs Liaison Com., 1984-90, Park Plz. Civic Adv. Com., 1985-86; Boston Employment Com., 1986-88; chmn. Mass. Realtors Pub. Policy Com., 1989; adv. com. Boston U. Sch. for Real Estate Studies, 1986-91 With USCGR, 1968—72. Named Greater Boston Realtor of Yr., 1984. Fellow: Mass. Hist. Soc.; mem.: Internat. Coun. Shop Ctrs., Greater Boston Bldg. Owners and Mgrs. Assn. (bd. dirs. 1979—88, pres. 1982), Greater Boston Real Estate Bd. (bd. dirs. 1982—89, pres. 1983), Mass. Assn. Realtors, Nat. Assn. Realtors, Boston Athenaeum (propr.), Somerset Club, The Country Club (gov.), Harvard Club NYC. Episcopalian. Home: 80 Parker Hill Ave Boston MA 02120 Office: Hunneman Comml Co 303 Congress St Boston MA 02111-2611

LUNDGREN, TERRY J., retail company executive; b. Long Beach, Calif., 1953; m. Nancy (div.); two children. BA, U. Ariz., 1974. From. v.p. Bullock's to pres. Bullock's Wilshire Federated Dept. Stores, Inc., NYC, 1975-88; chmn., CEO Neiman Marcus Stores Neiman Marcus Group Inc., 1990—94; chmn., CEO Federated Merchandising Group Federated Merchandising Group, 1994—98; pres., chief merchandising officer Macy's Inc. (formerly Federated Dept. Stores, Inc.), 1997—2002; COO Macy's Inc., 2002—03, pres., CEO, 2003—, chmn., 2004—. Bd. dirs. Dallas Symphony Orch., Dallas Citizens Coun. Office: Macy's Inc 7 W 7th St Cincinnati OH 45202*

LUNDIN, BENJAMIN W., religious studies scholar, political science scholar; b. Nashville, 1985; s. Keith and Linda L. BA in Religious Studies, Univ. NC, Chapel Hill, 2007; MPhil. student in Internat. Rels., Oxford Univ. Intern Rep. Jim Cooper (D-Tenn.); worked in pub. defender's office, Peru. Rhodes Scholar. Mem.: Chi Psi fraternity. Avocation: lacrosse.*

LUNDIN, NORMAN KENT, artist, educator; b. LA, Dec. 1, 1938; s. John R. and Louise A. (Marland) L.; m. Sylvia Johnson; children: Kelly Jean, Christopher David. BA, Sch. Art Inst. Chgo., 1961; M.F.A., U. Cin., 1963. Asst. to dir. Cin. Art Mus., 1962-63; instr. art U. Wash., Seattle, 1964-66, asst. prof., 1966-68, assoc. prof., 1968-75, prof., 1976—. Vis. artist Hornsey Coll. Art, London, 1969-70; vis. prof. Ohio State U., Columbus, 1975; prof. San Diego State U., 1978; vis. prof. U. Tex.-San Antonio, 1982, Chelsea Coll. Art, London, 1996. Exhibited one-man shows, Francine Seders Gallery, Seattle, Space, L.A., Jack Rasmussen Gallery, Washington, Allen Stone, N.Y.C., Adams Middleton Gallery, Dallas, Allport Gallery, San Francisco, Stephen Haller Fine Art, N.Y.C., 1987-94, Schmidt-Bingham Gallery, N.Y.C., 1997, Koplin Gallery, L.A., 1997, Koplin DelRio Gallery, Los Angeles, 2005; group shows include Mus. Modern Art, N.Y.C., Whitney Mus. Am. Art, N.Y.C., Denver Art Mus., Seattle Art Mus., San Joes Mus. Art, Ca, 1982-1983, Fine Art Mus., Seattle, 2000, San Francisco Mus. Modern Art Nat. Endowment Arts grantee; Fulbright-Hays grantee Norway, 1963-64; Tiffany Found. grantee, 1968; Ford. Found. grantee Soviet Union, Eastern Europe, 1978-79 Office: U Wash Sch Art Seattle WA 98105

LUNDING, CHRISTOPHER HANNA, lawyer; b. Evanston, Ill., June 15, 1946; s. Franklin J. and Virginia (Hanna) L.; children: Elizabeth, Nelson, Alexander, Andrew, Kirsten; m. Barbara J. Fontana, Aug. 19, 1989. BA, Harvard U., 1968; JD, Yale U., 1971. Bar: NY 1972, Fla. 1972, U.S. Supreme Ct. 1975. Law clk. to judge 2d Cir. U.S. Ct. Appeals, NYC, 1971-72; assoc. Cleary, Gottlieb, Steen & Hamilton LLP, NYC, 1973-79, ptnr., 1980—2004, sr. counsel, 2005—. Chmn. Legal Svcs. NYC, 1987—94. Chmn. Belle Haven Tax Dist., Greenwich, Conn., 1986-96, 2001-05. Fellow Am. Bar Found. (life); mem. NY County Lawyers Assn. (bd. dirs. 1988-94), Commodore Belle Haven Club. Office: Cleary Gottlieb Steen & Hamilton LLP One Liberty Plz Ste 3800 New York NY 10006 E-mail: CLunding@CGSH.com.

LUNDQUIST, C. DAVID, lawyer; b. Plainwell, Mich., Feb. 20, 1935; s. Leonard and Esther Lundquist; m. Georgia T. Townsend, Nov. 18, 1934; children: Anne E., Thomas D., Sarah J. Leskovec. AB, U. Mich., Ann Arbor, 1957; LLB, Duke U., Durham, NC, 1960; LLD (hon.), Adrian Coll., Mich., 1992. Trust officer Am. Nat. Bank & Trust Co., Kalamazoo, 1960—62; gen. sec., CEO United Meth. Ch. Gen. Coun. Ministries, Dayton, Ohio, 1986—2000. Trustee Bronson Meth. Hosp., Kalamazoo, 1983—86. Exec. com. World Meth. Coun., Lake Junaluska, NC, 1986—2000; truste Bronson Meth. Hosp., Kalamazoo, 1983—86. Methodist. Home: 5920 Wood Valley Rd Kalamazoo MI 49009 Home Phone: 269-372-2044.

LUNDQUIST, CHARLES ARTHUR, academic administrator; b. Webster, SD, Mar. 26, 1928; s. Arthur Reynald and Olive Esther (Parks) L.; m. Patricia Jean Richardson, Nov. 28, 1951; children: Clara Lee, Dawn Elizabeth, Frances Johanna, Eric Arthur, Gary Lars. BS, S.D. State U., 1949, DSc, 1979; PhD, U. Kans., 1953. Asst. prof. engrng. rsch. Pa. State U., 1953-54; sect. chief U.S. Army Ballistic Missile Agy., Huntsville, Ala., 1956-60; br. chief NASA-Marshall Space Flight Ctr., Huntsville, 1960-62; dir. Space Scis. Lab., 1973-81; asst. dir. sci. Smithsonian Astrophys. Obs., Cambridge, Mass., 1962-73; assoc. Harvard Coll. Obs., 1962-73; dir. rsch. U. Ala., Huntsville, 1982-90, assoc. v.p. for rsch., 1990-96, dir. consortium for materials devel. in space, 1985-98, dir. interactive projects office, 1999—. Editor: (with G. Veis) Smithsonian Institution Standard Earth, 1966, The Physics and Astronomy of Space Science, 1966, Skylab's Astronomy and Space Sciences, 1979. With US Army, 1954—56. Recipient Exceptional Sci. Achievement medal NASA, 1971, Hermann Oberth award AIAA, 1978. Mem. AAAS, Am. Geophys. Union, Am. Astron. Soc., Am. Phys. Soc., Nat. Speleological Soc. Home: 214 Jones Valley Dr SW Huntsville AL 35802-1724 Office: U Ala Research Inst Rm E-37 Huntsville AL 35899-0001 Office Phone: 256-824-2684. Business E-Mail: lundquc@email.uah.edu. E-mail: lundquist5@comcast.net.

LUNDQUIST, DANA RICHARD, health facility administrator; b. Mpls., Sept. 12, 1941; s. R. Dana and Mary Jane (Norton) L.; children: Brenda A., Sheila R. BA, Valparaiso U., 1963; postgrad., U. Hawaii, 1963-64, U. Colo., 1963; MBA, U. Chgo., 1966. Adminstrv. asst. U. Chgo. Hosps. and Clinics, 1966—67, asst. supt., 1967—68, asst. dir., 1968—70; officer, bd. dirs. affiliates Hamot Health Systems, Inc., Erie, Pa., 1970—92, pres. parent co., 1981—92, cons., 1992—97; sr. v.p. Highmark Blue Cross Blue Shield, 1993—97; exec. v.p. Hardware Hawaii, 1997—98. Lectr. grad. program in hosp. adminstrn. U. Chgo., 1967-70; mem. Erie County Hosp. Coun., 1978-92, pres., 1982; bd. dirs. Hosp. Coun. Western Pa., 1978-92, vice chmn.; exec. com. Pa. Coun. Tchg. Hosps., 1986-90; adv. coun. risk mgmt. Pa. Hosp. Ins. Co., 1982-90, bd. dirs. Vol. Hosps. Am. of Pa., 1985-92, chmn. bd.; bd. visitors The Behrend Coll., Pa. State U., 1990-92; bd. dirs. Pa. Med. Coll., 1991-92. Mem. Erie Conf. on Community Devel., 1981-92, bd. dirs., 1988-92; bd. dirs. N.W. Pa. Buy Right Coun., 1986-92, United Way Erie County, 1983-92; mem. pres.'s coun. Villa Maria Coll., Erie, 1981-90, bd. incorporators Gannon U., Erie, 1981-92; mem. governing bd. St. Paul's Luth. Ch., Erie, 1973-78, v.p., 1974-78; mem. Erie Down Town Coalition Steering Com., 1990-92, chmn., 1991-92, numerous other activities. Fellow Am. Coll. Healthcare Execs. (former regents adv. coun. Pa.); mem. Am. Hosp. Assn. (governing coun. sect. met. hosps. 1987, alt. ho. of dels. 1988), Hosp. Assn. Pa. (polit. action com. 1981-92), Pa. C. of C., U. Chgo. Hosp. Alumni Assn. (exec. com. 1967-70, 87-92, sec.-treas. 1988, pres. 1990-91), Rotary. Lutheran. Home and Office: 207 E Ohio St # 423 Chicago IL 60611 Personal E-mail: danalundquist@yahoo.com.

LUNDQUIST, JOHN MILTON, librarian, Egyptologist, author, travel writer, photographer; b. Twin Falls, Idaho, Sept. 22, 1938; s. Milton Rocine and Mildred (Toolson) L.; m. Suzanne Evertsen, Sept. 6, 1966 (div. July 1985); children: Jennifer, Lila, Eric, Margaret, John, Jack. BA in History, Portland State U., 1970; MLS, Brigham Young U., 1972; MA in Near Eastern Studies, U. Mich., 1974, PhD in Near Eastern Studies, 1983. Instr. anthropology and religious instrn. Brigham Young U., Provo, Utah, 1979-83, asst. prof. anthropology and religious instrn., 1983-85; mem. faculty New Sch. for Social Rsch., NYC, 1986-88; Susan and Douglas chief libr. Asian and Middle Eastern divsn. N.Y. Pub. Libr., NYC, 1985. Rschr. Archive for Rsch. in Archetypal Symbolism, N.Y.C., 1987—; lectr. Inst. for Asian Studies, Inc., N.Y.C., C.G. Jung Found., N.Y.; adj. assoc. prof. art history and archaeology Columbia U., N.Y.C., 1987-89; adj. assoc. prof. Near Eastern langs. and lit. NYU, 1987; adj. instr. grad. studies divsn. Fashion Inst. Tech., N.Y.C., 1996—; adj. instr. philosophy and religious studies Pace U., N.Y.C., 2002—; adj. prof. art history Sch. Visual Arts, N.Y.C., 2001—; spkr., lectr. in field; dir. excavation Am. Sch. Oriental Rsch., Tell Quarqur, Syria, 1981-85, field archaeologist, Syria, 1979-82; area supr. Am. Expedition to Tell Hadidi, Syria, summers 1974-76; extensive travel, rsch., field work China, Tibet, Japan, Hong Kong, Taiwan, India, Egypt, Syria, Jordan, Indonesia, others; guest scholar Japan Ctr. for Area Studies, Nat. Mus. Ethnology, Osaka, Mar. 1996. Author: The Temple: Meeting Place of Heaven and Earth, 1993, Japanese edit., 1994, Spanish edit., 1995, Portuguese edit., 1997, Babylon in European Writing and Art Civilizations of the Ancient Near East, 1995; contbr. articles to The N.Y. Times, United Airlines Hemispheres, and other publs.; translator langs. and lang. behavior abstracts; photography exhbns. include NY Pub. Libr., NYC, 1995-96, Asian-Am. Arts Ctr., NYC, 2000, Cathedral of St. John the Divine, NYC, 2001, Kent State U. Art Mus., 2001-02. Bd. advisors The Asian Classics Inst., 1995—, Art 21, 2005—. Mem. Internat. Assn. Orientalist Librs., Am. Inst. Archaeology (bd. govs. N.Y.C. chpt.), Am. Schs. Oriental Rsch. (corp. instnl. rep. 1985—), Oriental Club N.Y.C. (pres. 1992-95), East Side Conservative Club, Circumnavigators Club, Phi Kappa Phi. Republican. Mem. Lds Ch. Avocation: marathons. Office: NY Pub Libr Asian and Middle Eastern Divsn Fifth Ave and 42d St New York NY 10018 Home: Apt 525 33 Gold St New York NY 10038-2829 Home Phone: 212-566-7363; Office Phone: 212-930-0721. Business E-Mail: jlundquist@nypl.org.

LUNDQUIST, WEYMAN IVAN, lawyer; b. Worcester, Mass., July 27, 1930; s. Hilding Ivan and Florence Cecilia (Westerholm) L.; m. Joan Durrell, Sept. 15, 1956 (div. July 1977); children: Weyman, Erica, Jettora, Kirk; m. Kathryn E. Taylor, Dec. 28, 1978; 1 child, Derek. BA magna cum laude, Dartmouth Coll., 1952; LLB, Harvard U., 1955. Bar: Mass. 1955, Alaska 1961, Calif. 1963, Vt. 1994. Assoc. Thayer, Smith & Gaskill, Worcester, 1957-60; atty. U.S. Attys. Office, Mass. and Alaska, 1960-62; assoc. Heller, Ehrman, White & McAuliffe, San Francisco, 1963-65, ptnr., 1967—; counsel, v.p. State Mut. Life Ins. Co., Worcester, 1965-67. Vis. prof. environ. studies Dartmouth Coll., Hanover, NH, 1980, 84, adj. prof. Amos Tuck Bus. Sch., 1997—99, faculty advisor, 1998—; program chmn. 1990 Moscow Conf. on Law and Bilateral Econ. Rels.; mem. U.S. adv. com. Alaska/Can./Soviet No. Justice Conf., 1993—94, N.Y., San Francisco Cutting Edge Lawyer Liability Programs, 1989; assoc. dir. Inst. Arctic Studies, Dartmouth Coll., 1999—2003; bd. dirs. Univ. Press New Eng., 1996—2002, West Coast Magnetics, Stockton, Calif. Author: (fiction) The Promised Land, 1987, (nonfiction) The Art of Shaping the Case, 1999; contbr. articles to profl. jours. Trustee Natural Resources Def. Coun., 1982-91; faculty advisor Dartmouth Coll. women's lacrosse and soccer teams, 2000-. Sr. fellow Dickey Ctr. Internat. Understanding Dartmouth Coll., 2003, Inst. Artic Studies; recipient CPR Significant Achievement award, 1987. Fellow ABA (founder and chmn. litig. sect. 1978-79; mem. Soviet Bar Assn. liaison com. (chmn. 1986-96, co-chmn. spl. com. for study discovery abuse 1976-83, spl. com. on tort liability sys. 1981-84), Soviet legal dialogue com. (chmn. 1981-96, superfund 301e study group advisor to U.S. Congress 1983), Am. Coll. Trial Lawyers, Worcester County Bar Assn., Dartmouth Lawyers Assn. (founding mem.), Environ. Careers Orgn. (bd. dirs. 2001, chmn. 2002—04), Am. Antiquarian Soc. (life, councillor), Assn. Life Ins. Coun., U.S. Supreme Ct. Hist. Soc., Swedish Am. C. of C. (pres., bd. dirs. 1982-89). Avocations: squash, skiing, writing. Home: 16 Occum Rdg Hanover NH 03755-1410 Office: PO Box 5527 53 S Main St Ste 313 Hanover NH 03755-2022 Office Phone: 603-643-8610. Personal E-mail: wey@dartmouth.edu. Business E-Mail: wlundquist@hewm.com.

LUNDQVIST, HENRIK, professional hockey player; b. Are, Sweden, Mar. 2, 1982; Goalie Västra Frölunda HC, Swedish Elite League, 2000—05, NY Rangers, 2005—. Mem. Swedish Olympic Hockey Team, Torino, Italy, 2006. Named Player of Month, Eurohockey.net, 2005; recipient MetLife/Steven McDonald Extra Effort Award, 2006. Achievements include being a member of gold medal winning Swedish Hockey Team, Torino Olympics, Italy, 2006. Office: c/o NY Rangers 2 Pennsylvania Plaza New York NY 10121*

LUNDRIGAN, NICOLE M., lawyer; b. Piqua, Ohio, 1977; BA, U. Dayton, 1998; JD, Ohio Northern U., 2002. Bar: Ohio 2002, US Dist. Ct. Southern Dist. Ohio 2002, US Ct. of Appeals Sixth Cir. 2003. Assoc. Strauss & Troy, Cin. Named one of Ohio's Rising Stars, Super Lawyers, 2006. Mem.: Ohio State Bar Assn., Cin. Bar Assn., Dayton Bar Assn. Office: Strauss & Troy Federal Reserve Bldg 150 E Fourth St Cincinnati OH 45202-4018 Office Phone: 513-621-2120. Office Fax: 513-241-8259.

LUNDSAGER, MARGRETHE (MEG LUNDSAGER), federal official; b. Dec. 27, 1951; married; two children. Grad., Am. U., U. Md. With US Exec. Dirs. Office, IMF; spl. asst. to under sec. for internat. affairs US Dept. Treasury, Washington, 1987-90; dir. NSC staff Internat. Econ. Affairs Directorate, 1990-91; dir. Office Asian and Near East Nations US Dept. Treasury, Washington, 1991-95, dep. asst. sec. for trade & investment policy, 1996—2000, adv. to exec. dir., IMF, 2000, US alt. exec. dir. IMF, 2001—07, US exec. dir. to IMF, 2007—. Altantic fellow in pub. policy London Sch. Econs., 1995-96. Office: IMF 700 19th St NW Rm 13-318 Washington DC 20431*

LUNDSTEDT, SVEN BERTIL, behavioral and social scientist, educator; b. NYC, May 6, 1926; s. Sven David and Edith Maria L.; m. Jean Elizabeth Sanford, June 16, 1951; children: Margaret, Peter, Janet. AB, U. Chgo., 1952, PhD, 1955; SM, Harvard U., 1960. Lic. in psychology, N.Y., Ohio; cert. Council for Nat. Register of Health Services. Asst. dir. Found. for Research on Human Behavior, 1960-62; asst. prof. Case-Western Res. U., Cleve., 1962-64, assoc. prof., 1964-68; assoc. prof. adminstrv. sci. Ohio State U., Columbus, 1968-69, prof. pub. policy and mgmt., 1969—, Ameritech Research prof., 1987-89, prof. internat. bus. and pub. policy, 1988—, prof. mgmt. and human resources, 1990—2005, prof. emeritus, 2005—, mem. John Glenn Inst. for Pub. Svc. and Pub. Policy, 1999—, emeritus prof. pub. policy and mgmt., 2004—. Affiliate scientist Battelle PNL, 1974—; chmn. Batelle Endowment Program for Tech. and Human Affairs, 1976—80; mem. Univ. Senate, 2002—; dir. project on edn. of CEO Aspen Inst., 1978—80; advisor Task Force on Innovation, US Ho. of Reps., 1983—84; advisor Citizens Network for Fgn. Affairs, 1988—; mem. Am. Com. on US Soviet Rels., 1985—, chair trade and negotiation project; cons. E.I. duPont de Nemours & Co., B.F. Goodrich Co., Bell Tel. Labs., Battelle Meml. Inst., Nat. Fulbright Award Com.; invited spkr. Royal Swedish Acad. Scis., 1989. Author: Higher Education in Social Psychology, 1968; co-author: Managing Innovation, 1982, Managing Innovation and Change, 1989; author, editor: Telecommunications, Values and the Public Interest, 1990; contbr. articles to profl. jours. Pres., Cleve. Mental Health Assn., 1966-68; mem. Ohio Citizen's Task Force on Corrections, 1971-72. Served with U.S. Army, 1944-46 Harvard U. fellow, 1960; grantee Bell Telephone Labs., 1964-65, NSF, 1965-67, Kettering Found., 1978-80, Atlantic Richfield Found., 1980-82, German Marshall Fund of U.S. to conduct internat. ednl. joint ventures on econ. negotiations, Budapest, Hungary, 1990; recipient Ohio Ho. of Reps. award, 1986. Mem.: APA, Internat. Soc. Panetics (mem., sec. bd. govs., founding mem.), Am. Soc. for Pub. Adminstrn. (pres. Central Ohio chpt. 1975—77, founder, chmn. com. on bus. govt. relations 1977—79, editl. bd. Pub. Adminstrn. Rev. 1978—82), Am. Acad. Arts and Scis. (chmn. PIN com. on east/west trade negotiation), Internat. Inst. for Applied Systems Analysis (innovation task force, nat. adv. com. project. internat. negotiation with AAAS, founder, chmn. U.S. Midwest Assn. for IIASA 1986—, sr. social sci. advisor 1994—). Unitarian Universalist. E-mail: lundstedt.1@osu.edu.

LUNDSTROM, GILBERT GENE, bank executive, lawyer; b. Sept. 27, 1941; s. Vernon G. and Imogene (Jackett) L.; m. Joyce Elaine Ronin, June 26, 1965; children: Trevor A., Gregory G. BS, U. Nebr., 1964, JD, 1969; MBA, Wayne State U., 1966. Bar: U.S. Dist. Ct. (1st dist.) Nebr. 1969, Nebr. 1969, U.S. Ct. Appeals (5th cir.) 1970, U.S. Ct. Appeals (10th cir.) 1971, U.S. Ct. Appeals (8th cir.) 1974, U.S. Ct. Appeals (3d cir.) 1986. Ptnr. Woods & Aitken Law Firm, Lincoln, Nebr., 1969-93; CEO, chmn. bd. Tier One Bank, 1994—. Chmn., CEO Tier One Corp.; faculty law sch. U. Nebr., Lincoln, 1970-74; bd. dirs. Tier One Bank, TMS Corp. Ams., Sahara Enterprises, Inc., SMCO, Inc.; vice-chmn. Fed. Home Loan Bank Topeka, 1996-2002. Bd. dirs. Folsom Children's Zoo, Lincoln, 1979-83, St. Elizabeth Hosp. Found., 1998-2002, Tier One Charitable Found, Jr. Achievement Found., Nebr. Art Assn. Fellow Nebr. State Bar Assn.; mem. ABA, ATLA, Lincoln Bar Assn., Nebr. Bankers Assn. (bd. dirs.), Country Club of Lincoln, Firethorn County Club, Masons, Scottish Rite (33 degree), Lincoln C. of C. (bd. dirs.). Republican. Methodist. Home: 9519 Firethorn Ln Lincoln NE 68520-1459 Office: Tier One Bank 1235 N St Lincoln NE 68508-2083

LUNDSTROM, MARJIE, editor; Grad., U. Nebr. Columnist, editor, nat. corr. The Denver Post, 1981-89; with The Sacramento Bee, 1989-90, 91—; nat. corr. Gannett News Svc., Washington, 1990-91. Recipient Pulitzer Prize for nat. reporting, 1991. Office: The Sacramento Bee PO Box 15779 Sacramento CA 95852-0779 Business E-Mail: mlundstrom@sacbee.com.

LUNDY, AUDIE LEE, JR., lawyer; b. Columbus, Ga., Mar. 10, 1943; s. Audie Lee and Mary Blanche (Snipes) L.; m. Ann Porter, June 11, 1966; children: Travis Stuart, Katherine Porter. BA, Yale U., 1965; LLB magna cum laude, Columbia U., 1968. Bar: N.Y. 1968, D.C. 1976, Pa., 1988, Md. 1990. Assoc. firm White & Case, NYC, 1968-71, 74-75, London, 1971-74, Washington, 1975-78; asst. gen. counsel Campbell Soup Co., Camden, NJ, 1978, gen. counsel, 1979-88, v.p., gen. counsel, 1988-89; ptnr. Tydings & Rosenberg LLP, Balt., 1989—. Bd. mgrs. St. Christopher's Hosp. for Children, Phila., 1980-89, vice-chmn. 1986-89; trustee Food and Drug Law Inst., Washington, 1982-91, The Children's Guild, Inc., Balt., 1992-2005, chmn. 1997-99; chmn. Meritas Law Firms Worldwide, Mpls., 2005-07. Mem. ABA, Am. Soc. Internat. Law, Assn. Gen. Counsel (emeritus). Republican. Presbyterian. Clus: Merion Cricket Home: 203 Goodwood Gdns Baltimore MD 21210-2531 Office: Tydings & Rosenberg LLP 100 E Pratt St Baltimore MD 21202-1009 Office Phone: 410-752-9705. Business E-Mail: llundy@tydingslaw.com.

LUNDY, J(OSEPH) EDWARD, retired automobile company executive; b. Iowa, Jan. 6, 1915; s. Vern E. and Mary L. (Chambers) L. BA, U. Iowa, 1936. Fellow Princeton U., 1936-39, mem. econs. faculty, 1940-42, beginning as planning ofcl.; with Ford Motor Co., Dearborn, Mich., 1946-85, successively dir. fin. planning and analysis, gen. asst. contr., 1946-57, treas., 1957-61, v.p., contr., 1961-62, v.p. fin., 1962-67, exec. v.p., 1967-79, dir. and vice-chmn. fin. com., 1979-85. Dir. research and analysis Office Statis. Control, Hdqrs. USAAF, 1945 Served from pvt. to maj. USAAF, 1943-45. Decorated Legion of Merit. Mem. Dearborn Country Club, Phi Beta Kappa, Delta Upsilon. Clubs: Detroit Princeton. Roman Catholic. Home: 7 Brookwood Ln Dearborn MI 48120-1302

LUNDY, SADIE ALLEN, small business owner; b. Milton, Fla., Mar. 29, 1918; d. Stephen Grover and Martha Ellen (Harter) Allen; m. Wilson Tate Lundy, May 17, 1939 (div. 1962); children: Wilson Tate Jr., Houston Allen, Micheal David, Robert Douglas, Martha Jo-Ellen. Degree in acctg., Graceland Coll., 1938. Acct. Powers Furniture Co., Milton, 1939-40; acct., v.p. Lundy Oil Co., Milton, 1941-52; controller First Fed. Savs. & Loan, Kansas City, Mo., 1953-55, Herald Pub. Co., Indepenence, Mo., 1956-58; mgr. Baird & Son Toy Co., Kansas City, 1959-62; regional mgr. Emmons Jewelers NY, Kansas City, 1963-65; owner, pres. Lundy Tax Svc., Independence, 1965-85; corp. sec., treas., purchasing mgr. Optimation, Inc., Independence, 1974-85, mgr., 1985—, corp. sec., treas., 2006—; COO Wasber Industries LLC, Independence, 2001—; dir. ops., corp. sec., treas. ReEngineer Profit LLC, Independence, 2003—06. Contbr. articles to profl. jours. Mem. com. Neighborhood Coun., Independence, 1985. Mem.: Am. Bus. Women's Assn., Independence C. of C. (mem. com. 1965—85), Independence Women's Club. Republican. Cmty. Of Christ Ch. Avocations: counseling, swimming, bicycling. Home: PO Box 520238 Independence MO 64052-0238 Office: ReEngineer Profit LLC 704 NW Mock Blue Springs MO 64015 Office Phone: 816-228-2100. Business E-Mail: slundy@optonest.com. E-mail: slundy@comcast.net.

LUNDY, SHERMAN PERRY, secondary school educator; b. Kansas City, Mo., July 26, 1939; s. Loren F. and O. Metta (Brown) L.; m. Beverly J., Feb. 25, 1960; children: Paul, Carolyn. BA, U. Okla., 1963; MA, So. Meth. U., 1966; EdS, U. Iowa, 1975. Cert. tchr., Iowa. Tchr. Platte Canyon High Sch., Bailey, Colo., 1964-65, Lone Grove (Okla.) High Sch., 1966-68, Ardmore (Okla.) High Sch., 1968-69; tchr., sci. dept. chair Burlington (Iowa) High Sch., 1969—. Geologist Basic Materials Corp., Waterloo, Iowa, 1983—, Raid Quarries, Burlington, 1975-80. Contbr. articles to profl. jours.; author curriculum guide: Environmental Activities, 1975. Mem., commr. Regional Solid Waste Commn., Des Moines County, 1990—; mem., pres. Conservation Bd., Des Moines County, 1978-88; bd. dirs. Iowa Conservation Bd. Assn., 1984-85; mem. Civil Rights Commn., City of Burlington, 1970-76; pres. Burlington Trees Forever, 1998-99. With USMC, 1960-64. Recipient Silver Beaver Boy Scouts Am., 1975, Service Recognition, Des Moines County Conservation Bd., 1988, Project ESTEEM agt., Harvard/Smithsonian, 1992, Soil Conservation Water Shed Achievement award State of Iowa, 1998, DAR Award for Conservation, 1998, Environ. Educator of Yr. award U.S. EPA, Region 7, Iowa, 1998. Mem. Geol. Soc. Am. (North Cen. edn. com. 1989—), Iowa Acad. Sci. (edn. com. 1990-91, chair earth sci. tchrs. sect. 1993-94, exec. bd. 1992-94), Nat. Assn. Geology Tchrs. (Outstanding Earth Sci. Tchr. 1992, v.p. ctrl. sect. 1994-95, pres. ctrl. sect. 1996-98), Soc. Econ. and Sedimentary Geology, Geol. Soc. Iowa, Am. Chem. Soc. (Excellence in Sci. Tchg. award consortiums 1996, Chem. Cos. award), Unitarian Fellowship, Sons of Confederate Vets. (comdr. Camp 1759 1998—), SE Iowa Civil War Round Table (chair 1992-94). Unitarian Universalist. Avocations: history, stamp collecting/philately, fossil collecting. Home: 1103 Ellen St Cedar Falls IA 50613-2366

LUNDY, VICTOR ALFRED, architect, educator; b. NYC, Feb. 1, 1923; s. Alfred Henry and Rachel Lundy; m. Shirley Corwin, 1947 (div. 1959); children: Christopher Mark, Jennifer Alison; m. Anstis Manton Burwell, Sept. 19, 1960; 1 child, Nicholas Burwell. BArch, Harvard U., 1947, MArch, 1948. Registered architect, Tex., N.Y., Calif. Pvt. practice architecture, Sarasota, Fla., 1951-59, NYC, 1960-75; prin. Victor A. Lundy & Assocs., Inc., Houston, 1976-84; design. prin., v.p. HKS Inc., Dallas, 1984-90. Vis. prof. Grad. Sch. Design, Harvard U., Sch. Architecture, Yale U., Columbia U., U. Calif., Berkeley, Calif. Poly. State U. San Luis Obispo, U. Houston, U. Rome, others; U.S. specialist-architect in U.S.I.A. exhibit, USSR, 1965. Responsible for design St. Paul's Luth. Ch., Sarasota, 1959, new sanctuary, 1970, 1st Unitarian Ch. of Fairfield County, Westport, Conn., 1961, 1st Unitarian Congl. Soc., Hartford, Conn., 1964, Ch. of Resurrection, East Harlem Protestant Parish, N.Y.C., 1966, exhbn. bldg. and exhibit for AEC in S.Am. (Buenos Aires, Rio de Janeiro, Bogota, Santiago), 1967 (Silver medal for exhbn. Archtl. League N.Y. 1965), recreation shelters for Nat. Mus. History and tech., Smithsonian Instn., Washington, 1967, U.S. States Tax Ct. bldg. and pla., Washington, 1976, U.S. Embassy, Colombo, Sri Lanka, for Office of Fgn. Bldgs., Dept. State, 1983 (U.S. Presdl. Design Awards Program 1988, Fed. Design Achievement award), Austin Centre-Omni Hotel, Austin, Tex., 1984, One Congress Pla., Austin, Tex., 1984, Walnut Glen Tower, Dallas, 1985, Mack Ctr. II, Tampa, Fla., 1990, Greyhound Corp. Ctr., Phoenix, 1991, GTE Telephone Ops. World Hdqrs., Irving, Tex., 1991, Tex. A&M Found Hdqs., 1999, others; archtl. work represented in Berlin Internat. Archtl. Exposition, 1957, Sao Paulo Internat. Biennial Exposition, 1957, 5th Congress Union Internat. Des Architectes, Moscow, 1958, Expo '70 Exhbn., Osaka, Japan, 1970, travelling exhbn. of architecture in S.Am. Sgt. inf. U.S. Army, 1943-46, ETO. Decorated Purple Heart; recipient Gold medal award Buenos Aires Sesquicentennial Internat. Exhbn., 1960, Gold medal award Buenos Aires Sesquicentennial Internt.Exhbn., 1960; Silver medal Archtl. League N.Y., 1965; Charles Hayden Meml. Scholastic scholar, 1939-43, Edward H. Kendall scholar Harvard U., 1947-48, Rotch travelling scholar Boston Soc. Architects, 1948-50; travelling fellow Harvard U., 1948-50; Dept. State grantee, 1965. Fellow AIA. Avocations: painting, sculpture. Home: 701 Mulberry Ln Bellaire TX 77401-3805

LUNEMANN, JAN D., neurologist, researcher; b. Hanau, Germany, Oct. 22, 1972; s. Ewald Janssen and Erika Maria Lunemann; m. Anna Kloeting; children: Kea Philine, Lilli Sophia. MD, Humboldt U., Berlin, 1999. Resident Dept. Neurology, Berlin, 2000—04; postdoctoral fellow NIH, Bethesda, Md., 2004—05; postdoctoral assoc. The Rockefeller U., NYC, 2005—. Student rep. German sect. Internat. Physicians for Prevention Nuc. War, Berlin, 1994—99. Recipient Human Immunology award and fellowship, Dana Found./Irvington Inst. Immunlogical Rsch., 2006—07; scholar, Heinrich Boell Found., 1994—99; predoctoral rsch. scholar, German Rheumatism Rsch. Ctr., 1997, postdoctoral fellow, German Rsch. Soc., 2004—05, NIH, 2005—06. Mem.: NY Acad. Scis. (assoc.), German Neurol. Soc. (assoc.). Achievements include patents for TRAIL expression as a biomarker for interferon-beta response in patients with multiple sclerosis; research in the role of Epstein-Barr Virus in the pathogenesis of multiple sclerosis. Office: The Rockefeller U Box 390 1230 York Ave New York NY 10021 Office Phone: 212-327-8110.

LUNGREN, DANIEL EDWARD, congressman, former state attorney general; b. Long Beach, Calif., Sept. 22, 1946; s. John Charles and Lorain Kathleen (Youngberg) Lungren; m. Barbara Kolls, Aug. 2, 1969; children: Jeffrey Edward, Kelly Christine, Kathleen Marie. AB with honors cum laude, Notre Dame U., 1968; postgrad., U. So. Calif., 1968—69; JD, Georgetown U., 1971. Bar: Calif. 1972. Staff asst. to Senators George Murphy and William Brock US Senate, 1969—71; spl. asst. to co-chmn. Rep. Nat. Com., 1971—72, dir. spl. programs, 1971—72; from assoc. to ptnr. Ball, Hunt, Hart, Brown & Baerwitz, Long Beach, 1973—78; mem. US Congress from 42d Calif. dist., 1979—89, Rep. State Cen. Com. Calif., 1974—89; ptnr. Diepenbrock, Wulff, Plant & Hannegan, Sacramento, 1989—90; atty. gen. State of Calif., Sacramento, 1991—99; host, Dan Lungren Show Catholic Family Radio, San Diego; ptnr. Venable LLP, Washington, 1999—2004; mem. US Congress from 3rd Calif. dist., 2005—, Ho. Judiciary Com., Homeland Security Com., Budget Com. Chair Youth for Nixon campaign, Calif. Nat. syndicated radio talk show host, 1998. Committeeman Rep. Nat. Com., 1988—96; bd. dirs. ARC Boy's Club, Long Beach, 1976—88. Recipient Good Samaritan award, L.A. Coun. Mormon Chs., 1976; fellow Harvard Univ.'s Inst. Politics. Republican. Roman Catholic. Achievements include helped write and later defended in court California's landmark Three-Strikes-and-You're Out law; sponsored legis. against sexual predators which culminated in the state's Megan's Law giving people in Calif. the right to know if their children are at risk of predators in their own neighborhoods. Office: US Ho Reps 2448 Rayburn Ho Office Bldg Washington DC 20515-0503 Office Phone: 202-225-5716.*

LUNGSTRUM, JOHN W., federal judge; b. Topeka, Nov. 2, 1945; s. Jack Edward and Helen Alice (Watson) L.; m. Linda Eileen Ewing, June 21, 1969; children: Justin Matthew, Jordan Elizabeth, Alison Paige. BA magna cum laude, Yale Coll., 1967; JD, U. Kans., 1970. Bar: Kans. 1970, Calif. 1970, admitted to practice: US Dist. Ct. (Ctrl. Dist.) Calif., US Ct. Appeals (10th Cir.). Assoc. Latham & Watkins, LA, 1970-71; ptnr. Stevens, Brand, Lungstrum, Golden & Winter, Lawrence, Kans., 1972-91; U.S. Dist. judge Dist. of Kans., Kansas City, 1991—2001, chief judge, 2001—. Lectr. law U. Kans. Law Sch., 1973—; mem. faculty Kans. Bar Assn. Coll. Advocacy, Trial Tactics and Techniques Inst., 1983-86; chmn. Douglas County Rep. Ctrl. Com., 1975-81; mem. Rep. State Com.; del. State Rep. Conv., 1968, 76, 80; chair com. on ct. adminstrn. and case mgmt. Jud. Conf. US, 2000-05, mem. budget com., 2005-. Chmn. bd. dirs. Lawrence C. of C., 1990-91; pres. Lawrence United Fund, 1979; pres. Independence Days Lawrence, Inc., 1984, 85, Seem-to-be-Players, Inc., Lawrence Rotary Club, 1978-79; bd. dirs. Lawrence Soc. Chamber Music, Swarthout Soc. (corp. fund-raising chmn.); mem. Lawrence Art Commn., Williams Scholarship Fund, Lawrence League Women Voters, Douglas County Hist. Soc.; bd. trustees, stewardship chmn. Plymouth Congl. Ch.; pres. Lawrence Round Ball Club; coach Lawrence Summertime Basketball; vice chmn. U. Kans. Disciplinary Bd.; bd. govs. Kans Sch. Religion; bd. dirs. Kans. Day Club, 1980, 81. National Merit scholar, Yale Nat. scholar. Fellow Am. Bar Found.; mem. ABA (commn. Am. Jury 2004-05, past mem. litig. and ins. sect.), Douglas County Bar Assn., Johnson County Bar Assn., Wyandotte County Bar Assn., Kans. Bar Assn. (vice chair legis. com., subcom. litig., mem.CLE com.), U. Kans. Alumni Assn. (life), Judge Hugh Means Inn of Ct. (pres. 2005-), Phi Beta Kappa, Phi Gamma Delta, Phi Delta Phi. Avocations: basketball, hiking, skiing. Office: Robt J Dole US Courthouse Ste 517 500 State Ave Rm 517 Kansas City KS 66101-2400

LUNINE, JONATHAN IRVING, astronomer, educator; b. NYC, June 26, 1959; BS magna cum laude, U. Rochester, 1980; MS, Calif. Inst. Tech., 1983, PhD, 1985. Rsch. assoc. U. Ariz., Tucson, 1984-86, asst. prof. planetary scis., 1986-90; vis. asst. prof. UCLA, 1986, assoc. prof., 1990-95, prof., 1995—2003, prof. planetary sci. and physics, faculty mem. program in applied math., 1992—, chair theoretical astrophys. program, 2000—05. Interdisciplary scientist joint U.S.-European Cassini mission to Saturn and JWST mission, James Webb Space Telescope, 2002—; mem. com. planetary and lunar exploration space sci. bd. NAS, 1986—90; disting. vis. scientist Jet Propulsion Lab., 1997—; mem. exec. com. space studies bd. NRC, 1998—2002, chmn. com. origin and evolution life in universe space studies bd., 2000—02; mem. sci. coun. NASA Astrobiology Inst., 2000—03; chair solar sys. exploration subcom. NASA, 1990—94, 2003—05, mem. internat. Mars exploration adv. panel, 1993—94, mem. space sci. adv. com., 1990—95, 2003—05; vis. prof. Inst. Physics Interplanetary Space, Rome, 2005—06. Co-editor: (book) Protostars and Planets III, 1993; author: Earth: Evolution of, 1999, Astrobiology: A Multidisciplinary Approach, 2005; contbr. articles to profl. jours. Named one of 50 Emerging Leaders, Time Mag., 1994; recipient Cospar Zeldovich prize, Soviet Intercosmos and Inst. for Space Rsch., 1990, Arthur Adel award sci. achievement, No. Ariz. U., 2000; Galileo Circle fellow, U. Ariz., 2003. Fellow: AAAS, Am. Geophys. Union (Macelwane medal 1995); mem.: NAS (nat. assoc.), European Geophys. Soc., Internat. Coun. Sci. Unions, Internat. Acad. Astronautics, Am. Astron. Soc. (Harold C. Urey prize 1988), Sigma Xi. Avocation: hiking. Office: U Ariz Dept Planetary Scis PO Box 210092 Tucson AZ 85721-0092 Office Phone: 520-621-2789. Business E-Mail: jlunine@lpl.arizona.edu.

LUNING, THOMAS P., lawyer; b. St. Louis, Oct. 11, 1942; AB magna cum laude, Xavier U., 1964; JD, Georgetown U., 1967. Bar: D.C. 1968, Ill. 1968. Law clk. to Hon. Spottswood W. Robinson III and to ct. U.S. Ct. Appeals (D.C. cir.), 1967-68; atty. Schiff Hardin & Waite, Chgo. Mng. editor Georgetown Law Jour., 1966-67. Mem. ABA, Ill. State Bar Assn., Chgo. Bar Assn., 7th Cir. Bar Assn., Chgo. Coun. Lawyers. Office: Schiff Hardin & Waite 6600 Sears Tower Chicago IL 60606 E-mail: tluning@schiffhardin.com.

LUNN, STEVEN, automotive executive; Nat. cert. in Bus. Studies, Leeds Coll. Commerce, Eng.; postgrad. diploma in mgmt. studies; final diploma, Inst. Mktg. Dir. foundries and fuel sys. Rover Group, 1982; mng. dir. braking sys. Lucas Varity, mng. dir. light vehicle braking sys. divsn., 1996, dep. pres., COO; sr. v.p. ops. chassis sys. TRW Automotive, exec. v.p. automotive ops., exec. v.p., COO Livonia, Mich., 2002—. Office: TRW Automotive 12025 Tech Center Dr Livonia MI 48150*.

LUNSFORD, LAWRENCE DADE, medical educator; s. Lita Alexander Lunsford; m. Julianne Lunsford, Aug. 27, 1971; children: Stephanie Dade, Andrew Kirk. MD, Columbia U., NYC, 1974. Diplomate Am. Bd. Neurol. Surgery. Lars Leksell prof. neurological surgery U. Pitts., 1990—, prof. radiation oncology, 1991—97, prof., chmn. dept. neurol. surgery, 1997—2006. Recipient Jacob Fabrikant award, IRSA, 1997. Fellow: ACS (life); mem.: Internat. Stereotactic Radiosurgery Assn. (founder, 1st. pres. 1991—93). Achievements include first to Gamma knife brain surgery. Avocations: piano, golf, tennis, brittany spaniels. Office: B 400 Upmc 200 Lothrop St Pittsburgh PA 15213 Home Phone: 412-647-6781.

LUNSFORD, MIKE (MICHAEL CAMERON LUNSFORD), Internet company executive; b. NC, Dec. 5, 1967; Grad., MBA, U. N.C. Cons. Scott, Madden & Associates, Raleigh, NC, Anderson Consulting (now Accenture), Chgo.; exec. v.p. products Earthlink, Inc., Atlanta, exec. v.p. mktg., 2004—05, exec. v.p., pres. access & voice, 2005—, interim CEO, 2006—07. Office: Earthlink Inc 1375 Peachtree St Atlanta GA 30309 Business E-Mail: lunsford.support@corp.earthlink.net.*

LUNSFORD, W. BRUCE, health facility administrator and products executive; b. Nov. 11, 1947; m. Becky Lunsford, Aug. 29, 1970; children: Amy, Cindy, Brandy. BA, U. Ky., 1969; JD, Salmon P. Chase Coll. Law, 1974. CPA Ky., Ohio; bar: Ky. 1974, Ohio 1974. With Alexander Grant & Co., CPA, Cin., 1969—74, Keating, Muething and Klekamp Attys., Cin., 1974—79; dep. sec. Ky. Devel. Cabinet and Gov.'s Legis. Liaison, 1980—81; sec. Ky. Commerce Cabinet, 1981—83; of counsel, atty. Greenebaum Doll & McDonald, Louisville, 1984—91; chmn., pres., CEO Vencor Inc., Louisville, 1985—99; pres., CEO Ventas Inc., Louisville, 1998, chmn., 1998—. Bd. trustees U. Ky., 1983—87, Centre Coll., 1992—97, Shakertown at Pleasant Hill, Ky., Inc., 1992—; bd. trustees, sec. Bellarmine Coll., 1991—97; bd. govs. Salmon P. Chase Coll. Law, 1983—87; bd. dirs. Greater Louisville Fund for the Arts, 1990—97, Ky. Ctr. for the Arts Endowment Fund, Inc., 1992—97, Ky. Econs. Devel. Corp., 1989—, chmn., 1996—; bd. dirs., exec. com. Nat. City Bank, Ky., 1991—; bd. dirs. Res-Care, Inc., 1992—, Churchill Downs, Inc., 1995—, Nat. City Corp., 1995—; Fedn. Am. Health Sys., 1996—; bd. dirs. exec. com. Greater Louisville Econ. Devel. Partnership, 1992—. Named Entrepreneur of the Yr., Ky. and So. Ind., 1988, U. Ky. Bus. Leader of Yr., 1994; named to Kentuckiana Bus. Hall of Fame, 1993. Mem.: AICPA (Outstanding CPA in bus. and Ind. 1996), Omicron Delta Kappa. Office: Ventas Inc 10350 Ormsby Park Pl #300 Louisville KY 40223-6177

LUNT, LORA G., language educator, director; b. Princeton, NJ, Mar. 21, 1940; m. C. Richard K. Lunt; children: Emily Garland, Mary Jenney. BA in French with honors, Swarthmore Coll., 1962; MAT. in French, Johns Hopkins U., 1963; PhD in Arabic, Ind. U., 1978; PhD in French, McGill U., 2001. Instr. French U. Maine, Orono, 1963—64; ESL tchr. Peace Corps, Sfax, Tunisia, 1964—66; instr. French Canton Agrl. and Tech. Coll., NY, 1973; tchr. French Potsdam H.S., NY, 1973—80; adj. instr. French St. Lawrence U., Canton, NY, 1981; assoc. dean Arts and Scis. SUNY Potsdam, 1981—86, interim chair modern langs., 1987—88, instr. French, 1989—90, dir. internat. edn., 1990—. Editor: (book) The Potsdam Reader, 1982; contbr. articles newsletter N.E. Conf. Tchg. Fgn. Langs., 1988, articles including Institut des Belles Lettres Arabes, 1996; dir.: (grant project U.S. Dept. Edn.) Potsdam Coll. Fgn. Lang. Project, 1985, Potsdam Coll. Collaborative Project, 1989, (grant project U.S. Dept. State) Tunisia-SUNY Potsdam Bus. Edn. Partnership, 2002—06. Mem. World in Potsdam Diversity Festival, NY, 1998—; Clk. St. Lawrence Valley Friends Meeting, Potsdam, NY, 2000—01; Host Mother AFS, Potsdam, NY, 1977—78, 1983—84, 1987—88, Organizer of Bus Stop, 1987. Recipient Dictée Ameriques, Quebec, Can., 2002, Pres.'s Excellence Acad. Svc. award, SUNY Potsdam, 2000, Chancellor's award for excellence in profl. svc., SUNY, 2007. Mem.: Northeast MLA, Conseil Internat. des Etudes Francophones, NAFSA Orgn.Internat. Educators. Office: SUNY Potsdam 44 Pierrepont Ave Potsdam NY Office Phone: 315-267-2793. Office Fax: 315-267-2656. Business E-Mail: luntlg@potsdam.edu.

LUNT, OWEN RAYNAL, biologist, educator; b. El Paso, Tex., Apr. 8, 1921; s. Owen and Velma (Jackson) L.; m. Helen Hickman, Aug. 8, 1953; children: David, Carol, Janet. BA in Chemistry, 1947, PhD in Agronomy, 1951. Mem. faculty UCLA, 1951-93, prof. plant nutrition, 1964-72, prof. biology, 1972—, acting chmn. dept. biophysics, 1965-70, prof. emeritus, 1993; dir. Lab. Biomed. and Environ. Scis., 1968-93. Researcher in soil chemistry, fertility, plant physiology; tech. expert Internat. Atomic Energy Agy to Colombia, 1970, Kenya, 1983, Malaysia, 1985, Uruguay, 1987. Served with USN, 1944-46. Fellow Am. Soc. Agronomy, Soil Sci. Soc. Am.; Internat. Soc. Soil Sci., AAAS, Sigma Xi. Home and Office: 1200 Roberto Ln Los Angeles CA 90077-2334 Office Phone: 310-476-3597. *I was reared in a cheerful, harmonious family on a farm. During childhood, we were poor. We all had chores and the entire household was willing to work. The family was very generous with others who were less fortunate. Unwavering allegiance to high ethical and moral standards was expected. The whole family was active in the Mormon church. Neither parent had finished high school, but they read extensively. From an early age, I understood the family would support me in securing any educational objectives. In retrospect, I believe I had one of the best of starts.*

LUNTZ, MAURICE HAROLD, ophthalmologist; b. Capetown, South Africa, July 27, 1930; came to US, 1978; s. Montague Bernard and Sarah Miriam (Friedman) L.; m. Angela June Myerson, June 21, 1956; children: Melvyn Howard, Caryn Susan, David Sean. B Medicine B Surgery, Capetown U., 1952; MD, U. Witwatersrand, Johannesburg, South Africa, 1974. Diplomate Am. Bd. Ophthalmology. Lectr. ophthalmology Oxford U., England, 1960-62; prof., chmn. ophthalmology U. Witwatersrand, 1964-78; dir. ophthalmology Beth Israel Med. Ctr., NYC, 1978-88; chief glaucoma svc. Manhattan Eye, Ear & Throat Hosp., NYC, 1992—2002, bd. surgeon dir., 1993-95, pres. bd. surgeon dir., 1995—98; clin. prof. Mt. Sinai Sch. Medicine, NYC, 1978—2005, clin. prof. emeritus, 2005—; clin. prof. NYU, NYC, 2000—07. Adj. prof. NYU, 2007—; cons. Merck, Sharp & Dohme, NJ, 1980-82; chmn. Internat. Com. Ophthalmic Edn., 1974-90. Author: Uveitis, 1983, Glaucoma Surgery, 1984, 2d edit., 1995, Innovations in Diagnosis and Management of the Glaucomas, 2002; mem. editl. bd. Highlights Ophthalmology, Panama, 1970—, pres., 2002—; contbr. articles to profl. jour.; prodr. film Glaucoma Surveys, 1970. Fellow Royal Coll. Surgeons (Edinburgh), Coll. Surgeons South Africa (hon.); mem. Academia Ophthalmologica Internationalis, Order St. John Jerusalem (comdr. 2001—). Office: 550 Pk Ave New York NY 10021 Personal E-mail: Juneboy193@aol.com.

LUO, JIAN, engineering educator, researcher; s. Guangwu Luo and Qiaoling Wang; m. Qiong Jiang, Feb. 14, 2002; 1 child, Kevin J. BEng in Materials Sci. and Engring. with honors, Tsinghua U., Beijing, 1994; BEng in Electronics and Computer Tech., Tsinghua U., Beijing, China, 1994; MS in Materials Sci. and Engring., MIT, Cambridge, Mass., 1999; PhD in Ceramics, MIT, Cambridge, 2001. Mem. tech. staff Lucent Technologies, Inc. Bell Lab. & OFS Fitel/Furukawa Electric Co., Norcross, Ga., 2001—03; asst. prof. Clemson U., SC, 2003—; summer faculty rschr. Oak Ridge Nat. Lab., Tenn., 2005. Recipient CAREER award, Nat. Sci. Found., 2005, Ralph E. Powe Jr. Faculty Enhancement award, Oak Ridge Associated Universities, 2005, Faculty Excellence award, Clemson U. Bd. Trustees, 2006, 2007, Young Investigator award, Air Force Office Scientific Rsch., 2007. Mem.: Assn. Iron and Steel Tech., Minerals, Metals and Materials Soc., ASM Internat., Am. Ceramic Soc., Materials Rsch. Soc., Sigma Xi. Office: Clemson Univ 201 Olin Hall Clemson SC 29634 Office Phone: 864-656-5961. Office Fax: 864-656-1453. Personal E-mail: jluo@alum.mit.edu.

LUO, MICHAEL, journalist; b. 1976; BA, Harvard Univ., Cambridge, Mass. Intern Boston Bureau, AP; with Los Angeles Times; crime, law enforcement jour. Newsday, 1999—2001; nat. reporter NY Bureau, AP, 2001; now spl. projects reporter The New York Times. Contbr. articles Small Town Justice (Best Local Reporting, Livingston Awards, 2002, Polk Award for Criminal Justice Reporting, 2002). Office: The New York Times 229 W 43rd St New York NY 10036 E-mail: luo@nytimes.com.

LUONG, KHANH VINH QUOC, nephrologist, researcher; b. Cantho, Vietnam, Oct. 20, 1952; s. Hien Vinh Luong and Lieu Thi Huynh; m. Lan

Thi Hoang Nguyen, Oct. 15, 1981. MD, U. Kans., 1981. Diplomate Am. Bd. Internal Medicine, Am. Bd. Nephrology, Nat. Bd. Med. Examiners, Am. Coll. Ethical Physicians. Intern in internal medicine St. Elizabeth Med. Ctr., Northeastern Ohio U., Youngstown, 1981; resident internal medicine Tulane U. Hosp. Program, New Orleans, 1982-83, City of Faith Med. and Rsch. Ctr., Oral Roberts U., Tulsa, Okla., 1986-87; fellow in nephrology Cedars-Sinai Med. Ctr., UCLA Program in Nephrology, LA, 1987-90; pvt. practice Westminster, Calif., 1990—; clin. assoc. prof. family medicine U. So. Calif., Keck Sch. Medicine, LA, 2002—. Vis. asst. prof. medicine UCLA, 1989—90; clin. assoc. prof. family medicine Keck Sch. Medicine, U. So. Calif., LA, 2002—; presenter at nat. and internat. meetings. Contbr. articles to profl. jours. Nat. Kidney Found. So. Calif. fellow, 1989-90. Fellow ACP, Am. Coll. Endocrinology, Am. Coll. Allergy, Asthma and Immunology, Am. Coll. Nutrition, Am. Bd. Hosp. Physicians (diplomate), Am. Soc. Nephrology, Am. Assn. Clin. Endocrinologists, Am. Coll. Chest Physicians, Endocrine Soc., Am. Soc. Bone and Mineral Rsch., Assn. Vietnamese Physicians of the Free World, Vietnamese Med. Assn. in U.S., Vietnamese Am. Med. Rsch. Found. (pres.). Office: 14971 Brookhurst St Westminster CA 92683-5556 Office Phone: 714-839-5898.

LUONGO, C. PAUL, public relations executive; b. Winchester, Mass., Dec. 31, 1930; s. Carmine and Carmela (Gilberti) L. Grad., Cambridge Sch. Radio-TV, 1955; diploma, Bentley Coll., 1951; BSBA, Suffolk U., 1955; MBA, Babson Coll., 1956; AAS (hon.), Grahm Jr. Coll., 1970. Jr. exec. Raytheon Co., Lexington, Mass., 1956-59; account exec. Young & Rubicam, Inc., 1959-62; v.p. Copley Advt. Agy., Boston, 1962-64; pres. C. Paul Luongo Co., Boston, 1964—. Guest appearances include: (TV programs) Today Show, NBC-TV, 1984-89, Tomorrow Show, NBC-TV; TV-radio programs, Can.; author: America's Best!, 1980; contbr. syndicated newspaper-mag. features to Pub. Rels. Today; contbg. editor Travel Smart, N.Y., mo. newsletter. Founder Anthony Spinazzola Meml. Scholarship Found., Boston U., 1986-88; vol. U.S.S. Constn. Mus., Boston, Sta. WGBH-TV, Boston, TV Auctions, 1991-2000; mem. WORLDBOSTON, Boston, Mus. Fine Arts, Black Ships Festival, Inc., Newport, R.I.; pub. rels. dir. centennial ba. Belcourt Castle, Newport, 1994. With AUS, 1952-54. Mem. Boston Stockbrokers Club, Boston Advt. Club, Newcomen Soc. N.Am., Am. Inst. Wine and Food, Japan-Am. Soc. R.I., Neighborhood Assn. of Back Bay, Inc., Back Bay Assn., Suffolk U. Gen. Alumni Assn. (bd. dirs. 1994-98), James Beard Found., Friends of the Boston Pops. Address: 545 Boylston St 9th Fl Boston MA 02116 Office Phone: 617-266-4210. *I believe in the work ethic, integrity and the maximum utilization of time for work and recreational activities. I loathe prejudice in any form, dishonesty and indolent people.*

LUONGO, ROBERTO, professional hockey player; b. Montreal, Quebec, Canada, Apr. 4, 1979; Goaltender NY Islanders, 1999—2000, Florida Panthers, 2000—06, Vancouver Canucks, 2006—. Goaltender Team Can., World Championships, 2003, 04, Team Can., World Cup of Hockey, 2004. Named to NHL All-Star Game, 2004; recipient Mark Messier Leadership Award, 2007, Second All-Star Team, NHL, 2007. Achievements include being a member of gold medal winning Canadian World Championships Team, 2003, 2004; being a member of World Cup Champion Team Canada, 2004; setting NHL record for saves in a single season (2,303), 2004. Office: Vancouver Canucks 800 Griffiths Way Vancouver BC Canada*

LUONGO, STEPHEN EARLE, lawyer; b. Phila., June 15, 1947; s. Alfred Leopold and Dorothy West L.; m. Louise Anne Cipriani, Aug. 12, 1972; children: Peter James, Richard Stephen, Michael Paul. BS, U. Pa.; JD, Temple U. Bar: Pa. 1972, U.S. Dist. Ct. (ea. dist.) Pa. 1972. Assoc. atty. Blank, Rome, Comisky & McCauley, Phila., 1972-79, ptnr., 1979—, co.-chmn. corp. dept., 1988-93, mem. ptnr. bd., 1995—. Bd. dirs. Genesis Health Ventures, Inc., Kennett Suare, Pa., 1985-2000. Solicitor Merion Pk. Civic Assn., 1990-93. Mem. ABA, Am. Acad. Hosp. Attys., Pa. Bar Assn., Phila. Bar Assn., Nat. Assn. Coll. and Univ. Attys. Lodges: Order of Sons of Italy. Home: 215 Winding Way Merion Station PA 19066-1217 Office: Blank Rome Comisky & McCauley One Logan Sq Philadelphia PA 19103-6998

LUPERT, LESLIE ALLAN, lawyer; b. Syracuse, NY, May 24, 1946; s. Reuben and Miriam (Kaufman) L.; m. Roberta Gail Fellner, May 19, 1968; children: Jocelyn, Rachel, Susannah. BA, U. Buffalo, 1967; JD, Columbia U., 1971. Bar: N.Y. 1971. Ptnr. Orans Elsen & Lupert, NYC, 1971—. Contbr. articles to profl. jours. Mem. ABA, N.Y. State Bar Assn. (trial lawyers sect.), Assn. of Bar of City of N.Y. (com. fed. legislation 1977-80, profl. and jud. ethics com. 1983-86, com. on fed. cts. 1986-89, 95-96), Phi Beta Kappa. Office: Orans Elsen & Lupert LLP 875 3d Ave 28th Fl New York NY 10022 Office Phone: 212-586-2211. Business E-Mail: llupert@oellaw.com.

LUPIA, ARTHUR W., political science educator; b. Buffalo, May 20, 1964; BA in Econs., U. Rochester, 1986; MS in Social Sci., Calif. Inst. Tech., 1988, PhD in Social Sci., 1991. Asst. prof. polit. sci. U. Calif., San Diego, 1990-96, assoc. prof. polit. sci., 1996-98, prof. polit. sci., 1998—2001; sr. rsch. scientist, Inst. for Social Rsch. U. Mich., Ann Arbor, 2001—, prof. polit. sci., 2001—. Presenter in field; panelist San Diego Headliners, KNSD-TV, 1990; election analyst L.A. Times, 1987, 88, Sol Del Valle Cmty. Ctr., 1988, Remcho, Johannson and Purcell law firm, 1989. Author: (with Mathew D. McCubbins) The Democratic Dilemma: Can Citizens Learn What They Need to Know?, 1998; contbr. articles to profl. publs.; referee for numerous publs., including Econ. Inquiry, Games and Econ. Behavior, Jour. Instnl. and Theoretical Econs., Jour. of Law, Econs. and Orgn., Pub. Opinion Quar., NAS, others. Recipient Emerging Scholar award Am. Polit. Sci. Assn., 1996, award for initiatives in rsch. NAS, 1998; fellow Ctr. for Advanced Study in Behavioral Sci., 1999-2000, John Randolph Haynes and Dora Haynes fellow, 1989, Earle D. Anthony Grad. fellow, 1986; grantee NSF, 1994, 95, U. Calif.-San Diego, 1990, 91, 94, 96, 97, 98, Ctr. for European and German Studies, 1994, World Bank, 1997. Fellow Am. Acad. Arts & Scis.; mem. Am. Polit. Sci. Assn. (mem. exec. com. sect. on elections, public opinion and voting behavior 1996—, sec. on polit. economy, 1995—). Office: Inst for Social Rsch Univ Mich 426 Thompson St Rm 4252 Ann Arbor MI 48104-2321 E-mail: lupia@umich.edu.*

LUPIANI, DONALD ANTHONY, psychologist; b. NYC, June 7, 1946; s. Louis and Josephine (Boccia) L.; m. Linda Moyik, June 20, 1970; 1 child, Jennifer. BA, Iona Coll., 1968; MA, Columbia U., 1971, PhD, 1973; post-doctoral, Behavior Therapy Inst., White Plains, NY, 1976. Lic. psychologist, N.Y.; diplomat Am. Bd. Profl. Psychology, Am. Bd. Psychotherapy, Am. Acad. Behavioral Medicine, Intenat. Acad. Behavioral Medicine, Internat. Acad. Behavioral Medicine. Clin. assoc. Columbia U., NYC, 1974-85, Fordham U., Bronx, NY, 1979-81; dir. psychology and spl. edn. svcs. Riverdale Country Sch., Bronx, 1973-87; chief psychologist Franciscan Order of Priests, NYC, 1983—; pvt. practice Yonkers, NY, 1975—. Dir. spl. svcs. Riverdale Country Sch., Bronx., 1973-87; bd. dirs. St. Ursula Learning Ctr., Mt. Vernon, N.Y. Contbr. articles to profl. jours. Bd. dirs., mem. The St. Ursula Learning Ctr. Fellow Am. Orthopsychiat. Assn., Am. Coll. Psychology, Am. Acad. Sch. Psychology; mem. APA, N.Y. State Psychol. Assn., Westchester County Psychol. Assn. (chmn. ethics com. 1980-87). Roman Catholic. Avocations: woodworking, painting, drawing. Home and Office: 227 Mile Square Rd Yonkers NY 10701-5369

LUPIANI, JENNIFER LYNNE, school psychologist; b. Bronx, NY, Mar. 24, 1975; d. Donald Anthony and Linda Lupiani. BA, Boston Coll., 1993—97; MS in edn., Fordham U., 1997—2001, profl. diploma, 1997—2001, PhD, 1997—2004. Cert. school psychologist NY, 2001. Sch. psychologist Astor Child Guidance Ctr., Bronx, NY, 2001—02, Croton Harmon Sch. Dist., Croton-on-Hudson, NY, 2002—04; asst. psychologist Ind. Practice, Yonkers, NY, 1999—; sch. psychologist Putnam No. Westchester BOCES, Yorktown Heights, NY, 2002—, Hendrick Hudson Sch. Dist., Cortlandt Manor, NY, 2004—. Field specialist for applied behavior analysis Fordham U., New York, NY, 2001—02. Recipient Ted Bernstein award, NY Assn. of Sch. Psychologists, 2004, Lambda Xi Chpt. of Kappa Delta Pi, Fordham U., 2000, Golden Key Nat. Honor Soc., Boston Coll., 1995, Psi Chi, 1996. Mem.: NASP, NY Assn. of Sch. Psychologists, APA. Avocations: sewing, knitting, painting, swimming, travel. Home: 227 Mile Square Rd Yonkers NY 10701 Office: Furnace Woods Elementary Sch 239 Watch Hill Rd Cortlandt Manor NY 10567 Home Phone: 914-965-6883; Office Phone: 914-736-5416. Personal E-mail: jlupiani@aol.com.

LUPICA, MIKE (MICHAEL THOMAS LUPICA), sports columnist; b. Oneida, NY, May 11, 1952; s. Benedict and Lee; m. Taylor Lupica; 3 children. BA, Boston Coll., 1974. Corr. Boston Globe, 1970-74; columnist Boston Phoenix, 1971-75, Boston mag., 1974-75; feature writer Washington Star, 1974-75; basketball writer, columnist N.Y. Post, 1975-76; columnist N.Y. Daily News, 1980—; writer syndicated TV spls.; contbg. editor World Tennis, 1974-81. Contr.: (TV series) The Sports Reporters; host The Mike Lupica Show; author: (nonfiction) Reggie, 1984, Parcells, 1987, Mad as Hell: How Sports Got Away From the Fans and How We Get It Back, 1996, Summer of '98, 1999, (novels) Dead Air, 1986, Extra Credits, 1988, Limited Partner, 1990, Jump, 1996, Full Court Press, 2001, Red Zone, 2003, Wild Pitch, 2003, Too Far, 2004, Travel Team, 2004, Heat, 2006, Miracle on 49th Street, 2006; co-author: (nonfiction) Wait Till Next Year, 1988. Mem. Newspaper Guild Am. Achievements include youngest columnist (23 years old) to write for a major New York City newspaper. Office: NY Daily News 450 W 33rd St New York NY 10001

LUPIN, LOUIS MARTIN, lawyer; b. Mar. 1955; m. Margarita I. Lupin; children: Gabe, Daniel, Leanna. BA in Psych., Swarthmore Coll., 1977; JD, Stanford U., 1985. Bar: 1985. Assoc. Cooley, Godward, Castro, Huddleson & Tatum, San Francisco, 1985—92, ptnr., 1992—95; sr. legal counsel QUALCOMM Inc., San Diego, 1995—96, v.p., proprietary rights counsel, 1996—98, sr. v.p., proprietary rights counsel, 1998—2000, sr. v.p., gen. counsel, 2000—06, exec. v.p., gen. counsel, 2006—07. Exec. com. bd. visitors Stanford Law Sch. Mem.: San Francisco Bar Assn., Santa Clara County Bar Assn., ABA.*

LUPKIN, STANLEY NEIL, lawyer; b. Bklyn., Mar. 27, 1941; s. David B. and Sylvia (Strassman) L.; m. Anne Rachel Fischler, June 3, 1962; children: Jonathan Daniel, Deborah Eve. BA, Columbia Coll., NYC, 1962; LLB, NYU, 1966. Bar: NY 1966, US Dist. Ct. (so. and ea. dists.) NY 1970, US Ct. Appeals (2d cir.) 1970, US Supreme Ct. 1971. Asst. dist. atty., sr. trial atty., chief indictment bur. NY County Dist. Atty.'s Office, NYC, 1966-71; asst. commr. City of NY, 1966-71; 1st dep. commr., commr. Dept. Investigation, NYC, 1978-82; ptnr. Litman, Asche, Lupkin, Gioiella & Bassin, NYC, 1982-96; exec. v.p. Decision Strategies LLC, NYC, 1996—2004, Ackerman, Levine, Cullen, Brickman & Limmer, LLP, 2004—06; atty. Law Offices of Stanley N. Lupkin, 2006—. Mem. faculty Nat. Coll. Dist. Attys., Houston, 1974—75, FBI Nat. Acad., Quantico, Va., 1980—82. Co-author: Anatomy of A Municipal Franchise: N.Y.C. Bus Shelter Program, 1973-79, 1981; contbr. articles to profl. jours.; co-author: Independent Private Sector Inspectors General: Privately Funded Overseers of Public Integrity, 2006. Trustee, counsel Solomon Schechter Sch. of Queens, Flushing, NY, 1974—; mem. secondary schs. com. admissions office Columbia Coll., NYC, 1987-99. With USAR, 1963-69. Fellow: Theodore Roosevelt Inn of Ct., NY State Bar Found.; mem.: NACDL, Ind. Pvt. Sector Insps. Gen., Internat. Assn. Dir., NY Criminal Bar Assn., NY State Assn. Criminal Def. Lawyers, Assn. Bar City NY (chmn. com. on criminal justice ops. 1982—85, com. on criminal cts. 2001—), NY State Bar Assn. (chmn. com. on prosecution 1977—85, exec. com. criminal justice sect. 1977—2000, chmn. com. on def. 1985—2004, Prosecutor of Yr. award 1981), Soc. Columbia Grads. (v.p. 1989—98, dir. 1989—). Avocations: classical music, talmudic law. Office: 98 Cutter Mill Rd Great Neck NY 11021 Home Phone: 516-482-3070; Office Phone: 516-482-1223. Business E-Mail: slupkin@gnlaw.com.

LUPO, RAPHAEL V., lawyer; b. Washington, Oct. 15, 1941; BSEE, George Washington U., 1963, JD, 1968. Bar: Va. 1968, D.C. 1968, U.S. Dist. Ct. D.C. 1968, U.S. Dist. Ct. (ea. dist.) Va. 1969, U.S. Patent and Trademark Office, U.S. Claims Ct. 1969, U.S. Ct. Appeals ((D.C. cir.) 1968, U.S. Ct. Appeals (4th cir.) 1969, U.S. Ct. Appeals (fed. cir.) 1982, U.S. Ct. Customs and Patent Appeals 1969, U.S. Supreme Ct. 1969, U.S. Ct. Appeals 1982. Assoc. solicitor U.S. Patent and Trademark Office, 1969-77; dep. asst. gen. counsel for patents Dept. Energy, 1977-80; atty. Spencer & Kaye, Washington, 1980-82, Lupo Lipman & Lever, Washington, 1982-89, Willian Brinks Olds Hofer Gilson & Lione, P.C., Washington; ptnr., mem. firm exec. mgmt. com., IP dept. chair McDermott Will & Emery LLP, Washington. Adj. prof. George Washington U. Law Sch., 1992; speaker 6th Annual Jud. Conf. U.S. Ct. Appeals (Fed. cir.), 1988, 10th Annual Jud. Conf. U.S. Ct. Appeals (Fed. cir.), 1992-1998; presenter in field. Co-author: Patent Litigation and Strategy, 1999. Mem. ABA (contbr. Patent Litig. Strategies Handbook sect. Intellectual Property BNA 2000, co-chair Sedona conf. patent litig. 2004-05), Fed. Cir. Bar Assn. (presenter 2006), DC Bar, Va. State Bar, Am. Intellectual Property Law Assn. Office: McDermott Will & Emery LLP 600 13th St NW Fl 12-8 Washington DC 20005-3005 Office Phone: 202-756-8366. Office Fax: 202-756-8087. Business E-Mail: rlupo@mwe.com.

LUPONE, PATTI, actress; b. Northport, L.I., NY, Apr. 21, 1949; d. Orlando Joseph and Angela Louise (Patti) LuP.; m. Matt Johnston, 1988; 1 child, Joshua Luke. BFA, The Juilliard Sch., 1972. Off-Broadway prodns. include: The Woods, School for Scandal, The Lower Depths, Stage Directions; regional prodns. include: The Lady With The Torch, 2004, The Little Foxes, 2005, Anyone Can Whistle, 2005; Broadway prodns. include: Next Time I'll Sing to You, The Time of Your Life, The Three Sisters, The Robber Bridegroom, 1976 (Tony award nominee), The Water Engine, The Beggar's Opera, Edward II, The Baker's Wife, 1976, The Woods, 1977, Working, 1978, Catchpenny Twist, 1978, As You Like It, 1982, The Cradle Will Rock, 1983, Stars of Broadway, 1983, Edmond, 1982, Oliver, 1984; star Broadway musicals Evita, 1979 (Best Actress in Musical Tony award, 1980), Anything Goes, 1987, Pal Joey, 1995, Sweeney Todd, 2005, Gypsy, 2006; London prodns. Les Miserables, 1985, Sunset Boulevard, 1993; films include: King of the Gypsies, 1978, 1941, 1979, Fighting Back, 1982, Witness, 1985, Wise Guys, 1986, Driving Miss Daisy, 1989, Family Prayers, 1993, State and Maine, 1999, Just Looking, 1999, Bad Faith, 1999, The 24 Hour Woman, 1999, Summer of Sam, 1999, Bad Faith, 2000, State and Main, 2000, The Victim, 2001, Heist, 2001, City By the City, 2002; TV appearances include: Kitty, The Time of Your Life, Lady Bird in LBJ, 1987, The Water Engine, 1992, Family Prayers, 1993, The Song Spinner, 1995, Her Last Chance, 1996; TV series, Life Goes On, 1989-93, Falcone, 2000; TV guest appearances Law & Order, 1990, Frasier, 1993, Remember WENN, 1996, Saturday Night Live, 1998, Touched by an Angel, 2001, Oz, 2003, The Tony Danza Show, 2004, Will & Grace, 2005. Volunteer Craft and Folk Art Mus., 1999—2000. Named to Theatre Hall of Fame, 2007; recipient John Houseman award, 2006. First Am. actress to win an Olivier award in England, 1985. Office: ICM 40 W 57th St Fl 16 New York NY 10019-4098*

LUPTON, STEPHEN D., lawyer; b. 1944; LLB, Newcastle U., Eng., 1968. Bar: London 1970. Mgr. legal and secretarial svcs. UK divsn. GM Corp., 1968—72; sec., group legal adv. domestic appliance divsn. GEC Plc., 1972—75; European legal counsel NCH Corp., Irving, Tex., 1975—90; dir. legal svcs. Massey Ferguson Group Ltd. (acquired by AGCO Corp. 1994), 1990—94; dir. legal svcs. internat. AGCO Corp., Duluth, Ga., 1994—95, v.p., internat. counsel, 1995—99, sr. v.p., gen. counsel, 1999—2002, sr. v.p. corp. devel., gen. counsel, 2002—. Office: AGCO Corp 4205 River Green Pky Duluth GA 30096 Office Phone: 770-813-9200.*

LUPU, RADU, pianist; b. Galati, Romania, Nov. 30, 1945; s. Meyer and Ana (Gabor) Lupu. Attended Conservatoire, Moscow, USSR, 1961-69. Musician, US debut Cleve. Orch.; musician: (with worldwide maj. orchs.) Berlin Philharm., Vienna Philharm., Israel Philharm., Orch. de Paris, Concertgebouw, NY Philharm., Phila. Symphony Orch., Chgo. Symphony Orch., Cleve. Symphony Orch.; musician: (albums) Beethoven Cycle with Israel Philharmonic and Zubin Mehta, Mozart Sonatas for Violin and Piano with Szymon Goldberg, Schubert Lieder with Barbara Hendricks, Mozart and Schubert duets and Mozart Concerto for 2 pianos with Murray Perahia, Brahms Piano Concerto # 1, Mozart and Beethoven Quintets in E Flat, Schubert Piano Duets with Daniel Barenboim. Recipient 1st prize, Van Cliburn Internat. Piano Competition, 1966, Enescu Competition, 1967, Leeds Internat. Piano Competition, 1969, Abbiati prize, Italian Critic's Assn., 1989, 2006, Edison award, Schumann Kinderszenen, Kreisleriana, 1995, Grammy award for Schubert D960 and D664, 1995, Premio Internazionale Arturo Benedetti Michelangeli, 2006. Office Phone: 01608 810330. Business E-Mail: artists@harristurner.co.uk.

LUPULESCU, AUREL PETER, medical educator, researcher, physician; b. Manastiur, Banat, Romania, Jan. 1, 1923; came to US, 1967, naturalized, 1973; s. Peter Vichentie and Maria Ann (Dragan) L. MD magna cum laude, Sch. Medicine, Bucharest, Romania, 1950; MS in Endocrinology, U. Bucharest, 1965; PhD in Biology, U. Windsor, Ont., Can., 1976. Diplomate Am. Bd. Internal Medicine. Chief lab. investigations Inst. Endocrinology, Bucharest, 1950-67; rsch. assoc. SUNY Downstate Med. Ctr., 1968-69; asst. prof. medicine Wayne State U., 1969-72, assoc. prof., 1973—. Vis. prof. Inst. Med. Pathology, U. Rome, 1967; cons. VA Hosp., Allen Park, Mich., 1971-73; sr. cancer rsch. scientist Wayne State U., 1991—. Author: Steroid Hormones, 1958, Advances in Endocrinology and Metabolism, 1962, Experimental Pathophysiology of Thyroid Gland, 1963, Ultrastructure of Thyroid Gland, 1968, Effect of Calcitonin on Epidermal Cells and Collagen Synthesis in Experimental Wounds As Revealed by Electron Microscopy Autoradiography and Scanning Electron Microscopy, 1976, Hormones and Carcinogenesis, 1983, Hormones and Vitamins in Cancer Treatment, 1990, Cancer Cell Metabolism and Cancer Treatment, 2001; reviewer various sci. jours.; contbr. chpts., numerous articles to profl. publs. Recipient Lifetime Sci. Achievement award, Internat. Biographical Cr., 2003. Fellow Fedn. Am. Socs. for Exptl. Biology; mem. AMA, AAAS, Electron Microscopy Soc. Am., Soc. for Investigative Dermatology, NY Acad. Scis., Am. Soc. Cell Biology, Soc. Exptl. Biology and Medicine. Republican. Achievements include research on hormones and tumor biology; studies regarding role of hormones and vitamins in cancer treatment and prevention. Home: 21480 Mahon Dr Southfield MI 48075-7525 Office: Wayne State U Sch Medicine 540 E Canfield St Detroit MI 48201-1928

LUQUE, NANCY, lawyer; BA, San Diego St. Univ., Calif., 1973; JD, Univ. San Diego, 1976. Bar: Calif. 1976, DC 1989. Trial atty. Dept. Justice Antitrust Div., Washington, 1979—82; asst. US atty. US Dept. Justice, Washington, 1983—89; assoc. Washington Perito & Dubuc, 1989—91; ptnr. Katten Muchin Zavis, 1989—91, Reed Smith, Washington, 1995—2002, Luque Sheinbach, Washington, 2002—04, DLA Piper Rudnick Gray Cary US, LLP, Washington, 2004—. Chmn. ABA, Criminal Justice Section, White Collar Crime Com., Washington; past pres. Asst. US Atty. Assn. Editor: (Newsletter) White Collar Crime Com.; co-author: (Criminal Justice Magazine) Joint Defense Agreements: Protecting the Privilege and the Future, 1990, (Nat. Inst. HJealthcare Fraud, ABA) Grand Jury: Conflicts and Document Production, 1993, (Nat. Inst. Healthcare Fraud, ABA) Sentencing Guidelines, 1994. Office: DLA Piper Rudnick Gray Cary US LLP 1200 Nineteenth St NW Washington DC 20036-2412 E-mail: nancy.luque@dlapiper.com.

LURA, SUSAN, librarian; Children's libr. Pioneer Libr. System, Norman (Okla.) Pub. Libr. Recipient NY Times Libr. award, 2006. Office: Pioneer Libr Sys Norman Pub Libr 225 N Webster Norman OK 73069 Office Phone: 405-701-2600. Office Fax: 405-701-2608. E-mail: norman_library@pls.lib.ok.us.

LURAIN, JOHN ROBERT, III, gynecologist; b. Princeton, Ill., Oct. 27, 1946; s. John Robert Jr. and Elizabeth Helen (Grampp) L.; m. Nell Lee Snavely, June 14, 1969; children: Alice Elizabeth, Kathryn Anne. BA, Oberlin Coll., 1968; MD, U. N.C., 1972. Diplomate Am. Bd. Ob-Gyn., Am. Bd. Gynecologic Oncology. Resident in ob-gyn. U. Pitts./Magee-Womens Hosp., 1972-75; fellow in gynecologic oncology Roswell Park Cancer Inst., Buffalo, 1977-79; prof. gynecology and cancer rsch. Northwestern U., Feinberg Sch. Medicine, Chgo., 1979—; chief gyn. oncology svc. Northwestern Meml. Hosp., 1985—2004. Contbr. over 170 articles to profl. jours., chapters to books. Lt. comdr. USN, 1975-77. Fellow: Am. Coll. Ob-Gyn.; mem.: Internat. Soc. Study Trophoblastic Diseases, Internat. Gynecol. Cancer Soc., Am Soc. Colposcopy and Cervical Pathology, Ctrl. Assn. Ob-Gyn., Am. Soc. Clin. Oncology, Soc. Gynecologic Oncologists. Avocations: golf, tennis. Office: Northwestern U Med Sch 333 E Superior St Chicago IL 60611-3015 Home Phone: 708-383-4950; Office Phone: 312-926-7365. Business E-Mail: jlurain@nmff.org.

LURASCHI, WILLIAM R., utilities executive, lawyer; BS in Fin., U. Conn.; JD, Rutgers U. Assoc. Chadbourne & Parke LLP; gen. counsel The AES Corp., Arlington, Va., 1994—, sec., 1996—2002, v.p., 1998—2002, sr. v.p., 2002—03, exec. v.p., 2003—. Office: The Aes Corporation 4300 Wilson Blvd Ste 900 Arlington VA 22203-4168

LURENSKY, MARCIA ADELE, lawyer; b. Newton, Mass., May 4, 1948; BA magna cum laude, Wheaton Coll., 1970; JD, Boston Coll. Law Sch., 1973. Bar: Mass. 1973, D.C. 1990, U.S. Dist. Ct. (we. dist.) Wis. 1978, U.S. Dist. Ct. Mass. 1974, U.S. Ct. Appeals (1st cir.) 1974, U.S. Ct. Appeals (3d cir.) 1982, U.S. Ct. Appeals (4th cir.) 1984, U.S. Ct. Appeals (5th cir.) 1995, U.S. Ct. Appeals (8th cir.) 1985, U.S. Ct. Appeals (9th cir.) 1976, U.S. Ct. Appeals (10th cir.) 1995, U.S. Ct. Appeals (11th cir.) 1982, U.S. Ct. Appeals (fed. cir.) 1989, U.S. Claims Ct. 1989, U.S. Supreme Ct. 1979. Atty. U.S. Dept. Labor, Washington, 1974-90, Fed. Energy Regulatory Commn., U.S. Dept. Energy, Washington, 1990—. Mem. Phi Beta Kappa. Office: Fed Energy Regulatory Commn 888 1st St NE Washington DC 20426-0002

LUREY, MICHAEL S., lawyer; b. Chgo., Aug. 31, 1946; BS with distinction, Northwestern U., 1967; JD cum laude, Harvard U., 1970. Bar: Calif. 1971. Atty. Latham & Watkins, LA, 1970—88, co chair, 1988—91, ptnr., 1991—. Dir. Am. Bankruptcy Inst., 1982-88; bd. govs. Fin. Lawyers Conf., 1979-82, 85—, pres., 1988-89; contbr. workshops in field; counsel Intermark Inc. and Triton Group Ltd, NorthPoint Comm. Grp. Inc. Contbr. articles to profl. journs. Recipient Am.'s Leading Bus. Lawyers, Chambers USA, 2003—04, Am.'s Top 100, 2003, Internat. Who's Who of Bus. Lawyers, 2002. Mem. ABA (bus. bankruptcy com. corp. banking and bus. law sect. 1975—), LA County Bar Assn. (chmn. exec. com. commercial law and bankruptcy sect. 1981-82), Tau Beta Pi, Pi Mu Epsilon. Office: Latham & Watkins 633 W 5th St Ste 4000 Los Angeles CA 90071 Office Phone: 213-891-8304. Office Fax: 213-891-8763. Business E-Mail: michael.lurey@lw.com.

LURIA, MARTIN JAY, endocrinologist; b. Bklyn., Apr. 19, 1946; MD, NYU, 1971. Diplomate Am. Bd. Internal Medicine, Am. Bd. Endocrinology. Intern Kings County Hosp.-SUNY Downstate Med., 1971—72, resident in medicine, 1972—74; fellow in endocrinology Mt. Sinai Hosp., NYC, 1974—76; chief sect. endocrinology Monmouth Med. Ctr., Long Branch, NJ, 1976—. Attending physician dept. medicine Riverview Med. Ctr., Red Bank, NJ, 1976—; mem. courtesy staff Bayshore Cmty. Hosp., Holmdel, NJ, 1976—; consulting physician in endocrinology Ctrl. State Hosp., Freehold, NJ, 1976—. Named one of Top Drs., N.J. Monthly Mag., 2003, 2005, Castle Connolly, 2003, 2005. Fellow: Am. Coll. Endocrinology. Office: 170 Morris Ave Ste F Long Branch NJ 07740-6660 Home Phone: 732-222-1070; Office Phone: 732-222-8874.

LURIA, MARY MERCER, lawyer; b. Boston, Dec. 29, 1942; d. Albert and Mabel (Jacomb) Mercer; m. Nelson J. Luria, June 19, 1967. AB, Radcliffe Coll., 1964; LLB, Yale U., 1967. Bar: N.Y. 1968. Assoc. Simpson, Thacher & Bartlett, NYC, 1967-68, Hale & Dorr, Boston, 1968-69, Satterlee & Stephens, NYC, 1969-74, ptnr., 1974-86, Patterson, Belknap, Webb & Tyler, NYC, 1986-97, Davis & Gilbert, NYC, 1997—. Mem. ABA, N.Y. State Bar Assn., Assn. Bar City N.Y. Avocations: gardening, photography. Office: Davis & Gilbert 1740 Broadway Fl 20 New York NY 10019-4379 Office Phone: 212-468-4813. E-mail: mluria@dglaw.com.

LURIE, ALISON, writer; b. Chgo., Sept. 3, 1926; children: John, Jeremy, Joshua. AB, Radcliffe Coll., 1947. Lectr. English Cornell U., 1968-73, adj. assoc. prof. English Ithaca, NY, 1973-76, assoc. prof., 1976-79, prof., 1979—. Author: V.R. Lang: A Memoir, 1959, Love and Friendship, 1962, The Nowhere City, 1965, Imaginary Friends, 1967, Real People, 1969, The War Between the Tates, 1974, Only Children, 1979, The Language of Clothes, 1981, Foreign Affairs, 1984 (Pulitzer prize in fiction, 1985), The Truth About Lorin Jones, 1988, Don't Tell the Grownups, 1990, Women and Ghosts, 1994, The Last Resort, 1998, Familiar Spirits, 2001, Boys and Girls Forever, 2003, Truth and Consequences, 2005. Recipient award in lit. Am. Acad. Arts and Letters, 1978; fellow Yaddo Found., 1963-64, 66, Guggenheim Found., 1965, Rockefeller Found., 1967, Prix Femina Etranger, 1989. Mem.: Am. Acad. Arts and Letters (v.p. 2006—). Mailing: Am Acad Arts and Letters 633 West 155th St New York NY 10032 Business E-Mail: al28@cornell.edu.

LURIE, ALVIN DAVID, lawyer; b. NYC, Apr. 16, 1923; s. Samuel and Rose L.; m. Marian Weinberg, Aug. 21, 1944; children: James, Jeanne, Margery, Jonathan. AB, Cornell U., 1943, LLB, 1944. Bar: N.Y. 1944, D.C. 1978. Ptnr. Lurie & Rubin, NYC, 1961—68, Aranow, Brodsky, Bohlinger & Einhorn, NYC, 1968—74; asst. commr. for employee plans and exempt orgns. IRS, Washington, 1974—78; ptnr. Chadbourne, Parke, Whiteside & Wolff, NYC, 1978—84, Meyers, Tersigni, Lurie, Feldman & Gray, NYC, 1984—94; atty. Alvin D. Lurie, NYC, 1994—96; pres. Alvin D. Lurie, PC, Larchmont, NY, 1996—; of counsel The Wagner Law Group, Boston, 2006—; trustee N.Y. Ctr. Fin. Studies, 1980—. Mem. adv. bd. NYU Tax Inst., 1978-90; mem. adv. bd.Tax Mgmt., 1978—; mem. adv. bd. Tax Analysts and Advocates, 1995-2002; spl. counsel Small Bus. Coun. Am., 1978—; counsel N.Y. Soc. Fin. Svcs. Profls., 1978—. Author: Lurie's Commentaries on Pension Design, 1980, Lurie's Guide to VEBAs, 1983, Collected Commentaries on Pensions, 1984, ESOPs Made Easy, 1985; chair, editor NYU Rev. of Employee Benefits and Executive Compensation, 1998—; co-editor-in-chief Cornell Law Quar., 1943-44; editor-in-chief Pension & Benefit Power, 2002—; mem. editl. bd. LexisNexis Fed. Tax Libr., 2005; gen. editor LexisNexis Matthew Bender Fed. Income Taxation Retirement Plans, 2007—; contbr. articles to profl. jours. Fellow Am. Coll. Tax Counsel; mem. ABA (recipient Lifetime Employee Benefits Achievement award), NY State Bar Assn. (chmn. spl. com. pension simplification 1986—2004), Assn. Bar City NY, Am. Coll. Employee Benefits Counsel (charter), NY Bar Found. Office Phone: 914-834-6725. Personal E-mail: allurie@verizon.net. *Hard work, in intensive spurts, is my formula. The work must be varied, permitting application of different skills in constantly changing, creative ways. But one thing more is needed: carpe diem.*

LURIE, ANN LASALLE, foundation administrator; b. Fla. m. Robert H. Lurie (dec. 1990); 6 children. BS in Nursing, Univ. Fla. Former pub. health, pediatric intensive care nurse; pres. Lurie Investments, Chgo., 1990—; pres., treas. Ann and Robert H. Lurie Foundation, Chgo., 1992—; founding pres. Africa Infectious Disease (AID) Village Clinic, Kenya, 2002—. Bd. trustees Northwestern Univ. Named one of Top 10 Women in Philanthropy, Chgo. Sun-Times, 100 Most Influential Women, Crain's Chicago Bus., 2004; recipient Jane Addams History Maker award for distinction in social services. Office: Ann and Robert H Lurie Found Ste 1500 2 N Riverside Plz Chicago IL 60606

LURIE, RANAN RAYMOND, political cartoonist, artist, journalist; b. Port Said, Egypt, May 26, 1932; came to U.S., 1968, naturalized, 1974; s. Joseph and Rose (Sam) L. (parents Israeli citizens); m. Tamar Fletcher, Feb. 25, 1959; children: Rod, Barak, Daphne, Danielle. Student, Herzelia High Sch., Tel Aviv, Israel, 1949; student, Jerusalem Art Coll., 1951. Corr. Maariv Daily, 1950-52; features editor Hador Daily, 1953-54; editor-in-chief Tevel mag., 1954-55; staff polit. cartoonist Yedioth Aharonot Daily, 1955-66, Honolulu Advertiser, 1979; lectr. polit. cartooning U. Hawaii; univ. lectr. in fine arts, polit. cartoon and polit. analysis Am. Program Bur., Boston.; polit. cartoonist Time Internat. mag., 1994-97. Inventor 1st electronically syndicated bus.-news cartoon Lurie's Business World; 101 million readers of 1105 newspapers in 102 countries; 1999 Guiness Book of World Records; chief judge Internat. Cartoon Comp., Seoul, Korea, 1996, 97; sr. adj. fellow Ctr. Strategic and Internat. Studies, Washington. Author: Among the Suns, 1952, Lurie's Best Cartoons, 1961, Nixon Rated Cartoons, 1973, Pardon Me, Mr. President, 1974, Lurie's Worlds, 1980, So sieht es Lurie, 1981, Fed. Republic Germany, Lurie's Almanac (U.K.), 1982, (U.S.A.), 1983, Taro's International Politics, Japan, 1984, Lurie's Middle East, Israel, 1986; creator: The Uniting Painting, 1969; Cartoons used as guidelines in several encys., polit. sci. books.; 22 shows, Israel, Can., U.S., 1960-75, including, Exp 67, Can., Dominion Gallery, Montreal, Que., Can., Lim Gallery, Tel Aviv, 1965, Overseas Press Club, N.Y.C., 1962, 64, 75, U.S. Senate, Washington, Honolulu Acad. Fine Arts, 1979; represented by Circle Gallery, 1988-93; exhibited numerous group shows including, Smithsonian Instn., 1972, Circle Gallery, Washington, 1989; creator Japan's nat. cartoon symbol Taro-San, Taiwan's nat. cartoon symbol Cousin Lee; polit. cartoonist, Life Mag., N.Y.C., 1968-73, polit. cartoonist, interviewer, Die Welt, Bonn, W. Ger., 1980-81; contbr.: N.Y. Times, 1952—; contbg. editor, polit. cartoonist, Newsweek Internat., 1973-76, editor, polit. cartoonist, Vision Mag. of South Am., 1974-76, syndicated, United Features Syndicate, 1971-73; syndicated nationally by Los Angeles Times, also internationally by, N.Y. Times to over 260 newspapers, 1973-75, internationally by Editors Press Syndicate (345 newspapers), King Features Syndicate, 1975-83; syndicated in U.S. by Universal Press Syndicate, 1982-86, Cartoonews Internat. Syndicat, 1986—; polit. cartoonist, The Times of London, 1981-83, ABC's Nightline, 1991—, World News Show, 1993; sr. polit. analyst, editorial cartoonist Asahi Shimbun, Japan's largest daily newspaper, 1983-84; sr. analyst and polit. cartoonist U.S. News & World Report, 1984-85; chief editorial dir. Editors Press Service, 1985; joined staff MacNeil/Lehrer News Hour (PBS) as daily polit. cartoonist, analyst; editl. bd. Mid. East Quarterly, 1994—; creator, editor-in-chief Cartoon News Mag (now Cartoonews-.com), 1996-2000, editor-in-chief Cartoonews.com, 2000—, The Current Events Ednl. Mag., 1996—; polit. cartoonist Fgn. Affairs Mag., 2000-04. Chief judge Seoul (Republic of Korea) Internat. Cartoon Competition, 1996, 97. Served as maj. Combat Paratroop, Israeli Army Res., 1950-67. Recipient highest Israeli journalism award, 1954; U.S. Headliners award, 1972; named Outstanding Editorial Cartoonist of Nat. Cartoonist Soc., 1971-78; Salon award Montreal Cartoon, 1971; N.Y. Front Page award, 1972, 74, 77; cert. merit U.S. Publ. Designers, 1974; award Overseas Press Club, 1979; John Fischetti polit. cartoon award, 1984, 86; Ranan R. Lurie Internat. Polit. Cartoon ann. award created in his honor by Nat. Fedn. Hispanic Owned Newspapers, 1994, Ranan R. Lurie Internat. award for Polit. Cartooning created by U.N. Soc. of Writers, 1995, Annual Ranan Lurie Polit. Cartoon award created in his honor by U.N., 2000; recip. 1996 Hubert Humphrey 1st Amendment and Freedom of the Press Award, 1996; UN Corrs. Assn. Ranan Lurie Polit. Cartoon award created in his honor, 1999; nominated for Nobel Peace Prize, Cyprus, 2002. Mem. Soc. Profl. Journalists, Nat. Cartoonists Soc. Am., Assn. Editorial Cartoonists, Mensa, Overseas Press Club, Friars Club. Inventor 1st electronically animated TV news cartoon; creator 1st syndicated bus.-news cartoon Lurie's Business World; 104 million readers of 1,105 newspapers in 104 countries; 1999 Guiness Book of World Records. Office: Cartoonews Internat Trump Tower 721 5th Ave 60H New York NY 10022 Office Phone: 212-980-0855. E-mail: cartoonews@aol.com, luriestudioes@aol.com. *The moment of truth will come when the cartoonist gauges the margin of time from the day he drew the cartoon. Then he can see how correctly he has evaluated the situation through his work. Eventually, the simple facts and reality always win. Then it becomes apparent that wishful thinking is meaningless and the capacity to evaluate the project and even predict the events that are happening will eventually cement the professional status and integrity of the political cartoonist.*

LUSCH, CHARLES JACK, oncologist, director; b. Lehighton, Pa., Feb. 15, 1936; s. Charles Norman and Loretta (Gaumer) L.; m. Carole Faye Eckart, Aug. 17, 1957; children: Marjorie, Susan, Stephen, Robert. AB in Biology magna cum laude, Lafayette Coll., Easton, Pa., 1957; MD, Temple U., 1961. Diplomate in med. oncology, hematology, internal medicine, forensic medicine; diplomate Am. Bd. Forensic Medicine. Pres. Berks Hematology-Oncology Assocs., Reading, Pa., 1968—; chief sect. med. oncology and hematology Reading Hosp. and Med. Ctr., 1970—, asst. chief medicine, chmn. instl. rev. bd., 1986—, dir. continuing med. edn., 1987—, dir. oncology svcs., 1990—; dir. Pa. State Hemophilia Ctr., Reading Hosp. & Med. Ctr., 1973—; v.p. Lusch Motor Parts, Lehighton, Pa., 1975—; chief sect. med. oncology and hematology Cmty. Gen. Hosp., Reading, 1980—; med. dir. Pocono Internat. Raceway, 1980-85, Berks County Hospice, Berks County Vis. Nurse Assn., Reading, 1987—. Med. adv. com. Pa. Blue Shield, Camp Hill, Pa., 1987—; bd. dirs. Berks Home Health Car, Reading Cancer Ctr., Reading Hosp.; malpractice cons. Med. Protective Ins. Co., Ft. Wayne, Ind., 1985—; cons. in hematology and oncology Pottsville (Pa.) Hosp. and Good Samaritan Hosp., 1975—; clin. asst. prof. medicine Pa. Med. Sch., 1984—, Pa. State Med. Sch., 1981—, Pa. State Sch. Medicine, 2003—, Temple U. Med. Sch., clin. assoc. prof. 1990; clin. assoc. prof. medicine U. Pa., 2000—; sr. clin. instr. Mahnemann U. Med. Sch., 1968—; prin. investigator Ea. Coop Oncology Group, 1975-90, Nat. Surg. Adj. & Breast Project, 1986—. Contbr. articles to profl. jours.; editor The Med. Record (regional med. jour.), 1970-71. Advisor Future Physicians Am., Reading, 1965; bd. dirs. Berks County unit Am. Cancer Soc., Reading, 1968-78, Keystone Cmty. Blood Bank, Reading, 1970-80; adv. com. The Women's Ctr., Reading Hosp., 1987-88; mem. bd. divsn. ch. soc. Evang. Luth. Ch. Am., Chgo.; pres. ch. coun. Atonement Luth. Ch., Wyomissing, Pa.; pres. bd. dirs. Reading Symphony Orch., Pa., 2005—. Lt. comdr. USPHS, 1965-67. Fellow ACP; mem. Pa. Med. Soc. (commn. on continuing med. edn. 2007-), Pa. Soc. Hematology-Oncology (sec.-treas. 1986-87), Am. Soc. Clin. Oncology, Am. Soc. Hematology, Am. Fedn. Clin. Rsch., Acad. Hospice Physicians (publs. com. 1989—), U.S. Amateur Ballroom Dance Assn. (past pres. Reading chpt.), Sports Car Club Am., Phi Beta Kappa, Alpha Omega Alpha. Republican. Lutheran. Avocations: competition ballroom dancing, tennis, motor racing. Home: 1617 Meadowlark Rd Wyomissing PA 19610-2820 Office: Berks Hematology Oncology Assoc PO Box 16052 Reading PA 19612-6052 Home Phone: 610-372-3640; Office Phone: 610-374-4404. Personal E-mail: bolero36@aol.com.

LÜSCHEN, GÜNTHER RUDOLF FRIEDO, social sciences educator; b. Oldenburg, Germany, Jan. 21, 1930; s. Gustav Hermann Anton and Elsa Pauline Elisabeth (Magnus) Lüschen; m. Klara Maria Mertens, Dec. 22, 1958 (div. Aug. 1989); children: Birgit, Gerhard; m. Leila Antoun Sfeir, Nov. 18, 1989 (dec. July 2005); 1 child, Gerlinde. PhD, U. Graz, Austria, 1959; MA, U. Bonn, Germany, 1960; D (hon.), U. Jyvaskyla, Finland, 1990. Rsch. assoc. U. Cologne, Germany, 1961-64; assoc. prof. U. Bremen, Germany, 1965-72; prof. U. Ill., 1966-90, prof. emeritus, 1990—; prof. Tech. U. Aachen, Germany, 1982-89, U. Düsseldorf, Germany, 1990-95, 2001—, U. Ala., Birmingham, 1995-2001. Pres. Internat. Com. Sociology Sport/UNESCO, 1967—80, Rene-König-Gesellschaft, Cologne, Germany, 1993—96; mem. Rsch. Coun. Internat. Soc. Assn., 1966—74, 1982. Author: Sociology of Sport, 1967, Health Systems in the European Union, 1995, Methodology of Applied Sociology, 2005; co-author: Health Promotion Policy in Europe, 2000; editor: Deutsche Soziologie seit 1945, 1979, Das Moralische in der Soziologie, 1998; co-editor: Soziologie der Familie, 1970, Handbook of Social Science of Sport, 1981. Founder Polit. Action Group, Oldenburg, 1969. Recipient Fed. Merit Cross, German Pres., 1989, citation, Internat. Com. Sociology Sport, 1993, Nat. citation, N.Am. Sociology Sport; vis. scholar, U. Mich., 1960—61. Mem.: German Sociol. Assn., Am. Sociol. Assn., Midwest Sociol. Soc. (life), Internat. Sociol. Assn. (life). Avocations: tennis, guitar. Office: U Ill Dept Sociology 702 S Wright Urbana IL 61801 Home: Sodenstich 35a Oldenburg Germany Office Phone: 217-333-1951. Business E-Mail: lueschen@uiuc.edu.

LUSCOMBE, GEORGE A., II, lawyer; b. Jefferson, Iowa, Oct. 22, 1944; BS, U. Ill., 1966, JD, 1969; LLM, George Washington U., 1972. Bar: Ill. 1969, U.S. Supreme Ct. 1972, U.S. Claims Ct. 1972, D.C. 1972. Asst. br. chief legislation and regulations divsn. IRS Office Chief Counsel, 1972-73; ptnr. Mayer, Brown, Rowe & Maw, LLP, Chgo. Adj. prof. law IIT, 1987-93; speaker in field. Mem. ABA (chmn. com. depreciation and investment tax credit, sect. taxation 1980-82), Ill. State Bar Assn. (chmn. fed. tax sect. coun. 1991-92), Chgo. Bar Assn. (chmn. gen. income tax divsn., fed. tax com. 1977-79), D.C. Bar. Office: Mayer Brown Rowe & Maw LLP 71 S Wacker Dr Chicago IL 60606-4637 Office Phone: 312-701-7099.

LUSE, KIMBERLY ANN, radiologist, educator; b. Fort Thomas, Ky., July 4, 1963; d. James Herbert and Ramona Jean Miller; m. Evan Ray Luse, Sr., Nov. 11, 1988; children: Jessica Lee, Sara Jean, Evan Ray Luse, Jr., Hannah Kimberly. AS, No. Ky. U., 1985, BS, 1994; MEd, Xavier U., 1998; EdD in Edn. Founds., U. of Cin., 2002. Cert. educator Nat. Profl. Orgn., 2000. Coop. edn. coord. Cin. (Ohio) State Tech. and C.C., 1996—99; asst. prof. of clin. The U. of Cin., 1999—2003; dir. clin. rsch. program imaging Proscan Imaging, 2003—; exec. asst. to pres., sec. to bd. regents No. Ky. U., 2004—. Presdl. mgmt. intern Fed. Govt., 2002—; faculty advisor Student Advanced Med. Imaging Tech. Orgn. U. of Cin., Cin., 2002—; nat. presentor Am. Healthcare Radiology Administrators, New Orleans, 2002—, Hispanic Assn. Colls. and Univs., Phoeniz, 2005. Bd. dir. Am. Heart Assn., 2004—; bd. mem. Brighton Ctr., Newport, Ky., 2001. Mem.: Am. Soc. of Radiology, Leadership Ky. (class of 2005), Leadership No. Ky. (class of 2001, Grad. of the cohort for 2001 current alumni 2001). Home: 71 Hanover Place Fort Thomas KY 41075 Office: No Ky U Office of Pres 800 Lucas Adminstv Ctr Highland Heights KY 41099 Office Phone: 859-572-5172. E-mail: kimberly.luse@uc.edu, lusek1@nku.edu.

LUSHNIAK, BORIS D., public health service officer; b. Chgo. married; 2 children. MD, Northwestern Univ., 1983; MPH, Harvard Univ. Cert. Am. Bd. Family Practice, Am. Bd. Preventive Medicine, Am. Bd. Dermatology. Lt., Epidemic Intelligence Svc. Ctr. for Disease Control, Russia, Kosovo, Bangladesh; sr. med. officer, Divn. Surveillance, Hazard Evaluations, and Field Studies Nat. Inst. Occupational Safety and Health, Cin.; Chief Med. Officer, Off. of Counterterrorism Policy and Planning FDA, Washington, 2004—05, asst. commnr., 2005—06, asst. surgeon gen., rear adm., 2006—. Recipient Dr. William Beaumont award in Medicine, AMA, 2006. Office: Asst Surgeon General 5600 Fishers Ln Rockville MD 20857 Office Phone: 301-443-3574.*

LUSK, CODY, auto association executive; BA, U. Tex. Assoc. Nat. Rep. Congl. Com., Rep. Nat. Com.; legis. specialist U.S. Dept. Commerce; assoc. Am. Internat. Automobile Dealers Assn., dir. legis. affairs, 1995—2001, pres., 2006—; chief of staff to U.S. rep. Sam Johnson U.S. Ho. of Reps., 2002—06. Office: Am Internat Automobile Dealers Assn 211 N Union St Ste 300 Alexandria VA 22314 Office Phone: 703-519-7800. Office Fax: 703-519-7810. E-mail: goaiada@aiada.org.

LUSK, GLENNA RAE KNIGHT (MRS. EDWIN BRUCE LUSK), librarian; b. Aug. 16, 1935; d. Otis Harvey and Lou Zelle Knight; m. Bruce 2d Edwin Lusk, Nov. 28, 1970; m. John Earle Uhler, May 26, 1956; children: Anne Knight, Camille Allana. BS, La. State U., 1956, MS, 1963. Asst. libr. Iberville Parish Libr., Plaquemine, La., 1956—57, 1962—68; tchr. Iberville Parish Pub. Schs., Plaquemine, 1957—59, Plaquemines Parish Pub. Schs., Buras, La., 1959—61; dir. Iberville Parish Libr., Plaquemine, 1969—89. Chmn. La. State Bd. Libr. Examiners, 1979—89; pres. Camille Navarre Gallery, Ltd., Zachary, La., 1989—94. Author (with John E. Uhler Jr.): Cajun Country Cookin', 1966, Rochester Clarke Bibliography of Louisiana Cookery, 1966, Royal Recipes from the Cajun Country, 1969, Iberville Parish, 1970. Mem. Iberville Parish Econ. Devel. Coun., Plaquemine, 1970—71; sec. Iberville Parish Bicentennial Commn., 1973—; mem. La. Bicentennial Commn., 1974; bd. dirs. McHugh House Mus., 1991—92. Named Outstanding Young Woman Plaquemine, La. Jr. C. of C., 1970. Mem.: Capital Area Libr. (chmn. com. 1972—74), Riverland Libr. Assn. (sec. 1973—74), La. Libr. Assn. (sect. chmn. 1967—68). Republican. Episcopalian. Home: 13291 Legacy Ct Baton Rouge LA 70816-7936

LUSK, HARLAN GILBERT, national park superintendent, business executive; b. Jersey City, June 22, 1943; s. Harlan H. and Mary M. (Kuhl) L.; m. Catherine L. Rutherford, Oct. 11, 1986. BA in History, Gettysburg Coll., 1965, PhD (hon.), 2001. Supervisory historian Cape Hatteras Nat. Seashore, Manteo, NC, 1968; historian Nat. Pk. Svc., Washington, 1968-69; programs specialist So. Utah Group, Cedar City, 1968-70; pk. supt. Wolf Trap Farm Pk., Vienna, Va., 1970-72; supervisory pk. ranger Blue Ridge Pkwy., Roanoke, Va., 1972-74; pk. supt. Appomattox (Va.) Courthouse, Nat. Hist. Pk., 1974-76, Valley Forge (Pa.), Nat. Hist. Pk., 1976-81, Big Bend (Tex.) Nat. Pk., 1981-86, Glacier Nat. Pk., West Glacier, Mont., 1986-94; pk. supt. Albright Tng. Ctr. Grand Canyon Nat. Pk., Ariz., 1994-95; chief, Divsn. Tng. and Employee Nat. Park Svc., Washington, 1995-97; retired from park svc., 1997; chmn. Gil Lusk Assocs., 1997—; group mgr. The Cholla Group, 1997—. Organizer 1st regional conf. Rio Grande Border, States on Pks. and Wildlife, Laredo, Tex., 1985 Bd. dirs. Tech. Com. on Pks. and Recreation Cen. Va. Planning Dist., 1972-74, Fed. Exec. Assn. Roanoke Valley, 1972-74, Flathead Basin Commn., 1986-94, Flathead Conv. and Visitor Assn., 1986-94, Sonoran Inst., 1995-2001; prin. founder, 1st pres., Appomattox County Hist. Soc., 1974-76; trustee Sci. Mus. Assn. Roanoke Valley, 1972-74, Nature Conservancy Mont., 1994-1997; ex-officio Friends of Valley Forge, 1977-81; founder, ex-officio, bd. dirs. Valley Forge Pk. Interpretive Assn., 1977-81; founder Big Bend Area Travel Assn., chmn., 1984-86. Recipient Meritorious Svc. award. Dept. Interior, 1986, Disting. Svc. award, 1999. Mem. Glacier Natural History Assn. (ex officio 1986-94), Glacier Nat. Pk. Assocs. (founder, ex-officio 1989-94), George Wright Soc., Lions, Rotary. Avocations: golf, antiques, computers, collecting artwork, hiking. Home and Office: 1382 N Boyce Ave Green Valley AZ 85614-6259 Personal E-mail: hglusk@msn.com.

LUSK, PEGGY JUNE, retired counseling administrator; b. Springfield, Mo., Aug. 31, 1925; d. James G. and Cecile C. (Slagle) L. BA magna cum laude, Drury U., Springfield, 1947; MA, Syracuse U., NY, 1950; postgrad., U. Chgo., 1958—61. Field dir., camp dir. Girl Scouts U.S.A., Springfield, 1946-48; student dean Syracuse (N.Y.) U., 1948-50; resident counselor Winthrop Coll., Rock Hill, S.C., 1950-52; asst. dean women, instr. Ohio Wesleyan U., Delaware, 1952-58; asst. dean students U. Chgo., 1958-61; counselor, asst. prof. Rush Presbyn. St. Luke's Med. Ctr., Chgo., 1961-96, ret., 1996; on-call cons. in field, 1996—. Recipient Friend of Nursing award Rush U., Chgo., 1993; Danforth faculty fellow, 1956. Mem. AAUP, Nat. League for Nurisng, Am. Counseling and Pers. Assn., Am. Assn. Mental Health Workers, Nat. Assn. for Women in Edn., Am. Assn. for Higher Edn., Ill. Assn. for Women in Edn. (exec. bd., pres. 1977-79), Alumni Assn. Drury Coll. (pres. Chgo. chpt. 1961-63), Mortar Board. Avocations: classical music, gardening, bird study, camping. Office: Rush Presbyn St Lukes Med 1743 W Harrison St # 840 Chicago IL 60612-3823

LUSKIN, FREDERIC MICHAEL, psychologist, educator; b. NYC, May 5, 1954; BA, Binghamton U., 1976; MS, San Jose State, 1987; PhD, Stanford U., 1999. Cert. Lic. psychologist, marriage & family therapist, ednl. psychologist. Sch. psychologist, 1986—93; dir. Stanford Forgiveness Project Stanford U., 1996—2005; assoc. prof. Inst. Transpersonal Psychology, Palo Alto, Calif., 2003—06; rsch. assoc. Stanford U., 1999—2003. Author: Forgive for Good, 2002, Stress Free for Good, 2005. Office Phone: 650-208-7658. Business E-Mail: learningtoforgive@comcast.net.

LUSKIN, ROBERT DAVID, lawyer; b. Chgo., Jan. 21, 1950; s. Bert L. and S. Ruth (Katz) L.; m. Fairlea A. Sheehy, Aug. 23, 1975 (div. Mar. 2000); children: Peter Duncan, Charles Cassimer. BA magna cum laude, Harvard U., 1972, JD magna cum laude, 1979; postgrad., Oxford U., Eng., 1972-75. Bar: D.C. 1979, U.S. Ct. Appeals (1st, 2nd, 4th, 5th, 6th, 7th, 8th, 9th, 11th, D.C. and fed. cirs.) 1979, U.S. Supreme Ct., 1983. Law clk. to Hon. Louis F. Oberdorfer US Dist. Ct. for D.C., Washington, 1979-80; spl. counsel organized crime racketeering sect. US Dept. Justice, Washington, 1980-82; ptnr. Onek, Klein & Farr, Washington, 1982-89, Powell, Goldstein, Frazer & Murphy, Washington, 1989-93, Comey, Boyd & Luskin, Washington, 1993-99, Patton Boggs, LLP, 2000—, co-chmn., litig. dept. Lectr. in law U. Va. Sch. Law, 1992—. Rhodes scholar, 1972-75. Mem. ABA (chmn. RICO Forfeitures and Civil Remedies com. 1986-94, vice chmn. task force on forfeitures), Harvard Law Sch. Assn. Washington (former pres.). Office: Patton Boggs LLP 2550 M St NW Washington DC 20037 Home Phone: 202-965-9489; Office Phone: 202-457-6190. Business E-Mail: rluskin@pattonboggs.com.

LUSS, DAN, chemical engineering professor; b. Tel Aviv, May 5, 1938; came to U.S., 1963, naturalized, 1973; s. Manfred and Gertrude (Weinstein) L.; m. Amalia Rubin, Sept. 4, 1966; children: Noya, Limor. BS, Technion Inst. Tech., Haifa, Israel, 1960, MSc, 1963; PhD, U. Minn., 1966. Registered profl. engr., Tex. Asst. prof. chem. engring. U. Minn., Mpls., 1966-67, U. Houston, 1967-69, assoc. prof., 1969-72, prof., 1972—, chmn. dept., 1975-95, 99-00; assoc. dir. Tex. Ctr. for Superconductivity, 1988-92. Cons. to several chem. cos. Editor: Revs. in Chem. Engring.; mem. editorial bd. Sci. and Engring, Catalysis Rev., IEC Rsch. Fellow Am. Inst. Chem. Engrs. (Allan P. Colburn award 1973, Profl. Progress award 1979, Wilhelm award 1986, Founders award 2005, chmn. awards com., former mem. editl. bd. jour., former dir.), Am. Chem. Soc. (Honor Scroll award Indsl. Engring. Chemistry div. 1967); mem. NAE, Am. Soc. Engring. Edn.

(Curtis McGraw award 1977 3M-Chem. Engring. Lectureship award 1985). Home: 115 Stablewood Ct Houston TX 77024 Office: U Houston Dept Chem Engring Houston TX 77204-4004 Office Phone: 713-743-4305. Business E-Mail: dluss@uh.edu.

LUST, HERBERT COHNFELDT, III, securities trader; b. Chgo., Jan. 15, 1957; s. Herbert Cohnfeldt Lust II and Frances Ratcliffe Hutchins; m. Melani D'amore Espinosa, May 17, 1997; 1 child, Terry Grosvenor Hutchins. BA, NYU, 1976, MBA, 1986. Account rep., ltd. ptnr. Herzfeld & Stern, NYC, 1978-88; portfolio mgr. distressed investments Halcyon Investments, NYC, 1988-89; head distressed rsch. Bear Stearns & Co., NYC, 1990-94; co-head high yield dept. Furman Selz, NYC, 1994-95; head distressed rsch. Lehman Bros., NYC, 1995-97; bus. mgr. distressed securities Smith Barney, NYC, 1997-98, J.P. Morgan, NYC, 1998—. Author: Alexandera Finds Out. Home: 21 Hickory Dr Westport CT 06880-3807

LÜST, REIMAR, foundation president; b. Wuppertal, Germany, 1923; BS Physics, U. Frankfurt, Germany, 1949; Ph. D., Max-Planck Inst., Göttingen, Germany, 1955; Fulbright fellow, Enrico Fermi Inst. U. Chgo., Germany, 1955-56; Habilitation, U. Munich TH, Germany, 1959. Vis. prof. NYU, NYC, 1959-60; mem. Max-Planck-Inst. f. Physik u. Astrophysik, Munich, Germany, 1960; vis. prof. MIT, Cambridge, 1961, Cal. Tech., Pasadena, 1962; dir. ESRO (European Space Research Organization), 1962-64, Inst. f. Extraterrestr. Physik, Max-Planck-Inst. f. Physik u. Astrophysik, Garching b. Munich, Germany, 1963; aus. ord. prof. U. Munich, Germany, 1963-72; hon. prof. U. Munich TH, Germany, 1963-72; v.p. ESRO, Germany, 1968-70; chmn. Wissenschaftsrat, Germany, 1969-72; pres. Max-Planck-Gesellschaft zur Förderung der Wissenschaften, 1972-84; gen. dir. Europäische Weltraumorganisation, Paris, France, 1984-90; pres. Alexander von Humboldt-Stiftung, Bonn, Germany, 1989-99, hon. pres., 1999—; prof. U. Hamburg, Germany, 1992. Max-Planck-Inst., Göttingen, Physics, 1951-55, Fulbright Fellow, Enrico Fermi Inst., U. Chgo., 1955-56, 99-2004; chmn. bd. Internat. U. Bremen, 1999-2004 Hon. chmn. bd. govs. Internat. U. Bremen, 2005. Office: Humboldt Found Max Planck Inst Bundesstraße 53 D-20146 Hamburg Germany Home Phone: 040-2798514; Office Phone: 0049-40-41173-301. E-mail: cornelia.sengbusch@zmaw.de.

LUSTED, DONA SANDERS, music educator, consultant, organist; b. Washington, Oct. 2, 1951; d. Troy Harry and Rosemarie (Klemann) Sanders; m. Barry Emile Lusted, Nov. 7, 1982; children: Lori Marie, Luke Alan. Degree in ch. music, Evang. Landeskirchen Musik., Dusseldorf, Germany, 1969; BS in Music Edn. and German, Jacksonville State U., 1973; MM in Piano Performance, La. State U., 1975, PhD in Music, 1984. Instr. Northeastern Okla. State U., Tahlequah, 1975-76, Baker (La.) Mid. Sch., 1976-77; organist First United Meth Ch., Tahlequah, 1975-76; assoc. dir. music, organist Broadmoor United Meth. Ch., Baton Rouge, 1977—; pvt. music instr. Okla., Ala., La., 1969—; instr. La. State U., Baton Rouge, 1978-79. Dir. Summer Music and Arts/Theater Camp, Baton Rouge, 1987—; adjudicator Okla. Fedn. Music Clubs, Muskogee, 1976, Bayou-land Choral Festival, Nichols State U., Thibadoux, 1994, 2000, Baton Rouge Choral Soc., 1978-79; co-founder/co-dir. South La. chpt. Choristers Guild, 1994-2000. Mem. Am. Guild Organists, Music Tchrs. Nat. Assn., La. Fedn. Music Clubs, Baton Rouge Piano Tchrs. Methodist. Avocations: swimming, reading, travel. Home: 10709 Waverland Dr Baton Rouge LA 70815-5056 Office: Broadmoor United Meth Ch 10230 Mollylea Dr Baton Rouge LA 70815-4698 Office Phone: 225-924-6269. E-mail: dllb@juno.com.

LUSTICK, DAVID SCOTT, science educator, mathematics professor; s. Bernard Ruben and Renee Miriam Lustick; m. Doreen Michelle Marcks; children: Dakota Abraham, Avalon Gieselle, Troy Oliver. BS, Cornell U., Ithaca, NY, 1985; MEd, Harvard U., Cambridge, Mass., 1989; PhD, Mich. State U., East Lansing, 2005. Cert. Nat. Bd. Profl. Tchg. Standards, 1997. Tchr. sci. Escola Graduada, Sao Paulo, Brazil, 1991—99; assoc. dir. US-China ctr. rsch. ednl. excellence Mich. State U., East Lansing, Mich., 2004—05; asst. prof. sci. and math. edn. U. Mass., Lowell, 2005—. Office: U Massachusetts Lowell 61 Wilder St Lowell MA 01854 Home Phone: 603-883-2826; Office Phone: 978-934-4644. Office Fax: 978-934-3005; Home Fax: 978-934-3005. Business E-Mail: david_lustick@uml.edu.

LUSTIG, GRAHAM, performing company executive; b. London; Student, Royal Ballet. Joined Dutch Nat. Ballet, prin. dancer; co-founder Dance Advance; joined Sadler's Wells Royal Ballet (now Birmingham Royal Ballet), 1980, prin. dancer; artistic dir. Am. Repertory Ballet and Princeton Ballet Sch., 1999—. Choreographer-in-residence Washington Ballet; panelist Nat. Endowment Arts, 2003, Dance Grants and Policy panels, 2005. Choreographer Thanatos Instinct (Dutch Ministry on Culture award), (evening commd. works include) Peter Pan for Scottish Ballet, Uncertain Stages, George's Day Out and The Shrew for Introdans, D'Ensemble for No. Ballet Theatre, Appassionato for Singapore Dance Theatre, A Far Cry for Hartford Ballet, Borderlines for BalletMet. Bd. dirs. Choo-San Goh and H. Robert McGee; charter mem. Artists Coun. for Am. for Arts, 2003—. Recipient Dutch Ministry of Culture Award; grantee Winston Churchill Traveling Fellowship, 1987. Office: Am Repertory Ballet Co 301 N Harrison St Princeton NJ 08540-3512*

LUSTIG, M. BRUCE, rabbi; BA, U. Tenn.; MHL, Hebrew Union Coll.-Jewish Inst. Religion. Ordained Rabbi Hebrew Union Coll.-Jewish Inst. Religion. Sr. rabbi Washington Hebrew Congregation. Exec. dir. Israel Bonds of the Greater Wash. Area; mem. D.C. Mayors Faith Advisory Board. Mem. bd., DC div. American Cancer Soc. Named one of The Top 50 Rabbis in America, Newsweek Mag., 2007. Office: Washington Congregation 3935 Macomb Street NW Washington DC 20016*

LUSTIG, SUSAN GARDNER, occupational therapist; b. Beloit, Wis., Apr. 27, 1942; d. James and Sally Howell; m. Karl Lustig, Aug. 16, 1969 (div. 1997); children: Kurt, Daniel, Benjamin, David, Amy, Richard, Lauren. BS with distinction, U. Minn., 1965. Lic. occupl. therapist. Occupl. therapist Minn. State Hosp., Hastings, 1965—66; occupl. therapy cons. Hawaii Divsn. Vocat. Rehab., Honolulu, 1966—67; occupl. therapist Kaneohe State Hosp., Kaneohe, Hawaii, 1967, Minn. VA Hosp., Mpls., 1967—68, unit supr., 1968—70; chief occupl. therapist, mgr. occupl. therapy dept. Avery Health Care Sys., Newland, NC, 1997—2000; established occupl. therapy depts. Autumn Care Marion.Autumn Care, Drexel, NC, 2000—01, occupl. therapist, 2001—05, Yancey County Schs., 2005—07, Rehab. Sys. & Carolina Therapy Svcs., 2005—, Avery County Schs., 2007—. Mem Nat. Bd. Cert. Occupl. Therapy, 1997—; del. to Russia, People to People Amb. Program. Pres. LaSalle County Med. Aux., Ill., 1976—78; tutor, mentor Burke County Elem. Sch. Students; organist New Life Bapt. Ch., Newland, NC, 2003—, Crossmore 1st Bapt. Ch., NC, 1999—2001; organist, pianist, dir. of music Linville River Bapt. Ch., NC; organist, Sunday sch. tchr. Long Ridge Bapt. Ch., 2001—03; bd. dirs. Harrison County Sheltered Workshop, 1971—72, Ottawa Pub. Health Nursing, Ill., 1976—78, Cooking for Christ, 1998—2002, Heartland Christian Acad. Sch., 1986—88, Diversified Industries, Port Angeles, Wash., 1980—82. Mem.: N.C. Occupl. Therapy Assn., Nat. Bd. for Cert. of Occupl. Therapists, Am. Occupl. Therapy Assn. Republican. Baptist. Avocations: organ, gardening, woodcarving, ice skating, reading. Home: 15 Little Cow Camp Rd Newland NC 28657-8704

LUSTYK, MARY KATHLEEN, neuroscientist, educator; d. Vincent de Paul and Patricia Ann Burkhart; m. Michael John Lustyk, Dec. 12, 1993; children: Zachery Michael, Luke Vincent. BS in Psychology, U. Wash., 1988, PhD, 1992. Asst. prof. Seattle Pacific U., 1996—2000, assoc. prof. psychology, 2000—, adj. faculty, 1995. Affiliate assoc. prof. U. Wash. Sch. Nursing, Seattle; affiliate prof. U. Wash., 1996—; presenter in field. Contbr. articles and abstracts to profl. jours. Mem.: Stress and Anxiety Rsch. Sco., We. Psychol. Assn., Am. Psychol. Soc., APA, Psi Chi.

LUSZTIG, PETER ALFRED, dean, educator; b. Budapest, Hungary, May 12, 1930; s. Alfred Peter and Susan (Szabo) L.; m. Penny Bicknell, Aug. 26, 1961; children: Michael, Cameron, Carrie. B in Com., U. B.C., Vancouver, Can., 1954; MBA, U. Western Ont., London, Can., 1955; PhD, Stanford U., 1964. Asst. to comptroller B.C. Electric, Vancouver, 1955-57; instr. fin. U. B.C., 1957-60, asst. prof. fin., 1962-64, assoc. prof., 1965—68, Killam sr. research fellow, 1968-69, prof., 1968—95, dean faculty commerce, 1977-91, dean emeritus, 1995—. Trustee BC Health Benefit Trust; bd. dirs. Canfor Pulpco; fed. commr. BC Treaty Commn., 1995-2003; vis. prof. IMEDE, Switzerland, 1973-74, London Grad. Sch. Bur. Studies, 1968-69, Pacific Coast Banking Sch., 1977—1982; sr. advisor B.C. Ministry of Econ. Devel., Small Bus. and Trade, 1991. Author: Report of the Royal Commission on Automobile Insurance, 2 vols., 1968, Financial Management in a Canadian Setting, 6th rev. edit., 2001, Report of the Commission on the B.C. Tree Fruit Industry, 1990. Past bd. dirs. Vancouver Gen. Hosp. Ford Found. faculty dissertation fellow, Stanford U., 1964.

LUTE, DOUGLAS E., federal official, career military officer; b. Michigan City, Ind., 1952; m. Jane Holl Lute; 3 children. Grad., US Mil. Acad., West Point, NY, 1975; MPA, Harvard U., 1983; attended, British Amy Staff Coll. Advanced through ranks to lt. gen., 2006; ops. officer 2nd Cavalry Divsn.; comdr. 1st Squadron, 7th Cavalry, Ft. Hood, Tex., 1992—94; dir. strategic plans & policy (J-5) The Joint Staff, Washington; comdr. 2nd Armored Cavalry Regiment, Ft. Polk, La., 1998—2000; exec. asst. to Chmn. Joint Chiefs of Staff US Dept. Def., Washington, 2000—01; asst. divsn. comdr. First Infantry Divsn., Schweinfurt, Germany, 2001—03; comdr. Multi-Nat. Brigade East & "Task Force Falcon", Kosovo, 2002—03; dep. dir. ops. (J-3) US European Command, Stuttgart, Germany, 2003—04; dir. ops. (J-3) US Ctrl. Command, MacDill AFB, Fla., 2004—06, The Joint Staff, Washington, 2006—07; asst. to Pres., dep. nat. security adv. for Iraq & Afghanistan The White House, Washington, 2007—. Achievements include serving in Operation Desert Storm, 1990-91. Office: Nat Security Coun 600 Pennsylvania Ave NW Washington DC 20500*

LUTER, JOSEPH WILLIAMSON, III, meat packing and processing company executive; b. Smithfield, Va., 1940; married. BBA, Wake Forest Coll., 1962. Pres. Smithfield Packing Co., Arlington, Va., 1964—69, Bryce Mountain Resort Inc., 1969—75; with Smithfield Foods Inc., Arlington, 1975—, pres., 1975—86, 1989—, CEO, 1975—, chmn., 1977—. Lectr. Harvard Bus. Sch., Darden Grad. Sch. Bus., Univ. Va.; mem. exec. com. Am. Meat Inst. Trustee Wake Forest Univ. Office: Smithfield Foods Inc 200 Commerce St Smithfield VA 23430-1204*

LUTERMAN, GERALD, electronics company executive; married; 2 children. B.Commerce with honors in Econs., McGill U., Can., 1965; MBA, Harvard U., 1969. Chartered acct. With Booz Allen & Hamilton, 1969-71, prin., 1984-85; v.p., CFO Xomox Corp., 1971-80, pres. internat., 1980-83; v.p. fin. and planning payment sys. divsn. Am. Express Travel Related Svcs., 1985-87, sr. v.p. fin. and planning, 1987-90, exec. v.p. establishment svcs. divsn., 1990-91, exec. v.p., CFO consumer card divsn., 1992-96; sr. v.p., CFO, Arrow Electronics, Inc., Melville, N.Y., 1996-1999; sr. v.p., CFO KeySpan Energy, Bklyn., 1999—2002, exec. v.p., CFO, 2002—. Bd. dir. IKON Office Solutions Inc., Tech. Solutions Co., U.S. Shipping Partners; past chmn. fin. com Am. Gas Assn. Bd. dir. Lutheran Med. Ctr. Baker scholar, 1969, Kresge fellow, 1969. Mem.: Fin. Executives Inst., Edison Elec. Inst., Soc. Gas Lighters. Avocations: reading, jogging, golf, tennis, skiing. Office: KeySpan Corp One Metro Tech Ctr Brooklyn NY 11201-3850*

LUTES, BYRON B., retired surgeon; b. Highland, Mich., Feb. 28, 1923; s. Byron Joseph and Hazel Juanita Lutes; m. Dorothy F. Lutes (dec.); m. Catherine Lutes; children: Byron Jr., Brenda F., Heather F. MD, Wayne U., Detroit, 1949. Diplomate Am. Bd. Rectal Colon Surgeons. Pvt. practice rectal and colon surgeon, Detroit; chief surgery Blue Care Network, Saginaw, Mich. Capt. US Army, 1953—55. Recipient 50 Yr. award, State of Mich., 1999. Mem.: ACS, Mich. State Rectal Colon Surgeons (past pres.), Saginaw Med. Soc. Republican. Methodist. Avocation: raising and training American miniature horses. Home: 12215 Scott Freeland MI 48623

LUTES, DONALD HENRY, architect; b. San Diego, Mar. 7, 1926; s. Charles McKinley and Helen (Bjoraker) L.; m. Donnie Wageman, Aug. 14, 1949; children: Laura Jo, Gail Eileen, Dana Charles. BArch, U. Oreg., 2000. Pvt. archtl. practice, Springfield, Oreg., 1956-58; ptnr. John Amundson, Springfield, 1958-70; pres. Lutes & Amundson, Springfield, 1970-72; ptnr. Lutes/Sanetel, 1989—2000. Adj. assoc. prof. architecture U. Oreg., 1964-66, 89-2000; chmn. Springfield Planning Commn., 1954-65, 93-99, Urban Design and Devel. Corp., 1968-70, Eugene Non-Profit Housing, Inc., 1970 Architect: Springfield Pub. Library, 1957, Mt. Hood Community Coll, 1965-79, Shoppers Paradise Expt. in Downtown Revitalization, 1957. Chmn. Springfield United Appeal, 1959. Served to 1st lt. AUS, 1943-46, 51-52. Decorate Bronze Star; named Jr. 1st Citizen, Springfield C. of C., 1957, 1st Citizen, 1968, Disting. Citizen, 1995. Fellow AIA (bd. dirs. 1987-90, v.p. 1991, doc. com. 1993-2000, Northwest & Pacific Region medal hon. 2003); mem. Rotary, Theta Chi. Home: 778 Crest Ln Springfield OR 97477-3601

LUTES, JIM G. (JAMES LUTES), artist; b. Ft. Lewis, Wash., Dec. 5, 1955; s. James Gerald and Diane Gwendolyn (Schille) L.; m. Kimberly Ellen Piotrowski, Jan. 15, 1994. BA, Wash. State U., 1978; MFA, Art Inst. Chco., 1982. Assoc. prof. art Ill. State U., Normal, 1983-95. Vis. artist The Sch. of The Art Inst. Chgo., 1983—; adj. assoc. prof. U. Ill., Chgo., 1995. One-man shows include Dart Gallery, Chgo., 1986, 87, 88, 91, 92, Michael Kohn Gallery, L.A., 1989, Temple Gallery, Phila., 1990, Vera Van Laer Gallery, Knokke-Heist, Belgium, 1993, Mus. Contemporary Art, Chgo., 1994, others; group shows include Hyde Park Art Ctr., Chgo., 1983, Dart Gallery, 1984, The Corcoran Gallery Art, Washington, 1984-86, Walker Art Ctr., Mpls., 1985, Artists Space, N.Y.C., 1986, The Whitney Mus., N.Y.C., 1987, 2006 The Contemporary Arts Ctr., Cin., 1989, Evanston (Ill.) Art Ctr., 1991, 95, Katonah (N.Y.) Mus. Art, 1992, Klein Gallery, Chgo., 1993, Edward Thorp Gallery, N.Y.C., 1993, Vallery Carberry Gallery, 2006, several others; represented in permanent collections at The Progressive Corp., Pepper Pike, Ohio, Ill. State Mus., Springfield, The Ruttenberg Family Found., Chgo., Larry and Evelyn Aronson, Chgo., James and Edie Cloonan, Chgo., Howard and Donna Stone, Chgo., Mus. of Contemproary Art, Chgo., Mus. van Hendendaagee Kinst, Ghent, Belgium, Paul and Camille Oliver-Hoffman, Chgo. NEA grantee, 1993; recipient Awards in Visual Arts award, 1987, Louis Comfort Tiffany Found. award, 1993.

LUTGEN, ROBERT RAYMOND, newspaper editor; b. Fairmont, Minn., Oct. 27, 1949; s. William J. and Barbara Estella (Sanger) L.; m. Teresa L. Palm, July 17, 1971; children: Mark, Kyle, Laura. BA, Ctrl. Wash. State Coll., 1971. Reporter, asst. city editor Yakima (Wash.) Herald Republic, 1970-77; city editor Bryan (Tex.) Eagle, 1977-81, Texarkana (Tex.) Gazette, 1981-83, mng. editor, 1983-87; asst. mng. editor Ark. Dem., 1987-91; mng. editor Ark. Dem.-Gazette, 1991-99, Chattanooga Times Free Press, 1999—. Recipient Best News Story award, Editorial Writing award, Headline Writing award AP Mng. Editors Assn., 1985. Mem. Ark. AP (pres. 1989-90), Mng. Editors Assn. (bd. dirs. 1986-91). Avocations: travel, golf, reading. Home: 141 S Brent Dr Ringgold GA 30736-8243 Office: Chattanooga Times Free Press 400 E 11th St Chattanooga TN 37403-4203 E-mail: lutgen1@aol.com.

LUTH, WILLIAM CLAIR, geochemist, retired research manager; b. Winterset, Iowa, June 28, 1934; s. William Henry Luth and Ora Anna (Klingaman) Sorenson; m. Betty L. Heubrock, Aug. 23, 1953; children: Linda Diane, Robert William, Sharon Jean. BA in Geology, U. Iowa, 1958, MS in Geology, 1960; PhD in Geochemistry, Pa. State U., 1963. Rsch. assoc. in geochemistry Pa. State U., University Park, Pa., 1963-65; asst. prof. geochemistry MIT, Cambridge, Mass., 1965-68; assoc. prof. geology Stanford U., 1968-77, prof. geology, 1977-79; supr. geophysics div. Sandia Nat. Labs, Albuquerque, 1979-82, mgr. geoscis. dept., 1982-90; mgr. geoscis. rsch. program U.S. Dept. Energy, Washington, 1990-95, acting dir. divsn. engring. & geosci., 1994-95, dir. divsn. engring and geosci., 1996; ret., 1996. Geoscientist US ERDA/DOE Washington, 1976-78; faculty sabbatical Sandia Laboratories, Albuquerque, N. Mex., 1975, visiting staff mem. Los Alamos Nat. Lab, 1978. Contbr. articles to profl. jours. Served with U.S. Army, 1953-56. Grantee NSF, 1964-78, Alfred P. Sloan Rsch. fellow, 1966-67. Fellow: Mineralogical Soc. Am., Geological Soc. Am.; mem.: Am. Geophysical Union, Sigma Xi. Avocations: photography, travel. Home: 653 N 63d Pl Mesa AZ 85205-6745 Personal E-mail: wluth@cox.net.

LUTHER, DAVID BYRON, management consultant; b. Utica, NY, May 26, 1936; s. Everett David and Mary (Brown) Luther; m. Geraldine Frost; children: Leslie, Gregory, Valorie. BS, Syracuse U., 1958, MBA, 1961. Mfg. mgr. Corning Glass Works, 1962-74, dir. pers. resources, 1974-76, asst. corp. contr., 1976-78, dir. corp. planning, 1978-79, dir. info. svcs., 1979-80, v.p. pers., 1980-83, v.p. quality, 1983-85, sr. v.p., corp. dir. quality, 1985-94; founder, prin. Luther Quality Assocs., Corning, then Fairfield, Conn., 1994—. V.p. ops. Green Mountain Energy Resources, South Burlington, Vt., 1998—99; exec. in residence Syracuse U. Sch. Bus., 1994—96; mem. exec. session pub. sector mgmt. Harvard U. Kennedy Sch., 1998—2000; mem. conf. bd. steering com. Global Ctr. Performance Excellence; nat. chmn. Koalaty Kid Edn. Project; judge Malcolm Baldrige Nat. Quality Award, 1988—91. Fellow: Am. Soc. Quality (pres. 1994—95, chmn. 1995—96); mem.: Internat. Acad. Quality (v.p.). Office: Luther Quality Assoc PO Box 1008 Fairfield CT 06825 Home: 144 Stillson Rd PO 1008 Fairfield CT 06825 Office Phone: 203-333-5005. Personal E-mail: davidbluther@cs.com.

LUTHER, JON L., food service executive; b. 1943; m. Sharon Luther. BA in Hotel & Restaurant Mgmt., Paul Smith Coll., 1967; DCS (hon.), Bentley Coll., 2006. Various positions including pres. Davre's Restaurant ARA Svcs., Phila., 1967—81; pvt. cons., 1983—87; founder, pres. Benchmark Svcs., Inc., 1987—92; pres. CA One Svcs., Del. North Cos. Inc., 1992—97; pres. Popeyes Chicken & Biscuits AFC Enterprises, 1997—2002; CEO Dunkin' Brands, Inc., 2003—, chmn., 2006—. Bd. dirs. Women's Foodservice Forum. Recipient Golden Chain award, Nation's Restaurant News, 2005, Chain Leadership award, Chain mag., 2006, Silver Plate award, Internat. Foodservice Mfrs. Assn., 2007. Office: Dunkin Brands Inc 130 Royall St Canton MA 02021 Office Phone: 781-737-3000. Office Fax: 781-737-4000.*

LUTHER, THOMAS WILLIAM, retired dermatologist; b. Milw., Feb. 27, 1925; s. Elmer Charles and Ida Martha (Sohrweide) L.; m. Warrene E. Luther; children: Brian Thomas, Siri Karen Luther Witt. BS, U. Wis., 1947, MD, 1950. Diplomate Am. Bd. Dermatology. Intern West Suburban Hosp., Oak Park, Ill., 1950-51; resident VA Hosps., 1951-52, 55-56, U. Pa., 1954-55. Lt. USN, 1943-54. Fellow Am. Acad. Dermatology; mem. AMA, Wis. Med. Soc., Wis. Dermatologic Soc., Appleton Rotary. Avocations: archaeology, genealogy. Home: 1936 Palisades Dr Appleton WI 54915-1023 E-mail: tomandwarrene@aol.com.

LUTHER, WILLIAM P., former congressman; b. Fergus Falls, Minn., June 27, 1945; s. Leonard and Eleanor L.; m. Darlene Luther, Dec. 16, 1967; children: Alexander, Alicia. BS in Elec. Engring. with high distinction, U. Minn., 1967; JD cum laude, U. Minn. Law Sch., 1970. Judicial clerkship 8th cir. U.S. Ct. Appeals, 1970-71; atty. Dorsey & Whitney Law Firm, Mpls., 1971-74, William P. Luther Law Office, Mpls., 1974-83; founder, sr. ptnr. Luther, Ballenthin & Carruthers Law Firm, Mpls., 1983-92; state sen. 47th dist. State of Minn., 1977-94, asst. maj. leader, 1983-94; mem. U.S. Congress from 6th Minn. dist., 1995—2003; mem. commerce com., telecomm., trade & consumer protection, fin., hazardous materials subcoms. Democrat. Home: 12310 Singletree Ln Apt 2444 Eden Prairie MN 55344-7976

LUTHEY, GRAYDON DEAN, JR., lawyer, educator; b. Topeka, Sept. 18, 1955; s. Graydon Dean Sr. and S. Anne (Murphy) L.; m. Deborah Denise McCullough, May 26, 1979; children: Sarah Elizabeth, Katherine Alexandra. BA in Letters with highest honors, U. Okla., 1976, JD, 1979. Bar: Okla. 1979, U.S. Ct. Appeals (10th cir.) 1979, U.S. Dist. Ct. (no., we. and ea. dists.) Okla. 1980, U.S. Supreme Ct. 1982. Assoc. Jones, Givens, Gotcher, Bogan & Hilborne, Tulsa, 1979-84, ptnr., 1984-92, also bd. dirs.; ptnr. Hall, Estill, Hardwick, Gable, Golden & Nelson, Tulsa, 1992—, also bd. dirs. Adj. assoc. prof. U. Tulsa, 1985-87, adj. prof., 1987—; vis. fellow in theology Keble Coll., Oxford U., Eng., 1976; presiding judge Okla. Temporary Ct. Appeals, 1992-93; mem. Okla. Supreme Ct. Rules Com., 1992-94. Bd. dirs. Tulsa Ballet, 1987-2000; chmn. Tulsa Pub. faciltes Authority, 1990-93; trustee Episcopal Theol. Sem. of S.W., 1991-99, exec. com., 1992-99; vice chmn. Univ. Hosps. Authority, 1993-94, chmn. 1994-98, sec., 1998-99; chancellor Episcopal Diocese Okla., 1986-99; mem. bd. visitors U. Okla. Coll. Arts and Scis., 1997—; mem. State of Okla. Futures Auth., 1998-2002, chmn., 1999-2002; mem. adv. bd. U. Okla. Tulsa, 2003-. Master Am. Inns of Ct. (pres. 2007); fellow Am. Bar Found. (life, chmn. Okla. chpt. 2003-06, mem. nat. fellows rsch. adv. com.); mem. ABA, Okla. Bar Assn. (chmn. continuing legal edn. com. 1989-91), Tulsa County Bar Assn. (bd. dirs. 1983-89, Disting. Svc. award 1988), Am. Law Inst., Summit Club, So. Hills Country Club, Beta Theta Pi, Phi Beta Kappa, Omicron Delta Kappa. Office: Hall Estill Hardwick Gable Golden & Nelson 320 S Boston Ave Ste 400 Tulsa OK 74103-3704 Office Phone: 918-594-0437. Business E-Mail: dluthey@hallestill.com.

LUTHI, RANDALL B., federal agency administrator, former state legislator; b. Afton, Wyo., June 3, 1955; BS in Adminstrn. of Justice, U. Wyo., 1979, JD, 1982. Legis. asst. to Senator Alan K. Simpson US Senate; ptnr. Luthi & Voyles, Thayne, Wyo.; atty. Office Solicitor US Dept. Interior, 1986—90; sr. counselor environ. regulations, Office Gen. Counsel NOAA, 1990—93; mem. Wyo. Ho. Reps. from Dist. 21, Cheyenne, 1995—2006, spkr., 2005—06; dep. dir. US Fish & Wildlife Svc. US Dept. Interior, 2007, dir. Minerals Mgmt. Svc., 2007—. Mem. Judiciary com. Wyo. State Legis., Cheyenne, mem. Rules and Procedure com. Mem.: NCA, Wyo. Stockgrowers, Wyo. Bar Assn., D.C. Bar Assn., Farm Bur., Star Valley Rotary Club. Republican. Mem. Lds Ch. Office: Minerals Mgmt Svc US Dept Interior 1849 C St NW Washington DC 20240*

LUTHRINGSHAUSER, DANIEL RENE, manufacturing executive; b. Fontainebleau, France, July 23, 1935; came to U.S., 1937; s. Ernest Henri and Jeanne (Guerville) L.; m. Carol King; children: Mark Ernest, Heidi Elizabeth. BS, NYU, 1956, MBA, 1970. With exec. tng. program, internat. pub. relations Merck & Co. Inc., Rahway, N.J. and NYC, 1962-65; dep. mktg. dir. Merck Sharp & Dohme Internat., Brussels, 1965-66; mktg. service dir. Paris, 1966-69; gen. mgr. Merck Sharp & Dohme/Chibret, Paris, 1970-74; v.p. mktg. Merrell (France), Paris, 1974-78; v.p. gen. mgr.

Revlon Devel. Corp., Paris, 1978-82, Medtronic Europe, Paris, Africa, Middle East, 1982-86; v.p. internat. Medtronic Inc., Mpls., 1986-98; prin. DRL Internat. Cons., 1998—. Bd. dirs. Medtronic Found., Mpls., 1986—91, French-Am. C. of C., 2003—; chmn. Internat. Assn. of Prosthesis Mfrs., Paris, 1983—85; adj. prof. Grad. Sch. of Bus., Univ. St. Thomas. Bd. dirs. Am. Hosp. Paris, 1983-86, 94-95, Minn. Internat. Ctr., 1990—2003; mem. Am. Club Paris, 1970-80, Medtronic Found., Mpls., 1986-91. Served to capt. USAF, 1956-62. Recipient Gold medal Am. Mktg. Assn., 1956. Mem.: Mpls. Club, Ausable Club (Keene Valley, N.Y.). Avocations: gardening, golf, squash, skiing. Home: 480 Peavey Rd Wayzata MN 55391-1529 Office: PO Box 718 Wayzata MN 55391 Personal E-mail: dluthring@aol.com.

LUTHY, KARLEN E., adult nurse practitioner, educator; d. Lois G. Moffett; m. Michael J. Luthy; children: Michael R., Marc J. ADN, Utah Valley State Coll., 2000; BS in Cmty. Health Edn., Brigham Young U., Provo, Utah, 2003, MS, 2005; postgrad., Rush U., Chgo., 2007—. Advanced practice RN, Utah, 2005, RN Utah, 2000. RN Intermountain Healthcare, Provo, 1999—; FNP Vol. Care Clinic, Provo, 2005—; prof. Brigham Young U., 2005—. Guest lectr. Provo Sch. Dist., 2000—. Mem.: Nat. Student Nurse Assn., Am. Acad. Nurse Practitioners (licentiate), Nat. League Nursing (life), Sigma Theta Tau (v.p. 2006—), Phi Kappa Phi (life). Office: Brigham Young Univ 355 Swkt Provo UT 84602 Home Phone: 801-377-7988; Office Phone: 801-422-6683.

LUTHY, RICHARD GODFREY, environmental engineering educator; b. June 11, 1945; s. Robert Godfrey Luthy and Marian Ruth (Ireland) Haines; m. Mary Frances Sullivan, Nov. 22, 1969; children: Matthew Robert, Mara Catherine, Jessica Bethlin. BSChemE, U. Calif., Berkeley, 1967; MS in Ocean Engring., U. Hawaii, 1969; MSCE, U. Calif., Berkeley, 1974, PhDCE, 1976; DSc (hon.), Clarkson U., 2005. Registered profl. engr. Pa.; diplomate Am. Acad. Environ. Engrs. Rsch. asst. dept. civil engring. U. Hawaii, Honolulu, 1968-69; rsch. asst. div. san. and hydraulic engring. U. Calif., Berkeley, 1973-75; asst. prof. civil engring. Carnegie Mellon U., Pitts., 1975-80, assoc. prof., 1980-83, prof., 1983—, assoc. dean Carnegie Inst. Tech., 1986-89, head dept. civil and environ. engring., 1989-96, Lord prof. environ. engring., 1996-2000; Silas H. Palmer prof. dept. civil and environ. engring. Stanford (Calif.) U., 2000—, chmn. Dept. Civil and Environ. Engring., 2003—. Shimizu Corp. vis. prof. dept. civil engring. Stanford U., 1996-97; cons. sci. adv. bd. U.S. EPA, 1983-2004, Bioremediation Action com., 1990-92; cons. U.S. Dept. Energy, 1978-93, various pvt. industries; del. water sci. and tech. bd. NAE, Washington and Beijing, 1988; mem. tech. adv. bd. Remediation Techs., Inc., Concord, Mass., 1989-94, Fostin Capital, Pitts., 1991-94, Balt. Gas & Elec., 1992-95, Pa. Dept. Environ. Protection, 1994-96; mem. sci. adv. com. Hazardous Substance Rsch. Ctr. Stanford U., 1994-99; chair Gordon Rsch. Conf. Environ. Scis., 1994; Nat. Rsch. Coun. Commn. on Innovative Remediation Tech., Com. on Intrinsic Remediation, Com. on Bioavailabilty, Water Sci. and Tech. Bd., 1997-2004, chair, 2000-04. Contbr. articles to tech. and sci. jours. Chmn. NSF/Assn. Environ. Engring. Prof. Conf. on Fundamental Rsch. Directions in Environ. Engring, Washington, 1988. Lt. C.E. Corps, USN, 1969-72. Recipient George Tallman Ladd award Carnegie Inst. Tech., 1977; AT&T Indsl. Ecology Faculty fellow, 2005. Mem. ASCE (Pitts. sect. Prof. of Yr. award 1987), Nat. Acad. Engring., Assn. Environ. Engring. Sci. Profs. (pres. 1987-88, Nalco award 1978, 82, Engring. Sci. award 1988, 2005, Svc. award 1999), Water Environ. Fedn. (rsch. com. 1982-86, awards com. 1981-84, 89-94, std. methods com. 1977—, groundwater com. 1989-90, editor jour. 1989-92, Eddy medal 1980, McKee medal 2000), Water Environ. Rsch. Found. (bd. 2003—), Internat. Assn. on Water Quality (Foudners award U.S. Nat. Com. 1986, 93, orgnl. com. 16th Biennial Conf. Washington 1992), Am. Chem. Soc. (divsn. environ. chemistry, mem. editl. adv. bd. Environ. Sci. Tech. 1992-95). Presbyterian.

LUTI, BILL (WILLIAM JOSEPH LUTI), federal official, retired military officer; b. Boston, Nov. 13, 1953; s. William Vincent and Marjorie Louise (Barnes) L.; m. Donna Margaret King, Dec. 13, 1990; children: Lauren Marie, Natalie Rose. BA in History, The Citadel, 1975; MA in Nat. Security Affairs, U.S. Naval War Coll., 1986; MA in Internat. Rels., Salve Regina Coll., 1986; MA in Law and Diplomacy, PhD in Internat. Rels., Tufts U., 1990. Commd. ensign USN, 1975, advanced through grades to capt., 1997; flight student Naval Air Station, Pensacola, Fla., 1975-76; div. officer VQ-1 (EA-3B aircraft), Agana, Guam, 1976-79; asst. dept. head VAQ-131 (EA-6B aircraft), Oak Harbor, Wash., 1979-82; dept. head VAQ-135 (EA-6B), Oak Harbor, 1986-88; commanding officer VAQ-130 (EA-6B squadron) USN, Oak Harbor, 1991-93; admiral's aide U.S. Naval Acad., Annapolis, Md., 1982-85; dep. dir. Chief of Navel Ops. Exec. Panel, Alexandria, Va., 1993-96; congl. fellow Office of Spkr. of the House Hon. Newt Gingrich, Washington, 1996—97; comdr. USS GUAM USN, 1997—98; spl. advisor to v.p., nat. security affairs The White House, Washington, 2001, spl. asst. to Pres. & sr. dir. def. policy & strategy, 2005—; dep. under sec. near ea. & south Asian affairs US Dept. Def., Washington, 2001—05. Panelist Persian Gulf War Symposium, Naval Inst., Pensacola, 1992 Tchr.'s aide Hillcrest Elem. Sch., Oak Harbor, 1991-92. Decorated with Air medal U.S. Navy, Iraq, 1991. Mem. U.S. Naval Inst. (contbr. editor), Assn. of Naval Aviation, Phi Alpha Theta. Roman Catholic. Avocations: writing, golf, swimming.

LUTNICK, HOWARD WILLIAM, brokerage house executive; b. NY, July 14, 1961; s. Solomon and Jane Lutnick; m. Allison Lambert, June 10, 1994. BA in Econ., Haverford Coll., 1983. With Cantor Fitzgerald, L.P., NYC, 1983—, pres., CEO, 1991—, chmn., 1996—; founder, chmn., pres., CEO eSpeed, Inc., NYC, 1999—. Spkr. in field. Bd. mgrs. Zachary & Elizabeth M. Fisher Ctr. Alzheimer's Disease Rsch., Rockefeller U.; trustee Solomon R. Guggenheim Mus.; bd. trustee, exec. com. Intrepid Mus. Found.; bd. dir. Tate Gallery Projects Ltd., Tate Mus.; bd. mgrs. Haverford Coll. Named Most Valuable Player, Boomer Esiason Found., 1995; recipient Distinguished Pub. Svc. Award, Dept. Navy. Office: Cantor Fitzgerald LP 110 E 59th St Fl 25 New York NY 10022-1304 Office Fax: 212-829-4866.

LUTSYSHYN, OKSANA, concert pianist, organist; b. Sokal, Ukraine, July 22, 1964; d. Yaroslav and Lubov Lutsyshyn; m. Andrey Rafailovich Kasparov, Nov. 1, 1991. MusM, Moscow State Conservatory, 1987, MusD, 1991. Soloist and accompanist Chernovtsy State Philharmony, Chernovtsy, Ukraine, 1987—89; dir. ARK Mgmt., Bloomington, Ind., 1995—98; music dir., organist Prince Peace Luth. Ch., Virginia Beach, Va., 1999—; dir. Prince Peace Concert Series, 2000—. Pianist (concertizing) Concert Tours of Europe, Japan, Latin America, South Africa, South America and the United States, (recording) Andrey Kasparov's Toccata (Second prize Internat. Vienna Modern Masters Rec. Competition, 1997), (Grammy nomination, 1999), Recordings on VMM and CRS labels, (competition) William Kapell International Piano Competition (Prince George Coun. County Art prize, 1990), (recording) Appeared with violinist Joshua Bell and Josef Gingold in the BBC documentary, organist (organ recitals) Organ recitals throughout the United States and Ukraine. Bd. mem. Feldman Chamber Soc., Norfolk, Va., 2004—05; founding mem. Old Dominion U. Contemporary Musc. Ensemble, 1998—, Invencia Piano Duo, 2003—. Mem.: Coll. Music Soc. Home: 1460 Harmott Ave Norfolk VA 23509 Office: Prince Peace Luth Ch 424 Kings Grant Rd Virginia Beach VA 23452 Home Phone: 757-852-9072; Office Phone: 757-340-8420. Personal E-mail: oksana_lutsyshyn@yahoo.com.

LUTTER, CHARLES WILLIAM, JR., lawyer; b. Kenosha, Wis., July 12, 1944; s. Charles William and Eva (Kuyawa) L.; m. Carol Hamilton Ewing, July 13, 1974; children: Charles William III, Scott. BS, U. Wis., 1966; postgrad., U. Tex., 1972; JD, St. Mary's U., 1976. Bar: Tex. 1976, U.S. Dist. Ct. (no. dist.) 1977, U.S. Dist. Ct. (so. dist.) 1981, U.S. Dist. Ct. (we. dist.) 1985, U.S. Ct. Appeals (5th and 11th cir.) 1981. Gen. atty. fin. SEC, Atlanta, 1976-80, chief regulations br. Houston, 1980-83; ptnr. Byrnes & Martin, Houston, 1983-84, Martin, Shannon & Drought, Inc., San Antonio, 1984-87; sr. corp. atty. LaQuinta Motor Inns, Inc., San Antonio, 1987—90; v.p., assoc. gen. counsel, sec. United Svcs. Advisors, Inc., 1991—93, v.p., spl. counsel, sec. San Antonio, 1993—95, legal/operational cons., 1995—; counsel to trust and ind. trustees ICON Funds, 1996—, Lindbergh Funds, 1999—2005, Monteagle Funds, 2002—; of counsel MGL Cons. Corp., Houston, 2000—; chief compliance officer U.S. Global Accolade Funds and US Global Investors Funds, 2004—. Planning com. Ann. Securities Regulation Conf., SEC, Tex. Securities Bd., State Bar Tex., U. Tex. Law Sch., 1986—; initial exec. com. San Antonio Tech. Adv. Group, 1985-87; mem. target '90 Goals for San Antonio Sci. and Tech. Venture Task Force, 1985-90, exec. com. for forum on entrepreneurship, 1985-87; estate planning coun. Southwest Found. Biomed. Rsch., San Antonio, 1987-2003, U. Tex. Health Sci. Ctr., 1998—; arbitrator Nat. Assn. Securities Dealers, NY Stock Exch., Mcpl. Securities Rulemaking Bd. Contbr. articles to profl. jours. Scout leader Alamo Area coun. Boy Scouts Am., 1988—2006; bd. dirs. Boysville, San Antonio, 1989—, exec. com., 1995—99, 2005—, pres., 1999. Capt. USAF, 1966—71. Decorated Air medal (6). Mem. ABA, State Bar Tex. (securities and investment banking com. 1984—, ad hoc subcom. on securities activities of banks 1987-89, subcom. on rules of fair practce for Tex. broker-dealers 1990), Internat. Assn. for Fin. Planning (bd. dirs. and regulatory coord. San Antonio chpt. 1987-98), Investment Co. Inst. (SEC rules com. 1993-95), San Antonio Bar Assn., San Antonio Bar Found., U. Wis. Alumni Assn., Air Force Assn., John M. Harlan Soc., Kiwanis, Phi Delta Phi. Office: 103 Canyon Oaks Dr San Antonio TX 78232-1305 also: care MGL Cons Ste 10077 100 Grogan's Mill Rd The Woodlands TX 77380 E-mail: lutter@swbell.net.

LUTTER, PAUL ALLEN, lawyer; b. Chgo., Feb. 28, 1946; s. Herbert W. and Lois (Muller) L. BA, Carleton Coll., 1968; JD, Yale U., 1971. Bar: Ill. 1971, U.S. Tax Ct. 1986. Assoc. Ross & Hardies, Chgo., 1971-77, ptnr., 1978—2003, McGuire Woods, Chgo., 2003—04, Bryan Cave, Chgo., 2004—. Co-author: Illinois Estate Administration, 1993. Office: Bryan Cave 161 N Clark St Ste 4300 Chicago IL 60601 Home: 437 N Canal St Chicago IL 60610 Office Phone: 312-602-5121.

LUTTERODT, CLEMENT H., mathematician, educator; b. Nsawam, Ghana, Aug. 17, 1943; arrived in U.S., 1979; s. Samuel Augustus Christian Lutterodt and Olaonipekun Lutterodt (dec.); m. Sarah Anne French, Sept. 25, 1971; children: Tobias, Isabelle, Justine. BSc, U. Ghana, Legon, 1967, MSc, 1972; PhD, U. Birmingham, Eng., 1974. Lectr. U. Cape Coast, Ghana, 1973—78, sr. lectr., 1978—80; vis. asst. prof. U. South Fla., Tampa, 1980; asst. prof. Howard U., Washington, 1980—84, assoc. prof., 1984—90, prof., 1990—. Contbr. articles to profl. jours. Fellow, Internat. Ctr. for Theoretical Physics, 1971, Internat. Ctr. for Theoretical Physics, Miramare, Italy, 1975, 1977, 1980, 1988, 1999, 2000, others. Mem.: Math Assn. Am., NY Acad. Scis., Am. Math. Soc. Achievements include creation of the field of rational approximants in several complex variables. Avocations: ping pong/table tennis, walking, reading. Office: Howard Univ Dept Math 6th St NW Washington DC 20059 Personal E-mail: clemlutterodt@att.net.

LUTTIG, J(OHN) MICHAEL (JOHN MICHAEL LUTTIG), aerospace transportation executive, former federal judge; b. Tyler, Tex., June 13, 1954; s. John and Bobbie Luttig; m. Elizabeth Ann Luttig; children: Morgan, John. BA, Washington and Lee U., 1976; JD, U. Va., 1981. Asst. counsel to Pres. The White House, Washington, 1981—82; law clk. to Hon. Antonin Scalia US Ct. Appeals (DC Cir.), 1982—83; law clerk to Chief Justice Warren Burger US Supreme Ct., 1983—84, spl. asst. to Chief Justice Warren Burger, 1984—85; assoc. Davis Polk & Wardwell, 1985—89; prin. dep. asst. atty. gen., Office of Legal Counsel US Dept. Justice, 1989—90, asst. atty. gen., Office of Legal Counsel, counselor to atty. gen., 1990—91; judge US Ct. Appeals (4th Cir.), McLean, Va., 1991—2006; sr. v.p., gen. counsel The Boeing Co., Chgo., 2006—. Mem. Nat. Adv. Com. of Lawyers for Bush, 1988, Lawyers for Bush Com., 1988. Mem.: ABA, D.C. Bar Assn., Va. Bar Assn. Office: The Boeing Co 100 N Riverside Plz Chicago IL 60606*

LUTTIKHUIZEN, HENRY MARTIN, art historian, curator; b. Zeeland, Mich., Oct. 18, 1964; s. Marinus and Marian Luttikhuizen; m. Shari van Maastricht, July 11, 1986; children: Arie, Gabrielle. BA, Calvin Coll., 1986; PhD, U. Va., 1997. Prof. art history Calvin Coll., Grand Rapids, Mich., 1991—. Protestant. Office: Calvin College 3201 Burton SE Grand Rapids MI 49546 Office Phone: 616-526-6327. Business E-Mail: lutt@calvin.edu.

LUTTS, RALPH HERBERT, scholar, educator, museum administrator; b. Quincy, Mass., Jan. 7, 1944; s. Herbert Warren Lutts and Jean May (MacKenzie) Easton. BA in Biology, Trinity U., San Antonio, 1967; EdD, U. Mass., 1978. Curator, educator Mus. Sci., Boston, 1967-73; naturalist Hampshire Coll., Amherst, Mass., 1973-80, mem. natural sci. faculty, 1976-84; dir. Blue Hills Trailside Mus., Mass. Audubon Soc., Milton, 1980-90; dir. edn. Va. Mus. Natural History, Martinsville, 1990-92, dir. outreach divsn., 1992-94, rsch. assoc., 1994-97; mem. faculty Goddard Coll., Plainfield, Vt., 1995—, coord. MA concentration in environ. studies, 2002—, chair, faculty coun., 2005—06, trustee, 2007—; mem. adj. faculty U. Va., Charlottesville, 1995—2006; mem. adj. history faculty Va. Tech., 1998—. Pres. Alliance for Environ. Edn., 1988-89; founding pres. New Eng. Environ. Edn. Alliance, 1980-84; assoc. Ctr. for Animals and Pub. Policy, Tufts U. Sch. Vet. Medicine, North Grafton, Mass., 1989-90; dept. dir. mid-atlantic region Global Network of Environ. Edn. Ctrs., 1993-95; pres. Am. Nature Study Soc., 1995-97; founding mem. bd. dirs. Blue Ridge Heritage. Author: The Nature Fakers: Wildlife, Science and Sentiment, 1990; editor: The Wild Animal Story, 1998; founding editor New Eng. Jour. Environ. Edn., 1985-88; contbr. articles to profl. jours. Pres. Hitchcock Ctr. for Environ., Amherst, Mass., 1977-79; pres. New Eng. Environ. Edn. Alliance, 1980-82; treas. Mass. Environ. Edn. Soc., 1982-84; mem. Blue Hills citizens' adv. com. Met. Dist. Commn., 1988-89, mgmt. adv. com., 1989-90; mem. sec.'s adv. group on environ. edn. Mass. Exec. Office for Environ. Affairs, 1989-90; mem. exec. com. Patrick Environ. Awareness Group, 1998-99; assoc. dir. Patrick Soil and Water Conservation Dist., 2001-2002. Recipient New Eng. award for achievement New Eng. Founding Bd. Mem. Blue Ridge Heritage Environ. Edn. Alliance, 1989; Paul Harris fellow Rotary Internat. Mem. Am. Soc. Environ. History, Assn. for Study of Lit. and Environ., Forest History Soc. (Ralph W. Hidy award 1993), N.Am. Assn. Environ. Edn., Am. Nature Study Soc. (bd. dirs. 1990-98, pres. 1995-97), Authors Guild, Popular Culture Assn. (area chair 1993-95), Appalachian Studies Assn., Soc. for Conservation Biology

LUTTWAK, EDWARD NICOLAE, academic administrator, policy and business consultant, senior advisor; b. Arad, Transylvania, Nov. 4, 1942; came to U.S., 1972, naturalized, 1981; s. Josif Menashe and Clara (Baruch) L.; m. Dalya Iaari, Dec. 14, 1970; children: Yael Rachel, Joseph Emannuel. B.Sc. with honors, London Sch. Econs., 1964; PhD (Univ. fellow), Johns Hopkins U., 1975; D (hon.), U. Bath, Eng., 2004. Vis. prof. polit. sci. Johns Hopkins U., 1973-78; sr. fellow Georgetown U. Center Strategic and Internat. Studies, 1978-87, research prof. internat. security affairs, 1978-82, Burke chair in strategy, 1987—, dir. geo-econs., 1991-94, sr. fellow, 1994—; sr. fellow in preventive diplomacy Office of Sec. of Def., Nat. Security Coun. and Dept. State. Cons. Office of Sec. of Def., Nat. Security Coun., Dept. of Def. Army, Navy and U.S. Air Force, Fgn. (allied) Govs. and U.S., overseas bus. entities. Author: Coup d'Etat, 19 edits. including 12 for lang. translations, 1968-79, Dictionary of Modern War, 1971 (also Spanish edit.), The Political Uses of Sea Power, 1975 (also Japanese edit.), The Israeli Army, 1975, 85, (also Chinese edit.), The Grand Strategy of the Roman Empire, 1976 (also Hebrew, Italian and French edits.), Strategy and Politics: Collected Essays, 1980, The Grand Strategy of the Soviet Union, 1983 (also Italian and French edits.),The Pentagon and the Art of War: The Question of Military Reform, 1985 (also Italian, Japanese and Korean edits.), Strategy and History: Collected Essays, On the Meaning of Victory, 1986 (also Italian edit.), Strategy: The Logic of War and Peace, 1987 (also Chinese, French and Italian edits.), revised edit., 2001, 2d rev. edit., 2002, (with Stuart Koehl) Dictionary of Modern War, 1991 (also Italian edit.), The Endangered American Dream, 1993 (also French, Italian, German and Japanese edits.), (with G. Tremonti, Carlo Palanda) Il Fantasma della Poverta, 1995, (with Susanna Creperio) Cose e Davvero La Democrazia, 1996, Turbo Capitalism, U.K. edit., 1998, Turbo-Capitalism: Winners and Losers in the Global Economy, U.S. edit., 1999, French edit., 1999, Italian edit., 1999, Portuguese edit., 1999, Polish edit., 1999, German edit., 1999, Dutch edit., 1999, Japanese edit., 1999, Chinese edit., 1999, Taiwan edit., 1999, Spanish edit., 1999, La Renaissance De La Puissance Aerienne Strategique, 1999, Il Libro Della Liberta 2000 (with Susanna Creporop Verraiti), Strategy: The Logic of War and Peace, 2001, French edit., 2002, Italian edit., 2002, Hebrew edit., 2002; contbr. articles to Fgn. Affairs, London Rev. of Books, Times Lit. Supplement, Commentary National Interest Foreign Affairs Strategy: The Logic of War and Peace New, Revised and Enlarged Edit., 2001, translated edit. in Chinese, Estonian, French, German, Italian, Hebrew, Turkish. Independent. Jewish. Office: CSIS 1800 K St NW Washington DC 20006-2294

LUTVAK, MARK ALLEN, computer company executive; b. Chgo., Feb. 9, 1939; s. Joseph Issac and Jeanette Nettie (Pollock) L.; m. Gayle Helene Rotofsky, May 24, 1964; children: Jeffrey, Eric. BSEE, U. Mich., 1962; MBA, Wayne State U., Detroit, 1969. Sales rep. IBM Corp., 1962-64; from sales rep. to corp. product mgr. Burroughs Corp., Detroit, 1964-76; mgr. product mktg. Memorex Corp., Santa Clara, Calif., 1976-80, product program gen. mgr., 1980-81; dir. product mktg. Personal Computer divsn. Atari, Inc., Sunnyvale, Calif., 1981-83; dir. mktg., v.p. Durango Sys., San Jose, Calif., 1983-85; dir. mktg. ITTQUME Corp., San Jose, 1985-87; v.p. mktg. Optimem, Mountain View, Calif., 1987-88; dir. mktg. Priam Corp., San Jose, 1988-91; dir. Memorex, Santa Clara, 1991-94; pres. Synergistic Mktg., 1994—. Prof. Applied Mgmt. Center, Wayne State U., 1967-72, Walsh U., Troy, Mich., 1974-76, West Valley Coll., Saratoga, Calif., 1977-78. Trustee, pres. brotherhood Temple Emanuel, San Jose, 1979-80, pres. Mens Orgn. Cong. Peninsula Sinai, Foster City, 2005-07, CIRM Soc., 2005-07. Mem. IEEE, Soc. Applied Math., Alpha Epsilon Pi. Home: 899 Balboa Ln Foster City CA 94404-2931 Office Phone: 650-349-5123. Personal E-mail: mlutvak@sbcglobal.net.

LUTZ, FRANCIS CHARLES, dean, civil engineering educator; b. Pottsville, Pa., Apr. 5, 1944; s. Charles Henry and Pauline Anna (Weislo) L.; m. Evelyn Florence Zommer, Apr. 29, 1972; 1 child, Stephanie Diane BSCE, N.J. Inst. Tech., 1966; MSCE, NYU, 1967, PhD, 1971. Assoc. M. Disko Assocs., West Orange, NJ, 1970-72; asst. prof. civil engring. Worcester Poly. Inst., Mass., 1972-76, prof., 1980-96, assoc. dean, 1980-90, dean undergrad. studies, 1990-95; dean sch. sci., tech. & engring. Monmouth U., West Long Branch, NJ, 1996—. Cons. Council on Environ. Quality, Washington, 1974-75; reviewer NSF Co-editor: Studies in Science, Technology and Culture, Worcester Poly. Inst.; contbr. articles to profl. jours. Trustee Worcester Ctr. for Crafts, 1992-96; mem. Boston Fed. Exec. Bd., 1972-74, Cen. Mass. Regional Planning Commn., Worcester, 1975-77. Am. Council on Edn. fellow, 1988-89; honors scholar NYU. Mem. ASCE, Am. Soc. Engring. Edn., Boynton Assn. (pres. 1982, 83), JETS (bd. dirs.), Sigma Xi, Chi Epsilon. Office: Monmouth U Office of Dean Sch Sci Tech & Engring West Long Branch NJ 07764-1898 Office Phone: 732-571-3421. Business E-Mail: flutz@monmouth.edu.

LUTZ, FRANK WENZEL, education administration educator; b. St. Louis, Sept. 24, 1928; s. Vincent J. and Helen M. (Scrivens) L.; m. Susan Virginia Bleikamp, July 12, 1958; children: Paul E., Andrew C., Lynn S. AA, Harris Tchrs. Coll., 1948; BS, Washington U., 1950, MS, 1954, EdD, 1962. Instr. Washington U., St. Louis, 1961-62; from asst. to assoc. prof. NYU, NYC, 1964-68; dir. divsn. policy studies Pa. State U., State College, 1968-73, prof. edn. adminstrn., 1974-80; dean Sch. Edn. Eastern Ill. U., 1980-82, asst. to v.p., 1982-83; prof., dir. Ctr. Policy Studies Tex. A&M-Commerce, 1983—91, prof. edn. adminstrn., 1983—98, prof. emeritus, 1998; sr. nat. lectr. Nova S.E. U., Ft. Lauderdale, Fla., 1991-98; prof. edn. adminstrn. U. Tex.-Pan-Am., Edinburg, 1998—2002. Mem. adv. com. Opportunities Acad. Mgmt. Tng., Phila., 1975—90; mem., pres. Pattonville (Mo.) Sch. Bd., 1960—62; adv. bd. Nederland Columbine Clinic, 2001—03. Author seven books, numerous book chpts. in field; contbr. more than 200 articles to profl. jours. Chair Nederland Cmty. Ctr. Bd., 1998-2000; deacon 1st Presbyn. Ch., Commerce, Tex., 1989-91; clerk of session, Nederland Presbyn Ch., 2003-04. Doctoral fellow Washington U., 1960-61; grantee U.S. Office Edn., OEO. Mem. Am. Ednl. Rsch. Assn. (sec. Divsn. A 1970-72, dir. rsch. pre-session 1969, program com. 1970), Nederland C. of C. (bd. dirs. 2005—), Nederland Area Sr. Inc. (pres. bd. dirs. 2006—), Commerce Rotary (dist. 5810, pres. 1991-92, chair internat. svc. 1994-96, Found. award 1994, Paul Harris fellow), Peak-to-Peak Rotary (int. chair 2000—, Dist. 5450 world cmty. svc. and youth exch. com. 1999—, ambassadorial fellow com. 2006—, Rotarian of Yr. 1999-2001), Nederland C. of C. (bd. dirs. 2004—), Phi Delta Kappa (life, pres. Washington U. chpt. 1960, 1st v.p. East Tex. State U. chpt. 1985, sec. 2006, Lafferty Faculty Senate Disting. scholarship award 1996, Lifetime Achievement award 2006). Avocations: appaloosa horses, opera, classical music. Home: PO Box 51 Nederland CO 80466-0051 Personal E-mail: fslutz@msn.com.

LUTZ, JACOB A., III, (JAKE LUTZ), lawyer; b. Radford, Va., 1956; BS in Fin. with distinction, Va. Polytechnic Inst. State U., 1978; JD, Coll. William and Mary, 1981. Bar: Va. 1982, Tenn. 1987. Atty. FDIC, Washington, 1981—84, sr. regional atty. Atlanta, 1984—87; assoc. Borod & Huggins, Memphis, 1987—90; ptnr., chair fin. instns. Troutman Sanders LLP, Richmond, 1990—, chair bus. dept., 1994—99, mng. ptnr., 1999—2003. Mem. bd. visitors Va. Tech., 2000—, vice rector, 2004—06; chair Va. Bioinformatics Inst. Policy Bd., 2002—06; elder First Presbyn. Ch., Richmond. Mem.: ABA, Am. Bar Found., Tenn. Bar Assn., Va. Bar Assn. Office: Troutman Sanders LLP 1001 Haxall Point Richmond VA 23219 Office Phone: 804-697-1490. Office Fax: 804-698-6014. Business E-Mail: jake.lutz@troutmansanders.com.

LUTZ, JAMES GURNEY, lawyer; b. Cin., Sept. 18, 1933; s. Arthur Harold and Frances (Gurney) L.; children: Monica, Susan. JD, Duke U Law Sch, U. Cin., 1960. Bar: Ohio 1960, U.S. Dist. Ct. (so. dist.) Ohio 1961, U.S. Ct. Appeals (6th cir.) 1961, U.S. Tax Ct. 1975, U.S. Supreme Ct. 1975. Ptnr. Barbour, Kinpel & Allen, Cin., 1960-68; chief counsel E.C. Industries Inc., Cin., 1968-71; sr. ptnr. Lutz Cornetet Meyer & Rush, Cin., 1971—. Pres., bd. dirs. Motivation Dynamics Inc., Cin., 1978—85; gen. counsel Synchrocare Inc. Advisor, staff Hamilton County Vocat. Schs., Cin., 1968; advisor U. Cin. Coll., 1970-75; mem. adv. council Wyoming (Ohio) Bd. Edn., 1972-75; mem. bd. Ohio Pvt. Industry Coun., Columbus, 1975; gen. counsel S.W. Ohio Autistic Assn., Cin., 1980—. Mem. ABA, ATLA, Ohio Acad. Trial Lawyers, Ohio State Bar Assn., Cin. Bar Assn. Avocations: psychology, computer science. Office: Lutz Cornetet Meyer & Rush 123 Boggs Lane Cincinnati OH 45246-3289 E-mail: jlutz@lcmrlaw.com.

LUTZ, JEANNE V., elementary school educator; d. Theodore J. and Virginia R. Lutz. BS, SUNY, Cortland, 1972; MS, Adelphi U., Garden City, N.J., 1975. Tchr. grade 2 Sachem Consolidated Sch. Dist., Holbrook, NY, 1973—. Office Phone: 631-654-8690. Business E-Mail: jlutz@sachem.edu.

LUTZ, JOHN SHAFROTH, lawyer; b. San Francisco, Sept. 10, 1943; s. Frederick Henry and Helena Morrison (Shafroth) L.; m. Elizabeth Boschen, Dec. 14, 1968; children: John Shafroth, Victoria. BA, Brown U., 1965; JD, U. Denver, 1971. Bar: Colo. 1971, U.S. Dist. Ct. Colo. 1971, U.S. Ct. Appeals (2d cir.) 1975, D.C. 1976, U.S. Supreme Ct. 1976, U.S. Dist. Ct. (so. dist.) N.Y. 1977, U.S. Tax Ct. 1977, U.S. Ct. Appeals (10th cir.) 1979, N.Y. 1984, U.S. Ct. Appeals (9th cir.) 1990, U.S. Dist. Ct. (no. dist.) Calif. 1993. Trial atty. Denver regional office U.S. SEC, 1971-74; spl. atty. organized crime, racketeering sect. U.S. Dept. Justice (so. dist.) N.Y., 1974-77; atty. Kelly, Stansfield and O'Donnell, Denver, 1977-78; gen. counsel Boettcher & Co., Denver, 1987, spl. counsel, 1987-88, ptnr., 1988-93; of counsel LeBoeuf, Lamb, Greene and MacRae, LLP, Denver, 1993-94, ptnr., 1995—2001; dir. Fairfield and Woods, PC, Denver, 2002—. Spkr. on broker, dealer, securities law and arbitration issues. Contbr. articles to profl. jours. Bd. dirs. Cherry Creek Improvement Assn., 1980-84, Spalding Rehab. Hosp., 1986-89; dir. Recs. for the Blind and Dyslectic; chmn., vice-chmn. securities sub sect. Bus. Law Sect. of Colo. Bar, 1990, chmn., 1990-91. Lt. (j.g.) USNR, 1965-67. Mem. ABA, Colo. Bar Assn., Denver Bar Assn., Am. Law Inst., Securities Industry Assn. (life; state regulation com. 1982-86), Nat. Assn. Securities Dealers, Inc. (nat. arbitration com. 1987-91), St. Nicholas Soc. N.Y.C., Denver Law Club, Denver Country Club, Denver Athletic Club (dir. 1990-93), Univ. Club (Denver), Rocky Mountain Brown Club (founder, past pres.). Republican. Episcopalian. Office: Fairfield and Woods PC Wells Fargo Ctr 1700 Lincoln St #2400 Denver CO 80203 Office Phone: 303-894-4476. Business E-Mail: jlutz@fwlaw.com.

LUTZ, JOHN THOMAS, author; b. Dallas, Sept. 11, 1939; s. John Peter and Esther Jane (Gundelfinger) L.; m. Barbara Jean Bradley, Mar. 15, 1958; children: Steven, Jennifer, Wendy. Student, Meramec C.C., 1965; ArtsD, LittD, U. Mo., 2007. Author: The Truth of the Matter, 1971, Buyer Beware, 1976, Bonegrinder, 1977, Lazarus Man, 1979, Jericho Man, 1980, The Shadow Man, 1981; (with Steven Greene) Exiled, 1982; (with Bill Pronzini) The Eye, 1984, Nightlines, 1984, The Right to Sing the Blues, 1986, Tropical Heat, 1986, Ride the Lightning, 1987, Scorcher, 1987, Dancers Debt, 1988, Shadowtown, 1988, Kiss, 1988, Better Mousetraps (short story collection), 1988, Time Exposure, 1989, Flame, 1990, Diamond Eyes, 1990, SWF Seeks Same (Single White Female), 1990, Bloodfire, 1991, Hot, 1992, Dancing with the Dead, 1992, Spark, 1993, Thicker than Blood, 1993, (short story collection) Shadows Everywhere, 1994, Torch, 1994, Death by Jury, 1995, Burn, 1995, Lightning, 1996; (novel and screenplay) The Ex, 1996, Oops!, 1998; (with David August) Final Seconds, 1998; (short stories) Until You Are Dead, 1998, The Nudger Dilemmas, 2001, The Night Caller, 2001, The Night Watcher, 2002, The Night Spider, 2003, Endless Road, 2003; contbr. short stories and articles to mystery and private-eye mags. Darker Than Night, 2004, Fear the Night, 2005, Chill of Night, 2006, In for the Kill, 2007. Mem. Mystery Writers Am. (pres. 1991, Scroll 1981, 2003, Edgar award 1986), Pvt.-Eye Writers Am. (pres. 1988, 89, Shamus award 1982, 88, Life Achievement award 1995), Short Mystery Fiction Soc. (Golden Derringer Life Achievement award 2001). Democrat. Home and Office: 12444 Balwyck Ln Saint Louis MO 63131

LUTZ, MATTHEW CHARLES, oil industry executive, geologist; b. Bunkie, La., Mar. 28, 1934; s. John Matthew and Maxie Mae (Andrus) L.; m. Patricia Dawnn Feazel, Apr. 11, 1953; children: Matt Jr., Cyndy, Tracey, Clay. BS, U. Southwestern La., 1956. Various geol. profl. positions Tidewater-Getty Oil Co., 1956-71; asst. dist. geologist Getty Oil Co., Houston, 1971-73, dist. geologist Midland, Tex., 1973-78, ctrl. divsn. geologist Tulsa, 1978-80, offshore dist. exploration mgr. Houston, 1980, so. divsn. exploration mgr., 1980-82, gen. mgr. offshore exploration and prodn., 1982-83, exploration mgr. so. divsn., 1983-84; sr. v.p. exploration Enserch Exploration, Inc., Dallas, 1984-92, also bd. dirs.; vice chmn. and bus. devel. mgr. Hunter Resources, Inc., Irving, Tex., 1993-95, also bd. dirs.; vice chmn. exploration and bus. devel. mgr. Magnum Hunter Resources, Inc., Irving, 1995-97, chmn., exec. v.p., 1997—2001, bd. dirs., 1993—2005; cons., 2005—. Mem. Am. Assn. Petroleum Geologists, Houston Geol. Soc., Dallas Geol. Soc., Dallas Petroleum Club. Republican. Baptist. Avocations: golf, hunting, ranching.

LUTZ, NANCY COLE, educational consultant; b. Rockford, Ill., Sept. 23, 1936; d. Sanford and Mildred Cole; m. Raymond P. Lutz. BA in English Edn., U. N.Mex., 1958, MA in English Lit., 1964; EdD in Curriculum and Instrn., N.Mex. State U., 1969. English tchr. John Adams Jr. H.S., Albuquerque, 1958—61, Ames (Iowa) Sr. H.S., 1961—64; asst. prof. edn./reading U. Okla., Norman, 1969; clin. practical reading Cleveland County Mental Health, Norman, 1970—73; curriculum cons., dir. Learning Ctr. U. Tex., Dallas, 1973—80; pvt. ednl. cons. Dallas, 1979—. Mng. editor: Engring. Economist, 1974—77; editor: Tech. Impact Assessment, 1974. Curriculum cons. U. Houston, 1973—75; mem. edn. com. annual fund com. Santa Fe Opera Bd., 2001—; mem. stewardship com. First Presbyn. Ch., Santa Fe, 2004—; bd. mem. United Cerebral Palsy Am., NYC, 1984, United Cerebral Palsy, Dallas, 1973—80, pres., 1983—84. Grantee, State of Tex. Health and Edn. Adolescents, 1973—75. Mem.: Nat. Coun. Tchrs. Math., Coun. for Exceptional Children, Internat. Reading Assn., Sigma Alpha Iota, Pi Lambda Theta. Democrat. Avocations: opera, music, reading, gardening, hiking. Home and Office: 1230 Turquoise Trail Cerrillos NM 87010 Home Phone: 505-471-6709; Office Phone: 505-471-6709. Personal E-mail: nclutz@att.net.

LUTZ, RANDALL MATTHEW, lawyer; b. New Brunswick, NJ, June 1, 1945; s. Ralph P. and Gertrude (Goodman) L. BS with high honors, U. Md., 1967, JD, 1970. Bar: Md. 1970, U.S. Dist. Ct. Md. 1970, U.S. Ct. Appeals (4th cir.) 1970, U.S. Supreme Ct. 1975. Assoc. Burke, Gerber & Wilen, Balt., 1970-75; asst. atty. gen. State of Md., 1975-84; dir. criminal enforcement U.S. EPA, Washington, 1984-87; ptnr. Kaplan, Heyman, Greenberg, Engleman & Belgrade, Balt., 1987-90, Smith, Somerville & Case, LLC, Balt., 1990-98, Hodes, Ulman, Pessin & Katz, PA, Towson, Md., 1998—. Lectr. in field. Author: (column) Environmental Law jour.,1987-88. Mem. dist. cabinet Balt. area coun. Boy Scouts Am., 1974-75. Mem: ABA, Md. Bar Assn., Nat. Health Lawyers Assn. Office: Hodes Ulman Pessin & Katz PA 901 Dulaney Valley Rd Towson MD 21204-2600 Home Phone: 410-486-0156; Office Phone: 410-339-6744. E-mail: rlutz@hupk.com.

LUTZ, RAYMOND PRICE, retired industrial engineer, educator; b. Oak Park, Ill., Feb. 27, 1935; s. Raymond Price and Sibyl Elizabeth (Haralson) Lutz; m. Nancy Marie Cole, Aug. 23, 1958. BSME, U. N.Mex., Albuquerque, 1958, MBA, 1962; PhD, Iowa State U., Ames, 1964. Registered profl. engr., N.Mex., Okla. With Sandia Corp., Albuquerque, summers 1958-63; instr. mech. engring. U. N.Mex., 1958-62; from asst. to assoc. prof. indsl. engring. N.Mex. State U., 1964-68; prof. head indsl. engring. U. Okla., 1968-73; prof., acting dean U. Tex. Sch. Mgmt., Dallas, 1973-76, dean, 1976-78, exec. dean grad. studies and rsch., 1979-92, prof. ops. mgmt., 1992-2001, ret., 2001. Cons. Bell Telephone Labs., Tex. Instruments, Kennecott Corp., Bath Iron Works, Sabre, Inc., City of Dallas, Oklahoma City; cons. US Army, USAF, US Dept. Transp., LA and Seattle public schs.; shipbldg. productivity panel NRC Editor: The Engring. Economist, 1973-77, Indsl. Mgmt., 1983-87. Pres., bd. dirs. United Cerebral Palsy, Dallas, 1978, treas., 1984-88; bd. dirs., treas. Amigos Bibliographic Network, Dallas, 1984-90; chmn., bd. dirs. S.W. Police Inst., Dallas, 1980—; v.p., bd. dirs. Santa Fe Opera, 1988—, Dallas Opera, 1989-2001; pres. bd. Santa Fe Opera Found., 1993-2000, Santa Fe Women's Ensemble, 2005—; dirs. coun. Desert Chorale, 2005—. Fellow AAAS, Am. Inst. Indsl. Engrs. (v.p. industry and mgmt. divsns., trustee, dir. engring. economy divsn., systems engring. group); mem. Am. Soc. Engring. Edn. (chmn. engring. economy divsn., Eugene L. Grant award 1972), INFORMS, Dallas Classic Guitar Soc. (bd. dirs. 1993-96, v.p. 1994-96), Ops. Mgmt. Assn. (bd. dirs. 1994-98), Sigma Xi (bd. dirs. 1990-98, 99—2005, chmn. devel. 1992—, exec. com. 1992-95). Avocations: opera, hiking. Home: 1230 Turquoise Trl Cerrillos NM 87010-9716 Office Phone: 505-471-6709. Personal E-mail: rplutz@att.net.

LUTZ, ROBERT ANTHONY, automotive company executive; b. Zurich, Switzerland, Feb. 12, 1932; came to U.S., 1939; s. Robert H. and Marguerite (Schmid) L.; m. Betty D. Lutz, Dec. 12, 1956 (div. 1979); children: Jacqueline, Carolyn, Catherine, Alexandra; m. Heide Marie Schmid, Mar. 3, 1980 (div. Dec. 1992); m. Denise Ford, Apr. 17, 1994; 2 stepchildren. BS in Prodn. Mgmt., U. Calif., Berkeley, 1961, MBA in Mktg. with highest honors, 1962; LLD (hon.), Boston U., 1988; DM (hon.), Kettering U., 2003. Research assoc., sr. analyst IMEDE, Lausanne, Switzerland, 1962-63; sr. analyst forward planning GM, NYC, 1963-65, mgr. vehicle div. Paris, 1966-69; staff asst., mng. dir. Adam Opel, Russelsheim, Germany, 1965-66, asst. mgr. domestic sales, 1969, dir. sales Vorstand, 1969-70; v.p. Vorstand BMW, Munich, 1972-74; gen. mgr. Ford of Germany, Cologne, Germany, 1974-76; v.p. truck ops. Ford of Europe, Brentwood, Eng., 1976-77, pres., 1977-79, chmn., 1979-82, also bd. dirs.; exec. v.p. Ford Internat., Dearborn, Mich., 1982-84, Chrysler Motors Corp., Highland Park, Mich., 1986-88; pres. ops., pres., COO Chrysler Corp., Highland Park, Mich., 1988-96, vice chmn., 1996—98; chmn. Exide Corp., 1998—2002, pres., 1998—2000, CEO, 1998—2001; chmn. General Motors N. Am., 2001—05; pres. GM Europe, 2004; vice chmn., prod. devel. General Motors Corp., 2001—. Bd. dirs. Exide Technologies, 1998-, Kepner-Tregoe, Silicon Graphics, ASCOM, Switzerland; mem., former chmn. Hwy. Users Fedn. for Safety and Mobility. Author: Guts: The Seven Laws of Business That Made Chrysler the World's Hottest Car Company, 1998, Guts: 8 Laws of Business from One of the Most Innovative Business Leaders of our Time, 2003. Trustee: Mich. Cancer Found., USMC U. Found.; vice-chmn, bd. trustees, Marine Military Acad.; bd. dirs. United Way of Southeastern Mich.; mem. adv. bd. Walter A. Haas Sch. Bus., U. Calif., Berkeley, 1979—; chmn., The New Common School Found.; Capt. USMC, 1954-65. Named Alumnus of Yr., Sch. Bus., U. Calif., 1983; Kaiser Found. grantee, 1962. Mem. NAM (exec. com.), Phi Beta Kappa. Republican. Avocations: skiing, motorcycling, bicycling, helicopter flying, vintage cars, fixed-wing flying. Office: GM Corp PO Box 300 Detroit MI 48265-3000 also: Exide Technologies 3000 Montrose Ave Reading PA 19605-2751*

LUTZ, TAMARA JEAN, nursing consultant; d. Edward and Dorothy Lutz. AA, Kirkwood CC, Cedar Rapids, Iowa, 1983; B of Nursing, U. Iowa, 1985; M of Nursing, U. Wash., 1995. RN Iowa, registered Level I-II Neonatal Nurse. Commd. 2d lt. US Army, 1986, advanced through grades to maj., 1996; nurse methods analyst Gen. Leonard Wood Army Cmty. Hosp., Ft. Leonard Wood, Mo., 2002—04, joint commn. on accrediation of hospitals coord., 2004—05; behavioral mental health program developer US Army, Ft. Leonard Wood, Mo., 2005—06; case mgr. Prin. Fin. Group, 2006—. Cons. in field. Decorated Army Svc. Ribbon US Army, Nat. Def. Svc. medal with Bronze Star U.S. Army, Overseas Svc. Ribbon US Army, Achievement medals, Commendation medals, Humanitarian Svc. medal, Joint Svc. Commendation medal, Global War on Terrorism Svc. medal, Meritorius Svc. medal, Mil. Outstanding Vol. Svc. medal. Mem.: Nat. Assn. Healthcare Quality (cert.), Mo. League Nursing (assoc.), Sigma Theta Tau. Lutheran. Avocations: travel, reading, cross stitch. Home Phone: 573-774-2105. E-mail: tamara.lutz@yahoo.com.

LUTZ, TINA, apparel designer; Grad. in Fashion Design and Pattern Making, Esmod Fashion Sch., Paris. Designer, Paris, Tokyo, NYC, 1992—; co-owner, designer (with Marcia Patmos) Lutz & Patmos, NYC, 2000—. Work featured in Vogue, Elle, Cosmopolitan, Town & Country, WWD, Glamour, NY Mag., NY Times, Marie Claire; work shown in Cooper Hewitt Museum, Pasadena Museum of Calif. Arts, Royal Museum of Scotland, San Francisco Modern Museum of Art. Office: Lutz & Patmos Ste 406 425 W 13th New York NY 10014

LUTZKER, ELLIOT HOWARD, lawyer; b. Flushing, NY, Feb. 22, 1953; s. Stanley Lawrence and Mildred Lutzker; m. Jill Leslie Simon, Aug. 24, 1975; children: Stacey, Amanda. BA, SUNY, Stony Brook, 1974; JD, NY Law Sch., 1978. Bar: NY 1979, Fla. 1979, US Dist. Ct. (so. and ea. dists.) NY 1979. Atty. SEC, NYC, 1978-81; assoc. Bachner, Tally, Polevoy, Misher & Brinberg, NYC, 1981-85; ptnr. Snow Becker Krauss P.C., NYC, 1985—2004; counsel Robinson & Cole, LLP, NYC, 2004—06; ptnr. Phillips Nizer LLP, NYC, 2006—. Mem.: ABA (corp., banking law div.), NY State Bar Assn. (securities law com.). Jewish. Avocations: reading, sports. Home: 15 Kevin Ct Jericho NY 11753-1308 Office: Phillips Nizer LLP 666 Fifth Ave New York NY 10103 Office Phone: 212-841-0707. Business E-Mail: elutzker@phillipsnizer.com.

LUTZKER, JOEL E., lawyer; b. Queens, NY, Dec. 30, 1951; BA in Physics, cum laude, NYU, 1972, JD, 1975. Bar: NY 1976, Conn. 1977, US Patent & Trademark Office. Atty. Bryan & Bollo, Stamford, Conn., 1976—80, Amster, Rothstein & Ebenstein, NYC, 1985—2001; ptnr., intellectual property dept. Schulte Roth & Zabel LLP. Contbr. articles to profl. jour.; spkr. in field. Mem.: Intellectual Property Owner's Assn., Licensing Exec. Soc., Internat. Trade Commn. Trial Lawyers Assn., Am. Intellectual Property Law Assn., NY Intellectual Property Law Assn., ABA, NY State Bar Assn., Sigma Pi Sigma. Office: Schulte Roth & Zabel LLP 919 Third Ave New York NY 10022 Office Phone: 212-756-2520. Office Fax: 212-593-5955. Business E-Mail: joel.lutzker@srz.com.

LUVIANO, DAMIEN M., ophthalmologist; s. Damian and Teresa Luviano; m. Sonia Luviano, Mar. 6, 1999; children: Crystal, Hannah. BA with honors, U. Tex., Austin, 1997; MD, U. Tex., Dallas, 2003. Lic. physician Med. Bd. Calif., 2004, Tex. State Bd. Med. Examiners, 2004. Emergency triage dental specialist Harris County Dental Ctr., Houston, 1992—95; exec. asst. Enron Internat., Houston, 1996—97; tchr. HS Gary Job Corps., San Marcos, Tex., 1998; with chem. quality control Equistat, La Porte, Tex., 1999; gen. pediatric preceptor Parkland COPC Eastside Clinic, Dallas, 2000; intern neurology Childrens Hosp. Dallas, 2003; intern gen. surgery Meth. Hosp., Dallas, 2003—04, gen. surgeon, 2003—04; resident ophthalmology LA County, 2004—07; med. retina fellowship Vitreoretinal Cons., Houston, 2007—. Med. software cons. Skyscape website, Hudson, Mass., 2001—, Epocrates, San Mateo, Calif., 2004—; founder, pres. EyePalm website, LA, 2001—, OjosLatinos website, LA, 2004—. Author: Wills Eye Manual for Pocket PCs and PDAs, 2002; contbr. articles to profl. jours. Recruiter Prevent Blindness Am., Dallas, 2001—03; wish grantor Make-a-Wish Found., Dallas, 1998—2003. Dental specialist 10th med. detachment USAR, 1991—2000. Named one of Am.'s Top Surgeons, Consumer's Rsch. Coun. Am., 2007; scholar, Princeton Rev., 1998; Jesse Jones scholarship, U. Houston, 1994, Martin Luther King Jr. Cmty. Svc. scholarship, Southwestern Med. Sch., 2001, 2003. Master: Soc. Oftalmologos Latinos en Am. (pres. 2004); mem.: AMA (assoc.), ACS (assoc.), ACP (assoc.), ARVO, ORBIS, Am. Acad. Ophthalmology (cons. eye care registry 2006), Calif. Ophthalmology Soc., Am. Soc. Cataract and Refractive Surgery (scholarship 2005), Tex. Ophthal. Assn., Assn. Rsch. Vision in Ophthalmology, Tex. Med. Assn. (scholarship 1999), Am. Diabetes Assn., Smithsonian Nat. Postal Mus., Salk Inst., Ex-Students Assn. U. Tex. (hon.), Consumer Reports Rsch. Divsn. (assoc.). Independent. Methodist. Achievements include patents pending for mechanism and treatment of migraine headaches; invention of first ophthalmology photo atlas for PDAs. Avocations: stamp collecting/philately, travel, web page design, technology.

LUXENBERG, ARTHUR MARTIN, lawyer; b. NYC, Apr. 14, 1959; s. Irwin Eugene and Joan Florence (Aronson) L.; m. Randi Joy Beeber Luxenberg, Aug. 14, 1984; children: Elizabeth Jewel, Jacqueline Paige. Attended, Univ. Pa.; BA, Yeshiva Univ., NYC, 1981; JD, Cardozo Sch. Law, Yeshiva Univ., NYC, 1984. Bar: NY 1985, US Dist. Ct. (so. dist.) NY 1988, US Dist. Ct. (ea. dist.) NY 1988, US Ct. Appeals 2d cir. 1988. Assoc. law and appeals div. Morris J. Eisen P.C., NYC, 1984-86, dir. law and appeals div., 1986—; founding mem. & mng. ptnr. Weitz & Luxenberg, NYC, 1986—. Moot ct. judge Fordham U., NYC, 1987—88. Co-author: Practicing Law Institute Course Book, 1988. Trustee Schneider Children's Hosp.; v.p., mem. exec. bd. Young Israel of Great Neck, North Shore Hebrew Acad., pres.; mem. exec. com. Lawyers divsn. United Jewish Appeal; chmn. Days of Shame Holocaust Com., United Soup Kitchens; bd. dirs. U.S. Holocaust Mus., Mesorah Found., Juvenile Diabetes Found., Children's Med. Fund. Mem.: NY State Bar Assn., NY State Trial Lawyers Assn. (officer, 1st v.p.), Assn. Trial Lawyers City NY (bd. govs.), Trial Lawyers for Pub. Justice, Jewish Lawyers Guild (officer, bd. govs.). Office: Weitz & Luxenberg PC 180 Maiden Ln 17th Fl New York NY 10038-4925 Office Phone: 212-558-5500.

LUXENBERG, MALCOLM NEUWAHL, ophthalmologist, educator; b. Philipsburg, Pa., July 29, 1935; s. Maurice and Henrietta (Neuwahl) L.; m. Sandra Diane Rosen, June 16, 1957; children: Steven Neuwahl, Cathy Ann. Student, Tulane U., 1953-56; MD, U. Miami, Fla., 1960. Diplomate: Am. Bd. Ophthalmology. Intern Cin. Gen. Hosp., 1960-61; resident in neurology U. Vt. Affiliated Hosps., Burlington, 1961-63; resident in ophthalmology Bascom Palmer Eye Inst., U. Miami-Jackson Meml. Hosp., Miami, Fla., 1963-66; asst. prof. ophthalmology Coll. Medicine, U. Iowa, Iowa City, 1968-70; chief ophthalmology service VA Hosp., Iowa City, 1968-70; practice medicine specializing in ophthalmology West Palm Beach, Fla., 1970-72; clin. asst. prof. ophthalmology Bascom Palmer Eye Inst., Sch. Medicine, U. Miami, 1971-72; prof., chmn. dept. ophthalmology Med. Coll. Ga., Augusta, 1972-2000, prof. emeritus, 2000—. Cons. ophthalmology VA Hosp., Augusta, 1972—; sr. surgeon USPHS, 1966-68. Mem. editl. bd.: Archives of Ophthalmology, 1986-94. Recipient Outstanding Civilian Service Medal Dept. of Army, 1986. Mem. AMA, Am. Acad. Ophthalmology (hon. award 1986), Am. Ophthalmol. Soc., Assn. Univ. Profs. in Ophthalmology (pres. 1982-83), Ga. Soc. Ophthalmology, Med. Assn. Ga., Richmond County Med. Soc. Office: Med Coll Ga Dept Ophthalmology Augusta GA 30912 Home Phone: 706-736-5851; Office Phone: 706-721-1148.

LUXON, THOMAS HYATT, language educator, director; b. Darby, Pa., Apr. 26, 1954; s. Herbert Dawson and Doris Hyatt Luxon; m. Ivy Terry Schweitzer, June 15, 1988; children: Isaac Jesse Schweitzer Luxon, Rebekah Rosa Luxon Schweitzer. AB, Brown U., 1977; MA, U.Chgo., 1978, PhD, 1984. William Rainey Harper instr. U. Chgo., 1984—85; vis. asst. prof. English St. Lawrence U., Canton, NY, 1985—86; asst. prof. English Franklin and Marshall Coll., Lancaster, Pa., 1987—88, Dartmouth Coll., Hanover, NH, 1988—94, assoc. prof. English, 1994—2005, prof. English, 2005—; Cheheyl prof., dir. Dartmouth Ctr. for Advancement of Learning, Hanover, NH, 2004—. Author: Literal Figures: Puritan Allegory and the Reformation Crisis in Representation, 1995, Single Imperfection: Milton, Marriage and Friendship, 2005; editor: (online edit.) The John Milton Reading Room. Recipient Bess Award, Renascence Edits., 1998, Milton Reading Rm. Recognition award, Internet Scout Project, U. Wis., 1999, Webivore award, Learning Co., 1999, Swan award, Internet Shakespeare Edits., U. Victoria, BC, 2003; Charlotte W. Newcombe Dissertation fellowship, Woodrow Wilson Fellowship Found., 1983/1984, Ind. Study and Rsch. fellowship, Nat. Endowment for the Humanities, 1986-1987, Jr. Faculty fellowship, Dartmouth Coll., 1992, Cheheyl Fellowship in Tech. and Tchg., 2002, Russell Ladd Newcomb 1926 fellow, 2005-2006. Mem.: MLA, Milton Soc. of Am. (exec. com. 2004—), Internat. John Bunyan Soc. (pres. 2004—). Avocations: scuba diving, skiing, sailing. Office: Dartmouth Ctr Advancement of Learning 6247 Baker Berry Hanover NH 03755 Office Phone: 603-646-2655. Office Fax: 603-646-6906. E-mail: thomas.h.luxon@dartmouth.edu.

LUXTON, JANE CHARLOTTE, lawyer; b. Phila., June 25, 1951; d. Elvin L. and Charoltte M. (Herring) Luxton: m. Charles Matz Horn, May 29, 1976; children: Andrew Luxton Horn, Caroline Charlotte Horn. BA, Harvard U., 1973; JD, Cornell U., 1976. Bar: D.C. 1976. Atty. adv. to commr. FTC, Washington, 1976-78; trial atty. US Dept. Justice, Washington, 1978-81; assoc. Steptoe & Johnson LLP, Washington, 1981-86, Bell Atlantic, Washington, 1986-89; assoc., then ptnr. Prather Seeger Doolittle & Farmer, Washington, 1989-94; ptnr. Vedder Price, Kammholz PC, Washington, 1994-95, Seeger Potter Richardson Luxton Joselow & Brooks LLP, Washington, 1995-99, King & Spalding LLP, Washington, 1999—2007; gen. counsel, Nat. Oceanic & Atmospheric Adminstrn. (NOAA) US Dept. Commerce, Washington, 2007—. Mem. ABA, D.C. Bar Assn. Republican. Office: Nat Oceanic & Atmospheric Adminstrn (NOAA) US Dept Commerce 14th St & Constitution Ave Rm 6217 Washington DC 20230

LUYENDYK, BRUCE PETER, geophysicist, educator, academic administrator; b. Freeport, NY, Feb. 23, 1943; s. Pieter Johannes and Frances Marie (Blakeney) L.; 1 child, Loren Taylor Luyendyk. BS Geophysics, San Diego State Coll., 1965; PhD Marine Geophysics, Scripps Inst. Oceanography, 1969. Geophysicist Arctic Sci. and Tech. Lab. USN Electronics Lab. Ctr., 1965; lectr. San Diego State Coll., 1967-68; postgrad rsch. geologist Scripps Inst. Oceanography, 1969; postdoctoral fellow dept. geology and geophysics Woods Hole Oceanographic Instn., 1969-70, asst. scientist dept. geology and geophysics, 1970-73; asst. prof. U. Calif., Santa Barbara, 1973-75, assoc. prof., 1975-81, prof. dept. geol. scis., 1981—, acting dir. Inst. Crustal Studies, 1987-88, dir. Inst. Crustal Studies, 1988-97, chair dept. geol. scis., 1997—2003, assoc. dean, 2005—. Participant, chief sci. oceanographic cruises, geol. expdns.; coord. bd. So. Calif. Integrated GPS Network, 1997-2000. Editorial bd. Geology, 1975-79, Marine Geophysical Rschs., 1976-92, Jour. Geophysical Rsch., 1982-84, Tectonophysics, 1988-92, Pageoph, 1988-95; contbr. articles to profl. jours., chpts. to books, encys. Co-recipient Newcomb Cleveland prize AAAS, 1980; recipient Antarctic Svc. medal U.S. NSF, Dept. Navy, 1990, Disting. Alumni award San Diego State U., 1983, numerous rsch. grants, 1971—. Fellow Geol. Soc. Am., Am. Geophys. Union. Office: U Calif Santa Barbara Dept Earth Scis Santa Barbara CA 93106 Home Phone: 805-967-0259. Business E-Mail: luyendyk@geol.ucsb.edu.

LUYTEN, JAMES REINDERT, research institute director, oceanographer; b. Mpls., Dec. 26, 1941; s. Willem Jacob and Willemina (Miedema) L.; m. Meredith Fuller, June 18, 1966; children: Dylan, Laura, Elijah. AB, Reed Coll., 1963; AM, Harvard U., 1965, PhD, 1969. Rsch. fellow Harvard U., Cambridge, Mass., 1968-70; asst. scientist Woods Hole (Mass.) Oceanographic Instn., 1971-74, assoc. scientist, 1971-86, sr. scientist, 1986—, chmn. phys. oceanography, 1991-94, assoc. dir. rsch., 1994—96, sr. assoc. dir. & dir. rsch., 1996—2002, exec. v.p. & dir. rsch., 2002—05, exec. v.p., 2005—06, acting pres. & dir., 2006—. Vis. scientist Nat. Ctr. for Atmospheric Rsch., Boulder, Colo., 1983; mem. Naval Rsch. Adv. Com., 1997—2003. Mem.: Am. Meteorological Soc. (awards com. 1998—2003). Office: Woods Hole Oceanographic Instn Fenno House MS 40A 183 Oyster Pond Rd Woods Hole MA 02543 Office Fax: 508-457-2190, 508-457-2036. Business E-Mail: jluyten@whoi.edu.

LUZ, VIRGINIA OLIVAR, dietician; b. Antique, Philippines, May 21, 1934; came to U.S., 1960; d. Adriano and Expectacion Xavier (Salazar) Olivar; m. Zosimo Umali Luz, 1965; children: Cecilia Luz-Cariaga, Patricia Ann Luz-Holgado, Melinda M. Luz-Royall. BS in Nutrition, U. Philippines, 1957. Registered dietitian, Am. Dietetic Assn. Dietetic intern Brigham Women's Hosp., 1961-62; clin. dietitian Lemuell Shattuck Hosp., Jamaica Plain, Mass., 1962-63, Temple U. Hosp., Phila., 1963-65, Santa Cabrini Hosp., Montreal, Can., 1966-67, Roxborough Meml. Hosp., Phila., 1966; chief dietitian Nazareth Hosp., Phila., 1967-77; clin. dietitian Temple U. Hosp., Phila., 1977-87, Nazareth Hosp., Phila., 1994—; gen. renal nutritionist Biomed. Applications (name now Fresenius Med. Care), Phila., 1987—. Historian Mutya Philippine Dance Co., 1990—. Founder Mutya Philippine Dance Co., St. Augustine, Church Hall, Phila., 1990—; lectr., historian Pub. Grade Schs., Phila., 1963; pres. Filipino Am. Assn. Phila., Girard Avenue, 1980-82, Phila. Philippine Lions Club, 1982-84. Named Mother of Yr., Filipino Am. Assn. Phila., 1981; recipient Cultural Appreciation award Gov.'s Commn. on Heritage, Pa., 1995. Mem. Am. Dietetic Assn., Coun. on Renal Nurtition Network, Mutya Philippine Dance Co. Roman Catholic. Avocations: folklorist, modeling ethnic, drama, singing. Home: 706 Sunflower Ave Langhorne PA 19047-3748 Office: Nazareth Hosp & Fresnius Med Care 6201 Holme Ave Philadelphia PA 19152

LUZA, RADOMIR VACLAV, historian, educator; b. Prague, Czechoslovakia, Oct. 17, 1922; s. Vojtech V. and Milada (Vecera) L.; m. Libuse Ladislava Podhrazska, Feb. 5, 1949; children: Radomir V., Sabrina. JuDr, U. Brno, Czechoslovakia, 1948; MA, NYU, 1958, PhD, 1959. Assoc. prof. modern European history La. State U., New Orleans, 1966-67; prof. history Tulane U., New Orleans, 1967—. Scholar-in-residence Rockefeller Found., Bellagio Study Ctr., 1988; prof. gen. history Masaryk U., Brno, 1993—. Author: The Transfer of the Sudeten Germans, 1964, History of the International Socialist Youth Movement, 1970, (with V. Mamatey) A History of the Czechoslovak Republic, 1918-1948, 1973, Austro-German Relations in the Anschluss Era, 1975, Österreich und die Grossdeutsche Idee in der NS-Zeit, 1977, Geschichte der Tschechoslowakischen Republik 1918-1948, 1980, A History of the Resistance in Austria, 1938-1945, 1984, Der Widerstand in Österreich, 1938-1945, 1985, La République Tchécoslovaque 1918-1948, 1987, The Czechoslovak Social Democracy Abroad, 1948-1989, 2001, The Hitler Kiss: A Memoir of the Czech Resistance, 2002, Hitlerovo Objeti Chapters from the Czech Resistance, 2006; mem. editl. bd. East European Quar., Contemporary Austrian Studies. With Czech Resistance, 1939—45, WWII, col. Czech Army, 1995, ret. N, Czech Army. Recipient all Czechoslovak mil. decorations; prize Theodor Körner Found., Vienna, 1965, J. Hlavka Hon. medal Czechoslovak Acad. Arts and Scis., 1992, T.G. Masaryk medal Pres. of Czech Rep., 1996, Austrian Cross of Honor Sci. and Art I. Class, 1997, Meml. medal Czech Rep., 2000; grantee Social Rsch. Coun., Am. Philos. Soc., Coun. Learned Socs., Fulbright Com., NEH. Mem. Am. Hist. Assn., Czechoslovak History Conf. Home: 2313 Twin Silo Dr Blue Bell PA 19422-3281 Office: Tulane U Dept History New Orleans LA 70118 Office Phone: 215-699-4152. Personal E-mail: radomirprof@aol.com.

LY, HINH, science educator; arrived in U.S., 1987; s. Moc Ly and So Ngo; m. Yuying Liang. BS with honors, UCLA, 1995, MA with honors, 1998; PhD, U. N.C., 2000; postgrad., U. Calif., San Francisco, 2000—03. Asst. prof. dept. pathology and lab. medicine Emory U. Sch. Medicine, Atlanta, 2003—. Contbr. articles to profl. jours. Various scholarships, fellowships, and rsch. grants, NIH, Am. Cancer Soc., The Leukemia and Lymphoma Soc. Am., AA&MDSIF. Mem.: Am. Soc. for Microbiologists, Am. Soc. Hematology, Am. Assn. for Cancer Rsch. Achievements include research in hematology, virology and cancer biology. Office: Emory Univ Sch Medicine 615 Michael St Rm 105L Whitehead Bldg Atlanta GA 30322 Office Phone: 404-712-2841.

LYALL, KATHARINE CULBERT, former academic administrator, economist, educator; b. Lancaster, Pa., Apr. 26, 1941; d. John D. and Eleanor G. Lyall. BA in Econs., Cornell U., 1963, PhD in Econs., 1969; MBA, NYU, 1965. Economist Chase Manhattan Bank, NYC, 1963-65; asst. prof. econs. Syracuse U., 1969-72; assoc. prof. econs. Johns Hopkins U., Balt., 1972-77, dir. grad. program in pub. policy, 1979-81; dep. asst. sec. for econs. Office Econ. Affairs, HUD, Washington, 1977-79; v.p. acad. affairs U. Wis. Sys., 1981-85; prof. of econ. U. Wis., Madison, 1982—; acting pres. U. Wis. Sys., Madison, 1985-86, 91-92, exec. v.p., 1986-91, pres., 1992—2004, pres. emeritus, 2005—. Bd. dirs. Marshall & Ilsley Bank, Alliant, Carnegie Found. for Advancement of Tchg. Author: Reforming Public Welfare, 1976, Microeconomic Issues of the 70s, 1978, True Genius of America At Risk, 2006. Mem. Mcpl. Securities Rulemaking Bd., Washington, 1990-93. Mem. Am. Econ. Assn., Phi Beta Kappa. Business E-Mail: klyall@wisc.edu.

LYALL, LYNN, consumer products company executive; Sr. v.p. fin., info. svcs. & tech. Cadbury Schweppes, PLC; exec. v.p., CFO Blockbuster Entertainment, Inc.; exec. v.p. Alticor Inc., 1999—, CFO. Office: Alticor Inc 7575 Fulton St E Ada MI 49355

LYBARGER, JERRY, lawyer; b. 1947; BA, Northeast Mo. State U., 1969; JD, Calif. Western Sch. Law, 1972. Bar: 1973. Atty. Furniture Brands Internat., 1977—80, asst. gen. counsel, 1980—96, asst. gen. counsel, asst. sec., 1996—97, assoc. gen. counsel, dir. legal services, asst. sec., 1997—2000, gen. counsel, asst. sec., 2000—. Office: Furniture Brands Internat 101 S Hanley Rd Saint Louis MO 63105 E-mail: j.lybarger@furniturebrands.com.

LYBECKER, MARTIN EARL, lawyer; b. Lincoln, Nebr., Feb. 11, 1945; s. Earl Edward and Jeanette Frances (Kiefer) L.; m. Andrea Kristine Tollefson, Dec. 27, 1969; children: Carl Martin, Neil Anders. BBA, U. Wash., 1967, JD, 1970; LLM in Taxation, NYU, 1971; LLM, U. Pa., 1973. Bar: Wash. 1970, D.C. 1972, Pa. 1982. Atty. investment mgmt. div. SEC, Washington, 1972-75, assoc. dir. div., 1978-81; assoc. prof. SUNY, Buffalo, 1975-78; ptnr. Drinker Biddle & Reath, Washington, 1981-87, Ropes & Gray, Washington, 1987—2002, Wilmer Cutler Pickering Hale and Dorr LLP, Washington, 2002—. Adj. prof. Georgetown U., Washington, 1974-75; vis. assoc. prof. Duke U., Durham, N.C., 1977-78, sr. lecturing fellow in law, 2000—. Contbr. articles to law revs. Fellow U. Pa. Ctr. for Study of Fin. Instns., 1971-72. Mem.: ABA (mem. subcom. on investment cos. and investment advisers, mem. com. on fed. regulation of securities bus. law sect., former chmn. com. devels. in investment svcs. bus. law sect., former chmn. com. banking law), Am. Law Inst., Univ. Club. Washington. Home: 2806 Daniel Rd Bethesda MD 20815-3149 Office: Wilmer Cutler Pickering Hale and Dorr LLP 1875 Pennsylvannia Ave NW Washington DC 20006 Home Phone: 301-656-8337; Office Phone: 202-663-6240. Business E-Mail: martin.lybecker@wilmerhale.com.

LYCETT, SARA F. See **FINNEGAN, SARA**

LYDDANE, ANNE ALEXANDRA, retired writer; b. Washington, Nov. 24, 1917; d. John Clarence and Mildred Katherine (Linder) L. Student, Fla. State U., 1936-38. Staff writer Llewellyn Publs., St. Paul, 1976-96, ret., 1996. Tchr., lectr. Asheville (N.C.) C.C., 1986-96, Charlottesville (Va.) C.C., 1986-96; freelance spkr., lectr. throughout U.S., 1986-96. Author: Kaleidoscope, 1985, Astrological Color Magic and You, 1985, Travellers' Rest, 1991, Angels, Incorporated, 1995, Love Is An Energy That Never Dies, 2000. Avocations: swimming, travel, historical research, gardening, tutoring. Home: Apt 114 12105 Ambassador Dr Colorado Springs CO 80921-3647

LYDDANE, JOHN LAWRENCE ASHTON, lawyer; b. Aug. 22, 1947; s. Russell Hancock and Lucy Barnes (Ashton) L.; m. Virginia Ciurleo, Jan. 14, 1983; children: Ashley Elizabeth, Alexandra Marie, Ariel Ashton, Amanda Scott. AB, U. Rochester, 1969; JD, Syracuse U., 1972. Bar: N.Y. 1973, U.S. Dist. Ct. (no. dist.) N.Y. 1973, U.S. Dist. Ct. (so. and ea. dists.) N.Y. 1975, U.S. Ct. Appeals (2d cir.) 1975, U.S. Supreme Ct. 1976. Asst. atty. gen. N.Y. State, Albany, 1972—73; assoc. Harry H. Lipsig, NYC, 1973—75, Martin, Clearwater & Bell, NYC, 1975—78, ptnr., 1978—. Panelist Supreme Ct. Malpractice Panel, Bronx, 1979—87; commodore Belle Haven Club, 2002—03. Commr., clk. Belle Haven Tax Dist., 2005—; mem. U. Rochester Trustees Coun. Fellow: Am. Coll. Trial Lawyers; mem.: Belle Haven Club (commodore), Univ. Club (N.Y.C.). Republican. Episcopalian. Home: 29 Meadow Wood Dr Greenwich CT 06830-7023 Office: Martin Clearwater & Bell LLP 220 E 42nd St New York NY 10017-5806 Home Phone: 203-661-5862; Office Phone: 212-697-3122. E-mail: lyddaj@mcblaw.com.

LYDEN, DAVID CHARLES, oncologist, cell biologist; s. Thomas Francis and Lillian Denise Lyden. MD, Brown Med. Sch., Providence, 1989; PhD, U. Vt., Burlington, 1985. Pediatric residency Duke U. Med. Ctr., Durham, NC, 1989—92; pediat. hematology-oncology fellow and chief fellow Meml. Sloan-Kettering Cancer Ctr., NYC, 1992—95, clin. instr. pediat. neurooncology, 1995—99; asst. prof. pediat., cell and devel. biology Weill Med. Coll. Cornell U. and Meml. Sloan-Kettering Cancer Ctr., 2002—04, assoc. prof. pediat., cell and devel. biology, 2004—. Sci. advisor Children's Brain Tumor Found., NYC, 2000—; dir. cellular oncology Children's Cancer and Blood Found. Labs., 2002—. Contbr. scientific papers to profl. jour. Named Disting. Alumni, Brown Med. Sch., 2003; recipient Tchg. Sci. award, Harlem Children's Soc., 2004, Mahajani award, Nature, 2006; grantee, Children's Brain Tumor Found., 1998—2000, Emerald Found., 2001—, Nat. Cancer Inst. NIH, 2002—, NIH, 2002—, Theodore A. Rapp Found., 2003—, The Malcolm Wiener Found., 2006, NIH Clin. Rsch. Ctr., 2006, Princess Takamatsu Lectureship award, 2006; scholar, Doris Duke Charitable Found., 2000—03. Fellow: Linnean Soc. London; mem.: Internat. Soc. Biological Therapy of Cancer, Am. Soc. Cell Biology, Metastasis Rsch. Soc. (assoc.), Fulbright Assn., AAAS, Sigma Xi, Soc. Pediat. Rsch. (assoc.). Achievements include development of monoclonal antibodies that block the formation of new blood vessels in tumors and importantly block the nest of stem cells that are required to start metastasis in distant sites; discovery of first genes known as Id genes involved in angiogenesis or the formation of new blood vessels in tumors; two adult bone marrow-derived stem cells that contribute to the formation of new blood vessels in tumors; patents for Use of Vascular Endothelial Growth Factor Receptor 1 Cells in Treating and Monitoring Cancer and in Screening for Chemotherapeutics; first to discover the Pre-metastatic Niche or all the early events that take place in a distant organ preceding the implantation of tumor cells. Office: Dept Pediat Weill Cornell 515 E 71st St Box 284 New York NY 10021 Office Phone: 212-746-3941. Business E-Mail: dcl2001@med.cornell.edu.

LYDIC, GARRETT WALTON, elementary school educator; Edn. Tech. Cert., Del. Tech. & Cmty. Coll.; BS in Health Svc. Adminstrn., James Madison Univ., Harrisburg, Va., 1992, MS in Health, Fitness Promotion, 1995; MA in Tchg., Salisbury (Md.) State Univ., 2000. Adj. instr., kinesiology, human anatomy James Madison Univ., 1996—2001; tchr. Paul Lawrence Dunbar Elem. Sch., Laurel, Md., 2001; now tchr. North Laurel Elem. Sch., Laurel, Md. Named Del. Tchr. of Yr., 2006. Mem.: NEA, Laurel Edn. Assn., Nat. Fedn. State H.S. Assns., Internat. Assn. of Approved Basketball Officials. Office: North Laurel Elem Sch 300 Wilson St Laurel DE 19956 Business E-Mail: glydic@laurel.k12.de.us.*

LYDIC, MICHAEL LYNN, medical educator, obstetrician; b. Pitts., Mar. 21, 1963; s. Fred William and Marianne Lydic; m. Sandra Rosario Ortega, June 25, 1988; children: Michael Andrew, Maria Christina. MD, Hahnemann U., Phila., 1989. Lic. Gen. Ob-Gyn Am. Bd. Obstetricians and Gynecologists, 1998, Reproductive Endocrinology and Infertility Am. Bd. Obstetricians and Gynecologists, 2000. Physician Crozer Chester Med. Ctr., Chester, Pa., 1995—96; assoc. dir. Reproductive Endocrine Associates, San Diego, Calif., 1996—98; clin. asst. prof. SUNY-Stony Brook Sch. of Medicine, Dept Ob-Gyn, Divsn. Reproductive Endocrinology and Infertility, SUNY-Stony Brook Sch. of Medicine, Dept Ob/Gyn, Divsn. Reproductive Endocrinology, Stony Brook, NY, 1998—; med. student clerkship dir. SUNY Stonybrook Sch. of Medicine, Dept Ob/Gyn, Stony Brook, NY, 2004—. Named one of Nat. Top Drs., Castle Connolly Ltd., 2006. Mem.: Androgen Excess Soc. (licentiate), Soc. Reproductive Surgeons (licentiate), The Endocrine Soc. (licentiate), Am. Coll. Ob-Gyns (licentiate), Am. Soc. Reproductive Medicine (licentiate). Liberal. Roman Catholic. Achievements include research in use of chromium picolinate in treatment of polycystic ovarian syndrome. Avocations: guitar, music, drums. Office: SUNY UMC HSC T9-080 Dept Ob-Gyn Stony Brook NY 11794-8091 Office Phone: 631-444-2745. Office Fax: 631-444-7740. Business E-Mail: mlydic@notes2.cc.sunysb.edu.

LYDON, AMANDA, chef; Undergrad Harvard Univ. Chef Truc, Radius, Chez Henri, Cambridge, Mass., Metro Brasserie, Boston, 2001—, UpStairs on the Square. Nominee James Beard award, 2000; named Best New Chef, Boston Mag., 2000; named one of Best Young Chefs in Am., Food & Wine Mag., Boston's Rising Stars, StarChefs.com, 2006. Office: UpStairs on the Square 91 Winthrop St Cambridge MA 02138 Office Phone: 617-864-1933.

LYDON, NICHOLAS B. (NICK LYDON), biochemist, pharmaceutical executive, researcher; b. Feb. 27, 1957; BSc, U. Leeds, Eng.; PhD, U. Dundee, Scotland, 1984. With Schering Plough, 1985; oncology rsch. team Ciba-Geigy AG (now Novartis Pharmaceuticals AG), 1985—87; founder, pres., CEO Kinetix Pharmaceutical Inc. (acquired by Amgen, Inc.), Medford, Mass., 1997—2000; v.p. small molecule drug discovery Amgen, Inc., Thousand Oaks, Calif., 2000—03; with Verizon Pharmaceutical Co., Calif., 2002; founder Granite Biopharma LLC, Jackson Hole, Wyo. Past mem. Novartis Oncology Mgmt. Com.; bd. dirs. Ambit Biosciences; advisor Avalon Ventures. Recipient Sci. Prize, Warren Alpert Found., 2000, Bruce F. Cain Meml. award, Am. Assn. Cancer Rsch., 2002, Charles F. Kettering prize, GM Cancer Rsch. Found., 2002, Bruce F. Cain Meml. award, Am. Assn. Cancer Rsch., 2002. Achievements include development of leukemia drug, Gleevac, that effectively treats chronic megelogenous leukemia and other forms of cancer. Office: Avalon Ventures 888 Prospect St Ste 320 La Jolla CA 92037

LYDON, THOMAS J., federal judge; BA, U. Maine, 1952; LLB, Georgetown U., 1955, LLM, 1957. Bars: Maine, DC. Supervisory trial atty. US Dept. Justice, Washington, 1955—72; commr. US Ct. Claims, Washington, 1972—82; judge US Ct. Fed. Claims, Washington, 1982—87, sr. judge, 1987—. Served in USN, 1945—46. Office: US Ct of Fed Claims 717 Madison Pl NW Washington DC 20439-0002*

LYERLA, BRADFORD PETER, lawyer; b. Savanna, Ill., Aug. 2, 1954; s. Ralph Herbert and Nancy Lee (Nelson) L.; m. Marilyn Wyse, Aug. 18, 1979; 3 children. BA, U. Ill., 1976, JD, 1980. Bar: Ill. 1980, U.S. Dist. Ct. (no. dist.) Ill. 1980, U.S. Dist. Ct. (no. dist.) Ind. 1982, U.S. Dist. Ct. (no. dist.) Calif. 1991, U.S. Dist. Ct. (ctrl. dist.) Ill. 1991, U.S. Dist. Ct. (no. dist.) Tex. 1999, U.S. Dist. Ct. (ea. dist.) Wis. 2000, U.S. Dist. Ct. Nebr. 1998, U.S. Dist. Ct. Colo. 2004, U.S. Ct. Appeals (7th cir.) 1983, U.S. Ct. Appeals (fed. cir.) 1991, U.S. Ct. Appeals (2d cir.) 2002, U.S. Supreme Ct. 1995. Trial lawyer, Chgo.; sr. ptnr. Marshall, Gerstein & Borun, Chgo. Lectr. on litigation and intellectual property law. Author publications in field; editor U. Ill. Law Rev., 1978-80. Bd. dirs. North Suburban Bd. of the Heartland Alliance, Wilmette, Ill., 1987-96, pres. 1993-94; bd. dirs. Traveler's and Immigrant's Aid, Chgo., 1991-95; bd. dirs., sec. Youth Svcs. Project, Inc., Chgo., 1987-91; mem. U. Ill. Pres.'s Coun.; founding mem. Cribbett Soc., U. Ill. Coll. Law; mem. Saints Faith Hope and Charity, Winnetka, Ill. Recipient John Powers Crowley Justice award People's Uptown Law Ctr., 1989. Fellow Am. Bar Found. (life); mem. ABA (editor litigation sect. intellectual properties litigation quar. 1990—, intellectual property sect. com. on unfair competition litigation), Ill. Bar Assn. (sect. coun. gen. practice sect. 1984-85, intellectual property sect. 1989—, co-editor intellectual property newsletter 1989-95, chair 1996-97), Chgo. Bar Assn. (legal ethics), Am. Intellectual Property Law Assn. (antitrust and fed. lit. com.), Intellectual Property Law Assn. Chgo. (patent litigation), Univ. Club Chgo., Sunset Ridge Country Club, Phi Beta Kappa, Phi Kappa Phi. Office: Marshall Gerstein & Borun 233 S Wacker Dr 6300 Sears Tower Chicago IL 60606 Office Phone: 312-474-6300. E-mail: blyerla@marshallip.com.

LYERLY, ELAINE MYRICK, advertising executive; b. Charlotte, NC, Nov. 26, 1951; d. J.M. and Annie Mary (Myrick) L. AA in Advt. and Comml. Design, Cen. Piedmont Community Coll., 1972. Freelance designer Sta. WBTV, Charlotte, NC, 1972; fashion illustrator Matthews Belk, Gastonia, NC, 1972-73; designer Monte Curry Mktg. and Communication Svcs., Charlotte, 1973-74, exec. v.p., 1974-77; pres. Repro/Graphics, Charlotte, 1975-77, Lyerly Agy. Inc., Charlotte, 1977—. Organizing dir. First Trust Bank. Illustrator: Mister Cookie Breakfast Cookbook, 1985. Former chmn. regional blood com. Greater Carolinas chpt. ARC, 1990-93, mem. nat. implementation com., 1991, chair nat. conv., 2001, mem. nat. bd. govs., 2002-, Red Cross, nat. exec. com. and chair pub. support, nat. co-chair task force non-episodic fundraising, vice chmn. nat. bd. govs., 2006, 07; bd. dirs. United Way, 1996, YMCA, Women's Impact Fund, 2003-, Levine Mus. of New South; bd. dirs., chair Child Care Resources, Inc., 2003-, Women's Impact Fund, 2002-; mem. bd. advisors Belmont Abbey Coll. Named Bus. Woman of Yr., Shearson Lehman Hutton/Queens Coll., 1989, N.C. Young Careerist Bus. and Profl. Women's Club, 1981; recipient ACE award Women in Comms., 1993, CPCC Hagemeyer award, 1996, Schley Lyons Leadership Charlotte award, 1999, Bus. Jour. Top 25 Women of Achievement award 2001. Mem. Women Execs., Women Bus. Owners (adv. coun., Leadership award 1990, Woman Bus. Owner of Yr. award 1994), Pub. Rels. Soc. Am. (Counselors Acad. 1985—), Charlotte C. of C. (bd. dirs., diversity coun., long-range planning com., Bus. Woman of Yr. award 1985), Hadassah. Republican. Jewish. Office: Lyerly Agy Inc 4819 Park Rd Charlotte NC 28209-3274 E-mail: elyerly@lyerly.com.

LYFORD, CABOT, sculptor; b. Sayre, Pa., May 22, 1925; s. Frederic Eugene and Eleanor (Cabot) L.; m. Joan Ardyth Richmond, June 22, 1953; children: Matthew, Julia, Thaddeus. BFA, Cornell U., 1950. Exec. trainee NBC, NYC, 1952-54; producer and dir. J. Walter Thompson, NYC, 1954-57, Sta. WGBH-TV, Boston, 1957-59; program mgr. Sta. WENH-TV, Durham, N.H., 1959-63; chmn. Dept. Art The Phillips Exeter (N.H.) Acad., 1963-86. Prin. sculptures include pub. monuments in Portland, Maine and Portsmouth, N.H., Berwick, Maine; represented in permanent collections at Portland Mus., Chattanooga Mus., Indpls. Mus., Wichita (Kans.) Mus., Ogunquit (Maine) Mus., Currier Gallery, Manchester, N.H., Addison Gallery, Andover, Mass., Theme sculpture New Bedford (Mass.) Whaling Mus.e With inf. U.S. Army, 1943-46, PTO. Recipient Sculpture prize Nat. Design Acad., 1990. Home: 4 Fish Point Rd New Harbor ME 04554-4606 Office Phone: 207-677-2795.

LYFORD, RONALD LEE, music educator; s. Lowell Horace Lyford and Betty Louise Hufty. AA in arts, Clark Coll., 1965; BA in edn., Ctr. Wash. State Coll., 1967; MA in music edn., Ctrl. Wash. State Coll., 1973. Music tchr. Thorp Sch. Dist., Wash., 1967—68, Vancouver Sch. Dist., Wash., 1968—87, Oak Tree Sch., Forrest Grove, Oreg., 2002—03, Cornelias Luth. Sch., Oreg., 2002—03, Battle Ground Sch. Dist., Battle Ground, Wash., 2003, Nogales Sch. Dist., Ariz., 2004—06. Tchr. brass seminar, Germany, 1979—80; music festival judge Nogales Sch. Dist., Ariz., 2004—06, dir. Nogales elem. honor band, 2005—06. Performer: Brass Octet, 1979—80, German Band, 2006—07, Brit. Brass Band, 2006—07, Cmty. Band, 2006, (handbell choir) Chamber Orch., 2007. Treasurer Faith Bapt. Ch., Vancouver, Wash., 1984—94. Recipient Arion award, Battle Ground Sch. Dist., Wash., 1963. Mem.: NEA, Am. String Tchrs. Assn., Ariz. Music Educators Assn. Avocations: woodcarving, instrument repair, furniture refinishing. Office Phone: 520-223-0847. E-mail: ronlyford@aol.com.

LYJAK CHORAZY, ANNA JULIA, pediatrician, educator, retired health facility administrator; d. Walter and Cecilia (Swiatkowski) Lyjak; m. Chester John Chorazy, May 6, 1961; children: Paula Ann Chorazy Peters, Mary Ellen Chorazy-Cuccaro, Mark Edward Chorazy. BS, Waynesburg Coll., 1958; MD, Women's Med. Coll. Pa., 1960. Diplomate Am. Bd. Pediat. Intern St. Francis Gen. Hosp., Pitts., 1960-61; resident in pediat., tchg. fellow Children's Hosp. Pitts., 1961-63, pediatrician, devel. clinic, 1966-75; pediat. house physician Western Pa. Hosp., Pitts., 1963-66; med. dir. Rehab. Instn. Pitts., 1975-98, Children's Inst., Pitts., 1998—2001, interim med. dir., 2002—03. Clin. asst. prof. pediat. Children's Hosp. Pitts. and U. Pitts. Sch. Medicine, 1971—94, clin. assoc. prof. pediat., 1994—2001; pediat. cons. Children's Home Pitts., 1985—2001. Author chpts. to books. Co-chmn. EACH Joint Planning and Assessment, Pitts., 1980-85; mem. adv. com. 10th Nat. Conf. on Child Abuse, Pitts., 1993. Recipient Miracle Maker award, Children's Miracle Network, 1995, Disting. Alumni award, Waynesburg Coll., 2002. Fellow Am. Acad. Pediat.; mem. Pitts. Pediat. Soc. Avocations: reading, comedy, theater, music, opera. Home: 131 Washington Rd Pittsburgh PA 15221-4437 Home Phone: 412-242-2124. Personal E-mail: cjcajc@comcast.net.

LYLE, ROBERT EDWARD, chemist; b. Atlanta, Jan. 26, 1926; s. Robert Edward and Adaline (Cason) L.; m. Gloria Gilbert, Aug. 28, 1947 (dec. Dec. 1996); m. Anne Carroll Kohl, Aug. 1, 1997. BA, Emory U., 1945, MS, 1946; PhD, U. Wis., Madison, 1949. Asst. prof. Oberlin Coll., Ohio, 1949-51; asst. prof. U. N.H., Durham, 1951-53, assoc. prof., 1953-57, prof., 1957-76; prof., chmn. dept. chemistry U. North Tex., Denton, 1977-79; v.p. chemistry, chem. engr. S.W Rsch. Inst., San Antonio, 1979-91; v.p. GRL Cons., San Antonio, 1992—97, pres., 1997—. Vis. prof. U. Va., Charlottesville, 1973-74, U. Grenoble, France, 1976; adj. prof. Bowdoin Coll., Brunswick, Maine, 1975-79, U. Tex., San Antonio, 1985-2001. Mem. editl. bd. Index Chemicus, 1976—. USPHS fellow Oxford U., Eng., 1965; recipient honor scroll award Mass. chpt. Am. Inst. Chemistry, 1971; Harry and Carol Mosher co-awardee, 1986. Fellow AAAS; mem. Am. Chem. Soc. (councilor 1965-84, 86-92, medicinal chemistry divsn.), Royal Soc. Chemistry, Alpha Chi Sigma (editor Hexagon 1992-99, Kuebler award 1998). Methodist. Office: GRL Cons 12814 Kings Forest Dr San Antonio TX 78230-1511 Personal E-mail: geegeel@aol.com.

LYLE, VALARIE GAY, art educator, artist; d. James Franklin and Phyllis Eggers Lyle. BFA, Ringling Sch. Art Design, 1989; MFA, East Tenn. State U., 2001. Calendar editor Museums NY Mag., 1984—86, 1994—96; adj. art instr. East Tenn. State U., Johnson City, Tenn., 2001—03, N.E. State CC, Johnson City, 2002, Va. Highlands CC, Abingdon, 2003—04, Va. Intermont Coll., Bristol, 2005—. Art advisor, student art and lit. mag. The Mockingbird, East Tenn. State U., Johnson City, 2002—05. Exhibitions include Who We Are: The Figure in the 21st Century, A Difference of Opinion, Appalachian Corridors, Charleston, W.Va., The Figurative Gallery of Contemporary Art, From the Bar; New York City, 3.10 Exhibition by Peter Suschin, Nat. Conf. Edn. in Ceramic Arts, Bklyn. Waterfront Artists Coalition, Ise Foundation, NYC. Bd. mem. NC Folk Art Soc., 2004—05. Recipient Career Awards in Art, Nat. Soc. of Arts & Letters, Hono, HI, 1984, Gold Addy award of excellence, Tri-City Metro Advt.

Fedn., 2004, 2005; grantee Exhbn. grant, Artist's Space, 1991; scholar Outstanding Fine Arts Student Scholarship, Binney & Smith Artist Materials Mfg. Co., Ethel and Stanley Glen Scholarship, Ringling Sch. of art and Design, 1987, Richard & Va. Crossley Scholarship, Ringling Sch. Art & Design, 1988. Mem.: NC Folk Art Soc., Tenn. Assn. Craft Artists, Nat. Coun. Edn. in Ceramic Arts, Coll. Art Assn., Peter Pugger Clay Pugmills (spokesperson 2003—), Knoxville Contra Dancers, Women's Mus. Art, Phi Kappa Phi Honor Soc. Achievements include writing and publishing one of the first fine art electronic thesis which is still considered exemplary by the international community of Graduate School Deans. Home: 2045 Carolina Ave Bristol TN 37620 Office: E Tenn State U PO Box 70708 Johnson City TN 37620 Home Phone: 423-878-2857; Office Phone: 423-439-5712. Personal E-mail: val@vallyle.com. Business E-Mail: lylev@etsu.edu.

LYLES, MARK BRADLEY, advanced technology company executive, military officer; b. Paducah, Ky., Dec. 3, 1957; s. Kendall Smith Lyles and Charlotte Dean (Ruley) Martell; m. Catherine Lynn Gregg, Mar. 17, 1984 (div. 1995); children: Austin Bradley, Dahlon Patrick; m. Tammi Michele Pedersen, Aug. 4, 2006. AS, BS, BA in Cell Biology and Chemistry, Murray State U., Ky., 1978, MS, EdS in Analytical Chemistry, 1982; DMD in Dental Medicine, U. Louisville, 1986; PhD in Cellular and Structural Biology, U. Tex., San Antonio, 2001. Resident in oral and maxillofacial surgery U. Tex. Health Sci. Ctr., 1991-95; founder, chief exec. officer, pres. Talis Techs., Inc., San Antonio, 1992—; founder, pres., chief sci. officer Materials Evolution and Devel. U.S.A., Inc. (M.E.D. USA), San Antonio, 1993—. Presenter in field. Author, inventor of over 70 sci. papers and abstracts; contbr. articles to profl. jours. Comdr. USNR, 1983—, recalled to active duty USN, 2003—, dep. dir. M5B3 US Navy Bur. Medicine and Surgery, advanced through ranks to capt., 2007. Recipient Dentist-Scientist award Nat. Inst. Dental Rsch., 1991-98; Dept. Chemistry and Bd. Regents scholar Murray State U., 1975-77, Imagineer of Yr. award Mind Sci. Found., 1997; Grad. Coop. Edn. fellow Nat. Ctr. Toxicol. Rsch., EPA, FDA, 1979-80, Grad. fellow U. Louisville, 1981-82. Mem. Am. Coll. Oral and Maxillofacial Surgeons (Walter Lorenz Residents Rsch. award 1994), Acad. Osseointegration, Acad. Gen. Dentistry, Navy Inst., Assn. Mil. Surgeons US, Hon. Order Ky. Cols., Naval Res. Officers Assn., Phi Delta Kappa. Republican. Baptist. Achievements include invention of ultra-low density fused fibrous ceramics for industrial applications; implantable system for cell growth control; filters for polynuclear aromatic hydrocarbon containing smoke; research in use of fused fibrous ceramics in dental materials; over 20 national and international patents with 18 patents pending; recent patents in the use of DNA as a sunscreen, drug delivery and as a biomaterial; research in environmental toxicology. Avocations: rifle and pistol marksmanship, weight training, sailing, travel, Harley motorcycles. Office Phone: 210-724-9776. Personal E-mail: jawbrkr@texas.net. Business E-Mail: mark.lyles@med.navy.mil.

LYMAN, CHARLES EDSON, materials scientist, educator; b. Willimantic, Conn., Mar. 7, 1946; s. Edson Hunt and Sylvia (Hill) L.; m. Valerie Ann Livingston, Aug. 30, 1984. BS, Cornell U., 1968; PhD, MIT, 1974. Postdoctoral fellow dept. metallurgy Oxford (England) U., 1974-76; asst. prof. Rensselaer Poly. Inst., Troy, N.Y., 1976-80; staff scientist E.I. DuPont de Nemours, Wilmington, Del., 1980-84; assoc. prof. Lehigh U., Bethlehem, Pa., 1984-90, prof., 1990—. Electron microscopy steering com. Argonne Nat. Lab., Ill., 1984—. Author, editor: Scanning Electron Microscopy, X-Ray Microanalysis, and Analytical Electron Microscopy: A Laboratory Workbook, 1990; co-author: Scanning Electron Microscopy and X-ray Microanalysis, 2003; editor-in-chief: Microscopy and Microanalysis, 2000-; contbr. articles to profl. jours. Pres. Burnside Plantation Inc., 1993, Historic Bethlehem Inc., 1996—98. Mem. Microscopy Soc. Am. (pres. 1991), Microbeam Analysis Soc. (pres. 2000), Am. Soc. Materials Internat., Am. Chem. Soc. Home: 444 N New St Bethlehem PA 18018-5814 Office: Lehigh U Whitaker Lab 5 E Packer Ave Bethlehem PA 18015-3102 Office Phone: 610-758-4249. Business E-Mail: charles.lyman@lehigh.edu.

LYMAN, GARY HERBERT, epidemiologist, cancer researcher, educator; b. Buffalo, Feb. 24, 1946; s. Leonard Samuel and Beatrice Louise Lyman; children: Stephen Leonard, Christopher Henry. BA, SUNY, Buffalo, 1968, MD, 1972; MPH, Harvard U., 1982. Diplomate Am. Bd. Internal Medicine, Am. Bd. Oncology and Hematology. Resident in medicine U. NC, Chapel Hill, 1972-74; fellow in oncology Roswell Park Meml. Inst., Buffalo, 1974-77; rsch. instr. medicine SUNY Med. Sch., Buffalo, 1974-77; mem. faculty U. South Fla. Coll. Medicine, Tampa, 1977-2000, assoc. prof. medicine, 1980-86, prof. medicine, 1986-2000, dir. divsn. med. oncology, 1979-93, chief medicine H. Lee Moffitt Cancer and Rsch. Inst., 1985—93, prof. epidemiology and biostats., 1988-2000; Thomas Ordway prof. medicine divsn. hematology and oncology Albany (NY) Med. Coll., Union U., 2000—02, dir. Cancer Ctr., 2000—02; prof. biometry and stats. SUNY Sch. Pub. Health, 2000—02; prof. medicine, dept. medicine U. Rochester (NY) Sch. Medicine and Dentistry, 2002—; dir. health svcs. and outcomes rsch. James P. Wilmot Cancer Ctr., 2002—. Vis. prof. med. stats. London Sch. Hygiene and Tropical Medicine, 1997—98. Co-author: Geriatric Oncology, 1998, Comprehensive Geriatric Oncology, 1997, 2d edit., 2004, Breast Cancer: Transitional Therapeutic Strategies, 2007; contbr. chpts. to books, mre than 300 articles to profl. jours. Spl. fellow Leukemia Soc. Am., 1976-77; postdoctoral fellow biostats. Harvard U., 1981-82; spl. clin. rellow Roswell Park Meml. Inst., 1975-76. Fellow ACP, Am. Coll. Preventive Medicine, Am. Coll. Clin. Pharmacology, Royal Coll. Physicians (Edinburgh); mem. Am. Soc. Clin. Oncology. Achievements include research in cancer clinical trials, biostatistics, epidemiology and clinical decision analysis. Office: U Rochester Med Ctr Box 704 601 Elmwood Ave Rochester NY 14642 Business E-Mail: gary_lyman@urmc.rochester.edu.

LYMAN, KRISTIN M., music educator; BM with tchr. cert., Tex. Tech U., Lubbock, 1997, BM in Music Performance magna cum laude, 1998, postgrad.; MM in Percussion Performance, U. N.C., Greensboro, 2000. Elem. music specialist Zavala Magnet Elem. Sch., Odesea, Tex., 2002—06; dir. steel drum band and percussion ensemble Iles Elem., Lubbock, 2004—06; lectr. music Angelo State U., San Angelo, Tex., 2006—07. Percussion sect. tchr. and percussion ensemble coach Lubbock Youth Symphony Orch., 2002—05. Helen DeVitt Jones Assn. fellow, Tex. Tech U., 2006—07. Mem.: Percussive Arts Soc. (mem. young leaders forum 2005—). Home: 671 Sterling Park Cortland NY 13045 Personal E-mail: kristinmlyman@aol.com.

LYMAN, PEGGY, artistic director, dancer, choreographer, educator; b. Cin., June 28, 1950; d. James Louis and Anne Earlene (Weeks) Morner; m. David Stanley Lyman, Aug. 29, 1970 (div. 1979); m. Timothy Scott Lynch, June 21, 1982 (div. 1997); 1 child, Kevin Lynch; m. Richard R. Hayes, Feb. 26, 2005. BFA in Dance, U. Hartford, 2006. Solo dancer Cin. Ballet Co., 1964-68, Contemporary Dance Theater, 1970-71; chorus dancer N.Y.C. Opera, 1969-70; Radio City Music Hall Ballet Co., 1970; chorus singer, dancer Sugar, Broadway musical, NYC, 1971-73; prin. dancer Martha Graham Dance Co., NYC, 1973-88, rehearsal dir., 1989-90, assoc. rehearsal dir., 2005—; artistic dir. Martha Graham Ensemble, NYC, 1990-91; faculty Martha Graham Sch., 1975—; co-artistic dir. Dance Conn., Hartford, 1998-2000. Head dance divns. No. Ky. U., 1977—78; artistic dir. Peggy Lyman Dance Co., NYC, 1978—89; asst. prof. dance, guest choreographer Fla. State U., Tallahassee, 1982—89; guest choreographer So. Meth. U., Dallas, 1986; adjudicator Nat. Coll. Dance Festival Assn., 1983—; co-host To Make a Dance, QUBE cable TV, 1979; mem. guest faculty Am. Dance Festival, Durham, NC, 1984; site adjudicator NEA, 1982—84; tchr. Sch. Dance Conn., 1992—2004, East Conn. Concert Ballet, 1992—94; guest faculty Wesleyan U., Middletown, Conn., 1992; guest artist Conn. Coll., 1993; chair dance divsn. Hartt Sch., U. Hartford, Conn., 1994—2001, dir. dance divsn., Conn., 2002—04; freelance master tchr. internat. univs. Prin. dancer (TV spls.) Dance in America, 1976, 79, 84; guest with Rudolph Nureyev (CBS-TV) Invitation to the Dance, 1980; guest artist Theatre Choreographique Rennes, Paris, 1981, Rennes, France, 1983; Adelaide U., 1991; site dir. Martha Graham's Diversion of Angels for student concert U. Mich., 1992, Martha Graham's Panorama, U. Ill., Champaign-Urbana, 1993, Towson State U., 1997, Martha Graham's Diversion of Angels for Dutch Nat. Ballet, 1995, Diversion of Angels and Acts of Light for Dance Conn., 1998, Ballet Argentino, 1999, Lamentation For Ballet de Lorraine, 2004, The Hartt Sch. U. Hartford, 2007; choreographer: Conundrum (solo), 1982, Mantid (group), 1984, Roll, Spin, Draw, or Fold (group), 1984, Chope Dance (solo), 1985, Mirror's Edge (group), 1986, No Gavotte Bach (group), 1995, Interior Landscapes (group), 1997, Family Portrait (group), 1999, Yes, Is A World (group), 2002; co-creator (with John Feierabend) Move It (CD/DVD), 2003. Founding mem. Cin. Arts Coun., 1976-78. Mem. Am. Guild Mus. Artists. Office: care Martha Graham Sch Contemporary Dance 316 E 63d St New York NY 10021 Office Phone: 212-838-5886. Personal E-mail: peggylhayes@comcast.net.*

LYMAN, RICHARD WALL, foundation administrator, academic administrator, historian; b. Phila., Oct. 18, 1923; s. Charles M. and Aglae (Wall) Lyman; m. Elizabeth D. Schauffler, Aug. 20, 1947; children: Jennifer P., Holly Lyman Antolini, Christopher M., Timothy R. BA, Swarthmore Coll., 1947, LLD (hon.), 1974; MA, Harvard U., 1948, PhD, 1954, LLD (hon.), 1980, Washington U., St. Louis, 1971, Mills Coll., 1972, Yale U., 1975; LHD (hon.), U. Rochester, 1975, Coll. of Idaho, 1989. Teaching fellow, tutor, Harvard U., 1949-51; instr. Swarthmore Coll., 1952-53; instr., then asst. prof. Washington U., St. Louis, 1953-58; mem. faculty Stanford U., 1958-80, 88-91, prof. history, 1962-80, 88-91, Sterling prof., 1980-91, Sterling prof. emeritus, 1991—, assoc. dean Sch Humanities and Scis., 1964-66, v.p., provost, 1967-70, pres., 1970-80, pres. emeritus, 1980—, dir. Inst. Internat. Studies, 1988-91; pres. Rockefeller Found., 1980-88. Spl. corr. The Economist, London, 1953-56; bd. dirs. Coun. on Founds., 1982-88, Independent Sector, 1980-88, chair, 1983-86, Nat. Com. on U.S.-China Rels., 1986-92; dir. IBM, 1978-92, Chase Manhattan Corp., 1981-91. Author: The First Labour Government, 1957; editor: (with Lewis W. Spitz) Major Crises in Western Civilization, 1965, (with Virginia A. Hodgkinson) The Future of the Nonprofit Sector, 1989; editorial bd. Jour. Modern History, 1958-61. Mem. Nat. Coun. on Humanities, 1976-82, vice chmn., 1980-82; chmn. Commn. on Humanities, 1978-80; trustee Rockefeller Found., 1976-88, Carnegie Found. Advancement of Tchg., 1976-82, World Affairs Coun. of No. Calif., 1992-98; bd. dirs. Nat. Assn. Ind. Colls. and Univs., 1976-77, Assn. of Governing Bds. of Univs. and Colls., 1994-97, Am. Alliance for Rights and Responsiblities, 1993-2002; chmn. Assn. Am. Univs., 1978-79. With USAAF, 1943-46. Decorated officier Legion of Honor; recipient Clark Kerr award U. Calif., Berkeley, 1981; Fulbright fellow London Sch. Econs., 1951-52, hon. fellow, 1978—; Guggenheim fellow, 1959-60. Fellow Royal Hist. Soc.; mem. Am. Acad. Arts and Scis., Am. Hist. Assn., Council on Fgn. Relations, Am. Philos. Soc., Conf. Brit. Studies, Phi Beta Kappa. Office: Stanford U Sch Edn Stanford CA 94305-3096 Personal E-mail: rwlyman@hotmail.com.

LYMAN, WILLIAM WELLES, JR., retired architect; b. New London, Conn., Aug. 31, 1916; s. William Welles and Gladys Estelle (Latimer) L.; m. Margaret Helen Whittemore, July 12, 1941 (div. Sept. 1970); children: Cheryl, Steven, Philip, Susan, Donna, Patricia; m. Joan Evelyn Dalrymple, Sept. 26, 1970. BArch, U. Mich., 1939; MArch, Harvard U., Cambridge, Mass., 1940. Architect various orgns., Boston, 1941-42; pvt. practice Cambridge, Mass., 1947-53; chief designer Smith, Hinchman & Grylls, Detroit, 1953-56; architect Swanson Assocs., Bloomfield Hills, Mich., 1956-59, Smith & Smith Assocs., Royal Oak, Mich., 1959-62, Jickling Lyman & Powell Assocs., Inc., Birmingham, Mich., 1962-81, ret., 1981. Mem. faculty Harvard U., Cambridge, Mass., 1947-53; lectr. on early Am. furniture, 1975—. Pres. Cambridge Coun. PTAs, 1950-52, Harlan Sch. PTA, 1960-61; treas. Mass. Coun. for Better Schs., 1950-52; chmn. Citizens Elem. Curriculum Study Birmingham Pub. Schs., 1962-63; bd. dirs. South Oakland Symphony Soc., 1960-63, Birmingham Teen. Ctr., 1965-67, Birmingham Cmty. House, 1967-70, Profl. Skills Alliance, Detroit, 1973-75, Birmingham Hist. Bd., 1969-73, chmn., 1972-73; chmn. Birmingham Hist. Dist. Study Com., 1975-77, Cmty. Devel. Svcs., Portsmouth, NH, 1993-96; pres. Birmingham Hist. Soc., 1980-81, bd. dirs. 1967-70; chmn. acquisitions com. John W. Hunter House, 1974-82; bd. govs. Warner House Assn., Portsmouth, NH, 1983-91, chmn., 1986-88. U.S. Coast Guard, 1942-46. Fellow: AIA; mem.: York Pub. Libr. Assn. (trustee 1999—2002), Mich. Soc. Architects (pres. 1970). Unitarian Universalist. Home: 15 Victoria Ct York ME 03909-1454

LYN, JEAN, interior designer; b. Charlotte, NC, Nov. 22, 1946; d. Frederic C. and Justine Keith Mayer; m. Nicolae Umberto Pollcappelli, July 15, 1976 (div. Apr. 1982). AA, Stephen's Coll., 1966; BA with honors in Interior Arch., U. Ky., 1968. Designer Loeffler Johnson, Ludnberg, Pitts., 1970—73, Morganell-Heumann & Assocs., LA, 1973—76; design ptnr. Inventor Policappelli, 1976—81; prin., owner Jean Lyn & Assocs., 1981—. Achievements include design of copyright for eco homes; founder environmental endowments. Avocations: Bikram yoga, philosophy, hiking, bicycling, climbing. Office Phone: 480-585-9751.

LYNCH, BARBARA, chef, restaurant owner; b. 1964; m. Charles Petri. Head chef dinner cruise ship, Martha's Vineyard; chef Michaela's, Olives, Figs, Boston, Rocco's, Boston, 1993—95; exec. chef Galleria Italiana, Boston, 1995—98; chef, owner No. 9 Park, Boston, 1998—; owner B&G Oysters, Ltd., Boston, 2003—. Subject: (documentaries) Amuse Bouche - A Chef's Tale; Boston 24/7. Named Ten Best New Chefs, Food & Wine mag., 1996, Best Chef, Northeast, James Beard Found., 2003. Office: 9 Park St Boston MA 02108*

LYNCH, BENJAMIN LEO, oral surgeon, educator; b. Omaha, Dec. 29, 1923; s. William Patrick and Mary (Rauber) L.; m. Colleen D. Cook, Nov. 10, 1956; children: Kathleen Ann, Mary Elizabeth, Patrick, George, Martha, Estelle. BSD, Creighton U., Omaha, 1945, DDS, 1947, MA, 1953; fellow, U. Tex., 1947-48; MSD, Northwestern U., Evanston, Ill., 1954. Diplomate Am. Bd. Oral and Maxillofacial Surgery. Asst. instr. oral surgery Creighton U., 1948-50, instr., 1950-52, asst. prof., 1952-53; dean Creighton U. (Sch. Dentistry), 1954-61, assoc. prof. oral surgery, 1954—57, prof. oral surgery, 1957-86, prof. emeritus, 1986—, dir. oral surgery dept., 1954-67; also coordinator grad. and postgrad. programs; chief oral surgeon Douglas County Hosp., Omaha, 1951-63; pres. dental staff Children's Meml. Hosp., Omaha, 1952, 59, co-founder cleft palate team, 1959; chmn. dept. dentistry Bergan-Mercy Hosp., Omaha, 1963-68; exec. com., head dental staff Luth. Hosp., 1963—66; bd. dirs. Nebr. Dental Service Corp., 1972-78, pres., 1974-78; treas. Children's Meml. Hosp. Med. Staff, 1979—81. Guest lectr. Walter Reed Grad. Sch. Medicine, 1957-58. Active Omaha-Douglas County Health Bd., 1966-68, v.p., 1967, pres., 1968; exec. com. Nebr. divsn. Am. Cancer Soc., 1963-67; bd. dirs. Creighton U. Alumni Coun., Omaha chpt., 1989-91, Cath. Acad., Omaha, 2000—01; trustee United Cath. Social Svcs., 1989-95, chmn. devel. com., active Irish Fest, 1992—; alumni adv. bd. to dean Creighton U. Dental Sch., 1984—, vice chmn., 1992-93, chmn., 1993-94; pres. Creighton U. Graybackers, 1991-94. Served at Walter Reed US Army Med. Ctr., 1955-57. Recipient Alumni merit award Creighton U., 1978; named one of Ten Outstanding Young Omahans, 1952-53, 58; named to Nebr. Dental Hall of Fame, 1981 Fellow Am. Coll. Dentists (pres. Nebr. chpt. 1973-74); mem. Am. Soc. Oral Surgeons, Midwest Soc. Oral Surgeons, Nebr. Soc. Oral Surgeons (founder 1957, pres. 1961), Nebr. Dental Soc. (trustee 1964-66), Omaha Dist. Dent Soc. (pres. 1963-64), Am. Coll. Oral-Maxillofacial Surgeons (founding mem.), Nebr. Soc. Dental Anesthesiology (founder, 1st pres.), Alpha Sigma Nu, Omicron Kappa Epsilon, Delta Sigma Delta. Home: 509 S Happy Hollow Blvd Omaha NE 68106-1224

LYNCH, BEVERLY LOVE, language educator; b. Newport News, Va., Dec. 15, 1950; d. Eugene Stone and Beverly (Pennell) Love; m. Kevin Timothy Lynch, Aug. 25, 1973; children: Robyn Michelle, Perry Kevin. BA, Furman U., 1972; MA in Spanish, Middlebury Coll., 1973. Instr. Spanish South Brunswick (NJ) HS, 1974—79; translator North Plainfield (NJ) Bd. Edn., 1979—81; instr. Spanish Watkinson Sch., West Hartford, Conn., 1980—82, Bancroft Sch., Worcester, Mass., 1983—84, Far Hills (NJ) Country Day Sch., 1988—90, West Morris Ctrl. HS, Chester, NJ, 1990—. Mem.: Fgn. Lang. Educators NJ, Am. Coun. on the Tchg. Fgn. Lang., Am. Assn. Tchrs. Spanish and Portuguese, Harmonium Choral Soc. Methodist. Avocations: jogging, cross stitch, needlepoint, travel, singing. Office: West Morris Ctrl High Sch Bartley Rd Chester NJ 07930

LYNCH, BEVERLY PFEIFER, education and information studies educator; b. Moorhead, Minn. d. Joseph B. and Nellie K. (Bailey) Pfeifer; m. John A. Lynch, Aug. 24, 1968. BS, N.D. State U., 1957, L.H.D. (hon.); MS, U. Ill., 1959; PhD, U. Wis., 1972. Librarian Marquette U., 1959-60, 62-63; exchange librarian Plymouth (Eng.) Pub. Library, 1960-61; asst. head serials div. Yale U. Library, 1963-65, head, 1965-68; vis. lectr. U. Wis., Madison, 1970-71, U. Chgo., 1975; exec. sec. Assn. Coll. and Research Libraries, 1972-76; univ. librarian U. Ill.-Chgo., 1977-89; dean, prof. Grad. Sch. Libr. and Info. Sci. UCLA, 1989-94, prof. Grad. Sch. Edn. and Info. Studies, 1989—, dir. sr. fellows program, 1990—; interim pres. Ctr. for Rsch. Librs., Chgo., 2000-01; founding dir. Calif. Rare Book Sch., 2004—. Sr. fellow, vis. scholar UCLA, 1982. Author: (with Thomas J. Galvin) Priorities for Academic Libraries, 1982, Management Strategies for Libraries, 1985, Academic Library in Transition, 1989, Information Technology and the Remaking of the University Library, 1995. Recipient Cert. of Appreciation, Chinese Am. Librs. Assn., 2001; named Acad. Libr. of Yr., 1982, one of top sixteen libr. leaders in Am., 1990; fellow Indo-U.S. Subcommn. on Edn. and Culture, 1992-93; vis. scholar U. Nebr., 1981. Mem.: ALA (pres. 1985—86, coun. 1998—2004, chair 1999—2000, com. on accreditation 1999—2002, co-chair joint com. ALA, Soc. Am. Archivists and Am. Assn. Museums 2005—07), Bibliog. Soc. Am., Assn. for Study Higher Edn., Am. Sociol. Assn., Acad. Mgmt., Nat. Info. Stds. Org. (bd. dirs. 1996—2005, vice chair 1999—2001, chair 2001—03, co-chair organizing com. 4th China-US conf. 2007), Scottish Libr. Assn. (hon.), Book Club Calif., Grolier Club, Caxton Club, Phi Kappa Phi. Office: UCLA Grad Sch Edn Info Mailbox 951520 Los Angeles CA 90095-1520 Office Phone: 310-209-4294. Business E-Mail: bplynch@ucla.edu.

LYNCH, CAROL, special services director, psychologist, minister; d. Joseph Louis and Ellen (Birish) Dobkowski; 1 child, Eric Alexander. BA, William Paterson Coll., 1966; MA, NYU, 1970, PsyD, 1984. Lic. psychologist, N.J., N.Y. Tchr. Bloomfield (N.J.) Pub. Schs., 1966-68, psychologist, 1970-87; dir. spl. svcs. Waldwick (N.J.) Pub. Schs., 1987—, acting supt. schs., 1995-96, 98. Adj. clin. prof. NYU, N.Y.C., 1983-86 adj. prof. Montclair (N.J.) State Coll., 1984-85. Mem. prof. alumni coun. Sch. Edn., Health and Nursing, NYU, 1989—91; alumni coun. chair Sch. Edn., NYU, 1991—93, sec., 2002—03; trustee First Church of Religious Sci., 2001—, bd. trustees, 2002—, lic. practitioner, 2005, v.p., 2006—, staff minister, 2007—. NYU fellow, 1981-82; recipient Best Practice award N.J. State Dept. Edn. for Fast Families Program, 1995, Disting. Grad. Brian E. Tomlinson Meml. award NYU, 1995, Exemplary Practice award N.J. Adminstrs. Assn./N.J. Sch. Bds. "Crisis Response Initiative," 2002. Mem. APA (sch. psychology task force 1989-90), N.J. Psychol. Assn. (treas. 1985-86, Sch. Psychologist of Yr. 2003), Nat. Assn. Sch. Psychologists (del. 1984-88), N.J. Assn. Sch. Psychologists (pres. 1982-83, Sch. Psychologist of Yr. 2003), Ea. Ednl. Rsch. Assn. (pres. 1993-95), Bergen County Assn. Lic. Psychologists (bd. dirs. 1991-93), NYU Sch. Psychology Alumni Assn. (founder 1988-92), Ramapo Valley Adminstrs. (v.p. 1996-98, pres. 1998—). Avocations: skiing, antiques, tennis, gourmet cooking. Home: 124 Frank Ct Mahwah NJ 07430-2963 Office: Waldwick Pub Schs 155 Summit Ave Waldwick NJ 07463-2133 Office Phone: 201-652-5052. Personal E-mail: drcarollynch@msn.com. Business E-Mail: dr.carol.lynch@waldwick.k12.nj.us.

LYNCH, CATHERINE GORES, social services administrator; b. Waynesboro, Pa., Nov. 23, 1943; d. Landis and Pamela (Whitmarsh) Gores; m. Joseph C. Keefe, Nov. 29, 1981; children: Shannon Maria, Lisa Alison, Gregory T. Keefe, Michael D. Keefe. BA magna cum laude with honors, Bryn Mawr Coll., 1965; postgrad., Cornell U., 1966-67. Cert. police instr. Mayor's intern Human Resources Adminstrn., NYC, 1967; rsch. asst. Orgn. for Social and Tech. Innovation, Cambridge, Mass., 1967-69; cons. Ford Found., Bogota, Columbia, 1970; staff Nat. Housing Census, Nat. Bur. Statistics, Bogota, 1971; evaluator Foster Parent Plan, Bogota, 1972; rsch. staff FEDESARROLLO, Bogota, 1973-74; dir. Dade County Advocates for Victims, Miami, Fla., 1974-86; asst. to dep. dir. Dept. Human Resouces, Miami, 1986-87, computer liaison, 1987-88, asst. adminstr. placement svcs. program, 1988-89; exec. dir. Health Crisis Network, Miami, 1989-96; liaison HIV cmty. svc. State of Fla. Health and Rehab. Svcs., 1996-97; program ops. adminstr. adult protective svcs. Fla. Dept. Children and Families, 1997-2000; dir. grants mgmt. U. Miami Sch. Nursing, 2000—03; ann. giving and grants mgr. Audubon of Fla., 2003—05; dir. devel. svcs. Miami Children's Hosp. Found., 2005—. Guest lectr. local univs. Participant, co-chmn. various task forces rape, child abuse, incest, family violence, elderly victims of crime, nat. state, local levels, 1974-86, 1999-2000; developer workshops in field; participant, chair, co-chair task forces on HIV/AIDS impact; long term care, children and AIDS, AIDS orgnl. issues, 1991-96; mem. gov.'s task force on victims and witnesses, gov.'s task force on sex offenders and their victims, gov.'s Red Ribbon panel on AIDS, 1992-93, gov.'s interdepartmental work group, 1993-96; mem. ednl. rev. com. Am. Found AIDS Rsch., 1991-96; vice chair Metro-Dade HIV Svcs. Planning Coun., 1991-93; active Fla. HIV Svcs. Adv. Coun., 1991-96; rev. panel Fed. Spl. Projects of Nat. Significance, 1994, 96; adv. coun. Metro Dade Social Svcs., 1995-96; bd. dirs., v.p. Dade County Healthy Start Coalition, 2002—04; cert. expert witness on battered women syndrome in civil and criminal cts. Contbr. writings to field to publs. Recipient various pub. svcs. awards including WINZ Citizen of Day, 1979, Outstanding Achievement award Fla. Network Victim Witness Svcs., 1982, Pioneer award Metro-Dade Women's Assn., 1989; Fulbright scholar U. Central de Venezuela, Caracas, 1965-66; Lehman fellow Cornell U. Mem. Nat. Orgn. of Victim Assistance Programs (bd. dirs. 1977-83, Outstanding Program award 1984), Fla. Network of Victim/Witness Programs (bd. dirs., treas. 1980-81), Am. Soc. Pub. Adminstrs., Dade County Fedn. Health and Welfare Workers, Fla. Assn. Health and Social Svcs. (chpt. treas. 1979-80), LWV (bd. dirs. Dade County chpt. 1988-92, 2005—), Fla. Consortium Sch.-Based Health Ctrs. (sec. 2001-03). Office: Miami Children's Hosp Found 3000 SW 62d Ave Miami FL 33155 Office Phone: 786-268-1841. Business E-Mail: clynch@mchf.org.

LYNCH, CHARLES ALLEN, investment company executive, director; b. Denver, Sept. 7, 1927; s. Laurence J. and Louanna (Robertson) L.; divorced; children: Charles A., Tara O'Hara, Casey Alexander; m. Justine Bailey, Dec. 27, 1992. BS, Yale U., 1950. With E.I. duPont de Nemours & Co., Inc., Wilmington, Del., 1950—69, dir. mktg., 1965—69; corp. v.p. SCOA Industries, Columbus, Ohio, 1969—72; corp. exec. v.p., also mem. rotating bd. W.R. Grace & Co., NYC, 1972—78; chmn. bd., CEO, Saga Corp., Menlo Park, Calif., 1978—86; chmn., CEO, DHL Airways, Inc., Redwood City, Calif., 1986—88; pres., CEO Levolor Corp., 1988—89, chmn. exec. com. of bd. dirs., 1989—90; chmn. Market Value Ptnrs. Co., Menlo Park, Calif., 1990—95, 1999—. Bd. dirs. Sigaba Corp. Bd. dirs.

United Way, 1990-92, past chmn. Bay Area campaign, 1987; vice chmn., dir. Bay Area Coun.; past chmn. Calif. Bus. Roundtable; past chmn. bd. trustees Palo Alto Med. Found. Mem. Yale Club (N.Y.C.), Internat. Lawn Tennis Club, Menlo Country Club (Calif.), Pacific Union Club (San Francisco), Coral Beach and Tennis Club (Bermuda), Vintage Club (Indian Wells, Calif.), Menlo Circus Club. Republican. Home: 96 Ridge View Dr Atherton CA 94027-6464 Office: 333 Ravenswood Ave Ste Ag320 Menlo Park CA 94025-3453 Office Phone: 650-859-5884. Business E-Mail: clynch@mvp-co.com.

LYNCH, CHARLES ANDREW, chemicals executive; b. Bklyn., Jan. 6, 1935; s. Charles Andrew and Mary Martina (McEvoy) L.; m. Marilyn Anne Monaco, July 30, 1960; children: Nancy Callan, Cara Martina. BS, Manhattan Coll., 1956; PhD, U. Notre Dame, 1960. Rsch. chemist Esso Rsch. & Engring. Co., Linden, NJ, 1960-65; rsch. supr. organic chemistry divsn. FMC Corp., Balt., 1965-72, rsch. mgr. indsl. chemistry divsn. Princeton, NJ, 1972-74; exec. v.p. Am. Oil & Supply Co., Newark, 1974-80; tech. dir., dir. sales & mktg., dir. rsch. & bus. devel., v.p. tech. Hatco Corp., Fords, NJ, 1981-95; with Calivera Cons., 1995—; account exec. N.J. Commerce, Econ. Growth and Tourism Commn., 1997—2006; ret. Contbr. articles to profl. jours.; patentee in field (U.S. and foreign). Mem. Am. Chem. Soc., Soc. Tribologists and Lubrication Engrs. (chmn. N.Y. sect. 1980-81, 97-98), Ind. Lubricant Mfrs. Assn. (bd. dirs. 1985-88). Home Phone: 609-924-6655. E-mail: clynch@patmedia.net.

LYNCH, CHARLES THEODORE, SR., materials science engineering researcher, consultant, educator; b. Lima, Ohio, May 17, 1932; s. John Richard and Helen (Dunn) L.; m. Betty Ann Korkolis, Feb. 3, 1956; children: Karen Elaine Ostdiek, Charles Theodore Jr., Richard Anthony, Thomas Edward. BS, George Washington U., 1955; MS, U. Ill., 1957, PhD in Analytical Chemistry, 1960. Group leader ceramics div. Air Force Materials Lab., Wright-Patterson AFB, Ohio, 1962-66; lectr. in chemistry Wright State U., Dayton, Ohio, 1964-66; chief advanced metall. studies br. Air Force Materials Lab., Wright-Patterson AFB, Ohio, 1966-74, sr. scientist, 1974-81; head materials div. Office of Naval Rsch., Arlington, Va., 1981-85; pvt. practice cons. Washington, 1985-88; sr. engr. space ops. Vitro Corp., Washington, 1988-95, 96-98; cons. Burke, Va., 1996—; sr. cons. space ops. Marconi Systems Techs., Washington, 1998—99; v.p. RSC&L, Inc., Grayling, Mich., 1996—. USAF liaison mem. NMAB Panels on Solids Processing, Ion Implantation and Environ. Cracking, Washington, 1965-68, 78, 81; U.S. rep. AGARD structures and materials panel NATO, 1983-85. Co-author: Metal Matrix Composites, 1972; editor, author: Practical Handbook of Materials Science, 1989; editor: (series) Handbook of Materials Science, vol. I, 1974, vol. II, 1975, vol. III, 1975; vice chmn. editorial bd. Vitro Corp. Tech. Jour., 1989-92, chmn., 1993; contbr. articles to profl. jours. including Jour. Am. Ceramics Soc., Analytical Chemistry, Sci., Transactions AIME, Corr. Jour., Jour. Inorganic Chemistry, SAMPE, Jour. Less Common Metals. Mem., soloist George Washington U. Traveling Troubadours, Washington, 1950-55; choir dir. Trinity United Ch. of Christ, Fairborn, Ohio, 1966-81, Univ. Bapt. Ch., Champaign, Ill., 1957-60, Chapel II, Wright-Patterson AFB, Ohio, 1960-64; bd. dirs. Southport Home Owners' Assn., Burke, Va., 2002—; pres. Pub. Sch. PTO, 1967-69. 1st lt. USAF, 1960-62. Bailey scholar U. Ill., 1958-60; recipient Commendation medal USAF, 1962, Outstanding Achievement cert. NASA, 1992, award Soc. for Tech. Comm. Publ., 1993. Mem. Am. Chem. Soc. (treas. 1966-67, chmn. audit sect. 1967-68), ASM Internat. (sec. oxidation and corrosion com. 1980-81, chmn. 1981-82). Methodist. Achievements include patents for new corrosion inhibitors including encapsulated types, and for alkoxides and oxides; co-development of the refractory ceramic Zyttrite, the first high density translucent zirconia made from thermal or hydrolytic decomposition of mixed alkoxides followed by hot pressing; pioneered general approach of organometallic compounds as precursors of high purity, fine particulate, materials. Office: 5629 Kemp Ln Burke VA 22015-2041

LYNCH, CHARLOTTE ANDREWS, retired communications executive, consultant; b. Fall River, Mass., Mar. 25, 1928; d. Alan Hall and Florence (Worthen) Andrews; m. Francis Bradley Lynch, June 7, 1952; children: Sarah Faldetta, Richard, Stephen, William. AB in Philosophy, Radcliffe Coll., 1950; postgrad., U. Bridgeport, 1969-71. Adminstrv. asst. Mass. Congl. Confs. and Missionary Soc., Boston, 1951-52; journalist Town Crier newspaper, Westport, Conn., 1968; asst. dir. devel. Cape Cod Hosp., Hyannis, Mass., 1975-76; parish adminstr. S. Congl. Ch., Centerville, Mass., 1976-83; cons. to ethnic advt. agy. Loiminchay, Inc., NYC, 1992-98; ret. Mem. Radcliffe Club Cape Cod (v.p. 1990-97, pres. 1997-2000, exec. com. 1990-2000), Harvard Club of Boston. Republican. Roman Catholic. Avocation: travel.

LYNCH, CLIFFORD A., library and information scientist; PhD in Computer Sci., U. Calif., Berkeley. Various positions in divsn. library automation Office of Pres., Univ. Calif., 1979—87, dir. divsn. library automation, 1987—97; exec. dir. Coalition for Networked Information, Washington, 1997—. Adj. prof. Sch. Info. Mgmt. & Systems, Univ. Calif., Berkeley; mem. com. digital archiving Nat. Rsch. Council. Contbr. of over 100 chapters to books and articles to profl. jours. Fellow: AAAS, Nat. Info. Standards Org.; mem.: Am. Soc. Info. Sci. (past pres.). Office: Coalition for Networked Information 21 DuPont Cir Washington DC 20036 Office Phone: 202-296-5098. Office Fax: 202-872-0884. Business E-Mail: clifford@cni.org.

LYNCH, CONSTANCE, reading specialist; Guest spkr. WNYE, Bklyn., 1965, Bd. Edn., Bklyn., 1965, promotional policy adv. coun., 68; guest lectr., reading cons. Branch Coll., NYC, 1970. Author: Reflections, 1988, It Takes a Kitongoji, 1999, In Other Words, 2005, Reflections of the Day, 2005. Mem. MADD; vol. Charlotte County Retired Educator Assn., Port Charlotte, Fla., 1994—, v.p., 1995—99; vol. Unity Ch. of Peace, Port Charlotte, 1994—; mem. Christopher Reeves Found., Nat. Com. to Preserve Social Security and Medicare, Operation Smile. Recipient Life Mem. plaque, NAACP, 1994, Voice of Civil Rights cert., 2005. Mem.: Peace River Ctr. for Writers, Nat. Women's Hist. Mus., Charlotte County Retired Educators Assn., Am. Assn. U. Women, Nat. Fed. for the Blind, Girls' HS Alumni Assn. Democrat. Avocations: sewing, music, poetry, dance. Home: 26287 Copiapo Cir Punta Gorda FL 33983

LYNCH, DAVID K., film director, writer; b. Missoula, Mont., Jan. 20, 1946; s. Donald and Sunny L.; m. Peggy Reavey, 1967 (div. 1974); 1 child, Jennifer; m. Mary Fisk, June 21, 1977 (div. 1987); 1 child, Austin; m. Mary Sweeney, 2006 (separated); 1 child, Riley Sweeney Lynch. Student, Pa. Acad. Fine Arts, Phila. Co-screenwriter, dir.: (films) Eraserhead, 1978, The Elephant Man, 1980 (Acad. award), Dune, 1984; screenwriter, dir.: (films) Blue Velvet, 1986, Wild at Heart, 1990 (Palme d'Or, Cannes Internat. Film Festival), Twin Peaks: Fire Walk With Me, 1992, Lost Highway, 1997, Driven to It, 1999, The Straight Story, 1999, Mulholland Drive, 2001, Dumbland, 2002, Rabbits, 2002, Darkened Room, 2002, Inland Empire, 2006; co-dir.: Lumiere et compagnie, 1995; creator: (TV series) Twin Peaks, 1990, American Chronicles, 1990, On the Air, 1992, Hotel Room, 1993, (performance piece) Industrial Symphony #1, 1989. Am. Film Inst. grantee. Mem. Dirs. Guild Am. Office: Endeavor Talent Agy 9701 Wilshire Blvd Fl 10 Beverly Hills CA 90212-2010*

LYNCH, DAVID WILLIAM, physicist, retired educator; b. Rochester, NY, July 14, 1932; s. William J. and Eleanor (Fouratt) L.; m. Joan N. Hill, Aug. 29, 1954 (dec. Nov. 1989); children: Jean Louise, Richard William, David Allan; m. Glenys R. Bittick, Nov. 14, 1992. BS, Rensselaer Poly. Inst., 1954; MS, U. Ill., 1955, PhD, 1958. Asst. prof. physics Iowa State U., 1959-63, assoc. prof., 1963-66, prof., 1966—2003, chmn. dept., 1985-90, disting. prof. liberal arts and scis., 1985—; on leave at U. Hamburg, Germany; and U. Rome, Italy, 1968-69; sr. physicist Ames Lab. of Dept. of Energy; acting assoc. dir. Synchrotron Radiation Ctr., Stoughton, Wis., 1984. Vis. prof. U. Hamburg, summer 1974; dir. Microelectronics Rsch. Ctr., Iowa State U., 1995-99. Fulbright scholar U. Pavia, Italy, 1958-59. Fellow: Am. Phys. Soc.; mem.: AAAS. Achievements include research on solid state physics. Home: 2020 Elm Cir West Des Moines IA 50265-4294 Home Phone: 525-440-1716; Office Phone: 515-294-3476. Business E-Mail: dwl@ameslab.gov.

LYNCH, DENNIS JAMES, plastic surgeon; b. Bayonne, NJ, Aug. 5, 1939; s. Dennis J. Lynch and Eileen Mallon; m. Mary; children: Dennis, David, Sarah. BS, Villanova U., 1961; MD, Georgetown U. Med. Ctr., 1965. Diplomate Am. Bd. Surgery, Am. Bd. Plastic Surgery. Resident U. Pa., Phila., 1965—74; plastic surgeon Scott & White Clinic, Temple, Tex., 1974—. Dir. divsn. plastic surgery Tex. A&M Med. Sch., Temple, 1974-87, chair dept. surgery, 1990-2004; bd. dirs. Scott & White Clinic, 1981-95. Mem. AMA, Am. Coll. Surgeons, Am. Cleft Palate Assn., Am. Assn. Plastic Surgeons, Tex. Soc. Plastic Surgeons, Am. Soc. Plastic & Reconstructive Surgeons (pres. elect 1996—, pres. 1997), Am. Bd. Plastic Surgery. Roman Catholic. Avocations: tennis, sailing. Office: Scott & White Meml Hosp 2401 S 31st St Temple TX 76508-0001 Home Phone: 254-933-9342; Office Phone: 254-724-2321. Business E-Mail: djlynch@swmail.sw.org.

LYNCH, DICK, telecommunications industry executive; BEE, Lowell Technological Inst., 1970, MEE; completed postgraduate work, Wharton Sch. U. Pa., Johnson Sch. Mgmt. Cornell U. Variety of positions New England Telephone, 1972; gen. mgr. ops. Bell Atlantic Mobile, Harrisburg, Pa., exec. v.p., chief tech. officer, 1990—2000, Verizon Wireless (formerly Bell Atlantic Mobile), 2000—07, Verizon Communications, Inc., 2007—. Chmn. Wireless Data Forum; charter mem. exec. bd. Code Divsn. Multiple Access; guest lectr. at universities and conf. Mem. tech. adv. coun. Fed. Communications Comm. Mem.: IEEE (sr.; gen. chmn. Wireless Communication and Networking Conf. 2002). Achievements include patents in field. Office: Verizon Communications Inc 140 W St New York NY 10007*

LYNCH, DOUGLAS E., dean; b. Washington, May 7, 1964; s. William John Lynch and Gretchen Gail Holmes; m. Kuinera Jennifer De Kramer; 1 child, Cornelius. BA, Ariz. State U., 1987, postgrad., 1995; MBA, N.Y. U., NYC, 1991; MPhil, PhD, Columbia U., 2005. Intern U.S. Embassy, Stockholm, 1984, Gov.'s Office, Phoenix, 1985; exec. asst. Coll. Bd., NYC, 1989—95; asst. dir. Ariz. State U., Tempe, 1995—96; dir. mem. svcs. Coll. Bd., NYC, 1996—99; asst. dean N.Y. U., NYC, 1999—2004; vice dean U. Pa., Phila., 2004—. Author: Corporate-University Partnership, 2005; contbr. chapters to books. Mem. Goals 2000 Taskforce, Washington; with Congl. Nebr.-Based Commn., Washington. Recipient Pres. E-award, U.S. Dept. Commerce, 2002. Mem.: Am. Ednl. Rsch. Assn., Univ. Continuing Edn. Assn., Assn. Continuing Higher Edn. Democrat. Episcopalian. Office: Univ Pa 3700 Walnut St Philadelphia PA 19104 Office Phone: 215-573-5022. Business E-Mail: dougl@gse.upenn.edu.

LYNCH, FRANK THOMAS, aeronautical engineer, consultant; b. Binghamton, NY, Oct. 19, 1933; s. John Francis and Irene Elizabeth L.; m. Blanca Lynch, Dec. 10, 1966; children: Fernando, Maria, Monica, Manuel, Jose. BS in Aero. Engring., U. Notre Dame, 1955; postgrad., Cornell U., 1955-56. From propulsion airframe integration specialist to mgr. and sr. mgr. Douglas/McDonnell Douglas, Calif., 1956—93, program and technical mgr. integrated wing design Calif., 1993-99; sr. mgr. subsonic aerodynamics tech. devel. Douglas/McDonnell Douglas (now The Boeing Co.), Long Beach, Calif., 1993-99; pvt. practice Yorba Linda, Calif., 1999—. Chmn. NASA Aerodynamics adv. group, 1995-97, Airframe Sys. adv. group, 1997-2000, Aerospace Tech. adv. group, 1998-2000, sr. adv. staff to Rand, 2003. Contbr. numerous articles to profl. publs., including Jour. of Aircraft, Aero. Jour., Prog. Aero. Sci., others; presenter in field. Recipient Disting. Pub. Svc. medal NASA, 1994; technical fellow McDonnell Douglas/Boeing Corp., 1992. Mem.: AIAA (aerodynamics award 1999). Roman Catholic. Avocations: writing, travel. Home and Office: 5370 Via Maria Yorba Linda CA 92886-5014 Office Phone: 714-693-8797. Personal E-mail: aerofrank@sbcglobal.net.

LYNCH, GARY G., investment company executive, lawyer; b. Middletown, NY, July 25, 1950; BA, Syracuse U., 1972; JD, Duke U., 1975. Atty. SEC, 1976—89, dir., enforcement divsn., 1985—89; ptnr. Davis Polk & Wardwell, NYC, 1989—2001; gen. counsel Credit Suisse First Boston, NYC, 2001, vice chmn. rsch. and legal, 2002—05; chief legal officer, mem. mgmt. com. Morgan Stanley, NYC, 2005—. Named Phi Beta Kappa. Mem.: DC Bar Assn., NY State Bar Assn. Office: Morgan Stanley 1585 Broadway New York NY 10036*

LYNCH, GEORGE MICHAEL, auto parts manufacturing executive; b. Ft. Lauderdale, Fla., Apr. 7, 1943; s. Jack Traverse and Ruth Margarite (Koehler) L.; m. Carol Rollins, June 18, 1966; children: Kristin Ruth, Michael Scott. BSEE, Cornell U., 1965, MEE, 1966; MS in Indsl. Adminstrn., Carnegie-Mellon U., 1968. Fin. analyst, various supervisory positions Ford Motor Co., Dearborn, Mich., 1968-73, mgr. car product analysis, 1973-76, mgr. N.Am. ops. N.Am. contrs. analysis dept. office, 1976-77, mgr. programming and capacity dept., 1977-81, mgr. facilities and fin. staff mgmt. svcs., 1981-83, dir. fin. Ford of Australia, 1983-86, contr. Ford Tractor div. Troy, Mich., 1986-87; exec. v.p., chief fin. officer Ford New Holland, Inc., New Holland, Pa., 1987-97; v.p., contr. Dow Chem. Co., 1997-2000; exec. v.p., CFO Fed.-Mogul Corp., Southfield, Mich., 2000—. Mem. Orchard Lake Country Club, Birmingham Athletic Club (tennis chmn. 1977—), Phi Kappa Phi, Tau Beta Pi. Avocations: tennis, bicycling. Office: Fed Mogul Corp 26555 Northwestern Hwy Southfield MI 48034 Home: 2566 Kent Ridge Ct Bloomfield Hills MI 48301-2276 Office Phone: 248-354-9935.*

LYNCH, GERARD E., federal judge; b. NYC, Sept. 4, 1951; s. Gerard Norman and Marjorie Ann (Werner) L.; m. Karen Marisak, June 10, 1972; 1 child, Christopher Marisak Lynch. BA, Columbia U., 1972, JD, 1975. Bar: N.Y. 1976, U.S. Supreme Ct., U.S. Ct. Appeals (2d, 4th and D.C. cirs.). Law clk. US Ct. Appeals, NYC, 1975-76, US Supreme Ct., Washington, 1976-77; asst. U.S. atty. So. Dist. NY, NYC, 1980-83; chief criminal div. U.S. Dist. Ct. (so. dist.) NY, NYC, 1990-92; assoc. independent counsel Iran/Contra, 1988-90; asst. prof. Columbia U., NYC, 1977-80, assoc. prof., 1980-87, prof. law, 1987—96, vice dean, 1992—97, Paul J. Kellner prof. law, 1996—; of counsel Howard, Darby & Levin, NYC, 1992—2000; judge U.S. Dist. Ct. (So. Dist.), NYC, 2000—. Office: US Courthouse 40 Centre St Room 803 New York NY 10007 Office Phone: 212-805-0427.

LYNCH, HARRY JAMES, retired biologist; b. Glenfield, Pa., Jan. 18, 1929; s. Harry James and Rachel (McComb) L.; m. Pokum Lee Lynch. BS, Geneva Coll., Beaver Falls, Pa., 1957; PhD, U. Pitts., 1971; postgrad. Bio-Space Tech. Tng. Program, NASA and U. Va., 1970. Clin. chemist West Penn Hosp., Pitts., 1955-56; grad. teaching asst. U. Pitts., 1966-71, sr. teaching fellow, 1971; postdoctoral fellow MIT, Cambridge, 1973-75, rsch. assoc. dept. nutrition, lab. neuroendocrine regulation, 1973-75, lectr., 1976-81, rsch. scientist dept. brain and cognitive sci., 1982-92; ret., 1992. Contbr. more than 60 articles on the pineal gland to profl. jours. and books; patentee on implantable programmed microinfusion apparatus, 1981. With USN, 1950—54. NIH postdoctoral fellow 1971-73. Democrat. Avocation: study of animal behavior.

LYNCH, JESSICA, military officer; b. Palestine, W. Va., Apr. 26, 1983; d. Gregory O. and Deadra Lynch. Army Pvt. First Class, Hon. Med. Disability Discharge, 2003. Spokesperson Operation Purple. Decorated Purple Heart, Bronze Star, POW Medal; named West Virginian of Yr., 2003, Glamour Woman of Yr., 2003; recipient Heroes of Health award, 2003. Achievements include first POW/MIA recovered from Operation: Iraqi Freedom; subject of songs, poems, tributes, TV movies and reports; subject of Rick Bragg biography: I Am A Soldier Too: The Jessica Lynch Story, 2003; created the Jessica Lynch Found. to educate children of veterans.

LYNCH, JOHN BROWN, plastic surgeon, educator; b. Akron, Ohio, Feb. 5, 1929; s. John A. and Eloise L.; student Vanderbilt U., Nashville, Tenn., 1946-49; M.D., U. Tenn., Memphis, 1952; children: John Brown, Margaret Frances Lynch Callihan; m. Mary Joyce Burrus, Dec. 1, 1994. Rotating intern John Gaston Hosp., Memphis, Tenn., 1953-54; resident in gen. surgery U. Tex. Med. Br., Galveston, 1956-59, resident in plastic surgery, 1959-62, instr., 1962, asst. prof. surgery, 1962-67, asso. prof., 1967-72, prof., 1972-73; prof., plastic surgery, chmn. dept. plastic surgery Vanderbilt U. Med. Center, 1973—. Served as capt. USAF, 1954-56. Diplomate Am. Bd. Plastic Surgery (chmn.). Fellow ACS; mem. Singleton Surg. Soc. (pres. 1982-83), AMA, Am. Soc. Plastic and Reconstructive Surgeons (pres. 1983-84), Am. Assn. Plastic Surgeons, Plastic Surgery Research Council, Am. Cleft Palate Assn., Am. Burn Assn., Soc. Head and Neck Surgeons, Internat. Burn Assn., Pan Am. Med. Assn., Am. Cancer Soc. (pres. Galveston County, Tex., Chpt. 1968), So. Med. Assn. (pres.-elect 1983-84), Tenn. med. Assn., Nashville Acad. Medicine, Tenn. Soc. Plastic Surgeons, Southeastern Soc. Plastic Surgeons, Southeastern Surg. Soc., H. William Scott, Jr. Soc., Nashville Surg. Soc., Am. Soc. Maxillofacial Surgeons, So. Surg. Assn., Am. Surg. Assn., Sigma Xi. Contbr. numerous articles to med. publs.; editor: (with S.R. Lewis) Symposium on the Treatment of Burns, 1973. Home: 5810 Hillsboro Pike Nashville TN 37215-4602 Office: Vanderbilt Hospital Nashville TN 37232-0001 Personal E-mail: jblynchsr@bellsouth.net.

LYNCH, JOHN CHRISTOPHER, lawyer; b. Jacksonville, Fla., July 11, 1962; s. John Irving and Beverly Anne Beale Lynch; m. Anna Maria Szaz, Apr. 16, 1988; children: Flannery Elizabeth, Riley Davis. BA with honors, U. Va., Charlottesville, 1984; JD cum laude, Harvard U., Cambridge, Mass., 1988. Bar: NC 1993, Calif. 1988. Assoc. Wilson Sonsini Goodrich & Rosati, Palo Alto, Calif., 1988—92; ptnr. Wyrick Robbins Yates & Ponton LLP, Raleigh, NC, 1992—. Charter mem. The Indus Entrepreneurs, Research Triangle Park, NC, 2006—; bd. mem. Coun. for Entrepreneurial Devel., Durham, NC, 2002—. Democrat. Avocations: mountaineering, skiing, soccer. Office: Wyrick Robbins Yates & Ponton LLP Ste 300 4101 Lake Boone Trail Raleigh NC 27607 Office Phone: 919-781-4000. Business E-Mail: clynch@wyrick.com.

LYNCH, JOHN EDWARD, JR., lawyer; b. Lansing, Mich., May 3, 1952; s. John Edward and Miriam Ann (Hyland) L.; m. Brenda Jayne Clark, Nov. 16, 1984; children: John E. III, Robert C., David B., Patrick D., Jacqueline E. AB, Hamilton Coll., 1974; JD, Case Western Res. U., 1977. Bar: Conn. 1978, Ohio 1980, U.S. Dist. Ct. (no. dist.) Ohio 1980, U.S. Ct. Appeals (6th cir.) 1980, Tex. 2000. Assoc. Thompson, Weir & Barclay, 1977-78; law clk. U.S. Dist. Judge, Cleve., 1978-80; assoc. Squire, Sanders and Dempsey, Cleve., 1980-86, ptnr., 1986-96; v.p., gen. counsel, sec. Caliber System, Inc., Akron, Ohio, 1996-98; sr. v.p. gen. couns. BP America, Inc., 1998-99; assoc. gen. counsel Upstream Western Hemisphere BP, 1999—2002; assoc. gen. counsel Upstream GP&R Global BP, London, 2003—06; group compliance ethics officer BP PLC, London, 2006—. Master bencher Am. Inns of Ct. Found., 1987-98; mem. civil justice reform act adv. group U.S. Dist. Ct. (no. dist.) Ohio. Del. Hamilton Coll. Alumni Coun., 1992-97, regional chair alumni admissions, 1993—97; trustee The Cath. Charities Corp., 1995-97; mem. Cuyahoga County Rep. Exec. Com., Cleve., 1984—98; mem. Seton Soc. St. Vincent Hosp. Fund. Roman Catholic. Avocations: golf, jogging. Home: Chilton House Ravenscroft Rd St Georges Hill Weybridge Surrey KT13 0NX England Office: BP PLC 1 St James Sq London SW1Y 4PD England Home Phone: 44 1932 862 810; Office Phone: 44 1932 771709, 44 20 7496 4299. E-mail: lynchjl@bp.com.

LYNCH, JOHN F., lawyer; BSChemE, Rensselaer Poly. Inst., 1960; JD, Fordham U., 1964. Bar: DC, Fla., NY, Tex., Wash., registered: US Ct. Appeals, Fed. Cir., US Patent & Trademark Office, US Supreme Ct. Engr. Hercules Power Co.; atty. Monsanto Company; atty. & patent agent Union Carbide Corp.; ptnr. & mem. exec. com. Howrey Simon Arnold & White LLP, Houston. Author: Patent Litig.: Procedure & Tactics; contbr. articles to profl. jours. Named one of top 20 patent lawyers, Euromoney Legal Media Group's Best of the Best: 2000 Ed., 100 most influential lawyers in Am., Nat. Law Jour., 2000. Mem.: ABA, Wash. State Bar Assn., Tex. Bar Assn., Licensing Exec. Soc., Houston Bar Found., Houston Bar Assn., Fed. Cir. Bar Assn., Am. Intellectual Property Law Assn. Office: Howrey LLP 1111 Louisiana 25th Fl Houston TX 77002-5230 Home Phone: 360-437-7605. Office Fax: 713-787-1440. Business E-Mail: lynchj@howrey.com.

LYNCH, JOHN F., human resources specialist; b. Edinburgh; m. Sarajane Lynch; 3 children. Attended, Blairs Coll. Aberdeen, St. Andrews Coll. Mgmt. positions UK auto fin. GE Capital, 1991—94; HR leader GE Capital Fin. Europe, 1994—95; sr. HR leader GE Capital Glob. Consumer Fin., Stamford, Conn., 1995—2001; v.p. HR GE Medical Systems, Milw., 2001—04, GE Healthcare, London, 2004—07; sr. v.p. corp. HR GE, Fairfield, Conn., 2007—. Office: GE 3135 Easton Tpke Fairfield CT 06431*

LYNCH, JOHN H., governor; b. Waltham, Mass., Nov. 25, 1952; s. William and Margaret Lynch; m. Susan Lynch; children: Jacqueline, Julia, Hayden. BA, U. NH, 1974; MBA, Harvard Bus. Sch., 1979; JD, Georgetown U. Law Ctr., 1984. Dir. admissions Harvard Bus. Sch.; pres., CEO Knoll, Inc., 1994—2001; pres. The Lynch Group, Manchester, 2001—04; gov. State of N.H., Concord, 2005—. Bd. dirs. Capitol Ctr. for Arts; past-pres. alumni assn. U. N.H.; bd. dirs. Catholic Med. Ctr., Manchester, Mass., 1997—2003; mem. bd. trustees Univ. Sys. NH, 2000—, chmn. bd. trustees, 2001—04; coach youth soccer, hockey and baseball teams. Democrat. Office: Office of Governor State House 25 Capitol St Concord NH 03301 Office Phone: 603-271-2121. Office Fax: 603-271-7680.*

LYNCH, JOHN JAMES, lawyer; b. Evergreen Park, Ill., Aug. 22, 1945; s. John J. and Agnes (Daly) L.; m. Kathleen Russell, Aug. 15, 1970; children: Kerry, Elizabeth, Erin. BA, St. Mary of the Lake Sem., 1967; MA in Philosophy, DePaul U., Chgo., 1970, JD, 1973. Bar: Ill. 1973, U.S. Dist. Ct. (no. dist.) Ill. 1973, U.S. Ct. Appeals (7th cir.) 1976. Assoc. McKenna, Storer, Rowe, White & Haskell, Chgo., 1973-75, Haskell & Perrin, Chgo., 1975-77, ptnr., 1977-2000, Figliulo & Silverman, Chgo., 2000—. Pres. bd. trustees Village Western Springs, Ill., 2005—. Mem. ABA, Ill. State Bar Assn., Chgo. Bar Assn., Fedn. Def. and Corp. Counsel. Office: Figliulo & Silverman Ten S LaSalle St Ste 3600 Chicago IL 60603 Office Phone: 312-251-5280. E-mail: jlynch@fslegal.com.

LYNCH, JOHN PETER, lawyer; b. Chgo., June 5, 1942; s. Charles Joseph and Anne Mae (Loughlin) Lynch; m. Judy Godvin, Sept. 21, 1968; children: Julie, Jennifer. AB, Marquette U., 1964; JD, Northwestern U., 1967. Bar: Ill. 1967, U.S. Ct. Appeals (7th cir.) 1979, U.S. Ct. Appeals (5th cir.) 1976, U.S. Supreme Ct. 1979. Atty. Kirkland & Ellis, Chgo., 1970—73, ptnr., 1973—76, Hedlund, Hunter & Lynch, Chgo., 1976—82, Latham, Watkins, Hedlund, Hunter & Lynch, Chgo., 1982—85, Latham & Watkins, Chgo., 1985—, and vice chair, global litig. dept., also resident ptnr. Paris, 2001—. Former mem. exec. com. Latham & Watkins. Notes and Comments editor: Northwestern U. Law Rev., 1967. Mem. vis. com. Northwestern U. Law Sch. Lt. USN, 1968—71. Mem.: ATLA, ABA, Ill. Bar Assn., Order of Coif, Met. Club, Exec. Club, City Club. Home: 439 Sheridan Rd Kenilworth IL 60043-1220 Office: Latham & Watkins Ste 5800 Sears Tower 233 S Wacker Dr Chicago IL 60606 also: Latham & Watkins 53 quai d'Orsay 75007 Paris France

LYNCH, JOHN TERRENCE, professional football player; b. Hinsdale, Ill., Sept. 25, 1971; m. Linda; 1 child, Jake. Student, Stanford U. Safety Tampa Bay Buccaneers, 1993—2003, Denver Broncos, 2004—. Active San Diguieto Boys Club; creator Lynch's Safety Zone; founder Lynch Family Legacy Scholarship. Named to NFL Pro-Bowl, 1999—2002, 2004. Achievements include being a member of Super Bowl Champion Tampa Bay Buccaneers, 2003. Office: c/o Denver Broncos 13655 Broncos Pkwy Englewood CO 80112

LYNCH, JOHN THOMAS, retired science administrator, physicist; b. Washington, Mar. 21, 1938; s. John Thomas and Mary Ellen (Kaye) L.; m. Leslie Gray, June 22, 1959 (div. June 1972); children: John Thomas III, Michael Gray; m. Carol Rollins, July 5, 1980. BS in Physics, Va. Poly. Inst., 1963; MS in Physics, U. Wis., 1965, PhD, 1972. Lab. technician Nat. Bur. Standards, Washington, 1957-60; rsch. scientist U. Wis., Madison, 1965-78; staff Los Alamos (N.Mex.) Nat. Labs., 1978-81; program scientist NASA Hdqs., Washington, 1981-85; program dir. aeronomy and astrophysics Polar programs NSF, Washington, 1985-2000; ret., 2000. Contbr. articles to sci. jours. Recipient Antarctic svc. medal USN, 1986; named Disting. Alumni fellow dept. physics U. Wis., Madison, 2003; a mountain in Antarctica is named in his honor. Avocations: music, sailing. Personal E-mail: JLynch137@comcast.net.

LYNCH, JUNEANN M., medical/surgical nurse, nursing educator; d. Samuel Frendo and Iris Agatha Thompson; 1 child, Joel. RN cert., New Amsterdam Sch. Nursing, Guyana, 1984; cert. in midwifery, New Amsterdam Sch. Nursing, 1986. RN Calif., Wash. RN, charge nurse med./surg. and pediat. units New Amsterdam Hosp., Guyana, 1984—89, midwife, 1986—89; RN, midwife Dennery Hosp., Dennery, Saint Lucia, 1990—92; head nurse St. Lucia Cancer Soc., Castries, 1992—96; RN, midwife Tapion Hosp., Castries, 1996—99; RN Swedish Hosp., Seattle, 2000—01, Overlake Hosp., Bellevue, Wash., 2001—; RN instr. Edmonds C.C., Lynnwood, Wash., 2003—. Conf. rep. Nat. Network Health Career Programs in 2-Yr. Colls., Seattle; workshop rep. St. Lucia Cancer Soc., Castries, 1992—96; faculty student advisor for allied health edn. Edmonds C.C., 2004—; Edmonds C.C. rep. Dept. Health, Olympia, Wash., 2005; instr. Lake Washington Tech. Coll. Contbr. articles to profl. jours. Bible instr., New Amsterdam, 1971—89; ho. to ho. ministry Castries, 1989—99, Bellevue, 1999—. Named Best student in Midwifery, New Amsterdam Hosp., 1986; recipient cert. in piano, Trinity Coll. of Music, 1969. Mem.: Wash. State Nurses Assn. Avocations: music, dance, piano, reading, travel. Office: Edmonds CC 20000 68th Ave W Lynnwood WA 98036-5999 Office Phone: 425-460-1712. E-mail: juneann.lynch@edcc.edu.

LYNCH, KIRSTEN, food products executive; b. Chgo., 1968; BA, Ill. State U., 1990; MA, Washington U., St. Louis, 1990. With Kraft Foods, Chgo., 1996—; mktg. dir., Macaroni & Cheese Kraft Foods, Inc., 2005—. Avocation: snowboarding. Office: Kraft Foods Inc 3 Lakes Dr Northfield IL 60093 Office Phone: 847-646-2000, 847-646-0372. Office Fax: 847-646-6005. E-mail: klynch@kraft.com.*

LYNCH, KYLE THOMAS, lawyer; b. Glen Cove, NY, Aug. 5, 1974; BA, Hartwick Coll., 1996; AS, Johnson & Wales U., 1998; JD, Hofstra U., 2003. Bar: N.Y. 2004. Ptnr. Lynch Legal Assocs., LLP, Williston Park, NY, 2004—. Office: Lynch Legal Associates LLP 431 Willis Avenue Williston Park NY 11596 Home Phone: 516-746-2072; Office Phone: 516-746-2072. Office Fax: 516-248-2972. Business E-Mail: kylelynch@lynchlegal.com.

LYNCH, LORETTA E., lawyer, former prosecutor; b. Durham, NC, May 21, 1959; d. Lorenzo Lynch. Grad., Harvard Coll., 1981; JD, Harvard U., 1984. Bar: N.Y., U.S. Dist. Ct. (ea. dist. NY), U.S. Dist. Ct. (so. dist. NY), U.S. Ct. Appeals (2nd cir.). Litigation assoc. Cahill, Gordon & Reindel, 1984-90; with Office of U.S. Atty. for Ea. Dist. of N.Y., 1990—2001; chief L.I. offices, 1994-98; chief asst. U.S. States Atty., 1998—99; U.S. atty. ea. dist. N.Y. U.S. Dept. Justice, Bklyn., 2000—01; ptnr. Hogan & Hartson LLP, NYC, 2002—. Instr. Dept. Justice Criminal Trial Advocacy Prog.; adj. prof. St. John's Univ. Sch. Law; bd. dir. Fed. Reserve Bank N.Y., Office of the Appellate Defender; trustee Nat. Inst. Trial Advocacy; mem. Magistrate Judge Selection Panel Ea. Dist. N.Y., Judicial Screening Panel of Sen. Charles Schumer, NYC Charter Revision Commn., NY State Commn. on Jury, 2003—04; bd. advs. Brennan Ctr. for Justice, NYU Sch. Law. Author: White-Collar Crime: Counseling Corporate Clients Under Investigation, 2003. Bd. dirs. Nat. Inst. Law and Equity. Named one of Am.'s Top Black Lawyers, Black Enterprise Mag., 2003. Mem.: ABA (mem. sec. on litig.), Ea. Dist Com. on Civil Litigation, Fed. Bar. Coun., Assn. Bar N.Y.C. (chair Criminal Law Com.). Avocations: reading, tennis. Office: Hogan & Hartson 875 Third Ave New York NY 10022

LYNCH, LUCIA, language educator; d. Raul F. Soares Pinto and Silvia M. Lamoglia. BBA in Mktg., N.Ga. Coll., Dahlonega, 1986—88; M in Spanish Culture & Lang., U. Salamanca, Spain, 2003—04. Cert. tchr. Profl. Standards Commn., Ga., 2001. Instr. wellness, preventive medicine & fitness Northeast Ga. Med. Ctr., Gainesville, Ga., 1986—88; dir. Dept. Def., Schwaebisch Hall, Baden-Wuttemberg, Germany, 1989—93; tourism mgr. Berlichingen Aleman Panameno, Ciudad de Panama, 1994—95; fgn. lang. tchr. Va. L. Heard Elem. Sch., Savannah, Ga., 2000—06, Armstrong Atlantic State U., Savannah, 2004—05; substitute tchr. Dept. Def. Edn. Activity, Wiesbaden, Germany, 2007—. Parish coun. St. Frances Cabrini Ch., Savannah, 2006. Mem.: Am. Coun. Tchg. Fgn. Langs. (corr.). Roman Cath. Avocations: reading, travel, yoga. Home: Haideweg # 6 Sonnenberg-Wiesbaden 65191 Germany Home Phone: 49-611-1745635. Personal E-mail: lucialynch@hotmail.com.

LYNCH, LUKE DANIEL, JR., lawyer; b. Bklyn., Mar. 28, 1945; s. Luke Daniel and Marjorie Carol (Thien) L.; m. Nancy G. Ott, Sept. 19, 1970; children: Luke D. III, Bettina Anne. BA cum laude, Yale U., 1966; JD, Harvard U., 1969. Bar: N.Y. 1969, U.S. Dist. Ct. (so. dist.) N.Y. 1970. Assoc. Shearman & Sterling, NYC, 1969-78; spl. asst. U.S. Treasury Dept., Washington, 1978-79, assoc. gen. counsel, 1979-82; gen. counsel Chrysler Corp Loan Guaranty Bd., Washington, 1981-82; ptnr. D'Amato & Lynch, P.C., NYC, 1983—. Mem. ABA. Avocation: golf. Office: D'Amato & Lynch 70 Pine St Fl 41 New York NY 10270-0110

LYNCH, MATTHEW J., information technology executive, retail executive; Grad., No. Ariz. U., Coll. Engring. Tech. Software engr. Sperry Aerospace; info. sys. mgmt. Air Wis. Airlines, Am. West Airlines, Honeywell, Aerospace Electronics Sys., 1985—93; v.p., info. tech. svcs. Runzheimer Internat., 1993—98; v.p., oper. tech. svcs. ShopKo, Green Bay, Wis., 1998—2003, sr. v.p., chief info. officer, 2003—. Named one of Premier 100 IT Leaders, Computerworld, 2006. Office: ShopKo 700 Pilgrim Way Green Bay WI 54304

LYNCH, MICHAEL, lawyer, staffing company executive; BSBA, JD, Marquette U. Tax mgr. Arthur Andersen & Co.; dir. corp. tax Manpower, Inc., Milw., 1990—93, v.p. corp. tax, 1993, v.p. internat. support services., internat. gen. counsel, 1999—. Office: Manpower Inc 5301 N Ironwood Rd Milwaukee WI 53217*

LYNCH, MICHAEL A., health products executive; B, Cornell U. Sales rep. V. Mueller divsn. Cardinal Health, Inc., Dublin, Ohio, 1984—87, region mgr. Oper. Rm. divsn., 1987, v.p., gen. mgr. Thermal Bus. Grp., 1995, pres. Gloves divsn., pres. Med. Specialties, grp. pres. Med. Products Mfg. Office: Cardinal Health Inc 7000 Cardinal Pl Dublin OH 43017*

LYNCH, MONIQUE CHRISTINE, mathematics educator; b. Washington, Feb. 20, 1970; d. Verel Willard and Carol Sue Benson; m. John Patrick Lynch, July 17, 1999. BA, U. No. Colo., 1992; MA, U. Colo., 1996; PhD, George Mason U., 2003. Cert. Math Tchr. Va., 2000, Colo., 1992. Math. tchr. Englewood Pub. Schs., Colo., 1992—96; rsch. assn. CORD, Waco, Tex., 1996—97; math. curriculum specialist Ingenius, Englewood, 1997—98; math. tchr. Jefferson County Pub. Schs., Lakewood, Colo., 1998—99; continuing edn. mgr. Coun. for Exceptional Children, Reston, Va., 1999—2000; faculty, project mgr. George Mason U., Fairfax, Va., 2000—03; asst. prof. Salisbury U., Md., 2003—05; dir. of profl. devel. programs and svcs. Nat. Coun. of Tchrs. of Math., Reston, Va., 2005—. Freelance author, 1992—2003. Vol. Habitat for Humanity, Leesburg, Va., 2004. Doctoral Rsch. fellow, George Mason U., 2002-2003, PT3 grant, Tex. Instruments, 2003-2004. Mem.: Mathematics Assn. Am., Assn. Advancement Computers in Edn., Internat. Soc. Tech. in Edn., Nat. Coun. Tchrs. Math., Am. Ednl. Rsch. Assn. Avocations: rubber stamping cards, pottery painting, walking, scrapbooks. Home: 400 Salyor Way SW Leesburg VA 20175 Office: Nctm 1906 Association Dr Reston VA 20191 Home Phone: 703-777-5672; Office Phone: 703-620-9840 2150. Personal E-mail: drmlynch@yahoo.com. E-mail: mlynch@nctm.org.

LYNCH, NANCY ANN, computer scientist, educator; b. Bklyn., Jan. 19, 1948; d. Roland David and Marie Catherine (Adinolfi) Evraets; m. Dennis Christopher Lynch, June 14, 1969; children: Patrick, Kathleen (dec.), Mary. BS, Bklyn. Coll., 1968; PhD, MIT, 1972. Asst. prof. math. Tufts U., Medford, Mass., 1972-73, U. So. Calif., Los Angeles, 1973-76, Fla. Internat. U., Miami, 1976-77; assoc. prof. computer sci. Ga. Tech. U., Atlanta, 1977-82, MIT, Cambridge, 1982-86, prof. computer sci., 1986—, NEC prof. software sci. and engring., 1996—. Ellen Swallow Richards chair MIT, 1982-87, Cecil H. Green chair, 1994-96. Contbr. numerous articles to profl. jours. Recipient Adriaan van Wijngarden Achievement award for excellence in math. and computer sci., 2006. Fellow: Assn. Computing Machinery; mem.: NAE. Roman Catholic. Office: MIT 32-G668 Comp Sci & Artificial Intelligence Lab 32 Vassar St Cambridge MA 02139

LYNCH, PATRICK C., state attorney general; b. Providence, Feb. 4, 1965; s. Dennis and Irene Lynch; m. Christin Lynch; children: Kelsy, Graham. BA, Brown U., 1987; JD, Suffolk U., 1992. Bar: R.I. 1992, U.S. Dist. Ct. R.I. 1993. Clk. to Justice Joseph Rodgers Jr. RI Superior Ct., 1993—94; spl. asst. atty. gen. State of RI, Providence, 1994—99, atty. gen., 2003—; assoc. Tillinghast Licht Perkins Smith and Cohen, LLP, Providence, 1999—2003. Sec., bd. dirs. Advent House; bd. mem. Camp St. Cmty. Ministries, Brown Club, RI; mem. Brown Hall of Fame Com.; former pres. bd. St. Raphael. Mem.: RI Bar Assn. Democrat. Office: Office of Atty Gen 150 S Main St Providence RI 02903 Office Phone: 401-274-4400.*

LYNCH, PETER JOHN, retired dermatologist; b. Mpls., Oct. 22, 1936; s. Francis Watson and Viola Adeline (White) L.; m. Barbara Ann Lanzi, Jan. 18, 1964; children: Deborah, Timothy. Student, St. Thomas Coll., 1954-57; BS, U. Minn., 1958, MD, 1961. Intern U. Mich. Med. Ctr., 1961-62, resident in dermatology, 1962-65, asst. prof., then assoc. prof. dermatology, 1968-73; clin. instr. U. Minn., 1965; chief dermatology and venereal disease Martin Army Hosp., Columbus, Ga., 1966-68; asso. prof. to prof. dermatology U. Ariz., Tucson, 1973-86, chief sect. dermatology, 1973-86, asso. head dept. internal medicine, 1977-86; prof., head dermatology U. Minn. Med. Sch., Mpls., 1986-95; med. dir. ambulatory care U. Minn. Health Sys., 1993-95; prof., chmn. dept. dermatology U. Calif., Davis, 1995-2000, prof. emeritus, 2000—, tng. program dir., 2001—, Frederick G. Novy, Jr. prof., 2005—. Author: (with S. Epstein) Burckhardt's Atlas and Manual of Dermatology and Venereology, 1977, Dermatology for the House Officer, 1982, 3rd edit., 1994, (with W.M. Sams) Principles and Practice of Dermatology, 1992, 2nd edit., 1996, (with I.E. Edwards) Genital Dermatology, 1994. With AUS, 1966-68. Decorated Army Commendation Medal; recipient Disting. Service award for faculty U. Mich., 1970, Disting. Faculty award U. Ariz., 1981 Mem. Am. Acad. Dermatology (hon., bd. dirs. 1974-78, v.p. 1991-92), Assn. Profs. Dermatology (bd. dirs. 1976-80, pres. 1994-96), Internat. Soc. Study of Vulvar Disease (bd. dirs. 1976-79, pres. 1983), Soc. Investigative Dermatology, Am. Bd. Dermatology (bd. dirs. 1984-89), Gougerot Soc. (Bronze medal award), Alpha Omega Alpha. Democrat. Roman Catholic. Home: 425 Hartnell Pl Sacramento CA 95825-6615 Office: U Calif 3301 C St #1400 Sacramento CA 95816 E-mail: pjlynch@ucdavis.edu.

LYNCH, PETER K., education educator; b. Rockville Centre, NY; s. George W. and Veronica Rennie Lynch; m. Barbara Yates Lynch, Feb. 17, 1968. BA in English, Hofstra U., Hempstead, NY, 1965, MA in Secondary Edn., 1969, profl. diploma, 1975; EdD in Ednl. Leadership, St. John's U., Jamaica, NY, 1981. Tchr. English Baldwin HS, NY, 1966—75, dean of students, 1975—82, asst. prin., 1982, prin., 1982—88; asst. supt. Baldwin Pub. Schs., 1988—2001; prof. edn. Molloy Coll., Hempstead, 1999—. Mem. commn. secondary schs. Mid. States Assn., Phila., 1993—2001; mem. LI Sch. Leadership Bd., 2006—. Contbr. chapters to books. Mem. Baldwin Coun. Against Drug Abuse, 1975—, Baldwin Found. Edn., 1988—. Mem.: ASCD, Kappa Delta Pi, Phi Delta Kappa (treas. 1975—). Avocations: kayaking, swimming, photography, needlecrafts. Office: Molloy Coll 1000 Hemstead Ave Rockville Centre NY 11571 Office Phone: 516-678-5000.

LYNCH, PETER L., retail executive; m. Maddy Lynch; 2 children. BS in Fin., Nichols Coll. V.p., gen. mgr. Star Markets, Boston; pres. Acme Markets subs. Am. Stores Co., Malvern, Pa.; exec. v.p. ops. Albertson's Inc., Boise, Idaho, 1999-2000, pres., COO, 2000—03; pres., CEO Winn-Dixie Stores, Inc., Jacksonville, Fla., 2004, chmn., pres., CEO, 2006—. Mem. bd. dirs. Winn-Dixie Stores Inc, 2004—. Office: Winn-Dixie Stores Inc 5050 Edgewood Ct Jacksonville FL 32254*

LYNCH, ROBERT BERGER, retired lawyer, judge; b. LaCrosse, Wis., June 10, 1931; s. Jan P. and Eve (Berger) Lynch; m. Iris D. Healy; 1 child, Jan Fredrick. BS, U.S. Merchant Marine Acad., 1955; JD, U. of the Pacific, 1967. Bar: Calif. 1969, US Supreme Ct. 1972. Engr. AeroJet-Gen. Corp., Sacramento, 1955-61, proposal mgr., 1961-63, asst. contract adminstrn. mgr., 1963-66, contract adminstrn. mgr., 1967-70; pvt. practice Rancho Cordova, Calif., 1969—2000; ret., 2000. Instr. bus. law Solano C.C., 1977—79, San Joaquin Delta Coll., 1978—79; mediator family law panel Sacramento Superior Ct.; traffic and small claims pro tem judge Sacramento, 1997—2001; appointed presiding judge Mcpl. Ct., Bisbee, Ariz., 2001—02. Active charity fund-raising campaigns, Sacramento, 1966-68; mission com. St. Clements Episcopal Ch., Rancho Cordova, Calif., 1967-68; pres. bd. dirs., trustee Los Rios C.C. Dist., Calif., 1971-79; ch. advocate Diocese of No. Calif. Episcopal Ch., 1975; vestryman, reader St. Mark's Anglican Ch., Loomis, Calif., 2000-01; reader St. John the Divine Ch., Hereford, Ariz., 2002-; vice chancellor Diocese of Pacific and S.W., Anglican Rite, 2005; sub deacon St. John the Divine, 2007—. With USCG, 1949-51, USNR, 1951-80, N.G., 1988-91, maj. US Army, appt. col. US Vols., ret. Fellow: Calif. Rifle and Pistol Assn. (life); mem.: NRA, IEEE, Calif. Wildlife Fedn., Calif.-Am. Pistol and Rifle Assn., Mil. Officers Am. Assn., Marines Meml. Assn., Gun Owners Am., Internat. Turtle Club, Am. Legion. Personal E-mail: rblynch@dtg-llc.com.

LYNCH, ROBERT EMMETT, mathematics professor; b. Chgo., Feb. 5, 1932; s. Joseph Burke and Mildred Cecilia (Bildhauser) L.; m. Martha Bolling Hacker, Oct. 8, 1955; children: Barbara Ann, William Robert, Pamela Elizabeth. B of Engring. Physics, Cornell U., Ithaca, NY, 1954; MS, Harvard U., Cambridge, Mass., 1959, PhD, 1963. Sr. rsch. mathematician Gen. Motors Rsch. Lab., Warren, Mich., 1961-64; assoc. prof. computer sci. and math. U. Tex., Austin, 1964—67, Purdue U., West Lafayette, Ind., 1967-85, prof., 1985—; prof. emeritus, 1998—. Author: (with Garrett Birkhoff) Numerical Solution of Elliptic Problems, 1984; (with John R. Rice) Computers, Their Impact and Use/with Basic, 1975, Computers, Their Impact and Use/With Fortran, 1977, Computers, Their Impact and Use/with PL/1, 1978. Lt. USAF, 1955-57.

LYNCH, ROBERT MARTIN, lawyer, consultant; b. St. Louis, Mar. 28, 1950; s. Raymond Burns and Nancy Winn (Roeder) L.; m. Cynthia Kay Allmeyer, June 7, 1974; children: Christopher, Kelly, Stephanie. AB, St. Louis U., Mo., 1972, JD, 1975. Bar: Mo. 1975, DC 1985, Tex. 1992. Law clk. to presiding justice Mo. Ct. Appeals, St. Louis, 1975-76; atty. Southwestern Bell Telephone Corp., St. Louis, 1976-79, atty. network, 1979-83, gen. atty., 1983-88, v.p., asst. gen. counsel, 1988-91; v.p., gen. counsel Tex. office Southwestern Bell Telephone Co., Dallas, 1991-93, v.p., gen. counsel external affairs San Antonio, 1993-98; sr. v.p., gen. counsel external affairs SBC Comm., Inc., 1998—99, sr. v.p., gen. counsel bus. and consumer markets, 1999-2000; sr. v.p. gen. counsel SBC Ops., Inc., 2000—02; sr. v.p. assoc. gen. counsel SBC Ameritech, 2002—03; pvt. cons., 2003—06; counsel Devoto and Benbenek LLC, 2006—. Instr. paralegal studies St. Louis C.C., 1977-91; adj. prof. Webster U., St. Louis, 2005-. Mem. ABA, Tex. Bar, Dallas Bar Assn., Mo. Bar Assn. (adminstrv. law com. coun.), St. Louis Bar Assn. (chmn. adminstrv. law com. 1981-82), Am. Corp. Counsel Assn. (chmn. communications com. St. Louis chpt., chmn. law dept. mgmt. com. 1997-98, bd. dirs. 1999—). Republican. Avocations: racquetball, writing. Home: 206 Topton Way Saint Louis MO 63105-3638 Personal E-mail: blynch@sbcglobal.net. Business E-Mail: blynch@devotobenbenek.com.

LYNCH, SANDRA LEA, federal judge; b. Oak Park, Ill., July 31, 1946; d. Bernard Francis and Eugenia Tyus Lynch; married; 1 child. AB in Philosophy, Wellesley Coll., 1968; JD cum laude, Boston U., 1971. Bar: Mass. 1971, US Supreme Ct. 1974. Law clk. to Hon. Raymond J. Pettine US Dist. Ct., Providence; asst. atty. gen. Commonwealth of Mass., Boston, 1974; gen. counsel Mass. Dept. Edn., Boston, 1974—78; ptnr. Foley, Hoag & Eliot, Boston, 1978—95; judge 1st cir. US Ct. Appeals, Boston, 1995—. Instr. Boston Univ. Law Sch., 1973—74. Contbr. articles to profl. jours. Past co-chair leading industries com. Greater Boston C. of C. Recipient Disting. Alumnae award, Boston U. Law Sch., 1993, Wellesley Coll., 1997, Disting. Svc. award, Planned Parenthood, 1991. Mem.: ABA, Boston Bar Assn. (pres. 1992—93, Jud. Excellence award 2001), Mass. Bar Assn., Nat. Assn. Women Judges, Women's Forum. Office: US Ct Appeals One Courthouse Way Ste 8710 Boston MA 02210-3010*

LYNCH, STEPHEN F., congressman; b. Boston, Mar. 31, 1955; m. Margaret Lynch; 1 child, Victoria. BS, Wentworth Inst. of Tech., 1988; JD, Boston Coll., 1991; MPA, Harvard U., 1999. Ironworker US Steel Plant, General Motors, General Dynamics Shipyard, 1973—91; former atty. priv. practice; mem. Mass. Ho. Reps., Boston, 1994—96, Mass. Senate, Boston, 1996—2001, US Congress from 9th Mass. dist., 2001—, mem. fin. svc. com., govt. reform com. Co-founder Congressional Labor and Working Families Caucus. Mem.: Boston Ironworkers Union (pres. Local 7). Democrat. Roman Catholic. Office: US Ho of Reps 319 Cannon Ho Office Bldg Washington DC 20515-2109 Office Phone: 202-225-8273. Office Fax: 202-225-3984. E-mail: stephen.lynch@mail.house.gov.*

LYNCH, THOMAS JOSEPH, museum director; b. Omaha, Feb. 15, 1960; s. James Humphery and Patricia Mae (Gaughan) L. BA in History, U. Nebr., 1984. Mus. asst. Father Flanagan's Boys' Home, Boys Town, Nebr., 1986-88, mus. assoc., 1988-93; CEO, dir. Boys Town Hall of History and Fr. Flanagan's House, 1993—. Mem. adv. bd. RSVP; bd. dirs. Union Pacific R.R. Mus. Mem. Am. Assn. for State and Local History, Am. Mus. Assn., Nebr. Mus. Assn. (bd. dirs., former pres.), Nat. Hist. Landmark Stewards Assn. Office: Boys Town Hall of History 14057 Flanagan Blvd Boys Town NE 68010-7509 Business E-Mail: lyncht@boystown.org.

LYNCH, THOMAS PETER, retired investment company executive; b. NYC, May 3, 1924; s. Michael Joseph and Margaret Mary (Fitzgerald) L.; m. Madeleine D'Eufemia, June 3, 1950; children: Francine, Richard. Student, Syracuse U., 1943-44; BBA, Baruch Coll., 1947. Acct. Deloitte, Haskins & Sells, NYC, 1947-56; partner Bache & Co., NYC, 1956-61; v.p. E.F. Hutton Co. Inc., NYC, 1962-67; sr. v.p. E.F. Hutton Group Inc., 1967-72, exec. v.p., 1972-83, pres., dir., 1983-85; ret., 1985. Pres., dir. Cash Res. Mgmt. Inc., 1976-85 Served with U.S. Army, 1943-46. Decorated Bronze Star. Mem. AICPA, Fin. Execs. Inst., Canoe Brook Country Club, Baltusrol Golf Club, Johns Island Club, Morris County Golf Club.

LYNCH, THOMAS WIMP, lawyer; b. Monmouth, Ill., Mar. 5, 1930; s. William Brennan and Mildred Maurine (Wimp) L.; m. Elizabeth J. McDonald, July 30, 1952; children: Deborah, Michael, Maureen, Karen, Kathleen. BS in Geology, U. Ill., 1955, MS in Geology, 1958, JD, 1959. Bar: Ill. 1960, Okla. 1960, U.S. Supreme Ct. 1971, Tex. 1978. Staff atty. Amerada Hess Corp., Tulsa, 1959-72, asst. gen. counsel, 1972-75; mem. Hall, Estill, Hardwick, Gable, Collingsworth & Nelson, Tulsa, 1975; v.p., gen. counsel Tex. Pacific Oil Co., Inc., Dallas, 1975-80, Oryx Energy Co., Dallas, 1980-94; ret., 1994. Adj. prof. law U. Tulsa, 1974; trustee Ctr. Am. and Internat. Law, chmn., lectr. ann. Oil and Gas Short course, 1976-92; adv. bd. Oil and Gas Edn. Ctr.; chmn. Oil, Gas and Energy Resources Law sect. State Bar of Tex., 1995-96. Served with USN, 1948-49, U.S. Army, 1951-53. Mem. ABA, Okla. Bar Assn., Tex. Bar Assn., Dallas County Bar Assn. Roman Catholic.

LYNCH, TIMOTHY JEREMIAH-MAHONEY, lawyer, educator, theologian, realtor, writer; b. June 10, 1952; s. Joseph David and Margaret Mary (Mahoney) L. MS, JD in Taxation, Golden Gate U., 1981; MA, PhD in Modern European History, U. San Francisco, 1983; Licentiate, Inter-Am. Acad., Rio de Janeiro, 1988; PhD in Classics and Divinity/Theology, Harvard U., 1988; JSD in Constl. Law, Hastings Law Ctr., 1990. Bar: D.C. 1989, Calif., U.S. Ct. Appeals (2d cir.) 1989, U.S. Ct. Appeals (4th cir.) 1990; mem. Bar/Outer Temple/Comml. Bar of U.K.; European Econ. Ct. of 1st Instance. Legal bus., tax, counsel Lynch Real Estate, San Francisco, 1981-85; researcher, writer Kolb, Roche & Sullivan, San Francisco, 1986-88; chmn. internat. law dept. Timothy J.M. Lynch & Assocs., San Francisco, 1987-88, chmn., mng. dir. law dept., 1988—. Chmn., pres., CEO Lynch Real Estate Investment Corp., San Francisco, 1989—; ptnr. Lynch Investment Corp.; bd. lawyer/arbitrators Pacific Coast Stock Exch., NASD, 1994—; chmn. bd. Lynch Holdings Corp. Group; corp. counsel, sr. ptnr. L.A. Ctr. Internat. Comml. Arbitration, 1991—; vis. fellow classics, Inst. of Classical Studies, U. London; rsch. prof. Canon law and ecumenical ch. history grad. Theological Union U. Calif. Berkeley, 1992—; vis. scholar Patristic theology and classical philosophy of ecumenical doctrines, U. Laval, Quebec, Can., 1993—; vis. scholar Medieval ch. history U. Leeds, Eng., 1993-95; del. lectr. 24th Internat. Congress Arts Comms., Kreble Coll., Oxford U., 1997; arbitrator Iran-U.S. Claims Tribunal, The Hague, 1993; mem. internat. corp. adv. bd. J.P. Morgan and Co., N.Y.C.; bd. dirs. Morgan-Stanley Corp., N.Y.C.; chmn. Latin Am., African and Middle East Corp. Groups J.P. Morgan Internat., Corp.; adv. bd. Morgan Stanley Corp., N.Y.C.; mem. Orgn. Econ. Cooperation and Devel., mem. adv. com. Internat. Labor Orgn.; participant Forum/A Group of Internat. Leaders, Calif., 1995, mem. adv. bd. U.S.-Saudi Arabia Bus. Coun., OECD on

Industry and Fin., Paris, 1995, others; apptd. U.S. amb. Spl. Del. to Commn. Security/Coop. in Europe on Econ. and Pub. Reforms in Russian Republics; participant World Outlook Conf. on 21st Century, 1995; mem. Nat. Planning Assns., Washington, Brit.-North Am. Com. on Econ. and Pub. Policy Planning, Global Econ. Coun.; mem. adv. bd. Nat. Bus. Leadership Coun., Washington; mem. Arbitration Tribunal, Geneva; judge World Intellectual Property Orgns.; selected arbitrator, mem. tribunal; mem. arbitration bd., panel of arbitrators NAFTA Trade Policy; mem. adv. com. on private internat. law U.S. State Dept., Washington; mem. Dead Sea Scrolls Rsch. Project, 1998; mem. author and writers group on multi-vol. transl. series classical works from late Roman, medieval near eastern, patristic and early Christian ch. periods Princeton U., 1998, Cath. U. Am., 1998, U. Calif., Berkely, 1998; rsch. prof. Old and New Testament bibl. lit. commentary, 1998. Author: (10 vol. manuscript) History of Ecumenical Doctrines and Canon Law of Church; editorial bd. Internat. Tax Jour., 1993; author: Publishers National Endowment for Arts and Humanities Classical Translations: Latin, Greek, and Byzantine Literary Texts for Modern Theological-Philosophical Analysis of Social Issues; Essays on Issues of Religious Ethics and Social, Public Policy Issues, 1995, 96, others; editorial bd. Internat. Tax Jour., 1993, Melrose Press: Internat. Firm; contbr. articles to profl. jours. Dir., vice chmn. Downtown Assn. San Francisco; councillor, dir. Atlantic Coun. U.S., 1984—; corp. counsel, chmn. spl. arbitrator's tribunal on U.S.-Brazil trade, fin. and banking rels. Inter-Am. Comml. Arbitration Commn., Washington; chmn. nat. adv. com. U.S.-Mid. East rels. U.S. Mid. East Policy Coun., U.S. State Dept., Washington, 1989—; mem. Pres. Bush's Adv. Commn. on Econ. and Public Policy Priorities, Washington, 1989; mem. conf. bd. Mid. East Policy Coun., U.S. State Dept., Washington, 1994—; elected mem. Coun. of Scholars U.S. Libr. Congress, Washington; bd. dirs. Internat. Diplomacy Coun., San Francisco Opera, Ballet, Symphony Assns. Recipient Cmty. Svc. honors Mayor Dianne Feinstein, San Francisco, 1987, Leadership awards St. Ignatius Coll. Prep., 1984, Calif.'s Gold State award, 1990, AU-ABA Achievement award, 1990, Medal of Honor Order Internat. Ambs. Com. U.S. State Dept. and Foreign Svc. Inst., Washington D.C., World Lifetime Achievement award, Induction 20th Century Millenium Hall Fame and Dist. Leadership Hall Fame Am. Acad. Achievement, 1998, award Superior Talent in Bus. and Arts, Century Dist. Acheivement award, Am. Acad. Achievement, 1998, Internat. Cultural award, 1997, Presdl. Seal Honor, 1997, Decree Internat. Cultural Letters, 1997; named Civic Leader of Yr., Nat. Trust for Hist. Preservation, 1988, 89; named to Presdl. Order of Merit, 1991., Induction U.S. Lib. Congress 500 Leaders of Influence Hall Fame, 1998, Noble Installation Orders of Knighthood Royal British Legions by Queen Elizabeth II, 1998. Fellow World Jurist Assn., World Assn. Judges (Washington); mem. ATLA, Internat. Bar Assn. (various coms., internat. litigation, taxation, labor issue), Am. Arbitration Assn. (panelist, internat. decree), Am. Fgn. Law Assn. (various coms.), Am. Soc. Ch. History, Am. Inst. Archaeology (Boston), Pontifical Inst. Medieval Studies (Toronto, Can.), Am. Hist. Assn., Am. Philol. Assn., Inst. European Law, Medieval Acad. Am., U.S. Supreme Ct. Hist. Soc. (presdl. seal of honor, cultural diploma honor), J Canon Law Soc. U.S., Nat. Planning Assn., Nat. Assn. Scholars (Eminent Scholar of Yr. 1993), Netherlands Arbitration Inst. (mem. Gen. Panels of Arbitrators, mem. Permanent Ct. Arbitration), Calif. Coun. Internat. Trade (GATT com., tax com., legis. com.), Practicing Law Inst., Am. Fgn. Law Assn. (mem. editl. bd. Working Groups on Rsch. Jour. for Legal systems of Africa, Mid. East, Latin Am., EEC and Soviet Union), U.S.-China Bus. Coun. (export com., GATT com., banking and fin. com., import com.), Bay Area Coun. (corp. mem.), Nat. Acad. Conciliators (Spl. award), Internat. Bar (mem. U.S. Group on Model on Insolvency Corp. Acts), Ctr. Internat. Comml. Arbitration, Comml. Club (various positions), Am. Venture Capital Assn., Pacific Venture Capital Assn., Am. Soc. Internat. Law, Washington Fgn. Law Soc., Asia-Pacific Lawyers Assn., Soc. Profls. in Dispute Resolution, British Inst. Internat. and Comparative Law, Internat. Law Assn. (U.S. br.), Commercial Bar Assn. of United Kingdom (London), Inter-Pacific Bar Assn. (Tokyo; mem. arbitration intellectual property, consitutional taxation, labor, legal groups), Inst. European Law Faculty of Laws (United Kingdom), Urban Land Inst. Internat., Mid. East Inst. (Am.-Arab Affairs Coun.), Inter-Am. Bar Assn., 1987—, Calif. Trial Lawyers Assn., Ctr. Reformation Rsch. (co-chmn. Calif. State Com. on U.S-Mid. East Econ. and Polit. Rels.), Soc. Biblical Lit., Am. Acad. Arts and Letters, Am. Acad. Religion, World Lit. Acad., Coun. Scholars, Am. Com. on U.S.-Japan Rels., Japan Soc. No. Calif., Pan-Am. Assn. San Francisco, Soc. Indsl./Office Realtors, Assn. Entertainment Lawyers London, Royal Chartered Inst. Arbitrators (London), Soc. Indsl. and Office Realtors, Urban Land Inst., San Francisco Realtors Assn., Calif. Realtors Assn., Coun. Fgn. Rels., Chgo. Coun. Fgn. Rels., Conf. Bd., San Francisco Urban and Planning Assn., U.S. Trade Facilitation Coun., Asia Soc., Am. Petroleum Inst., Internat. Platform Assn., San Francisco C. of C. (bus. policy com., pub. policy com., co-chmn. congl. issues study group), Am. Inst. Diplomacy, Overseas Devel. Coun. (Mid. East, Russian Republics, Latin Am. studies group), Internat. Vis. Ctr. (adv. bd.), Fin. Execs. Inst., Nat. Assn. Corp. Dirs., Heritage Found. (bd. dirs.), Archaeological Inst. Am. (fellow coun. near east studies, Egyptology), Am. Literature Judicature Soc., Soc. of Biblical, Nat. Assn. Indsl. and Office Properties, World Literary Acad. (Cambridge, Eng.), Am. Acad. Arts & Letters, Am. Acad. Religion, Pres. Club, Nat. Assn. Bus. Economists, Villa Taverna Club, Palm Beach Yacht Club, Pebble Beach Tennis Club, Calif. Yacht Club, Commonwealth Club, City Club San Francisco, British Bankers Club, London, San Diego Track Club (registered athlete), Crow Canyon Country Club (bd. dirs.), Western Venture Capital Assn., Am. Venture Capital Assn., Authors Guild, Internat. Pen Soc., diplomate-delegate World Econ. Summit Conf., Paris, 1998, IOSECC Conf. Internat. Org. Securities Conf., Paris, 1998. Republican. Roman Catholic; Clubs: Crow Canyon Country Club, The Players. Avocations: theater, social entertainment events, opera, ballet, fine arts. Home: 501 Forest Ave Ste 804 Palo Alto CA 94301-2631

LYNCH, WILLIAM JOSEPH, lawyer; b. Providence, July 13, 1957; s. Dennis M. and Irene M. (MacIsaac) L.; m. Lynn M. Perna, Feb. 14, 1986; children: Jarred, Blair. BA, Brandeis U., 1979; JD, Suffolk U., 1982. Bar: R.I. 1982, U.S. Dist. Ct. R.I. 1984, U.S. Supreme Ct. 1988. Asst. atty. gen., dir. consumer protection Dept. Atty. Gen., Providence, 1983—85; lawyer Blais Cunningham Crowe & Chester, Pawtucket, RI, 1985—92, McIntyre, Tate, Lynch and Holt, Providence, 1992—. Mem. Pawtucket (R.I.) City Coun., 1986-92; vice chmn., dir. Sargent Rehab. Ctr., Providence, 1988—; dir. Boys & Girls Club, Pawtucket, 1988—, St. Raphael Acad., Pawtucket, 1989—; chmn. R.I. Dem. State Com., 1998—. Named R.I. Ethic Fellow R.I. Inst. for Internat. Sport, 1993. Office: McIntyre Tate Lynch and Holt 321 S Main St Providence RI 02903-7108 Office Phone: 401-351-7700.

LYNCH, WILLIAM REDINGTON, retired lawyer; b. NYC, Nov. 17, 1928; s. Francis Russell Vincent and Helen Adams (Barrett) L.; m. Mary Pomeroy Grant, Aug. 22, 1958; children: Melissa L. Woolford, Elizabeth Barrett, Cynthia Pomeroy, Kimberly Townsend, Sarah Phillips. Student, Phillips Exeter Acad., 1944-47; BA, Yale U., 1951; JD, Columbia U., 1958. Bar: N.Y. 1959, Conn. 1963. Assoc. Milbank Tweed Hadley & McCloy, NYC, 1958-62, Cummings & Lockwood, Stamford, Conn., 1962-66, ptnr., 1966—, ptnr. in charge Greenwich office, 1978-88. Bd. dirs. Greenwich Plaza Inc., 1970-74, Harrison & Ellis Inc., Cairo, Ga., 1985-87, Greenwich News Inc., 1986-90; chmn. ADM Mgmt. Corp., 1989-91. Chmn. Pub. Works Com., Greenwich, 1974-77, Greenwich United Way Campaign, 1975-76; vice chmn. Greenwich Bd. Edn., 1977-81, Rep. Town Meeting, 1967-77, dir., sec. Forum World Affairs, 1992-95. Lt. USNR, 1952-56. Mem. ABA, Conn. Bar Assn., Greenwich Bar Assn. (pres. 1979-80), Greenwich Field Club (pres. 1973-75), Round Hill Club (dir., sec. 1993-96). Congregationalist. Home: 100 Bedford Rd Greenwich CT 06831-2535

LYNCH, WILLIAM THOMAS, JR., advertising executive; b. Evergreen Park, Ill., Dec. 3, 1942; s. William T. and Loretta J. L.; m. Kathleen; children: Kelly, Maureen, Kim, Meagan, Molly. BA, Loras Coll., 1964; MBA, U. Iowa, 1966. Media trainee Leo Burnett Co. Inc., Chgo., 1966-68, asst. account exec., 1968-76, v.p., 1976-79, sr. v.p., 1979-82, exec. v.p., 1981—86; vice chmn. Leo Burnett USA, Chgo., 1985-89, chmn., CEO, 1987—91; pres. Leo Burnett Worldwide, Chgo., 1993; CEO, pres. Leo Burnett Worldwide, Leo Burnett Co. Inc., Chgo., 1993-97; pres., CEO Liam Holdings, Prospect Heights, Ill., 1997—. Bd. dirs. Pella Corp., Krispy Kreme Doughnut Corp., SEI Info. Tech., Smurfit-Stone Container Corp. Bd. dir. U. Chgo. Grad. Sch. Bus., Northwestern Meml. Found.; bd. dirs., mem. exec. com. Big Shoulders Archdiocese of Chgo., Loras Coll. Mem. Econ. Club Chgo., Comml. Club Chgo. Roman Catholic. Avocations: running, skiing, gardening, golf. Office: Liam Holdings 206 N Pine St Prospect Heights IL 60070-1524

LYNCH, WILLIAM WALKER, banker; b. Washington, Sept. 18, 1926; s. Talbott and Gertrude (Farrell) L.; m. Barbara Van Sant, Apr. 21, 1951; children: John S., William Walker, Franklin P., Mark F. BA, George Washington U., 1950. Vice pres., treas., dir. Met. Mortgage Co., Washington, 1950-55; dir., mem. exec. com. Prog. Fed. Savs. & Loan Assn., Washington, 1953-58; v.p., treas., dir. Anderson & Co., Inc., Washington, 1953-59; with First Bank of Fla., West Palm Beach, Fla., 1959-98, exec. v.p., 1966-89, pres., chief exec. officer, 1989-94, chmn. bd., 1994-98. Chmn. 1st Palm Beach Bancorp., 1994-98; mem. tournament com. 53d PGA Championship, 1971; mem. tournament com. 19th World Cup, Internat. Golf Assn., 1971, 69th PGA Championship, 1987; dist. dir. Fla. League Fin. Instns., 1991; dir. Fed. Home Loan Bank of Atlanta, 1991-94; bd. dirs. Fla. Bankers Assn., 1994. Treas. Herbert Hoover Dike Dedication com., 1960; Asst. treas. Fla. Kennedy-Johnson campaign, 1960; bd. dirs. Am. Cancer Soc., 1967-69, 79—, hon. life dir. local United Way, 1962-64; trustee Media Rsch, Ctr.; hon. trustee Parent's T.V. Coun. With USNR, 1944-46. Recipient Free Enterprise Companion medal Palm Beach Atlantic Coll., 1989. Mem. West Palm Beach C. of C. (bd. dirs. 1970), Kiwanis (bd. dirs. West Palm Beach club 1961, v.p. 1970-71, pres. 1971-72), No. Palm Beach Country Club, Pi Kappa Alpha. Republican. Roman Catholic. Home: 1032 Country Club Dr North Palm Beach FL 33408-3716

LYNCH, WILLIAM WRIGHT, JR., investment company executive, engineer; b. Dallas, Aug. 26, 1936; s. William Wright Sr. and Alma Martha (Hirsch) L.; m. June 11, 1960; children: Mary Margaret, Katherine. BSEE, U. Ariz., 1959; MBA, Stanford U., 1962. Pres. Ins. Bldg. Corp., Dallas, 1965-84; ptnr. Estacado Ptnrs., Dallas, 1985—, Encino Co., Dallas, 1970—, Cimarron Properties Co., Tucson, 1972-83. Pres., bd. dirs. Argus Realty Corp., Dallas, 1972—; bd. dirs. Lynch Properties Inc., Dallas, Lynch Investment Co., Dallas, Fleetwood Transp. Svcs., Inc., Dallas; adv. dir. Sun Valley Fruit Co., Albuquerque, 1993-1995, Hacienda Packing, Albuquerque, 1993-95, LTD Enersyst Devel. Ctr., Inc., Dallas, 1995-98, TEWA Mouldings, Albuquerque, 1997-2004. Bd. dirs. Dallas Symphony Orch., 1966-74, Dallas Civic Music, 1970-77, Ednl. Opportunities Inc., Dallas, 1973-90, Dallas Coun. World Affairs, 1990-96; trustee W. W. Lynch Found., Dallas, 1968—. Capt. U.S. Army, 1959-60. Mem.: M.O. Club (Tucson), Verandah Club, Brook Hollow Club. Republican. Episcopalian. Office: Lynch Investment Co Ste 1600 LB-16 1845 Woodall Rodgers Fwy Dallas TX 75201-2295 Personal E-mail: w.w.lynch@sbcglobal.net.

LYNCH-STIEGLITZ, JEAN, geophysicist, educator; b. Ithaca, NY, Sept. 4, 1965; d. Thomas Francis and Barbara Deutsch Lynch; m. Marc Stieglitz, June 9, 1991; children: Noah William Stieglitz, Amelia Henri Stieglitz. PhD, Columbia U., NYC, 1995. Asst. prof. Columbia U., Palisades, NY, 1996—2001, assoc. prof., 2001—03; assoc. prof. paleoclimatology Ga. Inst. Tech., Atlanta, 2003—. Contbr. scientific papers to profl. jours. Mem.: AAAS, Geol. Soc. Am., Am. Geophys. Union. Achievements include research in role of oceans in past climate change. Office: Ga Inst Tech 311 Ferst Dr Atlanta GA 30332 Office Phone: 404-894-3944.

LYND, LEE RYBECK, biology educator; b. Poughkeepsee, NY, May 9, 1958; s. Staughton and Alice (Niles) L.; m. Betsy Rybeck, June 21, 1980; children: Geordie Rybeck, Noah Staughton Rybeck. BS, Bates Coll., 1979; MS in Bacteriology, U. Wis., 1981; MS in Engring. Sciences, Thayer Sch. Engring., 1983; DEng, Thayer Sch., 1987. Rsch. asst. prof. Thayer Sch. Engring., Dartmouth, NH, 1987, asst. prof. engring., 1987-91, prof. engring., adj. asst. prof. biology, 1990—. Co-founder, chief scientific officer, dir., Mascoma Corp., Cambridge, Mass., 2005-; mgr., Link Found. Energy Fellowship prog., 1998-; prof. extraordinary microbiology, U. Stellenbosch, South Africa; mem. organizing com., Annual Symposium on Biotechnology for Fuels and Chemicals, 1992; mem. presdl. adv. com. on reducing greenhouse gas emissions from personal vehicles, 1994-95; co-leader, The Role of Biomass in America's Energy Future, 2003-; mem., R&D area coord., Biomass and Agr. Working Group of the Energy Future Coalition, 2003-2004; cons. in field. Assoc. editor, Biotechnology and Bioengineering, 1995-; contbr. articles to profl. jours. Bd. dirs. Muskeg Music, Lebanon, NH, 1983-87, Meriden, NH Players, 1985-91. Recipient Presdl. Young Investigator award NSF, 1990, Charles A. Lindbergh award (two-time winner), Charles D. Scott award, 2005, Lemelson-MIT award for sustainability, 2007; grantee USDA, 1990, Solar Energy Rsch. Inst., 1991, Howard Hughes Med. Inst., 1989. Mem. AAAS, Am. Chem. Soc., Am. Inst. Chem. Engrs., Am. Soc. for Microbiology. Democrat. Mem. Soc. Of Friends. Achievements include patents in distillation process for Ethanol; distillation process and apparatus; propagation of microbial cells on single carbon products. Office: Thayer Sch Engring 8000 Cummings Hall Hanover NH 03755-8000 Address: Mascoma Corp 161 First St 2nd Fl East Cambridge MA 02142 Office Phone: 603-646-2231. Fax: 617-868-0408. Business E-Mail: Lee.Lynd@Dartmouth.edu.*

LYNDRUP, PEGGY B., lawyer; b. Winnipeg, Can., Mar. 27, 1949; BS in Edn. magna cum laude, U. N.D., 1969; MEd, Kent State U., 1971; JD summa cum laude, U. Louisville, 1979. Bar: Ky. 1979, U.S. Dist. Ct. (we. dist.) Ky. 1979, U.S. Dist. Ct. (ea. dist.) Ky. 1981. Atty. Greenebaum Doll & McDonald, PLLC, Louisville, 1979—. Recipient Disting. Alumnus award, U. Louisville Sch. Law, 1989; Brandeis scholar. Mem. ABA, Louisville Bar Assn. (pres. 1989). Office: Greenbaum Doll & McDonald PLLC 3500 National City Tower Louisville KY 40202 Office Phone: 502-587-3626. Business E-Mail: pbl@gdm.com.

LYNDS, GAYLE HALLENBECK, writer; b. Omaha, June 23; d. Paul Duane and Marian Lucille (Tice) Hallenbeck; m. Thomas F. Stone, Aug. 14, 1966 (div. 1984); children: Paul F. Stone, Julia L. Stone; m. Dennis Lynds, Feb. 14, 1986. BA in Journalism, U. Iowa, Iowa City, 1967. Reporter Ariz. Rep., Phoenix, 1967; editor, rsch. asst. Iowa Ctr. for Edn. in Politics, Iowa City, 1968; editor GE-Tempo, Santa Barbara, Calif., 1968—71, Santa Barbara Mag., 1983—86, Prime Mag., Santa Barbara, 1986—89. Tchr. creative writing courses U. Calif., Santa Barbara, Pima Coll., Tucson, Asilomar Writing Conf., Monterey, Calif., So. Calif. Writers Conf., San Diego, others. Author: Masquerade, 1996, Mosaic, 1998; author: (with Robert Ludlum) The Hades Factor, 2000, The Paris Option, 2002, The Altman Code, 2003; author: The Coil, 2004, The Last Spymaster, 2006, Mesmerized, 2001; author: (contbr. first chpt., edited by Mardla Talley) I'd Kill For That, 2004. Mem. Authors Guild, Mystery Writers Am., Internat. Crime Writers, Internat. Thriller Writers, Inc. (co-founder and co-pres.)

LYNE, DOROTHY-ARDEN, secondary school educator; b. Orangeburg, NY, Mar. 9, 1928; d. William Henry and Janet More (Freston) Dean; m. Thomas Delmar Lyne, Aug. 16, 1952 (div. June 1982); children: James Delmar, Peter Freston, Jennifer Dean. BA, Ursinus Coll., Collegeville, Pa., 1949; MA, Tufts U., 1950. Assoc. editor World Peace Found., Boston, 1950-51; editorial assoc. Carnegie Endowment Internat. Peace, NYC, 1951-52; dir. Assoc. of Internat. Rels. Clubs, NYC, 1952-53; editor The Town Crier, Westport, Conn., 1966-68; editorial assoc. Machinery Allied Products Inst., Wash., 1959-63; tchr. Helen Keller Mid. Sch., Easton, Conn., 1967-89. Vice chmn. Cooperative Ednl. Svcs., Fairfield, 1983-85. Editor: Documents in American Foreign Rels., 1950, Current Rsch. in Internat. Affairs, 1951. Chmn. Westport Zoning Bd. of Appeals, 1976-80, Westport Bd. of Edn., 1985-87; vice chmn. Westport Bd. of Edn., 1980-85; mem. Westport Charter Revision Commn., 1966-67. Democrat. Episcopalian.

LYNE, SUSAN MARKHAM, multi-media company executive, former broadcast executive; b. Boston, Apr. 30, 1950; d. Eugene and Ruth (Lally) L.; m. George Crile III; children: Susan Markham, Jane Halle; stepchildren: Katherine Murphy, Elizabeth McCook. Assoc. editor City Mag., San Francisco, 1975-76; west coast editor New Times, San Francisco, 1976-77, mng. editor NYC, 1978, The Village Voice, NYC, 1978-82; v.p. creative devel. IPC Films, NYC, 1982-85; ptnr. Lazar/Lyne Films, NYC, 1985-86; founder Premiere mag., NYC, 1987-96, editor-in-chief, publication dir., 1987—96; exec. v.p. acquisitions, development, and new bus. Walt Disney Motion Picture Group, 1996—98; exec. v.p. movies and miniseries ABC Entertainment, 1998—2002, pres., 2002—04; pres., CEO Martha Stewart Living Omnimedia, Inc., 2004—. Bd. dirs. Lifetime Network, 1996—, Martha Stewart Living Omnimedia, Inc., 2004—, CIT, 2006—. Bd. dirs. Pub. Theater. Named one of 50 Women to Watch, Wall St. Jour., 2006. Mem. Am. Soc. Mag. Editors (bd. dirs. 1993-96). Oversaw the development of recent hits including "Desperate Housewives", "Lost" and "Extreme Makeover, Home Edition". Also guided other programs, including "8 Simple Rules for Dating My Teenage Daughter", "The Bachelor" and "Hope and Faith". Office: Martha Stewart Living Omnimedia Inc 11 W 42nd St New York NY 10036*

LYNEMA, EMILY, library and information scientist, university librarian; MLIS, U. Mich., 2005. Systems libr. for digital projects NC State U. Librs., Raleigh, 2005—, chair Endeca product team, 2005—. Named one of the Movers & Shakers, Libr. Jour., 2007; fellow, Digital Libr. Fedn. Forum, 2006. Achievements include development of Endeca ProFind platform. Office: NC U Librs DH Hill Libr Campus Box 7111 Raleigh NC 27695-7111 Office Phone: 919-513-8031. E-mail: emily_lynema@ncsu.edu.

LYNESS, JEFFREY MARC, psychiatrist, educator; b. Arlington, Va., June 18, 1960; married. BA, U. Rochester, 1983, MD, 1986. Diplomate Am. Bd. Psychiatry and Neurology, Am. Bd. Geriatric Psychiatry. Intern U. Rochester Med. Ctr., NY, 1986—87; resident Yale U., New Haven, 1987—90; fellow geriatric psychiatry U. Rochester Med. Ctr., Rochester, NY, 1990—91, sr. instr., fellow, 1990—93, asst. prof., 1993—99, assoc. prof., 1999—2006, chair third and fourth yr. instrn. com., 1996—2002, dir. program geriat. and neuropsychiatry, dir. med. student edn. psychiatry, 1999—, dir. geriatric psychiatry fellowship, 2000—, prof., 2006—, assoc. chair edn., 2007—. Author: Psychiatric Pearls, 1997. Recipient Young Investigator award, Nat. Alliance Rsch. Schizophrenia and Depression, 1999. Fellow: Gerontol. Soc. Am., Am. Psychiat. Assn. (Nancy C. A. Roeske, MD cert. Recognition 1997, Distinguished Fellow 2003); mem.: Internat. Psychogeriatrics Assn., Assn. Dirs. Med. Student Edn. Psychiatry, Internat. Coll. Geriatric Psychopharmacology, Am. Assn. Geriatric Psychiatry, Alpha Omega Alpha, Phi Beta Kappa. Office: U Rochester Med Ctr 300 Crittenden Blvd Rochester NY 14642

LYNETT, WILLIAM RUDDY, publishing and broadcast executive; b. Scranton, Pa., Jan. 18, 1947; s. Edward James and Jean O'Hara Lynett; m. Mary Jean Foley; children: Scott, Jennifer, Christopher P., Brigid P., Jean O. BS, U. Scranton, 1972. Pub. Scranton Times, 1966—; pres., chief exec. officer Shamrock Communications, Inc., 1971—; pres. Towanda Daily Rev., 1977-81, Owego Pennysaver Press, Inc., 1977-81. Owner, Pres. Mgmt. Program, Harvard U., 1990; vice-chmn. bd. dirs. WVIA TV. Bd. dirs. Cmty. Med. Ctr., Scranton, 1974—96; pres. Scranton Cultural Ctr.; chmn. Mayor's Libr. Fund Drive, 1974; chmn. spl. gifts divsn. Heart Fund, 1975; chmn. United Way of Lackawanna County, 1988; bd. govs. Scranton Area Found., chmn., 1996—97; trustee U. Scranton, 1990—96; chmn. Steamtown Nat. Pk. Grand Opening Com.; mem. exec. com. N.E. coun. Boy Scouts Am.; trustee Marywood Univ. Mem. Nat. Assn. Broadcasters, Pa. Assn. Broadcasters, Am. Newspaper Pubs. Assn., Pa. Newspaper Pubs. Assn., Pa. Newspaper Assn. (bd. dirs.), Greater Scranton C. of C. (chmn. membership drive 1980-81) Clubs: Scranton Country, Elks, K.C. Democrat. Roman Catholic. Office: 149 Penn Ave Scranton PA 18503-2022 Home Phone: 570-586-8088; Office Phone: 570-348-9107. E-mail: blynett@timesshamrock.com.

LYNGBYE, JØRGEN, hospital advisor, researcher; b. Andst, Denmark, July 23, 1929; arrived in Norway, 1988, permanent resident; s. Knud and Estrid Marie Schou (Nielsen) Lyngbye; m. Ulla von Holstein, July 15, 1967 (div. 1982); 1 child, Rie; m. Jintana Detwilaiphong, Jan. 3, 1994. MD, U. Copenhagen, 1956; PhD, U. Arhus, Denmark, 1969. Asst. U. Arhus, 1957-65; asst. prof. U. Copenhagen, 1966-72; sr. cons. Regional Hosp., Frederiksborg, Denmark, 1973-83, Førde, Norway, 1983; assoc. prof. molecular biology, 1984—89; prof. U. Thailand, 1990—91; dir. Regional Hosp., Molde, Norway, 1991—98; sci. advisor Copenhagen, 1999—. Author: Clinical Biochemistry, 1986, Twins--A Unique World Scenario, 1995, Norwegian Handbook of Laboratory Medicine, 1999, Danish Textbook of Laboratory Medicine, 2001, Niels Finsen, A Danish Nobel Prize Laureate, 2003, Ole Roemer, The Scientist, A Biography, 2004; contbr. articles to sci. jours. and newspapers. Sec. Danish Polit. Orgn., Copenhagen, 1977-81. Lt. Danish Army, 1951-66. Decorated WEO Order (Thailand); recipient prize Danish Sci. Soc., 1978, Prix Scientifique, France, 1980, prize Danish Soc. for Protection of Animals, 1987, Applied Physics award, 1993. Mem. Danish Med. Assn. (rep. 1978-83). Avocations: philosophy, mathematics, nuclear physics, music. Home Phone: 45-32576477. Personal E-mail: jin@c.dk.

LYNHAM, C(HARLES) RICHARD, manufacturing executive; b. Easton, Md., Feb. 24, 1942; s. John Cameron and Anna Louise (Lynch) L.; m. Elizabeth Joy Card, Sept. 19, 1964; children: Jennifer Beth, Thomas Richard. BME, Cornell U., 1965; MBA with distinction, Harvard U., 1969. Sales mgr. Nat. Carbide Die Co., McKeesport, Pa., 1969-71; v.p. sales Sinter-Met Corp., North Brunswick, NJ, 1971-72; sr. mgmt. analyst Am. Cyanamid Co., Wayne, NJ, 1972-74; gen. mgr. ceramics and additives div. Foseco Inc., Cleve., 1974-77, dir. mktg. steel mill products group, 1977-79; pres., chief exec. officer Exomet, Inc. subs. Foseco, Inc., Conneaut, Ohio, 1979-81, Fosbel Inc. subs. Foseco, Inc., Cleve., 1981-82; gen. mgr. splty. ceramics group Ferro Corp., Cleve., 1982-84, group v.p. splty. ceramics, 1984-92; owner, pres. Harbor Castings, Inc., North Canton, Ohio, 1992—, Island Castings, Inc., Muskegon, Mich., 2000—; owner, CEO Blue Ridge Castings, Inc., Piney Flats, Tenn., 2000—07. Bd. dirs. Western Res. Bancorp., Inc. Patentee foundry casting ladle, desulphurization of metals. Past pres. bd. trustees Hospice of Medina County; treas., past pres. bd. trustees Bridges Home Health Care. Capt. C.E. US Army, 1965—71. Decorated Bronze Star with one oak leaf cluster; recipient Frank H.T. Rhodes Exemplary Alumni Svc. award, Cornell U., 1999. Mem. Am. Foundrymen's Soc., Cornell U. Alumni Coun., Cornell U. Alumni Class 1963 (past v.p., past pres.), Cornell U. Alumni Fedn. (past pres., bd. dirs., past v.p.), Chippewa Yacht Club (commodore 1982), Cornell Club of N.E.

Ohio (past pres., bd. dirs.), Harbor Bay Yacht Club. Republican. Congregationalist. Avocations: sailing, genealogy. Home: 970 Hickory Grove Ave Medina OH 44256-1616 Office: Harbor Castings Inc 4321 Strausser St NW North Canton OH 44720-7144

LYNN, BRENDA, physical education educator; b. San Gabriel, Calif., Feb. 3, 1964; d. Richard Joseph and Charlene Sue Lynn. BS in Edn., Mo. We. State Coll., St. Joseph, 1987. Tchr. phys. edn. and coach Savannah R-III Sch. Dist., Mo., 1991—96; customer svc. and sales Pickup Palace, St. Joseph, 1996—2001; tchr. phys. edn. and health South Holt R-I Sch. Dist., Oregon, 2001—. Volleyball coach South Holt R-I Sch. Dist., Oregon, Mo., 2001—, coach Jr. H.S. basketball, 2001—05, mem. profl. devel. com., 2003—, chair profl. devel. com., 2005—06, mem. Character Plus leadership com., 2005—, sponsor smokebuster, 2004—, coach Jr. H.S. track, 2001—, sponosr jr. class, 2001—, mem. welfare com., 2005—. Mem.: AAHPERD, Mo. State Tchrs. Assn., Cmty. Tchrs. Assn. (v.p. 2006—), Mo. Alliance Health, Phys. Edn., Recreation and Dance. Office: S Holt RI Sch Dist 201 S Barbour St Oregon MO 64473

LYNN, C(HARLES) STEPHEN, franchising company executive; b. LaGrange, Ga., July 27, 1947; s. Charles Hubert and Norma Lee (Batey) L.; m. Milah Faith Pass, Sept. 4, 1976 BS in Indsl. Engring., Tenn. Tech. U., 1970; MBA, U. Louisville, 1973. Indsl. engr. Brown & Williamson Corp., Louisville, 1970-73; dir. distbn. div. Ky. Fried Chicken Corp., Louisville, 1973-77; pres., chief exec. officer MarQuest, Inc. subs. Century 21 Real Estate Corp., Irvine, Calif., 1978-80; v.p. Century 21 Real Estate Corp., Irvine, 1978-80; exec. v.p., dir., chief operating officer Burtson Corp., Marina Del Rey, Calif., 1980-83; chmn., pres., CEO Sonic Corp., Oklahoma City, 1983—95; also bd. dirs. Sonic Industries, Inc., Oklahoma City; pres., CEO Shoney's Corp., Nashville, 1995; chmn. Cummings Inc., Nashville, 1999—. Bd. dirs. Okla. Healthcare Corp., City Bank, Krispy Kreme Doughnuts Corp., Winston-Salem, NC, 2007—. Bd. dirs. Salvation Army, Oklahoma City, U. Okla. Sch. of Bus., Okla. Art Mus., Allied Arts, Oklahoma City U., Young Pres.'s Orgn., Bapt. Hosp. Found., Scope Ministry Internat., Tenn. Tech. Sch. Engring.; bd. trustees U. Louisville. Mem. Inst. Indsl. Engrs. (pres. 1973), Nat. Restaurant Assn., Internat. Franchise Assn. (bd. dirs. past chmn.), Okla. C. of C. (bd. dirs., past chmn.), Oklahoma City C. of C. (bd. dirs.), Nat. Cowboy Hall of Fame (bd. dirs.), Acad. State Goals, Fellowship Christian Athletes. Republican. Presbyterian. Avocations: tennis; basketball; reading; movies; travel. Office: Cummings Signs 4560 Trousdale Dr Nashville TN 37204*

LYNN, D. JOANNE, physician, researcher; b. Oakland, Md., July 2, 1951; d. John B. and Mary Dorcas (Clark) Harley; m. Barry W. Lynn; children: Christina, Nicholas. BS summa cum laude, Dickinson Coll., 1970; MD cum laude, Boston U., 1974; MA in Philosophy and Social Policy, George Washington U., 1981; MS Clin. Evaluative Scis., Dartmouth Coll., 1995. Diplomate Am. Bd. Internal Medicine. Resident internal Medicine The George Washington U. Med. Ctr., 1974-77; emergency rm. physician, triage physician Washington VA Hosp., 1977-78; faculty assoc. for medicine and humanities divsn. experimental programs George Washington U., Washington, 1978-81, dir. divsn. aging studies, 1988-92, prof. health care scis. and medicine, 1991-92, assoc. chairperson dept. health care scis., 1990-92, dir of the Ctr. to Improve the Care of the Dying, 1995-2000; prof. medicine, cmty. and family medicine, sr. assoc. Ctr. Evaluative Clin. Scis. Dartmouth-Hitchcock Med. Ctr., Hanover, NH, 1992-95, assoc. dir. Ctr. for Aging, 1992-95; dir. RAND Ctr. to Improve Care of the Dying, Arlington, Va., 2000—02; pres. Ams. for Better Care of the Dying, 1995—2005; dir. The Washington Home Ctr. for Palliative Care Studies, 2002—05; sr. natural scientist RAND, 2005—06; med. officer Ctr. Medicine and Med. Svcs., 2006—. Robert Wood Johnson clin. scholar George Washington U., 1977-78, sr. fellow Ctr. Health Policy Rsch., 1991-92; asst. dir. med. studies The Pres. Commn. for Study of Ethical Problems in Medicine and Biomed. and Behavioral Rsch., 1981-83; med. dir. The Washington Home, 1983-89, Hospice of Washington, 1979-91, George Washington Cancer Home Care Program and Home Health Svcs. of The Washington Home, 1990-92, staff physician, 1979-92; fellow Hastings Ctr., 1984—; mem. working group on guidelines for care of terminally ill, 1985-87, rsch. project on ethical issues in care and treatment of chronically ill, 1985-87, working group on new physician-patient relationship, 1991-94, v.p., 1987, chair fellows nominating com., 1991; mem. coordinating coun. on life-sustaining med. treatment decision making by cts. Nat. Ctr. State Cts., 1989-93; fellow Kennedy Inst., 1991; mem. geriat. and gerontology adv. com. Dept. Vet. Affairs, 1991-97; mem. bioethics com. Vets. Health Adminstrn., 1991-93; active Washington Area Seminar on Sci., Tech., and Ethics, 1982-92, Nat. Clin. Panel on High-Cost Hospice Care, Washington, 1991; presenter in field. Author: (with J. Harrold) Handbook for Mortals: Guidance for People Facing Serious Illness, 1999, (with A. Kabenell and J. Lynch Schuster) Improving Care for the End of Life: A Sourcebook for Health Care Managers and Clinicians, 2000, Sick to Death and Not Going to Take It Any More, 2004; author chpts. to books; mem. editl. bd. The Ency. of Bioethics, 1994-95; mem. adv. editl. bd. Biolaw, 1983, The Hospice Jour., 1984—, Med. Ethics for the Physician, 1985-92, Med. Humanities Rev., 1986—, Cambridge Quar., 1991-95; contbr. articles, revs. to profl. jours. Peter Jeffries and Jeanne Arnold scholar, 1973; recipient Wellington Parlin Sci. Scholarship award, 1979, Dr. Bertha Curtis prize Boston U. Med. Sch., 1974, Nat. Bd. award Med. Coll. Pa., 1992. Master ACP (mem. subcom. on aging 1986-91), Am. Geriatrics Soc. (mem. com. public policy 1983-98, mem. ethics com. 1988, chair subcom. on ethics and policy 1986, chair ethics com. 1991-98, bd. dirs. 1991-97); mem. AAAS, APHA, Am. Fedn. Clin. Rsch., Am. Health Care Assn. (mem. task force on AIDS 1987-89), Am. Hosp. Assn. (mem. spl. com. on biomedical ethics 1983-85, 89-94), Am. Med. Dirs. Assn., Am. Soc. Law and Medicine, Am. Coll. Health Care Adminstrs. (mem. nat. adv. com. wandering patients 1987-88), Nat. Inst. on Aging (mem. senile dementia of Alzheimer's type, mem. rsch. ethics task force 1981-82, Am. Geriatrics Soc. rep. 1984-86), Soc. Health and Human Values (mem. gov. coun. 1981-84), Inst. Medicine (mem. com. on future issues in med. tech. devel. 1992-94), N.H. Med. Soc., Soc. Health and Human Values (mem. gov. coun. 1981-84), Internat. Hospice Inst. (mem. physician's adv. com. 1984-86), Med. Soc. D.C. (mem. legis. affairs com. 1985-92, vice chairperson 1991-92), Soc. Gen. Internal Medicine (mem. editl. adv. bd. Jour. 1988-91), Inst. of Medicine, Americans for Better Care of the Dying (pres. 1994-2005) Home: 2318 Ashboro Dr Chevy Chase MD 20815-3055 Business E-Mail: JLynn@medicaring.org.

LYNN, DAVID G., biology and chemistry professor; AB in Chem., Univ. NC, Chapel Hill; PhD in Organic/Biological Chem., Duke Univ. Prof., chem. Univ. Chgo.; Asa Griggs Candler prof. chem, biology Emory Univ., Atlanta. Adv. bds. in genetics to bioorganic and natural products NIH; rsch. prof. Howard Hughes Med. Inst., 2002—. Adv. bd. Amyloid: The Journal of Protein Folding Disorders, and Current Organic Synthesis. Adv. bd. Ga. Citizens for Integrity in Sci. Edn. Recipient Camille and Henry Dreyfus Teacher-Scholar award, Howard Hughes Med. Inst. grant, 2002; fellow Am. Chem. Soc., 1988—89; grantee NIH Fellowship, Columbia Univ., Sloan Rsch. Fellowship. Office: Dept Chem Emory Univ 1515 Pierce Dr Atlanta GA 30322 Office Phone: 404-727-9348. Office Fax: 404-727-6586. Business E-Mail: dlynn2@emory.edu.

LYNN, DAVID LAWRENCE, music educator; b. Summit, NJ, Nov. 16, 1962; s. James David Lynn and Barbara Dean, George Dean (Stepfather) and Dianne Jean Lynn (Stepmother); m. Carol Jean Barnes, July 27, 1985; children: Melodie Christa, Ian Davis. BA in Music, Humboldt State U., Arcata, Calif., 1988. Single subject tchg. credential in music Calif. Music tchr. grades K-8 Union Hill Sch., Grass Valley, Calif., 1998—. Contemporary music dir. Nevada City (Calif.) United Meth. Ch., 1992—. Author, dir.: (plays) Rumpelstiltzkin, 2004, Little Red Robin Hood, 2005; actor: Jesus Christ Superstar, Fiddler on the Roof (Elly Award nominee for best male lead, 1999); music dir.: Godspell (Elly Award nominee for best musical dir., 1996), musician, arranger, prodr.: (CDs) PraySongs, 2001, Beloved Song, 1994, Spheres, 1989; composer: (suite of modern sacred music) FolkMass, 1985. Scholar Van Duzer Arts award and scholarship, Humboldt State U., 1988. Mem.: Calif. Music Educators Assn. Democrat. Methodist. Avocations: music composition and recording, community theatre. Office: Union Hill School Dist 11638 Colfax Hwy Grass Valley CA 95945

LYNN, EMERSON ELWOOD, JR., retired newspaper editor/publisher; b. Boulder, Colo., Aug. 18, 1924; s. Emerson Elwood and Ruth Merriman (Scott) L.; m. Mickey June Killough, Jan. 27, 1950; children: Emerson Killough, Michael Jay, Angelo Scott, Susan. BS, U. Chgo., 1947. Editor/pub. The Humboldt (Kans.) Union, 1951-58, The Bowie (Tex.) News, 1958-65, The Iola (Kans.) Register, 1965-2001. Chmn. Iola Industries, Inc.; mem. SEK, Inc.; chmn. bd. dirs. Huck Boyd Found., Manhattan, Kans., 2001-2002. Chmn. Allen County Hosp. Bd., Iola, 1970-77, adv. bd. Kans. Dept. Transp., Topeka, 1992-93; mem. panels on reform of probate code, Kans. Jud. Coun., others; mem. Pulitzer Prize Nominating Jury, 2000-20001. Sgt. USAF, 1942-46. Rotary Internat. fellow U. Melbourne, 1948-49. Mem. Rotary Internat. (pres.), Kans. Press Assn. (pres. 1979, Clyde Reed Master Editor award 1995), William Allen White Found. (pres. 1978). Republican. Presbyterian. Home: 821 S Buckeye St Iola KS 66749-3807 Office: The Iola Register 302 S Washington St Iola KS 66749-3255 Home Phone: 620-365-5665; Office Phone: 620-365-2111.

LYNN, EVELYN JOAN, state senator, consultant; b. NY, Feb. 2, 1930; d. Leo A. and Helen (Shep) Hoes. BA in Psychology, Queens Coll., NYC, 1950; MA English and Edn., Stetson U., 1969; EdD, U. Fla., 1979. Cons. for bus., edn. and govt., 1979—; rep. Fla. House, 1994—2002, Fla. Senate Dist. 7, Fla., 2002—. Bd. dirs. Edn. Commn. States; mem. So. Regional Edn. Bd. Mem. Nat. Coun. State Legislators (com. vice chair, mem. Blue Ribbon com.). Home: PO Box 4236 Ormond Beach FL 32175-4236 Office Phone: 386-238-3180. Business E-Mail: lynn.evelyn.web@FLsenate.gov.

LYNN, JEFFREY WHIDDEN, research physicist, educator; b. Hackensack, NJ, Mar. 2, 1947; s. Theodore John and Frances Whidden Lynn; m. Linda Mayo; children: Robert William, Heather Diane Hudspeth. BS, Ga. Inst. of Tech., 1969, MS, 1970, PhD, 1974. Rsch. fellow Oak Ridge Nat. Lab., Tenn., 1972—74; postdoctoral assoc. Brookhaven Nat. Lab., Upton, NY, 1974—76; prof. physics U. Md., College Park, 1976—97; rsch. scientist, fellow Nat. Inst. Stds. and Tech., Gaithersburg, Md., 1977—; fellow NIST, 2006—. Acting dir., founder Ctr. for Superconductivity Rsch., U. of Md., College Park, 1987—89; adj. prof. physics U. Md., College Park, 1997—. Author: (rsch. book) High Temperature Superconductivity (Stratton award, 2005); contbr. sci. revs. to profl. jours. Recipient Award for Sci. Achievement, Wash. Acad. of Scis., 1988, multiple grants, NSF, 1976—2003; fellow, Wash. Acad. of Scis., 1988. Fellow: Am. Phys. Soc. (exec. com. divsn. materials physics 1999—2002, chair topical group in magnetism 1999—2003, chair divsn. materials physics 2005—). Office: Nat Inst Stds and Tech NIST Ctr for Neutron Rsch Gaithersburg MD 20899-8562 Office Phone: 301-975-6246. E-mail: jeff.lynn@nist.gov.

LYNN, JOHN ERIC, nuclear physicist, researcher, consultant; arrived in U.S., 1985; s. William and Emily Lynn; m. Joyce Ward, Aug. 7, 1954; children: Shirley, David. BSc, U. Durham, 1953; DSc, U. Newcastle upon Tyne, 1970. Chartered physicist Inst. Physics, 1970. Group leader electron accelerator group U.K. Atomic Energy Authority, Harwell, England, 1971—78, head nuc. physics divsn., 1978—85, sr. individual merit scientist, 1977—89; fellow Argonne Nat. Lab., Ill., 1988—89; vis. staff mem. Los Alamos Nat. Lab., N.Mex., 1990—93; assoc. Sumner Assocs., Santa Fe, 1994—. Bd. mem. nuc. physics bd. Sci. Rsch. Coun., London, 1978—85. Author: (scientific monograph) Theory of Neutron Resonance Reactions. Fellow: Inst. Physics. Achievements include research in elucidation of the nature of different kinds of resonances in neutron reactions, especially in fission reactions and their relation to the shell structure effects in the fission barrier; application of neutron resonances to measuring quantum vibrational properties of crystalline materials; theoretical evaluation of fission and capture cross sections for applications ranging from nuclear astrophysics to nuclear criticality safety. Avocations: travel, piano. Office: Sumner Assoc Office 100 Cienega St Santa Fe NM 87501

LYNN, KARYL CHARNA (KARYL LYNN KOPELMAN ZIETZ), writer, filmmaker, critic, television producer; b. NYC, Oct. 11, 1943; d. Bernard and Vera Jeanne (Wantman) Kopelman; m. Neil J. Stone, Aug. 16, 1970 (div. 1975); m. Joachim Zietz, July 19, 1978 (div. 1994). BA in Chemistry, U. Pa., 1965; MA in Film and Broadcast Journalism, Am. U., 1980; spl. cert., Goettinger U., Germany, 1976. Rschr. Columbia Coll. Physicians and Surgeons, NYC, 1967-70, NIH, Bethesda, Md., 1971-72; producer, writer Am. Chem. Soc., Washington, 1976-78; prodr., rschr. Zweites Deutsches Fernsehen, Mainz, Germany, 1978-89; prodr. ORF-Austrian TV, 1980-84; prodr., reporter European Television Svc., Cologne, Germany, 1985-88; prodr., dir., corr. KOPE Prodns., Washington, 1985—. Lectr. Smithsonian Inst., Arts Club; site reporter NEA, 1994—95; lectr. Chautauqua Instn., 1998, Balt. Opera Guild, 2000, Italian Opera House Lecture Series, Washington, 2003, Italian Cultural Inst. (part of Italian Embassy), 2005, Italian Cultural Soc., 2004; book presenter in field. Author: Opera! Guide to Western Europe's Great Houses, 1991, Eastern Europe's and USSR's Great Opera Houses, 1992, Opera-Going in South America, 1993, Opera Companies and Houses of the United States: A Comprehensive, Illustrated Reference, 1994, The National Trust Guide to Great Opera Houses in America, 1996, Italian Opera Directory, 1998, Opera Companies and Houses of Western Europe, Canada, Australia, New Zealand: A Comprehensive Illustrated Reference, 1999, Breve Storia dei Teatri d'Opera Italiani, 2001, Italian Opera Houses and Festivals, 2005; prodr. (video) An Amish Portrait for USIA; prodr., dir., writer, interviewer documentary films; opera critic, feature writer, contbr. articles to Opera Now, Oper Orpheus Internat., Toronto Globe and Mail, Opera News, Musica and Arte: Quaderno del Museo Teatrale alla Scala, Opera-Opera. Mem. Music Critics Assn., Internat. Platform Assn., Am. Women in Radio and TV, Author's Guild, Assn. Ind. Video and Filmakers, Washington Ind. Writers, Contemporary Authors, Cosmos Club. Avocations: sailing, jogging, bicycling, tennis, foreign languages. Office: KOPE Prodns Palisades Sta PO Box 40103 Washington DC 20016-0103 Personal E-mail: rifiuti4u@aol.com.

LYNN, LARRY (VERNE LAURISTON LYNN), engineering executive; b. Seattle, Sept. 5, 1930; s. Eldin Verne and Irma (Tuell) Lynn; m. Emily Jean Badger, Oct. 4, 1952 (div. 1988); m. Shirley Marie Pieczynski, Sept. 27, 1988. BS in Physics, Tufts U., 1951. Assoc. divsn. head, mem. steering com. Lincoln Lab. M.I.T., Lexington, Mass., 1953-79; dir. defensive systems Office of the Undersecretary of Defense, Washington, 1979-81; dep. dir. Adv. Rsch. Project Agy., Washington, 1981-85; v.p., COO Atlantic Aerospace Electronics, Greenbelt, Md., 1985-93; dep. under sec. defense Office Sec. Defense, Washington, 1993-95, dir. def. adv. rsch. project agy., 1995-98; pres., owner, cons. Larry Lynn Assocs., Naples, Fla., 1998—. Mem Def. Sci. Bd. Contbr. articles to profl. jours. Lt. JG USNR, 1951-53. Fellow: IEEE (life); mem.: NAE. Home and Office: 480 15th Ave S Naples FL 34102-7437 Home Phone: 239-261-7619; Office Phone: 757-876-2558. Personal E-mail: larry.lynn@attglobal.net.

LYNN, LAURENCE EDWIN, JR., academic administrator, educator; b. Long Beach, Calif., June 10, 1937; s. Laurence Edwin and Marjorie Louise (Hart) L.; m. Patricia Ramsey Lynn; 1 dau., Katherine Bell; children from previous marriage— Stephen Louis, Daniel Laurence, Diana Jane, Julia Suzanne. AB, U. Calif., 1959; PhD (Ford Found. fellow), Yale, 1966. Dir., dep. asst. sec. def. (OASD/SA) Dept. Def., Washington, 1965-69; asst. for program analysis NSC, Washington, 1969-70; assoc. prof. bus. Grad. Sch. Bus., Stanford (Calif.) U., 1970-71, vis. prof. pub. policy, 1982-83; asst. sec. planning and evaluation HEW, Washington, 1971-73; asst. sec. program devel. and budget U.S. Dept. Interior, Washington, 1973-74; sr. fellow Brookings Instn., 1974-75; prof. pub. policy John Fitzgerald Kennedy Sch. Govt. Harvard U., Cambridge, Mass., 1975-83; dean Sch. Social Service Adminstrn. U. Chgo., 1983-88, prof., sch. of social svc. adminstrn. and Harris grad. sch. pub. policy studies, 1983—2002, dir. Ctr. for Urban Rsch. and Policy Studies, 1986—2002; dir. Mgmt. Inst., 1992-99; Sydney Stein, Jr. prof., 1997—2002; George H.W. Bush chair and prof. Bush Sch. Govt. and Pub. Svc., Tex A&M U., 2002—07. Author: Designing Public Policy, 1980, The State and Human Services, 1980, Managing the Public's Business, 1981, Managing Public Policy, 1987, Public Management as Art, Science and Profession, 1996, Teaching and Learning with Cases: A Guidebook, 1999, Public Management: Old and New, 2006; co-author: The President as Policymaker, 1981, Improving Governance: A New Logic for Empirical Research, 2001, Madison's Managers: Public Administration and the Constitution, 2006; contbr. articles to profl. jours. Bd. dirs. Chgo. Met. Planning Coun., 1984-89, Leadership Greater Chgo., 1989-92; mem. coun. of scholars Libr. of Congress, 1989-93. 1st lt. AUS, 1963-65. Recipient Sec. Def. Meritorious Civilian Svc. medal, Presdl. Cert. of Disting. Achievment, Vernon prize, best book award Acad. Mgmt., 1996. Fellow Nat. Acad. Public Adminstrn.; mem. Am. Soc. for Pub. Adminstn. (Dwight Walto award 2006, Paul Van Rider award, 2007), U. Calif. Alumni Assn., Coun. on Fgn. Rels., Assn. Pub. Policy Analysis and Mgmt. (past pres.), Pub. Mgmt. Rsch. Assn. (H. George Frederickson award 2005), Am. Polit. Sci. Assn. (Gaus award, 2007), Phi Beta Kappa. Office: 1081 Allen 4220 TAMU College Station TX 77843-4220 Personal E-mail: llynnjr@gmail.com.

LYNN, NAOMI B., academic administrator; b. NYC, Apr. 16, 1933; d. Carmelo Burgos and Maria (Lebron) Berly; m. Robert A. Lynn, Aug. 28, 1954; children: Mary Louise, Nancy Lynn Francis, Judy Lynn Chance, Jo-An Lynn Cooper. BA, Maryville Coll., Tenn., 1954; MA, U. Ill., 1958; PhD, U. Kans., 1970. Instr. polit. sci. Cen. Mo. State Coll., Warrensburg, Mo., 1966-68; asst. prof. Kans. State U., Manhattan, 1970-75, assoc. prof., 1975-80, acting dept. head, prof., 1980-81, head polit. sci. dept., prof., 1982-84; dean Coll. Pub. and Urban Affairs, prof. Ga. State U., Atlanta, 1984-91; chancellor U. Ill., Springfield, 1991-2001, chancellor emerita, 2001—. Cons. fed., state and local govts., Manhattan, Topeka, Altanta, 1981-91; bd. trustees Maryville Coll., 1997—. Author: The Fulbright Premise, 1973; editor: Public Administration, The State of Discipline, 1990, Women, Politics and the Constitution, 1990; contbr. articles and textbook chpts. to profl. pubs. Bd. dirs. United Way of Sangamon County, 1991-98, Ill. Symphony Orch., 1992-95, Urban League, 1993-99, Ill. State Mus. Soc., 2002-05; v.p. World Affairs Coun. Ctrl. Ill., 2006—. Recipient Disting. Alumni award Maryville Coll., 1986; fellow Nat. Acad. Pub. Adminstrn. Mem. Nat. Assn. Schs. Pub. Affairs and Adminstrn. (nat. pres.), Am. Soc. Pub. Adminstrn. (nat. pres. 1985-86, chair endowment bd. 2005—), Am. Polit. Sci. Assn. (mem. exec. coun. 1981-83, trustee 1993-96, Am. Assn. State Colls. and Univs. (bd. dirs.), Midwest Polit. Sci. Assn. (mem. exec. coun. 1976-79), Women's Caucus Polit. Sci. (pres. 1975-76), Greater Springfield C. of C. (bd. dirs. 1991-99, mem. U.S. Senate jud. nominations commn. State Ill. 1999-01), Pi Sigma Alpha (nat. pres.). Presbyterian. Personal E-mail: nblynn416@aol.com.

LYNN, ROBERT PATRICK, JR., lawyer; b. NYC, Nov. 17, 1943; s. Robert P. and Marie (Madeo) L.; m. Maria T. Zeccola, Nov. 18, 1967; children— Robert P. III, Stephanie M., Kerry Elizabeth. BA, Villanova U., 1965; JD, St. John's U., Bklyn., 1968. Bar: NY 1969, US Dist. Ct. (ea. dist.) NY 1975, US Ct. Appeals (1st cir.) 1978, US Ct. Appeals (2d cir.) 1975, US Supreme Ct. 1978. Assoc. Leboeuf, Lamb & Leiby, NYC, 1966-69; dep. town atty. Town of North Hempstead, Manhasset, NY, 1969-71; assoc. Sprague Dwyer Aspland & Tobin, Mineola, NY, 1971-75, ptnr., 1975-76; ptnr. Lynn & Ledwith, Garden City, NY, 1976-92; spl. prosecutor Inc. Village of Bayville, 1975-76; ptnr. Lynn and Gartner, LLP, 2006—. Bd. dir. Cath. Charities, 1971-89, chmn., 1982; vice chmn. Diocese of Rockville Centre Family Life Ctr., 1978-82. Mem. Nassau County Bar Assn., Suffolk County Bar Assn., NY State Bar Assn. Roman Catholic. Clubs: Wheatley Hills Golf Club (East Williston, NY); Lloyd Neck Bath (Lloyd Harbor, NY), La Romana Country Club (Dominican Rep.). Office: 330 Old Country Rd Ste 103 Mineola NY 11501-4143 also: Las Colinas 2 Casa de Campo La Romana Dominican Republic Home: 6 Richard Ln Huntington NY 11743-2354

LYNN, THEODORE STANLEY, lawyer; s. Irving and Sydell Lynn; m. Linda Isabel Freeman, July 21, 1968; children: Jessica, Douglas. AB, Columbia U., 1958; LLB, Harvard U., 1961; LLM, NYU, 1962; SJD, George Washington U., 1972. Law clk. to Hon. Bruce M. Forrester U.S. Tax Ct., Washington, 1962-64; tchg. fellow in law George Washington U., Washington, 1963-64; ptnr. Webster & Sheffield, NYC, 1964-90, Stroock & Stroock & Lavan LLP, NYC, 1991—. Consult Adminstrn. Conf. U.S., Washington, 1974—75; founding counsel Pension Real Estate Assn., Washington, 1981—84. Author: Real Estate Limited Partnerships, 3d ed, 1991, Real Estate Investment Trusts, 1994, 12th edit., 2007; contbr. articles to profl jours. Sec. Manhattan Sch. Dance, 1974—93; trustee Birch Wathen Lenox Sch., NYC, 1975—93; bd. dirs. Citizens Union, 1991—, vice-chair, 2001—04, treas., 2005—; dir. Sutton Area Cmty. Fund Inc., 1995—; treas., trustee Citizens Union Found, 2000—; bd. dirs. Daniel K. Thorne Found.; spl. asst. Mayor John V Lindsay, NYC, 1966—69; bd. dirs. Jewish Home and Hosp. Life Care Sys., 2003—, Manhattan Cmty. Bd. # 6, NYC, 1977—; trustee John Sellon Charitable Trust, 2002—. Mem.: Asn Bar City NY, Fed Bar Coun, Harvard Club, Univ Club. Office: Stroock & Stroock & Lavan 180 Maiden Ln Fl 17 New York NY 10038-4937 Office Phone: 212-806-6629.

LYNNE, MICHAEL, film company executive; b. 1941; m. Ninah Lynne; 2 children. BA in English Literature, Brooklyn Coll., 1961; JD, Columbia Law Sch., 1964. Atty. Barovick & Konecky; ptnr. Blumenthal & Lynne, 1960—80; counsel New Line Cinema, 1980—90, COO, pres., 1990—2001, co-chmn., co-CEO, 2001—. Bd. dirs. New Line Cinema, 1983—; mem. NY Bar. Exec. prodr.: (films) Lord of the Rings: The Fellowship of the Ring, 2001, Lord of the Rings: The Two Towers, 2002, Lord of the Rings: The Return of the King, 2003. Bd. mem. Museum of Modern Art, Citymeals-on-Wheels, Am. Museum of the Moving Image, Drawing Ctr.; chair Museum Com. of Guild Hall East Hampton; mem. bd. visitors Columbia Law Sch.; mem. dean's coun. Columbia U. Sch. Arts. Named one of 50 Most Powerful People in Hollywood, Premiere mag., 2002—06, Top 200 Collectors in the World, ARTnews Mag, 2004—. Avocation: Collector of contemporary art. Office: New Line Cinema Corp 888 7th Ave Fl 20 New York NY 10106-0001

LYNNE, SHELBY (SHELBY LYNN MOORER), country singer; b. Quantico, Va., Oct. 22, 1968; Singer: (albums) Sunrise, 1989, Tough All Over, 1990, Soft Talk, 1991, Temptation, 1993, Restless, 1995, I Am Shelby Lynne, 2000 (Grammy award best new artist, 2000), Love, Shelby, 2001, Identity Crisis, 2003, Suit Yourself, 2005, (singles) I'll Lie Myself to Sleep, 1990, Things Are Tough All Over, 1990, Feelin Kind of Lonely Tonight, 1993, (duet with George Jones) If I Could Bottle This Up, 1988; actor: (films) Walk the Line, 2005; (TV films) Another Pair of Aces: Three of a Kind, 1991; appearances (TV special) Willie Nelson and Friends,

Outlaws and Angles, (TV series) Nashville Now. Named best new female artist, ACM, 1991; recipient Horizon award, CMA, 1991. Office: Capital Records 1750 N Vine St Hollywood CA 90028

LYNNE-O'BRIEN, VINCENT, theater director, actor; b. East Orange, NJ, Dec. 11, 1935; s. Patrick A. and Mary (Gallagher) O'B. BBA, Seton Hall U., 1957. Artistic dir. Shoreline Youth Theatre, Madison, Conn., 1978-85, Shubert Acad., Shubert Theatre, New Haven, 1990-95; dir. Alliance Theatre, New Haven, 1977-88, Stratford Cmty. Svcs., 1986-88, Jewish Cmty. Svcs., New Haven, 1986-87. Appearances include (on Broadway) The Boy Friend, No Time for Sargeants, Fiorello, Golden Boy, Best Laid Plans, Sweet Charity, Billy, (regional theaters) West Side Story, Mass Appeal, Tribute, Odd Couple, You Can't Take It with You, Diary of Ann Frank, The Sea Gull, Cape Cod-Wellfleet, You Can't Take It with You, Cape Cod-Orleans, On Golden Pond, (TV shows) Studio One, U.S. Steel, I Remember Mama, Voice of Firestone, Lucy Arnaz Show, I Bonino, Search for Tomorrow; (TV movies) Princess Daisey, Prisoner without a Name, Cell without a Number, Empire Falls; theatrical films include The Long Grey Line, Ragtime, Ghost Busters, Godfather III, Other Peoples Money, Amistad; dir. Life With Father, Broadway Bound. Dir. Daniel Hand Drama Soc., 1975-85; bd. dirs. ABC Program, 1984-86, Madison Arts and Sci. Council, 1985-86; commr. conservation com. Town of Eastham, Mass. Mem. Actors Equity Assn., Screen Actors Guild, Am. Fedn. TV and Radio Artists, Madison C. of C. (bd. dirs. 1979-85), Eastham Conservation Commn. Roman Catholic. Avocations: tennis, travel. Home: 11080 SE 173rd Pl Summerfield FL 34491 E-mail: vinmort@xpinternet.net.

LYNTON, MICHAEL, film company executive; b. London, Jan. 1, 1960; s. Mark and Marion Lynton; m. Jamie Alter, 1993. AB in History and Lit., Harvard Coll., 1982; MBA, Harvard Bus. Sch., 1987. Assoc. mergers and acquisitions The First Boston Corp./Credit Suisse First Boston, 1982-85; pres. Disney Pub. The Walt Disney Co., 1987—92, pres. Hollywood Pictures, 1992—96; chmn., CEO, penguin group Pearson plc, NYC, 1996—2000; pres. AOL Internat., NYC, 2000—03; CEO AOL Europe, 2000—03; pres. Time Warner Internat. (formerly AOL Time Warner Internat.), NYC, 2002—03; chmn., CEO Sony Pictures Entertainment, Culver City, Calif., 2004—. Bd. dirs. JAMDAT, 2005—. Named one of 50 Most Powerful People in Hollywood, Premiere mag., 2004—06. Office: Sony Pictures Entertainment 10202 W Washington Blvd Culver City CA 90232

LYON, ANDREW BENNET, economist; b. Chgo. s. Richard M. and Rhee Lyon; m. Jennifer A. Sour, May 1987; 2 children. AB, Stanford U., 1980; PhD, Princeton U., 1986. Economist Jt. Com. on Taxation, U.S. Congress, Washington, 1985-87; asst. prof. dept. econs. U. Md., College Park, 1987-93, assoc. prof. dept. econs., 1993—2004; vis. fellow Brookings Inst., 1994-95. Sr. econ. Coun. Econ. Advisers, 1992-93; dep. asst. sec. tax analysis U.S. Treasury Dept., 2001-03; prin. PricewaterhouseCoopers LLP, 2004—. Author: Cracking the Code: Making Sense of the Corporate Alternative Minimum Tax, 1997; contbr. numerous articles to profl. jours. Nat. Bur. Econs. fellow, 1987-94. Mem. Am. Econ. Assn., Nat. Tax Assn. (Outstanding Doctoral Dissertation award 1986, Fed. Tax Com. 1991), Phi Beta Kappa. Office: Pricewaterhousecoopers 1914 11th St Nw Washington DC 20001-4114 Office Phone: 202-414-3865.

LYON, BRUCE ARNOLD, lawyer, educator; b. Sacramento, Sept. 24, 1951; s. Arnold E. and Arlene R. (Cox) L.; m. Patricia J. Gibson, Dec. 14, 1974; children: Barrett, Andrew. AB with honors, U. Pacific, 1974; JD, U. Calif.-Hastings Coll. Law, 1977. Bar: Calif. 1977, U.S. Dist. Ct. (ea. and no. dists.) Calif. 1977. Ptnr. Ingoglia, Marskey, Kearney & Lyon, Sacramento, 1977-84; sole practice Auburn, Calif., 1984-91; ptnr. Robinson, Robinson & Lyon, Auburn, 1991-98, Robinson, Lyon & Springford LLP, Auburn, 1999—2004; of counsel Robinson, Lyon & Fulton, Auburn, 2005—. Instr. in law Sierra Coll., Rocklin, Calif., 1983-98; mem. adminstrv. bd. Harvard Div. Sch., Cambridge, 2006-07. Mng. editor Comment, A Jour. of Comm. and Entertainment Law, 1974; contbr. articles to trade publs. Bd. dirs. Auburn Cmty. Found., Harvard Mediation Program; pres. Calif. Tule Elk Found. Mem.: ABA, Thurston Soc., Placer County Bar Assn., State Bar Calif., Native Sons of the Golden West, Mensa, Order of Coif. Business E-Mail: blyon@hds.harvard.edu.

LYON, CARL FRANCIS, JR., lawyer; b. Sumter, SC, May 9, 1943; s. Carl Francis and Sophie (Goldstrum) L.; m. Maryann Mercier; children—Barbara Ruth, Sarah Frances, Carl Francis, III. AB, Duke U., 1965, JD with honors, 1968. Bar: N.Y. 1969, D.C. 1977. Assoc., then ptnr. Mudge Rose Guthrie Alexander & Ferdon, NYC, 1968-95, mem. exec. com., 1986-87, 94-95; ptnr. Orrick Herrington & Sutcliffe, NYC, 1995—, mem. exec. com., 1998-2000. Contbr. articles to profl. publs. Mem. ABA (vice-chmn. spl. com. on energy fin. 1988-91), N.Y. State Bar Assn., D.C. Bar Asns., Am. Pub. Power Assn., Duke U. Law Alumni Coun., Order of Coif, Phi Alpha Delta. Office: Orrick Herrington Sutcliffe 666 5th Ave Rm 203 New York NY 10103-1798 Home Phone: 908-522-1413; Office Phone: 212-506-5180. Business E-Mail: cflyon@orrick.com.

LYON, CHARLES HERBERT RANDOLPH, investment banker; b. Durham, NC, June 5, 1943; m. Evelyn Howard, Aug. 21, 1965; children: William, Emily. AB, Princeton U., 1965; MBA, U. Va., 1967. Assoc., asst. v.p., v.p. The First Boston Corp., NYC, 1967-76, mng. dir., 1978-82, mng. dir., head of Midwest investment banking Chgo., 1982—92; dir. First Boston Europe, Ltd., London, 1976-78; mng. dir., co-founder Chgo. investment banking office J.P. Morgan & Co.; mng. dir., head Chgo. investment banking Lehman Brothers, 2001—05; vice chmn. Robert W. Baird & Co., Chgo., 2006—. Trustee, vice chmn. Chgo. Symphony Orch. Mem. Econ. Club of Chgo., Chgo. Club, Onwentsia Club (bd. dirs.), Old Elm Club, Chgo. Commonwealth Club, Commercial Club of Chgo. Avocations: skiing, golf. Office: Robert W Baird & Co Inc 227 W Monroe St Ste 2100 Chicago IL 60606 Office Phone: 312-609-4931.

LYON, DAVID WILLIAM, research executive; b. Lansing, Mich., Mar. 26, 1941; s. Herbert Reid and Mary Kathleen (Slack) L.; m. Catherine McHugh Dillon, July 8, 1967. BS, Mich. State U., 1963; M in City and Regional Planning, U. Calif., Berkeley, 1966, PhD, 1972. Regional economist Fed. Res. Bank Phila., 1969-71; rsch. dir. human and econ. resources The N.Y.C.-Rand Inst., 1972-75, v.p., 1975; sr. economist The Rand Corp., Santa Monica, Calif., 1975-77, dep. v.p., 1977-79, v.p. domestic rsch. divsn., 1979-93, v.p. external affairs, 1993-94; pres., CEO Pub. Policy Inst. Calif., 1994—. Adj. prof. U. Pa., 1975; mem. adv. bd. Inst. for Civil Justice, 1987-93, Rand-Urban Inst. Program for Rsch. on Immigration Policy, 1988-91, Drug Policy Rsch. Ctr., 1989-93, So. Calif. Health Policy Rsch. Consortium, 1989-94, Rand Ctr. for U.S.-Japan Rels., 1989-93, Rand Ctr. for Asia-Pacific Policy, 1993-95; dir. Coll. Environ. Design Coun., U. Calif., Berkeley, 1979-90; Walker-Ames lectr., U. Wash. Mem. publs. com. Rand Jour. Econs., 1984-94; contbr. articles to profl. jours. Bd. dirs. Ctr. for Healthy Aging, Santa Monica, 1985-94, pres., 1989-91; mem. com. fgn. rels. San Francisco, Calif., 1996—, adv. coun. Coll. Environ. Design, U. Calif., Berkeley, 2000-05. Mellon fellow in city planning, 1966-68; Econ. Devel. Adminstrn. grad. fellow, 1966. Mem. Coun. on Fgn. Rels., San Francisco Com. on Fgn. Rels., World Affairs Coun. No. Calif. (trustee 1999—), Japan Am. Soc. So. Calif. (bd. dirs. 1990-94), Japan Soc. No. Calif. (bd. dirs. 2000-), Asia Soc. (So. Calif. Ctr. adv. coun. 1988-2002), No. Calif. adv. bd. 2002—), Calif. Connected (cir. of advisors 2002-05), Pacific Coun. on Internat. Policy, Delta Phi Epsilon, Lambda Alpha Internat. Office: Pub Policy Inst Calif 500 Washington St Ste 800 San Francisco CA 94111-2919 Business E-Mail: lyon@ppic.org.

LYON, JAMES BURROUGHS, lawyer; b. NYC, May 11, 1930; s. Francis Murray and Edith May (Strong) L. BA, Amherst Coll., 1952; LLB, Yale U., 1955. Bar: Conn. 1955, U.S. Tax Ct. 1970. Asst. football coach Yale U., 1953-55; assoc. Murtha, Cullina LLP (and predecessor), Hartford, Conn., 1956-61, ptnr., 1961-96, counsel, 1996—. Adv. com., lectr. and session leader NYU Inst. on Fed. Taxation, 1973-86; mem. IRS Northeast Key Dist.'s Exempt Orgns. Liaison Group, Bklyn., 1993—. Mem. editl. bd. Conn. Law Tribune, 1988—. Chmn. 13th Conf. Charitable Orgn. N.Y.U. Inst. on Fed. Taxation, 1982; trustee Kingswood-Oxford Sch., 1961—91, chmn. bd. trustees, 1975—78, hon. trustee, 1991—; trustee Wadsworth Atheneum, Hartford, 1968—93, pres., 1981—84, hon. trustee, 1993—; exec. com., chmn. Amherst Coll. Alumni Coun., 1963—69, alumni trustee candidate, 1970; trustee Conn. River Mus., Essex, 1971—76; corporator Hartford Hosp., 1975—, St. Francis Hosp., Hartford, 1976—2007; trustee St. Francis Hosp. Found., 1991—2007; corporator Hartford Pub. Libr., 1979—; trustee Conn. Pub. Radio and TV, 1979—86; corporator Inst. Living, 1981—; trustee Ellen Burr McManus Trust, Hartford, 1987—98, Watkinson Libr., 1990—, Hartford YMCA, 1985—99; chmn. bd. trustees Old Sturbridge Village, 1991—93, hon. trustee, 2002—; bd. dirs. Conn. Policy and Econ. Com., Inc., 1991—98; mem. Conn. adv. com. New Eng. Legal Found., 1991—; mem. adv. com. Florence Griswold Mus., Old Lyme, Conn., 1991—; trustee Horace Bushnell Meml. Hall, Hartford, 1993—, sec., 1996—; trustee Ellen Battell Stoeckel Trust, Norfolk, Conn., 1994—; mem. N.E. regional coun. Nat. Club Assn., 1998—; trustee Conn. Jr. Republic, Litchfield, 2000—, Conn. Hist. Soc., 2000—06, sec., 2002—05, hon. trustee, 2006—; pres. Watkinson Libr., 2001—; mem. adv. bd. Tax Exempt Law Review, 2007—. Recipient Eminent Svc. medal Amherst Coll., 1967, Nathan Hale award Yale Club Hartford, 1982, Disting. Am. award No. Conn. chpt. Nat. Football Found. Hall of Fame, 1983, Community Svc. award United Way of the Capital Area, 1986, Disting. Alumnus award Kingswood Oxford Sch., 1998, Thomas Hooker award Ancient Burying Ground Assn., 2003; honored as a direct descendant of its founder Mary Lyon, Mt. Holyoke Coll., South Hadley, Mass. 1997. Fellow: ABA (co-chmn. subcom. on mus. and other cultural orgns. sect. of taxation 1988—, exempt orgn. com.), Am. Coll. Tax Counsel, Phi Beta Kappa; mem.: Am. Law Inst., Conn. State Srs. Golf Assn., Limestone Trout Club (East Canaan, CT), Town and County Club (Hartford), Univ. Club Hartford (pres. 1976—77), Mory's Assn. (New Haven), Wianno Club (Osterville, Mass.), Dauntless Club (Essex, Conn., pres. 1989—93), Union Club NYC, Yale Club NYC, Hartford Golf Club. Office: 185 Asylum St Hartford CT 06103-3408 Office Phone: 860-240-6007. Business E-Mail: jlyon@murthalaw.com.

LYON, JAMES KARL, German language educator; b. Rotterdam, Holland, Feb. 17, 1934; came to U.S., 1937; s. T. Edgar and Hermana (Forsberg) L.; m. Dorothy Ann Burton, Dec. 22, 1959; children: James, John, Elizabeth, Sarah, Christina, Rebecca, Matthew, Melissa. BA, U. Utah, 1958, MA, 1959; PhD, Harvard U., 1963. Instr. German Harvard U., Cambridge, Mass., 1962-63, asst. prof., 1966-71; assoc. prof. U. Fla., Gainesville, 1971-74; prof. U. Calif. San Diego, La Jolla, 1974-94, provost Eleanor Roosevelt Coll., 1987-94; prof. dept. Germanic and Slavic langs. Brigham Young U., Provo, Utah, 1994—. Vis. prof. U. Augsburg, Germany, 1993, 2005. Author: Konkordanz zur Lyrik Gottfried Benns, 1971, Bertolt Brecht and Rudyard Kipling, 1975, Brecht's American Cicerone, 1978, Bertolt Brecht in America, 1980, Brecht in den USA, 1994, Paul Celan and Martin Heidegger: An Unresolved Conversation 1951-1970, 2006. Capt. M.I., U.S. Army, 1963-66. NEH fellow, 1970, Guggenheim Found. fellow, 1974; Ford Found. grantee, 1988, 91. Mem. MLA, Am. Assn. Tchrs. German, Internat. Brecht. Soc., Phi Beta Kappa. Democrat. Mem. Lds Ch. Avocations: backpacking, fishing. Office: Brigham Young U Dept Germanic & Slavic Lang 3106 JFSB Provo UT 84602-6120 Business E-Mail: james_lyon@byu.edu.

LYON, MARTHA SUE, research engineer, retired military officer; b. Oct. 3, 1935; d. Harry Bowman and Erma Louise (Moreland) Lyon. BA in Chemistry, U. Louisville, 1959; MEd in Math., Northeastern Ill. U., 1974; postgrad., McGeorge Sch. Law, 1981-82, Northwestern Calif. U., 1999—, George Washington U., 1995—96. Cert. tchr. Ill., Ky. Rsch. assoc. U. Louisville Med. Sch., 1959-61, 62-63; commd. ensign USNR, 1965; advanced through grades to commr. USN, 1983; instr. instrumentation chemistry Northwestern U., Evanston, Ill., 1968-70; tchr. sci., chemistry, gifted math. Waukegan (Ill.) pub. schs., 1970-75; phys. scientist Libr. of Congress, Washington, 1975-76; rsch. engr. Lockheed Missiles & Space Co., Sunnyvale, Calif., 1976-77; instr., assoc. chmn. dept. physics U.S. Naval Acad., Annapolis, Md., 1977-80; analyst sys. analysis divsn. Office of Chief of Naval Ops. Staff, Washington, 1980-81; comdg. officer Naval Rsch. Ctr., Stockton, Calif., 1981-83; mem. faculty Def. Intelligence Coll., 1983-85; program mgr. Space and Naval Warfare Sys. Command, 1985-86; commdg. officer PERSUPPACT Memphis, 1986-88; program mgr. Space and Naval Warfare Sys. Command, 1988-91; sect. chief Def. Intelligence Agy., 1991-95. Chief marching divsn. Nat. Homecoming Parade and N.Y.C. Regional Parade Task Force Desert Storm, 1991; contractor mgr. supporting spl. asst. to Sec. of Def. for Gulf War Illnesses Investigations, 1997—98; pro bono work for Class Act Group; Fla. chpt. svc. officer, comdr. dist. 4 DAV. Mem. citizen rev. panel Fla. Foster Care Project Marion County, 1999; vet.'s advocate; mem. exec. com. Marion County Dem. Grantee, Am. Heart Assn., 1960—62, 1997—98, NSF, 1971, 1982. Mem.: Nat. Assn. Parliamentarians, Pvt. Investigators Assn. Va., Evidence Photographers' Internat. Coun., Internat. Soc. Bassists, Internat. Conf. Women in Sci. Engring. (protocol chair), Am. Soc. Photogrammetry, Am. Statis. Assn., Am. Fedn. Musicians, Soc. Women Engrs., Am. Chem. Soc., Mensa, Order Eastern Star, Delta Phi Alpha, Zeta Tau Alpha. Achievements include development of processes used in archival photography. E-mail: mslyon@att.net.

LYON, MARY LOU, retired secondary school educator; b. Wichita, Kans., Sept. 18, 1926; d. Theodore Joseph and Hazel Pearl (Johnson) Cochran; m. William Madison Lyon, Mar. 15, 1944 (div. July 1970); children: William Madison, Jr., Theodore Richard. AA, Coll. San Mateo, Calif., 1958; BA with distinction and honors, San Jose State U., Calif., 1960, lifetime secondary credential, 1961, MA, 1967. Cert. secondary edn. tchr., Calif. Tchr. Los Gatos (Calif.) HS, 1961, Blach Jr. HS Los Altos (Calif.) Elem. Dist., 1961-62, Homestead High, Fremont Union HS Dist., Cupertino, Calif., 1962—93, Metropolitan Adult Edn. Program, San Jose, 1986—. Tchr. San Jose State U. Extension, Cupertino, 1974-76, Fremont Union High Sch. Adult Edn., 1977; various offices Calif. Coun. for Social Studies, Sacramento, 1962-80; historian, photographer Anza Trek Observance Bicentennial, Santa Clara County (Calif.) Bicentennial Commn., 1975-76; cons. Calif. map Hearne Bros. Map Co., 1981; speaker Genealogical Soc., San Jose Hist. Mus., Calif. Hist. Soc., others. Author, editor (pamphlet) Social Sci. Rev., 1975-76; author numerous books on Santa Clara County, 2006, photographer (one-woman show) Cupertino Hist. Soc., 1975; photographer: (textbook) Addison Wesley, 1980; author: Some Women in Santa Clara County, 1996, Some More Women in Santa Clara County, 2001, Elisha Stephens of the Stephens-Murphy Party of 1844, 2005, Some Men in Santa Clara History, Cupertino, 2006, Early Cupertino by Arcadia, 2006. Chair of site & times Conf. Calif. hist. soc., 1985—; commr. Santa Clara County Hist. Heritage, 1994—2003; delegate Calif. State Sesquicentennial commn. for CCHS, 1998—2000; deacon Union Ch. of Cupertino; tchr. safe driving classes Am. Assn. Ret. Persons, 1995—. Recipient history honor, Phi Alpha Theta, 1959—60, Award of excellence for tchng. Calif. history, Conf. of Calif. Hist. Soc., 1973, Honored as an Achiever, Santa Clara County Penwomen, 1976, Coke Wood award, Conf. of Calif. Hist. Soc., 1994, 1997, award of merit, Calif. Pioneers of Santa Clara County, 1999, Pres. award, Conf. of Calif. Hist. Soc., 1999, 2002, 2007. Mem.: San Francisco Hist. Soc., Menlo Park Hist. Soc., Santa Clara County Pioneers (editor Trailblazer, historian), San Jose Hist. Soc. (cons.), Cupertino Hist. Soc., Nat. Oreg.-Calif. Trail. Assn., Oreg.-Calif. Trail. Assn. (publicity com. Calif.-Nev. Hawaii br. 1985—), Conf. Calif. Hist. Soc. (various offices 1973—, pres. 1983—84, organizer confs. 2005, co-chair no. symposium 2005), San Francisco Corral of Westerners (sheriff 1995, editor Signals from Telegraph Hill), San Jose Hist. Mus. Assn., Nat. Parks and Conservation Assn., Lewis & Clark Hist. Assn., Westerners Internat. (bd. dirs.). Democrat. Avocations: photography, travel, lecturing, western history. Home: 879 Lily Ave Cupertino CA 95014-4261 Personal E-mail: malyon_1999@yahoo.com.

LYON, NORMA DUFFIELD, sculptor, agriculturist; b. Nashville, July 29, 1929; d. Benton J. and Elsa (Walburn) Stong; m. Gaylord Joe Lyon, July 22, 1950; children: Emily, Mark, Eric, Michelle, Gregory, Valerie, Lori, Kurt, Douglas. BS, Iowa State U., 1951. AnSci sculptor Iowa State Fair, Des Moines, Ill. State Fair, Springfield, Kans. State Fair, Hutcheson, Mo. State Fair, Nat. Cattle Congress, Waterloo, 1960; cattle judge, 1960—; art tchr. gifted and talented, South Tama (Iowa) Sch., 1986—, elem. nutrition tchr., 1986—, Toldeo, Iowa, 1986—; mem. Iowa Vet. Medicine Bd., 1992-97. Prin. works include New Dairy Farm bronze statue, Iowa State U., 2007, numerous temporary and permanent sculptures in Iowa, Calif., Wis., Ariz., Kans., Tex., Ill., NY, Mo., Can.; illustrator pen and ink drawings for books. Mem. County Dem. Cen. Com., Tama, Friends of Extension ISU '91. Named Disting. Grad. Dairy Sci. Club, 1990, World Dairy Expo Woman of Yr., 1990, Iowa Master Farm Homemaker, 2004; recipient Pioneer award Nat. Dairy Shrine, 2000, Ralph Keeling award Iowa Dairy Industry, 2002. Mem. AAUW (treas. 1987-91), Iowa 4-H Found. (trustee 1986-91), Arts Coun. Tama-Toledo Area, Iowa Jersey Cattle Assn., Am. Jersey Cattle Club, Nat. Dairy Shrine (state membership chmn.), 4-H (hon.), Alpha Delta Pi. Roman Catholic. Avocations: music, knitting, reading, social concerns, religious edn. Home: 2621 K Ave Toledo IA 52342-9446

LYON, PHILIP KIRKLAND, lawyer; b. Warren, Ark., Jan. 19, 1944; s. Leroy and Maxine (Campbell) L.; children by previous marriage: Bradford F., Lucinda H., Bruce P., Suzette P., John P., Martin K., Meredith J.; m. Jayne Carol Jack, Aug. 12, 1982. JD with honors, U. Ark., 1967. Bar: Ark. 1967, U.S. Supreme Ct. 1970, Tenn. 1989. Sr. ptnr., dir. ops. House, Wallace, Nelson & Jewell, P.A., Little Rock, 1967-86; pres. Jack, Lyon & Jones, P.A., Little Rock and Nashville, 1986—2007; CEO, Jack, Lyon, Jones & Phillips, PLLC, 2007—. Instr. bus. law, labor law, govt. bus. and collective bargaining U. Ark., Little Rock, 1969-72; lectr. practice skills and labor law U. Ark. Law Sch., 1979-80; bd. dirs. labor program Ctr. Am. and Internat. Law; editl. bd. dirs. Entertainment Law and Fin., 1993-2004. Author: Arkansas Employment Law Desk Book, 1997; co-author: Schlei and Grossman Employment Discrimination Law, 2d edit., 1982; editor-in-chief Ark. Law Rev., 1966—67, bd. dirs., 1978—93, v.p., 1990—92; editor: Arkansas Employment Law Letter, 1995—, Arkansas Employment Law Ctr., 1998—. Mem. Ark. State C. of C. (bd. dirs. 1984-88), Greater Little Rock C. of C. (chmn. cmty. affairs com. 1982-84, minority bus. affairs 1985-89). Inaugural fellow Coll. Labor and Employment Lawyers, 1996; recipient Writing Excellence award Ark. Bar Found., 1980. Mem.: ABA (select com. liaison office fed. contract compliance programs 1982—92, select com. liaison EEOC 1984—92, co-chair ethics and profl. responsibility com. 2000—03, forum governing com. entertainment and sports industries 2006—, select com. immigration), Nashville Bar Assn. (entertainment law com., lawyers concerned for lawyers com., employment law com., governing com. 2006—), Tenn. Bar Assn. (lawyers helping lawyers com. 1989—, labor sect.), Ark. Bar Assn. (chmn. labor law com. 1977—78, chmn. labor law sect. 1978—79, chmn. lawyers helping lawyers com. 1988—94, Golden Gavel award 1978). Office: Jack Lyon Jones & Phillps PLLC 11 Music Cir S Ste 202 Nashville TN 37203-4335 also: Jack Lyon Jones & Phillips PLLC Shiloh Rd Jasper AR 72641-9744 Home: PO Box 121195 Nashville TN 37212 also: Owl Lyon Ranch HC 70 Box 478 Jasper AR 72641-9744 Office Phone: 615-259-4664. Business E-Mail: pklyon@jljnash.com. *One of the true secrets of success is to concentrate your efforts--for if you apply these efforts everywhere at once then you will accomplish very little anywhere.*

LYON, RICHARD, retired mayor, military officer; b. Pasadena, Calif., July 14, 1923; s. Norman Morais and Ruth (Hollis) L.; m. Cynthia Gisslin, Aug. 8, 1975; children: Patricia, Michael, Sean; children by previous marriage: Mary, Edward, Sally, Kathryn, Patrick (dec.), Susan. B.E., Yale U., 1944; MBA, Stanford U., 1953. Commd. ensign USN, 1944; advanced through grades to rear adm. SEAL, 1974; served as scout and raider in Pacific and China, World War II; with Underwater Demolition Team 5 in Korea; recalled to active duty as dep. chief Naval Res. New Orleans, 1978-81. Mem. Chief Naval Ops. Res. Affairs Adv. Bd., 1978-81; exec. v.p. Nat. Assn. Employee Benefits, Newport Beach, Calif., 1981-90; mem. Bd. Control, U.S. Naval Inst., 1978-81; pres. Civil Svc. Commn., San Diego County, 1990, Oceanside Unified Sch. Bd., 1991; mayor City of Oceanside, 1992-2000. Pres. bd. trustees Children's Hosp. Orange County, 1965, 72. Decorated Legion of Merit. Mem. Nat. Assn. Securities Dealers (registered prin.), Newport Harbor Yacht Club, Oceanside Yacht Club, Rotary (Anaheim, Calif. pres. 1966). Republican. Anglican. Home: 600 S The Strand Oceanside CA 92054-3902 Personal E-mail: lyonclan@cox.net.

LYON, RICHARD HAROLD, physicist, educator; b. Evansville, Ind., Aug. 24, 1929; s. Chester Clyde and Gertrude Lyon; m. Jean Wheaton; children: Katherine Lyon Davis, Geoffrey Cleveland, Suzanne Marie Riggle. AB, Evansville Coll., 1952; PhD in Physics (Owens-Corning fellow), MIT, 1955; DEng, U. Evansville, 1976. Asst. prof. elec. engring. U. Minn., Mpls., 1956-59; Mem. research staff Mass. Inst. Tech., 1955-56, lectr. mech. engring., 1963-69, prof. mech. engring., 1970-95, prof. emeritus, 1995—, head mechanics and materials div., 1981-86. NSF postdoctoral fellow U. Manchester, Eng., 1959-60; sr. scientist Bolt Beranek & Newman, Cambridge, 1960-66, v.p., 1966-70; chmn. Cambridge Collaborative, Inc., 1972-90; v.p. Grozier Pub., Inc., 1972; pres. Grozier Tech. Systems, 1976-82, RH Lyon Corp, 1976—; sr. scientist, Acentech, Inc., 2005. Author: Transportation Noise, 1974, Theory and Applications of Statistical Energy Analysis, 1975, 2d edit. (with R. DeJong), 1994, Machinery Noise and Diagnostics, 1987, Designing for Product Sound Quality, 2000; mem. editl. bd. Acoustical Soc. Japan, 1996—. Bd. dirs. Boston Light Opera, Ltd., 1975; mem. alumni bd. U. Evansville, 1988-94, trustee, 1995-98, chmn. ann. fund, 1996-97. Recipient Rayleigh medal Brit. Inst. Acoustics, 1995, Nat. Acad. Engring. award 1995, Disting. Alumni award U. Evansville, 1997, medal of Honor, U. Evansville, 2002, Gold medal Indian Acoustical Soc., 2003. Fellow: AAAS, Acoustical Soc. Am. (assoc. editor jour. 1967—74, exec. coun. 1976—79, v.p. 1989—90, pres. 1993—94, Silver medal in engring. acoustics 1998, Gold medal 2003), Internat. Inst. Acoustics and Vibrations (hon.); mem.: Brit. Inst. Acoustics (Rayleigh medal 1995), Nat. Acad. Engring. (tech. for a quiet Am. com. 2005—), Sigma Xi, Sigma Pi Sigma. Achievements include research and publications in fields of nonlinear random oscillations, energy transfer in complex structures, sound transmission in marine and aerospace vehicles, building acoustics, product sound quality, environmental noise, machinery diagnostics, home theater audio systems. Home: 60 Prentiss Ln Belmont MA 02478-2021 Office: RH Lyon Corp 60 Prentiss Lane Belmont MA 02478 Office Phone: 617-489-2112. Business E-Mail: rhlyon@lyoncorp.com.

LYON, SHARRON, retired church organist; b. Pontotoc, Miss., June 19, 1941; d. Richard and Faye Lyon. MusB, Union U., Jackson, Tenn., 1963; MusM, Vanderbilt U., Nashville, 1964. Sr. music editor-in-chief LifeWay Christian Resources, Nashville, 1973—2003; ch. organist First Bapt. Ch., Nashville, 1964—2004, ret., 2004. Recipient Disting. Music Alumnus,

Union U., 2003. Mem.: Bapt. Ch. Music Conf. (bd. mem. 1994—96), Am. Guild Organists (membership chair, editor 1963—2007). Home: 641 Old Hickory Blvd Unit #113 Brentwood TN 37027 Home Phone: 615-373-9820. Personal E-mail: sharronlyon@comcast.net.

LYON, THOMAS PEYTON, finance educator, consultant; b. Charleston, W.Va., Aug. 18, 1959; s. John Thomas and Joyce Glascock Lyon; m. Susan Virginia Hunter, Aug. 23, 1986 (div.); 1 child, Emily Asunta. BSE, Princeton U., NJ, 1981; MS, Stanford U., Calif., 1984, PhD, 1989. Prof. Ind. U., Bloomington, Ind., 1989—2004; vis. prof. U. Chgo., 1995—96; fulbright scholar Scuola Sant'Anna, Pisa, Italy, 1997; Gilbrt White fellow Resources for the Future, Washington, 2002—03; antitrust economist US Dept. Justice, Washington, 2003—04; prof. U. Mich., Ann Arbor, 2004—; dir. Erb Inst. Global Sustainable Enterprise, Ann Arbor, Mich., 2006—. Adv. bd. Nat. Renewable Energy Lab., Golden, Colo., 2005—. Author: (book) Corporate Environmentalism and Public Policy, 2004. Fellow, Olin Found., 1996—97. Mem.: Am. Econ. Assn. Avocations: swimming, backpacking, cello. Office: Univ Mich 701 Tappan St Ann Arbor MI 48109 Home Phone: 734-332-0541; Office Phone: 734-615-1639. Business E-Mail: tplyon@umich.edu.

LYON, WILFORD CHARLES, JR., insurance executive; b. Blackfoot, Idaho, June 1, 1935; s. Wilford Charles and Nellie Anna (Estenson) L.; m. Eleanor Perkins, Aug. 23, 1957; children: Katherine Ann, Wilford Charles III. BS, Ga. Inst. Tech., 1958; MA in Actuarial Sci., Ga. State Coll., 1962. Asst. v.p. Ind. Life and Accident Ins. Co., Jacksonville, Fla., 1963-69, asst. v.p., dir. methods and planning dept., 1969-70, v.p., home office coord., 1970-79, pres., chief adminstrv. officer, 1979-84, chmn. bd., CEO, 1984-96; ret., 1996. Exec. compensation com., audit com. Fla. Bank, Inc., 1997-2004; trustee, exec. com. Edward Waters Coll., Jacksonville, 1983-96, chmn., bd. visitors, 1993-96, 2001-02. Pres. Jacksonville Jaycees, 1966; trustee Gator Bowl Assn., Jacksonville, 1981—, pres., 1981, mem. fin. com. and selection com.; pres. Jacksonville C. of C., 1984; trustee Cmty. TV, Inc., Jacksonville, 1980-93, chmn., 1991-92, exec. com., 2001-02; trustee Univ. Hosp., Jacksonville, Inc., 1985-86; bd. trustees Jacksonville Cmty. Found., 1999-; bd. dirs. YMCA Fla.'s First Coast, 1985—, sec., 1986, vice-chmn., 1987, chmn., 1988, chmn. devel. com. 2004—; chmn. 1991 Nat. Vol. Week, Vol. Jacksonville, Inc.; pres. bd. Cypress Village, Inc., 1998-99; bd. dirs. Bolles Sch., 2001—; trustee Gooding Found., 2002—; deacon, elder, clk., trustee Presbyn. Ch. Recipient Disting Svc. award Jacksonville Jaycees, 1972, Jack Donnell award Outstanding Businessman of Yr., 1983, Dick Hutchinson award Sertoma Club South Jacksonville, 1972, Svc. to Mankind award, 1972, Boss of Yr. award Profl. Secs. Internat., 1972-73, Victory Crusade award Fla. Cancer Soc., 1969, Ins. Industry Cmty. Svc. award Jacksonville Assn. Life Underwriters, 1986, C.G. Snead Meml. award Jacksonville Assn. of Life Underwriters, 1991, Top Mgmt. award Sales and Mktg. Execs. of Jacksonville, 1990, Clanzel T. Brown award Jacksonville Urban League, 1991, Svc. to Youth award YMCA of Fla.'s First Coast, 1991, Humanitarian award NCCJ, 1994. Mem. Life Insurers Conf. (exec. com. 1981-91, chmn. membership com. 1981-86, sec. 1984-85, vice chmn. 1985-86, chmn. 1986-87), Am. Coun. Life Ins. (Fla. state v.p. 1981-96, bd. dirs. 1987-88, bd. dirs. Polit. Action Com. 1988-94), Southeastern Actuaries Club, Rotary Club Jacksonville (pres. Mandarin club 1977-78, Paul Harris fellow, dist. gov. 697 1985-86), Masons (33d degree), York Rite, Scottish Rite Bodies, Shriners (potentate Morocco Temple 1973, emeritus rep., investment com. 2005—). Republican. Home: 4035 Alhambra Dr W Jacksonville FL 32207

LYON, WILLIAM, SR., construction executive; b. 1923; Student, U. So. Calif. With Lyon & Son, Phoenix, 1945-50, William Lyon Devel. Co., Newport Beach, Calif., 1954-72, pres.; with William Lyon Co., Newport Beach, 1972—, now chmn. bd., CEO; and owner Martin Aviation, Orange County, Calif. Served to maj. gen. USAF, Pacific, European, Middle East theaters. WWII, pilot, 75 combat missions, Korean War. Decorated DSM, DFC, Air Medal, Presdl. Unit Citation, others. Office: William Lyon Co 4490 Von Karman Ave Newport Beach CA 92660-2000

LYONS, BRUCE MARTIN, lawyer; b. New Rochelle, NY, Sept. 22, 1942; s. Mildred Goodavitch; m. Madeline Lyons, Nov. 29, 1971 (div. 1981); m. Marcia Mae Lyons, June 8, 1983; children: Scott, Marc. BA, U. Miami, 1964, JD, 1967. Bar: Fla. 1967, US Dist. Ct. (so. dist. Fla.) 1967, US Fed. Ct. 1969, US Ct. Appeals (5th cir.) 1972, US Supreme Ct. 1976, US Ct. Appeals (11th cir.) 1981, Colo. 1993. Asst. county solicitor Broward County, 1967—71; mcpl. judge City of Coconut Creek, 1969—72; assoc. mcpl. judge City of Lauderdale Lakes, 1972—73; pres. Lyons & Sanders Chartered, Ft. Lauderdale, Fla. Adv. Nat. Criminal Justice Student Trial Advocacy Competition, 1990-91; trial practice instr. Nat. Coll. Criminal Def., Macon, Ga., 1991; mem. Broward County Narcotics Guidance Coun., 1971; master of the bench, Stephen R. Booher Inn of Ct.; spkr. in field. Contbr. articles to profl. jours. Dir. The Starting Place, Hollywood, Fla.; mem. Youth Leadership of Broward County, Juvenile Delinquency and Gang Prevention Coun., Narcotics Guidance Coun. of Broward County. Mem. ABA (criminal justice coun. 1992-93, 95, vice-chmn. CLE 1996-97, chmn.-elect criminal justice sect. 1998, chmn. 1999-2000, chmn. def. function com. 1989-92), NACDL (pres. 1986-87, dir. 1976-81, sec. 1982-83, 2nd v.p. 1984-85, pres. 1986-87, Robert C. Heeney award 1997), Broward County Criminal Def. Attys. Assn. (pres. 1988-89), Fla. Bar Assn. (mem. criminal rules com. 1988-89, exec. coun. criminal law sect. 1994), Broward County Bar Assn. (chmn. criminal law sect. 1976-77), Acad. Fla. Trial Lawyers (criminal law sect. chmn. 1974-76), Fed. Bar Assn., Fla. Assn. Criminal Def. Lawyers (dir. 1988-95), Am. Acad. Forensics Sci., Phi Delta Phi. Office: Lyons & Sanders Chartered 600 NE 3rd Ave Fort Lauderdale FL 33304-2618 Office Phone: 305-467-8700. Office Fax: 954-763-4856. E-mail: brucelyons@aol.com.*

LYONS, CATHY, computer company executive; BS in Bus. Adminstrn. and Mktg., U. Colo. Gen. mgr. LaserJet Solutions Grp. European Operation Hewlett-Packard Co., Bergamo, Italy, v.p., gen. mgr. Supplies Bus. Palo Alto, Calif., 1999—2001, v.p., gen. mgr. Inkjet Supplies Divsn., 2001—03, sr. v.p. bus. and imaging printing Imaging and Personal Systems Grp., 2003—05, exec. v.p., chief mktg. officer, 2005—07, exec. v.p. imaging & printing group strategic change mgmt., 2007—. Office: Hewlett Packard Co 3000 Hanover St Palo Alto CA 94304-1185 also: Hewlett Packard Co 11311 Chinden Blvd Boise ID 83714-1021

LYONS, CHAMP, JR., state supreme court justice; b. Boston, Dec. 6, 1940; m. Emily Lee Oswalt, 1967; children— Emily Olive, Champ III. AB, Harvard U., 1962; LL.B., U. Ala., 1965. Bar: Ala. 1965, U.S. Supreme Ct. 1973. Law clk. U.S. Dist. Ct., Mobile, Ala., 1965-67; assoc. Capell, Howard, Knabe & Cobbs, Montgomery, Ala., 1967-70, ptnr., 1970-76, Helmsing, Lyons, Sims & Leach, Mobile, 1976-98; legal advisor Hon. Fob James, Jr. Gov. State Ala., 1998; assoc. justice Supreme Ct. of Ala., Montgomery, 1998—. Mem. adv. commn. on civil procedure Ala. Supreme Ct., 1971-98, chmn., 1985-98. Author: Alabama Practice, 1973, 3d edit., 1996; contbr. articles to law jours. Mem. ABA, Ala. Bar Assn., Mobile Bar Assn. (pres. 1991), Am. Law Inst., Ala. Law Inst., Farrah Law Soc., Harvard U. Alumni Assn. (S.E. regional dir. 1988-91, v.p.-at-large 1992-94, 1st v.p. 1994-95, pres. 1995-96).

LYONS, CHARLES M., education educator, former academic administrator; b. Manchester, NH, Apr. 6, 1944; m. Barbara Lyons. BA, St. Francis Xavier U., 1966; MEd, U. Hartford, 1970; EdD, Boston U., 1978. Chair Dept. Profl. Edn. U. So. Maine, Portland, 1978—80, 1991—93, assoc. dean Coll. Edn., 1982—84, prof. Grad. Sch., 2006—; instr. U. Maine Sys., exec. dir. Office of Health Professions Edn., 1984—87, prof., 1994—, vice chancellor, 2001; interim pres. U. Maine, Presque Isle, 1986, Fort Kent, 1996—97, pres., 1997—2001, interim pres. Augusta, 2001, pres., 2001—05. Assoc. clin. prof. Dept. Cmty. Health Tufts Med. Sch., Medford, Mass., 1984—.

LYONS, CURTIS A., archivist; b. Alexandria, Va., Apr. 12, 1966; s. Kyle D. and Denna W. Lyons; m. Lisa A. Nieforth, Nov. 12, 2000; 1 child, Audrey E. BA in History and Polit. Sci., U. of Tenn., 1988, MA in History, 1998. Sr. libr. asst. U. of Tenn., Knoxville, 1988—93, archives specialist, 1993—98; head spl. collections and archives Va. Commonwealth U., Richmond, 1999—. Co-author: (pictorial history) Virginia Commonwealth University. Mem. Va. State Hist. Records Adv. Bd., 2004—; treas. Va. Civil Rights Movement Video Initiative, Richmond, 2001—. Recipient Archive of the New Dominion grant, Nat. Hist. Publs. and Records Commn., 2004. Office: Va Commonwealth Univ 901 Park Ave Richmond VA 23284-2033 Office Phone: 804-828-1108. Office Fax: 804-828-0151. E-mail: calyons@vcu.edu.

LYONS, DANIEL, editor, website blogger; Freelancer for various computer trade journals; freelancer NY Times Mag., GQ, Boston Globe, Detroit Free Press; sr. editor, enterprise computing and consumer electronics Forbes Mag., NYC, 1998—. Tchr. U. Mich., U. Toledo. Author: The Last Good Man, 1995, Dog Days, 1998, Options: The Secret Life of Steve Jobs, a Parody, 2007, (cover article for Forbes) Attack of the Blogs, 2006; blog writer floatingpoint.wordpress.com, mysterious blog writer fakesteve.blogspot.com (The Secret Diary of Steve Jobs), 2006—. Named one of 50 Who Matter Now, Business 2.0, 2007. Achievements include revealing on August 5, 2007 that he is the mysterious writer of blog site called fakesteve.blogspot.com (The Secret Diary of Steve Jobs). Office: Forbes Mag 60 5th Ave New York NY 10011

LYONS, DAVID BARRY, philosophy and law educator; b. NYC, Feb. 6, 1935; s. Joseph and Betty (Janower) L.; m. Sandra Yetta Nemiroff, Dec. 18, 1955; children— Matthew, Emily, Jeremy. Student, Cooper Union, 1952-54, 56-57; BA, Bklyn. Coll., 1960; MA (Gen. Electric Found. fellow), Harvard U., 1963, PhD (Woodrow Wilson dissertation fellow), 1963; postgrad., Oxford U., Eng., 1963-64. Asst. prof. philosophy Cornell U., Ithaca, NY, 1964-67, assoc. prof., 1967-71, prof., 1971-90, Susan Linn Sage prof. philosophy, 1990-95, chmn. dept. philosophy, 1978-84, prof. law, 1979-95, Boston U., 1995—, prof. philosophy, 1998—. Author: Forms and Limits of Utilitarianism, 1965, In the Interest of the Governed, 1973, Ethics and the Rule of Law, 1984, Moral Aspects of Legal Theory, 1993, Rights, Welfare, and Mill's Moral Theory, 1994; editor: Philos Rev., 1968-70, 73-75. Recipient Clark award Cornell U., 1976; Woodrow Wilson hon. fellow, 1960-61, Knox travelling fellow, 1963-64; Guggenheim fellow, 1970-71, Soc. for Humanities fellow, 1972-73, Nat. Endowment for Humanities fellow, 1977-78, 84-85, 93-94. Mem. Am. Philos. Assn., Am. Soc. Polit. and Legal Philosophy, Soc. Philosophy and Pub. Affairs. Office: Boston U Law Sch 765 Commonwealth Ave Boston MA 02215-1401 Home Phone: 617-524-2305; Office Phone: 617-353-3135. Business E-Mail: dbl@bu.edu.

LYONS, DENNIS GERALD, lawyer; b. Passaic, NJ, Nov. 20, 1931; s. Denis A.G. and Agnes C. (Dyt) L.; m. Anna Maria Nuñez, 1983; 1 child, Alexandra; children by previous marriage: Andrew, Sarah, Tessa. AB, Holy Cross Coll., 1952; JD, Harvard U., 1955. Bar: D.C. 1955, N.Y. 1956, U.S. Supreme Ct 1960. Law clk. U.S. Supreme Ct., Washington, 1958—60; assoc. Arnold & Porter, Washington, 1960—62, ptnr., 1963—; v.p., gen. counsel, dir. Gulf United Corp., Jacksonville, Fla., 1968—80; asst. sec. Braniff Airways, Dallas, 1966—77; trustee GMR Properties, Boston, 1971—81; dir. Gulf Broadcast Co., Dallas, 1983—86; vis. prof. law U. Va., Charlottesville, 1982—83. Pres. Harvard Law Rev., 1954-55 Served with USAF, 1955-58. Mem. ABA, Am. Law Inst. Office: Arnold & Porter 555 12th St NW Washington DC 20004-1206 Home Phone: 301-320-4117. Personal E-mail: lyonsden@erols.com. Business E-Mail: dennislyons@aporter.com.

LYONS, FRANCIS XAVIER, lawyer; b. Evanston, Ill., Apr. 1, 1962; s. Thomas George and Ruth Frances (Tobin) L.; m. Mary Patricia Rotunno, Apr. 25, 1992; children: Caroline Marie, Elizabeth Lahey, Frances Grace. BA in History, U. Minn., 1984; JD, Loyola U., Chgo., 1988. Bar: Ill. 1988, U.S. Dist. Ct. (no. dist.) Ill. 1989, U.S. Dist. Ct. (ctrl. dist.) Ill. 1990, U.S. Ct. Appeals (D.C. cir.) 1994, U.S. Dist. Ct. Nebr. 2006. Asst. atty. gen., gen. law divsn. Ill. Atty. Gen.'s Office, Chgo., 1988-93, asst. atty. gen. environ. control divsn., 1993-94; trial atty. environ. and natural resources divsn. Environ. Enforcement Sect., U.S. Dept. Justice, Washington, 1994-99; regional adminstr. U.S. EPA Region 5, Chgo., 1999-2001; ptnr. Gardner, Carton & Douglas, Chgo., 2001—05, Bell, Boyd, & Lloyd LLC, Chgo., 2005—. Mem. steering com. Dem. Leadership for 21st Century, Chgo., 1992-93; bd. dirs. Alliance for Great Lakes, Chgo.'s Environ. Fund; Capt. USAR. ret. Recipient Special Achievement and Commendation award U.S. Dept. Justice, Nat. Notable Achievement award EPA; named one of 40 Ill. Attys. Under 40 to Watch, Law Bull. Pub. Co., 2000, The Top Lawyers, Leading Lawyers Network, 2005, Ill. Super Lawyers, Chgo. (Ill.) Mag., 2006 Mem. ABA, Ill. Bar Assn. Chgo. Bar Assn., Cath. Lawyers Guild Chgo., Delta Tau Delta, Phi Alpha Delta. Office: Bell Boyd & Lloyd LLC 1615 L St NW Washington DC 20036 Office Phone: 312-807-4448. Office Fax: 312-827-8107. Business E-Mail: flyons@bellboyd.com.

LYONS, GENE MARTIN, political scientist, educator; b. Revere, Mass., Feb. 29, 1924; s. Abraham M. and Mary (Karger) L.; m. Micheline Pohl, Sept. 5, 1951; children: Catherine Anne, Daniel Eugene, Mark Lucien. BA, Tufts Coll., Medford, Mass., 1947; license en Scis. Politiques, Grad. Inst. Internat. Studies, Geneva, Switzerland, 1949; PhD, Columbia U., NYC, 1958. Mgmt. officer Internat. Refugee Orgn., Geneva, 1948-52; budget and adminstrv. officer UN Korean Reconstrn. Agy., 1952-56; mem. faculty Dartmouth Coll., 1957-94, prof. govt., 1965-94, dir. Pub. Affairs Center, 1961-66, 73-75, assoc. dean faculty social scis., 1974-78; rsch. fellow Dickey Ctr. Dartmouth Coll., Hanover, NH, 1994—. Vis. lectr. Sch. Mgmt. MIT, 1961-70; exec. sec. adv. com. govt. program behavioral scis. Nat. Acad. Scis., 1966-68; dir. dept. social scis. UNESCO, 1970-72; mem. US Nat. Commn. for UNESCO, 1975-80, vice chmn., 1977-78; adv. U.S. del. UNESCO 19th Gen. Conf., 1976, 20th Gen. Conf., 1978; US rep. to UNESCO European Conf., 1977; prof. associé U. Paris I, 1986; exec. dir. acad. council on the UN system, 1987-92. Author: Military Policy and Economic Aid: The Korean Case, 1961; co-author: (with J.W. Masland) Education and Military Leadership, 1959, (with L. Morton) Schools for Strategy, 1965, The Uneasy Partnership, 1969; editor, contbr. America: Purpose and Power, 1965, Social Science and the Federal Government, 1971; co-editor, contbr. Beyond Westphalia?, 1995, The United Nations System: The Policies of Member States, 1995, International Human Rights in the 21st Century, 2003—. Served with AUS, 1943—46. Mem. Acad. Coun. on UN System, Coun. on Fgn. Rels. Office: Dartmouth Coll Dickey Ctr Hanover NH 03755 Home: 16 Sterling Springs Wilder VT 05001 Office Phone: 603-646-0437. Business E-Mail: Gene.Lyons@Dartmouth.edu.

LYONS, JAMES EDWARD (JED), publishing executive; b. NYC, Feb. 7, 1952; s. James Vincent and Audrey Lucille (Garbers) L.; m. Blythe Mitchell Jones, June 6, 1981; children: James Edward Jr., Michael Davidson. BA cum laude, Bowdoin Coll., 1974. Advanceman and legis. asst. to Congressman William S. Cohen of Maine, Washington, 1972-75; pub. U. Press Am., Lanham, Md., 1975—, also bd. dirs.; pres. Madison Books, Inc., 1986—, U. Pub. Assocs. Inc., 1986—, Rowman and Littlefield Pubs., Inc., 1988—, Barnes and Noble Books, 1988—, Littlefield, Adams Quality Paperbacks, 1988—, Nat. Book Network, Inc. (divsn. Rowman and Littlefield Pubs.), 1986—, Scarecrow Press, Inc., 1995—, Vestal Press, 1997—, New Amsterdam Books, 1998—, Ivan R. Dee, 1998—, Lexington Books, Inc., 1998—. Nat. adv. com. to sec. HEW, 1974, The Derrydale Press, Inc., 1999—, Ardsley House, Pubs., 1999—, AltaMira Press, 1999—, Roberts Rinehart, 2000—, General Hall, 2000—, Madison House, 2000—, Sheed & Ward, 2002, Taylor Trade Pub., 2002, Gulf Pub., 2002, Republic of Tex. Press, 2003, Burnham Pubs., 2003, Collegiate Press, 2003, Jason Aronson, 2004, SR Books, 2004, Govt. Insts., 2004; panelist U.S. Dept. Edn., 1986-87; mem. USIA book and libr. adv. com., 1981-93; mem. bd. dir. Fidelity and Trust Bank, 2005-. Mem. Statue of Liberty-Ellis Island Centennial Commn., 1986-89; Presdl. appointee Nat. Commn. on Librs. and Info. Sci., 1991-93; trustee Georgetown U. Libr., 1981-92pres. St. Albans Sch. for Boys Parent's Club, 2002-03. Mem. Assn. Am. Pub. (exec. coun. profl. and scholarly pub. div. 1990-93, coll. div. faculty rels. com.), Soc. Scholarly Pub. (chmn. publ. com. 1979-80), Coun. on Fgn. Rels., Chief Execs. Orgn., Leaders Cir., Libr. of Congress (mem. exec. com. 2004-)Young Pres. Orgn. (bd. dir. 1994-99), Rolling Rock Club (Ligonier, Pa.), Chevy Chase Club, The Brook, Anglers Club of NY, Psi Upsilon. Presbyterian. Office: Rowman & Littlefield Pub Group National Book Network Ste 200 4501 Forbes Blvd Lanham MD 20706-4310 Office Phone: 301-459-3366. Office Fax: 301-429-5746. Business E-Mail: jlyons@rowman.com.

LYONS, JAMES ELLIOTT, lawyer; b. Lexington, Mo., Mar. 10, 1951; s. james Elliott and Elouise L.; m. Mary Jane McCarthy, June 30, 1979; children: Sean Austin, Caitlan Maureen. BA with honors, U. Mo., 1973; JD, NYU, 1976. Bar: Mo. 1976, N.Y. 1977, Calif. 1984. Assoc. Stinson Mag Thompson McEvers & Fizzell, Kansas City, Mo., 1976-77; assoc. Skadden, Arps, Slate et al., NYC, L.A., 1977-84; law clk. to Hon. Robert W. Sweet U.S. Dist. Ct. (so. dist.) N.Y., 1978; ptnr. Skadden, Arps, Slate et al., L.A. and San Francisco, 1984—. Mem. ABA, Los Angeles County Bar Assn., Bar Assn. San Francisco, Mo. Bar Assn., Phi Beta Kappa Democrat. Office: Skadden Arps Slate et al 4 Embarcadero Ctr Ste 3800 San Francisco CA 94111-5974

LYONS, JAMES M., lawyer; b. Joliet, Ill., Jan. 6, 1947; AB, Coll. Holy Cross, 1968; JD, DePaul U., 1971; LLD (hon.), U. Ulster, Belfast, Ireland, 2002. Bar: Colo. 1971, Ill. 1971, U.S. Dist. Ct. Colo. 1971, U.S. Dist. Ct. (no. dist.) Ill. 1971, U.S. Ct. Appeals (7th and 10th cirs.) 1971, U.S. Supreme Ct. 1971. Sr. trial ptnr., litigation & arbitration Rothgerber Johnson & Lyons LLP, Denver, 1971—. Mem. Colo. Supreme Ct. bd. law examiners, 1982-88; instr. Univ. Denver, Univ. Colo., Nat. Inst. Trial Advocacy; gen. counsel Clinton for Pres. Com., 1991-92, Office of Pres.-Elect, 1992-93; U.S. observer, Internat. Fund for Ireland, 1993-2001; spl. adv. to U.S. Pres. & Sec. State for econ. initiatives in Ireland & No. Ireland, 1997-2001; pres. Faculty of Fed. Advocates, US Dist. Ct. Colo. dist., 2003; vis. lectr. Univ. Ulster, No. Ireland, 2004; adj. prof. Univ. Denver, 2004. Assoc. editor DePaul Law Rev., 1970-71. Recipient St. Thomas More award, Catholic Lawyers Guild Colo., Learned Hand Nat. award, Am. Jewish Com., 1998. Fellow Am. Coll. Trial Lawyers, Internat. Acad. Trial Lawyers; master barrister Doyle's Inn chpt. Am. Inns of Ct.; mem. Ill. State Bar Assn., Colo. Bar Assn., Denver Bar Assn., Am. Bd. Trial Advocates. Office: Rothgerber Johnson & Lyons LLP Ste 3000 1 Tabor Ctr 1200 17th St Denver CO 80202 Office Phone: 303-623-9000. Office Fax: 303-623-9222. Business E-Mail: jlyons@rothgerber.com.

LYONS, JAMES RICHARD, research scientist; b. Buffalo, Dec. 17, 1960; s. James Richard and Dorothy Eileen Lyons; m. Alina Yurievna Smirnova, Jan. 27, 2005; 1 child, Elizaveta Catherine. BS in Elec. Engring. with honors, Rennselaer Polytechnic Inst., Troy, NY, 1983; MS in Elec. Engring. with honors, Ohio State U., Columbus, 1985; PhD in Planetary Sci., Calif. Inst. Tech., Pasadena, 1996. Postdoctoral fellow U. Calif., San Diego, 1997—98; rsch. scientist UCLA, 2000—. Contbr. articles to profl. jours. Origins of Solar Systems grant, NASA, 2003—06, Planetary Atmospheres grant, 2006—, Origins of Solar Sys. grant, 2006—, Exobiology/Evolutionary Biology grant, 2007—. Mem.: Am. Geophysical Union (assoc.). Achievements include research in the theory of oxygen and sulfur isotopes for Earth, Mars, and the solar system. Avocations: writing screenplays, photography. Home: 10660 Eastborne Ave Los Angeles CA 90024 Office: Univ Calif LA 595 Charles Young Dr E Los Angeles CA 90095-1567 Home Phone: 310-880-1992; Office Phone: 310-825-1021. Business E-Mail: jrl@ess.ucla.edu.

LYONS, JANIS E., bank executive; BBA in Fin., Cleve. State U., 1981, MBA, 1985. Adminstrv. asst. Bank Investment Divsn. Nat. City Corp., Cleve., 1978, bank investment officer, 1983, asst. v.p., budget dir., mgr. Internal Funds Transfer Pricing Sys. corp. treasury group, v.p., dir. investor rels., mgr. fin. comm., 1995—97, sr. v.p., 1997—, head corp. acctg., 1997—2000, corp. comptr., 2000—04, pres. Card Svcs., 2004—05, dir. Best In Class program office, 2005—06, chief risk officer enterprise risk reporting and analysis, 2006—. Bd. mem. Vis. Nurse Assn. Office: Nat City Corp Nat City Ctr 1900 E Ninth St Cleveland OH 44114-3484 Office Phone: 216-222-2000.*

LYONS, JERRY LEE, mechanical engineer; b. St. Louis, Apr. 2, 1939; s. Ferd H. and Edna T. Lyons Diploma in Mech. Engring., Okla. Inst. Tech., 1964; MSME, Southwest U., 1983, PhD in Engring. Mgmt., 1994. Registered profl. engr., Calif.; diplomate Am. Bd. Forensic Engring. and Tech., Am. Coll. Forensic Examiners in forensic engring. and tech. (life). Project engr. Harris Mfg. Co., St. Louis, 1965—70, Essex Cryogenics Industries, St. Louis, 1963—65, 1970—73; pres., chief exec. Yankee Ingenuity, Inc., Ft. Wayne, Ind., 1974—, pres., founder, engring. mgr., 1991—. Chmn. exec. bd. continuing engring. edn. in St. Louis for U. Mo., Columbia, 1980-81; bd. dirs. Intertech., Inc., Houston; cons. fluid power dept. Bradley U., Peoria, 1977-84, U. Wis., 1977—; mgr. engring. rsch. Chemetron Corp., St. Louis, 1973-77; v.p., gen. mgr. engring. R&D Essex Fluid Controls divsn. Essex Industries, Inc., St. Louis, 1977-90; pres. Lyons Pub. Co., St. Louis, 1983— Author: Home Study Series Course on Actuators and Accessories, 1977, The Valve Designers Handbook, 1983, The Lyons' Encyclopedia of Valves, 1975, 93, The Designers Handbook of Pressure Sensing Devices, 1980, Special Process Applications, 1980; co-author: Handbook of Product Liability, 1991; contbr. articles to profl. jours With USAF, 1957—62. Recipient Winston Churchill medal, 1988, Dwight D. Eisenhower Achievement Honor award, 1990; named Businessman of Week KEZK Radio, Eminent Churchill fellow Winston Churchill Wisdom Soc., Bus. Man of Yr., Rep. Nat. Com., 2003 Fellow ASME; mem. N.Y. Acad. Scis., Soc. Mfg. Engrs. (life, cert. product design, chmn. Mo. registration com. 1975-90, chmn. St. Louis chpt. 1979-80, internat. dir. 1982-84, 85-87, Engr. of Yr. 1984, internat. Merit award 1985), NSPE, Mo. Soc. Profl. Engrs., St. Louis Soc. Mfg. Engrs. (chmn. profl. devel., registration and cert. com. 1975-79), Instrument Soc. Am. (sr. life, control valve stability com. 1978-84), Computer and Automated Sys. Assn. (1st chmn. St. Louis chpt. 1980-81), St. Louis Engrs. Club (Merit award 1977, Wisdom Honor award 1987, Wisdom Hall of Fame 1987), Am. Security Coun. (committeeman 1976—), Nat. Fluid Power Assn. (com. pressure ratings 1975-77), Am. Legion. Lutheran. Achievements include patents in field. Home: 1719 Wisteria Pl Fort Wayne IN 46818-8812 Office: Innovative Controls Inc 2705 Camino Court Fort Wayne IN 46808 Personal E-mail: a1yankee@aol.com.

LYONS, JOHN DAVID, literature and language professor; b. Springfield, Mass., Oct. 14, 1946; AB, Brown U., 1967; MA, Yale U., 1968, PhD, 1972. Asst. prof. French, Italian and comparative lit. Dartmouth Coll., Hanover, NH, 1972-78, assoc. prof., 1978-82, prof., 1982-87, chmn. comparative lit. program, 1981-84, chmn., prof. dept. French and Italian, 1987; dir. Am. Univ. Ctr. for Film and Critical Studies, Paris, 1984-85; prof. French U. Va., Charlottesville, 1987-92, Commonwealth prof. French, 1993—, chmn. dept., 1989—92, 1998—99, 2005—. Vis. prof. U. Paris III, 2005. Author:

A Theatre of Disguise, 1978, The Listening Voice, 1982, Examplum, 1989, The Tragedy of Origins, 1996, Kingdom of Disorder, 1999, Before Imagination, 2005; co-editor: Mimesis: Mirror to Method, 1982, Dialectic of Discovery, 1983, Critical Tales, 1993; editor: Art, Architecture, Text: The Late Renaissance, 1985; assoc. editor Continuum, 1987—93, editor Academe, 1994—97, mem. editl. adv. bd. Philosophy and Literature, 1992—2002, French Forum. Recipient Robert Fish award for teaching Dartmouth Coll., 1978, Outstanding Tchr. award U. Va., 1996, Cchevalier Legion d'Honneur, 2007; Woodrow Wilson fellow, 1967, ACLS study fellow, 1978, NEH fellow, 1985-89, 92-93, ACLS contemplative practice fellow, 2002, J.S. Guggenheim fellow, 2002-03, Ctr. for Advanced Studies U. Va. fellow, 1987-89. Mem.: N.Am. Soc. for Seventeenth-Century French Lit. (pres. 2002).

LYONS, JOHN MATTHEW, telecommunications industry, broadcast executive; b. NYC, Nov. 5, 1948; s. Matthew Joseph and Anna (Coroneos) D.; m. Natalia Astakhova, Apr. 12, 1992; 1 child, Matthew. BSEE, Roosevelt U., Chgo., 1970, MSEE, 1976; PhD in Comm., Loyola U., Chgo., 1979; BSE, Century U., LA, 1981, MBA in Engrng. Mgmt., 1982; PhD in Broadcasting (hon.), Sicluna U. Found., 1987. Registered profl. engr. Engr., prodr. Sta. WRFM, NYC, 1965-69; sr. facilities planning and project engr. Sta. WWRL-Radio, NYC, 1969-76; sr. facilities planning project engr. Sta. WWRL/WRVR, NYC, 1976-78; asst. chief engr. Sta. WOR, Inc., NYC, 1978-80; chief engr. Sta. WRKS-FM, NYC, 1980-90; sr. project mgr. DSI Comm. (now. DSI RF Sys. Inc. Somerset, NJ), Kenilworth, NJ, 1990-94, Vista Engring. Corp., NYC, 1994—; mgr. telecom. and broadcast ops. The Durst Orgn., 2002—. Pvt. cons. 1994—; dir. Raritan Ctr. Internat. Teleport, NJ, 1992-94; chief engr. WLTW/WAXQ, 1996-2002; ind. broadcasting cons., 1994—; mem. World Dance and Dancesport Coun., 1997—; pres. Lyon Records, NY, 1971—, Short Lines Co., NY, 1980—; chmn. master antenna com. Empire State Bldg., NY, 1980-88, exec. com., 1988-98, chmn. 1998-2002, Condé Nast Tower, 1999—, chmn. advt. industry com., 2000—; bd. dirs. The Document Ctr., NY; cons. broadcasting and telecom.; ofcl. photographer U.S. Imperial Soc. Tchrs. of Dance, 1991—, Blackpool Dance Festival, 1992—. Prodr.: (radio broadcast) The Cuban Missile Crisis, 1962 (Peabody award 1963); exec. prodr. (broadcast series) Radio: The First 50 Years, 1970, Sta. WOR 60th Anniversary Program, 1982 (Armstrong award 1983, Internat. Radio Festival award 1983), Sta. WOR 65th Anniversary Program, 1983; photography editor Amateur Dancers mag., Ability Mag.; contbg. photographer to Dance Scene mag., Dance News, Eng.; photographer Dance Beat, U.S.A., Australian Dance Rev., Dance Action, U.S.A., Japan Dance News, U.S. Imperial Soc. Tchrs. Dance, 1991—. Chmn. media curriculum com. Westchester Cmty. Coll., NY, 1987—. With USAF, 1967-70. Fellow Soc. Broadcast Engrs. (sr., life cert., bd. dirs. 1974-78), Internat. Biog. Assn.; mem. IEEE, ASCAP, Nat. Assn. Radio and Telecom. Engrs. (cert.), Broadcast Music, Inc., Audio Engring. Soc., Assn. Fed. Comms. Cons. Engrs., Internat. Radio and TV Soc., VA Hosp. Radio and TV Guild (v.p. 1976-82, 84—, pres. 1982-84, chmn. exec. com. 1984—, Bennie award 1981), Broadcast Pioneers, Broadcast Music, Am. Inst. Plant Engrs., U.S. Amateur Ballroom Dancers Assn. (regional v.p. 1987-89, dir. for internat. liaison 1989—), Knights of Malta, 1986. Avocations: competitive ballroom dancing, photography. Home: 305 E 86th St New York NY 10028-4702 Office: The Durst Orgn 4 Times Sq New York NY 10036 E-mail: dpintl@aol.com.

LYONS, JOHN W(INSHIP), retired civilian military employee, chemist, consultant; b. Reading, Mass., Nov. 5, 1930; m. Grace Hanley, Nov. 28, 1953; children: John, Louis, Margaret, Mary Ann. AB in Chemistry, Harvard U., 1952; AM in Phys. Chemistry, Washington U., St. Louis, 1963, PhD in Phys. Chemistry, 1964. With Monsanto Co., 1955-73, group leader, sect. mgr. research dept., inorganic chems. div., 1962-69, mgr. comml. devel., head fire safety center, 1969-73; mem. ad hoc panel on fire research Nat. Bur. Standards, Washington, 1971-73; dir. Ctr. for Fire Rsch., 1973-77, Nat. Engrng. Lab., 1978-89, Nat. Inst. Standards and Tech., Gaithersburg, Md., 1990-93, Army Rsch. Lab., Adelphi, Md., 1993-98; ret., 1998. Co-chmn. U.S.-Japan Natural Resources Panel on Fire Rsch., 1975-78; mem. adv. com. on engring NSF, 1981-90; mem. bd. visitors Coll. Engring., U. Md., 1980-90, 99—2005, Biotech. Inst., 1999—2004; mem. adv. com. Naval Rsch. Lab., 1985; mem. com. on fed. labs. Office Sci. and Tech. Policy; mem. Nat. Rsch. Coun. Bd. on Army Sci. Tech.; chmn. standing com. on army tech. for Homeland Security; chmn. com. on hi-end computing NRC; disting. rsch. prof. Ctr. Tech. and Nat. Security Policy, Nat. Def. U. Author: Viscosity and Flow Measurement, 1963, The Chemistry and Uses of Fire Retardants, 1970; Fire, 1985; contbr. numerous articles to profl. publs. Chmn. blue ribbon com. on rsch. and pub. svc. U. Md., 1993. Recipient gold medal Dept. Commerce, 1977, President's Mgmt. Improvement award White House, 1977, President's Disting. Exec. Rank award, 1981, E.U. Condon award, 1986; Disting. Svc. award U. Md. Coll. Engring., 1990, Centennial medal, 1994; 1st ann. Outstanding Achievement award Fire Retardant Chem. Assn., 1994. Fellow AAAS, Washington Acad. Sci.; mem. Am. Chem. Soc. (chmn. St. Louis sect. 1971-72), Nat. Fire Protection Assn. (bd. dirs. 1978-84), ASTM (bd. dirs. 1985-87), Nat. Acad. Engring., Sigma Xi. E-mail: johnwlyons@gmail.com.

LYONS, MARY E., academic administrator; b. Calif. BA, Sonoma St. Univ., 1971; MA, San Diego St. Univ., 1976; PhD, Sonoma St. Univ., 1983. Prof. Franciscan School of Theology, Berkeley, Calif., 1984—90; pres. Calif. Maritime Acad., Vallejo, 1990-96, Coll. of St. Benedict, St. Joseph, Minn., 1996—2003, U. San Diego, 2003—. Office: Office of Pres U San Diego 5998 Alcala Pk San Diego CA 92110-2492 Office Phone: 619-260-4520. Office Fax: 619-260-6833. E-mail: president@sandiego.edu.

LYONS, MAXINE EVADNEY, small business owner, poet; b. Kingston, Jamaica, Nov. 7, 1962; arrived in U.S., 1995; d. Ezekiel West and Eunice May Hitnarinesingh; m. Norman W. Lyons, Dec. 31, 1989. AS, No. U. West Indies, Mandeville, Jamaica, 1985. Tchr. Continuation HS, Jamaica, 1980—81; sec. Precision Arts Ltd., Jamaica, 1986—88; sec., receptionist Speed-O-Graphic Printer, Jamaica, 1988—89; asst. mgr. Astra Hotel, Jamaica, 1990—91; sec. Jamaica Transformer Co., 1991—92. Owner Jamaica Pl., Bronx, 2000—; host poetry readings Xpressions Night Club, Bronx; resident poet Royal Radio 106.3 FM. TV appearance Good Day NY, 2002, Bronxnet TV, 2002 (named Small Bus. of Week, 2002); author: numerous poems; prodr. (poetry CD): My History as a Child. Recipient Shakespear trophy Excellence and medallion, 2003. Avocations: poetry, short stories, cooking, catering, music. Home: 3313 Eastchester Rd Bronx NY 10469 Office: Maroon Books PO Box 682 Bronx NY 10462 Office Phone: 917-557-3806. Personal E-mail: poettothemax@verizon.net, poettothemax@hotmail.com.

LYONS, MONA, lawyer; b. NYC, Jan. 10, 1950; BA, Coll. Potomac, 1972; JD, Catholic U. Am., 1975. Bar: DC 1975. Private practice, Washington. Named one of 75 Best Lawyers in Washington, Washingtonian Mag., 2002. Mem.: DC Bar. Office: Law Office of Mona Lyons 1666 Connecticut Ave NW Ste 500 Washington DC 20009 Office Phone: 202-387-7000. Office Fax: 202-387-7116.

LYONS, NICK, publishing executive; b. NYC, June 5, 1932; s. Nathan and Rose (Bernstein) Ress; m. Mari Blumenau, Sept. 1, 1957; children: Paul, Charles, Jennifer, Anthony. BS in Econs., U. Pa., 1953; MA in Am. Lit., U. Mich., 1961, PhD in Am. Lit., 1963. Prof. English Hunter Coll., NYC, 1961-88; exec. editor Crown Pubs., Inc., NYC, 1963-78; pres. Nick Lyons Books, NYC, 1979-84, Lyons & Burford, Pubs., NYC, 1984-98; chmn. bd. dirs. The Lyons Press, NYC, 1999—2001. Author: The Sony Vision, 1975, The Seasonable Angler, 1970, Bright Rivers, 1978, Confessions of a Fly Fishing Addict, 1988, Spring Creek, 1991, Full Creel, 2000; editor: The Gigantic Book of Fishing Stories, 2007. With U.S. Army, 1954-55. Avocation: fly fishing. Home: 342 W 84th St New York NY 10024-4202

LYONS, NONA MARY, adult education educator; d. Michael Peter Plessner and Norah Agnes Hennessy Plessner; m. Robert Francis Lyons, May 31, 1969. BA, St. John's U. Coll., Bklyn., 1955; MA, Fordham U., 1961; EdD, Harvard U., 1982. Cert. tchr. English NYC Pub. Schs., State of N.Y., Dept. of Edn., supt. NYC Pub. Schs., State of N.Y., Dept. of Edn. Tchr. N.Y.C. Pub. Schs., 1956—63; curriculum developer, project dir. Edn. Devel. Ctr., Cambridge, Mass., 1963—75; dir. curriculum and staff devel. Scarsdale (N.Y.) Pub. Schs., 1975—78; student/tchg. fellow Harvard Grad. Sch. of Edn., Cambridge, 1978—82, lectr., 1982—90; dir. of tchr. edn. Brown U., Providence, 1990—93, U. of So. Maine, Gorham, Maine, 1993—97; vis. assoc. prof. of edn. Dartmouth Coll., Hanover, NH, 1997—2001; vis. rsch. scholar Nat. U. of Ireland, Cork, 2000—. Prin. rschr., co-dir. Emma Willard Sch. Study of Adolescent Girls Harvard Grad. Sch. Edn. and Emma Willard Sch., Cambridge, Mass and Troy, NY, 1981—89; convener Portfolios in Tchg. and Tchr. Edn. Conf., Cambridge, 1994—2001; founder Spl. Interest Group of Am. Edn. Rsch. Assn.: Reflective Portfolios in Tchg. and Tchr. Edn., Washington; cons. developing a reflective portfolio to document tchg. at univ. level. Univ. Coll. Cork, Trinity Coll., Univ. Coll. Dublin, Dublin Inst. of Tech., St. Angela's Coll., Ireland, 2001—; vis. rsch. scholar Wellesley Ctr. for Rsch. on Women, 1996—97, Nat. U. Ireland, Cork, 2000—. Co-author (with Carol Gilligan and Trudy Hanmer): Making Connections: The Relational World of Adolescent Girls at Emma Willard School; author: With Portfolio in Hand: Validating the New Teacher Professionalism, The University as a Learning Organization; author, co-editor with Vicki LaBoskey: Narrative Inquiry in Practice: Advancing the Knowledge of Teaching (Book of the Yr., Am. Edn. Rsch. Assn., Narrative Spl. Interest Group, 2004); co-author: Women's Education; co-author: (with H. Freidus) (chpt.) International Handbook of Self-Study of Teaching and Teacher Edn. Practices, 2004. Mem. expert panel reviewer, sci. initiative Higher Edn. Authority, Ireland, 2003. Recipient Spencer fellowship, Spencer Found., NAE, 1987—89. Mem.: European Edn. Rsch. Assn., Edn. Studies Assn. Ireland, Am. Edn. Rsch. Assn. (editor-reviewer 2001—04). Achievements include research in Dialectic of Choice and Relectivity in Human Development. Avocations: sketching, writing family narratives, travel, cooking, coaching. Office: Nat U Ireland Cork Edn Dept Donovan's Rd Cork Ireland Personal E-mail: nonalyons@hotmail.com.

LYONS, OREN, Native American chieftain, conservationist; b. 1930; BA, Syracuse U., 1958, LLD (hon.). Lic. profl. boxing second NY. Mem. Onondaga Coun. of Chiefs of Six Nations of Iroquois Confederacy; Faithkeeper Turtle Clan of Onondaga Nation, 1970—; prof. Am. Studies SUNY, Buffalo, dir. Native Am. Studies Prog. Native Am. rep. Corp. for Pub. Broadcasting, 1974—; Six Nations rep. to sub-commn. on prevention of discrimination and protection of minorities Commn. on Human Rights, UN Econ. and Social Coun., Washington, 1976; mem. Human Rights Divsn. of UN; bd. dirs. Harvard Project on Am. Econ. Devel.; chmn. bd. dirs. Honoring Contbns. in Governance of Am. Indian Nations; mem. exec. com. World Forum of Spiritual and Parliamentary Leaders on Human Survival, Oxford, England, 1998; hon. bd. dirs., co-founder Native Am. Ctr. for the Living Arts, Niagara Falls, NY; mem. adv. bd. Native Am. Family Nurse Practitioner Prog.; spkr., presenter in field. Author: Exiled in the Land of the Free, 1992, Voice of Indigenous Peoples, 1992, Native People Address the United Nations, 1994; pub.: Daybreak Mag.; co-editor: Exiled in the Land of the Free. Named to Lacrosse Nat. Hall of Fame, 1993; recipient Ellis Island Congl. Medal of Honor, 1990, Howard E. Johnson award, 1991, Audubon medal, Nat. Audubon Soc., 1993. Mem.: Am. Arbitration Assn., Salt City Amateur Boxing Club (bd. dirs.), Onandaga Athletic Club (founding mem.). Avocations: Native American history, international indigenous affairs, contemporary indigenous issues, international environmental issues. Office: The Onondaga Nation PO Box 200 Nedrow NY 13120-0200 also: Dept Am Studies U Buffalo 1010 Clemens Hall Buffalo NY 14260-4630

LYONS, PAUL VINCENT, lawyer; b. Boston, July 19, 1939; s. Joseph Vincent and Doris Irene (Griffin) L.; m. Elaine Marie Hurley, July 13, 1968; children: Judith Marie, Maureen Patricia, Paula Anne, Joseph Hurley BS cum laude, Boston Coll., 1960; MBA, NYU, 1962; JD, Suffolk U., Boston, 1968. Bar: Mass. 1968, U.S. Dist. Ct. Mass. 1969, U.S. Cir. Ct. (1st cir.) 1969, U.S. Supreme Ct. 1991. Div. adminstrn. mgr. Pepsi-Cola Co., NYC, 1962-64; mem. bus. faculty Burdett Coll., Boston, 1964-68; atty. NLRB, Boston, 1968-73; assoc. Foley Hoag LLP, Boston, 1973-77, ptnr., 1978—. Mem. faculty Boston U., 1972-74. Mem. Town Meeting, Milton, Mass., 1986—2002, Pers. Bd., Milton, 1994—2004. Lt. US Army, 1960—62. Mem. ABA, Mass. Bar Assn., Boston Bar Assn. Office: Foley Hoag LLP 155 Seaport Blvd Boston MA 02210-2175 Office Phone: 617-832-1000. Business E-Mail: plyons@foleyhoag.com.

LYONS, PETER B., commissioner; b. Nev. BS in Physics & Math., U. Ariz., 1964; Ph.D in Nuclear Astrophysics, Calif. Inst. Tech., 1969. With Los Alamos Nat. Lab, 1969—96, dir., LANL Industrial Partnership Office, 1993—96; sci. adv. to Senator Peter Domenici US Senate, Washington, 1997—2005, adv., Energy and Natural Resources Com., 2002—05; commr. US Nuclear Regulatory Commn., Rockville, 2005—. Chmn. NATO Nuclear Effects Task Group; bd. dirs. Los Alamos Sch. Bd. Fellow: Am. Physical Soc. Office: US Nuclear Regulatory Commn One White Flint N Bldg 11555 Rockville Pike Rm 18G1 Rockville MD 20852

LYONS, PHILLIP MICHAEL, SR., insurance accounting and real estate executive; b. Gueydan, La., Nov. 22, 1941; s. Joseph Bosman and Elder (Richard) L.; children from previous marriage: Phillip M., Wilton J.; m. Regina Zoe (Malloy) Johnson, Aug. 15, 1991; stepchildren: Jennifer R. Johnson, Tracey L. Johnson Student, McNeese State Coll., 1959—62, Alvin Jr. Coll., 1964, Coll. Mainland, 1974; BBA, U. Houston, 1977, postgrad., 1984. CPA; cert. in employee benefit law. Adminstrv. trainee Am. Nat. Ins. Co., Galveston, Tex., 1965, asst. mgr., acting mgr. policy issue dept., 1966—67, mgr., 1967—71, mgr. pre-issue dept., sys. analyst, 1971—72, divsn. mgr., policyholder's svc. divsn., 1972—74, dir. ordinary policyholder's svc., 1974—76, dir. combination policy records, 1976—77; supervising acct. materials acctg. comptr.'s dept. Aramco Svcs. Co., Houston, 1977—79, ins. adviser treas.'s dept., 1979—80, adminstr. risk mgmt. and ins. divsn., treas.'s dept., 1980—87, sr. ins. advisor, 1988—98; sr. cons. employee benefits Equiva Svcs., Houston, 1998—99, adminstr. employee benefits fin. and contracts, 1999—2002; cons. fin., acctg., tax and employee benefits Houston, 2003—. Ptnr. Lyons Real Estate, Sulphur, La., 1966—; bd. dirs. Studio B, Inc., Houston Solicitor United Fund, 1966-69; pres. Alvin Youth Baseball Tex. League, 1982 Fellow Life Mgmt. Inst.; mem. AICPA, Tex. State CPA, Risk and Ins. Mgmt. Soc. (assoc. in risk mgmt.), Jr. C. of C. (bd. dirs. 1972, state bd. dirs. 1972-74, Sparkplug of Yr. 1972-73, Roadrunner of Yr. 1972-73), Masons, Shriners, KC Home: 223 W Sherwood Dr Alvin TX 77511-5109 also: 1012 S Stanford St Sulphur LA 70663-4824 Personal E-mail: pmlyons@houston.rr.com.

LYONS, RICHARD KENT, dean, finance educator; b. Palo Alto, Calif., Feb. 10, 1961; s. J. Richard and Ida (Primavera) L. BS in Bus. with highest honors, U. Calif., Berkeley, 1982; PhD in Econs., MIT, 1987. Rsch. analyst SRI Internat., Menlo Park, Calif., 1983-84; summer intern Orgn. for Econ. Cooperation & Devel., Paris, 1985, Bd. Govs., Fed. Res. System, Washington, 1986; asst. prof. Columbia U., NYC, 1987-91, assoc. prof., 1991-93; asst. prof. Haas Sch. Bus., U. Calif., Berkeley, 1993-96, assoc. prof., 1996—2000, prof., 2000—04, Sylvan Coleman Chair fin., 2004—, assoc. dean for academic affairs, 2004, acting dean, 2004—05, exec. assoc. dean, 2005—06; chief learning officer Goldman Sachs, NYC, 2006—. Vis. prof. U. Toulouse, France, Stockholm U., Sweden, London Sch. Econs., Found. for Advanced Info. and Rsch., Japan, U. Aix-Marseille, France; rsch. assoc. Nat. Bur. Econ. Rsch., Cambridge, Mass., 1989—; former chmn., dir. Matthews Asian Funds; former trustee iShares; cons. IMF, World Bank, Fed. Res. Bank, European Commn.; adv. bd. Econ. Policy Review, NYC. Assoc. editor Calif. Mgmt. Rev., Jour. Fin. Markets; contbr. articles to profl. jours. NSF grad. fellow, 1984. Mem. Am. Econ. Assn., Coun. on Fgn. Rels., Phi Beta Kappa, Beta Gamma Sigma, Sigma Alpha Epsilon. Democrat. Avocations: squash, guitar, French.

LYONS, ROBERT, information technology executive; BS in Internat. Rels., Georgetown Univ.; MS in Edn. Tech., Boston Coll.; MS in Econs., Univ. Minn.; PhD in Polit. Economy and Computational Game Theory, Univ. Calif., Berkeley. Co-founder, chief tech. officer Nextrials, Inc., San Ramon, Calif. Named one of Top 25 chief tech. officers, InfoWorld mag., 2007. Mem.: Clin. Data Interchange Standards Consortium, Drug Info. Assn. Office: Nextrials Inc 5000 Executive Pkwy Ste 540 San Ramon CA 94583 Office Phone: 925-355-3000. Office Fax: 925-355-3005. Business E-Mail: info@nextrials.com.

LYONS, SUSANNE D., former finance company executive; BA, Vassar Coll.; MBA, Boston Univ. Mgmt. positions through sr. v.p. brokerage mktg. Fidelity Investments, 1984—94; mgmt. positions through enterprise pres. retail services Charles Schwab & Co., 1994—2004; exec. v.p., chief mktg. officer Visa USA, San Francisco, 2004—07.*

LYONS, TERRENCE ALLAN, mining executive; b. Grand Prairie, Alta., Can., Aug. 1, 1949; s. Allan Lynnwood and Mildred Helen (Smith) L. B in Applied Sci., U. B.C., 1972; MBA, U. Western Ont., 1974. Registered profl. engr., B.C. Gen. mgr. Southwestern Drug Co., Vancouver, B.C., Canada, 1975-76; mgr. planning Versatile Corp., Vancouver, 1976-83, asst. v.p., 1983-86, v.p., dir., 1986-88; dir. B.C. Pacific Capital Corp., 1988—. Bd. dirs. Canaccord Capital Inc., Polaris Minerals Corp., Skye Resources, Inc.; chmn. Northgate Minerals Corp. Author articles on mfg. tech. Office: Northgate Minerals Corp Ste 406-815 Hornby St Vancouver BC Canada V6Z 2E6 Office Phone: 604-681-4004. Business E-Mail: tlyons@northgateminerals.com.

LYONS, THOMAS PATRICK, economics professor; b. Groton, Conn., Sept. 8, 1953; BA in Asian Studies, Cornell U., 1979, MA in Econs., 1982, PhD in Econs., 1983. Asst. prof. econs. Dartmouth Coll., Hanover, NH, 1983-87; vis. asst. prof. Cornell U., Ithaca, NY, 1986-88, asst. prof., 1988-91; assoc. prof., 1991-2000; dir. East Asia program Cornell U., Ithaca, NY, 1991-94, dir. undergrad. studies, econs., 1995—, prof., 2000—. Author: Economic Integration and Planning in Maoist China, 1987, China's War on Poverty, 1992, Economic Geography of Fujian: A Sourcebook, vols. 1 and 2, 1995, China Maritime Customs and China's Trade Statistics 1859-1948, 2003, Townships in Fujian, 1997-2003: Digital Maps and Data, 2006; contbr. articles to profl. jours. With USN, 1972—76. Grantee, Ford Found., 1987. Mem.: Assn. Am. Geographers, Assn. Asian Studies, Am. Econ. Assn. Office: Cornell U Dept Econs Uris Hall Ithaca NY 14853-7601 Home Phone: 607-387-3382; Office Phone: 607-255-9534. Business E-Mail: tpl4@cornell.edu.

LYRA, JON ROBERT, music educator, artist; b. Luke AFB, Ariz., May 20, 1956; s. Ray and Lucy Garcia Lyra; m. Judith Ellen Grames-Lyra, Feb. 14, 1997; m. Patricia Ann Espinoza (div.); 1 child, Jon David. AA, Allan Hancock Coll., 1978; BA, U. Calif., Santa Barbara, Calif., 1982. Cert. tchr. Calif. Music tutor Allan Hancock Coll., Santa Maria, Calif., 1977—78; graphics illustrator USAF, Peterson, Colo., 1985—88; counselor Stewart Learning Ctr., Lompoc, Calif., 1990; instr. Vocational Learning Ctr., Lompoc, 1991; sub. tchr. Lompoc Unified Sch. Dist., 1998—2006; music tchr. Lompoc Sch. Music, 2002—06. Substitute instrnl. asst. Lompoc Unified Sch. Dist., 1998—2006; piano tchr. Lompoc Sch. Music, 2002—06. Exhibitions include U. Calif. Santa Barbara Art Mus., 1981, Grossman Gallery, Lompoc, Calif., 1998, Cypress Gallery, 1998—2006. Mem. Cmty. Emergency Response Team, Lompoc, 2002—06. E-4 USAF, 1984—88, Peterson, Calif. Recipient Andrew Spooner Meml. award, Cabrillo H.S., 1975, Bank of Am. award, 1975, numerous 1st Pl. awards for artwork, 1972—2002; grantee, Allan Hancock Coll., 1978. Mem.: Lompoc Art Assn. (program com. chmn. 2002), Nat. Women's History Mus. Democrat. Cath. Avocations: digital photography, song writing, filmmaking, painting, travel. Office: Lompoc Sch Music 601 East Ocean Ave Ste 9 Lompoc CA 93436 Office Phone: 805-736-9933. E-mail: jonandjudith@earthlink.net, jonrobertandjudith@yahoo.com.

LYSNE, ALLEN BRUCE, laboratory director; b. Owen, Wis. s. Almond P. and Helen A. (Childs) L.; children: Michael, Bruce, Brooke. BS, U. N.D., 1960. Lic. med. technologist, N.D. Bd. Clin. Lab. Practice; cert. clin. lab. scientist, Nat. Cert. Agy. Clin. lab. dir USPHS Indian Hosp., Fort Yates, N.D., 1961-62; asst. dir. biochemistry Dr. Salsbury's Lab., Charles City, Iowa, 1962-63; clin. lab. dir Lake Region Clinic, Devils Lake, N.D., 1963-69; CEO Meml. Hosp. Assn., Maddock, N.D., 1969-75; asst. exec. dir. ops. N.D. Health Care Rev., Minot, 1976-80; regional mgr. Colo. Found. Med. Care, Pueblo, Denver, Colo., 1980-87; dir. diagnositc svcs. Cmty. Hosp., Hillsboro, N.D., 1988-92; clin. lab. dir. Carroll County Meml. Hosp., Carrollton, Mo., 1992—. Chmn. Coun. on Aging, Pueblo, 1980-87. Mem. Am. Chem. Soc., Am. Assn. Clin. Lab. Sci., Am. Assn. Clin. Chemistry, Sci. Pub. Interest, Mo. Assn. Clin. Lab. Sci., N.Y. Acad. Scis. Achievements include research in effectiveness, toxicity and safety of 2 new drugs for coccidioidomycosis.

LYSTAD, MARY HANEMANN (MRS. ROBERT LYSTAD), sociologist, writer; b. New Orleans, Apr. 11, 1928; d. James and Mary (Douglass) Hanemann; m. Robert Lystad, June 20, 1953; children: Lisa Douglass, Anne Hanemann, Mary Lunde, Robert Douglass, James Hanemann. AB cum laude, Newcomb Coll., 1949; MA, Columbia U., 1951; PhD, Tulane U., 1955. Postdoctoral fellow social psychology S.E. La. Hosp., Mandeville, 1955-57; field rsch. social psychology Ghana, 1957-58, South Africa and Swaziland, 1968, China, 1986; chief sociologist Collaborative Child Devel. Project, Charity Hosp. La., New Orleans, 1958-61; feature writer African div. Voice Am., Washington, 1964-73; program analyst NIMH, Washington, 1968-78, asso. dir. for planning and coordination div. spl. mental health programs, 1978-80; chief Nat. Ctr. for Prevention and Control of Rape, 1980-83, Ctr. Mental Health Studies of Emergencies, 1983-89; pvt. cons. specializing on mental health implications social and econ. problems Bethesda, Md., 1990—. Cons. on youth Nat. Goals Research Staff, White House, Washington, 1969-70. Author: (nonfiction) Social Aspects of Alienation, 1969, As They See It: Changing Values of College Youth, 1972, Violence at Home, 1974, A Child's World As Seen in His Stories and Drawings, 1974, From Dr. Mather to Dr. Seuss: 200 Years of American Books for Children, 1980, At Home in America, 1983; (fiction for children) Millicent the Monster, 1968, James the Jaguar, 1972, Jennifer Takes Over P.S. 94, 1972, Halloween Parade, 1973, That New Boy, 1973, Play Ball, 1997; editor: Innovations in Mental Health Services to Disaster Victims, 1985, Violence in the Home: Interdisciplinary Perspectives, 1986, Mental Health Response to Mass Emergencies: Theory and Practice, 1988. Recipient Spl. Recognition award USPHS, 1983, Alumna Centennial award Newcomb Coll., 1986. Home and Office: 4900 Scarsdale Rd Bethesda MD 20816-2440

LYTHCOTT, MARCIA A., newspaper editor; d. William and Florence; m. Stephen Lythcott (dec.). BA in journalism, U. Wisc., Madison. Assoc. food guide editor Chicago Tribune, Ill., editor, style section Ill., editor, home section Ill., 1993—94, op-ed editor Ill., 1995—. Office: Chicago Tribune 435 N Michigan Ave Chicago IL 60611-4066

LYTLE, BRUCE WHITNEY, cardiovascular surgeon; b. Mpls., Sept. 10, 1945; s. Francis Theodore and Dorothy L. (Whitney) L.; m. Ellen Suzanne Baker, Feb. 1970; children: Francis Theodore, Medora Suzanne. BA with great distinction, Stanford U., 1967; MD cum laude, Harvard Med. Sch., 1971. Diplomate Am. Bd. Surgery, Am. Bd. Thoracic Surgery. Surg. intern Mass. Gen. Hosp., Boston, 1971-72, third asst. resident in gen. surgery, 1972-73, second asst. resident, 1973-74, fourth yr. resident, 1974-75; sr. registrar in cardiothoracic surgery Shotley Bridge Hosp., No. Regional Health Authority, Eng., 1975-76; fifth yr. resident in surgery Mass. Gen. Hosp., Boston, 1976, chief resident in cardiovascular surgery, 1977; assoc. staff Dept. Thoracic and Cardiovascular Surgery The Cleve. Clinic Found., 1978-79, profl. staff Dept. Thoracic and Cardiovascular Surgery, 1979—. Contbr. over 200 articles to profl. med. jours. Mem. ACS, AMA, Am. Coll. Cardiology, Am. Heart Assn., Ohio Chpt. ACS, Ohio State Med. Assn., Am. Assn. for Thoracic Surgery, Cleve. Acad. Medicine, Soc. Thoracic Surgeons, Am. Surg. Assn. Office: Cleveland Clinic Found 9500 Euclid Ave # F25 Cleveland OH 44195-0002*

LYTLE, GARY R., telecommunications industry executive; 4 children. BA in Bus. Adminstrn., Mich. State U., East Lansing, MBA. Various govt. rels. positions including v.p. govt. affairs Mich. Bell, 1980—92; dir. fed. rels. Ameritech, 1992—94, v.p. fed. rels. Washington, 1994—99; cons. Lytle Consulting, 1999—2000; interim pres., CEO US Telecom Assn., 2000—01; sr. v.p. fed. rels. Qwest Comm. Internat., Inc., Washington, 2001—. Office: Qwest Comm Internat Inc 1275 K St NW Washington DC 20005 Office Phone: 202-408-8446.*

LYTLE, L(ARRY) BEN, insurance company executive, lawyer; b. Greenville, Tex., Sept. 30, 1946; children: Hugh, Larry. BS in Mgmt. Sci. and Indsl. Psychology, East Tex. State U., 1970; JD, Ind. U., 1980. Computer operator/programmer U.S. Govt., Ft. Smith, Ark., 1964-65; customer engr. Olivetti Corp., San Antonio, 1965-66; mgr. computer ops. and computer software LTV Electrosystems, Greenville, 1966-70; project mgr. electronic fin. system, dir. systems planning Assocs. Corp. N.Am., South Bend, Ind., 1970-75; asst. v.p. systems Am. Fletcher Nat. Bank, Indpls., 1975-76; with Anaheim Ins. Cos., Inc., Indpls., 1976-99; pres. Assoc. Ins. Cos., Inc., Indpls., 1987-99, COO, 1987-89, CEO, 1989-99. Chmn. bd. dirs. Anthem Cos., Inc., Acordia, Inc.; chmn. bd. dirs. AdminaStar, Inc., Health Networks Am., Inc., Novalis, Inc., Robinson-Conner Nev., Inc.; bd. dirs. The Shelby Ins. Group, Raffensperger, Hughes & Co., Inc., Indpls. Power and Light Co. Enterprises; mem. adv. bd. CID Venture Ptnrs., Ltd. Partnership; rschr., cons. state and fed. govt. orgns., including, Adv. Coun. on Social Security, Pepper Commn. of U.S. Congress, others. Chmn. health policy commn. State of Ind., Indpls., 1990-92; active various civic orgns., including United Negro Coll. Fund, Indpls. Mus. Art. Mem. ABA, Ind. Bar Assn., Indpls. Bar Assn., Ind. State C. of C. (bd. dirs.), Indpls. C. of C. (bd. dirs.). Home: PO Box 441830 Indianapolis IN 46244-1830

LYTLE, MICHAEL ALLEN, forensic criminologist, consultant; b. Salina, Kans., Oct. 22, 1946; s. Milton Earl and Geraldine Faye (Young) L.; div.; 1 child, Eric Alexander. BA, Ind. U., 1973; grad. cert., Sam Houston State U., Huntsville, Tex., 1977; MEd, Tex. A&M U., 1978; postgrad., 1978-80; student, Nat. Def. U., 1988. Substitute high sch. tchr., Butler Cty., KS, 1969; instr. criminal justice Cleve. State C.C., Tenn., 1974-77; adj. instr. criminal justice U. Tenn., Chattanooga, 1975-76; tchg. asst. Tex. A&M U. Sys., 1977-80, intern adminstrv. asst. Office Vice Chancellor Legal Affairs and Gen. Counsel, 1980, staff assoc. Office Chancellor, 1980-81, asst. to chancellor, 1981-83, asst. dir. govt. rels., 1983-84, spl. asst. to chancellor for fed. rels., 1984-87; dir. rsch. devel. and spl. asst. to v.p. for rsch. and grad. studies Syracuse U., NY, 1987, exec. dir. govt. rels. NY, 1987-89, sr. rsch. assoc. tech. and info. policy prog. Maxwell Sch. Citizenship and Pub. Affairs NY, 1987-92, dir. fed. rels. NY, 1989-92, adj. prof. internatl. bus. studies NY, 1990-92; prin. and sr. couns. The Erik Alexander Group, 1992-93; exec. dir. instl. devel. U. Tex., Brownsville, 1993-95, sr. lectr. criminal justice, 1995-97; rsch. fellow Office Undersec. Def., 1997; sr. rsch. assoc. Sci. Applications Internat. Corp., 1997-99; adj. prof. criminal justice Marymount U. and Lutheran Colls., Wash. Consortiums, 1999—; dep. mgr. tech. svcs. divsn. Sci. Applications Internat. Corp., 2000—06; asst. prof. criminal justice U. Tex., Brownsville, 2006—. Rep. Coun. on Fed. Rels., Assn. Am. Univs.; instl. rep. Rsch. Univs. Network; exec. dir. Tex. Com. for Employer Support of the Guard and Res., 1982-86; mem. U.S. Mexico Com. Philanthropy and the Border, 1994-95, militarily critical techs. adv. com. U.S. Internat. Bus. Studies, Tex. A&M Univ., 1986-87; res. asst. army attache to Rep. of Ireland, 1986-87; mem. exec. com. N.E. Parallel Architectures Ctr.; mem. Sec. of Army's adv. panel in ROTC affairs, 1988-92; cons. Nat. Inst. Justice, 2000—, Office of Victims of Crime, 2002—. Mem. editl. bd., Jour. Tech. Transfer, 1987-95, contbr. articles to profl. jours. Served with USAR, Vietnam and Bosnia. Trustee, Brownsville Hist. Mus. Assn., 1994-96. Decorated Legion of Merit, Bronze Star, Purple Heart, Meritorious Svc. medal with 2 oak leaf clusters, Joint Svc. Commendation medal, Army Commendation medal with 4 oak leaf clusters; recipient Disting. Alumni award Sam Houston State U., 2003. Fellow Inter-Univ. Seminar Armed Forces and Soc. Am. Coll. Forensic Examiners (life); mem. AAAS (bd. advs. nat. security and sci. comm. proj. mem. awd. sel. panel. sci. freedom and responsibilty), Nat. Assn. State Univs. and Land-Grant Colls. (vet. affairs and nat. svc. com.), Am. Soc. for Pub. Adminstrn. (exec. com. sect., past chair on Nat. Security and Def. Analysis), Atlantic Counc. U.S. (councilor), Forensic Sci. Soc., Acad. Criminal Justice Scis., Internat. Assn. for the Study of Organized Crime, Internat. Assn. Chief's Police, mem., US Attorney's Law Enforcement Coordinating Com., southern dist., Tex., 1995-97. Mem. Army and Navy Club, Capitol Hill Club, Sigma Xi, Phi Delta Kappa, Alpha Phi Sigma Republican. Episcopalian. Address: 206 Parkview Cir Harlingen TX 78550 Personal E-mail: malytle@aol.com.

LYTLE, WILLIAM DAVID, lawyer; b. Waynesville, Mo., Mar. 18, 1948; s. William R. and Ruth (Byler) L.; m. Barbara Carroll Louis, Aug. 29, 1970; children: Jeffrey, Kathryn. AB cum laude, Washington U., St. Louis, 1970, JD, 1973. Ptnr. Preston, Altman, Parlapiano, Keilbach & Lytle, Pueblo, Colo., 1974, Altman, Keilbach, Lytle, Parlapiano & Ware PC, Pueblo, Colo. Pres. Downtown Pueblo Assn., 1986. Mem. Colo. Bar Assn. (v.p. Denver chpt. 1985-86, chmn. com. on legal fee arbitration 1984-87, chmn. com. on law firm mgmt. 1979-80, pres.-elect, 2006-07), ABA, Pueblo County Bar Assn. Democrat. Roman Catholic. Office: Altman Keilbach Lytle Parlapiano & Ware PC 229 Colorado Ave PO Box 33 Pueblo CO 81002 Office Phone: 719-545-7325. Office Fax: 719-545-9437. E-mail: lytle@altman-keilbach.com.

LYTTON, BERNARD, urology educator; b. London, June 28, 1926; came to U.S., 1962; s. Morris and Pearl (Zuckerberg) L.; m. Norma M. Mendle, Oct. 28, 1963; children: Sharon, Simon, Timothy, Jennifer. MB, BS, U. London, 1948, FRCS, 1955. House officer, sr. registrar Royal London Hosp., 1948-50, 58-61; prof., chief urology Yale Univ. Sch. Medicine, New Haven, 1967-87, Donald Guthrie prof. surgery, 1987—96, prof. emeritus, 1996—, dir. Henry Koerner Ctr. Emeritus Faculty, 2001—; Master Jonathan Edwards Coll. Yale U., 1987-97. Squadron leader Royal Airforce Med. Br., Eng., 1950-52. Fellow, Kings Coll. Hosp., 1961—63. Fellow ACS; mem. Am. Urol. Assn. (Hugh Hampton Young award 1985, pres. New Eng. sect. 1974), Am. Assn. Genito-Urinary Surgeons (v.p. 2006, pres. 2007—), Clin. Soc. Genito-Urinary Surgeons (pres. 2000-01), Soc. Pelvic Surgeons. Avocations: tennis, skiing, history, hiking. Home: 21 Autumn St New Haven CT 06511-2220 Office: Yale U Sch Medicine Sect Urology PO Box 208041 New Haven CT 06520-8041 Office Phone: 203-785-2815. Business E-Mail: bernard.lytton@yale.edu.

LYTTON, ROBERT LEONARD, civil engineer, educator; b. Port Arthur, Tex., Oct. 23, 1937; s. Robert Odell and Nora Mae (Verrett) Lytton; m. Eleanor Marilyn Anderson, Sept. 9, 1961; children: Lynn Elizabeth, Robert Douglas, John Kirby. BSCE, U. Tex., 1960, MSCE, 1961, PhD, 1967. Registered profl. engr., Tex., La., land surveyor, La. Cowhand Slaughter Ranch, Douglas, Ariz., 1963; assoc. Dannenbaum and Assocs., Cons. Engrs., Houston, 1963—65; U.S. NSF fellow U. Tex., Austin, 1965—67, asst. prof., 1967—68; NSF fellow Australian Commonwealth Sci. & Indsl. Rsch. Orgn., Melbourne, Australia, 1969—70; assoc. prof. Tex. A&M U., College Station, 1971—76, prof., 1976—90, Wiley chair prof., 1990—95, dir. ctr. for infrastructure engring., 1995—, Benson chair prof., 1995—; divsn. head Tex. Transp. Inst., College Station, 1982—91, head infrastructure and transp. divsn. civil engring. dept., 1993—95. Bd. dir. MLA Labs., Inc., Austin, Lyric Tech., LLC, Houston; v.p., bd. dir. Electronic Pavement and Infrastructure Charting, Inc., MLAW Cons., Inc., Austin, Geostructural Tool Kit, Inc.; prin. investigator strategic hwy. rsch. program A005 rsch. project, 1990—93; keynote spkr. 5th Internat. Conf. Rsch. Inst. Labs. Materials Testing, Limoges, France, 2004. Active St. Vincent de Paul Soc., Houston, 1963—65, Redemptorist Lay Mission Soc., Melbourne, Australia, 1969—70. Capt. US Army, 1961—63. Named a Legend of PTI, 2004; named Soc. Am. Mil. Engrs. Outstanding Sr. Cadet, U. Tex., 1959, Trendsetter, Pub. Works Mag., 2005; recipient SAR medal of Honor, St. Mary's U., 1957, Disting. Mil. Grad. award, 1960, Hamilton Watch award, Coll. Engring., 1960, Everite Bursary award, Coun. Sci. and Indsl. Rsch., South Africa, 1984, Disting. Achievement award, Tex. A&M U. Assn. Former Students, 1996, Zachary Sr. Rschr. award, Tex. Transp. Inst., 1996. Fellow: ASCE (John B. Hawley award Tex. sect. 1966), Post-Tensioning Inst. (adv. bd., Named Legend of Post-Tensioning 2005); mem.: NSPE, Constrn. Users Round Table (Constrn. Innovation Forum NOVA award 2006), Found. Performance Assn. Houston (hon. life mem.), Internat. Soc. Asphalt Pavements, Tex. Soc. Profl. Engrs., Assn. Asphalt Paving Technologists, Internat. Soc. Soil Mechanics and Geotechnical Engring. (US rep. tech. com. TC-6 1987—, keynote adress 7th internat. conf. expansive soils 1992, keynote address 1st internat. conf. unsaturated soils 1995), Transp. Rsch. Bd. (chmn. com. A2LO6 1967—93, disting. lectr. 2000), Sigma Xi, Phi Kappa Phi, Tau Beta Pi, Chi Epsilon, Phi Kappa Delta. Roman Catholic. Achievements include patents for sys. identification, analysis of subsurface radar signals. Office: Tex A&M U 503A CE Tex Transp Inst Bldg College Station TX 77843-3136 Personal E-mail: rllytton@mail.com.

LYTTON, WILLIAM BRYAN, lawyer; b. St. Louis, Mo., Aug. 22, 1948; s. William Bryan and Josephine (Lamy) L.; m. Christine Mary Miller; children— William Bryan IV, Laura Miller. AB, Georgetown U., 1970; JD, Am. U., Washington, 1973. Bar: D.C. 1973, U.S. Ct. Appeals (7th cir.) 1975, U.S. Supreme Ct. 1978, Pa. 1979, U.S. Dist. Ct. (ea. dist.) Pa. 1979, U.S. Ct. Appeals (3d cir.) 1979. Legal counsel, legis. asst. US Senator Charles H. Percy, 1973-75; asst. U.S. atty. US Dist. Ct., Chgo., 1975-78, US Dist. Ct. (ea. dist.), Pa., 1978-83, dep. chief spl. prosecutions div. Pa., 1980, dep. chief criminal div. Pa., 1980, chief criminal div. Pa., 1980-81, 1st asst. U.S. atty. Pa., 1981-83; ptnr. Kohn, Savett, Klein & Graf, P.C., Phila., 1983-87, 87-89; chief counsel, staff dir. Spl. Investigation Commn., Phila., 1985-86; dep. spl. counsellor to Pres. of U.S., Washington, 1987; v.p., gen. counsel GE Aerospace, King of Prussia, Pa., 1989-93; v.p., assoc. gen. counsel Martin Marietta & Lockheed Martin, 1993-95; v.p. and gen. coun. Internat. Paper, Purchase, NY, 1996—99, sr. v.p., gen. counsel, 1999—2002; exec. v.p., gen. counsel Tyco Internat. Ltd., Portsmouth, NH, 2002—. Contbr. articles to profl. jours. Committeeman Republican Party, Chester County, Pa.; mem. Easttown Twp. Bd. Suprs., 1990-95. Mem. ABA, Am. Corp. Counsel Assn. (bd. dirs. 1997—). Office: Tyco Internat Ltd 273 Corporate Dr 100 Portsmouth NH 03801-6807